SURVEY OF RURAL INDIA

List of Volumes

SOUTH ZONE

Vol. 1 : Andhra Pradesh (A-J)
Vol. 2 : Andhra Pradesh (K-P)
Vol. 3 : Andhra Pradesh (Q-Z)
Vol. 4 : Karnataka
Vol. 5 : Kerala, Lekshdweep
Vol. 6 : Tamil Nadu (A-P)
Vol. 7 : Tamil Nadu (Q-Z), Pondicherry, Andaman & Nicobar Islands.

WEST ZONE

Vol. 8 : Gujrat, Dadra & Nagara and Haveli, Daman & Diu
Vol. 9 : Maharashtra
Vol. 10 : Maharashtra, Goa
Vol. 11 : Rajasthan

CENTRAL ZONE

Vol. 12 : Chhattisgarh
Vol. 13 : Madhya Pradesh
Vol. 14 : Madhra Pradesh
Vol. 15 : Uttar Pradesh
Vol. 16 : Uttar Pradesh
Vol. 17 : Uttar Pradesh

NORTH ZONE

Vol. 18 : Haryana, Delhi.
Vol. 19 : Himachal Pradesh, Jammu & Kashmir , Uttarakhand
Vol. 20 : Punjab, Chandigarh.

EAST ZONE

Vol. 21 : Bihar
Vol. 22 : Bihar
Vol. 23 : Jharkhand
Vol. 24 : Orrisa
Vol. 25 : West Bangal.

NORTH EAST ZONE

Vol. 26 : Assam, Sikkim
Vol. 27 : Arunachal Pradesh, Manipur, Meghalaya, Mizoram, Nagaland, Tripura.

SURVEY OF RURAL INDIA

A Comprehensive Study of Gram Panchayat and Community Development Block

In 27 Volumes

Volume 4

Karnataka

Editor

Dr. N. Seshagiri

GYAN

Survey of Rural India
Karnataka

ISBN : 978-81-212-1100-0 (Set)
ISBN : 978-81-212-1104-8 (Volume 4 : Karnataka)

Published in 2013 in India by
Gyan Publishing House
23, Main Ansari Road, Daryaganj,
New Delhi - 110002
Phones : 0091-011-23282060, 23261060
Fax : (011) 23285914
E-mail: books@gyanbooks.com
website: gyanbooks.com

Laser Type Setting : Rajender Vashist, Delhi
Printed at : Chawla Offset Printers, Delhi

Contents

List of Photographs

Preface

The Community Development Block in India is a demarcated rural area for administration and development. The area is administered by a Block Development Officer. A Community Development block covers several gram panchayats, which are local administrative unit at the village level. It was launched on a pilot basis in 1952 to provide for substantial streamlining of the country's agricultural sector, and for sustained improvements in systems of rural health and hygiene, rural education and communication among others. By the end of the First Five Year Plan period, there were 248 blocks which rapidly increased to around 3,000 blocks covering about seventy percent of the rural population in the country by the end of the Second Five Year Plan period. By 1964 there were 6,312 blocks covering the entire country.

India has travelled a considerable distance on the road to development since independence and has made significant progress in various sectors. However, new challenging demands have emerged calling for more integrated rural information. Acute shortage of basic facilities such as drinking water, medical support, education infrastructure is still felt in the face of over 27 per cent of rural population who are still facing poverty and essential sustenance. The Block Development Offices face daunting job of having to accelerate the development process and correct imbalances in tune with the wishes and aspirations of the rural people. Progressive policies and huge investments are being inducted by the Ministry of Rural Development at the Centre towards this, while State Governments are continuously upgrading their implementation machinery.

In addition, new paradigms like rural marketing by a host of retail and manufacturing enterprises as well as expanding technological infrastructure for telecommunication, IT, Transport and Energy among others are posing demands of new types of information on rural India.

Agriculture is a mainstay of the Indian economy. Agriculture and allied sectors contribute nearly 18 per cent of Gross Domestic Product (GDP) of India. Total area coverage under food grains has been reported as 123.22 million hectares. Out of 328.7 million hectares of geographical area of India about 142 million hectares is the net cultivated area. Of this, about 57 million hectare (40%) is irrigated and the remaining is rain fed. This area poses numerous problems for bringing about intensive agricultural production. Information on the four main river systems of India, feeding much of the irrigation schemes- The Himalayan Rivers, The Brahmaputra–centric Rivers, The Deccan Rivers and The Inland Rivers – has to be accurate enough to facilitate efficient irrigation planning.

The government has started focusing on the development of rural heath infrastructure. In the rural areas, services are provided through a network of integrated health and family welfare delivery system. An extensive network of about 3,500 Community Health Centers, 25,000 Primary Health Centers and 1,37,311 Sub-Centers have been set up to provide primary health care at the grassroots level. One sub-centre manned by one female and one male multipurpose worker covers a population of 5000 in plain areas and 3,000 in hilly, tribal, backward and difficult terrain areas. One Primary Health Centre covers a population of 30,000 in the plain areas and 20,000 in tribal and terrain areas. One Community Health Centre covers 80,000 to 1,20,000 Population.

Universalisation of Elementary Education (UEE) has been accepted as a national goal. The Ninth Five year plan envisages UEE to mean universal access, universal retention and universal achievement. As a result of the efforts made by the central and state governments, 94 per cent of country's rural population has primary schools within 1 Km. At the upper primary stage, 84 per cent of the rural population have a school within a distance of three kilometers.

The social milieu of India is not only vast but also diverse. We have tried to capture a representative sample of this diversity. Economic and social development of Scheduled Castes and Scheduled Tribes, who together comprise 24 per cent of the population, and other disadvantaged sections of our society, has called for special efforts, as provided for in the Constitution, of an unprecedented magnitude not faced by any other country in the world.

With deep satisfaction and a sense of accomplishment the book 'SURVEY OF RURAL INDIA (A COMPREHENSIVE STUDY OF GRAM PANCHAYAT AND COMMUNITY DEVELOPMENT BLOCK)' is presented to the readers in 27 Volumes. Such a massive work on Rural India has been commissioned in support of rural-oriented initiatives, containing a wide spectrum of information brought out in a single coherent publication.

All facts and figures have been diligently collected and very little has been left to chance or conjecture by meticulously adhering to documentation and professional standards. We cherish the hope that the twenty-seven volumes presented here will prove to be an invaluable companion to all researchers, scholars, planners, administrators, corporate investors, libraries, NGOs and all those who want to know about any of our Community Development Blocks.

Every detail of the information collected, collated and formatted has gone through meticulous validation checks and rechecks. In line with the constant evolution of the rural scenario, this encyclopedia too will have to be updated and improved in successive editions. A country as vast and complex as India is, there will always be scope for improving the work through suggestions, omissions and additions pointed out. We request the beneficiaries of this encyclopedia to so participate in its evolution.

We sincerely thank the Ministries/Departments of Agriculture, Rural Development, Textiles, Mines, Energy, Finance, Railways, Labour, Human Resource Development, Health and Family Welfare, Culture, Environment and Forest, Minority Affairs, Panchayti Raj, Parliamentary Affairs, Rural Development, Statistics, Tribal affairs, Water Resources, Women and Child Development, University Grants Commission, Law, Justice and Company Affairs, Tourism, Information and Broadcasting, Road Transport and Highways, Home Affairs, Social Justice and Empowerment, Science and Technology, Publication Division, Meteorological Department, Census Commissioner, Backward Classes Commission, Election Commission, Central Statistical Organisation, National Sample Survey Organisation, Anthropological Survey of India, Directorate General of Health Services, Archaeological Survey of India, Central Board of Irrigation and Power, State Statistical Officers, State Editors and gazetteers, State Librarians, Directors of State Information Centers and other connected with the government for the valuable material they have made available to us. We have studied the contents of a large number of published works and drawn from them. We owe a debt of gratitude to all such publishers, authors, editors and compilers. The credit for producing and furnishing authentic data actually goes to them. We have only weaved, consolidated and formatted the content of the information collected by them.

Gyan Publishing House went far beyond the normal call of publishers to give background support to the preparation of these volumes.

DISCLAIMER

This publication contains the collected, collated, formatted and validated information on Community Development Blocks (CD Block) of India on a best and sincere effort basis for presentation in a single encyclopedic work. This work does not constitute an advisory for research, analysis or investment planning, nor, in general, any professional advice. The reader should seek the services of appropriate specialists for such advice.

The information presented here is to be regarded as a first information service on any CDB. The reader should make his/her own deeper investigation of the information on any particular CDB, or state before making any decision or investment of any kind. The Editorial Board or the Publishers cannot be held responsible for loss, if any, incurred as result of specific planning or decision or investments made by the reader in pursuance of this work.

Dr. N. Seshagiri

1. Cashewnut. (C.D. Blocks : Karkal (District- Udupi) Kundapura (District – Udupi) Yellapur (District- Uttar Kannada) Ankola (Distrcit-Uttar Kannada)

2. Mango. C.D. Blocks : Sandur (District- Bellary) Kudligi (District- Bellary) Molakalmaru (District- Chitradurga)

3. Betel Leaf. C.D. Blocks : Hiriyur (District- Chitradurga) Sira (District- Tunkur) Hosdurga (District- Chitradurga)

4. Cotton. C.D. Blocks : Indi (District- Bijapur) Afzalpur (District- Gulbarga) Shorapur (District- Gulbarga)

5. Coconut. C.D. Blocks : Honavar (District- Uttar Kannada) Bhatkal (District- Uttar Kannada) Kundapura, (District- Udupi)

6. Red Chilli. C.D. Blocks : Haliyal (District- Uttara Kannada) Raybag (District- Belgaum) Hiriyur (District- Chitradurga)

7. Orange. C.D. Blocks : Virajpet (District- Kodagu) Mudigeri (District- Chikmagalur) Suliya (District- Dakshin Kannada)

8. Oil seed. (Maximum parts of the Karnataka)

9. Marvanthe Beach. C.D. Blocks : Udupi, (District- Udupi) Kundapura (District- Udupi)

10. Jog falls. C.D. Block : Sagar (District- Shimoga)

Introduction

Location

Karnataka in South-West India is the country's eighth largest State, situated on a tableland where the Western and Eastern Ghat ranges converge into the Nilgiri hill complex, the State of Karnataka is confined roughly within 11.5 degree North and 18.5 degree North latitudes and 74 degree East and 78.5 degree East longitude.

The State is bounded by Maharashtra and Goa States in the North and North-West; by the Arabian sea in the West; by Kerala and Tamilnadu States in the South and by the State of Andhra Pradesh in the East. The State extends to about 750 km from North to South and about 400 km from East to West, and covers an area of about 1,91,791 sq.km.

Karnataka has representatives of all types of variations in topography - high mountains, plateaus, residual hills and coastal plains. The State is enclosed by chains of mountains to its west, east and south. It consists mainly of plateau which has higher elevation of 600 to 900 metres above mean sea level. The entire landscape is undulating, broken up by mountains and deep ravines. Plain land of elevation less than 300 metres above mean sea level is to be found only in the narrow coastal belt, facing the Arabian Sea.

There are quite a few high peaks both in Western and Eastern Ghat systems with altitudes more than 1,500 metres. A series of cross-sections drawn from west to east across the Western Ghat generally exhibit, a narrow coastal plain followed to the east by small and short plateaus at different altitudes, then suddenly rising upto great heights.

Then follows the gentle east and east-north-west sloping plateau. Among the tallest peaks of Karnataka are the Mullayyana Giri (1,925 m), Bababudangiri (Chandradrona Parvata 1,894 m) and the Kudremukh (1,895 m) all in Chikmagalur Dt. and the Pushpagiri (1,908 m) in Kodagu Dt. There are a dozen peaks which rise above the height of 1,500 metres.

Physical Aspects

Physiograpically, Karnataka State forms part of two well defined macro regions of Indian Union; the Deccan Plateau and the Coastal plains and Islands. The State has **four physiographic regions** :

1. Northern Karnataka Plateau

Northern Karnataka Plateau comprises of the districts of Belgaum, Bidar, Bijapur and Gulbarga and is largely composed of the Deccan Trap. It represents a monotonous, treeless extensive plateau landscape with a general elevation of 300 to 600 metres from the mean sea level. However the river plains of the Krishna, the Bhima, the Ghataprabha and the Malaprabha with the intervening watersheds, the step like landscapes, lateritic scarpments, residual hills and ridges break the monotony of this extensive plateau. The general slope is towards the east. This region is largely covered with rich black cotton soils.

2. Central Karnataka Plateau

Central Karnataka Plateau covers the districts of Bellary, Chikmagalur, Chitradurga, Dharwad, Raichur and Shimoga. The region represents the transitional surface between the Northern Karnataka Plateau of Deccan Trap and southern Karnataka Plateau with relatively higher surface. By and large, this region represents the area of Tungabhadra basin. The general elevation varies between 450 and 700 metres. The general slope of this region is towards the east.

3. Southern Karnataka Plateau

The Southern Karnataka Plateau covers the districts of Bangalore, Bangalore Rural, Hassan, Kodagu, Kolar, Mandya, Mysore and Tumkur. This region largely covers the area of the Cauvery river basin lying in Karnataka. It is bounded by 600 metres contour and is characterised by a higher degree of slope. In the west and south, it is enclosed by the ranges of Western Ghats and the northern part is an interrupted but clearly identifiable high plateau.

In the east the valleys of the Cauvery and its tributaries open out to form undulating plains. The general elevation of the region varies from 600 to 900 metres. However, residual heights of 1,500 to 1,750 metres are found in the Biligirirangan hills of Mysore district and the Brahmagiri range of Kodagu district.

4. Karnataka Coastal Region

Karnataka coastal region forms are important part of Karnataka geography. The region covers the western ghats, edges of the Karnataka plateau, Uttar Kannada and Dakshin Kannada districts.

Climate

The State enjoys three main types of climates. For meteorological purposes, the State has been divided into three sub-divisions namely (a) Coastal Karnataka (Dakshina Kannada and Uttara Kannada districts), (b) North Interior Karnataka (Belgaum, Bidar, Bijapur, Dharwad, Gulbarga and Raichur districts) and (c) South Interior Karnataka (the remaining districts of Bangalore Rural, Bangalore, Bellary, Chikmagalur, Chitradurga, Kodagu, Hassan, Kolar, Mysore, Mandya, Shimoga and Tumkur districts).

The Tropical Monsoon climate covers the entire coastal belt and adjoining areas. The climate in this region is hot with excessive rainfall during the monsoon season i.e., June to September. The Southern half of the State experiences hot, seasonally dry tropical savana climate while most of the northern half experiences hot, semi-arid, tropical steppe type of climate. The climate of the State varies with the seasons.

The winter season from January to February is followed by summer season from March to May. The period from October to December forms the post-monsoon season. The period from October to March, covering the post-monsoon and winter seasons, is generally pleasant over the entire State except during a few spells of rain associated with north-east monsoon which affects the south-eastern parts of the State during October to December.

The months April and May are hot, very dry and generally uncomfortable. Weather tends to be oppressive during June due to high humidity and temperature. The next three months (July, August and September) are somewhat comfortable due to reduced day temperature although the humidities continue to be very high.

Hills

The Sahyadris mountain range run from Belgaum in the north to Mysore in the south. They form a triangular area in conjunction with the Eastern Ghats. The Ghats are only 305 to 610 meters in height in the middle but towards the south, they are quite tall and rise to a height of 1830 meters above sea level. It is here that the Nilgiris overlap the Ghats and at places, they rise to 2440 meters. Naturally at that height there are wooded areas and evergreen valleys, deep gorges, and pleasant plateaus. They lend themselves to the growth of plantations of different kinds which yield coffee, tea, areca nut, cashew nut and cardamom.

Rivers

The Kalinadi, the Gangavathi Bedti, the Tadri, and the Sharavati are the prominent rivers of North Karnataka. Sharavati is the shortest river and is famous for the mighty Jog Falls, the site of the hydel projects. All these rivers are west flowing and some of them are torrential streams which are in full flow in the monsoon.

Most of the major rivers of the state have their origin in the Ghats and flow eastwards towards the Bay of Bengal, through Andhra Pradesh or Tamil Nadu. Krishna with its tributaries like the Bhima and Ghataprabha and Tungabhadra is among these mighty rivers. The Kaveri river in the southern part of the state, which has its origin on Brahma Giri in Coorg, with its tributaries like the Shimsha, Hemavati, Kapila and others enters Tamil Nadu and is a major source of irrigation both in Karnataka and Tamil Nadu. It is a river of discord between the two states because of the great demand on its waters for the farmers in each of the two states and the matter often reaches emotional where politicians take over. The rivers Polar and Pennar in the eastern parts of the state are among the other important rivers.

The Krishna which originates in Maharashtra, is also a cause of dissension between Karnataka and Andhra Pradesh. The coast has several ports. Ports like Karwar, Ankola, Honavar and Bhatkal are situated at the mouth of the rivers where they fall into the Arabian sea. Mangalore and Malpe are important ports in the southern part of the state and the river of significance is the Netravathi. In ancient times these ports provided India's contacts, commercial and cultural with far way and near lands like Egypt and Sumeria.

Soils

Karnataka Light Soils (KLS): The light soils located in Mysore, Hassan, Shimoga, Coorg and Chitradurga districts constitute the light soils of Karnataka. The area is also called as Transitional zone with light soils and abundant rainfall suitable for tobacco cultivation. The crop is planted in the last week of April- May and harvested in July-August. The yields per hectare are around 1000 kgs. The varieties suitable are Special FCV, Bhavya, Swarna. The tobacco produced is light to medium bodied, lemon orange to orange in color, soft in nature, open grained. EEC Countries and some African and Middle East countries mostly prefer this variety of tobacco.

Annual Rain Fall

The state has a bitter-sweet relationship with rains. While its regions of Malnad and coastal Karnataka receive copious amount of rainfall; its north Bayaluseemae region in the Deccan Plateau is one of the most arid regions in the country. Most of the rains received in the state is during the monsoon season. Being an agrarian economy with a large percentage of its citizens engaged in agriculture, the failure of rains can have a crippling effect on the economy of the state. Apart from the benefits in agriculture, the Government of Karnataka has tried to avail other benefits of rainfall using scientific methods. An example of this is the project, *Rainwater Harvesting in Rural Karnataka* which is initiated by the Karnataka State Council for Science and Technology and is one of the largest rainwater harvesting projects in the world. Agumbe in the Shimoga district is known as one of the places with the highest annual rainfall in India. The average annual rainfall in the state is 1248 mm. The state is divided into three meteorological zones viz. North Interior Karnataka, South Interior Karnataka and Coastal Karnataka. Coastal Karnataka with an average annual rainfall of 3456 mm is one of the most rainy regions in the country. Contrasting this, the region of South Interior Karnataka and North Interior Karnataka receive only 1286 and 731 mm of average annual rainfall. The average annual rainfall in the districts of Karnataka varies from 562 mm in the Bagalkot district to 4119 mm in the Udupi district. Bagalkot, Chitradurga and Koppal are the districts which receive the least rainfall whereas Uttara Kannada, Dakshina Kannada and Udupi districts receive the heaviest rainfall.

Ground water

The state is covered by peninsular gneisses, granites, schists, & basalts along with sedimentaries of Kaldagi and Bhima groups. The recent alluvium is restricted to coastal areas and stream courses. The water bearing and yield characteristics in hard rock are primarily controlled by the extent of weathering and fracturing. In limestone areas, solution cavities impart secondary porosity. The yield of tube wells tapping hard rocks is as high as 50 m3/hr. The tube wells in sedimentaries can yield up to 15 m3/hr.

Dynamic Ground Water Resources	
Annual Replenishable Ground water Resource	15.93 BCM
Net Annual Ground Water Availability	15.30 BCM
Annual Ground Water Draft	10.71 BCM
Stage of Ground Water Development	70 %
Ground Water Development & Management	
Over Exploited	65 Talukas
Critical	3 Talukas
Semi- critical	14 Talukas

Forest and wildlife

The Forest department manages about 20.15% of the geographical area of the State. Forest have been classified as reserved forests, protected forests, unclassified forests, Villages forests, and private forests. There are 5 National Parks and 23 Wildlife sanctuaries. To overcome shortage of fuel wood, fodder and timber, degraded forests and waste lands are being developed. Emphasis is also being laid on the conservation, protection and development of the fragile eco-system of the Western Ghats. Several Wildlife protection schemes such as Project Tiger and Project Elephant are being implemented with the Central assistance. The concept of joint Forest Planning and Management applied to the 2 extrenally aided projects viz., Western Ghats Forestry and Environment project (DFID) and Forestry and Environment Project for Eastern Plains (JBIS) has resulted in village forest planning and management through establishment of Village Forest Committees. Japan Bank for International Cooperation has approved a new scheme called Karnataka Sustainable Forest Management and Bio-diversity project and it is being implemented from 2005-06 to 2012-13 throughout the state.

Communication

Road

Total road length of the state has increased from 83.749 km in 1971 to 2,15,849 km in 2007. The Karnataka Highways Improvement Project with World Bank assistance will improve 2375 kms of road, i.e. up gradation of 900 km and rehabilitation of 1475 kms comprising state highways and major district roads an estimated cost of Rs.2402.51 crores. Assistance is being provided under the Rural Infrastructure Development Fund for the construction and improvement of roads and bridge in the state.

Railways

A good rail network connects Bangalore to various parts of India. The major Indian cities connected with Bangalore through regular trains are Chennai, Mysore, New Delhi, Calcutta, and Mumbai.

The Western Ghats have long been a barrier for railways. But the state has 2,500 kilometres of one-metre-gauge and 160 kilometres of narrow-gauge line. Bangalore is the main centre of the network and connects with Chennai (formerly Madras) on the broad-gauge line.

Construction of the Konkan Railway was planned to connect Mangalore to Mumbai (formerly Bombay).

The line runs for 740 kilometres along the west coast of India. A direct rail link from New Delhi to Mangalore involves 45 hours of continuous travel. Mangalore is also the terminus of the railway line from Kerala.

Administration

Karnataka, like other Indian states, has a parliamentary system of government with two democratically elected houses, the Legislative Assembly and the Legislative Council. The Legislative Assembly consists of 224 members who are elected for five-year terms. The Legislative Council is a permanent body of 75 members with one-third (25 members) retiring every two years

The government of Karnataka is headed by the Chief Minister who is chosen by the ruling party members of the Legislative Assembly. The Chief Minister, along with the council of ministers, drives the legislative agenda and exercises most of the executive powers. However, the constitutional and formal head of the state is the Governor who is appointed for a five-year term by the President of India on the advice of the Union government. The people of Karnataka also elect 28 members to the Lok Sabha, the lower house of the Indian Parliament. The members of the state Legislative Assembly elect 12 members to the Rajya Sabha, the upper house of the Indian Parliament.

For administrative purposes, Karnataka has been divided into four revenue divisions, 49 sub-divisions, 29 districts, 175 taluks and 745 hoblies/revenue circles. The administration in each district is headed by a Deputy Commissioner who belongs to the Indian Administrative Service and is assisted by a number of officers belonging to Karnataka state services. The Deputy Commissioner of Police, an officer belonging to the Indian Police Service and assisted by the officers of the Karnataka Police Service, is entrusted with the responsibility of maintaining law and order and related issues in each district. The Deputy Conservator of Forests, an officer belonging to the Indian Forest Service, also serves the government. Sectoral development in the districts is looked after by the district head of each development department such as Public Works Department, Health, Education, Agriculture, Animal Husbandry, etc. The judiciary in the state consists of the Karnataka High Court (*Attara Kacheri*) in Bangalore, district and session courts in each district and lower courts and judges at the taluk level.

Gram Panchayat

The Panchayats are one of the oldest local governance institutions in rural Karnataka. This age old system of governance at the local level has gained much popularity in the current time. The Karnataka government is laying more and more importance on the Panchayati Raj, as it is often called. They believe that the local community should be provided with the recognition and the opportunity to set their own priorities as well as make their own strategies and implement them. In the state of Karnataka, the chief responsibility of the Rural Development and Panchayat Raj department lies in the implementation of the provisions of the Karnataka Panchayat Raj Act, 1993. This act aims at the achievement of the democratic decentralization especially for the rural areas. Panchayat Raj in Karnataka have a three-tier structural constitution: the Zilla Panchayats at the district level, the Taluka Panchayats at the sub-district level, the Gram Panchayats at the village level. In Karnataka you will get 27 Zilla Panchayats, 175 Taluka Panchayats, and 5659 Grama Panchayats.

Education

Out of every 100 children who join primary school in Karnataka in the first standard, by the sixth standard 50 children have left. Only 8 out of every 100 children finish twelve years of schooling. In rural areas the figure are even more dismal. Only 3 out of every 100 children who join school in the first standard finish twelve years of schooling.

In a study of government and corporation schools in South Bangalore was found that several students could not read and write Kannada even by the 6th standard. In the Government Lower Primary School in Gavipuram Guttahalli, for e.g. 33.4% of children in the third standard were unable to read and write Kannada alphabets. In the Government Model Primary School in Gavipuram Guttahalli, 24% of children in the second standard were unable to read and write.

Infrastructure Facilities in Schools

About 85% schools have 2 rooms or less, of these schools 38% have 50 children and 41% have 100 children enrolled. 89% schools have 2 or less teachers. A majority of the schools have books but the cramped conditions of the existing schools makes it impossible for their proper storage and effective utilisation. Only 36% of the schools have playgrounds which are in a usable condition, with 23.94% of the schools having drinking water, and 4.57 % having toilet facilities.

Medical

The Directorate of Health and Family Welfare Services is providing comprehensive health care and services to the people of the State through its network. The state has an extensive network of 293 (176 Government) hospitals, 1,297 Primary Health Centres, 622 Primary Health Units/dispensaries and 7,793 Sub-centres with more than 50,000 bed strength.Rural Health Programme: The state is following the National pattern of three-tier health infrastructure in rendering Primary Health Centres, Health Units, Community Health Centres and Sub-Centres. The policy of the Government is to establish one Primary Health Centre for every 30,000 population and one primary health unit for every 15-20 thousand population and a Sub-Centre for 5,000 population. The Community Health Centre (CHP) for every one lakh of population or one out of four P.H.Cs. to be formed to cater to the health care of the rural mas.

Maternal and Child Health Services :Great emphasis is laid on improving the health of the mother and child. Under these programmes, children are immunized against Tetanus, T.B, Polio, Measles, Diphtheria, Pertussis. Pregnant women too are immunized against Tetanus. Under the National programme of Prevention of Blindness, Vitamin 'A' concentrate is being distributed to the children.

Schools Health Programme: Medical examinations are conducted for children in all the primary and higher primary schools in the rural areas. Immunization against DT and TT, treatment of ailments, health education to teachers and students etc., are included in this School Health Programme.

Bank

The state of Karnataka, particularly the region comprising the coastal districts of Dakshina Kannada and Udupi is called as the **cradle of banking** in India.[1] This is because seven of the country's leading banks, Canara Bank, Syndicate Bank, Corporation Bank, Vijaya Bank, Karnataka Bank, Vysya Bank and the State Bank of Mysore originated from this state. The first five in the above list of banks were established in the districts of Udupi and Dakshina Kannada. These districts have one among the best distribution of banks in India - a branch for every 500 persons. Between 1880 and 1935, 22 banks were established in coastal Karnataka, nine of them in the city of Mangalore. The origin of banking in Karnataka's coastal region can be traced to the year 1868 when the Presidency Bank of Madras opened a branch to cater to the needs of British companies involved in exporting plantation produce. In the year 1912, the Indian Co-operative Societies Act in 1912 further energised the financial sector in this region leading to the establishment of a lot of co-operative societies. The freedom movement of India also played a crucial role as can be seen in the establishment of Karnataka Bank which was created as an offshoot of the swadeshi movement of 1905. These banks were earlier created to address the main sector in the economy i.e. agriculture but later they diversified to address other economical sectors as well. The Indian Government's notification of nationalisation of banks in the year 1969 and 1980, resulted in lot of these banks being nationalised with the Indian Government now owning some amount of control over these banks. As of today, State Bank of Mysore, Canara Bank, Vijaya Bank and Vysya Bank have their headquarters in Bangalore, Corporation Bank and Karnataka Bank are headquartered in Mangalore while Syndicate Bank is headquartered in Manipal. The entry of the private sector into the banking sector with aggressive marketing has led these banks to rethink some of their strategies. Earlier, banking was the main activity that was undertaken by these banks but due to the competition, they have been forced to diversify into other areas like insurance, equity and mutual funds. They have also been forced to upgrade their technology and introduce services like ATMs and online-banking transactions. As of March 2002, Karnataka had 4767 branches of different banks servicing the people of the state. The number of people served by each branch was 11,000 which is lesser than the national average of 16,000, thereby indicating better penetration of banking in the state.

Scheduled Castes

The total population of the state, as per 2001 Census is 52,850,562. Of this, 8,563,930 are Scheduled Castes (SCs). The SC population constitutes 16.2 per cent of the population of the state as a whole and 5.0 per cent of the SC population of the Country. The Scheduled Castes and Scheduled Tribes Order (Amendment) Act, 1976, has notified 101 SCs in Karnataka. This state has the highest number of SCs notified and living compared to other states/UTs of the Country. Two of the SCs namely, Adiya and Bant have been notified with area restriction. Adiya have been notified in Kodagu district only and Bant in Belgaum, Bijapur, Dharwad and Uttar Kannada districts.

The growth rate of SC population in the decade 1991-2001 at 16.2 per cent, is higher in comparison to the overall 17.5 per cent of the population of the state as a whole. At the individual SC level, Adi Karnataka, the largest SC have reported negative growth rate of 12.5 per cent. The second largest SC, Madiga have registered very high (259.2 per cent) growth. Due to the ethnic affinity, it is likely that a large number of Adi Karnataka have reported as Madiga, resulting in fluctuation in the growth rate.

Population - Size and Distribution (SC)

Of the 101 SCs, Adi Karnataka, Madiga, Banjara, Bhovi, Holaya, Adi Dravida and Bhambi together constitute 85.0 per cent of the SC population of the state. Adi Karnataka are numerically the largest SC with a population of 2,199,170, constituting 25.7 per cent of the state's SC population. They are followed by Madiga 1,305,976 (15.2 per cent), Banjara 997,338 (11.6 per cent), Bhovi 955,752 (11.2 per cent), Holaya 641,472 (7.5 per cent), Adi Dravida 616,332 (7.2 per cent) and Bhambi 564,599 (6.6 per cent). Forty one (41) SCs have returned population below 1000 in 2001 Census.

District wise distribution of SC population shows that Kolar district has the highest 26.5 per cent SC population, followed by Chamarajanagar (24.6 per cent), where as the least percentage of SC population (6.1 per cent) is recorded in the newly formed Udupi district.

As per the 2001 Census, 74.9 per cent and 25.1 per cent of the SC population are residing in rural and urban areas respectively. Among major SCs, Banjara have the highest (88.9 per cent) rural population, followed by Holaya (82.0 per cent), Bhambi (80.7 per cent), Madiga (80.3 per cent), Adi Karnataka (76.2 per cent) and Bhovi (74.9 per cent). But on the other hand, Adi Dravida have 62.8 per cent urban population.

Sex ratio (SC)

The overall sex ratio of the SC population of Karnataka is 973 females per 1000 males, which is marginally higher than 965 reported for the state population at 2001 Census.

The sex ratio of SC population has increased from 962 registered in 1991 Census. The Statement below shows sex ratio and child sex ratio (0-6) of SC population at the national, state and numerically the largest seven SCs in 2001 Census:

Age Groups	*All SCs India*	*All SCs (Karnataka)*	*Adi (Karnataka)*	*Madiga*	*Banjara*	*Bhovi*	*Holaya*	*Adi Dravida*	*Bhambi*
All Ages	936	973	976	979	938	973	969	988	992
0-6	938	960	968	969	944	969	948	961	970

The sex ratio as well as child sex ratio (0-6) of SC population of Karnataka is considerably higher than the corresponding national figures for SC population. At the individual caste level, Banjara and Holaya have lower sex ratio in overall and 0-6 age group populations, in comparison to the state SC population as well as other major SCs.

Literacy and educational level (SC)

Literacy and level of education are two basic indicators of the level of development achieved by a group/society. The literacy results in more awareness besides contributing to the overall improvement of health, hygiene and other social conditions. According to 2001 Census, percentage of literate persons (those who can read & write with understanding), aged 7 years and above, among SC population of Karnataka, is 52.9 per cent, which is lower than 66.6 per cent reported for the state population. The literacy data show that the SC population of the state has made significant improvement in literacy during the decade 1991-2001. The literacy rate, which was 38.1 per cent in 1991, has increased by 14.8 percentage points in 2001.

Among the major SCs, Adi Dravida have reported the highest 70.1 per cent literacy rate, followed by Adi Karnataka (56.7 per cent), Holaya (51.8 per cent), Bhovi (49.2 per cent), Bhambi (46.8 per cent), Madiga (45.7 per cent) and Banjara (43.0 per cent). The female literacy rate of 41.7 per cent among SC population is lower as compared to 56.9 per cent among state's female population. As in literacy rate, the highest and lowest female literacy rate of 46.9 per cent and 28.8 per cent have also been recorded among Adi Dravida and Banjara as well.

Out of total literates, 33.7 per cent are literates without any educational level or have attained below Primary level. The literates, who have attained education up to Primary level and Middle level, constitute 28.6 per cent and 13.9 per cent respectively. 18.8 per cent are having educational level up to Matric/ Higher Secondary etc. levels, implying that every 5th SC literate is a Matriculate. Literates with educational level of Graduation & above are 4.1 per cent. Individually, Holaya (5.9 per cent) and Adi Karnataka (4.3 per cent) have highest percentage of Graduation & above educational level.

From the above it also emerges that the drop out is more prominent in Middle level.

Population in the age group 5-14 years are the potential students. 64.7 per cent of the SC population in this age group is attending various educational institutions.

Educational levels attained by major SCs

Name of SC	*Literate without educational level*	*Below primary*	*Primary*	*Middle*	*Matric/Secondary/Higher Secondary Intermediate etc.*	*Technical & Non-technical diploma*	*Graduate & above*
All SCs	2.4	31.3	28.6	13.9	18.8	0.9	4.1
Adi Karnataka	2.1	26.3	29.4	16.9	20.3	0.8	4.3
Madiga	3.0	35.3	29.2	12.9	15.9	0.5	3.1
Banjara	3.2	41.2	25.1	10.6	14.9	1.1	4.0
Bhovi	2.7	34.9	30.4	12.6	15.6	0.8	2.9
Holaya	2.6	31.6	27.8	11.1	20.3	0.8	5.9
Adi Dravida	1.5	22.2	28.2	17.3	24.8	1.7	4.3
Bhambi	2.6	41.0	26.6	10.2	15.3	0.8	3.5

Economic activity Work Participation Rate (WPR) (SC)

The WPR of the state SC population is 46.3 per cent in 2001 Census, which is higher than 44.7 per cent reported in 1991 Census. In WPR, Karnataka SCs have sixth position after Mizoram (68.8 per cent), Manipur (51.4 per cent), Andhra Pradesh (50.5 per cent), Himachal Pradesh (48.9 per cent) and Tamil Nadu (48.1 per cent). The WPR for male has been 54 per cent and for females 38.4 per cent in 2001 Census. 14. At individual caste level, the WPR varies from the highest 48.5 per cent among Madiga to the lowest 41.6 per cent among Adi Dravida.

Category of Workers (SC)

There has been a decline in the main workers from 92.6 per cent in 1991 Census to 78.4 per cent in 2001 Census. This has resulted in corresponding increase in the marginal workers from 7.4 per cent in 1991 to 21.6 per cent in 2001. Out of total workers, 'agricultural labourers' constitute 43.8 per cent, which is lower than 1.8 percentage points when compared to 45.6 per cent registered at national level SC population. 'Other workers' accounts for 33.1 per cent and only 20.5 per cent have been returned as 'cultivators'. Remaining 2.5 per cent have been workers in 'household industry'.

At the individual caste level, Bhambi have recorded the highest 63.1 per cent agricultural labourers, followed by Madiga (57.9 per cent) where as the lowest 20.4 per cent has been registered in case of Adi Dravida.

Religion (SC)

Majority (96.1 per cent) of the SC population of the state are Hindus. There are 331,638 (3.9 per cent) Buddhists and 718 SC Sikh populations reported in the state. Among major SCs, Holaya have reported 34.1 per cent Buddhist population.

Scheduled Tribes

The total population of the state, as per 2001 Census is 52,850,562. Of this, 3,463,986 are Scheduled Tribes (STs). The ST population constitutes 6.6 per cent of the state population and 4.1 per cent of the country's ST population. Forty-nine STs have been notified in Karnataka by the Scheduled Castes and Scheduled Tribes Order (Amendment) Act, 1976 and by the Act 39 of 1991. This is the second highest number, next to Orissa (64) if compared with the number of STs notified in any other states/UTs of the Country. Five STs namely, Kammara, Kaniyan, Kuruba, Maratha and Marati have been notified with area restriction. Kuruba and Maratha have been notified only in Kodagu district, where as Marati in Dakshina Kannada, Kaniyan in Kollegal taluk of Chamarajanagar and Kammara in Dakshina Kannada districts..

Of the STs, two namely, Jenu Kuruba and Koraga are among the Primitive Tribal Groups (PTGs) of India having population of 29,828 and 16,071 respectively in 2001 Census. Jenu Kuruba are mainly distributed in Mysore, Kodagu and Bangalore districts, and Koraga in Dakshina Kannada and Dharward districts. In the present census, a low growth rate of 1.6 per cent and a negative growth rate of 1.5 per cent have been reported for the Jenu Kuruba and Koraga respectively.

The growth rate of ST population in the decade 1991-2001 at 80.8 per cent is considerably higher in comparison to the overall 17.5 per cent of state population. The steep growth of ST population is due to addition of Naik, Nayak, Beda, Bedar and Valmiki as subgroups of Naikda. The sub groups have been enumerated for the first time at the 2001 Census. Naikda, the largest ST have registered a higher growth rate 113.0 per cent, compared to 8.8 per cent during the decade (1981-1991).

Population: Size and Distribution (ST)

Naikda alone constitute 84.3 per cent of the ST population of the state. Gond 136,700 (3.9per cent), Koli Dhor 80,627 (2.3 per cent) and Marati 63,549 (1.8per cent) are of the second, third and fourth positions. 5. The ST population of Karnataka are primarily rural (84.7per cent). Among major STs, Koli Dhor have the highest (92.2per cent) rural population, followed by Gond (91.7per cent), Marati (90.8per cent) and Naikda (85.1per cent). District-wise distribution of ST population shows that they have been returned in all 27 districts of the state. But they are mainly concentrated in the districts of Bellary, Raichur, Mysore, Chitradurga, Belgaum, Davanagere and Kolar. The seven districts account for 54 per cent of the ST population of the state. The remaining 46 per cent ST populations are distributed in 20 districts.

Sex ratio (ST)

The overall sex ratio of the ST population of the state is 972, which is marginally higher than 965 reported for state population in 2001.The sex ratio of ST population has improved from 961 reported in 1991 Census. The statement showing comparative sex ratio at the national level and state level for ST population as a whole and the numerically largest four STs is given below :

Age Groups	*All STs (India)*	*All STs (Karnataka)*	*Naikda*	*Gond*	*Koli Dhor*	*Marati*
All Ages	978	972	973	949	944	1013
0-6	973	961	961	937	946	962

As shown in the statement above, the overall sex ratio as well as child sex ratio (0- 6) of ST population of Karnataka is lower than the corresponding national figures for ST population. At individual tribe level, Gond and Koli Dhor have lower sex ratio in total and 0-6 age group populations, in comparison to the state ST population as well as other major STs.

Literacy and educational level (ST)

Literacy and level of education are two basic indicators of the level of development achieved by a group/society. The literacy results in more awareness besides contributing to the overall improvement of health, hygiene and other social conditions. According to 2001 Census, percentage of literate persons (those who can read & write with understanding), aged 7 years and above, among ST population of Karnataka, is 48.3 per cent which is lower than 66.6 per cent reported for the state population as a whole. The literacy data show that the ST population of the state has made significant improvement during the decade 1991- 2001. The literacy rate, which was 36.0 per cent in 1991, has increased by 12.3 percentage points in 2001.

Educational levels attained by major STs

Name of ST	*Literate without educational level*	*Below primary*	*Primary*	*Middle*	*Matric/Secondary/Higher Secondary Intermediate etc.*	*Technical & Non-technical diploma*	*Graduate & above*
All STs	2.9	36.3	29.3	11.8	15.8	0.8	3.1
Naikda	2.9	36.8	28.9	12.0	15.6	0.8	3.0
Gond	4.5	32.6	29.2	9.8	19.2	1.0	3.6
Koil Dhor	4.0	37.2	28.8	9.2	17.0	0.7	3.0
Marati	0.7	31.4	35.9	12.0	16.7	0.4	2.9

Among the major STs, Marati are reported to have the highest 73.9 per cent literacy rate, followed by Gond (51.5per cent), Naikda (47.3 per cent) and Koli Dhor (46.5 per cent), The female literacy rate of 36.6 per cent among ST population is lower as compared to 56.9 per cent among state female population. Like literacy rate, the highest and lowest female literacy rates of 66.2 per cent and 32.2 per cent have been recorded among Marati and Koli Dhor.

Out of total literates, 39.2 per cent are literates without any educational level or have attained below Primary level. The literates, who have attained education up to Primary level and Middle level, constitute 29.3 per cent and 11.8 per cent respectively. 15.8 per cent of the literates are having educational level up to Matric/Higher Secondary etc. levels, implying that every 6th ST literate is a Matriculate. Literates with educational level of Graduation and above are 3.1 per cent. Individually, Gond (3.6 per cent) have the highest percentage of Graduation and above educational level.

From the above educational level table, it emerges that the drop out is prominent in Middle level.

Population in the age group 5-14 years are the

potential students. Only 59.3 per cent of the ST population in this age group is attending various educational institutions. In this regard, Marati, the fourth largest ST, have the highest 83.6 per cent school going children.

Economic activity Work Participation Rate (WPR) (ST)

The work participation rate (WPR) is the percentage of workers to the total population. The WPR of 49.4 per cent among the ST population in 2001 is higher than that of the state population (44.5 per cent). The WPR has increased from 47.8 per cent reported in 1991.The WPR at 56.8 per cent for males are higher than 41.7 per cent reported among females in 2001 Census.

At individual tribe level, the highest WPR of 55.1 per cent is reported for Marati, followed by Naikda (49.6 per cent), Koli Dhor (44.3 per cent) and Gond (42 per cent). The trend follows in case of WPR of female. Marati have the highest 48.4 per cent female work participation rate.

Category of Workers (ST)

There has been a decline in the main workers from 91.5 per cent in 1991 to 77.9 per cent in 2001 Census. This has resulted in corresponding increase in the marginal workers from 8.5 per cent in 1991 to 22.1 per cent in 2001. Out of total workers, 'agricultural labourers' constitute 43.2 per cent, which is higher by 6.3 percentage points when compared to 36.9 per cent registered at national level for ST population. 'Cultivators' account for 30.8 per cent and only 23.4 per cent has been returned as 'other workers'. Remaining 2.6 per cent have been workers in 'household industry'.

In the economic category, at individual tribe level, the highest percentage (50.9 per cent) of agricultural labourers is recorded for Koli Dhor. Naikda have the highest number of cultivators (33.1 per cent).

Religion (ST)

Hinduism is the predominant religion of ST population of the state. The Census data show that Hindus constitute 98.7 per cent, followed by Muslims 3,670 (0.1 per cent). The remaining population belongs to the category of 'other religions and persuasions' and 'religion not stated'.

Agriculture

The State has 66% Rural population and 55.60 per cent of workers are agricultural laborers. The State has 60% (114 lakh ha) cultivable land and 72% of the cultivable area is rain fed ; only 28% is under irrigation. The state has 10 Agro climatic Zones. The Red soil constituted major soil type, followed by Blank soil. The sown area of the state 51.7% of the total land. During 2007-08, food grain production is anticipated to be 117.35 lakh metric tons against the target of 119.70 lakh metric ton.

Irrigation

About 28% of the cultivable land in the state is under irrigation. During 2006-07, 23.21 hectares of land was covered by major and medium irrigation and 9.93 lakh hectare was covered by minor irrigation, constituting a total of 33.14 lakh hectares of irrigated area.

Irrigation place utmost significant part in obtaining increased yields from the land. The development of Irrigation in the state was slow and unsystematic during the pre independence era. However, there were some notable Irrigation works undertaken and completed during the pre-independence, such as Krishnaraja Sagar (which was the only major project completed prior to independence), Vijayanagar canals, Cauvery anicut Channels, Gokak canal, Vanivilasa Sagar, Markonahalli and Anjanapura. Though major projects like Tungabhadra, Bhadra and Ghataprabha stage-I were commenced prior to the plan period, their progress was slow and they got impetus only after their inclusion in the first five year plan.

There were more than 25,000 tanks scattered over erstwhile Mysore state. But in Bombay Karnataka and Hyderabad Karnataka areas, the number of such minor irrigation works are meager.

Large Dams

Moti -Talab : Year of completion Old Dam (10th century); River Local Stream Siddipet; Nearest city Mandya; Type TE; Height above lowest foundation (m) 24; Length of dam (m) 157; Volume content of dam (10^3m^3) NA ; Gross capacity of reservoir (10^3m^3) 2190.0; Effective capacity of reservoir (10^3m^3) NA ; Design purpose I, S; Designed spillway capacity (m^3/s) NA ; Cultivable command area (hectares) NA ; Estimated cost (Rs. million) NA ; Project irrigation potential (hectares) NA .

Madag dam: Year of completion 1867; River Kumudati; Nearest city Dharwar; Type TE; Height above lowest foundation (m) 44; Length of dam (m) 564; Volume content of dam (10^3m^3) NA; Gross capacity of reservoir (10^3m^3) 1590; Effective capacity of reservoir (10^3m^3) NA; Design purpose I; Designed spillway capacity (m^3/s) NA; Cultivable command area (hectares) NA; Estimated cost (Rs. million) NA; Project irrigation potential (hectares) NA.

Muchkudi: Year of completion 1884; River Local Stream; Nearest city Bagalkot; Type PG; Height above lowest foundation (m) 19; Length of dam (m) 158; Volume content of dam (10^3m^3) 18; Gross capacity of reservoir (10^3m^3) 1770.0; Effective capacity of reservoir (10^3m^3) NA; Design purpose I; Designed spillway capacity (m^3/s) NA; Cultivable command area (hectares) NA; Estimated cost (Rs. million) NA; Project irrigation potential (hectares) NA.

Unkal: Year of completion 1894; River Kalhalla; Nearest city Hubli; Type TE; Height above lowest foundation (m) 19; Length of dam (m) 831; Volume content of dam (10^3m^3) NA; Gross capacity of reservoir (10^3m^3) 4330; Effective capacity of reservoir (10^3m^3) NA; Design purpose S; Designed spillway capacity (m^3/s) NA; Cultivable command area (hectares) NA; Estimated cost (Rs. million) NA; Project irrigation potential (hectares) NA.

Vanivilas Sagar: Year of completion 190.7; River Vedavati; Nearest city Chitaldurg; Type PG; Height above lowest foundation (m) 50; Length of dam (m) 408; Volume content of dam (10^3m^3) 536; Gross capacity of reservoir (10^3m^3) 849600; Effective capacity of reservoir (10^3m^3) NA; Design purpose I, S; Designed spillway capacity (m^3/s) NA; Cultivable command area (hectares) NA; Estimated cost (Rs. million) NA; Project irrigation potential (hectares) NA.

Krishnarajasagar: Year of completion 1932; River Cauvery; Nearest city Mysore; Type PG; Height above lowest foundation (m) 43; Length of dam (m) 2621; Volume content of dam (10^3m^3) 849; Gross capacity of reservoir (10^3m^3) 1368847; Effective capacity of reservoir (10^3m^3) 1244210; Design purpose I, H; Designed spillway capacity (m^3/s) 9911; Cultivable command area (hectares) NA; Estimated cost (Rs. million) 63.4; Project irrigation potential (hectares) NA.

Chamrajsagar: Year of completion 1934; River Arkavathi & Kumudavathi; Nearest city Bangalore; Type PG; Height above lowest foundation (m) 49; Length of dam (m) 518; Volume content of dam (10^3m^3) NA; Gross capacity of reservoir (10^3m^3) 94730; Effective capacity of reservoir (10^3m^3) 85158; Design purpose S; Designed spillway capacity (m^3/s) 274; Cultivable command area (hectares) NA; Estimated cost (Rs. million) NA; Project irrigation potential (hectares) NA.

Anjanapur: Year of completion 1938; River Kumudavathi; Nearest city Shimoga; Type TE; Height above lowest foundation (m) 27; Length of dam (m) 1524; Volume content of dam (10^3m^3) NA; Gross capacity of reservoir (10^3m^3) 16500; Effective capacity of reservoir (10^3m^3) NA; Design purpose I; Designed spillway capacity (m^3/s) 611; Cultivable command area (hectares) NA; Estimated cost (Rs. million) 3.0; Project irrigation potential (hectares) NA.

Marconhalli: Year of completion 1941; River Shimsha; Nearest city Tumkur; Type PG, TE; Height above lowest foundation (m) 27; Length of dam (m) 1612; Volume content of dam (10^3m^3) NA; Gross capacity of reservoir (10^3m^3) 65800; Effective capacity of reservoir (10^3m^3) NA; Design purpose I; Designed spillway capacity (m^3/s) 1681; Cultivable command area (hectares) NA; Estimated cost (Rs. million) NA; Project irrigation potential (hectares) NA.

Nandargi: Year of completion 1942; River Local Stream; Nearest city Bijapur; Type TE; Height above lowest foundation (m) 18; Length of dam (m) 491; Volume content of dam (10^3m^3) 61; Gross capacity of reservoir (10^3m^3) 1490; Effective capacity of reservoir (10^3m^3) NA; Design purpose I; Designed spillway capacity (m^3/s) NA; Cultivable command area (hectares) NA; Estimated cost (Rs. million) NA; Project irrigation potential (hectares) NA.

Byramangala: Year of completion 1945; River Varisha-Bhavati; Nearest city Bangalore; Type TE; Height above lowest foundation (m) 22; Length of dam (m) 2287; Volume content of dam (10^3m^3) NA; Gross capacity of reservoir (10^3m^3) 21150; Effective capacity of reservoir (10^3m^3) NA; Design purpose I; Designed spillway capacity (m^3/s) 205; Cultivable command area (hectares) NA; Estimated cost (Rs. million) NA; Project irrigation potential (hectares) NA.

Kanva: Year of completion 1946; River Kanva; Nearest city Bangalore; Type TE; Height above lowest foundation (m) 27; Length of dam (m) 1422; Volume content of dam (10^3m^3) 212; Gross capacity of reservoir (10^3m^3) 27670; Effective capacity of reservoir (10^3m^3) NA; Design purpose I; Designed spillway capacity (m^3/s) I; Cultivable command area (hectares) 396; Estimated cost (Rs. million) NA; Project irrigation potential (hectares) NA.

Tungabhadra: Year of completion 1957; River Tungabhadra; Nearest city Hospet; Type PG, TE; Height above lowest foundation (m) 49; Length of dam (m) 2449; Volume content of dam (10^3m^3) 1155; Gross

TE-Earth; ER-Rockfill; PG-Gravity; CB-Buttress; VA-Arch; MV-Multi Arch; I-Irrigation; H-Hydro-electric; C-Flood Control; N-Navigation; S-Water Supply Recreational; R-Purposes; U.C.-Under Construction; L-Uncontrolled Spillway; V-Controlled Spillway; Gross capacity of reservoir ($10.^3m^3$)-Unit; Effective capacity of reservoir ($10.^3m^3$)-Unit; Volume content of dam ($10.^3m^3$)-Unit; Designed spillway capacity (m^3/s)-Unit.

capacity of reservoir (10^3m^3) 3767000; Effective capacity of reservoir (10^3m^3) 3701000; Design purpose I, H; Designed spillway capacity (m^3/s) 1840.8; Cultivable command area (hectares) 528981; Estimated cost (Rs. million) 762.2; Project irrigation potential (hectares) 364900.

Nugu: Year of completion 1958; River Nugu; Nearest city Mysore; Type TE, PG; Height above lowest foundation (m) 44; Length of dam (m) 635; Volume content of dam (10^3m^3) 341; Gross capacity of reservoir (10^3m^3) 154060; Effective capacity of reservoir (10^3m^3) 138711; Design purpose I; Designed spillway capacity (m^3/s) 566; Cultivable command area (hectares) NA; Estimated cost (Rs. million) 3100; Project irrigation potential (hectares) NA.

Kalaskope: Year of completion 1959; River Local Stream; Nearest city Bagalkot; Type TE; Height above lowest foundation (m) 18; Length of dam (m) 277; Volume content of dam (10^3m^3) NA; Gross capacity of reservoir (10^3m^3) 6820; Effective capacity of reservoir (10^3m^3) NA; Design purpose I; Designed spillway capacity (m^3/s) 863; Cultivable command area (hectares) NA; Estimated cost (Rs. million) 2.21; Project irrigation potential (hectares) 1140.

Areshankar: Year of completion 1960; River Tr.of Krishna; Nearest city Almatti; Type PG; Height above lowest foundation (m) 20; Length of dam (m) 1188; Volume content of dam (10^3m^3) NA; Gross capacity of reservoir (10^3m^3) 7160; Effective capacity of reservoir (10^3m^3) NA; Design purpose I; Designed spillway capacity (m3/s) NA; Cultivable command area (hectares) NA; Estimated cost (Rs. million) 2.15; Project irrigation potential (hectares) 1240.

Ramanahalli: Year of completion 1960; River Navelli Stream; Nearest city Bijapur; Type TE; Height above lowest foundation (m) 17; Length of dam (m) 1619; Volume content of dam (10^3m^3) 600; Gross capacity of reservoir (10^3m^3) 12740; Effective capacity of reservoir (10^3m^3) NA; Design purpose I; Designed spillway capacity (m^3/s) NA; Cultivable command area (hectares) NA; Estimated cost (Rs. million) 407; Project irrigation potential (hectares) 1940.

Bhadra :Year of completion 1963; River Bhadra; Nearest city Shimoga; Type PG; Height above lowest foundation (m) 72; Length of dam (m) 1790; Volume content of dam (10^3m^3) 779; Gross capacity of reservoir (10^3m^3) 2025871; Effective capacity of reservoir (10^3m^3) 1785151; Design purpose I, H; Designed spillway capacity (m^3/s) 3022; Cultivable command area (hectares) 97870; Estimated cost (Rs. million) 4800; Project irrigation potential (hectares) NA.

Talakalale (Sharavathy Project); Year of completion 1964; River Talakalale Stream; Nearest city Shimoga; Type PG; Height above lowest foundation (m) 62; Length of dam (m) 718; Volume content of dam (10^3m^3) 994; Gross capacity of reservoir (10^3m^3) 130000; Effective capacity of reservoir (10^3m^3) 56000; Design purpose H; Designed spillway capacity (m^3/s) 850; Cultivable command area (hectares) NA; Estimated cost (Rs. million) 25.3; Project irrigation potential (hectares) NA.

Linganamakki (Sharavathy Project): Year of completion 1965; River Sharavathy; Nearest city Shimoga; Type PG, TE; Height above lowest foundation (m) 61; Length of dam (m) 2582; Volume content of dam (10^3m^3) 14251; Gross capacity of reservoir (10^3m^3) 4418000; Effective capacity of reservoir (10^3m^3) 4276000; Design purpose H; Designed spillway capacity (m^3/s) 80.71; Cultivable command area (hectares) NA; Estimated cost (Rs. million) 2400; Project irrigation potential (hectares) NA.

Ambligola: Year of completion 1967; River Salur; Nearest city Shimoga; Type TE; Height above lowest foundation (m) 21; Length of dam (m) 684; Volume content of dam (10^3m^3) NA; Gross capacity of reservoir (10^3m^3) 11690; Effective capacity of reservoir (10^3m^3) NA; Design purpose I; Designed spillway capacity (m^3/s) 253; Cultivable command area (hectares) NA; Estimated cost (Rs. million) 12.27; Project irrigation potential (hectares) 2950.

Chikhole: Year of completion 1967; River Chikhole; Nearest city Chamrajanagar; Type TE; Height above lowest foundation (m) 29; Length of dam (m) 675; Volume content of dam (10^3m^3) 174; Gross capacity of reservoir (10^3m^3) 10669; Effective capacity of reservoir (10^3m^3) NA; Design purpose I; Designed spillway capacity (m^3/s) NA; Cultivable command area (hectares) NA; Estimated cost (Rs. million) 13.40; Project irrigation potential (hectares) 1620.

Nagathna: Year of completion 1967; River Kyadginalla; Nearest city Bijapur; Type TE; Height above ground level (m) 11; Length of dam (m) 2652; Volume content of dam (10^3m^3) NA; Gross capacity of reservoir (10^3m^3) 2775; Effective capacity of reservoir (10^3m^3) NA; Design purpose I; Designed spillway capacity (m^3/s) NA; Cultivable command area (hectares) NA; Estimated cost (Rs. million) 1.77; Project irrigation potential (hectares) 540.

Dharma: Year of completion 1968; River Dharma; Nearest city Mundgao; Type TE; Height above lowest foundation (m) 23; Length of dam (m) 142; Volume content of dam (10^3m^3) 42; Gross capacity of reservoir (10^3m^3) 23050; Effective capacity of reservoir (10^3m^3)

NA; Design purpose I; Designed spillway capacity (m^3/s) 556; Cultivable command area (hectares) NA; Estimated cost (Rs. million) 13.29; Project irrigation potential (hectares) 5660.

Hebbahalla: Year of completion 1968; River Hebbahalla; Nearest city Mysore; Type TE; Height above lowest foundation (m) 20; Length of dam (m) 863; Volume content of dam (10^3m^3) NA; Gross capacity of reservoir (10^3m^3) 11950; Effective capacity of reservoir (10^3m^3) NA; Design purpose I; Designed spillway capacity (m^3/s) NA; Cultivable command area (hectares) NA; Estimated cost (Rs. million) 4.73; Project irrigation potential (hectares) 1210.

Jambadahalla: Year of completion 1968; River Jambadahalla; Nearest city Tarikere; Type TE; Height above lowest foundation (m) 28; Length of dam (m) 935; Volume content of dam (10^3m^3) NA; Gross capacity of reservoir (10^3m^3) 37000; Effective capacity of reservoir (10^3m^3) NA; Design purpose I; Designed spillway capacity (m^3/s) 3398; Cultivable command area (hectares) NA; Estimated cost (Rs. million) 11.80; Project irrigation potential (hectares) 2430.

Mangla: Year of completion 1968; River Tr.of Karari; Nearest city Tumkur; Type TE; Height above lowest foundation (m) 12; Length of dam (m) 696; Volume content of dam (10^3m^3) NA; Gross capacity of reservoir (10^3m^3) 19030; Effective capacity of reservoir (10^3m^3) NA; Design purpose I; Designed spillway capacity (m^3/s) 566; Cultivable command area (hectares) NA; Estimated cost (Rs. million) 601; Project irrigation potential (hectares) 860.

Chandrampalli: Year of completion 1972; River Sarnala (Tr. of Bhima); Nearest city Gulbarga; Type TE; Height above lowest foundation (m) 29; Length of dam (m) 926; Volume content of dam (10^3m^3) 1599; Gross capacity of reservoir (10^3m^3) 34206; Effective capacity of reservoir (10^3m^3) 403; Design purpose I; Designed spillway capacity (m^3/s) 870; Cultivable command area (hectares) NA; Estimated cost (Rs. million) 2068; Project irrigation potential (hectares) 5220.

Hathi Koni Project: Year of completion 1973; River Hathi Koni (Tr.of Bhima); Nearest city Yadgir; Type TE; Height above lowest foundation (m) 27; Length of dam (m) 924; Volume content of dam (10^3m^3) NA; Gross capacity of reservoir (10^3m^3) 9976; Effective capacity of reservoir (10^3m^3) NA; Design purpose I; Designed spillway capacity (m^3/s) 377; Cultivable command area (hectares) NA; Estimated cost (Rs. million) 9.39; Project irrigation potential (hectares) 2150.

Malaprabha: Year of completion 1973; River Malaprabha; Nearest city Dharwar; Type PG; Height above lowest foundation (m) 56; Length of dam (m) 155; Volume content of dam (10^3m^3) 115; Gross capacity of reservoir (10^3m^3) 879800; Effective capacity of reservoir (10^3m^3) NA; Design purpose I; Designed spillway capacity (m^3/s) 5239; Cultivable command area (hectares) NA; Estimated cost (Rs. million) 99061; Project irrigation potential (hectares) 206,500.

Bachanki: Year of completion 1974; River Bachanki; Nearest city Hubli; Type TE; Height above lowest foundation (m) 23; Length of dam (m) 776; Volume content of dam (10^3m^3) 436; Gross capacity of reservoir (10^3m^3) 11120; Effective capacity of reservoir (10^3m^3) NA; Design purpose I; Designed spillway capacity (m^3/s) 326; Cultivable command area (hectares) NA; Estimated cost (Rs. million) 12.64; Project irrigation potential (hectares) 1940.

Kabini: Year of completion 1974; River Kabini; Nearest city Mysore; Type TE, PG; Height above lowest foundation (m) 58; Length of dam (m) 2733; Volume content of dam (10^3m^3) 3547; Gross capacity of reservoir (10^3m^3) 553000; Effective capacity of reservoir (10^3m^3) 396000; Design purpose I, H, S; Designed spillway capacity (m^3/s) 5494; Cultivable command area (hectares) NA; Estimated cost (Rs. million) 5700; Project irrigation potential (hectares) 94,700.

Kanakanala Project: Year of completion 1975; River Kanakanala; Nearest city Raichur; Type TE; Height above lowest foundation (m) 20; Length of dam (m) 781; Volume content of dam (10^3m^3) NA; Gross capacity of reservoir (10^3m^3) 7946; Effective capacity of reservoir (10^3m^3) 7013; Design purpose I; Designed spillway capacity (m^3/s) 499; Cultivable command area (hectares) 3237; Estimated cost (Rs. million) 9.7; Project irrigation potential (hectares) 2060.

Suvarnavathy: Year of completion 1978; River Suvarnavathy; Nearest city Mysore; Type TE, PG; Height above lowest foundation (m) 29; Length of Dam (m) NA; Volume content of dam (10^3m^3) 834; Gross capacity of reservoir (10^3m^3) 31152; Effective capacity of reservoir (10^3m^3) NA; Design purpose I; Designed spillway capacity (m^3/s) 799; Cultivable command area (hectares) NA Estimated cost (Rs. million) 41.50; Project irrigation potential (hectares) 2830.

Bommanhalli (Pick-up Dam-Kalinadi Project): Year of completion 1979; River Kali; Nearest city Dandeli; Type PG, TE; Height above lowest foundation (m) 28; Length of dam (m) 1030; Volume content of dam (10^3m^3) 496; Gross capacity of reservoir (10^3m^3) 136000; Effective capacity of reservoir (10^3m^3) 131120; Design purpose H; Designed spillway capacity (m^3/s) 9622;

Cultivable command area (hectares) NA; Estimated cost (Rs. million) 84.7; Project irrigation potential (hectares) NA.

Hidkal (Ghataprabha Project): Year of completion 1979; River Ghataprabha; Nearest city Belgaum; Type PG, TE; Height above lowest foundation (m) 60; Length of dam (m) 10183; Volume content of dam (10^3m^3) 7346; Gross capacity of reservoir (10^3m^3) 1449000; Effective capacity of reservoir (10^3m^3) 1387000; Design purpose I; Designed spillway capacity (m^3/s) 4616; Cultivable command area (hectares) NA; Estimated cost (Rs. million) 5100; Project irrigation potential (hectares) NA.

Almatti (Upper Krishna Project): Year of completion U.C.; River Krishna; Nearest city Bijapur; Type PG; Height above lowest foundation (m) 48; Length of dam (m) 1565; Volume content of dam (10^3m^3) 928; Gross capacity of reservoir (10^3m^3) 6425000; Effective capacity of reservoir (10^3m^3) 6092000; Design purpose I, H; Designed spillway capacity (m^3/s) 30989; Cultivable command area (hectares) 48561; Estimated cost (Rs. million) 558.4; Project irrigation potential (hectares) NA.

Amarja Irrigation Project: Year of completion U.C.; River Amarja; Nearest city Gulbarga; Type TE; Height above lowest foundation (m) 33; Length of dam (m) 860; Volume content of dam (10^3m^3) 1181; Gross capacity of reservoir (10^3m^3) 44010; Effective capacity of reservoir (10^3m^3) 40070; Design purpose I; Designed spillway capacity (m^3/s) 2811; Cultivable command area (hectares) NA; Estimated cost (Rs. million) 570; Project irrigation potential (hectares) NA.

Arkavathi: Year of completion U.C.; River Arkavathi; Nearest city Bangalore; Type TE; Height above ground level (m) 18; Length of dam (m) 488; Volume content of dam (10^3m^3) NA; Gross capacity of reservoir (10^3m^3) 26424; Effective capacity of reservoir (10^3m^3) NA; Design purpose I; Designed spillway capacity (m^3/s) NA; Cultivable command area (hectares) NA; Estimated cost (Rs. million) NA; Project irrigation potential (hectares) 3040.

Bellatha Sanahalla: Year of completion U.C.; River Local Stream; Nearest city Mysore; Type TE; Height above lowest foundation (m) 19; Length of dam (m) 113; Volume content of dam (10^3m^3) 50; Gross capacity of reservoir (10^3m^3) 671; Effective capacity of reservoir (10^3m^3) NA; Design purpose I; Designed spillway capacity (m^3/s) 145; Cultivable command area (hectares) NA; Estimated cost (Rs. million) NA; Project irrigation potential (hectares) NA.

Bennithora Irrigation Project: Year of completion U.C.; River Bennithora; Nearest city Gulbarga; Type TE, PG; Height above lowest foundation (m) 31; Length of dam (m) 1818; Volume content of dam (10^3m^3) NA; Gross capacity of reservoir (10^3m^3) 90482; Effective capacity of reservoir (10^3m^3) 81259; Design purpose I; Designed spillway capacity (m^3/s) 4791; Cultivable command area (hectares) NA; Estimated cost (Rs. million) 1600; Project irrigation potential (hectares) NA.

Bijjur: Year of completion U.C.; River Bijjur; Nearest city Kundapur; Type TE; Height above ground level (m) 21; Length of dam (m) 1616; Volume content of dam (10^3m^3) NA; Gross capacity of reservoir (10^3m^3) 16797; Effective capacity of reservoir (10^3m^3) NA; Design purpose I; Designed spillway capacity (m^3/s) NA; Cultivable command area (hectares) NA; Estimated cost (Rs. million) 19.50; Project irrigation potential (hectares) 1820.

Chakra (Chakra Project): Year of completion U.C.; River Chakra; Nearest city Shimoga; Type TE, ER; Height above lowest foundation (m) 84; Length of dam (m) 568; Volume content of dam (10^3m^3) 1715; Gross capacity of reservoir (10^3m^3) 219000; Effective capacity of reservoir (10^3m^3) 134000; Design purpose H; Designed spillway capacity (m^3/s) 1416; Cultivable command area (hectares) NA; Estimated cost (Rs. million) 116.10; Project irrigation potential (hectares) NA.

Gundal: Year of completion U.C.; River Gundal; Nearest city Kollegal; Type TE; Height above lowest foundation (m) 29; Length of Dam (m) NA; Volume content of dam (10^3m^3) NA; Gross capacity of reservoir (10^3m^3) 27442; Effective capacity of reservoir (10^3m^3) NA; Design purpose I; Designed spillway capacity (m^3/s) 463; Cultivable command area (hectares) NA; Estimated cost (Rs. million) 29.50; Project irrigation potential (hectares) 4050.

Hadagalla Tank: Year of completion U.C.; River Hadagalla Stream; Nearest city Gulbarga; Type TE; Height above lowest foundation (m) 13; Length of Dam (m) NA; Volume content of dam (10^3m^3) 87; Gross capacity of reservoir (10^3m^3) 2000; Effective capacity of reservoir (10^3m^3) NA; Design purpose I; Designed spillway capacity (m^3/s) NA; Cultivable command area (hectares) NA; Estimated cost (Rs. million) NA; Project irrigation potential (hectares) NA.

Harangi Res. Project: Year of completion U.C.; River Harangi; Nearest city Coorg; Type PG; Height above lowest foundation (m) 53; Length of dam (m) 846; Volume content of dam (10^3m^3) 538; Gross capacity of reservoir (10^3m^3) 240720; Effective capacity of reservoir

(10^3m^3) 228627; Design purpose I; Designed spillway capacity (m^3/s) 2730; Cultivable command area (hectares) NA; Estimated cost (Rs. million) 58000; Project irrigation potential (hectares) NA.

Harinala: Year of completion U.C.; River Harinala; Nearest city Belgaum; Type TE; Height above ground level (m) 21; Length of dam (m) 2271; Volume content of dam (10^3m^3) NA; Gross capacity of reservoir (10^3m^3) 949; Effective capacity of reservoir (10^3m^3) NA; Design purpose I; Designed spillway capacity (m^3/s) NA; Cultivable command area (hectares) NA; Estimated cost (Rs. million) 16.39; Project irrigation potential (hectares) 4350.

Hemavathy Res. Project: Year of completion U.C.; River Hemavathy; Nearest city Hassan; Type PG; Height above lowest foundation (m) 59; Length of dam (m) 4692; Volume content of dam (10^3m^3) 5420; Gross capacity of reservoir (10^3m^3) 1048000; Effective capacity of reservoir (10^3m^3) 963000; Design purpose I; Designed spillway capacity (m^3/s) 40.21; Cultivable command area (hectares) NA; Estimated cost (Rs. million) 12800; Project irrigation potential (hectares) NA.

Kohali Irrigation Tank: Year of completion U.C.; River Hirehalla; Nearest city Belgaum; Type TE; Height above lowest foundation (m) 14; Length of Dam (m) NA; Volume content of dam (10^3m^3) 10.4; Gross capacity of reservoir (10^3m^3) 2644; Effective capacity of reservoir (10^3m^3) NA; Design purpose I; Designed spillway capacity (m^3/s) 2711; Cultivable command area (hectares) NA; Estimated cost (Rs. million) NA; Project irrigation potential (hectares) NA.

Manchanabele Reservoir Project: Year of completion U.C.; River Arkavathy; Nearest city Bangalore; Type TE, PG; Height above lowest foundation (m) 34; Length of dam (m) 351; Volume content of dam (10^3m^3) 610; Gross capacity of reservoir (10^3m^3) 32000; Effective capacity of reservoir (10^3m^3) 27000; Design purpose I; Designed spillway capacity (m^3/s) 1545; Cultivable command area (hectares) NA; Estimated cost (Rs. million) 500; Project irrigation potential (hectares) NA.

Mani Dam (Varahi H.E. Project): Year of completion U.C.; River Varahi; Nearest city Shimoga; Type PG; Height above lowest foundation (m) 59; Length of dam (m) 505; Volume content of dam (10^3m^3) 790; Gross capacity of reservoir (10^3m^3) 1018470; Effective capacity of reservoir (10^3m^3) 928680; Design purpose H; Designed spillway capacity (m^3/s) 7588; Cultivable command area (hectares) NA; Estimated cost (Rs. million) 20500; Project irrigation potential (hectares) NA.

Mustrahally Tank: Year of completion U.C.; River Naihole; Nearest city K.G.F.; Type TE; Height above lowest foundation (m) 21; Length of dam (m) 197; Volume content of dam (10^3m^3) 93; Gross capacity of reservoir (10^3m^3) 24497; Effective capacity of reservoir (10^3m^3) NA; Design purpose I; Designed spillway capacity (m^3/s) 117; Cultivable command area (hectares) NA; Estimated cost (Rs. million) NA; Project irrigation potential (hectares) NA.

Narihalla Project: Year of completion U.C.; River Narihalla; Nearest city Bellary; Type TE; Height above lowest foundation (m) 32; Length of dam (m) 351; Volume content of dam (10^3m^3) 493; Gross capacity of reservoir (10^3m^3) 23000; Effective capacity of reservoir (10^3m^3) 21000; Design purpose I, S; Designed spillway capacity (m^3/s) 1237; Cultivable command area (hectares) 1400; Estimated cost (Rs. million) 350; Project irrigation potential (hectares) NA.

Narayanpur (Upper Krishna Project): Year of completion U.C.; River Krishna; Nearest city Lingsgur; Type TE, PG; Height above lowest foundation (m) 30; Length of dam (m) 10637; Volume content of dam (10^3m^3) 4586; Gross capacity of reservoir (10^3m^3) 1066000; Effective capacity of reservoir (10^3m^3) 863000; Design purpose I; Designed spillway capacity (m^3/s) 37944; Cultivable command area (hectares) 425000; Estimated cost (Rs. million) 4802; Project irrigation potential (hectares) NA.

New Irrigation Tank at Hosahalli: Year of completion U.C.; River Tr. of Tungabhadra; Nearest city Channagiri; Type TE; Height above lowest foundation (m) 20; Length of dam (m) 532; Volume content of dam (10^3m^3) NA; Gross capacity of reservoir (10^3m^3) 201; Effective capacity of reservoir (10^3m^3) NA; Design purpose I; Designed spillway capacity (m^3/s) 9; Cultivable command area (hectares) NA; Estimated cost (Rs. million) NA; Project irrigation potential (hectares) NA.

New Irrigation Tank at Huvinabhevi: Year of completion U.C.; River Tr. of Krishna; Nearest city Raichur; Type TE; Height above lowest foundation (m) 11; Length of dam (m) 545; Volume content of dam (10^3m^3) NA; Gross capacity of reservoir (10^3m^3) 1830; Effective capacity of reservoir (10^3m^3) NA; Design purpose I; Designed spillway capacity (m^3/s) 121; Cultivable command area (hectares) NA; Estimated cost (Rs. million) NA; Project irrigation potential (hectares) NA.

New Irrigation Tank at Janwada (West): Year of completion U.C.; River Tr. of Manjra; Nearest city Bidar; Type TE; Height above lowest foundation (m) 15; Length of Dam (m) NA; Volume content of dam (10^3m^3) NA; Gross capacity of reservoir (10^3m^3) 124; Effective capacity of reservoir (10^3m^3) NA; Design purpose I; Designed spillway capacity (m^3/s) 835; Cultivable command area (hectares) NA; Estimated cost (Rs. million) NA; Project irrigation potential (hectares) NA.

New Tank near Vederahalli: Year of completion U.C.; River Tr.of Cauvery; Nearest city Bangalore; Type TE; Height above lowest foundation (m) 29; Length of Dam (m) NA; Volume content of dam (10^3m^3) NA; Gross capacity of reservoir (10^3m^3) 4013; Effective capacity of reservoir (10^3m^3) NA; Design purpose I; Designed spillway capacity (m^3/s) 81; Cultivable command area (hectares) NA; Estimated cost (Rs. million) NA; Project irrigation potential (hectares) NA.

Savehaklu (Chakra Project): Year of completion U.C.; River Savehaklu; Nearest city Shimoga; Type TE; Height above lowest foundation (m) 53; Length of dam (m) 633; Volume content of dam (10^3m^3) 1493; Gross capacity of reservoir (10^3m^3) 154000; Effective capacity of reservoir (10^3m^3) 100000; Design purpose H; Designed spillway capacity (m^3/s) 176; Cultivable command area (hectares) NA; Estimated cost (Rs. million) 99.3; Project irrigation potential (hectares) NA.

Supa (Kalinadi Project): Year of completion U.C.; River Kali; Nearest city Dandeli; Type PG; Height above lowest foundation (m) 101; Length of dam (m) 322; Volume content of dam (10^3m^3) 1150; Gross capacity of reservoir (10^3m^3) 4418000; Effective capacity of reservoir (10^3m^3) 3977000; Design purpose H; Designed spillway capacity (m^3/s) 2830; Cultivable command area (hectares) NA; Estimated cost (Rs. million) 469.90; Project irrigation potential (hectares) NA.

Tarakka Reservoir Project: Year of completion U.C.; River Tarakka; Nearest city Kote; Type PG; Height above lowest foundation (m) 40; Length of dam (m) 180; Volume content of dam (10^3m^3) NA; Gross capacity of reservoir (10^3m^3) 112000; Effective capacity of reservoir (10^3m^3) 91000; Design purpose I; Designed spillway capacity (m^3/s) 1133; Cultivable command area (hectares) NA; Estimated cost (Rs. million) 81.7; Project irrigation potential (hectares) NA.

Tattihalla (Kalinadi Project): Year of completion U.C.; River Tattihalla (Tr.of Kali); Nearest city Dandeli; Type PG; Height above lowest foundation (m) 44; Length of dam (m) 1337; Volume content of dam (10^3m^3) 771; Gross capacity of reservoir (10^3m^3) 303000; Effective capacity of reservoir (10^3m^3) 251000; Design purpose H; Designed spillway capacity (m^3/s) 4730; Cultivable command area (hectares) NA; Estimated cost (Rs. million) 78.50; Project irrigation potential (hectares) NA.

Upper Mullamari Project: Year of completion U.C.; River Mullamari; Nearest city Bidar; Type TE; Height above lowest foundation (m) 33; Length of dam (m) 1879; Volume content of dam (10^3m^3) 593; Gross capacity of reservoir (10^3m^3) 21210; Effective capacity of reservoir (10^3m^3) 18864; Design purpose I; Designed spillway capacity (m^3/s) 651; Cultivable command area (hectares) NA; Estimated cost (Rs. million) 32.8; Project irrigation potential (hectares) NA.

Religion

Throughout its history, Karnataka has been the preferred sanctuary for a myriad of religions and faiths. Hinduism, Islam, Jainism, Sikhism and Christianity are the major religions in Karnataka. In a fine example of communal harmony, all these religions of Karnataka have peacefully co-existed over the years.

Hinduism: Of all the Karnataka religions, Hinduism enjoys an omnipresent stature. The succession of Hindu dynasties in Karnataka has patronized religious activities to a great extent while emphasizing on the building of temples and shrines. Within the confines of Hinduism, there are sects worshipping the deities of Lord Shiva and Vishnu. Banavasi, Basavakalyan, Udupi and Sringeri are the prominent Hindu pilgrimages of Karnataka.

Islam: Islam flourished in Karnataka with the emergence of powerful Muslim kingdoms. Besides spawning a plethora of monuments and forts, these dynasties established some of the magnificent mosques of Karnataka. With the creation of Deccan Sultanates and the invasion of Mughal rulers, Islam became the predominant religion in regions like Gulbarga and Bijapur. The Khwaja Bande Nawaz Durgah in Gulbarga is regarded as one of the holiest Muslim pilgrimages in Karnataka.

Jainism: Karnataka has been a hotbed for the religion of Jainism. Some of the most sacred Jain pilgrimages like Mudabidri and Shravanabelagola are located in Karnataka. The enormous statues of Lord Bahubali in Dharmasthala and Shravanabelagola attract Jain devotees in large numbers.

Sikhism: Sikhs are found in scattered locations of the state. The Gurudwara Nanak Jhira in Bidar is a prominent Sikh pilgrimage and this shrine was supposed to have been consecrated by Guru Nanak.

Christianity: Christianity is very much prevalent in Karnataka and some of India's most splendid churches are found in Mysore and Bangalore.

Distribution of Religion by Sex with Percentage of Total Population (State)

Religion	*T/R/U*	*Persons*	*Males*	*Females*	*%age*
Total Population	Total	52,850,562	26,898,918	25,951,644	100.00
	Rural	34,889,033	17,648,958	17,240,075	100.00
	Urban	17,961,529	9,249,960	8,711,569	100.00
Hindu	Total	44,300,304	22,537,633	21,762,671	83.82
	Rural	31,192,652	15,767,809	15,424,843	89.41
	Urban	13,107,652	6,769,824	6,337,828	72.98
Muslim	Total	6,460,522	3,301,316	3,159,206	12.22
	Rural	2,646,433	1,342,775	1,303,658	7.59
	Urban	3,814,089	1,958,541	1,855,548	21.23
Christian	Total	1,008,183	496,731	511,452	1.91
	Rural	328,124	163,446	164,678	0.94
	Urban	680,059	333,285	346,774	3.79
Sikh	Total	33,842	19,024	14,818	0.06
	Rural	13,772	7,550	6,222	0.04
	Urban	20,070	11,474	8,596	0.11
Buddhist	Total	400,499	210,028	190,471	0.76
	Rural	332,880	174,559	158,321	0.95
	Urban	67,619	35,469	32,150	0.38
Jain	Total	411,952	213,872	198,080	0.78
	Rural	218,511	113,312	105,199	0.63
	Urban	193,441	100,560	92,881	1.08
Other Religions	Total	115,448	58,710	56,738	0.22
	Rural	74,122	37,564	36,558	0.21
	Urban	41,326	21,146	20,180	0.23
Religion Not Stated	Total	119,812	61,604	58,208	0.23
	Rural	82,539	41,943	40,596	0.24
	Urban	37,273	19,661	17,612	0.21

Language

A great binding force here is language, which was the government's chief consideration while forming the boundary lines of Karnataka and other States in 1965. After Sanskrit, and Tamil, Kannada is the oldest Indian language, and is the State's official language. It is musical sounding, and has a number of words borrowed from Sanskrit as well as Persian and Urdu, and has in turn loaned certain words to Urdu and Marathi.

Urdu is spoken in Bijapur and Bidar in the north. In fact, it originated there during the period when it was part of the old state of Hyderabad, under the Nizam. Kannada is more logical than Sanskrit and Hindi, to the extent that gender is not an arbitrary matter. Objects which are inanimate belong to the neuter gender.

Tulu and Konkani are spoken languages only, used by the people living on the coast. Konkani is a full-fledged and expressive system. For written purposes, it handily borrows a script, such as the roman script in Goa, just north of the border of Karnataka, where Konkani is prevalent. Elsewhere, the Marathi or Kannada scripts are used.

The small and distinctive region of Coorg in Mangalore has its own language, Coorgi, which has resemblances to Tulu and Kannada. The Koudavas or Coorgis, are a distinct ethnic group with their own customs, cuisine and culture.

Literature

Creativity of human mind has found a generous expression in Karnataka in literature or art and architecture. Several literary forms in Kannada language have found remarkable exponents in Pampa, Ranna, Kumaravyasa or Sarvajna in the past and in K. V. Putappa, D. R. Bendre or Shivarama Karanth in the present.

History of Kannada Literature

Kannada is the language predominant in the state of Karnataka in India. Perhaps being the oldest language next to Sanskrit, Prakrit, and Tamil, Kannada country and language have a rich heritage. 'Kavirajamarga' of king Nripatunga (9th century A.D.) is believed to be the earliest literary work in Kannada. It is a treatise on poetics or a guide to poets indicating that Kannada was a fully developed literary language when Kavirajamarga (cu-ve-raa-ja-maarga) was composed. It refers to earlier linguists and poets whose works are not forthcoming.

But from epigraphical evidence it can be surmised that the spoken Kannada language evolved much earlier than the Halmidi inscription (c. 450 A.D.). Belonging to the Pro-Dravidian group it has close affinity with the Tamil language, prevalent now in the neighboring Tamil Nadu. But the language of the Halmidi inscription is highly Sanskritized.

Distribution of Language (State)

		Persons	*Males*	*Females*
Assamese	Total	829	573	256
	Rural	44	40	4
	Urban	785	533	252
Bengali	Total	20,926	12,331	8,595
	Rural	9,743	5,288	4,455
	Urban	11,183	7,043	4,140
Gujarati	Total	53,785	28,103	25,682
	Rural	9,304	4,835	4,469
	Urban	44,481	23,268	21,213
Hindi	Total	885,251	472,769	412,482
	Rural	576,149	299,172	276,977
	Urban	309,102	173,597	135,505
Kannada	Total	29,785,004	15,191,826	14,593,178
	Rural	23,253,783	11,795,764	11,458,019
	Urban	6,531,221	3,396,062	3,135,159
Kashmiri	Total	1,140	772	368
	Rural	39	30	9
	Urban	1,101	742	359
Konkani	Total	706,397	348,010	358,387
	Rural	395,800	194,285	201,515
	Urban	310,597	153,725	156,872
Malayalam	Total	757,030	397,802	359,228
	Rural	427,300	218,201	209,099
	Urban	329,730	179,601	150,129

		Persons	Males	Females
Manipuri	Total	272	180	92
	Rural	26	22	4
	Urban	246	158	88
Marathi	Total	1,640,020	832,832	807,188
	Rural	1,019,092	515,419	503,673
	Urban	620,928	317,413	303,515
Nepali	Total	4,702	3,044	1,658
	Rural	922	619	303
	Urban	3,780	2,425	1,355
Oriya	Total	5,474	3,923	1,551
	Rural	1,676	1,200	476
	Urban	3,798	2,723	1,075
Punjabi	Total	13,824	8,293	5,531
	Rural	982	720	262
	Urban	12,842	7,573	5,269
Sanskrit	Total	695	388	307
	Rural	424	235	189
	Urban	271	153	118
Sindhi	Total	13,930	6,979	6,951
	Rural	94	57	37
	Urban	13,836	6,922	6,914
Tamil	Total	1,728,361	896,809	831,552
	Rural	436,450	227,743	208,707
	Urban	1,291,911	669,066	622,845
Telugu	Total	3,325,062	1,699,250	1,625,812
	Rural	2,031,627	1,032,503	999,124
	Urban	1,293,435	666,747	626,688
Urdu	Total	4,480,038	2,293,424	2,186,614
	Rural	1,779,379	906,918	872,461
	Urban	2,700,659	1,386,506	1,314,153
Adi	Total	13	8	5
	Rural	6	2	4
	Urban	7	6	1
Angami	Total	13	8	5
	Rural	-	-	-
	Urban	13	8	5
Ao	Total	28	20	8
	Rural	6	4	2
	Urban	22	16	6
Arabic/Arbi	Total	2,875	1,535	1,340
	Rural	2,105	1,042	1,063
	Urban	770	493	277
Bhili/Bhilodi	Total	1,847	957	890
	Rural	559	289	270
	Urban	1,288	668	620
Bhotia	Total	188	188	-
	Rural	187	187	-
	Urban	1	1	-
Bodo/Boro	Total	15	9	6
	Rural	4	3	1
	Urban	11	6	5
Coorgi/Kodagu	Total	96,291	47,114	49,177
	Rural	73,454	36,135	37,319
	Urban	22,837	10,979	11,858
Dogri	Total	373	271	102
	Rural	27	27	-
	Urban	346	244	102
English	Total	15,675	7,673	8,002
	Rural	599	337	262
	Urban	15,076	7,336	7,740

		Persons	Males	Females
Gangte	Total	1	1	-
	Rural	-	-	-
	Urban	1	1	-
Garo	Total	13	3	10
	Rural	1	-	1
	Urban	12	3	9
Gondi	Total	397	208	189
	Rural	14	5	9
	Urban	383	203	180
Halabi	Total	3	-	3
	Rural	-	-	-
	Urban	3	-	3
Ho	Total	26	15	11
	Rural	-	-	-
	Urban	26	15	11
Jatapu	Total	1	-	1
	Rural	-	-	-
	Urban	1	-	1
Karbi/Mikir	Total	1	1	-
	Rural	-	-	-
	Urban	1	1	-
Khandeshi	Total	161	82	79
	Rural	145	75	70
	Urban	16	7	9
Kharia	Total	63	35	28
	Rural	61	34	27
	Urban	2	1	1
Khasi	Total	52	28	24
	Rural	11	4	7
	Urban	41	24	17
Kisan	Total	1	-	1
	Rural	-	-	-
	Urban	1	-	1
Koda/Kora	Total	12	9	3
	Rural	-	-	-
	Urban	12	9	3
Kom	Total	55	29	26
	Rural	55	29	26
	Urban	-	-	-
Konyak	Total	27	16	11
	Rural	-	-	-
	Urban	27	16	11
Korwa	Total	686	325	361
	Rural	363	170	193
	Urban	323	155	168
Koya	Total	6	3	3
	Rural	6	3	3
	Urban	-	-	-
Kui	Total	2	-	2
	Rural	-	-	-
	Urban	2	-	2
Kuki	Total	7	3	4
	Rural	-	-	-
	Urban	7	3	4
Kurukh/Oraon	Total	17	11	6
	Rural	4	2	2
	Urban	13	9	4
Lahnda	Total	4	2	2
	Rural	-	-	-
	Urban	4	2	2

		Persons	Males	Females
Limbu	Total	5	2	3
	Rural	-	-	-
	Urban	5	2	3
Lotha	Total	7	3	4
	Rural	-	-	-
	Urban	7	3	4
Lushai/Mizo	Total	103	59	44
	Rural	1	-	1
	Urban	102	59	43
Mishmi	Total	11	5	6
	Rural	-	-	-
	Urban	11	5	6
Monpa	Total	4	4	-
	Rural	4	4	-
	Urban	-	-	-
Munda	Total	3	1	2
	Rural	2	1	1
	Urban	1	-	1
Mundari	Total	1	-	1
	Rural	1	-	1
	Urban	-	-	-
Nicobarese	Total	5	5	-
	Rural	-	-	-
	Urban	5	5	-
Paite	Total	16	13	3
	Rural	8	7	1
	Urban	8	6	2
Santali	Total	11	10	1
	Rural	6	6	-
	Urban	5	4	1
Sema	Total	21	17	4
	Rural	-	-	-
	Urban	21	17	4
Sherpa	Total	4	2	2
	Rural	-	-	-
	Urban	4	2	2
Tangkhul	Total	5	5	-
	Rural	-	-	-
	Urban	5	5	-
Thado	Total	2	2	-
	Rural	-	-	-
	Urban	2	2	-
Tibetan	Total	23,182	13,493	9,689
	Rural	22,915	13,341	9,574
	Urban	267	152	115
Total of	Total	33,438	17,473	15,965
Other	Rural	9,596	4,965	4,631
Languages	Urban	23,842	12,508	11,334
Tripuri	Total	11	8	3
	Rural	-	-	-
	Urban	11	8	3
Tulu	Total	1,378,779	664,953	713,826
	Rural	1,016,439	485,219	531,220
	Urban	362,340	179,734	182,606

Distribution of Mother Toungue (State)

		Persons	Males	Females
Assamese	Total	819	564	255
	Rural	38	34	4
	Urban	781	530	251
Awadhi	Total	11	6	5
	Rural	-	-	-
	Urban	11	6	5
Badaga	Total	43	25	18
	Rural	8	5	3
	Urban	35	20	15
Banjari	Total	3,932	2,086	1,846
	Rural	3,092	1,590	1,502
	Urban	840	496	344
Bengali	Total	20,926	12,331	8,595
	Rural	9,743	5,288	4,455
	Urban	11,183	7,043	4,140
Bhojpuri	Total	669	480	189
	Rural	76	66	10
	Urban	593	414	179
Braj Bhasha	Total	244	122	122
	Rural	193	95	98
	Urban	51	27	24
Garhwali	Total	121	92	29
	Rural	42	36	6
	Urban	79	56	23
Gujarati	Total	43,849	23,072	20,777
	Rural	9,000	4,669	4,331
	Urban	34,849	18,403	16,446
Haryanvi	Total	228	152	76
	Rural	8	4	4
	Urban	220	148	72
Hindi	Total	270,280	154,131	116,149
	Rural	51,917	29,303	22,614
	Urban	218,363	124,828	93,535
Kachchhi	Total	1,147	574	573
	Rural	9	5	4
	Urban	1,138	569	569
Kaikadi	Total	310	161	149
	Rural	310	161	149
	Urban	-	-	-
Kannada	Total	29,775,374	15,186,878	14,588,496
	Rural	23,246,236	11,791,870	11,454,366
	Urban	6,529,138	3,395,008	3,134,130
Kashmiri	Total	1,133	765	368
	Rural	39	30	9
	Urban	1,094	735	359
Konkani	Total	700,274	344,987	355,287
	Rural	391,164	191,979	199,185
	Urban	309,110	153,008	156,102
Kumauni	Total	258	162	96
	Rural	-	-	-
	Urban	258	162	96
Labani	Total	2	1	1
	Rural	-	-	-
	Urban	2	1	1
Lamani/	Total	547,797	282,450	265,347
Lambadi	Rural	509,820	262,435	247,385
	Urban	37,977	20,015	17,962
Magadhi/	Total	31	24	7
Magahi	Rural	2	2	-
	Urban	29	22	7

		Persons	Males	Females
Maithili	Total	202	139	63
	Rural	17	17	-
	Urban	185	122	63
Malayalam	Total	733,596	385,905	347,691
	Rural	404,939	206,834	198,105
	Urban	328,657	179,071	149,586
Malvi	Total	28	12	16
	Rural	28	12	16
	Urban	-	-	-
Manipuri	Total	272	180	92
	Rural	26	22	4
	Urban	246	158	88
Marathi	Total	1,639,163	832,398	806,765
	Rural	1,018,798	515,271	503,527
	Urban	620,365	317,127	303,238
Marwari	Total	30,821	16,725	14,096
	Rural	682	390	292
	Urban	30,139	16,335	13,804
Mewari	Total	93	56	37
	Rural	32	16	16
	Urban	61	40	21
Nagpuria	Total	3	2	1
	Rural	2	1	1
	Urban	1	1	-
Nepali	Total	4,702	3,044	1,658
	Rural	922	619	303
	Urban	3,780	2,425	1,355
Nimadi	Total	1	1	-
	Rural	-	-	-
	Urban	1	1	-
Oriya	Total	4,889	3,622	1,267
	Rural	1,351	1,030	321
	Urban	3,538	2,592	946
Pahari	Total	51	29	22
	Rural	7	5	2
	Urban	44	24	20
Pawari/	Total	11	6	5
Powari	Rural	11	6	5
	Urban	-	-	-
Punjabi	Total	13,797	8,279	5,518
	Rural	982	720	262
	Urban	12,815	7,559	5,256
Rajasthani	Total	10,723	6,052	4,671
	Rural	685	429	256
	Urban	10,038	5,623	4,415
Sadan/Sadri	Total	11	11	-
	Rural	11	11	-
	Urban	-	-	-
Sanskrit	Total	695	388	307
	Rural	424	235	189
	Urban	271	153	118
Saurashtra/	Total	2,235	1,163	1,072
	Rural	43	29	14
	Urban	2,192	1,134	1,058
Sindhi	Total	12,736	6,375	6,361
	Rural	85	52	33
	Urban	12,651	6,323	6,328
Sugali	Total	45	24	21
	Rural	10	5	5
	Urban	35	19	16

		Persons	Males	Females
Tamil	Total	1,724,349	894,777	829,572
	Rural	434,130	226,576	207,554
	Urban	1,290,219	668,201	622,018
Telugu	Total	3,321,089	1,697,223	1,623,866
	Rural	2,029,829	1,031,594	998,235
	Urban	1,291,260	665,629	625,631
Urdu	Total	4,470,645	2,288,644	2,182,001
	Rural	1,774,439	904,419	870,020
	Urban	2,696,206	1,384,225	1,311,981
Vadari	Total	3,722	1,903	1,819
	Rural	1,587	808	779
	Urban	2,135	1,095	1,040
Yarava	Total	17,286	8,816	8,470
	Rural	17,079	8,731	8,348
	Urban	207	85	122
Yerukala/	Total	8	3	5
Yerukula	Rural	8	3	5
	Urban	-	-	-
Adi	Total	7	2	5
	Rural	6	2	4
	Urban	1	-	1
Adi	Total	6	6	-
Miniyong/	Rural	-	-	-
Miniyong	Urban	6	6	-
Angami	Total	12	7	5
	Rural	-	-	-
	Urban	12	7	5
Ao	Total	7	5	2
	Rural	6	4	2
	Urban	1	1	-
Arabic/Arbi	Total	2,875	1,535	1,340
	Rural	2,105	1,042	1,063
	Urban	770	493	277
Bhotia	Total	187	187	-
	Rural	187	187	-
	Urban	-	-	-
Bodo/Boro	Total	15	9	6
	Rural	4	3	1
	Urban	11	6	5
Coorgi/	Total	96,291	47,114	49,177
Kodagu	Rural	73,454	36,135	37,319
	Urban	22,837	10,979	11,858
Dangi	Total	7	3	4
	Rural	-	-	-
	Urban	7	3	4
Dogri	Total	373	271	102
	Rural	27	27	-
	Urban	346	244	102
English	Total	15,675	7,673	8,002
	Rural	599	337	262
	Urban	15,076	7,336	7,740
Gangte	Total	1	1	-
	Rural	-	-	-
	Urban	1	1	-
Garo	Total	3	1	2
	Rural	1	-	1
	Urban	2	1	1
Gondi	Total	163	81	82
	Rural	-	-	-
	Urban	163	81	82

		Persons	Males	Females
Halabi	Total	3	-	3
	Rural	-	-	-
	Urban	3	-	3
Ho	Total	26	15	11
	Rural	-	-	-
	Urban	26	15	11
Karbi/Mikir	Total	1	1	-
	Rural	-	-	-
	Urban	1	1	-
Kharia	Total	63	35	28
	Rural	61	34	27
	Urban	2	1	1
Khasi	Total	52	28	24
	Rural	11	4	7
	Urban	41	24	17
Kisan	Total	1	-	1
	Rural	-	-	-
	Urban	1	-	1
Koda/Kora	Total	10	7	3
	Rural	-	-	-
	Urban	10	7	3
Kokbarak	Total	11	8	3
	Rural	-	-	-
	Urban	11	8	3
Kom	Total	55	29	26
	Rural	55	29	26
	Urban	-	-	-
Konyak	Total	27	16	11
	Rural	-	-	-
	Urban	27	16	11
Korwa	Total	684	323	361
	Rural	363	170	193
	Urban	321	153	168
Koya	Total	6	3	3
	Rural	6	3	3
	Urban	-	-	-
Kui	Total	2	-	2
	Rural	-	-	-
	Urban	2	-	2
Kuki	Total	4	2	2
	Rural	-	-	-
	Urban	4	2	2
Kurukh/Oraon	Total	17	11	6
	Rural	4	2	2
	Urban	13	9	4
Limbu	Total	5	2	3
	Rural	-	-	-
	Urban	5	2	3
Lotha	Total	7	3	4
	Rural	-	-	-
	Urban	7	3	4
Lushai/Mizo	Total	103	59	44
	Rural	1	-	1
	Urban	102	59	43
Multani	Total	4	2	2
	Rural	-	-	-
	Urban	4	2	2
Munda	Total	3	1	2
	Rural	2	1	1
	Urban	1	-	1
Mundari	Total	1	-	1
	Rural	1	-	1
	Urban	-	-	-
Muria	Total	12	7	5
	Rural	-	-	-
	Urban	12	7	5
Nicobarese	Total	5	5	-
	Rural	-	-	-
	Urban	5	5	-
Paite	Total	16	13	3
	Rural	8	7	1
	Urban	8	6	2
Paradhi	Total	1,745	888	857
	Rural	513	260	253
	Urban	1,232	628	604
Pawri	Total	1	1	-
	Rural	-	-	-
	Urban	1	1	-
Santali	Total	11	10	1
	Rural	6	6	-
	Urban	5	4	1
Sema	Total	21	17	4
	Rural	-	-	-
	Urban	21	17	4
Sherpa	Total	4	2	2
	Rural	-	-	-
	Urban	4	2	2
Tangkhul	Total	5	5	-
	Rural	-	-	-
	Urban	5	5	-
Thado	Total	2	2	-
	Rural	-	-	-
	Urban	2	2	-
Tibetan	Total	23,182	13,493	9,689
	Rural	22,915	13,341	9,574
	Urban	267	152	115
Tulu	Total	1,377,810	664,456	713,354
	Rural	1,015,624	484,815	530,809
	Urban	362,186	179,641	182,545

Age wise Data (State)

Lakh

Age Ddistribution (in Percentage)									
	0 - 4 years			5 - 9 years			10 - 14 years		
	P	M	F	P	M	F	P	M	F
Total	11.4	11.3	11.4	12.7	12.5	12.8	12.0	11.9	12.1
Rural	11.9	11.9	11.8	13.1	13.0	13.2	12.1	12.1	12.1
Urban	10.3	10.1	10.5	11.8	11.5	12.0	11.7	11.4	11.9
	15 - 44 years			45 - 59 years			60 years and above		
	P	M	F	P	M	F	P	M	F
Total	45.9	45.9	45.9	10 .5	11.0	10.1	7.5	7.4	7.7
Rural	44.1	43.9	44.4	10.8	11.2	10.4	8.0	7.9	8.1
Urban	49.8	50.3	49.4	9.9	10.4	9.4	6.5	6.3	6.8

Disabled

Distribution of Disabled Persons by Type of Disabilty and Residence (in %)

State/ District	T/R/U	Total disabled population	In seeing	In speech	In hearing	In movement	Mental
Karnataka	T	940643	46.9	9.6	5.3	28.3	9.8
	R	661139	46.1	9.9	5.7	29.0	9.4
	U	279504	48.7	9.1	4.5	26.9	10.8
Belgaum	T	58900	30.5	11.0	6.1	40.2	12.3
	R	46070	29.1	11.1	6.7	41.2	11.9
	U	12830	35.3	10.5	4.1	36.4	13.7
Bagalkot *	T	28042	45.7	9.2	5.0	31.8	8.4
	R	21173	45.7	8.7	5.5	32.1	8.1
	U	6869	45.4	10.6	3.5	31.0	9.6
Bijapur	T	37315	51.0	8.5	4.2	27.1	9.2
	R	31041	52.5	8.6	4.3	25.9	8.6
	U	6274	43.1	8.2	3.8	32.7	12.1
Gulbarga	T	60657	46.5	8.8	5.1	31.9	7.6
	R	42354	42.0	9.4	6.0	34.8	7.7
	U	18303	57.0	7.3	2.9	25.2	7.6
Bidar	T	30224	44.0	8.5	4.9	34.1	8.5
	R	24814	44.5	8.4	5.3	33.6	8.3
	U	5410	41.6	9.1	3.3	36.5	9.6
Raichur	T	23349	47.1	9.0	5.0	30.7	8.2
	R	16243	41.0	9.8	6.0	34.4	8.8
	U	7106	61.0	7.3	2.7	22.2	6.7
Koppal *	T	21041	37.9	10.3	5.3	36.4	10.1
	R	17912	37.6	10.3	5.6	36.8	9.8
	U	3129	39.7	10.3	3.5	34.6	11.9
Gadag *	T	18355	39.9	8.7	6.5	35.4	9.5
	R	12867	44.8	8.8	5.7	32.7	8.1
	U	5488	28.6	8.7	8.3	41.7	12.7
Dharwad	T	23031	30.3	10.8	6.3	39.3	13.4
	R	11989	33.1	10.2	6.4	38.6	11.7
	U	11042	27.2	11.4	6.2	40.0	15.3
Uttara Kannada	T	28313	46.9	8.8	5.8	27.6	10.8
	R	21698	47.7	8.4	5.9	27.6	10.4
	U	6615	44.4	9.8	5.6	27.9	12.4
Haveri *	T	26635	42.1	10.3	5.2	31.4	11.0
	R	21252	42.6	10.7	4.8	31.2	10.7
	U	5383	40.4	8.6	6.5	32.1	12.4
Bellary	T	37270	48.6	9.1	4.3	29.4	8.6
	R	24396	45.3	9.2	4.8	32.8	8.0
	U	12874	55.0	9.1	3.4	22.9	9.6
Chitradurga	T	31971	48.7	10.1	5.3	27.9	8.1
	R	26307	47.6	10.5	5.7	27.8	8.3
	U	5664	53.8	8.0	3.1	27.9	7.1
Davanagere*	T	33904	45.8	10.3	4.5	29.5	9.9
	R	24689	48.2	9.8	4.7	28.1	9.2
	U	9215	39.4	11.8	3.9	33.3	11.7
Shimoga	T	26612	39.9	10.3	6.3	32.1	11.4
	R	19068	41.5	10.2	6.1	31.3	10.9
	U	7544	35.8	10.7	6.5	34.3	12.7
Udupi *	T	17050	39.5	12.9	4.7	24.8	17.9
	R	14777	40.6	13.2	4.7	24.4	17.0
	U	2273	32.6	11.3	4.8	27.5	23.9
Chikmagalur	T	25263	57.7	8.0	5.0	21.6	7.6
	R	20886	56.7	8.1	5.4	22.0	7.8
	U	4377	62.4	7.6	3.4	19.6	7.0
Tumkur	T	49391	46.1	11.4	5.8	27.7	9.0
	R	41178	45.4	11.5	6.2	27.9	9.0
	U	8213	49.6	11.1	3.9	26.2	9.1
Kolar	T	44426	45.5	10.6	5.6	28.0	10.4
	R	35540	45.3	10.6	5.7	28.3	10.2
	U	8886	46.2	10.8	5.2	26.6	11.2
Bangalore	T	94228	50.7	8.2	5.0	25.1	11.0
	R	13108	44.4	9.5	5.9	28.9	11.2
	U	81120	51.7	8.0	4.9	24.5	11.0
Bangalore Rural	T	39616	48.0	9.6	5.6	27.2	9.6
	R	32735	48.1	9.7	6.0	26.7	9.5
	U	6881	47.2	9.1	3.7	29.9	10.0
Mandya	T	41842	59.8	9.7	4.3	19.1	7.1
	R	35693	59.3	9.7	4.5	19.4	7.1
	U	6149	62.4	9.6	3.3	17.7	7.1
Hassan	T	29481	42.3	10.5	8.1	30.0	9.1
	R	25392	43.1	10.2	8.6	29.2	9.0
	U	4089	37.2	12.9	5.2	34.9	9.9
Dakshina Kannada	T	37999	52.2	8.6	4.3	20.6	14.2
	R	21978	46.4	9.6	5.1	23.6	15.2
	U	16021	60.2	7.2	3.3	16.4	12.9
Kodagu	T	7666	44.4	9.7	8.8	26.1	11.0
	R	6798	44.4	9.8	9.2	25.9	10.7
	U	868	44.2	8.9	5.8	28.1	13.0
Mysore	T	44094	54.6	11.0	5.8	20.1	8.5
	R	29972	55.5	10.7	5.8	20.3	7.8
	U	14122	52.8	11.7	5.8	19.8	9.9
Chamarajanagar*	T	23968	67.3	8.3	3.6	14.6	6.2
	R	21209	67.7	8.2	3.6	14.6	5.9
	U	2759	64.5	8.8	3.1	15.2	8.4

Drinking water

The State is endowed with limited water resources that are stressed and depleting. Different Sectoral demands are growing rapidly. Increase in population, urbanization, rapid industrialization and rising incomes are putting this resource under stress. Unless water resources are properly developed and managed, the State will face acute crisis within the next two decades. Serious destabilization of the water sector affecting the hydrology, economy and ecology of the State is likely.

Distribution of Household by Sources of Drinking Water

		Total	Rural	Urban
INDIA				
Tap	Total	70,448,827	33,583,755	36,865,072
	Within Premises	39,966,085	13,289,645	26,676,440
	Near Premises	24,998,605	16,908,647	8,089,958
	Away	5,484,137	3,385,463	2,098,674
Handpump	Total	68,456,319	59,736,874	8,719,445
	Within Premises	21,332,741	16,899,373	4,433,368
	Near Premises	36,605,076	33,442,465	3,162,611
	Away	10,518,502	9,395,036	1,123,466

Tubewell	Total	10,676,594	7,930,488	2,746,106
	Within Premises	3,138,814	1,583,518	1,555,296
	Near Premises	4,794,142	4,065,129	729,013
	Away	2,743,638	2,281,841	461,797
Well	Total	34,873,103	30,732,819	4,140,284
	Within Premises	9,961,068	7,618,694	2,342,374
	Near Premises	15,650,450	14,555,796	1,094,654
	Away	9,261,585	8,558,329	703,256
Tank, Pond, etc.	Total	1,936,671	1,769,496	167,175
	Within Premises	268,380	233,258	35,122
	Near Premises	860,293	798,155	62,138
	Away	807,998	738,083	69,915
River, Canal	Total	1,943,863	1,840,868	102,995
	Within Premises	0	0	0
	Near Premises	829,904	778,200	51,704
	Away	1,113,959	1,062,668	51,291
Spring	Total	1,415,997	1,283,098	132,899
	Within Premises	0	0	0
	Near Premises	614,404	539,449	74,955
	Away	801,593	743,649	57,944
Any other	Total	2,212,561	1,394,161	818,400
	Within Premises	136,181	74,259	61,922
	Near Premises	759,396	472,891	286,505
	Away	1,316,984	847,011	469,973
KARNATAKA				
Tap	Total	6,025,364	3,235,817	2,789,547
	Within Premises	2,468,101	750,419	1,717,682
	Near Premises	2,741,505	1,939,315	802,190
	Away	815,758	546,083	269,675
Handpump	Total	1,750,387	1,530,208	220,179
	Within Premises	108,065	71,271	36,794
	Near Premises	1,052,937	944,174	108,763
	Away	589,385	514,763	74,622
Tubewell	Total	876,001	609,016	266,985
	Within Premises	184,767	70,823	113,944
	Near Premises	403,499	320,805	82,694
	Away	287,735	217,388	70,347
Well	Total	1,268,913	1,038,380	230,533
	Within Premises	474,771	334,769	140,002
	Near Premises	436,551	390,357	46,194
	Away	357,591	313,254	44,337
Tank, Pond, etc.	Total	110,689	100,592	10,097
	Within Premises	7,894	6,884	1,010
	Near Premises	41,384	38,863	2,521
	Away	61,411	54,845	6,566
River, Canal	Total	111,748	105,028	6,720
	Within Premises	0	0	0
	Near Premises	46,156	41,960	4,196
	Away	65,592	63,068	2,524
Spring	Total	30,540	28,511	2,029
	Within Premises	0	0	0
	Near Premises	14,279	12,690	1,589
	Away	16,261	15,821	440
Any other	Total	58,491	27,621	30,870
	Within Premises	3,903	2,029	1,874
	Near Premises	13,032	7,579	5,453
	Away	41,556	18,013	23,543

Electrcity

Karnataka was the pioneer in establishing hydroelectric project in the country. Today, Karnataka has 7222.91 Power Generation Installed capacity and 31,229 Million Units of Electricity was generated in 2007-08.

Distribution of workers

Work participation rate		
	Total main Worker (in '000s)	*Total Marginal Worker (in '000s)*
Persons	17,292	1,595
Males	12,285	129
Females	5,007	1,466

Total Non-Worker (in '000s)			*Per cent main Worker engaged in Agricultural labour, Cultivation Livestock, Forestry, etc.*	
P	26,090	34.2	28.9	3.6
M	10,538	37.7	20.4	3.8
F	15,552	25.7	49.7	3.0

Fairs and Festivals

Adi Shaktyattmaka Sri Annapurneshvari : It is held at Horanadu in Chikmagalur area sometime in the month of March-April for one day.

Adi Shaktyattmaka Sri Annapurneshvari : It is held at Horanadu in Chikmagalur area sometime in the month of March-April for one day.

Adi Subrahmanyeshwara Jatra : It is held at Gonibeedu in Chikmagalur area in the month of March every year.

Baba Prabhu Jatra : It is held at Karaknali in Bidar area in the month of March for five days every year. Karaknali is about 42 kms. south-east of Humnabad town.

Balamuri Fair : Balamuri near Murnad is 18 kms. away from Madidri in Kadagu. One of the sacred places for the Kodavas, the well-known pilgrimage centre is on the banks of the Cauvery. It is here that the river changes her course to the right in a crescent curve. Hence, the name 'Balamuri'. From ancient times, it was known as 'Valampuri' a famous Shaiva centre.

Cauvery Festival : Talakaveri is the birth place of the sacred river, Cauvery. It is situated on the slopes of the Brahmagiri Hills.

The Cauvery *jatra* which begins on the Tula Sankramana day continues for one full month and is an event of great importance to the people of Coorg and the surrounding districts.

Chandralamba Jatra : Sonthi is a place in Chittapur taluk near Gulbarga though a small place has become renowned for its Chandralamba temple, which is visited by a large number of Hindus. In March-April every year, a *jatra* is held here.

Dabbaguli Basaveshwara Temple Jatra : Dubbaguli Basaveshwara temple *jatra* is held at Vanakanahalli in Bangalore district in the month of *Chaitra* (March-April). Vanakanahalli situated at a distance of five kms. to the south of Anekal appears to be an ancient place.

Dakke-Bali Festival : Padubidri near Dakshin Kannade, about 26 kms. from Udipi on the Udipi-Mangalore Road, was the seat of chiefs known as Ballalas. It has a *Brahmasthana*, a Mahalingeshwara temple and a Mahaganapati temple which are well-known. A religious festival called the *dakke-bali* is held in the *Brahmasthana* here once in two years.

Gadadam Venkataramanaswami Jatra : Gadadam Venkataramanaswami *jatra* is held at Devaragudipalli near Kotor in the month of *Vaishakha* (April-May) for seven days. Devaragudipalli, situated about 5 kms. from Bagepalli, has a well-known temple dedicated to Venkataramanaswamy.

Gaddi-Khader Wali Urs : Mukkunda, in Sindhanur taluk of Roichar area is situated on the banks of the Tungabhadra, nearby a hill, about 26 kms. from Sindhanur. An island in the river has the *dargah* of Gaddikhader Wali, where an annual *Urs* is held which attracts a large number of people.

Hagaranada Habba Jatra : Hagaranada Habba Jatra is held at Hiregouja in Chikmagalur district once in seven years for seven days. Hiregouja is 14 kms. north east of Chikmagalur town.

Haladamma Jatra : Marikoppa near Shimoga, about four kilometres west of Honnali town on Honnali-Shimoga Road, has a famous shrine dedicated to Haladamma. A *jatra* of the deity is held twice a year around March-April and September-October.

Imam Jaffar Urs : Savadi 28 kms. from Athani in Belgaum district. The place has a Virakta Matha and a *dargah* of Imam Jaffar, whose *Urs* is held at Davanada Hunnime where about 10,000 people assemble. There is also a stone mosque of considerable antiquity.

Inam Dattatreya Peetha Festival : Inam Dattatreya Peetha, is situated on Baba-Budan Giri at a distance of about 30 kms. north of Chikmagalur town. An annual *jatra* or *urs*, which is held under the auspices of the *peetha* for three days after the holi festival according to Hindu calendar, is attended by both Hindus and Muslims.

Jagannath Maharaj Fair : An annual fair is held at Rajeshvar near Bidar in honour of Saint Jagannath Maharaj in the month of April.

Rajeshvar is a place about 20 kms. south-east of Basavakalyan town.

Jain Basadis Jatra : Narasimharajapura in Chikmagalur district, previously called Yedehalli, is 88 kms. north-west of Chikmagalur town, 54 kms. west of Tarikere town. 42 kms. south-west of Bhadravali town and 330 kms. north-west of Bangalore City.

Kadasiddheshwara and Maradi Matha Jatra : Kadasiddheshwara Matha jatra is held at Konnur in Belgaum district in about the month of April every year.

Konnur 11 kilometres from Gokak, located on the right bank of the river Ghataprabha is one of the earliest settlements in the district.

Kadlurayya Fair : The Kadlurayya fair is held at Kadlur in Raichur district in the month of Margashira (December) and attracts a good number of people.

Ladle Moray Mushaik Urs : Ladle Moray Mushaik Urs is observed at Aland in the month of 9 Rabi-us-Sani for four days.

Lakshmi Jatra : Lakshmi jatra is held at Hattargi in Belgaum district.

Madarsab Bavasaburs : Madarsab Bavasaburs Urs in held at Ammangi in Belgaum district every year.

Madeppa Swami Jatra : Madeppa Swami jatra is held at Narayanapur near Bidar, in about the month of July for two days.

Nadavali Festival : Nadavali festival is held at the temple of Manjumatha at Dharmasthala near Dakshina Kannada district once in twelve years, for thirteen days.

Naganatha Devara Jatra : Naganatha Devara jatra is held at Hallikhed near Bidar in about the month of October for three days.

Obaleshvara Jatra : Obaleshvara jatra is held at Gopala near Chikmagalur around the month of February-March every year.

Padmavati Utsava : Padmavati utsava is held at Ugar Khurd, Belgaum area in about the month of May every year.

Padmavatiamma Rathotsava : Padmavatiamma Rathotsava is observed at the temple of Padmavati at Humcha near Shimoga around the month of March every year.

Ramalinga Temple Jatra : Ramalinga temple jatra is held at Tavadi near Belgaum in the month of Shravana (July-August).

Rajarajeshwari Temple Car Festival : Rajarajeshwari temple car festival is held at Polali near Dakshina Kannada district every year.

Sadanandaswami Festival : Sadanandaswami festival is held at Sadananda Saraswati Matha at Basavakalyan near Bidar in the month of July every year.

Sadashiva Car Festival : Sadashiva temple car festival is held at Surathkal near Dakshina Kannada around the month of December every year.

Teppotsava Festival : Teppotsava festival is held at

Madagadakere near Shimoga around the month of February every year.

Teru-Malleshwara Jatra : The jatra of Teru-Malleshwara is celebrated for a week from the full moon day of Magha (January - February) at Hiriyur, near Chitradurga.

Uchchangi Amma Temple Dasara Festival : There is a well-known temple of Uchchangi-amma at Uchchangidurga in Bellary district. The Dasara festival is held in this temple and is largely attended.

Udumaradi Ranganatha Car Festival : A car festival is observed at the temple of lord Udumaradi Ranganatha at Devarahalli near Shimoga around the month of March-April for five days.

Vadiraja Jatra : Vadiraja jatra is held at Sonda near Uttara Kannada for one day in the months of April-May every year.

Vairamudi Festival : The Vairamudi festival is observed at Melkote near Mandya in the month of Chaitra (March-April) for 6 days in the honour of Lord Cheluvaraya-swamy.

Yoganarasimhaswamy Jatra : Yoganarasimhaswamy jatra is held at Gorur in Hassan district about January-February for a period of 15 days.

Zahiruddin Shah Urs : An annual Urs is held at Hadikere near Chikmagalur in honour of Zahiruddin Shah at his dargah for two days. Hadikere is about six kilometres north of Tarikore town.

Zinda Shah Madar Urs : An Urs in honour of Zinda Shah Madar is held at Kohinoor-Pahad near Bidar in the month of Jamadilawwal for four days.

Abbreviations

BCM	: Billion Cubic Meter	NA	: Not Available
C	: Flood Control	NH	: National Highway
C.D. Block	: Community Development Block	O.G	: Outgrowth
CB	: Buttress	PG	: Gravity
ER	: Rockfill	R	: Purposes
GP	: Gram Panchayat	S	: Water Supply Recreational
GDP	: Gross Domestic Product	SC	: Scheduled Caste
H	: Hydro-electric	SH	: State Highway
HAM	: Hectare Meter	Sqs. Kms	: Square Kilometers
HQ	: Headquarters	ST	: Scheduled Tribes
I	: Irrigation	TE	: Earth
L	: Uncontrolled Spillway	U	: C.-Under Construction
MCM	: Million Cubic Meter	UE	: Universalisation of Elementary Education
MM	: Millimeter	VA	: Arch
MV	: Multi Arch	V	: Controlled Spillway
N	: Navigation	WRP	: Work Participation Rate

AFZALPUR

Afzalpur C.D. Block lies in the western part of Gulbarga district.It is a part of Afzalpur taluka. The Block is located at a distance of 46 kms. from district H.Q. (Gulbarga). There are 93 villages in the block with the total Pop. of 160,702 persons. Area of the C.D Block is 1301.73 sq. kms. It is bounded by taluk Aland on north, district Bijapur and taluk Jevargi on south, taluk Gulbarga on east, district Bijapur on west, and it has common boundary with the state of Maharashtra on north.

Communications:

Roadways : S.H-22: Direction- Akalkot to Gulbarga, Nearest Villages- Mannur, Karajagi, Ramnagar, Bhankalga, Shirwad, Gour (K), Gour (B), Afzalpur (Rural), Matoli, Mallabad, Atnoor, Shivajinagar, Ingalgi (B), Chowdapur, Gobbur (B), Gobbur (K), Hawanur, Chinmmgera.

Railway Station: Villages- Kulali, Gudur.

River: Bhima Nadi- Nearest Villages- Mannur, Kodagnur, Shivoor, Udchan, Algi (B), Bhosga, Hiriyal, Dudangi, Mangaroli, Soan, Afzalpur (Rural), Banhatti, Shivpur, Kesapur, Hinchgera, Kalur, Batgera, Guolnur, Ingalgi (K), Hawalga, Ghatterga,Kolnur, Guddewadi, D.Ghangapur, Banderwad, Chinmmgera, Teghalli, Siragi, Taklu, Umerga, Sagnur, Kirsavalgi, Chinmalla, Kekarsawalgi. Awarja Nadi- Nearest Villages- Tellur, Karkanahalli, Batgera, Goudgaon, Kognur, Diksanga (B), Karbhosga, Madra (K),Dannur, Madra (B), Badnalli, Ingalgi (B), Awarad, D. Ghangapur, Chowdapur.

Annual Rainfall: Normal Rianfall 777 mm.

Ground Water: Availability of the Ground Water in the Basin is 8439 H.A.M. and the utilization is 4052 H.A.M. It belongs to Over Exploited category. Depth to water level 2 to 20 meter below the ground. Most of the wells go down in summer months, according to the Ground Water Estimation Committee.

Soils: Deep Black, Medium Black Soil, Shallow Soil and Lateritic Soil.

Natural Division : It falls in the Lower Bhima Valley of the Northern Karnataka Plateau.

Administration:

Division: Gulbarga. Parliamentary Constituency: 5 Gulbarga (SC). District: Gulbarga. Taluka: Afzalpur. Assembly Constituency: 34 Afzalpur. Gram Panchayat: 22.

Regional Area Development Boards: The Hyderabad-Karnataka Area Development Board.

Border Villages: (State: Maharashtra)- Mannur, Vithalnagar, Mashal, Jevargi(B), Jevargi (K), Karajagi, Ramnagar, Belurgi, Badadal, Arjungi.

Fairs: Dattatraya Maharaj Jatra: Dattatraya Maharaj jatra is held at Ghangapur near Gulbarga in the month of magha (Feb).Ghangapur is a pilgrim centre in Afzalpur taluk 16 kms. in Gulbarga south of Ghangapur railway station on the Chennai-Mumbai railway route. It is highly venerated by the Hindus of both Karnatakaand Maharashtra States. The sacred temple of Shri Narasimha Saraswathi Datta Maharaj is situated here. Pilgrims visit Ghangapurthroughout the year to worship at the temple and also to take holy bath at the confluence of the river Amerja and Bhima. There are two large Dharmashalas for the use of pilgrims. It is estimated that on an average 500 pilgrims visit this place daily to worship the Dattatraya Paduka. Around the month of February, a big jatra is held at this place at which one lakh pilgrims congregate.Government road transport buses are run from Ghangapur railway station to this place every day. For the pilgrims, this place is known as Deval Ghangapur.

Villages: 93 **Inhabited:** 89 **Uninhabited:** 4

Ranking	District	State	National
Area	9	51	221
Population	9	119	1539
Sex Ratio	10	147	3497
Child Sex Ratio	6	121	3538
Literacy Rate	2	147	4610
Density	10	144	5919
Work Participation Rate	9	153	3379

Gram Panchayats:

Mannur, Mashal, Badadal, Revoor (B), Kognur, Gudur, Bhairamadgi, Belurgi, Karajagi, Udchan, Gour(B), Mallabad, Atnoor, Chowdapur, Gobbur(B), Bidnur, Banderwad, D.Ghangapur, Anur, Algi(B), Kalur, Hasargundgi.

Amenities:

Education: Primary School in 89 villages, Middle school in 58 villages, Matriculation or Secondary School in 22 villages, namely Mannur, Mashal, Jevargi(B), Jevargi (K), Karajagi, Shivoor, Udchan, Belurgi, Badadal, Revoor (K), Revoor (B), Mallabad, Ghatterga, Gudur, Neeloor, Bhairamadgi, Atnoor, D.Ghangapur, Gobbur (B), Banderwad, Chinmmgera, Sagnur.

Higher Secondary or Pre University Courses or Intermediate or Junior College in 2 villages of the CD Block,, namely Karajagi, Udchan.

College in 0 village, Adult Literacy Center in 4 villages.

Medical: Hospital in 1 village, Dispensary in 11 villages, Health Center in 10 villages, Sub Center in 35 villages, Maternity and Child Welfare Center in 3 villages, Community health workers in 30 villages.

The Villages having Hospital or Dispensary or Health Center are Mannur, Karajagi, Udchan, Belurgi, Revoor (B), Kalur, Ghatterga, Atnoor, D.Ghangapur, Chowdapur, Banderwad.

Drinking Water: Tap water in 63 villages, Tank water in 6 villages, Well water in 49 villages, Tubewell in 50 villages and more than one source in 88 villages.

Bank: Banking facility in 15 villages, namely, Mannur, Mashal, Karajagi, Udchan, Revoor (K) Revoor (B), Kalur, Gudur, Atnoor, D.Ghangapur Chowdapur, Gobbur (B), Banderwad, Hasargundgi Sagnur.

Credit Society in 14 villages Agricultural Credit Society in 13 Non-Agricultural Credit Society in 0 village.

Others: Power supply in 89 villages, Cinema hall in 0 village, sport club in 4 villages, Stadium or Auditorium or Community Hall in 89 villages, Post Office in 44 villages.

There are 65 villages having bus facilities.

Villages with most of facilities: Mannur, Mashal Karajagi, Udchan, Revoor (K), Revoor (B), Kalur Atnoor, D.Ghangapur, Chowdapur, Gobbur (B) Banderwad, Hasargundgi, Sagnur.

Villages without Amenities (Education): None..

Scheduled Castes: Out of the total population of 160736 persons, 28607 persons (17.8%) belong to Scheduled Castes. The villages having less than 10% SC population are Mannur, Vithalnagar, Diksanga (K), Ramnagar, Shivoor Udchan, Hiriyal, Mangaroli, Matoli, Shivpur, Kesapur Badnalli, Awarad, Awarhalli.

The village having more than 50% SC population is None.

Sex ratio of Scheduled Caste population is 485.

Scheduled Castes Literates and Illiterates by Sex:

	Persons	Males	Females
Literate	9,896	6,647	3,249
Illiterate	18,711	8,099	10,612
Literacy rate	41.9	54.6	28.4
Graduate	334	304	30

Scheduled Castes (Dominant):

Holaya etc., Banjara etc., Madiga, Bhovi Generic Castes etc.

For their cultural identity please see Appendix-I

Villages without Scheduled Castes: There are 7 villages without any scheduled caste population.

Scheduled Tribes: Out of the total population of 160736 persons, 3667 persons (2.28%) belong to Scheduled Tribes. The villages having less than 10% ST population are Mannur, Vithalnagar, Mashal, Jevargi(B), Jevargi (K) Nanderga, Telloni, Diksanga (K), Karajagi, Ramnagar Kodagnur, Shivoor, Udchan, Bhankalga, Shirwad Algi (K), Algi (B), Bhosga, Hiriyal, Dudangi Mangaroli, Soan, Gour (K), Gour (B), Belurgi Arjungi, Kulali, Revoor (K), Revoor (B), Chincholi Haliyal, Matoli, Mallabad, Bilwad (K), Tellur, Anur Kesapur, Hinchgera, Kalur, Bilwad (B), Karkanahalli Batgera, Guolnur, Hawalga, Ghatterga, Kolnur Guddewadi, Sidnur, Ankalga, Goudgaon, Kognur, Gudur Neeloor, Bhairamadgi, Diksanga (B), Karbhosga Bhognalli, Atnoor, Madra (K), Dannur, Madra (B) Wadhalli, Shivajinagar, Badnalli, Ingalgi (B) Awarad, Chowdapur, Gobbur (B), Gobbur (K), Hawanur Awarhalli, Banderwad, Chinmmgera, Teghalli Hasargundgi, Huvinhalli, Siragi, Taklu, Umerga Sagnur, Kirsavalgi, Chinmalla, Kekarsawalgi.

The villages having more than 50% ST population are None.

Sex ratio of Scheduled tribe population is 473.

Scheduled Tribes Literates and Illiterates by Sex:

	Persons	Males	Females
Literate	1,431	936	495
Illiterate	2,236	995	1,241
Literacy rate	47.0	59.1	33.9
Graduate	39	33	6

Scheduled Tribes (Dominant):

Koli Dhor etc., Koya etc., Gond etc., Naikda etc. Iruliga

For their cultural identity please see Appendix-II

Villages without Scheduled Tribes: There are 69 villages without any scheduled tribe population.

Literates and Illiterates by Sex (Total Population):

	Persons	Males	Females
Literate	66,455	43,053	23,402
Illiterate	94,281	39,394	54,887
Literacy rate	50	63	36
Graduate	1,993	1,748	245

Agriculture: ***Distribution of villages according to land use:*** Out of 93 villages, Total area (in hectare) is 130173, out of that 87.68 percent is cultivable and 5.01 percent of the cultivable area is irrigated.

Sources of Irrigation (Hectares): Government Canal 0, Private Canal 0, Well without Electricity 14.16, Well with Electricity 3400.07, Tubewell without Electricity 90.41, Tubewell with Electricity 1078.79, Tank 9.81, River 1074.32, Lake 0, Waterfall 0, Others 46.63.

Villages with population of 5000 to 9999: Mashal, Karajagi, Udchan, D.Ghangapur, Gobbur (B).

Villages with population of 10000 and above: Mannur.

Distribution of Workers:

	Persons	Males	Females	WPR
Cultivators	21,534	17,815	3,719	30.91
Agricultural Labour	34,688	14,334	20,354	49.79
Household Industry	1,896	1,301	595	2.72
Other Workers	11,544	9,304	2,240	16.57

Main Workers	49,103	36,751	12,352	70.49
Marginal Workers	20,559	6,003	14,556	29.51
Total Workers	69,662	42,754	26,908	

Religion: Major Religious Communities:

	Persons	Males	Females	Sex Ratio
Hindu (80.89%)	130,017	66,757	63,260	948
Muslim (12.2%)	19,610	9,950	9,660	971
Christian (0.06%)	98	52	46	885
Sikh (0.01%)	12	6	6	1,000
Buddhists (6.13%)	9,855	5,097	4,758	933
Jain (0.18%)	292	156	136	872

Agewise Data:

	Persons	Males	Females	Sex Ratio
All ages	160,736	82,447	78,289	950
0-14	62,296	31,792	30,504	959
15-44	67,339	35,367	31,972	904
45-79	29,618	14,558	15,060	1034
80+	1,353	653	700	1072
Age not stated	130	77	53	688

Languages (Dominant):
Kannada, Urdu, Hindi, Marathi, Telugu

Disabled Population:

	Persons	Males	Females	%
Total Disabled	2,534	1,400	1,134	
In Seeing	898	417	481	35.44
In Speech	264	152	112	10.42
In Hearing	151	82	69	5.96
In Movement	952	593	359	37.57
Mentally	269	156	113	10.62

ALAND

Aland C.D. Block lies in the north-western part of Gulbarga district. It is a part of Aland taluka. The Block is located at a distance of 43 kms. from district headquarters (Gulbarga). There are 136 villages in the block with the total population of 259,530 persons. Area ofthe CD Block is 1716.90 sq.kms. It is bounded by district Bidar on north, taluk Afzalpur on south, taluk Gulbarga on east, and it has common boundary with the state of Maharashtra on north, south and west.

Communications:

Roadways : S.H.-10: Direction- Wagdari to Gulbarga, Nearest Villages- Aland (Rural), Khanapur, Jamga.J, Shakhapur, Yelinawadgi, Bolani, Hiroli, Sarasamba, Nagelagaon, Allapur (H), Sawleshwar, Ladchincholi, Nellur, Kadganchi, Sunthnoor. S.H.-11: Direction- Basavakalyan to Ladmugli, Nearest Villages- Ladmugli, Ambalga. S.H.-32: Direction- Aland to Umarga and Mahagaon, Nearest Vill.- Khajuri, Rudrawadi, Bableshwar, Bangerga, Chitali, Sangunda, Belamogi, Karhari, Salgera (V.K.), Ladmugli, Ambalga, Dhammur, Madki, Telekuni, Tadkal, Haltadkal, Walwandwadi, Munhalli, Mamdapur, Aland (Rural).

Railway Station: Villages- Benisirur.

River: Benithora Nadi- Nearest Villages- Nandgur, Kota-nhiperga, Bharked, Sangunda, Madki, Hodal, Mudadga, Wagdhari, Betjewargi, Sawalgi (K), Bilgunda, Bhodhan, Apchand,Chinchansur. Awarja Nadi- Nearest Villages- Tadola, Khandala, Matki, Hebli, Jeerhalli, Shakhapur, Jidga, Gulhalli, Rajwal, Sangolgi,Bhusnoor, Korhalli, Kadganchi, Nimberga, Battarga, Dhangapur, Devanti, Jawali.D, Hithal Sirur, Kudki.

Annual Rainfall: Normal Rianfall 777 mm.

Ground Water: Availability of the Ground Water in the Basin is 10055 H.A.M. and the utilization is 3186 H.A.M. It belongs to Over Expoited category. Depth to water level 2 to 20 meter below the ground. Most of the wells go down in summer months, according to the Ground Water Estimation Committee.

Soils: Deep Black, Medium Black Soil, Shallow Soil and Lateritic Soil.

Natural Division : It falls in the Aland-Chincholi Tract of Trappeai Outcrops of the Northern Karnataka Plateau.

Administration:

Division: Gulbarga. Parliamentary Constituency: 5 Gulbarga (SC), 7 Bidar (SC). District: Gulbarga. Taluka: Aland. Assembly Constituency: 34 Afzalpur, 46 Aland. Gram Panchayat: 39.

Regional Area Development Boards: The Hyderabad-Karnataka Area Development Board.

Border Villages: (State: Maharashtra)- Jamga Khandala, Alanga, Sirur (G), Gadlegaon, Khajuri, Jawalga (J), Tugaon, Hodlur, Subhashnagar, Nandgur, Khandala, Nirgudi, Matki, Chincholi (K), Chincholi (B), Hiroli, Sarasamba, Bhimpur, Kamanhalli, Ningdhalli, Kerur, Madan Hipperga, Nimbal, Khedomerga, Tadola, Annur.

Fairs and Festival: Ladle Moray Mushaik Urs: Ladle Moray Mushaik Urs is observed at Aland in the month of 9 Rabi-us-Sanifor four days. Aland is also the headquarters of a taluk of the same name, situated 45 kms. north-west of the district headquarters town of Gulbarga. Prior to the integration of jagirs in the former Hyderabad State, the town was administered by paigah administrators through an officer known as Duam Talukdar. The place has many historical relics. A stone inscription in Aland speaks of its association with king Tribhuvana Malla Vikramaditya of the 11th century. In the 15th century, a Russian explorer seems to have visited Aland and noted that the place was a centre of 1,000 villages called Aland Sasira. It is also noted as a pilgrim centre for many Hindus. It has the samadhi of an eminent saint, Shri Raghava Chaitanya Maharaj Paratpar Guru. Shri Hastamalakacharya, who was the guru of Shri Shankaracharya, is said to have lived here for some time. Muslims from all over the Karnataka congregate at Aland every year to pray at the Dargah of Ladle-Mushaik.

Villages: 136 **Inhabited:** 135 **Uninhabited:** 1

Ranking	District	State	National
Area	3	15	82
Population	2	32	172
Sex Ratio	9	135	3232
Child Sex Ratio	10	171	5062
Literacy Rate	1	138	4265
Density	2	20	5518
Work Participation Rate	4	126	773

Gram Panchayats:

Nirgudi, Alanga, Khajuri, Hodlur, Rudrawadi, Belamogi, Salgera (V.K.), Ambalga, Ladmugli, Kamalanagar, Tadkal, Kinnisultan, Hiroli, Sarasamba, Padsawali, Munhalli, Bhodhan, Hallisalgar, Sawleshwar, Jidga, Kodalhangerga, Narona, Chinchansur, Sirchand, Gola (B), Korhalli, Bhusnoor, Kawalga, Dargasirur, Madan Hipperga, Dhuttagaon, Kadganchi, Dhangapur, Hadalgi, Nimbal, Yelsangi, Madiyal, Nimberga, Sunthnoor.

Amenities:

Education: Primary School in 135 villages, Middle school in 123 villages, Matriculation or Secondary School in 40 villages, namely Alanga, Khajuri, Hodlur, Kotanhipperga, Rudrawadi, Matki, Salegaon, Kinnisultan, Belamogi, Salgera (V.K.), Ambalga, Mudadga, Kamalanagar, Bhodhan, Narona, Chinchansur, Padsawali, Tadkal, Munhalli, Jamga.J, Jidga, Sangolgi, Kodalhangerga, Hiroli, Sarasamba, Sawleshwar, Dargasirur, Madan Hipperga, Nimbal, Kawalga, Bhusnoor, Korhalli, Dhuttagaon, Ladchincholi, Kadganchi, Nimberga, Dhangapur, Madiyal, Hadalgi, Yelsangi.

Higher Secondary or Pre University Courses or Intermediate or Junior College in 11 villages of the CD Block,, namely Khajuri, Salgera (V.K.), Narona, Chinchansur, Munhalli, Madan Hipperga, Dhuttagaon, Kadganchi, Nimberga, Dhangapur, Yelsangi.

College in 0 village, Adult Literacy Center in 38 villages.

Medical: Hospital in 3 villages, Dispensary in 14 villages, Health Center in 17 villages, Sub Center in 50 villages, Maternity and Child Welfare Center in 8 villages, Community health workers in 29 villages.

The Villages having Hospital or Dispensary or Health Center are Khajuri, Jawalga (J), Salegaon, Salgera (V.K.), Narona, Chinchansur, Padsawali, Aland (Rural), Hiroli, Sarasamba, Ningdhalli, Bhusnoor, Korhalli, Gola (B), Kadganchi, Nimberga, Jawali.D.

Drinking Water: Tap water in 109 villages, Tank water in 13 villages, Well water in 125 villages, Tubewell in 87 villages and more than one source in 134 villages.

Bank: Banking facility in 20 villages, namely, Khajuri, Rudrawadi, Kinnisultan, Salgera (V.K.) Ladmugli, Madki, Kamalanagar, Narona, Apchand Chinchansur, Hebli, Tadkal, Hallisalgar Aland (Rural), Sarasamba, Madan Hipperga, Bhusnoor Kadganchi, Nimberga, Madiyal.

Credit Society in 29 villages Agricultural Credit Society in 28 Non-Agricultural Credit Society in 1 village.

Others: Power supply in 135 villages, Cinema hall in 2 villages sport club in 4 villages, Stadium or Auditorium or Community Hall in 135 villages, Post Office in 85 villages.

There are 110 villages having bus facilities.

Villages with most of facilities: Khajuri Rudrawadi, Kinnisultan, Salgera (V.K.), Ladmugli Kamalanagar, Narona, Chinchansur, Tadkal Hallisalgar, Aland (Rural), Sarasamba Madan Hipperga, Bhusnoor, Kadganchi, Nimberga Madiyal.

Villages without Amenities (Education): None..

Scheduled Castes: Out of the total population of 261891 persons, 63682 persons (24.32%) belong to Scheduled Castes. The villages having less than 10% SC population are Kotanhipperga, Bhodhan, Telekuni, Haltadkal Nasirwadi, Kamanhalli, Allapur.J.

The villages having more than 50% SC population are Jamga Khandala, Subhashnagar, Madki, Honhalli Mamdapur, Aland (Rural), Sangolgi, Vijaynagar Sharananagar.

Sex ratio of Scheduled Caste population is 488.

Scheduled Castes Literates and Illiterates by Sex:

	Persons	Males	Females
Literate	22,627	15,026	7,601
Illiterate	41,055	17,554	23,501
Literacy rate	42.9	55.8	29.4
Graduate	756	721	35

Scheduled Castes (Dominant):

Holaya etc., Banjara etc., Madiga, Samagara, Bhovi

For their cultural identity please see Appendix-I

Village without Scheduled Castes: There is 1 village without any scheduled caste population.

Scheduled Tribes: Out of the total population of 261891 persons, 6035 persons (2.3%) belong to Scheduled Tribes. The villages having less than 10% ST population are Jamga Khandala, Tadola, Alanga, Sirur (G), Gadlegaon Khajuri, Tugaon, Annur, Hodlur, Subhashnagar Nandgur, Kotanhipperga, Jamga Ruderwadi, Rudrawadi Bableshwar, Bangerga, Nirgudi, Matki, Teerth

Salegaon, Chitali, Kinnisultan, Kanmas, Bharked Sangunda, Belamogi, Karhari, Salgera (V.K.) Ladmugli, Kalkutga, Kudmud, Ambalga, Dhammur, Madki Hodal, Murdi, Mudadga, Wagdhari, Betjewargi Kamalanagar, Sawalgi (K), Bilgunda, Bhodhan Gunjbablad, Narona, Sangolgi (C), Jawalga, Apchand Sirchand, Chinchansur, Rikkenalur, Keriambalga Chincholi (K), Chincholi (B), Padsawali, Hebli Telekuni, Honhalli, Tadkal, Haltadkal, Sukarwadi Walwandwadi, Degaon, Kunisangavi, Munhalli Hallisalgar, Mamdapur, Aland (Rural), Jeerhalli Khanapur, Jamga.J, Jidga, Gulhalli, Sangolgi Kodalhangerga, Yelinawadgi, Bolani, Hiroli Sarasamba, Nagelagaon, Chalgera, Bhimpur, Kamanhalli Sakkerga, Sawleshwar, Kinihabas, Mogha (B) Khatarbad, Ikkalki, Allapur.J, Mogha (K), Ambewad Ningdhalli, Kerur, Dargasirur, Madan Hipperga Nimbal, Madgunki, Zalki, Zalki (K), Kawalga Bhusnoor, Vijaynagar, Korhalli, Dhuttagaon Ladchincholi, Nellur, Dhannur, Tellur, Gola (B) Kadganchi, Sunthnoor, Bomanhalli, Nimberga, Battarga Devanti, Jawali.D, Hithal Sirur, Madiyal, Hadalgi Yelsangi, Benisirur, Kudki, Sharananagar, Vaijapur.

The villages having more than 50% ST population are None.

Sex ratio of Scheduled tribe population is 480.

Scheduled Tribes Literates and Illiterates by Sex:

	Persons	Males	Females
Literate	2,187	1,456	731
Illiterate	3,848	1,683	2,165
Literacy rate	43.8	55.6	30.8
Graduate	45	44	1

Scheduled Tribes (Dominant):

Gond etc., Naikda etc., Koli Dhor etc., Pardhi etc. Generic Tribes etc.

For their cultural identity please see Appendix-II

Villages without Scheduled Tribes: There are 81 villages without any scheduled tribe population.

Literates and Illiterates by Sex (Total Population):

	Persons	Males	Females
Literate	113,550	72,976	40,574
Illiterate	148,341	60,986	87,355
Literacy rate	52	65	38
Graduate	3,089	2,783	306

Agriculture: ***Distribution of villages according to land use:*** Out of 136 villages, Total area (in hectare) is 171690, out of that 91.83 percent is cultivable and 4.86 percent of the cultivable area is irrigated.

Sources of Irrigation (Hectares): Government Canal 20.24, Private Canal 0, Well without Electricity 258.83, Well with Electricity 6575.49, Tubewell without Electricity 149.79, Tubewell with Electricity 607.76, Tank 48.56, River 0, Lake 0, Waterfall 0, Others 0.

Villages with population of 5000 to 9999: Khajuri, Narona, Chinchansur, Madan Hipperga Bhusnoor, Kadganchi, Nimberga, Madiyal.

Villages with population of 10000 and above: None

Distribution of Workers:

	Persons	Males	Females	WPR
Cultivators	46,957	33,435	13,522	33.37
Agricultural Labour	74,218	27,768	46,450	52.75
Household Industry	3,065	1,830	1,235	2.18
Other Workers	16,458	13,468	2,990	11.7
Main Workers	95,759	63,243	32,516	68.06
Marginal Workers	44,939	13,258	31,681	31.94
Total Workers	140,698	76,501	64,197	

Religion: Major Religious Communities:

	Persons	Males	Females	Sex Ratio
Hindu (79.33%)	207,747	106,497	101,250	951
Muslim (9.13%)	23,899	12,085	11,814	978
Christian (0.04%)	108	49	59	1,204
Sikh (0%)	6	4	2	500
Buddhists (10.44%	27,349	13,914	13,435	966
Jain (0.19%)	490	260	230	885

Agewise Data:

	Persons	Males	Females	Sex Ratio
All ages	261,891	133,962	127,929	955
0-14	100,627	51,612	49,015	950
15-44	108,173	56,294	51,879	922
45-79	50,515	24,886	25,629	1030
80+	2,432	1,090	1,342	1231
Age not stated	144	80	64	800

Languages (Dominant):

Kannada, Urdu, Hindi, Marathi, Telugu

Disabled Population:

	Persons	Males	Females	%
Total Disabled	5,533	3,154	2,379	
In Seeing	2,044	991	1,053	36.94
In Speech	515	294	221	9.31
In Hearing	351	174	177	6.34
In Movement	2,142	1,419	723	38.71
Mentally	481	276	205	8.69

ALUR

Alur C.D. Block lies in the western part of Hassan distr ict. It is a part of Alur tehsil. The Block is located at a distance of 12 kms. from district headquarters (Hassan). There are 259 villages in the block with the total population of 79,998 persons. Area of the C.D. Block is 420.85 sq. kms. It is bounded by taluks Belur and Hassan on north, district Kodagu and Arkalgud on south, taluk Hassan on east, and Sakleshpur on west.

Communications:

Roadways : NH- 48: Direction- Sakleshpur to Hassan, Neare st Villages- Rangenahalli, Honnavalli, Channahalli, Shank aranahalli, Kanadahalli, Palya, Singapura, Samadale, Bijjanahalli, Bachanahalli, Soppinahalli, Mavanoor, Yadur, Neralakere, Chowlagere, Byrapura, Bharathavalli.

River: Yagachi Nadi- Nearest Villages- Jannapura, J. Thimmanahalli, Chikkanagalu, C.Hosahalli, Bellur, Ummade varahalli, Bandithimmanahalli, Togaranahalli, Doddakanaga l(Kanagal), Basavanapura, Hosapura, Hunasavalli, Mudigere, Kavalikere, Mavanoor, Kiragadalu, Kadalu, Muthige, Chakanahalli, Karigodanahalli, Hasaganur, Kenchanahalli, Kadabagala, Chittanahalli, Merve, Ramanahalli, Sulagodu, Mandira, Malenahalli Kavalu, Ganjigere, Appagowdanahalli, Holemaragodanahalli. Hemavati Nadi- Nearest Villages- Kithagalale, Kodagalavadi, Hyaragalale, Kithagere, Bigat hur, Harihalli, Bembaluru, Kaganoor, Kaganoor Estate, Siragavara, Hemmige, Sulagodu, Huskuru, Magadihalli, Bharathur, Kattehosur, Nagavara, Samasoge, Lakkondanaha lli, Ajjagodanahalli, Muddanahalli, Devanayakanahalli, Kalasetty Beedu, Rajapura, Siddapura, Bandimallenahalli.

Annual Rainfall: Normal Rianfall 962.3 mm.

Ground Water: Availability of the Ground Water in the Basin is 18.13 H.A.M. and the utilization is 10.98 H. A.M. It belongs to Safe category. Depth to water level 2 to 20 meter below the ground. Most of the wells go down in summer months, according to the Ground Water Estimation Committee.

Soils: Red Soil, Red Sandy Soil, Mixed Soil and Silty Clay Soil.

Natural Division : It falls in Cauvery-Hemavati Basin of the Southern Karnataka Plateau.

Administration:

Division: Mysore. Parliamentary Constituency: 16 Hassan. District: Hassan. Taluka: Alur. Assembly Constituency: 199 Sakleshpur (SC). Gram Panchayat: 15.

Regional Area Development Boards: The Maland Aera Development Board.

Fairs: Lakshmijanardhanaswamy Jatra: It at Palya near Hassan is held on Poornima day (full-moon day) of Phalguna (April) for a period of ten days. Palya, the headquarters of the Hobli of the same name in Alur taluk, is situated on the Bangalore-Mangalore road about 8 kilometres, from Alur town. It has Lakshmijanardhana, Rameshvara and Tripurantakeshvara temples. The original structure of Lakshmijanardhana temple was perhaps constr ucted during the early part of the 14th century. The prakara walls and the minor shrines in the prakara were probably built during the Paleyagar period. The main image of the Lakshmijanardhana temple is peculiar in design and goes back to about the 11th Century A.D. The structure of the Rameshvara temple appears to belong to the 19th century though the Rameshvara linga in the main cell may perhaps be older. The Tripurantakeshvara temple appears like a present-day country house of tiles but enshrines 17th century sculptures. To the south-east of the village, there was a Jaina basti which was built some time during the late Vijayanagara period as evidenc ed by some of its architectural remains.

Nageshwaraswamy Jatra: It is held at Nauili near Hassan in about April every year for a period of seven days.

Navilahalli—which means peacock village—is situated at a distance of 22.5 kms. from Alur on the Banavase-Mag ge road. It is in Kenchammana-Hosakote hobli of Alur taluk. The Maharajanadurga fort is also closeby. Nearby there is a small hill called Parvathammana-Betta with a small temple of Shiva-Paravathi amidst beautiful scene ry. It is about 3,300 feet above the sea level and has a huge precipitous rock. On it, are seen the remains of an old fort. The fort is an octagonal structure conta ining a pond, a few powder magazines and other adjuncts. The plan of the fort is beautifully shown on the roof of the first gate. From the top of the hill, a good view can be had of the country around. According to a local legend, Veera Raja, a Paleyagar of this area, once ate the flesh of his own son without knowing it to be so. When he came to know of this, he committed suicide by jumping down, from a galloping horse, into a deep hollow. Further, it is said that for this reason the place came to be called Magana Tinda Maharajanadurga. There is a secret passage leading out of the fort. Two Persian inscriptions are to be seen near a tomb at the foot of the hill.

Villages: 259 **Inhabited:** 250 **Uninhabited:** 9

Ranking	District	State	National
Area	8	169	1818
Population	8	165	4108
Sex Ratio	7	27	992
Child Sex Ratio	3	9	920
Literacy Rate	6	64	2052
Density	8	86	4882
Work Participation Rate	7	85	2002

Gram Panchayats:

Taluru, Doddakanagal, Hunasavalli, Kanathur, Madabalu, Palya, Byrapura, Kadalu, Hanchur , Abbana, Mallapura, Karagodu, Magge, Kundur, Ganjigere .

Amenities:

Education: Primary School in 167 villages, Middle school in 68 villages, Matriculation or Secondary School in 16 villages, namely Mallapura, Abbana, Magge, Karagodu, Kamathi,

Hullahalli, Chikkanagalu, Kanathur, Palya, Nidanur, Nalluru, Doddakanagal(Kanagal), Hanchur, Kundur, Kadalu, Ganjigere.

Higher Secondary or Pre University Courses or Intermediate or Junior College in 1 village of the CD Block,, namely Karagodu.

College in 0 village, Adult Literacy Center in 2 villages.

Medical: Hospital in 0 village, Dispensary in 8 villages, Health Center in 4 villages, Sub Center in 18 villages, Maternity and Child Welfare Center in 2 villages, Community health workers in 1 village.

The Villages having Hospital or Dispensary or Health Center are Mallapura, Magge, Karagodu, Karjuvalli, Palya, Doddakanagal(Kanagal), Kadabagala, Ganjigere.

Drinking Water: Tap water in 90 villages, Tank water in 240 villages, Well water in 200 villages, Tubewell in 92 villages and more than one source in 247 villages.

Bank: Banking facility in 9 villages, namely, Mallapura, Magge, Karagodu, Madabalu, Kanathur Bhavasavalli, Palya, Hanchur, Channapura.

Credit Society in 10 villages Agricultural Credit Society in 10 Non-Agricultural Credit Society in 0 village.

Others: Power supply in 250 villages, Cinema hall in 1 village, sport club in 0 village, Stadium or Auditorium or Community Hall in 0 village, Post Office in 32 villages.

There are 106 villages having bus facilities.

Villages with most of facilities: Mallapura, Magge Madabalu, Kanathur, Palya, Hanchur, Channapura.

Villages without amenities (Education):

Hyaragalale, Bigathur, Hydur, Anigalale, Bembaluru, Kaganoor Estate, Kakkehalli, Karadibetta Estate, Halasooru, Halliyur, Madagodu, Hachagodanahalli, Mallenahalli, Bekkadi, Dhaturu, Magadihalli, Kodagathavalli, Kattehosur, Nagavara, Bilagavalli, Lakkammanahalli, Chennenahalli, Nilavagilu, Kuppe Hosahalli, Beerakanahalli, Kallakere, Kadadaravalli, Megatavalli, Madanahalli, Gowlakatte, Yerehalli, Virupapura, Yelaganahalli, Kittaganamane, Siddapura, Kenchanahalli Pura, Thippapura, Dindagatta, Boodanahalli, Basavanahalli, Channahalli, Shankaranahalli, Hosahalli, Bandikere, Kottiganahalli, Muddanaikanahallipura, Harohalli, Vasudevarahalli, Baliganahalli, Imatipura, Gollara Thimmanahalli, Vajarahalli, Bijjanahalli, Dadadahalli, Alur (Rural), Kiggatta, Basavanapura, Channapura, Aniganahalli, Bommachavalli, Hanjihalli, Chattanahalli, Devihalli, Kithabur, Govindanahalli, Turuganahalli, Pattana, Kabbinahalli, Sathagala, Muthige, Chakanahalli, Kenchanahalli, Yadavanahalli, Devarajanahalli, Cheekanahalli, Kamenahalli, Mandira, Malenahalli Kavalu, Malenahalli, Samasoge, Lakkondanahalli, Ajjagodanahalli, Kalasetty Beedu..

Scheduled Castes: Out of the total population of 79938 persons, 20188 persons (25.25%) belong to Scheduled Castes.

The villages having less than 10% SC population are Hydur, Kaganoor, Hosahalli, Karadibetta Estate Hachagodanahalli, Mallenahalli, Bekkadi, Magge Magadihalli, Kanigere, Purabyravanahalli, Kattehosur Bilagavalli, Hunase, Chennenahalli, Beerakanahalli Kallakere, Chikkote, Kerehalli, Thimmanahalli Gowlakatte, Madagere, Yerehalli, Kallahalli Kittaganamane, Kolavanahalli, Kenchanahalli Pura Thippapura, Dindagatta, Shankaranahalli, Palya Chigaluru, Bandikere, Singapura, Danihalli Harohalli, Vasudevarahalli, Balluru, Kaggaravalli Beechalapura, Bandithimmanahalli Gollara Thimmanahalli, Vajarahalli, Kenchanahalli Machenahalli, Alur (Rural), Kiggatta, Basavanapura Rajanahalli, Mavanoor, Byrapura, Amalepura Moodanahalli, Aniganahalli, Bommachavalli Manchenahalli, Kundur, Devarapura, Sanenahalli Devihalli, Bhaktharavalli, Govindanahalli K.Hosahalli, Hotanahallipura, Turuganahalli Bettadahalli, Kabbinahalli, Sathagala, Thimmanahalli Kenchanahalli, Chittanahalli, Yadavanahalli Ramanahalli, Devarajanahalli, Cheekanahalli Kamenahalli, Garighatta, Malenahalli, Kyathanahalli Lakkondanahalli, Ganjigere, Siddapura.

The villages having more than 50% SC population are Kithagalale, Hyaragalale, Nagavara, Bosmanahalli Halliyur, Hiduvanahalli, Maranayakanahalli Thippapura, Bommanamane, Bellavara, Ajjenahalli Kamathi, Neelanahalli, J.Thimmanahalli Yelaganahalli, Hollahalli, Kongavalli, Honnavalli Boodanahalli, Basavanahalli, Hosahalli, Bettahalli Gekaravalli, Togaranahalli, Mudigere, Neralakere Byaba, Hanjihalli, Muthige, Kariganahalli Malenahalli Kavalu, Muddanahalli.

Sex ratio of Scheduled Caste population is 508.

Scheduled Castes Literates and Illiterates by Sex:

	Persons	Males	Females
Literate	8,486	5,052	3,434
Illiterate	11,702	4,889	6,813
Literacy rate	48.8	59.2	38.8
Graduate	102	85	17

Scheduled Castes (Dominant):

Adi Karnataka, Madiga, Adi Dravida, Bhovi, Moger

For their cultural identity please see Appendix-I

Villages without Scheduled Castes: There are 61 villages without any scheduled caste population.

Scheduled Tribes: Out of the total population of 79938 persons, 1674 persons (2.09%) belong to Scheduled Tribes. The villages having less than 10% ST population are Kithagalale, Hyaragalale, Kithagere, Mallapura Bigathur, Harihalli, Nagavara, Hadya, Kadlur, Hydur Honkaravalli, Anigalale, Malagalale, Bosmanahalli Muthige, Bembaluru, Kaganoor, Kaganoor Estate Siragavara, Hemmige, Sulagodu, Kakkehalli, Kudidale Hosahalli, Karadibetta Estate, Halasooru, Halliyur Dyathapura, Madagodu, Jinagaravalli, Hiduvanahalli Abbana, Maranayakanahalli, Hachagodanahalli Mallenahalli, Bekkadi, Dhaturu, Thippapura Navilahalli, Magge, Karagodu, Yadehalli Nanjapura Kanive Basavanahalli, Neragalale, Huskuru Magadihalli, Hulasinahalli, Kanigere, Adibylu Kodagathavalli, Hanjalige, Bharathur Purabyravanahalli, Kattehosur, Nagavara, Madihalli Lakkammanahalli, Bommanamane, Bellavara Chennenahalli, Samudravalli, Kuppe Hosahalli Ajjenahalli, Kamathi, Kadadaravalli, Hullahalli Chikkote, Megatavalli, Belame, Kerehalli Madanahalli, Thimmanahalli, Neelanahalli, Karjuvalli Taluru, Kuppe, Jannapura, J.Thimmanahalli Chikkanagalu, C.Hosahalli, Kumbarahalli, Gowlakatte Madagere, Yerehalli, Virupapura, Yelaganahalli Kallahalli, Hollahalli, Madabalu, Manjalagodu Kongavalli, Heddurga, Kittaganamane, Kolavanahalli Murudur, Siddapura, Kanathur, Bhavasavalli Toragaravalli, Kenchanahalli Pura, Belluru Rangenahalli, Honnavalli, Dindagatta, Boodanahalli Basavanahalli, Channahalli, Shankaranahalli Kanadahalli, Palya, Hosahalli, Nidanur, Chigaluru Singodanahalli, Bandikere, Singapura, Kottiganahalli Danihalli, Manikyathanahalli, Singatakere Muddanaikanahallipura, Nalluru, Bettahalli Harohalli, Vasudevarahalli, Baliganahalli Ballurpura, Balluru, Sindhuvalli, Beechalapura Sugganahalli, Nakalgod, Bellur, Ummadevarahalli Bandithimmanahalli, Gekaravalli Gollara Thimmanahalli, Vajarahalli, Hosahalli Kenchanahalli, Samadale, Bijjanahalli, Bachanahalli Soppinahalli, Machenahalli, Dadadahalli Hanthanamane, Alur (Rural), Kiggatta, Togaranahalli Doddakanagal(Kanagal), Katihalli, Somapura Basavanapura, Hosapura, Kirahalli, Hunasavalli Mudigere, Rajanahalli, Kavalikere, Mavanoor, Yadur Neralakere, Chowlagere, Byrapura, Byaba, Byaba Kaval Hosuru, Rayasamudra, Channapura, Bharathavalli Kiragadalu, Billagaravalli, Kuduravalli, Amalepura Gangara, Moodanahalli, Aniganahalli, Bommachavalli Manchenahalli, Hanjihalli, Hanchur, Chattanahalli Maniganahalli, Honnenahalli, Santhebasavanahalli Thippanahalli, Kundur, Devarapura, Channapura Thimmalapura, Hanumanahalli, Sanenahalli Valagarahalli, Devihalli, Bhaktharavalli, Kithabur Govindanahalli, K.Hosahalli, Hotanahallipura Turuganahalli, Bettadahalli, Kabbinahalli, Kadalu Sathagala, Muthige, Thimmanahalli, Chakanahalli Karigodanahalli, Hasaganur, Kariganahalli Kenchanahalli, Kadabagala, Yadavanahalli, Merve Ramanahalli, Devarajanahalli, Cheekanahalli Kamenahalli, Tattekere, Garighatta, Sulagodu Mandira, Malenahalli Kavalu, Malenahalli Basavanahalli, Thippanahalli, Nelligere Kyathanahalli, Samasoge, Lakkondanahalli Ajjagodanahalli, Muddanahalli, Kalasetty Beedu Ganjigere, Appagowdanahalli, Siddapura.

The villages having more than 50% ST population are None.

Sex ratio of Scheduled tribe population is 517.

Scheduled Tribes Literates and Illiterates by Sex:

	Persons	Males	Females
Literate	742	444	298
Illiterate	932	365	567
Literacy rate	52.3	64.4	40.8
Graduate	8	7	1

Scheduled Tribes (Dominant):

Naikda etc., Meda, Gond etc., Hasalaru, Paniyan

For their cultural identity please see Appendix-II

Villages without Scheduled Tribes: There are 222 villages without any scheduled tribe population.

Literates and Illiterates by Sex (Total Population):

	Persons	Males	Females
Literate	45,242	26,106	19,136
Illiterate	34,696	13,745	20,951
Literacy rate	64	75	54
Graduate	1,263	979	284

Agriculture: ***Distribution of villages according to land use:*** Out of 259 villages, Total area (in hectare) is 42085, out of that 62.5 percent is cultivable and 34.98 percent of the cultivable area is irrigated.

Sources of Irrigation (Hectares): Government Canal 102.81, Private Canal 10, Well without Electricity 25.4, Well with Electricity 142.7, Tubewell without Electricity 71.4, Tubewell with Electricity 96.1, Tank 7709.47, River 54.53, Lake 0, Waterfall 243.71, Others 744.28.

Villages with population of 5000 to 9999: None

Villages with population of 10000 and above: None

Distribution of Workers:

	Persons	Males	Females	WPR

Cultivators	18,501	12,264	6,237	45.15
Agricultural Labour	6,333	2,231	4,102	15.46
Household Industry	473	242	231	1.15
Other Workers	15,669	9,445	6,224	38.24
Main Workers	34,040	22,834	11,206	83.07
Marginal Workers	6,936	1,348	5,588	16.93
Total Workers	40,976	24,182	16,794	

Religion: Major Religious Communities:

	Persons	Males	Females	Sex Ratio
Hindu (94.16%)	75,267	37,349	37,918	1,015
Muslim (3.07%)	2,458	1,373	1,085	790
Christian (2.4%)	1,918	952	966	1,015
Sikh (0.07%)	58	56	2	36
Buddhists (0.07%)	59	30	29	967
Jain (0.02%)	16	8	8	1,000

Agewise Data:

	Persons	Males	Females	Sex Ratio
All ages	79,938	39,851	40,087	1006
0-14	23,686	12,031	11,655	969
15-44	40,298	20,007	20,291	1014
45-79	15,084	7,404	7,680	1037
80+	788	361	427	1183
Age not stated	82	48	34	708

Languages (Dominant):

Kannada, Tulu, Urdu, Malayalam, Tamil

Disabled Population:

	Persons	Males	Females	%
Total Disabled	1,427	757	670	
In Seeing	564	267	297	39.52
In Speech	143	67	76	10.02
In Hearing	91	38	53	6.38
In Movement	514	324	190	36.02
Mentally	115	61	54	8.06

ANEKAL

Anekal C.D. Block lies in the south-eastern part of Bangalore district. It is a part of Anekal taluka. The Block is located at a distance of 35 kms. from district headquarters (Bangalore). There are 233 villages in the block with the total population of 240,636 persons. Area of the C.D. Block is 520.08 sq. kms. It is bounded by taluk Bangalore South and district Bangalore Rural on north, district Bangalore Rural on east, district Bangalore Rural and Bangalore South taluk on west. It has common boundary with the state of Tamil Nadu on south and east.

Communications:

Roadways : N.H.-7: Direction- Bangalore to Chennai, Nearest Villages- Veerasandra, Kammasandra, Chandapura, Chandra pura -Chatrakane, Kittaganahalli, Banahalli, Thirumagond anahalli, Balagaranahalli, Neralur, Yadavanahalli, Krishn asagara, Giddenahalli, Attibele. N.H-207: Direction- Varthur to Attibele, Nearest Villages- Dommasandra, Thigala Chowdadenahalli, Chikkavaderapura, Heggondahalli, Halasahalli Tippasandra, Chambenahalli, Yamare, Sompura, S.Medihalli, Tyayakana Halli, Billapura, Buragunte, Sarjapura, Bidaraguppe, Indlabele, Attibele.

S.H-35: Direction- Anekal to Attibele, Nearest Villages- Mayasandra, M.Medihalli, Bhaktipura, Arehalli, Attibele, Thattanahalli, Haldenahalli, Bestammanahalli, Karpur, Bidaragere. S.H-86 A: Direction- Bangalore to Hosur, Nearest Villages- Bannerughatta, Gollahalli, Kalkere, Laxmipura, Mantapa, Jangal Palya, Begihalli, Nallasandra, Amani Bidarakere, Harapanahalli, Jigani, Koppa Gate, Haragadde, Mada Patna, Kumbaranahalli, Suragajakkanahal li, Gowrenahalli, Honnakalasapura, Hasaruvani, Anekal (Rural), Hompalaghatta, Gudnahalli, Geratiganabele, Submangala, Muthagatti, Channena Agrahara, Samandur.

Railway Station: Villages- Janatha Colony, Huskur, Avala halli, Haldenahalli, Karpur.

River: Pinakini Nadi- Nearest Villages- Seeganaikanahalli, Madappanahalli, Deshapande Guttahalli, Banahalli, Mugalur, Kugur, Panditana Agrahara, Mattanahalli.

Annual Rainfall: Normal Rianfall 816.4 mm.

Ground Water: Availability of the Ground Water in the Basin is 16769 H.A.M. and the utilization is 33027 H. A.M. It belongs to Over Exploited category. Depth to water level 2 to 20 meter below the ground. Most of the wells go down in summer months, according to the Ground Water Estimation Committee.

Soils: Laterite soils, occur on undulating terrain forming plain to gently sloping topography of peninsular gneissic region. It is mainly covered in Anekal taluk and western parts of Bangalore North and south taluks.

Natural Division : It falls in Bangalore Plateau of the Southern Karnataka Plateau.

Administration:

Division: Bangalore. Parliamentary Constituency: Bangalo re- III. District: Bangalore. Taluka: Anekal. Assembly Constituency: 175 Bommanahalli, 177 Anekal (SC). Gram Panchayat: 32.

Border Villages: (State: Tamil Nadu)- Byalahalli, Adigarak-allahalli, Billapura, Sarjapura, Thindlu, Gudighattanahalli, Mattanahalli, Halehalli, Kodlipura, Dasanapura, Bidarag uppe, Chikkanahalli, Attibele, Ballur, Maranaikanahalli, Thammanaikanahalli, Bidarakadahalli, Kalanaikanahalli, Solur, Menasiganahalli, Gudnahalli, Chikkanahatti, Great-iganabele, Submangala, Channena Agrahara, Samandur.

Fairs: Dabbaguli Basaveshwara Temple Jatra: The jatra is held at Vanakanahalli in the month of Chaitra (March-April). Vanakanahalli situated at a distance of five kms. to the south of Anekal appears to be an ancient place.

Someshwara Jatra: Someshwara Jatra is held at Anekal near Bangalore in the month of April every year. Anekal is situated about 36 kms. from Bangalore.

Thimmarayaswamy Jatra: It is held at Anekal near Bangalo re in the month of April every year. On the outskirts of the town on the Hosur Road is the temple of Thimmaray aswamy. Many temple parts were brought from a village called Halehalli and the temple reconstructed.

Venkataramana Car Festival: The car festival of God Venkataramana is held during Kamana Hunnime, Phalgun Poornima (March) at Muthanallur near Bangalore. Muthanal lur situated at a distance of eight kms. from Sarjapur is described by local enthusiasts as Muttunallur uru or the town of pearl like paddy.

Villages: 233 **Inhabited:** 225 **Uninhabited:** 8

Ranking	District	State	National
Area	2	163	1414
Population	2	45	287
Sex Ratio	3	174	5294
Child Sex Ratio	2	90	3070
Literacy Rate	3	40	1442
Density	3	159	2381
Work Participation Rate	2	3	3751

Gram Panchayats:

Kudlu, Huskur, Yamare, Neriga, Dommasandra , Mugalur, Sarjapura, Handenahalli, Muthanallur, Hebbagodi, Hulimangala, Bannerughatta, Mantapa, Kalbalu, Jigani, Hennagara, Bommasandra, Chandapura, Neralur, Bidaraguppe, Attibele, Ballur, Mayasandra, Byagadadenahalli, Marasur, Haragadde, Ragihalli, Indlawadi, Suragajakkanahalli , Vanakanahalli, Karpur, Samandur.

Amenities:

Education: Primary School in 177 villages, Middle school in 72 villages, Matriculation or Secondary School in 15 villages, namely Jigani, Hennagara, Huskur, Muthanallur, Dommasandra, Halasahalli Thippasandra, Sarjapura, Kugur, Chandapura, Mayasandra, Attibele, Byagadadenahalli, Marasur, Solur, Muthagatti.

Higher Secondary or Pre University Courses or Intermediate or Junior College in 5 villages of the CD Block,, namely Sarjapura, Chandapura, Iggalur, Attibele, Indlawadi.

College in 1 village, Adult Literacy Center in 2 villages., College is in village, namely Sarjapura.

Medical: Hospital in 2 villages, Dispensary in 9 villages, Health Center in 8 villages, Sub Center in 28 villages, Maternity and Child Welfare Center in 5 villages, Community health workers in 0 village.

The Villages having Hospital or Dispensary or Health Center are Bannerughatta, Kalbalu, Ragihalli, Jigani, Haragadde, Kudlu, Muthanallur, Sarjapura, Attibele.

Drinking Water: Tap water in 115 villages, Tank water in 94 villages, Well water in 48 villages, Tubewell in 125 villages and more than one source in 188 villages.

Bank: Banking facility in 16 villages, namely, Bannerughatta, Kalkere, Jigani, Hulimangala Rajapura, Hennagara, Huskur, Dommasandra Handenahalli, Sarjapura, Kugur, Chandapura, Jigala Attibele, Marasur, Anekal (Rural).

Credit Society in 27 villages Agricultural Credit Society in 17 Non-Agricultural Credit Society in 3 villages.

Others: Power supply in 214 villages, Cinema hall in 9 villages sport club in 225 villages, Stadium or Auditorium or Communi Hall in 225 villages, Post Office in 30 villages.

There are 156 villages having bus facilities.

Villages with most of facilities: Bannerughatta Jigani, Hulimangala, Hennagara, Huskur, Dommasandra Handenahalli, Sarjapura, Chandapura, Attibele Marasur, Anekal (Rural).

Villages without amenities (Education):
Gollahalli, Vaderahalli, Jangal Palya, Hullukasavanahalli, Amani Bidarakere, Kadajakkanahalli, Giddenahalli, J.Bingipura, Koppa Gate, Mada Patna, Nosenur Gollahalli, Dyavasandra, Seethanaikana Halli, Hinnakki, Janatha Colony, Bhovi Palya (Shanthi Pur), Gottamaranahalli, Thigala Chowdadenahalli, Chikkavaderapura, Chikkadunnasandra, Kotiganahalli, Tyayakana Halli, Byalahalli, Nagen Agrahara, Seeganaikanahalli, Deshapande Guttahalli, Banahalli, Gudighattanahalli, Kammasandra, Vaddara Palya, Andapura, Chandrapura -Chatrakane, Krishnasagara, Muthasandra, Chikkanahalli, Indlawadipura, Thammanaikanahalli, Agasa Thimmanahalli, Kunmadivala, Naganaikanahalli, Bandapura, Marasur Agrahara, Amani Doddakere, Hasaruvani, Patnagere Gollahalli, Kalanaikanahalli, Chikkanahatti, Kurubarahatti..

Scheduled Castes: Out of the total population of 241160 persons, 73473 persons (30.47%) belong to Scheduled Castes. The villages having less than 10% SC population are Halesampigehalli, Jangal Palya, J.Bingipura Maragondahalli, Nosenur Gollahalli, Gattahalli Dommasandra, Nagen Agrahara, Banahalli, Mugalur Gudighattanahalli, Gollahalli, Andapura Chandrapura -Chatrakane, Thimmasandra Chikkanahalli, Agasa Thimmanahalli, Amani Doddakere Singasandra, Chikkanahatti, Kurubarahatti.

The villages having more than 50% SC population are Bhoothanahalli, Hullukasavanahalli, Hullahalli Ramasandra, Giddenahalli, Koppa Gate Seethanaikana Halli, Hosahalli, Kudlu, Choodasandra Janatha Colony, Avalahalli, Singena Agrahara Ramnaikanahalli, Yamare, Sompura, Kotiganahalli Tyayakana Halli, Gonighattapura Deshapande Guttahalli, Kuthaganahalli, Vaddara Palya Krishnasagara, Muthasandra, Arehalli, Soppahalli Sonnanayakanapura, Adur, Dodda Hagade Naganaikanahalli, Kammasandra Agrahara Anekal (Rural), Patnagere Gollahalli, Solur Hompalaghatta, Aravantigepura, Rachamanahalli Channena Agrahara.

Sex ratio of Scheduled Caste population is 490.

Scheduled Castes Literates and Illiterates by Sex:

	Persons	Males	Females
Literate	36,063	21,556	14,507
Illiterate	37,410	15,882	21,528
Literacy rate	57.1	67.1	46.7
Graduate	904	783	121

Scheduled Castes (Dominant):

Adi Karnataka, Bhovi, Madiga, Adi Dravida Banjara etc.

For their cultural identity please see Appendix-I

Villages without Scheduled Castes: There are 20 villages without any scheduled caste population.

Scheduled Tribes: Out of the total population of 241160 persons, 4914 persons (2.04%) belong to Scheduled Tribes.

The villages having less than 10% ST population are Kannaikana Agrahara, Bilwaradahalli, Bannerughatta Gollahalli, Kalkere, Vaderahalli, Laxmipura Halesampigehalli, Mantapa, Jangal Palya, Begihalli Nallasandra, Hullukasavanahalli, Sakalawara Hullahalli, Ramasandra, Harapanahalli, Bukkasagara Giddenahalli, J.Bingipura, Vaderamanchanahalli Jigani, Koppa, Koppa Gate, S.Bingipura, Hulimangala Maragondahalli, Thirupalya, Yarandahalli, Vabasandra Nanjapura, Kyalasanahalli, Bande Nalla Sandra Haragadde, Mada Patna, Konasandra, Bommandahalli Nosenur Gollahalli, Nosenur, Dyavasandra Seethanaikana Halli, Rajapura, Masthena Halli Hinnakki, Hennagara, Hosahalli, Kachanaikanahalli Ramakrishnapura, Kudlu, Choodasandra, Rayasandra Gattahalli, Janatha Colony, Chikkanagamangala Bhovi Palya (Shanthi Pur), Gulimangala, Huskur Avalahalli, Chokkasandra, Harohalli, Kaggalipura Gottamaranahalli, Singena Agrahara, Narayanaghatta Muthanallur, Ali Bommasandra, Samanahalli Chikkathimmasandra, Gopasandra, Kommasandra Dommasandra, Thigala Chowdadenahalli Chikkavaderapura, Heggondahalli Halasahalli Thippasandra, Chikkanekkundi Nekkundi Dommasandra, Kathriguppe, Ramnaikanahalli Chambenahalli, Yamare, Sompura, Kadagrahara B.Hosahalli, Bikkanahalli, Sollepura, Handenahalli Kotiganahalli, S.Medihalli, Tyayakana Halli Byalahalli, Adigarakallahalli, Billapura, Buragunte Sarjapura, Ittangur, Volagerekallahalli Chikkadasarahalli, Gonighattapura, Neriga Janthagondanahalli, Nagen Agrahara Seeganaikanahalli, Madappanahalli, Banahalli Mugalur, Kugur, Kamanahalli, Kuthaganahalli Doddathimmasandra, Thindlu, Mahal Chowdadenahalli Gudighattanahalli, Panditana Agrahara, Gollahalli Veerasandra, Kammasandra, Vaddara Palya, Andapura Ramasagara, Heelalige, Chandapura Chandrapura -Chatrakane, Kittaganahalli, Banahalli Iggalur, Thirumagondanahalli, Balagaranahalli Neralur, Laxmi Sagara, Bendiganahalli Adigondanahalli, Guddahatti, Yadavanahalli Itchangur, Muthasandra, Kamblipura, Mayasandra M.Medihalli, Halehalli, Kodlipura, Dasanapura Bhaktipura, Arehalli, Manchanahalli, Jigala, Arenur Bidaraguppe, Chikkanahalli, Indlabele, Attibele Ballur, Maranaikanahalli, Soppahalli, Kumbaranahalli Suragajakkanahalli , Sonnanayakanapura, Adur Indlawadi, Indlawadipura, Thammanaikanahalli Chikka Hosahalli, Agasa Thimmanahalli, A Medihalli Gowrenahalli, Honnakalasapura, Sidihosakote Kempavaderahalli, Dodda Hagade, Kunmadivala Byagadadenahalli, Marasur, Naganaikanahalli Madivala, Bandapura, Marasur Agrahara, Thattanahalli Avadadenahalli, Kammasandra Agrahara, Hasaruvani Anekal (Rural), Sunavara, Patnagere Gollahalli Kalanaikanahalli, Solur, Menasiganahalli Vanakanahalli, Singasandra, Telagarahalli Hompalaghatta, Gudnahalli, Chikkanahatti Geratiganabele, Submangala, Muthagatti Kurubarahatti, Haldenahalli, Kaval Hosahalli Chikka Hagade, Aravantigepura, Bestammanahalli Karpur, Bidaragere, Rachamanahalli Channena Agrahara, Samandur.

The villages having more than 50% ST population are None.

Sex ratio of Scheduled tribe population is 480.

Scheduled Tribes Literates and Illiterates by Sex:

	Persons	Males	Females
Literate	2,071	1,266	805
Illiterate	2,843	1,287	1,556

Literacy rate	50.1	58.4	40.9
Graduate	57	46	11

Scheduled Tribes (Dominant):

Naikda etc., Iruliga, Hakkipikki

Generic Tribes etc., Irular

For their cultural identity please see Appendix-II

Villages without Scheduled Tribes: There are 132 villages without any scheduled tribe population.

Literates and Illiterates by Sex (Total Population):

	Persons	Males	Females
Literate	143,180	85,871	57,309
Illiterate	97,980	41,278	56,702
Literacy rate	68	77	58
Graduate	5,895	4,623	1,272

Agriculture: ***Distribution of villages according to land use:*** Out of 233 villages, Total area (in hectare) is 52008, out of that 69.19 percent is cultivable and 20.26 percent of the cultivable area is irrigated.

Sources of Irrigation (Hectares): Government Canal 40.94, Private Canal 0, Well without Electricity 8.71, Well with Electricity 51.13, Tubewell without Electricity 12.87, Tubewell with Electricity 3625.14, Tank 3023, River 22.2, Lake 4.05, Waterfall 0, Others 502.25.

Villages with population of 5000 to 9999:

Jigani, Dommasandra, Sarjapura.

Villages with population of 10000 and above:

Attibele.

Distribution of Workers:

	Persons	Males	Females	WPR
Cultivators	23,853	20,224	3,629	22.71
Agricultural Labour	18,849	10,070	8,779	17.94
Household Industry	3,334	2,103	1,231	3.17
Other Workers	59,004	45,202	13,802	56.17
Main Workers	85,813	67,560	18,253	81.7
Marginal Workers	19,227	10,039	9,188	18.3
Total Workers	105,040	77,599	27,441	

Religion: Major Religious Communities:

	Persons	Males	Females	Sex Ratio
Hindu (93.18%)	224,718	118,281	106,437	900
Muslim (5.14%)	12,397	6,699	5,698	851
Christian (1.05%)	2,521	1,380	1,141	827
Sikh (0.03%)	84	52	32	615
Buddhists (0.41%)	982	497	485	976
Jain (0.03%)	67	37	30	811

Agewise Data:

	Persons	Males	Females	Sex Ratio
All ages	241,160	127,149	114,011	897
0-14	71,412	36,533	34,879	955
15-44	125,260	67,254	58,006	862
45-79	41,847	22,044	19,803	898
80+	2,401	1,191	1,210	1016
Age not stated	240	127	113	890

Languages (Dominant):

Kannada, Telugu, Tamil, Urdu, Hindi

Disabled Population:

	Persons	Males	Females	%
Total Disabled	4,157	2,410	1,747	
In Seeing	2,065	1,150	915	49.68
In Speech	372	197	175	8.95
In Hearing	165	94	71	3.97
In Movement	1,118	733	385	26.89
Mentally	437	236	201	10.51

ANKOLA

Ankola C.D. Block lies in the central west part of Uttara Kannada district. It is a part of Ankola taluka. The Block is located at a distance of 34 kms. from district headquarters (Karwar). There are 86 villages in the block with the total population of 75,405 persons. Area of the C.D. Block is 902.14 sq. kms. It is bounded by taluks Karwar and Yellapur on north, taluk Kumta on south, taluk Sirsi on east, and Lakshadweep sea on west.

Communications:

Roadways : N.H-17 : Direction- Panaji to Mangalore, Nearest Villages- Harwada, Sakalbena, Aversa, Hattikeri, Algeri, Baleguli, Nellurkanchinbail, Bole, Shetgeri, Talgadde, Belse, Shirur, Devigadde, Ulware, Balale. N.H-63: Direction- Ankola to Hubli, Nearest Villages- Algeri, Bogribail, Navagadde, Adlur, Heggar Makkigadde, Agsur, Kavalalli, Sunksal, Hebbul, Kodlagadde.

Railway Station: Village: Hosgadde.

River: Kandani Halla Nadi- Nearest Villages- Harwada, Sakalbena, Aversa, Hattikeri, Belekeri, Nellurkanchinbail, Heggarnikotebavi, Gule, Kendige, Shikliturli, Mallani, Sheveguli. Bedti Nadi- Nearest Villages- Kodlagadde, Shevakar, Heggar, Kalleshwar, Halvalli. Gangavali Nadi- Nearest Villages- Kattinhakkal, Kavalalli, Sunksal, Hebbul, Dongri, Kodlagadde, Halvalli, Kammani, Kanagil, Hichkad, Hadav, Bilehoingi, Manjaguni, Agragon, Shirur, Joog, Kamge, Sagadgeri, Ulware, Kodsani, Vasar Kudrige, Mogta, Andle, Moralli, Shirgunji, Gundabala, Hillur, Kuntgani.

Reserved Forest: Nearest Villages- Harwada, Sakalbena, Belekeri, Bhavikeri, Berde, Nellurkanchinbail, Heggarni kotebavi, Gule, Kendige, Shikliturli, Mallani, Sheveguli, Navagadde, Adlur, Marugadde, Heggar Makkigadde, Agsur, Kavalalli, Kattinhakkal, Sunksal, Hebbul, Dongri, Kodla gadde, Shevakar, Heggar, Kalleshwar, Halvalli, Kammani, Talgadde, Belse, Vasar, Kudrige, Moralli, Shirgunji, Gundabala, Hillur, Kuntgani, Manigadde, Achave, Kabgal, Brahmur.

Annual Rainfall: Normal Rianfall 3554.6 mm.

Ground Water: Availability of the Ground Water in the Basin is 6406 H.A.M. and the utilization is 849 H.A. M. It belongs to Safe category. Depth to water level 5 to 20 meter below the ground. Most of the wells go down in summer months, according to the Ground Water Estimation Committee.

Soils: Coastal Alluvial Soil.

Natural Division : It falls partly in Karwar-Honawar Coast and Western Ghats of the Karnataka Coast (Western Coastal Region).

Coastal Villages: (Lakshadeep Sea)- Harwada, Belekeri, Bhavikeri, Nadibag, Belambar, Wadibogri, Honnebail, Manjaguni.

Administration:

Division: Belgaum. Parliamentary Constituency: 12 Uttara Kannada . District: Uttara Kannada. Taluka: Ankola.Assembly Constituency: 77 Karwar, 78 Kumta. Gram Panchayat: 19.

Regional Area Development Boards: The Maland Aera Development Board.

Fairs: Bandi Habba Festival: It is held to win the goodw ill of Gods and deities (Ammas) who preside over crops. These Gods have no images. During the festival, the small metal water vessels called kalashas or gindis are set for them on an alter-like stone platform in the village temple which is called Kalashadevasthan. The priests of these kalasha temples are Gunagas (potte rs). It is said that in ancient days the deities were placed in a bandi or cart with four wheels and the proce ssion of deity was taking place. Hence the festival is called Bandi Habba. The remains of these bandis are even now seen in some temples of the district. The festi val is popular in the coastal areas and specially in Uttara Kannada Ankola seeme, Gokaran seeme and Chandavara seeme of the district.

Bhandi Habba Jatra: Bhandi Habba (Bhoomi Davate-Shanta Durga, jatra is held annually in the month of May at Aversa near Uttara Kannada for seven days. Aversa a place about four kms. from Ankola is having a Katyayini Basens hwara temple which is the Kuladevata of many Gauda Saraswats. The main idol and other deities are said to have been brought from Goa in early 16th century.

Katyayani Devi Jatra: It is held at Aversa near Uttara Kannada in the month of October for three days. Aversa four kilometres from Ankola is having a Katyayini Banesh wara temple which is the Kuladevata of many Gauda Saraswats.

Lakshminarayana Deva Jatra: It is held at Aversa near Uttara Kannada for one day in the month at November. Aversa, four kms. from Ankola is having a Katyayini Baneshwara temple which is the Kuladevata of many Gauda Saraswats. Mahadeva Jatra: It is held at Ankola in the month of November for two days. Ankola, a taluk Headquarters, 34 kms. from Karwar of rich antiquity, is the home of Halakki Bokkals. The place name is derived from a forest shrub ankole (Alanglum Iamarckil) grown on the coastal hillside and worshipped by the Halakki Vokkals as a totem.

Mahadeva Temple Jatra: It is held at Ulware near Uttara Kannada during Chaitra Purnima (March-April). Ulware, 8.2 kms. from Ankola, is on the bank of the Gangavali and the place name literally means a ferry in Kannada. The place is approachable by road from Madangeri (Ankola taluk) and also by crossing the Gangavali river by means of a ferry from Shirur (Ankola).

Syed Hasan Shah Quadri Urs: At Taksmeshwara, a place 10 kms. from Ankola near Uttara Kannada, there are three dargahs ascribed to Syed Hasan Shah Quadri, Shah Fata and Shah Mokka and Urs is held at the latter dargahs, when nearly 5000 people participate.

Vithoba Jatra: It is held at Aversa near Uttara Kannada in the month of November for one day. Aversa four kms. from Ankola has Katyayini Bareshwara temple which is the Kuladevata of many Gauda Saraswats.

Villages: 81 **Inhabited:** 80 **Uninhabited:** 1

Ranking	District	State	National
Area	4	99	546
Population	7	166	4269
Sex Ratio	7	94	2429
Child Sex Ratio	1	6	691
Literacy Rate	6	21	827
Density	2	11	6224
Work Participation Rate	9	168	515

Gram Panchayats:

Harwada, Aversa, Belekeri, Hattikeri, Sunksal, Dongri, Achave, Hillur, Agsur, Belse, Vandige, Algeri, Bhavikeri, Bobruwada, Belambar, Shetgeri, Agragon, Sagadgeri, Mogta.

Amenities:

Education: Primary School in 65 villages, Middle school in 43 villages, Matriculation or Secondary School in 14 villages, namely Harwada, Aversa, Belekeri, Bhavikeri, Algeri, Agsur, Shetgeri, Belambar, Manjaguni, Agragon, Belse, Mogta, Moralli, Hillur.

Higher Secondary or Pre University Courses or Intermediate or Junior College in 2 villages of the CD Block,, namely Aversa, Agsur.

College in 0 village, Adult Literacy Center in 0 village.

Medical: Hospital in 0 village, Dispensary in 3 villages, Health Center in 5 villages, Sub Center in 11 villages,

Maternity and Child Welfare Center in 0 village, Community health workers in 0 village.
The Villages having Hospital or Dispensary or Health Center are Harwada, Belse, Achave.
Drinking Water: Tap water in 38 villages, Tank water in 9 villages, Well water in 78 villages, Tubewell in 0 village and more than one source in 69 villages.
Bank: Banking facility in 19 villages, namely, Sakalbena, Aversa, Belekeri, Bhavikeri, Agsur Sunksal, Kodlagadde, Heggar, Kalleshwar, Bhasgod Manjaguni, Belse, Shirur, Ulware, Vasar Kudrige Andle, Balale, Hillur, Kuntgani.
Credit Society in 22 villages Agricultural Credit Society in 21 Non-Agricultural Credit Society in 4 villages.
Others: Power supply in 72 villages, Cinema hall in 0 village, sport club in 0 village, Stadium or Auditorium or Community Hall in 0 village, Post Office in 35 villages.
There are 60 villages having bus facilities.
Villages with most of facilities: Sakalbena Belekeri, Agsur, Kodlagadde, Belse, Andle, Hillur.
Villages without amenities (Education): Varilbena, Baleguli, Berde, Nellurkanchinbail, Heggarnikotebavi, Lakkeguli, Kendige, Shikliturli, Mallani, Sheveguli, Navagadde, Kogre, Shinganmakki, Kanagil, Takatgeri..
Scheduled Castes: Out of the total population of 75411 persons, 4585 persons (6.08%) belong to Scheduled Castes.
The villages having less than 10% SC population are Harwada, Varilbena, Sakalbena, Aversa, Hattikeri Belekeri, Bhavikeri, Bogribail, Berde Nellurkanchinbail, Heggarnikotebavi, Gule, Lakkeguli Kendige, Shikliturli, Mallani, Sheveguli, Navagadde Adlur, Marugadde, Heggar Makkigadde, Agsur Kavalalli, Kattinhakkal, Sunksal, Hebbul, Dongri Kodlagadde, Shevakar, Heggar, Kalleshwar, Halvalli Kammani, Nadibag, Poojgeri, Hosgadde, Bhasgod Belambar, Wadibogri, Honnebail, Shinganmakki, Hadav Bilehoingi, Manjaguni, Hegre, Adigon, Talgadde Shirur, Joog, Kamge, Devigadde, Ulware, Kodsani Andle, Karebail, Takatgeri, Kenkanishivapur, Moralli Shirgunji, Gundabala, Manigadde, Kabgal, Brahmur.
The village having more than 50% SC population is None.
Sex ratio of Scheduled Caste population is 503.
Scheduled Castes Literates and Illiterates by Sex:

	Persons	Males	Females
Literate	2,578	1,491	1,087
Illiterate	2,007	789	1,218
Literacy rate	66.4	77.8	55.3
Graduate	46	31	15

Scheduled Castes (Dominant):
Ager, Halsar etc., Bhovi, Halleer, Chalavadi etc.
For their cultural identity please see Appendix-I
Villages without Scheduled Castes: There are 40 villages without any scheduled caste population.
Scheduled Tribes: Out of the total population of 75411 persons, 113 persons (0.15%) belong to Scheduled Tribes.
The villages having less than 10% ST population are Harwada, Varilbena, Sakalbena, Aversa, Hattikeri Belekeri, Bhavikeri, Algeri, Baleguli, Bogribail Berde, Nellurkanchinbail, Heggarnikotebavi, Gule Lakkeguli, Kendige, Shikliturli, Mallani, Sheveguli Navagadde, Adlur, Marugadde, Heggar Makkigadde Agsur, Kavalalli, Kattinhakkal, Sunksal, Hebbul Dongri, Kodlagadde, Shevakar, Heggar, Kalleshwar Halvalli, Kammani, Nadibag, Poojgeri, Hosgadde, Bole Shetgeri, Bhasgod, Kogre, Belambar, Wadibogri Honnebail, Shinganmakki, Surve, Kanagil, Hichkad Hadav, Bilehoingi, Manjaguni, Agragon, Hegre, Adigon Talgadde, Belse, Shirur, Joog, Kamge, Devigadde Sagadgeri, Ulware, Kodsani, Vasar Kudrige, Mogta Andle, Balale, Karebail, Takatgeri, Kenkanishivapur Moralli, Shirgunji, Gundabala, Hillur, Kuntgani Manigadde, Achave, Kabgal, Brahmur.
The villages having more than 50% ST population are None.
Sex ratio of Scheduled tribe population is 381.
Scheduled Tribes Literates and Illiterates by Sex:

	Persons	Males	Females
Literate	34	29	5
Illiterate	79	41	38
Literacy rate	39.1	51.8	16.1
Graduate	1	1	0

Scheduled Tribes (Dominant):
Naikda etc., Chenchu etc., Generic Tribes etc. Gond etc.
For their cultural identity please see Appendix-II
Villages without Scheduled Tribes: There are 74 villages without any scheduled tribe population.
Literates and Illiterates by Sex (Total Population):

	Persons	Males	Females
Literate	48,442	27,937	20,505
Illiterate	26,969	10,326	16,643
Literacy rate	73	83	63
Graduate	2,296	1,565	731

Agriculture: ***Distribution of villages according to land use:*** Out of 81 villages, Total area (in hectare) is 90214, out of that 9.6 percent is cultivable and 11.38 percent of the cultivable area is irrigated.
Sources of Irrigation (Hectares): Government Canal 0, Private Canal 1.17, Well without Electricity 429.55, Well with

Electricity 112.33, Tubewell without Electricity 0.81, Tubewell with Electricity 0, Tank 26.61, River 2.18, Lake 0, Waterfall 0, Others 416.92.

Villages with population of 5000 to 9999: Bhavikeri.

Villages with population of 10000 and above: None

Distribution of Workers:

	Persons	Males	Females	WPR
Cultivators	18,298	10,588	7,710	42.08
Agricultural Labour	8,278	3,606	4,672	19.04
Household Industry	860	546	314	1.98
Other Workers	16,050	10,533	5,517	36.91
Main Workers	29,479	20,879	8,600	67.79
Marginal Workers	14,007	4,394	9,613	32.21
Total Workers	43,486	25,273	18,213	

Religion: Major Religious Communities:

	Persons	Males	Females	Sex Ratio
Hindu (98.72%)	74,442	37,759	36,683	972
Muslim (0.84%)	630	331	299	903
Christian (0.44%)	332	170	162	953
Sikh (0.01%)	5	2	3	1,500
Buddhists (0%)	-	-	-	-
Jain (0%)	-	-	-	-

Agewise Data:

	Persons	Males	Females	Sex Ratio
All ages	75,411	38,263	37,148	971
0-14	21,239	10,890	10,349	950
15-44	38,016	19,582	18,434	941
45-79	15,517	7,519	7,998	1064
80+	603	251	352	1402
Age not stated	36	21	15	714

Languages (Dominant):

Kannada, Konkani, Hindi, Urdu, Marathi

Disabled Population:

	Persons	Males	Females	%
Total Disabled	1,890	1,033	857	
In Seeing	1,014	507	507	53.65
In Speech	152	91	61	8.04
In Hearing	71	35	36	3.76
In Movement	491	310	181	25.98
Mentally	162	90	72	8.57

ARKALGUD

Arkalgud C.D. Block lies in the southern part of Hassan district. It is a part of Arkalgud taluka. The Block is located at a distance of 30 kms. from district headquarters (Hassan). There are 296 villages in the block with the total population of 184,059 persons. Area of the C.D. Block is 666.61 sq. kms. It is bounded by taluks Alur and Hassan on north, districts Mysore and Kodagu on south, taluk Hole Narsipur on east, and district Kodagu on west.

Communications:

Roadways : SH- 8: Direction- Sanivarsante to Holenarsipur, Nearest Villages- Mallipatna, Kelagalale, Boodanur, Hippali, Shiradanahalli, Darikongalale, Bobbagalale, Chowragallu, Vijapura Forest, Vijapura, Chikkarakalagud, Adike Bommanahalli, Arakalgud (Rural), Kellur, Honnavalli, Devarahalli, Devarahalli Kaval, Chikkagavanahalli, Doddagavanahalli, Bychanahalli, Goravanahalli, Hethagowdanahalli, Kallimuddanahalli, Paramahamsa Chakanahalli. SH- 21: Direction- Piriyapatna to Hassan, Nearest Villages- Arakalgud (Rural), Shambunathapura, Ankanaikanahalli, Neralahalli, Voddarahalli, Machagodanahalli, Madihalli, Mokali, Malalikere, Muthige, Chikkamagge, Doddamagge, Baragur, Nilavagilu, Mugalur, Muthugada Hosur, Hirehalli, Kotavalu, Ramanathapura, Ragupathi, Koppal, Mallarajapatna, Mallinathapura, Maradibasavanahalli, Gangoor, J. Hosahalli, Kathihalu, Ragimarur, Mallapura.

Railway Station: Narasinakuppe, Chikanahalli, Kenchinahalli.

River: Hemavati Nadi- Nearest Villages- Nelabahalli, Majjigepura, Honganoor, Konapura, Shanubhoganahalli, Ulivala, Ankanaikanahalli Kaval, Voddarahalli, Maradi, Honnagowdanahalli, Athini, Hebbale, Bolakyathanahalli, Anniganahalli, Ganganahalli, Haradoor. Cauvery Nadi- Nearest Villages- Kadavinahosahalli, Sheegodu, Saragoor, Ullenahalli, Konanur, Vodavana Hosahalli, Kattepura, Bandipalya, Gabbali, Madapura, Uttaranalakolavai Hantha, Ramanathapuranala Hantha, Basavapatna Hantha, Mathigodu, Rudrapatnanala Hantha, Bettasoge Hantha, Basavanahalli Hantha, Keralapura.

Canal: Nearest Villages- Saragoor, Ullenahalli, Konanur, Vodavana Hosahalli, Kattepura Bangarahalli, Yadiyur, Navile, Uttaranalakolavai Hantha, Kotavalu, Ragupathi Koppal, Mallarajapatna, Mallinathapura, Gangoor, J.Hosahalli, Ramanathapuranala Hantha, Moole Hosahalli, Basavapatna, Basavapatna Hantha, Mathigodu, Hanyalu, Rudrapatna, Rudrapatnanala Hantha, Bommanahalli, Bettasoge Hantha, Anandoor, Kantapura, Basavanahalli Hantha, Halekeralapura, Honnenahalli, Keralapura, Doramballi.

Annual Rainfall: Normal Rianfall 870.3 mm.

Ground Water: Availability of the Ground Water in the Basin is 46.79 H.A.M. and the utilization is 18.48 H.A.M. It belongs to Over Exploited category. Depth to water level 2 to 20 meter below the ground. Most of the wells go down in summer months, according to the Ground Water Estimation Committee.

Soils: Red Soil, Red Sandy Soil, Mixed Soil and Silty Clay Soil.

Natural Division : It falls in Cauvery-Hemavati Basin of the Southern Karnataka Plateau.

Administration:
Division: Mysore. Parliamentary Constituency: 16 Hassan. District: Hassan. Taluka: Arkalgud. Assembly Constituen cy: 198 Arkalgud. Gram Panchayat: 29.
Regional Area Development Boards: The Maland Aera Development Board.
Fairs: Kolalu Gopalakrishanaswamy Car Festival: It held at Konanur for about five days about the month of Febru ary. Konanur a town on the left bank of the Cauvery in Arkalgud taluk and also the headquarters of the hobli of the same name, is about 25 kms. north of Arkalgud town.
Lakshminarasimhaswamy Jatra: It held at Arkalgud in the month of march for two days. Arkalgud is the headqu arters town of the taluk of the same name and is situated 30 kms. south of Hassan on the Hassan-Periyapatna and Kodlipet-Holenarsipur roads. The Hemavathy forms the entire northern boundary of the taluk, while the Cauvery runs through a portion of the south.
Prasanna Subramanyaswamy Festival: It is held at Ramana thapura near Hassan for a period of ten days during Novem ber-December. Ramanathapura is a place, 20 kms. from Arkalgud town and 50 kms. from Hassan town.

Villages: 296 **Inhabited:** 278 **Uninhabited:** 18

Ranking	District	State	National
Area	6	139	1001
Population	4	103	953
Sex Ratio	5	24	956
Child Sex Ratio	4	11	973
Literacy Rate	7	98	3002
Density	7	77	3782
Work Participation Rate	1	32	1878

Gram Panchayats:
Voddarahalli, Hebbale, Ganjalagodu, Bychanahalli, Honnavalli, Vijapura Forest, Mallipatna, Holalagodu, Kattimallenahalli, Santhemarur, Yalagathavalli, Doddamagge, Hulikallu, Doddabemmathi, Handrangi, Chikkahalli, Agrahara, Belavadi, Basavapatna, Ramanathapura, Konanur , Bannur, Saragoor, Kattepura, Kalenahalli, Keralapura, Rudrapatna, Gangoor, Lakkur.
Amenities:
Education: Primary School in 240 villages, Middle school in 99 villages, Matriculation or Secondary School in 29 villages, namely Mallipatna, Doddabemmathi, Adike Bommanahalli, Honnavalli, Hebbale, Bychanahalli, Maravalalu, Hulikallu, Doddamagge, Dadadahalli, Santhemarur, Dummi, Belavadi, Handrangi, Kesavathur, Bannur, Beeranahalli Kaval, Saragoor, Konanur, Kattepura, Ramanathapura, Gangoor, Basavapatna, Ragimarur, Sompura, Rudrapatna, Keragodu, Lakkur, Keralapura.
Higher Secondary or Pre University Courses or Intermediate or Junior College in 11 villages of the CD Block,, namely Mallipatna, Bychanahalli, Maravalalu, Doddamagge, Dummi, Konanur, Kattepura, Basavapatna, Sompura, Lakkur, Keralapura.
College in 1 village, Adult Literacy Center in 0 village., College is in village, namely Konanur.
Medical: Hospital in 2 villages, Dispensary in 21 villages, Health Center in 10 villages, Sub Center in 50 villages, Maternity and Child Welfare Center in 7 villages, Community health workers in 6 villages.
The Villages having Hospital or Dispensary or Health Center are Mallipatna, Doddabemmathi, Hebbale, Hethagowdanahalli, Hulikallu, Doddamagge, Parasanahalli, Santhemarur, Bellame (Mariyanagara), Handrangi, Bannur, Siddapura, Konanur , Kattepura, Ramanathapura, Gangoor, J.Hosahalli, Basavapatna, Hanyalu, Rudrapatna, Lakkur, Keralapura.
Drinking Water: Tap water in 215 villages, Tank water in 244 villages, Well water in 241 villages, Tubewell in 153 villages and more than one source in 267 villages.
Bank: Banking facility in 29 villages, namely, Mallipatna, Sompura, Ittapatna, Madanur Hennur Kongalale, Maragowdanahalli, Pemmanahalli Chikkabemmathi, Yadiyuru, Lingadahalli, Dadadahalli Doddabemmathi, Bychanahalli, Muddanahalli, Hulikallu Doddamagge, Bannur, Siddapura, Saragoor, Konanur Chikkahalli, Kattepura, Yaladahalli, Navile Ramanathapura, Shiradanahalli, Basavapatna Rudrapatna, Keralapura.
Credit Society in 28 villages Agricultural Credit Society in 23 Non-Agricultural Credit Society in 20 villages.
Others: Power supply in 276 villages, Cinema hall in 5 villages sport club in 0 village, Stadium or Auditorium or Community Hall in 0 village, Post Office in 47 villages.
There are 157 villages having bus facilities.
Villages with most of facilities: Mallipatna Hennur Kongalale, Doddabemmathi, Hulikallu Doddamagge, Bannur, Siddapura, Saragoor, Konanur Kattepura, Ramanathapura, Basavapatna, Rudrapatna Keralapura.
Villages without amenities (Education):
Baisoor Forest, Dasanapura, Nelabahalli, Majjigepura, Honganoor, Kamanahalli, Konapura, Dharmapura, Shanubhoganahalli, Bagadalu, Sompura, Muduganur Kaval, Dadadahalli, Jakkahalli, Ragibychanahalli, Jogihosahalli, Mallenahalli, Puttana Hosahalli, Ulivala, Kanive Kaval, Devarahalli Kaval, Basavanahalli Kaval, Ankanathapura, Heelagere, Ankanahalli, Malenahalli,

Sabbathi, Beeranahalli, Kerehosahalli, Bandipalya, Navile, Kotavalu, Ragupathi Koppal, Maradibasavanahalli, Naganahalli, Rudrapatnanala Hantha, Bommanahalli, Kutakamarati Kaval..

Scheduled Castes: Out of the total population of 184789 persons, 37752 persons (20.43%) belong to Scheduled Castes. The villages having less than 10% SC population are Baisoor Forest, Basavanahalli, Dasanapura Nelabahalli, Majjigepura, Honganoor, Konapura Shanubhoganahalli, Beejaghatta, Darikongalale Masarangala, Mathra, Bagadalu, Maragowdanahalli Pemmanahalli, Chikkabemmathi, Yadiyuru Kakodanahalli, Jakkahalli, Ragibychanahalli Jogihosahalli, Vijapura, Mallenahalli, Ulivala Ankanaikanahalli Kaval, Adike Bommanahalli Thattekere, Harohalli, Madapura, Siddapura Kyathanahalli, Neralahalli, Madihalli, Siddapura Chikkagavanahalli, Chikkanahalli, Boranahalli Keshavapura, Bychanahalli, Hethagowdanahalli Haradoor, Basavanahlli, Kallubyadrahalli Ankanathapura, Shanbhoganahalli, Lingapura Kortikere Kaval, Mallapura, Bittagodanahalli Devipura, Dollenahalli, Bandiganahalli, Hennur Heelagere, Sulagodu-Somavara, Tarigalale Hindlahalli, Ankanahalli, Honnaganahalli, Karagallu Bettagalale, Hodenoor, Handrangi, Malenahalli Akkalavadi, Bislahalli, Kurubara Abbur, Aregallu Beeranahalli Kaval, Ramenahalli, Kadavinahosahalli Siddapura, Kerehosahalli, Chikkahalli Vodavana Hosahalli, Bandipalya, Madapura Gabbali Kaval, Navile, Ramanathapura Ragupathi Koppal, Mallarajapatna Maradibasavanahalli, Anjaneya Hosahalli, Naganahalli Kathihalu, Haralahalli, Mallapura, Rudrapatna Jittenahalli, Keragodu, Kantapura, Halekeralapura Keralapura.

The villages having more than 50% SC population are Dadadahalli, Kendinne Kaval, Dharmapura, Mudigere Holalagodu, Ambigodanahlli, Muduganur Kaval Dadadahalli, Kanive Kaval, Devarahalli Kaval Goravanahalli, Basavanahalli Kaval, Magge Kaval Chikkamagge, Dadadahalli, Santhemarur, Lakshmipura Belikarpuravalli, Paramahamsa Chakanahalli Muddanahalli, Beeranahalli, Yaladahalli Rudrapatnanala Hantha, Yachana Kuppe Kutakamarati Kaval.

Sex ratio of Scheduled Caste population is 499.

Scheduled Castes Literates and Illiterates by Sex:

	Persons	Males	Females
Literate	15,873	9,834	6,039
Illiterate	21,879	9,078	12,801
Literacy rate	48.3	59.8	36.8
Graduate	263	236	27

Scheduled Castes (Dominant):

Adi Karnataka, Madiga, Generic Castes etc., Bhovi Adi Dravida

For their cultural identity please see Appendix-I

Villages without Scheduled Castes: There are 64 villages without any scheduled caste population.

Scheduled Tribes: Out of the total population of 184789 persons, 2214 persons (1.2%) belong to Scheduled Tribes. The villages having less than 10% ST population are Madalapura, Koti Agrahara, Magodu, Mallipatna Kelagalale, Boodanur, Hippali, Baisoor Forest Baisoor, Basavanahalli, Dadadahalli, Shiradanahalli Manajur, Dasanapura, Kendinne Kaval, Hosahalli Nelabahalli, Majjigepura, Honganoor, Kamanahalli Konapura, Dharmapura, Shanubhoganahalli, Beejaghatta Mudigere, Darikongalale, Masarangala, Bobbagalale Chowragallu, Musavathur, Aladahalli, Mathra Bagadalu, Magalu, Hondaravally, Holalagodu, Sompura Ittapatna, Madanur, Hennur Kongalale Maragowdanahalli, Pemmanahalli, Chikkabemmathi Yadiyuru, Nilakunda, Singanakuppe Abbur Machagowdanahalli, Kollangi, Kallur Ambigodanahlli, Muduganur Kaval, Gerukuppe Lingadahalli, Dadadahalli, Doddabemmathi, Jakkahalli Arasikatte Kaval, Heggadihalli, Mudaganur Ragibychanahalli, Jogihosahalli, Allapatna Vijapura Forest, Vijapura, Mallenahalli Puttana Hosahalli, Chowdenahalli, Ulivala Ankanaikanahalli Kaval, Chikkarakalagud Adike Bommanahalli, Aremadanahalli, Thattekere Harohalli, Mundagodu, Madapura, Siddapura Kyathanahalli, Kattimallenahalli, Shambunathapura Ankanaikanahalli, Neralahalli, Voddarahalli, Maradi Nygere, Kashipura, Cholenahalli, Banadahalli Ramenahalli, Tejur, Kanive Kaval, Madihalli, Mokali Malalikere, Muthige, Honnavalli, Nelamane Garighatta, Siddapura, Honnagowdanahalli, Athini Narasinakuppe, Devarahalli, Devarahalli Kaval Chikkagavanahalli, Doddagavanahalli, Chikkanahalli Hullangala, Kenchenahalli, Boranahalli, Hebbale Bolakyathanahalli, Anniganahalli, Ganganahalli Mallithammanahalli, Muddanahalli, Keshavapura Bychanahalli, Goravanahalli, Maravalalu Hethagowdanahalli, Ganjalagodu, Haradoor Basavanahlli, Basavanahalli Kaval, Muddanahalli Kallubyadrahalli, Kallimuddanahalli, Ankanathapura

Madikehosahalli, Somanahalli, Kaniyar, Bettadahalli Magge Kaval, Chikkamagge, Doddamagge, Baragur Kodakahalli, Shanbhoganahalli, Parasanahalli Dadadahalli, Shanavinakuppe, Santhemarur, Illahalli Dummi, Lakshmipura, Muddanahalli, Koratikere Nilavagilu, Mugalur, Muthugada Hosur, Agrahara Doddahalli, Lingapura, Belikarpuravalli Kotekarpuravalli, Kortikere Kaval, Ibbadi, Mallapura Mallithammanahalli, Bittagodanahalli, Rangapura Paramahamsa Chakanahalli, Devipura, Yagati Yalagathavalli, Ajjur, Vaddarahalli, Hanemaranahalli Karahalli, Belavadi, Seebahalli, Ankanahalli Thattavalu, Dollenahalli, Hanagallu Shanubhoganahalli, Mallappanahalli, Bandiganahalli Hennur, Heelagere, Sulagodu-Somavara, Tarigalale Channigarayana Abbur, Hindlahalli, Heggathur Ankanahalli, Honnaganahalli, Karagallu, Bettagalale Bellame (Mariyanagara), Hodenoor, Chikkabommenahalli Majjanahalli, Handrangi, Malenahalli, Kesavathur Sabbathi, Bidarur, Kabbaligere, Lakkanahalli Muddanahalli, Akkalavadi, Doddabommenahalli Kurubara Abbur, Bannur, Kantenahalli Kaval, Aregallu Kantenahalli, Beeranahalli Kaval, Beeranahalli Ramenahalli, Kadavinahosahalli, Sheegodu, Siddapura Saragoor, Ullenahalli, Kerehosahalli, Konanur Chikkahalli, Konapura, Hirehalli, Vodavana Hosahalli Kattepura, Bandipalya, Gabbali, Gabbali Kaval Yaladahalli, Koodalur, Kotavalu, Bilaguli Ramanathapura, Ragupathi Koppal, Mallinathapura Hampapura, Gangoor, J.Hosahalli, Moole Hosahalli Basavapatna, Anjaneya Hosahalli, Naganahalli Mathigodu, Vaddarahalli, Kathihalu, Ragimarur Haralahalli, Mallapura, Sompura, Hanyalu, Rudrapatna Rudrapatnanala Hantha, Bommanahalli, Kanana Koppal Garudanahalli, Yachana Kuppe, Jittenahalli Kalenahalli, Bettasoge, Anandoor, Keragodu Maduranahalli, Kantapura, Basavanahalli Halekeralapura, Honnenahalli, Boodanur, Keralapura.

The villages having more than 50% ST population are None.

Sex ratio of Scheduled tribe population is 502.

Scheduled Tribes Literates and Illiterates by Sex:

	Persons	Males	Females
Literate	1,000	603	397
Illiterate	1,214	499	715
Literacy rate	51.6	62.6	40.7
Graduate	21	21	0

Scheduled Tribes (Dominant):

Naikda etc., Gond etc., Hakkipikki Generic Tribes etc., Soligaru

For their cultural identity please see Appendix-II

Villages without Scheduled Tribes: There are 242 villages without any scheduled tribe population.

Literates and Illiterates by Sex (Total Population):

	Persons	Males	Females
Literate	95,556	56,820	38,736
Illiterate	89,233	35,260	53,973
Literacy rate	59	70	47
Graduate	2,830	2,222	608

Agriculture: ***Distribution of villages according to land use:*** Out of 296 villages, Total area (in hectare) is 66661, out of that 62.78 percent is cultivable and 33.68 percent of the cultivable area is irrigated.

Sources of Irrigation (Hectares): Government Canal 8618.45, Private Canal 39.34, Well without Electricity 51.42, Well with Electricity 600.05, Tubewell without Electricity 4.84, Tubewell with Electricity 397.69, Tank 3423.79, River 136.37, Lake 0, Waterfall 99.12, Others 723.27.

Villages with population of 5000 to 9999: Konanur.

Villages with population of 10000 and above: None

Distribution of Workers:

	Persons	Males	Females	WPR
Cultivators	64,657	40,634	24,023	67.49
Agricultural Labour	18,391	6,673	11,718	19.2
Household Industry	1,513	815	698	1.58
Other Workers	11,237	8,033	3,204	11.73
Main Workers	73,113	50,826	22,287	76.32
Marginal Workers	22,685	5,329	17,356	23.68
Total Workers	95,798	56,155	39,643	

Religion: Major Religious Communities:

	Persons	Males	Females	Sex Ratio
Hindu (96.78%)	178,839	89,090	89,749	1,007
Muslim (2.35%)	4,349	2,188	2,161	988
Christian (0.44%)	822	403	419	1,040
Sikh (0%)	2	1	1	1,000
Buddhists (0.01%)	11	5	6	1,200
Jain (0.01%)	18	10	8	800

Agewise Data:

	Persons	Males	Females	Sex Ratio
All ages	184,789	92,080	92,709	1007
0-14	55,635	27,874	27,761	996
15-44	90,530	44,835	45,695	1019
45-79	36,215	18,260	17,955	983
80+	2,200	994	1,206	1213
Age not stated	209	117	92	786

Languages (Dominant):

Kannada, Urdu, Telugu, Tamil, Coorgi/Kodagu

Disabled Population:

	Persons	Males	Females	%

Total Disabled	2,963	1,661	1,302	
In Seeing	1,315	715	600	44.38
In Speech	307	176	131	10.36
In Hearing	213	108	105	7.19
In Movement	868	545	323	29.29
Mentally	260	117	143	8.77

ARSIKERE

Arsikere C.D. Block lies in the north-eastern part of Hassan district. It is a part of Arsikere tehsil. The Block is located at a distance of 42 kms. from district headquarters (Hassan). There are 369 villages in the block with the total population of 257,840 persons. Area of the C.D. Block is 1253.93 sq. kms. It is bounded by districts Chikmagalur and Tumkur on north, taluks Belur, Hassan and Channarayapatna on south, district Tumkur on east, and district Chikmagalur on west.

Communications:

Roadways : NH- 206: Direction- Shimoga to Tumkur, Nearest Villages- Agrahara, Uppinahalli, Chikkarehalli, Basavan ahalli, Byrapura, Banavara, Salapura, Masthihalli, Chaluv anahalli, Byragondanahalli, Shanthanahalli, Sydrahalli, Kallanaikanahalli, Jajuru, Arasikere (Rural), Kodihalli, Kellangere, Laxmidevarahalli, Honnasettihalli, Pannasam udra, Rangapura Kaval, Saluparahalli, Hunsekatte, Mylnaha lli, Hiriyalu. SH- 7: Direction- Arsikere to Channarayapatna, Nearest Villages- Habbanaghatta Kaval, Thirupathihalli, Habbanaghatta, Thalalur, Mududi, Borehalli, Chogachagere, Lalanakere, Honnakumaranahalli, Jakkanahalli, Gandasi,Chik kagandsi, Honnenahalli, Basavanapura, Doddayaraganalu. SH- 58: Direction-Villages- Belur to Madhugiri, Athigudda Kaval, Javagal, Savanthanahalli,, Maladevihalli, Sankihalli, Neelagiri Kaval, Kodihalli, Narasipura, Kelaginahosahalli, Arakere, Beluvalli, Kenkerehalli, Suledimmanahalli, Haruvanahalli, Mallapura, Banavara, Khandilinganahalli, Kachighatta, Kardihalli, Shanegere, Pura, Arehalli, Shankaranahalli (Garudana Giri), Kallu Sadarahalli, Karadihalli, Somasettihalli, Ahamedpura, Kallugundi, Hallithimmanahalli, Magenahalli, Kanakatte. SH- 68 A: Direction- Hassan to Tiptur, Nearest Villages- Nagarahalli, Lalanakere, Honnakumaranahalli, Jakkanahalli, Gandasi, Huragalavadi, Honnenahalli, Kondenalu, Marasettihalli, Narammanahalli, Lakkihalli Kaval, Bidare Kaval, Kenkere.

Railway Station: Villages- Bagilaghatta, Kachighatta.

Canal: Nearest Villages- Boochenahalli Kaval, Guddenaha lli, Kamenahalli, Sompura, S.Diggenahalli, Nerlige, Thimm anahalli, Kuruvanka, Kondavagilu, Kempasagara, Puralehalli, Harathanahalli, Siddapura, Venkatapura.

Annual Rainfall: Normal Rianfall 733.3 mm.

Ground Water: Availability of the Ground Water in the Basin is 101.29 H.A.M. and the utilization is 88.88 H.A.M. It belongs to Semi Critical category. Depth to water level 2 to 20 meter below the ground. Most of the wells go down in summer months, according to the Ground Water Estimation Committee.

Soils: Red Soil, Red Sandy Soil, Mixed Soil and Silty Clay Soil.

Natural Division : It falls partly in Arsikere Uplands and Gandasi-Hirisave Plateau of the Southern Karnataka Plateau.

Administration:

Division: Mysore. Parliamentary Constituency: 16 Hassan. District: Hassan. Taluka: Arsikere. Assembly Constituen cy: 194 Arsikere, 195 Belur. Gram Panchayat: 45.

Regional Area Development Boards: The Bailu Seeme Area Development Board.

Fairs: Venkataramanaswami Car Festival: The car festival of Venkataramanaswami temple held at Malckal-Tirupati around the month of July for a period of one week. Malck al-Tirupati, situated on the Hirckal hills close to Arsik ere, is about 3 kms. from Arsikere town and about 44 kms. from Hassan town. It is well-known for the Venkata ramanaswami temple, which is on the top of the hill on the northern side. A flight of 1,700 steps leads to the temple. There is also a large temple of Govindarajas wami at the foot of the hills. Both the temples are frequ ently visited by a large number of devotees throughout the year. An annual car festival is held which is well attended.

Villages: 369 **Inhabited:** 339 **Uninhabited:** 30

Ranking	District	State	National
Area	1	53	241
Population	1	33	190
Sex Ratio	8	33	1344
Child Sex Ratio	8	106	3319
Literacy Rate	1	34	1278
Density	5	62	4652
Work Participation Rate	5	72	1606

Gram Panchayats:

Kanakatte, Shankaranahalli, Madalu, Kallugundi, Shanegere, Narasipura, Doddametikurke, Rampura, Jayachamarajapura, Kuruvanka, Banavara, Kachighatta, Arakere, Bendekere, Puralehalli, Kamasamudra, Dummenahalli, Aggunda, Jajuru, Hiriyur, Kolagunda, Nerlige, Javagal, Bandur, Handralu, Undiganalu, Murundi, Geejihalli, Belagumba, Thalalur, Harnahalli , Karagunda, Kalyadi, Habbanaghatta, Yadavanahalli, Mududi, Rangapura, Bageshpura, Gandasi, Heggatta, Kenkere, Kondenalu, Lalanakere, Bagivalu, Chogachagere.

Amenities:

Education: Primary School in 309 villages, Middle school in

191 villages, Matriculation or Secondary School in 61 villages, namely Javagal, S.Diggenahalli, Nerlige, Handralu, Undiganalu, Kalyadi, Kolagunda, Arakere, Kurudahalli, Karagunda, Haralahalli, Nagenahalli, Banavara, Hiriyur, Byragondanahalli, Shanegere, Nagasamudra, Hosahalli, Bendekere, Chikkammanahalli, Puralehalli, Kallu Sadarahalli, Kallugundi, Kanakatte, Hirisadarahalli, Nagavedi, Haralakatta, Doddametikurke, Madalu, Kittanakere, Kadalamagge, Jayachamarajapura, Singenahalli, Kamasamudra, Rampura, Chikkur, Yadapura, Bommanahalli, Murundi, Annanaikanahalli, Harnahalli *, Thalalur, Aggunda, Dummenahalli, Pannasamudra, Thalalatore, Belagumba, Hunsekatte, Bilenahalli, Bageshpura, Mududi, Nagarahalli, Chogachagere, Gandasi, Bachenahalli, Heggatta, Doddayaraganalu, Bagivalu, Kondenalu, Yadavanahalli, Kenkere.

Higher Secondary or Pre University Courses or Intermediate or Junior College in 11 villages of the CD Block,, namely Javagal, Banavara, Kallu Sadarahalli, Hirisadarahalli, Doddametikurke, Madalu, Kittanakere, Jayachamarajapura, Harnahalli *, Gandasi, Kenkere.

College in 3 villages, Adult Literacy Center in 19 villages., Colleges are in villages, namely Javagal, Gandasi, Kenkere.

Medical: Hospital in 2 villages, Dispensary in 32 villages, Health Center in 17 villages, Sub Center in 54 villages, Maternity and Child Welfare Center in 15 villages, Community health workers in 9 villages.

The Villages having Hospital or Dispensary or Health Center are Javagal, Nerlige, Handralu, Undiganalu, Vrundavanahalli, Kalyadi, Kolagunda, Arakere, Beluvalli, Karagunda, Byalekere, Banavara, Pura, Nagasamudra, Kuruvanka, Kallu Sadarahalli, Kallugundi, Madalu, Jayachamarajapura, Shashivala, Chikkur, Yadapura, Harnahalli *, Geejihalli, Thalalatore, Belagumba, Bageshpura, Halagenahalli, Lalanakere, Gandasi, Bagivalu, Kondenalu.

Drinking Water: Tap water in 184 villages, Tank water in 134 villages, Well water in 214 villages, Tubewell in 281 villages and more than one source in 315 villages.

Bank: Banking facility in 23 villages, namely, Javagal, Undiganalu, Kolagunda, Banavara, Arehalli Kuruvanka, Kallugundi, Kanakatte, Nagavedi Haralakatta, Doddametikurke, Kittanakere Jayachamarajapura, Kamasamudra, Chikkur Kallanaikanahalli, Harnahalli *, Aggunda, Belagumba Bageshpura, Chogachagere, Gandasi, Kenkere.

Credit Society in 28 villages Agricultural Credit Society in 21 Non-Agricultural Credit Society in 3 villages.

Others: Power supply in 329 villages, Cinema hall in 6 villages sport club in 2 villages, Stadium or Auditorium or Community Hall in 0 village, Post Office in 77 villages.

There are 202 villages having bus facilities.

Villages with most of facilities: Javagal Undiganalu, Kolagunda, Banavara, Kuruvanka Kallugundi, Kanakatte, Doddametikurke, Kittanakere Jayachamarajapura, Kamasamudra, Chikkur Harnahalli *, Aggunda, Belagumba, Bageshpura Chogachagere, Gandasi, Kenkere.

Villages without amenities (Education): Athigudda Kaval, Boochenahalli Kaval, Devihalli, Nayakanakere, K.Diggenahalli, Kenganahalli, Kelaginahosahalli, Upparkalenahalli, Rangapura Kaval, Hanumanahalli, Thippanahalli, Doddenahalli, Shanthanahalli, Rangapura, Siddapura, Hallithimmanahalli, Mallapura, Basavanahalli, Mallenahalli, Arasikere (Rural), Karlahalli, Kenchenahalli, Pura, Rangapura Kaval, Nagathihalli, Singenahalli, Bagooranahalli, Thimmalapura, Lingapura, Bandihalli..

Scheduled Castes: Out of the total population of 257878 persons, 48524 persons (18.82%) belong to Scheduled Castes. The villages having less than 10% SC population are Doddaghatta, Boochenahalli Kaval, Guddenahalli Savanthanahalli, Nerlige, Thimmanahalli, Sankihalli Mosale, Kodihalli, Dhananjayapura Chikkalinganahalli, Nayakanakere, Vrundavanahalli Kalyadi, Kurubarahalli, Kenganahalli, Narasipura Chikkajjikattehalli, Thavarehalli, Singanahalli Moodnahalli, Haralahalli, Byalekere, Doddenahalli Vaderahalli, Suledimmanahalli, Uppinahalli Venkatapura, Basavanahalli, Byrapura, Hanumanahalli Thippanahalli, Mallapura, Banavara, Salapura Bisalehalli, Kanihalli, Masthihalli, Rampura Chaluvanahalli, Doddenahalli, Ganjigere, Pura Yarehalli, Sunkadahalli, Shanthanahalli Basavarajapura, Byadarahalli, Chikkammanahalli Anandanahalli, Kondavagilu, Siddapura, Venkatapura Valehalli, Giri Bommanahalli, Somasettihalli Ahamedpura, Hallithimmanahalli, Gollarahalli Sathanagere, Kasuvanahalli, Kanakatte Yachagondanahalli, Dibbur, Chikkondihalli, Jannavara Ramanahalli, Mallapura, Byrapura, Hosahalli Donanakatte, Kumbaraghatta, Maddarahalli Chikkametikurke, Chikkalkur, Jayachamarajapura Basavanahalli, Yarigenahalli, Singenahalli Thudikenahalli, Thumbapura, Gollarahalli Nagathihalli, Javanahalli, Mannamakanahalli Yelavare, Muddaranganahalli, Arasikere (Rural)

Bandihalli, Kodihalli, Thirupathihalli, Vitalapura
Guttinakere, Doddenahalli, Belavathahalli
Hebbaranahalli, Makanahalli, Sulekere, Dasihalli
Somenahalli, Karlahalli, Chandlapura, Kenchenahalli
Pura, Kunighattahalli, Jotimallapura, Annapura
Ajjanahalli, Thippanahalli, Kallukere
Rangapura Kaval, Gollarahalli, Rangapura Kaval
Saluparahalli, Hunsekatte, Kammaraghatta, Hosahalli
Ramjihalli, Kadehalli, Bilenahalli, Appenahalli
Bageshpura, Jeenakerehalli, Nagathihalli
Cheelanahalli, Jogenahalli, Bommachihalli
Mahadevarahalli, Rangapura Kaval, Halagenahalli
Bisalehalli, Gollarahalli, Singenahalli, Nagarahalli
Manjenahalli, Kudukundi, Chogachagere, Lalanakere
Honnakumaranahalli, Jakkanahalli, Gandasi
Dasenahalli, Bachenahalli, Jeekanahalli
Bagooranahalli, Heggatta, Gundakallahalli
Huragalavadi, Honnenahalli, Thimmalapura
Doddayaraganalu, Yaraganalu, Hirisamudra, Hiriyalu
Bagivalu, Lingapura, Aladahalli, Karimaranahalli
Mangalapura, Kondenalu, Ugranahalli, Hullekere
Somenahalli, Mallenahalli, Shivapura
Jalagaranahalli, Mallapura, Kenkere.

The villages having more than 50% SC population are Athigudda Kaval, Neelagiri Kaval, Devihalli
Thirupathihalli, Thimmalapura, Upparkalenahalli
Gollarahalli, Kachighatta, Bettadapura, Hariharapura
Chikkabanavara, Lingodanahalli, Kurubarahalli
Sydrahalli, Maratagere, Puralehalli, Harathanahalli
Yadapura, Bommanahalli, Maladevihalli, Muddanahalli
Karehalli, Bommenahalli, Narayanaghattahalli
Thalalatore, Mylnahalli, Rangapura Kaval, Bandihalli.

Sex ratio of Scheduled Caste population is 497.

Scheduled Castes Literates and Illiterates by Sex:

	Persons	Males	Females
Literate	21,709	13,171	8,538
Illiterate	26,815	11,244	15,571
Literacy rate	51.9	62.6	41.1
Graduate	373	330	43

Scheduled Castes (Dominant):

Banjara etc., Bhovi, Madiga, Adi Karnataka
Sudugadu Siddha

For their cultural identity please see Appendix-I

Villages without Scheduled Castes: There are 112 villages without any scheduled caste population.

Scheduled Tribes: Out of the total population of 257878 persons, 8052 persons (3.12%) belong to Scheduled Tribes.

The villages having less than 10% ST population are Doddaghatta, Athigudda Kaval, Javagal
Boochenahalli Kaval, Guddenahalli, Kamenahalli
S.Kallahalli, S.Diggenahalli, Savanthanahalli
Thimmanahalli, Maladevihalli, Sankihalli, Mosale
Neelagiri Kaval, Kodihalli, Dhananjayapura
Linglapura, Bandur, Handralu, Devihalli, Undiganalu
Chikkalinganahalli, Nayakanakere, Vrundavanahalli
Kalyadi, Halekalyadi, Deshani, Kurubarahalli
Kenganahalli, Thirupathihalli, Mavuthanahalli
Kolagunda, Narasipura, Melinahosahalli
Chikkajjikattehalli, Chikkalinganahalli
Thavarehalli, Maragondanahalli, Kelaginahosahalli
Arakere, Beluvalli, Thimmalapura, Upparkalenahalli
Madanahalli, Singanahalli, Matadahosahalli
Govindapura , Gollarahalli, Karagunda, Madapura
Vaderahalli, Haralahalli, Byalekere, Kamalapura
Nagenahalli, Rangapura Kaval, Doddenahalli
Bevinahalli, Vaderahalli, Kenkerehalli
Suledimmanahalli, Bagilaghatta, Agrahara
Uppinahalli, Venkatapura, Chikkarehalli
Basavanahalli, Hanumanahalli, Thippanahalli
Thondiganahalli, Manakathur, Mallapura, Banavara
Salapura, Kachighatta, Kenchanahalli, Byrambudi
Bisalehalli, Bettadapura, Hiriyur, Kanihalli
Hariharapura, Korenahalli, Rampura, Byragondanahalli
Chikkabanavara, Kardihalli, Shanegere, Doddenahalli
Ganjigere, Pura, Arehalli, Nagasamudra, Hosahalli
Yarehalli, Lingodanahalli, K.G.Agrahara
Sunkadahalli, Kurubarahalli, Kommaraghatta
Bendekere, Sydrahalli, Shanthanahalli
Basavarajapura, Rangapura, Kuruvanka, Thippaghatta
Byadarahalli, Maratagere, Chikkammanahalli
Mylnahalli, Kempasagara, Puralehalli, Harathanahalli
Siddapura, Venkatapura, Byrapura
Shankaranahalli (Garudana Giri), Karadihalli
Giri Bommanahalli, Somasettihalli, Ahamedpura
Kallugundi, Narasipura, Honnakatta, Sathanagere
Magenahalli, Kasuvanahalli, Yachagondanahalli
Dibbur, Chikkondihalli, Soppinahalli
Hirisadarahalli, Kyathanahalli, Jannavara
Ramanahalli, Mallapura, Nagavedi, Byrapura
Doddaghatta, Haralakatta, Doddametikurke, Madalu
Hosahalli, Kittanakere, Donanakatte, Kumbaraghatta
Bennigundihalli, Shankaranahalli, Kadalamagge
Chikkametikurke, Holalakere, Chikkalkur
Jayachamarajapura, Basavanahalli, Kasuvanahalli
Paduvanahalli, Kamasamudra, Mallenahalli
Thudikenahalli, Thumbapura, Gollarahalli
Melenahalli, Rampura, Shashivala, Sankodanahalli
Chikkur, Layalapura, Kallanaikanahalli, Nagathihalli
Jajuru, Katikere, Yadapura, Javanahalli
Bommanahalli, Murundi, Annanaikanahalli

Mannamakanahalli, Harnahalli *, Yelavare
Habbanaghatta Kaval, Geejihalli, Muddaranganahalli
Muddanahalli, Arasikere (Rural), Karehalli
Bommenahalli, Bandihalli, Thirupathihalli
Vitalapura, Guttinakere, Doddenahalli
Belavathahalli, Hebbaranahalli, Makanahalli
Habbanaghatta, Thalalur, Narayanaghattahalli
Laxmidevarahalli, Sulekere, Aggunda, Shankaranahalli
Dasihalli, Somenahalli, Chandlapura, Dummenahalli
Kenchenahalli, Pura, Harlakatta, Adihalli
Honnasettihalli, Pannasamudra, Challapura
Honnenahalli, Kunighattahalli, T.Kodihalli
Jotimallapura, Annapura, Thalalatore, Thimmalapura
Ajjanahalli, Thippanahalli, Belagumba, Kallukere
Rangapura Kaval, Sanklapura, Gollarahalli
Rangapura Kaval, Annenahalli, Saluparahalli
Hunsekatte, Mylnahalli, Rangenahalli
Rangapura Kaval, Mootikere, Kammaraghatta, Hosahalli
Ramjihalli, Kadehalli, Bageshpura, Jeenakerehalli
Nandihalli, B. Hosahalli, Nagathihalli
Chittanahalli, Cheelanahalli, Jogenahalli, Adihalli
Manjenahalli Kaval, Bommachihalli, Mahadevarahalli
Rangapura Kaval, Halagenahalli, Mududi, Bisalehalli
Borehalli, Gollarahalli, Mangalapura, Singenahalli
Channapura, Nagarahalli, Manjenahalli, Kudukundi
Chogachagere, Lalanakere, Honnakumaranahalli
Jakkanahalli, Gandasi, Chikkagandsi, Dasenahalli
Bachenahalli, Jogenahalli, Jeekanahalli
Bagooranahalli, Heggatta, Gundakallahalli
Huragalavadi, Honnenahalli, Honnenahalli
Vadagarahalli, Thimmalapura, Basavanapura
Doddayaraganalu, Yaraganalu, Hirisamudra, Hiriyalu
Bagivalu, Lingapura, Aladahalli, Karimaranahalli
Mangalapura, Kondenalu, Ugranahalli, Marasettihalli
Hullekere, Channaikanahalli, Somenahalli
Yadavanahalli, Mallenahalli, Shivapura, Sannenahalli
Jalagaranahalli, Narammanahalli, Mallapura
Bidare Kaval, Bandihalli, Kenkere.

The villages having more than 50% ST population are Kurudahalli, Valehalli, Hallithimmanahalli Singenahalli.

Sex ratio of Scheduled tribe population is 494.

Scheduled Tribes Literates and Illiterates by Sex:

	Persons	Males	Females
Literate	4,247	2,507	1,740
Illiterate	3,805	1,565	2,240
Literacy rate	60.2	70.7	49.6
Graduate	73	61	12

Scheduled Tribes (Dominant):

Naikda etc., Meda, Soligaru, Generic Tribes etc. Hakkipikki

For their cultural identity please see Appendix-II

Villages without Scheduled Tribes: There are 256 villages without any scheduled tribe population.

Literates and Illiterates by Sex (Total Population):

	Persons	Males	Females
Literate	158,564	90,512	68,052
Illiterate	99,314	38,762	60,552
Literacy rate	69	79	60
Graduate	4,892	3,978	914

Agriculture: ***Distribution of villages according to land use:*** Out of 369 villages, Total area (in hectare) is 125393, out of that 58.17 percent is cultivable and 16.35 percent of the cultivable area is irrigated.

Sources of Irrigation (Hectares): Government Canal 886.05, Private Canal 0, Well without Electricity 33.09, Well with Electricity 909.26, Tubewell without Electricity 50.6, Tubewell with Electricity 6546.88, Tank 2088.02, River 4, Lake 0, Waterfall 43.72, Others 1368.71.

Villages with population of 5000 to 9999:
Javagal, Banavara, Harnahalli *.

Villages with population of 10000 and above: None

Distribution of Workers:

	Persons	Males	Females	WPR
Cultivators	84,234	54,380	29,854	61.31
Agricultural Labour	28,851	10,382	18,469	21
Household Industry	3,234	1,991	1,243	2.35
Other Workers	21,077	15,982	5,095	15.34
Main Workers	103,340	75,184	28,156	75.21
Marginal Workers	34,056	7,551	26,505	24.79
Total Workers	137,396	82,735	54,661	

Religion: Major Religious Communities:

	Persons	Males	Females	Sex Ratio
Hindu (96.06%)	247,709	124,108	123,601	996
Muslim (3.5%)	9,023	4,576	4,447	972
Christian (0.07%)	169	84	85	1,012
Sikh (0.02%)	54	20	34	1,700
Buddhists (0.01%)	26	16	10	625
Jain (0.09%)	220	111	109	982

Agewise Data:

	Persons	Males	Females	Sex Ratio
All ages	257,878	129,274	128,604	995
0-14	69,433	35,303	34,130	967
15-44	126,739	62,897	63,842	1015
45-79	58,201	29,455	28,746	976
80+	3,342	1,522	1,820	1196
Age not stated	163	97	66	680

Languages (Dominant):
Kannada, Telugu, Urdu, Hindi, Marathi

Disabled Population:

	Persons	Males	Females	%
Total Disabled	4,981	2,699	2,282	
In Seeing	2,151	1,086	1,065	43.18
In Speech	534	292	242	10.72
In Hearing	480	223	257	9.64
In Movement	1,375	872	503	27.6
Mentally	441	226	215	8.85

ATHNI

Athni C.D. Block lies in the north-eastern part of Belgaum district. It is a part of Athni taluka. The Block is located at a distance of 150 kms. from district headquarters (Belgaum). There are 108 villages in the block with the total population of 420,447 persons. Area of the C.D. Block is 1987.47 sq. kms. It is bounded by districts Bijapur and Bagalkot on east, taluks Chikodi and Raybag and district Bagalkot on south, and it has common boundary with the state of Maharashtra on north and west.

Communications:

Roadways : S.H-12: Direction- Chikodi to Bijapur, Nearest Villages- Kagawad, Jugul, Shahapur, Shiraguppi, Shedbal, Lokur, Mangasuli, Navalihal, Koulgudd, Mole, Muragundi, Devaradderahatti, Athani (Rural), Telsang, Fadatarawadi, Aigali,Yakkanchi, Badachi, Desairatti, Khotanatti, Aratal, Badagi, Yallammawadi. S.H-31: Direction- Gokak to Dapalapur, Nearest Villages- Anantapur, Bevanoor, Kiranagi, Balligeri, Gundewadi, Parthanahalli, Athani (Rural), Sankonahatti, Hulagabali, Darur, Halyal, Avarkhod, Khavatkoppa, Sankaratti.

Railway Station: Shedbal, Ugar Khurd.

River: Krishna Nadi- Nearest Villages- Mangavati, Jugul, Shahapur, Molwad, Kusnal, Ugar Budruk, Ugar Khurd, Ainapur, Krishna Kittur, Banajawad, Hulagabali, Nadi-Ingalgaon, Teerth,Saptasagar, Darur, Halyal, Avarkhod, Naganur P.A., Khavatkoppa, Shegunshi, Dodwad, Satti, Nandeshwar, Mahishwadgi, Janawad, Savadi, Shirahatti, Junjarwad. Agrani Nadi- Nearest Villages- Khilegaon, Ajur, Tawashi, Naganur P.A., Shirur, Sambaragi, Kallotti, Kiranagi, Gundewadi, Shivanoor, Agrani-Ingalgaon, Abbihal, Parthanahalli, Mavinahatti, Katral, Ainapur, Banajawad, Muragundi, Masarguppi, Devaradderahatti, Tangadi, Shinal, Hulagabali. Don Nadi- Nearest Villages- Kakamari, Kottalgi, Bannur, Telsang. Canal: Nearest Villages- Anantapur, Tawashi, Naganur P.A., Kagawad, Jugul, Shahapur, Shiraguppi, Molwad, Kusnal, Ugar Budruk, Ugar Khurd, Farida Khanawadi, Manga Mole, Ainapur.

Annual Rainfall: Normal Rianfall 513.8 mm.

Ground Water: Availability of the Ground Water in the Basin is15716 H.A.M. and the utilization is 21518 H.A.M. It belongs to Over Exploited category. Depth to water level 2 to 20 meter below the ground. Most of the wells go down in summer months, according to the Ground Water Estimation Committee.

Soil: Red Soil, Black Soil.

Natural Division : It falls partly in the Athni Upland and Krishna Ghatprabha Irrigated Tract of the Northern Karnataka Plateau.

Administration:

Division: Belgaum. Parliamentary Constituency: 1Chikodi. District: Belgaum. Taluka: Athni. Assembly Constituency: 3 Athni, 4 Kagawad. Gram Panchayat: 51.

Regional Area Development Boards: The Bailu Seeme Area Development Board.

Border Villages: (State: Maharashtra)- Pandegaon, Malabad, Aralihatti, Bammanal, Vishnuvadi, Siddewadi, Kempwad, Kakamari, Ramateerth, Kohalli, Adalatti, Khilegaon, Ajur, Anantapur, Kottalgi, Balligeri, Shahpur, Jugal, Kagawad, Mangavatti, Shedbad, Lokur, Mangasulhi.

Fairs: Basavanna Jatra: It is held at Khilegaon around the month of March-April for five days. Khilegaon, 38 kilometer from Athani, situated on the border of Maharashtra is a place of pilgrimage. The place has temples dedicated to Basavanna, Hanumanta, Motu Basaveshwara and Sangamanatha. The Basavanna temple is a huge complex with a garbhagriha (modern) having a Nandi and also statues built by Bijapur rulers, recently renovated completely. Surrounding the temple inside the wide prakara are small shrines of Karaveerappa, Akkamahadevi, Huchchappa, Dhavalappa, Hanumanta, Kadasiddheshwara (Linga) and Bharamappa. The annual jatra takes place for five days beginning from Ugadi Padya, when more than 10,000 people assemble. There is a huge kalyana mantapa also.

Mahboob Subhani Baghdadi Urs: It is held at Athani near Belgaum in the north after Moharram every year.

Maradi Basaveshwar Jatra: It is held at Dodwad near Belgaum in the month of May every year. Dodwad is a place with considerable antiquity. According to a record of Dodwad its agrahara was founded by Kadamba Permadi and it was under Navalgunda Kampana. The place is referred to by Captain Moor in 1790 as a pretty large place with good looking newly repaired fortifications. The place has a Veerabhadra temple immediately after the agase (entrance) of the village. The Veerabhadra image is about one metre tall flanked by Ganapathi and a standing female deity. An inscription in front of the temple has a Jaina Tirthankara at the top portion and is of later Chalukyas dated in the 1081 AD, badly damaged and seems to record a gift by a Mahasamanta.

Masabti Urs: It is held at Jugal near Belgaum in the month of Rajjab. Jugal, is about 45 kms. fom Athani, located on the bank of Krishna river. The place has a dargah of a lady,

Masabti and the Urs is held in the month of Rajjab when a huge gathering is seen. Masabti is described as the wife of the Pir at the dargah of Miraj, and both hailed from Bidar. Across the river Krishna (two kilometres from Jugal) towards north (in Maharashtra) is the celebrated pilgrim centre Khidrapur which has a huge and marvellous later Chalukyan monument in honour of Kopeshwar (or Kopnath).

Padmavati Utsava: It is held at Ugar Khurd, Belgaum area in about the month of May every year. Ugar Khurd 34 kms. from Athani on the left bank of the Krishna is a famous industrial centre. The name of the place, Ugar is attributed to the God Ugreshwara who is also called Mahadeva. The place has temples dedicated to Ugreshwara, Vithoba, Vishwanatha, Raghavendra Matha, Venkateshwara and Ganapati. The Mahadeva or Ugreshwara on the river bank in the old township area, though renovated has the stellar garbhagriha of Chalukyan times intact. The Vishwantha temple in later Chalukyan style is completely renovated, but only the door frame of the garbhagriha is retained.

Sangameshwara Jatra: It is held at Adhalli near Belgaum around the month of October-November every year. Adhalli which is at a distance of 18 kms. from Athani situated on a left deviation road from the Athani-Bijapur road, appears to be an old place. The has temples of Hanumanta, Shankarlinga, etc. The Hanumanta temple, a stone structure built recently has its garbhagriha in a slight depression. Outside the temple is a Saptamatrika panel built in the wall.

Santoobai Jatra: It is held at Kagwad in the month of Magha (February-March) every year. Kagwad 30 kms. from Athani approachable from Shedbal Railway Station is a place with considerable antiquity. Its place name is attributed to the local deity Kaggodaraya, a Jaina deity. But a village (bada) with red soil (kaga or masari) appears to be the origin of the place name.The place has temples dedicated to Kaggodaraya (Jaina),Ganapati, Maruti and Santubai. The Kaggodaraya temple (also basti) has a renovated mukhamantapa and a garbhagriha. The garbhagriha has images of Kaggodaraya along with his female companion Kalamma. (Some identify these with Brahmanatha and Padmavati). Sayed Ummer Quadri Urs: It is held at Ainapur near Belgaum during the Bakrid every year. Ainapur 24 kms. from Athani is an ancient place on the bank of the Krishna. The place has a mosque (renovated) and a dargah ascribed to Syed Ummer Quadri. The Urs is held three days following 'Bakrid' when nearly 2,000 people assemble.

Shivayogi Jatra: It is held at Athani near Belgaum around the months of January-February every year. The place has temples dedicated to Amritalingeshwara, Ramalinga, Kalmeshwara, Narasimha, Siddeshwara, Hanumanta, Ganapati, etc.The finest among them is the Amritalingeshwara temple, a monument of Later Chalukyan style with profuse carvings and highly artistic pillars in the Navaranga. The temple has a garbhagriha, a navaranga and a fallen (renovated) mukhamantapa. The entrance of the navaranga has pierced windows. The exterior of the garbhagriha has fine figures and designs in high relief.

Siddeshwar Jatra: It is held at Ainapur around the month of January every year. Ainapur, 24 kms. from Athani is an ancient place located on the bank of the river Krishna. The earliest reference to the place was in 1639 when the German traveller notices as 'Eynatour'. The place has temples dedicated to Brahmadeva, Vishwanatha, Siddeshwara (Gramadevata),Venkataramana, Hanumanta, Ramalinga, etc.

Siddeshwara Temple Jatra: It is held at Athani near Belgaum around the month of January every year. The Siddeshwara temple on the Bijapur road is the gramadevata and the domed temple is completely renovated by the Adilshahis. The remains of an earlier structure like Chalukyan pillars are built into the wall. Annual jatra and a cattle fair is held in January when about 75,000 people assemble.

Siddharameshwara Jatra: It is held at Shedbal near Belgaum during Shivaratri (February-March). Shedbal 27 kms. from Athani on the Bangalore-Miraj railway lines mentioned as 'Shedambala' in a record of 1143 A.D. from Miral (Maharashtra).The place has temples dedicated to Basavanna, Hanumanta, Vithoba and Yellamma. The Basavanna temple is in later Vijayanagara style. The navaranga (granite) pillars are square shaped. There is a shrine of Siddhara meshwara in its premises. The annual jatra is held during Shivaratri when more than 10,000 people assemble. Yellamma Devi Jatra: It is held at Kokatnur near Belgaum around the months of January-February for fifteen days and over one lakh people assemble. Kokatnur eight kms. from Athani located in a bowl shaped area is a place of rich antiquity. The place name Kokatnur is found mentioned as "Korggatanur", an agrahara in two inscriptions from the same place. The place has temples like the Papanasi, Siddharameshwara, Kadasiddheshwara, Amritlinge shwara, Veerabhadra, Mallikarjuna, Appayyaswami, Durgavva, Beerappa, etc. The Papanasi temple (also locally called Kalmeshwara) is built on the bank of the Papanasinala and appears to be the earliest structure.

Yellamma Jatra: It is held at Telsang near Belgaum around the months of October-November. Telsang 35 kms. from Athani is mentioned as "Tilasanga" in various records. It was a celebrated centre for learning in those days and is repeatedly referred as Mahagrahara". The place has temples dedicated to Satyappa-Sannappa, Vithoba, Venkataramana, Shankaralinga, Maruti, Yellamma, Durgavva, Kalmeshwara of Kalalinga and Basavanna. The Satyappa-Sannappagudi built out of the Chalukyan temple material used to create five dolmen like shrines in which several stones are worshipped.

Villages: 108 **Inhabited:** 108 **Uninhabited:** 0

Ranking	District	State	National
Area	1	6	53
Population	2	2	6
Sex Ratio	8	148	3596
Child Sex Ratio	9	170	5033
Literacy Rate	6	92	2848
Density	2	28	4561
Work Participation Rate	7	69	991

Gram Panchayats:
Shirur, Khilegaon, Anantapur, Sambaragi, Aralihatti, Madabhavi, Jambagi, Gundewadi, Malabad, Balligeri, Parthanahalli, Muragundi, Kempwad, Mangasuli, Shedbal , Kagawad, Jugul, Shiraguppi, Ugar Budruk, Kusnal, Ugar Khurd, Ainapur, Mole, Tangadi, Athani (Rural) , Yelihadalagi, Adahalli, Kohalli, Kakamari, Kottalgi, Telsang, Aratal, Aigali, Kokatnoor, Katageri, Nandagaon, Halyal, Hulagabali, Krishna Kittur, Saptasagar, Nadi-Ingalgaon, Darur, Sankaratti, Naganur P.K., Shegunshi, Satti, Nandeshwar, Mahishwadgi, Savadi, Shirahatti, Junjarwad.

Amenities:
Education: Primary School in 108 villages, Middle school in 102 villages, Matriculation or Secondary School in 42 villages, namely Khilegaon, Anantapur, Malabad, Tawashi, Shirur, Sambaragi, Aralihatti, Balligeri, Gundewadi, Madabhavi, Kagawad, Jugul, Shiraguppi, Molwad, Ugar Budruk, Ugar Khurd, Shedbal, Lokur, Mangasuli, Kempwad, Mole, Ainapur, Krishna Kittur, Muragundi, Shinal, Sankonahatti, Nadi-Ingalgaon, Saptasagar, Halyal, Khavatkoppa, Sankaratti, Shegunshi, Satti, Kakamari, Kottalgi, Telsang, Aigali, Adahalli, Yelihadalagi, Kokatnoor, Ghatanatti, Shirahatti.
Higher Secondary or Pre University Courses or Intermediate or Junior College in 9 villages of the CD Block,, namely Anantapur, Sambaragi, Shivanoor, Madabhavi, Kagawad, Ugar Khurd, Ainapur, Telsang, Aigali.
College in 2 villages, Adult Literacy Center in 8 villages., Colleges are in villages, namely Kagawad, Ainapur.
Medical: Hospital in 0 village, Dispensary in 4 villages, Health Center in 14 villages, Sub Center in 55 villages, Maternity and Child Welfare Center in 5 villages, Community health workers in 20 villages.
The Villages having Hospital or Dispensary or Health Center are Muragundi, Tangadi, Kakamari, Kottalgi.

Drinking Water: Tap water in 75 villages, Tank water in 26 villages, Well water in 59 villages, Tubewell in 41 villages and more than one source in 103 villages.
Bank: Banking facility in 26 villages, namely, Khilegaon, Anantapur, Malabad, Madabhavi, Kagawad Jugul, Shiraguppi, Molwad, Ugar Budruk, Ugar Khurd Shedbal, Mangasuli, Mole, Ainapur, Athani (Rural) Shinal, Hulagabali, Halyal, Sankaratti, Satti Telsang, Aigali, Adalatti, Adahalli, Kokatnoor Shirahatti.
Credit Society in 66 villages Agricultural Credit Society in 64 Non-Agricultural Credit Society in 3 villages.
Others: Power supply in 108 villages, Cinema hall in 6 villages sport club in 2 villages, Stadium or Auditorium or Community Hall in 0 village, Post Office in 86 villages.
There are 101 villages having bus facilities.
Villages with most of facilities: Khilegaon Anantapur, Malabad, Madabhavi, Kagawad, Jugul Shiraguppi, Ugar Budruk, Ugar Khurd, Shedbal Mangasuli, Mole, Ainapur, Athani (Rural), Hulagabali Halyal, Sankaratti, Satti, Telsang, Aigali, Adahalli Kokatnoor, Shirahatti.
Villages without Amenities (Education): None..
Scheduled Castes: Out of the total population of 420912 persons, 60335 persons (14.33%) belong to Scheduled Castes.
The villages having less than 10% SC population are Pandegaon, Anantapur, Tawashi, Aralihatti, Bammanal Vishnuvadi, Jakkaratti, Jambagi, Kiranagi, Tevaratti Siddewadi, Mavinahatti, Chamakeri, Bedarahatti, Mole Athani (Rural) , Nadi-Ingalgaon, Avarkhod Radderahatti, Savadi, Ramateerth, Kannal Fadatarawadi, Kèskaradaddi, Adalatti, Desairatti Khotanatti, Halalli, Badagi, Dhabadhabahatti Buralatti, Katageri, Kodaganoor, Suttatti.
The village having more than 50% SC population is None.
Sex ratio of Scheduled Caste population is 494.
Scheduled Castes Literates and Illiterates by Sex:

	Persons	Males	Females
Literate	26,838	16,948	9,890
Illiterate	33,497	13,603	19,894
Literacy rate	53.1	66.3	39.5
Graduate	951	856	95

Scheduled Castes (Dominant):
Holaya etc., Bhambi etc., Samagara, Mahar etc. Madiga
For their cultural identity please see Appendix-I
Villages without Scheduled Castes: There are 2 villages without any scheduled caste population.
Scheduled Tribes: Out of the total population of 420912

persons, 11557 persons (2.75%) belong to Scheduled Tribes. The villages having less than 10% ST population are Pandegaon, Khilegaon, Ajur, Anantapur, Malabad Bevanoor, Tawashi, Naganur P.A., Shirur, Sambaragi Aralihatti, Vishnuvadi, Jakkaratti, Jambagi Kiranagi, Balligeri, Gundewadi, Shivanoor, Madabhavi Tevaratti, Siddewadi, Hanamapur, Agrani-Ingalgaon Abbihal, Parthanahalli, Mavinahatti, Chamakeri Kagawad, Mangavati, Jugul, Shahapur, Shiraguppi Molwad, Kusnal, Ugar Budruk, Ugar Khurd Farida Khanawadi, Lokur, Mangasuli, Kempwad Navalihal, Koulgudd, Mole, Katral, Ainapur Krishna Kittur, Banajawad, Muragundi, Masarguppi Devaradderahatti, Athani (Rural) , Tangadi, Shinal Sankonahatti, Hulagabali, Nadi-Ingalgaon, Teerth Saptasagar, Darur, Halyal, Avarkhod, Naganur P.K. Khavatkoppa, Sankaratti, Shegunshi, Dodwad, Satti Mahishwadgi, Janawad, Ramateerth, Kakamari, Kottalgi Bannur, Telsang, Kannal, Fadatarawadi, Aigali Kohalli, Keskaradaddi, Adalatti, Adahalli, Yakkanchi Desairatti, Khotanatti, Aratal, Halalli, Badagi Yallammawadi, Dhabadhabahatti, Kokatnoor, Buralatti Katageri, Kodaganoor, Nandagaon, Ghatanatti, Balawad Shirahatti, Junjarwad, Suttatti.

The villages having more than 50% ST population are None.

Sex ratio of Scheduled tribe population is 485.

Scheduled Tribes Literates and Illiterates by Sex:

	Persons	Males	Females
Literate	3,940	2,546	1,394
Illiterate	7,617	3,402	4,215
Literacy rate	40.9	51.4	29.8
Graduate	65	59	6

Scheduled Tribes (Dominant):

Naikda etc., Koli Dhor etc., Koraga, Kadu Kuruba Pardhi etc.

For their cultural identity please see Appendix-II

Villages without Scheduled Tribes: There are 35 villages without any scheduled tribe population.

Literates and Illiterates by Sex (Total Population):

	Persons	Males	Females
Literate	212,363	129,278	83,085
Illiterate	208,549	86,783	121,766
Literacy rate	60	71	48
Graduate	7,233	6,159	1,074

Agriculture: ***Distribution of villages according to land use:*** Out of 108 villages, Total area (in hectare) is 198747, out of that 91.79 percent is cultivable and 37.38 percent of the cultivable area is irrigated.

Sources of Irrigation (Hectares): Government Canal 3581.88, Private Canal 0, Well without Electricity 1197.05, Well with Electricity 26319.38, Tubewell without Electricity 1147.26, Tubewell with Electricity 8278.43, Tank 907.3, River 26685.92, Lake 0, Waterfall 0, Others 80.94.

Villages with population of 5000 to 9999:
Anantapur, Madabhavi, Jugul, Shiraguppi, Ugar Budruk Mole, Hulagabali, Saptasagar, Darur, Shegunshi Satti, Savadi, Kottalgi, Telsang, Aigali, Kohalli Kokatnoor, Nandagaon, Shirahatti.

Villages with population of 10000 and above:
Kagawad, Ugar Khurd, Shedbal , Mangasuli, Ainapur Athani (Rural).

Distribution of Workers:

	Persons	Males	Females	WPR
Cultivators	110,507	71,126	39,381	49.35
Agricultural Labour	82,722	35,373	47,349	36.94
Household Industry	3,522	2,317	1,205	1.57
Other Workers	27,175	20,589	6,586	12.14
Main Workers	164,721	116,741	47,980	73.56
Marginal Workers	59,205	12,664	46,541	26.44
Total Workers	223,926	129,405	94,521	

Religion: Major Religious Communities:

	Persons	Males	Females	Sex Ratio
Hindu (82.99%)	349,327	179,129	170,198	950
Muslim (7.49%)	31,532	16,136	15,396	954
Christian (0.02%)	97	52	45	865
Sikh (0%)	12	5	7	1,400
Buddhists (0.04%)	173	79	94	1,190
Jain (9.28%)	39,062	20,296	18,766	925

Agewise Data:

	Persons	Males	Females	Sex Ratio
All ages	420,912	216,061	204,851	948
0-14	145,909	75,825	70,084	924
15-44	188,988	97,699	91,289	934
45-79	81,170	40,346	40,824	1012
80+	4,681	2,088	2,593	1242
Age not stated	164	103	61	592

Languages (Dominant):

Kannada, Marathi, Urdu, Telugu, Hindi

Disabled Population:

	Persons	Males	Females	%
Total Disabled	4,807	2,660	2,147	
In Seeing	1,397	693	704	29.06
In Speech	662	356	306	13.77
In Hearing	334	166	168	6.95
In Movement	1,657	1,031	626	34.47
Mentally	757	414	343	15.75

AURAD

Aurad C.D. Block lies in the northern part of Bidar district. It is a part of Aurad taluka. The Block is located at a distance of 48 kms. from district headquarters (Bidar). There are 152 villages in the block with the total population of 228,910 persons. Area of the C.D. Block is 1217.54 sq. kms. It is bounded by taluks Bhalki and Bidar on south, and it has common boundary with the state of Maharashtra on north and west, and with state of Andhra Pradesh on north and east.

Communications:

Roadways : S.H-4: Direction- Nanded to Bidar, Nearest Villages- Madnoor, Kamalnagar, Murg (K), Diggi, Holesamudra, Sawali, Sangam. S.H-15: Direction- Digular to Bidar, Nearest Villages- Wanmarpalli, Badalgaon, Narayanpur, Aurad (Rural), Tuljapur, Boral, Kappekeri, Chatnal, Jeerga(B), Santhpur, Shambelli, Mustapur, Kaudgaon, Alur (B), Pashapur, Ballur Janwada, Koutha (K), Koutha (B).

River: Manjra Nadi- Nearest Villages- Horandi, Sonala, Kalgapur, Hulsoor, Khed, Sangam, Balat (B), Halhalli, Nidoda, Nittur (K), Hedgapur, Dhupatmahagaon, Manganpur, Babli, Bachepalli, Ladha, Duduknal, Khanapur, Kushnoor Gadi, Ballur, Janwada, Koutha (K), Koutha (B), Kandgoal.

Annual Rainfall: Normal Rianfall 735 mm.

Ground Water: Availability of the Ground Water in the Basin is 7361.03 H.A.M. and the utilization is 1826. 20 H.A.M. It belongs to Over Exploited category. Depth to water level 2 to 20 meter below the ground. Most of the wells go down in summer months, according to the Ground Water Estimation Committee.

Soils: Black Soils and Lateritic Soils.

Natural Division : It falls partly in Manjra-Karanja Basin of the Northern Karnataka Plateau.

Administration:

Division: Gulbarga. Parliamentary Constituency: 7 Bidar (SC). District: Bidar. Taluka: Aurad. Assembly Constituency: 52 Aurad (SC). Gram Panchayat: 38.

Regional Area Development Boards: The Hyderabad - Karnataka Area Development Board.

Border Villages: (State: Maharashtra)- Chikli Udgir, Mukhed, Nandi Bijalgaon, Bawalgaon, Hokrana, Ganganbid, Ganeshpur (Udgir), Hangerga, Bonthi, Murki, Madnoor, Hakyal, Ramdiyal, Kamalnagar, Murg (K), Balur, Horandi, Huliyal, Ekamba, Duduknal, Wanmarpalli, Badalgaon, Narayanpur, Narasimhapur, Allapur, Sundhal, Jaknal, Nandiyal, Manoor (K). (State: Andhra Pradesh)- Karanji (K), Raipalli, Lingadhalli(Jukal), Naganpalli, Chintaki, Ashoknagar, Ujani, Sunknal, Chikli Janwada, Jambgi (B), Kandgoal, Vijayanagar, Wallepur.

Fairs: Amareshara Jatra: Amareshara Jatra is held at Aurad in Bidar area in the month of February-March for seven days. Aurad about 42 kms. north of Bidar town, is the headquarters of the taluk of the same name. It has a well-known temple of Amareshvar, the jatra of which is held for seven days in February-March every year. This festival attracts a large gathering. Bidar is also an important centre of cattle trade, therefore a cattle fair is also organized on this occasion.

Mahadeva Fair: Santhapur, about 11 kms. south-east of Aurad, has the headquarters of the Aurad Taluk Development Board. It has an ancient temple of Mahadeva under the auspices of which an annual fair is held for three days around the month of April.

Sangameshvara Jatra: It is held at Sangam in Bidar area in the month of about February-March. Sangam a place about 32 kms. south-west of Aurad, lies at the confluence of the Karanja and the Manjra river. There is an ancient shrine here of Sangameshvara. On the right and left sides of the walls of the mantapa, in front of the garbhagriha, there are paintings of some figures done in modern times which are pointed out as those of Gangadhareshvara, Akka-Mahadevi, Narayana, Neelambike, Ganapathi,Lakshmi and Basaveshvara. A jatra is held here for a week at the time of the Shivaratri festival.

Shaik Saheb Urs: Chintaki about 16 kms. south-east of Aurad is noted for the dargah of Shaik saheb in whose honour an annual urs is held for about two days.

Villages: 152 **Inhabited:** 151 **Uninhabited:** 1

Ranking	District	State	National
Area	1	58	270
Population	4	58	372
Sex Ratio	3	140	3396
Child Sex Ratio	4	114	3426
Literacy Rate	2	109	3270
Density	3	166	4906
Work Participation Rate	5	89	4101

Gram Panchayats:

Chikli Udgir, Hokrana, Bonthi, Dabka(Chawar), Murki, Chimegaon, Bhandar Kumta, Badalgaon, Ekamba, Belkuni Chaudhri, Dongaon Makta, Madnoor, Kamalnagar, Diggi, Torna, Mudhole(B), Sundhal, Nagmarpalli, Chintaki, Eklora, K0Rekal, Holesamudra, Sonala, Khed, Chandoori, Balat (B), Kushnoor Thana, Belkuni Bhopalgad, Santhpur, Jojna, Chikli Janwada, Wadgaon Deshmukh, Shambelli, Hedgapur, Dhupatmahagaon, Ladha, Jambgi(B), Koutha (B).

Amenities:

Education: Primary School in 148 villages, Middle school in 79 villages, Matriculation or Secondary School in 28 villages, namely Hokrana, Dabka(Chawar), Malegaon, Madnoor, Khatgaon, Dongaon Makta, Belkuni Bhopalgad, Torna, Kamalnagar, Holesamudra, Sonala, Hulsoor, Mudhole(B),

Sangam, Kushnoor Thana, Belkuni Chaudhri, Nagur Babji, Hedgapur, Dhupatmahagaon, Ekamba, Sundhal, Chintaki, Santhpur, Wadgaon Deshmukh, Jambgi(B), Khanapur, Koutha(K), Koutha (B).

Higher Secondary or Pre University Courses or Intermediate or Junior College in 7 villages of the CD Block,, namely Dabka(Chawar), Kamalnagar, Sonala, Kushnoor Thana, Chintaki, Santhpur, Koutha (B).

College in 2 villages, Adult Literacy Center in 19 villages., Colleges are in villages, namely Kamalnagar, Nagur Babji.

Medical: Hospital in 3 villages, Dispensary in 11 villages, Health Center in 10 villages, Sub Center in 48 villages, Maternity and Child Welfare Center in 5 villages, Community health workers in 17 villages.

The Villages having Hospital or Dispensary or Health Center are Dabka(Chawar), Wagangera, Dongaon Makta, Kamalnagar, Kushnoor Thana, Hedgapur, Dhupatmahagaon, Sundhal, Chintaki, Nandi Nagoor, Jeerga(B), Wadgaon Deshmukh.

Drinking Water: Tap water in 113 villages, Tank water in 76 villages, Well water in 143 villages, Tubewell in 106 villages and more than one source in 148 villages.

Bank: Banking facility in 22 villages, namely, Hokrana, Aknapur, Dabka(Chawar), Murki, Torna Kamalnagar, Sonala, Mudhole(B), Kushnoor Thana Belkuni Chaudhri, Eklora, Mahadongaon, Manoor (K) Chintaki, Ashoknagar, Gandhinagar, Chikli Janwada Santhpur, Wadgaon Deshmukh, Jambgi(B), Koutha (B) Vijayanagar.

Credit Society in 41 villages Agricultural Credit Society in 35 Non-Agricultural Credit Society in 17 villages.

Others: Power supply in 150 villages, Cinema hall in 1 village, sport club in 151 villages, Stadium or Auditorium or Community Hall in 151 villages, Post Office in 72 villages.

There are 113 villages having bus facilities.

Villages with most of facilities: Hokrana Dabka(Chawar), Murki, Torna, Kamalnagar, Sonala Mudhole(B), Kushnoor Thana, Belkuni Chaudhri, Eklora Chintaki, Chikli Janwada, Santhpur, Wadgaon Deshmukh Jambgi(B).

Villages without amenities (Education):

Aurad (Rural), Raipalli, Khasimpur Borgi..

Scheduled Castes: Out of the total population of 229490 persons, 61547 persons (26.82%) belong to Scheduled Castes.

The villages having less than 10% SC population are Muthkhed (Chondi Mukhed), Aknapur, Basnal, Kalgapur Sangam, Rakshiyal(B), Babli, Kappekeri, Raipalli Yengunda, Lingadhalli(Jukal), Kaudgaon, Kandgoal.

The villages having more than 50% SC population are Ganganbeed, Bonthi, Handikhera, Malegaon, Huliyal Narasimhapur, Aurad (Rural), Ashoknagar, Gandhinagar Vijayanagar.

Sex ratio of Scheduled Caste population is 484.

Scheduled Castes Literates and Illiterates by Sex:

	Persons	Males	Females
Literate	24,937	15,831	9,106
Illiterate	36,610	15,929	20,681
Literacy rate	49.4	60.6	37.3
Graduate	1,011	907	104

Scheduled Castes (Dominant):

Banjara etc., Madiga, Holaya etc., Mang etc. Mahar etc.

For their cultural identity please see Appendix-I

Villages without Scheduled Castes: There are 4 villages without any scheduled caste population.

Scheduled Tribes: Out of the total population of 229490 persons, 20764 persons (9.05%) belong to Scheduled Tribes.

The villages having less than 10% ST population are Chikli Udgir, Mukhed, Nandi Bijalgaon, Bawalgaon Hokrana, Muthkhed (Chondi Mukhed), Aknapur Ganeshpur (Udgir), Dabka(Chawar), Hangerga, Bonthi Bhandar Kumta, Chimegaon, Wagangera, Handikhera Malegaon, Karkhiyal, Dangargaon, Madnoor, Ramdiyal Khatgaon, Dongaon Makta, Bhavani Bijalgaon, Torna Kotgyal, Rampur, Kamalnagar, Murg (K), Horandi Chandeshwar, Diggi, Basnal, Koryal, Kalgapur Hulsoor, Sawali, Mudhole (K), Lingadhalli (Udgir) Bembra, K0Rekal, Sangam, Halhalli, Kushnoor Thana Belkuni Chaudhri, Maskal, Nagur Babji, Hedgapur Manganpur, Babli, Bachepalli, Ladha, Hassikeri Huliyal, Ekamba, Badalgaon, Narayanpur, Narasimhapur Ganeshpur, Jamlapur, Gondgaon, Khandikeri Aurad (Rural), Mohmadapur, Allapur, Tegumpur Tuljapur, Mungnal, Mahadongaon, Kappekeri, Sundhal Jaknal, Manoor (K), Nagmarpalli, Karanji (B) Raipalli, Itgiyal, Khasimpur, Lingadhalli(Jukal) Ashoknagar, Lingadhalli(Karamungi), Jojna Nagoor (Muzafar), Gandhinagar, Ujani, Sunknal Chatnal, Jeerga(B), Santhpur, Jeerga (K) Khasimpur Borgi, Borgi (Janwada), Wadgaon Deshmukh Jambgi(B), Belur (Narayan-Khed), Sorhalli, Khanapur Ballur Janwada, Vijayanagar.

The villages having more than 50% ST population are None.

Sex ratio of Scheduled tribe population is 485.

Scheduled Tribes Literates and Illiterates by Sex:

	Persons	Males	Females
Literate	8,356	5,230	3,126
Illiterate	12,408	5,458	6,950

Literacy rate	48.4	58.9	37.3
Graduate	238	214	24

Scheduled Tribes (Dominant):
Gond etc., Koli Dhor etc., Generic Tribes etc.
Naikda etc., Chodhara
For their cultural identity please see Appendix-II
Villages without Scheduled Tribes: There are 31 villages without any scheduled tribe population.
Literates and Illiterates by Sex (Total Population):

	Persons	Males	Females
Literate	110,913	68,864	42,049
Illiterate	118,577	48,695	69,882
Literacy rate	57	70	45
Graduate	4,904	4,259	645

Agriculture: ***Distribution of villages according to land use:*** Out of 152 villages, Total area (in hectare) is 121754.83, out of that 84.59 percent is cultivable and 3.2 percent of the cultivable area is irrigated.
Sources of Irrigation (Hectares): Government Canal 443.61, Private Canal 0, Well without Electricity 3.24, Well with Electricity 927.52, Tubewell without Electricity 43.19, Tubewell with Electricity 371.71, Tank 1249.85, River 258.67, Lake 0, Waterfall 0, Others 0.
Villages with population of 5000 to 9999: Kamalnagar.
Villages with population of 10000 and above: None
Distribution of Workers:

	Persons	Males	Females	WPR
Cultivators	33,190	23,184	10,006	35.72
Agricultural Labour	37,880	16,860	21,020	40.77
Household Industry	2,376	1,276	1,100	2.56
Other Workers	19,465	15,803	3,662	20.95
Main Workers	66,432	48,438	17,994	71.5
Marginal Workers	26,479	8,685	17,794	28.5
Total Workers	92,911	57,123	35,788	

Religion: Major Religious Communities:

	Persons	Males	Females	Sex Ratio
Hindu (80.93%)	185,716	95,064	90,652	954
Muslim (8.35%)	19,173	9,798	9,375	957
Christian (1.55%)	3,568	1,809	1,759	972
Sikh (0%)	3	3	-	-
Buddhists (7.75%)	17,789	9,221	8,568	929
Jain (0.05%)	120	64	56	875

Agewise Data:

	Persons	Males	Females	Sex Ratio
All ages	229,490	117,559	111,931	952
0-14	86,684	44,193	42,491	961
15-44	96,563	50,370	46,193	917
45-79	43,141	21,514	21,627	1005
80+	2,818	1,314	1,504	1145
Age not stated	284	168	116	690

Languages (Dominant):
Kannada, Marathi, Hindi, Urdu, Telugu
Disabled Population:

	Persons	Males	Females	%
Total Disabled	5,065	2,864	2,201	
In Seeing	2,400	1,264	1,136	47.38
In Speech	441	247	194	8.71
In Hearing	252	138	114	4.98
In Movement	1,556	983	573	30.72
Mentally	416	232	184	8.21

BADAMI

Badami C.D. Block lies in the southern part of Bagalkot district. It is a part of Badami taluka. The Block is located at a distance of 49 kms. from district headquarters (Bagalkot). There are 149 villages in the block with the total population of 214,871 persons. Area of the C.D. Block is 1389.15 sq. kms. It is bounded by taluksBagalkot and Hungund on north, district Gadag on south, district Koppal and taluk Hungund on east, district Belgaum and taluk Mudhol on west.
Communications:
Roadways : N.H-218: Direction- Hubli to Bijapur, Nearest Villages- Hoolageri, Yaragoppa Inam, Agasarakoppa, Kerur (Rural), Kadapatti S.K., Halageri, Ugalawat, Mamatageri, Hanamasagar, Kallapur S.K., Chirlakoppa, Khanapur S.K., Somanakoppa, Beeranur, Govanakoppa. S.H-14: Direction-Ramdurg to Hungund, Nearest Villages- Chimmalagi, Mangalagudda, Katapur, Neelagund, Kakanur, Chimmanakatti,Chirlakoppa, Khanapur S.K., Muttalageri, Bankaneri, Narasapur, Kulageri, Kutakanakeri, Kendur, Nandikeshwar, Bhadra Nayakan Jalihal, Bachinagudd, Pattadakall, Shirabadagi, Adagal , Badami (Rural), Yaragoppa S.B, Timmapur S.N.,
Railway Station: Villages- Hirebudihal, Lakhamapur, Adagal
River: Mal Prabha Nadi- Nearest Villages- Injanawari, Haladu Allur S.P., Asangi, Kotnalli, Kataginahalli, Layadagundi, Subbalahunashi, Nagaral S.P., Chimmalagi, Mangalagudda, Katapur, Karalakoppa, Haganur, Alur S.K., Talakawad, Govanakoppa, Wadawatti, Kalas, Kittaliulla, Hebballi, Nandikeshwar, Bhadra Nayakan Jalihal, Bachinagudd, Gonal, Shirabadagi, Mangalur, Govanaki, Nelwagi, Navilahole, Hirenasabi, Chikkanasabi, Cholachagudda, Neeralagi, Thaminal, Katharaki, Khyad, Manneri, Jakanur, Beeranur, Pattadakall, Nagaral [S.B.], Dhanakashirur.
Reserved Forest: Nearest Villages- Yandigeri, Karadigudd S.A.,Kerakalamatti, Kagalagomba, Sulikeri, Hoolageri, Krishnapur, Kalabandakeri, Anawal, Hosakoti, Kainakatti, Narenur, Malagi, Maninagar, Mattikatti, Hanamaneri (G), Kadapatti S.K., Hullikeri Inam, Halakurki, Jammanakatti, Hulasageri, Katageri, Hangaragi, Kelawadi, Lingapur,

Timasagar, Khanapur S.P., Murudi, Hirebudihal, Hansanoor, Raghapur, Hanapur S.P., Saraswathinagar, Hullikeri S.P., Kotnalli, Kataginahalli, Layadagundi, Subbalahunashi, Nagaral S.P., Chimmalagi, Katapur, Neeralakeri, Haligeri, Halageri, Ugalawat, Mustigeri, Karadigudda S.N., Neelagund, Mamatageri, Kallapur S.K, Tappasakatti,Kakanur, Chimmanakatti, Chirlakoppa, Khanapur S.K., Muttalageri, Mallapur, Lakhamapur, Belawalakoppa, Bankaneri, Kulageri, Karalakoppa, Haganur, Alur S.K., Talakawad, Beeranur, Govanakoppa, Wadawatti, Kittali, Sulla, Hebballi, Mumaraddikoppa, Hiremuchalagudda, Chikkamuchalagudda, Bedarabudihal, Kutakanakeri, Kendur, Nandikeshwar, Bhadra Nayakan Jalihal, Bachinagudd, Pattadakall, Gonal, Shirabadagi, Mangalur, Adagal, Kabbalageri, Badami (Rural), Navilahole, Hosur, Hirenasabi, Chikkanasabi, Cholachagudda, Yaragoppa S.B, Budihal, Neeralagi, Thaminal, Katharaki, Khyad, Belur, Jalihal, G. Mallapur,Anantagiri, Nasagunni.

Annual Rainfall: Normal Rianfall 516.2 mm.

Ground Water: Availability of the Ground Water in the Basin is (Information not avablable) H.A.M. and the utilization is (Information not avablable) H.A.M. It belongs to (Information not avablable) category. Depth to water level 5 to 20 meter below the ground.Most of the wells go down in summer months, according to the Ground Water Estimation Committee.

Natural Division : It falls in the Badami Hills of the Northern Karnataka Plateau.

Soils: Black and Red Soils.

Administration:

Division: Belgaum. Parliamentary Constituency: 3 Bagalkot. District: Bagalkot. Taluka: Badami. Assembly Constituency: 24 Bagalkot. Gram Panchayat: 22.

Regional Area Development Boards: The Bailu Seeme Area Development Board.

Fairs: Mahakuteshvara Fair: Nandikeshvara (Badami taluk), a garden town is 5 kms. east of Badami near Bijapur and is of great archaeological interest. In one of the inscriptions found in the Badami caves, there is a mention of Lanjigeshvara, which may be the present Nandikeshvara. Close by is Mahakuta, the site of numerous temples and linga. The enclosure in which the Mahakuta temples are located, are accessible from the Badami side down a steep flight of stones, at the foot of which is a doorway guarded by door-keepers and are said to be figures of the demons, Vatapi and Ilaval. The enclosure, which is bounded by a stone wall is small but contains numerous temples in various styles chiefly Chalukyan and Dravidian. In the middle of the enclosure is a pond called Vishnu Pushkarini Tirtha, said to have been built by the sage Agastya. In the pond is a mantapa containing a handsome four-faced image of Brahma. The Mahakuteshva ra temple has six inscriptions, all on pillars. One, dated in the reign of the Western Chalukya king, Vijayaditya (696-733) records a gift by a courtesan; another dated 934 A.D. records a grant by Bappuvarasa, a chiefof Katak and the third records the gift of a pillar as a votive offering. The other three inscriptions are of no particular interest. Mahakuta is known as "Dakshina Kashi". The Mahakuteshvara fair is held every year, when about 15,000 people assemble.

Shakhambari Devi Fair: Cholachagud is a place about 6 kms. south of Badami taluk near Bijapur. It is an ancient place. There are inscriptions dating back to eighth century A.D. The chief object of interest is the temple of Banashankari or Shakhambari Devi worshipped as the goddess of Forest. An important fair is heldevery year and about 75,000 people attend it. There is a perennial tank in front of the temple. The old temple was in the Dravidian style and it has been rebuilt in a modern style. The present temple is a granite building with a small dome.

Shivayoga Mandira Fair: An annual fair is held at Shivayoga Mandira near Bijapur in the month of Jan-Feb for five days, in honour of Hangal Kumaraswamy. Shivayoga Mandira situated on the bank of the Malaprabha, is about 10 kms. east of Badam in Bijapur district. Mahakuta Nandikeshvara, Banashankari and Pattadakal are also close by amidst ideal natural surroundings and in the viscinity of ancient temples and historical places, an ashrama was established here in the first decade of the twentieth century by the efforts of the late Hangal Kumaraswamiji and Ilkal Mahantaswamiji. Spiritual and religious training, with an orientation for social service, is given here. There are caves for yoga-sadhanaand mantapas for meditation.

Ramalinga Car Festival: It takes place every year on the Seventh day of the bright half of Phalguna (February-March) at Aihole near Bijapur. Aihole or Aiholli or Aivalli (Hungund taluk) is a very old place of great architectural interest containing several temples within its crumbling walls that enclose a space little more than 500 metres across and many more in the open fields outside. In all, there are about 70 temples at this place. It is situated on the Malaprabha river, 20 kms. south-west of Hungund and 35 east of Badami. The name Aivalli, which apparently is Ayyavole, the 'priests' holy village or noble place (similar to Sanskrit Aryapura), has given rise to the legend that Parashurama, after fulfilling his vow of avenging his father's murder, came to the Malaprabha and washed his axe and at the sight of the river, the water of which had become red, cried "Ai,ai! Holi" (Ah! the river!). There is a fine old temple of Ramalinga and the car festival of this temple takes place every year on the seventh day of the bright half of Phalguna

(February-March). A grant inscription is carved on the rock on the river bank. Between this rock and the village are the remains ofa paved street and on both sides are the ruins of many temples. On a hill facing the village is a temple called Meguti. It is built in the southern or Dravidian style of architecture.

Sangameshvara Fair: Hungund is the headquarters of the Hungund taluk near Bijapur. Most of the wells in Hungund are impregnated with sulphured hydrogen. On the hill overlooking the town are the remains of a Jaina temple called Meguti. The temple pillars are square, massive and of unusual design. In the town just below the hill is the temple of Ramalingadeva with 16 Chalukyan pillars, square and tulip-shaped. A fair in honour of god Sangameshvara is held in the town every year. A type of yellow talc is found on the hill overlooking the town. This was perhaps the reason for its old name honna kunda or honna gunda meaning abounding in gold.

Sangameshvara Fair: Sangam is a place in Hungund taluk of Bijapur area at the meeting of the Malaprabha and the Krishna river about 16 kms. of Hungund. On Chalukyan style the linga in the temple is greatly revered. Sangam is looked upon as an important holy place. It is said that Basaveshvara had his education here and that, after his return from Kalyana, he became one with Kudala Sangama Deva here. A yearly fair is held in the month of April-May near by the Rakkasa-Tangadgi, the place where the fateful battle of 1565 A.D. took place.

Villages: 149 **Inhabited:** 149 **Uninhabited:** 0

Ranking	District	State	National
Area	1	42	185
Population	3	75	521
Sex Ratio	1	32	1259
Child Sex Ratio	2	63	2527
Literacy Rate	3	144	4503
Density	3	74	5490
Work Participation Rate	6	123	1817

Gram Panchayats:

Neerabudihal, Sulikeri, Hoolageri, Anawal, Fakeerabudihal, Hullikeri Inam, Halakurki, Jammanakatti, Katageri, Kelawadi, Kotikall, Haladur, Parwati, Hansanoor, Layadagundi, Nagaral.S.P., Neeralakeri, Mustigeri, Neelagund, Mamatageri, Kakanur, Khanapur S.K., Muttalageri, Kittali, Hebballi, Nandikeshwar, Pattadakall, Mangalur, Adagal , Hosur, Cholachagudda, Katharaki, Belur, Jalihal.

Amenities:

Education: Primary School in 114 villages, Middle school in 118 villages, Matriculation or Secondary School in 25 villages, namely Neerabudihal, Ganganabudihal, Kagalagomba, Anawal, Halakurki, Katageri, Kelawadi, Hansanoor, Nagaral.S.P., Raddera Timmapur, Haligeri, Ugalawat, Mustigeri, Neelagund, Kakanur, Khanapur S.K., Govanakoppa, Hebballi, Kutakanakeri, Pattadakall, Hosur, Cholachagudda, Katharaki, Belur, Jalihal.

Higher Secondary or Pre University Courses or Intermediate or Junior College in 3 villages of the CD Block,, namely Neerabudihal, Ganganabudihal, Belur.

College in 1 village, Adult Literacy Center in 3 villages., College is in village, namely Belur.

Medical: Hospital in 1 village, Dispensary in 8 villages, Health Center in 10 villages, Sub Center in 42 villages, Maternity and Child Welfare Center in 6 villages, Community health workers in 65 villages.

The Villages having Hospital or Dispensary or Health Center are Narenur, Kelawadi, Thogunashi, Saraswathinagar, Mustigeri, Kakanur, Khanapur S.K., Kulageri, Nandikeshwar, Katharaki, Jalihal.

Drinking Water: Tap water in 112 villages, Tank water in 71 villages, Well water in 107 villages, Tubewell in 32 villages and more than one source in 142 villages.

Bank: Banking facility in 17 villages, namely, Neerabudihal, Kerakalamatti, Anawal, Katageri Asangi, Teggi, Mustigeri, Neelagund, Kakanur Khanapur S.K., Hebballi, Nandikeshwar, Pattadakall Cholachagudda, Thaminal, Belur, Jalihal.

Credit Society in 23 villages Agricultural Credit Society in 22 Non-Agricultural Credit Society in 0 village.

Others: Power supply in 145 villages, Cinema hall in 1 village, sport club in 0 village, Stadium or Auditorium or Community Hall in 0 village, Post Office in 77 villages.

There are 143 villages having bus facilities.

Villages with most of facilities: Neerabudihal Kerakalamatti, Anawal, Katageri, Mustigeri Neelagund, Kakanur, Khanapur S.K., Hebballi Nandikeshwar, Pattadakall, Cholachagudda, Belur Jalihal.

Villages without amenities (Education): Karadigudd S.A., Sheeparamatti, Gubberakoppa, Kerur (Rural), Saganur, Kadapatti S.K, Injanawari, Asangi, Kotnalli, Aladakatti, Bankaneri, Mumaraddikoppa, Bedarabudihal, Badami (Rural) *, Nagaral [S.B], Chikkanasabi, Budihal, Anantagiri, Nasagunni..

Scheduled Castes: Out of the total population of 214869 persons, 28607 persons (13.31%) belong to Scheduled Castes. The villages having less than 10% SC population are Hanamaneri Inam, Yandigeri, Karadigudd S.A. Neerabudihal, Jalageri, Kalabandakeri, Anawal

Hosakoti, Kainakatti, Sheeparamatti, Bellikindi Fakeerabudihal, Malagi, Gubberakoppa, Saganur Hanamaneri (G), Jammanakatti, Hulasageri, Katageri Hangaragi, Khazibudihal, Kelawadi, Lingapur Timasagar, Injanawari, Padanakatti, Khanapur.S.P. Murudi, Teggi, Hirebudihal, Lakkasakoppa Konkanakoppa, Kotnalli, Kataginahalli Subbalahunashi, Nagaral.S.P., Neeralakeri Raddera Timmapur, Ugalawat, Mustigeri Karadigudda.S.N., Mamatageri, Hanamasagar Kallapur.S.K, Chimmanakatti, Chirlakoppa Khanapur S.K., Somanakoppa, Aladakatti, Muttalageri Lakhamapur, Belawalakoppa, Bankaneri, Narasapur Kulageri, Karalakoppa, Alur .S.K., Talakawad Beeranur, Kalas, Hebballi, Hiremuchalagudda Chikkamuchalagudda, Kutakanakeri, Nandikeshwar Bhadra Nayakan Jalihal, Bachinagudd, Pattadakall Shirabadagi, Mangalur, Govanaki, Nelwagi Kabbalageri, Badami (Rural) * , Navilahole Neeralagi, Guddada Mallapur, Nasagunni.

The villages having more than 50% SC population are Krishnapur, Chinchalakatti, Saraswathinagar Anantagiri.

Sex ratio of Scheduled Caste population is 504.

Scheduled Castes Literates and Illiterates by Sex:

	Persons	Males	Females
Literate	9,717	6,701	3,016
Illiterate	18,890	7,498	11,392
Literacy rate	42.0	58.6	25.7
Graduate	238	225	13

Scheduled Castes (Dominant):

Bhambi etc., Banjara etc., Bhovi, Chalavadi etc. Chenna Dasar etc.

For their cultural identity please see Appendix-I

Villages without Scheduled Castes: There are 4 villages without any scheduled caste population.

Scheduled Tribes: Out of the total population of 214869 persons, 22578 persons (10.51%) belong to Scheduled Tribes.

The villages having less than 10% ST population are Kadarakoppa, Hanamaneri Inam, Yandigeri Neerabudihal, Ganganabudihal, Kagalagomba Krishnapur, Sheeparamatti, Jangawad, Bellikindi Hawalakhod, Fakeerabudihal, Narenur, Agasarakoppa Yankanchi, Gubberakoppa, Maninagar, Mattikatti Saganur, Hanamaneri (G), Kadapatti S.K, Hulasageri Katageri, Hangaragi, Khazibudihal, Lingapur Timasagar, Haradolli, Budanagad, Injanawari, Haladur Allur. S.P., Padanakatti, Parwati, Thogunashi, Teggi Hirebudihal, Lakkasakoppa, Konkanakoppa, Hansanoor Hanapur.S.P., Saraswathinagar, Hullikeri.S.P. Layadagundi, Nagaral.S.P., Chimmalagi, Mangalagudda Katapur, Neeralakeri, Raddera Timmapur, Haligeri Ugalawat, Mustigeri, Mamatageri, Kallapur.S.K Tappasakatti, Kakanur, Chimmanakatti, Chirlakoppa Khanapur S.K., Somanakoppa, Mallapur, Timmapur S.N. Kulageri, Karalakoppa, Haganur, Alur .S.K. Talakawad, Beeranur, Wadawatti, Kittali, Sulla Hebballi, Hiremuchalagudda, Chikkamuchalagudda Nandikeshwar, Bhadra Nayakan Jalihal, Bachinagudd Pattadakall, Gonal, Shirabadagi, Mangalur Badami (Rural) * , Navilahole, Hosur, Hirenasabi Cholachagudda, Yaragoppa.S.B, Budihal, Jakanur Neeralagi, Thaminal, Katharaki, Khyad, Manneri Dhanakashirur, Jalihal, Guddada Mallapur.

The villages having more than 50% ST population are None.

Sex ratio of Scheduled tribe population is 497.

Scheduled Tribes Literates and Illiterates by Sex:

	Persons	Males	Females
Literate	7,614	5,135	2,479
Illiterate	14,964	6,212	8,752
Literacy rate	41.3	55.7	26.9
Graduate	129	118	11

Scheduled Tribes (Dominant):

Naikda etc., Meda, Pardhi etc., Koli Dhor etc. Kurumans

For their cultural identity please see Appendix-II

Villages without Scheduled Tribes: There are 23 villages without any scheduled tribe population.

Literates and Illiterates by Sex (Total Population):

	Persons	Males	Females
Literate	89,545	59,224	30,321
Illiterate	125,324	48,357	76,967
Literacy rate	50	67	34
Graduate	2,593	2,269	324

Agriculture: ***Distribution of villages according to land use:*** Out of 149 villages, Total area (in hectare) is 138915, out of that 64.85 percent is cultivable and 17.3 percent of the cultivable area is irrigated.

Sources of Irrigation (Hectares): Government Canal 5693.32, Private Canal 111.75, Well without Electricity 618.98, Well with Electricity 1881.47, Tubewell without Electricity 364.61, Tubewell with Electricity 2877.19, Tank 407.39, River 2441.36, Lake 4.13, Waterfall 337.52, Others 841.76.

Villages with population of 5000 to 9999: Belur, Jalihal.

Villages with population of 10000 and above: None

Distribution of Workers:

	Persons	Males	Females	WPR
Cultivators	32,201	25,239	6,962	30.5

Agricultural Labour	52,759	18,189	34,570	49.98
Household Industry	3,591	2,224	1,367	3.4
Other Workers	17,019	12,852	4,167	16.12
Main Workers	72,984	49,847	23,137	69.13
Marginal Workers	32,586	8,657	23,929	30.87
Total Workers	105,570	58,504	47,066	

Religion: Major Religious Communities:

	Persons	Males	Females	Sex Ratio
Hindu (93.61%)	201,134	100,753	100,381	996
Muslim (5.37%)	11,546	5,755	5,791	1,006
Christian (0.66%)	1,412	691	721	1,043
Sikh (0.01%)	11	6	5	833
Buddhists (0%)	3	2	1	500
Jain (0.04%)	77	38	39	1,026

Agewise Data:

	Persons	Males	Females	Sex Ratio
All ages	214,869	107,581	107,288	997
0-14	80,832	41,205	39,627	962
15-44	93,504	47,831	45,673	955
45-79	38,764	17,905	20,859	1165
80+	1,647	583	1,064	1825
Age not stated	122	57	65	1140

Languages (Dominant):
Kannada, Hindi, Urdu, Telugu, Marathi

Disabled Population:

	Persons	Males	Females	%
Total Disabled	4,373	2,360	2,013	
In Seeing	1,879	888	991	42.97
In Speech	376	207	169	8.6
In Hearing	314	157	157	7.18
In Movement	1,490	938	552	34.07
Mentally	314	170	144	7.18

BAGALKOT

Bagalkot C.D. Block lies in the east-central part of Bagalkot district. It is a part of Bagalkot taluka. The Block is located at a distance of 00 kms. from district H.Q. (Bagalkot). There are 96 villages in the block with the total population of 156,274 persons.Area of the C.D. Block is 897.13 sq. kms. It is bounded by taluk Bilgi and district Bijapur on north, taluk Badami on south, taluk Hungund on east, and taluk Mudhol on west.

Communications:

Roadways : N.H-13: Direction- Bijapur to Chitradurga, Nearest Villages- Chebbi, Nagasampagi, Nagaral, Nainegali, Mankani, Sutagundar, Domanal, Bommanagi, C.Myageri, Handaragala, Mudavinkop, Chitaginakopp, Devalapur (SM.). N.H-218: Direction- Hubli to Bijapur, Nearest Villages- Yadahalli, Anadinni, Gaddankeri, Simikeri. S.H-20: Belgaum to Hungund, Direction-Nearest Villages- Kaladgi, Govindkopp, Chebbi, Yadahalli, Anadinni, Gaddankeri, Simikeri, Tulasigeri, Khajjidoni, Mallapur,Honnakatti, Bevinamatti-S.Haveli, Sirur.

Railway Station: Villages- Alur, Dharmnagar, Jadramakunti, Kadalimatti.

River: Krishna Nadi- Nearest Villages- Hiregulabal, Chikkgulabal, Mastihal, Alur, Sitimani, Manahalli, Hosur, Nagasampagi, Nagaral, Nainegali, Mankani, Sutagundar, Domanal, Bommanagi, Chick Myageri, Handaragala, Hire Myageri. Ghatprabha Nadi- Nearest Villages- Udagatti, Sharadal, Ankalagi, Kaladgi, Govindkopp, Hire-Sansi, Chikk-Sansi, Devanal, Sokanadgi, Chebbi, Yadahalli, Muranal, Anadinni, annidinni, Honaralli, Sorakopp, Nakargundi, Sindagi, Kadampur, Yankachi, Sidnal, Andamuranal, Salagundi, Talagihal, Ilal, Hire-Hodlur, Chick Hodlur, Veerapur, Siraguppi, Chikkmuramatti, Hiremuramatti, Muttatti, Hiregulabal, Bennur, Sangondi, Mugalalli, Bagalkot (Rural), Kirasur.

Reserved Forest: Nearest Villages- Govindkopp, Honaralli, Sorakop, Nakargundi, Sindagi, Kadampur, Yankachi, Sidnal, Andamuranal, Salagundi, Tulasigeri, Chickka-Shellikeri, Hire-Shellikeri, Talagihal, Ilal, Hire-Hodlur, Basavanagar, Chikkgulabal, Mastihal, Alur, Dharmnagar, Chick Sitimani, Rampur, Timmapur, Jadramakunti, Siraguppi, Bennur, Sangondi, Mugalalli, Lavaleshavar, Achanur, Bilkerur, Mallapur, Kirasur, Kadalimatti, Mudapaljivi, Mannikatti, Honnakatti, Bevinamatti-S.Haveli, Sigikeri, Niralkeri, Sirur.

Annual Rainfall: Normal Rianfall 635.05 mm.

Ground Water: Availability of the Ground Water in the Basin is (Information not avablable) H.A.M. and the utilization is (Information not avablable) H.A.M. It belongs to (Information not avablable) category. Depth to water level 5 to 20 meter below the ground. Most of the wells go down in summer months, according to the Ground Water Estimation Committee.

Soils: Black and Red Soils.

Natural Division : It falls partly in the Upper Krishna Valley and the Ghatprabha Irrigated Tract of the Northern Karnataka Plateau.

Administration:

Division: Belgaum. Parliamentary Constituency: 3 Bagalkot. District: Bagalkot.Taluka: Bagalkot. Assembly Constituency: 24 Bagalkot. Gram Panchayat: 22.

Regional Area Development Boards: The Bailu Seeme Area Development Board.

Villages: 96 **Inhabited:** 95 **Uninhabited:** 1

Ranking	District	State	National
Area	5	101	556
Population	5	127	1677
Sex Ratio	2	35	1350
Child Sex Ratio	5	136	3875
Literacy Rate	2	125	3843

Density	4	96	5159
Work Participation Rate	3	98	2251

Gram Panchayats:
Kaladgi, Yadahalli, Kadampur, Muranal , Gaddankeri , Tulasigeri, Khajjidoni, Chickka-Shellikeri, Hiregulabal, Rampur, Bennur, Mugalalli, Bilkerur, Nainegali, Sutagundar, Bhagavati, Kadalimatti, Hallur, Bevoor, Benakatti, Niralkeri, Sirur.

Amenities:
Education: Primary School in 91 villages, Middle school in 77 villages, Matriculation or Secondary School in 21 villages, namely Kaladgi, Kadampur, Muranal, Gaddankeri, Khajjidoni, Hiregulabal, Sitimani, Siraguppi, Bennur, Mugalalli, Bilkerur, Nainegali, Sutagundar, Chick Myageri, Bhagavati, Hallur, Bevoor, Benakatti, Muchakhandi, Niralkeri, Sirur.
Higher Secondary or Pre University Courses or Intermediate or Junior College in 4 villages of the CD Block,, namely Kaladgi, Gaddankeri, Bevoor, Sirur.
College in 2 villages, Adult Literacy Center in 18 villages., Colleges are in villages, namely Bevoor, Sirur.
Medical: Hospital in 2 villages, Dispensary in 1 village, Health Center in 5 villages, Sub Center in 28 villages, Maternity and Child Welfare Center in 1 village, Community health workers in 18 villages.
The Villages having Hospital or Dispensary or Health Center are Kaladgi, Rampur, Achanur.
Drinking Water: Tap water in 83 villages, Tank water in 57 villages, Well water in 48 villages, Tubewell in 37 villages and more than one source in 92 villages.
Bank: Banking facility in 6 villages, namely, Kaladgi, Gaddankeri, Sutagundar, Bevoor, Benakatti Sirur.
Credit Society in 16 villages Agricultural Credit Society in 14 Non-Agricultural Credit Society in 3 villages.
Others: Power supply in 95 villages, Cinema hall in 2 villages, sport club in 0 village, Stadium or Auditorium or Community Hall in 0 village, Post Office in 48 villages.
There are 89 villages having bus facilities.
Villages with most of facilities: Kaladgi Gaddankeri, Sutagundar, Bevoor, Benakatti, Sirur.
Villages without amenities (Education): Honaralli, Chick Hodlur..
Scheduled Castes: Out of the total population of 156283 persons, 29783 persons (19.06%) belong to Scheduled Castes.
The villages having less than 10% SC population are Udagatti, Sharadal, Kaladgi, Govindkopp, Hire-Sansi Devanal, Chebbi, Anadinni, Kadampur, Sidnal Salagundi, Gaddankeri, Hire-Shellikeri, Talagihal Muttatti, Manahalli, Hosur, Sutagundar Chick Myageri, Handaragala, Devalapur (S.M.) Honnakatti, Bevinamatti-S.Haveli.
The villages having more than 50% SC population are Durganagar, Basavanagar, Dharmnagar, Chick Sitimani Lavaleshavar, Durgadevinagar, Neelanagar.
Sex ratio of Scheduled Caste population is 503.

Scheduled Castes Literates and Illiterates by Sex:

	Persons	Males	Females
Literate	10,471	7,191	3,280
Illiterate	19,312	7,626	11,686
Literacy rate	43.7	60.7	27.0
Graduate	263	243	20

Scheduled Castes (Dominant):
Banjara etc., Bhambi etc., Chalavadi etc., Bhovi Holaya etc.
For their cultural identity please see Appendix-I
Villages without Scheduled Castes: There are 4 villages without any scheduled caste population.
Scheduled Tribes: Out of the total population of 156283 persons, 11891 persons (7.61%) belong to Scheduled Tribes.
The villages having less than 10% ST population are Udagatti, Ankalagi, Kaladgi, Govindkopp, Hire-Sansi Chikk-Sansi, Devanal, Chebbi, Yadahalli, Anadinni Honaralli, Sorakopp, Nakargundi, Sindagi, Kadampur Yankachi , Sidnal, Andamuranal, Salagundi, Muranal Gaddankeri, Chickka-Shellikeri, Durganagar Talagihal, Ilal, Hire-Hodlur, Chick Hodlur Chikkmuramatti, Hiremuramatti, Muttatti, Hiregulabal Basavanagar, Chikkgulabal, Mastihal, Alur Dharmnagar, Chick Sitimani, Sitimani, Rampur Timmapur, Jadramakunti, Siraguppi, Bennur, Sangondi Mugalalli, Lavaleshavar, Achanur, Manahalli, Hosur Nagasampagi, Nagaral, Nainegali, Mankani, Sutagundar Domanal, Bommanagi, Chick Myageri, Handaragala Hire Myageri, Mudavinkopp, Chitaginakopp Devalapur (S.M.), Kadalimatti, Hallur, Sangapur Bodanayakdinni, Choudapur, Bhairamatti, Benakatti Mannikatti, Sigikeri, Durgadevinagar, Sirur Neelanagar.
The villages having more than 50% ST population are None.
Sex ratio of Scheduled tribe population is 501.

Scheduled Tribes Literates and Illiterates by Sex:

	Persons	Males	Females
Literate	4,372	2,914	1,458
Illiterate	7,519	3,023	4,496
Literacy rate	44.7	59.9	29.7
Graduate	120	112	8

Scheduled Tribes (Dominant):
Naikda etc., Pardhi etc., Koli Dhor etc., Meda

Koraga

For their cultural identity please see Appendix-II

Villages without Scheduled Tribes: There are 31 villages without any scheduled tribe population.

Literates and Illiterates by Sex (Total Population):

	Persons	Males	Females
Literate	70,292	45,735	24,557
Illiterate	85,991	32,591	53,400
Literacy rate	54	70	38
Graduate	2,630	2,283	347

Agriculture: ***Distribution of villages according to land use:*** Out of 96 villages, Total area (in hectare) is 89713, out of that 77.4 percent is cultivable and 13.08 percent of the cultivable area is irrigated.

Sources of Irrigation (Hectares): Government Canal 500.43, Private Canal 0.11, Well without Electricity 0, Well with Electricity 598.66, Tubewell without Electricity 0, Tubewell with Electricity 5485.31, Tank 69.46, River 2373.44, Lake 0, Waterfall 45.45, Others 8.09.

Villages with population of 5000 to 9999:

Bevoor.

Villages with population of 10000 and above:

Kaladgi, Sirur.

Distribution of Workers:

	Persons	Males	Females	WPR
Cultivators	21,778	16,042	5,736	29.19
Agricultural Labour	34,389	11,962	22,427	46.1
Household Industry	2,051	1,314	737	2.75
Other Workers	16,384	12,959	3,425	21.96
Main Workers	56,369	38,800	17,569	75.56
Marginal Workers	18,233	3,477	14,756	24.44
Total Workers	74,602	42,277	32,325	

Religion: Major Religious Communities:

	Persons	Males	Females	Sex Ratio
Hindu (91.89%)	143,603	71,937	71,666	996
Muslim (7.39%)	11,553	5,831	5,722	981
Christian (0.02%)	35	21	14	667
Sikh (0.01%)	12	7	5	714
Buddhists (0.14%)	217	107	110	1,028
Jain (0.02%)	36	17	19	1,118

Agewise Data:

	Persons	Males	Females	Sex Ratio
All ages	156,283	78,326	77,957	995
0-14	56,888	29,187	27,701	949
15-44	69,662	35,555	34,107	959
45-79	28,595	13,148	15,447	1175
80+	1,043	387	656	1695
Age not stated	95	49	46	939

Languages (Dominant):

Kannada, Hindi, Urdu, Marathi, Telugu

Disabled Population:

	Persons	Males	Females	%
Total Disabled	2,911	1,561	1,350	
In Seeing	1,193	575	618	40.98
In Speech	265	150	115	9.1
In Hearing	168	72	96	5.77
In Movement	1,053	637	416	36.17
Mentally	232	127	105	7.97

BAGEPALLI

Bagepalli C.D. Block lies in the northern part of Kolar distri ct. It is a part of Bagepalli taluka. The Block is located at a distance of 85 kms. from district headquarters (Kolar). There are 229 villages in the block with the total population of 149,403 persons. Area of the C.D. Block is 930.45 sq. kms. It is bounded by taluks Gudiba nda, Sidlaghatta and Chintamani on south. It has common boundary with the state of Andhra Pradesh on north, east and west.

Communications:

Roadways : N.H.-7: Direction- Ananthapur to Bangalore, Nearest Villages- Adiganapalli, Narepalli, Hosahudya, Bagepalli (Rural), Etigaddapalli, Gantamvarapalli, Kondareddipalli, Matteddaladinne, Kothakote, Paragodu, Mangasandra. S.H.-5: Direction- Mangasanda to Chintamani, Nearest Villages- Kondamvaripalli, Etigaddapalli, Ganta mvarapalli, Karkur, Gundlapalli, Devaragudipalli, Mallasa ndra, Yellampalli, Maddalakane, Reddyvaripalli, Kanagamak alapalli, Muthinapalli, Meruvapalli, Nallamallepalli, Mittemari.

River: Chitravati Nadi- Nearest Villages- Hosahudya, Digavabandlakere, Bagepalli (Rural), Etigaddapalli, Matteddaladinne, Kothakote, Paragodu, Karkur, Makireddy palli, Solimakalapalli, Buttivaripalli, Arigepalli, Thumm epalli, Kanagamakalapalli. Vandaman Nadi- Nearest Village s- Digavagollapalli, Nallaguttapalli, Arigevarigutta, Gollavaripalli, Mukkaravaripalli, Ramaswamypalli, Kondo rupalli, Rascheruvu, Kammaravaripalli, Musaliganapalli, Kadirennagarikote, Kottampalli, Kondamvaripalli.

Reserved Forest: (Vandaman R.F.): Nearest Villages- Vasanthapura, Agatamdike, Sujanampalli, Bandakindapalli, Vangyaralapalli, Mallepalli, Digavagollapalli, Arigevarigutta, Mukkaravaripalli, Dugginaikanapalli.

Annual Rainfall: Normal Rianfall 662.15 mm.

Ground Water: Availability of the Ground Water in the Basin is (Information not avablable) H.A.M. and the utilization is (Information not avablable) H.A.M. It belongs to (Information not avablable) category. Depth to water level 5 to 20 meter below the ground. Most of the wells go down in summer months, according to the Ground Water Estimation Committee.

Soils: Red Soils.

Natural Division : It falls in Gudibanda-Bagepalli Highla nds and Sidlaghatta-Sriniwaspur Uplands of the Southern Karnataka Plateau.

Administration:

Division: Bangalore. Parliamentary Constituency: 27 Bangalore (SC). District: Kolar. Taluka: Bagepalli. Assembly Constituency: 140 Bagepalli. Gram Panchayat: 24.

Regional Area Development Boards: The Bailu Seeme Area Development Board.

Border Villages: (State: Andhra Pradesh)- Mumadivaripalli, Thathannagaridinne, Pesalaparthi, Kothakoti, Kolimpalli, Madakavaripalli, Ramanodupalli, Kokkuvarupalli, Chinth amakala Dinne, Marganakunte, Devikunte, G.Cherlopalli, Gorthipalli, Sajjupalli, Guntipalli, Guttapalya, Naraya naswamykote, Narasapura, Jinajirlu, Pothepalli, Gulur, G. Maddepalli, Kavalaganganadinne, Krishnapura, Puttapa rthi, Abakavaripalli, Adiganapalli, Hosahudya, Gawnipalli, Sujanampalli, Bandakindapalli, Chemulavaripalli, Boyipa lli, Gandamvaripalli, Narayanareddypalli, Ugranampalli, Billur, Narayanampalli, Ramaswamypalli, Thimmaiahgaripa lli, Kondorupalli, Rascheruvu, Kottampalli, Kondamvaripal li, Chakavelu, Sajjalavaripalli, Buttayyagarapalli, Ooduv aripalli, Debbaravaripalli, Zinkapalli, Machanapalli, Peddarajupalli, Byrappalli, Nimmakayilapalli, Chelur, Hosahudya.

Fairs: Gadadam Venkataramanaswami Jatra: It is held at Devaragudipalli near Kotor in the month of Vaishakha (April-May) for seven days. Devaragudipalli, situated about 5 kms. from Bagepalli, has a well known temple dedicated to Venkataramanaswamy.

Villages: 229 **Inhabited:** 212 **Uninhabited:** 17

Ranking	District	State	National
Area	1	96	508
Population	9	132	1878
Sex Ratio	3	75	2088
Child Sex Ratio	10	116	3403
Literacy Rate	11	158	4896
Density	3	15	5401
Work Participation Rate	11	116	607

Gram Panchayats:

Kothakoti, Marganakunte, Gorthipalli, Thimmampalli, Gulur, Nallappareddipalli, Gantamvarapalli ., Paragodu, Devaragudipalli, Thollapalli, Billur, Rascheruvu, Chakavelu, Puligal, Naremaddepalli, Somanathapura, Pathapalya, Yellampalli, Kanagamakalapalli, Mittemari, Joolapalya, Palyakere, Nallaguttapalli, Chelur.

Amenities:

Education: Primary School in 175 villages, Middle school in 67 villages, Matriculation or Secondary School in 16 villages, namely Marganakunte, Gulur, Thimmampalli, Bagepalli (Rural), Yellampalli, Lagumaddepalli, Achepalli, Mittemari, Billur, Nallaguttapalli, Naremaddepalli, Pathapalya, Chakavelu, Nallaguttapalli, Palyakere, Chelur.

Higher Secondary or Pre University Courses or Intermediate or Junior College in 1 village of the CD Block,, namely Chelur.

College in 1 village, Adult Literacy Center in 1 village., College is in village, namely Gulur.

Medical: Hospital in 3 villages, Dispensary in 10 villages, Health Center in 7 villages, Sub Center in 26 villages, Maternity and Child Welfare Center in 4 villages, Community health workers in 1 village.

The Villages having Hospital or Dispensary or Health Center are Marganakunte, Gulur, Motakapalli, Naravalapalli, Kanampalli, G. Maddepalli, Kondamvaripalli, Devaragudipalli, Mittemari, Joolapalya, Billur, Pathapalya, Chakavelu.

Drinking Water: Tap water in 104 villages, Tank water in 15 villages, Well water in 33 villages, Tubewell in 88 villages and more than one source in 161 villages.

Bank: Banking facility in 10 villages, namely, Kolimpalli, Marganakunte, Thimmampalli Bagepalli (Rural), Yellampalli, Mittemari, Billur Somanathapura, Chakavelu, Chelur.

Credit Society in 17 villages Agricultural Credit Society in 14 Non-Agricultural Credit Society in 2 villages.

Others: Power supply in 209 villages, Cinema hall in 5 villages sport club in 0 village, Stadium or Auditorium or Community Hall in 0 village, Post Office in 24 villages.

There are 119 villages having bus facilities.

Villages with most of facilities: Marganakunte Thimmampalli, Yellampalli, Mittemari, Billur Somanathapura, Chakavelu, Chelur.

Villages without amenities (Education):

Pesalaparthi, Ramanodupalli, G.Cherlopalli, Guntipalli, Kammaravaripalli, Boyinavaripalli, Roddamvaripalli, Pathabagepalli, Kondamvaripalli, Matteddaladinne, Mynaganapalli, Potlavaripalli, Reddyvaripalli, Papinaikanapalli, Sridharavaripalli, Bommasandra, Bandakindapalli, Chemulavaripalli, Narayanareddypalli, Babenayakanapalli, Mukkaravaripalli, Gummalapalli, Berigollapalli, Cheemanagaripalli, Gopanavaripalli, Thimmaiahgaripalli, Venteeravandlapalli, Buddalavaripalli, Debbaravaripalli, Yagavanetiguntapalli, Yerrayyagaripalli, Gundlapalli, Pemmaiahgaripalli..

Scheduled Castes: Out of the total population of 149570 persons, 40629 persons (27.16%) belong to Scheduled Castes.

The villages having less than 10% SC population are Kolimpalli, Pokamakalapalli, G.Cherlopalli Kammaravaripalli, Boyinavaripalli, Marasanapalli Pothepalli, Kanampalli, Bagepalli (Rural) Etigaddapalli, Poolavaripalli, Matteddaladinne Kammaravaripalli, Peddathumkepalli, Gollapalli Tenkaimakalapalli, Reddyvaripalli, Meruvapalli Paipalya, Gummalapalli, Venkatapura, Pulukuntlapalli Kuntlapalli, Battalapalli, Vasanthapura Chemulavaripalli, Boyipalli, Gandamvaripalli Ugranampalli, Nallaguttapalli, Mukkaravaripalli Jangalapalli, Berigollapalli, Pathakote, Gujjepalli Kamasanepalli, Devalavaripalli, Gundamvaripalli Kurubarapalli, Gopanavaripalli, Thimmaiahgaripalli Kammaravaripalli, Kallarollapalli, Ragimakalapalli Nallasanampalli, Bellalampalli, Doddipalli Digavanettakuntlapalli, Yerrayyagaripalli Peddarajupalli, Chigateegalagutta, Gundlapalli Pemmaiahgaripalli, Byrappalli.

The villages having more than 50% SC population are Sajjupalli, Roddamvaripalli, Nallappareddipalli Saddupalli, Abakavaripalli, Adiganapalli, Narepalli Gawnipalli, Pathabagepalli, Penamala, Achepalli Booragamadagu, Bodikadirepalli, Agatamdike Narayanareddypalli, Babenayakanapalli, Lakkasandra Doddivaripalli, Myakalapalli, Debbaravaripalli Kondikonda, Jalipigaraipalli, Mandampalli.

Sex ratio of Scheduled Caste population is 495.

Scheduled Castes Literates and Illiterates by Sex:

	Persons	Males	Females
Literate	12,363	8,186	4,177
Illiterate	28,266	12,345	15,921
Literacy rate	35.2	46.2	23.9
Graduate	154	150	4

Scheduled Castes (Dominant):

Bhovi, Adi Karnataka, Madiga, Banjara etc. Chalavadi etc.

For their cultural identity please see Appendix-I

Villages without Scheduled Castes: There are 44 villages without any scheduled caste population.

Scheduled Tribes: Out of the total population of 149570 persons, 26022 persons (17.4%) belong to Scheduled Tribes.

The villages having less than 10% ST population are Pesalaparthi, Guntipalli, Thattanagaripalli Kammaravaripalli, Boyinavaripalli, Marasanapalli Malakacheruvu, Sadlavaripalli, Thimmampalli G. Maddepalli, Abakavaripalli, Adiganapalli Narepalli, Hosahudya, Gawnipalli, Yegavabandlakere Pathabagepalli, Kadirannagaripalli Gantamvarapalli ., Matteddaladinne, Paragodu Srinivasapura, Mynaganapalli, Penamala, Kaganapalli Dasiahgaripalli, Shankavarampalli, Lagumaddepalli Buttivaripalli, Arigepalli, Reddyvaripalli Meruvapalli, Nallamallepalli, Achepalli Chakkampalli, Chinampalli, Bodikadirepalli Dugginaikanapalli, Pulukuntlapalli, Bandakindapalli Chemulavaripalli, Gandamvaripalli Narayanareddypalli, Babenayakanapalli, Bandarlapalli Mallepalli, Digavagollapalli, Arigevarigutta Mukkaravaripalli, Gummalapalli, Naremaddepalli Jangalapalli, Berigollapalli, Kamasanepalli Singappagaripalli, Cheemanagaripalli, Lakkasandra Doddivaripalli, Yeragudi, Gopanavaripalli Narayanampalli, Thimmaiahgaripalli, Kondorupalli Rascheruvu, Kammaravaripalli, Kadirennagarikote Venteeravandlapalli, Kallarollapalli Buddalavaripalli, Kottampalli, Chakavelu Sajjalavaripalli, Ooduvaripalli, Ragimakalapalli Myakalapalli, Nallasanampalli, Debbaravaripalli Venkatapura, Kondikonda, Nallaguttapalli Bathalavarapalli, Jalipigaraipalli Digavanettakuntlapalli, Mandampalli, Peddur Gundlapalli, Nimmakayilapalli, Chelur, Hosahudya.

The villages having more than 50% ST population are Kolimpalli, Madakavaripalli, Chinthamakala Dinne Pokamakalapalli, Devikunte, G.Cherlopalli M.Cherlopalli, Gollapalli, Giriyapalli, Gummalapalli Venkatapura, Sridharavaripalli, Kuntlapalli Battalapalli, Vasanthapura, Dugginaikanapalli Gundamvaripalli, Musaliganapalli, Bellalampalli Ramojupalli, Yerrayyagaripalli, Gollapalli Pemmaiahgaripalli.

Sex ratio of Scheduled tribe population is 491.

Scheduled Tribes Literates and Illiterates by Sex:

	Persons	Males	Females
Literate	8,449	5,551	2,898
Illiterate	17,573	7,696	9,877
Literacy rate	37.6	48.4	26.3
Graduate	94	87	7

Scheduled Tribes (Dominant):

Naikda etc., Hakkipikki, Yerava Generic Tribes etc., Soligaru

For their cultural identity please see Appendix-II

Villages without Scheduled Tribes: There are 53 villages without any scheduled tribe population.

Literates and Illiterates by Sex (Total Population):

	Persons	Males	Females
Literate	61,912	39,228	22,684
Illiterate	87,658	36,390	51,268
Literacy rate	47	60	35

Graduate	1,497	1,314	183

Agriculture: ***Distribution of villages according to land use:*** Out of 229 villages, Total area (in hectare) is 93045, out of that 47.34 percent is cultivable and 22.61 percent of the cultivable area is irrigated.

Sources of Irrigation (Hectares): Government Canal 25.07, Private Canal 0, Well without Electricity 38.23, Well with Electricity 1447.62, Tubewell without Electricity 221.63, Tubewell with Electricity 4203.16, Tank 3334, River 18.79, Lake 0, Waterfall 0, Others 672.33.

Villages with population of 5000 to 9999: Chelur.

Villages with population of 10000 and above: None

Distribution of Workers:

	Persons	Males	Females	WPR
Cultivators	43,944	26,699	17,245	51.75
Agricultural Labour	26,814	10,125	16,689	31.58
Household Industry	1,417	905	512	1.67
Other Workers	12,739	9,024	3,715	15
Main Workers	66,425	41,965	24,460	78.23
Marginal Workers	18,489	4,788	13,701	21.77
Total Workers	84,914	46,753	38,161	

Religion: Major Religious Communities:

	Persons	Males	Females	Sex Ratio
Hindu (93.47%)	139,801	70,656	69,145	979
Muslim (6.39%)	9,565	4,854	4,711	971
Christian (0.05%)	75	40	35	875
Sikh (0%)	1	-	1	-
Buddhists (0%)	-	-	-	-
Jain (0%)	1	1	-	-

Agewise Data:

	Persons	Males	Females	Sex Ratio
All ages	149,570	75,618	73,952	978
0-14	46,004	23,725	22,279	939
15-44	70,460	34,982	35,478	1014
45-79	31,565	16,167	15,398	952
80+	1,347	632	715	1131
Age not stated	194	112	82	732

Languages (Dominant):
Telugu, Kannada, Urdu, Hindi, Marathi

Disabled Population:

	Persons	Males	Females	%
Total Disabled	2,981	1,609	1,372	
In Seeing	1,303	664	639	43.71
In Speech	302	177	125	10.13
In Hearing	219	121	98	7.35
In Movement	881	506	375	29.55
Mentally	276	141	135	9.26

BANGALORE NORTH

Bangalore North C.D. Block lies in the north-western part of Bangalore district. It is a part of Bangalore North taluka. The Block is located at a distance of 00 kms. from district headquarters (Bangalore). There are 225 villages in the block with the total population of 223,660 persons. Area of the C.D. Block is 514.74 sq. kms. It is bounded by district Bangalore Rural on north, west and east, and taluk Bangalore South on south and east.

Communications:

Roadways : N.H.-4: Direction- Tumkur to Chennai, Nearest Villages- Makali, Adakamaranahalli, Dasanapura, Madanaiy akanahalli, Madavara, Siddanahosahalli. N.H-7: Direction- Chennai to Ananthapur, Nearest Villages- Navarathna Agrahara, Meenakunte, Bettahalasur, Chikkajala, Doddajala, Sonapanahalli, Kattigenahalli. S.H-9: Direction- Hindupur to Yelahanka, Nearest Villages- Kadathanamale, Marasandra Amanikere, Suradenpura, Vishwanathapura, Sriramanahalli, Sadenahalli, Adiganahalli, Rajanukunte, Honenahalli, Adde, Singanayakanahalli, Avalahalli, Harohalli, Ananthapura. S.H-17 E: Direction- Singanayakanahtion- Magadi to Bangalore, Villages-Kadabagere, Machohalli, Kachohalli, Hosahalli Gollarapalya, Kodigehalli, Seegehalli. SH-39: Direction- Dod Ballapur to Bangalore, Nearest Villages- Chikkabanavara, Ganigarahalli, Chikkasandra, Hesaraghatta Grass Farm, Dasenahalli,Ivar Kandapura, Hesaraghatta, Kodagi Thirumalapura, Hurali Chikkanahalli, Tharabana Halli, Sasiveghatta, Soladevanahalli, Kumbarahalli.

Railway Station: Villages- Adiganahalli, Rajanukunte, Sasiveghatta, Soladevanahalli, Bettahalasur, Doddajala.

River: Arkavati Nadi- Nearest Villages- Muniyanapalya, Alur, Kuduragere, Hanumantha Sagara, Heggadadevanapura, Makali, Adakamaranahalli, Gowdahalli, Harokyathanahalli, Madanaiyakanahalli, Siddanahosahalli, Dombarahalli, Gavipalya, Kadaranahalli, Sondekoppa, Nagasandra, Malla sandra, Ravuthanahalli, Kammasandra, Bettahalli, Kittana Halli, Giddenahalli, Kadabagere, Byandahalli, Hesaraghat ta, Kodagi Thirumalapura, Tharabana Halli, Sasiveghatta.

Reserved Forest: Nearest Villages- Manchappanahosahalli, Maralakunte, Dasanayakanahalli, Marenahalli, Marasandra, Challamakunte.

Annual Rainfall: Normal Rianfall 836 mm.

Ground Water: Availability of the Ground Water in the Basin is 6650 H.A.M. and the utilization is 13176 H. A.M. It belongs to Over Expoited category. Depth to water level 2 to 20 meter below the ground. Most of the wells go down in summer months, according to the Ground Water Estimation Committee.

Soils: Red Loamy Soils, it is seen in the eastern and southern parts of the block.

Natural Division : It falls in Bangalore Plateau of the Southern Karnataka Plateau.

Administration:

Division: Bangalore. Parliamentary Constituency: 24 Bangalore- 1, 23 Bangalore Rural. District: Bangalore. Taluka: Bangalore North. Assembly Constituency: 150 Bangalore North, 152 Bayatara, 153. Yesuanthapura, 154 Yanapura Pallangere, 155 Dasarahalli. Gram Panchayat: 33.

Fairs and Festivals: Keshava Navaratri Utsava: Popularly called "Keshava Navaratri" are held at Sondekoppa in the month of Phalguna (February-March). Sondekoppa or 'Sontekoppa' of the inscriptions appears (10 kms. from Nelamangala) to be an agrahara under the Hoysala. In the outskirts of the village is an old Ishwara temple in the fort area, from the garbhagriha walls are evident ly seen. The navaranga and mukhamantapa have been built in Vijayanagara style. The east entrance of the temple is closed and the new entrance to the south has the mukhamantapa, addition made later by the Vijayanagara rulers. The dwajasthambha of the temple is in front of the closed east entrance. The pillars of the mukhaman tapa have fine relief sculptures depicting many social themes like dancing girls, duelling and other figures like Matsyendra, Shanmukha, etc. Facing this temple across the road is a huge tank.

Villages: 225 **Inhabited:** 217 **Uninhabited:** 8

Ranking	District	State	National
Area	3	164	1439
Population	3	66	434
Sex Ratio	1	170	4512
Child Sex Ratio	3	94	3144
Literacy Rate	1	26	972
Density	1	137	2540
Work Participation Rate	3	7	3227

Gram Panchayats:

Sonnenahalli, Arakere, Rajanukunte, Bettahalasur, Chikkajala, Doddajala, Bandi Kodige Halli, Bagalur, Marenahalli, Kattigenahalli, Hunasamaranahalli, Sonnappanahalli, Gantiganahalli, Singanayakanahalli, Shivakote, Hesaraghatta, Gopalapura, Huskur, Huralichikkanahalli, Kasagattapura, Doddabettahalli , Abbigere, Chikkabanavara, Alur, Dasanapura, Madanaiyakanahalli, Madavara, Doddabidarakallu, Kittana Halli, Sondekoppa, Machohalli, Kodigehalli, Herohalli.

Amenities:

Education: Primary School in 191 villages, Middle school in 93 villages, Matriculation or Secondary School in 26 villages, namely Totagere, Huskur, Makali, Madanaiyakanahalli, Madavara, Sondekoppa, Ravuthanahalli, Kadabagere, Machohalli, Chikkabanavara, Abbigere, Kodigehalli, Kakolu, Sreeramanahalli, Rajanukunte, Ivar Kandapura, Hesaraghatta, Kasagattapura, Tarahunase, Nellukunte, Chikkajala, Doddajala, Bagalur, Bandi Kodige Halli, Singanayakanahalli, Vaderahalli.

Higher Secondary or Pre University Courses or Intermediate or Junior College in 10 villages of the CD Block,, namely Mathahalli, Madavara, Gangondanahalli, Machohalli, Chikkabanavara, Kodigehalli, Rajanukunte, Krishnarajapura, Hesaraghatta, Tarahunase.

College in 6 villages, Adult Literacy Center in 34 villages., Colleges are in villages, namely Krishnarajapura, Hesaraghatta, Soladevanahalli, Tarahunase, Bettahalasur, Chokkanahalli.

Medical: Hospital in 0 village, Dispensary in 5 villages, Health Center in 8 villages, Sub Center in 38 villages, Maternity and Child Welfare Center in 7 villages, Community health workers in 2 villages.

The Villages having Hospital or Dispensary or Health Center are Makali, Machohalli, Handrahalli, Singanayakanahalli, Gantiganahalli.

Drinking Water: Tap water in 97 villages, Tank water in 61 villages, Well water in 56 villages, Tubewell in 83 villages and more than one source in 156 villages.

Bank: Banking facility in 10 villages, namely, Alur, Dasanapura, Madanaiyakanahalli, Sondekoppa Rajanukunte, Hesaraghatta, Bettahalasur, Mylanahalli Bagalur, Singanayakanahalli.

Credit Society in 12 villages Agricultural Credit Society in 12 Non-Agricultural Credit Society in 2 villages.

Others: Power supply in 210 villages, Cinema hall in 1 village, sport club in 217 villages, Stadium or Auditorium or Communi Hall in 217 villages, Post Office in 32 villages.

There are 139 villages having bus facilities.

Villages with most of facilities: Dasanapura Madanaiyakanahalli, Sondekoppa, Rajanukunte, Bagalur Singanayakanahalli.

Villages without amenities (Education): Kodipalya, Seshagiri Rao Palya, Mariyanapalya, Venkatapura, Narayanappana Palya, Gollarapalya, K.G.Srikantapura, Gattisiddanahalli, Thirumalapura, Hesaraghatta Grass Farm, Lingarajapura, Byanahalli, Papanahalli, Chokkanahalli, Chikkanahalli, Dummanur, Gollahalli, Challamakunte, Govindapura, Jarakbandekaval, Shamarajpura, Manchenahalli, Vasudevapura..

Scheduled Castes: Out of the total population of 223031 persons, 49539 persons (22.21%) belong to Scheduled Castes. The villages having less than 10% SC population are Shamabhattara Palya, Rampalya, Huskur Agrahara Palya, Hosahalli Palya, Huchana Palya Seshagiri Rao Palya, Mariyanapalya, Narasipura

Muniyanapalya, Vaderahalli, Totadaguddadahalli Hanumantha Sagara, Narayanappana Palya Madanaiyakanahalli, Siddanahosahalli, Gollarapalya Kammasandra, K.G.Srikantapura, Gattisiddanahalli Giddenahalli, Kadabagere, Bylakonenahalli Ganigarahalli, Abbigere, Chikkasandra, Sidedahalli Kariobanahalli, Handrahalli, Kannahalli Kadathanamale, Chokkanahalli, Rajanukunte Kalenahalli, Krishnarajapura, Hesaraghatta Kodagi Thirumalapura, Madhugirihalli, Kasagattapura Sasiveghatta, Channahalli, Byanahalli, Nellukunte Muthugada Halli, Begur, Meesaganahalli, Chagalahatti Dummanur, Govindapura, Shamarajpura, Medi Agrahara Kempanahalli, Vasudevapura, Srinivasapura.

The villages having more than 50% SC population are Govindapura, Kodipalya, Thammenahalli, Shivanapura Nagasandra, Somashetti Halli, Myadarahalli Seegehalli, Suradenpura, Channasandra, Seeresandra Seethakempanahalli, Hesaraghatta Grass Farm Chokkanahalli, Maranayakana Halli, Byappanahalli Gollahalli, Challamakunte.

Sex ratio of Scheduled Caste population is 491.

Scheduled Castes Literates and Illiterates by Sex:

	Persons	Males	Females
Literate	25,588	15,271	10,317
Illiterate	23,951	9,956	13,995
Literacy rate	60.1	70.5	49.3
Graduate	489	415	74

Scheduled Castes (Dominant):

Adi Karnataka, Madiga, Bhovi, Adi Dravida Bhambi etc.

For their cultural identity please see Appendix-I

Villages without Scheduled Castes: There are 29 villages without any scheduled caste population.

Scheduled Tribes: Out of the total population of 223031 persons, 7446 persons (3.34%) belong to Scheduled Tribes.

The villages having less than 10% ST population are Gopalapura, Kukkanahalli, Shamabhattara Palya Totagere, Bommasettihalli, Syadamipalya, Bethanagere Rampalya, Huskur, Agrahara Palya, Hosahalli Palya Govindapura, Honnasandra, Huchana Palya, Pillahalli Nagarur, Kodipalya, Seshagiri Rao Palya Mariyanapalya, Narasipura, Torenagasandra Muniyanapalya, Vaderahalli, Alur, Kudur[illegible] Thammenahalli, Totadaguddadahalli, Hanumantha Sagara Heggadadevanapura, Makali, Adakamaranahalli Dasanapura, Gejjagadahalli, Hullegowdanahalli Byregowdanahalli, Venkatapura, Lakkenahalli Kenganahalli, Shivanapura, Gowdahalli Harokyathanahalli, Narayanappana Palya Madanaiyakanahalli, Madavara, Siddanahosahalli Dombarahalli, Kadaranahalli, Avverahalli, Hunnigere Sondekoppa, Nagasandra, Mallasandra, Gollarapalya Ravuthanahalli, Kammasandra, Lakshmipura K.G. Lakkenahalli, Vaddarahalli, Bettahalli Kittana Halli, Gattisiddanahalli, Giddenahalli Kadabagere, Byandahalli, Machohalli, Kachohalli Chikkabanavara, Ganigarahalli, Somashetti Halli Lakshmipura, Abbigere, Guddahalli, Myadarahalli Chikkasandra, Sidedahalli, Thirumalapura Doddabidarakallu, Kariobanahalli Hosahalli Gollarapalya, Kodigehalli, Seegehalli Manganahalli, Ullalu, Gidadakonenahalli Sonnenahalli, Challahalli, Haniyur, Kakkehalli Nellukunte, Marasandra Amanikere, Suradenpura Adde Vishwanathapura, Arakere, Byrapura Channasandra, Kamakshipura, Seeresandra, Byatha Kakolu, Budumanahalli, Shanubhoganahalli Chokkanahalli, Sreeramanahalli, Sadenahalli Adiganahalli, Rajanukunte, Ittagallpura, Dibburu Koluvarayanahalli, Seethakempanahalli Hesaraghatta Grass Farm, Dasenahalli, Kalenahalli Mathkur, Linganahalli, Muthagada Halli Madappanahalli, Krishnarajapura, Mylappanahalli Lingarajapura, Shivakote, Ivar Kandapura Hesaraghatta, Guddadahalli, Kodagi Thirumalapura Thammarasanahalli, Madhugirihalli, Mavallipura Bylakere, Kondashetti Halli, Kasagattapura Hurali Chikkanahalli, Sasiveghatta, Soladevanahalli Kumbarahalli, Kempapura, Kalathammanahalli Guniagrahara, Tarahunase, Gadenahalli Tharabanahalli, Meenakunte, Papanahalli Thimmasandra, Nellukunte, Bettahalasur Chokkanahalli, Chikkajala, Maranayakana Halli Doddajala, Settigere, Muthugada Halli, Begur Meesaganahalli, Huttanahalli, Hosahalli Sonnappanahalli, Kattigenahalli, Sathnur Byappanahalli, Chagalahatti, Bagalur Huvinayakanahalli, Bandi Kodige Halli, Hunachur Dummanur, Singahalli, Gollahalli, Arebinnamangala Mahadevakodigehalli, Manchappanahosahalli Maralakunte, Dasanayakanahalli, Marenahalli Marasandra, Challamakunte, Honnenahalli Nagadasanahalli, Muddanahalli, Singanayakanahalli Avalahalli, Gantiganahalli, Harohalli Ramagondanahalli, Jarakbandekaval, Shamarajpura Medi Agrahara, Vaderahalli, Veerasagara Kempanahalli, Ananthapura, Kenchenahalli Manchenahalli, Vasudevapura, Srinivasapura Bellahalli, Chokkanahalli.

The villages having more than 50% ST population are Bylakonenahalli, Channahalli, Byanahalli Bilmaranahalli.

Sex ratio of Scheduled tribe population is 493.

Scheduled Tribes Literates and Illiterates by Sex:

	Persons	Males	Females
Literate	3,938	2,324	1,614
Illiterate	3,508	1,450	2,058
Literacy rate	61.4	71.1	51.3
Graduate	91	73	18

Scheduled Tribes (Dominant):

Naikda etc., Soligaru, Generic Tribes etc., Iruliga Kadu Kuruba

For their cultural identity please see Appendix-II

Villages without Scheduled Tribes: There are 110 villages without any scheduled tribe population.

Literates and Illiterates by Sex (Total Population):

	Persons	Males	Females
Literate	139,790	81,601	58,189
Illiterate	83,241	34,013	49,228
Literacy rate	72	81	62
Graduate	5,675	4,256	1,419

Agriculture: ***Distribution of villages according to land use:*** Out of 225 villages, Total area (in hectare) is 51474, out of that 66.5 percent is cultivable and 31.14 percent of the cultivable area is irrigated.

Sources of Irrigation (Hectares): Government Canal 200.35, Private Canal 26.38, Well without Electricity 127.67, Well with Electricity 748.17, Tubewell without Electricity 180.17, Tubewell with Electricity 3580.15, Tank 1722.99, River 0, Lake 0, Waterfall 0, Others 4074.463.

Villages with population of 5000 to 9999: Madanaiyakanahalli, Chikkabanavara, Ullalu Hesaraghatta, Bagalur.

Villages with population of 10000 and above: None

Distribution of Workers:

	Persons	Males	Females	WPR
Cultivators	26,999	18,463	8,536	26.33
Agricultural Labour	20,762	9,497	11,265	20.25
Household Industry	3,721	1,605	2,116	3.63
Other Workers	51,064	39,308	11,756	49.8
Main Workers	81,631	60,920	20,711	79.6
Marginal Workers	20,915	7,953	12,962	20.4
Total Workers	102,546	68,873	33,673	

Religion: Major Religious Communities:

	Persons	Males	Females	Sex Ratio
Hindu (92.87%)	207,126	107,413	99,713	928
Muslim (4.67%)	10,417	5,356	5,061	945
Christian (1.79%)	3,997	2,094	1,903	909
Sikh (0.04%)	80	43	37	860
Buddhists (0.06%)	125	59	66	1,119
Jain (0.09%)	204	109	95	872

Agewise Data:

	Persons	Males	Females	Sex Ratio
All ages	223,031	115,614	107,417	929
0-14	66,664	34,050	32,614	958
15-44	115,265	59,914	55,351	924
45-79	38,718	20,478	18,240	891
80+	2,172	1,076	1,096	1019
Age not stated	212	96	116	1208

Languages (Dominant):

Kannada, Telugu, Urdu, Tamil, Hindi

Disabled Population:

	Persons	Males	Females	%
Total Disabled	3,669	2,124	1,545	
In Seeing	1,383	766	617	37.69
In Speech	357	196	161	9.73
In Hearing	300	159	141	8.18
In Movement	1,206	786	420	32.87
Mentally	423	217	206	11.53

BANGALORE SOUTH

Bangalore South C.D. Block lies in the south-western part of Bangalore district. It is a part of Bangalore south taluka. The Block is located at a distance of 00 kms. from district headquarters (Bangalore). There are 241 villages in the block with the total population of 313,397 persons. Area of the C.D. Block is 616.57 sq. kms. It is bounded by taluk Bangalore north and district Bangalore Rural on north, taluk Anekal and district Bangalore Rural on south, district Bangalore Rural on east and west.

Communications:

Roadways : N.H.-4: Direction- Bangalore to Chennai, Nearest Villages- Huskur, Nimbekaipura, Avalahalli, Veerenahalli, Bandapura, Konadasapura, Katamnallur. N.H-7: Direction- Bangalore to Chennai, Nearest Villages- Basapura, Beratena Agrahara, Chikkathoguru, Doddathoguru, Konappana Agrahara. N.H-207: Direction- Katamanallur to Attibele, Nearest Villages- Konadasapura, Katamnallur, Goravigere, Khaji Sonnenahalli, Kannamangala, Chikkabanahalli, Kadugodi Plantation, Belathur, Seegehalli. N.H-209: Direction- Banagalore to Kanakpura, Nearest Villages- Badamanavarthekaval, Agara, Gabbalalu, Thalaghattapura, Vajarahalli, Raghuvanahalli, Doddakallasandra, Mallasandra, Uttarahalli -Manavarthekaval, Kaggalipura, Nelaguli, K. Chudahalli, Somanahalli, Nettigere, Ravugodlu. S.H-17: Direction- Mysore to Bangalore, Nearest Villages- Chalaghatta, Kumbalagodu, Kaniminike, Kambipura. S. H-17 E: Direction- Magadi to Bangalore, Nearest Villages- Tavakadahalli, Honniganahatti, Channenahalli, Kurubarahalli, Bychaguppe, Devamachahalli Narayanapura, Devama chohalli, Marenahalli, Gangappanahalli, Thippagondanahalli, Kempagondanahalli, Cholanaikanahalli, Peddanapalya, Tavarekere. S.H-86 A: Direction- Bangalore to Anekal, Nearest Villages- Pillaganahalli, Basavanapura, Hommade vanahalli.

River: South Pinakini Nadi- Nearest Villages- Goravigere, Khaji Sonnenahalli, Kannamangala, Seegehalli, Nagondah alli. Arkavati Nadi- Nearest Villages- Jogerahalli, Gange nahalli, Varthur Narasimhapura, Varthur, Honniganahatti, Kurubarahalli.

Annual Rainfall: Normal Rianfall 970 mm.

Ground Water: Availability of the Ground Water in the Basin is 6267 H.A.M. and the utilization is 11896 H. A.M. It belongs to Over Exploited category. Depth to water level 2 to 20 meter below the ground. Most of the wells go down in summer months, according to the Ground Water Estimation Committee.

Soils: Red Loamy Soils, it is seen in the eastern and southern parts of the block.

Natural Division : It falls in Bangalore Plateau of the Southern Karnataka Plateau.

Administration:

Division: Bangalore. Parliamentary Constituency: Bangalo re- I, 26 Bangalore- III Bangalore Rural. District: Banga lore. Taluka: Bangalore South. Assembly Constituency: 153 Yeshavanthapura, 175 Bommanahalli, 176 Bangalore South. Gram Panchayat: 47.

Fairs: Bhavani Shankara Jatra: It is held during Shivaratri (February) at Vasanthapura. Vasanthapura is an interior place about 14 kms. from Bangalore at the Konana Kunte cross (Bangalore-Kanakapura Road).

Brahma Rathotsava: It is held at Vasanthapura in the month of Magha (January-February).

Channarayaswamy Temple Festival: It is held at the Venka taramana temple at Agara near Bangalore in the month of March for one day. Agara situated about 13 kms. from Bangalore is a place as old as of the Ganga times.

Chennaraysawamy Jatra: The jatra is held for ten days in honour of Chennarayaswamy beginning from Ratha Saptami at Varthur near Bangalore. Varthur a place about 9 kms. from Bangalore was perhaps a celebrated agrahara founded by Ganga Ereyapparasa.

Muneshwara Jatra: It is held at Kengeri near Bangalore in the month at Chaitra (March-APril). It attracts large number of people and is situated about 16 kms. from Bangalore on the Bangalore-Mysore Highway.

Villages: 241 **Inhabited:** 226 **Uninhabited:** 15

Ranking	District	State	National
Area	1	150	1113
Population	1	9	48
Sex Ratio	2	173	4946
Child Sex Ratio	1	57	2501
Literacy Rate	2	28	1113
Density	2	151	2184
Work Participation Rate	1	1	3608

Gram Panchayats:

Cholanaikanahalli, Tavarekere , Sulikere, Uttarahalli, Subramanyapura, Konanakunte, Doddakallasandra, Kothnur, Gottikere, Begur, Bellandur, Horamavu, Horamavu Agara, Thanisandra, Dasarahalli, Kothnur Narayanapura, Kannur, Doddagubbi, Bidarahalli, Mandur, Avalahalli, Doddabanahalli, Seegehalli, Channasandra, Hagadur, Ramagondanahalli, Sorahunase, Varthur, Gunjur, Panathur, Doddakannalli, Kodathi, Konappana Agrahara, Doddathoguru, Basavanapura, Anjanapura, Thalaghattapura, Hemmigepura, Ramohalli, Chunchanakuppe, Chikkanahalli, Kumbalagodu, Kumbalagodu Gollahalli, Agara, Kaggalipura, Somanahalli, Tharalu.

Amenities:

Education: Primary School in 193 villages, Middle school in 112 villages, Matriculation or Secondary School in 31 villages, namely Channenahalli, Thippagondanahalli, Tavarekere, Chunchanakuppe, Ganapathihalli, Dodderi, Sulikere, Ramohalli, Doddabele, Kumbalagodu Gollahalli, Badamanavarthekaval, Raghuvanahalli, Doddakallasandra, Kaggalipura, Nelaguli, Somanahalli, Begur, Doddagubbi, Bilishivale, Bidarahalli, Jothipura, Huskur, Avalahalli, Kannamangala, Belathur, Kothnur, Thanisandra, Kalkere, Kaikondahalli, Ramagondanahalli, Varthur.

Higher Secondary or Pre University Courses or Intermediate or Junior College in 7 villages of the CD Block,, namely Kurubarahalli, Ramohalli, Kammanahalli, Hommadevanahalli, Doddagubbi, Raghuvanahalli, Varthur.

College in 7 villages, Adult Literacy Center in 8 villages., Colleges are in villages, namely Kurubarahalli, Kumbalagodu, Somanahalli, Hommadevanahalli, Raghuvanahalli, Kothnur Narayanapura, Kaikondahalli.

Medical: Hospital in 0 village, Dispensary in 5 villages, Health Center in 13 villages, Sub Center in 38 villages, Maternity and Child Welfare Center in 9 villages, Community health workers in 6 villages.

The Villages having Hospital or Dispensary or Health Center are Thippagondanahalli, Tavarekere , Agara, Somanahalli, Chandrasekarapura, Maragondanahalli, Mandur, Avalahalli, Siddapura, Varthur.

Drinking Water: Tap water in 170 villages, Tank water in

104 villages, Well water in 65 villages, Tubewell in 63 villages and more than one source in 169 villages.

Bank: Banking facility in 19 villages, namely, Thippagondanahalli, Tavarekere, Ramohalli Kumbalagodu, Badamanavarthekaval, Agara, Kaggalipura Tharalu, Somanahalli, Ravugodlu, Begur Konappana Agrahara, Bidarahalli, Avalahalli Horamavu, Bellandur, Panathur, Varthur, Gunjur.

Credit Society in 27 villages Agricultural Credit Society in 13 Non-Agricultural Credit Society in 2 villages.

Others: Power supply in 220 villages, Cinema hall in 6 villages, sport club in 226 villages, Stadium or Auditorium or Community Hall in 226 villages, Post Office in 49 villages.

There are 185 villages having bus facilities.

Villages with most of facilities: Thippagondanahalli Tavarekere, Ramohalli, Kumbalagodu Badamanavarthekaval, Agara, Kaggalipura, Somanahalli Ravugodlu, Begur, Konappana Agrahara, Bidarahalli Avalahalli, Horamavu, Bellandur, Panathur, Varthur Gunjur.

Villages without amenities (Education):
Devamachahalli Narayanapura, Yalachaguppe Ramapura, Sulivara Ramapura, Vadahalli, Kurubarapalya, Kethohalli Narasimhapura, Kethohalli Ramapura, Kolur Gururayanapura, Kolur Nanjundapura, Seshagiripura, M.Krishnasagara, Kommaghatta - Krishnasagara, Venkatapura, Gudimavu, Vasanthanahalli, Thurahalli, Hosahalli, Raghuvanapalya, Mallasandra, Uttarahalli -Manavarthekaval, Alakabelalu, Sunkadakatte, Chandrasekarapura, Yelenahalli, Naganathapura, Chikkasandra, Anagalapura, Kammasandra, Shringaripura, Kodigehalli, Bidare Agrahara, Ambalipura, Chikkakannalli..

Scheduled Castes: Out of the total population of 312946 persons, 70576 persons (22.55%) belong to Scheduled Castes. The villages having less than 10% SC population are Naganahalli, Jogerahalli, Channenahalli Devamachahalli Narayanapura, Gangappanahalli Kempagondanahalli, Madapatna, Peddanapalya Yalachaguppe Ramapura, Sulivara Ramapura, Vadahalli Muddaiahnapalya, Kethohalli Narasimhapura Kolur Nanjundapura, Sonnenahalli, Bheemanakuppe Kommaghatta - Krishnasagara, Chalaghatta Kumbalagodu, Kambipura, Ganakal, Somapura Kengeri Gollahalli, Vasanthanahalli Lingadheeranahalli, Seegehalli, Doddakallasandra Alahalli, Uttari, Naganayakanahalli, Alakabelalu Thattaguppe, Chandrasekarapura, Begur Parappana Agrahara, Naganathapura, Chikkathoguru Basavanapura, Konappana Agrahara, Chikkasandra Bendiganahalli, Bidare Agrahara, Bandapura Kannamangala, Nagareshwara - Nagenahalli Kothnur Narayanapura, Geddalahalli, Kalkere K.Channasandra, Ambalipura, Ramagondanahalli.

The villages having more than 50% SC population are Kethohalli Ramapura, Chikkellur, Maligondanahalli Varahasandra, Thippasandra, Gulakamale Doddanagamangala, Vittasandra, Mittaganahalli Kada Agrahara, Anagalapura, Halehalli Raghuvanahalli, Kodigehalli, Bommenahalli Nimbekaipura, Dommasandra, Kadugodi Plantation Kadabeesanahalli, Bhoganahalli, Balagere Hadosiddapura, Sulikunte.

Sex ratio of Scheduled Caste population is 493.

Scheduled Castes Literates and Illiterates by Sex:

	Persons	Males	Females
Literate	36,453	21,410	15,043
Illiterate	34,123	14,387	19,736
Literacy rate	60.3	69.7	50.5
Graduate	794	650	144

Scheduled Castes (Dominant):
Adi Karnataka, Bhovi, Madiga, Adi Dravida Generic Castes etc.

For their cultural identity please see Appendix-I

Villages without Scheduled Castes: There are 31 villages without any scheduled caste population.

Scheduled Tribes: Out of the total population of 312946 persons, 5715 persons (1.83%) belong to Scheduled Tribes. The villages having less than 10% ST population are Naganahalli, Jogerahalli, Gangenahalli, Varthur Honniganahatti, Channenahalli, Kurubarahalli Bychaguppe, Devamachahalli Narayanapura Devamachohalli, Marenahalli, Gangappanahalli Thippagondanahalli, Madapatna, Cholanaikanahalli Ganukal, Peddanapalya, Tavarekere Yalachaguppe Ramapura, Yelachaguppe, Puradapalya Doddamaranahalli, Ajjanahalli, Huluvenahalli Sulivara, Sulivara Ramapura, Chikkanahalli Kurubarapalya, Donnenahalli, Byalalu, Chunchanakuppe Ganapathihalli, Muddaiahnapalya, Punagumaranahalli Kethohalli, Kethohalli Narasimhapura Kethohalli Ramapura, Kolur Gururayanapura, Dodderi Kolur Nanjundapura, Kolur, Seshagiripura, Chikkellur M.Krishnasagara, Kenchanapura, Sonnenahalli Ramasandra, Sulikere, Maragondanahalli Maligondanahalli, Ramohalli, Bheemanakuppe Kommaghatta - Krishnasagara, Chalaghatta Kumbalagodu, Kaniminike, Thagachaguppe, Kambipura Venkatapura, Doddabele, Hemmigepura, Ganakal

Somapura, Varahasandra, Kengeri Gollahalli, Gudimavu
Kumbalagodu Gollahalli, Hampapura, Thippur, Gonipura
Vasanthanahalli, Gangasandra, Devagere
Badamanavarthekaval, Chinnakurchi, Seegehalli, Agara
Thurahalli, Vasanthapura, Gabbalalu, Hosahalli
Thalaghattapura, Vajarahalli, Raghuvanahalli
Doddakallasandra, Raghuvanapalya, Pillaganahalli
Kembathahalli, Gollahalli, Alahalli, Thippasandra
Anjanapura, Uttarahalli -Manavarthekaval
O.B.Chudahalli, Kaggalipura, Uttari, Nelaguli
Tharalu, Gulakamale, Alakabelalu, Somanahalli
Ravugodlu, Sunkadakatte , Thattaguppe, Vaddarapalya
Chandrasekarapura, Yelenahalli, Begur, Basapura
Parappana Agrahara, Naganathapura, Doddanagamangala
Chikkathoguru, Vittasandra, Mylasandra, Kammanahalli
Basavanapura, Hommadevanahalli, Bettadasanapura
Doddathoguru, Konappana Agrahara, Mittaganahalli
Kadusonnappanahalli, Yerappanahalli, Chikkasandra
Gundur, Kada Agrahara, Bandebommasandra, Anagalapura
Nadagowdagollahalli, Chikkagubbi, Kannur, Byrathi
Doddagubbi, Bilishivale, Rampura, Adur, Varanasi
Maragondanahalli, Halehalli, Kithiganur
Hirandahalli, Bidarahalli, Byappanahalli
Kammasandra, Shringaripura, Jothipura
Thirumenahalli, Hancharahalli, Raghuvanahalli
Kodigehalli, Mandur, Bendiganahalli, Lagumenahalli
Bommenahalli, Huskur, Nimbekaipura, Cheemasandra
Avalahalli, Veerenahalli, Kurudusonnenahalli
Dommasandra, Doddabanahalli, Bidare Agrahara
Bandapura, Konadasapura, Katamnallur, Goravigere
Khaji Sonnenahalli, Kannamangala, Chikkabanahalli
Kumbena Agrahara, Kadugodi Plantation, Belathur
Seegehalli, Rachenahalli
Nagareshwara - Nagenahalli, Kothnur
Kothnur Narayanapura, Thanisandra, Geddalahalli
Horamavu Agara, Horamavu, Kyalasanahalli, Kalkere
K.Channasandra, Nagondahalli, Bellandur
Kariyammana Agrahara, Kadabeesanahalli, Panathur
Devara Beesana Halli, Kaikondahalli, Ambalipura
Haralur, Kasavanahalli, Junnasandra
Halanayakanahalli, Chikkakannalli, Doddakannalli
Bhoganahalli, Thubarahalli, Siddapura
Ramagondanahalli, Valepura, Sorahunise, Varthur
Balagere, Gunjur, Kachamaranahalli, Chikkabellandur
Mulluru, Hadosiddapura, Chikkanayakanahalli, Kodathi
Sulikunte.

The villages having more than 50% ST population are None.

Sex ratio of Scheduled tribe population is 484.

Scheduled Tribes Literates and Illiterates by Sex:

	Persons	Males	Females
Literate	3,001	1,737	1,264
Illiterate	2,714	1,214	1,500
Literacy rate	61.7	69.2	53.7
Graduate	69	55	14

Scheduled Tribes (Dominant):

Naikda etc., Iruliga, Soligaru, Gowdalu
Kadu Kuruba

For their cultural identity please see Appendix-II

Villages without Scheduled Tribes: There are 107 villages without any scheduled tribe population.

Literates and Illiterates by Sex (Total Population):

	Persons	Males	Females
Literate	191,561	111,730	79,831
Illiterate	121,385	51,708	69,677
Literacy rate	71	79	62
Graduate	8,819	6,331	2,488

Agriculture: ***Distribution of villages according to land use:*** Out of 241 villages, Total area (in hectare) is 61657, out of that 62.98 percent is cultivable and 24.14 percent of the cultivable area is irrigated.

Sources of Irrigation (Hectares): Government Canal 72.75, Private Canal 20.23, Well without Electricity 368.89, Well with Electricity 1520.84, Tubewell without Electricity 258.53, Tubewell with Electricity 2220.43, Tank 2543.86, River 11.03, Lake 0, Waterfall 0, Others 2359.58.

Villages with population of 5000 to 9999:

Alahalli, Kaggalipura, Belathur, Thanisandra
Varthur.

Villages with population of 10000 and above:

Konappana Agrahara.

Distribution of Workers:

	Persons	Males	Females	WPR
Cultivators	26,294	18,923	7,371	19.08
Agricultural Labour	18,355	9,894	8,461	13.32
Household Industry	4,696	2,584	2,112	3.41
Other Workers	88,482	66,019	22,463	64.2
Main Workers	118,317	87,479	30,838	85.84
Marginal Workers	19,510	9,941	9,569	14.16
Total Workers	137,827	97,420	40,407	

Religion: Major Religious Communities:

	Persons	Males	Females	Sex Ratio
Hindu (87.26%)	273,090	142,682	130,408	914
Muslim (7.41%)	23,202	12,014	11,188	931
Christian (4.69%)	14,687	7,705	6,982	906
Sikh (0.06%)	173	101	72	713
Buddhists (0.21%)	644	337	307	911
Jain (0.04%)	119	73	46	630

Agewise Data:

	Persons	Males	Females	Sex Ratio

All ages	312,946	163,438	149,508	915
0-14	94,989	48,180	46,809	972
15-44	164,485	86,761	77,724	896
45-79	50,005	26,700	23,305	873
80+	2,731	1,395	1,336	958
Age not stated	736	402	334	831

Languages (Dominant):
Kannada, Telugu, Tamil, Urdu, Hindi

Disabled Population:

	Persons	Males	Females	%
Total Disabled	5,282	3,019	2,263	
In Seeing	2,378	1,269	1,109	45.02
In Speech	512	286	226	9.69
In Hearing	313	161	152	5.93
In Movement	1,470	931	539	27.83
Mentally	609	372	237	11.53

BANGARAPET

Bangarapet C.D. Block lies in the southern part of Kolar district. It is a part of Bangarapet taluka. The Block is located at a distance of 18 kms. from district headqu arters (Kolar). There are 383 villages in the block with the total population of 225,413 persons. Area of the C.D. Block is 799.26 sq. kms. It is bounded by taluks Kolar and Mulbagal on north, taluk Malur on west. It has common boundary with the state of Tamil Nadu on south, and the state of Andhra Pradesh on south-east and east.

Communications:
Roadways : S.H.-5: Direction- Kolar to Bangarapet, Nearest Villages- Pakarahalli, Hudukula, Chikka Ankandahalli, Kuppanhalli, Haliganahalli, Karabele, Beerandahalli, Yelaburgi, Dodda Ankandhalli.
Railway Station: Villages- Hudukula, Vattigal, Thanimadagu.
River: Palar Nadi- Nearest Villages- Thambarlahalli, Jaimangala, Maddinayakanahalli, Chinnapalli, Kallikuppa, Vaddahalli, Hangala, Natha, Thimmasandra, Iyyappalli Amanikere, Nallur, Ankathattahalli, Hulkuru, Kavaraganah alli, Koolur, Doddakari Majara Kambampalli, Kodihalli, Bethamangala, Pootharajanahalli, Deverahalli, Mahadevap ura, Gopenahalli, Annasagara, Mustoor, Thathepalli, Malla palli, Kadaripura, Papenahalli, Ramasagara, Veerasandra, Thimmapura, Kannur,, Kangandlahalli, Ihvarahalli, Golla guruanahalli, Thathareddihalli, Thongalakuppa, Doddagandl ahalli, Chinchandlahalli, Bennavara, Srinivasasandra.
Markanda Halla Nadi- Nearest Villages- Balamande, Palam adagu, Thamatamakanahalli, Kanumanahalli, Yerragola.
Koppakere Halla Nadi- Nearest Villages- Balamande, Kendo dimande, Dodapannandahalli, Dasaramale, Bodapatti, Chikk apannanndahalli, Rathenahalli, Keerumande, Chamanahalli.
Reserved Forest: Nearest Villages- Mustrahalli, Kadarina tha, Sakarasanhalli, Thalur, Donimadagu, Bathlahalli. (Kamasandra R.F.): Nearest Villages- Pataramagulla, Mutanuru, Godagumande, Gullahalli, Balamande, Palamada gu, Thamatamakanahalli, Kanumanahalli, Yerragola.
Annual Rainfall: Normal Rianfall 793.29 mm.
Ground Water: Availability of the Ground Water in the Basin is (Information not avablable) H.A.M. and the utilization is (Information not avablable) H.A.M.
It belongs to (Information not avablable) category.
Depth to water level 5 to 20 meter below the ground.
Most of the wells go down in summer months, according to the Ground Water Estimation Committee.
Soils: Red Soils.
Natural Division : It falls in Kolar-Bangarapet Rugged Tract of the Southern Karnataka Plateau.
Administration:
Division: Bangalore. Parliamentary Constituency: 28 Kolar (SC). District: Kolar. Taluka: Bangarapet. Assembly Constituency: 146 Robertsonpet (SC), 147 Bangarapet (SC). Gram Panchayat: 37.
Regional Area Development Boards: The Bailu Seeme Area Development Board.
Border Villages: (State: Andhra Pradesh)- Ramasandra, Thanimadagu, Boggilahalli, Mustrahalli, Donimadagu, Bathlahalli, Pooganahalli , Kadiriganakoppa, Thathepalli, Jadamakanhalli, Panthanahalli, Mothakapalli, Thongalak uppa, Dalavaihosahalli, Karadaguru, Karadiganahalli, Thookal, Keerthikuppa, Banagere, Doddakallahalli , Lakki nayakanahalli, Kempapura, Chokarabande, Kattenagasandra, Kururu, Allikallu, Neelagirihalli, Madivala-Majara Kothur, Maradagatta, Sanganahalli, Doddagandlahalli, Chinchandlahalli, Bennavara, Mittakothur, Srinivasasand ra, Nagakuppa, Krishnarajapura, Peelavara. (State Tamil Nadu)- Pataramagulla, Muthanuru, Thamatamakanahalli, Kanumanahalli, Doddapannandahalli, Chikkapannanndahalli, Kadarinatha, Thalur.
Fairs: Bangara-Tirupati Jatra: Guttahalli situated on the left bank of the river Palar near the Kolar Gold Fields-Mulbagal road and the Bethamangala lake in Bangar pet taluk, is well-known for its Venkataramanaswamy temple built on the top of a hillock. The place is also popula rly called as 'Bangara-Tirupati' or 'Chinna-Tirupati' by virtue of its being at a short distance from the gold fields. According to a legend, Sage Bhrigu had his ashram at this place. Hundreds of devotees from far and near visit the temple, especially on Saturdays. An impressive gopura and a spacious choultry were const ructed here recently at a considerable cost. Other amenit ies have also been improved and the place is becoming popular as a holiday resort as well. A large number of marriages are celebrated at this holy place. A jatra

with a cattle fair held here in the month of Magha is well attended.

Villages: 383 **Inhabited:** 355 **Uninhabited:** 28

Ranking	District	State	National
Area	6	122	728
Population	3	64	412
Sex Ratio	7	84	2306
Child Sex Ratio	6	42	2073
Literacy Rate	6	106	3162
Density	11	97	3720
Work Participation Rate	2	28	2297

Gram Panchayats:
Sulikunte, Chikka Ankandahalli, Mavahalli, Hunukunda, Gollahalli, Hulkuru, Sundrapalya, N.G. Hulkur, Vengasandra, Ramasagara, Bethamangala, Kammasandra, Ghattakamadenahalli, Doddurkarpanhalli, Karahalli , Inorahosahalli, Hulibele, Desihalli , Chinnakote, Doddavalagamadhi, Magondi, Alambadi, Budikote, Gullahalli, Yelesandra, Kethaganahalli, Kamasamudra, Balamande, Thoppanahalli, Donimadagu, Ghattamadamangala, Marikuppa, Parandahalli, Kyasamballi, Kangandlahalli, Jakkarasanakuppa, Srinivasasandra.

Amenities:
Education: Primary School in 270 villages, Middle school in 123 villages, Matriculation or Secondary School in 15 villages, namely Hanchala, Madamangala, Guttahalli, Karamangala, Budikote, Gullahalli, Balamande, Doddapannandahalli, Thoppanahalli, Ghattakamadenahalli, Badamakanhalli, Bethamangala, Sundrapalya, N.G. Hulkur, Kyasamballi.
Higher Secondary or Pre University Courses or Intermediate or Junior College in 3 villages of the CD Block,, namely Hunukunda, Madamuthanhalli, Bethamangala.
College in 5 villages, Adult Literacy Center in 19 villages., Colleges are in villages, namely Mittamalahalli, Hunukunda, Madamuthanhalli, Doddachinnapalli, Yethur.
Medical: Hospital in 4 villages, Dispensary in 1 village, Health Center in 8 villages, Sub Center in 41 villages, Maternity and Child Welfare Center in 15 villages, Community health workers in 13 villages.
The Villages having Hospital or Dispensary or Health Center are Sulikunte, Chalganahalli, Hunukunda, Madamuthanhalli, Doddarahalli, Mustoor, Lakkinayakanahalli.
Drinking Water: Tap water in 204 villages, Tank water in 92 villages, Well water in 174 villages, Tubewell in 237 villages and more than one source in 311 villages.
Bank: Banking facility in 18 villages, namely, Hudukula, Hulibele, Alambadi, Karimanahalli Budikote, Hoshalli, Doddapannandahalli, Dasaramale Bodapatti, Thoppanahalli, Kamandahalli, Doddarahalli Doddachinnapalli, Doddavalagamadhi, Badamakanhalli Sundrapalya, Kyasamballi, Kempapura.
Credit Society in 22 villages Agricultural Credit Society in 20 Non-Agricultural Credit Society in 2 villages.
Others: Power supply in 336 villages, Cinema hall in 9 villages sport club in 8 villages, Stadium or Auditorium or Community Hall in 7 villages, Post Office in 52 villages.
There are 219 villages having bus facilities.
Villages with most of facilities: Hudukula Hulibele, Budikote, Doddapannandahalli Thoppanahalli, Doddachinnapalli, Doddavalagamadhi Sundrapalya, Kyasamballi, Kempapura.
Villages without amenities (Education):
Kumbaragollahalli, Ramapuradinne, Voggayahnadinne, Haliganahalli, Akshantaragollahalli, Ramanayakanhalli, Byadabele, Karabele, Goravanahalli, Kasipura, Hanumanthapura, Koppa, Singarahalli, Chakkaranahalli, Bendiganahalli, Hurlahalli, Chikkanallaguttahalli, Varadapura, Kodagurki, Kadaripura, Chintagumnahalli, Poojarahalli, Suriganahalli, Guttahalli, Godagumande, Kendodimande, Dasaramale, Kanthepura, Dimbaladebbanahalli, Doddamarihalli, Lakkenahalli, Arimanahalli, Ramasandra, Bathlur, Chinnakamanahalli, Bompalli, Rathenahalli, Bangaranatha, Thalur, Manchenahalli, Maliyangurki, Chikkakrimanahalli, Iymarasapura, Byraganahalli, Krishnarajapura, Gattarayagadahalli, Mallampalli -Ryagadahalli, Nakkanahalli, Kallikuppa, Thongal, Surapalli, Baliganahalli, Keelukambali, Bynepalli, Chinnapalli, Dharmakrishnepalli, Doddakari Majara Kambampalli, Thippaboyenahalli, Kothapalya, Peddampalli, Chimalabandahalli, Kaggilahalli, Batavarahalli, Allikunte-Kadirenahalli, Lakshmisagar, Nagalapalli, Kogilahalli, Gollaguruanahalli, Nakkanahalli, Kachimittahalli, Keerthikuppa, Ballagere, Lakkinayakanahalli, Settikunte, Mittakothur, Krishnarajapura..
Scheduled Castes: Out of the total population of 225650 persons, 71233 persons (31.57%) belong to Scheduled Castes. The villages having less than 10% SC population are Kumbaragollahalli, Ramapuradinne, Dodda Ankandhalli Yaluvahalli, Goravanahalli, Kasipura, Maravahalli Bendiganahalli, Chikkanallaguttahalli, Debbanhalli Budikote, Pacharalahalli, Dinnekothur, Hunakaldoddi Kadaripura, Upasapura, Chembenahalli, Suriganahalli Hoshalli, Muthanuru, Boppanhalli, Godagumande Yerragola, Kendodimande, Doddapannandahalli Dasaramale, Bodapatti, Doddamarihalli, Vattigal

Kongarahalli, Ramasandra, Thanimadagu, Boggilahalli
Mustrahalli, Gundaralahalli, Bathlur, Bhuvanahalli
Bandarlahalli, Sakarasanhalli, Thalur, Chalganahalli
Iymarasapura, Nakkanahalli, Doddakambali, Bynepalli
Maddinayakanahalli, Dharmakrishnepalli, Kodihalli
Kothur, Kalavihosahalli, Kadaripura, Kachimittahalli
Lakkinayakanahalli, Madivala-Majara Kothur
Mittakothur.

The villages having more than 50% SC population are Voggayahnadinne, Hudukula, Chikka Ankandahalli Akshantaragollahalli, Ramanayakanhalli, Karabele Kanivekallu, Hanumanthapura, Benganur, Keelukoppa Koppa, Thatnahalli, Singarahalli, Chakkaranahalli Hirekarapanahalli, Chickkakarapanahalli, Atthigere Varadapura, Makarahalli, Sanganahalli, Gajiga Srirangabandahalli, Kodagurki, Muduguli Chintagumnahalli, Buvanahalli, Yachamanahalli Sontiganahalli, Poojarahalli, Garudakempanahalli Nagenahalli, Kanthepura, Boyisonnenahalli Kavaraganahalli, Thammenhalli, Ajjapalli Byraganahalli, Gattarayagadahalli, Peddapalli M. Kothur, Giddegowdanahalli, Lakshmisagara Chinnapalli, Kallikuppa, Siddareddy Dinne Gollahalli, Iyyappalli, Betkur, Chimalabandahalli Kaggilahalli, Muddegowdanahalli, Batavarahalli Adampalli, Allikunte-Kadirenahalli, Beernakuppa N.G. Hulkur, Mahadevapura , Lakshmisagar Panthanahalli, Thimmapura, Nagalapalli, Kogilahalli Kangandlahalli, Dalavaihosahalli, Nakkanahalli Kasireddigandlahalli, Keerthikuppa, Neelagirihalli.

Sex ratio of Scheduled Caste population is 496.

Scheduled Castes Literates and Illiterates by Sex:

	Persons	Males	Females
Literate	32,075	19,863	12,212
Illiterate	39,158	16,045	23,113
Literacy rate	52.7	64.7	40.4
Graduate	549	466	83

Scheduled Castes (Dominant):

Adi Karnataka, Bhovi, Chalavadi etc., Adi Dravida Koracha

For their cultural identity please see Appendix-I

Villages without Scheduled Castes: There are 53 villages without any scheduled caste population.

Scheduled Tribes: Out of the total population of 225650 persons, 8167 persons (3.62%) belong to Scheduled Tribes. The villages having less than 10% ST population are Kumbaragollahalli, Mageri, Hanchala, Ramapuradinne Voggayahnadinne, Pakarahalli, Hudukula, Vattrakunte Byranayakanahalli, Venugopalapura, Bhavarahalli Chikka Ankandahalli, Kuppanhalli, Haliganahalli Siddanahalli, Akshantaragollahalli, Madamangala Mugalabele, Sulikunte, Ramanayakanhalli Madigarahalli, Honnenahalli, Madivala, Byadabele Karabele, Margal, Iythandahalli, Nernahalli Karahalli, Yelaburgi, Dodda Ankandhalli, Kanimbele Guttahalli, Karamangala, Thyranahalli, Goravanahalli Oombathguli, Kasipura, Inorahosahalli, Kanivekallu Hanumanthapura, Hunasanahalli, Benganur, Neralekere Soregowdanakote, Keelukoppa, Maravahalli, Koppa Huvrasanahalli, Hulibele, Thoraganadoddi, Nethibele Abbigirihosahalli, Thumatagere, Kadirenahalli Hosakote, Thatnahalli, Chikkavalagamadi Singarahalli, Harohalli, Chakkaranahalli Bendiganahalli, Magondi, Hirekarapanahalli Banahalli, Chickkakarapanahalli, Atthigere Hurlahalli, Paravanahalli, Varadapura, Makarahalli Kondanahalli, Sanganahalli, Junjanahalli, Gajiga Alambadi, Karimanahalli, Budikote Srirangabandahalli, Marandahalli, Pacharalahalli Dinnekothur, Kodagurki, Hunakaldoddi Puttrasonnenahalli, Muduguli, Chintagumnahalli Mooganahalli, Dodderi, Buvanahalli, Yachamanahalli Sontiganahalli, Poojarahalli, Kotaramagulla Suriganahalli, Garudakempanahalli, Kadirenahalli Nagenahalli, Guttahalli, Pataramagulla, Muthanuru Boppanhalli, Godagumande, Doddur, Pura, Palamadagu Thamatamakanahalli, Kanumanahalli, Yerragola Kendodimande, Doddapannandahalli, Dasaramale Bodapatti, Boyinahalli, Ukkarahalli, Kanthepura Dimbaladebbanahalli, Boyisonnenahalli, Pitchahalli Tavarekere, Appenahalli, Kethaganahalli Nallaguttahalli, Vattigal, Kamasamudra, Janagutta Lakkenahalli, Bodagurki, Yelachamande, Narinetha Kongarahalli, Nadampalli, Bodenahalli, Arimanahalli Ramasandra, Boggilahalli, Mustrahalli Gundaralahalli, Bathlur, Bhuvanahalli, Rathenahalli Keerumande, Bangaranatha, Chamanahalli Bandarlahalli, Thoppanahalli, Kalavanchi Polenahalli, Kundarasanahalli, Kadarinatha, Thalur Donimadagu, Bathlahalli, Chalganahalli, Mavahalli Kamandahalli, Vadandahalli, Mittamalahalli Pitchaguntrahalli, Kavaraganahalli, Thammenhalli Ajjapalli, Maliyangurki, Kesaranhalli Chikkakrimanahalli, Doddachinnapalli, Iymarasapura Doddavalagamadhi, Buragamakanahalli, Byraganahalli Krishnarajapura, Ghattakamadenahalli Gattarayagadahalli, Peddapalli, Yerranaganahalli Chinnapalli, Mallampalli -Ryagadahalli, Nakkanahalli Kallikuppa, Thongal, M. Kothur, Surapalli Baliganahalli, Giddegowdanahalli, Chinnanagahalli

Keelukambali, Bynepalli, Lakshmisagara Ghattamadamangala, Kanganallur, Thambarlahalli Jaimangala, Maddinayakanahalli, Chinnapalli Kallikuppa, Kogilahalli, Vaddahalli, Battarakuppa Dharmakrishnepalli, Siddareddy Dinne, Nayanahalli Hangala, Natha, Thimmasandra, Gollahalli Badamakanhalli, Ysandra, Iyyappalli, Nallur Ankathattahalli, Hulkuru, Venkatapura Kavaraganahalli, Betkur, Gennerahalli, Nernahalli Koolur, Doddakari Majara Kambampalli, Doddakari Kodihalli, Kothur, Bethamangala, Thippaboyenahalli Kothapalya, Chigarapura, Kadiregowdanakote Reddihalli, Peddampalli, Kammasandra Chimalabandahalli, Nagisettihalli, Kaggilahalli Gorlachinnapalli, Bommandahalli, Byatarayanahalli Pootharajanahalli, Deverahalli, Jangamanahalli Muddegowdanahalli, Batavarahalli, Adampalli Garudadrihalli, Allikunte-Kadirenahalli Chaliganhalli, Kambampalli, Beernakuppa Kaveranahalli, Buchepalli , Nachandahalli Kalavihosahalli, Sundrapalya, Thallapalli Kodigepalli, Surnahalli, Gandodihalli, Pooganahalli Kadiriganakoppa, N.G. Hulkur, Vengasandra Rayasandra, Pillagondanahalli, Vaddarahalli Mahadevapura , Sarvareddihalli, Gopenahalli Annasagara, Mustoor, Lakshmisagar, Thathepalli Jadamakanhalli, Panthanahalli, Mallapalli Kadaripura, Papenahalli, Ramasagara, Veerasandra Thimmapura, Nagalapalli, Baluvanahalli, Kyasamballi Billerahalli, Kannur, Kogilahalli, Kangandlahalli Gollaguruanahalli, Thathareddihalli, Mothakapalli Thongalakuppa, Dalavaihosahalli, Karadaguru Nakkanahalli, Kasireddigandlahalli, Jakkarasanakuppa Kachimittahalli, Madivala, Karadiganahalli, Thookal Banagere, Ballagere, Byatarayanahalli, Kempapura Chokkarabande, Kururu, Allikallu, Neelagirihalli Madivala-Majara Kothur, Maradagatta, Yethur Chinchandlahalli, Bennavara, Mittakothur Krishnarajapura.

The villages having more than 50% ST population are Desihlli, Debbanhalli, Kadaripura, Thanimadagu Kurubarahalli, Lakkinayakanahalli.

Sex ratio of Scheduled tribe population is 500.

Scheduled Tribes Literates and Illiterates by Sex:

	Persons	Males	Females
Literate	3,143	2,009	1,134
Illiterate	5,024	2,072	2,952
Literacy rate	45.5	57.9	33.0
Graduate	35	31	4

Scheduled Tribes (Dominant):

Naikda etc., Soligaru, Palliyan, Gond etc.
Kadu Kuruba

For their cultural identity please see Appendix-II

Villages without Scheduled Tribes: There are 247 villages without any scheduled tribe population.

Literates and Illiterates by Sex (Total Population):

	Persons	Males	Females
Literate	112,454	68,750	43,704
Illiterate	113,196	45,586	67,610
Literacy rate	58	70	46
Graduate	2,583	2,087	496

Agriculture: ***Distribution of villages according to land use:*** Out of 383 villages, Total area (in hectare) is 79926, out of that 62.18 percent is cultivable and 36.96 percent of the cultivable area is irrigated.

Sources of Irrigation (Hectares): Government Canal 579.12, Private Canal 15.88, Well without Electricity 272.65, Well with Electricity 2340.14, Tubewell without Electricity 61.53, Tubewell with Electricity 6899.15, Tank 3712.95, River 130.88, Lake 0, Waterfall 0, Others 4353.93.

Villages with population of 5000 to 9999: Bethamangala.

Villages with population of 10000 and above: None

Distribution of Workers:

	Persons	Males	Females	WPR
Cultivators	45,365	28,430	16,935	40.94
Agricultural Labour	35,558	15,197	20,361	32.09
Household Industry	1,980	845	1,135	1.79
Other Workers	27,897	21,811	6,086	25.18
Main Workers	89,976	59,936	30,040	81.21
Marginal Workers	20,824	6,347	14,477	18.79
Total Workers	110,800	66,283	44,517	

Religion: Major Religious Communities:

	Persons	Males	Females	Sex Ratio
Hindu (93.31%)	210,559	106,607	103,952	975
Muslim (6.22%)	14,030	7,243	6,787	937
Christian (0.4%)	900	411	489	1,190
Sikh (0%)	10	5	5	1,000
Buddhists (0%)	5	2	3	1,500
Jain (0.03%)	69	35	34	971

Agewise Data:

	Persons	Males	Females	Sex Ratio
All ages	225,650	114,336	111,314	974
0-14	75,503	38,034	37,469	985
15-44	102,838	52,231	50,607	969
45-79	44,129	22,490	21,639	962
80+	3,011	1,481	1,530	1033
Age not stated	169	100	69	690

Languages (Dominant):
Telugu, Kannada, Urdu, Tamil, Marathi

Disabled Population:

	Persons	Males	Females	%
Total Disabled	3,947	2,232	1,715	
In Seeing	1,826	1,020	806	46.26
In Speech	430	241	189	10.89
In Hearing	192	104	88	4.86
In Movement	1,065	657	408	26.98
Mentally	434	210	224	11

BANTVAL

Bantval C.D. Block lies in the south-western part of Dakshina Kannada district. It is a part of Bantval taluka. The Block is located at a distance of 24 kms. from district headquarters (Mangalore). There are 79 villages in the block with the total population of 306,414 persons. Area of the C.D. Block is 695.11 sq. kms. It is bounded by taluks Beltangadi and Mangalore on north, taluks Puttur and Beltangadi on east, and taluk Mangalore on west. It has common boundary with the state of Kerala on south.

Communications:

Roadways : NH- 48: Direction- Mangalore to Hassan, Nearest Villages- Kallige, Munnuru, Narikombu, Golthamajal, Balthila, Kadeshwalya, Mani, Peraje, Biliyur, Perne, Kedila. SH- 64: Direction- Bantval to Beltangadi, Neare st Villages- Amtady, Mudanadugodu, Navoor, Kavalpadur, Kadabettu, Moodapadukodi, Pilathabettu, Kavalmudur. SH- 88: Direction- Mani to Puttur, Nearest Villages- Mani, Peraje, Kedila, Netlamudnur, Idkidu, Kula. SH- 88 C: Direction- Golthamajal to Hosdurga, Nearest Villag es- Golthamajal, Veerakamba, Vittal, Alike, Kepu, Punacha.

River: Gurpur Nadi- Nearest Villages- Karpe, Sangabettu, Arala, Ajjibettu, Kariyangala, Badaga Bellur, Ammunje. Natravati Nadi- Nearest Villages- Navoor, Sarapady, Maninalkur, Munnuru, Sajipanadu, Sajipapadu, Narikombu, Shambhoor, Balthila, Barimar, Kadeshwalya, Biliyur.

Reserved Forest: Nearest Villahges- Veerakamba, Ananthadi, Mani, Netlamudnur. (Kalanjimale R.F.): Nearest Village s- Kolnadu, Vittal, Vittalpadanur, Salethur, Karopady, Kanyana, Alike. (Kodkamale R.F.): Nearest Villages-

Annual Rainfall: Normal Rianfall 4615.34 mm.

Ground Water: Availability of the Ground Water in the Basin is (Information not avablable) H.A.M. and the utilization is (Information not avablable) H.A.M. It belongs to (Information not avablable) category. Depth to water level 5 to 20 meter below the ground. Most of the wells go down in summer months, according to the Ground Water Estimation Committee.

Natural Division : It falls partly in Kundapur-Mangalore Coast and Bainduru-Bantval Plain of the Karnataka Coast (Western Coastal Region).

Administration:

Division: Mysore. Parliamentary Constituency: 17 Dakshina Kannada. District: Dakshina Kannada. Taluka: Bantval. Assembly Constituency: 204 Mangalore, 205 Bantval, 206 Puttur. Gram Panchayat: 47.

Regional Area Development Boards: The Maland Aera Development Board.

Border Villages: (State: Kerala)- Kairangala, Naringana, Balepuni, Ira, Kolnadu, Salethur, Karopady, Kanyana, Peruvai, Manila, Alike, Kepu, Punacha.

Fairs: Rajarajeshwari Temple Car Festival: It is held at Polali every year. Polali, about 12 kms. north-west of the Buntwal Cross Road, formerly kown as "Pulingapura" is a hamlet of Kariangala village.

Syed Baba Fakruddin Urs: Ajilamogaru near Dakshina Kannada about 20 kms. east of Buntwal has an old mosque which was built by an Ajila chief. It is said, he was cured of a disease by a Persian Saint by the name Syed Baba Fakruddin who had settled for some time in the village. Under the auspices of this mosque, an annual Urs is held.

Thirumala Venkataramana Temple Rathotsava: It is held at Buntwal near Dakshina Kannada. Buntwal, is the headqu arters of a taluk of the same name and is situated at a distance of about 25 kms. to the east of Mangalore, on the northern bank of the Netravati river. There are three noted temples here, viz., Venkataramana, Seeth arama and Mahalingeshwara. Closeby, there is a large hill called Narahari Parvata with a temple.

Venkataramana Temple Laksha Deepotsava: Pane-Mangalore near Dakshina Kannada, about six kms. to the south of Buntwal, is situated on the bank of the Netravati river and is connected with Buntwal by a bridge across the river. It is a trading centre. An attractive Laksha-Deep otsava function is held here annually at the Venkataramana temple.

Villages: 79 **Inhabited:** 79 **Uninhabited:** 0

Ranking	District	State	National
Area	4	134	926
Population	1	14	60
Sex Ratio	3	12	547
Child Sex Ratio	1	70	2690
Literacy Rate	2	4	291
Density	2	19	2496
Work Participation Rate	2	5	723

Gram Panchayats:

Kariyangala, Badaga Bellur, Rayee, Sangabettu, Kukkipady, Chennaithodi, Pilathabettu, Panjikal, Amtady, Meremajalu, Pudu, Thumbe, Narikombu, Navoor, Kavalpadur, Kavalmudur, Badagakajekar, Uli, Sarapady, Balthila, Munnuru (Sajipura), Sajipamuda, Sajipanadu,

Phajeer, Kurnad, Ira, Manchi, Golthamajal, Mani, Kadeshwalya, Perne, Kedila, Ananthadi, Veerakamba, Balepuni, Naringana, Kolnadu, Vittalpadanur, Idkidu, Vittal, Vittalmudnoor, Kepu, Alike, Kanyana, Karopady, Peruvai, Punacha.

Amenities:

Education: Primary School in 78 villages, Middle school in 75 villages, Matriculation or Secondary School in 31 villages, namely Sangabettu, Kukkipady, Rayee, Koila, Ajjibettu, Pilimogru, Navoor, Kavalpadur, Pilathabettu, Uli, Maninalkur, Tenkabellur, Ammunje, Kallige, Kurnad, Naringana, Sajipamuda, Manchi, Golthamajal, Balthila, Kadeshwalya, Kolnadu, Mani, Biliyur, Perne, Vittal, Kanyana, Manila, Alike, Kepu, Punacha.

Higher Secondary or Pre University Courses or Intermediate or Junior College in 13 villages of the CD Block,, namely Sangabettu, Chennaithodi, Kavalpadur, Pilathabettu, Maninalkur, Ammunje, Kurnad, Sajipamuda, Perne, Vittal, Kanyana, Alike, Kepu.

College in 3 villages, Adult Literacy Center in 9 villages., Colleges are in villages, namely Chennaithodi, Pilimogru, Vittal.

Medical: Hospital in 4 villages, Dispensary in 31 villages, Health Center in 17 villages, Sub Center in 67 villages, Maternity and Child Welfare Center in 8 villages, Community health workers in 36 villages.

The Villages having Hospital or Dispensary or Health Center are Pilimogru, Kavalpadur, Irvathur, Pilathabettu, Uli, Kariyangala, Tenkabellur, Ammunje, Kallige, Munnuru, Sajipanadu, Chelur, Kurnad, Kairangala, Naringana, Balepuni, Ira, Sajipamuda, Amtoor, Manchi, Balthila, Kolnadu, Bolanthuru, Mani, Biliyur, Perne, Kedila, Vittal, Vittalpadanur, Salethur, Kanyana, Alike, Kepu, Punacha.

Drinking Water: Tap water in 76 villages, Tank water in 57 villages, Well water in 79 villages, Tubewell in 79 villages and more than one source in 79 villages.

Bank: Banking facility in 38 villages, namely, Karpe, Sangabettu, Kukkipady, Amtady, Chennaithodi Navoor, Kavalpadur, Pilathabettu, Sarapady Badagakajekar, Uli, Maninalkur, Kariyangala Badaga Bellur, Kallige, Kurnad, Kairangala Narikombu, Manchi, Golthamajal, Balthila, Barimar Kadeshwalya, Kolnadu, Veerakamba, Mani, Kedila Netlamudnur, Vittal, Salethur, Karopady, Kanyana Manila, Alike, Idkidu, Kula, Kepu, Punacha.

Credit Society in 30 villages Agricultural Credit Society in 27 Non-Agricultural Credit Society in 7 villages.

Others: Power supply in 79 villages, Cinema hall in 1 village, sport club in 7 villages, Stadium or Auditorium or Community Hall in 1 village, Post Office in 74 villages.

There are 76 villages having bus facilities.

Villages with most of facilities: Karpe Sangabettu, Amtady, Chennaithodi, Navoor, Kavalpadur Pilathabettu, Sarapady, Badagakajekar, Uli Maninalkur, Kariyangala, Badaga Bellur, Kallige Kurnad, Kairangala, Narikombu, Manchi, Golthamajal Balthila, Barimar, Kadeshwalya, Kolnadu, Veerakamba Mani, Kedila, Netlamudnur, Vittal, Salethur Karopady, Kanyana, Manila, Alike, Idkidu, Kepu Punacha.

Villages without amenities (Education): Irvathur..

Scheduled Castes: Out of the total population of 306734 persons, 15682 persons (5.11%) belong to Scheduled Castes. The villages having less than 10% SC population are Karpe, Sangabettu, Eliyanadugodu, Kukkipady, Rayee Arala, Kuriyala, Amtady, Panjikal, Koila Chennaithodi, Kudambettu, Budoli, Mudanadugodu Navoor, Kadabettu, Moodapadukodi , Pilathabettu Kavalmudur, Sarapady, Badagakajekar, Tenkakajekar Uli, Maninalkur, Kariyangala, Badaga Bellur Tenkabellur, Ammunje, Meremajalu, Kodman, Kallige Munnuru, Sajipanadu, Sajipapadu, Chelur, Kurnad Phajeer, Kairangala, Naringana, Balepuni, Ira Sajipamuda, Narikombu, Shambhoor, Manchi Golthamajal, Balthila, Barimar, Kolnadu, Bolanthuru Veerakamba, Mani, Peraje, Biliyur, Kedila Netlamudnur, Vittal, Vittalpadanur, Karopady Kanyana, Peruvai, Manila, Alike, Idkidu, Kula Vittalmudnoor, Kepu, Punacha.

The village having more than 50% SC population is None.

Sex ratio of Scheduled Caste population is 502.

Scheduled Castes Literates and Illiterates by Sex:

	Persons	Males	Females
Literate	9,060	5,093	3,967
Illiterate	6,622	2,721	3,901
Literacy rate	65.1	73.0	57.1
Graduate	125	87	38

Scheduled Castes (Dominant):

Moger, Adi Dravida, Baira, Nalakeyava, Holaya etc.

For their cultural identity please see Appendix-I

Villages without Scheduled Castes: There are 2 villages without any scheduled caste population.

Scheduled Tribes: Out of the total population of 306734 persons, 14400 persons (4.69%) belong to Scheduled Tribes. The villages having less than 10% ST population are Sangabettu, Eliyanadugodu, Kukkipady, Rayee, Arala Kuriyala, Amtady, Panjikal, Koila, Chennaithodi

Ajjibettu, Kudambettu, Pilimogru, Budoli Mudanadugodu, Navoor, Kavalpadur, Kadabettu Moodapadukodi , Irvathur, Pilathabettu, Kavalmudur Devasyapadur, Sarapady, Badagakajekar, Tenkakajekar Uli, Kariyangala, Badaga Bellur, Tenkabellur Ammunje, Meremajalu, Kodman, Kallige, Munnuru Sajipanadu, Sajipapadu, Chelur, Kurnad, Phajeer Kairangala, Naringana, Balepuni, Ira, Sajipamuda Amtoor, Narikombu, Shambhoor, Manchi, Golthamajal Balthila, Barimar, Kadeshwalya, Kolnadu, Bolanthuru Veerakamba, Ananthadi, Mani, Biliyur, Perne, Kedila Netlamudnur, Vittal, Vittalpadanur, Salethur Karopady, Kanyana, Peruvai, Manila, Alike, Idkidu Kula.

The villages having more than 50% ST population are None.

Sex ratio of Scheduled tribe population is 498.

Scheduled Tribes Literates and Illiterates by Sex:

	Persons	Males	Females
Literate	9,511	5,269	4,242
Illiterate	4,889	1,963	2,926
Literacy rate	73.4	81.1	65.7
Graduate	283	192	91

Scheduled Tribes (Dominant):

Marati, Naikda etc., Koraga, Malaikudi Generic Tribes etc.

For their cultural identity please see Appendix-II

Villages without Scheduled Tribes: There are 3 villages without any scheduled tribe population.

Literates and Illiterates by Sex (Total Population):

	Persons	Males	Females
Literate	215,987	116,255	99,732
Illiterate	90,747	35,139	55,608
Literacy rate	80	88	73
Graduate	7,017	4,526	2,491

Agriculture: ***Distribution of villages according to land use:*** Out of 79 villages, Total area (in hectare) is 69511, out of that 35.99 percent is cultivable and 56.03 percent of the cultivable area is irrigated.

Sources of Irrigation (Hectares): Government Canal 0, Private Canal 0, Well without Electricity 2263.95, Well with Electricity 5592.4, Tubewell without Electricity 53.6, Tubewell with Electricity 1381.25, Tank 17, River 0, Lake 0, Waterfall 0, Others 4706.55.

Villages with population of 5000 to 9999:

Amtady, Munnuru, Phajeer, Naringana, Ira, Sajipamuda Narikombu, Manchi, Golthamajal, Balthila, Veerakamba Vittalpadanur, Karopady, Kanyana, Alike, Kepu Punacha.

Villages with population of 10000 and above:

Kolnadu, Vittal.

Distribution of Workers:

	Persons	Males	Females	WPR
Cultivators	12,014	8,607	3,407	6.94
Agricultural Labour	11,115	7,826	3,289	6.42
Household Industry	5,262	1,490	3,772	3.04
Other Workers	144,821	73,097	71,724	83.61
Main Workers	155,321	84,174	71,147	89.67
Marginal Workers	17,891	6,846	11,045	10.33
Total Workers	173,212	91,020	82,192	

Religion: Major Religious Communities:

	Persons	Males	Females	Sex Ratio
Hindu (65.4%)	200,617	98,545	102,072	1,036
Muslim (27.78%)	85,223	42,251	42,972	1,017
Christian (6.39%)	19,606	9,932	9,674	974
Sikh (0%)	4	4	-	-
Buddhists (0%)	5	3	2	667
Jain (0.37%)	1,140	578	562	972

Agewise Data:

	Persons	Males	Females	Sex Ratio
All ages	306,734	151,394	155,340	1026
0-14	89,283	45,579	43,704	959
15-44	153,410	74,574	78,836	1057
45-79	60,673	29,706	30,967	1042
80+	2,308	983	1,325	1348
Age not stated	1,060	552	508	920

Languages (Dominant):

Tulu, Others, Malayalam, Konkani, Kannada

Disabled Population:

	Persons	Males	Females	%
Total Disabled	5,599	2,985	2,614	
In Seeing	2,733	1,374	1,359	48.81
In Speech	580	298	282	10.36
In Hearing	245	128	117	4.38
In Movement	1,255	771	484	22.41
Mentally	786	414	372	14.04

BASAVAKALYAN

Basavakalyan C.D. Block lies in the south-western part of Bidar district. It is a part of Basavakalyan taluka. The Block is located at a distance of 84 kms. From district headquarters (Bidar). There are 115 villages in the block with the total population of 240,779 persons. Area of the C.D. Block is 1189.23 sq. kms. It is bounded by taluk Bhalki on north, district Gulbarga on south, taluks Bhalki and Homnabad on east, and it has common boundary with the state of Maharashtra on west.

Communications:

Roadways : N.H-9: Direction- Solapur to Homnabad, Nearest Villages- Narayanapur, Yerandi, Kouiyal, Tadola, Rajeshwar, Handriyal (Kalyan), Nirgudi, Manhalli, Ghotala, Halli, Sastapur, Chandakpur. SH-11: Direction- Mahagaon to

Nilanga, Nearest Villages- Mirkhal, Hulsoor, Gadigondgaon, Belura, Basavakalyan (R), Gour, Betbalkunda, Yerandi, Hatyal, Bagduri, Mudbi, Eklora, Hamunagar, Maisalga.
River: Benithora Nadi- Nearest Villages- Gadlegaon (K), Sirgur, Hattarga (Sarhad), Chitkota (K), Gilagili.
Manjra Nadi- Nearest Villages- Mirkhal, Hulsoor.
Annual Rainfall: Normal Rianfall 830 mm.
Ground Water: Availability of the Ground Water in the Basin is 8079.03 H.A.M. and the utilization is 3856.56 H.A.M. It belongs to Over Exploited category. Depth to water level 2 to 20 meter below the ground. Most of the wells go down in summer months, according to the Ground Water Estimation Committee.
Soils: Black Soils and Lateritic Soils.
Natural Division : It falls partly in the Manjra-Karanja Basin and Homnabad-Kamthana Lateritic Tract of the Northern Karnakata Plateau.
Administration:
Division: Gulbarga. Parliamentary Constituency: 7 Bidar (SC).District: Bidar. Taluka: Basavakalyan. Assembly Constituency: 47 Basavakalyan, 48 Homnabad.
Gram Panchayat: 36.
Regional Area Development Boards: The Hyderabad-Karnataka Area Development Board.
Border Villages: (State: Maharashtra)- Kotmal, Mirkhal, Gutti, Gour, Khandala, Partapur, Talbhog, Morkhandi, Manhalli, Ghotala, Jajanmugli, Ramteerth (K), Honnali, Ekamba, Dhamuri, Ujlam, Gadlegaon (K), Sirgur, . Hattarga (Sarhad)
Fairs: Amruthakunda Jatra: Amruthakunda jatra is held at Chandakapur in Bidar area in the month of March for three days.Chandakapur is about 20 kilometers south-west of Basavakalyan town. According to a legend, Ramachandra, the hero of Ramayana, camped at this place during his exile. There are two ponds called Amrit-Kund and Seeta-Nahani kund, had shrines of Ramalingeshvara, Somal ingeshvara and Revanasiddeshvara. An annual jatra is held for Ramalingeshvara about the month of March.There is also a shrine of Chandikadevi after whose name this place is called.
Basava-Jayanti Fair: It is held at Basavakalyan in Bidar area about April-May for three days. Basavakalyan was until recently known as Kalyani and Kalyan and has been also called Qasba Kalyanabad in some Bahamani records. Situated about 80 kms. south west of Bidar town, it is the headquarters of the taluk of the same name. This place came to prominence towards the close of the tenth century A.D. when the capital of the later Western Chalukyas was shifted here from Malkhed. It extended over a large area and attained great status as the metropolis of an empire, as a centre of wealth and prosperity, as a seat of learning and as an abode of spiritual wisdom haloed by illustrious saints like Basaveshvara, Allama Prabhu, Akka-Mahadevi, Channabasavanna and Siddha-ranma. Vijnaneshvara, the renowned law-giver, and the author of a highly valued treatise on law known as Mitakshara, was at the court of Chalukya Vikramaditya VI. He goes into raptures while describing the splendours of the capital city of Kalyana and exclaims that no other city like Kalyana existed in the past or present and would never exist in future. The great Sanskrit poet Bilhana who wrote Vikramankadeva Charita also adorned the court of Vikramaditya VI and he too has sung the an extensive empire till the end of the twelfth century with a Chalukyas ruled few yearswhen the Kalachuris had seized Western was at this place that there was the upsurge of the revolutionary Sharana (Veerashaiva) movement led by later Allama Prabhu and their associates, which attracted like- terms. The persons from various parts of India. The illustrious Sharanas, who came, from all strata of the society composed glowing Vachanas here and founded the "Anubhava Mantapa" where inimitable minded Basaveshvara. power. It break of a glory of this city in they carried on deliberations. Thisprotestant movement, which aimed at radical religious and socialreforms, gained formidable popular strength. When the traditiona lists and the imperial power headed by Kalachuri Bijjala clashed with it and made voilent attempts to suppress it, there was anupheaval which shook up the imperial authority and brought abouta different chain of social and political events.
Channabasaveshvara Jatra: Harkud in Bidar distirct lies about 35kms. south-west of Basavakalyan town. It has a well-known matha (monastery) of Channabasaveshvara in honour of whom a jatra takes place about the month of January when wrestling matches are also held.
Jagannath Maharaj Fair: An annual fair is held at Rajeshvar near Bidar in honour of Saint Jagannath Maharajin the month of April. Rajeshvar is a place about 20 kms. south-east of Basavakalyan town. It has a temple of Ramalingeshvara and another of Mallinatha, also called Mallikarjuna built recently. Out of the two,that of Ramalingeshvara, which is a stone structure, deserves a special mention. Its floor and roofs are built with large slabs of black stones. There is a marble image of Nandi. The place has the shrine of Saint Jagannath Maharaj in honour of whom an annual fair is held about April.
Madeppa Swami Jatra: Madeppa Swami jatra is held at Narayanapur near Bidar, in about the month of July for two days. Narayanapur is an important ancient place three kms. east of Basavakalyan town. Its name has been mentio

ned as Tribhuvana-tilaka Shri Rama Narayanapura & Raya-Narayanapura in inscriptions. Probably, Rayanarayana was one of the titles of a Chalukyan King. The village has a Shiva temple of the Chalukyan times, constructed with a trikutachala (three-cell). Only its garbhagriha and a pillared mantapa are now remaining and they too are in a dilapidated condition. There are some fine mananike-like figures in different poses. It appears that the presiding deity of this temple was originally Vishnu. The place has ruins of several other shrines also. Relics of many images are lying scattered in the vicinity of the local tank. There are a few small shrines of Amba-Bhavani, Ishavara, Hanuman, Lakshmi & Madeppa Swami. An annual jatra is held here in honour of Madeppa Swami for two days in the month of July. Recently, two exquisite female figures of stone came to light at this place.

Mahadeva Jatra: Mahadeva jatra is held at Goria near Bidar in the month of about March-April for two days. Gorta situated about 18 kms., north-east of Basavakalyan town, has been called Gorante in inscriptions. It was an agrahara village and a centre of learning. There was a Rudreshvara temple near the present Hanuman shrine said to have been constructed by Rudra Mishra, a precept or of Chalukya Vikramaditya VI. There were also Nagares hvara and Malleshwara temples and Jain basadis. The place has an old Mahadeva temple constructed in rock stones. Each of the pillars of this temple is made of a single stone. The temple has a ruined Mantapa called Nrtakiya Mantapa which has a sculpture of Nandi. Under the auspic es of this temple an annual jatra takes place for two days about March-April. There are also shrines of Gorakn ath and Mahalakshmi, the annual fairs of which attract a large gathering of devotees.

Hazarath Syed Tajuddin Bagsawar Urs: It is held at Basav akalyan near Bidar in the month of Shwwal for five days. Basavakalyan was until recently known as Kalyani and Kalyan and has been also called Qusba Kalyanabad in some Bahamani records.

Sadanandaswami Festival: It is held at Sadananda Saraswa ti Matha at Basavakalyan near Bidar in the month of July every year.

Sharana Basaveshvara Fair: It is held at Kinni near Bidar around the month of February for three days. Kinni is about 22 kms. south-east of Basavakalyan town, where a well-known annual fair is held in honour of Sharana Basaveshvara about February.

Veerabhadreshvara Fair: The Veerabhadreshvara fair is held at Partapur near Bidar around the month of March. Partapur about three kms. north-east of Basavakalyan town, is known for ruins of Shiva temples of the Chalukya times. Perhaps, the name of this place is derived from one of the Chalukyan titles, which was Pratapa-Chakravar ti. A handsome Chalukyan image of Surya (the Sun god), which was found here, is now kept at the Goswami Matha in Basavakalyan town. It is carved in a standing posture and its workmanship is admirable. The Veerabhadreshvara shrine here, which is of recent times, holds an annual fair about the month of March.

Zinda Shah Madar Urs: An Urs in honour of Zinda Shah Madar is held at Kohinoor-Pahad near Bidar in the month of Jamadilawwal for four days. Kohinoor previously called Kolur and Kollur, is about 35 kms. south-west of Basava kalyan town. It has a dargah (tomb shrine) of Hazrat Zindashah Madar, which is held in high reverence. An annual Urs is held in honour of the saint for three days.

Villages: 115 **Inhabited:** 112 **Uninhabited:** 3

Ranking	District	State	National
Area	2	63	290
Population	1	46	288
Sex Ratio	1	97	2511
Child Sex Ratio	5	153	4268
Literacy Rate	3	111	3297
Density	1	150	4697
Work Participation Rate	4	77	3598

Gram Panchayats:

Mirkhal, Hulsoor, Gorta (B), Muchalam, Gadigondgaon, Belura, Betbalkunda, Dhanura (K), Kitta, Partapur, Morkhandi, Ghotala, Chendakapur, Matala, Sastapur, Narayanapur, Rajola, Tadola, Rajeshwar, Islampur, Nirgudi, Yerandigi, Gundur, Algood, Ujlam, Ladwanti, Bhosga, Mudbi, Yerbagh, Kherda (B), Harkood, Batgera, Kohinoor, Eklora, Kalkora.

Amenities:

Education: Primary School in 109 villages, Middle school in 108 villages, Matriculation or Secondary School in 27 villages, namely Mirkhal, Hulsoor, Belura, Muchalam, Gorta (B), Partapur, Morkhandi, Narayanapur, Kitta, Yerandi, Rajola, Rajeshwar, Yerbagh, Kherda (B), Ghotala, Sastapur, Mantala, Chandakpur, Algood, Ujlam, Ladwanti, Batgera, Kohinoor, Mudbi, Harkud, Maisalga, Hipparga(Bag).

Higher Secondary or Pre University Courses or Intermediate or Junior College in 4 villages of the CD Block,, namely Hulsoor, Rajeshwar, Mantala, Mudbi.

College in 0 village, Adult Literacy Center in 4 villages.

Medical: Hospital in 3 villages, Dispensary in 11 villages, Health Center in 10 villages, Sub Center in 43 villages, Maternity and Child Welfare Center in 2 villages, Community health workers in 24 villages.

The Villages having Hospital or Dispensary or Health Center are Mirkhal, Hulsoor, Gadigondgaon, Muchalam, Dhanura (K), Kitta, Rajeshwar, Ghotala, Mantala, Mudbi, Harkud.

Drinking Water: Tap water in 58 villages, Tank water in 1 villages, Well water in 112 villages, Tubewell in 73 villages and more than one source in 112 villages.

Bank: Banking facility in 19 villages, namely, Mirkhal, Hulsoor, Belura, Muchalam, Dhanura (K) Partapur, Morkhandi, Kitta, Yerandi, Rajeshwar Sastapur, Mantala, Chandakpur, Algood, Ujlam, Bhosga Ladwanti, Mudbi, Harkud.

Credit Society in 37 villages Agricultural Credit Society in 31 Non-Agricultural Credit Society in 6 villages.

Others: Power supply in 112 villages, Cinema hall in 1 village, sport club in 112 villages, Stadium or Auditorium or Community Hall in 112 villages, Post Office in 60 villages.

There are 94 villages having bus facilities.

Villages with most of facilities: Mirkhal, Hulsoor Belura, Muchalam, Dhanura (K), Partapur, Morkhandi Kitta, Yerandi, Rajeshwar, Sastapur, Mantala Chandakpur, Algood, Ujlam, Bhosga, Ladwanti, Mudbi Harkud.

Villages without amenities (Education): Laheshwar, Bhaknal, Sungahana..

Scheduled Castes: Out of the total population of 241125 persons, 52982 persons (21.97%) belong to Scheduled Castes.

The villages having less than 10% SC population are Quaderabad, Toglur, Laheshwar, Ghoga, Kamlewadi Honnali, Handriyal (Raj), Ujlam, Batgera, Khanapur B Sungahana.

The village having more than 50% SC population is None.

Sex ratio of Scheduled Caste population is 489.

Scheduled Castes Literates and Illiterates by Sex:

	Persons	Males	Females
Literate	22,302	14,273	8,029
Illiterate	30,680	12,812	17,868
Literacy rate	51.0	64.2	37.4
Graduate	849	762	87

Scheduled Castes (Dominant):

Holaya etc., Banjara etc., Madiga, Mahar etc., Bhovi

For their cultural identity please see Appendix-I

Villages without Scheduled Castes: There are 4 villages without any scheduled caste population.

Scheduled Tribes: Out of the total population of 241125 persons, 46767 persons (19.4%) belong to Scheduled Tribes.

The villages having less than 10% ST population are otmal, Mirkhal, Machanal, Hulsoor, Soldabka uaderabad, Gutti, Mustapur, Limbapur, Kadepur Khandala, Betbalkunda, Janapur, Partapur, Rajola Handriyal (Kalyan), Mangrool, Islampur, Yerbagh Umapur, Kamlewadi, Chittakaldev, Honnali Handriyal (Raj), Wadderga, Ekamba, Dhamuri Gadlegaon (K), Sirgur, Chitkota (K), Attur, Saidapur Hatyal, Hamunagar, Harkud, Sarjawalga, Hipparga(Bag).

The villages having more than 50% ST population are None.

Sex ratio of Scheduled tribe population is 489.

Scheduled Tribes Literates and Illiterates by Sex:

	Persons	Males	Females
Literate	17,970	11,765	6,205
Illiterate	28,797	12,117	16,680
Literacy rate	46.9	60.4	32.9
Graduate	356	325	31

Scheduled Tribes (Dominant):

Koli Dhor etc., Gond etc., Naikda etc.

Generic Tribes etc., Iruliga

For their cultural identity please see Appendix-II

Villages without Scheduled Tribes: There are 14 villages without any scheduled tribe population.

Literates and Illiterates by Sex (Total Population):

	Persons	Males	Females
Literate	115,320	72,115	43,205
Illiterate	125,805	50,312	75,493
Literacy rate	57	71	43
Graduate	3,809	3,341	468

Agriculture: ***Distribution of villages according to land use:***
Out of 115 villages, Total area (in hectare) is 118923, out of that 76.09 percent is cultivable and 8.06 percent of the cultivable area is irrigated.

Sources of Irrigation (Hectares): Government Canal 217.49, Private Canal 42.23, Well without Electricity 14.6, Well with Electricity 5626.63, Tubewell without Electricity 98.62, Tubewell with Electricity 841.63, Tank 438.36, River 13.35, Lake 0, Waterfall 0, Others 0.

Villages with population of 5000 to 9999:
Mirkhal, Belura, Narayanapur, Mantala, Ujlam Kohinoor.

Villages with population of 10000 and above:
Hulsoor, Rajeshwar.

Distribution of Workers:

	Persons	Males	Females	WPR
Cultivators	35,191	24,716	10,475	34.29
Agricultural Labour	41,294	17,082	24,212	40.24
Household Industry	2,385	1,465	920	2.32
Other Workers	23,759	18,373	5,386	23.15
Main Workers	75,686	52,748	22,938	73.75
Marginal Workers	26,943	8,888	18,055	26.25
Total Workers	102,629	61,636	40,993	

Religion: Major Religious Communities:

	Persons	Males	Females	Sex Ratio
Hindu (77.7%)	187,358	95,186	92,172	968
Muslim (11.07%)	26,692	13,556	13,136	969
Christian (0.14%)	345	178	167	938
Sikh (0%)	-	-	-	-
Buddhists (9.43%)	22,733	11,520	11,213	973
Jain (0.04%)	96	50	46	920

Agewise Data:

	Persons	Males	Females	Sex Ratio
All ages	241,125	122,427	118,698	970
0-14	93,215	47,896	45,319	946
15-44	98,952	50,512	48,440	959
45-79	45,800	22,507	23,293	1035
80+	2,967	1,399	1,568	1121
Age not stated	191	113	78	690

Languages (Dominant):

Kannada, Marathi, Telugu, Urdu, Hindi

Disabled Population:

	Persons	Males	Females	%
Total Disabled	6,320	3,605	2,715	
In Seeing	2,937	1,462	1,475	46.47
In Speech	480	268	212	7.59
In Hearing	364	194	170	5.76
In Movement	2,062	1,411	651	32.63
Mentally	477	270	207	7.55

BASAVANA BAGEVADI

Basavana Bagevadi C.D. Block lies in the southern part of Bijapur dist.. It is a part of Basavana Bagevadi taluka. The Block is located at a distance of 43 kms. from district headquarters (Bijapur). There are 125 villages in the block with the total population of 274,632 persons. Area of the C.D. Block is 1852.00 sq. kms. It is bounded by taluks Bijapur and Sindgi on north,district Bagalkot on south, taluk Muddebihal on east, and taluk Bijapur on west.

Communications:

Roadways : N.H-13: Direction- Bijapur to Hospet, Nearest Villages- Kudgi, Golasangi, Budni, Hunashyal (P.C.), Beeraladinni, Unnibhavi, Wandal, Benal R.C, Devalapur, Gonal R.C., Nidagundi, Managuli, Muttagi. N.H-218: Direction- Hubli to Bijapur, Nearest Villages- Mulawad, Ronihal, Kubakaddi, Hallada Gennur,Garasangi (K.D.), Kolhar (Old). S.H-41: Direction- Indi to Muddebihal, Nearest Villages- Ingaleshwar, Markabbinahalli, Satihal, Basaveshwar Nagar, Ramnagar, Utnal, Dindawar, Kudari Salawadgi, Karibhanthnal, Hunashyal (P.B.), Huvinahippargi, Byakod, Agasabal, Solawadagi, Jayawadgi. S.H-41B: Direction- Managuli to Huvinahippargi, Nearest Villages- Managuli, Yarnal, Hunashyal (P.B.), Huvinahippargi, Sankanal.

Raliway Station: Villages- Mulawad, Telgi, Bisalakoppa (R.C.), Benal R.C., Almatti, Kudgi.

River: Krishna Nadi- Nearest Villages- Kolhar (Old), Baluti . R.C., Halerolli.R.C., Siddanath R.C., Bisalakoppa (R.C.), Gani R.C., Maradagi (R.C.), Majarekoppa (R.C.), Chimmalgi R.C., Almatti , Marimatti R.C., Araladinni. Don Nadi- Nearest Villages- Mulaw ad, Managuli, Ukkali, Neginal, Mullal, Bommanahalli, Bisanal, Donur, Markabbinahalli, Satihal, Basaveshwar Nagar, Bhairawadgi, Yalwar,Kadakol, Sindgeri (Old), Chabanur, Sasanur.

Annual Rainfall: Normal Rianfall 584 mm.

Ground Water: Availability of the Ground Water in the Basin is 9318.08 H.A.M. and the utilization is 6401.40 HAM It belongs to Over Exploited category. Depth to water level 2 to 20 meter below the ground. Most of the wells go down in summer months, according to the Ground Water Estimation Committee.

Soils: Black Soils, Mixed Soils.

Natural Division : It falls partly in the Bijapur-Basavana Bagevadi Upland and the Upper Krishna Valley of the Northern Karnataka Plateau.

Administration:

Division: Belgaum. Parliamentary Constituency: 24 Bijapur. District: Bijapur. Taluka: Basavana Bagevadi. Assembly Constituency: 27 Devar Hippargi, 28 Basalvana Bagavadi. Gram Panchayat: 38.

Regional Area Development Boards: The Bailu Seeme Area Development Board.

Villages: 125 **Inhabited:** 121 **Uninhabited:** 4

Ranking	District	State	National
Area	4	8	65
Population	4	26	131
Sex Ratio	2	124	3061
Child Sex Ratio	3	150	4219
Literacy Rate	1	129	3906
Density	1	134	5582
Work Participation Rate	1	131	3176

Gram Panchayats:

Mulwad, Talewad, Kudgi, Masuti, Malghan, Ronihal, Kolhar (Old), Hanamapur, Telgi, Golasangi, Arasangi, Chimmalgi R.C, Beeraladinni, Wandal, Almatti , Nidagundi, Managuli, Ukkali, Donur, Ingaleshwar, Masabinal, Yarnal, Muttagi, Mannur, Hebbal, Markabbinahalli, Satihal, Dindawar, Yalwar, Sasanur, Wadawadagi, Kudari Salawadgi, Hunashyal (P.B.), Huvinahippargi, Byakod, Narasalgi, Kanakal, Itagi.

Amenities:

Education: Primary School in 112 villages, Middle school in 98 villages, Matriculation or Secondary School in 36 villages, namely Mulawad, Kudgi, Masuti, Malghan, Ronihal, Kolhar (Old), Hanamapur, Tadalgi, Telgi, Golasangi,

Hunashyal (P.C.), Wandal, Nidagundi, Managuli, Ukkali, Bisanal, Donur, Ingaleshwar, Masabinal, Yarnal, Muttagi, Hebbal, Markabbinahalli, Satihal, Bhairawadgi, Yalwar, Somnal, Sasanur, Wadawadagi, Kudari Salawadgi, Hunashyal (P.B.), Huvinahippargi, Narasalgi, Jayawadgi, Kanakal, Itagi.

Higher Secondary or Pre University Courses or Intermediate or Junior College in 14 villages of the CD Block,, namely Kudgi, Kolhar (Old), Telgi, Golasangi, Nidagundi, Managuli, Bisanal, Ingaleshwar, Masabinal, Muttagi, Wadawadagi, Huvinahippargi, Jayawadgi, Kanakal.

College in 1 village, Adult Literacy Center in 6 villages., College is in village, namely Nidagundi.

Medical: Hospital in 0 village, Dispensary in 10 villages, Health Center in 11 villages, Sub Center in 51 villages, Maternity and Child Welfare Center in 8 villages, Community health workers in 14 villages.

The Villages having Hospital or Dispensary or Health Center are Kolhar (Old), Telgi, Managuli, Ukkali, Hebbal, Markabbinahalli, Wadawadagi, Kudari Salawadgi, Huvinahippargi, Itagi.

Drinking Water: Tap water in 63 villages, Tank water in 48 villages, Well water in 101 villages, Tubewell in 64 villages and more than one source in 115 villages.

Bank: Banking facility in 9 villages, namely, Kolhar (Old), Telgi, Nidagundi, Managuli, Ukkali Muttagi, Wadawadagi, Huvinahippargi, Itagi.

Credit Society in 35 villages Agricultural Credit Society in 33 Non-Agricultural Credit Society in 1 village.

Others: Power supply in 120 villages, Cinema hall in 2 villages, sport club in 121 villages, Stadium or Auditorium or Community Hall in 121 villages, Post Office in 65 villages.

There are 99 villages having bus facilities.

Villages with most of facilities: Kolhar (Old) Telgi, Nidagundi, Managuli, Ukkali, Muttagi Wadawadagi, Huvinahippargi, Itagi.

Villages without amenities (Education): Shankarnagar, Garasangi (B.K.), Marimatti R.C, Krishnapur, Basaveshwar Nagar, Sevalalnagar, Basaveshwar Nagar, Ramnagar, Nagaraldon..

Scheduled Castes: Out of the total population of 274730 persons, 51652 persons (18.8%) belong to Scheduled Castes.

The villages having less than 10% SC population are Kolhar (Old), Asangi (B.K.), Siddanath R.C Bhaganagar, Cheeraldinni, Arasangi, Beeraladinni Yambatnal, Nandihal P.U., Mukartihal, Ivanagi Satihal, Bhairawadgi, Nagaraldon, Sasanur Hunashyal (P.B.), Huvinahippargi, Rajanal.

The villages having more than 50% SC population are Shankarnagar, Maradagi (R.C), Marimatti R.C Krishnapur, Basaveshwar Nagar, Sevalalnagar Basaveshwar Nagar, Ramnagar, Ambalanur.

Sex ratio of Scheduled Caste population is 494.

Scheduled Castes Literates and Illiterates by Sex:

	Persons	Males	Females
Literate	17,193	11,925	5,268
Illiterate	34,459	14,219	20,240
Literacy rate	40.8	55.9	25.3
Graduate	599	534	65

Scheduled Castes (Dominant):

Banjara etc., Bhambi etc., Holaya etc., Bhovi Holar etc.

For their cultural identity please see Appendix-I

Villages without Scheduled Castes: There are 5 villages without any scheduled caste population.

Scheduled Tribes: Out of the total population of 274730 persons, 5625 persons (2.05%) belong to Scheduled Tribes.

The villages having less than 10% ST population are Mulawad, Kalgurki, Talewad, Kudgi, Shankarnagar Masuti, Malghan, Ronihal, Kubakaddi, Hallada Gennur Garasangi (K.D.), Kolhar (Old), Garasangi (B.K.) Asangi (B.K.), Asangi (K.D.), Kurubaradinni Nagaradinni, Mattihal, Baluti . R.C, Halerolli.R.C. Hanamapur, Siddanath R.C, Bhaganagar, Tadalgi Cheeraldinni, Telgi, Golasangi, Budni, Sulakhod Arasangi, Gani R.C, Maradagi (R.C) Majarekoppa (R.C), Akalwadi, Seekalwadi, Gudadinni Hunashyal (P.C.), Beeraladinni, Unnibhavi, Wandal Benal R.C, Marimatti R.C, Araladinni , Gonal R.C. Nidagundi, Managuli, Ukkali, Yambatnal, Neginal Mullal, Bommanahalli, Bisanal, Donur, Ingaleshwar Krishnapur, Masabinal, Deginal, Basaveshwar Nagar Hattarkihal, Nandihal P.U., Yarnal, Muttagi Takkalki, Nagawad, Mannur, Hangargi, Abbihal, Hebbal Sevalalnagar, Uppaladinni, Nagur, Ivanagi, Hanchinal Markabbinahalli, Rabinal, Basaveshwar Nagar Ramnagar, Utnal, Dindawar, Bhairawadgi, Yalwar Kamankeri, Budihal, Kadakol, Nandihal (P.H.) Sindgeri (Old), Somnal, Chabanur, Sasanur Wadawadagi, Nagaralhuli, Hulabenchi Kudari Salawadgi, Karibhanthnal, Hunashyal (P.B.) Huvinahippargi, Byakod, Agasabal, Sankanal Narasalgi, Solawadagi, Jayawadgi, Kannal, Kanakal Ambalanur, Halihal, Kodaganur, Byalyal, Bidanal Itagi, Jeeralabhavi.

The villages having more than 50% ST population are None.

Sex ratio of Scheduled tribe population is 479.

Scheduled Tribes Literates and Illiterates by Sex:

	Persons	Males	Females
Literate	2,142	1,493	649
Illiterate	3,483	1,440	2,043
Literacy rate	45.5	60.2	29.2
Graduate	62	52	10

Scheduled Tribes (Dominant):
Naikda etc., Pardhi etc., Chenchu etc., Dubla etc. Bhil etc.
For their cultural identity please see Appendix-II
Villages without Scheduled Tribes: There are 68 villages without any scheduled tribe population.
Literates and Illiterates by Sex (Total Population):

	Persons	Males	Females
Literate	124,060	79,854	44,206
Illiterate	150,670	60,353	90,317
Literacy rate	54	68	39
Graduate	5,311	4,561	750

Agriculture: ***Distribution of villages according to land use:*** Out of 125 villages, Total area (in hectare) is 185200, out of that 91.89 percent is cultivable and 6.84 percent of the cultivable area is irrigated.
Sources of Irrigation (Hectares): Government Canal 650.94, Private Canal 127.48, Well without Electricity 224.72, Well with Electricity 6144.96, Tubewell without Electricity 23.93, Tubewell with Electricity 2284.93, Tank 835.7, River 1342.35, Lake 0.52, Waterfall 0, Others 0.
Villages with population of 5000 to 9999:
Mulawad, Kudgi, Golasangi, Ukkali, Ingaleshwar Masabinal, Muttagi, Kudari Salawadgi, Huvinahippargi.
Villages with population of 10000 and above:
Kolhar (Old), Araladinni , Nidagundi, Managuli.
Distribution of Workers:

	Persons	Males	Females	WPR
Cultivators	38,356	29,522	8,834	31.28
Agricultural Labour	57,254	22,696	34,558	46.69
Household Industry	4,662	3,124	1,538	3.8
Other Workers	22,349	17,534	4,815	18.23
Main Workers	92,060	63,979	28,081	75.08
Marginal Workers	30,561	8,897	21,664	24.92
Total Workers	122,621	72,876	49,745	

Religion: Major Religious Communities:

	Persons	Males	Females	Sex Ratio
Hindu (87.06%)	239,178	122,060	117,118	960
Muslim (12.37%)	33,974	17,331	16,643	960
Christian (0.05%)	148	78	70	897
Sikh (0.01%)	15	12	3	250
Buddhists (0.04%)	118	63	55	873
Jain (0.07%)	192	93	99	1,065

Agewise Data:

	Persons	Males	Females	Sex Ratio
All ages	274,730	140,207	134,523	959
0-14	102,115	52,909	49,206	930
15-44	118,237	60,899	57,338	942
45-79	51,479	25,176	26,303	1045
80+	2,566	1,044	1,522	1458
Age not stated	333	179	154	860

Languages (Dominant):
Kannada, Urdu, Hindi, Marathi, Telugu
Disabled Population:

	Persons	Males	Females	%
Total Disabled	5,295	3,066	2,229	
In Seeing	2,485	1,431	1,054	46.93
In Speech	442	235	207	8.35
In Hearing	235	124	111	4.44
In Movement	1,658	1,023	635	31.31
Mentally	475	253	222	8.97

BELGAUM

Belgaum C.D. Block lies in the south western part of Belgaum district. It is a part of Belgaum taluka. The Block is located at a distance of 00 kms. from district headquarters (Belgaum). There are 120 villages in the block with the total population of 308,878 persons. Area of the C.D. Block is 868.25 sq. kms. It is boundedby taluk Hukeri on north, taluk Khanapur on south, taluks Sampgaon and Gokak on east, and it has common boundary with the state of Maharashtra on west.

Communications:
Roadways : N.H-4: Direction- Poona to Bangalore, Nearest Villages- Sutagatti, Ningenhatti, Bhutaramanahatti, Ramdurg, Halabhavi, Heggere, Bambarge, Honaga, Tarihal, Halaga, Bastawad, Shaganamatti, Kondaskoppa, Kamakarahatti, Kolikopp,Bagewadi. N.H-4A: Direction- Belgaum to Khanapur, Nearest Villages- Waghawade, Desur, Zad-Shahapur. S.H-20: Direction-Chandgad to Bagalkot, Nearest Villages- Sulge (Uchagaon), Kallehol, Uchagaon, Turamari, Bachi, Kudremani, Karadiguddi, Marihal, Sulebhavi, Modge, Balekundri (B.K), Honnihal, Balekundri (K.H), Sambra, Mutga, Nilaji. S.H-31: Direction- Khanapur to Bail Hongal, Nearest Villages- Bagewadi, Bhendigeri, Gajapati, Badas (K.H).
Railway Station: Villages- Desur, Sulge (Yellur), Khanagaon (B.K).
River: Ghatprabha Nadi- Nearest Villages- Parsenahatti, Sutagatti, Maranhol. Mogitra Nadi- Nearest Villages- Santibastawad, Ranakunde, Waghawade, Desur, Zad-Shahapur. Markandeya Nadi- Nearest Villages- Heggere, Kadoli, Alatage, Goundawad, Honaga, Sonatti, Nandi, Kenchanatti, Gutti, Harankol, Rangadholi, Mannur, Ambewadi, Kallehol, Uchagaon, Sonoli, Belgundi, Yalebail, Rakaskop, Belvatti, Badas (Inam), Baknur.
Reserved Forest: Nearest Villages- Nandi, Kenchanatti,

Gutti,Panagutti, Harankol, Rangadholi, Hudali, Otamadu (Kabalapur),Kabalapur (Bharmyanatti), Kalakhamb, Muchandi, Aste, Chandgad,Kiniye, Karle, Navage, Santibastawad, Bahadarwadi, Ranakunde,Khanagaon (K.H.), Khanagaon (B.K), Chandur, Tumarguddi.

Annual Rainfall: Normal Rianfall 1284.3 mm.

Ground Water: Availability of the Ground Water in the Basin is 9620 H.A.M. and the utilization is 6495 H.A. M. It belongs to Safecategory. Depth to water level 2 to 5 meter below the ground. Most of the wells go down in summer months, accordingto the Ground Water Estimation Committee.

Soil: Red Soil, Black Soil.

Natural Division : It falls partly in the Gokak-Saundatti Hills andthe Malaprabha Basin of the Northern Karnataka Plateau.

Administration:

Division: Belgaum. Parliamentary Constituency: 1 Chikodi, 2 Belgaon. District: Belgaum. Taluka: Belgaum. Assembly Constituency: 10 Yemkanmardi (ST), Belgaum Rural. Gram Panchayat: 54.

Regional Area Development Boards: The Maland Aera Development Board.

Border Villages: (State: Maharashtra)- Parsenahatti, Ningenhatti, Kurihal (K.H), Kattanabhavi, Bodakyanhatti, Handiganur, Mahalenahatti, Bekkinakeri, Attiwad, Maranhol, Kallehol, Uchagaon, Bachi, Kudremani, Sonoli, Belgundi, Yalebail, Rakaskop, Dhamne S.Bailur, Belvatti, Badas (Inam), Baknur.

Fairs: Belli Basavanna Jatra: It is held at Hirebagewadi in about the month of March-April every year. Hirebagewadi 19 kms. From Belgaum has temples dedicated to Prabhedevaru, Veerabhadra (old), Belli Basavana and Gramadevata. The Prabhudevaragudi is described as built in memory of Allama Prabhu's visit to the place.

Lakshmi Temple Jatra: It is held at Sulebhavi near Belgaum in the month of Phalguna (December) for nine days. Sulebhavi 16 kilometres from Belgaum is a railway station. The place name is attributed to a prostitute with the same name. The place has temples dedicated to Lakshmidevi, Kalmeshwara, Maruti, Basavanna, Banashankari and Ganapati (1707). The Lakshmi temple a tiled structure has fine wood work and the wooden pillars and doors frames are nailed with hundreds of coins offered to thedeity. The jatra in this temple is held once in five years in the month of Phalguna for nine days in which about 20,000 people assemble.The Kalmeshwara temple in later Vijayanagara style has a garbhagriha and a navaranga. Beside the temple is a Veerashaiva matha having a gadduge of a saint (name lost) who is described as hailing from Varanasi.

Revanasiddheshwara Jatra: It is also held at Sulebhavi during the month of March-April. The jatra in this temple is held once in five year.

Sharif Sayed Mohamed Gouse Quadri Urs: It is held at Hirebagewadi. about 19 kms. from Belgaum. The place has two mosques and a dargah ascribed to Sharif Sayed Mohamed Ghose Khadri (hailed from Arkad), and the Urs is held after fifteen days of the Belli Basavanna jatra when about 50,000 people assemble. The pir is described as a disciple of Hazrath Shah Khadri. The followers of the Pir are drawn from different parts of the country (mostly Hindus) from places like Konkan, Maharashtra, etc.

Villages: 120 **Inhabited:** 119 **Uninhabited:** 1

Ranking	District	State	National
Area	10	108	597
Population	6	12	58
Sex Ratio	6	100	2562
Child Sex Ratio	7	159	4468
Literacy Rate	2	65	2078
Density	8	129	3050
Work Participation Rate	2	12	3076

Gram Panchayats:

Bambarge, Halabhavi, Honaga, Kadoli, Kedanur, Handiganur, Agasage, Bekkinakeri, Uchagaon, Ambewadi, Kangrali (K.H.), Kangrali (B.K.), Kakati , Rangadholi, Hudali, Tumarguddi, Marihal, Sulebhavi, Balekundri (B.K), Balekundri (K.H), Aste, Muchandi, Nilaji, Mutga, Sambra, Mastamardi, Halaga, Bastawad, Dhamane S.Belgaum, Yellur, Machche, Peeranwadi, Mandoli, Benakanahalli, Hindalgi, Sulge (Uchagaon), Turamari, Kudremani, Belgundi, Bijagarni, Belvatti, Kiniye, Santibastawad, Desur, Sulge (Yellur), Nandihalli, Kanvi Karvinakoppa, Tarihal, Aralikatti, Bagewadi, Mutnal, Bhendigeri, Ankalagi (Badalankalagi), Badas (K.H).

Amenities:

Education: Primary School in 119 villages, Middle school in 103 villages, Matriculation or Secondary School in 50 villages, namely Halabhavi, Bambarge, Handiganur, Kedanur, Mannikeri, Agasage, Kadoli, Alatage, Honaga, Hudali, Muchandi, Bekkinakeri, Gojage, Mannur, Ambewadi, Sulge (Uchagaon), Kallehol, Uchagaon, Turamari, Kudremani, Belgundi, Bijagarni, Rakaskop, Belvatti, Kiniye, Karle, Santibastawad, Ranakunde, Waghawade, Desur, Sulge (Yellur), Nandihalli, Zad-Shahapur, Yellur, Marihal, Sulebhavi, Modge, Balekundri (K.H), Sambra, Mutga, Nilaji, Basarikatti, Halaga, Bastawad, Aralikatti, Bagewadi, Kanvi Karvinakoppa, Ankalagi (Badalankalagi), Gajapati, Mutnal.

Higher Secondary or Pre University Courses or Intermediate or Junior College in 3 villages of the CD Block,, namely Hudali, Sambra, Bagewadi.
College in 0 village, Adult Literacy Center in 5 villages.
Medical: Hospital in 0 village, Dispensary in 1 village, Health Center in 11 villages, Sub Center in 46 villages, Maternity and Child Welfare Center in 1 village, Community health workers in 19 villages.
The Village having Hospital or Dispensary or Health Center is Baknur.
Drinking Water: Tap water in 72 villages, Tank water in 6 villages, Well water in 86 villages, Tubewell in 9 villages and more than one source in 107 villages.
Bank: Banking facility in 13 villages, namely, Bhutaramanahatti, Kadoli, Hudali, Uchagaon, Yellur Marihal, Sulebhavi, Balekundri (B.K), Sambra Basarikatti, Halaga, Bagewadi, Kanvi Karvinakoppa.
Credit Society in 44 villages Agricultural Credit Society in 28 Non-Agricultural Credit Society in 2 villages.
Others: Power supply in 119 villages, Cinema hall in 2 villages, sport club in 1 village, Stadium or Auditorium or Community Hall in 1 village, Post Office in 62 villages.
There are 113 villages having bus facilities.
Villages with most of facilities: Bhutaramanahatti Kadoli, Hudali, Uchagaon, Yellur, Marihal, Sulebhavi Balekundri (B.K), Sambra, Basarikatti, Halaga Bagewadi, Kanvi Karvinakoppa.
Villages without Amenities (Education): None..
Scheduled Castes: Out of the total population of 309101 persons, 17264 persons (5.59%) belong to Scheduled Castes.
The villages having less than 10% SC population are Sutagatti, Ningenhatti, Godihal, Bhutaramanahatti Ramdurg, Halabhavi, Heggere, Bambarge, Kurihal (K.H) Kattanabhavi, Bodakyanhatti, Handiganur Mahalenahatti, Chalvenahatti, Kedanur, Mannikeri Kadoli, Alatage, Honaga, Nandi, Kenchanatti Panagutti, Gutti, Harankol, Rangadholi, Hudali Otamadu (Kabalapur), Kabalapur (Bharmyanatti) Kalakhamb, Muchandi, Aste, Bekkinakeri, Attiwad Maranhol, Mannur, Ambewadi, Sulge (Uchagaon) Kallehol, Uchagaon, Kudremani, Sonoli, Belgundi Bokanur, Savagaon, Mandoli, Rakaskop Dhamne S.Bailur, Belvatti, Badas (Inam), Baknur Kiniye, Karle, Navage, Santibastawad, Bahadarwadi Ranakunde, Waghawade, Desur, Sulge (Yellur) Rajahansagad, Nandihalli, Nagenahatti, Yellur Dhamane S.Belgaum, Yaramale, Khanagaon (K.H.) Khanagaon (B.K), Chandur, Tumarguddi, Karadiguddi Marihal, Sulebhavi, Yaddalabhavi-Hatti, Modge Balekundri (B.K), Honnihal, Sambra, Mutga, Nilaji Shindoli, Basarikatti, Chandanhosur, Tarihal Mastamardi, Halaga, Bastawad, K0Ndaskoppa Kamakarahatti, Kolikopp, Hulikatti, Bassapur Aralikatti, Bagewadi, Sutgatti (Ah) Kanvi Karvinakoppa, Ankalagi (Badalankalagi) Bhendigeri, Badas (K.H), Kukadoli, Mutnal.
The village having more than 50% SC population is None.
Sex ratio of Scheduled Caste population is 498.
Scheduled Castes Literates and Illiterates by Sex:

	Persons	Males	Females
Literate	8,592	5,388	3,204
Illiterate	8,672	3,278	5,394
Literacy rate	59.0	74.1	43.9
Graduate	287	241	46

Scheduled Castes (Dominant):
Mahar etc., Holaya etc., Madiga, Bhambi etc. Banjara etc.
For their cultural identity please see Appendix-I
Villages without Scheduled Castes: There are 14 villages without any scheduled caste population.
Scheduled Tribes: Out of the total population of 309101 persons, 35857 persons (11.6%) belong to Scheduled Tribes.
The villages having less than 10% ST population are Kurihal (B.K), Handiganur, Chalvenahatti, Kedanur Mannikeri, Agasage, Kadoli, Alatage, Sonatti Chandgad, Bekkinakeri, Attiwad, Maranhol, Mannur Ambewadi, Sulge (Uchagaon), Kallehol, Uchagaon Turamari, Bachi, Sonoli, Belgundi, Bokanur, Savagaon Mandoli, Bijagarni, Yalebail, Rakaskop Dhamne S.Bailur, Belvatti, Badas (Inam), Kiniye Karle, Kuttalawadi, Ranakunde, Desur, Sulge (Yellur) Rajahansagad, Nandihalli, Nagenahatti, Zad-Shahapur Yellur, Dhamane S.Belgaum, Khanagaon (K.H.) Karadiguddi, Sulebhavi, Modge, Balekundri (B.K) Honnihal, Balekundri (K.H), Sambra, Mutga, Nilaji Shindoli, Basarikatti, Mavinakatti, Halaga, Bastawad Shaganamatti, K0Ndaskoppa, Kamakarahatti, Bassapur Aralikatti, Bagewadi, Sutgatti (Ah) Ankalagi (Badalankalagi), Hulikavi, Bhendigeri Gajapati, Kukadoli, Virapankoppa, Mutnal.
The villages having more than 50% ST population are Ramdurg, Halabhavi, Heggere, Mahalenahatti, Nandi Kenchanatti, Panagutti, Gutti, Rangadholi Otamadu (Kabalapur), Kabalapur (Bharmyanatti) Chandur, Tumarguddi, Yaddalabhavi-Hatti.
Sex ratio of Scheduled tribe population is 501.
Scheduled Tribes Literates and Illiterates by Sex:

	Persons	Males	Females
Literate	10,934	7,198	3,736

Illiterate	24,923	10,707	14,216
Literacy rate	37.4	49.7	25.3
Graduate	90	78	12

Scheduled Tribes (Dominant):
Naikda etc., Koli Dhor etc., Meda, Kadu Kuruba Bhil etc.
For their cultural identity please see Appendix-II
Villages without Scheduled Tribes: There are 23 villages without any scheduled tribe population.
Literates and Illiterates by Sex (Total Population):

	Persons	Males	Females
Literate	169,028	101,165	67,863
Illiterate	140,073	55,805	84,268
Literacy rate	64	76	52
Graduate	4,991	3,975	1,016

Agriculture: ***Distribution of villages according to land use:*** Out of 120 villages, Total area (in hectare) is 86825, out of that 65.7 percent is cultivable and 13.9 percent of the cultivable area is irrigated.
Sources of Irrigation (Hectares): Government Canal 128.28, Private Canal 18.51, Well without Electricity 193.71, Well with Electricity 3873.34, Tubewell without Electricity 103.19, Tubewell with Electricity 3500.63, Tank 35.29, River 37.19, Lake 20.23, Waterfall 0, Others 20.63.
Villages with population of 5000 to 9999:
Halabhavi, Kadoli, Honaga, Hudali, Muchandi Uchagaon, Dhamane S.Belgaum, Marihal, Sulebhavi Balekundri (K.H), Halaga, Bastawad Kanvi Karvinakoppa.
Villages with population of 10000 and above:
Yellur, Sambra, Bagewadi.
Distribution of Workers:

	Persons	Males	Females	WPR
Cultivators	60,650	36,674	23,976	42.95
Agricultural Labour	30,859	9,816	21,043	21.85
Household Industry	5,181	3,569	1,612	3.67
Other Workers	44,511	40,058	4,453	31.52
Main Workers	119,714	85,166	34,548	84.78
Marginal Workers	21,487	4,951	16,536	15.22
Total Workers	141,201	90,117	51,084	

Religion: Major Religious Communities:

	Persons	Males	Females	Sex Ratio
Hindu (91.12%)	281,660	142,860	138,800	972
Muslim (5.72%)	17,671	9,068	8,603	949
Christian (0.4%)	1,250	656	594	905
Sikh (0.01%)	45	28	17	607
Buddhists (0.04%)	114	57	57	1,000
Jain (2.39%)	7,384	3,812	3,572	937

Agewise Data:

	Persons	Males	Females	Sex Ratio
All ages	309,101	156,970	152,131	969
0-14	104,127	53,420	50,707	949
15-44	143,392	73,537	69,855	950
45-79	58,681	28,801	29,880	1037
80+	2,690	1,098	1,592	1450
Age not stated	211	114	97	851

Languages (Dominant):
Kannada, Marathi, Urdu, Hindi, Telugu
Disabled Population:

	Persons	Males	Females	%
Total Disabled	3,667	2,093	1,574	
In Seeing	1,093	571	522	29.81
In Speech	389	199	190	10.61
In Hearing	157	72	85	4.28
In Movement	1,564	1,018	546	42.65
Mentally	464	233	231	12.65

BELLARY

Bellary C.D. Block lies in the eastern part of Bellary district. It is a part of Bellary taluka. The Block is located at a distance of 00 kms. from district headquarters (Bellary). There are 103 villages in the block with the total population of 308,429 persons. Area of the C.D. Block is 1609.67 sq. kms. It is bounded by taluk Siruguppa on north, taluks Sandur and Hospet on west. It has common boundary with the state of Andhra Pradesh on south and east.
Communications:
Roadways : N.H-63: Direction- Hospet to Gooty, Nearest Villages- Kudathini, Veniveerapura, Chaganur, Kolagallu, Bevinahalli, Bisalahalli, Kakkabevinahalli, Amarapura, Godehal, Tegginabudihal, Meenahalli, Joladarasi, Paramadevanahalli. S.H-19: Direction- Challakere to Siruguppa, Nearest Villages- Singadevanahalli, Byluru, Sindegeri, Dammur, Kolur, Somasamudra, Sidaragadda, Bellary [R], Honnahalli, Halakundi. S.H-29: Direction- Kampli to Kudathini, Nearest Villages- Thimmalapura, Kudathini. S.H-42: Direction- Joladarsi to Anantapur, Nearest Villages- Joladarasi, Chellagurki.
Railway Station: Villages- Kudathini, Karekal Veerapura, Kolagallu, Meenahalli, Sidiginamola, Paramadevanahalli.
River: Hagari Nadi- Nearest Villages- Hirehadagali, Basarakodu, Karichedu, Moka, Gotur, Kallukutiganahalu, Banapura, Vannenur, Sindhavalam, Bennikallu, Yerragudi, Dasara Nagenahalli, Tambrahalli, Byradevanahalli, Chaganur, Gollanaganahalli, Byalachinte, Asundi, Godehal, Tegginabudihal, Meenahalli, Sidiginamola, Paramadevanahalli, Yalpi Kaggalu, Lingadevanahalli, Yalpi, Kuntanahal, Tolamamidi, Kammarchedu, Chandur, Rupanagudi, Rayapura.
Canal: Nearest Villages- Nelludi, Kotal Camp, Emmiganur, Havinahal Veerapura, Genikihal, Mustagatta, Chitiginahalu, Karikeri, Somalapura, Orvai, Guttiganur, Pattanasaragu,

Kurugodu, Siddammanahalli, Yelubemchi, Thimmalapura, Kudathini, Veniveerapura, Sindegeri, Dammur Kaggal, Chanahal, Hirehadagali, Karichedu, Handihal, Gudadur, Dammur, Korlagundi, Kolur, Somasamudra, Sidaragadda, Moka, Gotur, Kallukutiganahalu, Masudipura, Banapura, Vannenur, Sindhavalam, Mokagonahal, Bommanahal, Jalihal,Tambrahalli, Byradevanahalli, Gollanaganahalli, Byal achinte, Kolagallu, Patrabudhihal, Aladahalli, Sanjeevarayan akote, Bobbukunta, Burranayakanahalli, Yettinabudihal.

Reserved Forest: Nearest Villages- Thimmalapura, Kuda thini. (Moka R.F.): Nearest Villages- Bennikallu, Yerragudi, Dasara Nagenahalli. (Bellary R.F.): Nearest Villages- Belagal, Honnahalli, Halakundi. (Moncheri R.F.): Nearest Villages- Halakundi, Mincheri, Sanjeevarayanakote, Burra nayakanahalli, Yettinabudihal.

Annual Rainfall: Normal Rianfall 642.2 mm.

Ground Water: Availability of the Ground Water in the Basin is (Information not avablable) H.A.M. and the utilization is (Information not avablable) H.A.M.
It belongs to (Information not avablable) category.
Depth to water level 5 to 20 meter below the ground.
Most of the wells go down in summer months, according to the Ground Water Estimation Committee.

Soils: Black and Red Sandy Soils.

Natural Division : It falls partly in Middle Tungabhadra Valley, Lower Vedavati (Hagari) Valley and Sandur Highla nds of the Central Karnataka Plateau.

Administration:

Division: Gulbarga. Parliamentary Constituency: 9 Bellary (ST). District: Bellary. Taluka: Bellary. Assembly Constituency: 91 Kampli (ST), 93 Bellary (ST). Gram Panchayat: 40.

Regional Area Development Boards: The Hyderabad - Karnataka Area Development Board.

Border Villages: (State: Andhra Pradesh)- Hirehadagali, Basarakodu, Sindhavalam, Mokagonahal, Bommanahal, Jali hal, Tambrahalli, Karekal, Karekal Veerapura, Halakundi, Sidiginamola, Joladarasi, Chellagurki, Yalpi, Kuntanahal, Yettinabudihal, Chandur, Rupanagudi, Rayapura.

Villages: 103 **Inhabited:** 99 **Uninhabited:** 4

Ranking	District	State	National
Area	1	23	104
Population	1	13	59
Sex Ratio	5	80	2245
Child Sex Ratio	3	53	2305
Literacy Rate	6	165	5224
Density	4	38	4852
Work Participation Rate	1	82	1178

Gram Panchayats:

Nelludi, Emmiganur, Havinahal Veerapura, Genikihal, Sindegeri, Dammur, Handihal, Basarakodu, Vannenur, Yerragudi, Mokagonahal, Karekal, Sidiginamola, Chellagurki, Rupanagudi, Paramadevanahalli, Byradevanahalli, Moka, Korlagundi, Kappagallu, Sirivaram, Sanganakal , Amarapura, Shankarabanda, Yettinabudihal, Sanjeevarayanakote, Sidaragadda, Kolur, Somasamudra, Kolagallu , Halakundi , Belagal, Yarringaligi, Badanahatti, Kurugodu, Kallukamba, Siddammanahalli, Kudathini, Yelubenchi, Orvai.

Amenities:

Education: Primary School in 77 villages, Middle school in 70 villages, Matriculation or Secondary School in 20 villages, namely Nelludi, Kotal Camp, Emmiganur, Havinahal Veerapura, Kallukamba, Kurugodu, Kudathini, Dammur, Korlagundi, Sidaragadda, Moka, Banapura, Sanganakal, Kolagallu, Bellary[R], Halakundi, Sidiginamola, Joladarasi, Chellagurki, Rupanagudi.
Higher Secondary or Pre University Courses or Intermediate or Junior College in 4 villages of the CD Block,, namely Kurugodu, Kudathini, Moka, Bellary[R].
College in 2 villages, Adult Literacy Center in 1 village., Colleges are in villages, namely Byalachinte, Bellary[R].

Medical: Hospital in 10 villages, Dispensary in 30 villages, Health Center in 13 villages, Sub Center in 49 villages, Maternity and Child Welfare Center in 4 villages, Community health workers in 23 villages.
The Villages having Hospital or Dispensary or Health Center are Emmiganur, Havinahal Veerapura, Orvai, Kurugodu, Siddammanahalli, Kudathini, Vaddahatti, Chanahal, Dammur, Kolur, Yarringaligi, Somasamudra, Moka, Vannenur, Sindhavalam, Bennikallu, Mokagonahal, Yerragudi, Sanganakal, Chaganur, Karekal, Halakundi, Mincheri, Sanjeevarayanakote, Kakkabevinahalli, Sidiginamola, Joladarasi, Paramadevanahalli, Chellagurki, Yettinabudihal.

Drinking Water: Tap water in 82 villages, Tank water in 8 villages, Well water in 28 villages, Tubewell in 17 villages and more than one source in 91 villages.

Bank: Banking facility in 26 villages, namely, Nelludi, Kotal Camp, Emmiganur, Genikihal Kallukamba, Kurugodu, Kudathini, Dammur Kaggal Dammur, Korlagundi, Kolur, Yarringaligi, Somasamudra Sidaragadda, Moka, Mokagonahal, Sirivaram Sanganakal, Chaganur, Kolagallu, Tegginabudihal Joladarasi, Chellagurki, Shankarabanda, Ibrampura Yettinabudihal.
Credit Society in 21 villages Agricultural Credit Society in 20 Non-Agricultural Credit Society in 0 village.

Others: Power supply in 99 villages, Cinema hall in 7 villages,

sport club in 99 villages, Stadium or Auditorium or Community Hall in 99 villages, Post Office in 64 villages.
There are 95 villages having bus facilities.

Villages with most of facilities: Nelludi Kotal Camp, Emmiganur, Genikihal, Kallukamba Kurugodu, Kudathini, Dammur, Korlagundi, Kolur Yarringaligi, Sidaragadda, Moka, Mokagonahal Sanganakal, Chaganur, Kolagallu, Joladarasi Chellagurki, Shankarabanda, Ibrampura Yettinabudihal.

Villages without amenities (Education): Kyadigehal, Mustagatta, Chitiginahalu, Karikeri, Lakshmipura, Singadevanahalli, Dammur Kaggal, Handihal, Somasamudra, Vannenur, Byradevanahalli, Gollanaganahalli, Honnahalli, Asundi, Tegginabudihal, Meenahalli, Lingadevanahalli, Tolamamidi, Burranayakanahalli, Chandur, Rayapura..

Scheduled Castes: Out of the total population of 308728 persons, 57289 persons (18.56%) belong to Scheduled Castes.
The villages having less than 10% SC population are Mustagatta, Chitiginahalu, Karikeri, Somalapura Dammur Kaggal, Basarakodu, Handihal, Dammur Masudipura, Sindhavalam, Gollanaganahalli Bisalahalli, Andralu, Godehal, Shankarabanda Burranayakanahalli, Chandur, Rupanagudi.
The village having more than 50% SC population is None.
Sex ratio of Scheduled Caste population is 498.

Scheduled Castes Literates and Illiterates by Sex:

	Persons	Males	Females
Literate	14,467	10,333	4,134
Illiterate	42,822	18,413	24,409
Literacy rate	31.4	44.7	18.0
Graduate	207	184	23

Scheduled Castes (Dominant):
Adi Karnataka, Madiga, Bhovi, Chalavadi etc.
Banjara etc.

For their cultural identity please see Appendix-I

Villages without Scheduled Castes: There are 6 villages without any scheduled caste population.

Scheduled Tribes: Out of the total population of 308728 persons, 73802 persons (23.91%) belong to Scheduled Tribes.
The villages having less than 10% ST population are Kotal Camp, Emmiganur, Havinahal Veerapura Kyadigehal, Chitiginahalu, Guttiganur, Pattanasaragu Kallukamba, Lakshmipura, Thimmalapura Singadevanahalli, Gudadur, Masudipura, Mokagonahal Dasara Nagenahalli, Sanganakal, Janikunte, Andralu Mincheri, Kakkabevinahalli, Amarapura Tegginabudihal, Bobbukunta.
The villages having more than 50% ST population are Mustagatta, Karikeri, Somalapura, Hirehadagali Basarakodu, Yerragudi, Tambrahalli, Byalachinte Meenahalli, Paramadevanahalli, Kuntanahal Burranayakanahalli.
Sex ratio of Scheduled tribe population is 495.

Scheduled Tribes Literates and Illiterates by Sex:

	Persons	Males	Females
Literate	17,915	12,943	4,972
Illiterate	55,887	24,347	31,540
Literacy rate	29.7	42.5	16.6
Graduate	192	176	16

Scheduled Tribes (Dominant):
Naikda etc., Generic Tribes etc., Gond etc.
Bhil etc., Gowdalu

For their cultural identity please see Appendix-II

Villages without Scheduled Tribes: There are 7 villages without any scheduled tribe population.

Literates and Illiterates by Sex (Total Population):

	Persons	Males	Females
Literate	115,770	76,300	39,470
Illiterate	192,958	80,009	112,949
Literacy rate	45	59	31
Graduate	2,602	2,243	359

Agriculture: ***Distribution of villages according to land use:***
Out of 103 villages, Total area (in hectare) is 160967, out of that 83.97 percent is cultivable and 50.31 percent of the cultivable area is irrigated.

Sources of Irrigation (Hectares): Government Canal 62388.87, Private Canal 550.06, Well without Electricity 29.81, Well with Electricity 2238.43, Tubewell without Electricity 0, Tubewell with Electricity 1423.33, Tank 0.38, River 593.58, Lake 22.26, Waterfall 0, Others 754.64.

Villages with population of 5000 to 9999:
Genikihal, Badanahatti, Siddammanahalli, Korlagundi Kolur, Somasamudra, Sidaragadda, Kappagallu, Moka Sirivaram, Sanganakal.

Villages with population of 10000 and above:
Emmiganur, Kurugodu, Kudathini, Kolagallu.

Distribution of Workers:

	Persons	Males	Females	WPR
Cultivators	61,585	40,207	21,378	38.56
Agricultural Labour	77,298	33,621	43,677	48.39
Household Industry	2,031	1,192	839	1.27
Other Workers	18,817	14,345	4,472	11.78
Main Workers	139,989	83,283	56,706	87.64
Marginal Workers	19,742	6,082	13,660	12.36
Total Workers	159,731	89,365	70,366	

Religion: Major Religious Communities:

	Persons	Males	Females	Sex Ratio

Hindu (92.51%)	285,603	144,516	141,087	976
Muslim (7.06%)	21,785	11,113	10,672	960
Christian (0.16%)	479	240	239	996
Sikh (0%)	9	5	4	800
Buddhists (0%)	2	1	1	1,000
Jain (0.01%)	36	17	19	1,118

Agewise Data:

	Persons	Males	Females	Sex Ratio
All ages	308,728	156,309	152,419	975
0-14	119,504	61,013	58,491	959
15-44	138,523	70,594	67,929	962
45-79	48,659	23,832	24,827	1042
80+	1,819	739	1,080	1461
Age not stated	223	131	92	702

Languages (Dominant):

Kannada, Telugu, Urdu, Hindi, Marathi

Disabled Population:

	Persons	Males	Females	%
Total Disabled	5,021	2,839	2,182	
In Seeing	2,286	1,235	1,051	45.53
In Speech	496	289	207	9.88
In Hearing	195	102	93	3.88
In Movement	1,603	967	636	31.93
Mentally	441	246	195	8.78

BELTANGADI

Beltangadi C.D. Block lies in the north-eastern part of Dakshina Kannada district. It is a part of Beltangadi taluka. The Block is located at a distance of 57 kms. from district headquarters (Mangalore). There are 80 villages in the block with the total population of 239, 141 persons. Area of the C.D. Block is 1366.72 sq. kms. It is bounded by district Udupi and Chikmagalur on north, taluks Bantval and Puttur on south, districts Hassan and Chikmagalur on east, taluks Mangalore and Bantval on west.

Communications:

Roadways : NH-48: Direction- Mangalore to Hassan, Nearest Village- Rekhya. SH- 37: Direction- Karkal to Shirady, Nearest Villages- Naravi, Kuthluru, Sulkeri, Kokradi, Kudyadi, Navara, Badagakaranduru, Pilya, Tenkakaranduru, Padangady, Kuvettu, Ujire, Kalamanja, Belalu, Dharmast hala, Patrame, Kokkada. SH- 64: Direction- Bantaval to Chikmagalur, Nearest Villages- Charmadi, Kanyady, Maladi, Sonandur, Kuvettu, Ujire, Kalamanja, Mundaje, Neriya, Kukkala, Parenky, Chibidre. SH- 66 A: Direction- Mudbid ri to Kuvettu, Nearest Villages- Hosangadi, Venooru, Karimanelu, Moodukodi, Nittade, Kukkedi, Padangady, Gardadi, Kuvettu.

River: Shishila Nadi- Nearest Villages- Shishila, Nidle, Patrame, Kokkada, Hathyadka, Rekhya, Shibaje. Netravati Nadi- Nearest Villages- Charmadi, Kalamanja, Mundaje, Thekkaru, Barya, Ilanthila, Mogru, Bandaru, Belalu, Dharmasthala, Chibidre, Patrame. Aniyur Hole Nadi- Nearest Villages- Nearest Village- Neriya. Neriya Hole Nadi- Nearest Villages- Neriya, Dharmasthala, Chibidre, Puduvettu, Kalanja, Nidle, Patrame. Gunderi Hole Nadi- Nearest Villages- Gunduri, Bajire, Kukkedi, Gardadi. Aladangadi Hole Nadi- Nearest Villages- Hosangadi, Arambodi, Gunduri, Venooru, Karimanelu, Moodukodi, Andinje, Nittade. Kela Hole Nadi- Nearest Villages- Marodi, Nravi, Kashipatna, Badakodi, Hosangadi, Arambodi. Gundia Hole Nadi- Nearest Village- Rekhya.

Reserved Forest: (Charmadi Kanapadi R.F.): Nearest Villages- Mithabagilu, Malavanthige, Charmadi, Kadirudyavara, Mundaje, Chibidre. (Dharmastala Mundaje R.F.): Nearest Villages- Dharmasthala, Chibidre, Kalanja, Nidle. (Dadan thamale R.F.): Nearest Villages- Bandaru, Belalu, Dharmas thala. (Nidhi R.F.): Nearest Villages- Nidle, Patrame, Kokkada, Hathyadka. (Kodemale R.F.): Nearest Villages- Marodi, Naravi. (Naravi R.F.): Nearest Villages- Naravi, Kuthluru, Sulkeri, Kokradi, Navara, Sulkerimogru, Shirl alu, Savanalu, Navooru, Mithabagilu, Malavanthige, Indabe ttu, Nada, Laila. (Miyar R.F.): Nearest Villages- Shishila, Kalanja. (Shiradi Shishilla R.F.): Nearest Villages- Shishila, Kalanja, Rekhya, Shibaje. (Nanjimalai R.F.): Nearest Villages- Andinje, Kudyadi, Pilya, Nittade, Nalkuru, Gardadi.

Annual Rainfall: Normal Rianfall 3593.17 mm.

Ground Water: Availability of the Ground Water in the Basin is (Information not avablable) H.A.M. and the utilization is (Information not avablable) H.A.M. It belongs to (Information not avablable) category. Depth to water level 5 to 20 meter below the ground. Most of the wells go down in summer months, according to the Ground Water Estimation Committee.

Natural Division : It falls partly in Western Ghats (Daks hina Kannada) and Beltangadi Dissected zone of the Karnat aka Coast (Western Coastal Region).

Administration:

Division: Mysore. Parliamentary Constituency: 17 Dakshina Kannada. District: Dakshina Kannada. Taluka: Beltangadi. Assembly Const.: 200 Baltangadi. Gram Panchayat: 43.

Regional Area Development Boards: The Maland Aera Development Board.

Fairs: Ananta Vrata: Bailangadi district is situated at a distance of 22 kms. from Belthangady. It was once the seat of a family of local chiefs called Moolas. They had authority over twelve magancs around this place. There is an old ruined palace about three kilometers from this place. In a field opposite to this building are fifteen tombs said to be those of the Moola chiefs.

Two other tombs made of fine black stone stand a little apart. They are said to be those of Somala Devi, a Moola princess, and a Banga Chief whom she married. According to a tragic story told about her, there was a bitter fight between herself and her husband on account of such a minor cause as to the place assigned to her in the course of a religious function called 'Ananta Vrata'. This is stated to have led to a fierce battle between the two in which the Banga Raja was killed. But though the queen won the battle, she repented for the tragic event and committed suicide. Under the Moolas, the place had a considerable population and was noted for the manufacture of bell-metal vessels. There is a basadi to the north-west of the place and it appears from an inscription, on one of its pillars, that it was renovated in 1611 A.D.

Laksha Deepotsava Festival: It is held at the temple of Manjunatha at Dharmasthala in the month of November-De cember every year. Dharmasthala, a famous place of pilgri mage about 75 kilometres from Mangalore and about 16 kilometres from Belthangady, is on the Mangalore-Charmadi Road..

Nadavali Festival: It is held at the temple of Manjumatha at Dharmasthala district once in twelve years, for thirteen days. Dharmasthala, a famous place of pilgrimage about 75 kms. from Mangalore and about 16 kms. from Belthangady, is on the Mangalore-Charmadi road. About three kilometres from Dharmasthala flows the Netravati river in which the pilgrims have a bath. The place is surrounded by a picturesque fringe of hill, rice fields and areca and coconut gardens.

Villages: 80 **Inhabited:** 80 **Uninhabited:** 0

Ranking	District	State	National
Area	1	43	195
Population	3	51	301
Sex Ratio	2	7	444
Child Sex Ratio	4	119	3508
Literacy Rate	5	13	473
Density	4	65	5144
Work Participation Rate	4	97	1648

Gram Panchayats:

Naravi, Aladangady, Marodi, Kashipatna, Hosangadi, Arambodi, Venooru, Andinje, Kukkedi, Maladi, Madanthyaru, Barya, Thannirpantha, Machina, Kuvettu, Padangady, Balenja, Shirlalu, Melanthabettu, Laila, Kaliya, Kaniyooru, Ilanthila, Bandaru, Belalu, Koyyur, Ujire, Nada, Indabettu, Mithabagilu, Malavanthige, Charmadi, Mundaje, Kalamanja (Nidgale), Dharmasthala, Patrame, Kokkada, Nidle, Puduvettu, Neriya, Shishila, Hathyadka (Arasinamakki), Shibaje.

Amenities:

Education: Primary School in 80 villages, Middle school in 77 villages, Matriculation or Secondary School in 31 villages, namely Naravi, Kokradi, Hosangadi, Venooru, Badagakaranduru, Malavanthige, Charmadi, Indabettu, Nada, Laila, Padangady, Kuvettu, Koyyur, Ujire, Mundaje, Thotathadi, Neriya, Kukkala, Parenky, Kaliya, Kaniyooru, Puthila, Karaya, Mogru, Bandaru, Belalu, Dharmasthala, Kalanja, Nidle, Kokkada, Hathyadka.

Higher Secondary or Pre University Courses or Intermediate or Junior College in 5 villages of the CD Block,, namely Maladi, Ujire, Kukkala, Parenky, Kaniyooru.

College in 1 village, Adult Literacy Center in 18 villages., College is in village, namely Ujire.

Medical: Hospital in 2 villages, Dispensary in 17 villages, Health Center in 13 villages, Sub Center in 54 villages, Maternity and Child Welfare Center in 7 villages, Community health workers in 13 villages.

The Villages having Hospital or Dispensary or Health Center are Arambodi, Venooru, Andinje, Shirlalu, Badagakaranduru, Charmadi, Nada, Laila, Padangady, Maladi, Sonandur, Koyyur, Ujire, Mundaje, Neriya, Kaliya, Kaniyooru, Thannirpantha, Dharmasthala, Chibidre.

Drinking Water: Tap water in 73 villages, Tank water in 16 villages, Well water in 80 villages, Tubewell in 65 villages and more than one source in 80 villages.

Bank: Banking facility in 28 villages, namely, Marodi, Naravi, Venooru, Andinje, Shirlalu Badagakaranduru, Kukkedi, Indabettu, Kanyady, Nada Laila, Maladi, Kuvettu, Ujire, Mundaje, Kukkala Parenky, Machina, Kaliya, Kaniyooru, Belalu Dharmasthala, Chibidre, Shishila, Nidle, Kokkada Hathyadka, Rekhya.

Credit Society in 21 villages Agricultural Credit Society in 19 Non-Agricultural Credit Society in 5 villages.

Others: Power supply in 80 villages, Cinema hall in 0 village, sport club in 1 village, Stadium or Auditorium or Community Hall in 0 village, Post Office in 70 villages.

There are 76 villages having bus facilities.

Villages with most of facilities: Marodi, Naravi Venooru, Andinje, Shirlalu, Badagakaranduru Indabettu, Kanyady, Nada, Laila, Maladi, Kuvettu Ujire, Mundaje, Kukkala, Parenky, Machina, Kaliya Kaniyooru, Belalu, Dharmasthala, Chibidre, Shishila Kokkada, Hathyadka, Rekhya.

Villages without Amenities (Education): None..

Scheduled Castes: Out of the total population of 239189 persons, 21386 persons (8.94%) belong to Scheduled Castes.

The villages having less than 10% SC population are Kuthluru, Gunduri, Karimanelu, Moodukodi, Kudyadi Sulkerimogru, Bajire, Kukkedi, Nalkuru, Balenja Thenkakaranduru, Navooru, Mithabagilu, Malavanthige Charmadi, Kadirudyavara, Kanyady, Nada, Munduru Maladi, Kuvettu, Odilnala, Ujire, Kalamanja, Mundaje Thotathadi, Neriya, Parenky, Machina, Kaliya Nyayatarpu, Thannirpantha, Puthila, Thekkaru, Barya Karaya, Ilanthila, Urvalu, Mogru, Chibidre Puduvettu, Kalanja, Rekhya.

The village having more than 50% SC population is None.

Sex ratio of Scheduled Caste population is 505.

Scheduled Castes Literates and Illiterates by Sex:

	Persons	Males	Females
Literate	10,957	6,185	4,772
Illiterate	10,429	4,391	6,038
Literacy rate	58.9	67.4	50.7
Graduate	121	86	35

Scheduled Castes (Dominant):

Holaya etc., Moger, Nalakeyava, Generic Castes etc. Samagara

For their cultural identity please see Appendix-I

Villages without Scheduled Castes: There are 0 village without any scheduled caste population.

Scheduled Tribes: Out of the total population of 239189 persons, 12478 persons (5.22%) belong to Scheduled Tribes.

The villages having less than 10% ST population are Marodi, Naravi, Sulkeri, Kokradi, Savya, Peradi Kashipatna, Hosangadi, Arambodi, Gunduri, Venooru Moodukodi, Andinje, Kudyadi, Sulkerimogru, Shirlalu Karambaru, Badagakaranduru, Pilya, Nittade, Bajire Kukkedi, Nalkuru, Balenja, Thenkakaranduru, Navooru Mithabagilu, Charmadi, Indabettu, Kanyady, Nada Laila, Munduru, Melanthabettu, Padangady, Gardadi Maladi, Sonandur, Kuvettu, Odilnala, Koyyur, Ujire Kalamanja, Thotathadi, Kukkala, Parenky, Machina Kaliya, Nyayatarpu, Kaniyooru, Thannirpantha Puthila, Thekkaru, Barya, Karaya, Ilanthila, Urvalu Mogru, Bandaru, Belalu, Dharmasthala, Chibidre Puduvettu, Kalanja, Patrame, Kokkada, Hathyadka Rekhya, Shibaje.

The villages having more than 50% ST population are None.

Sex ratio of Scheduled tribe population is 502.

Scheduled Tribes Literates and Illiterates by Sex:

	Persons	Males	Females
Literate	7,644	4,197	3,447
Illiterate	4,834	2,019	2,815
Literacy rate	69.3	76.9	61.8
Graduate	138	99	39

Scheduled Tribes (Dominant):

Malaikudi, Marati, Naikda etc., Kudiya etc., Koraga

For their cultural identity please see Appendix-II

Villages without Scheduled Tribes: There are 3 villages without any scheduled tribe population.

Literates and Illiterates by Sex (Total Population):

	Persons	Males	Females
Literate	161,165	86,311	74,854
Illiterate	78,024	31,330	46,694
Literacy rate	77	85	70
Graduate	5,228	3,299	1,929

Agriculture: ***Distribution of villages according to land use:***

Out of 80 villages, Total area (in hectare) is 136672, out of that 25.8 percent is cultivable and 54.8 percent of the cultivable area is irrigated.

Sources of Irrigation (Hectares): Government Canal 384.46, Private Canal 239.68, Well without Electricity 3821.47, Well wi Electricity 3904.22, Tubewell without Electricity 147.44, Tubewell with Electricity 1856.1, Tank 539.74, River 2409.64, Lake 0, Waterfall 380.16, Others 5637.93.

Villages with population of 5000 to 9999:

Laila, Kuvettu, Neriya, Ilanthila, Dharmasthala.

Villages with population of 10000 and above:

Ujire.

Distribution of Workers:

	Persons	Males	Females	WPR
Cultivators	13,774	10,379	3,395	11.05
Agricultural Labour	11,898	8,424	3,474	9.55
Household Industry	41,185	2,525	38,660	33.04
Other Workers	57,794	47,357	10,437	46.36
Main Workers	107,815	62,874	44,941	86.49
Marginal Workers	16,836	5,811	11,025	13.51
Total Workers	124,651	68,685	55,966	

Religion: Major Religious Communities:

	Persons	Males	Females	Sex Ratio
Hindu (72.79%)	174,111	85,246	88,865	1,042
Muslim (17.86%)	42,725	20,958	21,767	1,039
Christian (7.54%)	18,043	9,270	8,773	946
Sikh (0%)	6	3	3	1,000
Buddhists (0.02%)	59	28	31	1,107
Jain (1.71%)	4,086	2,055	2,031	988

Agewise Data:

	Persons	Males	Females	Sex Ratio
All ages	239,189	117,641	121,548	1033
0-14	71,356	36,415	34,941	960
15-44	119,847	57,265	62,582	1093
45-79	45,820	22,968	22,852	995
80+	1,977	899	1,078	1199
Age not stated	189	94	95	1011

Languages (Dominant):
Tulu, Others, Malayalam, Kannada, Konkani

Disabled Population:

	Persons	Males	Females	%
Total Disabled	4,253	2,400	1,853	
In Seeing	1,810	961	849	42.56
In Speech	406	224	182	9.55
In Hearing	237	129	108	5.57
In Movement	1,065	655	410	25.04
Mentally	735	431	304	17.28

BELUR

Belur C.D. Block lies in the north-western part of Hassan district. It is a part of Belur taluka. The Block is located at a distance of 37 kms. from district headquart ers (Hassan). There are 383 villages in the block with the total population of 162,855 persons. Area of the C.D. Block is 840.51 sq. kms. It is bounded by taluk Arsikere and district Chikmagalur on north, taluks Sakle shpur and Alur on south, taluks Arsikere, Hassan and Alur on east, and district Chikmagalur on west.

Communications:

Roadways : SH- 21: Direction- Halebeedu to Hassan, Nearest Villages- Halebeedu, Siddapura, Hulikere, Rajagere, Girikallahalli, Komaranahalli, Thattehalli, Shivapura Kaval, Mayagodanahalli, Illenahalli, Adagooru, Kumarihal li. SH- 57: Direction- Chikmagalur to Hassan, Nearest Villages- Karagada, Yakkasettihalli, Channapura, Shettig ere, Kanaikanahalli, Danikanahalli, Chikkabyadigere, Rayapura, Nettekere, Mudigere, Mallikarjunapura, Ramenah alli, Ibbedu, Ballenahalli, Chilkur, Ramachandrapura, Shivayogipura, Madihalli, Hagare, Hagaremudibetta, Kaval, Angadihalli, Basavapura, Mulenahalli, Suledevarah alli. SH- 58: Direction- Mudigere to Banawar, Nearest Villages- Cheekanahalli, Hunuganahalli, Hirigadde, Kuppa godu, Kogodu, Hanjihalli, Naganhalli, Mathihalli, Bellotte, Tholalu, Navilahalli, Alur, Konerlu, Ballur, Nidagodu, Gotravalli, Bantenahalli, Rayapura, Lakshmipura, Mudige re, Sompura, M. Hunsekere, Hebbalu, Kallahalli Kaval, Kallahalli Kaval (A.M.), Kallahalli, Cheelanaikanahalli, Jodi, Thippanahalli, Mayagowdanahalli, Huvenahalli, Halebeedu, Kallibore Kaval, Chatchatnahalli.

River: Hemavati Nadi- Nearest Villages- Thumbadevanahal li, Hosahalli, Goravanahalli, Narvey, Sulagalale. Yagachi Nadi- Nearest Villages- Malur, Keethur, Sanenahalli, Madvapura, Muthugadalu, Madapura, Marur, Somanahalli, Chunchanahalli, Dabbe, Madagodu, H. Hosahalli, Singapura, Devalapura, Iravalli, Agasaravalli, I. Hunsekere, Govinahalli, Mundaghatta, Bommadihalli, Sugalur, Surapura, Shanuboganahalli, Kudlur, Kanaikanahalli, Danikanahalli, Chikkabyadigere, Attalgere, Rayapura, Bitravalli, Mallapura, Prasadihalli, Ranaghatta, Nettekere, Surapura, Hadlagere, Hosahalli, Harohalli, Pura, Chomanahalli, Thattegere, Konaikanahalli Jodi, Hiruguppe, Hanike, Thendegere, Bommenahalli, Chandanahalli, Mallarahosahal li, Jinnenahalli, Paduvalalu, Jinigenahalli, Doddihalli.

Canal: Nearest Villages- Keethur, Sanenahalli, Madvapura, Muthugadalu, Maravathi, Madapura, Marur, Somanahalli, Chunchanahalli, Chikkamedur, H. Hosahalli, Singapura, Devalapura, Iravalli, Agasaravalli, I. Hunsekere, Govin ahalli, Mundaghatta, Kabbinamane, Bommadihalli, Surapura, Shanuboganahalli, Yamasandi, Kudlur, Kanaikanahalli, Danikanahalli, Chikkabyadigere, Attalgere, Rayapura, Nettekere, Surapura, Hosahalli, Harohalli, Chomanahalli, Konaikanahalli Jodi, Gorur, Hiruguppe, Hanike, Thendege re, Bommenahalli, Chikkamedur.

Annual Rainfall: Normal Rianfall 882.7 mm.

Ground Water: Availability of the Ground Water in the Basin is 47.17 H.A.M. and the utilization is 34.96 H. A.M. It belongs to Safe category. Depth to water level 5 to 20 meter below the ground. Most of the wells go down in summer months, according to the Ground Water Estimation Committee.

Soils: Red Soil, Red Sandy Soil, Mixed Soil and Silty Clay Soil.

Natural Division : It falls in Cauvery-Hemavati Basin of the Southern Karnataka Plateau.

Administration:

Division: Mysore. Parliamentary Constituency: 16 Hassan. District: Hassan. Taluka: Belur. Assembly Constituency: 195 Belur. Gram Panchayat: 383.

Regional Area Development Boards: The Maland Aera Development Board.

Fairs: Channakeshavaswamy Car Festival: The car festival of Sri Channakeshavaswamy is held at Belur near Hassan in about the month of March-April for a period of 12 days. Belur is situated on the bank of Yagachi river, about 38. 6 kms. north-west of Banavara. It is at the junction of Hassan-Chikmagalur and Banavara-Mudigere roads. Belur, which has marvellous temples, is a famous tourist centre and is also a place of pilgrimage. It is an ancient city which had various names such as Velap uri, Velur and Belahur and was also called Dakshina Varan asi. The main temples of Channakeshava and Kappe Channig araya were erected during the reign of the great Hoysala king Vishnuvardhana in the twelfth century A.D. The Channakeshava temple, which was caused to be constructed by Vishnuvardhana to commemorate his victories, is surrounded by other temples, namely, those of Kappe, Channigaraya, Somanayaki, Andal and others and various mantapas. The image of Channakeshava or Vijayanarayana is about 12 feet in height from the ground to the top of the torana. On the jambs of the eastern door of the main temple are sculptured the images of Manniatha and Rathi, which are rare figures in temples of this type.

Pushpagiri Mallikarjunaswamy Car Festival: It is held at Siddapura near Hassan for one day about October. Siddapura in the Halebid hobli of Belur taluk, is about a km. from Halebid and about 16 kms. from Belur town. There is a temple of Mallikarjunaswamy at this place, popularly known as Pushpagiri Sri Mallikarjunaswamy temple. This is a major temple. The car festival is held during the month of kartika every year. A large number of devotees gather here on the occasion.

Villages: 383 **Inhabited:** 355 **Uninhabited:** 28

Ranking	District	State	National
Area	5	114	642
Population	5	117	1457
Sex Ratio	4	19	914
Child Sex Ratio	6	75	2767
Literacy Rate	5	62	1992
Density	6	69	4803
Work Participation Rate	6	81	1693

Gram Panchayats:

Narayanapur, Hanike, Rajanasiriyur, Chatchatnahalli, Kodihalli, Gangur, Ghattadahalli, Gonisomenahalli, Halebeedu, Hebbalu, Bantenahalli , Yamasandi , Kalleri, Dabbe, Chikkamedur, Sanyasihalli, Ibbedu, Yalahanka, Savasihalli, Adagooru, Hagare, Andale, Kogilamane, Kushavara, Tholalu, Hunuganahalli, Cheekanahalli, Malasavara, Anughatta, Bikkodu, Madaghatta, Hulugundi, Kesagodu, Lakkunda, Arehalli , Thumbadevanahalli, Narvepete.

Amenities:

Education: Primary School in 265 villages, Middle school in 122 villages, Matriculation or Secondary School in 22 villages, namely Cheekanahalli, Sanenahalli, Narvey, Bellotte, Tholalu, Arehalli, Gendehalli, Bennur, Hanumidi, Hebbalu, Rajanasiriyur, Halebeedu, Kodihalli, Rajagere, Ghattadahalli, Appihalli, Sanenahalli, Hosahalli, Ibbedu, Hagare, Adagooru, Bikkodu.

Higher Secondary or Pre University Courses or Intermediate or Junior College in 3 villages of the CD Block,, namely Arehalli, Halebeedu, Hagare.

College in 1 village, Adult Literacy Center in 39 villages., College is in village, namely Halebeedu.

Medical: Hospital in 0 village, Dispensary in 17 villages, Health Center in 7 villages, Sub Center in 44 villages, Maternity and Child Welfare Center in 1 village, Community health workers in 34 villages.

The Villages having Hospital or Dispensary or Health Center are Cheekanahalli, Narvey, Vatehalli, Balaguli, Echala Halli, Arehalli, I. Hunsekere, Karagada, Appagodanahalli, Chatchatnahalli, Mathighatta, Appihalli, Chatnahalli, Sanenahalli, Bikkodu, Kesagodu, Rajanahalli.

Drinking Water: Tap water in 159 villages, Tank water in 294 villages, Well water in 248 villages, Tubewell in 156 villages and more than one source in 345 villages.

Bank: Banking facility in 15 villages, namely, Cheekanahalli, Dabbe, Tholalu, Arehalli, Kalleri Bennur, Hebbalu, Halebeedu, Harubihalli Ghattadahalli, Ballenahalli, Hagare, Adagooru Bikkodu, Ankihalli.

Credit Society in 12 villages Agricultural Credit Society in 11 Non-Agricultural Credit Society in 1 village.

Others: Power supply in 354 villages, Cinema hall in 0 village, sport club in 0 village, Stadium or Auditorium or Community Hall in 0 village, Post Office in 50 villages.

There are 168 villages having bus facilities.

Villages with most of facilities: Cheekanahalli Tholalu, Arehalli, Bennur, Hebbalu, Halebeedu Harubihalli, Ghattadahalli, Ballenahalli, Hagare Adagooru, Bikkodu, Ankihalli.

Villages without amenities (Education):
Kumbarahalli, Chunganahalli, Madvapura, Marur, Malalakeshavi, Devarakeshavi, Hirigadde, Kanahalli, Umbalagodu, Baladakallu, Hosahalli, Narvepete, Heggadde, Balaguli, Madenahalli, Gurgihalli, Hanjihalli, Menasinamane, Navilahalli, Sullakki, Boovanahalli, Shettihalli, Dolanamane, Kittavara, Adagunchanahalli, Malahalli, Heggadihalli, Hulukodu, Muddanahalli, Bilagavalli, Chataki, Angajanahalli, Bindenahalli, Balaguppe, Kallahalli, Mundaghatta, Melanahalli, N. Hosahalli, Gollenahalli, Honnenahalli Kaval, Lakshmipura, Hakkihalli, Kallahalli, Chikkanahalli, Maranahalli, Minuganahalli, Idahalla Kaval, Laxmipura, Ammanagudi Kaval, Thendekere Jodi, Konaikanahalli Jodi, Keshavapura, Mallapura, Shivapura Kaval, Devarahalli, Illenahalli, Dasagodanahalli, Kumarihalli, Mallavalli, Chandapura, Karadagodu, Chokanahalli, Challenahalli, Baliganahalli, Ginnanamane, Honnemane, Arekaravalli, Moovala, Kalanamata, Bandahalli, Kodaganahalli, Gummanahalli, Heddaravalli, Shingaravalli, Mahala, Hosahalli, Pura, Chatnahalli, Neelanahalli, Bolenahalli, Lakkenahalli, Kodihalli, Bilaguli, Andur, Krishnapura, Jinigenahalli, Madavalli..

Scheduled Castes: Out of the total population of 163527 persons, 47969 persons (29.33%) belong to Scheduled Castes. The villages having less than 10% SC population are

Banasavalli, Madvapura, Chunchanahalli
Malalakeshavi, Devarakeshavi, Kogodu, Bakkaravalli
Kanahalli, Narvepete, Hosamane, Balaguli
Madenahalli, Gurgihalli, Mathihalli, Haralakatte
Navilahalli, Boovanahalli, Shettihalli, Echala Halli
Dolanamane, Adagunchanahalli, Malahalli, Hulukodu
Bilagavalli, Surukodu, Chataki, Kumbarahalli
Mandalamane, Nidagodu (A.C.), Angajanahalli
Bindenahalli, Biranagodu, Chinnenahalli
N. Hosahalli, Channapura, Machanaikanahalli
Utpatanahalli, Lakshmipura, Channapura, Kachihalli
Prasadihalli, Hakkihalli, Kallahalli, Shivaladahalli
Veeradevanahalli, Jodi Thippanahalli, Karikattehalli
Mayagowdanahalli, Kyathalapura, Yalahanka, Siddapura
Kodihalli, Chatchatnahalli, Gonisomenahalli
Girikallahalli, Jogihalli, Suranaikanahalli
Hirihalli, Maranahalli, Kondli, Kabbigarahalli
Minuganahalli, Appihalli, Kanakenahalli
Idahalla Kaval, Laxmipura, Ammanagudi Kaval
Ballenahalli, Chilkur, Thattegere
Konaikanahalli Jodi, Ramachandrapura, Thendegere
Bommenahalli, Keshavapura, Panditanahalli
Holabagere, Adavibantenahalli, Devarahalli
Illenahalli, Dasagodanahalli, Umadevihalli
Kumarihalli, Mallavalli, Kiragadalu, Chandapura
Karadagodu, Honnemane, Venktipete, Kalanamata
Somanahalli, Bandahalli, Mahala, Pura, Bolenahalli
Lakkenahalli, Intitholalu, Bilaguli, Jinigenahalli.

The villages having more than 50% SC population are Kanadur, Chunganahalli, Madapura, Umbalagodu Goravanahalli, Sulagalale, Heggadde, Bommenahalli Menasinamane, Tholalu, Alur, Konerlu, Mailahalli Gangavara, Kadegarje, Mallapura, Thalagodu, Marur Madagodu, Kudumanahalli, Balaguppe, Singapura I. Hunsekere, Govinahalli, Mundaghatta, Kabbinamane Ballur, Hosahalli, Shanuboganahalli, Kelahalli Kodanahalli, Yakkasettihalli, Malenahalli Shettihalli, Danikanahalli, Chikkabyadigere, Kerlur Mavinakere, Sanyasihalli, Ranaghatta, Nettekere Sompura, Appagodanahalli, Chikkanahalli Ponnathapura, Devihalli, Kallibore Kaval Vaddarahalli, Somenahalli, Thendekere Jodi, Pura Chomanahalli, Hulugundi, Mallapura, Mulenahalli Shivapura Kaval, Kowri, Mugalihalli, Bommadihalli Chowdanahalli, Ginnanamane, Holalu, Neelanahalli Kerlur, Rajanahalli, Madaghatta, Andur, Yedehalli Mallarahosahalli, Madavalli.

Sex ratio of Scheduled Caste population is 502.

Scheduled Castes Literates and Illiterates by Sex:

	Persons	Males	Females
Literate	19,513	11,787	7,726
Illiterate	28,456	12,109	16,347
Literacy rate	47.4	57.5	37.4
Graduate	270	227	43

Scheduled Castes (Dominant):
Adi Karnataka, Bhovi, Madiga, Chalavadi etc.
Generic Castes etc.

For their cultural identity please see Appendix-I

Villages without Scheduled Castes: There are 95 villages without any scheduled caste population.

Scheduled Tribes: Out of the total population of 163527 persons, 3748 persons (2.29%) belong to Scheduled Tribes. The villages having less than 10% ST population are Cheekanahalli, Hunuganahalli, Kanadur, Chunganahalli Malur, Keethur, Banasavalli, Madvapura, Muthugadalu Maravathi, Madapura, Marur, Somanahalli Kotiganahalli, Chunchanahalli, Dabbe, Malalakeshavi Bettadakeshavi, Devarakeshavi, Hirigadde, Kuppagodu Kogodu, Bakkaravalli, Malasavara, Umbalagodu Baladakallu, Murahalli, Thumbadevanahalli, Hosahalli Goravanahalli, Narvey, Sulagalale, Narvepete Uddamanahalli, Koralagadde, Heggadde, Byadane Hosamane, Balaguli, Utholalu, Nandagodanahalli Madenahalli, Gurgihalli, Doddasalavara Chikkasalavara, Bommenahalli, Hirihasade, Hanjihalli Naganhalli, Mathihalli, Bellotte, Menasinamane Tholalu, Haralakatte, Navilahalli, Alur, Konerlu Mailahalli, Sullakki, Kandavara, Boovanahalli Shettihalli, Echala Halli, Gangavara, Chikkahasade Kanaguppe, Anughatta, Dolanamane, Kittavara Adagunchanahalli, Malahalli, Arehalli, Heggadihalli Hirigarje, Lingapura, Mallapura, Hulukodu, Ballavara Muddanahalli, Bilagavalli, Surukodu, Thalagodu Marur, Chataki, Gendehalli, Kumbarahalli Mandalamane, Nidagodu (A.C.), Kalleri, Angajanahalli Magehalli, Madagodu, H. Hosahalli, Kudumanahalli Bindenahalli, Biranagodu, Balaguppe, Aduvalli Byadra Somanahalli, Kallahalli, Aggadalu, Singapura Devalapura, Iravalli, Vaginakere, Agasaravalli I. Hunsekere, Govinahalli, Mundaghatta, Kabbinamane Bommadihalli, Chikkamedur, Sugalur, Gabbalagodu Benninamane, Karikihalli, Melanahalli, Ballur Hosahalli, Chinnenahalli, Nidagodu, Surapura Doddamedur, Shanuboganahalli, Yamasandi, Kudlur N. Hosahalli, Bennur, Kelahalli, Hanumidi Narayanapur, Kodanahalli, Karagada, Yakkasettihalli Channapura, Shettigere, Malenahalli, Gollenahalli Honnenahalli Kaval, Honnenahalli, Shettihalli Doddabyadigere, Muthuganne, Koratikere Kanaikanahalli, Machanaikanahalli, Danikanahalli

Chikkabyadigere, Bantenahalli, Rayapura, Bitravalli
Utpatanahalli, Kerlur, Lakshmipura, Channapura
Mavinakere, Nittor, Kachihalli, Sanyasihalli
Mallapura, Prasadihalli, Hirikole, Chikkole
Ranaghatta, Nettekere, Surapura, Sompura
M. Hunsekere, Hebbalu, Thimmanahalli, Jogihalli
Hakkihalli, Hullenahalli, Appagodanahalli
Kallusettihalli, Kallahalli, Shivaladahalli
Chikkanahalli, Cheelanaikanahalli
Jodi Thippanahalli, Rajanasiriyur, Karikattehalli
Mayagowdanahalli, Halebeedu, Kattesomenahalli
Ponnathapura, Kyathalapura, Chikkammanahalli
Yalahanka, Mallikarjunapura, Devihalli, Siddapura
Hulikere, Kodihalli, Kallibore Kaval
Chatchatnahalli, Gonisomenahalli, Rajagere
Girikallahalli, Harubihalli, Vaddarahalli
Komaranahalli, Ghattadahalli, Mathighatta
Shivanenahalli, Jogihalli, Suranaikanahalli
Hirihalli, Maranahalli, Kodihalli, Kondli
Kabbigarahalli, Minuganahalli, Appihalli
Kanakenahalli, Chatnahalli, Gangur, Sanenahalli
Idahalla Kaval, Hadlagere, Hosahalli, Laxmipura
Ramenahalli, Ibbedu, Ibbedu Hosahalli, Somenahalli
Ammanagudi Kaval, Ajjenahalli, Thendekere Jodi
Ballenahalli, Chilkur, Kallusettihalli, Harohalli
Pura, Chomanahalli, Thattegere, Konaikanahalli Jodi
Gorur, Mugalihalli, Andale, Ramachandrapura
Veerapura, Shivayogipura, Handralu, Hanike
Thendegere, Bommenahalli, Hulugundi, Halthore
Keshavapura, Madihalli, Hagare, Kalyanapura
Siddanahalli, Panditanahalli, Mallapura, Savasihalli
Mulenahalli, Suledevarahalli, Adavibantenahalli
Shivapura Kaval, Shivapura, Devarahalli, Aladahalli
Kodihalli, Illenahalli, Kyathanakere
Dasagodanahalli, Umadevihalli, Thirumalanahalli
Adagooru, Kumarihalli, Mallavalli, Kowri, Kushavara
Kiragadalu, Mugalihalli, Thagare, Kogilamane
Bommadihalli, Chowdanahalli, Mogasavara, Malliganur
Chandapura, Bakravalli, Karadagodu, Chokanahalli
Challenahalli , Baliganahalli, Jagaboranahalli
Ginnanamane, Honnemane, Nidumanahalli, Bikkodu
Huskur, Arekaravalli, Venktipete, Moovala, Mathavara
Kalanamata, Chikkabiccodu, Somanahalli, Bandahalli
Kodaganahalli, Lakkunda, Irakaravalli, Ankihalli
Gummanahalli, Heddaravalli, Shingaravalli, Hirivate
Holalu, Mahala, Hosahalli, Pura, Chatnahalli
Neelanahalli, Kesagodu, Kerlur, Bolenahalli
Lakkenahalli, Rajanahalli, Hemmidaganahalli
Intitholalu, Kodihalli, Madaghatta, Bilaguli
Malagere, Chandanahalli, Andur, Yedehalli
Danaikanahalli, Mallarahosahalli, Paduvalalu
Jinigenahalli, Madavalli, Doddihalli.

The villages having more than 50% ST population are None.

Sex ratio of Scheduled tribe population is 507.

Scheduled Tribes Literates and Illiterates by Sex:

	Persons	Males	Females
Literate	1,451	848	603
Illiterate	2,297	998	1,299
Literacy rate	46.3	55.6	37.5
Graduate	25	18	7

Scheduled Tribes (Dominant):

Naikda etc., Hakkipikki, Hasalaru, Meda
Generic Tribes etc.

For their cultural identity please see Appendix-II

Villages without Scheduled Tribes: There are 309 villages without any scheduled tribe population.

Literates and Illiterates by Sex (Total Population):

	Persons	Males	Females
Literate	92,772	52,657	40,115
Illiterate	70,755	28,740	42,015
Literacy rate	65	74	55
Graduate	2,631	1,921	710

Agriculture: ***Distribution of villages according to land use:*** Out of 383 villages, Total area (in hectare) is 84051, out of that 63.52 percent is cultivable and 30.51 percent of the cultivable area is irrigated.

Sources of Irrigation (Hectares): Government Canal 254.85, Private Canal 0, Well without Electricity 0, Well with Electricity 642.47, Tubewell without Electricity 45.81, Tubewell with Electricity 2086.39, Tank 9275.03, River 27.78, Lake 0, Waterfall 49.68, Others 3907.82.

Villages with population of 5000 to 9999:
Arehalli, Halebeedu.

Villages with population of 10000 and above: None

Distribution of Workers:

	Persons	Males	Females	WPR
Cultivators	47,829	30,645	17,184	55.85
Agricultural Labour	14,549	5,502	9,047	16.99
Household Industry	970	680	290	1.13
Other Workers	22,286	13,644	8,642	26.02
Main Workers	72,586	47,274	25,312	84.76
Marginal Workers	13,048	3,197	9,851	15.24
Total Workers	85,634	50,471	35,163	

Religion: Major Religious Communities:

	Persons	Males	Females	Sex Ratio
Hindu (93.14%)	152,309	75,777	76,532	1,010
Muslim (5.33%)	8,721	4,343	4,378	1,008
Christian (0.84%)	1,380	711	669	941
Sikh (0%)	3	2	1	500

Buddhists (0.02%)	38	19	19	1,000
Jain (0.28%)	460	238	222	933

Agewise Data:

	Persons	Males	Females	Sex Ratio
All ages	163,527	81,397	82,130	1009
0-14	48,054	24,448	23,606	966
15-44	81,706	40,211	41,495	1032
45-79	32,016	15,928	16,088	1010
80+	1,641	748	893	1194
Age not stated	110	62	48	774

Languages (Dominant):
Kannada, Urdu, Tulu, Telugu, Tamil

Disabled Population:

	Persons	Males	Females	%
Total Disabled	3,069	1,581	1,488	
In Seeing	1,420	682	738	46.27
In Speech	260	145	115	8.47
In Hearing	365	160	205	11.89
In Movement	740	446	294	24.11
Mentally	284	148	136	9.25

BHADRAVATI

Bhadravati C.D. Block lies in the south-eastern part of Shimoga district. It is a part of Bhadravati taluka. The Block is located at a distance of 40 kms. from district headquarters (Shimoga). There are 145 villages in the block with the total population of 178,219 persons. Area of the C.D. Block is 623.43 sq. kms. It is bounded by district Davanagere on north and east, district Chikmagalur on south, taluk Shimoga, districts Davanage re and Chikmaglaur on west.

Communications:

Roadways : N.H-13: Direction- Shimoga to Channagiri, Nearest Villages- Danayakapura, Holehonnuru, Kannekoppa, Jambaraghatta, Arahatholalu, Mudalavittalapura, Koppa, Yedehalli, Kenganalu, Agaradahalli, Hanchinasiddapura. N.H-206: Direction- Shimoga to Tumkur, Nearest Villages- Hallikere, Barandooru, Karehalli. S.H-50: Direction- Bhadravati to Channagiri, Nearest Villages- Arebilachi, Hosuru, Nagoli, Kallapura, Sitaramapura, Veerapura, Thiplapura, Aralihalli, Athigunda, Kudligere, Kodihalli, Kottadalu.

Railway Station: Villages- Masarahalli, Hallikere.

River: Bhadra Nadi- Nearest Villages- Sidlipura, Danaya kapura, Holehonnuru, Kannekoppa, Koppa, Holebyranahalli, Agasanahalli, Dasarakallahalli, Aradottilu, Thallikatte, Nagathibelagalu, Kagekodamagge, Baballi, Mathighatta, Tadasa, Donabaghatta, Holeneralakere, Barandooru, Bomm enahalli, Honnehatti, Goneebeedu, Malligenahalli, Singanam ane, Vadiyuru,, Nellisara, Malenahalli, Chikkagoppenahalli, Ganguru, Balemaranahalli. Tungabhadra Nadi- Nearest Villages- Nimbegondi, Vaderapura, Anaveri, Mangote, Nagasamudra, Sidlipura, Sannyasikodamagge.

Canal: Nearest Villages- Danayakapura, Kannekoppa, Jamba raghatta, Kerebeeranahalli, Mudalavittalapura, Yammehatti, Agasanahalli, Dasarakallahalli, Aradottilu, Chandanakere, Yedehalli, Agaradahalli, Bhadrapura, Basavapura, Harog undi, Bommanakatte, Kallihal, Thimmlapura, Arebilachi, Danavadi, Nagoli, Belligere, Thallikatte, Nagathibelaga lu, Hosahalli, Sitaramapura, Kagekodamagge, Veerapura, Thiplapura, Komaranahalli, Devarahalli, Kachagondanahal li, Devaranarasipura, Koralakoppa, Guninarasipura, Yareha lli, Antaragange, Bisilamane, Guddadaneralakere, Basalika tte, Athigunda, Kudligere, Kottadalu, Kenchammanahalli, Ukkunda, Koppadalu, Bilaki, Masarahalli, Mavinakere, Barandooru, Bommenahalli, Karehalli, Hadlaghatta, Siriy ur, Veerapura, Kalanakattel Hiriyur, Tharikatte, Kambadala Hosuru, Honnehatti, Thammadihalli, Goneebeedu, Malligen ahalli, Thavaraghatta, Singanamane, Vadiyuru, Nellisara, Malenahalli, Chikkagoppenahalli.

Annual Rainfall: Normal Rianfall 769.4 mm.

Ground Water: Availability of the Ground Water in the Basin is 102.3 MCM and the utilization is 36.94 MCM. It belongs to Safe category. Depth to water level 2 to 10 meter below the ground. Most of the wells go down in summer months, according to the Ground Water Estimati on Committee.

Soils: Reddish to Brownish Clayey Loam.

Natural Division : It falls partly in Upper Tungabhadra Valley and Tirthahalli Rolling Tract of the Central Karnataka Plateau.

Administration:

Division: Bangalore. Parliamentary Constituency: 14 Shimoga. District: Shimoga. Taluka: Bhadravati. Assembly Constituency: 111 Shimoga Rural (SC), 112 Bhadravati. Gram Panchayat: 39.

Regional Area Development Boards: The Maland Aera Development Board.

Fairs: Lakshminarasimha Car Festival: It is held at Bhadravati near Shimoga in about the month of May every year.

Villages: 145 **Inhabited:** 138 **Uninhabited:** 7

Ranking	District	State	National
Area	7	148	1103
Population	1	108	1086
Sex Ratio	6	102	2566
Child Sex Ratio	7	158	4424
Literacy Rate	7	52	1789
Density	7	162	3681
Work Participation Rate	1	27	3819

Gram Panchayats:
Mangote, Anaveri, Nimbegondi, Sydarakallahalli,

Gudumagatta, Mydolalu, Sidlipura, Holehonnuru, Yammehatti, Arahatholalu, Yedehalli, Agaradahalli, Kallihal, Arakere, Marasettyhalli, Dasarakallahalli, Nagathibelagalu, Arebilachi, Kudligere, Athigunda, Aralihalli, Kagekodamagge, Tadasa, Donabaghatta, Bilaki, Kallahalli, Kambadala Hosuru, Singanamane, Thavaraghatta, Hiriyur, Aralikoppa, Karehalli, Barandooru, Mavinakere, Yarehalli, Antaragange, Veerapura, Komaranahalli, Dodderi.

Amenities:

Education: Primary School in 112 villages, Middle school in 76 villages, Matriculation or Secondary School in 22 villages, namely Nimbegondi, Anaveri, Mydolalu, Sannyasikodamagge, Holehonnuru, Dasarakallahalli, Yedehalli, Agaradahalli, Kallihal, Marasettyhalli, Arebilachi, Sitaramapura, Aralihalli, Devarahalli, Antaragange, Kudligere, Donabaghatta, Barandooru, Karehalli, Hunasekatte, Hiriyur, Goneebeedu.

Higher Secondary or Pre University Courses or Intermediate or Junior College in 7 villages of the CD Block,, namely Anaveri, Holehonnuru, Bommanakatte, Kallihal, Danavadi, Sitaramapura, Barandooru.

College in 3 villages, Adult Literacy Center in 1 village., Colleges are in villages, namely Holehonnuru, Bommanakatte, Danavadi.

Medical: Hospital in 0 village, Dispensary in 11 villages, Health Center in 8 villages, Sub Center in 16 villages, Maternity and Child Welfare Center in 7 villages, Community health workers in 19 villages.

The Villages having Hospital or Dispensary or Health Center are Nimbegondi, Sydarakallahalli, Anaveri, Mydolalu, Holehonnuru, Hanumanthapura, Arebilachi, Yarehalli, Barandooru, Hiriyur, Aralikoppa.

Drinking Water: Tap water in 67 villages, Tank water in 36 villages, Well water in 103 villages, Tubewell in 93 villages and more than one source in 129 villages.

Bank: Banking facility in 14 villages, namely, Nimbegondi, Anaveri, Holehonnuru, Kannekoppa Agaradahalli, Kallihal, Marasettyhalli, Arebilachi Veerapura, Aralihalli, Devarahalli, Bilaki Barandooru, Hiriyur.

Credit Society in 29 villages Agricultural Credit Society in 18 Non-Agricultural Credit Society in 13 villages.

Others: Power supply in 132 villages, Cinema hall in 7 villages, sport club in 138 villages, Stadium or Auditorium or Community Hall in 138 villages, Post Office in 34 villages.

There are 101 villages having bus facilities.

Villages with most of facilities: Nimbegondi Anaveri, Holehonnuru, Agaradahalli, Kallihal Arebilachi, Veerapura, Aralihalli, Barandooru Hiriyur.

Villages without amenities (Education): Kurubaravittalapura, Jangamarahalli, Mallapura, Koppa, Kenganalu, Hanchinasiddapura, Bhadrapura, Basavapura, Nagoli, Hosahalli, Majjigenahalli, Thiplapura, Guninarasipura, Kottadalu, Yammedoddi, Balekatte, Varavinakere, Gangooru, Koppadalu, Navile Basavapura, Somenakoppa, Huliyar Ramenakoppa, Honnehatti, Malligenahalli, Thavaraghatta, Malenahalli..

Scheduled Castes: Out of the total population of 178327 persons, 42258 persons (23.7%) belong to Scheduled Castes.

The villages having less than 10% SC population are Diggenahalli, Arisinaghatta, Danayakapura Holehonnuru, Jambaraghatta, Mudalavittalapura Holebyranahalli, Yammehatti, Dasarakallahalli Kenganalu, Basavapura, Gowdarahalli, Majjigenahalli Thiplapura, Guninarasipura, Kottadalu Nettakallahatti, Yammedoddi, Gangooru, Koppadalu Tadasa, Donabaghatta, Holeneralakere, Masarahalli Kenchenahalli, Hallikere, Sanklipura, Thammadihalli Malligenahalli.

The villages having more than 50% SC population are Adrihalli, Indiranagara, Malligenahalli Bommanakatte, Hosuru, Kalpanahalli, Komaranahalli Dodderi, Kenchammanahalli, Hathikatte, Bilaki Kalinganahalli, Somenakoppa, Huliyar Ramenakoppa Nanjapura, Nellisara, Aralikoppa, Ganguru.

Sex ratio of Scheduled Caste population is 497.

Scheduled Castes Literates and Illiterates by Sex:

	Persons	Males	Females
Literate	18,620	11,320	7,300
Illiterate	23,638	9,933	13,705
Literacy rate	51.5	62.3	40.6
Graduate	513	426	87

Scheduled Castes (Dominant):

Bhovi, Adi Karnataka, Banjara etc., Madiga Adi Dravida

For their cultural identity please see Appendix-I

Villages without Scheduled Castes: There are 19 villages without any scheduled caste population.

Scheduled Tribes: Out of the total population of 178327 persons, 8442 persons (4.73%) belong to Scheduled Tribes.

The villages having less than 10% ST population are Nimbegondi, Kurubaravittalapura, Diggenahalli Adrihalli, Vaderapura, Anaveri, Indiranagara Gudumagatta, Jangamarahalli, Mangote, Nagasamudra Mallapura, Mydolalu, Kallajjanalu, Malligenahalli Thadasa, Sidlipura, Sannyasikodamagge, Kanasinakatte Danayakapura, Holehonnuru, Kannekoppa

Kerebeeranahalli, Mudalavittalapura, Koppa Yammehatti, Agasanahalli, Dasarakallahalli Aradottilu, Yedehalli, Bommanakatte, Kallihal Thimmlapura, Marasettyhalli, Hosuru, Belligere Thallikatte, Nagathibelagalu, Hosahalli Kalpanahalli, Sitaramapura, Kagekodamagge, Baballi Gowdarahalli, Majjigenahalli, Veerapura, Thiplapura Aralihalli, Komaranahalli, Devarahalli Kachagondanahalli, Devaranarasipura, Koralakoppa Guninarasipura, Yarehalli, Antaragange Guddadaneralakere, Athigunda, Kudligere, Kottadalu Nettakallahatti, Dodderi, Yammedoddi, Balekatte Varavinakere, Kenchammanahalli, Ukkunda, Koppadalu Padmenahalli, Hathikatte, Mathighatta, Tadasa Donabaghatta, Bilaki, Navile Basavapura Majjigenahalli, Holeneralakere, Masarahalli Mavinakere, Kenchenahalli, Hallikere, Barandooru Bommenahalli, Karehalli, Kalinganahalli, Hadlaghatta Somenakoppa, Kallahalli, Siriyur, Veerapura Sanklipura, Huliyar Ramenakoppa, Hunasekatte Kalanakatte, Nanjapura, Hiriyur, Tharikatte Kambadala Hosuru, Honnehatti, Thammadihalli Goneebeedu, Malligenahalli, Thavaraghatta Singanamane, Nellisara, Malenahalli Chikkagoppenahalli, Aralikoppa, Ganguru Balemaranahalli.

The villages having more than 50% ST population are None.

Sex ratio of Scheduled tribe population is 490.

Scheduled Tribes Literates and Illiterates by Sex:

	Persons	Males	Females
Literate	4,085	2,400	1,685
Illiterate	4,357	1,904	2,453
Literacy rate	56.2	65.5	46.7
Graduate	125	107	18

Scheduled Tribes (Dominant):

Naikda etc., Meda, Gowdalu, Kurumans, Irular

For their cultural identity please see Appendix-II

Villages without Scheduled Tribes: There are 51 villages without any scheduled tribe population.

Literates and Illiterates by Sex (Total Population):

	Persons	Males	Females
Literate	102,032	58,164	43,868
Illiterate	76,295	32,402	43,893
Literacy rate	66	74	57
Graduate	4,215	3,227	988

Agriculture: ***Distribution of villages according to land use:***

Out of 145 villages, Total area (in hectare) is 62343, out of that 43.97 percent is cultivable and 79.06 percent of the cultivable area is irrigated.

Sources of Irrigation (Hectares): Government Canal 18691.95, Private Canal 0, Well without Electricity 2.44, Well with Electricity 543.22, Tubewell without Electricity 65.64, Tubewell with Electricity 857.62, Tank 549.74, River 545.33, Lake 0, Waterfall 0, Others 416.86.

Villages with population of 5000 to 9999:

Arebilachi, Donabaghatta, Singanamane.

Villages with population of 10000 and above: None

Distribution of Workers:

	Persons	Males	Females	WPR
Cultivators	21,462	19,012	2,450	27.92
Agricultural Labour	37,667	21,330	16,337	48.99
Household Industry	2,016	1,031	985	2.62
Other Workers	15,736	11,685	4,051	20.47
Main Workers	64,926	48,291	16,635	84.45
Marginal Workers	11,955	4,767	7,188	15.55
Total Workers	76,881	53,058	23,823	

Religion: Major Religious Communities:

	Persons	Males	Females	Sex Ratio
Hindu (85.44%)	152,367	77,150	75,217	975
Muslim (13.64%)	24,330	12,567	11,763	936
Christian (0.54%)	955	492	463	941
Sikh (0.01%)	16	10	6	600
Buddhists (0.04%)	76	40	36	900
Jain (0.05%)	88	40	48	1,200

Agewise Data:

	Persons	Males	Females	Sex Ratio
All ages	178,327	90,566	87,761	969
0-14	56,383	28,764	27,619	960
15-44	89,284	45,415	43,869	966
45-79	31,293	15,762	15,531	985
80+	1,204	536	668	1246
Age not stated	163	89	74	831

Languages (Dominant):

Kannada, Urdu, Tamil, Telugu, Hindi

Disabled Population:

	Persons	Males	Females	%
Total Disabled	3,092	1,732	1,360	
In Seeing	1,379	697	682	44.6
In Speech	286	152	134	9.25
In Hearing	253	134	119	8.18
In Movement	871	581	290	28.17
Mentally	303	168	135	9.8

BHALKI

Bhalki C.D. Block lies in the west central part of Bidar district. It is a part of Bhalki taluka. The Block is located at a distance of 42 kms. from district headquarters (Bidar). There are 133 villages in the block with the total population of 221,918 persons. Area of the C.D. Block is 1082.12 sq. kms. It is bounded by taluk

Aurad on north, taluks Basavakalyan and Homnabad on south, taluk Bidar on east, and it has common boundary with the state of Mahrashtra on north and west.

Communications:

Roadways : S.H-4: Direction- Nanded to Bidar, Nearest Villages- Alandi, Hunjialandi, Kalasdhal, Walsang, Ambes angu, Hupla, Ahmadabad, Kotgiyalwadi, Kommelkunda, Paigampur, Halbarga, Dhanura, Khanapur, Malchapur. S.H-11: Direction-Nilanga to Basavakalyan, Nearest Vill.- Jamkhandi. S.H-19: Direction- Homnabad to Bidar, Nearest Villages- Tugaon (Chalkapur), Byalhalli, Kamalpur, Halhalli.

Railway Station: Villages- Dongapur, Jaigaon, Talwada (K), Halbarga.

River: Manjra Nadi- Nearest Vill.- Kasara Tugaon Wadi, Shivani, Lakhangaon, Atnoor, Sompur, Talwada (Mara tha), Bhatsangvi, Dongapur, Alandi, Hunjialandi, Hachi, Kamath, Beeri, Nagral, Kodli, Nittur, Hajnal, Gornal, Chandapur, Dongargi. Karanja Nadi- Nearest Villages- Jirgyal, Wagalgaon, Khudawandpur, Saigaon, Inchur, Bhats angvi, Thamgyal Wadi, Bhatambra, Gorchincholi, Nideban, Anandwadil, Eklaspur, Gubyal, Koroor, Ramteerthwadi, Bhalki (R), Dadgi, Harnal, Kuntesirsi, Chikalchanda, Maroor, Joldabka, Kurubkhelgi, Dawargaon, Masimadu, Nelwad, Chalkapur, Tugaon (Chalkapur), Kanji, Hunji (K), Godihipperga, Byalhalli, Kamalpur.

Resrved Forest: Nearest Villages- Kosam, Halhipperga, Halbarga, Dhanura, Khanapur, Malchapur.

Annual Rainfall: Normal Rianfall 859 mm.

Ground Water: Availability of the Ground Water in the Basin is 8704.76 H.A.M. and the utilization is 4432. 94 H.A.M. It belongs to Over Exploited category. Depth to water level 2 to 20 meter below the ground. Most of the wells go down in summer months, according to the Ground Water Estimation Committee.

Soils: Black Soils and Lateritic Soils.

Natural Division : It falls in Manjra-Karanja Basin of the Northern Karnataka Plateau.

Administration:

Division: Gulbarga. Parliamentary Constituency: 7 Bidar (SC). District: Bidar. Taluka: Bhalki. Assembly Constitu ency: 51 Bhalki. Gram Panchayat: 35.

Regional Area Development Boards: The Hyderabad - Karna taka Area Development Board.

Border Villages: (State: Maharashtra)- Tugaonhalsi, Alwai, Yellammawadi, Mankeshwar, Atterga, Wanjarkhada, Jamkhandi, Kasara Tugaon Wadi, Shivani, Lakhangaon.

Fairs: Bhalkeshvara Jatra: It is held at Bhalki around the month of March-April for eight-days. There are old Veerasaiva monasteries known as Channabasava Hirematha, Bhalkeshvara Matha and Mahanteshvara Matha.

Hanuman Fair: A fair is held at Tugaon near Bidar in honour of Hanuman in about the month of April for two days. The river Karanja flows close to this village. During the month of Phalguna (February-March), devotees assemble on the banks of this river and offer worship to a Shivalinga here. A fair is held in honour of Hanum an for about two days in April.

Mailara Lingeswara Devara Jatra: Mailara Lingeswara Devara jatra is held at Khanapur near Bidar around the month of December-Jan. for 30 days. Khanapur popularly called Mailara, is about 26 kms. south-east of Bhalki town. It is said that the eastern main gate of the temple was erected by Ahilyabai Holkar who donated some lands to the temple. The temple is situated in the midst of fine natural surroundings on the bank of a pond at a short distance from a stream. A jatra is held here around December-January for four days, which is attended by people from various parts of Bidar and Gulbarga area and also from the neighbouring districts of Andhra Prade sh and Maharashtra.

Moola-Chalkamma Jatra: Moola-Chalkamma jatra is held at Chalkapur near Bidar, twice a year the month of Octob er and April for two days. Chalkapur lies about 30 kms. south-east of Bhalki town. There is a temple of Chalka mmana which has some impressive modern wall paintings of various saints and deities. The Chalkammana-gudda (hill), which is nearby, has small shrines of Moola-Chal kamma twice a year, in October and April. Another fair takes place here for Hanuman in about April.

Rameshvara Puja Festival: It is observed at Aliabad near Bidar, twice a year in about the months of Augus t-September and February-March every year. Aliabad is about seven kilometres north-west of Bidar town. It has a temple dedicated to Ishvara, also called Rameshvara, in front of which there is a natural water-spring and a pond called "Papanash" (destroyer of sins).

Revappayya Swami Jatra: It is held at Nawadgi near Bidar in the month of December every year for three days. Nawadgi is about 12 kms. south-west of Bhalki town, the birth-place of a famous sharana named Revappayya who lived a few decades back. It has his samadhi over which a building has been constructed. Under the auspices of this shrine, a fair is held for three days around the month of December every year.

Siddeshwara Fair: It is held at Siddeshwar near Bidar around the month of March-April for two days. Siddeshwar located about nineteen kilometres south-east of Bhalki town, is noted for its temple of Siddeshwara. Just near this place of worship, there is the samadhi of Imam

Sahib who was a devotee of Siddeshwara. He is held in high respect by the local people. The temple holds an annual fair in March-April for two days.
Siddhalingeshwara Jatra: It is held at Salgaon near Bidar around the months of February - March. Salgaon is at a distance of 24 kms. north-west of Bhalki town and has a temple dedicated to Hanuman, in veneration of whom a jatra is held about October - November. There is also a temple of Siddhalingeshwara here under the auspices of which a jatra is held about February-March which is attended by a large gathering.
Veerabhadra Jatra: It is held at Bhatambra near Bidal around the month of April-May for two days. Bhatambra is about 8 kms. north-west of Bhalki town. It has an old, large and strong fort. The place has a temple of Veerbhadra which holds an annual jatra for two days during April-May and a Gurubasaveshvara Matha.

Villages: 133 **Inhabited:** 130 **Uninhabited:** 3

Ranking	District	State	National
Area	3	73	365
Population	5	67	449
Sex Ratio	2	130	3117
Child Sex Ratio	3	108	3342
Literacy Rate	1	82	2681
Density	2	165	4659
Work Participation Rate	3	73	4098

Gram Panchayats:
Alwai, Kalsar Tugaon, Lakhangaon, Dongapur, Beeri (B), Telgaoon, Methimelkunda, Mehkar, Tugaonhalsi, Wanjarkhada, Saigaon, Inchur, Bhatambra, Ambesangi, Nittur, Balur, Gorchincholi, Morambi, Madkatti, Dadgi, Talwada (K), Konmelkunda, Halbarga, Siddeshwar, Kurubkhelgi, Warwatti, Dawargaon, Joldabka, Janti, Dhanura, Kanji, Khatak Chincholi, Chalkapur, Byalhalli, Malchapur.

Amenities:

Education: Primary School in 130 villages, Middle school in 87 villages, Matriculation or Secondary School in 31 villages, namely Alwai, Mehkar, Saigaon, Kesarjawalga, Ladha, Kalsar Tugaon, Lakhangaon, Kaknal, Dongapur, Bhatambra, Beeri, Nittur, Ambesangu, Balur, Gorchincholi, Kotgiyalwadi, Madkatti, Talwada (K), Joldabka, Siddeshwar, Warwatti, Kurubkhelgi, Dawargaon, Khatak Chincholi, Chalkapur, Kommelkunda, Halbarga, Janti, Dhanura, Kanji, Halhalli.
Higher Secondary or Pre University Courses or Intermediate or Junior College in 4 villages of the CD Block,, namely Bhatambra, Nittur, Gornal, Halbarga.
College in 1 village, Adult Literacy Center in 48 villages., College is in village, namely Nittur.

Medical: Hospital in 0 village, Dispensary in 12 villages, Health Center in 11 villages, Sub Center in 44 villages, Maternity and Child Welfare Center in 2 villages, Community health workers in 26 villages.
The Villages having Hospital or Dispensary or Health Center are Lakhangaon, Dongapur, Bhatambra, Beeri, Kotgiyal, Dadgi, Warwatti, Dawargaon, Khatak Chincholi, Kommelkunda, Halbarga, Kanji, Byalhalli.

Drinking Water: Tap water in 97 villages, Tank water in 28 villages, Well water in 129 villages, Tubewell in 94 villages and more than one source in 130 villages.

Bank: Banking facility in 21 villages, namely, Alwai, Saigaon, Kalsar Tugaon, Lakhangaon, Alandi Bhatambra, Nittur, Kotgiyal, Hupla, Balur Gorchincholi, Dadgi, Joldabka, Siddeshwar Kurubkhelgi, Khatak Chincholi, Chalkapur, Halbarga Dhanura, Kanji, Byalhalli.
Credit Society in 41 villages Agricultural Credit Society in 36 Non-Agricultural Credit Society in 7 villages.

Others: Power supply in 130 villages, Cinema hall in 0 village, sport club in 130 villages, Stadium or Auditorium or Communi Hall in 130 villages, Post Office in 56 villages.
There are 106 villages having bus facilities.

Villages with most of facilities: Alwai, Saigaon Kalsar Tugaon, Lakhangaon, Alandi, Bhatambra, Nittur Kotgiyal, Hupla, Gorchincholi, Dadgi, Siddeshwar Kurubkhelgi, Khatak Chincholi, Chalkapur, Halbarga Dhanura, Kanji, Byalhalli.

Villages without Amenities (Education): None..

Scheduled Castes: Out of the total population of 221949 persons, 48026 persons (21.64%) belong to Scheduled Castes.
The villages having less than 10% SC population are None..
The village having more than 50% SC population is None.
Sex ratio of Scheduled Caste population is 491.

Scheduled Castes Literates and Illiterates by Sex:

	Persons	Males	Females
Literate	21,156	13,226	7,930
Illiterate	26,870	11,201	15,669
Literacy rate	53.0	65.0	40.4
Graduate	789	698	91

Scheduled Castes (Dominant):
Holaya etc., Madiga, Banjara etc., Mahar etc. Mang etc.

For their cultural identity please see Appendix-I

Villages without Scheduled Castes: There are 3 villages without any scheduled caste population.

Scheduled Tribes: Out of the total population of 221949

persons, 21324 persons (9.61%) belong to Scheduled Tribes. The villages having less than 10% ST population are Tugaonhalsi, Alwai, Yellammawadi, Mankeshwar Atterga, Gunjarga, Srimali, Bolegaon, Nardasangam Mehkar, Wanjarkhada, Jamkhandi, Kongli, Jirgyal Halsilakmadevi, Rachappagondgaon, Kuntegaon, Ladha Kalsar Tugaon, Lakhangaon, Atnoor, Sompur Talwada (Maratha), Kaknal, Bhatsangvi, Dongapur Alandi, Hachi Kamath, Bhatambra, Telgaon, Jaigaon Shamsheerpur, Kalasdhal, Beeri, Kodli, Nittur Hajnal, Gornal, Kotgiyal, Walsang, Siddapur, Hupla Keroor, Ahmadabad, Jainapur, Khasimpur, Dongargi Nideban, Kotgiyalwadi, Ganeshpurwadi, Eklaspur Koroor, Kotgira, Ramteerthwadi, Dharajwadi, Kardhyal Talwada (K), Saidapurwadi, Kuntesirsi, Chikalchanda Joldabka, Siddeshwar, Bylhalli, Warwatti, Mavinhalli Nawadgi, Dawargaon, Bardapur, Secundrabad, Nelwad Chitta, Tugaon (Chalkapur), Kommelkunda, Paigampur Nagoor, Allabad, Kosam, Tarnalli, Nelgi, Dhanura Sevanagar, Khanapur, Rudnoor.

The villages having more than 50% ST population are None.

Sex ratio of Scheduled tribe population is 487.

Scheduled Tribes Literates and Illiterates by Sex:

	Persons	Males	Females
Literate	9,353	5,896	3,457
Illiterate	11,971	5,052	6,919
Literacy rate	52.3	64.3	39.7
Graduate	302	280	22

Scheduled Tribes (Dominant):

Gond etc., Koli Dhor etc., Naikda etc.

Generic Tribes etc., Kokna etc.

For their cultural identity please see Appendix-II

Villages without Scheduled Tribes: There are 24 villages without any scheduled tribe population.

Literates and Illiterates by Sex (Total Population):

	Persons	Males	Females
Literate	113,908	70,774	43,134
Illiterate	108,041	42,579	65,462
Literacy rate	60	74	47
Graduate	4,776	4,240	536

Agriculture: *Distribution of villages according to land use:* Out of 133 villages, Total area (in hectare) is 108212, out of that 82.05 percent is cultivable and 7.47 percent of the cultivable area is irrigated.

Sources of Irrigation (Hectares): Government Canal 1371.44, Private Canal 0, Well without Electricity 26.96, Well with Electricity 3203.8, Tubewell without Electricity 48.55, Tubewell with Electricity 1091.55, Tank 36.45, River 841.94, Lake 7.39, Waterfall 0, Others 4.24.

Villages with population of 5000 to 9999: Mehkar, Bhatambra, Khatak Chincholi, Dhanura.

Villages with population of 10000 and above: None

Distribution of Workers:

	Persons	Males	Females	WPR
Cultivators	30,064	21,834	8,230	33.24
Agricultural Labour	41,662	19,154	22,508	46.06
Household Industry	1,760	1,193	567	1.95
Other Workers	16,971	13,412	3,559	18.76
Main Workers	67,999	48,125	19,874	75.17
Marginal Workers	22,458	7,468	14,990	24.83
Total Workers	90,457	55,593	34,864	

Religion: Major Religious Communities:

	Persons	Males	Females	Sex Ratio
Hindu (78.28%)	173,740	88,605	85,135	961
Muslim (9.44%)	20,949	10,783	10,166	943
Christian (0.96%)	2,141	1,084	1,057	975
Sikh (0%)	4	-	4	-
Buddhists (10.1%)	22,412	11,479	10,933	952
Jain (0.05%)	119	69	50	725

Agewise Data:

	Persons	Males	Females	Sex Ratio
All ages	221,949	113,353	108,596	958
0-14	81,688	41,638	40,050	962
15-44	94,448	49,076	45,372	925
45-79	42,875	21,237	21,638	1019
80+	2,643	1,237	1,406	1137
Age not stated	295	165	130	788

Languages (Dominant):

Kannada, Marathi, Urdu, Hindi, Telugu

Disabled Population:

	Persons	Males	Females	%
Total Disabled	4,895	2,814	2,081	
In Seeing	2,166	1,144	1,022	44.25
In Speech	372	206	166	7.6
In Hearing	289	164	125	5.9
In Movement	1,644	1,053	591	33.59
Mentally	424	247	177	8.66

BHATKAL

Bhatkal C.D. Block lies in the southern most part of Uttara Kannada district. It is a part of Bhatkal taluka. The Block is located at a distance of 126 kms. from district headquarters (Karwar). There are 60 villages in the block with the total population of 107,140 persons. Area of the C.D. Block is 339.26 sq. kms. It is bounded by taluk Honavar on north, district Udupi on south, district Shimoga on east, and Lakshadweep sea on west.

Communications:

Roadways : N.H-17 : Direction- Honavar to Mangalore, Nearest Villages- Bailur, Mavalli, Kaikini, Bengre, Shirali, Heble, Hadin, Purvarga, Yelavadikavoor, Belke.

River: Venkatapura Nadi- Nearest Villages- Shirali, Heble, Belalkhanda, Kitre, Antravalli, Hudil, Badabag, Agga, Henjale, Hasarvalli, Hallyani, Bastigalmigte (Koppa).

Reserved Forest: Nearest Villages- Mavalli, Kaikini, Koppa, Hudil, Badabag, Agga, Henjale, Hasarvalli, Hally ani, Murkodi, Hadavalli.

Annual Rainfall: Normal Rianfall 4145.6 mm.

Ground Water: Availability of the Ground Water in the Basin is 3284 H.A.M. and the utilization is 990 H.A. M. It belongs to Safe category. Depth to water level 2 to 10 meter below the ground. Most of the wells go down in summer months, according to the Ground Water Estimation Committee.

Soils: Coastal Alluvial Soils.

Natural Division : It falls partly in Karwar-Honavar Coast and Western Ghats (Uttar Kannada) of the Karnataka Coast.

Coastal Villages: (Lakshadeep Sea)- Bailur, Mavalli, Kaikini, Bengre, Shirali, Heble, Jali, Karikal, Talgod, Belni, Mundalli, Bastigalamigte (Hadin), Hadin, Gorte, Belke.

Administration:

Division: Belgaum. Parliamentary Constituency: 12 Uttara Kannada. District: Uttara Kannada. Taluka: Bhatkal. Assembly Constituency: 79 Bhatkal. Gram Panchayat: 25.

Regional Area Development Boards: The Maland Aera Development Board.

Fairs: Mahaganapati Rathotsava Festival: It is held at Shirali near Uttara Kannada for one day around April, when nearly one lakh people assemble. Shirali, a place of considerable antiquity is six kms. away from Bhatkal on the national highway between Bhatkal and Honavar to the north of the Venktapur river.

Mari Jatra: The Mari Gudi jatra is held at Bhatkal near Uttara Kannada in about the month of July-August for two days when nearly one lakh people assemble. Bhatkal, 126 kms. from Karwar, located at the southern-most point of the district has a hoary past.

Maruti Car Festival: Maruti is the gramadevata of Bhatkal town near Uttara Kannada, and his newly renovated temple is in the heart of the town. The car festival of this temple takes place during Ramanavami (March-April) for three days. There are eight other Maruti shrines in the town in its eight directions with this gramadevata temple as the nucleus. Other temples of the place are the Shanteri Kamakshi, the Parashurama Damodara, the Venkataramana, the Kalikamba, the Gopala Krishna and the Dattatreya which are all of recent times or recently renovated.

Murdeshwara Rathotsava Festival: It is held at Murdeshwa ra near Uttara Kannada for three days in about January every year. Murdeshwara, a holy place, described as linked with Gokarn (one of the panchakshetras), is 16 kms. from Bhatkal near Uttara Kannada and has a huge beautiful temple on a hillock on the sea shore, formerly separated from the main land, now connected by a small foot bridge across an estuary.

Sadashivgad Pir Urs: An Urs is held in the month of saffar at Bhatkal near Uttara Kannada in memory of the Pir of Sadashivgad. Bhatkal has sizeable Muslim populat ion and they are called Navayats, mostly engaged in trade, and the town has a variety of residential buildings, with superb wooden workmanship and new enterprising people.

Villages: 60 **Inhabited:** 60 **Uninhabited:** 0

Ranking	**District**	**State**	**National**
Area	11	173	2370
Population	4	159	3243
Sex Ratio	1	8	452
Child Sex Ratio	4	35	1758
Literacy Rate	9	41	1483
Density	10	172	3382
Work Participation Rate	1	22	4408

Gram Panchayats:

Bailur, Mavalli, Koppa, Kaikini, Bengre, Shirali, Heble, Muttalli, Jali, Mavinkurve, Mundalli, Yelavadikavoor, Belke, Konar, Marukeri, Hadavalli.

Amenities:

Education: Primary School in 44 villages, Middle school in 25 villages, Matriculation or Secondary School in 7 villages, namely Mavalli, Bengre, Shirali, Heble, Purvarga, Marukeri, Belke.

Higher Secondary or Pre University Courses or Intermediate or Junior College in 2 villages of the CD Block,, namely Mavalli, Shirali.

College in 0 village, Adult Literacy Center in 1 village.

Medical: Hospital in 0 village, Dispensary in 3 villages, Health Center in 4 villages, Sub Center in 9 villages, Maternity and Child Welfare Center in 1 village, Community health workers in 15 villages.

The Villages having Hospital or Dispensary or Health Center are Shirali, Jali, Konar.

Drinking Water: Tap water in 4 villages, Tank water in 17 villages, Well water in 59 villages, Tubewell in 4 villages and more than one source in 38 villages.

Bank: Banking facility in 7 villages, namely, Mavalli, Kaikini, Shirali, Jali, Kotkhanda, Herur Konar.

Credit Society in 10 villages Agricultural Credit Society in 8

Non-Agricultural Credit Society in 4 villages.
Others: Power supply in 58 villages, Cinema hall in 2 villages, sport club in 0 village, Stadium or Auditorium or Community Hall in 0 village, Post Office in 18 villages.
There are 43 villages having bus facilities.
Villages with most of facilities: Mavalli, Kaikini Shirali, Jali, Konar.
Villages without amenities (Education): Taggorgod, Bastigalamigte (Hadin), Behalli, Agga, Bastigalmigte (Koppa), Murkodi, Golibilur, Bilurmane, Voni Bagil, Devastan Megthe, Kurandur, Kerehittal, Bese, Kaggundi, Hejjil, Mugali..
Scheduled Castes: Out of the total population of 107196 persons, 12452 persons (11.62%) belong to Scheduled Castes.
The villages having less than 10% SC population are Bailur, Mavalli, Koppa, Taggorgod, Jali, Talgod Bastigalamigte (Hadin), Hadin, Chavathani, Purvarga Behalli, Mudbhatkal, Muttalli, Talan, Belalkhanda Kitre, Antravalli, Hudil, Badabag, Agga, Henjale Hallyani, Bastigalmigte (Koppa), Murkodi, Marukeri Kotkhanda, Hadeel, Golibilur, Yelavadikavoor, Herur Hadlur, Konar, Bilurmane, Hadavalli, Devastan Megthe Kurandur, Kulawadi, Aravakki, Kerehittal, Bese Hallari, Benandoor, Kaggundi, Hejjil, Kekkod, Mugali Nuz.
The village having more than 50% SC population is None.
Sex ratio of Scheduled Caste population is 506.
Scheduled Castes Literates and Illiterates by Sex:

	Persons	Males	Females
Literate	7,569	4,423	3,146
Illiterate	4,883	1,733	3,150
Literacy rate	68.9	81.6	56.6
Graduate	144	106	38

Scheduled Castes (Dominant):
Moger, Bakad, Halleer, Godda, Bakuda
For their cultural identity please see Appendix-I
Villages without Scheduled Castes: There are 27 villages without any scheduled caste population.
Scheduled Tribes: Out of the total population of 107196 persons, 7936 persons (7.4%) belong to Scheduled Tribes.
The villages having less than 10% ST population are Bailur, Mavalli, Kaikini, Bengre, Shirali, Heble Taggorgod, Karikal, Talgod, Mavinkurve, Belni Mundalli, Bastigalamigte (Hadin), Hadin, Chavathani Purvarga, Behalli, Mudbhatkal, Muttalli, Belalkhanda Badabag, Agga, Henjale, Bastigalmigte (Koppa) Murkodi, Yelavadikavoor, Gorte, Belke Devastan Megthe, Kurandur, Kulawadi, Aravakki Kerehittal, Hallari, Benandoor, Hejjil, Kekkod Mugali.
The villages having more than 50% ST population are Kitre, Hallyani, Marukeri, Hadlur, Bilurmane Voni Bagil.
Sex ratio of Scheduled tribe population is 500.
Scheduled Tribes Literates and Illiterates by Sex:

	Persons	Males	Females
Literate	3,898	2,263	1,635
Illiterate	4,038	1,705	2,333
Literacy rate	57.0	66.4	47.7
Graduate	29	27	2

Scheduled Tribes (Dominant):
Gond etc., Naikda etc., Hasalaru, Barda Generic Tribes etc.
For their cultural identity please see Appendix-II
Villages without Scheduled Tribes: There are 18 villages without any scheduled tribe population.
Literates and Illiterates by Sex (Total Population):

	Persons	Males	Females
Literate	62,668	34,899	27,769
Illiterate	44,528	17,834	26,694
Literacy rate	68	77	59
Graduate	1,645	1,154	491

Agriculture: ***Distribution of villages according to land use:*** Out of 60 villages, Total area (in hectare) is 33926, out of that 19.26 percent is cultivable and 12.21 percent of the cultivable area is irrigated.
Sources of Irrigation (Hectares): Government Canal 4, Private Canal 0.31, Well without Electricity 25.68, Well with Electricity 600.73, Tubewell without Electricity 0, Tubewell with Electricity 21.99, Tank 0, River 34.81, Lake 0, Waterfall 0, Others 114.43.
Villages with population of 5000 to 9999: Bailur, Kaikini, Bengre, Heble.
Villages with population of 10000 and above: Mavalli, Shirali.
Distribution of Workers:

	Persons	Males	Females	WPR
Cultivators	8,001	5,267	2,734	18.73
Agricultural Labour	6,356	1,570	4,786	14.88
Household Industry	389	222	167	0.91
Other Workers	27,979	21,617	6,362	65.49
Main Workers	30,793	25,207	5,586	72.07
Marginal Workers	11,932	3,469	8,463	27.93
Total Workers	42,725	28,676	14,049	

Religion: Major Religious Communities:

	Persons	Males	Females	Sex Ratio
Hindu (81.31%)	87,163	42,988	44,175	1,028
Muslim (15.77%)	16,910	8,128	8,782	1,080
Christian (2.72%)	2,921	1,514	1,407	929

Sikh (0%)	1	1	-	-
Buddhists (0.01%)	7	2	5	2,500
Jain (0.16%)	174	91	83	912

Agewise Data:

	Persons	Males	Females	Sex Ratio
All ages	107,196	52,733	54,463	1033
0-14	36,585	18,515	18,070	976
15-44	52,508	25,427	27,081	1065
45-79	17,441	8,503	8,938	1051
80+	613	264	349	1322
Age not stated	49	24	25	1042

Languages (Dominant):
Kannada, Urdu, Konkani, Marathi, Malayalam

Disabled Population:

	Persons	Males	Females	%
Total Disabled	2,207	1,191	1,016	
In Seeing	1,030	492	538	46.67
In Speech	260	134	126	11.78
In Hearing	90	44	46	4.08
In Movement	623	398	225	28.23
Mentally	204	123	81	9.24

BIDAR

Bidar C.D. Block lies in the eastern part of Bidar distr ict. It is a part of Bidar taluka. The Block is located at a distance of 00 kms. from district headquarters (Bidar). There are 134 villages in the block with the total population of 231,239 persons. Area of the C.D. Block is 857.19 sq. kms. It is bounded by taluk Aurad on north, taluk Homnabad on south, taluks Bhalki and Homnabad on west, and it has common boundary with the state of Andhra Pradesh on north and east.

Communications:

Roadways : N.H-9: Direction- Solapur to Hyderabad, Nearest Villages- Rekulgi, Bambalgi, Bapur, Magdal, Markunda, Bhangoor. S.H-4: Direction- Nanded to Zahirabad, Neare st Villages- Shahpur, Goonalli, Kapplapur (A), Chondi, Kolhar (K), Atwal. S.H-15: Direction- Aurad to Chincholi, Nearest Villages- Imampur, Janwada, Markhal, Zamistanp ur, Kamthana, Ayazpur, Yadlapur, Qutubabad, M. Mirzapur, Kasimpur (Pan), Kadwad, Kasimpur (Chitgoppa), Chatnalli, Bagdal, Indira Nagar, Bapur, Magdal. S.H-19: Direction- Gulbarga to Bidar, Nearest Villages- Kolhar (K), Andura, Khadernagar, Kolhar (B).

River: Manjra Nadi- Nearest Villages- Sangvi, Yarnhalli (Pahilwan), Bompalli, Yarnalli (Deshmukh), Islampur, Imampur, Hippalgaon, Chambool, Naulaspur, Sirimandal, Nematabad, Allapur, Janwada, Chimkod, Chillargi, Jampad, Ambalpad. Karanja Nadi: Nearest Villages- Ranjolkheni, Sangolgi, Nelwad, Baugi, Sirsi (A), Hochaknalli, Aurad (S), Bagdal, Bahirnalli, Nidwancha, Indira Nagar, Paterp alli, Barur, Dharmapur, Hokrana(B), Hokrana(K), Sindhol, Rekulgi, Bambalgi, Bapur, Magdal, Markunda, Bhangoor, Rajgera.

Reserved Forest: (Honnakheri): Nearest Villages- Gumtapur, Honnakheri, Chondi, Chouli, Kolhar (K), Atwal. (Chitta R.F.): Nearest Villages- Amlapur, Chitta, Kapplapur (A), Zamistanpur, Ayazpur, Qutubabad, Telang - Mirzapur, Ghodepalli. (Shahpur R.F.): Nearest Villages- Shahpur, Goonalli.

Annual Rainfall: Normal Rianfall 860 mm.

Ground Water: Availability of the Ground Water in the Basin is 6803.43 H.A.M. and the utilization is 7110. 60 H.A.M. It belongs to Over Exploited category. Depth to water level 10 to 20 meter below the ground. Most of the wells go down in summer months, according to the Ground Water Estimation Committee.

Soils: Black Soils and Lateritic Soils.

Natural Division : It falls partly in Manjra-Karanja Basin and Homnabad-Kamthana Lateritic Tract of the North ern Karnataka Plateau.

Administration:

Division: Gulbarga. Parliamentary Constituency: 7 Bidar (SC). District: Bidar. Taluka: Bidar. Assembly Constitue ncy: 49 Bidar South, 50 Bidar. Gram Panchayat: 33.

Regional Area Development Boards: The Hyderabad - Karnataka Area Development Board.

Border Villages: (State: A.P.)- Sirimandal, Nematabad, Allapur, Chimkod, Chillargi, Jampad, Ambalpad, Almaspur, Immamabad, Ashtoor, Sultanpur (J), Shahpur, Goonalli, Chitta, Ghodepalli, Manhalli, Barur, Dharmapur, Hokrana (B), Hokrana (K), Bhangoor, Rajgera.

Fairs: Ahmad Shah Wali Bahamani Urs: Ahmad Shah Wali Bahamani Urs, also called as "Adlama Prabhu Jatra" is held at Ashtoor for three days commencing on the twentie th of the month in which the Holi festival is held. Ashto or is about four kilometers east of Bidar town in the lowlands.

Baba Prabhu Jatra: It is held at Karkaknali in Bidar area in the month of March for five days every year. Karaknali is about 42 kms. south-east of Humnabad town, has the samadhi of Bakka Prabhu, a famed saint, and a temple dedicated to him. A Jatra is held for five days in March for paying homage to him.

Dattananda Maharaj Fair: It is held at Tajlapur in about the month of January for two days. Tajlapur, popularly called also as Dattanagar, is south-east of Bidar. There is a matha of Dattananda Swamiji and shrines of Ishvara (also called Dakshinamurthy) Hanuman and Ganesha.There is a small cave inside the matha which is said to contain the samadhis of Swami Dattananda Maharaj and his disciples. A fair is held in honour of Dattananda Maharaj for two days about January.

Mahadeva Temple Festival: Shamrajapur, which was formerly called Agrahara, is about two kilometres North of Bidar town. A large temple built here recently contains an impressive Anantshayana image of the Chalukyan period. The figure of Vishnu as Anantashayana is reclining on the couch of Adishesha, the primordial serpent. An image of Brahma with four faces is found sitting on a lotus that has emerged from the nabhi (navel) of Vishnu. On one of the prabhavalis of Vishnu, there are elegant carvings of the ten divine incarnations. At the end of the icon is goddess Lakshmi. An annual festival is held under the auspices of this temple for a day about the month of February. The place has also a shrine of Mahadeva.

Panduranga Fair: A fair is held at Sadhughat near Bidar for seven days around the month of March. Sadhughat situates about ten kms. south-west of Bidar town. There are shrines of Panduranga and Hanuman and two samadhis, one belonging to Eknath Maharaj and the other to Siddhu pant Maharaj. A fair is held here for seven days about March. Annual aradhana ceremony in honour of Siddhupant Maharaj takes place about October.

Shripatananda Atmananda Swamiji Jatra: It is held at Bagdal near Bidar around the month of July. Bagdal is about 24 kms. south-west of Bidar town. It has a shrine containing the samadhi (tomb) of a reputed saint named Shripatananda Atmananda Swamiji who is stated to have composed songs in several languages. In his honour, an annual jatra is held about July. There is a another shrine dedicated to Pandurana Maharaj under the auspices of which also a jatra takes place about September for three days every year.

Venkateshwara Jatra: It is held at Chintalgera about the month of January every year for two days. Chintalgera is at a distance of about 22 kms. south of Bidar town. Under the auspices of the local temple of Veerabhadra, an annual jatra is held here. On the hill closeby is situated a shrine of Venkateshwara, under the auspices of which an annual fair is held about January.

Villages: 134 **Inhabited:** 124 **Uninhabited:** 10

Ranking	District	State	National
Area	5	111	618
Population	3	57	358
Sex Ratio	5	144	3463
Child Sex Ratio	1	49	2246
Literacy Rate	5	131	3926
Density	5	174	3864
Work Participation Rate	1	37	4466

Gram Panchayats:
Yarnhalli (Pahilwan), Chambool, Chimkod, Chillargi, Janwada, Aliamber, Kaplapur(A), Aliabad , Markhal, Gadgi, Malegaon, Ashtoor, Kolhar (K), Andura, Sangolgi, Kamthana, Amlapur, Malkapur, Chitta, Yadlapur, Mandaknalli, Ranjolkheni, Sirsi (A), Kadwad, Nagora, Manhalli, Chatnalli, Aurad (S), Rekulgi, Bagdal, Markunda, Sindhole, Barur.

Amenities:

Education: Primary School in 122 villages, Middle school in 65 villages, Matriculation or Secondary School in 17 villages, namely Yarnhalli (Pahilwan), Chambool, Janwada, Gadgi, Malegaon, Kapplapur (A), Kolhar (K), Andura, Kamthana, Ranjolkheni, Kadwad, Aurad (S), Bagdal, Nidwancha, Manhalli, Rekulgi, Markunda.

Higher Secondary or Pre University Courses or Intermediate or Junior College in 5 villages of the CD Block,, namely Janwada, Chimkod, Kamthana, Bagdal, Manhalli. College in 0 village, Adult Literacy Center in 35 villages.

Medical: Hospital in 1 village, Dispensary in 7 villages, Health Center in 7 villages, Sub Center in 40 villages, Maternity and Child Welfare Center in 1 village, Community health workers in 18 villages.

The Villages having Hospital or Dispensary or Health Center are Chillargi, Gornalli(B), Honnakheri, Bagdal, Nidwancha, Yakatpur, Rekulgi.

Drinking Water: Tap water in 91 villages, Tank water in 43 villages, Well water in 117 villages, Tubewell in 107 villages and more than one source in 121 villages.

Bank: Banking facility in 20 villages, namely, Aliamber, Chambool, Sirimandal, Janwada, Chillargi Gadgi, Ashtoor, Chitta, Kapplapur (A), Atwal, Andura Kamthana, Ranjolkheni, Madaknalli, Sirkatnalli Bagdal, Nagora, Manhalli, Bambalgi, Rajgera.

Credit Society in 43 villages Agricultural Credit Society in 38 Non-Agricultural Credit Society in 15 villages.

Others: Power supply in 123 villages, Cinema hall in 1 village, sport club in 124 villages, Stadium or Auditorium or Communi Hall in 124 villages, Post Office in 52 villages.

There are 103 villages having bus facilities.

Villages with most of facilities: Aliamber Chambool, Sirimandal, Janwada, Chillargi, Gadgi Ashtoor, Chitta, Kapplapur (A), Andura, Kamthana Ranjolkheni, Madaknalli, Sirkatnalli, Bagdal, Nagora Manhalli, Bambalgi.

Villages without amenities (Education): Imampur, Chintalgera..

Scheduled Castes: Out of the total population of 231283 persons, 43508 persons (18.81%) belong to Scheduled Castes. The villages having less than 10% SC population are

Yarnalli (Deshmukh), Imampur, Chambool, Nematabad Mahamdapur, Daddapur, Fathepur, Malegaon, Hamilapur Shamrajapur, Tajlapur, Soupur, Immamabad Mirzapur Taj, Malkapur, Sultanpur (J), Kapplapur (A) Atwal, Kolhar (B), Bellura, Kamthana, Ranjolkheni Kasimpur (Pan), Aurad (S), Telang - Mirzapur Manhalli, Chintalgera, Sindhol.

The villages having more than 50% SC population are Chikpet, Sippalgeri, Kabirwada, Odwada, Honnakheri Indira Nagar, Gandhi Nagar.

Sex ratio of Scheduled Caste population is 483.

Scheduled Castes Literates and Illiterates by Sex:

	Persons	Males	Females
Literate	17,121	10,713	6,408
Illiterate	26,387	11,788	14,599
Literacy rate	47.8	57.7	37.1
Graduate	694	616	78

Scheduled Castes (Dominant):

Holaya etc., Madiga, Banjara etc., Bhovi, Mahar etc.

For their cultural identity please see Appendix-I

Villages without Scheduled Castes: There are 15 villages without any scheduled caste population.

Scheduled Tribes: Out of the total population of 231283 persons, 37451 persons (16.19%) belong to Scheduled Tribes.

The villages having less than 10% ST population are Siddapur, Sangvi, Yarnhalli (Pahilwan), Bompalli Rajnal, Sirimandal, Nematabad, Mahamdapur, Janwada Daddapur, Chikpet, Nawadgeri, Mamankeri, Sippalgeri Jampad, Hamilapur, Shamrajapur, Kabirwada, Odwada Tajlapur, Ghumma, Rasoolabad, Almaspur, Mirzapur Taj Malkapur, Amlapur, Honnakheri, Chouli, Andura Nizampur, Secundrapur, Bakchawadi, Bellura Zamistanpur, Yadlapur, Ranjolkheni, Nelwad, Baugi Madaknalli, Malik Mirzapur, Hochaknalli, Sirkatnalli Bagdal, Bahirnalli, Indira Nagar, Manhalli, Gouspur Barur, Dharmapur, Gandhi Nagar, Markunda, Bhangoor.

The villages having more than 50% ST population are None.

Sex ratio of Scheduled tribe population is 490.

Scheduled Tribes Literates and Illiterates by Sex:

	Persons	Males	Females
Literate	14,477	9,352	5,125
Illiterate	22,974	9,763	13,211
Literacy rate	46.5	58.6	33.7
Graduate	342	304	38

Scheduled Tribes (Dominant):

Gond etc., Koli Dhor etc., Generic Tribes etc.
Naikda etc., Chodhara

For their cultural identity please see Appendix-II

Villages without Scheduled Tribes: There are 22 villages without any scheduled tribe population.

Literates and Illiterates by Sex (Total Population):

	Persons	Males	Females
Literate	103,469	64,298	39,171
Illiterate	127,814	54,270	73,544
Literacy rate	54	65	42
Graduate	3,726	3,229	497

Agriculture: ***Distribution of villages according to land use:*** Out of 134 villages, Total area (in hectare) is 85719.77, out of that 65.55 percent is cultivable and 20.45 percent of the cultivable area is irrigated.

Sources of Irrigation (Hectares): Government Canal 269.77, Private Canal 134.23, Well without Electricity 259.98, Well witl Electricity 5122.79, Tubewell without Electricity 420.63, Tubewell with Electricity 4335.12, Tank 278.44, River 372.74, Lake 0, Waterfall 0, Others 296.23.

Villages with population of 5000 to 9999:
Janwada, Kamthana, Bagdal, Manhalli.

Villages with population of 10000 and above: None

Distribution of Workers:

	Persons	Males	Females	WPR
Cultivators	17,741	13,849	3,892	20.01
Agricultural Labour	39,223	19,294	19,929	44.25
Household Industry	1,913	1,175	738	2.16
Other Workers	29,769	24,046	5,723	33.58
Main Workers	69,810	50,336	19,474	78.75
Marginal Workers	18,836	8,028	10,808	21.25
Total Workers	88,646	58,364	30,282	

Religion: Major Religious Communities:

	Persons	Males	Females	Sex Ratio
Hindu (61.1%)	141,307	72,268	69,039	955
Muslim (22.92%)	53,004	27,317	25,687	940
Christian (6.88%)	15,919	8,138	7,781	956
Sikh (0.01%)	12	6	6	1,000
Buddhists (7.16%)	16,561	8,568	7,993	933
Jain (0.05%)	106	51	55	1,078

Agewise Data:

	Persons	Males	Females	Sex Ratio
All ages	231,283	118,568	112,715	951
0-14	91,040	46,172	44,868	972
15-44	98,044	51,417	46,627	907
45-79	39,386	19,616	19,770	1008
80+	2,311	1,087	1,224	1126
Age not stated	502	276	226	819

Languages (Dominant):
Kannada, Urdu, Telugu, Marathi, Hindi

Disabled Population:

	Persons	Males	Females	%
Total Disabled	4,177	2,420	1,757	
In Seeing	1,662	843	819	39.79

In Speech	436	233	203	10.44
In Hearing	171	98	73	4.09

In Movement	1,509	991	518	36.13
Mentally	399	255	144	9.55

BIJAPUR

Bijapur C.D. Block lies in the western part of Bijapur district. It is a part of Bijapur taluka. The Block is located at a distance of 00 kms. from district headquarters (Bijapur). There are 118 villages in the block with the total population of 315,574 persons. Area of the C.D. Block is 2560.57 sq. kms. It is bounded by taluk Indi on north, district Bagalkot on south, taluks Sindgi and Basavana Bagevadi on east, districts Belgaum and Bagalkot on west, and it hascommon boundary with the state of Maharashtra on north.

Communications:

Roadways : N.H-13: Direction- Solapur to Chitradurga, NearestVillages- Arakeri, Baratagi, Makanapur, Domanal, Bommanalli, Tidagundi, Kannal, Bijapur (Rural), Hittinahalli. N.H-218: Direction- Hubli to Bijapur, Nearest Villages- Mahal Bagayat , Jumnal, Honaganahalli, Karjol, Dudihal. S.H-12: Direction- Athni to Sindgi, Nearest Villages-Babanagar, Honawad, Tajapur(H), Tikota, Toravi, Ainapur, Buranpur, Madhabhavi, Tikota. Lalbahadur Shastrinagar, Kaggod, Mahatmagandhinagar, Indiranagar, Shivanagi, Hadagali, Kumatagi, Honnutagi, Kaulagi. S.H-12A: Direction- Jath to Bijapur, Nearest Villages- Kanamadi, Bijjaragi, Siddapur, Babanagar, S.H-65: Direction- Jamkhandi to Bijapur, Nearest Villages- Khatijapur, Bijapur (Rural), Sarawad, Babaleshwar, Arjunagi, Halagani, Yakkundi.

Railway Station: Villages- Minchinal, Ramnagar, Jumnal, Honaganahalli.

River: Don Nadi- Nearest Villages- Kanamadi, Bijjaragi, Babanagar, Honawad, Kotyal, Tajapur (H), Tikota, Kaggod, Kumatagi, Honnutagi, Kaulagi, Ukumanal, Bijapur (Rural), Hittinahalli, Katakanahalli, Dasyal, Dhanyal, Kanamuchanal, Sarawad, Honaganahalli, Savanalli, Tonsyal, Babaleshwar, Nidoni, Kakhandaki. Krishna Nadi- Nearest Villages- Babalad, Shirabur, Kanabur, Chikka-Galagali, Jambagi(H), Hosur, Sutagundi, Devara-Gennur, Lingadalli, Jainapur, Bellubbi, Hangaragi.

Annual Rainfall: Normal Rianfall 565 mm.

Ground Water: Availability of the Ground Water in the Basin is 13936.16 H.A.M. and the utilization is 7229.09 H.A.M. It belongs to Over Expoited category. Depth to water level 2 to 20 meter below the ground. Most of the wells go down in summer months, according to the Ground Water Estimation Committee.

Soils: Black Soils.

Natural Division : It falls partly in the Bijapur-Basavana Bagewadi Upland and Upper Krishna Valley of the Northern Karnataka Plateau.

Administration:

Division: Belgaum. Parliamentary Constituency: 4 Bijapur. District: Bijapur. Taluka: Bijapur. Assembly Constituency: 29 Babaleswar, 31 Naglhan (SC). Gram Panchayat: 46.

Regional Area Development Boards: The Bailu Seeme Area Development Board.

Border Villages: (State: Maharashtra)- Kanamadi, Bijjaragi, Alaginal, Gonasagi, Kallakavatagi, Hubanur, Indiranagar, Yatnal, Jalageri, Arakeri, Madasanal, Kannur, Shirnal.

Villages: 118 **Inhabited:** 118 **Uninhabited:** 0

Ranking	District	State	National
Area	1	2	33
Population	2	7	44
Sex Ratio	4	159	3813
Child Sex Ratio	2	140	3974
Literacy Rate	4	142	4403
Density	2	146	5921
Work Participation Rate	5	154	3422

Gram Panchayats:

Kanamadi, Bijjaragi, Gonasagi, Takkalaki, Jalageri, Arakeri, Baratagi, Lohagaon, Siddapur, Babanagar, Honawad, Kotyal, Tajapur(H), Tikota, Toravi, Kannur, Makanapur, Tidagundi, Gunaki, Nagathan, Aliyabad, Jambagi(A), Aheri(Bheri), Ainapur , Madhabhavi, Shivanagi, Hadagali, Honnutagi, Hittinahalli, Hegadihal, Kumathe, Sarawad, Honaganahalli, Babaleshwar, Nidoni, Arjunagi, Halagani, Kambagi, Kakhandaki, Karjol, Bolachikkalaki, Gunadal, Hosur, Devara-Gennur, Jainapur, Mamadapur.

Amenities:

Education: Primary School in 112 villages, Middle school in 108 villages, Matriculation or Secondary School in 48 villages, namely Kanamadi, Bijjaragi, Gonasagi, Kallakavatagi, Hubanur, Jalageri, Arakeri, Lohagaon, Sevalalnagar, Babanagar, Honawad, Tajapur(H), Tikota, Toravi, Navarasapur, Kannur, Domanal, Bommanalli, Tidagundi, Kannal, Gunaki, Minchinal, Ramnagar, Nagathan, Honnalli, Aheri(Bheri), Ainapur, Buranpur, Kaggod, Mahatmagandhinagar, Shivanagi, Hadagali, Honnutagi, Hittinahalli, Utnal, Katakanahalli, Hegadihal, Sarawad, Honaganahalli, Babaleshwar, Nidoni, Arjunagi, Halagani, Kakhandaki, Gunadal, Tajapur, Jainapur, Mamadapur.

Higher Secondary or Pre University Courses or Intermediate or Junior College in 5 villages of the CD Block,, namely Bijjaragi, Honawad, Tikota, Nagathan, Babaleshwar.

College in 2 villages, Adult Literacy Center in 21 villages., Colleges are in villages, namely Tikota, Babaleshwar.

Medical: Hospital in 2 villages, Dispensary in 8 villages, Health Center in 9 villages, Sub Center in 63 villages, Maternity and Child Welfare Center in 3 villages, Community health workers in 45 villages.

The Villages having Hospital or Dispensary or Health Center are Kanamadi, Dhanaragi, Tikota, Toravi, Navarasapur, Sarawad, Gunadal, Kanabur.

Drinking Water: Tap water in 82 villages, Tank water in 51 villages, Well water in 112 villages, Tubewell in 92 villages and more than one source in 117 villages.

Bank: Banking facility in 9 villages, namely, Kanamadi, Lohagaon, Honawad, Tikota, Nagathan Jambagi(A), Honnutagi, Sarawad, Kambagi.

Credit Society in 42 villages Agricultural Credit Society in 42 Non-Agricultural Credit Society in 2 villages.

Others: Power supply in 116 villages, Cinema hall in 1 village, sport club in 118 villages, Stadium or Auditorium or Community Hall in 118 villages, Post Office in 76 villages.

There are 111 villages having bus facilities.

Villages with most of facilities: Kanamadi Lohagaon, Honawad, Tikota, Nagathan, Jambagi(A) Honnutagi, Sarawad, Kambagi.

Villages without amenities (Education):
Narasimhanagar, Mahal Bagayat, Rajajinagar, Bijapur (Rural), Chintamaninagar, Hanchinal(Pm)..

Scheduled Castes: Out of the total population of 315457 persons, 73897 persons (23.43%) belong to Scheduled Castes.

The villages having less than 10% SC population are Alaginal, Babanagar, Honawad, Kotyal, Tajapur(H) Madasanal, Gunaki, Nagathan, Gugadaddi, Honnalli Rambhapur , Shivanagi, Katakanahalli, Sarawad Hokkundi, Nandyal, Madagunaki, Tajapur, Uppala-Dinni Hangaragi.

The villages having more than 50% SC population are Hubanur, Indiranagar, Jalageri, Baratagi Hanchinal(Ph), Sevalalnagar, Navarasapur Narasimhanagar, Makanapur, Ramnagar, Mahal Bagayat Rajajinagar, Lalbahadur Shastrinagar Mahatmagandhinagar, Indiranagar, Basavanagar.

Sex ratio of Scheduled Caste population is 486.

Scheduled Castes Literates and Illiterates by Sex:

	Persons	Males	Females
Literate	27,356	18,723	8,633
Illiterate	46,541	19,255	27,286
Literacy rate	44.7	59.5	29.0
Graduate	1,083	997	86

Scheduled Castes (Dominant):
Banjara etc., Holaya etc., Bhambi etc., Holar etc. Bhovi

For their cultural identity please see Appendix-I

Villages without Scheduled Castes: There are 0 village without any scheduled caste population.

Scheduled Tribes: Out of the total population of 315457 persons, 3725 persons (1.18%) belong to Scheduled Tribes.

The villages having less than 10% ST population are Kanamadi, Bijjaragi, Alaginal, Gonasagi Kallakavatagi, Hubanur, Indiranagar, Yatnal Takkalaki, Jalageri, Arakeri, Baratagi Hanchinal(Ph), Lohagaon, Sevalalnagar, Dhanaragi Siddapur, Babanagar, Honawad, Kotyal, Tajapur(H) Tikota, Navarasapur, Madasanal, Kannur, Shirnal Narasimhanagar, Makanapur, Domanal, Bommanalli Tidagundi, Kannal, Gunaki, Minchinal, Ramnagar Nagathan, Gugadaddi, Inganal, Aliyabad, Dyaberi Hunsyal, Honnalli, Jambagi(A), Aheri(Bheri) Mahal Bagayat , Khatijapur, Rambhapur , Ainapur Buranpur, Madhabhavi, Rajajinagar Lalbahadur Shastrinagar, Kaggod, Mahatmagandhinagar Ankalagi, Indiranagar, Shivanagi, Hadagali, Kumatagi Honnutagi, Kaulagi, Ukumanal, Bijapur (Rural) Jumnal, Hittinahalli, Katakanahalli, Basavanagar Kumathe, Nagaral, Dasyal, Dhanyal, Sarawad Honaganahalli, Savanalli, Tonsyal, Babaleshwar Nidoni, Arjunagi, Hokkundi, Tiganibidare, Halagani Yakkundi, Katral, Nandyal, Kambagi, Madagunaki Shegunashi, Kakhandaki, Karjol, Dudihal Bolachikkalaki, Gunadal, Kengalagutti, Babalad Shirabur, Kanabur, Chikka-Galagali, Jambagi(H) Hosur, Sutagundi, Devara-Gennur, Devapur, Kodabagi Tajapur, Lingadalli, Jainapur, Mangalur Hanchinal(Pm), Mamadapur, Uppala-Dinni, Bellubbi Hangaragi.

The villages having more than 50% ST population are None.

Sex ratio of Scheduled tribe population is 472.

Scheduled Tribes Literates and Illiterates by Sex:

	Persons	Males	Females
Literate	1,053	727	326
Illiterate	2,672	1,240	1,432
Literacy rate	34.5	44.5	23.0
Graduate	28	27	1

Scheduled Tribes (Dominant):
Naikda etc., Kadu Kuruba, Koli Dhor etc. Jenu Kuruba, Pardhi etc.

For their cultural identity please see Appendix-II

Villages without Scheduled Tribes: There are 65 villages without any scheduled tribe population.

Literates and Illiterates by Sex (Total Population):

	Persons	Males	Females
Literate	134,104	86,059	48,045

Illiterate	181,353	76,212	105,141
Literacy rate	51	63	37
Graduate	5,399	4,797	602

Agriculture: ***Distribution of villages according to land use:*** Out of 118 villages, Total area (in hectare) is 256057, out of that 91.76 percent is cultivable and 12.63 percent of the cultivable area is irrigated.

Sources of Irrigation (Hectares): Government Canal 362.4, Private Canal 526.39, Well without Electricity 0, Well with Electricity 13431.05, Tubewell without Electricity 0, Tubewell with Electricity 12221.61, Tank 1268.82, River 1852.88, Lake 0, Waterfall 0, Others 6.13.

Villages with population of 5000 to 9999:
Kanamadi, Bijjaragi, Jalageri, Arakeri, Honawad Tajapur(H), Kannur, Nagathan, Shivanagi, Sarawad Nidoni, Kakhandaki.

Villages with population of 10000 and above:
Tikota, Babaleshwar.

Distribution of Workers:

	Persons	Males	Females	WPR
Cultivators	50,687	38,321	12,366	37.09
Agricultural Labour	61,223	27,172	34,051	44.8
Household Industry	3,216	2,141	1,075	2.35
Other Workers	21,525	17,410	4,115	15.75
Main Workers	101,422	73,869	27,553	74.22
Marginal Workers	35,229	11,175	24,054	25.78
Total Workers	136,651	85,044	51,607	

Religion: Major Religious Communities:

	Persons	Males	Females	Sex Ratio
Hindu (88.88%)	280,373	144,412	135,961	941
Muslim (10.44%)	32,944	16,743	16,201	968
Christian (0.06%)	183	100	83	830
Sikh (0%)	8	4	4	1,000
Buddhists (0.08%)	264	138	126	913
Jain (0.39%)	1,222	638	584	915

Agewise Data:

	Persons	Males	Females	Sex Ratio
All ages	315,457	162,271	153,186	944
0-14	116,562	60,445	56,117	928
15-44	135,998	70,840	65,158	920
45-79	59,207	29,288	29,919	1022
80+	3,216	1,440	1,776	1233
Age not stated	474	258	216	837

Languages (Dominant):
Kannada, Urdu, Hindi, Marathi, Telugu

Disabled Population:

	Persons	Males	Females	%
Total Disabled	8,500	5,151	3,349	
In Seeing	5,128	3,189	1,939	60.33
In Speech	688	364	324	8.09
In Hearing	293	138	155	3.45
In Movement	1,669	1,041	628	19.64
Mentally	722	419	303	8.49

BILGI

Bilgi C.D. Block lies in the north-eastern part of Bagalkot district. It is a part of Bilgi taluka. The Block is located at a distance of 25 kms. from district headquarters (Bagalkot). There are 71 villages in the block with the total population of 126,379 persons. Area of the C.D. Block is 787.72 sq. kms.It is bounded by taluk Jamkhandi and district Bijapur on north, taluk Bagalkot on south and east, taluks Jamkhandi and Mudhol on west.

Communications:

Roadways : N.H-218: Direction- Kerur to Bijapur, Nearest Villages- Bilgi (Rural), Korti, Badagandi, Sunaga, Mannikeri, Tummarmatti, Anagawadi.

River: Krishna Nadi- Nearest Villages- Galagali, Rabkavi, Chowdapur,Chickhanchinal, Kolur, Mundaganur, Yadahalli, Gulbal, Budihal(S.G.), Badgi, Girgaon, Gudadinni, Hanchinal (Inam), Ballur, Kontikal, Sonna, Dhawaleshwar, Garadadinni, Korti, Govinadinni, Takkalki, Rolli, Gundanapalli, Heggur, Lingapur S.R, Godihal, Chinvalkoppa, Muttaladinni, Koppa S.R, Hadarihal, Beerkabbi, Kamadal, Mangur, Chicksangam.
Ghatprabha Nadi- Nearest Villages- Algundi, Koppa (S.K), Katarki, Lingapur (S.K), Shiraguppi, Beerkabbi, Kamadal, Mangur, Chicksangam, Kandagal, Honnihal, Badardinni, Yettinatti, Herkal, Venkatapura, Kundargi, Bavalatti, Kovalli, Budhihal(S.H), Anagawadi.

Canal: Nearest Villages- Amalzari, Rabkavi, Chowdapur, Yadahalli, Gulbal, Bisnal, Shivanagar, Ramapratappa Nagar, Nagaral, Siddapur, Teggi, Bilgi (Rural), Badagandi, Rolli, Algundi, Koppa (S.K), Katarki, Lingapur(S.K), Shiraguppi, Durgapura, Janamatti, Sunaga , Mannikeri, Girisagar, Muttaladinni, Koppa S.R, Honnihal, Herkal, Tolamatti Tummarmatti, Dattapura, Venkatapura, Kundargi, Bavalatti, Kovalli.

Reserved Forest: Nearset Villages- Amalzari, Yadahalli, Gulbal, Bisnal, Shaktinagar, Shivanagar, Ramapratappa Nagar, Teggi, Bilgi (Rural), Arakeri, Durgapura, Janamatti, Sunaga, Herkal, Tolamatti, Tummarmatti, Dattapura, Bavalatti, Kovalli, Anagawadi, Kadapatti, Yelligutti.

Annual Rainfall: Normal Rianfall 468.4 mm.

Ground Water: Availability of the Ground Water in the Basin is (Information not avablable) H.A.M. and the utilization is (Information not avablable) H.A.M. It belongs to (Information not avablable) category. Depth to water level 5 to 20 meter below the ground.Most of the wells go down in summer months, according to the Ground Water Estimation Committee.

Natural Division : It falls partly in the Upper Krishna Valley and the Ghatprabha Irrigated Tract of the Northern Karnataka Plateau.

Soils: Black and Red Soils.

Administration:

Division: Belgaum. Parliamentary Constituency: 3 Bagalkot. District: Bagalkot. Taluka: Bilgi. Assembly Constituency: 22 Bilgi, 24 Bagalkot. Gram Panchayat: 20.

Regional Area Development Boards: The Bailu Seeme Area Development Board.

Villages: 71 **Inhabited:** 69 **Uninhabited:** 2

Ranking	District	State	National
Area	6	125	750
Population	6	147	2632
Sex Ratio	3	39	1397
Child Sex Ratio	3	115	3390
Literacy Rate	6	152	4717
Density	2	67	5404
Work Participation Rate	5	117	1664

Gram Panchayats:

Galagali, Kolur, Yadahalli, Siddapur, Teggi, Badgi, Hanchinal(Inam), Sonna, Korti, Heggur, Algundi, Katarki, Arakeri, Sunaga , Girisagar, Kandagal, Honnihal, Herkal, Kundargi, Anagawadi,.

Amenities:

Education: Primary School in 66 villages, Middle school in 54 villages, Matriculation or Secondary School in 11 villages, namely Galagali, Siddapur, Teggi, Korti, Badagandi, Algundi, Sunaga, Girisagar, Herkal, Kundargi, Anagawadi.

Higher Secondary or Pre University Courses or Intermediate or Junior College in 11 villages of the CD Block,, namely Galagali, Shivanagar, Siddapur, Teggi, Badagandi, Algundi, Sunaga, Girisagar, Herkal, Kundargi, Anagawadi.

College in 2 villages, Adult Literacy Center in 8 villages., Colleges are in villages, namely Algundi, Kundargi.

Medical: Hospital in 1 village, Dispensary in 8 villages, Health Center in 4 villages, Sub Center in 21 villages, Maternity and Child Welfare Center in 4 villages, Community health workers in 23 villages.

The Villages having Hospital or Dispensary or Health Center are Galagali, Rabkavi, Teggi, Arakeri, Mannikeri, Girisagar, Kundargi, Anagawadi.

Drinking Water: Tap water in 38 villages, Tank water in 49 villages, Well water in 17 villages, Tubewell in 22 villages and more than one source in 64 villages.

Bank: Banking facility in 7 villages, namely, Amalzari, Galagali, Katarki, Sunaga, Girisagar Kundargi, Anagawadi.

Credit Society in 15 villages Agricultural Credit Society in 15 Non-Agricultural Credit Society in 1 village.

Others: Power supply in 68 villages, Cinema hall in 1 village, sport club in 0 village, Stadium or Auditorium or Community Hall in 0 village, Post Office in 36 villages.

There are 58 villages having bus facilities.

Villages with most of facilities: Amalzari Galagali, Katarki, Sunaga, Girisagar, Kundargi Anagawadi.

Villages without amenities (Education):
Chinvalkoppa, Kamadal, Mangur..

Scheduled Castes: Out of the total population of 126542 persons, 22681 persons (17.92%) belong to Scheduled Castes.

The villages having less than 10% SC population are Budihal(S.G.), Bisnal, Nagaral, Teggi, Ballur Dhawaleshwar, Garadadinni, Takkalki, Rolli Lingapur.S.R, Algundi, Lingapur(S.K), Shiraguppi Hadarihal, Yettinatti, Tolamatti, Yelligutti.

The villages having more than 50% SC population are Shaktinagar, Shivanagar, Ramapratappa Nagar Durgapura, Dattapura, Venkatapura.

Sex ratio of Scheduled Caste population is 510.

Scheduled Castes Literates and Illiterates by Sex:

	Persons	Males	Females
Literate	6,577	4,407	2,170
Illiterate	16,104	6,712	9,392
Literacy rate	35.8	49.1	23.1
Graduate	143	132	11

Scheduled Castes (Dominant):

Bhambi etc., Banjara etc., Holaya etc., Madiga Chalavadi etc.

For their cultural identity please see Appendix-I

Villages without Scheduled Castes: There are 6 villages without any scheduled caste population.

Scheduled Tribes: Out of the total population of 126542 persons, 13592 persons (10.74%) belong to Scheduled Tribes.

The villages having less than 10% ST population are Amalzari, Galagali, Rabkavi, Chickhanchinal, Kolur Mundaganur, Gulbal, Budihal(S.G.), Shaktinagar Shivanagar, Ramapratappa Nagar, Badgi, Girgaon Ballur, Kontikal, Sonna, Dhawaleshwar, Garadadinni Bilgi (Rural), Korti, Govinadinni, Badagandi Takkalki, Rolli, Gundanapalli, Heggur, Lingapur.S.R Chinvalkoppa, Koppa(S.K), Katarki, Durgapura Mannikeri, Girisagar, Muttaladinni, Koppa S.R Beerkabbi, Kamadal, Mangur, Kandagal, Honnihal Badardinni, Yettinatti, Tolamatti, Tummarmatti Dattapura, Venkatapura, Kundargi, Bavalatti Budhihal(S.H), Anagawadi, Kadapatti.

The villages having more than 50% ST population are

None.

Sex ratio of Scheduled tribe population is 503.

Scheduled Tribes Literates and Illiterates by Sex:

	Persons	Males	Females
Literate	3,895	2,656	1,239
Illiterate	9,697	4,093	5,604
Literacy rate	34.9	48.1	22.0
Graduate	83	80	3

Scheduled Tribes (Dominant):

Naikda etc., Koli Dhor etc., Generic Tribes etc.
Kadu Kuruba, Barda

For their cultural identity please see Appendix-II

Villages without Scheduled Tribes: There are 23 villages without any scheduled tribe population.

Literates and Illiterates by Sex (Total Population):

	Persons	Males	Females
Literate	51,525	33,332	18,193
Illiterate	75,017	30,141	44,876
Literacy rate	49	63	35
Graduate	1,583	1,427	156

Agriculture: ***Distribution of villages according to land use:*** Out of 71 villages, Total area (in hectare) is 78772, out of that 69.66 percent is cultivable and 43.15 percent of the cultivable area is irrigated.

Sources of Irrigation (Hectares): Government Canal 14045.24, Private Canal 470.54, Well without Electricity 131.19, Well with Electricity 1245.22, Tubewell without Electricity 12.07, Tubewell with Electricity 4232.67, Tank 31.97, River 2403.21, Lake 0.8, Waterfall 0, Others 1105.81.

Villages with population of 5000 to 9999:
Galagali, Girisagar.

Villages with population of 10000 and above: None

Distribution of Workers:

	Persons	Males	Females	WPR
Cultivators	20,271	14,275	5,996	32.18
Agricultural Labour	30,786	12,169	18,617	48.88
Household Industry	1,854	1,085	769	2.94
Other Workers	10,074	7,576	2,498	15.99
Main Workers	48,500	30,904	17,596	77
Marginal Workers	14,485	4,201	10,284	23
Total Workers	62,985	35,105	27,880	

Religion: Major Religious Communities:

	Persons	Males	Females	Sex Ratio
Hindu (90.97%)	115,111	57,703	57,408	995
Muslim (8.58%)	10,851	5,487	5,364	978
Christian (0.03%)	36	16	20	1,250
Sikh (0.02%)	23	13	10	769
Buddhists (0.02%)	29	18	11	611
Jain (0.03%)	44	23	21	913

Agewise Data:

	Persons	Males	Females	Sex Ratio
All ages	126,542	63,473	63,069	994
0-14	46,646	23,677	22,969	970
15-44	56,701	28,655	28,046	979
45-79	22,139	10,738	11,401	1062
80+	970	355	615	1732
Age not stated	86	48	38	792

Languages (Dominant):
Kannada, Urdu, Hindi, Marathi, Telugu

Disabled Population:

	Persons	Males	Females	%
Total Disabled	2,911	1,552	1,359	
In Seeing	1,571	772	799	53.97
In Speech	213	111	102	7.32
In Hearing	180	88	92	6.18
In Movement	721	453	268	24.77
Mentally	226	128	98	7.76

BYADGI

Byadgi C.D. Block lies in the central south part of Haveri district. It is a part of Byadgi taluka. The Block is located at a distance of 16 kms. from district headquarters (Haveri). There are 66 villages in the block with the total population of 102,221 persons. Area of the C.D. Block is 433.14 sq. kms. It is bounded by taluk Haveri on north, taluk Hirekerur on south,

Communications:

Roadways : N.H-4: Direction- Hubli to Bangalore, Nearest Villages- Gundenahalli, Kadamanahalli, Motebennur, Chattra.

Railway Station: Villages- Motebennur, Byadgi (Rural).

Annual Rainfall: Normal Rianfall 592 mm.

Ground Water: Availability of the Ground Water in the Basin is 30.83 MCM and the utilization is 37.04 MCM It belongs to Over Exploited category. Depth to water level 10 to 20 meter below the ground. Most of the wells go down in summer months, according to the Ground Water Estimation Committee.

Soils: Red Sandy Soil, Medium Soil, Deep Black Soil, Red Loamy Soil and Lateritic Soil.

Natural Division : It falls partly in Barad Basin and Byadagi-Hirekerur Rocky Knobs of the Central Karnataka Plateau.

Administration:

Division: Belgaum. Parliamentary Constituency: 10 Haveri. District: Haveri. Taluka: Byadgi. Assembly Constituency: 85 Bayadgi. Gram Panchayat: 20.

Regional Area Development Boards: The Maland Aera Development Board.

Villages: 66 **Inhabited:** 64 **Uninhabited:** 2

Ranking	District	State	National
Area	7	168	1754

Population	7	160	3394
Sex Ratio	3	162	3851
Child Sex Ratio	4	40	2019
Literacy Rate	2	33	1242
Density	2	75	4244
Work Participation Rate	5	51	1848

Gram Panchayats:
Kaginelli, Hedigonda, Mallur, Motebennur, Gundenahalli, Kalledvar, Budapanahalli, Masangi, Kerawadi, Kummur, Hirehalli, Chikkabasur, Ghalapuji, Sudambi, Hireanaji, Tadas, Shidenur, Bannihatti, Kadaramandalagi, Bisalahalli.

Amenities:
Education: Primary School in 60 villages, Middle school in 53 villages, Matriculation or Secondary School in 18 villages, namely Kaginelli, Hedigonda, Chikkabasur, Masanagi, Kerawadi, Ghalapuji, Guddada Mallapur, Sudambi, Hireanaji, Gundenahalli, Kalledevar, Motebennur, Mallur, Kadaramandalagi, Shidenur, Lakamaji Koppa, Anur, Bisalahalli.
Higher Secondary or Pre University Courses or Intermediate or Junior College in 4 villages of the CD Block,, namely Chikkabasur, Motebennur, Shidenur, Bisalahalli.
College in 0 village, Adult Literacy Center in 0 village.
Medical: Hospital in 0 village, Dispensary in 3 villages, Health Center in 4 villages, Sub Center in 22 villages, Maternity and Child Welfare Center in 0 village, Community health workers in 6 villages.
The Villages having Hospital or Dispensary or Health Center are Budapanahalli, Kadaramandalagi, Anur.
Drinking Water: Tap water in 46 villages, Tank water in 10 villages, Well water in 0 village, Tubewell in 37 villages and more than one source in 56 villages.
Bank: Banking facility in 9 villages, namely, Kaginelli, Chikkabasur, Sudambi, Tadas, Motebennur Mallur, Kadaramandalagi, Shidenur, Shivajinagar.
Credit Society in 12 villages Agricultural Credit Society in 10 Non-Agricultural Credit Society in 3 villages.
Others: Power supply in 61 villages, Cinema hall in 0 village, sport club in 0 village, Stadium or Auditorium or Community Hall in 0 village, Post Office in 21 villages.
There are 57 villages having bus facilities.
Villages with most of facilities: Kaginelli Chikkabasur, Sudambi, Tadas, Motebennur, Mallur Kadaramandalagi, Shidenur.
Villages without amenities (Education): Sevanagar, Shivapur, Shivajinagar..
Scheduled Castes: Out of the total population of 102281 persons, 11726 persons (11.46%) belong to Scheduled Castes.
The villages having less than 10% SC population are Kaginelli, Bannihalli, Ingalagondi, Kasambi Chikkabasur, Hirehalli, Kummur, Thippalapur Masanagi, Angaragatti, Hirenandihalli, Chinnikatti Muttur, Beeranakoppa, Ghalapuji, Attikatti Guddada Mallapur, Thimmapur, Sudambi, Hireanaji Gundenahalli, Kadamanahalli, Kengond, Kalledevar Alalageri, Khurdha Kodihalli, Shankripura, Mallur Gummanahalli, Ramgondanahalli, Belakeri, Bannihatti Timmenahalli.
The village having more than 50% SC population is None.
Sex ratio of Scheduled Caste population is 471.
Scheduled Castes Literates and Illiterates by Sex:

	Persons	Males	Females
Literate	5,211	3,467	1,744
Illiterate	6,515	2,732	3,783
Literacy rate	52.2	65.1	37.5
Graduate	115	102	13

Scheduled Castes (Dominant):
Bhambi etc., Banjara etc., Bhovi, Madiga, Korama
For their cultural identity please see Appendix-I
Villages without Scheduled Castes: There are 4 villages without any scheduled caste population.
Scheduled Tribes: Out of the total population of 102281 persons, 14399 persons (14.08%) belong to Scheduled Tribes.
The villages having less than 10% ST population are Kaginelli, Ingalagondi, Dasanakoppa, Chikkabasur Nellikoppa, Masanagi, Kerawadi, Chinnikatti Chikkalli, Sudambi, Dhulikoppa, Chikkanaji Gundenahalli, Sevanagar, Shivapur, Khurdha Kodihalli Mallur, Chattra, Gummanahalli, Ramgondanahalli Lakamaji Koppa, Kollapur, Shivajinagar, Katenahalli Timmenahalli.
The villages having more than 50% ST population are None.
Sex ratio of Scheduled tribe population is 484.
Scheduled Tribes Literates and Illiterates by Sex:

	Persons	Males	Females
Literate	7,391	4,667	2,724
Illiterate	7,008	2,760	4,248
Literacy rate	59.4	72.3	45.4
Graduate	190	177	13

Scheduled Tribes (Dominant):
Naikda etc., Koraga, Kadu Kuruba, Meda
For their cultural identity please see Appendix-II
Villages without Scheduled Tribes: There are 9 villages without any scheduled tribe population.
Literates and Illiterates by Sex (Total Population):

	Persons	Males	Females

Literate	61,509	36,607	24,902
Illiterate	40,772	16,034	24,738
Literacy rate	70	80	58
Graduate	1,633	1,435	198

Agriculture: ***Distribution of villages according to land use:*** Out of 66 villages, Total area (in hectare) is 43314, out of that 78.13 percent is cultivable and 11.66 percent of the cultivable area is irrigated.

Sources of Irrigation (Hectares): Government Canal 0, Private Canal 0, Well without Electricity 0, Well with Electricity 0, Tubewell without Electricity 0, Tubewell with Electricity 2665.59, Tank 1026.79, River 0, Lake 0, Waterfall 0, Others 0.

Villages with population of 5000 to 9999: Motebennur, Kadaramandalagi.

Villages with population of 10000 and above: None

Distribution of Workers:

	Persons	Males	Females	WPR
Cultivators	20,993	15,604	5,389	40.21
Agricultural Labour	24,883	10,273	14,610	47.66
Household Industry	1,029	620	409	1.97
Other Workers	5,301	4,464	837	10.15
Main Workers	37,020	26,701	10,319	70.91
Marginal Workers	15,186	4,260	10,926	29.09
Total Workers	52,206	30,961	21,245	

Religion: Major Religious Communities:

	Persons	Males	Females	Sex Ratio
Hindu (87.5%)	89,493	46,148	43,345	939
Muslim (11.46%)	11,725	5,957	5,768	968
Christian (0.24%)	249	135	114	844
Sikh (0.01%)	10	6	4	667
Buddhists (0%)	2	1	1	1,000
Jain (0.55%)	562	271	291	1,074

Agewise Data:

	Persons	Males	Females	Sex Ratio
All ages	102,281	52,641	49,640	943
0-14	33,598	17,317	16,281	940
15-44	48,923	25,446	23,477	923
45-79	18,925	9,530	9,395	986
80+	785	309	476	1540
Age not stated	50	39	11	282

Languages (Dominant):
Kannada, Urdu, Hindi, Coorgi/Kodagu, Marathi

Disabled Population:

	Persons	Males	Females	%
Total Disabled	1,573	864	709	
In Seeing	668	345	323	42.47
In Speech	146	85	61	9.28
In Hearing	66	40	26	4.2
In Movement	506	293	213	32.17
Mentally	187	101	86	11.89

CHALLAKERE

Challakere C.D. Block lies in the northern part of Chitr adurga district. It is a part of Challakere taluka. The Block is located at a distance of 29 kms. from district headquarters (Chitradurga). There are 195 villages in the block with the total population of 275,757 persons. Area of the C.D. Block is 2036.74 sq. kms. It is bounded by taluk Molakalmuru and district Bellary on north, taluk Hiriyur on south, district Tumkur on east, district Davanagere, and taluk Chitradurga on west. It has common boundary with the state of A.P.on south and east.

Communications:

Roadways : S.H-19: Direction- Hiriyur to Molakalmuru, Nearest Villages- Hirehalli, Obannanahalli Kaval, Manne kote, Thalaku, Giriyammanahalli, Chikkaammanahalli, Budnahatti, Nagaramgere, Siddapura, Lakshmipura, Kammathmarikunte, Hotteppanahalli, Mummadisagara (B), Sanikere, Heggere.

S.H-48: Direction- Chitradurga to Pavagada, Nearest Villages- Nannivala, Challakere(Rural), Vidupanakunte, Meerasabihalli, Bommasamudra, Dodderi, Nagaramgere, Kurudihalli, Ramajogihalli, Balenahalli, Nandanahalli, Dyavaranahalli, Purlahalli, Suranahalli, Chowluru, Viswanathapura, Parasuramapura, Gowripura, Pillahalli, Siddheswaranadurga, Mahadevapura, Parashuramapura Kaval, Kyadigunte.

Railway Station: Village- Balenahalli.

River:;Garani Halla Nadi- Nearest Villages- Kaluvehalli, Kyatagondanahalli, Yadalagatta, Bharamasagara, Rangavv anahalli, Visweswarapura, Karikere, Vidupanakunte, Meeras abihalli, Dodderi, Chikkamadhure, Hiremadhure, Sevalalnag ar, Kammathmarikunte, Re.Halli, Gopanahalli, Mummadisag ara (B), Sanikere, Ganjigunte, Lakumagondanahalli, Nagago ndanahalli. Vedavati Nadi- Nearest Villages- Bhoganahalli, Basapura, Renukapura, Mylanahalli, Gudihalli, Kasavigon danahalli, Thappagondanahalli, Katamdevarakote, Donehalli Kaval, Vaderahalli, Bomberahalli, Devara Marikunte, Nallurahalli, Lakumagondanahalli, Moduru Kaval, Moduru, Jajuru Kaval, Jajur, Nagagondanahalli, Haligondanahalli, Haravigondanahalli, Pagadalabande, Bommanakunte, Junjar agunte, Chattekamba, Matasamudra, Chanammanagathihalli, Suranahalli, Chowluru, Viswanathapura, Parasuramapura, Gosikere Kaval, Gosikere, Konigarahalli Kaval, Konigara halli, Yalagatta, Belagere, Kyathanamale, Kalamarahalli, Gorlathu, Torebeeranahalli.

Annual Rainfall: Normal Rianfall 568.3 mm.

Ground Water: Availability of the Ground Water in the Basin is 10879.45 H.A.M. and the utilization is 11970. 98 H.A.M. It belongs to Over Expoited category. Depth to water level 2 to 20 meter below the ground. Most of the wells go down in summer months, according to the Ground Water Estimation Committee.

Soils: Deep and Shallow black soils, mixed red and black soil, red loamy and sandy soils.

Natural Division : It falls in Middle Vedavati (Hagari) Basin of the Central Karnataka Plateau.

Administration:

Division: Bangalore. Parliamentary Constituency: 18 Chitradurga (SC). District: Chitradurga. Taluka: Challak ere. Assembly Constituency: 98 Challakere (ST), 99 Chitra durga, 102 Holalkere (SC). Gram Panchayat: 36.

Regional Area Development Boards: The Bailu Seeme Area Development Board.

Border Villages: (State: A. P.)- Bandethimmalapura, Mallasamudra, Devarahalli, Bhoganahalli, Basapura, Renukapura, Katamdevarakote, Donehalli Kaval, Obalapura Kaval, Obalapura, Chikkabadihalli, Doddabadihalli, Doneh alli, Thippareddyhalli, Jajuru Kaval, Pagadalabande, Pagadalabande Kaval, Putloorahalli Kaval, Korlakunte, Gowripura, Pillahalli, Siddheswaranadurga, Doddachellur, Kadegude, Kyadigunte.

Fairs: Maremma Jatra: The jatra is held at Goura samudra in Challakere taluk of Chitradurga area, in the month at Bhadrapad (August-September). This jatra is quite famous and a large volume of business is transacted during this jatra.

Tipperudraswamy Car Festival: It is held for three days in the month of Phalguna (March) at Nayakanahatti near Challakere taluk, of Chitradurga. Nayakanhatti formerly called Hatti, the place is situated about 20 kms. north-west of Challakere. The place contains a celebrated tomb and a temple dedicated to a great saint of the Lingayats, named Tippe Rudrayya, who is said to have lived about 250 years ago and wrought miracles. He is also said to have become the spiritual preceptor of the Hatti Paleyagars. The large sums of money bestowed upon him by the faithful were devoted to the elargement and repair of tanks, and for other works of public benefit, which endeared him to the people. An annual festival is held in honour of the sant, which attracts a large number of people. The place has a big tank, perhaps one of the biggest in the district, with a fine broad bund said to have been built by the saint.

Villages: 195 **Inhabited:** 185 **Uninhabited:** 10

Ranking	District	State	National
Area	1	5	48
Population	1	23	105
Sex Ratio	4	136	3275
Child Sex Ratio	3	120	3536
Literacy Rate	5	119	3579
Density	2	43	5712
Work Participation Rate	5	142	1333

Gram Panchayats:

Abbaiahnahalli, Mallurahalli, Hirehalli, Gowrasamudra, Devareddyhalli, Renukapura, Obalapura, Mylanahalli, Ghataparthi, Byadareddyhalli, Mannekote, Thalaku, Thimmappaiahnahalli, Mahadevapura, Naikanahatti, Gowdagere, Nelagetanahatti, Neralagunte, Budnahatti, Doddaullarthi, Jajur, Pagadalabande, Channammanagathihalli, Meerasabihalli, Dodderi, Nagaramgere , Somaguddu, Nannivala, Ramajogihalli, Sanikere, Gopanahalli, Devara Marikunte, Chowluru, Parasuramapura, Mahadevapura, Siddheswaranadurga, Doddachellur, Thimmannanayakanakote, Belagere.

Amenities:

Education: Primary School in 164 villages, Middle school in 134 villages, Matriculation or Secondary School in 50 villages, namely Torekolammanahalli, Abbaiahnahalli, Mustalagummi, Mallurahalli, Naikanahatti, Mahadevapura, Thimmappaiahnahalli, Nelagetanahatti, Hirehalli, Hanumanthanahalli, Gowrasamudra, Devareddyhalli, Byadareddyhalli, Ghataparthi, Renukapura, Chitranayakanahalli, Thimmannanahalli, Thalaku, Doddaullarthi, Kaluvehalli, Obalapura, Thippareddyhalli, Nannivala, Meerasabihalli, Nagaramgere, Siddapura, Somaguddu, Ramajogihalli, Balenahalli, Hiremadhure, Devara Marikunte, Gopanahalli, Sanikere, Kaparahalli, Jajur, Pagadalabande, Junjaragunte, Channammanagathihalli, Suranahalli, Chowluru, Parasuramapura, Siddheswaranadurga, Mahadevapura, Gosikere, Belagere, Hulikunte, Kalamarahalli, Thimmannanayakanakote, Doddachellur, Kyadigunte.

Higher Secondary or Pre University Courses or Intermediate or Junior College in 11 villages of the CD Block,, namely Naikanahatti, Byadareddyhalli, Renukapura, Thalaku, Meerasabihalli, Siddapura, Gopanahalli, Parasuramapura, Belagere, Thimmannanayakanakote, Kyadigunte.

College in 3 villages, Adult Literacy Center in 0 village., Colleges are in villages, namely Naikanahatti, Meerasabihalli, Parasuramapura.

Medical: Hospital in 7 villages, Dispensary in 20 villages, Health Center in 13 villages, Sub Center in 34 villages, Maternity and Child Welfare Center in 4 villages, Community health workers in 3 villages.

The Villages having Hospital or Dispensary or Health Center are Abbaiahnahalli, Mallurahalli,

Thimmappaiahnahalli, Thippaiahnakote, Hirehalli, Mallasamudra, Ghataparthi, Chennaganahalli, Doddaullarthi, Obalapura, Nannivala, Challakere(Rural), Meerasabihalli, Hiremadhure, Parasuramapura, Siddheswaranadurga, Mahadevapura, Belagere, Hulikunte, Thimmannanayakanakote.

Drinking Water: Tap water in 71 villages, Tank water in 19 villages, Well water in 6 villages, Tubewell in 63 villages and more than one source in 110 villages.

Bank: Banking facility in 17 villages, namely, Giddapura, Katrikenahatti, Hirehalli Chitranayakanahalli, Chennaganahalli, Thalaku Ullarthi Kaval, Obalapura, Meerasabihalli, Sanikere Jajur, Parasuramapura, Mahadevapura, Yalagatta Belagere, Thimmannanayakanakote, Kyadigunte.

Credit Society in 25 villages Agricultural Credit Society in 23 Non-Agricultural Credit Society in 2 villages.

Others: Power supply in 185 villages, Cinema hall in 3 villages, sport club in 1 village, Stadium or Auditorium or Community Hall in 0 village, Post Office in 61 villages.

There are 147 villages having bus facilities.

Villages with most of facilities: Giddapura Hirehalli, Chennaganahalli, Thalaku, Obalapura Meerasabihalli, Sanikere, Jajur, Parasuramapura Mahadevapura, Belagere, Thimmannanayakanakote.

Villages without amenities (Education):
Baramasagara (B), Rekhalagere Kaval (B), Kavalanahalli, Kamplisagara (B), Bheemanakere, Varavoo Kaval, Henjimuttenahalli, Banavigondanahalli, Ullarthi Kaval, Donehalli Kaval, Chikkabadihalli, Kannenahalli (B), Mummadisagara (B), Badavanahalli (B), Lakumagondanahalli, Moduru Kaval, Pagadalabande Kaval, Viswanathapura, Gosikere Kaval, Konigarahalli Kaval, Belagere Kaval..

Scheduled Castes: Out of the total population of 283651 persons, 65039 persons (22.93%) belong to Scheduled Castes.

The villages having less than 10% SC population are Koradihalli, Mustalagummi, Chowlakere, Buklorahalli Dasaramuthenahalli, Kavalanahalli Bhairanayakanahatti, Obaiahnahatti, Ramasagara Sarjavvanahalli, Varavoo Kaval, Katrikenahatti Gowrasamudra Kaval, Henjimuttenahalli Banavigondanahalli, Chikkaullarti, Ullarthi Kaval Kaluvehalli, Katamdevarakote, Donehalli Kaval Doddabadihalli, Challakere(Rural), Bommasamudra Kannenahalli (B), Kasturi Thimmanahalli Badavanahalli (B), Moduru, Jajuru Kaval, Jajur Pagadalabande Kaval, Thimmannanahalli Viswanathapura, Konigarahalli, Belagere Kaval.

The villages having more than 50% SC population are Rekhalagere, Rekhalagere Kaval (B) Thimmappaiahnahalli, Kereyagalahalli Jambaiahnahalli, Bheemanakere, Manamainahatti Harishchandranayakana Halli, Veeradimmanahalli Nandanahalli, Sevalalnagar, Kammathmarikunte Dyavaranahalli, Lakumagondanahalli, Moduru Kaval Matasamudra, Parashuramapura Kaval, Chowlur Kaval Konigarahalli Kaval, Kyathanamale.

Sex ratio of Scheduled Caste population is 488.

Scheduled Castes Literates and Illiterates by Sex:

	Persons	Males	Females
Literate	27,433	17,492	9,941
Illiterate	37,606	15,794	21,812
Literacy rate	49.7	61.9	36.9
Graduate	778	708	70

Scheduled Castes (Dominant):
Madiga, Banjara etc., Bhovi, Adi Karnataka Chalavadi etc.

For their cultural identity please see Appendix-I

Villages without Scheduled Castes: There are 30 villages without any scheduled caste population.

Scheduled Tribes: Out of the total population of 283651 persons, 82615 persons (29.13%) belong to Scheduled Tribes.

The villages having less than 10% ST population are Torekolammanahalli, Jogihatti, Jambaiahnahalli Thippaiahnakote, Bheemanakere, Devarahalli Gowripura, Manamainahatti, Chikkahalli Henjimuttenahalli, Basapura Harishchandranayakana Halli, Kyatagondanahalli Thappagondanahalli, Chikkabadihalli Challakere(Rural), Gorlakatte, Visweswarapura Meerasabihalli, Bommasamudra, Siddapura, Somaguddu Nandanahalli, Chikkamadhure, Sevalalnagar Kammathmarikunte, Hotteppanahalli Kasturi Thimmanahalli, Dyavaranahalli, Nallurahalli Chikkenahalli, Badavanahalli Kaval (B), Gopanahalli Mummadisagara (B), Ganjigunte, Heggere, Kaparahalli Jadekunte, Badavanahalli (B), Lakumagondanahalli Haravigondanahalli, Pagadalabande Pagadalabande Kaval, Bommanakunte, Junjaragunte Thimmannanahalli, Matasamudra, Suranahalli, Chowluru Pillahalli, Obanahalli, Chowlur Kaval Gosikere Kaval, Konigarahalli Kaval, Konigarahalli Yalagatta, Belagere, Hulikunte, Belagere Kaval Kyathanamale, Kalamarahalli, Gorlathu Torebeeranahalli, Doddabeeranahalli.

The villages having more than 50% ST population are Koradihalli, Maleboranahatti, Mustalagummi Chowlakere, Buklorahalli, Mallurahalli Baramasagara (B), Dasaramuthenahalli

Guntakolammanahalli, Kavalanahalli Bhairanayakanahatti, Hirekere Kaval Bheemagondanahalli, Kamplisagara (B), Giddapura Obaiahnahatti, Ramasagara, Gajjaganahalli, Ramadurga Sarjavvanahalli, Nelagetanahatti, Varavoo Kaval Katavvanahalli, Katrikenahatti, Varavoo, Hirehalli Gowrasamudra, Bukkambudi, Banavigondanahalli Giriyammanahalli, Chikkaullarti, Ullarthi Kaval Kaluvehalli, Kasavigondanahalli, Donehalli Kaval Nannivala, Bomberahalli, Moduru, Jajuru Kaval Putloorahalli, Thimmannanayakanakote.

Sex ratio of Scheduled tribe population is 487.

Scheduled Tribes Literates and Illiterates by Sex:

	Persons	Males	Females
Literate	33,881	21,733	12,148
Illiterate	48,734	20,631	28,103
Literacy rate	48.3	60.5	35.5
Graduate	818	729	89

Scheduled Tribes (Dominant):

Naikda etc., Generic Tribes etc., Meda

For their cultural identity please see Appendix-II

Villages without Scheduled Tribes: There are 31 villages without any scheduled tribe population.

Literates and Illiterates by Sex (Total Population):

	Persons	Males	Females
Literate	134,914	83,633	51,281
Illiterate	148,737	61,527	87,210
Literacy rate	56	67	43
Graduate	4,427	3,874	553

Agriculture: ***Distribution of villages according to land use:*** Out of 195 villages, Total area (in hectare) is 203674, out of that 60.97 percent is cultivable and 12.31 percent of the cultivable area is irrigated.

Sources of Irrigation (Hectares): Government Canal 0, Private Canal 0, Well without Electricity 20.55, Well with Electricity 495.34, Tubewell without Electricity 194.55, Tubewell with Electricity 13715.83, Tank 864.91, River 0, Lake 0, Waterfall 0, Others 0.

Villages with population of 5000 to 9999: Hirehalli, Ghataparthi, Nannivala, Parasuramapura.

Villages with population of 10000 and above: Naikanahatti.

Distribution of Workers:

	Persons	Males	Females	WPR
Cultivators	58,906	39,344	19,562	39.56
Agricultural Labour	63,339	23,929	39,410	42.54
Household Industry	6,695	3,593	3,102	4.5
Other Workers	19,966	15,579	4,387	13.41
Main Workers	116,985	73,244	43,741	78.56
Marginal Workers	31,921	9,201	22,720	21.44
Total Workers	148,906	82,445	66,461	

Religion: Major Religious Communities:

	Persons	Males	Females	Sex Ratio
Hindu (96.54%)	273,827	140,176	133,651	953
Muslim (2.86%)	8,120	4,098	4,022	981
Christian (0.02%)	47	24	23	958
Sikh (0.03%)	95	50	45	900
Buddhists (0.01%)	30	14	16	1,143
Jain (0.02%)	48	20	28	1,400

Agewise Data:

	Persons	Males	Females	Sex Ratio
All ages	283,651	145,160	138,491	954
0-14	97,015	49,541	47,474	958
15-44	128,240	65,580	62,660	955
45-79	55,164	28,412	26,752	942
80+	2,676	1,314	1,362	1037
Age not stated	556	313	243	776

Languages (Dominant):

Kannada, Telugu, Urdu, Hindi, Coorgi/Kodagu

Disabled Population:

	Persons	Males	Females	%
Total Disabled	5,537	3,245	2,292	
In Seeing	2,662	1,521	1,141	48.08
In Speech	658	387	271	11.88
In Hearing	264	143	121	4.77
In Movement	1,462	935	527	26.4
Mentally	491	259	232	8.87

CHAMARAJANAGAR

Chamarajanagar C.D. Block lies in the western part of Chamarajanagar district. It is a part of Chamarajanagar tehsil. The Block is located at a distance of 00 kms. from district headquarters (Chamarajanagar). There are 184 villages in the block with the total population of 276,083 persons. Area of the C.D. Block is 1210.23 sq. kms. It is bounded by district Mysore on north, taluks Kollegal and Yelandur on east, and taluk Gundlupet on west. It has common boundary with the state of Tamil Nadu on South.

Communications:

Roadways : NH- 209: Direction- Coimbatore to Yelandur, Nearest Villages- Desavalli, Santhemarahalli, Kempanapu ra, Mangala, Kiragasur, Madapura, Chamarajanagar [R], Masagapura, Haradanahalli, Bandigere, Ankanasettypura, Venkataiahna Chatra, Bevinathalapura, Srirangapura, Haradanahalli District Forest II, Attagulipura, Punajan ur. SH- 17 B: Direction- Nanjangud to Chamarajanagar, Nearest Villages- Badanaguppe, Bendaravady, Muthige, Bedarapura, Mariyala, Gangavadi, Chamarajanagar [R], Kadahalli, Heggavadi.

Railway Station: Badanaguppe, Mutige, Mariyala, Gangavadi.

River: Suvarnavati Nadi- Nearest Villages- Kempanapura, Singanapura, Kannegala, Gulipura, Homma, Kotamballi, Kudalur, Boodithittu, Basavanapura, Byadamudlu, Basavap ura, Bandigowdanahalli, Bommanahalli, Hosahalli, Alur, Mallupura, Saraguru, Chandakavadi, Kodimole, Hebbasur, Dollipura, Kanikere, Karadihalla, Haradanahalli District Forest II, Hongalavadi.

Canal: Nearest Villages- Byadamudlu, Basavapura, Ankanas ettypura, Venkataiahna Chatra, Amachavadi, Kodiugane, Bevinathalapura, Srirangapura, Haradanahalli, District Forest, Malledevanahalli, Ayyanapura, Dollipura, Kanikere, Haradanahalli District Forest II, Punajur State Forest.

Annual Rainfall: Normal Rianfall 782 mm.

Ground Water: Availability of the Ground Water in the Basin is 1275 H.A.M. and the utilization is 7513 H.A. M. It belongs to Safe category. Depth to water level 2 to 10 meter below the ground. Most of the wells go down in summer months, according to the Ground Water Estimation Committee.

Soils: Red Soils, Black Soils and Mixed Soils.

Natural Division : It falls partly in Kabbani-Cauvery Valley, Cauvery Forested Region & Gundlupet-Chamraraja nagar Plateau of the Southern Karnataka Plateau.

Administration:

Division: Mysore. Parliamentary Constituency: 22 Mysore Purab, 21 Mysore Paschim. District: Chamarajanagar. Taluka: Gundlupet. Assembly Constituency: 222 Kollegal (SC), 223 Chamarajanagar, 224 Gundlupet. Gram Panchayat: 42.

Regional Area Development Boards: The Maland Area Development Board.

Border Villages: (State: Tamil Nadu)- Yaraganhalli, Yanagumba, Vaddarahalli, Mudala Hosahalli, Arakalavadi, Chowdahalli, Vaddagalapura, Yalachagere, Bisalavadi, Bandigowdanahalli, Bommanahalli, Haradanahalli District Forest II, Honnegowdanahalli, Kulluru, Punajur State Forest, Punajanur, Mukanapalya.

Villages: 184 **Inhabited:** 171 **Uninhabited:** 13

Ranking	District	State	National
Area	3	62	278
Population	2	25	124
Sex Ratio	2	61	1856
Child Sex Ratio	1	2	228
Literacy Rate	4	164	5171
Density	3	147	4337
Work Participation Rate	2	58	3461

Gram Panchayats:

Navilur, Bagali, Demahalli, Ummathur, Kuderu, Santhemarahalli, Kempanapura, Erasavadi, Masanapura, Gulipura, Mangala, Bhogapura, Badanaguppe, Mukkadahalli, Heggotara, Madapura, Kudalur , Alur, Kagalavadi, Honganoor, Jyothigowdanapura, Nagavalli, Chandakavadi, Hebbasur, Doddamole, Haradanahalli, Shivapura, Nanjedevanapura, Harave, Maliyuru, Kulagana, Sagade, Udigala, Amachavadi, Venkataiahna Chatra, Attagulipura, Punajanur, Bisalavadi, Honnahalli, Kothalavadi, Arakalavadi, Yaraganhalli.

Amenities:

Education: Primary School in 148 villages, Middle school in 97 villages, Matriculation or Secondary School in 28 villages, namely Navilur, Ganaganur, Ummathur, Kuderu, Santhemarahalli, Honganoor, Mangala, Bhogapura, Badanaguppe, Mariyala, Madapura, Handarakalli, Ramasamudra Rural, Aralikatte, Harave, Nanjedevanapura, Udigala, Thammadahalli, Kothalavadi, Venkataiahna Chatra, Amachavadi, Arakalavadi, Kodiugane, Bisalavadi, Alur, Kagalavadi, Nagavalli, Chandakavadi.

Higher Secondary or Pre University Courses or Intermediate or Junior College in 3 villages of the CD Block,, namely Kuderu, Harave, Venkataiahna Chatra.

College in 0 village, Adult Literacy Center in 30 villages.

Medical: Hospital in 4 villages, Dispensary in 4 villages, Health Center in 18 villages, Sub Center in 5 villages, Maternity and Child Welfare Center in 2 villages, Community health workers in 19 villages.

The Villages having Hospital or Dispensary or Health Center are Ummathur, Santhemarahalli, Honganoor, Mangala, Kothalavadi, Bisalavadi.

Drinking Water: Tap water in 121 villages, Tank water in 34 villages, Well water in 40 villages, Tubewell in 166 villages and more than one source in 162 villages.

Bank: Banking facility in 19 villages, namely, Navilur, Ummathur, Kuderu, Santhemarahalli, Mangala Badanaguppe, Kudalur, Chamarajanagar [R] Ramasamudra Rural, Kulagana, Udigala Venkataiahna Chatra, Amachavadi, Arakalavadi Bisalavadi, Alur, Kagalavadi, Nagavalli Chandakavadi.

Credit Society in 79 villages Agricultural Credit Society in 27 Non-Agricultural Credit Society in 48 villages.

Others: Power supply in 169 villages, Cinema hall in 10 village sport club in 0 village, Stadium or Auditorium or Community Hall in 0 village, Post Office in 122 villages.

There are 127 villages having bus facilities.

Villages with most of facilities: Ummathur, Kuderu Santhemarahalli, Mangala, Badanaguppe, Udigala Venkataiahna Chatra, Amachavadi, Arakalavadi Bisalavadi, Alur, Kagalavadi, Nagavalli

Chandakavadi.

Villages without amenities (Education):
Nanjarajapura, Thimmegowdanapalya, Melmala, Sappaiahnapura, Gangavadi, Somasamudra, Kattepura, Munachanahalli, Managanahalli, Basavanapura, Kaggalipura, Hangarepura, Maduvinabeedu, Kotaganahalli, Kuthanapura, Shindaiahanapura, Chowdahalli, Yalachagere, Hagalabele, Haradanahalli District Forest, Devarajapura, Kanikere, Karadihalla..

Scheduled Castes: Out of the total population of 277013 persons, 67816 persons (24.48%) belong to Scheduled Castes. The villages having less than 10% SC population are Aldur, Mudala Agrahara, Kasturu, Kannegala Kallipura, Thimmegowdanapalya, Hanahalli, Gangavadi Chamarajanagar [R], Masagapura, Somasamudra Kattepura, Munachanahalli, Managanahalli Ramasamudra Rural, Doddamole, Aralikatte, Maliyuru Bettadapura, Sagade, Kaggalipura, Nanjedevanapura Veeranapura, Hangarepura, Kengaki, Kumachahalli Maduvinabeedu, Uganedahundi, Haradanahalli Bandigere, Byadamudlu, Kotaganahalli, Bokkepura Narasamangala, Kuthanapura, Meluru, Shindaiahanapura Vaddarahalli, Chowdahalli, Yalachagere, Hagalabele Mallupura, Kodimole, Hanchithalapura, Kokkanahalli Puttanapura, Haradanahalli District Forest, Kanikere Karadihalla, Punajanur.

The villages having more than 50% SC population are Kavudavadi, K.Mookahalli, Suthur, Chatipura Nanjarajapura, Honganoor, Yadapura, Uthavalli Mallaiahnapura, Heggavadi, Devalapura, Achattipura Kodiugane, Haradanahalli District Forest Ii Hongalavadi, Mukanapalya.

Sex ratio of Scheduled Caste population is 493.

Scheduled Castes Literates and Illiterates by Sex:

	Persons	Males	Females
Literate	28,365	16,612	11,753
Illiterate	39,451	17,757	21,694
Literacy rate	47.5	54.7	40.0
Graduate	1,193	1,031	162

Scheduled Castes (Dominant):

Adi Karnataka, Madiga, Banjara etc., Bhovi, Korama

For their cultural identity please see Appendix-I

Villages without Scheduled Castes: There are 42 villages without any scheduled caste population.

Scheduled Tribes: Out of the total population of 277013 persons, 27068 persons (9.77%) belong to Scheduled Tribes. The villages having less than 10% ST population are Aldur, Navilur, Ganaganur, Jannur, Thelanur Kavudavadi, Kamaravadi, Demahalli, Mudala Agrahara Kuderu, Heggavadi, Heggavadipura, Desavalli Basavatti, Santhemarahalli, Kempanapura K.Mookahalli, Kasturu, Boodamballi, Erasavadi Chatipura, Kallipura, H.Mookahalli, Kotamballi Rechamballi, Nanjarajapura, Gangavadi Thimmegowdanapalya, Yalakkur, Hanahalli, Mangala Sappaiahnapura, Kellamballi, Bendaravady, Muthige Bedarapura, Gangavadi, Kiragasur, Madapura Handarakalli, Kudalur, Chamarajanagar [R] Masagapura, Kadahalli, Somasamudra, Yadapura Shivapura, Sanegala, Uthavalli, Mallaiahnapura Boodithittu, Basavanapura, Ramasamudra Rural Doddamole, Heggavadi, Bujaganapura, Aralikatte Kebbepura, Chikkabegur, Hirebegur, Kilalipura Mukkadahalli, Govindavadi, Harave, Maliyuru Mudnakodu, Bettadapura, Kethahalli, Kalanahundi Veeranapura, Hangarepura, Udigala, Kumachahalli Devalapura, Maduvinabeedu, Badagalapura, Katnavadi Kothalavadi, Bandigere, Byadamudlu, Ankanasettypura Venkataiahna Chatra, Kotaganahalli, Bokkepura Narasamangala, Kuthanapura, Madalavadi, Yaraganhalli Shindaiahanapura, Yanagumba, Achattipura Vaddarahalli, Mudala Hosahalli, Manchagundipura Linganapura, Chowdahalli, Vaddagalapura, Honnahalli Yalachagere, Hagalabele, Channappanapura, Kodiugane Bevinathalapura, Srirangapura, Basthipura Bandigowdanahalli, Bommanahalli, Alur, Mallupura Saraguru, Kagalavadi, Kodimole, Hebbasur Hanchithalapura, Kokkanahalli, Puttanapura, Nallur Haradanahalli District Forest, Ayyanapura Devarajapura, Dollipura, Kanikere, Karadihalla Haradanahalli District Forest Ii, Hongalavadi Attagulipura, Mukanapalya.

The villages having more than 50% ST population are Kannegala, Melmala, Kaggalipura, Yanagahalli Bedaguli.

Sex ratio of Scheduled tribe population is 504.

Scheduled Tribes Literates and Illiterates by Sex:

	Persons	Males	Females
Literate	8,280	4,992	3,288
Illiterate	18,788	8,438	10,350
Literacy rate	34.7	42.0	27.5
Graduate	125	115	10

Scheduled Tribes (Dominant):

Naikda etc., Soligaru, Generic Tribes etc., Meda Sholaga

For their cultural identity please see Appendix-II

Villages without Scheduled Tribes: There are 100 villages without any scheduled tribe population.

Literates and Illiterates by Sex (Total Population):

	Persons	Males	Females
Literate	111,436	65,734	45,702
Illiterate	165,577	73,859	91,718
Literacy rate	45	53	38
Graduate	3,649	3,139	510

Agriculture: ***Distribution of villages according to land use:*** Out of 184 villages, Total area (in hectare) is 121023, out of that 53.35 percent is cultivable and 28.11 percent of the cultivable area is irrigated.

Sources of Irrigation (Hectares): Government Canal 1895.75, Private Canal 0, Well without Electricity 24.59, Well with Electricity 923.8, Tubewell without Electricity 378.56, Tubewell with Electricity 12621.42, Tank 2306.72, River 0, Lake 0, Waterfall 0, Others 0.

Villages with population of 5000 to 9999:
Ummathur, Honganoor, Mangala, Amachavadi, Nagavalli Hebbasur.

Villages with population of 10000 and above: None

Distribution of Workers:

	Persons	Males	Females	WPR
Cultivators	35,104	31,244	3,860	27.71
Agricultural Labour	64,659	37,880	26,779	51.04
Household Industry	4,851	2,842	2,009	3.83
Other Workers	22,058	16,747	5,311	17.41
Main Workers	91,548	72,657	18,891	72.27
Marginal Workers	35,124	16,056	19,068	27.73
Total Workers	126,672	88,713	37,959	

Religion: Major Religious Communities:

	Persons	Males	Females	Sex Ratio
Hindu (91.76%)	254,192	128,080	126,112	985
Muslim (1.79%)	4,970	2,505	2,465	984
Christian (1%)	2,778	1,392	1,386	996
Sikh (0%)	1	1	-	-
Buddhists (5.21%)	14,433	7,286	7,147	981
Jain (0.06%)	166	82	84	1,024

Agewise Data:

	Persons	Males	Females	Sex Ratio
All ages	277,013	139,593	137,420	984
0-14	75,937	38,120	37,817	992
15-44	137,567	68,967	68,600	995
45-79	59,523	30,663	28,860	941
80+	3,039	1,375	1,664	1210
Age not stated	947	468	479	1024

Languages (Dominant):
Kannada, Urdu, Hindi, Tamil, Telugu

Disabled Population:

	Persons	Males	Females	%
Total Disabled	8,126	4,781	3,345	
In Seeing	5,545	3,248	2,297	68.24
In Speech	683	377	306	8.41
In Hearing	249	116	133	3.06
In Movement	1,116	741	375	13.73
Mentally	533	299	234	6.56

CHANNAGIRI

Channagiri C.D. Block lies in the southern part of Davan agere district. It is a part of Channagiri taluka. The Block is located at a distance of 61 kms. from district headquarters (Davanagere). There are 249 villages in the block with the total population of 273,845 persons. Area of the C.D. Block is 1185.68 sq. kms. It is bounded by taluks Davanangere and Honnali on north, district Chikmagalur on south, districts Chikmagalur and Chitradu rga on east, taluk Honnali and district Shimoga on west.

Communications:

Roadways : N.H-13: Direction- Shimoga to Chitradurga, Nearest Villages- Thimlapura (Jodi), Hagedahalli, Chann eshapura, Mavinakatte, Dondraghatta, Sunnagere, Chikkulik ere, Machanaikanahalli, Kaval, Machanaikanahalli, Channag iri (Rural), Honnebagi, Garaga, Madapura, Hebbalagere, Benkikere, Narashettihalli S.H-48: Direction- Honnali to Chitradurga, Nearest Villages- Daginakatte, Hosakere, Sringarabagu, Kanchugaranahalli, Mohidinpura, Vylipura, Hosahalli, Rudrapura, Chickkbennur, Santhebennur, Hosah alli, Doddabbigere, Sulekere, Kerebilachi, Somlapura, Channapura, Jakkali. S.H-50: Direction- Bhadravati to Channagiri, Nearest Villages- Chikkulikere, Ajjihalli, Haronahalli, Yarehalli, Gopanhal, K.Ganadakatte, Joladalu.

Canal: Nearest Villages- Doddaghatta, Ramagondanahalli, Uduva, Kabbala, Siddapura, Komaranahalli, Yekkegondi, Kallenahalli, Thopenahalli, Medikere, Mangenahalli, Belliganodu, Chikkakogalur, Gollarahalli, Somanahalu, Santhebennur, Sulekere, Kerebilachi, Somlapura, Kashipu ra, Hallimallapura.

Annual Rainfall: Normal Rianfall 804 mm.

Ground Water: Availability of the Ground Water in the Basin is 14811.56 H.A.M. and the utilization is 13611. 51 H.A.M. It belongs to Over Exploited category. Depth to water level 2 to 20 meter below the ground. Most of the wells go down in summer months, according to the Ground Water Estimation Committee.

Soils: Red Sandy Soils and Black Soils.

Natural Division : It falls in Channagiri Plateau of the Central Karantaka Plateau.

Administration:

Division: Bangalore. Parliamentary Constituency: 13 Davanagere. District: Davanagere. Taluka: Channagiri. Assembly Constituency: 108 Maya Konda (SC), 109 Channagiri. Gram Panchayat: 61.

Regional Area Development Boards: The Maland Aera Development Board.

Fairs: Hanuman Jatra: It is held at Ajjihalli at Shimoga area in around the month of April every year. Ajjihalli is about three kms. to the south-west of Channagiri town. It is reputed for its sculptors who are good at statue-making in stone, metals and wood and castings. It has a temple of Hanuman in whose honour a jatra is held about April every year.
Keteshvar Temple Festival: It is held annually during Shivaratri (February-March) at Channagiri. Channagiri about 43 kms. north-east of Shimoga city, is the headqu arters town of the taluk of the same name. From inscripti ons, it would appear that in early times, this part was in the possession of the Gangas and was governed from Asandi which is in the present Chikmagalur district. In the 12th century, it formed a part of the Chalukyan dominions and was included in the Nolambavadi-32,000 province over which the Pandyas of Uchehangi ruled. Under Vijayanagar, it was a part of the Uchchangi distri ct and was attached to Santhebennur. Later, it passed into the hands of the Keladi Nayakas. It was named Chann agiri after queen Channammaji who created the fort and granted the place as an estate to her sister.
Siddeshwara Festival: It is held at Sulekere near Shimoga around the months of February-March every year. Sulekere, is about 20 kms. north of Channagiri town. At the east end of the embankment of the Shantisagar tank here, there is a small hillock on which is situated an intere sting temple dedicated to Siddeshwara. An inscription in the temple bears a date corresponding to 1546 A.D.
Udumaradi Ranganatha Car Festival: A car festival is observed at the temple of Lord Udumaradi Ranganatha at Devarahalli near Shimoga around the month of March-Ap ril for five days. Devarahalli, about 12 kms. north-east of Channagiri town, has a small mud hill known as Udumar adi on which is situated a temple dedicated to Ranganatha. The hill is called Udumaradi because according to the Sthalapurana, an iguana (udu) came from a long distance. Ranganatha is represented by a round stone marked with the figures of a discus and a conch. Behind it is a linga of the shape of an arrow, and above it a small figure of Keshava, said to have set up by the Vijayanaga ra king Krishnadeva Raya. A car festival takes place around the month of April.

Villages: 249 **Inhabited:** 209 **Uninhabited:** 40

Ranking	District	State	National
Area	2	64	294
Population	1	28	134
Sex Ratio	5	137	3296
Child Sex Ratio	6	123	3598
Literacy Rate	3	61	1920
Density	6	164	4308
Work Participation Rate	4	57	3941

Gram Panchayats:
Kariganur, Kathalgere, Belalagere , Thyavanige, Nalkudre, Kempanahalli, Tanigere, Medikere, Navilehalu, Basavapatna, Kotehalu, Daginakatte, Chiradoni, Kogaloor, Siddanamatha, Belliganodu, Karekatte, Kabbala, Kamsagara, Kanivebilchi, Mallapura, Santhebennur, Doddabbigere, Somlapura, Kerebilachi, Rudrapura, Nilogallu, Komaranahalli, Kondadahalli, Kakanur, Nuggehalli, Devarahalli, Kagathur, Ittige, Nallur, Bulsagara, Chikgangoor, Kortikere, Agarabannihatti, Hiremalali, Channeshapura, Mudigere, Garaga, Hodigere, Hebbalagere, Honnebagi, Ajjihalli, Haronahalli, Thippagondanahalli, Vaddanalu, Kanchiganahalu, Rajagondanahalli, Goppenahalli, Joladalu, Malahalu, Maravanji, Nellihanklu, Thavarekere, Durvigere, Lingadahalli, Pandomatti.

Amenities:

Education: Primary School in 179 villages, Middle school in 111 villages, Matriculation or Secondary School in 80 villages, namely Daginakatte, Yalodahalli, Belalagere, Sangahalli, Chikkakurubarahalli, Marabanahalli, Kotehalu, Harosagara, Hosakere, Nilogallu, Komaranahalli, Kamsagara, Chiradoni, Kanivebilchi, Rudrapura, Kathalgere, Kariganur, Arehalli, Thyavanige, Nalkudre, Navilehalu, Doddaghatta, Kogaloor, Kempanahalli, Tanigere, Maradi, Siddanamatha, Thopenahalli, Medikere, Belliganodu, Santhebennur, Doddabbigere, Kulenur, Kakanur, Arlikatte, Kerebilachi, Kagathur, Somlapura, Karekatte, Alur, Channapura, Chikkuda, Hireuda, Devarahalli, Kondadahalli, Nuggehalli, Neethigere, Ramenahalli, Yeragattihalli, Hiregangoor, Chikgangoor, Kortikere, Arasinaghatta, Hatti, Gullehalli, Nallur, Thilineerkatte, Billahalli, Hiremalali, Chikkamadalu, Ajjihalli, Joladalu, Rajagondanahalli, Hodigere, Hebbalagere, Benkikere, Pandomatti, Vaddanalu, Kanchiganahalu, Bettakaduru, Goppenahalli, Malahalu, Maravanji, Medugondanahalli, Jammapura, Kodagikere, Durvigere, Thavarekere, Mugalihalli, Gangondanahalli.
Higher Secondary or Pre University Courses or Intermediate or Junior College in 17 villages of the CD Block,, namely Belalagere, Komaranahalli, Chiradoni, Kanivebilchi, Kariganur, Thyavanige, Nalkudre, Kogaloor, Santhebennur, Kerebilachi, Kagathur, Karekatte, Chikgangoor, Nallur, Joladalu, Kanchiganahalu, Thavarekere.

College in 3 villages, Adult Literacy Center in 0 village., Colleges are in villages, namely Santhebennur, Kerebilachi, Channagiri (Rural).

Medical: Hospital in 15 villages, Dispensary in 14 villages, Health Center in 15 villages, Sub Center in 59 villages, Maternity and Child Welfare Center in 16 villages, Community health workers in 34 villages.

The Villages having Hospital or Dispensary or Health Center are Daginakatte, Belalagere , Hosakere, Komaranahalli, Chiradoni, Kanivebilchi, Kathalgere, Kadaranahalli, Thyavanige, Nalkudre, Tanigere, Medikere, Santhebennur, Kerebilachi, Kagathur, Mallapura, Nuggehalli, Chikgangoor, Kortikere, Nallur, Channagiri (Rural), Durvigere, Thavarekere.

Drinking Water: Tap water in 129 villages, Tank water in 45 villages, Well water in 76 villages, Tubewell in 118 villages and more than one source in 182 villages.

Bank: Banking facility in 12 villages, namely, Daginakatte, Hosakere, Kathalgere, Thyavanige Santhebennur, Kerebilachi, Nallur Channagiri (Rural), Kukwada, Hodigere, Goppenahalli Thavarekere.

Credit Society in 4 villages Agricultural Credit Society in 1 Non-Agricultural Credit Society in 1 village.

Others: Power supply in 209 villages, Cinema hall in 6 villages, sport club in 1 village, Stadium or Auditorium or Community Hall in 0 village, Post Office in 56 villages.

There are 151 villages having bus facilities.

Villages with most of facilities: Daginakatte Hosakere, Kathalgere, Thyavanige, Santhebennur Kerebilachi, Nallur, Channagiri (Rural), Hodigere Goppenahalli, Thavarekere.

Villages without amenities (Education): Bulnaikanahalli, Hirekurubarahalli, Kadaranahalli, Thyavanige Thanda, Ramagondanahalli, Uduva, Kamanahalli, Kallenahalli, Chikkakogalur, Chikkabbigere, Kenchapura, Neethigere Camp, Siddapura, Garagadakatte, N.Basavanahalli, Hagedahalli, Machanaikanahalli, Gopanhal, K.Ganadakatte, Kukwada, Shivpuradal, Ganduganahanklu, Benakanahalli, Kalkere, Veerapura, Karkikere, Athigatta..

Scheduled Castes: Out of the total population of 273995 persons, 66727 persons (24.35%) belong to Scheduled Castes.

The villages having less than 10% SC population are Harlipura, Reddihalli , Sangahalli, Uduva Giriyapura, Bhimanere, Maradi, Yekkegondi Mangenahalli, Gollarahalli, Somanahalu, Nagenahalli Kerebilachi, Mallapura, Alur, Jakkali Ramagondanahalli, Devarahalli, Kondadahalli Nuggehalli, Bommenahalli, Chikkadevarahalli Kenchapura, Siddapura, Hatti, Sripura, Akalikatti Astapanahalli, Garagadakatte, Byranahalli Bussenahalli, Channeshapura, Gurupura Machanaikanahalli Kaval, Machanaikanahalli, Gopanhal Dandigenahalli, Honnebagi, Honnaikanahalli, Madapura Mahadevapura, Malahalu, Ubrani, Basavapura Mugalihalli, Masanikere, Athigatta.

The villages having more than 50% SC population are Marabanahalli, Bulnaikanahalli, Benakanahalli Madhuranaikanahalli, Hirekurubarahalli, Hosahalli Rudrapura, Kavalithanda, Kadaranahalli Thyavanige Thanda, Miyapura, Kabbala, Kamanahalli Chickkbennur, Chikkabbigere, Sulekere, Kashipura Hallimallapura, Ramenahalli, Neethigere Camp Arasinaghatta, Rangapura, Thilineerkatte N.Basavanahalli, Shivagangehalli, Chiradoni Thimlapura, Chennenahalli, Chikkamadalu, Hagedahalli Mavinakatte, Madenahalli, Channagiri (Rural) Laxmisagara, Haronahalli, Benkikere, Ganduganahanklu Komaranahalli, Penasamudra, Beedugondanahalli Kalkere, Hanumalapura, Chikkamalali, Veerapura Nellihanklu, Kolkere, Karkikere.

Sex ratio of Scheduled Caste population is 489.

Scheduled Castes Literates and Illiterates by Sex:

	Persons	Males	Females
Literate	26,592	16,731	9,861
Illiterate	40,135	17,365	22,770
Literacy rate	46.7	57.6	35.3
Graduate	867	784	83

Scheduled Castes (Dominant):

Banjara etc., Adi Karnataka, Bhovi, Madiga, Koracha

For their cultural identity please see Appendix-I

Villages without Scheduled Castes: There are 52 villages without any scheduled caste population.

Scheduled Tribes: Out of the total population of 273995 persons, 35668 persons (13.02%) belong to Scheduled Tribes.

The villages having less than 10% ST population are Harlipura, Sangahalli, Chikkakurubarahalli Marabanahalli, Kotehalu, Sagarapet, Hosakere Sringarabagu, Benakanahalli, Madhuranaikanahalli Chiradoni, Hirekurubarahalli, Kanivebilchi Hosahalli, Kavalithanda, Kathalgere, Kariganur Kadaranahalli, Arehalli, Thyavanige Thanda, Miyapura Navilehalu, Uduva, Kabbala, Kamanahalli, Bhimanere Tanigere, Kallenahalli, Gollarahalli, Somanahalu Chickkbennur, Santhebennur, Nagenahalli Chikkabbigere, Dodderikatte, Arlikatte, Kerebilachi Kashipura, Mallapura, Karekatte, Channapura Ramagondanahalli, Devarahalli, Honnemaradahalli

Bommenahalli, Neethigere, Chikkadevarahalli Ramenahalli, Yeragattihalli, Neethigere Camp Chikgangoor, Kortikere, Siddapura, Somasettihalli Arasinaghatta, Hatti, Rangapura, Gullehalli, Sripura Akalikatti, Nallur, Thilineerkatte, Garagadakatte N.Basavanahalli, Shivagangehalli, Chiradoni Byranahalli, Galihalli, Billahalli, Bussenahalli Donihalli, Thimlapura, Chennenahalli, Hiremalali Hagedahalli, Madenahalli, Chikkulikere, Muddenahalli Channagiri (Rural), Laxmisagara, Ajjihalli Haronahalli, Shivpuradal, Malligere, Mavinahole Thippagondanahalli, Honnebagi, Settihalli, Madapura Benkikere, Halakanhalu, Pandomatti, Narashettihalli Benakanahalli, Bannihatti, Komaranahalli Kanchiganahalu, Mahadevapura, Penasamudra Goppenahalli, Maravanji, Medugondanahalli Beedugondanahalli, Hanumalapura, Chikkasandi, Khaggi Chikkamalali, Ubrani, Shankaripura, Veerapura Thavarekere, Mugalihalli, Nellihanklu, Kolkere Gondhihosalli.

The villages having more than 50% ST population are Reddihalli , Eraganahalli, Uppanaikanahalli Mangenahalli, Chikkakogalur, Anapura, Astapanahalli Machanaikanahalli, Gopanhal, Dandigenahalli Honnaikanahalli, Bettakaduru, Athigatta.

Sex ratio of Scheduled tribe population is 491.

Scheduled Tribes Literates and Illiterates by Sex:

	Persons	Males	Females
Literate	17,047	10,361	6,686
Illiterate	18,621	7,805	10,816
Literacy rate	54.8	65.4	43.8
Graduate	619	533	86

Scheduled Tribes (Dominant):

Naikda etc., Hakkipikki, Meda, Generic Tribes etc. Jenu Kuruba

For their cultural identity please see Appendix-II

Villages without Scheduled Tribes: There are 78 villages without any scheduled tribe population.

Literates and Illiterates by Sex (Total Population):

	Persons	Males	Females
Literate	155,359	90,486	64,873
Illiterate	118,636	49,736	68,900
Literacy rate	65	74	56
Graduate	7,099	5,992	1,107

Agriculture: ***Distribution of villages according to land use:*** Out of 249 villages, Total area (in hectare) is 118568, out of that 60.89 percent is cultivable and 39.78 percent of the cultivable area is irrigated.

Sources of Irrigation (Hectares): Government Canal 14289.63, Private Canal 0, Well without Electricity 2.17, Well with Electricity 275.73, Tubewell without Electricity 273.9, Tubewell with Electricity 11886.94, Tank 1288.84, River 5.7, Lake 0, Waterfall 0, Others 695.74.

Villages with population of 5000 to 9999: Thyavanige, Santhebennur, Kerebilachi, Nallur.

Villages with population of 10000 and above: None

Distribution of Workers:

	Persons	Males	Females	WPR
Cultivators	48,252	41,574	6,678	41.25
Agricultural Labour	45,920	22,066	23,854	39.25
Household Industry	3,174	2,083	1,091	2.71
Other Workers	19,641	13,880	5,761	16.79
Main Workers	87,458	69,778	17,680	74.76
Marginal Workers	29,529	9,825	19,704	25.24
Total Workers	116,987	79,603	37,384	

Religion: Major Religious Communities:

	Persons	Males	Females	Sex Ratio
Hindu (88.35%)	242,086	123,775	118,311	956
Muslim (11.01%)	30,176	15,565	14,611	939
Christian (0.07%)	182	85	97	1,141
Sikh (0%)	1	1	-	-
Buddhists (0%)	1	1	-	-
Jain (0.02%)	44	24	20	833

Agewise Data:

	Persons	Males	Females	Sex Ratio
All ages	273,995	140,222	133,773	954
0-14	83,684	42,564	41,120	966
15-44	134,163	68,754	65,409	951
45-79	52,283	26,993	25,290	937
80+	2,738	1,310	1,428	1090
Age not stated	1,127	601	526	875

Languages (Dominant):

Kannada, Urdu, Telugu, Hindi, Marathi

Disabled Population:

	Persons	Males	Females	%
Total Disabled	4,620	2,764	1,856	
In Seeing	2,263	1,322	941	48.98
In Speech	434	240	194	9.39
In Hearing	207	124	83	4.48
In Movement	1,260	819	441	27.27
Mentally	456	259	197	9.87

CHANNAPATNA

Channapatna C.D. Block lies in the southern part of Bangalore Rural district. It is a part of Channapatna tehsil. The Block is located at a distance of 59 kms. from district headquarters (Bangalore). There are 145 villages in the block with the total population of 189, 002 persons. Area of the C.D. Block is 534.96 sq. kms. It is bounded by district Tumkur and taluk Ramanagaram on north, district Mandya and taluk Kanakapura on south, taluks Ramanagaram and Kanakapura on east, and district Mandya on west.

Communication

Roadways : S.H-17: Direction- Mandya to Bangalore, Nearest Villages- Koluru, Dhabanagunda, Mudigere, Settihalli, Malur, Mathikere, Mudigere Plantation, Vandaraguppe, Honniganahalli, Chikkamannugudde State Forest.

Railway Station: Villages- Settihalli, Vandaraguppe, Chikkamannugudde State Forest.

River: Shimsha Nadi- Nearest Villages- Iggaluru, Nelama kanahalli, Saraguru. Kanva Nadi- Nearest Villages- Dasava ra, Malur, Hottiganahosahalli, Malurpatna, Mylanayakanaha lli, Thore Hosur, Patlu, Abbur, Yelehosahalli, Kudlur, Santhemogenahalli, Malagalu, Hosahalli, Akkur, Nagapura, Somanathapura, Mangadahalli, Hunasanahalli, Kondapura, Banagahalli, Sogala, Harokoppa, Madapura, Bananthahalli, Halehalli, Ambadahalli, Nunnuru, Neralur, Saraguru, Nelamakanahalli, Yalethotadahalli, Yaliyur.

Canal: Nearest Villages- Dasavara, Kannasandra, Thavatan ahallidoddi, Huluvady, Mankunda, Devarahalli, Anigere, Nagavara, Chikkenahalli, Mylanayakanahalli, Patlu, Komananahalli, Yelehosahalli, Cholamaranahalli, Devaraho sahalli, Rampura, Honniganahalli.

Annual Rainfall: Normal Rianfall 868.8 mm.

Ground Water: Availability of the Ground Water in the Basin is (Information not avablable) H.A.M. and the utilization is (Information not avablable) H.A.M.

It belongs to (Information not avablable) category.

Depth to water level 5 to 20 meter below the ground.

Most of the wells go down in summer months, according to the Ground Water Estimation Committee.

Natural Division : It falls in Cauvery Forested Region of the Southern Karnataka Plateau.

Administration:

Division: Bangalore. Parliamentary Constituency: 23 Bangalore Rural. District: Bangalore Rural. Taluka: Channapatna. Assembly Constituency: 185 Channapatna. Gram Panchayat: 32.

Regional Area Development Boards: The Bailu Seeme Area Development Board.

Villages: 145 **Inhabited:** 134 **Uninhabited:** 11

Ranking	District	State	National
Area	5	159	1364
Population	3	97	875
Sex Ratio	1	43	1550
Child Sex Ratio	4	92	3013
Literacy Rate	7	112	3329
Density	7	127	3080
Work Participation Rate	1	13	3003

Gram Panchayats:

Mandya Bommanayakanahalli, Makali, Dasavara, Nagavara, Bevooru, Byadarahalli, Mylanayakanahalli, Thittamaranahalli, Rampura, Vandaraguppe, Thagachakere, Neelasandra, Honganur, Kudlur, Malur, Mathikere, Mudigere, Malurpatna, Chakkere, Akkur, Banagahalli, Sogala, Sulleri, Harokoppa, Iggaluru, Yalethotadahalli, Byadarahalli, Kodamballi, Virupakshipura, Banduru Valagerehalli, Bhoohalli, Singarajapura.

Amenities:

Education: Primary School in 129 villages, Middle school in 96 villages, Matriculation or Secondary School in 27 villages, namely Makali, Dasavara, Mandya Bommanayakanahalli, Honnayakanahalli, Bevooru, Byadarahalli, Chakkere, Mathikere, Belakere, Malurpatna, Nagavara, Mylanayakanahalli, Abbur, Vandaraguppe, Thattekere, Lalaghatta, Honganur, Brahmanipura, Sulleri, Hosahalli, Aralalasandra, Harokoppa, Iggaluru, Yalethotadahalli, Byadarahalli, Kodamballi, Singarajapura.

Higher Secondary or Pre University Courses or Intermediate or Junior College in 10 villages of the CD Block,, namely Bevooru, Byadarahalli, Chakkere, Mathikere, Belakere, Vandaraguppe, Honganur, Hosahalli, Aralalasandra, Byadarahalli.

College in 3 villages, Adult Literacy Center in 0 village., Colleges are in villages, namely Bevooru, Thubinakere, Vandaraguppe.

Medical: Hospital in 1 village, Dispensary in 12 villages, Health Center in 14 villages, Sub Center in 49 villages, Maternity and Child Welfare Center in 1 village, Community health workers in 3 villages.

The Villages having Hospital or Dispensary or Health Center are Dasavara, Siddanahalli, Mylanayakanahalli, Thimmasandra, Santhemogenahalli, Honganur, Neelasandra, Kodipura, Sanabanahalli, Soudahalli, Yalethotadahalli, Jagadapura.

Drinking Water: Tap water in 126 villages, Tank water in 2 villages, Well water in 56 villages, Tubewell in 94 villages and more than one source in 131 villages.

Bank: Banking facility in 14 villages, namely, Dasavara, Bevooru, Mudigere, Malur Mudigere Plantation, Kannamangala, Vandaraguppe Honganur, Hosahalli, Akkur, Sadahalli, Neralur Kodamballi, Singarajapura.

Credit Society in 23 villages Agricultural Credit Society in 23 Non-Agricultural Credit Society in 1 village.

Others: Power supply in 132 villages, Cinema hall in 4 villages sport club in 0 village, Stadium or Auditorium or Community Hall in 134 villages, Post Office in 39 villages.

There are 108 villages having bus facilities.

Villages with most of facilities: Dasavara Bevooru, Mudigere, Malur, Kannamangala, Vandaraguppe Honganur, Hosahalli, Neralur, Kodamballi Singarajapura.

Villages without amenities (Education): Ammallydoddi, Gendemadu, Chikkamannugudde State Forest, Soudahalli, Halehalli..

Scheduled Castes: Out of the total population of 188997 persons, 34874 persons (18.45%) belong to Scheduled Castes. The villages having less than 10% SC population are Makali, Nayidolle, Harohallidoddi, Byranayakanahalli Ammallydoddi, Gowdagere, Siddanahalli Mandya Bommanayakanahalli, Kannasandra Thavatanahallidoddi, Byadarahalli, Guddehosuru Devarahalli, Seebanahalli, Mudigere Mudigere Plantation, Thubinakere, Thore Hosur, Patlu Komananahalli, Kannamangala, Gendemadu, Bommanahalli Thattekere, Kodipura, Sanabanahalli, Doddanahalli Ankushanahalli, Agrahara Valagerehalli, Sulleri Akkur, Nagapura, Somanathapura Banduru Valagerehalli, Aralalasandra , Soudahalli Hunasanahalli, Kondapura, Banagahalli, Krishnapura Madapura, Bananthahalli, Halehalli, Ambadahalli Nunnuru, Siddapura, Karekoppa, Shanubhoganahalli Kodihosahalli, Bukkasagara.

The villages having more than 50% SC population are Cholamaranahalli, Chikkamannugudde State Forest Thimmasandra, Mangalawarpet, Neelakantanahalli Neelasandra, Mallamgere, Kallapura, Bachahalli Honniganahalli.

Sex ratio of Scheduled Caste population is 493.

Scheduled Castes Literates and Illiterates by Sex:

	Persons	Males	Females
Literate	17,201	10,439	6,762
Illiterate	17,673	7,254	10,419
Literacy rate	55.6	66.6	44.2
Graduate	599	520	79

Scheduled Castes (Dominant):

Adi Karnataka, Bhovi, Generic Castes etc., Madiga Korama

For their cultural identity please see Appendix-I

Villages without Scheduled Castes: There are 30 villages without any scheduled caste population.

Scheduled Tribes: Out of the total population of 188997 persons, 599 persons (0.32%) belong to Scheduled Tribes. The villages having less than 10% ST population are Kadaramangala, Makali, Nayidolle, Dasavara, Kelagere Harohallidoddi, Byranayakanahalli, Ammallydoddi Gowdagere, Siddanahalli, Mandya Bommanayakanahalli Aralapura, Honnayakanahalli, Thimmasandra, Bevooru Kannasandra, Thavatanahallidoddi, Thavatanahalli Byadarahalli, Guddehosuru, Thenkanahalli, Huluvady Mankunda, Devarahalli. Anigere, Seebanahalli, Koluru Dhabanagunda , Mudigere, Settihalli, Malur Hottiganahosahalli, Chakkere, Sankalagere, Mathikere Mudigere Plantation, Belakere, Marchanahalli, Kukkur Govindanahalli, Koornagere, Thubinakere, Chakkalur Malurpatna, Nagavara, Chikkenahalli, Mogenahalli Mylanayakanahalli, Thore Hosur, Patlu, Komananahalli Abbur, Yelehosahalli, Kannamangala, Vandaraguppe Cholamaranahalli, Devarahosahalli, Rampura Gendemadu, Honniganahalli Chikkamannugudde State Forest, Bommanahalli Thagachakere, Thimmasandra, Thattekere, Lalaghatta Mangalawarpet, Neelakantanahalli, Kudlur Santhemogenahalli, Honganur, Sunnaghatta Neelasandra, Kodipura, Sanabanahalli, Brahmanipura Mallamgere, Doddanahalli, Ankushanahalli Agrahara Valagerehalli, Sulleri, Avverahalli Malagalu, Hosahalli, Akkur, Nagapura, Somanathapura Virupakshipura, Banduru Valagerehalli, Dyavapatna Aralalasandra , Menasiganahalli, Vitalenahalli Virupasandra, Soudahalli, Mangadahalli, Ballapatna Hunasanahalli, Kondapura, Banagahalli, Sogala Sadahalli, Krishnapura, Garakahalli, Harokoppa Madapura, Bananthahalli, Halehalli, Ambadahalli Nunnuru, Neralur, Iggaluru, Saraguru Nelamakanahalli, Yalethotadahalli, Yaliyur Siddapura, Kallapura, Jagadapura, Byadarahalli Bachahalli, Kodamballi, Voddarahalli, Honniganahalli Karekoppa, Shanubhoganahalli, Byrasettihalli Singarajapura, Haniyur, Kodihosahalli, Bhoohalli Ujjanahalli, Bukkasagara.

The villages having more than 50% ST population are None.

Sex ratio of Scheduled tribe population is 487.

Scheduled Tribes Literates and Illiterates by Sex:

	Persons	Males	Females
Literate	204	139	65
Illiterate	395	168	227
Literacy rate	41.5	53.1	28.3
Graduate	12	12	0

Scheduled Tribes (Dominant):

Iruliga, Soligaru, Bavacha etc., Naikda etc., Meda

For their cultural identity please see Appendix-II

Villages without Scheduled Tribes: There are 125 villages without any scheduled tribe population.

Literates and Illiterates by Sex (Total Population):

	Persons	Males	Females

Literate	95,929	57,302	38,627
Illiterate	93,068	37,638	55,430
Literacy rate	57	68	46
Graduate	3,550	3,042	508

Agriculture: ***Distribution of villages according to land use:*** Out of 145 villages, Total area (in hectare) is 53496, out of that 61.12 percent is cultivable and 34.79 percent of the cultivable area is irrigated.

Sources of Irrigation (Hectares): Government Canal 1007.16, Private Canal 23.88, Well without Electricity 4.12, Well with Electricity 338.94, Tubewell without Electricity 48.56, Tubewell with Electricity 6406, Tank 3534.47, River 0, Lake 0, Waterfall 0, Others 11.31.

Villages with population of 5000 to 9999: Malur, Honganur.

Villages with population of 10000 and above: None

Distribution of Workers:

	Persons	Males	Females	WPR
Cultivators	44,166	30,694	13,472	48.55
Agricultural Labour	24,757	11,970	12,787	27.22
Household Industry	2,144	881	1,263	2.36
Other Workers	19,895	14,459	5,436	21.87
Main Workers	77,561	53,891	23,670	85.27
Marginal Workers	13,401	4,113	9,288	14.73
Total Workers	90,962	58,004	32,958	

Religion: Major Religious Communities:

	Persons	Males	Females	Sex Ratio
Hindu (98.42%)	186,002	93,419	92,583	991
Muslim (1.32%)	2,491	1,265	1,226	969
Christian (0.12%)	226	117	109	932
Sikh (0%)	2	2	-	-
Buddhists (0.01%)	10	6	4	667
Jain (0%)	7	4	3	750

Agewise Data:

	Persons	Males	Females	Sex Ratio
All ages	188,997	94,940	94,057	991
0-14	51,500	26,165	25,335	968
15-44	93,635	46,870	46,765	998
45-79	41,490	20,896	20,594	986
80+	2,269	951	1,318	1386
Age not stated	103	58	45	776

Languages (Dominant):
Kannada, Telugu, Urdu, Tamil, Hindi

Disabled Population:

	Persons	Males	Females	%
Total Disabled	4,874	2,696	2,178	
In Seeing	2,394	1,244	1,150	49.12
In Speech	458	254	204	9.4
In Hearing	327	156	171	6.71
In Movement	1,283	815	468	26.32
Mentally	412	227	185	8.45

CHANNARAYAPATNA

Channarayapatna C.D. Block lies in the eastern part of Hassan district. It is a part of Channarayapatna taluka. The Block is located at a distance of 37 kms. from district headquarters (Hassan). There are 385 villages in the block with the total population of 243, 610 persons. Area of the C.D. Block is 1033.61 sq. kms. It is bounded by taluk Arsikere and district Tumkur on north, district Mandya and taluk Hole Narsipur on south, districts Tumkur and Mandya on east, taluks Hassan and Hole Narsipur on west.

Communications:

Roadways : NH- 48: Direction- Hassan to Nelamangala, Nearest Villages- Baladare, Dandiganahalli, Avareningana koppal, Muddanahalli, Hirihalli, Appenahalli, Yeliyur, Uppinahalli, Chowdenahalli, Baragur, Doddamathighatta, Hosur, Aralabaragur, Katrighatta, Kerechikenahalli, Belasinda, Guramaranahalli, Chamadihalli, Shettihalli, Jogipura, Malavanaghatta, Gowdagere, Gulihonnenahalli, Madihalli, Chikkonahalli, Honnenahalli, Heggadihalli, Bookanabetta, Hirisave, Metikere, Byadarahalli, Thoobin akere, Kirisave, Kodibelagola, Mattanavile, Rajapura. SH- 7: Direction- Arsikere to Krishnarajpet, Nearest Villages- Nettekere, Sathenahalli, Ankenahalli, Gyarahal li, Jakkenahalli, Y.Singenahalli, Baragur, Doddamathighat ta, Alagodanahalli, Kurikaval, Kundur Mallenahalli, Mudan ahalli, Chamarajapura, Byadarahalli, Darasighatta, Madaba, Cholenahalli, Adagur, Mallenahalli, Yachenahalli, Devas thana Kalenahalli. SH- 8: Direction- Holenarsipur to Hirisave, Nearest Villages- Bindenahalli, Bindenahalli Kaval, Kagganti Kaval, Mancheganahalli, A.Kalenahalli, Chikkaganni, Gullahalli , Doddaganni, Yachenahalli, Kaggali Kaval, Devasthana Kalenahalli, Guramaranahalli, C.R.Patna Amanikere, Bindenahalli, Janivara Amanikere, Shravaneri, Janivara, Booka, Hirisave, Arakere, Sorekay ipura, Mathigatta, Hadenahalli, B.Cholenahalli, Bastihalli, Rachenahalli, Jinnathapura, Shravanabelgola (Rural), Sanenahalli, S. Hosahalli , Sundahalli, M. Hosur, Madane, Juttanahalli, Mallenahalli, Beeranahalli, Chalya.

River: Hemavati Nadi- Nearest Villages- Kachenahalli, Kumbenahalli, Agrahara, Cholenahalli, Somadevarapura, A.Kalenahalli, Chikkaganni, Doddaganni.

Canal: Nearest Villages- Hampanahalli, Kalenahalli, Paduvanahalli, Noranakki, Bindenahalli, Honnashettyhalli, K. Singenahalli, Thejigere, Kachenahalli, Kumbenahalli, Chittanahosahalli, Agrahara, Cholenahalli, Somadevarapu ra, A.Kalenahalli, Chikkaganni, Gullahalli , Nallur, Doddaganni, Dadadahalli, Cholenahalli, Adagur, Yaduvanah alli, Janivara Amanikere, Pyalasamudra, Jattenahalli,

Shravaneri, Janivara.
Annual Rainfall: Normal Rianfall 771.5 mm.
Ground Water: Availability of the Ground Water in the Basin is 112.54 H.A.M. and the utilization is 85.84 H.A.M. It belongs to Over Exploited category. Depth to water level 2 to 10 meter below the ground. Most of the wells go down in summer months, according to the Ground Water Estimation Committee.
Soils: Red Soil, Red Sandy Soil, Mixed Soil and Silty Clay Soil.
Natural Division : It falls partly in Gandasi-Hirisave Plateau and Cauvery-Hemavati Basin of the Southern Karnataka Plateau.
Administration:
Division: Mysore. Parliamentary Constituency: 16 Hassan. District: Hassan. Taluka: Channarayapatna. Assembly Constituency: 193 Sharavana Belagola, 197 Hole Narsipur. Gram Panchayat: 40.
Fairs: Ammadevaru Car Festival: It is held at Arakere in about March every year for one day. Arakere is a place in Banavara hobli of Arsikere taluk in Hassan area. There are two temples, namely, Chanukeshava temple and Ramesh vara temples, at this place. The former is a trikutachala or three-celled temple.
Lakshmi Narasimhaswamy Jatra: It is held at Nuggihalli, in about March-April every.year for a period of seven days. Nuggihalli, the headquarters of the Hobli of the same name in Channarayapatna taluk, is on the Channaraya patna-Tiptur road about 20 kms. from the taluk headquarters.
Gommateshwara Mahamasthakabhishekha: Mahamasthakabhishekha of Gommateshwara and connected festivals at the Jaina Matha and temples are held in about March once in twelve years only for a period of 13 days at Shravanabelgola. This occasion attracts a large number of people from all over India.
Jain Matha's Jatra: It is held at Shravanabelgola in about March-April for a period of ten days. Shravanabel gola a well-known place of pilgrimage for the Jains and of great cultural interest in general, is situated at a distance of 12 kms. from Bangalore-Mangalore road, in Channarayapatna taluk and is about 13 kms. to the south-east of the taluk headquarters.
Villages: 385 **Inhabited:** 374 **Uninhabited:** 11

Ranking	District	State	National
Area	2	77	405
Population	2	44	272
Sex Ratio	2	11	512
Child Sex Ratio	5	59	2435
Literacy Rate	4	58	1882
Density	3	44	4251
Work Participation Rate	4	52	1390

Gram Panchayats:
Kembalu, Anathi, Karehalli, Navile, S.Shivara, Kabbali, Didaga, Akkanahalli, Nuggehalli , Tagadur, M.Shivara, Sathenahalli, Kundur, Bagur , Byadarahalli, Jambur, Belagihalli, Jinnenahalli, Balaganchi, Hirisave, Mattinavile, Kalkere, Baladare, Baragur, Gulasinda, Dindagur, Gowdagere, Mathigatta, Juttanahalli, Sundahalli, Bekka, Janivara, Devasthana Kalenahalli, Anekere, Noranakki, Kumbenahalli, Nallur, Kantharajapura, Shravanabelgola (Rural) , Dammaningala.
Amenities:
Education: Primary School in 338 villages, Middle school in 181 villages, Matriculation or Secondary School in 38 villages, namely Baladare, Sathenahalli, Kundur, Baragur, Anekere, Paduvanahalli, Bidare, M.Shivara, K.Byrapura, Kembalu, Valagerehalli, Anathi, Honnanakoppal, Byadarahalli, Bagur, Obalapura, Navile, Karehalli, Chikkaganni, Doddaganni, Gowdagere, Kalkere, Tagadur, Hulikere, Nuggehalli, S.Shivara, Akkanahalli, Kabbali, Didaga, Hirisave, Honnashettihalli, Byadarahalli, Kantharajapura, Jinnenahalli, Shravanabelgola (Rural), Dammaningala, Mattanavile, Juttanahalli.
Higher Secondary or Pre University Courses or Intermediate or Junior College in 8 villages of the CD Block,, namely Baladare, Kembalu, Anathi, Bagur, Chikkaganni, Nuggehalli, Hirisave, Shravanabelgola (Rural).
College in 2 villages, Adult Literacy Center in 0 village., Colleges are in villages, namely Nuggehalli, Shravanabelgola (Rural).
Medical: Hospital in 0 village, Dispensary in 38 villages, Health Center in 17 villages, Sub Center in 77 villages, Maternity and Child Welfare Center in 10 villages, Community health workers in 14 villages.
The Villages having Hospital or Dispensary or Health Center are Chowlagala, Sathenahalli, Uppinahalli, Alagodanahalli, Anekere, Balaghatta, Bidare, M.Shivara, Kembalu, Valagerehalli, Anathi, Adihalli, Bagur, Chikkonahalli, Navile, B.Byrapura, Karehalli, Chikkaganni, Vaddarahalli, Sathenahalli, Gowdagere, Kalkere, Tagadur, Nuggehalli, Rampura, S.Shivara, Yachanaghatta, Channagonahalli, Ganjigere, Hosur, Akkanahalli, Thoti, Hirisave, Kantharajapura, Shravanabelgola (Rural) , Dammaningala, Basavanahalli, Mattanavile, Dadigatta.
Drinking Water: Tap water in 160 villages, Tank water in 198 villages, Well water in 284 villages, Tubewell in 253 villages and more than one source in 347 villages.

Bank: Banking facility in 27 villages, namely, Anekere, Bidare, Basavanapura, M.Shivara, Bagur Karehalli, Chikkaganni, Kalkere, Nuggehalli, Rampura S.Shivara, Hosahalli, Yachanaghatta, Ganjigere Hosur, Kabbali, Didaga, Hirisave, Honnashettihalli Honnamaranahalli, Chikkabilithi, Vaddarahalli Hiribilithi, Shravanabelgola (Rural), K.Hosahalli Mattanavile, Juttanahalli.

Credit Society in 40 villages Agricultural Credit Society in 38 Non-Agricultural Credit Society in 5 villages.

Others: Power supply in 365 villages, Cinema hall in 3 villages, sport club in 1 village, Stadium or Auditorium or Community Hall in 0 village, Post Office in 66 villages.

There are 218 villages having bus facilities.

Villages with most of facilities: Anekere, Bidare Bagur, Karehalli, Kalkere, Nuggehalli, Kabbali Didaga, Hirisave, Vaddarahalli Shravanabelgola (Rural), Mattanavile, Juttanahalli.

Villages without amenities (Education): Avareninganakoppal, Doothanur Kaval, Appenahalli, Aralabaragur, Hampanahalli, Kagganti Kaval, Mancheganahalli, Thejigere, Kalenahalli, Thippalapura, Papanaghatta, Kashipura, Chamarajapura, Darasighatta, Mallenahalli, Yachenahalli, Kaggali Kaval, Yaduvanahalli, Bisalahalli, Pyalasamudra, Hosur, Gowdagere Kaval, Lakkarasanahalli, Duggenahalli, Hosur, Basavanapura, Mandaleekanahalli, Hammanahalli, Makanahalli, Balaganchi Amanikere, Bekkadamanikere, Uthenahalli, Majjanahalli, Basavanahalli, Dasarahalli, Beeranahalli..

Scheduled Castes: Out of the total population of 243590 persons, 24907 persons (10.22%) belong to Scheduled Castes. The villages having less than 10% SC population are D.Samudravalli, Sajjekoppalu, Sannenahalli Sattigodanahalli, Somanathanahalli, Tenkanahalli Dandiganahalli, Avareninganakoppal, Muraranahalli Doothanur Kaval, Chikkarade, Doddakarade, Belaguli Chowlagala, Tarabenahalli, Varanahalli, Nettekere Sathenahalli, Thippur, Gyarahalli, Thimmalapura Madalapura, Annenahalli, Muddanahalli, Hirihalli Appenahalli, Yeliyur, Uppinahalli, Chowdenahalli Baragur, Doddamathighatta, Gejjegaranahalli Katrighatta, Channapura, Anekere, Nambihalli Hampanahalli, Kalenahalli, Nadanahalli, Narayanapura Bindenahalli, Bindenahalli Kaval, Mancheganahalli Honnashettyhalli, Kachenahalli, Kumbenahalli Agrahara, Agrahara, Narayanapura, Madaguddanahalli Balaghatta, Bidare, Chikkarasanahalli, K.Dasapura Lakkihalli, Banavase, Kalenahalli, Krishnapura Halasinahalli, Darshihalli, Maragur, Somenahalli Kamanahalli, Kakkihalli, K.Byrapura, Kembalu Beechagondanahalli, Valagerehalli, Thippalapura Papanaghatta, Honnanakoppal, Chattanahalli Baktaravalli, Kallumallenahalli, Kashipura Govinakere, Mudanahalli, Byadarahalli, Darasighatta Maruvanahalli, Dyavanahalli, Chikkonahalli Rechihalli, Channenahalli, Nagenahalli, Chikkaganni Gullahalli , Nallur, Doddaganni, Dadadahalli, Adagur Yachenahalli, Devasthana Kalenahalli Kerechikenahalli, Belasinda, Gulasinda Chikkanayakanahalli, P.Dasapura, Gollara Hosahalli Vaddarahalli, Karimaranahalli, Chikkagondanahalli Gundasetty Halli, Yaduvanahalli, Bisalahalli Jattenahalli, Baralu, Janivara, Chamadihalli Shettihalli, Sathenahalli, Sorekaipura, Devigere Nandipura, K.Kalenahalli, Bediganahalli Malavanaghatta, Anthanahalli, Gowdagere Gowdagere Kaval, Valageresomanahalli, Somalapura Harosomanahalli, Tavarekere, Tenkanahalli J.Madihalli, Chowdenahalli, Rangapura Rayasamudra Kaval, Honna Maranahalli Jambur Amanikere, Hulikere, Bananakere, Karekere Muddanahalli, Nuggehalli, M.Dasapura, A.Belaguli Narenahalli, Dyavalapura, Rampura, Hosahalli Yachanaghatta, Duggenahalli, Channagonahalli, Hosur Neralakere, Shettihalli, Joisaramavinahalli Basavanapura, Chinnenahalli, Dodderi, Kavalhosur Maradihalli, Dasarahalli, Mandaleekanahalli Mukikere, Ungragere, Pura, Nari Halli Thuppada Halli, K.Kamana Ghatta, D. Tumukur Bidarakere, Ugenahalli, Hammanahalli, Mellahalli Ullavalli, Jinnenahalli, Belagihalli, Bookanabetta Booka, Makanahalli, Kabbinakere, Honnashettihalli Mudibetta Kaval, Gowdarahalli, Yalanahalli Byadarahalli, Thoobinakere, Kollenahalli, Arakere Sorekayipura, Channenahalli (Channahalli) Kamaravalli, Boregowdana Koppalu, Ayyarahalli Kirisave, Thimmalapura, Balaganchi Amanikere Vaddarahalli, Jinnenahalli, Hadenahalli B.Cholenahalli, Manchenahalli, Hosur, Halebelagola Parama, Bastihalli, Rachenahalli, Jinnathapura Shravanabelgola (Rural) , Kabbalu Sugganahalli Koppal, K.Hosahalli, Dinka Majjanahalli, Kothanaghatta, Aruvanahalli Kantirayapura, Sanenahalli, S. Hosahalli , Sundahalli Kempinakote, Gullenahalli, Kasaranahalli, Huligere M. Hosur, Dasarahalli, Beeranahalli, Korenahalli Kumbenahalli, Dadigatta.

The villages having more than 50% SC population are

Hosur, Joisarahalli, C.Honnenahalli
Muddanahalli Kaval, Kallesomanahalli, Appenahalli
Pyalasamudra, Mavinahalli, Bhoovanahalli, Tagadur
Hullenahalli, Dodderi Kaval, Bekkadamanikere.
Sex ratio of Scheduled Caste population is 507.

Scheduled Castes Literates and Illiterates by Sex:

	Persons	Males	Females
Literate	11,861	6,936	4,925
Illiterate	13,046	5,354	7,692
Literacy rate	54.6	65.2	44.5
Graduate	227	193	34

Scheduled Castes (Dominant):
Adi Karnataka, Bhovi, Madiga, Sudugadu Siddha Korama

For their cultural identity please see Appendix-I

Villages without Scheduled Castes: There are 82 villages without any scheduled caste population.

Scheduled Tribes: Out of the total population of 243590 persons, 1717 persons (0.7%) belong to Scheduled Tribes. The villages having less than 10% ST population are D.Samudravalli, Sajjekoppalu, Sannenahalli Sattigodanahalli, B.Samudravalli, Baladare Tenkanahalli, Dandiganahalli, Avareninganakoppal Muraranahalli, Doothanur Kaval, Chikkarade Doddakarade, Belaguli, Chowlagala, Tarabenahalli Varanahalli, Nettekere, Sathenahalli, Thippur Ankenahalli, Kundur, Gyarahalli, Thimmalapura Madalapura, Annenahalli, Muddanahalli, Vagarahalli Hirihalli, Appenahalli, Yeliyur, Jakkenahalli Y.Singenahalli, Uppinahalli, Chowdenahalli, Baragur Chikkamathighatta, Doddamathighatta, Hosur Alagodanahalli, Gejjegaranahalli, Aralabaragur Katrighatta, Sagathavalli, Channapura, Anekere Malenahalli, Nambihalli, Hampanahalli, Kalenahalli Nadanahalli, Narayanapura, Paduvanahalli, Noranakki Bindenahalli, Bindenahalli Kaval, Kagganti Kaval Mancheganahalli, Honnashettyhalli, K. Singenahalli Thejigere, Pothanahalli, Kachenahalli, Kumbenahalli Chittanahosahalli, Agrahara, Cholenahalli A.Kalenahalli, Agrahara, Narayanapura, Kurikaval Joisarahalli, Madaguddanahalli, Balaghatta Balehalli, Bidare, Basavanapura, Chikkarasanahalli K.Dasapura, Lakkihalli, C.Honnenahalli, M.Shivara Hongehalli, Agasarahalli, Banavase, Kalenahalli Krishnapura, Halasinahalli, Darshihalli, Maragur Somenahalli, Kamanahalli, Kalamaranahalli Kakkihalli, K.Byrapura, Kembalu, Hullenahalli Beechagondanahalli, Valagerehalli, Kodihalli Thippalapura, Papanaghatta, Anathi, Honnanakoppal Chattanahalli, Adihalli, Chokenahalli, Chowvenahalli Baktaravalli, Muddanahalli Kaval, Kallumallenahalli Kashipura, Govinakere, Dyavanoor, Kooradahalli Kumbarahalli, Kundur Mallenahalli, Mudanahalli Chamarajapura, Byadarahalli, Darasighatta, Madaba Maruvanahalli, Bagur, Dyavanahalli, Daddihalli Chowdenahalli, Honnenahalli, Obalapura Kallesomanahalli, Kamanayakanahalli, Chikkonahalli Appenahalli, Navile, Rechihalli, B.Byrapura Karehalli, Channenahalli, Thimmalapura, Nagenahalli Chikkaganni, Gullahalli , Nallur, Doddaganni Dadadahalli, Cholenahalli, Adagur, Mallenahalli Yachenahalli, Kaggali Kaval, Devasthana Kalenahalli Kerechikenahalli, Belasinda, Gulasinda Chikkanayakanahalli, Byaladakere, Kuruvanka P.Dasapura, Gollara Hosahalli, Vaddarahalli Kalasinda, Karimaranahalli, Chikkagondanahalli Bandihalli, Gundasetty Halli, Bindenahalli Yaduvanahalli, Bisalahalli, Pyalasamudra Jattenahalli, Baralu, Shravaneri, Janivara Chamadihalli, Shettihalli, Aralapura, Dindagur Sathenahalli, Sorekaipura, Devigere, Soppinahalli Nandipura, Jogipura, K.Kalenahalli, Bediganahalli Hosur, Malavanaghatta, Anthanahalli, Gowdagere Gowdagere Kaval, Valageresomanahalli, Badakanahalli Somalapura, Harosomanahalli, Nettikere, Tavarekere Tenkanahalli, Jambur, J.Madihalli, Kalkere Chowdenahalli, Avverahalli, Mavinahalli Bhoovanahalli, Heggadigere, Tagadur Lakkarasanahalli, Rangapura, Rayasamudra Kaval Virupakshapura, Honna Maranahalli, Jambur Amanikere Hulikere, Athihalli, Kaggere, M.Honnenahalli Bananakere, Hebbalalu, Karekere, Muddanahalli Samudravalli, Nuggehalli, M.Dasapura, Hoovinahalli A.Belaguli, Hullenahalli, Narenahalli, Dyavalapura Rampura, S.Shivara, Hosahalli, Yachanaghatta Duggenahalli, Channagonahalli, Ganjigere, Hosur Neralakere, Mullkere, Shettihalli Joisaramavinahalli, Basavanapura, Kattigehalli Baddikere, Chinnenahalli, Dodderi, Gulihonnenahalli Madihalli, Chikkonahalli, Dodderi Kaval, Kavalhosur Maradihalli, Akkanahalli, Sosalagere, Kanuvanaghatta Masakanahalli, Duggenahalli, Dasarahalli, Kabbali Mandaleekanahalli, Mukikere, Bilikere, Ungragere Madalagere Kaval, Madalagere, Nimbihalli, Pura Nari Halli, Thuppada Halli, Didaga, K.Kamana Ghatta D. Tumukur, Bidarakere, Ugenahalli, Hammanahalli Karikyathanahalli, Mellahalli, Ullavalli, Hosahalli Naganahalli, Jinnenahalli, Thoti, Belagihalli Honnenahalli, Heggadihalli, Bookanabetta, Booka Hirisave, Metikere, Makanahalli, Kabbinakere

Honnashettihalli, Mudibetta Kaval, Gowdarahalli Honnamaranahalli, Yalanahalli, Byadarahalli Thoobinakere, Kollenahalli, Sorekayipura, Mathigatta Bommenahalli, Channenahalli (Channahalli) Kamaravalli, Cholamballi, Boregowdana Koppalu Ayyarahalli, Sabbanahalli, Kothanahalli, Kirisave Thimmalapura, Balaganchi Amanikere, Balaganchi Chikkabilithi, Vaddarahalli, Hiribilithi Kantharajapura, Jinnenahalli, Hadenahalli B.Cholenahalli, Manchenahalli, Ragibommenahalli Kodibelagola, Hosur, Halebelagola, Shivapura, Bekka B. Honnenahalli, Parama, Bekkadamanikere, Bastihalli Rachenahalli, Jinnathapura, Shravanabelgola (Rural) Uthenahalli, Halumathighatta, Kabbalu Sugganahalli Koppal, Sugganahalli, Gurigaranahalli Aladahalli, K.Hosahalli, Dinka, D. Honnenahalli Dammaningala, Majjanahalli, Kothanaghatta K.Bommenahalli, Aruvanahalli, Kantirayapura Sanenahalli, S. Hosahalli , Sundahalli Basavanahalli, Kempinakote, Gullenahalli Mattanavile, Mallasettyhalli, Rajapura Kasaranahalli, Huligere, Poomadihalli, M. Hosur Madane, Ankanahalli, Juttanahalli, Mallenahalli Dasarahalli, Beeranahalli, Chalya, Korenahalli Kumbenahalli, Dadigatta.

The villages having more than 50% ST population are None.

Sex ratio of Scheduled tribe population is 492.

Scheduled Tribes Literates and Illiterates by Sex:

	Persons	Males	Females
Literate	868	519	349
Illiterate	849	353	496
Literacy rate	57.6	67.7	47.1
Graduate	23	18	5

Scheduled Tribes (Dominant):

Naikda etc., Soligaru, Meda, Generic Tribes etc. Hakkipikki

For their cultural identity please see Appendix-II

Villages without Scheduled Tribes: There are 327 villages without any scheduled tribe population.

Literates and Illiterates by Sex (Total Population):

	Persons	Males	Females
Literate	142,102	82,185	59,917
Illiterate	101,488	37,842	63,646
Literacy rate	65	77	54
Graduate	4,182	3,424	758

Agriculture: ***Distribution of villages according to land use:***

Out of 385 villages, Total area (in hectare) is 103361, out of that 70.17 percent is cultivable and 26.05 percent of the cultivable area is irrigated.

Sources of Irrigation (Hectares): Government Canal 4987.55, Private Canal 102, Well without Electricity 251.79, Well with Electricity 2861.32, Tubewell without Electricity 357.47, Tubewell with Electricity 6301.3, Tank 2026.22, River 4.05, Lake 0, Waterfall 199.01, Others 1797.18.

Villages with population of 5000 to 9999: Shravanabelgola (Rural).

Villages with population of 10000 and above: None

Distribution of Workers:

	Persons	Males	Females	WPR
Cultivators	102,154	59,174	42,980	77
Agricultural Labour	15,303	5,355	9,948	11.54
Household Industry	1,373	964	409	1.03
Other Workers	13,834	10,033	3,801	10.43
Main Workers	111,852	71,665	40,187	84.31
Marginal Workers	20,812	3,861	16,951	15.69
Total Workers	132,664	75,526	57,138	

Religion: Major Religious Communities:

	Persons	Males	Females	Sex Ratio
Hindu (97.42%)	237,303	116,718	120,585	1,033
Muslim (1.4%)	3,407	1,756	1,651	940
Christian (0.44%)	1,063	534	529	991
Sikh (0.01%)	19	9	10	1,111
Buddhists (0.01%)	29	17	12	706
Jain (0.48%)	1,172	702	470	670

Agewise Data:

	Persons	Males	Females	Sex Ratio
All ages	243,590	120,027	123,563	1029
0-14	65,216	32,913	32,303	981
15-44	119,591	58,584	61,007	1041
45-79	55,302	26,973	28,329	1050
80+	3,291	1,453	1,838	1265
Age not stated	190	104	86	827

Languages (Dominant):

Kannada, Urdu, Telugu, Coorgi/Kodagu, Tamil

Disabled Population:

	Persons	Males	Females	%
Total Disabled	4,082	2,152	1,930	
In Seeing	1,782	818	964	43.66
In Speech	415	219	196	10.17
In Hearing	322	159	163	7.89
In Movement	1,209	779	430	29.62
Mentally	354	177	177	8.67

CHIK BALLAPUR

Chikballapur C.D. Block lies in the north-western part of Kolar district. It is a part of Chikballapur taluka. The Block is located at a distance of 60 kms. from district headquarters (Kolar). There are 251 villages in the block with the total population of 129,288 persons. Area of the C.D. Block is 634.67 sq. kms. It is bounded by taluk Gudibanda on north, district Bangalore Rural on south, taluk Sidlaghatta on east, and taluk Gauribida nur and district Bangalore Rural on west.

Communications:

Roadways : N.H.-7: Direction- Ananthapur to Bangalore, Nearest Villages- Nandanaganahalli, Gantiganahudya, Yalagalahalli, Peresandra, Aroor, Kakalachinte, Bandaha lli, Doddapyalagurki, Samasenahalli, Maraganahalli, Byapp anahalli, Guvalakanahalli, Amani Poornasagarakere, Ballag ere, Devasthanadahosahalli, Hunegallu, Burugamakalahalli, Honnenahalli, Harobande, Marasanahalli, Amani Manchanab elekere, Jadalathimmanahalli, Yaluvahalli , Beedaganahalli, Amani Doddamaralikere, Varamallenahalli, Chadulapura, Thumukalahalli , Kothanoor, Chokkahalli. S.H.-58: Direct ion- Gauribidanur to Sidlaghatta, Nearest Villages- Thipp enahalli, Amani Manchanabelekere, Anakanur, Patrenahalli, Bommenahalli, Kolimenahalli, Posettihalli, Bandammanaha lli, Gollahalli, Motlur, Nallakadirenahalli, Amani Gopala krishnakere, Marimakalahalli, Andarlahalli, Varadahalli, Nayanahalli, Jathavara, Jathavara-Hosahalli, Thammanaya kanahalli, Hosahudya. S.H.-74: Direction- Nelamangla to Kolar, Nearest Villages- Singadikadirenahalli, Sulthanp et, Madakuhosahalli, Nandi Hills, Nandi, Kuppahalli, Devisettihalli, Yaluvahalli , Amani Doddamaralikere, Doddamaralli. S.H.-74 A: Direction- Bangalore to Chikbal lapur, Nearest Villages- Kandavara, Thirnahalli, Chikkamu ddenahalli, Naremmanahalli, Kuduvathi, Angatta, Nandi, Mavahalli.

Railway Station: Villages- Devisettihalli, Jathavara, Kalinayakana-Kondenahalli.

River: Penner Nadi- Nearest Villages- Bommenahalli, Posettihalli, Bandammanahalli, Gollahalli, Nallakadirena halli, Chokkanahalli, Gurukulanagenahalli, Balakuntahalli, Chikkanahalli, Jakkalamadagu.

Reserved Forest: (Haristala R.F.): Nearest Villages- Koothanahalli, Aroor, Settigere, Bandahalli, Haristhala, Chikkapayalagurki, Doddapyalagurki, Samasenahalli.

Annual Rainfall: Normal Rianfall 801.6 mm.

Ground Water: Availability of the Ground Water in the basin is (Information not avablable) H.A.M. and the utilization is (Information not avablable) H.A.M.. belongs to (Information not avablable) category. Depth to water level 5 to 20 meter below the ground. Most of the wells go down in summer months, according the Ground Water Estimation Committee.

Soils: Red Soils.

Natural Division : It falls in Sidlaghatta-Sriniwaspur uplands of the Southern Karnataka Plateau.

Administration:

Division: Bangalore. Parliamentary Constituency: 27 Bangalore (SC). District: Kolar. Taluka: Chik Ballapur. Assembly Constituency: 141 Chikballapur.

Gram Panchayat: 22.

Regional Area Development Boards: The Bailu Seeme Area Development Board.

Fairs and Festivals: Nandishwara Jatra: It is held at Nandi near Kolar in the month of Jan.-Feb. and attended by about 1 lakh persons. Nandi is in Chikballapur taluk at the north-eastern base of Nandidurga. It is the headquarters of the Nandi hobli. It contains a large temple dedicated to Bhoga-Nandishvara, which is surrounded by a number of Chola inscriptions in the grantha character. The foundation is much older as is evident from one Pallava and several Chola inscriptions that are found in its courtyard. The place was for some years a British milita ry station, a regiment being stationed between Nandi and Sultanpet from 1799 to 1808.

Villages: 251 **Inhabited:** 223 **Uninhabited:** 28

Ranking	District	State	National
Area	10	146	1074
Population	10	141	2298
Sex Ratio	10	112	2732
Child Sex Ratio	9	76	2799
Literacy Rate	4	101	3081
Density	7	37	4516
Work Participation Rate	8	66	1165

Gram Panchayats:

Kammaguttahalli, Peresandra, Aroor, Mandikal , Gollahalli, Doddapyalagurki, Dibbur, Harobande, Avalagurki, Thippenahalli , Posettihalli , Muddenahalli, Nandi, Kuppahalli, Doddamaralli, Agalagurki , Kondenahalli, Ajjavara, Patrenahalli, Manchanabele, Angarekanahalli, Hosahudya.

Amenities:

Education: Primary School in 153 villages, Middle school in 74 villages, Matriculation or Secondary School in 13 villages, namely Renumakalahalli, Peresandra, Mandikal, Reddy Gollavarahalli, Gollahalli, Thippenahalli, Marasanahalli, Dibbur, Muddenahalli, Nandi, Kolavanahalli, Nugathihalli, Hosahudya.

Higher Secondary or Pre University Courses or Intermediate or Junior College in 3 villages of the CD Block,, namely Peresandra, Muddenahalli, Kuduvathi.

College in 0 village, Adult Literacy Center in 1 village.

Medical: Hospital in 1 village, Dispensary in 2 villages, Health Center in 6 villages, Sub Center in 28 villages, Maternity and Child Welfare Center in 0 village, Community health workers in 1 village.

The Villages having Hospital or Dispensary or Health Center are Mandikal , Marasanahalli, Kandavara.

Drinking Water: Tap water in 131 villages, Tank water in 20 villages, Well water in 42 villages, Tubewell in 124 villages and more than one source in 189 villages.

Bank: Banking facility in 19 villages, namely, Peresandra, Mandikal, Yerramaranahalli, Parenahalli Anemadagu, Kethenahalli, Settigere, Gollahalli Renumakalahalli, Avalagurki, Manchanabele Puttathimmanahalli, Dibbur, Posettihalli, Agalagurki Varadahalli, Ramachandra Hosur, Yennur Kadirenahalli Hosahudya.

Credit Society in 14 villages Agricultural Credit Society in 12 Non-Agricultural Credit Society in 3 villages.

Others: Power supply in 212 villages, Cinema hall in 2 villages, sport club in 0 village, Stadium or Auditorium or Community Hall in 0 village, Post Office in 37 villages.

There are 202 villages having bus facilities.

Villages with most of facilities: Peresandra Mandikal, Kethenahalli, Gollahalli, Avalagurki Manchanabele, Dibbur, Posettihalli, Agalagurki.

Villages without amenities (Education): R.Kambalahalli, R.Chokkanahalli, Kommalamari, Bommaganahalli, Karakamakalahalli, Ropparlahalli, Muddalahalli, P.Chokkanahalli, Jonnalakunte, Madinayakanahalli, Hosahalli, Gantiganahudya, Lakshmipathihalli, Amani Reddihallikere, Nallaguttahalli, Hanumanthapura, Dorabure, Yadarlahalli, Parenahalli, Yarrapapanahalli, Doddihalli, Kachakadatha, Bisaigarahalli, Bandahalli, H.Kurubarahalli, Papinayakanahalli, Reddihalli, Beeraganahalli, Maraganahalli, Byappanahalli, Naduvanahalli, Venkatapura, Lakkanayakanahalli, Billappavanagenahalli, Burugamakalahalli, Gondihalli, Ankanagondi, Byrojanahalli, Nallenahalli, Kalavara, Ethamakalahalli, Akalathimmanahalli, D.Kurubarahalli, Kolimenahalli, Gollahalli, Kandavara, Gantiganahalli, Naremmanahalli, Madakuhosahalli, Nandi Hills, Chikkasagarahalli, Mavahalli, Jadalathimmanahalli, Beedaganahalli, Amani Doddamaralikere, Varamallenahalli, Nakkalabachahalli, Sonnapura, Marimakalahalli, Mannarapura, Marthammanahalli, Balajigapade, Yennur Kadirenahalli, Obalenahalli..

Scheduled Castes: Out of the total population of 136154 persons, 40599 persons (29.82%) belong to Scheduled Castes. The villages having less than 10% SC population are Udagirinallappanahalli, Siddaganahalli Nagasanahalli, R.Kambalahalli, Renumakalahalli Ropparlahalli, Jonnalakunte, Lakshmipathihalli Amani Reddihallikere, Yadarlahalli, Sadenahalli Haristhala, Beeraganahalli, Soolikunte Naduvanahalli, Mogalakuppe, Venkatapura Billappavanagenahalli, Burugamakalahalli Pavandahalli, Byrojanahalli, Nallenahalli Amani Kandavarakere, Thandramaradahalli Akalathimmanahalli, Rayappanahalli, D.Kurubarahalli Hiriyannahalli, Kadadibbur, Avalahalli Angarekanahalli, Kolimenahalli, Bandammanahalli Gollahalli, Nasikuntehosur, Kanivenarayanapura Muddenahalli, Chikkamuddenahalli, Varamallenahalli Thumukalahalli , Cheedachikkanahalli , Yalehalli Jathavara, Marthammanahalli, Obalenahalli.

The villages having more than 50% SC population are Ramapatna, Chikkanareppanahalli, Bommaganahalli Karakamakalahalli, Madinayakanahalli Chikkanagavalli, Gantiganahudya, Boyanahalli Bommahalli, Nallaguttahalli, Doddihalli Kachakadatha, H.Kurubarahalli, Papinayakanahalli Ramaganaparthy, Golladoddi, Nallaguttapalya Settivarahalli, Lakkanayakanahalli, Ankanagondi Harobande, Lingasettipura, Ethamakalahalli, Motlur Nallakadirenahalli, Gurukulanagenahalli Balakuntahalli, Bandahalli, Kandavara Singadikadirenahalli, Mavahalli, Kuppahalli Chikkakadiganahalli, Thowdanahalli Nakkalabachahalli , Sonnapura, Marimakalahalli Balajigapade.

Sex ratio of Scheduled Caste population is 495.

Scheduled Castes Literates and Illiterates by Sex:

	Persons	Males	Females
Literate	15,646	9,814	5,832
Illiterate	24,953	10,706	14,247
Literacy rate	45.3	56.2	34.2
Graduate	254	235	19

Scheduled Castes (Dominant):

Madiga, Adi Karnataka, Bhovi, Adi Dravida Chalavadi etc.

For their cultural identity please see Appendix-I

Villages without Scheduled Castes: There are 53 villages without any scheduled caste population.

Scheduled Tribes: Out of the total population of 136154 persons, 14639 persons (10.75%) belong to Scheduled Tribes. The villages having less than 10% ST population are Ramapatna, R.Kambalahalli, R.Chokkanahalli Chikkanareppanahalli, Kommalamari, Bommaganahalli Renumakalahalli, Karakamakalahalli, Ropparlahalli Muddalahalli , Jonnalakunte, Madinayakanahalli Hosahalli, Chikkanagavalli, Nandanaganahalli Gantiganahudya, Yalagalahalli, Boyanahalli Kammathanahalli, Bommahalli, Amani Reddihallikere Nallaguttahalli, Koduru, Koothanahalli, Peresandra Aroor, Hanumanthapura, Kakalachinte

Yarrapapanahalli, Doddihalli, Nallappanahalli
Bhogaparthi, Addagal, Kachakadatha, H.Kurubarahalli
Papinayakanahalli, Dasarenahalli, Reddihalli
Beeraganahalli, Reddy Gollavarahalli, Ramaganaparthy
Maraganahalli, Byappanahalli, Yalagere, Gongadipura
Ittappanahalli, Gollahalli, Soolikunte
Naduvanahalli, Inam Inchenahalli, Renumakalahalli
Settivarahalli, Chalakayalaparthi
Lakkanayakanahalli, Soppahalli
Billappavanagenahalli, Devasthanadahosahalli
Hunegallu, Burugamakalahalli, Gondihalli, Arikere
Pavandahalli, Ankanagondi, Nallenahalli
Thippenahalli , Kanajenahalli, Dinnehosahalli
Gerahalli, Mustoor, Harobande, Lingasettipura
Marasanahalli, Manchanabele, Sabbenahalli
Patrenahalli, Thandramaradahalli
Adavigollavarahalli, Puttathimmanahalli, Gundlagurki
Akalathimmanahalli, Rayappanahalli, D.Kurubarahalli
Hiriyannahalli, Nellimaradahalli, Kathriguppe
Maralakunte, Cheemanahalli, Badaniganahalli
Bommenahalli, Kolimenahalli, Posettihalli
Bandammanahalli, Motlur, Nallakadirenahalli
Gurukulanagenahalli, Balakuntahalli, Chikkanahalli
Bandahalli, Bachahalli, Kandavara, Thirnahalli
Chikkamuddenahalli, Singadikadirenahalli
Chikkasagarahalli, Nandi, Mavahalli
Jadalathimmanahalli, Arasanahalli, Kuppahalli
Devisettihalli, Yaluvahalli , Amani Doddamaralikere
Doddamaralli, Chadulapura, Thumukalahalli , Kothanoor
Agalagurki , Bannikuppe, Cheedachikkanahalli
Chikkakadiganahalli, Kolavanahalli, Bommenahalli
Kanithahalli, Thowdanahalli, Nakkalabachahalli
Sonnapura, Marimakalahalli, Andarlahalli
Muthukadahalli, Varadahalli, Nayanahalli
Nugathihalli, Thimmanahalli, Kondenahalli
Kadaseegenahalli, Nelamakalahalli, Keshavara
Doddakirugumbi , Jathavara-Hosahalli
Thammanayakanahalli, Marthammanahalli, Balajigapade
Ramachandra Hosur, Yennur Kadirenahalli
Obalenahalli.

The villages having more than 50% ST population are Udagirinallappanahalli, Siddaganahalli, Gudisihalli Sadenahalli, Venkatapura, Amani Kandavarakere Kadadibbur, Avalahalli, Kandakanahalli, Korlahalli Nasikuntehosur, Kanivenarayanapura, Varamallenahalli Yalehalli.

Sex ratio of Scheduled tribe population is 492.

Scheduled Tribes Literates and Illiterates by Sex:

	Persons	Males	Females
Literate	5,977	3,657	2,320
Illiterate	8,662	3,777	4,885
Literacy rate	48.0	58.3	37.5
Graduate	55	49	6

Scheduled Tribes (Dominant):

Naikda etc., Meda, Kadu Kuruba, Iruliga, Hakkipikki

For their cultural identity please see Appendix-II

Villages without Scheduled Tribes: There are 114 villages without any scheduled tribe population.

Literates and Illiterates by Sex (Total Population):

	Persons	Males	Females
Literate	68,710	41,545	27,165
Illiterate	67,444	27,751	39,693
Literacy rate	58	69	47
Graduate	1,969	1,627	342

Agriculture: ***Distribution of villages according to land use:*** Out of 251 villages, Total area (in hectare) is 63467, out of that 46.61 percent is cultivable and 32.66 percent of the cultivable area is irrigated.

Sources of Irrigation (Hectares): Government Canal 364.6, Private Canal 25.9, Well without Electricity 52.24, Well with Electricity 1314.6, Tubewell without Electricity 210.15, Tubewell with Electricity 5685.63, Tank 1202.88, River 0, Lake 0, Waterfall 0, Others 804.57.

Villages with population of 5000 to 9999: None

Villages with population of 10000 and above: None

Distribution of Workers:

	Persons	Males	Females	WPR
Cultivators	31,795	20,602	11,193	43.52
Agricultural Labour	26,172	11,889	14,283	35.83
Household Industry	1,401	718	683	1.92
Other Workers	13,686	8,813	4,873	18.73
Main Workers	64,112	39,294	24,818	87.76
Marginal Workers	8,942	2,728	6,214	12.24
Total Workers	73,054	42,022	31,032	

Religion: Major Religious Communities:

	Persons	Males	Females	Sex Ratio
Hindu (96.05%)	130,775	66,569	64,206	965
Muslim (3.46%)	4,706	2,386	2,320	972
Christian (0.31%)	420	204	216	1,059
Sikh (0.01%)	7	6	1	167
Buddhists (0.03%)	36	16	20	1,250
Jain (0.02%)	21	11	10	909

Agewise Data:

	Persons	Males	Females	Sex Ratio
All ages	136,154	69,296	66,858	965
0-14	43,673	22,411	21,262	949
15-44	63,491	32,114	31,377	977
45-79	27,321	13,923	13,398	962
80+	1,617	815	802	984
Age not stated	52	33	19	576

Languages (Dominant):
Kannada, Telugu, Urdu, Tamil, Hindi
Disabled Population:

	Persons	Males	Females	%
Total Disabled	2,220	1,245	975	
In Seeing	920	482	438	41.44
In Speech	245	135	110	11.04
In Hearing	132	66	66	5.95
In Movement	703	451	252	31.67
Mentally	220	111	109	9.91

CHIKMAGALUR

Chikmagalur C.D. Block lies in the east central part of Chikmagalur district. It is a part of Chikmagalur taluka. The Block is located at a distance of 00 kms. from district headquarters (Chikmagalur). There are 229 villages in the block with the total population of 193,423 persons. Area of the C.D. Block is 1581.50 sq. kms. It is bounded by taluks Narasimharajapura and Tarikere on north, taluk Mudigere and district Hassan on south, taluk Kadur and district Hassan on east, and taluk Narsimharajapura on west.

Communications:

Roadways : S.H.-57: Direction- Tarikere to Belur, Nearest Villages- Athigiri, Thogarihankal, Gonakal, Galipooje, Suruguppe, Dasarahalli, Arasinaguppe, Bindiga, Hebballi, Hosahalli, Aralaguppe, Allampura, Hiremagalur, Karthi kere, Mugulavalli, Magadi, Kabbikere, Nagarahalli. S. H.-58: Direction- Belur to Banavar, Nearest Villages- Kottigenahalli, Kurubara Boodi Halu, Shankaranahalli. S.H.-64: Direction- Bantwal to Kadur, Nearest Villages- Mathavara, Dambadahalli, Siragunda, Mugathihalli, Kuruva ngi, Churchugudde Kaval, Jakerikaval, Kenkere, Uddeboran ahalli, Thadabenahalli, Kengenahalli, Karehalli, Kurichik kanahalli, Hiregowja, Dasarahalli, Devarahalli, Halelakya, Vasthare, Aladagudde, Huluvale, Kuduvalli, Chithavalli, Siravolalu, Kelagoor, Machagondanahalli, Handi.

River: Bhadra Nadi- Nearest Villages- Siragola, Bidare, Devadana, Huigere, Heggarmathavani.

Canal: Nearest Villages- Kuduvalli, Malalur, Thiruguna, Boodanike, Kundur, Kambihalli, Hadihalli, Haluvalli, Big ganahalli, Mavinakere, Mathikere, Banavara, Gangalagodu.

Canal: Thiruguna, Boodanike, Kundur, Bigganahalli, Mavina kere, Matikere, Gangalagodu, Kambihalli, Hadialli, Haluvalli, Chitavalli, Samse, Neradi, Hachadamane,Vajuval, Banavara,

Annual Rainfall: Normal Rianfall 845.5 mm.

Ground Water: Availability of the Ground Water in the Basin is 8317 H.A.M. and the utilization is 3798 H.A. M. It belongs to Safe category. Depth to water level 2 to 20 meter below the ground. Most of the wells go down in summer months, according to the Ground Water Estimation Committee.

Soils: Red Loamy and Sandy Soils.

Natural Division : It falls partly in Kudremukh-Bababudan Forested Hilly zone and Chikmagalur-Mudigere Rolling Humid Belt of the Central Karnataka Plateau.

Administration:

Division: Mysore. Parliamentary Constituency: 15 Udupi. District: Chikmagalur. Taluka: Chikmagalur. Assembly Constituency: 123 Siringeri, 124 Mudegere (SC), 125 Chikmagalur. Gram Panchayat: 47.

Regional Area Development Boards: The Maland Aera Development Board.

Fairs : Adi-Gaddige Shri Guru Dattatreya Phalahara Matha festival: Muttinapura, situated on the Baba-Budan hill range is 20 kms. north of Chikmagalur town. It has Adi-G addige Shri Guru Dattatreya Phalahara Matha and a temple dedicated to Prasanna Virupaksheshvara.

Bhola-Rameshvara Jatra: It is held at Chikmagalur in about the month of April for one day. Chikmagalur, situa ted in a fertile valley, south of the Bala Budan range of hills, about 248 kms. north-west of Bangalore, 39 kms. south-west of Kadur, 56 kms. south of Tarikere and 120 kms. south of Shimoga.

Bhoomi-Hunnime Festival: During the Deepavali season, "Bhoomi-Hunnime" festival is celebrated by the farmers of Sringeri, Mudigere, Koppa, Narasmharajapura and Chikm agalur taluks of Chikmagalur area.

Kattimaramma Jatra: It is held at Chikmagalur in about the month of April for one day.

Chaudeshvari Jatra: Mattavara near Chikmagalur, five kms. south-west of Chikmagalur town, has an ancient Parshvanatha basadi. An annual jatra of the Chaudeshvari is held for two days during September-October.

Hagaranada Habba Jatra: It is held at Hiregouja once in Seven Years for Seven days. Hiregouja is 14 kms. north-east of Chikmagalur town.

Hazrat Khaja Bunnabi Urs: At Gorigundi, which is a hamlet of Devadana village near Chikmagalur. Hazrat Khaja Bunnabi Urs is held annually in the month of Rabi-u l-Sani. The dargah is said to be more than a hundred years old.

Huligere Dodda Matha Festival: Huligere near Chikmagalur is about 23 kms. to the south of Kadur. It has a Veeras haiva monastery called Huligere Dodda Matha which is said to be connected with the Kallumaradi Matha of Sakrepatna.

Kodandarama Temple Jatra: It is held at Hiremagalur-Chik magalur in about the month of February every year. Hirema galur, which was until recently a separate village, is now a part of Chikmagalur town.

Kollapura-Mahalakshmi Jatra: It is held at Chikmagalur

in about the month of May-June for one day every year.
Lakshminarayana Kotarotsava Festival: It is held at Ishvarahalli near Chikmagalur in about the month of January every year. Ishvarahalli, 27 kms. east of Chikma galur town, has a temple dedicated to Lakshminarayana which was once a trikutachala structure.
Malluramma Jatra: It is held at Jagara near Chikmagalur in about the month of February for two days. Jagara, the headquarters of the hobli of the same name, situated amidst coffee plantations and enchanting natural scenar ies and paddy fields, is at a distance of about 30 kms. north-west of Chikmagalur town.
Markandeshvara Temple Jatra: It is held at Devadana near Chikmagalur around the month of February for three days. Devadana, located at a distance of 43 kms. north-w est of Chikmagalur town is on the right Bhadra.
Mullappaswami Jatra: It is held at Baba-Budangiri near Chikmagalur around the month of February-March for three days. The old name of Baba- Budangiri range of hills is Chandra-Drona Parvata.
Nirvanaswami Matha Jatra: It is held at Aralaguppe near Chikmagalur around the month of April every year. Aralag uppe is eight kilometres north-west of Chikmagalur town. It has a temple of Deveeramma who is much venerated by the local people.
Rameshvara Jatra: It is held at Kotevuru near Chikmagalur around the month of March for three days. Kotevuru 21 kms. south-west of Chikmagalur town, is noted for its ancient inscriptions.
Ranganathaswamy Jatra: It is held at Hiremagalur-Chikmag alur in about the month of April for five days every year.
Revanasiddheshvara Jatra: Sindigere near Chikmagalur called after Sindhamma a Jaina lady, is 32 kms. east of Chikmagalur. There is also a temple of Revanasiddhesh vara under the auspices of which an annual jatra is held for four days about March.

Villages: 229 **Inhabited:** 218 **Uninhabited:** 11

Ranking	District	State	National
Area	1	25	114
Population	2	93	774
Sex Ratio	5	38	1410
Child Sex Ratio	3	58	2451
Literacy Rate	4	29	1138
Density	3	125	5926
Work Participation Rate	4	155	2947

Gram Panchayats:
Bidare, Melinahuluvathi, Thogarihankal, Bilekallahalli, Mallenaalli, Inam Dattathreya Peeta, Shiravase, Kadavanthi, Byaravalli, Lakkamanahalli, Hiregowja, Hirekolale, Devadana, Avathi, Allampura, Dasarahalli, Lakya, Beekanahalli (Rural) , Indavara, Thalihalla, Basaravalli, Huigere, Bygoor, Mylimane, Sindigere, Machenahalli, Belawadi, Kalasapura, Marle, Aradavalli, Karthikere, Thegur, Mugathihalli, Anoor, Doddamagaravalli, Vasthare, Amble, Mugulavalli, Eswarahalli, Kurubara Boodi Halu , Malalur, Kuduvalli , Aldur, Kelagoor, Bigganahalli, Sathihalli, Basagal.

Amenities:
Education: Primary School in 96 villages, Middle school in 89 villages, Matriculation or Secondary School in 30 villages, namely Devadana, Saragodu, Thogarihankal, Shiravase, Byaravalli, Avathi, Bindiga, Mugathihalli, Hiremagalur *, Hiregowja, Lakya, Kanivehalli, Sindigere, Kalasapura, Belawadi, Kurubara Boodi Halu, Thalihalla, Mylimane, Anoor, Vasthare, Basagal, Chikkamagaravalli, Hawalli, Aldur, Kelagoor, Machagondanahalli, Kesavinamane, Mugulavalli, Marle, Malalur.
Higher Secondary or Pre University Courses or Intermediate or Junior College in 2 villages of the CD Block,, namely Mylimane, Aldur.
College in 0 village, Adult Literacy Center in 27 villages.
Medical: Hospital in 2 villages, Dispensary in 18 villages, Health Center in 9 villages, Sub Center in 22 villages, Maternity and Child Welfare Center in 15 villages, Community health workers in 12 villages.
The Villages having Hospital or Dispensary or Health Center are Kadavanthi, Hyarambi, Shiravase, Inam Dattathreya Peeta, Byaravalli, Avathi, Bindiga, Aralaguppe, Kalasapura, Belawadi, Kurubara Boodi Halu , Anoor, Vasthare, Hawalli, Kelagoor, Machagondanahalli, Amble, Bigganahalli.
Drinking Water: Tap water in 146 villages, Tank water in 51 villages, Well water in 164 villages, Tubewell in 57 villages and more than one source in 191 villages.
Bank: Banking facility in 30 villages, namely, Kadavanthi, Devadana, Thogarihankal, Melinahuluvathi Shiravase, Inam Dattathreya Peeta, Byaravalli Avathi, Hirekolale, Dambadahalli, Siragunda Mugathihalli, Nallur, Thegur, Hiremagalur * Uddeboranahalli, Hiregowja, Lakya, Kalasapura Belawadi, Kurubara Boodi Halu, Thalihalla, Mylimane Kuduvalli, Chikkamagaravalli, Aldur, Kelagoor Machagondanahalli, Amble, Mugulavalli.
Credit Society in 23 villages Agricultural Credit Society in 23 Non-Agricultural Credit Society in 4 villages.
Others: Power supply in 218 villages, Cinema hall in 2 villages sport club in 218 villages, Stadium or Auditorium or Communi Hall in 218 villages, Post Office in 50 villages.

There are 131 villages having bus facilities.

Villages with most of facilities: Kadavanthi Devadana, Shiravase, Inam Dattathreya Peeta Byaravalli, Avathi, Kalasapura, Belawadi Kurubara Boodi Halu, Aldur, Kelagoor Machagondanahalli, Amble, Mugulavalli.

Villages without amenities (Education): Basapura, Bikkarane, Manaboor, Heggarmathavani, Melagiri, Kesavinamane, Athigiri, Melinahuluvathi, Kesave, Jagara, Gonakal, Malagaru, Pandaravalli, Nagenahalli, Suruguppe, Masagali, Bagamane, Makodu, Karagoor, Bettadamalali, Pura, Basaravalli, Iydahalli, Aniganahalli, Havare, Devarahalli, Arenoor, Thotadahalli, Mavinahalli, Arebidacoor Estate, Dasarahalli, Hebballi, Huliyarahalli, Hosahalli, Karadihallikaval, Iyanahalli, Hampapura, Hukkunda, Dambadahalli, Siragunda, Dumagere, Chikmagalur (Rural), Churchugudde Kaval, Kamenahallikaval, Padamane, Jakkerikaval, Srinivasapura, Gungarahalli, Kenkere, Thadabenahalli, Karisiddanahalli, Kengenahalli, Karehalli, Balenahalli, Lakkamanahalli, Kurichikkanahalli, Dasarahalli, Devarahalli, Chikkagowja, Kabbigarahalli, Ganadalu, Halelakya, Boochenahallikaval, Sevalal Nagara, Payagondanahalli, Annindadike, Kallahalli, Shankaranahalli, Subramanyadahalli, Govindapura, Kottigenahalli, Jakkanahalli, Ilehole, Basagodu, Hancharavalli, Mylimane Estate, Kotevooru, Thoranamavu, Gowthameshwara, Guddenahalli, Aladagudde, Nandikere, Huluvale, Mahaji, Siravolalu, Thondavalli, Valagarehalli, Thadagase, Samse, Halasumane, Neradi, Hachadamane, Vajuvalli, Vataganahalli, Kelagani, Kesavinahaklu, Haliyur, Donagudige, Yelagudige, Balehalli, Aradavalli, Ramanahalli, Hejjiganahalli, Bikkemane, Kenchenahalli, Thiruguna, Boodanike, Kundur, Tagadoor, Haluvalli, Mavinakere, Nagarahalli..

Scheduled Castes: Out of the total population of 194314 persons, 51149 persons (26.32%) belong to Scheduled Castes. The villages having less than 10% SC population are Heggarmathavani, Melagiri, Dattathreyapeeta Masagali, Basaravalli, Havare, Arenoor, Hebballi Huliyarahalli, Iyanahalli, Chikmagalur (Rural) Kamenahallikaval, Jakkerikaval, Srinivasapura Karisiddanahalli, Karehalli, Balenahalli, Kunnalu Lakkamanahalli, Kurichikkanahalli, Dasarahalli Devarahalli, Chikkagowja, Shirabadige Kabbigarahalli, Ganadalu, Halelakya, Kyathanabeedu Kanivehalli, Machenahalli, Payagondanahalli Annindadike, Belawadi, Kallahalli, Kurubarahalli Shankaranahalli, Subramanyadahalli, Narasipura Vaddarahalli, Govindapura, Kottigenahalli Kurubara Boodi Halu , Aladagudde, Mahaji, Siravolalu Arenahalli, Samse, Neradi, Vajuvalli, Vataganahalli Kelagani, Kesavinahaklu, Ramanahalli, Gangalagodu Kabbikere.

The villages having more than 50% SC population are Bisagnimutt, Nagenahalli, Suruguppe, Mavinahalli Arebidacoor Estate, Hosahalli, Aralaguppe, Dumagere Gungarahalli, Boochenahallikaval, Sevalal Nagara Jakkanahalli, Channagondanahalli, Basagodu Hancharavalli, Nandikere, Huluvale, Thadagase Donagudige, Magadi, Boodanike.

Sex ratio of Scheduled Caste population is 504.

Scheduled Castes Literates and Illiterates by Sex:

	Persons	Males	Females
Literate	24,159	14,263	9,896
Illiterate	26,990	11,125	15,865
Literacy rate	55.5	66.2	45.1
Graduate	306	241	65

Scheduled Castes (Dominant):

Adi Karnataka, Adi Dravida, Banjara etc., Madiga Bhovi

For their cultural identity please see Appendix-I

Villages without Scheduled Castes: There are 43 villages without any scheduled caste population.

Scheduled Tribes: Out of the total population of 194314 persons, 4930 persons (2.54%) belong to Scheduled Tribes. The villages having less than 10% ST population are Siragola, Bidare, Boggase, Kadavanthi, Basapura Devadana, Hyarambi, Huigere, Bikkarane, Saragodu Heggarmathavani, Madla, Hipla, Melagiri Kesavinamane, Athigiri, Thogarihankal Melinahuluvathi, Kesave, Suguduvani, Shiravase Jagara, Dattathreyapeeta, Gonakal, Muthinapura Bisagnimutt, Malagaru, Pandaravalli Inam Dattathreya Peeta, Nagenahalli, Galipooje Suruguppe, Beranagodu, Masagali, Saragoor Byaravalli, Baganeheddalu, Makodu, Danihalli Karagoor, Bettadamalali, Pura, Iydahalli Aniganahalli, Bygoor, Avathi, Keremakki, Havare Devarahalli, Hangaravalli, Hirekolale, Thotadahalli Mavinahalli, Arebidacoor Estate, Dasarahalli Arasinaguppe, Bindiga, Halasabalu, Hebballi Huliyarahalli, Hosahalli, Aralaguppe, Chikkolale Indavara, Allampura, Karadihallikaval, Iyanahalli Hampapura, Beekanahalli (Rural), Hukkunda, Mathavara Dambadahalli, Siragunda, Dumagere, Mugathihalli Gavanahalli (Rural, Nallur , Thegur Chikmagalur (Rural), Hiremagalur *, Karthikere

Kuruvangi, Churchugudde Kaval, Kamenahallikaval Padamane, Jakkerikaval, Srinivasapura, Gungarahalli Sarapanahalli, Bilekallahalli, Kenkere Uddeboranahalli, Thadabenahalli, Karisiddanahalli Kengenahalli, Balenahalli, Lakkamanahalli Sadarahalli, Kurichikkanahalli, Hiregowja Dasarahalli, Devarahalli, Chikkagowja, Beeranahalli Shirabadige, Kabbigarahalli, Devagondanahalli Ganadalu, Lakya, Halelakya, Kyathanabeedu Kanivehalli, Sindigere, Boochenahallikaval Sevalal Nagara, Machenahalli, Bhaktharahalli Kalasapura, Payagondanahalli, Annindadike, Galihalli Eswarahalli, Belawadi, Kallahalli, Kurubarahalli Shankaranahalli, Subramanyadahalli, Narasipura Vaddarahalli, Govindapura, Kottigenahalli Kurubara Boodi Halu , Thalihalla, Jakkanahalli Channagondanahalli, Joladalu, Ilehole, Basagodu Hedadalu, Hancharavalli, Mylimane, Mylimane Estate Anoor, Koduvalli, Kotevooru, Gowthameshwara Aladagudde, Nandikere, Huluvale, Mahaji, Kuduvalli Chithavalli, Siravolalu, Thondavalli, Valagarehalli Arenahalli, Thadagase, Samse, Hachadamane Kesavinahaklu, Haliyur, Chikkamagaravalli, Bannur Donagudige, Hawalli, Aldur, Kelagoor, Yelagudige Sathihalli, Kesavinamane, Kadrimidri, Amble Mugulavalli, Aradavalli, Ramanahalli, Hoskote, Marle Magadi, Hejjiganahalli, Biggadevanahalli, Malalur Bikkemane, Kenchenahalli, Billenahalli, Thiruguna Boodanike, Kundur, Tagadoor, Kambihalli, Hadihalli Haluvalli, Bigganahalli, Mavinakere, Mathikere Banavara, Gangalagodu, Kabbikere, Nagarahalli.

The villages having more than 50% ST population are None.

Sex ratio of Scheduled tribe population is 521.

Scheduled Tribes Literates and Illiterates by Sex:

	Persons	Males	Females
Literate	2,177	1,281	896
Illiterate	2,753	1,080	1,673
Literacy rate	53.2	65.0	42.3
Graduate	23	16	7

Scheduled Tribes (Dominant):

Hasalaru, Naikda etc., Meda, Generic Tribes etc. Hakkipikki

For their cultural identity please see Appendix-II

Villages without Scheduled Tribes: There are 126 villages without any scheduled tribe population.

Literates and Illiterates by Sex (Total Population):

	Persons	Males	Females
Literate	118,730	67,105	51,625
Illiterate	75,584	30,359	45,225
Literacy rate	70	80	61
Graduate	3,883	2,677	1,206

Agriculture: ***Distribution of villages according to land use:*** Out of 229 villages, Total area (in hectare) is 158150, out of that 43.9 percent is cultivable and 5.11 percent of the cultivable area is irrigated.

Sources of Irrigation (Hectares): Government Canal 22.01, Private Canal 0, Well without Electricity 13.39, Well with Electricity 120.71, Tubewell without Electricity 5.76, Tubewell with Electricity 423.14, Tank 2947.94, River 0, Lake 0, Waterfall 0, Others 17.44.

Villages with population of 5000 to 9999: None

Villages with population of 10000 and above: None

Distribution of Workers:

	Persons	Males	Females	WPR
Cultivators	22,892	19,238	3,654	25.02
Agricultural Labour	9,526	4,132	5,394	10.41
Household Industry	1,299	875	424	1.42
Other Workers	57,775	33,233	24,542	63.15
Main Workers	76,629	52,459	24,170	83.75
Marginal Workers	14,863	5,019	9,844	16.25
Total Workers	91,492	57,478	34,014	

Religion: Major Religious Communities:

	Persons	Males	Females	Sex Ratio
Hindu (92.08%)	178,925	89,599	89,326	997
Muslim (5.72%)	11,106	5,648	5,458	966
Christian (1.66%)	3,217	1,652	1,565	947
Sikh (0.01%)	24	15	9	600
Buddhists (0.24%)	466	247	219	887
Jain (0.07%)	135	74	61	824

Agewise Data:

	Persons	Males	Females	Sex Ratio
All ages	194,314	97,464	96,850	994
0-14	58,633	29,810	28,823	967
15-44	98,864	49,013	49,851	1017
45-79	34,881	17,689	17,192	972
80+	1,603	744	859	1155
Age not stated	333	208	125	601

Languages (Dominant):

Kannada, Tulu, Tamil, Urdu, Malayalam

Disabled Population:

	Persons	Males	Females	%
Total Disabled	4,772	2,604	2,168	
In Seeing	2,764	1,436	1,328	57.92
In Speech	376	205	171	7.88
In Hearing	276	125	151	5.78
In Movement	1,032	671	361	21.63
Mentally	324	167	157	6.79

CHIKNAYAKANHALLI

Chiknayakanhalli C.D. Block lies in the western part of Tumkur district. It is a part of Chiknayakanhalli taluka. The Block is located at a distance of 62 kms. from district headquarters (Tumkur). There are 234 villages in the block with the total population of 187, 179 persons. Area of the C.D. Block is 1108.48 sq. kms. it is bounded by district Chitradurga on north, taluk Tiptur on south, taluks Sira and Gubbi on east, districts Chikmagalur and Hassan on west.

Communications:

Roadways : S.H.-19: Direction- Bellaary to Turuvekere, Nearest Villages- Devarahalli, Kenkere, Huliyar Amanike re, Gowdagere, Ballekatte, Huliyar, Kallahalli, Avalagere, Byrapura, Chikkabidare, Doddabidare, Pochkatte, Maraluh allada Kaval, Salakatte, Muddenahalli, Aladakatte, Byalak ere, Savigehalli, Maligehalli, Dasihalli, Dabbeghatta, Kadenahalli, Byraganahalli, Jayachamarajapura, Tharaben ahalli, Bydarahalli, Krishnasagarakere, Nagenahalli, Halgona. S.H.-19 A: Direction- Hosadurg to Keresuragondan ahalli, Nearest Villages- Yalanadu, Singapura, Bhattaraha lli, Keresuragondanahalli. S.H.-58: Direction- Chikmagalur to Sira, Nearest Villages- Naduvanahalli, Doddahullenaha lli, Bommenahalli, Halumalledevara, Kaval, Doddayannegere, Chikkayannegere, Salapura, Dinkanahalli, Koragere, Keresuragondanahalli, Keshavapura, Huliyar, Amanikere, Gowdagere, Kampanahalli, Yagachihalli, Gandalu, Boranak anive, Hoisalakatte, Bellara, Maruhole, Karehalli, Ballek atte, Huliyar, Thimmalapura.

River: Karetore Nadi- Nearest Villages- Marenadu, Ambarapura, Boranakanive, Muthugadahalli, Bellara, Lakkenahalli, Maruhole.

Canal: Nearest Villages- Dasudi, Marenadu, Ambarapura, Dabbagunte, Boranakanive, Hoisalakatte, Muthugadahalli, Maruhole, Kurihalli Kaval.

Annual Rainfall: Normal Rianfall 728.5 mm.

Ground Water: Availability of the Ground Water in the Basin is 10940.97 H.A.M. and the utilization is 12542. 39 H.A.M. It belongs to Over Exploited category. Depth to water level 2 to 20 meter below the ground. Most of the wells go down in summer months, according to the Ground Water Estimation Committee.

Soils: Red Sandy Soil.

Natural Division : It falls partly in Tumkur Kunigal and Tiptur Turuvekere plateaus of the Sourthern Karnataka plateau.

Administration:

Division: Bangalore. Parliamentary Constituency: 19 Tumkur. District: Tumkur. Taluka: Chiknayakanhalli. Assembly Constituency: 128 Chiknayakanhalli. Gram Panchayat: 28.

Regional Area Development Boards: The Bailu Seeme Area Development Board.

Fairs and Festivals: Siddharameshwara Belpatri Vahanam: It is held at Yellanadu near Tumkur around the month of October for three days.

Haliyur Shri Anjaneyaswami Jatra: It is held at Chiknaya kanahalli near Tumkur about the month of April for seven days. Chiknayakanahalli, a town situated north-west of the Tumkur town on the Turuvekere-Huliyar road, about 16 kms. of the Bangalore-Shimoga road, and about 20 kms. north of Banasandra Railway Station, is the headqua rters of the taluk of the same name.

Villages: 234 **Inhabited:** 221 **Uninhabited:** 13

Ranking	District	State	National
Area	5	71	341
Population	7	99	900
Sex Ratio	4	62	1840
Child Sex Ratio	2	39	1909
Literacy Rate	3	37	1335
Density	9	90	5251
Work Participation Rate	8	101	2125

Gram Panchayats:

Dasudi, Hoisalakatte, Gandalu, Kenkere, Yalanadu, Doddayannegere, Koragere, Thimmalapura, Huliyar, Barakanahalu, Thimmanahalli, Kandikere, Doddabidare, Handanakere, Chowlakatte, Belaguli, Ramanahalli, Muddenahalli, Baragur, Mathighatta, Malligere, Kuppuru, Theerthapura, Honnebagi, Dugadihalli, Settikere, Jayachamarajapura, Godekere.

Amenities:

Education: Primary School in 182 villages, Middle school in 119 villages, Matriculation or Secondary School in 40 villages, namely Bommenahalli, Baragihalli, Puradakatte, Handanakere, Harenahalli, Kamalapura, Belaguli, Baragur, Mathighatta, Bevinahalli, Bangaragere, Dasudi, Dabbagunte, Yalanadu, Kurihatti, Gandalu, Boranakanive, Bellara, Yarehalli, Huliyar, Shegebagi, Chikkabidare, Pochkatte, Barakanahalu, Vaddanakallahalli, Thimmanahalli, Kandikere, Maraluhallada Kaval, Ramanahalli, Katharikehal, Theerthapura, Barasidlahalli, Muddenahalli, Anekatte, Kuppuru, Settikere, Sasalu, Malagondanahalli, Jayachamarajapura, Godekere.

Higher Secondary or Pre University Courses or Intermediate or Junior College in 7 villages of the CD Block,, namely Handanakere, Mathighatta, Boranakanive, Huliyar, Thimmanahalli, Settikere, Godekere.

College in 2 villages, Adult Literacy Center in 1 village., Colleges are in villages, namely Mathighatta, Huliyar.

Medical: Hospital in 1 village, Dispensary in 4 villages, Health Center in 9 villages, Sub Center in 36 villages,

Maternity and Child Welfare Center in 1 village, Community health workers in 4 villages.
The Villages having Hospital or Dispensary or Health Center are Handanakere, Mathighatta, Melanahalli, Gowdagere, Kurihatti, Huliyar, Theerthapura.
Drinking Water: Tap water in 63 villages, Tank water in 37 villages, Well water in 71 villages, Tubewell in 75 villages and more than one source in 147 villages.
Bank: Banking facility in 15 villages, namely, Handanakere, Belaguli, Baragur, Mathighatta, Kenkere Yalanadu, Hoisalakatte, Yarehalli, Huliyar Thimmanahalli, Kandikere, Theerthapura, Settikere Vaderahalli, Jayachamarajapura.
Credit Society in 11 villages Agricultural Credit Society in 10 Non-Agricultural Credit Society in 3 villages.
Others: Power supply in 221 villages, Cinema hall in 4 villages, sport club in 221 villages, Stadium or Auditorium or Community Hall in 221 villages, Post Office in 43 villages.
There are 148 villages having bus facilities.
Villages with most of facilities: Handanakere Belaguli, Mathighatta, Yalanadu, Hoisalakatte Huliyar, Thimmanahalli, Kandikere, Theerthapura Settikere.
Villages without amenities (Education): Salapura, Otikere Thimmalapura, Ankasandra Kavalu, Daggenahalli, Keshavapura, Huliyar Amanikere, Volagerehalli, Kallenahalli, Sangenahalli, Taredahalli, Kurihalli Kaval, Kopparigehalu, Balenahalli, Chikkabelavadi, Ganganaikanahalli, Uppalekanahalli, Gopagondanahalli, Madanahalli, Akkanahalli, Yerekatte, Pura, Thonnalapura, Pinnenahalli, Yarehalli, Chikkenahalli, Dasihalli, Bagayathu, Bavanahalli, Melanahalli, Byateranganahalli, Thammadihalli, Siddaramanagara, Pemmaladevarahalli, Lakmagondanahalli, Panajanahalli, Byraganahalli, Krishnasagarakere, Nagenahalli, Manchekatte..
Scheduled Castes: Out of the total population of 187233 persons, 33764 persons (18.03%) belong to Scheduled Castes.
The villages having less than 10% SC population are Choragondanahalli, Naduvanahalli, Doddahullenahalli Bommenahalli, Doddayannegere, Salapura, Puradakatte Ramaghatta, Handanakere, Honnasettihalli Lingadahalli, Hutchanahalli, Kanakere, Bheemasandra Davanadahosahalli, Rangenahalli, Yarakatte Dasihalli, Chattasandra, Ankasandra, Thammadihalli Yalanadu, Singapura, Keresuragondanahalli Keshavapura, Huliyar Amanikere, Volagerehalli Kurihatti, Kampanahalli, Yagachihalli Muthugadahalli, Huliyar, Thoresuragondanahalli Thimmalapura, Shegebagi, Nandihalli, Kodihalli Sangenahalli, Kurihalli Kaval, Kopparigehalu Balenahalli, Chikkabelavadi, Gantenahalli Ganganaikanahalli, Kandikere, Gotigenahalli Gowrasagara, Uppalekanahalli, Gopagondanahalli Sadarahalli, Madanahalli, Janehar, Harogondanahalli Akkanahalli, Thimmalapura, Doddaramapura Barasidlahalli, Kottigal, Thonnalapura, Byalakere Pinnenahalli, Kallenahalli, Yarehalli, Anekatte Navile, Karehalli, Marasandra, Chikkenahalli Maligehalli, Dasihalli, Hosahalli, Gollarahalli Melanahalli, Chunganahalli, Byateranganahalli Kodalagara, Kadenahalli, Benakanakatte Kurubarahalli, Manchasandra, Madihalli, Gowdanahalli Siddaramanagara, Settikere, Vaderahalli, Ajjenahalli Makuvalli, Gopalanahalli, Pemmaladevarahalli Thigalanahalli, Krishnasagarakere, Bagganahalli Manchekatte, Bullenahalli, Sondenahalli.
The villages having more than 50% SC population are Kengalapura, Bandrehalli, Otikere Thimmalapura Mallenahalli, Somanahalli, Motihalli, Boranakanive Karehalli, Barakanahalu, Taredahalli Maraluhallada Kaval, Kamanahalli, Aladakatte Panajanahalli, Kantalagere.
Sex ratio of Scheduled Caste population is 493.
Scheduled Castes Literates and Illiterates by Sex:

	Persons	Males	Females
Literate	16,106	9,663	6,443
Illiterate	17,658	7,449	10,209
Literacy rate	54.8	65.0	44.4
Graduate	338	288	50

Scheduled Castes (Dominant):
Adi Karnataka, Banjara etc., Bhovi, Madiga
Adi Dravida
For their cultural identity please see Appendix-I
Villages without Scheduled Castes: There are 56 villages without any scheduled caste population.
Scheduled Tribes: Out of the total population of 187233 persons, 15576 persons (8.32%) belong to Scheduled Tribes.
The villages having less than 10% ST population are Kidukanahalli, Choragondanahalli, Naduvanahalli Bommenahalli, Halumalledevara Kaval, Doddayannegere Chikkayannegere, Baragihalli, Sabbenahalli Hallithimmalapura, Puradakatte, Handanakere Chowlakatte, Honnasettihalli, Lakshmipura Gopalapura, Harenahalli, Lingadahalli, Hutchanahalli Kanakere, Bheemasandra, Davanadahosahalli Kamalapura, Bandrehalli, Soralamavu, Rangenahalli Otikere Thimmalapura, Niruvagal, Yarakatte, Belaguli Devarahalli, Tarikatte, Baragur, Ankasandra Kavalu

Yallenahalli, Daggenahalli, Dasihalli, Tagacheghatta Bevinahalli, Chattasandra, Mallenahalli, Upparahalli Ankasandra, Bangaragere, Marenadu, Dabbagunte Nulenoor, Somanahalli, Guruvapura, Kenkere Thammadihalli, Yalanadu, Bhattarahalli, Motihalli Dinkanahalli, Koragere, Keresuragondanahalli Keshavapura, Huliyar Amanikere, Volagerehalli Gowdagere, Kurihatti, Kampanahalli, Yagachihalli Gandalu, Boranakanive, Kallenahalli, Muthugadahalli Lakkenahalli, Maruhole, Karehalli, Yarehalli Ballekatte, Huliyar, Thoresuragondanahalli Thimmalapura, Nandihalli, Kallahalli, Avalagere Byrapura, Doddabidare, Kodihalli, Pochkatte Siddalakatte, Sangenahalli, Barakanahalu Taredahalli, Vaddanakallahalli, Balenahalli Bhyralinganahalli, Thimmanahalli, Badakegudlu Kandikere, Gotigenahalli, Mallenahalli, Gowrasagara Uppalekanahalli, Maraluhallada Kaval, Salakatte Gopagondanahalli, Kamanahalli, Sadarahalli Ramanahalli, Madanahalli, Ajjigudde Harogondanahalli, Akkanahalli, Theerthapura Chikkaramapura, Pura, Aladakatte, Lakmenahalli Thonnalapura, Byalakere, Savigehalli, Kallenahalli Yarehalli, Karehalli, Marasandra, Chikkenahalli Maligehalli, Dasihalli, Bagayathu, Hosahalli Melanahalli, Dugadihalli, Bachihalli, Chunganahalli Byateranganahalli, Kadenahalli, Thammadihalli Benakanakatte, Dibbadahalli, Manchasandra, Madihalli Hesarahalli, Siddaramanagara, Balenahalli, Settikere Vaderahalli, Ajjenahalli, Somalapura, Makuvalli Gopalanahalli, Sasalu, Pemmaladevarahalli Agasarahalli, Gyarehalli, Lakmagondanahalli Panajanahalli, Malagondanahalli, Kantalagere Byraganahalli, Tharabenahalli, Bydarahalli Krishnasagarakere, Nagenahalli, Halgona, Somanahalli Godekere, Naduvanahalli.

The villages having more than 50% ST population are Doddahullenahalli, Madapura, Handiganadu Hanumanthanahalli, Janehar, Thimmalapura, Madanamadu Yerekatte, Kottigal.

Sex ratio of Scheduled tribe population is 496.

Scheduled Tribes Literates and Illiterates by Sex:

	Persons	Males	Females
Literate	9,017	5,212	3,805
Illiterate	6,559	2,645	3,914
Literacy rate	65.3	75.0	55.6
Graduate	117	102	15

Scheduled Tribes (Dominant):

Naikda etc., Hakkipikki, Meda, Generic Tribes etc.

For their cultural identity please see Appendix-II

Villages without Scheduled Tribes: There are 101 villages without any scheduled tribe population.

Literates and Illiterates by Sex (Total Population):

	Persons	Males	Females
Literate	114,063	65,378	48,685
Illiterate	73,170	28,972	44,198
Literacy rate	69	79	59
Graduate	3,749	3,023	726

Agriculture: ***Distribution of villages according to land use:*** Out of 234 villages, Total area (in hectare) is 110848, out of that 60.95 percent is cultivable and 17.13 percent of the cultivable area is irrigated.

Sources of Irrigation (Hectares): Government Canal 0, Private Canal 0, Well without Electricity 0, Well with Electricity 489.34, Tubewell without Electricity 57.21, Tubewell with Electricity 8367.01, Tank 2030.19, River 0, Lake 0, Waterfall 246.5, Others 380.12.

Villages with population of 5000 to 9999:

Kenkere.

Villages with population of 10000 and above:

Huliyar.

Distribution of Workers:

	Persons	Males	Females	WPR
Cultivators	47,795	33,541	14,254	50.04
Agricultural Labour	21,653	8,239	13,414	22.67
Household Industry	4,882	2,038	2,844	5.11
Other Workers	21,193	15,357	5,836	22.19
Main Workers	72,185	53,633	18,552	75.57
Marginal Workers	23,338	5,542	17,796	24.43
Total Workers	95,523	59,175	36,348	

Religion: Major Religious Communities:

	Persons	Males	Females	Sex Ratio
Hindu (92.12%)	172,479	86,903	85,576	985
Muslim (5.1%)	9,550	4,853	4,697	968
Christian (0.04%)	73	37	36	973
Sikh (0%)	-	-	-	-
Buddhists (0.01%)	12	7	5	714
Jain (0.1%)	183	101	82	812

Agewise Data:

	Persons	Males	Females	Sex Ratio
All ages	187,233	94,350	92,883	984
0-14	51,532	26,133	25,399	972
15-44	92,575	46,049	46,526	1010
45-79	40,768	21,015	19,753	940
80+	2,171	1,036	1,135	1096
Age not stated	187	117	70	598

Languages (Dominant):

Kannada, Urdu, Hindi, Telugu, Marathi

Disabled Population:

	Persons	Males	Females	%

Total Disabled	3,880	2,153	1,727	
In Seeing	1,640	873	767	42.27
In Speech	446	255	191	11.49
In Hearing	265	129	136	6.83
In Movement	1,151	697	454	29.66
Mentally	378	199	179	9.74

CHIKODI

Chikodi C.D. Block lies in the north-western part of Belgaum district. It is a part of Chikodi taluka. The Block is located at a distance of 72 kms. from district headquarters (Belgaum). There are 131 villages in the block with the total population of 450,583 persons. Area of the C.D. Block is 1221.83 sq. kms. It is bounded by Athni taluka on north, it has common boundary with the state of Maharashtra on north and west, taluk Hukeri on south, taluks Raybag and Gokak on east.

Communications:

Roadways: N.H-4: Direction- Poona to Sankeshwar, Nearest Villages- Koganoli, Hanabarawadi, Naganur, Yamagarni, Soundalga, Yarnal, Nippani (Rural), Gavan, Tavadi. S.H-12: Direction- Sankeshwar to Athni, Nearest Villages- Manjari, Ankali, Shiddapurwadi, Kadapur, Kerur, Roopanal, Hirekudi, Chikodi (Rural), Karoshi, Jainapur, Wadral, Majalatti. S.H-18: Direction-Kankouli to Mudhol, Nearest Villages- Kodni, Gayakanawadi, Nippani (Rural), Chikodi (Rural), Navalihal, Kuppanawadi, Peerawadi, Pattankudi, Yadyanawadi, Dhulaganawadi, Kuthali, Kothali, Chinchani, Umrani, Itnal, Nagaramunnoli, Belkud, Belagali, Kabbur, Jodatti.

Railway Station: Villages- Meerapurhatti, Jaganur.

River: Krishna Nadi- Nearest Villages- Kallol, Yadurwadi, Chandur, Chandur-Tek, Yadur, Hosa Yedur, Ingali, Manjari, Nagaramunnoli, Belkud, Belagali, Kabbur, Jodatti.

Annual Rainfall: Normal Rianfall 678.6 mm.

Ground Water: Availability of the Ground Water in the Basin is 23559 H.A.M. and the utilization is 18425 H.A.M. It belongs to Over Exploited category. Depth to water level 2 to 20 meter below the ground. Most of the wells go down in summer months, according to the Ground Water Estimation Committee.

Soil: Red Soil, Black Soil.

Natural Division : It falls in Krishna Ghatprabha Irrigated Tract of the Northern Karnataka Plateau.

Administration:

Division: Belgaum. Parliamentary Constituency: 1 Chikodi. District: Belgaum. Taluka: Chikodi. Assembly Constituency: 1 Sadalga, 2 Chikodi, 6 Raybag (SC) Gram Panchayat: 65.

Regional Area Development Boards: The Bailu Seeme Area Development Board.

Border Villages: (with State Maharashtra)- Hadnal, Sulagaon, Mattiwade, Bhatnaganur, Kurli, Koganoli, Hanchinal (K.S.), Budihal, Kodni, Gayakanawadi, Shirguppi, Budulmukh, Shendur, Manakapur, Kasanal, Donewadi, Boragaon, Sadalaga (Rural), Karadaga,(Rural), Karadaga,(Rural), Karadaga,(Rural), Karadaga,Mangur, Gajabarwadi, Shivapurawadi, Malikwad, Examba, Kallol,Yadurwadi, Chandur, Chandur - Tek.

Fairs and Festival: Aranya Siddheshwara Jatra: Aranya Siddheshwara jatra is held at Kerur in the month of Phalguna (March) for five days. Kerur is eight kms. from Chikodi, is mentioned as 'Kerevur' in a Chalukyan record from the same place dated saka 1071. The place has temples dedicated to Mahadeva, Aranya Siddheshwara, Hanumanta, Kalmeshwara, Lakshmi, Basavanna, Kere Siddhadavaru and Vithoba. The Mahadeva temple has a garbhagriha, an ardhamantapa and a navaranga. The navaranga pillars have Kalashamotif and the ceiling has a Bhuvaneshwari decorated with Ashtadikpalas. The Aranya Siddheshwara temple in the outskirts of the village, has small shrines of Malesiddha, Amukha Siddha and Bhutala Siddha. The Kalmeshwara (old) is renovated. Inside the temple are placed sculptures of Vishnu, Umamaheshwara, Saptamatrikas, etc (all in later Chalukyan style). There are two herostones and one Mahasati stone. There is one private compound. There are two stone elephants, said to be of a tank called Anekere. The Lakshmi temple has a Kalabhairava and Kubera (late Vijayanagara time) images. The Dyamavva temple has a huge painted wooden statue, seated on a lion. Nearby, remains of an old Bharmappa temple, broken pieces of a Kannada inscription and a broken Bhairava image are found. An inscription slab built into the platform of the Hanumanta temple dated Saka 1071 is of Chalukyas of Kalyana and it records gifts of land, house, etc, to god Mulasthana Koppeshwara of Kerevur Agrahara in Koravalli-150. The donors were Jayadevayya, Jayasimhadeva who was governing the Koondi-3,000, Ratta Kattamadeva and Hemmadidevaras who was administering Koravalli-150 from Gokage when Kalachuri Bijjala was in charge of (melalke) of Koondi-3,000. Another fragment of an inscription built into the wall of the Bharamappa temple speaks of a person who was highly learned, in the characters of about 12th century. Beeredeva Jatra: It is held at Examba in the month of Magha (January-February) every year. Examba 11 kms. From Chikodi is a place with considerable antiquity. Examba was in the Koravalli Kampana. The Adinatha Basti (built in 1155) in later Chalukyan style has a garbhagriha and an aradhamantapa and a spacious navaranga. It has an inscription belonging to the rule of Kalachuri Bijjala and is dated 1165 A.D. It refers to a Shilahara chief Vijayaditya as the subordinate of the king. A herostone here dated 1139 A.D. is also of Bijjalla's time and records the death of one Padevala Jinna. Other two bastis of the place are of Shantinatha and Neminatha (both fallen). The former was built by an officer of Shilahara Vijayditya when they were administering from Valavada. A record dated 1235 A.D. from the same place states that kesiyamayya Dannayaka made a grant of land for feeding a house with the consent of Ratta Lakshmidevarasa. Other monuments of the place are Adinatha and (Svetambara) Vasupujya bastis and temples of Vithala, Ganapathi, Yellamma, Mahadeva, Beeredeva (big one) and Dattatreya. The jatra of Beeredeva is held during Magha when nearly 50,000 people assemble. Hind Kesari (wrestler) and Sripati Kanchinal belong to this place. The place has a mosque and a dargah ascribed to Panand Pir (Adilshahi times) and Urs is held in Chaitra Annually when about 10,000 people assemble. Bhairoba Jatra: It is held at Akkol in Belgaum area is about the month of Chaitra (January-February) every year. Akkol, ten kilometers from Nipani, with the suffixkol standing for Kola or a tank, has temples dedicated to Mahadeva, (Balekundri) Panth Mandira, Maruti, Bhairoba, Beeroba, Yellamma, Lakshmi Naraynan (old), Margubai and Padmavati. The Mahadeva temple is an old stone structure. Halasiddhanatha Jatra: :It is held at Appachiwadi in about the month of October every year. Appachiwadi located at two kms. from Kurli and 16 kms. from Nipani, is a pilgrimage centre for the Nath Panthis as it has the samadhi of Halasiddhanatha of the Nath Panth. This Samadhi built in Indo-Islamic style has a central dome and two other small domes with minars in the front. Halasiddhanatha is believed to have expired in Saka 1734 (1812 AD). There is another tomb of Bhimabai Shintre, a devotee of the saint. Khaza Kabir Peer and Mahboob Subhani Urs: Kerur is a place situated about eight kilometres from Chikodi town. The place has a mosque and two dargahs ascribed to Hyderabad Khaza Kabir Peer and Mahboob Subhani (chilla) and the urs is held in the months of Akhr and Dastgir respectively, when 2,000 people assemble. Mahalakshmi Jatra: The Mahalakshmi jatra is held at Pattankudi in the month of Ashwayuja (September). Pattankudi five kilometres from Nipani has temples dedicated to Mahadeva (Matha), Yellamma (two), Mahalakshmi (huge), Bharamappa, Vithoba (two) and Maruti. The Mahalakshmi shrine renovated and expanded recently is said to have been built during the 16th century. The annual jatra takes place on the first Friday or Tuesday before Ashwayuja Amavasya.

Mahboob Subhani Baghadadi Urs: Mahboob Suhani Baghdadi (Dastagir) Urs is held at Nipani near Belgaum in the month of Rabi-ul-Akhar for eleven days. Nipani is 24 kms. from Chikodi, located on the Pune-Bangalore highway is a town of recent growth, very near to the Maharashtra border. The earliest mention of the place is around 1800 A.D. when its Desai Siddojiaro Nimbalkar also called Appa Saheb was engaged in the siege of Nerli fort between Sankeshvar and Hukeri.

Gayib Peer Sheban Urs: Khadaklat located on Chikodi-Nipani road is a place with considerable antiquity. The place has a mosque and a dargah ascribed to Gayib Peer Sheban. The Urus is held annually when about 10,000 people assemble.

Pamalinga Temple Jatra: Ramalinga temple jatra is held at Tavadi near Belgaum in the month of Shravana (July-August). Tavadi, five kilometres from Nipani or Tavandi or Stavanidhi as variedly called is a celebrated Jaina centre, addressed by Jains as 'Sri Atishayakshetra'. The place can be reached after a deviation to the right from Sankeshwar-Nipani (highway) road. The place has the famous Brahmadeva temple complex in later Chalukyan style with five small shrines in a row. But, the Brahmadeva temple is the earliest with a garbhagriha, an ardhamantapa and a navaranga. Shantigiri Jatra: Kothali about 10 kms. from Chikodi has a recently created Jaina centre atop a small hillock locally called Shantigiri. The entrance to this huge open air complex has a beautiful gateway. There are the three standing, statues of Chandraprabha, Shantinatha and Mahavira all in white marble installed on an elevated Siddeshwara Jatra: Siddeshwara jatra is held at Kabbur once in three years in the month of Shravana (July-August). Kabbur 19 kms. from Chikodi has been referred as Piriya Agrahara Karburu in a record of Ratta Kartavirya dated Saka 1126, found on a pillar in the Kalmeshwara temple of the same place. The placename might have originated from karbu (kabbu) sugar cane, which is even today grown in the area. The place has a huge Kalmeshwara temple in later Chalukyan style with three garbhagrihas (trikutachala), a spacious navaranga and a separate spacious mukhamantapa.

Sri Atishayakshetra Jatra : It is held at Tavadi near Belgaum in the months of Vaishakha (March-April) for three days. Tavadi five kilometres from Nipani, or Tavandi or Stavanidhi as variedly called is a celebrated Jaina centre, addressed by Jains as"Sri Atishayakshetra". The place has the famous Brahmadeva temple complex in later Chalukyan style with five small shrines in a row. But, the Brahmadeva temple is earliest with a garbhagriha, an ardhamantapa and a navaranga. The garbhagriha has a short shikhara in earlier style and the pilla rs of the navaranga are lathe-turned. The Parshwanatha image (enshrined separately) is a fine standing statue in imitation of later Chalukyan style. An inscription of its pedestal dated 1400 A.D. states that the image was carved by one Jinnoja Chintamani Parshwanatha in thirteen characters.

Veerabhadra-Virupaksha Jatra: It is held at Yadur near Belgaum in the month of Chaitra (March-April). Yadur is a place on the northern bank of the Krishna, 19 kms. from Chikodi. It is called so as it is on the left bank, edaduru, or perhaps yedeyuru place of dasoha. It is famous pilgrim centre, having the Veerabhadra temple and this deity is the kuladevata of Lingayats and brahmins. This Veerabhadra-Virupaksha Linga, originally housed in a trikutachala stone temple of the Seuna (Yadava) times, now empty, found in the south-west corner of the compound or the prakara of the present temple, is housed in a new structure, about 300 years old, of brick and mortar, installed in a depressed garbhagriha which has entrance from three sides.

Villages: 131 **Inhabited:** 131 **Uninhabited:** 0

Ranking	District	State	National
Area	5	57	269
Population	1	1	3
Sex Ratio	9	152	3698
Child Sex Ratio	10	175	5714
Literacy Rate	1	56	1833
Density	5	104	2925
Work Participation Rate	1	11	2363

Gram Panchayats:

Koganoli, Adi, Benadi, Kunnur, Mangur, Barwad, Karadaga, Manakapur, Boragaon, Janwad, Shiradwad, Shamanewadi, Bedkihal, Bhoj, Hunnaragi, Sidnal, Soundalga, Appachiwadi, Kurli, Yamagarni, Jatrat, Akkol, Mamadapur (Kl), Galatga, Shirgaon, Nej, Malikwad, Examba, Kallol, Yadur, Chandur, Manjari, Ingali, Ankali, Kadapur, Kerur, Hirekudi, Nanadi, Nagaral, Khadaklat, Chikalwal, Lakhanapur, Kodni , Shirguppi, Shendur, Yarnal , Pattankudi, Walki, Nainglaj, Navalihal, Kothali, Chinchani, Jainapur, Hattarwat, Wadral, Mugali, Karoshi, Umrani, Jodakurli, Nagaramunnoli, Belkud, Bambalwad, Karagaon, Kabbur, Jaganur.

Amenities:

Education: Primary School in 128 villages, Middle school in 122 villages, Matriculation or Secondary School in 37 villages, namely Kurli, Koganoli, Benadi, Akkol, Jatrat, Soundalga, Tavadi, Boragaon, Shiradwad, Karadaga, Mangur, Bhoj, Hunnaragi, Sidnal, Galatga, Bedkihal, Nej, Examba, Kallol, Chandur, Ingali, Manjari, Ankali, Kerur, Hirekudi, Shirgaon, Khadaklat, Navalihal, Pattankudi, Kothali, Chinchani, Nagaramunnoli, Bambalwad, Karoshi, Majalatti, Karagaon, Kabbur.

Higher Secondary or Pre University Courses or Intermediate or Junior College in 8 villages of the CD Block,, namely Budihal, Karadaga, Bedkihal, Nej, Examba, Kallol, Ankali, Majalatti.

College in 1 village, Adult Literacy Center in 3 villages., College is in village, namely Bedkihal.

Medical: Hospital in 0 village, Dispensary in 4 villages, Health Center in 16 villages, Sub Center in 67 villages, Maternity and Child Welfare Center in 9 villages, Community health workers in 47 villages.

The Villages having Hospital or Dispensary or Health Center are Manakapur, Nej, Sankanwadi, Majalatti.

Drinking Water: Tap water in 87 villages, Tank water in 16 villages, Well water in 75 villages, Tubewell in 105 villages and more than one source in 129 villages.

Bank: Banking facility in 39 villages, namely, Kurli, Koganoli, Hanchinal (K.S.), Benadi, Jatrat Adi, Yamagarni, Soundalga, Yarnal, Manakapur Boragaon, Sadalaga (Rural), Shiradwad, Karadaga Barwad, Gajabarwadi, Shivapurawadi, Bhoj, Sidnal Mamadapur (Kl), Galatga, Bedkihal, Shamanewadi, Nej Nanadi, Malikwad, Examba, Kallol, Yadur, Hosa Yedur Ingali, Ankali, Kerur, Hirekudi, Khadaklat Pattankudi, Nagaramunnoli, Karoshi, Kabbur.

Credit Society in 73 villages Agricultural Credit Society in 56 Non-Agricultural Credit Society in 16 villages.

Others: Power supply in 131 villages, Cinema hall in 13 village sport club in 2 villages, Stadium or Auditorium or Community Hall in 0 village, Post Office in 90 villages.

There are 128 villages having bus facilities.

Villages with most of facilities: Kurli, Koganoli Hanchinal (K.S.), Benadi, Jatrat, Adi, Yamagarni Soundalga, Yarnal, Manakapur, Boragaon, Shiradwad Karadaga, Barwad, Bhoj, Mamadapur (Kl), Galatga Bedkihal, Shamanewadi, Nej, Nanadi, Malikwad, Examba Kallol, Yadur, Hosa Yedur, Ingali, Ankali, Kerur Hirekudi, Khadaklat, Pattankudi, Nagaramunnoli Karoshi, Kabbur.

Villages without amenities (Education):

Nippani (Rural), Sadalaga (Rural), Chikodi (Rural)..

Scheduled Castes: Out of the total population of 456495 persons, 70506 persons (15.45%) belong to Scheduled Castes. The villages having less than 10% SC population are Bolewadi, Gayakanawadi, Shendur, Nippani (Rural) Amalzari, Tavadi, Donewadi, Boragaonwadi Sadalaga (Rural), Janwad, Mangur, Shivapurawadi Bhimapurwadi, Vadagol (Rural), Nanadiwadi, Nanadi Yadurwadi, Chandur - Tek, Yadur, Shiddapurwadi Chikodi (Rural), Kuppanawadi, Shiragaonwadi Thapakarwadi, Manuchiwadi, Peerawadi, Yadyanawadi Itnal, Wadral, Khajagoudanhatti, Kenchanatti

Jodatti, Vijayanagar, Pogatyanatti, Jaganur Mamadapur (Kk).

The village having more than 50% SC population is None.

Sex ratio of Scheduled Caste population is 488.

Scheduled Castes Literates and Illiterates by Sex:

	Persons	Males	Females
Literate	35,470	22,608	12,862
Illiterate	35,036	13,466	21,570
Literacy rate	58.9	73.6	43.6
Graduate	1,407	1,221	186

Scheduled Castes (Dominant):

Holaya etc., Mahar etc., Bhambi etc., Holar etc. Mang etc.

For their cultural identity please see Appendix-I

Villages without Scheduled Castes: There are 7 villages without any scheduled caste population.

Scheduled Tribes: Out of the total population of 456495 persons, 4495 persons (0.98%) belong to Scheduled Tribes.

The villages having less than 10% ST population are Hadnal, Sulagaon, Mattiwade, Bhatnaganur, Kurli Appachiwadi, Koganoli, Hanabarawadi Hanchinal (K.S.), Benadi, Bolewadi, Akkol, Padlihal Jatrat, Adi, Bhivashi, Naganur, Yamagarni, Soundalga Budihal, Kodni, Gayakanawadi, Shirguppi, Pangeri (B) Budulmukh, Shendur, Gondikuppi, Yarnal, Amalzari Gavan, Tavadi, Manakapur, Kasanal, Donewadi Boragaon, Boragaonwadi, Sadalaga (Rural), Janwad Shiradwad, Karadaga, Barwad, Mangur, Kunnur Gajabarwadi, Shivapurawadi, Bhoj, Hunnaragi, Sidnal Mamadapur (Kl), Bhimapurwadi, Galatga, Bedkihal Shamanewadi, Vadagol (Rural), Nej, Nagaral Nanadiwadi, Nanadi, Malikwad, Examba, Kallol Yadyanawadi, Yadurwadi, Chandur, Chandur - Tek Yadur, Hosa Yedur, Ingali, Manjari, Ankali Shiddapurwadi, Kadapur, Jodakurli, Kerur, Roopanal Hirekudi, Chikodi (Rural), Kuppanawadi, Girgaon Shirgaon, Shiragaonwadi, Khadaklat, Thapakarwadi Pangire (A), Rampur, Chikalwal, Manuchiwadi Sankanwadi, Navalihal, Peerawadi, Pattankudi Yadyanawadi, Dhulaganawadi, Kuthali, Kothali Chinchani, Handyanwadi, Umrani, Itnal, Nagaramunnoli Belkud, Bambalwad, Kungatolli, Karoshi, Jainapur Toranahalli, Bidrahalli, Hattarwat, Mangnur, Wadral Majalatti, Khajagoudanhatti, Mugali, Kamatyanahatti Bennihalli, Karagaon, Donawad, Hanchinal (K.K.) Belagali, Kenchanatti, Meerapurhatti, Kabbur Jodatti, Vijayanagar, Pogatyanatti, Jaganur Mamadapur (Kk).

The villages having more than 50% ST population are None.

Sex ratio of Scheduled tribe population is 499.

Scheduled Tribes Literates and Illiterates by Sex:

	Persons	Males	Females
Literate	1,914	1,210	704
Illiterate	2,581	1,044	1,537
Literacy rate	49.9	62.5	37.1
Graduate	50	45	5

Scheduled Tribes (Dominant):

Naikda etc., Koli Dhor etc., Meda, Kadu Kuruba Bhil etc.

For their cultural identity please see Appendix-II

Villages without Scheduled Tribes: There are 70 villages without any scheduled tribe population.

Literates and Illiterates by Sex (Total Population):

	Persons	Males	Females
Literate	258,522	156,929	101,593
Illiterate	197,973	77,668	120,305
Literacy rate	66	78	53
Graduate	9,753	8,328	1,425

Agriculture: ***Distribution of villages according to land use:*** Out of 131 villages, Total area (in hectare) is 122183.74, out of that 83.86 percent is cultivable and 35.45 percent of the cultivable area is irrigated.

Sources of Irrigation (Hectares): Government Canal 5782.15, Private Canal 0, Well without Electricity 1167.47, Well with Electricity 9967.21000000001, Tubewell without Electricity 332.(Tubewell with Electricity 5273.21, Tank 603.11, River 12159.05, Lake 19.45, Waterfall 0, Others 1022.41.

Villages with population of 5000 to 9999:

Kurli, Koganoli, Benadi, Akkol, Jatrat, Soundalga Manakapur, Karadaga, Mangur, Kunnur, Bedkihal Shamanewadi, Nej, Ingali, Kadapur, Hirekudi Pattankudi, Nagaramunnoli, Karoshi, Kabbur, Jaganur.

Villages with population of 10000 and above:

Boragaon, Bhoj, Galatga, Examba, Manjari, Ankali Kerur, Khadaklat.

Distribution of Workers:

	Persons	Males	Females	WPR
Cultivators	101,659	68,167	33,492	45.43
Agricultural Labour	76,775	35,089	41,686	34.31
Household Industry	5,999	3,482	2,517	2.68
Other Workers	39,314	31,311	8,003	17.57
Main Workers	180,883	129,463	51,420	80.84
Marginal Workers	42,864	8,586	34,278	19.16
Total Workers	223,747	138,049	85,698	

Religion: Major Religious Communities:

	Persons	Males	Females	Sex Ratio
Hindu (85.06%)	388,285	199,355	188,930	948
Muslim (5.9%)	26,925	13,754	13,171	958

Christian (0.03%)	158	81	77	951
Sikh (0.01%)	53	29	24	828
Buddhists (0.64%)	2,941	1,533	1,408	918
Jain (8.12%)	37,054	19,305	17,749	919

Agewise Data:

	Persons	Males	Females	Sex Ratio
All ages	456,495	234,597	221,898	946
0-14	142,881	75,370	67,511	896
15-44	210,144	108,439	101,705	938
45-79	98,064	48,308	49,756	1030
80+	5,048	2,279	2,769	1215
Age not stated	358	201	157	781

Languages (Dominant):
Kannada, Marathi, Urdu, Telugu, Hindi

Disabled Population:

	Persons	Males	Females	%
Total Disabled	5,729	3,284	2,445	
In Seeing	1,698	872	826	29.64
In Speech	690	382	308	12.04
In Hearing	342	191	151	5.97
In Movement	2,208	1,413	795	38.54
Mentally	791	426	365	13.81

CHINCHOLI

Chincholi C.D. Block lies in the north-eastern part of Gulbarga district. It is a part of Chincholi taluka. The Block is located at a distance of 85 kms. From district headquarters (Gulbarga). There are 148 villages in the block with the total population of 206,319 persons. Area of the CD Block is 1536.70 sq. kms. It is boundedby district Bidar on north, taluks Sedam and Chitapur on south, taluks Gulbarga and Chitapur on west, and it has common boundary with the state of A.P., on north and east.

Communications:

Roadways : S.H-15: Direction- Sedam to Bidar, Nearest Villages- Tumkunta, Kollur, Nagaidlai, Patpalli, Fathepur, Konchawaram, Neemahosalli, Daultapur, Chimmaidlai, Dastapur, Sulepeth, Penchganpalli, Keroli, Kordampalli, Nidugunda, Venkatapur, Hovinhalli, Siroli. S.H-32: Direction- Mahagaon to Sulepeth, Nearest Villages- Ainapur, Benkeppalli, Salgar Basanthpur, Yetabarpur, Salebeernhalli, Kudhalli, Hasargundgi, Yalmamdi, Channur, Chimmanchod, Nawadgi, Sulepeth.

River: Kagna Nadi- Nearest Villages- Halkoda, Potangal, Jettur.Mullamari Nadi- Nearest Villages- Jettur, Chatarsal, Karachkhed,Ghanpur, Burugpalli, Bhaktampalli, Sangam[K], Ganganpalli, Polakpalli, Ainoli, Garampalli, Tajlapur, Iragpalli,Garagpalli, Pardarmotakpalli, Anwar, Neemahosalli, Degalmadi, Karakmukli,Goudanhalli, Chimmanchod, Tajlapur.

Reserved Forest: Nearest Villages- Bhunyar[K], Khanapur, Ainapur, Salgar Basanthpur, Yetabarpur, Salebeernhalli, Tumkunta, Hasargundgi, Gurampalli, Nagarhal, Dhuttarga, Gongi, Chandankera, Narnal, Chimmanchod, Tajlapur, Marpalli, palli, Kusrampalli, Gottamgotta[K], Gottamgotta, Sangapur, Katangidda, Srinagar, Venkatapur, Dharmasagar, Chandrampalli,Kollur, Nagaidlai, Ainoli, Bhikkanhalli, Burugdoddi, Linganagar,Bhonaspur, Shivrampur, Magdam-pur, Shivredpalli, Konchawaram,Jilwarsha, Chindnoor, Lachmasagar, Mambapur, Hanum-annagar,Shadipur, Bhoglingdhalli, Kalbhavi, Chikkalingadhalli, Somlingadhalli, Bhairampalli, Miryan, Gandhinagar, Rummungud, Karakmukli, Tadpalli, Allapur, Seri, JNagar, Kodli, Nawadgi.

Annual Rainfall: Normal Rianfall 777 mm.

Ground Water: Availability of the Ground Water in the Basin is 7601 H.A.M. and the utilization is 2332 H.A.M. It belongs to Over Exploited category. Depth to water level 2 to 20 meter below the ground. Most of the wells go down in summer months, according to the Ground Water Estimation Committee.

Soils: Deep Black, Medium Black Soil, Shallow Soil and Lateritic Soil.

Natural Division : It falls partly in the Aland-Chincholi Tract of Trappean Outcrops, and the Kagna Basin of the Northern Karnataka Plateau.

Administration:

Division: Gulbarga. Parliamentary Constituency: 7 Bidar (SC). District: Gulbarga. Taluka: Chincholi. Assembly Constituency: 42 Chincholi (SC). Gram Panchayat: 32.

Regional Area Development Boards: The Hyderabad-Karnataka Area Development Board.

Border Villages: (State: Andhra Pradesh)- Tumkunta, Kusrampalli, Manikpur, Gottamgotta, Sangapur, Katangidda, Srinagar, Venkatapur, Nagaidlai, Linganagar, Bhonaspur, Shiv-rampur, Magdampur, Konchawaram, Pochawaram, Jilwarsha, Chindnoor, Shadipur, Yakatpur, Nirchalma, Chikkalingadhalli, Somlingadhalli, Kallur Road, Bhairampalli, Miryan, Sangam[K], Ghanpur, Burugpalli, Chatarsal, Halkoda, Potangal, Jettur.

Fairs: Khudawande Numa Hussaini Urs: It is observed at Chincholi near Gulbarga on 15 Shavval for two days. Chincholi is the headquarters of the taluk of the same name in the north-eastern part of the Gulbarga district. The town is surroun-ded by hills and the valleys are rich in laterite and black soils. In the rearrangement of boundaries in 1905, Chincholi taluk recei-ved a few villages from Kodangal. Once the entire taluk belonged to Nawab Alam Ali Kairoz, a jagirdar. Chincholi town is on the banks of the Mullamari river. There is a fine Dargah here which is visited by a large number of Muslims. There is an imposing building, the Raja's Palace, which is also worth a visit. The Raimanghad temple here attracts as large number of pilgrims.

Villages: 148 **Inhabited:** 137 **Uninhabited:** 11

Ranking	District	State	National
Area	8	30	128
Population	8	82	613
Sex Ratio	6	68	1964
Child Sex Ratio	7	133	3821
Literacy Rate	4	159	4924
Density	3	35	5786
Work Participation Rate	8	144	1160

Gram Panchayats:
Ainapur, Salgar Basanthpur, Chengta, Gadilingdhalli , Salebeernhalli, Nagaidlai, Venkatapur, Hasargundgi, Chimmanchod , Chandankera, Karakmukli, Degalmadi, Ainoli, Konchawaram, Shadipur, Pastpur, Mogha, Rummungud, Ratkal, Chimmaidlai, Polakpalli, Anwar, Sulepeth, Hodebeeranhalli, Kodli, Halcher, Gadikeshwar, Keroli, Miryan, Karachkhed, Nidugunda, Siroli.

Amenities:
Education: Primary School in 128 villages, Middle school in 62 villages, Matriculation or Secondary School in 18 villages, namely Bhunyar[B], Benkeppalli, Tumkunta, Ranapur, Tajlapur, Nagaidlai, Patpalli, Fathepur, Bhikkanhalli, Pochawaram, Mogha, Karakmukli, Ratkal, Kodli, Sulepeth, Gadikeshwar, Nidugunda, Raikod.
Higher Secondary or Pre University Courses or Intermediate or Junior College in 2 villages of the CD Block,, namely Indarpadhosali, Sulepeth.
College in 0 village, Adult Literacy Center in 28 villages.
Medical: Hospital in 3 villages, Dispensary in 6 villages, Health Center in 16 villages, Sub Center in 8 villages, Maternity and Child Welfare Center in 26 villages, Community health workers in 42 villages.
The Villages having Hospital or Dispensary or Health Center are Benkeppalli, Yetabarpur, Tajlapur, Gandhinagar, Rummungud, Mogha, Pastpur, Karakmukli, Ratkal, Kodli, Nidugunda.
Drinking Water: Tap water in 62 villages, Tank water in 28 villages, Well water in 106 villages, Tubewell in 37 villages and more than one source in 124 villages.
Bank: Banking facility in 8 villages, namely, Tajlapur, Fathepur, Pochawaram, Ratkal, Sulepeth Nidugunda, Chintpalli, Rudnoor.
Credit Society in 27 villages Agricultural Credit Society in 23 Non-Agricultural Credit Society in 1 village.
Others: Power supply in 133 villages, Cinema hall in 4 villages, sport club in 8 villages, Stadium or Auditorium or Community Hall in 137 villages, Post Office in 52 villages.
There are 100 villages having bus facilities.
Villages with most of facilities: Tajlapur Fathepur, Ratkal, Sulepeth, Nidugunda, Chintpalli.
Villages without amenities (Education): Chengta, Gottamgotta[K] *, Sangapur, Srinagar, Antwaram, Hanumannagar, Bhoglingdhalli, Khairtapur, Moranhal..
Scheduled Castes: Out of the total population of 206502 persons, 70023 persons (33.91%) belong to Scheduled Castes.
The villages having less than 10% SC population are Nagarhal, Kotga, Gottamgotta[K] *, Fathepur Khairtapur, Moranhal, Iragpalli, Venkatapur.
The villages having more than 50% SC population are Bhunyar[K], Khanapur, Benkeppalli, Salgar Basanthpur Yetabarpur, Gadilingdhalli, Ranapur, Kusrampalli Sangapur, Srinagar, Venkatapur, Dharmasagar Bhikkanhalli, Linganagar, Shivredpalli, Chindnoor Hanumannagar, Shadipur, Bhoglingdhalli, Kalbhavi Bhairampalli, Gandhinagar, Huvinbhavi, Tadpalli Seri, Jawaharnagar, Korvi.
Sex ratio of Scheduled Caste population is 490.

Scheduled Castes Literates and Illiterates by Sex:

	Persons	Males	Females
Literate	20,837	14,244	6,593
Illiterate	49,186	21,455	27,731
Literacy rate	36.6	49.2	23.6
Graduate	502	470	32

Scheduled Castes (Dominant):
Banjara etc., Holaya etc., Madiga, Bhovi, Mala
For their cultural identity please see Appendix-I
Villages without Scheduled Castes: There are 15 villages without any scheduled caste population.
Scheduled Tribes: Out of the total population of 206502 persons, 4917 persons (2.38%) belong to Scheduled Tribes.
The villages having less than 10% ST population are Chengta, Bhunyar[B], Bhunyar[K], Khanapur, Ainapur Benkeppalli, Salgar Basanthpur, Yetabarpur, Tumkunta Hasargundgi, Gurampalli, Nagarhal, Yalmamdi, Channur Gadilingdhalli, Kotga, Dhuttarga, Gongi, Pangarga Chandankera, Ranapur, Sasargaon, Narnal, Chimmanchod Tajlapur, Shikarm0Takpalli, Garampalli, Kusrampalli Gottamgotta[K] *, Sangapur, Srinagar, Venkatapur Dharmasagar, Kollur, Nagaidlai, Patpalli, Fathepur Ainoli, Bhikkanhalli, Antwaram, Linganagar Shivrampur, Magdampur, Shivredpalli, Konchawaram Pochawaram, Jilwarsha, Chindnoor, Lachmasagar Hanumannagar, Shadipur, Bhoglingdhalli, Kalbhavi Chincholi [R], Neemahosalli, Goudanhalli Indarpadhosali, Anwar, Polakpalli, Chikkalingadhalli Somlingadhalli, Ganganpalli, Kallur Road Bhairampalli, Miryan, Mukramba, Hulsgud, Gandhinagar Rummungud, Mogha, Rustumpur, Dhotikol, Khudavandpur Karakmukli, Hudadhalli, Chimmaidlai, Dastapur

Yelakpalli, Khairtapur, Moranhal, Huvinbhavi Ganjgera, Chinkunta, Tadpalli, Allapur, Jawaharnagar Sunthan, Ratkal, Kanchanhal, Kodli, Nawadgi Wazirgaon, Kudhalli, Hosalli, Tegaltippi, Halcher Korvi, Hodebeeranhalli, Sulepeth, Pardarmotakpalli Bhaktampalli, Garagpalli, Bedagpalli, Penchganpalli Kupnoor, Gadikeshwar, Benkanhalli, Bhantanahalli Keroli, Kordampalli, Iragpalli, Ghanpur, Burugpalli Karachkhed, Nidugunda, Venkatapur, Chintpalli Raikod, Bhootpur, Rudnoor, Hovinhalli, Siroli Halkoda, Potangal, Jettur.

The villages having more than 50% ST population are None.

Sex ratio of Scheduled tribe population is 488.

Scheduled Tribes Literates and Illiterates by Sex:

	Persons	Males	Females
Literate	1,900	1,254	646
Illiterate	3,017	1,263	1,754
Literacy rate	46.4	60.5	32.0
Graduate	57	50	7

Scheduled Tribes (Dominant):

Gond etc., Naikda etc., Koli Dhor etc., Kadu Kuruba Koraga

For their cultural identity please see Appendix-II

Villages without Scheduled Tribes: There are 93 villages without any scheduled tribe population.

Literates and Illiterates by Sex (Total Population):

	Persons	Males	Females
Literate	80,813	52,561	28,252
Illiterate	125,689	51,706	73,983
Literacy rate	47	61	33
Graduate	2,155	1,880	275

Agriculture: ***Distribution of villages according to land use:*** Out of 148 villages, Total area (in hectare) is 153670, out of that 69.3 percent is cultivable and 5.68 percent of the cultivable area is irrigated.

Sources of Irrigation (Hectares): Government Canal 3220.35, Private Canal 0, Well without Electricity 42.97, Well with Electricity 1253.24, Tubewell without Electricity 27.98, Tubewell with Electricity 110.59, Tank 507.58, River 873.6, Lake 0, Waterfall 0, Others 9.3.

Villages with population of 5000 to 9999: Chimmanchod, Ainoli, Kodli, Sulepeth, Nidugunda.

Villages with population of 10000 and above: None

Distribution of Workers:

	Persons	Males	Females	WPR
Cultivators	32,943	23,535	9,408	31.05
Agricultural Labour	51,340	17,519	33,821	48.39
Household Industry	2,819	1,448	1,371	2.66
Other Workers	18,985	14,394	4,591	17.9
Main Workers	76,114	49,806	26,308	71.75
Marginal Workers	29,973	7,090	22,883	28.25
Total Workers	106,087	56,896	49,191	

Religion: Major Religious Communities:

	Persons	Males	Females	Sex Ratio
Hindu (81.08%)	167,430	84,560	82,870	980
Muslim (14.29%)	29,510	14,846	14,664	988
Christian (0.58%)	1,205	624	581	931
Sikh (0.01%)	20	7	13	1,857
Buddhists (3.24%)	6,700	3,374	3,326	986
Jain (0.02%)	40	19	21	1,105

Agewise Data:

	Persons	Males	Females	Sex Ratio
All ages	206,502	104,267	102,235	981
0-14	82,692	42,345	40,347	953
15-44	85,046	43,526	41,520	954
45-79	36,678	17,448	19,230	1102
80+	1,895	842	1,053	1251
Age not stated	191	106	85	802

Languages (Dominant):

Kannada, Hindi, Urdu, Telugu, Marathi

Disabled Population:

	Persons	Males	Females	%
Total Disabled	4,107	2,253	1,854	
In Seeing	1,535	763	772	37.38
In Speech	446	243	203	10.86
In Hearing	281	134	147	6.84
In Movement	1,515	940	575	36.89
Mentally	330	173	157	8.04

CHINTAMANI

Chintamani C.D. Block lies in the northern part of Kolar district. It is a part of Chintamani taluka. The Block is located at a distance of 33 kms. from district headqu arters (Kolar). There are 400 villages in the block with the total population of 205,790 persons. Area of the C.D. Block is 876.93 sq. kms. It is bounded by taluk Bagepalli on north, taluks Kolar and Srinivaspur on south, taluk Chintamani on east, and taluk Sidlaghatta on west. It has common boundary with the state of Andhra Pradesh on north and east.

Communications:

Roadways : S.H.-5: Direction- Bagepalli to Kolar, Nearest Villages- Shettihalli, Kethanaikanahalli, Nalamachanahalli, Chickamunimangala, Venkatapura, Doddamunimangala, Srinivasapura, Mohamadpura, Nayanahalli, Nagasandra-gadde, Yerranayanahalli, Chetlapalligadde, Kallahalli, Kuruti halli, Kachihalli, Hadigere, Jodi Brahmanadinne, Ramenaha lli, Gadadhasanahalli, Kuruburu, Mylandahalli, Seekallu. S.H.-58: Direction- Sidlaghatta to Mulbagal, Nearest Villages- Yeraseegehalli, Thinakallu, Ulavakayalahalli,

Amitiganahalli, Chorapalli, Upparapete, Konappalli, Gopasandra, Booragamakalahalli, Oolavadi, Madikere, Doddaganjur, Nakalapalligadde, Siddimata, Brahmanagadde, Singanahalli. S.H.-82: Direction- Bangalore to Madanapa lli, Nearest Villages- Dandupalya, Marinaikanahalli, Nandiganahalli, Kodigivaripalli, Jogyanahalli, Kolimivar ipalli, Goppalli, Kendanahalli, Perumachanahalli, Chapura, Battiganahalli, Santhekallahalli , Hirepalya, Vaizakuru, Hosahalli (Jodi), Talagavara, Banahalli, Konganahalli, Oolavadi, Hebbari, Imareddihalli, Kambampalli, Madikere, Chetlapalligadde, Kallahalli, Katamachnahalli, Chinnasa ndra, Munganahalli, Kurutihalli.

Railway Station: Village- Doddanatha.

River: Papagni Nadi- Nearest Villages- Yenigadale, Chinn epalli, Balareddihalli, Vangimalu, Gundalahalli, Kenchepa lli, Chokkanahalli, Ulibele, Amani Thimmasanikere, Konepa lli, Burudugunte, Kadirenahalli, Maniyaramuddalahalli, Devaganahalli, Gajalavarahalli, Korlaparthi, Kuthappana halli, Papathimmanahalli, Bandenahalli, Basavapura, Appas anihalli, Mutamakalahalli, Nandanavana. Chitravati Nadi- Nearest Villages- Chilakalanerpu, Beedalahalli, Hosahudya, T.Gollahalli, Gadigivarahalli, Deshamvaripalli, Thuluv anuru, Devapalli, Nallaguttahalli, Yenigadale, Minchalaha lli, Vangimalu, Burudugunte.

Annual Rainfall: Normal Rianfall 747.39 mm.

Ground Water: Availability of the Ground Water in the Basin is (Information not avablable) H.A.M. and the utilization is (Information not avablable) H.A.M.
It belongs to (Information not avablable) category.
Depth to water level 5 to 20 meter below the ground.
Most of the wells go down in summer months, according to the Ground Water Estimation Committee.

Soils: Red Soils.

Natural Division : It falls in Sidlaghatta-Sriniwaspuri Uplands of the Southern Karnataka Plateau.

Administration:

Division: Bangalore. Parliamentary Constituency: 28 Kolar (SC). District: Kolar. Taluka: Chintamani. Assembly Constituency: 142 Sidlaghatta, 143 Chintamani. Gram Panchayat: 34.

Regional Area Development Boards: The Bailu Seeme Area Development Board.

Border Villages: (State: Andhra Pradesh)- Chilakalanerpu, Minchalahalli, Kukkaladinne, Chinnepalli, Balareddihalli, Anakalamadagu, Billandlahalli, Bodigundlapalli, Sunnap pagutta, Yenumalapadi, Kambalapalli, Konapura, Devapalli.

Villages: 400 **Inhabited:** 339 **Uninhabited:** 61

Ranking	District	State	National
Area	3	107	587
Population	4	83	626
Sex Ratio	9	98	2472
Child Sex Ratio	7	45	2153
Literacy Rate	9	117	3555
Density	4	18	4266
Work Participation Rate	5	53	700

Gram Panchayats:
Burudugunte, Chilakalanerpu, Yenigadale , Kadadalamari, Batlahalli, Mudalagollahalli, Raghuttahalli, Kencharlahalli, Mittahalli, Korlaparthi, Shettihalli, Kotagal, Iragampalli, Yegavakote, Pedduru, Nandiganahalli, Murugamalla, Bhoomi Setti Halli, Kagathi, Konappalli, Kathriguppe, Upparapete, Masthenahalli, Kaiwara, Talagavara, Santhekallahalli , Perumachanahalli , Chinnasandra, Hirekattigenahalli, Kuruburu, Munganahalli, Oolavadi, Doddaganjur, Anoor.

Amenities:

Education: Primary School in 268 villages, Middle school in 110 villages, Matriculation or Secondary School in 24 villages, namely Chilakalanerpu, T.Gollahalli, Yenigadale, Burudugunte, Korlaparthi, Nandanahosahalli, Kencharlahalli, Kadadalamari, Munganahalli, Batlahalli, Iragampalli, Yegavakote, Murugamalla, K.Raguttahalli, Kaiwara, Kadirapura, Santhekallahalli, Talagavara, Hirekattigenahalli, Kariyapalli, Doddaganjur, Anoor, Kuruburu, Doddabommanahalli.
Higher Secondary or Pre University Courses or Intermediate or Junior College in 4 villages of the CD Block,, namely Nimmakayalahalli, Kaiwara, Booragamakalahalli, Bathalahalli.
College in 3 villages, Adult Literacy Center in 4 villages., Colleges are in villages, namely Vegalapalli, Gollapalli, Yendapalli.

Medical: Hospital in 6 villages, Dispensary in 4 villages, Health Center in 12 villages, Sub Center in 42 villages, Maternity and Child Welfare Center in 17 villages, Community health workers in 4 villages.
The Villages having Hospital or Dispensary or Health Center are Chilakalanerpu, Batlahalli, Gollapalli, Iragampalli, Doddakarakamakalahalli, Kaiwara, Bachhappanahalli, Santhekallahalli , Surrappanahalli, Talagavara.

Drinking Water: Tap water in 148 villages, Tank water in 52 villages, Well water in 39 villages, Tubewell in 159 villages and more than one source in 238 villages.

Bank: Banking facility in 15 villages, namely, Chilakalanerpu, Yenigadale, Burudugunte Kencharlahalli, Iragampalli, Mudalagollahalli Yegavakote, Pedduru, Murugamalla, Kotagal, Kaiwara

Talagavara, Oolavadi, Doddaganjur, Kuruburu.
Credit Society in 12 villages Agricultural Credit Society in 11 Non-Agricultural Credit Society in 0 village.

Others: Power supply in 321 villages, Cinema hall in 3 villages, sport club in 2 villages, Stadium or Auditorium or Community Hall in 0 village, Post Office in 45 villages.

There are 255 villages having bus facilities.

Villages with most of facilities: Chilakalanerpu Yenigadale, Burudugunte, Kencharlahalli, Iragampalli Mudalagollahalli, Yegavakote, Pedduru, Murugamalla Kotagal, Kaiwara, Talagavara, Oolavadi, Doddaganjur.

Villages without amenities (Education): Thirumalapura, Beedalahalli, Kukkaladinne, Chokkanahalli, Amani Thimmasanikere, Maniyaramuddalahalli, Agraharahalli, Changavarahalli, Gurrampalli, Yarrapalli, Gonenahalli, Gowdanahalli, Cheemalagutta, Yerrapalli, Eathamakalhalli, Bhoopanahalli, Guttapalya, Gunthurugadde, Gondivarihalli, Dokkachintalapalli, Bodigundlahalli, Domalapalli, Kappalli, Bynahalli, Annepalli, Yerramantapalli, Duganarepalli, Chalamakote, Gollapalli, Jogyanahalli, Gollahalli, Dwarapalli, Karakamakalagadde, Kodigehalli, Thippanahalli, Jagathanahalli, Vasanthahalli, Kurlapalligadde, Korlahalli, Yeraseegehalli, Booragamakalahalli, Gubalahalli, Ulavakayalahalli, Subbarayanapet, Chorapalli, Upparapete, Nagasandragadde, Amani Keelukuntekere, Guttahalli, Bodaguru, Kendanahalli, Chapura, Vaddihalli, Bachhappanahalli, Surrappanahalli, Gownigadde, Marimakalahalli, Diguru, Byreddihalli, Chetlapalligadde, Doddanatha, Gidadakodihalli, Jodi Brahmanadinne, Naindrahalli, Bandarlahalli, Hosahalli, Ramenahalli..

Scheduled Castes: Out of the total population of 205791 persons, 54491 persons (26.48%) belong to Scheduled Castes. The villages having less than 10% SC population are Dwarapalli, Kukkaladinne, Konepalli, Annapalli Yaramareddihalli, Polanayakanahalli, Kariyapalli Somakalahalli, Konapura, Yerrapalli , Bhoopanahalli Guddampalli, Pasalanaikanahalli, Vempalli Gunthurugadde, Kondavenakapalli, Byrasandra Gondivarihalli, Dokkachintalapalli, Bodigundlahalli Thummalapalli, Kanagamakalapalli, Agrahara C. Kurupalli , Murugamalla, Annepalli Yerramantapalli, Gollapalli, Jogyanahalli Karakamakalagadde, Kethanaikanahalli, Yeshwanthapura Hussainpura, Thippanahalli, Adepalli, Srinivasapura Lakshmidevikote, Yeraseegehalli, Ulavakayalahalli Amani Keelukuntekere, Bodaguru, Perumachanahalli Shamarao Hospete, Kadirapura, Akkimangala Bachhappanahalli, Hirepalya, Subbarayanapete Muthukadahalli, Nernakallu, Marimakalahalli, Kagathi Byreddihalli, Cheemanahalli, Kachihalli, Siddimata Doddanatha, Singanahalli, Jodi Brahmanadinne.

The villages having more than 50% SC population are Thirumalapura, Thuluvanuru, Kadirenahalli Agraharahalli, Settinayanahalli, Nandanahosahalli Yarrapalli, Gonenahalli, Gowdanahalli Bodigundlapalli, Gudivabanahalli, Eathamakalhalli Vegalapalli, Seetharamapura, Naravamakalahalli Gudisilahalli, Yerrakote, Domalapalli, Duganarepalli Chalamakote, Bodanamari, Sujjanahalli, Anakallu Chowdadenahalli, Kurlapalligadde, Gubalahalli Guttahalli, Munthakadirenahalli, Narayanahalli Chapura, Bathalahalli, Chetlapalligadde , Gollahalli Suladenahalli, Gajalahalli, Viswanathapura.

Sex ratio of Scheduled Caste population is 496.

Scheduled Castes Literates and Illiterates by Sex:

	Persons	Males	Females
Literate	20,575	13,178	7,397
Illiterate	33,916	14,283	19,633
Literacy rate	43.8	55.5	31.8
Graduate	316	287	29

Scheduled Castes (Dominant):
Madiga, Adi Karnataka, Bhovi, Adi Dravida Chalavadi etc.

For their cultural identity please see Appendix-I

Villages without Scheduled Castes: There are 91 villages without any scheduled caste population.

Scheduled Tribes: Out of the total population of 205791 persons, 25478 persons (12.38%) belong to Scheduled Tribes. The villages having less than 10% ST population are Thirumalapura, Beedalahalli, Hosahudya, T.Gollahalli Devapalli, Yenigadale , Kukkaladinne, Chinnepalli Balareddihalli, Bommepalli, Gundalahalli Kenchepalli, Chokkanahalli, Ulibele Amani Thimmasanikere, Konepalli, Annapalli Kadirenahalli, Maniyaramuddalahalli, Devaganahalli Gajalavarahalli, Korlaparthi, Kuthappanahalli Papathimmanahalli, Bandenahalli, Basavapura Appasanihalli, Agraharahalli, Kodegandlu, Nadampalli Chintamakalahalli, Settinayanahalli, Kommepalli Mittahalli, Nandanavana, Kattigenahalli Nandanahosahalli, Rangenahalli, Yaramareddihalli Changavarahalli, Seegalagutta, Amitahalli Gurrampalli, Yarrapalli, Gonenahalli, Gowdanahalli Kencharlahalli, Anakalamadagu, Kadadalamari Bodigundlapalli, Hanumaigaripalli, Kariyapalli Cheemalagutta, Somakalahalli, Bodampalli Channarayanahalli, Yenumalapadi, Kambalapalli

Batlahalli, Yesagalahalli, Madamangala
Nagarajahosahalli, Kondliganahalli, Yerrapalli
Gudivabanahalli, Eathamakalhalli, Raghuttahalli
Brahmanahalli, Vegalapalli, Gollapalli, Yendapalli
Mindigal, Bhoopanahalli, Seetharamapura
Nallagutlahalli, Iragampalli, Guntipalli
Mudalagollahalli, Yerraigaripalli, Myakapothalahalli
Neelappalli, Naravamakalahalli, Gudisilahalli
Gondivarihalli, Gudumarlahalli, Maniganahalli
Kadirappanaiakanakote, Pedduru, Korakonahalli
Kothapalli, Kothahudya, Agrahara, Domalapalli
C. Kurupalli , Nimmakayalahalli, Yerramantapalli
Duganarepalli, Chalamakote, Gollapalli, Barlahalli
Gandraganahalli, Goppalli, Gollahalli, Narasapura
Sujjanahalli, Anakallu, Nalamachanahalli
Chickamunimangala, Chowdadenahalli, Jagathanahalli
K.Raguttahalli, Vasanthahalli, Kurlapalligadde
Kothur, Venkatapura, Korlahalli, Booragamakalahalli
Kempadenahalli, Guttahalli, Ulavakayalahalli
Amitiganahalli, Upparapete, Vaddahalli, Konappalli
Chokkanahalli, Munthakadirenahalli, Bukkanahalli
Amani Keelukuntekere, Hulugummanahalli, Guttahalli
Bodaguru, Mylapura, Narayanahalli, Nagadenahalli
Chapura, Shamarao Hospete, Kaiwara, Masthenahalli
Atturu, Kadirapura, Bachhappanahalli, Hirepalya
Vaizakuru, Beerajenahalli, Virupakshapura
Hosahalli (Jodi), Talagavara, Banahalli
Konganahalli, Gunnahalli, Muthukadahalli
Madabahalli, Nernakallu, Chikkakattigenahalli
Madarakallu, Byalahalli, Jangamapura, Rachapura
Hirekattigenahalli, Jeedarahalli, Gownigadde
Singasandra, Marimakalahalli, Badagavarahalli
Diguru, Kagathi, Byreddihalli, Chokkareddihalli
Kariyapalli, Gopasandra, Booragamakalahalli
Oolavadi, Bachuvarihalli, Bathalahalli, Hebbari
Imareddihalli, Cheemanahalli, Madikere
Chetlapalligadde , Kallahalli, Chinnasandra
Munganahalli, Kurutihalli, Kachihalli, Gollahalli
Doddaganjur, Siddimata, Kodadhavadi , Doddanatha
Hosuru, Kodihalli, Gidadakodihalli, Alambagiri
Suladenahalli, Naindrahalli, Channakeshavapura
Nidagurki, Bandarlahalli, Gajalahalli, Hosahalli
Kootharajanahalli, Gadadhasanahalli, Yadahalli
Mylandahalli, Viswanathapura, Doddapura
Krishnammanahosahalli, Doddabommanahalli.

The villages having more than 50% ST population are
Deshamvaripalli, Marabahalli, Konapura
Kanchinayakanahalli, Pasalanaikanahalli
Kondavenakapalli, Puligundlahalli, Bodigundlahalli
Kanagamakalapalli, Kanisettyhalli, Annepalli
Doddakarakamakalahalli, Kurumarlahalli, Dwarapalli
Karakamakalagadde, Kethanaikanahalli, Yeshwanthapura
Hussainpura, Kodigehalli, Adepalli, Gownipalli
Yeraseegehalli, Kavalaganahalli, Nallaguttahalli
Mallikapura, Marapalli, Jodi Brahmanadinne
Ramenahalli.

Sex ratio of Scheduled tribe population is 494.

Scheduled Tribes Literates and Illiterates by Sex:

	Persons	Males	Females
Literate	9,880	6,231	3,649
Illiterate	15,598	6,652	8,946
Literacy rate	45.0	56.1	33.6
Graduate	116	106	10

Scheduled Tribes (Dominant):
Naikda etc., Generic Tribes etc., Kadu Kuruba
Gowdalu, Hakkipikki

For their cultural identity please see Appendix-II

Villages without Scheduled Tribes: There are 178 villages without any scheduled tribe population.

Literates and Illiterates by Sex (Total Population):

	Persons	Males	Females
Literate	99,953	61,566	38,387
Illiterate	105,838	42,900	62,938
Literacy rate	56	68	43
Graduate	2,596	2,210	386

Agriculture: ***Distribution of villages according to land use:*** Out of 400 villages, Total area (in hectare) is 87693, out of that 51.23 percent is cultivable and 23.24 percent of the cultivable area is irrigated.

Sources of Irrigation (Hectares): Government Canal 13.87, Private Canal 0, Well without Electricity 13.15, Well with Electricity 453.19, Tubewell without Electricity 88.81, Tubewell with Electricity 6387.69, Tank 3109.1, River 28.4, Lake 0, Waterfall 0, Others 348.81.

Villages with population of 5000 to 9999:
Kaiwara.

Villages with population of 10000 and above: None

Distribution of Workers:

	Persons	Males	Females	WPR
Cultivators	57,212	34,064	23,148	49.45
Agricultural Labour	34,040	12,928	21,112	29.42
Household Industry	3,242	1,904	1,338	2.8
Other Workers	21,204	14,778	6,426	18.33
Main Workers	88,897	57,318	31,579	76.84
Marginal Workers	26,801	6,356	20,445	23.16
Total Workers	115,698	63,674	52,024	

Religion: Major Religious Communities:

	Persons	Males	Females	Sex Ratio
Hindu (91.73%)	188,767	95,670	93,097	973
Muslim (8.04%)	16,537	8,580	7,957	927

Christian (0.17%)	344	150	194	1,293
Sikh (0%)	-	-	-	-
Buddhists (0.01%)	11	6	5	833
Jain (0.01%)	12	4	8	2,000

Agewise Data:

	Persons	Males	Females	Sex Ratio
All ages	205,791	104,466	101,325	970
0-14	65,111	33,397	31,714	950
15-44	95,853	48,276	47,577	986
45-79	42,224	21,566	20,658	958
80+	2,490	1,168	1,322	1132
Age not stated	113	59	54	915

Languages (Dominant):

Telugu, Kannada, Urdu, Hindi, Marathi

Disabled Population:

	Persons	Males	Females	%
Total Disabled	3,804	2,159	1,645	
In Seeing	1,892	1,019	873	49.74
In Speech	390	226	164	10.25
In Hearing	151	80	71	3.97
In Movement	956	597	359	25.13
Mentally	415	237	178	10.91

CHITAPUR

Chitapur C.D. Block lies in the central part of Gulbarga district. It is a part of Chitapur taluka. The Block is located at a distance of 52 kms from district headquarters (Gulbarga). There are 125 villages in the block with the total population of 238,766 persons. Area of the C.D. Block is 1635.57 sq. kms. It is bounded by taluk Chincholi and Gulbarga on north, taluk Shahpur and Yadgir on south, taluks Chincholi and Sedam on east, taluks Gulbarga, Jevargi and Shahpur on west.

Communications:

Roadways : S.H-10: Direction- Gulbarga to Sedam, Nearest Villages- Hadnoor, Mutpa, Madbol, Gundagurthi, Evani, Dandothi, Malkood. S.H-15: Nearest Village- Bhimanhalli. S.H- 32: Direction-Mahagaon to Sulepeth, Nearest Villages- Herur (K), Watwati, Revai, Kandagol, Sugur (K).

Railway Station: Villages- Martur, Gola (K).

River: Bhima Nadi- Nearest Villages- Hongunta, Kadhalli, Kundanoor, Chamnoor, Kadaboor,, Kolkunda, Malag (N), Turnur, Maradgi, Kollur, Sonthi, Kanganahalli, Hulandgera, Banhatti. Kagna Nadi- Nearest Vill.- Pethsirur, Belgumpa, Evani, Dandothi, Mutga, Katamdevarhalli, Shankerwadi, Malgatti, Gola (K), Ingalgi, Hongunta, Kundanur, Jeevangi, Kaddargi, Bhagodi, Mudbol, Margol. Benithora Nadi- Nearest Villages- Kannadgi, Herur (K),Kandagol, Shelgi, Kalhipperga, Banbi, Chincholi (H), Gotur, Kalgi, Donnur, Arjamga, Tengli, Savathkhed, Jeevanmardgi, Tonchi, Kamaknoor, Hebbal, Bennur (K), Kansoor, Malaghan, Kalgurthi, Tonsinhalli (T), Malkood.

Reserved Forest: (Yadgir): Nearest Villages- Hannikere, Alhalli, Allur (K), Allur (B), Dandgund, Ladlapur, Sanknoor, Shiva Nagar, Balgere, Yagapur.

Annual Rainfall: Normal Rianfall 777 mm.

Ground Water: Availability of the Ground Water in the Basin is 7985 H.A.M. and the utilization is 1818 H.A.M. It belongs to Over Exploited category. Depth to water level 5 to 10 meter below the ground. Most of the wells go down in summer months, according to the Ground Water Estimation Committee.

Soils: Deep Black, Medium Black Soil, Shallow Soil and Lateritic Soil.

Natural Division : It falls partly in the Aland-Chincholi Tract of Trappean Outcrops, Kagna Basin and Lower Bhima Valley of the Northern Karnataka Plateau.

Administration:

Division: Gulbarga. Parliamentary Constituency: 5 Gulbarga (SC), 7 Bidar (SC), 5 Gulbarga (SC). Dist.: Gulbarga. Taluka: Chitapur. Assembly Const.: 40 Chitapur (SC), 42 Chinchodi (SC), 43 Gulbarga Rural (SC). Gram Panchayat:35 .

Regional Area Development Boards: The Hyderabad-Karnataka Area Development Board.

Fairs: Kaleshwara Jatra: Kalgi in Chitapur taluk near Gulbarga is a Hindu pilgrim centre where a jatra is held about May every year. There are two temples, Kaleshwar temple and Narsimha temple.Throughout the year, pilgrims visit this place to worship the deities.Kalgi has a panchayat and is 32 kms. station which is on the Wadi-Secunderabad broad gauge section. The Government transport buses run to this place.

Chandralamba Jatra: Sonthi is a place in Chitapur taluk near Gulbarga, though a small place it has become renowned for its Chandralamba temple, which is visited by a large number of Hindus. In March-April every year, a jatra is held here. The temple faces east and is in circular shape. On either side of the main entrance, there are huge mantaps, beyond which there is a broad open space nearly 30 ft. wide. The mantaps are so constructed as to hold some 2,000 pilgrims at a time. In the centre of this enclosure, the sanctum-sanctorum of the Goddess is situated,with the main opening facing east. The outer prakaras are used bydevotees to sing in the praise of the presiding deity. It is said on historical author ity that the great dynasty of the western Chalukyas worshipped Chandralamba as their family deity. Even to this day the Goddess is the family deity of several communities near Gulbarga. In the inner courtyard of this celebrated temple, there are Dwadasha lingas, together with the images of Mahakali, Mahalakshmi and Saraswathi. In addition to the temple of Chandralamba, pilgrims go to the Sri Markandeya temple, the Marthanda Bhairava and the samadhi of Sri Vishwambhara Dikshit.

Villages: 125 **Inhabited:** 122 **Uninhabited:** 3

Ranking	District	State	National
Area	6	20	96
Population	6	52	305
Sex Ratio	4	64	1902
Child Sex Ratio	3	93	3019
Literacy Rate	6	167	5605
Density	8	130	5612
Work Participation Rate	7	136	3089

Gram Panchayats:

Arankal, Kandagol, Hebbal, Chincholi (H), Gotur, Kalgi, Rajapur, Kodadur, Korwar, Madbol, Tengli, Gundagurthi, Pethsirur, Dandothi, Bhagodi, Martur, Bhankur , Tonsinhalli, Malgatti, Diggaon, Ravoor, Hongunta, Ingalgi, Wadi, Kamarwadi, Satnoor, Alhalli, Halkatta, Kadaboor, Ladlapur, Allur (B), Bhimanhalli, Yagapur, Nalwar, Kollur, Sonthi.

Amenities:

Education: Primary School in 121 villages, Middle school in 77 villages, Matriculation or Secondary School in 20 villages, namely Revai, Kandagol, Kalgi, Tengli, Kodadur, Mangalgi, Hebbal, Korwar, Pethsirur, Gundagurthi, Dandothi, Martur, Hongunta, Gandhinagar, Ravoor, Diggaon, Alhalli, Bhimanhalli, Nalwar, Kollur.

Higher Secondary or Pre University Courses or Intermediate or Junior College in 4 villages of the CD Block,, namely Kalgi, Hebbal, Gundagurthi, Ravoor.

College in 1 village, Adult Literacy Center in 16 villages., College is in village, namely Ravoor.

Medical: Hospital in 7 villages, Dispensary in 16 villages, Health Center in 13 villages, Sub Center in 44 villages, Maternity and Child Welfare Center in 10 villages, Community health workers in 22 villages.

The Villages having Hospital or Dispensary or Health Center are Sugur (K), Kalgi, Tengli, Salhalli, Mangalgi, Hebbal, Korwar, Mugulnagaon, Maha Nagar, Pethsirur, Gundagurthi, Tonsinhalli (T), Malgatti, Hongunta, Margol, Mogla, Alhalli, Nalwar, Kollur.

Drinking Water: Tap water in 53 villages, Tank water in 26 villages, Well water in 96 villages, Tubewell in 31 villages and more than one source in 108 villages.

Bank: Banking facility in 22 villages, namely, Arankal, Revai, Kalgi, Tengli, Kodadur, Mugulnagaon Maha Nagar, Gundagurthi, Dandothi, Tonsinhalli (T) Kundanoor, Bhagodi, Margol, Mogla, Itga, Ravoor Alhalli, Kolkunda, Malag (N), Nalwar, Turnur, Kollur. Credit Society in 20 villages Agricultural Credit Society in 20 Non-Agricultural Credit Society in 8 villages.

Others: Power supply in 121 villages, Cinema hall in 4 villages sport club in 20 villages, Stadium or Auditorium or Community Hall in 122 villages, Post Office in 66 villages.

There are 81 villages having bus facilities.

Villages with most of facilities: Arankal, Kalgi Tengli, Kodadur, Mugulnagaon, Maha Nagar Gundagurthi, Dandothi, Tonsinhalli (T), Ravoor Alhalli, Nalwar, Kollur.

Villages without amenities (Education): Mavinsur..

Scheduled Castes: Out of the total population of 238532 persons, 66845 persons (28.02%) belong to Scheduled Castes. The villages having less than 10% SC population are Rajapur, Arjamga, Nippani, Alura, Bammanhalli Hossur, Allur (B), Dandgund, Sanknoor, Banhatti.

The villages having more than 50% SC population are Mavinsur, Bhedsur, Sanjay Nagar, Sugur (K) Mugulnagaon, Maha Nagar, Seva Nagar, Devapur Shiva Nagar, Balgere, Yagapur, Turnur, Kollur Hulandgera.

Sex ratio of Scheduled Caste population is 492.

Scheduled Castes Literates and Illiterates by Sex:

	Persons	Males	Females
Literate	18,154	12,014	6,140
Illiterate	48,691	21,940	26,751
Literacy rate	33.4	43.6	22.9
Graduate	425	374	51

Scheduled Castes (Dominant):

Banjara etc., Holaya etc., Madiga, Bhovi Generic Castes etc.

For their cultural identity please see Appendix-I

Villages without Scheduled Castes: There are 4 villages without any scheduled caste population.

Scheduled Tribes: Out of the total population of 238532 persons, 4560 persons (1.91%) belong to Scheduled Tribes. The villages having less than 10% ST population are Kannadgi, Herur (K), Watwati, Arankal, Revai Mavinsur, Bhedsur, Sanjay Nagar, Shelgi, Kalhipperga Hulgera, Banbi, Chincholi (H), Sugur (K), Gotur Kalgi, Bharatnoor, Rajapur, Donnur, Arjamga, Tengli Salhalli, Kodadur, Malag (K), Mangalgi, Nippani Savathkhed, Jeevanmardgi, Tonchi, Kamaknoor, Hebbal Bennur (K), Kansoor, Malaghan, Korwar, Hadnoor Wacha, Muchakhed, Kalgurthi, Indankal, Mattimudu Mutpa, Madbol, Sangavi, Bennur (B), Mugulnagaon Maha Nagar, Pethsirur, Belgumpa, Gundagurthi Dandothi, Tonsinhalli (T), Malkood, Martur Devantegnur, Aldihal, Seva Nagar, Mutga Katamdevarhalli, Shankerwadi, Taranhalli Tonsinhalli, Malgatti, Gola (K), Ingalgi, Hongunta

Kadhalli, Kundanoor, Kadaboor, Balwadgi, Jeevangi Kaddargi, Bhagodi, Mudbol, Margol, Mogla, Itga Yergal, Gandhinagar, Ravoor, Kardal, Satnoor Diggaon, Bhankalga, Dongaon, Halkatta, Kamarwadi Hannikere, Alhalli, Allur (K), Ramteerth, Rajola Bhimanhalli, Allur (B), Dandgund, Devapur, Konchur Kolkunda, Malag (N), Nalwar, Sanknoor, Shiva Nagar Balgere, Yagapur, Sugur (N), Turnur, Maradgi, Kollur Sonthi, Kanganahalli, Hulandgera, Banhatti Tarkaspet, Rampurhalli.

The villages having more than 50% ST population are None.

Sex ratio of Scheduled tribe population is 490.

Scheduled Tribes Literates and Illiterates by Sex:

	Persons	Males	Females
Literate	1,121	760	361
Illiterate	3,439	1,566	1,873
Literacy rate	30.0	40.2	19.6
Graduate	14	14	0

Scheduled Tribes (Dominant):

Naikda etc., Koli Dhor etc., Gond etc., Meda Kadu Kuruba

For their cultural identity please see Appendix-II

Villages without Scheduled Tribes: There are 68 villages without any scheduled tribe population.

Literates and Illiterates by Sex (Total Population):

	Persons	Males	Females
Literate	81,293	52,616	28,677
Illiterate	157,239	67,651	89,588
Literacy rate	41	53	29
Graduate	2,086	1,749	337

Agriculture: ***Distribution of villages according to land use:***

Out of 125 villages, Total area (in hectare) is 163557, out of that 81.35 percent is cultivable and 0.65 percent of the cultivable area is irrigated.

Sources of Irrigation (Hectares): Government Canal 195.16, Private Canal 0, Well without Electricity 137.85, Well with Electricity 378.79, Tubewell without Electricity 38.85, Tubewell with Electricity 22.18, Tank 18.04, River 57.73, Lake 0, Waterfall 0, Others 15.95.

Villages with population of 5000 to 9999:

Kalgi, Dandothi, Ingalgi, Hongunta, Kollur.

Villages with population of 10000 and above:

Ravoor, Nalwar.

Distribution of Workers:

	Persons	Males	Females	WPR
Cultivators	29,320	22,108	7,212	27.83
Agricultural Labour	44,419	18,114	26,305	42.17
Household Industry	2,180	1,378	802	2.07
Other Workers	29,417	20,843	8,574	27.93
Main Workers	83,251	55,620	27,631	79.03
Marginal Workers	22,085	6,823	15,262	20.97
Total Workers	105,336	62,443	42,893	

Religion: Major Religious Communities:

	Persons	Males	Females	Sex Ratio
Hindu (74.49%)	177,671	89,505	88,166	985
Muslim (15.58%)	37,161	18,814	18,347	975
Christian (0.68%)	1,632	836	796	952
Sikh (0.01%)	35	18	17	944
Buddhists (8.42%)	20,079	10,109	9,970	986
Jain (0.09%)	217	103	114	1,107

Agewise Data:

	Persons	Males	Females	Sex Ratio
All ages	238,532	120,267	118,265	983
0-14	97,073	49,866	47,207	947
15-44	97,518	49,550	47,968	968
45-79	41,818	19,911	21,907	1100
80+	1,818	777	1,041	1340
Age not stated	305	163	142	871

Languages (Dominant):

Kannada, Urdu, Hindi, Telugu, Marathi

Disabled Population:

	Persons	Males	Females	%
Total Disabled	4,709	2,497	2,212	
In Seeing	2,129	983	1,146	45.21
In Speech	409	239	170	8.69
In Hearing	272	132	140	5.78
In Movement	1,613	999	614	34.25
Mentally	286	144	142	6.07

CHITRADURGA

Chitradurga C.D. Block lies in the northern part of Chitradurga district. It is a part of Chitradurga taluka. The Block is located at a distance of 00 kms. from district headquarters (Chitradurga). There are 190 villages in the block with the total population of 250,967 persons. Area of the C.D. Block is 1353.06 sq. kms.

It is bounded by district Davanagere on north, taluks Hiriyur and Holalkere on south, taluks Challakere and Hiriyur on east, district Davanagere and taluk Holalkere on west.

Communications:

Roadways : N.H-4: Direction- Davanagere to Bangalore, Nearest Villages- Bevinahalli, Kasavanahalli, Heggere, Bharamasagara, Yemmehatti, Hampanur, Kolahal, Jatlahalli, Chikkabennur, Hirebennur, Cheelangi, Kalkunte, Beerava ra, Katralu, Iyyanahalli, K. Ballekatte, Lakshmisagara, Vijapura, Maraghatta, Guttinadu, Seebara, Doddasiddavva nahalli, Kunchiganahal, Sevapura, Medakeripura, Matadakur ubarahatti, Kavadigarahatti, Ingaladalu. N.H-13: Shimoga to Hospet, Direction- Nearest Villages- Chikkagondanahal li, Turuvanur, Madanaikanahalli, Chikkappanahalli, Vijapu ra, Chikkalaghatta, Hullur, Singapura, Guddadarangavvanah alli, Pillekerenahalli, Mallapura, Janukonda, Jagadalipura, Jalikatte, Kirubanakallu, Huligundi, Attikatte, Pandar ahalli. S.H-48: Direction- Honnali to Challakere, Nearest Villages- Bommenahalli, Hireguntanur, Haliyur, Kurubarah alli , Thurebailu, Dindadahalli, Palya, Bheemasamudra, Dyamavvanahalli, Toparamalige, Doddasiddavvanahalli, Medakeripura, Kavadigarahatti, Siddapura, Katihalli, Manangi.

River: Chinna Hagira Nadi- Nearest Villages- Chippinake re, Chikkagondanahalli, Surenahalli, Sultanipura, Rimmagh atta, Papenahalli, Rayannanahalli, Katralu, Vaddanahalli, Iyyanahalli. Janaga Halla Nadi- Nearest Villages- Sadar ahalli, Chikkapura, Hosahalli, Kyasapura, Hireguntanur, Chikkaguntanur, Haliyur, Rottihalli, Thurebailu, Bheema samudra, Bettadanagenahalli.

Canal: Nearest Villages- Siddavvanadurga, Baligatte, Beeravara, Katralu, Vaddanahalli, Hireguntanur, Thureba ilu, Dindadahalli, Palya, Malali, Bheemasamudra.

Annual Rainfall: Normal Rianfall 670.0 mm

Ground Water: Availability of the Ground Water in the Basin is 7857.30 H.A.M. and the utilization is 11970. 98 H.A.M. It belongs to Over Expoited category. Depth to water level 2 to 20 meter below the ground. Most of the wells go down in summer months, according to the Ground Water Estimation Committee.

Soils: Deep and Shallow black soils, mixed red and black soil, red loamy and sandy soils.

Natural Division : It falls partly in Middle Vedavati (Hagari) Basin, Chitradurga-Hosadurga Hills and Devangere Plateau of the Central Karnataka Plateau.

Administration:

Division: Bangalore. Parliamentary Constituency: 18 Chitradurga (SC). District: Chitradurga. Taluka: Chitrad urga. Assembly Constituency: 98 Challakere (ST), 99 Chitr adurga, 103 Holalkere (SC). Gram Panchayat: 36.

Regional Area Development Boards: The Bailu Seeme Area Development Board.

Fairs: Murugimatha Festival: The Murugimatha festival is observed at Chitradurga on the 11th day of Ashvina (September-October), Chitradurga, a district headquarters is about 180 kms. north-west of Bangalore is a place, of religious importance.

Villages: 190 **Inhabited:** 165 **Uninhabited:** 25

Ranking	District	State	National
Area	3	46	199
Population	2	36	227
Sex Ratio	6	160	3807
Child Sex Ratio	2	95	3135
Literacy Rate	2	59	1884
Density	6	122	4949
Work Participation Rate	1	92	2870

Gram Panchayats:

Kogunde, Kalgere, Issamudra, Yelagodu, Chikkagondanahalli, Turuvanur, Kunabevu, Madanaikanahalli, Muddapura, Chikkabennur, Kolahal, Bharamasagara, Alagavadi, Sirigere, Alaghatta, Lakshmisagara, Iyyanahalli, Guddadarangawanahalli, Belaghatta, Dyamawanahalli, Medakeripura, Gonur, Medehalli, Matadakurubarahatti, Cholagatta, Siddapura, Hireguntanur, Bommenahalli, Bheemasamudra, Hallur, Janukonda, Annehal, Sondekola, Ingaladalu, Doddasiddawanahalli, Jampannanakanakote.

Amenities:

Education: Primary School in 162 villages, Middle school in 114 villages, Matriculation or Secondary School in 47 villages, namely Bahadurghatta, Kadehude, Kalgere, Issamudra, Yelagodu, Basavanashivanakere, Bharamasagara, Hampanur, Chikkabennur, Cheelangi, Alagavadi, Sirigere, Muddapura, Chikkagondanahalli, Turuvanur, Kunabevu, Haikal, Madanaikanahalli, Sultanipura, Belaghatta, Katralu, Lakshmisagara, Vijapura, Alaghatta, Dyamavvanahalli, Guttinadu, Kyasapura, Hunasekatte, Kadleguddu, Hireguntanur, Haliyur, Kurubarahalli, Hullur, Bheemasamudra, Guddadarangavvanahalli, Dyamavvanahalli, Doddasiddavvanahalli, Medakeripura, Mallapura, Matadakurubarahatti, Siddapura, Janukonda, Jampannanaikanakote, Sondekola, Godabanahal, Annehal, Kenne Hadlu.

Higher Secondary or Pre University Courses or Intermediate or Junior College in 10 villages of the CD Block,, namely Bharamasagara, Alagavadi, Sirigere, Chikkagondanahalli, Turuvanur, Haikal, Hireguntanur, Bheemasamudra, Doddasiddavvanahalli, Janukonda.

College in 1 village, Adult Literacy Center in 1 village., College is in village, namely Sirigere.

Medical: Hospital in 3 villages, Dispensary in 15 villages, Health Center in 14 villages, Sub Center in 28 villages, Maternity and Child Welfare Center in 2 villages, Community health workers in 5 villages.

The Villages having Hospital or Dispensary or Health Center are Kadehude, Kalgere, Rangavvanahalli, Kasavanahalli, Bharamasagara, Kolahal, Gowrammanahalli, Alagavadi, Doddiganahal, Kunabevu, K. Ballekatte, Bheemasamudra, Guddadarangavvanahalli, Jampannanaikanakote, Godabanahal.

Drinking Water: Tap water in 70 villages, Tank water in

20 villages, Well water in 2 villages, Tubewell in 93 villages and more than one source in 151 villages.

Bank: Banking facility in 18 villages, namely, Bevinahalli, Bharamasagara, Chikkabennur, Sirigere Muddapura, Chikkagondanahalli, Turuvanur, Haikal Baggalurangavvanahalli, Belaghatta, Hireguntanur Kurubarahalli, Hullur, Bheemasamudra Guddadarangavvanahalli, Dyamavvanahalli Doddasiddavvanahalli, Godabanahal.

Credit Society in 32 villages Agricultural Credit Society in 24 Non-Agricultural Credit Society in 0 village.

Others: Power supply in 165 villages, Cinema hall in 2 villages, sport club in 0 village, Stadium or Auditorium or Community Hall in 1 village, Post Office in 52 villages.

There are 149 villages having bus facilities.

Villages with most of facilities: Bharamasagara Sirigere, Muddapura, Chikkagondanahalli, Turuvanur Haikal, Belaghatta, Hireguntanur, Bheemasamudra Guddadarangavvanahalli, Doddasiddavvanahalli Godabanahal.

Villages without amenities (Education):
Sriramanagara, Ragalobanahalli, Kirubanakallu..

Scheduled Castes: Out of the total population of 251336 persons, 64979 persons (25.85%) belong to Scheduled Castes.

The villages having less than 10% SC population are Bahadurghatta, Haralakatte, Adavigollarahalli Gowrammanahalli, Lingavvanagatihalli, Halavudara Pudukalahalli, Jammenahalli, Ragalobanahalli Chikkajagalur, Rimmaghatta, Pelorahatti Dyamavvanahalli, Guttinadu, Megalahalli, Nallikatte Bheemasamudra, Kallenahalli, Mallanakatte Kavadigarahatti.

The villages having more than 50% SC population are Kariyannanahalli, Hosapete, Sriramanagara Bevinahalli, Rangavvanahalli, Bedarashivanakere Kasavanahalli, Eshwaranagara, Halerangapura Doddiganahal, Chikkappanahalli, Papenahalli Vaddanahalli, Siddavvanahalli, Palya, N.Ballikatte Malali, Bettadanagenahalli, Sevapura, Sevalalnagar Obannanahalli, Nandipura, Kakkeharavu, Doddapura.

Sex ratio of Scheduled Caste population is 489.

Scheduled Castes Literates and Illiterates by Sex:

	Persons	Males	Females
Literate	29,225	18,245	10,980
Illiterate	35,754	14,942	20,812
Literacy rate	53.1	64.7	40.9
Graduate	869	766	103

Scheduled Castes (Dominant):

Madiga, Bhovi, Banjara etc., Adi Karnataka Adi Dravida

For their cultural identity please see Appendix-I

Villages without Scheduled Castes: There are 32 villages without any scheduled caste population.

Scheduled Tribes: Out of the total population of 251336 persons, 52045 persons (20.71%) belong to Scheduled Tribes.

The villages having less than 10% ST population are Kodihalli, Kariyannanahalli, Kalgere, Issamudra Kakabalu, Sriramanagara, Bevinahalli, Dyapanahalli Rangavvanahalli, Haralakatte, Ajjappanahalli Hullehal, Bastihalli, Bedarashivanakere, Heggadehalu Kasavanahalli, Bharamasagara, Yemmehatti, Hampanur Eshwaranagara, Gowrammanahalli, Halerangapura Seegehalli, Jammenahalli, Doddiganahal, Bagenahal Iyyanahalli, Alaghatta, Guttinadu, Echalanagenahalli Chikkapura, Hosahalli, Hunasekatte, Chikkaguntanur Kurubarahalli , Thirumalapura, Hullur, Thurebailu Palya, N.Ballikatte, Singapura, Pallavagere Sajjanakere, Toparamalige, Doddasiddavvanahalli Sevapura, Medakeripura, Megalahalli Matadakurubarahatti, Kavadigarahatti, Siddapura Manangi, Dalavaihalli, Jalikatte, Kirubanakallu Sevalalnagar, Obannanahalli, Nandipura Uppanaikanahalli, Godabanahal, Mahadevanakatte Doddapura.

The villages having more than 50% ST population are Byalahal, Heggere, Lingavvanagatihalli Pudukalahalli, Hosarangapura, Palakihalli Medakeripura, Bommavvanagathihalli, Muddapura Ragalobanahalli, Chikkajagalur, Hunesekatte Pelorahatti, Kalkunte, Megalahalli, Kallenahalli Gonur.

Sex ratio of Scheduled tribe population is 486.

Scheduled Tribes Literates and Illiterates by Sex:

	Persons	Males	Females
Literate	26,748	16,633	10,115
Illiterate	25,297	10,099	15,198
Literacy rate	59.6	72.2	46.3
Graduate	723	636	87

Scheduled Tribes (Dominant):

Naikda etc., Meda, Generic Tribes etc., Kadu Kuruba Chenchu etc.

For their cultural identity please see Appendix-II

Villages without Scheduled Tribes: There are 42 villages without any scheduled tribe population.

Literates and Illiterates by Sex (Total Population):

	Persons	Males	Females
Literate	142,455	85,164	57,291
Illiterate	108,881	44,095	64,786
Literacy rate	65	76	54
Graduate	5,438	4,540	898

Agriculture: ***Distribution of villages according to land use:*** Out of 190 villages, Total area (in hectare) is 135306, out of that 70.98 percent is cultivable and 11.73 percent of the cultivable area is irrigated.

Sources of Irrigation (Hectares): Government Canal 0, Private Canal 0, Well without Electricity 0, Well with Electricity 60, Tubewell without Electricity 31.39, Tubewell with Electricity 11129.12, Tank 49.57, River 0, Lake 0, Waterfall 0, Others 0.

Villages with population of 5000 to 9999:
Bharamasagara, Dyamavvanahalli, Doddasiddavvanahalli Matadakurubarahatti.

Villages with population of 10000 and above:
Turuvanur.

Distribution of Workers:

	Persons	Males	Females	WPR
Cultivators	50,757	37,794	12,963	42.61
Agricultural Labour	45,956	18,940	27,016	38.58
Household Industry	1,770	1,111	659	1.49
Other Workers	20,625	15,398	5,227	17.32
Main Workers	94,481	66,100	28,381	79.32
Marginal Workers	24,627	7,143	17,484	20.68
Total Workers	119,108	73,243	45,865	

Religion: Major Religious Communities:

	Persons	Males	Females	Sex Ratio
Hindu (94.71%)	238,052	122,311	115,741	946
Muslim (4.34%)	10,920	5,710	5,210	912
Christian (0.08%)	201	102	99	971
Sikh (0.04%)	99	60	39	650
Buddhists (0.02%)	40	23	17	739
Jain (0.02%)	53	30	23	767

Agewise Data:

	Persons	Males	Females	Sex Ratio
All ages	251,336	129,259	122,077	944
0-14	80,109	41,122	38,987	948
15-44	119,508	61,496	58,012	943
45-79	48,798	25,219	23,579	935
80+	2,685	1,282	1,403	1094
Age not stated	236	140	96	686

Languages (Dominant):
Kannada, Telugu, Urdu, Hindi, Tamil

Disabled Population:

	Persons	Males	Females	%
Total Disabled	5,598	3,352	2,246	
In Seeing	2,735	1,644	1,091	48.86
In Speech	580	332	248	10.36
In Hearing	283	148	135	5.06
In Movement	1,553	996	557	27.74
Mentally	447	232	215	7.98

DAVANAGERE

Davanagere C.D. Block lies in the central part of Davana gere district. It is a part of Davanagere taluka. The Block is located at a distance of 00 kms. from district headquarters (Davanagere). There are 166 villages in the block with the total population of 237,885 persons. Area of the C.D. Block is 880.28 sq. kms. It is bounded by taluks Harihar and Harapanahalli on north, taluk Channagiri on south, district Chitradurga and taluk Jagalur on east, taluks Honalli and Harihar on west.

Communications:

Roadways : N.H-4: Direction- Dharwad to Bangalore, NearestVillages- Neelanahalli, Doddabathi, Vaddinahalli, Honnur, Kalapanahalli, Chattobanahalli, Mallashettihalli, Kogganur, Hulapanakatte, Anagodu, Halavarthy, Hunase katte, Lakkamuthenahalli, Nirthadi, Panchenahalli, Hebbalu. S.H-19 A: Direction- Anagodu to Holalkere, Nearest Villages- Anagodu, Nerlegi, Ganganakatte, Sultanipura, Kodaganur, Annapura, Dindadahalli, Doddamagadi, Hindasa katte, Mayakonda.

Railway Station: Villages- Tholahunse, Hanumanahalli, Kodaganur, Mayakonda.

River: Tungabhadra Nadi- Nearest Villages- Siriganahalli, Balluru, Jadaganahalli, Nagarasanahalli. Syagali Halla Nadi- Nearest Villages- Mudahadadi, Hadadi, Vaderahalli, Siriganahalli, Kanagondanahalli, Kolenahalli, Kukkavada, Giriyapura, Hanumanahalli, Bullapura, Mayakonda, Donkan ahalli, Likikere, Turuvanahalu, Honnamaradi, Gonivada, Huvinamadu, Syagale, Kandagal, Kodihalli, Malalakere, Bada, Vitalapura, Vantihal, Anaberu. Haritra Nadi- Nearest Villages- Siriganahalli, Balluru, Jadaganahalli, Nagarasanahalli. Hagari Nadi- Kurudi, Hemmanabethur.

Canal: Nearest Villages- Doddabathi, Devarahatti, Putaka nahalu, Bethuru, Kadajji, Mallapura, Nagarakatte, Shirama gondanahalli, Naganur, Belavanur, Chandrenahalli, Srikris hnanagara, Igoor, Giriyavvanahalli, Boragondanahalli, Honnur, Kalapanahalli, Pamenahalli, Tholahunse, Rangavv anahalli, Kurki, Chattobanahalli, Chikkatogaleri, Hiretog aleri, Kabburu, Madakeripura, Kaluru, Dyamenahalli, Bada, Vitalapura, Shankaranahalli, Anaberu, Nalkunda.

Annual Rainfall: Normal Rianfall 589 mm.

Ground Water: Availability of the Ground Water in the Basin is 10576.79 H.A.M. and the utilization is 6439. 13 H.A.M.. It belongs to Over Exploited category. Depth to water level 5 to 20 meter below the ground. Most of the wells go down in summer months, according to the Ground Water Estimation Committee.

Soils: Red Sandy Soils and Black Soils.

Natural Division : It falls in Devangere Plateau of the Central Karnataka Plateau.

Administration:

Division: Bangalore. Parliamentary Constituency: 13 Davanagere. District: Davanagere. Taluka: Davanagere. Assembly Constituency: 106 Davanagere North, 107 Davana gere. Gram Panchayat: 40.

Fairs and Festivals: Durgamma Jatra: It is one of the most important jatras of Karnataka. It is held at Davangere, once in two years in the month of Phalguna (February-March), at which more than a lakh people congregate.

Villages: 166 **Inhabited:** 153 **Uninhabited:** 13

Ranking	District	State	National
Area	4	105	580
Population	2	53	308
Sex Ratio	4	134	3208
Child Sex Ratio	4	91	3037
Literacy Rate	1	48	1735
Density	4	138	3859
Work Participation Rate	2	36	3228

Gram Panchayats:
Kakkaragolla, Arasapura, Kadlebalu, Avaragolla, Doddabathi, Bethuru, Kadajji, Alur, Hemmanabethur, Anaji, Basavanahalu, Igoor, Hulikatte, Kandanakovi, Honnur, Shiramagondanahalli , Mudahadadi, Belavanur, Tholahunse, Gudalu, Anagodu, Kurki, Hadadi, Kanagondanahalli, Kaidale, Nerlegi, Hebbalu, Naraganahalli, Kodaganur, Attigere, Gopanahal, Kukkavada, Matti, Likikere, Malalakere, Bada, Mayakonda , Anaberu, Syagale, Kandagal, Hutchavvanahalli.

Amenities:

Education: Primary School in 136 villages, Middle school in 113 villages, Matriculation or Secondary School in 40 villages, namely Doddabathi, Avaragolla, Kakkaragolla, Arasapura, Shiramagondanahalli, Naganur, Belavanur, Hadadi, Kukkavada, Kaidale, Turuchagatta, Srikrishnanagara, Igoor, Anaji, Honnur, Tholahunse, Kurki, Anagodu, Nerlegi, Ganganakatte, Halavarthy, Gummanur, Mandaluru, Hebbalu, Yaravvanagathihalli, Kuntapalanahalli, Kolkunte, Annapura, Hutchavvanahalli, Mayakonda, Kabburu, Ramagondanahalli, Kashipura, Likikere, Honnamaradi, Matti, Syagale, Malalakere, Anaberu, Nalkunda.

Higher Secondary or Pre University Courses or Intermediate or Junior College in 23 villages of the CD Block,, namely Doddabathi, Arasapura, Kadlebalu, Malagondanahalli, Bethuru, Kadajji, Nagarakatte, Belavanur, Hadadi, Kukkavada, Igoor, Alur, Anaji, Hulikatte, Kurki, Anagodu, Gopanahal, Kodaganur, Attigere, Likikere, Syagale, Kandagal, Bada.

College in 8 villages, Adult Literacy Center in 2 villages., Colleges are in villages, namely Doddabathi, Kakkaragolla, Kukkavada, Anagodu, Mayakonda, Attigere, Likikere, Bada.

Medical: Hospital in 21 villages, Dispensary in 15 villages, Health Center in 13 villages, Sub Center in 45 villages, Maternity and Child Welfare Center in 13 villages, Community health workers in 1 village.

The Villages having Hospital or Dispensary or Health Center are Doddabathi, Kakkaragolla, Arasapura, Kadlebalu, Kadajji, Jarikatte, Hadadi, Kanagondanahalli, Kukkavada, Igoor, Anaji, Hulikatte, Honnur, Anagodu, Nerlegi, Hebbalu, Naraganahalli, Sri Rangaiahnamatti, Kodaganur, Mayakonda , Likikere, Huvinamadu, Syagale, Kandagal, Bada, Anaberu, Nalkunda.

Drinking Water: Tap water in 87 villages, Tank water in 7 villages, Well water in 5 villages, Tubewell in 143 villages and more than one source in 148 villages.

Bank: Banking facility in 29 villages, namely, Kakkaragolla, Bethuru, Hadadi, Kukkavada, Igoor Anaji, Hemmanabethur, Thumbigere, Honnur Kandanakovi, Anagodu, Gudalu, Hebbalu, Naraganahalli Gopanahal, Echagatta, Kodaganur, Hutchavvanahalli Mayakonda, Attigere, Kashipura, Likikere, Matti Syagale, Kandagal, Kodihalli, Bada, Anaberu Nalkunda.

Credit Society in 16 villages Agricultural Credit Society in 12 Non-Agricultural Credit Society in 4 villages.

Others: Power supply in 151 villages, Cinema hall in 1 village, sport club in 1 village, Stadium or Auditorium or Community Hall in 0 village, Post Office in 52 villages.

There are 130 villages having bus facilities.

Villages with most of facilities: Kakkaragolla Bethuru, Hadadi, Kukkavada, Igoor, Anaji Hemmanabethur, Honnur, Kandanakovi, Anagodu, Hebbalu Naraganahalli, Gopanahal, Echagatta, Kodaganur Mayakonda, Likikere, Matti, Syagale, Kandagal, Bada Anaberu, Nalkunda.

Villages without amenities (Education):
Agasanakatte, Basavanahatti, Vaderahalli, Bullapura, Gandamuktenahalli, Sriramanagara, Katanaikana Hosahalli, Rangavvanahalli, Sri Rangaiahnamatti, Hanumanahalli, Jamapannanahalli, Madakeripura, Vaderahalli..

Scheduled Castes: Out of the total population of 238000 persons, 55844 persons (23.46%) belong to Scheduled Castes. The villages having less than 10% SC population are Agasanakatte, Neelanahalli, Basavanahatti Chikkabudihalu, Devarahatti, Ramapura, Jarikatte Hadadi, Batlekatte, Vaderahalli, Jadaganahalli Kanagondanahalli, Kolenahalli, Giriyapura, Kaidale

Turuchagatta, Mallekatte, Rangavvanahalli Karilakkanahalli, Rudranakatte, Kenchammanahalli Mandaluru, Lakkamuthenahalli, Dindadahalli, Rampura Vaderahalli, Giddenahalli, Vitalapura.

The villages having more than 50% SC population are Arasapura, Obajjihalli, Nagarakatte, Javalagatta Sriramanagara, Gollarahatti, Katanaikana Hosahalli Pamenahalli, Chattobanahalli, Jammapura Doddarangavvanahalli, Hosahalli, Chinnasamudra Sri Rangaiahnamatti, Hanumanahalli, Echagatta Jamapannanahalli, Doddamagadi, Bullapura, Hedne.

Sex ratio of Scheduled Caste population is 492.

Scheduled Castes Literates and Illiterates by Sex:

	Persons	Males	Females
Literate	23,722	14,626	9,096
Illiterate	32,122	13,746	18,376
Literacy rate	50.2	61.0	39.1
Graduate	658	588	70

Scheduled Castes (Dominant):

Banjara etc., Madiga, Bhovi, Adi Karnataka Beda Jangam etc.

For their cultural identity please see Appendix-I

Villages without Scheduled Castes: There are 18 villages without any scheduled caste population.

Scheduled Tribes: Out of the total population of 238000 persons, 33911 persons (14.25%) belong to Scheduled Tribes.

The villages having less than 10% ST population are Halebathi, Doddabathi, Avaragolla, Kodihalli Kakkaragolla, Arasapura, Obajjihalli, Basavanahatti Chikkabudihalu, Devarahatti, Malagondanahalli Putakanahalu, Kadajji, Nagarakatte, Ramapura Lingadahalli, Shiramagondanahalli, Jarikatte Mudahadadi, Javalagatta, Vaderahalli, Jadaganahalli Kanagondanahalli, Kolenahalli, Kukkavada, Giriyapura Naikanahalli, Bullapura, Vaddinahalli Srikrishnanagara, Basavanahalu, Boragondanahalli Sriramanagara, Mallekatte, Dyamavvanahalli Chikkavvanagathihalli, Katanaikana Hosahalli Tholahunse, Rangavvanahalli, Mallashettihalli Narasipura, Siddanur, Agasanakatte, Rudranakatte Jammapura, Kandanakovi, Pavadarangavvanahalli Hulapanakatte, Doddarangavvanahalli, Nerlegi Hosahalli, Lakkamuthenahalli, Chinnasamudra Sri Rangaiahnamatti, Obannanahalli, Gopanahal Echagatta, Jamapannanahalli, Sultanipura Doddamagadi, Bullapura, Hutchavvanahalli, Kabburu Madakeripura, Vaderahalli, Kaluru, Attigere Ramagondanahalli, Honnamaradi, Matti, Giddenahalli Anaberu, Kyatanahalli.

The villages having more than 50% ST population are Mallapura, Giriyapura, Lingapura, Karilakkanahalli Katihalli, Chikkatogaleri, Kalkere, Kodihalli Vitalapura.

Sex ratio of Scheduled tribe population is 493.

Scheduled Tribes Literates and Illiterates by Sex:

	Persons	Males	Females
Literate	16,782	10,148	6,634
Illiterate	17,129	7,030	10,099
Literacy rate	57.2	68.0	46.1
Graduate	396	341	55

Scheduled Tribes (Dominant):

Naikda etc., Meda, Konda Kapus, Bavacha etc. Generic Tribes etc.

For their cultural identity please see Appendix-II

Villages without Scheduled Tribes: There are 36 villages without any scheduled tribe population.

Literates and Illiterates by Sex (Total Population):

	Persons	Males	Females
Literate	136,785	79,925	56,860
Illiterate	101,215	41,730	59,485
Literacy rate	66	76	56
Graduate	4,964	4,172	792

Agriculture: ***Distribution of villages according to land use:*** Out of 166 villages, Total area (in hectare) is 88028, out of that 77.74 percent is cultivable and 51.24 percent of the cultivable area is irrigated.

Sources of Irrigation (Hectares): Government Canal 23394.23, Private Canal 0, Well without Electricity 0, Well with Electricity 0, Tubewell without Electricity 33.08, Tubewell with Electricity 10411.42, Tank 0, River 0, Lake 0, Waterfall 1, Others 1231.03.

Villages with population of 5000 to 9999: Doddabathi, Bethuru, Hadadi, Mayakonda , Likikere.

Villages with population of 10000 and above: None

Distribution of Workers:

	Persons	Males	Females	WPR
Cultivators	39,565	31,853	7,712	36.33
Agricultural Labour	50,325	24,822	25,503	46.22
Household Industry	1,767	1,204	563	1.62
Other Workers	17,233	13,302	3,931	15.83
Main Workers	89,536	64,168	25,368	82.23
Marginal Workers	19,354	7,013	12,341	17.77
Total Workers	108,890	71,181	37,709	

Religion: Major Religious Communities:

	Persons	Males	Females	Sex Ratio
Hindu (94.26%)	224,336	114,664	109,672	956
Muslim (5.02%)	11,936	6,089	5,847	960
Christian (0.22%)	533	284	249	877
Sikh (0%)	4	3	1	333
Buddhists (0%)	2	-	2	-

Jain (0.07%)	165	90	75	833

Agewise Data:

	Persons	Males	Females	Sex Ratio
All ages	238,000	121,655	116,345	956
0-14	73,584	37,488	36,096	963
15-44	117,452	60,457	56,995	943
45-79	44,131	22,453	21,678	965
80+	2,270	938	1,332	1420
Age not stated	563	319	244	765

Languages (Dominant):
Kannada, Hindi, Urdu, Telugu, Tamil

Disabled Population:

	Persons	Males	Females	%
Total Disabled	4,232	2,550	1,682	
In Seeing	2,022	1,190	832	47.78
In Speech	437	243	194	10.33
In Hearing	204	122	82	4.82
In Movement	1,189	774	415	28.1
Mentally	380	221	159	8.98

DEVADURGA

Devadurga C.D. Block lies in the northern part of Raichur district. It is a part of Devadurga taluka. The Block is located at a distance of 57 kms. from district headqu arters (Raichur). There are 188 villages in the block with the total population of 182,082 persons. Area of the C.D. Block is 1507.05 sq. kms. It is bounded by district Gulbarga on north, taluk Lingsugur and Manvi on south, taluk Raichur on east, and taluk Lingsugur on west.

Communications:

Roadways : S.H-15: Direction- Jevargi to Raichur, Nearest Villages- Wagadambli, Huvinhadgi, Joladhadgi, Devadurga (Rural), Sasvigera, Devergud, Chickhonkuni, Hirehonkuni, Miyapur, Masarkal, Khanapur, Amrapur, Sunkeshwarhal, Kakkargal, Gabbur, Jinnapur. S.H-19: Direction- Lingsug ur to Shorapur, Nearest Village- Veergot.

River: Krishna Nadi- Nearest Villages- Veergot, Bunkaldo ddi, Chinchodi, Lingadhalli, Chapalki, Mudgot, Buddinni, Bagur, Herundi, Anchesugur, Gopalpur, Wagadambli, Huvin hadgi, Joladhadgi, Dondambli, Benkal, Konchapli, Mydargol, Karkihalli, Paratpur, Kopper, Kurkihalli, Yatgal, Herur, Anjal, Nilvanji, Itagi, Gagal, Gugal, Chickraikumpi, Hireraikumpi, Madarkal, Apprahal, Baswantpur.

Canal: Nearest Villages- Huligud,, Madarkal, Devergud, Sunnadkal, Galag, Khardigud, Ramdurg, Maladkal, Ganekal, Neelgal, Jagatkal, Markamdinni, Jagir-Jadaldinni, Yerma rus, Heggaddinni.

Reserved Forest: (Lingsugur): Nearest Villages- Veergot, Bunkaldoddi, Chinchodi, Jalhalli, Yerkamandoddi, Yergud da, Bassapur, Hosur Siddapur, Bommanhalli, Suladgud, Mundargi, Somanmardi, Naglapur, Gandhal, Ooti, Sunnadkal, Devadurga (Rural), Karegud, Venglapur, Samudra, Nimbaid oddi, Guddad Irabgera, Kelgin Irabgera, Kachapur, Kothdod di, Chikkaldoddi, Benkal, Malkamdinni, Mallinaikandoddi, Piligund, Arkera, Kyadigera.

Annual Rainfall: Normal Rianfall 632 mm.

Ground Water: Availability of the Ground Water in the Basin is 65.93 H.A.M. and the utilization is 20.29 H. A.M. It belongs to Over Exploited category. Depth to water level 2 to 20 meter below the ground. Most of the wells go down in summer months, according to the Ground Water Estimation Committee.

Soils: Mixed Red and Black Soils.

Natural Division : It falls partly in the Middle Krishna Valley, Middle Tungabhadra Valley and the Arkera-Mudgal-Kanakgiri Upland of the Central Karnataka Plateau.

Administration:

Division: Gulbarga. Parliamentary Constituency: 6 Raichur (ST). District: Raichur. Taluka: Devadurga. Assembly Constituency: 56 Devdurga (ST). Gram Panchayat: 28. Regional Area Development Boards: The Hyderabad - Karnataka Area Development Board.

Villages: 188 **Inhabited:** 173 **Uninhabited:** 15

Ranking	District	State	National
Area	4	32	140
Population	5	88	692
Sex Ratio	4	59	1776
Child Sex Ratio	2	19	1200
Literacy Rate	5	173	5916
Density	5	157	5800
Work Participation Rate	4	147	3740

Gram Panchayats:

Chinchodi, Jalhalli, Hosur Siddapur, Karadigudda, Mundargi, Gandhal, Palkanmardi, Galag, Alkod, Benderganekal, Kelgin Irabgera, Karegud, Dondambli, Kopper, Gugal, Hemanal, Hirebudur, Jerbandi, Masarkal, Mustoor, Kothdoddi, Arkera, Kyadigera, Jagir-Jadaldinni, Ramdurg, Gabbur, Maladkal, Nagaddinni.

Amenities:

Education: Primary School in 53 villages, Middle school in 51 villages, Matriculation or Secondary School in 9 villages, namely Jalhalli, Galag, Konchapli, Kopper, Masarkal, Masihal, Gabbur, Arkera, Jagir-Jadaldinni.

Higher Secondary or Pre University Courses or Intermediate or Junior College in 1 village of the CD Block,, namely Gabbur.

College in 0 village, Adult Literacy Center in 10 villages.

Medical: Hospital in 2 villages, Dispensary in 8 villages, Health Center in 10 villages, Sub Center in 31 villages,

Maternity and Child Welfare Center in 16 villages, Community health workers in 31 villages.

The Villages having Hospital or Dispensary or Health Center are Jalhalli, Galag, Dondambli, Kopper, Karegud, Chickhonkuni, Masarkal, Ramdurg, Gabbur, Alkod, Kyadigera.

Drinking Water: Tap water in 86 villages, Tank water in 43 villages, Well water in 129 villages, Tubewell in 51 villages and more than one source in 159 villages.

Bank: Banking facility in 10 villages, namely, Jalhalli, Mundargi, Galag, Kopper, Masarkal, Gugal Chickraikumpi, Ramdurg, Gabbur, Arkera.

Credit Society in 13 villages Agricultural Credit Society in 13 Non-Agricultural Credit Society in 4 villages.

Others: Power supply in 172 villages, Cinema hall in 2 villages, sport club in 173 villages, Stadium or Auditorium or Community Hall in 173 villages, Post Office in 42 villages.

There are 100 villages having bus facilities.

Villages with most of facilities: Jalhalli Mundargi, Galag, Kopper, Masarkal, Ramdurg, Gabbur.

Villages without amenities (Education): Veergot, Lingadhalli, Mudgot, Bagur, Herundi, Navilgudda, Jambaldinni, Medinapur, Yergudda, Bassapur, Bommanhalli, Timmapur, Parapur, Amrapur, Suladgud, Mandalgud, Gajaldinni, Mukanhal, Ganajali, Katmalli, Huligud, Kakkaldoddi, Kamaldinni, Mudvaigaddi, Mykaldoddi, Bhogiramangund, Naglapur, Ooti, Madarkal, Devergud, Mudalagund, Sunnadkal, Chadkalgudda, Anchesugur, Wagadambli, Huvinhadgi, Benkal, Mydargol, Karkihalli, Paratpur, Kurkihalli, Yatgal, Herur, Salkyapur, Gopendeverhalli, Nagarhal, Arshangi, Ramanhal, Hunur, Hemnhal, Nagargund, Anjal, Nilvanji, Venglapur, Samudra, Nimbaidoddi, Guddad Irabgera, Kelgin Irabgera, Mansagal, Kotigud, Sasvigera, Kardigudda, Sugarhal, Jerbandi, Kamdhal, Devergud, Yermasal, Chickhonkuni, Guntarhal, Matpalli, Itagi, Gagal, Gugal, Chickraikumpi, Apprahal, Baswantpur, Bommanhal, Kolur, Budinhal, Hanchinhal, Hirekudalgi, Chickkudalgi, Honnatagi, Amrapur, Ingaladhal, Aldharti, Khardigud, Pandyan, Kachapur, Pilikal, Chikkaldoddi, Yeldoddi, Teggihal, Shakapur, Jinnapur, Hungunbad, Gajjibhavi, Jaradbandi, Honkatmalli, Kardona, Malkamdinni, Mallinaikandoddi, Piligund, Hal-Jadaldinni, Mailapur, Mallapur, Bhumangund, Adkalgud, Anwar, Shavantgal, Nagoli, Buddinni, Rekalmardi..

Scheduled Castes: Out of the total population of 200463 persons, 40689 persons (20.3%) belong to Scheduled Castes.

The villages having less than 10% SC population are Bunkaldoddi, Yergudda, Bassapur, Hosur Siddapur Timmapur, Gajaldinni, Devatgal, Katmalli, Huligud Mudvaigaddi, Naglapur, Ooti, Madarkal, Mudalagund Wagadambli, Joladhadgi, Konchapli, Mydargol Gopendeverhalli, Anjal, Nilvanji, Nimbaidoddi Guddad Irabgera, Gagal, Chickraikumpi, Chickkudalgi Maseedpur, Pandyan, Kachapur, Pilikal, Teggihal Chintalkunta, Govindpalli, Mallinaikandoddi Piligund, Mailapur, Mallapur, Bhumangund, Adkalgud Anwar, Shavantgal, Malledevergud, Jutmardi Nagaddinni.

The villages having more than 50% SC population are Suladgud, Sasvigera, Gundgurthi, Aldharti, Yeldoddi Kardona, Kyadigera, Bandegud.

Sex ratio of Scheduled Caste population is 498.

Scheduled Castes Literates and Illiterates by Sex:

	Persons	Males	Females
Literate	10,036	6,853	3,183
Illiterate	30,653	13,591	17,062
Literacy rate	30.7	41.7	19.6
Graduate	192	173	19

Scheduled Castes (Dominant):

Madiga, Banjara etc., Chalavadi etc., Bhambi etc. Bhovi

For their cultural identity please see Appendix-I

Villages without Scheduled Castes: There are 26 villages without any scheduled caste population.

Scheduled Tribes: Out of the total population of 200463 persons, 69131 persons (34.49%) belong to Scheduled Tribes.

The villages having less than 10% ST population are Bagur, Herundi, Medinapur, Amrapur, Gajaldinni Dondambli, Yatgal, Herur, Hunur, Mansagal, Jerbandi Yermasal, Matpalli, Apprahal, Baswantpur, Bommanhal Budinhal, Honnatagi, Amrapur, Ingaladhal Sunkeshwarhal, Aldharti, Khardigud, Gabbur Maseedpur, Ganekal, Neelgal, Pilikal, Govindpalli.

The villages having more than 50% ST population are Mudgot, Navilgudda, Bassapur, Hosur Siddapur Bommanhalli, Timmapur, Parapur, Devatgal, Huligud Mudvaigaddi, Bhogiramangund, Somanmardi, Naglapur Ooti, Devergud, Mudalagund, Sunnadkal, Chadkalgudda Konchapli, Mydargol, Karkihalli, Ramanhal, Nagargund Anjal, Karegud, Venglapur, Samudra, Nimbaidoddi Guddad Irabgera, Kelgin Irabgera, Kotigud Kardigudda, Chickraikumpi, Hanchinhal, Kachapur Chikkaldoddi, Chintalkunta, Jaradbandi Mallinaikandoddi, Piligund, Mailapur, Mallapur Bhumangund, Adkalgud, Anwar, Akalkumpi Malledevergud, Jutmardi, Buddinni, Markamdinni.

Sex ratio of Scheduled tribe population is 498.

Scheduled Tribes Literates and Illiterates by Sex:

	Persons	Males	Females
Literate	15,031	10,503	4,528
Illiterate	54,100	24,223	29,877
Literacy rate	26.9	37.4	16.3
Graduate	155	145	10

Scheduled Tribes (Dominant):

Naikda etc., Jenu Kuruba, Meda, Chenchu etc.
Kadu Kuruba

For their cultural identity please see Appendix-II

Villages without Scheduled Tribes: There are 19 villages without any scheduled tribe population.

Literates and Illiterates by Sex (Total Population):

	Persons	Males	Females
Literate	59,917	40,097	19,820
Illiterate	140,546	60,836	79,710
Literacy rate	37	49	24
Graduate	1,205	1,071	134

Agriculture: ***Distribution of villages according to land use:*** Out of 188 villages, Total area (in hectare) is 150705, out of that 74.79 percent is cultivable and 4.85 percent of the cultivable area is irrigated.

Sources of Irrigation (Hectares): Government Canal 1431.71, Private Canal 0, Well without Electricity 40.1, Well with Electricity 2144.58, Tubewell without Electricity 42.88, Tubewell with Electricity 627.73, Tank 678.48, River 481.06, Lake 2.5, Waterfall 0, Others 18.2.

Villages with population of 5000 to 9999:
Galag, Gabbur, Arkera, Kyadigera.

Villages with population of 10000 and above:
Jalhalli.

Distribution of Workers:

	Persons	Males	Females	WPR
Cultivators	27,047	24,646	2,401	33.01
Agricultural Labour	40,038	16,946	23,092	48.86
Household Industry	1,221	866	355	1.49
Other Workers	13,633	9,644	3,989	16.64
Main Workers	49,310	39,447	9,863	60.18
Marginal Workers	32,629	12,655	19,974	39.82
Total Workers	81,939	52,102	29,837	

Religion: Major Religious Communities:

	Persons	Males	Females	Sex Ratio
Hindu (91.01%)	182,443	91,882	90,561	986
Muslim (8.23%)	16,506	8,293	8,213	990
Christian (0.3%)	601	306	295	964
Sikh (0.01%)	16	8	8	1,000
Buddhists (0.29%)	590	291	299	1,027
Jain (0%)	5	3	2	667

Agewise Data:

	Persons	Males	Females	Sex Ratio
All ages	200,463	100,933	99,530	986
0-14	85,079	43,460	41,619	958
15-44	81,509	41,453	40,056	966
45-79	32,775	15,611	17,164	1099
80+	990	360	630	1750
Age not stated	110	49	61	1245

Languages (Dominant):
Kannada, Urdu, Hindi, Telugu, Marathi

Disabled Population:

	Persons	Males	Females	%
Total Disabled	3,520	1,901	1,619	
In Seeing	1,631	780	851	46.34
In Speech	326	183	143	9.26
In Hearing	285	129	156	8.1
In Movement	1,028	667	361	29.2
Mentally	250	142	108	7.1

DEVANAHALLI

Devanahalli C.D. Block lies in the north eastern part of Bangalore Rural district. It is a part of Devanahalli taluka. The Block is located at a distance of 35 kms. from district headquarters (Bangalore). There are 214 villages in the block with the total population of 132, 224 persons. Area of the C.D. Block is 418.60 sq. kms. It is bounded by district Kolar on north, district Bangalore on south, taluk Hosakote and district Kolar on east, taluk Dod Ballapur and district Bangalore on west.

Communications:

Roadways : N.H.-7: Direction- Bangalore to Kurnool. Nearest Villages- Mudugurki, Hosahudya, Thatamachanahalli Amani kere, Venkatagirikote, Bullahalli, Dasarahalli, Avathi, Attibele, Abachikkanahalli, Lalagondanahalli, Hire Amanikere, Upparahalli, Sanne, Amanikere, Chikkasanne, Kannamangala, Udayagiri, Akkalenahalli Mallena - Halli, Boovanahalli. N.H.-207: Direction- Dod Ballapur to Hosak ote, Nearest Villages- Byadarahalli, Byradenahalli, Beera sandra, Vishwanathapura, Solur, Lakshmipura, Setterahalli, Devenahalli, Boodihal, Southegowdanahalli, Srothreyathe llohalli, Haralur, Channahalli, Nallur, Mallepura, Balepu ra, Kachipura. SH-74A- Direction- Devanahalli to Nandi Hills, Nearest Villages- Devenahalli, Attibele, Maligenahalli, Vaderahalli, Kodagurki, Yambarahalli, Yerrappanahalli, Kempathimmanahalli, Moodiganahalli, Karahalli, Karahalli Amanikere, Kottigethimmanahal

Railway Station: Village- Avathi.

River: Pinakin Nadi- Nearest Villages- Bidalapura, Bidal apura Amanikere, Devanayakanahalli, Budigere Amanikere, Budigere, Handrahalli, Gangavara Chowdappana Halli, Somathanahalli.

Reserved Forest: (S G Kaval R.F.): Nearest Villages- Gollahalli, Narayanapura, Sambaragiddada Kavalu,

Chinnappanayakana Hosur, Ranganathapura, Chikkenahalli.

Annual Rainfall: Normal Rianfall 907.3 mm.

Ground Water: Availability of the Ground Water in the Basin is (Information not avablable) H.A.M. and the utilization is (Information not avablable) H.A.M.
It belongs to (Information not avablable) category.
Depth to water level 5 to 20 meter below the ground.
Most of the wells go down in summer months, according to the Ground Water Estimation Committee.

Natural Division : It falls in Bangalore Plateau of the Southern Karnataka Plateau.

Administration:

Division: Bangalore. Parliamentary Constituency: 27 Bangalore- IV (SC). District: Bangalore Rural. Taluka: Devanahalli. Assembly Constituency: 179 Devanahalli (SC). Gram Panchayat: 21.

Regional Area Development Boards: The Bailu Seeme Area Development Board.

Villages: 214 **Inhabited:** 187 **Uninhabited:** 27

Ranking	District	State	National
Area	8	170	1833
Population	8	143	2425
Sex Ratio	6	150	3600
Child Sex Ratio	5	101	3278
Literacy Rate	3	49	1769
Density	2	82	3378
Work Participation Rate	3	21	1941

Gram Panchayats:

Koira, Karahalli, Venkatagirikote, Bijjawara, Gudla Muddenahalli, Harohalli, Avathi, Bidalur, Vishwanathapura, Kundana, Jalige, Kannamangala, Anneswara, Bettakote, Budigere, Gangavara Chowdappanahalli, Nallur, Channahalli, Yaleyur, Channarayapatna.

Amenities:

Education: Primary School in 163 villages, Middle school in 106 villages, Matriculation or Secondary School in 20 villages, namely Karahalli, Koira, Vishwanathapura, Kundana, Thindlu, Jalige, Venkatagirikote, Bijjawara, Narayanapura, Sadahalli, Kannamangala, Yaleyur, Channarayapatna, Channahalli, Bettakote, Reddihalli, Nallur, Mallepura, Budigere, Somathanahalli.
Higher Secondary or Pre University Courses or Intermediate or Junior College in 5 villages of the CD Block,, namely Vishwanathapura, Channahalli, Reddihalli, Mallepura, Budigere.
College in 1 village, Adult Literacy Center in 0 village., College is in village, namely Vishwanathapura.

Medical: Hospital in 1 village, Dispensary in 5 villages, Health Center in 10 villages, Sub Center in 32 villages, Maternity and Child Welfare Center in 0 village, Community health workers in 0 village.
The Villages having Hospital or Dispensary or Health Center Are Moodiganahalli, Karahalli, Koira, Kundana, Hegganahalli.

Drinking Water: Tap water in 57 villages, Tank water in 33 villages, Well water in 43 villages, Tubewell in 137 villages and more than one source in 142 villages.

Bank: Banking facility in 8 villages, namely, Karahalli, Vishwanathapura, Aradeshahalli, Avathi Sadahalli, Channarayapatna, Nallur, Budigere.
Credit Society in 84 villages Agricultural Credit Society in 16 Non-Agricultural Credit Society in 66 villages.

Others: Power supply in 183 villages, Cinema hall in 0 village, sport club in 0 village, Stadium or Auditorium or Community Hall in 187 villages, Post Office in 35 villages.
There are 121 villages having bus facilities.

Villages with most of facilities: Karahalli Vishwanathapura, Aradeshahalli, Avathi, Sadahalli Channarayapatna, Nallur, Budigere.

Villages without amenities (Education): Kottigethimmanahalli, Vajarahalli, Chapparadahalli, Gejjaguppe, Vaderahalli, Lakshmipura, Devenahalli, Abachikkanahalli, Sanne Amanikere, Bandaramanahalli, Doddappanahalli, Jogahalli, Udayagiri, Akkalenahalli Mallena - Halli, Hiriganahalli, Palya, Papanahalli, Bettakote Amanikere, Hosahalli, Nallur Amari, Bidalapura Amanikere, Baladimmanahalli..

Scheduled Castes: Out of the total population of 132380 persons, 35245 persons (26.62%) belong to Scheduled Castes.
The villages having less than 10% SC population are Kottigethimmanahalli, Sonnenahalli, Maragondanahalli Solur, Gonur, Holerahalli, Yaluvahalli Guduvanahalli, Dodda Thattamangala, Bidalur Abachikkanahalli, Lalagondanahalli, Binnamangala Chikkachimanahalli, Thimmegowdana Hosahalli, Palya Jogahalli, Yerthiganahalli, Rayasandra, Hyadala Mattabaralu, Bammanahalli, Thellohalli Agrahara Palya, Agalakote, Bettakote Amanikere, Hosahalli Nallappanahalli, Bidalapura Amanikere, Jonnahalli Baladimmanahalli, Kondenahalli.
The villages having more than 50% SC population are Meesaganahalli, Moodiganahalli, Venkatapura Dyavarahalli, Chikkannanahosahalli, Indrasanahalli Hegganahalli, Singrahalli, Devaganahalli Irigenahalli, Gollahalli, Chinnappanayakana Hosur Shettahalli, Chandenahalli, Thimmanahalli Gejjaguppe, Devenahalli, Kurubarakunte, Boodihal Hiriganahalli, Konaginabele, Muddenahalli, Haralur Mallepura.

Sex ratio of Scheduled Caste population is 492.

Scheduled Castes Literates and Illiterates by Sex:

	Persons	Males	Females
Literate	16,055	9,795	6,260
Illiterate	19,190	8,126	11,064
Literacy rate	53.0	63.6	42.0
Graduate	217	195	22

Scheduled Castes (Dominant):

Adi Karnataka, Adi Dravida, Madiga, Bhovi
Holaya etc.

For their cultural identity please see Appendix-I

Villages without Scheduled Castes: There are 42 villages without any scheduled caste population.

Scheduled Tribes: Out of the total population of 132380 persons, 15648 persons (11.82%) belong to Scheduled Tribes.

The villages having less than 10% ST population are Ramanathapura, Thylagere, Moodiganahalli, Karahalli Kottigethimmanahalli, Mayasandra, Koira Byadarahalli, Shanappanahalli, Vajarahalli Mangondanahalli, Aruvanahalli, Chapparadahalli Doddagollahalli, Byradenahalli, Chikkobanahalli Beerasandra, Vishwanathapura, Kundana Chinnakempanahalli, Alurdoddanahalli, Sunnagatta Bachahalli, Venkatapura, Lingadeeragollahalli Dyavarahalli, Thindlu, Pandithapura, Juttanahalli Maragondanahalli, Chikkannanahosahalli, Jalige Bettenahalli, Kamenahalli, Indrasanahalli Hegganahalli, Nagamangala, Chowdenahalli, Ilathore Singrahalli, Neraganahalli Arasanahalli Peddanahalli, Devaganahalli Doddasagarahalli, Mudugurki, Hosahudya Venkatagirikote, Irigenahalli, Hosahalli, Gollahalli Gonur, Bijjawara, Narayanapura, Ranganathapura Gudla Muddenahalli, Doddamuddenahalli, Thimmahalli Harohalli, Bullahalli, Byrapura, Chikkanahalli, Pura Kommasandra, Bhattrenahalli, Shettahalli Yaluvahalli, Guduvanahalli, Thimmanahalli Gaddadanagenahalli, Gejjaguppe, Dharmapura Yambarahalli, Dasarahalli, Avathi, Gobbarakunte Vaderahalli, Kurubarakunte, Lalagondanahalli Binnamangala, Gokare, Boodihal, Bommawara Chikkachimanahalli, Uganavadi Thimmegowdana Hosahalli, Bandaramanahalli, Palya Doddappanahalli, Sadahalli, Kannamangala, Udayagiri Bychapura, Gangamuthanahalli, Thammenahalli, Yaleyur Hyadala, Hiriganahalli, Bediganahalli Srothreyathellohalli, Naganayakanahalli Doddakurubarahalli, Ibasapura, Gopasandra Konaginabele, Varadenahalli, Papanahalli Cheemachanahalli, Muddenahalli, Haralur Bettakote Amanikere, Bettakote, Reddihalli Hosahalli, Nallur Amari, Nallur, Nallappanahalli Mallepura, Balepura, Bidalapura Bidalapura Amanikere, Devanayakanahalli Mallenahalli, Bhatramarenahalli, Kaggalahalli Budigere, Handrahalli, Gangavara Chowdappana Halli Somathanahalli.

The villages having more than 50% ST population are Sonnenahalli, Holerahalli, Venkatenahalli Chikka Thattamangala, Kempathimmanahalli Akkalenahalli Mallena - Halli, Yerthiganahalli Boovanahalli, Arasinakunte, Rayasandra, Mattabaralu Bammanahalli, Agalakote, Jonnahalli Baladimmanahalli, Kondenahalli.

Sex ratio of Scheduled tribe population is 487.

Scheduled Tribes Literates and Illiterates by Sex:

	Persons	Males	Females
Literate	7,735	4,706	3,029
Illiterate	7,913	3,319	4,594
Literacy rate	57.2	67.9	45.9
Graduate	103	93	10

Scheduled Tribes (Dominant):

Naikda etc., Yerava, Generic Tribes etc., Gowdalu Kurumans

For their cultural identity please see Appendix-II

Villages without Scheduled Tribes: There are 93 villages without any scheduled tribe population.

Literates and Illiterates by Sex (Total Population):

	Persons	Males	Females
Literate	76,508	45,462	31,046
Illiterate	55,872	22,484	33,388
Literacy rate	66	76	55
Graduate	1,967	1,688	279

Agriculture: ***Distribution of villages according to land use:*** Out of 214 villages, Total area (in hectare) is 41860, out of that 65.8 percent is cultivable and 38.61 percent of the cultivable area is irrigated.

Sources of Irrigation (Hectares): Government Canal 0, Private Canal 0, Well without Electricity 0, Well with Electricity 327.01, Tubewell without Electricity 212.69, Tubewell with Electricity 6051.06, Tank 1095.93, River 0, Lake 33.59, Waterfall 1233.38, Others 1681.38.

Villages with population of 5000 to 9999: Budigere.

Villages with population of 10000 and above: None

Distribution of Workers:

	Persons	Males	Females	WPR
Cultivators	29,170	20,370	8,800	42.95
Agricultural Labour	21,394	9,977	11,417	31.5
Household Industry	1,144	575	569	1.68

Other Workers	16,210	10,413	5,797	23.87
Main Workers	55,603	37,613	17,990	81.87
Marginal Workers	12,315	3,722	8,593	18.13
Total Workers	67,918	41,335	26,583	

Religion: Major Religious Communities:

	Persons	Males	Females	Sex Ratio
Hindu (97.63%)	129,237	66,284	62,953	950
Muslim (1.81%)	2,402	1,274	1,128	885
Christian (0.29%)	386	196	190	969
Sikh (0%)	-	-	-	-
Buddhists (0.06%)	81	40	41	1,025
Jain (0%)	6	5	1	200

Agewise Data:

	Persons	Males	Females	Sex Ratio
All ages	132,380	67,946	64,434	948
0-14	39,534	20,239	19,295	953
15-44	65,005	33,067	31,938	966
45-79	26,195	13,824	12,371	895
80+	1,517	748	769	1028
Age not stated	129	68	61	897

Languages (Dominant):

Kannada, Telugu, Tamil, Urdu, Coorgi/Kodagu

Disabled Population:

	Persons	Males	Females	%
Total Disabled	2,504	1,393	1,111	
In Seeing	1,067	550	517	42.61
In Speech	254	139	115	10.14
In Hearing	161	87	74	6.43
In Movement	768	495	273	30.67
Mentally	254	122	132	10.14

DHARWAD

Dharwad C.D. Block lies in the north-western part of Dharwad district. It is a part of Dharwad taluka. The Block is located at a distance of 00 kms. from district headquarters (Dharwad). There are 118 villages in the block with the total population of 202,517 persons. Area of the C.D. Block is 1022.75 sq. kms. It is bounded by district Belgaum on north and west, district Uttara Kannada, taluks Kalghatgi and Hubli on south, taluks Navalgund and Hubli on east.

Communications:

Roadways : N.H-4: Direction- Belgaum to Hubli, Nearest Villages- Hale Tegur, Tegur, Neeralakatti, Kummanayakana koppa, Shinganahalli, Venkatapur, Guledakoppa, Kotur, Belur, Narendra, Kumbapur-m-Narendra, Mummigatti, Hirem alligawad. S.H-28: Direction- Haliyal to Hebsur, Nearest Villages- Mavinakoppa, Holtikoti, Bommarsikoppa, Murakat ti, Devarhubli, Halligeri, Lakamanahalli, Salakinkoppa, Baad, Nigadi, Benkankatti, Mansur, Hebballi, Govankoppa, Ghongadikoppa, Maradagi, Somapur (Allapur), Shivalli. S.H-34: Direction- Londa to Hubli Dharwad, Nearest Villages- Kadabagatti, Hindasgeri, Kogilageri, Kumbarkop pa, Kumbarganvi, Aravatagi, Honnapur , Daddikamalapur, Mandihal, Mugad, Kyarkoppa, Kelgeri. S.H-65: Direction- Hubli-Dharward to Bijapur, Nearest Villages- Kamalapur, Dharwad (Rural), Harobelavadi, Amminabhavi, Marewad. S.H-93: Direction- Khanapur to Siddapur,Nearest Village- Kadabagatti.

Railway Station: Villages- Kogilageri, Kumbarganvi, Waravanagalavi, Mugad, Kyarkoppa.

Reserved Forest: Nearest Villages- Belur, Heggeri, Ramap ur, Kumbarganvi, Aravatagi, Dori, Benachi, Honnapur, War avanagalavi, Daddikamalapur, Mandihal, Mugad, Kalakeri, Holtikoti, Devagiri-M-Kyarkoppa, Murakatti, Halligeri, Mummigatti, Chikkamalligwad.

Annual Rainfall: Normal Rianfall 772 mm.

Ground Water: Availability of the Ground Water in the Basin is 8823.76 H.A.M. and the utilization is 3441. 18 H.A.M. It belongs to Over Exploited category. Depth to water level 2 to 20 meter below the ground. Most of the wells go down in summer months, according to the Ground Water Estimation Committee.

Soils: Loamy and Kankary Soils.

Natural Division : It falls partly in the Dharwad-Gadag Plateau and Kalghatgi-Lakshmeshwar Residual Hills of the Central Karnataka Plateau.

Administration:

Division: Belgaum. Parliamentary Constituency: 11 Dharwad. District: Dharwad. Taluka: Dharwad. Assembly Constitue ncy: 71 Dharwad, 75 Kalghatgi. Gram Panchayat: 37.

Regional Area Development Boards: The Maland Aera Devel opment Board.

Fairs: Lakshminarayana Temple: It is held at Dharwar in about the month of (September-October). The Lakshmina rayana temple, located in Javali Peth, was built by one Shri Srinivas Tippanna Tikare. The structure is an ordin ary one and is maintained by the Bhavsar Ksatriya Samaj. An annual fair takes place during the Navaratra festival (September-October) and attracts large crowds to the temple. The god is shown in different incarnations (avat ars) during these days.

Villages: 118 **Inhabited:** 109 **Uninhabited:** 9

Ranking	District	State	National
Area	2	80	422
Population	1	86	658
Sex Ratio	2	146	3481
Child Sex Ratio	1	83	2898
Literacy Rate	4	107	3204
Density	4	46	4753
Work Participation Rate	3	78	1408

Gram Panchayats:

Madanabhavi, Tadakod, Hangarki, Kotabagi, Uppinbetageri, Harobelavadi, Pudakalakatti, Lokur, Garag, Kotur, Tegur, Aravatagi, Kadabagatti, Benachi, Honnapur , Ramapur, Belur, Mummigatti, Kurabagatti, Yadwad, Karadigudda, Amminabhavi, Kanakur, Marewad, Narendra, Kyarkoppa, Mandihal, Mugad, Kalakeri, Halligeri, Devarhubli, Nigadi, Managundi, Yerikoppa, Maradagi, Hebballi, Shivalli.

Amenities:

Education: Primary School in 98 villages, Middle school in 72 villages, Matriculation or Secondary School in 16 villages, namely Tadakod, Tegur, Garag, Yadwad, Kotur, Narendra, Honnapur, Mugad, Devarhubli, Nigadi, Yerikoppa, Uppinbetageri, Karadigudda, Amminabhavi, Hebballi, Somapur (Allapur).

Higher Secondary or Pre University Courses or Intermediate or Junior College in 3 villages of the CD Block,, namely Garag, Uppinbetageri, Hebballi.

College in 0 village, Adult Literacy Center in 0 village.

Medical: Hospital in 3 villages, Dispensary in 4 villages, Health Center in 6 villages, Sub Center in 39 villages, Maternity and Child Welfare Center in 1 village, Community health workers in 25 villages.

The Villages having Hospital or Dispensary or Health Center are Mulamutta!, Balageri, Durgadakeri, Honnapur , Kalakeri, Nigadi, Yerikoppa.

Drinking Water: Tap water in 64 villages, Tank water in 42 villages, Well water in 38 villages, Tubewell in 38 villages and more than one source in 99 villages.

Bank: Banking facility in 10 villages, namely, Thimmapur-M-Tadakod, Agasanahalli Kumbapur-M-Narendra, Balageri, Durgadakeri, Mugad Mummigatti, Nigadi, Hanamanakoppa, Hebballi.

Credit Society in 25 villages Agricultural Credit Society in 25 Non-Agricultural Credit Society in 2 villages.

Others: Power supply in 108 villages, Cinema hall in 1 village, sport club in 2 villages, Stadium or Auditorium or Community Hall in 0 village, Post Office in 44 villages.

There are 106 villages having bus facilities.

Villages with most of facilities: Thimmapur-M-Tadakod Agasanahalli, Durgadakeri, Mugad, Mummigatti, Nigadi Hanamanakoppa, Hebballi.

Villages without amenities (Education): Shedbal, Kummanayakanakoppa, Kumbapur-M-Narendra, Balageri, Holtikoti, Dharwad (Rural), Lakamanahalli, Saibankoppa..

Scheduled Castes: Out of the total population of 202671 persons, 12118 persons (5.98%) belong to Scheduled Castes. The villages having less than 10% SC population are Madanabhavi, Hosatti, Khanapur-M-Tadakod Thimmapur-M-Tadakod, Tadakod, Jeeragiwad, Kotabagi Kallur, Lokur, Hangarki, Mugali, Tegur, Dubbanamardi Agasanahalli, Garag, Kurabagatti, Shibaragatti Yadwad, Mangalagatti, Kummanayakanakoppa Shinganahalli, Guledakoppa, Kotur Devagiri-M-Narendra, Lakamapur, Dasanakoppa Narendra, Heggeri, Kumbapur-M-Narendra, Hulikeri Kadabagatti, Hindasgeri, Balageri, Kogilageri Kumbarkoppa, Durgadakeri, Kallapur, Hosawal Veerapur, Ramapur, Kumbarganvi, Aravatagi, Benachi Waravanagalavi, Daddikamalapur, Mandihal, Mugad Kalakeri, Mavinakoppa, Holtikoti Devagiri-M-Kyarkoppa, Kyarkoppa, Lalagatti Murakatti, Devarhubli, Halligeri, Ambalikoppa Chikkamalligwad, Hiremalligawad, Kelgeri, Kamalapur Lakamanahalli, Salakinkoppa, Baad, Mallur , Nigadi Benkankatti, Mansur, Managundi, Nayakanahulikatti Saibankoppa, Kalle, Kabbenur, Hanamanhal Harobelavadi, Uppinbetageri, Hanamanakoppa Pudakalakatti, Karadigudda, Amminabhavi, Marewad Kavalgeri, Chandanmatti, Talwai, Vanahalli, Hebballi Govankoppa, Ghongadikoppa, Maradagi Somapur (Allapur), Shivalli.

The village having more than 50% SC population is None.

Sex ratio of Scheduled Caste population is 494.

Scheduled Castes Literates and Illiterates by Sex:

	Persons	Males	Females
Literate	4,899	3,189	1,710
Illiterate	7,219	2,940	4,279
Literacy rate	48.5	62.0	34.4
Graduate	93	83	10

Scheduled Castes (Dominant):

Bhambi etc., Chalavadi etc., Bhovi, Korama Sudugadu Siddha

For their cultural identity please see Appendix-I

Villages without Scheduled Castes: There are 21 villages without any scheduled caste population.

Scheduled Tribes: Out of the total population of 202671 persons, 13673 persons (6.75%) belong to Scheduled Tribes. The villages having less than 10% ST population are Madanabhavi, Hosatti, Khanapur-M-Tadakod Thimmapur-M-Tadakod, Tadakod, Jeeragiwad, Kotabagi Kallur, Lokur, Hangarki, Shedbal, Mugali, Hale Tegur Tegur, Bogur, Garag, Shibaragatti, Neeralakatti Kummanayakanakoppa, Shinganahalli, Venkatapur Guledakoppa, Kotur, Devagiri-M-Narendra, Lakamapur Narendra, Kumbapur-M-Narendra, Khanapur-M-Narendra Hulikeri, Kadabagatti, Balageri, Kogilageri Kumbarkoppa, Durgadakeri, Hosawal, Veerapur, Amboli

Dori, Benachi, Daddikamalapur, Mandihal, Mugad Kalakeri, Mavinakoppa, Devagiri-M-Kyarkoppa Kyarkoppa, Lalagatti, Devarhubli, Chikkamalligwad Kelgeri, Kamalapur, Lakamanahalli, Nigadi Benkankatti, Yerikoppa, Kalle, Kabbenur, Hanamanhal Harobelavadi, Uppinbetageri, Hanamanakoppa Pudakalakatti, Karadigudda, Amminabhavi Thimmapura-M-Amminabhavi, Marewad, Kavalgeri Chandanmatti, Kanakur, Talwai, Vanahalli, Hebballi Dandikoppa, Govankoppa, Maradagi, Somapur (Allapur) Shivalli.

The villages having more than 50% ST population are None.

Sex ratio of Scheduled tribe population is 488.

Scheduled Tribes Literates and Illiterates by Sex:

	Persons	Males	Females
Literate	5,122	3,239	1,883
Illiterate	8,551	3,756	4,795
Literacy rate	44.6	55.4	33.4
Graduate	80	71	9

Scheduled Tribes (Dominant):

Naikda etc., Meda, Kadu Kuruba, Pardhi etc., Koraga

For their cultural identity please see Appendix-II

Villages without Scheduled Tribes: There are 23 villages without any scheduled tribe population.

Literates and Illiterates by Sex (Total Population):

	Persons	Males	Females
Literate	99,574	61,227	38,347
Illiterate	103,097	42,714	60,383
Literacy rate	58	69	46
Graduate	2,393	2,036	357

Agriculture: ***Distribution of villages according to land use:*** Out of 118 villages, Total area (in hectare) is 102275, out of that 73.22 percent is cultivable and 5.55 percent of the cultivable area is irrigated.

Sources of Irrigation (Hectares): Government Canal 473.07, Private Canal 0, Well without Electricity 51.22, Well with Electricity 354.55, Tubewell without Electricity 93.34, Tubewell with Electricity 2376.8, Tank 339.95, River 13.6, Lake 0, Waterfall 0, Others 450.19.

Villages with population of 5000 to 9999:

Tadakod, Garag, Narendra, Uppinbetageri.

Villages with population of 10000 and above:

Amminabhavi, Hebballi.

Distribution of Workers:

	Persons	Males	Females	WPR
Cultivators	42,113	28,498	13,615	40.04
Agricultural Labour	40,157	16,984	23,173	38.18
Household Industry	3,086	1,861	1,225	2.93
Other Workers	19,810	15,324	4,486	18.84
Main Workers	89,488	58,717	30,771	85.09
Marginal Workers	15,678	3,950	11,728	14.91
Total Workers	105,166	62,667	42,499	

Religion: Major Religious Communities:

	Persons	Males	Females	Sex Ratio
Hindu (84.58%)	171,410	87,952	83,458	949
Muslim (12.33%)	24,982	12,694	12,288	968
Christian (0.07%)	143	80	63	788
Sikh (0.01%)	24	10	14	1,400
Buddhists (0.02%)	31	18	13	722
Jain (2.46%)	4,993	2,635	2,358	895

Agewise Data:

	Persons	Males	Females	Sex Ratio
All ages	202,671	103,941	98,730	950
0-14	69,371	35,357	34,014	962
15-44	95,727	49,807	45,920	922
45-79	35,771	17,933	17,838	995
80+	1,649	754	895	1187
Age not stated	153	90	63	700

Languages (Dominant):

Kannada, Urdu, Marathi, Telugu, Hindi

Disabled Population:

	Persons	Males	Females	%
Total Disabled	3,594	1,997	1,597	
In Seeing	1,406	715	691	39.12
In Speech	326	184	142	9.07
In Hearing	195	107	88	5.43
In Movement	1,270	754	516	35.34
Mentally	397	237	160	11.05

DOD BALLAPUR

Dod Ballapur C.D. Block lies in the northern part of Bangalore Rural district. It is a part of Dod Ballapur taluka. The Block is located at a distance of 40 kms. from district headquarters (Bangalore). There are 297 villages in the block with the total population of 190, 431 persons. Area of the C.D. Block is 778.31 sq. kms. It is bounded by district Kolar on north, district Bangalore and taluk Nelamangala on south, taluk Devanaha lli and district Kolar on east, district Tumkur and taluk Nelamangala on west.

Communications:

Roadways : N.H-207: Direction- Sompura to Devanahalli, Nearest Villages- Nagadenahalli, Adinarayana Hosahalli, Ragunathapura, Thammasettihalli, Shivapura, Talagavara, Mandibyadarahalli, Kesthur, Kodigehalli, Kurubarahalli, Sonnenahalli, Kugonahalli, Naranahalli, Doddabelavangala, Chikkabelavangala, Mugenahalli, Kattiihosahalli, Tubak unte, Muttugadahalli, Hulikunte, Tharabanahalli, Doddahej jaji, Rameswara, Chunchegowdanahosahalli. S.H-9: Directio n- Hindpur to Bangalore, Nearest Villages- Gunjur, Kelagi najuganahalli, Melinajuganahalli, Melinanaikaradahalli, Allalasandra, Tapasihalli, Bachchahalli, Shivalinga Pura, Thirumagondanahalli, Kantanakunte, Vaddarahalli, Palanjogihalli, Amani Palankere, Hasanghatta, Hosahudya, Bisuvanahalli, Yellupura, Veerapura, Thippapura, Basett ihalli. S.H-74: Direction- Nelamangala to Chik Ballapur, Nearest Villages- Heggadihalli, Tapasipura, Machagonda halli, Chowgondanahalli, Beedikere, Beedikere Agrahara, Kurubarahalli, Udanahalli, Thimmasandra, Rajaghatta Amanikere, Rajaghatta, Linganahalli, Dasagondanahalli, Konaghatta, Pindakuru Thimmanahalli, Muthasandra, Karen ahalli, Alahalli, Aralamallige, S.M. Gollahalli, Thippapu ra, Madagondanahalli, Gejjigadahalli, Karim Sonnenahalli, Kadanur, Mallohalli, Kannamangala , Puttenahalli, Kanas avadi, Marasandra, Ramadevanahalli, Kallodu, Madhure, Madhure Amanikere, Channadevi Agrahara.

Railway Station: Villages- Gunjur, Kelaginajuganahalli, Melinanaikaradahalli, Thirumagondanahalli, Vaddarahalli, Thippapura.

Annual Rainfall: Normal Rianfall 837.11 mm.

Ground Water: Availability of the Ground Water in the Basin is (Information not avablable) H.A.M. and the utilization is (Information not avablable) H.A.M.
It belongs to (Information not avablable) category.
Depth to water level 5 to 20 meter below the ground.
Most of the wells go down in summer months, according to the Ground Water Estimation Committee.

Natural Division : It falls in Bangalore Plateau of the Southern Karnataka Plateau.

Administration:

Division: Bangalore. Parliamentary Constituency: 27 Bangalore- IV (SC). District: Bangalore Rural. Taluka: Dod Ballapur. Assembly Constituency: 179 Devanahalli (SC), 180 Dod Ballapur. Gram Panchayat: 29.

Regional Area Development Boards: The Bailu Seeme Area Development Board.

Fairs and Festivals: Bhimeshwara Jatra: It is held at Makali in Bangalore on the day of Makara Sankranti Makali located on the right bank of (13 kms. from Banga lore) the Arkavati is a place with enchanting surroundings.

Villages: 297 **Inhabited:** 277 **Uninhabited:** 20

Ranking	District	State	National
Area	3	127	774
Population	2	95	841
Sex Ratio	5	131	3098
Child Sex Ratio	3	81	2891
Literacy Rate	4	51	1788
Density	3	83	4148
Work Participation Rate	6	47	1979

Gram Panchayats:

Sasalu, Aroodi, Hosahalli, Melinajuganahalli, Tubagere, Melekote, Heggadihalli, Konaghatta, Rajaghatta, Kantanakunte, Hadonahalli, Thippur, Kodigehalli, Hanabe, Sakkaregollahalli, Bhaktharahalli, Hulikunte, Doddabelavangala, Hadripura, Kesthur, Dargajogihalli , Aralamallige, Kadanur, Honnavara, Kanasavadi, Channadevi Agrahara, Dodda Tumkur, Majarahosahalli, Basettihalli .

Amenities:

Education: Primary School in 250 villages, Middle school in 121 villages, Matriculation or Secondary School in 21 villages, namely Aroodi, Hosahalli, Sasalu, Channaveeranahalli, Gunjur, Tubagere, Melekote, Kantanakunte, Rajaghatta, Konaghatta, Kadathippur, Hanabe, Sakkaregollahalli, Koligere, Doddabelavangala, Hulikunte, Kadanur, Mallohalli, Purusanahalli, Kanasavadi, Marasandra.
Higher Secondary or Pre University Courses or Intermediate or Junior College in 6 villages of the CD Block,, namely Aroodi, Hosahalli, Doddabelavangala, Hulikunte, Kanasavadi, Marasandra.
College in 1 village, Adult Literacy Center in 4 villages., College is in village, namely Karenahalli.

Medical: Hospital in 3 villages, Dispensary in 6 villages, Health Center in 15 villages, Sub Center in 41 villages, Maternity and Child Welfare Center in 0 village, Community health workers in 2 villages.
The Villages having Hospital or Dispensary or Health Center are Sasalu, Melekote, Hanabe, Gundasandra, Sonnenahalli, Doddahejjaji, Kodihalli.

Drinking Water: Tap water in 64 villages, Tank water in 35 villages, Well water in 11 villages, Tubewell in 184 villages and more than one source in 188 villages.

Bank: Banking facility in 8 villages, namely, Aroodi, Hosahalli, Tubagere, Melekote, Rajaghatta Hanabe, Doddabelavangala, Kanasavadi.
Credit Society in 24 villages Agricultural Credit Society in 22 Non-Agricultural Credit Society in 0 village.

Others: Power supply in 269 villages, Cinema hall in 5 villages sport club in 0 village, Stadium or Auditorium or Community Hall in 277 villages, Post Office in 43 villages.
There are 178 villages having bus facilities.

Villages with most of facilities: Aroodi Hosahalli, Tubagere, Melekote, Rajaghatta, Hanabe Doddabelavangala, Kanasavadi.

Villages without amenities (Education):
K.G.Devapala, Yaramuddenahalli, Tekalahalli, Hosanagenahalli, Bommenahalli, Narasapura, Ankonahalli, Kadlapanahalli, K.G.Lakkasandra, Chokkanahalli, Sevanagara, Shivalinga Pura, Naraganahalli, Kavalahalli, Masthimmanahalli,

Kachahalli, Muttugadahalli, Beedikere Agrahara, Thammasettihalli, Srinivasapura, Veerapura, Kolipura, Badrapura, Kangalapura, Kadathippenahalli, Chikkahejjaji Amanikere, Junnasandra..

Scheduled Castes: Out of the total population of 190554 persons, 47241 persons (24.79%) belong to Scheduled Castes. The villages having less than 10% SC population are K.G.Devapala, Kallukunte, Yaramuddenahalli, Hosakote Bankenahalli, Makali, Ojenahalli, Bommenahalli Kadakunte, Lingadaveeranahalli, Kilarlahalli Harohalli, Machenahalli, Garudagallu, Singenahalli Ganadalu, Todalabande, Lakkenahalli, Ankonahalli Mallegowdanahalli, Kadabyadarahalli Mugachinnenahalli, K.G.Lakkasandra, Mukkadigatta Chokkanahalli, Somasettihalli, Srinivasapura Majarahosahalli, Allalasandra, Sothenahalli Kavalahalli, Bhumenahalli, Chikkarayappanahalli Channapura, Tapasipura, Masthimmanahalli, Kachahalli Hireanaguddadahalli, Kurubarahalli Dandu Dasakodigehalli, Thammasettihalli Srinivasapura, Karenahalli, Ekasipura K.G. Kuntanahalli, Yellupura, Kolipura Sirigondanahalli, Konenahalli, Thambenahalli Bommanahalli, Chikkakalenahalli, Gundlahalli Kadathippenahalli, Mallanaikanahalli, Muttugadahalli Tharabanahalli, Chikkahejjaji Amanikere Chikkahejjaji, Gandragolipura, Nallenahalli Uddichikkanahalli, Puttenahalli, Kallodu Junnasandra.

The villages having more than 50% SC population are Vabasandra, Hosanagenahalli, Alappanahalli Narasapura, Suthahalli, Durgenahalli, Gedlapalya Kelaginanaikaradahalli, Melinanaikaradahalli Sevanagara, Shivalinga Pura, Naraganahalli Muttugadahalli, Beedikere Agrahara, Medihalli Sonnappanahalli, Galipuje, Kakkehalli, Obadenahalli Bhaktharahalli, Doddamankanala, Karim Sonnenahalli.

Sex ratio of Scheduled Caste population is 494.

Scheduled Castes Literates and Illiterates by Sex:

	Persons	Males	Females
Literate	21,573	13,299	8,274
Illiterate	25,668	10,588	15,080
Literacy rate	53.3	64.8	41.5
Graduate	333	302	31

Scheduled Castes (Dominant):

Madiga, Adi Karnataka, Bhovi, Adi Dravida Banjara etc.

For their cultural identity please see Appendix-I

Villages without Scheduled Castes: There are 61 villages without any scheduled caste population.

Scheduled Tribes: Out of the total population of 190554 persons, 10593 persons (5.56%) belong to Scheduled Tribes. The villages having less than 10% ST population are Gowdanakunte, Aroodi, K.G.Devapala, Yaramuddenahalli Tekalahalli, Jakkenahalli, Ujjani, Bankenahalli Ojenahalli, Hosanagenahalli, Sonnenahalli Bommenahalli, Kadakunte, Kottige Machenahalli K.G.Thammaganahalli, Lingadaveeranahalli Kilarlahalli, Harohalli, Sriramanahalli Machenahalli, Garudagallu, Singenahalli, Ganadalu Sasalu, Todalabande, Alappanahalli, Lakkenahalli Narasapura, Ankonahalli, Bhaktharahalli, Adakavala Mallegowdanahalli, Kadlapanahalli, Benakinamadugu Sulikunte, Channaveeranahalli, Jaligere, Byrapura Suthahalli, Melinajuganahalli, Lagumenahalli K.G.Lakkasandra, Kallukote, Hiremuddenahalli Durgenahalli, Gedlapalya, Subraya Nagenahalli Kelaginanaikaradahalli, Chokkanahalli, Cheelenahalli Kalludevanahalli, Somasettihalli, Srinivasapura Siravara, Sevanagara, Nellukunte, Kamalur Antharahalli, Tapasihalli, Bachchahalli Shivalinga Pura, Thirumagondanahalli, Hadonahalli Lakshmidevipura, Karnala, Naraganahalli, Tubagere Sothenahalli, Kavalahalli, Bhumenahalli, Marahalli Melekote, Doddarayappanahalli, Channapura Heggadihalli, Tapasipura, Gantiganahalli, Kuruvigere Masthimmanahalli, Kachahalli, Muttugadahalli Kanchiganala, Beedikere, Beedikere Agrahara Udanahalli, Gulyanandigunda , Sonnamaranahalli Maralenahalli, Honnaghatta, Kolur, Kantanakunte Vaddarahalli, Medihalli, Thogarighatta, Thimmasandra Rajaghatta, Konaghatta, Nagadenahalli, Ragunathapura Thammasettihalli, Sonnappanahalli, Shivapura Mallathahalli, Palanjogihalli, Hasanghatta Madagondahalli, Talagavara, Galipuje, Neralaghatta Mandibyadarahalli, Kesthur, Kodigehalli Kurubarahalli, Srinivasapura, Kakkehalli, Nagasandra Karenahalli, Alahalli , Jakkasandra, Menasi Kuntanahalli, S.M. Gollahalli, Ekasipura Chikka Tumkur, Majarahosahalli, Jinkebachchahalli K.G. Kuntanahalli, Hosahudya, Yellupura, Veerapura Thippapura, Basettihalli , Varadanahalli Arehalli Guddadahalli, Obadenahalli Sirigondanahalli, Badrapura, Konenahalli Kangalapura, Sankarasanahalli, Buchanahalli Thambenahalli, Halekote, Bommanahalli, Galibilikote Vanigarahalli, Thippur, Hanabe, Gundasandra Madeswara, Bhaktharahalli, Lingapura Bheemarauthanahalli, Chikkakalenahalli Sakkaregollahalli, Gundlahalli, Mudlakalenahalli

Kadathippenahalli, Chikkamankanala, Doddamankanala Kamana Agrahara, Akkathammanahalli, Sonnenahalli Jodi Karapura, Chikkanahalli, Shravanur, Naranahalli Doddabelavangala, Chikkabelavangala, Mugenahalli Kattiihosahalli, Tubakunte, Muttugadahalli Appkarenahalli, Hulikunte, Tharabanahalli Kasaghatta, Ambalagere, Karepura Chikkahejjaji Amanikere, Hadripura Madhurana Hosahalli, Rameswara Chunchegowdanahosahalli, Huskur, Bokipura Kalludevanahalli, Honnadevipura, Puttaiana Agrahara Syakaldevanapura, Muppadighatta, Narasaihna Agrahara Madagondanahalli, Gejjigadahalli, Byrasandra Dodda Tumkur, Karim Sonnenahalli, Kadanur Mallohalli, Isthur, Gandragolipura, Gulya Purusanahalli, Badrapura, Halenahalli, Nallenahalli Honnavara, Doddavadagere, Kammasandra Chikkavadagere, Nagenahalli, Kenjiganahalli Uddichikkanahalli, Jodithimasandra, Kanasavadi Ramadevanahalli, Kallodu, K.G. Sastry Palya Kodihalli, Junnasandra, Madhure, Channadevi Agrahara.

The villages having more than 50% ST population are Makali, Kadabyadarahalli, Hireanaguddadahalli Kurubarahalli, Kolipura.

Sex ratio of Scheduled tribe population is 491.

Scheduled Tribes Literates and Illiterates by Sex:

	Persons	Males	Females
Literate	5,348	3,181	2,167
Illiterate	5,245	2,212	3,033
Literacy rate	59.1	69.4	48.5
Graduate	93	75	18

Scheduled Tribes (Dominant):

Naikda etc., Kadu Kuruba, Kurumans

Generic Tribes etc., Meda

For their cultural identity please see Appendix-II

Villages without Scheduled Tribes: There are 156 villages without any scheduled tribe population.

Literates and Illiterates by Sex (Total Population):

	Persons	Males	Females
Literate	109,689	65,577	44,112
Illiterate	80,865	31,767	49,098
Literacy rate	66	77	54
Graduate	3,110	2,609	501

Agriculture: ***Distribution of villages according to land use:*** Out of 297 villages, Total area (in hectare) is 77831, out of that 64.47 percent is cultivable and 21.89 percent of the cultivable area is irrigated.

Sources of Irrigation (Hectares): Government Canal 846.68, Private Canal 0, Well without Electricity 30.95, Well with Electricity 89.58, Tubewell without Electricity 71.03, Tubewell with Electricity 5294.9, Tank 1704.98, River 0, Lake 129.64, Waterfall 1777.12, Others 1037.93.

Villages with population of 5000 to 9999: None

Villages with population of 10000 and above: None

Distribution of Workers:

	Persons	Males	Females	WPR
Cultivators	48,357	32,249	16,108	49.74
Agricultural Labour	23,657	8,672	14,985	24.34
Household Industry	3,055	1,617	1,438	3.14
Other Workers	22,143	16,323	5,820	22.78
Main Workers	76,872	53,240	23,632	79.08
Marginal Workers	20,340	5,621	14,719	20.92
Total Workers	97,212	58,861	38,351	

Religion: Major Religious Communities:

	Persons	Males	Females	Sex Ratio
Hindu (97.19%)	185,206	94,603	90,603	958
Muslim (2.29%)	4,355	2,242	2,113	942
Christian (0.3%)	566	288	278	965
Sikh (0.01%)	15	9	6	667
Buddhists (0.02%)	30	17	13	765
Jain (0.01%)	20	12	8	667

Agewise Data:

	Persons	Males	Females	Sex Ratio
All ages	190,554	97,344	93,210	958
0-14	57,981	29,466	28,515	968
15-44	90,302	46,263	44,039	952
45-79	39,861	20,472	19,389	947
80+	2,219	1,044	1,175	1125
Age not stated	191	99	92	929

Languages (Dominant):

Kannada, Telugu, Urdu, Hindi, Tamil

Disabled Population:

	Persons	Males	Females	%
Total Disabled	3,872	2,221	1,651	
In Seeing	1,715	903	812	44.29
In Speech	363	193	170	9.38
In Hearing	191	109	82	4.93
In Movement	1,225	809	416	31.64
Mentally	378	207	171	9.76

GADAG

Gadag C.D. Block lies in the central part of Gadag distr ict. It is a part of Gadag taluka. The Block is located at a distance of 00 kms. from district headquarters (Gadag). There are 64 villages in the block with the total population of 159,214 persons. Area of the C.D. Block is 1041.46 sq. kms. It is bounded by taluk Ron on north, taluk Shirhatti on south, district Koppal, taluks Mundargi and Ron on east, district Dharwad and taluk Shirhatti on west.

Communications:

Roadways : N.H-63: Direction- Hubli to Bellary, Nearest Villages- Dundur, Harlapur, Timmapur, Adavisomapur, Sambhapur, Lakkundi, Hulkoti, Binkadakatti, Asundi, Kalasapur. S.H-6: Direction- Lakshmeshwar to Gajendragarh, Nearest Villages- Hirekoppa, Benakanakoppa, Neeralagi, Kotumachagi, Nagasamudra, Kanaginahal, Asundi, Kalasapur, Pandurangapur, Malasamudra, Nagavi, Kanavi, Harti, Mulgund (Rural), Seethalahari.

Railway Station: Villages- Balaganur, Hombal, Harlapur, Hulkoti.

River: Panjarjalla Nadi: Nearest Villages- Hombal, Venka tapur (H.S.), Binkadakatti, Gadag (Rural).

Reserved Forest: Nearest Villages- Sambhapur, Jalashanka rnagar, Balajinagar, Papanashi, Lakkundi, Binkadakatti, Asundi, Kalasapur, Brahmandapur, Kabalayata Katti, Venkatapur (Inam), Soratur, Hanganakatti, Mahalingeshwarapur.

Annual Rainfall: Normal Rianfall 665.7 mm.

Ground Water: Availability of the Ground Water in the Basin is 5710 H.A.M. and the utilization is 708 H.A. M. It belongs to Over Exploited category. Depth to water level 5 to 20 meter below the ground. Most of the wells go down in summer months, according to the Ground Water Estimation Committee.

Soils: Medium to deep black soils.

Natural Division : It falls partly in the Dharwad-Gadag Plateau, Kalghatgi-Lakshmeshwar Residual Hills and the Middle Tungabhadra Valley of the Central Karnataka Plateau.

Administration:

Division: Belgaum. Parliamentary Constituency: 11 Dharwad, 10 Haveri, 3 Bagalkot. District: Gadag. Taluka: Gadag. Assembly Constituency: 66 Gadag, 67 Ron, 68 Nargund. Gram Panchayat: 25.

Regional Area Development Boards: The Bailu Seeme Area Development Board.

Villages: 64 **Inhabited:** 61 **Uninhabited:** 3

Ranking	District	State	National
Area	2	75	400
Population	2	122	1586
Sex Ratio	2	113	2779
Child Sex Ratio	1	25	1542
Literacy Rate	2	69	2221
Density	4	56	5517
Work Participation Rate	2	125	1527

Gram Panchayats:

Lingadhal, Balaganur, Kadadi, Huilgol, Hombal, Belahod, Chikkahandigol, Binkadakatti, Neeralagi, Kotumachagi, Harlapur, Kanaginahal, Hatalageri, Asundi, Hulkoti, Kurtakoti, Antur, Chinchalli, Harti, Nagavi, Adavisomapur, Lakkundi, Beladhadi, Yalishirur, Soratur.

Amenities:

Education: Primary School in 48 villages, Middle school in 48 villages, Matriculation or Secondary School in 22 villages, namely Lingadhal, Balaganur, Kadadi, Huilgol, Hombal, Belahod, Chikkahandigol, Kotumachagi, Harlapur, Timmapur, Jalashankarnagar, Lakkundi, Hulkoti, Asundi, Kurtakoti, Antur, Brahmandapur, Beladhadi, Kanavi, Harti, Chinchalli, Soratur.

Higher Secondary or Pre University Courses or Intermediate or Junior College in 4 villages of the CD Block,, namely Kadadi, Timmapur, Lakkundi, Hulkoti.

College in 1 village, Adult Literacy Center in 0 village., College is in village, namely Hulkoti.

Medical: Hospital in 7 villages, Dispensary in 6 villages, Health Center in 7 villages, Sub Center in 30 villages, Maternity and Child Welfare Center in 3 villages, Community health workers in 24 villages.

The Villages having Hospital or Dispensary or Health Center are Lingadhal, Balaganur, Kadadi, Hombal, Chikkahandigol, Kotumachagi, Narasapur, Papanashi, Hulkoti, Chinchalli, Yalishirur, Soratur.

Drinking Water: Tap water in 44 villages, Tank water in 29 villages, Well water in 49 villages, Tubewell in 45 villages and more than one source in 59 villages.

Bank: Banking facility in 16 villages, namely, Lingadhal, Balaganur, Gavarawad, Huilgol, Hombal Kanaginahal, Harlapur, Timmapur, Adavisomapur Lakkundi, Hulkoti, Malasamudra, Kurtakoti, Nagavi Harti, Soratur.

Credit Society in 34 villages Agricultural Credit Society in 33 Non-Agricultural Credit Society in 6 villages.

Others: Power supply in 58 villages, Cinema hall in 1 village, sport club in 1 village, Stadium or Auditorium or Community Hall in 0 village, Post Office in 35 villages.

There are 59 villages having bus facilities.

Villages with most of facilities: Lingadhal Balaganur, Huilgol, Hombal, Kanaginahal, Harlapur Timmapur, Adavisomapur, Lakkundi, Hulkoti Malasamudra, Kurtakoti, Nagavi, Harti, Soratur.

Villages without amenities (Education): Chikkoppa, Hirekoppa, Gadag (Rural), Pandurangapur, Bentur, Siddarameshwara Nagar, Shirol, Venkatapur (Inam), Mulgund (Rural), Mahalingeshwarapur..

Scheduled Castes: Out of the total population of 158931 persons, 24507 persons (15.42%) belong to Scheduled Castes. The villages having less than 10% SC population are Balaganur, Hombal, Venkatapur (H.S.), Chikkahandigol Shagoti, Dundur, Chikkoppa, Kiritageri, Narasapur Kanaginahal, Timmapur, Hatalageri, Sambhapur

Papanashi, Lakkundi, Hirehandigol, Binkadakatti Gadag (Rural), Kurtakoti, Antur, Kanavi, Harti Shirol, Venkatapur (Inam), Mulgund (Rural), Soratur Hanganakatti.

The villages having more than 50% SC population are Jalashankarnagar, Balajinagar, Pandurangapur Siddarameshwara Nagar, Brahmandapur, Nabhapur Kabalayata Katti, Mahalingeshwarapur.

Sex ratio of Scheduled Caste population is 492.

Scheduled Castes Literates and Illiterates by Sex:

	Persons	Males	Females
Literate	9,325	6,294	3,031
Illiterate	15,182	6,159	9,023
Literacy rate	45.7	60.5	30.4
Graduate	226	208	18

Scheduled Castes (Dominant):

Banjara etc., Bhambi etc., Bhovi, Chalavadi etc. Madiga

For their cultural identity please see Appendix-I

Villages without Scheduled Castes: There are 7 villages without any scheduled caste population.

Scheduled Tribes: Out of the total population of 158931 persons, 10933 persons (6.88%) belong to Scheduled Tribes.

The villages having less than 10% ST population are Lingadhal, Balaganur, Kadadi, Gavarawad, Huilgol Hombal, Belahod, Chikkahandigol, Chikkoppa Hirekoppa, Kiritageri, Benakanakoppa, Kotumachagi Nagasamudra, Narasapur, Kanaginahal, Harlapur Timmapur, Adavisomapur, Sambhapur, Jalashankarnagar Balajinagar, Papanashi, Lakkundi, Hirehandigol Hulkoti, Binkadakatti, Gadag (Rural), Asundi Pandurangapur, Malasamudra, Nagavi Siddarameshwara Nagar, Brahmandapur, Nabhapur Kanavi, Harti, Neelagund, Chinchalli, Hosur Shirunja, Kabalayata Katti, Yalishirur Mulgund (Rural), Soratur, Mahalingeshwarapur.

The villages having more than 50% ST population are None.

Sex ratio of Scheduled tribe population is 488.

Scheduled Tribes Literates and Illiterates by Sex:

	Persons	Males	Females
Literate	5,260	3,391	1,869
Illiterate	5,673	2,208	3,465
Literacy rate	55.5	70.0	40.3
Graduate	163	145	18

Scheduled Tribes (Dominant):

Naikda etc., Pardhi etc., Kadu Kuruba, Dubla etc. Meda

For their cultural identity please see Appendix-II

Villages without Scheduled Tribes: There are 14 villages without any scheduled tribe population.

Literates and Illiterates by Sex (Total Population):

	Persons	Males	Females
Literate	86,455	53,765	32,690
Illiterate	72,476	27,141	45,335
Literacy rate	63	77	49
Graduate	3,164	2,674	490

Agriculture: ***Distribution of villages according to land use:*** Out of 64 villages, Total area (in hectare) is 104146, out of that 84.6 percent is cultivable and 3.53 percent of the cultivable area is irrigated.

Sources of Irrigation (Hectares): Government Canal 176.04, Private Canal 0, Well without Electricity 2.51, Well with Electricity 1005.93, Tubewell without Electricity 9, Tubewell with Electricity 1780.95, Tank 5.37, River 0, Lake 61.12, Waterfall 0, Others 70.87.

Villages with population of 5000 to 9999:

Hombal, Kotumachagi, Hulkoti, Soratur.

Villages with population of 10000 and above:

Lakkundi, Kurtakoti.

Distribution of Workers:

	Persons	Males	Females	WPR
Cultivators	30,574	20,413	10,161	37.01
Agricultural Labour	34,917	13,525	21,392	42.26
Household Industry	2,103	1,260	843	2.55
Other Workers	15,024	12,377	2,647	18.18
Main Workers	68,027	44,032	23,995	82.34
Marginal Workers	14,591	3,543	11,048	17.66
Total Workers	82,618	47,575	35,043	

Religion: Major Religious Communities:

	Persons	Males	Females	Sex Ratio
Hindu (87.75%)	139,458	70,966	68,492	965
Muslim (10.78%)	17,133	8,736	8,397	961
Christian (0.12%)	187	99	88	889
Sikh (0.01%)	13	7	6	857
Buddhists (0.14%)	216	104	112	1,077
Jain (0.52%)	831	428	403	942

Agewise Data:

	Persons	Males	Females	Sex Ratio
All ages	158,931	80,906	78,025	964
0-14	52,100	26,483	25,617	967
15-44	75,358	39,401	35,957	913
45-79	30,123	14,491	15,632	1079
80+	1,241	471	770	1635
Age not stated	109	60	49	817

Languages (Dominant):

Kannada, Hindi, Urdu, Telugu, Marathi

Disabled Population:

	Persons	Males	Females	%
Total Disabled	3,276	1,759	1,517	

In Seeing	1,472	708	764	44.93
In Speech	303	157	146	9.25
In Hearing	157	76	81	4.79

In Movement	1,110	672	438	33.88
Mentally	234	146	88	7.14

GANGAWATI

Gangawati C.D. Block lies in the south-eastern part of Koppal district. It is a part of Gangawati taluka. The Block is located at a distance of 50 kms. from district headquarters (Koppal). There are 157 villages in the block with the total population of 303,679 persons. Area of the C.D. Block is 1318.38 sq. kms. It is bound ed by district Raichur and taluk Kushtagi on north, district Bellary on south, districts Bellary and Raichur on east, taluks Yelbarga and Koppal on west.

Communications:

Roadways : S.H-23: Direction- Koppal to Sindhnur, Nearest Villages- Dasanhal, Venkatagiri, Lingadhalli, Yemmigudda, Mukkumpi, Hire, Benkal , Chikka Benkal, Basapattana, Gangawati (Rural), Marli, Sriramanagar, Hebbal, Acharna rsapur, Danapur, Jangamarkalgudi, Pannapur, Karatgi, Juratgi , Marlanahalli, Gundur, Krishnapur, Siddapur, Bargur. S.H-29: Direction- Gangawati to Kampli and Lingsugur, Nearest Villages- Hulihyder, Sirwar, Hanmanhal, Kanakapura, Varankhed, Kanakgiri, Sulekal, Tippanhal, Malkanmardi, Arlahalli, Kesarhatti, Gangawati (Rural), Herur, Gonal, Batterhanchnal, Jangamarkalgudi, Achalapur, Ayodhya, Chikka Jantkal.

River: Tungabhadra Nadi- Nearest Villages- Tirmalapur, Sangapur, Anjanhalli, Virupapuragaddi, Hanmanhalli, Nagarhalli, Jantkal (Kalan), Vipra, Virpapur, Rajapur, Singangund, Basvandurg, Ramdurg, Anegundi, Hebbal, Danapur, Ayodhya, Chikka Jantkal , Mustur, Kuntoji, Jamapur, Ulenoor, Bennur, Nandihalli, Kakkargol, Shalignoor.

Canal: Nearest Villages- Battarnarsapur, Kesarhatti, Arhal, Dasanhal, Hire Benkal , Basapattana, Laxmipur, Rangapur, Tirmalapur, Anjanhalli, Temba, Mallapur, Rampur, Kesakihanchnal, Guldal, Herur, Chikka Dankankal , Jeeralkalgudi, Hire Dankankal, Gudur, Mylapur, Bevinhal, Pannapur, Karatgi, Challur, Somanhal, Budugumpa, Timmapur, Halsamudra, Kakkargol.

Reserved Forest: (Agoli R.F.): Nearest Villages- Bommasagara,Ramdurg, Chikka Madinal, Hire Madinal , Hampasadurg, Agoli, Venkatagiri, Banderhal, Gaddi, Lingadhalli,Yemmigudda, Mukkumpi, Hire Benkal , Chikka Benkal, Basapattana, Laxmipur, Temba, Mallapur.

Annual Rainfall: Normal Rianfall 571.92 mm.

Ground Water: Availability of the Ground Water in the Basin is 28649 H.A.M. and the utilization is 6393 H. A.M. It belongs to Over Exploited category. Depth to water level 5 to 20 meter below the ground. Most of the wells go down in summer months, according to the Ground Water Estimation Committee.

Soils: Black Cotton Soil.

Natural Division : It falls partly in the Arkera-Mudgal-K anakgiri Upland and Middle Tungabhadra Valley of the Central Karnataka Plateau.

Adminisrtation:

Division: Gulbarga. Parliamentary Constituency: 8 Koppal. District: Koppal. Taluka: Gangawati. Assembly Constituency: 61 Kanakagiri (SC), 62 Gangawati. Gram Panchayat: 38.

Regional Area Development Boards: The Hyderabad - Karnataka Area Development Board.

Fairs: Kanaka Chalapathi Temple Jatra: An annual jatra associated with the Kanakaehalapathi temple at Kanakgiri near Raichur held in the month of Phalguna (Feb.-March) is largely attended. Kanakgiri in Gangawati taluk, is an ancient place, situated on the Gangawati-Lingsugur road, about 22 kms. from Gangawati. It is surrounded on three sides by two streams and was formerly the chief town of a principality of Bedar Rajas, founded by Parasappa Naik during the days of the Vijayanagara rule. Kanakgiri Fair: The Kanakgiri fair held at Gangawati in around the month of March for two days. Gangawati, headquarters town of the Gangawati taluk, is about 15 kms. to the north of Auegundi. It is said that former ly it was known as Neelavati. The Tungabhadra flows at a short distance of about 3.5 kms. from here. Gangawati has been a centre of developmental activities under the Tungabhadra Project. It has an old matha of Sri Muddusangaswami and a temple of Viroopaksha built by a Vijayanagara king.

Villages: 157 **Inhabited:** 148 **Uninhabited:** 9

Ranking	District	State	National
Area	4	50	214
Population	1	15	63
Sex Ratio	1	41	1543
Child Sex Ratio	3	77	2781
Literacy Rate	4	154	4739
Density	4	109	4304
Work Participation Rate	1	55	2591

Gram Panchayats:

Gouripur, Hulihyder, Hire Khed, Kardona, Navali, Bevinhal, Karatgi, Challur, Chikka Dankankal , Sulekal, Kanakgiri, Chikka Madinal , Muslapur, Agoli, Venkatagiri, Chikka Benkal, Basapattana, Mallapur, Anegundi, Sangapur, Chikka Jantkal , Waddarhatti , Herur, Kesarhatti, Hanwal, Hosekera, Marli, Danapur, Sriramanagar, Gundur, Hulkihal, Marlanahalli, Budugumpa, Yerdona, Bennur, Ulenoor, Siddapur,

Mustur.

Amenities:

Education: Primary School in 134 villages, Middle school in 90 villages, Matriculation or Secondary School in 15 villages, namely Hulihyder, Kanakgiri, Udamkal, Basapattana, Anegundi, Herur, Marli, Sriramanagar, Navali, Karatgi, Marlanahalli, Budugumpa, Siddapur, Mustur, Ulenoor.

Higher Secondary or Pre University Courses or Intermediate or Junior College in 2 villages of the CD Block,, namely Kanakgiri, Karatgi.

College in 1 village, Adult Literacy Center in 0 village., College is in village, namely Karatgi.

Medical: Hospital in 8 villages, Dispensary in 17 villages, Health Center in 12 villages, Sub Center in 38 villages, Maternity and Child Welfare Center in 3 villages, Community health workers in 12 villages.

The Villages having Hospital or Dispensary or Health Center are Hulihyder, Muslapur, Obalbanda, Chikka Madinal , Kanakgiri, Agoli, Arhal, Mallapur, Anegundi, Hanwal, Hosekera, Navali, Karatgi, Challur, Budugumpa, Halsamudra, Bennur, Nandihalli.

Drinking Water: Tap water in 58 villages, Tank water in 56 villages, Well water in 40 villages, Tubewell in 46 villages and more than one source in 136 villages.

Bank: Banking facility in 19 villages, namely, Hulihyder, Muslapur, Kanakgiri, Basapattana, Sanapur Anegundi, Herur, Hanwal, Hosekera, Marli Sriramanagar, Chikka Jantkal, Navali, Karatgi Challur, Marlanahalli, Budugumpa, Gundur, Siddapur.

Credit Society in 30 villages Agricultural Credit Society in 27 Non-Agricultural Credit Society in 8 villages.

Others: Power supply in 148 villages, Cinema hall in 8 villages, sport club in 148 villages, Stadium or Auditorium or Community Hall in 148 villages, Post Office in 57 villages.

There are 103 villages having bus facilities.

Villages with most of facilities: Hulihyder Muslapur, Kanakgiri, Basapattana, Sanapur, Anegundi Herur, Hanwal, Hosekera, Marli, Sriramanagar Chikka Jantkal, Navali, Karatgi, Challur Marlanahalli, Budugumpa, Gundur, Siddapur.

Villages without amenities (Education): Ingaldal, Rampur, Jalihuda, Kardigudda, Hire Madinal, Yemmigudda, Laxmipur, Krishnapur, Rajapur, Singangund, Guldal, Achalapur, Hatti, Krishnapur..

Scheduled Castes: Out of the total population of 304942 persons, 53445 persons (17.53%) belong to Scheduled Castes.

The villages having less than 10% SC population are Hosgudda, Guddadur, Varankhed, Devlapur, Basrihal Somsagara, Ramdurg, Obalbanda, Jalihuda Chikka Madinal , Naglapur, Neerloti, Chikka Khed Hire Khed, Malligwad, Benkanhal, Bankapur Kardigudda, Hire Madinal , Hampasadurg Battarnarsapur, Banderhal, Hire Benkal , Hanmanhalli Rajapur, Singangund, Kesakihanchnal, Acharnarsapur Achalapur, Bunhatti, Eachanhal, Uddihal, Kyarihal Sankanhal, Kardona, Mallapur, Akalkumpi, Wadki Adapura, Bhairapura, Chikka Dankankal , Gudur Mylapur, Yerdona, Halsamudra, Kottankal, Jamapur Ulenoor, Kakkargol.

The villages having more than 50% SC population are Advibhavi, Ingaldal, Bommasagara, Laxmipur Krishnapur, Nagarhalli, Chirchanagudda.

Sex ratio of Scheduled Caste population is 502.

Scheduled Castes Literates and Illiterates by Sex:

	Persons	Males	Females
Literate	13,406	9,166	4,240
Illiterate	40,039	17,442	22,597
Literacy rate	31.4	43.3	19.7
Graduate	172	151	21

Scheduled Castes (Dominant):

Madiga, Bhovi, Banjara etc., Bhambi etc. Chalavadi etc.

For their cultural identity please see Appendix-I

Villages without Scheduled Castes: There are 17 villages without any scheduled caste population.

Scheduled Tribes: Out of the total population of 304942 persons, 49536 persons (16.24%) belong to Scheduled Tribes.

The villages having less than 10% ST population are Sirwar, Kanakapura, Devlapur, Ingaldal, Muslapur Bommasagara, Obalbanda, Kanakgiri, Kalkera Benkanhal, Sulekal, Tippanhal, Bankapur, Kardigudda Arlahalli, Battarnarsapur, Kesarhatti, Venkatagiri Hire Benkal , Laxmipur, Sangapur, Virupapuragaddi Chickrampur, Krishnapur, Hosalli, Singangund Markumbi, Herur, Batterhanchnal, Hanwal Sriramanagar, Hebbal, Danapur, Jangamarkalgudi Achalapur, Ayodhya, Eachanhal, Uddihal, Navali Jeeralkalgudi, Bevinhal, Pannapur, Budugumpa Timmapur, Gundur, Krishnapur, Siddapur, Bargur Mustur, Kuntoji, Jamapur, Bennur, Shalignoor.

The villages having more than 50% ST population are Layadhunsi, Varankhed, Basrihal, Parapur, Hire Khed Malligwad, Katapur (Khalsa), Hire Madinal Lingadhalli, Yemmigudda, Kesakihanchnal, Kyarihal Mallapur, Akalkumpi, Hatti, Wadki, Bhairapura, Gudur Tondihal, Halsamudra.

Sex ratio of Scheduled tribe population is 499.

Scheduled Tribes Literates and Illiterates by Sex:

	Persons	Males	Females

Literate	14,716	10,307	4,409
Illiterate	34,820	14,493	20,327
Literacy rate	37.0	52.0	22.1
Graduate	149	136	13

Scheduled Tribes (Dominant):

Naikda etc., Iruliga, Meda, Generic Tribes etc. Bhil etc.

For their cultural identity please see Appendix-II

Villages without Scheduled Tribes: There are 16 villages without any scheduled tribe population.

Literates and Illiterates by Sex (Total Population):

	Persons	Males	Females
Literate	122,631	78,065	44,566
Illiterate	182,311	75,080	107,231
Literacy rate	49	62	35
Graduate	3,034	2,521	513

Agriculture: ***Distribution of villages according to land use:*** Out of 157 villages, Total area (in hectare) is 131838, out of that 70.37 percent is cultivable and 43.25 percent of the cultivable area is irrigated.

Sources of Irrigation (Hectares): Government Canal 30773.78, Private Canal 143.53, Well without Electricity 0, Well with Electricity 338.87, Tubewell without Electricity 0, Tubewell with Electricity 7431.16, Tank 75.2, River 566.68, Lake 0, Waterfall 0, Others 793.67.

Villages with population of 5000 to 9999:

Basapattana, Herur, Hanwal, Hosekera, Marli Sriramanagar, Bevinhal, Marlanahalli, Yerdona Budugumpa, Gundur, Siddapur, Mustur.

Villages with population of 10000 and above:

Kanakgiri, Karatgi.

Distribution of Workers:

	Persons	Males	Females	WPR
Cultivators	39,170	31,785	7,385	27.86
Agricultural Labour	72,378	30,117	42,261	51.48
Household Industry	2,898	1,757	1,141	2.06
Other Workers	26,159	19,156	7,003	18.6
Main Workers	103,545	71,823	31,722	73.64
Marginal Workers	37,060	10,992	26,068	26.36
Total Workers	140,605	82,815	57,790	

Religion: Major Religious Communities:

	Persons	Males	Females	Sex Ratio
Hindu (89.39%)	272,577	136,891	135,686	991
Muslim (9.69%)	29,545	14,815	14,730	994
Christian (0.4%)	1,222	629	593	943
Sikh (0%)	12	6	6	1,000
Buddhists (0.01%)	25	9	16	1,778
Jain (0.04%)	118	63	55	873

Agewise Data:

	Persons	Males	Females	Sex Ratio
All ages	304,942	153,145	151,797	991
0-14	121,317	61,864	59,453	961
15-44	135,400	68,101	67,299	988
45-79	46,307	22,447	23,860	1063
80+	1,691	616	1,075	1745
Age not stated	227	117	110	940

Languages (Dominant):

Kannada, Telugu, Urdu, Hindi, Tamil

Disabled Population:

	Persons	Males	Females	%
Total Disabled	5,852	3,310	2,542	
In Seeing	2,498	1,347	1,151	42.69
In Speech	621	370	251	10.61
In Hearing	286	143	143	4.89
In Movement	1,873	1,127	746	32.01
Mentally	574	323	251	9.81

GAURIBIDANUR

Gauribidanur C.D. Block lies in the north-western part of Kolar district. It is a part of Gauribidanur taluka. The Block is located at a distance of 93 kms. from district headquarters (Kolar). There are 239 villages in the block with the total population of 240,538 persons. Area of the C.D. Block is 887.59 sq. kms. It is bounded by district Tumkur on north, district Bangalore Rural on south, taluks Gudibanda and Chikballapur on east, and district Tumkur on west. It has common boundary with the state of Andhra Pradesh on north.

Communications:

Roadways : S.H.-9: Direction- Bangalore to Hindupur, Nearest Villages- Kudumalakunte, Doddakurugodu, Yerrahalli, Chikkakurugodu, Puttapurlahalli, Kalludi, Madanahalli, Mittenahalli, Vedalaveni, Veeralagollahalli, Alakapura, Pothenahalli, Thippaganahalli, Kothur, Kallinaikanahalli, Basavapura, Thondebhavi, Kamalapura. S.H.-58: Direction- Sira to Chikballapur, Nearest Villages- Kurudi, Ranganahalli, Kadaranahalli, Bommasettihalli, Jeerigepete, Mudigere, Hossur, Bhaktarahalli, Hirebidanur, Gundapura, Kadalaveni, Moorumanehalli, Kurubarahalli, Cheegatagere, Gangasandra, Beeramangala, Bisalahalli, Arasalbande, Kondenahalli, P.Nagenahalli, Arkunda, Pura, Manchenahalli, Budivanthanahalli, Gidaganahalli, Kanaganakoppa.

Railway Station: Nearest Villages- Doddakurugodu, Yerrahalli, Thondebhavi.

River: Kumadvati Nadi- Nearest Villages- Hampasandra, Balagere, Ramapura, Bommasettihalli, Jeerigepete, Mudigere, Kurugodu Tammanahalli, Dinamagattanahalli, Kenkere, Narasimhanahalli, Singanahalli, Kondapura, Gedare, Kamaganahalli, Idagur, Vychakurahalli, Kadalaveni, Vedalaveni, Kuntachikkanahalli, G.Bommasandra, Allipura, Pulaganahalli, Veerammanahalli, Taridalu, Dyavasandra. Penner Nadi- Nearest Villages- Babenahalli, Doddakurugodu,

Yerrahalli, Chikkakurugodu, H.Nagasandra, Kadaranahalli, Kalludi, Hirebidanur, Madanahalli, Veeralagollahalli, Moorumanehalli, Kurubarahalli, Cheegatagere, Alakapura, Nandiganahalli, Rayarekalahalli, Hanumenahalli, Bisalah alli, Guvvalahalli, Chennabyrenahalli, Dwaraganahalli, Rayamakalahalli, Arasalbande, Kondenahalli, P.Nagenahal li, Arkunda, Pura, Manchenahalli, Budivanthanahalli, Gidaganahalli, Varavani, Gowdagere, Kanaganakoppa, Addekoppa, Shampura.

Annual Rainfall: Normal Rianfall 755.91 mm.

Ground Water: Availability of the Ground Water in the Basin is (Information not avablable) H.A.M. and the utilization is (Information not avablable) H.A.M.
It belongs to (Information not avablable) category.
Depth to water level 5 to 20 meter below the ground.
Most of the wells go down in summer months, according to the Ground Water Estimation Committee.

Soils: Red Soils.

Natural Division : It falls in Upper Penner Basin and Gudibanda-Bagepalli Highlands of the Southern Karnataka Plateau.

Administration:

Division: Bangalore. Parliamentary Constituency: 27 Bangalore (SC). District: Kolar. Taluka: Gauribidanur. Assembly Constituency: 139 Gauribidanur, 141 Chikballap ur. Gram Panchayat: 37.
Border Villages: (State: A.P.)- Chandanadur, Halaganahalli, Babenahalli, Kudumalakunte, Doddakurugodu, Gowdas andra, Jarabandahalli, Huchodanahalli, Hunasenahalli, Myalya, Maripadagu, Mudalodu, Jeelakunte, Sadarlahalli, Mallenahalli, Payannanahalli, Nagaragere, Pillaguttahal li, Mattavalahalli, Kantharlahalli, Bandarlahalli.

Villages: 239 **Inhabited:** 219 **Uninhabited:** 20

Ranking	District	State	National
Area	2	102	570
Population	1	47	292
Sex Ratio	11	123	2981
Child Sex Ratio	8	69	2634
Literacy Rate	7	113	3399
Density	5	24	3848
Work Participation Rate	4	35	874

Gram Panchayats:
Ramapura, Idagur, Halaganahalli, Doddakurugodu, Bychapura, Myalya, Mudalodu, Nagaragere, Kothur, Vatadahosahalli, Nakkalahalli, Darinaikanapalya, Hudugur, Chikkakurugodu, Kadalaveni, Kurudi, Sonaganahalli, Hossur, Mudigere, Gedare, G.Bommasandra, Hirebidanur , Gangasandra, B.Bommasandra, Namagondlu, Jarabandahalli, Minakanagurki, Manchenahalli, Gowdagere, Pura, Alakapura, Taridalu, Allipura, Bevinahalli, Thondebhavi, Kallinaikanahalli, Halehalli.

Amenities:

Education: Primary School in 187 villages, Middle school in 115 villages, Matriculation or Secondary School in 27 villages, namely Anudi, Kurudi, Ramapura, Hossur, Machenahalli, Gedare, Chandanadur, Doddakurugodu, Idagur, Kadalaveni, Gangasandra, Myalya, Mudalodu, Nagaragere, Bandarlahalli, Vatadahosahalli, Nakkalahalli, Hudugur, Darinaikanapalya, Namagondlu, Alakapura, Allipura, Taridalu, Thondebhavi, Kondenahalli, Manchenahalli, Halehalli.
Higher Secondary or Pre University Courses or Intermediate or Junior College in 5 villages of the CD Block,, namely Hossur, Vatadahosahalli, Darinaikanapalya, Thondebhavi, Manchenahalli.
College in 0 village, Adult Literacy Center in 0 village.

Medical: Hospital in 3 villages, Dispensary in 10 villages, Health Center in 10 villages, Sub Center in 42 villages, Maternity and Child Welfare Center in 21 villages, Community health workers in 13 villages.
The Villages having Hospital or Dispensary or Health Center are Kurudi, Ramapura, Hossur, Doddakurugodu, Nagaragere, Hudugur, Darinaikanapalya, Mallasandra, Kallinaikanahalli, Manchenahalli.

Drinking Water: Tap water in 153 villages, Tank water in 27 villages, Well water in 25 villages, Tubewell in 93 villages and more than one source in 188 villages.

Bank: Banking facility in 19 villages, namely, Hampasandra, Kurudi, Ramapura, Hossur, Gedare Doddakurugodu, Chikkakurugodu, Hirebidanur, Hudugur Vaddenahalli, Namagondlu, Alakapura, Nandiganahalli Rayarekalahalli, Allipura, Thondebhavi, Bisalahalli Manchenahalli, Shampura.
Credit Society in 28 villages Agricultural Credit Society in 26 Non-Agricultural Credit Society in 5 villages.

Others: Power supply in 211 villages, Cinema hall in 7 villages sport club in 0 village, Stadium or Auditorium or Community Hall in 0 village, Post Office in 57 villages.
There are 127 villages having bus facilities.

Villages with most of facilities: Hampasandra Kurudi, Ramapura, Hossur, Gedare, Doddakurugodu Chikkakurugodu, Hudugur, Namagondlu, Alakapura Allipura, Thondebhavi, Manchenahalli.

Villages without amenities (Education):
Papaganahalli, Jeerigepete, Jodigurrappanahalli, Kurugodu Thammanahalli, Dinamagattanahalli, Naduvalahalli, Goddavalahalli, Kondapura, Babenahalli, Nasakuntahalli, Moorumanehalli, Kantharlahalli, Channarayanahalli, Muchatlahalli,

Mopurahalli, Chikkamallenahalli, Muddalahalli, Siddenahalli, Puttegowdanadinne, Reddydyavarahalli, Komarlahalli, Agraharahosahalli, Uchalagollahalli, Nulagummanahalli, Gondihalli, Budivanthanahalli, Cheelenahalli, Budagathimmanahalli..

Scheduled Castes: Out of the total population of 240582 persons, 61589 persons (25.6%) belong to Scheduled Castes. The villages having less than 10% SC population are Balagere, Gollahalli, Dronakunte, Kadaranahalli Papaganahalli, Bhaktarahalli, Yerrapothenahalli Jodigurrappanahalli, Hale Upparahalli Kurugodu Thammanahalli, Babenahalli, Nasakuntahalli Malenahalli, Udamalodu, Sadarlahalli, Payannanahalli Bandarlahalli, Channarayanahalli, Kerevolaginahalli Muddalahalli, Lakkasandra, Bachareddyhalli Lakshmanapura, Chinchanahalli, Kadiradevarahalli Puttegowdanadinne, Budigenahalli, Jakkenahalli Allipura, Komarlahalli, Agraharahosahalli Dyavasandra, Kambalahalli, Bhumenahalli Uchalagollahalli, Mindenahalli, Bhumenahalli Hanumanthapura, Dinnenahalli, Gondihalli M.Nagenahalli, Hosahalli, Nagarabhavi.

The villages having more than 50% SC population are Ranganahalli, Naduvalahalli, Goddavalahalli Yerrahalli, Moorumanehalli, Mallenahalli Sabbanahalli, Narlahalli, Chikkamallenahalli Kodihalli, Cholasettyhalli, Gulaganjihalli Nandiganahalli, Mallasandra, Yerragunte Basavanahalli, Guvvalahalli, Kodiganahalli P.Nagenahalli, Gollahalli, Budivanthanahalli Gowdagere, Alas Thimmanahalli.

Sex ratio of Scheduled Caste population is 489.

Scheduled Castes Literates and Illiterates by Sex:

	Persons	Males	Females
Literate	21,762	13,827	7,935
Illiterate	39,827	17,644	22,183
Literacy rate	41.6	51.6	31.0
Graduate	461	425	36

Scheduled Castes (Dominant):

Adi Karnataka, Madiga, Bhovi, Adi Dravida Banjara etc.

For their cultural identity please see Appendix-I

Villages without Scheduled Castes: There are 47 villages without any scheduled caste population.

Scheduled Tribes: Out of the total population of 240582 persons, 37812 persons (15.72%) belong to Scheduled Tribes. The villages having less than 10% ST population are Jodibisilahalli, Hosa Upparahalli, Balagere, Anudi Kurudi, Gollahalli, Dronakunte, Kadaranahalli Bhaktarahalli, Yerrapothenahalli, Hale Upparahalli Kurugodu Thammanahalli, Dinamagattanahalli Narasimhanahalli, Naduvalahalli, Goddavalahalli Konaganahalli, Kondapura, Gedare, Kamaganahalli Babenahalli, Kudumalakunte, Yerrahalli, Konapura Nasakuntahalli, Devaganahalli, H.Nagasandra Malenahalli, Hirebidanur, Udamalodu Veeralagollahalli, Moorumanehalli, Cheegatagere Gangasandra, Saganahalli, Hunasenahalli, Maripadagu Jeelakunte, Sadarlahalli, Mallenahalli Payannanahalli, Kantharlahalli, Kothur Hanumenahalli, Gotlakunte, Mopurahalli, Sabbanahalli Narlahalli, Chikkamallenahalli, Kodihalli Cholasettyhalli, Muddalahalli, Chimakalahalli Virupasandra, Narasapura, Hulikunte, Anagattahalli Siddenahalli, Kadabur, Cheelammanahalli, Venkatapura Puttegowdanadinne, Budigenahalli, Gundlahalli Kuntachikkanahalli, Alakapura, Nandiganahalli Rayarekalahalli, Bevinahalli, Yerragunte, Allipura Pulaganahalli, Veerammanahalli, Komarlahalli Nachikunte, Chikkamallekere, Kambalahalli Basavanahalli, Kothur, Kallinaikanahalli, Kamalapura Charakamittenehalli, Mindenahalli, Beeramangala Bisalahalli, Guvvalahalli, Rayamakalahalli Kondenahalli, P.Nagenahalli, Bhumenahalli Gollahalli, Hanumanthapura, Pidachalahalli Nulagummanahalli, Gondihalli, M.Nagenahalli Hosahalli, Manchenahalli, Gidaganahalli Chinnagenahalli, Kanaganakoppa, Shampura Upparahalli, Halehalli, Alas Thimmanahalli Guyyalahalli, Marimakalahalli, Budagathimmanahalli.

The villages having more than 50% ST population are Singanahalli, Machenahalli, Huchodanahalli Mattavalahalli, Krishnarajapura, Lakkasandra Golachinnenahalli, Lakshmanapura, Chinchanahalli Agraharahosahalli, Doddamallekere, Dwaraganahalli Nagarabhavi.

Sex ratio of Scheduled tribe population is 493.

Scheduled Tribes Literates and Illiterates by Sex:

	Persons	Males	Females
Literate	16,356	10,190	6,166
Illiterate	21,456	8,976	12,480
Literacy rate	50.3	61.8	38.4
Graduate	329	291	38

Scheduled Tribes (Dominant):

Naikda etc., Hakkipikki, Generic Tribes etc. Jenu Kuruba, Meda

For their cultural identity please see Appendix-II

Villages without Scheduled Tribes: There are 55 villages without any scheduled tribe population.

Literates and Illiterates by Sex (Total Population):

	Persons	Males	Females
Literate	118,150	71,756	46,394
Illiterate	122,432	51,000	71,432
Literacy rate	57	67	45
Graduate	3,558	2,954	604

Agriculture: ***Distribution of villages according to land use:*** Out of 239 villages, Total area (in hectare) is 88759, out of that 58.33 percent is cultivable and 32.16 percent of the cultivable area is irrigated.

Sources of Irrigation (Hectares): Government Canal 284.099986, Private Canal 25.29, Well without Electricity 212.874134, Well w Electricity 790.818164, Tubewell without Electricity 1115.160895, Tubewell with Electricity 8925.628875, Tank 4306.46739, River 0, Lake 0, Waterfall 0, Others 987.785045.

Villages with population of 5000 to 9999:
Hossur, Allipura, Manchenahalli.

Villages with population of 10000 and above: None

Distribution of Workers:

	Persons	Males	Females	WPR
Cultivators	60,294	37,873	22,421	45.57
Agricultural Labour	48,319	20,465	27,854	36.52
Household Industry	3,942	1,769	2,173	2.98
Other Workers	19,755	14,291	5,464	14.93
Main Workers	109,681	67,195	42,486	82.9
Marginal Workers	22,629	7,203	15,426	17.1
Total Workers	132,310	74,398	57,912	

Religion: Major Religious Communities:

	Persons	Males	Females	Sex Ratio
Hindu (90.99%)	218,897	111,657	107,240	960
Muslim (8.45%)	20,333	10,409	9,924	953
Christian (0.2%)	476	249	227	912
Sikh (0.01%)	14	6	8	1,333
Buddhists (0.01%)	32	20	12	600
Jain (0.24%)	574	288	286	993

Agewise Data:

	Persons	Males	Females	Sex Ratio
All ages	240,582	122,756	117,826	960
0-14	74,264	37,868	36,396	961
15-44	111,853	56,625	55,228	975
45-79	51,835	26,998	24,837	920
80+	2,333	1,105	1,228	1111
Age not stated	297	160	137	856

Languages (Dominant):
Kannada, Telugu, Urdu, Hindi, Marathi

Disabled Population:

	Persons	Males	Females	%
Total Disabled	4,443	2,480	1,963	
In Seeing	1,893	984	909	42.61
In Speech	604	317	287	13.59
In Hearing	264	130	134	5.94
In Movement	1,293	834	459	29.1
Mentally	389	215	174	8.76

GOKAK

Gokak C.D. Block lies in the east central part of Belgaum district. It is a part of Gokak taluka. The Block is located at a distance of 65 kms. from district headquart ers (Belgaum). There are 131 villages in the block with the total population of 400,785 persons. Area of the C.D. Block is 1473.36 sq. kms. It is bounded by taluk Raybag and district Bagalkot on north, taluk Sampgaon and Parasgad on south, district Bagalkot, and taluk Ramdurg and Parasgad on east, taluk Belgaum and Hukeri on west.

Communications:

Roadways : S.H-18: Direction- Chikodi to Mudhol, Nearest Villages-Mudalgi (Rural), Gurlapur, Hallur. SH-31: Direction-Sampgaon to Terdal, Nearest Villages- Naganur, Mudalgi (Rural), Gurlapur, Hallur, Jokanatti, Kallolli, Arabhavi, Lolasur, Nallanati, Sanganakeri, Hanamapur, Gokak (Rural), Maladinni, Benachinamaradi, Kolavi, Ginimar Hosur, Hulikatti, Khanagaon, Nabapur, Devagoudanahatti.

Railway Station: Villages- Mallapur (P.G.), Suladhal.

River: Ghatprabha Nadi- Munyal, Konnur (Rural), Shivapur, Dhupadal, Lolasur, Basaligundi, Nallanatti, Balobal, Beerangaddi, Hunshyal (P.G.), Waderatti, Hunshyal (P.Y.), Bisanakoppa, Dhavaleshwar, Aralimatti, Avaradi, Hale Yaragudri, Bairanatti, Sunadholi, Tigadi, Talakatnal, Udagatti, Hadiginal, Kalarkoppa, Melavanki, Chigadolli, Adibatti. Didda Halla Nadi- Nearest Vill.-Gulaganjikoppa, Yadwad. Kanvi Nadi- Nearest Villages- Maladinni, Upparatti, Mamadapur, Ajjanakatti, Chikkanandi, Herenandi, Hirehatti, Jamanal, Melavanki. Markandeya Nadi- Nearest Villages- Konnur (Rural), Molmanatti, Godachinamalaki, Gokak (Rural), Shigiholi, Gaddiholi, Kundargi.

Canal: Nearest Villages- Dandapur, Rajapur, Duradundi, Ganeshwadi, Badigwad, Pamaladinnil, Mallapur (P.G.), Dhupadal, Shindikurbet, Arabhavi, Lolasur, Basaligundi, Nallanatti, Sanganakeri, Hanamapur, Balobal, Beerangaddi, Hunshyal (P.G.), Waderatti.

Reserved Forest: Nearest Villages- Konnur (Rural), Molmanatti, Godachinamalaki, Gokak (Rural), Maladinni, Benachinamaradi, Kolavi, Tavag, Benachinamardi, Urabinahatti, Shigiholi, Musalamari, Mallapur S.A., Iranattti, Telaginahati, Kaitanal, Ginimar Hosur, Hulikati, Hanamapur, Panchanaikanatti, Herenandi, Makkalageri, Pudakalkatti, Khanagaon,Midakanatti, Rajanakati, Ankalgi, Lagameshwar, Gujanal, Yaddalgudd, Budihal, Suladhal, Panjanatti, Kesappanatti, Nabapur, Shiltibhavi, Hirehatti, Jamanal.

Annual Rainfall: Normal Rianfall 507.6 mm.

Ground Water: Availability of the Ground Water in the Basin is 16082 H.A.M. and the utilization is 15895 H.A.M. It belongs to Over Expoited category. Depth to water level 2 to 20 meter below the ground. Most of the wells go down in summer months, according to the Ground Water Estimation Committee.

Soil: Red Soil, Black Soil.

Natural Division : It falls partly in the Krishna Ghatprabha Irrigated Tract and the Gokak-Saundatti Hills of the Northern Karnataka Plateau.

Administration:

Division: Belgaum. Parliamentary Constituency: 2 Belgaum. District: Belgaum. Taluka: Gokak. Assembly Constituency: 8 Arabhavi, 9 Gokak. Gram Panchayat: 51.

Regional Area Development Boards: The Bailu Seeme Area Development Board.

Fairs: Ahmad Shah Urs: It is held at Gokak in the month of Moharram Annually. Gokak, 65 kms. from Belgaum is located in between the South bank of the Ghataprabha and an hill-fort locally called Malikarjuna or Panchmigudda or Maliksaheb gudda. Adavisiddeshwara Matha Jatra: It is held at Ankalgi in the month of Februry for five days every year. Ankalgi 30 kms. from Gokak, a place located on the bank of the Markandeya is a celebrated Veerashaiva Centre. The place has temples dedicated to Lakshmi, Basaveshwara (recent) and Maruti. The Adavisiddeshwara Matha is named after the famous Veerashaiva saint Adavisiddeshwara who lived here about two hundred years ago.The Matha has the gadduge of Sri Adviswami and behind it is that of Siddeshwara Swami (the guru of the former). The Matha has shrines of Veerabhadra, Akkamahadevi and Ishwara. The Matha has a fine lecture hall and well designed balconies with walls adorned with modern paintings and has fine wood work. Annual jatra of the Matha is held during Shivaratri for five days when a huge cattle fair is also held, which attracts nearly 20,000 people.

Pir Shah Hussain Khufari Barijan Qadri Urs: Konnur near Belgaum is located about 11 kms. from Gokak town, on the right bank of the river Ghataprabha. There is a famous temple of lord Chikaleshwara. Near the Chikaleshwara temple is a dargah ascribed to Pir Shah Hussain Khufari Barijan Qadri and the urs is held annually when about 5,000 people assemble. Another dargah ascribed to Gayabi sab is on the station road and one more to Pathan Sab near the Kadasiddheshwara Matha. The place has two mosques and the Jama Masjid is of the Adil Shahi times.

Subodharanga Jatra: It is held at Mudalgi around the month of March-April. Mudalgi, 32 kms. from Gokak has an old Vithoba temple. Though renovated it is Later Chalukyan as materials like lathe-turned pillar, doorway, etc., are seen and the old plan is retained. It has a garbhagriha, ardhamantapa and navaranga. The huge sukanasa pendant of the shikhara is fixed in a wall of the navaranga, and a modern statue of Maruti is affixed in its centre. It has a Kadambanagara shikhara over the garbhagriha. Other temples of the place, all recent, are the Basavanna, Hanumanta, Yellavva, Subodharanga and the Eerappa.

Chattibasaveswar Jatra: It is held at Yadwad near Belgaum in the month of March every year.Yadawad, 43 kms. From Gokak is a place with rich antiquity. The place was under the Tasgaon Patwardhans for long. The place has temples dedicated to Basavanna, Harideva, Bennekrishna, Rameshwara, Sri Raghavendra Matha and Narayana. The Harideva temple as locally described appears to be an old Jaina basti in later Chalukyan style.

Durdundeeshwara Jatra: It is held at Arabhavi near Belgaum in about the month of March-April for three days every year. Arabhavi, six kms. from Gokak is a celebrated Veerashaiva centre. In 1791, Captain Moor identified it as Aarbyengh and describes that the place was having beautiful mango groves around a stupendous building which is ornamented with sculptures. The chief attraction of the place is the Durdundeeshwara Matha built in red sand stone. This colossal stone structure with massive pillars and sloped mchajjas decorated with stone chains, etc., is a fine onument. It has a garbhagriha, and an open mantapa.

Kadasiddheshwara and Maradi Matha Jatra: It is held at Konnur inabout the month of April every year. Konnur 11 kilometres from Gokak, located on the right bank of the river Ghataprabha is one of the earliest settle ments in the district.

Kalbhairava Jatra: It is held at Handibadagnatha near Belgaum in about the month of February-March for two days every year. Handibadagnatha, 24 kms. from Khanapury a celebrated Nathapanthi centre is situated atop a huge hill which is more than about 650 metres high.To reach this beautiful spot one has to travel on the Khanapur-Londa road upto Kumbarda and take deviation to the left to walk in an irregular forest route for about 5 kms. in a serpentine fashion. The Matha, founded by the Nathapanthis about 900 years ago at this place is called the Handibadaganatha Matha. There is a wooden structure with a profusely carved doorway said to have been renovated by Rani Chennamma of Kutur. The garbagriha has the statue of Handibadaganatha, seated on a horse, resembling Revantha.

Kallolappa Jatra: It is held at Kallolli near Belgaum in about the month of December for fifteen days every year. Kallolli 11 kms.from Gokak is called Kallole in a Ratta inscription. The place has the famous temple of Kallolappa (Maruti) which is mainly of the Vodda community. Other temples of the place are, the Ramalinge shwara, Kalmeshwara, Yellamma, Dyamavva, Durgavva, Beerappa, Siddharudha and the Sadashiva. The huge Kallolappa temple is an ordinary structure and in front of which in an enclosure is a queer status of Katamuttappa, standing with folded hands. There is also the head of a Jinabimba, in a shrine near the temple. The Ramalingeshwara temple in later Chalukyan style has a garbhagriha, an ardhamantapa, a navaranga and a mukhamantapa.

Lakshmi Jatra: It is held at Kundargi. Kundargi 32 kms.from Gokak located on the bank of the Markandeya river is a place of considerable antiquity. The place has temples dedicated to Lakshmi, Basavanna, Bharamappa, Hanumanta and Mallikarjuna. It is locally described that the capital of the deepasthambha (about 10 metres in height) facing the Lakshmi (Kunduravva) temple canoscillate.

Mahalingeshwar Jatra: It is held at Gokak falls near Belgaum around the month of February every year and is attended by 20,000 persons. Gokak Falls are six kms. from Gokak. Located right on the main road, is a celebrated tourist centre in the district.

Mallikarjuna Jatra: It is held at Yogikolla near Belgaum in the month of Shravana (July-August) every year. Yogikolla, also Googikolla, 6 kms. from Gokak is an enchanting spot and religious centre. The place name is derived from googi (owl) and kolla (valley) which is in-between the horse-shoe shaped rocky hill ranges. In the middle of the hill is a cave-opening and one has to ascend 800 to 900 steps to reach this spot where beneath a huge rock roofing is the Mallikarjuna Linga and the image of Boramma (Bharamaramba) is seated on a Nandi. Beneath this cave is the hidden place of origin of a stream which comes out from an outlet where a Nandi's face is fixed and it falls into a rocky base from a height of just eight metres. Viewing from this mid-cave one can witness the aerial view of the deep valley amidst green as well as rocky surroundings where the river Markandeya flows. Annual jatra of Mallikarjuna is held on the last Monday of Shravana 20,000 people assemble.

Villages: 131 **Inhabited:** 131 **Uninhabited:** 0

Ranking	District	State	National
Area	4	36	150
Population	3	3	8
Sex Ratio	2	79	2260
Child Sex Ratio	4	141	4026
Literacy Rate	10	141	4402
Density	7	110	3839
Work Participation Rate	6	34	2609

Gram Panchayats:

Mallapur (P.G.), Pamaladinni, Badigwad, Duradundi, Rajapur, Tukkanatti, Naganur, Shivapur, Hallur, Munyal, Dharmatti, Masaguppi, Waderatti, Kallolli, Hunshyal (P.G.), Balobal, Nallanatti, Arabhavi, Shindikurbet, Dhupadal, Nandagaon, Konnur (Rural) , Lolasur, Melavanki, Udagatti, Talakatnal, Sunadholi, Hunshyal (P.Y.), Dhavaleshwar, Avaradi, Kuligod, Yadwad, Kalliguddi, Koujalgi, Gosabal, Betageri, Mamadapur, Maladinni, Kolavi, Tavag, Benachinamardi, Kundargi, Akkatangerahal, Ankalgi, Gujanal, Suladhal, Madawal, Khanagaon, Shiltibhavi, Makkalageri, Herenandi.

Amenities:

Education: Primary School in 131 villages, Middle school in 111 villages, Matriculation or Secondary School in 38 villages, namely Tukkanatti, Naganur, Gurlapur, Hallur, Khanatti, Dharmatti, Kallolli, Duradundi, Mallapur (P.G.), Nandagaon, Shivapur, Molmanatti, Dhupadal, Shindikurbet, Arabhavi, Balobal, Hunshyal (P.G.), Waderatti, Masaguppi, Maladinni, Mamadapur, Kolavi, Tavag, Benachinamardi, Shigiholi, Kundargi, Akkatangerahal, Madawal, Khanagaon, Ankalgi, Shiltibhavi, Avaradi, Yadwad, Kuligod, Sunadholi, Melavanki, Betageri, Koujalgi.

Higher Secondary or Pre University Courses or Intermediate or Junior College in 8 villages of the CD Block,, namely Naganur, Kallolli, Konnur (Rural), Balobal, Waderatti, Urabinahatti, Ankalgi, Yadwad.

College in 6 villages, Adult Literacy Center in 2 villages., Colleges are in villages, namely Tukkanatti, Kallolli, Mallapur (P.G.), Arabhavi, Mamadapur, Shiltibhavi.

Medical: Hospital in 1 village, Dispensary in 5 villages, Health Center in 16 villages, Sub Center in 42 villages, Maternity and Child Welfare Center in 2 villages, Community health workers in 1 village.

The Villages having Hospital or Dispensary or Health Center are Hallur, Dhupadal, Mamadapur, Makkalageri, Koujalgi.

Drinking Water: Tap water in 82 villages, Tank water in 24 villages, Well water in 28 villages, Tubewell in 58 villages and more than one source in 114 villages.

Bank: Banking facility in 19 villages, namely, Naganur, Gurlapur, Hallur, Kallolli, Mallapur (P.G.) Dhupadal, Shindikurbet, Arabhavi, Mamadapur, Tavag Khanagaon, Ankalgi, Nabapur, Yadwad, Kuligod Sunadholi, Betageri, Kaparatti, Koujalgi.

Credit Society in 57 villages Agricultural Credit Society in 52 Non-Agricultural Credit Society in 8 villages.

Others: Power supply in 131 villages, Cinema hall in 6 villages sport club in 1 village, Stadium or Auditorium or Community Hall in 0 village, Post Office in 69 villages.

There are 126 villages having bus facilities.

Villages with most of facilities: Naganur

Gurlapur, Hallur, Kallolli, Mallapur (P.G.) Dhupadal, Shindikurbet, Mamadapur, Tavag, Khanagaon Ankalgi, Yadwad, Kuligod, Betageri, Koujalgi.

Villages without Amenities (Education): None..

Scheduled Castes: Out of the total population of 401006 persons, 38116 persons (9.51%) belong to Scheduled Castes.

The villages having less than 10% SC population are Dandapur, Tukkanatti, Mudalgi (Rural), Gurlapur Dharmatti, Gujanatti, Rajapur, Duradundi, Ganeshwadi Pamaladinni, Molmanatti, Lolasur, Basaligundi Nallanatti, Sanganakeri, Hanamapur, Hunshyal (P.G.) Fulagaddi, Masaguppi, Godachinamalaki, Shingalapur Gokak (Rural), Maladinni, Upparatti, Maradishivapur Mamadapur, Ajjanakatti, Benachinamaradi, Kolavi Tavag, Benachinamardi, Urabinahatti, Shigiholi Gaddiholi, Kundargi, Dhasanatti, Musalamari Mallapur. S.A., Dum Urabinahatti, Akkatangerahal Madawal, Iranattti, Telaginahatti, Kaitanal Ginimar Hosur, Hanamapur, Panchanaikanatti Makkalageri, Pudakalkatti, Midakanatti, Rajanakatti Arabhavi-Dhavalatti, Ankalgi, Lagameshwar Yaddalgudd, Budihal, Suladhal, Panjanatti Kesappanatti, Nabapur, Devagoudanahatti, Shiltibhavi Hirehatti, Jamanal, Venkatapur, Gulaganjikoppa Kamankatti, Timmapur, Bairanatti, Sunadholi Lakshmeshwar, Shiddapurahatti, Tigadi, Talakatnal Hadiginal, Kalarkoppa, Melavanki, Adibatti, Tapashi Betageri, Kemmankol, Kaparatti, Bilakundi, Mannikeri.

The village having more than 50% SC population is None.

Sex ratio of Scheduled Caste population is 499.

Scheduled Castes Literates and Illiterates by Sex:

	Persons	Males	Females
Literate	14,177	9,228	4,949
Illiterate	23,939	9,873	14,066
Literacy rate	45.1	58.9	31.4
Graduate	409	360	49

Scheduled Castes (Dominant):

Bhambi etc., Korama, Samagara, Madiga, Bhovi

For their cultural identity please see Appendix-I

Villages without Scheduled Castes: There are 12 villages without any scheduled caste population.

Scheduled Tribes: Out of the total population of 401006 persons, 40012 persons (9.98%) belong to Scheduled Tribes.

The villages having less than 10% ST population are Dandapur, Tukkanatti, Naganur, Mudalgi (Rural) Gurlapur, Hallur, Shivapur, Khanatti, Munyal Kamaladinni, Rangapur, Dharmatti, Patagundi Gujanatti, Jokanatti, Kallolli, Rajapur, Duradundi Ganeshwadi, Badigwad, Pamaladinni, Mallapur (P.G.) Khanapur, Mutnal, Nandagaon, Shivapur, Dhupadal Shindikurbet, Arabhavi, Lolasur, Basaligundi Nallanatti, Sanganakeri, Hanamapur, Balobal Beerangaddi, Hunshyal (P.G.), Masaguppi, Maladinni Upparatti, Maradishivapur, Mamadapur Benachinamaradi, Kolavi, Dum Urabinahatti, Hulikatti Hanamapur, Chikkanandi, Makkalageri, Nabapur Devagoudanahatti, Hunshyal (P.Y.), Bisanakoppa Dhavaleshwar, Aralimatti, Avaradi, Hale Yaragudri Venkatapur, Yaragudri, Gulaganjikoppa, Kamankatti Kopadatti, Yadwad, Timmapur, Kuligod, Bairanatti Sunadholi, Lakshmeshwar, Honakuppi, Shiddapurahatti Tigadi, Hadiginal, Kalarkoppa, Melavanki, Chigadolli Adibatti, Betageri, Bilakundi, Gosabal, Bagarnal Mannikeri, Koujalgi, Radderatti, Kalliguddi.

The villages having more than 50% ST population are Konnur (Rural), Gaddiholi, Dhasanatti, Kaitanal Ginimar Hosur, Pudakalkatti, Khanagaon, Rajanakatti Arabhavi-Dhavalatti, Lagameshwar, Gujanal Yaddalgudd, Panjanatti, Kesappanatti, Jamanal.

Sex ratio of Scheduled tribe population is 498.

Scheduled Tribes Literates and Illiterates by Sex:

	Persons	Males	Females
Literate	13,988	9,636	4,352
Illiterate	26,024	10,441	15,583
Literacy rate	42.3	58.2	26.3
Graduate	202	177	25

Scheduled Tribes (Dominant):

Naikda etc., Koli Dhor etc., Iruliga, Kathodi etc. Generic Tribes etc.

For their cultural identity please see Appendix-II

Villages without Scheduled Tribes: There are 25 villages without any scheduled tribe population.

Literates and Illiterates by Sex (Total Population):

	Persons	Males	Females
Literate	169,400	108,795	60,605
Illiterate	231,606	94,196	137,410
Literacy rate	51	65	37
Graduate	5,211	4,445	766

Agriculture: ***Distribution of villages according to land use:*** Out of 131 villages, Total area (in hectare) is 147336, out of that 78.19 percent is cultivable and 40.87 percent of the cultivable area is irrigated.

Sources of Irrigation (Hectares): Government Canal 26994.82, Private Canal 476.8, Well without Electricity 798.74, Well with Electricity 6719.69, Tubewell without Electricity 109.33, Tubewell with Electricity 5214.66, Tank 971.66, River 4991.13, Lake 0, Waterfall 150.21, Others 658.02.

Villages with population of 5000 to 9999:

Tukkanatti, Hallur, Rajapur, Duradundi, Pamaladinni

Dhupadal, Arabhavi, Hunshyal (P.G.), Waderatti Mamadapur, Benachinamaradi, Tavag, Ankalgi, Yadwad Kuligod, Melavanki, Koujalgi.

Villages with population of 10000 and above:
Naganur, Kallolli, Mallapur (P.G.), Shindikurbet.

Distribution of Workers:

	Persons	Males	Females	WPR
Cultivators	83,701	57,790	25,911	44.95
Agricultural Labour	70,360	27,307	43,053	37.79
Household Industry	5,764	3,331	2,433	3.1
Other Workers	26,378	22,017	4,361	14.17
Main Workers	150,051	103,620	46,431	80.58
Marginal Workers	36,152	6,825	29,327	19.42
Total Workers	186,203	110,445	75,758	

Religion: Major Religious Communities:

	Persons	Males	Females	Sex Ratio
Hindu (91.32%)	366,192	185,392	180,800	975
Muslim (7.01%)	28,099	14,253	13,846	971
Christian (0.2%)	812	295	517	1,753
Sikh (0%)	13	8	5	625
Buddhists (0%)	19	11	8	727
Jain (1.2%)	4,819	2,494	2,325	932

Agewise Data:

	Persons	Males	Females	Sex Ratio
All ages	401,006	202,991	198,015	975
0-14	151,320	77,934	73,386	942
15-44	177,579	90,298	87,281	967
45-79	68,781	33,281	35,500	1067
80+	3,071	1,340	1,731	1292
Age not stated	255	138	117	848

Languages (Dominant):
Kannada, Urdu, Marathi, Telugu, Hindi

Disabled Population:

	Persons	Males	Females	%
Total Disabled	6,627	3,784	2,843	
In Seeing	1,889	960	929	28.5
In Speech	693	385	308	10.46
In Hearing	552	272	280	8.33
In Movement	2,877	1,844	1,033	43.41
Mentally	616	323	293	9.3

GUBBI

Gubbi C.D. Block lies in the central south part of Tumkur district. It is a part of Gubbi taluka. The Block is located at a distance of 18 kms. from district headquarters (Tumkur). There are 346 villages in the block with the total population of 239,342 persons. Area of the C.D. Block is 1216.63 sq. kms. It is bounded by taluk Sira on north, taluks Turuvekere and Kunigal on south, taluk Tumkur on east, taluks Chiknayakanhalli, Tiptur and Turuvekere on west.

Communications:

Roadways : N.H.-206: Direction- Tiptur to Timkur, Nearest Villages- Harenahalli, Ankapura, Sagaranahalli, Kundaranahalli, Sopanahalli, Thimmalpalya A, Yellapura, Kanchiganahalli, Doddaguni, Hindiganahalli, Bonehallada Kaval, Bidarehalla Kaval, Babiganahalli, Karchalli, Nittur, Nittur Amanikere, Bagur, Mathighatta , Benchagere, Mukanahallipatna, Singonahalli, Mudigere, Mukanahallipatna Amanikere, Kallipalya, Gubbi (Rural), Herur.

Railway Station: Villags- Pura.

River: Shimsaha Nadi- Nearest Villages- Mudigere, Mukanahallipatna Amanikere, Kallipalya Adagoor, Dhulanahalli, Prabhuvanahalli, Halegubbi, Gubbiamanikere, Madenahalli, Kadaba, Belavatha, Ambarapura, Gulenahalli, Honnasettyhalli, Yadavanahalli, Varahasandra, Benkana Gondi, Vadavana, Ghatta, Melekallahalli, Manchihalli, Pendaranahalli, Bittagondanahalli, Kadabagadde Kaval, Belur, K.Kallahalli, Kallur, Chamanahalli, Bochihalli, Bilinandi, Jannenahalli.

Annual Rainfall: Normal Rianfall 739.2 mm.

Ground Water: Availability of the Ground Water in the Basin is 10732.49 H.A.M. and the utilization is 9504.56 H.A.M. It belongs to Over Expolited category. Depth to water level 5 to 20 meter below the ground. Most of the wells go down in summer months, according to the Ground Water Estimation Committee.

Soils: Red Sandy Soil.

Natural Division : It falls partly in Tumkur-Kunigal Plateau, Tiptur-Turuvekere Plateau and Chiknayakanahalli -Sira Scrubby Upland of the Southern Karnataka Plateau.

Administration:

Division: Bangalore. Parliamentary Constituency: 19 Tumkur. District: Tumkur. Taluka: Gubbi. Assembly Constituency: 130 Turuvekere, 135 Gubbi. Gram Panchayat: 33.

Regional Area Development Boards: The Bailu Seeme Area Development Board.

Fairs and Festivals: Channabasaveshwaraswami Jatra: It is held at Gubbi about February-March for seven days. Gubbi is situated about 20 kilometers west of Tumkur town, on the Bangalore-Poona railway line and the Bangalore-Shimoga road. It is said to have been founded over 400 years ago by the Gauda of Hosahalli, 3.5 kms distant, and was formerly called 'Amaragondapura'. He claimed to be a descendant of Honnappa Gauda, a hereditary chief of the Nonabas who lived about 700 years ago and owned an area yielding a revenue of 3,000 pagodas. The family first made a tributary by the Mysore Rajas, to whom it paid 500 pagodas a year. Haidar increased the tribute to 2,500 leaving them little better than renters and Tipu dispossessed them altogether.

Villages: 346 **Inhabited:** 328 **Uninhabited:** 18

Ranking	District	State	National

Area	3	59	272
Population	3	48	294
Sex Ratio	5	72	2064
Child Sex Ratio	6	66	2622
Literacy Rate	5	47	1715
Density	6	40	4770
Work Participation Rate	7	80	1289

Gram Panchayats:
Shivapura, Hagalavadi, Manchaladore, Ankasandra, Nallur, Irakasandra, Chelur, Hosakere, Alalaghatta, Kondli, Doddaguni, Thyagatur, Muganayakanakote, Bidaré, Mukanahallipatna, Ammanaghatta, Nittur, Marasettyhalli, Belavatha, Herur, Adagoor, Hosahalli.G, Koppa, Kadaba, Peddanahalli, Kallur, Kunnala, Hindisgere, Chandrashekarapura, Idagoor, Mavinahalli, Changavi, Kodigehalli.

Amenities:

Education: Primary School in 265 villages, Middle school in 159 villages, Matriculation or Secondary School in 46 villages, namely Manchaladore, Hagalavadi, Hosakere, Alalaghatta, Bettadahalli, Devarahalli, Ankasandra, Ranganahalli, Madenahalli, Chelur, Kodiyala, Nandihalli C., Bidare, Mannemariamruth Mahalkaval, Haradagere, Somalapura, Muganayakanakote, Adalagere, Thyagatur, N.Ramapura, Kundaranahalli, Doddaguni, Neralekere, Nittur, Thippur, Ammanaghatta, Lakkenahalli, Mukanahallipatna, Kallipalya, Adagoor, Prabhuvanahalli, Herur, Hodalur, Hosahalli.G, Nagasandra, Kodigehalli, Athikatte, Kadaba, Koppa, Mathighatta, Benkana Gondi, Melekallahalli, Kallur, Hindisgere, Chandrashekarapura, Idagoor.

Higher Secondary or Pre University Courses or Intermediate or Junior College in 12 villages of the CD Block,, namely Manchaladore, Hagalavadi, Alalaghatta, Bettadahalli, Chelur, Nandihalli C., Bidare, Kondli, Mavinahalli, Nittur, Kadaba, Chandrashekarapura.

College in 2 villages, Adult Literacy Center in 1 village., Colleges are in villages, namely Adalagere, Nittur.

Medical: Hospital in 1 village, Dispensary in 10 villages, Health Center in 9 villages, Sub Center in 34 villages, Maternity and Child Welfare Center in 2 villages, Community health workers in 1 village.

The Villages having Hospital or Dispensary or Health Center are Manchaladore, Alalaghatta, Bettadahalli, Bidare, Haradagere, Muganayakanakote, Adalagere, Doddaguni, B.Kodihalli, Mavinahalli.

Drinking Water: Tap water in 157 villages, Tank water in 2 villages, Well water in 8 villages, Tubewell in 15 villages and more than one source in 167 villages.

Bank: Banking facility in 16 villages, namely, Manchaladore, Hosakere, Ankasandra, Thogarigunte Chelur, Kachenahalli, Bidare, Gowripura Muganayakanakote, Halasina Nagenahalli, Doddaguni Nittur, Kadaba, Kallur, Mavinahalli Chandrashekarapura.

Credit Society in 46 villages Agricultural Credit Society in 31 Non-Agricultural Credit Society in 32 villages.

Others: Power supply in 328 villages, Cinema hall in 8 villages sport club in 328 villages, Stadium or Auditorium or Communi Hall in 328 villages, Post Office in 73 villages.

There are 204 villages having bus facilities.

Villages with most of facilities: Manchaladore Ankasandra, Kachenahalli, Bidare, Muganayakanakote Doddaguni, Nittur, Kadaba, Kallur, Mavinahalli Chandrashekarapura.

Villages without amenities (Education): Anehalli, Malenahalli, Harthi, Rangapura.M., Gedlahalli.G, Mathikere, Rangapura.G., Chittappanahalli, Mallasandra Katte, Marehalladakaval, Pura, Karigondanahalli, Arehalli, Yere Kaval, Mudlahalli, Jakkanahalli, Kempanahalli, Gadiyankanahalli, Kasimata, Manemarinagudi Kaval, Bidare Amanikere, Bidare Raja Kaval, Karadikallu, Echala Kaval, Kallanahalli, Muddanahalli, Kalasanahalli, Gyara Halli, M.Hosahalli, Banniganahalli, Jogihalli, Thyagatur Amanikere, Ankapura, Rajanapanche, Sigehalli, Babiganahalli, Ammanahalli, Nittur Amanikere, Harnahalli, Bisalahalli, Badakana Palya, Mukanahallipatna Amanikere, Byadagere, Ingalda Kaval, Dodderi, Basthikatte Kaval, Kodimallenahalli, Haragaladevgudda Kaval, B.Kodihalli, K.Ramapura, Thogrighatta, Kattiginahalli, Kadaba Amanikere, Kenchaviranahalli, Shankaradevihalli, Hanumanthapura, Mavinahalli Amanikere, Amanikere, Chikkayadiyur, Chandrasekharapura Bagayat, Beeramaranahalli, Abbanakuppe..

Scheduled Castes: Out of the total population of 239608 persons, 38780 persons (16.18%) belong to Scheduled Castes. The villages having less than 10% SC population are Anehalli, Shivarampura, Bodathimmanahalli Malenahalli, Jogihalli, Kuntaramanahalli, Harthi Rangapura.M., Nallur, Gedlahalli.G, Kurihalli Guddenahalli, Mathikere, Rangapura.G., Obalapura Chittappanahalli, Kodihalli, Mallasandra Katte Marehalladakaval, Yakkalakatte, Appannanahalli Unganala, Karigondanahalli, Shivanehalli Thevadihalli, Thimmalapura, Yere Kaval, Mudlahalli Jakkanahalli, Bettadahalli, D0Ddahedegehalli Thogarigunte, Revanalu, Kurubarahalli, Jogihalli

Kempanahalli, Gadiyankanahalli, Chelur Amanikere Malimachana Kunte, Nallur, Anupanakunte Sorekayipente, Patravathanahalli, Thonachanahalli Byadanakatte, Yenne Kattee, Seegenahalli Kadabettanahalli, Muginahunase, Kasimata, Nimbekatte Chindigere, Kaggere, Bidare Amanikere, Jainarahalli Bidare Raja Kaval, Guddadahallii, Boragondanahalli Guddada Obalapura, Echala Kaval, Kallanahalli Bhogasandra, Muddanahalli, Bandanahalli, Sagasandra Kalasanahalli, M.Hosahalli, Mathikere, Basavapatna Mallenahalli, Somalapura, Sankapura, Jogihalli Mudla Palya, Mavinahalli, Harenahalli, N.Hosahalli Virupakshipura, Samudranakote, Muddapura, Thyagatur Muganayakanakote Amanikere, Thyagatur Amanikere Ankapura, Sagaranahalli, Rajanapanche, Sopanahalli Yellapura, Doddaguni, Hindiganahalli, Dindigadahalli Sigehalli, Thaggihalli, Babiganahalli, Ammanahalli Bandihalli, Nittur Amanikere, Parasanahalli Kenchanahalli, Gollahalli, Thippur, Varadenahalli Bisalahalli, Badakana Palya Mukanahallipatna Amanikere, Dhulanahalli Chikkonahalli, Gubbiamanikere, Dodderi, Gopalapura Surigenahalli, Voddarahalli, Kalenahalli, B.Ramapura Haragaladevgudda Kaval, Peramasandra Janakadevanahalli, Gangasnadra, B.Kodihalli Kadasettyhalli, K.Ramapura, Ambarapura, Gulenahalli Yadavanahalli, Chakenahalli, Lingammanahalli Kunnala, Hallenahalli, Kadaba Amanikere Peddanahalli, Kunaghatta, Varahasandra Benkana Gondi, V.Kodihalli, Kenchaviranahalli Harivesandra .K, Kamba Sandra, Belur, K.Kallahalli Chamanahalli, Bochihalli, Bilinandi, Bukkasagara Changavi Kaval, Shankaradevihalli, Nettikere Mavinahalli, Mavinahalli Amanikere, Ungra, Hulekere Hindisgere, Amanikere, Hurulagere Chandrasekharapura Bagayat, Horakere, Kenchanahalli Mathikere, Adakekere, Idagoor, Beeramaranahalli Bellahalli, Cheelanahalli, Abbanakuppe.

The villages having more than 50% SC population are Pura, Sirivallehalli, Madapura, Banniganahalli Musakondli, Kodinagenahalli, Bidarehalla Kaval Harnahalli, Bilekal Palya, Harivesandra Bikkegudda Kaval, Byadagere.

Sex ratio of Scheduled Caste population is 493.

Scheduled Castes Literates and Illiterates by Sex:

	Persons	Males	Females
Literate	19,251	11,371	7,880
Illiterate	19,529	8,288	11,241
Literacy rate	56.8	66.3	47.0
Graduate	436	394	42

Scheduled Castes (Dominant):

Adi Karnataka, Madiga, Adi Dravida, Bhovi Chalavadi etc.

For their cultural identity please see Appendix-I

Villages without Scheduled Castes: There are 117 villages without any scheduled caste population.

Scheduled Tribes: Out of the total population of 239608 persons, 17362 persons (7.25%) belong to Scheduled Tribes.

The villages having less than 10% ST population are Anehalli, Malenahalli, Jogihalli, Yarabahalli Kuntaramanahalli, Harthi, Rangapura.M., Nallur, Mata Kurihalli, Guddenahalli, Hagalavadi, Mathikere Rangapura.G., Madalapura, Obalapura, Shivapura Chittappanahalli, Kodihalli, Mallasandra Katte Marehalladakaval, Appannanahalli, Pura Karigondanahalli, Arehalli, Shivanehalli Thevadihalli, Thimmalapura, Yere Kaval, Alalaghatta Mudlahalli, Jakkanahalli, Benehalli, Bettadahalli Talekoppa, D0Ddahedegehalli, Devarahalli Ranganahalli, Anthapura, Maranahalli, Sanabanahalli Kempanahalli, Pinnenahalli, Sangenahalli Gadiyankanahalli, Chelur Amanikere Malimachana Kunte, Nallur, Byadanakatte Yenne Kattee, Chelur, Kachenahalli, Seegenahalli Kadabettanahalli, Muginahunase, Kodiyala, Kasimata Nimbekatte, Harivesandra, Irakasandra, Nandihalli C. Chindigere, Kaggere, Bidare Amanikere, Bidare Gowripura, Bidare Raja Kaval, Konanakallu Guddadahallii, Boragondanahalli, Madapura Karadikallu, Echala Kaval, Kallanahalli, Haradagere Bhogasandra, Muddanahalli, Kalasanahalli Gyara Halli, M.Hosahalli, Mathikere, Idakanahalli Basavapatna, Mallenahalli, Somalapura, Sankapura Banniganahalli, Bommarasanahalli, Mudla Palya Kondli, Mavinahalli, Musakondli, Yemmedoddi Honnenahalli, Badavana Palya, Handanahalli Adalagere, Muddapura, Thyagatur Muganayakanakote Amanikere, Halasina Nagenahalli Madanaghatta, Hesarahalli, N.Ramapura Kodinagenahalli, Thyagatur Amanikere, Bommenahalli Ankapura, Sagaranahalli, Kundaranahalli Kallenahalli, Rajanapanche, Sopanahalli Thimmalpalya.A, Yellapura, Hindiganahalli Neralekere, Dindigadahalli, Sigehalli Bidarehalla Kaval, Babiganahalli, Bandihalli Nittur Amanikere, Benchagere, Harnahalli, Pura Parasanahalli, Nandihalli, Gollahalli, Thippur Ammanaghatta, Varadenahalli, Lakkenahalli Bychenahalli, Chowkenahalli, Bisalahalli Doddanetagunte, Badakana Palya, Bilekal Palya

Chikkanetagunte, Honnavalli, Harivesandra, Rayavara Singonahalli, Mudigere, Mukanahallipatna Amanikere Kallipalya, Dhulanahalli, Halegubbi, Chikkonahalli Kittadakuppe, Hodalur, Gubbiamanikere, Thorehalli Madenahalli, Ingalda Kaval, Kattigenahalli Hosahalli.G, Dodderi, Basthikatte Kaval Bikkegudda Kaval, Muddanahalli, Gopalapura Surigenahalli, Surigenahalli Kaval, Voddarahalli Nagasandra, Kodigehalli, Kalenahalli, Donnere Kodimallenahalli, Peramasandra, Badenahalli Gangasnadra, Athikatte, Bennur, B.Kodihalli Karigondanahalli, Kadasettyhalli, K.Ramapura, Kadaba Adagondanahalli, Thogrighatta, Belavatha, Ambarapura Gulenahalli, Honnasettyhalli, Kattiginahalli, Koppa Konanakere, Yadavanahalli, Dasarakallahalli Byalahalli, Byadaramallenahalli, Konemadenahalli Jeeganahalli, Chakenahalli, Lingammanahalli, Kunnala Hallenahalli, Yalachihalli, Byadagere Kadaba Amanikere, Peddanahalli, Mathighatta Kunaghatta, Varahasandra, Benkana Gondi Vadavana Ghatta, Melekallahalli, Manchihalli Pendaranahalli, Bittagondanahalli, V.Kodihalli Kenchaviranahalli, Harivesandra .K, Kamba Sandra Belur, K.Kallahalli, Kallur, Chamanahalli, Bilinandi Ankalakoppa, Hindisgere Kaval, Changavi Kaval Changavi, Dollenahalli, Averahalli Shankaradevihalli, Manikuppe, Nettikere Hanumanthapura, Mavinahalli, Mavinahalli Amanikere Ungra, Hulekere, Hindisgere, Chandrashekarapura Padugudi, Amanikere, Chikkayadiyur, Kodagihalli.C Chandrasekharapura Bagayat, Horakere, Kenchanahalli Mathikere, Adakekere, Idagoor, Beeramaranahalli Bellahalli, Borappanapalya, Cheelanahalli Naranahalli, Abbanakuppe.

The villages having more than 50% ST population are Bodathimmanahalli, Unganala, Thogarigunte, Revanalu Kallugudi, Anupanakunte, Katanahalli, Jalaguni Patravathanahalli, Sagasandra, Kanchiganahalli Haragaladevgudda Kaval, Aremaranahalli.

Sex ratio of Scheduled tribe population is 494.

Scheduled Tribes Literates and Illiterates by Sex:

	Persons	Males	Females
Literate	9,325	5,423	3,902
Illiterate	8,037	3,363	4,674
Literacy rate	60.9	70.1	51.4
Graduate	166	135	31

Scheduled Tribes (Dominant):

Naikda etc., Generic Tribes etc., Soligaru, Yerava Hakkipikki

For their cultural identity please see Appendix-II

Villages without Scheduled Tribes: There are 179 villages without any scheduled tribe population.

Literates and Illiterates by Sex (Total Population):

	Persons	Males	Females
Literate	140,606	81,059	59,547
Illiterate	99,002	39,988	59,014
Literacy rate	66	76	57
Graduate	4,331	3,571	760

Agriculture: ***Distribution of villages according to land use:*** Out of 346 villages, Total area (in hectare) is 121663, out of that 59.49 percent is cultivable and 25.48 percent of the cultivable area is irrigated.

Sources of Irrigation (Hectares): Government Canal 521.66, Private Canal 0, Well without Electricity 16.06, Well with Electricity 834.21, Tubewell without Electricity 135.49, Tubewell with Electricity 12463.52, Tank 4119.19, River 33.78, Lake 11.13, Waterfall 0, Others 299.57.

Villages with population of 5000 to 9999:
Kallur.

Villages with population of 10000 and above: None

Distribution of Workers:

	Persons	Males	Females	WPR
Cultivators	76,408	50,608	25,800	58.59
Agricultural Labour	34,061	11,350	22,711	26.12
Household Industry	5,212	2,350	2,862	4
Other Workers	14,737	11,481	3,256	11.3
Main Workers	99,611	69,252	30,359	76.38
Marginal Workers	30,807	6,537	24,270	23.62
Total Workers	130,418	75,789	54,629	

Religion: Major Religious Communities:

	Persons	Males	Females	Sex Ratio
Hindu (94.1%)	225,482	113,904	111,578	980
Muslim (5.41%)	12,958	6,536	6,422	983
Christian (0.03%)	71	37	34	919
Sikh (0%)	1	1	-	-
Buddhists (0%)	1	1	-	-
Jain (0.17%)	411	202	209	1,035

Agewise Data:

	Persons	Males	Females	Sex Ratio
All ages	239,608	121,047	118,561	979
0-14	69,318	35,029	34,289	979
15-44	114,793	57,820	56,973	985
45-79	52,637	26,782	25,855	965
80+	2,668	1,301	1,367	1051
Age not stated	192	115	77	670

Languages (Dominant):
Kannada, Urdu, Marathi, Telugu, Hindi

Disabled Population:

	Persons	Males	Females	%
Total Disabled	4,018	2,251	1,767	

In Seeing	1,691	905	786	42.09
In Speech	482	266	216	12
In Hearing	194	93	101	4.83
In Movement	1,252	791	461	31.16
Mentally	399	196	203	9.93

GUDIBANDA

Gudibanda C.D. Block lies in the northern part of Kolar district. It is a part of Gudibanda taluka. The Block is located at a distance of 100 kms. from district headq uarters (Kolar). There are 105 villages in the block with the total population of 40,146 persons. Area of the C.D. Block is 226.51 sq. kms. It is bounded by taluk Bagepalli on north, taluk Chik Ballapur on south, taluk Sidlaghatta and Bagepalli on east, and taluk Gauribidanur on west. It has common boundary with the state of Andhra Pradesh on north.

Communications:

Roadways : N.H.-7: Direction- Bangalore to Ananthpur, Nearest Villages- Chendur, Kalkipapanadinne, Bhogenahalli, Doddakurubarahalli, Yerralakkenahalli, Kodiganahalli, Ramaganahalli, Doddanancherlu, Singanahalli, Uppakuntah alli, Kurubarahosa Halli, Ragimakalahalli, Bandarlahalli, Gopuradahalli, Lakshmisagara, Varlakonda.

River: Kushavari Nadi- Nearest Villages- Pulasanivoddu, Nilugumba, Kadenahalli Dinne, Nimmalahalli, Kadehalli, Hampasandra, Lakshmanapura, Benneparthi. Chitravati Nadi- Nearest Villages- Bhogenahalli, Doddakurubarahalli, Thirumani, Doddanancherlu, Thummenahalli, Katenahalli, Kadirisettihalli, Chikkanancherlu.

Annual Rainfall: Normal Rianfall 776.48 mm.

Ground Water: Availability of the Ground Water in the Basin is (Information not avablable) H.A.M. and the utilization is (Information not avablable) H.A.M. It belongs to (Information not avablable) category. Depth to water level 5 to 20 meter below the ground. Most of the wells go down in summer months, according to the Ground Water Estimation Committee.

Soils: Red Soils.

Natural Division : It falls in Sub-micro regions of Gudib anda-Bagepalli Highlands and Sidlaghatta-Sriniwaspur Uplands of the Southern Karnataka Plateau.

Administration:

Division: Bangalore. Parliamentary Constituency: 27. Bangalore (SC). District: Kolar. Taluka: Gudibanda. Assembly Constituency: 140 Bagepalli. Gram Panchayat: 7.

Regional Area Development Boards: The Bailu Seeme Area Development Board.

Border Villages: (State: Andhra Pradesh)- Bullasandra, Yellodu, Yerrahalli, Nilugumba, Kadenahalli Dinne.

Villages: 105 **Inhabited:** 85 **Uninhabited:** 20

Ranking	District	State	National
Area	11	175	3718
Population	11	174	5597
Sex Ratio	5	78	2145
Child Sex Ratio	5	37	1839
Literacy Rate	10	137	4260
Density	2	13	4883
Work Participation Rate	9	86	566

Gram Panchayats:

Yellodu, Hampasandra, Ullodu, Beechaganahalli, Thirumani, Varlakonda, Somenahalli.

Amenities:

Education: Primary School in 68 villages, Middle school in 31 villages, Matriculation or Secondary School in 4 villages, namely Yellodu, Hampasandra, Somenahalli, Varlakonda. Higher Secondary or Pre University Courses or Inter-mediate or Junior College in 0 village of the CD Block, College in 1 village, Adult Literacy Center in 2 villages., College is in village, namely Somenahalli.

Medical: Hospital in 0 village, Dispensary in 5 villages, Health Center in 1 village, Sub Center in 9 villages, Maternity and Child Welfare Center in 0 village, Community health workers in 0 village.
The Villages having Hospital or Dispensary or Health Center are Yellodu, Hampasandra, Chendur, Beechaganahalli, Somenahalli.

Drinking Water: Tap water in 67 villages, Tank water in 43 villages, Well water in 37 villages, Tubewell in 63 villages and more than one source in 73 villages.

Bank: Banking facility in 7 villages, namely, Chowtakuntahalli, Yellodu, Hampasandra, Kambalahalli Thirumani, Beechaganahalli, Somenahalli.
Credit Society in 8 villages Agricultural Credit Society in 8 Non-Agricultural Credit Society in 2 villages.

Others: Power supply in 80 villages, Cinema hall in 2 villages, sport club in 2 villages, Stadium or Auditorium or Community Hall in 0 village, Post Office in 10 villages.
There are 36 villages having bus facilities.

Villages with most of facilities: Hampasandra Thirumani, Beechaganahalli.

Villages without amenities (Education): Kadenahalli Dinne, Palaigarahalli, Kantharlahalli, Amani Byrasagara, Chadumanahalli, Somalapura, Chowtathimmanahalli, Gerumaradahalli, Myakalahalli, Pulavamakalahalli, Nallojanahalli, Kadirisettihalli, Chikkanancherlu, Singanahalli, Uppakuntahalli, Singanadinne, Giddappanahalli..

Scheduled Castes: Out of the total population of 43021 persons, 11200 persons (26.03%) belong to Scheduled Castes. The villages having less than 10% SC population are

Sanjeevarayanahalli, Adinarayanahalli
Palaigarahalli, Amani Byrasagara, Vabasandra
Gerumaradahalli, Aligadirenahalli, Hale Gudibanda
Bathalahalli, Nichanabandahalli, Chikkakurubarahalli
Nallojanahalli, Chikkanancherlu, Jambigemaradahalli
Pavajenahalli, Singanadinne, Iragareddihalli
Polampalli, Jangalahalli, Medimakalahalli.

The villages having more than 50% SC population are Yerrahalli, Kadenahalli Dinne, Benneparthi Kondareddihalli, Chadumanahalli, Somalapura Brahmanarahalli, Dhumakuntahalli, Thummenahalli Singanahalli, Uppakuntahalli, Giddappanahalli.

Sex ratio of Scheduled Caste population is 498.

Scheduled Castes Literates and Illiterates by Sex:

	Persons	Males	Females
Literate	3,881	2,439	1,442
Illiterate	7,319	3,186	4,133
Literacy rate	40.6	50.8	30.4
Graduate	58	57	1

Scheduled Castes (Dominant):

Adi Karnataka, Bhovi, Adi Dravida, Chalavadi etc. Madiga

For their cultural identity please see Appendix-I

Villages without Scheduled Castes: There are 30 villages without any scheduled caste population.

Scheduled Tribes: Out of the total population of 43021 persons, 6353 persons (14.77%) belong to Scheduled Tribes.

The villages having less than 10% ST population are Bullasandra, Yerrahalli, Nilugumba
Kadenahalli Dinne, Kadehalli, Sanjeevarayanahalli
Pasapalodu, Kondareddihalli, Kondavalahalli
Kataiahgarahalli, Kantharlahalli, Amani Byrasagara
Chadumanahalli, Somalapura, Machavalahalli
Chowtathimmanahalli, Aligadirenahalli
Brahmanarahalli, Hale Gudibanda, Bathalahalli
Myakalahal'i, Pulavamakalahalli, Yelakalarallahalli
Dhumakuntahalli, Doddakurubarahalli, Kambalahalli
Yerralakkenahalli, Kondavabanahalli
Chikkakurubarahalli, Nallojanahalli, Ramaganahalli
Thummenahalli, Katenahalli, Gummareddihalli
Kammadike, Kadirisettihalli, Chikkanancherlu
Puradahalli, Jambigemaradahalli, Singanahalli
Uppakuntahalli, Bandarlahalli, Pavajenahalli
Singanadinne, Giddappanahalli, Medimakalahalli
Lakshmisagara, Someswara, Geggilarallahalli
Thimmenahalli.

The villages having more than 50% ST population are Palaigarahalli, Nichanabandahalli, Chendur Jangalahalli.

Sex ratio of Scheduled tribe population is 489.

Scheduled Tribes Literates and Illiterates by Sex:

	Persons	Males	Females
Literate	2,430	1,543	887
Illiterate	3,923	1,701	2,222
Literacy rate	44.6	55.4	33.3
Graduate	36	34	2

Scheduled Tribes (Dominant):

Naikda etc., Soligaru, Pardhi etc., Hakkipikki Generic Tribes etc.

For their cultural identity please see Appendix-II

Villages without Scheduled Tribes: There are 43 villages without any scheduled tribe population.

Literates and Illiterates by Sex (Total Population):

	Persons	Males	Females
Literate	19,246	11,962	7,284
Illiterate	23,775	9,796	13,979
Literacy rate	52	64	40
Graduate	515	441	74

Agriculture: ***Distribution of villages according to land use:*** Out of 105 villages, Total area (in hectare) is 22651, out of that 60.54 percent is cultivable and 30.6 percent of the cultivable area is irrigated.

Sources of Irrigation (Hectares): Government Canal 143.53, Private Canal 10.02, Well without Electricity 85.32, Well with Electricity 446.9, Tubewell without Electricity 75.88, Tubewell with Electricity 1503.96, Tank 1890.19, River 27.9, Lake 0, Waterfall 0, Others 12.82.

Villages with population of 5000 to 9999: None

Villages with population of 10000 and above: None

Distribution of Workers:

	Persons	Males	Females	WPR
Cultivators	10,428	7,375	3,053	42.79
Agricultural Labour	10,917	3,676	7,241	44.79
Household Industry	294	193	101	1.21
Other Workers	2,734	1,928	806	11.22
Main Workers	17,971	11,611	6,360	73.73
Marginal Workers	6,402	1,561	4,841	26.27
Total Workers	24,373	13,172	11,201	

Religion: Major Religious Communities:

	Persons	Males	Females	Sex Ratio
Hindu (95.98%)	41,293	20,911	20,382	975
Muslim (3.94%)	1,694	828	866	1,046
Christian (0.02%)	10	6	4	667
Sikh (0.01%)	3	-	3	-
Buddhists (0%)	-	-	-	-
Jain (0%)	1	1	-	-

Agewise Data:

	Persons	Males	Females	Sex Ratio
All ages	43,021	21,758	21,263	977
0-14	13,537	6,990	6,547	937

15-44	19,831	9,828	10,003	1018
45-79	9,126	4,683	4,443	949
80+	480	227	253	1115
Age not stated	47	30	17	567

Languages (Dominant):
Telugu, Kannada, Urdu, Hindi, Marathi
Disabled Population:

	Persons	Males	Females	%
Total Disabled	870	488	382	
In Seeing	379	196	183	43.56
In Speech	88	47	41	10.11
In Hearing	47	25	22	5.4
In Movement	282	178	104	32.41
Mentally	74	42	32	8.51

GULBARGA

Gulbarga C.D. Block lies in the northern part of Gulbarga district. It is a part of Gulbarga taluka. The Block is located at a distance of (oo) kms. from district headquarters (Gulbarga). There are 140 villages in the block with the total population of 247,161 persons. Area of the C.D. Block is 1666.02 sq. kms. It is bounded by district Bidar on north, taluk Jevargi on south, taluks Chitapur and Chincholi on east, taluks Afzalpur, Aland and district Bidar on west.

Communications:
Roadways : S.H-10: Direction- Aland to Sedam, Nearest Villages- Srinivas Saradgi, Kalagnoor, Sannur, Pallapur, Shaikroza, Azadpur, Kusnoor, Naganhalli, Hatkunda, Pattan, Syed Chincholi,Taj, Sultanpur, Keribhosga, Sindagi, Savalgi (B). S.H-19: Direction-Shahpur to Homnabad, Nearest Villages- Dongeragaon,Kinnisadak, Bhimnal, Bachnal, Rajanhal, Kamalapur, Mahagaon,Navadgi (K), Navadgi (B), Kurikota, Ankalga, Sirgapur, Awrad (B), Tawargera, Kapnoor, Uplaon, Sitnoor, Nandikur, Sirnoor,Farhatabad, Siradgi (Bhatad), Balwad, Naddisinur, Ferozabad.S.H-22: Direction- Afzalpur to Gulbarga, Nearest Villages- Kollur,Hadgilharuti, Sirasgi. S.H-32: Direction- Mudbi to Sulepeth, Nearest Villages- Mahagaon, Holkunda, Tadkal, Kathalli, Kurikota,Nagoora.
Railway Station: Villages- Nandoor (K), Savalgi (B).
River: Bhima Nadi- Nearest Villages- Farhatabad, Hagargundagi,Holkunda, Tadkal, Kathalli, Kurikota, Maniyal, Belgumpa (K), Basavapattana, Aurad (K), Siradgi (Bhatad), Naddisinur, Herur (B),Ferozabad, Somnathahalli,Nadvinhalli.
Benithora Nadi- Nearest Villages- Mahagaon, Kurikota, Siradhone,Bhusangi, Kannura, Ankalga, Sirgapur, Tondkal, Yankanchi,Harkanchi, Kadbur, Nagoora, Harsoor
Reserved Forest: (Bachnal): Nearest Villages- Dongeragaon,Marguthi, Bhimnal,Bachnal, Dinshikurnur, Kalmud, Sonth.$Annual
Rainfall:$ Normal Rianfall 777 mm
.**Ground Water:** Availability of the Ground Water in the Basin is 10799 H.A.M. and the utilization is 2551 H.A.M. It belongs to Over Expoited category. Depth to water level 5 to 20 meter below the ground. Most of the wells down in summer months, according to the Ground Water Estimation Committee
.**Soils:** Deep Black, Medium Black Soil, Shallow Soil and Lateritic Soil.
Natural Division : It falls partly in the Aland-Chincholi Tract of Trappean Outcrops, Kagna Basin, Gurmatkal Scrub by Upland and Lower Bhima Valley of the North Karnataka Plateau.
Regional Area Development Boards: The Hyderabad - Karnataka Area Development Board.
Administration:
Division: Gulbarga. Parliamentary Constituency: 5 Gulbarga (SC). District: Gubarga.Taluka: Gulbarga. Assembly Constituency: 43 Gulbarga Rural (SC), 44 Gulbarga Dakshin. Gram Panchayat: 36.
Fairs: Syed Jalaluddin Chanda Khadri Urs: It is observed at Gogi near Gulbarga in the month of 10 Shaban (3). Gogi is about 10 kms. from Shahapur. It contains a big masjid and several tombs dating back to the Adil Shahi rule. Every year in the month of Shaban, an Urs takes place here when nearly five thousand pilgrims attend.
Villages: 140 **Inhabited:** 136 **Uninhabited:** 4

Ranking	District	State	National
Area	5	18	92
Population	5	43	264
Sex Ratio	8	118	2900
Child Sex Ratio	9	146	4157
Literacy Rate	3	150	4670
Density	9	133	5601
Work Participation Rate	6	134	3168

Gram Panchayats:
Dongeragaon, Kinnisadak, Sonth, Marguthi, Okali, Kamalapur, Kalmud, Jeevangi, Holkunda, Mahagaon, Bablad (T.K.), Kurikota, Nagoora, Harsoor, Awrad (B), Kumsi, Kalhangerga, Bhimanhalli, Bhopal Tegnur, Taj Sultanpur, Pattan, Savalgi (B), Srinivas Saradgi, Sannur, Kusnoor, Sirasgi , Melkunda (B), Kadni, Nandikur, Nandoor (K), Khandal, Farhatabad, Kiranagi, Kawalga (B), Herur (B), Ferozabad.
Amenities:
Education: Primary School in 133 villages, Middle school in 99 villages, Matriculation or Secondary School in 24 villages, namely Dongeragaon, Marguthi, Kamalapur, Kalmud, Sonth, Mahagaon, Kurikota, Nagoora, Kalhangerga, Awrad (B), Harsoor, Srinivas Saradgi, Kusnoor, Nandoor (K), Pattan, Taj Sultanpur, Savalgi (B),

Melkunda (B), Sirnoor, Khandal, Farhatabad, Hagargundagi, Herur (B), Kiranagi.
Higher Secondary or Pre University Courses or Intermediate or Junior College in 6 villages of the CD Block,, namely Marguthi, Kamalapur, Mahagaon, Harsoor, Jaferabad, Farhatabad.
College in 1 village, Adult Literacy Center in 29 villages., College is in village, namely Kamalapur.
Medical: Hospital in 3 villages, Dispensary in 13 villages, Health Center in 12 villages, Sub Center in 44 villages, Maternity and Child Welfare Center in 9 villages, Community health workers in 26 villages.
The Villages having Hospital or Dispensary or Health Center are Dongeragaon, Kamalapur, Mahagaon, Kalhangerga, Awrad (B), Srinivas Saradgi, Sannur, Nandikur, Nandoor (B), Savalgi (B), Farhatabad, Ferozabad, Kiranagi.
Drinking Water: Tap water in 88 villages, Tank water in 40 villages, Well water in 120 villages, Tubewell in 92 villages and more than one source in 130 villages.
Bank: Banking facility in 14 villages, namely, Kamalapur, Sonth, Mahagaon, Belkotta, Kurikota Kumsi, Harsoor, Srinivas Saradgi, Kusnoor, Pattan Savalgi (B), Farhatabad, Hagargundagi, Kiranagi.
Credit Society in 24 villages Agricultural Credit Society in 23 Non-Agricultural Credit Society in 2 villages.
Others: Power supply in 136 villages, Cinema hall in 1 village, sport club in 9 villages, Stadium or Auditorium or Community Hall in 136 villages, Post Office in 58 villages.
There are 113 villages having bus facilities.
Villages with most of facilities: Kamalapur, Sonth Mahagaon, Kurikota, Kumsi, Harsoor, Srinivas Saradgi Kusnoor, Pattan, Savalgi (B), Farhatabad Hagargundagi, Kiranagi.
Villages without amenities (Education):
Navadgi (K), Pallapur, Garoor (K)..
Scheduled Castes: Out of the total population of 245414 persons, 73669 persons (30.02%) belong to Scheduled Castes.
The villages having less than 10% SC population are Navadgi (K), Pallapur, Kapnoor, Kadnal, Kadni Sirasgi, Jogur, Siradgi (Bhatad), Ferozabad.
The villages having more than 50% SC population are Warnihal, Malsapur, Marmanchi, Bhimnal, Bachnal Rajanhal, Dinshikurnur, Kawanhalli, Kalmud Kinnisarposh, Keroor, Srinivas Saradgi, Kalagnoor Kusnoor, Panegaon, Nandoor (B), Machnal, Garoor (K).
Sex ratio of Scheduled Caste population is 487.

Scheduled Castes Literates and Illiterates by Sex:

	Persons	Males	Females
Literate	25,279	16,795	8,484
Illiterate	48,390	21,011	27,379
Literacy rate	42.3	54.7	29.2
Graduate	876	788	88

Scheduled Castes (Dominant):
Holaya etc., Banjara etc., Madiga, Bhovi Generic Castes etc.
For their cultural identity please see Appendix-I
Villages without Scheduled Castes: There are 6 villages without any scheduled caste population.
Scheduled Tribes: Out of the total population of 245414 persons, 5335 persons (2.17%) belong to Scheduled Tribes.
The villages having less than 10% ST population are Warnihal, Dongeragaon, Gobburwadi, Nilkod, Patwada Malsapur, Dhorjambga, Marmanchi, Marguthi, Bhimnal Bachnal, Okali, Rajanhal, Navanihal, Kamalapur Dinshikurnur, Antapnhal, Belura, Kawanhalli, Kalmud Sonth, Kinnisarposh, Belkotta, Dastapur, Navadgi (K) Navadgi (B), Holkunda, Jeevangi, Gogi, Tadkal Kathalli, Kurikota, Siradhone, Bhusangi, Kannura Yalvanthi (B), Kagganmardi, Ankalga, Sirgapur Tondkal, Yankanchi, Kadbur, Nagoora, Ashta Kalhangerga, Jamga (B), Kumsi, Bannura, Awrad (B) Tawargera, Ganjalnkhed, Belura (J), Malgathi Bhopal Tegnur, Keroor, Halsultanpur, Harsoor Venkatbennur, Khajikotnur, Kalbenur Srinivas Saradgi, Kalagnoor, Zhapur, Pala, Sannur Bolewad, Jaferabad, Pallapur, Kapnoor, Uplaon Hagargi, Azadpur, Kusnoor, Naganhalli *, Udnoor Panegaon, Sitnoor, Nandikur, Kesratgi, Nandoor (K) Dharmapur, Nandoor (B), Hatkunda, Pattan Bhimanhalli, Syed Chincholi, Taj Sultanpur Keribhosga, Sindagi, Bablad Sindagi, Savalgi (B) Hunsihadgil, Melkunda (B), Kadnal, Machnal, Malni Kollur, Melkunda (K), Hadgilharuti, Kadni Garoor (K), Garoor (B), Minajgi, Tadtegnoor, Sirnoor Khandal, Itga Khandal, Farhatabad, Hagargundagi Kawalga (B), Jogur, Maniyal, Herur (B), Belgumpa (K) Basavapattana, Kawalga (K), Aurad (K) Siradgi (Bhatad), Tilgul, Balwad, Naddisinur Ferozabad, Somnathahalli, Nadvinhalli, Kiranagi.
The villages having more than 50% ST population are None.
Sex ratio of Scheduled tribe population is 479.

Scheduled Tribes Literates and Illiterates by Sex:

	Persons	Males	Females
Literate	1,759	1,153	606
Illiterate	3,576	1,628	1,948
Literacy rate	40.6	51.0	29.3
Graduate	48	42	6

Scheduled Tribes (Dominant):

Gond etc., Naikda etc., Koli Dhor etc., Pardhi etc.
Kadu Kuruba

For their cultural identity please see Appendix-II

Villages without Scheduled Tribes: There are 91 villages without any scheduled tribe population.

Literates and Illiterates by Sex (Total Population):

	Persons	Males	Females
Literate	100,320	64,761	35,559
Illiterate	145,094	60,310	84,784
Literacy rate	49	63	36
Graduate	3,246	2,765	481

Agriculture: ***Distribution of villages according to land use:*** Out of 140 villages, Total area (in hectare) is 166602, out of that 89.5 percent is cultivable and 2.73 percent of the cultivable area is irrigated.

Sources of Irrigation (Hectares): Government Canal 108.91, Private Canal 27.4, Well without Electricity 175.29, Well with Electricity 2909.27, Tubewell without Electricity 15.24, Tubewell with Electricity 489.24, Tank 222.34, River 41.58, Lake 74.77, Waterfall 0, Others 5.26.

Villages with population of 5000 to 9999:
Kamalapur, Mahagaon, Srinivas Saradgi, Taj Sultanpur Farhatabad, Kiranagi.

Villages with population of 10000 and above: None

Distribution of Workers:

	Persons	Males	Females	WPR
Cultivators	32,798	24,907	7,891	30.33
Agricultural Labour	49,048	19,573	29,475	45.35
Household Industry	2,302	1,510	792	2.13
Other Workers	24,000	17,363	6,637	22.19
Main Workers	78,710	54,002	24,708	72.78
Marginal Workers	29,438	9,351	20,087	27.22
Total Workers	108,148	63,353	44,795	

Religion: Major Religious Communities:

	Persons	Males	Females	Sex Ratio
Hindu (78.52%)	192,703	98,046	94,657	965
Muslim (12.07%)	29,632	15,181	14,451	952
Christian (0.24%)	583	278	305	1,097
Sikh (0.03%)	72	46	26	565
Buddhists (8.31%)	20,385	10,485	9,900	944
Jain (0.08%)	203	96	107	1,115

Agewise Data:

	Persons	Males	Females	Sex Ratio
All ages	245,414	125,071	120,343	962
0-14	97,601	50,145	47,456	946
15-44	102,906	53,150	49,756	936
45-79	42,559	20,649	21,910	1061
80+	2,070	960	1,110	1156
Age not stated	278	167	111	665

Languages (Dominant):
Kannada, Hindi, Urdu, Marathi, Telugu

Disabled Population:

	Persons	Males	Females	%
Total Disabled	4,385	2,527	1,858	
In Seeing	1,756	921	835	40.05
In Speech	410	240	170	9.35
In Hearing	219	102	117	4.99
In Movement	1,625	1,037	588	37.06
Mentally	375	227	148	8.55

GUNDLUPET

Gundlupet C.D. Block lies in the western part of Chamraj anagar district. It is a part of Gundlupet taluka. The Block is located at a distance of 40 kms. from district headquarters (Chamarajanagar). There are 158 villages in the block with the total population of 186,527 persons. Area of the C.D. Block is 1397.46 sq. kms. It is bound ed by district Mysore on north and west, and taluk Chamar ajanagar on east. It has common boundary with the state of Kerala on west, and with the state of Tamil Nadu on south and east.

Communications:

Roadways : NH- 212: Direction- Calicut to Mysore, Nearest Villages- Arepura, Hirikati, Chikkati, Thondavadi, Begur, Taggalur, Raghavapura, Garaganahalli, Agathagowdanahalli, Halladamadahalli, Malavalli, Bendagalli, Veeranapura, Madrahalli, Bheemanabeedu, Kuthanur, Madahalli, Panjana halli, Dumdasanapura, Vijayapura, Berambadi State Forest, Channamallipura, Maddur, Bachanahalli, Berambadi, Kanne gala. SH- 17: Direction- Ootacamund to Gundlupet, Nearest Villages- Kuthanur, Managalli, Putthanapura, Basavapura, Hangala, Siddaianapura, Maguvinahallimel Kamanahalli, Bandipura, Bandipura State Forest.

River: Mugu Hole Nadi- Nearest Village- Berambadi State Forest. Mavina Hole Nadi- Nearest Village- Berambadi State Forest. Kagal Hole Nadi- Nearest Villages- Bandipu ra State Forest, Kaniyanapura. Moyar Hole Nadi- Nearest Village- Bandipura District Forest.

Canal: Nearest Villages- Chikkati, Thondavadi, Bhogganap ura, Kamarahalli, Berambadi, Kannegala.

Forest and Reserved Forest: (Nenekatte Sandalwood R.F.)- Nearest Villages- Mukha Halli, Madahalli, Madrahalli, Nenekatte, Baragi. (Bolegaudanakatte Reserved Forest)- Nearest Villages-Yadavanahalli, Kotekere.

Annual Rainfall: Normal Rianfall 754 mm.

Ground Water: Availability of the Ground Water in the Basin is 12264 H.A.M. and the utilization is 16195 H. A.M. It belongs to Safe category. Depth to water level 2 to 10 meter below the ground. Most of the wells go down in summer months, according to the Ground Water Estimation Committee.

Soils: Red Soils, Black Soils and Mixed Soils.
Natural Division : It falls partly in Gundlupet-Chamrajna gar Plateau and Heggadadevankote-Bandipur Forest Upland of the Southern Karnataka Plateau.
Administration:
Division: Mysore. Parliamentary Constituency: 21 Mysore Paschim. District: Chamarajanagar. Taluka: Gundlupet. Assembly Constituency: 224 Gundlupet. Gram Panchayat:30.
Regional Area Development Boards: The Maland Aera Development Board.
Border Villages: (State: Tamil Nadu)- Berambadi State Forest, Kaniyanapura, Bandipura State Forest, Bandipura District Forest. (State Kerala)- Berambadi State Forest.
Villages: 158 **Inhabited:** 140 **Uninhabited:** 18

Ranking	District	State	National
Area	2	39	181
Population	3	100	911
Sex Ratio	1	56	1715
Child Sex Ratio	2	47	2139
Literacy Rate	3	161	5049
Density	2	103	5793
Work Participation Rate	3	146	2356

Gram Panchayats:
Horeyala, Chikkati, Nitre, Somahalli, Begur, Kotekere, Raghavapura, Alathur, Agathagowdanahalli, Kabbahalli, Balachavady, Kelasur, Padagur, Bannithalapura, Nenekatte, Baragi, Bachahalli, Berambadi, Kannegala, Bheemanabeedu, Annur, Shindanapura, Terakanambi, Bommanahalli, Kodasoge, Bommalapura, Hundipura, Shivapura, Hangala, Mangala.
Amenities:
Education: Primary School in 115 villages, Middle school in 80 villages, Matriculation or Secondary School in 18 villages, namely Horeyala, Chikkati, Begur, Somahalli, Garaganahalli, Kabbahalli, Baragi, Chikkathuppur, Padagur, Terakanambi, Kodasoge, Bommanahalli, Vaddagere, Kannegala, Hangala, Shivapura, Bommalapura, Bachahalli.
Higher Secondary or Pre University Courses or Intermediate or Junior College in 4 villages of the CD Block,, namely Begur, Somahalli, Terakanambi, Bommalapura.
College in 0 village, Adult Literacy Center in 0 village.
Medical: Hospital in 1 village, Dispensary in 13 villages, Health Center in 15 villages, Sub Center in 9 villages, Maternity and Child Welfare Center in 6 villages, Community health workers in 17 villages.
The Villages having Hospital or Dispensary or Health Center are Nitre, Begur, Belachalavadi, Somahalli, Madapattana, Kabbahalli, Baragi, Nenekatte, Vijayapura, Bommanahalli, Devarahalli, Hundipura, Bachahalli, Mangala.
Drinking Water: Tap water in 99 villages, Tank water in 41 villages, Well water in 52 villages, Tubewell in 114 villages and more than one source in 128 villages.
Bank: Banking facility in 23 villages, namely, Horeyala, Hirikati, Begur, Kotekere, Somahalli Agathagowdanahalli, Kabbahalli, Alathur, Baragi Nenekatte, Chikkathuppur, Vijayapura, Mudagur Terakanambi, Bommanahalli, Vaddagere, Berambadi Putthanapura, Hangala, Bommalapura, Ankahalli Bachahalli, Mangala.
Credit Society in 81 villages Agricultural Credit Society in 28 Non-Agricultural Credit Society in 78 villages.
Others: Power supply in 136 villages, Cinema hall in 7 villages sport club in 0 village, Stadium or Auditorium or Community Hall in 2 villages, Post Office in 76 villages.
There are 112 villages having bus facilities.
Villages with most of facilities: Horeyala, Begur Somahalli, Kabbahalli, Baragi, Nenekatte, Vijayapura Terakanambi, Bommanahalli, Hangala, Bommalapura Bachahalli, Mangala.
Villages without amenities (Education):
Ballahalli, Parvathanapura, Devalapura, Honakanahalli, Vaddarahalli, Talale, Hosur, Managalli, Vijayapura Amani, Kandegaladahosahalli, Belakuppe, Thodipura, Kengavadi, Berambadi State Forest, Lakkipura, Kunagahalli, Hangaladahosahalli, Karle, Siddapura, Passaiahnapura, Kaniyanapura, Lokkere, Bandipura, Bandipura State Forest..
Scheduled Castes: Out of the total population of 186742 persons, 37230 persons (19.94%) belong to Scheduled Castes.
The villages having less than 10% SC population are Thondavadi, Thoravalli, Taggalur, Ballahalli Parvathanapura, Manchahalli, Garaganahalli Chikanapura, Hunasinapura, Hakkalapura, Sampigepura Deshipura, Devalapura, Honakanahalli, Vaddarahalli Bannithalapura, Talale, Hosur, Dumdasanapura Vijayapura, Vijayapura Amani, Kodahalli, Balachavady Triyambakapura, Sheelavanthapura, Somanapura Thodipura, Daribegur, Kengavadi, Kadabur, Malapura Berambadi State Forest, Maddur, Lakkipura, Kallipura Devarahalli, Basavapura, Vaddana Hosahalli Hangalapura, Siddaianapura, Vadeyanapura Kaligowdanahalli, Shettahalli, Lokkere, Jakkahalli Bandipura State Forest, Yelachatti.
The villages having more than 50% SC population are Savakanahalli, Ramaiahnapura, Yeriyur, Heggavadi Hangaladahosahalli, Bendaravadi, Passaiahnapura

Mangala.

Sex ratio of Scheduled Caste population is 497.

Scheduled Castes Literates and Illiterates by Sex:

	Persons	Males	Females
Literate	15,219	9,097	6,122
Illiterate	22,011	9,629	12,382
Literacy rate	46.3	54.8	37.6
Graduate	417	355	62

Scheduled Castes (Dominant):

Adi Karnataka, Madiga, Bhovi, Adi Dravida Bhambi etc.

For their cultural identity please see Appendix-I

Villages without Scheduled Castes: There are 44 villages without any scheduled caste population.

Scheduled Tribes: Out of the total population of 186742 persons, 18562 persons (9.94%) belong to Scheduled Tribes. The villages having less than 10% ST population are Hosapura, Yadavanahalli, Arepura, Hirikati Thoravalli, Nitre, Kamarahalli, Begur, Belachalavadi Bettadamadahalli, Taggalur, Ballahalli, Madapattana Parvathanapura, Raghavapura, Savakanahalli, Hasaguli Garaganahalli, Agathagowdanahalli, Halladamadahalli Chikanapura, Hunasinapura, Hakkalapura, Heggadahalli Kallahalli, Sampigepura, Kabbahalli, Alathur Deshipura, Devalapura, Honakanahalli, Malavalli Bendagalli, Vaddarahalli, Veeranapura, Madrahalli Nenekatte, Hongahalli, Bheemanabeedu, Kuthanur Madahalli, Panjanahalli, Kilagere, Kelasurupura Hosur, Dumdasanapura, Vijayapura, Doddathuppur Shindanapura, Bettahalli, Annur, Kodahalli Kandegaladahosahalli, Kandegala, Padagur, Paramapura Hooradahalli, Mudagur, Shyanadrahalli, Lakkur Guruvinapura, Balachavady, Triyambakapura, Belakuppe Huttur, Depapura, Sheelavanthapura, Thodipura Daribegur, Karakalamadahalli, Bommanahalli Kengavadi, Ramaiahnapura, Kadabur, Chirakanahalli Vaddagere, Yeriyur, Malapura, Kundakere Berambadi State Forest, Channamallipura, Kannegala Honnegowdanahalli, Hangaladahosahalli, Devarahalli Putthanapura, Basavapura, Vaddana Hosahalli Bendaravadi, Hangalapura, Siddaianapura, Karle Shivapura, Hullepura, Vadeyanapura, Belavadi Hundipura, Siddapura, Passaiahnapura Kaligowdanahalli, Kebbepura, Shettahalli, Ankahalli Bachahalli, Lokkere, Mangala.

The villages having more than 50% ST population are Thondavadi, Somanapura, Maddur, Lakkipura Kaniyanapura, Bandipura State Forest.

Sex ratio of Scheduled tribe population is 502.

Scheduled Tribes Literates and Illiterates by Sex:

	Persons	Males	Females
Literate	6,186	3,890	2,296
Illiterate	12,376	5,361	7,015
Literacy rate	37.8	47.8	27.8
Graduate	137	125	12

Scheduled Tribes (Dominant):

Naikda etc., Soligaru, Jenu Kuruba, Kadu Kuruba Meda

For their cultural identity please see Appendix-II

Villages without Scheduled Tribes: There are 90 villages without any scheduled tribe population.

Literates and Illiterates by Sex (Total Population):

	Persons	Males	Females
Literate	76,962	46,907	30,055
Illiterate	109,780	47,074	62,706
Literacy rate	46	56	36
Graduate	1,997	1,743	254

Agriculture: ***Distribution of villages according to land use:*** Out of 158 villages, Total area (in hectare) is 139746, out of that 38.58 percent is cultivable and 18.81 percent of the cultivable area is irrigated.

Sources of Irrigation (Hectares): Government Canal 27.8, Private Canal 0, Well without Electricity 40.21, Well with Electricity 2320.15, Tubewell without Electricity 399.33, Tubewell with Electricity 6956.41, Tank 57.97, River 0, Lake 0, Waterfall 0, Others 337.94.

Villages with population of 5000 to 9999: Terakanambi, Hangala.

Villages with population of 10000 and above: None

Distribution of Workers:

	Persons	Males	Females	WPR
Cultivators	34,046	28,344	5,702	36.06
Agricultural Labour	45,451	21,399	24,052	48.14
Household Industry	2,516	1,437	1,079	2.66
Other Workers	12,400	9,522	2,878	13.13
Main Workers	71,259	52,674	18,585	75.48
Marginal Workers	23,154	8,028	15,126	24.52
Total Workers	94,413	60,702	33,711	

Religion: Major Religious Communities:

	Persons	Males	Females	Sex Ratio
Hindu (97.15%)	181,417	91,328	90,089	986
Muslim (0.64%)	1,193	617	576	934
Christian (0.1%)	187	109	78	716
Sikh (0%)	8	2	6	3,000
Buddhists (1.95%)	3,640	1,778	1,862	1,047
Jain (0.05%)	101	49	52	1,061

Agewise Data:

	Persons	Males	Females	Sex Ratio
All ages	186,742	93,981	92,761	987
0-14	50,098	25,411	24,687	972

15-44	92,357	45,814	46,543	1016
45-79	41,720	21,532	20,188	938
80+	2,271	1,054	1,217	1155
Age not stated	296	170	126	741

Languages (Dominant):
Kannada, Hindi, Tamil, Telugu, Urdu
Disabled Population:

	Persons	Males	Females	%
Total Disabled	4,134	2,384	1,750	
In Seeing	2,639	1,521	1,118	63.84
In Speech	367	195	172	8.88
In Hearing	190	90	100	4.6
In Movement	716	453	263	17.32
Mentally	222	125	97	5.37

HADAGALLI

Hadagalli C.D. Block lies in the south-western part of Bellary district. It is a part of Hadagalli taluka. The Block is located at a distance of 144 kms. from district headquarters (Bellary). There are 57 villages in the block with the total population of 144,616 persons. Area of the C.D. Block is 927.99 sq. kms. It is bounded by districts Koppal and Gadag on north, districts Davan gere and Haveri on south, taluk Hagari Bommanahalli on east, and district Haveri on west.

Communications:
Roadways : S.H-2: Direction- Haveri to Harapanahalli, Nearest Villages- Mylar, Kuravathi, Harivi Basapura, Harivi. S.H-25: Direction- Harapanahalli to Hagaribom-manahalli, Nearest Villages- Mahajanadahalli, Ittigi.
River: Tungabhadra Nadi- Nearest Villages- Byalhunsi, Makarabbi, Holalu, Mylar, Kuravathi , Harivi Basapura, Harivi, Angoor, Magala, Rangapura, Thimalapura, Nowli, Kotanakal, Kombli, Sovinahalli, Hakandi, Kalvi West, Hirabannimatti.
Reserved Forest: Nearest Villages- Thimalapura, Nowli, Halathimalapura, Ayyanahalli, Uppanayakanahalli, Thippa pura, Shivalinganahalli, Thamalapura, Musuvinakallahalli. (Hyarada R.F.): Nearest Villages- Holalu, Hyarada, Kuravathi , Harivi Basapura. (Koilaragatti R.F.): Nearest Villages- Kombli, Sovinahalli, Koilaragatti, Hiremallina keri. (Sogi R.F.): Nearest Villages- Nagathi Basapura, Komaranahalli, Hugulura, Sogi, Varakanhalli, Advimallan akeri. (Thumbinakere R.F.): Nearest Villages- Katebennuru, Thumbinakeri, Hirehadagalli, Veerapura, Dasanahalli, Pothalakatti, Beerabbi.
Annual Rainfall: Normal Rianfall 615.5 mm.
Ground Water: Availability of the Ground Water in the Basin is (Information not avablable) H.A.M. and the utilization is (Information not avablable) H.A.M. It belongs to (Information not avablable) category. Depth to water level 5 to 20 meter below the ground. Most of the wells go down in summer months, according to the Ground Water Estimation Committee.
Soils: Black and Red Sandy Soils.
Natural Division : It falls partly in Middle Tungabhadra Valley and Chikka Hagary Valley of the Central Karnataka Plateau.
Administration:

Division: Gulbarga. Parliamentary Constituency: 9 Bellary (ST). District: Bellary. Taluka: Hadagally. Assembly Constituency: 88 Hadagalli (SC). Gram Panchayat: 24.
Regional Area Development Boards: The Hyderabad - Karnataka Area Development Board.
Villages: 57 **Inhabited:** 56 **Uninhabited:** 1

Ranking	**District**	**State**	**National**
Area	6	97	513
Population	7	135	2035
Sex Ratio	4	77	2158
Child Sex Ratio	1	21	1391
Literacy Rate	1	95	2964
Density	5	48	5474
Work Participation Rate	5	121	1423

Gram Panchayats:
Kombli, Sovinahalli, Kalvi West, Hiremallinakeri, Holagundi, Uttangi, Ittigi, Mahajanadahalli, Sogi, Nandihalli, Devagondanahalli, Nagathi Basapura, Mannera Masalavada, Hagaranur, Hirehadagalli, Dasanahalli, Hyarada, Kuravathi , Mylar, Holalu, Kattebennuru, Makarabbi, Magala, Nowli.
Amenities:
Education: Primary School in 46 villages, Middle school in 40 villages, Matriculation or Secondary School in 15 villages, namely Hirehadagalli, Holalu, Mylar, Hyarada, Kuravathi, Magala, Kombli, Halathimalapura, Mannera Masalavada, Komaranahalli, Hugulura, Sogi, Uttangi, Advimallanakeri, Ittigi.
Higher Secondary or Pre University Courses or Inter-mediate or Junior College in 9 villages of the CD Block,, namely Hirehadagalli, Holalu, Mylar, Kombli, Sovinahalli, Halathimalapura, Nagathi Basapura, Holagundi, Hugulura.
College in 5 villages, Adult Literacy Center in 1 village., Colleges are in villages, namely Mylar, Kombli, Halathimalapura, Hagaranur, Hugulura.
Medical: Hospital in 0 village, Dispensary in 7 villages, Health Center in 9 villages, Sub Center in 9 villages, Maternity and Child Welfare Center in 0 village, Community health workers in 2 villages.
The Villages having Hospital or Dispensary or Health Center are Holalu, Magala, Nagathi Basapura, Mannera Masalavada, Nandihalli, Sogi, Ittigi.

Drinking Water: Tap water in 32 villages, Tank water in 20 villages, Well water in 7 villages, Tubewell in 15 villages and more than one source in 47 villages.

Bank: Banking facility in 16 villages, namely, Byalhunsi, Makarabbi, Hirehadagalli, Manihalli Holalu, Mylar, Hyarada, Kuravathi, Harivi, Magala Kombli, Hagaranur, Nagathi Basapura, Sogi, Uttangi Ittigi.

Credit Society in 15 villages Agricultural Credit Society in 15 Non-Agricultural Credit Society in 3 villages.

Others: Power supply in 56 villages, Cinema hall in 4 villages, sport club in 56 villages, Stadium or Auditorium or Community Hall in 56 villages, Post Office in 3 villages.

There are 52 villages having bus facilities.

Villages with most of facilities: Holalu, Hyarada Magala, Nagathi Basapura, Sogi, Ittigi.

Villages without amenities (Education): Thumbinakeri, Manihalli, Dombrahalli, Dasanahalli, Harivi Basapura, Kotihal, Rangapura, Thippapura, Vyasamallapura, Mudenur..

Scheduled Castes: Out of the total population of 144704 persons, 35285 persons (24.38%) belong to Scheduled Castes.

The villages having less than 10% SC population are Katebennuru, Manihalli, Veerapura, Budanur Dasanahalli, Hyarada, Harivi Basapura, Harivi Rangapura, Ayyanahalli, Nagathi Basapura, Nandihalli Uttangi, Mahajanadahalli.

The villages having more than 50% SC population are Thumbinakeri, Dombrahalli, Kalvi West, Dasarahalli Vyasamallapura, Thamalapura, Komaranahalli.

Sex ratio of Scheduled Caste population is 497.

Scheduled Castes Literates and Illiterates by Sex:

	Persons	Males	Females
Literate	10,979	7,419	3,560
Illiterate	24,306	10,341	13,965
Literacy rate	38.5	51.6	25.2
Graduate	239	226	13

Scheduled Castes (Dominant):

Banjara etc., Adi Karnataka, Madiga, Bhovi Sillekyathas

For their cultural identity please see Appendix-I

Villages without Scheduled Castes: There are 3 villages without any scheduled caste population.

Scheduled Tribes: Out of the total population of 144704 persons, 11434 persons (7.9%) belong to Scheduled Tribes.

The villages having less than 10% ST population are Byalhunsi, Katebennuru, Thumbinakeri, Hirehadagalli Holalu, Mylar, Dombrahalli, Kuravathi Harivi Basapura, Harivi, Beerabbi, Magala, Rangapura Thimalapura, Sovinahalli, Hakandi, Kalvi West Dasarahalli, Ayyanahalli, Uppanayakanahalli Thippapura, Devagondanahalli, Nagathi Basapura Shivalinganahalli, Mannera Masalavada Vyasamallapura, Thamalapura, Komaranahalli Holagundi, Mudenur, Nandihalli, Hugulura, Sogi Uttangi, Varakanhalli, Mahajanadahalli, Ittigi.

The villages having more than 50% ST population are None.

Sex ratio of Scheduled tribe population is 495.

Scheduled Tribes Literates and Illiterates by Sex:

	Persons	Males	Females
Literate	5,238	3,273	1,965
Illiterate	6,196	2,502	3,694
Literacy rate	54.1	66.9	41.0
Graduate	102	87	15

Scheduled Tribes (Dominant):

Naikda etc., Meda, Generic Tribes etc., Koraga Bhil etc.

For their cultural identity please see Appendix-II

Villages without Scheduled Tribes: There are 6 villages without any scheduled tribe population.

Literates and Illiterates by Sex (Total Population):

	Persons	Males	Females
Literate	72,430	44,344	28,086
Illiterate	72,274	28,833	43,441
Literacy rate	59	71	46
Graduate	2,386	2,050	336

Agriculture: ***Distribution of villages according to land use:*** Out of 57 villages, Total area (in hectare) is 92799, out of that 75.44 percent is cultivable and 15.97 percent of the cultivable area is irrigated.

Sources of Irrigation (Hectares): Government Canal 152.45, Private Canal 0, Well without Electricity 0, Well with Electricity 20.23, Tubewell without Electricity 0, Tubewell with Electricity 5719.16, Tank 530.19, River 3570.92, Lake 0, Waterfall 0, Others 1186.85.

Villages with population of 5000 to 9999: Hirehadagalli, Holalu, Magala, Holagundi, Uttangi Ittigi.

Villages with population of 10000 and above: None

Distribution of Workers:

	Persons	Males	Females	WPR
Cultivators	22,784	17,268	5,516	30.49
Agricultural Labour	41,855	16,326	25,529	56.02
Household Industry	1,558	972	586	2.09
Other Workers	8,522	6,787	1,735	11.41
Main Workers	58,262	36,621	21,641	77.97
Marginal Workers	16,457	4,732	11,725	22.03
Total Workers	74,719	41,353	33,366	

Religion: Major Religious Communities:

	Persons	Males	Females	Sex Ratio
Hindu (94.33%)	136,505	69,013	67,492	978
Muslim (4.67%)	6,764	3,456	3,308	957
Christian (0.06%)	91	40	51	1,275
Sikh (0.01%)	10	5	5	1,000
Buddhists (0%)	1	1	-	-
Jain (0.19%)	282	131	151	1,153

Agewise Data:

	Persons	Males	Females	Sex Ratio
All ages	144,704	73,177	71,527	977
0-14	52,879	27,008	25,871	958
15-44	64,251	33,064	31,187	943
45-79	26,466	12,667	13,799	1089
80+	998	383	615	1606
Age not stated	110	55	55	1000

Languages (Dominant):
Kannada, Hindi, Urdu, Telugu, Marathi

Disabled Population:

	Persons	Males	Females	%
Total Disabled	2,682	1,563	1,119	
In Seeing	1,044	590	454	38.93
In Speech	273	157	116	10.18
In Hearing	163	81	82	6.08
In Movement	948	594	354	35.35
Mentally	254	141	113	9.47

HAGARIBOMMANAHALLI

Hagaribommanahalli C.D. Block lies in the south-western part of Bellary district. It is a part of Hagaribommanah alli taluka. The Block is located at a distance of 105 kms. from district headquarters (Bellary). There are 56 villages in the block with the total population of 159,900 persons. Area of the C.D. Block is 974.14 sq. kms. It is bounded by district Koppal on north, district Davangere and taluk Kudligi on south, taluks Hospet and Sandur on east, and taluk Hadagalli on west.

Communications:

Roadways : S.H-25: Direction- Harapanahali to Hospet, Nearest Villages- Marabbihal, Varadapura, Kadlabalu, Pinjara Heggadal, Hampapatna, Kachinabandi, Hagaribom-manahalli, Chintrapalli, Kannehalli, Nellukudri , Ulavathi, Haregondanahalli.

Railway Station: Village- Kadlabalu.

River: Chikka Hagari Nadi- Nearest Villages- Hiresobati, Bachigondanahalli, Kadlabalu, Hagaribommanahalli, Chintrapalli, Nellukudri, Ulavathi, Haregondanahalli, Malvi, Kogali, Alabur. Tungabhadra Nadi- Nearest Villag es- Hampasagara, Enigi, Basarakodu, Bannigola, Seeganahal li, Rameswara Bandi, Muthukur, Kithanur, Thambrahalli, Bachigondanahalli, Anandadevanahalli , Ankasamudra, Bellahunshi, Marabbihal, Narayanadevarakeri , Mudlapura , Varadapura.

Canal: Nearest Villages- Hiresobati, Bachigondanahalli, Byasigaderl, Kadlabalu, Hagaribommanahalli, Chintrapalli, Ulavathi, Haregondanahalli, Malvi.

Reserved Forest: (Bennikal): Nearest Villages- Varalihal li, Kallahalli, Bennikal. (Nandibanda R.F.): Nearest Villages- Varadapura, Vyasapura , Halagapura. (Sivapura R.F.): Nearest Villages- Halagapura, Anekal, Dasmapura, Hosakeri.

Annual Rainfall: Normal Rianfall 642.2 mm.

Ground Water: Availability of the Ground Water in the Basin is (Information not avablable) H.A.M. and the utilization is (Information not avablable) H.A.M.. It belongs to (Information not avablable) category. Depth to water level 5 to 20 meter below the ground. Most of the wells go down in summer months, according to the Ground Water Estimation Committee.

Soils: Black and Red Sandy Soils.

Natural Division : It falls partly in Middle Tungabhadra Valley, Sandur Highlands, Kudligi Scrubby Uplands and Chikka Hagari Valley of the Central Karnataka Plateau.

Administration:

Division: Gulbarga. Parliamentary Constituency: 9 Bellary (ST). District: Bellary. Taluka: Hagaribommanahalli. Assembly Constituency: 88 Hadagalli (SC), 90 Hagaribomm anahalli (SC). Gram Panchayat: 22.

Regional Area Development Boards: The Hyderabad - Karnataka Area Development Board.

Villages: 56 **Inhabited:** 53 **Uninhabited:** 3

Ranking	District	State	National
Area	4	85	459
Population	4	120	1558
Sex Ratio	3	71	2037
Child Sex Ratio	7	161	4571
Literacy Rate	2	105	3140
Density	7	126	5334
Work Participation Rate	4	106	2986

Gram Panchayats:
Hampasagara , Bannigola, Thambrahalli, Muthukur, Bachigondanahalli , Marabbihal, Hampapatna, Halagapura, Dasmapura, Hansi, Bennikal, Ambli, Alabur, Kogali, Malvi, Chintrapalli, Hagaribommanahalli, Kadlabalu, Byasigaderi , Sonna, Morigeri, Bannikal.

Amenities:

Education: Primary School in 46 villages, Middle school in 45 villages, Matriculation or Secondary School in 20 villages, namely Hampasagara, Bannikal, Moregeri, Sonna, Rameswara Bandi, Thambrahalli, Bachigondanahalli, Marabbihal, Kadlabalu, Hampapatna, Vyasapura,

Hagaribommanahalli, Chintrapalli, Haregondanahalli, Malvi, Dasmapura, Hansi, Bennikal, Kogali, Ambli.

Higher Secondary or Pre University Courses or Intermediate or Junior College in 7 villages of the CD Block,, namely Moregeri, Thambrahalli, Kadlabalu, Hagaribommanahalli, Chintrapalli, Haregondanahalli, Kogali.

College in 3 villages, Adult Literacy Center in 3 villages., Colleges are in villages, namely Kadlabalu, Hagaribommanahalli, Haregondanahalli.

Medical: Hospital in 0 village, Dispensary in 11 villages, Health Center in 7 villages, Sub Center in 23 villages, Maternity and Child Welfare Center in 5 villages, Community health workers in 7 villages.

The Villages having Hospital or Dispensary or Health Center are Hampasagara , Bannikal, Moregeri, Muthukur, Ankasamudra, Kadlabalu, Hampapatna, Hagaribommanahalli, Chintrapalli, Hansi, Bennikal, Kogali, Alabur.

Drinking Water: Tap water in 44 villages, Tank water in 36 villages, Well water in 14 villages, Tubewell in 41 villages and more than one source in 50 villages.

Bank: Banking facility in 17 villages, namely, Hampasagara, Enigi, Bannikal, Moregeri, Bannigola Muthukur, Kithanur, Thambrahalli, Bachigondanahalli Marabbihal, Hampapatna, Vyasapura Hagaribommanahalli, Chintrapalli, Ulavathi, Hosakeri Hansi.

Credit Society in 22 villages Agricultural Credit Society in 19 Non-Agricultural Credit Society in 8 villages.

Others: Power supply in 53 villages, Cinema hall in 6 villages, sport club in 53 villages, Stadium or Auditorium or Community Hall in 53 villages, Post Office in 6 villages.

There are 47 villages having bus facilities.

Villages with most of facilities: Hampasagara Bannikal, Moregeri, Bannigola, Thambrahalli Bachigondanahalli, Marabbihal, Hampapatna Hagaribommanahalli, Chintrapalli.

Villages without amenities (Education): Yenagi Basapura, Adivikyadigihalli, Seeganahalli, Varadapura, Guledahalu, Kachinabandi, Kogali-Samatu Kodihalli..

Scheduled Castes: Out of the total population of 159886 persons, 29941 persons (18.73%) belong to Scheduled Castes.

The villages having less than 10% SC population are Hanumagondanahalli, Gaddikeri, Adivikyadigihalli Narayanadevarakeri , Kannehalli, Malvi, Varalihalli Upparagatta, Dasmapura, Hansi, Ambli.

The village having more than 50% SC population is None.

Sex ratio of Scheduled Caste population is 497.

Scheduled Castes Literates and Illiterates by Sex:

	Persons	Males	Females
Literate	9,598	6,497	3,101
Illiterate	20,343	8,571	11,772
Literacy rate	40.6	55.0	26.2
Graduate	180	167	13

Scheduled Castes (Dominant):

Adi Karnataka, Banjara etc., Bhovi, Sudugadu Siddha Madiga

For their cultural identity please see Appendix-I

Villages without Scheduled Castes: There are 6 villages without any scheduled caste population.

Scheduled Tribes: Out of the total population of 159886 persons, 21716 persons (13.58%) belong to Scheduled Tribes.

The villages having less than 10% ST population are Yenagi Basapura, Adivikyadigihalli , Sonna, Kithanur Thambrahalli, Hiresobati, Bachigondanahalli Marabbihal, Varadapura, Byasigaderi , Vyasapura Guledahalu, Hagaribommanahalli, Anekal, Kannehalli Nellukudri , Ulavathi, Haregondanahalli, Malvi Upparagatta, Sree Rama Nagar, Alabur, Ambli.

The villages having more than 50% ST population are None.

Sex ratio of Scheduled tribe population is 497.

Scheduled Tribes Literates and Illiterates by Sex:

	Persons	Males	Females
Literate	8,836	5,417	3,419
Illiterate	12,880	5,507	7,373
Literacy rate	49.3	60.8	37.9
Graduate	189	161	28

Scheduled Tribes (Dominant):

Naikda etc., Meda, Gond etc.

For their cultural identity please see Appendix-II

Villages without Scheduled Tribes: There are 5 villages without any scheduled tribe population.

Literates and Illiterates by Sex (Total Population):

	Persons	Males	Females
Literate	77,353	47,379	29,974
Illiterate	82,533	33,391	49,142
Literacy rate	58	71	45
Graduate	2,508	2,051	457

Agriculture: ***Distribution of villages according to land use:*** Out of 56 villages, Total area (in hectare) is 97414, out of that 60.63 percent is cultivable and 29.52 percent of the cultivable area is irrigated.

Sources of Irrigation (Hectares): Government Canal 2777.75, Private Canal 0.81, Well without Electricity 221.4, Well with Electricity 699.35, Tubewell without Electricity 60.7, Tubewell with Electricity 11504.86, Tank 2018.58, River 151.76,

Lake 0, Waterfall 0, Others 0.

Villages with population of 5000 to 9999:
Hampasagara , Moregeri, Bachigondanahalli, Kadlabalu Hagaribommanahalli.

Villages with population of 10000 and above:
Chintrapalli.

Distribution of Workers:

	Persons	Males	Females	WPR
Cultivators	21,990	18,004	3,986	30.52
Agricultural Labour	35,500	13,701	21,799	49.28
Household Industry	2,129	1,156	973	2.96
Other Workers	12,422	10,307	2,115	17.24
Main Workers	58,520	39,549	18,971	81.23
Marginal Workers	13,521	3,619	9,902	18.77
Total Workers	72,041	43,168	28,873	

Religion: Major Religious Communities:

	Persons	Males	Females	Sex Ratio
Hindu (91.58%)	146,427	73,912	72,515	981
Muslim (7.54%)	12,050	6,142	5,908	962
Christian (0.06%)	97	42	55	1,310
Sikh (0%)	3	2	1	500
Buddhists (0.01%)	8	5	3	600
Jain (0.23%)	370	193	177	917

Agewise Data:

	Persons	Males	Females	Sex Ratio
All ages	159,886	80,770	79,116	980
0-14	62,286	32,168	30,118	936
15-44	70,842	36,164	34,678	959
45-79	25,440	11,942	13,498	1130
80+	1,245	445	800	1798
Age not stated	73	51	22	431

Languages (Dominant):
Kannada, Urdu, Hindi, Telugu, Marathi

Disabled Population:

	Persons	Males	Females	%
Total Disabled	2,915	1,673	1,242	
In Seeing	1,094	580	514	37.53
In Speech	252	147	105	8.64
In Hearing	128	68	60	4.39
In Movement	1,205	754	451	41.34
Mentally	236	124	112	8.1

HALIYAL

Haliyal C.D. Block lies in the north-eastern part of Uttara Kannada district. It is a part of Haliyal taluka. The Block is located at a distance of 155 kms. from district headquarters (Karwar). There are 129 villages in the block with the total population of 80,316 persons. Area of the C.D. Block is 820.83 sq. kms. It is bounded by districts Belgaum and Dharwad on north, taluk Yellapur on south, district Dharwad on east, and taluk Supa on west.

Communications:

Roadways : S.H-28: Direction- Supa to Dharwad, Nearest Villages- Haregali, Ajgarni, Vitnal, Bedarshirgur, Babli kop, Niralagi, Domagera, Alur, Ajgaon, Kesrolli, Halsi, Kerwad (H), Magwad, Buzurkanchanalli, Tatwanagi. S. H-93: Direction- Shimoga to Khanapur, Nearest Villages- Bablikop, Narnalli, Addigere, Bhagawati, Malawadi, Karlk atta, Kesrolli, Halsi, Kurigadde, Siddapur, Sambrani, Bukkankoppa, Nilwani, Madnalli, Dusagi, Muttalmuri, Antrolli, Tergaon, Havagi, Kerwad (H).

River: Kalinadi Nadi- Nearest Villages- Kumbarkop, Kerwad(Dandeli), Kariyampali, Badakanshirda, Harnoda, Mainal, Chimnalli, Malawad, Kalbhavi, Amga, Gutti, Donshirgur, Badashirgur, Bommanalli, Kegdal, Vincholli, Addigere, Balshettikop. Tattihalla Nadi- Nearest Villages- Kesrolli, Halsi, Kurigadde, Siddapur, Kumbarkop, Pura, Arshingeri, Kalginkop, Dodkop, Mavinkop, Dusagi, Muttalmuri, Antrolli, Hunswad, Kalasapur Mangalawad, Khamdolli, Chibbalgeri, Guledkop, Belwatgi, Dongrikop, Murkwad, Golehalli, Malwadi, Mugadkop, Janaga, Chinagin kop, Jatga, Basawalli, Kawalwad, Tergaon, Havagi, Hampehalli.

Annual Rainfall: Normal Rianfall 1166.3 mm.

Ground Water: Availability of the Ground Water in the Basin is 6319 H.A.M. and the utilization is 1238 H.A. M. It belongs to Safe category. Depth to water level 5 to 20 meter below the ground. Most of the wells go down in summer months, according to the Ground Water Estimation Committee.

Soils: Lateritic Soil.

Natural Division : It falls in the Yellapur-Dandeli Forest of the Karnataka Coast (Western Coastal Region).

Administration:

Division: Belgaum. Parliamentary Constituency: 12 Uttara Kannada. District: Uttara Kannada. Taluka: Haliyal. Assembly Constituency: 76. Gram Panchayat: 20.

Regional Area Development Boards: The Maland Aera Development Board.

Fairs: Basaveshwara Jatra: Basaveshvara jatra is held at Haliyal near Uttara Kannada for one day in about February-March every year.

Dandelappa Jatra: It is held at Dandeli near Uttara Kannada in about the month of October every year. Dande, a hobli centre, 21 kms. from Haliyal and 157 kms. from Karwar near Uttara Karnada is a famous industrial centre of the district.

Dyamavva Jatra: Gundolli, a place about 15 kms. from Haliyal near Uttara Kannada of considerable antiquity, has temples of Kalamma (grama-devata), Dyamavva,

Maddidyamavva (atop a small hill), Ishwara (near the tank), Maruti, Karevva, etc. The jatra of Dyamavva is held during April-May once in 12 years which attracts more than 10,000 people. The Ishwara of Kalmeshwara now in brick appears to be an ancient temple. Near this temple there are many antiquities such as three statues of Ganapati, one of Surya, etc. There are some broken hero-stones in the place.

Hanuman Jayanti Jatra: It is held at Tergaon near Uttara Kannada in the month of April. Tergaon 14 kms. from Haliyal is considerably a big place. The Kalmeshwara temple here which has two hero-stones and two mahasati-s tones in its precincts and on the banks of the local tank there are two more hero-stones..

Kavalelinga Jatra: It is held at Kavale Caves near Uttara Kannada in about the month of February-March. Kavale Caves about 37 kms. from Haliyal on the ridge of tall hills amdist captivating forest surroundings. This spot can be approached either by crossing the Nagjhari stream (from Power House) and climbing nearly 1,000 steps or through the Dandeli Game Sanctuary via Panasolli. From this village, one has to cover 12 kilometres distance and then descend 350 steps to reach the spot.

Someshwara Jatra: It is held at Kawalwad near Uttar Kannada in the month of Shravana (July-August).Kawalwad, is about 19 kms. from Haliyal on the Haliyal Kalaghati Road. It is known as Kahulawada in one of the two inscri ptions found in the place. The Someshwara temple here is a huge ancient structure recently renovated.

Umarali Urs: Haliyal, a taluk centre near Uttara Kannada has six mosques and three dargahs, and of these the Kasba area mosque is considerably old and the building is ascribed to Adilshahi times. Of the rest, two were built during the nineteenth century and the remaining are recent constructions. The dargah of Umar Ali, a saint of Adilshahi days, attracts a gathering of 5,000 people during its annual Urs held 10 days after Bakrid in the month Zul Haj. Near the Munsiff court there is the tomb of one Haidarshah in whose honour a Urs is held a day earlier to Umar Ali's Urs.

Villages: 129 **Inhabited:** 111 **Uninhabited:** 18

Ranking	District	State	National
Area	6	116	675
Population	6	164	4098
Sex Ratio	9	120	2879
Child Sex Ratio	3	31	1631
Literacy Rate	11	94	2955
Density	3	14	6149
Work Participation Rate	7	166	569

Gram Panchayats:

Yedoga, Mangalawad, Arlwad, Madnalli, Tergaon, Havagi, Tatwanagi, Buzurkanchanalli, Chibbalgeri, Nagshetikop, Murkwad, Belwatgi, Janaga, Gundolli, Kesrolli, Alur, Ambikanagar, Bhagawati, Sambrani, Kawalwad.

Amenities:

Education: Primary School in 88 villages, Middle school in 39 villages, Matriculation or Secondary School in 6 villages, namely Yedoga, Bhagawati, Gundolli, Mangalawad, Tergaon, Murkwad.

Higher Secondary or Pre University Courses or Intermediate or Junior College in 1 village of the CD Block,, namely Murkwad.

College in 0 village, Adult Literacy Center in 0 village.

Medical: Hospital in 0 village, Dispensary in 1 village, Health Center in 5 villages, Sub Center in 14 villages, Maternity and Child Welfare Center in 0 village, Community health workers in 0 village.

The Village having Hospital or Dispensary or Health Center is Buzurkanchanalli.

Drinking Water: Tap water in 64 villages, Tank water in 35 villages, Well water in 65 villages, Tubewell in 8 villages and more than one source in 95 villages.

Bank: Banking facility in 9 villages, namely, Bhagawati, Gundolli, Sambrani, Mangalawad, Tergaon Buzurkanchanalli, Nagshetikop, Belwatgi, Murkwad.

Credit Society in 7 villages Agricultural Credit Society in 6 Non-Agricultural Credit Society in 2 villages.

Others: Power supply in 98 villages, Cinema hall in 1 village, sport club in 0 village, Stadium or Auditorium or Community Hall in 0 village, Post Office in 30 villages.

There are 77 villages having bus facilities.

Villages with most of facilities: Bhagawati Gundolli, Sambrani, Mangalawad, Tergaon Buzurkanchanalli, Belwatgi, Murkwad.

Villages without amenities (Education): Kesrodaga, Singatgeri, Bidrolli, Channapur, Baloga, Satmani, Gutti, Badashirgur, Vincholli, Tatgera, Kesrolli, Halsi, Kumbarkop, Pura, Arshingeri, Chotakanshirda, Mundki, Malwad, Ambodaga, Kalasapur, Tegnalli, Guttibail, Dongrikop..

Scheduled Castes: Out of the total population of 80350 persons, 4917 persons (6.12%) belong to Scheduled Castes. The villages having less than 10% SC population are Haregali, Vitnal, Bedarshirgur, Handli, Ramapur Modalgera, Bidrolli, Timmapur, Channapur, Niralagi Baloga, Satmani, Jawalli, Domagera, Alur Kariyampali, Badakanshirda , Harnoda, Rayapattan Kalbhavi, Gutti, Badashirgur, Narnalli, Bommanalli Kegdal, Vincholli, Addigera, Bhagawati, Bhimanalli

Tatgera, Gardolli, Karlkatta, Ajga0N, Kesrolli Halsi, Kurigadde, Siddapur, Kumbarkop, Tippingeri Pura, Arshingeri, Kalginkop, Gundolli, Sambrani Balshettikop, Chotakanshirda, Nilwani, Hosur Adikehosur, Dodkop, Jatgahosur, Tattigeri, Mundki Arlwad, Homnalli, Madnalli, Dusagi, Muttalmuri Antrolli, Hunswad, Satnalli, Malwad, Ambodaga, Pala Kalasapur, Mangalawad, Tergaon, Magwad Buzurkanchanalli, Tatwanagi, Jogankop, Bhanasageri Tegnalli, Alolli, Khamdolli, Chibbalgeri Nagshetikop, Ghadiyal, Shivapur, Belwatgi, Golehalli Malwadi, Mugadkop, Khurd Kanchanalli, Janaga, Jatga Basawalli, Nandigadda, Kawalwad, Hampehalli.

The village having more than 50% SC population is None.

Sex ratio of Scheduled Caste population is 496.

Scheduled Castes Literates and Illiterates by Sex:

	Persons	Males	Females
Literate	2,296	1,443	853
Illiterate	2,621	1,034	1,587
Literacy rate	57.0	71.0	42.8
Graduate	53	42	11

Scheduled Castes (Dominant):

Bhovi, Kotegar etc., Korama, Chalavadi etc. Bhambi etc.

For their cultural identity please see Appendix-I

Villages without Scheduled Castes: There are 50 villages without any scheduled caste population.

Scheduled Tribes: Out of the total population of 80350 persons, 1394 persons (1.73%) belong to Scheduled Tribes.

The villages having less than 10% ST population are Haregali, Gobral, Kesrodaga, Vitnal, Ambewadi Bedarshirgur, Ramapur, Modalgera, Bidrolli, Yedoga Timmapur, Channapur, Niralagi, Baloga, Satmani Jawalli, Domagera, Alur, Kyatangera Kerwad (Dandeli), Kariyampali, Badakanshirda Harnoda, Mainal, Rayapattan, Kalbhavi, Kulgi, Gutti Badashirgur, Narnalli, Bommanalli, Vincholli Addigera, Bhagawati, Bhimanalli, Tatgera, Gardolli Gadagera, Karlkatta, Agasalkatta, Ajga0N, Kesrolli Halsi, Kurigadde, Siddapur, Kumbarkop, Tippingeri Pura, Arshingeri, Kalginkop, Gundolli, Sambrani Balshettikop, Chotakanshirda, Bukkankoppa, Nilwani Ajminal, Hosur, Adikehosur, Dodkop, Jatgahosur Tattigeri, Mundki, Arlwad, Homnalli, Dusagi Muttalmuri, Antrolli, Hunswad, Satnalli, Malwad Ambodaga, Pala, Kalasapur, Mangalawad, Tergaon Havagi, Kerwad (H), Magwad, Buzurkanchanalli Tatwanagi, Ammankop, Jogankop, Bhanasageri, Tegnalli Alolli, Khamdolli, Chibbalgeri, Guttibail Nagshetikop, Mundwad, Ghadiyal, Guledkop, Belwatgi Dongrikop, Murkwad, Golehalli, Malwadi, Mugadkop Khurd Kanchanalli, Janaga, Jatga, Basawalli Nandigadda, Kawalwad, Hampehalli.

The villages having more than 50% ST population are None.

Sex ratio of Scheduled tribe population is 494.

Scheduled Tribes Literates and Illiterates by Sex:

	Persons	Males	Females
Literate	571	347	224
Illiterate	823	359	464
Literacy rate	48.5	57.8	38.8
Graduate	10	10	0

Scheduled Tribes (Dominant):

Naikda etc., Kadu Kuruba, Bhil etc., Meda Jenu Kuruba

For their cultural identity please see Appendix-II

Villages without Scheduled Tribes: There are 87 villages without any scheduled tribe population.

Literates and Illiterates by Sex (Total Population):

	Persons	Males	Females
Literate	39,611	24,343	15,268
Illiterate	40,739	16,614	24,125
Literacy rate	59	71	46
Graduate	719	579	140

Agriculture: ***Distribution of villages according to land use:*** Out of 129 villages, Total area (in hectare) is 82083, out of that 24.41 percent is cultivable and 15.87 percent of the cultivable area is irrigated.

Sources of Irrigation (Hectares): Government Canal 1709.09, Private Canal 0, Well without Electricity 0, Well with Electricity 131.44, Tubewell without Electricity 0, Tubewell with Electricity 811.4, Tank 1508.14, River 236.97, Lake 4.55, Waterfall 0, Others 0.

Villages with population of 5000 to 9999: None

Villages with population of 10000 and above: None

Distribution of Workers:

	Persons	Males	Females	WPR
Cultivators	25,301	14,869	10,432	57.69
Agricultural Labour	9,659	3,474	6,185	22.02
Household Industry	1,227	870	357	2.8
Other Workers	7,673	5,918	1,755	17.49
Main Workers	36,470	22,963	13,507	83.15
Marginal Workers	7,390	2,168	5,222	16.85
Total Workers	43,860	25,131	18,729	

Religion: Major Religious Communities:

	Persons	Males	Females	Sex Ratio
Hindu (86.88%)	69,808	35,667	34,141	957
Muslim (7.7%)	6,185	3,087	3,098	1,004
Christian (3.43%)	2,757	1,360	1,397	1,027

Sikh (0.01%)	6	2	4	2,000
Buddhists (0%)	1	1	-	-
Jain (1.89%)	1,519	805	714	887

Agewise Data:

	Persons	Males	Females	Sex Ratio
All ages	80,350	40,957	39,393	962
0-14	28,259	14,268	13,991	981
15-44	36,789	18,969	17,820	939
45-79	14,574	7,391	7,183	972
80+	677	302	375	1242
Age not stated	51	27	24	889

Languages (Dominant):
Marathi, Kannada, Urdu, Konkani, Hindi

Disabled Population:

	Persons	Males	Females	%
Total Disabled	1,515	855	660	
In Seeing	550	279	271	36.3
In Speech	108	68	40	7.13
In Hearing	104	56	48	6.86
In Movement	589	367	222	38.88
Mentally	164	85	79	10.83

HANGAL

Hangal C.D. Block lies in the western part of Haveri district. It is a part of Hangal taluka. The Block is located at a distance of 32 kms. from district headquarters (Haveri). There are 151 villages in the block with the total population of 205,299 persons. Area of the C.D. Block is 753.15 sq. kms. It is bounded by taluk Shiggaon on north, district Shimoga and taluk Hirekerur on south, taluks Savanur, Haveri and Byadgi on east, and district Uttara Kannada on west.

Communications:

Roadways : S.H-1: Direction- Shikarpur to Shiggaon, Nearest Villages- Nellikoppa, Badamgatti, Yalavatti, Nitaginakoppa, Gundur, Maharajpet, Rathnapur, Kargudri, Malligar, Savasgi, Girishinkoppa, Gejjihalli, Mavakoppa, Dyamankoppa (Sarkar), Mudur, Kondoji, Makarvalli, Hirekounshi,Gondi, Sevalal, Balur, Hanamapur. S.H-2: Direction-Sirsi to Haveri, Nearest Villages- Hanumanakoppa, Gadiyankanahalli, Mavakoppa, Balihalli, Harlakoppa, Sammasgi, Janginakoppa, Channapur (M) Adur, Adur, Kodiyellapur, Shingapur, Balambeed, Havanagi, Gururayapatna, Sevalal, Balur, Akki Alur.

River: Varada Nadi- Nearest Villages- Harvi, Kudal, Naregal, Wardi, Shyadaguppi, Makarvalli, Gondi, Adur, Shingapur, Sheegihalli (Shingahalli), Tumarikoppa, Lakamapur (M) Adur, Balambeed, Havanagi, Veerapura, Hirehullal, Chikkahullal, Basapur (M) Adur, Somapur, Malagund, Wasan, Kusnur, Kanneshwar, Arashinguppi, Sheshagiri, Honkan, Lakmapur (Inam), Byathanal.

Canal: Nearest Villages- Naregal, Kalvekallapur, Nellibeed, Jakkanaikankoppa, Kanchinegalur, Araleshwar, Kalveyellapur, Hotanhalli, Akkivalli, Surleshwar, Dolleshwar, Girishinkoppa, Gejjihalli, Sringeri, Savikeri, Hanumanakoppa, Hirur, Gadiyankanahalli, Channapur (M), Adur, Balambeed, Havanagi, Akki Alur, Malagund.

Reserved Forest: Nearest Villages- Hirekanagi, Bidarakoppa, Chikkeri, Kamanhalli, Manthagi, Savikeri, Hanumanakoppa, Hirur, Gadiyankanahalli, Mavakoppa, Dyamankopa (Sarkar), Balihalli, Harlakoppa, Neralgi (Inam), Hulaginahalli, Konankoppa, Kyasanur, Shirgoda, Janginakoppa, Mudur, Kondoji, Shyadaguppi, Makarvalli, Hanamapur, Arashinguppi, Sheshagiri, Honkan. (Hullati R.F.): Nearest Villages- Yaliwal, Bailwal, Hullatti, Dasharatkoppa, Gadegundiyellapur, Cheeranahalli, Gudagudi, Thimmapur (M) Nidasangi, Ramathirtha, Baichavalli, Handihal.

Annual Rainfall: Normal Rianfall 592 mm.

Ground Water: Availability of the Ground Water in the Basin is 78.21 MCM and the utilization is 30.20 MCM. It belongs to Over Exploited category. Depth to water level 10 to 20 meter below the ground. Most of the wells go down in summer months, according to the Ground Water Estimation Committee.

Soils: Red Sandy Soil, Medium Soil, Deep Black Soil, Red Loamy Soil and Lateritic Soil.

Natural Division : It falls partly in Barada Basin and Byadagi-Hirekerur Rocky Knobs of the Central Karnataka Plateau.

Administration:

Division: Belgaum. Parliamentary Constituency: 10 Haveri. District: Haveri. Taluka: Hangal. Assembly Constituency: 82 Hangal. Gram Panchayat: 40.

Regional Area Development Boards: The Maland Aera Development Board.

Villages: 151 **Inhabited:** 150 **Uninhabited:** 1

Ranking	District	State	National
Area	4	131	826
Population	2	84	627
Sex Ratio	1	139	3328
Child Sex Ratio	3	41	2013
Literacy Rate	3	44	1638
Density	7	123	3827
Work Participation Rate	1	33	2884

Gram Panchayats:

Hullatti, Bommanahalli, Yalavatti, Masankatti, Kudal, Maranabeed, Belagalapeth, Kargudri, Baichavalli, Kopparsikoppa, Savasgi, Kanchinegalur, Naregal, Sheegihalli-Shingapur , Adur, Balambeed, Araleshwar, Surleshwar, Hirekanagi, Manthagi, Hirur, Gejjihalli, Akkialur, Havanagi, Hirehullal, Herur, Uppanshi,

Somasagara, Kusnur, Malagund, Kallapur, Shirgoda, Sammasgi, Chikkounshi Hosur, Gondi, Shyadaguppi, Honkan, Kelavarkoppa, Tilavalli, Kirwadi.

Amenities:

Education: Primary School in 143 villages, Middle school in 106 villages, Matriculation or Secondary School in 23 villages, namely Bommanahalli, Maranabeed, Naregal, Belagalapeth, Baichavalli, Kadashettihalli, Kopparsikoppa, Araleshwar, Hirekanagi, Shirgoda, Chikkounshi Hosur, Shyadaguppi, Gondi, Adur, Balambeed, Akki Alur, Herur, Uppanshi, Kalkeri, Kusnur, Sheshagiri, Tilavalli, Kirwadi.

Higher Secondary or Pre University Courses or Intermediate or Junior College in 6 villages of the CD Block,, namely Bommanahalli, Belagalapeth, Araleshwar, Adur, Akki Alur, Tilavalli.

College in 1 village, Adult Literacy Center in 7 villages., College is in village, namely Akki Alur.

Medical: Hospital in 3 villages, Dispensary in 8 villages, Health Center in 10 villages, Sub Center in 43 villages, Maternity and Child Welfare Center in 2 villages, Community health workers in 26 villages.

The Villages having Hospital or Dispensary or Health Center are Belagalapeth, Kopparsikoppa, Sammasgi, Shirgoda, Chikkounshi Hosur, Gondi, Adur, Havanagi, Akki Alur, Kalkeri.

Drinking Water: Tap water in 121 villages, Tank water in 31 villages, Well water in 35 villages, Tubewell in 22 villages and more than one source in 128 villages.

Bank: Banking facility in 28 villages, namely, Bommanahalli, Hospet, Neeralgi (M) Adur, Harvi Maranabeed, Masankatti, Dyamankoppa (Inam) Nitaginakoppa, Aladakatti, Kudal, Naregal Belagalapeth, Baichavalli, Kopparsikoppa, Araleshwar Manthagi, Hirur, Mavakoppa, Sammasgi, Shirgoda Chikkounshi Hosur, Gondi, Adur, Akki Alur, Kallapur Kusnur, Sheshagiri, Tilavalli.

Credit Society in 25 villages Agricultural Credit Society in 22 Non-Agricultural Credit Society in 6 villages.

Others: Power supply in 148 villages, Cinema hall in 6 villages, sport club in 0 village, Stadium or Auditorium or Community Hall in 0 village, Post Office in 41 villages.

There are 130 villages having bus facilities.

Villages with most of facilities: Bommanahalli Harvi, Maranabeed, Masankatti, Nitaginakoppa Aladakatti, Naregal, Belagalapeth, Baichavalli Kopparsikoppa, Araleshwar, Manthagi, Hirur, Sammasgi Shirgoda, Chikkounshi Hosur, Gondi, Adur, Akki Alur Kallapur, Kusnur, Sheshagiri, Tilavalli.

Villages without amenities (Education): Chandragiri, Negavanigi, Sivajipur, Satenhalli, Mattihalli, Gururayapatna, Sevalal..

Scheduled Castes: Out of the total population of 205741 persons, 29431 persons (14.3%) belong to Scheduled Castes.

The villages having less than 10% SC population are Yaliwal, Bommanahalli, Hanamasagar, Badamgatti Walageri, Harvi, Haranagiri, Maranabeed, Masankatti Belavatti (Hunasikatti), Yalavatti, Hullatti Gadegundiyellapur, Hasanabadi, Basapur (M) Nidasangi Yallur, Nitaginakoppa, Gundur, Aladakatti Chandragiri, Bhingapur, Allapur, Kudal, Naregal Wardi, Belagalapeth, Gudagudi, Ramathirtha Baichavalli, Shirmapur (M) Adur, Kadashettihalli Kanchinegalur, Kopparsikoppa, Gazipur, Araleshwar Hotanhalli, Akkivalli, Kuntanhosahalli, Hosahalli Gotagodi, Handihal, Surleshwar, Dolleshwar Girishinkoppa, Kamanhalli, Manthagi, Hanumanakoppa Hirur, Dyamankoppa (Sarkar), Harlakoppa, Sammasgi Hulaginahalli, Shirgoda, Gondi, Channapur (M) Adur Adur, Sankrikoppa, Kodiyellapur, Shingapur Sheegihalli (Shingahalli), Tumarikoppa Lakamapur (M) Adur, Balambeed, Havanagi, Balur Veerapura, Hirehullal, Herur, Chikkahullal Tavargoppa, Basapur (M) Adur, Somapur, Malagund Kallapur, Yallapur (Inam), Kusnur, Somasagara Mulathalli, Kelavarkoppa, Lakmapur (Inam), Byathanal Tilavalli, Yathinhalli (M) Tilavalli, Koppagondankop.

The villages having more than 50% SC population are Nellikoppa, Janagundikoppa, Dasharatkoppa Negavanigi, Sivajipur, Rathnapur, Hulaginakoppa Bidarakoppa, Sringeri, Mavakoppa, Neralgi (Inam) Mattihalli, Konankoppa, Kyasanur, Janginakoppa Kondoji, Gururayapatna, Sevalal, Hanamapur Karekyathanahalli, Malapur, Hallibail, Kalguddi.

Sex ratio of Scheduled Caste population is 485.

Scheduled Castes Literates and Illiterates by Sex:

	Persons	Males	Females
Literate	13,034	8,436	4,598
Illiterate	16,397	6,729	9,668
Literacy rate	52.3	65.7	38.1
Graduate	297	274	23

Scheduled Castes (Dominant):

Bhovi, Banjara etc., Bhambi etc., Chalavadi etc. Korama

For their cultural identity please see Appendix-I

Villages without Scheduled Castes: There are 12 villages without any scheduled caste population.

Scheduled Tribes: Out of the total population of 205741 persons, 17942 persons (8.72%) belong to Scheduled Tribes.

The villages having less than 10% ST population are

Yaliwal, Bommanahalli, Hanamasagar, Nellikoppa Hospet, Neeralgi (M) Adur, Harvi, Haranagiri Masankatti, Janagundikoppa, Yalavatti, Bailwal Hullatti, Gadegundiyellapur, Yallur, Gundur Bhingapur, Hombli, Allapur, Kudal, Naregal, Wardi Kalvekallapur, Nellibeed, Belagalapeth, Negavanigi Sivajipur, Maharajpet, Ramathirtha, Rathnapur Kargudri, Kadashettihalli, Kopparsikoppa, Gazipur Hulaginakoppa, Satenhalli, Malligar, Kuntanhosahalli Hosahalli, Hirekanagi, Bidarakoppa, Surleshwar Dolleshwar, Girishinkoppa, Kamanhalli, Laxmipur Sagarvalli, Sringeri, Hanumanakoppa, Hirur Gadiyankanahalli, Dyamankoppa (Sarkar), Harlakoppa Sammasgi, Neralgi (Inam), Mattihalli, Kyasanur Shirgoda, Chikkounshi Hosur, Janginakoppa, Mudur Gondi, Channapur (M) Adur, Adur, Shingapur Lakamapur (M) Adur, Gururayapatna, Sevalal, Balur Akki Alur, Veerapura, Herur, Uppanshi, Kalkeri Tavargoppa, Somapur, Kallapur, Hanamapur Yallapur (Inam), Kusnur, Somasagara Guddad Mattihalli, Dommanala, Hirebasur Karekyathanahalli, Byathanal, Malapur, Tilavalli Hallibail, Kalguddi, Yathinhalli (M) Tilavalli.

The villages having more than 50% ST population are None.

Sex ratio of Scheduled tribe population is 490.

Scheduled Tribes Literates and Illiterates by Sex:

	Persons	Males	Females
Literate	8,779	5,480	3,299
Illiterate	9,163	3,667	5,496
Literacy rate	57.4	70.1	44.1
Graduate	193	179	14

Scheduled Tribes (Dominant):

Naikda etc., Koraga, Iruliga, Kadu Kuruba, Meda

For their cultural identity please see Appendix-II

Villages without Scheduled Tribes: There are 36 villages without any scheduled tribe population.

Literates and Illiterates by Sex (Total Population):

	Persons	Males	Females
Literate	117,253	68,723	48,530
Illiterate	88,488	36,637	51,851
Literacy rate	67	76	57
Graduate	3,028	2,509	519

Agriculture: ***Distribution of villages according to land use:*** Out of 151 villages, Total area (in hectare) is 75315, out of that 75.78 percent is cultivable and 35.65 percent of the cultivable area is irrigated.

Sources of Irrigation (Hectares): Government Canal 5842.47, Private Canal 40.47, Well without Electricity 0, Well with Electricity 6.96, Tubewell without Electricity 0, Tubewell with Electricity 2794.09, Tank 10412.04, River 1191.4[illegible] Lake 0, Waterfall 0, Others 26.45.

Villages with population of 5000 to 9999:

Tilavalli.

Villages with population of 10000 and above:

Akki Alur.

Distribution of Workers:

	Persons	Males	Females	WPR
Cultivators	36,124	29,973	6,151	37.72
Agricultural Labour	45,492	21,259	24,233	47.5
Household Industry	2,370	1,681	689	2.47
Other Workers	11,792	10,003	1,789	12.31
Main Workers	72,869	55,678	17,191	76.08
Marginal Workers	22,909	7,238	15,671	23.92
Total Workers	95,778	62,916	32,862	

Religion: Major Religious Communities:

	Persons	Males	Females	Sex Ratio
Hindu (80.27%)	165,152	84,649	80,503	951
Muslim (17.96%)	36,956	18,797	18,159	966
Christian (0.05%)	109	56	53	946
Sikh (0%)	3	2	1	500
Buddhists (0%)	1	1	-	-
Jain (1.27%)	2,611	1,398	1,213	868

Agewise Data:

	Persons	Males	Females	Sex Ratio
All ages	205,741	105,360	100,381	953
0-14	69,844	35,601	34,243	962
15-44	98,750	51,085	47,665	933
45-79	35,503	17,969	17,534	976
80+	1,501	626	875	1398
Age not stated	143	79	64	810

Languages (Dominant):

Kannada, Urdu, Hindi, Telugu, Marathi

Disabled Population:

	Persons	Males	Females	%
Total Disabled	3,740	2,171	1,569	
In Seeing	1,520	808	712	40.64
In Speech	407	243	164	10.88
In Hearing	197	108	89	5.27
In Movement	1,164	756	408	31.12
Mentally	452	256	196	12.09

HARAPANAHALLI

Harapanahalli C.D. Block lies in the northern part of Davana gere district. It is a part of Harapanahalli taluka. The Block is located at a distance of 52 kms. from district headquarters (Davanagere). There are 80 villages in the block with the total population of 226,831 persons. Area of the C.D. Block is 1395.84 sq. kms. It is bounded by district Bellary on north, taluks Harihar and Davana gere on south, taluk Jagalur and district Bellary on east, districts Haveri and Bellary on west.

Communications:

Roadways : S.H-2: Direction- Haveri to Machihalli, Nearest Villages- Neelagunda, Ittigudi, Kunchur, Halavagal, Machihalli. S.H-40: Direction- Kudligi to Harapanahalli, Nearest Vill.- Nichapura, Adavihalli, Bennihalli, Niluvanji, Pruthveswara. S.H-25: Direction- Harihar to Hospet, Nearest Villages- Neelagunda, Ananthanahalli, Kodihalli, Bagali, Sringarathota, Kanvihalli, Nandibevoor, Chirast

River: Tungabhadra Nadi- Nearest Villages- Halavagal, Tavaragundi, Nittur Basapura, Nittur, Kadathi. Chikka HagariNadi- Nearest Villages- Bennihalli, Sasvihalli, Mathihalli, Aladahalli, Hagari Gudihalli, Hosakote, Budihal, Madihalli, Anajigeri, Ramaghatta.

Reserved Forest: (Ahigilawada R.F.): Nearest Villages- Kadathi, Yerbalu, Aligilawada, Shivapur. (Neelagunda R.F.): Nearest Villages- Neelagunda, Ittigudi, Aligilawada, Shivapur, Chirasthahalli, Machihalli, Neelagunda, Ittig udi, Chirasthahalli, Machihalli. (Hyarada R.F.): Nearset Villages- Chennahalli, Harakanahal, Hulikatti, Kannayaka nahalli, Arasanahal, K.Kallahalli, Kunchur, Halavagal. (Togarikatti R.F.): Nearest Villages- Hulikatti, Kannay akanahalli, Madalageri, Togarikatti. (Jajkalgudda R.F.): Nearest Villages- Kodihalli, Bagali, Sringarathota, Kayakadahalli, Nichapura, Kanvihalli, Kongana Hossur, Mydur, Chigateri, Pruthveswara. (Jittinakatti R.F.): Nearest Villages- Muttigi, Komaranahalli, Kambatrahalli, Nichavvanahalli, Kadabageri, Gundagathi, Sevanagar, Yadihalli, Kyarakatti, Towdur, Punabagatta,. Kanchikeri, Hallikeri. (Uchangidurga R.F.): Nearest Villages- Punab agatta, Kanchikeri, Hiremegalageri, Uchangidurga. (Sogi R.F.): Nearest Villages- Togarikatti, Kulahalli, Kodihalli, Kanvihalli.

Annual Rainfall: Normal Rianfall 507 mm.

Ground Water: Availability of the Ground Water in the Basin is 11946.14 H.A.M. and the utilization is 11370. 59 H.A.M. It belongs to Over Exploited category. Depth to watcr level 5 to 20 meter below the ground. Most of the wells go down in summer months, according to the Ground Water Estimation Committee.

Soils: Red Sandy Soils and Black Soils.

Natural Division : It falls partly in Harapanahalli Scrub by Uplands and Chikka Hagari Valley of the Central Karnat aka Plateau.

Administration:

Division: Bangalore. Parliamentary Constituency: 13 Davanagere. District: Davanagere. Taluka: Harapanahalli. Assembly Constituency: 103 Jagalpur (ST). Gram Panchayat:35.

Regional Area Development Boards: The Hyderabad - Karnataka Area Development Board.

Villages: 80 **Inhabited:** 80 **Uninhabited:** 0

Ranking	District	State	National
Area	1	40	182
Population	3	62	396
Sex Ratio	2	122	2946
Child Sex Ratio	2	84	2884
Literacy Rate	6	123	3743
Density	2	73	5357
Work Participation Rate	5	109	1797

Gram Panchayats:

Madalageri, Nandibevoor, Kulahalli, Harakanahal, Bagali, Mydur, Chigateri, Togarikatti, K.Kallahalli, Adavihalli, Bennihalli, Mathihalli, Sasvihalli, Neelagunda, Kunchur, Halavagal, Nittur, Chirasthahalli, Gundagathi, Nichavvanahalli, Kadabageri, Arsikeri, Yadihalli, Duggavatti, Teligi, Towdur, Hosakote, Punabagatta, Kanchikeri, Ragimasalawada, Singrihalli, Anajigeri, Uchangidurga, Hiremegalageri, Chatnihalli.

Amenities:

Education: Primary School in 76 villages, Middle school in 67 villages, Matriculation or Secondary School in 27 villages, namely Togarikatti, Neelagunda, Bagali, Mydur, Chigateri, Gajapura, Bennihalli, Hikkimgeri, Kadabageri, Sasvihalli, Mathihalli, Kunchur, Halavagal, Kadathi, Machihalli, Gundagathi, Teligi, Duggavatti, Arsikeri, Madihalli, Anajigeri, Punabagatta, Kanchikeri, Singrihalli, Laxmipura, Hiremegalageri, Uchangidurga.

Higher Secondary or Pre University Courses or Intermediate or Junior College in 8 villages of the CD Block,, namely Togarikatti, Mathihalli, Kunchur, Halavagal, Teligi, Madihalli, Singrihalli, Uchangidurga.

College in 0 village, Adult Literacy Center in 0 village.

Medical: Hospital in 13 villages, Dispensary in 8 villages, Health Center in 10 villages, Sub Center in 48 villages, Maternity and Child Welfare Center in 10 villages, Community health workers in 17 villages.

The Villages having Hospital or Dispensary or Health Center are Chennahalli, Hulikatti, Nandibevoor, Chigateri, Bennihalli, Kadabageri, Sasvihalli, Mathihalli, K.Kallahalli, Halavagal, Gundagathi, Teligi, Ragimasalawada, Arsikeri, Punabagatta, Kanchikeri, Hiremegalageri, Uchangidurga.

Drinking Water: Tap water in 48 villages, Tank water in 2 villages, Well water in 3 villages, Tubewell in 30 villages and more than one source in 54 villages.

Bank: Banking facility in 16 villages, namely, Harakanahal, Neelagunda, Bagali, Nandibevoor

Chigateri, Bennihalli, Mathihalli, Halavagal Gundagathi, Teligi, Ragimasalawada, Arsikeri Madihalli, Kanchikeri, Hiremegalageri, Uchangidurga.

Credit Society in 1 village Agricultural Credit Society in 0 Non-Agricultural Credit Society in 1 village.

Others: Power supply in 80 villages, Cinema hall in 4 villages, sport club in 0 village, Stadium or Auditorium or Community Hall in 0 village, Post Office in 55 villages.

There are 74 villages having bus facilities.

Villages with most of facilities: Harakanahal Neelagunda, Bagali, Nandibevoor, Chigateri Bennihalli, Mathihalli, Halavagal, Gundagathi Teligi, Ragimasalawada, Arsikeri, Madihalli Kanchikeri, Hiremegalageri, Uchangidurga.

Villages without amenities (Education):
Chennahalli, Myalikatti, Thimalapura..

Scheduled Castes: Out of the total population of 226886 persons, 53901 persons (23.76%) belong to Scheduled Castes.

The villages having less than 10% SC population are Ananthanahalli, Myalikatti, Madapura, Kodihalli Kayakadahalli, Nichapura, Adavihalli, Niluvanji Komaranahalli, Kambatrahalli, Joislingapura Aladahalli, Ittigudi, Tavaragundi, Nittur Basapura Madihalli, Sathur.

The villages having more than 50% SC population are Chennahalli, Kannayakanahalli, Bapujinagar, Shivapur Towdur, Laxmipura , Ramaghatta.

Sex ratio of Scheduled Caste population is 489.

Scheduled Castes Literates and Illiterates by Sex:

	Persons	Males	Females
Literate	18,188	12,182	6,006
Illiterate	35,713	15,374	20,339
Literacy rate	40.8	53.7	27.5
Graduate	489	458	31

Scheduled Castes (Dominant):

Banjara etc., Madiga, Bhovi, Adi Karnataka Bhambi etc.

For their cultural identity please see Appendix-I

Villages without Scheduled Castes: There are 6 villages without any scheduled caste population.

Scheduled Tribes: Out of the total population of 226886 persons, 37164 persons (16.38%) belong to Scheduled Tribes.

The villages having less than 10% ST population are Chennahalli, Harakanahal, Kannayakanahalli Bapujinagar, Togarikatti, Myalikatti, Narayanapura Kulahalli, Bagali, Sringarathota, Kayakadahalli Nandibevoor, Kongana Hossur, Mydur, Gajapura Bennihalli, Niluvanji, Sasvihalli, Arasanahal K.Kallahalli, Ittigudi, Tavaragundi, Nittur Basapura Kadathi, Shivapur , Machihalli, Siriganahalli Towdur, Thimalapura, Budihal, Madihalli.

The villages having more than 50% ST population are Ananthanahalli, Komaranahalli, Kambatrahalli Nichavvanahalli.

Sex ratio of Scheduled tribe population is 492.

Scheduled Tribes Literates and Illiterates by Sex:

	Persons	Males	Females
Literate	13,438	8,508	4,930
Illiterate	23,726	10,373	13,353
Literacy rate	43.0	53.6	32.1
Graduate	210	192	18

Scheduled Tribes (Dominant):

Naikda etc., Generic Tribes etc., Dubla etc., Meda Kadu Kuruba

For their cultural identity please see Appendix-II

Villages without Scheduled Tribes: There are 7 villages without any scheduled tribe population.

Literates and Illiterates by Sex (Total Population):

	Persons	Males	Females
Literate	105,164	65,293	39,871
Illiterate	121,722	50,427	71,295
Literacy rate	55	66	42
Graduate	2,957	2,622	335

Agriculture: ***Distribution of villages according to land use:***
Out of 80 villages, Total area (in hectare) is 139584, out of that 70.16 percent is cultivable and 14.87 percent of the cultivable area is irrigated.

Sources of Irrigation (Hectares): Government Canal 2195.8, Private Canal 0, Well without Electricity 0, Well with Electricity 1.62, Tubewell without Electricity 0, Tubewell with Electricity 10025.81, Tank 975.02, River 80.94, Lake 0, Waterfall 0, Others 1283.76.

Villages with population of 5000 to 9999:
Chigateri, Halavagal, Teligi, Towdur, Arsikeri Punabagatta, Hiremegalageri, Uchangidurga.

Villages with population of 10000 and above: None

Distribution of Workers:

	Persons	Males	Females	WPR
Cultivators	39,067	30,734	8,333	34.19
Agricultural Labour	56,800	22,028	34,772	49.72
Household Industry	3,821	1,794	2,027	3.34
Other Workers	14,560	10,749	3,811	12.74
Main Workers	82,171	56,151	26,020	71.92
Marginal Workers	32,077	9,154	22,923	28.08
Total Workers	114,248	65,305	48,943	

Religion: Major Religious Communities:

	Persons	Males	Females	Sex Ratio
Hindu (92.54%)	209,961	107,158	102,803	959
Muslim (4.25%)	9,632	4,922	4,710	957
Christian (0.03%)	70	37	33	892

Sikh (0%)	8	5	3	600
Buddhists (0%)	1	1	-	-
Jain (0.05%)	117	53	64	1,208

Agewise Data:

	Persons	Males	Females	Sex Ratio
All ages	226,886	115,720	111,166	961
0-14	82,051	41,787	40,264	964
15-44	103,574	53,551	50,023	934
45-79	39,041	19,420	19,621	1010
80+	1,903	797	1,106	1388
Age not stated	317	165	152	921

Languages (Dominant):
Kannada, Hindi, Urdu, Telugu, Coorgi/Kodagu

Disabled Population:

	Persons	Males	Females	%
Total Disabled	4,596	2,607	1,989	
In Seeing	2,317	1,279	1,038	50.41
In Speech	452	239	213	9.83
In Hearing	184	90	94	4
In Movement	1,187	745	442	25.83
Mentally	456	254	202	9.92

HARIHAR

Harihar C.D. Block lies in the western part of Davanagere district. It is a part of Harihar taluka. The Block is located at a distance of 14 kms. from district headqu arters (Davanagere). There are 84 villages in the block with the total population of 157,878 persons. Area of the C.D. Block is 461.74 sq. kms. It is bounded by taluk Harapanahalli on north, taluk Honnali on south, taluks Davanagere and Harapanahalli on east, and district Haveri on west.

Communications:
Roadways : N.H-4: Direction- Dharwad to Bangalore, Village- Doggalli. S.H-25: Direction- Honnali to Hospet, Nearest Villages- Kumbalur, Nandi Tavare, Malebennur, Komaranahalli, Koppa, Yakkegondi, Byaladahalli, Belludi, Hanagawadi, Mahajenahalli, Bhyranahalli, Dheetur, Hotti genahalli, Kurubarahalli, Karalahalli.

River: Tungabhadra Nadi- Nearest Villages- Huliginahole, Ingalagondi, Dhulehole, Nandigavi, Bilasanur, Hosahalli, Yalehole, Ukkadagathri, Malalahalli, Palya, Vasana, Nandigudi, Govinahalu, Baggadanahalu, Muginagondi, Thimlapura, Rajanahalli, Halasabalu, Bhyranahalli, Dheet ur, Pamenahalli, Chikkabidre, Sarathi. Haridra Nadi- Nearest Villages- Nandi Tavare, Kunibelakere, Budihalu, Guladahalli, Sanklipura, Halasabalu, Haraganahalli, Nagenahalli, Ramathirtha, Rayapura, Bhanuvalli, Yakkego ndi, Byaladahalli, Belludi, Hanagawadi, Mahajenahalli, Salaganahalli, Kadlegondi, Devarabelakere.

Canal: Nearest Villages- Bilasanur, Hosahalli, Kamalapura, Kadaranaikanahalli, Yalavatti, Jigali, Hallihalu, Kambathanahalli, Kokkanur, Hindasaghatte, Govinahalu, Bevinahalli, Vadera Basapura, Kumbalur, Nittur, Maleben nur, Komaranahalli, Dibadahalli, Halivana, Mudalabasapura, Thimlapura, Rajanahalli, Ramathirtha, Bhanuvalli, Lakkasettihalli.

Annual Rainfall: Normal Rianfall 579 mm.

Ground Water: Availability of the Ground Water in the Basin is 6317.29 H.A.M. and the utilization is 2966. 95 H.A.M. It belongs to Over Exploited category. Depth to water level 5to 20 meter below the ground. Most of the wells go down in summer months, according to the Ground Water Estimation Committee.

Soils: Red Sandy Soils and Black Soils.

Natural Division : It falls in Middle Tungabhadra Valley of the Central Karnataka Plateau.

Administration:
Division: Bangalore. Parliamentary Constituency: 13 Davanagere. District: Davanagere. Taluka: Harihar. Assem bly Constituency: 105 Harihar. Gram Panchayat: 25.

Fairs and Festivals: Sangameshvara Jatra: It is held around the month of March at Harihar near Chitradurga. Harihar is an ancient town situated on the right bank of the Tungab It is the headquarters of the taluk bearing the same name, and it is only 15 kms. west of Davangere. According to a legend, this spot was the capital or stronghold of a giant named Guha or Guhasura, the limits of whose territory were Uchchangi-durga in the east, Govinahal in the south, Mudunur in the west and Airani in the north. Guhasura, having by his penance, obtained from Brahma a boon of exemption from death at the hands of either Hari or Hara, became trouble some to both gods and men. On a request by the latter, Hari and Hara,in order to counteract the spell, combined themselves into one form of Harihara and destroyed him. The descent of this incarnation was at Kudlur, now Harihara, the place of confluence of the Tungabhadra and Harihara, where the 'god's footprints' are still shown. The giant while dying prayed that the place might be named after him, whence it came to be called Guharanya Kshetra.

Villages: 84 **Inhabited:** 75 **Uninhabited:** 9

Ranking	**District**	**State**	**National**
Area	6	166	1641
Population	5	123	1617
Sex Ratio	6	155	3707
Child Sex Ratio	5	98	3198
Literacy Rate	4	73	2326
Density	5	161	3171
Work Participation Rate	1	17	3818

Gram Panchayats:

Sarathi, Kondajji, Guttur, Haralapura , Rajanahalli, Hanagawadi, Yalehole, Nandigavi, Belludi, Bannikodu, Bhanuvalli, Sirigere, Vasana, Kadaranaikanahalli, Yalavatti, Bevinahalli, Salakatte, Devarabelakere, Kunibelakere, Kumbalur, Jigali, Kokkanur, Malebennur, Haralahalli, Halivana.

Amenities:

Education: Primary School in 72 villages, Middle school in 60 villages, Matriculation or Secondary School in 21 villages, namely Dhulehole, Bilasanur, Sirigere, Ukkadagathri, Nandigudi, Jigali, Kokkanur, Kumbalur, Nandi Tavare, Kunibelakere, Budihalu, Malebennur, Halivana, Guladahalli, Rajanahalli, Bhanuvalli, Belludi, Sarathi, Kondajji, Bannikodu, Devarabelakere.

Higher Secondary or Pre University Courses or Intermediate or Junior College in 5 villages of the CD Block,, namely Sirigere, Kumbalur, Malebennur, Kondajji, Devarabelakere.

College in 2 villages, Adult Literacy Center in 0 village., Colleges are in villages, namely Malebennur, Kondajji.

Medical: Hospital in 3 villages, Dispensary in 13 villages, Health Center in 7 villages, Sub Center in 29 villages, Maternity and Child Welfare Center in 7 villages, Community health workers in 5 villages.

The Villages having Hospital or Dispensary or Health Center are Ukkadagathri, Vasana, Nandigudi, Kadaranaikanahalli, Kokkanur, Muginagondi, Kumbalur, Malebennur, Halivana, Bhanuvalli, Belludi, Kondajji, Bannikodu, Bevinahalli.

Drinking Water: Tap water in 55 villages, Tank water in 18 villages, Well water in 22 villages, Tubewell in 11 villages and more than one source in 66 villages.

Bank: Banking facility in 9 villages, namely, Vasana, Kokkanur, Kumbalur, Nandi Tavare, Malebennur Bhanuvalli, Belludi, Sarathi, Kondajji.

Credit Society in 1 village Agricultural Credit Society in 0 Non-Agricultural Credit Society in 0 village.

Others: Power supply in 75 villages, Cinema hall in 7 villages, sport club in 0 village, Stadium or Auditorium or Community Hall in 0 village, Post Office in 18 villages.

There are 70 villages having bus facilities.

Villages with most of facilities: Vasana, Kokkanur Kumbalur, Malebennur, Bhanuvalli, Belludi, Sarathi.

Villages without amenities (Education): Kambathanahalli, Rayapura, Mahajenahalli..

Scheduled Castes: Out of the total population of 157910 persons, 21047 persons (13.33%) belong to Scheduled Castes. The villages having less than 10% SC population are Huliginahole, Ingalagondi, Kamalapura, Malalahalli Hallihalu, Kambathanahalli, Govinahalu Guddada Thumminakatte, Bevinahalli, Vadera Basapura Malebennur, Koppa, Dibbadahalli, Halivana Guladahalli, Sanklipura, Thimlapura, Halasabalu Haraganahalli, Nagenahalli, Rayapura Lakkasettihalli, Byaladahalli, Mahajenahalli Dheetur, Pamenahalli, Chikkabidre, Kurubarahalli Karalahalli, Bullapura, Bevinahalli.

The village having more than 50% SC population is None.

Sex ratio of Scheduled Caste population is 491.

Scheduled Castes Literates and Illiterates by Sex:

	Persons	Males	Females
Literate	7,651	4,835	2,816
Illiterate	13,396	5,874	7,522
Literacy rate	43.1	53.6	32.2
Graduate	173	154	19

Scheduled Castes (Dominant):

Madiga, Bhovi, Adi Karnataka, Banjara etc.
Beda Jangam etc.

For their cultural identity please see Appendix-I

Villages without Scheduled Castes: There are 16 villages without any scheduled caste population.

Scheduled Tribes: Out of the total population of 157910 persons, 17746 persons (11.24%) belong to Scheduled Tribes. The villages having less than 10% ST population are Nandigavi, Hosahalli, Kamalapura, Palya, Vasana Nandigudi, Kambathanahalli, Muginagondi Vadera Basapura, Kumbalur, Nandi Tavare Kunibelakere, Adapura, Nittur, Malebennur Komaranahalli, Dibbadahalli, Sanklipura Mallanaikanahalli, Haralahalli, Thimlapura Halasabalu, Nagenahalli, Rayapura, Lakkasettihalli Yakkegondi, Byaladahalli, Mahajenahalli, Dheetur Pamenahalli, Chikkabidre, Karalahalli, Kenchanahalli Kondajji, Shamshipura, Bannikodu, Kadlegondi Mittlakatte.

The villages having more than 50% ST population are None.

Sex ratio of Scheduled tribe population is 490.

Scheduled Tribes Literates and Illiterates by Sex:

	Persons	Males	Females
Literate	7,944	4,964	2,980
Illiterate	9,802	4,095	5,707
Literacy rate	51.9	63.3	39.9
Graduate	183	167	16

Scheduled Tribes (Dominant):

Naikda etc., Gond etc., Koya etc., Meda
Generic Tribes etc.

For their cultural identity please see Appendix-II

Villages without Scheduled Tribes: There are 20 villages without any scheduled tribe population.

Literates and Illiterates by Sex (Total Population):

	Persons	Males	Females
Literate	85,565	50,910	34,655
Illiterate	72,345	30,221	42,124
Literacy rate	63	73	52
Graduate	2,543	2,155	388

Agriculture: ***Distribution of villages according to land use:*** Out of 84 villages, Total area (in hectare) is 46174, out of that 78.45 percent is cultivable and 76.99 percent of the cultivable area is irrigated.

Sources of Irrigation (Hectares): Government Canal 20804.11, Private Canal 0, Well without Electricity 0, Well with Electricity 375.53, Tubewell without Electricity 96.02, Tubewell with Electricity 2986.19, Tank 117.3, River 2855.74, Lake 0, Waterfall 0, Others 652.78.

Villages with population of 5000 to 9999:
Sirigere, Bhanuvalli, Belludi.

Villages with population of 10000 and above:
Malebennur.

Distribution of Workers:

	Persons	Males	Females	WPR
Cultivators	21,966	19,287	2,679	32.38
Agricultural Labour	30,339	16,386	13,953	44.72
Household Industry	1,897	942	955	2.8
Other Workers	13,633	10,436	3,197	20.1
Main Workers	58,227	43,054	15,173	85.84
Marginal Workers	9,608	3,997	5,611	14.16
Total Workers	67,835	47,051	20,784	

Religion: Major Religious Communities:

	Persons	Males	Females	Sex Ratio
Hindu (89.27%)	140,974	72,443	68,531	946
Muslim (9.82%)	15,514	7,946	7,568	952
Christian (0.06%)	93	40	53	1,325
Sikh (0%)	1	-	1	-
Buddhists (0%)	-	-	-	-
Jain (0.05%)	72	43	29	674

Agewise Data:

	Persons	Males	Females	Sex Ratio
All ages	157,910	81,131	76,779	946
0-14	51,247	26,249	24,998	952
15-44	78,266	40,518	37,748	932
45-79	27,082	13,792	13,290	964
80+	1,217	510	707	1386
Age not stated	98	62	36	581

Languages (Dominant):
Kannada, Urdu, Telugu, Hindi, Gondi

Disabled Population:

	Persons	Males	Females	%
Total Disabled	3,400	1,986	1,414	
In Seeing	1,641	956	685	48.26
In Speech	328	182	146	9.65
In Hearing	174	84	90	5.12
In Movement	978	612	366	28.76
Mentally	279	152	127	8.21

HASSAN

Hassan C.D. Block lies in the central part of Hassan district. It is a part of Hassan taluka. The Block is located at a distance of 00 kms. from district headquart ers (Hassan). There are 391 villages in the block with the total population of 229,711 persons. Area of the C.D. Block is 907.75 sq. kms. It is bounded by taluks Belur and Arsikere on north, taluks Arkalgud and Holenar sipur on south, taluk Channarayapatna on east, and taluk Alur on west.

Communications:

Roadways : NH- 48: Direction- Mangalore to Channarayapatna, Nearest Villages- Anachihalli, Eachalahalli, Thimmanahalli, Kandali, Doddamandiganahalli, Devarayapatna, B.Kattihalli, Gavenahalli, Bustenahalli, Kasturavalli, Kenchatavalli, Boovanahalli, Chikkagenigere, Heggadihalli, Upparahosahalli, Ranganathapura, Shanthigrama, Addihalli, Madenur, Hittalaladahalli. SH- 21: Direction- Halebeedu to Arakalgud, Nearest Villages- Kondajji, Seege,Rayapura, Madihalli, Ballenahalli, Devihalli, Kakkehalli, Thimmanahalli, Salagame, Mugganahalli, Govindapura, Ramadevarahalla Kaval, Singapatna, Hanumanthapura, Kabbinahalli, Agile, Perumanahalli, Kokkanagatta, Sankalapura, S.Thattekere, Thattekere, Bittagowdanahalli, Hullenahalli, Chikkakondagola, Chikka Honnenahalli, Haralahalli, Gyarahalli, Kanchamaranahalli, Doddakondagula, Changaravalli, Kattaya, Bommenahalli, Padumanahalli, Beekanahalli, Konapura, Gorur, Uduvare, Chikkanayakanahalli, Henavanahalli Kaval, Kodaramanahalli, Byadarahalli, KattayaKaval. SH- 57: Direction- Belur to Hole Narispur, Nearest Villages- Chikkagadduvalli, Sanenahalli, Seegegudda Kaval, Kadadaravalli, Ibdane, Bommenahalli, Chinnenahalli,Handinakere, Kokkanagatta, Nagathavalli, Sankalapura , Hassan (Rural), Uddur, Huvinahalli Kaval, Kittane,Kallenahalli, Chikkamallenahalli, Doddamallenahalli, Bastihalli, Konthagodanahalli, Ganigarahosahalli, Kanchanahalli, Samudravalli, Kowsika, Sathenahalli, Mosale, Hosahalli. SH- 68 A: Direction- B.Kattihalli to Tiptur, Nearest Villages- Mahadevarahalli, Cheeranahalli, Koravangala, Chikkakadalur, Hirikadlur, Kittanakere, B.Devihalli, Dudda, Bommenahalli, Attavara, Channammanahalli, Attavara Hosahalli, Manjenahalli Kaval, Doddapura, B. Kattihalli, Boovanahalli, Sankenahalli.

Railway Station: Direction- Nearest Villages- Koravangala

Aduvalli, Ambuga, Kowsika, Hosahalli.

River: Yagachi Nadi- Nearest Villages- Kalenahalli, Bylahalli, Kanavanahalli, Eachalahalli, Thimmanahalli, Kandali, Haluvagilu, Anniganahalli, Thamaganahalli, Muttanahalli, Rahuthanahalli, Kallahalli, Malligavalu, Kattehosahalli, Malliganahalli, Uppahalli, Myadarahalli, Honnammanahalli, Gadenahalli, Bilagunda, Settihalli, Chowdavalli, Changaravalli, Sidala Hosahalli, Hiriganah alli, Anjaneyapura, Oorumundalahosahalli, Konapura. Hemav ati Nadi- Nearest Villages- Gorur, Ramagatta, Thyagatur, Banavase, Nayakarahalli, Karle Kaval, Mukundur Hosahalli, Mukundur.

Canal: Direction- Nearest Villages- Haluvagilu, Annigana halli, Malligavalu, Kattehosahalli, Honnammanahalli, Gadenahalli, Bilagunda, Gorur, Ramagatta, Thyagatur, Devihalli, Avverahalli, Banavase, Nayakarahalli, Karle, Sattigarahalli, Karle Kaval.

Annual Rainfall: Normal Rianfall 790.4 mm.

Ground Water: Availability of the Ground Water in the Basin is 59.95 H.A.M. and the utilization is 49.34 H. A.M. It belongs to Over Expoited category. Depth to water level 2 to 20 meter below the ground. Most of the wells go down in summer months, according to the Ground Water Estimation Committee.

Soils: Red Soil, Red Sandy Soil, Mixed Soil and Silty Clay Soil.

Natural Division : It falls partly in Arsikere, Gandasi-H irisave Plateau and Cauvery-Hemavati Basin of the Southern Karnataka Plateau.

Administration:

Division: Mysore. Parliamentary Constituency: 16 Hassan. District: Hassan. Taluka: Hassan. Assembly Constituency: 196 Hassan, 197 Hole Narsipur, 199 Sakleshpur. Gram Panchayat: 40.

Regional Area Development Boards: The Maland Aera Development Board.

Fairs: Channakeshavaswamy Jatra: It is held at Hassan in about May-June every year for a perod of 42 days. Hassan is the headquarters town of the district. The original town was at the adjacent village of Chennapatna, which was founded in the 11th century A.D. by Bukkanna Nayaka or Bukka Nayaka, said to be a Chola officer deput ed to put down some refractory chieftains in the neighbou rhood of this place. In this enterprise, he succeeded so well that he received permission to erect a fort and petta on the site of his encampment. He named the place Channapatna, the handsome city, and made the large tank between it and Hassan. After a prosperous rule of 43 years, Bukka Nayaka died and was succeeded by his son Buchi Nayaka who, after six years, was followed by his son Chennappa Nayaka and he was followed after 45 years by his son Bucha Nayaka. The latter died after about 50 years without leaving any male issue.

Hasanamba Temple Jatra: It is held at Hassan in the month of October. Hassan is the headquarters town of the district. The original town was at the adjacent village of Chennapatna, which was founded in the 11th century A.D. by Bukkanna Nayaka or Bukka Nayaka.

Virupakshaswamy Jatra: It at Doddagaddavalli near Hassan is held around April for a period of six days. Doddagadd avalli is situated about 16 kms. from Hassan town on the way to Belur. At Girimardihalli on the way to Doddag addavalli from the main road, there is a temple of Hariha reshvara. The image of the deity of this temple is said to be an udbhavamurty. A jatra is held here every year on the Mahanavami day. There are also images of two other goddesses in this temple known as Lakkamma and Chowdamma. The Lakshmidevi temple at Doddagaddavalli is situated in a courtyard enclosed by an old stone wall. At the corners of the enclosures are four small shrines surmounted by stone towers and Hoysala crests. This temple was built by a merchant named Kullahana Rahuta in 1114 A.D. four years before the Channakeshava temple at Belur. The inscription compares the architect Naniyoja to Vishwakarma, the architect of the gods. The presiding deity of the temple has been called Dakshi na Kolhapuradamma and the village as Dakshina Kolhapura.

Yoganarasimhaswamy Jatra: It is held at Gorur about January-February for a period of 15 days. Gorur is a place in Hassan taluk about 9 kms. north of Akalgud and is situated on the bank of the river Hemavathy. There is a temple of Yoga-Narasimha on the left bank, facing west. It was built after about 1586 A.D. Though the temple is architecturally not important, its situati on on the bank of the river with a flight of steps leading down to the bed of the river, presents a fascinating appearance. The image of the chief deity, which is of Hoysala workmanship, sitting in yoga posture on a pedestal.

Villages: 391 **Inhabited:** 367 **Uninhabited:** 24

Ranking	District	State	National
Area	4	98	536
Population	3	60	384
Sex Ratio	3	15	649
Child Sex Ratio	7	107	3309
Literacy Rate	2	35	1309
Density	1	16	4063
Work Participation Rate	2	43	637

Gram Panchayats:

Yalagunda, Nittur, Kuduragundi, Honnavara,

Basavagatta, Attavara, Dudda, Kabbali, Salagame, Seege , Ugane, Bylahalli, Huvinahalli Kaval, Tejur, Haralahalli, Koravangala, Melagodu, Heragu, Madenur, Shanthigrama, Boovanahalli, B.Kattihalli , Satyamangala, Handinakere, Kandali, Thattekere, Doddagenigere, Jagaravalli, Markuli, Kowsika , Hanumanthapura, Shankaranahalli, Settihalli , Kattaya, Ambuga, Mosale-Hosahalli, Ankapura, Channangihalli, Gorur, Karle.

Amenities:

Education: Primary School in 333 villages, Middle school in 163 villages, Matriculation or Secondary School in 52 villages, namely Bylahalli, Kyathanahalli, Doddagadduvalli, Seege, Salagame, Yalagunda, Nittur, Bidaradahalli, Kuduragundi, Honnavara, Chikkakadalur, Basavagatta, Dudda, Gadenahalli, Melagodu, Heragu, Attavara Hosahalli, Handinakere, Kandali, Haluvagilu, Hanumanthapura, Agile, Thattekere, Guddenahalli, Kuppahalli, Chikkakondagola, Doddakondagula, Doddapura, B.Kattihalli, Gavenahalli, Aduvalli, Boovanahalli, Lakshmisagara, Kallahalli, Settihalli, Kattaya, Gorur, Byadarahalli, Karle, Kabbathi, Kittane, Ankapura, Konthagodanahalli, Kanchanahalli, Kowsika, Doddagenigere, K.Hirihalli, Hosahalli, Markuli, Shanthigrama, Hongere, Madenur.

Higher Secondary or Pre University Courses or Intermediate or Junior College in 9 villages of the CD Block,, namely Nittur, Bidaradahalli, Dudda, Boovanahalli, Gorur, K.Hirihalli, Hosahalli, Shanthigrama, Hongere.

College in 1 village, Adult Literacy Center in 44 villages., College is in village, namely Gorur.

Medical: Hospital in 1 village, Dispensary in 29 villages, Health Center in 14 villages, Sub Center in 65 villages, Maternity and Child Welfare Center in 14 villages, Community health workers in 3 villages.

The Villages having Hospital or Dispensary or Health Center are Doddagadduvalli, Kakkehalli, Salagame, Nittur, Muthathi, Honnavara, Kodihalli, Basavagatta, Dudda, Melagodu, Mavinahalli, Boovanahalli, Dundanayakanahalli, Settihalli, Kattaya, Gorur, Karle, Kittane, Ankapura, Ganigarahosahalli, Kanchanahalli, Kowsika, Doddagenigere, K.Hirihalli, Hosahalli, Muthigehirihalli, Markuli, Shanthigrama, Madenur.

Drinking Water: Tap water in 217 villages, Tank water in 267 villages, Well water in 230 villages, Tubewell in 259 villages and more than one source in 327 villages.

Bank: Banking facility in 20 villages, namely, Bylahalli, Salagame, Nittur, Anugavalli, Haranahalli Heragu, Eachalahalli, Kandali, Kuppahalli Settihalli, Kattaya, Gorur, Karle, Kowsika Hosahalli, Markuli, Shanthigrama, Bengatta, Karekere Karekere Kaval.

Credit Society in 39 villages Agricultural Credit Society in 38 Non-Agricultural Credit Society in 4 villages.

Others: Power supply in 338 villages, Cinema hall in 2 villages sport club in 0 village, Stadium or Auditorium or Community Hall in 0 village, Post Office in 52 villages.

There are 196 villages having bus facilities.

Villages with most of facilities: Bylahalli Salagame, Nittur, Heragu, Kandali, Kuppahalli Settihalli, Kattaya, Gorur, Karle, Kowsika Hosahalli, Markuli, Shanthigrama, Karekere.

Villages without amenities (Education): Kanavanahalli, Siddapura, Seegegudda Kaval, Mugganahalli, Govindapura, Sajjenahalli, Kanakere, Machikatte, Rangapura Kaval, Karebore Kaval, Koravangala Kaval, Kenchanahalli, Channammanahalli, S.Thattekere, Hullenahalli, Chikkamandiganahalli, Haralahalli, Gendekatte Forest, Muttanahalli, Rahuthanahalli, Kattehosahalli, Madihalli, Changaravalli, Hiriganahalli, Virupanahalli, Doranahosahalli, Dasalapur, Gaddehosahalli, Mani Kaval, Hasuvinabetta Kaval, Buntarahalli, Perumenahalli, Malali Kaval, Byadarahalli Kaval..

Scheduled Castes: Out of the total population of 227885 persons, 35263 persons (15.47%) belong to Scheduled Castes. The villages having less than 10% SC population are Kanavanahalli, Gowdagere, Heggadihalli Thimmanahalli, Siddapura, Devagondanahalli Veerapura, Hosahalli, Bommenahalli, Chinnenahalli Gullenahalli, Kondajji Koppal, Thimmanahalli Salagame, Aladahalli, Mugganahalli, Govindapura Narsipura, Mandiganahalli, Ramadevarapura Chowdenahalli, Beekanahalli, Bommenahalli, Kanakere Machikatte, Dyapalapura, Ubbenahalli, Rangenahalli Muddalapura, Bhogarahalli, Kuduragundi Lingarasanahalli, Vedavathi, M.Devihalli Chikkamenahalli, Somanahalli, Chikkakadalur Anugavalli, Chigatihalli, Hullenahalli, Basavagatta B.Byrapura, Kittanakere, B.Devihalli, Jakkenahalli Chikkaboovanahalli, Bandihalli, Chakanahalli Gadenahalli, Halasinahalli, Dyalapura, Handrangi Yogihalli, Kammarige, K.Honnenahalli, Krishnapura Kanajanahalli, Haranahalli, Kenchanahalli H.Dyavalapura, Valagerehalli, Savankanahalli Honnammanahalli, Attavara, Channammanahalli Siddapura, Rudradevarahalli, Mudigere Attavara Hosahalli, Bittahalli, Arasihalli Gowdagere, Varthikere, Nanjedevara Kaval

Yathinakatte, Thimmanahalli, Maragodanahalli Anniganahalli, Hanumanthapura, Agile, Kokkanagatta Nagathavalli, S.Thattekere, Narihalli, Hullenahalli Hassan (Rural), Uddur, Huvinahalli Kaval Huvinahalli, Hachagowdanahalli, Chikkakondagola Chikka Honnenahalli, Haralahalli, Gyarahalli Kanchamaranahalli, Doddahonnenahalli, B.Kattihalli Gavenahalli, Aduvalli, Gendekatte Forest Bustenahalli, Kasturavalli, Samudravalli Gekaravalli, Sankenahalli, Rahuthanahalli Kattehosahalli, Uppahalli, Myadarahalli, Madihalli Changaravalli, Hiriganahalli, Dornahalli Virupanahalli, Gopanahalli, Bommenahalli Anjaneyapura, Beekanahalli, Ramagatta, Devihalli Varadalapura, Hirigowdanahalli, Avverahalli Banavase, Ankanahalli, Dasalapur, Channangihalli Hulihalli, Jakkanahalli, Kittane, Chikkamallenahalli Doddamallenahalli, Ammagodanahalli, Thimmanahalli Konthagodanahalli, Kanchanahalli, Samudravalli Chikkabasavanahalli, Doddabasavanahalli Kachanayakanahalli, Doddahonnenahalli Chikkagenigere, Doddagenigere, Guduganahalli Narayanapura, Hanchihalli, Danayakanahalli Hasuvinabetta Kaval, Muthigehirihalli, Banavase Heggadihalli, Thyavihalli, Ranganathapura Halasinahalli, Dummagere, Kallugeduganahalli Nagenahalli, Malali Kaval, Bandihalli Mallanayakanahalli, Bengatta, Devihalli, Addihalli Byadarahalli Kaval, K.Byadarahalli, Muddanahalli Madenur, Karekere, Junjanahalli, Holalu, Melalli Nellakkihalli, Hosur, Ballenahalli, Jagaravalli Bijemaranahalli, B.Hosahalli.

The villages having more than 50% SC population are Kamenahalli, Gullenahalli, Chikkagadduvalli Mallenahalli, Seegegudda Kaval, Kadadaravalli Idalla Kaval, Nagenahalli, Bidaradahalli Doddenahalli, Singatagere, Hangarahalli Rangapura Kaval, Koravangala Kaval Manjenahalli Kaval, Kabbinahalli, Parasanahalli Jinnenahalli, Oorumundalahosahalli Ganigarahosahalli, Gaddehosahalli, Karekere Kaval.

Sex ratio of Scheduled Caste population is 503.

Scheduled Castes Literates and Illiterates by Sex:

	Persons	Males	Females
Literate	17,158	10,078	7,080
Illiterate	18,105	7,438	10,667
Literacy rate	56.5	67.1	46.1
Graduate	373	300	73

Scheduled Castes (Dominant):

Adi Karnataka, Madiga, Bhovi, Banjara etc. Adi Dravida

For their cultural identity please see Appendix-I

Villages without Scheduled Castes: There are 111 villages without any scheduled caste population.

Scheduled Tribes: Out of the total population of 227885 persons, 2296 persons (1.01%) belong to Scheduled Tribes. The villages having less than 10% ST population are Kalenahalli, Bylahalli, Kanavanahalli, Chatranahalli Kamenahalli, Gundasettihalli, Gullenahalli Madvapura, Kalla Halli, Kalathammanahalli, Ugane Kyathanahalli, Dassur, Gowdagere, Doddagadduvalli Chikkagadduvalli, Heggadihalli, Thimmanahalli Siddapura, Anuganalu, Mallenahalli, Maranahalli Devagondanahalli, Sanenahalli, Seegegudda Kaval Kondajji, Seege , Veerapura, Kadadaravalli, Ibdane Hosahalli, Bommenahalli, Chinnenahalli, Attihalli Shanka, Yalagondanahalli, Gullenahalli Kalludevarahalli, Kondajji Koppal, Rayapura Madihalli, Ballenahalli, Devihalli, Kakkehalli Thimmanahalli, Salagame, Aladahalli, Mugganahalli Govindapura, Narsipura, Kadaga, Sundenahalli Hommagodnahalli, Haruvanahalli, Mandiganahalli Sajjenahalli, Ramadevarapura, Chowdenahalli Beekanahalli, Idalla Kaval, Kanakere, Soppinahalli Nagenahalli, Mallanayakanahalli, Yalagunda Machikatte, Dyapalapura, Kelavathi, Nittur Bidaradahalli, Ubbenahalli, Doddenahalli Singatagere, Rangenahalli, Muddalapura Somanahalli Kaval, Bhogarahalli, Kuduragundi Lingarasanahalli, Hangarahalli, Rangapura Kaval Thirupathihalli, Vedavathi, M.Devihalli, Muthathi Chikkamenahalli, Thimmanahalli, Honnavara, Poomagame Somanahalli, K.Hosahalli, Kabbali, Krishnapura Mahadevarahalli, Cheeranahalli, Koravangala Chikkakadalur, H.Mylahalli, Hirikadlur, Kodihalli Anugavalli, Hullenahalli, Basavagatta, B.Byrapura Karebore Kaval, Kittanakere, B.Devihalli, Dudda Uddurahalli, Jakkenahalli, Koravangala Kaval Chikkaboovanahalli, Kommanahalli, Thendihalli G.Mylanahalli, Bandihalli, Chakanahalli, Gadenahalli Halasinahalli, Dyalapura, Handrangi, Yogihalli Melagodu, Kammarige, Mayasamudra, K.Honnenahalli Krishnapura, Kanajanahalli, Haranahalli Hampanahalli, Kenchanahalli, Hariharapura H.Dyavalapura, Heragu, Valagerehalli, Savankanahalli Honnammanahalli, Bommenahalli, Attavara Channammanahalli, Siddapura, Thimmalapura Rudradevarahalli, Attavara Hosahalli Manjenahalli Kaval, Anehalli, Bittahalli, Arasihalli Gowdagere, H.Byarapura, Varthikere

Nanjedevara Kaval, Handinakere, Yathinakatte
Anachihalli, Eachalahalli, Thimmanahalli, Kandali
Haluvagilu, Maragodanahalli, Anniganahalli
Bidarakere, Singapatna, Hanumanthapura, Kabbinahalli
Agile, Doddabaganahalli, Perumanahalli, Kokkanagatta
Nagathavalli, Sankalapura , S.Thattekere, Thattekere
Narihalli, Bittagowdanahalli, Hullenahalli
Chikkamandiganahalli, Doddamandiganahalli
Devarayapatna, Guddenahalli, Hassan (Rural), Uddur
Huvinahalli Kaval, Huvinahalli, Mugalur, Agalahalli
Janivara, Kuppahalli, Hachagowdanahalli, Korahalli
Tejur, Chikkakondagola, Chikka Honnenahalli
Haralahalli, Mavinahalli, Gyarahalli, Rachenahalli
Kanchamaranahalli, Doddakondagula, Yadiyur
Doddahonnenahalli, Chitnahalli, Nidudi, Doddapura
B.Kattihalli, Gavenahalli, Aduvalli
Gendekatte Forest, Bustenahalli, Kasturavalli
Kenchatavalli, Samudravalli, Gekaravalli
Boovanahalli, Sankenahalli, Lakshmisagara
Thamaganahalli, Muttanahalli, Rahuthanahalli
Kallahalli, Malligavalu, Kattehosahalli
Malliganahalli, Uppahalli, Myadarahalli, Gadenahalli
Shankaranahalli, Bilagunda, Dundanayakanahalli
Ballekere, Madihalli, Settihalli, Chowdavalli
Changaravalli, Sidala Hosahalli, Hiriganahalli
Muddanahalli, Dornahalli, Parasanahalli
Virupanahalli, Gopanahalli, Mallappanahalli
Golenahalli, Javenahalli, Doranahosahalli, Kattaya
Bommenahalli, Jinnenahalli, Anjaneyapura
Oorumundalahosahalli, Padumanahalli, Beekanahalli
Gorur, Ramagatta, Thyagatur, Devihalli, Uduvare
Chikkanayakanahalli, Henavanahalli Kaval
Kodaramanahalli, Byadarahalli, Varadalapura
Avverahalli, Banavase, Nayakarahalli, Karle
Sattigarahalli, Jodi Mallappanahalli, Ankanahalli
Dasalapur, Kabbathi, Channangihalli, Kattaya Kaval
Chikkabaganahalli, Hulihalli, Hyarane, Jakkanahalli
Kittane, Bachihalli, Maranayakanahalli, Ankapura
Seegur, Malledevarapura, Mukundur Hosahalli
Mukundur, Guddadatheranya, Kallenahalli
Chikkamallenahalli, Doddamallenahalli, Kurubarahalli
Ammagodanahalli, Thimmanahalli, Bastihalli, Ambuga
Konthagodanahalli, Ganigarahosahalli, Kanchanahalli
Samudravalli, Kowsika, Chikkabasavanahalli
Doddabasavanahalli, Kachanayakanahalli
Doddahonnenahalli, Chikkagenigere, Doddagenigere
Doddaladahalli, Savanthanahalli, Sathenahalli
Gaddehosahalli, K.Hirihalli, Guduganahalli
Narayanapura, Mosale, Hosahalli, Mani Kaval
Hanchihalli, Halenahalli, Danayakanahalli
Hasuvinabetta Kaval, Muthigehirihalli, Buntarahalli
Marenahalli, Huluvare, Banavase, Markuli, Chigahalli
Heggadihalli, Thyavihalli, Perumenahalli
Upparahosahalli, Ranganathapura, Shanthigrama
Hongere, Halasinahalli, Dummagere, Muthige
Kallugeduganahalli, Nagenahalli, Malali Kaval
Bandihalli, Mallanayakanahalli, Bengatta, Devihalli
Addihalli, Byadarahalli Kaval, K.Byadarahalli
Kanive Aladahalli, Muddanahalli, Madenur
Hittalaladahalli, Karekere, Junjanahalli, Holalu
Melalli, Nellakkihalli, Hosur, Karekere Kaval
Ballenahalli, Melagodanahalli, Bijemaranahalli
B.Hosahalli.

The villages having more than 50% ST population are None.

Sex ratio of Scheduled tribe population is 490.

Scheduled Tribes Literates and Illiterates by Sex:

	Persons	Males	Females
Literate	1,025	648	377
Illiterate	1,271	522	749
Literacy rate	51.1	63.3	38.3
Graduate	32	23	9

Scheduled Tribes (Dominant):

Naikda etc., Soligaru, Generic Tribes etc.
Hakkipikki, Kadu Kuruba

For their cultural identity please see Appendix-II

Villages without Scheduled Tribes: There are 343 villages without any scheduled tribe population.

Literates and Illiterates by Sex (Total Population):

	Persons	Males	Females
Literate	139,525	79,199	60,326
Illiterate	88,360	33,616	54,744
Literacy rate	69	80	59
Graduate	4,788	3,559	1,229

Agriculture: ***Distribution of villages according to land use:*** Out of 391 villages, Total area (in hectare) is 90775, out of that 61.9 percent is cultivable and 32.42 percent of the cultivable area is irrigated.

Sources of Irrigation (Hectares): Government Canal 1027.31, Private Canal 15.52, Well without Electricity 123.25, Well with Electricity 633.73, Tubewell without Electricity 26.29, Tubewell with Electricity 2535.7, Tank 6707.2, River 224.83, Lake 993.35, Waterfall 641.85, Others 5254.39.

Villages with population of 5000 to 9999: None

Villages with population of 10000 and above: None

Distribution of Workers:

	Persons	Males	Females	WPR
Cultivators	92,499	50,129	42,370	70.65
Agricultural Labour	15,107	4,423	10,684	11.54
Household Industry	1,050	515	535	0.8

Other Workers	22,264	17,093	5,171	17.01
Main Workers	103,156	65,924	37,232	78.79
Marginal Workers	27,764	6,236	21,528	21.21
Total Workers	130,920	72,160	58,760	

Religion: Major Religious Communities:

	Persons	Males	Females	Sex Ratio
Hindu (97.24%)	221,586	109,622	111,964	1,021
Muslim (1.26%)	2,873	1,497	1,376	919
Christian (0.89%)	2,025	991	1,034	1,043
Sikh (0%)	8	6	2	333
Buddhists (0%)	6	3	3	1,000
Jain (0.18%)	405	206	199	966

Agewise Data:

	Persons	Males	Females	Sex Ratio
All ages	227,885	112,815	115,070	1020
0-14	63,765	32,377	31,388	969
15-44	114,504	56,116	58,388	1040
45-79	46,871	23,092	23,779	1030
80+	2,610	1,157	1,453	1256
Age not stated	135	73	62	849

Languages (Dominant):

Kannada, Urdu, Telugu, Tamil, Hindi

Disabled Population:

	Persons	Males	Females	%
Total Disabled	4,465	2,385	2,080	
In Seeing	1,875	861	1,014	41.99
In Speech	428	241	187	9.59
In Hearing	386	181	205	8.65
In Movement	1,376	886	490	30.82
Mentally	400	216	184	8.96

HAVERI

Haveri C.D. Block lies in the east central part of Haveri district. It is a part of Haveri taluka. The Block is located at a distance of 00 kms. from district headqu arters (Haveri). There are 89 villages in the block with the total population of 196,051 persons. Area of the C.D. Block is 778.42 sq. kms. It is bounded by district Gadag and taluk Savanur on north, taluks Byadgi and Ranibennur on south, district Bellary on east, and taluk Hangal on west.

Communications:

Roadways : N.H-4: Direction- Dharwad to Bangalore, Nearest Villages- Naganur, Varadahalli, Devagiri, Hombardi, Devagiri Yellapur, Totadayellapur, Nelogal, Kallihal. S.H-2: Direction- Sirsi to Harapanahalli, Nearest Villa ges- Venkatapur, Aladakatti, Hosalli-M-Adur, Gourapur-M-Adur, Kulenur, Sangur, Basavanakatti, Yattinahalli, Jangam anakop, Agadi, Budagatti, Malapur, Kanavalli, Haleritti, Basapur, Guttal, Havanur, Haunshi, Shyakar, Shivanagar.

Railway Station: Villages- Kolur, Totadayellapur.

River: Tungabhadra Nadi- Nearest Villages- Meundi, Taredahalli, Guilagundi, Galaganath, Havanur, Haunshi, Shyakar, Haralahalli, Kancharagatti. Varada Nadi- Neare st Villages- Naganur, Varadahalli, Devagiri, Benchihalli, Venkatapur, Sangur, Bidaragaddi, Kolur, Karjagi, Ramapur, Agasanamatti, Konana Tambigi, Kesaralli, Melmuri, Handiganur, Koradur, Mannur, Guilagundi, Neeralagi-M-Guttal, Gudur, Halagi, Maradur, Kittur, Channur, Hosaritti, Akkur, Kodabal, Marol, Belavigi, Galaganath.

Reserved Forest: Karjagi, Basavanakatti, Ganajur, Yattin ahalli, Jangamanakop, Agadi, Katenahalli, Hosaritti, Neglur, Bommanakatti, Haleritti, Basapur, Guttal, Shivan agar, Bharadi, Kuragund.

Annual Rainfall: Normal Rianfall 592 mm.

Ground Water: Availability of the Ground Water in the Basin is 59.24 MCM and the utilization is 61.61 MCM It belongs to Over Exploited category. Depth to water level 10 to 20 meter below the ground. Most of the wells go down in summer months, according to the Ground Water Estimation Committee.

Soils: Red Sandy Soil, Medium Soil, Deep Black Soil, Red Loamy Soil and Lateritic Soil.

Natural Division : It falls partly in Barad Basin, Byadag i-Hirekerur Rocky Knobs and Middle Tungabhadra Valley of the Central Karnataka Plateau.

Administration:

Division: Belgaum. Parliamentary Constituency: 10 Haveri. District: Haveri. Taluka: Haveri. Assembly Constituency: 84 Haveri (SC), 85 Byadgi. Gram Panchayat: 31.

Regional Area Development Boards: The Bailu Seeme Area Development Board.

Villages: 89 **Inhabited:** 89 **Uninhabited:** 0

Ranking	District	State	National
Area	3	126	772
Population	4	92	745
Sex Ratio	7	167	4342
Child Sex Ratio	2	26	1563
Literacy Rate	6	77	2581
Density	5	101	4047
Work Participation Rate	2	41	2343

Gram Panchayats:

Naganur, Devagiri, Kolur, Karjagi, Yalagachi, Konana Tambigi, Handiganur, Halagi, Marol, Belavigi, Meundi, Neglur, Hosaritti, Agadi, Devihosur, Sangur, Kulenur, Aladakatti, Kallihal, Katenahalli, Kanavalli, Basapur, Guttal, Havanur, Haunshi, Kancharagatti, Kuragund, Hombardi, Kanakapur, Kurabagonda, Kabbur.

Amenities:

Education: Primary School in 86 villages, Middle school in 74 villages, Matriculation or Secondary School in 21 villages,

namely Varadahalli, Devihosur, Aladakatti, Sangur, Kabbur, Kurabagonda, Karjagi, Handiganur, Yalagachi, Agadi, Katenahalli, Hanumanahalli, Kanavalli, Meundi, Kittur, Hosaritti, Marol, Belavigi, Neglur, Guttal, Havanur.

Higher Secondary or Pre University Courses or Intermediate or Junior College in 4 villages of the CD Block,, namely Kabbur, Karjagi, Hosaritti, Guttal.

College in 0 village, Adult Literacy Center in 0 village.

Medical: Hospital in 1 village, Dispensary in 7 villages, Health Center in 8 villages, Sub Center in 34 villages, Maternity and Child Welfare Center in 3 villages, Community health workers in 11 villages.

The Villages having Hospital or Dispensary or Health Center are Devihosur, Hombardi, Karjagi, Hosaritti, Belavigi, Neglur, Guttal, Havanur.

Drinking Water: Tap water in 71 villages, Tank water in 9 villages, Well water in 0 village, Tubewell in 23 villages and more than one source in 38 villages.

Bank: Banking facility in 10 villages, namely, Devagiri, Devihosur, Sangur, Kurabagonda, Karjagi Agadi, Hosaritti, Belavigi, Neglur, Guttal.

Credit Society in 31 villages Agricultural Credit Society in 29 Non-Agricultural Credit Society in 4 villages.

Others: Power supply in 87 villages, Cinema hall in 2 villages, sport club in 2 villages, Stadium or Auditorium or Community Hall in 0 village, Post Office in 32 villages.

There are 84 villages having bus facilities.

Villages with most of facilities: Devagiri Devihosur, Sangur, Kurabagonda, Karjagi, Agadi Hosaritti, Belavigi, Neglur, Guttal.

Villages without amenities (Education):
Shivajinagar, Shiddeshwar Nagar, Rajivnagar..

Scheduled Castes: Out of the total population of 196434 persons, 23169 persons (11.79%) belong to Scheduled Castes.

The villages having less than 10% SC population are Naganur, Devagiri, Benchihalli, Venkatapur Devihosur, Hosalli-M-Adur, Gourapur-M-Adur, Kulenur Sangur, Bidaragaddi, Timmapur-M-Adur Najikalakamapur, Bujruk Kodihalli Chikkalingadahalli, Kabbur, Hirelingadahalli, Kolur Karjagi, Ramapur, Agasanamatti, Konana Tambigi Kesaralli, Melmuri, Shirmapur, Ganajur, Jangamanakop Agadi, Timmenhalli, Malapur, Totadayellapur Kanakapur, Hanumanahalli, Gudisalkoppa, Taredahalli Gudur, Maradur, Channur, Hosaritti, Akkur, Guttal Havanur, Shyakar, Haralahalli, Kancharagatti Timmapur-M-Guttal, Bharadi, Kuragund.

The villages having more than 50% SC population are Shivajinagar, Shiddeshwar Nagar, Shivanagar Rajivnagar.

Sex ratio of Scheduled Caste population is 491.

Scheduled Castes Literates and Illiterates by Sex:

	Persons	Males	Females
Literate	7,565	5,010	2,555
Illiterate	15,604	6,775	8,829
Literacy rate	39.3	50.9	27.2
Graduate	165	148	17

Scheduled Castes (Dominant):
Bhambi etc., Banjara etc., Bhovi, Madiga Chalavadi etc.

For their cultural identity please see Appendix-I

Villages without Scheduled Castes: There are 6 villages without any scheduled caste population.

Scheduled Tribes: Out of the total population of 196434 persons, 20044 persons (10.2%) belong to Scheduled Tribes.

The villages having less than 10% ST population are Varadahalli, Devihosur, Aladakatti, Bidaragaddi Najikalakamapur, Hombardi, Kabbur, Shivajinagar Shiddeshwar Nagar, Benakanahalli, Hirelingadahalli Kallapur, Karjagi, Kesaralli, Melmuri, Handiganur Koradur, Shirmapur, Yalagachi, Basavanakatti Machapur, Devagiri Yellapur, Yattinahalli Jangamanakop, Timmenhalli, Malapur, Nelogal Kallihal, Kanavalli, Gudisalkoppa Neeralagi-M-Guttal, Gudur, Halagi, Maradur, Channur Hosaritti, Kodabal, Belavigi, Neglur, Havanur Kancharagatti, Timmapur-M-Guttal, Shivanagar Rajivnagar.

The villages having more than 50% ST population are None.

Sex ratio of Scheduled tribe population is 478.

Scheduled Tribes Literates and Illiterates by Sex:

	Persons	Males	Females
Literate	8,953	5,839	3,114
Illiterate	11,091	4,629	6,462
Literacy rate	52.1	64.7	38.2
Graduate	217	194	23

Scheduled Tribes (Dominant):
Naikda etc., Koraga, Kadu Kuruba, Meda Koli Dhor etc.

For their cultural identity please see Appendix-II

Villages without Scheduled Tribes: There are 12 villages without any scheduled tribe population.

Literates and Illiterates by Sex (Total Population):

	Persons	Males	Females
Literate	102,932	63,066	39,866
Illiterate	93,502	38,575	54,927
Literacy rate	61	72	49
Graduate	2,904	2,414	490

Agriculture: ***Distribution of villages according to land use:*** Out of 89 villages, Total area (in hectare) is 77842, out of that 85.73 percent is cultivable and 13.27 percent of the cultivable area is irrigated.

Sources of Irrigation (Hectares): Government Canal 0, Private Canal 0, Well without Electricity 0, Well with Electricity 95.5, Tubewell without Electricity 6.19, Tubewell with Electricity 5734.35, Tank 188.73, River 2646.17, Lake 0, Waterfall 0, Others 186.16.

Villages with population of 5000 to 9999:
Devagiri, Devihosur, Karjagi, Agadi, Kanavalli Hosaritti, Neglur, Havanur.

Villages with population of 10000 and above:
Guttal.

Distribution of Workers:

	Persons	Males	Females	WPR
Cultivators	30,323	23,570	6,753	31.66
Agricultural Labour	49,767	23,623	26,144	51.96
Household Industry	2,252	1,397	855	2.35
Other Workers	13,429	11,428	2,001	14.02
Main Workers	79,912	54,744	25,168	83.44
Marginal Workers	15,859	5,274	10,585	16.56
Total Workers	95,771	60,018	35,753	

Religion: Major Religious Communities:

	Persons	Males	Females	Sex Ratio
Hindu (84.97%)	166,915	86,369	80,546	933
Muslim (13.93%)	27,357	14,161	13,196	932
Christian (0.11%)	210	100	110	1,100
Sikh (0.02%)	38	21	17	810
Buddhists (0.01%)	24	13	11	846
Jain (0.32%)	638	325	313	963

Agewise Data:

	Persons	Males	Females	Sex Ratio
All ages	196,434	101,641	94,793	933
0-14	67,823	34,670	33,153	956
15-44	92,116	48,517	43,599	899
45-79	34,767	17,686	17,081	966
80+	1,584	694	890	1282
Age not stated	144	74	70	946

Languages (Dominant):
Kannada, Urdu, Hindi, Marathi, Coorgi/Kodagu

Disabled Population:

	Persons	Males	Females	%
Total Disabled	4,028	2,345	1,683	
In Seeing	1,770	1,001	769	43.94
In Speech	430	238	192	10.68
In Hearing	174	83	91	4.32
In Movement	1,232	782	450	30.59
Mentally	422	241	181	10.48

HEGGADADEVANKOTE

Heggadadevankote C.D. Block lies in the south-western part of Mysore district. It is a part of Heggadadevankote taluka. The Block is located at a distance of 52 kms. from district headquarters (Mysore). There are 281 villages in the block with the total population of 230, 572 persons. Area of the C.D. Block is 1612.28 sq. kms. It is bounded by taluk Hunsur on north, district Chamar ajanagar, and taluks Mysore and Nanjangud on east, distri ct Kodagu on west. It has common boundary with the state of Kerala on south and west.

Communications:

Roadways : SH-17 D: Direction- Tellicherry to Mysore, Nearest Villages- Gudumanahalli, Hyrige, Matakere, Manuganahalli, Yarahalli, Seeranahundi, Kollegowdanahalli, Yarahallikaval, Iruvidi, Nayakanahundi, Madapura, Kolagala, Holehundi, Karigala, Hommaragahalli, Hampapura, Kohala, Marchahalli, Pura, Jinnahalli, Kanchamalli, Chamahalli, Antharasanthe, Nuralakuppe, Anagatti, Krish narajapura, Ragalakuppe, Antharasanthe Plantation, N. Belathur, Huralipura, Nisna, Karapura, Thenekallu, Udbur, Melukote, Kakanakote Forest, Kadegadde, Vadakanamala, Timmanihosahalli, Doddabyranakuppe, Chikkabyranakuppe, Anemala, Netkalhundi, Hosur, Golur, Machur, Begurjungle.

River: Kabbani Nadi- Nearest Villages- Hyrige, Matakere, Boppanahalli, Hebbalaguppe, Hulikura, Thumbasoge, Thoravalli, Itna, Nayakanahundi, Madapura, Kolagala, Holehundi, Karigala, Hommaragahalli, Jinnahalli, Hirena ndi, Kanchamalli, Chikkanandi, Hatwal, Chakkur, Moleyur (Kalihundi), Shankahalli, K.Belthur, Kulya, Halemanchaha lli, Manchahalli, Kallasaragur, Kunnapatna, Lakkur (B), Bidagalu , Saragur, Kothegala, Nilavagilu, Magudilu, Pura, Nerale, Beechanahalli, Jeeyara, Machare, Krishnarajapura, Ragalakuppe, Honnurkuppe, Badanakuppe, Hosaholalu, Magge, Sundapura, N.Belathur, Nisna, Malali, Sogahalli, Jaganakote, Kanakanahalli, N. Begur, Beeramballi, Hosah alli, Gundathur, K.Gandathur, Iyyanapura, Thenekallu, Udbur, Melukote, Kakanakote Forest, Kadegadde, Vadakana mala, Timmanihosahalli, Dodabyranakuppe, Chikabyranaku ppe, Anmala, Netkalhundi, Hosur, Golur, Machur, Begurjun gle, Kittur (Therani Manti), Uyyamballi, Bidarahalli, Agathuru, Sagare, Singapatna. Nuge Hole Nadi- Nearest Villages- Kattehunsur, Kallambalu, Kundur, Halasur, Chamalapura, Bennagere, Mullur, Jatagathipura, Beerwal, B.Kote, Nandinathapura, Lakkasoge, Shambugowdanah alli, Lakshmanapura, Muthigechikkathalalu, Hunasur, Mugut hanamule, Siddapura, Baragi, Vaderahalli, Heggudlu, Konan alathuru, Huskur , Hariyalapura, Iyyanapura, Byrapura, Kandalike, Hosakote, Beguru, Inur Marigudi Jungle, Kudagi, Kurnagala, Alanahalli. Nagar Hole Nadi- Nearest Villages- Metikuppe Forest, Amani Jungle, Hunasekuppe,

Hirehalli, Antharasanthe, Metikuppe Forest. Sarat Hole Nadi- Nearest Villages- Amani Jungle, Hunasekuppe, Penjahalli, Hirehalli, Heggadadevankote (Rural), Belagan ahallikaval, Belaganahalli, Gudumanahalli, Hyrige, Matake re, Manuganahalli, Kattemanuganahalli, Heggadapura, Akkad

Canal: Nearest Villages- Haropura, Voddaragudi, Heggadade vankote (Rural), Belaganahallikaval, Belaganahalli, Malara, Gudumanahalli, Hyrige, Matakere, Thumbasoge, Thoravalli, Itna, Nayakanahundi, Chottanahalli, Madapura, Kolagala, Kattehunsur, Kallambalu, Kundur, Halasur, Chamalapura, Bennagere, Changowdanahalli, Jatagathipura, Beerwal, Nilavagilu, Magudilu, Mullur, Nerale, Pura, Beechanahalli.

Annual Rainfall: Normal Rianfall 904 mm.

Ground Water: Availability of the Ground Water in the Basin is 9518.08 H.A.M. and the utilization is 3554. 44 H.A.M. It belongs to Over Exploited category. Depth to water level 2 to 10 meter below the ground. Most of the wells go down in summer months, according to the Ground Water Estimation Committee.

Soils: Red Sandy Soils, Red Loamy Soils and Deep Black Soils.

Natural Division : It falls partly in Kabbani Cauvery Valley and Heggadadevankote-Bandipur Forested Upland of the Southern Karnataka Plateau.

Administration:

Division: Mysore. Parliamentary Constituency: 21 Mysore Paschim. District: Mysore. Taluka: Heggadadevankote. Assembly Constituency: 213 Heggadadevankote (ST). Gram Panchayat: 32.

Regional Area Development Boards: The Maland Aera Development Board.

Border Villages: (State: Kerala)- Kakanakote Forest, Kadegadde, Vadakanamala, Thimmanihosahalli, Anemala, Doddabyranakuppe, Chikkabyranakuppe, Netkalhundi, Hosur, Golur, Machur, Begurjungle, Inur Marigudi Jungle.

Villages: 281 **Inhabited:** 243 **Uninhabited:** 38

Ranking	District	State	National
Area	1	22	102
Population	4	55	338
Sex Ratio	3	89	2342
Child Sex Ratio	1	5	591
Literacy Rate	4	136	4256
Density	2	64	5621
Work Participation Rate	7	137	1631

Gram Panchayats:

Bheemanahalli, Annur, Savve, Chikkereyur, Kyathanahalli, Alanahalli, Gollanabeedusagur, Kanchamall, Hampapura, Madapura, Hurige, Chakkodanahalli, Hirehalli, Naganahalli, K. Belthur, Manuganahalli, Hebbalaguppe, Thumbasoge, Nuralakuppe, Antharasanthe , Beechanahalli , Bidarahalli, Sagare, Saragur, Kallambalu, Mullur, Hanchipura, Hegganur , N. Belathur , N. Begur , Doddabyranakuppe, B. Matagere, Muthigechikkathalalu.

Amenities:

Education: Primary School in 196 villages, Middle school in 106 villages, Matriculation or Secondary School in 26 villages, namely Annur, Savve, Metikuppe, Naganahalli, Hebbalaguppe, Thumbasoge, Kyathanahalli, Bachegowdanahalli, Madapura, Hommaragahalli, Kanchamalli, K.Belthur, Manuganahalli, Kallambalu, Bidagalu, Saragur, Mullur, Muthigechikkathalalu, Baragi, Antharasanthe, Beechanahalli, Halemagge, Kenchanahalli, Hosahalli, Kittur (Therani Manti), B. Matagere.

Higher Secondary or Pre University Courses or Intermediate or Junior College in 4 villages of the CD Block,, namely Naganahalli, Saragur, Beechanahalli, Kittur (Therani Manti).

College in 1 village, Adult Literacy Center in 0 village., College is in village, namely Kittur (Therani Manti).

Medical: Hospital in 0 village, Dispensary in 7 villages, Health Center in 13 villages, Sub Center in 66 villages, Maternity and Child Welfare Center in 2 villages, Community health workers in 18 villages.

The Villages having Hospital or Dispensary or Health Center are Naganahalli, Hebbalaguppe, Saragur, Antharasanthe, Beechanahalli, Kenchanahalli, N. Begur.

Drinking Water: Tap water in 129 villages, Tank water in 58 villages, Well water in 84 villages, Tubewell in 128 villages and more than one source in 200 villages.

Bank: Banking facility in 20 villages, namely, Annur, Heggadadevankote (Rural), Naganahalli Hebbalaguppe, Thumbasoge, Kyathanahalli, Madapura Hommaragahalli, Hampapura, Chakkur, K.Belthur Saragur, Mullur, Antharasanthe, Beechanahalli N.Belathur, N. Begur, Kittur (Therani Manti), Sagare B. Matagere.

Credit Society in 242 villages Agricultural Credit Society in 11 Non-Agricultural Credit Society in 29 villages.

Others: Power supply in 242 villages, Cinema hall in 6 villages sport club in 0 village, Stadium or Auditorium or Community Hall in 0 village, Post Office in 51 villages.

There are 170 villages having bus facilities.

Villages with most of facilities: Annur Naganahalli, Hebbalaguppe, Thumbasoge, Kyathanahalli Madapura, Hommaragahalli, Hampapura, Chakkur

K.Belthur, Saragur, Mullur, Antharasanthe Beechanahalli, N.Belathur, N. Begur, Sagare B. Matagere.

Villages without amenities (Education): Yelehundikaval, Sollapura, Bommalapura, Metikuppe Forest, Gudumanahalli, Manuganahalli, Akkadevanahalli, Yarahallikaval, Hulikurakaval, Masanakuppe, Ankanahalli, Yennegerekaval, Thandasipura, Gangadahalli, M. Mallahalli, Kethahalli, Kalkodu, Kadasur, Doddakereyur, Kodichamanahalli, Mallahalli, Doddakerekaval, Garikekattekaval, Bettahalli, Iruvidi, Chottanahalli, Bennagere, Chillahalli, Hunasur, Muguthanamule, Vaderahalli, Pura, Antharasanthe Plantation, Honnurkuppe, Kalasuru, Thimmanihosahalli, Netkalhundi, Bettadavarehundi, Lingenahalli, Heggudlu, Hariyalapura, Vallahalli, Seegevadi, Moleyurukaval, Kebbepura, Chikkabesuge, Inur Marigudi Jungle..

Scheduled Castes: Out of the total population of 233885 persons, 63596 persons (27.19%) belong to Scheduled Castes. The villages having less than 10% SC population are Musker, Agasanahundi, Bommalapura, Haropura Metikuppe, Metikuppe Forest, Chakahalli Belaganahalli, Gudumanahalli, Akkadevanahalli Naganahalli, Motha, Hulikura, Halladamanuganahalli Gollanabeedusaragur, Ankanahalli, Muddaiahnahundi Yennegerekaval, Thandasipura, Gangadahalli Sindenahalli, M. Mallahalli, Kaniyanahundi Kethahalli, Kalkodu, Kadasur, Doddakereyur Kodichamanahalli, Mallahalli, Doddakerekaval Bachegowdanahalli, Garikekattekaval, Bettahalli Iruvidi, Nayakanahundi, Karehundi, Kanchamalli Chamahalli, Shankahalli, Manchahalli, Kundur Puradakatte, Halasur, Bennagere, Chiilahalli Muthigechikkathalalu, Baragi, Vaderahalli Beechanahalli, Ragalakuppe, Antharasanthe Plantation Honnurkuppe, Hosaholalu, Sogahalli, Hosahalli K.Gandathur, Kakanakote Forest, Kadegadde Vadakanamala, Thimmanihosahalli, Doddabyranakuppe Chikkabyranakuppe, Anemala, Netkalhundi, Hosur Golur, Machur, Bettadavarehundi, Agathuru Singapatna, Thelagumasahalli, Beddalapura, Huskur Hariyalapura, Kandalike, Hosakote, Seegevadi Kebbepura, Nadahadi, Chikkabesuge, Moleyuru Hirehalli, Alanahalli, Channagundi, Alalahalli.

The villages having more than 50% SC population are Sollapura, Voddaragudi, Malara, Matakere Krishnapurakaval, Yarahallikaval, Chowdahalli Jakkahalli, Masanakuppe, Kandegowdanapura, Bannavadi Holehundi, Kohala, Marchahalli, Muddanahalli Hunsahalli, Lanke, Hoovinakola, Nallur Changowdanahalli, Hadanur, Hunasur, Muguthanamule Anagatti, Jeeyara, Krishnarajapura, Halemagge Jaganakote, Kenchanahalli, Uyyamballi Nanjanathapura, Lingenahalli, Devalapura, Hullemala Vallahalli, Beguru, Moleyurukaval, Kurnagala.

Sex ratio of Scheduled Caste population is 494.

Scheduled Castes Literates and Illiterates by Sex:

	Persons	Males	Females
Literate	25,250	15,108	10,142
Illiterate	38,346	17,094	21,252
Literacy rate	46.5	55.0	37.8
Graduate	504	462	42

Scheduled Castes (Dominant):

Adi Karnataka, Madiga, Bhovi, Banjara etc.
Adi Dravida

For their cultural identity please see Appendix-I

Villages without Scheduled Castes: There are 90 villages without any scheduled caste population.

Scheduled Tribes: Out of the total population of 233885 persons, 49390 persons (21.12%) belong to Scheduled Tribes. The villages having less than 10% ST population are Rajegowdanahundi, Yelehundikaval, Padukotekava Sollapura, Siddapura, Agasanahundi, Bommalapura Hosahalli, Kodaseege, Chakkodanahalli, Penjahalli Belaganahallikaval, Belaganahalli, Malara Gudumanahalli, Manuganahalli, Yarahalli Kattemanuganahalli, Dasanapura, Akkadevanahalli Naganahalli, Machanayakanahalli, Seeranahundi Krishnapurakaval, Kollegowdanahalli, Yarahallikaval Shirmahalli, Chowdahalli, Jakkahalli, Heggadahalli Halladamanuganahalli, Kattehundi Gollanabeedusaragur, Gollanabeedu, Masanakuppe Ankanahalli, Muddaiahnahundi, Yennegerekaval Thandasipura, Gangadahalli, Alanahalli, Devalapura Sindenahalli, M. Mallahalli, Kaniyanahundi Kethahalli, Kalkodu, Kadasur, Kyathanahalli Kandegowdanapura, Chamalapura, Bannavadi Jompanahalli, Chikkereyur, Doddakereyur Kodichamanahalli, Mallahalli, Doddakerekaval Garikekattekaval, Bettahalli, Iruvidi, Nayakanahundi Chottanahalli, Holehundi, Hampapura, Kohala Marchahalli, Pura, Karehundi, Hirenandi, Kanchamalli Chikkanandi, Chamahalli, Moleyur (Kalihundi) Shankahalli, Muddanahalli, Adahalli, Kulya Hunaganahalli, Manuganahalli, Manchahalli Hunsahalli, Lanke, Hoovinakola, Kattehunsur Kallambalu, Kundur, Bidagalu , Nallur, Hanchipura Bennagere, Changowdanahalli, Chillahalli, Hadanur

Hunasur, Muguthanamule, Siddapura, Baragi, Anagatti Yelamathur, Jeeyara, Manchegowdanahalli Antharasanthe Plantation, Honnurkuppe, Badanakuppe Hosaholalu, Malali, Jaganakote, Kalasuru Kenchanahalli, Uyyamballi, Bettadavarehundi Kandegala, Nanjanathapura, Hegganur, Lingenahalli Thelagumasahalli, Devalapura, Hullemala, Beddalapura Haleyuru, Narasipura, Hariyalapura, Vallahalli B. Matagere, Kandalike, Hosakote, Beguru Moleyurukaval, Nadahadi, Bankavadi, Chikkabesuge Moleyuru, Hirehalli, Kudagi, Kurnagala, Channagundi.

The villages having more than 50% ST population are Savve, Metikuppe Forest, Chakahalli, Itna, Kunigalu Bachegowdanahalli, K.Belthur, Puradakatte Kunnapatna, Halasur, Vaderahalli, Beechanahalli Hosahalli, K.Gandathur, Kakanakote Forest, Kadegadde Vadakanamala, Thimmanihosahalli, Chikkabyranakuppe Anemala, Netkalhundi, Hosur, Golur, Machur Kittur (Therani Manti), Agathuru, Sagare, Singapatna Heggudlu, Huskur , Seegevadi, Kebbepura Inur Marigudi Jungle.

Sex ratio of Scheduled tribe population is 500.

Scheduled Tribes Literates and Illiterates by Sex:

	Persons	Males	Females
Literate	17,427	10,660	6,767
Illiterate	31,963	14,042	17,921
Literacy rate	41.7	50.9	32.5
Graduate	222	207	15

Scheduled Tribes (Dominant):

Naikda etc., Jenu Kuruba, Soligaru, Yerava Kadu Kuruba

For their cultural identity please see Appendix-II

Villages without Scheduled Tribes: There are 117 villages without any scheduled tribe population.

Literates and Illiterates by Sex (Total Population):

	Persons	Males	Females
Literate	104,065	62,245	41,820
Illiterate	129,820	56,291	73,529
Literacy rate	52	61	42
Graduate	2,207	1,888	319

Agriculture: ***Distribution of villages according to land use:*** Out of 281 villages, Total area (in hectare) is 161228, out of that 37.44 percent is cultivable and 13.36 percent of the cultivable area is irrigated.

Sources of Irrigation (Hectares): Government Canal 5909.58, Private Canal 2.98, Well without Electricity 181.47, Well with Electricity 829.43, Tubewell without Electricity 17.4, Tubewell with Electricity 635.51, Tank 266.32, River 578.45, Lake 0, Waterfall 0, Others 85.81.

Villages with population of 5000 to 9999: Saragur.

Villages with population of 10000 and above: None

Distribution of Workers:

	Persons	Males	Females	WPR
Cultivators	63,170	41,415	21,755	52.28
Agricultural Labour	42,535	19,216	23,319	35.2
Household Industry	1,331	707	624	1.1
Other Workers	13,794	10,854	2,940	11.42
Main Workers	99,432	65,182	34,250	82.29
Marginal Workers	21,398	7,010	14,388	17.71
Total Workers	120,830	72,192	48,638	

Religion: Major Religious Communities:

	Persons	Males	Females	Sex Ratio
Hindu (92.55%)	216,465	109,545	106,920	976
Muslim (2.43%)	5,683	2,986	2,697	903
Christian (1.01%)	2,370	1,223	1,147	938
Sikh (0.01%)	24	21	3	143
Buddhists (1.66%)	3,882	1,994	1,888	947
Jain (1.69%)	3,954	1,998	1,956	979

Agewise Data:

	Persons	Males	Females	Sex Ratio
All ages	233,885	118,536	115,349	973
0-14	75,827	37,693	38,134	1012
15-44	113,829	57,924	55,905	965
45-79	41,818	21,778	20,040	920
80+	2,205	1,004	1,201	1196
Age not stated	206	137	69	504

Languages (Dominant):

Kannada, Telugu, Tamil, Urdu, Malayalam

Disabled Population:

	Persons	Males	Females	%
Total Disabled	4,914	2,747	2,167	
In Seeing	2,878	1,513	1,365	58.57
In Speech	467	261	206	9.5
In Hearing	298	166	132	6.06
In Movement	919	605	314	18.7
Mentally	352	202	150	7.16

HIREKERUR

Hirekerur C.D. Block lies in the southern part of Haveri district. It is a part of Hirekerur taluka. The Block is located at a distance of 37 kms. from district headqu arters (Haveri). There are 128 villages in the block with the total population of 196,560 persons. Area of the C.D. Block is 795.79 sq. kms. It is bounded by taluks Hangal and Byadgi on north, district Shimoga on south and west, and districts Davanagere, Shimoga and taluk Ranibennur on east.

Communications: ***Roadways :***

River: Tungabhadra Nadi- Nearest Villages- Kirageri, Chatnalli, Puradakeri, Hallur, Shankaranahalli.

Canal: Nearest Villages- Veerapur, Masur, Ramatirta, Khandibagur, Tippaikoppa, Bellur, Hiremoraba, Chikkamor aba, Chapparadahalli, Yaliwal, Malagi, Kanvishidgeri, Yattinahalli-M-Masur, Kodamaggi, Thirumaiapura.

Reserved Forest: Nearest Villages- Dudihalli, Channalli, Gundagatti, Waraha, Nidanegila, Bannihatti, Khandibagur, Bellur, Chapparadahalli, Yaliwal, Malagi, Kanvishidgeri, Jokanala, Kadur, Bullapur, Chatnalli, Chikkabbar, Hirek abbur, Galaginakatti, Tadakanahalli, Halliyal, Kenchayiko ppa, Medur, Angaragatti, Yattinahalli-M-Masur, Kodamaggi, Gangaikoppa.

Annual Rainfall: Normal Rianfall 592 mm.

Ground Water: Availability of the Ground Water in the Basin is 66.64 MCM and the utilization is 56.65 MCM. It belongs to Over Exploited category. Depth to water level 10 to 20 meter below the ground. Most of the wells go down in summer months, according to the Ground Water Estimation Committee.

Soils: Red Sandy Soil, Medium Soil, Deep Black Soil, Red Loamy Soil and Lateritic Soil.

Natural Division : It falls partly in Byadagi-Hirekerur Rocky Knobs and Middle Tungabhadra Valley of the Central Karnataka Plateau.

Administration:

Division: Belgaum. Parliamentary Constituency: 10 Haveri. District: Haveri. Taluka: Hirekerur. Assembly Constituency: 86 Hirekerur. Gram Panchayat: 37.

Regional Area Development Boards: The Maland Aera Development Board.

Villages: 128 **Inhabited:** 125 **Uninhabited:** 3

Ranking	District	State	National
Area	2	123	733
Population	3	91	743
Sex Ratio	2	141	3381
Child Sex Ratio	1	22	1483
Literacy Rate	1	22	867
Density	6	114	4117
Work Participation Rate	3	45	2667

Gram Panchayats:

Kachavi, Madlur, Satenahalli, Haunsabhavi, Bhogavi, Chinnamulagund, Aralikatti, Aladageri, Sutakoti, Chikkaonati, Chikkerur, Betakerur, Yattinahalli-M-Kod, Abalur, Kod, Hullatti, Neshwi, Kudapali, Makari, Shiragambi, Tawaragi, Buradikatti, Channalli, Ingalagondi, Rattihalli, Kadur, Hallur, Hirekabbur, Tadakanahalli, Kanvishidgeri, Hiremoraba, Masur, Nidanegila, Kodamaggi, Medur, Nagawand, Anaji.

Amenities:

Education: Primary School in 123 villages, Middle school in 86 villages, Matriculation or Secondary School in 29 villages, namely Kachavi, Madlur, Chinnamulagund, Haunsabhavi, Chikkonati, Bhogavi, Abalur, Yattinahalli-M-K0D, Betakerur, Chikkerur, Yallapur, Balambid, Kod, Aladageri, Neshwi, Tawaragi, Hosalli, Nidanegila, Masur, Doddagubbi, Kudapali, Rattihalli, Shiragambi, Kadur, Chikkabbar, Maidur, Hallur, Anaji, Guddadamadapur.

Higher Secondary or Pre University Courses or Intermediate or Junior College in 9 villages of the CD Block,, namely Haunsabhavi, Chikkerur, Kod, Masur, Kudapali, Rattihalli, Medur, Hallur, Anaji.

College in 2 villages, Adult Literacy Center in 79 villages., Colleges are in villages, namely Haunsabhavi, Rattihalli.

Medical: Hospital in 0 village, Dispensary in 7 villages, Health Center in 8 villages, Sub Center in 44 villages, Maternity and Child Welfare Center in 1 village, Community health workers in 66 villages.

The Villages having Hospital or Dispensary or Health Center are Yattinahalli-M-K0D, Lingadevarakoppa, Veerapur, Kadur, Tadakanahalli, Medur, Hallur.

Drinking Water: Tap water in 83 villages, Tank water in 35 villages, Well water in 23 villages, Tubewell in 62 villages and more than one source in 116 villages.

Bank: Banking facility in 9 villages, namely, Haunsabhavi, Yattinahalli-M-K0D, Chikkerur, Kod Masur, Kudapali, Rattihalli, Tadakanahalli Yattinahalli-M-Masur.

Credit Society in 41 villages Agricultural Credit Society in 41 Non-Agricultural Credit Society in 6 villages.

Others: Power supply in 124 villages, Cinema hall in 5 villages sport club in 0 village, Stadium or Auditorium or Community Hall in 0 village, Post Office in 46 villages.

There are 111 villages having bus facilities.

Villages with most of facilities: Haunsabhavi Yattinahalli-M-K0D, Chikkerur, Kod, Masur, Kudapali Rattihalli, Tadakanahalli.

Villages without Amenities (Education): None..

Scheduled Castes: Out of the total population of 196586 persons, 25341 persons (12.89%) belong to Scheduled Castes. The villages having less than 10% SC population are Haunsabhavi, Dasanakoppa, Satenahalli, Divagihalli Sutakoti, Abalur, Betakerur, Chikkerur, Arikatti Aladakatti, Kalagonda, Balambid, Somanahalli Basarihalli, Kod, Ujanipur, Shanakaranahalli-M-Kod Aladageri, Yalawadahalli, Neshwi, Timalapur Gangapur, Hosalli, Gundagatti, Veerapur, Masur Ramatirta, Khandibagur , Tippaikoppa, Hireyadachi Makari, Doddagubbi, Yadagod, Badasangapur, Kudapali Sannagubbi, Rattihalli, Shiragambi, Ingalagondi

Satagihalli, Hiremoraba, Chikkamoraba, Malagi Totaganti, Jokanala, Kadur, Bullapur, Kirageri Chatnalli, Puradakeri, Chikkabbar, Galaginakatti Halliyal, Medur, Hosakatti, Hallur, Kamalapur Guddadamadapur.

The villages having more than 50% SC population are Kargi, Apinakoppa, Jyavalli, Shitikonda, Babapur Sevalayanagar, Nidanegila, Bannihatti, Bellur Kenchayikoppa.

Sex ratio of Scheduled Caste population is 489.

Scheduled Castes Literates and Illiterates by Sex:

	Persons	Males	Females
Literate	12,256	7,766	4,490
Illiterate	13,085	5,186	7,899
Literacy rate	56.9	70.2	42.8
Graduate	315	279	36

Scheduled Castes (Dominant):

Bhambi etc., Banjara etc., Bhovi, Chalavadi etc. Madiga

For their cultural identity please see Appendix-I

Villages without Scheduled Castes: There are 12 villages without any scheduled caste population.

Scheduled Tribes: Out of the total population of 196586 persons, 21238 persons (10.8%) belong to Scheduled Tribes.

The villages having less than 10% ST population are Purakondikoppa, Kachavi, Chinnamulagund, Wadenapur Haunsabhavi, Satenahalli, Yammiganur, Sutakoti Abalur, Yattinahalli-M-K0D, Shiramanakoppa Betakerur, Chikkerur, Jyavalli, Yallapur, Shitikonda Dammalli, Godachikonda, Dhupadahalli, Nulageri Hadrihalli, Hire Mattur, Kod, Shanakaranahalli-M-Kod Babapur, Lingadevarakoppa, Waderahalli, Mavinatop Gangapur, Hosalli, Dudihalli, Sevalayanagar Kalvihalli, Channalli, Gundagatti, Waraha Nidanegila, Bannihatti, Masur, Ramatirta Khandibagur , Bellur, Chikkayadachi, Doddagubbi Yadagod, Kudapali, Hiremadapur, Sannagubbi Rattihalli, Shiragambi, Ingalagondi, Hiremoraba Yaliwal, Malagi, Parvata Shidgeri, Kanvishidgeri Puradakeri, Chikkabbar, Hirekabbur, Tadakanahalli Halliyal, Kenchayikoppa, Angaragatti Yattinahalli-M-Masur, Kodamaggi, Gangaikoppa, Maidur Hallur, Kamalapur.

The villages having more than 50% ST population are None.

Sex ratio of Scheduled tribe population is 489.

Scheduled Tribes Literates and Illiterates by Sex:

	Persons	Males	Females
Literate	11,703	7,202	4,501
Illiterate	9,535	3,651	5,884
Literacy rate	63.8	76.7	50.4
Graduate	321	285	36

Scheduled Tribes (Dominant):

Naikda etc., Koraga, Meda, Kadu Kuruba, Iruliga

For their cultural identity please see Appendix-II

Villages without Scheduled Tribes: There are 18 villages without any scheduled tribe population.

Literates and Illiterates by Sex (Total Population):

	Persons	Males	Females
Literate	124,152	72,719	51,433
Illiterate	72,434	28,006	44,428
Literacy rate	73	83	62
Graduate	4,454	3,692	762

Agriculture: ***Distribution of villages according to land use:*** Out of 128 villages, Total area (in hectare) is 79579, out of that 78.76 percent is cultivable and 18.46 percent of the cultivable area is irrigated.

Sources of Irrigation (Hectares): Government Canal 1168.72, Private Canal 0, Well without Electricity 0, Well with Electricity 109.11, Tubewell without Electricity 0, Tubewell with Electricity 5002.57, Tank 3515.44, River 1777.09, Lake 0, Waterfall 0, Others 0.

Villages with population of 5000 to 9999: Haunsabhavi, Chikkerur, Kod, Masur.

Villages with population of 10000 and above: Rattihalli.

Distribution of Workers:

	Persons	Males	Females	WPR
Cultivators	38,998	29,718	9,280	41.2
Agricultural Labour	41,560	17,648	23,912	43.91
Household Industry	2,213	1,685	528	2.34
Other Workers	11,883	9,602	2,281	12.55
Main Workers	74,466	53,203	21,263	78.67
Marginal Workers	20,188	5,450	14,738	21.33
Total Workers	94,654	58,653	36,001	

Religion: Major Religious Communities:

	Persons	Males	Females	Sex Ratio
Hindu (85.33%)	167,742	85,850	81,892	954
Muslim (13.54%)	26,620	13,752	12,868	936
Christian (0.13%)	247	131	116	885
Sikh (0%)	3	2	1	500
Buddhists (0%)	5	1	4	4,000
Jain (0.16%)	318	165	153	927

Agewise Data:

	Persons	Males	Females	Sex Ratio
All ages	196,586	100,725	95,861	952
0-14	62,090	31,548	30,542	968
15-44	95,729	49,379	46,350	939
45-79	36,920	18,926	17,994	951
80+	1,622	741	881	1189

Age not stated	225	131	94	718

Languages (Dominant):

Kannada, Urdu, Hindi, Telugu, Marathi

Disabled Population:

	Persons	Males	Females	%
Total Disabled	3,691	2,136	1,555	
In Seeing	1,664	898	766	45.08
In Speech	396	207	189	10.73
In Hearing	183	97	86	4.96
In Movement	1,070	707	363	28.99
Mentally	378	227	151	10.24

HIRIYUR

Hiriyur C.D. Block lies in the southern part of Chitradu rga district. It is a part of Hiriyur taluka. The Block is located at a distance of 42 kms. from district headqu arters (Chitradurga). There are 158 villages in the block with the total population of 215,890 persons. Area of the C.D. Block is 1684.09 sq. kms. It is bounded by taluks Chitradurga and Challakere on north, district Tumkur on south and east, taluks Hosdurga, Holalkere and Chitradurga on west. It has common boundary with the state of Andhra Pradesh on east.

Communications:

Roadways : N.H-4: Direction- Chitrdurga to Bangalore, Nearest Villages- Palavvanahalli, Burujanaroppa, Maradi halli, Aimangala, Thadapinachinnammana Halli, Guilalu, Giddaobanahalli, Metikurke, Yaradakatte, Myakalurahalli, Hiriyur (Rural), Patrehalli Kasturirangappenahalli, Bagganadu, Vaddanahalli, Rayabommanahalli, Adivala, Anesidri, Javanagondanahalli. S.H-19: Direction- Turuve kere to Challakere, Nearest Villages- Gollahalli, Khandik ere, Yaraballi, Kalavibagi, Harthikote, Gannayakanahalli, Balenahalli, Hemadala, Myakalurahalli, Babbur, Hiriyur (Rural), Doddaghatta, Hindasakatte, Uduvalli, Hulugalaku nte, Somerahalli, Challamadu, Iddalanagenahalli, Yelladak ere, Arasinagundi, Ulivinahal, Halumadenahalli. S.H-24: Direction- Hosdurga to Hemavathi, Nearest Villages- Beerenahalli, Yaradakatte, Abbinahole, Khandenahalli, Halagaladdi, Parasuramadevarakote, Amanitalav, Shravana gere, Hariyabbe, Gollahalli, Chillahalli, Eswaragere, Devarakotta, Byadarahalli, Venukalgudda, Dharmapura, Bharamagiri, Yarekenagenahalli, Kunikere, Mayasandra, Huchavvanahalli, Babbur, Maskal, Sevalalnagar, Kambadah alli, Vanivilasapura, Myakenahalli, Koodlahalli.

River: Karetore Nadi- Nearest Villages- Huvinahole, Myadanahole, Kundalagura, Thimmalapura, Koodlahalli, Samudradahalli, Javanagondanahalli, Kariyala, Obalapura, Kilaradahalli. Vedavati Nadi- Nearest Villages- Shidlai ahnakote, Sangenahalli, Bidarakere, Bhagavathikere, Toreo benahalli, Abbinahole, Devarakotta, Byadarahalli, Yareken agenahalli, Kunikere, Mayasandra, Huchavvanahalli, Babbur, Maskal, Hiriyur (Rural), Lakkavvanahalli, Doddaghatta, Katrikenahalli, Kurubarahalli, Kambadahalli, Vanivilasa pura, Myakenahalli, Paremenahalli, Patrehalli, Alur, Kasavanahalli, Nandihalli, Pitlali, Yelanadu, Koodlahalli, Toresal Nagenahalli, Uppalagere, Ranganathapura.

Canal: Nearest Villages- Beerenahalli, Gannayakanahalli, Hemadala, Ambalagere, Toreobenahalli, Abbinahole, Byada rahalli, Kundalagura, Kunikere, Mayasandra, Huchavvanahal li, Babbur, Maskal, Bochapura, Sevalalnagar, Hiriyur (Rural), Lakkavvanahalli, Doddaghatta, Paremenahalli, Somerahalli, Indiranagar, Lakkanahal, Alur, Kasavanahal li, Yerachikkenahalli, Pitlali, Yelanadu, Koodlahalli, Toresal Nagenahalli, Samudradahalli, Uppalagere, Rangan athapura, Boranakunte, Vaddanahalli, Rayabommanahalli, Adivala.

Annual Rainfall: Normal Rianfall 601.5 mm.

Ground Water: Availability of the Ground Water in the Basin is 13363.79 H.A.M. and the utilization is 13841. 12 H.A.M. It belongs to Over Expoited category. Depth to water level 2 to 20 meter below the ground. Most of the wells go down in summer months, according to the Ground Water Estimation Committee.

Soils: Deep and Shallow black soils, mixed red and black soil, red loamy and sandy soils.

Natural Division : It falls partly in Middle Vedavati (Hagari) Valley, Kanchipura Scrubby Upland and Chitradur

Administration:

Division: Bangalore. Parliamentary Constituency: 18 Chitradurga (SC). District: Chitradurga. Taluka: Hiriyur. Assembly Constituency: 100 Hiriyur. Gram Panchayat: 32.

Regional Area Development Boards: The Bailu Seeme Area Development Board.

Border Villages: (State: Andhra Pradesh)- Hosakere, Khandenahalli.

Fairs: Maremma Jatra: It is held for five days at Marika nive in Hiriyur taluk of Chitradurga area in the month of Vaishakha (March-April). Marekanive is situated at a distance of about 50 kms. from the Hosadurga Road railway station on the Bangalore-Poona line. Near this village is a large artificial lake called the 'Vanivilas Sagar' which has been constructed by putting up a dam across the river.

Teru-Malleshwara Jatra: The jatra of Teru-Malleshwara is celebrated for a week from the full moon day of Magha (January - February) at Hiriyur, near Chitradurga. Hiriy ur was founded probably in the sixteenth century by a chief of Mayasamudra named Keshava Nayaka.

Villages: 158 **Inhabited:** 154 **Uninhabited:** 4

Ranking	District	State	National

Area	2	17	87
Population	3	74	513
Sex Ratio	3	127	3048
Child Sex Ratio	4	134	3888
Literacy Rate	4	87	2789
Density	4	93	5859
Work Participation Rate	6	149	2158

Gram Panchayats:
Burujana Roppa, Maradihalli, Madakarinaikanakote, Yaraballi, Rangenahalli, Kanajanahalli, Khandenahalli, Parasuramadevarakote, Dharmapura, Hariyabbe, Abbinahole, Harthikote, Aimangala, Sooragondanahalli, Metikurke, Gannayakanahalli, Maskal, Eswaragere, Ikkanur, Ranganthapura, Yelanadu, Babbur, Kunikere, Vanivilasapura, Adivala, Kasturirangappenahalli, Javanagondahahalli, Gowadanahalli, Uduvalli, Yelladakere, Dindavara, Kariyala.

Amenities:

Education: Primary School in 140 villages, Middle school in 103 villages, Matriculation or Secondary School in 36 villages, namely Chikkasiddavvanahalli, Palavvanahalli, Burujanaroppa, Maradihalli, Madakarinaikana Kote, Sondekere, Yaraballi, Aimangala, Guilalu, Mallappanahalli, Harthikote, Hulithotlu, Gannayakanahalli, Hemadala, Rangenahalli, Sugur, Kanajanahalli, Khandenahalli, Hariyabbe, Devarakotta, Byadarahalli, Huvinahole, Dharmapura, Ikkanur, Kunikere, Maskal, Vanivilasapura, Uduvalli, Alur, Yelanadu, Uppalagere, Adivala, Gowadanahalli, Javanagondanahalli, Dindavara, Yelladakere.

Higher Secondary or Pre University Courses or Intermediate or Junior College in 10 villages of the CD Block,, namely Maradihalli, Yaraballi, Aimangala, Rangenahalli, Hariyabbe, Dharmapura, Vanivilasapura, Uduvalli, Yelanadu, Javanagondanahalli.

College in 2 villages, Adult Literacy Center in 0 village., Colleges are in villages, namely Aimangala, Dharmapura.

Medical: Hospital in 3 villages, Dispensary in 8 villages, Health Center in 14 villages, Sub Center in 18 villages, Maternity and Child Welfare Center in 0 village, Community health workers in 5 villages.

The Villages having Hospital or Dispensary or Health Center are Sondekere, Aimangala, Bharamapura, Mallappanahalli, Kanajanahalli, Hariyabbe, Byadarahalli, Yelanadu.

Drinking Water: Tap water in 116 villages, Tank water in 70 villages, Well water in 39 villages, Tubewell in 28 villages and more than one source in 137 villages.

Bank: Banking facility in 20 villages, namely, Maradihalli, Yaraballi, Aimangala, Kalavibagi Metikurke, Beerenahalli, Upparahalli, Hariyabbe Chillahalli, Byadarahalli, Dharmapura, Maskal Kambadahalli, Vanivilasapura, Patrehalli, Uppalagere Adivala, Javanagondanahalli, Dindavara, Yelladakere.

Credit Society in 44 villages Agricultural Credit Society in 31 Non-Agricultural Credit Society in 18 villages.

Others: Power supply in 154 villages, Cinema hall in 5 villages sport club in 0 village, Stadium or Auditorium or Community Hall in 0 village, Post Office in 62 villages.

There are 129 villages having bus facilities.

Villages with most of facilities: Maradihalli Yaraballi, Aimangala, Hariyabbe, Byadarahalli Dharmapura, Maskal, Vanivilasapura, Adivala Javanagondanahalli, Dindavara, Yelladakere.

Villages without amenities (Education): Jodipura, Kumbarakatte, Amanitalav, Appasamudra, Thimmalapura, Yarekenagenahalli, Bochapura, Myakenahalli, Kattehole, Lakkanahal, Yerachikkenahalli, Bagganadu Kaval, Rayabommanahalli..

Scheduled Castes: Out of the total population of 215913 persons, 55176 persons (25.55%) belong to Scheduled Castes.

The villages having less than 10% SC population are Jodipura, Maddanakunte, Yelakurnahalli, Kumbarakatte Hulithotlu, Goguddu, Gudunurhalli, Sangenahalli Upparahalli, Yelagondanahalli, Salhunse Parasuramadevarakote, Amanitalav, Yennegere Appasamudra, Thimmalapura, Ikkanur, Mayasandra Bochapura, Hiriyur (Rural), Nandihalli Yerachikkenahalli, Vaddanahalli, Madenahalli Anesidri, Kariyala, Layaradasarahalli, Arasinagundi Halumadenahalli, Kilaradahalli.

The villages having more than 50% SC population are Gudihalli, Bharamagiri, Sevalalnagar, Kambadahalli Myakenahalli, Indiranagar, Patrehalli Rayabommanahalli, Ganjalagunte, Challamadu Obalapura, Ulivinahal, Veeravvanagathihalli.

Sex ratio of Scheduled Caste population is 486.

Scheduled Castes Literates and Illiterates by Sex:

	Persons	Males	Females
Literate	24,485	15,456	9,029
Illiterate	30,691	12,900	17,791
Literacy rate	51.5	63.1	39.1
Graduate	673	580	93

Scheduled Castes (Dominant):

Madiga, Bhovi, Adi Karnataka, Banjara etc. Chalavadi etc.

For their cultural identity please see Appendix-I

Villages without Scheduled Castes: There are

20 villages without any scheduled caste population.

Scheduled Tribes: Out of the total population of 215913 persons, 21091 persons (9.77%) belong to Scheduled Tribes. The villages having less than 10% ST population are Burujanaroppa, Maradihalli, Ramajogihalli Maddanakunte, Talavatti, Maradidevigere Kumbarakatte, Giddaobanahalli, Mallappanahalli Salabommanahalli, Kalavibagi, Golagondanahalli Kariobenahalli, Sooragondanahalli, Gudihalli Beerenahalli, Yaradakatte, Balenahalli, Gudunurhalli Rangenahalli, Shidlaiahnakote, Sangenahalli Bidarakere, Upparahalli, Abbinahole Yelagondanahalli, Gulya, Hosahalli, Salhunse, Sugur Khandenahalli, Halagaladdi, Parasuramadevarakote Amanitalav, Shravanagere, Hariyabbe, Mungasavalli Gollahalli, Chillahalli, Eswaragere, Byadarahalli Huvinahole, Venukalgudda, Dharmapura, Benkanahalli Sakkara, Yennegere, Appasamudra, Myadanahole Kundalagura, Kurubarahalli, Yarekenagenahalli Kunikere, Huchavvanahalli, Myakalurahalli Sevalalnagar, Lakkavvanahalli, Doddaghatta Katrikenahalli, Kurubarahalli, Kambadahalli Vanivilasapura, Myakenahalli, Paremenahalli Uduvalli, Hulugalakunte, Somerahalli, Indiranagar Lakkanahal, Patrehalli, Nandihalli Yerachikkenahalli, Pitlali, Samudradahalli Ranganathapura, Boranakunte, Kasturirangappenahalli Gorladaku, Bagganadu Kaval, Vaddanahalli Rayabommanahalli, Adivala, Ganjalagunte, Challamadu Madenahalli, Malagondanahalli, Katanayakanahalli Javanagondanahalli, Obalapura, Dindavara Layaradasarahalli, Handiganadu, Ulivinahal Halumadenahalli, Sheshappanahalli, Pilali Veeravvanagathihalli, Lakkenahalli, Mavinamadu Kilaradahalli.

The villages having more than 50% ST population are Yelakurnahalli, Toreobenahalli, Thimmalapura Hiriyur (Rural), Bagganadu, Iddalanagenahalli Arasinagundi.

Sex ratio of Scheduled tribe population is 492.

Scheduled Tribes Literates and Illiterates by Sex:

	Persons	Males	Females
Literate	11,046	6,731	4,315
Illiterate	10,045	3,987	6,058
Literacy rate	59.8	71.3	47.8
Graduate	307	269	38

Scheduled Tribes (Dominant):

Naikda etc., Meda, Gond etc.

For their cultural identity please see Appendix-II

Villages without Scheduled Tribes: There are 33 villages without any scheduled tribe population.

Literates and Illiterates by Sex (Total Population):

	Persons	Males	Females
Literate	112,911	68,054	44,857
Illiterate	103,002	42,177	60,825
Literacy rate	60	71	49
Graduate	4,297	3,683	614

Agriculture: ***Distribution of villages according to land use:*** Out of 158 villages, Total area (in hectare) is 168409, out of that 68.4 percent is cultivable and 15.58 percent of the cultivable area is irrigated.

Sources of Irrigation (Hectares): Government Canal 5868.63, Private Canal 0, Well without Electricity 28.24, Well with Electricity 598.77, Tubewell without Electricity 0, Tubewell with Electricity 8239.61, Tank 2947.52, River 268.2, Lake 0, Waterfall 0, Others 0.

Villages with population of 5000 to 9999:

Kanajanahalli, Maskal, Adivala.

Villages with population of 10000 and above: None

Distribution of Workers:

	Persons	Males	Females	WPR
Cultivators	44,139	30,785	13,354	40.63
Agricultural Labour	41,455	17,880	23,575	38.16
Household Industry	4,263	1,652	2,611	3.92
Other Workers	18,772	13,504	5,268	17.28
Main Workers	88,737	57,109	31,628	81.69
Marginal Workers	19,892	6,712	13,180	18.31
Total Workers	108,629	63,821	44,808	

Religion: Major Religious Communities:

	Persons	Males	Females	Sex Ratio
Hindu (93.83%)	202,601	103,491	99,110	958
Muslim (5.05%)	10,897	5,474	5,423	991
Christian (0.02%)	46	28	18	643
Sikh (0.03%)	74	46	28	609
Buddhists (0.01%)	18	11	7	636
Jain (0.06%)	136	67	69	1,030

Agewise Data:

	Persons	Males	Females	Sex Ratio
All ages	215,913	110,231	105,682	959
0-14	66,546	34,248	32,298	943
15-44	102,839	51,915	50,924	981
45-79	44,252	22,956	21,296	928
80+	2,152	1,040	1,112	1069
Age not stated	124	72	52	722

Languages (Dominant):

Kannada, Telugu, Urdu, Hindi, Tamil

Disabled Population:

	Persons	Males	Females	%
Total Disabled	5,485	3,066	2,419	
In Seeing	2,647	1,405	1,242	48.26

In Speech	544	306	238	9.92
In Hearing	400	199	201	7.29

In Movement	1,427	891	536	26.02
Mentally	467	265	202	8.51

HOLALKERE

Holakere C.D. Block lies in the southern part of Chitradurga district. It is a part of Holalkere taluka. The Block is located at a distance of 32 kms. from district headquarters (Chitradurga). There are 202 villages in the block with the total population of 184,186 persons. Area of the C.D. Block is 1098.11 sq. kms. It is bounded by district Davanagere and taluk Chitradurga on north, district Chikmagalur and taluk Hosdurga on south, taluk Hiriyur on east, and district Davanagere on west.

Communications:

Roadways : N.H-13: Direction- Shimoga to Chitradurga, Nearest Villages- Malladihalli, Basapura, N.Mallapura, Dummi, Gundimadu, Halehalli, Kudineerakatti, Holalkere (Rural), Amanahal, Arehalli, Arehalli Kaval, Chitrahalli, T. Nulenur, Banjagondanahalli, Kengunte, Shivaganga, T.Yemmiganur. S.H-19 A: Direction- Mayakonda to Hosdurga, Nearest Villages- Andanur, Ingaladahalli, Bande Bommenahalli, Gyarehalli, Tyagadahalli, Muthugaduru, Kutvihalli, Sasalu, B.Durga, Gunjiganur, Rangavvanahalli, Honnakaluve, Gunderi Kaval, Bommanakatte, Lokadolalu, Thirumalapura, Viswanathanahalli, Dodderikatti, Chikkajajur, Kotehal, Banagere, Narayanagondanahalli, Uganekatte, Adanur, Padigatte, Cheeranahalli, Holalkere (Rural). S.H-48: Direction- Honnali to Chitradurga, Nearest Villages- Mallenahalli, Vishvanathanahalli, Dandigenahalli, Kalagatta, Sasalu, B.Durga, Kallavvanagathihalli, Shanubhoganahalli, Hirekandavadi.

Railway Station: Villages- Muthugaduru, Chikkajajur, Kotehal, Ramagiri, Bidarakere, Hanumanakatte, Gundimadu, Arehalli, Arehalli Kaval, Amruthapura, Kashipura, Gowripura.

River: Hire Halla Nadi- Nearest Villages- Ramagatta, Abradasikatte, Kengunte, Malladihalli, N.Mallapura, Dogganal, Dummi, Shivapura.

Annual Rainfall: Normal Rianfall 654.1 mm.

Ground Water: Availability of the Ground Water in the Basin is 11052.88 H.A.M. and the utilization is 13776.28 H.A.M. It belongs to Over Expoited category. Depth to water level 2 to 10 meter below the ground. Most of the wells go down in summer months, according to the Ground Water Estimation Committee.

Soils: Deep and Shallow black soils, mixed red and black soil, red loamy and sandy soils.

Natural Division : It falls partly in Chitradurga-Hosadurga Hills and Devangere Plateau of the Central Karnataka Plateau.

Administration:

Division: Bangalore. Parliamentary Constituency: 18 Chitradurga (SC). District: Chitradurga. Taluka: Holalkere. Assembly Constituency: 102 Holalkere (SC). Gram Panchayat: 29.

Regional Area Development Boards: The Bailu Seeme Area Development Board.

Villages: 202 **Inhabited:** 166 **Uninhabited:** 36

Ranking	District	State	National
Area	5	72	356
Population	5	104	985
Sex Ratio	2	111	2727
Child Sex Ratio	6	145	4153
Literacy Rate	1	43	1622
Density	1	25	5288
Work Participation Rate	2	104	938

Gram Panchayats:

Andanur, Muthugaduru, B. Durga, Gunjiganur, Chikkajajur, Chitrahalli, T. Nulenur, Shivaganga, Adanur, Chikkayemmiganur, Hireyemmiganur, Dummi, Malladihalli, Shivapura, Arehalli, Madderu, Horakeredevarapura, Tekalavatti, Upparigenahalli, Talya, Gunderi, R. Nulenur, Talikatti, Ramagiri, Viswanathanahalli, Narayanagondanalli, Gangasamudra, Thuppadahalli, Bidarakere.

Amenities:

Education: Primary School in 163 villages, Middle school in 97 villages, Matriculation or Secondary School in 28 villages, namely Muthugaduru, Vishvanathanahalli, B.Durga, Hirekandavadi, Chikkajajur, Kodagavalli, Hireyemmiganur, Malladihalli, R.Nulenur, Dummi, Kalkere, Rangapura, Talikatti, Ramagiri, Narayanagondanahalli, Gowdihalli, Kenchapura, Chikkandavadi, Shivapura, Holalkere (Rural), Gunderi, Viswanathanahalli, Amruthapura, Kashipura, Chitrahalli, Talya, Horakeredevarapura, Upparigenahalli.

Higher Secondary or Pre University Courses or Intermediate or Junior College in 10 villages of the CD Block,, namely Chikkajajur, Malladihalli, Ramagiri, Narayanagondanahalli, Amruthapura, Kashipura, Chitrahalli, Talya, Horakeredevarapura, Upparigenahalli.

College in 2 villages, Adult Literacy Center in 1 village., Colleges are in villages, namely Chikkajajur, Ramagiri.

Medical: Hospital in 3 villages, Dispensary in 12 villages, Health Center in 8 villages, Sub Center in 25 villages, Maternity and Child Welfare Center in 0 village, Community health workers in 2 villages.

The Villages having Hospital or Dispensary or Health Center are Bande Bommenahalli, B.Durga, Malladihalli, Narayanagondanahalli, Gowdihalli, Thuppadahalli, Shivapura, Malenahalli, Gunderi, Chitrahalli, Talya, Gulihosahalli.

Drinking Water: Tap water in 53 villages, Tank water in 35 villages, Well water in 10 villages, Tubewell in 86 villages and more than one source in 121 villages.

Bank: Banking facility in 18 villages, namely, Muthugaduru, Sasalu, B.Durga, Hirekandavadi Chikkajajur, Chikkayemmiganur, Malladihalli R.Nulenur, Rangapura, Talikatti, Ramagiri Narayanagondanahalli, Hulemalali, Thirumalapura Chitrahalli, Shivaganga, Talya, Horakeredevarapura.

Credit Society in 18 villages Agricultural Credit Society in 18 Non-Agricultural Credit Society in 2 villages.

Others: Power supply in 166 villages, Cinema hall in 2 villages, sport club in 0 village, Stadium or Auditorium or Community Hall in 0 village, Post Office in 48 villages.

There are 118 villages having bus facilities.

Villages with most of facilities: Muthugaduru Sasalu, B.Durga, Chikkajajur, Malladihalli R.Nulenur, Talikatti, Ramagiri, Narayanagondanahalli Chitrahalli, Shivaganga, Talya, Horakeredevarapura.

Villages without amenities (Education): Chikkayemmiganur Kaval, N.Mallapura, Makunte..

Scheduled Castes: Out of the total population of 183192 persons, 46900 persons (25.6%) belong to Scheduled Castes.

The villages having less than 10% SC population are Ingaladahalli, Gyarehalli, Kagalagere Vishvanathanahalli, Dandigenahalli Sringeri-Hanumanahalli, Chikkayemmiganur Kaval Hosahalli, Malladihalli, Dasikatte, Talikatte Kaval Talikatti, T.Vaderahalli, Narayanagondanahalli Gowdihalli, Gangasamudra, Kanivehalli, Mallenahalli Arabagatta, G.Vaderahalli, Apparasanahalli Dasarahalli Inam, Harenahalli, Agrahara, Kunugali Malkapura, Basavapura, Amruthapura, Gowripura Brahmapura, Echaghatta, Pampapura, Nellikatte Sangenahalli, Hulikere, Upparigenahalli.

The villages having more than 50% SC population are Tanigehalli, Kutvihalli, Kalagatta Chikkajajur Kaval, Honnakaluve, Iyyanahalli Kadur Kaval, Dasarahalli, Nandihalli, Kalkere Uganekatte, Muddapura, Jakkanahalli, Makunte Garaga Forest, Kudineerakatti, Holalkere (Rural) Gunderi Kaval, Lingadahalli, Kashipura, Nagaraghatta Borenahalli, Ramenahalli, T.Yemmiganur, Hunasepanche Kasavanahalli, Neralakatte, Giddanahalli.

Sex ratio of Scheduled Caste population is 491.

Scheduled Castes Literates and Illiterates by Sex:

	Persons	Males	Females
Literate	20,407	12,642	7,765
Illiterate	26,493	11,229	15,264
Literacy rate	51.1	62.3	39.5
Graduate	487	430	57

Scheduled Castes (Dominant):

Madiga, Bhovi, Banjara etc., Adi Karnataka, Koracha

For their cultural identity please see Appendix-I

Villages without Scheduled Castes: There are 49 villages without any scheduled caste population.

Scheduled Tribes: Out of the total population of 183192 persons, 21594 persons (11.79%) belong to Scheduled Tribes.

The villages having less than 10% ST population are Hiriyur, Gyarehalli, Muthugaduru, Mallenahalli Dandigenahalli, Kallavvanagathihalli, Hirekandavadi Chikkajajur Kaval, Honnakaluve Sringeri-Hanumanahalli, Iyyanahalli, Kadur Kaval Dasarahalli, Nandihalli, Anthapura, Kadur Chikkajajur, Hireyemmiganur, Ajjikyatanahalli Chikkayemmiganur, Hosahalli, Abradasikatte, Kengunte Malladihalli, Basapura, R.Nulenur, Dummi, Kalkere Talikatti, T.Vaderahalli, Gollarahalli Narayanagondanahalli, Uganekatte, Gowdihalli Rangaiahnadurga Kaval, Kenchapura, Devarahosahalli Kanivehalli, Muddapura, Bidarakere, Mallenahalli Arabagatta, G.Vaderahalli, Gundasamudra Jakkanahalli, Channasamudra, Bommenahalli Hanumanakatte, Arasanaghatta, Makunte, Garaga Forest Adanur, Padigatte, Agrahara, Shivapura, Kunugali Punajur, Cheeranahalli, Halehalli, Kudineerakatti Holalkere (Rural), Arehalli Kaval, Gunderi Kaval Lokadolalu, Thirumalapura, Gunderi, Edehalli Viswanathanahalli, Santhenahalli, Basavapura Thirumalapura, Lingadahalli, Thodranal, Amruthapura Kashipura, Gowripura, Kondapura, Chitrahalli T. Nulenur, Brahmapura, Mahadevapura, Shivaganga Borenahalli, Ramenahalli, Nellikatte, Madderu T.Yemmiganur, Sirappanahalli, Talya, Mathigatta Horakeredevarapura, Kanivejogihalli, Kasavanahalli Sangenahalli, Kereyagalahalli, Gollarahalli Chowdagondanahalli, Nandanahosur, Neralakatte Papenahalli, Budipura, Halenahalli, Upparigenahalli Gulihosahalli.

The villages having more than 50% ST population are Ingaladahalli, Kagalagere, Vishvanathanahalli Chikkayemmiganur Kaval, Chikkanakatti Talikatte Kaval, Dasarahalli Inam, Malkapura Malenahalli Kaval, Pampapura, Ghattihosahalli.

Sex ratio of Scheduled tribe population is 494.

Scheduled Tribes Literates and Illiterates by Sex:

	Persons	Males	Females
Literate	11,398	6,859	4,539
Illiterate	10,196	4,058	6,138
Literacy rate	60.4	72.0	48.6
Graduate	365	311	54

Scheduled Tribes (Dominant):

Naikda etc., Kadu Kuruba, Dubla etc.

For their cultural identity please see Appendix-II

Villages without Scheduled Tribes: There are 64 villages without any scheduled tribe population.

Literates and Illiterates by Sex (Total Population):

	Persons	Males	Females
Literate	107,614	63,320	44,294
Illiterate	75,578	29,898	45,680
Literacy rate	67	78	56
Graduate	5,054	4,259	795

Agriculture: ***Distribution of villages according to land use:***
Out of 202 villages, Total area (in hectare) is 109811, out of that 55.16 percent is cultivable and 13.56 percent of the cultivable area is irrigated.

Sources of Irrigation (Hectares): Government Canal 0, Private Canal 0, Well without Electricity 0, Well with Electricity 80, Tubewell without Electricity 0, Tubewell with Electricity 7248.49, Tank 887.13, River 0, Lake 0, Waterfall 0, Others 0.

Villages with population of 5000 to 9999:
Chikkajajur, Talikatti.

Villages with population of 10000 and above: None

Distribution of Workers:

	Persons	Males	Females	WPR
Cultivators	51,584	34,527	17,057	50.83
Agricultural Labour	35,864	13,413	22,451	35.34
Household Industry	1,768	1,109	659	1.74
Other Workers	12,259	8,916	3,343	12.08
Main Workers	71,495	49,749	21,746	70.46
Marginal Workers	29,980	8,216	21,764	29.54
Total Workers	101,475	57,965	43,510	

Religion: Major Religious Communities:

	Persons	Males	Females	Sex Ratio
Hindu (95.82%)	175,538	89,331	86,207	965
Muslim (1.86%)	3,405	1,714	1,691	987
Christian (0.05%)	83	46	37	804
Sikh (0.02%)	44	20	24	1,200
Buddhists (0.01%)	23	10	13	1,300
Jain (0.08%)	138	72	66	917

Agewise Data:

	Persons	Males	Females	Sex Ratio
All ages	183,192	93,218	89,974	965
0-14	53,064	27,191	25,873	952
15-44	89,127	44,871	44,256	986
45-79	38,640	19,980	18,660	934
80+	2,164	1,072	1,092	1019
Age not stated	197	104	93	894

Languages (Dominant):
Kannada, Telugu, Hindi, Urdu, Coorgi/Kodagu

Disabled Population:

	Persons	Males	Females	%
Total Disabled	3,792	2,246	1,546	
In Seeing	1,840	1,070	770	48.52
In Speech	349	191	158	9.2
In Hearing	237	123	114	6.25
In Movement	1,053	694	359	27.77
Mentally	313	168	145	8.25

HOLE NARSIPUR

Hole Narsipur C.D. Block lies in the south-eastern part of Hassan district. It is a part of Hole Narsipur taluka. The Block is located at a distance of 31 kms. from district headquarters (Hassan). There are 249 villages in the block with the total population of 148,050 persons. Area of the C.D. Block is 598.96 sq. kms. It is bounded by taluks Hassan and Channarayapatna on north, district Mysore on south, districts Mandya and Mysore on east, taluks Hassan and Arkalgud on west.

Communications:

Roadways : SH- 8: Direction- Arkalgud to Channarayapatna, Nearest Villages- Boovanahalli, Hirehalli, Ankanahalli, Doddabyagathavalli, Sankanahalli, Nagalapura, Krishnapu ra, Holenarasipura (Rural), Thattekere, Sunkalhosur, Mangalapura, Mudalahippe, Jakkavalli, Ulivala, Singapura. SH- 57: Direction- Hassan to Mysore, Nearest Villages- Nyamanahalli, Amanidoddakere, Hangarahalli, Mavinakere, Amanichikkere, Halekote, Channapura, Kamasamudra, Kat tebelaguli, Yalleshapura, Beemanahalli, Chikknahalli, Hireb elaguli, Kadavinakote, Hantha, Kadavinakote, Chikkchagaha lli, S.Ankanahalli, Peddanahalli, Hullahalli, Alagodanaha lli, Chikkakadnur, C.Hindalahalli, Doddahalli, Kaval, Kabbur, Bachanahalli, Doddakadanur, Yadegowdanahalli, Honnenahalli, Marahalli, Marahalli Kaval, Doddahalli, Ragithalli Kaval.

Railway Station: Villages- Hangarahalli, Haralahalli, Annechakenahalli, Mavinakere, Sravanur.

River: Hemavati Nadi- Nearest Villages- Hanumanahalli, Haralahalli, Mavinakere, Kamasamudra, Hirebelaguli, Kadavinakote Hantha, Kadavinakote, Kadavinahosahalli, Kadavinah0Sahalli Hantha, Bagivalu Hantha, Hoovinahalli, Hoovinahalli, Hantha, Kumkumadahosur, Sagar, Sagar Hantha, Gulisathenahalli Hantha, Marasettihalli, Maraset tihalli Hantha, Kattehosahalli Hantha, Mallasamudra Hantha, Maragowdanahalli, Paduvalahippe, Makavalli, Kattahalli, Dakshinanala, Holenarasipura (Rural), Gondi Mallenahalli,

Thattekere, Mangalapura, Mudalahippe, Maranayakanahalli, Ediganahosur, Gunje, Somanahalli, Jakkavalli, Hangraho sur, Ulivala, Singapura Nala, Volambige, Kattehosur, Mulekalenahalli, Kadavinabachanahalli, Nagarthi, Kodihal li, Nagarthi Amanikere.

Canal: Nearest Villages- Kattebelaguli Hantha, Yalleshap ura Hantha, Yalleshapura, Hirebelaguli, Hirebelaguli Hantha, Kadavinakote Hantha, Kadavinakote, Kadavinahosahalli, Kadavinah0Sahalli Hantha, Bagivalu, Bagivalu Hantha, Hoovinahalli, Hoovinahalli Hantha, Beechenahalli Hantha, Hadavanahalli Hantha, Unnenahalli Hantha, Kumkumadahosur, Gulisathenahalli, Sagar, Sagar Hantha, Gulisathenahalli Hantha, Marasettihalli, Marasettihalli Hantha, Kattehosahalli Hantha, Kattahalli, Kattehosahalli, Mallasamudra Hantha, Ankanathapura, Chikkabyagathavalli, Shivapura, Dakshinanala, Nagalapura, Chittanahalli, Holenarasipura (Rural), Gondi Mallenahalli, Thattekere, Sunkalhosur, Mangalapura, Thirumalapura, Amanihirekere, Mallappanahalli, Gaddehosur, Mudalahippe.

Annual Rainfall: Normal Rianfall 760.2 mm.

Ground Water: Availability of the Ground Water in the Basin is 59.22 H.A.M. and the utilization is 42.32 H. A.M. It belongs to Over Expoited category. Depth to water level 2 to 10 meter below the ground. Most of the wells go down in summer months, according to the Ground Water Estimation Committee.

Soils: Red Soil, Red Sandy Soil, Mixed Soil and Silty Clay Soil.

Natural Division : It falls partly in Gandasi-Hirisave Plateau and Cauvery-Hemavati Basin of the Southern Karnataka Plateau.

Administration:

Division: Mysore. Parliamentary Constituency: 16 Hassan. District: Hassan. Taluka: Hole Narsipur. Assembly Constituency: 197 Hole Narsipur, 198 Arkalgud. Gram Panchayat: 26.

Fairs: Lakshminarasimhaswamy Car Festival: It held at Hole Narsipur in about March for a period of six days. Hole Narsipur, the headquarters of the taluk of the same name issituated on the bank of the Hemavathy river about 32 kms. south-east of Hassan town on the Mysore-Hassan road.

Villages: 249 **Inhabited:** 209 **Uninhabited:** 40

Ranking	District	State	National
Area	7	152	1177
Population	6	133	1921
Sex Ratio	6	26	987
Child Sex Ratio	1	4	472
Literacy Rate	8	102	3088
Density	4	60	4111
Work Participation Rate	3	44	1571

Gram Panchayats:
Malali, Doddakunche, Kodihalli, Hariharapura, Halekote, Hangarahalli, Maragowdanahalli, Kattebelaguli, Bagivalu, Mudalahippe, Mallappanahalli, Sankanahalli, Doddabyagathavalli, Keragodu, Ichanahalli, Sravanur, Nagaranahalli, Doddakadanur, Tathanahalli, Odanahalli, Niduvani, Bidarakka, Kyathanahalli, Halli Mysore, Anekannambadi, Doddahalli.

Amenities:

Education: Primary School in 184 villages, Middle school in 99 villages, Matriculation or Secondary School in 25 villages, namely Hangarahalli, Halekote, Yalleshapura, Malali, Hariharapura, Doddakunche, Mavanoor, Hadavanahalli, Hirehalli, Paduvalahippe, Sankanahalli, Yalechagahalli, Mudalahippe, Gubbi, Keragodu, Niduvani, Somanahalli, Haragodanahalli, Tathanahalli, Halli Mysore, Doddakadanur, Devaramuddanahalli, Anekannambadi, Doddahalli, Nagaranahalli.
Higher Secondary or Pre University Courses or Intermediate or Junior College in 6 villages of the CD Block,, namely Halekote, Doddakunche, Haragodanahalli, Halli Mysore, Doddakadanur, Doddahalli.
College in 0 village, Adult Literacy Center in 2 villages.

Medical: Hospital in 0 village, Dispensary in 8 villages, Health Center in 11 villages, Sub Center in 34 villages, Maternity and Child Welfare Center in 0 village, Community health workers in 1 village.
The Villages having Hospital or Dispensary or Health Center are Hariharapura, Doddakunche, Mudalahippe, Uddurhosahalli, Somanahalli, Doddakadanur, Devaramuddanahalli, Doddahalli.

Drinking Water: Tap water in 144 villages, Tank water in 104 villages, Well water in 92 villages, Tubewell in 132 villages and more than one source in 205 villages.

Bank: Banking facility in 16 villages, namely, Hangarahalli, Halekote, Bagivalu, Theranya Hariharapura, Doddakunche, Hadavanahalli Paduvalahippe, Yalechagahalli, Mudalahippe, Gubbi Muddanahalli, Somanahalli, Halli Mysore Doddakadanur, Doddahalli.
Credit Society in 29 villages Agricultural Credit Society in 15 Non-Agricultural Credit Society in 1 village.

Others: Power supply in 207 villages, Cinema hall in 3 villages sport club in 0 village, Stadium or Auditorium or Community Hall in 0 village, Post Office in 28 villages.
There are 139 villages having bus facilities.

Villages with most of facilities: Hangarahalli

Halekote, Bagivalu, Theranya, Hariharapura
Doddakunche, Hadavanahalli, Paduvalahippe
Yalechagahalli, Mudalahippe, Gubbi, Somanahalli
Halli Mysore, Doddakadanur, Doddahalli.

Villages without amenities (Education):
Nyamanahalli, Kattebelaguli Hantha,
Kadavinakote Hantha, Beeranahalli, Misiganahalli,
Laxmipura, Shivapura, Ontigudda Kaval,
Kattehosahalli, Shivapura, Galipura Kaval,
Sunkalhosur, Thirumalapura, Gulladapura, Hullahalli,
Srimatada Kaval, Hangrahosur, Kattehosur, Kuri Kaval,
Gummanaladahosahalli, Upparahosahalli,
Shankarasettihalli, Doddahalli Kaval, Kodihalli,
Ganjikuppahalli..

Scheduled Castes: Out of the total population of 148220 persons, 26406 persons (17.82%) belong to Scheduled Castes.
The villages having less than 10% SC population are
Nyamanahalli, Hangarahalli, Hanumanahalli
Haralahalli, Kinnarahalli, Channapura, Beemanahalli
Kadavinakote Hantha, Bagivalu, Malali, Parasanahalli
Gavisomanahalli, Arekalhosahalli, Hariharapura
Beeranahalli, Hoovinahalli, Kallenahalli
Misiganahalli, Laxmipura, Bittagowdanahalli
Banukuppe, Shivapura, Athichowdenahalli
Ontigudda Kaval, Kurubarahalli, Hosahalli
Hadavanahalli, Unnenahalli, Kattehosahalli
Hirehalli, Ankavalli, Paduvalahippe
Doddabyagathavalli, Shivapura, Galipura Kaval
Haralahalli, Mangalapura, Thirumalapura
Mallenahalli, Honnavara, S.Ankanahalli, Peddanahalli
Gulladapura, Aladahalli, Hullahalli, Mallappanahalli
Gaddehosur, Srimatada Kaval, Maranayakanahalli
Gunje, Somanahalli, Jakkavalli, Hangrahosur
Adikekerehosur, Volambige, Kattehosur, Jakkanahalli
Gopanahalli, Cholenahalli, Machagowdanahalli
Bandiganahalli, Bediganahalli, Hadya
Motanayakanahalli, Somanahalli, Sidlahalli
Kogilahalli, Malanayakanahalli, Guddenahalli
H.Hindalahalli, Malliganahalli
Tejur Mayagowdanahalli, Alagodanahalli, Chikkakadnur
Kallahalli, Halli Mysore, Singanakuppe
Gummanaladahosahalli, Devaraguddenahalli
Shankarasettihalli, Doddahalli Kaval, Mallenahalli
Annechakenahalli, Bantarathalalu, Arehalli
Kodihalli, Sravanur, Gulaganjihalli, Neggalahalli
Yadegowdanahalli, Marahalli, Donanaghatta
Doddahalli, Maluganahalli, Kotiganahosur
Mudalamayigowdanahalli.
The villages having more than 50% SC population are
Kattebelaguli, Thavanandi, Kallenahalli Kaval
Chigahalli, Mundanahalli, Chittanahalli, Ichanahalli
Galipura, Laxmipura, Muddanahalli, Kuri Kaval
Ganjikuppahalli.
Sex ratio of Scheduled Caste population is 497.

Scheduled Castes Literates and Illiterates by Sex:

	Persons	Males	Females
Literate	12,394	7,686	4,708
Illiterate	14,012	5,597	8,415
Literacy rate	54.0	66.6	41.3
Graduate	264	236	28

Scheduled Castes (Dominant):
Adi Karnataka, Madiga, Bhovi, Generic Castes etc.
Adi Dravida

For their cultural identity please see Appendix-I

Villages without Scheduled Castes: There are 81 villages without any scheduled caste population.

Scheduled Tribes: Out of the total population of 148220 persons, 3025 persons (2.04%) belong to Scheduled Tribes.
The villages having less than 10% ST population are
Nyamanahalli, Kabbinahalli, Hangarahalli
Basavanayakanahalli, Hanumanahalli, Haralahalli
Mavinakere, Halekote, Kinnarahalli
Machagowdanahalli, Haradanahalli, Kyathanahalli
Channapura, Kamasamudra, Kattebelaguli
Kattebelaguli Hantha, Yalleshapura, Beemanahalli
Chikknahalli, Hirebelaguli, Kadavinakote Hantha
Kadavinakote, Kadavinahosahalli, Bagivalu
Bettadasathenahalli, Sigaranahalli, Thavanandi
Boranahalli, Ankanahalli, Sabbanahalli
Karaganahalli, Malali, Parasanahalli
Gavisomanahalli, Theranya, Chakenahalli
Arekalhosahalli, Hariharapura, Beeranahalli
Kallenahalli Kaval, Hoovinahalli, Beechenahalli
Borehosur, Pillenahalli, Kallenahalli, Misiganahalli
Mavanoor, Laxmipura, Bittagowdanahalli, Banukuppe
Shivapura, Kamenahalli, Athichowdenahalli
Ontigudda Kaval, Kurubarahalli, Kodihalli
Hale Kunche, Hosahalli, Vaddarahalli, Hadavanahalli
Kumkumadahosur, Gulisathenahalli, Unnenahalli
Marasettihalli, Kattehosahalli, Mallasamudra
Boovanahalli, Hirehalli, Ankanahalli, Gangoor
Ankavalli, Maragowdanahalli, Paduvalahippe
Makavalli, Kattahalli, Chikkabyagathavalli
Doddabyagathavalli, Chigahalli, Bandisettihalli
Mundanahalli, Billenahalli, Sankanahalli, Shivapura
Nagalapura, Krishnapura, Chittanahalli, Ichanahalli
Byadarahalli, Galipura Kaval, Galipura
Yalechagahalli, Haralahalli, Laxmipura
Gondi Mallenahalli, Thattekere, Sunkalhosur
Mangalapura, Thirumalapura, Chikkchagahalli

Mallenahalli, Lakkur, Honnavara, Kongalabeedu
S.Ankanahalli, Peddanahalli, Gulladapura, Aladahalli
Hullahalli, Mallappanahalli, Beeranahalli
Tevadahalli, Gaddehosur, Mudalahippe
Srimatada Kaval, Maranayakanahalli, Gunje
Somanahalli, Ulivala, Singapura, Adikekerehosur
Volambige, Kattehosur, Mulekalenahalli, Gubbi
Uddurhosahalli, Keragodu, Muddanahalli, Jakkanahalli
Gopanahalli, Cholenahalli, Ramenahalli
Machagowdanahalli, Bandiganahalli, Godagundi
Bediganahalli, Kuppe, Niduvani, Odanahalli, Hadya
Gejjiganahalli, Motanayakanahalli, Somanahalli
Bidarakka, Sidlahalli, Nerale, Kogilahalli
Malanayakanahalli, Badakyathanahalli, Guddenahalli
Jakanahalli, Kuri Kaval, Mangalavadi, Kyathanahalli
H.Hindalahalli, Malliganahalli, Tejur
Tejur Mayagowdanahalli, Tathanahalli, Menaganahalli
Alagodanahalli, Chikkakadnur, C.Hindalahalli
Dalagowdanahalli, Kallahalli, Halli Mysore, Gohalli
Singanakuppe, Makaballi, Mukkanahalli
Gummanaladahosahalli, Devaraguddenahalli
Upparahosahalli, Shankarasettihalli
Doddahalli Kaval, Kabbur, Bachanahalli, Mallenahalli
Annechakenahalli, Bantarathalalu, Arehalli
Havinamaranahalli, Kadavinabachanahalli
Devaramuddanahalli, Nagarthi, Kodihalli
Gulaganjihalli, Hirithalalu, Rangenahalli
Neggalahalli, Yadegowdanahalli, Honnenahalli
Marahalli, Donanaghatta, Doddahalli
Ragithalli Kaval, Nagaranahalli, Ganjikuppahalli
Maluganahalli, Kotiganahosur, Mudalamayigowdanahalli.

The villages having more than 50% ST population are None.

Sex ratio of Scheduled tribe population is 502.

Scheduled Tribes Literates and Illiterates by Sex:

	Persons	Males	Females
Literate	1,398	869	529
Illiterate	1,627	637	990
Literacy rate	52.4	65.3	39.5
Graduate	12	12	0

Scheduled Tribes (Dominant):

Naikda etc., Soligaru, Generic Tribes etc.
Jenu Kuruba, Hakkipikki

For their cultural identity please see Appendix-II

Villages without Scheduled Tribes: There are 206 villages without any scheduled tribe population.

Literates and Illiterates by Sex (Total Population):

	Persons	Males	Females
Literate	76,120	46,529	29,591
Illiterate	72,100	27,359	44,741
Literacy rate	58	72	45
Graduate	1,764	1,500	264

Agriculture: ***Distribution of villages according to land use:*** Out of 249 villages, Total area (in hectare) is 59896, out of that 65.02 percent is cultivable and 33.39 percent of the cultivable area is irrigated.

Sources of Irrigation (Hectares): Government Canal 10325.08, Private Canal 47.15, Well without Electricity 23.08, Well with Electricity 113.04, Tubewell without Electricity 6.87, Tubewell with Electricity 663.53, Tank 1226.99, River 372.16, Lake 0, Waterfall 0, Others 227.24.

Villages with population of 5000 to 9999: None

Villages with population of 10000 and above: None

Distribution of Workers:

	Persons	Males	Females	WPR
Cultivators	51,002	32,667	18,335	64.79
Agricultural Labour	20,133	5,977	14,156	25.58
Household Industry	824	494	330	1.05
Other Workers	6,760	5,370	1,390	8.59
Main Workers	55,648	40,175	15,473	70.69
Marginal Workers	23,071	4,333	18,738	29.31
Total Workers	78,719	44,508	34,211	

Religion: Major Religious Communities:

	Persons	Males	Females	Sex Ratio
Hindu (97.52%)	144,541	72,085	72,456	1,005
Muslim (1.78%)	2,640	1,291	1,349	1,045
Christian (0.1%)	151	72	79	1,097
Sikh (0%)	2	2	-	-
Buddhists (0.01%)	18	11	7	636
Jain (0.01%)	10	4	6	1,500

Agewise Data:

	Persons	Males	Females	Sex Ratio
All ages	148,220	73,888	74,332	1006
0-14	44,669	22,468	22,201	988
15-44	71,762	35,857	35,905	1001
45-79	30,010	14,790	15,220	1029
80+	1,658	714	944	1322
Age not stated	121	59	62	1051

Languages (Dominant):

Kannada, Urdu, Telugu, Tamil, Marathi

Disabled Population:

	Persons	Males	Females	%
Total Disabled	2,569	1,466	1,103	
In Seeing	1,025	523	502	39.9
In Speech	313	189	124	12.18
In Hearing	172	90	82	6.7
In Movement	829	534	295	32.27
Mentally	230	130	100	8.95

HOMNABAD

Homnabad C.D. Block lies in the southern part of Bidar district. It is a part of Homnabad taluka. The Block is located at a distance of 50 kms. from district headqu arters (Bidar). There are 87 villages in the block with the total population of 234,074 persons. Area of the C.D. Block is 950.56 sq. kms. It is bounded by taluk Bhalki on north, district Gulbarga on south, taluk Bidar on east, taluk Basavakalyan on west, and it has common boundary with the state of Andhra Pradesh on east.

Communications:

Roadways : N.H-9: Direction- Solapur to Hyderbad, Nearest Villages- Molkhera, Gadawanti, Maniknagar, Kappargaon, Hudgi, Homnabad (Rural), Hippargaon, Wadankera, Taimadgi,Mangalgi, Boral, Mannaekhalli. S.H-15: Direction- Chincholi to Bidar, Nearest Villages- Bashirapur, Boral, Meenkhera, Bemalkheda, Polakpalli, Changler. S.H-19: Direction- Gulbarga to Bidar, Nearest Villages- Chinkera, Jalasangi, Kabeerabad, Hallikhed (B), Benchincholi, Gadawanti, Maniknagar, Dhumansoor, Hudgi, Hallikhed (K), Kallur.

River: Karanja Nadi- Nearest Villages- Nearest Villages- Sindbandigi, Dakulgi.

Reserved Forest: (Devgir): Nearest Villages- Muthangi, Bashirapur, Madargi, Bhadrapur, Devgir, Alipur, Bemalkh eda, Polakpalli, Karpakpalli, Changler, Saidapur, Karaknalli.

Annual Rainfall: Normal Rianfall 849 mm.

Ground Water: Availability of the Ground Water in the Basin is 9646.00 H.A.M. and the utilization is 5781. 82 H.A.M. It belongs to Over Exploited category. Depth to water level 5 to 20 meter below the ground. Most of the wells go down in summer months, according to the Ground Water Estimation Committee.

Soils: Black Soils and Lateritic Soils.

Natural Division : It falls partly in Manjra-Kharanja Basin and Homnabad-Kamthana Lateritic Tract of the North ern Karnataka Plateau.

Administration:

Division: Gulbarga. Parliamentary Constituency: 7 Bidar (SC). District: Bidar. Taluka: Homnabad. Assembly Consti tuency: 48 Homnabad, 49 Bidar south. Gram Panchayat: 33.

Regional Area Development Boards: The Hyderabad - Karnataka Area Development Board.

Border Villages: (State: Andhra Pradesh)- Bemalkheda, Saidapur, Karaknalli, Udamnalli.

Fairs: Baloba Fair: It is held at Chitaguppa in the month of August every year. Chitaguppa is an important Place situated 12 kms. south-east of Humnabad town. An important annual event here is a fair held to venerate Baloba about the month of August. There is an ancient cave said to be of Sharana Madivalappa. It has the samad hi of another saint named Mahaduappa Devershi who died in 1967. He was a celibate and was much venerated by the people of the surrounding areas. His life-size marble statue has been installed in his matha at Chitaguppa by the gowlis (dairy men).

Ismail Khadri Urs: It is held at Ghodwadi near Bidir in the month of Muharram for one day. Ghodwadi also called Ghodwadi Shareef about 21 kms. north-west of Humnabad town, has the dargah of a well-known Muslim saint named Ismail Khadri in whose honour an Urs is held every year in the month of Muharram.

Molige Marayya Jatra: An annual jatra is held in honour of Saint Molige Marayya near Bidar. Molige, seven kms. west of Humnabad town, is noted for a spacious and beautiful cave of a famous Veerashaiva saint called Molige Marayya. He was a ruling chief from Kashmir and his original name was Raja Mahadeva. He gave up his all and came to Kalyana (now Basavakalyan) being attract ed by the teachings of Basaveshvara and lived a saintly lite. For his living, he was doing molige-kayaka (occupa tion of fetching pieces of fire-wood from the jungle and selling). An annual jatra is held here in his honour.

Hanuman Jatra: It is held of Bhimalkheda near Bidar around the month of April every year. Bhimalkheda is about 41 kms. south-east of Hamnabad town. It has an ancient cave in which some sharanas are said to have meditated and two temples, one dedicated to Veerabhadra and the other to Hanuman. A jatra is held for Hanuman in about the month of April.

Manikprabhu Jayanti: A jatra is held at Manik Nagar near Bidar in honour of saint Manikprabhu around the month of December for four days. Manik Nagar situated amidst idyllic surroundings about three kms. north-west of Humnabad town, is a fine modern village.

Hassan Peer Urs: Nandgaon eight kms. north-east of Humnabad town, is noted for the tomb-shrine of saint Karibasaveshvara and Venkamma Jatra: It is held at Hudgi in around the month of April-May every year. Hudgi is an important progressive place about five kms. east of Humnabad town. The village has a noted Veerashaiva matha which is giving encouragement to Sanskrit education. Two temples here of Karibasveshvara and Venkamma hold a jatra about April-May of every year.

Naganatha Devara Jatra: It is held at Hallikhed near Bidar in about the month of October for three days. Hallikhed situated about 22 kms. north-east of Humnabad town, was formerly the headquarters of paigah of Ikbat-u d-Dowla. The place is noted also for its temple of Nagana thaswami and its annual jatra which is held about October. In front of the temple of Naganathaswami, a samadhi for the child was constructed which is venerated by people of the area. There is another temple of Sangamesh vara which has at present no idol of the presiding deity. There is a shrine dedicated to Vishvambharanand Swamiji, which holds an annual fair about January.

Syed Salar Makhdum Husain Urs: An Urs is held in honour of Saint Salar Makhdum in the month of Rajab for two days at Chitaguppa near Bidar. Chitaguppa is an important town situated 12 kms. south east of Humnabad town. It was formerly the headquarters of the Paigah taluk held by Nawab Moinuddowla and was also, known as Moinabad. There is a dargah (tomb) of a saint Salar Makdoom, in honour of whom an annual Urs takes place for two days. There is another dargah of Karimulla Shah for whom also an annual Urs is held.

Veerabhadreshvara Jatra: It is held at Humnabad near Bidar in the month of about January-February for seven days. Humnabad previously called Jayasinga-pura, situated at a distance of 52 kms. south-west of Bidar town, is the taluk headquarters town of the same name and a trade centre. It is said to have been built by a Chalu kya king Jayasimha in 1040 A.D. There is a well-known old temple of Veerabhadreshvara here facing east. Veerab hadra has a sword in his right hand and hero's valiant shield with silver covering in his left.

Villages: 87 **Inhabited:** 82 **Uninhabited:** 5

Ranking	**District**	**State**	**National**
Area	4	91	482
Population	2	56	339
Sex Ratio	4	143	3458
Child Sex Ratio	2	89	2970
Literacy Rate	4	120	3653
Density	4	170	4136
Work Participation Rate	2	46	4314

Gram Panchayats:

Ghodwadi, Ghatboral, Chandanalli, Sultanabad, Dakulgi, Hallikhed (B), Dubbalgundi, Sedol, Kankatta, Benchincholi, Maniknagar, Dhumansoor, Nandagaon, Madargaon, Sitalgera, Hudgi, Taimadgi, Sindankera, Kallur, Hallikhed (K), Itga, Belkera, Mangalgi, Mannaekhalli, Udabal, Nirna, Meenkhera, Kodambal, Mustari, Muthangi, Changler, Bemalkheda, Udamnalli.

Amenities:

Education: Primary School in 82 villages, Middle school in 72 villages, Matriculation or Secondary School in 24 villages, namely Ghatboral, Ghodwadi, Dubalgundi, Chandanalli, Kankatta, Sedol, Jalasangi, Hallikhed (B), Sindbandigi, Benchincholi, Gadawanti, Maniknagar, Nandagaon, Kappargaon, Hudgi, Hallikhed (K), Kallur, Taimadgi, Kodambal, Muthangi, Mannaekhalli, Meenkhera, Bemalkheda, Changler.

Higher Secondary or Pre University Courses or Intermediate or Junior College in 10 villages of the CD Block,, namely Ghatboral, Dubalgundi, Hallikhed (B), Hudgi, Taimadgi, Rampur, Nirna, Mannaekhalli, Bemalkheda, Changler.

College in 2 villages, Adult Literacy Center in 6 villages., Colleges are in villages, namely Hallikhed (B), Mannaekhalli.

Medical: Hospital in 6 villages, Dispensary in 11 villages, Health Center in 9 villages, Sub Center in 31 villages, Maternity and Child Welfare Center in 8 villages, Community health workers in 3 villages.

The Villages having Hospital or Dispensary or Health Center are Ghatboral, Ghodwadi, Dubalgundi, Hallikhed (B), Hudgi, Hallikhed (K), Taimadgi, Nirna, Mannaekhalli, Bemalkheda, Changler.

Drinking Water: Tap water in 71 villages, Tank water in 5 villages, Well water in 79 villages, Tubewell in 22 villages and more than one source in 81 villages.

Bank: Banking facility in 13 villages, namely, Ghatboral, Dubalgundi, Hallikhed (B), Allura Sitalgera, Hallikhed (K), Taimadgi, Kodambal, Nirna Muthangi, Mannaekhalli, Bemalkheda, Changler.

Credit Society in 49 villages Agricultural Credit Society in 27 Non-Agricultural Credit Society in 39 villages.

Others: Power supply in 81 villages, Cinema hall in 4 villages, sport club in 82 villages, Stadium or Auditorium or Communit Hall in 82 villages, Post Office in 51 villages.

There are 71 villages having bus facilities.

Villages with most of facilities: Ghatboral Dubalgundi, Hallikhed (B), Hallikhed (K), Taimadgi Kodambal, Nirna, Muthangi, Mannaekhalli, Bemalkheda Changler.

Villages without Amenities (Education): None..

Scheduled Castes: Out of the total population of 233651 persons, 51848 persons (22.19%) belong to Scheduled Castes.

The villages having less than 10% SC population are Hunsnal, Maniknagar, Dhumansoor, Nagankera, Nirna Bashirapur, Mannaekhalli.

The village having more than 50% SC population is None.

Sex ratio of Scheduled Caste population is 486.

Scheduled Castes Literates and Illiterates by Sex:

	Persons	Males	Females
Literate	20,550	13,111	7,439
Illiterate	31,298	13,513	17,785
Literacy rate	48.1	59.8	35.8
Graduate	1,114	992	122

Scheduled Castes (Dominant):

Holaya etc., Madiga, Banjara etc., Bhovi Beda Jangam etc.

For their cultural identity please see Appendix-I

Villages without Scheduled Castes: There are 5 villages without any scheduled caste population.

Scheduled Tribes: Out of the total population of 233651 persons, 43823 persons (18.76%) belong to Scheduled Tribes. The villages having less than 10% ST population are Ghodwadi, Hunsnal, Mugnoor, Warwatti (K), Namdapur Hallikhed (B), Atiwal, Dakulgi, Hilalpur, Bothagi Allura, Madgul, Madargi, Bhadrapur, Devgir, Alipur Changler.

The villages having more than 50% ST population are None.

Sex ratio of Scheduled tribe population is 486.

Scheduled Tribes Literates and Illiterates by Sex:

	Persons	Males	Females
Literate	16,735	11,019	5,716
Illiterate	27,088	11,505	15,583
Literacy rate	46.3	59.1	32.7
Graduate	524	489	35

Scheduled Tribes (Dominant):

Gond etc., Koli Dhor etc., Koya etc., Naikda etc. Generic Tribes etc.

For their cultural identity please see Appendix-II

Villages without Scheduled Tribes: There are 7 villages without any scheduled tribe population.

Literates and Illiterates by Sex (Total Population):

	Persons	Males	Females
Literate	107,115	67,300	39,815
Illiterate	126,536	52,446	74,090
Literacy rate	55	68	42
Graduate	4,963	4,267	696

Agriculture: *Distribution of villages according to land use:* Out of 87 villages, Total area (in hectare) is 95056, out of that 66.65 percent is cultivable and 19.55 percent of the cultivable area is irrigated.

Sources of Irrigation (Hectares): Government Canal 184.14, Private Canal 0, Well without Electricity 38.67, Well with Electricity 7709.52, Tubewell without Electricity 303.15, Tubewell with Electricity 216.12, Tank 42.16, River 0, Lake 0, Waterfall 0, Others 3894.42.

Villages with population of 5000 to 9999: Ghatboral, Dubalgundi, Hudgi, Kodambal, Nirna Mannaekhalli, Bemalkheda.

Villages with population of 10000 and above: Hallikhed (B).

Distribution of Workers:

	Persons	Males	Females	WPR
Cultivators	20,304	15,849	4,455	22.33
Agricultural Labour	42,696	19,599	23,097	46.96
Household Industry	2,476	1,561	915	2.72
Other Workers	25,450	20,350	5,100	27.99
Main Workers	65,650	47,727	17,923	72.2
Marginal Workers	25,276	9,632	15,644	27.8
Total Workers	90,926	57,359	33,567	

Religion: Major Religious Communities:

	Persons	Males	Females	Sex Ratio
Hindu (67.32%)	157,287	80,682	76,605	949
Muslim (20.86%)	48,730	24,911	23,819	956
Christian (1.54%)	3,598	1,849	1,749	946
Sikh (0.01%)	22	11	11	1,000
Buddhists (9.52%)	22,248	11,399	10,849	952
Jain (0.05%)	107	55	52	945

Agewise Data:

	Persons	Males	Females	Sex Ratio
All ages	233,651	119,746	113,905	951
0-14	92,345	47,153	45,192	958
15-44	99,083	51,811	47,272	912
45-79	39,525	19,545	19,980	1022
80+	2,369	1,063	1,306	1229
Age not stated	329	174	155	891

Languages (Dominant):

Kannada, Urdu, Marathi, Telugu, Hindi

Disabled Population:

	Persons	Males	Females	%
Total Disabled	4,357	2,527	1,830	
In Seeing	1,881	984	897	43.17
In Speech	359	203	156	8.24
In Hearing	229	118	111	5.26
In Movement	1,555	1,029	526	35.69
Mentally	333	193	140	7.64

HONAVAR

Honavar C.D. Block lies in the south-western part of Uttara Kannada district. It is a part of Honavar taluka. The Block is located at a distance of 95 kms. from district headquarters (Karwar). There are 93 villages in the block with the total population of 142,466 persons. Area of the C.D. Block is 745.52 sq. kms. It is bounded by taluk Kumta on north, taluk Bhatkal and district Shimoga on south, taluk Siddapur and district Shimoga on east, and Lakshadweep Sea on west.

Communications:

Roadways : N.H-17 : Direction- Mangalore to Karwar, Nearest Villages- Haldipur, Karki, Kasarkod, Apsarkonda, Kelginoor, Kankichitta, Gunavante, Melin-Idgunji, Manki, Tumbebeela, Sulebil. N.H-206 : Direction- Honavar to Sagar, Nearest Villages- Hosakuli, Mugwa, Arolli-Mundagod, Kulakod, Nirwattikodla, Hadinbal, Kharwa, Jalwal Karki, Kervalli, Jalwalli, Melinamudkani, Adkar, Herangadi, Upponi, Hanehallikabbinahakkal, Hulegar, Saralagi, Nagarabastikeri. S.H-48: Direction- Kumta to Siddapur, Nearest Villages- Chandavar, Kadnir.

River: Mugali Nadi- Nearest Villages- Hosad, Berolli, Hadinbal, Mutta, Gundabala, Hirebail, Janna Kadkal, Chikkankod, Kharwa, Koodla. Sharavati Nadi- Nearest Villages- Haldipur, Pavinakurve, Karki, Mugwa, Kasarkod, Kankichitta, Hosapatna, Malkod, Kelgin-Idgunji, Melin-I dgunji, Balkur, Heggar, Kelgin-Mannige, Anilgod, Beranki, Kodani, Birangod, Magod, Kulakod, Mavinkurva, Mandalakurve, Molkod, Hosad, Berolli, Nagre, Padukuli, Jalwal Karki, Kervalli, Jalwalli, Kelgina-Mudkani, Adkar, Herangadi, Upponi, Mahime, Hanehallikabbinahakkal, Hulegar, Saralagi, Kudrige, Nagarabastikeri. Kalkatti Hole Nadi- Nearest Villages- Khandodi, Nagarabastikeri, Hadgeri.

Reserved Forest: Nearest Villages- Chandavar, Kadnir, Hodke Shiroor, Kekkar, Kadtoka, Aunsalli, Kadle, Nilkod, Salkod, Hosakuli, Malkod, Gunavante, Kelgin-Idgunji, Melin-Idgunji, Balkur, Heggar, Kelgin-Mannige, Talgod, Manki, Dabbod, Melin-Mannige, Hinnur, Anilgod, Beranki, Kodani, Birangod, Magod, Adukal, Hadikal, Sampolli, Kota, Tumbebeela, Sulebil, Herali, Kuchodi, Adekekuli, Ashikeri, Mutta, Gundabala, Hirebail, Hosgod, Janna Kadkal, Heravali, Jalwalli, Tumbolli, Herangadi, Mahime, Hanehallikabbinahakkal, Hulegar, Saralagi, Kudrige, Shirkur, Khandodi, Nagarabastikeri, Begodi, Hadgeri.

Annual Rainfall: Normal Rianfall 3672.5 mm.

Ground Water: Availability of the Ground Water in the Basin is 4604 H.A.M. and the utilization is 1642 H.A. M. It belongs to Safe category. Depth to water level 2 to 10 meter below the ground. Most of the wells go down in summer months, according to the Ground Water Estimation Committee.

Soils: Coastal Alluvial Soil

Natural Division : It falls partly in Karwar-Honavar Coast, Western Ghats (Uttara Kannada) and Sirsi-Siddapur Dissected Humid Tract of the Karnataka Coast.

Coastal Villages: (Lakshadeep Sea)- Haldipur, Pavinakurve, Karki, Kasarkod, Apsarkonda, Gunavante, Manki.

Administration:

Division: Belgaum. Parliamentary Constituency: 12 Uttara Kannada. District: Uttara Kannada. Taluka: Honavar. Assembly Constituency: 79 Bhatkal. Gram Panchayat: 24.

Regional Area Development Boards: The Maland Aera Development Board.

Fairs: Ahmad-Bava Fakki Urs: There are two dargahs in Karki on way from Honavar described as of Ahmad Fakki and Bava Fakki whose Urs takes place in Rabbil Ahker being attended by about 5,000 people. Qawali programmes are arranged on the occasion. The place has long quiet beach extending as far as Hadipur.

Keshavanarayana Jatra: It is held at Kadtoka in the month of April. Kadtoka 14 kms. from Honavar is mentioned as Kadatoke in an inscription. The place has temples dedicated to Keshavanaryana, Narsimha and Elukopparige Gudi (where there is a Jattiga stone).

Lakshminarayana Jatra: It is held at Manki near Uttra Kannada for three days in the month of the Magha (Januar y-February) every year. Manki a hobli centre (11 kms. from Honavar), a place of considerable antiquity, was a celebrated Jaina centre during 14th and 15th centuries.

Maha Ganapati Jatra: It is held at Idgunji near Uttara Kannada for one day in the month of January every year. Idgunji, 10 kms. from Honavar near Uttarada Kanna is a place of hoary past, and is also mentioned as Idakunja and Kunjavana, and also called as Idugunjige in an inscr iption at the same place dated 1348 A.D.

Muda Ganapati Jatra: It is held at Karki near Uttara Kannada for two days in about the month of April-May. Karki five kilometres from Honavar on the Honavar-Kumta road must have been an agrahara as there are over 500 houses of Havyaka Brahmanas. It vied with Gokarn in matters of scholarly pursuits. The place name is derived from karki a tree found mostly in Uttara Kannada, also called hinari (Celtis cinnamomesca Lindl). The Chennakes hava temple here is a post-Vijayanagar building, and its ceiling has carvings of Ramayana scenes. The tile roofed Muda Ganapati temple is towards Haldipur.

Ramachandra Bharti Jatra: It is held at Kekkar near Uttara Kannada on the day of Ramanavami. Kekkar is a place situated about 5 kms. from Honavar, of considerab le antiquity, has temples dedicated to Lakshminarasimha (or the Kekkar Matha), Vishnu, Vinayaka, Carbatte Vinaya ka, Ammanavara gudi, etc. Near the Kekkar Matha is a small tank surrounding which are several samadhis and a statue of Vishnu of Vijayanagar times. The Matha belongs to the Havyaka Brahmanas and is a huge establishment. There is the samadhi of Ramachandra Bharati in the Matha.

Shambhulingeshwara Jatra: It is held at Gunavante near Uttara Kannada in the month of April every year. Gunavan te 8 kms. from Honavar finds a mention in Skandapurana wherein it is treated as one among the panchakshetras on a par with Gokarn. It has the famous Gunavanteshwara temple.

Venkataramana Jatra: It is held at Honavar near Uttara Kannada for two days in the month of April every year. Honavar a taluk centre 93 kms. from Karwar is a place on the banks of the Sharavati and a port town, one of great antiquity. The name might have originated from the plant Honnavari also called Tangadi in Kannada (Cass ia auriculata, Linn).

Villages: 93 **Inhabited:** 92 **Uninhabited:** 1

KARNATAKA

Ranking	District	State	National
Area	7	132	842
Population	1	137	2103
Sex Ratio	2	25	968
Child Sex Ratio	9	163	4627
Literacy Rate	5	19	722
Density	11	173	4860
Work Participation Rate	3	83	4413

Gram Panchayats:
Haldipur, Navilgone, Kadtoka, Chandavar, Salkod, Chikkankod, Kharwa, Mavinkurva, Hadinbal, Mugwa, Hosakuli, Kadle, Karki, Kasarkod, Kelginoor, Melin-Idgunji, Manki, Balkur, Jalwalli, Herangadi, Upponi, Kodani, Kudrige, Nagarabastikeri.

Amenities:
Education: Primary School in 84 villages, Middle school in 60 villages, Matriculation or Secondary School in 20 villages, namely Mallapur, Hodke Shiroor, Kadtoka, Haldipur, Karki, Salkod, Mugwa, Kasarkod, Gunavante, Kelgin-Idgunji, Manki, Anilgod, Magod, Hosad, Hadinbal, Gundabala, Kharwa, Herangadi, Kudrige, Nagarabastikeri.
Higher Secondary or Pre University Courses or Intermediate or Junior College in 6 villages of the CD Block,, namely Kadtoka, Haldipur, Salkod, Mugwa, Melin-Idgunji, Manki.
College in 0 village, Adult Literacy Center in 0 village.
Medical: Hospital in 0 village, Dispensary in 5 villages, Health Center in 6 villages, Sub Center in 10 villages, Maternity and Child Welfare Center in 2 villages, Community health workers in 0 village.
The Villages having Hospital or Dispensary or Health Center are Chandavar, Kadtoka, Manki, Hosad, Hirebail.
Drinking Water: Tap water in 20 villages, Tank water in 33 villages, Well water in 92 villages, Tubewell in 4 villages and more than one source in 92 villages.
Bank: Banking facility in 24 villages, namely, Mallapur, Chandavar, Kadtoka, Navilgone, Haldipur Karki, Salkod, Hosakuli, Mugwa, Kasarkod, Gunavante Melin-Idgunji, Balkur, Manki, Kodani, Magod Mavinkurva, Hadinbal, Chikkankod, Kharwa, Jalwalli Herangadi, Kudrige, Nagarabastikeri.
Credit Society in 19 villages Agricultural Credit Society in 18 Non-Agricultural Credit Society in 4 villages.
Others: Power supply in 91 villages, Cinema hall in 2 villages, sport club in 0 village, Stadium or Auditorium or Community Hall in 0 village, Post Office in 46 villages.
There are 51 villages having bus facilities.
Villages with most of facilities: Chandavar Kadtoka, Navilgone, Haldipur, Karki, Salkod, Mugwa Kasarkod, Balkur, Manki, Kharwa, Herangadi.
Villages without amenities (Education):
Kankichitta, Heggar, Kelgin-Mannige, Sulebil, Mandalakurve, Kelgina-Mudkani, Hanehallikabbinahakkal, Hulegar..
Scheduled Castes: Out of the total population of 142507 persons, 6737 persons (4.73%) belong to Scheduled Castes.
The villages having less than 10% SC population are Mallapur, Chandavar, Kadnir, Hodke Shiroor, Madageri Navilgone, Aunsalli, Kadle, Pavinakurve, Duggur Vandoor, Nilkod, Salkod, Mugwa, Kasarkod, Apsarkonda Kelginoor, Kankichitta, Hosapatna , Malkod Gunavante, Kelgin-Idgunji, Melin-Idgunji, Balkur Heggar, Kelgin-Mannige, Talgod, Manki, Gudemakki Hinnur, Anilgod, Beranki, Kodani, Birangod, Magod Balemet, Adukal, Hadikal, Sampolli, Kota, Tumbebeela Sulebil, Kuchodi, Adekekuli, Ashikeri Arolli-Mundagod, Kulakod, Mavinkurva, Mandalakurve Molkod, Hosad, Berolli, Nagre, Nirwattikodla Hadinbal, Mutta, Gundabala, Hirebail, Hosgod Janna Kadkal, Chikkankod, Heravali, Kharwa, Koodla Padukuli, Jalwal Karki, Kervalli, Jalwalli, Tumbolli Kelgina-Mudkani, Adkar, Herangadi, Upponi, Mahime Hanehallikabbinahakkal, Hulegar, Saralagi, Shirkur Khandodi, Nagarabastikeri, Begodi, Hadgeri.
The village having more than 50% SC population is None.
Sex ratio of Scheduled Caste population is 495.

Scheduled Castes Literates and Illiterates by Sex:

	Persons	Males	Females
Literate	3,345	1,953	1,392
Illiterate	3,392	1,452	1,940
Literacy rate	57.2	66.4	47.9
Graduate	49	33	16

Scheduled Castes (Dominant):
Mukri, Halleer, Moger, Halsar etc., Holaya etc.
For their cultural identity please see Appendix-I
Villages without Scheduled Castes: There are 36 villages without any scheduled caste population.
Scheduled Tribes: Out of the total population of 142507 persons, 234 persons (0.16%) belong to Scheduled Tribes.
The villages having less than 10% ST population are Mallapur, Chandavar, Kadnir, Hodke Shiroor, Kekkar Kadtoka, Madageri , Navilgone, Aunsalli, Kadle Haldipur, Pavinakurve, Karki, Duggur, Vandoor Nilkod, Salkod, Hosakuli, Mugwa, Kasarkod Apsarkonda, Kelginoor, Kankichitta, Hosapatna Malkod, Gunavante, Kelgin-Idgunji, Melin-Idgunji Balkur, Heggar, Kelgin-Mannige, Talgod, Manki

Gudemakki, Dabbod, Melin-Mannige, Hinnur, Anilgod Beranki, Kodani, Birangod, Magod, Balemet, Adukal Hadikal, Sampolli, Kota, Tumbebeela, Sulebil Kuchodi, Adekekuli, Ashikeri, Arolli-Mundagod Kulakod, Mavinkurva, Mandalakurve, Molkod, Hosad Berolli, Nagre, Nirwattikodla, Hadinbal, Mutta Gundabala, Hirebail, Hosgod, Janna Kadkal Chikkankod, Heravali, Kharwa, Koodla, Padukuli Jalwal Karki, Kervalli, Jalwalli, Tumbolli Melinamudkani, Kelgina-Mudkani, Adkar, Herangadi Upponi, Mahime, Hanehallikabbinahakkal, Hulegar Saralagi, Kudrige, Shirkur, Khandodi Nagarabastikeri, Begodi, Hadgeri.

The villages having more than 50% ST population are None.

Sex ratio of Scheduled tribe population is 517.

Scheduled Tribes Literates and Illiterates by Sex:

	Persons	Males	Females
Literate	119	57	62
Illiterate	115	56	59
Literacy rate	57.8	59.4	56.4
Graduate	3	3	0

Scheduled Tribes (Dominant):

Hasalaru, Gond etc., Naikda etc., Malasar Gamit etc.

For their cultural identity please see Appendix-II

Villages without Scheduled Tribes: There are 68 villages without any scheduled tribe population.

Literates and Illiterates by Sex (Total Population):

	Persons	Males	Females
Literate	92,439	50,734	41,705
Illiterate	50,068	20,278	29,790
Literacy rate	74	82	66
Graduate	3,489	2,396	1,093

Agriculture: ***Distribution of villages according to land use:*** Out of 93 villages, Total area (in hectare) is 74552, out of that 11.69 percent is cultivable and 51.95 percent of the cultivable area is irrigated.

Sources of Irrigation (Hectares): Government Canal 187, Private Canal 0, Well without Electricity 42.66, Well with Electricity 2970.8, Tubewell without Electricity 53.4, Tubewell with Electricity 0, Tank 0, River 0, Lake 0, Waterfall 0, Others 1517.64.

Villages with population of 5000 to 9999:
Karki, Kasarkod.

Villages with population of 10000 and above:
Haldipur, Manki.

Distribution of Workers:

	Persons	Males	Females	WPR
Cultivators	8,741	6,344	2,397	15.21
Agricultural Labour	6,344	2,813	3,531	11.04
Household Industry	1,164	819	345	2.02
Other Workers	41,236	30,680	10,556	71.73
Main Workers	46,113	36,017	10,096	80.22
Marginal Workers	11,372	4,639	6,733	19.78
Total Workers	57,485	40,656	16,829	

Religion: Major Religious Communities:

	Persons	Males	Females	Sex Ratio
Hindu (82.61%)	117,728	58,999	58,729	995
Muslim (9.94%)	14,165	6,754	7,411	1,097
Christian (7.25%)	10,327	5,100	5,227	1,025
Sikh (0.03%)	39	31	8	258
Buddhists (0%)	7	2	5	2,500
Jain (0.11%)	152	83	69	831

Agewise Data:

	Persons	Males	Females	Sex Ratio
All ages	142,507	71,012	71,495	1007
0-14	42,473	21,727	20,746	955
15-44	68,965	33,947	35,018	1032
45-79	29,758	14,729	15,029	1020
80+	1,251	575	676	1176
Age not stated	60	34	26	765

Languages (Dominant):

Kannada, Konkani, Urdu, Marathi, Malayalam

Disabled Population:

	Persons	Males	Females	%
Total Disabled	3,527	1,929	1,598	
In Seeing	1,879	979	900	53.27
In Speech	342	176	166	9.7
In Hearing	153	78	75	4.34
In Movement	773	484	289	21.92
Mentally	380	212	168	10.77

HONNALI

Honnali C.D. Block lies in the southern part of Davanage re district. It is a part of Honnali taluka. The Block is located at a distance of 54 kms. from district headqu arters (Davanagere). There are 173 villages in the block with the total population of 206,916 persons. Area of the C.D. Block is 860.10 sq. kms. It is bounded by taluks Harihar and Haveri on north, district Shimoga on south, taluks Davanagere and Channagiri on east, and district Shimoga on west.

Communications:

Roadways : S.H-25: Direction- Hospet to Shimoga, Villages- Arakere, Narasagondanahalli, Masadi, Belimallur, Gollarahalli, Honnali(Rural), Sunkadakatte, Devanayaka nahalli, Didagur, Haralahalli, Govinakovi, Kuruva, Gorava rakatte, Chilurkadadakatte, Dodderi, Chilur, Akkathangera katte, Tavaragopagondanahalli. S.H-26: Direction- Hosanag ar to Honnali, Nearest Villages- Machagondanahalli, Soval anga, Surahonne, Nyamati, Basavapura, Danihalli, Deve koppa, Salubalu, Veerapura, Sogilu, Madanabhavi, Soratur, H.Kadadakatte, Honnali(Rural), Hiremata. S.H-48: Direct ion- Shikarpur to Chitradurga, Nearest Villages- Jeenahal li, Kathige, Boodihalu, Soratur, H.Kadadakatte, Gollaraha lli, Devarahonnali, Thakkanahalli, Kammaragatte, Hanuma pura, Honnali(Rural), Hunesehalli, Benakanahalli.

River: Tungabhadra Nadi- Nearest Villages- Konanathale, Haraganahalli, Hiregonigere, Chickagonigere, Kotemallur, Belimallur, Gollarahalli, Devarahonnali, Thakkanahalli, Kammaragatte, Holeharalahalli, Narasimhapura, Balleshwa ra, Konayakanahalli, Anjanapura, Honnali (Rural), Devanaya kanahalli, Holemadapura, Bidaragadde, Didagur, Haralahalli, Govinakovi, Kuruva, Marigondanahalli, Achuthapura, Kotehalu, Goravarakatte, Chilur, Thaggehalli, Malali, Hirebasur, Beeragondanahalli, Chikkabasur, Benakanahalli, Hottyapura, Rampura, Bullapura, Iyanoor, Sasavehallil, Mavinakote, Bommenahalli, Hosahalli, Huralihalli, Bagav adi, Lingapura, Hanagavadi.

Canal: Nearest Villages- Arabagatte, Hanumasagara, Kotem allur, Vijayapura, Belimallur, Gollarahalli, Devarahonnali, Thakkanahalli, Kammaragatte, Anjaneyapura , Basavapura, Gantyapura, Kundur, Yakkanahalli, Chikkahalivana, Yareh alli, Nelahonne, Kumblur, Balamuri, Narasimhapura, Balles hwara, Konayakanahalli, Anjanapura, Honnali (Rural), Hirem ata, Sunkadakatte, Maragondanahalli, Didagur, Haralahalli, Basavanahalli, Govinakovi, Arehalli, Bijogatte, Sevalal Nagar , Kuruva, Chilurkadadakatte, Kengatte, Dodderi, Chilur, Akkathangerakatte, Tavaragopagondanahalli, Chikkabasur, Hunesehalli, Benakanahalli, Vijayapura , Ujjanipura, Sadashivapura, Sasavehalli, Mavinakote, Hanumanahalli, Kamalapura, Kulagatte, Channambapura, Hunsagatta, Jalikatte, Kyasainakere.

Annual Rainfall: Normal Rianfall 673 mm.

Ground Water: Availability of the Ground Water in the Basin is 10145.2 H.A.M. and the utilization is 5446. 92 H.A.M. It belongs to Over Exploited category. Depth to water level 2 to 20 meter below the ground. Most of the wells go down in summer months, according to the Ground Water Estimation Committee.

Soils: Red Sandy Soils and Black Soils.

Natural Division : It falls partly in Sub-micro regions of Channagiri Plateau and Upper Tungabhadra Valley of the Central Karnataka Plateau.

Administration:

Division: Bangalore. Parliamentary Constituency: 13 Davanagere. District: Davanagere. Taluka: Honnali. Assem bly Constituency: 110 Honnali. Gram Panchayat: 47.

Regional Area Development Boards: The Maland Aera Development Board.

Fairs and Festivals: Channappaswami Matha Festival: Hirematha about a kilometer from the Honnali town, is on the Honnali-Nyamati-Shikaripur Road. It has a Veerashaiva monastery called the Channappa-swami Matha headed by a Viraktaswami. The matha has a spacious stone structure with massive stone pillars, a large compound and a lofty dhwaja-stambha. It is stated to have been founded several centuries back by Jadeya Shankara Mahaswami who was the pontiff of the Shrishaila Jagadguru Peetha. His disciple Shri Channamallikarajuna-swami was the first head of this monastery. Within the premises of the matha, there are shrines dedicated to Channamalikarjuna, Veera bhadra and Chowdeshvari and also an Anubhava Mantapa. An annual car festival is held here. The matha has established Shri Channappaswami Samskrita, Veda and Jyotisha Pathashala. It is publishing annually a Panchanga.

Haladamma Jatra: Marikoppa near Shimoga, about four kilometers west of Honnali town on Honnali-Shimoga Road, has a famous shrine dedicated to Haladamma. A jatra of the deity is held twice a year around March-Apr il and September-October.

Kartikotsava Festival: Kartikotsava festival is held at Kammaragatte near Shimoga in about the month of October-November. Kammaragatte is about six kms. from Honnali town towards the east. The name of the village means "blacksmiths platform". According to a local legend, the village was 'Karmahara-kshetra' where Parashurama washed his blood stained axe. Helavanakatte Giriyamma, a famous saint, is said to have spent the last days of her life here. The spot where she is believed to have died is called bandahole where annually a kartikotsa va is celebrated by the villagers. There is an Anjaneya temple on the bank of the Tunga river which is much frequented for worship.

Kuruvadagadde Jatra: Kuruvadagadde jatra is held at Kuruva near Shimoga in about the month of March-April every year. Kuruva about ten kilometres south-east of Honnali, on the river Tungabhadra, is on Honnali-Shimoga Road. Near this place, there is a Rameshvara temple on an island in the Tungabhadra river known as Kuruvadag adde. A large stone lamp pillar with fortresses faces its south door. This is a small temple constructed origi nally during the Chalukyan times. There are several inscr iptions in the premises of the temple, the oldest of which is of the 36th year of the Chalukya Vikrama era, i.e., A.D. 1142. The Hoysalas, Scunas (Yadavas) and the Vijayanagar kings have also left their records here. An annual jatra of this temple takes place about March-April.

Villages: 173 **Inhabited:** 153 **Uninhabited:** 20

Ranking	District	State	National

Area	5	109	612
Population	4	81	605
Sex Ratio	3	128	3052
Child Sex Ratio	1	67	2637
Literacy Rate	2	54	1814
Density	3	119	4200
Work Participation Rate	3	49	2719

Gram Panchayats:
Hiregonigere, Arakere, Thimalapura, Yakkanahalli, Kulambi, Bannikodu, Mukthenahalli, Kumblur, Kundur, Masadi, Belimallur, Hanumasagara, Kathige, Hathur, Gopagondanahalli, Kammaragatte, Benakanahalli, Beeragondanahalli, Arabagatte, H.Kadadakatte, Soratur, Kenchikoppa, Guddehalli, Belaguthi, Yaraganal, Surahonne, Nyamati, Basavanahalli, Haralahalli, Govinakovi, Rampura, Sasavehalli, Kulagatte, Kyasainakere, Hosahalli, Hunsagatta, Chilurkadadakatte, Vaderahathur, Ganganakote, Chinnikatte, Sovalanga, Chatnahalli, Palavanahalli, Kunkova, Chilur, Lingapura, Tavaragopagondanahalli, Honnali(Rural) .

Amenities:
Education: Primary School in 138 villages, Middle school in 95 villages, Matriculation or Secondary School in 35 villages, namely Jeenahalli, Belaguthi, Chinnikatte, Sovalanga, Nyamati, Chatnahalli, Vaderahathur, Kathige, Kenchikoppa, Arabagatte, Soratur, Hathur, Dodderahalli, Hiregonigere, Arakere, Belimallur, Tharaganahalli, Kundur, Yakkanahalli, Yarachikkanahalli, Bannikodu, Kulambi, Kumblur, Devanayakanahalli, Govinakovi, Marigondanahalli, Kotehalu, Chilur, Benakanahalli, Ujjanipura, Sasavehalli, Kulagatte, Lingapura, Hanagavadi, Kyasainakere.
Higher Secondary or Pre University Courses or Intermediate or Junior College in 7 villages of the CD Block,, namely Jeenahalli, Nyamati, Kundur, Kulambi, Balamuri, Devanayakanahalli, Sasavehalli.
College in 4 villages, Adult Literacy Center in 3 villages., Colleges are in villages, namely Nyamati, Kundur, Hiremata, Sasavehalli.
Medical: Hospital in 7 villages, Dispensary in 14 villages, Health Center in 6 villages, Sub Center in 37 villages, Maternity and Child Welfare Center in 6 villages, Community health workers in 5 villages.
The Villages having Hospital or Dispensary or Health Center are Belaguthi, Chinnikatte, Rameswara, Nyamati, Palavanahalli, Vaderahathur, Kathige, Madenahalli, Arabagatte, Gopagondanahalli, Mukthenahalli, Kumblur, Govinakovi, Marigondanahalli, Chilur, Benakanahalli, Sasavehalli, Kyasainakere.
Drinking Water: Tap water in 94 villages, Tank water in 19 villages, Well water in 17 villages, Tubewell in 84 villages and more than one source in 137 villages.
Bank: Banking facility in 8 villages, namely, Belaguthi, Sovalanga, Nyamati, Kundur, Kulambi Chilur, Benakanahalli, Sasavehalli.
Credit Society in 7 villages Agricultural Credit Society in 2 Non-Agricultural Credit Society in 2 villages.
Others: Power supply in 153 villages, Cinema hall in 6 villages sport club in 0 village, Stadium or Auditorium or Community Hall in 0 village, Post Office in 52 villages.
There are 146 villages having bus facilities.
Villages with most of facilities: Belaguthi Sovalanga, Nyamati, Kundur, Kulambi, Chilur Benakanahalli, Sasavehalli.
Villages without amenities (Education):
Naraginakere, Kullahalli, Thirtharampura, Kyathinkoppa, Gundichatnahalli, Lakkienkoppa, Manganakoppa, Boodihalu, Basavapura, Sevalalnagara, Narasimhapura, Malladevarakatte, Sevalal Nagar, Sadashivapura..
Scheduled Castes: Out of the total population of 207024 persons, 42491 persons (20.52%) belong to Scheduled Castes.
The villages having less than 10% SC population are Hosakoppa, Kullahalli, Chinnikatte, Rameswara Kudurekonda, Surahonne, Nyamati, Kodikoppa Chatnahalli, Kenchiganahalli, Gadikatte, Kathige Boodihalu, Arundi, Kodachagondanahalli, Madanabhavi Hosakatte, Dodderahalli, Chikkerahalli Haraganahalli, Narasagondanahalli, Belimallur Kammaragatte, Bevinahalli, Yakkanahalli, Bannikodu Mukthenahalli, Thimmenahalli, Kengalahalli, Kulambi Balamuri, Balleshwara, Konayakanahalli, Hiremata Malladevarakatte, Ganganakote, Kotehalu, Thaggehalli Malali, Chikkabasur, Rampura, Hanumanahalli Kulagatte, Hunsagatta, Byranahalli, Chilapura Hattehalu.
The villages having more than 50% SC population are Thirtharampura, Siddapura, Belalakatte Gundichatnahalli, Lakkienkoppa, Machagondanahalli Salubalu, Mussenalu, Kooganahalli, Hanumasagara Chickagonigere, Vijayapura , Anjaneyapura Gantyapura, Neralagundi, Sevalalnagara , Kankanahalli Sevalal Nagar , Kengatte, Vijayapura , Sadashivapura Channanahalli.
Sex ratio of Scheduled Caste population is 491.
Scheduled Castes Literates and Illiterates by Sex:

	Persons	Males	Females
Literate	16,758	10,735	6,023

Illiterate	25,733	10,912	14,821
Literacy rate	46.6	58.4	34.2
Graduate	401	349	52

Scheduled Castes (Dominant):

Banjara etc., Madiga, Bhovi, Adi Karnataka, Koracha

For their cultural identity please see Appendix-I

Villages without Scheduled Castes: There are 32 villages without any scheduled caste population.

Scheduled Tribes: Out of the total population of 207024 persons, 15662 persons (7.57%) belong to Scheduled Tribes.

The villages having less than 10% ST population are Naraginakere, Hosakoppa, Kullahalli, Guddehalli Jeenahalli, Belaguthi, Thirtharampura, Kyathinkoppa Siddapura, Joga, Gundichatnahalli, Suragondanakoppa Lakkienkoppa, Bidarahalli, Rameswara, Yaraganal Machagondanahalli, Sovalanga, Kodatalu, Surahonne Danihalli, Doddethenahalli, Kodikoppa, Salubalu Sogilu, Manganakoppa, Kenchiganahalli, Palavanahalli Mussenalu, Kooganahalli, Kathige, Madenahalli Boodihalu, Thuglahalli, Kenchikoppa Kodachagondanahalli, Madanabhavi, Arabagatte Soratur, H.Kadadakatte, Hosakatte, Hathur Dodderahalli, Chikkerahalli, Somanamallapura Gopagondanahalli, Hanumasagara, Chickagonigere Kotemallur, Vijayapura , Arakere, Narasagondanahalli Masadi, Gollarahalli, Devarahonnali, Thakkanahalli Anjaneyapura , Basavapura, Singatagere, Gantyapura Bevinahalli, Sevalalnagara , Thimalapura, Kundur Yakkanahalli, Yarehalli, Yarachikkanahalli Bannikodu, Kengalahalli, Kulambi, Nelahonne Marikoppa, Narasimhapura, Balleshwara Konayakanahalli, Hiremata, Malladevarakatte Sunkadakatte, Devanayakanahalli, Holemadapura Bidaragadde, Haralahalli, Basavanahalli, Govinakovi Kankanahalli, Ganganakote, Bijogatte, Sevalal Nagar Kuruva, Chilurkadadakatte, Kengatte, Dodderi, Chilur Tavaragopagondanahalli, Thaggehalli, Malali Hunesehalli, Benakanahalli, Vijayapura , Ujjanipura Sadashivapura, Hottyapura, Rampura, Bullapura Iyanoor, Sasavehalli, Mavinakote, Hanumanahalli Hosahalli, Bagavadi, Lingapura, Hanagavadi Channambapura, Hunsagatta, Kyasainakere Channanahalli, Chilapura, Hattehalu.

The villages having more than 50% ST population are None.

Sex ratio of Scheduled tribe population is 494.

Scheduled Tribes Literates and Illiterates by Sex:

	Persons	Males	Females
Literate	7,511	4,535	2,976
Illiterate	8,151	3,394	4,757
Literacy rate	55.4	65.8	44.6
Graduate	129	113	16

Scheduled Tribes (Dominant):

Naikda etc., Meda, Jenu Kuruba, Kadu Kuruba Generic Tribes etc.

For their cultural identity please see Appendix-II

Villages without Scheduled Tribes: There are 63 villages without any scheduled tribe population.

Literates and Illiterates by Sex (Total Population):

	Persons	Males	Females
Literate	118,419	70,023	48,396
Illiterate	88,605	35,680	52,925
Literacy rate	66	76	55
Graduate	4,359	3,627	732

Agriculture: ***Distribution of villages according to land use:*** Out of 173 villages, Total area (in hectare) is 86010, out of that 65.46 percent is cultivable and 32.53 percent of the cultivable area is irrigated.

Sources of Irrigation (Hectares): Government Canal 11844.33, Private Canal 195.13, Well without Electricity 14.04, Well with Electricity 349.15, Tubewell without Electricity 282.77, Tubewell with Electricity 3525.44, Tank 972.67, River 992.67, Lake 0, Waterfall 0, Others 143.38.

Villages with population of 5000 to 9999: Belaguthi, Surahonne, Nyamati, Kundur.

Villages with population of 10000 and above: None

Distribution of Workers:

	Persons	Males	Females	WPR
Cultivators	39,974	31,718	8,256	40.12
Agricultural Labour	43,317	19,571	23,746	43.48
Household Industry	2,296	1,637	659	2.3
Other Workers	14,041	11,157	2,884	14.09
Main Workers	79,624	58,214	21,410	79.92
Marginal Workers	20,004	5,869	14,135	20.08
Total Workers	99,628	64,083	35,545	

Religion: Major Religious Communities:

	Persons	Males	Females	Sex Ratio
Hindu (91.74%)	189,920	96,897	93,023	960
Muslim (6.87%)	14,219	7,303	6,916	947
Christian (0.05%)	113	55	58	1,055
Sikh (0%)	4	2	2	1,000
Buddhists (0%)	2	1	1	1,000
Jain (0.33%)	684	353	331	938

Agewise Data:

	Persons	Males	Females	Sex Ratio
All ages	207,024	105,703	101,321	959
0-14	63,180	32,028	31,152	973
15-44	102,145	52,817	49,328	934
45-79	39,405	19,852	19,553	985
80+	1,882	774	1,108	1432

Age not stated	412	232	180	776

Languages (Dominant):

Kannada, Urdu, Hindi, Telugu, Tamil

Disabled Population:

	Persons	Males	Females	%
Total Disabled	4,265	2,525	1,740	
In Seeing	1,882	1,063	819	44.13
In Speech	427	235	192	10.01
In Hearing	218	133	85	5.11
In Movement	1,317	854	463	30.88
Mentally	421	240	181	9.87

HOSAKOTE

Hosakote C.D. Block lies in the north-eastern part of Bangalore Rural district. It is a part of Hosakote taluka. The Block is located at a distance of 26 kms. from district headquarters (Bangalore). There are 296 villages in the block with the total population of 186,393 perso ns. Area of the C.D. Block is 533.47 sq. kms. It is bound ed by district Kolar on north and east, district Bangalore and taluk Devanahalli on west. It has common boundary with the state of Tamil Nadu on south.

Communications:

Roadways : N.H.-4: Direction- Bangalore to Cheenai, Nearest Villages- Yelachahalli, Manchappanahalli, Thavarekere, Banamakanahalli, Gangapura, Venkatapura, Mugabala, Poojaramanahalli, Mugabala Hosahalli, Mylapura, Valagere pura, Channapura, Gottipura, Attur, Nidagatta, Doddanalla la Plantation, Halasahalli, Kolathur, Dodda Amanikere. N.H.-207: Direction- Devanahalli to Hosakote, Nearest Villages- Ramapura, Kadaranapura, Sulibele, Valagerepura, Attibele, Yenagunte, Yethinavadeyarapura, Kammasandra, Hasigala, Thimmasandra, Shivadenahalli, Lakkondahalli, Shankanipura, Alappanahalli, Upparahalli, Chikka Amanik ere, Kumbalahalli, Kallahalli. S.H.-35: Direction- Hosakote to Sidlaghatta, Nearest Villages- Theneyur, Chikkakurub arahalli, Dyavasandra, Bendiganahalli, Chikkaralagere, Thammarasanahalli, Aralagere Amanikere, Gullahalli, Chowdasandra, Vanamanahalli, Kamblipura, Ekarajapura, Nagarenahalli, Chikkakoliga, Sompura, Sonnadenahalli, Yelachanayakanapura, Doddahullur, Chikkahullur, Chokkah alli, Hullur Amanikere. S.H.-82: Direction- Hosakote to Madanapalli, Nearest Villages- Gundrahalli, Bheemakkanah alli, Hindiganala, Tharabahalli, Chikkondahalli, Banahalli, Geddalahallipura, Nandagudi, Sarakar, Vaddahalli, Chokasandra, Karapanahalli, Mumynahosahalli, K.Sathyawa ra, D.Settihalli, Doddenahalli, Sonnadenahalli, Yelachana yakanapura, Doddahullur, Chikkahullur, Chokkahalli, Chola ppanahalli, Malimakanapura, Dasarathimmanahalli, Pillagum pe, Hullur Amanikere.

Railway Station: Village- Devanagondi.

River: Dakshina Pinakini Nadi- Nearest Villages- Bathiga nahalli, Nallaganahalli, Ankonahalli, Arasanahalli, Ramap ura, Kadaranapura, Sulibele, Attibele, Yenagunte, Kammasa ndra, Hasigala, Timmasandra, Lakkondahalli, Shankanipura, Alappanahalli, Upparahalli, Chikka Amanikere, Dodda Amanikere, Sarakariguttahalli, Doddagattiganabbe, Bhakth arahalli, Mallasandra, Koralur, Naganayakanakote, Harohal li, Thimmadahalli, Kotur, Muthasandra, Bellikere, Bylahal li, Muthkur, Muthakadahalli, Thathnur, Thiruvaranga, Bagur, Gundur.

Canal: Nearest Villages- Doddaharadi Plantation, Hosahar di, Dodda Amanikere, Sarakariguttahalli, Doddagattiganabbe, Bhaktharahalli, Mallasandra, Koralur, Poojena Agrahara, Thirumalasettihalli, Samethanahalli, Naganayakanakote.

Annual Rainfall: Normal Rianfall 869.97 mm.

Ground Water: Availability of the Ground Water in the Basin is (Information not avablable) H.A.M. and the utilization is (Information not avablable) H.A.M. It belongs to (Information not avablable) category. Depth to water level 5 to 20 meter below the ground. Most of the wells go down in summer months, according to the Ground Water Estimation Committee.

Natural Division : It falls in Bangalore Plateau of the Southern Karnataka Plateau.

Administration:

Division: Bangalore. Parliamentary Constituency: 27 Bangalore- IV (SC). District: Bangalore Rural. Taluka: Hosakote. Assembly Constituency: 178 Hosakote. Gram Panchayat: 26.

Regional Area Development Boards: The Bailu Seeme Area Development Board.

Border Villages: (State: Tamil Nadu)- Gundur, Siddanapura, Shivanapura.

Fairs: Nageshwara Temple Jatra: It is held at Bagur near Bangalore in the month of Vaishaka (April-May), mentioned severally as Bempur, Veppur, Behur or Beyur in inscriptions (13 kms. from Bangalore) is perhaps one of the very old towns in Karnataka. It was the headq uarters of a Nadu then, popularly called Bempur-12 under the Gangas. According to a hero-stone (now preserved in Bangalore Museum) the place was ruled by a Ganga officer Nagattara, who in about 890 A.D. fell in a war between Ganga Ereyapa and Nolamba Bira Mahendra, while attacking the elephants in the army of the Nolamba prince Ayyapadeva. This record (Bn 83), besides giving the above details also states that the war was fought at a place called Tumbepadi. It is now preserved in Bangalo re Museum and had a very detailed depiction of a terrible war scene relief. The record states that Nagattara's son Iruga received crown from King Ereyappa. The place is also considered a pre-historic site as once fields full of ash-pits containing bones and of pottery were found. It is also said that several circular ovens built of bricks had been erected for the manufacture of glass bangles. The Nageshwara temple complex here consists of five Lingas enshrined separately known as Nageshwara, Nagareshwara, Choleshwara, Karneshwara and Kamateshwara.

Villages: 296 **Inhabited:** 255 **Uninhabited:** 41

Ranking	District	State	National
Area	6	161	1372
Population	4	101	919
Sex Ratio	8	169	4385
Child Sex Ratio	7	149	4235
Literacy Rate	2	42	1559
Density	6	121	3116
Work Participation Rate	2	16	2858

Gram Panchayats:

Sulibele, Doddaralagere, Ittasandra, Nelavagilu, Bylanarasapura, Nandagudi, Shivanapura, Kamblipura, Giddappanahalli, Lakkondahalli, Kumbalahalli, Doddahullur, Mugabala, Thavarekere, Doddanallala, Orohalli, Jadigenahalli, Doddagattiganabbe, Samethanahalli, Muthasandra, Ganagalur, Kalkunte Agrahara, Anugondahalli, Devanagondi, Vagata , Khajihosahalli.

Amenities:

Education: Primary School in 223 villages, Middle school in 116 villages, Matriculation or Secondary School in 22 villages, namely Bendiganahalli, Sulibele, Sonnahallipura, Begur, Nelavagilu, Nandagudi, Korati, Hedakanahalli, Shivanapura, Thavarekere, Mugabala, Nidagatta, Doddanallala, Jadigenahalli, Vagata, Vagata Agrahara, Kolathur, Doddagattiganabbe, Thirumalasettihalli, Devalapura, Anugondahalli, Kalkunte Agrahara.

Higher Secondary or Pre University Courses or Intermediate or Junior College in 3 villages of the CD Block,, namely Sulibele, Nandagudi, Devalapura.

College in 0 village, Adult Literacy Center in 1 village.

Medical: Hospital in 0 village, Dispensary in 3 villages, Health Center in 12 villages, Sub Center in 42 villages, Maternity and Child Welfare Center in 2 villages, Community health workers in 11 villages.

The Villages having Hospital or Dispensary or Health Center are Shivanapura, Mugabala, Haralur.

Drinking Water: Tap water in 116 villages, Tank water in 48 villages, Well water in 19 villages, Tubewell in 101 villages and more than one source in 179 villages.

Bank: Banking facility in 9 villages, namely, Sulibele, Nelavagilu, Nandagudi, Thavarekere Mugabala, Jadigenahalli, Lakkondahalli Malimakanapura, Kalkunte Agrahara.

Credit Society in 46 villages Agricultural Credit Society in 14 Non-Agricultural Credit Society in 10 villages.

Others: Power supply in 250 villages, Cinema hall in 1 village, sport club in 2 villages, Stadium or Auditorium or Community Hall in 255 villages, Post Office in 42 villages.

There are 202 villages having bus facilities.

Villages with most of facilities: Sulibele Nelavagilu, Nandagudi, Thavarekere, Mugabala Jadigenahalli, Lakkondahalli, Kalkunte Agrahara.

Villages without amenities (Education): Chikkakurubarahalli, Shantanapura, Bathiganahalli, Nallaganahalli, Siddanahalli, Kodipura, Yethinavadeyarapura, Thimmasandra, Kempapura, Agrahara Vaddahalli, Medur, Yeshvanthapura, Doddaganahalli, Gullenahalli, Mumynahosahalli, Ankonahalli, Chinnathimmanagolla Halli, Gerahalli, Halasakaipura, Channapura, Thimmapura, Ambalipura, Kurubara Gollahalli, Devara Gollahalli, Chikka Amanikere, Sonnadenahalli, Yelachanayakanapura, Dodda Amanikere, Appajipura, Thimmadahalli, Gullakaipura, Bylahalli..

Scheduled Castes: Out of the total population of 186107 persons, 44930 persons (24.14%) belong to Scheduled Castes.

The villages having less than 10% SC population are Chikkakurubarahalli, Kachipuradakambada Beedu Shantanapura, Bathiganahalli, Nallaganahalli Ankonahalli, Ramapura, Thammarasanahalli, Kodipura Valagerepura, Ekarajapura, Chikkakoliga, Doddakoliga Sonnebychanahalli, Bheemakkanahalli, Chikkondahalli Banahalli, Geddalahallipura, Agrahara Vaddahalli Doddaganahalli, Bylanarasapura, Gundrahalli Sathigenahalli, Gullenahalli, Ankonahalli, Gerahalli Doddanallurahalli, Nakkanahalli, Chinnandahalli Mylapura, Nidagatta, Thimmapura, Belamangala Kattigenahalli, Hunasehalli, Doddadasarahalli Bommanabande, Upparahalli, Chikka Amanikere Kumbalahalli, Kurubarahalli, Yelachanayakanapura Chikkahullur, Chikkanallurahalli, Dasarahalli Thimmadahalli, Gullakaipura, Siddanapura Shivanapura, Maramgere.

The villages having more than 50% SC population are Shivadenahalli, Yethinavadeyarapura, Bandahalli Bisanahalli, Lingapura, Chikkanallala, Halasakaipura Mugabala Hosahalli, Channapura, Yelachammanahalli Kurubara Gollahalli, Govindapura, Kacharakanahalli Tharabahalli, Devara Gollahalli, Sompura Sonnadenahalli, Sarakariguttahalli, Bhodanahosahalli Obalapura, Hemmandahalli, Banarahalli

Muthakadahalli, Thiruvaranga.

Sex ratio of Scheduled Caste population is 491.

Scheduled Castes Literates and Illiterates by Sex:

	Persons	Males	Females
Literate	21,951	13,347	8,604
Illiterate	22,979	9,525	13,454
Literacy rate	56.8	67.9	45.3
Graduate	458	413	45

Scheduled Castes (Dominant):

Adi Karnataka, Madiga, Adi Dravida, Bhovi Holaya etc.

For their cultural identity please see Appendix-I

Villages without Scheduled Castes: There are 62 villages without any scheduled caste population.

Scheduled Tribes: Out of the total population of 186107 persons, 6787 persons (3.65%) belong to Scheduled Tribes. The villages having less than 10% ST population are Thimmappanahalli, Theneyur, Chikkakurubarahalli Anupahalli, Esthur Hosahalli, Ralkunte, Esthur Cheemasandra, Bendiganahalli, Chikkaralagere Kachipuradakambada Beedu, Shantanapura Bathiganahalli, Ankonahalli, Arasanahalli, Ramapura Kadaranapura, Thammarasanahalli, Doddaralagere Thammarayasandra Agrahara, Hosadimbahalli Bhuvanahalli, Gullahalli, Bettahalli Giddappanahalli, Attibele, Yenagunte Yethinavadeyarapura, Sadappanahalli, M.Sathyawara Kammasandra, Hasigala, Thimmasandra, Shivadenahalli Sonnahallipura, Kempapura, Kamblipura, Nagarenahalli Chikkakoliga, Doddakoliga, Muthukadahalli Sonnebychanahalli, Bagalur, Gundrahalli, Ittasandra Hosavenkatapura, Hindiganala, Tharabahalli Chikkondahalli, Arehalli, Yethinavadeyarapura Nelavagilu, Sarakanur, Siddanahalli Geddalahallipura, Ramagovindapura Agrahara Vaddahalli, Medur, K.Settihalli, Karahalli Yeshvanthapura, Doddaganahalli, N.Hosahalli Muddenahalli, Chokkasandra, Mothakadahalli Kondrahalli, Bylanarasapura, Sathigenahalli Bandahalli, Huluvanahalli, Oblahalli, Gullenahalli Shivanapura, Karapanahalli, Mumynahosahalli K.Sathyawara, D.Settihalli, Doddenahalli Ankonahalli, Chinnathimmanagolla Halli Mallyappanahalli, Bisanahalli, Bheemapura Chikkanahalli, Yelachahalli, Manchappanahalli Kalappanahalli, Thavarekere, Lingapura, Beerahalli Hethakki, Agasarahalli, Marasandahalli Banamakanahalli, Gangapura, Nakkanahalli, Mugabala Poojaramanahalli, Chikkanallala, Dabbagunte Halasakaipura, Mugabala Hosahalli, Mylapura Valagerepura, Channapura, Attur, Nidagatta Doddanallala, Guguttahalli, Thimmapura, Ummalu Doddadenahalli, Alagondahalli, Yelachammanahalli Appasandra, Injanahalli, Ambalipura, Attivatta Solur, Orohalli, Doddathaggali, Chikkathaggali Thaggali Hosahalli, Gonakanahalli, Belamangala Jadigenahalli, Haralur, Vadigehalli, Kattigenahalli Kurubara Gollahalli, Govindapura, Vagata Vagata Agrahara, Jinnagara, Devasettihalli Kodihalli, Bisanahalli, Kacharakanahalli, Kanekallu Hunasehalli, Makanahalli, Doddadasarahalli Paramanahalli, Tharabahalli, Thindlu, Khajihosahalli Honachanahalli, Kamarasanahalli, Devara Gollahalli Lakkondahalli, Vabasandra, Shankanipura Alappanahalli, Upparahalli, Chikka Amanikere Kumbalahalli, Kallahalli, Kurubarahalli, Sompura Sonnadenahalli, Yelachanayakanapura, Doddahullur Chikkahullur, Chokkahalli, Malimakanapura Dasarahalli, Halasahalli, Kolathur, Kannurahalli Ganagalu, Pethanahalli, Sarakariguttahalli Doddagattiganabbe, Bhaktharahalli, Mallasandra Koralur, Appajipura, Naduvathi, Poojena Agrahara Chikkagattiganabbe, Cheemandahalli Thirumalasettihalli, Samethanahalli Bhodanahosahalli, Doddadunnasandra, Devalapura Devanagondi, Lingadeeramallasandra, Somalapura Medihalli, Devanagondi Hosahalli, Obalapura Anugondahalli, Hemmandahalli, Naganayakanakote Harohalli, Thimmadahalli, Ajjagondahalli, Kotur Gullakaipura, Muthasandra, Bellikere, Bylahalli Muthkur, Yedagondahalli, Medimallasandra Handenahalli, Banarahalli, S.Narayanakere Kalkunte Agrahara, Arehalli, Muthakadahalli Thathnur, Thiruvaranga, Bagur, Gundur, Siddanapura Shivanapura, Maramgere, Ganagalur.

The villages having more than 50% ST population are None.

Sex ratio of Scheduled tribe population is 488.

Scheduled Tribes Literates and Illiterates by Sex:

	Persons	Males	Females
Literate	3,264	1,999	1,265
Illiterate	3,523	1,479	2,044
Literacy rate	56.5	67.7	44.9
Graduate	57	49	8

Scheduled Tribes (Dominant):

Naikda etc., Kadu Kuruba, Generic Tribes etc., Meda Kudiya etc.

For their cultural identity please see Appendix-II

Villages without Scheduled Tribes: There are 199 villages without any scheduled tribe population.

Literates and Illiterates by Sex (Total Population):

	Persons	Males	Females
Literate	108,875	64,524	44,351
Illiterate	77,232	31,801	45,431
Literacy rate	67	77	57
Graduate	2,795	2,349	446

Agriculture: ***Distribution of villages according to land use:*** Out of 296 villages, Total area (in hectare) is 53347, out of that 64.24 percent is cultivable and 29.97 percent of the cultivable area is irrigated.

Sources of Irrigation (Hectares): Government Canal 42.62, Private Canal 0, Well without Electricity 0, Well with Electricity 756.87, Tubewell without Electricity 280.37, Tubewell with Electricity 5969.85, Tank 1773.78, River 63.94, Lake 151.66, Waterfall 0, Others 1232.13.

Villages with population of 5000 to 9999: Sulibele.

Villages with population of 10000 and above: None

Distribution of Workers:

	Persons	Males	Females	WPR
Cultivators	34,998	24,406	10,592	39.56
Agricultural Labour	21,308	10,474	10,834	24.09
Household Industry	2,856	1,915	941	3.23
Other Workers	29,295	20,508	8,787	33.12
Main Workers	73,392	52,617	20,775	82.97
Marginal Workers	15,065	4,686	10,379	17.03
Total Workers	88,457	57,303	31,154	

Religion: Major Religious Communities:

	Persons	Males	Females	Sex Ratio
Hindu (87.9%)	163,597	84,546	79,051	935
Muslim (11.66%)	21,692	11,326	10,366	915
Christian (0.2%)	376	211	165	782
Sikh (0.03%)	53	31	22	710
Buddhists (0.01%)	18	9	9	1,000
Jain (0.01%)	19	9	10	1,111

Agewise Data:

	Persons	Males	Females	Sex Ratio
All ages	186,107	96,325	89,782	932
0-14	58,304	29,883	28,421	951
15-44	90,109	46,811	43,298	925
45-79	35,013	18,280	16,733	915
80+	2,404	1,194	1,210	1013
Age not stated	277	157	120	764

Languages (Dominant): Kannada, Telugu, Urdu, Tamil, Hindi

Disabled Population:

	Persons	Males	Females	%
Total Disabled	3,512	1,984	1,528	
In Seeing	1,556	840	716	44.31
In Speech	352	184	168	10.02
In Hearing	192	100	92	5.47
In Movement	990	625	365	28.19
Mentally	422	235	187	12.02

HOSANAGARA

Hosanagara C.D. Block lies in the southern part of Shimoga district. It is a part of Hosanagara taluka. The Block is located at a distance of 73 kms. from district headquarters (Shimoga). There are 204 villages in the block with the total population of 109,977 persons. Area of the C.D. Block is 1392.86 sq. kms. It is bounded by taluk Sagar on north, taluk Tirthahalli on south, taluk Shimoga on east, district Udupi and taluk Sagar on west.

Communications:

Roadways : S.H-1: Direction- Tirthahalli to Sagar, Nearest Villages- Nevatoor, Balur, Govatoor, Baruve, Malavalli, Halandur, Jamballi, Huligadde, Amrutha, Kallur, Mugadthi, Kanabandur, Karagodu. S.H-26: Direction- Kollur to Shimoga, Nearest Villages- Nagodi, Sutha, Salageri, Ganganakoppa, Varakodu , Mavinakoppa, M.Guddekoppa, Mumbaru, Kusgundi, Chikkajeni, Govatoor, Kerehalli, Benavalli, Baruve, Arasalu, Basavapura, Haniya, Kukkod Agasaramane, Ramachandrapura, Melina Besige, Nellunde, Behalli, Kodur, Yalagallu, Hirejeni, Tariga, Manjagalale, Adagodi, Hosur, Mathikai, Bhramanavada, Aramane Koppa, Byse, Mudugoppa (Nagara), Kodase, Hilukunji.

Railway Station: Villages- Kenchanala, Arasalu.

River: Varahi Nadi- Nearest Villages- Nidagodu, Sulagodu, Hummadagallu, Gubbiga, Begadali. Haridravati Nadi- Nearest Villages- Hosakoppa, Churda, Veerabhadrapura, Kanagodu, Nelagalale, Gudodi, Thotada Koppa, Amachi, Gubbiga, Baniga, Majavana, Hulusale Malavalli, Haridravati, Alageri Mandri, Dombekoppa, Shunti Koppa, Muthala, Hiremaithe, Nanjavalli. Sharavati Nadi- Nearest Villages- Badenagara, Hosanadu, Andagoli, Horoyathige, Hosakoppa, Halethota, Neelakantanathota, K.Honnekoppa, Dumma, Mulagadde, Malali, Manasette, L.Guddekoppa , Tenkabylu, Suta, Salageri, H.Honne Koppa, Ganganakoppa, Balekoppa, Kargadi, Agasaramane, Ramachandrapura, Goragodu, Thogare, Magodu, Hebburli, Aramane Koppa, Brahmanatharuve, Kumbatti, Mudugoppa (Nagara), Kodase, Kukkod.

Reserved Forest: Nearest Villages- Nagodi, Manjagalale, Hebburli, Hosur, Mathikai, Kattinahole, Kilandur Jungle, Bhramanavada, Aramane, Koppa, Byse, Malali, Karimane, Khyrugundha.

Annual Rainfall: Normal Rianfall 3201.30 mm.

Ground Water: Availability of the Ground Water in the Basin is 133.02 MCM and the utilization is 15.67 MCM. It belongs to Safe category. Depth to water level 5 to 20 meter below the ground. Most of the wells go down in summer months, according to the Ground Water Estimati on Committee.

Soils: Reddish to Brownish Clayey Loam.

Natural Division : It falls partly in Sagar-Sorab-Shikarpur Rolling Humid Region, Shimoga Forested Hills and Weste

Administration:

Division: Bangalore. Parliamentary Constituency: 14 Shimoga. District: Shimoga. Taluka: Hosanagara. Assembly Constituency: 117 Sagar. Gram Panchayat: 29.

Regional Area Development Boards: The Maland Aera Development Board.

Fairs: Kartikotsava: Kartikotsava is observed at Nagar near Shimoga in the month of November every year. Nagar is about 15 kms. south of Hosanagar town and about 86 kms. west of Shimoga city. It was originally a small village called Bidarahalli (bamboo-village) from the nature of the forest around and contained a temple of Neelkantha managed by a Brahmin named Honna-Kambali Bhatta.

Mahaganpati Kartikotsava: It is observed annually at Hosanagar near Shimoga in about the month of November. Hosanagar, previously called Kallurkatte, about 70 kms. west of Shimoga city, is a taluk headquarters which was shifted from Nagar to Kallurkatte in 1898. The place is situated in the midst of splendid natural scenery. Several roads from this place connect other parts of the malnad, semi-malnad and coastal areas of the State. The place is noted for arecanut trade.

Marikamba Jatra: Marikamba jatra is held at Hosanagar Shimoga area in around the month of February for one day. Hosanagar, previously called Kallurkatte, about 70 kms. west of Shimoga city, is a taluk headquarters town.

Neelakantheshvara Jatra: It is held at Nagar near Shimo ga around the month of April. Nagar, is about 15 kms. south of Hosanagar town and about 86 kms. west of Shimoga city. It was originally a small village called Bidarahalli (bamboo-village) from the nature of the forest around and contained a temple of Neelakantha managed by a Brahmin named Honna-Kambali Bhatta.

Padmavatiamma Rathotsava: Padmavatiamma Rathotsava is observed at the temple of Padmavati at Humcha near Shimo ga around the month of March every year. Humcha situated at a distance of about 60 kms. south-west of Shimoga city and 21 kms. south-east of Hosanagar, is a hobli headquarters.

Villages: 204 **Inhabited:** 201 **Uninhabited:** 3

Ranking	District	State	National
Area	2	41	183
Population	7	156	3156
Sex Ratio	2	28	1028
Child Sex Ratio	4	43	2124
Literacy Rate	3	24	929
Density	6	160	6234
Work Participation Rate	6	170	3779

Gram Panchayats:

Nagodi, Hosur, Jeni, Purappe Mane, Haridravati, Harathalu, Maruthipura, M.Guddekoppa, Melina Besige, Aramane Koppa, Karimane, Khyrugundha , Sulagodu, Yadur, Andagadoduru, Mudugoppa (Nagara), Thrinive, Sonale, Mumbaru, Kodur, Chikkajeni, Humcha, Amrutha, Heddaripura, Rippanpete, Balur, Kenchanala, Arasalu, Bellur.

Amenities:

Education: Primary School in 133 villages, Middle school in 83 villages, Matriculation or Secondary School in 18 villages, namely Nagodi, Ganganakoppa, Kanagodu, Maruthipura, Alageri Mandri, Govatoor, Arasalu, Bellur, Sonale, Kodur, Humcha, Jamballi, Amrutha, Mugadthi, Kattinahole, Mudugoppa (Nagara), Khyrugundha, Yadur. Higher Secondary or Pre University Courses or Intermediate or Junior College in 6 villages of the CD Block,, namely Nagodi, Kanagodu, Govatoor, Kodur, Amrutha, Yadur.

College in 0 village, Adult Literacy Center in 9 villages.

Medical: Hospital in 1 village, Dispensary in 10 villages, Health Center in 6 villages, Sub Center in 19 villages, Maternity and Child Welfare Center in 1 village, Community health workers in 12 villages.

The Villages having Hospital or Dispensary or Health Center are Nagodi, Thotada Koppa, Purappe Mane, Alageri Mandri, Harathalu, Bellur, Thrinive, Sonale, Kodur, Hosur.

Drinking Water: Tap water in 25 villages, Tank water in 6 villages, Well water in 180 villages, Tubewell in 47 villages and more than one source in 190 villages.

Bank: Banking facility in 13 villages, namely, Nagodi, Maruthipura, Govatoor, Baruve, Sonale, Kodur Humcha, Manjagalale, Malali, Mudugoppa (Nagara) Khyrugundha, Sulagodu, Yadur.

Credit Society in 24 villages Agricultural Credit Society in 22 Non-Agricultural Credit Society in 1 village.

Others: Power supply in 190 villages, Cinema hall in 1 village, sport club in 201 villages, Stadium or Auditorium or Communi Hall in 201 villages, Post Office in 50 villages.

There are 135 villages having bus facilities.

Villages with most of facilities: Nagodi Maruthipura, Govatoor, Baruve, Sonale, Kodur, Humcha Mudugoppa (Nagara), Yadur.

Villages without amenities (Education): Kallodi, Bydur, Kesare, Andagoli, Horoyathige, Hosakoppa,

Churda, Veerabhadrapura, Halethota, Neelakantanathota, K.Honnekoppa, Manasette, L.Guddekoppa, Tenkabylu, Salageri, H.Honne Koppa, Varakodu, Kalur, Kalikapura, Holagodu, Gudodi, Sidiyapura, Aragodi, Kachigebylu, Hulusale Malavalli, H.Kallukoppa, Dodda Bilagodu, Nandri, Chikkabilagodu, Devara Honnekoppa, P. Kallukoppa, H.Hunasavalli, Bilagodu, Amachi, Menase, K.Hunasavalli, Harathalu, Hosahalli, Karakki, Adavalli, Chikkajeni, Kalasetti Koppa, Mugute Koppa, Alavalli, Haramballi, Kargadi, Kukkod Agasaramane, Melina Besige, Devarasalike, Nellunde, Kalluvidi Abbigalla, Bori Koppa, Iragodu, Hiriyogi, Behalli, H. Kunnur, Malali Koppa, Nagarahalli, Halandur, Karagodu, Magodu, Kilandur Jungle, Kadiggere, Hummadagallu, Gubbiga, Karigallu, Begadali..

Scheduled Castes: Out of the total population of 109957 persons, 9839 persons (8.95%) belong to Scheduled Castes. The villages having less than 10% SC population are Hebbige, Koteshirur, Kallodi, Bydur, Jala, Hosanadu Kesare, Andagoli, Horoyathige, Churda Neelakantanathota, K.Honnekoppa, Manasette L.Guddekoppa , Tenkabylu, H.Honne Koppa, Varakodu Gerupura, Kalur, Kalikapura, Jeni, Holagodu Basavapura, Kanagodu, Nelagalale, Gudodi Thotada Koppa, Sidiyapura, Mumbaru, Gubbiga, Baniga Hosakesare, Hulusale Malavalli, Echala Koppa H.Kallukoppa, Dodda Bilagodu, Chikkabilagodu Hebbylu, Devara Honnekoppa, P. Kallukoppa H.Hunasavalli, Bilagodu, Amachi, Heelagodu, Menase Muthala, Adavalli, K.Kunnur, Chikkajeni, Hiremaithe Kalasetti Koppa, Nanjavalli, Halugudde, Balur Nerala Mane, Kukakalale, Bilki, Govatoor Mugute Koppa, Kerehalli, Madapura, Benavalli Haramballi, Thammadikoppa, Basavapura, Harohithlu Kalase, Masakani, Dobylu, Bellur, Gubbiga, Haniya Balekoppa, Kargadi, Vasave, Devarasalike, Varamballi Thrinive, Thogare, Kalluvidi Abbigalla, Billodi Bori Koppa, Sonale, Kolagi, Iragodu, Hiriyogi Behalli, Yalagallu, Shakavalli, Savanthur Honne Bylu, Kadasoor, Malur, H. Kunnur, Hirejeni Karigerasu, Malali Koppa, Halandur, Kalkoppa, Tariga Kolavalli, Huligadde, Amrutha, Bidharalli, Mugadthi Talale, Vadahosalli, Manjagalale, Adagodi, Magodu Hebburli, Hosur, Kilandur Jungle, Bhramanavada Aramane Koppa, Kumbatti, Basavanabyana, Byse, Malali Karimane, Kilandur , Kadiggere, Mudugoppa (Nagara) Kodase, Belur, Anadagadoduru, Kabale, Ryave Kolavadi, Ginikallu, Nidagodu, Sulagodu, Kavari Karigallu, Koranakote, Begadali, Kattekoppa.

The village having more than 50% SC population is None.

Sex ratio of Scheduled Caste population is 493.

Scheduled Castes Literates and Illiterates by Sex:

	Persons	Males	Females
Literate	4,890	2,833	2,057
Illiterate	4,949	2,157	2,792
Literacy rate	58.1	66.7	49.3
Graduate	113	86	27

Scheduled Castes (Dominant):

Adi Karnataka, Bhovi, Moger, Bhambi etc.

Adi Dravida

For their cultural identity please see Appendix-I

Villages without Scheduled Castes: There are 74 villages without any scheduled caste population.

Scheduled Tribes: Out of the total population of 109957 persons, 1827 persons (1.66%) belong to Scheduled Tribes. The villages having less than 10% ST population are Nagodi, Hebbige, Koteshirur, Kallodi, Bydur, Jala Hosanadu, Kesare, Andagoli, Horoyathige, Hosakoppa Churda, Veerabhadrapura, Halethota Neelakantanathota, K.Honnekoppa, Dumma, Mulagadde Malali, Manasette, L.Guddekoppa , Tenkabylu, Sutha Salageri, H.Honne Koppa, Ganganakoppa, Varakodu Mavinakoppa, Gerupura, Kalur, Masagalli, Kalikapura Jeni, Holagodu, Basavapura, Kanagodu, Nelagalale Gudodi, Thotada Koppa, Melina Sampalli, Sidiyapura Punaje, M.Guddekoppa, Mumbaru, Muthur, Aragodi Kachigebylu, Gubbiga, Baniga, Maruthipura Hosakesare, Majavana, Hulusale Malavalli Echala Koppa, H.Kallukoppa, Purappe Mane Dodda Bilagodu, Nandri, Chikkabilagodu, Hebbylu Devara Honnekoppa, Haridravati, P. Kallukoppa H.Hunasavalli, Bilagodu, Amachi, Heelagodu Alageri Mandri, Dombekoppa, Menase, K.Hunasavalli Harathalu, Shunti Koppa, Muthala, Hosahalli, Karakki Kusgundi, Adavalli, K.Kunnur, Chikkajeni, Hiremaithe Kalasetti Koppa, Nanjavalli, Halugudde, Nevatoor Balur, Nerala Mane, Kukakalale, Bilki, Govatoor Mugute Koppa, Kerehalli, Belanduru, Madapura Alavalli, Masarur, Kenchanala, Benavalli, Baruve Malavalli, Haramballi, Thammadikoppa, Arasalu Basavapura, Harohithlu, Kalase, Masakani, Dobylu Bellur, Gubbiga, Haniya, Balekoppa, Kargadi Kukkod Agasaramane, Ramachandrapura, Melina Besige Vasave, Devarasalike, Varamballi, Goragodu, Nellunde Thrinive, Thogare, Kalluvidi Abbigalla, Billodi Bori Koppa, Sonale, Kolagi, Iragodu, Kodur Yalagallu, Shakavalli, Savanthur, Nivane, Anegadde Honne Bylu, Malur, H. Kunnur, Hirejeni, Karigerasu

Malali Koppa, Nagarahalli, Humcha, Halandur Jamballi, Kalkoppa, Tariga, Kolavalli, Huligadde Amrutha, Kammachi, Bidharalli, Kallur, Mugadthi Kanabandur, Karagodu, Talale, Kagachi, Vadahosalli Adagodi, Magodu, Hebburli, Hosur, Mathikai Kattinahole, Kilandur Jungle, Bhramanavada, Kumbatti Basavanabyana, Byse, Malali, Karimane, Kilandur Kadiggere, Mudugoppa (Nagara), Hilukunji, Belur Kabale, Khyrugundha, Ryave, Kolavadi, Ginikallu Nidagodu, Sulagodu, Kavari, Yadur, Hummadagallu Gubbiga, Karigallu, Begadali.

The villages having more than 50% ST population are None.

Sex ratio of Scheduled tribe population is 501.

Scheduled Tribes Literates and Illiterates by Sex:

	Persons	Males	Females
Literate	819	455	364
Illiterate	1,008	456	552
Literacy rate	52.3	59.4	45.5
Graduate	21	15	6

Scheduled Tribes (Dominant):

Hasalaru, Naikda etc., Koraga, Maleru , Hakkipikki

For their cultural identity please see Appendix-II

Villages without Scheduled Tribes: There are 138 villages without any scheduled tribe population.

Literates and Illiterates by Sex (Total Population):

	Persons	Males	Females
Literate	69,451	38,627	30,824
Illiterate	40,506	16,201	24,305
Literacy rate	72	81	64
Graduate	2,697	1,953	744

Agriculture: ***Distribution of villages according to land use:*** Out of 204 villages, Total area (in hectare) is 139286, out of that 13.65 percent is cultivable and 43.5 percent of the cultivable area is irrigated.

Sources of Irrigation (Hectares): Government Canal 188.09, Private Canal 0, Well without Electricity 1.52, Well with Electricity 192.89, Tubewell without Electricity 4, Tubewell with Electricity 348.73, Tank 5189.24, River 323.06, Lake 46.14, Waterfall 12.96, Others 1966.62.

Villages with population of 5000 to 9999: None

Villages with population of 10000 and above: None

Distribution of Workers:

	Persons	Males	Females	WPR
Cultivators	17,452	13,598	3,854	36.45
Agricultural Labour	16,858	8,862	7,996	35.21
Household Industry	1,245	640	605	2.6
Other Workers	12,324	9,842	2,482	25.74
Main Workers	38,590	29,509	9,081	80.6
Marginal Workers	9,289	3,433	5,856	19.4
Total Workers	47,879	32,942	14,937	

Religion: Major Religious Communities:

	Persons	Males	Females	Sex Ratio
Hindu (93.16%)	102,441	51,076	51,365	1,006
Muslim (4.75%)	5,224	2,564	2,660	1,037
Christian (1.61%)	1,765	904	861	952
Sikh (0%)	5	3	2	667
Buddhists (0%)	-	-	-	-
Jain (0.31%)	339	199	140	704

Agewise Data:

	Persons	Males	Females	Sex Ratio
All ages	109,957	54,828	55,129	1005
0-14	30,930	15,779	15,151	960
15-44	56,480	27,677	28,803	1041
45-79	21,355	10,781	10,574	981
80+	1,080	528	552	1045
Age not stated	112	63	49	778

Languages (Dominant):

Kannada, Urdu, Malayalam, Konkani, Marathi

Disabled Population:

	Persons	Males	Females	%
Total Disabled	1,578	881	697	
In Seeing	582	316	266	36.88
In Speech	179	96	83	11.34
In Hearing	123	55	68	7.79
In Movement	471	302	169	29.85
Mentally	223	112	111	14.13

HOSDURGA

Hosdurga C.D. Block lies in the southern part of Chitradurga district. It is a part of Hosdurga taluka. The Block is located at a distance of 65 kms. from district headquarters (Chitradurga). There are 225 villages in the block with the total population of 196,831 persons. Area of the C.D. Block is 1332.42 sq. kms. It is bounded by taluk Holalkere on north, districts Chikmagalur and Tumkur on south, taluk Hiriyur on east, and district Chikamagalur on west.

Communications:

Roadways : S.H-19: Direction- Huliyur to Huliyur, Nearest Villages- Kudurekanive Forest, Chikkabyladakere, Doddabyladakere. S.H-19 A: Direction- Holalkere to Huliyur, Nearest Villages- Beesanahalli, Kabbala, Mavinakatte, Herur, Kumbaragatte, Devigere, Guthikatte, Janthikolalu, Madhure, Chinnapura, Shivanekatte, Rangapura, Nagenahalli, Bokikere, Byrapura, Kumaranakanive, Kyadigere, Kaval, Goravigondanahalli, Kellodu, Hosural, Aralahalli, Malappanahalli, Somasandra, Kainaduval Kaval, Neralakere, Naigere, Heggere, Banapura, Sriramapura, Hagalakere, Muttagundi, Menasinadu, Sirigondanahalli. S.H-24: Direction- Tarikere to Hiriyur, Nearest Villages- Shivanekatte,

Aralihalli, Bokikere, Goravinakal, Srirangapura (Jodi), Hosahalli, Hunavinadu, Peelapura, Neeragunda, Hurulihal li, Adrikatte, Malali, Lakkihalli, Devapura, Masanihalli, Rangavvanahalli, Ramajjanahalli, Madadakere, Seeranakatte.

Railway Station: Chikkamanahalli.

River: Vedavati Nadi- Nearest Villages- Attigatta, Bagas ettihalli, Koratikere, Ballalasamudra Kaval, Kadadanakere, Karalamavinahalli, Mettinahole, Kannagondi, Kellodu, Alagatta, Ballalasamudra, Handanakere, Hosural, Muttagundi.

Annual Rainfall: Normal Rianfall 702.8 mm.

Ground Water: Availability of the Ground Water in the Basin is 9376.88 H.A.M. and the utilization is 7395. 25 H.A.M. It belongs to Over Exploited category. Depth to water level 2 to 20 meter below the ground. Most of the wells go down in summer months, according to the Ground Water Estimation Committee.

Soils: Deep and Shallow black soils, mixed red and black soil, red loamy and sandy soils.

Natural Division : It falls partly in Kanchipura Scrubby Upland, Upper Vedavati (Hagari) Basin and Chitradurga-Ho sadurga Hills of the Central Karnataka Plateau.

Administration:

Division: Bangalore. Parliamentary Constituency: 18 Chitradurga (SC). District: Chitradurga. Taluka: Hosdurga. Assembly Constituency: 101 Hosdurga. Gram Panchayat: 33.

Regional Area Development Boards: The Bailu Seeme Area Development Board.

Villages: 225 **Inhabited:** 198 **Uninhabited:** 27

Ranking	District	State	National
Area	4	49	211
Population	4	90	734
Sex Ratio	1	81	2254
Child Sex Ratio	1	14	1090
Literacy Rate	3	70	2234
Density	3	81	5591
Work Participation Rate	4	133	1937

Gram Panchayats:

Doddakittadahalli, Lakkihalli, Janakal, Doddagatta, Hebballi, Madadakere, Devigere, Mallapanahalli, Devapura, Athimage, Madhure, Anivala, Bagur, Hunavinadu, Bokikere , Mathodu, Guddadaneralakere, Kellodu, Karehalli, Kanchipura, Chikkabyladakere, Doddathekalavatti, Ballalasamudra, Kabbala, Kainadu, Neralakere, Belagur, Sriramapura, Heggere, Tandaga, Kurubarahalli, Sanihalli, Kangavalli.

Amenities:

Education: Primary School in 181 villages, Middle school in 121 villages, Matriculation or Secondary School in 46 villages, namely Kabbala, Mavinakatte, Hebballi, Devigere, Kondapura, Mallapanahalli, Anivala, Madhure, Shivanekatte, Bagur, Bokikere, Kappagere, Channasamudra, Neeragunda, Sanihalli, Marabagatta, Malali, Kellodu, Doddagatta, Goolihatti, Janakal, Devapura, Athimage, Madadakere, Alagatta, Ballalasamudra, Aralahalli, Somasandra, Neralakere, Garaga, Belagur, Tandaga, Somenahalli, Gavirangapura, Heggere, Sriramapura, Vengalapura, Kachapura, Karehalli, Mathodu, Guddadaneralakere, Doddathekalavatti, Bukkasagara, Kanchipura, Chikkabyladakere, Kittadal.

Higher Secondary or Pre University Courses or Intermediate or Junior College in 14 villages of the CD Block,, namely Mallapanahalli, Anivala, Madhure, Malali, Doddagatta, Janakal, Madadakere, Neralakere, Belagur, Gavirangapura, Sriramapura, Mathodu, Doddathekalavatti, Kittadal.

College in 2 villages, Adult Literacy Center in 0 village., Colleges are in villages, namely Gavirangapura, Sriramapura.

Medical: Hospital in 4 villages, Dispensary in 14 villages, Health Center in 8 villages, Sub Center in 21 villages, Maternity and Child Welfare Center in 2 villages, Community health workers in 8 villages.

The Villages having Hospital or Dispensary or Health Center are Hebballi, Mallapanahalli, Kangavalli, Doddagatta, Madadakere, Alagatta, Ballalasamudra, Krishnapura, Neralakere, Tandaga, Somenahalli, Heggere, Mathodu, Doddathekalavatti, Bukkasagara.

Drinking Water: Tap water in 50 villages, Tank water in 4 villages, Well water in 6 villages, Tubewell in 155 villages and more than one source in 166 villages.

Bank: Banking facility in 14 villages, namely, Mallapanahalli, Bagur, Sanihalli, Janakal Madadakere, Ballalasamudra, Belagur, Tandaga Sriramapura, Karehalli, Mathodu, Doddathekalavatti Kanchipura, Kittadal.

Credit Society in 15 villages Agricultural Credit Society in 15 Non-Agricultural Credit Society in 0 village.

Others: Power supply in 198 villages, Cinema hall in 2 villages sport club in 0 village, Stadium or Auditorium or Community Hall in 0 village, Post Office in 60 villages.

There are 126 villages having bus facilities.

Villages with most of facilities: Mallapanahalli Bagur, Janakal, Madadakere, Ballalasamudra, Belagur Tandaga, Sriramapura, Mathodu, Doddathekalavatti Kanchipura, Kittadal.

Villages without amenities (Education):

Kumbaragatte, Dasarahalli, Rangapura, Byrapura, Ballalasamudra Kaval, Karalamavinahalli,

Thimmalapura, Handanakere, Sirigepura, Ballalasamudrakere Kaval, Grantapura, Agrahara, Sujikal Amanikere, Banapura, Kudurekanive Forest, Gollarahalli, Mugilodu..

Scheduled Castes: Out of the total population of 196957 persons, 38975 persons (19.79%) belong to Scheduled Castes. The villages having less than 10% SC population are Thumbinakere, Mavinakatte, Dasarahalli, Kondapura Kadivanakatte, Jammapura, Burudekatte, Kundur Iyalapura, Mantenahalli (Jodi), Lakkenahalli Kanivesangenahalli, Rangapura, Nagenahalli Palyadahalli, Srirangapura, Kabbinakere, Settyhalli Kodihalli, Honnekere, Aralihalli, Bokikere Hosahalli, Hunavinadu, Kurubarahalli, Adrikatte Machenahalli, Goravigondanahalli, Jogammanahalli Lingadhahalli, Attigatta, Kyadigere Adavi Sangenahalli, Bagasettihalli, Koratikere Kannagondi, Thanigekal, Kodihalli, Thimmalapura Ulavinagondi, Malappanahalli, Mathur, Kodihalli Bommenahalli, Bachavara, Mengasandra Chikkahullenahalli, Grantapura, Kadavagere, Agrahara Naigere, Nagaragere, Kerehosahalli, Kurubarahalli Somenahalli, Mallihalli, Sujikal, Goolihalli Heggere, Banapura, Kachapura, Kudurekanive Forest Ajjikamasagara, Thippenahalli, Nagathihalli Agasarahalli, Kasappanahalli, Doddakarpuradakatte Kappanaikanahalli, Balenahalli, Gollarahalli Mugilodu, Bydarahalli, Jayasuvarnapura.

The villages having more than 50% SC population are Beesanahalli, Devigere, Chinnapura Karalamavinahalli, Sevanagara, Devapura Colony Galabenahalli, Rangavvanahalli, Athimage Handanakere, Ballalasamudrakere Kaval, Krishnapura Gollarahalli, Yadagatta, Hariyanahalli, Singenahalli Ganjigere, Giriyapura, Naganaikanakatte.

Sex ratio of Scheduled Caste population is 494.

Scheduled Castes Literates and Illiterates by Sex:

	Persons	Males	Females
Literate	15,763	9,745	6,018
Illiterate	23,212	9,966	13,246
Literacy rate	47.1	57.5	36.4
Graduate	261	238	23

Scheduled Castes (Dominant):

Bhovi, Madiga, Adi Karnataka, Banjara etc., Koracha

For their cultural identity please see Appendix-I

Villages without Scheduled Castes: There are 59 villages without any scheduled caste population.

Scheduled Tribes: Out of the total population of 196957 persons, 15945 persons (8.1%) belong to Scheduled Tribes. The villages having less than 10% ST population are Nagarakatte, Beesanahalli, Kabbala, Hebballi Krishnapura, Kumbaragatte, Devigere, Dasarahalli Janthikolalu, Kondapura, Kadivanakatte, Chikkayagati Mallapanahalli, Chikkamanahalli, Burudekatte Anivala, Kundur, Iyalapura, Mantenahalli (Jodi) Lakkenahalli, Madhure, Kanivesangenahalli Chinnapura, Shivanekatte, Nagenahalli, Bagur Palyadahalli, Srirangapura, Ballekere, Kabbinakere Settyhalli, Kodihalli, Honnekere, Aralihalli Goravinakal, Srirangapura (Jodi), Hosahalli Sodaranal, Byrapura, Peelapura, Neeragunda Sanihalli, Hurulihalli, Adrikatte, Marabagatta Machenahalli, Goravigondanahalli, Jogammanahalli Lingadhahalli, Attigatta, Adavi Sangenahalli Kangavalli, Aladahalli, Bagasettihalli, Koratikere Ballalasamudra Kaval, Kadadanakere Karalamavinahalli, Mettinahole, Kannagondi, Kellodu Doddagatta, Duggavara, Goolihatti, Sevanagara Sannakittadahalli, Hullukatti, Kodihalli Devapura Colony, Benakanahalli, Banasihalli Galabenahalli, Devapura, Masanihalli Rangavvanahalli, Athimage, Ramajjanahalli Madadakere, Seeranakatte, Alagatta, Ballalasamudra Thimmalapura, Handanakere, Ulavinagondi, Kalkere Aralahalli, Malappanahalli, Tumbinakere, Kabbala Mallenahalli (Jodi), Mathur, Sirigepura, Kodihalli Ballalasamudrakere Kaval, Bommenahalli, Krishnapura Thonechenahalli, Kainadu, Bachavara, Gollarahalli Mengasandra, Arenahalli, Grantapura, Sadarahalli Neralakere, Agrahara, Naigere, Nagaragere Haragondanahalli, Mylarapura, Yadagatta, Garaga Kerehosahalli, Belagur, Hariyanahalli, Singenahalli Tandaga, Kurubarahalli, Somenahalli, Mallihalli Sujikal, Sujikal Amanikere, Goolihalli Gavirangapura, Heggere, Banapura, Sriramapura Kachapura, Hagalakere, Muttagundi, Menasinadu Ganjigere, Karehalli, Ajjikamasagara, Arehalli Siddagondanahalli, Agasarahalli, Ittigehalli Guddadaneralakere, Laxmidevarahalli, Giriyapura Sirigondanahalli, Doddathekalavatti, Bukkasagara Chikkathekalavatti, Kaggalakatte, Chikkabyladakere Kittadal, Naganaikanakatte, Bydarahalli Doddabyladakere, Jayasuvarnapura.

The villages having more than 50% ST population are Rangapura, Kurubarahalli, Kyadigere Veeravvanagathihalli, Iyyanahalli, Kadavagere Kudurekanive Forest, Thippenahalli, Nagathihalli Kasappanahalli, Gollarahalli.

Sex ratio of Scheduled tribe population is 500.

Scheduled Tribes Literates and Illiterates by Sex:

	Persons	Males	Females
Literate	7,619	4,583	3,036
Illiterate	8,326	3,396	4,930
Literacy rate	54.9	65.4	44.1
Graduate	120	106	14

Scheduled Tribes (Dominant):

Naikda etc., Gowdalu

For their cultural identity please see Appendix-II

Villages without Scheduled Tribes: There are 94 villages without any scheduled tribe population.

Literates and Illiterates by Sex (Total Population):

	Persons	Males	Females
Literate	109,638	64,935	44,703
Illiterate	87,319	34,797	52,522
Literacy rate	63	74	52
Graduate	3,593	2,984	609

Agriculture: ***Distribution of villages according to land use:*** Out of 225 villages, Total area (in hectare) is 133242, out of that 54.11 percent is cultivable and 6.31 percent of the cultivable area is irrigated.

Sources of Irrigation (Hectares): Government Canal 0, Private Canal 0, Well without Electricity 0, Well with Electricity 18.12, Tubewell without Electricity 0, Tubewell with Electricity 4503.57, Tank 26.16, River 0, Lake 0, Waterfall 0, Others 0.

Villages with population of 5000 to 9999:

Belagur, Sriramapura.

Villages with population of 10000 and above: None

Distribution of Workers:

	Persons	Males	Females	WPR
Cultivators	52,279	35,636	16,643	51.41
Agricultural Labour	29,401	10,499	18,902	28.91
Household Industry	1,966	1,163	803	1.93
Other Workers	18,035	13,694	4,341	17.74
Main Workers	78,493	56,176	22,317	77.2
Marginal Workers	23,188	4,816	18,372	22.8
Total Workers	101,681	60,992	40,689	

Religion: Major Religious Communities:

	Persons	Males	Females	Sex Ratio
Hindu (96.36%)	189,789	96,134	93,655	974
Muslim (2.64%)	5,200	2,613	2,587	990
Christian (0.01%)	24	13	11	846
Sikh (0.02%)	48	23	25	1,087
Buddhists (0.01%)	18	9	9	1,000
Jain (0.06%)	109	53	56	1,057

Agewise Data:

	Persons	Males	Females	Sex Ratio
All ages	196,957	99,732	97,225	975
0-14	57,457	29,108	28,349	974
15-44	95,819	48,395	47,424	980
45-79	41,661	21,228	20,433	963
80+	1,925	950	975	1026
Age not stated	95	51	44	863

Languages (Dominant):

Kannada, Telugu, Hindi, Urdu, Tamil

Disabled Population:

	Persons	Males	Females	%
Total Disabled	3,938	2,352	1,586	
In Seeing	1,899	1,168	731	48.22
In Speech	421	239	182	10.69
In Hearing	202	110	92	5.13
In Movement	1,110	690	420	28.19
Mentally	306	145	161	7.77

HOSPET

Hospet C.D. Block lies in the western part of Bellary district. It is a part of Hospet taluka. The Block is located at a distance of 65 kms. from district headquarters (Bellary). There are 74 villages in the block with the total population of 153,184 persons. Area of the C.D. Block is 812.26 sq. kms. It is bounded by district Koppal on north, taluk Sandur on south, taluks Siruguppa and Bellary on east, district Koppal and taluk Hagaribommanahalli on west.

Communications:

Roadways : N.H-13: Direction- Koppal to Kudligi, Nearest Villages- Danapuram, Mariyammanahalli, Mariyammanahalli Thanda, Danayakanakere, Gollarahalli, Haravanahalli, Telugubalu, Chilakanahatti, Thimmalapura, Hosur, Jambunathanahalli. N.H-63: Direction- Bijapur to Bellary, Nearest Villages- Ingaligi, Vadrahalli, Papinayakanahalli, Byluvadigeri, Gundlavaddigeri, Kakubal, Dharmasagara, Kottiginahal, Gadiganur, Buvvanahalli, Gonahal. S.H-25: Direction- Kotturu to Mariyammanahalli, Nearest Villages- Mariyammanahalli, Nandibanda, Mariyammanahalli Thanda. S.H-29: Direction- Gangawati to Bellary, Nearest Villages- Muddapura No.10, Devasamudra, Metri, Devalapura.

Railway Station: Villages- Nagalapura, Byluvadigeri, Gundlavaddigeri, Gadiganur.

River: Tungabhadra Nadi- Nearest Villages- Hosakota, Hosur, Narasapura, Kalghatta, Danapur, Hampi, Nimbapura, Venkatapura, Bukkasagara, Belugoduhal, Arlihalli, Sanapura, Muddapura No.2, Ittigi, Ramasagara.

Canal: Nearest Villages- Nagenahalli, Venkatapura, Bukkasagara, Seetharama Tanda, Malapanagudi, Arlihalli, Muddapura No.10, Ramasagara, Kanvithimmalapura, Devasamudra, Jowku, Metri, Upparahalli, Devalapura, Jeeriganuru, Gonahal, Belugoduhal.

Reserved Forest: (Bandri R.F.): Nearest Villages- Haravanahalli, Basavanadurga, Byalakundi, Garga, Telugubalu. (Billakallu R.F.): Nearest Villages- Seetharama

Tanda, Ingaligi, Vadrahalli, Papinayakanahalli, Byluvadigeri, Gundlavaddigeri, Kakubal, Dharmasagara, Kottiginahal, Gadiganur, Buvvanahalli, Gonahal, Upparahalli, Devalapura. (Bukkasagara R.F.): Nearest Villages- Venkatapura, Bukkasagara, Ramasagara, Kanvithimmalapura, Metri. (Gunda R.F.): Nearest Villages- Danapuram, Nagalapura, Jambunathanahalli, Rajapura, Kallahalli. (Sivapura R.F.): Nearest Villages- Chilakanahatti, T.Basapura, Vantigodu, Thimmalapura.

Annual Rainfall: Normal Rianfall 649.84 mm.

Ground Water: Availability of the Ground Water in the Basin is (Information not avablable) H.A.M. and the utilization is (Information not avablable) H.A.M.
It belongs to (Information not avablable) category.
Depth to water level 5 to 20 meter below the ground.
Most of the wells go down in summer months, according to the Ground Water Estimation Committee.

Soils: Black and Red Sandy Soils.

Natural Division : It falls partly in Middle Tungabhadra Valley, Sandur Highlands, Kudligi Scrubby Uplands and Chikka Hagari Valley of the Central Karnataka Plateau.

Administration:

Division: Gulbarga. Parliamentary Constituency: 9 Bellary (ST). District: Bellary. Taluka: Hospet. Assembly Const ituency: 89 Hagaribommanahalli (SC), 90 Hospet, 91 Kampli (ST). Gram Panchayat: 23.

Regional Area Development Boards: The Hyderabad - Karnataka Area Development Board.

Villages: 74 **Inhabited:** 68 **Uninhabited:** 6

Ranking	District	State	National
Area	7	117	695
Population	6	129	1760
Sex Ratio	2	50	1623
Child Sex Ratio	2	46	2135
Literacy Rate	5	160	4980
Density	2	34	4896
Work Participation Rate	2	88	1112

Gram Panchayats:

Hosur , Nagenahalli, Malapanagudi, Hampi, Bukkasagara, Ramasagara, Muddapura No.10, Sanapura, Devasamudra, Hampadevanahalli, Sugginahalli, Devalapura, Metri, Gadiganur, Seetharama Tanda, Byluvadigeri, Papinayakanahalli, Kallahalli, Danapuram, Mariyammanahalli, Danayakanakere, Nagalapura, Chilakanahatti.

Amenities:

Education: Primary School in 46 villages, Middle school in 45 villages, Matriculation or Secondary School in 11 villages, namely Danapuram, Mariyammanahalli, Nagalapura, Telugubalu, Bukkasagara, Malapanagudi, Papinayakanahalli, Gadiganur, Ramasagara, Devasamudra, Chikkajaiganur.
Higher Secondary or Pre University Courses or Intermediate or Junior College in 4 villages of the CD Block,, namely Vyasanakeri, Danapuram, Mariyammanahalli, Mariyammanahalli Thanda.
College in 0 village, Adult Literacy Center in 2 villages.

Medical: Hospital in 0 village, Dispensary in 4 villages, Health Center in 5 villages, Sub Center in 21 villages, Maternity and Child Welfare Center in 1 village, Community health workers in 2 villages.
The Villages having Hospital or Dispensary or Health Center are Danapuram, Chilakanahatti, Kakubal, Devasamudra.

Drinking Water: Tap water in 48 villages, Tank water in 38 villages, Well water in 37 villages, Tubewell in 64 villages and more than one source in 68 villages.

Bank: Banking facility in 9 villages, namely, Danapuram, Mariyammanahalli, Kaddirampura, Hampi Dharmasagara, Gadiganur, Ramasagara, Metri Devalapura.
Credit Society in 8 villages Agricultural Credit Society in 8 Non-Agricultural Credit Society in 2 villages.

Others: Power supply in 68 villages, Cinema hall in 1 village, sport club in 68 villages, Stadium or Auditorium or Community Hall in 68 villages, Post Office in 2 villages.
There are 56 villages having bus facilities.

Villages with most of facilities: Danapuram Mariyammanahalli, Hampi, Gadiganur, Ramasagara Metri, Devalapura.

Villages without amenities (Education):
T.Basapura, Hosur, Kallirampura, Narasapura, Belagodu, Gudioblapura, Rajapura, Kalghatta, Singanathanahalli, Krishnapura, Venkatapura, Gundlavaddigeri, Kottiginahal, Buvvanahalli, Belugoduhal, Arlihalli, Hirejaiganur, Hampadevanahalli, Upparahalli, Jeeriganuru, Gonahal, Sankalapuram..

Scheduled Castes: Out of the total population of 153499 persons, 40360 persons (26.29%) belong to Scheduled Castes.
The villages having less than 10% SC population are Telugubalu, Hosur, Kallirampura, Belagodu, Rajapura Singanathanahalli, Krishnapura, Ingaligi, Kakubal Gadiganur, Kanvithimmalapura, Upparahalli Jeeriganuru, Sankalapuram.
The villages having more than 50% SC population are Mariyammanahalli Thanda, T.Basapura, Kallahalli Danapura, Seetharama Tanda, Vadrahalli, Arlihalli.
Sex ratio of Scheduled Caste population is 498.

Scheduled Castes Literates and Illiterates by Sex:

	Persons	Males	Females
Literate	11,475	7,854	3,621
Illiterate	28,885	12,422	16,463
Literacy rate	35.3	48.4	22.2
Graduate	168	150	18

Scheduled Castes (Dominant):

Madiga, Banjara etc., Bhovi, Adi Karnataka Chalavadi etc.

For their cultural identity please see Appendix-I

Villages without Scheduled Castes: There are 10 villages without any scheduled caste population.

Scheduled Tribes: Out of the total population of 153499 persons, 30242 persons (19.7%) belong to Scheduled Tribes. The villages having less than 10% ST population are Venkatapura, Nandibanda, Mariyammanahalli Thanda T.Basapura, Kalghatta, Danapura, Singanathanahalli Krishnapura, Bukkasagara, Vadrahalli Gundlavaddigeri, Belugoduhal, Arlihalli, Sanapura Ittigi, Muddapura No.10, Ramasagara, Metri Jeeriganuru, Gonahal, Sankalapuram.

The villages having more than 50% ST population are Chilakanahatti, Hosur, Kallirampura, Narasapura Belagodu, Upparahalli.

Sex ratio of Scheduled tribe population is 501.

Scheduled Tribes Literates and Illiterates by Sex:

	Persons	Males	Females
Literate	9,286	5,921	3,365
Illiterate	20,956	9,171	11,785
Literacy rate	37.4	48.0	27.0
Graduate	175	144	31

Scheduled Tribes (Dominant):

Naikda etc., Hakkipikki, Meda, Kathodi etc. Generic Tribes etc.

For their cultural identity please see Appendix-II

Villages without Scheduled Tribes: There are 10 villages without any scheduled tribe population.

Literates and Illiterates by Sex (Total Population):

	Persons	Males	Females
Literate	59,871	38,013	21,858
Illiterate	93,628	39,164	54,464
Literacy rate	47	59	34
Graduate	1,699	1,359	340

Agriculture: ***Distribution of villages according to land use:*** Out of 74 villages, Total area (in hectare) is 81226, out of that 51.08 percent is cultivable and 43.78 percent of the cultivable area is irrigated.

Sources of Irrigation (Hectares): Government Canal 12150.96, Private Canal 0, Well without Electricity 107.04, Well with Electricity 1498.11, Tubewell without Electricity 48.58, Tubewell with Electricity 1710.04, Tank 1319.62, River 397.49, Lake 40.39, Waterfall 141.63, Others 749.

Villages with population of 5000 to 9999:

Danapuram, Malapanagudi, Ramasagara, Devasamudra.

Villages with population of 10000 and above:

Mariyammanahalli.

Distribution of Workers:

	Persons	Males	Females	WPR
Cultivators	21,228	14,501	6,727	26.67
Agricultural Labour	42,122	18,178	23,944	52.92
Household Industry	2,044	951	1,093	2.57
Other Workers	14,208	9,953	4,255	17.85
Main Workers	69,631	40,773	28,858	87.47
Marginal Workers	9,971	2,810	7,161	12.53
Total Workers	79,602	43,583	36,019	

Religion: Major Religious Communities:

	Persons	Males	Females	Sex Ratio
Hindu (91.26%)	140,078	70,384	69,694	990
Muslim (7.88%)	12,098	6,152	5,946	967
Christian (0.3%)	462	220	242	1,100
Sikh (0.01%)	11	10	1	100
Buddhists (0%)	3	3	-	-
Jain (0.08%)	120	60	60	1,000

Agewise Data:

	Persons	Males	Females	Sex Ratio
All ages	153,499	77,177	76,322	989
0-14	60,111	30,607	29,504	964
15-44	68,836	34,903	33,933	972
45-79	23,494	11,246	12,248	1089
80+	924	343	581	1694
Age not stated	134	78	56	718

Languages (Dominant):

Kannada, Telugu, Urdu, Hindi, Tamil

Disabled Population:

	Persons	Males	Females	%
Total Disabled	3,291	1,823	1,468	
In Seeing	1,734	906	828	52.69
In Speech	242	130	112	7.35
In Hearing	178	89	89	5.41
In Movement	915	574	341	27.8
Mentally	222	124	98	6.75

HUBLI

Hubli C.D. Block lies in the central part of Dharwad district. It is a part of Hubli taluka. The Block is located at a distance of 15 kms. from district headquarters (Dharwad). There are 58 villages in the block with the total population of 128,315 persons. Area of the C.D. Block is 629.45 sq. kms. It is bounded by taluks Dharwad and Navalgund on north, district Haveri, taluks Kalghatgi and Kundgol on south, taluks Navalgund and Kundgol, dist. Gadag on east, taluks Dharwad and Kalghatgi on west.

Communications:

Roadways : N.H-4: Direction- Dharwad to Bangalore, NearestVillages- Gabbur, Budarsingi, Kotgondhunshi, Adargunchi,Murarhalli, Nulvi, Sherewad, Pale, Chebbi, Warur, Palikop, Tirumalkoppa, Agadi. N.H-63: Direction- Kalghatgi to Gadag, Nearest Villages- Bommapur, Kusugal, Bhandiwad,Mantur, Shirguppi, Gangiwal, Anchatgeri. N.H-218: Direction- Hubli-Dharwad to Bijapur, Nearest Villages- Bengeri,Nagashettikop, Byahatti, Kirasur, Kusugal. S.H-28:Direction- Dharwad to Hebsur, Nearest Vill.- Sulla, Byahatti, Hebsur, Kirasur.

River: Bedti Nadi- Nearest Villages- Gabbur, Mavanur, Katnur, Channapur, Ramapur, Inam-Veerapur, Giriyal, Belegali, Karadikop, Kurdikeri.

Raliway Station: Villages- Kirasur, Kusugal.

Reserved Forest: Nearest Villages- A.Timmasagar, Kirasur, Devargudihal, Parasapur, Anchatgeri, Mavanur, Katnur, Channapur, Inam-Veerapur.

Annual Rainfall: Normal Rianfall 772 mm.

Ground Water: Availability of the Ground Water in the Basin is 4536.887 H.A.M. and the utilization is 1552. 674 H.A.M.. It belongs to Over Exploited category. Depth to water level 5 to 20 meter below the ground. Most of the wells go down in summer months, according to the Ground Water Estimation Committee.

Soils: Loamy and Kankary Soils.

Natural Division : It falls in the Dharwad-Gadag Plateau of the Central Karnataka Plateau.

Administration:

Division: Belgaum. Parliamentary Constituency: 11 Dharwad. District: Dharwad. Taluka: Hubli. Assembly Constituency: 69 Navalgund, 70 Kundgol. Gram Panchayat: 19.

Regional Area Development Boards: The Bailu Seeme Area Development Board.

Villages: 58 **Inhabited:** 51 **Uninhabited:** 7

Ranking	District	State	National
Area	5	147	1089
Population	4	146	2570
Sex Ratio	4	157	3742
Child Sex Ratio	4	129	3726
Literacy Rate	3	72	2249
Density	3	45	4678
Work Participation Rate	2	74	1395

Gram Panchayats:

Sulla, Byahatti, Hebsur, Ingalhalli, Kusugal, Rayanal , Anchatgeri, Katnur, Adargunchi, Halyal, Mantur, Shirguppi, Koliwad, Nulvi, Belegali, Karadikop, Warur, Chebbi, B.Aralikatti.

Amenities:

Education: Primary School in 33 villages, Middle school in 34 villages, Matriculation or Secondary School in 21 villages, namely Gopankop, Bengeri, Tarihal, Gokul, Bommapur, Sulla, Byahatti, Hebsur, Kirasur, Kusugal, Ingalhalli, Bhandiwad, Halyal, Shirguppi, Koliwad, Rayanal, Katnur, Nulvi, B.Aralikatti, Warur, Tirumalkoppa.

Higher Secondary or Pre University Courses or Intermediate or Junior College in 5 villages of the CD Block,, namely Gopankop, Hebsur, Rayanal, Nulvi, B.Aralikatti.

College in 0 village, Adult Literacy Center in 1 village.

Medical: Hospital in 3 villages, Dispensary in 15 villages, Health Center in 6 villages, Sub Center in 5 villages, Maternity and Child Welfare Center in 2 villages, Community health workers in 2 villages.

The Villages having Hospital or Dispensary or Health Center are Bommapur, Byahatti, Hebsur, Kirasur, Ingalhalli, Bhandiwad, Mantur, Nagarhalli, Shirguppi, Anchatgeri, Adargunchi, Nulvi, B.Aralikatti, Warur, Agadi.

Drinking Water: Tap water in 41 villages, Tank water in 11 villages, Well water in 8 villages, Tubewell in 8 villages and more than one source in 30 villages.

Bank: Banking facility in 13 villages, namely, Bengeri, Byahatti, Hebsur, Kirasur, Kusugal Ingalhalli, Bhandiwad, Halyal, Shirguppi, Koliwad Nulvi, B.Aralikatti, Warur.

Credit Society in 24 villages Agricultural Credit Society in 23 Non-Agricultural Credit Society in 5 villages.

Others: Power supply in 50 villages, Cinema hall in 1 village, sport club in 3 villages, Stadium or Auditorium or Community Hall in 0 village, Post Office in 4 villages.

There are 49 villages having bus facilities.

Villages with most of facilities: Bengeri Byahatti, Hebsur, Kusugal, Ingalhalli, Bhandiwad Shirguppi, Koliwad, B.Aralikatti, Warur.

Villages without amenities (Education): Parasapur, Gangiwal, Mavanur, Budarsingi, Kotgondhunshi, Murarhalli, Channapur, Chavargudd, Ramapur, Giriyal, Kamplikop..

Scheduled Castes: Out of the total population of 128380 persons, 9097 persons (7.09%) belong to Scheduled Castes. The villages having less than 10% SC population are Gopankop, Bengeri, Tarihal, Gokul, Bommapur, Sulla Byahatti, Hebsur, Kirasur, Kusugal, Ingalhalli Bhandiwad, Mantur, Halyal, Nagarhalli, Shirguppi Umachigi, Koliwad, Malligwad, Devargudihal Parasapur, Rayanal, Gangiwal, Kotgondhunshi Adargunchi, Murarhalli, Katnur, Ramapur, Belegali Nulvi, Sherewad, Pale, Bommasamudra, Karadikop Kamplikop, B.Aralikatti, Palikop, Agadi.

The village having more than 50% SC population is None.

Sex ratio of Scheduled Caste population is 497.

Scheduled Castes Literates and Illiterates by Sex:

	Persons	Males	Females
Literate	3,421	2,260	1,161
Illiterate	5,676	2,318	3,358
Literacy rate	45.5	59.9	31.0
Graduate	61	53	8

Scheduled Castes (Dominant):

Bhambi etc., Chalavadi etc., Bhovi, Madiga Chenna Dasar etc.

For their cultural identity please see Appendix-I

Villages without Scheduled Castes: There are 12 villages without any scheduled caste population.

Scheduled Tribes: Out of the total population of 128380 persons, 6184 persons (4.82%) belong to Scheduled Tribes. The villages having less than 10% ST population are Gopankop, Bengeri, Tarihal, Gokul, Bommapur, Sulla Byahatti, Hebsur, Kirasur, Kusugal, Ingalhalli Bhandiwad, Mantur, Halyal, Nagarhalli, Shirguppi Umachigi, Rayanal, Gangiwal, Anchatgeri, Mavanur Budarsingi, Adargunchi, Murarhalli, Katnur Channapur, Chavargudd, Ramapur, Giriyal, Belegali Nulvi, Sherewad, Pale, Bommasamudra, Karadikop Chebbi, B.Aralikatti, Palikop, Tirumalkoppa, Agadi.

The villages having more than 50% ST population are None.

Sex ratio of Scheduled tribe population is 479.

Scheduled Tribes Literates and Illiterates by Sex:

	Persons	Males	Females
Literate	2,493	1,625	868
illiterate	3,691	1,594	2,097
Literacy rate	47.4	59.4	34.4
Graduate	55	46	9

Scheduled Tribes (Dominant):

Naikda etc., Pardhi etc., Kadu Kuruba, Meda Jenu Kuruba

For their cultural identity please see Appendix-II

Villages without Scheduled Tribes: There are 14 villages without any scheduled tribe population.

Literates and Illiterates by Sex (Total Population):

	Persons	Males	Females
Literate	69,364	42,681	26,683
Illiterate	59,016	23,319	35,697
Literacy rate	63	76	50
Graduate	1,886	1,593	293

Agriculture: ***Distribution of villages according to land use:***

Out of 58 villages, Total area (in hectare) is 62945, out of that 77.98 percent is cultivable and 7.33 percent of the cultivable area is irrigated.

Sources of Irrigation (Hectares): Government Canal 2675.89, Private Canal 0, Well without Electricity 0, Well with Electricity 43.32, Tubewell without Electricity 8.13, Tubewell with Electricity 637.58, Tank 40.1, River 0, Lake 0, Waterfall 0, Others 192.85.

Villages with population of 5000 to 9999:

Sulla, Hebsur, Kusugal, Adargunchi, Nulvi.

Villages with population of 10000 and above:

Byahatti.

Distribution of Workers:

	Persons	Males	Females	WPR
Cultivators	25,279	17,516	7,763	37.7
Agricultural Labour	26,865	10,127	16,738	40.07
Household Industry	1,314	853	461	1.96
Other Workers	13,592	11,519	2,073	20.27
Main Workers	53,810	36,956	16,854	80.25
Marginal Workers	13,240	3,059	10,181	19.75
Total Workers	67,050	40,015	27,035	

Religion: Major Religious Communities:

	Persons	Males	Females	Sex Ratio
Hindu (82.29%)	105,641	54,207	51,434	949
Muslim (15.42%)	19,796	10,210	9,586	939
Christian (0.07%)	96	53	43	811
Sikh (0.02%)	24	14	10	714
Buddhists (0.13%)	169	97	72	742
Jain (1.67%)	2,140	1,150	990	861

Agewise Data:

	Persons	Males	Females	Sex Ratio
All ages	128,380	66,000	62,380	945
0-14	41,116	21,019	20,097	956
15-44	62,245	32,428	29,817	919
45-79	23,843	12,027	11,816	982
80+	1,127	502	625	1245
Age not stated	49	24	25	1042

Languages (Dominant):

Kannada, Urdu, Marathi, Telugu, Coorgi/Kodagu

Disabled Population:

	Persons	Males	Females	%
Total Disabled	2,049	1,163	886	
In Seeing	646	350	296	31.53
In Speech	215	123	92	10.49
In Hearing	146	66	80	7.13
In Movement	798	482	316	38.95
Mentally	244	142	102	11.91

HUKERI

Hukeri C.D. Block lies in the west-central part of Belgaum district. It is a part of Hukeri taluka. The Block is located at a distance of 50 kms. from district headquarters (Belgaum). There are 123 villages in the block with the total population of 304,710 persons. Area of the C.D. Block is 942.84 sq. kms. It is bounded by taluk Chikodi on north, taluk Belgaum on south, taluk Gokak on east, and it has Common Boundary with the state of Maharashtra on South and west.

Communications:

Roadways : N.H-4: Direction- Poona to Belgaukm, Nearest Villages- Shippur, Hittani, Honnihalli, Kanagale, Sollapur, Bad, Alur (K.M), Akkiwat, Sankeshwar (R), Gotur, Hebbal, Chikalgud, U Khanapur, Hanchinal, Thanahattargi, Dadabanahatti, Mangutti, Benakanholi, Biranholi. S.H-12: Direction- Sankeshwar to Chikodi, Nearest Villages- Borgal, Amminbhavi, Ammanagi, Nidasoshi, Kamatanur.

Railway Station: Villages- Yallapur, Karguppi.

River: Ghatprabha Nadi- Nearest Villages- Shirdhan, Zangatihal, Gudas, Kotabagi, Awargol, Noginhal, Sultanpur, Ingali, Hidkal, Hospet, Naganur K.D. , Aldhal, Bidrewadi, Shettihalli, Salamwadi, Khavanewadi, Modage, Daddi, Ramewadi, Wantmuri. Markandeya Nadi- Pachapur, Gumchinmardi, Mavanur.

Reserved Forest: Nearest Villages- Yarnal, Chilbhavi, Aralikatti,Shindihatti, Naganur K.M., Naganur K.D., Aldhal, Biranholi, Islampur, Shahabandar, Chikkaladinni, Gutagudi, Gejapati, Rajakatti, Shirur, Hagedal, Basapur, Wantmuri, Yallapur, Karguppi, Bannibagi, Bagarnal, Rustumpur.

Annual Rainfall: Normal Rianfall 658.4 mm.

Ground Water: Availability of the Ground Water in the Basin is 17331 H.A.M. and the utilization is 13257 H. A.M. It belongs to Safe category. Depth to water level 5 to 20 meter below the ground. Most of the wells go down in summer months, according to the Ground Water Estimation Committee.

Soil: Red Soil, Black Soil.

Natural Division : It falls in the Krishna Ghatprabha rrigated Tract of the Northern Karnataka Plateau.

Administration:

Division: Belgaum. Parliamentary Constituency: 1 Chikodi. District: Belgaum. Taluka: Hukeri. Assembly Constituenc y: 7 Hukeri, 10 Yemkanmardi (ST). Gram Panchayat: 51.

Regional Area Development Boards: The Maland Aera Development Board.

Border Villages: (State: Maharashtra)- Rashing, Bugate-alur, Hadalga, Bhairapur, Shekinhosur, Konankeri, Sollapur, Sankeshwar (R), Gotur, Hebbal, Chikalgud, U Khanapur, Thanahattargi, Dadabanahatti, Mangutti, Bolasyanahatti, Naganur K.M., Naganur K.D., Aldhal, Bidrewadi, Attihal, Kot,Bellanki, Dhondagatti, Shettihalli, Modage, Ramewadi.

Fairs: Gajalingeshwara Jatra: It is held at Ghodgeri near Belgaum in about the month of February every year. Ghodgeri, 22 kms. from Hukeri is very near the Gokak Rd . railway station and is a place of considerable antiquity. The place has temples dedicated to Ramalinga, Niravanappa, Gajalingeshwara, Neelakantheshwara, Lakshmi and Maruti. The Ramalingeshwara temple in later Chaluky an style has a garbhagriha (star shaped), shukanasa and a navaranga.

Lakshmi Jatra: It is held at Hattargi in about the month of February once in three years. Hattargi 12 kms. From Hukeri on the Pune-Bangalore highway has temples dedicated to Shikhareshwara, Kalmeshwara, Lakshmi, Parameshwara, Hanumanta, Brahmadeva and Siddheshwara. The Shikhareshwara temple is a beautiful later Chalukyan monument and has a trikutachala but only two garbhagrihas remainand the one to the left of the central garbhagriha is totally fallen. The garbhagriha has a rekhanagara shikhara, the only shikhara of the kind in the district. The main garbhagriha has a Shivalinga and the other one is empty.

Lakshmi Temple Jatra: It is held at Ullagaddi Khanapur near Belgaum. Ullagaddi Khanapur, ten kilometres from Sankeshwar, located on the national highway, is named to differentiate it from Khanapur. The place has temples dedicated to Hanumanta, Lakshmi, Ishwara, Basaveshwara and Yellamma. The Hanumanta temple has a Nishidi stone, engraved with inscription and another inscription slab is built into the wall of the same temple (both unpublished). The Lakshmi temple is a big structure recently built. Beside the garbhagriha is a broken image of Lakshmi in Chalukyan style. The jatra in honour of the Goddess is held annually in which about 20,000 people assemble. There is a Mahaveera basti (recent). The place has a Siddhadevara Matha. In the outskirts of the village amidst fields in a well are found broken antiquities like images of Surya, Vishnu, a hero-stone and a Linga.

Madarsab Bavasaburs: It is held at Ammangi every year. Ammangi 10 kilometres from Hukeri is a place of conside rable antiquiting. The place has the mosque and a dargah ascribed to Madarsab Bavasab and the Urs is held annually when about 5,000 people assemble.

Shankaralinga Jatra: It is held at Sankeshwar near Belgaum around the month of February for 5 days every year. Sankeshwar 12 kms. from Hukeri and situated on the bank of the Hiranyakeshi on the Bangalore-Pune Highway is a place with considerable antiquity. Traditional accounts call the place as Sankyeshwara's. There are two Ratta inscriptions at the place dated 1199 and 1202 of Kartaveeryta IV and Mallikarjuna. The place has temples dedicated to Shankaralinga, Narayana, Lakshmi, Maruti, Vithoba, Banashankari, Beerappa, Basavanna and Dattatreya. The Shankaralinga temple on the bank of the Hiranyakeshi is a complex structure with a garbhagriha (star-shaped). an ardhamantapa, a navaranga and a mukhamantapa.

Siddeshwara Jatra: It is held at Hattargi near Belgaum around the month of March for three days. Hattargi 12 kms. from Hukeri on the Pune-Bangalore highway has temples dedicated to Shikareshwara, Kalmeshwara, Lakshmi, Parameshwara, Hanumata, Brahmadeva and Siddeshwara. The Shikhareshwara temple is a beautiful later Chalukyan monument and has a trikutachata but only two garbhagriha remain and the one to the left of the central garbhagriha is totally fallen. The garbhagriha has a rekhanagara shikhara, the only shikhara of the kind in the district. The main garbhagriha has a Shivalinga and the other one is empty. The Kalmeshwara temple is another later Chalukyan monument with a garbhagriha, ardhamantapa, and a navaranga (with no ceiling).

Veerabhadra Jatra: It is held at Hattargi near Belgaum around the month of March-April every year. Hattargi 12 kms.from Hukeri on the Pune-Bangalore highway has temples dedicated to Shikhareshwara, Kalmeshwara, Lakshmi, Parameshwara, Hanumanta, Brahmadeya and Siddheshwara. The Shikhareshwara temple is a beautiful later Chalukyan monument and has a trikutachala but only two garbhagri has remain and the one to the left of the central garbhagriha is totally fallen.

Villages: 123 **Inhabited:** 123 **Uninhabited:** 0

Ranking	District	State	National
Area	9	94	488
Population	7	16	64
Sex Ratio	5	96	2500
Child Sex Ratio	6	160	4467
Literacy Rate	5	89	2829
Density	6	105	3325
Work Participation Rate	4	19	2416

Gram Panchayats:

Bugatealur, Mattiwade, Hittani, Kanagale, Bad, Kesti, Borgal, Nidasoshi, Ankale, Haragapur, Konankeri, Sollapur, Gotur, Kamatanur, Ammanagi, Yadgud, Yalimunoli, Nerli, Hebbal, Kochari, Bastawad, Beniwad, Madihalli, Hulloli. Bellambi, Sarapur, Bagewadi, Gudas, Kotabagi, Sultanpur, Hosur, Badkundri, Kurni, Hanchinal, U Khanapur, Thanahattargi, Yemakanmardi, Mangutti, Naganur K.D. , Daddi, Kot, Salamwadi, Islampur, Shahabandar, Basapur, Karguppi, Rustumpur, Pachapur, Hospet, Ghodageri, Mavanur.

Amenities:

Education: Primary School in 120 villages, Middle school in 100 villages, Matriculation or Secondary School in 36 villages, namely Mattiwade, Naganur K.S., Kanagale, Sollapur, Bad, Kesti, Nidasoshi, Nerli, Hebbal, Kochari, U Khanapur, Kurni, Yadgud, Bellambi, Bagewadi, Shirdhan, Gudas, Yalimunoli, Shiragaon, Awargol, Sultanpur, Yargatti, Hospet, Ghodageri, Thanahattargi, Yemakanmardi, Mangutti, Naganur K.M., Kot, Salamwadi, Modage, Daddi, Islampur, Basapur, Pachapur, Mavanur.

Higher Secondary or Pre University Courses or Intermediate or Junior College in 10 villages of the CD Block,, namely Hebbal, Kurni, Yadgud, Bagewadi, Hidkal, Hospet, Ghodageri, Thanahattargi, Yemakanmardi, Pachapur.

College in 2 villages, Adult Literacy Center in 10 villages., Colleges are in villages, namely Hebbal, Yemakanmardi.

Medical: Hospital in 0 village, Dispensary in 3 villages, Health Center in 13 villages, Sub Center in 51 villages, Maternity and Child Welfare Center in 2 villages, Community health workers in 60 villages.

The Villages having Hospital or Dispensary or Health Center are Hebbal, Hospet, Thanahattargi.

Drinking Water: Tap water in 72 villages, Tank water in 6 villages, Well water in 76 villages, Tubewell in 84 villages and more than one source in 120 villages.

Bank: Banking facility in 25 villages, namely, Honnihalli, Kanagale, Karajage, Haragapur, Bad Alur (K.M), Kesti, Amminbhavi, Ammanagi, Nidasoshi Ankale, Hebbal, U Khanapur, Bellambi, Bagewadi Gudas, Hukkeri (Rural), Hidkal, Hospet Thanahattargi, Yemakanmardi, Dadabanahatti, Daddi Basapur, Pachapur.

Credit Society in 57 villages Agricultural Credit Society in 52 Non-Agricultural Credit Society in 4 villages.

Others: Power supply in 123 villages, Cinema hall in 5 villages sport club in 0 village, Stadium or Auditorium or Community Hall in 0 village, Post Office in 63 villages.

There are 119 villages having bus facilities.

Villages with most of facilities: Honnihalli Kanagale, Karajage, Haragapur, Bad, Alur (K.M) Kesti, Amminbhavi, Ammanagi, Nidasoshi, Ankale Hebbal, U Khanapur, Bellambi, Bagewadi, Gudas Hospet, Thanahattargi, Yemakanmardi, Dadabanahatti Daddi, Basapur, Pachapur.

Villages without amenities (Education):

Sankeshwar (R), Jabapur (R), Hukkeri (Rural)..

Scheduled Castes: Out of the total population of 304765 persons, 41040 persons (13.47%) belong to Scheduled Castes. The villages having less than 10% SC population are Mattiwade, Rashing, Bugatealur, Bhairapur Honnihalli, Akkiwat, Sankeshwar (R), Masarguppi U Khanapur, Kurniwadi, Shirhatti (Kh), Hulloli Hanjanatti, Jabapur (R), Hukkeri (Rural), Bastawad

Chilbhavi, Aralikatti, Ankalgudiketra, Yemakanmardi
Jinaral, Gudaganahatti, Mastiholi, Dadabanahatti
Benakanholi, Bolasyanahatti, Aldhal, Bidrewadi
Attihal, Kot, Dhondagatti, Salamwadi, Khavanewadi
Modage, Ramewadi, Biranholi, Islampur, Shahabandar
Chikkaladinni, Gutaguddi, Gejapati, Rajakatti
Hagedal, Basapur, Wantmuri, Yallapur, Karguppi
Bannibagi, Bagarnal, Rustumpur, Pachapur, Mavanur.

The village having more than 50% SC population is None.

Sex ratio of Scheduled Caste population is 497.

Scheduled Castes Literates and Illiterates by Sex:

	Persons	Males	Females
Literate	19,014	12,044	6,970
Illiterate	22,026	8,614	13,412
Literacy rate	54.3	68.5	40.0
Graduate	652	579	73

Scheduled Castes (Dominant):

Holaya etc., Bhambi etc., Mahar etc., Holar etc. Samagara

For their cultural identity please see Appendix-I

Villages without Scheduled Castes: There are 8 villages without any scheduled caste population.

Scheduled Tribes: Out of the total population of 304765 persons, 37950 persons (12.45%) belong to Scheduled Tribes.

The villages having less than 10% ST population are Shippur, Hittani, Mattiwade, Naganur K.S., Rashing Bugatealur, Hadalga, Bhairapur, Kanagale, Karajage Sollapur, Haragapur, Bad, Alur (K.M), Akkiwat, Kesti Borgal, Amminbhavi, Handigud, Ammanagi, Nidasoshi Ankale, Sankeshwar (R), Kamatanur, Nerli, Masarguppi Gavanal, Hebbal, Kochari, Chikalgud, Kurniwadi Arjunwad, Yadgud, Shelapur, Bellambi, Shirhatti (Bk) Sarapur, Shirhatti (Kh), Bagewadi, Kadhatti Shirdhan, Zangatihal, Gudas, Kotabagi, Hulloli Hullolihatti, Hanjanatti, Yalimunoli, Jabapur (R) Hukkeri (Rural), Madihalli, Raxi, Shiragaon, Awargol Noginhal, Sultanpur, Beniwad, Madamakkanal, Bastawad Hosur, Ingali, Hidkal, Hospet, Shindihatti Hattialur, Nadigudiketra, Ankalgudiketra, Ghodageri Yemakanmardi, Gudaganahatti, Dhondagatti Shettihalli, Salamwadi, Khavanewadi, Modage, Daddi Ramewadi, Basapur.

The villages having more than 50% ST population are Chilbhavi, Aralikatti, Jinaral, Dadabanahatti Benakanholi, Bolasyanahatti, Aldhal, Bidrewadi Biranholi, Chikkaladinni, Gutaguddi, Gejapati Rajakatti, Hagedal, Wantmuri, Bannibagi, Rustumpur.

Sex ratio of Scheduled tribe population is 497.

Scheduled Tribes Literates and Illiterates by Sex:

	Persons	Males	Females
Literate	12,585	8,590	3,995
Illiterate	25,365	10,489	14,876
Literacy rate	39.8	54.0	25.5
Graduate	168	150	18

Scheduled Tribes (Dominant):

Naikda etc., Koli Dhor etc., Kadu Kuruba, Meda Bhil etc.

For their cultural identity please see Appendix-II

Villages without Scheduled Tribes: There are 35 villages without any scheduled tribe population.

Literates and Illiterates by Sex (Total Population):

	Persons	Males	Females
Literate	155,081	95,524	59,557
Illiterate	149,684	59,180	90,504
Literacy rate	60	73	46
Graduate	4,980	4,197	783

Agriculture: ***Distribution of villages according to land use:*** Out of 123 villages, Total area (in hectare) is 94284, out of that 69.29 percent is cultivable and 24.95 percent of the cultivable area is irrigated.

Sources of Irrigation (Hectares): Government Canal 2582.79, Private Canal 0, Well without Electricity 179.08, Well with Electricity 6842.27, Tubewell without Electricity 21.82, Tubewell with Electricity 2931.59, Tank 22.66, River 3630.03, Lake 0, Waterfall 0, Others 85.6.

Villages with population of 5000 to 9999: Kanagale, Sollapur, Ammanagi, Nidasoshi, Hebbal U Khanapur, Kurni, Bagewadi, Yalimunoli Thanahattargi, Yemakanmardi, Mangutti, Pachapur.

Villages with population of 10000 and above: None

Distribution of Workers:

	Persons	Males	Females	WPR
Cultivators	66,921	43,642	23,279	45.53
Agricultural Labour	49,993	21,119	28,874	34.01
Household Industry	4,514	2,752	1,762	3.07
Other Workers	25,561	20,530	5,031	17.39
Main Workers	120,718	81,785	38,933	82.13
Marginal Workers	26,271	6,258	20,013	17.87
Total Workers	146,989	88,043	58,946	

Religion: Major Religious Communities:

	Persons	Males	Females	Sex Ratio
Hindu (87.67%)	267,194	135,534	131,660	971
Muslim (7.75%)	23,620	11,954	11,666	976
Christian (0.07%)	219	114	105	921
Sikh (0%)	4	4	-	-
Buddhists (0.13%)	399	210	189	900
Jain (4.06%)	12,368	6,388	5,980	936

Agewise Data:

	Persons	Males	Females	Sex Ratio

All ages	304,765	154,704	150,061	970
0-14	99,843	51,771	48,072	929
15-44	139,178	70,796	68,382	966
45-79	62,276	30,601	31,675	1035
80+	3,308	1,443	1,865	1292
Age not stated	160	93	67	720

Languages (Dominant):
Kannada, Marathi, Urdu, Telugu, Hindi

Disabled Population:

	Persons	Males	Females	%
Total Disabled	4,253	2,347	1,906	
In Seeing	1,232	594	638	28.97
In Speech	515	265	250	12.11
In Hearing	311	156	155	7.31
In Movement	1,644	1,035	609	38.66
Mentally	551	297	254	12.96

HUNGUND

Hungund CD.Block lies in the south-eastern part of Bagalkot district. It is a part of Hungund taluka. The Block is located at a distance of 48 kms. from district H.Q. (Bagalkot). There are 71 villages in the block with the total population of 217,082 persons. Area of the C.D. Block is 1337.46 sq. kms. It is bounded by taluk Bagalkot and district Bijapur on north, districts Koppal and Raichur on south, district Raichur on east, taluks Badami and Bagalkot on west.

Communications:

Roadways : N.H-13: Direction- Bijapur to Chitradurga, Nearest Vill.- Huvanur, Kengalkadapatti, Belgal, Timmapur, Hungund (Rural), Amarawati, Chinnapur (S.T.), Herur, Tondihal, Gudur (S.B.), Hanamanal, Gonal (S.B.), Hirekodagali, Gugalmari. S.H-6: Direction- Hanamasagar to Ilkal, Nearest Vill.- Hireupnal, Balakundi, Ishwarnagar. S.H-6A: Direction- Kushtagi to Hanamanal, Nearest Vill.- Gudur (S.B.), Hanamanal, Gonal (S.B.), Chickkodagali, Hirekodagali. S.H-14: Direction- Badami to Hirebadawadgi, Nearest Villages- Bhimanagad, Chikanal, Gudur, Vadageri, Ilal, Nagur, Yadahalli, Chittawadgi, Bannihatti, Hirebadawadgi, Hungund (Rural). S.H-20: Direction- Bagalkot to Lingsugur, Nearest Villages- Kamatgi, Hiremagi, Ramathal, Aminagad, Rakkasagi, Bevinamatti, Hireyaranakeri, Chickyaranakeri, Hirebadawadgi, Amarawati, Nandavadgi, Hireadapur, Hiresinganagutti, Tumba, Kesarabhavi, Chinnapur (S.T.), Chicksinganagutti. S.H-41A: Direction- Hungund to Muddebihal, Nearest Villages- Hungund (Rural), Dhannur, Ramawadgi.

River: Malprabha Nadi- Nearest Villages- Kamatgi, Suralikal, Basawanal, Muganur, Budihal (S.K.), Budihal (Inam), Bevinal, Hiremagi, Madapur, Ramathal, Huvinahalli, Mullur, Kalligudda, Nimbalgundi, Aiahole, Chilapur, Benakanavari, Siddanakolla, Chickmagi, Khairwadgi, Papathanal, Hiremalagavi, Chickmalagavi, Ganjihal, Nandanoor, Huvanur, Varagodadinni, Kengalkadapatti, Sangam, Khajagal, Bisanalkoppa, Belgal, Medinapur, Hadagali, Kamadatta, Adihal. Krishna Nadi- Nearest Villages- Katagur, Turadagi, Bisaladinni, Valakaladinni, Chowdakamaladinni, Sangam, Adihal, Yemmihatti, Dhannur, Hullalli, Koppa (S.M.), Marol, Havaragi, Koujaganur, Anapakatti, Iddalgi, Indawar, Islampur.

Reserved Forest: Nearest Villages- Kamatgi, Basarikatti, Kadiwal, Kallapur, Hiremagi, Madapur, Ramathal, Huvinahalli, Mullur, Aiahole, Aminagad, Rakkasagi, Gorjnal, Tallikeri, Kelur, Chilapur, Benakanavari, Ilal, Siddanakolla, Upnal (S.C.), Bhimanagad, Chikanal, Gudur, Muradi, Gandal, Dammur,Vadageri, Huliginal, Kalagonal.

Annual Rainfall: Normal Rianfall 591.24 mm.

Ground Water: Availability of the Ground Water in the Basin is (Information not avablable) HAM and the utilization is (Information not avablable) H.A.M. It belongs to (Information not avablable) category. Depth to water level 5 to 20 meter below the ground.Most of the wells go down in summer months, according to the Ground Water Estimation Committee.

Soils: Black and Red Soils.

Natural Division : It falls partly in the Upper Krishna Valley and the Badami Hills of the Northern Karnataka Plateau.

Administration:

Division: Belgaum. Parliamentary Constituency: 3 Bagalkot. District: Bagalkot. Taluka: Hungund. Assembly Const.: 24 Bagalkot, 25 Hungund. Gram Panchayat: 30.

Regional Area Development Boards: The Bailu Seeme Area Development Board.

Fairs: Mahanataswami Fair: It is a centre of the weaving and dyeing industries in the district, specially famous for its sarees. There are three temples, one of Banashankari, another of Basavanna and the third of Vyankonda. The first two temples are modern in the open style and have architectural interest. The third is a solid stone structure. The pillars are said to have been brought from Aihole. The stone roof is carved into the battens in imitation of old temples but the front of the temple is open. The town has two high schools. There is a Veerashaiva Matha here presided over by a Virakta Swami called Mahantaswami. The founder of the Matha was a great saint who is remembered even today by all sections of the people in the area. A fair is held annually in honour of Mahantaswami.

Villages: 162 **Inhabited:** 161 **Uninhabited:** 1

Ranking	District	State	National
Area	2	48	207
Population	2	72	499
Sex Ratio	4	42	1548

Child Sex Ratio	4	131	3817
Literacy Rate	1	118	3577
Density	5	120	5365
Work Participation Rate	4	111	2835

Gram Panchayats:
Kamatgi, Muganur, Hiremagi, Aiahole, Aminagad, Rakkasagi, Sulibhavi, Kelur, Chikanal, Gudur, Vadageri, Ganjihal, Sangam, Belgal, Chittaragi, Nagur, Dhannur, Marol, Karadi, Amarawati, Binjawadgi, Budihal (S.K.), Jambaladinni, Nandavadgi, Hiresinganagutti, Kandgal, Gorbal , Hire-Otageri, Balakundi, Hirekodagali.

Amenities:
Education: Primary School in 157 villages, Middle school in 95 villages, Matriculation or Secondary School in 26 villages, namely Kamatgi, Muganur, Hiremagi, Aiahole, Aminagad, Sulibhavi, Kelur, Gudur, Ganjihal, Sangam, Iddalgi, Chittaragi, Bevinamatti, Nagur, Hirebadawadgi, Dhannur, Marol, Havaragi, Karadi, Amarawati, Ghattiganur, Nandavadgi, Hiresinganagutti, Tumba, Kandgal, Hirekodagali.
Higher Secondary or Pre University Courses or Intermediate or Junior College in 10 villages of the CD Block,, namely Kamatgi, Aminagad, Sulibhavi, Ganjihal, Sangam, Chittaragi, Nagur, Dhannur, Karadi, Kandgal.
College in 2 villages, Adult Literacy Center in 12 villages., Colleges are in villages, namely Kamatgi, Aminagad.
Medical: Hospital in 2 villages, Dispensary in 14 villages, Health Center in 12 villages, Sub Center in 42 villages, Maternity and Child Welfare Center in 2 villages, Community health workers in 63 villages.
The Villages having Hospital or Dispensary or Health Center are Kamatgi, Muganur, Aminagad, Sulibhavi, Gudur, Sangam, Chittaragi, Chittawadgi, Chickbadawadgi, Dhannur, Marol, Kodihal, Karadi, Amarawati, Nidasanur.
Drinking Water: Tap water in 91 villages, Tank water in 68 villages, Well water in 103 villages, Tubewell in 45 villages and more than one source in 161 villages.
Bank: Banking facility in 13 villages, namely, Kamatgi, Aiahole, Sulibhavi, Gudur, Ganjihal, Sangam Chittaragi, Nagur, Dhannur, Karadi, Nandavadgi Hiresinganagutti, Kandgal.
Credit Society in 20 villages Agricultural Credit Society in 19 Non-Agricultural Credit Society in 1 village.
Others: Power supply in 161 villages, Cinema hall in 3 villages, sport club in 1 village, Stadium or Auditorium or Community Hall in 0 village, Post Office in 65 villages.
There are 156 villages having bus facilities.
Villages with most of facilities: Kamatgi, Aiahole Sulibhavi, Gudur, Ganjihal, Sangam, Chittaragi Nagur, Dhannur, Karadi, Nandavadgi, Hiresinganagutti Kandgal.
Villages without amenities (Education): Khairwadgi, Hungund (Rural), Ishwarnagar, Sevalalnagar..
Scheduled Castes: Out of the total population of 217129 persons, 35055 persons (16.14%) belong to Scheduled Castes. The villages having less than 10% SC population are Kadiwal Kallapur, Suralikal, Amblikoppa, Bevinal Mullur, Kyadiggeri, Sulibhavi, Chilapur Benakanavari, Siddanakolla, Bhimanagad, Chikanal Muradi, Gandal, Dammur, Ilal, Huvanur, Valakaladinni Khajagal, Hadagali, Kalagonal, Hireyaranakeri Chickyaranakeri, Yadahalli, Chickbadawadgi, Virapur Yemmihatti, Koppa(S.M.), Koujaganur, Anapakatti Kamaladinni, Kodihal, Revadihal, Turamari, Chatnihal Malagihal, Chicksinganagutti, Hanamanal, Sankalapur.
The villages having more than 50% SC population are Hungund (Rural), Balakundi, Ishwarnagar Sevalalnagar, Chickkodagali.
Sex ratio of Scheduled Caste population is 504.

Scheduled Castes Literates and Illiterates by Sex:

	Persons	Males	Females
Literate	11,008	7,670	3,338
Illiterate	24,047	9,708	14,339
Literacy rate	39.3	55.7	23.4
Graduate	345	299	46

Scheduled Castes (Dominant):
Bhambi etc., Banjara etc., Chalavadi etc., Bhovi Madiga
For their cultural identity please see Appendix-I
Villages without Scheduled Castes: There are 5 villages without any scheduled caste population.
Scheduled Tribes: Out of the total population of 217129 persons, 8754 persons (4.03%) belong to Scheduled Tribes. The villages having less than 10% ST population are Kamatgi, Basarikatti, Kadiwal Kallapur, Yeranaikanal Suralikal, Basawanal, Amblikoppa, Muganur Budihal (S.K.), Budihal (Inam), Bevinal, Hiremagi Madapur, Huvinahalli, Mullur, Nimbalgundi, Aiahole Kyadiggeri, Kunabenchi, Aminagad, Rakkasagi Sulibhavi, Tallikeri, Kelur, Chilapur, Benakanavari Siddanakolla, Gudur, Muradi, Vadageri, Ilal Chickmagi, Khairwadgi, Papathanal, Hiremalagavi Chickmalagavi, Ganjihal, Huvanur, Varagodadinni Kengalkadapatti, Katagur, Turadagi, Bisaladinni Valakaladinni, Chowdakamaladinni, Sangam, Khajagal Iddalgi, Bisanalkoppa, Belgal, Hadagali, Kirasur Timmapur, Chittaragi, Gangur, Huliginal, Kalagonal

Bevinamatti, Hireyaranakeri, Honnarahalli, Nagur Yadahalli, Chittawadgi, Chickbadawadgi, Virapur Bannihatti, Hirebadawadgi, Hungund (Rural) Kamadatta, Adihal, Yemmihatti, Hullalli, Koppa(S.M.) Marol, Havaragi, Koujaganur, Anapakatti, Indawar Islampur, Amarawadgi, Chinnapur (S.K.), Dasbal Kesarapenti, Vadergonal, Kamaladinni, Kadiwal(Inam) Jalakamaladinni, Pochapur, Kodihal, Karadi, Palti Chintakamaladinni, Revadihal, Bekamaladinni, Hagedal Ramawadgi, Amarawati, Binjawadgi, Ghattiganur Hemawadgi, Turamari, Tariwal, Budihal (S.K.) Benakanadoni, Chamalapur, Kambalihal, Hirehunakunti Chatnihal, Malagihal, Nidasanur, Gadisunkapur Chikadapur, Nandavadgi, Harnapur, Hireadapur Hiresinganagutti, Tumba, Kesarabhavi Chinnapur (S.T.), Herur, Gopsani, Chicksinganagutti Krishnapur, Gonal (S.K.), Kandgal, Vajjal, Tondihal Gorbal, Gudur (S.B.), Hanamanal, Gonal (S.B.) Hireupnal, Balakundi, Ishwarnagar, Sankalapur Sevalalnagar, Chickkodagali, Hirekodagali Gonal (S.T.), Maratgeri, Somalapur.

The villages having more than 50% ST population are None.

Sex ratio of Scheduled tribe population is 493.

Scheduled Tribes Literates and Illiterates by Sex:

	Persons	Males	Females
Literate	3,424	2,411	1,013
Illiterate	5,330	2,026	3,304
Literacy rate	47.7	66.7	28.5
Graduate	74	67	7

Scheduled Tribes (Dominant):

Naikda etc., Koli Dhor etc., Meda, Pardhi etc. Gond etc.

For their cultural identity please see Appendix-II

Villages without Scheduled Tribes: There are 55 villages without any scheduled tribe population.

Literates and Illiterates by Sex (Total Population):

	Persons	Males	Females
Literate	100,475	66,358	34,117
Illiterate	116,654	42,699	73,955
Literacy rate	56	73	38
Graduate	3,493	2,982	511

Agriculture: ***Distribution of villages according to land use:*** Out of 162 villages, Total area (in hectare) is 133746, out of that 82.9 percent is cultivable and 4.52 percent of the cultivable area is irrigated.

Sources of Irrigation (Hectares): Government Canal 0, Private Canal 0, Well without Electricity 21.89, Well with Electricity 1151.76, Tubewell without Electricity 1, Tubewell with Electricity 930.36, Tank 453.98, River 2430.99, Lake 0, Waterfall 0, Others 24.68.

Villages with population of 5000 to 9999:

Sulibhavi, Kandgal.

Villages with population of 10000 and above:

Kamatgi, Aminagad, Gudur.

Distribution of Workers:

	Persons	Males	Females	WPR
Cultivators	26,979	21,409	5,570	27.24
Agricultural Labour	40,184	13,361	26,823	40.57
Household Industry	10,719	6,241	4,478	10.82
Other Workers	21,168	16,520	4,648	21.37
Main Workers	69,831	50,325	19,506	70.5
Marginal Workers	29,219	7,206	22,013	29.5
Total Workers	99,050	57,531	41,519	

Religion: Major Religious Communities:

	Persons	Males	Females	Sex Ratio
Hindu (90.94%)	197,461	99,217	98,244	990
Muslim (8.03%)	17,427	8,731	8,696	996
Christian (0.08%)	173	86	87	1,012
Sikh (0.01%)	26	15	11	733
Buddhists (0%)	3	2	1	500
Jain (0.05%)	117	60	57	950

Agewise Data:

	Persons	Males	Females	Sex Ratio
All ages	217,129	109,057	108,072	991
0-14	79,520	40,788	38,732	950
15-44	96,852	49,592	47,260	953
45-79	39,051	18,067	20,984	1161
80+	1,605	556	1,049	1887
Age not stated	101	54	47	870

Languages (Dominant):

Kannada, Urdu, Hindi, Telugu, Marathi

Disabled Population:

	Persons	Males	Females	%
Total Disabled	3,510	1,916	1,594	
In Seeing	1,545	761	784	44.02
In Speech	334	191	143	9.52
In Hearing	156	73	83	4.44
In Movement	1,213	749	464	34.56
Mentally	262	142	120	7.46

HUNSUR

Hunsur C.D. Block lies in the western part of Mysore district. It is a part of Hunsur taluka. The Block is located at a distance of 43 kms. from district headquarters (Mysore). There are 213 villages in the block with the total population of 214,245 persons. Area of the C.D. Block is 886.17 sq. kms. It is bounded by taluk Krishnarajanagara on north, taluk Heggadadevankote on south, taluks Mysore and Heggadadevankote on east, and Piriyapatna taluk on west.

Communications:

Roadways : SH- 57: Direction- Mallinathapura to Krishnara janagara, Nearest Villages- Krishnapura, Siriyurunala, Bolanahalli, Mallinathapura. SH- 88: Direction- Piriyap atna to Mysore, Nearest Villages- Atthikuppe, Chilkunda, Kallahalli, Tammadahalli, Nilavagilukaval, Adiganahalli, Mookanahalli, Kebbe Koppalu, Bannikuppe, Somanahalli, Beejaganahalli, Doddahunsur, Nilavagilu, Mallinathapura, Rangaiahnakoppalu, Kuppekolagatta, Bilikere, Bilikereka val, Hullenahalli, Manuganahalli, Doddakadanahalli, Chikk adanahalli, Ankanahalli. SH- 88 A: Direction- Virajpet to Adiganahalli, Nearest Villages- Direction- Nearest Villages- Vadlimanuganahalli, Harinahalli, Muthurayana Hosahalli, Kallahalli, Adiganahalli, Kallahallikaval, Hunasegala, Muthurayana, Hosahalli Kaval, Karnakuppe.

River: Lakshmantirtha Nadi- Nearest Villages- Belthur, Kattemalalavadi, Krishnapura, Ramenahalli, Chennasoge, Hosakote, Vaddambalu, Heggandur, Hanagodu, Kiranguru, Parekoppalu, Beeranahallikaval, Beeranahalli, Kudlur, Hanagodunala, Haralahalli, Hindugodlu, Dasanapura, Doddahejjurkaval, Abburu, Sindenahalli, Negathur, Habbar akuppe K.G, Billanahosahalli, Konanahosahalli, Kolavige, Mudaganur, Chikkahejjur, Doddahejjur, Veeranahosahalli Jungle, Kirijaji, Mookanahalli, Ramapatna, Kattemalalava dinala, Hagaranahalli, Nilavagilu, Govindanahallinala, Chikkahunsur, Nallurunala, Ayarahalli, Harohalli, Husen pura, Husenpuranala.

Canal: Nearest Villages- Gavadagere, Kattemalalavadi, Agrahara, Hodakekattekaval, Pinnikyathanahalli, Undavadi, Hejjodlu, Attiguppe, Krishnapura, Siriyuru, Siriyuruna la, Kiranguru, Parekoppalu, Kottigekaval, Ummathur, Hanag odunala, Penjahallikaval, Haralahalli, Madahalli, Varanchi Or, Gurupura, Kirijaji, Mookanahalli, Kirasodlu, Kattem alalavadinala, Thondalu , Hagaranahalli, Rayanahalli, Govindanahallinala, Chikkahunsur, Govindanahalli, Hanch ya, Nallurunala, Hanumanthapuranala, Aspathrekaval, Uddur nala, Udduru, Nadappanahalli, Husenpura, Husenpuranala, Shravananahalli, Shsnubhoganahalli, Lakkur, Bolanahalli, Kempanahalli, Mallinathapura, Rangaiahnakoppalu, Kuppek olagatta, Uyyigondanahalli, Tarikalkaval, Kuttavadi, Mudlapura.

Annual Rainfall: Normal Rianfall 761 mm.

Ground Water: Availability of the Ground Water in the Basin is 5639.75 H.A.M. and the utilization is 3238. 51 H.A.M. It belongs to Over Exploited category. Depth to water level 2 to 20 meter below the ground. Most of the wells go down in summer months, according to the Ground Water Estimation Committee.

Soils: Red Sandy Soils, Red Loamy Soils and Deep Black Soils.

Natural Division : It falls partly in Heggadadevankote-Ba ndipur Forested Upland, Kabbani-Cauvery Valley.

Administration:

Division: Mysore. Parliamentary Constituency: 21 Mysore Paschim. District: Mysore. Taluka: Hunsur. Assembly Constituency: 212 Hunsur. Gram Panchayat: 30.

Regional Area Development Boards: The Maland Aera Development Board.

Villages: 213 **Inhabited:** 192 **Uninhabited:** 21

Ranking	District	State	National
Area	3	103	573
Population	5	76	576
Sex Ratio	4	119	2877
Child Sex Ratio	3	27	1543
Literacy Rate	3	127	3864
Density	1	10	4232
Work Participation Rate	6	50	474

Gram Panchayats:

Harave, Hirikyathanahalli, Gavadagere, Mullur, Bolanahalli, Halebeedu, Manuganahalli, Bilikere, Maraduru, Kattemalalavadi, Kothegala, Chilkunda, Kallahalli, Karnakuppe, Thattekere, Govindanahalli, Beejaganahalli, Bannikuppe, Gagenahalli, Challahalli, Dharmapura, Uddurkaval, Aspathrekaval, Ummathur, Hanagodu, Meralakuppe, Doddahejjur, Uyyigondanahalli, Karimuddanahalli, Singaramaranahalli (Aswalu).

Amenities:

Education: Primary School in 172 villages, Middle school in 99 villages, Matriculation or Secondary School in 24 villages, namely Ramenahalli, Hirikyathanahalli, Mulluru, Gavadagere, Kothegala, Chilkunda, Thattekere, Karnakuppe, Hanagodu, Neralakuppe, Doddahejjur, Varanchi Or Gurupura, Kalkunike, Maraduru, Bannikuppe, Doddahunsur, Aspathrekaval, Rathnapuri, Gagenahalli, Gerasanahalli, Husenpura, Bilikere, Challahalli, Karimuddanahalli.

Higher Secondary or Pre University Courses or Intermediate or Junior College in 5 villages of the CD Block,, namely Hanagodu, Doddahunsur, Rathnapuri, Bilikere, Karimuddanahalli.

College in 1 village, Adult Literacy Center in 0 village., College is in village, namely Doddahunsur.

Medical: Hospital in 3 villages, Dispensary in 10 villages, Health Center in 12 villages, Sub Center in 46 villages, Maternity and Child Welfare Center in 2 villages, Community health workers in 20 villages.

The Villages having Hospital or Dispensary or Health Center are Harave, Mulluru, Undavadi, Kothegala, Kallahalli, Karnakuppe, Doddahunsur, Ayarahalli, Bolanahalli, Bilikere.

Drinking Water: Tap water in 144 villages, Tank water in

45 villages, Well water in 79 villages, Tubewell in 114 villages and more than one source in 162 villages.

Bank: Banking facility in 32 villages, namely, Hirikyathanahalli, Gavadagere, Kattemalalavadi Habbanakuppe, Chilkunda, Kallahalli, Thattekere Karnakuppe, Heggandur, Hanagodu, Ummathur Doddahejjur, Varanchi Or Gurupura, Kalkunike Bannikuppe, Somanahalli, Doddahunsur, Nilavagilu Aspathrekaval, Rathnapuri, Udduru, Gagenahalli Gerasanahalli, Husenpura, Shsnubhoganahalli Bilikere, Manuganahalli, Haradanahalli, Challahalli Dharmapura, Karimuddanahalli, Kuttavadi.

Credit Society in 192 villages Agricultural Credit Society in 25 Non-Agricultural Credit Society in 65 villages.

Others: Power supply in 192 villages, Cinema hall in 10 villages, sport club in 1 village, Stadium or Auditorium or Community Hall in 0 village, Post Office in 45 villages.

There are 171 villages having bus facilities.

Villages with most of facilities: Hirikyathanahalli Gavadagere, Kattemalalavadi, Chilkunda, Kallahalli Thattekere, Karnakuppe, Hanagodu, Doddahejjur Varanchi Or Gurupura, Kalkunike, Bannikuppe Somanahalli, Doddahunsur, Nilavagilu, Aspathrekaval Rathnapuri, Udduru, Gagenahalli, Shsnubhoganahalli Bilikere, Manuganahalli, Dharmapura Karimuddanahalli, Kuttavadi.

Villages without amenities (Education): Hodakekattekaval, Pinnikyathanahalli, Siriyurunala, Chilkundakaval, Hulaganahalli, Kallahallikaval, Beeranahallikaval, Hanagodunala, Habbanakuppe K.G, Billanahosahalli, Konanahosahalli, Veeranahosahalli, Madahallikaval, Bommalapura, Khayam Gutta Gudishetti Halli, Annarayapura, Dhythyanakerekaval, Basthimadanahalli, Sulekerekaval, Mudlapura..

Scheduled Castes: Out of the total population of 210026 persons, 39106 persons (18.62%) belong to Scheduled Castes. The villages having less than 10% SC population are Ramenahalli, Harave, Hirikyathanahalli Manchabayanahalli, Jabagere, Gavadagere Manuganahalli, Honnenahalli, Marurkaval, Moduru Belthur, Hodakekattekaval, Maragowdanahalli Pinnikyathanahalli, Undavadi, Attiguppe, Krishnapura Siriyurunala, Habbanakuppe, Kothegala, Kanagal Hulaganahalli, Vadlimanuganahalli, Nilavagilukaval Kallahallikaval, Angatahalli, Ramenahalli Chennasoge, Vaddambalu, Heggandur, Kamegowdanahalli Gowdikere, Uduvepura, Kallaboochahalli Beeranahallikaval, Kudlur, Kottigekaval Hanagodunala, Haralahalli, Dasanapura, Abburu Sindenahalli, Kachuvinahalli, Neralakuppe Habbanakuppe K.G, Billanahosahalli, Konanahosahalli Kolavige, Chikkahejjur, Veeranahosahalli Kurubarahosahalli, Kalkunike, Ramapatna, Kirasodlu Maraduru, Govindanahalli, Hanchya, Rathnapuri Madahallikaval, Maralaiahna Koppalu, Ayarahalli Shravananahalli, Shsnubhoganahalli, Bolanahalli Kempanahalli, Vaddarahalli, Halladakallahalli Boochahalli, Bommalapura, Sabbanahalli Mallinathapura, Hullenahalli, Manuganahalli Handanahalli, Haradanahalli, Shankahalli, Hallikere Khayam Gutta Gudishetti Halli, Benkipura, Gohalli Annarayapura, Basthimadanahalli, Karimuddanahalli Halladakoppalu, Tarikallu, Kudineerumuddanahalli Kuttavadi, Sonahalli.

The villages having more than 50% SC population are Chilkundakaval, Naganahalli, Beeranahalli Hagaranahalli, Somanahalli, Doddahunsur Doddabeechanahalli, Maranahalli, Tharikalnala.

Sex ratio of Scheduled Caste population is 492.

Scheduled Castes Literates and Illiterates by Sex:

	Persons	Males	Females
Literate	15,915	9,779	6,136
Illiterate	23,191	10,104	13,087
Literacy rate	47.3	57.0	37.2
Graduate	343	308	35

Scheduled Castes (Dominant):

Adi Karnataka, Madiga, Bhovi, Korama Generic Castes etc.

For their cultural identity please see Appendix-I

Villages without Scheduled Castes: There are 62 villages without any scheduled caste population.

Scheduled Tribes: Out of the total population of 210026 persons, 35801 persons (17.05%) belong to Scheduled Tribes. The villages having less than 10% ST population are Chikkadiganahalli, Mulluru, Hulyalu, Manuganahalli Mylamburu, Marurkaval, Chittikyathanahalli Sannenahalli, Thippalapura, Belthur, Agrahara Hodakekattekaval, Biligere, Maragowdanahalli Pinnikyathanahalli, Hejjodlu, Attiguppe, Siriyuru Siriyurunala, Habbanakuppe, Chilkundakaval Yamagumbha, Atthikuppe, Chilkunda, Hulaganahalli Kallahalli, Naganahalli, Nilavagilukaval Adiganahalli, Kallahallikaval, Angatahalli Chennasoge, Thattekere, Hunasegala, Karnakuppe Hyrige, Honnenahalli, Heggandur, Gowdikere Kademanuganahalli, Kallaboochahalli, Hanagodu Kiranguru, Beeranahalli, Kudlur, Hanagodunala Penjahallikaval, Hindugodlu, Sindenahalli, Negathur Kachuvinahalli, Mudaganur, Kalkunike, Kirijaji

Mookanahalli, Ramapatna, Kirasodlu, Thondalu Hagaranahalli, Rayanahalli, Kebbe Koppalu Somanahalli, Uyyigowdanahalli, Beejaganahalli Doddahunsur, Hanchya, Aspathrekaval, Rathnapuri Uddurkaval, Udduru, Gagenahalli, Harohalli Gerasanahalli, Husenpura, Shravananahalli Shsnubhoganahalli, Mydanahalli, Vaddarahalli Bettadur, Halladakallahalli, Boochahalli Bommalapura, Mallinathapura, Rangaiahnakoppalu Kuppekolagatta, Jeenahalli, Devarahalli Manuganahalli, Chikkadanahalli, Ankanahalli Doddabeechanahalli, Chikkabeechanahalli Haradanahalli, Shankahalli, Vaderahosahalli Hallikere, Khayam Gutta Gudishetti Halli, Thippur Challahalli, Dhythyanakerekaval, Basthimadanahalli Aswalu, Maranahalli, Gejjaiahnavaddaragudi Halladakoppalu, Tharikalnala, Kudineerumuddanahalli Uyyigondanahalli, Tarikalkaval, Mudlapura, Devagalli Sonahalli, Yalachanahalli.

The villages having more than 50% ST population are Manchabayanahalli, Tammadahalli, Kottigekaval Dasanapura, Neralakuppe, Habbanakuppe K.G Billanahosahalli, Kolavige, Veeranahosahalli Madahalli, Maralaiahna Koppalu, Bolanahalli Sabbanahalli, Hullenahalli, Handanahalli, Benkipura Gohalli.

Sex ratio of Scheduled tribe population is 491.

Scheduled Tribes Literates and Illiterates by Sex:

	Persons	Males	Females
Literate	13,950	8,847	5,103
Illiterate	21,851	9,377	12,474
Literacy rate	45.2	56.2	33.8
Graduate	239	220	19

Scheduled Tribes (Dominant):

Naikda etc., Jenu Kuruba, Soligaru, Hakkipikki Bhil etc.

For their cultural identity please see Appendix-II

Villages without Scheduled Tribes: There are 85 villages without any scheduled tribe population.

Literates and Illiterates by Sex (Total Population):

	Persons	Males	Females
Literate	98,232	59,631	38,601
Illiterate	111,794	47,418	64,376
Literacy rate	54	64	43
Graduate	2,349	1,968	381

Agriculture: ***Distribution of villages according to land use:***

Out of 213 villages, Total area (in hectare) is 88617, out of that 47.91 percent is cultivable and 19.56 percent of the cultivable area is irrigated.

Sources of Irrigation (Hectares): Government Canal 4603.6, Private Canal 3.3, Well without Electricity 38.45, Well with Electricity 651.44, Tubewell without Electricity 33.86, Tubewell with Electricity 1730.82, Tank 513.46, River 74.76, Lake 0, Waterfall 0, Others 629.76.

Villages with population of 5000 to 9999:

Kattemalalavadi, Aspathrekaval.

Villages with population of 10000 and above: None

Distribution of Workers:

	Persons	Males	Females	WPR
Cultivators	76,255	46,203	30,052	63.31
Agricultural Labour	31,157	12,688	18,469	25.87
Household Industry	1,132	605	527	0.94
Other Workers	11,896	8,620	3,276	9.88
Main Workers	86,546	58,848	27,698	71.86
Marginal Workers	33,894	9,268	24,626	28.14
Total Workers	120,440	68,116	52,324	

Religion: Major Religious Communities:

	Persons	Males	Females	Sex Ratio
Hindu (92.75%)	194,802	99,045	95,757	967
Muslim (3.76%)	7,891	4,027	3,864	960
Christian (0.7%)	1,464	767	697	909
Sikh (0.01%)	17	11	6	545
Buddhists (1.27%)	2,671	1,572	1,099	699
Jain (0.03%)	57	28	29	1,036

Agewise Data:

	Persons	Males	Females	Sex Ratio
All ages	210,026	107,049	102,977	962
0-14	65,461	33,023	32,438	982
15-44	103,164	52,871	50,293	951
45-79	39,102	20,054	19,048	950
80+	2,030	975	1,055	1082
Age not stated	269	126	143	1135

Languages (Dominant):

Kannada, Urdu, Telugu, Marathi, Tamil

Disabled Population:

	Persons	Males	Females	%
Total Disabled	3,635	1,980	1,655	
In Seeing	2,145	1,092	1,053	59.01
In Speech	401	229	172	11.03
In Hearing	197	97	100	5.42
In Movement	641	423	218	17.63
Mentally	251	139	112	6.91

INDI

Indi C.D. Block lies in the northern part of Bijapur district. It is a part of Indi taluka. The Block is located at a distance of 50 kms. from district headquarters (Bijapur). There are 133 villages in the block with the total population of 325,285 persons. Area of the C.D. Block is 2199.28 sq. kms. It is bounded by taluk Bijapur on south, distt. Gulbarga and taluk Sindgi on east, and it has common boundary with the state of Maharashtra on north and west.

Communications:

Roadways : N.H-13: Direction- Bijapur to Solapur, Nearest Villages- Dhulikhed (Old), Halasangi, Yelgi [P.H.], Ballolli, Zalaki, Arajanal, Gundawan, Kapanimbargi, Sonakanahalli, Horti, Halagunaki, Basanal, Agasanal. S.H-41: Direction- Pandharapur to Devara Hippargi, Nearest Villages- Shiradon, Hala Halli, Chadchan, Jeerankalgi, Godihal, Bardol, Ballolli, Jevoor, Zalaki, Budihal,Anjutagi, Gundawan, Indi, (Rural), Vasantanagar, Rugi, Tennihalli, Gornal, Tamba.

Railway Station: Villages- Padanur, Lachyan, Ahirasang, Choragi, Nimbal [K.D.], Kyatanakeri.

River: Bhima Nadi- Nearest Villages- Dasur, Umraj, Nivargi, Sankha (Old), Umrani, (Old), Takali, Taddewadi, Shirnal, Dhulikhed (Old), Chanegaon, Shiragur Khalasa, Hingani, Baragudi, Padanur , Shiragur Inam (Old), Agarkhed, Gubbewad, Mannur, Bhuyar, Nagarhalli, Khedgi, Rodagi, Govindapu, Maragur, Anachi.

Canal: Nearest Villages- Golasar, Miragi, Arjunagi [B.K.], Marasanahalli, Shirshyad.

Annual Rainfall: Normal Rianfall 595 mm.

Ground Water: Availability of the Ground Water in the Basin is 14657.65 H.A.M. and the utilization is 11217.88 HAM It belongs to Over Exploited category. Depth to water level 2 to 5 meter below the ground. Most of the wells go down in summer months, according to the Ground Water Estimation Committee.

Soils: Black Soils.

Natural Division : It falls partly in the Lower Bhima Valley and the Bijapur- Basavana Bagevadi Upland of the Northern Karnataka Plateau.

Administration:

Division: Belgaum. Parliamentary Constituency: 3 Bijapur. District: Bijapur. Taluka: Indi.Assembly Constituency: 32 Indi, 33 Sindgi. Gram Panchayat: 44.

Regional Area Development Boards: The Bailu Seeme Area Development Board.

Border Villages: (State: Maharashtra)- Dasur, Umraj, Govindapur, Revathagaon, Shiradon, Hala Halli, Nivargi, Sankha (Old), Umrani (Old), Chadchan, Konkanagaon, Jeerankalgi, Takali, Taddewadi, Maragur, Shirnal, Dhulikhed (Old), Chanegaon, Shiragur Khalasa, Anachi, Nimbargi, Jigajeevani, Kataral, Kanakanal, Mahaveernagar, Inchageri, Hingani, Baragudi, Padanur, Shiragur Inam (Old), Gubewad.

Villages: 133 **Inhabited:** 129 **Uninhabited:** 4

Ranking	District	State	National
Area	2	3	42
Population	1	6	40
Sex Ratio	5	171	4585
Child Sex Ratio	5	165	4794
Literacy Rate	3	135	4229
Density	3	154	5606
Work Participation Rate	2	135	3697

Gram Panchayats:

Revathagaon, Nivargi, Umrani (Old), Hatta Halli, Chadchan, Dhulikhed (Old), Halasangi, Loni [B.K.], Bardol, Nimbargi, Jigajeevani, Inchageri, Nandaragi, Ballolli, Zalaki, Bhatagunaki, Padanur , Lachyan, Ahirasang, Anjutagi, Hadalasang, Koluragi, Horti, Babalad, Hanjagi, Nimbal [K.D.], Basanal, Tadavalga, Atharga, Benakanahalli, Agarkhed, Hirebevanur, Alur, Chickbevanur, Khedgi, Lalasangi, Salotgi, Rugi, Tennihalli, Naad[K.D.], Miragi, Shirshyad, Masali[B.K.], Tamba.

Amenities:

Education: Primary School in 121 villages, Middle school in 112 villages, Matriculation or Secondary School in 50 villages, namely Umraj, Revathagaon, Shiradon, Nivargi, Umrani (Old), Hatta Halli, Chadchan, Taddewadi, Dhulikhed (Old), Halasangi, Loni [B.K.], Bardol, Nimbargi, Jigajeevani, Inchageri, Satalagaon[P.B.], Nandaragi, Ballolli, Jevoor, Zalaki, Bhatagunaki, Padanur, Lachyan, Ahirasang, Anjutagi, Hadalasang, Savalsang, Horti, Halagunaki, Chavadihal, Hanjagi, Nimbal [K.D.], Nimbal [B.K.], Agasanal, Tadavalga, Atharga, Shirkanahalli, Bolegaon, Agarkhed, Hirebevanur, Chickbevanur, Nagarhalli, Salotgi, Masali[K.D.], Naad[K.D.], Golasar, Miragi, Shirshyad, Masali[B.K.], Tamba.

Higher Secondary or Pre University Courses or Intermediate or Junior College in 16 villages of the CD Block,, namely Nivargi, Chadchan, Halasangi, Loni [B.K.], Bardol, Nimbargi, Ballolli, Bhatagunaki, Ahirasang, Horti, Atharga, Bolegaon, Nagarhalli, Salotgi, Shirshyad, Tamba.

College in 5 villages, Adult Literacy Center in 14 villages., Colleges are in villages, namely Chadchan, Loni [B.K.], Horti, Bolegaon, Tamba.

Medical: Hospital in 0 village, Dispensary in 3 villages, Health Center in 11 villages, Sub Center in 53 villages, Maternity and Child Welfare Center in 3 villages, Community health workers in 31 villages.

The Villages having Hospital or Dispensary or Health Center are Chadchan, Jevoor, Basanal.

Drinking Water: Tap water in 96 villages, Tank water in 35 villages, Well water in 121 villages, Tubewell in 92 villages and more than one source in 129 villages.

Bank: Banking facility in 8 villages, namely, Chadchan, Dhulikhed (Old), Loni [B.K.], Bhatagunaki Khedgi, Salotgi, Naad[B.K.], Arjunagi [B.K.].

Credit Society in 50 villages Agricultural Credit Society in 47

Non-Agricultural Credit Society in 5 villages.
Others: Power supply in 129 villages, Cinema hall in 3 villages, sport club in 129 villages, Stadium or Auditorium or Community Hall in 129 villages, Post Office in 76 villages.
There are 105 villages having bus facilities.
Villages with most of facilities: Chadchan Dhulikhed (Old), Loni [B.K.], Bhatagunaki, Khedgi Salotgi.
Villages without amenities (Education):
Shiragur Khalasa, Mahaveernagar, Hanumanagar, Vijayanagar, Nehrunagar, Ramanagar, Gandhinagar, Wade..
Scheduled Castes: Out of the total population of 322505 persons, 60542 persons (18.77%) belong to Scheduled Castes.
The villages having less than 10% SC population are Umraj, Taddewadi, Shirnal, Anachi, Manankalgi Loni [B.K.], Dhumakanal, Padanur , Deginal Shirkanahalli, Bolegaon, Gubbewad, Tennihalli Masali[K.D.], Rodagi, Arjunagi [B.K.], Teggihalli Sangogi, Masali[B.K.], Kenginal, Bhanthanal.
The villages having more than 50% SC population are Kanchinal, Shiragur Khalasa, Mahaveernagar Hadalasang, Vijayanagar, Rajanal, Lingadalli Nehrunagar, Ramanagar, Gandhinagar.
Sex ratio of Scheduled Caste population is 482.
Scheduled Castes Literates and Illiterates by Sex:

	Persons	Males	Females
Literate	23,460	15,810	7,650
Illiterate	37,082	15,573	21,509
Literacy rate	46.4	60.4	31.4
Graduate	965	883	82

Scheduled Castes (Dominant):
Holaya etc., Banjara etc., Bhambi etc., Samagara Bhovi
For their cultural identity please see Appendix-I
Villages without Scheduled Castes: There are 4 villages without any scheduled caste population.
Scheduled Tribes: Out of the total population of 322505 persons, 5770 persons (1.79%) belong to Scheduled Tribes.
The villages having less than 10% ST population are Dasur, Umraj, Govindapur, Revathagaon, Shiradon Hala Halli, Nivargi, Sankha (Old), Umrani (Old) Hatta Halli, Havinal, Chadchan, Konkanagaon Jeerankalgi, Godihal, Kanchinal, Karur, Takali Taddewadi, Maragur, Dhulikhed (Old) Shiragur Khalasa, Anachi, Nandral, Halasangi Yelgi [P.H.], Manankalgi, Gotyal, Loni [B.K.] Bardol, Nimbargi, Jigajeevani, Kataral, Kanakanal Mahaveernagar, Inchageri, Hanumanagar Satalagaon[P.B.], Dhumakanal, Shiganapur, Nandaragi Ballolli, Jevoor, Zalaki, Mailar, Arajanal Bhatagunaki, Bhairunagi, Hingani, Baragudi, Padanur Lachyan, Loni (K.D), Budihal, Anjutagi, Gundawan Kapanimbargi, Sonakanahalli, Hadalasang, Vijayanagar Savalsang, Koluragi, Horti, Halagunaki, Kudagi Choragi, Chavadihal, Babalad, Hanjagi, Nimbal [K.D.] Nimbal [B.K.], Deginal, Basanal, Agasanal, Kotnal Kyatanakeri, Lingadalli, Tadavalga, Atharga Shirkanahalli, Benakanahalli, Ganavalga, Bolegaon Shiragur Inam (Old), Agarkhed, Gubbewad, Mannur Hirebevanur, Alur, Mavinalli, Chickbevanur, Ingalgi Nehrunagar, Nagarhalli, Lalasangi, Satalagaon (P.I) Salotgi, Rugi, Tennihalli, Gornal, Masali[K.D.] Ramanagar, Naad[B.K.], Naad[K.D.], Golasar Shivapur [K.H.], Rodagi, Miragi, Hanchinal Arjunagi [K.H.], Arjunagi [B.K.], Teggihalli Shirshyad, Sangogi, Masali[B.K.], Bannihatti, Tamba Shivapur [B.K.], Kenginal, Gandhinagar, Wade Bhanthanal.
The villages having more than 50% ST population are None.
Sex ratio of Scheduled tribe population is 488.
Scheduled Tribes Literates and Illiterates by Sex:

	Persons	Males	Females
Literate	2,085	1,341	744
Illiterate	3,685	1,616	2,069
Literacy rate	44.5	55.7	32.6
Graduate	58	56	2

Scheduled Tribes (Dominant):
Koli Dhor etc., Naikda etc., Kadu Kuruba Pardhi etc., Koraga
For their cultural identity please see Appendix-II
Villages without Scheduled Tribes: There are 81 villages without any scheduled tribe population.
Literates and Illiterates by Sex (Total Population):

	Persons	Males	Females
Literate	140,420	90,602	49,818
Illiterate	182,085	76,761	105,324
Literacy rate	52	65	38
Graduate	6,035	5,490	545

Agriculture: ***Distribution of villages according to land use:***
Out of 133 villages, Total area (in hectare) is 219928, out of that 91.51 percent is cultivable and 16.9 percent of the cultivable area is irrigated.
Sources of Irrigation (Hectares): Government Canal 291.38, Private Canal 0, Well without Electricity 98.35, Well with Electricity 16497.5, Tubewell without Electricity 113.8, Tubewell with Electricity 8651.35, Tank 1772, River 4816.6, Lake 0, Waterfall 0, Others 1762.57.
Villages with population of 5000 to 9999:

Halasangi, Loni [B.K.], Bardol, Anjutagi, Horti Hanjagi, Tadavalga, Atharga, Agarkhed, Rugi, Tamba.

Villages with population of 10000 and above:
Chadchan, Salotgi.

Distribution of Workers:

	Persons	Males	Females	WPR
Cultivators	51,552	39,778	11,774	37.87
Agricultural Labour	60,680	27,267	33,413	44.57
Household Industry	3,201	2,246	955	2.35
Other Workers	20,713	16,893	3,820	15.21
Main Workers	109,065	78,447	30,618	80.11
Marginal Workers	27,081	7,737	19,344	19.89
Total Workers	136,146	86,184	49,962	

Religion: Major Religious Communities:

	Persons	Males	Females	Sex Ratio
Hindu (88.17%)	284,352	147,685	136,667	925
Muslim (10.89%)	35,125	18,167	16,958	933
Christian (0.02%)	75	38	37	974
Sikh (0.01%)	22	11	11	1,000
Buddhists (0.28%)	905	436	469	1,076
Jain (0.31%)	1,014	517	497	961

Agewise Data:

	Persons	Males	Females	Sex Ratio
All ages	322,505	167,363	155,142	927
0-14	120,291	62,223	58,068	933
15-44	137,768	72,595	65,173	898
45-79	60,862	30,750	30,112	979
80+	3,239	1,584	1,655	1045
Age not stated	345	211	134	635

Languages (Dominant):
Kannada, Urdu, Hindi, Marathi, Telugu

Disabled Population:

	Persons	Males	Females	%
Total Disabled	7,554	4,900	2,654	
In Seeing	4,077	2,724	1,353	53.97
In Speech	590	342	248	7.81
In Hearing	315	162	153	4.17
In Movement	1,956	1,317	639	25.89
Mentally	616	355	261	8.15

JAGALUR

Jagalur C.D. Block lies in the eastern part of Davanagere district. It is a part of Jagalur taluka. The Block is located at a distance of 48 kms. from district headqu arters (Davanagere). There are 171 villages in the block with the total population of 144,088 persons. Area of the C.D. Block is 963.44 sq. kms. It is bounded by distr ict Bellary and taluk Harapanahalli on north, district Chitradurga on south and east, taluks Davangere and Harapanahalli on west.

Communications:
Roadways : N.H-13: Direction- Chitradurga to Hospet, Nearest Villages- Kananakatte, Madamuthnahalli, Hiremall anahole, Huchavvanahalli, Bangarakkanagudda, Mudlamachikere, Donnehalli, Bennehalli, Bommagatta, Kalledevarapura, Sangenahalli.

River: Hagari Nadi- Nearest Villages- Basavanakote, Asagodu, Thuppadahalli, Kurubanahalli. Chinna Hagari Nadi- Nearest Villages- Chikkamallanahole, Thumbaraguddu, Mallapura, Kamandalagondi, Dibbadahalli, Taitone, Salah alli, Halehalli, Hiremallanahole, Mudlamachikere, Siddiha lli, Donnehalli, Dyamalinganahalli, Bennehalli, Bommagatta, Kalledevarapura, Sangenahalli.

Canal: Nearest Villages- Sokke, Chikkabantanahalli, Gopalapura, Gadimakunte, Mallapura, Kamandalagondi, Halehalli, Hiremallanahole, Donnehalli, Jammapura, Bomma kkanahalli, Bennehalli, Kalledevarapura, Sangenahalli.

Annual Rainfall: Normal Rianfall 495 mm.

Ground Water: Availability of the Ground Water in the Basin is 5330.12 H.A.M. and the utilization is 5834. 64 H.A.M. It belongs to Over Exploited category. Depth to water level 5 to 20 meter below the ground. Most of the wells go down in summer months, according to the Ground Water Estimation Committee.

Soils: Red Sandy Soils and Black Soils.

Natural Division : It falls partly in Jagalur-Molakalmuru Upland and Devangere Plateau of the Central Karnataka Plateau.

Administration:
Division: Bangalore. Parliamentary Constituency: 13 Davanagere. District: Davanagere. Taluka: Jagalur. Assem bly Constituency: 103 Jagalur (ST). Gram Panchayat: 22.

Regional Area Development Boards: The Bailu Seeme Area Development Board.

Villages: 171 **Inhabited:** 140 **Uninhabited:** 31

Ranking	**District**	**State**	**National**
Area	3	89	470
Population	6	136	2052
Sex Ratio	1	104	2583
Child Sex Ratio	3	88	2956
Literacy Rate	5	78	2603
Density	1	1	5565
Work Participation Rate	6	129	60

Gram Panchayats:
Basavanakote, Gurusiddapura, Sokke, Kyasenahalli, Hosakere, Diddige, Asagodu, Pallagatte, Kenchenahalli, Hanumanthapura, Anabur, Hiremallanahole, Donnehalli, Devikere, Bilichodu, Halekal, Guttidurga, Bistuvalli, Mustur, Kalledevarapura, Thoranagatte, Bidarakere.

Amenities:

Education: Primary School in 126 villages, Middle school in 80 villages, Matriculation or Secondary School in 24 villages, namely Basavanakote, Gurusiddapura, Ujjappavaderahalli, Sokke, Hosakere, Gowripura, Pallagatte, Asagodu, Marikunte, Devikere, Bilichodu, Halekal, Chaduragolla, Guttidurga, Hanumanthapura, Anabur, Chikkamallanahole, Mallapura, Hiremallanahole, Mustur, Donnehalli, Bidarakere, Thoranagatte, Kalledevarapura.
Higher Secondary or Pre University Courses or Intermediate or Junior College in 4 villages of the CD Block,, namely Sokke, Bilichodu, Kamandalagondi, Mustur.
College in 0 village, Adult Literacy Center in 0 village.
Medical: Hospital in 7 villages, Dispensary in 5 villages, Health Center in 8 villages, Sub Center in 30 villages, Maternity and Child Welfare Center in 11 villages, Community health workers in 12 villages.
The Villages having Hospital or Dispensary or Health Center are Basavanakote, Sokke, Pallagatte, Asagodu, Marikunte, Rastemachikere, Bilichodu, Halekal, Jagalur Rural, Huchavvanahalli, Kalledevarapura.
Drinking Water: Tap water in 35 villages, Tank water in 13 villages, Well water in 3 villages, Tubewell in 87 villages and more than one source in 96 villages.
Bank: Banking facility in 9 villages, namely, Basavanakote, Sokke, Hosakere, Pallagatte, Devikere Bilichodu, Anabur, Mallapura, Bidarakere.
Credit Society in 6 villages Agricultural Credit Society in 6 Non-Agricultural Credit Society in 0 village.
Others: Power supply in 140 villages, Cinema hall in 2 villages, sport club in 0 village, Stadium or Auditorium or Community Hall in 0 village, Post Office in 39 villages.
There are 111 villages having bus facilities.
Villages with most of facilities: Basavanakote Sokke, Hosakere, Pallagatte, Devikere, Bilichodu Anabur, Mallapura, Bidarakere.
Villages without amenities (Education):
Medakeripura, Katenahalli, Krishnapura, Seetharasanahalli, Venkatapura, Jayaramanahalli, Badabasavanahalli, Kolamaghatta, Kurubanahalli, Channapura, Ajjabommanahalli, Narasimharajapura, Maddarasanakatte..
Scheduled Castes: Out of the total population of 144139 persons, 35525 persons (24.65%) belong to Scheduled Castes.
The villages having less than 10% SC population are Magadi, Chikkabantanahalli, Lakkampura, Katenahalli Krishnapura, Hirebannihatti, Gowdikatte, Kanakuppe Seetharasanahalli, Gowdagondanahalli, Venkatapura Hanumavvanagathihalli, Chikkammanahatti Giddanakatte, Kenchammanagathihalli Badabasavanahalli, Guddadalingana Halli Palanaikanakote, Kurubanahalli, Iyyanahalli Kasturipura, Halekal, Rangapura, Hanumanthapura Goguddu, Thimmalapura, Madamuthnahalli, Dibbadahalli Siddammanahalli, Mudlamachikere, Kamagethanahalli Santhemuddapura, Mathadadyamavvanahalli Maddarasanakatte, Thoranagatte, Bommakkanahalli Sangenahalli.
The villages having more than 50% SC population are Agasanahalli, Jadanakatte, Huchangipura, Obalapura Kotadagudda, Channapura, Baggenahalli Malammanahalli, Narenahalli, Chaduragolla Narasimharajapura, Kortikere, Somanahalli Byatagaranahalli, Jyothipura, Kamandalagondi Huchavvanahalli, Bangarakkanagudda, Kattigehalli Gowrammanahalli.
Sex ratio of Scheduled Caste population is 493.

Scheduled Castes Literates and Illiterates by Sex:

	Persons	Males	Females
Literate	15,529	9,866	5,663
Illiterate	19,996	8,129	11,867
Literacy rate	51.9	65.1	38.4
Graduate	350	322	28

Scheduled Castes (Dominant):
Bhovi, Madiga, Adi Karnataka, Banjara etc.
Adi Dravida
For their cultural identity please see Appendix-I
Villages without Scheduled Castes: There are 46 villages without any scheduled caste population.
Scheduled Tribes: Out of the total population of 144139 persons, 35622 persons (24.71%) belong to Scheduled Tribes.
The villages having less than 10% ST population are Basavanakote, Jadanakatte, Ujjappavaderahalli Chikkabantanahalli, Katenahalli, Seetharasanahalli Venkatapura, Chikka-Ujjini, Hanumavvanagathihalli Diddige, Pallagatte, Kenchammanagathihalli Badabasavanahalli, Obalapura, Marikunte Kolamaghatta, Katenahalli, Medakerehalli Suraddihalli, Kotadagudda, Channapura, Baggenahalli Malammanahalli, Meldaginakere, Ajjabommanahalli Narenahalli, Muggidaragihalli, Halekal, Muchanur Chaduragolla, Narasimharajapura, Sagalagatte Halavadandi, Somanahalli, Byatagaranahalli Jyothipura, Anabur, Goguddu, Uddagatta Bharamasamudra, Mallapura, Kamandalagondi Hiremallanahole, Huchavvanahalli, Bangarakkanagudda Siddammanahalli, Siddihalli, Rastemakunte Kattigehalli, Maddarasanakatte, Gowrammanahalli Thoranagatte, Bennehalli.
The villages having more than 50% ST population are

Magadi, Lakkampura, Krishnapura, Hirebannihatti Gowdikatte, Kanakuppe, Gowdagondanahalli Tamalihalli, Byranaikanahalli, Guddadalingana Halli Palanaikanakote, Kurubanahalli, Basavapura Iyyanahalli, Bullanahalli, Kasturipura Vysyagondanahalli, Settigondanahalli, Rangapura Kasavanahalli, Doddabommanahalli, Thimmalapura Kananakatte, Kamagethanahalli, Marenahalli Lingannanahalli, Gopagondanahalli, Bommakkanahalli Sangenahalli.

Sex ratio of Scheduled tribe population is 489.

Scheduled Tribes Literates and Illiterates by Sex:

	Persons	Males	Females
Literate	15,720	9,903	5,817
Illiterate	19,902	8,291	11,611
Literacy rate	52.7	65.1	39.7
Graduate	294	268	26

Scheduled Tribes (Dominant):

Naikda etc., Generic Tribes etc.

For their cultural identity please see Appendix-II

Villages without Scheduled Tribes: There are 51 villages without any scheduled tribe population.

Literates and Illiterates by Sex (Total Population):

	Persons	Males	Females
Literate	74,818	45,234	29,584
Illiterate	69,321	28,005	41,316
Literacy rate	61	73	49
Graduate	2,035	1,764	271

Agriculture: ***Distribution of villages according to land use:*** Out of 171 villages, Total area (in hectare) is 96344, out of that 64.67 percent is cultivable and 12.64 percent of the cultivable area is irrigated.

Sources of Irrigation (Hectares): Government Canal 0, Private Canal 0, Well without Electricity 0, Well with Electricity 0, Tubewell without Electricity 0, Tubewell with Electricity 7875.61, Tank 0, River 0, Lake 0, Waterfall 0, Others 0.

Villages with population of 5000 to 9999: Bilichodu.

Villages with population of 10000 and above: None

Distribution of Workers:

	Persons	Males	Females	WPR
Cultivators	45,469	27,200	18,269	50.77
Agricultural Labour	34,421	12,882	21,539	38.44
Household Industry	965	544	421	1.08
Other Workers	8,701	6,462	2,239	9.72
Main Workers	65,065	39,429	25,636	72.65
Marginal Workers	24,491	7,659	16,832	27.35
Total Workers	89,556	47,088	42,468	

Religion: Major Religious Communities:

	Persons	Males	Females	Sex Ratio
Hindu (95.15%)	137,147	69,685	67,462	968
Muslim (4.22%)	6,086	3,103	2,983	961
Christian (0.01%)	17	11	6	545
Sikh (0%)	1	1	-	-
Buddhists (0%)	-	-	-	-
Jain (0.1%)	141	63	78	1,238

Agewise Data:

	Persons	Males	Females	Sex Ratio
All ages	144,139	73,239	70,900	968
0-14	50,163	25,680	24,483	953
15-44	65,350	33,640	31,710	943
45-79	27,017	13,231	13,786	1042
80+	1,528	637	891	1399
Age not stated	81	51	30	588

Languages (Dominant):

Kannada, Telugu, Urdu, Hindi, Marathi

Disabled Population:

	Persons	Males	Females	%
Total Disabled	3,576	2,118	1,458	
In Seeing	1,777	1,023	754	49.69
In Speech	334	181	153	9.34
In Hearing	185	106	79	5.17
In Movement	1,000	642	358	27.96
Mentally	280	166	114	7.83

JAMKHANDI

Jamkhandi C.D. Block lies in the northern part of Bagalkte distt.. It is a part of Jamkhandi taluka. The Block is located at a distance of 68 kms. from district H.Q. (Bagalkot). There are 71 villages in the block with the total population of 256,665 persons. Area of the C.D. Block is 1134.67 sq. kms. It is bounded by distt. Belgaum and Bijapur on north, taluk Mudhol and district Belgaum on south, district Bijapur and taluk Bilgi on east, and district Belgaum on west. and taluk Bilgi on east, and

Communications:

Roadways : S.H-65: Direction- Mudhol to Bijapur, Nearest Villages- Sanal, Alagur, Kumbarhal, Jamkhandi (Rural), Hulyal, Siddapur, Todalbagi, Chikkalaki, Chikkapadasalgi, Kavatagi.

River: Krishna Nadi- Nearest Villages- Tamadaddi, Halingali, Madanamatti, Asangi, Kulhalli, Hipparagi, Shiraguppi, Maigur, Muttur, Kankanawadi, Kadakol, Sanal, Alagur, Kunchanur, Jamkhandi (Rural), Jakanur, Chingundi, Shurpali, Jambag.(KD), Jambag.(B.K.), Takkod, Takkalaki, Hirepadasalgi, Naganur, Chikkapadasalgi, Kavatagi, Janawad, Bidari.

Canal: Nearest Villages- Terdal (Rural), Kulhalli, Hipparagi, Madarkhandi, Bandigani, Yallatti, Jagadal, Banhatti (Rural), Hosur, Hangandi, Sasalatti, Kaltippi, Golbhavi, Yaragatti,

Chimmad, Navalgi, Shiraguppi, Maigur, Albal, Kunchanur, Kumbarhal, Jamkhandi (Rural), Hunnur, Ramateerth, Mareguddi, Konnur, Gani, Budni.

Reserved Forest: Nearest Vill.- Halingali, Madarkhandi, Rabkavi (Rural), Hangandi, Kalhalli, Kunchanur, Ramateerth, Jakanur, Chingundi, Linganur, Hunashikatti, Hulyal, Siddapur, Konnur, Tungal, Kuragod, Kajibilgi, Gothe, Kannolli, Savalagi, Todalbagi, Jamkhandi (Rural).

Annual Rainfall: Normal Rianfall 551.4 mm.

Ground Water: Availability of the Ground Water in the Basin is (Information not avablable) H.A.M. and the utilization is (Information not avablable) H.A.M. It belongs to (Information not avablable) category. Depth to water level 5 to 20 meter below the ground. Most of the wells go down in summer months, according to the Ground Water Estimation Committee.

Natural Division : It falls partly in the Upper Krishna Valley and the Ghatprabha Irrigated Tract of the Northern Karnataka Plateau.

Soils: Black and Red Soils.

Administration:

Division: Belgaum. Parliamentary Constituency: 3 Bagalkot. District: Bagalkot. Taluka: Jamkhandi. Assembly Const.: 20 Terdol, 21 Jamkhandi. Gram Panchayat: 32.

Fairs and Festivals: Lakshmi Devi Mandira Festival: Muttur in Jamkhandi taluka is a small but beautiful garden-town situated on the southern bank of the Krishna river, 10 kilometres north of Jamkhandi. The town is well-known for the beautiful and well-built Lakshamidevi Mandira. A yearly festival is held on Makara Sankranti day.

Villages: 71 **Inhabited:** 71 **Uninhabited:** 0

Ranking	District	State	National
Area	3	66	320
Population	1	34	197
Sex Ratio	6	125	3062
Child Sex Ratio	6	155	4277
Literacy Rate	4	148	4615
Density	6	136	4357
Work Participation Rate	1	60	3201

Gram Panchayats:

Halingali, Asangi , Kulhalli, Hipparagi, Madarkhandi, Jagadal, Hangandi, Sasalatti , Golbhavi, Chimmad, Navalgi, Maigur, Muttur, Kankanawadi, Alagur, Kunchanur, Kumbarhal , Kadapatti, Hunnur , Linganur, Hulyal, Konnur, Tungal, Gothe, Kannolli, Savalagi, Shurpali, Jambagi.(B.K.), Todalbagi, Hirepadasalgi, Chikkapadasalgi, Bidari.

Amenities:

Education: Primary School in 68 villages, Middle school in 63 villages, Matriculation or Secondary School in 21 villages, namely Terdal (Rural), Halingali, Kulhalli, Hipparagi, Jagadal, Sasalatti, Chimmad, Navalgi, Albal, Kadapatti, Hunnur, Linganur, Hulyal, Mareguddi, Tungal, Gothe, Kalbilagi, Savalagi, Todalbagi, Chikkapadasalgi, Bidari.

Higher Secondary or Pre University Courses or Intermediate or Junior College in 4 villages of the CD Block,, namely Hipparagi, Hunnur, Savalagi, Todalbagi.

College in 2 villages, Adult Literacy Center in 2 villages., Colleges are in villages, namely Savalagi, Todalbagi.

Medical: Hospital in 0 village, Dispensary in 19 villages, Health Center in 6 villages, Sub Center in 38 villages, Maternity and Child Welfare Center in 0 village, Community health workers in 29 villages.

The Villages having Hospital or Dispensary or Health Center are Terdal (Rural), Madanamatti, Asangi, Hipparagi, Yallatti, Chimmad, Navalgi, Kalhalli, Muttur, Alagur, Kumbarhal, Kadapatti, Hunnur, Linganur, Gothe, Kalbilagi, Gadyal, Naganur, Chikkalaki.

Drinking Water: Tap water in 45 villages, Tank water in 38 villages, Well water in 51 villages, Tubewell in 42 villages and more than one source in 67 villages.

Bank: Banking facility in 14 villages, namely, Halingali, Hipparagi, Sasalatti, Navalgi, Muttur Alagur, Jakanur, Hulyal, Konnur, Gothe, Savalagi Todalbagi, Hirepadasalgi, Bidari.

Credit Society in 36 villages Agricultural Credit Society in 32 Non-Agricultural Credit Society in 1 village.

Others: Power supply in 71 villages, Cinema hall in 1 village, sport club in 0 village, Stadium or Auditorium or Community Hall in 0 village, Post Office in 59 villages.

There are 67 villages having bus facilities.

Villages with most of facilities: Halingali Hipparagi, Sasalatti, Navalgi, Muttur, Alagur Jakanur, Hulyal, Konnur, Gothe, Savalagi, Todalbagi Hirepadasalgi, Bidari.

Villages without amenities (Education): Kalhatti, Rabkavi (Rural), Ramateerth..

Scheduled Castes: Out of the total population of 256694 persons, 41449 persons (16.15%) belong to Scheduled Castes.

The villages having less than 10% SC population are Kalhatti, Hipparagi, Banhatti (Rural) Rabkavi (Rural), Kaltippi, Jamkhandi (Rural) Kuragod, Kajibilgi, Kalbilagi, Gadyal, Adihudi.

The village having more than 50% SC population is None.

Sex ratio of Scheduled Caste population is 506.

Scheduled Castes Literates and Illiterates by Sex:

	Persons	Males	Females

Literate	12,503	8,159	4,344
Illiterate	28,946	12,335	16,611
Literacy rate	37.2	49.5	25.4
Graduate	338	316	22

Scheduled Castes (Dominant):
Holaya etc., Bhambi etc., Madiga, Korama, Bhovi
For their cultural identity please see Appendix-I
Villages without Scheduled Castes: There are 2 villages without any scheduled caste population.
Scheduled Tribes: Out of the total population of 256694 persons, 3888 persons (1.51%) belong to Scheduled Tribes.
The villages having less than 10% ST population are Kalhatti, Terdal (Rural), Tamadaddi, Halingali Madanamatti, Asangi, Kulhalli, Hipparagi Madarkhandi, Bandigani, Yallatti, Jagadal Banhatti (Rural), Hosur, Rabkavi (Rural), Hangandi Sasalatti , Kaltippi, Golbhavi, Yaragatti, Chimmad Navalgi, Kalhalli, Maigur, Kankanawadi, Albal Hanchinal, Kadakol, Sanal, Alagur, Kunchanur Kumbarhal, Jamkhandi (Rural), Kadapatti, Hunnur Ramateerth, Chingundi, Linganur, Hunashikatti Hulyal, Siddapur, Mareguddi, Konnur, Gani, Budni Tungal, Kuragod, Kajibilgi, Gothe, Kalbilagi, Gadyal Kannolli, Savalagi, Tubachi, Shurpali Jambagi.(K.D.), Jambagi.(B.K.), Takkod, Takkalaki Adihudi, Todalbagi, Hirepadasalgi, Naganur Chikkalaki, Chikkapadasalgi, Kavatagi, Janawad Bidari.
The villages having more than 50% ST population are None.
Sex ratio of Scheduled tribe population is 489.
Scheduled Tribes Literates and Illiterates by Sex:

	Persons	Males	Females
Literate	1,248	822	426
Illiterate	2,640	1,164	1,476
Literacy rate	39.1	51.0	27.0
Graduate	18	16	2

Scheduled Tribes (Dominant):
Naikda etc., Koli Dhor etc., Koraga, Jenu Kuruba Meda
For their cultural identity please see Appendix-II
Villages without Scheduled Tribes: There are 34 villages without any scheduled tribe population.
Literates and Illiterates by Sex (Total Population):

	Persons	Males	Females
Literate	105,472	66,258	39,214
Illiterate	151,222	64,767	86,455
Literacy rate	50	61	37
Graduate	2,855	2,616	239

Agriculture: ***Distribution of villages according to land use:***
Out of 71 villages, Total area (in hectare) is 113467, out of that 79.34 percent is cultivable and 53.33 percent of the cultivable area is irrigated.
Sources of Irrigation (Hectares): Government Canal 20391.67, Private Canal 282.17, Well without Electricity 1001.84, Well with Electricity 6581.34, Tubewell without Electricity 187.51, Tubewell with Electricity 4353.27, Tank 1232.09, River 13977.04, Lake 0, Waterfall 0, Others 0.
Villages with population of 5000 to 9999:
Terdal (Rural), Halingali, Asangi, Kulhalli Hipparagi, Jagadal, Hangandi, Sasalatti , Chimmad Navalgi, Alagur, Hunnur, Konnur, Tungal, Gothe Savalagi, Todalbagi, Hirepadasalgi, Bidari.
Villages with population of 10000 and above: None
Distribution of Workers:

	Persons	Males	Females	WPR
Cultivators	46,837	34,631	12,206	41.57
Agricultural Labour	46,969	22,382	24,587	41.69
Household Industry	3,978	2,697	1,281	3.53
Other Workers	14,876	12,058	2,818	13.2
Main Workers	91,566	64,300	27,266	81.28
Marginal Workers	21,094	7,468	13,626	18.72
Total Workers	112,660	71,768	40,892	

Religion: Major Religious Communities:

	Persons	Males	Females	Sex Ratio
Hindu (86.42%)	221,834	112,935	108,899	964
Muslim (6.36%)	16,335	8,452	7,883	933
Christian (0.04%)	97	58	39	672
Sikh (0%)	9	4	5	1,250
Buddhists (0.06%)	161	84	77	917
Jain (6.65%)	17,065	8,876	8,189	923

Agewise Data:

	Persons	Males	Females	Sex Ratio
All ages	256,694	131,025	125,669	959
0-14	97,004	49,944	47,060	942
15-44	114,004	58,465	55,539	950
45-79	43,301	21,557	21,744	1009
80+	2,286	1,004	1,282	1277
Age not stated	99	55	44	800

Languages (Dominant):
Kannada, Urdu, Marathi, Hindi, Telugu
Disabled Population:

	Persons	Males	Females	%
Total Disabled	3,879	2,226	1,653	
In Seeing	1,793	1,000	793	46.22
In Speech	350	166	184	9.02
In Hearing	163	75	88	4.2
In Movement	1,189	777	412	30.65
Mentally	384	208	176	9.9

JEVARGI

Jevargi C.D. Block lies in the west central part of Gulbarga district.It is a part of Jevargi taluka. The Block is located at a distance of 44 kms. from district headquarters (Gulbarga). There are 159 villages in the block with the total population of 215,651 persons. Area of the C.D. Block is 1811.98 sq. kms. It is bounded by taluks Afzalpur and Gulbarga on north, taluks Shorapur and Shahpur on south, taluks Chitapur and Shahpur on east, and district Bijapur and taluk Afzalpur on west.

Communications:

Roadways : S.H-12: Direction- Sindgi to Jevargi, Nearest Villages- Mandewal, Indiragandhinagar, Gudur S.Nelogi, Billad, Jeratgi, Needalgi, Hipperga S.Nelogi, Janiwar, Jevargi (B) (Rural), Ravnoor, Mavnoor, Kalhangerga, Soan. S.H-16: Direction- Bijapur to Shahpur, Nearest Villages- Magengera, Allapur, Biryalhissa, Malli, Nagarhalli S.Malli, Mallbad. S.H-19: Direction- Shahpur to Gulbarga, Nearest Villages- Raddewadgi, Kellur, Aurad, Halgattarga, Murganoor, Kattisangavi, Sigarthalli, Ganwar, Mudbal (B), Mudbal (K).

River: Chinamgeri Nadi- Nearest Villages- Kudalgi, Mandewal,Gudur S.Nelogi, Billad, Mayoor, Balwandgi, Jeratgi, Mulhalli, Ranjangi, Needalgi, Kadkol, Jamberhal, Halgattarga, Murganoor, Aralgundgi, Konsirasgi, Telegbal, Yedrami, Sumbad, Dumadri, Kachapur, Akhandhalli, Malli, Wadgera. Bhima Nadi- Nearest Villages- Hullur, Harnal (K), Mogan Itga, Ankalga, Sidnal, Gulihal, Itga, Bhosga (K), Bhosga (B), Jalihal, Hanchinal S.Nelogi, Bedarhalli, Kudalgi, Yenkanchi, Mahur, Kallur (B), Kallur (K), Nelogi, Balwandgi,Narayanpur,Desangi, Badnihal, Kutnoor,Harwal, Rasangi, Handnoor, Banmi, Kobal, Kudi, Hipperga-Kona, Manderwad, Kolkur, Raddewadgi, Kattisangavi, Madri, Yangunti, Naribole, Rajwal, Malla (B), Malla (K), Honnal, Hotinmadu, Hanchinal Bhari, Rampur.

Annual Rainfall: Normal Rianfall 777 mm.

Ground Water: Availability of the Ground Water in the Basin is 9600 H.A.M. and the utilization is 2685 H.A.M. It belongs to Over Exploited category. Depth to water level 2 to 20 meter below the ground. Most of the wells go down in summer months, according to the Ground Water Estimation Committee.

Soils: Deep Black, Medium Black Soil, Shallow Soil and Lateritic Soil.

Natural Division : It falls partly in the Lower Bhima Valley and the Shorapur-Shahpur Upland of the Northern Karnataka Plateau.

Administration:

Division: Gulbarga. Parliamentary Constituency: 5 Gulbarga (SC). District: Gulbarga. Taluka: Jevargi. AssemblyConstituency: 35 Jevargi. Gram Panchayat: 33.

Regional Area Development Boards: The Hyderabad-Karnataka Area Development Board.

Villages: 159 **Inhabited:** 145 **Uninhabited:** 14

Ranking	District	State	National
Area	2	10	69
Population	7	73	511
Sex Ratio	7	101	2551
Child Sex Ratio	8	147	4149
Literacy Rate	5	166	5505
Density	6	87	5964
Work Participation Rate	10	156	2029

Gram Panchayats:

Itga, Ankalga, Kudi, Kolkur, Harwal, Nelogi, Kallur (K), Balwandgi, Jeratgi, Mandewal, Hipperga S.Nelogi, Soan, Gudur S.Andola, Naribole, Andola, Kellur, Harnur, Aralgundgi, Kuknoor, Alur, Ijeri, Yalwar, Ganwar, Biryal (B), Kadkol, Yedrami, Yalgod, Bilwar, Magengera, Malli, Kuralgera, Wadgera, Balbatti.

Amenities:

Education: Primary School in 145 villages, Middle school in 69 villages, Matriculation or Secondary School in 18 villages, namely Ankalga, Nelogi, Mandewal, Jeratgi, Hipperga S.Nelogi, Kolkur, Aralgundgi, Yedrami, Magengera, Malli, Wadgera, Ijeri, Alur, Bilwar, Naribole, Andola, Ganwar, Biryal (B).

Higher Secondary or Pre University Courses or Intermediate or Junior College in 1 village of the CD Block,, namely Yedrami.

College in 0 village, Adult Literacy Center in 8 villages.

Medical: Hospital in 4 villages, Dispensary in 20 villages, Health Center in 21 villages, Sub Center in 47 villages, Maternity and Child Welfare Center in 6 villages, Community health workers in 16 villages.

The Villages having Hospital or Dispensary or Health Center are Hullur, Harnal (K), Mogan Itga, Ankalga, Sidnal, Itga, Bhosga (K), Bhosga (B), Hanchinal S.Nelogi, Kudalgi, Jeratgi, Hipperga S.Nelogi, Gounahalli, Aralgundgi, Yedrami, Magengera, Kuralgera, Wadgera, Bilwar, Jamkhandi, Balbatti, Rajwal, Andola, Ganwar, Biryal (B), Rampur.

Drinking Water: Tap water in 42 villages, Tank water in 20 villages, Well water in 99 villages, Tubewell in 32 villages and more than one source in 134 villages.

Bank: Banking facility in 17 villages, namely, Hullur, Harnal (K), Ankalga, Sidnal, Itga Bhosga (K), Bhosga (B), Nelogi, Mandewal, Narayanpur Jeratgi, Kuranhalli, Aralgundgi, Yedrami, Malli Ijeri, Balbatti.

Credit Society in 29 villages Agricultural Credit Society in 29 Non-Agricultural Credit Society in 0 village.

Others: Power supply in 144 villages, Cinema hall in 4 villages, sport club in 40 villages, Stadium or Auditorium or Community Hall in 145 villages, Post Office in 66 villages.

There are 92 villages having bus facilities.

Villages with most of facilities: Hullur Harnal (K), Ankalga, Itga, Bhosga (K), Bhosga (B) Nelogi, Mandewal, Jeratgi, Aralgundgi, Yedrami Malli, Ijeri, Balbatti.

Villages without Amenities (Education): None..

Scheduled Castes: Out of the total population of 216075 persons, 43240 persons (20.01%) belong to Scheduled Castes.

The villages having less than 10% SC population are Mogan Itga, Yenkanchi, Kallur (B), Gudur S.Nelogi Balwandgi, Narayanpur, Desangi, Raddewadgi, Mavnoor Hanchinal S.Sulekhan, Jamberhal, Kuknoor Biryalhissa, Somnathhalli, Anadgi, Sigarthalli.

The village having more than 50% SC population is None.

Sex ratio of Scheduled Caste population is 493.

Scheduled Castes Literates and Illiterates by Sex:

	Persons	Males	Females
Literate	11,362	7,763	3,599
Illiterate	31,878	14,165	17,713
Literacy rate	32.9	44.5	21.0
Graduate	270	251	19

Scheduled Castes (Dominant):

Holaya etc., Banjara etc., Madiga, Bhovi Bhambi etc.

For their cultural identity please see Appendix-I

Villages without Scheduled Castes: There are 17 villages without any scheduled caste population.

Scheduled Tribes: Out of the total population of 216075 persons, 10454 persons (4.84%) belong to Scheduled Tribes.

The villages having less than 10% ST population are Hullur, Harnal (K), Mogan Itga, Ankalga, Sidnal Bhosga (K), Bhosga (B), Hanchinal S.Nelogi, Kudalgi Yenkanchi, Mahur, Kallur (B), Kallur (K), Nelogi Mandewal, Indiragandhinagar, Gudur S.Nelogi, Billad Mayoor, Balwandgi, Belur, Narayanpur, Yatnoor Jeratgi, Desangi, Badnihal, Ranjangi, Needalgi Kuranhalli, Hipperga S.Nelogi, Handnoor, Banmi Kobal, Kudi, Hipperga-Kona, Manderwad, Kolkur Raddewadgi, Janiwar, Ravnoor, Mavnoor, Kalhangerga Soan, Heggnal, Neeralkod, Hanchinal S.Sulekhan Kellur, Mansivangi, Shakapur, Kadkol, Jamberhal Halgattarga, Murganoor, Aralgundgi, Kummanasirasgi Wastari, Kuknoor, Konsirasgi, Telegbal, Yedrami Saidapur, Harnal (B), Hangerga (B), Sumbad, Dumadri Kachapur, Yatnal, Hanchinal S.Yedrami, Ainapur Magengera, Kondguli, Allapur, Biryalhissa, Malli Kuralgera, Nagarhalli S.Malli, Wadgera, Bennur Gobberwadgi, Kasrbhosga, Mutkod, Jawalga Somnathhalli, Gogihal, Kakhandki, Alur, Warvi Karkihalli, Yalgod, Anadgi, Nandihalli, Sathkhed Niradgi, Maradgi S.Madarki, Bilwar, Mangaloor Kachur, Shivapur, Jamkhandi, Konnur, Balbatti Amberkhed, Channur, Gudur S.Andola, Kattisangavi Madri, Yangunti, Malla (B), Andola, Jainapur Chigarhalli, Sigarthalli, Ganwar, Honnal, Hotinmadu Rampur, Maradgi S.Andola, Padgadhalli, Mudbal (B) Mudbal (K), Varchanhalli.

The villages having more than 50% ST population are None.

Sex ratio of Scheduled tribe population is 496.

Scheduled Tribes Literates and Illiterates by Sex:

	Persons	Males	Females
Literate	2,673	1,908	765
Illiterate	7,781	3,361	4,420
Literacy rate	31.5	44.5	18.2
Graduate	54	47	7

Scheduled Tribes (Dominant):

Naikda etc., Koli Dhor etc., Gond etc., Kadu Kuruba Iruliga

For their cultural identity please see Appendix-II

Villages without Scheduled Tribes: There are 70 villages without any scheduled tribe population.

Literates and Illiterates by Sex (Total Population):

	Persons	Males	Females
Literate	74,941	50,465	24,476
Illiterate	141,134	59,300	81,834
Literacy rate	42	56	28
Graduate	1,892	1,696	196

Agriculture: ***Distribution of villages according to land use:***

Out of 159 villages, Total area (in hectare) is 181198, out of that 89.17 percent is cultivable and 1.45 percent of the cultivable area is irrigated.

Sources of Irrigation (Hectares): Government Canal 552.79, Private Canal 0, Well without Electricity 392.25, Well with Electricity 1071.36, Tubewell without Electricity 23.06, Tubewell with Electricity 4.11, Tank 124.44, River 172.91, Lake 0, Waterfall 0, Others 0.

Villages with population of 5000 to 9999:

Nelogi, Yedrami, Ijeri.

Villages with population of 10000 and above: None

Distribution of Workers:

	Persons	Males	Females	WPR
Cultivators	30,334	24,630	5,704	29.47
Agricultural Labour	55,486	19,791	35,695	53.91

Household Industry	1,738	1,108	630	1.69
Other Workers	15,365	11,582	3,783	14.93
Main Workers	74,103	49,731	24,372	72
Marginal Workers	28,820	7,380	21,440	28
Total Workers	102,923	57,111	45,812	

Religion: Major Religious Communities:

	Persons	Males	Females	Sex Ratio
Hindu (78%)	168,549	85,666	82,883	968
Muslim (14.53%)	31,393	15,904	15,489	974
Christian (0.08%)	171	88	83	943
Sikh (0%)	5	4	1	250
Buddhists (6.67%)	14,414	7,318	7,096	970
Jain (0.1%)	214	103	111	1,078

Agewise Data:

	Persons	Males	Females	Sex Ratio
All ages	216,075	109,765	106,310	969
0-14	89,762	46,367	43,395	936
15-44	87,671	45,261	42,410	937
45-79	36,952	17,420	19,532	1121
80+	1,516	596	920	1544
Age not stated	174	121	53	438

Languages (Dominant):

Kannada, Urdu, Hindi, Telugu, Marathi

Disabled Population:

	Persons	Males	Females	%
Total Disabled	3,255	1,830	1,425	
In Seeing	1,108	538	570	34.04
In Speech	392	211	181	12.04
In Hearing	189	93	96	5.81
In Movement	1,290	818	472	39.63
Mentally	276	170	106	8.48

KADUR

Kadur C.D. Block lies in the eastern part of Chikmagalur district. It is a part of Kadur taluka. The Block is located at a distance of 40 kms. from district headquart ers (Chikmagalur). There are 312 villages in the block with the total population of 235,689 persons. Area of the C.D. Block is 1415.74 sq. kms. It is bounded by taluk Tarikere and district Chitradurga on north, taluk Chikmagalur and District Hassan on south, districts Chitradurga, Tumkur and Hassan on east, taluks Tarikere and Chikmagalur on west.

Communications:

Roadways : N.H.-206: Direction- Honavar to Tumkur, Nearest Villages- Doddagatta, Birurkaval (Rural), Galihalli, Jodithimmapura, Hanumapura, Nagadevarahalli, Birur (Rural), Ullinagur (Rural), Kadurhalli, Tangli, Nagdiyat hkaval, G.Thimmapura, Gedlehalli, Vaderahalli, Mathigatta, Kuppalu, Anche Chomanahalli, Mallappanahalli, Linglapu ra, Karehalli.D. S.H.-24: Direction- Ajjampur to Hosadurga, Nearest Villages- Antharagatte, Hullehalli, Sanklapura, C.Dasarahalli. S.H.-64: Direction- Chikmagalur to Kadur, Nearest Villages- Yemmedoddi, Dodabukkasagara, Kadur (Rural), Chikapatnagere, Saraswathipura, Kamasagara, Channapura, Ramanahalli, Hasthinapura, Kariyanahalli, Chikkabukkasagara, Sakrepatna, Kaluvehalli. S.H.-58: Nearest Villages- Panchanahalli, Thimlapura, B.T.Mallenahalli.

Railway Station: Villages- Hosahalli (Rural), Halladaha lll, Devanurkaval.

River: Veda Nadi- Nearest Villages- G.Madapura, Garje, G.Byrapura, Siriyappanahalli, Chokkapura, Vittalapura, Thippagondanahalli, Kandagadahalli, Mallidevihalli, Yalambalse, Biluvalakaval, Malleshwara (Rural), Mallapp anahalli (Rural), Haruvanahalli (Rural), Gopisettyhalli, Dombarahalli, Kadurhalli , Tangli, Macheri, Bhoothanaha lli, Chandrapura, Muddenahalli, Chikkatangli, Pattanagere, Kurubagere, Karehallikaval, Heelapura, Brahmasamudra, Gubbihalli, Banur, Chattnapalya, Sakrepatna, Kaluvehalli, L. Agrahara, Agrahara. Vedavati Nadi- Nearest Villages- Chowlihiriyur, Kukkasamudra, Bannihatti, Jammapura, Yaradakere G, Vokkalagere, Y.Basavanahalli, P.Mallapura, Pura, Garje, Yagati, Bukkanagundi, Siriyappanahalli, Chikkanayakanahalli, Seethapura, Sanehalli, Bokkmallana halli, Yalambalse, Sadarahalli, Madalu, Y.Mallapura, Doddanayakanahalli, Lakkenahalli, Kariyanahalli, Devanur kaval, Shanabinagundi, Laxmisagara, Kuppalu, Yaradakere, Y.Basavanahalli, Huligundi, Banannahalli, Sevanagar, Mangenahalli, Kambenahalli, Kabballi, Nagarahalu, Bolanahalli, Gedlehalli, Virupanahalli, Tandreborekaval.

Canal: Nearest Villages- Kalkere, Kallahalli, Chowlihiriyur, E.Timmapura, P.Kodihalli, P.Mallapura, Pura, Hiregarje, Yaradakere, Keresanthe, Lakkashettyhalli, Mallagatta, S. Kodihalli, Sevanagar, Hallikerekaval, Bolanahalli, Devanur, Gedlehalli, Virupanahalli, Nidaghatta, Siddara halli, Lingadahalli Jodi, Chatnahalli, Tandreborekaval.

Annual Rainfall: Normal Rianfall 620.3 mm.

Ground Water: Availability of the Ground Water in the Basin is 9654 H.A.M. and the utilization is 8465 H.A. M. It belongs to Semi Critical category. Depth to water level 2 to 20 meter below the ground. Most of the wells go down in summer months, according to the Ground Water Estimation Committee.

Soils: Red Loamy and Sandy Soils.

Natural Division : It falls in Upper Vedavati Basin of the Central Karnataka Plateau.

Administration:

Division: Mysore. Parliamentary Constituency: 15 Udupi, 16 Hassan. District: Chikmagalur. Taluka: Kadur. Assembly Constituency: 125 Chikmagalur, 127 Kadur.

Gram Panchayat: 59.

Regional Area Development Boards: The Maland Aera Development Board.

Fairs: Antaraghattamma Jatra: Antaraghattamma Jatra is held at Birur in about the month of January for three days. Birur is seven kilometers north-west of Kadur, 47 kms. north-east of Chikmagalur, 22 kms. south-east of Tarikere and abour 213 kms. north-east of Bangalore.

Beeralingeshvara Jatra: It is held at Asandi once in twelve years for fifteen days. Asandi is at a distance of about 20 kms. north-east of Kadur town and eight kilometers east of Ajjampura town in Tarikere taluk. About 14 inscriptions and a few notable structures have been found here.

Beeredevaru Jatra: It is held at Birur once in twelve years for fifteen days. Birur is seven kilometers north-west of Kadur.

Channakeshava Jatra: It is held at Kadur in around the month of June for four days every year Kadur is headquar ters town of the taluk of the same name, is at a distance of 28 kms. south-east of Tarikere town, 39 kms. north-ea st of Chikmagalur town, 47 kms. south-east of Bhadravati town and 206 kms. north-west of Bangalore city.

Chaudeshvari Festival: Nagadevanahalli is an uninhabited village 10 kms. north-west of Kadur town and about three kms. west of Birur town. There are two temples here, one of Chaudeshvari and the other of Anjaneya. The first is noted for its oracular ceremony held on full-mo on days. Special poojas are performed of Chaudeshvari during the Navaratri festival, and in the month of Kartika (October-November) deepotsava is celebrated.

Durgambika Jatra: Durgambika jatra is held at Antaraghat ta in around the month of February-March for ten days every year. Antaraghatta is 25 kms. north-east of Kadur town. It has a popular temple of goddess Durgambika which is also called Antaraghattamma and Chamundeshvari.

Honnaralamma Jatra: Honnaralamma jatra is held at Malles hvara near Chikmagalur in about the month of March-April for eight days. Malleshvara lies two kilometers east of Kadur town. It is said to derive its name from Mallas ura, "a giant who was harassing the local people and who was subdued by Shri Ramachandra". The Mallideva temple here is ascribed to the 12th century A.D.

Kalikamaba Jatra: Karehalli is 19 kms. south-east of Kadur town. There are two old popular temples here, one of Kalikamba and the other of Veerabhadra. It is said that the images in them are udbhava-murtis. The jatra of Kalikamba is held in March for two days.

Katte- Holeyamma Jatra: It is held at Patnagere around the month of March every year. Patnagere called Nagaravati in olden days, is seven kilometres south of Kadur town. To the north of the village, ruins of an old mud fort-w all, which appears to belong to about the 17th century A.D., are found. There are temples in this village dedicated to Lakshminarayana, Ballakki Narasimha and Katte-Holeyamma also called Doddamma.

Lakshmikanta Temple Jatra: It is held at Devanur near Chikmagalur in about the month of April-May for eight days. Devanur lies at a distance of 17 kilometres by railway from Kadur on the Miraj-Bangalore line, and 21 kms. to the south-west of Kadur town by road. The place is called so as it is noted for temples.

Lokaparameshvari Temple Jatra: It is held at Halamattauru in about the month of April for two days. Halamattauru, 21 kms. north-west of Koppa town, has a temple dedicated to Lokaparameshvari with shrines of Channakeshvara, Bhavanishankara and Ganapati. What is called moola-vigr aha, which is here an anthill, and the utsava-moorti have separate shrines. The anthill is fairly high. An annual jatra of the temple is held for two days about April.

Mailaralinga Jatra: It is held at Birur Chikmagalur area around the month of September-October every year. Birur is seven kilometres north-west of Kadur.

Malleshvara Jatra: It is held at Hirenalluru near Chikm agalur in around the month of April for five days. Hirena lluru, the headquarters of the Hubli situated about 13 kms. north-east of Kadur town is an ancient place.

Malli karjunaswamy Jatra: Keresante near Chikmagalur is 18 kms. south-east of Kadur town. On the top of the hill, there is a temple of Ishvara locally called Mallikarjun aswamy. The Shivalinga here, which is said to have been naturally formed, faces south. An annual jatra of this temple takes place for 20 days about January, at the time of which a cattle fair is also held. The place has also ruins of the temples of Veerabhadra, Janardana and Shambulingeshvara.

Prasanma-Mallikarjuna Temple Jatra: Pura near Chik-magalur situated on the left bank of the river Vedavati, is 26 kms. north-east of Kadur town. There is an old spacio us temple here dedicated to Prasanna-Mallikarjuna. An annual jatra of the temple is held for five days around March.

Shakuna Ranganathaswami Jatra: It is held at Sakrepatna near Chikmagalur around the month of January for nine days every year. Sakrepatna which is sometimes also called Sakharayapatna, is 17 kms. south-west of Kadur town.

Veerabhadra Jatra: It is held at Birur near Chikmagalur around the month of January - February for about nine days. There are several shrines and temples here. The jatra of Beeradevaru takes place once in twelve years for fifteen days. An annual jatra of Veerabharda is held about January-February for about nine days. There is a shrine of Antara-ghattamma, the annual jatra of which also is held for three days about January. There is also a temple of Mailaralinga here, the jatra of which is held on the Mahanavami day (September-October) when a customary oracular ceremony is held.

Villages: 312 **Inhabited:** 284 **Uninhabited:** 28

Ranking	District	State	National
Area	2	38	173
Population	1	54	326
Sex Ratio	6	69	2038
Child Sex Ratio	2	44	2145
Literacy Rate	7	55	1821
Density	4	128	5291
Work Participation Rate	1	105	3010

Gram Panchayats:
Jodithimmapura, Hirenalluru, Giriyapura, Asandi, Antharagatte, Kalkere, Chowlihiriyur, Vokkalagere, Chikkaballekere, Pura, Bislere, Basuru, Kamanakere, Hullehalli, Balliganur, Biluvala, Garje, Yagati, Hochihalli, Ganganahalli, Kunkanadu, Udugere, Yalambalse, Malleshwara (Rural) , Chikkangala, Yemmedoddi, Saraswathipura, Kadurhalli , Tangli, Y.Mallapura, Annegere, Uligere, Niduvalli, Panchanahalli, Thimlapura, Annegere, K.Bidre, Yaradakere, Ballekere, Pattanagere, Bisalehalli, Sakrepatna, Banur, Jigenehalli, Hochihalli, Cheelanahalli, Mathigatta, Singatagere, S.Madapura, Somanahalli, Keresanthe, Chikkadevanur, Devanur, Nagarahalu, Nidaghatta, Nagenahalli, Pillenahalli, Halikere, S.Bidre.

Amenities:

Education: Primary School in 149 villages, Middle school in 124 villages, Matriculation or Secondary School in 57 villages, namely Balliganur, Birur (Rural), Chikkangala, Giriyapura, Asandi, Antharagatte, Kalkere, Hirenalluru, Chowlihiriyur, Chikkaballekere, Basuru, Kamanakere, Bislere, P.Kodihalli, Yaradakere.G, Vokkalagere, Garje, Yagati, Hochihalli, Honnenahalli, Udugere, Kunkanadu, Vaderahalli, Uligere, Yalambalse, Y.Mallapura, Annegere, Saraswathipura, Dombarahalli, G.Thimmapura, Channapura, Bisalehalli, Gedlehalli, Jigenehalli, Mathigatta, Yaradakere, Garugadahalli, K.Bidre, Keresanthe, Singatagere, Niduvalli, Panchanahalli, Annegere, Somanahalli, Muthanagere, Thimlapura, Hochihalli, Banur, Sakrepatna, Pillenahalli, Nagenahalli, Devanur, Nidaghatta, Chandrashekarapura, Halikere, Lingadahalli Jodi, S.Bidre.

Higher Secondary or Pre University Courses or Intermediate or Junior College in 8 villages of the CD Block,, namely Birur (Rural), Antharagatte, Chowlihiriyur, Yagati, Singatagere, Sakrepatna, Devanur, Nidaghatta. College in 4 villages, Adult Literacy Center in 2 villages., Colleges are in villages, namely Birur (Rural), Chowlihiriyur, Singatagere, Panchanahalli.

Medical: Hospital in 10 villages, Dispensary in 29 villages, Health Center in 17 villages, Sub Center in 34 villages, Maternity and Child Welfare Center in 14 villages, Community health workers in 28 villages.

The Villages having Hospital or Dispensary or Health Center are Hogrehalli, Yemmedoddi, Asandi, Hirenalluru, Chowlihiriyur, Chikkaballekere, Basuru, Garje, Yagati, Udugere, Kunkanadu, Uligere, Yalambalse, G.Thimmapura, Muddenahalli, Ganganahalli, K.Bidre, Keresanthe, Singatagere, Niduvalli, Panchanahalli, Bittenahalli, Annegere, Somanahalli, S.Madapura, Thimlapura, B.T.Mallenahalli, Sakrepatna, Devanur, Nidaghatta, Halikere.

Drinking Water: Tap water in 148 villages, Tank water in 131 villages, Well water in 211 villages, Tubewell in 169 villages and more than one source in 233 villages.

Bank: Banking facility in 20 villages, namely, Antharagatte, Hirenalluru, Chowlihiriyur Vokkalagere, Yagati, Kunkanadu, Yalambalse Bisalehalli, K.Bidre, Singatagere, Panchanahalli Annegere, B.T.Mallenahalli, Shanabinagundi, Banur Sakrepatna, Devanur, Nidaghatta, Swamykatte, S.Bidre. Credit Society in 18 villages Agricultural Credit Society in 17 Non-Agricultural Credit Society in 3 villages.

Others: Power supply in 284 villages, Cinema hall in 6 villages sport club in 284 villages, Stadium or Auditorium or Communi Hall in 284 villages, Post Office in 54 villages. There are 133 villages having bus facilities.

Villages with most of facilities: Hirenalluru Chowlihiriyur, Vokkalagere, Yagati, Kunkanadu Yalambalse, K.Bidre, Singatagere, Panchanahalli Annegere, Sakrepatna, Devanur, Nidaghatta.

Villages without amenities (Education):
Doddagatta, Karehalli, Birurkaval (Rural), Inglaranahalli, Galihalli, Horithimmanahalli, Hanumapura, Dogihalli, Nagadevarahalli, Devarahalli Kaval, Aladahalli, Ullinagur (Rural), Lingalapura, Hireyangala, Outhanahalli, Gollarahalli, Channenahalli, Govindapura, Kannenahalli, K.Chomanahalli, Hullehalli, Gummanahalli, Siddapura, Siddegowdanahalli, Gadaganahalli, Hirenallurukaval, Basurukaval, Aadigere, Hosahalli Kalli, Kallahalli,

Kurubarahalli, E.Timmapura, Ganganahalli, Hanumanahalli, Gedlehalli, Marulanahalli, Jammapura, Mavinahalli, Chinakarahalli, M.Jakkanahalli, Y.Basavanahalli, P.Mallapura, Hiregarje, Rampura, G.Jakkanahalli, G.Madapura, Harisamudra, Keremelenahalli, Hanumanahalli, Bukkanagundi, Chokkapura, Vittalapura, Chikkanayakanahalli, Aladahalli, Sanehalli, Kandagadahalli, Soorapura, Doddanayakanahalli, K.Basavanahalli, Biluvalakaval, Aladahalli, Kurubarahalli, Malleshwara (Rural), Mallappanahalli (Rural), Haruvanahalli (Rural), Kachapura, Gopisettyhalli, Macheri, Bhoothanahalli, Chandrapura, Muddenahalli, Chikkatangli, Kanagondanahalli, Maradihalli, Ramanahalli, Kurubagere, Karehalli, Vaderahalli, Kurubarahalli, Yarehalli, Karehallikaval, Heelapura, Banjenahalli, Devarahalli, Lakkenahalli, Y.Basavanahalli, Kasuvanahalli, Muddenahalli, B.Basavanahalli, Thaggihallikaval, G.Bommenahalli, B.Bommenahalli, B.Mallenahalli, Lalithanagar, Banannahalli, D.Hosahalli, Kerehindinakaval (Kanakatte), Thubinakere, Ramanahalli, Pattadevarahalli, Mathihalli, Santhekerehalli, Mallappanahalli, Linglapura, Sevanagar, S. Kodihalli, Laxmipura, Devarahalli, Siddaramanahalli, M.Mallenahalli, Hasthinapura, Kariyanahalli, Chikkabukkasagara, Mangenahalli, Laxmisagara, Jadakanakatte, Halladahalli, Chattnapalya, Kaluvehalli, L. Agrahara, Manjihalli, Hallikerekaval, Bolanahalli, Kurubarahalli, Mallappanahalli, Bommenahalli.S, Thippagondanalli, Gedlehalli, Siddarahalli, Kanchugaranahalli, Gangabasavanahalli, Hudugerehalli, Swamykatte, Honnenahalli..

Scheduled Castes: Out of the total population of 235890 persons, 46361 persons (19.65%) belong to Scheduled Castes.

The villages having less than 10% SC population are Hoovinahalli, Karehalli, Inglaranahalli, Galihalli Jodithimmapura, Dogihalli, Nagadevarahalli Devarahalli Kaval, Birur (Rural), Byagadihalli Hireyangala, Kannenahalli, Giriyapura K.Chomanahalli, Hullehalli, C.Dasarahalli, Siddapura Siddegowdanahalli, Gadaganahalli, Hirenallurukaval M.Chomanahalli, Narasipura, Basurukaval, Aadigere Hireballekere, Hurukanahalli, Hosahalli Kalli H.Thimmapura, Kallahalli, Kurubarahalli Hanumanahalli, Gedlehalli, Bantiganahalli K.Dasarahalli, Marulanahalli, Chikkabasur, Bislere Jammapura, P.Kodihalli, Chinakarahalli M.Jakkanahalli, Y.Basavanahalli, P.Mallapura Hiregarje, Rampura, G.Jakkanahalli, G.Madapura Garje, Harisamudra, Somanahalli, Keremelenahalli Hanumanahalli, Bukkanagundi, Chokkapura Chikkanayakanahalli, Guddehalli, Vaderahalli Kothigere, Muglikatte, Kandagadahalli, Yalambalse Soorapura, Yalagundanahalli, Doddanayakanahalli Chattanahalli, K.Basavanahalli, Chowdlapura Biluvalakaval, Aladahalli, Nagagondanahalli Biluvala, Kurubarahalli, Kachapura, Gopisettyhalli Dombarahalli, Kallapura, Bhoothanahalli, Channapura Bisalehalli, Kurubagere, Karehalli, Vaderahalli Cheelanahalli, Alagatta, Yarehalli, Jigenehalli Panchehosahalli, Banjenahalli, Devarahalli Kariyanahalli, Hyaralagatta, Muddenahalli B.Basavanahalli, Thaggihallikaval, Ganganahalli B.Mallenahalli, K.Bidre, Kallelinganahalli Banannahalli, S.Basavanahalli, Kanchagallu D.Hosahalli, Thubinakere, Ramanahalli, Shettyhalli Pattadevarahalli, Mallappanahalli, Rangapura Siddaramanahalli, Kundur, M.Mallenahalli Mangenahalli, Laxmisagara, Halladahalli Pillenahalli, Nagenahalli, Agrahara, Manjihalli Hallikerekaval, Chikkadevanur, Kurubarahalli Machegundanahalli, Bommenahalli.S, Thippagondanalli Kamenahalli, Gedlehalli, Nidaghatta, Siddarahalli Chandrashekarapura, Gangabasavanahalli Hudugerehalli, Swamykatte, Kethumaranahalli Honnenahalli, S.Bidre.

The villages having more than 50% SC population are Birurkaval (Rural), Horithimmanahalli, B.Kodihalli Aladahalli, E.Timmapura, Ganganahalli, Seethapura Mallidevihalli, Thuruvanahalli, Ramanahalli Beeranahalli, Karehallikaval, Yaradakere Y.Basavanahalli, B.Bommenahalli, Lalithanagar Kerehindinakaval (Kanakatte), Anche Chomanahalli Sevanagar, Laxmipura, Hasthinapura, Brahmasamudra Chattnapalya, L. Agrahara, Bolanahalli Mallappanahalli, Byadarahalli.

Sex ratio of Scheduled Caste population is 494.

Scheduled Castes Literates and Illiterates by Sex:

	Persons	Males	Females
Literate	19,943	12,119	7,824
Illiterate	26,418	11,342	15,076
Literacy rate	49.6	59.6	39.4
Graduate	441	390	51

Scheduled Castes (Dominant):

Banjara etc., Madiga, Bhovi, Adi Karnataka, Korama

For their cultural identity please see Appendix-I

Villages without Scheduled Castes: There are 113 villages without any scheduled caste population.

Scheduled Tribes: Out of the total population of 235890

persons, 4418 persons (1.87%) belong to Scheduled Tribes. The villages having less than 10% ST population are Hoovinahalli, Doddagatta, Karehalli, Yarehalli Hullehalli, Birurkaval (Rural), Inglaranahalli Galihalli, Jodithimmapura, Horithimmanahalli Hanumapura, B.Kodihalli, Dogihalli, Nagadevarahalli Devarahalli Kaval, Balliganur, Aladahalli Hogrehalli, Birur (Rural), Byagadihalli Ullinagur (Rural), Lingalapura, Hireyangala Gollarahalli, Hyaralagatta, Yemmedoddi Dodabukkasagara, Channenahalli, Govindapura Kannenahalli, Chikkangala, Giriyapura, Chikkanalluru Asandi, K.Chomanahalli, Hullehalli, Sanklapura Kalkere, Gummanahalli, C.Dasarahalli, Siddapura Siddegowdanahalli, Gadaganahalli, Hirenalluru Hirenallurukaval, M.Chomanahalli, Melenahalli Narasipura, Basurukaval, Aadigere, Hireballekere Hurukanahalli, Hosahalli Kalli, Hadagalu H.Thimmapura, Kallahalli, Kurubarahalli Chowlihiriyur, E.Timmapura, Ganganahalli Chikkaballekere, Hanumanahalli, Gedlehalli, Arehalli Basuru, Kamanakere, Bantiganahalli, K.Dasarahalli Marulanahalli, Chikkabasur, Gowdanakattehalli Jammapura, Mavinahalli, P.Kodihalli Donnekoranahalli, Narasipura, Yaradakere.G Vokkalagere, M.Kodihalli, Chinakarahalli M.Jakkanahalli, Byregondanahalli, Y.Basavanahalli P.Mallapura, Pura, Hiregarje, G.Jakkanahalli G.Madapura, Garje, Yagati, Harisamudra, Hochihalli Somanahalli, Maravanji, Honnenahalli, Udugere Keremelenahalli, Hanumanahalli, Bukkanagundi Chokkapura, Vittalapura, Chikkanayakanahalli Seethapura, Guddehalli, Kunkanadu, Aladahalli Vaderahalli, Uligere, Kothigere, Muglikatte Sanehalli, Kandagadahalli, Mallidevihalli Yalambalse, Soorapura, Madalu, Yalagundanahalli Y.Mallapura, Doddanayakanahalli, Chattanahalli Annegere, K.Basavanahalli, Thuruvanahalli Chowdlapura, Uppunse, Biluvalakaval, Aladahalli Nagagondanahalli, Biluvala, Kurubarahalli Malleshwara (Rural), Mallappanahalli (Rural) Haruvanahalli (Rural), Chikapatnagere, Kachapura Saraswathipura, Kamasagara, Gopisettyhalli Dombarahalli, Kadurhalli , Tangli, Macheri Kallapura, Muddenahalli, Chikkatangli Kanagondanahalli, G.Thimmapura, Maradihalli Pattanagere, Channapura, Ramanahalli, Bisalehalli Kurubagere, Ballekere, Gedlehalli, Karehalli Beeranahalli, Vaderahalli, Kurubarahalli Cheelanahalli, Alagatta, Yarehalli, Karehallikaval Heelapura, Jigenehalli, Panchehosahalli Banjenahalli, Devarahalli, Mathigatta, Lakkenahalli Kariyanahalli, Kuppalu, Yaradakere, Y.Basavanahalli Alagatta, Hyaralagatta, Muddenahalli B.Basavanahalli, Thaggihallikaval, G.Bommenahalli Uppinahalli, Ganganahalli, Garugadahalli B.Bommenahalli, B.Mallenahalli, K.Bidre Lalithanagar, Kallelinganahalli, Huligundi Banannahalli, Keresanthe, Mallagatta, Singatagere S.Basavanahalli, Kanchagallu, D.Hosahalli Kerehindinakaval (Kanakatte), Niduvalli Panchanahalli, Thubinakere, Ramanahalli Bittenahalli, Annegere, Shettyhalli Pattadevarahalli, Mathihalli, Santhekerehalli Anche Chomanahalli, Mallappanahalli, Linglapura Sevanagar, S. Kodihalli, Laxmipura, Rangapura S.Madapura, Siddaramanahalli, Muthanagere Thimlapura, M.Mallenahalli, Hasthinapura Kariyanahalli, Chikkabukkasagara, Brahmasamudra Gubbihalli, Hochihalli, Gundasagara, Mangenahalli Shanabinagundi, Laxmisagara, Karehalli.D Jadakanakatte, Halladahalli, Kabballi, Byladalu Banur, Chattnapalya, Sakrepatna, Kaluvehalli Pillenahalli, Nagenahalli, L. Agrahara, Agrahara Hallikerekaval, Bolanahalli, Devanur, Chikkadevanur Kurubarahalli, Mallappanahalli, Machegundanahalli Bommenahalli.S, Thippagondanalli, Kamenahalli Gedlehalli, Nidaghatta, Siddarahalli Chandrashekarapura, Halikere, Kanchugaranahalli Gangabasavanahalli, Byadarahalli, Hudugerehalli Swamykatte, Kethumaranahalli, Lingadahalli Jodi Chatnahalli, Tandreborekaval, Honnenahalli, S.Bidre.

The villages having more than 50% ST population are None.

Sex ratio of Scheduled tribe population is 490.

Scheduled Tribes Literates and Illiterates by Sex:

	Persons	Males	Females
Literate	2,253	1,356	897
Illiterate	2,165	898	1,267
Literacy rate	58.2	68.6	47.4
Graduate	36	29	7

Scheduled Tribes (Dominant):

Naikda etc., Generic Tribes etc., Gowdalu, Meda Koraga

For their cultural identity please see Appendix-II

Villages without Scheduled Tribes: There are 241 villages without any scheduled tribe population.

Literates and Illiterates by Sex (Total Population):

	Persons	Males	Females
Literate	137,229	79,832	57,397

Illiterate	98,661	39,310	59,351
Literacy rate	66	76	55
Graduate	4,296	3,481	815

Agriculture: ***Distribution of villages according to land use:*** Out of 312 villages, Total area (in hectare) is 141574, out of that 63.61 percent is cultivable and 13.24 percent of the cultivable area is irrigated.

Sources of Irrigation (Hectares): Government Canal 745.34, Private Canal 0, Well without Electricity 39.11, Well with Electricity 126.42, Tubewell without Electricity 289.13, Tubewell with Electricity 7031.43, Tank 2820.02, River 0, Lake 0, Waterfall 0, Others 870.33.

Villages with population of 5000 to 9999: Yemmedoddi, Sakrepatna.

Villages with population of 10000 and above: None

Distribution of Workers:

	Persons	Males	Females	WPR
Cultivators	60,325	45,794	14,531	53.53
Agricultural Labour	32,805	12,709	20,096	29.11
Household Industry	2,455	1,621	834	2.18
Other Workers	17,114	12,011	5,103	15.19
Main Workers	84,609	65,027	19,582	75.08
Marginal Workers	28,090	7,108	20,982	24.92
Total Workers	112,699	72,135	40,564	

Religion: Major Religious Communities:

	Persons	Males	Females	Sex Ratio
Hindu (95.04%)	224,182	113,202	110,980	980
Muslim (3.09%)	7,290	3,695	3,595	973
Christian (0.18%)	429	225	204	907
Sikh (0%)	2	2	-	-
Buddhists (0.13%)	300	151	149	987
Jain (0%)	11	6	5	833

Agewise Data:

	Persons	Males	Females	Sex Ratio
All ages	235,890	119,142	116,748	980
0-14	64,211	32,741	31,470	961
15-44	117,094	58,085	59,009	1016
45-79	51,425	26,782	24,643	920
80+	2,839	1,351	1,488	1101
Age not stated	321	183	138	754

Languages (Dominant): Kannada, Hindi, Telugu, Urdu, Tamil

Disabled Population:

	Persons	Males	Females	%
Total Disabled	4,775	2,833	1,942	
In Seeing	2,455	1,437	1,018	51.41
In Speech	475	264	211	9.95
In Hearing	277	152	125	5.8
In Movement	1,191	781	410	24.94
Mentally	377	199	178	7.9

KALGHATGI

Kalghatgi C.D. Block lies in the south-western part of Dharwad district. It is a part of Kalghatgi taluka. The Block is located at a distance of 35 kms. from district headquarters (Dharwad). There are 87 villages in the block with the total population of 122,302 persons. Area of the C.D. Block is 658.93 sq. kms. It is bounded by taluk Dharwad on north, district Uttara Kannada on south and west, district Haveri, taluks Hubli and Kundgol on east.

Communications:

Roadways : N.H-63: Direction- Ankola to Hubli, Nearest Villages- Chalamatti, Kadankoppa, Ugginakeri, Hirehonnih alli, Kamadhenu, Mishrikoti, Harogeri, Dastikoppa, Ramanal, Madkihonnihalli, Devikoppa, Galaginakatti, Junjanbail, Sangatikoppa.

River: Bedti Nadi- Nearest Villages- Kamadhenu, Mishriko ti, Harogeri, Bhogenagarkoppa, Ramanal, Sangedevarkoppa, Madkihonnihalli, Galaginakatti, Belavantra, Hanamapur, Aladakatti, Singanahalli, Tambur, Shiddanabhavi, Bagadageri, Hindasgeri, Shivanapur, Tavargeri, Bammigatti.

Reserved Forest: Nearest Villages- Hulakoppa, Neerasagar, Devalingikoppa, Dasanur, Lingankoppa, Galagi, Karlakoppa, Dhummawad, Kudalgi, Tumarikoppa, Kalakundi, Sangameshwar,Masalikatti, Sulikatti, Hatakinhal, Dimbavalli, Nehru Nagar, Devikoppa, Galaginakatti. (Bendalagatti R.F.): Nearest Villages- Yammihatti, Arebasankoppa, Hasarambi, Kurankoppa, Chalamatti, Hullambi, Rajajinagar, Astakatti, Bendalgatti.

Annual Rainfall: Normal Rianfall 772 mm.

Ground Water: Availability of the Ground Water in the Basin is 5732.105 H.A.M. and the utilization is 2011. 809 H.A.M. It belongs to Over Exploited category. Depth to water level 5 to 10 meter below the ground. Most of the wells go down in summer months, according to the Ground Water Estimation Committee.

Soils: Loamy and Kankary Soils.

Natural Division : It falls partly in the Dharwad-Gadag Plateau and Kalghatgi-Lakshmeshwar Residual Hills of the Central Karnataka Plateau.

Administration:

Division: Belgaum. Parliamentary Constituency: 11 Dharwad. District: Dharwad. Taluka: Kalghatgi. Assembly Constit uency: 75 Kalghatgi. Gram Panchayat: 27.

Regional Area Development Boards: The Maland Aera Deve opment Board.

Villages: 87 **Inhabited:** 87 **Uninhabited:** 0

Ranking	District	State	National
Area	3	141	1017
Population	5	150	2800
Sex Ratio	5	168	4331

Child Sex Ratio	5	167	4867
Literacy Rate	5	114	3401
Density	2	5	4950
Work Participation Rate	4	93	238

Gram Panchayats:
Galagi, Gambyapur, G. Basavankoppa, Devalingikoppa, Dhummawad, Kurankoppa, Ugginakeri, Mishrikoti, Hirehonnihalli, Muttagi, Begur, Sangameshwar, Sulikatti, Devikoppa, Dastikoppa, Madkihonnihalli, Ganjigatti, Surasettikoppa, Guddad Hulikatti, Tabakadhonnihalli, Jinnur, Belavantra, Tambur, Tavargeri, Mukkall , Beeravalli, Bammigatti.

Amenities:

Education: Primary School in 78 villages, Middle school in 62 villages, Matriculation or Secondary School in 7 villages, namely Galagi, Hirehonnihalli, Mishrikoti, Tumarikoppa, Devikoppa, Mukkall, Bammigatti.
Higher Secondary or Pre University Courses or Intermediate or Junior College in 4 villages of the CD Block,, namely Galagi, Mishrikoti, Tumarikoppa, Devikoppa.
College in 0 village, Adult Literacy Center in 2 villages.

Medical: Hospital in 2 villages, Dispensary in 8 villages, Health Center in 5 villages, Sub Center in 26 villages, Maternity and Child Welfare Center in 0 village, Community health workers in 4 villages.
The Villages having Hospital or Dispensary or Health Center are Hulakoppa, Dhummawad, Hirehonnihalli, Sangameshwar, Ganjigatti, Surasettikoppa, Solargoppa, Mukkall.

Drinking Water: Tap water in 67 villages, Tank water in 0 villages, Well water in 5 villages, Tubewell in 15 villages and more than one source in 67 villages.

Bank: Banking facility in 8 villages, namely, Hulakoppa, Muttagi, Hirehonnihalli, Mishrikoti Tumarikoppa, Ganjigatti, Tabakadhonnihalli Bammigatti.
Credit Society in 29 villages Agricultural Credit Society in 29 Non-Agricultural Credit Society in 0 village.

Others: Power supply in 87 villages, Cinema hall in 1 village, sport club in 0 village, Stadium or Auditorium or Community Hall in 0 village, Post Office in 24 villages.
There are 83 villages having bus facilities.

Villages with most of facilities: Hulakoppa Muttagi, Hirehonnihalli, Mishrikoti, Tumarikoppa Ganjigatti, Tabakadhonnihalli, Bammigatti.

Villages without amenities (Education):
Karlakoppa, Shivanagar, Rangapur, Kandli, Nehru Nagar, Shiddanabhavi, Hulaginakoppa, Rajajinagar, Rajivanagar..

Scheduled Castes: Out of the total population of 122336 persons, 12138 persons (9.92%) belong to Scheduled Castes.
The villages having less than 10% SC population are Hulakoppa, Kannenaikankoppa, Basavarsikoppa Devalingikoppa, Dasanur, Jammihal, Lingankoppa Galagi, Karlakoppa, Yammihatti, B.Shigigatti Hasarambi, Muttagi, Bangittigudihal, Kurankoppa Kadankoppa, Ugginakeri, Hirehonnihalli, Dhulikoppa Hullambi, Begur, Kamadhenu, Kudalgi, Tumarikoppa Rangapur, Ramanal, Sangedevarkoppa, Madkihonnihalli Kalakundi, Sangameshwar, Masalikatti, Sulikatti Hatakinhal, Kandli, Dimbavalli, Devikoppa Galaginakatti, Belavantra, Hanamapur, Aladakatti Tambur, Shiddanabhavi, Bagadageri, Surasettikoppa Parasapur, Malkankoppa, Hindasgeri, Jinnur Shivanapur, Somanakoppa, Dyavankonda K. Hunishikatti, Tabakadhonnihalli Bullanaikanahulikatti, Guddad Hulikatti, Mukkall Yalavadal, Tavargeri, Bammigatti, Aralihonda Astakatti.
The village having more than 50% SC population is None.
Sex ratio of Scheduled Caste population is 492.

Scheduled Castes Literates and Illiterates by Sex:

	Persons	Males	Females
Literate	4,164	2,727	1,437
Illiterate	7,974	3,443	4,531
Literacy rate	41.8	53.4	29.6
Graduate	74	64	10

Scheduled Castes (Dominant):
Bhambi etc., Banjara etc., Bhovi, Chalavadi etc. Madiga

For their cultural identity please see Appendix-I

Villages without Scheduled Castes: There are 3 villages without any scheduled caste population.

Scheduled Tribes: Out of the total population of 122336 persons, 6873 persons (5.62%) belong to Scheduled Tribes.
The villages having less than 10% ST population are Hulakoppa, Basavarsikoppa, G. Basavankoppa Lingankoppa, Galagi, Karlakoppa, Gambyapur B.Shigigatti, Hasarambi, Muttagi, Kurankoppa Chalamatti, Kadankoppa, Ugginakeri, Hirehonnihalli Dhulikoppa, Shivanagar, Hullambi, Begur, Bisaralli Mishrikoti, Bhogenagarkoppa, Kudalgi, Tumarikoppa Rangapur, Dastikoppa, Sangedevarkoppa Madkihonnihalli, Kalakundi, Sangameshwar Masalikatti, Sulikatti, Kandli, Dimbavalli Nehru Nagar, Devikoppa, Belavantra, Hanamapur Aladakatti, Singanahalli, Junjanbail, Sangatikoppa Tambur, Shiddanabhavi, Hulaginakoppa, Ganjigatti Surasettikoppa, Dyamapur, Parasapur, Malkankoppa

Jinnur, Dyavankonda, K. Hunishikatti Bullanaikanahulikatti, Beeravalli, Bammigatti Aralihonda, Nelliharvi, Rajajinagar, Rajivanagar Bendalgatti.

The villages having more than 50% ST population are None.

Sex ratio of Scheduled tribe population is 470.

Scheduled Tribes Literates and Illiterates by Sex:

	Persons	Males	Females
Literate	2,637	1,712	925
Illiterate	4,236	1,929	2,307
Literacy rate	45.6	56.0	33.9
Graduate	19	18	1

Scheduled Tribes (Dominant):

Naikda etc., Kadu Kuruba, Meda, Irular

For their cultural identity please see Appendix-II

Villages without Scheduled Tribes: There are 20 villages without any scheduled tribe population.

Literates and Illiterates by Sex (Total Population):

	Persons	Males	Females
Literate	58,472	36,292	22,180
Illiterate	63,864	27,002	36,862
Literacy rate	57	68	44
Graduate	1,115	945	170

Agriculture: *Distribution of villages according to land use:*
Out of 87 villages, Total area (in hectare) is 65893, out of that 61.2 percent is cultivable and 8.88 percent of the cultivable area is irrigated.

Sources of Irrigation (Hectares): Government Canal 346.77, Private Canal 0, Well without Electricity 0, Well with Electricity 7.28, Tubewell without Electricity 0, Tubewell with Electricity 2273.41, Tank 915.68, River 39.42, Lake 0, Waterfall 0, Others 0.

Villages with population of 5000 to 9999:
Mishrikoti.

Villages with population of 10000 and above: None

Distribution of Workers:

	Persons	Males	Females	WPR
Cultivators	32,590	21,084	11,506	46.3
Agricultural Labour	24,748	8,983	15,765	35.16
Household Industry	1,670	1,077	593	2.37
Other Workers	11,374	9,139	2,235	16.16
Main Workers	53,463	36,049	17,414	75.96
Marginal Workers	16,919	4,234	12,685	24.04
Total Workers	70,382	40,283	30,099	

Religion: Major Religious Communities:

	Persons	Males	Females	Sex Ratio
Hindu (88.84%)	108,685	56,195	52,490	934
Muslim (8.12%)	9,932	5,167	4,765	922
Christian (0.58%)	711	378	333	881
Sikh (0.01%)	8	5	3	600
Buddhists (0.29%)	360	196	164	837
Jain (1.78%)	2,182	1,131	1,051	929

Agewise Data:

	Persons	Males	Females	Sex Ratio
All ages	122,336	63,294	59,042	933
0-14	42,603	21,971	20,632	939
15-44	58,458	30,508	27,950	916
45-79	20,383	10,403	9,980	959
80+	816	371	445	1199
Age not stated	76	41	35	854

Languages (Dominant):
Kannada, Urdu, Marathi, Hindi, Telugu

Disabled Population:

	Persons	Males	Females	%
Total Disabled	2,072	1,190	882	
In Seeing	513	269	244	24.76
In Speech	188	99	89	9.07
In Hearing	190	94	96	9.17
In Movement	911	571	340	43.97
Mentally	270	157	113	13.03

KANAKAPURA

Kanakapura C.D. Block lies in the southern part of Bangalore Rural district. It is a part of Kanakapura tehsil. The Block is located at a distance of 56 kms. from district headquarters (Bangalore). There are 259 villages in the block with the total population of 289,578 persons. Area of the C.D. Block is 1599.24 sq. kms. It is bounded by district Bangalore and taluk Ramanagaram on north, district Chamarajanagar on south, district Bangalore on east, district Mandya, taluk Channapatna on west. It has common boundary with the state of Tamil Nadu on east.

Communications:

Roadways : N.H.-209: Direction- Chamrajanagar to Bangalore, Nearest Villages- Hosakote, Gabbadi Kaval, Gabbadi, Kaggalahalli, Vaderahalli, Yadamadu, Marasandra, Harohalli, Devarakaggalahalli, Maralagere, Cheeluru, Jakkasandra, Keeranagere, Tungani, Rayasandra, Agrahara, Kallahalli, Shivanahalli, Anjanapura, Seegekote, Thotahalli, Mudalaswamikuppe, Honiganahalli, Kemmale, Satanur, Yadugowdanahalli, Achalu. S.H.-3: Direction- Ramanagaram to State of Tamil Nadu, Nearest Villages- Singasandra, Doddamuduwadi, Anajawadi, Chikkamuduwadi, Allimaranahalli, Ganalu, Aralalusandra, Thammasandra, Aralalu, Kanakapura (Rural), Bekuppe, Nidagallu Aralasandra, Narayanapura, Kebbehalli, Kuthagale, Garalapura, Doddakabbahalli, Tattiguppe, Yeramgere, Kodihalli, Balepura, Hosadurga , Thattikere, Hunsanahalli, Ganganahalli, Hunasanakodihalli. S.H.-86 B: Direction- Kanakpura to the southern bound of the

Block, Nearest Villages- Aralalu, Chokasandra, Bekuppe, Tigalarahosahalli, Horalagallu, Kunuru, Marale Bekuppe, Mahimanahalli, Alahalli, Uyyamballi, Cheelandavadi Forest, Hegganuru, Heligehalli, Haroshivanahalli.

River: Cauvery Nadi- Nearest Villages- Cheelandavadi Forest, Hyra, Mugguru Forest. Arkavati Nadi- Nearest Villages- Singasandra, Doddamuduwadi, Bandiganahalli, Allimaranahalli, Ramapura, Agrahara, Aralalusandra, Tigalarahalli, Thammasandra, Kallahalli, Virupasandra, Cheeranakuppe, Aralalu, Kanakapura (Rural), Chokasandra, Bekuppe, Tigalarahosahalli, Horalagallu, Kunuru, Nidaga llu, Nidagallu Aralasandra, Kebbehalli, Margadevanagundi, Kutagale, Ganalu, Anajawadi, Chikkamuduwadi, Kokkareho sahalli, Hukundha, Mullahalli, Nallahalli, Cheelandavadi Forest, Purushagondanahalli, Madarahalli, Gollahalli, Arekoppa, Haroshivanahalli, Bennegodlu, Mahalli, Mugguru Forest.

Canal: Nearest Villages- Kolliganahalli, Kadasikoppa, Kurubarhalli, Bandiganahalli, Haravathipalya, Aratabele, Chikkakalbalu, Bannikuppe, Cheeluru, Allimaranahalli, Ramapura, Tungani, Agrahara, Aralalusandra.

Reserved Forest: (Bananthimari R.F.): Nearest Villages- Vaded oddi, Udarahalli, Murkani, Somedyapanahalli, Muradihosaha lli, Banthamari State Forest, Allimaranahalli, Dollahalli, Aralalusandra, Tigalarahalli, Thammasandra, Kanakapura (Rural), Ramanahalli, Kuthagondanahalli. (G. Gudda R. F.): Nearest Villages- Paduvanagere, Ballagere, Guthalah onase, Ajjegowdanavalase, Bachahalli, Rayasandra.

Annual Rainfall: Normal Rianfall 805.51 mm.

Ground Water: Availability of the Ground Water in the Basin is (Information not avablable) H.A.M. and the utilization is (Information not avablable) H.A.M.
It belongs to (Information not avablable) category.
Depth to water level 5 to 20 meter below the ground.
Most of the wells go down in summer months, according to the Ground Water Estimation Committee.

Natural Division : It falls partly in Cauvery Forested Region and Bangalore Plateau of the Southern Karnataka Plateau.

Administration:

Division: Bangalore. Parliamentary Constituency: 23 Bangalore Rural. District: Bangalore Rural. Taluka: Kanakapura. Assembly Constituency: 183 Ramanagaram, 184 Kanakapura. Gram Panchayat: 43.

Regional Area Development Boards: The Bailu Seeme Area Development Board.

Border Villages: (State: Tamil Nadu)- Kolalugundi, Kalla nakuppe, Sheetalavadi, Kattarinatha, Yalachavadi, Bantana lu, Therubeedi, Bilikal Forest, Mahalli, Mugguru Forest, Mugguru, Gattigunda, Kolagondanahalli, Manjilnatha, Yalachahalli, Basavapatna Veerasandra, Belidale, Bannim ukkodlu, Honniganahalli, Chikkmukodlu, Ganganahalli, Hunasanakodihalli.

Villages: 259 **Inhabited:** 239 **Uninhabited:** 20

Ranking	District	State	National
Area	1	24	108
Population	1	21	84
Sex Ratio	7	154	3696
Child Sex Ratio	8	164	4787
Literacy Rate	8	133	4017
Density	4	94	5021
Work Participation Rate	8	95	2218

Gram Panchayats:
Kottagalu, Kolliganahalli, Harohalli, Kaggalahalli, Dyavasandra, Banavasi, Yalachavadi, Doddamaralawadi, Thokasandra, T.Hosahalli, Cheeluru, Doddamuduwadi, Chikkamuduwadi, Allimaranahalli, Tungani, Kallahalli, Budiguppe, Somedyapanahalli, Choodahalli, Kabbal, Honniganahalli, Kadahalli, Sathanur, Arekattedoddi, Achalu, Shivanahalli , Bekuppe, Narayanapura, Chakanahalli, Arakere, Mullahalli, Marale Bekuppe, Dodda Alahalli, Uyyamballi, Nallahalli, Hukundha, Gollahalli, Bannimukkodlu, Kodihalli, Herandyappanahalli, Hosadurga , Kolagondanahalli, Hunsanahalli.

Amenities:

Education: Primary School in 182 villages, Middle school in 119 villages, Matriculation or Secondary School in 27 villages, namely Kadasikoppa, Harohalli, Chikkakalbalu, Cheeluru, Thokasandra, Banavasi, Doddamaralawadi, Chikkamuduwadi, Tungani, Tigalarahalli, Shivanahalli, Kanakapura (Rural), Thenganayakanahalli, Kambasagara, Attihalli, Sathanur, Marale Bekuppe, Hukundha, Nallahalli, Alahalli, Uyyamballi, Gollahalli, Herandyappanahalli, Kolagondanahalli, Kodihalli, Hosadurga, Hunsanahalli.
Higher Secondary or Pre University Courses or Intermediate or Junior College in 7 villages of the CD Block,, namely Harohalli, Thenganayakanahalli, Sathanur, Alahalli, Herandyappanahalli, Kodihalli, Hunsanahalli.
College in 0 village, Adult Literacy Center in 43 villages.

Medical: Hospital in 1 village, Dispensary in 9 villages, Health Center in 16 villages, Sub Center in 63 villages, Maternity and Child Welfare Center in 6 villages, Community health workers in 20 villages.
The Villages having Hospital or Dispensary or Health Center are Harohalli, Chikkamuduwadi, Choodahalli, Sathanur, Alahalli, Cheelandavadi Forest, Bijjahalli, Hosadurga , Hunsanahalli.

Drinking Water: Tap water in 106 villages, Tank water in 43 villages, Well water in 62 villages, Tubewell in 198 villages and more than one source in 217 villages.

Bank: Banking facility in 13 villages, namely, Kolliganahalli, Harohalli, Jakkasandra Doddamaralawadi, Chikkamuduwadi, Thammasandra Kabbal, Honniganahalli, Sathanur, Alahalli Kodihalli, Hosadurga, Hunsanahalli.

Credit Society in 35 villages Agricultural Credit Society in 33 Non-Agricultural Credit Society in 1 village.

Others: Power supply in 235 villages, Cinema hall in 5 villages, sport club in 2 villages, Stadium or Auditorium or Community Hall in 239 villages, Post Office in 51 villages.

There are 200 villages having bus facilities.

Villages with most of facilities: Kolliganahalli Harohalli, Jakkasandra, Doddamaralawadi Chikkamuduwadi, Thammasandra, Kabbal, Alahalli Kodihalli, Hosadurga, Hunsanahalli.

Villages without amenities (Education): Gabbadi Kaval, Yadamadu, Bettahalli Kaval, Gullahatti Kaval, Belaguli, Chulakanakere Kaval, Keeranagere, Chikkadevarahalli, Hosahalli, Gadaranahalli, T.Maniyambal, Marasarahalli, Huyalappanahalli, Bheemasandra, Vadedoddi, Udarahalli, Belikothanur, Muradihosahalli, Dollahalli, Agrahara, Aranakuppe, Anjanapura, Nidagallu Aralasandra, Tailuru Forest, Virupasandra, Honnahalli, Mallapura, Arehosahalli, Anamanahalli, Naripura, S00Ligere, Konanagundi, Makkalandha, Chikkamudude, Chikkakoppa, Veerasandra, Vadakekatte, Madarahalli, Bennegodlu, Mahalli, Mugguru Forest, Mugguru, K.Gollahalli, Ajjabasavanahalli, Tattiguppe, Bommasandra, Yeramgere, Balepura, Guddaveerana Hosahalli, Hunasalanatha, Kudigalane, Balagondanahalli..

Scheduled Castes: Out of the total population of 290148 persons, 58481 persons (20.16%) belong to Scheduled Castes.

The villages having less than 10% SC population are Pichanakere, Kadasikoppa, Gabbadi Kaval, Gabbadi Yadamadu, Kadujakkasandra, Marasandra Hulugondanahalli, Kurubarhalli, Haravathipalya Aratabele, Belaguli, Chikkakalbalu, Bannikuppe Devarakaggalahalli, Bheemasandra, Dyavasandra Keeranagere, Malligemetlu, Ballagere, Gadaranahalli Goduru, Billiganakuppe, Marasarahalli, Sheetalavadi Bheemasandra, Bantanalu, Sundagatta, Udarahalli Basavanahalli, Muradihosahalli, Dollahalli Rayasandra, Tigalarahalli, Aranakuppe, Baradanahalli Virupasandra, Bekuppe, Horalagallu Nidagallu Aralasandra, Honnahalli, Suranahalli Hosahalli, Mallapura, Kachavanahalli, Anamanahalli Naripura, Halasinamaradahalli, Sasalapura Mudalaswamikuppe, Chikkamudude, Yadamaranahalli Margadevanagundi, Kuthagale, Hukundha, Nallahalli Mahimanahalli, Uyyamballi, Cheelandvadi, Hoolya Vadakekatte, Madarahalli, Mugguru Forest, Doddaguli Hanchiguli, Herandyappanahalli, Thippur Ajjabasavanahalli, Belidale, Bommasandra Channasandra, Salabanni, Kempalanatha, Hunasalanatha Irlapodu, Ganganahalli.

The villages having more than 50% SC population are Bettahalli Kaval, Gullahatti Kaval Chikkadevarahalli, Devarahalli, Kattarinatha Linganapura, Vadedoddi, Aralalu, Anjanapura Chokasandra, Nidagallu, Sambapura, S00Ligere Dunthuru, Purushagondanahalli, Bennegodlu, Arakere K.Gollahalli, Bijjahalli, Mallapura Balagondanahalli.

Sex ratio of Scheduled Caste population is 488.

Scheduled Castes Literates and Illiterates by Sex:

	Persons	Males	Females
Literate	24,379	15,072	9,307
Illiterate	34,102	14,890	19,212
Literacy rate	47.4	57.2	37.1
Graduate	586	525	61

Scheduled Castes (Dominant):

Adi Karnataka, Banjara etc., Bhovi, Madiga, Korama

For their cultural identity please see Appendix-I

Villages without Scheduled Castes: There are 38 villages without any scheduled caste population.

Scheduled Tribes: Out of the total population of 290148 persons, 5330 persons (1.84%) belong to Scheduled Tribes.

The villages having less than 10% ST population are Pichanakere, Gollahalli, Kolliganahalli, Kadasikoppa Yerehalli, Medamaranahalli, Mudenahalli, Hosakote Gabbadi Kaval, Gabbadi, Kaggalahalli, Vaderahalli Yadamadu, Bettahalli Kaval, Gottigehalli Gullahatti Kaval, Kadujakkasandra, Marasandra Harohalli, Hulugondanahalli, Kurubarhalli Doddakalbalu, Kottagalu, Singasandra, Doddamuduwadi Bandiganahalli, Haravathipalya, Aratabele, Belaguli Chikkakalbalu, Bannikuppe, Devarakaggalahalli Chulakanakere Kaval, Bheemasandra, Dyavasandra Konasandra, Cheeluru, Jakkasandra, Keeranagere Chikkadevarahalli, T.Hosahalli, Paduvanagere Doddasadenahalli, Chakkasadenahalli, Malligemetlu Ballagere, Guthalahonase, Ajjegowdanavalase Mavathoor, Bachahalli, M.Maniyambal, Thokasandra Hosahalli, Devarahalli, Chikkamaralavadi Anehosahalli, Avaremala, Gadaranahalli, Attikuppe

Goduru, Billiganakuppe, Thattekere, Kolalugundi T.Maniyambal, Banavasi, Marasarahalli Doddamaralawadi, Huyalappanahalli, Sheetalavadi Kattarinatha, Yalachavadi, Bheemasandra, Bantanalu Sundagatta, Anajawadi, Chikkamuduwadi, Vadedoddi Udarahalli, Murkani, Belikothanur, Basavanahalli Somedyapanahalli, Mallappana Hosahalli Muradihosahalli, Allimaranahalli, Ganalu, Ramapura Tungani, Rayasandra, Anmanahalli, Agrahara Aralalusandra, Tigalarahalli, Thammasandra Kallahalli, Aranakuppe, Baradanahalli, Virupasandra Chakanahalli, Kerelallusandra, Cheeranakuppe Aralalu, Shivanahalli, Kanakapura (Rural) Ramanahalli, Anjanapura, Seegekote , Chokasandra Bekuppe, Tigalarahosahalli, Horalagallu, Kunuru Nidagallu, Nidagallu Aralasandra, Kebbehalli Chikkabettahalli, Goravinapura, Kanchanahalli, Alur Tailuru Forest, Choodahalli, Thenganayakanahalli Virupasandra, Honnahalli, Suranahalli, Kambasagara Kabbal, Hosahalli, Attihalli, Gerahalli Bommanahalli, Thotahalli, Mallapura, Arehosahalli Kachavanahalli, Dalimba, Anamanahalli, Naripura Sasalapura, Mudalaswamikuppe, Honniganahalli Kemmale, Sathanur, Achalu, Nagarasanakote, Halasuru Kadahalli, Harihara, Sambapura, S00Ligere, Boohalli Dunthuru, Chikkalahalli, Chikkamudude, Nayakanahalli Marale Bekuppe, Margadevanagundi, Kuthagale Kokkarehosahalli, Hukundha, Chikkakoppa, Mullahalli Nallahalli, Mahimanahalli, Alahalli, Uyyamballi Cheelandvadi, Cheelandavadi Forest, Hegganuru Heligehalli, Vadakekatte, Purushagondanahalli Madarahalli, Gollahalli, Doddakoppa, Kotekoppa Arekoppa, Haroshivanahalli, Bennegodlu Mugguru Forest, Garalapura, Arakere, Doddaguli Halasuru, Hanchiguli, Kebre, K.Gollahalli Herandyappanahalli, Thippur, Yakkuli Ajjabasavanahalli, Doddakabbahalli, Tattiguppe Bijjahalli, Gattigunda, Kolagondanahalli, Yeramgere Kodihalli, T.Gollahalli, Channasandra, Mallapura Balepura, Hosadurga , Salabanni Guddaveerana Hosahalli, Kempalanatha, Halanatha Hunasalanatha, Kudigalane, Irlapodu, Bannimukkodlu Honniganahalli, Chikkmukodlu, Thattikere Balagondanahalli, Hunsanahalli, Ganganahalli Hunasanakodihalli.

The villages having more than 50% ST population are None.

Sex ratio of Scheduled tribe population is 477.

Scheduled Tribes Literates and Illiterates by Sex:

	Persons	Males	Females
Literate	1,561	969	592
Illiterate	3,769	1,819	1,950
Literacy rate	34.5	40.9	27.4
Graduate	15	10	5

Scheduled Tribes (Dominant):

Iruliga, Soligaru, Naikda etc., Meda, Irular

For their cultural identity please see Appendix-II

Villages without Scheduled Tribes: There are 160 villages without any scheduled tribe population.

Literates and Illiterates by Sex (Total Population):

	Persons	Males	Females
Literate	136,870	82,736	54,134
Illiterate	153,278	66,367	86,911
Literacy rate	53	63	43
Graduate	3,496	2,914	582

Agriculture: ***Distribution of villages according to land use:*** Out of 259 villages, Total area (in hectare) is 159924, out of that 43.53 percent is cultivable and 21.24 percent of the cultivable area is irrigated.

Sources of Irrigation (Hectares): Government Canal 635.84, Private Canal 0, Well without Electricity 278.87, Well with Electricity 2392.27, Tubewell without Electricity 152.18, Tubewell with Electricity 8204.78, Tank 2244.49, River 166.64, Lake 0, Waterfall 0, Others 709.1.

Villages with population of 5000 to 9999:

Sathanur, Kodihalli.

Villages with population of 10000 and above:

Harohalli.

Distribution of Workers:

	Persons	Males	Females	WPR
Cultivators	78,414	52,461	25,953	52.95
Agricultural Labour	34,626	14,953	19,673	23.38
Household Industry	3,123	1,619	1,504	2.11
Other Workers	31,932	20,968	10,964	21.56
Main Workers	111,677	77,871	33,806	75.41
Marginal Workers	36,418	12,130	24,288	24.59
Total Workers	148,095	90,001	58,094	

Religion: Major Religious Communities:

	Persons	Males	Females	Sex Ratio
Hindu (96.44%)	279,824	143,731	136,093	947
Muslim (2.37%)	6,884	3,531	3,353	950
Christian (0.81%)	2,357	1,245	1,112	893
Sikh (0%)	6	4	2	500
Buddhists (0.14%)	403	212	191	901
Jain (0.08%)	221	150	71	473

Agewise Data:

	Persons	Males	Females	Sex Ratio
All ages	290,148	149,103	141,045	946
0-14	85,177	44,252	40,925	925
15-44	138,029	70,740	67,289	951

45-79	62,494	32,114	30,380	946
80+	4,052	1,781	2,271	1275
Age not stated	396	216	180	833

Languages (Dominant):
Kannada, Hindi, Urdu, Telugu, Tamil

Disabled Population:

	Persons	Males	Females	%
Total Disabled	6,503	3,612	2,891	
In Seeing	3,309	1,745	1,564	50.88
In Speech	681	380	301	10.47
In Hearing	427	218	209	6.57
In Movement	1,458	923	535	22.42
Mentally	628	346	282	9.66

KARKAL

Karkal C.D. Block lies in the south-eastern part of Udupi district. It is a part of Karkal taluka. The Block is located at a distance of 40 kms. from district headqu arters (Udupi). There are 50 villages in the block with the total population of 179,453 persons. Area of the C.D. Block is 1049.53 sq. kms. It is bounded by district Shimoga and taluk Kundapur on north, district Dakshina Kannada on south, district Chikmagalur on east, and taluk Udupi on west.

Communications:

Roadways : N.H.-13: Direction- Karkal to Mudigere & Mudbidri, Nearest Villages- Kervashe, Mala, Kanthavara, Sanoor, Miyar, Mudar, Nallur, Irvathuru. S.H-25: Direction- Karkal to Shimoga, Nearest Villages- Nadpalu, Hebri, Mudrady, Varanga, Marne, Hirgana, Kukkundoor. S.H.-25 A: Direction- Udupi to Hebli, Nearest Villages- Nadpalu, Hebri, Shivapura. S.H.-37: Direction- Udupi to Beltanga di, Nearest Villages- Ninjoor, Palli, Kallya, Nitte, Eedu, Nallur. S.H.-52: Direction- Hosangara to Nadpadu, Nearest Villages- Kuchchur, Nadpalu. S.H.-66: Direction- Nadsal to Karkal, Nearest Villages- Kallya, Nitte, Nandalike, Belman, Inna, Bola, Kedinje, Sanoor. S.H.-66 A: Direction- Mulki to Belman, Nearest Villages- Belman, Mulladka, Mundkuru.

River: Sita Nadi- Nearest Villages- Belenje, Kuchchur, Nadpalu, Hebri, Chara. Jarvattu Halla Nadi- Nearest Villages- Hebri, Shivapura, Mudrady. Yenne Hole Nadi- Nearest Villages- Kukkuje, Marne, Yerlapady, Hirgana, Hermunde, Jarkala, Kervashe, Mala, Durga, Mudar. Sudda Hole Nadi- Nearest Villages- Kowdoor, Palli, Kallya, Kukkundoor, Sooda. Mulki Nadi- Nearest Villages- Nitte, Inna, Mundkuru, Bola, Kanthavara, Sanoor, Miyar.

Reserved Forest: Nearest Villages- Kuchchur, Hebri, Mudrady, Varanga, Marne, Hirgana, Hermunde, Andaru, Shirlal, Jarkala, Kervashe, Kanajaru, Neere, Durga, Nallur, Renjala. (Andar R.F.): Nearest Villages- Mala, Mudar, Nooralbettu, Eedu. (Someshwar R.F.): Nearest Villages- Nadpalu, Kabbinale.

Annual Rainfall: Normal Rianfall 4008.76 mm.

Ground Water: Availability of the Ground Water in the Basin is 22365 H.A.M. and the utilization is 8868 H. A.M. It belongs to Safe category. Depth to water level 5 to 10 meter below the ground. Most of the wells go down in summer months, according to the Ground Water Estimation Committee.

Soils: Red Lateritic Soil.

Natural Division : It falls partly in Kundapur-Mangalore Coast, Bainduru-Bantval Plain and Western Ghats (Dakshina Kannada) of the Karnataka Coast.

Administration:

Division: Mysore. Parliamentary Constituency: 15 Udupi. District: Udupi. Taluka: Karkal. Assembly Constituency: 122 Karkal. Gram Panchayat: 29.

Regional Area Development Boards: The Maland Aera Development Board.

Villages: 50 **Inhabited:** 50 **Uninhabited:** 0

Ranking	**District**	**State**	**National**
Area	2	74	390
Population	3	106	1032
Sex Ratio	2	2	46
Child Sex Ratio	3	78	2841
Literacy Rate	2	6	296
Density	1	107	5196
Work Participation Rate	3	100	2533

Gram Panchayats:
Kuchchur, Hebri, Shivapura, Mudrady, Nadpalu, Varanga, Kadthala, Marne, Yerlapady, Neere, Palli, Bailoor, Hirgana, Shirlal, Durga, Kukkundoor, Nitte, Belman, Inna, Mundkuru, Bola, Kanthavara, Sanoor, Miyar, Mudar, Mala, Nallur, Renjala, Eedu.

Amenities:

Education: Primary School in 49 villages, Middle school in 48 villages, Matriculation or Secondary School in 25 villages, namely Kuchchur, Hebri, Shivapura, Mudrady, Varanga, Kukkuje, Marne, Hirgana, Shirlal, Mala, Neere, Kowdoor, Palli, Kukkundoor, Nitte, Sooda, Belman, Inna, Mundkuru, Kanthavara, Sanoor, Miyar, Durga, Mudar, Eedu.

Higher Secondary or Pre University Courses or Intermediate or Junior College in 9 villages of the CD Block,, namely Hebri, Varanga, Kukkuje, Palli, Nitte, Belman, Mundkuru, Sanoor, Mudar.

College in 2 villages, Adult Literacy Center in 4 villages., Colleges are in villages, namely Hebri, Nitte.

Medical: Hospital in 3 villages, Dispensary in 16 villages, Health Center in 14 villages, Sub Center in 44 villages,

Maternity and Child Welfare Center in 1 village, Community health workers in 7 villages.
The Villages having Hospital or Dispensary or Health Center are Nadpalu, Hebri, Mudrady, Varanga, Marne, Neere, Kowdoor, Kukkundoor, Nandalike, Sooda, Belman, Inna, Mundkuru, Durga, Mudar, Eedu.
Drinking Water: Tap water in 44 villages, Tank water in 32 villages, Well water in 50 villages, Tubewell in 26 villages and more than one source in 50 villages.
Bank: Banking facility in 22 villages, namely, Belenje, Nadpalu, Kerebettu, Kabbinale, Yellare Kukkuje, Yerlapady, Hermunde, Shirlal, Jarkala, Mala Neere, Kowdoor, Ninjoor, Kallya, Nitte, Sooda, Inna Kedinje, Kanthavara, Sanoor, Mudar.
Credit Society in 15 villages Agricultural Credit Society in 11 Non-Agricultural Credit Society in 3 villages.
Others: Power supply in 50 villages, Cinema hall in 1 village, sport club in 0 village, Stadium or Auditorium or Community Hall in 0 village, Post Office in 46 villages.
There are 49 villages having bus facilities.
Villages with most of facilities: Belenje, Nadpalu Kabbinale, Kukkuje, Yerlapady, Hermunde, Shirlal Jarkala, Mala, Neere, Kowdoor, Ninjoor, Kallya Nitte, Sooda, Inna, Kedinje, Kanthavara, Sanoor Mudar.
Villages without amenities (Education): Kerebettu..
Scheduled Castes: Out of the total population of 180482 persons, 15660 persons (8.68%) belong to Scheduled Castes.
The villages having less than 10% SC population are Belenje, Kuchchur, Nadpalu, Hebri, Chara, Kerebettu Shivapura, Mudrady, Kabbinale, Varanga, Yellare Marne, Hirgana, Hermunde, Andaru, Shirlal, Jarkala Kervashe, Kanajaru, Bailoor, Ninjoor, Kallya, Sooda Belman, Inna, Mulladka, Mundkuru, Bola, Kanthavara Sanoor, Nooralbettu.
The village having more than 50% SC population is None.
Sex ratio of Scheduled Caste population is 501.
Scheduled Castes Literates and Illiterates by Sex:

	Persons	Males	Females
Literate	8,412	4,636	3,776
Illiterate	7,248	3,186	4,062
Literacy rate	61.9	68.8	55.2
Graduate	102	80	22

Scheduled Castes (Dominant):
Adi Dravida, Moger, Paravan, Holaya etc., Bhovi
For their cultural identity please see Appendix-I
Villages without Scheduled Castes: There are 0 village without any scheduled caste population.
Scheduled Tribes: Out of the total population of 180482 persons, 9748 persons (5.4%) belong to Scheduled Tribes.
The villages having less than 10% ST population are Kerebettu, Mudrady, Varanga, Padukudoor, Kukkuje Marne, Yerlapady, Hirgana, Hermunde, Jarkala Kervashe, Mala, Kanajaru, Neere, Bailoor, Kowdoor Ninjoor, Kukkundoor, Nitte, Nandalike, Sooda, Belman Inna, Mulladka, Mundkuru, Bola, Kedinje, Kanthavara Sanoor, Miyar, Mudar, Nooralbettu, Eedu, Nallur Renjala, Irvathuru.
The villages having more than 50% ST population are None.
Sex ratio of Scheduled tribe population is 507.
Scheduled Tribes Literates and Illiterates by Sex:

	Persons	Males	Females
Literate	6,110	3,247	2,863
Illiterate	3,638	1,554	2,084
Literacy rate	72.0	78.4	65.9
Graduate	100	64	36

Scheduled Tribes (Dominant):
Marati, Malaikudi, Koraga, Naikda etc.
Generic Tribes etc.
For their cultural identity please see Appendix-II
Villages without Scheduled Tribes: There are 2 villages without any scheduled tribe population.
Literates and Illiterates by Sex (Total Population):

	Persons	Males	Females
Literate	128,691	63,678	65,013
Illiterate	51,791	20,391	31,400
Literacy rate	80	86	75
Graduate	4,741	2,744	1,997

Agriculture: ***Distribution of villages according to land use:*** Out of 50 villages, Total area (in hectare) is 104953, out of that 24.13 percent is cultivable and 36.11 percent of the cultivable area is irrigated.
Sources of Irrigation (Hectares): Government Canal 0, Private Canal 0, Well without Electricity 980.93, Well with Electricity 1834.67, Tubewell without Electricity 2.42, Tubewell with Electricity 41.11, Tank 35.37, River 1653.92, Lake 0, Waterfall 0, Others 4594.87.
Villages with population of 5000 to 9999:
Hebri, Marne, Mala, Mundkuru, Sanoor, Miyar, Mudar Nallur.
Villages with population of 10000 and above:
Kukkundoor, Nitte.
Distribution of Workers:

	Persons	Males	Females	WPR
Cultivators	21,478	11,806	9,672	23.8
Agricultural Labour	12,958	6,716	6,242	14.36
Household Industry	21,229	2,142	19,087	23.52
Other Workers	34,589	26,664	7,925	38.32

Main Workers	79,564	43,737	35,827	88.16
Marginal Workers	10,690	3,591	7,099	11.84
Total Workers	90,254	47,328	42,926	

Religion: Major Religious Communities:

	Persons	Males	Females	Sex Ratio
Hindu (87.32%)	157,603	73,038	84,565	1,158
Muslim (4.16%)	7,501	3,766	3,735	992
Christian (6.47%)	11,670	5,408	6,262	1,158
Sikh (0.02%)	35	13	22	1,692
Buddhists (0.01%)	18	6	12	2,000
Jain (2.01%)	3,625	1,824	1,801	987

Agewise Data:

	Persons	Males	Females	Sex Ratio
All ages	180,482	84,069	96,413	1147
0-14	49,278	25,063	24,215	966
15-44	86,278	38,658	47,620	1232
45-79	42,478	19,283	23,195	1203
80+	2,392	1,037	1,355	1307
Age not stated	56	28	28	1000

Languages (Dominant):
Tulu, Konkani, Kannada, Marathi, Malayalam

Disabled Population:

	Persons	Males	Females	%
Total Disabled	2,744	1,497	1,247	
In Seeing	1,024	503	521	37.32
In Speech	337	197	140	12.28
In Hearing	129	66	63	4.7
In Movement	746	461	285	27.19
Mentally	508	270	238	18.51

KARWAR

Karwar C.D. Block lies in the western part of Uttara Kannada district. It is a part of Karwar taluka. The Block is located at a distance of 00 kms. from district headquarters (Karwar). There are 53 villages in the block with the total population of 77,822 persons. Area of the C.D. Block is 685.17 sq. kms. It is bounded by Supa taluk on north, Laksha Dweep Sea on south with taluk Ankola, taluk Yellapur on east, the sea encloses it on west, and it has common boundary with the State of Goa on north.

Communications:

Roadways : N.H-17: Direction- Panaji to Ankola, Nearest Villages- Majali, Arga, Todur, Amadalli. S.H-6: Directio n- Karwar to Yellapur, Nearest Villages- Kadiye, Katar, Kerwadi, Mallapur, Virje, Kuchegar, Hartuga, Kaiga, Kinnar, Kadwad, Makheri, Shirwad, Siddar, Wailwada, Naitisavar, Bargal, Devalmakki. S.H-95: Direction- Chitakula to Supa, Nearest Villages- Kolage, Sawantwada, Hotegali, Hankon, Gopashitta, Ghadasai, Ulga, Bhaire, Gotegali, Kadra.

Railway Station: Village- Shirwad.

River: Kalinadi- Nearest Villages- Hosali, Kanasgiri, Madhewada, Hotegali, Hankon, Gopashitta, Hankonjoog, Halgejoog, Bolshitta, Ghadasai, Ulga, Kadiye, Katar, Kerwadi, Bhaire, Gotegali, Mallapur, Virje, Kadra, Kuchegar, Hartuga, Balemane, Devakar, Kaiga, Kinnar, Kadwad, Makheri, Shirwad, Siddar, Wailwada.

Reserved Forest: Nearest Villages- Angadi, Hotegali, Maigini, Hankon, Gopashitta, Ghadasai, Bhaire, Goyar, Kamargaon, Lande, Gotegali, Mallapur, Virje, Kadra, Kuchegar, Hartuga, Balemane, Devakar. (Naiti R.F.): Nearest Villages- Shirwad, Belur, Shirve, Nivli, Nagekove, Arga, Chendiye, Todur, Amadalli.

Annual Rainfall: Normal Rianfall 3209.0 mm.

Ground Water: Availability of the Ground Water in the Basin is 2016 H.A.M. and the utilization is 745 H.A. M. It belongs to Safe category. Depth to water level 2 to 5 meter below the ground. Most of the wells go down in summer months, according to the Ground Water Estimation Committee.

Soils: Lateritic Soil.

Natural Division : It falls partly in the Karwar-Honavar Coast and Western Ghats (Uttara Kannada) of the Karnataka Coast (Western Coastal Region).

Coastal Villages: (Lakshadeep Sea)- Majali, Arga, Chendiye.

Administration:

Division: Belgaum. Parliamentary Constituency: 12 Uttara Kannada. District: Uttara Kannada. Taluka: Karwar. Assem bly Constituency: 77 Karwar. Gram Panchayat: 18.

Regional Area Development Boards: The Maland Aera Devel opment Board.

Border Villages: (State: Goa)- Majali, Angadi, Hotegali, Maigini, Gopashitta, Bhaire, Goyar, Kamargaon, Lande.

Fairs and Festival: Mahamya Jatra: It is held at Kadra for one dayin the month of October every year. Kadra Mahamaya jatra is located at the foot of the Anshi Ghat, about 32 kilometres from Karwar. During Deepavali, a jatra is heldin honour of Mahamaya for 12 days when about 5,000 people assemble.

Saint Karimuddin Urs: An annual Urs is held in Sadashivg ad near Uttara Kannad in honour of Saint Karimuddin Ghous e-e-Azam Abdul Quadir Jilani in the Muslim month of Saffar for one day.

Shejjeshwara Jatra: It is held at Shejwad for two days in the month of February. Shejwad 10 kms. from Karwar is a place of considerable antiquity. The Shejjeshwara (Siddeshwar) is a Later Chalukyan temple with a star-sha ped garbhagriha which is completely renovated.

Sri Kshetra Baad Matha Festivals: Sri Kshetra Baad Matha (or Guru Matha), Karwar near Uttara Kannada celebrates a number of Hindu festivals throughout the year in honour of Dattatreya. Vastralankara, Bhajanas, Purana, Keertana, Vahanotsava, Ashtavadhana seve, etc., are the important features of festivals.

Villages: 52 **Inhabited:** 51 **Uninhabited:** 1

Ranking	District	State	National
Area	8	137	946
Population	9	168	4361
Sex Ratio	3	51	1643
Child Sex Ratio	7	105	3323
Literacy Rate	1	8	337
Density	8	169	6082
Work Participation Rate	5	162	4252

Gram Panchayats:

Majali, Mudgeri, Chitakula ,Madhewada, Hankon, Gotegali,Kadra, Mallapur, Kerwadi, Ghadasai, Wailwada, Kinnar, Kadwad, Shirwad, Arga, Chendiye, Amadalli, Devalmakki.

Amenities:

Education: Primary School in 50 villages, Middle school in 31 villages, Matriculation or Secondary School in 21 villages, namely Angadi, Hotegali, Hankon, Hankonjoog, Halgejoog, Ghadasai, Ulga, Katar, Gotegali, Mallapur, Virje, Kadra, Kinnar, Kadwad, Shirwad, Siddar, Wailwada, Naitisavar, Devalmakki, Chendiye, Amadalli. Higher Secondary or Pre University Courses or Intermediate or Junior College in 4 villages of the CD Block,, namely Majali, Ulga, Kerwadi, Siddar.

College in 3 villages, Adult Literacy Center in 0 village., Colleges are in villages, namely Ulga, Kerwadi, Siddar.

Medical: Hospital in 0 village, Dispensary in 6 villages, Health Center in 5 villages, Sub Center in 6 villages, Maternity and Child Welfare Center in 1 village, Community health workers in 2 villages.

The Villages having Hospital or Dispensary or Health Center are Majali , Hankon , Ulga , Kadra , Todur , Amadalli.

Drinking Water: Tap water in 26 villages, Tank water in 18 villages, Well water in 49 villages, Tubewell in 1 village and more than one source in 47 villages.

Bank: Banking facility in 11 villages, namely, Majali, Sawantwada, Ghadasai, Ulga, Virje, Kadra Kaiga, Kadwad, Shirwad, Chendiye, Amadalli.

Credit Society in 9 villages Agricultural Credit Society in 8 Non-Agricultural Credit Society in 1 village.

Others: Power supply in 43 villages, Cinema hall in 0 village, sport club in 0 village, Stadium or Auditorium or Community Hall in 0 village, Post Office in 31 villages.

There are 40 villages having bus facilities.

Villages with most of facilities: Majali, Ghadasai Ulga, Virje, Kadra, Kadwad, Shirwad, Chendiye Amadalli.

Villages without amenities (Education): Balemane..

Scheduled Castes: Out of the total population of 72852 persons, 2884 persons (3.96%) belong to Scheduled Castes.

The villages having less than 10% SC population are Majali , Angadi , Mudgeri Hosali, Kanasgiri, Kolage, Arav , Sawantwada Madhewada, Hotegali , Maigini , Hankon Gopashitta , Hankonjoog Halgejoog , Bolshitta Ghadasai , Ulga , Kadiye Katar , Kerwadi , Bhaire Goyar , Kamargaon , Lande Gotegali , Mallapur , Virje Kuchegar , Hartuga , Balemane Devakar , Kaiga , Kinnar Makheri , Shirwad , Siddar Naitisavar , Bargal , Belur Devalmakki , Shirve , Nivli Nagekove , Arga , Chendiye Todur , Amadalli.

The village having more than 50% SC population is None.

Sex ratio of Scheduled Caste population is 491.

Scheduled Castes Literates and Illiterates by Sex:

	Persons	Males	Females
Literate	1,761	1,012	749
Illiterate	1,123	456	667
Literacy rate	71.6	80.6	62.1
Graduate	118	71	47

Scheduled Castes (Dominant):

Bhovi, Halsar etc., Ager, Bhambi etc., Banjara etc.

For their cultural identity please see Appendix-I

Villages without Scheduled Castes: There are 16 villages without any scheduled caste population.

Scheduled Tribes: Out of the total population of 72852 persons, 2906 persons (3.99%) belong to Scheduled Tribes.

The villages having less than 10% ST population are Majali , Angadi , Mudgeri Hosali, Kanasgiri, Kolage, Hotegali , Maigini Hankon , Gopashitta Hankonjoog , Halgejoog Bolshitta , Ghadasai , Kadiye Kerwadi , Bhaire , Goyar Kamargaon , Lande , Gotegali Mallapur , Virje , Kadra Kuchegar , Hartuga , Balemane

Devakar , Kinnar , Kadwad
Shirwad , Siddar , Naitisavar
Bargal , Belur , Devalmakki
Shirve , Nivli , Nagekove
Arga , Chendiye , Todur
Amadalli.

The villages having more than 50% ST population are None.

Sex ratio of Scheduled tribe population is 530.

Scheduled Tribes Literates and Illiterates by Sex:

	Persons	Males	Females
Literate	2,198	1,145	1,053
Illiterate	708	220	488
Literacy rate	82.1	91.8	73.6
Graduate	211	121	90

Scheduled Tribes (Dominant):

Kokna etc., Naikda etc., Malasar, Kota, Gond etc.

For their cultural identity please see Appendix-II

Villages without Scheduled Tribes: There are 24 villages without any scheduled tribe population.

Literates and Illiterates by Sex (Total Population):

	Persons	Males	Females
Literate	51,549	28,988	22,561
Illiterate	21,303	7,637	13,666
Literacy rate	79	89	70
Graduate	3,357	1,985	1,372

Agriculture: ***Distribution of villages according to land use:*** Out of 52 villages, Total area (in hectare) is 68517, out of that 10.92 percent is cultivable and 11.48 percent of the cultivable area is irrigated.

Sources of Irrigation (Hectares): Government Canal 184.19, Private Canal 0, Well without Electricity 147.08, Well with Electricity 503.79, Tubewell without Electricity 0, Tubewell with Electricity 0, Tank 0, River 0, Lake 0, Waterfall 0, Others 24.53.

Villages with population of 5000 to 9999:

Majali , Virje , Amadalli.

Villages with population of 10000 and above: None

Distribution of Workers:

	Persons	Males	Females	WPR
Cultivators	7,315	4,411	2,904	23.94
Agricultural Labour	4,399	2,103	2,296	14.4
Household Industry	1,138	852	286	3.72
Other Workers	17,699	13,565	4,134	57.93
Main Workers	21,518	16,300	5,218	70.43
Marginal Workers	9,033	4,631	4,402	29.57
Total Workers	30,551	20,931	9,620	

Religion: Major Religious Communities:

	Persons	Males	Females	Sex Ratio
Hindu (92.29%)	67,232	33,747	33,485	992
Muslim (3.06%)	2,227	1,172	1,055	900
Christian (4.57%)	3,327	1,662	1,665	1,002
Sikh (0.04%)	30	21	9	429
Buddhists (0%)	1	1	-	-
Jain (0.02%)	17	11	6	545

Agewise Data:

	Persons	Males	Females	Sex Ratio
All ages	72,852	36,625	36,227	989
0-14	18,217	9,400	8,817	938
15-44	37,395	19,247	18,148	943
45-79	16,488	7,656	8,832	1154
80+	715	298	417	1399
Age not stated	37	24	13	542

Languages (Dominant):

Konkani, Kannada, Urdu, Tamil, Telugu

Disabled Population:

	Persons	Males	Females	%
Total Disabled	1,816	1,029	787	
In Seeing	833	441	392	45.87
In Speech	165	90	75	9.09
In Hearing	134	80	54	7.38
In Movement	450	298	152	24.78
Mentally	234	120	114	12.89

KHANAPUR

Khanapur C.D. Block lies in the south-western part of Belgaum district. It is a part of Khanapur taluka. The Block is located at a distance of 26 kms. from district headquarters (Belgaum).There are 219 villages in the block with the total population of 220,315 persons. Area of the C.D. Block is 1726.57 sq.kms. It is bounded by taluk Belgaum on north, district Uttara Kannada on south, district Dharwad and taluk Sampgaon on east, and it has common boundary with the state of Maharashtra on west and north, and with state of Goa on west.

Communications:

Roadways : N.H-4 A: Direction- Anmod to Belgaum, Nearest Villages- Ramgurwadi, Ganebail, Nittur, Idalhond, Ankale, Hattar Gunji, Halakarni, Rumewadi, Karambal, Akrali, Mohiset, Kirawale (K.G.), Sangargali, Honakal, Gangawali, Savargali, Shindholli, Manikwadi, Gunji, Kamatage,Watre, Manjarpai (K.G.). S.H-31: Direction- Goa to Bagewadi, Nearest Villages- Kanakumbi, Chorla, Parwad, Betne, Amate, Kalmani, Olamani, Jamboti, Daroli, Otoli, Alloli-Kansoli, Modekop, Nagurda, Harasanwadi, Bacholi, Ramgurwadi, Devalatti, Jainkoppa, Lokoli, Baragaon, Dukkarwadi, Halakarni, Kuppatagiri, Khanapur (Rural), Doddahosur, Kamsinkop, Parishwad. S.H-34: Direction- Karwar to Dharwad, Nearest Villages- Mundwad-Pimpale, Gharli, Chinchewadi, Tarawad, Suwatawadi, Kumbarda, Nagaragali,Tavargatti, Bhistenatti,

Godholi, Linganmath, Gundolli. S.H-93: Direction-Khanapur to Siddapur, Nearest Villages-Karambal, Koundal, Hebbal, Navage,Mouje Nandgad Zunjawad K.Nandagad, Kasabanandgad, Bekwad,Junjwad (K.G.), Bidi, Mangenkop-Alias Ghosenatti, Adi, Golihalli, Kukenatti Alias (Ramapur), Surapur, Kakkeri, Linganmath, Gundolli.

Railway Station: Villages- Bacholi, Idalhond, Gunji, Jambegali, Tavargatti.

River: Malprabha Nadi- Nearest Villages- Kanakumbi, Bailur, Betne, Talawade, Golyali, Torali, Amate, Kalmani, Habbanatti, Devachihatti, Uchawade, Kusamalli, Olamani, Jamboti, Kanjale, Amboli, Nilawade, Daroli, Otoli, Malai, Alloli-Kansoli, Modekop, Thirthkunde, Katagali, Devalatti, Manasapur, Asoga, Rumewadi, Karambal, Jalage, Kuppatagiri, Khanapur (Rural), Balogi, Yadoga, Lakkebail, Kamsinkop, Parishwad, Hire-Hattiholi, Chikkahattiholi, Jikanur, Karvinkop, Chikkamanoli, Hiremanoli, Chikadinkop, Kagganagi, Kodachwad, Vaddebail, Chapagaon, Karalga, Itagi, Shedegali. Mandavi Nadi- Nearest Villages- Amagaon, Chapoli, Mugawade, Kabanali, Kavale, Holda, Kelil, Gavali, Pastoli, Kongale, Nerase.

Reserved Forest: Nearset Villages- Chikhale, Betne, Talawade, Golyali, Betageri, Torali, Amate, Gawase, Amagaon, Chapoli, Kalmani, Bailur, Jamboti, Mugawade, Kabanali, Kanjale, Navage, Mouje Nandgad, Nerase, Haruri, Shedegali, Gangawali, Savargali, Shindholli, Dhokegali, Manikwadi, Gunji, Kamatage, Diggegali, Jatage, Karanjal, Padalwadi, Halasal, Anagadi, Kapoli (K.G.), Potoli, Shivathan, Shindholi (K.H.), Shindholli (B.K.), Bhatewadi, Malwad, Ghotagali, Bijagarni, Halashi, Halaga, Merada, Karajagi, Kirhalashi, Hattarwad, Bhuranaki, Maskenahatti, Balagund, Tavargatti, Bhistenatti, Godholi, Chunchwad Deshanur, Mohare, Hanabar Hatti, Hoskoti, Mastamaradi, Hogarti, Degaon, Honnapur, Kulavalli.

Annual Rainfall: Normal Rianfall 1859.1 mm.

Ground Water: Availability of the Ground Water in the Basin is 14234 H.A.M. and the utilization is 4518 H.A.M. It belongs to Safe category. Depth to water level 2 to 20 meter below the ground. Most of the wells go down in summer months, according to the Ground Water Estimation Committee.

Soil: Red Soil, Black Soil.

Natural Division : It falls partly in the Malaprabha Basin and the Khanapur Forest of the Northern Karnataka Plateau.

Administration:

Division: Belgaum. Parliamentary Constituency: 12 Uttara Kannada. District: Belgaum. Taluka: Khanapur. Assembly Constituency: 14 Khanapur. Gram Panchayat: 51.

Regional Area Development Boards: The Maland Aera Development Board.

Border Villages: (State: Maharashtra)- Huland, Chigule, Kanakumbi, Chorla, Parwad, Chikhale, Talawade, Golyali, Betageri, Bailur. (State: Goa)- Chorla, Parwad, Chikhale, Amagaon, Holda, Kelil, Mendil.

Fairs and festival: Bishtadevi Jatra: It is held at Kakkeri in around the month of October for three days every year. Kakkeri 30 kms.from Khanapur situated on the Khanapur-Haliyal road and 10 kms. from Alnawar station is associated with famous Veerashaiva Sharana Dohara Kakkaya, who is believed to have died here in a scuffle with Kalachuri army on his way to Ulvi from Kalyana in the company of Chennabasavanna. His gadduge (concrete structure)amidst the fields stands testimony to this. The gadduge has a small garbhagriha which has a considerably old seated stone image of Kakkayya with Chauri bearers on both the sides. He is engaged in Linga worship.

Gajbar Sab, Sabu Sayida And Khadirshah Urs: Khanapur located on the Belgaum-Panaji road at a distance of 28 kms. from Belgaum is a commercial centre. It has been the taluk headquarters since 1829 when the office was shifted from Bidi, as a consequence of the burning of the Taluk kacheri by Sangolli Rayanna. Some people from the place are said to have been associated with the Supa Uprising of 1858-59. The place Khanapur is said to be named ater a Bijapur officer Khan Bahadur.The place has a fort which has now completely vanished. There are totally six mosques and the Jamia mosque in the Sayida galli is described as built by Khan Bahadur of Bijapur. The place has three dargahs ascribed to Gajbar Sab (chilla), Sabu Sayida (near the Sayidagalli Mosque) and Khadir Shah. The Urs is held in the month of Rajjab and nearly 1,000 people assemble when qawaliprogrammes are also held.

Galageshwara Temple Jatra: It is held at Asoga in around the month of Feb-Mar every year. Asoga, five kilometers from Khanapur located on the left bank of the Malaprabha river is a fine picnic spot with pictures que surroundings. The name of the place is mentioned as 'Asoke' in an inscription on a hero-stone (broken) which is in 12th century character found near the Ramalinga at the same place. The Asoge plates of Kadamba Jayakeshi dated 1113 A.D. record a grant by the king of the village Kupattoggarika (modern Kuppatageri) to one Shiva sakti, for the worship of God Galageshwara and other charities. At Baloge (Khanapur tq), there is a Galageshwara temple which might be the same as mentioned in the record. Asoga has a Ramalinga temple, a tiled structure (completely renovated) on the bank of the Malaprabha. The temple has a mukhamantapa, a spacious hall and a grabhagriha.

Kalmeshwara Jatra: It is held at Gunji every year. Gunji 13 kms. from Khanapur located on the Belgaum-Panaji highway has a temple dedicated to Kalmeshwara, Ganapati, Ravalanatha, Mavulidevi (recent and tiled), etc. The Kalmeshwara temple with only a garbhagriha appears to be old, as the Shivalinga Pitha has later Chalukyan features. It has been completely renovated and there is a mound and remains of an old temple are lying all around the area. The Ganapati temple is also recently renovated. It is locally described that this sculpture of Ganapati and that of a Vishnu and a Shivalinga were found beside the temple under a mound. The Shivalinga and Vishnu (of later Chalukyan style) are placed inside the garbhagriha of the Ganapati temple. The Ravalanatha temple is a fine modern cement structure.

Kulakumbi Jatra: It is held at Kankumbi near Belgaum in about the month of February for three days. Kankumbi 38 kms. from Khanapur is located amidst thick forest and has a pleasant location.

Lakshmi Temple Jatra: Kirhalshi near Belgaum, 19 kms. from Khanapur area, situated on the Khanapur-Nagargali road appears to be an old town under the Goa Kadambas. The place name appears to correspond with Halshi, which is hardly six kilometres from here. In the terrier of the village, across the fields there is a Kallappangudi, built in laterite.It has a later Chalukyan Shivalinga and many broken antiquities are lying all around the place. There is a mound near which is a plain inscription slab, and this appears to have been a Vishnu temple.

Lakshmi Temple Jatra: It is held at Ullagaddi Khanapur near Belgaum. Ullagaddi Khanapur, ten kilometres from Sankeshwar, located on the national highway, is named to differentiate it from Khanapur. The place has temples dedicated to Hanumanta, Lakshmi, Ishwara, Basaveshwara and Yellamma. The Hanumanta temple has a Nishidi stone, engraved with inscription and another inscription slab is built into the wall of the same temple (both unpublished).

Mahuli Devi Jatra: It is held at Gunji near Belgaum in around the month of October for three days every year. Gunji is 13 kms. from Khanapur located on the Belgaum-Panaji highway. It has temples dedicated to Kalmeshwara, Ganapathi, Ravalanatha, Mavulidevi (recent and tiled), etc. The Kalmeshwara temple with only agarbhagriha appear to be old, as the Shivalinga Pitha has later Chalukyan features.

Narasimha Jatra: It is held at Halshi around the month of November for three days every year when nearly twenty thousand people assemble. Halshi 14 kms. south-west of Khanapur called Palasika, Palashi and Halasige in inscriptions, is a place with rich antiquity. The name appears to have been derived from palasha in Sanskrit (Butea frondosa, Koen; muttuga in Kannada). It was the secondary capital of the early Kadambas (seven copper plates of theirs werelocated here) and a minor capital under the Goa Kadambas who ruled between 980-1250 A.D. It is one of the oldest towns in the district with many monuments. During the days of early Kadambas, it was a centre confluence of Jainism, Vaishnavism and Shaivism.

Rampurpeth Jatra: It is held at Jamboti near Belgaum. Jamboti 17 kms. from Khanapur is situated atop an evergreen hilly forest surroundings. The traditional belief is that it was the birth place of Jambavati the daughter of Jambuvanta. Bears were once abundant in the Forest surrounding the place.

Ravalanatha Temple Jatra: It is held at Gunji near Belgaum during Dasara (October-November) for five days. Gunji 13 kms. from Khanapur located on the Belgaum-Panaji highway has temples dedicated to Kalmeshwara, Ganapati, Ravalanatha, Mavulidevi (recent and tiled), etc. The Kalmeshwara temple with only a garbhagriha appears to be old, as the Shivalinga Pitha has later Chalukyan features. It has been completely renovated and there is a mound and remains of an old temple are lying all around the area. The Ganapati temple is also recently renovated. It is locally described that this sculpture of Ganapati and that of a Vishnu and Shivalinga were found beside the temple under a mound. The Shivalinga and Vishnu (of later Chalukyan style) are placed inside the garbhagriha of the Ganapati temple. The Ravalanatha temple is a fine modern cement structure. In front of this temple are placed five hero-stones. Another tiled Shiva temple in the outskirts of the village has a huge Shivalinga.

Shankara Narayana Car Festival: It is held at Halshi near Belgaum in the month of Ashwayuja Shuddha Poornima (September-October) every year. Halshi 14 kms. south-west of Khanapur called Palasika, Palashi and Halasige in inscriptions, is a place with rich antiquity. The name appears to have been derived from Palasha in Sanskrit (Butea Frondosa, Koen, Muttunga in Kannada). It was the secondary capital of the early Kadambas (seven copper plates of them were located here) and a minor capital under the Goa Kadambas who ruled between 980-1250 A.D. It is one of the oldest towns in the district with many monuments. During the days of early Kadambas it was a centre of confluence of Jainism, Vaishnavism and Shaivism. The place has temples dedicated to Bhuvaraha Narasimha, Kapileswara, Suvarneshwara, Kalmeshwara, Hatakeshwara (Gramadevata), Gokarneshwara and a Jaina basti. The Bhuvaraha Narasimha temple is a huge complex built in the later Chalukyan style, with two garbhagrihas facing each other. The temple was originally single shrined, but during later periods another garbhagriha was added.

Villages: 219 **Inhabited:** 218 **Uninhabited:** 1

Ranking	District	State	National
Area	2	14	79
Population	9	68	466
Sex Ratio	1	34	1348
Child Sex Ratio	1	125	3577
Literacy Rate	3	66	2087
Density	4	89	5864
Work Participation Rate	10	151	2099

Gram Panchayats:
Parwad, Kanakumbi, Golyali, Bailur, Amate, Jamboti, Nilawade, Nagurda, Ramgurwadi, Nittur, Idalhond, Garlagunji, Topinkatti, Devalatti, Parishwad, Hire-Hattiholi, Hiremanoli, Kodachwad, Chapagaon, Lokoli, Baragaon, Halakarni, Karambal, Manturga, Nerase, Shiroli, Gunji, Shindholli, Hebbal, Bekwad, Kadatanbagewadi, Itagi, Gandigwad, Kerwad, Mangenkop-Alias Ghosenatti, Bidi, Nanjankodal, Halashi, Kasabanandgad, Mouje Nandgad, Bijagarni, Kapoli (K.G.), Mohiset, Londa, Ghotagali, Halaga, Nagaragali, Godholi, Bhuranaki, Kakkeri, Linganmath.

Amenities:

Education: Primary School in 213 villages, Middle school in 117 villages, Matriculation or Secondary School in 26 villages, namely Kanakumbi, Bailur, Olamani, Jamboti, Alloli-Kansoli, Ganebail, Idalhond, Garlagunji, Devalatti, Karambal, Parishwad, Chapagaon, Karalga, Mouje Nandgad, Bekwad, Itagi, Gandigwad, Manturga, Gunji, Kapoli (K.G.), Shivathan, Halashi, Halaga, Bidi, Godholi, Kakkeri.

Higher Secondary or Pre University Courses or Intermediate or Junior College in 3 villages of the CD Block,, namely Parishwad, Mouje Nandgad, Itagi.

College in 1 village, Adult Literacy Center in 65 villages., College is in village, namely Mouje Nandgad.

Medical: Hospital in 0 village, Dispensary in 4 villages, Health Center in 10 villages, Sub Center in 38 villages, Maternity and Child Welfare Center in 1 village, Community health workers in 19 villages.

The Villages having Hospital or Dispensary or Health Center are Ganebail, Kadatanbagewadi, Gandigwad, Godholi.

Drinking Water: Tap water in 63 villages, Tank water in 32 villages, Well water in 119 villages, Tubewell in 53 villages and more than one source in 164 villages.

Bank: Banking facility in 14 villages, namely, Kanakumbi, Jamboti, Garlagunji, Parishwad Mouje Nandgad, Tolagi, Itagi, Gandigwad, Gunji Nagaragali, Halashi, Bidi, Kakkeri, Linganmath.

Credit Society in 41 villages Agricultural Credit Society in 30 Non-Agricultural Credit Society in 5 villages.

Others: Power supply in 212 villages, Cinema hall in 1 village, sport club in 2 villages, Stadium or Auditorium or Community Hall in 0 village, Post Office in 53 villages.

There are 134 villages having bus facilities.

Villages with most of facilities: Kanakumbi Jamboti, Garlagunji, Parishwad, Mouje Nandgad Tolagi, Itagi, Gandigwad, Halashi, Bidi, Kakkeri Linganmath.

Villages without amenities (Education): Budase, Khanapur (Rural), Holda, Kelil, Bhistenatti..

Scheduled Castes: Out of the total population of 220345 persons, 15340 persons (6.96%) belong to Scheduled Castes. The villages having less than 10% SC population are Huland, Kanakumbi, Chorla, Parwad, Chikhale, Betne Talawade, Golyali, Betageri, Torali, Amate, Gawase Amagaon, Chapoli, Habbanatti, Devachihatti, Bailur Morab, Uchawade, Kusamalli, Olamani, Jamboti Kapoli K.Chapoli, Budase, Mugawade, Kabanali Kanjale, Amboli, Daroli, Otoli, Malavi Alloli-Kansoli, Modekop, Thirthkunde, Nagurda Harasanwadi, Ramgurwadi, Ganebail, Idalhond Garlagunji, Singinkop, Ankale, Khemewadi, Nidagal Topinkatti, Bidarbhavi, Devalatti, Jainkoppa, Lokoli Sannahosur, Bhandargali, Baragaon, Dukkarwadi Mudewadi, Hattar Gunji, Rumewadi, Koundal, Jalage Kuppatagiri, Khanapur (Rural), Yadoga Hire-Hattiholi, Jikanur, Chikkamanoli, Hiremanoli Chikadinkop, Vaddebail, Allehol, Shivoli, Karalga Hebbal, Navage, Mouje Nandgad, Channewadi Bhuttewadi, Zunjawad K.Nandagad, Khairwad, Hadalaga Deminkop, Banki-Basarikatti, Bekwad, Kadatanbagewadi Tolagi, Bogur, Gandigwad, Holda, Kelil, Mendil Degaon, Gavali, Pastoli, Kongale, Jamagaon Hemmadaga, Abanali, Nerase, Manturga, Teregali Shiroli, Dongargaon, Warkhadpatye, Akrali, Mohiset Kirawale (K.G.), Ambewadi, Sangargali, Tivoli Haruri, Shedegali, Honakal, Gangawali, Savargali Shindholli, Dhokegali, Manikwadi, Gunji, Kamatage Watre, Ghose (K.H.), Diggegali, Jatage Bhalake (K.H.), Bhalake(B.K), Karanjal, Halasal Anagadi, Kapoli (K.G.), Ghose (B.K.), Potoli Machali, Satanali, Manjarpai (K.G.), Mundwad-Pimpale Gharli, Chinchewadi, Kodagai, Shivathan Shindholi (K.H.), Shindholli (B.K.), Bhatewadi Malwad, Ghotagali, Devarai, Tarawad, Suwatawadi Kumbarda, Bamanakop, Jambegali, Bastawad, Sulegali Nagaragali, Mendegali, Halaga, Merada, Karajagi Kirhalashi, Gundapi, Sagare, Nanjankodal, Doddebail Bidi, Hindalagi, Hulikottal Mangenkop-Alias Ghosenatti, Adi, Chankebail, Gastoli

Maskenahatti, Balagund, Tavargatti, Bhistenatti Godholi, Chunchwad, Kukenatti Alias (Ramapur) Kerwad (Gundyanati), Kakkeri, Linganmath, Gundolli Godageri.

The village having more than 50% SC population is None.

Sex ratio of Scheduled Caste population is 503.

Scheduled Castes Literates and Illiterates by Sex:

	Persons	Males	Females
Literate	7,046	4,500	2,546
Illiterate	8,294	3,130	5,164
Literacy rate	54.4	70.1	39.0
Graduate	176	145	31

Scheduled Castes (Dominant):

Chalavadi etc., Mahar etc., Bhambi etc., Madiga Bhovi

For their cultural identity please see Appendix-I

Villages without Scheduled Castes: There are 60 villages without any scheduled caste population.

Scheduled Tribes: Out of the total population of 220345 persons, 9282 persons (4.21%) belong to Scheduled Tribes.

The villages having less than 10% ST population are Huland, Chigule, Kanakumbi, Chorla, Parwad, Chikhale Betne, Talawade, Golyali, Betageri, Torali, Gawase Amagaon, Chapoli, Kalmani, Devachihatti, Bailur Morab, Uchawade, Kusamalli, Olamani, Jamboti Kapoli K.Chapoli, Budase, Mugawade, Kabanali Kanjale, Nilawade, Daroli, Malavi, Alloli-Kansoli Modekop, Nagurda, Harasanwadi, Bacholi, Ramgurwadi Ganebail, Idalhond, Garlagunji, Singinkop, Ankale Khemewadi, Nidagal, Topinkatti, Devalatti, Jainkoppa Lokoli, Sannahosur, Bhandargali, Baragaon Dukkarwadi, Mudewadi, Hattar Gunji, Halakarni Manasapur, Asoga, Rumewadi, Karambal, Koundal Jalage, Kuppatagiri, Khanapur (Rural), Doddahosur Balogi, Yadoga, Lakkebail, Kamsinkop, Parishwad Gadikop, Hire-Hattiholi, Chikkahattiholi, Jikanur Karvinkop, Chikkamanoli, Chikadinkop, Kagganagi Kodachwad, Vaddebail, Chapagaon, Allehol, Shivoli Karalga, Hebbal, Navage, Mouje Nandgad, Channewadi Bhuttewadi, Zunjawad K.Nandagad, Kasabanandgad Khairwad, Hadalaga, Deminkop, Avarolli Banki-Basarikatti, Bekwad, Hire-Angrolli, Bogur Holda, Kelil, Mendil, Degaon, Gavali, Pastoli Kongale, Jamagaon, Hemmadaga, Abanali, Manturga Shiroli, Dongargaon, Warkhadpatye, Akrali, Mohiset Ambewadi, Sangargali, Tivoli, Haruri, Shedegali Honakal, Gangawali, Savargali, Shindholli, Dhokegali Manikwadi, Gunji, Watre, Ghose (K.H.), Diggegali Jatage, Bhalake (K.H.), Bhalake(B.K), Shimpewadi Karanjal, Padalwadi, Halasal, Anagadi, Kapoli (K.G.) Potoli, Machali, Satanali, Manjarpai (K.G.) Mundwad-Pimpale, Gharli, Chinchewadi, Kodagai Shivathan, Shindholi (K.H.), Shindholli (B.K.) Bhatewadi, Malwad, Ghotagali, Devarai, Tarawad Suwatawadi, Kumbarda, Bamanakop, Jambegali, Bastawad Sulegali, Bijagarni, Halashi, Mendegali, Halaga Merada, Karajagi, Kirhalashi, Hattarwad, Gundapi Sagare, Nanjankodal, Doddebail, Junjwad (K.G.), Bidi Hindalagi, Chick-Angrolli, Hulikottal, Handur Kasamalagi, Mangenkop-Alias Ghosenatti, Adi Golihalli, Chankebail, Gastoli, Bhuranaki Maskenahatti, Balagund, Tavargatti, Godholi Chunchwad, Karikatti, Kukenatti Alias (Ramapur) Kerwad (Gundyanati), Surapur, Kakkeri, Linganmath Gundolli, Godageri, Pur.

The villages having more than 50% ST population are None.

Sex ratio of Scheduled tribe population is 492.

Scheduled Tribes Literates and Illiterates by Sex:

	Persons	Males	Females
Literate	2,903	1,931	972
Illiterate	6,379	2,782	3,597
Literacy rate	37.8	49.2	25.9
Graduate	32	29	3

Scheduled Tribes (Dominant):

Naikda etc., Meda, Koli Dhor etc., Bavacha etc. Bhil etc.

For their cultural identity please see Appendix-II

Villages without Scheduled Tribes: There are 137 villages without any scheduled tribe population.

Literates and Illiterates by Sex (Total Population):

	Persons	Males	Females
Literate	120,531	71,989	48,542
Illiterate	99,814	38,464	61,350
Literacy rate	64	77	52
Graduate	3,200	2,600	600

Agriculture: ***Distribution of villages according to land use:*** Out of 219 villages, Total area (in hectare) is 172657, out of that 31.63 percent is cultivable and 25.92 percent of the cultivable area is irrigated.

Sources of Irrigation (Hectares): Government Canal 711.39, Private Canal 53.09, Well without Electricity 984.01, Well with Electricity 1964.47, Tubewell without Electricity 54.35, Tubewell with Electricity 5498.32, Tank 1476.5, River 2120.37, Lake 56.88, Waterfall 0, Others 1234.23.

Villages with population of 5000 to 9999:

Mouje Nandgad, Itagi, Gandigwad.

Villages with population of 10000 and above: None

Distribution of Workers:

	Persons	Males	Females	WPR
Cultivators	50,526	30,763	19,763	46.44
Agricultural Labour	37,390	14,002	23,388	34.36
Household Industry	2,767	1,795	972	2.54
Other Workers	18,122	15,568	2,554	16.66
Main Workers	83,877	55,491	28,386	77.09
Marginal Workers	24,928	6,637	18,291	22.91
Total Workers	108,805	62,128	46,677	

Religion: Major Religious Communities:

	Persons	Males	Females	Sex Ratio
Hindu (88.19%)	194,331	97,120	97,211	1,001
Muslim (7.1%)	15,644	8,025	7,619	949
Christian (1.79%)	3,946	1,976	1,970	997
Sikh (0%)	8	4	4	1,000
Buddhists (0.09%)	193	104	89	856
Jain (2.61%)	5,755	2,978	2,777	933

Agewise Data:

	Persons	Males	Females	Sex Ratio
All ages	220,345	110,453	109,892	995
0-14	74,427	38,034	36,393	957
15-44	99,223	49,636	49,587	999
45-79	44,594	21,898	22,696	1036
80+	1,985	822	1,163	1415
Age not stated	116	63	53	841

Languages (Dominant):

Marathi, Kannada, Urdu, Konkani, Telugu

Disabled Population:

	Persons	Males	Females	%
Total Disabled	3,592	2,054	1,538	
In Seeing	1,093	558	535	30.43
In Speech	298	150	148	8.3
In Hearing	200	93	107	5.57
In Movement	1,546	1,015	531	43.04
Mentally	455	238	217	12.67

KOLAR

Kolar C.D. Block lies in the southern part of Kolar district. It is a part of Kolar taluka. The Block is located at a distance of 00 kms. from district headquart ers (Kolar). There are 361 villages in the block with the total population of 228,485 persons. Area of the C.D. Block is 774.70 sq. kms. It is bounded by taluks Chintamani and Srinivaspur on north, taluks Malur and Bangarapet on south, taluks Mulbagal and Srinivaspur on east, district Bangalore Rural and taluk Sidlaghatta on west.

Communications:

Roadways : N.H.-4: Direction- Bangalore to Chennai, Nearest Villages- Kurki, Narasapura, Bellur, Chakarasanahalli, Byrasandra, Ramabhadrapura, Uddappanahalli, Lakshmisaga ra, Ramasandra, Kendatti, Gollahalli, Nagalapura, Arabiko thanur, Kendatti, Chunchedenahalli, Kaparasiddanahalli, Maderahalli, Chowdadenahalli, Kumbarahalli, Kondarajana halli, Ammerahalli, Seesandra, Nernahalli, Yanadahalli, Rasthe Thambihalli, Thambihalli, Ajjapalli, Kembodi, Chadumanahalli, Kalahastipura, Vadagur, Venkatapura. S.H.-5: Direction- Chintamani to Bangarapet, Nearest Villages- Balagere, Mullahalli, Settimadamangala, Chitna halli, Thotli, Bommasandra, Sugatur, Hanumanthapura, Uppakunte, Jangamagurjenahalli, Arahalli, Moorandahalli, Barandahalli, Kodi Kannur, Gajaladinne, Basavanatha, Doddahasala, Chikkahasala, Dimba. S.H.-74: Direction- Chikballapur to Kolar, Nearest Villages- Balanagenahalli, Hullankallu, Perjenahalli, Harjenahalli, Maliyappanaha lli, Madivala, Kurugal, Singihalli, Vemagal, Channappanah alli, Medihala, Kondenahalii, Sujjanahalli, Dhanamatanaha lli, Mallasandra, Talagunda, Chokkahalli, Hogari Gollahal li, Garudanahalli, Seepura, Sangondahalli, Joohalli , Hogari. S.H.-82: Direction- Hosakote to Chintamani, Neare st Villages- Beechagondahalli, Orati Agrahara.

Railway Station: Villages- Jannaghatta, Yadahalli.

River: Palar Nadi- Nearest Villages- Jannaghatta, Yadaha lli, Chaldiganahalli, Kadahalli, Karenahalli, Mylasandra Amanikere, Kyalanur, Kyalanur Amanikere, Thippenahalli, Seethi, Matapura, Kadagattur, Raghupathi Agrahara, Byrandahalli, Veerapura, Rajakallahalli, Settihalli, Thokalagatta, Hullankallu, Matnahalli, Ankathatti, Chitnahalli, Thotli, Urati, Agrahara, Thurandahalli, Janna-ghatta, Obenahalli, Gowdahalli, Sugatur, Kolakunjanahalli, Somambudi Amanikere, Naganala, Vanarasi, Muduvadi, Kondenahalli, Nukkanahalli, Mallasandra, Arinaganahalli, Bellambari, Somasastri Hosur, Gangatta, Nayakarahalli, Chillapalli, Kuduvanahalli, Chillapalli Amanikere, Krishnarajapura, Shanubhoganahalli, Manighatta, Vittappa nahalli, Yanadahalli, Rasthe, Thambihalli, Huthur, Holali, Somambudi Agrahara, Gottihalli, Muduvadi Hosahalli, Siresandra.

Annual Rainfall: Normal Rianfall 959.61 mm.

Ground Water: Availability of the Ground Water in the Basin is (Information not avablable) H.A.M. and the utilization is (Information not avablable) H.A.M. It belongs to (Information not avablable) category. Depth to water level 5 to 20 meter below the ground. Most of the wells go down in summer months, according to the Ground Water Estimation Committee.

Soils: Red Soils.

Natural Division : It falls in Sidlaghatta-Srinivaspur Upland of the Southern Karnataka Plateau.

Administration:

Division: Bangalore. Parliamentary Constituency: 28 Kolar (SC). District: Kolar. Taluka: Kolar. Assembly Constituency: 144 Srinivaspur, 147 Bangarapet, 148 Kolar.

Gram Panchayat: 36.

Regional Area Development Boards: The Bailu Seeme Area Development Board.

Fairs: Iralappa Festival: Vanarasi, in Kolar taluk, is about 10 kms. north of Kolar town. A large annual festival is held here for 10 days in the month of Chait ra in honour of Iralappa, when about 20,000 people assemb le and a cattle fair takes place to which about 20,000 heads of cattle are brought for sale.

Kolaramma Fair: A large fair takes place at Kolar every Thursday in honour of Kolaramma.

Markandeshwaraswamy Jatra: It is held at Vokkaleri near Kolar in about the month of February attended by about 50,000 persons. On the Vokkaleri hill, there is a temple dedicated to Markandeshwaraswamy.

Jatra is held every year for ten days in the month of Magha, a large cattle fair, which attracts about 30,000 heads of cattle, also takes place. Several copper plates of the eighth century, which threw a flood light on the exploits of the Chalukyas and contempora ry political events in the south, were discovered at this place.

Villages: 361 **Inhabited:** 327 **Uninhabited:** 34

Ranking	District	State	National
Area	7	128	782
Population	2	59	378
Sex Ratio	6	83	2299
Child Sex Ratio	3	20	1323
Literacy Rate	1	74	2336
Density	8	51	3581
Work Participation Rate	1	25	1468

Gram Panchayats:

Ammanallur , Madderi, Madanahalli, Thotli, Jannaghatta, Muduvadi, Holur, Itharasanahalli, Thoradevandahalli, Urigili, Sugatur, Settihalli, Seethi, Kyalanur, Channasandra, Kurugal, Vemagal, Belamarnahalli, Chowdadenahalli, Sulur, Arahalli, Marjenahalli, Manighatta, Huthur, Vadagur, Gaddekannur, Kondarajanahalli , Arabikothanur, Narasapura, Bellur, Vokkaleri, Muduvathi, Begli Hosahalli, Doddahasala, Harati, Shapur.

Amenities:

Education: Primary School in 284 villages, Middle school in 145 villages, Matriculation or Secondary School in 27 villages, namely Ammanallur, Kyalanur, Madderi, Vemagal, Medihala, Narasapura, Sulur, Talagunda, Arabikothanur, Vokkaleri, Parswaganahalli, Madanahalli, Thotli, Sugatur, Muduvadi, Holur, Nayakarahalli, Annihalli, Manighatta, Thoradevandahalli, Begli Hosahalli, Dimba Chamanahalli, Kembodi, Huthur, Bhatrahalli, Shapur, Harati.

Higher Secondary or Pre University Courses or Intermediate or Junior College in 5 villages of the CD Block,, namely Kyalanur, Vemagal, Muduvathi, Sugatur, Harohalli.

College in 2 villages, Adult Literacy Center in 3 villages., Colleges are in villages, namely Doddaiyyur, Harohalli.

Medical: Hospital in 1 village, Dispensary in 7 villages, Health Center in 10 villages, Sub Center in 46 villages, Maternity and Child Welfare Center in 3 villages, Community health workers in 1 village.

The Villages having Hospital or Dispensary or Health Center are Ammanallur , Kyalanur, Madderi, Byappanahalli, Annihalli, Seesandra, Thambihalli, Kembodi, Chamarahalli.

Drinking Water: Tap water in 215 villages, Tank water in 66 villages, Well water in 46 villages, Tubewell in 92 villages and more than one source in 189 villages.

Bank: Banking facility in 16 villages, namely, Kyalanur, Madderi, Kamandahalli, Belamarnahalli Vemagal, Medihala, Muduvathi, Vokkaleri, Sugatur Kondasandra, Holur, Kamadenahalli, Keelukote Kembodi, Huthur, Haratimallandahalli.

Credit Society in 8 villages Agricultural Credit Society in 8 Non-Agricultural Credit Society in 1 village.

Others: Power supply in 308 villages, Cinema hall in 4 villages sport club in 1 village, Stadium or Auditorium or Community Hall in 2 villages, Post Office in 43 villages.

There are 255 villages having bus facilities.

Villages with most of facilities: Kyalanur Madderi, Belamarnahalli, Vemagal, Medihala Vokkaleri, Sugatur, Holur, Kamadenahalli, Keelukote Kembodi, Huthur.

Villages without amenities (Education):

K.G.Mylasandra, Sarkari Kyalanur, Devarahalli, Kadripura, Girijampete, Nandikamanahalli, Kalva, Chikkavallabi, Garudapalya, Ramabhadrapura, Yantrakaipura, Kendatti Gollahalli, Horakere, Kaparasiddanahalli, Seegahalli, Nagalapura Gollahalli, Papenahalli, Sambapura, Pindipapanahalli, Somambudi Agrahara, Channapura, Obenahalli, Talagondapurahalli, Jodi Holur, Chillapalli, Garudapalya, Krishnarajapura, Thippasandra, Ganeshapura, Kolar Amanikere, Bettadahosahalli, Kolathammanahalli, Begli, Chinnenahalli, Dimba, Kurubarahalli, Bandur Krishnapura, Nernahalli, Girnahalli, Charaladinne, Siresandra, Haralakunte..

Scheduled Castes: Out of the total population of 228686 persons, 64929 persons (28.39%) belong to Scheduled Castes.
The villages having less than 10% SC population are Orati Agrahara, K.G.Mylasandra, Raghupathi Agrahara Veerapura, Perjenahalli, Manchandahalli Bhuvanahalli, Chikkavallabi, Chokkapura, Garudapalya Ramabhadrapura, Mallasandra, Yantrakaipura Appasandra, Achatnahalli, Kendatti Gollahalli Madivala, Horakere, Talagunda, Chokkahalli Doddaiyyur, Guddanapura, Maderahalli, Banakanahalli Betta Benajanahalli, Papenahalli, Sambapura Channapura, Settikunte, Obenahalli, Urigili Jodi Holur, Kondasandra, Dodda Kurubarahalli Kuduvanahalli, Besthenahalli, Gangarasanahalli Thippasandra, Ganeshapura, Kolar Amanikere, Joohalli Bettadahosahalli, Keelukote, Petechamanahalli Gajaladinne, Basavanatha, Kallipura Bandur Krishnapura, Rasthe Thambihalli, Thambihalli Charaladinne.
The villages having more than 50% SC population are Bellahalli, Veerenahalli, Maniyanahalli Seethappanahalli, Pacharlahalli, Iragasandra Chandrasekarapura, Danavahalli, Sonnenahalli Nagalapura, Kaparasiddanahalli, Guttahalli Chikkanahalli, Nernahalli, Dandiganahalli Mullahalli, Pindipapanahalli, Madavagurjenahalli Kolakunjanahalli, Somambudi Amanikere Hanumanthapura, Uppakunte, Havalegowdana Hosur Mallasandra, Moorandahalli, Poovandahalli Marjenahalli, Tamaka, Chinnapura, Barandahalli Chinnenahalli, Kooteri, Dimba Chamanahalli Ramasandra, Channarayapura, Nandamballi, Haralakunte.
Sex ratio of Scheduled Caste population is 496.

Scheduled Castes Literates and Illiterates by Sex:

	Persons	Males	Females
Literate	29,590	18,434	11,156
Illiterate	35,339	14,306	21,033
Literacy rate	53.4	66.0	40.7
Graduate	802	707	95

Scheduled Castes (Dominant):
Adi Karnataka, Bhovi, Adi Dravida, Chalavadi etc. Koracha

For their cultural identity please see Appendix-I

Villages without Scheduled Castes: There are 58 villages without any scheduled caste population.

Scheduled Tribes: Out of the total population of 228686 persons, 11609 persons (5.08%) belong to Scheduled Tribes.
The villages having less than 10% ST population are Padiganahalli, Chaldiganahalli, Ammanallur Krishnapura, Nachahalli, Kadahalli, Karenahalli Bellahalli, Beechagondahalli, Orati Agrahara Channasandra, K.G.Mylasandra, Sarkari Kyalanur Thippenahalli, Marjenahalli, Veerenahalli Cholaghatta, Maniyanahalli, Jambapura, Devarahalli Seethappanahalli, Pacharlahalli, Bedli, Kadripura Iragasandra, Madderi, Madderi Mallandahalli Matapura, Raghupathi Agrahara, Raghupathi Hosahalli Chanjimale, Veerapura, Rajakallahalli, Settihalli Girijampete, Thokalagatta, Purahalli, Hullankallu Perjenahalli, Harjenahalli, Manchandahalli Chandrasekarapura, Korati Mallandahalli Belamarnahalli, Thoranakambadahalli, Vemagal Channappanahalli, Bettahosapura, Handrahalli Nandikamanahalli, Dhanamatanahalli, Guttahalli Danavahalli, Dinnehosahalli, Kalkere Chowdadenahalli, Chokkapura, Garudapalya, Kurki Narasapura, Sonnenahalli, Chakarasanahalli Byrasandra, Ramabhadrapura, Uddappanahalli Lakshmisagara, Yantrakaipura, Krishnapura Appasandra, Achatnahalli, Khajikallahalli Kendatti Gollahalli, Madivala, Horakere, Sulur Pemmasettihalli, Nuggalapura, Talagunda, Chokkahalli Hogari Gollahalli, Challahalli, Nagalapura, Kendatti Doddaiyyur, Chunchedenahalli, Kaparasiddanahalli Chowdadenahalli, Mangasandra, Chaluvanahalli Seegahalli, Nagalapura Gollahalli, Thyavanahalli Banakanahalli, Koothandahalli, Markandapura Betta Benajanahalli, Chikkanahalli, Konepura Koragondahalli, Jangalahalli, Papenahalli, Muduvathi Nernahalli, Settiganahalli, Settikothanur, Vokkaleri Thirumalakoppa, Chinnapura, Sambapura Dandiganahalli, Parswaganahalli, Vadagere Settivarahalli, Balagere, Mullahalli Settimadamangala, Pindipapanahalli, Haleri Matnahalli, Somambudi Agrahara, Ankathatti Channapura, Chitnahalli, Urati Agrahara, Kakinatha Settikunte, Kembathanahalli, Kithandur, Gottihalli Thurandahalli, Jannaghatta, Obenahalli, Kallur Bommasandra, Gowdahalli, Sugatur, Madavagurjenahalli Kolakunjanahalli, Somambudi Amanikere, Naganala Urigili, Bussanahalli, Talagondapurahalli Byappanahalli, Hanumanthapura, Uppakunte Jangamagurjenahalli, Vanarasi, Muduvadi Muduvadi Hosahalli, Thotliganahalli, Jannapalli Annenahalli, Ghatta Halli, Kondasandra Havalegowdana Hosur, Dadireddihalli, Jaderi, Holur Chikka Kurubarahalli, Somasandra Dodda Kurubarahalli, Kondenahalli, Nukkanahalli Mallasandra, Arinaganahalli, Bellambari, Gangatta Aralimaradahosahalli, Kammasandra, Nayakarahalli

Chillapalli, Besthenahalli, Mathikunte, Annihalli
Garudapalya, Thondala, Gangarasanahalli
Krishnarajapura, Shanubhoganahalli, Manighatta
Gooliganahalli, Nenumanahalli, Byalahalli
Thippasandra, Karahalli, Agnihalli, Seepura
Hoohalli, Arahalli, Moorandahalli, Ganeshapura
Beeramanahalli, Yadahalli, Thoradevandahalli
Veerapura, Poovandahalli, Yalavara, Marjenahalli
Yalachipura, Kamadenahalli, Koothandahalli
Varadenahalli, Gaddekannur, Tamaka, Kolar Amanikere
Chinnapura, Hodalavadi, Barandahalli, Kodi Kannur
Kadripura, Sangondahalli, Joohalli , Hogari
Bettadahosahalli, Paparajanahalli, Keelukote
Kondarajanahalli, Harohalli, Petechamanahalli
Gajaladinne, Basavanatha, Kodi Ramasandra
Honnenahalli, Kallipura, Ekamballi, Doddahasala
Chikkahasala, Chatrakodihalli, Begli Hosahalli
Kolathammanahalli, Begli, Begli Benjenahalli
Chinnenahalli, Cholaghatta, Singondahalli, Kooteri
Dimba, Kurubarahalli, Parehosahalli
Bandur Krishnapura, Iragasandra, Seesandra
Nernahalli, Vittappanahalli, Yanadahalli
Rasthe Thambihalli, Thambihalli, Ramasandra
Ajjapalli, Kembodi, Chadumanahalli, Kalahastipura
Vadagur, Channarayapura, Belaganahalli, Huthur
Holali, Hollamballi, Doddnahalli, Girnahalli
Thimmasandra, Nadupalli, Shillangere, Bhatrahalli
Jangamabasapura, Abbani, Charaladinne, Shapur
Siresandra, Nandamballi, Thippasandra, Haralakunte
Haratimallandahalli, Kenchapura, Harati
Kotiganahalli, Hale Somarasanahalli, Patna
Agrahara Somarasanahalli, Neelakantapura.

The villages having more than 50% ST population are None.

Sex ratio of Scheduled tribe population is 501.

Scheduled Tribes Literates and Illiterates by Sex:

	Persons	Males	Females
Literate	5,365	3,284	2,081
Illiterate	6,244	2,514	3,730
Literacy rate	54.2	66.2	42.1
Graduate	95	83	12

Scheduled Tribes (Dominant):

Naikda etc., Generic Tribes etc., Meda, Palliyan Kadu Kuruba

For their cultural identity please see Appendix-II

Villages without Scheduled Tribes: There are 222 villages without any scheduled tribe population.

Literates and Illiterates by Sex (Total Population):

	Persons	Males	Females
Literate	123,858	74,819	49,039
Illiterate	104,828	41,034	63,794
Literacy rate	63	75	50
Graduate	4,041	3,423	618

Agriculture: ***Distribution of villages according to iand use:*** Out of 361 villages, Total area (in hectare) is 77470, out of that 57.79 percent is cultivable and 35.87 percent of the cultivable area is irrigated.

Sources of Irrigation (Hectares): Government Canal 201.81, Private Canal 5.08, Well without Electricity 106.2, Well with Electricity 1047.78, Tubewell without Electricity 119.74, Tubewell with Electricity 9492.9, Tank 3083.15, River 11.14, Lake 0, Waterfall 0, Others 1991.18.

Villages with population of 5000 to 9999:
Kyalanur.

Villages with population of 10000 and above: None

Distribution of Workers:

	Persons	Males	Females	WPR
Cultivators	44,459	27,146	17,313	36.99
Agricultural Labour	34,946	15,131	19,815	29.08
Household Industry	2,963	1,540	1,423	2.47
Other Workers	37,819	25,371	12,448	31.47
Main Workers	99,658	63,519	36,139	82.92
Marginal Workers	20,529	5,669	14,860	17.08
Total Workers	120,187	69,188	50,999	

Religion: Major Religious Communities:

	Persons	Males	Females	Sex Ratio
Hindu (93.88%)	214,689	108,603	106,086	977
Muslim (5.52%)	12,619	6,560	6,059	924
Christian (0.25%)	573	293	280	956
Sikh (0.01%)	15	8	7	875
Buddhists (0.01%)	15	5	10	2,000
Jain (0.01%)	28	14	14	1,000

Agewise Data:

	Persons	Males	Females	Sex Ratio
All ages	228,686	115,853	112,833	974
0-14	72,549	36,441	36,108	991
15-44	107,687	54,613	53,074	972
45-79	45,239	23,227	22,012	948
80+	2,954	1,443	1,511	1047
Age not stated	257	129	128	992

Languages (Dominant):

Kannada, Telugu, Urdu, Tamil, Hindi

Disabled Population:

	Persons	Males	Females	%
Total Disabled	4,027	2,354	1,673	
In Seeing	1,651	923	728	41
In Speech	436	238	198	10.83
In Hearing	209	104	105	5.19
In Movement	1,264	820	444	31.39
Mentally	467	269	198	11.6

KOLLEGAL

Kollegal C.D. Block lies in the eastern part of Chamarajanagar district. It is a part of Kollegal taluka. The Block is located at a distance of 36 kms. from district headquarters (Chamarajanagar). There are 139 villages in the block with the total population of 284,070 persons. Area of the C.D. Block is 2812.22 sq. kms. It is bounded by districts Mandya and Bangalore Rural on north, districts Mandya, Mysore and taluks Chamarajanagar and Yelandur on west. It has common boundary with the state of Tamil Nadu on north, south and east.

Communications:

Roadways : NH-212: Direction- Mysore to Kollegal, Nearest Villages- C.M.Samudra, Sathegala, Dhanagere, Uganiya, Saragur, Jinakanahalli, Tagarapura, Alahalli, Chilakavadi, Kunthur, Teramballi, Agrahara, Uttamballi, Siddayyanapura. NH-209: Direction- Malawalli to Kollegal, Villages- Sathegala, Dhanagere, Uganiya, Saragur, Jinakanahalli, Agrahara, Siddayyanapura. NH-212: Nearest Villages- Hosamalangi, Tagarapura, Chilakavadi, Kunthur, Teramballi, Mullur, Uttamballi SH- 17 A: Direction- Hasanur to Kollegal, Nearest Villages- M.Halli, Haravanapura, Lakshmipura, Siddayyanapura, Linganapura, Modahalli, Channalinganahalli, Chikkamalapura, Kandayyanapalya, Lokkanahalli, Andipalya, Arabigere-85, Huthur, Bylur, Madhuvanahalli Beat, Lokkanahalli East Beat.

River: Cauvery Nadi- Nearest Villages- C.M. Samudra, Sathegala, Dhanagere, Tellanur, Saragur, Mullur, Hampapura, Dasanapura, Harale, Agrahara, Ponnachi, Sathegala Beat, Cauvery Beat, Saggayam 'B' Beat, Saggayam 'A' Beat, Saggayam 'C' Beat, Martalli 'B' Beat, Indiganatha B' Beat, Palar Beat, Gopinatham Beat, Indiganatha 'A' Beat, Bejjalane 'A' Beat. Palar Nadi- Nearest Villages- Hoogya, Martalli 'A' Beat, Martalli 'B' Beat, Minnya B' Beat, Doddani Beat, Indiganatha 'B' Beat. Dolla Halla Nadi- Nearest Villages- Chikkinduvadi, Saragur, Jinakanahalli, Gundegala, Madhuvanahalli, Haravanapura, Doddinduvadi, Lakshmipura, Agrahara, Siddayyanapura, Modahalli, Bellaji Beat, Gundal 'A' Beat, Gundal 'B' Beat, Kannur Beat, Lokkanahalli West Beat, Surapura Beat, Arepalya Beat. Uduthorai Halla Nadi- Nearest Villages- Ajjipura, Cowdalli, Suleri Palya, Ganganadoddi, Bylore West Beat, Rudrapuram Beat, Dinnahalli Beat, Kurahatti Hosur Beat, Huthur, Arabigere-85, P.G. Palya Beat, Saggayam 'B' Beat.

Reserved Forest: Nearest Villages- Sathegala, Uganiya, Tellanur, Chikkilur, Ikkadahalli, Palya, Hondarabalu, Haravanapura, Lakshmipura, Kunagalli, Arepalya, Jakkalli, Thimmarajipura, Alagumole, Bandalli, Channalinganahalli, Chikkamalapura, Kandayyanapalya, Lokkanahalli, Arabigere-85, P.G. Palya, Huthur, Bylur, Minya, Hoogya, Dantalli, Changadi, Ponnachi, Mahadeshwarabetta, Doddalathur, Changadarahalli, Dinnahalli, Bylore 'West' Beat, Bylore East' Beat, Uttur Beat, P.G. Palya Beat, Mavathur 'A' Beat, Mavathur 'B' Beat, Bellaji Beat, Gundal 'A' Beat, Gundal 'B' Beat, Lokkanahalli West Beat, Surapura Beat, Arepalya Beat, Bandalli 'B' Beat, Bandalli 'A' Beat, Kothanur 'A' Beat, Kothanur 'B' Beat, Sathegala Beat, Mathipura Beat, Cauvery Beat, Saggayam 'A' Beat, Saggayam 'C' Beat, Channur Beat, Martalli 'A' Beat, Martalli B' Beat, Ramapuram Beat, Satyamangala 'A' Beat, Satyamangala 'B' Beat, Hugyam Beat, Minnya 'A' Beat, Minnya B' Beat, M.Malai Beat, Doddani Beat, Indiganatha 'B' Beat, Palar Beat, Gopinatham Beat, Alambadi Beat, Bijjalane'B' Beat, Changadi Beat. (Cowdalli R.F.): Nearest Villages- Shagya, Goreyur, D.M.Samudra, Ellemala, Ajjipura, Arabigere-75, Kurahatti Hosur, Settahalli, Bhadrayyanahalli, Cowdalli, Rudrapuram Beat, Saggayam 'B' Beat, Kurahatti Hosur Beat. (Hanur R.F.): Nearest Villages- Udanur, Siragodu, Hanur, DM Samudra, Ellemala, Ajjipura, Andipalya, Suleri Palya, Ganganadoddi, Ellemala Beat, Lokkanahalli East Beat, Hanur Beat, Dinnahalli Beat.

Annual Rainfall: Normal Rianfall 770.02 mm.

Ground Water: Availability of the Ground Water in the Basin is 13089 H.A.M. and the utilization is 11275 H.A.M. It belongs to Safe category. Depth to water level 2 to 20 meter below the ground. Most of the wells go down in summer months, according to the Ground Water Estimation Committee.

Natural Division : It falls partly in Cauvery Forested Region and Kabbani-Cauvery Valley of the Southern Karnataka Plateau.

Administration:

Division: Mysore. Parliamentary Constituency: 22 Mysore Purab, 23 Bangalore Rural. District: Cham arajanagar. Taluka: Kollegal. Assembly Constituency: 221 Hanur, 222 Kollegal (SC). Gram Panchayat: 37.

Regional Area Development Boards: The Maland Aera Development Board.

Border Villages: (State: Tamil Nadu)- Bylur, Minya, Hoogya, Dantalli, Ponnachi, Mahadeshwarabetta, Martalli, Bylore 'West' Beat, Saggayam 'B' Beat, Kurahatti Hosur Beat, Martalli 'A' Beat, Martalli 'B' Beat, Hugyam Beat, Minnya 'A' Beat, Minnya 'B' Beat, M.Malai Beat, Doddani Beat, Indiganatha 'B' Beat, Palar Beat, Gopinatham Beat, Indiganatha 'A' Beat, Bijjalane'B' Beat, Bejjalane A' Beat. Beat, Doddani Beat, Indiganatha 'B' Beat, Palar Beat, Gopinatham Beat, Indiganatha 'A' Beat, Bijjalane'B' Beat, Bejjalane 'A' Beat, Martalli 'A' Beat, Martalli 'B' Beat.

Villages: 139 **Inhabited:** 85 **Uninhabited:** 54

Ranking	District	State	National
Area	1	1	29
Population	1	22	101
Sex Ratio	4	149	3603
Child Sex Ratio	4	144	4095
Literacy Rate	1	146	4608
Density	1	88	6127
Work Participation Rate	4	165	2067

Gram Panchayats:
Sathegala, Tellanur, Shagya, Bandalli, Chikkilur, Palya, Dhanagere, Harale, Siddayyanapura, Madhuvanahalli, Doddinduvadi, Singanallur, Kongarahalli, Mangala, Managalli, Kannur, Hondarabalu, Mullur, Tagarapura, Kunthur, Kunagalli, Chikkamalapura, Hanur, Ellemala, Ajjipura, Cowdalli, Kurahatti Hosur, Ponnachi, Mahadeshwarabetta, Martalli, Ramapura, Suleri Palya, Lokkanahalli, Dinnahalli, P.G.Palya, Huthur, Hoogya.

Amenities:

Education: Primary School in 78 villages, Middle school in 67 villages, Matriculation or Secondary School in 24 villages, namely Sathegala, Dhanagere, Palya, Madhuvanahalli, Singanallur, Tagarapura, Chilakavadi, Mullur, Kunagalli, Mangala, Goreyur, Bandalli, Managalli, Hanur, Ajjipura, Lokkanahalli, P.G.Palya, Hoogya, Ponnachi, Kurahatti Hosur, Cowdalli, Dinnahalli, Ramapura, Martalli.

Higher Secondary or Pre University Courses or Intermediate or Junior College in 4 villages of the CD Block,, namely Hanur, Lokkanahalli, Ramapura, Martalli.

College in 1 village, Adult Literacy Center in 0 village., College is in village, namely Hanur.

Medical: Hospital in 1 village, Dispensary in 11 villages, Health Center in 16 villages, Sub Center in 3 villages, Maternity and Child Welfare Center in 5 villages, Community health workers in 3 villages.

The Villages having Hospital or Dispensary or Health Center are Sathegala, Doddinduvadi, Kongarahalli, Thimmarajipura, Bandalli, Hanur, P.G.Palya, Mahadeshwarabetta, Cowdalli, Ramapura, Martalli.

Drinking Water: Tap water in 69 villages, Tank water in 23 villages, Well water in 81 villages, Tubewell in 80 villages and more than one source in 84 villages.

Bank: Banking facility in 13 villages, namely, Sathegala, Singanallur, Bandalli, Hanur Lokkanahalli, Arabigere-85, P.G.Palya, Huthur Hoogya, Mahadeshwarabetta, Cowdalli, Ramapura Martalli.

Credit Society in 43 villages Agricultural Credit Society in 17 Non-Agricultural Credit Society in 37 villages.

Others: Power supply in 85 villages, Cinema hall in 13 villages sport club in 0 village, Stadium or Auditorium or Community Hall in 0 village, Post Office in 67 villages.

There are 69 villages having bus facilities.

Villages with most of facilities: Sathegala Bandalli, Hanur, Lokkanahalli, P.G.Palya, Huthur Hoogya, Mahadeshwarabetta, Cowdalli, Ramapura Martalli.

Villages without amenities (Education):
C.M.Samudra, Haravanapura, Lakshmipura, Boodabalu, Bataguppa, Hullepura, Modahalli..

Scheduled Castes: Out of the total population of 284231 persons, 78049 persons (27.46%) belong to Scheduled Castes.

The villages having less than 10% SC population are Lakshmipura, Arepalya, Jakkalli, Alagumole Bataguppa, Siragodu, Gangadharakatte, Arabigere-85 Huthur, Minya, Changadi, Bhadrayyanahalli.

The villages having more than 50% SC population are Jinakanahalli, Gundegala, Haravanapura, Harale Siddayyanapura, Boodabalu, Mangala, Chikkamalapura Ganganadoddi, Dinnahalli.

Sex ratio of Scheduled Caste population is 483.

Scheduled Castes Literates and Illiterates by Sex:

	Persons	Males	Females
Literate	31,383	18,786	12,597
Illiterate	46,666	21,529	25,137
Literacy rate	46.5	54.0	38.5
Graduate	1,451	1,208	243

Scheduled Castes (Dominant):
Adi Karnataka, Madiga, Banjara etc., Bhovi, Korama

For their cultural identity please see Appendix-I

Villages without Scheduled Castes: There are 55 villages without any scheduled caste population.

Scheduled Tribes: Out of the total population of 284231 persons, 28599 persons (10.06%) belong to Scheduled Tribes.

The villages having less than 10% ST population are C.M.Samudra, Uganiya, Tellanur, Chikkilur Chikkinduvadi, Jinakanahalli, Gundegala, Hondarabalu Madhuvanahalli, Haravanapura, Doddinduvadi Singanallur, Kongarahalli, Lakshmipura, Tagarapura Alahalli, Chilakavadi, Kunthur, Teramballi Uttamballi, Siddayyanapura, Thimmarajipura Boodabalu, Mangala, Alagumole, Goreyur, Managalli Byranatha, Chinchalli, Bataguppa, Hullepura Belathur, Siragodu, Hanur, D.M.Samudra, Ellemala Ajjipura, Anapura, Gangadharakatte Channalinganahalli, Chikkamalapura, Kandayyanapalya Lokkanahalli, P.G.Palya, Hoogya, Arabigere-75 Changadi, Mahadeshwarabetta, Kurahatti Hosur Settahalli, Bhadrayyanahalli, Doddalathur

Changadarahalli, Suleri Palya, Ganganadoddi Dinnahalli, Ramapura, Martalli.

The villages having more than 50% ST population are None.

Sex ratio of Scheduled tribe population is 492.

Scheduled Tribes Literates and Illiterates by Sex:

	Persons	Males	Females
Literate	9,045	5,614	3,431
Illiterate	19,554	8,911	10,643
Literacy rate	37.0	45.2	28.5
Graduate	165	152	13

Scheduled Tribes (Dominant):

Naikda etc., Soligaru, Generic Tribes etc., Meda Kaniyan etc.

For their cultural identity please see Appendix-II

Villages without Scheduled Tribes: There are 75 villages without any scheduled tribe population.

Literates and Illiterates by Sex (Total Population):

	Persons	Males	Females
Literate	122,395	73,403	48,992
Illiterate	161,836	72,539	89,297
Literacy rate	50	58	41
Graduate	4,236	3,483	753

Agriculture: ***Distribution of villages according to land use:*** Out of 139 villages, Total area (in hectare) is 281222, out of that 23.23 percent is cultivable and 31.96 percent of the cultivable area is irrigated.

Sources of Irrigation (Hectares): Government Canal 6436.98, Private Canal 129.5, Well without Electricity 1168.35, Well with Electricity 7272.82, Tubewell without Electricity 91.43, Tubewell with Electricity 4202.4, Tank 1282.34, River 12.71, Lake 0, Waterfall 0, Others 281.34.

Villages with population of 5000 to 9999:

Tellanur, Palya, Madhuvanahalli, Doddinduvadi Kongarahalli, Mullur, Kunagalli, Shagya, Bandalli Hanur, Ajjipura, Arabigere-85, Huthur, Hoogya Ponnachi, Cowdalli, Suleri Palya, Ramapura.

Villages with population of 10000 and above:

Sathegala, Mahadeshwarabetta, Martalli.

Distribution of Workers:

	Persons	Males	Females	WPR
Cultivators	47,449	34,171	13,278	33.1
Agricultural Labour	61,140	30,958	30,182	42.65
Household Industry	4,459	1,755	2,704	3.11
Other Workers	30,297	21,811	8,486	21.14
Main Workers	108,667	74,467	34,200	75.81
Marginal Workers	34,678	14,228	20,450	24.19
Total Workers	143,345	88,695	54,650	

Religion: Major Religious Communities:

	Persons	Males	Females	Sex Ratio
Hindu (87.28%)	248,086	127,406	120,680	947
Muslim (3.35%)	9,511	4,945	4,566	923
Christian (5.51%)	15,669	7,973	7,696	965
Sikh (0%)	12	8	4	500
Buddhists (2.74%)	7,777	4,035	3,742	927
Jain (0.01%)	31	16	15	938

Agewise Data:

	Persons	Males	Females	Sex Ratio
All ages	284,231	145,942	138,289	948
0-14	87,701	45,179	42,522	941
15-44	138,311	70,845	67,466	952
45-79	54,941	28,357	26,584	937
80+	2,761	1,268	1,493	1177
Age not stated	517	293	224	765

Languages (Dominant):

Kannada, Tamil, Telugu, Urdu, Hindi

Disabled Population:

	Persons	Males	Females	%
Total Disabled	7,262	4,697	2,565	
In Seeing	5,113	3,407	1,706	70.41
In Speech	552	308	244	7.6
In Hearing	276	141	135	3.8
In Movement	935	616	319	12.88
Mentally	386	225	161	5.32

KOPPA

Koppa C.D. Block lies in the western part of Chikmagalur district. It is a part of Koppa taluka. The Block is located at a distance of 95 kms. from district headquart ers (Chikmagalur). There are 80 villages in the block with the total population of 82,548 persons. Area of the C.D. Block is 570.15 sq. kms. It is bounded by distr ict Shimoga on north, taluk Mudigere on south, taluk Narsimharajapura on east, taluk Sringeri and district Shimoga on west.

Communications:

Roadways : N.H.-13: Direction- Sringeri to Trithahalli, Nearest Villages- Yadadanti, Hariharapura, Kunimakki, Asagodu, Thammadavalli, Hirekodige, Kelakuli, Kumbarkoppa, Addada, Ammadi Estate, Koppa (Rural).

River: Tunga Nadi- Nearest Villages- Chavalamane, Halma thur, Bhandigadi, Hariharapura, Kunimakki, Thammadavalli, Bhuyanakote, Bomlapura, Addada, Narasipura, Belagola. Sita Nadi- Nearest Villages- Bhuyanakote, Heddase, Belagola, Thuluvinakoppa, Belawadi, Lokanathapura, Kulur, Jayapura, Yelemadalu, Murugadde, Herur, Hillikere, Devagodu.

Annual Rainfall: Normal Rianfall 2640.7 mm.

Ground Water: Availability of the Ground Water in the Basin is 3041 H.A.M. and the utilization is 441 H.A. M. It belongs to Safe category. Depth to water level 2 to 20 meter below the ground. Most of the wells go down in summer months, according to the Ground Water Estimation Committee.

Soils: Red Loamy and Sandy Soils.

Natural Division : It falls partly in Sringeri-Koppa Rolling Humid Tract and Kudremukh-Bababudan Forested Hilly zone of the Central Karnataka Plateau.

Administration:

Division: Mysore. Parliamentary Constituency: 15 Udupi. District: Chikmagalur. Taluka: Koppa. Assembly Constitu ency: 123 Sringeri. Gram Panchayat: 22.

Regional Area Development Boards: The Maland Aera Development Board.

Fairs: Bhoomi-Hunnime Festival: During the Deepavali season, "Bhoomi-Hunnime" festival is celebrated by the farmers of Sringeri, Mudigere, Koppa, Narasmharajapura and Chikmagalur taluks of Chikmagalur area.

Kashi-Visveshvara Jatra: Narve, a hamlet of Narasipura in Chikmagalur district is situated on the bank of the river Tunga nine kilometres south-west of Koppa.

Neelakantheshvara Pooja Festival: It is held at Jambitti ge near Chikmagalur around the month of Kartik (October-N ovember) and on the Maha Shivaratri day. Jambittige, a Hamlet of Hariharapura, is at a distance of two kms. from the main 'Jambittige' means natural bricks of laterite, a geological formation.

Sharadamba Car Festival: It is held at Hariharapura near Chikmagalur around the month of April-May for one day. Hariharapura, situated on the left bank of the river Tunga, ten kms. west of Koppa town, in the headqua rters of the hobli of the same name.

Siddeshvaraswami Jatra: Kelakuli which lies about 11 kms. north-east of Koppa town, has fine natural scenery and a temple of Siddheshwara which was renovated about for decades back. The Siddheshwara linga is in a small, brass-metalled mantapa which is built around it. There is a separate utsava-murti. An oracular ceremony called Gana-Darshana is held at this temple on Saturdays, which attracts a large gathering. An annual jatra of Siddeshwa raswami is held for three days about March.

Veerabhadra Jatra: It is held at Koppa near Chikmagalur around the month of April for two days. Koopa, 90 kms. north-west of Chikmagalur town, is the headquarters of the taluk of the same name. A stream called by the local people as 'Musurihalla' flows adjacent to the town. The Veerabhadra temple here, is a small stone construction consisting of a garbhagriha which is surmou nted by a tower, a sukanasi and a porch.

Villages: 80 **Inhabited:** 80 **Uninhabited:** 0

Ranking	District	State	National
Area	6	156	1262
Population	5	163	4014
Sex Ratio	4	36	1360
Child Sex Ratio	7	122	3578
Literacy Rate	2	12	465
Density	6	148	5624
Work Participation Rate	3	138	3488

Gram Panchayats:

Chavalamane, Hirekodige, Kesave, Harandur , Koppa , Bhandigadi, Nilavagilu, Shanuvalli, Hariharapura, Bintravalli , Nuggi, Marithotlu, Narasipura, Asagodu, Bhuvanakote, Thuluvinakoppa, Hiregadde, Jayapura, Agalagandi, Guddethota, Herur, Honnagundi.

Amenities:

Education: Primary School in 54 villages, Middle school in 50 villages, Matriculation or Secondary School in 14 villages, namely Chavalamane, Bhandigadi, Nilavagilu, Hariharapura, Bomlapura, Hirekodige, Thalamakki, Narasipura, Nuggi, Agalagandi, Jayapura, Byredevaru, Herur, Attikudige.

Higher Secondary or Pre University Courses or Inter-mediate or Junior College in 3 villages of the CD Block,, namely Chavalamane, Hariharapura, Jayapura.

College in 1 village, Adult Literacy Center in 0 village., College is in village, namely Hariharapura.

Medical: Hospital in 0 village, Dispensary in 3 villages, Health Center in 4 villages, Sub Center in 6 villages, Maternity and Child Welfare Center in 4 villages, Community health workers in 4 villages.

The Villages having Hospital or Dispensary or Health Center are Chavalamane, Bhandigadi, Hariharapura, Koppa (Rural).

Drinking Water: Tap water in 51 villages, Tank water in 32 villages, Well water in 56 villages, Tubewell in 34 villages and more than one source in 73 villages.

Bank: Banking facility in 13 villages, namely, Chavalamane, Shanuvalli, Hariharapura, Bhuyanakote Hirekodige, Koppa (Rural), Narasipura, Lokanathapura Jayapura, Hiregadde, Yelemadalu, Guddethota Honnagundi.

Credit Society in 10 villages Agricultural Credit Society in 8 Non-Agricultural Credit Society in 3 villages.

Others: Power supply in 80 villages, Cinema hall in 2 villages, sport club in 80 villages, Stadium or Auditorium or Communit Hall in 80 villages, Post Office in 25 villages.

There are 52 villages having bus facilities.

Villages with most of facilities: Chavalamane Hariharapura, Bhuyanakote, Koppa (Rural), Jayapura.

Villages without amenities (Education):

Devarahalli, Shirakaradi, Makkikoppa, Hosur, Heggaru, Heggadde, Shankarapura, Kuppali, Yadadanti,

Thammadavalli, Kagga, Ammadi Estate, Talamakki Estate, Herambapura, Machikoppa, Udana, Belagola, Belawadi, Karimane, Kalasapura, Murugadde, Vate Bachalakan, Bethadakolalu, Herthanakudige, Hillikere, Sthirur..

Scheduled Castes: Out of the total population of 82667 persons, 15793 persons (19.1%) belong to Scheduled Castes. The villages having less than 10% SC population are Devarahalli, Shirakaradi, Halmathur, Honagaru Makkikoppa, Hosur, Nilavagilu, Heggaru, Heggadde Shankarapura, Shanuvalli, Kuppali, Yadadanti Bolapura, Gunavanthe, Kumbarkoppa, Kagga, Kesave Herambapura, Udana, Belawadi, Huligaradi, Haralane Megur, Herthanakudige, Hillikere.

The village having more than 50% SC population is None.

Sex ratio of Scheduled Caste population is 495.

Scheduled Castes Literates and Illiterates by Sex:

	Persons	Males	Females
Literate	8,245	4,816	3,429
Illiterate	7,548	3,154	4,394
Literacy rate	60.3	70.1	50.3
Graduate	125	102	23

Scheduled Castes (Dominant):

Adi Karnataka, Adi Dravida, Bhovi, Mundala Generic Castes etc.

For their cultural identity please see Appendix-I

Villages without Scheduled Castes: There are 13 villages without any scheduled caste population.

Scheduled Tribes: Out of the total population of 82667 persons, 4113 persons (4.98%) belong to Scheduled Tribes. The villages having less than 10% ST population are Chavalamane, Devarahalli, Shirakaradi, Halmathur Honagaru, Makkikoppa, Hosur, Bhandigadi, Nilavagilu Heggaru, Heggadde, Shankarapura, Kodur, Shanuvalli Bilagadde, Kuppali, Melbilre, Yadadanti Hariharapura, Kunimakki, Asagodu, Thammadavalli Bhuyanakote, Heddase, Bomlapura, Bolapura Hirekodige, Kelakuli, Gunavanthe, Kumbarkoppa, Kagga Addada, Ammadi Estate, Harandur, Kesave, Thalamakki Talamakki Estate, Koppa (Rural), Narasipura, Kunchur Marithotlu, Somlapura, Bintravalli, Nuggi, Tanudi Herambapura, Machikoppa, Udana, Belagola Thuluvinakoppa, Belawadi, Karimane, Kalasapura Lokanathapura, Hosuru, Heggaru, Jayapura, Hiregadde Adigebylu, Yelemadalu, Murugadde, Vate Bachalakan Byredevaru , Bethadakolalu, Herthanakudige, Herur Hillikere, Sthirur, Devagodu.

The villages having more than 50% ST population are None.

Sex ratio of Scheduled tribe population is 490.

Scheduled Tribes Literates and Illiterates by Sex:

	Persons	Males	Females
Literate	2,408	1,381	1,027
Illiterate	1,705	716	989
Literacy rate	66.7	75.3	57.8
Graduate	64	47	17

Scheduled Tribes (Dominant):

Gowdalu, Hasalaru, Naikda etc., Maleru Generic Tribes etc.

For their cultural identity please see Appendix-II

Villages without Scheduled Tribes: There are 28 villages without any scheduled tribe population.

Literates and Illiterates by Sex (Total Population):

	Persons	Males	Females
Literate	56,598	30,928	25,670
Illiterate	26,069	10,499	15,570
Literacy rate	78	85	70
Graduate	2,953	1,907	1,046

Agriculture: ***Distribution of villages according to land use:*** Out of 80 villages, Total area (in hectare) is 57015, out of that 37.27 percent is cultivable and 14.89 percent of the cultivable area is irrigated.

Sources of Irrigation (Hectares): Government Canal 31.88, Private Canal 314.72, Well without Electricity 10.11, Well with Electricity 171.74, Tubewell without Electricity 0, Tubewell with Electricity 140.72, Tank 613.74, River 111.12, Lake 0, Waterfall 22.26, Others 1747.4.

Villages with population of 5000 to 9999: None

Villages with population of 10000 and above: None

Distribution of Workers:

	Persons	Males	Females	WPR
Cultivators	7,338	5,988	1,350	19.54
Agricultural Labour	8,916	4,709	4,207	23.75
Household Industry	912	505	407	2.43
Other Workers	20,382	13,518	6,864	54.28
Main Workers	31,410	22,065	9,345	83.65
Marginal Workers	6,138	2,655	3,483	16.35
Total Workers	37,548	24,720	12,828	

Religion: Major Religious Communities:

	Persons	Males	Females	Sex Ratio
Hindu (88.24%)	72,942	36,539	36,403	996
Muslim (6.64%)	5,485	2,757	2,728	989
Christian (4.31%)	3,566	1,788	1,778	994
Sikh (0.01%)	5	3	2	667
Buddhists (0.19%)	157	77	80	1,039
Jain (0.4%)	328	178	150	843

Agewise Data:

	Persons	Males	Females	Sex Ratio
All ages	82,667	41,427	41,240	995

0-14	22,375	11,432	10,943	957
15-44	42,855	21,001	21,854	1041
45-79	16,592	8,548	8,044	941
80+	759	393	366	931
Age not stated	86	53	33	623

Languages (Dominant):
Kannada, Tulu, Malayalam, Konkani, Urdu
Disabled Population:

	Persons	Males	Females	%
Total Disabled	2,081	1,383	698	
In Seeing	1,246	864	382	59.88
In Speech	142	86	56	6.82
In Hearing	72	42	30	3.46
In Movement	415	272	143	19.94
Mentally	206	119	87	9.9

KOPPAL

Koppal C.D. Block lies in the southern part of Koppal district. It is a part of Koppal taluka. The Block is located at a distance of 00 kms. from district headquarters (Koppal). There are 151 villages in the block with the total population of 249,640 persons. Area of the C.D. Block is 1364.10 sq. kms. It is bounded by taluk Yelbarga on north, district Bellary on south, taluk Gangawati on east, and district Gadag on west.

Communications:

Roadways : N.H-13: Direction- Kushtagi to Chitradurga, Nearest Villages- Shahapur, Hiresulikeri, Achartimmapur, Hosur, Metgal, Arsinkera, Wanballary, Kukanpalli, Dhangaldoddi, Budugumpa, Sulthanpur, Kerihalli, Shivapur, Agalkera, Hitnal, Bullapur, Kampasagar, Hosahalli, Holemudlapur. N.H-63: Direction- Hubli to Hintal & Koppal, Nearest Villages- Halgera, Ginigera, Rudrapura, Kanakapur, Basapur, Kidadhal, Koppal (Rural), Dadegal, Kolur, Bevinhalli, Hitnal, Bullapur, Hosahalli, Holemudlapur. S.H-6A: Direction- Kushtagi to Koppal, Nearest Villages- Hatti, Chilwadgi, Ojanhalli, Tankankal, Koppal (Rural), Kodadhal, Chamalapura, Irkalgada, Taad Kanakapur, Yelamgera, Kardigudda, Lebgera. S.H-23: Direction- Ginigera to Gangawati, Nearest Villages- Gabbur, Ginigera, Kanakapur, Dhangaldoddi, Amarapur, Budugumpa, Bilebhavi, Indargi, Jabbalgudda, Guldahalli, Kerihalli.

River: Tungabhadra Nadi- Nearest Villages- Dombarhalli, Belur, Keslapur, Halwagali, Nilogipur, Tigari, Hunkuntiakkapur, Katarkigudlanur, Bochanhalli, Hosahalli, Neeralgi, Mattur, Hireboganhal, Gondbal, Hyati Mellikeri, Lachankera, Chikboganhal, Karkihalli, Narayanpet, Attivatti, Mohammad Nagar, Shivapur, Hirekhasankandi, Chikkasankandi, Hulgi, Munirabad (Rural), Holemudlapur. Hire Halla Nadi- Nearest Villages- Katrahalli, Hiresindogi, Chiksindogi, Dombarhalli, Madinur, Devlapur, Chilwadgi, Naregal, Yettinhatti, Ojanhalli, Dadegal, Kolur, Mangalapur, Horthatanhal, Gunhalli, Muddaballi, Budihal, Gondbal, Mudlapur, Kinhal.

Canal: Nearest Villages- Basapur, Rajarampet, Ayodhya, Bandiharlapur, Shivapur, Agalkera, Hitnal, Bullapur, Kampasagar, Hosahalli, Holemudlapur.

Railway Station: Halgera, Bullapur.

Annual Rainfall: Normal Rianfall 571.92 mm.

Ground Water: Availability of the Ground Water in the Basin is 14684 H.A.M. and the utilization is 9932 H. A.M. It belongs to Over Exploited category. Depth to water level 5 to 20 meter below the ground. Most of the wells go down in summer months, according to the Ground Water Estimation Committee.

Soils: Black Cotton Soil.

Natural Division : It falls partly in the Arkera-Mudgal-Kanakgiri Upland and Middle Tungabhadra Valley of the Central Karnataka Plateau.

Administration:

Division: Gulbarga. Parliamentary Constituency: 8 Koppal. District: Koppal. Taluka: Koppal. Assembly Constituency: 62 Gangawati, 64 Koppal. Gram Panchayat: 35.

Regional Area Development Boards: The Hyderabad - Karnataka Area Development Board.

Fairs: Gavisiddheshwara Jatra: The Gavisiddheshwara jatra is held at Koppal near Raichur in about the month of January for 11 days. A cattle show is also held as an adjunct to the religious fair. Koppal is situated on the left bank of Hirehalla, a tributary of the Tungabhadra, and is on the Guntakal-Hubli railway line. Until 1949, it was the chief town of the jagir of Nawab Salar Jung, which consisted of the Koppal and Yelburga taluks. It has an old and noted Veerashaiva matha, which runs also two high schools, a free boarding home and an Arts and Science times as can be seen from the numerous Sanskrit, Prakrit and Kannada inscriptions dating from the times of Ashoka onwards, found here.

Huligemma Temple Jatra: An annual big jatra is held under the auspices of Huligemma temple at Munirabad near Raichur. Munirabad in Koppal Taluk, is about eight kms. from Hospet. An inscription dated in the year 1088 A.D. found here mentions that this place was gifted to one Chanvedi (Chaturvedi) Bhatta, by the Chalukya king Vikramaditya VI. The former constructed an irrigation canal from the Tungabhadra river. Hulige is the old name of this place, called Vyaghrapuri in Sanskrit.

It has a temple dedicated to Huligemma, which appears to have been built originally in the thirteenth century. There is a dhwajasthamba, which is of a height of about 25 feet, in front of the temple. Within the compound of the temple there is a shrine of Parashurama. Nearby is a group of Panchalingeshwara shrines, only one of which is in a good state of preservation. There is also a Jaina basadi. Annually, a big jatra is held under the auspices of the Huligemma temple.

Villages: 151 **Inhabited:** 144 **Uninhabited:** 7

Ranking	District	State	National
Area	2	44	196
Population	2	39	240
Sex Ratio	4	73	2103
Child Sex Ratio	1	48	2222
Literacy Rate	1	128	3880
Density	3	78	4988
Work Participation Rate	2	94	1893

Gram Panchayats:
Kawaloor, Hatti, Alwandi, Bochanhalli, Betgera, Mattur, Katarkigudlanur , Bisarhalli, Hiresindogi, Gondbal, Kolur, Halgera, Ojanhalli, Bhagyanagar, Lebgera, Madinur, Kinhal, Irkalgada, Hasgal, Chikbommanhal, Indargi, Tawargera, Budugumpa, Bandiharlapur, Shivapur, Hulgi, Munirabad (Dam), Hosahalli, Hitnal, Agalkera, Guldahalli, Ginigera, Hireboganhal, Kunikera, Bahaddurbandi.

Amenities:

Education: Primary School in 136 villages, Middle school in 99 villages, Matriculation or Secondary School in 22 villages, namely Kawaloor, Halgera, Hiresindogi, Bisarhalli, Alwandi, Betgera, Katarkigudlanur, Ginigera, Koppal (Rural), Gondbal, Hyati, Hirebommanhal, Chilkmukki, Irkalgada, Kinhal, Kukanpalli, Budugumpa, Bandiharlapur, Agalkera, Hitnal, Hulgi, Munirabad (Rural).

Higher Secondary or Pre University Courses or Intermediate or Junior College in 4 villages of the CD Block,, namely Alwandi, Koppal (Rural), Kinhal, Munirabad (Rural).

College in 1 village, Adult Literacy Center in 61 villages., College is in village, namely Koppal (Rural).

Medical: Hospital in 5 villages, Dispensary in 16 villages, Health Center in 13 villages, Sub Center in 41 villages, Maternity and Child Welfare Center in 5 villages, Community health workers in 65 villages.

The Villages having Hospital or Dispensary or Health Center are Hiresindogi, Alwandi, Betgera, Ginigera, Koppal (Rural), Hirebommanhal, Irkalgada, Kinhal, Kukanpalli, Kamanur, Indargi, Basapur, Mohammad Nagar, Hitnal, Hulgi, Munirabad (Rural), Hosahalli.

Drinking Water: Tap water in 95 villages, Tank water in 55 villages, Well water in 24 villages, Tubewell in 41 villages and more than one source in 117 villages.

Bank: Banking facility in 13 villages, namely, Hunkuntiakkapur, Bochanhalli, Bhairapur, Kutganhalli Koppal (Rural), Gunhalli, Budihal, Hirebommanhal Chilkmukki, Kinhal, Dhangaldoddi, Achalapur Munirabad (Rural).

Credit Society in 33 villages Agricultural Credit Society in 18 Non-Agricultural Credit Society in 7 villages.

Others: Power supply in 144 villages, Cinema hall in 9 villages sport club in 144 villages, Stadium or Auditorium or Communi Hall in 144 villages, Post Office in 54 villages.

There are 125 villages having bus facilities.

Villages with most of facilities: Hunkuntiakkapur Bochanhalli, Bhairapur, Kutganhalli, Koppal (Rural) Gunhalli, Hirebommanhal, Chilkmukki, Kinhal Munirabad (Rural).

Villages without amenities (Education): Rudrapura, Sulthanpur, Ayodhya, Attivatti, Bullapur..

Scheduled Castes: Out of the total population of 249776 persons, 43743 persons (17.51%) belong to Scheduled Castes.

The villages having less than 10% SC population are Hanwal, Wadganhal, Halgera, Katrahalli, Chiksindogi Belgatti, Hatti, Tigari, Bhairapur, Kampli Moranhalli, Devlapur, Kutganhalli, Rudrapura, Kolur Mangalapur, Horthatanhal, Gunhalli, Bahaddurbandi Gondbal, Sidaganhalli, Achartimmapur, Challari Chikbommanhal, Ganganhal, Uplapur, Chiksulikeri Metgal, Wanballary, Irkalgada, Wadderhatti, Abbigeri Tawargera, Lebgera, Sangapur, Bhimanur, Dhangaldoddi Amarapur, Jabbalgudda, Kerihalli, Rajarampet Ayodhya, Attivatti, Mohammad Nagar, Bevinhalli Chikkasankandi, Bullapur.

The villages having more than 50% SC population are Hydernagar, Kunikera, Hiresulikeri, Jinnapur Hosahalli, Kenchandoni, Taad Kanakapur, Sulthanpur Chandragiri, Achalapur.

Sex ratio of Scheduled Caste population is 499.

Scheduled Castes Literates and Illiterates by Sex:

	Persons	Males	Females
Literate	12,934	8,767	4,167
Illiterate	30,809	13,133	17,676
Literacy rate	37.8	51.4	24.3
Graduate	156	138	18

Scheduled Castes (Dominant):
Madiga, Bhambi etc., Banjara etc., Bhovi Chenna Dasar etc.

For their cultural identity please see Appendix-I

Villages without Scheduled Castes: There are 18 villages without any scheduled caste population.

Scheduled Tribes: Out of the total population of 249776

persons, 23982 persons (9.6%) belong to Scheduled Tribes. The villages having less than 10% ST population are Gudigera, Hanwal, Wadganhal, Halgera, Katrahalli Hiresindogi, Chiksindogi, Bisarhalli, Bikanhalli Mainahalli, Alwandi, Raghunathanhalli, Hydernagar Bhairapur, Kampli, Moranhalli, Mattur, Madinur Devlapur, Kalkera, Naregal, Yettinhatti, Ojanhalli Tankankal, Gabbur, Ginigera, Lingadahalli, Shahapur Rudrapura, Kanakapur, Allanagar, Basapur Koppal (Rural), Kolur, Mangalapur, Horthatanhal Bahaddurbandi, Halwarti, Hireboganhal, Kunikera Hoshalli, Muddaballi, Gondbal, Karkihalli Achartimmapur, Hirebommanhal, Hasgal, Chilkmukki Kodadhal, Chamalapura, Gosaldoddi, Jinnapur, Metgal Hosahalli, Kenchandoni, Wadderhatti, Hanmanhatti Mudlapur, Kinhal, Taad Kanakapur, Yelamgera Tawargera, Kamanur, Lebgera, Sangapur, Bhimanur Halahalli, Dhangaldoddi, Amarapur, Budugumpa Bilebhavi, Sulthanpur, Chandragiri, Nageshanahalli Jabbalgudda, Guldahalli, Kerihalli, Achalapur Attivatti, Mohammad Nagar, Agalkera, Bevinhalli Chikkasankandi, Hitnal, Bullapur, Kampasagar, Hulgi. The villages having more than 50% ST population are Hanmanhalli, Sidaganhalli, Halekunta, Rajarampet Ayodhya.

Sex ratio of Scheduled tribe population is 490.

Scheduled Tribes Literates and Illiterates by Sex:

	Persons	Males	Females
Literate	9,216	6,192	3,024
Illiterate	14,766	6,048	8,718
Literacy rate	47.4	62.6	31.7
Graduate	123	101	22

Scheduled Tribes (Dominant):

Naikda etc., Generic Tribes etc., Meda, Iruliga Maleru

For their cultural identity please see Appendix-II

Villages without Scheduled Tribes: There are 25 villages without any scheduled tribe population.

Literates and Illiterates by Sex (Total Population):

	Persons	Males	Females
Literate	109,905	70,552	39,353
Illiterate	139,871	55,709	84,162
Literacy rate	54	68	39
Graduate	2,850	2,260	590

Agriculture: ***Distribution of villages according to land use:*** Out of 151 villages, Total area (in hectare) is 136410, out of that 69.04 percent is cultivable and 20.59 percent of the cultivable area is irrigated.

Sources of Irrigation (Hectares): Government Canal 3483.27, Private Canal 0, Well without Electricity 8.51, Well with Electricity 2810.29, Tubewell without Electricity 8.04, Tubewell with Electricity 11343.67, Tank 1454.32, River 144.25, Lake 29.15, Waterfall 0, Others 109.65.

Villages with population of 5000 to 9999:

Kawaloor, Alwandi, Kinhal, Hosahalli.

Villages with population of 10000 and above:

Koppal (Rural).

Distribution of Workers:

	Persons	Males	Females	WPR
Cultivators	35,130	26,857	8,273	29.2
Agricultural Labour	54,937	19,609	35,328	45.66
Household Industry	4,386	2,574	1,812	3.65
Other Workers	25,867	19,000	6,867	21.5
Main Workers	94,609	61,273	33,336	78.63
Marginal Workers	25,711	6,767	18,944	21.37
Total Workers	120,320	68,040	52,280	

Religion: Major Religious Communities:

	Persons	Males	Females	Sex Ratio
Hindu (91.48%)	228,504	115,407	113,097	980
Muslim (7.66%)	19,122	9,725	9,397	966
Christian (0.14%)	356	180	176	978
Sikh (0.01%)	34	25	9	360
Buddhists (0.01%)	27	15	12	800
Jain (0.19%)	481	250	231	924

Agewise Data:

	Persons	Males	Females	Sex Ratio
All ages	249,776	126,261	123,515	978
0-14	100,830	51,750	49,080	948
15-44	108,010	55,062	52,948	962
45-79	39,059	18,720	20,339	1086
80+	1,612	586	1,026	1751
Age not stated	265	143	122	853

Languages (Dominant):

Kannada, Urdu, Hindi, Telugu, Marathi

Disabled Population:

	Persons	Males	Females	%
Total Disabled	3,941	2,226	1,715	
In Seeing	1,267	650	617	32.15
In Speech	443	238	205	11.24
In Hearing	204	94	110	5.18
In Movement	1,655	1,021	634	41.99
Mentally	372	223	149	9.44

KORATAGERE

Koratagere C.D. Block lies in the eastern part of Tumkur district. It is a part of Koratagere taluka. The Block is located at a distance of 26 kms. from district headqu arters (Tumkur). There are 251 villages in the block with the total population of 147,031 persons. Area of the C.D. Block is 650.96 sq. kms. It is bounded by taluk Madhugiri on north, taluk Tumkur and district Bangalore Rural on south, districts Kolar and Bangalore Rural on east, and taluk Sira on west.

Communications:

Roadways : S.H.-3: Direction- Madhugiri to Bangalore, Nearest Villages- Baleveeranahalli, Golladevarahalli, Pemmedevarahalli, Dasarahalli, Muggondanahalli, Tumbadi, Musuvinakallu, Kambadahalli, Kamenahalli, Hosahalli, Mudlapanne, Malleshapura, Nagenhalli G., Doddenahalli, Tannenahalli, Manur Thimmanahalli, Chikkapalanahalli, Siddapura, Neelagondanahalli, Irakasandra, Vaddarahalli, D.Nagenahalli. S.H.-33: Direction- Tumkur to Koratagere, Nearest Villages- Bukkapatna, Agrahara, Tharati, Kallug uttarahalli, Jampenahalli. S.H.-58: Direction- Madhugiri to Gauribidanur, Nearest Villages- Byrenahalli, Rayavara, Arasapura, Agrahara, Madenahalli.

River: Suvarnamukhi Nadi- Nearest Villages- Cheelagonda nahalli, Obaladevarahalli, Kathinagenahalli, Gowraganahal li, Reddihalli Venkatapura, Reddihalli, Kyashavara, Byren ahalli, Rayavara, Akkirampura. Garudachala Nadi- Nearest Villages- Holavanahalli, Shakuni Thimmanahalli, Lankenah alli, Budamaranahalli, Bhaktarahalli, Majara Agraharam, Alapanahalli, Chikkasaggere, Cheelenahalli, Madya Venka tapura, Mavattur, Majara Hosahalli. Jayamagali Nadi- Nearest Villages- Kereyagalahalli, Byrenahalli, Rayavara, Bychapura, Chikkanahalli, Hosahalli, Goravanahalli, Hanumenahalli, Akkirampura, Sompura, Holavanahalli, Duggenahalli, Honnaranahalli, Chikkovalli, Thumbuganaha lli, Kodlahalli, Shakuni Thimmanahalli, Malenahalli, Thitha Venkatapura, Kambadahalli, Kenganapalya, Theetha, Melehalli, Veerapura, Maracharahalli, K.G.Bevinahalli, Yarapanahalli, Sankenahalli, Karidugganahalli.

Canal: Nearest Villages- Malenahalli, Kambadahalli, Bhaktarahalli, Polenahalli, Doddasaggere, Obaladevarahal li, Chikkasaggere, Cheelenahalli, Madya, Venkatapura, Lingapura, Mavattur, Majara Hosahalli.

Annual Rainfall: Normal Rianfall 755.12 mm.

Ground Water: Availability of the Ground Water in the Basin is 8362.48 H.A.M. and the utilization is 15294. 56 H.A.M. It belongs to Over Exploited category. Depth to water level 2 to 20 meter below the ground. Most of the wells go down in summer months, according to the Ground Water Estimation Committee.

Soils: Red Loamy Soil.

Natural Division : It falls partly in Madhugiri Hills, Upper Pennar Basin and Tumkur-Kunigal Plateau of the Southern Karnataka Plateau.

Administration:

Division: Bangalore. Parliamentary Constituency: 19 Tumkur. District: Tumkur. Taluka: Koratagere. Assembly Constituency: 134 Koratagere (SC). Gram Panchayat: 23.

Regional Area Development Boards: The Bailu Seeme Area Development Board.

Fairs: Anjaaneyaswami Jatra: Shri Anjaneyaswami Jatra is held at Kyamenahalli about the month of February or March for twelve days. K[illegible]enahalli in Koratagere taluk of Tumkur area about a kilometer from Holavanahalli. It is well-known on account of the big annual Jatra of its Shri Anjaneyaswami temple. A cattle fair is also held here on the occasion.

Villages: 251 **Inhabited:** 236 **Uninhabited:** 15

Ranking	District	State	National
Area	10	144	1030
Population	10	134	1953
Sex Ratio	8	110	2674
Child Sex Ratio	8	126	3643
Literacy Rate	6	76	2570
Density	1	12	4356
Work Participation Rate	2	59	519

Gram Panchayats:

Thovinakere, Boodagavi, Tumbadi, Voddagere, Akkirampura, Bychapura, Arasapura, Bommaladevipura, Holavanahalli, Kyamenahalli, Hulikunte, Bukkapatna, Kuramkote, Agrahara, Hanchihalli, Theetha, Doddasaggere, Mavattur, Neelagondanahalli, Yalerampura, Vajjankurike, Chinnahalli, Kolala.

Amenities:

Education: Primary School in 188 villages, Middle school in 101 villages, Matriculation or Secondary School in 23 villages, namely Kabbigere, Thovinakere, Junjuramanahalli, Manuvinakurike, Kuramkote, Mallekavu, Bukkapatna, Voddagere, Tumbadi, Goravanahalli, Byrenahalli, Akkirampura, Godrahalli, Holavanahalli, Bommaladevipura, Doddasaggere, Theetha, Duddanahalli, Neelagondanahalli, Pathaganahalli, Yalerampura, Kolala, Yalachagere.

Higher Secondary or Pre University Courses or Intermediate or Junior College in 7 villages of the CD Block,, namely Thovinakere, Tumbadi, Holavanahalli, Theetha, Neelagondanahalli, Irakasandra, Kolala.

College in 1 village, Adult Literacy Center in 0 village., College is in village, namely Thovinakere.

Medical: Hospital in 1 village, Dispensary in 8 villages, Health Center in 7 villages, Sub Center in 32 villages, Maternity and Child Welfare Center in 1 village, Community health workers in 1 village.

The Villages having Hospital or Dispensary or Health Center are Thovinakere, Pemmedevarahalli, Byrenahalli, Akkirampura, Doddasaggere, Maracharahalli, Duddanahalli, Yalerampura.

Drinking Water: Tap water in 153 villages, Tank water in 4 villages, Well water in 11 villages, Tubewell in 18

villages and more than one source in 152 villages.
Bank: Banking facility in 12 villages, namely, Thovinakere, Kurihalli, Tumbadi, Byrenahalli Akkirampura, Buddenahalli, Holavanahalli, Mavattur Theetha, Neelagondanahalli, Yalerampura, Kolala.
Credit Society in 23 villages Agricultural Credit Society in 16 Non-Agricultural Credit Society in 13 villages.
Others: Power supply in 236 villages, Cinema hall in 6 villages, sport club in 236 villages, Stadium or Auditorium or Community Hall in 236 villages, Post Office in 36 villages.
There are 139 villages having bus facilities.
Villages with most of facilities: Kurihalli Tumbadi, Byrenahalli, Akkirampura, Holavanahalli Mavattur, Theetha, Yalerampura, Kolala.
Villages without amenities (Education):
Obanahalli, Bisadihalli, Doddasanjevegowdanapalya, Venkataramanahalli, Devarahalli, Kanive Hosahalli, Gattithimmanahalli, Kumatenahalli, Venkannanahalli, Jagannathapura, Baleveeranahalli, Golladevarahalli, Biradenahalli, Musuvinakallu, Kamenahalli, Hosahalli, Kongenahalli, Chikkegowdanahalli, Chigaranahalli, Kurubarahalli, Harapagondanahalli, Sonnenahalli, Hosahalli, Byadarahalli, Gangenahalli, Malenahalli, Majara Agrahara, Avadharanahalli, Obaladevarahalli, Hulisoppinahalli, Melehalli, Yarapanahalli, Siddapura, Byrasandra, Thigalarahalli, Obanayakanapalya, Majara Hosahalli, Yalamarahalli, Mudlakerepalya, Hanumanthapura, Lakkaiahnapalya, Gadamenahalli, Madhavarayanapalya, Rangapura, Byatarayanapalya, Kantevaderahalli, K.Bevinahalli, Challalu..
Scheduled Castes: Out of the total population of 147297 persons, 33434 persons (22.7%) belong to Scheduled Castes.
The villages having less than 10% SC population are Bisadihalli, Doddasanjevegowdanapalya Venkataramanahalli, Devarahalli, Kanive Hosahalli Badamuddanapalya, Gattithimmanahalli, Kumatenahalli Dogganahalli, Gowjagal, Hanchimallanahalli Venkannanahalli, Kambadahalli, Channapatna Gatlagollahalli, Gowrikallu, Tharati, Navilakurike Kalluguttarahalli, Jampenahalli, Baleveeranahalli Golladevarahalli, Yattugonahalli, Tumbadi Kathinagenahalli, Hosahalli, Bajjanahalli Kongenahalli, Chikkegowdanahalli, Chigaranahalli Hanumenahalli, Kurubarahalli, Buddenahalli Godrahalli, Pannenahalli, Kyamenahalli Harapagondanahalli, Sonnenahalli, Hosahalli Honnaranahalli, Chikkovalli, Lingadaveeranahalli Byadarahalli, Gangenahalli, Bhaktarahalli Polenahalli, Obaladevarahalli, Channavaderahalli Singalikapura, Hulisoppinahalli, Kenganapalya Gaddobanahalli, Yarapanahalli, Manur Thimmanahalli Chikkapalanahalli, Karidugganahalli, Maragondanaguni Thigalarahalli, Vengalammanahalli, Motagondanahalli Obanayakanapalya, M.Bevinahalli, Upasapura Yalamarahalli, Byragondlu, Veerasagara Byadara Agrahara, Yalerampura, Mudlakerepalya Vaddarahalli, Bychenahalli, Thimmanayakanahalli Thimmasandra, Lakkaiahnapalya, Kaluvehalli Rahutanahalli, Madhavarayanapalya, Rangapura Katenahalli, Byatarayanapalya, Kantevaderahalli Narasapura, K.Bevinahalli, Challalu.
The villages having more than 50% SC population are Gattalahalli, Gondihalli, Bukkapatna, Jagannathapura Pemmedevarahalli, Muggondanahalli Tumbadi Gollahalli, Obaladevarahalli, Malapanahalli Gantiganahalli, Kamarajanahalli Reddihalli Venkatapura, Reddihalli, Rayavara Sirigonahalli, Avadharanahalli, Honnenahalli Siddapura, Majara Hosahalli, Hanumanthapura Sunkadahalli, Mitrahalli.
Sex ratio of Scheduled Caste population is 490.
Scheduled Castes Literates and Illiterates by Sex:

	Persons	Males	Females
Literate	14,891	9,213	5,678
Illiterate	18,543	7,850	10,693
Literacy rate	51.1	62.0	39.8
Graduate	377	344	33

Scheduled Castes (Dominant):
Madiga, Adi Karnataka, Bhovi, Adi Dravida Banjara etc.
For their cultural identity please see Appendix-I
Villages without Scheduled Castes: There are 66 villages without any scheduled caste population.
Scheduled Tribes: Out of the total population of 147297 persons, 14246 persons (9.67%) belong to Scheduled Tribes.
The villages having less than 10% ST population are Ajjenahalli, Chikkannanahalli, Bisadihalli Doddasanjevegowdanapalya, Mudigowdanahalli Surenahalli, Devarahalli, Thovinakere, Kurihalli Dasalakunte, Jonigarahalli, Badamuddanapalya Doddegowdanapalya, Gattithimmanahalli, Boodagavi Junjuramanahalli, Manuvinakurike, Shambonahalli Kurubarahalli, Holathalu, Dogganahalli Hanchimallanahalli, Venkannanahalli, Herajenahalli Gattalahalli, Baraka, Channarayanadurga, Gowrikallu Jagannathapura, Tharati, Navilakurike, Jampenahalli Baleveeranahalli, Pemmedevarahalli, Dasarahalli Kalkere, Garaga Doddi, Cheelagondanahalli Kurudugonahalli, Muggondanahalli, Tumbadi Gollahalli

Tumbadi, Biradenahalli, Musuvinakallu, Kambadahalli
Devarahalli, Obaladevarahalli, Malapanahalli
Buruganahalli, Kathinagenahalli, Hosahalli
Koratagere (Rural), Hulikunte, Hulugonahalli
Gantiganahalli, Kongenahalli, Kamarajanahalli
Chikkegowdanahalli, Chigaranahalli, Madavara
Reddihalli Venkatapura, Reddihalli, Kyashavara
Rayavara, Arasapura, Agrahara, Chikkanahalli
Hanumenahalli, Akkirampura, Kurubarahalli, Sompura
Buddenahalli, Madenahalli, Thogarigatta
Pannenahalli, Duggenahalli, Harapagondanahalli
Thimmanahalli, Thumbuganahalli
Shakuni Thimmanahalli, Sirigonahalli, Muddenahalli
Lingadaveeranahalli, Lankenahalli, Malenahalli
Theetha Venkatapura, Kambadahalli, Bhaktarahalli
Majara Agrahara, Alapanahalli, Avadharanahalli
Obaladevarahalli, Chikkasaggere, Cheelenahalli
Madya Venkatapura, Lingapura, Minasandra
Channavaderahalli, Mavattur, Sriramanahalli
Doddapalanahalli, Honnenahalli, Hoskote
Tannenahalli, A.Venkatapura, Kenganapalya
Gaddobanahalli, Melehalli, Maracharahalli
Puttasandra, Yarapanahalli, Sankenahalli
Manur Thimmanahalli, Chikkapalanahalli, Siddapura
Neelagondanahalli, Karidugganahalli, Byrasandra
Vengalammanahalli, Motagondanahalli
Obanayakanapalya, M.Bevinahalli, Majara Hosahalli
Yalamarahalli, Belladahalli, Lakkamuthanahalli
Buchenahalli, Veerasagara, Byadara Agrahara
Yalerampura, Mudlakerepalya, Vaddarahalli
Bychenahalli, Hanumanthapura, Singrihalli
Hanumanthagiri, Huluvangala, Thimmanayakanahalli
Gadamenahalli, Sunkadahalli, Vaderahalli
Kaluvehalli, Puradahalli, Rahutanahalli, Omachihalli
Madhavarayanapalya, Kolala, Rangapura, Katenahalli
Mitrahalli, Kantevaderahalli, Narasapura
Malagonahalli, K.Bevinahalli, Challalu, Yalachagere.

The villages having more than 50% ST population are Kumatenahalli, Chikkovalli, Gangenahalli Thigalarahalli, Bheemasagara.

Sex ratio of Scheduled tribe population is 490.

Scheduled Tribes Literates and Illiterates by Sex:

	Persons	Males	Females
Literate	6,957	4,186	2,771
Illiterate	7,289	3,073	4,216
Literacy rate	56.0	65.8	45.7
Graduate	164	135	29

Scheduled Tribes (Dominant):

Naikda etc., Hakkipikki, Generic Tribes etc.

For their cultural identity please see Appendix-II

Villages without Scheduled Tribes: There are 100 villages without any scheduled tribe population.

Literates and Illiterates by Sex (Total Population):

	Persons	Males	Females
Literate	79,449	47,553	31,896
Illiterate	67,848	27,380	40,468
Literacy rate	61	72	50
Graduate	2,671	2,262	409

Agriculture: ***Distribution of villages according to land use:*** Out of 251 villages, Total area (in hectare) is 65096, out of that 63.92 percent is cultivable and 19.83 percent of the cultivable area is irrigated.

Sources of Irrigation (Hectares): Government Canal 0, Private Canal 0, Well without Electricity 16.89, Well with Electricity 520.01, Tubewell without Electricity 111.25, Tubewell with Electricity 5805.08, Tank 1797.59, River 0, Lake 0, Waterfall 0, Others 1.01.

Villages with population of 5000 to 9999:
Holavanahalli.

Villages with population of 10000 and above: None

Distribution of Workers:

	Persons	Males	Females	WPR
Cultivators	47,450	29,503	17,947	55.66
Agricultural Labour	23,705	8,697	15,008	27.8
Household Industry	2,322	930	1,392	2.72
Other Workers	11,779	8,410	3,369	13.82
Main Workers	67,719	42,846	24,873	79.43
Marginal Workers	17,537	4,694	12,843	20.57
Total Workers	85,256	47,540	37,716	

Religion: Major Religious Communities:

	Persons	Males	Females	Sex Ratio
Hindu (95.47%)	140,630	71,532	69,098	966
Muslim (4.14%)	6,098	3,107	2,991	963
Christian (0.02%)	25	12	13	1,083
Sikh (0%)	2	1	1	1,000
Buddhists (0%)	2	2	-	-
Jain (0.26%)	383	194	189	974

Agewise Data:

	Persons	Males	Females	Sex Ratio
All ages	147,297	74,933	72,364	966
0-14	42,445	21,803	20,642	947
15-44	68,937	34,713	34,224	986
45-79	34,036	17,479	16,557	947
80+	1,778	880	898	1020
Age not stated	101	58	43	741

Languages (Dominant):

Kannada, Urdu, Hindi, Telugu, Marathi

Disabled Population:

	Persons	Males	Females	%
Total Disabled	3,234	1,829	1,405	

In Seeing	1,494	792	702	46.2
In Speech	397	232	165	12.28
In Hearing	180	96	84	5.57

In Movement	873	554	319	26.99
Mentally	290	155	135	8.97

KRISHNARAJANAGARA

Krishnarajanagara C.D. Block lies in the northern part of Mysore district. It is a part of Krishnarajanagara taluka. The Block is located at a distance of 40 kms. from district headquarters (Mysore). There are 178 villages in the block with the total population of 208, 552 persons. Area of the C.D. Block is 596.01 sq. kms. It is bounded by district Hassan on north, taluks Mysore and Hunsur on south, district Mandya on east, district Hassan and taluk Piriyapatna on west.

Communications:

Roadways **:** SH-57: Direction- Hassan to Mysore, Nearest Villages- Guluvinaattiguppe, Arakere, Munjanaha lli, Valagerehalli, Battiganahalli, Bherya, Sugganahalli, Hosa Agrahara, Bommenahalli, Chikkavoddaragudi, Arjunah alli, Manchanahalli, Hampapura, Goragundi, Kantenahalli, Arakere, Dornahalli.

Railway Station: Villages- Hampapura, Hosa Agrahara, Arjunahalli Lalamdevanahalli, Hosahalli.

River: Cauvery Nadi- Nearest Villages- Hebsur, Saraguru, Pashupathi, Kedaga, Mavanur, Laxmipura, Bevinahalli, Mirle, Kallahalli, Gandhanahalli, Adaguru, Galigekere, Manchanahalli, Chenga, Hampapura, Sanyasipura, Kolurhan tha, Hadyahantha, Diddahalli, Hosur, Kuppehantha, Kuppe, Mavathur Hantha, Byadarahalli Hantha, Kappadihantha, Chandagalhantha, Katnalhantha, Degganahalli, Kanugana Halli, Thippur, Chamalapura, Goragundi, Hosahalli. Laksh mantirtha Nadi- Nearest Villages- Kallahalli, Mulepetlu, Marchahalli, Hosahalli, Hangaraboyanahalli, Mallahalli.

Canal: Nearest Villages- Kallimuddanahalli, Ankanahalli, Saligrama, Chikkanayakanahalli, Ballur, Bylapura, Kench anahalli, Narachanahalli, Halemirle, Natanahalli, Shyabalu, Malanaikanahalli, Mirle, Beechanahalli, Hosa, Agrahara, Bommenahalli, Gandhanahalli, Chikkavoddaragudi, Galigek ere, Arjunahalli, Manchanahalli, Kaggaliborekaval, Chenga, Hampapura, Abburu, Vallambudi, Karthalu, Hullehosur, Thandre, Hanasogehantha, Hanasoge, Chikkahanasoge, Bandahalli, Kolur, Kolurhantha, Kaggala, Nadappanahalli, Damanahalli, Hadya, Hadyahanta, Sakkare, Mayigowdanah alli, Kuppehantha, Sreeramapura, Kuppe, Kestur, Kanchagar akoppalu, Malali, Mavathur Hantha, Byadarahalli Hantha, Kappadihantha, Chandagalhantha, Venkatapura, Buvanahalli, Bachahalli, Hebbal, Hebbal Kaval, Chandagal, Katnalhan tha, Katnal, Cheernahalli, Beeranahalli, Byadarahalli, Siddapura, Mavathur, Kanugana Halli, Thippur, Bannikuppe, Kamenahalli, Kaggere, Goragundi, Yedathore, Manuganaha lli, Mudalakoppalu, Lalanahalli, Narayanapura, Sathigrama, Southanahalli, Kallahalli, Basavarajapura, Hosahalli, Chowkahalli, Kantenahalli, Kalenahalli, Arakere, Dornah alli, Hangaraboyanahalli.

Annual Rainfall: Normal Rianfall 741 mm.

Ground Water: Availability of the Ground Water in the Basin is 3259.43 H.A.M. and the utilization is 1259. 23 H.A.M. It belongs to Over Exploited category. Depth to water level 2 to 10 meter below the ground. Most of the wells go down in summer months, according to the Ground Water Estimation Committee.

Soils: Red Sandy Soils, Red Loamy Soils & Deep Black Soils.

Natural Division : It falls in Cauvery Valley of the Southern Karnataka Plateau.

Administration:

Division: Mysore. Parliamentary Constituency: 21 Mysore Paschim. District: Mysore. Taluka: Krishnarajanagar. Assembly Constituency: 211 Krishnarajanagara. Gram Panchayat: 31.

Villages: 178 **Inhabited:** 156 **Uninhabited:** 22

Ranking	**District**	**State**	**National**
Area	6	153	1183
Population	7	80	592
Sex Ratio	1	48	1634
Child Sex Ratio	7	103	3248
Literacy Rate	2	115	3422
Density	3	117	3104
Work Participation Rate	2	14	2687

Gram Panchayats:

Haradanahalli, Karpuravalli, Thandre, Meluru, Munjanahalli, Bherya, Hosa Agrahara, Narachanahalli, Ankanahalli, Saligrama, Laxmippura, Honnenahalli, Hanasoge, Channamgere, Mayigowadanahalli, Haleyuru, Mirle, Gandhanahalli, Adaguru, Thippur, Hampapura, Kuppehantha, Chandagal, Kaggere, Hebbal, Kestur, Hosakote, Mavathur, Byadarahalli, Lalamdevanahalli, Dornahalli.

Amenities:

Education: Primary School in 146 villages, Middle school in 85 villages, Matriculation or Secondary School in 30 villages, namely Kalammana Koppalu, Haradanahalli, Saligrama, Chikkanayakanahalli, Thandre, Meluru, Mirle, Bherya, Hosa Agrahara, Kakanahalli, Gandhanahalli, Adaguru, Hampapura, Thandre, Hanasoge, Channamgere, Hadya, Diddahalli, Hosur, Haleyuru, Ankanahalli, Kuppe, Kestur, Hosakote, Hebbal, Chandagal, Mavathur, Thippur, Kaggere, Dornahalli.

Higher Secondary or Pre University Courses or Intermediate or Junior College in 6 villages of the CD Block,,

namely Saligrama, Mirle, Bherya, Hosa Agrahara, Hosur, Kestur.

College in 1 village, Adult Literacy Center in 0 village., College is in village, namely Saligrama.

Medical: Hospital in 0 village, Dispensary in 8 villages, Health Center in 9 villages, Sub Center in 52 villages, Maternity and Child Welfare Center in 1 village, Community health workers in 18 villages.

The Villages having Hospital or Dispensary or Health Center are Hebsur, Saligrama, Meluru, Gandhanahalli, Adaguru, Hampapura, Channamgere, Kestur.

Drinking Water: Tap water in 134 villages, Tank water in 58 villages, Well water in 127 villages, Tubewell in 119 villages and more than one source in 150 villages.

Bank: Banking facility in 24 villages, namely, Rampura, Saligrama, Ballur, Laxmipura, Natanahalli Mirle, Beechanahalli, Bherya, Hosa Agrahara Chikkavoddaragudi, Galigekere, Hampapura, Hanasoge Hadya, Hosur, Haleyuru, Chibukahalli, Hebbal Byadarahalli, Mavathur, Thippur, Narayanapura Hosahalli, Dornahalli.

Credit Society in 156 villages Agricultural Credit Society in 11 Non-Agricultural Credit Society in 60 villages.

Others: Power supply in 156 villages, Cinema hall in 8 villages, sport club in 0 village, Stadium or Auditorium or Community Hall in 0 village, Post Office in 49 villages.

There are 121 villages having bus facilities.

Villages with most of facilities: Saligrama Natanahalli, Mirle, Bherya, Hosa Agrahara Chikkavoddaragudi, Hampapura, Hanasoge, Hadya, Hosur Haleyuru, Hebbal, Byadarahalli, Mavathur, Thippur Narayanapura.

Villages without amenities (Education): Sanabinakuppe, Bevinahalli, Hulleborekaval, Alambadikaval, Vallambudi, Kuppehantha, Kappadihantha, Bachahalli, Huralikamena Halli, Manuganahalli..

Scheduled Castes: Out of the total population of 208566 persons, 30474 persons (14.61%) belong to Scheduled Castes.

The villages having less than 10% SC population are Kulume Hosuru, Munduru, Kalammana Koppalu Sanabinakuppe, Hebsur, Gummanahalli, Yaladahalli Moodalabeedu, Ankanahalli, Kedaga, Ballur Bevinahalli, Thandreankanahalli, Kuppahalli Kenchanahalli, Sankanahalli, Bachahalli, Natanahalli Malanaikanahalli, Mirle, Beechanahalli, Hosuru Arakere, Battiganahalli, Sambaravalli Mandiganahalli, Sugganahalli, Alambadikaval Gandhanahalli, Kanchinakere, Adaguru. Galigekere Manchanahalli, Kaggaliborekaval, Abburu, Vallambudi Karthalu, Thandre, Hanasoge, Sakkare, Diddahalli Hosur, Kuppehantha, Ankanahalli, Benaganahalli Kestur, Hosakote, Kappadihantha, Buvanahalli Bachahalli, Chandagal, Katnal, Cheernahalli Madhuvanahalli, Maragowdanahalli, Madahalli Huralikamena Halli, Adaganahalli, Degganahalli Kanugana Halli, Thippur, Manuganahalli, Sathigrama Marchahalli, Kalenahalli.

The villages having more than 50% SC population are Hulleborekaval, Somanahalli, Kakanahalli Sanyasipura, Nijaganahalli, Goragundi, Southanahalli Hangaraboyanahalli.

Sex ratio of Scheduled Caste population is 497.

Scheduled Castes Literates and Illiterates by Sex:

	Persons	Males	Females
Literate	12,430	7,663	4,767
Illiterate	18,044	7,677	10,367
Literacy rate	46.9	57.5	36.1
Graduate	346	311	35

Scheduled Castes (Dominant):

Adi Karnataka, Madiga, Generic Castes etc.

Adi Dravida, Korama

For their cultural identity please see Appendix-I

Villages without Scheduled Castes: There are 52 villages without any scheduled caste population.

Scheduled Tribes: Out of the total population of 208566 persons, 13955 persons (6.69%) belong to Scheduled Tribes.

The villages having less than 10% ST population are Bettahalli, Maluganahalli, Kulume Hosuru, Munduru Kalammana Koppalu, Seegavalu, Haradanahalli Sanabinakuppe, Karpuravalli, Dadadahalli, Lakkikuppe Hebsur, Saraguru, Pashupathi, Gummanahalli Honnenahalli, Yaladahalli, Moodalabeedu Kallimuddanahalli, Ankanahalli, Saligrama Chikkanayakanahalli, Kedaga, Ballur, Laxmipura Bylapura, Bevinahalli, Kuppahalli, Mudiguppe Kenchanahalli, Thandre, Katnalu, Meluru Sankanahalli, Bachahalli, Kurubahalli Yalemuddanahalli, Kodiyala, Hanumanahalli Narachanahalli, Halemirle, Natanahalli Malanaikanahalli, Mirle, Beechanahalli Hulleborekaval, Guluvinaattiguppe, Arakere, Gerudada Somanahalli, Battiganahalli, Bherya, Sambaravalli Mandiganahalli, Sugganahalli, Haramballi Alambadikaval, Doddavaddaragudi, Bommenahalli Kakanahalli, Gandhanahalli, Chikkavoddaragudi Kanchinakere, Maragowdanahalli, Adaguru Manchanahalli, Kaggaliborekaval, Sanyasipura, Abburu Vallambudi, Karthalu, Thandre, Yaremanuganahalli Chikkahanasoge, Bandahalli, Kolur, Kaggala

Nadappanahalli, Dammanahalli, Sakkare Mayigowdanahalli, Diddahalli, Hosur, Kuppehantha Sreeramapura, Haleyuru, Ankanahalli, Gudduganahalli Somanahalli, Benaganahalli, Kogilur, Chibukahalli Kuppe, Kestur, Kanchagarakoppalu, Nijaganahalli Kappadihantha, Buvanahalli, Bachahalli, Hebbal Cheernahalli, Beeranahalli, Madhuvanahalli Byadarahalli, Siddapura, Gowdenahalli, Mavathur Maragowdanahalli, Madahalli, Huralikamena Halli Degganahalli, Kamenahalli, Goragundi, Manuganahalli Mudalakoppalu, Lalanahalli, Narayanapura Southanahalli, Mulepetlu, Lalamdevanahalli Basavarajapura, Hosahalli, Chowkahalli, Kalenahalli Basavapatna.

The villages having more than 50% ST population are None.

Sex ratio of Scheduled tribe population is 497.

Scheduled Tribes Literates and Illiterates by Sex:

	Persons	Males	Females
Literate	6,633	4,125	2,508
Illiterate	7,322	2,891	4,431
Literacy rate	53.8	66.8	40.8
Graduate	159	140	19

Scheduled Tribes (Dominant):

Naikda etc., Gond etc., Generic Tribes etc.
Jenu Kuruba, Sholaga

For their cultural identity please see Appendix-II

Villages without Scheduled Tribes: There are 103 villages without any scheduled tribe population.

Literates and Illiterates by Sex (Total Population):

	Persons	Males	Females
Literate	103,994	62,619	41,375
Illiterate	104,572	42,262	62,310
Literacy rate	56	68	45
Graduate	3,763	3,236	527

Agriculture: ***Distribution of villages according to land use:*** Out of 178 villages, Total area (in hectare) is 59601, out of that 67.93 percent is cultivable and 41.02 percent of the cultivable area is irrigated.

Sources of Irrigation (Hectares): Government Canal 15111.36, Private Canal 0, Well without Electricity 9.49, Well with Electricity 364.4, Tubewell without Electricity 3.24, Tubewell with Electricity 381.43, Tank 556.14, River 12.14, Lake 0, Waterfall 0, Others 115.22.

Villages with population of 5000 to 9999:
Mirle, Gandhanahalli, Haleyuru, Kestur.

Villages with population of 10000 and above:
Saligrama.

Distribution of Workers:

	Persons	Males	Females	WPR
Cultivators	58,870	41,618	17,252	57.63
Agricultural Labour	28,567	12,541	16,026	27.97
Household Industry	932	604	328	0.91
Other Workers	13,780	10,891	2,889	13.49
Main Workers	78,709	60,156	18,553	77.05
Marginal Workers	23,440	5,498	17,942	22.95
Total Workers	102,149	65,654	36,495	

Religion: Major Religious Communities:

	Persons	Males	Females	Sex Ratio
Hindu (96.71%)	201,713	101,364	100,349	990
Muslim (2.44%)	5,088	2,625	2,463	938
Christian (0.24%)	496	234	262	1,120
Sikh (0%)	6	4	2	500
Buddhists (0.02%)	34	20	14	700
Jain (0.34%)	709	356	353	992

Agewise Data:

	Persons	Males	Females	Sex Ratio
All ages	208,566	104,881	103,685	989
0-14	59,531	30,170	29,361	973
15-44	103,130	51,846	51,284	989
45-79	43,411	21,785	21,626	993
80+	2,379	1,016	1,363	1342
Age not stated	115	64	51	797

Languages (Dominant):
Kannada, Urdu, Telugu, Marathi, Tamil

Disabled Population:

	Persons	Males	Females	%
Total Disabled	4,392	2,387	2,005	
In Seeing	2,400	1,208	1,192	54.64
In Speech	481	292	189	10.95
In Hearing	281	127	154	6.4
In Movement	885	576	309	20.15
Mentally	345	184	161	7.86

KRISHNARAJPET

Krishnarajpet C.D. Block lies in the western part of Mandya district. It is a part of Krishnarajpet tehsil. The Block is located at a distance of 56 kms. from district headquarters (Mandya). There are 316 villages in the block with the total population of 225,284 persons. Area of the C.D. Block is 898.72 sq. kms. It is bounded by district Hassan on north, district Mysore on south, taluks Pandavapura and Nagamangala on east, districts Hassan and Mysore on west.

Communications:

Roadways : S.H.-7: Direction- Channarayapatna to Pandavapura, Nearest Villages- Bolamaranahalli, Anegola, Anchebeeranahalli, Mandalekanahalli, Uddinamallanahosur, Tholasi, Ankanahalli, Vaddarahalli, Basavanahalli, Laxmipura, Kikkeri, Kikkeri Amanikere, Kodimaranahalli, Hodakahalli, Chikkalale, Oochanahalli, Honnenahalli, Murukanahalli,

Maradahalli, Hadanur, Thendekere, Anchanahalli, Anchemu ddanahalli, Cheekanahalli, Hirikalale, Theganahalli, Pura, Chikkonahalli, Krishnarajpet (Rural), Hemmanahalli, Agasarahalli, Jakkanahalli.

Railway Station: Villages- Mandagere, Karthalu, Beeraval li, Saxibeedu, Voddaragudi.

River: Cauvery Nadi- Nearest Villages- Sangapura, Ambig arahalli, Varahanathakallahalli, Bookahalli, Poovanahalli, Mavinakere, B. Hosakote, Gopalapura, Hosur, Heraganahal li. Hemavati Nadi- Nearest Villages- Gondihalli, Madapura nala, Madapura, Halemadapura, Ganadahalli, Gudehosahalli, Kadahemmige, Dananahalli, Bidaranalli, Margonahalli, Dabbeghatta, Kalenahalli, Borapura, Manikanahalli, Voddarahalli, Kuppahalli, Biliganahalli, Bandihole, Gattiganahalli, Laxmipura, Kurnenahalli, Hariharapura, Dammalapura, Bomenahalli, Chikkamandagere, Bevinahalli, Gaddehosur, Honnenahalli, Mallenahalli, Moodanahalli, Natanahalli, Chandagonahalli, Karthalu, Hosagadde, V.Hosur, Laxmipura, Dudukanahalli, Akkihebbal, Alambadi, Basavanahalli, Guduganahalli, Somanathapura, Mambahalli, Kattekyathanahalli, Belathur, Ambigarahalli, Mellahalli, Doddayachenahalli, Maduvinakodi, Maddikyachenahalli, Kudalakuppe, Kallahalli, Poovanahalli.

Canal: Nearest Villages- Gondihalli, Madapuranala, Madap ura, Halemadapura, Ganadahalli, Chinnenahalli, Kotahalli, Dananahalli, Dabbeghatta, Kalenahalli, Borapura, Manika nahalli, Voddarahalli, Kuppahalli, Biliganahalli, Bandiho le, Gattiganahalli, Laxmipura, Bellibettadakaval, Kurnena halli, Thernenahalli, Hariharapura, Dammalapura, Bomenah alli, Mandagere, Gaddehosur, Honnenahalli, Mallenahalli, Moodanahalli, Nandipura, Natanahalli, Chandagonahalli, Karthalu, Beeravalli, Saxibeedu, Hosagadde, Dudukanahal li, Dadadahalli, Akkihebbal, Machaholalu, Singanahalli, Mudlapura, Jainahalli, Alambadi Kaval, Mellahalli, Doddayachenahalli, Maduvinakodi, Maddikyachenahalli, Kudalakuppe.

Annual Rainfall: Normal Rianfall 735.2 mm.

Ground Water: Availability of the Ground Water in the Basin is 11920.20 H.A.M. and the utilization is 9089. 43 H.A.M. It belongs to Over Expoited category. Depth to water level 2 to 20 meter below the ground. Most of the wells go down in summer months, according to the Ground Water Estimation Committee.

Soils: Red Sandy Loams to Red Clay Loam.

Natural Division : It falls in Cauvery-Hemavati Valley of the Southen Karnataka Plateau.

Administration:

Division: Mysore. Parliamentary Constituency: 20 Mandaya. District: Mandaya. Taluka: Krishnarajpet. Assembly Constituency: 192 Krishnarajpet. Gram Panchayat: 34.

Fairs and Festivals: Kikkeramma Festival: The festival is observed at Kikkeri near Madya in honour of goddess Kikke ramma. Kikkeri in Krishnarajpet taluk 10 kilometres from Krishnarajpet town and 15 kilometres from Shravana Belgo la. According to a legend, the village was so named after a tribesman called 'Keeka'. The Brahmeshvara temple at this place is a fine specimen of Hoysala style of architecture. It was constructed in A.D. 1171, during the rule of the Hoysala king Narasimha I, by a lady named Bammare-Nayakiti. This ornate structure has some special features. The sides of the temple are convex viewed from outside and bulge out so that the interior dimensions are widened beyond the base. The deep indenat ation of the horizontal courses in the basement and the knife-edge to which the cornices have been brought are also interesting points. It is a single-celled temple and has an impressive and lofty stone tower.

Villages: 316 **Inhabited:** 297 **Uninhabited:** 19

Ranking	District	State	National
Area	2	100	550
Population	4	63	411
Sex Ratio	2	16	745
Child Sex Ratio	1	30	1591
Literacy Rate	3	88	2797
Density	4	99	4062
Work Participation Rate	6	42	2315

Gram Panchayats:

Anegola, Madapura, Ikanahalli, Laxmipura, Kikkeri, Dabbeghatta, Mandagere, Chowdenahalli, Bharathipura, Aghalaya, Santhebachnahalli, Ranganathapura Cross, Sarangi, Hirikalale, Makavalli, Beeravalli, Bandihole, Agrahara Bachahalli, Sindaghatta, Haralahalli, Seelanere, Hariharapura, Akkihebbal, Maduvinakodi, Ballekere, Thendekere, Vittalapura, Alambadi Kaval, Somanahalli, Ganjigere, Bukkanakere, Ichanahalli, Ballenahalli, Murukanahalli.

Amenities:

Education: Primary School in 261 villages, Middle school in 154 villages, Matriculation or Secondary School in 23 villages, namely Madapura, Kikkeri, Santhebachahalli, Aghalaya, Billenahalli, Sarangi, Ballekere, Sindaghatta, Seelanere, Chattamgere, Makavalli, Bandihole, Mandagere, Beeravalli, Saxibeedu, Akkihebbal, Somanahalli, Maduvinakodi, Ballekere, Vittalapura, Bukanakere, Ganjigere, Ballenahalli.

Higher Secondary or Pre University Courses or Intermediate or Junior College in 5 villages of the CD Block,, namely Kikkeri, Sindaghatta, Seelanere, Hariharapura, Akkihebbal.

College in 0 village, Adult Literacy Center in 0 village.

Medical: Hospital in 15 villages, Dispensary in 14 villages, Health Center in 19 villages, Sub Center in 39 villages, Maternity and Child Welfare Center in 6 villages, Community health workers in 13 villages.
The Villages having Hospital or Dispensary or Health Center are Madapura, Anegola, Margonahalli, Govindanahalli, Kikkeri, Sarangi, Kaigonahalli, Chikkanayakanahalli, Navilumaranahalli, Seelanere, Heggadahalli, Makavalli, Shravanahalli, Bevinahalli, Mandagere, Alenahalli, Ballenahalli, Somanahalli, Maduvinakodi, Ballekere, Haliyur, Vittalapura, Bukanakere, Ballenahalli.
Drinking Water: Tap water in 152 villages, Tank water in 159 villages, Well water in 263 villages, Tubewell in 188 villages and more than one source in 273 villages.
Bank: Banking facility in 21 villages, namely, Anegola, Sasalu, Kikkeri, Santhebachahalli, Aghalaya Kodagahalli, Bharathipura, Sindaghatta, Seelanere Thendekere, Mallenahalli, Biliganahalli, Bandihole Hosaholalu, Mandagere, Akkihebbal, Somanahalli Mellahalli, Vittalapura, Bukanakere, Ganjigere.
Credit Society in 33 villages Agricultural Credit Society in 27 Non-Agricultural Credit Society in 6 villages.
Others: Power supply in 276 villages, Cinema hall in 4 villages, sport club in 0 village, Stadium or Auditorium or Community Hall in 0 village, Post Office in 55 villages.
There are 169 villages having bus facilities.
Villages with most of facilities: Anegola, Kikkeri Santhebachahalli, Aghalaya, Sindaghatta, Seelanere Thendekere, Bandihole, Mandagere, Akkihebbal Somanahalli, Vittalapura, Bukanakere, Ganjigere.
Villages without amenities (Education):
Madapuranala, Echaluguddekaval, Basavanahalli, Kallanakere, Kikkeri Amanikere, Borapura, Hodakahalli, Jakkanahalli, Hadavanahalli, Aghalaya Kaval, Halagehosahalli, Machahalli, Mallenahalli, Ankanathapura, Kodihalli, Hathimaranahalli, Uygonahalli, Harinahalli, Kodihalli, Billaramanahalli, Dammalapura, Maniganahalli, Uddinaborekaval, Honnenahalli, Mallenahalli, Kyathanahalli, Ballenahalli, Buvanahalli, Aralakuppe..
Scheduled Castes: Out of the total population of 225665 persons, 27225 persons (12.06%) belong to Scheduled Castes.
The villages having less than 10% SC population are Madapuranala, Madapura, Halemadapura, Ganadahalli Gudehosahalli, Kadahemmige, Bolamaranahalli, Anegola Doddatharahalli, Ooginahalli, Echaluguddekaval Chinnenahalli, Dananahalli, Bidaranalli Govindanahalli, Uddinamallanahosur, Ikanahalli Sasalu, Devarahalli, Bhadranakoppalu, Ankanahalli Laxmipura, Mariyanahosur, Dabbeghatta Chujjalakyathanahalli, Kalenahalli, Dorenahalli Kikkeri, Boovanahalli, Sollepura, Kikkeri Amanikere Kodimaranahalli, Chowdenahalli, Ramanahalli Borapura, Kariganahalli, Hodakahalli, Settihalli Manganahosahalli, Kundur, Marenahalli, Ganganahalli Haleathiguppe, Chottanahalli, Ramanakoppalu Hadavanahalli, Chikkakyathnahalli, Amchahalli Aghalaya, Chikkasomanahalli, Aghalaya Kaval Hosahalli, Kodagahalli, Mavinakatte Koppalu Adihalli, Yeladahalli, Mallenahalli, Bikkasandra Laxmipura, Somenahalli, Ranganathapura, Dasagolapura Hethagonahalli, Shyarahalli, Ballekere, Jothanapura Molenahalli (B), Mallenahalli, Ankanathapura Kodihalli, Maruvanahalli, Chikkanayakanahalli Hathimaranahalli, Singapura, Hemmadahalli Karathanahalli, Shivapura, Honnenahalli Murukanahalli, Bommanaykanahalli, Chowda Ghatta Maradahalli, Ramanahalli, Rajaghatta, Anchanahalli Anchemuddanahalli, Voddarahalli, Kuppahalli Heggadahalli, Makavalli, Gangenahalli, Margonahalli Chilladahalli, Komanahalli, Pura, Chikkonahalli Mallenahalli, Biliganahalli, Sadugonahalli Chikkahosahalli, Agrahara Bachahalli Bommanayakanahalli, Kodihalli, Guddenahalli Bandaboyanahalli, Hemmanahalli, Hosaholalu Kurnenahalli, Dammalapura, Kommenahalli Maniganahalli, Mathighatta, Chikkamandagere Shravanahalli, Bevinahalli, Honnenahalli Mallenahalli, Alenahalli, Chowdasamudra Hangaramuddanahalli, Beekanahalli, Manchibeedu Nandipura, Ballenahalli, Natanahalli, Beeravalli Gubbahalli, Dudukanahalli, Voddaragudi, Dadadahalli Akkihebbal, Singanahalli, Mudlapura, Guduganahalli Somanahalli, Pura (S), Kattekyathanahalli, Belathur Sangapura, Mellahalli, Doddayachenahalli Maddikyachenahalli, Ballekere, Hosur (M) Agasarahalli, Modur, Buvanahalli, Natanahalli Vittalapura, Kudalakuppe, Kallahalli, Aralakuppe Bettadahosur, Ichanahalli, Bukanakere, Hosahalli Bookahalli, Mathikere, Athuppe, Doddagadiganahalli Machagonahalli, Ballenahalli, Murukanahalli Rajenahalli, Poovanahalli, Mavinakere.
The villages having more than 50% SC population are Mandalekanahalli, Gangenahalli, Lingapura Jakkanahalli, Halagehosahalli, Kundanahalli Bellibettadakaval, Billaramanahalli, Hariharapura Nargonahalli, Uddinaborekaval, Kyathanahalli Arenahalli, B. Hosakote.

Sex ratio of Scheduled Caste population is 500.

Scheduled Castes Literates and Illiterates by Sex:

	Persons	Males	Females
Literate	12,248	7,362	4,886
Illiterate	14,977	6,237	8,740
Literacy rate	51.8	62.7	41.0
Graduate	206	189	17

Scheduled Castes (Dominant):

Adi Karnataka, Madiga, Bhovi, Generic Castes etc. Korama

For their cultural identity please see Appendix-I

Villages without Scheduled Castes: There are 92 villages without any scheduled caste population.

Scheduled Tribes: Out of the total population of 225665 persons, 4910 persons (2.18%) belong to Scheduled Tribes. The villages having less than 10% ST population are Gondihalli, Madapuranala, Madapura, Halemadapura Ganadahalli, Gudehosahalli, Kadahemmige Bolamaranahalli, Anegola, Doddatharahalli Chikkatharahalli, Anchebeeranahalli Mandalekanahalli, Ooginahalli, Echaluguddekaval Chinnenahalli, Kotahalli, Dananahalli, Bidaranalli Margonahalli, Govindanahalli, Uddinamallanahosur Tholasi, Ikanahalli, Sasalu, Yeladahalli Devarahalli, Bhadranakoppalu, Ankanahalli Vaddarahalli, Basavanahalli, Laxmipura Mariyanahosur, Thenginaghatta, Dabbeghatta Chujjalakyathanahalli, Kalenahalli, Dorenahalli Kikkeri, Gangenahalli, Boovanahalli, Madahalli Kallanakere, Sollepura, Kikkeri Amanikere Kodimaranahalli, Chowdenahalli, Ramanahalli Beechanahalli, Borapura, Manikanahalli, Lingapura Hodakahalli, Chikkalale, Settihalli, Jakkanahalli Manganahosahalli, Kundur, Marenahalli, Ganganahalli Achamanahalli, Haleathiguppe, Halasinahalli Nagaragatta, Narayanapura, Chottanahalli Ramanakoppalu, Doddakyathnahalli, Chikkakyathnahalli Santhebachahalli, Hubbanahalli, Amchahalli Nayasinganahalli, Aghalaya, Doddasomanahalli Chikkasomanahalli, Aghalaya Kaval, Hosahalli Lokanahalli, Kodagahalli, Appanahalli, Malagur Singapura, Mavinakatte Koppalu, Halagehosahalli Adihalli, Doddaharanahalli, Yeladahalli Bharathipura, Annechakanahalli, Koratikere Mallenahalli, Goravi, Billenahalli, Harapanahalli Bikkasandra, Nayakanahalli, Laxmipura, Somenahalli Ranganathapura, Dasagolapura, Shyarahalli Machahalli, Sarangi, Kaigonahalli, Jaginakere Jothanapura, Chikkaharanahalli, Kotagahalli Dugganahalli, Boppanahalli, Molenahalli (B) Mallenahalli, Kyathanahalli, Ankanathapura Vasanthapura, Mylanahalli, Rayasamudra, Kodihalli Sindaghatta, Maruvanahalli, Chikkanayakanahalli Hathimaranahalli, Uygonahalli, Haralahalli Singapura, Hemmadahalli, Karathanahalli, Byrapura Shivapura, Byaladakere, Chattenahalli, Hiralahalli Oochanahalli, Honnenahalli, Murukanahalli Naduboganahalli, Hakkimanchnahalli Bommanaykanahalli, Chowda Ghatta, Sheerbillenahally Navilumaranahalli, Guduganahalli, Seelanere Maradahalli, Hadanur, Ramanahalli Paduvabagalu Manchana Halli, Rajaghatta K.G.Kodihalli, Chattamgere, Malkonahalli, Thendekere Anchanahalli, Thagadur, Anchemuddanahalli, Ballekere Hunusanahalli, Cheekanahalli, Bommalapura Voddarahalli, Heggadahalli, Makavalli, Hirikalale Gangenahalli, Kadumenasa, Margonahalli, Nagarur Valageremenasa, Chilladahalli, Harinahalli Theganahalli, Komanahalli, Pura, Chikkonahalli Kundanahalli, Mallenahalli, Biliganahalli, Bandihole Laxmipura, Bellibettadakaval, Sadugonahalli Chikkahosahalli, Agrahara Bachahalli Bommanayakanahalli, Kallahalli, Areboppanahalli Guddenahalli, Anuvinakatte, Bandaboyanahalli Hemmanahalli, Hosaholalu, Billaramanahalli Kathrighatta, Kurnenahalli, Thernenahalli Hariharapura, Dammalapura, Kommenahalli, Yadahalli Maniganahalli, Mathighatta, Chowdenahalli Nargonahalli, Kamanahalli, Uddinaborekaval Chikkamandagere, Shravanahalli, Bevinahalli Mandagere, Gaddehosur, Honnenahalli, Mallenahalli Moodanahalli, Alenahalli, Kyathanahalli Chowdasamudra, Hangaramuddanahalli, Beekanahalli Arenahalli, Manchibeedu, Nandipura, Ballenahalli Natanahalli, Beeravalli, Saxibeedu, Gubbahalli Dudukanahalli, Voddaragudi, Machaholalu, Mudlapura Jainahalli, Alambadi, Ipanahalli, Guduganahalli Somanathapura, Mambahalli, Somanahalli Kattekyathanahalli, Belathur, Sangapura Ambigarahalli, Mellahalli, Doddayachenahalli Maduvinakodi, Maddikyachenahalli, Ballekere, Haliyur Hosur (M), Jakkanahalli, Bannanakere, Modur Buvanahalli, Natanahalli, Vittalapura, Kudalakuppe Kallahalli, Yagachaguppe, Aralakuppe, B.Bachahalli Bettadahosur, Bannenahalli, Ichanahalli, Bukanakere Hosahalli, Chikkadiganahalli , Varahanathakallahalli Bookahalli, Ganjigere, Mudigere, Mathikere, Athuppe Chokanahalli, Doddagadiganahalli, Machagonahalli Ballenahalli, Murukanahalli, Rajenahalli, Mavinakere Kabbalagerepura, B. Hosakote, Heraganahalli.

The villages having more than 50% ST population are None.

Sex ratio of Scheduled tribe population is 487.

Scheduled Tribes Literates and Illiterates by Sex:

	Persons	Males	Females
Literate	2,527	1,567	960
Illiterate	2,383	954	1,429
Literacy rate	59.0	71.4	46.0
Graduate	90	74	16

Scheduled Tribes (Dominant):

Naikda etc., Soligaru, Generic Tribes etc., Meda Hakkipikki

For their cultural identity please see Appendix-II

Villages without Scheduled Tribes: There are 244 villages without any scheduled tribe population.

Literates and Illiterates by Sex (Total Population):

	Persons	Males	Females
Literate	118,891	70,340	48,551
Illiterate	106,774	41,606	65,168
Literacy rate	60	72	48
Graduate	3,236	2,738	498

Agriculture: ***Distribution of villages according to land use:*** Out of 316 villages, Total area (in hectare) is 89872, out of that 63.22 percent is cultivable and 41 percent of the cultivable area is irrigated.

Sources of Irrigation (Hectares): Government Canal 13917.47, Private Canal 0, Well without Electricity 351.64, Well with Electricity 1345.77, Tubewell without Electricity 212.54, Tubewell with Electricity 2838.24, Tank 2274.43, River 46.18, Lake 6.82, Waterfall 125.53, Others 2032.9.

Villages with population of 5000 to 9999: None

Villages with population of 10000 and above: None

Distribution of Workers:

	Persons	Males	Females	WPR
Cultivators	76,269	51,998	24,271	67.41
Agricultural Labour	23,115	8,725	14,390	20.43
Household Industry	2,215	1,142	1,073	1.96
Other Workers	11,535	7,926	3,609	10.2
Main Workers	91,508	64,595	26,913	80.88
Marginal Workers	21,626	5,196	16,430	19.12
Total Workers	113,134	69,791	43,343	

Religion: Major Religious Communities:

	Persons	Males	Females	Sex Ratio
Hindu (97.77%)	220,632	109,406	111,226	1,017
Muslim (1.85%)	4,178	2,113	2,065	977
Christian (0.02%)	49	27	22	815
Sikh (0.01%)	16	6	10	1,667
Buddhists (0%)	2	2	-	-
Jain (0.01%)	25	13	12	923

Agewise Data:

	Persons	Males	Females	Sex Ratio
All ages	225,665	111,946	113,719	1016
0-14	65,765	33,060	32,705	989
15-44	108,776	53,677	55,099	1026
45-79	48,141	23,866	24,275	1017
80+	2,799	1,233	1,566	1270
Age not stated	184	110	74	673

Languages (Dominant):

Kannada, Urdu, Telugu, Tamil, Marathi

Disabled Population:

	Persons	Males	Females	%
Total Disabled	5,968	3,505	2,463	
In Seeing	3,979	2,288	1,691	66.67
In Speech	532	302	230	8.91
In Hearing	179	101	78	3
In Movement	958	637	321	16.05
Mentally	320	177	143	5.36

KUDLIGI

Kudligi C.D. Block lies in the southern part of Bellary district. It is a part of Kudligi taluka. The Block is located at a distance of 70 kms. from district headqu arters (Bellary). There are 91 villages in the block with the total population of 227,368 persons. Area of the C.D. Block is 1528.92 sq. kms. It is bounded by Hagaribommanahalli and Sandur taluks on north, district Davanagere on south, district Chitradurga on east, taluk Hagaribommanahalli and district Davanagere on west.

Communications:

Roadways : N.H-13: Nearest Villages- Sivapura, Bande Basapura Tanda, Ammanakeri, Kuppinakeri, Moraba, Kak kuppi, Adavi Sooravvanahalli, Kadekolla, M.B.Iyyanahalli, Kyasanakere, Amalapura, Banavikal, Harakabhavi, Bellika tti, S. Imadapura, Hosahalli, Hulikere, Alur. S.H-2: Direction- Kudligi to Melkalmuru, Nearest Villages- Ammanakeri, Kakkuppi, Harudi, Chandrasekarapura, Rama durg, Srikantapura Thanda, Gudekota, Kasapura, Sidegallu. S.H-40: Direction- Harapanahalli to Kudligi, Nearest Villages- Motikal Tanda, Kandagal, Gajapura, Chapparada halli, K.Iyyanahalli, Haralu, Kuppinakeri.

Railway Station: Villages- Bevoor, Dhoopadahalli.

River: Marur Vanka Nadi- Nearest Villages- Chapparadah alli, K.Iyyanahalli, Haralu, Kannanayakanakatte, Joladaku dligi , Nagarakatti, Thoolahalli, Ujjini. Pedda Vanka Nadi- Nearest Villages- Chikkajogi Tanda, Gundumunugu, Hurlihalu, Meenakeri, Kumathi, Bellikatti. Chinna Hagiri Nadi- Nearest Villages- Uradihalli, Chitrathagundu, Kombihalli, Meenakeri, Kumathi, Hudem, Thippehalli, Kallahalli.

Canal: Nearest Villages- Gandabommanahalli, Uradihalli, Yekkigundi, Chitrathagundu.

Reserved Forest: (Appainahalli R.F.): Villages- Mahad evarapura, Appainahalli. (Godekota R.F.): Nearest Village s- Srikantapura Thanda, Mahadevarapura, Appainahalli, Gudekota. (Bannikal R.F.): Villages- Dhoopadahalli, K.Basapura Tanda, Thimmalapura, Kandagal, Boppalapura. (Chirilri R.F.): Nearest villages- Thimmalapura, Kanda gal, Gajapura, Chiribi, Rampura, Nagalapura. (Chornur R.F.): Nearest Villages- Ramadurg, Kudureduvu. (Sidegallu R.F.): Nearest Villages- Chandrasekarapura, Srikantapura Thanda, Gudekota, Kasapura, Sidegallu, Narasimhagiri, Belligatta, Yerralinganahalli, Gandabommanahalli, Uradi halli. (Halasgara R.F.): Nearest Villages- Mahadevarapura, Halasagara, Gudekota, Kasapura. (Hosahalli R.F.): Nerae st Villages- S. Imadapura, Hosahalli, Lokikere, Jummobana halli, Poojarahalli. (Hulikunta R.F.): Nearest Villages- Jermali, Narasimhagiri, Belligatta, Hulikunta, Kadekolla. (Jermali R.F.): Neraest Villages- Kadekolla, Amalapura, Banavikal, Jermali. (Jummobanahalhi R.F.): Nearest Vill.- Gundumunugu, Hurlihalu, Kumathi, Jummobanahalli, Hudem, Poojarahalli. (Kakoppi R.F.): Nearest Villages- Gundinahole, Ammanakeri, Nagalapura, Kakkuppi, Adavi Sooravvanahalli, Harudi, Ramadurg. (Nimbalage R.F.): Neraest Villages- Nimbalageri, Harakabhavi, Bellikatti. (Sumadakal R.F.): Neraest Villages- Hirevaddarahalli, Kalapura, Ujjini, Sunkadakal, Palayyanakota, C.Imadapura, Chowdapura, Solladahalli, Nagenahalli, Mangapura, Nimbalageri.

Annual Rainfall: Normal Rianfall 597.1 mm.

Ground Water: Availability of the Ground Water in the Basin is (Information not avablable) H.A.M. and the utilization is (Information not avablable) H.A.M. It belongs to (Information not avablable) category. Depth to water level 5 to 20 meter below the ground. Most of the wells go down in summer months, according to the Ground Water Estimation Committee.

Soils: Black and Red Sandy Soils.

Natural Division : It falls partly in Kudligi Scrubby Uplands and Chikka Hagari Valley of the Central Karnataka Plateau.

Administration:

Division: Gulbarga. Parliamentary Constituency: 9 Bellary (ST). District: Bellary. Taluka: Hudligi. Assembly Constituency: 95 Sandur (ST), 96 Kudligi (ST). Gram Panchayat: 33.

Regional Area Development Boards: The Hyderabad - Karnataka Area Development Board.

Villages: 91 **Inhabited:** 89 **Uninhabited:** 2

Ranking	District	State	National
Area	2	31	132
Population	2	61	387
Sex Ratio	6	133	3148
Child Sex Ratio	6	109	3344
Literacy Rate	3	110	3280
Density	3	36	5577
Work Participation Rate	6	130	1162

Gram Panchayats:
Sivapura, Hireheggadahal, Kandagal, Badaladuku, Moraba, Jermali, Belligatta, Ramadurg, Gudekote, Appenahalli, Gandabommanahalli, Chiratagundu, Hudem, Poojarahalli, Alur, Jummobanahalli, Hurlihalu, Gundumunugu, Makanaduku, Hosahalli, Hirekumbalagunta, Harakabhavi, Banavikal, Chowdapura, Sooladahalli, Nimbalageri, Ujjini, Thoolahalli, Kalapura, Rampura, K.Iyyanahalli, Hyalya, Dhoopadahalli.

Amenities:

Education: Primary School in 66 villages, Middle school in 66 villages, Matriculation or Secondary School in 22 villages, namely Dhoopadahalli, Rampura, K.Iyyanahalli, Nagarakatti, Thoolahalli, Ujjini, Hireheggadahal, Chandrasekarapura, Mahadevarapura, Gudekota, Narasimhagiri, M.B.Iyyanahalli, Chikkajogi Tanda, Hurlihalu, Chitrathagundu, Banavikal, Solladahalli, Nimbalageri, Harakabhavi, Hosahalli, Alur, Hudem.
Higher Secondary or Pre University Courses or Intermediate or Junior College in 6 villages of the CD Block,, namely Ujjini, Gudekota, Chikkajogi Tanda, Hurlihalu, Hosahalli, Alur.
College in 1 village, Adult Literacy Center in 16 villages., College is in village, namely Alur.

Medical: Hospital in 1 village, Dispensary in 10 villages, Health Center in 9 villages, Sub Center in 47 villages, Maternity and Child Welfare Center in 2 villages, Community health workers in 10 villages.
The Villages having Hospital or Dispensary or Health Center are Dhoopadahalli, Haralu, Nagarakatti, Ujjini, Sivapura, Gudekota, Chikkajogi Tanda, Chowdapura, Harakabhavi, Hudem.

Drinking Water: Tap water in 66 villages, Tank water in 36 villages, Well water in 30 villages, Tubewell in 40 villages and more than one source in 87 villages.

Bank: Banking facility in 12 villages, namely, Dhoopadahalli, Thoolahalli, Ujjini, Ramadurg Gudekota, Chikkajogi Tanda, Chitrathagundu Banavikal, Solladahalli, Nimbalageri, Hosahalli Hudem.
Credit Society in 21 villages Agricultural Credit Society in 19 Non-Agricultural Credit Society in 6 villages.

Others: Power supply in 89 villages, Cinema hall in 6 villages, sport club in 89 villages, Stadium or Auditorium or Communit Hall in 89 villages, Post Office in 61 villages.

There are 86 villages having bus facilities.

Villages with most of facilities: Dhoopadahalli Thoolahalli, Ujjini, Ramadurg, Gudekota Chikkajogi Tanda, Chitrathagundu, Banavikal Solladahalli, Nimbalageri, Hosahalli, Hudem.

Villages without amenities (Education): Kodihalli, Sirinayakanahalli, Boppalapura, Gundinahole, Kuppinakeri, Nagalapura, Harudi, Srikantapura Thanda, Kasapura, Kombihalli, Meenakeri, Palayyanakota, Kyasanakere, Nagenahalli, S. Imadapura, Ranganathanahalli, Byluthumbaraguddi, Poojarahalli, Thippehalli, Kallahalli..

Scheduled Castes: Out of the total population of 227633 persons, 46182 persons (20.29%) belong to Scheduled Castes. The villages having less than 10% SC population are Chiribi, Kodihalli, Sirinayakanahalli Chapparadahalli, Sivapura, Nagalapura, Moraba Kakkuppi, Adavi Sooravvanahalli, Sidegallu Chitrathagundu, Palayyanakota, Nagenahalli Nimbalageri, Hulikere.

The villages having more than 50% SC population are Motikal Tanda, K.Basapura Tanda, Thimmalapura Bande Basapura Tanda, Gundinahole Srikantapura Thanda, Kasapura, Chikkajogi Tanda.

Sex ratio of Scheduled Caste population is 493.

Scheduled Castes Literates and Illiterates by Sex:

	Persons	Males	Females
Literate	18,386	11,993	6,393
Illiterate	27,796	11,435	16,361
Literacy rate	48.9	63.1	34.5
Graduate	335	314	21

Scheduled Castes (Dominant):

Adi Karnataka, Banjara etc., Bhovi, Madiga, Koracha

For their cultural identity please see Appendix-I

Villages without Scheduled Castes: There are 5 villages without any scheduled caste population.

Scheduled Tribes: Out of the total population of 227633 persons, 65005 persons (28.56%) belong to Scheduled Tribes. The villages having less than 10% ST population are Motikal Tanda, Bevoor, Dhoopadahalli K.Basapura Tanda, Thimmalapura, Kandagal, Kodihalli Sirinayakanahalli, K.Iyyanahalli, Haralu Kannanayakanakatte, Joladakudligi , Thoolahalli Hireheggadahal, Bande Basapura Tanda, Gundinahole Belligatta, Chikkajogi Tanda, Mangapura, Bellikatti S. Imadapura, Ranganathanahalli, Byluthumbaraguddi Kenchamallanahalli, Kallahalli.

The villages having more than 50% ST population are Nagalapura, Adavi Sooravvanahalli, Narasimhagiri Hulikunta, Yerralinganahalli, Gandabommanahalli Uradihalli, Chitrathagundu, Meenakeri, Kumathi Palayyanakota, Solladahalli, Nagenahalli Jummobanahalli, Thippehalli.

Sex ratio of Scheduled tribe population is 492.

Scheduled Tribes Literates and Illiterates by Sex:

	Persons	Males	Females
Literate	24,668	16,297	8,371
Illiterate	40,337	16,758	23,579
Literacy rate	46.5	60.6	32.0
Graduate	285	268	17

Scheduled Tribes (Dominant):

Naikda etc., Generic Tribes etc., Meda, Soligaru

For their cultural identity please see Appendix-II

Villages without Scheduled Tribes: There are 8 villages without any scheduled tribe population.

Literates and Illiterates by Sex (Total Population):

	Persons	Males	Females
Literate	108,647	68,368	40,279
Illiterate	118,986	47,947	71,039
Literacy rate	57	71	43
Graduate	2,748	2,409	339

Agriculture: ***Distribution of villages according to land use:*** Out of 91 villages, Total area (in hectare) is 152892, out of that 59.14 percent is cultivable and 9.91 percent of the cultivable area is irrigated.

Sources of Irrigation (Hectares): Government Canal 233.78, Private Canal 0, Well without Electricity 0, Well with Electricity 1314.38, Tubewell without Electricity 242.82, Tubewell with Electricity 4857.81, Tank 2316.08, River 0, Lake 0, Waterfall 0, Others 0.

Villages with population of 5000 to 9999: Ujjini, Gudekota, Solladahalli, Hosahalli, Hudem.

Villages with population of 10000 and above: None

Distribution of Workers:

	Persons	Males	Females	WPR
Cultivators	56,107	37,070	19,037	47.71
Agricultural Labour	45,185	14,476	30,709	38.42
Household Industry	3,651	2,006	1,645	3.1
Other Workers	12,661	8,888	3,773	10.77
Main Workers	99,715	58,465	41,250	84.79
Marginal Workers	17,889	3,975	13,914	15.21
Total Workers	117,604	62,440	55,164	

Religion: Major Religious Communities:

	Persons	Males	Females	Sex Ratio
Hindu (95.87%)	218,239	111,514	106,725	957
Muslim (3.39%)	7,723	3,942	3,781	959
Christian (0.02%)	45	24	21	875
Sikh (0%)	3	2	1	500
Buddhists (0.06%)	128	66	62	939
Jain (0%)	11	4	7	1,750

Agewise Data:

	Persons	Males	Females	Sex Ratio
All ages	227,633	116,315	111,318	957
0-14	91,065	46,847	44,218	944
15-44	96,785	49,841	46,944	942
45-79	37,873	18,796	19,077	1015
80+	1,771	757	1,014	1339
Age not stated	139	74	65	878

Languages (Dominant):

Kannada, Telugu, Hindi, Urdu, Coorgi/Kodagu

Disabled Population:

	Persons	Males	Females	%
Total Disabled	4,482	2,660	1,822	
In Seeing	1,966	1,097	869	43.86
In Speech	460	267	193	10.26
In Hearing	256	138	118	5.71
In Movement	1,492	982	510	33.29
Mentally	308	176	132	6.87

KUMTA

Kumta C.D. Block lies in the south-eastern part of Uttara Kannada district. It is a part of Kumta taluka. The Block is located at a distance of 72 kms. from district headquarters (Karwar). There are 119 villages in the block with the total population of 111,274 persons. Area of the C.D. Block is 564.45 sq. kms. It is bounded by taluk Ankola on north, taluk Honavar on south, taluks Sirsi and Siddapur on east, and Lakshadweep sea on west.

Communications:

Roadways : N.H-17: Direction- Karwar to Mangalore, Villages- Madangeri, Yennemadi, Hiregutti, Morba, Kolim anjaguni, Betkuli, Kurigadde, Bargi, Chatrakurve, Kodkani, Paduvani, Yattinabail, Mirjan, Divgi, Manaki, Antravalli, Handigona, Talgod, Kadekodi, Math, Horbhag. S.H-48: Direction- Kumta to Siddapur, Nearest Villages- Valgalli, Kalkeri, Harodi, Kujalli, Hegle, Muroor, Hosad, Kandava lli, Bangane, Mudgi, Basolli, Santeguli, Hegde-Hosalli, Bastikeri, Divalli, Santagal, Soppinahosalli, Medini. S.H-69: Direction- Kumta to Sirsi, Nearest Villages- Divgi, Antravalli, Alkod, Bellangi, Kodambale, Harita.

River: Tadri Nadi- Nearest Villages- Gokarn, Naranapur, Nagarbail, Toregazani, Torke Hittalmakki, Madangeri, Yennemadi, Hiregutti, Midlagazani, Morba, Aghanashini, Kagal, Hubbangeri, Baad, Gudeangadi, Holanagadde, Manik atta, Halkar, Kelaginstala, Betkuli, Bargigazani, Savalku rve, Keppekurve, Masurkurve, Pattubele, Tannirhonda, Aigalkurve, Lukkeri, Hegde, Chatrakurve, Kodkani, Paduva ni, Mirjan, Divgi, Manaki, Antravalli, Toppalgutta, Uppin pattana, Shirgunji, Malwalli, Karkimakki, Kallabbe, Kanda valli, Kavalodi Kanakale, Holavalli, Kalve, Bangane, Mudgi, Basolli, Santeguli, Bastikeri, Divalli, Soppinaho salli, Morse, Medini. Benni Halla Nadi- Nearest Villages- Bangane, Morse.

Reserved Forest: Nearest Villages- Sandolli-Muttolli, Yana, Alvalli, Muroor, Kallabbe, Kandavalli, Kavalodi, Kanakale, Holavalli, Kalve, Chimmolli, Bangane, Mudgi, Basolli, Santeguli, Hegde-Hosalli, Bastikeri, Divalli, Santagal, Haravalli, Abbolli, Hindbail, Honagere, Ullur math, Algar, Mudnalli, Soppinahosalli, Medini. (S. Hos..'i R.F.): Nearest Villages- Mugvekanvadi, Nagur, Kadkod, Yelavalli, Nilkod, Antravalli, Alkod, Santur, Bhandival, Uppinpattana, Shirgunji, Hebbali, Malwalli, Kujalli, Hegle.

Annual Rainfall: Normal Rianfall 3466.3 mm.

Ground Water: Availability of the Ground Water in the Basin is 4155 H.A.M. and the utilization is 1453 H.A. M. It belongs to Safe category. Depth to water level 5 to 20 meter below the ground. Most of the wells go down in summer months, according to the Ground Water Estimation Committee.

Soils: Coastal Alluvial Soil.

Natural Division : It falls partly in Karwar-Honawar Coast and Western Ghats of the Karnataka Coast (Western Coastal Region).

Coastal Villages: (Lakshadeep Sea)- Nadumaskeri, Harumask eri, Bhavikodla, Gokarn, Kagal, Hubbangeri, Baad, Gudeang adi, Holanagadde, Handigona, Talgod, Kadekodi, Math, Devagiri, Horbhag.

Administration:

Division: Belgaum. Parliamentary Constituency: 12 Uttara Kannada. District: Uttara Kannada. Taluka: Kumta. Assemb ly Constituency: 79 Bhatkal. Gram Panchayat: 20.

Regional Area Development Boards: The Maland Aera Development Board.

Fairs: Bhairveshwara Jatra: It is held at Yan in Uttara Kannada area during Shivaratri (February-March). Yan is about 24 kms. from Kumta and 45 kms. from Sirsi. One has to walk a distance of 9 kms. through the irregul ar forest route which is open only during summer. This leads to a steep valley and then crossing the Vaddi Pass the spot can be reached. The place can also be reached from Sirsi, via Devimane ghat and Harita and also from Hegdekatta one can reach by walking 9 kms. crossing the steep ghats.

Dharanatha Jatra: It is held at Dhareshwar near Uttara Karnada for one day in the month of January. Dhareshwar, an ancient place 5 kms. from Kumta is one of the pancha kshetras associated with Gokarn. The place name has a traditional interpretation which says that Ravana while dislodging the box of the atmalinga at Gokarn threw away the dora or string packing the box and the place where the dora fell came to be known as Doreshwara. The Dhareshwara temple is a huge fine later Chalukyan temple with garbhagriha, ardhamantapa, two navarangas and one mukhamantapa.

Mahabaleshwara Devara Jatra: It is held at Gokarn for one day in the month of March every year. Gokarn a Hobli centre 38 kms. from Kumta, is one of the ancient holy places situated on the coast. The name of the place Gokarn literally means a 'Cow's Ear' as the the landscape here is formed in that shape by two rivers the Aghana shini and the Gangavali on either sides of the town and the Arabian sea at the west.

Pir Syed Ahmad-Shah Qadri Urs: An urs in honour of Peer Syed Ahmad-Shah Qadri is held at Mirjan near Uttara Kannada. Mirjan placed about 10 kms. from Kumta.

Pir Hazarat Kaka Rafiq Ali-Ullah Urs: An urs in honour of Pir Hazrat Kaka Rafiq Ali-Ullah is held at Mirjan near Uttara Kannada. Mirjan is 10 kms. from Kumta.

Sri Shantika Parameshwari Devi Festival: There are a number of special festivals celebrated in honour of Sri Shantika Parameshwari Devi (Sri Bhoomi Devate) at Kumta, gadi habba (boundary to offer charu (boiled rice mixed with kumkum) to ward off evils is observed on any Tuesday other than third Tuesday in Ashadha month of Uttarayana. Sapta prahara bhajana seva is a seva of devotees irrespective of caste and creed, a non-stop bhajan for 21 hours on Bhadrapad shoddha chaturdashi.

Venkataramana Devara Jatra: Venkataramana Devara jatra is held at Kumta near Uttara Kannada for one day in the month of February every year. Kumta 80 kms. from Karwar is a place of considerable antiquity. It is belie ved that the place name is derived from the local deity Kumbhateswara.

Villages: 118 **Inhabited:** 111 **Uninhabited:** 7

Ranking	District	State	National
Area	10	158	1288
Population	2	153	3122
Sex Ratio	5	86	2318
Child Sex Ratio	6	79	2873
Literacy Rate	3	11	450
Density	9	171	4757
Work Participation Rate	2	79	4399

Gram Panchayats:

Nadumaskeri, Hanehalli, Gokarn, Torke, Hiregutti Bargi, Kagal, Baad, Kodkani, Mirjan, Alkod, Divgi, Hegde, Holanagadde, Kalbhag , Devagiri, Valgalli, Kujalli, Mur0OR, Santeguli.

Amenities:

Education: Primary School in 93 villages, Middle school in 55 villages, Matriculation or Secondary School in 16 villages, namely Nadumaskeri, Bankikodla, Gokarn, Hiregutti, Kagal, Chitragi, Bargi, Lukkeri, Kodkani, Divgi, Devagiri, Holegadde, Urkeri, Alvalli, Muroor, Santeguli.

Higher Secondary or Pre University Courses or Intermediate or Junior College in 2 villages of the CD Block,, namely Gokarn, Baad.

College in 1 village, Adult Literacy Center in 0 village., College is in village, namely Gokarn.

Medical: Hospital in 0 village, Dispensary in 1 village, Health Center in 8 villages, Sub Center in 9 villages, Maternity and Child Welfare Center in 0 village, Community health workers in 0 village.

The Villages having Hospital or Dispensary or Health Center are Bhavikodla, Bankikodla, Gokarn, Kavalodi.

Drinking Water: Tap water in 32 villages, Tank water in 21 villages, Well water in 108 villages, Tubewell in 9 villages and more than one source in 94 villages.

Bank: Banking facility in 15 villages, namely, Bankikodla, Gokarn, Madangeri, Hiregutti, Kagal Baad, Gudeangadi, Hegde, Kodkani, Mirjan, Alkod Muroor, Karkimakki, Santeguli, Medini.

Credit Society in 30 villages Agricultural Credit Society in 20 Non-Agricultural Credit Society in 15 villages.

Others: Power supply in 110 villages, Cinema hall in 1 village, sport club in 0 village, Stadium or Auditorium or Community Hall in 0 village, Post Office in 45 villages.

There are 76 villages having bus facilities.

Villages with most of facilities: Bankikodla Gokarn, Hiregutti, Kagal, Gudeangadi, Kodkani Mirjan, Alkod, Muroor, Santeguli.

Villages without amenities (Education): Naranapur, Manikatta, Pattubele, Tannirhonda, Toppalgutta, Yedatare, Harita, Handigona, Kundguni, Math, Madki Bail, Chimmolli, Mudgi, Hegde-Hosalli, Haravalli, Abbolli, Hindbail, Algar..

Scheduled Castes: Out of the total population of 111327 persons, 6745 persons (6.06%) belong to Scheduled Castes. The villages having less than 10% SC population are Nadumaskeri, Harumaskeri, Bhavikodla, Bankikodla Hoskeri, Kadime, Gonehalli, Bidrageri, Gokarn Naranapur, Toregazani, Torke, Hittalmakki, Madangeri Kolimanjaguni, Aghanashini, Kagal, Hubbangeri Gudeangadi, Holanagadde, Manikatta, Chitragi Betkuli, Kurigadde, Bargi, Bargigazani, Pattubele Tannirhonda, Aigalkurve, Lukkeri, Chatrakurve Kodkani, Paduvani, Mugvekanvadi, Nagur, Kadkod Yattinabail, Mirjan, Divgi, Manaki , Antravalli Toppalgutta, Alkod, Yedatare, Bellangi Sandolli-Muttolli, Yana, Kodambale, Harita, Santur Bhandival, Shirgunji, Hebbail, Malwalli, Talgod Kundguni, Math, Devagiri, Horbhag, Kalkeri, Harodi

Kujalli, Hegle, Alvalli, Madki Bail, Muroor Karkimakki, Kallabbe, Hosad, Kandavalli, Kavalodi Holavalli, Kalve, Chimmolli, Bangane, Mudgi, Basolli Santeguli, Hegde-Hosalli, Bastikeri, Divalli Santagal, Haravalli, Abbolli, Hindbail, Honagere Ullurmath, Algar, Mudnalli, Soppinahosalli, Morse Medini.

The village having more than 50% SC population is None.

Sex ratio of Scheduled Caste population is 497.

Scheduled Castes Literates and Illiterates by Sex:

	Persons	Males	Females
Literate	3,587	2,074	1,513
Illiterate	3,158	1,318	1,840
Literacy rate	61.5	71.2	51.8
Graduate	44	39	5

Scheduled Castes (Dominant):

Mukri, Halleer, Ager, Halsar etc.

Generic Castes etc.

For their cultural identity please see Appendix-I

Villages without Scheduled Castes: There are 52 villages without any scheduled caste population.

Scheduled Tribes: Out of the total population of 111327 persons, 41 persons (0.04%) belong to Scheduled Tribes. The villages having less than 10% ST population are Nadumaskeri, Harumaskeri, Bhavikodla, Bankikodla Hanehalli, Hoskeri, Kadime, Gonehalli, Bidrageri Gokarn, Naranapur, Toregazani, Torke, Hittalmakki Madangeri, Yennemadi, Hiregutti , Morba Kolimanjaguni, Aghanashini, Kagal, Hubbangeri, Baad Gudeangadi, Holanagadde, Manikatta, Halkar, Chitragi Betkuli, Kurigadde, Bargi, Bargigazani, Pattubele Tannirhonda, Aigalkurve, Lukkeri, Hegde, Chatrakurve Kodkani, Paduvani, Mugvekanvadi, Nagur, Kadkod Yelavalli, Yattinabail, Mirjan, Nilkod, Divgi Manaki , Antravalli, Toppalgutta, Alkod, Yedatare Bellangi, Sandolli-Muttolli, Yana, Kodambale, Harita Anegundi, Santur, Bhandival, Uppinpattana, Shirgunji Hebbail, Malwalli, Handigona, Talgod, Kundguni Kadekodi, Math, Devagiri, Horbhag, Holegadde, Harnir Urkeri, Valgalli, Kalkeri, Harodi, Konalli, Kujalli Hegle, Alvalli, Madki Bail, Muroor, Karkimakki Kallabbe, Hosad, Kandavalli, Kavalodi, Kanakale Holavalli, Kalve, Chimmolli, Bangane, Mudgi, Basolli Santeguli, Hegde-Hosalli, Bastikeri, Divalli Santagal, Haravalli, Abbolli, Hindbail, Honagere Ullurmath, Algar, Mudnalli, Soppinahosalli, Morse Medini.

The villages having more than 50% ST population are None.

Sex ratio of Scheduled tribe population is 463.

Scheduled Tribes Literates and Illiterates by Sex:

	Persons	Males	Females
Literate	22	14	8
Illiterate	19	8	11
Literacy rate	66.7	77.8	53.3
Graduate	1	0	1

Scheduled Tribes (Dominant):

Naikda etc., Gond etc., Kadu Kuruba, Koraga Chenchu etc.

For their cultural identity please see Appendix-II

Villages without Scheduled Tribes: There are 113 villages without any scheduled tribe population.

Literates and Illiterates by Sex (Total Population):

	Persons	Males	Females
Literate	76,406	42,881	33,525
Illiterate	34,921	13,510	21,411
Literacy rate	78	86	69
Graduate	3,826	2,623	1,203

Agriculture: ***Distribution of villages according to land use:*** Out of 118 villages, Total area (in hectare) is 56245, out of that 18.32 percent is cultivable and 22.84 percent of the cultivable area is irrigated.

Sources of Irrigation (Hectares): Government Canal 38.12, Private Canal 12.64, Well without Electricity 330.43, Well with Electricity 1270.13, Tubewell without Electricity 0, Tubewell with Electricity 0, Tank 6.8, River 19.48, Lake 0, Waterfall 22.32, Others 607.69.

Villages with population of 5000 to 9999:

Hegde.

Villages with population of 10000 and above:

Gokarn.

Distribution of Workers:

	Persons	Males	Females	WPR
Cultivators	9,226	6,976	2,250	20.26
Agricultural Labour	8,550	4,346	4,204	18.78
Household Industry	748	542	206	1.64
Other Workers	27,012	20,201	6,811	59.32
Main Workers	34,004	27,307	6,697	74.67
Marginal Workers	11,532	4,758	6,774	25.33
Total Workers	45,536	32,065	13,471	

Religion: Major Religious Communities:

	Persons	Males	Females	Sex Ratio
Hindu (92.47%)	102,941	52,112	50,829	975
Muslim (6.02%)	6,704	3,404	3,300	969
Christian (1.41%)	1,567	816	751	920
Sikh (0%)	1	1	-	-
Buddhists (0%)	2	1	1	1,000
Jain (0.08%)	86	41	45	1,098

Agewise Data:

	Persons	Males	Females	Sex Ratio
All ages	111,327	56,391	54,936	974
0-14	31,536	16,152	15,384	952
15-44	54,153	27,573	26,580	964
45-79	24,517	12,122	12,395	1023
80+	1,081	524	557	1063
Age not stated	40	20	20	1000

Languages (Dominant):
Kannada, Konkani, Urdu, Hindi, Marathi

Disabled Population:

	Persons	Males	Females	%
Total Disabled	2,313	1,330	983	
In Seeing	1,158	635	523	50.06
In Speech	201	110	91	8.69
In Hearing	94	54	40	4.06
In Movement	621	393	228	26.85
Mentally	239	138	101	10.33

KUNDAPURA

Kundapura C.D. Block lies in the northern part of Udupi district. It is a part of Kundapura taluka. The Block is located at a distance of 38 kms. from district headquarters (Udupi). There are 99 villages in the block with the total population of 348,777 persons. Area of the C.D. Block is 1545.75 sq. kms. It is bounded by districts Uttara Kannada and Shimoga on north, taluks Udupi and Karkal on south, district Shimoga on east, and Lakshadweep sea on west.

Communications:

Roadways : N.H-17: Direction- Karwar to Udupi, Nearest Villages- Shiroor, Yedthare, Paduvari, Uppunda, Bijoor, Nandanavana, Kergal, Kirimanjeshwar, Kambadakone, Navunda, Badakere, Maravante, Hadavu, Trashi, Hosadu, Gujjadi, Tallur, Kattabelthoor, Hemmadi, Hangaloor, Koteshwar, Beejadi, Gopadi, Vakwadi, Thekkatte. S.H.-26: Direction- Idurkunhadi to Hosanagara, Nearest Villages- Kollur, Jadkal. S.H.-52: Direction- Panduvahi to Someshwara, Nearest Villages- Yedthare, Kalthodu, Thagarasi, Byndoor, Yeljith, Golihole, Jadkal, Kenchanoor, Gulvadi, Karkunje, Vandse, Idurkunhadi, Chittoor, Hosoor, Kavrady, Ampar, Shankaranarayana, Kulanje, Harady (28), Halady (76), Hengavalli, Belve, Albadi, Madammakki.

River: Varahi Nadi- Nearest Villages- Hosangadi, Machattu, Ulloor 74, Kulanje, Rattadi. Haladi Nadi- Nearest Villages- Uppinakudru, Tallur, Hattiangadi, Gulvadi, Kavrady, Halnad, Ampar, Shankaranarayana, Kulanje, Anagalli, Basrur, Balkur, Japthi, Molahalli, Hardally-Mandally, Harady (28), Halady (76). Kubja Nadi- Nearest Villages- Gulvadi, Kodladi, Kavrady, Ampar, Siddapur, Ajri, Kamalashile, Edmoge. Kollur Nadi- Nearest Villages- Navunda, Badakere, Maravanthe, Hadavu, Nada, Heroor, Kalthodu, Golihole, Jadkal, Trashi, Hosadu, Gujjadi, Gangolli, Hakladi, Senapur, Harkoor, Aloor, Idurkunhadi. Dasanakatte Nadi- Nearest Villages- Halady (76), Hengavalli, Belve, Albadi, Shedimane, Rattadi, Kulanje. Chakara Nadi- Nearest Villages- Mudoor, Kattabelthoor, Hemmadi, Hakladi, Kundabarandadi, Noojadi, Devalkunda, Karkunje, Vandse, Chittoor, Keradi, Bellal, Kodladi, Ajri, Kamalashile. Sita Nadi- Nearest Village- Belve.

Reserved Forest: (Ballimane R.F.): Villages- Shedimane, Amasebailu, Madammakki. (Haroor R.F.): Nearest Villages- Ulloor [11], Navunda, Nada, Heroor, Harkoor, Aloor. (Kadike R.F.): Nearest Villages- Byndoor, Shiroor. (Karani R.F.): Nearest Villages- Thagarasi, Byndoor, Yeljith, Kollur, Golihole. (Kuresgudde R.F.): Nearest Villages- Kalthodu, Golihole. (Koratikal Bare R.F.): Nearest Villages- Golihole, Jadkal. (Megani R.F.): Nearest Village- Kollur. (Madi Bare R.F.): Nearest Villages- Kollur, Jadkal. (Hulimishe Pare R.F.): Nearest Villages- Kalthodu, Jadkal. (Mettukallugudde R.F.): Nearest Villages- Siddapur, Hosangadi. (Tombattu R.F.): Nearest Villages- Noojadi, Idurkunhadi, Hosangadi, Machattu, Rattadi, Amasebailu. (Mudugal Pare R.F.): Nearest Villages- Vandse, Chittoor, Hosoor, Keradi, Bellal. (Naganakal Bare R.F.): Nearest Villages- Mudoor, Hallihole. (Surikodlu R.F.): Nearest Villages- Ulloor 74, Amasebailu.

Annual Rainfall: Normal Rianfall 4164.97 mm.

Ground Water: Availability of the Ground Water in the Basin is 12952 H.A.M. and the utilization is 4198 H.A.M. It belongs to Safe category. Depth to water level 2 to 10 meter below the ground. Most of the wells go down in summer months, according to the Ground Water Estimation Committee.

Soils: Sandy Soil.

Natural Division : It falls partly in Kundapur-Mangalore Coast, Bainduru-Bantval Plain & Western Ghats (Dakshina Kannada) of the Karnataka Coast (Western Coastal Region). Coastal Villages: (Lakshadeep Sea)- Shiroor, Paduvari, Uppunda, Nandanavana, Kergal, Kirimanjeshwar, Navunda, Maravanthe, Trashi, Hosadu, Gujjadi, Gangolli, Koteshwar, Beejadi, Gopadi, Vakwadi, Thekkatte.

Administration:

Division: Mysore. Parliamentary Constituency: 15 Udupi. District: Udupi. Taluka: Kundapura. Assembly Constituency: 118 Byndoor, 119 Kundapura. Gram Panchayat: 56. Regional Area Development Boards: The Maland Aera Development Board.

Fairs and Festivals: Brahmi-Durga Parameshwari Temple Car Festival: Kamalashile about 44 kms. to the north-east of taluk headquarters, is noted for its temple of Brahmi-Durga Parameshwari and also a small cave on a hill about one kilometer from the temple. The bed of the cave slopes downwards and stops at a well called Nagateertha. A car festival of the temple is held around the month of April.

Durgaparameshwari Jatra: It is held at Uppunda Dakshina Kannada area every year. Uppunda, about 28 kms. north-west of Coondapur, has an old temple dedicated to Durga-pa rameshwari. Its old name was Uppugunda. There are three inscriptions of some archaeological importance in this temple.

Shankaranarayanan Teertha Jatra: Shankaranarayana about 32 kms. to the east of Coondapur, is traditionally called also as Krodhashetra and is one of the seven places of pilgrimage in the region, referred to in the Skanda Purana, Shankaranarayana means Shiva and Vishnu. According to a legend, a sage named Krodha performed penance here and a spot with a cave here is shown as having been the site of his ashrama.

Shanteri Jogavva Matha Festival: A festival in connection with the Krishna Janmashtami is held around the month of July-August every year. Hemmadi, which was formely called as Hemapura, is about seven kilometres to the north of Coondapur on the highway. It has a matha established by Shanteri Jogavva. Ramavallabhadas, a saint, his disciple Krishnadas Gosavi came here about 300 years back and popularised some keerthanas on Lord Krishna. Later Ramavallabhadas went to Mallapura in North Kanara and accepted Avadi as one of his disciples, and was responsible for the establishment of the Avadi Matha.

Villages: 99 **Inhabited:** 99 **Uninhabited:** 0

Ranking	District	State	National
Area	1	28	125
Population	2	5	24
Sex Ratio	1	1	30
Child Sex Ratio	2	64	2581
Literacy Rate	3	18	682
Density	3	167	4366
Work Participation Rate	2	62	4172

Gram Panchayats:

Shiroor, Yedthare , Paduvari, Uppunda, Byndoor , Bijoor, Kergal, Kambadakone, Kirimanjeshwar, Kalthodu, Kollur, Golihole, Heroor, Navunda, Maravanthe, Nada, Aloor, Jadkal, Keradi, Chittoor, Vandse, Hakladi, Trashi, Gujjadi, Gangolli, Hemmadi, Tallur, Hattiangadi, Karkunje, Hallihole, Ajri, Ampar, Kavrady, Balkur, Basrur, Anagalli, Hangaloor, Koteshwar, Beejadi, Kumbashi , Koni, Thekkatte, Beloor, Kedoor, Kalavara, Hombady-Mandadi, Molahalli, Hardally-Mandally, Shankaranarayana, Siddapur, Hosangadi, Amasebailu, Halady (76), Hengavalli, Belve, Madammakki.

Amenities:

Education: Primary School in 99 villages, Middle school in 93 villages, Matriculation or Secondary School in 39 villages, namely Shiroor, Yedthare, Uppunda, Kergal, Kambadakone, Navunda, Maravanthe, Nada, Byndoor, Kollur, Jadkal, Mudoor, Gangolli, Uppinakudru, Tallur, Hemmadi, Hakladi, Gulvadi, Karkunje, Hosoor, Kodladi, Kavrady, Ampar, Shankaranarayana, Siddapur, Kamalashile, Hosangadi, Machattu, Koteshwar, Vakwadi, Thekkatte, Beloor, Kedoor, Kalavara, Basrur, Molahalli, Halady (76), Albadi, Amasebailu.

Higher Secondary or Pre University Courses or Intermediate or Junior College in 14 villages of the CD Block,, namely Yedthare, Uppunda, Kergal, Kambadakone, Navunda, Byndoor, Gangolli, Vandse, Shankaranarayana, Hosangadi, Koteshwar, Thekkatte, Basrur, Molahalli.

College in 3 villages, Adult Literacy Center in 13 villages., Colleges are in villages, namely Byndoor, Shankaranarayana, Basrur.

Medical: Hospital in 12 villages, Dispensary in 31 villages, Health Center in 7 villages, Sub Center in 76 villages, Maternity and Child Welfare Center in 4 villages, Community health workers in 47 villages.

The Villages having Hospital or Dispensary or Health Center are Shiroor, Yedthare, Kirimanjeshwar, Navunda, Nada, Kollur, Jadkal, Mudoor, Hakladi, Karkunje, Aloor, Kavrady, Ampar, Hosangadi, Hangaloor, Koni, Koteshwar, Thekkatte, Beloor, Kumbashi , Asodu, Kalavara, Anagalli, Basrur, Balkur, Hombady-Mandadi, Korgi, Molahalli, Hardally-Mandally, Harady (28), Hengavalli, Belve, Shedimane, Amasebailu.

Drinking Water: Tap water in 88 villages, Tank water in 74 villages, Well water in 99 villages, Tubewell in 67 villages and more than one source in 99 villages.

Bank: Banking facility in 55 villages, namely, Yedthare, Paduvari, Uppunda, Bijoor, Navunda Badakere, Maravanthe, Hadavu, Heranjal, Byndoor Yeljith, Jadkal, Mudoor, Trashi, Gujjadi, Gangolli Uppinakudru, Tallur, Hattiangadi, Kanyana, Hemmadi Senapur, Harkoor, Noojadi, Devalkunda, Kenchanoor Karkunje, Aloor, Chittoor, Hosoor, Halnad, Ampar Shankaranarayana, Siddapur, Ulloor 74, Kulanje Hangaloor, Koni, Koteshwar, Gopadi, Vakwadi Thekkatte, Beloor, Kumbashi, Asodu, Kalavara, Japthi Korgi, Hallady-Harkadi, Yedyadi-Mathyadi, Molahalli Hengavalli, Belve, Shedimane, Madammakki.

Credit Society in 49 villages Agricultural Credit Society in 18

Non-Agricultural Credit Society in 13 villages.

Others: Power supply in 99 villages, Cinema hall in 5 villages, sport club in 2 villages, Stadium or Auditorium or Community Hall in 0 village, Post Office in 91 villages.

There are 97 villages having bus facilities.

Villages with most of facilities: Yedthare Paduvari, Uppunda, Bijoor, Navunda, Badakere Maravanthe, Hadavu, Byndoor, Jadkal, Mudoor, Trashi Gujjadi, Uppinakudru, Tallur, Hattiangadi, Kanyana Hemmadi, Senapur, Harkoor, Noojadi, Devalkunda Kenchanoor, Karkunje, Aloor, Chittoor, Halnad, Ampar Shankaranarayana, Siddapur, Ulloor 74, Kulanje Hangaloor, Koni, Koteshwar, Gopadi, Vakwadi Thekkatte, Beloor, Kumbashi, Asodu, Kalavara, Korgi Hallady-Harkadi, Yedyadi-Mathyadi, Molahalli Hengavalli, Belve, Shedimane.

Villages without Amenities (Education): None..

Scheduled Castes: Out of the total population of 348829 persons, 19249 persons (5.52%) belong to Scheduled Castes.

The villages having less than 10% SC population are Shiroor, Yedthare, Paduvari, Uppunda, Bijoor Nandanavana, Kergal, Kirimanjeshwar, Kambadakone Ulloor [11], Navunda, Badakere, Maravanthe, Hadavu Nada, Heroor, Kalthodu, Heranjal, Thagarasi, Byndoor Yeljith, Kollur, Golihole, Jadkal, Mudoor, Hosadu Gangolli, Tallur, Kattabelthoor, Hemmadi, Hakladi Senapur, Harkoor, Kundabarandadi, Noojadi Devalkunda, Kenchanoor, Gulvadi, Karkunje, Vandse Aloor, Idurkunhadi, Chittoor, Hosoor, Keradi, Bellal Kodladi, Kavrady, Shankaranarayana, Siddapur, Ajri Kamalashile, Edmoge, Hosangadi, Machattu, Ulloor 74 Kulanje, Hangaloor, Koni, Koteshwar, Beejadi Vakwadi, Thekkatte, Ulthoor, Asodu, Anagalli, Basrur Balkur, Japthi, Yedyadi-Mathyadi, Molahalli Hardally-Mandally, Harady (28), Halady (76) Hengavalli, Belve, Albadi, Shedimane, Rattadi Amasebailu, Madammakki.

The village having more than 50% SC population is None.

Sex ratio of Scheduled Caste population is 513.

Scheduled Castes Literates and Illiterates by Sex:

	Persons	Males	Females
Literate	11,069	6,075	4,994
Illiterate	8,180	3,299	4,881
Literacy rate	65.8	74.5	57.6
Graduate	205	151	54

Scheduled Castes (Dominant):

Adi Dravida, Bhovi, Samagara, Bellara, Koosa

For their cultural identity please see Appendix-I

Villages without Scheduled Castes: There are 1 village without any scheduled caste population.

Scheduled Tribes: Out of the total population of 348829 persons, 10908 persons (3.13%) belong to Scheduled Tribes.

The villages having less than 10% ST population are Shiroor, Yedthare, Paduvari, Uppunda, Bijoor Nandanavana, Kergal, Kirimanjeshwar, Kambadakone Ulloor [11], Navunda, Badakere, Maravanthe, Hadavu Nada, Kalthodu, Heranjal, Thagarasi, Mudoor, Trashi Hosadu, Gujjadi, Gangolli, Uppinakudru, Tallur Hattiangadi, Kanyana, Kattabelthoor, Hemmadi Hakladi, Senapur, Harkoor, Kundabarandadi, Noojadi Devalkunda, Kenchanoor, Gulvadi, Karkunje, Vandse Aloor, Idurkunhadi, Chittoor, Hosoor, Keradi, Bellal Kavrady, Halnad, Ampar, Shankaranarayana, Siddapur Ajri, Hosangadi, Machattu, Ulloor 74, Hangaloor Koni, Koteshwar, Beejadi, Gopadi, Vakwadi, Thekkatte Ulthoor, Beloor, Kedoor, Kumbashi , Asodu, Kalavara Kandavara, Anagalli, Basrur, Balkur, Japthi Hombady-Mandadi, Korgi, Heskathoor, Hallady-Harkadi Yedyadi-Mathyadi, Molahalli, Hardally-Mandally Harady (28), Halady (76), Hengavalli, Belve, Albadi Shedimane, Rattadi, Madammakki.

The villages having more than 50% ST population are None.

Sex ratio of Scheduled tribe population is 503.

Scheduled Tribes Literates and Illiterates by Sex:

	Persons	Males	Females
Literate	5,374	3,019	2,355
Illiterate	5,534	2,398	3,136
Literacy rate	57.9	65.9	50.0
Graduate	51	45	6

Scheduled Tribes (Dominant):

Marati, Koraga, Naikda etc., Gond etc.

Generic Tribes etc.

For their cultural identity please see Appendix-II

Villages without Scheduled Tribes: There are 13 villages without any scheduled tribe population.

Literates and Illiterates by Sex (Total Population):

	Persons	Males	Females
Literate	231,360	117,762	113,598
Illiterate	117,469	42,774	74,695
Literacy rate	75	84	67
Graduate	7,827	5,218	2,609

Agriculture: ***Distribution of villages according to land use:*** Out of 99 villages, Total area (in hectare) is 154575, out of that 30.26 percent is cultivable and 38.33 percent of the cultivable area is irrigated.

Sources of Irrigation (Hectares): Government Canal 0, Private Canal 80.04, Well without Electricity 1308.84, Well witl Electricity 3813.66, Tubewell without Electricity 102.11,

Tubewell with Electricity 221.04, Tank 79.51, River 1654.46, Lake 104.77, Waterfall 4003.5, Others 6562.88.

Villages with population of 5000 to 9999:

Yedthare, Paduvari, Bijoor, Kirimanjeshwar, Navunda Maravanthe, Gujjadi, Kavrady, Shankaranarayana Siddapur, Koteshwar, Beejadi, Basrur.

Villages with population of 10000 and above:

Shiroor, Uppunda, Gangolli.

Distribution of Workers:

	Persons	Males	Females	WPR
Cultivators	39,259	20,867	18,392	26.64
Agricultural Labour	39,852	15,794	24,058	27.04
Household Industry	9,779	2,912	6,867	6.63
Other Workers	58,499	45,900	12,599	39.69
Main Workers	114,368	75,154	39,214	77.6
Marginal Workers	33,021	10,319	22,702	22.4
Total Workers	147,389	85,473	61,916	

Religion: Major Religious Communities:

	Persons	Males	Females	Sex Ratio
Hindu (89.63%)	312,639	142,926	169,713	1,187
Muslim (6.96%)	24,282	11,703	12,579	1,075
Christian (3.35%)	11,683	5,805	5,878	1,013
Sikh (0%)	13	9	4	444
Buddhists (0%)	4	2	2	1,000
Jain (0.03%)	102	54	48	889

Agewise Data:

	Persons	Males	Females	Sex Ratio
All ages	348,829	160,536	188,293	1173
0-14	102,461	51,885	50,576	975
15-44	166,346	71,212	95,134	1336
45-79	76,331	36,005	40,326	1120
80+	3,607	1,395	2,212	1586
Age not stated	84	39	45	1154

Languages (Dominant):

Kannada, Konkani, Urdu, Malayalam, Marathi

Disabled Population:

	Persons	Males	Females	%
Total Disabled	5,511	2,847	2,664	
In Seeing	2,393	1,100	1,293	43.42
In Speech	745	386	359	13.52
In Hearing	233	98	135	4.23
In Movement	1,295	797	498	23.5
Mentally	845	466	379	15.33

KUNDGOL

Kundgol C.D. Block lies in the south-eastern part of Dharwad district. It is a part of Kundgol taluka. The Block is located at a distance of 37 kms. from district headquarters (Dharwad). There are 58 villages in the block with the total population of 140,202 persons. Area of the C.D. Block is 651.36 sq. kms. It is bounded by taluks Hubli and Navalgund on north, district Haveri on south, district Gadag on east, district Haveri and taluk Hubli on west.

Communications:

Roadways : N.H-4 : Direction- Poona to Bangalore, Nearest Villages- Ramanakoppa, Jigalur, Belligatti.

Railway Station: Villages- Kundgol (Rural), Saunshi, Gudgeri.

Annual Rainfall: Normal Rianfall 772 mm.

Ground Water: Availability of the Ground Water in the Basin is 3387 H.A.M. and the utilization is 937.3835 H.A.M. It belongs to Over Exploited category. Depth to water level 5 to 20 meter below the ground. Most of the wells go down in summer months, according to the Ground Water Estimation Committee.

Soils: Loamy and Kankary Soils.

Natural Division : It falls in the Dharwad-Gadag Plateau of the Central Karnataka Plateau.

Administration:

Division: Belgaum. Parliamentary Constituency: 11 Dharwad. District: Dharwad. Taluka: Kundgol. Assembly Constitue ncy: 70 Kundgol. Gram Panchayat: 22.

Regional Area Development Boards: The Bailu Seeme Area Development Board.

Fairs: Nirvaneshwara Jatra: Ghodgeri 22 kms. from Hukeri is very near to Gokak Road Railway Station and is a place of considerable antiquity. The place has temples dedicated to Ramalinga, Niravanappa, Gajalingeshwara, Neelakantheshwara, Lakshmi and Maruti. The Ramalingeshw ara temple in later Chalukyan style has a garbhagriha (star shaped), shukanasa and a navaranga. The navaranga pillars are in granite with both circular and square cross-sections.

Villages: 58 **Inhabited:** 57 **Uninhabited:** 1

Ranking	District	State	National
Area	4	143	1029
Population	2	138	2152
Sex Ratio	3	156	3743
Child Sex Ratio	3	124	3602
Literacy Rate	1	63	2037
Density	5	47	4511
Work Participation Rate	1	65	1421

Gram Panchayats:

Gudenakatti, Yaraguppi, Rottigawad, Hirenarti, Shirur, Betadur, Yaliwal, Kubihal, Kamadolli, Saunshi, Yaribudihal, Hiregunjal, Haralapur, Gudgeri, Hireharakuni, Bujruk Tarlaghatta, Ingalagi, Gurunahalli, Ramanakoppa, Mattigatti, Goudgeri, Kalas.

Amenities:

Education: Primary School in 57 villages, Middle school in 51 villages, Matriculation or Secondary School in 17 villages, namely Pura, Yaliwal, Kamadolli, Bujruk Tarlaghatta, Kubihal, Ingalagi, Yaraguppi, Rottigawad, Mullahalli, Hirenarti, Bardwad, Hiregunjal, Yaribudihal, Saunshi, Gudgeri, Haralapur, Kalas.

Higher Secondary or Pre University Courses or Intermediate or Junior College in 5 villages of the CD Block,, namely Yaliwal, Kamadolli, Kubihal, Hiregunjal, Gudgeri.

College in 2 villages, Adult Literacy Center in 0 village., Colleges are in villages, namely Rottigawad, Gudgeri.

Medical: Hospital in 0 village, Dispensary in 4 villages, Health Center in 5 villages, Sub Center in 24 villages, Maternity and Child Welfare Center in 2 villages, Community health workers in 4 villages.

The Villages having Hospital or Dispensary or Health Center are Rottigawad, Bardwad, Yaribudihal, Gudgeri.

Drinking Water: Tap water in 42 villages, Tank water in 26 villages, Well water in 21 villages, Tubewell in 9 villages and more than one source in 50 villages.

Bank: Banking facility in 8 villages, namely, Yaliwal, Kamadolli, Kubihal, Ingalagi, Yaraguppi Yaribudihal, Saunshi, Kalas.

Credit Society in 29 villages Agricultural Credit Society in 29 Non-Agricultural Credit Society in 0 village.

Others: Power supply in 57 villages, Cinema hall in 3 villages, sport club in 3 villages, Stadium or Auditorium or Community Hall in 0 village, Post Office in 27 villages.

There are 56 villages having bus facilities.

Villages with most of facilities: Yaliwal Kamadolli, Kubihal, Ingalagi, Yaraguppi, Yaribudihal Saunshi, Kalas.

Villages without Amenities (Education): None..

Scheduled Castes: Out of the total population of 140213 persons, 12029 persons (8.58%) belong to Scheduled Castes.

The villages having less than 10% SC population are Pura, Gudenakatti, Shirur, Devanur, Yaliwal Hanchinal, Kamadolli, Hireharakuni Bujruk Tarlaghatta, Kubihal, Vithalapur, Hosakatti Ramanakoppa, Malali, Gurunahalli, Hirebudihal Ramapur, Kunkur, Teertha, Mattigatti, Ingalagi Yaraguppi, Rottigawad, Kodliwad, Chikkanarti Mullahalli, Benakanahalli, Hirenarti, Chakalabbi Bardwad, Bagawad, Chikkagunjal, Yaribudihal, Saunshi Pasupathihal, Sultanapur, Kalas, Rattigeri Sankalipur.

The village having more than 50% SC population is None.

Sex ratio of Scheduled Caste population is 488.

Scheduled Castes Literates and Illiterates by Sex:

	Persons	Males	Females
Literate	4,495	3,019	1,476
Illiterate	7,534	3,134	4,400
Literacy rate	44.6	58.9	29.9
Graduate	85	77	8

Scheduled Castes (Dominant):

Bhambi etc., Chalavadi etc., Banjara etc., Bhovi Madiga

For their cultural identity please see Appendix-I

Villages without Scheduled Castes: There are 2 villages without any scheduled caste population.

Scheduled Tribes: Out of the total population of 140213 persons, 10026 persons (7.15%) belong to Scheduled Tribes.

The villages having less than 10% ST population are Pura, Gudenakatti, Shirur, Bilebal, Betadur, Yaliwal Hanchinal, Kamadolli, Hireharakuni Bujruk Tarlaghatta, Bullappanakoppa, Kubihal Hosakatti, Ramanakoppa, Malali, Hirebudihal, Ramapur Kunkur, Jigalur, Belligatti, Teertha, Ingalagi Yarinarayanpur, Yaraguppi, Mullahalli, Benakanahalli Hirenarti, Basapur, Bardwad, Bagawad, Hiregunjal Hosahalli, Gudgeri, Kalas, Mandiganal, Rattigeri Goudgeri, Sankalipur.

The villages having more than 50% ST population are None.

Sex ratio of Scheduled tribe population is 489.

Scheduled Tribes Literates and Illiterates by Sex:

	Persons	Males	Females
Literate	4,484	2,966	1,518
Illiterate	5,542	2,162	3,380
Literacy rate	52.4	67.8	36.4
Graduate	96	86	10

Scheduled Tribes (Dominant):

Naikda etc., Pardhi etc., Koraga, Kadu Kuruba Generic Tribes etc.

For their cultural identity please see Appendix-II

Villages without Scheduled Tribes: There are 6 villages without any scheduled tribe population.

Literates and Illiterates by Sex (Total Population):

	Persons	Males	Females
Literate	77,633	47,941	29,692
Illiterate	62,580	24,149	38,431
Literacy rate	64	77	51
Graduate	2,219	1,923	296

Agriculture: ***Distribution of villages according to land use:***

Out of 58 villages, Total area (in hectare) is 65136, out of that 89.83 percent is cultivable and 0.29 percent of the cultivable area is irrigated.

Sources of Irrigation (Hectares): Government Canal 18.82,

Private Canal 0, Well without Electricity 0, Well with Electricity 30.53, Tubewell without Electricity 0, Tubewell with Electricity 19.37, Tank 46.51, River 0, Lake 1.36, Waterfall 0, Others 50.38.

Villages with population of 5000 to 9999:
Yaliwal, Kamadolli, Gudgeri, Kalas.

Villages with population of 10000 and above:
Saunshi.

Distribution of Workers:

	Persons	Males	Females	WPR
Cultivators	27,939	19,947	7,992	38.11
Agricultural Labour	36,264	15,781	20,483	49.47
Household Industry	1,459	1,081	378	1.99
Other Workers	7,647	6,607	1,040	10.43
Main Workers	62,018	40,599	21,419	84.6
Marginal Workers	11,291	2,817	8,474	15.4
Total Workers	73,309	43,416	29,893	

Religion: Major Religious Communities:

	Persons	Males	Females	Sex Ratio
Hindu (81.31%)	114,007	58,567	55,440	947
Muslim (15.86%)	22,238	11,524	10,714	930
Christian (0.04%)	50	24	26	1,083
Sikh (0.01%)	12	4	8	2,000
Buddhists (0.33%)	458	222	236	1,063
Jain (1.02%)	1,425	722	703	974

Agewise Data:

	Persons	Males	Females	Sex Ratio
All ages	140,213	72,090	68,123	945
0-14	44,493	22,769	21,724	954
15-44	67,635	35,433	32,202	909
45-79	26,904	13,366	13,538	1013
80+	1,119	491	628	1279
Age not stated	62	31	31	1000

Languages (Dominant):
Kannada, Urdu, Telugu, Marathi, Coorgi/Kodagu

Disabled Population:

	Persons	Males	Females	%
Total Disabled	1,972	1,133	839	
In Seeing	569	286	283	28.85
In Speech	217	124	93	11
In Hearing	129	56	73	6.54
In Movement	806	529	277	40.87
Mentally	251	138	113	12.73

KUNIGAL

Kunigal C.D. Block lies in the south-eastern part of Tumkur district. It is a part of Kunigal taluka. The Block is located at a distance of 40 kms. from district headquarters (Tumkur). There are 314 villages in the block with the total population of 204,891 persons. Area of the C.D. Block is 974.73 sq. kms. It is bounded by taluks Turuvekere. Gubbi and Tumkur on north, districts Mandya and Bangalore Rural on south, district Bangalore Rural on east, taluk Turuvekere and district Mandya on west.

Communications:

Roadways : N.H.-48: Direction- Hassan to Nelamangal, Nearest Villages- Nademavinapura, Siddapura, Byaladakere, Jaladagere, Koppa, Vaddarakatte Kaval, Avaragere, Kaggere, Singonahalli, Thippur, Chakenahalli, Beeragonah alli, Yediyur, Nittur, Gantaganahalli, Kenkere, Boralinga napalya, Bidanagere, Jodi Krishnaraja Sagara , Lakshmidevi, Hantha, Belidevalaya, Sarakari Krishnaraja. S.H.-33: Direction- Maddur to Timkur, Nearest Villages- Halugonah alli, Chikkamalalavadi, Kurudihalli, Voddarakuppe, Baktha rahalli, Kothagere Amanikere, Kothagere, Honnenahalli, Kurudihalli Chaturbaga, Ramabanada Hantha, Gangadahalli, Kunigal Bagayath, Kothipura, Herur Kanchagalapura, Arakere, Gavimata, Hanumapura, Kadamatikere, T. Hosaha lli, Tharikere, Santhemavathur, Kadarapura, Kempanahalli, Doddamavathur, Bolenahalli, Madappanahalli, Beeragonaha lli, Hosahalli, Hasige Hobli, Lakkashettypura, Kampalapura, Shringarasagra, Huliyurdurga, P. Honnamachanahalli, Hunuganahalli, Nidasale.

River: Shimsaha Nadi- Nearest Villages- Shingatihalli, Chikkamadure, Gottikere, Thattekere, Beeragonahalli, Hosahalli, Y. Hampapura, Ragihalli, Yediyur, Chikkanaha lli, Kurubarashettihalli, Kachanahalli, Kodavathi, Markon ahalli, Sunnadapura, Hanumapura, Kadashettyhalli, Besinele, Kaggalapura, Thorehalli, Bettahalli, Chikkajjanahalli, Doddakallahalli, Valagerepura, Chandanahalli, Arjunahal li, Yadavanne, Ungra, Pallerayanahalli, Bommenahalli, Kodavathi, Byranaikanahalli.

Canal: Nearest Villages- Begur, Begur Amanikere, Markona halli, Sunnadapura, Tubinakere, Devarayanapalya, Madihalli, Hosahalli, Mallapura, Sondekoppe, Kodagihalli, Hanumap ura, Kadashettyhalli, Besinele, Kaggalapura, Thorehalli, Raghavana Hosur, Korati, Handalagere, Bettahalli, Chikk ajjanahalli, Padavagere, Halagere, Honnamachanahalli, Voddarahalli, Kuppe, Sanaba, Kantanahalli, Kodihalli, Sanabagatta, Byadagere, Kagganahalli, Keelara, Palleray anahalli, Madagonahalli.

Annual Rainfall: Normal Rianfall 740.49 mm.

Ground Water: Availability of the Ground Water in the Basin is 12326.67 H.A.M. and the utilization is 7910. 28 H.A.M. It belongs to Over Expoited category. Depth to water level 2 to 10 meter below the ground. Most of the wells go down in summer months, according to the Ground Water Estimation Committee.

Soils: Red Loamy Soil.

Natural Division : It falls in Tumkur-Kunigal Plateau of the Southern Karnataka Plateau.

Administration:
Division: Bangalore. Parliamentary Constituency: 20 Mandaya. District: Tumkur. Taluka: Kunigal. Assembly Constituency: 131 Kunigal. Gram Panchayat: 36.
Regional Area Development Boards: The Bailu Seeme Area Development Board.
Fairs: Kaggere Jatra: It is held at Kaggere in the month of March for two days. Kaggere in Kunigal taluk, is the place where Tontada-Siddhalinga is said to have been absorbed in the practice of yoga or meditation, so much so that ant-hills grew around him.
Siddhalingeshwaraswami Jatra: It is held at Yedeyur near Tumkur in the month of March for five days. The Siddhalingeshwara temple at this place, facing north, is a large structure constructed in the Dravidian style of architecture and has the gaddige (samadhi or tomb) of Tontada-Siddhalinga, a celebrated Veerashaiva spiritu al teacher and auther who lived in the fifteenth century.
Villages: 314 **Inhabited:** 294 **Uninhabited:** 20

Ranking	District	State	National
Area	6	84	457
Population	6	85	629
Sex Ratio	1	6	432
Child Sex Ratio	1	18	1185
Literacy Rate	9	96	2989
Density	8	63	4574
Work Participation Rate	5	71	1616

Gram Panchayats:
Nagasandra, Madikehalli, Baktharahalli, Taredakuppe, Bagenahalli, Kothagere, Belidevalaya, Nademavinapura, Koppa, Yediyur, Markonahalli, Kodagihalli, Kaggere, T. Hosahalli, Herur, Begur, Yeliyur, Kithanamangala, Santhemavathur, K. Honnamachanahalli, Amruthur, Jinnagara, Padavagere, Yadavanne, Kodavathi, Halevoor, Hosahalli, Ippadi, Kempanahalli, Huthridurga, Hosahalli, Chowdanakuppe, Huliyurdurga, Nidasale, Ujjani, Thavarekere.
Amenities:
Education: Primary School in 253 villages, Middle school in 161 villages, Matriculation or Secondary School in 43 villages, namely Doddamadure, Nagasandra, Kaggere, Basavanamathikere, Yediyur, Singonahalli, Taredakuppe, Shettikere, Baktharahalli, Gunnagare, Janagere, Bommenahalli, Yeliyur, Hosur, Kempanahalli, Seenappanahalli, Huthridurga, Yelagalavadi, Belidevalaya, Gavimata, Santhemavathur, Modur, Kodavathi, Markonahalli, Holalagunda, Kodagihalli, Amruthur, Jinnagara, Honnamachanahalli, Sanaba, Valagerepura, Sanabagatta, Hanchipura, Yadavanne, Ankanahalli, Chowdanakuppe, Kodavathi, Huliyurdurga, Thavarekere, Devasandra, Ujjani, P. Honnamachanahalli, Nidasale.
Higher Secondary or Pre University Courses or Intermediate or Junior College in 11 villages of the CD Block,, namely Nagasandra, Kaggere, Yediyur, Baktharahalli, Huthridurga, Amruthur, Bettahalli, Shringarasagra, Huliyurdurga, Thavarekere, Nidasale.
College in 0 village, Adult Literacy Center in 0 village.
Medical: Hospital in 0 village, Dispensary in 11 villages, Health Center in 8 villages, Sub Center in 42 villages, Maternity and Child Welfare Center in 0 village, Community health workers in 0 village.
The Villages Having Hospital or Dispensary or Health Center are Doddamadure, Nagasandra, Nademavinapura, Yeliyur, Kithanamangala Amanikere, Santhemavathur, Honnamachanahalli, Ankanahalli, Thavarekere, Ujjani, Nidasale.
Drinking Water: Tap water in 128 villages, Tank water in 4 villages, Well water in 3 villages, Tubewell in 20 villages and more than one source in 33 villages.
Bank: Banking facility in 13 villages, namely, Nagasandra, Yediyur, Baktharahalli, Huthridurga Santhemavathur, Amruthur, Honnamachanahalli Yadavanne, Chowdanakuppe, Halevoor, Huliyurdurga Ujjani, Nidasale.
Credit Society in 26 villages Agricultural Credit Society in 16 Non-Agricultural Credit Society in 3 villages.
Others: Power supply in 294 villages, Cinema hall in 4 villages sport club in 294 villages, Stadium or Auditorium or Communi Hall in 294 villages, Post Office in 77 villages.
There are 155 villages having bus facilities.
Villages with most of facilities: Nagasandra Yediyur, Baktharahalli, Huthridurga, Santhemavathur Amruthur, Yadavanne, Chowdanakuppe, Halevoor Huliyurdurga, Ujjani, Nidasale.
Villages without amenities (Education):
Mavinahalli, M. Huruliborasandra, Kantanahalli Mavinahalli, Vaddarakatte Kaval, Dasanapura, Hosahalli, Y. Hampapura, Chikkanahalli, Singonahalli Agrahara, Nademavinapurada Ane Hantha, Chikkamalalavadi Chathurbaga, Shettikere Chathurbaga, Dasanapura, Rangaswamy Bettada Kaval, Nagalapura, Kurudihalli Chathurbaga, Devasthanada Dasanapura, Taremaradapalya, Beemanapura, Gantaganahalli, Gangadahalli, Kunigal (Rural), Begur Amanikere, Herur Kanchagalapura, Kithanamangala Chaturbhaga, Kallanaikanahalli, Hosur, Kithagatta, Taggikuppe, Devarayanapalya, Narayanapura, Hosapura, Kaggalapura, Yachanahalli, Kachonahalli, Shettipura, Voddarahalli, Voddarakempapura, Sonnaikanahalli, Lakkashettypura,

Gangapura..

Scheduled Castes: Out of the total population of 205687 persons, 27436 persons (13.34%) belong to Scheduled Castes. The villages having less than 10% SC population are Chottanahalli, Jiddigere, Heddigere, Shettibeedu Thuruganoor, Hurulagere, Mavinahalli Devarakannasandra, M. Huruliborasandra, Kodipalya Shingatihalli, Hulivana, Hulipura Kantanahalli Mavinahalli, Byadarahalli, Thuvekere Hadonahalli, Siddapura, Mallanaikanahalli, Gottikere Thattekere, Vaddarakatte Kaval, Avaragere, Thippur Y. Hampapura, Chikkanahalli, Mantya Singonahalli Agrahara, Vanigere Kaval Chikkamalalavadi, Taredakuppe, Naganahalli Kurudihalli, Voddarakuppe, Bommadigere Menasinahalli, Madikehalli, Nagalapura, Janagere Hosahalli, Kothagere, Kurudihalli Chathurbaga Bagenahalli, Nilathahalli Kaval, Kempasagara Somedevarapalya, A. Hosahalli, Kogatta, Kundur Rajagere, Devasthanada Dasanapura, Kathrigatta Hosur, Taremaradapalya, Beemanapura, Gujjenahalli Thippanaikanahalli, Kadasinganahalli, Hunusekuppe Gangadahalli, Kunigal (Rural), Mallagatta Byranaikanahalli, Channapura, Kothipura Begur Amanikere, Herur Kanchagalapura, Chottanahalli Arakere, Hanumapura, Kadamathikere Kithanamangala Amanikere, Kithanamangala Chaturbhaga Hithalahalli, Yachagatta, Arepalya, Budanahalli Hosur, Taggikuppe, Tubinakere, Devarayanapalya Narayanapura, Hosapura, Hosahalli, Sondekoppe Kodagihalli, Kadashettyhalli, Besinele, Kaggalapura Kerengor, Shanuboganahalli, Puttanapalya, Beligere Hosakere, Kachonahalli, Bettahalli, Voddarahalli Kuppe, Sanaba, Kantanahalli, Sanabagatta, Byadagere Kagganahalli, Hanchipura, Yadavanne, Ungra Lakshmipura, Doddamavathur, Chikkamavathur Nagathihalli, Ankanahalli, Voddarakempapura Guddethippasandra, K.G. Muthenahalli, Singonahalli Kebballi, Sugganahalli, Pura, Bommenahalli Byranaikanahalli, Lakkashettypura, Kampalapura Kenkere, Huliyurdurga, Kenchanahalli, Kachihalli Yelekadak[illegible] Devasandra, Hithalapura, Hunuganahalli Chalamasandra.

The villages having more than 50% SC population are Nademavinapurada Ane Hantha Rangaswamy Bettada Kaval, Naganahalli, Lalapura Kallanaikanahalli, Kachanahalli, Yachanahalli Raghavana Hosur, Benavara, Sonnaikanahalli Gangapura.

Sex ratio of Scheduled Caste population is 512.

Scheduled Castes Literates and Illiterates by Sex:

	Persons	Males	Females
Literate	12,570	7,443	5,127
Illiterate	14,866	5,937	8,929
Literacy rate	52.5	64.1	41.7
Graduate	174	147	27

Scheduled Castes (Dominant):

Adi Dravida, Adi Karnataka, Madiga, Bhovi Chalavadi etc.

For their cultural identity please see Appendix-I

Villages without Scheduled Castes: There are 58 villages without any scheduled caste population.

Scheduled Tribes: Out of the total population of 205687 persons, 2231 persons (1.08%) belong to Scheduled Tribes. The villages having less than 10% ST population are Chottanahalli, Vogaragere, Jiddigere, Heddigere Shettibeedu, Kotekere, Thuruganoor, Hurulagere Mavinahalli, Devarakannasandra, Yellapura Kanchagalapura, Madhure Kaval, M. Huruliborasandra Kodipalya, Shingatihalli, Chikkamadure, Doddamadure Hulivana, Hulipura, Nagasandra Kantanahalli Mavinahalli, Kantanahalli, Byadarahalli Thuvekere, Hadonahalli, Kannaguni, Nademavinapura Siddapura, Byaladakere, Manavalli, Mallanaikanahalli Gottikere, Thattekere, Jaladagere, Koppa Vaddarakatte Kaval, Avaragere, Kaggere, Dasanapura Kattigehalli, Basavanamathikere, Singonahalli Thippur, Chakenahalli, Beeragonahalli, Hosahalli Y. Hampapura, Ragihalli, Chikkanahalli, Mangala Mantya, Singonahalli Agrahara Nademavinapurada Ane Hantha, Gowdagere Huruliborasandra, Singonahalli, Vanigere Kaval Kamanahalli, Doddamalalavadi, Halugonahalli Chikkamalalavadi, Chikkamalalavadi Chathurbaga Taredakuppe, Sulekuppe Kaval, Sulekuppe, Naganahalli Shettikere Chathurbaga, Shettikere, Kurudihalli Voddarakuppe, Baktharahalli, Vanigere, Rayagonahalli Gunnagare, Madike Kannasandra, Bommadigere Dasanapura, Rangaswamy Bettada Kaval, Menasinahalli Madikehalli, Nagalapura, Janagere, Kodihalli Hosahalli, Kothagere Amanikere, Kothagere Honnenahalli, Kurudihalli Chathurbaga, Bagenahalli Sobaganahalli, Nilathahalli Kaval, Kempasagara Nilathahalli, Mavinakatte, Somedevarapalya Gottikere, Kallanaikanahalli, A. Hosahalli, Alkere Kogatta, Bommenahalli, Bukkasagara, Yeliyur, Kundur Rajagere, Sondalagere, Huthri, Thattasandra Devasthanada Dasanapura, Kathrigatta, Hosur Huluvagilu, Taremaradapalya, Beemanapura Kempanahalli, Nittur, Gantaganahalli, Gujjenahalli

Hosakere, Kadaramanahalli, Thippanaikanahalli
Seenappanahalli, Kadasinganahalli, Muganapura
Yelachavadi Gullahallipura, Huthridurga
Lingadevarana Palya, Hodagatta, Yelagalavadi
Hosahalli, Giddadasanapura, Naganahalli, Hunusekuppe
Ippadi, Kenkere, Boralinganapalya, Muthugadahalli
Gangadahalli, Kunigal (Rural), Mallagatta
Kutharahalli, Byranaikanahalli, Channapura, Begur
Shettigehalli, Kothipura, Begur Amanikere
Herur Kanchagalapura, Belidevalaya, Urukehalli
Chottanahalli, Theppasandra, Lalapura, Herur
Arakere, Hanumapura, Kadamathikere
Kithanamangala Amanikere, Kithanamangala Chaturbhaga
Hithalahalli, Kithanamangala, T. Hosahalli
Yachagatta, Dasanapura, Borasandra, Tharikere
Handalakuppe, Hangrahalli, Santhemavathur, Arepalya
Kadarapura, Kempanahalli, Kallanaikanahalli
Heggadathihalli, Modur, Hosur, Budanahalli
Pavasandra, Kurubarashettihalli, Hosur, Kithagatta
Kachanahalli, Taggikuppe, Kodavathi, Markonahalli
Tubinakere, Devarayanapalya, Madihalli, Sankenapura
Narayanapura, Holalagunda, Hosapura, Hosahalli
Mallapura, Sondekoppe, Kodagihalli, Chinnahalli
Hanumapura, Kadashettyhalli, Besinele, Thorehalli
Kerengor, Shanuboganahalli, Yachanahalli, Amruthur
Puttanapalya, Raghavana Hosur, Korati, Handalagere
Beligere, Hosakere, Bettahalli, Padavagere
Jinnagara, Shettipura, Halagere, Honnamachanahalli
Voddarahalli, Kuppe, Sanaba, Kantanahalli
Doddakallahalli, Valagerepura, Benavara, Kodihalli
Sanabagatta, Byadagere, Kagganahalli, Keelara
Hanchipura, Chandanahalli, Arjunahalli, Yadavanne
Ungra, Lakshmipura, Kichavadi, Madagonahalli
Doddamavathur, Chikkamavathur, Madappanahalli
Nagathihalli, Yedehalli, Byadarahalli, Neelasandra
Herohalli, Ankanahalli, Chikkonahalli, Chowdanakuppe
Guddethippasandra, K.G. Muthenahalli, Singonahalli
Hosahalli, Hasige Hobli, Halevoor, Kebballi
Sonnaikanahalli, Sugganahalli, Pura, Bommenahalli
Kodavathi, Byranaikanahalli, Bandihalli
Lakkashettypura, Kenkere, Shringarasagra
Huliyurdurga, Benachakallu, Hangarahalli, Hulikatte
Kenchanahalli, Gangapura, Kempanahalli, Handalagere
Thavarekere, Kachihalli, Byadarahalli, Yelekadakalu
Devasandra, Ujjani, Hithalapura
P. Honnamachanahalli, Hunuganahalli, Nidasale
Shivanahalli, Chalamasandra.

The villages having more than 50% ST population are None.

Sex ratio of Scheduled tribe population is 488.

Scheduled Tribes Literates and Illiterates by Sex:

	Persons	Males	Females
Literate	1,036	613	423
Illiterate	1,195	530	665
Literacy rate	53.4	61.4	44.9
Graduate	32	28	4

Scheduled Tribes (Dominant):

Naikda etc., Soligaru, Iruliga, Meda, Hakkipikki

For their cultural identity please see Appendix-II

Villages without Scheduled Tribes: There are 240 villages without any scheduled tribe population.

Literates and Illiterates by Sex (Total Population):

	Persons	Males	Females
Literate	106,699	62,274	44,425
Illiterate	98,988	38,853	60,135
Literacy rate	59	70	48
Graduate	1,956	1,644	312

Agriculture: ***Distribution of villages according to land use:*** Out of 314 villages, Total area (in hectare) is 97473, out of that 56.4 percent is cultivable and 29.69 percent of the cultivable area is irrigated.

Sources of Irrigation (Hectares): Government Canal 3871.55, Private Canal 0, Well without Electricity 68.5, Well with Electricity 562.89, Tubewell without Electricity 202.83, Tubewell with Electricity 6465.33, Tank 4909.18, River 6, Lake 0, Waterfall 0, Others 216.34.

Villages with population of 5000 to 9999:
Huliyurdurga.

Villages with population of 10000 and above: None

Distribution of Workers:

	Persons	Males	Females	WPR
Cultivators	79,233	44,394	34,839	72.74
Agricultural Labour	11,818	4,798	7,020	10.85
Household Industry	3,151	1,407	1,744	2.89
Other Workers	14,727	10,874	3,853	13.52
Main Workers	102,518	59,824	42,694	94.11
Marginal Workers	6,411	1,649	4,762	5.89
Total Workers	108,929	61,473	47,456	

Religion: Major Religious Communities:

	Persons	Males	Females	Sex Ratio
Hindu (93.81%)	192,945	94,821	98,124	1,035
Muslim (6.09%)	12,529	6,196	6,333	1,022
Christian (0.04%)	78	44	34	773
Sikh (0%)	5	3	2	667
Buddhists (0%)	1	1	-	-
Jain (0.02%)	38	16	22	1,375

Agewise Data:

	Persons	Males	Females	Sex Ratio
All ages	205,687	101,127	104,560	1034
0-14	61,369	30,991	30,378	980

15-44	92,155	44,228	47,927	1084
45-79	49,210	24,498	24,712	1009
80+	2,753	1,277	1,476	1156
Age not stated	200	133	67	504

Languages (Dominant):
Kannada, Urdu, Telugu, Marathi, Hindi
Disabled Population:

	Persons	Males	Females	%
Total Disabled	4,756	2,625	2,131	
In Seeing	2,427	1,310	1,117	51.03
In Speech	483	265	218	10.16
In Hearing	343	165	178	7.21
In Movement	1,101	673	428	23.15
Mentally	402	212	190	8.45

KUSHTAGI

Kushtagi C.D. Block lies in the northern part of Koppal district. It is a part of Kushtagi taluka. The Block is located at a distance of 55 kms. from district headqu arters (Koppal). There are 177 villages in the block with the total population of 218,079 persons. Area of the C.D. Block is 1354.92 sq. kms. It is bounded by districts Bagalkot and Raichur on north, district Gadag, taluks Yelbarga and Gangawati on south, district Raich ur and taluka Gangawati on east, and district Bagalkot on west.

Communications:
Roadways : N.H-13: Direction- Bijapur to Chitradurga, Nearest Villages- Mensageri, Kyadiguppa, Kadekoppa, Timmanhatti, Nadavalkoppa, Kalkeri, Upparbasapur, Kawal bodur, Vanageri, Kushtagi (Rural), Kandakur. S.H-6: Direct ion- Ilkal to Kushtagi, Nearest Villages- Hanamsagar, Mudhotagi, Develapur, Malkapur, Hosalli, Zhunjalkoppa, Chalgera, Talugeri, Nidsesi. S.H-6 A: Direction- Koppal to Kyadiguppa, Nearest Villages- Kyadiguppa, Kadekoppa, Dotihal, Kesoor, Nadavalkoppa, Kalkeri, Upparbasapur, Mankalkeri, Hesrur, Bijakal, Vanageri, Tekkalki, Kushtagi (Rural), Nerebenchi, Kurbanhal. SH-14: Direction- Badami to Hungund, Nearest Villages- Katapur, Turkanur, Kadoor, Yerigonhal, Antarthana. S.H-29: Direction- Gangawati to Lingsugur, NearestVillages- Kilarhatti, Konapur, Umlirampur, Narinhal,Vitalapur, Tawargera, Manedhal. SH-30: Direction- Ron to Sindhnur, Nearest Villages- Chicknandihal, Hireba nnigol, Yelburthi, Kushtagi (Rural), Nidsesi, Byalihal, Madalgatti, Kandakur, Gumgeri, Ganganhal, Hiremannapur, Hanchinhal, Nawalhalli, Nandapur, Vithalapur, Tawargera.
Reserved Forest: (Hanamsagar R.F.): Nearest Villages- Gudadurkal, Mannerhal, Beelagi, Kabbargi, Chandragiri, Mavinitagi, Hanamsagar.
Annual Rainfall: Normal Rianfall 571.92 mm.
Ground Water: Availability of the Ground Water in the Basin is 10919 H.A.M. and the utilization is 4253 H. A.M. It belongs to Over Exploited category. Depth to water level 5 to 20 meter below the ground. Most of the wells go down in summer months, according to the Ground Water Estimation Committee.
Soils: Black Cotton Soil.
Natural Division : It falls partly in the Kustagi-Yelbarga Plateau and Arkera-Mudgal-Kanakgiri Upland of the Centr al Karnataka Plateau.
Administration:
Division: Gulbarga. Parliamentary Constituency: 8 Koppal. District: Koppal. Taluka: Kushtagi. Assembly Constituen cy: 60 Kushtagi. Gram Panchayat: 28.
Regional Area Development Boards: The Hyderabad - Karnataka Area Development Board.
Fairs: Adavirayanagudi Jatra: The Adavirayanagadi Jatra held at Kushtagi in Raichur area about the month of June last for 10 days when thousands of Hindus gather there to offer worship. Kushtagi headquarters the taluk of the same name, is about 150 kms. west of Raichur. It is an notable commercial centre. The Adaviraya Jatra held here annually is an important fair.
Someshwara Jatra: Pura, in Kushtagi taluk is noted for its fine and spacious temple of Someshwara which has 'Kotilingas', where annually a big jatra is held in the month of Shravana.

Villages: 177 **Inhabited:** 164 **Uninhabited:** 13

Ranking	District	State	National
Area	3	45	198
Population	4	70	488
Sex Ratio	2	58	1761
Child Sex Ratio	2	52	2294
Literacy Rate	3	153	4719
Density	2	55	5395
Work Participation Rate	3	115	1516

Gram Panchayats:
Nilogal, Tuggaldoni, Hanmanhal, Jagir Gadadur , Malgitti, Hiregonnagar, Yerigeri, Hanamsagar, Kabbargi, Katapur, Hulgera, Advibhavi, Chalgera, Benkanhal, Hirebannigol, Kordakera, Talugeri, Bijakal, Dotihal, Kyadiguppa, Mudenoor, Jumlapur, Kilarhatti, Tawargera, Manedhal, Sanganhal, Hiremannapur, Kandakur.
Amenities:
Education: Primary School in 155 villages, Middle school in 108 villages, Matriculation or Secondary School in 15 villages, namely Nilogal, Hanmanhal, Malgitti, Yerigeri, Hulgera, Hanamsagar, Chalgera, Kordakera, Mudenoor, Dotihal, Hiremannapur, Nawalhalli, Jumlapur, Tawargera, Huliyapur.
Higher Secondary or Pre University Courses or Inter-

mediate or Junior College in 4 villages of the CD Block,, namely Hanmanhal, Hanamsagar, Dotihal, Tawargera. College in 0 village, Adult Literacy Center in 11 villages.

Medical: Hospital in 1 village, Dispensary in 9 villages, Health Center in 9 villages, Sub Center in 32 villages, Maternity and Child Welfare Center in 23 villages, Community health workers in 12 villages.

The Villages having Hospital or Dispensary or Health Center are Hanmanhal, Hiregonnagar, Hulgera, Hanamsagar, Chalgera, Dotihal, Kesoor, Madalgatti, Hiremannapur, Tawargera.

Drinking Water: Tap water in 56 villages, Tank water in 25 villages, Well water in 91 villages, Tubewell in 67 villages and more than one source in 148 villages.

Bank: Banking facility in 10 villages, namely, Hanmanhal, Hulgera, Hanamsagar, Chalgera, Mudenoor Dotihal, Hiremannapur, Tawargera, Manedhal Sanganhal.

Credit Society in 21 villages Agricultural Credit Society in 17 Non-Agricultural Credit Society in 3 villages.

Others: Power supply in 164 villages, Cinema hall in 3 villages, sport club in 164 villages, Stadium or Auditorium or Community Hall in 164 villages, Post Office in 51 villages.

There are 134 villages having bus facilities.

Villages with most of facilities: Hanmanhal Hulgera, Hanamsagar, Chalgera, Mudenoor, Dotihal Hiremannapur, Tawargera, Manedhal, Sanganhal.

Villages without amenities (Education): Yelbunchi, Mavinitagi, Zhunjalkoppa, Parasapur, Donnegudda, Bisnhal, Rampur(Jagir), Umlirampur, Zhoolkunti..

Scheduled Castes: Out of the total population of 218148 persons, 28501 persons (13.06%) belong to Scheduled Castes.

The villages having less than 10% SC population are Rampur, Vakkandurga, Mittalkod, Nilogal, Bommanhal Basapur, Bilekal, Shadalgera, Tuggaldoni, Nirlakoppa Masbinkurbanhal, Pattalchinti, Guddadadevalapur Konapur, Paramanhatti, Jagir Gadadur , Mastkatti Gadchinti, Timmanhatti, Yerigeri, Gorbihal Hiregonnagar, Varikal, Kumblavati, Yelbunchi Mugnoor, Katapur, Kalgonhal, Yerigonhal, Puratageri Mannerhal, Kabbargi, Chandragiri, Develapur Hanamageri, Miyapur, Timmanhatti, Hosalli, Madikera Zhoolkatti, Topalkatti, Talugeri, Kalalbandi Parasapur, Bisnhal, Kankoppa, Kordakera Chicknandihal, Hirebannigol, Yelburthi, Banhatti Benchamatti, Kudloor, Matur, Dotihal, Rampur(Jagir) Nidsesi, Gorvarbenchamatti, Byalihal, Shakapur Nerebenchi, Kurbanhal, Neerloti, Nagarhal, Kidadur Umlirampur, Narinhal, Garjanhal, Zhoolkunti Gudadhanamsagar, Bachinhal, Chickmukrtinhal Mettinhal, Ganganhal, Hiretemminhal, Homminhal.

The village having more than 50% SC population is None.

Sex ratio of Scheduled Caste population is 497.

Scheduled Castes Literates and Illiterates by Sex:

	Persons	Males	Females
Literate	9,041	6,261	2,780
Illiterate	19,460	8,088	11,372
Literacy rate	39.9	55.1	24.7
Graduate	203	183	20

Scheduled Castes (Dominant):

Madiga, Bhambi etc., Banjara etc., Bhovi Beda Jangam etc.

For their cultural identity please see Appendix-I

Villages without Scheduled Castes: There are 23 villages without any scheduled caste population.

Scheduled Tribes: Out of the total population of 218148 persons, 30524 persons (13.99%) belong to Scheduled Tribes.

The villages having less than 10% ST population are Rampur, Bilekal, Shadalgera, Tuggaldoni Pattalchinti, Jagir Gadadur , Malgitti, Habalkatti Venkatapur, Gudadurkal, Chickgonnagar, Yelbunchi Mugnoor, Katapur, Kalgonhal, Kadoor, Yerigonhal Huchnoor, Puratageri, Bandargal, Sebankatti Mannerhal, Mavinitagi, Hanamsagar, Mudhotagi Develapur, Miyapur, Mensageri, Kyadiguppa, Kadekoppa Timmanhatti, Malkapur, Hosalli, Zhunjalkoppa Madikera, Zhoolkatti, Chalgera, Talugeri, Kalalbandi Donnegudda, Kankoppa, Hirebannigol, Sirguppa, Megur Banhatti, Benchamatti, Mudenoor, Kudloor, Balutagi Jalihal, Matur, Dotihal, Kesoor, Kawalbodur, Hesrur Ryawanki, Basapur(M), Gonhal(K), Madapur Rampur(Jagir), Gudadur(M), Tengunti, Vanageri Tekkalki, Nidsesi, Gorvarbenchamatti, Byalihal Nerebenchi, Kurbanhal, Gumgeri, Hanchinhal, Sasvihal Muddalgundi, Myadardokki, Umlirampur, Narinhal Garjanhal, Nandapur, Vithalapur, Tawargera Huliyapur, Chickmukrtinhal, Pura, Hongaddi.

The villages having more than 50% ST population are Basapur, Nirlakoppa, Gorbihal, Tumrikoppa Hanamageri, Bisnhal, Chicknandihal, Ganganhal Nagarhal, Idlapur, Mettinhal, Kanhal, Hadagli Virupapur, Hiremukartihal.

Sex ratio of Scheduled tribe population is 492.

Scheduled Tribes Literates and Illiterates by Sex:

	Persons	Males	Females
Literate	9,991	7,106	2,885
Illiterate	20,533	8,395	12,138
Literacy rate	41.1	57.9	24.0
Graduate	130	118	12

Scheduled Tribes (Dominant):
Naikda etc., Generic Tribes etc., Koli Dhor etc. Gond etc., Kadu Kuruba
For their cultural identity please see Appendix-II

Villages without Scheduled Tribes: There are 31 villages without any scheduled tribe population.

Literates and Illiterates by Sex (Total Population):

	Persons	Males	Females
Literate	86,910	58,818	28,092
Illiterate	131,238	51,037	80,201
Literacy rate	49	66	32
Graduate	2,180	1,860	320

Agriculture: ***Distribution of villages according to land use:*** Out of 177 villages, Total area (in hectare) is 135492, out of that 82.86 percent is cultivable and 7.39 percent of the cultivable area is irrigated.

Sources of Irrigation (Hectares): Government Canal 197.45, Private Canal 0, Well without Electricity 2.02, Well with Electricity 2446.98, Tubewell without Electricity 0.8, Tubewell with Electricity 4972.69, Tank 88.53, River 0, Lake 0, Waterfall 211.66, Others 371.91.

Villages with population of 5000 to 9999:
Hiremannapur.

Villages with population of 10000 and above:
Hanamsagar, Tawargera.

Distribution of Workers:

	Persons	Males	Females	WPR
Cultivators	46,821	32,552	14,269	43.57
Agricultural Labour	41,181	11,338	29,843	38.32
Household Industry	4,253	2,604	1,649	3.96
Other Workers	15,213	11,602	3,611	14.16
Main Workers	77,775	51,330	26,445	72.37
Marginal Workers	29,693	6,766	22,927	27.63
Total Workers	107,468	58,096	49,372	

Religion: Major Religious Communities:

	Persons	Males	Females	Sex Ratio
Hindu (92.4%)	201,562	101,354	100,208	989
Muslim (6.93%)	15,108	7,747	7,361	950
Christian (0.03%)	72	31	41	1,323
Sikh (0%)	10	6	4	667
Buddhists (0%)	-	-	-	-
Jain (0.04%)	93	52	41	788

Agewise Data:

	Persons	Males	Females	Sex Ratio
All ages	218,148	109,855	108,293	986
0-14	90,497	46,090	44,407	963
15-44	90,773	46,490	44,283	953
45-79	35,303	16,676	18,627	1117
80+	1,403	498	905	1817
Age not stated	172	101	71	703

Languages (Dominant):
Kannada, Urdu, Coorgi/Kodagu, Hindi, Telugu

Disabled Population:

	Persons	Males	Females	%
Total Disabled	4,065	2,320	1,745	
In Seeing	1,532	790	742	37.69
In Speech	403	222	181	9.91
In Hearing	236	122	114	5.81
In Movement	1,535	983	552	37.76
Mentally	359	203	156	8.83

LINGSUGUR

Lingsugur C.D. Block lies in the north-western part of Raichur district. It is a part of Lingsugur taluka. The Block is located at a distance of 93 kms. from district headquarters (Raichur). There are 191 villages in the block with the total population of 247,326 persons. Area of the C.D. Block is 1926.15 sq. kms. It is bounded by districts Bijapur and Gulbarga on north, district Koppal and taluk Sindhnur on south, taluks Devadurga, Manvi and Sindhnur on east, and district Bagalkot on west.

Communications:

Roadways : S.H-19: Direction- Lingsugur to Sindhnur, Nearest Villages- Aidanhal, Yalagaladinni , Lingsugur (Rural), Gadgi, Pai Doddi, Golpalli, Gurgunta, Devar-Bhupur, Yaradona, Honnahalli, Kotha, Sante-Kellur, Muslikarlkunti, Bendarkarlkunti, Ankusadoddi, Mudwal, Venkatapur, Maski. S.H-20: Direction- Belgaum to Raichur, Nearest Villages- Lukkihal (Big), Kannapur Hatti, Mudgal (Rural), Amdihal, Bellihal, Huligudda, Karadakal, Hunkunti, Lingsugur(Rural), Kuppigudda, Sarjapur, Gonwar, Chick-Hesarur, Kadadarahal, Teribhavi, Buddinni, Gudihal. S.H-29: Direction- Mudgal to Gangawati, Nearest Villages- Mudgal (Rural), Piklihal, Ulimeshwar, Vyakarnhal, Nagalapur, Chattar, Todki, Kumarkhed, Hadagali. S.H-41: Direction- Muddebihal to Lingsugur, Nearest Villages- Chittapur, Bendona, Anahosur, Eachanhal, Kesarhatti, Karadakal, Adavibhavi, Neeralkera.

River: Krishna Nadi- Nearest Villages- Upanhal, Ankanhal, Tondihal, Mallapur, Chittapur, Nowli, Kamaldinni, Jawoor (Small), Jawur (Big), Roudal Banda, Sunkal, Halbhavi, Jaldurga, Yalgundi, Yaragudi, Kadadargaddi, Hanchinal, Shilahalli, Gonwatla, Guntagola, Ramalooti, Aidbhavi, Tanmankal, Gadgi. Maski Halla Nadi- Nearest Villages- Ramatnal, Byalihal, Wandali, Turadgi, Hunoor, Makapur, Talekat, Marli, Piklihal, Ulimeshwar, Vyakarnhal, Nagalapur, Heggapur, Mattur, Kunikellur, Mittikellur, Katagal, Uskihal, Nagalapur (D), Dabbermadu, Maraldinni, Mudaldinni, Sultanpur, Jakker-Madu, Vyasa Nandihal, Kannal, Timmapur, Dignaikanbhavi, Benkanhal, Belladamaradi, Venkatapur, Maski, Hadagali.

Reserved Forest: (Lingsugur): Nearest Villages- Gonwatla,

Guntagola, Ramalooti, Aidbhavi, Tanmankal, Raidurga, Gadgi, Golpalli, Hosagudda, Benchaldoddi, Gurgunta, Paramapur, Devar-Bhupur, Yaradona, Phoolabhavi, Honnahalli, Machanur, Yalaghatta.

Annual Rainfall: Normal Rianfall 564 mm.

Ground Water: Availability of the Ground Water in the Basin is 85.88 H.A.M. and the utilization is 40.56 H. A.M.. It belongs to Over Exploited category. Depth to water level 2 to 20 meter below the ground. Most of the wells go down in summer months, according to the Ground Water Estimation Committee.

Soils: Mixed Red and Black Soils.

Natural Division : It falls partly in the Middle Krishna Valley, Middle Tungabhadra Valley and the Arkera-Mudgal-Kanakgiri Upland of the central Karnataka Plateau.

Administration:

Division: Gulbarga. Parliamentary Constituency: 6 Raichur (ST), 8 Koppal. District: Raichur. Taluka: Lingsugur. Assembly Constituency: 57 Lingsugur (SC), 59 Maski (ST). Gram Panchayat: 35.

Regional Area Development Boards: The Hyderabad - Karna taka Area Development Board.

Fairs: Amareshwara Jatra and Fair: The Amareshwara Jatra in Lingsugur taluk, is held for three days in the month of March. It attracts a large number of persons. This fair is held at Devarbhupur and is highly popular with the Veerashaivas of the area. Devarbhupur, in Lingsugur taluk, about 15 kilometers from Lingsugur, is noted for its Amareshvara temple and jaggery trade. The temple is beautifully situated amidst hillocks which have green foliage. Under the auspices of this temple, annually a big jatra takes place in the month of Phalguna when a cattle fair is also held.

Yellamma Temple Jatra: Nagai is a place of religious and archaeological interest, situated 2 kms. from the Chitapur railway station on the Wadi-Secunderabad secti on of the Central Railway. In the past it had assumed importance as a seat of learning. Nagai is also noted for its inscriptions, many of which reveal the state of the country in the hoary past. There is a temple in Nagai erected on 61 pillars with nice carvings and built in the Jain style. In front of the temple, a recta ngular pillar, seven feet in height, contains an interest ing inscription relating to the Chalukyan rule. There are also several old temples at this place. The Yellamma temple is visited by pilgrims from all over the Karnataka state and also from outside.

Villages: 191 **Inhabited:** 186 **Uninhabited:** 5

Ranking	**District**	**State**	**National**
Area	1	7	61
Population	3	40	251
Sex Ratio	5	67	1977
Child Sex Ratio	5	56	2378
Literacy Rate	2	162	5125
Density	4	98	5856
Work Participation Rate	5	148	2301

Gram Panchayats:

Nagarhal, Baiyapur, Narakaladinni, Anahosur, Roudal Banda, Gorebal, Eachanhal, Mavinbhavi, Kachapur, Uppar Nandihal, Amdihal, Hunoor, Bannigol, Nagalapur, Talekhan, Kannal, Mattur, Kalapur, Honnahalli, Guntagola, Devar-Bhupur, Pai Doddi, Gurgunta, Goudur, Kotha, Hatti, Roudala Banda, Anwari, Gejjelagatta, Sarjapur, Sante-Kellur, Ankusadoddi, Maraldinni, Medikinhal, Maski.

Amenities:

Education: Primary School in 59 villages, Middle school in 22 villages, Matriculation or Secondary School in 18 villages, namely Nagarhal, Khairwadgi, Sajjalagudda, Mudgal(Rural), Amdihal, Nagalapur, Roudal Banda, Anahosur, Eachanhal, Sarjapur, Guntagola, Gurgunta, Goudur, Anwari, Gejjelagatta, Sante-Kellur, Maski, Medikinhal.

Higher Secondary or Pre University Courses or Intermediate or Junior College in 3 villages of the CD Block,, namely Sajjalagudda, Mudgal(Rural), Maski.

College in 1 village, Adult Literacy Center in 3 villages., College is in village, namely Hanumangudda(Hosur).

Medical: Hospital in 2 villages, Dispensary in 12 villages, Health Center in 13 villages, Sub Center in 36 villages, Maternity and Child Welfare Center in 1 village, Community health workers in 28 villages.

The Villages having Hospital or Dispensary or Health Center are Nagarhal, Sajjalagudda, Makapur, Roudal Banda, Jungi-Rampur, Gorebal, Anahosur, Gurgunta, Anwari, Gejjelagatta, Mattur, Maski, Medikinhal.

Drinking Water: Tap water in 75 villages, Tank water in 79 villages, Well water in 158 villages, Tubewell in 152 villages and more than one source in 181 villages.

Bank: Banking facility in 8 villages, namely, Nagarhal, Mudgal(Rural), Roudal Banda, Anahosur Gurgunta, Yaradona, Sante-Kellur, Maski.

Credit Society in 19 villages Agricultural Credit Society in 19 Non-Agricultural Credit Society in 1 village.

Others: Power supply in 186 villages, Cinema hall in 4 villages sport club in 186 villages, Stadium or Auditorium or Communi Hall in 186 villages, Post Office in 50 villages.

There are 165 villages having bus facilities.

Villages with most of facilities: Nagarhal

Mudgal(Rural), Roudal Banda, Anahosur, Gurgunta Sante-Kellur, Maski.

Villages without amenities (Education): Upanhal, Ankanhal, Tondihal, Halkawatgi, Palgal Dinni, Tumbalgaddi, Rampur, Bhogapur, Baiyapur, Bandisunkapur, Bommanhal, Komnur, Lukkihal(Big), Lukkihal(Small), Uppar Nandihal, Killar Hatti, Ashihal, Advibhavi (Mudgal), Kannapur Hatti, Jantapur, Yerdihal(Khurd), Yerdihal(Big), Bellihal, Adapur, Komlapur, Ramatnal, Byalihal, Wandali, Turadgi, Arya-Bhogapur, Hunoor, Talekat, Marli, Piklihal, Ulimeshwar, Heggapur, Chattar, Todki, Kumarkhed, Nowli, Jawoor(Small), Jungi-Rampur, Upperi (Small), Sunkal, Halbhavi, Yargunti, Upperi(Big), Toral Benchi, Nandihal, Bendona, Narakaladinni, Julgudda, Kesarhatti, Jalibenchi, Mincheri, Aidanhal, Yalagaladinni, Adavibhavi, Margatnal, Chitranhal, Amarawati, Basapur, Buddinni, Sanbal, Jaldurga, Yalgundi, Yaragudi, Kadadargaddi, Hanchinal, Shilahalli, Gonwatla, Ramalooti, Aidbhavi, Tanmankal, Raidurga, Gadgi, Pai Doddi, Golpalli, Yarjanti, Bandebhavi, Hosagudda, Benchaldoddi, Chikaldoddi, Paramapur, Devar-Bhupur, Phoolabhavi, Medinapur, Machanur, Kaddona, Tawag, Mallapur, Hosur, Chikka Nagnur, Veerapur, Hire Hesarur, Kadadarahal, Teribhavi, Buddinni, Kunikellur, Mittikellur, Muslikarlkunti, Bendarkarlkunti, Mudwal, Katagal, Uskihal, Nagalapur(D), Dabbermadu, Maraldinni, Mudaldinni, Sultanpur, Jakker-Madu, Vyasa Nandihal, Timmapur, Tirthabhavi, Dignaikanbhavi, Nirlooti, Advibhavi(Maski), Benkanhal, Belladamaradi, Venkatapur, Antargangi (Big), Myadarnal, Antargangi (Small), Bailgudda, Sompur, Desai-Bhogapur, Kamandaldinni..

Scheduled Castes: Out of the total population of 247478 persons, 54760 persons (22.13%) belong to Scheduled Castes.

The villages having less than 10% SC population are Upanhal, Tondihal, Tumbalgaddi, Bandisunkapur Sajjalagudda, Komnur, Uppar Nandihal Advibhavi (Mudgal), Bellihal, Komlapur, Ramatnal Arya-Bhogapur, Makapur, Piklihal, Ulimeshwar Kumarkhed, Jawoor(Small), Jawoor(Big), Roudal Banda Upperi (Small), Yargunti, Upperi(Big), Toral Benchi Bendona, Yalagaladinni , Adavibhavi , Gundasagar Gonwar, Amarawati, Basapur, Hoovinabhavi, Buddinni Jaldurga, Yalgundi, Yaragudi, Kadadargaddi Hanchinal, Ramalooti, Aidbhavi, Tanmankal, Raidurga Yarjanti, Bandebhavi, Chikaldoddi , Gurgunta Gudadanhal, Mallapur, Hosur, Chikka Nagnur, Buddinni Mittikellur, Ankusadoddi, Katagal, Nagalapur(D) Sultanpur, Tirthabhavi, Belladamaradi Antargangi (Small), Baggalgudda.

The villages having more than 50% SC population are Ashihal, Mudgal(Rural), Heggapur, Chattar Jungi-Rampur, Gorebal, Kesarhatti, Mincheri Karadakal, Sanbal, Gonwatla, Hosagudda, Paramapur Maraldinni, Advibhavi(Maski), Benkanhal, Sompur Hadagali, Kamandaldinni.

Sex ratio of Scheduled Caste population is 495.

Scheduled Castes Literates and Illiterates by Sex:

	Persons	Males	Females
Literate	16,949	11,661	5,288
Illiterate	37,811	15,993	21,818
Literacy rate	39.0	53.2	24.5
Graduate	296	273	23

Scheduled Castes (Dominant):

Banjara etc., Madiga, Bhovi, Chalavadi etc. Bhambi etc.

For their cultural identity please see Appendix-I

Villages without Scheduled Castes: There are 16 villages without any scheduled caste population.

Scheduled Tribes: Out of the total population of 247478 persons, 47303 persons (19.11%) belong to Scheduled Tribes.

The villages having less than 10% ST population are Ankanhal, Tondihal, Halkawatgi, Palgal Dinni Tumbalgaddi, Rampur, Nagarhal, Bhogapur, Baiyapur Bandisunkapur, Bommanhal, Lukkihal(Big) Lukkihal(Small), Uppar Nandihal, Killar Hatti Ashihal, Kannapur Hatti, Mudgal(Rural), Jantapur Yerdihal(Khurd), Yerdihal(Big), Amdihal, Bellihal Kansavi, Komlapur, Ramatnal, Byalihal, Hunoor Talekat, Marli, Bannigol, Piklihal, Ulimeshwar Nagalapur, Nowli, Kamaldinni, Chittapur Jawoor(Small), Jawoor(Big), Roudal Banda Jungi-Rampur, Gorebal, Nandihal, Bendona Hanumangudda(Hosur), Anahosur, Kesarhatti, Kalapur Aidanhal, Yalagaladinni , Karadakal, Neeralkera Margatnal, Chitranhal, Gundasagar, Mavinbhavi Bhupur, Kallilingsugur, Hunkunti, Kuppigudda Amarawati, Buddinni, Sanbal, Shilahalli, Gudadanhal Medinapur, Tawag, Chikka Nagnur, Nilogal Chukanahatti, Chick-Hesarur, Kadadarahal, Teribhavi Gudihal, Sante-Kellur, Sultanpur, Jakker-Madu Advibhavi(Maski), Naraga Benchi, Sompur, Hadagali Baggalgudda, Kamandaldinni.

The villages having more than 50% ST population are Kumarkhed, Halbhavi, Upperi(Big), Adavibhavi , Rampur Yalgundi, Yaragudi, Kadadargaddi, Ramalooti Pai Doddi, Golpalli, Yarjanti, Bandebhavi Chikaldoddi , Phoolabhavi, Hosur, Katagal, Uskihal

Nagalapur(D), Tirthabhavi, Belladamaradi Antargangi (Small).

Sex ratio of Scheduled tribe population is 495.

Scheduled Tribes Literates and Illiterates by Sex:

	Persons	Males	Females
Literate	11,936	8,591	3,345
Illiterate	35,367	15,285	20,082
Literacy rate	32.0	45.5	18.1
Graduate	111	103	8

Scheduled Tribes (Dominant):

Naikda etc., Gond etc., Kadu Kuruba

Generic Tribes etc., Koraga

For their cultural identity please see Appendix-II

Villages without Scheduled Tribes: There are 26 villages without any scheduled tribe population.

Literates and Illiterates by Sex (Total Population):

	Persons	Males	Females
Literate	92,332	62,130	30,202
Illiterate	155,146	62,812	92,334
Literacy rate	46	61	30
Graduate	2,176	1,876	300

Agriculture: ***Distribution of villages according to land use:*** Out of 191 villages, Total area (in hectare) is 192615, out of that 78.3 percent is cultivable and 4.74 percent of the cultivable area is irrigated.

Sources of Irrigation (Hectares): Government Canal 0, Private Canal 0, Well without Electricity 57.08, Well with Electricity 3887.58, Tubewell without Electricity 78.83, Tubewell with Electricity 1980.2, Tank 682.03, River 275.37, Lake 0, Waterfall 0, Others 186.6.

Villages with population of 5000 to 9999: None

Villages with population of 10000 and above:

Gurgunta, Maski.

Distribution of Workers:

	Persons	Males	Females	WPR
Cultivators	42,366	35,092	7,274	36.84
Agricultural Labour	54,109	14,866	39,243	47.06
Household Industry	2,892	1,755	1,137	2.52
Other Workers	15,621	12,605	3,016	13.58
Main Workers	69,878	54,543	15,335	60.77
Marginal Workers	45,110	9,775	35,335	39.23
Total Workers	114,988	64,318	50,670	

Religion: Major Religious Communities:

	Persons	Males	Females	Sex Ratio
Hindu (90.54%)	224,074	112,978	111,096	983
Muslim (8.77%)	21,713	11,098	10,615	956
Christian (0.14%)	355	189	166	878
Sikh (0%)	1	-	1	-
Buddhists (0.03%)	86	42	44	1,048
Jain (0.01%)	32	19	13	684

Agewise Data:

	Persons	Males	Females	Sex Ratio
All ages	247,478	124,942	122,536	981
0-14	103,859	53,431	50,428	944
15-44	102,770	52,378	50,392	962
45-79	39,543	18,660	20,883	1119
80+	1,147	382	765	2003
Age not stated	159	91	68	747

Languages (Dominant):

Kannada, Hindi, Urdu, Telugu, Marathi

Disabled Population:

	Persons	Males	Females	%
Total Disabled	3,417	1,916	1,501	
In Seeing	1,599	847	752	46.8
In Speech	319	176	143	9.34
In Hearing	173	77	96	5.06
In Movement	1,070	660	410	31.31
Mentally	256	156	100	7.49

MADDUR

Maddur C.D. Block lies in the eastern part of Mandya district. It is a part of Maddur tehsil. The Block is located at a distance of 18 kms. from district headquarters (Mandya). There are 160 villages in the block with the total population of 263,248 persons. Area of the C.D. Block is 599.20 sq. kms. It is bounded by district Tumkur on north, taluk Malavalli on south, district Bangalore Rural on east, taluks Nagamangala and Mandya on west.

Communications:

Roadways : SH.-17: Direction- Mysore to Bangalore, Nearest Villages- Rudrakshipura, Nidaghatta, Madapuradadoddi, Somanahalli, Mobbalagere, Gejjalagere, Goravanahalli, Kudaragundi, K.Kodihalli, Agralinganahalli. SH-33: Direction- Malavalli to Tumkur, Nearest Villages- Mallanayakanahalli, Mallanakuppe, Dundanahalli, Kesthur, Tubinakere, Machahalli, Athaguru, Thore Settihalli, Yaraganahalli, Hanumanthapura, Hemmanahalli, Huluganahalli, Somanahalli, Goravanahalli, Kudaragundi, Channasandra, Sadolalu, Borapura, Huligerepura, Doddarasinakere , Chatradahosahalli, Chikkarasinakere, Mellahalli, Manigere.

Railway Station: Villages- Huluganahalli, Shivapura.

River: Shimsha Nadi- Nearest Villages- Kowdley, Yadavanahalli, Bekkalale, Kirangur, Halehalli, Mudya, Thaggahalli, Keelaghatta, N.Kodihalli, Nilvagilu, Mudigere, Marasinganahalli, Hosakere, Kothana Halli, Navile, Byaladakere, Hebberalu, Doddankanahalli, Chikkankanahalli, Kesthur, Tubinakere,, Thore Settihalli, Yaraganahalli, Chamanahalli, Kadalipura, Huluganahalli, Somanahalli, Vaidyanathapura, K.Kodihalli, Agralinganahalli, Buddaguppe, Alur, Neelakantanahalli, Hagalahalli, Nagarakere, Malagaranahalli, Ajjahalli, Kabbare, Chunchagahalli, Hulikere, K.

Bellur, Thore Chakanahalli, Kyathaghatta, Bannahalli, Koolagere, Madenahalli, Thore Bommanahalli, Mudenahalli, S.Hagalahalli.

Canal: Nearest Villages- Keelaghatta, V.Ballekere, Guloo ru, Maraliga, N.Kodihalli, Nilvagilu, Mudigere, Konasale, Chottanahalli, Besagarahalli, Marasinganahalli, Hosakere, Kothana Halli, Belathur, Rampura, Shankarapura, Doddan kanahalli, Chikkankanahalli, Kesthur, Tubinakere, Athaguru, Thore Settihalli, Yaraganahalli, Hanumanthapura, Kadal ur, Hemmanahalli, Rudrakshipura, Thylur, Sollepura, Volag arehalli, Chamanahalli, Kadalipura, Somanahalli, Maddur Rural, Mobbalagere, Hosahalli, Gejjalagere, Goravanahalli, Kudaragundi, Channasandra, Buddaguppe, Alur, Neelakant anahalli, Hagalahalli, Nagarakere, Sadolalu, Borapura, Huligerepura, Malagaranahalli, Ajjahalli, Sabbanahalli, Yadaganahalli, Haralahalli, Doddarasinakere , Chatradah osahalli, Chikkarasinakere, Thore Chakanahalli, Kyathagha tta, Karkahalli, Alabujanahalli, Mellahalli, Karadakere, K. Settihalli, Gopanahalli, Bujavalli, Kadukothanahalli, Yaladahalli, Bidarahosahalli, Manigere, Annur, Menasage re, Boppasamudra, Honnaikanahalli, S.Honnalagere.

Annual Rainfall: Normal Rianfall 706.1 mm.

Ground Water: Availability of the Ground Water in the Basin is 6962.10 H.A.M. and the utilization is 1778. 22 H.A.M. It belongs to Over Expoited category. Depth to water level 2 to 10 meter below the ground. Most of the wells go down in summer months, according to the Ground Water Estimation Committee.

Soils: Red Sandy Loams to Red Clay Loam.

Natural Division : It falls partly in Nagamangala Plateau and Shimsha Basin of the Southern Karnataka Plateau.

Administration:

Division: Mysore. Parliamentary Constituency: 20 Mandya. District: Mandya. Taluka: Maddur. Assembly Constituency :187 Maddur, 191 Nagamangala. Gram Panchayat: 42.

Fairs:: Madduramma Temple Jatra: It is dedicated to the village goddess Madduramma as the goddess is presiding over Maddur whereas Hasanamba is the goddess presiding over Hassan. The goddesses' aids are seven sisters,as represe nted by seven natural stones which are in a line in the open ground and protrude a few inches above the ground level, the central ones being bigger than in houses; so they are in the open in a pond-like basin in front of a mantapa, an oblong platform in mortar being built around them. A jatra is held every year.

Narasimhaswamy Jatra: It is held at Maddur near Mandya in the month of Vaishaka (April) for seven days. Maddur is a town on the right bank of the Shimsha river, about 50 kms. north-east of Mysore, on the Bangalore-Mysore railway rank and the Bangalore-Mysore road. According to a legend, it was originally named Arjunapuri after Arjuna, a Pandava prince, who arrived there on pilgrimage. The Shimsha also bears the name of Kadamaba, from a rishi who resided on its banks. Under the Gangavadi, and in later times Vishnuvardhana Hoysala is stated to have made it an agrahara town and given the same to Srivaishnava Brahmins. The agrahara was called 'Naras imha-Chaturvedi Mangalam'. He is also said to have built the Maddur tank and the temple of Varadaraja. The fort was taken in 1617 by the Dalavayi of Mysore, during the reign of raja Wodeyar, and was later rebuilt by Haidar Ali. It was dismantled by Lord Cornwallis in 1791 on his march to Srirangapatna.

Villages: 160 **Inhabited:** 153 **Uninhabited:** 7

Ranking	District	State	National
Area	5	151	1176
Population	2	31	163
Sex Ratio	4	63	1897
Child Sex Ratio	6	174	5350
Literacy Rate	5	108	3205
Density	5	112	2498
Work Participation Rate	1	6	2634

Gram Panchayats:

Kowdley, Bekkalale, Hosagavi, Abalavadi, Koppa, Thaggahalli, Huthagere, Mallanakuppe (Gate), Kesthur, Nilvagilu, Maraliga, Bidarakote, Besagarahalli, Hosakere, Athaguru, Kadalur, Nidaghatta, Somanahalli, Hemmanahalli, Chamanahalli, Volagarehalli, Gejjalagere, Goravanahalli, Alur, K. Honnalagere, Nagarakere, Sadolalu, Chikkarasinakere, Doddarasinakere, Madarahalli, Yadaganahalli, K. Settihalli, Kadukothanahalli, Bidarahalli, Bharati Nagar, Annur, Menasagere, Kyathagatta, K. Bellur, Koolagere, Thorebommanahalli, S.I. Honnalagere.

Amenities:

Education: Primary School in 144 villages, Middle school in 112 villages, Matriculation or Secondary School in 35 villages, namely Kowdley, Bekkalale, Hosagavi, Koppa, Hurugalavadi, Nambinayakana Halli, Bidarakote, Gulooru, Maraliga, Nilvagilu, Besagarahalli, Navile, Mallanakuppe, Chikkankanahalli, Kesthur, Athaguru, Kadalur, Thylur, Volagarehalli, Somanahalli, Maddur Rural, Gejjalagere, K. Honnalagere, Madarahalli, Yadaganahalli, Doddarasinakere, Chikkarasinakere, Kyathaghatta, Madenahalli, Mellahalli, Karadakere, Kadukothanahalli, Bidarahosahalli, Annur, S.Hagalahalli.

Higher Secondary or Pre University Courses or Intermediate or Junior College in 10 villages of the CD Block,,

namely Koppa, Kesthur, Volagarehalli, Somanahalli, Maddur Rural, K. Honnalagere, Doddarasinakere, Mellahalli, Annur, S.Hagalahalli.

College in 6 villages, Adult Literacy Center in 1 village., Colleges are in villages, namely Koppa, Besagarahalli, Hosakere, Mellahalli, Bidarahalli, Bidarahosahalli.

Medical: Hospital in 11 villages, Dispensary in 7 villages, Health Center in 18 villages, Sub Center in 53 villages, Maternity and Child Welfare Center in 14 villages, Community health workers in 5 villages.

The Villages having Hospital or Dispensary or Health Center are Kowdley, Bekkalale, Kirangur, Haralakere, Kuntanahalli, Bidarakote, Besagarahalli, Volagarehalli, K. Honnalagere, Yadaganahalli, Chatradahosahalli, Kothipur, Koolagere, Kadukothanahalli, Annur, S.Hagalahalli.

Drinking Water: Tap water in 138 villages, Tank water in 84 villages, Well water in 141 villages, Tubewell in 142 villages and more than one source in 152 villages.

Bank: Banking facility in 27 villages, namely, Kowdley, Hosagavi, Koppa, Bidarakote, Besagarahalli Hosakere, Hebberalu, Kesthur, Hemmanahalli Nidaghatta, Somanahalli, Gejjalagere Vaidyanathapura, Alur, K. Honnalagere Malagaranahalli, Madarahalli, Yadaganahalli Shingatageri, Doddarasinakere, Kothipur, Koolagere Mellahalli, Bidarahosahalli, Manigere, S.Honnalagere S.Hagalahalli.

Credit Society in 64 villages Agricultural Credit Society in 51 Non-Agricultural Credit Society in 14 villages.

Others: Power supply in 152 villages, Cinema hall in 4 villages, sport club in 2 villages, Stadium or Auditorium or Community Hall in 1 village, Post Office in 53 villages.

There are 111 villages having bus facilities.

Villages with most of facilities: Kowdley Hosagavi, Koppa, Bidarakote, Besagarahalli Hebberalu, Kesthur, Nidaghatta, Somanahalli Gejjalagere, K. Honnalagere, Madarahalli Yadaganahalli, Shingatageri, Doddarasinakere Mellahalli, S.Honnalagere, S.Hagalahalli.

Villages without amenities (Education): Naganahalli, Hosahalli, Agralinganahalli, Ajjahalli, Hannahalli Doddi..

Scheduled Castes: Out of the total population of 264262 persons, 33676 persons (12.74%) belong to Scheduled Castes. The villages having less than 10% SC population are Bolare, Kirangur, D. Malligere, Haralakere, Mudya Thaggahalli, T.Ballekere, Ankushapura, Kuntanahalli Hurugalavadi, Nambinayakana Halli, Bidarakote V.Ballekere, D.Hosahalli, Mudigere, Mullahalli Konasale, Besagarahalli, Hosakere, Belathur, Rampura Shankarapura, Byaladakere, Harakana Halli Lingasandra, Kundanakuppe, Mallanayakanahalli Dundanahalli, Chikkankanahalli, Thore Settihalli Hanumanthapura, Maradevanahalli, Hosahalli Rudrakshipura, Sollepura, Kadalipura, Huluganahalli Maddur Rural, Hosahalli, Channasandra Vaidyanathapura, Agralinganahalli, Buddaguppe Byadrahalli, Hagalahalli, Nagarakere, Uppinakere Sadolalu, Borapura, Sompura, Malagaranahalli Ajjahalli, Chunchagahalli, Madarahalli, Kadilavagilu Shingatageri, Haralahalli, Doddarasinakere Chatradahosahalli, Kyathaghatta, Aruvanahalli Koolagere, Madenahalli, Mellahalli, Karadakere Arechakanahalli, Bidarahalli, Thore Bommanahalli.

The village having more than 50% SC population is None.

Sex ratio of Scheduled Caste population is 501.

Scheduled Castes Literates and Illiterates by Sex:

	Persons	Males	Females
Literate	15,714	9,301	6,413
Illiterate	17,962	7,500	10,462
Literacy rate	52.8	63.2	42.7
Graduate	579	499	80

Scheduled Castes (Dominant):

Adi Karnataka, Madiga, Bhovi, Generic Castes etc. Korama

For their cultural identity please see Appendix-I

Villages without Scheduled Castes: There are 21 villages without any scheduled caste population.

Scheduled Tribes: Out of the total population of 264262 persons, 1142 persons (0.43%) belong to Scheduled Tribes. The villages having less than 10% ST population are Bolare, Kowdley, Yadavanahalli, Bekkalale, Kirangur Halehalli, Somanahalli, D. Malligere, Hosagavi Maramgere, Haralakere, Mudya, Thaggahalli T.Ballekere, Avverahalli, Abalavadi, Ankushapura Koppa, Chikkonahalli, Keelaghatta, Kuntanahalli Hurugalavadi, Nambinayakana Halli, Bidarakote V.Ballekere, Gulooru, D.Hosahalli, Maraliga N.Kodihalli, Nilvagilu, Mudigere, Mullahalli Haralahalli, Konasale, Chottanahalli, Besagarahalli Marasinganahalli, Hosakere, Kothana Halli, Belathur Rampura, Shankarapura, Navile, Byaladakere Hebberalu, Ankanathapura, Harakana Halli Lingasandra, Kundanakuppe, Mallanayakanahalli Mallanakuppe, Naganahalli, Dundanahalli, Huthagere Doddankanahalli, Chikkankanahalli, Kesthur Tubinakere, Machahalli, Alamsettahalli, Athaguru

Thore Settihalli, Yaraganahalli, Hanumanthapura Maradevanahalli, Hosahalli, Kadalur, Hemmanahalli Rudrakshipura, Nidaghatta, Madapuradadoddi, Thippur Madanaikanahalli, Thylur, Sollepura, Volagarehalli Deshahalli, Chamanahalli, Kadalipura, Huluganahalli Somanahalli, Maddur Rural, Hosahalli, Gejjalagere Goravanahalli, Kudaragundi, Channasandra Vaidyanathapura, K.Kodihalli, Agralinganahalli Buddaguppe, Dadaga, Alur, Byadrahalli, Chandahalli K. Honnalagere, Bheemanakere, Neelakantanahalli Hagalahalli, Nagarakere, Uppinakere, Sadolalu Borapura, Huligerepura, Sompura, Malagaranahalli Ajjahalli, Kabbare, Chunchagahalli, Hulikere Hallikere, K.Bellur, Ambarahalli, Madarahalli Kadilavagilu, Sabbanahalli, Yadaganahalli Shingatageri, Haralahalli, Doddarasinakere Chatradahosahalli, Chikkarasinakere Thore Chakanahalli, Kyathaghatta, Bannahalli Aruvanahalli, Kothipur, Koolagere, Madenahalli Karkahalli, Alabujanahalli, Mellahalli, Gudigere Karadakere, K. Settihalli, Arechakanahalli Gopanahalli, Bujavalli, Kadukothanahalli Yaladahalli, Bidarahalli, Bidarahosahalli, Manigere Annur, Menasagere, Boppasamudra, Thore Bommanahalli Hannahalli Doddi, Mudenahalli, Honnaikanahalli S.Honnalagere, S.Hagalahalli.

The villages having more than 50% ST population are None.

Sex ratio of Scheduled tribe population is 496.

Scheduled Tribes Literates and Illiterates by Sex:

	Persons	Males	Females
Literate	519	306	213
Illiterate	623	269	354
Literacy rate	52.6	61.5	43.7
Graduate	27	22	5

Scheduled Tribes (Dominant):

Naikda etc., Soligaru, Meda, Generic Tribes etc. Yerava

For their cultural identity please see Appendix-II

Villages without Scheduled Tribes: There are 111 villages without any scheduled tribe population.

Literates and Illiterates by Sex (Total Population):

	Persons	Males	Females
Literate	135,720	79,455	56,265
Illiterate	128,542	53,785	74,757
Literacy rate	58	67	48
Graduate	5,846	4,928	918

Agriculture: ***Distribution of villages according to land use:***

Out of 160 villages, Total area (in hectare) is 59920, out of that 70.46 percent is cultivable and 52.98 percent of the cultivable area is irrigated.

Sources of Irrigation (Hectares): Government Canal 17110.97, Private Canal 0, Well without Electricity 105.79, Well with Electricity 687.34, Tubewell without Electricity 105.09, Tubewell with Electricity 1450.09, Tank 1513.9, River 8.4, Lake 0, Waterfall 0, Others 1385.95.

Villages with population of 5000 to 9999:

Kesthur, Doddarasinakere , Mellahalli.

Villages with population of 10000 and above:

Besagarahalli.

Distribution of Workers:

	Persons	Males	Females	WPR
Cultivators	64,470	47,208	17,262	49.22
Agricultural Labour	41,458	17,154	24,304	31.65
Household Industry	3,033	1,481	1,552	2.32
Other Workers	22,015	15,667	6,348	16.81
Main Workers	98,603	72,243	26,360	75.28
Marginal Workers	32,373	9,267	23,106	24.72
Total Workers	130,976	81,510	49,466	

Religion: Major Religious Communities:

	Persons	Males	Females	Sex Ratio
Hindu (97.56%)	257,820	130,004	127,816	983
Muslim (1.48%)	3,899	1,973	1,926	976
Christian (0.27%)	715	347	368	1,061
Sikh (0%)	2	-	2	-
Buddhists (0.36%)	950	471	479	1,017
Jain (0.01%)	30	18	12	667

Agewise Data:

	Persons	Males	Females	Sex Ratio
All ages	264,262	133,240	131,022	983
0-14	73,394	37,742	35,652	945
15-44	131,314	65,792	65,522	996
45-79	55,765	28,015	27,750	991
80+	3,321	1,429	1,892	1324
Age not stated	468	262	206	786

Languages (Dominant):

Kannada, Urdu, Tamil, Telugu, Marathi

Disabled Population:

	Persons	Males	Females	%
Total Disabled	6,497	3,651	2,846	
In Seeing	3,554	1,980	1,574	54.7
In Speech	678	379	299	10.44
In Hearing	345	155	190	5.31
In Movement	1,431	881	550	22.03
Mentally	489	256	233	7.53

MADHUGIRI

Madhugiri C.D. Block lies in the north-eastern part of Tumkur district. It is a part of Madhugiri taluka. The Block is located at a distance of 42 kms. from district headquarters (Tumkur). There are 320 villages in the block with the total population of 238,096 persons. Area of the C.D. Block is 1122.44 sq. kms. It is bound ed by taluk Koratagere on south, district Kolar on east, and taluk Sira on west. It has common boundary with the state of Andhra Pradesh on north, east and west.

Communications:

Roadways : S.H.-3: Direction- Pavagada to Koratagere, Nearest Villages- Kyathagondanahalli, Bidarekere Kaval, Bidarakere, Nallekamanahalli, Medigeshi, Chinnenahalli, Veerachinnenahalli, Bedattur, Neelihalli, Thippagondana halli, Galihalli, Hosakere, Lakshmidevipura, Basavanahalli, Avaragal, Chikkanahalli, Karamaradi, Jadegondnahalli, Vaderahalli, Basavanahalli, Giddenahalli, Madhugiri (Rural), Harihararoppa, Chinakavajra. S.H.-58: Direction- Sira to Gauribidanur, Nearest Villages- Kunnahalli, Dodderi, Badavanahalli, Kurihalli, Kanapanaikanahalli, Bettadaranganahalli, Appanahalli, Lakshmipura, Adavikat anahalli, S.M.Gollahalli, Dabbeghatta, Hariharapura, Girigondanahalli, Badavanahalli Amrutmahal Kaval, Siddap ura, Gundlahalli, Ranganaikana Roppa, Doddaviragondanaha lli, Chinakavajra, Sogenahalli, Pujarahalli, Puttenahalli, Veerannanahalli, Settihalli, Maraballi, Ranganahalli, Mekethimmanahalli, Nitrahalli, Kodagadala.

River: Kumudvati Nadi- Nearest Villages-Vingalamanaha lli, Kasinaikanahalli, Thirumaladevarahalli, Nagenahalli, Parthihalli, Channavara, Gundagal, Yaragunte, Kadagathur, Yakaralahalli, Kalidevapura, Sravandanahalli, Thingalur. Jayamangali Nadi- Nearest Villages- Vitalapura, Chikk adalavatta, Shanaganahalli, Polenahalli, Muddenahalli, Theriyur, Annenahalli, Masarapadi, Hosahalli, Reddihalli, Jalihalli, Muthyalammanahalli, Kodigenahalli, Suranagena halli, Kalenahalli, Kempapura, Chikkamalur, Veeranagenah alli, Immadagondanahalli, Obalapura, Puruvara, Haralapura, Sankapura, Ramanahalli, Doddahosahalli, Gamkaralahalli, Taggihalli, Handralu, Byalya, Shiganagondanahalli, Chikkahosahalli, Hanumanthapura, Nitrahalli, Nanjapura, Kodagadala.

Canal: Nearest Villages- Pujarahalli, Madenahalli, Mudda ppanapalya, Angadithimanapalya, Hanumanahalli, Kavanadala, Gubalagutte, Kunigal Thimmanahalli, Bisadikariyanahalli, Kurumanakote-Thimmanapalya.

Annual Rainfall: Normal Rianfall 745.36 mm.

Ground Water: Availability of the Ground Water in the Basin is 7131.24 H.A.M. and the utilization is 13312. 69 H.A.M. It belongs to Over Exploited category. Depth to water level 2 to 20 meter below the ground. Most of the wells go down in summer months, according to the Ground Water Estimation Committee.

Soils: Red Loamy Soil.

Natural Division : It falls partly in Madhugiri Hills and Upper Pennar Basin of the Southern Karnataka Plateau.

Administration:

Division: Bangalore. Parliamentary Constituency: 19 Tumkur. District: Tumkur. Taluka: Madhugiri. Assembly Constituency: 138 Madhugiri. Gram Panchayat: 39.

Regional Area Development Boards: The Bailu Seeme Area Development Board.

Border Villages: (State: Andhra Pradesh)- R.Gollahalli, Reddihalli, Sattigenahalli, Lakshmipura, Mallanaikanaha lli, Mallanaikanahalli Kaval, Ayyanahalli, Benakanahalli, Narappanahalli, Kyathagondanahalli, Bidarekere Kaval, Bidarakere, Yammethimmanahalli, Sravanagudi, Medigeshi, Kasapura, Bramhadevarahalli Kaval, Brahmadevarahalli, Bedattur, Appenahalli, Dyavagondanahalli, Hosahalli, Karenahalli, Hosakere, Gampalahalli, K.Appenahalli, K.Krishnapura, Neralekere, Basmangi Kaval, Basavanahalli, Karpenhalli, Singiravathanahalli, Kittagali, Sajje Hosahalli, Karenahalli, Chambenahalli, Pulamaghatta, Rantavalalu, Kempachannenahalli, Mandathimmanahalli, Malagondanahalli, Thadi, Itakadibbanahalli, Thondoti, Doddadalavatta, Vitalapura, Chikkadalavatta, Muddenahal li, Vengalammanahalli, Kasinaikanahalli Thirumaladevarahalli, Nagenahalli, Parthihalli, Kadagath ur, Yakaralahalli, Bachenahalli, Thingalur.

Fairs: Dandi Marammana Jatra: It is held at Madhugiri in the month of February for ten days, a town situated about 40 kms. north of the Tumkur town.

Villages: 320 **Inhabited:** 298 **Uninhabited:** 22

Ranking	District	State	National
Area	4	67	327
Population	4	49	295
Sex Ratio	6	106	2638
Child Sex Ratio	4	62	2542
Literacy Rate	8	93	2926
Density	4	30	4539
Work Participation Rate	3	68	1060

Gram Panchayats:

Reddihalli, Medigeshi, Bedattur, Itakadibbanahalli, Chikkadalavatta, Kadagathur, Singanahalli, Doddayalkur, Garani, Chinnenahalli, Sajje Hosahalli, Rantavalalu, Neralekere, Hosakere, Brahmasamudra, Kodigenahalli, Kalidevapura, Doddamalur, Chikkamalur, Kodlapura, Ganjalagunte, Maruvekere, Siddapura, Kotagaralahalli, Chandragiri, Badavanahalli, Rangapura, Dodderi, Dabbeghatta, Doddaveeragondanahalli, Bijavara, Puruvara, Kondavadi, Byalya, Kavanadala, Chinakavajra, Kodagadala, Meuddenahalli, Gondihalli.

Amenities:

Education: Primary School in 252 villages, Middle school in

144 villages, Matriculation or Secondary School in 44 villages, namely Reddihalli, Mallanaikanahalli, Medigeshi, Chinnenahalli, Bedattur, Hosakere, Neralekere, Karpenhalli, Sajje Hosahalli, Rantavalalu, Kotagaralahalli, Sodenahalli, Jakkenahalli, Dodderi, Badavanahalli, Dabbeghatta, Kavanadala, Ganjalagunte, Bandrehalli, Bijavara, Bhaktarahalli, Vaderahalli, Siddapura, Settihalli, Itakadibbanahalli, Thippapura, Garani, Doddayalkur, Polenahalli, Theriyur, Singanahalli, Kodigenahalli, Gundagal, Kadagathur, Chikkamalur, Sravandanahalli, Kodlapura, Immadagondanahalli, Puruvara, Gondihalli, Byalya, G.Agrahara, Nitrahalli, Kodagadala.

Higher Secondary or Pre University Courses or Intermediate or Junior College in 11 villages of the CD Block,, namely Medigeshi, Sajje Hosahalli, Rantavalalu, Dodderi, Kavanadala, Itakadibbanahalli, Thippapura, Kodigenahalli, Kodlapura, Puruvara, Byalya.

College in 1 village, Adult Literacy Center in 0 village., College is in village, namely Kodigenahalli.

Medical: Hospital in 1 village, Dispensary in 5 villages, Health Center in 10 villages, Sub Center in 45 villages, Maternity and Child Welfare Center in 0 village, Community health workers in 3 villages.

The Villages having Hospital or Dispensary or Health Center are Medigeshi, Sajje Hosahalli, Itakadibbanahalli, Garani, Kondavadi.

Drinking Water: Tap water in 149 villages, Tank water in 60 villages, Well water in 112 villages, Tubewell in 139 villages and more than one source in 232 villages.

Bank: Banking facility in 35 villages, namely, Medigeshi, Hosakere, Kempachannenahalli Mayagondanahalli, Kotagaralahalli, Badavanahalli Dabbeghatta, Kavanadala, Itakadibbanahalli, Garani Sobenahalli, Muddeneralekere, Varadanahalli Muddenahalli, Vengalammanahalli, Kasinaikanahalli Thirumaladevarahalli, Nagenahalli, Parthihalli Annenahalli, Masarapadi, Singanahalli, Jalihalli Muthyalammanahalli, Kodigenahalli, Gundagal Yaragunte, Kadagathur, Yakaralahalli, Bachenahalli Venkatapura, Sravandanahalli, Thingalur, Puruvara Byalya.

Credit Society in 38 villages Agricultural Credit Society in 29 Non-Agricultural Credit Society in 13 villages.

Others: Power supply in 298 villages, Cinema hall in 8 villages, sport club in 298 villages, Stadium or Auditorium or Community Hall in 298 villages, Post Office in 57 villages.

There are 159 villages having bus facilities.

Villages with most of facilities: Medigeshi Hosakere, Kotagaralahalli, Badavanahalli Dabbeghatta, Kavanadala, Itakadibbanahalli, Garani Gundagal, Puruvara, Byalya.

Villages without amenities (Education): Mallanaikanahalli Kaval, Bramhadevarahalli Kaval, Kallenahalli, Dyavagondanahalli, Galihalli, K.Krishnapura, Badaobanahalli, Karenahalli, Kempachannenahalli, Mandathimmanahalli, Sarjammanahalli, Madaliyarhalli, Ummanahalli, Pemmanahalli, Lakshmipura, Adavikatanahalli, Begurdasarahalli, Krishnapura, Venkateshapura, Bommethimmanahalli, Angadithimanapalya, Kattijogipalya, Kurumanakote-Thimmanapalya, Chikkanahalli, K.G.Thippapura, Lakshmipura, Panne, Giddenahalli, Jogihalli, Chickegowdanaroppa, Palyadahalli, Puttenahalli, Malagondanahalli, Tummalu, Nallahalli, Varadanahalli, Yaragunte, Dasarahalli, Beeranahalli, Shivapura, Obalapura, Thimmasandra, Narasapura, Ramanahalli, Halethimmanahalli, Mekethimmanahalli..

Scheduled Castes: Out of the total population of 239580 persons, 57274 persons (23.91%) belong to Scheduled Castes. The villages having less than 10% SC population are Sattigenahalli, Lakshmipura, Narappanahalli Yammethimmanahalli, Sravanagudi, Nagalapura Veerachinnenahalli, Appenahalli, Neelihalli Kallenahalli, Gollahalli.R., Badaobanahalli Basavanahalli, Basmangi Kaval, Karenahalli Chambenahalli, Kodiramapura, Vitalapura Boramuthanahalli, Vajradahalli, Bhoothanahalli Ummanahalli, Kanapanaikanahalli, Lakshmipura Begurdasarahalli, Sanjeevapura, Girigondanahalli Banagarahalli, Krishnapura, Veerannanahalli Obalihalli, Bommethimmanahalli, Lingasandra Muddappanapalya, Goddanapalya, Borekunte Ranganapalya, Angadithimanapalya, Sheebaianapayla Kattijogipalya, Gidadagalahalli Kunigal Thimmanahalli, Kurumanakote-Thimmanapalya Chickathimmanahalli, Kambadahalli, Marithimmanahalli Midatarahalli, Amaravathi, K.G.Thippapura Lakshmipura, Tavakadahalli, Kambatanahalli, Panne Venkatapura, Banavenahalli, Giddenahalli, Jogihalli Chickegowdanaroppa, Hosahalli, Kuppachariroppa Thungoti, Somalapura, Gurammanakatte, Harihararoppa Chinakavajra, Palyadahalli, Puttenahalli Chowlahalli, Kantanahalli, Tummalu, Shanaganahalli Bydarahalli, Channamallanahalli, Nallahalli Yaramallanahalli, Huvinahalli, Varadanahalli Vengalammanahalli, Nagenahalli, Annenahalli, Gutte Jalihalli, Muthyalammanahalli, Yaragunte Yakaralahalli, Bachenahalli, Suranagenahalli

Venkatapura, Jogihalli, Kamsanahalli, Dasarahalli
Govindanahalli, Beeranahalli, Chunchenahalli
Shivapura, Obalapura, Thimmasandra, Narasapura
Sankapura, Aralimaradahalli, Siddanahalli
Raghuvanahalli, Chikkathimmanahalli, Yarranapalya
Ranganahalli, Ejihalli, Shiganagondanahalli
Chikkahosahalli, Nanjapura, Kulumenahalli.

The villages having more than 50% SC population are
Ayyanahalli, Bramhadevarahalli Kaval
Dyavagondanahalli, Karenahalli, Thippagondanahalli
K.Krishnapura, Sodenahalli, Bittanakurke
Pemmanahalli, Gopagondnahalli, Sanjeevapura
Bandrehalli, Veerannanahalli, Malagondanahalli
Dadagondanahalli, Byrapura, Handralu, G.Agrahara
Mekethimmanahalli, Hanumanthapura.

Sex ratio of Scheduled Caste population is 489.

Scheduled Castes Literates and Illiterates by Sex:

	Persons	Males	Females
Literate	24,577	15,521	9,056
Illiterate	32,697	13,760	18,937
Literacy rate	49.5	61.1	37.4
Graduate	760	692	68

Scheduled Castes (Dominant):

Madiga, Bhovi, Adi Karnataka, Chalavadi etc.
Banjara etc.

For their cultural identity please see Appendix-I

Villages without Scheduled Castes: There are 84 villages without any scheduled caste population.

Scheduled Tribes: Out of the total population of 239580 persons, 28277 persons (11.8%) belong to Scheduled Tribes.

The villages having less than 10% ST population are
R.Gollahalli, Reddihalli, Sattigenahalli
Ayyanahalli, Benakanahalli, Narappanahalli
Bidarekere Kaval, Yammethimmanahalli
Nallekamanahalli, Nagalapura
Bramhadevarahalli Kaval, Brahmadevarahalli
Veerachinnenahalli, Bedattur, Appenahalli
Neerakallu, Krishnapura, Kallenahalli
Thippagondanahalli, Galihalli, K.Appenahalli
Gollahalli.R., K.Krishnapura, Badaobanahalli
Neralekere, Katagondanahalli, Lakshmidevipura
Dasenahalli, Basavanahalli, Karpenhalli
Singiravathanahalli, Sajje Hosahalli, Karenahalli
Chambenahalli, Pulamaghatta, Rantavalalu
Kodiramapura, Kempachannenahalli, Mandathimmanahalli
Jeevagondanahalli, Vitalapura, Boramuthanahalli
Sodenahalli, Shivanagere, Jakkenahalli
Sarjammanahalli, Thonachagondanahalli, Bittanakurke
Bhoothanahalli, Ummanahalli, Nagenahallii
Badavanahalli, Rangapura, Kanapanaikanahalli
Pemmanahalli, Appanahalli, Lakshmipura, Hariharapura
Begurdasarahalli, Thimmalapura, Giriyammanapalya
Sanjeevapura, Girigondanahalli, Banagarahalli
Krishnapura, Venkateshapura, Sidadaragal, Obalihalli
Bommethimmanahalli, Pujarahalli, Lingasandra
Madenahalli, Muddappanapalya, Goddanapalya
Ranganapalya, Angadithimanapalya, Hanumanahalli
Kavanadala, Kattijogipalya, Gubalagutte
Kunigal Thimmanahalli, Kurumanakote-Thimmanapalya
Achenahalli, Kambadahalli, Marithimmanahalli
Chikkanahalli, Gopagondnahalli, Amaravathi
Sanjeevapura, K.G.Thippapura, Shambonahalli
Bandrehalli, Maruvekere, Tavakadahalli, Bijavara
Kambatanahalli, Karamaradi, Panne, Bhaktarahalli
Banavenahalli, Jadegondnahalli, Vaderahalli
Basavanahalli, Giddenahalli, Jogihalli, Siddapura
Gundlahalli, Ranganaikana Roppa
Doddaveeragondanahalli, Kuppachariroppa, Thungoti
Somalapura, Gurammanakatte, Harihararoppa
Muddaiahnapalya, Palyadahalli, Mallenahalli
Sogenahalli, Puttenahalli, Veerannanahalli
Maraballi, Pulamachi, Malagondanahalli, Chowlahalli
Thadi, Itakadibbanahalli, Kantanahalli, Tummalu
Thondoti, Doddadalavatta, Shanaganahalli, Obalapura
Thippapura, Bydarahalli, Gullahalli, Sadarahalli
Srinivasapura, Garani, Nallahalli, Yaramallanahalli
Huvinahalli, Yaragunte, Muddeneralekere
Varadanahalli, Thirumaladevarahalli, Nagenahalli
Masarapadi, Yaragunte, Bachenahalli, Byrapura
Suranagenahalli, Venkatapura, Kempapura, Jogihalli
Dasarahalli, Bommenahalli, Sravandanahalli
Thingalur, Badakanahalli, Girigondanahalli, Talakere
Veeranagenahalli, Govindanahalli, Beeranahalli
Shivapura, Immadagondanahalli, Obalapura, Narasapura
Sankapura, Aralimaradahalli, Halethimmanahalli
Raghuvanahalli, Chikkathimmanahalli, Doddahosahalli
Yarranapalya, Gamkaralahalli, Handralu, Byalya
G.Agrahara, Ranganahalli, Ejihalli, Chikkahosahalli
Hunasavadi, Nanjapura, Sunnavadi, Battikere
Kulumenahalli, Naveladaku.

The villages having more than 50% ST population are
Mallanaikanahalli Kaval, Hosahalli, Basavanahalli
Basmangi Kaval, Vajradahalli, Veerannanahalli
Chickathimmanahalli, Lakshmipura, Vitalapura, Gutte
Jalihalli, Muthyalammanahalli.

Sex ratio of Scheduled tribe population is 491.

Scheduled Tribes Literates and Illiterates by Sex:

	Persons	Males	Females
Literate	13,426	8,336	5,090
Illiterate	14,851	6,071	8,780

Literacy rate	54.3	66.2	41.9
Graduate	292	272	20

Scheduled Tribes (Dominant):
Naikda etc., Generic Tribes etc., Kadu Kuruba Hakkipikki, Dubla etc.
For their cultural identity please see Appendix-II
Villages without Scheduled Tribes: There are 109 villages without any scheduled tribe population.
Literates and Illiterates by Sex (Total Population):

	Persons	Males	Females
Literate	124,322	76,011	48,311
Illiterate	115,258	45,759	69,499
Literacy rate	59	71	47
Graduate	4,025	3,498	527

Agriculture: ***Distribution of villages according to land use:*** Out of 320 villages, Total area (in hectare) is 112244, out of that 60.41 percent is cultivable and 26.3 percent of the cultivable area is irrigated.
Sources of Irrigation (Hectares): Government Canal 95.51, Private Canal 32.7, Well without Electricity 128.54, Well with Electricity 2293.67, Tubewell without Electricity 170.88, Tubewell with Electricity 7422.56, Tank 5918.94, River 103.05, Lake 0, Waterfall 40.14, Others 1628.28.
Villages with population of 5000 to 9999: Kodigenahalli.
Villages with population of 10000 and above: None
Distribution of Workers:

	Persons	Males	Females	WPR
Cultivators	57,199	39,425	17,774	43.55
Agricultural Labour	52,789	20,174	32,615	40.2
Household Industry	4,187	1,442	2,745	3.19
Other Workers	17,152	12,705	4,447	13.06
Main Workers	94,672	63,501	31,171	72.09
Marginal Workers	36,655	10,245	26,410	27.91
Total Workers	131,327	73,746	57,581	

Religion: Major Religious Communities:

	Persons	Males	Females	Sex Ratio
Hindu (96.92%)	232,208	118,094	114,114	966
Muslim (2.88%)	6,897	3,435	3,462	1,008
Christian (0.02%)	45	23	22	957
Sikh (0.01%)	34	23	11	478
Buddhists (0%)	1	1	-	-
Jain (0.07%)	178	87	91	1,046

Agewise Data:

	Persons	Males	Females	Sex Ratio
All ages	239,580	121,770	117,810	967
0-14	71,500	36,501	34,999	959
15-44	110,917	55,958	54,959	982
45-79	54,085	27,780	26,305	947
80+	2,799	1,398	1,401	1002
Age not stated	279	133	146	1098

Languages (Dominant):
Kannada, Telugu, Urdu, Hindi, Tamil
Disabled Population:

	Persons	Males	Females	%
Total Disabled	4,148	2,300	1,848	
In Seeing	1,592	812	780	38.38
In Speech	566	284	282	13.65
In Hearing	277	137	140	6.68
In Movement	1,304	850	454	31.44
Mentally	409	217	192	9.86

MADIKERI

Madikeri C.D. Block lies in the western part of Kodagu district. It is a part of Madikeri taluka. The Block is located at a distance of 00 kms. from district headqu arters (Madikeri). There are 67 villages in the block with the total population of 109,261 persons. Area of the C.D. Block is 1435.35 sq. kms. It is bounded by district Dakshina Kannada and taluk Somvarpet on north, taluk Virajpet on south, and taluk Somvarpet on east. It has common boundary with the state of Kerala on south and west.
Communications:
Roadways : SH- 27: Direction- Somvarpet to Virajpet, Nearest Villages- Mekeri, Biligeri, Kaggodlu, Hakathoor, Makkandur, Karnangeri, Kanthur, Mutharmudi, M. Badaga, Kiggalu. SH- 88: Direction- Puttur to Piriyapatna, Nearest Villages- Kundalpadi Peraje, Sampaje, Made, Katakeri (Rural), Mekeri, Monnangeri, Karnangeri, Ibniv alvadi (Rural). SH- 88 B: Direction- Madikeri to Virajpet, Nearest Village- Kadagadalu.
Rivers: Cauvery Nadi- Villages- Thannimani, Bhagamanda la, Kundacheri, Kopatti, B.Badaga, Bengooru, Karugunda, Hodavada, Hoddur, M. Badaga, Kiggalu, Sodluru, Kattemadu, Arekadu, Yemmemadu, Napoklu, Paloor, Balamuri. Hundrotu Hole Nadi- Nearest Village- Sannapulikotu (No.2). Polin gom Puzha Nadi- Nearest Village- Sannapulikotu (No.2).
Reserved Forest: (Kadamakal R.F.): Nearest Vill.- Kalooru, Hammiyala, Galibeedu, Monnangeri. (Padinalknad Ghat R.F.): Nearest Villages- Cherangala, Sannapulikotu (No.2), Aiyangeri, Naladi, Yevakapadi, Chelavara, Karada. (Patt ighat R.F.): Nearest Villages- Karike, Thannimani, Bhagam andala, Bettathur, Kundalpadi Peraje, Melchembu, Sampaje, Monnangeri.
Annual Rainfall: Normal Rianfall 3082 mm.
Ground Water: Availability of the Ground Water in the Basin is 102.24 MCM and the utilization is 2829.32 MCM. It belongs to Safe category. Depth to water level 2 to 10 meter below the ground. Most of the wells go down in summer months, according to the Ground Water Estimati

on Committee.

Soils: Reddish brown forest soil, Yellowish grey to greyish sandy loam soils and mixed soils.

Natural Division : It falls partly in Patti-Brahmagiri Ghats and Somvarpet-Virajpet Rolling Humid Region of Southern Karnataka Plateau.

Administration:

Division: Mysore. Parliamentary Constituency: 21 Mysore Paschim. **District**: Kodagu. Taluka: Madukeri. Assembly Constituency: 208 Madikeri, 209 Virajpet.

Gram Panchayat:22.

Regional Area Development Boards: The Maland Aera Development Board.

Border Villages: (State: Kerala)- Karike, Cherangala, Sannapulikotu (No.2), Aiyangeri, Kundalpadi Peraje, Naladi, Yevakapadi, Chelavara, Karada.

Fairs: Balamuri Fair: Balamuri near Murnad is 18 kms. away from Madikeri. One of the sacred places for the Kodavas, the well-known pilgrimage centre is on the bank of the Cauvery. It is here that the river changes her course to the right in a crescent curve. Hence, the name 'Balamuri'. From ancient times, it was known as 'Valampuri' a famous Shaiva centre.

Bhagandeshwara Temple Fair: It is held at Bhagandeshwara in Kodagu area in about the month of November-December every year. Bhagandeshwara is a well known pilgrimage centre of sanctity not only for the Kodavas but also for other Hindus and is 29 kms. away from Madikeri.

Mahalingeshwara Fair: It is held at Paluru near Kodagu in about the month of May every year. Paluru is an ancient pilgrimage centre on the bank of the river Cauvery and is about 18 kms. from Madikeri, near Napokalu. The ancient name according to an eleventh century inscription found here is Palayuru. The temple of Mahali ngeshwara is built in the Kerala style of architecture.

Pir Hazarat Ganje Gauhar Ali Shah Urs: It is held at Madikeri near Kodagu in the month of Ramzan.

Arif-ul-Hassa Urf Syed Sikander Ali Shah Urs; Arif-Ul-Ha ssa Urf Syed Sikander Ali Shah Urs was held at Madikeri in the month of Rabia-Ul-Aulal.

Villages: 67 **Inhabited:** 67 **Uninhabited:** 0

Ranking	District	State	National
Area	2	37	165
Population	3	157	3169
Sex Ratio	2	22	937
Child Sex Ratio	1	3	315
Literacy Rate	1	3	242
Density	2	91	6245
Work Participation Rate	3	172	2126

Gram Panchayats:

Karike, Peraje, Chembu, Sampaje, Galibeedu, Makkandur, Kalakeri Nidugane, Made, Kundacheri, Bhagamandala, Bengooru, Bettageri, Kadagadalu, Maragodu, Hakathoor, Kanthur, Hoddur, Napoklu, Ballamavati, Kunjila, Konanjageri, Nariyandada.

Amenities:

Education: Primary School in 67 villages, Middle school in 50 villages, Matriculation or Secondary School in 18 villages, namely Karike, Bhagamandala, Bengooru, Bettageri, Kundalpadi Peraje, Melchembu, Sampaje, Made, Hakathoor, Galibeedu, Maragodu, Kanthur, Nelji, Kunjila, Napoklu, Konanjageri, Nariyandada, Arapattu. Higher Secondary or Pre University Courses or Intermediate or Junior College in 10 villages of the CD Block,, namely Bhagamandala, Bengooru, Sampaje, Made, Galibeedu, Maragodu, Kanthur, Ballamavati, Yemmemadu, Napoklu.

College in 2 villages, Adult Literacy Center in 4 villages., Colleges are in villages, namely Bhagamandala, M. Badaga.

Medical: Hospital in 3 villages, Dispensary in 7 villages, Health Center in 6 villages, Sub Center in 37 villages, Maternity and Child Welfare Center in 1 village, Community health workers in 0 village.

The Villages having Hospital or Dispensary or Health Center are Karike, Bhagamandala, Sampaje, Kanthur, Peroor, Ballamavati, Bethu.

Drinking Water: Tap water in 45 villages, Tank water in 14 villages, Well water in 61 villages, Tubewell in 32 villages and more than one source in 64 villages.

Bank: Banking facility in 34 villages, namely, Karike, Thannimani, Cherangala, Sannapulikotu (No.2) Kolagadalu, B.Badaga, Melchembu, Heravanadu, Mekeri Hakathoor, Kalooru, Hammiyala, Mukkodlu, Galibeedu Karnangeri, Ibnivalvadi (Rural), Kadagadalu Maragodu, Hoskeri, Kanthur, Kumbaladalu, Hodavada Kiggalu, Sodluru Kattemadu, Arekadu, Naladi Yevakapadi, Kokeri, Kolakeri, Balamuri, Kirundadu Nariyandada, Karada, Arapattu.

Credit Society in 45 villages Agricultural Credit Society in 43 Non-Agricultural Credit Society in 7 villages.

Others: Power supply in 67 villages, Cinema hall in 0 village, sport club in 10 villages, Stadium or Auditorium or Communit Hall in 1 village, Post Office in 54 villages.

There are 61 villages having bus facilities.

Villages with most of facilities: Karike Thannimani, Cherangala, Sannapulikotu (No.2) Kolagadalu, Melchembu, Mekeri, Hakathoor, Kalooru Mukkodlu, Galibeedu, Ibnivalvadi (Rural), Kanthur Sodluru Kattemadu, Arekadu, Yevakapadi, Nariyandada.

Villages without Amenities (Education): None..

Scheduled Castes: Out of the total population of 109516 persons, 11408 persons (10.42%) belong to Scheduled Castes. The villages having less than 10% SC population are Thannimani, Cherangala, Sannapulikotu (No.2) Bhagamandala, Kopatti, Bettathur, Kolagadalu Singathuru, B.Badaga, Aiyangeri, Kundalpadi Peraje Melchembu, Sampaje, Made, Katakeri (Rural), Mekeri Biligeri, Kalooru, Hammiyala, Mukkodlu, Monnangeri Maragodu, Hodavada, Naladi, Peroor, Ballamavati Yemmemadu, Nelji, Kunjila, Kokeri, Kolakeri, Napoklu Paloor, Bethu, Kirundadu, Arapattu.

The village having more than 50% SC population is None.

Sex ratio of Scheduled Caste population is 509.

Scheduled Castes Literates and Illiterates by Sex:

	Persons	Males	Females
Literate	5,920	3,228	2,692
Illiterate	5,488	2,371	3,117
Literacy rate	60.2	67.0	53.7
Graduate	64	45	19

Scheduled Castes (Dominant):

Adi Karnataka, Pale, Moger, Holaya etc., Bhovi

For their cultural identity please see Appendix-I

Villages without Scheduled Castes: There are 4 villages without any scheduled caste population.

Scheduled Tribes: Out of the total population of 109516 persons, 6358 persons (5.81%) belong to Scheduled Tribes. The villages having less than 10% ST population are Cherangala, Sannapulikotu (No.2), Kundacheri Kopatti, Kolagadalu, Singathuru, B.Badaga, Bengooru Karugunda, Bettageri, Aiyangeri, Katakeri (Rural) Heravanadu, Aruvathoklu, Mekeri, Kaggodlu, Hakathoor Kalooru, Hammiyala, Mukkodlu Kalakeri Nidugane (Rural), Hebbettageri, Makkandur Karnangeri, Ibnivalvadi (Rural), Kadagadalu Maragodu, Hoskeri, Kanthur, Mutharmudi, Kumbaladalu Hodavada, Hoddur, M. Badaga , Kiggalu, Arekadu Peroor, Ballamavati, Yemmemadu, Nelji, Kunjila Chelavara, Kokeri, Kolakeri, Napoklu, Paloor, Bethu Balamuri, Konanjageri, Kirundadu, Nariyandada Arapattu.

The villages having more than 50% ST population are None.

Sex ratio of Scheduled tribe population is 502.

Scheduled Tribes Literates and Illiterates by Sex:

	Persons	Males	Females
Literate	3,248	1,790	1,458
Illiterate	3,110	1,376	1,734
Literacy rate	59.1	65.3	53.0
Graduate	31	20	11

Scheduled Tribes (Dominant):

Maratha, Kudiya etc., Naikda etc., Yerava Jenu Kuruba

For their cultural identity please see Appendix-II

Villages without Scheduled Tribes: There are 2 villages without any scheduled tribe population.

Literates and Illiterates by Sex (Total Population):

	Persons	Males	Females
Literate	77,440	40,944	36,496
Illiterate	32,076	13,593	18,483
Literacy rate	81	86	76
Graduate	3,804	2,207	1,597

Agriculture: ***Distribution of villages according to land use:*** Out of 67 villages, Total area (in hectare) is 143535, out of that 33.35 percent is cultivable and 7.26 percent of the cultivable area is irrigated.

Sources of Irrigation (Hectares): Government Canal 0, Private Canal 0, Well without Electricity 0, Well with Electricity 3.49, Tubewell without Electricity 847.44, Tubewell with Electricity 243.7, Tank 584.89, River 883.22, Lake 0, Waterfall 0, Others 914.52.

Villages with population of 5000 to 9999: None

Villages with population of 10000 and above: None

Distribution of Workers:

	Persons	Males	Females	WPR
Cultivators	4,935	3,202	1,733	8.98
Agricultural Labour	2,339	1,307	1,032	4.26
Household Industry	764	277	487	1.39
Other Workers	46,932	29,038	17,894	85.38
Main Workers	49,189	31,568	17,621	89.48
Marginal Workers	5,781	2,256	3,525	10.52
Total Workers	54,970	33,824	21,146	

Religion: Major Religious Communities:

	Persons	Males	Females	Sex Ratio
Hindu (80.63%)	88,303	43,863	44,440	1,013
Muslim (17.48%)	19,139	9,588	9,551	996
Christian (1.81%)	1,980	1,032	948	919
Sikh (0.01%)	7	2	5	2,500
Buddhists (0.01%)	6	4	2	500
Jain (0.03%)	29	17	12	706

Agewise Data:

	Persons	Males	Females	Sex Ratio
All ages	109,516	54,537	54,979	1008
0-14	31,240	15,758	15,482	982
15-44	52,822	25,900	26,922	1039
45-79	24,305	12,350	11,955	968
80+	1,125	518	607	1172
Age not stated	24	11	13	1182

Languages (Dominant):

Kannada, Coorgi/Kodagu, Malayalam, Tulu, Tamil

Disabled Population:

	Persons	Males	Females	%
Total Disabled	1,465	797	668	
In Seeing	515	271	244	35.15
In Speech	159	84	75	10.85
In Hearing	147	81	66	10.03
In Movement	434	263	171	29.62
Mentally	210	98	112	14.33

MAGADI

Magadi C.D. Block lies in the northern part of Bangalore Rural district. It is a part of Magadi tehsil. The Block is located at a distance of 49 kms. from district headqu arters (Bangalore). There are 286 villages in the block with the total population of 175,962 persons. Area of the C.D. Block is 793.61 sq. kms. It is bounded by distr ict Tumkur on north and west, taluk Ramanagaram on south, taluk Nelamangala and district Bangalore on east.

Communications:

Roadways : N.H-48: Direction- Hassan to Nelamangala, Nearest Villages- Raghunathapura, Baganigerekaval, Bagan igere, Dandenahalli, Talekere, Siddapura, Machohalli, Madigondanahalli, Kannasandra, Narasandra, Surappanahal li, Marur, Tubarapalya, Soluru, Kannasandra, Lakkenahalli, Koramangala, Beeravara, Kudaluru. S.H-3: Direction- Shivaganga to Ramanagaram, Nearest Villages- Alur, Mooga nahalli, Banavadi, Udakunte, Muppenahalli, Kanikenahalli, Goruru, Lingenahalli, Beeravara, Kudaluru, Gudemaranaha lli, Shidaganahalli, Harthi, Singripalya, Belagumba, Thim masandra, Thirumale, Gummasandra, Melanahalli, Somak kanamutta, Attingere, Matha, Nayakanapalya, Hanchikuppe, Karlamangala, Guddahalli, Savanadurga State Forest. S.H-17 E: Direction- Magadi to Bangalore, Nearest Villa ges- Thirumale, Vengalappanahalli, Maralagondala, Chikkat horepalya, Thagachaguppe, Bachenahatti, Adakamaranahalli, Varadenahalli, Shanubhoganahalli, Kallur, Karlamangala.

River: Arkavati Nadi- Nearest Villages- Kallur, Singadas anahalli, Veerapura, Doddamaskal, Chikkamaskal, Awerahalli, Manchanabele.

Reserved Forest: (Bantara Kuppe R.F.): Nearest Villages- Torechannohalli, Malluru, Motagondanahalli, Bommanahalli, Bhantrakuppe, Mummenahalli, Gollarapalya, Bachenahatti.

Annual Rainfall: Normal Rianfall 876.62 mm.

Ground Water: Availability of the Ground Water in the Basin is (Information not avablable) H.A.M. and the utilization is (Information not avablable) H.A.M. It belongs to (Information not avablable) category. Depth to water level 5 to 20 meter below the ground. Most of the wells go down in summer months, according to the Ground Water Estimation Committee.

Natural Division : It falls in Cauvery Forested Region of the Southern Karnataka Plateau.

Administration:

Division: Bangalore. Parliamentary Constituency: 27 Bangalore- IV (SC), 23 Bangalore Rural. District: Bangal ore. Taluka: Magadi. Assembly Constituency: 181 Nelamangala (SC), 182 Magadi. Gram Panchayat: 32.

Regional Area Development Boards: The Bailu Seeme Area Development Board.

Villages: 286 **Inhabited:** 274 **Uninhabited:** 12

Ranking	District	State	National
Area	2	124	741
Population	5	111	1111
Sex Ratio	2	44	1529
Child Sex Ratio	2	68	2604
Literacy Rate	6	81	2633
Density	1	61	4395
Work Participation Rate	7	63	1595

Gram Panchayats:

Chikkahalli, Kannanur, Srigiripura, Banavadi, Bittasandra, Lakkenahalli, Motagondanahalli, Gudemaranahalli, Soluru, Madigondanahalli, Adarangi, Kudur, Hulikal, Hullenahalli, Shankighatta, Thippasandra, Biskuru, Narasandra, Chikkamudigere, Kalari Kaval, Kalya, Thaggikuppe, Belagumba, Nethenahalli, Sathanur, Agalakote, Seegekuppe, Mathikere, Ajjanahalli, Madabal, Hanchikuppe, Bachenahatti.

Amenities:

Education: Primary School in 159 villages, Middle school in 101 villages, Matriculation or Secondary School in 31 villages, namely Gangonahalli, Hullenahalli, Hebbalalu, Thippasandra, Baganigere, Sugganahalli, Chikkamaskal, Srigiripura, Hulikal, Kudur, Madigondanahalli, Narasandra, Biskuru, Alur, Kempapura, Yannegere, Arasinakunte, Soluru, Gudemaranahalli, Motagondanahalli, Kalya, Kempasagara, Bachenahatti, Madabal, Hulikatte, Chakrabavi, Gattipura, Seegekuppe, Ajjanahalli, Hanchikuppe, Manchanabele. Higher Secondary or Pre University Courses or Inter- mediate or Junior College in 2 villages of the CD Block,, namely Hullenahalli, Hulikatte. College in 1 village, Adult Literacy Center in 5 villages., College is in village, namely Soluru.

Medical: Hospital in 0 village, Dispensary in 4 villages, Health Center in 15 villages, Sub Center in 49 villages, Maternity and Child Welfare Center in 0 village, Community health workers in 6 villages. The Villages having Hospital or Dispensary or Health Center are Gundigere, Banavadi, Motagondanahalli,

Chakrabavi, Gejjagaraguppe, Hanchikuppe.

Drinking Water: Tap water in 38 villages, Tank water in 53 villages, Well water in 73 villages, Tubewell in 166 villages and more than one source in 223 villages.

Bank: Banking facility in 8 villages, namely, Tavarekere, Thippasandra, Hulikal, Kudur, Narasandra Soluru, Gudemaranahalli, Hanchikuppe.

Credit Society in 56 villages Agricultural Credit Society in 36 Non-Agricultural Credit Society in 0 village.

Others: Power supply in 272 villages, Cinema hall in 0 village, sport club in 0 village, Stadium or Auditorium or Community Hall in 274 villages, Post Office in 54 villages.

There are 191 villages having bus facilities.

Villages with most of facilities: Tavarekere Thippasandra, Hulikal, Kudur, Narasandra, Soluru Gudemaranahalli, Hanchikuppe.

Villages without amenities (Education): Honnapura, Raghuvanapalya, Sannenahalli, Yallapura, Palyadahalli, Sankighatta Kaval, Kamasagara, Annaiahsastripalya, Baganigerekaval, Dandenahalli, Siddapura, Iyandahalli, Marisomanahalli, Janigere, Srinivasapura, Dollenahalli, Mallappanahalli, Kempapura, Thoreramanahalli, Thammenahalli, Parvathapura, Byrapura, Aladakatte, Bisalahalli, K.G.Krishnapura, Muthasagara, Kaduramanahalli, Surappanahalli, Kempohalli, Hanumapura, Mylanahalli, Mallapura, Byrasandra, Muppenahalli, Hemapura, Rangenahalli, Kuppemala, Chikkenahalli, Gangenapura, Bittasandra, Thimmasandra, Ombathanakunte, Tubarapalya, Lingenahalli, Parvathapalya, Hosahalli, Beeravara, Kudaluru, Somedevanahalli, Byadarahalli, Pemmanahalli, Kodihalli, Thirumalapura, Kothagondanahalli, Thorechannohalli, Marenahalli, Bommanahalli, Varadohalli, Kalari, Hujagal, Rangenahalli, Shidaganahalli, Kanchugaranahalli, Gudepalya, Upparthi, Halashettihalli, Juttanahalli, Harohalli, Voddarapalya, Hosahalli, Karagadahalli, Bettadasipalya, Singripalya, Magadi (Rural), Thatavalu, Viswanathapura, Dandigepura, Kondahalli, Balekatte, Melanahalli, Somakkanamutta, Vengalappanahalli, Gollarapalya, Adakamaranahalli, Varadenahalli, Singadasanahalli, Pura (Gattipura), Subbasastripalya, Karlahalli, Basavenahalli, Thyagadarepalya, Sannenahalli, Huluvenahalli, Maraludevanapura, Varthenahalli, Mallenahalli, Alalakuppe, Sadamaranahalli, Koramangala, S.Bydarahalli, Lakkasandra, Kotagarahalli, Annekaranahalli, Kalyanadevramatha, Rangacharipalya, Papasastripalya, Guddahalli, Polohalli, Savanadurga State Forest, Nelapatna, Doddamaskal, Chikkamaskal, Awerahalli..

Scheduled Castes: Out of the total population of 177386 persons, 35690 persons (20.12%) belong to Scheduled Castes. The villages having less than 10% SC population are Chikkahalli, Doddahalli, Basavanapalya, Gangonahalli Raghuvanapalya, Narayanapura, Kalyani Kaval Annaiahsastripalya, Raghunathapura, Baganigerekaval Siddapura, Angajanahalli, Kenchanahalli Doddasomanahalli, Janigere, Srinivasapura Mallasandra, Chikkamaskal, Dollenahalli, Hosahalli Gundigere, Hanchibasavanapalya, Thammenahalli Gollahalli, Kenchanapura, Aladakatte Madigondanahalli, Narasandra, Marur, Kempohalli Manniganahalli, Kalluhattipalya, Kempapura Yannegere, Chikkenahalli, Gangenapura, Kanikenahalli Ramanahalli, Tubarapalya, Parvathapalya, Koramangala Somedevanahalli, Hyaganahalli, Byadarahalli Uddandahalli, Marikuppe, Naganahalli, Thirumalapura Kothagondanahalli, Marenahalli, Bommanahalli Varadohalli, Kodipalya, Rangenahalli Kanchugaranahalli, Gudepalya, Kalya, Kalari Kaval Halashettihalli, Voddarapalya, Bettadasipalya Byadarahalli, Thimmasandra, Magadi (Rural), Sathanur Donakuppe, Agalakote, Dandigepura, Balekatte Udavigere, Nethenahalli, Gummasandra, Melanahalli Somakkanamutta, Shambhudevanahalli, Karlahalli Basavenahalli, Thyagadarepalya, Balenahalli Maraludevanapura, Sadamaranahalli, Neralavadi Gerahalli, Annekaranahalli, Nayakanapalya Rangacharipalya, Papasastripalya, Karlamangala Guddahalli, Polohalli, Veerapura, Dabbaguli.

The villages having more than 50% SC population are Yallapura, Sankighatta Kaval, Marisomanahalli Kaduramanahalli, Hanumapura, Mallapura, Muppenahalli Narasapura, Rangenahalli, Kalyanapura, Kodihalli Thorechannohalli, Bhantrakuppe, Harohalli Karagadahalli, Singripalya, Viswanathapura Vengalappanahalli, Chikkathorepalya, Sannenahalli Heligehalli, Lakkasandra, Kalyanadevramatha Doddamaskal, Manchanabele.

Sex ratio of Scheduled Caste population is 500.

Scheduled Castes Literates and Illiterates by Sex:

	Persons	Males	Females
Literate	16,440	9,845	6,595
Illiterate	19,250	7,988	11,262
Literacy rate	52.7	63.2	42.3
Graduate	247	213	34

Scheduled Castes (Dominant):

Madiga, Adi Karnataka, Adi Dravida, Bhovi Chalavadi etc.

For their cultural identity please see Appendix-I

Villages without Scheduled Castes: There are 51 villages without any scheduled caste population.

Scheduled Tribes: Out of the total population of 177386 persons, 4951 persons (2.79%) belong to Scheduled Tribes. The villages having less than 10% ST population are Chikkahalli, Doddahalli, Basavanapalya, Gangonahalli Raghuvanapalya, Sannenahalli, Yallapura Beechanahalli, Hullenahalli, Hebbalalu Muthagadahalli, Palyadahalli, Sankighatta Kaval Neralekere, Narayanapura, Kalyani Kaval, Chikkakalya Kamasagara, Thippasandra, Annaiahsastripalya Raghunathapura, Baganigerekaval, Baganigere Dandenahalli, Talekere, Siddapura, Machohalli Kempapura, Angajanahalli, Doddamudigere, Iyandahalli Chikkamudigere, Kalkere, Kenchanahalli Marisomanahalli, Doddasomanahalli, Janigere Srinivasapura, Mallasandra, Shivanasandra Sugganahalli, Kenkere, Kannanur, Chowdibegur Naganahalli, Chikkamaskal, Dollenahalli, Hosahalli Veerasagara, Srigiripura, Mallappanahalli Marasandra, Hulikal, Gundigere, Kempapura Bettahalli, Adarangi, Veerapura, Ajjahalli, Kagimadu Thoreramanahalli, Hanchibasavanapalya, Thammenahalli Kudur, Lakkenahalli, Kodihalli, Gollahalli, Byrapura Mallligunte, Kenchanapura, Aladakatte Madigondanahalli, Kannasandra, Narasandra Bisalahalli, K.G.Krishnapura, Muthasagara, Biskuru Kaduramanahalli, Surappanahalli, Marur, Dommanakatte Kempohalli, Manniganahalli, Chilur, Hanumapura Mylanahalli, Alur, Mooganahalli, Mallapura Shiraganahalli, Banavadi, Byrasandra, Udakunte Kalluhattipalya, Palanahalli, Shanthapura Muppenahalli, Kempapura, Narasapura, Hemapura Rangenahalli, Kuppemala, Yannegere, Chikkenahalli Vaddarahalli, Gangenapura, Bittasandra Kanikenahalli, Goruru, Ramanahalli, Thattekere Channohalli, Thimmasandra, Arasinakunte Ombathanakunte, Tubarapalya, Soluru, Lingenahalli Parvathapalya, Kannasandra, Lakkenahalli, Hosahalli Koramangala, Beeravara, Kudaluru, Chikkasoluru Kalyanapura, Somedevanahalli, Hyaganahalli Byadarahalli, Gudemaranahalli, Garageswarapura Marikuppe, Basavenahalli, Pemmanahalli, Naganahalli Thirumalapura, Kothagondanahalli, Thorechannohalli Malluru, Marenahalli, Motagondanahalli, Bommanahalli Bhantrakuppe, Mummenahalli, Varadohalli, Kalari Kodipalya, Halasinganahalli, Hujagal, Nagasettihalli Byalakere, Rangenahalli, Shidaganahalli, Harthi Kanchugaranahalli, Gudepalya, Dubbagottige Thaggikuppe, Mayanaikanahalli, Vitalapura, Kalya Basavapatna, Kalari Kaval, Upparthi, Sripathihalli Halashettihalli, Juttanahalli, Harohalli Voddarapalya, Chandurayanahalli, Hosahalli Karagadahalli, Bychapura, Bettadasipalya Singripalya, Belagumba, Byadarahalli, Panakanakallu Thimmasandra, Thirumale, Magadi (Rural), Thatavalu Viswanathapura, Kempasagara, Sathanur, Donakuppe Halasabele, Agalakote, Dandigepura, Tubinakere Kondahalli, Balekatte, Udavigere, Nethenahalli Gummasandra, Melanahalli, Somakkanamutta Vengalappanahalli, Maralagondala, Chikkathorepalya Gollarapalya, Thagachaguppe, Bachenahatti Adakamaranahalli, Varadenahalli, Shanubhoganahalli Kallur, Singadasanahalli, Managallu, Madabal Pura (Gattipura), Subbasastripalya, Karlahalli Basavenahalli, Thyagadarepalya, Nagamangala Balenahalli, Huluvenahalli, Heligehalli, Mathikere Maraludevanapura, Hulikatte, Varthenahalli Alalakuppe, Chakrabavi, Gattipura, Sadamaranahalli Koramangala, Seegekuppe, Kalludevanahalli S.Bydarahalli, Belagavadi, Gejjagaraguppe Lakkasandra, Neralavadi, Kotagarahalli, Gerahalli Guddalahalli, Ajjanahalli, Annekaranahalli Attingere, Kalyanadevramatha, Hanchikuppe Rangacharipalya, Papasastripalya, Karlamangala Guddahalli, Polohalli, Veerapura, Doddamaskal Chikkamaskal, Awerahalli, Dabbaguli, Manchanabele.

The villages having more than 50% ST population are None.

Sex ratio of Scheduled tribe population is 495.

Scheduled Tribes Literates and Illiterates by Sex:

	Persons	Males	Females
Literate	2,352	1,391	961
Illiterate	2,599	1,109	1,490
Literacy rate	54.0	63.3	44.6
Graduate	46	34	12

Scheduled Tribes (Dominant):

Naikda etc., Iruliga, Generic Tribes etc., Soligaru Meda

For their cultural identity please see Appendix-II

Villages without Scheduled Tribes: There are 203 villages without any scheduled tribe population.

Literates and Illiterates by Sex (Total Population):

	Persons	Males	Females
Literate	95,741	56,534	39,207
Illiterate	81,645	32,544	49,101
Literacy rate	61	72	50
Graduate	2,443	2,010	433

Agriculture: ***Distribution of villages according to land use:***

Out of 286 villages, Total area (in hectare) is 79361, out of that 61.9 percent is cultivable and 17.29 percent of the cultivable area is irrigated.

Sources of Irrigation (Hectares): Government Canal 710.72, Private Canal 0, Well without Electricity 145.39, Well with Electricity 901.2, Tubewell without Electricity 67.52, Tubewell with Electricity 1820.73, Tank 3138.07, River 45.73, Lake 4.32, Waterfall 0, Others 1657.86.

Villages with population of 5000 to 9999: Kudur.

Villages with population of 10000 and above: None

Distribution of Workers:

	Persons	Males	Females	WPR
Cultivators	56,443	35,262	21,181	59.55
Agricultural Labour	19,881	6,150	13,731	20.98
Household Industry	4,059	2,168	1,891	4.28
Other Workers	14,395	10,455	3,940	15.19
Main Workers	63,712	48,356	15,356	67.22
Marginal Workers	31,066	5,679	25,387	32.78
Total Workers	94,778	54,035	40,743	

Religion: Major Religious Communities:

	Persons	Males	Females	Sex Ratio
Hindu (93.18%)	165,280	82,935	82,345	993
Muslim (5.57%)	9,876	5,012	4,864	970
Christian (0.29%)	522	262	260	992
Sikh (0%)	8	3	5	1,667
Buddhists (0.03%)	52	24	28	1,167
Jain (0.17%)	293	144	149	1,035

Agewise Data:

	Persons	Males	Females	Sex Ratio
All ages	177,386	89,078	88,308	991
0-14	51,155	25,979	25,176	969
15-44	81,767	40,458	41,309	1021
45-79	41,745	21,387	20,358	952
80+	2,522	1,153	1,369	1187
Age not stated	197	101	96	950

Languages (Dominant):

Kannada, Urdu, Telugu, Marathi, Gujarati

Disabled Population:

	Persons	Males	Females	%
Total Disabled	4,198	2,398	1,800	
In Seeing	2,006	1,060	946	47.78
In Speech	424	230	194	10.1
In Hearing	261	140	121	6.22
In Movement	1,141	760	381	27.18
Mentally	366	208	158	8.72

MALAVALLI

Malavalli C.D. Block lies in the south-eastern part of Mandya district. It is a part of Malavalli taluk. The Block is located at a distance of 29 kms. from district headquarters (Mandya). There are 186 villages in the block with the total population of 245,545 persons. Area of the C.D. Block is 807.38 sq. kms. It is bounded by taluks Mandya, Maddur, and district Bangalore Rural on north, districts Mysore and Chamarajanagar on south, district Bangalore Rural on east, district Mysore and taluk Mandya on west.

Communications:

Roadways : NH-209: Direction- Malavalli to Kollegal to Kanakapura, Nearest Villages- Malavalli(Rural), Nidaghat ta, Ankanahalli, Gowdagere, Hadli, Hullagala, Banasamudra, Halasahalli, Basavanpura, Nadakalapura, Megalapura, Attuvanahalli, Marehalli, Dalavaikodihalli, Deveerahalli, Gundapura, Hosapetebasavapura, Hagadur, Halaguru, Chillapura, Thorekadanahalli, Pandithahalli, Bachanahalli, Mallikyathanahalli, Belakavadi, Hosahalli, Dasanadoddi. SH-33: Direction- Mddur to Malavalli, Nearest Villages- Talagavadi, Kagepura, Koregala, Maganur, Nelamakanahalli, Gulagatta, Malavalli(Rural). SH-86: Direction- Mysore to Malavalli, Nearest Villages- Settahalli, Muganakoppalu, Nenanuru, Markalu, Kirugavalu, Honaganahalli, Kalkuni, Huvinakoppalu, Sujjalur, Uppanahalli, Yamaduru, Ragibom manahalli.

River: Cauvery Nadi- Nearest Villages- Ganalu, Basavego wdanadoddi, Muthathi, Netkal, Belakavadi, Purigali, Maral ahalli, Ballagere, Somanahalli. Shimsha Nadi- Nearest Villages- Chandupura, M.Shivapura, Huskur, Kaladevanahal li, Hosapura, Aslishivapura, Belathur, Yethambadi, Anthar avalli, Dadamahalli, Kiragasur, Banasamudra, Kaggalipura, Konnapura, Halasahalli, Dhanagur, Savandipura, Sagyasar agur, Ankanahalli, Maragowdanahalli, Thorekadanahalli, Halagapura, Madahalli, Ganalu, Basavana Betta Forest.

Canal: Nearest Villages- Mikkere, Bheemanahalli, Hittana halli, Muganakoppalu, Ganiganapura, Banduru, Kallarepura, Nenanuru, Doranahalli, Upanahalli, Yamaduru, Ragibomma nahalli, Avverahalli, Kebbepura, Maliyur, Jogipura, Agasa napura, Banagahalli, Huskur, Kaladevanahalli, Antharavalli, Hullahalli, Hullagala, Dadamahalli, Kiragasur, Banasam udra, Konnapura, Halasahalli, Dhanagur, Gramadevatepura, Basavanpura, Nadakalapura, Alada Halli, Gajanur, Voddar ahalli, Marehalli, Ravani, Devalinganapura, Doddaboovalli, Kyathanahalli, Kundur, Pandithahalli, Bachanahalli, Belakavadi, Kiragasur, Kadabahalli, Saraguru, Hanavadi, Purigali, Hullamballi, Ballagere, Somanahalli, Kaggalipura.

Reserved Forest: (Basavanabetta R.F.): Nearest Villags- Dhana gur, Ganalu, Bydarahalli, Solaba, Basavanahalli, Dalanaka tte, Basavegowdanadoddi, Talavadi, Majjigemallanahatti, Muthathi.

Annual Rainfall: Normal Rianfall 703.8 mm.

Ground Water: Availability of the Ground Water in the Basin is 5852.31 H.A.M. and the utilization is 4089.

54 H.A.M. It belongs to Over Expoited category. Depth to water level 5 to 20 meter below the ground. Most of the wells go down in summer months, according to the Ground Water Estimation Committee.

Soils: Red Sandy Loams to Red Clay Loam.

Natural Division : It falls partly in Shimsha Basin and Cauvery Forested Tract of the Southern Karnataka Plateau.

Administration:

Division: Mysore. Parliamentary Constituency: 20 Mandya. District: Mandya. Taluka: Malavalli. Assembly Constitue ncy: 186 Malavalli (SC). Gram Panchayat: 39.

Fairs:

Lakshminarasimhia Jatra: It is held at Marehalli near Mandya. Marehalli is about a kilometre from Malavalli town. It appears to be an old agrahara town. The large Lakshminarasimha temple of this place is called "Rajashr aya-Vinnagaram" in an inscription. "Rajashraya" being a title of the Chola king Rajaraja (985-1012), the temple seems to have been built by him or during his reign. The sukhanasi has still the original short Chola pillars. In a shrine to the north of the pond, there are some early Chalukyan pillars also. It has a handsome figure of Lakshmi-Narasimha seated in sukhasana. The temple was evidently restored during the Hoysala and Vijayanagar days. The annual jatra held during the month of May or June in connection with Rathothsava of the temple attracts a large number of people.

Villages: 186 **Inhabited:** 168 **Uninhabited:** 18

Ranking	District	State	National
Area	3	120	713
Population	3	41	261
Sex Ratio	7	109	2699
Child Sex Ratio	3	132	3835
Literacy Rate	7	132	3994
Density	6	131	3482
Work Participation Rate	4	23	3092

Gram Panchayats:

Chikkamulagudu, Mikkere, Hittanahalli, Dugganahalli, Banduru, Thalagavadi, Nelamakanahalli, Kandegala, Agasanapura, Huskur, Yethambadi, Nittur, Lingapatna, Dalavaikodihalli, Hosaperebasavapura, Halaguru, Thorekadanahalli, Bydarahalli, Dhanagur, Halasahalli, Hadli, Nidaghatta, Marehalli, Ragibommanahalli, Settahalli, Kirugavalu, Bendaravadi, Kalkuni, Sujjalur, Kyathanahalli, Kundur, Chottanahalli, Pandithahalli, Belakavadi, Hosahalli, Boppagowdanapura, Saraguru, Purigali, Kaggalipura.

Amenities:

Education: Primary School in 157 villages, Middle school in 118 villages, Matriculation or Secondary School in 38 villages, namely Veerajipura, Hittanahalli, Dugganahalli, Thalagavadi, Maganur, Banduru, Nenanuru, Kirugavalu, Kalkuni, Sujjalur, Uppanahalli, Ragibommanahalli, Nelamakanahalli, Kandegala, Malavalli(Rural), Hadli, Kodipura, Agasanapura, Yethambadi, Halasahalli, Gajanur, Kunthur, Nittur, Maragowdanahalli, Dalavaikodihalli, Halaguru, Thorekadanahalli, Ganalu, Bydarahalli, Doddaboovalli, Kundur, Pandithahalli, Chottanahalli, Netkal, Belakavadi, Boppagowdanapura, Saraguru, Purigali.

Higher Secondary or Pre University Courses or Intermediate or Junior College in 5 villages of the CD Block,, namely Veerajipura, Kirugavalu, Malavalli(Rural), Halaguru, Belakavadi.

College in 3 villages, Adult Literacy Center in 1 village., Colleges are in villages, namely Veerajipura, Kirugavalu, Purigali.

Medical: Hospital in 26 villages, Dispensary in 9 villages, Health Center in 22 villages, Sub Center in 49 villages, Maternity and Child Welfare Center in 6 villages, Community health workers in 36 villages.

The Villages having Hospital or Dispensary or Health Center are Chikkamulagudu, Bheemanahalli, Hittanahalli, Dugganahalli, Banduru, Kirugavalu, Ragibommanahalli, Kandegala, Agasanapura, Yethambadi, Dadamahalli, Nittur, Dalavaikodihalli, Halaguru, Chillapura, Doddaboovalli, Kundur, Shiramalli, Manchanapura, Chandahalli, Hebbani, Kanikahalli, Udape Boovalli, Muttanahalli, Saraguru, Purigali, Ballagere, Kodagahalli, Haladasanahalli.

Drinking Water: Tap water in 125 villages, Tank water in 90 villages, Well water in 150 villages, Tubewell in 77 villages and more than one source in 163 villages.

Bank: Banking facility in 14 villages, namely, Chikkamulagudu, Hittanahalli, Thalagavadi Kirugavalu, Kalkuni, Amrutheswaranahalli, Kodipura Halasahalli, Dhanagur, Megalapura, Halaguru Bydarahalli, Belakavadi, Purigali.

Credit Society in 47 villages Agricultural Credit Society in 33 Non-Agricultural Credit Society in 9 villages.

Others: Power supply in 166 villages, Cinema hall in 11 village sport club in 1 village, Stadium or Auditorium or Community Hall in 0 village, Post Office in 49 villages.

There are 116 villages having bus facilities.

Villages with most of facilities: Chikkamulagudu Hittanahalli, Kirugavalu, Kalkuni, Kodipura Halasahalli, Dhanagur, Halaguru, Bydarahalli Belakavadi, Purigali.

Villages without amenities (Education):

Honaganahalli, Devalinganapura, Ankanahalli,

Halagapura, Muthalakatte, Dalanakatte, Mallikyathanahalli, Malagalali, Udape Boovalli..

Scheduled Castes: Out of the total population of 245958 persons, 49625 persons (20.18%) belong to Scheduled Castes. The villages having less than 10% SC population are Veerajipura, Maganahalli, Bheemanahalli, Thalagavadi Muganakoppalu, Ganiganapura, Madahalli, Banduru Uppanahalli, Hangrapura, Surakahalli Nelamakanahalli, Appugowdana Halli, Kaluveeranahalli Gulagatta, Malavalli(Rural), Ankanahalli Amrutheswaranahalli, Kodipura, Banagahalli Yethambadi, Hullahalli, Channipura, Hullagala Linganapura, Gramadevathepura, Kamsagara, Thuraganur Alada Halli, Devalinganapura, Savandipura Lingapatna, Nittur, Nitthur Kodihalli, Karadahalli Handanahalli, Deveerahalli, Kempainadoddi Gollarahalli, Chikkayelachagere, Halagapura Madahalli, Muthalakatte, Muthathi, Kundur Chandahalli, Dabbahalli, Mallikyathanahalli Nanjanayanapura, Hebbani, Manchanahalli, Dasanadoddi Thenkahalli, Kadabahalli, Thigadahalli.

The villages having more than 50% SC population are Settahalli, Huvinakoppalu, Ganaganuru, Koonanapura Konnapura, Attuvanahalli, Juganahalli, Chillapura Solaba, Dalanakatte, Basavegowdanadoddi, Shiramalli Bachanahalli, Manchanapura, Dyavapatna, Malagalali Mallinathapura, Hanavadi, Ballagere.

Sex ratio of Scheduled Caste population is 497.

Scheduled Castes Literates and Illiterates by Sex:

	Persons	Males	Females
Literate	23,676	13,949	9,727
Illiterate	25,949	10,988	14,961
Literacy rate	54.2	63.6	44.7
Graduate	1,006	849	157

Scheduled Castes (Dominant):

Adi Karnataka, Madiga, Bhovi, Generic Castes etc. Korama

For their cultural identity please see Appendix-I

Villages without Scheduled Castes: There are 46 villages without any scheduled caste population.

Scheduled Tribes: Out of the total population of 245958 persons, 1435 persons (0.58%) belong to Scheduled Tribes. The villages having less than 10% ST population are Chikkamulagudu, Veerajipura, Maganahalli, Mikkere Ramandur, Anasale, Bheemanahalli, Hittanahalli Dugganahalli, Devipura, Thalagavadi, Kagepura Koregala, Maganur, Settahalli, Muganakoppalu Ganiganapura, Sasiyalapura, Madahalli, Hullegala Banduru, Kallarepura, Nenanuru, Markalu, Doranahalli Kirugavalu, Deshavalli, Bendaravadi, Honaganahalli Kalkuni, Huvinakoppalu, Sujjalur, Uppanahalli Yamaduru, Ragibommanahalli, Ganaganuru, Hangrapura Avverahalli, Maliyur, Hanakola, Surakahalli Nelamakanahalli, Appugowdana Halli, Kaluveeranahalli Kandegala, Gulagatta, Malavalli(Rural), Nidaghatta Ankanahalli, Gowdagere, Amrutheswaranahalli Kembuthagere, Sahalli, Hadli, Kodipura, Koonanapura Jogipura, Agasanapura, Banagahalli, Huskur, Hosapura Belathur, Yethambadi, Antharavalli, Hullahalli Channipura, Hullagala, Dadamahalli, Banasamudra Kaggalipura, Konnapura, Halasahalli, Dhanagur Linganapura, Gramadevathepura, Basavanpura Nadakalapura, Megalapura, Kamsagara, Thuraganur Attuvanahalli, Alada Halli, Gajanur, Voddarahalli Marehalli, Ravani, Devalinganapura, Savandipura Sagyasaragur, Nitturhalasahalli, Kunthur, Lingapatna Nittur, Ankanahalli, Maragowdanahalli Nitthur Kodihalli, Karadahalli, Vodeyarabasapura Handanahalli, Juganahalli, Balehonniga Dalavaikodihalli, Deveerahalli, Kempainadoddi Gundapura, Hagadur, Gollarahalli, Halaguru Chillapura, Thorekadanahalli, Nanjapura Chikkayelachagere, Halagapura, Doddayelachagere Madahalli, Ganalu, Bydarahalli, Solaba Basavanahalli, Dalanakatte, Basavegowdanadoddi Doddaboovalli, Kyathanahalli, Kundur, Shiramalli Pandithahalli, Bachanahalli, Manchanapura Chottanahalli, Chandahalli, Dabbahalli, Netkal Mallikyathanahalli, Belakavadi, Kiragasur, Vasuvalli Hokkarahalli, Nanjanayanapura, Dyavapatna, Hosahalli Hebbani, Manchanahalli, Dasanadoddi, Kanchugahalli Malagalali, Thenkahalli, Kadabahalli, Mallinathapura Kaggala, Kanikahalli, Udape Boovalli, Thigadahalli Boppagowdanapura, Muttanahalli, Saraguru, Hanavadi Purigali, Hullamballi, Chikka Abbagilu, Ballagere Somanahalli, Kodagahalli, Haladasanahalli Kaggalipura.

The villages having more than 50% ST population are None.

Sex ratio of Scheduled tribe population is 493.

Scheduled Tribes Literates and Illiterates by Sex:

	Persons	Males	Females
Literate	492	290	202
Illiterate	943	437	506
Literacy rate	40.7	47.8	33.5
Graduate	17	14	3

Scheduled Tribes (Dominant):

Meda, Soligaru, Naikda etc., Generic Tribes etc. Kadu Kuruba

For their cultural identity please see Appendix-II

Villages without Scheduled Tribes: There are 142 villages without any scheduled tribe population.

Literates and Illiterates by Sex (Total Population):

	Persons	Males	Females
Literate	115,275	68,128	47,147
Illiterate	130,683	56,991	73,692
Literacy rate	53	62	44
Graduate	3,825	3,253	572

Agriculture: ***Distribution of villages according to land use:*** Out of 186 villages, Total area (in hectare) is 80738, out of that 60.69 percent is cultivable and 42.36 percent of the cultivable area is irrigated.

Sources of Irrigation (Hectares): Government Canal 14755.18, Private Canal 0, Well without Electricity 229.57, Well with Electricity 1527.59, Tubewell without Electricity 238.4, Tubewell with Electricity 3257.11, Tank 80.07, River 10, Lake 12, Waterfall 0, Others 647.76.

Villages with population of 5000 to 9999: Kirugavalu, Kalkuni, Halaguru, Belakavadi.

Villages with population of 10000 and above: None

Distribution of Workers:

	Persons	Males	Females	WPR
Cultivators	49,251	39,441	9,810	42.43
Agricultural Labour	37,824	17,792	20,032	32.59
Household Industry	2,296	1,039	1,257	1.98
Other Workers	26,692	18,431	8,261	23
Main Workers	87,748	67,261	20,487	75.6
Marginal Workers	28,315	9,442	18,873	24.4
Total Workers	116,063	76,703	39,360	

Religion: Major Religious Communities:

	Persons	Males	Females	Sex Ratio
Hindu (94.46%)	232,320	118,207	114,113	965
Muslim (3.2%)	7,876	3,990	3,886	974
Christian (0.18%)	449	235	214	911
Sikh (0%)	1	-	1	-
Buddhists (2%)	4,907	2,470	2,437	987
Jain (0.01%)	25	13	12	923

Agewise Data:

	Persons	Males	Females	Sex Ratio
All ages	245,958	125,119	120,839	966
0-14	71,430	36,412	35,018	962
15-44	117,897	59,986	57,911	965
45-79	52,741	26,974	25,767	955
80+	3,642	1,616	2,026	1254
Age not stated	248	131	117	893

Languages (Dominant):
Kannada, Urdu, Telugu, Tamil, Hindi

Disabled Population:

	Persons	Males	Females	%
Total Disabled	5,626	3,352	2,274	
In Seeing	3,280	1,984	1,296	58.3
In Speech	535	297	238	9.51
In Hearing	297	155	142	5.28
In Movement	1,086	679	407	19.3
Mentally	428	237	191	7.61

MALUR

Malur C.D. Block lies in the south-western part of Kolar district. It is a part of Malur taluka. The Block is located at a distance of 28 kms. from district headquarters (Kolar). There are 363 villages in the block with the total population of 178,268 persons. Area of the C.D. Block is 635.65 sq. kms. It is bounded by district Bangalore Rural, taluks Kolar and Bangarapet on north, taluk Bangarapet on east, and district Bangalore Rural on west. It has common boundary with the state of Tamil Nadu on south.

Communications:

Roadways :

Railway Station: Villages- Tekal, Kavalagiriyanahalli.

Annual Rainfall: Normal Rianfall 793.29 mm.

Ground Water: Availability of the Ground Water in the Basin is (Information not avablable) H.A.M. and the utilization is (Information not avablable) H.A.M. It belongs to (Information not avablable) category. Depth to water level 5 to 20 meter below the ground. Most of the wells go down in summer months, according to the Ground Water Estimation Committee.

Soils: Red Soils.

Natural Division : It falls in Kolar-Bangarpet Rugged Tract of the Southern Karnataka Plateau.

Administration:

Division: Bangalore. Parliamentary Constituency: 28 Kolar (SC). District: Kolar. Taluka: Malur. Assembly Constituency: 149 Malur. Gram Panchayat: 28.

Regional Area Development Boards: The Bailu Seeme Area Development Board.

Border Villages: (State: Tamil Nadu)- Sampangere, Alambadi, Siddanahalli, Tharabahalli, Voppachahalli, Madamangala, Yakkadoddi, Dadinayakanadoddi, Bennagatta, Bantahalli, Ahanya, Bitnahalli, Halehalli, Appaiana Agrahara, Chavaramangala, Suggondahalli, Anikarahalli, Malkanahalli, Thrunasi, Krishnapura, Bedisettihalli, Duduvanahalli, Kothigutlahalli, Kondanahalli.

Fairs and Festivals: Prasanna Venkataramanaswami Jatra: Chikka-Tirupati in Malur taluk well-known as a place of pilgrimage. The Shrinivasa temple at this place is a fairly large structure with a prakara on enclosure and a spacious courtyard in front. The image of god Varada, who is named Shrinivasa, is well carved.

Sappalam Jatra: Toranahalli in Malur taluk is known for its

temple of the goddess Sappalamma, so called because she is among other things believed to cure the cattle of disease. A jatra, lasting for seven days, is held on a large-scale in her honour every year in the dark fortnight of the month of Pushya (about January). It attracts a large number of people. Many devotees make vows to the goddess and attend the jatra for fulfilling them. In the cattle fair held on the occasion of the jatra, as many as about 50,000 heads of cattle are brought for sale.

Villages: 363 **Inhabited:** 306 **Uninhabited:** 57

Ranking	District	State	National
Area	9	145	1070
Population	6	107	1065
Sex Ratio	8	90	2404
Child Sex Ratio	2	17	1152
Literacy Rate	2	99	3009
Density	10	95	3729
Work Participation Rate	3	30	2244

Gram Panchayats:

Thorna Halli, Abbenahalli, Shivarapatna, Hungenahalli, Doddashivara, Chikkakunthur, Kondasettihalli, Kugatiganahalli, Tekal, Banahalli, Nutuve, Huladenahalli, Araleri, Santhehalli, Madivala, Nosagere, Hulimangalahosakote, Lakkur, Chikkathirupathy, Jayamangala, Kudiyanur, Rajenahalli, Hasandahalli, Baliganahalli, Dadinayakanadoddi, Masthi, Thrunasi, Dinnahalli.

Amenities:

Education: Primary School in 241 villages, Middle school in 105 villages, Matriculation or Secondary School in 19 villages, namely Thorna Halli, Shivarapatna, Ramenahalli, Anepura, Abbenahalli, Doddashivara, Huralagere, Chikkakunthur, Tharanahalli, Sonnappanahatti, Kudiyanur, Lakkur, Chikkathirupathy, Dadinayakanadoddi, Rajenahalli, Masthi, Tekal, Huladenahalli, Doddanaikanahalli.

Higher Secondary or Pre University Courses or Intermediate or Junior College in 6 villages of the CD Block,, namely Shivarapatna, Ramenahalli, Lakkur, Chikkathirupathy, Masthi, Tekal.

College in 1 village, Adult Literacy Center in 1 village., College is in village, namely Ramenahalli.

Medical: Hospital in 4 villages, Dispensary in 6 villages, Health Center in 5 villages, Sub Center in 40 villages, Maternity and Child Welfare Center in 1 village, Community health workers in 9 villages.

The Villages having Hospital or Dispensary or Health Center are Shivarapatna, Doddashivara, Santhehalli, Chikkathirupathy, Dadinayakanadoddi, Masthi, Kavalagiriyanahalli, Huladenahalli, Thoralakki.

Drinking Water: Tap water in 176 villages, Tank water in 101 villages, Well water in 80 villages, Tubewell in 201 villages and more than one source in 250 villages.

Bank: Banking facility in 12 villages, namely, Shivarapatna, Yeswanthapura, Kudiyanur Chikkathirupathy, Hasandahalli, Masthi, Dinnahalli Nidaramangala, Kavalagiriyanahalli, Huladenahalli Thoralakki, Nutuve.

Credit Society in 22 villages Agricultural Credit Society in 14 Non-Agricultural Credit Society in 3 villages.

Others: Power supply in 285 villages, Cinema hall in 5 villages sport club in 1 village, Stadium or Auditorium or Community Hall in 1 village, Post Office in 32 villages.

There are 184 villages having bus facilities.

Villages with most of facilities: Shivarapatna Yeswanthapura, Kudiyanur, Chikkathirupathy Hasandahalli, Masthi, Dinnahalli Kavalagiriyanahalli, Huladenahalli, Thoralakki Nutuve.

Villages without amenities (Education): Jodipura, Vardenahalli, Obalapura, M.Sonnahalli, Gangapura, Kadasonnahalli, Kothakota Thimmanahalli, Chokkondahalli, Gangasandra, Nallappanahalli, Upavasapura, Kanachikkanahalli, Patitganahalli, Veerapura, Alubavikothur, Kundenahalli, Geragadenahalli, Hanumanthapura, Yarapasettihalli, Gaddamsonnahalli, Marasettihalli, Linganahalli, Halkempanahalli, Thuragalur, Lakkurhosahalli, Koppathimmanahalli, Kadumuthsandra, Bagursonnahalli, Byrasandra, Madamangala, Kadadanahalli, Harohalli, Byappanahatti, Sinkanahalli, Keshavanahatti, Balanaikanadoddi, M.Upparahalli, Bandahatti, Guddadahosahalli, Tholasanadoddi, Halepalya, Rajavarahalli, Thirtha Bandahatti, Pichaguntrahalli, Halehalli, Byappanahalli, Ajjappanahalli, Palya, Kothigutlahalli, Karagahalli, Kempasandra, Halliganahalli, Byrathanahallipura, Thotagowdana Halli, Kondarajanahalli, Korachanoor, Hosabalahalli, Haleballahalli, Ojarahalli, Yalesandra, Manchakal, Guruvalagollahalli..

Scheduled Castes: Out of the total population of 179194 persons, 46949 persons (26.2%) belong to Scheduled Castes. The villages having less than 10% SC population are Thorna Halli, Mindahalli, Seethappanahalli Shivarapatna, Jodipura, Ramenahalli Chikkasabbenahalli, Kondarahalli, Chavvenahalli Doddakunthur, Haripura, Kothakota Thimmanahalli Gangasandra, Hanumanayakanahalli, Lakkenahalli Yeswanthapura, Upavasapura, Veerapura, Kodur

Kodaginabele, Geragadenahalli, Angasettihalli
Bingipura, Hanumanthapura, Gaddamsonnahalli
Tharanahalli, Linganahalli, Halkempanahalli
Medahatti, Upparahalli, Lakkurhosahalli
Koppathimmanahalli, Kodur, Jagadenahalli, Gonur
Sinkanahalli, Nallandahalli, Muthenahatti
Natuvarahalli, Rayasandra, Chickadanavahalli
Pemmadoddi, Voosarahalli, Halepalya, Yelesandra
Malkanahalli, Thyaganadoddi, Durasandahalli
Byappanahalli, Ajjappanahalli, Ganiganahalli
Ramasagara, Kothigutlahalli, Karagahalli
Kadirenahalli, Obatti, Gollahalli, Byrathanahalli
Kondasettihalli, Bettahalli, Kondarajanahalli
Kempanahalli, Pudisettihalli, Gopasandra
Hosabalahalli , Haleballahalli, Settihalli
Yalesandra, Manchakal, Thoralakki, Nutuve.

The villages having more than 50% SC population are
Gerupura, Dombarahalli, Korachanoor
Seethanaikanahalli, Kambipura, Hizuvanahalli
Vardenahalli, Obalapura, Madivala, Lingapura
Chikkapura, Madanahatti , Kurandahalli, Mangapura
Marasettihalli, Kadumuthsandra, Bagursonnahalli
Alambadi, Chalaganahalli, Kadavanapura, Indumangala
Byappanahatti, Mathangapura, Thippasandra
Obatti Agrahara, Balanaikanadoddi, Gollahalli
Bandahatti, Varadapura, Rajavarahalli , Karisandra
Nidamakanahalli, Kugatiganahalli, Thotagowdana Halli
Mittiganahalli, Korachanoor, Chickamale
Jinagathimmanahalli, Ojarahalli, Animittnahalli.

Sex ratio of Scheduled Caste population is 498.

Scheduled Castes Literates and Illiterates by Sex:

	Persons	Males	Females
Literate	20,273	12,439	7,834
Illiterate	26,676	11,121	15,555
Literacy rate	50.6	61.8	39.2
Graduate	425	374	51

Scheduled Castes (Dominant):

Adi Karnataka, Bhovi, Adi Dravida, Chalavadi etc.
Koracha

For their cultural identity please see Appendix-I

Villages without Scheduled Castes: There are 89 villages without any scheduled caste population.

Scheduled Tribes: Out of the total population of 179194 persons, 18345 persons (10.24%) belong to Scheduled Tribes.

The villages having less than 10% ST population are
Sonnanaikanahalli, Byranahalli, Gerupura
Dombarahalli, Karinaikanahalli, Korachanoor
Thambihalli, Seethanaikanahalli, Kambipura, Agrahara
Anepura, Hizuvanahalli, Nambiganahalli
Chikkasabbenahalli, Vardenahalli, Abbenahalli
M.Sonnahalli, Kondarahalli, Bellavi, Hedaginabele
Channigarayapura, Gangapura, Irabanahalli, Madivala
Harohalli, Lingapura, Chavvenahalli, Doddashivara
Doddasabbenahalli, Kadasonnahalli, Puramakanahalli
Haripura, Vadaganahalli, Chikkashivara
Doddakadathur, Kothakota Thimmanahalli
Chokkondahalli, Gangasandra, Lakkenahalli
Boppanahalli, Chikkapura, Pitchaguntrahalli
Marasandra, Huralagere, Upavasapura, Byalahalli
Kurandahalli, Nosagere, Kanachikkanahalli
Purasanahalli, Patitganahalli, Mangapura, Channakal
Dyapasandra, Neelakanta Agrahara, Sonnahalli, Kateri
Kodaginabele, Chikkakunthur, Alubavikothur
Kundenahalli, Araleri, Hanumanthapura
Yarapasettihalli, Gaddamsonnahalli, Tharanahalli
Mylandahalli, Ramapura, Linganahalli
Halkempanahalli, Kudiyanur, Manisettihalli
Nariganahalli, Hulkur, Chakanahalli, Barugur
Dommalur, Arasanahalli, Hulimangalahosakote
Lakkurhosahalli, Seethanaikanahalli
Koppathimmanahalli, Kodur, Pura, Yattakodi
Kadumuthsandra, Lakkur, Kodihalli, Minasandra
Jayamangala, Jagadenahalli, Bagursonnahalli
Anchemuskur, Chikkathirupathy, Kalkere, Sampangere
Alambadi, Sonnur, Chowdadenahalli, Gonur
Channigarayapura, Arinagatta, Byrasandra
Chikka Iggaluru, Chalaganahalli, Voppachahalli
Dadinayakanadoddi, Bennagatta, Bantahalli, Ahanya
Padavanahalli, Kadadanahalli, Mirupanahalli
Nagapura, Baliganahalli, Kadavanapura, Indumangala
Dinneri, Harohalli, Byappanahatti, Obatti
Mathangapura, Sinkanahalli, Adikarahatti
Nallandahalli, Rajenahalli, Sonnappanahatti
Keshavanahatti, Thippasandra, Obatti Agrahara
Thuruvalahatti, Gollahalli, Chikkakallahalli
M.Hosahalli, M.Upparahalli, Byranadoddi, Bandahatti
Varadapura, Guddadahosahalli, Tholasanadoddi
Rayasandra, Doddadanavahalli, Voosarahalli
Rajavarahalli , Thirtha Bandahatti, Masthi
Bitnahalli, Halehalli, Chavaramangala, Suggondahalli
Thrunasi, Thyaganadoddi, Karisandra, Shamasettyhalli
Krishnapura, Kanchala, Byappanahalli
Sorakayalahalli, Ganiganahalli, Karagahalli
Nidaramangala, Karangutta, Nakkanahalli
Kuntanahalli, Kempasandra, Agalakote, Veerakaputra
Kadirenahalli, Janganahalli, Kugatiganahalli
Chinnapaganahalli, Agara, Gollahalli
Thotagowdana Halli, Kondasettihalli, Hunasikote
Balleri, Ullerahalli, Somasandra, Mittiganahalli
Yaluvahalli, Bettahalli, Makarahalli , Tekal

Kondarajanahalli, Korachanoor, Kavalagiriyanahalli Kempanahalli, Pudisettihalli, Doddamale, Yaluvaguli Dasarahalli, Gopasandra, Hosabalahalli Haleballahalli, Chickamale, Kurnahosahalli Huladenahalli, Seethahalli, Jinagathimmanahalli Ojarahalli, Settihalli, Yalesandra, Kshethranahalli Nellahalli, Animittnahalli, Doddanaikanahalli.

The villages having more than 50% ST population are Ramenahalli, Veerapura, Geragadenahalli Angasettihalli, Bingipura, Upparahalli, Muthenahatti Pemmadoddi, Yelesandra, Pichaguntrahalli Malkanahalli, Palya, Kothigutlahalli, Vurugurki Obatti, Byrathanahallipura, Manchakal.

Sex ratio of Scheduled tribe population is 498.

Scheduled Tribes Literates and Illiterates by Sex:

	Persons	Males	Females
Literate	7,148	4,532	2,616
Illiterate	11,197	4,684	6,513
Literacy rate	46.0	57.9	33.9
Graduate	76	67	9

Scheduled Tribes (Dominant):

Naikda etc., Generic Tribes etc., Hakkipikki, Kota Palliyan

For their cultural identity please see Appendix-II

Villages without Scheduled Tribes: There are 184 villages without any scheduled tribe population.

Literates and Illiterates by Sex (Total Population):

	Persons	Males	Females
Literate	90,821	54,674	36,147
Illiterate	88,373	36,206	52,167
Literacy rate	59	70	47
Graduate	2,387	2,020	367

Agriculture: ***Distribution of villages according to land use:*** Out of 363 villages, Total area (in hectare) is 63565, out of that 67.12 percent is cultivable and 24.27 percent of the cultivable area is irrigated.

Sources of Irrigation (Hectares): Government Canal 149.29, Private Canal 0, Well without Electricity 43.38, Well with Electricity 317.96, Tubewell without Electricity 9.39, Tubewell with Electricity 6104.74, Tank 2292.44, River 1, Lake 0, Waterfall 0, Others 1436.16.

Villages with population of 5000 to 9999: Masthi.

Villages with population of 10000 and above: None

Distribution of Workers:

	Persons	Males	Females	WPR
Cultivators	35,644	25,342	10,302	40.23
Agricultural Labour	30,584	13,077	17,507	34.51
Household Industry	3,128	1,399	1,729	3.53
Other Workers	19,255	13,605	5,650	21.73
Main Workers	66,644	46,648	19,996	75.21
Marginal Workers	21,967	6,775	15,192	24.79
Total Workers	88,611	53,423	35,188	

Religion: Major Religious Communities:

	Persons	Males	Females	Sex Ratio
Hindu (94.11%)	168,640	85,462	83,178	973
Muslim (5.73%)	10,274	5,269	5,005	950
Christian (0.08%)	139	68	71	1,044
Sikh (0.01%)	10	6	4	667
Buddhists (0.02%)	27	17	10	588
Jain (0.02%)	28	16	12	750

Agewise Data:

	Persons	Males	Females	Sex Ratio
All ages	179,194	90,880	88,314	972
0-14	58,979	29,722	29,257	984
15-44	82,644	41,675	40,969	983
45-79	35,026	18,219	16,807	922
80+	2,376	1,182	1,194	1010
Age not stated	169	82	87	1061

Languages (Dominant):

Kannada, Telugu, Tamil, Urdu, Marathi

Disabled Population:

	Persons	Males	Females	%
Total Disabled	3,495	1,929	1,566	
In Seeing	1,697	880	817	48.56
In Speech	343	194	149	9.81
In Hearing	167	95	72	4.78
In Movement	916	569	347	26.21
Mentally	372	191	181	10.64

MANDYA

Mandya C.D. Block lies in the central part of Mandya district. It is a part of Mandya tehsil. The Block is located at a distance of 00 kms. from district headquart ers (Mandya). There are 183 villages in the block with the total population of 274,687 persons. Area of the C.D. Block is 694.35 sq. kms. It is bounded by taluk Nagamangala on north, taluks Shrirangapattana, Malavalli and district Mysore on south, taluk Maddur on east, and taluk Pandavapura on west.

Communications:

Roadways : S.H.-17: Direction- Mysore to Bangalore, Nearest Villages- Kiragandur, Mandya (Rural), Sathanur, Ummadah alli, Budanur, Hanakere, Halasagere, B.Gowdagere, Yelacha kanahalli, Ragimuddanahalli, Kalenahalli, Yeliyur, Y. Yarahalli, Sundahalli, Indavalu, Guthalu.

Railway Station: Village- Hanakere.

River: Lokapavani Nadi- Nearest Villages- Ankuppe, Honne madu, Chikkagangavadi, Thippapura, G.Hoshalli, Javanahalli, Mallenahalli, Gerahalli(B), Billenahalli.

Canal: Nearest Villages- Machagowdanahalli, Ganiga,

Shivapura, Chikkakothagere, Gorakabalhosahalli, Guthagan ahalli, Chakanahalli, Doddakothagere, Karekatte, Baby, Doddagarudanahalli, Chokanahalli, Upparakanahalli, Gudigenahalli, Muddamgere, Hongalimutt, Alakere, Keelara, Hulivana, Nallahalli, Honnayakanahalli, Chikkabanasavadi, S.I.Kodihalli, Jeegundipatna, Chamalapura, Sowdenahalli, Maranahalli, M.Kebbahalli, Gunnaikanahalli, Shambonaha lli, H. Malligere, Goravale, Sampahalli, Chandagal, Shivh alli, Maradipura, Madla, Dudda, Kannahatti, Hullenahalli, Jayapura, Mallegere, Hulikere, Madchakanahalli, Bilaguli, Ummadahalli, Bellundagere, udanur, Hyadarahalli, Thumb akere, Kachigere, Hanakere, B.Gowdagere, Kannalli, Yeliyur, Y. Yarahalli, Sundahalli, Hullukere, Lalankere, Mothah.

Annual Rainfall: Normal Rianfall 765.7 mm.

Ground Water: Availability of the Ground Water in the Basin is 10367.12 H.A.M. and the utilization is 1250. 79 H.A.M. It belongs to Over Expoited category. Depth to water level 2 to 10 meter below the ground. Most of the wells go down in summer months, according to the Ground Water Estimation Committee.

Soils: Red Sandy Loams to Red Clay Loam.

Natural Division : It falls partly in Nagamangala Plateau and Shimsha Basin of the Southern Karnataka Plateau.

Administration:

Division: Mysore. Parliamentary Constituency: 20 Mandya. District: Mandya. Taluka: Mandya . Assembly Constituenc y: 188 Pandavpura, 189 Mandya, 190 Shrirangapattana. Gram Panchayat: 45.

Fairs:

Janardanaswami Temple Car Festival: The Janardanaswami temple in Mandya is considered a place of great sanctity and thousands of devotees visit the temple all the year round. The car festival of the temple is celebrated in the month of April or May of each year and attracts more than one lakh people. Several viragals have been found in Mandya and Chikka Mandya. Mandya town, which is the headquarters of the district, is situated 35 kms. north-east of Mysore on the Bangalore-Mysore railway line and the Bangalore-Mysore road. The importan ce of Mandya grew after the construction of the Krishnar ajasagar dam.

Venkataramanaswami Car Festival: The car festival of Venkataramanaswami temple held at Malckal Tirupati around the month of July lasts for a period of one week. Malckal-Tir upati, situated on the Hirckal hills close to Arsikere, is about 3 kms. from Arsikere town and about 44 kms. from Hassan town. It is well-known for the Venkatarama naswami temple, which is on the top of the hill on the northern side. A flight of 1,700 steps leads to the temple. There is also a large temple of Govindarajaswami at the foot of the hills. Both the temples are frequently visited by a large number of devotees throughout the year. An annual car festival is held which is well attended.

Villages: 183 **Inhabited:** 174 **Uninhabited:** 9

Ranking	District	State	National
Area	4	135	930
Population	1	27	133
Sex Ratio	6	92	2456
Child Sex Ratio	7	173	5352
Literacy Rate	4	97	2996
Density	7	143	2764
Work Participation Rate	3	10	3347

Gram Panchayats:

G. Malligere, Muthegere, Basaralu, Kambadahalli, Shivapura, Chandagalu, Hallerere, Baby, Doddagarudanahalli, Upparakanahalli, Mudagandur, Bevakal, Dudda, B. Hosur, Keregodu, Maragowdanahalli, Hodaghatta, Alakere, Keelara, Hulivana, H. Malligere, Shivhalli, Hullenahalli, Gandalu, Holalu, Gopalapura, Sathanur, Ummadahalli, Thubenakere, Hanakere, B.Gowdagere, Budanur, Mandya (Rural) , Chandagal, Yeliyur, Indavalu, Belur, Kannalli, Sunagahalli, Thaggahalli, Haluvadi, Santhekasalagere, Bevinahalli, Kothathi, Mangala.

Amenities:

Education: Primary School in 164 villages, Middle school in 123 villages, Matriculation or Secondary School in 38 villages, namely Muthegere, Shivapura, Hallegere, Tavarekere, Basaralu, Baby, Keregodu, Maragowdanahalli, Hodaghatta, Alakere, Keelara, Hulivana, K.Gowdagere, B.Hosur, G.Malligere, Mudagandur, Holalu, Chandagal, Gandalu, Dudda, Hulikere, Mandya (Rural), Kommerahalli, Sathanur, Ummadahalli, Budanur, Hanakere, Kannalli, Yelachakanahalli, Yeliyur, Indavalu, Kothathi, Guthalu, Thaggahalli, Mangala, Hebbakavadi, Thimmanahosur, Sunagahalli.

Higher Secondary or Pre University Courses or Intermediate or Junior College in 7 villages of the CD Block,, namely Basaralu, K.Gowdagere, Bilidegilu, Dudda, Kommerahalli, Mangala, Thimmanahosur.

College in 3 villages, Adult Literacy Center in 7 villages., Colleges are in villages, namely Basaralu, Baby, Kommerahalli.

Medical: Hospital in 23 villages, Dispensary in 16 villages, Health Center in 28 villages, Sub Center in 68 villages, Maternity and Child Welfare Center in 39 villages, Community health workers in 37 villages.

The Villages having Hospital or Dispensary or Health Center are Muthegere, Shivapura, Hallegere, Basaralu, Manuganahalli, Keregodu, Maragowdanahalli, Keelara,

Hulivana, Doddabanasavadi, B.Hosur, G.Malligere, Mudagandur, Goravale, Holalu, Chandagal, Shivhalli, Dudda, Mandya (Rural), Sathanur, Thumbakere, Kachigere, Hanakere, Kannalli, Kothathi, Belur, Thaggahalli, Mangala, Thimmanahosur.

Drinking Water: Tap water in 138 villages, Tank water in 87 villages, Well water in 148 villages, Tubewell in 94 villages and more than one source in 167 villages.

Bank: Banking facility in 38 villages, namely, Ganiga, Hallegere, Basaralu, Doddagarudanahalli Upparakanahalli, Keregodu, Maragowdanahalli, Keelara K.Gowdagere, B.Hosur, G.Malligere, Sowdenahalli H. Malligere, Goravale, Holalu, Chandagal, Gandalu Shivhalli, Madla, Dudda, Hulikere, Madchakanahalli Mandya (Rural), Kommerahalli, Sathanur, Ummadahalli Budanur, Hanakere, Halasagere, B.Gowdagere, Yeliyur Indavalu, Kothathi, Santhekasalagere, Guthalu Boothana Hosur, Thaggahalli, Mangala.

Credit Society in 44 villages Agricultural Credit Society in 40 Non-Agricultural Credit Society in 4 villages.

Others: Power supply in 173 villages, Cinema hall in 12 villages, sport club in 5 villages, Stadium or Auditorium or Community Hall in 1 village, Post Office in 65 villages.

There are 149 villages having bus facilities.

Villages with most of facilities: Hallegere Basaralu, Doddagarudanahalli, Upparakanahalli Keregodu, Maragowdanahalli, Keelara, K.Gowdagere B.Hosur, G.Malligere, H. Malligere, Goravale, Holalu Chandagal, Gandalu, Shivhalli, Dudda, Hulikere Madchakanahalli, Mandya (Rural), Kommerahalli Sathanur, Ummadahalli, Budanur, Hanakere B.Gowdagere, Yeliyur, Indavalu, Kothathi Santhekasalagere, Guthalu, Boothana Hosur Thaggahalli, Mangala.

Villages without amenities (Education): Heggadathahalli, Bidarkatte, Manuganahalli, Hongalimutt, Jeegundipatna, Ankuppe, Maralekere, Devarayapatna, Halasagere..

Scheduled Castes: Out of the total population of 274433 persons, 36241 persons (13.21%) belong to Scheduled Castes.

The villages having less than 10% SC population are Nanjenahalli, Kodagahalli, Hullahalli, Ankushapura Bennatti, Vaddarahalli, Heggadathahalli Kambadahalli, Balenahalli, Ganiga, Chikkakothagere Chandagalu, Rayashettipura, Thangalagere Guthaganahalli, Karekatte, Bidarkatte, Tavarekere Tharanagere, Madveeranahalli, Tirumalapura Gundapura, Kenchanahalli, Harakadahalli, Nandihalli Manuganahalli, Hanaganahalli, Hodagatta Ganthagowdanahalli, G.Kebbahalli, Hanchahalli Shivara, Danayakanapura, Muddamgere, Eachagere Doddabanasavadi, Honnayakanahalli, Chikkabanasavadi Bilidegilu, Jeegundipatna, Ankuppe, Honnemadu Maralekere, Chikkagangavadi, Thippapura, G.Hoshalli Javanahalli, Billenahalli, Bevakal, Bettahalli M. Honnenahalli, Managanahalli, M.Hosahalli Maranahalli, Gunnaikanahalli, Goravale Beeregowdanahalli, B.Hosahalli, Mallanayakanakatte Hadya, Maradipura, Dudda, Kannahatti, Devarayapatna Hullenahalli, Hulikere, Maradevanahalli Maranachakanahalli, Gopalapura, Sathanur Bellundagere, Thumbakere, Kachigere, Halasagere Nodekoppalu, Yeliyur, Indavalu, Hullukere, Lalankere Santhekasalagere, Kyathumgere, Cheeranahalli Kammanaiyakanhalli, Boothana Hosur, Belur, Haluvadi Hebbakavadi, Thimmanahosur, T.Mallegere.

The village having more than 50% SC population is None.

Sex ratio of Scheduled Caste population is 498.

Scheduled Castes Literates and Illiterates by Sex:

	Persons	Males	Females
Literate	17,396	10,285	7,111
Illiterate	18,845	7,921	10,924
Literacy rate	54.5	64.4	44.5
Graduate	624	528	96

Scheduled Castes (Dominant):

Adi Karnataka, Madiga, Adi Dravida, Bhovi, Korama

For their cultural identity please see Appendix-I

Villages without Scheduled Castes: There are 33 villages without any scheduled caste population.

Scheduled Tribes: Out of the total population of 274433 persons, 1379 persons (0.5%) belong to Scheduled Tribes.

The villages having less than 10% ST population are Nanjenahalli, Muthegere, Kodagahalli, Nayakanahalli Hullahalli, Ankushapura, Bennatti, Shanbhoganahalli Vaddarahalli, Heggadathahalli, Muddanaghatta Naragalu, Marasinganahalli, Kambadahalli Balenahalli, Machagowdanahalli, Ganiga, Shivapura Chikkakothagere, Gorakabalhosahalli, Chandagalu Rayashettipura, Challanayakanahalli, Hallegere Chikkaballi, Mayappanahalli, Thangalagere Guthaganahalli, Chakanahalli, Doddakothagere Karekatte, Bidarkatte, Tavarekere, Tharanagere Madveeranahalli, Tirumalapura, Basaralu, Gundapura Kenchanahalli, Harakadahalli, M.Hatna, Hunuganahalli Nandihalli, Manuganahalli, Hanaganahalli, Hodagatta Baby, Doddagarudanahalli, Chokanahalli Upparakanahalli, Gudigenahalli, Ganthagowdanahalli G.Kebbahalli, Hanchahalli, Keregodu Maragowdanahalli, Hodaghatta, Danayakanapura

Muddamgere, Hongalimutt, Alakere, Eachagere, Keelara Hulivana, Doddabanasavadi, Nallahalli Chikkabanasavadi, S.I.Kodihalli, K.Gowdagere Bilidegilu, B.Hosur, Jeegundipatna, Chamalapura Ankuppe, Honnemadu, G.Malligere, Maralekere Chikkagangavadi, Thippapura, G.Hoshalli, Javanahalli Mallenahalli, Billenahalli, Bevakal, B. Hatna Beechanahalli, Bettahalli, M. Honnenahalli Bommanahalli, Managanahalli, Mudagandur, M.Hosahalli Sowdenahalli, Maranahalli, M.Kebbahalli Gunnaikanahalli, Shambonahalli, H. Malligere Goravale, Sampahalli, Beeregowdanahalli, B.Hosahalli Holalu, Kiragandur, Chandagal, Mallanayakanakatte Gandalu, Hadya, Shivhalli, Maradipura, Madla, Dudda Kannahatti, Devarayapatna, Hullenahalli, Jayapura Mallegere, Hulikere, Madchakanahalli, Bilaguli Maradevanahalli, Maranachakanahalli, Avverahalli Panakanahalli, Mandya (Rural), Gopalapura H.Kodihalli, Honaganahalli, Kommerahalli, Sathanur Ummadahalli, Bellundagere, Budanur, Thumbakere Kachigere, Hanakere, Halasagere, B.Gowdagere Kannalli, Nodekoppalu, Yelachakanahalli Ragimuddanahalli, Uramarkasalagere, Kalenahalli Yeliyur, Y. Yarahalli, Sundahalli, Indavalu Bevinahalli, Hullukere, Kothathi, Lalankere Mothahalli, Santhekasalagere, Kyathumgere, Guthalu Cheeranahalli, Kammanaiyakanhalli, Boothana Hosur Belur, Kabbanahalli, Thaggahalli, Haluvadi, Mangala Hebbakavadi, Lokasara, Pura, Thimmanahosur Marasinganahalli, T.Mallegere, Sunagahalli, Hemmige.

The villages having more than 50% ST population are None.

Sex ratio of Scheduled tribe population is 495.

Scheduled Tribes Literates and Illiterates by Sex:

	Persons	Males	Females
Literate	517	302	215
Illiterate	862	395	467
Literacy rate	42.3	49.2	35.4
Graduate	15	12	3

Scheduled Tribes (Dominant):

Naikda etc., Soligaru, Meda, Generic Tribes etc. Hakkipikki

For their cultural identity please see Appendix-II

Villages without Scheduled Tribes: There are 126 villages without any scheduled tribe population.

Literates and Illiterates by Sex (Total Population):

	Persons	Males	Females
Literate	143,424	84,137	59,287
Illiterate	131,009	55,110	75,899
Literacy rate	59	68	49
Graduate	5,507	4,711	796

Agriculture: ***Distribution of villages according to land use:***
Out of 183 villages, Total area (in hectare) is 69435, out of that 67.62 percent is cultivable and 50.89 percent of the cultivable area is irrigated.

Sources of Irrigation (Hectares): Government Canal 18456.16, Private Canal 0, Well without Electricity 50.12, Well with Electricity 1470.34, Tubewell without Electricity 29.34, Tubewell with Electricity 885.51, Tank 820.49, River 84.54, Lake 0, Waterfall 0, Others 2096.64.

Villages with population of 5000 to 9999:
Keregodu, Keelara, Holalu, Mandya (Rural), Budanur Santhekasalagere.

Villages with population of 10000 and above: None

Distribution of Workers:

	Persons	Males	Females	WPR
Cultivators	63,983	50,581	13,402	50.34
Agricultural Labour	38,967	19,777	19,190	30.66
Household Industry	2,348	1,461	887	1.85
Other Workers	21,805	14,788	7,017	17.16
Main Workers	114,835	82,200	32,635	90.35
Marginal Workers	12,268	4,407	7,861	9.65
Total Workers	127,103	86,607	40,496	

Religion: Major Religious Communities:

	Persons	Males	Females	Sex Ratio
Hindu (98.7%)	270,866	137,452	133,414	971
Muslim (0.54%)	1,492	755	737	976
Christian (0.12%)	334	154	180	1,169
Sikh (0%)	8	6	2	333
Buddhists (0.51%)	1,408	723	685	947
Jain (0.01%)	32	17	15	882

Agewise Data:

	Persons	Males	Females	Sex Ratio
All ages	274,433	139,247	135,186	971
0-14	76,567	39,559	37,008	936
15-44	139,139	70,570	68,569	972
45-79	55,217	27,471	27,746	1010
80+	3,148	1,446	1,702	1177
Age not stated	362	201	161	801

Languages (Dominant):
Kannada, Tamil, Telugu, Urdu, Marathi

Disabled Population:

	Persons	Males	Females	%
Total Disabled	5,608	3,277	2,331	
In Seeing	3,249	1,907	1,342	57.94
In Speech	613	335	278	10.93
In Hearing	214	105	109	3.82
In Movement	1,108	708	400	19.76
Mentally	424	222	202	7.56

MANGALORE

Mangalore C.D. Block lies in the western part of Dakshina Kannada district. It is a part of Mangalore taluka. The Block is located at a distance of (00) kms. from district headquarters (Mangalore). There are 88 villages in the block with the total population of 281,743 persons. Area of the C.D. Block is 587.84 sq. kms. It is bounded by district Udupi on north, taluks Bantval and Beltanga di on east, and Lakshadweep sea on west. It has common boundary with the state of Kerala on south.

Communications:

Roadways : NH- 13: Direction- Mangalore to Karkal, NearestVillages- Badagumijaru, Tenkamijar, Thodaru, Puthige, Beluvai, Padumarnadu, Muduperar, Kandavara, Badagaulipady, Tenkayedapadavu, Badagayedapadavu, Thiruvail, Bondath ila. NH- 17: Direction- Udupi to Kasargod, Nearest Villages- Bellairu, Padupanamboor, Pavanje, Haleangady, Arkula, Talapady.

NH- 48: Direction- Mangalore to Bantaval.

Nearest Vi;;ages- Bellairu, Padupanamboor, Pavanje, Haleangady, Arkula, Talapady. SH- 37: Nearest Village- Nellikaru. SH- 64 A: Direction- Mulki to Beltangadi, Nearest Villages- Kilpady, Bellairu, Thokur-(10), Talipady, Aikala, Menna Bettu, Kemral, Kallamundkooru, Niddodi, Badagumijaru, Puthige. SH- 66 A: Direction- Mangalore to Udupi, Nearest Villages- Talipady, Elinje, Aikala, Menna Bettu, Nadugodu, Badagayekkaru, Tenkayekkar, Permude, Kenjar, Malavoor, Kondemula.

River: Mulki Nadi- Nearest Villages- Athikari Bettu, Karnire, Balkunje, Ulipady, Padupanamboor, Sasihithlu, Pavanje, Elinje, Kadandale, Kallamundkooru. Natravati Nadi- Nearest Villages- Arkula, Amblamogru, Harekala, Pavoor, Boliyar. Gurpur Nadi- Nearest Villages- Kenjar, Malavoor, Adyapady, Kandavara, Kolavooru, Muthuru, Mogaru, Tankaulipady, Addur, Thiruvail, Ulaibettu, Mallur. Panchamogaruholi Nadi- Nearest Villages- Ervuailu, Puchhamoguru, Shirthadi, Mantrady, Killenjaru.

Reserved Forest: Villages- Thodaru, Puchhamoguru, Hosabettu, Kellaputhige, Daregudde, Panapila, Nellikaru.

Annual Rainfall: Normal Rianfall 3852 mm.

Ground Water: Availability of the Ground Water in the Basin is (Information not avablable) H.A.M. and the utilization is (Information not avablable) H.A.M. It belongs to (Information not avablable) category. Depth to water level 5 to 20 meter below the ground. Most of the wells go down in summer months, according to the Ground Water Estimation Committee.

Coastal Villages: (Lakshadeep Sea)- Padupanamboor, Sasihi thlu, Pavanje.

Natural Division : It falls partly in Kundapur-Mangalore Coast and Bainduru-Bantval Plain of the Karnataka Coast (Western Coastal Region).

Administration:

Division: Mysore. Parliamentary Constituency: 17 Dakshina Kannada. District: Dakshina Kannada. Taluka: Mangalore. Assembly Constituency: 201 Surathkal, 202 Mangalore City North, 203 Mangalore City south. Gram Panchayat: 49.

Regional Area Development Boards: The Maland Aera Development Board.

Border Villages: (State: Kerala)- Talapady, Kinnya.

Fairs: Mangaladevi Temple Festival: It is held during Navratri (October -November) for about 10 days in Mangal ore. Otherwise locally known as 'Kodial Bunder' it is the headquarters of the district and is situated on the backwaters formed by the convergent mouths of the Netravati and Gurpur rivers consequently, it has waters on the south and west sides.

Manjunatha Temple Festival: It is held in around the month of November at Mangalore for three days every year.

Sadashiva Car Festival: It is held at Surathkal around the month of December every year. Surathkal is situated on the Mangalore-Mulki Road, 14 kms. from Mangalore.

Villages: 88 **Inhabited:** 88 **Uninhabited:** 0

Ranking	District	State	National
Area	5	155	1209
Population	2	24	111
Sex Ratio	1	4	157
Child Sex Ratio	3	117	3446
Literacy Rate	1	2	226
Density	5	113	2310
Work Participation Rate	1	2	2648

Gram Panchayats:

Kilpady, Balkunje, Kinnigoli, Padupanamboor, Haleangady, Chellairu, Kemral, Mennabettu, Aikala, Paladka, Kallamundkooru, Surinje, Bala, Permude, Tenkayekkar, Muchur, Puthige, Beluvai, Padumarnadu, Daregudde, Nellikaru, Shirthadi, Hosabettu, Badagayedapadavu, Tenkamijar, Paduperar, Bajpe, Jokatte, Malavoor, Mudushedde, Kandavara, Ganjimatha, Kuppepadavu, Gurupur, Thiruvail, Ulaibettu, Neermarga, Adyar, Kannur, Bajala, Munnur, Amblamogru, Harekala, Pavoor, Boliyar, Konaje, Belma, Someshwar, Kotekara, Talapady, Kinnya, Manjanady.

Amenities:

Education: Primary School in 87 villages, Middle school in 83 villages, Matriculation or Secondary School in 40 villages, namely Athikari Bettu, Balkunje, Shimanthur, Haleangady, Thokur-(10), Talipady, Menna Bettu, Kemral, Nadugodu, Kondemula, Kadandale,

Kallamundkooru, Niddodi, Badagumijaru, Puchhamoguru, Hosabettu, Beluvai, Moodumarnadu, Daregudde, Nellikaru, Valpadi, Shirthadi, Madya, Surinje, Kalavar, Kenjar, Kolambe, Adyapady, Badagaulipady, Tenkayedapadavu, Killenjaru, Muthuru, Tankaulipady, Thiruvail, Bondathila, Arkula, Harekala, Konaje, Belma, Talapady.

Higher Secondary or Pre University Courses or Intermediate or Junior College in 5 villages of the CD Block,, namely Haleangady, Talipady, Kondemula, Tenkayedapadavu, Bondathila.

College in 3 villages, Adult Literacy Center in 12 villages., Colleges are in villages, namely Haleangady, Aikala, Kondemula.

Medical: Hospital in 2 villages, Dispensary in 29 villages, Health Center in 17 villages, Sub Center in 64 villages, Maternity and Child Welfare Center in 13 villages, Community health workers in 30 villages.

The Villages having Hospital or Dispensary or Health Center are Balkunje, Kollur, Shimanthur, Kilpady, Sasihithlu, Haleangady, Thokur-(10), Talipady, Menna Bettu, Kemral, Kondemula, Kallamundkooru, Puthige, Beluvai, Madya, Adyapady, Kandavara, Tenkayedapadavu, Killenjaru, Addur, Thiruvail, Bondathila, Mallur, Amblamogru, Harekala, Pavoor , Boliyar, Konaje, Belma, Talapady, Manjanady.

Drinking Water: Tap water in 82 villages, Tank water in 27 villages, Well water in 88 villages, Tubewell in 84 villages and more than one source in 88 villages.

Bank: Banking facility in 28 villages, namely, Athikari Bettu, Shimanthur, Sasihithlu, Haleangady Thokur-(10), Talipady, Aikala, Menna Bettu Kondemula, Kadandale, Kallamundkooru, Niddodi Badagumijaru, Hosabettu, Beluvai, Nellikaru Shirthadi, Tenkayekkar, Permude, Kolambe Badagaulipady, Tenkayedapadavu, Killenjaru Thiruvail, Arkula, Konaje, Belma, Talapady.

Credit Society in 17 villages Agricultural Credit Society in 10 Non-Agricultural Credit Society in 5 villages.

Others: Power supply in 88 villages, Cinema hall in 1 village, sport club in 1 village, Stadium or Auditorium or Community Hall in 1 village, Post Office in 75 villages.

There are 88 villages having bus facilities.

Villages with most of facilities: Athikari Bettu Shimanthur, Sasihithlu, Haleangady, Thokur-(10) Talipady, Aikala, Menna Bettu, Kondemula, Kadandale Kallamundkooru, Niddodi, Badagumijaru, Hosabettu Beluvai, Nellikaru, Shirthadi, Tenkayekkar, Permude Kolambe, Badagaulipady, Tenkayedapadavu, Killenjaru Thiruvail, Arkula, Konaje, Belma, Talapady.

Villages without amenities (Education): Kilenjur..

Scheduled Castes: Out of the total population of 281777 persons, 17538 persons (6.22%) belong to Scheduled Castes.

The villages having less than 10% SC population are Athikari Bettu, Karnire, Balkunje, Ulipady, Kollur Shimanthur, Bellairu, Padupanamboor, Sasihithlu Pavanje, Haleangady, Talipady, Elathur, Elinje Kemral, Koikude, Kilenjur, Nadugodu, Kadandale Kallamundkooru, Niddodi, Badagumijaru, Tenkamijar Ervuailu, Puchhamoguru, Hosabettu, Puthige Kellaputhige, Surinje, Delanthabettu, Badagayekkaru Tenkayekkar, Permude, Kalavar, Paduperar, Kompadavu Muchur, Muduperar, Kolambe, Kandavara, Badagaulipady Tenkayedapadavu, Badagayedapadavu, Killenjaru Kolavooru, Muthuru, Mogaru, Tankaulipady, Addur Thiruvail, Bondathila, Ulaibettu, Mallur, Arkula Amblamogru, Harekala, Pavoor , Boliyar, Konaje Belma, Talapady, Kinnya, Manjanady.

The village having more than 50% SC population is None.

Sex ratio of Scheduled Caste population is 498.

Scheduled Castes Literates and Illiterates by Sex:

	Persons	Males	Females
Literate	10,888	6,006	4,882
Illiterate	6,650	2,794	3,856
Literacy rate	70.0	77.2	62.8
Graduate	240	148	92

Scheduled Castes (Dominant):

Adi Dravida, Mundala, Moger, Godda, Holaya etc.

For their cultural identity please see Appendix-I

Villages without Scheduled Castes: There are 2 villages without any scheduled caste population.

Scheduled Tribes: Out of the total population of 281777 persons, 6091 persons (2.16%) belong to Scheduled Tribes.

The villages having less than 10% ST population are Athikari Bettu, Karnire, Balkunje, Ulipady, Kollur Kavathar, Shimanthur, Kilpady, Bellairu Padupanamboor, Sasihithlu, Pavanje, Haleangady Thokur-(10), Talipady, Elathur, Elinje, Aikala Menna Bettu, Kemral, Koikude, Panja, Attur, Kilenjur Nadugodu, Kondemula, Kadandale, Paladka Kallamundkooru, Niddodi, Badagumijaru, Tenkamijar Thodaru, Puchhamoguru, Hosabettu, Beluvai Padumarnadu, Moodumarnadu, Kellaputhige, Daregudde Panapila, Nellikaru, Valpadi, Padukonaje Moodukonaje, Shirthadi, Mantrady, Madya, Surinje Delanthabettu, Badagayekkaru, Tenkayekkar, Permude Kalavar, Kenjar, Malavoor, Paduperar, Kompadavu Muchur, Muduperar, Kolambe, Adyapady, Kandavara Badagaulipady, Tenkayedapadavu, Badagayedapadavu

Killenjaru, Kolavooru, Muthuru, Mogaru, Tankaulipady Addur, Thiruvail, Bondathila, Ulaibettu, Mallur Arkula, Amblamogru, Harekala, Pavoor , Boliyar Konaje, Belma, Talapady, Kinnya, Manjanady.

The villages having more than 50% ST population are None.

Sex ratio of Scheduled tribe population is 514.

Scheduled Tribes Literates and Illiterates by Sex:

	Persons	Males	Females
Literate	3,729	1,932	1,797
Illiterate	2,362	1,029	1,333
Literacy rate	70.0	75.3	65.1
Graduate	104	69	35

Scheduled Tribes (Dominant):

Marati, Koraga, Naikda etc., Hakkipikki Generic Tribes etc.

For their cultural identity please see Appendix-II

Villages without Scheduled Tribes: There are 5 villages without any scheduled tribe population.

Literates and Illiterates by Sex (Total Population):

	Persons	Males	Females
Literate	203,709	105,673	98,036
Illiterate	78,068	29,797	48,271
Literacy rate	82	89	75
Graduate	8,101	4,629	3,472

Agriculture: ***Distribution of villages according to land use:*** Out of 88 villages, Total area (in hectare) is 58784, out of that 50.81 percent is cultivable and 47.3 percent of the cultivable area is irrigated.

Sources of Irrigation (Hectares): Government Canal 221.45, Private Canal 65.08, Well without Electricity 1022.97, Well with Electricity 4545.04, Tubewell without Electricity 220.26, Tubewell with Electricity 1731.83, Tank 285.63, River 1204.38, Lake 1.92, Waterfall 8.09, Others 4822.45.

Villages with population of 5000 to 9999:

Talipady, Puthige, Beluvai, Badagaulipady Tenkayedapadavu, Addur, Thiruvail, Harekala, Pavoor Konaje, Talapady, Manjanady.

Villages with population of 10000 and above: None

Distribution of Workers:

	Persons	Males	Females	WPR
Cultivators	13,127	9,248	3,879	9.5
Agricultural Labour	13,547	8,572	4,975	9.8
Household Industry	48,091	3,347	44,744	34.8
Other Workers	63,432	53,850	9,582	45.9
Main Workers	123,474	68,697	54,777	89.35
Marginal Workers	14,723	6,320	8,403	10.65
Total Workers	138,197	75,017	63,180	

Religion: Major Religious Communities:

	Persons	Males	Females	Sex Ratio
Hindu (65.04%)	183,262	87,398	95,864	1,097
Muslim (24.4%)	68,745	33,954	34,791	1,025
Christian (9.7%)	27,346	12,909	14,437	1,118
Sikh (0.01%)	36	24	12	500
Buddhists (0.1%)	281	146	135	925
Jain (0.71%)	2,006	988	1,018	1,030

Agewise Data:

	Persons	Males	Females	Sex Ratio
All ages	281,777	135,470	146,307	1080
0-14	80,098	40,855	39,243	961
15-44	139,283	66,034	73,249	1109
45-79	59,545	27,462	32,083	1168
80+	2,684	1,030	1,654	1606
Age not stated	167	89	78	876

Languages (Dominant):

Tulu, Konkani, Others, Malayalam, Kannada

Disabled Population:

	Persons	Males	Females	%
Total Disabled	5,975	3,084	2,891	
In Seeing	2,703	1,264	1,439	45.24
In Speech	561	297	264	9.39
In Hearing	297	138	159	4.97
In Movement	1,488	887	601	24.9
Mentally	926	498	428	15.5

MANVI

Manvi C.D. Block lies in the south-central part of Raich ur district. It is a part of Manvi taluka. The Block is located at a distance of 46 kms. from district headqu arters (Raichur). There are 171 villages in the block with the total population of 292,985 persons. Area of the C.D. Block is 1790.59 sq. kms. It is bounded by taluks Devadurga and Raichur on north, taluk Sindhnur on south, taluk Raichur on east, taluk Lingsugur on west, and it has common boundary with the state of Andhra Pradesh on south.

Communications:

Roadways : S.H-20: Direction- Lingsugur to Raichur, Neare st Villages- Eklasapur, Watgal, Ameengad, Kotekal, Pamank allur, Kowtal, Hire, Hanagi, Chikka Hanagi, Potapur, Goldinni, Malat, Narabanda, Murkigudda, Nawalkal, Sirwar, Jakkal Dinni, Atnur. S.H-23: Direction- Sindhunr to Raichur, Nearest Villages- Kallur, Neermanvi, Kapgal, Bettadur, Kurdi, Nandihal, Manvi [R], Yarmal Doddi, Rajaldinni, Jeenur, Potanhal, Bhogawati, Hire Kotankal, Uralgaddi, Muddamgaddi.

River: Maski Halla Nadi- Nearest Villages- Hire Kadboor, S.Ramal Dinni, Kabberhal, Hanchanhal, Nalgamdinni, Pannur Jagir, Yedival, Belwat, Utaknur, Tadkal, Jeenur, Potanhal, Uralgaddi, Muddamgaddi, Kharabadinni, Eralgad di, Devipur. Tungabhadra Nadi- Nearest Villages- Pannuru, Arnalli, Rajalbanda, Tammapur, Jukur, Rajoli, Daddal,

Katarki, Madlapur, Chikalparvi, Yedival.

Canal: Nearest Villages- Gudihal, Irkal, Basapur, Parasa pur, Nandihal, Joladarasi, Halapur, Nagaldinni, Hire Kadboor, Goge Hebbal, Kowtal, Goldinni, Chikkabadardinni, Dewatgal, Malat, Nawalkal, Hosur N, Nugdoni, Bagalwad, Sirwar, Kadadinni, Rajalbanda, Tammapur, Jukur, Rajoli.

Reserved Forest: (Kotwal): Nearest Villages- Yatgal, Kachapur, Eklasapur, Nelkola, Ameengad, Kotekal, Pamank allur, Timmapur, Hussainpur, Kowtal.

Annual Rainfall: Normal Rianfall 640 mm.

Ground Water: Availability of the Ground Water in the Basin is 234.53 H.A.M. and the utilization is 23.83 H.A.M. It belongs to Over Exploited category. Depth to water level 2 to 20 meter below the ground. Most of the wells go down in summer months, according to the Ground Water Estimation Committee.

Soils: Mixed Red and Black Soils.

Natural Division : It falls partly in the Middle Tungabha dra Valley and the Arkera-Mudgal-Kanakgiri Upland of the Central Karnataka Plateau.

Administration:

Division: Gulbarga. Parliamentary Constituency: 6 Raichur (ST), 8 Koppal. District: Raichur. Taluka: Manvi. Assem bly Constituency: 53 Raichur Rural (ST), 55 Manvi (ST), 59 Maski (ST). Gram Panchayat: 36.

Regional Area Development Boards: The Hyderabad - Karnataka Area Development Board.

Border Villages: (State: Andhra Pradesh)- Pannuru, Arnal li, Rajalbanda, Tammapur, Jukur, Rajoli, Daddal, Katarki, Madlapur, Chikalparvi, Yedival.

Fairs: Karemma Jatra: Karemma jatra held at Manvi in about the month of January for two days. Manvi is a place of pilgrimage for Hindus, where several fairs and festivals are held. It has a well known temple of Jagannathaswami. It is also the birth place of Jagannath aswami who spread the bhakti cult.

Mahamalleshappa Jatra: It is held at Manvi near Raichur in about the month of January. Manvi is a place of pilgr image for Hindus, where several fairs and festivals are held. It has a well known temple of Jagannathaswami. It is also the birth place of Jagannatha Dasa who spread the bhakti cult.

Sanjeevaraya Jatra: Sanjeevaraya jatra, held at Manvi near Raichur in about the month of December. Manvi is a place of pilgrimage for Hindus, where several fairs and festivals are held. It has a well known temple of Jagannathaswami who spread the bhakti cult.

Yellamma Jatra: It is held at Manvi near Raichur in the month of February for seven days. Manvi is a place of pilgrimage for Hindus, where several fairs and festiv als are held. It has a well known temple of Jagannathaswa mi. It is also the birth place of Jagannatha Deva who spread the Bhakti cult.

Villages: 171 **Inhabited:** 164 **Uninhabited:** 7

Ranking	District	State	National
Area	2	11	73
Population	2	20	81
Sex Ratio	2	37	1393
Child Sex Ratio	4	38	1829
Literacy Rate	3	168	5664
Density	2	57	5340
Work Participation Rate	2	107.	1528

Gram Panchayats:

Ameengad, Pamankallur, Halapur, Toran Dinni, Kowtal, Heera, Hire Hanagi, Malat, Nawalkal, Sirwar, Atnur, Kallur, Ganadinni, Madagiri, Chagbhavi, Gud-Dinni.K, Ballatgi, Janekal, Nakkunda, Bagalwad, Byagwat, Utaknur, Potanhal, Hire Kotankal, Chikkotankal, Madlapur, Bhogawati, Sangapur, Harvi, Neermanvi, Sadapur, Kapgal, Kurdi, Sunkeswara, Gorkal, Aroli.

Amenities:

Education: Primary School in 59 villages, Middle school in 57 villages, Matriculation or Secondary School in 12 villages, namely Pamankallur, Halapur, Kowtal, Ballatgi, Bagalwad, Sirwar, Madagiri, Neermanvi, Kurdi, Byagwat, Potanhal, Hire Kotankal.

Higher Secondary or Pre University Courses or Inter-mediate or Junior College in 3 villages of the CD Block,, namely Kowtal, Bagalwad, Sirwar.

College in 0 village, Adult Literacy Center in 6 villages.

Medical: Hospital in 5 villages, Dispensary in 12 villages, Health Center in 9 villages, Sub Center in 45 villages, Maternity and Child Welfare Center in 3 villages, Community health workers in 5 villages.

The Villages having Hospital or Dispensary or Health Center are Watgal, Pamankallur, Harvapur, Irkal, Kowtal, Ballatgi, Bagalwad, Sirwar, Rajalbanda, Chikalparvi, Byagwat, Hire Kotankal.

Drinking Water: Tap water in 103 villages, Tank water in 11 villages, Well water in 68 villages, Tubewell in 21 villages and more than one source in 158 villages.

Bank: Banking facility in 12 villages, namely, Pamankallur, Toran Dinni, Kowtal, Bagalwad, Sirwar Kallur, Hokrani, Harvi, Neermanvi, Kapgal Chikalparvi, Potanhal.

Credit Society in 24 villages Agricultural Credit Society in 24 Non-Agricultural Credit Society in 2 villages.

Others: Power supply in 164 villages, Cinema hall in 2 villages sport club in 164 villages, Stadium or Auditorium or Communi Hall in 164 villages, Post Office in 54 villages.

There are 122 villages having bus facilities.

Villages with most of facilities: Pamankallur Toran Dinni, Kowtal, Bagalwad, Sirwar, Kallur, Harvi Neermanvi, Chikalparvi, Potanhal.

Villages without amenities (Education): Yatgal, Kachapur, Eklasapur, Nelkola, Kotekal, Anandgal, Harvapur, Tupdoor, Benchamardi, Hilalpur, Chilkaragi, Irkal, Basapur, Parasapur, Joladarasi, Jangamarhalli, Yeddal Dinni, M.Ramaldinni, Nagaldinni, Hire Kadboor, Jinnapur, S.Ramal Dinni, Tuggal Dinni, Goge Hebbal, Chikkadinni, Malkapur, Sunknoor, Hiredinni, Malladgudda, Donamaradi, Huda, Bomsandoddi, Kasan Doddi, Donmardi, Buddinni, Toppal Doddi, Timmapur, Hussainpur, Saidapur, U. Gud-Dinni, Chikka Hanagi, Potapur, Goldinni, Chikkabadardinni, Dewatgal, Bullapur, Kalamgere, Wadwatti, Patakam Doddi, Narabanda, Hunched, Murkigudda, Marata, Hire-Badardinni, Gavigat, Aldhal, Shakapur, Singaddinni, Jambaldinni, Halli, Hokrani, Bommanahal, Bevinur, Tupdur. K, Mallige Madugu, Naslapur, Chimlapur, Govinadoddi, Advi Khanapur, Kambalanetti, Murharpur, Pannuru, Arnalli, Tammapur, Jukur, Nandihal, Manvi [R], Rabbankal, Daddal, Katarki, Burhanpur, Buddinni, Rangdhal, Mustoor, Yarmal Doddi, Jutlapur, Hosur Umli, Chikkotankal, Nalgamdinni, Pannur Jagir, Yedival, Badlapur, Belwat, Dhotarbandi, Udbal, Jeenur, Karegudda, Amarawati, Muddamgaddi, Kharabadinni, Eralgaddi, Devipur..

Scheduled Castes: Out of the total population of 293106 persons, 57699 persons (19.69%) belong to Scheduled Castes.
The villages having less than 10% SC population are Kachapur, Nelkola, Kotekal, Gudihal, Parasapur Joladarasi, Nagaldinni, S.Ramal Dinni, Huda Bomsandoddi, Kasan Doddi, Donmardi, Buddinni Toppal Doddi, Timmapur, Chikka Hanagi, Potapur Goldinni, Dewatgal, Bullapur, Singaddinni, Kadadinni Bevinur, Naslapur, Walkam Dinni, Sadapur, Korvi Rajalbanda, Tammapur, Rajoli, Manvi [R], Rabbankal Daddal, Katarki, Burhanpur, Buddinni, Jutlapur Nalgamdinni, Badlapur, Utaknur, Bhogawati.
The village having more than 50% SC population is None.
Sex ratio of Scheduled Caste population is 500.

Scheduled Castes Literates and Illiterates by Sex:

	Persons	Males	Females
Literate	13,929	9,570	4,359
Illiterate	43,770	19,283	24,487
Literacy rate	30.0	41.3	18.7
Graduate	271	246	25

Scheduled Castes (Dominant):
Madiga, Chalavadi etc., Bhovi, Banjara etc.
Bhambi etc.

For their cultural identity please see Appendix-I

Villages without Scheduled Castes: There are 16 villages without any scheduled caste population.

Scheduled Tribes: Out of the total population of 293106 persons, 73265 persons (25%) belong to Scheduled Tribes.
The villages having less than 10% ST population are Ameengad, Anandgal, Harvapur, Parasapur, Joladarasi Hanchanhal, Malkapur, Hiredinni, Donamaradi Chincharaki, Toppal Doddi, Kowtal, Potapur Kalamgere, Sannahosur, Kallur, Bommanahal, Naslapur Kurdi, Kambalanetti, Gorkal, Murharpur, Arnalli Buddinni, Utaknur, Dhotarbandi, Udbal, Tadkal Amarawati.
The villages having more than 50% ST population are Yatgal, Kachapur, Nelkola, Kotekal, Nagaldinni Jinnapur, S.Ramal Dinni, Tuggal Dinni, Huda Bomsandoddi, Kasan Doddi, Chikka Hanagi Patakam Doddi, Marata, Bevinur, Tupdur. K, Kardigud Mallige Madugu, Govinadoddi, Bettadur, Walkam Dinni Sadapur, Korvi, Tammapur, Rajoli, Daddal, Rangdhal Rajaldinni, Chikkotankal, Nalgamdinni, Yedival Badlapur, Jeenur, Devipur.
Sex ratio of Scheduled tribe population is 501.

Scheduled Tribes Literates and Illiterates by Sex:

	Persons	Males	Females
Literate	15,383	11,073	4,310
Illiterate	57,882	25,516	32,366
Literacy rate	25.7	37.2	14.3
Graduate	139	132	7

Scheduled Tribes (Dominant):
Naikda etc., Meda, Jenu Kuruba, Kathodi etc.
Koraga

For their cultural identity please see Appendix-II

Villages without Scheduled Tribes: There are 8 villages without any scheduled tribe population.

Literates and Illiterates by Sex (Total Population):

	Persons	Males	Females
Literate	98,475	64,399	34,076
Illiterate	194,631	82,603	112,028
Literacy rate	41	53	28
Graduate	2,366	2,050	316

Agriculture: ***Distribution of villages according to land use:*** Out of 171 villages, Total area (in hectare) is 179059, out of that 85.31 percent is cultivable and 30.29 percent of the cultivable area is irrigated.

Sources of Irrigation (Hectares): Government Canal 41422.28, Private Canal 0, Well without Electricity 40.65, Well with Electricity 832.43, Tubewell without Electricity 54.63,

Tubewell with Electricity 2250.93, Tank 226.76, River 870.31, Lake 0, Waterfall 0, Others 565.58.

Villages with population of 5000 to 9999:
Ballatgi, Bagalwad, Kallur, Harvi, Neermanvi, Kurdi Byagwat, Hire Kotankal.

Villages with population of 10000 and above:
Kowtal, Sirwar.

Distribution of Workers:

	Persons	Males	Females	WPR
Cultivators	43,044	34,813	8,231	29.4
Agricultural Labour	85,867	35,857	50,010	58.65
Household Industry	2,079	1,249	830	1.42
Other Workers	15,416	11,554	3,862	10.53
Main Workers	114,835	73,513	41,322	78.44
Marginal Workers	31,571	9,960	21,611	21.56
Total Workers	146,406	83,473	62,933	

Religion: Major Religious Communities:

	Persons	Males	Females	Sex Ratio
Hindu (90.18%)	264,315	132,509	131,806	995
Muslim (9.22%)	27,028	13,601	13,427	987
Christian (0.19%)	571	284	287	1,011
Sikh (0%)	6	3	3	1,000
Buddhists (0.03%)	99	45	54	1,200
Jain (0.02%)	52	28	24	857

Agewise Data:

	Persons	Males	Females	Sex Ratio
All ages	293,106	147,002	146,104	994
0-14	117,053	59,469	57,584	968
15-44	128,535	64,858	63,677	982
45-79	45,960	22,051	23,909	1084
80+	1,354	513	841	1639
Age not stated	204	111	93	838

Languages (Dominant):
Kannada, Telugu, Urdu, Hindi, Marathi

Disabled Population:

	Persons	Males	Females	%
Total Disabled	2,976	1,666	1,310	
In Seeing	1,029	510	519	34.58
In Speech	325	193	132	10.92
In Hearing	175	83	92	5.88
In Movement	1,128	691	437	37.9
Mentally	319	189	130	10.72

MOLAKALMURU

Molakalmuru C.D. Block lies in the northern part of Chitradurga district. It is a part of Molakalmuru taluka. The Block is located at a distance of 87 kms. from district headquarters (Chitradurga). There are 89 villages in the block with the total population of 112,517 persons. Area of the C.D. Block is 693.38 sq. kms. It is bounded by district Bellary on north, taluk Challakere on south, and district Bellary on west. It has common boundary with the state of Andhra Pradesh on north and east.

Communications:
Roadways : S.H-2: Direction- Kudligi to Molakamuru, Nearest Villages- Hirekerehalli, Talavarahalli, Bommalinganahalli, Yerajinnenahalli, Hanagal, Sulenahalli. S.H-19: Direction- Challakere to Bellary, Nearest Villages- Bommadevarahalli, Thammenahalli, Swamikere, Rajapura, Obalapura, Konapura, Bommakkanahalli, Murudi, Kerekopura, Rampura, Devasamudra, Ramasagara, Gowrasamudra, Heruru, Chikkerahalli, Amakundi, Nagasamudra, Katanaikanahalli, Guddadahalli, Byrapura, Obalapura, Hirekerehalli, Hanagal, Yerrenahalli, Rayapura, Adavimallapura, Tumkurlahalli, Kamara Kaval, Mathigarahalli, Bommagondanakere.
River: Chinna Hagari Nadi- Nearest Villages- Venkatapura, Urthal, Ramasagara, Veerapura, Gowrasamudra, Heruru, Siddapura, Machenahalli, Bhatrahalli, Chikkerahalli, Amakundi, Nagasamudra, Byrapura, Obalapura, Hirekerehalli, Talavarahalli, Rangaiahnadurga, Bommalinganahalli, Matadajogihalli, Iyanahalli, Siddaiahnakote, Yerapothajogihalli, Chikkumthi, Chikkobanahalli, Puraboranahalli. Gonde Halla Nadi- Nearest Villages- Karadihalli, Sirekola, Swamikere, Pokkurthi, Nallareddikondapura, Obalapura, Bommakkanahalli, Murudi.
Canal: Nearest Villages- Rampura, Basapura, Ramasagara, Siddapura.
Annual Rainfall: Normal Rianfall 593.5 mm.
Ground Water: Availability of the Ground Water in the Basin is 5092.89 H.A.M. and the utilization is 2341 H.A.M. It belongs to Over Expoited category. Depth to water level 5 to 20 meter below the ground. Most of the wells go down in summer months, according to the Ground Water Estimation Committee.
Soils: Deep and Shallow black soils, mixed red and black soil, red loamy and sandy soils.
Natural Division : It falls in Jagalur-Molakalmuru Upland and Middle Vedavati (Hagari) Basin of the Central Karnataka Plateau.
Administration:
Division: Bangalore. Parliamentary Constituency: 18 Chitradurga (SC). District: Chitradurga. Taluka: Molakalmuru. Assembly Constituency: 97 Mokalmaru (ST). Gram Panchayat: 16.
Regional Area Development Boards: The Bailu Seeme Area Development Board.
Border Villages: (State: Andhra Pradesh)- Melinakanive, Bommadevarahalli, Thammenahalli, Kanakuppe, Karadihalli, Sirekola, Hosanagalapura, Pennammanahalli, Urthal, Siddapura, Machenahalli, Nagasamudra, Konsagara.
Fairs: Pamadevaru Car Festival: Bemmaghatta near Molak

almaru taluk of Chitradurga, a car festival is celebrated in honour of Ramadevaru in the month of Phalguna (February-March), at which more than 75,000 people participate.

Villages: 89 **Inhabited:** 78 **Uninhabited:** 11

Ranking	District	State	National
Area	6	136	931
Population	6	152	3082
Sex Ratio	5	151	3657
Child Sex Ratio	5	138	3896
Literacy Rate	6	145	4579
Density	5	111	5364
Work Participation Rate	3	110	2615

Gram Panchayats:
Santhegudda, Thammenahalli, Jahagirbuddenahalli, Rampura, Devasamudra, Siddapura, Nagasamudra, Chikkerahalli, Hirekerehalli, Hanagal, Rayapura, Tumkurlahalli, Nerlahalli, Konsagara, Kondlahalli, Bommagondanakere.

Amenities:

Education: Primary School in 69 villages, Middle school in 51 villages, Matriculation or Secondary School in 14 villages, namely Bandravi, Rampura, Devasamudra, Siddapura, Chikkerahalli, Nagasamudra, Hanagal, Siddaiahnakote, Rayapura, Tumkurlahalli, Chikkobanahalli, Bommagondanakere, Kondlahalli, Konsagara.
Higher Secondary or Pre University Courses or Intermediate or Junior College in 2 villages of the CD Block,, namely Rampura, Bommagondanakere.
College in 1 village, Adult Literacy Center in 0 village., Colleges is in village, namely Bommagondanakere.

Medical: Hospital in 2 villages, Dispensary in 2 villages, Health Center in 3 villages, Sub Center in 17 villages, Maternity and Child Welfare Center in 2 villages, Community health workers in 0 village.
The Villages having Hospital or Dispensary or Health Center are Karadihalli, Devasamudra, Siddapura, Nagasamudra.

Drinking Water: Tap water in 37 villages, Tank water in 29 villages, Well water in 13 villages, Tubewell in 45 villages and more than one source in 66 villages.

Bank: Banking facility in 10 villages, namely, Kanakuppe, Basapura, Devasamudra, Nagasamudra Katanaikanahalli, Tuppadakkanahalli, Marlahalli Bommagondanakere, Mogalahalli, Netrenahalli.
Credit Society in 16 villages Agricultural Credit Society in 12 Non-Agricultural Credit Society in 4 villages.

Others: Power supply in 78 villages, Cinema hall in 3 villages, sport club in 0 village, Stadium or Auditorium or Community Hall in 1 village, Post Office in 23 villages.
There are 53 villages having bus facilities.

Villages with most of facilities: Basapura Devasamudra, Nagasamudra, Katanaikanahalli Bommagondanakere, Mogalahalli, Netrenahalli.

Villages without amenities (Education):
Chinivaladagudda, Obalapura, Rangaiahnadurga, Mahimenahatti, Tuppadakkanahalli, Matadajogihalli, Donetammenahalli, Harvinadoddi, Duppi..

Scheduled Castes: Out of the total population of 112609 persons, 23266 persons (20.66%) belong to Scheduled Castes.
The villages having less than 10% SC population are Bandravi, Santhegudda, Bommadevarahalli, Kanakuppe Kelaginakanive, Malleharavu, Nallareddikondapura Konapura, Murudi, Chinivaladagudda, Vittalapura Urthal, Veerapura, Heruru, Katanaikanahalli Obalapura, Talavarahalli, Rangaiahnadurga Mahimenahatti, Matadajogihalli, Iyanahalli, Gundluru Tumkurlahalli, Donetammenahalli, Yerapothajogihalli Duppi, Netrenahalli.
The villages having more than 50% SC population are Vaderahalli, Chikkerahalli, Yerajinnenahalli Tuppadakkanahalli, Siddaiahnakote.
Sex ratio of Scheduled Caste population is 482.

Scheduled Castes Literates and Illiterates by Sex:

	Persons	Males	Females
Literate	8,057	5,349	2,708
Illiterate	15,209	6,694	8,515
Literacy rate	42.3	54.6	29.3
Graduate	239	222	17

Scheduled Castes (Dominant):
Adi Karnataka, Madiga, Bhovi, Koracha Beda Jangam etc.

For their cultural identity please see Appendix-I

Villages without Scheduled Castes: There are 26 villages without any scheduled caste population.

Scheduled Tribes: Out of the total population of 112609 persons, 42821 persons (38.03%) belong to Scheduled Tribes.
The villages having less than 10% ST population are Thammenahalli, Rajapura, Obalapura, Bommakkanahalli Murudi, Pennammanahalli, Thimmalapura, Kerekondapura Basapura, Vaderahalli, Venkatapura, Veerapura Chikkanahalli, Byrapura, Obalapura Tuppadakkanahalli, Siddaiahnakote, Gundluru Mogalahalli, Kondlahalli.
The villages having more than 50% ST population are Bandravi, Melinakanive, Bommadevarahalli, Kanakuppe Kelaginakanive, Malleharavu, Konapura Chinivaladagudda, Vittalapura, Urthal, Ramasagara Heruru, Katanaikanahalli, Guddadahalli Talavarahalli, Rangaiahnadurga, Mahimenahatti Hanagal, Matadajogihalli, Iyanahalli, Yerrenahalli

Rayapura, Sulenahalli, Marlahalli, Nerlahalli Tumkurlahalli, Donetammenahalli, Yerapothajogihalli Chikkumthi, Harvinadoddi, Surammanhalli Mathigarahalli, Duppi, Marammanahalli, Netrenahalli.

Sex ratio of Scheduled tribe population is 487.

Scheduled Tribes Literates and Illiterates by Sex:

	Persons	Males	Females
Literate	13,204	9,110	4,094
Illiterate	29,617	12,874	16,743
Literacy rate	37.6	50.3	24.0
Graduate	303	276	27

Scheduled Tribes (Dominant):

Naikda etc., Generic Tribes etc.

For their cultural identity please see Appendix-II

Villages without Scheduled Tribes: There are 16 villages without any scheduled tribe population.

Literates and Illiterates by Sex (Total Population):

	Persons	Males	Females
Literate	46,752	30,124	16,628
Illiterate	65,857	27,718	38,139
Literacy rate	50	62	36
Graduate	1,504	1,316	188

Agriculture: ***Distribution of villages according to land use:*** Out of 89 villages, Total area (in hectare) is 69338, out of that 51.13 percent is cultivable and 17.93 percent of the cultivable area is irrigated.

Sources of Irrigation (Hectares): Government Canal 77.86, Private Canal 0, Well without Electricity 45.27, Well with Electricity 271.86, Tubewell without Electricity 0, Tubewell with Electricity 4896.56, Tank 1055.24, River 0, Lake 0, Waterfall 0, Others 8.21.

Villages with population of 5000 to 9999:

Rampura, Nagasamudra, Kondlahalli, Konsagara.

Villages with population of 10000 and above: None

Distribution of Workers:

	Persons	Males	Females	WPR
Cultivators	17,106	12,610	4,496	32.6
Agricultural Labour	22,563	9,380	13,183	43
Household Industry	3,268	1,816	1,452	6.23
Other Workers	9,541	6,923	2,618	18.18
Main Workers	42,962	27,723	15,239	81.87
Marginal Workers	9,516	3,006	6,510	18.13
Total Workers	52,478	30,729	21,749	

Religion: Major Religious Communities:

	Persons	Males	Females	Sex Ratio
Hindu (94.57%)	106,497	54,727	51,770	946
Muslim (4.87%)	5,480	2,790	2,690	964
Christian (0.03%)	33	18	15	833
Sikh (0.02%)	25	15	10	667
Buddhists (0.02%)	21	11	10	909
Jain (0.04%)	43	15	28	1,867

Agewise Data:

	Persons	Males	Females	Sex Ratio
All ages	112,609	57,842	54,767	947
0-14	43,247	22,262	20,985	943
15-44	49,563	25,342	24,221	956
45-79	18,904	9,821	9,083	925
80+	828	375	453	1208
Age not stated	67	42	25	595

Languages (Dominant):

Kannada, Telugu, Urdu, Marathi, Tamil

Disabled Population:

	Persons	Males	Females	%
Total Disabled	1,957	1,166	791	
In Seeing	735	403	332	37.56
In Speech	221	134	87	11.29
In Hearing	126	72	54	6.44
In Movement	716	469	247	36.59
Mentally	159	88	71	8.12

MUDDEBIHAL

Muddebihal C.D. Block lies in the south-eastern part of Bijapur district. It is a part of Muddebihal taluka. The Block is located at adistance of 85 kms. From district headquarters (Bijapur). There are 153 villages in the block with the total population of 199,202 persons. Area of the C.D. Block is 1489.66 sq. kms. It is boundedby taluks Sindgi and Basavana Bagewadi on north, districts Bagalkot and Raichur on south,district Gulbarga on east, and Basavana Bagewadi taluk on west.

Communications:

Roadways : N.H-13: Direction- Hindgund to Bijapur, NearestVillage- Yalgur. S.H-41: Direction- Indi to Lingsugur, Nearest Villages- Bidarkundi, Agasabal, Dhavalagi, Hallur, Kavadimatti, Jangamural, Aremural, Sarur, Hiremural, Budihal (P.Naltawad), Nagarabetta, Nalatawad, Siddapur P.Naltawad, Khanikeri, Sultanpur. S.H-41A: Direction- Hungund to Muddevihal, Nearest Villages- Shirol, Mudnal, Nebageri, Banoshi, Gangur, Tangadagi.

River: Krishna Nadi- Nearest Villages- Balabatti, Yalgur, Kashinakunti, Budihal (P N), Masuti. Kalagi, Mudur, Kandaganur, Handargall, Nagaral, Devoor, Gangur, Kamaldinni, Kunchaganur, Tangadagi, Amaragol, Hadagali, Bailkur, Madari, Garasangi, Hunakunti, Kapanur, Bangaragund, Rakkasagi, Baladinni, Karkur, Takkalaki, Ingalagi, Bachihal, Siddapur P.Naltawad, Khanikeri, Sultanpur, Khanapur, Bijjur. Don Nadi- Nearest Villages- Hirur,Tumbagi, Bommanahalli, Bolawad, Fatepur P.Talikoti, Guttihal, Minajagi, Talikoti (Rural) , Harnal, Hadaginal, Nagur.

Annual Rainfall: Normal Rianfall 577 mm.

Ground Water: Availability of the Ground Water in the Basin is 6053.81 H.A.M. and the utilization is 3701.45 H.A.M. It belongs to Over Exploited category. Depth to water level 2 to 20 meter below the ground. Most of the wells go down in summer months, according to the Ground Water Estimation Committee.

Soils: Black Soils, Mixed Soils and Red S

Natural Division : It falls partly in the Bijapur-Basavana Bagevadi Upland and the Upper Krishna Valley of the Northern Karnataka Plateau.

Administration:

Division: Belgaum. Parliamentary Constituency: 4 Bijapur. District: Bijapur. Taluka: Muddebihal. Assembly Constituency: 27 Devi Hippargi. Gram Panchayat: 31.

Regional Area Development Boards: The Bailu Seeme Area Development Board.

Villages: 153 **Inhabited:** 145 **Uninhabited:** 8

Ranking	District	State	National
Area	5	33	146
Population	5	89	714
Sex Ratio	1	60	1820
Child Sex Ratio	1	137	3878
Literacy Rate	2	130	3922
Density	4	155	5791
Work Participation Rate	4	145	3708

Gram Panchayats:

Hullur, Bidarkundi, Basarkod, Rudagi, Dhavalagi, Konnur, Madikeshirur, Ingalgeri, Bavoor, Yalgur, Kalagi, Yarazeri, Hadalageri, Kuntoji, Kavadimatti, Kolur, Tangadagi, Alur, Advisomnal, Hiremural, Rakkasagi, Nalatawad, Nagabenal, Bijjaur, Hirur, Tumbagi, Bhantnur, Minajagi, Kodaganur, Salawadagi, Mukihal.

Amenities:

Education: Primary School in 137 villages, Middle school in 116 villages, Matriculation or Secondary School in 25 villages, namely Hullur, Balabatti, Bidarkundi, Basarkod, Dhavalagi, Konnur, Madikeshirur, Ingalgeri, Lingadalli, Kandaganur, Kuntoji, Kolur, Tangadagi, Amaragol, Alur, Jangamural, Sarur, Kesapur, Rakkasagi, Nalatawad, Hirur, Tumbagi, Minajagi, Kodaganur, Salawadagi.

Higher Secondary or Pre University Courses or Intermediate or Junior College in 4 villages of the CD Block,, namely Dhavalagi, Nalatawad, Hirur, Salawadagi.

College in 1 village, Adult Literacy Center in 1 village., College is in village, namely Salawadagi.

Medical: Hospital in 0 village, Dispensary in 7 villages, Health Center in 11 villages, Sub Center in 47 villages, Maternity and Child Welfare Center in 3 villages, Community health workers in 36 villages.

The Villages having Hospital or Dispensary or Health Center are Balabatti, Bidarkundi, Basarkod, Dhavalagi, Konnur, Yalgur, Kalagi, Hiremural.

Drinking Water: Tap water in 31 villages, Tank water in 19 villages, Well water in 132 villages, Tubewell in 110 villages and more than one source in 142 villages.

Bank: Banking facility in 4 villages, namely, Masuti, Tangadagi, Alur, Minajagi.

Credit Society in 32 villages Agricultural Credit Society in 32 Non-Agricultural Credit Society in 1 village.

Others: Power supply in 145 villages, Cinema hall in 1 village, sport club in 145 villages, Stadium or Auditorium or Communi Hall in 145 villages, Post Office in 69 villages.

There are 134 villages having bus facilities.

Villages with most of facilities: Masuti Tangadagi, Alur, Minajagi.

Villages without amenities (Education): Venkateshnagar, Tapalkatti, Madinal, Gonal (P.N.), Sultanpur, Huvinahalli, Karaganur, Fatepur P.Talikoti..

Scheduled Castes: Out of the total population of 199214 persons, 38890 persons (19.52%) belong to Scheduled Castes.

The villages having less than 10% SC population are Chondi, Nadahalli, Gudnal, Chirchankal, Yarazeri Nagaral, Hadalageri, Abbihal, Banoshi, Kamaldinni Hadagali, Madari, Garasangi, Jakkeral, Donkamadu Gonal S.Hirur, Hokrani, Wanakihal, Jangamural Malagaladinni, Khilarahatti, Mavinbhavi, Arasanal Hosahalli, Kyatanal, Balaganur, Maileshwar, Maskanal Kaladevanahalli, Shivapur.

The villages having more than 50% SC population are Koppa, Venkateshnagar, Tapalkatti, Lingadalli Hagaragund, Geddalamari, Vijayanagar.

Sex ratio of Scheduled Caste population is 501.

Scheduled Castes Literates and Illiterates by Sex:

	Persons	Males	Females
Literate	13,864	9,515	4,349
Illiterate	25,026	9,890	15,136
Literacy rate	43.5	60.2	27.1
Graduate	379	355	24

Scheduled Castes (Dominant):

Bhambi etc., Banjara etc., Holaya etc., Bhovi Holar etc.

For their cultural identity please see Appendix-I

Villages without Scheduled Castes: There are 9 villages without any scheduled caste population.

Scheduled Tribes: Out of the total population of 199214 persons, 6786 persons (3.41%) belong to Scheduled Tribes.

The villages having less than 10% ST population are

Gudadinni, Koppa, Hullur, Balabatti, Venkateshnagar Tapalkatti, Chalami, Jettagi, Madinal, Gonal (P.N.) Bidarkundi, Basarkod, Siddapur P.Talikoti Gundakarjagi, Rudagi, Agasabal, Hallur, Madikeshirur Nadahalli, Taranal, Gudihal, Balawat, Ingalgeri Handral, Vanahalli, Lingadalli, Kuchabal, Bavoor Gudnal, Jammaladinni, Devarhulagabal, Hagaragund Kashinakunti, Budihal (P N), Wadawadagi, Masuti Kalagi, Mudur, Kandaganur, Chirchankal, Geddalamari Harindral, Yarazeri, Handargall, Nagaral Gonal S.Handral, Hadalageri, Kuntoji, Abbihal Kavadimatti, Mudnal, Nebageri, Kolur, Vijayanagar Banoshi, Devoor, Gangur, Kamaldinni, Kunchaganur Tangadagi, Amaragol, Hadagali, Bailkur, Madari Yaragalla, Garasangi, Hunakunti, Alur, Inchagal Kyatanadoni, Donkamadu, Advi Somnal, Advi Hulagabal Gonal S.Hirur, Hokrani, Jalapur, Wanakihal Jangamural, Aremural, Sarur, Hiremural Budihal (P.Naltawad), Malagaladinni, Chavanbhavi Khilarahatti, Mavinbhavi, Nagarabetta, Arasanal Nerabenchi, Bangaragund, Rakkasagi, Baladinni Takkalaki, Ghalapuji, Lotageri, Nalatawad, Nagabenal Sultanpur, Khanapur , Chokavi, Hirur, Tumbagi Hosahalli, Huvinahalli, Kyatanal, Gotakhindaki Bhantnur, Peerapur, Shellagi, Gadi Somanal Bommanahalli, Bolawad, Fatepur P.Talikoti, Guttihal Tamadaddi, Balaganur, Minajagi, Kodaganur, Lakkundi Salawadagi, Maileshwar, Bilebhavi, Maskanal, Harnal Hadaginal, Kaladevanahalli, Mukihal, Shivapur, Nagur.

The villages having more than 50% ST population are None.

Sex ratio of Scheduled tribe population is 493.

Scheduled Tribes Literates and Illiterates by Sex:

	Persons	Males	Females
Literate	2,587	1,744	843
Illiterate	4,199	1,696	2,503
Literacy rate	46.1	62.1	30.1
Graduate	55	47	8

Scheduled Tribes (Dominant):

Naikda etc., Koli Dhor etc., Chodhara, Kadu Kuruba Chenchu etc.

For their cultural identity please see Appendix-II

Villages without Scheduled Tribes: There are 76 villages without any scheduled tribe population.

Literates and Illiterates by Sex (Total Population):

	Persons	Males	Females
Literate	89,416	59,208	30,208
Illiterate	109,798	41,146	68,652
Literacy rate	54	71	36
Graduate	2,834	2,535	299

Agriculture: ***Distribution of villages according to land use:*** Out of 153 villages, Total area (in hectare) is 148966, out of that 85.85 percent is cultivable and 4.76 percent of the cultivable area is irrigated.

Sources of Irrigation (Hectares): Government Canal 0, Private Canal 0, Well without Electricity 0, Well with Electricity 2228.09, Tubewell without Electricity 0, Tubewell with Electricity 1261.06, Tank 503.96, River 1970.54, Lake 18.39, Waterfall 0, Others 107.34.

Villages with population of 5000 to 9999: None

Villages with population of 10000 and above: Nalatawad.

Distribution of Workers:

	Persons	Males	Females	WPR
Cultivators	26,173	21,814	4,359	31.21
Agricultural Labour	37,563	14,603	22,960	44.79
Household Industry	2,531	1,645	886	3.02
Other Workers	17,596	13,363	4,233	20.98
Main Workers	57,820	43,976	13,844	68.95
Marginal Workers	26,043	7,449	18,594	31.05
Total Workers	83,863	51,425	32,438	

Religion: Major Religious Communities:

	Persons	Males	Females	Sex Ratio
Hindu (90.41%)	180,110	90,659	89,451	987
Muslim (9.04%)	18,005	9,127	8,878	973
Christian (0.02%)	32	21	11	524
Sikh (0%)	2	1	1	1,000
Buddhists (0%)	6	1	5	5,000
Jain (0.24%)	476	249	227	912

Agewise Data:

	Persons	Males	Females	Sex Ratio
All ages	199,214	100,354	98,860	985
0-14	75,035	38,585	36,450	945
15-44	84,961	43,577	41,384	950
45-79	37,576	17,552	20,024	1141
80+	1,465	542	923	1703
Age not stated	177	98	79	806

Languages (Dominant):

Kannada, Urdu, Hindi, Telugu, Marathi

Disabled Population:

	Persons	Males	Females	%
Total Disabled	3,342	1,815	1,527	
In Seeing	1,349	676	673	40.37
In Speech	352	181	171	10.53
In Hearing	186	87	99	5.57
In Movement	1,052	653	399	31.48
Mentally	403	218	185	12.06

MUDHOL

Mudhol C.D. Block lies in the western part of Bagalkot district. It is a part of Mudhol taluka. The Block is located at a distance of 52 kms. from district headquarters (Bagalkot). There are 78 villages in the block with the total population of 201,787 persons. Area of the C.D. Block is 945.54 sq. kms. It is bounded by taluksJamkhandi and Bilgi on north, district Belgaum on south and west, taluks Bilgi, Bagalkot and Badami on east.

Communications:

Roadways : S.H-18: Direction- Chikodi to Mudhol, Nearest Villages- Koganoli, Saidapur, Bisanal, Kesrakoppa, Budni (PD), Belagali , Mugalkhod, Soragoan, Malali, Mudhol (Rural). SH20: Belgaum to Hungund, Nearest Villages- Lokapur, Chikkur, Bhantnur, Badnur, Dadanatti, Mallapur(P.L), Laxanatti, Jalikatti (BK), Jadar-Aralikati, Saidpur, Bisanal, Kesrakopa, Budni (PD), Belagali, Mugalkhod, Soragoan, Malali. S.H-65: Direction-Jamkhandi to Ramdurg, Nearest Villages- Shirol, Malapur,Zunjarakopp, Mudhol (Rural), Chinchakhandi (K.D), Jeeragal,Kasba Jambgi (B.K), Muddapur, Petlur, Timmapur, Hebbal, Naganapur, Lokapur, Varchagal, Palkimanya.

River: Ghatprabha Nadi- Nearest Villages- Akkimaradi, Nandagoan, Soragoan, Malali, Nagaral, Marapur, Dhavaleshwar, Mallapur (P.J), Mirji, Vantigodi, Channal, Ranjanagi, Uttur, Jaliber, Rugi, Zunjarakopp, Mudhol (Rural),Gulgal, Jambagi, Chinchakhandi (B.K), Chinchakhandi(K.D),Jeeragal, Ingalagi, Yadahalli, Baragi, Alagundi (B.K), Budni (B.K.), Machaknur, Budni Khurd, Bidri, Antapur, Jambgi (K.D), Kasba Jambgi (B.K), Muddapur, Timmapur, Hebbal, Chitrabanukoti, Chikkur, Bhantnur, Junnur, Badnur.

Canal: Nearest Villages- Saidapur, Madhabhavi, Bisanal, Mahalingapur (Rural), Belagali , Mugalkhod, Kulali, Shirol, Soragoan, Malali, Nagaral, Akkimaradi, Sanganatti, Zunjarakopp, Mudhol (Rural), Budni(P.M), Mantur, Kishori, Halagali, Baragi, Jeeragal, Ingalagi, Yadahalli, Vajjaramatti, Alagundi (B.K), Budni (B.K.), Machaknur, Bidri, Antapur, Malapur, Dhavaleshwar, Melligeri.

Reserved Forest: Nearest Villages- Kishori, Melligeri, Gulgal Jambagi, Chinchakhandi (B.K), Chincakh andi(K.D), Jeeragal, Kasba, Jambgi(B.K), Petlur, Ningapur, Halagali.

Annual Rainfall: Normal Rianfall 525.6 mm

Ground Water: Availability of the Ground Water in the Basin is (Information not avablable) H.A.M. and the utilization is (Information not avablable) H.A.M. It belongs to (Information not avablable) category. Depth to water level 5 to 20 meter below the ground. Most of the wells go downin summer months, according to the Ground Water Estimation Committee.

Natural Division : It falls partly in the Upper Krishna Valley and the Ghatprabha Irrigated Tract of the Northern Karnataka Plateau.

Soils: Black and Red Soils.

Administration:

Division: Belgaum. Parliamentary Constituency: 3 Bagalkot. District: Bagalkot. Taluka: Mudhol. Assembly Const.: 20 Terdal, 19 Mudhol (SC). Gram Panchayat: 25.

Regional Area Development Boards: The Other Areas.

Villages: 78 **Inhabited:** 78 **Uninhabited:** 0

Ranking	District	State	National
Area	4	93	485
Population	4	87	665
Sex Ratio	5	70	2023
Child Sex Ratio	1	50	2221
Literacy Rate	5	151	4692
Density	1	52	4537
Work Participation Rate	2	67	1480

Gram Panchayats:

Saidapur, Madhabhavi, Kesrakoppa, Belagali , Mugalkhod, Kulali, Shirol, Malali, Nagaral, Dhavaleshwar, Vantigodi, Uttur, Mantur, Halagali, Metgud, Chinchakhandi(K.D), Ingalagi, Vajjaramatti, Machaknur, Kasba Jambgi(B.K), Hebbal, Bhantnur, Dadanatti, Laxanatti, Lokapur.

Amenities:

Education: Primary School in 64 villages, Middle school in 69 villages, Matriculation or Secondary School in 18 villages, namely Saidapur, Belagali, Mugalkhod, Nagaral, Dhavaleshwar, Mirji, Uttur, Mudhol(Rural), Mantur, Halagali, Metgud, Gulgal Jambagi, Ingalagi, Yadahalli, Kasba Jambgi(B.K), Bhantnur, Dadanatti, Lokapur.

Higher Secondary or Pre University Courses or Intermediate or Junior College in 1 village of the CD Block,, namely Lokapur.

College in 0 village, Adult Literacy Center in 50 villages.

Medical: Hospital in 1 village, Dispensary in 9 villages, Health Center in 6 villages, Sub Center in 20 villages, Maternity and Child Welfare Center in 0 village, Community health workers in 15 villages.

The Villages having Hospital or Dispensary or Health Center are Belagali , Malali, Mirji, Mantur, Metgud, Yadahalli, Vajjaramatti, Bhantnur, Lokapur.

Drinking Water: Tap water in 71 villages, Tank water in 28 villages, Well water in 40 villages, Tubewell in 30 villages and more than one source in 77 villages.

Bank: Banking facility in 13 villages, namely, Saidapur, Belagali, Mugalkhod, Shirol, Uttur, Mantur Halagali, Metgud, Chinchakhandi(K.D), Machaknur Muddapur, Hosakoti, Lokapur.

Credit Society in 27 villages Agricultural Credit Society in 25 Non-Agricultural Credit Society in 6 villages.

Others: Power supply in 77 villages, Cinema hall in 1 village, sport club in 0 village, Stadium or Auditorium or Community Hall in 0 village, Post Office in 43 villages.

There are 74 villages having bus facilities.

Villages with most of facilities: Saidapur Belagali, Mugalkhod, Shirol, Uttur, Mantur, Halagali Metgud, Chinchakhandi(K.D), Machaknur, Muddapur Hosakoti, Lokapur.

Villages without amenities (Education): Zunjarakopp, Mallapur(P.L), Jadar-Aralikatti, Byadar-Aralikatti..

Scheduled Castes: Out of the total population of 201855 persons, 36069 persons (17.87%) belong to Scheduled Castes.

The villages having less than 10% SC population are Mallapur(P.J), Mudhol(Rural), Antapur, Bommanbudni Chitrabanukoti, Junnur, Dadanatti, Laxanatti Jadar-Aralikatti, Byadar-Aralikatti.

The village having more than 50% SC population is None.

Sex ratio of Scheduled Caste population is 513.

Scheduled Castes Literates and Illiterates by Sex:

	Persons	Males	Females
Literate	9,790	6,415	3,375
Illiterate	26,279	11,165	15,114
Literacy rate	33.5	45.4	22.4
Graduate	156	144	12

Scheduled Castes (Dominant):

Bhambi etc., Banjara etc., Holaya etc., Samagara Korama

For their cultural identity please see Appendix-I

Village without Scheduled Castes: There is 1 village without any scheduled caste population.

Scheduled Tribes: Out of the total population of 201855 persons, 9597 persons (4.75%) belong to Scheduled Tribes.

The villages having less than 10% ST population are Saidapur, Madhabhavi, Bisanal, Kesrakoppa Budni(P.D), Mahalingapur(Rural), Belagali , Mugalkhod Kulali, Shirol, Malapur, Soragoan, Malali, Nagaral Akkimaradi, Nandagoan, Sanganatti, Marapur Dhavaleshwar, Mirji, Vantigodi, Channal, Ranjanagi Uttur, Jaliber, Rugi, Zunjarakopp, Mudhol(Rural) Budni(P.M), Metgud, Gulgal Jambagi Chinchakhandi(B.K), Chinchakhandi(K.D), Jeeragal Ingalagi, Baragi, Marikatti, Vajjaramatti Alagundi(B.K), Budni (B.K.), Antapur, Jambgi(K.D) Kasba Jambgi(B.K), Petlur, Ningapur, Halaki Bommanbudni, Timmapur, Hebbal, Chikkur, Chawadapur Naganapur, Kanasageri, Dadanatti, Hosakoti Mallapur(P.L), Laxanatti, Lokapur, Jalikatti(B.K) Varchagal, Jalikatti(K.D).

The villages having more than 50% ST population are None.

Sex ratio of Scheduled tribe population is 502.

Scheduled Tribes Literates and Illiterates by Sex:

	Persons	Males	Females
Literate	3,078	2,038	1,040
Illiterate	6,519	2,737	3,782
Literacy rate	38.4	51.1	25.9
Graduate	52	49	3

Scheduled Tribes (Dominant):

Naikda etc., Koli Dhor etc., Bhil etc., Dubla etc. Generic Tribes etc.

For their cultural identity please see Appendix-II

Villages without Scheduled Tribes: There are 22 villages without any scheduled tribe population.

Literates and Illiterates by Sex (Total Population):

	Persons	Males	Females
Literate	82,998	52,706	30,292
Illiterate	118,857	49,232	69,625
Literacy rate	49	62	36
Graduate	2,328	2,070	258

Agriculture: ***Distribution of villages according to land use:*** Out of 78 villages, Total area (in hectare) is 94554, out of that 86.28 percent is cultivable and 58.2 percent of the cultivable area is irrigated.

Sources of Irrigation (Hectares): Government Canal 24499.37, Private Canal 0, Well without Electricity 110.08, Well with Electricity 5215.36, Tubewell without Electricity 7.53, Tubewell with Electricity 9253.77, Tank 0, River 8366.43, Lake 0, Waterfall 0, Others 29.23.

Villages with population of 5000 to 9999: Saidapur, Mugalkhod, Kulali, Malali, Nagaral Dhavaleshwar, Mantur.

Villages with population of 10000 and above: Belagali , Shirol, Lokapur.

Distribution of Workers:

	Persons	Males	Females	WPR
Cultivators	38,812	28,671	10,141	37.9
Agricultural Labour	47,653	18,111	29,542	46.54
Household Industry	2,595	1,555	1,040	2.53
Other Workers	13,341	10,347	2,994	13.03
Main Workers	77,710	54,068	23,642	75.89
Marginal Workers	24,691	4,616	20,075	24.11
Total Workers	102,401	58,684	43,717	

Religion: Major Religious Communities:

	Persons	Males	Females	Sex Ratio
Hindu (93.21%)	188,141	94,992	93,149	981
Muslim (6.05%)	12,216	6,154	6,062	985
Christian (0.03%)	66	39	27	692
Sikh (0%)	5	2	3	1,500

Buddhists (0.1%)	209	111	98	883
Jain (0.37%)	742	399	343	860

Agewise Data:

	Persons	Males	Females	Sex Ratio
All ages	201,855	101,938	99,917	980
0-14	74,265	37,791	36,474	965
15-44	91,793	46,585	45,208	970
45-79	33,994	16,832	17,162	1020
80+	1,617	633	984	1555
Age not stated	186	97	89	918

Languages (Dominant):
Kannada, Urdu, Marathi, Hindi, Telugu

Disabled Population:

	Persons	Males	Females	%
Total Disabled	3,589	1,956	1,633	
In Seeing	1,705	861	844	47.51
In Speech	300	150	150	8.36
In Hearing	175	89	86	4.88
In Movement	1,122	705	417	31.26
Mentally	287	151	136	8

MUDIGERE

Mudigere C.D. Block lies in the southern part of Chikmag alur district. It is a part of Mudigere taluka. The Block is located at a distance of 32 kms. from district headqu arters (Chikmagalur). There are 140 villages in the block with the total population of 124,198 persons. Area of the C.D. Block is 1116.44 sq. kms. It is bounded by taluks Sringeri, Koppa, Narasimharajapura and Chikmagalur on north, district Dakshina Kannada on south, district Hassan on east, and district Udupi on west.

Communications:

Roadways : S.H.-58: Direction- Mudigere to Belur. Nearest Villages- Halekote, Mudigere (Rural), Daradahalli, Muthi gepura, Hoisalalu, Kammaragodu, Gonibeedu, G.Agrahara, Nidagodu, Anajooru, Chinniga. S.H.-64: Direction- Mangal ore to Chikmagalur, Nearest Villages- Balur, Attigere, Banakal, Kudahalli, Taruve, Bankenahalli, Baggasagodu, Phalguni, Halike, Kolur, Halekote, Hesagal , Kollibylu, Karadagodu, Bilagola, Mudigere (Rural), Bidarahalli, Lokavalli, Kaduvalli. S.H.-66: Direction- karkal to Attigere, Nearest Villages- Samse, Thanudi, Thalagodu, Kalasa, Ambinakodige, Hadivoni, Coove, Balur Estate, Markal, Niduvale, Balur, Attigere.

River: Bhadra Nadi- Nearest Villages- Samse, Kalakodu, Thanudi, Kalasa, Ambinakodige, Hemmakki, Idkani, Kalm ane, Hadivoni, Coove. Hemavati Nadi- Nearest Villages- Jogannanakere, Hanthuru, G.Agrahara, Nidagodu, Anajooru, Uggehalli, Angadi, Harmakki, Bettadamane, Chinniga, Udase, G.Hanumanahalli, G.Hosahalli, Chakkodige, Hegrav alli, Chimmatagere, Hiresigara.

Annual Rainfall: Normal Rianfall 2172.8 mm.

Ground Water: Availability of the Ground Water in the Basin is 5675 H.A.M. and the utilization is 2303 H.A. M. It belongs to Safe category. Depth to water level 5 to 20 meter below the ground. Most of the wells go down in summer months, according to the Ground Water Estimation Committee.

Soils: Red Loamy and Sandy Soils.

Natural Division : It falls partly in Kudremukh-Bababudan Forested Hilly zone and Chikmagalur-Mudigere Rolling Belt of the Central Karnataka Plateau.

Administration:

Division: Mysore. Parliamentary Constituency: 15 Udupi. District: Chikmagalur. Taluka: Chikmagalur. Assembly Constituency: 124 Mudigere (SC). Gram Panchayat: 29.

Regional Area Development Boards: The Maland Aera Development Board.

Fairs: Adi Shaktyattmaka Sri Annapurneshvari: It is held at Horanadu in Chikmagalur area sometime in the month of March-April for one day. Horanadu, 68 kilometers north-west of Mudigere town and 8 kilometers north-west of Kalasa, is situated in the midst of enchanting natural scenery and is surrounded by small hills.

Adi Subrahmanyeshwara Jatra: It is held at Gonibeedu in Chikmagalur area in the month of March every year.

Anjaneya Jatra: It is held at Mudigere in about the month of April for three days. Mudigere is 30 kms. south -east of Ajjampura town.

Bhoomi-Hunnime Festival: During the Deepavali season, "Bhoomi-Hunnime" festival is celebrated by the farmers of Sringeri, Mudigere, Koppa, Narasmharajapura and Chikm agalur taluks of Chikmagalur area.

Kalabhairava Jatra: It is held at Durgadahalli near Chikmagalur in about the month of February-March for three days every year. Durgadahalli is 25 kms. west of Mudigere town.

Devi Jatra: It is held at Devavrunda in about the month of February-March every year. Devavrunda, about 24 kms. south-west of Mudigere town, appears to have been a noted place for the worship of goddess Lakshmi during the period of the Gangas of Talakad.

Girija-Kalyanotsava Festival: It is held at Kalasa in around the month of Kartika (October-November) for two days. Kalasa an old agrahara settlement, also called Mavinakere and Kalasapuri is the headquarters of the hobli of the same name, 60 kms. west of Mudigere town.

Villages: 140 **Inhabited:** 140 **Uninhabited:** 0

Ranking	District	State	National
Area	4	69	335
Population	4	148	2714
Sex Ratio	2	21	933

Child Sex Ratio	5	82	2859
Literacy Rate	6	53	1802
Density	1	54	6045
Work Participation Rate	5	158	1507

Gram Panchayats:
Hornadu, Thotadur, Idkani, Coove, Kundur, Hesagal, Nandipura, Makonahalli, Mudigere (Rural), Bidarahalli, Phalguni, B.Hosahalli, Banakal, Balur, Niduvale, Javali, Sunkasale, Marasanige, Kalasa, Samse, Taruve, Tripura, Bettagere, Daradahalli, Gonibeedu, Chinniga, Hanthuru, Kirugunda, Urubage.

Amenities:
Education: Primary School in 58 villages, Middle school in 50 villages, Matriculation or Secondary School in 12 villages, namely Samse, Kalasa, Javali, Banakal, Kundur, Bettagere, Hesagal, Kannapura, Daradahalli, Gonibeedu, Angadi, Chinniga.
Higher Secondary or Pre University Courses or Intermediate or Junior College in 4 villages of the CD Block,, namely Kalasa, Banakal, Kundur, Hesagal.
College in 0 village, Adult Literacy Center in 0 village.
Medical: Hospital in 5 villages, Dispensary in 16 villages, Health Center in 11 villages, Sub Center in 21 villages, Maternity and Child Welfare Center in 12 villages, Community health workers in 0 village.
The Villages having Hospital or Dispensary or Health Center are Samse, Kalasa, Kelagur Estate, Sunkasale, Javali, Banakal, Kundur, B.Hosahalli, Gutti, Bilagola, Daradahalli, Jogannanakere, Halekere, Hanthuru, Gonibeedu, Devarunda, Gowdahalli, Bettadamane.
Drinking Water: Tap water in 92 villages, Tank water in 30 villages, Well water in 70 villages, Tubewell in 13 villages and more than one source in 103 villages.
Bank: Banking facility in 14 villages, namely, Samse, Kalasa, Sunkasale, Javali, Niduvale, Attigere Banakal, B.Hosahalli, Pattaduru, Kannapura Mudigere (Rural), Daradahalli, Gonibeedu, Gowdahalli.
Credit Society in 12 villages Agricultural Credit Society in 12 Non-Agricultural Credit Society in 0 village.
Others: Power supply in 140 villages, Cinema hall in 2 villages, sport club in 140 villages, Stadium or Auditorium or Community Hall in 140 villages, Post Office in 40 villages.
There are 83 villages having bus facilities.
Villages with most of facilities: Samse, Kalasa Sunkasale, Javali, Banakal, B.Hosahalli, Daradahalli Gonibeedu, Gowdahalli.
Villages without amenities (Education): Thanudi, Ambinakodige, K.Kelagur, Edur, Balige, Aramane Thalagur, Bilagali, Kalmane, Hadivoni, Koradathalgur, Kelagur, Abrugodige Estate, Kelagur Estate, Halagadaka Estate, Madugundi, Megur, Balur Estate, Alekhan Estate, Darshana, Kannagere, Kudahalli, Binnadi, Taruve, Barimale Estate, Kogile, Kotrakere, Bankenahalli, Mularahalli, Hesagodu, Ousana, Kolur, Hyragudde, Pattaduru, Halekote, Kenjige Estate, Kenjige, Guddada Estate, Thatkola, Naduvinamadkal, Kademadkal, Indravalli, Nandipura, Bommenahalli, Sangamapura, Karabylu, Mudasasi, Ghattadahalli, Kollibylu, Karadagodu, Lokavalli Estate, Lokavalli, Beejavalli, Kaduvalli, Gabbahalli, Pura, Kellur, Kunnahalli, Kesavalalu Estate, Muthigepura, Halase, Chattanahalli, Byduvalli, Byduvalli Estate, Halekere, Halekere Estate, Kanachuru Estate, Chandrapura, G.Agrahara, Nidagodu, Anajooru, Uggehalli, Hemmadi, U.Hosahalli, Hosakere, Byrapura, Byrapura Estate, Harmakki, Kannehalli, G.Hanumanahalli, Chakkodige, Hegravalli, Chimmatagere..
Scheduled Castes: Out of the total population of 124350 persons, 32144 persons (25.85%) belong to Scheduled Castes.
The villages having less than 10% SC population are Ambinakodige, Halagadaka Estate, Kudahalli Mularahalli, Guddada Estate, Naduvinamadkal Indravalli, Malahalli, Kolugodu, Sangamapura Karadagodu, Beejavalli, Pura, Chattanahalli Byduvalli, Nidagodu, Gowdahalli, Hemmadi.
The villages having more than 50% SC population are Balur Estate, Bankenahalli, Tripura, Kolur Kademadkal, Kesavalalu Estate, Halase, Angadi Kirugunda.
Sex ratio of Scheduled Caste population is 509.
Scheduled Castes Literates and Illiterates by Sex:

	Persons	Males	Females
Literate	12,097	7,224	4,873
Illiterate	20,047	8,544	11,503
Literacy rate	44.4	54.6	34.8
Graduate	126	98	28

Scheduled Castes (Dominant):
Adi Karnataka, Banjara etc., Mundala, Adi Dravida Generic Castes etc.
For their cultural identity please see Appendix-I
Villages without Scheduled Castes: There are 7 villages without any scheduled caste population.
Scheduled Tribes: Out of the total population of 124350 persons, 12518 persons (10.07%) belong to Scheduled Tribes.
The villages having less than 10% ST population are Thotadur, K.Kelagur, Edur, Idkani, Durgadahalli Balige, Kalmane, Koradathalgur, Maliganadu, Kelagur Abrugodige Estate, Kelagur Estate, Sunkasale

Halagadaka Estate, Megur, Balur Estate, Javali Markal, Balur, Attigere, Banakal, Darshana Kudahalli, Binnadi, Taruve, Barimale Estate, Kogile Bankenahalli, Baggasagodu, Halike, Bettagere Tripura, Gutti, Hesagodu, Ousana, Kolur, Bakki Hyragudde, Pattaduru, Halekote, Hanumanahalli Naduvinamadkal, Kademadkal, Nandipura, Kolugodu Bommenahalli, Sangamapura, Karabylu, Karadagodu Bilagola, Mudigere (Rural), Bidarahalli, Lokavalli Beejavalli, Kaduvalli, Gabbahalli, Pura, Kellur Kadidal, Jogannanakere, Muthigepura, Halase Chattanahalli, Gowthahalli, Urubage, Byduvalli Halekere, Halekere Estate, Kanachuru Kanachuru Estate, Hanthuru, Gonibeedu, Anajooru Uggehalli, Angadi, Devarunda, Gowdahalli, Hemmadi U.Hosahalli, Hosakere, Byrapura, Byrapura Estate Mekanagadde, Bettadamane, Chinniga, Udase Chakkodige, Kirugunda, Hiresigara.

The villages having more than 50% ST population are None.

Sex ratio of Scheduled tribe population is 506.

Scheduled Tribes Literates and Illiterates by Sex:

	Persons	Males	Females
Literate	5,391	3,188	2,203
Illiterate	7,127	2,994	4,133
Literacy rate	50.1	60.2	40.3
Graduate	33	25	8

Scheduled Tribes (Dominant):

Hasalaru, Gowdalu, Naikda etc., Malaikudi Generic Tribes etc.

For their cultural identity please see Appendix-II

Villages without Scheduled Tribes: There are 25 villages without any scheduled tribe population.

Literates and Illiterates by Sex (Total Population):

	Persons	Males	Females
Literate	71,313	39,978	31,335
Illiterate	53,037	21,953	31,084
Literacy rate	66	74	57
Graduate	2,797	1,776	1,021

Agriculture: ***Distribution of villages according to land use:*** Out of 140 villages, Total area (in hectare) is 111644, out of that 39.59 percent is cultivable and 0.09 percent of the cultivable area is irrigated.

Sources of Irrigation (Hectares): Government Canal 32.37, Private Canal 0, Well without Electricity 0, Well with Electricity 0, Tubewell without Electricity 0, Tubewell with Electricity 3.68, Tank 2.16, River 0, Lake 0, Waterfall 0, Others 0.

Villages with population of 5000 to 9999:

Samse.

Villages with population of 10000 and above:

Kalasa.

Distribution of Workers:

	Persons	Males	Females	WPR
Cultivators	9,297	6,797	2,500	14.17
Agricultural Labour	5,259	2,712	2,547	8.01
Household Industry	988	478	510	1.51
Other Workers	50,081	28,615	21,466	76.31
Main Workers	59,783	36,475	23,308	91.1
Marginal Workers	5,842	2,127	3,715	8.9
Total Workers	65,625	38,602	27,023	

Religion: Major Religious Communities:

	Persons	Males	Females	Sex Ratio
Hindu (87.26%)	108,505	53,761	54,744	1,018
Muslim (7.25%)	9,013	4,632	4,381	946
Christian (3.65%)	4,541	2,343	2,198	938
Sikh (0.01%)	12	9	3	333
Buddhists (0.01%)	8	4	4	1,000
Jain (1.72%)	2,135	1,122	1,013	903

Agewise Data:

	Persons	Males	Females	Sex Ratio
All ages	124,350	61,931	62,419	1008
0-14	35,395	17,822	17,573	986
15-44	65,010	31,938	33,072	1036
45-79	22,526	11,473	11,053	963
80+	1,098	514	584	1136
Age not stated	321	184	137	745

Languages (Dominant):

Kannada, Tulu, Malayalam, Urdu, Konkani

Disabled Population:

	Persons	Males	Females	%
Total Disabled	3,361	1,926	1,435	
In Seeing	2,242	1,271	971	66.71
In Speech	201	110	91	5.98
In Hearing	148	74	74	4.4
In Movement	540	343	197	16.07
Mentally	230	128	102	6.84

MULBAGAL

Mulbagal C.D. Block lies in the south-eastern part of Kolar district. It is a part of Mulbagal taluka. The Block is located at a distance of 30 kms. from district headquarters (Kolar). There are 343 villages in the block with the total population of 187,034 persons. Area of the C.D. Block is 805.34 sq. kms. It is bounded by taluk Srinivaspur on north-west, taluk Bangarapet on south, and taluk Kolar on west. It has common boundary with the state of Andhra Pradesh on north and east.

Communications:

Roadways : N.H.-4: Direction- Bangalore to Chennai, Nearest Villages- Kurubarahalli, Ananthapur, Jammanahalli,

Chikkamadenahalli, V.Guttahalli, Devarayasamudra, Kammad atti Kamanur, Kappalamadagu, Srirangapura, N.Vaddahalli, Chikkapadmaghatta, Padmaghatta, Tatikal, Batrahalli, Darenahalli, Seegehalli, Vittalapura, Nangali, Halekoppa, Mudigere. S.H.-58: Direction- Srinivaspur to Venkatagir ikota, Nearest Villages- Kuthandahalli, Bestarahalli, Mudiyanur, Kondihalli, Doddagurki, Rachabandahalli, Sangondahalli, Kadukachanahalli, Kadripura, Sonnavadi, Kavathanahalli, Gumlapura, Chokkadoddi, D.Kurubarahalli, J.Agrahara, Mopurahalli, Mallanayakanahalli, Appikonden ahalli, Chukkanahalli, Ethurahalli, Thimmaravathanahalli, Charakurahalli, Kogileri, Karavireddihalli, V.Kurubarahalli.

Annual Rainfall: Normal Rianfall 875.38 mm.

Ground Water: Availability of the Ground Water in the Basin is (Information not avablable) H.A.M. and the utilization is (Information not avablable) H.A.M. It belongs to (Information not avablable) category. Depth to water level 5 to 20 meter below the ground. Most of the wells go down in summer months, according to the Ground Water Estimation Committee.

Soils: Red Soils.

Natural Division : It falls partly in Sidlaghatta-Sriniva spur Upland and Kolar-Bangarpet Rugged Tract of the Southern Karnataka Plateau.

Administration:

Division: Bangalore. Parliamentary Constituency: 28 Kolar (SC). District: Kolar. Taluka: Mulbagal. Assembly Constituency: 145 Mulbagal (SC). Gram Panchayat: 30.

Regional Area Development Boards: The Bailu Seeme Area Development Board.

Border Villages: (State: Andhra Pradesh)- Nachagundlahal li, Mugavanahalli, V.Hosahalli, Honnikere, Nachahalli, Byadarahalli, Rajendrahalli, Chandamamanahalli, Doddath ihalli, Kirumani, Ubbandlahalli, S.Ananthapura, Punyahalli, Thammiareddihalli, Hebbani, H.Byappalli, M.Gollahalli, Sunnapakunte, Nagavara, Byatanur, Nangali, N.Chamakalah alli, Gonikuppa, Jallapalli, Chinnabalepalli, T.Kurubarah alli, Thippadoddi, Ugani, Kasuvuganahalli, Jeeyapalli, Payastanahalli, Ramachandrapura , K.Byappalli, Sinigeha lli, Kothuru, Bovibikkanahalli, Appikondenahalli, Chukkan ahalli, Ethurahalli, Thimmaravathanahalli, Sivanapura, Vaddaguttahalli, Appenahalli, Kuppandahalli, Byrasandra, Abbihalli.

Fairs: Hazarat Baba Hyderwali Urs: An Urs in honour of Hazarat Baba Hyderwali is held for three days in the month of January-February, attended by about 20, 000 persons. Mulbagal is an important town about 25 kms. north-east of Kolar on the old Bangalore-Chenn ai road by the Mugli pass.

Prasana Someshwaraswami Jatra: Prasana Someshwarasw amijatra held at Madivala in Mulbagal Taluk in the month of December-January for five days. The Someshwaraswami temple at Madivala is, one of the more ornate temples in the district, built in many respects on the lines of the Someshvara temple of Kurudumale.

Ramalingeshwaraswami Jatra: It is held at Avani near Kolar about the month of February or March for seven days. Avani in Mulbagal taluk is a hill about 12 kms. south-west of Mulbagal town.

Someshwaraswami Jatra: It is held at Mulbagal in the month of Vaishakha (April-May) for five days. The name 'Mulbagal' seems to be derived from 'Muḍalabagalu', meaning eastern gate in Kannada, the place being situated on the eastern pass from the table-land of Mysore to the temple of Tirupati.

Villages: 343 **Inhabited:** 314 **Uninhabited:** 29

Ranking	District	State	National
Area	5	121	720
Population	5	98	899
Sex Ratio	1	53	1661
Child Sex Ratio	4	32	1611
Literacy Rate	8	116	3488
Density	9	59	4288
Work Participation Rate	6	54	1551

Gram Panchayats:

Agara, Gollahalli, Gudipalli, Rajendrahalli, Hebbani, Mustoor, Byrakur, Amblikal , Kurudamale, Mudiyanur, Uthanur, Hanamanahalli, Kappalamadagu, Alangur, Nangali, Mudigere, Gummakal, Pichaguntalahalli, Sonnavadi, Balla, Avani, Devarayasamudra , Oorakuntemittur, Angondahalli, Mothakapalli, Tayalur, Emmenatha, Mallanayakanahalli, Thimmaravathanahalli, Doolapalli.

Amenities:

Education: Primary School in 266 villages, Middle school in 108 villages, Matriculation or Secondary School in 19 villages, namely Gokunte, Gollahalli, Mudiyanur, Uthanur, Hanamanahalli, Devarayasamudra, Kasipura, Avani, Oorakuntemittur, Emmenatha, Yaluvahalli, N.Vaddahalli, Hebbani, Byrakur, Mustoor, Nangali, Rayalamanadinne, Mallanayakanahalli, Tayalur.

Higher Secondary or Pre University Courses or Intermediate or Junior College in 5 villages of the CD Block,, namely Gollahalli, Gudipalli, Byrakur, Nangali, Tayalur.

College in 1 village, Adult Literacy Center in 2 villages., College is in village, namely Byrakur.

Medical: Hospital in 3 villages, Dispensary in 12 villages, Health Center in 8 villages, Sub Center in 42 villages,

Maternity and Child Welfare Center in 1 village, Community health workers in 10 villages.

The Villages having Hospital or Dispensary or Health Center are Agara, Gokunte, Amblikal, Madaghatta, Kurudamale, Uthanur, Avani, Kannasandra, Alangur, Rajendrahalli, Hebbani, Gudipalli, Byrakur.

Drinking Water: Tap water in 193 villages, Tank water in 44 villages, Well water in 81 villages, Tubewell in 118 villages and more than one source in 246 villages.

Bank: Banking facility in 16 villages, namely, Gokunte, Mandikal, Amblikal, Uthanur, Avani, Balla Nagasandra, Padmaghatta, Hebbani, Gudipalli, Byrakur Nangali, N.Chamakalahalli, Dommasandra Mallanayakanahalli, Tayalur.

Credit Society in 24 villages Agricultural Credit Society in 19 Non-Agricultural Credit Society in 2 villages.

Others: Power supply in 309 villages, Cinema hall in 6 villages, sport club in 2 villages, Stadium or Auditorium or Community Hall in 0 village, Post Office in 45 villages.

There are 213 villages having bus facilities.

Villages with most of facilities: Gokunte Amblikal, Uthanur, Avani, Balla, Hebbani, Gudipalli Byrakur, Nangali, Mallanayakanahalli, Tayalur.

Villages without amenities (Education):
Kondenahalli, Chakethimmanadinne, Chikkanadinne, Kondathimmanahalli, Jangama Kannasandra, Kenchanahalli, V.Nagireddihalli, Bettagerahalli, S.I.Ananthapura, Chikkahonasettihalli, Doddahonasettihalli, Pichaguntlahalli, Minajenahalli, Marakalagatta, Bhumanahalli, Chikkapadmaghatta, Chinthlahalli, Darenahalli, Vittalapura, Thurakarahalli, Narasipurdinne, Veerasandra, G.Kodihalli, Chandamamanahalli, M.Chamakalahalli, Bhimanavoddu, Nagenahalli, Bommadasanahalli, Jamdadi Obenahalli, Gonikuppa, Kakkaladoddi, Chikkagollahalli, Chinnabalepalli, T.Kurubarahalli, Matsanahalli, Jeenankunte, Krishnapura, Thimmapura, Chukkanahalli, Dasepalli, Agara, Jowgupalli, Korevenuru, Kondihalli, Yadapalli, Ganiganakoppa..

Scheduled Castes: Out of the total population of 187269 persons, 58312 persons (31.14%) belong to Scheduled Castes.

The villages having less than 10% SC population are S.Bisanahalli, Nachahalli, Murakanakunte Kondenahalli, Kondathimmanahalli, Kunibande Madaghatta, Pombarahalli, Nallandahalli, Banahalli Chikkahonasettihalli, Gottikunte, Badenahalli Koravenur, Maraheru , Anehalli, Chinthlahalli Darenahalli, Vittalapura, Narasipurdinne Chapurahalli, Chandamamanahalli, M.Chamakalahalli M.Byapalli, Kambamdinne, Bhimanavoddu Bommadasanahalli, Jamdadi Obenahalli, Ganganahalli Thondahalli, N.Chamakalahalli, Kakkaladoddi Doddagollahalli, Chinnabalepalli, T.Kurubarahalli Ugani, Matsanahalli, Myalapura, Jeenankunte Krishnapura, Settikal, Kothuru, Kogileri, Dasepalli Yalachepalli, Jowgupalli, Kondihalli, Ganiganakoppa Abbihalli.

The villages having more than 50% SC population are Harapanayakanahalli, Jangama Kannasandra Kuthandahalli, Bettagerahalli, Krishnapura Yanadigollahalli, Jammanahalli, Doddamadenahalli Doddiganahalli, Keeluholali, Cholangunte, Vijalapura S.I.Ananthapura, Asali Attikunte, Kumadenahalli Sringeri Chadumanahalli, Kondenahalli, Kempapura Doddahonasettihalli, Yalagondahalli, Minajenahalli Ramenallur, Yadahalli, Kannatha, Kannasandra Padakasti, Jogalakasti, Sheshapura, Reddihalli Bandahalli, Nagasandra, Veerasettihalli Kurubarahalli, Sunnangur, Iragamuthanahalli Bevahalli, Marandahalli, Batrahalli Chalumanayakanahalli, Thoradi, Chamareddihalli Kasavireddihalli, Veerasandra, Pichaguntalahalli Kaggalanatha, Sunnapakunte, Poojenahalli Dasarahalli, B.Kurubarahalli, Kerasamangala Mudigere, Seegehalli, Seegehosahalli Chikkagollahalli, Kasuvuganahalli, Nagamangala Vajranagenahalli, Thimmapura, Puttenahalli V.Kurubarahalli, Sanyasipalli.

Sex ratio of Scheduled Caste population is 498.

Scheduled Castes Literates and Illiterates by Sex:

	Persons	Males	Females
Literate	23,337	14,807	8,530
Illiterate	34,975	14,442	20,533
Literacy rate	47.2	59.6	34.6
Graduate	536	484	52

Scheduled Castes (Dominant):
Adi Karnataka, Bhovi, Adi Dravida, Koracha Chenna Dasar etc.

For their cultural identity please see Appendix-I

Villages without Scheduled Castes: There are 52 villages without any scheduled caste population.

Scheduled Tribes: Out of the total population of 187269 persons, 7112 persons (3.8%) belong to Scheduled Tribes.

The villages having less than 10% ST population are Gokunte, Nachagundlahalli, V.Hosahalli, Honnikere Murakanakunte, Kondenahalli, Gollahalli, Mandikal Koladevi , Nichanakunte, J.Vommasandra, Gujjanahalli Chakethimmanadinne, Chikkanadinne, Gujjamarandahalli Arahalli, Duggasandra, Tavarekere Harapanayakanahalli, Vommasandra, Kondathimmanahalli

Kalikere, Amblikal , Balasandra, Sangasandra
Madaghatta, Kurudamale, Jangama Kannasandra
Kuthandahalli, Bestarahalli, Mudiyanur
Kenchanahalli, Uthanur, Sivanarahalli
V.Nagireddihalli, Pombarahalli, Nallandahalli
Bandarahalli, Majara Agrahara, Nalluru
Hanamanahalli, Bettagerahalli, Bheeampura, Meleri
Krishnapura, Alaganahalli, Vaniganahalli, Kondihalli
K.G.Lakshmisagara, Yanadigollahalli, Doddagurki
Rachabandahalli, Banahalli, Kurubarahalli
Ananthapur, Jammanahalli, V.Guttahalli
Doddamadenahalli, Varadaganahalli, Devarayasamudra
Kammadatti Kamanur, Bellamballi, Doddiganahalli
Keeluholali, Hosakere, Cholangunte, Vijalapura
S.I.Ananthapura, Asali Attikunte, Kumadenahalli
Settibanakanahalli, Mallakachanahalli
Sringeri Chadumanahalli, Kondenahalli, Kasipura
Ganjigunte, Avani, Batlabavanahalli, Kempapura
Chikkahonasettihalli, Doddahonasettihalli, Putheri
Chiyandahalli, Yalagondahalli, Pichaguntlahalli
Marakalagatta, Ramenallur, Oorakuntemittur, Chitheri
Yadahalli, Kagganahalli, Balla
Kuruba Chadumanahalli, Kannatha, Melagani
Sangondahalli, Kadukachanahalli, Keelagani
Gottikunte, Badenahalli, Tirumanahalli, Kannasandra
Emmenatha, Padakasti, Jogalakasti, Sheshapura
Channapura, Reddihalli, Bandahalli, Nagasandra
Veerasettihalli, Kurubarahalli, Angondahalli
Honaganahalli, Belapanahalli, Gopasandra
Bommasandra, Koravenur, Sunnangur, Iragamuthanahalli
Bevahalli, Yaluvahalli, Maraheru , Anehalli
Marandahalli, Hosahalli, Kappalamadagu
Kenchanahalli, Srirangapura, N.Vaddahalli
Chikkapadmaghatta, Padmaghatta, Tatikal
Bachamakalhalli, Chinthlahalli, Yachana Kogileri
Batrahalli, Mannenahalli, Allalasandra
Chikkabandahalli, Darenahalli, Seegehalli
Chalumanayakanahalli, Siddaghatta, Lingapura
Kadripura, Vittalapura, Thoradi, Thurakarahalli
Sonnavadi, Narasipurdinne, Doddabandahalli
Chamareddihalli, Kasavireddihalli, Veerasandra
Alangur, Palurahalli, Challapally
Doddathammanahalli, Yarraginnenahalli
Lakkisettyhalli, Pichaguntalahalli, P.Gangapura
Kavathanahalli, Khadripura, Manchiganahalli
Gumlapura, Kaggalanatha, G.Kodihalli, G.Vaddahalli
Byadarahalli , Rajendrahalli, Chandamamanahalli
Doddathihalli, Cheekurgundlahalli, Naganahalli
Kirumani, S.Ananthapura, Punyahalli
Thammiareddihalli, Bangavadi, Hebbani, H.Byappalli
M.Gollahalli, H.Kodihalli, Sunnapakunte
M.Chamakalahalli, M.Byapalli, Kadenahalli
Pethandahalli, Budaderu, C.Hosahalli, Kambamdinne
Bhimanavoddu, Gudipalli, Nagenahalli
Bommadasanahalli, Kamsanahalli, Jamdadi Obenahalli
Ganganahalli, Cheekur, Dasarahalli, Byrakur
Lakkadoddi, Perumakanahalli, Kerasamangala, Mustoor
Byatanur, Nangali, Thondahalli, Halekoppa
Mallekuppa, Venkatapura, Mudigere, N.Chamakalahalli
Kakkaladoddi, Seegehalli, Seegehosahalli
Chikkagollahalli, Jallapalli, Thippadoddi, Ugani
Patrahalli, Soorakunte, Matsanahalli, Nernahalli
Gummakal, Yadahalli, G.Marandahalli, Payastanahalli
Ramachandrapura , Myalapura, Mittahalli
Rayalamanadinne, Puli Obereddihalli, Nagamangala
Chokkadoddi, Jeenankunte, Vajranagenahalli
Krishnapura, Settikal, K.Byappalli, Sinigehalli
Bevanatha, Thimmapura, D.Kurubarahalli, J.Agrahara
Belaganehalli, Mopurahalli, Mallanayakanahalli
Puttenahalli, Appikondenahalli, Chukkanahalli
Ethurahalli, Thimmaravathanahalli, Kogileri
Appenahalli, Karavireddihalli, V.Kurubarahalli
Kuppandahalli, Gaddam Chinnepalli, Byrasandra
Yalachepalli, Doolapalli, Agara, Jowgupalli, Tayalur
Madivala, Meltayalur, Mothakapalli, Achampalli
Jangamahosahalli, Mindahalli, Korevenuru, Kondihalli
Somarasanahalli, Madderi, Kuppampalya, Yadapalli
Ganiganakoppa, Abbihalli.

The villages having more than 50% ST population are
Nachahalli, Kunibande, Chapurahalli
Hiranyagowdanahalli, Gonikuppa, Chinnabalepalli
T.Kurubarahalli, Doddaguttahalli, Kothuru
Kapabikkanahalli, Dasepalli.

Sex ratio of Scheduled tribe population is 493.

Scheduled Tribes Literates and Illiterates by Sex:

	Persons	Males	Females
Literate	2,947	1,911	1,036
Illiterate	4,165	1,692	2,473
Literacy rate	48.3	61.6	34.6
Graduate	37	32	5

Scheduled Tribes (Dominant):

Naikda etc., Generic Tribes etc., Palliyan, Irular
Iruliga

For their cultural identity please see Appendix-II

Villages without Scheduled Tribes: There are 243 villages without any scheduled tribe population.

Literates and Illiterates by Sex (Total Population):

	Persons	Males	Females
Literate	90,205	55,690	34,515
Illiterate	97,064	38,491	58,573

Literacy rate	56	69	43
Graduate	2,644	2,251	393

Agriculture: ***Distribution of villages according to land use:*** Out of 343 villages, Total area (in hectare) is 80534, out of that 54.9 percent is cultivable and 32.61 percent of the cultivable area is irrigated.

Sources of Irrigation (Hectares): Government Canal 100.3, Private Canal 10.92, Well without Electricity 314.05, Well with Electricity 2888.61, Tubewell without Electricity 134.08, Tubewell with Electricity 4389.94, Tank 5322.89, River 23.34, Lake 0.8, Waterfall 0, Others 1233.35.

Villages with population of 5000 to 9999: Nangali.

Villages with population of 10000 and above: None

Distribution of Workers:

	Persons	Males	Females	WPR
Cultivators	42,938	26,279	16,659	44.24
Agricultural Labour	32,103	13,456	18,647	33.08
Household Industry	2,792	1,077	1,715	2.88
Other Workers	19,227	14,399	4,828	19.81
Main Workers	76,259	48,359	27,900	78.57
Marginal Workers	20,801	6,852	13,949	21.43
Total Workers	97,060	55,211	41,849	

Religion: Major Religious Communities:

	Persons	Males	Females	Sex Ratio
Hindu (91.2%)	170,781	85,743	85,038	992
Muslim (8.29%)	15,533	7,949	7,584	954
Christian (0.31%)	574	299	275	920
Sikh (0%)	-	-	-	-
Buddhists (0.04%)	79	44	35	795
Jain (0%)	4	2	2	1,000

Agewise Data:

	Persons	Males	Females	Sex Ratio
All ages	187,269	94,181	93,088	988
0-14	61,367	30,894	30,473	986
15-44	85,863	42,845	43,018	1004
45-79	37,450	19,196	18,254	951
80+	2,389	1,138	1,251	1099
Age not stated	200	108	92	852

Languages (Dominant): Kannada, Telugu, Urdu, Tamil, Marathi

Disabled Population:

	Persons	Males	Females	%
Total Disabled	3,968	2,190	1,778	
In Seeing	2,252	1,170	1,082	56.75
In Speech	305	178	127	7.69
In Hearing	191	84	107	4.81
In Movement	867	570	297	21.85
Mentally	353	188	165	8.9

MUNDARGI

Mundargi C.D. Block lies in the south-eastern part of Gadag district. It is a part of Mundargi taluka. The Block is located at a distance of 39 kms. from district headquarters (Gadag). There are 58 villages in the block with the total population of 96,032 persons. Area of the C.D. Block is 877.43 sq. kms. It is bounded by taluk Gadag and district Koppal on north, district Bellary on south, district Koppal on east, taluks Gadag and Shirhatti on west.

Communications:

Roadways : N.H-63: Gadag to Bellary, Direction- Nearest Villages- Halligudi, Hallikeri.

Railway Station: Village- Halligudi.

River: Tungabhadra Nadi- Nearest Villages- Nagarahalli, Hesarur, Kakkur, Korlhalli, Gangapur, Bidarahalli, Vithalapur, Gumgol, Hammigi, Sheernahalli, Shingatalur.

Reserved Forest: Nearest Villages- Shivajinagar, Kadampur, Shingatarayanakeri, Dindur, Attikatti, Kappatagiri, Doni, Meundi, Hirewaddatti, Chikkawaddatti, Guddadbudih al, Maruthinagar, Kelur, Harogeri, Bagewadi, Kalkeri, Sevalalnagar, Bidnal, Korlhalli, Gangapur, Jyalawadgi, Mallikarjunapura, Mundawad, Vithalapur, Hammigi, Shingatalur.

Annual Rainfall: Normal Rianfall 489.0 mm.

Ground Water: Availability of the Ground Water in the Basin is 4848 H.A.M. and the utilization is 443 H.A. M. It belongs to Over Exploited category. Depth to water level 2 to 20 meter below the ground. Most of the wells go down in summer months, according to the Ground Water Estimation Committee.

Soils: Medium to deep black soils.

Natural Division : It falls partly in the Kalghatgi-Laksh meshwar Residual Hills and the Middle Tungabhadra Valley of the Central Karnataka Plateau.

Administration:

Division: Belgaum. Parliamentary Constituency: 10 Haveri. District: Gadag. Taluka: Mundargi. Assembly Constituenc y: 65 Shirahatti, 67 Ron. Gram Panchayat: 15.

Regional Area Development Boards: The Bailu Seeme Area Development Board.

Villages: 58 **Inhabited:** 54 **Uninhabited:** 4

Ranking	District	State	National
Area	4	106	586
Population	4	161	3591
Sex Ratio	4	117	2820
Child Sex Ratio	5	152	4274
Literacy Rate	5	91	2839
Density	1	23	6055
Work Participation Rate	5	159	832

Gram Panchayats:

Shingatarayanakeri, Alur, Hallikeri, Meundi, Dambal, Doni, Hirewaddatti, Harogeri, Hesarur, Korlhalli, Kalkeri, Bagewadi, Bidarahalli, Hammigi, Shingatalur.

Amenities:

Education: Primary School in 48 villages, Middle school in 42 villages, Matriculation or Secondary School in 12 villages, namely Halligudi, Venkatapur, Alur, Doni, Dambal, Baradur, Hirewaddatti, Bagewadi, Kalkeri, Korlhalli, Hammigi, Shingatalur.

Higher Secondary or Pre University Courses or Intermediate or Junior College in 4 villages of the CD Block,, namely Alur, Dambal, Kalkeri, Shingatalur.

College in 0 village, Adult Literacy Center in 30 villages.

Medical: Hospital in 0 village, Dispensary in 3 villages, Health Center in 7 villages, Sub Center in 22 villages, Maternity and Child Welfare Center in 2 villages, Community health workers in 36 villages.

The Villages having Hospital or Dispensary or Health Center are Doni, Harogeri, Kalkeri.

Drinking Water: Tap water in 28 villages, Tank water in 4 villages, Well water in 34 villages, Tubewell in 33 villages and more than one source in 53 villages.

Bank: Banking facility in 20 villages, namely, Kadampur, Shirur, Halligudi, Hallikeri, Venkatapur Alur, Doni, Dambal, Meundi, Baradur, Hirewaddatti Harogeri, Bagewadi, Kalkeri, Bidnal, Hesarur Korlhalli, Bidarahalli, Hammigi, Shingatalur.

Credit Society in 4 villages Agricultural Credit Society in 2 Non-Agricultural Credit Society in 3 villages.

Others: Power supply in 54 villages, Cinema hall in 1 village, sport club in 0 village, Stadium or Auditorium or Community Hall in 0 village, Post Office in 26 villages.

There are 53 villages having bus facilities.

Villages with most of facilities: Kadampur, Shirur Halligudi, Hallikeri, Venkatapur, Alur, Doni, Dambal Meundi, Baradur, Hirewaddatti, Harogeri, Bagewadi Kalkeri, Bidnal, Hesarur, Korlhalli, Bidarahalli Hammigi, Shingatalur.

Villages without amenities (Education):

Shivajinagar, Kappatagiri, Maruthinagar, Ashakiran..

Scheduled Castes: Out of the total population of 95946 persons, 19329 persons (20.15%) belong to Scheduled Castes.

The villages having less than 10% SC population are Jantli, Halligudi, Venkatapur, Eklasapur, Haitapur Meundi, Guddadbudihal, Muradi, Kelur, Mustik0Ppa Maktumpur, Tippapur, Bennihalli, Hesarur, Kakkur Gangapur, Mundawad, Gumgol, Sheernahalli.

The villages having more than 50% SC population are Shivajinagar, Dindur, Attikatti, Kappatagiri Maruthinagar, Venkateshnagar, Sevalalnagar Ashakiran.

Sex ratio of Scheduled Caste population is 488.

Scheduled Castes Literates and Illiterates by Sex:

	Persons	Males	Females
Literate	6,948	4,719	2,229
Illiterate	12,381	5,175	7,206
Literacy rate	44.2	59.0	28.9
Graduate	126	115	11

Scheduled Castes (Dominant):

Banjara etc., Bhambi etc., Bhovi, Madiga Chalavadi etc.

For their cultural identity please see Appendix-I

Villages without Scheduled Castes: There are 8 villages without any scheduled caste population.

Scheduled Tribes: Out of the total population of 95946 persons, 8392 persons (8.75%) belong to Scheduled Tribes.

The villages having less than 10% ST population are Shivajinagar, Shirur, Jantli, Halligudi, Hallikeri Alur, Dindur, Kappatagiri, Doni, Dambal, Eklasapur Meundi, Baradur, Tambragundi, Hirewaddatti Maruthinagar, Mustik0Ppa, Kalkeri, Tippapur Virapapur, Venkateshnagar, Sevalalnagar, Bidnal Bennihalli, Nagarahalli, Ashakiran, Korlhalli Jyalawadgi, Mallikarjunapura, Bidarahalli Vithalapur, Hammigi.

The villages having more than 50% ST population are None.

Sex ratio of Scheduled tribe population is 496.

Scheduled Tribes Literates and Illiterates by Sex:

	Persons	Males	Females
Literate	4,124	2,656	1,468
Illiterate	4,268	1,571	2,697
Literacy rate	58.0	74.4	41.5
Graduate	76	67	9

Scheduled Tribes (Dominant):

Naikda etc., Generic Tribes etc., Chodhara Bhil etc., Pardhi etc.

For their cultural identity please see Appendix-II

Villages without Scheduled Tribes: There are 13 villages without any scheduled tribe population.

Literates and Illiterates by Sex (Total Population):

	Persons	Males	Females
Literate	48,446	30,692	17,754
Illiterate	47,500	18,191	29,309
Literacy rate	60	74	44
Graduate	1,089	945	144

Agriculture: ***Distribution of villages according to land use:***

Out of 58 villages, Total area (in hectare) is 87743, out of that 76.32 percent is cultivable and 11.23 percent of the cultivable area is irrigated.

Sources of Irrigation (Hectares): Government Canal 214.33, Private Canal 0, Well without Electricity 0, Well with Electricity 224.53, Tubewell without Electricity 0, Tubewell with Electricity 3079.09, Tank 2556.09, River 1443.09, Lake 0, Waterfall 0, Others 0.

Villages with population of 5000 to 9999:
Doni, Hirewaddatti.

Villages with population of 10000 and above:
Dambal.

Distribution of Workers:

	Persons	Males	Females	WPR
Cultivators	20,173	14,364	5,809	39.05
Agricultural Labour	24,871	9,025	15,846	48.14
Household Industry	995	646	349	1.93
Other Workers	5,625	4,690	935	10.89
Main Workers	41,735	26,692	15,043	80.78
Marginal Workers	9,929	2,033	7,896	19.22
Total Workers	51,664	28,725	22,939	

Religion: Major Religious Communities:

	Persons	Males	Females	Sex Ratio
Hindu (91.03%)	87,342	44,525	42,817	962
Muslim (7.88%)	7,561	3,832	3,729	973
Christian (0.02%)	15	8	7	875
Sikh (0.01%)	13	4	9	2,250
Buddhists (0.01%)	14	14	-	-
Jain (0.18%)	171	86	85	988

Agewise Data:

	Persons	Males	Females	Sex Ratio
All ages	95,946	48,883	47,063	963
0-14	34,539	17,662	16,877	956
15-44	43,974	22,903	21,071	920
45-79	16,696	8,062	8,634	1071
80+	703	235	468	1991
Age not stated	34	21	13	619

Languages (Dominant):
Kannada, Hindi, Urdu, Telugu, Marathi

Disabled Population:

	Persons	Males	Females	%
Total Disabled	1,687	932	755	
In Seeing	542	263	279	32.13
In Speech	149	92	57	8.83
In Hearing	175	94	81	10.37
In Movement	665	409	256	39.42
Mentally	156	74	82	9.25

MUNDGOD

Mundgod C.D. Block lies in the eastern part of Uttara Kannada district. It is a part of Mundgod taluka. The Block is located at a distance of 150 kms. from district headquarters (Karwar). There are 91 villages in the block with the total population of 74,536 persons. Area of the C.D. Block is 656.08 sq. kms. It is bounded by district Dharwad on north, taluk Sirsi on south, district Haveri on east, and taluk Yellapur on west.

Communications:

Roadways : S.H-2: Direction- Sirsi to Haveri, Nearest Villages- Borangudda, Yemagalli. S.H-6: Direction- Yella pur to Savanur, Nearest Villages- Ugginkeri, Gunjavati, Mainalli, Balehalli, Kusur, Tattilli (Mundgod), Kargolli, Teginkoppa, Kundargi, Sanavalli, Bappalgundi, Salgaon. S.H-69: Direction- Kumta to Dharwad, Nearest Villages- Wadagatta, Bachanaki, Nyasargi, Kavalakoppa, Salgaon, Hirehalli, Chigalli, Katur, Shinganahalli, Hulihonda, orangudde, Hudelkoppa, Bhadrapura, Pala, Kalkoppa, Naginkeri, Siddapur, Malgi, Kop (Gotgudi), Gotagudi, Jangeri, Hoskoppa.

River: Bedti Nadi- Yerebail, Hulihonda, Agadi, Nandikat ta, Mainalli, Hungunda. Koulgi Nadi- Nearest Villages- Mainalli, Sanavalli, Lakkolli, Basavanakoppa, Rayanalli, Andalgi, Kavalakoppa, Salgaon, Tattalli (Katur).

Canal: Nearest Villages- Nandikatta, Kusur, Indoor, Hungunda, Bachanaki, Kopp (Ind).

Annual Rainfall: Normal Rianfall 1176.8 mm.

Ground Water: Availability of the Ground Water in the Basin is 6041 H.A.M. and the utilization is 1370 H.A. M. It belongs to Safe category. Depth to water level 5 to 20 meter below the ground. Most of the wells go down in summer months, according to the Ground Water Estimation Committee.

Soils: Black Cotton Soil.

Natural Division : It falls partly in Yellapur-Dandeli Forest and the Sirsi-Siddapur Dissected Humid Tract of the Karnataka Coast (Western Coastal Region).

Administration:

Division: Belgaum. Parliamentary Constituency: 12 Uttara Kannada. District: Uttar Kannada. Taluka: Mundgod. Assem bly Constituency: 81 Yellapur. Gram Panchayat: 13.

Regional Area Development Boards: The Maland Aera Development Board.

Fairs: Basavanna Devara Jatra: Basavanna Devara jatra is held at Mundgod in Uttara Kannada area for one day in the month of April. Mundgod is in the up-ghat region at a distance of 165 kilometers north-east of Karwar. Hundelkoppa Mukappa Swamy Jatra: It is held at Pala near Uttara Kannada during the Basava-jayenti. Pala is situated at the junction of Mundgod-Sirsi and Hangal-Hubli Road (30 kms. from Mundgod). The place is believed to be an army cantonment in good old days called Paleya in the Hiriya-Hingalige division. A hero-stone here dated 1270 was installed by Chalagamunda, the nalaprabhu of Paleya under Vira Mahadeva of the Devagiri Seuna family. Another hero-stone of the same period records the death of Kalagunda, the son of Somagavunda, the nalaprabhu of Hiriya-Hingalige.

Rameshwara Jatra: It is held at Bedasgaon near Uttara Kannada for one day in the month of February. Bedasgaon is a place of historical importance and is approachable via Malgi on the Sirsi-Hubli road. The name of the place is mentioned as Badasagame in an inscription found here on a broken slab inside the Boppeshvaradeva temple, which dated back to 1163 A.D. (of Kalachuri Bijjanadeva).

Razaqshah Vali Urs: It is held at Mundgod for one day in the month of April. Mundgod at a distance of 161 kms. north east of Karwar, has a mosque built during Hyder's period, extended by Tipu. On the opposite side of this mosque there is a small shrine called Khadir-lin ga, worshipped by both Hindus and Muslims. Perhaps it was connected with a saint from Dharwad area. There is a dargah built in 18th century in the memory of Razak -Shah-Wali Ulla.

Villages: 91 **Inhabited:** 84 **Uninhabited:** 7

Ranking	District	State	National
Area	9	142	1021
Population	8	167	4301
Sex Ratio	11	175	6215
Child Sex Ratio	5	55	2426
Literacy Rate	8	39	1396
Density	5	108	6025
Work Participation Rate	4	157	2573

Gram Panchayats:

Nandikatta, Hungunda, Bachanki, Indoor, Gunjavati, Chowdalli, Salgaon, Chigalli, Katur, Bedasgaon, Kodambi , Pala, Malgi.

Amenities:

Education: Primary School in 65 villages, Middle school in 38 villages, Matriculation or Secondary School in 6 villages, namely Indoor, Salgaon, Chigalli, Katur, Pala, Malgi. Higher Secondary or Pre University Courses or Intermediate or Junior College in 2 villages of the CD Block,, namely Katur, Malgi.

College in 0 village, Adult Literacy Center in 0 village.

Medical: Hospital in 0 village, Dispensary in 1 village, Health Center in 3 villages, Sub Center in 13 villages, Maternity and Child Welfare Center in 0 village, Community health workers in 21 villages.

The Village having Hospital or Dispensary or Health Center is Tattilli (Mundgod).

Drinking Water: Tap water in 35 villages, Tank water in 8 villages, Well water in 72 villages, Tubewell in 11 villages and more than one source in 76 villages.

Bank: Banking facility in 15 villages, namely, Nandikatta, Indoor, Hungunda, Tattilli (Mundgod) Chowdalli, Kalkeri, Chigalli, Katur, Pala, Atabail Shanvalli, Ummachagi, Bedasgaon, Bekkod, Malgi.

Credit Society in 12 villages Agricultural Credit Society in 9 Non-Agricultural Credit Society in 2 villages.

Others: Power supply in 78 villages, Cinema hall in 0 village, sport club in 0 village, Stadium or Auditorium or Community Hall in 0 village, Post Office in 20 villages.

There are 52 villages having bus facilities.

Villages with most of facilities: Nandikatta Indoor, Hungunda, Chowdalli, Kalkeri, Chigalli Katur, Pala, Bedasgaon, Malgi.

Villages without amenities (Education): Balehalli, Tattilli (Mundgod), Kargolli, Teginkoppa, Pur, Bappalgundi, Ganadahalli, Tattalli (Katur), Kallalli, Ammatgar, Hulihonda, Hudelkoppa, Ingalki, Hostot, Halaharavi, Naginkeri, Siddapur, Gotagudi, Kyadgikop..

Scheduled Castes: Out of the total population of 74565 persons, 10695 persons (14.34%) belong to Scheduled Castes.

The villages having less than 10% SC population are Yerebail, Hulihonda, Gunjavati, Mainalli, Balehalli Hungunda, Kopp (Ind), Tattilli (Mundgod), Chowdalli Pur, Sanavalli, Bappalgundi, Byanalli, Kalkeri Andalgi, Kavalakoppa, Hirehalli, Chigalli, Chipageri Ganadahalli, Chitgeri, Chalgeri, Katur, Mudasali Maragadi, Hulihonda, Oralgi, Hudelkoppa, Veerapur Pala, Ingalki, Kalkoppa, Kurli, Togralli, Atabail Kanchikoppa, Shanvalli, Ummachagi, Hostot Halaharavi, Balekoppa, Bekkod, Gotagudi, Haraganalli Borangudda.

The villages having more than 50% SC population are Agadi, Kargolli, Tamyankoppa, Kundargi, Nagnoor Doddaharvalli, Naginkeri.

Sex ratio of Scheduled Caste population is 487.

Scheduled Castes Literates and Illiterates by Sex:

	Persons	Males	Females
Literate	4,887	3,047	1,840
Illiterate	5,808	2,442	3,366
Literacy rate	55.4	67.1	43.0
Graduate	80	70	10

Scheduled Castes (Dominant):

Bhovi, Banjara etc., Bhambi etc., Halsar etc. Chalavadi etc.

For their cultural identity please see Appendix-I

Villages without Scheduled Castes: There are 17 villages without any scheduled caste population.

Scheduled Tribes: Out of the total population of 74565 persons, 3286 persons (4.41%) belong to Scheduled Tribes.

The villages having less than 10% ST population are Yerebail, Nandikatta, Ugginkeri, Gunjavati, Mainalli Balehalli , Kusur, Indoor, Hungunda, Wadagatta

Bachanaki, Kopp (Ind), Tattilli (Mundgod), Kargolli Tamyankoppa, Kyasankeri, Teginkoppa, Pur, Nyasargi Kundargi, Sanavalli, Ajjihalli, Lakkolli, Malavalli Byanalli, Kalkeri, Basavanakoppa, Andalgi Kavalakoppa, Salgaon, Hirehalli, Chigalli, Chipageri Ganadahalli, Tattalli (Katur), Kallalli, Nagnoor Chitgeri, Chalgeri, Ammatgar, Attangi, Doddaharvalli Katur, Mudasali, Alalli, Maragadi, Shinganahalli Hulihonda, Oralgi, Hudelkoppa, Veerapur, Bhadrapura Kalkoppa, Kurli, Togralli, Atabail, Kanchikoppa Shanvalli, Ummachagi, Hostot, Bedasgaon, Halaharavi Balekoppa, Bekkod, Naginkeri, Siddapur, Malgi, Kolgi Haraganalli, Veerapur, Jangeri, Hoskoppa, Borangudda Kyadgikop.

The villages having more than 50% ST population are None.

Sex ratio of Scheduled tribe population is 484.

Scheduled Tribes Literates and Illiterates by Sex:

	Persons	Males	Females
Literate	1,591	963	628
Illiterate	1,695	732	963
Literacy rate	57.6	67.9	46.8
Graduate	21	18	3

Scheduled Tribes (Dominant):

Naikda etc., Koraga, Chenchu etc., Kadu Kuruba Meda

For their cultural identity please see Appendix-II

Villages without Scheduled Tribes: There are 41 villages without any scheduled tribe population.

Literates and Illiterates by Sex (Total Population):

	Persons	Males	Females
Literate	43,482	27,489	15,993
Illiterate	31,083	13,154	17,929
Literacy rate	69	79	56
Graduate	820	585	235

Agriculture: ***Distribution of villages according to land use:*** Out of 91 villages, Total area (in hectare) is 65608, out of that 18.81 percent is cultivable and 23.94 percent of the cultivable area is irrigated.

Sources of Irrigation (Hectares): Government Canal 599.45, Private Canal 56.65, Well without Electricity 8.1, Well with Electricity 67.98, Tubewell without Electricity 0, Tubewell with Electricity 427.7, Tank 1792.63, River 0, Lake 0, Waterfall 0, Others 4.05.

Villages with population of 5000 to 9999: Nandikatta.

Villages with population of 10000 and above: None

Distribution of Workers:

	Persons	Males	Females	WPR
Cultivators	16,562	10,918	5,644	46.64
Agricultural Labour	11,729	5,361	6,368	33.03
Household Industry	703	423	280	1.98
Other Workers	6,515	4,764	1,751	18.35
Main Workers	27,084	19,099	7,985	76.27
Marginal Workers	8,425	2,367	6,058	23.73
Total Workers	35,509	21,466	14,043	

Religion: Major Religious Communities:

	Persons	Males	Females	Sex Ratio
Hindu (71.16%)	53,063	27,319	25,744	942
Muslim (12.38%)	9,232	4,729	4,503	952
Christian (1.47%)	1,099	559	540	966
Sikh (0.01%)	11	8	3	375
Buddhists (14.22%	10,606	7,724	2,882	373
Jain (0.68%)	505	276	229	830

Agewise Data:

	Persons	Males	Females	Sex Ratio
All ages	74,565	40,643	33,922	835
0-14	25,156	13,184	11,972	908
15-44	36,931	20,934	15,997	764
45-79	11,845	6,228	5,617	902
80+	598	278	320	1151
Age not stated	35	19	16	842

Languages (Dominant):

Kannada, Tibetan, Urdu, Marathi, Telugu

Disabled Population:

	Persons	Males	Females	%
Total Disabled	1,863	1,086	777	
In Seeing	787	423	364	42.24
In Speech	130	82	48	6.98
In Hearing	174	112	62	9.34
In Movement	574	358	216	30.81
Mentally	198	111	87	10.63

MYSORE

Mysore C.D. Block lies in the northern part of Mysore district. It is a part of Mysore taluka. The Block is located at a distance of 00 kms. from district headquarters (Mysore). There are 143 villages in the block with the total population of 238,610 persons. Area of the C.D. Block is 683.74 sq. kms. It is bounded in the north by taluks Krishnarajanagara and Tirumakudal-Narisnur, and district Mandya, in the south by taluks Heggadadeva nkote and Nanjamgud, in the east by taluks Tirumakudal-N arsipur and Nanjamgud, and in the west by taluks Krishnar ajanagara, Hunsur and Heggadadevankote.

Communications:

Roadways : NH- 212: Direction- Mysore to Gundlupet and Kollegal, Nearest Villages- Nadanahalli, Bandipalya, Kuppaluru, Mandakalli, Ballahalli, Kadakola, Bhugathaga lli, Chikkahalli, Choranahalli, Varuna, Puttegowdanahundi, Chatnahalli, Madhavagere, Keelanapura, Megalapura, Hongate, Duddagere, Marase, Madaragalli, Inam-Uthanahalli.

SH-17: Direction- Mysore to Bangalore, Nearest Villages- Naganahalli, Laxmipura, Kalastavadi, Sidalingapura, Kesare. SH- 17 D: Direction- Heggadadevankote to Mysore, Nearest Villages- Halalu, Chowdahalli, Kenchalagudu, Baradanap ura, Daripura, Danagalli, Udburu, Jayapura, Chikkanahalli, Harohalli, Mandanahalli, Gujjegowdanapura. SH- 86: Direction- Mysore to Malavalli, Nearest Villages- Nadana halli, Bhugathagalli, Vajamangala, Harohalli, Varakodu. SH- 88: Direction- Hunsur to Mysore, Nearest Villages- Karakanahalli, Elwala, Koorgalli, Belavadi, Nagawala. Railway Station: Yedahalli, Kallurunaganahalli, Amachawadi, Huyilalu, Naganahalli, Kadakola.

River: Kabbani Nadi- Nearest Villages- Inam-Uthanahalli, Kuppegala, Yadakola. Cauvery Nadi- Nearest Villages- Yedahalli, Hosakote, Kallinathapura, Anandur, Subramanya pura, Undavadi. Lakshmantirtha Nadi- Nearest Villages- Ramanahalli, Cholenahalli, Hosakote, Amachawadi, Hunnavaili.

Canal: Nearest Villages- K.Hemmanahalli, Madagalli, Shyadanahalli, Naganahalli, Laxmipura, Kalasthavadi, Siddalingapura, Kesare, Basavanahalli, Kemmannupura, Maratikyathanahalli, Kergalli, Harohalli, Madhavagere, Keelanapura, Inam-Uthanahalli, Kuppegala, Yadakola.

Reserved Forest: Nearest Villages- Hosahundi, Jayapura, Arasinakere, Lalithadripura, Sarakariuthanahalli. (Chik kanahalli R.F.): Nearest Villages- Mavinahalli, Chikkanah alli, Harohalli, Gumachanahalli, S. Kallahalli, Maddur.

Annual Rainfall: Normal Rianfall 798 mm.

Ground Water: Availability of the Ground Water in the Basin is 6774.49 H.A.M. and the utilization is 1489. 04 H.A.M. It belongs to Over Expoited category. Depth to water level 2 to 20 meter below the ground. Most of the wells go down in summer months, according to the Ground Water Estimation Committee.

Soils: Red Sandy Soils, Red Loamy Soils and Deep Black Soils.

Natural Division : It falls partly in Kabbani-Cauvery Valley, Mysore-Piriyapatna and Cauvery Valley of the Southern Karnataka Plateau.

Administration:

Division: Mysore. Parliamentary Constituency: 22 Mysore Purab. District: Mysore. Taluka: Mysore. Assembly Constituency: 215 Chamundeshwari, 219 Varuna. Gram Panchayat: 35.

Fairs: Dasara Festival: The Dasara in Mysore is observed as a semi-religious function. It falls usually in October, but sometimes towards the close of September.

Nandi Basaveshwaraswamy Jatra: It is held at Maddur in the month of Magha (January-February) for seven days. Madura is a town on the right bank of the Shimsha river, about 50 kms. north-east of Mysore, on the Bangalore-My sore railway route and the Bangalore-Mysore road.

Villages: 143 **Inhabited:** 131 **Uninhabited:** 12

Ranking	District	State	National
Area	5	138	949
Population	3	50	299
Sex Ratio	6	161	3875
Child Sex Ratio	6	86	2906
Literacy Rate	6	149	4646
Density	6	158	3105
Work Participation Rate	3	15	3745

Gram Panchayats:

Anandur, Gungralchatra, Elwala, Koorgalli, Naganahalli, Siddalingapura, Rammanahalli , Hanchya , Harohalli, Vajamangala, Alanahalli , Hinkal , Belavadi, Nagawala, Doddamaragowdanahalli, Mallahalli (B), Bhogadi, Srirampura , Chamundibetta, Hosahundi, Varuna, Keelanapura, Yadakola, Mosambayanahalli, Devalapura, Kadakola, Sindhuvalli, Udburu, Danagalli, Gopalapura, Harohalli, Marballi, Doora, Someshwarapura, Jayapura, Metagalli , Dattagalli , Hebbalu, Belvata.

Amenities:

Education: Primary School in 124 villages, Middle school in 97 villages, Matriculation or Secondary School in 26 villages, namely Kallurunaganahalli, Elwala, Koorgalli, Doddamaragowdanahalli, Naganahalli, Siddalingapura, Kesare, Hanchya, Mandakalli, Mallahalli, Kergalli, Nagarthahalli, Danagalli, Udburu, Sindhuvalli, Jayapura, Harohalli, Doora, Kadakola, Harohalli, Varakodu, Varuna, Keelanapura, Megalapura, Devalapura, Yadakola.

Higher Secondary or Pre University Courses or Intermediate or Junior College in 2 villages of the CD Block,, namely Devalapura, Yadakola.

College in 0 village, Adult Literacy Center in 0 village.

Medical: Hospital in 2 villages, Dispensary in 10 villages, Health Center in 13 villages, Sub Center in 37 villages, Maternity and Child Welfare Center in 4 villages, Community health workers in 13 villages.

The Villages having Hospital or Dispensary or Health Center are Kallurunaganahalli, Elwala, Naganahalli, Laxmipura, Danagalli, Jayapura, Harohalli, Harohalli, Devalapura, Inam-Uthanahalli.

Drinking Water: Tap water in 108 villages, Tank water in 45 villages, Well water in 65 villages, Tubewell in 113 villages and more than one source in 125 villages.

Bank: Banking facility in 22 villages, namely, Dadadakallahalli, Mydanahalli, Elwala, Belavadi K.Hemmanahalli, Doddamaragowdanahalli, Naganahalli

Siddalingapura, Mallahalli, Kergalli, Danagalli Udburu, Jayapura, Harohalli, Mandanahalli, Kadakola Harohalli, Varuna, Duddagere, Devalapura, Ayarahalli Yadakola.

Credit Society in 131 villages Agricultural Credit Society in 15 Non-Agricultural Credit Society in 49 villages.

Others: Power supply in 131 villages, Cinema hall in 7 villages, sport club in 0 village, Stadium or Auditorium or Community Hall in 0 village, Post Office in 40 villages.

There are 121 villages having bus facilities.

Villages with most of facilities: Elwala, Belavadi Doddamaragowdanahalli, Naganahalli, Mallahalli Kergalli, Danagalli, Udburu, Jayapura, Harohalli Kadakola, Harohalli, Varuna, Devalapura, Ayarahalli Yadakola.

Villages without amenities (Education): Kallurunaganahalli Kaval, Basavanahalli, Ayyajayyanahundi, Halalu, Javanahalli, Choganahalli, Madaragalli..

Scheduled Castes: Out of the total population of 239262 persons, 42640 persons (17.82%) belong to Scheduled Castes. The villages having less than 10% SC population are Yedahalli, Kallinathapura, Anandur, Chikkanahalli Kallurunaganahalli Kaval, S.Hemmanahalli, Amachawadi Yelachahalli, Karakanahalli, Koorgalli, Huyilalu Nagawala, Manikyapura, K.Hemmanahalli, Jettihundi Doddamaragowdanahalli, Nuggahalli, Gohalli Rammanahalli, Basavanahalli, Hosahundi Ayyajayyanahundi, Halalu, Javanahalli, Mallahalli Ballahalli, Kergalli, Baradanapura, Daripura, Udburu Kellahalli, Chikkanahalli, Gumachanahalli Kadanahalli, Thoreyanakaturu, Kadakola, Harohalli Varakodu, Chikkahalli, Puttegowdanahundi Madhavagere, Megalapura, Hongate, Choganahalli Gudumadanahalli, Marase, Kumbarahalli, Madaragalli Koodanahalli, Ayarahalli, Kiralu, Mosambayanahalli.

The villages having more than 50% SC population are Bommenahalli, Kuppaluru, Devagalli, S. Kallahalli Chatnahalli, Inam-Uthanahalli.

Sex ratio of Scheduled Caste population is 491.

Scheduled Castes Literates and Illiterates by Sex:

	Persons	Males	Females
Literate	17,897	10,640	7,257
Illiterate	24,743	11,050	13,693
Literacy rate	49.1	57.3	40.6
Graduate	360	316	44

Scheduled Castes (Dominant):

Adi Karnataka, Madiga, Adi Dravida, Bhovi Generic Castes etc.

For their cultural identity please see Appendix-I

Villages without Scheduled Castes: There are 37 villages without any scheduled caste population.

Scheduled Tribes: Out of the total population of 239262 persons, 32331 persons (13.51%) belong to Scheduled Tribes. The villages having less than 10% ST population are Kallinathapura, Anandur, Undavadi, Chikkanahalli Kallurunaganahalli Kaval, Kallurunaganahalli Dadadakallahalli, Megalapura, Mydanahalli Karakanahalli, Rattanahalli, Elwala, Koorgalli Belavadi, Huyilalu, Bommenahalli, Manikyapura K.Hemmanahalli, Jettihundi, Nuggahalli Shettinayakanahalli, Gohalli, Shyadanahalli Naganahalli, Laxmipura, Siddalingapura, Kesare Hanchya, Basavanahalli, Nadanahalli, Hosahundi Bandipalya, Kuppaluru, Ayyajayyanahundi, Halalu Chowdahalli, Gurur, Mandakalli, Madahalli Javanahalli, Mallahalli, Ballahalli Maratikyathanahalli, Kergalli, Yadahalli Nagarthahalli, Devagalli, Mullur, Anagalli Gopalapura, Mavinahalli, Baradanapura, Daripura Danagalli, Kalalavadi, Dadadahalli, Sindhuvalli Thaluru, Murudagalli, Kellahalli, Chikkanahalli Harohalli, S. Kallahalli, Maddur, Mandanahalli Kadanahalli, Gujjegowdanapura, Doora, Doddakaturu Doddakanya, Chikkakanya, Byathahalli, Bhugathagalli Vajamangala, Varakodu, Chikkahalli, Lalithadripura Sarakariuthanahalli, Choranahalli, Varuna Puttegowdanahundi, Chatnahalli, Madhavagere Keelanapura, Megalapura, Hongate, Duddagere Pillahalli, Dandikere, Choganahalli, Jantagalli Marasettihalli, Hadajana, Gudumadanahalli, Marase Devalapura, Kumbarahalli, Koodanahalli, Kiralu Mosambayanahalli, Hosahalli, Inam-Uthanahalli Kuppegala, Yadakola.

The villages having more than 50% ST population are Amachawadi, Kumarabeedu, Rammanahalli, Kenchalagudu Udburu, Gumachanahalli, Thoreyanakaturu.

Sex ratio of Scheduled tribe population is 488.

Scheduled Tribes Literates and Illiterates by Sex:

	Persons	Males	Females
Literate	9,730	5,984	3,746
Illiterate	22,601	10,574	12,027
Literacy rate	35.2	42.5	27.7
Graduate	121	113	8

Scheduled Tribes (Dominant):

Naikda etc., Soligaru, Meda, Hakkipikki Generic Tribes etc.

For their cultural identity please see Appendix-II

Villages without Scheduled Tribes: There are 70 villages without any scheduled tribe population.

Literates and Illiterates by Sex (Total Population):

	Persons	Males	Females
Literate	102,243	61,852	40,391
Illiterate	137,019	61,316	75,703
Literacy rate	49	58	40
Graduate	2,739	2,178	561

Agriculture: ***Distribution of villages according to land use:*** Out of 143 villages, Total area (in hectare) is 68374, out of that 69 percent is cultivable and 13.53 percent of the cultivable area is irrigated.

Sources of Irrigation (Hectares): Government Canal 2026.32, Private Canal 0, Well without Electricity 96.21, Well with Electricity 686.38, Tubewell without Electricity 11.83, Tubewell with Electricity 2894.32, Tank 538.83, River 112.05, Lake 0, Waterfall 0, Others 15.73.

Villages with population of 5000 to 9999:
Elwala, Koorgalli, Kesare, Rammanahalli, Danagalli Udburu, Kadakola, Harohalli.

Villages with population of 10000 and above: None

Distribution of Workers:

	Persons	Males	Females	WPR
Cultivators	40,723	31,077	9,646	39.31
Agricultural Labour	19,309	9,104	10,205	18.64
Household Industry	985	630	355	0.95
Other Workers	42,580	34,486	8,094	41.1
Main Workers	86,408	67,813	18,595	83.41
Marginal Workers	17,189	7,484	9,705	16.59
Total Workers	103,597	75,297	28,300	

Religion: Major Religious Communities:

	Persons	Males	Females	Sex Ratio
Hindu (97.78%)	233,958	120,526	113,432	941
Muslim (1.1%)	2,626	1,342	1,284	957
Christian (0.39%)	936	411	525	1,277
Sikh (0.01%)	12	7	5	714
Buddhists (0.49%)	1,167	598	569	952
Jain (0.06%)	133	62	71	1,145

Agewise Data:

	Persons	Males	Females	Sex Ratio
All ages	239,262	123,168	116,094	943
0-14	76,746	38,826	37,920	977
15-44	116,810	60,501	56,309	931
45-79	43,062	22,568	20,494	908
80+	2,456	1,169	1,287	1101
Age not stated	188	104	84	808

Languages (Dominant):
Kannada, Telugu, Urdu, Tamil, Malayalam

Disabled Population:

	Persons	Males	Females	%
Total Disabled	4,071	2,332	1,739	
In Seeing	2,294	1,255	1,039	56.35
In Speech	448	232	216	11
In Hearing	191	105	86	4.69
In Movement	827	551	276	20.31
Mentally	311	189	122	7.64

NAGAMANGALA

Nagamangala C.D. Block lies in the northern part of Mandya district. It is a part of Nagamangala tehsil. The Block is located at a distance of 40 kms. from district headquarters (Mandya). There are 367 villages in the block with the total population of 174,764 persons. Area of the C.D. Block is 1034.65 sq. kms. It is bounded by district Tumkur on north, taluks Pandavapura and Mandya on south, taluk Maddur and district Tumkur on east, district Hassan and taluk Krishnarajpet on west.

Communications:

Roadways : N.H.-48: Direction- Hassan to Nelamangala, Nearest Villages- Sanaba, Belluru, Devihalli, Agachahalli, Kannagatta, Bommanahalli, Javaranahalli, Hatna, Gondihalli, Kalinganahalli, Channapura, Beechanahalli, Irubanahalli, Kanchinakote, Karabylu, Nelligere, Halalu, Gowdarahalli, Thirumalapura, Honnadevihalli, Kadabahalli, Varahasandra, Dadaga, A.Nagathihalli, Avverahalli, Chikkonahallipura, Lalankere,, Yeladahalli. S.H.-19: Direction- Shrirangapattana to Challakere, Nearest Villages- Ambaljeeranahalli, Chunchanahalli, Yalachikere, Laxmipura, Belluru, Vaddarahalli, Thavarekere, Karijeeranahalli, Karabylu, Nelligere, Yeladahalli, Cholasandra, Vaderapura, Ramadevanahalli, Anchebuvanahalli, Byranahalli, Kachenahalli, Anche Chittanahalli, Mulkatte, Chowdenahalli, Tolali, K.Mallenahalli, Honnabettadahosur, Sirapatna, A.Sriramanahalli, B. Settihalli, Konanur, Bramhadevarahalli, Kavadihalli, Mallegowdanahalli, Samakahalli, Guddenahalli, Chinya, Honakere, Sreeraghurampura, Karadya.

River: Vira Vaishnava Nadi- Nearest Villages- Ambaljeeranahalli, Mudagere, Laxmipura, Belluru, Bommanahalli, Vaddarahalli, Thavarekere, Karijeeranahalli, Kanchinakote, Karabylu, Nelligere, Toremavinakere, Hampapura, Halalu, Vaderahalli, Kadumanchenahalli, Hosahalli, Doddajataka, Dumma Sandra, Ankanahalli, Kavalugundi, Doddaguni, Katriguppe, Shivanahalli, Bitagonahalli, Mugutigundi, Doddenahalli, Abbagere, Mallasandra, Yadavanahalli, Yeladahalli, Tolasikombri. Shimsha Nadi- Nearest Villages- Toremallanayakanahalli, Doddauppla, Hadamgere, Ballekere, Beemanahalli, Arakere, Settahalli, Kudagabalu, Kellenahalli, Sampanahalli, Cholenahalli, Sunaganahalli, Maddenahatti, Hanchipura.

Canal: Nearest Villages- Padavalapatna, Sankanahalli, Gangasamudra, Gollarahalli, Deverahosur, Ijjalagatta, Kuppahalli, Ganganahalli, Vaddarahalli.

Annual Rainfall: Normal Rianfall 686.5 mm.

Ground Water: Availability of the Ground Water in the

Basin is 13267.46 H.A.M. and the utilization is 2843. 73 H.A.M. It belongs to Over Exploited category. Depth to water level 2 to 20 meter below the ground. Most of the wells go down in summer months, according to the Ground Water Estimation Committee.

Soils: Red Sandy Loams to Red Clay Loam.

Natural Division : It falls in Nagamangala Plateau of the Southern Karnataka Plateau.

Administration:

Division: Mysore. Parliamentary Constituency: 20 Mandaya. District: Mandaya. Taluka: Nagamangala. Assembly Consti tuency: 191 Nagamangala. Gram Panchayat: 27.

Fairs: Brahmadeva Jatra: Kambadahalli in Nagamangala taluk is about a kilometer south of Bindiganavale. This is a holy place of the Jains and gets its name from its tall Brahmadeva pillar (kamba) standing on a high platf orm to the north of the Panchakuta Basti. This elegant pillar is about 50 feet high and is made of hard dark grey soapstone. Its pedestal is octagonal and has eight Dikpalakas carved on it. On the top is a seated figure of Brahma facing east.

Chunchanagiri Jatra: Popularly known as Adi-Chunchanagiri Matha. The Chunchanagiri hill in Nagamangala taluk situated at a distance of about 5 kms. from Bellur, is a noted place of pilgrimage. On the hill are two natural cave temples dedicated to Siddheshvara and Somes hvara, as also a Gangadhareshvara temple of the Paleyagar period. There are panchalingas, several toranas, mantapas and shrines and a Matha of Sappesvami. Figures of Shiva, Nandis, Anjaneya, Yogis performing tapas and pairs of feet of gurus also adorn the hill.

Janardhanaswamy Festival: An annual festival is observed for 7 days in the month of Marghashira Purnima (Decembe r) at Bindiganavale, in honour of lord Janardhanaswamy. Bindiganavale is a place in Nagamangala taluk and is the headquarters of the hobli of the same name. The Keshava temple at this place is a plain structure built in the Dravidian style of architecture. A Garuda image here is believed to be of special sanctity. It has many devotees who make vows to it and some of them name their children after it. The eyes of this Garuda are formed of two saligrama stones.

Madheshwaraswamy Jatra: It is held at Panduapatra near Mandya in the month of Magha (January-February) for three days. Paduapatra is about 10 kms. in the west of Nagamangala. About 3 kms. to the west of this place is a huge boulder called Pandavara-kalli, it is said that Pandava princes lived here for some time during their exile. There are three large and several other small viragals in the place. One of them has a wood carving with three panels of figures-sculptures, depicti ng the hero fighting, being conveyed to Kailasa and his worshipping a linga. There are two inscriptions on the under-surface of the boulder stating that Sri Ramanu jacharya performed penance there.

Saumyakeshava Temple Festival : Nagamangala is an old town situated on the Srirangapatna-Sira road 35 kms. to the north-east of Pandavapura railway station and 50 kms. north of Mysore. It is the headquarters of the taluk of the same name. It was a place of considerable importance even from the days of the Hoysalas. A line of chiefs of the Lohita family continued to rule the Nagamangala area till the end of the fifteenth century or longer. The outer fort was erected in 1578 by Jagadeva Raya of Channapatna (Bangalore district), of whose kingdom Nagamangala was one of the chief towns. It was captured in 1630 by Chamaraja Wodeyar of Mysore. The town was reduced to ruins in 1792 by a Maratha army under Parashuram Bhau.

Villages: 367 **Inhabited:** 345 **Uninhabited:** 22

Ranking	District	State	National
Area	1	76	404
Population	5	112	1171
Sex Ratio	1	9	461
Child Sex Ratio	2	71	2689
Literacy Rate	2	84	2719
Density	3	71	5253
Work Participation Rate	7	102	1767

Gram Panchayats:

Kadabahalli, Arni, Chunchanahalli, Kalinganahalli, Nelligere, Belluru (Rural), Javaranahalli, Gondenahalli, Lalankere, Bindiganavile, Honnavara, Doddabala, Mayigonahalli, Anchebuvanahalli, Thuppadamadu, Palagrahara, Haradanahalli, Devaramallanayakanahalli, Devalapura, Beemanahalli, Karadahalli, Mannahalli, Bramhadevarahalli, Kanthapura, Bogadi, Chinya, Honakere.

Amenities:

Education: Primary School in 259 villages, Middle school in 145 villages, Matriculation or Secondary School in 34 villages, namely Honnenahalli, Arni, Chunchanahalli, Belluru, Javaranahalli, Thavarekere, Kadabahalli, Heraganahalli, Alisandra, Gondenahalli, Bindiganavile, Honnavara, Madihalli, K.Mallenahalli, Vaderapura, Hulikere, Mayigonahalli, Bettadamallenahalli, Gaddebuvanahalli, Dodda Jakkana Halli, Mylarapatna, Haradanahalli, Ramenahalli, Kotebetta, Devalapura, Thattahalli, Karadahalli, Settahalli, G.Bommanahalli, Tiruganahalli, Bogadi, Kanthapura, Bramhadevarahalli,

Chinya.

Higher Secondary or Pre University Courses or Intermediate or Junior College in 10 villages of the CD Block,, namely Chunchanahalli, Belluru, Javaranahalli, Kadabahalli, Bindiganavile, Tolali, Gaddebuvanahalli, Devalapura, Bogadi, Chinya.

College in 5 villages, Adult Literacy Center in 0 village., Colleges are in villages, namely Chunchanahalli, Javaranahalli, Kadabahalli, Tolali, Upparahalli.

Medical: Hospital in 10 villages, Dispensary in 7 villages, Health Center in 11 villages, Sub Center in 40 villages, Maternity and Child Welfare Center in 11 villages, Community health workers in 10 villages.

The Villages having Hospital or Dispensary or Health Center are Manchenahalli, Chunchanahalli, Belluru, Javaranahalli, Byadarahosahalli, Kadabahalli , Garudanahalli, Bindiganavile, Kelagere, Gaddebuvanahalli, Muthsandra, Bogadi, Ijjalagatta, Honakere.

Drinking Water: Tap water in 166 villages, Tank water in 170 villages, Well water in 314 villages, Tubewell in 208 villages and more than one source in 327 villages.

Bank: Banking facility in 21 villages, namely, Devaramavinakere, Arni, Belluru, Javaranahalli Vaderahalli, Kadabahalli, Bindiganavile, Kelagere Thuppadamadu, S.Mutsandra, Devalapura, Muthsandra Karadahalli, Hullenahalli, Bogadi, Kanthapura Chottakyatanahalli, Chagatahalli, J.Hosur, Chinya Honakere.

Credit Society in 11 villages Agricultural Credit Society in 10 Non-Agricultural Credit Society in 1 village.

Others: Power supply in 329 villages, Cinema hall in 3 villages, sport club in 2 villages, Stadium or Auditorium or Community Hall in 0 village, Post Office in 51 villages.

There are 140 villages having bus facilities.

Villages with most of facilities: Arni, Belluru Javaranahalli, Kadabahalli, Bindiganavile Muthsandra, Kanthapura, Honakere.

Villages without amenities (Education): M.Kodihalli, Bannadahalli, Mylanahalli, Dyamasandra, Adakatahalli, Nagalapura, Yalachikere, Bananahalli, Mantanahalli, Kannagatta, Doddagatta, Karijeeranahalli, Byadarahosahalli, Beechanahalli, Hampapura, Kadumanchenahalli, Hosahalli, Krishnapura, Kuppe, Kavalugundi, Katriguppe, Bitagonahalli, Jogipura, Hadenahalli, Kamadihalli, Turubanahalli, Byadarahalli, Mallenahalli, Byadagere, Gangarahalli, Hosur, Jennenahalli, Vaddarahalli, Kesavinakatte, Mellahalli, Karadahalli, Neelakantanahalli, Arehalli, Honnudikehalli, Kendanahalli, Veerasandra, Mallarajapura, Manchenahalli, Tyapenahalli, Chowdenahalli, Gundakallu Hosur, Nagamangala (Rural), Tolasikombri, Sirapura, S.Mutsandra, Hiduva, Kuntanakoppalu, H.N.Kaval, Dum Jakkanahalli, Kellenahalli, Cholenahalli, Hosahalli, Mavinakere, Hanchipura, S.Channapura, B.Shanboganahalli, Koravanagundi, Ayitanahalli, Gollarahalli, Deverahosur, Sirapatna, Madahallikaval, Lingammanahalli, Arealpahalli, B. Settihalli, Maradipura, Hettagonahalli, Somanahalli, Honnahalli..

Scheduled Castes: Out of the total population of 174718 persons, 20849 persons (11.93%) belong to Scheduled Castes. The villages having less than 10% SC population are Shikaranahalli, Devaramavinakere, Tondahalli Maniyur, Honnenahalli, Siddapura, M.Kodihalli Manchenahalli, Chandanahalli, Bannadahalli Kokkaranahosahalli, Chabbanahalli, Ankanahalli Mylanahalli, Hullenahalli, Chakenahalli, Sanaba Dyamasandra, Adakatahalli, G.Nagatihalli Mantanahalli, Agachahalli, Kannagatta, Chamalapura Bommanahalli, Javaranahalli, Vaddarahalli Byrasandra, Bettadakote, Gondihalli, Channapura Beechanahalli, Karabylu, Nelligere, Hampapura Vaderahalli, Kadumanchenahalli, Hosahalli Volagerepura, Krishnapura, Kuppe, Dumma Sandra Ankanahalli, Kavalugundi, Doddaguni, Katriguppe Bitagonahalli, Honnadevihalli, Cholenahalli Heraganahalli, Alisandra, A.Nagathihalli Avverahalli, Chikkonahallipura, Hadenahalli Metimellahalli, Bommanahalli, Thittanahosahalli Halladahosahalli, Bettadahalli, Gondenahalli Kuchahalli, Haralahalli, Anechannapura, Lalankere Chattenahalli, Ballavalli, Byadarahalli Bindiganavile, Narugondanahalli, Gulkaihosahalli Mallenahalli, Koppa, Kenchagonahalli, Doddabala Hosur, Gunjenahalli, Jennenahalli, Kodihalli Irakanagatta, Beechanahalli, Honnenahalli, Bonagere Masgonahalli, Satenahalli, Hanumanahalli Kesavinakatte, Sannenahalli, Seegahalli, Cholasandra Vaderapura, Begamangala, Karadahalli, Kadagere Neelakantanahalli, Honnudikehalli, Byranahalli Kendanahalli, Anche Chittanahalli, Mallarajapura Huvinahalli, Mayigonahalli, Shivanahalli Manchenahalli, Padavalachittanahalli, P. Neralakere Chowdenahalli, Upparahalli, Hosahalli, Palagrahara Gundakallu Hosur, Kasuvinahalli, Nagamangala (Rural) Bettadamallenahalli, Beereswarapura, Mallasandra Tolasikombri, Dodda Chikkana Halli Dodda Jakkana Halli, Haradanahalli, Hiduva H.Kodihalli, Dandebala, H.Bommanahalli

J.Chikkanahalli, Tubinakere, Hadamgere, Muthsandra
Kuntanakoppalu, H.N.Kaval, Thattahalli
Dum Jakkanahalli, Karadahalli, Bindenahalli
Beemanahalli, Arakere, Kudagabalu, Cholenahalli
Hosahalli, Somanahalli, Mavinakere, Hanchipura
S.Channapura, Mallasandra, B.Shanboganahalli
Sukadore, Maranayakanahalli, Tiruganahalli
Kallenahalli, Bogadi, Kalenahalli, Honnabettadahosur
Sirapatna, A.Sriramanahalli, Jodi Neralakere
Kalludevanahalli, Madahallikaval, Chikkayagati
Mannahalli, Burudugunte, Arealpahalli, Konanur
Chottakyatanahalli, Gejjehosahalli, Balenahalli
Kanagonahalli, Vaddarahalli, A. Shanboganahalli
Maradipura, Chagatahalli, Hettagonahalli
Tenginabaga, T.Channapura, Koppa, Mallegowdanahalli
Samakahalli, Guddenahalli, J.Hosur, Advikatte
Chinya, Sreeraghurampura, Gotakahalli, Gudehosahalli
Machalagatta.

The villages having more than 50% SC population are Byadarahosahalli, Thirumalapura, Dasagalapura Deverahosur, Lingammanahalli, B.Sriramanahalli.

Sex ratio of Scheduled Caste population is 508.

Scheduled Castes Literates and Illiterates by Sex:

	Persons	Males	Females
Literate	9,779	5,767	4,012
Illiterate	11,070	4,490	6,580
Literacy rate	54.2	65.3	43.5
Graduate	179	153	26

Scheduled Castes (Dominant):

Adi Karnataka, Bhovi, Madiga, Korama, Adi Dravida

For their cultural identity please see Appendix-I

Villages without Scheduled Castes: There are 92 villages without any scheduled caste population.

Scheduled Tribes: Out of the total population of 174718 persons, 1585 persons (0.91%) belong to Scheduled Tribes.

The villages having less than 10% ST population are
Shikaranahalli, Devaramavinakere, Tondahalli
Maniyur, Siddapura, M.Kodihalli, Manchenahalli
Chandanahalli, Bannadahalli, Arni
Kokkaranahosahalli, Chabbanahalli, Ankanahalli
Mylanahalli, Hullenahalli, Chakenahalli, Sanaba
Dyamasandra, Adakatahalli, Thigalanahalli
Srirangapura, Ambaljeeranahalli, Mudagere
Chunchanahalli, Yalachikere, Byaladakere
G.Nagatihalli, Ganasandra, Bananahalli, Laxmipura
Belluru, Mantanahalli, Devihalli, Agachahalli
Kannagatta, Chamalapura, Maradevanahalli
Govindagatta, Doddagatta, Suranahalli, Bommanahalli
Javaranahalli, Vaddarahalli, Thavarekere
Karijeeranahalli, Koppa, Byrasandra, Bettadakote
Byadarahosahalli, Bilagunda, Hatna, Gondihalli
Kalinganahalli, Channapura, Beechanahalli
Irubanahalli, Kanchinakote, Karabylu, Nelligere
Toremavinakere, Hampapura, Halalu, Thirumalapura
Vaderahalli, Hosahalli, Doddajataka, Volagerepura
Chikkajataka, Krishnapura, Kuppe, Ankanahalli
Kavalugundi, Doddaguni, Katriguppe, Shivanahalli
Bitagonahalli, Honnadevihalli, Kadabahalli
Cholenahalli, Heraganahalli, Jogipura, Alisandra
Varahasandra, Dadaga, A.Nagathihalli, Avverahalli
Chikkonahallipura, Hadenahalli, Metimellahalli
Bommanahalli, Thittanahosahalli, Kamadihalli
D.Kodihalli, Halladahosahalli, Doddenahalli
Bettadahalli, Gondenahalli, Kuchahalli, Haralahalli
Anechannapura, Lalankere, Chattenahalli, Ballavalli
Bidarakere, Turubanahalli, Byadarahalli
Garudanahalli, Bindiganavile, Narugondanahalli
Gulkaihosahalli, Kurdikere, Mallenahalli, Byadagere
Koppa, Kenchagonahalli, Gangarahalli, Doddabala
Hosur, Ramachandra Agrahara, Addihalli, Kambadahalli
B.Mallenahalli, Buvanahalli, Gunjenahalli
H.Kyatanahalli, Honnavara, Madihalli, Jennenahalli
Kodihalli, K.Mallenahalli, Machanaikanahalli
Irakanagatta, Kanchanahalli, Beechanahalli
Honnenahalli, Bonagere, Masgonahalli, Satenahalli
Vaddarahalli, Hanumanahalli, Gidavinachannapura
Gidavinahosahalli, Kesavinakatte, Sannenahalli
Mellahalli, Kabbinakere, Yeladahalli, Seegahalli
Cholasandra, Vaderapura, Begamangala
Ramadevanahalli, Karadahalli, Kannenahalli, Kelagere
Gowdarahalli, Cholenahalli, Kadagere
Neelakantanahalli, Naraganahalli, Arehalli
Honnudikehalli, Anchebuvanahalli, Byranahalli
Karagere, Kodagahalli, Yagatahalli, Kendanahalli
Halthi, Veerasandra, Kachenahalli
Anche Chittanahalli, Hulikere, Mallarajapura
Huvinahalli, Mayigonahalli, Naragallu, Shivanahalli
Padavalamallenahalli, Chikkonahalli, Manchenahalli
Padavalachittanahalli, P. Neralakere, Padavalapatna
Kallukomari, Tyapenahalli, Ankushapura, Mulkatte
Chowdenahalli, Tolali, Upparahalli, Byadarahalli
Hosahalli, Palagrahara, Gundakallu Hosur
Kasuvinahalli, Nagamangala (Rural)
Bettadamallenahalli, Sankanahalli, K.Mallenahalli
Gaddebuvanahalli, Hullekere, Beereswarapura
Mallasandra, Yadavanahalli, Dodda Chikkana Halli
Ankanahalli, Toremallanayakanahalli
Dodda Jakkana Halli, Sirapura, Dadamudike
Mylarapatna, S.Mutsandra, Haradanahalli, Hiduva
Doddauppla, Devaramadahalli, Devarahalli

Ramenahalli, H.Kodihalli, Dandebala, H.Bommanahalli Nalkundi, Kotebetta, Dondemadahalli, J.Chikkanahalli Devaramallanayakana Halli, Tubinakere, Hadamgere Ballekere, Devalapura, Muthsandra, Kuntanakoppalu H.N.Kaval, Thattahalli, Dum Jakkanahalli Dandiganahalli, Karadahalli, Hullenahalli Bindenahalli, Beemanahalli, Gollarahalli, Kasalagere Mallinathapura, Thibbanahalli, Arakere, Settahalli Kudagabalu, Kellenahalli, Sampanahalli, Cholenahalli Sunaganahalli, Hosahalli, Somanahalli G.Bommanahalli, Maddenahatti, Hanchipura Muddanahalli, Matadabuvanahalli, S.Channapura Bommanayakanahalli, Mallasandra, B.Shanboganahalli Handenahalli, Thattekere, Sukadore Maranayakanahalli, Kalligundi, Tiruganahalli Koravanagundi, Hindasahalli, Madahalli, Kallenahalli Bogadi, Manchipatna, Karikyathanahalli, Ayitanahalli Kalenahalli, Kanthapura, Gangasamudra, Gollarahalli Deverahosur, Juttanahalli, Honnabettadahosur Sirapatna, A.Sriramanahalli, Jodi Neralakere Kalludevanahalli, Madahallikaval, Doddayagati Chikkayagati, Lingammanahalli, Mannahalli Burudugunte, Arealpahalli, B. Settihalli, Konanur Chottakyatanahalli, Ijjalagatta, Kuppahalli Gejjehosahalli, Uyanahalli, B.Sriramanahalli Balenahalli, Jodi Alpahalli, Kanagonahalli Kemmanahalli, Ganganahalli, Vaddarahalli A. Shanboganahalli, Maradipura, Bramhadevarahalli Chagatahalli, Hettagonahalli, Huraliganganahalli Tenginabaga, T.Channapura, Gangavadi, Koppa Kavadihalli, Mallegowdanahalli, Samakahalli Guddenahalli, Somanahalli, J.Hosur, Honnahalli Advikatte, Chinya, Honakere, Busamudra Sreeraghurampura, Gotakahalli, Karadya Gudehosahalli, Chowdagonahalli, Machalagatta.

The villages having more than 50% ST population are None.

Sex ratio of Scheduled tribe population is 474.

Scheduled Tribes Literates and Illiterates by Sex:

	Persons	Males	Females
Literate	612	396	216
Illiterate	973	437	536
Literacy rate	45.6	56.2	34.0
Graduate	10	10	0

Scheduled Tribes (Dominant):

Naikda etc., Hakkipikki, Soligaru, Meda Generic Tribes etc.

For their cultural identity please see Appendix-II

Villages without Scheduled Tribes: There are 305 villages without any scheduled tribe population.

Literates and Illiterates by Sex (Total Population):

	Persons	Males	Females
Literate	93,108	55,182	37,926
Illiterate	81,610	30,787	50,823
Literacy rate	60	73	48
Graduate	2,454	1,975	479

Agriculture: ***Distribution of villages according to land use:*** Out of 367 villages, Total area (in hectare) is 103465, out of that 51.53 percent is cultivable and 15.77 percent of the cultivable area is irrigated.

Sources of Irrigation (Hectares): Government Canal 1289.75, Private Canal 5.4, Well without Electricity 396.38, Well with Electricity 850.35, Tubewell without Electricity 105.58, Tubewell with Electricity 1781.58, Tank 2649.47, River 66.25, Lake 30.57, Waterfall 32.83, Others 1198.86.

Villages with population of 5000 to 9999: Belluru.

Villages with population of 10000 and above: None

Distribution of Workers:

	Persons	Males	Females	WPR
Cultivators	65,024	37,291	27,733	71
Agricultural Labour	10,413	3,266	7,147	11.37
Household Industry	1,482	815	667	1.62
Other Workers	14,669	10,208	4,461	16.02
Main Workers	76,222	48,630	27,592	83.22
Marginal Workers	15,366	2,950	12,416	16.78
Total Workers	91,588	51,580	40,008	

Religion: Major Religious Communities:

	Persons	Males	Females	Sex Ratio
Hindu (97.02%)	169,505	83,298	86,207	1,035
Muslim (2.18%)	3,816	2,018	1,798	891
Christian (0.18%)	314	102	212	2,078
Sikh (0.01%)	25	15	10	667
Buddhists (0.02%)	43	22	21	955
Jain (0.53%)	932	476	456	958

Agewise Data:

	Persons	Males	Females	Sex Ratio
All ages	174,718	85,969	88,749	1032
0-14	51,283	26,303	24,980	950
15-44	80,615	39,072	41,543	1063
45-79	40,032	19,346	20,686	1069
80+	2,591	1,147	1,444	1259
Age not stated	197	101	96	950

Languages (Dominant):

Kannada, Urdu, Telugu, Tamil, Marathi

Disabled Population:

	Persons	Males	Females	%
Total Disabled	4,948	2,740	2,208	
In Seeing	2,687	1,431	1,256	54.3
In Speech	485	269	216	9.8

In Hearing	295	144	151	5.96
In Movement	1,078	687	391	21.79

Mentally	403	209	194	8.14

NANJANGUD

Nanjangud C.D. Block lies in the south-eastern part of Mysore district. It is a part of Nanjangud taluka. The Block is located at a distance of 24 kms. from district headquarters (Mysore). There are 190 villages in the block with the total population of 310,195 persons. Area of the C.D. Block is 969.20 sq. kms. It is bounded by taluks Mysore and Heggadadevankote on north, district Chamarajanagar on south, and on east with taluk Tirumak udal-Narsipur, and taluk Heggadadevankote on west.

Communications:

Roadways : NH-212: Direction- Mysore to Gundlupet, Nearest Villages- Yechagalli, Thandavapura, Chikkaiahnachatra, Basavanapura, Kathavadipura, Deveerammanahalli, Uppinah alli, Kalale, Muddahalli, Sindhuvalli, Sindhuvallipura, Yelachagere, Hunasanalu. SH- 17 B: Direction- Nanjangud to Chamarajanagar, Nearest Villages- Nanjangud(Rural), Golur, Geekahalli, Badanavalu, Veeredevanapura, Kodinar asipura, Basavattige, Chikkakowlande, Nerale, Doddakowlan de, Konanapura.

Railway Station: Villages- Badanavalu, Jhandarapura, Konanoor, Doddakowlande.

River: Kabbani Nadi- Nearest Villages- Haradanahalli, Madanahalli, Kanenur, Hullahalli, Belale, Motha, Rampura, Kembal, Bidaragoodu, Maraluru, Goddanapura, Yechagalli, Chikkaiahnachatra, Basavanapura, Hejjige, Thoremavu, Immavu, Hulimavu, Bokkahalli, Hadinaru, Moodahalli, Alathur, Hosakote, Thumnerale, Thumneralekaval, Nandigu nda, Alambur, Saragooru, Nagarle, Kupparavalli, Suthur, Jeemaralli, Bilugali, Jodihariharapura (Igli), Thayuru, Kongahalli, Heggadahalli, Byalaru, Debur, Kallahalli, Kathavadipura, Nanjangud(Rural), Mullur, Horalavadi. Gundal Nadi- Nearest Villages- Deveerammanahalli, Devar asanahalli, Gonathagala, Uppinahalli, Kalale, Hedathale, Hemmaragala, Kumbarahalli, Hosapura, Koodlapura, Bagooru, Tharadale, Mallahalli. Nugu Nadi- Nearest Villages- Madanahalli, Kappasoge, Motha, Nellithalapura, Akala, Kadaburu, Shettahalli, Mangalore, Uganiya, Kadajetti, Ariyur, Jalahalli.

Canal: Nearest Villages- Kanenur, Hullahalli, Belale, Huskur, Karya, Kurihundi, Kappasoge, Nellithalapura, Shettahalli, Mangalore, Duggahalli, Chamanamadanahalli, Madapura, Haginavalu, Kaggalur, Melagalli, Uganiya, Kadajetti, Hura, Yedahalli, Hadya, Ariyur, Jalahalli, Kandegala, Thelanur, Gadiguddadakaval, Rampura, Kembal, Bidaragoodu, Maraluru, Yechagalli, Thandavapura, Chikka iahnachatra, Basavanapura, Hejjige, Thoremavu, Immavu, Hulimavu, Hadinaru, Moodahalli, Alathur, Hosakote, Tumnerale, Nandigunda, Alambur, Saragooru, Haniyamballi, Kalmahalli, Nagarle, Kupparavalli, Suthur, Jeemaralli, Bilugali, Jodihariharapura (Igli), Thayuru, Biligere, Belagunda, Kongahalli, Heggadahalli, Byalaru, Debur, Kallahalli, Kathavadipura, Devarasanahalli, Geekahalli, Mullur, Horalavadi, Gonathagala, Kalale, Karlapura, Harathale, Kanipura, Volagere, Hosakote (Masage), Yecha gundlu, Muddahalli, Sindhuvalli, Kurahatti, Hedathale.

Reserved Forest: Nearest Villages- Kaladevanahalli, Mallahalli, Channapatna, Thelanur, Gadiguddadakaval, Kallahalli, Kellupura, Karlapura, Hosaveedukaval, Hosav eedu, Maduvinahalli, Devarayasettipura.

Annual Rainfall: Normal Rianfall 697 mm.

Ground Water: Availability of the Ground Water in the Basin is 7127.87 H.A.M. and the utilization is 5187. 94 H.A.M. It belongs to Over Exploited category. Depth to water level 2 to 10 meter below the ground. Most of the wells go down in summer months, according to the Ground Water Estimation Committee.

Soils: Red Sandy Soils, Red Loamy Soils and Deep Black Soils.

Natural Division : It falls partly in Kabbani-Cauvery Valley and Heggadadevankote-Bandipur Forested Upland of the Southern Karnataka Plateau.

Administration:

Division: Mysore. Parliamentary Constituency: 21 Mysore Paschim, 22 Mysore Purab. District: Mysore. Taluka: Nanjangud. Assembly Constituency: 214 Nanjangud (SC), 219 Varuna. Gram Panchayat: 45.

Villages: 190 **Inhabited:** 176 **Uninhabited:** 14

Ranking	District	State	National
Area	2	87	466
Population	1	10	50
Sex Ratio	2	88	2361
Child Sex Ratio	2	10	934
Literacy Rate	7	163	5172
Density	5	149	3339
Work Participation Rate	4	20	3513

Gram Panchayats:

Rampura, Hullahalli, Shiramalli, Heggadahalli, Debur, Maraluru, Thandavapura, Hejjige, Horalavadi, Hulimavu, Hadinaru, Hosakote, Thumnerale, Thayuru, Suthur, Biligere, Nagarle, Mallupura, Devarasanahalli, Deveerammanahalli, Kalale, Haginavalu, Kurihundi, Haradanahalli, Nellithalapura, Duggahalli, Navilur, Sindhuvalli, Hedathale, Badanavalu, Devanur, Thagadooru, Karya, Dasanooru, Konanoor, Doddakowlande, Nerale, Hemmaragala, Koodlapura, Kasuvinahalli, Kallare, Hura, Hadya,

Hediyala, Devarayasettipura.

Amenities:

Education: Primary School in 168 villages, Middle school in 128 villages, Matriculation or Secondary School in 32 villages, namely Hullahalli, Karya, Kappasoge, Kadaburu, Haginavalu, Kadajetti, Hura, Maduvinahalli, Hediyala, Thandavapura, Hejjige, Thoremavu, Hadinaru, Hosakote, Nagarle, Suthur, Thayuru, Thagadooru, Heggadahalli, Devarasanahalli, Golur, Badanavalu, Kalale, Hosakote (Masage), Kasuvinahalli, Devanur, Karya, Hemmaragala, Koodlapura, Doddakowlande, Konanoor, Dasanooru.

Higher Secondary or Pre University Courses or Intermediate or Junior College in 4 villages of the CD Block,, namely Hullahalli, Hediyala, Devanur, Doddakowlande.

College in 0 village, Adult Literacy Center in 0 village.

Medical: Hospital in 1 village, Dispensary in 8 villages, Health Center in 15 villages, Sub Center in 64 villages, Maternity and Child Welfare Center in 2 villages, Community health workers in 0 village.

The Villages having Hospital or Dispensary or Health Center are Hullahalli, Hura, Maduvinahalli, Maraluru, Kasuvinahalli, Hedathale, Nerale, Koodlapura.

Drinking Water: Tap water in 133 villages, Tank water in 64 villages, Well water in 126 villages, Tubewell in 94 villages and more than one source in 164 villages.

Bank: Banking facility in 32 villages, namely, Hullahalli, Shiramalli, Kurihundi, Nellithalapura Hura, Hallare, Hadya, Hediyala, Yechagalli Thandavapura, Chikkaiahnachatra, Thoremavu, Hadinaru Hosakote, Nagarle, Suthur, Biligere, Thagadooru Chinnamballi, Heggadahalli, Veeredevanapura, Kalale Sindhuvalli, Surahalli, Kasuvinahalli, Hunasanalu Devanur, Hemmaragala, Koodlapura, Doddakowlande Dasanooru, Thoravalli.

Credit Society in 176 villages Agricultural Credit Society in 32 Non-Agricultural Credit Society in 68 villages.

Others: Power supply in 176 villages, Cinema hall in 10 villages, sport club in 0 village, Stadium or Auditorium or Community Hall in 0 village, Post Office in 80 villages.

There are 159 villages having bus facilities.

Villages with most of facilities: Hullahalli Kurihundi, Nellithalapura, Hura, Hediyala Thandavapura, Chikkaiahnachatra, Hadinaru, Hosakote Nagarle, Suthur, Thagadooru, Veeredevanapura, Kalale Kasuvinahalli, Devanur, Koodlapura, Doddakowlande Dasanooru, Thoravalli.

Villages without amenities (Education): Kongahallikaval, Mangalore, Bhogavaluvadeyanapura, Hosaveedukaval, Kurahattikaval, Srikantanagar, Ramasettipura, Paduvala Agrahara..

Scheduled Castes: Out of the total population of 311991 persons, 71608 persons (22.95%) belong to Scheduled Castes.

The villages having less than 10% SC population are Karya, Mangalore, Madapura, Kaggalur, Yedahalli M. Kongahalli, Bhogavaluvadeyanapura, Hosaveedukaval Kembal, Bidaragoodu, Maraluru, Yechagalli Thandavapura, Adakanahalli, Chikkaiahnachatra Hadinaru, Kurahattikaval, Alambur, Madahalli Mallupura, Srikantanagar, Handhvinahalli Bendagahalli, Lakshmanapura, Hunasanalu Kakkarahatti, Hemmaragala, Hosapura, Bagooru Hampapura, Gattavadipura, Haraganapur, Ramasettipura Thoravalli.

The villages having more than 50% SC population are Kongahallikaval, Channapatna, Jalahalli Hadanuruvadeyanapura, Kalmahalli, Belagunda Devarasanahalli, Mullur, Kodinarasipura, Konanapura.

Sex ratio of Scheduled Caste population is 496.

Scheduled Castes Literates and Illiterates by Sex:

	Persons	Males	Females
Literate	27,790	16,310	11,480
Illiterate	43,818	19,783	24,035
Literacy rate	45.0	52.3	37.5
Graduate	724	636	88

Scheduled Castes (Dominant):

Adi Karnataka, Madiga, Bhovi, Generic Castes etc. Bhambi etc.

For their cultural identity please see Appendix-I

Villages without Scheduled Castes: There are 30 villages without any scheduled caste population.

Scheduled Tribes: Out of the total population of 311991 persons, 45239 persons (14.5%) belong to Scheduled Tribes.

The villages having less than 10% ST population are Haradanahalli, Madanahalli, Kanenur, Shiramalli Huskur, Kurihundi, Motha, Kongahallikaval, Katur Nellithalapura, Akala, Rajur, Shettahalli, Mangalore Yalehalli, Duggahalli, Chamanamadanahalli, Ambale Kaggalur, Kadajetti, Yedahalli, M. Kongahalli Malkundi, Mallahalli, Channapatna, Ariyur, Jalahalli Kandegala, Kellupura, Bhogavaluvadeyanapura Hosaveedu, Maduvinahalli, Hediyala Hadanuruvadeyanapura, Devarayasettipura, Rampura Maraluru, Goddanapura, Thandavapura, Hebya Adakanahalli, Basavanapura, Hejjige, Thoremavu Immavu, Hulimavu, Moodahalli, Nandigundapura Nandigunda, Alambur, Haniyamballi, Kalmahalli Jeemaralli, Jodihariharapura (Igli) Eswaragowdanahalli, Haropura, Gejjiganahalli Kahalli, Kalkunda, Biligere, Belagunda, Kirugunda

Madahalli, Srikantanagar, Kamahalli, Kongahalli Heggadahalli, Byalaru, Kathavadipura, Handhvinahalli Deveerammanahalli, Devarasanahalli, Golur, Mullur Bendagahalli, Badanavalu, Veeredevanapura Kodinarasipura, Uppinahalli, Karlapura, Volagere Muddahalli, Kurahatti, Sindhuvallipura, Navilur Makanapura, Depegowdanapura, Krishnapura Lakshmanapura, Hunasanalu, Basavattige, Varahalli Kakkarahatti, Banooru, Hadya, Chunchanahalli, Nerale Hemmaragala, Hosapura, Koodlapura, Bagooru Tharadale, Hampapura, Haraganapur, Gattavadi Doddakowlande, Konanoor, Konanapura Paduvalamarahalli, Ramasettipura, Hanumanapura Paduvala Agrahara, Doddahomma, Chikkahomma Thoravalli.

The villages having more than 50% ST population are Ibjala, Belale, Kappasoge, Madapura, Kembal Kurahattikaval, Gonahalli, Kalale, Hedathale Kumbarahalli, Mallahalli.

Sex ratio of Scheduled tribe population is 500.

Scheduled Tribes Literates and Illiterates by Sex:

	Persons	Males	Females
Literate	14,481	8,686	5,795
Illiterate	30,758	13,947	16,811
Literacy rate	36.9	44.3	29.6
Graduate	332	289	43

Scheduled Tribes (Dominant):

Naikda etc., Jenu Kuruba, Soligaru, Kadu Kuruba Meda

For their cultural identity please see Appendix-II

Villages without Scheduled Tribes: There are 84 villages without any scheduled tribe population.

Literates and Illiterates by Sex (Total Population):

	Persons	Males	Females
Literate	123,576	73,597	49,979
Illiterate	188,415	84,538	103,877
Literacy rate	45	53	37
Graduate	3,289	2,834	455

Agriculture: ***Distribution of villages according to land use:*** Out of 190 villages, Total area (in hectare) is 96920, out of that 73.87 percent is cultivable and 28.37 percent of the cultivable area is irrigated.

Sources of Irrigation (Hectares): Government Canal 15162.7, Private Canal 0, Well without Electricity 33.95, Well with Electricity 643.48, Tubewell without Electricity 92.98, Tubewell with Electricity 2690.77, Tank 8.99, River 0, Lake 0, Waterfall 0, Others 0.

Villages with population of 5000 to 9999: Hullahalli, Thandavapura, Hadinaru, Thagadooru Kalale, Hedathale.

Villages with population of 10000 and above: None

Distribution of Workers:

	Persons	Males	Females	WPR
Cultivators	52,468	45,088	7,380	37.53
Agricultural Labour	60,212	33,030	27,182	43.07
Household Industry	1,582	870	712	1.13
Other Workers	25,536	20,767	4,769	18.27
Main Workers	109,685	87,764	21,921	78.46
Marginal Workers	30,113	11,991	18,122	21.54
Total Workers	139,798	99,755	40,043	

Religion: Major Religious Communities:

	Persons	Males	Females	Sex Ratio
Hindu (96.24%)	300,267	152,171	148,096	973
Muslim (2.03%)	6,344	3,285	3,059	931
Christian (0.18%)	546	291	255	876
Sikh (0%)	1	-	1	-
Buddhists (1.43%)	4,457	2,190	2,267	1,035
Jain (0.03%)	108	58	50	862

Agewise Data:

	Persons	Males	Females	Sex Ratio
All ages	311,991	158,135	153,856	973
0-14	92,711	46,516	46,195	993
15-44	152,556	77,480	75,076	969
45-79	63,206	32,613	30,593	938
80+	3,343	1,437	1,906	1326
Age not stated	175	89	86	966

Languages (Dominant):

Kannada, Urdu, Telugu, Tamil, Coorgi/Kodagu

Disabled Population:

	Persons	Males	Females	%
Total Disabled	5,568	3,103	2,465	
In Seeing	3,145	1,651	1,494	56.48
In Speech	606	325	281	10.88
In Hearing	292	147	145	5.24
In Movement	1,092	719	373	19.61
Mentally	433	261	172	7.78

NARASIMHARAJAPURA

Narsimharajapura C.D. Block lies in the north-western part of Chikmagalur district. It is a part of Narsimhara japura taluka. The Block is located at a distance of 88 kms. from district headquarters (Chikmagalur). There are 58 villages in the block with the total population of 58,183 persons. Area of the C.D. Block is 731.80 sq. kms. It is bounded by district Shimoga on north, taluk Mudigere on south, taluks Chikmagalur, Tarikere and district Shimoga on east, taluk Koppa and district Shimoga on west.

Communications:

Roadways : S.H.-66: Direction- Karkal to Kattigehar, Nearest Villages- Magundi.

River: Bhadra Nadi- Nearest Villages- Kusabur, Arambali,

Vittala, Haledanivasa, Lingapura, Soosalavani, Balekoppa, Mensur, Hiluvalli, Ravoor, Nagalapura, Shiragalale, Handur, Bilalkoppa, Salur, Nandigave, Varkate, Sarya, Hebbe, Alehalli, Aduvalli, Kolale, Muduguni, B.Kanabur, Karehadlu, Bannur, Magundi. Tunga Nadi- Nearest Villages- Kanive, Konakere, Muthinakoppa, K.Kanabur.

Annual Rainfall: Normal Rianfall 1423.9 mm.

Ground Water: Availability of the Ground Water in the Basin **is 5204** H.A.M. and the utilization is 717 H.A.M. **It belongs** to Safe category. Depth to water level 2 to **10 meter** below the ground. Most of the wells go down in summer months, according to the Ground Water Estimation Committee.

Soils: Red Loamy and Sandy Soils.

Natural Division : It falls in Kudremukh-Bababudan Forested Hilly zone of the Central Karnataka Plateau.

Administration:

Division: Mysore. Parliamentary Constituency: 15 Udupi. District: Chikmagalur. Taluka: Narsimharajapura. Assembly Constituency: 123 Sringeri. Gram Panchayat: 14.

Regional Area Development Boards: The Maland Aera Development Board.

Fairs: Bhoomi-Hunnime Festival: During the Deepavali season, "Bhoomi-Hunnime" festival is celebrated by the farmers of Sringeri, Mudigere, Koppa, Narasmharajapura and Chikmagalur taluks of Chikmagalur area.

Jain Basadis Jatra: Narasimharajapura previously called Yedehalli, is 88 kms. north-west of Chikmagalur town, 54 kms. west of Tarikere town, 42 kms. south-west of Bhadravali town and 330 kms. north-west of Bangalore City. Till 1882, it was the headquarters of Lakkavalli taluk, and then till 1897 of the Yedehalli sub-taluk was called so, because a Shivachara monastery here was providing free food to travellers. The new name Narasimharajapura was given to Yedehalli in commemoration of the visit of Yuvaraja Kanthirava Narasimharaja Wodeyar to this place in 1915.

Veera Shaiva Matha Festival: Balehonnur which is a part of Balehonnur-Kanabur near Chikmagalur, is situated on the left bank of the river Bhadra at a distance of about 32 kms. south of Narasimharajapura town. There is a ruined fort near the river Bhadra. There are some inscriptions which have been engraved on the boulders of the river dated about 1090 A.D. The river in which these rocks are is apparently called as the Tunga. Actually it is its twin stream, i.e., the Bhadra. After they join at some distance from here, the combined river is called the Tungabhadra. One of the boulders is called Bommanakallu, perhaps because of a Jaina figure on it.

Villages: 58 **Inhabited:** 58 **Uninhabited:** 0

Ranking	District	State	National
Area	5	133	864
Population	6	171	4921
Sex Ratio	1	13	620
Child Sex Ratio	1	1	68
Literacy Rate	3	17	615
Density	2	124	6232
Work Participation Rate	6	169	2928

Gram Panchayats:

Muthinakoppa, Kadahinabylu, Mensur , Nagalapura , Gubbiga, Seethur, Bale, Honnekudige, Kanur, Karekeshwara, Aduvalli, B.Kanabur, Bannur, Magundi.

Amenities:

Education: Primary School in 35 villages, Middle school in 35 villages, Matriculation or Secondary School in 11 villages, namely Muthinakoppa, K.Kanabur, Kadahinabylu, Mensur, Bellur, Aralikoppa, Bale, Aduvalli, Karekeshwara, B.Kanabur, Magundi.

Higher Secondary or Pre University Courses or Intermediate or Junior College in 2 villages of the CD Block,, namely Muthinakoppa, K.Kanabur.

College in 0 village, Adult Literacy Center in 0 village.

Medical: Hospital in 1 village, Dispensary in 3 villages, Health Center in 4 villages, Sub Center in 6 villages, Maternity and Child Welfare Center in 5 villages, Community health workers in 18 villages.

The Villages having Hospital or Dispensary or Health Center are Karekeshwara, B.Kanabur, Magundi.

Drinking Water: Tap water in 55 villages, Tank water in 56 villages, Well water in 58 villages, Tubewell in 56 villages and more than one source in 58 villages.

Bank: Banking facility in 5 villages, namely, Muthinakoppa, Aduvalli, Karekeshwara, B.Kanabur Magundi.

Credit Society in 15 villages Agricultural Credit Society in 15 Non-Agricultural Credit Society in 2 villages.

Others: Power supply in 58 villages, Cinema hall in 1 village, sport club in 58 villages, Stadium or Auditorium or Community Hall in 58 villages, Post Office in 23 villages.

There are 51 villages having bus facilities.

Villages with most of facilities: Muthinakoppa Karekeshwara, B.Kanabur, Magundi.

Villages without amenities (Education): Kanive, Byrapura, Aramballi, Vittala, Haledanivasa, Lingapura, Balekoppa, Nerlukoppa, Hiluvalli, Ravoor, Nagalapura, Shiragalale, Handur, Bilalkoppa, Salur, Dandubittahara, Sarya, Hebbe, Hathbur, Shedagaru, Sankse, Davana, Karehadlu..

Scheduled Castes: Out of the total population of 58175 persons, 8872 persons (15.25%) belong to Scheduled Castes.

The villages having less than 10% SC population are Konakere, Muthinakoppa, Madaboor, Kadahinabylu Aramballi, Vittala, Haledanivasa, Soosalavani Balekoppa, Nerlukoppa, Badagabylu, Hiluvalli Nagalapura, Shiragalale, Honnekudige, Salur Nandigave, Varkate, Sarya, Mallandaru, Hathbur Bellur, Konodi, Kamalapura, Shedagaru, Gubbiga Aralikoppa, Bale, Sankse, Vaggade, Alehalli Muduguni.

The village having more than 50% SC population is None.

Sex ratio of Scheduled Caste population is 508.

Scheduled Castes Literates and Illiterates by Sex:

	Persons	Males	Females
Literate	4,247	2,412	1,835
Illiterate	4,625	1,954	2,671
Literacy rate	56.3	65.0	47.9
Graduate	56	44	12

Scheduled Castes (Dominant):

Adi Karnataka, Bhovi, Adi Dravida, Chalavadi etc. Sillekyathas

For their cultural identity please see Appendix-I

Villages without Scheduled Castes: There are 3 villages without any scheduled caste population.

Scheduled Tribes: Out of the total population of 58175 persons, 1888 persons (3.25%) belong to Scheduled Tribes.

The villages having less than 10% ST population are Konakere, Muthinakoppa, K.Kanabur, Byrapura, Kusabur Madaboor, Kadahinabylu, Aramballi, Vittala Haledanivasa, Lingapura, Soosalavani, Balekoppa Nerlukoppa, Badagabylu, Shimse, Mensur, Hiluvalli Ravoor, Nagalapura, Shiragalale, Honnekudige, Handur Bilalkoppa, Salur, Dandubittahara, Varkate, Sarya Hebbe, Mallandaru, Hathbur, Bellur, Konodi Shedagaru, Gubbiga, Echikere, Aralikoppa, Bale Sankse, Kanur, Vaggade, Haluvari, Davana, Alehalli Aduvalli, Karekeshwara, Megaramakki, Kolale B.Kanabur, Karehadlu, Bannu , Halsur, Magundi.

The villages having more than 50% ST population are None.

Sex ratio of Scheduled tribe population is 503.

Scheduled Tribes Literates and Illiterates by Sex:

	Persons	Males	Females
Literate	1,026	582	444
Illiterate	862	356	506
Literacy rate	63.3	71.9	54.8
Graduate	21	16	5

Scheduled Tribes (Dominant):

Hasalaru, Naikda etc., Gowdalu, Maleru , Malaikudi

For their cultural identity please see Appendix-II

Villages without Scheduled Tribes: There are 21 villages without any scheduled tribe population.

Literates and Illiterates by Sex (Total Population):

	Persons	Males	Females
Literate	38,152	20,516	17,636
Illiterate	20,023	8,260	11,763
Literacy rate	76	82	69
Graduate	1,405	899	506

Agriculture: ***Distribution of villages according to land use:*** Out of 58 villages, Total area (in hectare) is 73180, out of that 18.7 percent is cultivable and 22.9 percent of the cultivable area is irrigated.

Sources of Irrigation (Hectares): Government Canal 0, Private Canal 207.31, Well without Electricity 555.72, Well with Electricity 248.14, Tubewell without Electricity 16.21, Tubewell with Electricity 113.64, Tank 1177.42, River 207.21, Lake 33.67, Waterfall 0, Others 573.46.

Villages with population of 5000 to 9999: B.Kanabur.

Villages with population of 10000 and above: None

Distribution of Workers:

	Persons	Males	Females	WPR
Cultivators	6,921	5,244	1,677	25.21
Agricultural Labour	8,024	4,218	3,806	29.22
Household Industry	767	479	288	2.79
Other Workers	11,744	7,638	4,106	42.77
Main Workers	24,025	16,308	7,717	87.5
Marginal Workers	3,431	1,271	2,160	12.5
Total Workers	27,456	17,579	9,877	

Religion: Major Religious Communities:

	Persons	Males	Females	Sex Ratio
Hindu (78.41%)	45,614	22,460	23,154	1,031
Muslim (9.16%)	5,326	2,646	2,680	1,013
Christian (12.28%)	7,141	3,619	3,522	973
Sikh (0%)	-	-	-	-
Buddhists (0.01%)	8	3	5	1,667
Jain (0.05%)	31	17	14	824

Agewise Data:

	Persons	Males	Females	Sex Ratio
All ages	58,175	28,776	29,399	1022
0-14	16,646	8,252	8,394	1017
15-44	30,154	14,683	15,471	1054
45-79	10,846	5,592	5,254	940
80+	469	216	253	1171
Age not stated	60	33	27	818

Languages (Dominant):

Kannada, Malayalam, Tulu, Tamil, Urdu

Disabled Population:

	Persons	Males	Females	%
Total Disabled	1,362	841	521	

In Seeing	740	493	247	54.33
In Speech	107	61	46	7.86
In Hearing	57	25	32	4.19

In Movement	328	192	136	24.08
Mentally	130	70	60	9.54

NARGUND

Nargund C.D. Block lies in the north-western part of Gadag district. It is a part of Nargund taluka. The Block is located at a distance of 56 kms. from district headquarters (Gadag). There are 35 villages in the block with the total population of 60,096 persons. Area of the C.D. Block is 415.66 sq. kms. It is bounded by distr icts Belgaum and Bagalkot on north, district Dharwad on south, taluk Ron on east, and district Belgaum on west.

Communications:

Roadways : N.H-218: Direction- Hubli to Bijapur, Nearest Villages- Somapur, Arban, Kalakeri, Konnur, Bhairana Hatti. S.H-30: Direction- Nargund to Ron, Nearest Village s- Somapur, Madagunaki, Hadali, Surkod.

River: Malprabha Nadi- Nearest Villages- Lakhamapur, Belleri, Vasan, Konnur, Budihal, Kappali, Kallapur, Shirol. Benni Halla Nadi- Nearest Villages- Muganur, Banahatti, Kurlageri, Radder Naganur, Khanapur, Gangapur, Hadali, Surkod.

Canal: Nearest Villages- Sankadal, Chikkanargund, Dandap ur, Peth, Somapur, Arban, Vasan, Konnur, Madagunaki, Hadali.

Annual Rainfall: Normal Rianfall 545 mm.

Ground Water: Availability of the Ground Water in the Basin is 1474 H.A.M. and the utilization is 237 H.A. M. It belongs to Over Exploited category. Depth to water level 5 to 10 meter below the ground. Most of the wells go down in summer months, according to the Ground Water Estimation Committee.

Soils: Medium to deep black soils.

Natural Division : It falls in the Dharward-Gadag Plateau of the Central Karnataka Plateau.

Administration:

Division: Belgaum. Parliamentary Constituency: 3 Bagalkot. District: Gadag. Taluka: Nargund. Assembly Constituenc y: 68 Nargund. Gram Panchayat: 12.

Regional Area Development Boards: The Bailu Seeme Area Development Board.

Villages: 35 **Inhabited:** 34 **Uninhabited:** 1

Ranking	District	State	National
Area	5	171	1848
Population	5	170	4853
Sex Ratio	5	132	3094
Child Sex Ratio	2	97	3191
Literacy Rate	1	68	2194
Density	3	42	5630
Work Participation Rate	3	139	1311

Gram Panchayats:

Chikkanargund, Hirekoppa, Vasan, Konnur, Shirol, Radder Naganur, Hadali, Bhairana Hatti, Kanakikop, Hunashikatti, Banahatti, Surkod.

Amenities:

Education: Primary School in 30 villages, Middle school in 28 villages, Matriculation or Secondary School in 7 villages, namely Hirekoppa, Chikkanargund, Jagapur, Banahatti, Konnur, Shirol, Hadali.

Higher Secondary or Pre University Courses or Inter-mediate or Junior College in 4 villages of the CD Block,, namely Banahatti, Konnur, Shirol, Hadali.

College in 0 village, Adult Literacy Center in 1 village.

Medical: Hospital in 0 village, Dispensary in 3 villages, Health Center in 4 villages, Sub Center in 14 villages, Maternity and Child Welfare Center in 2 villages, Community health workers in 8 villages.

The Villages having Hospital or Dispensary or Health Center are Chikkanargund, Nargund(Rural), Radder Naganur.

Drinking Water: Tap water in 16 villages, Tank water in 20 villages, Well water in 12 villages, Tubewell in 21 villages and more than one source in 29 villages.

Bank: Banking facility in 11 villages, namely, Sankadal, Benakanakoppa, Chikkanargund, Kanakikop Nargund(Rural), Kalakeri, Banahatti, Konnur, Shirol Hadali, Surkod.

Credit Society in 17 villages Agricultural Credit Society in 16 Non-Agricultural Credit Society in 3 villages.

Others: Power supply in 33 villages, Cinema hall in 1 village, sport club in 0 village, Stadium or Auditorium or Community Hall in 0 village, Post Office in 12 villages.

There are 27 villages having bus facilities.

Villages with most of facilities: Sankadal Chikkanargund, Kanakikop, Banahatti, Konnur, Shirol Hadali, Surkod.

Villages without amenities (Education): Dandapur, Somapur, Nargund(Rural), Arban..

Scheduled Castes: Out of the total population of 60118 persons, 5026 persons (8.36%) belong to Scheduled Castes. The villages having less than 10% SC population are Kurugovinakoppa, Chikkanargund, Kanakikop Gurlakatti, Dandapur, Somapur, Arban, Jagapur Siddapur, Hunashikatti, Kalakeri, Kurlageri Lakhamapur, Belleri, Vasan, Konnur, Gangapur Bhairana Hatti, Madagunaki, Hadali, Surkod.

The village having more than 50% SC population is None.

Sex ratio of Scheduled Caste population is 489.

Scheduled Castes Literates and Illiterates by Sex:

	Persons	Males	Females
Literate	1,979	1,325	654
Illiterate	3,047	1,241	1,806
Literacy rate	47.4	62.4	31.8
Graduate	50	48	2

Scheduled Castes (Dominant):

Bhambi etc., Chalavadi etc., Bhovi

Chenna Dasar etc., Korama

For their cultural identity please see Appendix-I

Villages without Scheduled Castes: There are 4 villages without any scheduled caste population.

Scheduled Tribes: Out of the total population of 60118 persons, 3508 persons (5.84%) belong to Scheduled Tribes. The villages having less than 10% ST population are Sankadal, Benakanakoppa, Kurugovinakoppa, Hirekopppa Chikkanargund, Gurlakatti, Dandapur, Somapur Nargund(Rural), Siddapur, Hunashikatti, Muganur Banahatti, Kurlageri, Lakhamapur, Vasan, Konnur Budihal, Kappali, Kallapur, Shirol, Radder Naganur Bhairana Hatti, Hadali, Surkod.

The villages having more than 50% ST population are None.

Sex ratio of Scheduled tribe population is 480.

Scheduled Tribes Literates and Illiterates by Sex:

	Persons	Males	Females
Literate	1,627	1,114	513
Illiterate	1,881	711	1,170
Literacy rate	54.3	71.4	35.8
Graduate	33	27	6

Scheduled Tribes (Dominant):

Naikda etc., Pardhi etc., Generic Tribes etc.

Dubla etc., Iruliga

For their cultural identity please see Appendix-II

Villages without Scheduled Tribes: There are 6 villages without any scheduled tribe population.

Literates and Illiterates by Sex (Total Population):

	Persons	Males	Females
Literate	32,531	20,626	11,905
Illiterate	27,587	10,075	17,512
Literacy rate	63	79	47
Graduate	1,060	909	151

Agriculture: ***Distribution of villages according to land use:*** Out of 35 villages, Total area (in hectare) is 41566, out of that 92.4 percent is cultivable and 73.98 percent of the cultivable area is irrigated.

Sources of Irrigation (Hectares): Government Canal 27092.32, Private Canal 0, Well without Electricity 0, Well with Electricity 70.96, Tubewell without Electricity 0, Tubewell with Electricity 247.46, Tank 0, River 539.79, Lake 0, Waterfall 0, Others 463.63.

Villages with population of 5000 to 9999:

Konnur, Shirol.

Villages with population of 10000 and above: None

Distribution of Workers:

	Persons	Males	Females	WPR
Cultivators	16,811	10,245	6,566	53.4
Agricultural Labour	10,579	4,300	6,279	33.6
Household Industry	1,104	667	437	3.51
Other Workers	2,989	2,344	645	9.49
Main Workers	29,146	16,941	12,205	92.58
Marginal Workers	2,337	615	1,722	7.42
Total Workers	31,483	17,556	13,927	

Religion: Major Religious Communities:

	Persons	Males	Females	Sex Ratio
Hindu (89.1%)	53,568	27,310	26,258	961
Muslim (8.82%)	5,302	2,733	2,569	940
Christian (0.02%)	15	12	3	250
Sikh (0.02%)	14	8	6	750
Buddhists (0.02%)	12	6	6	1,000
Jain (0.39%)	234	125	109	872

Agewise Data:

	Persons	Males	Females	Sex Ratio
All ages	60,118	30,701	29,417	958
0-14	20,654	10,495	10,159	968
15-44	27,877	14,624	13,253	906
45-79	11,069	5,347	5,722	1070
80+	423	184	239	1299
Age not stated	95	51	44	863

Languages (Dominant):

Kannada, Urdu, Hindi, Marathi, Oriya

Disabled Population:

	Persons	Males	Females	%
Total Disabled	1,265	727	538	
In Seeing	630	353	277	49.8
In Speech	110	57	53	8.7
In Hearing	52	25	27	4.11
In Movement	365	226	139	28.85
Mentally	108	66	42	8.54

NAVALGUND

Navalgund C.D. Block lies in the north-eastern part of Dharwad district. It is a part of Navalgund taluka. The Block is located at a distance of 45 kms. from district headquarters (Dharwad). There are 58 villages in the block with the total population of 128,732 persons. Area of the C.D. Block is 1027.49 sq. kms. It is bounded by districts Belgaum and Gadag on north, taluks Kundgol and Hubli on south, district Gadag on east, district Belgaum and taluks Dharwad and Hubli on west.

Communications:

Roadways : N.H-63: Direction- Hubli to Gadag, Nearest Villages- Kondikoppa, Nalavadi, Bhadrapur, Annigeri (Rural). N.H-218: Direction- Hubli to Bijapur, Nearest Villages- Amaragol, Belavatagi, Yamanur, Kumaragoppa, Arekurahatti, Kalawad, Kalawad.

Railway Station: Villages- Kondikoppa, Dundur.

River: Yaran Halla Nadi- Nearest Villages- Siswinahalli, Bhadrapur, Annigeri (Rural). Raddi Halla Nadi- Nearest Villages- Manakawad, Nalavadi, Amaragol, Belavatagi, Padesur, Yamanur, Kumaragoppa, Arekurahatti, Karlawad, Kalawad, Kadadahalli, Arahatti, Tadahal, Kongawad, Sotakanal, Naganur, Gudisagar, Nagarahalli, Ballarawad. Saval Halla Nadi- Nearest Villages- Shelawadi, Khannur, Navalli, Tuppadakurahatti, Kittur, Adnur, Hallikeri, Saswihalli, Kondikoppa, Annigeri (Rural). Handganhalla Nadi- Nearest Villages- Arahatti, Tadahal, Bhoganur, Naikanur. Benni Halla Nadi- Nearest Villages- Amaragol, Belavatagi, Padesur, Yamanur, Kumaragoppa, Arekurahatti, Karlawad, Kalawad, Kadadahalli, Arahatti, Tadahal, Kongawad, Sotakanal, Naganur, Gudisagar, Nagarahalli, Ballarawad. Tuparni Halla Nadi- Nearest Villages- Shirur, Gummagol, Morab.

Annual Rainfall: Normal Rianfall 772 mm.

Ground Water: Availability of the Ground Water in the Basin is 6676.85 H.A.M. and the utilization is 3116. 897 H.A.M. It belongs to Over Exploited category. Depth to water level 5 to 20 meter below the ground. Most of the wells go down in summer months, according to the Ground Water Estimation Committee.

Soils: Loamy and Kankary Soils.

Natural Division : It falls in the Dharwad-Gadag Plateau of the Central Karnataka Plateau.

Administration:

Division: Belgaum. Parliamentary Constituency: 11 Dharwad. District: Dharwad. Taluka: Navalgund. Assembly Constit uency: 69 Navalgund. Gram Panchayat: 22.

Villages: 58 **Inhabited:** 57 **Uninhabited:** 1

Ranking	District	State	National
Area	1	79	413
Population	3	144	2557
Sex Ratio	1	142	3359
Child Sex Ratio	2	102	3272
Literacy Rate	2	71	2243
Density	1	2	5895
Work Participation Rate	5	152	187

Gram Panchayats:

Shirur, Gummagol, Shirkol, Javoor, Hebbal, Alagawadi, Belavatagi, Gudisagar, Tadahal, Naikanur, Shelawadi, Tuppadakurahatti, Ibrahimpur, Yamanur, Halakusugal, Tirlapur, Morab, Kalawad, Hallikeri, Bhadrapur, Siswinahalli, Nalavadi.

Amenities:

Education: Primary School in 47 villages, Middle school in 52 villages, Matriculation or Secondary School in 12 villages, namely Javoor, Alagawadi, Shirkol, Morab, Arekurahatti, Tadahal, Shelawadi, Tuppadakurahatti, Adnur, Hallikeri, Siswinahalli, Nalavadi.

Higher Secondary or Pre University Courses or Intermediate or Junior College in 3 villages of the CD Block,, namely Morab, Shelawadi, Tuppadakurahatti.

College in 0 village, Adult Literacy Center in 2 villages.

Medical: Hospital in 0 village, Dispensary in 7 villages, Health Center in 4 villages, Sub Center in 27 villages, Maternity and Child Welfare Center in 1 village, Community health workers in 11 villages.

The Villages having Hospital or Dispensary or Health Center are Shirur, Hanashi, Hebbal, Alagawadi, Amaragol, Morab, Shelawadi.

Drinking Water: Tap water in 32 villages, Tank water in 39 villages, Well water in 1 village, Tubewell in 0 village and more than one source in 20 villages.

Bank: Banking facility in 9 villages, namely, Alagawadi, Amaragol, Shirkol, Morab, Tirlapur Arekurahatti, Shelawadi, Hallikeri, Nalavadi.

Credit Society in 37 villages Agricultural Credit Society in 37 Non-Agricultural Credit Society in 0 village.

Others: Power supply in 57 villages, Cinema hall in 0 village, sport club in 1 village, Stadium or Auditorium or Community Hall in 0 village, Post Office in 34 villages.

There are 55 villages having bus facilities.

Villages with most of facilities: Alagawadi Amaragol, Shirkol, Morab, Tirlapur, Arekurahatti Shelawadi, Hallikeri, Nalavadi.

Villages without amenities (Education): Kumaragoppa, Kadadahalli, Sotakanal, Nagarahalli, Dundur..

Scheduled Castes: Out of the total population of 128736 persons, 9299 persons (7.22%) belong to Scheduled Castes. The villages having less than 10% SC population are Shirur, Gummagol, Byalal, Javoor, Alagawadi Amaragol, Gobbaragumpi, Halakusugal, Ballur, Shirkol Morab, Talimorab, Tirlapur, Padesur, Yamanur Kumaragoppa, Arekurahatti, Karlawad, Sotakanal Naganur, Gudisagar, Datanal, Shelawadi, Khannur Ibrahimpur, Tuppadakurahatti, Kittur, Adnur Hallikeri, Nagarahalli, Basapur, Ballarawad, Bennur Dundur, Siswinahalli, Manakawad, Nalavadi, Bhadrapur Majjigudda, Saidapur.

The village having more than 50% SC population is None.

Sex ratio of Scheduled Caste population is 490.

Scheduled Castes Literates and Illiterates by Sex:

	Persons	Males	Females
Literate	3,655	2,459	1,196
Illiterate	5,644	2,287	3,357
Literacy rate	46.9	61.9	31.3
Graduate	66	63	3

Scheduled Castes (Dominant):

Bhambi etc., Chalavadi etc., Bhovi, Madiga
Chenna Dasar etc.

For their cultural identity please see Appendix-I

Villages without Scheduled Castes: There are 2 villages without any scheduled caste population.

Scheduled Tribes: Out of the total population of 128736 persons, 7445 persons (5.78%) belong to Scheduled Tribes. The villages having less than 10% ST population are Shirur, Gummagol, Byalal, Javoor, Alagawadi Amaragol, Belavatagi, Halakusugal, Ballur, Shirkol Morab, Talimorab, Tirlapur, Yamanur, Arekurahatti Chilakawad, Kalawad, Belahar, Kadadahalli, Arahatti Kongawad, Sotakanal, Naganur, Gudisagar, Bhoganur Datanal, Shelawadi, Ibrahimpur, Navalli Tuppadakurahatti, Kittur, Hallikeri, Nagarahalli Basapur, Kondikoppa, Bennur, Dundur, Manakawad Nalavadi, Bhadrapur.

The villages having more than 50% ST population are None.

Sex ratio of Scheduled tribe population is 485.

Scheduled Tribes Literates and Illiterates by Sex:

	Persons	Males	Females
Literate	3,115	2,070	1,045
Illiterate	4,330	1,765	2,565
Literacy rate	49.3	63.5	34.1
Graduate	47	43	4

Scheduled Tribes (Dominant):

Naikda etc., Pardhi etc., Kadu Kuruba, Gond etc.
Generic Tribes etc.

For their cultural identity please see Appendix-II

Villages without Scheduled Tribes: There are 3 villages without any scheduled tribe population.

Literates and Illiterates by Sex (Total Population):

	Persons	Males	Females
Literate	69,653	43,573	26,080
Illiterate	59,083	22,377	36,706
Literacy rate	63	77	48
Graduate	2,211	1,969	242

Agriculture: ***Distribution of villages according to land use:***

Out of 58 villages, Total area (in hectare) is 102749, out of that 86.01 percent is cultivable and 34.44 percent of the cultivable area is irrigated.

Sources of Irrigation (Hectares): Government Canal 29670.26, Private Canal 0, Well without Electricity 0, Well with Electricity 24.33, Tubewell without Electricity 0, Tubewell with Electricity 58.67, Tank 0, River 76.89, Lake 0, Waterfall 0, Others 601.45.

Villages with population of 5000 to 9999:

Alagawadi, Morab, Tirlapur, Shelawadi.

Villages with population of 10000 and above: None

Distribution of Workers:

	Persons	Males	Females	WPR
Cultivators	33,603	22,216	11,387	44.04
Agricultural Labour	33,399	12,594	20,805	43.77
Household Industry	1,170	754	416	1.53
Other Workers	8,133	6,436	1,697	10.66
Main Workers	58,913	37,205	21,708	77.21
Marginal Workers	17,392	4,795	12,597	22.79
Total Workers	76,305	42,000	34,305	

Religion: Major Religious Communities:

	Persons	Males	Females	Sex Ratio
Hindu (89.59%)	115,329	59,143	56,186	950
Muslim (8.9%)	11,455	5,820	5,635	968
Christian (0.03%)	37	19	18	947
Sikh (0.01%)	7	3	4	1,333
Buddhists (0.26%)	336	160	176	1,100
Jain (0.64%)	821	416	405	974

Agewise Data:

	Persons	Males	Females	Sex Ratio
All ages	128,736	65,950	62,786	952
0-14	41,484	21,102	20,382	966
15-44	60,159	31,621	28,538	903
45-79	25,845	12,693	13,152	1036
80+	1,196	504	692	1373
Age not stated	52	30	22	733

Languages (Dominant):

Kannada, Urdu, Telugu, Coorgi/Kodagu, Marathi

Disabled Population:

	Persons	Males	Females	%
Total Disabled	2,302	1,289	1,013	
In Seeing	833	414	419	36.19
In Speech	276	159	117	11.99
In Hearing	107	64	43	4.65
In Movement	846	521	325	36.75
Mentally	240	131	109	10.43

NELAMANGALA

Nelamangala C.D. Block lies in the northern part of Bangalore Rural district. It is a part of Nelamangala taluka. The Block is located at a distance of 28 kms. from district headquarters (Bangalore). There are 243 villages in the block with the total population of 149, 239 persons. Area of the C.D. Block is 507.50 sq. kms.

It is bounded by district Tumkur on north, district Bangalore on south, on east with taluk Dod Ballapur, district Tumkur and taluk Magadi on west.

Communications:

Roadways : N.H.-4: Direction- Tumkur to Bangalore, Nearest Villages- Halenijagal, Lakkuru, Sompura, Bharathipura, Yedehalli, Chandanahosahalli, Srinivasapura, Nijagal, Kengalkempohalli, Billanakote, Gundenahalli, Hanumanthap ura, Mahimapura, Kuluvanahalli, Thippagundanahalli, Dod deri, T.Begur, Malonagathihalli, Marohalli, Vajarahalli, Arasinakunte, Visveswarapura, Basavanahalli, Budihal, Tonachinakuppe, Bommanahalli, Byadarahalli. N.H.-48: Direction- Hassan to Nelamamgala, Nearest Villages- Jakkasandra, Visveswarapura, Srinivasapura, K.Kempalinga nahalli, Bhavikere, Mallarabanavadi,, Vaddarapalya, Hanch ipura, Dodakarenahalli, Bhusandra, Mahadevapura, Hanuma napalya, Sitaram Bhattarapalya, Yentiganahalli, Koratagere, Lingenahalli. N.H.-207: Direction- Sompura to Dod Balla pur, Nearest Villages- Nidavanda, Sompura, Thimanaikanah alli, Pemmanahalli, Krishnarajapura, Adihosahalli, Madden ahalli, Manne, Makanakuppe, Muddalinganahalli, Obalapura, Lakshmanapura. S.H.-3: Direction- Magadi to Koratagere, Nearest Villages- Halenahalli, Jajoor, Makenahalli, Bugadihalli, Narasipura, Nijagal Kempohalli, Channohalli, Imchanahalli, Maddenahalli, Lakkuru, Sompura, Chandana hosahalli, Bargenahalli, Honnenahalli, Shivagange, Naraya napura, Basavapatna, Kambal. S.H.-74: Direction- Nelaman gala to Dod Ballapur, Nearest Villages- Byrasettihalli, Arjunabettahalli, Gollahalli, Hydalu, Mylanahalli, Kanugondanahalli, Krishnarajapalya, Visveswarapura, Basavanahalli.

Railway Station: Villages- Nidavanda, Lakkuru, Sompura, Makanakuppe, Doddabele, Gollahalli.

River: Kumdavati Nadi- Nearest Villages- Koratagere, Lingenahalli, Honnasandra, Krishnarajapura, Bidanapalya, Chowdasandra, Kothanahalli, Avalakuppe, Hosahalli, Goravanahalli, Soladevanahalli, Narasimhapalya, Kanuvanahalli.

Annual Rainfall: Normal Rianfall 890.04 mm.

Ground Water: Availability of the Ground Water in the Basin is (Information not avablable) H.A.M. and the utilization is (Information not avablable) H.A.M. It belongs to (Information not avablable) category. Depth to water level 5 to 20 meter below the ground. Most of the wells go down in summer months, according to the Ground Water Estimation Committee.

Natural Division : It falls in Cauvery Forested Region of the Southern Karnataka Plateau.

Administration:

Division: Bangalore. Parliamentary Constituency: 27 Bangalore- IV (SC). District: Bangalore Rural. Taluka: Nelamangala. Assembly Constituency: 181 Nelamangala (SC). Gram Panchayat: 22.

Regional Area Development Boards: The Bailu Seeme Area Development Board.

Villages: 243 **Inhabited:** 230 **Uninhabited:** 13

Ranking	District	State	National
Area	7	165	1470
Population	7	131	1875
Sex Ratio	4	129	3064
Child Sex Ratio	6	128	3716
Literacy Rate	1	31	1201
Density	8	140	3584
Work Participation Rate	4	26	3282

Gram Panchayats:

Agalakuppa, Narasipura, Maralakunte, Kodigehalli, Manne, Sompura, Honnenahalli, Shivagange, Kuluvanahalli, Kalalghatta, Thyamagondlu, Doddabele, Hasurahalli, T.Begur, Arebommanahalli, Srinivasapura, Budihal, Basavanahalli, Visveswarapura, Yentiganahalli, Soladevanahalli, Arasinakunte.

Amenities:

Education: Primary School in 106 villages, Middle school in 86 villages, Matriculation or Secondary School in 28 villages, namely Halenahalli, Yelekyathanahalli, Maralakunte, Heggunda, Narasipura, Devarahosahalli, Nidavanda, Sompura, Billanakote, Shivagange, Kambal, Maragondanahalli, Manne, Makanakuppe, Doddabele, Byranaikanahalli, Chikkanahalli, Thyamagondlu, Kuluvanahalli, Arebommanahalli, T.Begur, Mandigere, Byrasettihalli, Gollahalli, Arasinakunte, Madalakote, Mallarabanavadi, Yentiganahalli.

Higher Secondary or Pre University Courses or Intermediate or Junior College in 6 villages of the CD Block,, namely Yelekyathanahalli, Sompura, Shivagange, Thyamagondlu, Byrasettihalli, Gollahalli.

College in 2 villages, Adult Literacy Center in 8 villages., Colleges are in villages, namely Yelekyathanahalli, Madalakote.

Medical: Hospital in 1 village, Dispensary in 9 villages, Health Center in 9 villages, Sub Center in 38 villages, Maternity and Child Welfare Center in 3 villages, Community health workers in 35 villages.

The Villages having Hospital or Dispensary or Health Center are Kuruvel Thimmanahalli, Yelekyathanahalli, Sompura, Hasurahalli, Honnarayanahalli, Thimmasandra, Byrasandra, Yentiganahalli, Mantanakurchi.

Drinking Water: Tap water in 124 villages, Tank water in 7 villages, Well water in 30 villages, Tubewell in 140 villages and more than one source in 184 villages.

Bank: Banking facility in 5 villages, namely, Sompura, Shivagange, Thyamagondlu, Kuluvanahalli T.Begur.
Credit Society in 51 villages Agricultural Credit Society in 21 Non-Agricultural Credit Society in 40 villages.
Others: Power supply in 230 villages, Cinema hall in 1 village, sport club in 0 village, Stadium or Auditorium or Community Hall in 230 villages, Post Office in 35 villages.
There are 152 villages having bus facilities.
Villages with most of facilities: Sompura Shivagange, Thyamagondlu, Kuluvanahalli, T.Begur.
Villages without amenities (Education): Jajoor, Makenahalli, Kuruvel Thimmanahalli, Bennegere, Chikkannanahalli, Hulleharve, Madaga, Chikkanapalya, Giriyanapalya, Bettadahosahalli, Ramanahalli, Kallunaikanahalli, Imchanahalli, Thattekere, Maddenahalli, Thimmanaikanahalli, Pemmanahalli, Bharathipura, Yedehalli, Chandanahosahalli, Kengal, Kengalkempohalli, Avverahalli, Gottikere, Gowrapura, Narayanapura, Basavapatna, Gantehosahalli, Guruvanahalli, Kasaragatta, Melekattiganoor, Geddalahalli, Aladahalli, Gundenahalli, Hanumanthapura, Sirganahalli, Mannerampura, Venkatapura, Somasagara, Karimaranahalli, Mavinakunte, Jakkasandra, Adihosahalli, Maddenahalli, Kenchanapura, Mavinakommenahalli, Doddachannohalli, Lakshmanapura, Thippasettihalli, Karehalli, Gulapura, Nimbenahalli, Lakkappanahalli, Guddegowdana Channohalli, Narasapura, Gundenahalli, Totanahalli, Kodipalya, Bidalur, Harvesandra, Lakkenahalli, Mahimapura, Karenahalli, Halkur, Govindapura, Pallarahalli, Lakkasandra, Thalekere, Minnapura, Krishnarajapalya, Marohalli, Byranahalli, Yeramanchanahalli, Tyagadahalli, Arjunabettahalli, Narasimanapalya, Narayanaraopalya, Machonaikanahalli, Ananthapura, Koolipura, Mallapura, Gangadharanapalya, Viranaanjipura, Krishnarajapura, Agasarahalli, Araledibba, Aralasandra, Geddalahalli, Bommanahalli, Ghandragulupura, Kenchanahalli, Hajipalya, Obanaikanahalli, Vaddarapalya, Kodappanahalli, Balaguruvanapalya, Bhoosandra, Hanumanapalya, Sitaram Bhattarapalya, Koratagere, Lingenahalli, Kadukarenahalli, Bhattarahalli, Krishnarajapura, Bidanapalya, Kothanahalli, Hosahalli, Narasimhapalya, Kanuvanahalli, Banasavadi, Gorinabele, Mantanakurchi..
Scheduled Castes: Out of the total population of 149593 persons, 36166 persons (24.18%) belong to Scheduled Castes.
The villages having less than 10% SC population are Kuruvel Thimmanahalli, Yelekyathanahalli, Bennegere Chikkannanahalli, Madaga, Giriyanapalya, Bugadihalli Ramanahalli, Halenijagal, Biragondanahalli Kallunaikanahalli, Thimmanaikanahalli, Veerasagara Sripathihalli, Kuthagatta, Hosahalli, Billanakote Gowrapura, Guruvanahalli, Geddalahalli, Venkatapura Karimaranahaili, Jakkasandra, Appagondanahalli Adihosahalli, Kodigehalli, Ballagere Mavinakommenahalli, Thippasettihalli, Hasurahalli Guddegowdana Channohalli, Karenahalli Kempapura Agrahara, Arebommanahalli, Govindapura Pallarahalli, Thippagundanahalli, T.Begur Malonagathihalli, Bolamaranahalli, Narayanaraopalya Kanugondanahalli, Krishnarajapura, Agasarahalli Tirumalapura, Geddalahalli, Bommanahalli Viraraghuvanapalya, Hajipalya, Balaguruvanapalya Yentiganahalli, Koratagere, Kadukarenahalli Krishnarajapura, Kothanahalli, Avalakuppe, Hosahalli Soladevanahalli, Narasimhapalya, Kanuvanahalli Bolamaranahalli.
The villages having more than 50% SC population are Chikkanapalya, Bettadahosahalli, Imchanahalli Govindapura, Maddenahalli, Honnenahalli Srinivasapura, Avverahalli, Gottikere, Narayanapura Gantehosahalli, Maragondanahalli, Kerekattiganoor Gundenahalli, Sirganahalli, Mavinakunte, Makanakuppe Kenchanapura, Lakshmanapura, Biragundanahalli Karehalli, Totanahalli, Kodihalli, Harvesandra Machonaikanahalli, Ananthapura, Mallapura Vaddarapalya, Sitaram Bhattarapalya, Lingenahalli Bidanapalya, Gorinabele.
Sex ratio of Scheduled Caste population is 496.
Scheduled Castes Literates and Illiterates by Sex:

	Persons	Males	Females
Literate	19,326	11,391	7,935
Illiterate	16,840	6,829	10,011
Literacy rate	61.3	71.8	50.7
Graduate	422	361	61

Scheduled Castes (Dominant):
Adi Karnataka, Madiga, Bhovi, Adi Dravida Chalavadi etc.
For their cultural identity please see Appendix-I
Villages without Scheduled Castes: There are 46 villages without any scheduled caste population.
Scheduled Tribes: Out of the total population of 149593 persons, 5662 persons (3.78%) belong to Scheduled Tribes.
The villages having less than 10% ST population are Halenahalli, Kuruvel Thimmanahalli, Bennegere Benchanahalli, Maralakunte, Chikkannanahalli Hulleharve, Baragoor, Madaga, Chikkanapalya Giriyanapalya, Kuntbommanahalli, Dasenahalli Heggunda, Bugadihalli, Narasipura, Bettadahosahalli

Halenijagal, Devarahosahalli, Kamalapura
Biragondanahalli, Kallunaikanahalli, Nijagal
Channohalli, Imchanahalli, Govindapura, Thattekere
Maddenahalli, Lakkuru, Sompura, Thimmanaikanahalli
Pemmanahalli, Bharathipura, Yedehalli
Chandanahosahalli, Kengal, Veerasagara, Kuthagatta
Bargenahalli, Honnenahalli, Srinivasapura
Kengalkempohalli, Billanakote, Avverahalli
Gottikere, Shivagange, Gowrapura, Narayanapura
Basavapatna, Kambal, Gantehosahalli, Guruvanahalli
Machenahalli, Kasaragatta, Maragondanahalli
Kerekattiganoor , Geddalahalli, Aladahalli
Gundenahalli, Hanumanthapura, Sirganahalli
Mannerampura, Venkatapura, Somasagara
Karimaranahalli, Mavinakunte, Goraghatta
Jakkasandra, Appagondanahalli, Adihosahalli
Maddenahalli, Kannohalli, Makanakuppe
Muddalinganahalli, Obalapura, Kodigehalli
Kenchanapura, Tadasigatta, Mavinakommenahalli
Doddachannohalli, Tavarekere, Lakshmanapura
Biragundanahalli, Thippasettihalli, Karehalli
Doddabele, Gulapura, Nimbenahalli, Vadakunte
Lakkappanahalli, Byranaikanahalli, Chikkanahalli
Guddegowdana Channohalli, Isuvanahalli, Narasapura
Gundenahalli, Thyamagondlu, Totanahalli, Kodipalya
Kodihalli, Kalalghatta, Harvesandra, Alunaikanahalli
Mahimapura, Kuluvanahalli, Karenahalli, Sulkunte
Kempapura Agrahara, Arebommanahalli
Kodigebommanahalli, Halkur, Honnarayanahalli
Thimmasandra, Govindapura, Pallarahalli, Lakkasandra
Thalekere, Byadarahalli, Thippagundanahalli, Dodderi
Govenahalli, Minnapura, Jakkanahalli
Krishnarajapalya, Varadanaikanahalli, T.Begur
Malonagathihalli, Marohalli, Byranahalli
Yeramanchanahalli, Mandigere, Tyagadahalli
Bettahalli, Bolamaranahalli, Byrasettihalli
Arjunabettahalli, Gollahalli, K.G. Srinivasapura
Mylanahalli, Narasimanapalya, Narayanaraopalya
Machonaikanahalli, Kachanahalli, Ananthapura
Kanugondanahalli, Koolipura, Vajarahalli
Arasinakunte, Mallapura, Jakkasandra, Visveswarapura
Gangadharanapalya, Virananjipura, Budihal
Tonachinakuppe, Krishnarajapura, Agasarahalli
Araledibba, Tirumalapura, Aralasandra, Madalakote
Kempohalli, Geddalahalli, Huralihalli, Bommanahalli
Viraraghuvanapalya, Byadarahalli, Ghandragulupura
Yelachagere, Kenchanahalli, Byrasandra
Chikmaranahalli, Hajipalya, Srinivasapura
K.Kempalinganahalli, Bhavikere, Mallarabanavadi
Vaddarapalya, Kodappanahalli, Hanchipura
Doddakarenahalli, Balaguruvanapalya, Bhoosandra
Mahadevapura, Hanumanapalya, Sitaram Bhattarapalya
Yentiganahalli, Koratagere, Lingenahalli
Kadukarenahalli, Honnasandra, Bhattarahalli
Manchenahalli, Krishnarajapura, Bidanapalya
Chowdasandra, Avalakuppe, Hosahalli, Goravanahalli
Kanuvanahalli, Banasavadi, Bolamaranahalli
Gorinabele, H.Kempalinganahalli, Mantanakurchi.

The villages having more than 50% ST population are None.

Sex ratio of Scheduled tribe population is 497.

Scheduled Tribes Literates and Illiterates by Sex:

	Persons	Males	Females
Literate	3,265	1,892	1,373
Illiterate	2,397	957	1,440
Literacy rate	66.1	75.8	56.1
Graduate	82	68	14

Scheduled Tribes (Dominant):

Naikda etc., Jenu Kuruba, Generic Tribes etc.
Maleru , Kadu Kuruba

For their cultural identity please see Appendix-II

Villages without Scheduled Tribes: There are 148 villages without any scheduled tribe population.

Literates and Illiterates by Sex (Total Population):

	Persons	Males	Females
Literate	92,166	53,602	38,564
Illiterate	57,427	22,748	34,679
Literacy rate	70	80	60
Graduate	3,037	2,397	640

Agriculture: ***Distribution of villages according to land use:*** Out of 243 villages, Total area (in hectare) is 50750, out of that 68.58 percent is cultivable and 17.46 percent of the cultivable area is irrigated.

Sources of Irrigation (Hectares): Government Canal 0, Private Canal 0, Well without Electricity 0, Well with Electricity 24.61, Tubewell without Electricity 43.46, Tubewell with Electricity 3422.64, Tank 2516.56, River 0, Lake 0, Waterfall 0, Others 68.51.

Villages with population of 5000 to 9999: Thyamagondlu.

Villages with population of 10000 and above: None

Distribution of Workers:

	Persons	Males	Females	WPR
Cultivators	31,851	21,907	9,944	46.01
Agricultural Labour	13,922	5,515	8,407	20.11
Household Industry	3,080	1,363	1,717	4.45
Other Workers	20,375	15,867	4,508	29.43
Main Workers	56,174	39,652	16,522	81.14
Marginal Workers	13,054	5,000	8,054	18.86
Total Workers	69,228	44,652	24,576	

Religion: Major Religious Communities:

	Persons	Males	Females	Sex Ratio
Hindu (92.4%)	138,222	70,431	67,791	963
Muslim (6.53%)	9,765	5,113	4,652	910
Christian (0.17%)	253	122	131	1,074
Sikh (0.02%)	25	18	7	389
Buddhists (0%)	7	6	1	167
Jain (0.11%)	165	69	96	1,391

Agewise Data:

	Persons	Males	Females	Sex Ratio
All ages	149,593	76,350	73,243	959
0-14	43,186	22,014	21,172	962
15-44	73,686	37,597	36,089	960
45-79	30,704	15,717	14,987	954
80+	1,866	936	930	994
Age not stated	151	86	65	756

Languages (Dominant):

Kannada, Urdu, Telugu, Tamil, Hindi

Disabled Population:

	Persons	Males	Females	%
Total Disabled	3,262	1,859	1,403	
In Seeing	1,536	796	740	47.09
In Speech	309	180	129	9.47
In Hearing	164	87	77	5.03
In Movement	939	632	307	28.79
Mentally	314	164	150	9.63

PANDAVAPURA

Pandavapura C.D. Block lies in the southern part of Mandya district. It is a part of Pandavapura tehsil. The Block is located at a distance of 29 kms. from district headquarters (Mandya). There are 171 villages in the block with the total population of 156,772 persons. Area of the C.D. Block is 522.90 sq. kms. It is bounded by taluk Nagamangala on north, district Mysore and taluk Shrirangapattana on south, taluks Mandya and Shrir angapattana on east, and taluk Krishnarajpet on west.

Communications:

Roadways : S.H.-7: Direction- Krishnarajpet to Shrirangapa ttana, Nearest Villages- Kurubaramanchanahalli, Kanaganah alli, Morasanahalli, Kurubaramallenahalli, Chinakurali, Honaganahalli, Kanivekoppalu, Hulkere, Vaddarahalli, Hullikere Koppalu, Chagasettihalli, Kurubarabettahalli, Shamboonahalli, Damadahalli, Kennalu, Manchanahalli, Yelekere. S.H.-19: Direction- Challakere to Shrirangapat tana, Nearest Villages- Nyamanahalli, Amruthi, Jakkanahal li, M. Shettihalli, Manikyanahalli, Bellale, Neelanahalli, Mahadeshwarapura, Rangapura, Seeranahalli, Ingalaguppe, Thirumalasagara Chatra, Koranahalli, Haralahalli, Panda vapura (Hirode) Rural, Beerasettihalli, Banaghatta, Kodih alli Hosur, Kennalu.

Railway Station: Villages- Dodda Byadarahalli, Kennalu.

River: Cauvery Nadi- Nearest Villages- Kaggalipura, Malligere, Anthanahalli, Giriyarahalli, Kannambadi, Chikkayarahalli, Duddaghatta, Katterinala, Seethapura, Aralakuppenala, Chaluvarasanakoppal, Yenne Hole Koppal, Puttayyanakoppalu. Lokapavani Nadi- Nearest Villages- Sangapura, Bolenahalli, Menagara, Sunkathonnur, Madrahalli, Nallahalli, Kalenahalli, Anavalu, Nuggahal li, Kurahatti, Vadesamudra, Talasasana, Kanagana Maradi, Thirumalapura, Pattasomanahalli, Narahalli, Madake Patna, Chikkamaralli.

Canal: Nearest Villages- Kalenahalli, Anavalu, Haganahal li, Katteri, Chikkayarahalli, Duddaghatta, Seethapura, Aralakuppe, Haravu, Hosa Koppal, Chaluvarasanakoppal, Koranahalli, Ganadahosur, Nuggahalli, Kurahatti, Vadesamu dra, Talasasana, Thirumalapura, Madake Patna, Hiremarali, Chikkade, Pattasomanahalli, Thyavadahalli, Pandavapura (Hirode) Rural, Beerasettihalli, Bevinakuppe, Banaghatta, Chagasettihalli, Shyadanahalli, Molenahalli, Mandibetta halli, Kurubarabettahalli, Shamboonahalli, Harohalli , Damadahalli, Kennalu, Yelekere, Ukkada, Kyathanahalli.

Annual Rainfall: Normal Rianfall 645.9 mm.

Ground Water: Availability of the Ground Water in the Basin is 10303.26 H.A.M. and the utilization is 2858. 00 H.A.M. It belongs to Over Expoited category. Depth to water level 2 to 20 meter below the ground. Most of the wells go down in summer months, according to the Ground Water Estimation Committee.

Soils: Red Sandy Loams to Red Clay Loam.

Natural Division : It falls in Cauvery-Hemavati Valley of the Southern Karnataka Plateau.

Administration:

Division: Mysore. Parliamentary Constituency: 20 Mandaya. District: Mandaya. Taluka: Pandavapura . Assembly Const ituency: 188 Pandavpura. Gram Panchayat: 24.

Fairs: Sayyad Salar Masud Sahib Urs: It is held at Tonnur in the month of Rajjab. Tonnur is also called Tondabur. It is in Pandavapura taluk, at the southern foot of the Yadugiri hills, about 17 kilometres north-west of Srirangapatna. It was a provincial capital of the Hoysal as. There is the well-known Dargah of Sayyad Salar Masud Sahib on a small hillock nearby. It bears the date of 760 Hijri corresponding to 1358 A.D. The central square of the hall, which is quite plain, has a fine bulbous-sh aped dome. Several of the pillars, which are of Hindu source, bear figures of gods. Near the gate are some mahasati stones and closeby are two small tombs which, it is said, are of some relations of Tipu. In the month of Rajjab, an annual Urs is held here, which is well-attended. Vairamudi Festival: It is observed at Melkote near Mandya in the month of Chaitra (March-April) for 6 days in the honour of Lord Cheluvaraya-swamy. Melkote or Melu kote in Pandavapura taluk is one of the principal sacred places in the State. The place is known as Tirunarayanap ura. It is built on rocky hills named Yadavagiri or Yadug iri. It is about 45 kms. from Mysore city. Early in the twelth century, the great Srivaishnava Saint Sri Ramanuj acharya, who hailed from Tamilnadu, took up his residence at Melkote and lived there, for about fourteen years. It thus became a prominent centre of the Srivaishnava sect of Brahmins, who obtained from the Hoysala king Vishnuvardhana, who has become a follower of the Acharya, an assignment of the fertile tracts of land in the neighbourhood, especially of the Ashta Grains, on either bank of the river Cauvery.

Villages: 171 **Inhabited:** 142 **Uninhabited:** 29

Ranking	District	State	National
Area	6	162	1401
Population	6	126	1663
Sex Ratio	3	29	1074
Child Sex Ratio	4	154	4261
Literacy Rate	6	122	3736
Density	2	58	3526
Work Participation Rate	5	24	1532

Gram Panchayats:
Balaghatta, Melukote (Rural) , Jakkanahalli, Manikyanahalli, Narayanapura, Laxmi Sagar, Halebeedu, Sunkathonnur, Thirumalasagara Chatra, Chinakurali, Gummanahalli, Honaganahalli, Dinka, Bannangadi, Kurubarabettahalli, Hiremarali, Kanagana Maradi, Dodda Byadarahalli, Chikkade, Kennalu, Kyathanahalli, Haravu, Aralakuppe, Katteri.

Amenities:

Education: Primary School in 128 villages, Middle school in 86 villages, Matriculation or Secondary School in 15 villages, namely Melukote, Jakkanahalli, Bellaie, Laxmi Sagar, Sunkathonnur, Narayanapura, Chinakurali, Bannangadi, Katteri, Aralakuppe, Chikkabyadarahalli, Thirumalapura, Hiremarali, Kurubarabettahalli, Ukkada.

Higher Secondary or Pre University Courses or Intermediate or Junior College in 4 villages of the CD Block,, namely Bellale, Chinakurali, Kyathanahalli, Puttayyanakoppalu.

College in 0 village, Adult Literacy Center in 4 villages.

Medical: Hospital in 5 villages, Dispensary in 6 villages, Health Center in 10 villages, Sub Center in 34 villages, Maternity and Child Welfare Center in 6 villages, Community health workers in 0 village.

The Villages having Hospital or Dispensary or Health Center are Melukote, Jakkanahalli, Bellale, Narayanapura, Chinakurali, Aralakuppe, Thonnur, Thirumalasagara Chatra, Chikkabyadarahalli, Thirumalapura.

Drinking Water: Tap water in 82 villages, Tank water in 82 villages, Well water in 129 villages, Tubewell in 52 villages and more than one source in 135 villages.

Bank: Banking facility in 13 villages, namely, Melukote, Jakkanahalli, Bellale, Sunkathonnur Chinakurali, Bannangadi, Aralakuppe, Haravu Dodda Byadarahalli, Chikkade, Kurubarabettahalli Kennalu, Kyathanahalli.

Credit Society in 60 villages Agricultural Credit Society in 36 Non-Agricultural Credit Society in 33 villages.

Others: Power supply in 138 villages, Cinema hall in 5 villages sport club in 3 villages, Stadium or Auditorium or Community Hall in 1 village, Post Office in 38 villages.

There are 86 villages having bus facilities.

Villages with most of facilities: Melukote Jakkanahalli, Sunkathonnur, Chinakurali, Bannangadi Aralakuppe, Haravu, Dodda Byadarahalli Kurubarabettahalli, Kennalu, Kyathanahalli.

Villages without amenities (Education):
G. Singapura, Madrahalli, Huligere, Molenahalli, Moodanahalli, Madake Patna, Rangana Koppal, Bijjanahalli, Shyadanahalli..

Scheduled Castes: Out of the total population of 156699 persons, 18397 persons (11.74%) belong to Scheduled Castes. The villages having less than 10% SC population are B.Kodagahalli, Naranapura, Madenahalli, Melukote Garudapura, Doddighatta, Kadenahalli, Devarahalli Kajji Koppal, Arakanakere, Sangapura, Anunahalli Borapura, Shamboonahalli, M. Shettihalli Manikyanahalli, Neelanahalli, Laxmi Sagar Mahadeshwarapura, Menagara, Halebeedu S. Kodagahalli, Sunkathonnur, Madrahalli Kalenahalli, Huligere, Hosahalli, Kuppahalli Chittanahalli, G.Shettihalli, Yeregowdanahalli Kodala, Kadaba, Dodda Bhoganahalli, Illenahalli Kanaganahalli, Morasanahalli, Lingapura Chikkaboganahalli, Kurubaramallenahalli Valalekatte Koppal, Dinka Settihalli, Moodanahalli Kanivekoppalu, Madarahalli, Bannangadi, Bindahalli Sundahalli, Haganahalli, Katteri, Seethapura Aralakuppe, Chaluvarasanakoppal, Yenne Hole Koppal Hulkere, Kenchanahalli, Pattanagere, Thonnur Ingalaguppe, Ganadahosur, Nuggahalli, Kurahatti Agatahalli, Dodda Byadarahalli, Hiremarali Bevinakuppe, Banaghatta, Kodihalli Hosur Hullikere Koppalu, Chagasettihalli Kurubarabettahalli, Kennalu, Kyathanahalli.

The villages having more than 50% SC population are Talekere, Molenahalli, Alpahalli, Madake Patna Haralahalli, Bijjanahalli.

Sex ratio of Scheduled Caste population is 507.

Scheduled Castes Literates and Illiterates by Sex:

	Persons	Males	Females
Literate	7,426	4,448	2,978
Illiterate	10,971	4,617	6,354
Literacy rate	46.6	56.8	36.7
Graduate	153	116	37

Scheduled Castes (Dominant):

Adi Karnataka, Madiga, Bhovi, Holaya etc., Korama

For their cultural identity please see Appendix-I

Villages without Scheduled Castes: There are 47 villages without any scheduled caste population.

Scheduled Tribes: Out of the total population of 156699 persons, 1694 persons (1.08%) belong to Scheduled Tribes.

The villages having less than 10% ST population are G. Singapura, Gujagonahalli, Talekere Pagade Kallahalli, Ramapura, B.Kodagahalli Balaghatta, Naranapura, Madenahalli, Melukote Kanagonahalli, Garudapura, Doddighatta, Kadalagere Kadenahalli, Gowdagere, Devarahalli, Jakkanahalli Kajji Koppal, Arakanakere, Sangapura, Bolenahalli Narahalli, Anunahalli, Borapura, Shamboonahalli Nyamanahalli, Amruthi, M. Shettihalli Manikyanahalli, Bellale, Neelanahalli, Laxmi Sagar Mahadeshwarapura, Hosakote, Menagara, Halebeedu Athiganahalli, Sunkathonnur, Madrahalli, Nallahalli Kalenahalli, Anavalu, Singapura, Huligere, Hosahalli Maramahalli, Valagere Devarahalli, Kuppahalli Chittanahalli, G.Shettihalli, Yeregowdanahalli Kodala, Kamanayakanahalli, Narayanapura Nallenahalli, Kadaba, Sanaba, Thirumalapura Dodda Bhoganahalli, Illenahalli, Molenahalli Kurubaramanchanahalli, Kanaganahalli, Morasanahalli Lingapura, Chikkaboganahalli, Kurubaramallenahalli Chinakurali, Gummanahalli, Valalekatte Koppal, Dinka Dinka Settihalli, Moodanahalli, Honaganahalli Kanivekoppalu, Madarahalli, Bebibettadakaval, Beby Jagate Mallenahalli, Alpahalli, Bannangadi Bindahalli, Sundahalli, Malligere, Anthanahalli Basthihalli, Haganahalli, Katteri, Chikkayarahalli Seethapura, Aralakuppe, Haravu, Chaluvarasanakoppal Yenne Hole Koppal, Hulkere, Kenchanahalli Desavahalli, Pattanagere, Thonnur, Ingalaguppe Thirumalasagara Chatra, Baleathiguppe, Ganadahosur Nuggahalli, Kurahatti, Vadesamudra, Agatahalli Dodda Byadarahalli, Talasasana, Chikkabyadarahalli Kanagana Maradi, Thirumalapura, Madake Patna Chikkamaralli, Hiremaralli, Chikkade Pattasomanahalli, Haralahalli, Bevinakuppe Banaghatta, Kodihalli Hosur, Sankanahalli Rangana Koppal, Chandre, Bijjanahalli, Vaddarahalli Hullikere Koppalu, Chagasettihalli, Shyadanahalli Mandibettahalli, Kurubarabettahalli, Shamboonahalli Damadahalli, Kennalu, Manchanahalli, Yelekere Ukkada, Kyathanahalli.

The villages having more than 50% ST population are None.

Sex ratio of Scheduled tribe population is 502.

Scheduled Tribes Literates and Illiterates by Sex:

	Persons	Males	Females
Literate	661	377	284
Illiterate	1,033	467	566
Literacy rate	44.4	50.6	38.2
Graduate	10	7	3

Scheduled Tribes (Dominant):

Naikda etc., Hakkipikki, Meda, Soligaru Generic Tribes etc.

For their cultural identity please see Appendix-II

Villages without Scheduled Tribes: There are 128 villages without any scheduled tribe population.

Literates and Illiterates by Sex (Total Population):

	Persons	Males	Females
Literate	75,298	44,604	30,694
Illiterate	81,401	33,616	47,785
Literacy rate	55	65	44
Graduate	2,559	2,112	447

Agriculture: ***Distribution of villages according to land use:*** Out of 171 villages, Total area (in hectare) is 52290, out of that 60.53 percent is cultivable and 51.63 percent of the cultivable area is irrigated.

Sources of Irrigation (Hectares): Government Canal 6942.52, Private Canal 0, Well without Electricity 327.95, Well with Electricity 1814.68, Tubewell without Electricity 47.78, Tubewell with Electricity 1362.86, Tank 639.32, River 242.01, Lake 515.11, Waterfall 45.85, Others 4404.52.

Villages with population of 5000 to 9999: Gummanahalli, Kennalu.

Villages with population of 10000 and above: None

Distribution of Workers:

	Persons	Males	Females	WPR
Cultivators	52,789	33,142	19,647	63.28
Agricultural Labour	18,146	7,893	10,253	21.75
Household Industry	1,183	655	528	1.42
Other Workers	11,306	8,435	2,871	13.55
Main Workers	66,283	47,289	18,994	79.45
Marginal Workers	17,141	2,836	14,305	20.55
Total Workers	83,424	50,125	33,299	

Religion: Major Religious Communities:

	Persons	Males	Females	Sex Ratio
Hindu (98.36%)	154,127	76,917	77,210	1,004
Muslim (1.08%)	1,687	860	827	962
Christian (0.1%)	153	80	73	913
Sikh (0%)	5	2	3	1,500
Buddhists (0.31%)	478	238	240	1,008
Jain (0.04%)	66	28	38	1,357

Agewise Data:

	Persons	Males	Females	Sex Ratio
All ages	156,699	78,220	78,479	1003
0-14	44,528	22,544	21,984	975
15-44	77,476	38,608	38,868	1007
45-79	32,733	16,186	16,547	1022
80+	1,845	817	1,028	1258
Age not stated	117	65	52	800

Languages (Dominant):
Kannada, Telugu, Urdu, Tamil, Marathi

Disabled Population:

	Persons	Males	Females	%
Total Disabled	3,889	2,333	1,556	
In Seeing	2,418	1,470	948	62.18
In Speech	358	207	151	9.21
In Hearing	136	57	79	3.5
In Movement	722	468	254	18.57
Mentally	255	131	124	6.56

PARASGAD

Parasgad C.D. Block lies in the south-eastern part of Belgaum district. It is a part of Parasgad taluka. The Block is located at a distance of 86 kms. from district headquarters (Belgaum). There are 132 villages in the block with the total population of 273,533 persons. Area of the C.D. Block is 1555.25 sq. kms. It is bounded by taluk Gokak on north, district Dharwad on south, taluk Ramdurg and districts Gadag and Dharwad on east, and taluk Sampgaon on west. The headquarters Complex is located at Saundatti-Yellamma.

Communications:
Roadways : S.H-20: Direction- Belgaum to Bagalkot, Nearest Villages- Korakoppa, Sattigeri, Yarazarvi, Budigoppa, Yaragatti, Soppadla, Rainapur, Nugganatti, Tadasalur, Gundlur, Chachadi, Gontamar, Halaki. S.H-65: Direction- Dharwad to Ramdurg, Nearest Villages- Inamhongal, Manikatti, Hireulligeri, S.Yellamma (R), Kuravinakoppa, Inam, Hoolikatti, Ramanagar, Basidoni, Shirasangi, Kallapur, Govanakoppa, Hooli

River: Malprabha Nadi- Nearest Villages- Mallur, Matolli, Ingalagi, Yenagi, Sutagatti, Hittanagi, Govanakoppa K.Y., Bomagadikopa, Chakrageri, Karlakatti, Dhupdal, Goravanakolla Yakkundim, Badli, Katral, Ganiyal, Nadavinahalli, Shindhogi, Kenchalarkop, Gurlhosur, Shingarkop, Asundi, Soundatti-Yella mma (Rural), Manolli, Teggihal, Jakabal, Kitadal, Vatnal, Artagall, Basaragi Inam, Bhandara Halli, Hallur, Hirur, Kadihalli

Reserved Forest: Nearest Villages- Bolakadabi, Yarazarvi, Budigoppa, Aladakatti K.M, Nugganatti, Tallur, Somapur, Jalikatti, Shrirangapur, Madlur, Mabanur, Hirebudanur, Malagali, Tadasalur, Halaki, Mahantheshnagar, Jangamabudagati, Shivanagar, Murgod, Girinagar, Rudrapur, Karimani, Sogal, Kagihal, Chakrageri, Karlakatti, Venkateshnagar, Aladakatti K.Y, Badli, Katral, Ganiyal, Manolli, Taredakoppa, Bhandara Halli, Hallur, Shindhogi, Vatnal, Goravanakolla, Kuravinakoppa , Katamalli, Yakkeri, Gorabal

Annual Rainfall: Normal Rianfall 503.6 mm.

Ground Water: Availability of the Ground Water in the Basin is 11543 H.A.M. and the utilization is 13347 H. A.M. It belongs to Over Exploited category. Depth to water level 2 to 20 meter below the ground. Most of the wells go down in summer months, according to the Ground Water Estimation Committee.

Soil: Red Soil, Black Soil.

Natural Division : It falls partly in the Krishna Ghatprabha Irrigated Tract and Gokak-Saundatti Hills of the Northern Karnataka Plateau.

Administration:

Division: Belgaum. Parliamentary Const.: 2 Belgaum. Distt.: Belgaum. Taluka: Parasgad. Assembly Constituency: 16 Bailhongal, 17 Saundatti Yellama. Gram Panchayat:43.

Regional Area Development Boards: The Maland Aera Development Board.

Fairs: Dhuredundeshwara Matha Car Festival: It is held at Murgod near Belgaum in the month of Phalguna (February-March)every year. Murgod, 10 kms. from Bailhongal is a very interestingtown with its religious importance. The name of the place is mentioned as Mudugade in inscriptions. The place has a huge Mallikarjuna temple in later Chalukyan style with a garbhagriha, ardhamantapa, a spacious navaranga and two mukhamantapas. The garbhagriha temple has a Kadambanagara shikhara. The ceiling of the navaranga has a Bhuvaneshwari decorated with several floral designs. Kalamma Temple Festival: It is held at Sirasangi near Belgaum in about the month of March-April for five days. Sirasangi 20 kms. from Saundatti located in a valley is a place of rich antiquity. The name of the place is mentioned as 'Rishishringapura' or Pirishingi or Hirishingi in two records from the same place dated 1148 of Jagadekamalla and another dated 1186 of Someshwara IV. It was a noted commercial centre of antiquity. The place has temples dedicated to Kalmeshwara and Bhairaveshwara or Kalamma. The Kalmeshwara temple is a trikutachala in Later Chalukyan style. It has three garbhagrihas, an ardhamantapa (only at the central sanctum), a common navaranga and an open mukhamantapa. Thecentral garbhagriha has a Shivalinga locally called Kalmeshwara or Kamateshwara.

Panchalingeshwara Car Festival: Panchalingeshwara Car festival at Manoli near Belgaum is during Shivaratri (February-March) every year. Manoli (Parasgad tq, 14 kms. from Saundatti), surrounded by the Malaprabha is a place of rich antiquity. The name of the place has been mentioned as Munipura or Munivalli, in a stone inscription dated Saka 1145 of Yadava Singhana. It must have been a centre where the Jaina Munis stayed and the noted scholar Pushpadanta is described as stayed at this place. The place is also called Shinde Manoli as Kolhapur Sardar Shinde built a fort here. The place has temples dedicated to Panchalingeshwara, Banashankari,Murulinga, Tarakeshwara, Mallikarjuna, Renuka and Rudra Muneshwara in a single huge complex and also Venkatesha,Vithoba, Shiva-lingeshwara, Hanumanta and Udachavva (in fort) Veera-bhadreshwara, Hariharaeshwara Ganapati and Kalamma.

Shivayogi Car Festival: It is held at Inchal near Belgaum around the months of March-April every year. Inchal 45 kms. from Saundatti and six kms. from Bailhongal has temples called to Karigudi or Ramalinga, Digavva, Veerabhadra, Dymavva, Hanumanta, Kalmeshwara or Bhairaveshwara, Nagalingeshwara and Mallaiah.

Someshwara Jatra: It is held at Sogal near Belgaum in the month of March for three days. Sogal 16 kilometres from Bailhongal, is a place with considerable antiquity. The place name is ascribed to a sage Sugola Muni who is believed to have lived here but one inscription speaks of "Sovala". It has a number of big and small temples and is of great antiquarian interest. The temple dedicated to Someshwara has a garbhagriha, an ardhamantapa, a navaranga and a mukhamantapa. The garbhagriha has an elaborately carved doorway and there are pierced windows on either sides. The garbhagriha has a Shivalinga as well as stone image. The temple is of Rashtrakuta times. The navaranga has square and octagonal pillars and six of them are cylindrical. The square pillars of the navaranga have relief motifs of Narasimha, Varaha, Vishnu, Brahma, Bhairava, Surya, Tandavashiva, Chandra, Gajasurasamhara, Rati-Manmatha, Chouri-bears and Durga, etc.

The Shikhara over the garbhagriha is a renovated Kadambanagara, the pendants of the Shukanasa has images of Brahma, Shiva and Vishnu. Near the temple is a later Chalukyan inscription dated Saka 902. Next to this is a Kalayanamantapa where the marriage of Shiva and Parvati is described to have taken place with old statue of Panchanana, Shiva and Parvati. Shiva with basinga and other traditional ornaments. There are Ashtadikpalakas like Yama, Agni, Ishanya, Indra all broken lying near this building, all fine examples of artistic accomplishments of the period. To the right of the Someshwara temple is a Veerabhadra shrine, with a new image inside, a broken statue of later Chalukyan times is also found.

Villages: 132 **Inhabited:** 121 **Uninhabited:** 11

Ranking	District	State	National
Area	3	27	120
Population	8	29	136
Sex Ratio	7	105	2646
Child Sex Ratio	2	135	3884
Literacy Rate	7	121	3719
Density	3	72	5121
Work Participation Rate	8	96	1796

Gram Panchayats:

Akkisagar, Mugalihal, Sattigeri, Madamageri, Kotur, Kadabi, Hirebudanur, Chachadi, Tadasalur, Yarazarvi, Yaragatti, Soppadla, Tallur, Murgod, Harugoppa, Inchal, Marakumbi, Rudrapur, Hosur, Mallur, Yakkundi, Badli, Madlur, Manolli, Teggihal, Artagall, Shindhogi, Gorabal, Shirasangi, Kagadal, Hoolikatti, Hooli, Goravanakolla, Asundi, Sutagatti, Karikatti, Sangreshkoppa, Inamhongal, Betasur, Ugaragol , Hirekumbi, Chulaki, Hanchinal.

Amenities:

Education: Primary School in 119 villages, Middle school in 91 villages, Matriculation or Secondary School in 26 villages, namely Mugalihal, Shivapur, Kadabi, Yarazarvi, Yaragatti, Soppadla, Tallur, Hirebudanur, Chachadi, Inchal, Harugoppa, Murgod, Chikkoppa K.M., Hosur, Sutagatti, Asundi, Karikatti, Sangreshkoppa, Inamhongal, Ugaragol, Hirekumbi, Hanchinal, Manolli, Shirasangi, Hoolikatti, Hooli.

Higher Secondary or Pre University Courses or Intermediate or Junior College in 7 villages of the CD Block,, namely Kadabi, Yaragatti, Inchal, Murgod, Hirekumbi, Manolli, Hoolikatti.

College in 0 village, Adult Literacy Center in 12 villages.

Medical: Hospital in 2 villages, Dispensary in 6 villages, Health Center in 13 villages, Sub Center in 38 villages, Maternity and Child Welfare Center in 1 village, Community health workers in 14 villages.

The Villages having Hospital or Dispensary or Health Center are Mugalihal, Sutagatti, Karlakatti, Shirasangi, Hooli, Chulaki, Kagadal.

Drinking Water: Tap water in 98 villages, Tank water in 31 villages, Well water in 45 villages, Tubewell in 61 villages and more than one source in 112 villages.

Bank: Banking facility in 15 villages, namely, Kotur, Kadabi, Yaragatti, Tallur, Chachadi, Murgod

Hosur, Hittanagi, Inamhongal, Ugaragol, Hanchinal Manolli, Teggihal, Shirasangi, Hoolikatti.

Credit Society in 59 villages Agricultural Credit Society in 58 Non-Agricultural Credit Society in 10 villages.

Others: Power supply in 120 villages, Cinema hall in 6 villages, sport club in 1 village, Stadium or Auditorium or Community Hall in 3 villages, Post Office in 59 villages.

There are 117 villages having bus facilities.

Villages with most of facilities: Kadabi Yaragatti, Tallur, Chachadi, Murgod, Hosur Inamhongal, Ugaragol, Hanchinal, Manolli, Teggihal Shirasangi, Hoolikatti.

Villages without amenities (Education):

Soundatti - Yellamma (Rural), Dugabal..

Scheduled Castes: Out of the total population of 273538 persons, 23006 persons (8.41%) belong to Scheduled Castes.

The villages having less than 10% SC population are Akkisagar, Dasanal, Mellikeri, Mugalihal Govanakoppa K.S., Tavalageri, Kurabagatti, Kodliwad Itnal, Gudamakeri, Yaraganavi, Madamageri, Shivapur Goraguddi, Kadabi, Bolakadabi, Yarazarvi, Budigoppa Rainapur, Aladakatti K.M, Nugganatti, Tallur Somapur, Jalikatti, Shrirangapur, Benakatti, Madlur Mabanur, Chikkabudanur, Kutaranatti, Hirebudanur Tadasalur, Chachadi, Gontamar, Mutawad, Inchal Harugoppa, Murgod, Rudrapur, Karimani Chikkoppa K.M., Hosur, Sogal, Ingalagi, Sutagatti Hittanagi, Karlakatti, Katral, Kenchalarkop Gurlhosur, Shingarkop, Asundi, Karikatti Kencharamanahal, Yadahalli, Sangreshkoppa Chikkulligeri, Inamhongal, Hireulligeri Soundatti - Yellamma (Rural), Yadravi, Betasur Dugabal, Hirekumbi, Dhaderkoppa, Manolli, Teggihal Jakabal, Kitadal, Artagall, Basaragi Inam Taredakoppa, Bhandara Halli, Hallur, Hirur Goravanakolla, Kuravinakoppa , Gorabal, Basidoni Kallapur, Haralakatti, Manikatti, Hoolikatti, Hooli Chikkumbi, Chulaki, Kagadal.

The villages having more than 50% SC population are Mahantheshnagar, Jangamabudagatti, Shivanagar Girinagar, Venkateshnagar, Aladakatti K.Y Renukanagar, Ramanagar, Katamalli.

Sex ratio of Scheduled Caste population is 495.

Scheduled Castes Literates and Illiterates by Sex:

	Persons	Males	Females
Literate	8,623	5,927	2,696
Illiterate	14,383	5,685	8,698
Literacy rate	45.8	62.4	28.9
Graduate	196	174	22

Scheduled Castes (Dominant):

Bhambi etc., Banjara etc., Korama, Bhovi Chalavadi etc.

For their cultural identity please see Appendix-I

Villages without Scheduled Castes: There are 21 villages without any scheduled caste population.

Scheduled Tribes: Out of the total population of 273538 persons, 32080 persons (11.73%) belong to Scheduled Tribes.

The villages having less than 10% ST population are Akkisagar, Dasanal, Mellikeri, Mugalihal Govanakoppa K.S., Itnal, Korakoppa, Sattigeri Yaragatti, Soppadla, Rainapur, Jalikatti, Jeevapur Shrirangapur, Madlur, Mabanur, Gontamar, Inchal Harugoppa, Jangamabudagatti, Shivanagar, Girinagar Hirekoppa K.M., Marakumbi, Hosur, Matolli, Ingalagi Yenagi, Sutagatti, Karlakatti, Venkateshnagar Aladakatti K.Y, Badli, Katral, Kenchalarkop, Mugali Asundi, Karikatti, Kencharamanahal, Yadahalli Sangreshkoppa, Chikkulligeri, Inamhongal, Yadravi Betasur, Ugaragol, Dugabal, Hirekumbi, Renukanagar Manolli, Teggihal, Jakabal, Kitadal, Artagall Bhandara Halli, Hallur, Hirur, Shindhogi, Vatnal Ramanagar, Kallapur, Govanakoppa Inam, Haralakatti Hoolikatti, Chikkumbi, Achamatti.

The villages having more than 50% ST population are None.

Sex ratio of Scheduled tribe population is 492.

Scheduled Tribes Literates and Illiterates by Sex:

	Persons	Males	Females
Literate	10,681	7,486	3,195
Illiterate	21,399	8,824	12,575
Literacy rate	39.9	55.3	24.1
Graduate	135	119	16

Scheduled Tribes (Dominant):

Naikda etc., Meda, Koli Dhor etc., Kadu Kuruba Gond etc.

For their cultural identity please see Appendix-II

Villages without Scheduled Tribes: There are 33 villages without any scheduled tribe population.

Literates and Illiterates by Sex (Total Population):

	Persons	Males	Females
Literate	125,917	80,621	45,296
Illiterate	147,621	58,416	89,205
Literacy rate	55	69	40
Graduate	3,802	3,193	609

Agriculture: ***Distribution of villages according to land use:*** Out of 132 villages, Total area (in hectare) is 155525, out of that 76.72 percent is cultivable and 30.01 percent of the cultivable area is irrigated.

Sources of Irrigation (Hectares): Government Canal 21268.65, Private Canal 330.78, Well without Electricity 1432.31, Well with Electricity 3629.5, Tubewell without Electricity 599.83, Tubewell with Electricity 8295.15, Tank 18.21, River 131.93, Lake 0, Waterfall 4.04, Others 90.9.

Villages with population of 5000 to 9999:
Sattigeri, Yaragatti, Inchal, Hosur, Karlakatti Ugaragol, Hanchinal, Hooli.

Villages with population of 10000 and above:
Murgod, Manolli.

Distribution of Workers:

	Persons	Males	Females	WPR
Cultivators	56,343	39,315	17,028	41.3
Agricultural Labour	54,620	20,546	34,074	40.04
Household Industry	4,211	2,704	1,507	3.09
Other Workers	21,242	17,387	3,855	15.57
Main Workers	110,889	74,487	36,402	81.29
Marginal Workers	25,527	5,465	20,062	18.71
Total Workers	136,416	79,952	56,464	

Religion: Major Religious Communities:

	Persons	Males	Females	Sex Ratio
Hindu (89.79%)	245,622	124,811	120,811	968
Muslim (9.27%)	25,365	12,918	12,447	964
Christian (0.03%)	76	40	36	900
Sikh (0%)	-	-	-	-
Buddhists (0.02%)	44	24	20	833
Jain (0.57%)	1,567	801	766	956

Agewise Data:

	Persons	Males	Females	Sex Ratio
All ages	273,538	139,037	134,501	967
0-14	97,915	50,293	47,622	947
15-44	123,526	63,483	60,043	946
45-79	49,677	24,188	25,489	1054
80+	2,314	1,008	1,306	1296
Age not stated	106	65	41	631

Languages (Dominant):
Kannada, Urdu, Hindi, Marathi, Telugu

Disabled Population:

	Persons	Males	Females	%
Total Disabled	4,610	2,525	2,085	
In Seeing	1,444	687	757	31.32
In Speech	485	266	219	10.52
In Hearing	354	176	178	7.68
In Movement	1,860	1,136	724	40.35
Mentally	467	260	207	10.13

PAVAGADA

Pavagada C.D. Block lies in the northern part of Tumkur district. It is a part of Pavagada taluka. The Block is located at a distance of 96 kms. from district headqu arters (Tumkur). There are 147 villages in the block with the total population of 218,202 persons. Area of the C.D. Block is 1351.41 sq. kms. It is bounded by district Chitradurga on west, it has common boundary with the state of Andhra Pradesh on north, south, east and west.

Communications:

Roadways : S.H.-3: Direction- Dharmavaram to Madhugiri, Nearest Villages- Nagalapura, Chikkahalli, Hanumanabetta, Soolanaikanahalli, Gangasagara, Kamanadurga, Buddaredd ihalli, Kenchaganahalli, Palavalli, Veerammanahalli, Thimmapura, Pavagada (Rural), Kanivenahalli, Rajavanthi. S.H.-48: Direction- Chitradurga to Penukonda, Nearest Villages- Rangasamudra, Kenchammanahalli, Jadenahalli, Vadanakal, Doddenahalli, Obalapura, Bellibatlu, Shilapura, Madlerahalli, Kotagudda, Kadapalakere, B. Achammanah alli, Bommathanahalli, Pavagada (Rural), Kadamalakunte, Kodamadagu, Gundlahalli.

River: Penner Nadi- Nearest Villages- Vaddarevu, Kyathaganakere, Thimmammanahalli, Kambalahalli, Nagalamadike, Pendlijeevi, Bugadur, Gummagatta.

Reserved Forest: Nearest Villages- Sasalukunte, Vadanakal, Mugadalbetta, Devalakere, Pavagada (Rural), Kadamalaku nte, Chikkanayakanahalli, Veeralagondi. (Kamanadurga R.F.): Nearest Villages- Nagalapura, Chikkahalli, Kamana durga, Bettadakelaginahalli. (Kotagudda R.F.): Nearest Villages- Thippaiahnadurga, B. Hosahalli, Obalapura, Maridasanahalli, Rachamaranahalli, Singareddihalli, Kashipura, Shilapura, Madlerahalli, Kotagudda. (Nidigal R.F.): Nearest Villages- Rangasamudra, Doddenahalli, Hottebommanahalli, Nidagal, Bellibatlu, Thimmalapura, Siddappanakatte, Rangappanahalli, Mummadisagara, Nyayadagunte, Kondetimmanahalli. (Yerrammanahalli R.F.) : Nearest Villages- Thippaganahalli, Hosadurga, Soolanaikanahalli, Yerrammanahalli, Thippaiahnadurga.

Annual Rainfall: Normal Rianfall 611.95 mm.

Ground Water: Availability of the Ground Water in the Basin is 8736.09 H.A.M. and the utilization is 7877. 25 H.A.M. It belongs to Over Exploited category. Depth to water level 2 to 10 meter below the ground. Most of the wells go down in summer months, according to the Ground Water Estimation Committee.

Soils: Red Sandy Soil.

Natural Division : It falls in Pavagada Uplands and Upper Pennar Basin of the Southern Karnataka Plateau.

Administration:

Division: Bangalore. Parliamentary Constituency: 18 Chitradurga (SC). District: Tumkur. Taluka: Pavagada. Assembly Constituency: 137 Pavagada (SC). Gram Panchayat: 33.

Regional Area Development Boards: The Bailu Seeme Area Development Board.

Border Villages: (State: A. P.)- Marammanahalli,

Jalodu, Gowdathimmanahalli, Dalavaihalli, Bheemanakunte, Nagalapura, Chikkahalli, Y.N.Hosakote, Achammanahalli, Thippaganahalli, B. Hosahalli, Rangasamudra, Sasalukunte, Polenahalli, Vadanakal, Kamanadurga, Bettadakelaginaha lli, Vaddarevu, Kyathaganakere, Kambalahalli, Srirangapura, Gyadigunte, Pendlijeevi, Bugadur, Thirumani, Balasamud ra, Vollur, Rayacharlu, Indiranagar, Ryapte (Ryaade), Hussainpura, Kyathaganahalli, Hottebommanahalli, Muddag anahalli, Gollanakunte, Thimmalanaikanabetta, Arasikere, Thumakunte, Mangalavada, Madde, Karekyathanahalli, Kothur, Thimmalanaikanakote, Kadamalakunte, Aralikunte, Kodamadagu, Sunkarlakunte, Chikanayakanahalli, Kanname di, Veeralagondi, Rajavanthi, R.Hosakote (Jodi), Jajuraya nahalli, J.Ranganathapura, Venkatapura, Neralekunte, Dommathamari, Gummagatta, Kanakapura, Gowdeti, Macharajanahalli, Virupasamudra.

Fairs: Anjaneyaswami Jatra: Shri Anjaneyaswami Jatra, is held at Gondihalli in the month of May for eight days. Gondihalli in Pavagada Taluk of Tumkur district is famous for the Anjaneya Temple.

Shanimahatmadevara Jatra: It is held at Pavagada near Tumkur about January-February. Pavagada is a town situat ed at the southern base of the hill so named, about 96 kms. north of the Tumkur town on the road from Madhugiri. Pavagada or Pavu-gonda, snake hill (Pavu means snake in old Kannada) is said to have been so named from a remarkable stone that was discovered there with the figure of a snake upon it.

Villages: 147 **Inhabited:** 145 **Uninhabited:** 2

Ranking	District	State	National
Area	2	47	202
Population	5	69	486
Sex Ratio	9	126	3030
Child Sex Ratio	9	143	4089
Literacy Rate	10	124	3817
Density	3	22	5382
Work Participation Rate	10	113	808

Gram Panchayats:

Achammanahalli, Y.N.Hosakote , Siddapura, Pothaganahalli, Chikkahalli, Kamanadurga, Bettadakelaginahalli, Vollur, Thirumani, Ryapte (Ryaade), Nagalamadike, Palavalli, Ponnasamudra, Kotagudda, Budibetta, Maridasanahalli, Rangasamudra, Vadanakal, Sasalukunte, Nyayadagunte, Arasikere, Mangalavada, Kondethimmanahalli, Gujjanadu, Chennakeshavapura, Kannamedi, Byadanur, Naliganahalli, Pavagada (Rural) , Rajavanthi, Venkatapura, Virupasamudra, Dommathamari.

Amenities:

Education: Primary School in 133 villages, Middle school in 97 villages, Matriculation or Secondary School in 26 villages, namely Siddapura, Chikkahalli, Pothaganahalli, Y.N.Hosakote, Rangasamudra, Kenchammanahalli, Maridasanahalli, Gangasagara, Nagalamadike, Hosahalli, Thirumani, Vollur, Bellibatlu, Kotagudda, Mugadalbetta, Nyayadagunte, Gollanakunte, Hosahalli, Kondethimmanahalli, Arasikere, Kadapalakere, Pavagada (Rural), Gundlahalli, Byadanur, Veeralagondi, Gummagatta.

Higher Secondary or Pre University Courses or Intermediate or Junior College in 9 villages of the CD Block,, namely Y.N.Hosakote, Vadanakal, Thirumani, Kotagudda, Arasikere, Mangalavada, Pavagada (Rural), Gundlahalli, Venkatapura.

College in 2 villages, Adult Literacy Center in 0 village., Colleges are in villages, namely Y.N.Hosakote, Kotagudda.

Medical: Hospital in 0 village, Dispensary in 3 villages, Health Center in 8 villages, Sub Center in 4 villages, Maternity and Child Welfare Center in 4 villages, Community health workers in 2 villages.

The Villages having Hospital or Dispensary or Health Center are Kotagudda, Kondethimmanahalli, Kilarlahalli.

Drinking Water: Tap water in 126 villages, Tank water in 6 villages, Well water in 12 villages, Tubewell in 23 villages and more than one source in 131 villages.

Bank: Banking facility in 19 villages, namely, Y.N.Hosakote, Vadanakal, Maridasanahalli Ponnasamudra, Nagalamadike, Palavalli, Thirumani Kotagudda, Siddappanakatte, Nyayadagunte Kondethimmanahalli, Chennakeshavapura, Arasikere Mangalavada, Pavagada (Rural), Venkatapura Neralekunte, Dommathamari, Gummagatta.

Credit Society in 24 villages Agricultural Credit Society in 24 Non-Agricultural Credit Society in 4 villages.

Others: Power supply in 145 villages, Cinema hall in 6 villages sport club in 145 villages, Stadium or Auditorium or Communi Hall in 145 villages, Post Office in 61 villages.

There are 116 villages having bus facilities.

Villages with most of facilities: Y.N.Hosakote Vadanakal, Maridasanahalli, Nagalamadike, Palavalli Thirumani, Kotagudda, Kondethimmanahalli Mangalavada, Pavagada (Rural), Venkatapura.

Villages without amenities (Education): Jadenahalli, K.Sevalapura, Upparahalli, Thappaganadoddi, Indiranagar, Thimmalapura, Kashipura, Madlerahalli, Bommanagathihalli, Siddappanakatte, Rangappanahalli, Mummadisagara..

Scheduled Castes: Out of the total population of 218187

persons, 61979 persons (28.41%) belong to Scheduled Castes. The villages having less than 10% SC population are Yerrammanahalli, Pennobanahalli, Jadenahalli Vaddarevu, Annadanapura, Thimmalapura Bommanagathihalli, Siddappanakatte, Rangappanahalli Mummadisagara, Muddaganahalli, Uddagatta, Palkunte Kotabande, Krishnagiri, Chittaganahalli R.Hosakote (Jodi).

The villages having more than 50% SC population are Nagalapura, Dalavaihalli, K.Sevalapura, Hosahalli Veerammanahalli, Srirangapura, Upparahalli Indiranagar, Kodigehalli, Hosahalli B. Achammanahalli, Jajurayanahalli J.Ranganathapura.

Sex ratio of Scheduled Caste population is 487.

Scheduled Castes Literates and Illiterates by Sex:

	Persons	Males	Females
Literate	21,759	14,482	7,277
Illiterate	40,220	17,313	22,907
Literacy rate	41.3	53.6	28.4
Graduate	556	527	29

Scheduled Castes (Dominant):

Madiga, Bhovi, Banjara etc., Adi Karnataka Adi Dravida

For their cultural identity please see Appendix-I

Villages without Scheduled Castes: There are 11 villages without any scheduled caste population.

Scheduled Tribes: Out of the total population of 218187 persons, 36677 persons (16.81%) belong to Scheduled Tribes. The villages having less than 10% ST population are Jalodu, Bheemanakunte, Thimmammanahalli, Kunihalli Pothaganahalli, Jadenahalli, Singareddihalli Talamaradahalli, Gangasagara, Kanikalabande Vaddarevu, Dalavaihalli, Kyathaganakere K.Sevalapura, Hosahalli, Buddareddihalli Kenchaganahalli, Upparahalli, Annadanapura Indiranagar, Kyathaganahalli, Bommanagathihalli Siddappanakatte, Mummadisagara, Nyayadagunte Kodigehalli, Muddaganahalli, Gollanakunte, Hosahalli Konanakurike, Devarabetta, Davadabetta, Hariharapura Thimmalanaikanabetta, Jangamarahalli, Marur, Kothur Kadapalakere, B. Achammanahalli, Bommathanahalli Pavagada (Rural), Balammanahalli, Palkunte, Byadanur Kotabande, Krishnagiri, Kilarlahalli R.Hosakote (Jodi), Jajurayanahalli, J.Ranganathapura Gummagatta, Virupasamudra.

The villages having more than 50% ST population are Dalavaihalli, Hosadurga, Hanumanabetta, Rangasamudra Doddenahalli, Hanumanthanahalli, Rachamaranahalli Hottebommanahalli, Nidagal, Bellibatlu, Thimmalapura Madlerahalli, Rangappanahalli, Budasanahalli Uddagatta.

Sex ratio of Scheduled tribe population is 490.

Scheduled Tribes Literates and Illiterates by Sex:

	Persons	Males	Females
Literate	16,468	10,430	6,038
Illiterate	20,209	8,276	11,933
Literacy rate	51.8	64.2	38.9
Graduate	454	404	50

Scheduled Tribes (Dominant):

Naikda etc., Generic Tribes etc., Yerava, Koraga

For their cultural identity please see Appendix-II

Villages without Scheduled Tribes: There are 19 villages without any scheduled tribe population.

Literates and Illiterates by Sex (Total Population):

	Persons	Males	Females
Literate	102,468	64,369	38,099
Illiterate	115,719	47,013	68,706
Literacy rate	54	67	41
Graduate	3,351	2,978	373

Agriculture: ***Distribution of villages according to land use:*** Out of 147 villages, Total area (in hectare) is 135141, out of that 67.05 percent is cultivable and 16.75 percent of the cultivable area is irrigated.

Sources of Irrigation (Hectares): Government Canal 0, Private Canal 0, Well without Electricity 51.52, Well with Electricity 2742.67, Tubewell without Electricity 146.9, Tubewell with Electricity 6024.69, Tank 2089.8, River 11, Lake 0, Waterfall 0, Others 4109.3.

Villages with population of 5000 to 9999:
Byadanur.

Villages with population of 10000 and above:
Y.N.Hosakote.

Distribution of Workers:

	Persons	Males	Females	WPR
Cultivators	48,333	31,187	17,146	40.06
Agricultural Labour	51,555	20,205	31,350	42.73
Household Industry	5,264	3,196	2,068	4.36
Other Workers	15,506	11,393	4,113	12.85
Main Workers	88,671	56,196	32,475	73.49
Marginal Workers	31,987	9,785	22,202	26.51
Total Workers	120,658	65,981	54,677	

Religion: Major Religious Communities:

	Persons	Males	Females	Sex Ratio
Hindu (96.93%)	211,491	107,984	103,507	959
Muslim (2.92%)	6,379	3,238	3,141	970
Christian (0.02%)	53	27	26	963
Sikh (0%)	6	3	3	1,000
Buddhists (0%)	2	-	2	-
Jain (0.03%)	71	38	33	868

Agewise Data:

	Persons	Males	Females	Sex Ratio
All ages	218,187	111,382	106,805	959
0-14	69,102	35,542	33,560	944
15-44	102,900	52,067	50,833	976
45-79	43,880	22,644	21,236	938
80+	2,141	1,042	1,099	1055
Age not stated	164	87	77	885

Languages (Dominant): Kannada, Telugu, Hindi, Urdu, Marathi

Disabled Population:

	Persons	Males	Females	%
Total Disabled	4,049	2,361	1,688	
In Seeing	1,630	882	748	40.26
In Speech	543	321	222	13.41
In Hearing	255	150	105	6.3
In Movement	1,275	816	459	31.49
Mentally	346	192	154	8.55

PIRIYAPATNA

Piriyapatna C.D. Block lies in the north-western part of Mysore district. It is a part of Piriyapatna taluka. The Block is located at a distance of 64 kms. from district headquarters (Mysore). There are 203 villages in the block with the total population of 209,100 persons. Area of the C.D. Block is 808.21 sq. kms. It is bounded by district Hassan and taluk Krishnarajanagara on north, district Kodagu on south and west, taluks Hunsur and Krishnarajanagara on east.

Communications:

Roadways : SH- 21: Direction- Virajpet to Arkalgud, Nearest Villages- Halaganahalli, Suragahalli, Gorahalli, Betta dakaval, Bettadapura, Kurgallu, Seegekorekaval, Eachuru, Seeguru, Hitnahalli, Hitnehebbagilu, Avarekaiguddadakav al, Kaggundi, Haravemallarajapatna, Habatoor, Ankanahalli, Rajapura, Ichanahalli, Mummadikaval, Anechowkur Forest. SH- 88: Direction- Madikeri to Hunsur, Nearest Villages- Koppa, Giragur, Bylakuppe, Handiguddadakaval, Kiranalli, Basalapura, Kampalapura, Borehosahalli, Alanahalli, Manchedevanahalli, Kundanahalli, Mallinathapura, Hunasa vadi, Chittenahalli, Chowdenahalli, Halepetekantapura, Abbur, Tatanahalli, Harilapura. SH-88 A: Direction- Virajpet to Hunsur, Nearest Villages- Anechowkur Forest, Malangi, Chowkur, Sathyagala, Bekya, Ittagalli, Panchav alli, Uthenahalli, Alalur, Kachuvanahalli Jungle.

Railway Station: Bhoganahalli, R. Hosahalli, R.Thunga.

River: Cauvery Nadi- Nearest Villages- K. Basavanahalli, Kanagal, Chamarayanakote, Sulekote, Shanuboganahalli, Doddakamaravalli, Chikkamaravalli, Dindagadu, Avarthi, Koppa, Giragur, Doddahosur, Lingapura, Doddaharve Forest.

Reserved Forest: (Dodharve R.F.): Nearest Villages- Doddahosur, Aralikumari, Lingapura, Doddaharve Forest, Doddaharve, Naviloor, Lingapura Forest, Ayarabeedu, Bemmathi, Lingapura.

Annual Rainfall: Normal Rianfall 858 mm.

Ground Water: Availability of the Ground Water in the Basin is 5613.61 H.A.M. and the utilization is 2349. 99 H.A.M. It belongs to Safe category. Depth to water level 2 to 20 meter below the ground. Most of the wells go down in summer months, according to the Ground Water Estimation Committee.

Soils: Red Sandy Soils, Red Loamy Soils and Deep Black Soils.

Natural Division : It falls partly in Heggadadevankote-Ba ndipur Forested Upland and Mysore Piriyapatna Plateau of the Southern Karnataka Plateau.

Administration:

Division: Mysore. Parliamentary Constituency: 21 Mysore Paschim. District: Mysore. Taluka: Piriyapatna. Assembly Constituency: 210 Piriyapatna. Gram Panchayat: 26. Regional Area Development Boards: The Maland Aera Development Board.

Villages: 203 **Inhabited:** 197 **Uninhabited:** 6

Ranking	District	State	National
Area	4	119	710
Population	6	77	583
Sex Ratio	7	165	4304
Child Sex Ratio	4	36	1874
Literacy Rate	1	104	3135
Density	4	135	3973
Work Participation Rate	5	39	3184

Gram Panchayats:

Kanagal, Halaganahalli, Chapparadahalli, Doddakamaravalli, Channakalkaval, Chikkanerale, Bettadapura, Bettada Thunga, Attigodu, Kithoor, Handitavalli, Ravandur, Bhuvanahalli, Koppa, Bylakuppe, Komalapura, Hitnehebbagilu, R.Thunga, Doddabyalalu , Makodu, Kampalapura, Chittenahalli, Hunasavadi, Muthur, Malangi, Panchavalli.

Amenities:

Education: Primary School in 174 villages, Middle school in 107 villages, Matriculation or Secondary School in 33 villages, namely Kanagal, Chamarayanakote, Haranahalli, Avarthi, Koppa, Giragur, Bylakuppe, Gollarahosahalli, Basavanayeni, Halaganahalli, Harinahalli, Maradoor, Kithoor, Bettadapura, Bhuvanahalli, Komalapura, Barse, Honnenahalli, Ravandur, Kellur, Makodu, Malaganakere, M. Settihalli, Kalkere, Doddabyalalu, Javanikuppe, Hitnehebbagilu, Kampalapura, Kundanahalli, Hunasavadi, Chittenahalli, Piriyapatna (Rural), Panchavalli.

Higher Secondary or Pre University Courses or Intermediate or Junior College in 4 villages of the CD Block,, namely Kanagal, Kithoor, Bettadapura, Ravandur.
College in 5 villages, Adult Literacy Center in 2 villages., Colleges are in villages, namely Malaganakere, M. Settihalli, Kalkere, Javanikuppe, Piriyapatna (Rural).
Medical: Hospital in 15 villages, Dispensary in 23 villages, Health Center in 20 villages, Sub Center in 48 villages, Maternity and Child Welfare Center in 8 villages, Community health workers in 9 villages.
The Villages having Hospital or Dispensary or Health Center are Chikkanerale, Doddanerale, Doddakamaravalli, Benagal, Koppa, Bylakuppe, Kailasapura, Sangarasettyhalli, Melur, Maradoor, Kithoor, Bettada Thunga, Bettadapura, Konasur, Komalapura, Ravandur, Arenahalli, Bhoganahalli, R. Hosahalli, Makodu, Malaganakere, M. Settihalli, Kalkere, Doddabyalalu , Javanikuppe, Hitnehebbagilu, Kampalapura, Panchavalli.
Drinking Water: Tap water in 133 villages, Tank water in 156 villages, Well water in 154 villages, Tubewell in 132 villages and more than one source in 190 villages.
Bank: Banking facility in 37 villages, namely, Kanagal, Chapparadahalli, Chikkanerale Doddakamaravalli, Koppa, Bylakuppe, Kailasapura Halaganahalli, Attigodu, Melur, Maradoor, Kithoor Bettada Thunga, Bettadapura, Bhuvanahalli Komalapura, N. Settihalli, Ravandur, Haralahalli Bhoganahalli, Kellur, R. Hosahalli, Makodu Aithanahalli, Seeguru, Doddabyalalu, Chikkabyalalu Hitnehebbagilu, Kandegala, Kampalapura, Hunasavadi Chittenahalli, Muthur, Piriyapatna (Rural), Abbur Bekya, Panchavalli.
Credit Society in 197 villages Agricultural Credit Society in 35 Non-Agricultural Credit Society in 58 villages.
Others: Power supply in 197 villages, Cinema hall in 13 villages, sport club in 5 villages, Stadium or Auditorium or Community Hall in 2 villages, Post Office in 57 villages.
There are 145 villages having bus facilities.
Villages with most of facilities: Kanagal Chapparadahalli, Chikkanerale, Doddakamaravalli Koppa, Bylakuppe, Halaganahalli, Attigodu, Melur Maradoor, Kithoor, Bettada Thunga, Bettadapura Komalapura, Ravandur, Bhoganahalli, R. Hosahalli Makodu, Doddabyalalu, Hitnehebbagilu, Kampalapura Hunasavadi, Chittenahalli, Muthur Piriyapatna (Rural), Panchavalli.
Villages without amenities (Education): Hegathur, Rasimartikaval, Haleyur, Doddahonnurkaval, Guddenahalli, Lakshmipura, Navilukodikaval, Hiremalali, Kodihalli, Manchedevanahalli, Avarekaiguddadakaval, Senabinakuppe, Kodihalli.K.G, Kamanahalli, Koralahosahalli, Chowdenahalli, Rajivagrama, Halepetekantapura, Kalethimmanahalli, Rajapura, Anechowkur Forest, Halasoor, Ittagalli..
Scheduled Castes: Out of the total population of 209330 persons, 35078 persons (16.76%) belong to Scheduled Castes.
The villages having less than 10% SC population are Kambipura, Hegathur, Gariguddakaval Gudibhadranahosahalli, Rasimartikaval Rajanabelaguli, Shanuboganahalli, Ambalare Byadarabilaguli, Chikkanerale, Kesarakere, Bilagunda Dindagadu, Doddahosur, Guddenahalli Gulledahalla Jungle, Handiguddadakaval Gollarahosahalli, Kailasapura, Aralikumari Lingapura, Basavanayeni, Halaganahalli, Haradur Kowlanahalli, Harinahalli, Sangarasettyhalli Navilukodikaval, Attigodu, Thammadahalli, Kothavalli Hiremalali, Chikkamalali, Bettadapura, Bhuvanahalli Komalapura, Billahalli, Eachuru, N. Settihalli Arenahalli, Bhoganahalli, Makodu, Kalkere Hitnahalli, Manchedevanahalli, R.Thunga, Javanikuppe Hitnehebbagilu, Neralakuppe, Senabinakuppe G.Basavanahalli, Hemmige, Kodihalli.K.G, Kaggundi Dodda Vaddarakere, Chikkavaddarakere, Kiranalli Manchedevanahalli, Kamanahalli, Ayarabeedu Chittenahalli, Naralapura, Kirangoor, Lingapura Rajivagrama , Magali, Piriyapatna (Rural) Kalethimmanahalli, Kogilavadi, Rajapura, Laxmipura Anechowkur Forest, Abbalathi, Malangi, Halasoor.
The villages having more than 50% SC population are Vaddarabylakuppe, Benagal, Doddahonnurkaval Maradiyur, M. Hosahalli, Doddaharve Forest, Anivalu Naganahalli, Makanahalli, Begur, Mummadikaval Sathyagalakaval.
Sex ratio of Scheduled Caste population is 492.
Scheduled Castes Literates and Illiterates by Sex:

	Persons	Males	Females
Literate	13,824	8,626	5,198
Illiterate	21,254	9,209	12,045
Literacy rate	46.0	56.5	35.2
Graduate	271	241	30

Scheduled Castes (Dominant):
Adi Karnataka, Madiga, Bhovi, Korama, Bhambi etc.
For their cultural identity please see Appendix-I
Villages without Scheduled Castes: There are 32 villages without any scheduled caste population.
Scheduled Tribes: Out of the total population of 209330 persons, 15689 persons (7.49%) belong to Scheduled Tribes.

The villages having less than 10% ST population are K. Basavanahalli, Manuganahalli, Chamarayanakote Kambipura, Hegathur, Gariguddakaval Gudibhadranahosahalli, Rasimartikaval Rajanabelaguli, Hunasethoppalu, Ganganakuppe Adagoor, Shanuboganahalli, Ambalare Vaddarabylakuppe, Chapparadahalli, Haleyur Haranahalli, Tharikal, Doddanerale, Kesarakere Bilagunda, Doddakamaravalli, Chikkamaravalli Avarthi, Sunkadahalli, Benagal, Doddahonnurkaval Maradiyur, Giragur, Guddenahalli, Bylakuppe Doddahonnur, Gulledahalla Jungle, Thirumalapura Poonadahalli, Gollarahosahalli, Lakshmipura Kailasapura, Aralikumari, Doddaharve Forest Doddaharve, Basavanayeni, Halaganahalli, Suragahalli Haradur, Anivalu, Kowlanahalli, Harinahalli Sangarasettyhalli, Navilukodikaval, Naganahalli Attigodu, Melur, Maradoor, Kithoor, Galaganakere Kothavalli, Hiremalali, Bettada Thunga, Bettadapura Konasur, Joganahalli, Bhuvanahalli, Bekkare, Kanoor Komalapura, Billahalli, Seegekorekaval, Eachuru Barse, Nandipura, N. Settihalli, Nilangala Kelaganahalli, Honnenahalli, Bhavalalu, Handitavalli Nagaraghatta, Ravandur, Haralahalli, Arenahalli Bhoganahalli, Kodihalli, Kellur, R. Hosahalli Makodu, Malaganakere, Dorekere, Seeguru, Hitnahalli Manchedevanahalli, Doddabyalalu , Javanikuppe Makanahalli, Chikkabyalalu, Sundavalu, Aswalu Hitnehebbagilu, Avarekaiguddadakaval, Telaginakuppe K. Haralahalli, Neralakuppe, Senabinakuppe Kandegala, G.Basavanahalli, Hemmige, Kodihalli.K.G Kaggundi, Dodda Vaddarakere, Chikkavaddarakere Kiranalli, Basalapura, Kampalapura, Naviloor Mallinathapura, Hunasavadi, Kamanahalli Boothanahalli, Koralahosahalli, Belathur Chittenahalli, Chowdenahalli, Channenahalli Kirangoor, Muthur, Magali, Halepetekantapura Haravemallarajapatna, Piriyapatna (Rural) Thimakapura, Begur, Kalethimmanahalli, Sulagodu Ankanahalli, Rajapura, Tatanahalli, Harilapura Hunasekuppe, Ichanahalli, Mummadikaval, Chowkur Halasoor, Sathyagalakaval, Sathyagala, Bekya Ittagalli, Panchavalli, Alalur.

The villages having more than 50% ST population are Charapura, Lingapura, Lingapura, Rajivagrama Abbalathi.

Sex ratio of Scheduled tribe population is 493.

Scheduled Tribes Literates and Illiterates by Sex:

	Persons	Males	Females
Literate	6,382	3,902	2,480
Illiterate	9,307	4,054	5,253
Literacy rate	47.5	57.4	37.4
Graduate	95	82	13

Scheduled Tribes (Dominant):

Naikda etc., Jenu Kuruba, Soligaru, Meda, Bhil etc.

For their cultural identity please see Appendix-II

Villages without Scheduled Tribes: There are 88 villages without any scheduled tribe population.

Literates and Illiterates by Sex (Total Population):

	Persons	Males	Females
Literate	105,704	64,973	40,731
Illiterate	103,626	43,284	60,342
Literacy rate	58	69	46
Graduate	4,546	3,990	556

Agriculture: ***Distribution of villages according to land use:*** Out of 203 villages, Total area (in hectare) is 80821, out of that 61.41 percent is cultivable and 18.84 percent of the cultivable area is irrigated.

Sources of Irrigation (Hectares): Government Canal 2201.92, Private Canal 0, Well without Electricity 123.85, Well with Electricity 386.96, Tubewell without Electricity 33.52, Tubewell with Electricity 569.59, Tank 2869.09, River 6.07, Lake 0, Waterfall 0, Others 1994.48.

Villages with population of 5000 to 9999: Doddaharve, Bettadapura.

Villages with population of 10000 and above: None

Distribution of Workers:

	Persons	Males	Females	WPR
Cultivators	63,868	42,552	21,316	66.23
Agricultural Labour	17,639	7,548	10,091	18.29
Household Industry	997	661	336	1.03
Other Workers	13,923	9,880	4,043	14.44
Main Workers	82,751	57,461	25,290	85.82
Marginal Workers	13,676	3,180	10,496	14.18
Total Workers	96,427	60,641	35,786	

Religion: Major Religious Communities:

	Persons	Males	Females	Sex Ratio
Hindu (86.97%)	182,056	91,953	90,103	980
Muslim (5.81%)	12,166	6,142	6,024	981
Christian (0.36%)	758	400	358	895
Sikh (0%)	4	1	3	3,000
Buddhists (6.4%)	13,389	9,293	4,096	441
Jain (0.02%)	34	20	14	700

Agewise Data:

	Persons	Males	Females	Sex Ratio
All ages	209,330	108,257	101,073	934
0-14	65,632	33,260	32,372	973
15-44	104,124	54,798	49,326	900
45-79	37,448	19,243	18,205	946
80+	1,961	858	1,103	1286

Age not stated	165	98	67	684

Languages (Dominant):
Kannada, Tibetan, Urdu, Telugu, Tamil
Disabled Population:

	Persons	Males	Females	%
Total Disabled	3,586	2,100	1,486	
In Seeing	1,914	1,112	802	53.37
In Speech	331	188	143	9.23
In Hearing	269	139	130	7.5
In Movement	809	508	301	22.56
Mentally	263	153	110	7.33

PUTTUR

Puttur C.D. Block lies in the southern part of Dakshina Kannada district. It is a part of Puttur taluka. The Block is located at a distance of 48 kms. from district headquarters (Mangalore). There are 67 villages in the block with the total population of 217,964 persons. Area of the C.D. Block is 964.97 sq. kms. It is bounded by taluk Beltangadi and district Hassan on north, taluk Sulya on south, district Hassan on east, taluk Bantaval on west. It has common boundary with the state of Kerala on south-west.

Communications:
Roadways : NH- 48: Direction- Mangalore to Hassan, Nearest Villages- Nekkiladi, Uppinangady, Bajathuru, G0Lithattu, Konalu, Nelyadi, Kowkradi, Ichlampady, Konaje, Shirady, Noojibalthila. SH- 37: Direction- Kokkada to Subramanya, Nearest Villages- Kowkradi, Ichlampady, Renjilady, Bilinele, Bantra, Kutrupadi, Aithoor. SH- 88: Direction- Mangalore to Madikeri, Nearest Villages- Kabaka (Rural), Aryapu (Rural), Kemminje (Rural), Kedambady, Olamogru, Ariyadka, Madnooru, Kuriya, Nettanigemudnoor, Kolthige.
Railway Station: Villages- Bilinele, Kaniyoor, Kodimbala Savanur, Narimogru.
River: Natravati Nadi- Nearest Villages- Nekkiladi, Uppinangady, Bajathuru, G0Lithattu. Uppar Hole Nadi- Nearest Villages- Golithattu, Konalu. Kumarldhari Nadi- Nearest Villages- Kunthoor, Charvaka, Kudmaru, Alankaru, Savanur, Dolpady, Shanthigodu. Kote Halla Nadi- Nearest Village- Bilinele. Bilanile Hole Nadi- Nearest Villages- Kutrupadi, Dolpady, Kadaba, Kodimbala, 102, Nekkilady, Aithoor. Komlar Hole Nadi- Nearest Villages- Kombaru, Bilinele. Bhagi Hole Nadi- Nearest Village- Aithoor. Gowri Hole Nadi- Nearest Villages- Savanur, Punachpady, Palthadi, Narimogru, Shanthigodu, Sarve, Keyyur. Uppar Hole Nadi- Nearest Villages- Golithattu, Konalu. Badanad ka Hole Nadi- Nearest Villages- Balnadu (Rural), Irde. Kodimbala Nadi- Nearest Village- Shirady. Kabbinala Nadi- Nearest Village- Shirady. Badra Halla Nadi- Nearest Villages- Chickamudnoor (Rural), Bellipadi, Kemminje (Rural), Narimogru, Shanthigodu.
Reserved Forest: (Anegundi): Nearest Villages- Madnooru, Nettanigemudnoor, Kolthige. (Kanijarmale R.F.): Nearest Villages- Ariyadka, Keyyur, Madnooru, Kolthige. (Bagimal ai R.F.): Nearest Villages- Kombaru, Bilinele, Aithoor. (Kiddu R.F.): Nearest Villages- Kombaru, Bilinele, Aithoor. (Kombar R.F.): Nearest Villages- Konaje, Shirib agilu, Noojibalthila, Renjilady, Kombaru. (Ballery R. F.): Nearest Villages- Balnadu (Rural), Aryapu (Rural), Olamogru, Bettampady. (Bantage R.F.): Nearest Villages- Panaje, Bettampady, Badagannur, Nidpalli, Paduvannur. (Kanndaka R.F.): Nearest Villages- Paduvannur, Nettanig emudnoor. (Kodimbala R.F.): Nearset Village- Shirady. (Konaje R.F.): Nearest Villages- Konaje, Shiribagilu, Noojibalthila, Renjilady. (Kunthur R.F.): Nearest Villa ges- Nelyadi, Perabe, Kunthoor, Ballya, Kutrupadi, Kadaba. (Dolpadi R.F.): Nearest villages- Kutrupadi, Dolpady, Kadaba. (Suvarmale R.F.): Nearest Villages- Alanthaya, Konalu, Nelyadi, Perabe. (Narimogaru R.F.): Nearest Villages- Chickamudnoor (Rural), Bellipadi, Hirebandadi, Koila, Narimogru, Shanthigodu. (Raikadamale R.F.): Nearest Villages- Charvaka, Kaniyoor, Dolpady.
Annual Rainfall: Normal Rianfall 3961.16 mm.
Ground Water: Availability of the Ground Water in the Basin is (Information not avablable) H.A.M. and the utilization is (Information not avablable) H.A.M. It belongs to (Information not avablable) category. Depth to water level 5 to 20 meter below the ground. Most of the wells go down in summer months, according to the Ground Water Estimation Committee.
Natural Division : It falls partly in Bainduru-Bantval Plain and Beltangadi Dissected zone of the Karnataka Coast (Western Coastal Region).
Administration:
Division: Mysore. Parliamentary Constituency: 17 Dakshina Kannada. District: Dakshina Kannada. Taluka: Puttur. Assembly Constituency: 206 Puttur, 207 Sulya (SC). Gram Panchayat: 37.
Regional Area Development Boards: The Maland Aera Development Board.
Border Villages: (State: Kerala)- Irde, Panaje, Bettamp ady, Badagannur, Nidpalli, Paduvannur, Nettanigemudnoor.
Fairs: Mahalingeshwara Temple Rathotsava: It is held at Puttur temples here, the Mahalingeshwara temple is the oldest. This temple has an inscribed slab of the time of the Vijayanagara king Pratapa Devaraya dated in the shaka year 1353. Other important temples here are of Venkataramana, Mahamaya, Radhakrishna and Bhavani Shankara.

Sahasralingeshwara Jatra: It is held at Uppinangad.
An old renowned temple of Lakshmi-Venkatramana stands
An old renowned temple of Lakshmi-Venkatramana stands
and the Kumaradhara. It was recently renovated. There is another temple dedicated to Sahasralingeshwara by the side of the Lakshmi-Venkataramana temple. In 1800, after the fall of Srirangapatna, two rebels Subba Rao and Vittala Heggasde, had made armed attempts to capture this place.

Villages: 67 **Inhabited:** 67 **Uninhabited:** 0

Ranking	District	State	National
Area	2	88	469
Population	4	71	489
Sex Ratio	4	18	902
Child Sex Ratio	2	74	2766
Literacy Rate	4	9	411
Density	1	4	4360
Work Participation Rate	3	61	212

Gram Panchayats:
Kabaka , Balnadu, Bannur, Kodimbady, Nekkiladi, Uppinangady, Hirebandadi, Aryapu, Panaje, Bettampady, Olamogru, Mundoor, Narimogru, Koila, Ramakunja, Bajathuru, G0Lithattu, Nelyadi, Perabe, Alankaru, Savanur, Kedambady, Ariyadka, Badagannur, Nettanigemudnoor, Belandoor, Kowkradi, Kaniyoor, Kutrupadi, Noojibalthila, Shirady, Kadaba, Mardala (Bantra), Aithoor, Kombaru, Bilinele, Kolthige.

Amenities:
Education: Primary School in 67 villages, Middle school in 67 villages, Matriculation or Secondary School in 32 villages, namely Kabaka (Rural), Kodimbady, Chickamudnoor (Rural), Bellipadi, Nekkiladi, Uppinangady, Bajathuru, Konalu, Nelyadi, Shirady, Ramakunja, Kunthoor, Noojibalthila, Bilinele, Bantra, Alankaru, Savanur, Kaniyoor, Dolpady, Kadaba, Balnadu (Rural), Sarve, Olamogru, Panaje, Bettampady, Ariyadka, Keyyur, Badagannur, Nidpalli, Paduvannur, Nettanigemudnoor, Kolthige.
Higher Secondary or Pre University Courses or Intermediate or Junior College in 11 villages of the CD Block,, namely Uppinangady, Nelyadi, Ramakunja, Noojibalthila, Savanur, Kadaba, Balnadu (Rural), Panaje, Bettampady, Keyyur, Nettanigemudnoor.
College in 2 villages, Adult Literacy Center in 2 villages., Colleges are in villages, namely Uppinangady, Bettampady.
Medical: Hospital in 2 villages, Dispensary in 27 villages, Health Center in 12 villages, Sub Center in 56 villages, Maternity and Child Welfare Center in 8 villages, Community health workers in 23 villages.
The Villages having Hospital or Dispensary or Health Center are Kabaka (Rural), Uppinangady, Nelyadi, Shirady, Koila, Ballya, Bantra, Kudmaru, Alankaru, Savanur, Palthadi, Kaniyoor, Kadaba, Kodimbala, Aithoor, Narimogru, Sarve, Kedambady, Irde, Panaje, Bettampady, Ariyadka, Keyyur, Madnooru, Badagannur, Nidpalli, Paduvannur, Nettanigemudnoor, Kolthige.
Drinking Water: Tap water in 63 villages, Tank water in 36 villages, Well water in 67 villages, Tubewell in 67 villages and more than one source in 67 villages.
Bank: Banking facility in 30 villages, namely, Kabaka (Rural), Bellipadi, Uppinangady, Bajathuru G0Lithattu, Nelyadi, Shirady, Koila, Noojibalthila Renjilady, Bilinele, Kutrupadi, Charvaka, Alankaru Savanur, Kaniyoor, Kadaba, Kodimbala Balnadu (Rural), Aryapu (Rural), Kuriya, Sarve Mundoor, Kedambady, Olamogru, Irde, Panaje Bettampady, Madnooru, Nettanigemudnoor.
Credit Society in 31 villages Agricultural Credit Society in 30 Non-Agricultural Credit Society in 11 villages.
Others: Power supply in 67 villages, Cinema hall in 4 villages, sport club in 4 villages, Stadium or Auditorium or Community Hall in 0 village, Post Office in 57 villages.
There are 66 villages having bus facilities.
Villages with most of facilities: Kabaka (Rural) Bellipadi, Uppinangady, Bajathuru, G0Lithattu Nelyadi, Shirady, Koila, Noojibalthila, Renjilady Bilinele, Kutrupadi, Charvaka, Alankaru, Savanur Kaniyoor, Kadaba, Kodimbala, Balnadu (Rural) Aryapu (Rural), Kuriya, Sarve, Mundoor, Kedambady Olamogru, Irde, Panaje, Bettampady, Madnooru Nettanigemudnoor.
Villages without Amenities (Education): None..
Scheduled Castes: Out of the total population of 218002 persons, 26808 persons (12.3%) belong to Scheduled Castes.
The villages having less than 10% SC population are Kabaka (Rural), Padnoor (Rural), Nekkiladi Uppinangady, Bajathuru, G0Lithattu, Konalu, Kowkradi Ichlampady, Shiribagilu, Koila, Bilinele, Bantra Savanur, Balnadu (Rural), Narimogru, Irde, Panaje Badagannur.
The village having more than 50% SC population is None.
Sex ratio of Scheduled Caste population is 487.

Scheduled Castes Literates and Illiterates by Sex:

	Persons	Males	Females
Literate	13,591	7,940	5,651
Illiterate	13,217	5,823	7,394
Literacy rate	58.6	66.8	49.9

Graduate	114	97	17

Scheduled Castes (Dominant):
Moger, Holaya etc., Adi Dravida, Baira, Ajila
For their cultural identity please see Appendix-I
Villages without Scheduled Castes: There are 0 village without any scheduled caste population.
Scheduled Tribes: Out of the total population of 218002 persons, 11601 persons (5.32%) belong to Scheduled Tribes.
The villages having less than 10% ST population are Kabaka (Rural), Kudipadi, Padnoor (Rural) Bannur (Rural), Kodimbady, Chickamudnoor (Rural) Bellipadi, Hirebandadi, Uppinangady, Bajathuru G0Lithattu, Konalu, Nelyadi, Kowkradi, Ichlampady Konaje, Shirady, Shiribagilu, Koila, Ramakunja Haleneranki, Perabe, Kunthoor, Ballya, Noojibalthila Renjilady, Kombaru, Bilinele, Bantra, Kutrupadi Charvaka, Kudmaru, Alankaru, Savanur, Punachpady Palthadi, Belandoor, Kaimana, Kaniyoor, Dolpady Kadaba, Kodimbala, 102 Nekkilady, Aithoor Aryapu (Rural), Kuriya, Kemminje (Rural), Narimogru Shanthigodu, Sarve, Mundoor, Kedambady, Olamogru Ariyadka, Keyyur, Madnooru, Nettanigemudnoor Kolthige.
The villages having more than 50% ST population are None.
Sex ratio of Scheduled tribe population is 500.
Scheduled Tribes Literates and Illiterates by Sex:

	Persons	Males	Females
Literate	7,427	4,140	3,287
Illiterate	4,174	1,666	2,508
Literacy rate	72.7	80.9	64.5
Graduate	182	138	44

Scheduled Tribes (Dominant):
Marati, Naikda etc., Malaikudi, Koraga, Meda
For their cultural identity please see Appendix-II
Villages without Scheduled Tribes: There are 4 villages without any scheduled tribe population.
Literates and Illiterates by Sex (Total Population):

	Persons	Males	Females
Literate	148,244	80,426	67,818
Illiterate	69,758	28,101	41,657
Literacy rate	78	86	71
Graduate	5,231	3,474	1,757

Agriculture: ***Distribution of villages according to land use:***
Out of 67 villages, Total area (in hectare) is 96497, out of that 32.77 percent is cultivable and 52.73 percent of the cultivable area is irrigated.
Sources of Irrigation (Hectares): Government Canal 0, Private Canal 0, Well without Electricity 5666.12, Well with Electricity 4840.35, Tubewell without Electricity 300.91, Tubewell with Electricity 2787.08, Tank 77.74, River 770.92, Lake 0, Waterfall 791.5, Others 1439.11.
Villages with population of 5000 to 9999:
Hirebandadi, Uppinangady, Bajathuru, Koila Kodimbala, Aryapu (Rural), Narimogru, Olamogru Keyyur, Nettanigemudnoor, Kolthige.
Villages with population of 10000 and above: None
Distribution of Workers:

	Persons	Males	Females	WPR
Cultivators	5,182	3,187	1,995	3.99
Agricultural Labour	2,241	1,297	944	1.73
Household Industry	36,239	2,772	33,467	27.93
Other Workers	86,088	62,278	23,810	66.35
Main Workers	103,542	61,033	42,509	79.8
Marginal Workers	26,208	8,501	17,707	20.2
Total Workers	129,750	69,534	60,216	

Religion: Major Religious Communities:

	Persons	Males	Females	Sex Ratio
Hindu (73.26%)	159,714	79,796	79,918	1,002
Muslim (21.19%)	46,188	22,635	23,553	1,041
Christian (5.11%)	11,149	5,612	5,537	987
Sikh (0.01%)	13	6	7	1,167
Buddhists (0%)	9	4	5	1,250
Jain (0.37%)	802	410	392	956

Agewise Data:

	Persons	Males	Females	Sex Ratio
All ages	218,002	108,527	109,475	1009
0-14	64,573	32,832	31,741	967
15-44	109,022	53,261	55,761	1047
45-79	42,385	21,437	20,948	977
80+	1,850	898	952	1060
Age not stated	172	99	73	737

Languages (Dominant):
Tulu, Malayalam, Kannada, Others, Konkani
Disabled Population:

	Persons	Males	Females	%
Total Disabled	3,282	1,825	1,457	
In Seeing	1,230	707	523	37.48
In Speech	316	171	145	9.63
In Hearing	220	107	113	6.7
In Movement	944	577	367	28.76
Mentally	572	263	309	17.43

RAICHUR

Raichur C.D. Block lies in the eastern part of Raichur district. It is a part of Raichur taluka. The Block is located at a distance of 00 kms. from district headqu arters (Raichur). There are 160 villages in the block with the total population of 207,947 persons. Area of the C.D. Block is 1479.55 sq. kms. It is bounded by district Gulbarga on north, taluks Devadurga and Manvi on west, and it has common boundary with the state of

Andhra Pradesh on north, south and east.

Communications:

Roadways : S.H-13: Direction- Adoni to Hyderabad, Nearest Villages- Hegsanhalli, Deosugur, Yegnur, Yermarus, Raich ur (Rural), Sidrampur, Maliabad, Mittimalkapur, Chicksugur, Kuknoor, Gonwar, Tuntapur, Yergera, Gunjhalli, Karebud ur, Hanchinhal, Gillesugur Tungabhadra. S.H-15: Direction- Devadurga to Kalmala, Nearest Villages- Sultanpur, Murhanpur, Kalmala, J. Venktapur. S.H-20: Direction- Lingsugur to Raichur, Nearest Villages- Askihal, Kalmala, Hunsihalhuda. S.H-23: Direction-Karnataka Manvi to Hunsihalhuda, Nearest Village- Hunsihalhuda.

Raliway Station: Villages- Chicksugur, Matmari.

River: Tungabhadra Nadi- Nearest Villages- Kataknur, Kotigud (D), Bichal, Tungabhadra, Bullapur, Chickmanchal, Gunderveli, Naddigaddimalkapur, Gangwar, Talmari. Krishna Nadi- Nearest Villages- Arshanagi, Gurjapur, Kadlur, Karekal, Deosugur, Ganjhalli, Korvihal, Ramgaddi, Korthkunda, Dongarampur, Mangigaddi, Korvakhurd, Agrah ar, Korvakala, Budidipad, Kurtipli, Athkur.

Canal: Nearest Villages- Rampur, Hosur, Murhanpur, Halve nktapur, Kalmala, J. Venktapur, Gonhal, Hunsihalhuda, Kataknur, Hanmapur, Kotigud (D), Bichal, Yedlapur, Gandhal, Gillesugur, Tungabhadra, Bullapur, Gunderveli, Buddinni, Idapnur, Meerapur, Mirzapur, Talmari.

Reserved Forest: Nearest Villages- Raichur (Rural), Sidrampur, Maliabad, Asapur.

Annual Rainfall: Normal Rianfall 688 mm

Ground Water: Availability of the Ground Water in the Basin is 86.92 H.A.M. and the utilization is 29.31 H. A.M.. It belongs to Over Exploited category. Depth to water level 2 to 10 meter below the ground. Most of the wells go down in summer months, according to the Ground Water Estimation Committee.

Soils: Mixed Red and Black Soils.

Natural Division : It falls partly in the Middle Krishna Valley and the Middle Tungabhadra Valley of the Central Karnataka Plateau.

Administration:

Division: Gulbarga. Parliamentary Constituency: 6 Raichur (ST). District: Raichur. Taluka: Raichur. Assembly Constituency: 53 Raichur Rural (ST), 54 Raichur. Gram Panchayat: 31.

Regional Area Development Boards: The Hyderabad - Karnataka Area Development Board.

Border Villages: (State: Andhra Pradesh)- Kadlur, Karekal, Deosugur, Ganjhalli, Korvihal, Ramgaddi, Korthkunda, Dongarampur, Mangigaddi, Korvakhurd, Agrahar, Korvakala, Budidipad, Kurtipli, Athkur, Gajral, Yapaldinni, Palwal doddi, Arsigera, Wadlamdoddi, Mandalgera, Singnodi, Bapur, Undral Doddi, Masdoddi, Julamgera, Kothdoddi, Maldoddi, Hanmapur, Kotigud (D), Bichal, Tungabhadra, Bullapur, Chickmanchal, Gunderveli, Naddigaddimalkapur, Gangwar, Idapnur, Meerapur, Mirzapur, Talmari.

Fairs: Basavanna Temple Jatra: It is held at Korva in Raichur area. Korva in Raichur taluk is a beautiful island surrounded by the Krishna river, about 25 kilomet ers of Raichur. It is looked upon as a holy place and is popularly known as Naradagadde, where sage Narada is said to have performed penance. A fine road has been laid from Raichur to this place which has been also electrified. It has a temple dedicated to Narada, a famous Veerashaiva Matha, the samadhi of Vairagya Channa basavaswamy who lived about four centuries ago and was well-known for his mystic wisdom, a Shivayoga Peetha and a Basavanna temple. The annual jatra at this place attracts a large number of people and a cattle fair is also held at the time, when there is a brisk trade especially in blankets, brass vessels, bullocks and carts. Just near Naradagadde, there is Koormagadde (Kurum akshetra or Kuravakala) which has a Dattatraya Peetha and the samadhi of Sripadavallbaha Swami. It is said to be the original place of Dattatraya. It has a temple dedicated to him which is visited by devotees from far and near.

Kadlurayya Fair: The Kadlurayya fair, held at Kadlur in the month of Margashira (December) and attracts a good number of people.

Kadlur in Raichur taluk, is looked upon as a sacred place. To the north of this place, the Bhima joins the Krishna. According to an inscription found at Chikalpar vi, the Vijayanagara king Krishnadevaraya visited this pilgrim centre with his family and offered worship.

Narada-Gadde Fair: One of the most important pilgrim centres for the Hindus in the Raichur area is Narada-Gadde, which is about 20 kms. from Raichur. It is surrounded by the Krishna river and the place is held sacred. The annual fair held in the month of Phalguna, (February-Mar ch) attracts thousands of pilgrims. It is looked upon as a holy place and is popularly known as Naradagadde, where sage Narada is said to have performed penance. A fine road has been laid from Raichur to this place which has been also electrified.

Syed Shams Alam Hussainali Urs: The Syed Shams Alam Hussainali Urs held about August is a great Muslim festi val. Muslims from all over the district and also from outside congregate at Raichur on this occasion to offer prayers.

Veerabhadra Jatra: It is held at Devarsugur near Raichur in the month of Margashiva (December). Devarsugur, in

Raichur taluk situated on the right bank of the Krishna river, is noted for its Sugureshvara or Veerabhadra temple. The annual jatra of this temple held in the month of Margashira, attracts a large number of people.

Villages: 160 **Inhabited:** 147 **Uninhabited:** 13

Ranking	District	State	National
Area	5	35	149
Population	4	78	588
Sex Ratio	3	47	1621
Child Sex Ratio	1	8	885
Literacy Rate	4	172	5818
Density	1	31	5687
Work Participation Rate	3	141	1061

Gram Panchayats:

Kadlur, Deosugur, Yedlapur, Chicksugur, Shakwadi, Sagamkunta, Athkur, Yapaldinni, Chandrabanda, Singnodi, Baidoddi, Bijangera, Manslapur, Jegarkal, J. Venktapur, Kalmala, Mamdapur, Merchathal, Matmari, Bichal, Purtipali, Kamlapur, Mittimalkapur, Lingankhan Doddi, Jambaldinni, Yergera, Gunjhalli, Gillesugur, Gandhal, Idapnur, Talmari.

Amenities:

Education: Primary School in 64 villages, Middle school in 60 villages, Matriculation or Secondary School in 15 villages, namely Deosugur, Yapaldinni, Chandrabanda, Singnodi, Jegarkal, Sultanpur, Halvenktapur, Kalmala, Khanapur, Udamgal, Naglapur, Gunjhalli, Matmari, Gillesugur, Idapnur.

Higher Secondary or Pre University Courses or Intermediate or Junior College in 2 villages of the CD Block,, namely Deosugur, Gunjhalli.

College in 0 village, Adult Literacy Center in 0 village.

Medical: Hospital in 1 village, Dispensary in 6 villages, Health Center in 9 villages, Sub Center in 36 villages, Maternity and Child Welfare Center in 1 village, Community health workers in 12 villages.

The Villages having Hospital or Dispensary or Health Center are Wadloor, Chicksugur, Yergera, Gandhal, Idapnur, Meerapur.

Drinking Water: Tap water in 79 villages, Tank water in 11 villages, Well water in 31 villages, Tubewell in 10 villages and more than one source in 119 villages.

Bank: Banking facility in 8 villages, namely, Wadloor, Mangigaddi, Arsigera, Chicksugur J. Venktapur, Manjerla, Midgaldinni, Moodaldinni.

Credit Society in 21 villages Agricultural Credit Society in 21 Non-Agricultural Credit Society in 0 village.

Others: Power supply in 146 villages, Cinema hall in 1 village, sport club in 147 villages, Stadium or Auditorium or Community Hall in 147 villages, Post Office in 60 villages.

There are 132 villages having bus facilities.

Villages with most of facilities: Chicksugur J. Venktapur, Manjerla.

Villages without amenities (Education): Gurjapur, Timmapur. G, Hanmapur, Hemberhal, Meerapur, Timmapur. H, Srinivaspur, Karekal, Rangapur, Nagalapur, Wadloor, Hanumandoddi, Ibrahimdoddi, Korvihal, Ramgaddi, Korthkunda, Mamadadoddi, Yergunta, Sagamkunta, Madmandoddi, Raldoddi, Waddepalli, Mangigaddi, Korvakhurd, Agrahar, Korvakala, Budidipad, Kurtipli, Gajral, Appandoddi, Kothdoddi, Palwaldoddi, Nagandoddi, Ganmur, Shakwadi, Polkamdoddi, Katlatkur, Kadgamdoddi, Arsigera, Wadlamdoddi, Mandalgera, Sanknur, Kurabdoddi, Wadwati, Ghousenagar, Bolmandoddi, Sidrampur, Bijangera, Rajalbanda, Ayazpur, Bapur, Undral Doddi, Mallapur, Fathepur, Gonhal, Hunsihalhuda, Pesaldinni, Arlibenchi, Kamlapur, Tuntapur, Murkidoddi, Masdoddi, Julamgera, Gadhar, Alkur, Midgaldinni, Puchaldinni, Kannedoddi, Kothdoddi, Maldoddi, Moodaldinni, Kataknur, Yedlapur, Karebudur, Hanchinhal, Tungabhadra, Bullapur, Chickmanchal, Gunderveli, Buddinni, Meerapur, Mirzapur..

Scheduled Castes: Out of the total population of 208976 persons, 41099 persons (19.67%) belong to Scheduled Castes. The villages having less than 10% SC population are Srinivaspur, Nagalapur, Hanumandoddi, Ibrahimdoddi Ramgaddi, Raldoddi, Mangigaddi, Agrahar, Kurtipli Appandoddi, Palwaldoddi, Kadgamdoddi, Wadlamdoddi Mallapur, Kuknoor, Arlappanahuda, Hunsihalhuda Pesaldinni, Arlibenchi, Jalibenchi, Anwar Lingankhan Doddi, Mallapur, Kannedoddi, Kothdoddi Maldoddi, Matmari, Moodaldinni, Heerapur, Kataknur Bichal, Yedlapur, Chickmanchal, Idapnur, Meerapur Mirzapur.

The village having more than 50% SC population is None.

Sex ratio of Scheduled Caste population is 495.

Scheduled Castes Literates and Illiterates by Sex:

	Persons	Males	Females
Literate	10,582	7,455	3,127
Illiterate	30,517	13,311	17,206
Literacy rate	31.2	43.5	18.6
Graduate	184	163	21

Scheduled Castes (Dominant):

Madiga, Bhovi, Bhambi etc., Generic Castes etc. Chalavadi etc.

For their cultural identity please see Appendix-I

Villages without Scheduled Castes: There are 24 villages without any scheduled caste population.

Scheduled Tribes: Out of the total population of 208976 persons, 43690 persons (20.91%) belong to Scheduled Tribes. The villages having less than 10% ST population are Arshanagi, Timmapur. G, Hanmapur, Hemberhal Meerapur, Bevin Benchi, Kadlur, Karekal, Yedlapur Nagalapur, Hegsanhalli, Deosugur, Wadloor Hanumandoddi, Ganjhalli, Korvihal, Ramgaddi Korthkunda, Mamadadoddi, Yergunta, Sagamkunta Raldoddi, Mangigaddi, Korvakhurd, Agrahar, Korvakala Gajral, Yapaldinni, Kothdoddi, Polkamdoddi, Arsigera Wadlamdoddi, Yegnur, Sanknur, Kurabdoddi Ghousenagar, Bolmandoddi, Rajalbanda, Mallapur Jegarkal, Chicksugur, Merched, Hospet, Arlappanahuda Raghunathanhalli, Sultanpur, Halvenktapur, Kalmala J. Venktapur, Fathepur, Mamdapur, Nelhal, Pesaldinni Merchathal, Asapur, Arlibenchi, Gonwar, Julamgera Jambaldinni, Naglapur, Kannedoddi, Heerapur Hanmapur, Yedlapur, Gunderveli, Gangwar.

The villages having more than 50% ST population are Ibrahimdoddi, Madmandoddi, Kurtipli, Nagandoddi Kuknoor, Anwar, Lingankhan Doddi, Kataknur Hanchinhal, Buddinni, Naddigaddimalkapur.

Sex ratio of Scheduled tribe population is 497.

Scheduled Tribes Literates and Illiterates by Sex:

	Persons	Males	Females
Literate	8,437	6,183	2,254
Illiterate	35,253	15,777	19,476
Literacy rate	23.6	34.3	12.7
Graduate	74	73	1

Scheduled Tribes (Dominant):

Naikda etc., Generic Tribes etc., Gond etc., Yerava Iruliga

For their cultural identity please see Appendix-II

Villages without Scheduled Tribes: There are 30 villages without any scheduled tribe population.

Literates and Illiterates by Sex (Total Population):

	Persons	Males	Females
Literate	66,530	45,117	21,413
Illiterate	142,446	59,970	82,476
Literacy rate	38	52	25
Graduate	1,375	1,201	174

Agriculture: ***Distribution of villages according to land use:*** Out of 160 villages, Total area (in hectare) is 147955, out of that 75.09 percent is cultivable and 17.22 percent of the cultivable area is irrigated.

Sources of Irrigation (Hectares): Government Canal 9719.11, Private Canal 75.67, Well without Electricity 234.93, Well with Electricity 3113.92, Tubewell without Electricity 101.17, Tubewell with Electricity 294.72, Tank 3734.7, River 1711.74, Lake 62.32, Waterfall 0, Others 80.12.

Villages with population of 5000 to 9999: Kalmala, Yergera, Gunjhalli.

Villages with population of 10000 and above: None

Distribution of Workers:

	Persons	Males	Females	WPR
Cultivators	33,094	24,989	8,105	30.5
Agricultural Labour	58,981	22,310	36,671	54.35
Household Industry	1,838	1,044	794	1.69
Other Workers	14,604	11,137	3,467	13.46
Main Workers	81,926	50,907	31,019	75.5
Marginal Workers	26,591	8,573	18,018	24.5
Total Workers	108,517	59,480	49,037	

Religion: Major Religious Communities:

	Persons	Males	Females	Sex Ratio
Hindu (89.9%)	187,860	94,459	93,401	989
Muslim (8.1%)	16,922	8,526	8,396	985
Christian (1.87%)	3,902	1,954	1,948	997
Sikh (0.01%)	11	7	4	571
Buddhists (0.01%)	16	7	9	1,286
Jain (0%)	5	3	2	667

Agewise Data:

	Persons	Males	Females	Sex Ratio
All ages	208,976	105,087	103,889	989
0-14	82,464	42,187	40,277	955
15-44	92,071	46,534	45,537	979
45-79	33,377	15,906	17,471	1098
80+	973	416	557	1339
Age not stated	91	44	47	1068

Languages (Dominant):

Kannada, Telugu, Urdu, Hindi, Marathi

Disabled Population:

	Persons	Males	Females	%
Total Disabled	2,778	1,560	1,218	
In Seeing	1,023	530	493	36.83
In Speech	246	142	104	8.86
In Hearing	165	81	84	5.94
In Movement	1,084	661	423	39.02
Mentally	260	146	114	9.36

RAMANAGARAM

Ramanagaram C.D. Block lies in the southern part of Bangalore Rural district. It is a part of Ramanagaram tehsil. The Block is located at a distance of 49 kms. from district headquarters (Bangalore). There are 133 villages in the block with the total population of 157, 713 persons. Area of the C.D. Block is 619.21 sq. kms. It is bounded by taluk Magadi and district Bangalore on north, taluk Channapatna on south, taluk Kanakapura and district Bangalore on east, district Tumkur and taluk Channapatna on west.

Communications:

Roadways : S.H-3: Direction- Magadi to Kanakpura, Nearest

Villages- Doddasulikere, Lakshmipura, Melehalli, Ibbalak ahalli, Arehalli, Chikkasulikere, Bommachanahalli, Harisa ndra, Hallimala, Jeeganahalli, Siddalakallu, Hunasanahalli, Nagohalli, Kunagal, Achalu, Channamanahalli, Achalu Forest, Kylancha, Hulikeregunnur, Subkere, Kotahalli.
S.H-17: Direction- Mysore to Bangalore, Nearest Village s- Archikarahalli, Voderahalli, Basavanapura, Kethohalli, Madapura, Mayaganahalli, Kempanahalli, Hejjala, Seshagi rihalli, Manchanayakanahalli, Hulthar State Forest, Kallu gopahalli, Kenchanakuppe, Bidadi, Billakempanahalli, Lakshmisagara, Bhimenahalli, Channamanahalli, Vibhuthikere.
Railway Station: Village- Mayaganahalli, Bidadi.
River: Arkavati Nadi- Nearest Villages- Hagalahalli, Bommachanahalli, Sugganahalli, Harisandra, Hallimala, Jeeganahalli, Hulthar State Forest, Siddalakallu, Hunas anahalli, Nagohalli, Kunagal, Achalu, Channamanahalli, Kylancha, Hulikeregunnur, Kotahalli.
Canal: Nearest Villages- Ramanahalli, Gopahalli, Byraman gala, Ittamadu.
Annual Rainfall: Normal Rianfall 978.28 mm.
Ground Water: Availability of the Ground Water in the Basin is (Information not avablable) H.A.M. and the utilization is (Information not avablable) H.A.M.
It belongs to (Information not avablable) category.
Depth to water level 5 to 20 meter below the ground.
Most of the wells go down in summer months, according to the Ground Water Estimation Committee.
Natural Division : It falls partly in Bangalore Plateau and Cauvery Forested Region of the Southern Karnataka Plateau.
Administration:
Division: Bangalore. Parliamentary Constituency: 23 Bangalore Rural. District: Bangalore Rural. Taluka: Ramanagaram. Assembly Constituency: 182 Magadi, 183 Ramanagaram. Gram Panchayat: 23.
Regional Area Development Boards: The Bailu Seeme Area Development Board.
Villages: 133 **Inhabited:** 123 **Uninhabited:** 10

Ranking	District	State	National
Area	4	149	1110
Population	6	121	1584
Sex Ratio	3	114	2842
Child Sex Ratio	1	12	1039
Literacy Rate	5	80	2625
Density	5	106	3998
Work Participation Rate	5	40	2492

Gram Panchayats:
Doddagangawadi, Akkur, Jalamangala, Kutagal, Shanubhoganahalli, Bilagumba, Harisandra, Lakshmipura, Sugganahalli, Kenchanakuppe, Bannikuppe, Bidadi, Manchanayakanahalli, Kanchugaranahalli, Byramangala, Ittamadu, Mayaganahalli, Hunasanahalli, Vibhuthikere, Bannikuppe, Hulikeregunnur, Kylancha, Gopahalli.
Amenities:
Education: Primary School in 116 villages, Middle school in 99 villages, Matriculation or Secondary School in 38 villages, namely Akkur, Virupasandra, Jalamangala, Tadikavagilu, Lakshmipura, Melehalli, Yerehalli, Doddagangawadi, Kutagal, Kyasapura, Chamanahalli, Hagalahalli, Sugganahalli, Hallimala, Bilagumba, Doddamannugudde Forest, Madapura, Mayaganahalli, Ganakallu, Bannikuppe, Kurubara Karenahalli, Kumbalagudu State Forest, Hejjala, Hirehalli, Bidadi, Kodiyala Karenahalli, Uragahalli, Byramangala, K.G.Gollarapalya, Hunasanahalli, Hebbakodi, Annahalli, Kunagal, Vibhuthikere, Kylancha, Bannikuppe, Lakkojanahalli, Hulikeregunnur.
Higher Secondary or Pre University Courses or Intermediate or Junior College in 7 villages of the CD Block,, namely Jalamangala, Tadikavagilu, Kutagal, Bilagumba, Doddamannugudde Forest, Bidadi, Kunagal.
College in 0 village, Adult Literacy Center in 0 village.
Medical: Hospital in 0 village, Dispensary in 8 villages, Health Center in 11 villages, Sub Center in 36 villages, Maternity and Child Welfare Center in 2 villages, Community health workers in 1 village.
The Villages having Hospital or Dispensary or Health Center are Akkur, Kolamaranakuppe, Yerehalli, Sugganahalli, Bidadi, Byramangala, Hosur, Manchegowdanapalya.
Drinking Water: Tap water in 99 villages, Tank water in 76 villages, Well water in 74 villages, Tubewell in 75 villages and more than one source in 114 villages.
Bank: Banking facility in 9 villages, namely, Akkur, Jalamangala, Lakshmipura, Kutagal Sugganahalli, Lakkasandra, Bidadi, Kylancha Bannikuppe.
Credit Society in 48 villages Agricultural Credit Society in 26 Non-Agricultural Credit Society in 24 villages.
Others: Power supply in 123 villages, Cinema hall in 1 village, sport club in 1 village, Stadium or Auditorium or Community Hall in 123 villages, Post Office in 30 villages.
There are 110 villages having bus facilities.
Villages with most of facilities: Akkur Jalamangala, Lakshmipura, Kutagal, Sugganahalli Lakkasandra, Bidadi, Kylancha, Bannikuppe.
Villages without amenities (Education):
Keshavapura, Dharapura, Lakshmisagara, Bhimenahalli,

Mandalahalli, Yerepalya, Ivagilu..

Scheduled Castes: Out of the total population of 158953 persons, 31009 persons (19.51%) belong to Scheduled Castes.

The villages having less than 10% SC population are Akkur, Lakshmipura, Ibbalakahalli, Yerehalli Thalawadi, Dasarahalli, Anumanahalli, Danaikanapura Chowdeshwarihalli, Arehalli, Chikkasulikere Keshavapura, Jeeganahalli, Kothipura, Voderahalli Basavanapura, Ganakallu, Kumbalagudu State Forest Hirehalli, Borehalli, Muddapura Karenahalli, Bidadi Bhimenahalli, Doddakuntanahalli, Mandalahalli Chikkakuntanahalli, Yerepalya, Ivagilu, Hosur Siddalakallu, Hunasanahalli, Nagohalli Channamanahalli, Chikkenahalli, Vibhuthikere Kavanapura, Hosadoddi, Thenginakallu, Nelamale K.G.Hosahalli.

The villages having more than 50% SC population are Doddamannugudde Forest, Kenjigarahalli, Bethimgere Kallugopahalli, Kumbapura, Shivanahalli Kurubarahalli, Ammanapura.

Sex ratio of Scheduled Caste population is 488.

Scheduled Castes Literates and Illiterates by Sex:

	Persons	Males	Females
Literate	14,912	9,070	5,842
Illiterate	16,097	6,809	9,288
Literacy rate	54.9	65.1	44.2
Graduate	379	334	45

Scheduled Castes (Dominant):

Adi Karnataka, Bhovi, Madiga, Banjara etc.
Beda Jangam etc.

For their cultural identity please see Appendix-I

Villages without Scheduled Castes: There are 20 villages without any scheduled caste population.

Scheduled Tribes: Out of the total population of 158953 persons, 4763 persons (3%) belong to Scheduled Tribes.

The villages having less than 10% ST population are Akkur, Virupasandra, Chikkagangawadi, Jalamangala Tadikavagilu, Ankanahalli, Kolamaranakuppe Kempavaderahalli, Melehalli, Ibbalakahalli Thalawadi, Doddagangawadi, Dasarahalli, Kutagal Shanubhoganahalli, Anumanahalli, Kyasapura Chamanahalli, Danaikanapura, Chowdeshwarihalli Arehalli, Hagalahalli, Bommachanahalli, Sugganahalli Lakkasandra, Harisandra, Hallimala, Bilagumba Keshavapura, Jeeganahalli, Doddamannugudde Forest Archikarahalli, Basavanapura, Kethohalli, Madapura Dharapura, Mayaganahalli, Kempanahalli Kenjigarahalli, Ganakallu, Kempadyapanahalli Bethimgere, Kurubara Karenahalli, Hejjala Seshagirihalli, Manchanayakanahalli, Vajarahalli Avaragere, Hirehalli, Borehalli, Kakaramanahalli Muddapura Karenahalli, Hulthar State Forest Kallugopahalli, Kenchanakuppe, Bidadi Kethiganahalli, Billakempanahalli, Lakshmisagara Bhimenahalli, Talakuppe, Doddakuntanahalli Kodiyala Karenahalli, Mandalahalli, Yerepalya Shanumangala, Banandur, Heggadagere, Ivagilu Uragahalli, Ramanahalli, Gopahalli, Byramangala Ittamadu, Abbanakuppe, Bannigiri, Hosur Kanchugaranahalli, Kempaiahnapalya, Allalasandra Siddalakallu, Hunasanahalli, Hebbakodi Manchegowdanapalya, Bennahalli, Annahalli, Nagohalli Kunagal, Achalu, Channamanahalli, Kumbapura Chikkenahalli, Vibhuthikere, Lakkappanahalli Kylancha, Ankanahalli, Bannikuppe, Shivanahalli Jakkanahalli, Kavanapura, Lakkojanahalli, Hosadoddi Thenginakallu, Kurubarahalli, Ammanapura, Nelamale K.G.Hosahalli, Hulikeregunnur, Subkere.

The villages having more than 50% ST population are None.

Sex ratio of Scheduled tribe population is 490.

Scheduled Tribes Literates and Illiterates by Sex:

	Persons	Males	Females
Literate	1,602	981	621
Illiterate	3,161	1,448	1,713
Literacy rate	39.7	47.6	31.5
Graduate	21	19	2

Scheduled Tribes (Dominant):

Iruliga, Naikda etc., Hakkipikki, Meda
Bavacha etc.

For their cultural identity please see Appendix-II

Villages without Scheduled Tribes: There are 73 villages without any scheduled tribe population.

Literates and Illiterates by Sex (Total Population):

	Persons	Males	Females
Literate	85,503	50,693	34,810
Illiterate	73,450	30,298	43,152
Literacy rate	61	71	51
Graduate	2,729	2,303	426

Agriculture: ***Distribution of villages according to land use:*** Out of 133 villages, Total area (in hectare) is 61921, out of that 57.1 percent is cultivable and 25.02 percent of the cultivable area is irrigated.

Sources of Irrigation (Hectares): Government Canal 1421.77, Private Canal 0, Well without Electricity 8.44, Well with Electricity 2507.79, Tubewell without Electricity 315.26, Tubewell with Electricity 2655.94, Tank 483.61, River 176.69, Lake 234.7, Waterfall 4.04, Others 1038.52.

Villages with population of 5000 to 9999:
Bidadi.

Villages with population of 10000 and above: None

Distribution of Workers:

	Persons	Males	Females	WPR
Cultivators	39,856	25,745	14,111	50.39
Agricultural Labour	15,700	7,251	8,449	19.85
Household Industry	1,549	796	753	1.96
Other Workers	21,996	15,846	6,150	27.81
Main Workers	67,337	45,851	21,486	85.13
Marginal Workers	11,764	3,787	7,977	14.87
Total Workers	79,101	49,638	29,463	

Religion: Major Religious Communities:

	Persons	Males	Females	Sex Ratio
Hindu (98.07%)	155,880	79,289	76,591	966
Muslim (1.4%)	2,227	1,251	976	780
Christian (0.19%)	309	168	141	839
Sikh (0.07%)	105	54	51	944
Buddhists (0%)	4	4	-	-
Jain (0.04%)	64	33	31	939

Agewise Data:

	Persons	Males	Females	Sex Ratio
All ages	158,953	80,991	77,962	963
0-14	45,544	23,174	22,370	965
15-44	78,246	39,665	38,581	973
45-79	32,859	17,059	15,800	926
80+	2,055	960	1,095	1141
Age not stated	249	133	116	872

Languages (Dominant):

Kannada, Telugu, Urdu, Hindi, Tamil

Disabled Population:

	Persons	Males	Females	%
Total Disabled	4,010	2,331	1,679	
In Seeing	2,167	1,259	908	54.04
In Speech	333	175	158	8.3
In Hearing	234	114	120	5.84
In Movement	929	588	341	23.17
Mentally	347	195	152	8.65

RAMDURG

Ramdurg C.D. Block lies in the eastern part of Belgaum district. It is a part of Ramdurg taluka. The Block is located at a distance of 102 kms. from district H.Q. (Belgaum). There are 115 villages in the block with the total Pop. of 190,616 persons. Area of the CD. Block is 1212.67 sq. kms. It is bounded by taluk Gokak and district Bagalkot on north, taluk Parasgad and district Gadag on south, districts Bagalkot and Gadag on east, taluk Parasgad and Gokak on west.

Communications:

Roadways : S.H-14: Direction- Ramdurg to Badami, Nearest Villages- Karadigudda, M.Timmapur, Halagatti, Mudakavi, Idagal, Hosakeri, Kilabanur, Ghatakanur. S.H-20: Direction- Belgaum to Bagalkot, Nearest Villages- K.Chandargi, M. Chandargi, Channatti, Gudakatti, Boodanur, Kullur, Panchagaon. Beedaki, Venktapur, Sidnal. SH-65: Direction- Saundatti Yellamma to Bijapur, Nearest Villages- Hosakoti, Tondikatti, Chippalkatti, Batakurki, Aneguddi, Mudenur, Halagatti, Rankalkoppa, Dodamangadi, Mullur, Mudenkopa, Kadlikoppa. S.H-218: Nearest Village- Godachi.

River: Malprabha Nadi- Nearest Villages- Halagatti, Idagal, Lingadal, Hiremulangi, Chikkamulangi, Benur, Chiktadashi, Hiretadashi, Kankanwadi, Sunnal, Khanapeth, Gonaganur, Bochabal, Mallapur, Maganur, K.Junipet, Halolli, Ramapur, Haletoragal, Turanur, Kilabanur, Rankalkopa, Dodamangadi, Chinchakhandi, Ghatakanur, Kolachi, Huligoppa, Gonnagar, Maradagi, Hampiholi, Awaradi, Sangal.

Canal: Nearest Villages- Kolachi, Huligoppa, Gonnagar, Maradagi, Hampiholi, Awaradi, Sangal, Kalhal.

Reserved Forest: Nesrest Villages- Hanamapur S.U., Umatar, M.Timmapur, M.Khanapur, M.Kallapur, Krishnanagar, Kalamad, Mudakavi, Idagal, Hiremulangi, Hosakeri.

Annual Rainfall: Normal Rianfall 529.6 mm.

Ground Water: Availability of the Ground Water in the Basin is 7214 H.A.M. and the utilization is 11370 H.A.M. It belongs to Over Expoited category. Depth to water level 10 to 20 meter below the ground. Most of the wells go down in summer months, according to the Ground Water Estimation Committee.

Natural Division : It falls in the Krishna Ghatprabha Irrigated Tract of the Northern Karnataka Plateau.

Soil: Red Soil, Black Soil.

Administration:

Division: Belgaum. Parliamentary Const.: 2 Belgaum. District: Belgaum. Taluka: Ramdurg. Assembly Const.: 18 Ramdurg. Gram Panchayat: 35.

Regional Area Development Boards: The Bailu Seeme Area Development Board.

Fairs: Shakhambari Devi Jatra: It is held at Sureban around themonth of February. Sureban, 13 kms. From Ramdurg, is a place of historical importance closely associated with Nargund Revolt of 1858 and is called Manihal-Sureban. It is in this place where C J Manson then the political agent of the southeren Maratha countrywas assassinated by Baba Saheb of Nargund on 29 May1858 when Manson was camping here in a Maruti temple. In his honour, a cenotaph was erected by the British here. A noted highly revered exponent of Advaitha philosophy Sri Shivananda Swamy of Gadag and his son Sri Atmanandaswami had come from this place. The place has samadhi of Atmananda in addition to temples of Chowdeshwari, Vithoba and Shivanand Ashrama. A memorial pillar in memory of 1857 martyrs is now erected here in front of the Vithoba temple. Shabrikolla (three kilometres from Sureban), is a fine valley situated amidst hilly surroundings. The place is named after Shabari; the temple is also called Shabari of Ramayana fame and she is said to have extended hospitality to Rama during his visit here. A bagari fruit tree is also shown within the precincts of the temple. The deity in the temple is Shakhambari who must have been corrupted as Shabari. Shakambari or Banashankari is the family deity of weavers who are found in large numbers in the area. The temple has a garbhagriha, an ardhamantapa and a navarangawith lathe-turned pillars and a huge mukhamantapa of a later date, though the original temple is in later Chalukyan style.

Veerabhadra Jatra: It is held at Godachi near Belgaum around the month of December every year. Godachi 14 kms. from Ramdurga is a celebrated pilgrim centre with temples like Veerabhadra, Kalamma and Maruti. The Veerabhadra temple in Vijayanagar style has a garbhagriha (with Chalukyan doorway) and a spacious mukhamantapa. The Veerabhadra image is recent. Marriages are held in the temple in good number. People from Kolhapur and other cities visit this place daily, and especially on Amavasya or Poornima days. The annual jatra is held in honour of Veerabhadra in the month of December when more than 50,000 people assemble.

Venkateshwara Jatra: It is held at Ramdurg near Belgaum around the month of April. Ramdurg is situated at a distance of about 104 kms. east of Belgaum on the right bank of the Malaprabha, surrounded by hill ranges. It is said that the earlier name of the place was Bhujabala durga, a fort built by Shivaji. Parts of the fort are still seen. It was named Ramdurg when one of the rulers here it in the palace. Rama, it is said had earlier built it in the palace.

Rama, it is said had earlier built the fort and many neighbouring places associated with the Ramayana like Shabarikolla are identified. The Venka teshwara temple here, also called Ramadeva on the river bank was built by the native rulers. There are also temples dedicated to Ganesha, Shankarlinga, Narayana,Maruti, Amba Bhavani, Durgadevi, all said to be about 200 years old. There are also Mathas with gadduges of Yechchaarappaswamy and Maleyappaswamy, the mystic yogis who sanctified the place by their miracles. There are modern temples of Gramadevata (Dyamavva), Basavanna, Panduranga, Vithala, Akkamahadevi and the Raghavendra Matha. In addition,there are two Veerashaiva mathas viz, Virakta Matha and Shivamurtheshwara Matha. The well built bathing ghats, constructed about 100 years ago in the western part of the town known as Padukote has number of shrines. At the annual jatras in honour of Venkateshwara (Ugadi) and Sankamma (April) about20,000 devotees congregate.

Villages: 115 **Inhabited:** 114 **Uninhabited:** 1

Ranking	District	State	National
Area	6	60	274
Population	10	94	837
Sex Ratio	3	93	2435
Child Sex Ratio	3	139	3958
Literacy Rate	9	140	4308
Density	1	27	5455
Work Participation Rate	9	119	971

Gram Panchayats:

Hulkund, Chippalkatti, Tondikatti, Hosakoti, Udapudi, Kadampur, Hirekoppa K.S., K.Chandargi, Godachi, Bannur, Dadibhavi Salapur , Batakurki, Nandihal, Hanamapur S.U., Mudenur, Sunnal, Narasapur, Katakol, Toranagatti, Chunchanur, K.Junipeth, Haletoragal, Turanur , Halagatti, Mudakavi, Hosakeri, Idagal, Gonnagar, Sureban, Ghatakanur, Mullur, Kittur, Manihal, Awaradi, Sangal.

Amenities:

Education: Primary School in 113 villages, Middle school in 78 villages, Matriculation or Secondary School in 20 villages, namely Hulkund, Kunnal, Hosakoti, Hirekoppa K.S., K.Chandargi, M.Chandargi, Boodanur, Kullur, Dadibhavi Salapur, Batakurki, Nandihal, Mudenur, Mudakavi, Hiremulangi, Godachi, Katakol, Toranagatti, Sureban, Manihal, Mullur.

Higher Secondary or Pre University Courses or Intermediate or Junior College in 4 villages of the CD Block,, namely Hulkund, Hirekoppa K.S., Katakol, Sureban.

College in 0 village, Adult Literacy Center in 14 villages.

Medical: Hospital in 0 village, Dispensary in 3 villages, Health Center in 6 villages, Sub Center in 36 villages, Maternity and Child Welfare Center in 1 village, Community health workers in 22 villages.

The Villages having Hospital or Dispensary or Health Center are K.Chandargi, Haletoragal, Mullur.

Drinking Water: Tap water in 57 villages, Tank water in 22 villages, Well water in 53 villages, Tubewell in 58 villages and more than one source in 110 villages.

Bank: Banking facility in 8 villages, namely, Hulkund, Hosakoti, K.Chandargi, Boodanur, Batakurki Katakol, Sureban, Manihal.

Credit Society in 29 villages Agricultural Credit Society in 28 Non-Agricultural Credit Society in 4 villages.

Others: Power supply in 113 villages, Cinema hall in 1 village, sport club in 1 village, Stadium or Auditorium or Community Hall in 0 village, Post Office in 53 villages.

There are 113 villages having bus facilities.

Villages with most of facilities: Hulkund Hosakoti, K.Chandargi, Boodanur, Batakurki, Katakol

Sureban, Manihal.

Villages without amenities (Education): Gudakatti..

Scheduled Castes: Out of the total population of 190763 persons, 26919 persons (14.11%) belong to Scheduled Castes.

The villages having less than 10% SC population are Kunnal, Guttigoli, Chippalkatti, Chikkoppa K.S. K.Chandargi, Kamanakoppa, Bijaguppi, Channatti Gudakatti, Kadampur, Beedaki, Venktapur, Udapudi Gudagumnal, Rokkadakatti, Naganur, Batakurki Aneguddi, Umatar, M.Khanapur, M.Kallapur, Mudenur Halagatti, Mudakavi, Hiremulangi, Hosakeri, Bennur Hiretadashi, Sidnal, Godachi, Narasapur, Bannur Sunnal, Chilamur, Katakol, Chunchanur, Hanama Sagar Khanapeth, Gonaganur, Bochabal, Mallapur, K.Junipeth Turanur, Rankalkoppa, Dodamangadi, Ghatakanur Kolachi, Huligoppa, Gonnagar, Maradagi, Manihal Jalikatti, Lakhanayakanakoppa, Kallur, Mullur Kadlikoppa, Kittur, Revadikoppa, Shivapeth, Awaradi Chikkoppa S.K., Kalhal.

The villages having more than 50% SC population are Shivanakote, Somapur, Timmapur S.A., Chennapur Shirasapur, Chetan Nagar, Krishnanagar, Kalamad Sarakote Devapur, Venkateshwarnagar, Gokulnagar Durganagar, Ramapur.

Sex ratio of Scheduled Caste population is 499.

Scheduled Castes Literates and Illiterates by Sex:

	Persons	Males	Females
Literate	8,955	6,196	2,759
Illiterate	17,964	7,298	10,666
Literacy rate	41.3	57.3	25.4
Graduate	188	175	13

Scheduled Castes (Dominant):

Bhambi etc., Banjara etc., Bhovi, Korama, Madiga

For their cultural identity please see Appendix-I

Villages without Scheduled Castes: There are 9 villages without any scheduled caste population.

Scheduled Tribes: Out of the total population of 190763 persons, 7276 persons (3.81%) belong to Scheduled Tribes.

The villages having less than 10% ST population are Hulkund, Kunnal, Budnikhurd, Kamakeri, Guttigoli Hosakoti, Tondikatti, Bhagojikoppa, Hirekoppa K.S. Chikkoppa K.S., Murakatnal, K.Chandargi, Gudagoppa M.Chandargi, Kamanakoppa, Bijaguppi, Channatti Gudakatti, Kadampur, Boodanur, Kullur, Panchagaon Beedaki, Venktapur, Shivanakote, Udapudi, Gudagumnal Rokkadakatti, Dadibhavi Salapur , Naganur, Somapur Batakurki, Nandihal, Timmapur S.A., Chennapur Shirasapur, Chetan Nagar, Soppadla, Hanamapur S.U. Umatar, Karadigudda, M.Timmapur, M.Khanapur M.Kallapur, Krishnanagar, Kalamad, Mudenur Halagatti, Idagal, Lingadal, Hiremulangi Chikkamulangi, Hosakeri, Bennur, Chiktadashi Hiretadashi, Kesaragoppa, Totagatti, Sidnal Narasapur, Bannur, Sarakote Devapur Venkateshwarnagar, Obalapur, Gokulnagar, Durganagar Aribenchi, Sunnal, Chilamur, Katakol, Toranagatti Ujjinakoppa, Padamandi, Chunchanur, Hanama Sagar Gonaganur, Bochabal, K.Junipeth, Halolli, Ramapur Haletoragal, Turanur, Rankalkoppa, Dodamangadi Chinchakhandi, Ghatakanur, Kolachi, Sureban, Manihal Jalikatti, Lakhanayakanakoppa, Kallur, Mullur Kittur, Shivapeth, Awaradi, Chikkoppa S.K., Kalhal.

The villages having more than 50% ST population are None.

Sex ratio of Scheduled tribe population is 492.

Scheduled Tribes Literates and Illiterates by Sex:

	Persons	Males	Females
Literate	2,709	1,849	860
Illiterate	4,567	1,844	2,723
Literacy rate	44.7	60.2	28.8
Graduate	42	39	3

Scheduled Tribes (Dominant):

Naikda etc., Koli Dhor etc., Meda, Kadu Kuruba Iruliga

For their cultural identity please see Appendix-II

Villages without Scheduled Tribes: There are 46 villages without any scheduled tribe population.

Literates and Illiterates by Sex (Total Population):

	Persons	Males	Females
Literate	81,876	53,520	28,356
Illiterate	108,887	43,264	65,623
Literacy rate	51	66	36
Graduate	2,459	2,145	314

Agriculture: ***Distribution of villages according to land use:*** Out of 115 villages, Total area (in hectare) is 121267, out of that 78.31 percent is cultivable and 25.39 percent of the cultivable area is irrigated.

Sources of Irrigation (Hectares): Government Canal 13561.34, Private Canal 0, Well without Electricity 53.83, Well with Electricity 2524.09, Tubewell without Electricity 155.81, Tubewell with Electricity 3904.91, Tank 403.26, River 2808.26, Lake 0, Waterfall 183.53, Others 516.37.

Villages with population of 5000 to 9999:

Chunchanur, Manihal.

Villages with population of 10000 and above:

Katakol.

Distribution of Workers:

	Persons	Males	Females	WPR
Cultivators	39,194	26,799	12,395	39.07
Agricultural Labour	39,236	13,384	25,852	39.11

Household Industry	4,516	2,819	1,697	4.5
Other Workers	17,368	13,053	4,315	17.31
Main Workers	82,643	52,126	30,517	82.38
Marginal Workers	17,671	3,929	13,742	17.62
Total Workers	100,314	56,055	44,259	

Religion: Major Religious Communities:

	Persons	Males	Females	Sex Ratio
Hindu (91.88%)	175,276	88,920	86,356	971
Muslim (7.6%)	14,490	7,374	7,116	965
Christian (0.01%)	21	12	9	750
Sikh (0%)	1	1	-	-
Buddhists (0%)	3	2	1	500
Jain (0.1%)	193	92	101	1,098

Agewise Data:

	Persons	Males	Females	Sex Ratio
All ages	190,763	96,784	93,979	971
0-14	70,355	36,285	34,070	939
15-44	85,512	43,682	41,830	958
45-79	33,310	16,144	17,166	1063
80+	1,499	627	872	1391
Age not stated	87	46	41	891

Languages (Dominant):

Kannada, Hindi, Urdu, Telugu, Marathi

Disabled Population:

	Persons	Males	Females	%
Total Disabled	3,229	1,821	1,408	
In Seeing	894	438	456	27.69
In Speech	301	182	119	9.32
In Hearing	252	108	144	7.8
In Movement	1,452	902	550	44.97
Mentally	330	191	139	10.22

RANIBENNUR

Ranibennur C.D. Block lies in the south-eastern part of Haveri district. It is a part of Ranibennur taluka. The Block is located at a distance of 30 kms. from district headquarters (Haveri). There are 107 villages in the block with the total population of 208,405 persons. Area of the C.D. Block is 854.05 sq. kms. It is bounded by taluks Haveri and district Bellary on north, district Davanagere and taluk Hirekerur on south, district Hirek erur on east, and taluk Byadgi on west.

Communications:

Roadways : N.H-4: Direction- Haveri to Banglore, Nearest Villages- Chalageri, Karur, Yennihosahalli, Waderayanaha lli, Kakol, Venkatapur, Kajjari, Kunabev, Hulihalli, Shrinivasapur, Magod, Kamadod, Devagondanakatti, Makanur, Kawalettu, Nalawagal.

Railway Station: Villages- Chalageri, Karur, Kunabev.

River: Tungabhadra Nadi- Nearest Villages- Choudayya Danapur, Chandapur, Chikka Kuravatti, Haranagiri, Kudrih al, Heeladahalli, Belur, Udagatti, Medleri, Somlapur, Konanatambigi, Hirebidari, Airani, Nadiharalalli, Holea nveri, Makanur, Kawalettu, Nalawagal, Nagenahalli, Mudenur, Kotihal, Fattepur, Kusagatti.

Reserved Forest· Nearest Villages- Hanumapur, Yellapur T.Honnatti.

Annual Rainfall: Normal Rianfall 592 mm.

Ground Water: Availability of the Ground Water in the Basin is 74.06 MCM and the utilization is 72.75 MCM It belongs to Over Exploited category. Depth to water level 10 to 20 meter below the ground. Most of the wells go down in summer months, according to the Ground Water Estimation Committee.

Soils:: Red Sandy Soil, Medium Soil, Deep Black Soil, Red Loamy Soil and Lateritic Soil.

Natural Division : It falls partly in Byadagi-Hirekerur Rocky Knobs and Middle Tungabhadra Valley of the Central Karnataka Plateau.

Administration:

Division: Belgaum. Parliamentary Constituency: 10 Haveri. District: Haveri. Taluka: Ranibennur. Assembly Constituency: 85 Bayadgi, 87 Ranibennur. Gram Panchayat: 35. Regional Area Development Boards: The Bailu Seeme Area Development Board.

Villages: 107 **Inhabited:** 107 **Uninhabited:** 0

Ranking	District	State	National
Area	1	112	626
Population	1	79	590
Sex Ratio	4	163	3995
Child Sex Ratio	5	96	3202
Literacy Rate	4	60	1915
Density	4	80	4151
Work Participation Rate	4	48	1936

Gram Panchayats:

Hanumapur, Honnatti, Chikkakuravatti, Haranagiri, Belur , Gudagur, Guddaguddapur, Kajjari, Kakol, Asundi, Medleri, Aremallapur, Hirebidari, Airani, Karur, Chalageri, Kamadod, Haligeri, Benakanakond, Joisaraharalahalli, Ukkund, Sunakalbidari, Billahalli, Antaravalli, Itagi, Makanur, Kawalettu, Kodiyala, Mudenur, Kotihal, Kuppelur, Malanaikanahalli, Tumminakatti.

Amenities:

Education: Primary School in 102 villages, Middle school in 82 villages, Matriculation or Secondary School in 29 villages, namely Haranagiri, Gudagur, Belur, Medleri, Hirebidari, Aremallapur, Chalageri, Karur, Nadiharalalli, Kakol, Kajjari, Guddaguddapur, Honnatti, Asundi, Ukkund, Joisaraharalahalli, Benakanakond, Sunakalbidari, Kamadod, Haligeri,

Itagi, Antaravalli, Billahalli, Makanur, Kawalettu, Mudenur, Kotihal, Kuppelur, Tumminakatti.

Higher Secondary or Pre University Courses or Intermediate or Junior College in 8 villages of the CD Block,, namely Aremallapur, Chalageri, Honnatti, Sunakalbidari, Haligeri, Itagi, Mudenur, Tumminakatti.

College in 1 village, Adult Literacy Center in 0 village., College in village, namely Sunakalbidari.

Medical: Hospital in 6 villages, Dispensary in 12 villages, Health Center in 14 villages, Sub Center in 42 villages, Maternity and Child Welfare Center in 3 villages, Community health workers in 40 villages.

The Villages having Hospital or Dispensary or Health Center are Airani, Karur, Kajjari, Honnatti, Yerekuppi, Sarvanda, Veerapur, Ukkund, Joisaraharalahalli, Sunakalbidari, Hediyal, Itagi, Billahalli, Lingadalli, Mudenur, Tumminakatti.

Drinking Water: Tap water in 80 villages, Tank water in 32 villages, Well water in 2 villages, Tubewell in 17 villages and more than one source in 101 villages.

Bank: Banking facility in 13 villages, namely, Haranagiri, Medleri, Aremallapur, Chalageri, Kakol Honnatti, Kerimallapur, Sunakalbidari, Haligeri Antaravalli, Makanur, Kuppelur, Tumminakatti.

Credit Society in 34 villages Agricultural Credit Society in 34 Non-Agricultural Credit Society in 1 village.

Others: Power supply in 102 villages, Cinema hall in 4 villages, sport club in 2 villages, Stadium or Auditorium or Community Hall in 0 village, Post Office in 44 villages.

There are 100 villages having bus facilities.

Villages with most of facilities: Haranagiri Medleri, Aremallapur, Chalageri, Kakol, Honnatti Sunakalbidari, Haligeri, Antaravalli, Makanur Kuppelur, Tumminakatti.

Villages without amenities (Education):

Venkatapur, Padmavathipur, Shrinivasapur, Kusagatti..

Scheduled Castes: Out of the total population of 208641 persons, 30967 persons (14.84%) belong to Scheduled Castes.

The villages having less than 10% SC population are Choudayya Danapur, Chandapur, Chikka Kuravatti Kudrihal, Gangapur, Somlapur, Yallapur T.Medleri Aremallapur, Yakalasapur, Karur, Yennihosahalli Waderayanahalli, Kakol, Shidaganahal, Yattinahalli Guddadanveri, Asundi, Laxmapur, Ukkund Joisaraharalahalli, Guddadahosahalli, Hediyal Devagondanakatti, Itagi, Krishnapur, Antaravalli Billahalli, Konanatali, Godihal, Yalabadigi Lingadalli, Holeanveri, Malakanahalli, Hanumanahalli Kawalettu, Nalawagal, Kotihal, Nitapalli Hiremaganur, Kooli, Chikkamaganur, Sannasangapur Badabasapur, Malanaikanahalli, Timmenahalli Fattepur, Tumminakatti, Kusagatti.

The villages having more than 50% SC population are Ramapur, Channapur, Venkatapur, Hullatti Padmavathipur, Shrinivasapur, Ranibennur (Rural) Veerapur.

Sex ratio of Scheduled Caste population is 484.

Scheduled Castes Literates and Illiterates by Sex:

	Persons	Males	Females
Literate	11,358	7,608	3,750
Illiterate	19,609	8,359	11,250
Literacy rate	44.1	57.2	30.2
Graduate	228	200	28

Scheduled Castes (Dominant):

Bhambi etc., Banjara etc., Madiga, Bhovi Chalavadi etc.

For their cultural identity please see Appendix-I

Villages without Scheduled Castes: There are 12 villages without any scheduled caste population.

Scheduled Tribes: Out of the total population of 208641 persons, 21605 persons (10.36%) belong to Scheduled Tribes.

The villages having less than 10% ST population are Hanumapur, Nukapur, Choudayya Danapur, Chandapur Chikka Kuravatti, Ramapur, Heeladahalli, Udagatti Ankasapur, Channapur, Medleri, Somlapur Konanatambigi, Yallapur T.Medleri, Aremallapur Airani, Khanderayanahalli, Waderayanahalli Hulikatti, Kakol, Venkatapur, Guddaguddapur Yellapur T.Honnatti, Honnatti, Kerimallapur, Kunabev Hulihalli, Padmavathipur, Hunashikatti Shrinivasapur, Ranibennur (Rural), Yerekuppi Laxmapur, Veerapur, Joisaraharalahalli, Benakanakond Sunakalbidari, Guddadahosahalli, Guddadabevinahalli Magod, Kusagur, Haligeri, Itagi, Manakur Antaravalli, Billahalli, Danoagihalli (Dandigihalli) Godihal, Yalabadigi, Nandihalli, Makanur, Kawalettu Mudenur, Sannasangapur, Menashinahal, Timmenahalli Tumminakatti.

The villages having more than 50% ST population are Bevinahalli, Yakalasapur, Krishnapur, Nalawagal Nagenahalli, Fattepur, Kusagatti.

Sex ratio of Scheduled tribe population is 486.

Scheduled Tribes Literates and Illiterates by Sex:

	Persons	Males	Females
Literate	11,226	7,087	4,139
Illiterate	10,379	4,008	6,371
Literacy rate	60.2	73.8	45.8
Graduate	334	297	37

Scheduled Tribes (Dominant):

Naikda etc., Koraga, Generic Tribes etc.
Koli Dhor etc.
For their cultural identity please see Appendix-II
Villages without Scheduled Tribes: There are 19 villages without any scheduled tribe population.
Literates and Illiterates by Sex (Total Population):

	Persons	Males	Females
Literate	117,548	71,357	46,191
Illiterate	91,093	36,194	54,899
Literacy rate	65	77	53
Graduate	4,324	3,453	871

Agriculture: ***Distribution of villages according to land use:*** Out of 107 villages, Total area (in hectare) is 85405, out of that 73.48 percent is cultivable and 15.84 percent of the cultivable area is irrigated.
Sources of Irrigation (Hectares): Government Canal 302.79, Private Canal 0, Well without Electricity 168.18, Well with Electricity 491.32, Tubewell without Electricity 108.86, Tubewell with Electricity 4405.17, Tank 3.25, River 4459.19, Lake 0, Waterfall 0, Others 0.
Villages with population of 5000 to 9999: Medleri, Chalageri, Karur, Haligeri, Kawalettu Tumminakatti.
Villages with population of 10000 and above: None
Distribution of Workers:

	Persons	Males	Females	WPR
Cultivators	29,610	23,811	5,799	28
Agricultural Labour	51,758	21,932	29,826	48.95
Household Industry	5,278	2,628	2,650	4.99
Other Workers	19,100	15,848	3,252	18.06
Main Workers	82,761	57,444	25,317	78.26
Marginal Workers	22,985	6,775	16,210	21.74
Total Workers	105,746	64,219	41,527	

Religion: Major Religious Communities:

	Persons	Males	Females	Sex Ratio
Hindu (93.52%)	195,121	100,593	94,528	940
Muslim (5.82%)	12,152	6,234	5,918	949
Christian (0.09%)	195	104	91	875
Sikh (0.01%)	18	10	8	800
Buddhists (0%)	1	1	-	-
Jain (0.07%)	148	78	70	897

Agewise Data:

	Persons	Males	Females	Sex Ratio
All ages	208,641	107,551	101,090	940
0-14	67,798	34,746	33,052	951
15-44	101,311	52,784	48,527	919
45-79	37,610	19,153	18,457	964
80+	1,583	698	885	1268
Age not stated	339	170	169	994

Languages (Dominant):
Kannada, Hindi, Urdu, Telugu, Coorgi/Kodagu
Disabled Population:

	Persons	Males	Females	%
Total Disabled	3,965	2,269	1,696	
In Seeing	1,838	1,007	831	46.36
In Speech	421	238	183	10.62
In Hearing	188	94	94	4.74
In Movement	1,158	722	436	29.21
Mentally	360	208	152	9.08

RAYBAG

Raybag C.D. Block lies in the north-eastern part of Belgaum district. It is a part of Raybag taluka. The Block is located at a distance of 105 kms. from district headquarters (Belgaum).There are 59 villages in the block with the total population of 311,761 persons. Area of the C.D. Block is 946.85 sq. kms.It is bounded by taluk Athni and Chikodi on north, taluk Chikodi and Gokak on south, district Bagalkot and taluk Athani on east, and taluk Chikodi on west.

Communication

Roadways : S.H-12: Direction- Chikodi to Athni, Nearest Villages- Soundatti, Nasalapur. S.H-18: Direction- Chikodi to Mudhol, Nearest Villages- Jodahatti, Bhendwad, Mantur, Nipanal, Kankanawadi, Kappalguddi. S.H-31: Direction-Athni to Gokak, Nearest Villages- Koligudda, Harugeri, Badabyakud, Hidakal, Khanadal, Itanal.
Railway Station: Villages- Chinchali, Nagaral, Kudachi (Rural). **River:** Krishna Nadi- Nearest Villages- Soundatti, Diggewadi (Old), Jalalpur, Bhiradi, Chinchali, Nasalapur, Kudachi (Rural), Gundwad, Shiragur, Paramanandwadi, Khemalapur, Siddapur. Canal: Nearest Villages- Soundatti, Raibag (Rural), Yadrav, Kanchakarawadi, Nasalapur, Bommanal, Mantur, Nipanal, Kankanawadi, Kudachi (Rural), Yelpratti, Siddapur, Koligudda, Harugeri, Badabyakud, Alakhanur, Nilaji, Suttatti, Bekkeri, Hidakal, Nidagundi, Alagawadi, Mugalkhod, Savasuddi, Katakbhavi, Devapur-hatti, Itanal, Marakudi, Palbhavi, Sultanpur, Handigund.
Annual Rainfall: Normal Rianfall 491.7 mm.
Ground Water: Availability of the Ground Water in the Basin is 19049 H.A.M. and the utilization is 16513 H.A.M. It belongs to Over Exploited category. Depth to water level 10 to 20 meter below the ground. Most of the wells go down in summer months, according to the Ground Water Estimation Committee.
Soil: Red Soil, Black Soil.
Natural Division : It falls in the Krishna Ghatprabha Irrigated Tract of Northern Karnataka Plateau.
Administration:
Division: Belgaum. Parliamentary Constituency: 1 Chikodi. District: Belgaum. Taluka: Raybag Assembly Constituency:

5 Kudachi (SC), 6 Raybag (SC). Gram Panchayat: 33.

Fairs: Basavanna Temple Jatra: It is held at Nandikurli in the month of Shravana (July-August) every year. Nandikurli is a village ten kilometers from Raybag on the banks of a stream locally called Karkanadi. The village has temples and shrines of Basavanna, Hanumanta, Siddheswaras Beerapa, Lakshmi Taladappa, Marugadevi and Santoobai Matha. There are also two mosques and one basti which is new, but the Parshwanatha statue in the sanctum has an inscription on the pedestal of the Kalyana Chalukya times. Kudachi's Urs: Kudachi near Belgaum, about 20 kms. From Raybag located on the right bank of the river Krishna is a celebrated pilgrim centre due to its dargahs. The place name could be ascribed to flora kodachi or godachi in Kannada (Zizyphus xylupyrus, Wild). The place is described as the birth-place of Alla-ud-din, the founder of the Bahmani dynasty. It has four prominent dargahs on the bank of the Krishna. One is ascribed to a lady hazarath Masaheba Ashrafe Dojahan who came from Arabia or Baghdad about 800 years ago. The Urs is held in the month of Rajjab when about one lakh people assemble. Mayakka Jatra: It is held at Chinchali near Belgaum district in the month of Magha Poornima (January-February), for seven days.

Chinchali is a celebrated pilgrim centre with considerable antiquity and is located on the bank of the Krishna. There is a pilgrim centre of Mayakkadevi visited by hundreds daily and the village proper has a very big temple dedicated to the Goddess.It has two garbhagrihas facing each other, diagonally. The main sanctum has the image of Mayakka and the other garbhagriha has the image of Hiridevi described as the sister of Mayakka. The mukhamantapa is built in wood which has many artistic designs.

Sheik Bahudin Jisdi Urs: Raybag is located about 96 kms. from the district headquarters. The place has a Jamia Masjid named after Ranadaula Khan. This masjid has an Arabic inscription on the facade dated 1629 A.D. It states that one Bijapur officer, Amin Mustafa Khan built the mosque. This is a fine structure with an imposing central dome and two minarets in the front. Raybag has two dargahs, one ascribed to Sheikh Bahudin Jisdi also called Langoti Wali, the urs is held Annually in the month of Saffar, when about 2,000 people assemble. Another dargah is ascribed to a Hukeri Pir and no Urs is held.

Siddeshwara Temple Car Festival: It is held at Raybag near Belgaum in the months of Shravana (July-August) every year.Raybag 96 kms. from Belgaum is a place with rich antiquity.The place name is mentioned as 'Baga' or 'Puvina Baga' in several inscriptions (to distinguish it from Tadala Bage) located nearby.Taluk Raybag has been referred to as a Ghatikasthana in an inscription dated Saka 1185 from Hannikeri wherein the name of the place is mentioned as Tenkalu Bagi. Kannada poet Rajaditya hailed from this place and he mentions it as Poovina Bage under Agalenadu. The place has temples dedicated to Siddeshwara, Somanatha, Bankanatha, Hanumanta (two), Dattatreya, Vithala, Narasimha and Ambabai. The Siddeshwara temple is the gramdevata with a garbhagriha and an open mukhamantapa and is described as built by the Peshwas.The mukhamantapa has three entrances and arches connecting the pillars. The garbhagriha hasa Shivalinga.

Yellamma Jatra: Saundatti 78 kms. from Belgaum is one of the oldest towns and celebrated pilgrim centre earlier under the Bhaisas and later under the Rattas. It was the original capital of the Rattas who flourished between the tenth and the thirteenth centuries. The place has temples dedicated to Ankeshwara, Puradeshwara, Nagarkere Mallikarjuna, Venkateshwara (huge temple), Veerabhadra, Ulvi Basaveshwara, Mouneshwara and Dyamavva. The Puradeshwara temple in Later Chalukyan style is a trikutachala with three ardhamantapas, a common navaranga and two mukhamantapas. All the three garbhagrihas with pierced windows have Shivalingas.

Yellamma Jatra: It is held at Yellammanagudda in the months of Chaitra (March-April) Margashiva (November-December).Yellammanagudda five kms. from Saundatti takes its name from the deity Yellamma temple atop. This temple of the later Chalukyan style has its stelar garbhagriha intact with small relief sculptures of seated Tirthankar as at three points of the miniature decorative shikharas on the outer wall. The temple can be entered either from its front or from its two sides at points very near the garbhagriha.

Yellinga Maharaja Math: Mugalkod 21 kms. from Raybag near Belgaum is mentioned as "Mugulikodu" in the spurious Bhol plates literally meaning hill (kodu) of mugali tree (Mimiusops elengi, Linn).The place has temples dedicated to Hanumanta, Basavanna, Chennabasavanna, Beeredevaru (two).Taladappa and the Adivappana Matha. The Matha of Yellinga Maharaja who was a disciple of Siddappa Maharaj of Lachchana is a huge complex with many interesting stucco sculptures. The matha has occupied an area of nearly 23 acres and has two gudduges ascribed to Yellinga Maharaja (expired in 1986) and Siddhappa Maharaja, the guru of the former. Annual jatra is held on Sri Ramanavami.

Villages: 59 **Inhabited:** 59 **Uninhabited:** 0

Ranking	District	State	National
Area	8	92	483
Population	5	11	51
Sex Ratio	10	153	3706
Child Sex Ratio	8	166	4828

Literacy Rate	8	126	3856
Density	10	156	3279
Work Participation Rate	3	18	3730

Gram Panchayats:
Nasalapur, Soundatti, Diggewadi (Old), Bhiradi, Chinchali, Kudachi (Rural) , Shiragur , Paramanandwadi , Khemalapur, Koligudda, Harugeri, Alakhanur, Nilaji, Morab, Bekkeri, Raibag (Rural) , Nandikurali, Mekhali, Hubbarwadi, Bhendwad, Byakud, Nidagundi, Alagawadi, Hidakal, Savasuddi, Katakbhavi, Nipanal, Kankanawadi, Itanal, Mugalkhod, Palbhavi, Kappalguddi, Handigund.

Amenities:

Education: Primary School in 59 villages, Middle school in 55 villages, Matriculation or Secondary School in 20 villages, namely Soundatti, Diggewadi (Old), Bhiradi, Chinchali, Nasalapur, Bhendwad, Kankanawadi, Gundwad, Shiragur, Paramanandwadi, Khemalapur, Koligudda, Harugeri, Morab, Alagawadi, Hidakal, Mugalkhod, Savasuddi, Itanal, Handigund.

Higher Secondary or Pre University Courses or Intermediate or Junior College in 6 villages of the CD Block,, namely Chinchali, Paramanandwadi, Harugeri, Hidakal, Mugalkhod, Katakbhavi.

College in 0 village, Adult Literacy Center in 24 villages.

Medical: Hospital in 0 village, Dispensary in 2 villages, Health Center in 8 villages, Sub Center in 34 villages, Maternity and Child Welfare Center in 35 villages, Community health workers in 45 villages.

The Villages having Hospital or Dispensary or Health Center are Bhendwad, Yabaratti.

Drinking Water: Tap water in 52 villages, Tank water in 4 villages, Well water in 24 villages, Tubewell in 16 villages and more than one source in 58 villages.

Bank: Banking facility in 13 villages, namely, Soundatti, Chinchali, Nasalapur, Mekhali, Bhendwad Nipanal, Kankanawadi, Paramanandwadi, Harugeri Morab, Hidakal, Mugalkhod, Handigund.

Credit Society in 34 villages Agricultural Credit Society in 31 Non-Agricultural Credit Society in 4 villages.

Others: Power supply in 59 villages, Cinema hall in 6 villages, sport club in 0 village, Stadium or Auditorium or Community Hall in 0 village, Post Office in 43 villages.

There are 58 villages having bus facilities.

Villages with most of facilities: Soundatti Chinchali, Nasalapur, Mekhali, Bhendwad, Nipanal Kankanawadi, Paramanandwadi, Harugeri, Morab Hidakal, Mugalkhod, Handigund.

Villages without Amenities (Education): None..

Scheduled Castes: Out of the total population of 311828 persons, 55980 persons (17.95%) belong to Scheduled Castes.

The villages having less than 10% SC population are Maradi, Biranal, Mavinhonda, Girinaikwadi Kudachi (Rural), Paramanandwadi , Yelpratti Badabyakud, Suttatti, Marakudi.

The village having more than 50% SC population is None.

Sex ratio of Scheduled Caste population is 491.

Scheduled Castes Literates and Illiterates by Sex:

	Persons	Males	Females
Literate	21,998	14,142	7,856
Illiterate	33,982	14,356	19,626
Literacy rate	47.6	60.1	34.6
Graduate	765	700	65

Scheduled Castes (Dominant):

Holaya etc., Bhambi etc., Chenna Dasar etc. Samagara, Bhovi

For their cultural identity please see Appendix-I

Villages without Scheduled Castes: There are 0 village without any scheduled caste population.

Scheduled Tribes: Out of the total population of 311828 persons, 5694 persons (1.83%) belong to Scheduled Tribes.

The villages having less than 10% ST population are Soundatti, Diggewadi (Old), Jalalpur, Bhiradi Chinchali, Raibag (Rural), Kanchakarawadi, Yadrav Nasalapur, Nandikurali, Kempatti, Mekhali, Maradi Devanakatti, Budihal, Bavachi, Hubbarwadi, Nagaral Bommanal, Biranal, Byakud, Mavinhonda, Girinaikwadi Bhendwad, Mantur, Kankanawadi, Kudachi (Rural) Gundwad, Shiragur , Paramanandwadi , Khemalapur Yelpratti, Siddapur, Koligudda, Yabaratti, Harugeri Nilaji, Suttatti, Morab, Bekkeri, Nidagundi Alagawadi, Bastwad, Hidakal, Mugalkhod, Khanadal Savasuddi, Katakbhavi, Devapurhatti, Itanal Marakudi, Palbhavi, Sultanpur, Handigund Kappalguddi.

The villages having more than 50% ST population are None.

Sex ratio of Scheduled tribe population is 487.

Scheduled Tribes Literates and Illiterates by Sex:

	Persons	Males	Females
Literate	1,927	1,262	665
Illiterate	3,767	1,661	2,106
Literacy rate	41.4	53.7	28.9
Graduate	35	29	6

Scheduled Tribes (Dominant):

Naikda etc., Koli Dhor etc., Generic Tribes etc. Pardhi etc., Meda

For their cultural identity please see Appendix-II

Villages without Scheduled Tribes: There are

23 villages without any scheduled tribe population.

Literates and Illiterates by Sex (Total Population):

	Persons	Males	Females
Literate	139,758	86,615	53,143
Illiterate	172,070	73,605	98,465
Literacy rate	54	65	42
Graduate	4,512	3,997	515

Agriculture: ***Distribution of villages according to land use:*** Out of 59 villages, Total area (in hectare) is 94685, out of that 88.07 percent is cultivable and 74.57 percent of the cultivable area is irrigated.

Sources of Irrigation (Hectares): Government Canal 28020.67, Private Canal 184.14, Well without Electricity 85.06, Well with Electricity 18578.93, Tubewell without Electricity 100, Tubewell with Electricity 7615.25, Tank 0, River 7524.99, Lake 0, Waterfall 0, Others 73.13.

Villages with population of 5000 to 9999: Soundatti, Bhiradi, Raibag (Rural), Nasalapur Nandikurali, Mekhali, Nipanal, Paramanandwadi Alakhanur, Morab, Bekkeri, Nidagundi, Savasuddi Itanal, Palbhavi, Handigund.

Villages with population of 10000 and above: Chinchali, Kankanawadi, Kudachi (Rural), Harugeri Hidakal, Mugalkhod.

Distribution of Workers:

	Persons	Males	Females	WPR
Cultivators	62,317	48,569	13,748	47.95
Agricultural Labour	50,952	24,880	26,072	39.2
Household Industry	2,905	2,026	879	2.24
Other Workers	13,796	10,795	3,001	10.61
Main Workers	104,420	81,496	22,924	80.34
Marginal Workers	25,550	4,774	20,776	19.66
Total Workers	129,970	86,270	43,700	

Religion: Major Religious Communities:

	Persons	Males	Females	Sex Ratio
Hindu (86.98%)	271,230	139,244	131,986	948
Muslim (7.2%)	22,449	11,550	10,899	944
Christian (0.02%)	68	37	31	838
Sikh (0%)	-	-	-	-
Buddhists (0.03%)	102	51	51	1,000
Jain (5.47%)	17,048	8,901	8,147	915

Agewise Data:

	Persons	Males	Females	Sex Ratio
All ages	311,828	160,220	151,608	946
0-14	119,060	61,734	57,326	929
15-44	138,457	71,788	66,669	929
45-79	51,420	25,416	26,004	1023
80+	2,817	1,235	1,582	1281
Age not stated	74	47	27	574

Languages (Dominant): Kannada, Urdu, Marathi, Telugu, Hindi

Disabled Population:

	Persons	Males	Females	%
Total Disabled	3,682	2,166	1,516	
In Seeing	939	478	461	25.5
In Speech	485	284	201	13.17
In Hearing	201	103	98	5.46
In Movement	1,557	1,017	540	42.29
Mentally	500	284	216	13.58

RON

Ron C.D. Block lies in the north-eastern part of Gadag distr ict. It is a part of Ron taluka. The Block is located at a distance of 48 kms. from district headquarters (Gadag). There are 93 villages in the block with the total population of 181,141 persons. Area of the C.D. Block is 1117.84 sq. kms. It is bounded by districts Koppal and Bagalkot on north, district Koppal and taluk Gadag on south, district Koppal on east, taluk Nargund and district Dharwad on west.

Communications:

Roadways : S.H-6: Direction- Gadag to Gajendragarh, Nearest Villages- Budihal, Maranabasari, Nidagundi, Rajur, Purthageri, Kodaganur. S.H-30: Direction- Nargund to Sindhnur, Nearest Villages- Yavagala, Kaujageri, Belavan aki, Mallapur, Sandigawad, Bhasalapur, Chikkmannur, Jigal ur, Hosalli, Itagi, Bevinakatti, Sudi, Dindur, Rajur, Purthageri, Goudageri, Gogeri, Nagarashikoppa, Matarangi.

Railway Station: Villages- Holealur, Belavanaki, Mallapur.

River: Benni Halla Nadi- Nearest Villages- Menasigi, H. Mannur, Asuti, Karamadi, Megur, Bhopalapur, Malawad, Hadagali- S-Yavagal, Yavagala. Malprabha Nadi- Nearest Villages- Gulagundi, Hole Mannur, Gadgoli, Holealur, Kuruvinakoppa, Amaragol.

Annual Rainfall: Normal Rianfall 613.1 mm.

Ground Water: Availability of the Ground Water in the Basin is 6128 H.A.M. and the utilization is 1062 H.A. M. It belongs to Over Exploited category. Depth to water level 10 to 20 meter below the ground. Most of the wells go down in summer months, according to the Ground Water Estimation Committee.

Soils: Medium to deep black soils.

Natural Division : It falls in the Dharwad-Gadag Plateau of the Central Karnataka Plateau.

Administration:

Division: Belgaum. Parliamentary Constituency: 10 Haveri, 3 Bagalkot. District: Gadag. Taluka: Ron. Assembly Constituency: 67 Ron, 68 Nargund. Gram Panchayat: 30.

Regional Area Development Boards: The Bailu Seeme Area Development Board.

Villages: 93 **Inhabited:** 93 **Uninhabited:** 0

Ranking	District	State	National
Area	1	68	333
Population	1	105	1021
Sex Ratio	1	54	1662
Child Sex Ratio	3	111	3395
Literacy Rate	3	75	2542
Density	5	68	5370
Work Participation Rate	1	112	1674

Gram Panchayats:
Menasigi, Hole Mannur, Holealur, Hunagundi, Madalagiri, Hirehal, Shantagiri, Mushigeri, Lakkalakatti, Kuntoji, Gogeri, Rampur, Rajur, Sudi, Itagi, Kotabal, Kurahatti, Hullur, Asuti, Yavagala, Belavanaki, Mallapur, Chikkmannur, Nidagundi, Halakeri, Jakkali, Abbigeri, Savadi, Hadagali -S- Dambal, Kurudagi.

Amenities:

Education: Primary School in 93 villages, Middle school in 83 villages, Matriculation or Secondary School in 26 villages, namely Menasigi, Holealur, B-S-Beler, Benahal, Hullur, Asuti, Yavagala, Kaujageri, Belavanaki, Mallapur, Madalagiri, Hirehal, Shantagiri, Mushigeri, Kotabal, Savadi, Itagi, Sudi, Yarebeleri, Abbigeri, Jakkali, Nidagundi, Lakkalakatti, Nagendragad, Rajur, Gogeri.

Higher Secondary or Pre University Courses or Intermediate or Junior College in 6 villages of the CD Block,, namely Holealur, Hullur, Kaujageri, Belavanaki, Sudi, Yarebeleri.

College in 1 village, Adult Literacy Center in 0 village., College is in village, namely Holealur.

Medical: Hospital in 0 village, Dispensary in 7 villages, Health Center in 7 villages, Sub Center in 33 villages, Maternity and Child Welfare Center in 0 village, Community health workers in 10 villages.

The Villages having Hospital or Dispensary or Health Center are Menasigi, Yavagala, Mushigeri, Savadi, Itagi, Maranabasari, Rajur.

Drinking Water: Tap water in 70 villages, Tank water in 22 villages, Well water in 9 villages, Tubewell in 35 villages and more than one source in 79 villages.

Bank: Banking facility in 22 villages, namely, Menasigi, Hole Mannur, Holealur, Hullur, Asuti Bhopalapur, Malawad, Yavagala, Belavanaki Madalagiri, Hirehal, Mushigeri, Hiremannur Chikkmannur, Savadi, Itagi, Sudi, Gujmagadi Abbigeri, Jakkali, Maranabasari, Nidagundi.

Credit Society in 31 villages Agricultural Credit Society in 27 Non-Agricultural Credit Society in 7 villages.

Others: Power supply in 93 villages, Cinema hall in 2 villages, sport club in 2 villages, Stadium or Auditorium or Community Hall in 0 village, Post Office in 48 villages.

There are 87 villages having bus facilities.

Villages with most of facilities: Menasigi Holealur, Hullur, Asuti, Malawad, Yavagala Belavanaki, Madalagiri, Hirehal, Mushigeri Hiremannur, Chikkmannur, Savadi, Itagi, Sudi Gujmagadi, Abbigeri, Jakkali, Maranabasari Nidagundi.

Villages without Amenities (Education): None..

Scheduled Castes: Out of the total population of 181091 persons, 24631 persons (13.6%) belong to Scheduled Castes. The villages having less than 10% SC population are Hole Mannur, Amaragol, Hunagundi, Hullur, Melmath Megur, Bhopalapur, Hadagali- S-Yavagal, Yavagala Belavanaki, Sandigawad, Honnapur, Madalagiri Hirehal, Mushigeri, Gulaguli, Honniganur, Tallihal Kurahatti, Hosalli, Dyamhunashi, Bevinakatti Gujmagadi, Jakkali, Budihal, Maranabasari, Kalakapur Amaragatti, Nagendragad, Vadegol, Myakalzeri Kuntoji, Gogeri.

The village having more than 50% SC population is None.

Sex ratio of Scheduled Caste population is 497.

Scheduled Castes Literates and Illiterates by Sex:

	Persons	Males	Females
Literate	9,348	6,398	2,950
Illiterate	15,283	6,002	9,281
Literacy rate	46.5	63.1	29.6
Graduate	245	228	17

Scheduled Castes (Dominant):
Bhambi etc., Banjara etc., Chalavadi etc., Bhovi Madiga

For their cultural identity please see Appendix-I

Villages without Scheduled Castes: There are 0 village without any scheduled caste population.

Scheduled Tribes: Out of the total population of 181091 persons, 11379 persons (6.28%) belong to Scheduled Tribes. The villages having less than 10% ST population are Karkikatti, Gulagundi, Menasigi, Gadgoli, Holealur Kuruvinakoppa, Amaragol, Hole Hadagali, B-S-Beler Hunagundi, Benahal, Somanakatti, Hullur, Asuti Karamadi, Bhopalapur, Malawad, Hadagali- S-Yavagal Yavagala, Kaujageri, Belavanaki, Mallapur Sandigawad, Honnapur, Basarakod , Nainapur Madalagiri, Hirehal, Balagod, Sarjapur, Kalliganur Chickalagundi, Yerekurubanal, Honniganur, Mugali Mudenagudi, Arahunashi, Bhasalapur, Chikkmannur Savadi, Jigalur, Hosalli, Itagi, Dyamhunashi Bevinakatti, Sudi, Hadagali -S- Dambal, Gujmagadi

Kurudagi, Yarebeleri, Nagaral, Abbigeri, Jakkali Budihal, Kalakapur, Nidagundi, Halakeri, Rudrapur Amaragatti, Lakkalakatti, Jigeri, Vadegol Myakalzeri, Benachamatti, Kuntoji, Dindur, Rajur Purthageri, Goudageri, Gogeri, Matarangi, Chilzeri Rampur, Hirekoppa.

The villages having more than 50% ST population are None.

Sex ratio of Scheduled tribe population is 493.

Scheduled Tribes Literates and Illiterates by Sex:

	Persons	Males	Females
Literate	5,272	3,446	1,826
Illiterate	6,107	2,326	3,781
Literacy rate	55.0	71.2	38.4
Graduate	185	162	23

Scheduled Tribes (Dominant):

Naikda etc., Pardhi etc., Generic Tribes etc. Iruliga, Meda

For their cultural identity please see Appendix-II

Villages without Scheduled Tribes: There are 9 villages without any scheduled tribe population.

Literates and Illiterates by Sex (Total Population):

	Persons	Males	Females
Literate	94,574	60,115	34,459
Illiterate	86,517	30,965	55,552
Literacy rate	61	78	45
Graduate	3,695	3,186	509

Agriculture: ***Distribution of villages according to land use:*** Out of 93 villages, Total area (in hectare) is 111784, out of that 93.09 percent is cultivable and 8.47 percent of the cultivable area is irrigated.

Sources of Irrigation (Hectares): Government Canal 3178.44, Private Canal 0, Well without Electricity 0, Well with Electricity 215.68, Tubewell without Electricity 56.64, Tubewell with Electricity 4496.39, Tank 285.83, River 212.3, Lake 32, Waterfall 0, Others 335.76.

Villages with population of 5000 to 9999: Holealur, Belavanaki, Savadi, Sudi, Abbigeri Nidagundi.

Villages with population of 10000 and above: None

Distribution of Workers:

	Persons	Males	Females	WPR
Cultivators	33,874	24,430	9,444	36.75
Agricultural Labour	43,862	14,666	29,196	47.58
Household Industry	2,230	1,458	772	2.42
Other Workers	12,213	9,867	2,346	13.25
Main Workers	73,767	45,876	27,891	80.03
Marginal Workers	18,412	4,545	13,867	19.97
Total Workers	92,179	50,421	41,758	

Religion: Major Religious Communities:

	Persons	Males	Females	Sex Ratio
Hindu (91.84%)	166,323	83,594	82,729	990
Muslim (7.21%)	13,049	6,628	6,421	969
Christian (0.03%)	51	25	26	1,040
Sikh (0%)	3	1	2	2,000
Buddhists (0.01%)	10	4	6	1,500
Jain (0.11%)	197	98	99	1,010

Agewise Data:

	Persons	Males	Females	Sex Ratio
All ages	181,091	91,080	90,011	988
0-14	62,045	31,681	30,364	958
15-44	81,741	42,409	39,332	927
45-79	35,767	16,421	19,346	1178
80+	1,400	483	917	1899
Age not stated	138	86	52	605

Languages (Dominant):

Kannada, Hindi, Urdu, Telugu, Marathi

Disabled Population:

	Persons	Males	Females	%
Total Disabled	4,296	2,344	1,952	
In Seeing	2,281	1,146	1,135	53.1
In Speech	362	207	155	8.43
In Hearing	207	104	103	4.82
In Movement	1,141	707	434	26.56
Mentally	305	180	125	7.1

SAGAR

Sagar C.D. Block lies in the western part of Shimoga district. It is a part of Sagar taluka. The Block is located at a distance of 72 kms. from district headquarters (Shimoga). There are 238 villages in the block with the total population of 137,526 persons. Area of the C.D. Block is 1771.04 sq. kms. It is bounded by district Uttara Kannada and taluk Sorab on north, district Udupi and taluk Hosanagara on south, taluks Shimoga and Shikarpur on east, and district Uttara Kannada on west.

Communications:

Roadways : N.H-206: Direction- Honavar to Shimoga, Villages- Talavata, Hiremane, Talaguppa, Martur, Hunasuru, Balegaru, Shiruru, Sunkadevarakoppa, Kelaginagolagodu, Hosakoppa, Shiravanthe, Kugve, Dombe, Nadahalli Kai , Shiravala, Yalagalale, Balasagodu, Yalavarsi, Jambagar, Nadamanchale, Banadakoppa, Puradasara, Hotalasara, Hakkarekoppa, Ulluru, Nanditale, Kaspadi, Nedaravalli, Jambekoppa, Hosagunda, Iginabylum, Channashettikoppa, Hosur, Adur, Tavarehalli, Mumbalu, Malanduru, Anandapuram, Yadehalli, Achapura, Khyra, Gilalagundi, Neerakodu.
S.H-1: Direction- Tirthahalli to Shikarpur, Nearest Villages- Mumbalu, Narasipura, Gowja Swasthi, Gowja Sarkari, Bhyrapura, Malanduru, Yadehalli, Achapura.
Railway Station: Villages- Talaguppa, Kanle, Nadamanchale,

Ulluru, Balegundi, Kelaginamane, Yadehalli.
River: Varada Nadi- Nearest Villages- Kanle, Sydur, Tadagalale, Shuntikoppa, Hirenellur, Baradavalli, Kugve, Adaranthe, Masuru, Keladi, Shiravala. Sharavati Nadi- Nearest Villages- Iduvani, Kanuthota, Heravale, Karumane, Aralagodu, Kopparige, Banumane, Honnemaradu, Hebbe bylu, Baligere, Nitlihalethota, Talaguppa, Marthur, Bellanne, Devasa, Nadamalla, Kagarasu, Kippadi, Ambaragodlu, Benkatavalli, Nadavaddalli, Chikkamattur, Hunalamadike, Mattikoppa, Induvalli, Kattinakaru, Kaluru, Valagere, Kalasavalli, Hosahalli, Avade, Araballi, Brahmana Keppi ge, Chimale, Nadakeppige, Kiruvase, Baruve. Haridravati Nadi- Nearest Villages- Heggattu, Gijaga, Bilagodi, Seetur, Hebbase, Kippadi, Kolur, Kanike, Kabbanadakoppa, Godekoppa, Satalalu, Induvalli. Mavin Hole Nadi- Nearest Villages- Shuntikoppa, Chikkanellur, Beluru, Malve, Madasuru.
Reserved Forest: Nearest Villages- Balige, Kattinakaru, Channagonda, Valagere, Chadaravalli, Karani, Kodanavalli, Kudaruru, Tumari , Maluru, Adagalale, Marati, Valur, Shankanna Shanubhog, Talagodu, Chimale.
Annual Rainfall: Normal Rianfall 2175.11 mm.
Ground Water: Availability of the Ground Water in the Basin is 102 MCM and the utilization is 36.94 MCM. It belongs to Safe category. Depth to water level 5 to 10 meter below the ground. Most of the wells go down in summer months, according to the Ground Water Estimati on Committee.
Soils: Reddish to Brownish Clayey Loam.
Natural Division : It falls partly in Sagar-Sorab-Shikarp ur Rolling Humid Region and Western Ghats (Shimoga) of the Central Karnataka Plateau.
Administration:
Division: Bangalore. Parliamentary Constituency: 14 Shimoga. District: Shimoga. Taluka: Sagar. Assembly Constituency: 116 Sorab, 117 Sagar. Gram Panchayat: 35.
Regional Area Development Boards: The Maland Aera Development Board.
Fairs and Festivals : Aghoreshwara Jatra: It is held at Ikkeri inabout the month of March-April for three days. Ikkeri is a hamlet of Aralikoppa about three kilometers to the south of Sagar town and about 76 kilometers to the north of Shimoga.
Mahaganapati Car Festival: It is held at Siddhi Vinayaka temple at Sagar near Shimoga on Chaitra-Shudda Chowti (about March-April) for four days. Sagar about 72 kms. , north-west of Shimoga city, is the headquarters of the Sagar taluk and Sagar Sub-division and a railway station.
Marikamba Jatra: Marikamba jatra is held at Sagar near Shimoga in about the month of April, once in three years. Sagar is about 72 kms. north-west of Shimoga city. There is a temple dedicated to Marikamba, the jatra of which is held once in three years around the month of April. There is a mrittika brindavana of Raghavendras wami of mantralaya which is much venerated. Shri Narayana shrama founded by Brahmananda in 1944 is located on the bank of the Varada river about a kilometre from the Sagar railway station.
Rameshwara Jatra: It is held at Keladi in the month of Phalguna-Shuddha Padyami (January). Keladi is situated at a distance of six kms. north of the Sagar town. It was the first capital of an illustrious line of kings known as the Keladi Nayakas.They subsequently shifted their capital to Ikkeri and then to Bidanur. At almost the northern end of the village, there is a large courty ard which is enclosed in modern tiled verandahs. In the middle of the courtyard stand three temples; they are Rameshvara temple which is in the centre, Veerabhadra temple which is to the right and Parvati temple which is to the left. The Parvati temple is actually a separate building built apart. But the other two touch each other and have a common railing between them.
Villages: 238 **Inhabited:** 230 **Uninhabited:** 8

Ranking	District	State	National
Area	1	13	76
Population	5	140	2214
Sex Ratio	3	45	1545
Child Sex Ratio	5	60	2530
Literacy Rate	2	20	826
Density	4	118	6238
Work Participation Rate	7	171	2697

Gram Panchayats:
Aralagodu, Bhanukuli, Talavata, Talaguppa, Marthur, Kanle, Sydur, Hirenellur, Masuru, Keladi, Malve, Padavagodu, Barur, Thyagarthi, Nadakalasi, Bhimaneri , Shiravanthe, Khandika, Yadajigalemane, Kalmane, Ulluru, Hirebilagunji, Gowthampura, Achapura, Anandapuram, Yadehalli, Hosur, Bhimanakone, Avinahalli, Tumari , Channagonda, Kudaruru, Shankanna Shanubhog, Kolur, Heggodu.
Amenities:
Education: Primary School in 105 villages, Middle school in 91 villages, Matriculation or Secondary School in 24 villages, namely Bhanukuli, Talaguppa, Kanle, Sydur, Hirenellur, Shiravanthe, Kugve, Masuru, Keladi, Ulluru, Barur, Theppagodu, Laviggere, Bhimanakone, Iginabylu, Thyagarthi, Gowthampura, Anandapuram, Achapura, Kolur, Avinahalli, Yadajigalemane, Kudaruru, Tumari.

Higher Secondary or Pre University Courses or Intermediate or Junior College in 9 villages of the CD Block,, namely Talaguppa, Kugve, Barur, Bhimanakone, Gowthampura, Anandapuram, Yadehalli, Avinahalli, Kudaruru.

College in 2 villages, Adult Literacy Center in 10 villages., Colleges are in villages, namely Anandapuram, Yadehalli.

Medical: Hospital in 0 village, Dispensary in 10 villages, Health Center in 10 villages, Sub Center in 35 villages, Maternity and Child Welfare Center in 30 villages, Community health workers in 21 villages.

The Villages having Hospital or Dispensary or Health Center are Nagavalli, Aralagodu, Talaguppa, Marthur, Kanle, Sydur, Hirenellur, Madasuru, Heggodu, Anandapuram, Avinahalli, Lingadahalli, Kudaruru.

Drinking Water: Tap water in 41 villages, Tank water in 12 villages, Well water in 228 villages, Tubewell in 50 villages and more than one source in 214 villages.

Bank: Banking facility in 18 villages, namely, Talaguppa, Kanle, Hirenellur, Khandika, Masuru Keladi, Malve, Padavagodu, Ulluru, Barur Bhimanakone, Heggodu, Thyagarthi, Anandapuram Avinahalli, Channagonda, Kudaruru, Tumari.

Credit Society in 32 villages Agricultural Credit Society in 26 Non-Agricultural Credit Society in 2 villages.

Others: Power supply in 230 villages, Cinema hall in 1 village, sport club in 230 villages, Stadium or Auditorium or Community Hall in 230 villages, Post Office in 60 villages.

There are 164 villages having bus facilities.

Villages with most of facilities: Talaguppa, Kanle Hirenellur, Masuru, Keladi, Ulluru, Barur Bhimanakone, Heggodu, Thyagarthi, Anandapuram Avinahalli, Kudaruru, Tumari.

Villages without amenities (Education):
Urulagallu, Nelahari, Balige, Gudihithalu, Kanapagaru, Brahmana Ilakalale, Aravade, Bidarur, Kanuthota, Karumane, Kopparige, Honnemaradu, Baligere, Nitlihalethota, Bellanne, Arehada, Sasaravalli, Kibbachalu, Balegaru, Shiruru, Sunkadevarakoppa, Kelaginagolagodu, Hosakoppa, Dombe, Nadahalli Kai, Shettisara, Sangala, Eli, Mankodu, Kambalikoppa, Yalagalale, Balasagodu, Yalavarsi, Jambagar, Balagodu, Marasa, Marur, Kerodi, Harogoppa, Banadakoppa, Puradasara, Hotalasara, Brahmanachitratte, Hakkarekoppa, Naragodu, Halavagodu, Guthanahalli, Malla, Henagere, Mathikoppa, Mavinasara, Athavadi, Mundigesara, Hythuru, Heggattu, Gijaga, Hiremane, Kanumane, Kaspadi, Jambekoppa, Ballibylu, Chipli, Byadarakoppa, Chikkabilagunji, Thyagarthi Sarkari, Kudigere, Sampalli, Kotekoppa, Tumari Koppa, Saragunda, Gantinakoppa, Yebbodi, Tavarehalli, Nadavalli, Danandur, Kannur Sarkari, Iruvakki, Khyra, Tangalavadi, Kerehithalu, Lakkavalli, Devasa, Kesavinamane, Hedatri, Kagarasu, Seetur, Hebbase, Kippadi, Ambaragodlu, Hulakodu, Nadavaddalli, Chikkamattur, Hunalamadike, Mattikoppa, Besur, Kabbanadakoppa, Ginivara, Gulehalli, Kuruva Ri, Udri, Brahmana Bedur, Mankalale, Aralikoppa, Haleikkeri, Koppalagadde, Thirtha, Godekoppa, Satalalu, Kaptemane, Induvalli, Channagonda, Bobbige, Hosahalli, Araballi, Adagalale, Marati, Valur, Talagodu, Chimale, Nadakeppige, Kiruvase..

Scheduled Castes: Out of the total population of 138294 persons, 13836 persons (10%) belong to Scheduled Castes. The villages having less than 10% SC population are Urulagallu, Kanuru, Nagavalli, Nelahari, Balige Gudihithalu, Bhanukuli, Kanapagaru, Talakalale Brahmana Ilakalale, Muppane, Aravade, Bidarur Iduvani, Kanuthota, Heravale, Karumane, Aralagodu Kopparige, Honnemaradu, Baligere, Nitlihalethota Hiremane, Marthur, Bellanne, Arehada, Sasaravalli Kibbachalu, Hunasuru, Balegaru, Kanle, Sydur Tadagalale, Shuntikoppa, Sunkadevarakoppa, Hulegaru Hosakoppa, Shiravanthe, Baradavalli, Kugve, Dombe Nadahalli Kai , Shettisara, Adaranthe, Chikkanellur Beluru, Shiravala, Analekoppa, Malve, Sulagodu Bhimaneri, Mankodu, Kambalikoppa, Balasagodu Yalavarsi , Jambagar, Marasa, Madasuru, Marur Kerodi, Harogoppa, Banadakoppa, Puradasara Hotalasara, Brahmanachitratte, Hakkarekoppa, Ulluru Balegundi, Shiraguppe, Naragodu, Bilisiri, Jambani Mullakere, Barur, Guthanahalli, Theppagodu Shedtikere, Kerekoppa, Henagere, Athavadi Channiganathota, Mundigesara, Hythuru, Heggattu Hebbarige, Bilagodi, Malali, Kanumane, Hongodu Nanditale, Jambekoppa, Madarasanakoppa, Ballibylu Hosagunda, Iginabylu, Chipli, Byadarakoppa Chikkabilagunji, Thyagarthi Sarkari , Belandur Sampalli, Channashettikoppa, Hosur, Tumari Koppa Mumbalu, Narasipura, Nadavalli, Bhyrapura Hireharaka, Danandur, Kannur Sarkari, Iruvakki Gilalagundi, Maradavalli, Kesavinamane, Kagarasu Hebbase, Kippadi, Benkatavalli, Nadavaddalli Chikkamattur, Hunalamadike, Kuruva Ri, Avinahalli Udri, Brahmana Bedur, Yadajigalemane, Mankalale Aralikoppa, Koppalagadde, Thirtha, Godekoppa Kaptemane, Kattinakaru, Channagonda, Kaluru Valagere, Chadaravalli, Honagallu, Bobbige, Karani

Kodanavalli, Kudaruru, Kalasavalli, Hosahalli
Araballi, Maluru, Adagalale, Marati, Valur
Nadakeppige, Kiruvase.

The village having more than 50% SC population is None.

Sex ratio of Scheduled Caste population is 493.

Scheduled Castes Literates and Illiterates by Sex:

	Persons	Males	Females
Literate	6,957	4,072	2,885
Illiterate	6,879	2,943	3,936
Literacy rate	58.4	67.6.	49.0
Graduate	133	106	27

Scheduled Castes (Dominant):

Adi Karnataka, Chalavadi etc., Bhambi etc., Bhovi
Moger

For their cultural identity please see Appendix-I

Villages without Scheduled Castes: There are 72 villages without any scheduled caste population.

Scheduled Tribes: Out of the total population of 138294 persons, 3186 persons (2.3%) belong to Scheduled Tribes.

The villages having less than 10% ST population are
Urulagallu, Kanuru, Nelahari, Gudihithalu, Bhanukuli
Kanapagaru, Aravade, Mandavalli, Bidarur, Iduvani
Kanuthota, Heravale, Aralagodu, Kopparige
Honnemaradu, Baligere, Talavata, Talaguppa, Marthur
Hosahalli, Kibbachalu, Hunasuru, Balegaru, Kanle
Sydur, Tadagalale, Shuntikoppa, Hirenellur, Shiruru
Sunkadevarakoppa, Hulegaru, Hosakoppa, Shiravanthe
Baradavalli, Kugve, Dombe, Nadahalli Kai , Shettisara
Adaranthe, Masuru, Chikkanellur, Keladi, Shiravala
Analekoppa, Sangala, Eli, Malve, Sulagodu, Bhimaneri
Mankodu, Kambalikoppa, Yalagalale, Balasagodu
Yalavarsi , Jambagar, Balagodu, Marasa, Madasuru
Padavagodu, Marur, Kerodi, Nadakalasi
Brahmanamanchale, Nadamanchale, Harogoppa
Puradasara, Hotalasara, Brahmanachitratte
Hakkarekoppa, Balegundi, Shiraguppe, Naragodu
Bilisiri, Halavagodu, Jambani, Mullakere, Barur
Guthanahalli, Korlikoppa, Theppagodu, Laviggere
Malla, Neechadi, Kelaginamane, Shedtikere, Kerekoppa
Henagere, Mathikoppa, Bhimanakone, Mavinasara
Athavadi, Channiganathota, Heggodu, Honnesara
Mundigesara, Hythuru, Heggattu, Hebbarige, Gijaga
Bilagodi, Hiremane, Malali, Hongodu, Nanditale
Kaspadi, Nedaravalli, Jambekoppa, Madarasanakoppa
Ballibylu, Hosagunda, Iginabylu, Chipli
Byadarakoppa, Chikkabilagunji, Hirebilagunji
Thyagarthi, Thyagarthi Sarkari , Belandur, Kudigere
Sampalli, Kotekoppa, Channashettikoppa, Hosur, Adur
Tumari Koppa, Saragunda, Gantinakoppa, Yebbodi
Tavarehalli, Mumbalu, Narasipura, Gowthampura
Nadavalli, Bhyrapura, Hireharaka, Danandur
Kannur Sarkari, Kannur Inam, Malanduru, Anandapuram
Yadehalli, Iruvakki, Achapura, Khyra, Tangalavadi
Gilalagundi, Kerehithalu, Lakkavalli, Devasa
Kesavinamane, Hedatri , Kagarasu, Seetur, Hebbase
Kippadi, Ambaragodlu, Hulakodu, Benkatavalli
Nadavaddalli, Chikkamattur, Hunalamadike, Mattikoppa
Besur, Kolur, Kanike, Kabbanadakoppa, Ginivara
Gulehalli, Kuruva Ri, Avinahalli, Udri
Brahmana Bedur, Yadajigalemane, Mankalale
Aralikoppa, Kalmane, Haleikkeri, Koppalagadde
Lingadahalli, Thirtha, Hosur, Genasinakuni, Satalalu
Kaptemane, Induvalli, Kattinakaru, Channagonda
Kaluru, Valagere, Chadaravalli, Honagallu, Bobbige
Karani, Kodanavalli, Kudaruru, Brahmana Keppige
Maluru, Adagalale, Marati, Valur
Shankanna Shanubhog, Chimale, Nadakeppige, Kiruvase
Baruve.

The villages having more than 50% ST population are None.

Sex ratio of Scheduled tribe population is 504.

Scheduled Tribes Literates and Illiterates by Sex:

	Persons	Males	Females
Literate	1,676	994	682
Illiterate	1,510	585	925
Literacy rate	60.8	71.7	49.8
Graduate	16	14	2

Scheduled Tribes (Dominant):

Hasalaru, Gond etc., Naikda etc., Meda, Kadu Kuruba

For their cultural identity please see Appendix-II

Villages without Scheduled Tribes: There are 162 villages without any scheduled tribe population.

Literates and Illiterates by Sex (Total Population):

	Persons	Males	Females
Literate	88,453	50,364	38,089
Illiterate	49,841	19,107	30,734
Literacy rate	73	83	63
Graduate	3,445	2,565	880

Agriculture: ***Distribution of villages according to land use:*** Out of 238 villages, Total area (in hectare) is 177104, out of that 17.41 percent is cultivable and 43.63 percent of the cultivable area is irrigated.

Sources of Irrigation (Hectares): Government Canal 71.29, Private Canal 0, Well without Electricity 26, Well with Electricity 289.65, Tubewell without Electricity 9.23, Tubewell with Electricity 19.43, Tank 8543.84, River 842.15, Lake 0, Waterfall 1129.45, Others 2534.49.

Villages with population of 5000 to 9999: None

Villages with population of 10000 and above: None

Distribution of Workers:

	Persons	Males	Females	WPR
Cultivators	32,706	21,291	11,415	48.82
Agricultural Labour	17,614	7,931	9,683	26.29
Household Industry	958	670	288	1.43
Other Workers	15,709	12,481	3,228	23.45
Main Workers	56,964	40,335	16,629	85.04
Marginal Workers	10,023	2,038	7,985	14.96
Total Workers	66,987	42,373	24,614	

Religion: Major Religious Communities:

	Persons	Males	Females	Sex Ratio
Hindu (91.89%)	127,077	63,751	63,326	993
Muslim (3.35%)	4,634	2,376	2,258	950
Christian (1.31%)	1,808	944	864	915
Sikh (0.02%)	27	12	15	1,250
Buddhists (0.01%)	9	5	4	800
Jain (3.26%)	4,507	2,274	2,233	982

Agewise Data:

	Persons	Males	Females	Sex Ratio
All ages	138,294	69,471	68,823	991
0-14	39,382	20,064	19,318	963
15-44	70,779	35,457	35,322	996
45-79	26,939	13,397	13,542	1011
80+	1,120	508	612	1205
Age not stated	74	45	29	644

Languages (Dominant):
Kannada, Urdu, Marathi, Malayalam, Konkani

Disabled Population:

	Persons	Males	Females	%
Total Disabled	2,704	1,544	1,160	
In Seeing	1,165	616	549	43.08
In Speech	243	149	94	8.99
In Hearing	176	97	79	6.51
In Movement	868	546	322	32.1
Mentally	252	136	116	9.32

SAKLESHPUR

Shakleshpur C.D. Block lies in the south-western part of Hassan district. It is a part of Shakleshpur tehsil. The Block is located at a distance of 40 kms. from district headquarters (Hassan). There are 227 villages in the block with the total population of 110,456 persons. Area of the C.D. Block is 1029.83 sq. kms. It is bound ed by taluk Belur and district Chikmagalur on north, districts Dakshina Kannada and Kodagu on south, taluk Alur and district Kodagu on east, districts Dakshina Kannada and Chikmagalur on west.

Communications:

Roadways : N.H-48: Direction- managalore to Hassan, Nearest Villages- Heggadde, Kollahalli, Saklespur (Rural), Anemahal,, Devihalli, Donigal, Kumbardi Estate, Kesagan ahalli, Hallibylu, Matasagara Coffee Estate, Matasagara, Gulagalale, Gantebommanahalli, Aluvalli, Yadehalli, Bage, Ballu, Hasugavalli, Chikkanayakanahalli, Banavase. S.H-27: Direction- Kasaganahalli to Madikeri, Nearest Villages- Kesaganahalli, Hullahalli Estate, Hullahalli, Kyanahalli, Haragarahalli, Byakaravalli, Neekanahalli, Kamanahalli, Vaddarahalli, Kurubathur, Yadavarahalli, Bellur, Nidigere, Magalu, Kerodi.

Railway Station: Villages- Donigal, Ballu, Yadekumari.

River: Hemavati Nadi- Nearest Villages- Acharadi, Hadige, Madanapura, Mavinahalli, Dabbegadde, Hebbasale, Hennali, Baikere, Doddanagara, Achangi, Malali, Saklespur (Rura l), Cowdahalli, Chikkasathigala, Doddasathigala, Ramenaha lli, Halebelur, Ibbadi, Byakaravalli, Nallulli, Shanthapu ra, Kanigalamane, Vadaru , Bellur, Nidigere, Magalu. Jayaparvathi Halla Nadi- Nearest Villages- Hirimande, Kogaravalli, Hanjagodanahalli Estate, Hanjagodanahalli, Hurudi, Maragunda, Hodachahalli, Kumarahalli. Bilaha Halla Nadi- Nearest Villages- Kerodi, Thontalapura, Yeslur. Gandahalli Hole Nadi- Nearest Villages- Thadakalu, Hanase, Hanase Estate, Echalabeedu. Giri Halla Nadi- Nearest Villages- Arini, Bisle State Forest, Arini Estate. Add Hole Nadi- Nearest Villages- Balehalla, Bajumane Estate, Battekumari, Yathahalla, Arini, Bisle State Forest. Kabbinale Hole Nadi- Nearest Village- Kumarahalli.

Annual Rainfall: Normal Rianfall 2050.3 mm.

Ground Water: Availability of the Ground Water in the Basin is 72.51 H.A.M. and the utilization is 36.26 H. A.M. It belongs to Safe category. Depth to water level 2 to 10 meter below the ground. Most of the wells go down in summer months, according to the Ground Water Estimation Committee.

Soils: Red Soil, Red Sandy Soil, Mixed Soil and Silty Clay Soil.

Natural Division : It falls partly in Cauvery-Hemavati Basin and Manjrabad Ghats of the Southern Karnataka Plateau.

Administration:

Division: Mysore. Parliamentary Constituency: 16 Hassan. District: Hassan. Taluka: Sakleshpur. Assembly Constitu ency: 199 Sakleshpur (SC). Gram Panchayat: 227.

Regional Area Development Boards: The Maland Aera Development Board.

Fairs: Sakleshwaraswamy Temple Jatra: The temple Jatra held around February-March for a period of nine days at Sakleshpur town near Hassan. Sakleshpur is situated on the right bank of the Hemavathy river about 90 kms. west of Hassan town on the Bangalore-Mang alore road. The town derives its name from a temple on the bank of the river dedicated to Sakleshvara (Sakala-I shvara, i.e., the fragmentary Ishvara, the linga having a small chip or dent). The temple is a comparatively modern Dravidian building. According to a puranic account, a sakala or piece of the linga came out when someone began to cook on it inadvertantly. He then repented for his action in having damaged the linga and built a shrine for it.

Villages: 227 **Inhabited:** 222 **Uninhabited:** 5

Ranking	District	State	National
Area	3	78	410
Population	7	154	3127
Sex Ratio	1	5	418
Child Sex Ratio	2	7	755
Literacy Rate	3	38	1381
Density	2	33	6073
Work Participation Rate	8	161	1100

Gram Panchayats:

Devaladakere, Hanbal, Kyamanahalli, Hebbasale , Biradahalli, Halasulige, Udevara, Belagodu, Ballu, Bage, Malali , Anemahal, Heggadde, Kyanahalli, Byakaravalli, Kuniganahalli, Kurubathur, Valalahalli, Hongadahalla, Hethur, Igoor , Yeslur , Changadihalli , Uchangi, Vanagoor, Hosur.

Amenities:

Education: Primary School in 154 villages, Middle school in 93 villages, Matriculation or Secondary School in 19 villages, namely Hurudi, Hanbal, Heggadde, Achangi, Udevara, Belagodu, Bage, Ballu, Kurubathur, Hiriyur, Hongadahalla, Vanagoor, Hethur, Uchangi, Kalale, Changadihalli, Maragalli, Doddakundur, Yeslur.

Higher Secondary or Pre University Courses or Intermediate or Junior College in 2 villages of the CD Block,, namely Hethur, Maragalli.

College in 0 village, Adult Literacy Center in 1 village.

Medical: Hospital in 0 village, Dispensary in 8 villages, Health Center in 9 villages, Sub Center in 37 villages, Maternity and Child Welfare Center in 1 village, Community health workers in 0 village.

The Villages having Hospital or Dispensary or Health Center are Devaladakere, Kadumane Estate, Kumbardi, Chikkasathigala, Halebelur, Belagodu, Hethur, Changadihalli.

Drinking Water: Tap water in 135 villages, Tank water in 24 villages, Well water in 167 villages, Tubewell in 74 villages and more than one source in 221 villages.

Bank: Banking facility in 17 villages, namely, Devaladakere, Hanbal, Kumarahalli, Heggadde Kelagalale, Balagodu, Belagodu, Bage, Ballu Banavase, Kurubathur, Hongadahalla, Hethur Chikkallur, Uchangi, Changadihalli, Yeslur.

Credit Society in 9 villages Agricultural Credit Society in 9 Non-Agricultural Credit Society in 0 village.

Others: Power supply in 222 villages, Cinema hall in 1 village, sport club in 0 village, Stadium or Auditorium or Community Hall in 0 village, Post Office in 50 villages.

There are 134 villages having bus facilities.

Villages with most of facilities: Devaladakere Hanbal, Heggadde, Kelagalale, Belagodu, Bage Kurubathur, Hongadahalla, Hethur, Uchangi Changadihalli, Yeslur.

Villages without amenities (Education): Hirimande, Kogaravalli, Bachanahalli Avare Kadu Estate, Maragadi, Hodachahalli, Dabbegadde, Mavinakolu, Raxidi Estate, Kumarahalli, Kirehalli, Magadi, Kadabanahalli, Hasade, Hosur Estate, Saklespur (Rural), Devihalli, Kumbardi Estate, Kesaganahalli, Hullahalli Estate, Hallibylu, Iragalu, Cowdahalli, Ramenahalli, Echalvalli Estate, Matasagara Coffee Estate, Kogaravalli, Bugadahalli, Shanthapura, Kanigalamane, Sidigalale, Lakkunda, Sundavalli, Kudanahalli, Gantebommanahalli, Menasumakki, Hosakere, Kiruhunse, Kelavalli, Yadekumari, Vaddarahalli, Yadavarahalli, Echalapura, Ummathur, Bannahalli, Battekumari, Jedigadde, Boranamane, Bisle State Forest, Kumathahalli, Maragathur, Vanagoor Estate, Halliyur *, Igoor Estate, Athiganahalli, Gowdarabylu, Palahalli, Banagere, Hadalkerehalli, Hulagathur Estate, Hosakote Estate, Thadakalu, Hanase Estate, Kalale Estate, Kadlur, Sundahalli, Heggadihalli, Mathur, Saragahalli..

Scheduled Castes: Out of the total population of 111169 persons, 34417 persons (30.96%) belong to Scheduled Castes.

The villages having less than 10% SC population are Hodachahalli, Hadige Estate, Kumarahalli Kadabanahalli, Kollahalli, Kumbardi Estate Hallibylu, Iragalu, Lakkunda, Gantebommanahalli Harakanahalli, Yadekumari, Hiridanahalli Chinnahalli, Vaddarahalli, Bannahalli, Bobbanahalli Hosahalli, Balehalla, Battekumari, Yathahalla Jedigadde, Boranamane, Arini, Bisle State Forest Arini Estate, Yaragalli, Kumathahalli, Vanagoor Byagadihalli, Konabanahalli, Gowdarabylu Doddakallur, Palahalli, Goddu, Banagere, Mageri Thambalagere, Hulagathur Estate, Hanase Estate Kadlur, Manjur, Mathur.

The villages having more than 50% SC population are Hirimande, Kogaravalli, Hanjagodanahalli Estate Hanjagodanahalli, Bachanahalli Avare Kadu Estate Maragadi, Kadumane Estate, Manjanahalla Estate

Hennali, Halasulige, Hosur Estate, Malali
Saklespur (Rural), Devihalli, Kalagane
Chikkasathigala, Doddasathigala, Ramenahalli, Ibbadi
Hebbanahalli, Sundavalli, Kudanahalli, Menasumakki
Ballu, Chikkanayakanahalli, Bandihalli, Rajendrapura
Igoor Estate, Hadalkerehalli, Herur, Hosakote Estate
Thontalapura.

Sex ratio of Scheduled Caste population is 514.

Scheduled Castes Literates and Illiterates by Sex:

	Persons	Males	Females
Literate	14,442	8,397	6,045
Illiterate	19,975	8,321	11,654
Literacy rate	49.1	59.3	39.7
Graduate	136	115	21

Scheduled Castes (Dominant):

Adi Karnataka, Moger, Adi Dravida
Generic Castes etc., Banjara etc.

For their cultural identity please see Appendix-I

Villages without Scheduled Castes: There are 26 villages without any scheduled caste population.

Scheduled Tribes: Out of the total population of 111169 persons, 1476 persons (1.33%) belong to Scheduled Tribes.

The villages having less than 10% ST population are
Hirimande, Kogaravalli, Hanjagodanahalli Estate
Devaladakere, Hanjagodanahalli, Hurudi, Acharadi
Bachanahalli, Bachanahalli Avare Kadu Estate, Hanbal
Maragadi, Neekanahalli, Nelagalli, Maragunda
Hodachahalli, Achanahalli, Makkihalli, Hadige Estate
Jambardi, Agani, Kyamanahalli, Agalahatti
Mavinahalli , Dabbegadde, Mavinakolu, Raxidi Estate
Kadumane Estate, Kumarahalli, Manjanahalla Estate
Kadumane, Heggadde, Hebbasale, Ganadahcle, Hennali
Baikere, Biradahalli, Kelagalale, Magadi
Kadabanahalli, Jannapura, Doddanagara, Achangi
Hasade, Halasulige, Masuvalli, Hosur Estate
Kollahalli, Malali, Saklespur (Rural), Anemahal
Devihalli, Donigal, Kumbardi, Nadahalli
Kumbardi Estate, Kesaganahalli, Hullahalli Estate
Kalagane, Hallibylu, Iragalu, Cowdahalli
Chikkasathigala, Doddasathigala, Ramenahalli
Kabbinagadde, Echalvalli Estate
Matasagara Coffee Estate, Matasagara, Kogaravalli
Siddapura, Halebelur, Ibbadi, Janekere, Hullahalli
Kyanahalli, Bugadahalli, Aluvalli, Kadagaravalli
Kalaginamanchahalli, Haragarahalli, Byakaravalli
Arekere, Sullakki, Kamanahalli, Nallulli
Shanthapura, Kanigalamane, Balagodu, Udevara
Kesaguli, Mathigalale, Kiruvale, Hebbanahalli
Sidigalale, Sundavalli, Kudanahalli, Golagonde
Kendanamane, Gulagalale, Gantebommanahalli, Aluvalli
Kakanamane, Belagodu, Eswarahalli, Menasumakki
Yadehalli, Bage, Hosakere, Ballu, Hasugavalli
Chikkanayakanahalli, Banavase, Jammanahalli
Halekere, Harakanahalli, Kiruhunse, Vadaru
Kelavalli, Heggove, Adarvalli, Kuniganahalli
Bandihalli, Hosagadde, Rajendrapura, Yadekumari
Hiridanahalli, Chinnahalli, Bommanakere
Vaddarahalli, Kurubathur, Yadavarahalli, Bellur
Nidigere, Echalapura, Ummathur, Hadlahalli
Bannahalli, Hiriyur, Karadigala, Valalahalli
Bobbanahalli, Hosahalli, Hongadahalla, Balehalla
Battekumari, Yathahalla, Jedigadde, Markalli
Hadlahalli, Athihalli, Boranamane, Arini
Arini Estate, Mankanahalli, Yaragalli, Kumathahalli
Maragathur, Vanagoor, Vanagoor Estate, Byagadihalli
Bachalli, Hethur, Konabanahalli, Halliyur *, Hadya
Igoor Estate, Yadakere, Athiganahalli, Doddanahalli
Hennali, Gowdarabylu, Magalu, Kumbarahalli
Kothanahalli, Chikkallur, Kerodi, Doddakallur, Igoor
Chikkakundur, Lakkunda, Karagoor, Palahalli, Goddu
Kongahalli, Banagere, Mageri, Thambalagere
Hadalkerehalli, Hulagathur, Uchangi, Vodahalli
Hulagathur Estate, Herur, Hosakote, Hosakote Estate
Kowkudi, Thadakalu, Kalale, Hanase, Hanase Estate
Echalabeedu, Kalale Estate, Hosur, Kadlur, Narur
Manjur, Sundahalli, Santhahalli, Changadihalli
Heggadihalli, Maragalli, Mathur, Doddakundur
Saragahalli, Thontalapura, Yeslur.

The villages having more than 50% ST population are None.

Sex ratio of Scheduled tribe population is 505.

Scheduled Tribes Literates and Illiterates by Sex:

	Persons	Males	Females
Literate	599	365	234
Illiterate	877	365	512
Literacy rate	47.4	58.4	36.6
Graduate	12	10	2

Scheduled Tribes (Dominant):

Naikda etc., Hasalaru, Meda, Generic Tribes etc.
Malaikudi

For their cultural identity please see Appendix-II

Villages without Scheduled Tribes: There are 150 villages without any scheduled tribe population.

Literates and Illiterates by Sex (Total Population):

	Persons	Males	Females
Literate	66,785	36,781	30,004
Illiterate	44,384	17,844	26,540
Literacy rate	69	77	60
Graduate	2,181	1,549	632

Agriculture: *Distribution of villages according to land use:*

Out of 227 villages, Total area (in hectare) is 102983, out of that 46.7 percent is cultivable and 24.63 percent of the cultivable area is irrigated.

Sources of Irrigation (Hectares): Government Canal 0, Private Canal 0, Well without Electricity 1.61, Well with Electricity 5.71, Tubewell without Electricity 0, Tubewell with Electricity 0, Tank 0, River 0, Lake 0, Waterfall 0, Others 11838.32.

Villages with population of 5000 to 9999: None

Villages with population of 10000 and above: None

Distribution of Workers:

	Persons	Males	Females	WPR
Cultivators	11,399	6,985	4,414	18.79
Agricultural Labour	5,823	2,393	3,430	9.6
Household Industry	589	360	229	0.97
Other Workers	42,856	24,166	18,690	70.64
Main Workers	54,859	32,722	22,137	90.43
Marginal Workers	5,808	1,182	4,626	9.57
Total Workers	60,667	33,904	26,763	100

Religion: Major Religious Communities:

	Persons	Males	Females	Sex Ratio
Hindu (90.23%)	100,307	49,133	51,174	1,042
Muslim (5.68%)	6,314	3,203	3,111	971
Christian (2.38%)	2,650	1,346	1,304	969
Sikh (0.01%)	9	6	3	500
Buddhists (1.34%)	1,495	736	759	1,031
Jain (0.03%)	32	16	16	1,000

Agewise Data:

	Persons	Males	Females	Sex Ratio
All ages	111,169	54,625	56,544	1035
0-14	31,806	15,989	15,817	989
15-44	56,665	27,585	29,080	1054
45-79	21,760	10,650	11,110	1043
80+	865	367	498	1357
Age not stated	73	34	39	1147

Languages (Dominant):

Kannada, Tulu, Malayalam, Tamil, Urdu

Disabled Population:

	Persons	Males	Females	%
Total Disabled	1,836	995	841	
In Seeing	818	411	407	44.55
In Speech	182	101	81	9.91
In Hearing	150	71	79	8.17
In Movement	497	320	177	27.07
Mentally	189	92	97	10.29

SAMPGAON

Sampgaon C.D. Block lies in the southern part of Belgaum district. It is a part of Sampgaon taluka. The Block is located at a distance of 48 kms. from district H.Q. (Belgaum). There are 132 villages in the block with the total population of 313,220 persons. Area of the C.D. Block is 1109.67 sq. kms. It is bounded by taluk Gokak on north, distt.Dharwad on south, taluk Parasgad on east, taluks Khanapur and Belgaum on west. The headquarters Complex is located at Bail Hongal.

Communications:

Roadways : N.H-4: Direction- Belgaum to Dharwad, Nearest Villages- M.K.Hubli, Dastikoppa, Kadrolli, Hulikatti Kariyat Ambadagatti, Honnidibba, Ambadagatti, Bachanakeri, Ugarkhod, Shigihalli Kariyat, Ambadagatti, Timmapur, Kittur, Marigeri, Dombarkoppa. SH-20: Direction- Belgaum to Bagalkot, Nearest Vill.- Mohare, Nesargi, Koldur, Mekalmaradi, Kalkuppi, Som-anatti, Mattikoppa, Hogarti, Hanamana Hatti, Sutagatti. S.H-31: Direction- Bailhongal to Gokak, Nearest Villages- Nesargi, Mallapur Kariyat Nesargi, Ujjanatti, Hanabar Hatti, Sunakumpi, Vannur, Madanbhavi, Muraki Bhavi, Nagnur, Benachinamardi, Chick-Bagewadi, Tigadi, Gaddikurvinkoppa, Mardinagalapur, Kallur, Sampagaon (BAIL HONGAL), Sanikoppa, Chivatagundi, Devalapur, Bailwad.

River: Malprabha Nadi- Nearest Villages- Holihosur, Kuragund, Neginhal, Kesarkoppa, Amarapur, M.K.Hubli, Veerapur, Marganakoppa, Dastikoppa, Kadrolli, Hunshikatti, Turamari, Amatur, Korvikoppa, Wakkund, Chikkmulakur, Hiremulakur, Bevinkoppa, Holinagalapur, Gudadur, Sangolli, Garjur, Kenganoor, Jalikoppa, Arawalli, Lingadahalli, Budihal, Mugabasav, Belawadi.

Annual Rainfall: Normal Rianfall 664.5 mm.

Ground Water: Availability of the Ground Water in the Basin is 9427 H.A.M. and the utilization is 9148 H.A.M.. It belongs to Over Exploited category. Depth to water level 5 to 20 meter below the ground. Most of the wells go down in summer months, according to the Ground Water Estimation Committee.

Soil: Red Soil, Black Soil.

Natural Division : It falls in the Malaprabha Basin of the Northern Karnataka Plateau.

Administration:

Division: Belgaum. Parliamentary Constituency: 12 Uttara Kannada, 2 Belgaum. District: Belgaum. Taluka: Sampgaon. Assembly Constituency: 15 Kittur, 16 Bailhongal. Gram Panchayat.

Regional Area Development Boards: The Maland Aera Development Board.

Fairs: Adrishyananda Math Jatra: It is held in honour of Lord Adrishyappa at Kadrolli in Belgaum area in about the month of January every year. Kadrolli 19 kms. From Bailhongal is a place with considerable antiquity. The name of the place is mentioned as Kadaravalli in two records of the place dated Saka 1075 A.D. and 1098 A.D. of

Chalukyan ruler Bhuvanikamalla and Tribhuvanamalla resepectively. The name of the place ascribed to a fight (kadana) between Chennabasavanna and Kalachuri army appears to be not correct as it was so named even earlier. The place has temples of Veerabhadra, Hanumantadeva, Dyamavva and Rudradeva. Basavanna Temple Jatra: It is held at Turamari during Shivaratri (February-March) for 15 days. Turamari 35 kms. from Bailhongal located at the foot of a small flat hillock is an enchanting picnic spot. The place has temples dedicated to Ramalingeshwara, Honnatavva, Hasavanna (new), Hanumanta and Dyamavva (two). The Ramalingeshwara temple structure on the side of the hillock and the Panipeetha and the Linga appear to be Chalukyan in style. Ishwara Temple Car Festival: It is held on Vishaka Poornima (April) at Mugatkhan Hubil near Belgaum. Mugutkhan Hubli 26 kms. from Bailhongal, is a place on the Bangalore-Pune highway. The place is named after Bijapur officer Mugutkhan who died here. The place appears in a Devagiri Yadava Copper place dated 1249 wherein, it is stated that a minister reigning at Mudgal granted lands in Bagewadi village in the Hubballi-12 unit. The place has temples dedicated to Ashwathanarasimha, Ishwara, Vithoba, Kamleshwara and Gramadevte. Siddeshwara Temple Jatra: It is held at Siddhanakolla near Belgaum around the month of December. Siddhanakolla, a quiet and enchanting place three kilometres from Kallur, is situated at the bottom of a huge steep rock of a long hill range. The cave opening is only about one square metre and the area in front of it is about three square metres with a perennial source of water trickling from the rock. Veerabhadra Jatra: It is held at Kadrolli near Belgaum around the month of March-April every year. Kadrolli 19 kms. from Bailhongali is a place with considerable antiquity. The name of the place is mentioned as Kadaravalli in two records of the place dated Saka 1075 A.D. and 1098 A.D. of Chalukyan ruler Bhuvanaikamalla and Tribhuvanamalla respectively.

Villages: 132 **Inhabited:** 131 **Uninhabited:** 1

Ranking	District	State	National
Area	7	70	339
Population	4	8	47
Sex Ratio	4	95	2505
Child Sex Ratio	5	142	4083
Literacy Rate	4	79	2608
Density	9	132	3723
Work Participation Rate	5	29	3157

Gram Panchayats:

Deshanur, Hanabar Hatti, Vannur, Mekalmaradi, Nesargi, Muraki Bhavi, Sutagatti, Hannikeri, Marikatti, Chick-Bagewadi, Tigadi, Bhavihal, Nagnur, Bailwad, Chivatagundi, Sampagaon, Mardinagalapur, M.K.Hubli, Holihosur, Neginhal, Devalapur, Amatur, Anigol, Wakkund, Udikeri, Belawadi, Kenganoor, Sangolli, Pattihal K.B., Holinagalapur, Turamari, Hunshikatti, Kadrolli, Dastikoppa, Devarashigihalli, Ambadagatti, Kalabhavi, Khodanapur, Hirenandihalli, Ugarkhod, Tigadolli, Bailur, Degaon, Kulavalli, Nichanaki, Kittur, Awaradi, Turakarshigihalli, Budrakatti, Govanakoppa, Dodawad.

Amenities:

Education: Primary School in 130 villages, Middle school in 100 villages, Matriculation or Secondary School in 41 villages, namely Deshanur, Nesargi, Mallapur Kariyat Nesargi, Hanabar Hatti, Hoskoti, Mastamaradi, Vannur, Mekalmaradi, Sutagatti, Muraki Bhavi, Nagnur, Hannikeri, Marikatti, Chick-Bagewadi, Tigadi, Sampagaon (Bail Hongal), Neginhal, M.K.Hubli, Devarashigihalli, Hunshikatti, Turamari, Kalabhavi, Ambadagatti, Tigadolli, Hirenandihalli, Degaon, Kittur, Bailwad, Devalapur, Wakkund, Bevinkoppa, Sangolli, Kenganoor, Mugabasav, Udikeri, Belawadi, Pattihal K.B., Turakarshigihalli, Budrakatti, Chikkabellikatti, Dodawad.

Higher Secondary or Pre University Courses or Intermediate or Junior College in 10 villages of the CD Block,, namely Nesargi, Vannur, Neginhal, M.K.Hubli, Kittur, Bailwad, Devalapur, Wakkund, Belawadi, Dodawad. College in 4 villages, Adult Literacy Center in 4 villages., Colleges are in villages, namely Nesargi, Kittur, Belawadi, Dodawad.

Medical: Hospital in 0 village, Dispensary in 7 villages, Health Center in 14 villages, Sub Center in 44 villages, Maternity and Child Welfare Center in 8 villages, Community health workers in 89 villages.

The Villages having Hospital or Dispensary or Health Center are Yaragoppa, Marikatti, Sampagaon (Bail Hongal), Turamari, Ambadagatti, Bailwad, Wakkund.

Drinking Water: Tap water in 112 villages, Tank water in 8 villages, Well water in 25 villages, Tubewell in 13 villages and more than one source in 124 villages.

Bank: Banking facility in 15 villages, namely, Deshanur, Nesargi, Vannur, Nagnur Sampagaon (Bail Hongal), Neginhal, Kesarkoppa Khodanapur, Ugarkhod, Dematti, Bailur, Kittur Sangolli, Udikeri, Dodawad.

Credit Society in 63 villages Agricultural Credit Society in 57 Non-Agricultural Credit Society in 10 villages.

Others: Power supply in 131 villages, Cinema hall in 6 villages, sport club in 0 village, Stadium or Auditorium or Community Hall in 0 village, Post Office in 68 villages.
There are 127 villages having bus facilities.
Villages with most of facilities: Deshanur Nesargi, Vannur, Nagnur, Sampagaon (Bail Hongal) Neginhal, Kesarkoppa, Khodanapur, Ugarkhod, Bailur Kittur, Sangolli, Udikeri, Dodawad.
Villages without amenities (Education): Ujjanatti..
Scheduled Castes: Out of the total population of 313061 persons, 19783 persons (6.32%) belong to Scheduled Castes.
The villages having less than 10% SC population are Deshanur, Mohare, Nesargi, Koldur Mallapur Kariyat Nesargi, Hanabar Hatti, Gajaminhal Hoskoti, Mastamaradi, Sunakumpi, Vannur, Mekalmaradi Kalkuppi, Somanatti, Madanbhavi, Mattikoppa, Hogarti Hanamana Hatti, Sutagatti, Bairanatti, Yaraguddi Lakkundi, Muraki Bhavi, Nagnur, Bhavihal, Yaragoppa Jakkanaikanakoppa, Hannikeri, Hiremele, Marikatti Ganikoppa, Shigihalli Kariyat Sampagaon Giriyal Kariyat Bagewadi, Benachinamardi Chick-Bagewadi, Gaddikurvinkoppa, Mardinagalapur Holihosur, Kuragund, Pattihal Kariyat Sampagaon Sampagaon (Bail Hongal), Yaradal, Kesarkoppa Amarapur, M.K.Hubli, Veerapur, Dastikoppa, Kadrolli Hunshikatti, Turamari, Kadatnal, Savatagi Khodanapur, Kalabhavi, Kotabagi Hulikatti Kariyat Ambadagatti, Honnidibba Ambadagatti, Ugarkhod, Dematti, Chikkanadihalli Hirenandihalli, Jamalur, Metyal, Awaradi Mallapur Kariyat Ambadagatti Shigihalli Kariyat Ambadagatti, Degaon, Channapur Kittur, Yettinkeri, Shivanur, Marigeri, Dombarkoppa Honnapur, Kulavalli, Katri Daddi, Sanikoppa Chivatagundi, Bailwad, Devalapur, Amatur, Anigol Korvikoppa, Wakkund, Chikkmulakur, Bevinkoppa Gudadur, Sangolli, Arawalli, Lingadahalli, Budihal Mugabasav, Udikeri, Belawadi, Pattihal K.B. Turakarshigihalli, Kadasagatti, Bidaragaddi Budrakatti, Govanakoppa, Chikkabellikatti, Gudikatti Dodawad.
The village having more than 50% SC population is None.
Sex ratio of Scheduled Caste population is 488.
Scheduled Castes Literates and Illiterates by Sex:

	Persons	Males	Females
Literate	8,261	5,447	2,814
Illiterate	11,522	4,680	6,842
Literacy rate	50.2	64.5	35.0
Graduate	217	171	46

Scheduled Castes (Dominant):
Bhambi etc., Madiga, Chalavadi etc., Bhovi, Korama
For their cultural identity please see Appendix-I
Villages without Scheduled Castes: There are 10 villages without any scheduled caste population.
Scheduled Tribes: Out of the total population of 313061 persons, 28467 persons (9.09%) belong to Scheduled Tribes.
The villages having less than 10% ST population are Deshanur, Ujjanatti, Mekalmaradi, Mattikoppa Sutagatti, Bairanatti, Yaraguddi, Muraki Bhavi Nagnur, Bhavihal, Yaragoppa, Hiremele Benachinamardi, Chick-Bagewadi, Tigadi Gaddikurvinkoppa, Mardinagalapur, Kallur, Holihosur Pattihal Kariyat Sampagaon, Sampagaon (Bail Hongal) Yaradal, Neginhal, Kesarkoppa, Amarapur, M.K.Hubli Veerapur, Marganakoppa, Dastikoppa, Kadrolli Hunshikatti, Turamari, Kadatnal, Kulamanatti Savatagi, Khodanapur, Kotabagi Hulikatti Kariyat Ambadagatti, Ambadagatti, Tegur Tigadolli, Ugarkhod, Dematti, Chikkanadihalli Hirenandihalli, Jamalur, Metyal, Awaradi Mallapur Kariyat Ambadagatti, Bassapur Shigihalli Kariyat Ambadagatti, Timmapur, Basarkhod Degulhalli, Bailur, Degaon, Giriyal-Kariyat Channapur, Kittur, Yettinkeri, Nichanaki, Shivanur Marigeri, Dombarkoppa, Honnapur, Sanikoppa Chivatagundi, Amatur, Anigol, Korvikoppa, Wakkund Chikkmulakur, Hiremulakur, Bevinkoppa, Holinagalapur Sangolli, Garjur, Kenganoor, Mugabasav, Udikeri Belawadi, Pattihal K.B., Siddasamudra Hirebellikatti, Turakarshigihalli, Kadasagatti Bidaragaddi, Budrakatti, Govanakoppa Chikkabellikatti, Dodawad, Nanagundikoppa.
The villages having more than 50% ST population are None.
Sex ratio of Scheduled tribe population is 491.
Scheduled Tribes Literates and Illiterates by Sex:

	Persons	Males	Females
Literate	10,509	7,158	3,351
Illiterate	17,958	7,330	10,628
Literacy rate	44.4	59.4	28.8
Graduate	117	99	18

Scheduled Tribes (Dominant):
Naikda etc., Meda, Koli Dhor etc., Kadu Kuruba Bhil etc.
For their cultural identity please see Appendix-II
Villages without Scheduled Tribes: There are 23 villages without any scheduled tribe population.
Literates and Illiterates by Sex (Total Population):

	Persons	Males	Females

Literate	161,996	98,771	63,225
Illiterate	151,065	60,168	90,897
Literacy rate	61	73	48
Graduate	4,886	3,993	893

Agriculture: ***Distribution of villages according to land use:*** Out of 132 villages, Total area (in hectare) is 110967, out of that 76.25 percent is cultivable and 18 percent of the cultivable area is irrigated.

Sources of Irrigation (Hectares): Government Canal 1781.38, Private Canal 0, Well without Electricity 7.98, Well with Electricity 706.91, Tubewell without Electricity 15.22, Tubewell with Electricity 11782.79, Tank 763.26, River 127.52, Lake 0, Waterfall 0, Others 46.53.

Villages with population of 5000 to 9999:
Deshanur, Nesargi, Nagnur, Tigadi
Sampagaon (Bailhongal), Neginhal, Kadrolli, Wakkund
Belawadi, Dodawad.

Villages with population of 10000 and above:
M.K.Hubli, Kittur.

Distribution of Workers:

	Persons	Males	Females	WPR
Cultivators	49,846	38,859	10,987	35.28
Agricultural Labour	65,172	29,112	36,060	46.12
Household Industry	5,856	3,728	2,128	4.14
Other Workers	20,429	16,770	3,659	14.46
Main Workers	112,331	79,892	32,439	79.5
Marginal Workers	28,972	8,577	20,395	20.5

Total Workers	141,303	88,469	52,834	

Religion: Major Religious Communities:

	Persons	Males	Females	Sex Ratio
Hindu (87.14%)	272,788	138,439	134,349	970
Muslim (9.7%)	30,355	15,386	14,969	973
Christian (0.09%)	284	135	149	1,104
Sikh (0.01%)	19	13	6	462
Buddhists (0.02%)	48	27	21	778
Jain (2.59%)	8,097	4,198	3,899	929

Agewise Data:

	Persons	Males	Females	Sex Ratio
All ages	313,061	158,939	154,122	970
0-14	105,958	54,500	51,458	944
15-44	143,478	73,155	70,323	961
45-79	60,631	29,907	30,724	1027
80+	2,845	1,287	1,558	1211
Age not stated	149	90	59	656

Languages (Dominant):
Kannada, Urdu, Telugu, Marathi, Coorgi/Kodagu

Disabled Population:

	Persons	Males	Females	%
Total Disabled	5,874	3,380	2,494	
In Seeing	1,728	839	889	29.42
In Speech	600	348	252	10.21
In Hearing	379	200	179	6.45
In Movement	2,611	1,678	933	44.45
Mentally	556	315	241	9.47

SANDUR

Sandur C.D. Block lies in the central part of Bellary district. It is a part of Sandur taluka. The Block is located at a distance of 48 kms. from district headquarters (Bellary). There are 89 villages in the block with the total population of 157,003 persons. Area of the C.D. Block is 1228.23 sq. kms. It is bounded by taluk Hospet on north, taluk Kudligi on south, taluk Bellary and district Chitradurga on east, taluks Hospet and Hagari Bommanahalli on west. It has common boundary with the state of Andhara Pradesh on east.

Communications:

Roadways : N.H-13: Direction- Hospet to Chitradurga, Nearest Villages- Hulikunta 73. N.H-63: Direction- Hospet to Bellary, Nearest Villages- Kurekuppa, Toranagal. S.H-29: Direction- Gangawati to Bellary, Nearest Village- Daroji. S.H-40: Direction-Kudligi to Torangal, Nearest Villages- North Eastern Block(F), Swamymalai Block (F), Somalapur, Bandri, Chikkakeriyaginahalli, Hirekeriyaginahalli, Yeswanthanagar, Krishnanagar, Taranagar, Sankarapur, Bhujanganagar, Kurekuppa, Toranagal, Vaddu, Nagalapur, Shro.Gangalapur, Gowripur, Bannihatti.

Railway Station: Villages- Swamymalai Block (F), Swamy Halli, Yerriahanahalli, Yeswanthanagar, Kurekuppa, Daroji, Toranagal.

River: Narihalla Nadi- Nearest Villages- Talur, Shro. Basapur, Kurekuppa, Vaddu, Nagalapur, Shro.Gangalapur, Bannihatti.

Canal: Nearest Villages- Kurekuppa, Daroji, Toranagal.

Reserved Forest: (Donimalai): Nearest Villages- Tonisigeri, Muraripur, Taranagar, Sankarapur, Bhujanganagar, Narasingapur, Ranjitpur, Vittalnagar, Deogiri, Narayanapur, Joga, Talur, Nagalapur, Shro.Gangalapur, Gowripur, Kodalu, Antapur, Marutala, Lingadahalli, Ayyanahalli, Ubbalagundi, Malapur, Avinamadugu, Rampur, Rajapur. Thimlapur. (Kakkuppi R.F.): Nearest Villages- Sovenahalli, Agrahara, Genatikatte, Chornur, Devarabudenahalli. (Metriki R.F.): Nearest Villages- Yerabanahalli, Chikkantapur, Appalapur, Antapur, Avinamadugu, Thumati, Vittalapur, Gangalapur, Rampur, Rajapur, 55 Mallapura, Timlapur, Metriki, Gundlahalli, Ramasagar, Lakkalahalli, Hanumanahalli. (North Eastren Block R.F.): Nearest Villages- Siddapur, Radhanagar, Suseelnagar, Dowlatpur, Krishnanagar, Muraripur, Sankarapur, Bhujanganagar, Joga. (Ramgad R.F.): Nearest Villages- Ramanmalai Block (F), Swamymalai Block (F), Ramgad, Jaisingapur, Emmihatti, Siddapur, Radhanagar, Suseelnagar, Dowlatpur, Krishnanagar. (Siva

pura R.F.): Nearest Villages- Bandri, Mallapura 72, Hulik unta 73, Chikkakeriyaginahalli, Hirekeriyaginahalli.
(Somalapur R.F.): Nearest Villages- Somalapur, Bandri, Nidugurthi, Mallapura 72, Ankammanahal, Yeswanthanagar.
(Toranagal R.F.): Nearest Village- Toranagal.
Annual Rainfall: Normal Rianfall 510.46 mm.
Ground Water: Availability of the Ground Water in the Basin is (Information not avablable) H.A.M. and the utilization is (Information not avablable) H.A.M.
It belongs to (Information not avablable) category.
Depth to water level 5 to 20 meter below the ground.
Most of the wells go down in summer months, according to the Ground Water Estimation Committee.
Soils: Black and Red Sandy Soils.
Natural Division : It falls in Sandur Highlands of the Central Karnataka Plateau.
Administration:
Division: Gulbarga. Parliamentary Constituency: 9 Bellary (ST). District: Bellary. Taluka: Sandur. Assembly Const ituency: 95 Sandur (ST). Gram Panchayat: 21.
Regional Area Development Boards: The Hyderabad - Karnataka Area Development Board.
Border Villages: (State: Andhra Pradesh)- Thumati, Vitta lapur, Gangalapur, Metriki, Gundlahalli, Lakkalahalli.
Fairs and Festovals: Kumaraswami Festival: The famous picturesque Kumaraswami temple is about 12 kms. away from the Sandur town near Bellary and is situated on the wooded slopes at the head of a ravine. A legend says that Karthikeya (Kumaraswami) on his way to the south from Kailasa rested here with sage Agastya. Twice in five years, the 'Mahayatra' of the deity is celebrated and this attracts pilgrims from various parts. According to a legend, Kumaraswami, the son of Shiva, killed a demon named Tarakasura who dwelt on the Sandur hills. There are a few sati stones and several inscriptions in the temple. Among the epigraphs, the most interesting one is of the time of the Hoisala king Ballala II dated in the year 1206 A.D. It refers to gifts made formerly for offerings to the Shanmukha temple by the Rashtrakuta king Krishna III.

Villages: 89 **Inhabited:** 76 **Uninhabited:** 13

Ranking	District	State	National
Area	3	56	263
Population	5	124	1650
Sex Ratio	7	145	3437
Child Sex Ratio	4	87	2897
Literacy Rate	4	155	4760
Density	6	92	5861
Work Participation Rate	7	150	2157

Gram Panchayats:
Suseelnagar, Krishnanagar, Bhujanganagar , Taranagar, Vaddu, Kurekuppa, Daroji, Toranagal, Antapur, Vittalapur, Metriki, Narasingapur , Deogiri, Gollalingammanahalli, Bommagatta, Chornur, Sovenahalli, Kalingeri, Bandri, Nidugurthi, Yeswanthanagar.
Amenities:
Education: Primary School in 50 villages, Middle school in 43 villages, Matriculation or Secondary School in 14 villages, namely Bandri, Gollalingammanahalli, Sovenahalli, Chornur, Bommagatta, Yeswanthanagar, Taranagar, Bhujanganagar, Ranjitpur, Deogiri, Kurekuppa, Daroji, Toranagal, Vittalapur.
Higher Secondary or Pre University Courses or Intermediate or Junior College in 0 village of the CD Block, College in 0 village, Adult Literacy Center in 2 villages.
Medical: Hospital in 2 villages, Dispensary in 12 villages, Health Center in 5 villages, Sub Center in 28 villages, Maternity and Child Welfare Center in 3 villages, Community health workers in 3 villages.
The Villages having Hospital or Dispensary or Health Center are Bandri, Gollalingammanahalli, Chornur, Yeswanthanagar, Jaisingapur, Suseelnagar, Karthikeshwar, Deogiri, Daroji, Toranagal, Antapur, Ubbalagundi, Metriki.
Drinking Water: Tap water in 58 villages, Tank water in 37 villages, Well water in 28 villages, Tubewell in 25 villages and more than one source in 64 villages.
Bank: Banking facility in 7 villages, namely, Chornur, Shro.Oblapur, Taranagar, Daroji, Toranagal Antapur, Metriki.
Credit Society in 8 villages Agricultural Credit Society in 8 Non-Agricultural Credit Society in 2 villages.
Others: Power supply in 76 villages, Cinema hall in 0 village, sport club in 76 villages, Stadium or Auditorium or Community Hall in 76 villages, Post Office in 12 villages.
There are 62 villages having bus facilities.
Villages with most of facilities: Chornur Taranagar, Daroji, Toranagal, Antapur, Metriki.
Villages without amenities (Education): Somalapur, Mallapura 72, Ankammanahal, Kanakapur .B.C., Jodikasinayakanahalli, Thippanamaradi, Shro.Oblapur, Devarabudenahalli, Ramgad, Vittalnagar, Shro.Gangalapur, Gowripur, Bannihatti, Yerabanahalli, Marutala, Lingadahalli, Malapur, Avinamadugu, Thumati, Gangalapur, Rampur, 55 Mallapura, Thimlapur, Gundlahalli, Ramasagar, Lakkalahalli..
Scheduled Castes: Out of the total population of 156998 persons, 27616 persons (17.59%) belong to Scheduled Castes. The villages having less than 10% SC population are

Somalapur, Mallapura 72, Hirekeriyaginahalli Ankammanahal, Tonisigeri, Kanakapur .B.C. Jodikasinayakanahalli, Thippanamaradi, Agrahara Shro.Oblapur, Yeswanthanagar, Siddapur, Krishnanagar Muraripur, Shro.Basapur, Vaddu, Shro.Gangalapur Gowripur, Yerabanahalli, Lingadahalli, Malapur Avinamadugu, 55 Mallapura, Metriki, Gundlahalli Ramasagar.

The village having more than 50% SC population is None.

Sex ratio of Scheduled Caste population is 496.

Scheduled Castes Literates and Illiterates by Sex:

	Persons	Males	Females
Literate	8,454	5,777	2,677
Illiterate	19,162	8,150	11,012
Literacy rate	38.7	52.5	24.6
Graduate	136	125	11

Scheduled Castes (Dominant):

Adi Karnataka, Bhovi, Banjara etc., Madiga, Koracha

For their cultural identity please see Appendix-I

Villages without Scheduled Castes: There are 17 villages without any scheduled caste population.

Scheduled Tribes: Out of the total population of 156998 persons, 46693 persons (29.74%) belong to Scheduled Tribes.

The villages having less than 10% ST population are Devaramallapur, Gowripur, Dowlatpur, Krishnanagar Bhujanganagar, Ranjitpur, Daroji, Vaddu, Nagalapur Shro.Gangalapur, Bannihatti, Kodalu, Yerabanahalli Marutala, Vittalapur, Thimlapur.

The villages having more than 50% ST population are Mallapura 72, Hulikunta 73, Hirekeriyaginahalli Ankammanahal, Tonisigeri, Kanakapur .B.C. Yerriahanahalli, Jodikasinayakanahalli, Agrahara Shro.Oblapur, Ramgad, Siddapur, Muraripur Narasingapur, Vittalnagar, Gowripur, Lingadahalli Malapur, 55 Mallapura, Ramasagar, Lakkalahalli.

Sex ratio of Scheduled tribe population is 492.

Scheduled Tribes Literates and Illiterates by Sex:

	Persons	Males	Females
Literate	14,252	9,531	4,721
Illiterate	32,441	14,191	18,250
Literacy rate	37.8	49.8	25.4
Graduate	158	135	23

Scheduled Tribes (Dominant):

Naikda etc., Generic Tribes etc., Gowdalu, Meda Soligaru

For their cultural identity please see Appendix-II

Villages without Scheduled Tribes: There are 16 villages without any scheduled tribe population.

Literates and Illiterates by Sex (Total Population):

	Persons	Males	Females
Literate	62,698	40,617	22,081
Illiterate	94,300	39,847	54,453
Literacy rate	49	61	35
Graduate	2,094	1,575	519

Agriculture: *Distribution of villages according to land use:*

Out of 89 villages, Total area (in hectare) is 122823, out of that 32.02 percent is cultivable and 17.72 percent of the cultivable area is irrigated.

Sources of Irrigation (Hectares): Government Canal 1574.81, Private Canal 16.19, Well without Electricity 205.45, Well with Electricity 1020.93, Tubewell without Electricity 85.51, Tubewell with Electricity 1522.09, Tank 997.04, River 0, Lake 0, Waterfall 0, Others 1548.47.

Villages with population of 5000 to 9999:

Bandri, Chornur, Yeswanthanagar, Taranagar, Daroji Toranagal, Vaddu.

Villages with population of 10000 and above:

Kurekuppa.

Distribution of Workers:

	Persons	Males	Females	WPR
Cultivators	25,084	19,349	5,735	33.69
Agricultural Labour	26,843	7,332	19,511	36.05
Household Industry	1,218	721	497	1.64
Other Workers	21,314	16,796	4,518	28.63
Main Workers	57,274	40,758	16,516	76.92
Marginal Workers	17,185	3,440	13,745	23.08
Total Workers	74,459	44,198	30,261	

Religion: Major Religious Communities:

	Persons	Males	Females	Sex Ratio
Hindu (89.15%)	139,967	71,523	68,444	957
Muslim (9.94%)	15,601	8,169	7,432	910
Christian (0.3%)	468	267	201	753
Sikh (0.02%)	35	28	7	250
Buddhists (0.01%)	15	7	8	1,143
Jain (0.02%)	28	15	13	867

Agewise Data:

	Persons	Males	Females	Sex Ratio
All ages	156,998	80,464	76,534	951
0-14	62,945	32,175	30,770	956
15-44	69,422	36,309	33,113	912
45-79	23,574	11,478	12,096	1054
80+	924	428	496	1159
Age not stated	133	74	59	797

Languages (Dominant):

Kannada, Urdu, Telugu, Hindi, Tamil

Disabled Population:

	Persons	Males	Females	%
Total Disabled	2,949	1,660	1,289	
In Seeing	1,424	738	686	48.29

In Speech	269	158	111	9.12
In Hearing	125	73	52	4.24

In Movement	895	563	332	30.35
Mentally	236	128	108	8

SAVANUR

Savanur C.D. Block lies in the northern part of Haveri district. It is a part of Savanur taluka. The Block is located at a distance of 23 kms. from district headqu arters (Haveri). There are 65 villages in the block with the total population of 108,407 persons. Area of the C.D. Block is 533.54 sq. kms. It is bounded by districts Dharwad, Gadag and taluk Shiggaon on north, taluk Haveri on south, district Gadag and taluk Haveri on east, taluks Hangal and Shiggaon on west.

Communications:

Roadways : N.H-4: Direction- Dharwad to Bangalore, Nearest Villages- Savoor, Tevaramellihalli, Kunimellihalli. S.H-6: Direction- Shiggaon to Gadag, Nearest Villages- Allipura, Bevinahalli, Gundur, Hosa Neeralgi-M-Karadgi (New), Savanur (Rural), Yelavigi, Huvinshigli, Paramawadi.

Railway Station: Nearest Villages- Yelavigi, Hattimattur, Jallapur.

River: Varada Nadi- Nearest Villages- Tondur, Melligatti, Halasur, Kunimellihalli, Mannangi, Hiremaralihalli, Chikkamaralihalli, Dombaramattur, Kalasur, Mantagani, Kalakoti, Hiremugadur, Neeralagi-Mahal-Karadgi , Chikka mugadur, Aralihalli.

Reserved Forest: Nearest Villages- Hesarur, Siddapur, Hiremaralihalli.

Annual Rainfall: Normal Rianfall 592 mm.

Ground Water: Availability of the Ground Water in the Basin is 45.00 MCM and the utilization is 14.17 MCM It belongs to Over Expoited category. Depth to water level 10 to 20 meter below the ground. Most of the wells go down in summer months, according to the Ground Water Estimation Committee.

Soils: Red Sandy Soil, Medium Soil, Deep Black Soil, Red Loamy Soil and Lateritic Soil.

Natural Division : It falls partly in Barada Basin of the Central Karnataka Plateau.

Administration:

Division: Belgaum. Parliamentary Constituency: 10 Haveri. District: Haveri. Taluka: Savanur. Assembly Constituency: 83 Shiggaon, 84 Haveri (SC). Gram Panchayat: 20.
Regional Area Development Boards: The Maland Aera Development Board.

Villages: 65 **Inhabited:** 65 **Uninhabited:** 0

Ranking	District	State	National
Area	6	160	1371
Population	6	158	3201
Sex Ratio	6	166	4287
Child Sex Ratio	6	113	3433
Literacy Rate	7	86	2756
Density	3	76	4694
Work Participation Rate	7	75	1855

Gram Panchayats:
Mantrodi, Karadagi, Chillur Badni, Yelavigi, Huvinshigli, Hesarur, Kadakola, Shirabadgi, Teggihalli, Kurubaramallur, Huralikuppi, Jallapur, Hattimattur, Ichangi, Hiremaralihalli, Tondur, Tevaramellihalli, Kunimellihalli, Kalasur, Hiremugadur.

Amenities:

Education: Primary School in 64 villages, Middle school in 56 villages, Matriculation or Secondary School in 13 villages, namely Karadagi, Mantrodi, Huralikuppi, Tevaramellihalli, Kunimellihalli, Yelavigi, Huvinshigli, Shirabadgi, Kadakola, Hattimattur, Jallapur, Dombaramattur, Hiremugadur.
Higher Secondary or Pre University Courses or Intermediate or Junior College in 2 villages of the CD Block,, namely Karadagi, Hattimattur.
College in 0 village, Adult Literacy Center in 0 village.

Medical: Hospital in 0 village, Dispensary in 3 villages, Health Center in 4 villages, Sub Center in 23 villages, Maternity and Child Welfare Center in 0 village, Community health workers in 1 village.
The Villages having Hospital or Dispensary or Health Center are Kadakola, Ichangi, Kalasur.

Drinking Water: Tap water in 24 villages, Tank water in 0 villages, Well water in 0 village, Tubewell in 64 villages and more than one source in 62 villages.

Bank: Banking facility in 7 villages, namely, Huralikuppi, Tevaramellihalli, Yelavigi, Kadakola Ichangi, Hattimattur, Hiremugadur.
Credit Society in 16 villages Agricultural Credit Society in 15 Non-Agricultural Credit Society in 3 villages.

Others: Power supply in 65 villages, Cinema hall in 0 village, sport club in 0 village, Stadium or Auditorium or Community Hall in 0 village, Post Office in 27 villages.
There are 63 villages having bus facilities.

Villages with most of facilities: Huralikuppi Tevaramellihalli, Yelavigi, Kadakola, Ichangi Hattimattur, Hiremugadur.

Villages without amenities (Education):
Savanur (Rural)..

Scheduled Castes: Out of the total population of 108322 persons, 16999 persons (15.69%) belong to Scheduled Castes. The villages having less than 10% SC population are Madapur, Gonala, Karadagi, Mantrodi, Chillur Hosa Neeralgi-M-Karadgi (New), Teggihalli

Savanur (Rural), Fakir Nandihalli, Chikkaboodihal Bardur, Challal, Tallihalli, Hosalli-M-Karadgi Melligatti, Kurubaramallur, Kalmadavu Tevaramellihalli, Halasur, Kunimellihalli, Mannangi Yelavigi, Huvinshigli, Basavankoppa, Siddapur Naikerur, Honikop, Shirabadgi, Vadnikoppa, Kadakola Kaliwal, Jallapur, Ichala Yellapur, Kalasur Mantagani, Aralihalli.

The villages having more than 50% SC population are Allipura, Paramawadi, Maruthipura, Shevalalpur Bhairapur.

Sex ratio of Scheduled Caste population is 488.

Scheduled Castes Literates and Illiterates by Sex:

	Persons	Males	Females
Literate	5,828	3,907	1,921
Illiterate	11,171	4,798	6,373
Literacy rate	41.3	53.9	28.0
Graduate	79	73	6

Scheduled Castes (Dominant):

Banjara etc., Bhambi etc., Bhovi, Madiga, Korama

For their cultural identity please see Appendix-I

Villages without Scheduled Castes: There are 3 villages without any scheduled caste population.

Scheduled Tribes: Out of the total population of 108322 persons, 11114 persons (10.26%) belong to Scheduled Tribes.

The villages having less than 10% ST population are Jekenakatti, Madapur, Gonala, Karadagi, Allipura Bevinahalli, Nandihalli, Mannur, Savanur (Rural) Fakir Nandihalli, Challal, Tondur, Tevaramellihalli Halasur, Yelavigi, Basavankoppa, Hesarur, Siddapur Paramawadi, Maruthipura, Shirabadgi, Shevalalpur Vadnikoppa, Kadakola, Bhairapur, Krishnapur Hattimattur, Ichala Yellapur, Kamal Bangadi Timmapur Hiremugadur.

The villages having more than 50% ST population are None.

Sex ratio of Scheduled tribe population is 482.

Scheduled Tribes Literates and Illiterates by Sex:

	Persons	Males	Females
Literate	4,772	3,034	1,738
Illiterate	6,342	2,720	3,622
Literacy rate	50.9	63.0	38.2
Graduate	77	68	9

Scheduled Tribes (Dominant):

Naikda etc., Koraga, Generic Tribes etc.
Koli Dhor etc., Iruliga

For their cultural identity please see Appendix-II

Villages without Scheduled Tribes: There are 8 villages without any scheduled tribe population.

Literates and Illiterates by Sex (Total Population):

	Persons	Males	Females
Literate	55,493	34,133	21,360
Illiterate	52,829	21,887	30,942
Literacy rate	60	72	48
Graduate	1,237	1,074	163

Agriculture: ***Distribution of villages according to land use:***
Out of 65 villages, Total area (in hectare) is 53354, out of that 91.65 percent is cultivable and 6.71 percent of the cultivable area is irrigated.

Sources of Irrigation (Hectares): Government Canal 0, Private Canal 0, Well without Electricity 0, Well with Electricity 0, Tubewell without Electricity 0, Tubewell with Electricity 2463.24, Tank 3.24, River 820.02, Lake 0, Waterfall 0, Others 0.

Villages with population of 5000 to 9999:
Karadagi, Hattimattur.

Villages with population of 10000 and above: None

Distribution of Workers:

	Persons	Males	Females	WPR
Cultivators	18,099	14,540	3,559	33.25
Agricultural Labour	29,672	13,816	15,856	54.51
Household Industry	1,837	672	1,165	3.37
Other Workers	4,827	4,186	641	8.87
Main Workers	43,655	30,626	13,029	80.2
Marginal Workers	10,780	2,588	8,192	19.8
Total Workers	54,435	33,214	21,221	

Religion: Major Religious Communities:

	Persons	Males	Females	Sex Ratio
Hindu (83.18%)	90,098	46,549	43,549	936
Muslim (15.35%)	16,627	8,645	7,982	923
Christian (0.04%)	46	29	17	586
Sikh (0%)	-	-	-	-
Buddhists (0%)	-	-	-	-
Jain (0.43%)	463	245	218	890

Agewise Data:

	Persons	Males	Females	Sex Ratio
All ages	108,322	56,020	52,302	934
0-14	37,809	19,217	18,592	967
15-44	50,915	27,031	23,884	884
45-79	18,857	9,447	9,410	996
80+	696	296	400	1351
Age not stated	45	29	16	552

Languages (Dominant):
Kannada, Urdu, Hindi, Telugu, Marathi

Disabled Population:

	Persons	Males	Females	%
Total Disabled	1,887	1,087	800	
In Seeing	733	392	341	38.84
In Speech	197	120	77	10.44
In Hearing	80	46	34	4.24

In Movement	666	399	267	35.29	Mentally	211	130	81	11.18

SEDAM

Sedam C.D. Block lies in the eastern part of Gulbarga district. It is a part of Sedam taluka. The Block is located at a distance of 52 kms. from district headquarters (Gulbarga). There are 117 villages in the block with the total population of 155,974 persons. Area ofthe C.D. Block is 987.92 sq. kms. It is bounded by taluks Chitapur and Chincholi on north, taluk Yadgir on south, taluk Chitapur on west, and it has common boundary with the state of Andhra Pradesh on east.

Communications:

Roadways : S.H-10: Direction- Gulbarga to Kodangal, Nearest Villages- Samkhed, Mugnoor, Malkhed (J), Hoshalli, Neelhalli, Konkanhalli, Sedam (Rural), Batgera(B), Injepalli, Kontanpalli, Batgera(K), Adki, Nagasanpalli, Gundepalli(K), Bannur, Lingampalli,Mudhole, Kadlapur, Khanderayanpalli, Ribbanpalli. S.H-15: Direction- Yadgir to Chincholi, Nearest Villages- Surwar, Telkur,Satpatanhalli, Sedam (Rural), Batgera(B), Kachwar, Turkbommanhalli, Allhalli, Kalkhamb, Hanmanhalli, Kodla, Gudanhalli, Hulgoal, Handerki.

Railway Station: Villages- Nrupathanga.

River: Kagna Nadi- Nearest Villages- Samkhed, Sangavi (M), Tottanhalli, Meenhabal, Kukunda, Yadga, Kachur, Mugnoor, Surwar, Telkur, Habal (T), Lohada, Hayyal, Yadhalli, Satpatanhalli, Bibhalli, Taranhalli, Arebommanhalli, Beeranhalli, Hunsanhalli, Bijjanhalli, Malkhed (J), Shahabajpur, Shankerajpur, Pakhal, Chandapur, Venkatapur, Gaddanna, Motakpalli, Kishtapur.Kamlavati Nadi- Nearest Villages- Bibhalli, Taranhalli, Sedam (Rural), Batgera(B), Injepalli, Batgera(K), Kachwar,Turkbommanhalli, Madhwar, Ranjole, Hanmanhalli, Sindhanmadu, Bhutpur, Jakanpalli, Gundahalli(B), Turnur, Devnoor, Dugnoor, Kolkunda, Malkapalli, Motakpalli, Shaklatpalli, Itkal.

Reserved Forest: (Yadgir): Nearset Villages- Madna, Nadepalli,Kadtal, Kompalli, Gajalapur, Chandapur, Venkatapur.

Annual Rainfall: Normal Rianfall 777 mm.

Ground Water: Availability of the Ground Water in the Basin is 8153 HAM and the utilization is 1069 HAM It belongs to Over Exploited category. Depth to water level 5 to 20 meter below the ground. Most of the wells go down in summer months, according to the Ground Water Estimation Committee.

Soils: Deep Black, Medium Black Soil, Shallow Soil and Lateritic Soil.

Natural Division : It falls in the Kagna Basin of the Northern Karnataka Plateau.

Administration:

Division: Gulbarga. Parliamentary Constituency: 5 Gulbarga (SC). District: Gulbarga. Taluka: Sedam. Assembly Constituency: 41 Sedam. Gram Panchayat: 23.

Regional Area Development Boards: The Hyderabad-Karnataka Area Development Board.

Border Villages: (State: Andhra Pradesh)- Habal (T), Madkal, Sompalli, Rajola (K),.Ernapalli, Bomdepalli, Indira Nagar, Mallabad, Anantapur, Ribbanpalli, Silarkot, Medak, Gangarawalpalli, Kanagadda, Yenagundi, Hayyal.

Fairs: Madhuva Matha Festival: Malkhed, known historically as'Manyakheta' is on the banks of the Kagna river in Sedam taluk. Malkhed is about 35 kilometres by road from district headquarters town and is on the Gulbarga-Sedam road. The nearest railway station is Malkhed Road, five kilometres away on the Wadi-Secunderabad broad gauge route of the Central Railway.About 10 kilometres east of Malkhed lies the taluk headquarters town of Sedam. Malkhed was once the flourishing capital of the Rashtrakuta monarchs who reigned for over two centuries from A.D. 753. The period of Rashtrakuta ascendancy in the Deccan markedone of the most brilliant periods in Indian history. No other ruling dynasty of the Deccan played such a dominant part in the history of India till the rise of the Marathas in the 17th century.'Amoghavarsha' who ascended in 814 A.D. developed the city. It lost importance after the fall of the Rashtrakutas. Once a sprawling city with palaces and gardens, it is now reduced to the level of an ordinary village with a meagre population. There are remains of old forts. The place is venerated by members of the Madhva faith as it has a samadhi of Tikacharya, the famous commentatorof Sri Madhvacharya's works.

Villages: 117 **Inhabited:** 109 **Uninhabited:** 8

Ranking	District	State	National
Area	10	83	447
Population	10	128	1685
Sex Ratio	1	14	634
Child Sex Ratio	2	33	1589
Literacy Rate	8	171	5752
Density	4	49	5443
Work Participation Rate	2	118	1451

Gram Panchayats:

Malkhed (J), Kukunda, Telkur, Kurgunta, Neelhalli, Udgi, Batgera (B), Madkal, Adki, Lingampalli, Ribbanpalli, Mudhole, Ranjole, Kodla, Jakanpalli, Madna, Medak, Kolkunda, Handerki, Dugnoor, Motakpalli, Itkal, Kanagadda.

Amenities:

Education: Primary School in 107 villages, Middle school in 59 villages, Matriculation or Secondary School in 16 villages,

namely Meenhabal, Habal (T), Malkhed (J), Nrupathanga, Neelhalli, Batgera(B), Adki, Ranjole, Kodla, Madna, Handerki, Kolkunda, Mudhole, Motakpalli, Kanagadda, Itkal.

Higher Secondary or Pre University Courses or Intermediate or Junior College in 1 village of the CD Block,, namely Mudhole.

College in 0 village, Adult Literacy Center in 59 villages.

Medical: Hospital in 2 villages, Dispensary in 10 villages, Health Center in 10 villages, Sub Center in 27 villages, Maternity and Child Welfare Center in 11 villages, Community health workers in 12 villages.

The Villages having Hospital or Dispensary or Health Center are Malkhed (J), Nrupathanga, Kodla, Madna, Kolkunda, Mudhole, Ribbanpalli, Motakpalli, Kanagadda, Itkal.

Drinking Water: Tap water in 68 villages, Tank water in 29 villages, Well water in 87 villages, Tubewell in 63 villages and more than one source in 107 villages.

Bank: Banking facility in 8 villages, namely, Malkhed (J), Nrupathanga, Adki, Kodla, Kolkunda Mudhole, Motakpalli, Kanagadda.

Credit Society in 8 villages Agricultural Credit Society in 4 Non-Agricultural Credit Society in 0 village.

Others: Power supply in 107 villages, Cinema hall in 2 villages, sport club in 10 villages, Stadium or Auditorium or Community Hall in 109 villages, Post Office in 38 villages.

There are 60 villages having bus facilities.

Villages with most of facilities: Malkhed (J) Nrupathanga, Adki, Kodla, Kolkunda, Mudhole Motakpalli, Kanagadda.

Villages without amenities (Education): Bilkal..

Scheduled Castes: Out of the total population of 156026 persons, 42248 persons (27.08%) belong to Scheduled Castes.

The villages having less than 10% SC population are Arebommanhalli, Rajivnagar, Bhimnagar Turkbommanhalli, Gopanapalli(K).

The villages having more than 50% SC population are Samkhed, Lohada, Nrupathanga, Batgera(K), Madhwar Jawahar Nagar, Indira Nagar, Rudrawaram, Mailwar Kadtal, Gajalapur, Venkatapur.

Sex ratio of Scheduled Caste population is 499.

Scheduled Castes Literates and Illiterates by Sex:

	Persons	Males	Females
Literate	9,072	6,122	2,950
Illiterate	33,176	15,039	18,137
Literacy rate	26.3	35.6	17.1
Graduate	181	161	20

Scheduled Castes (Dominant):

Madiga, Banjara etc., Holaya etc., Bhovi Bhambi etc.

For their cultural identity please see Appendix-I

Villages without Scheduled Castes: There are 9 villages without any scheduled caste population.

Scheduled Tribes: Out of the total population of 156026 persons, 4129 persons (2.65%) belong to Scheduled Tribes.

The villages having less than 10% ST population are Samkhed, Sangavi (M), Tottanhalli, Meenhabal Kukunda, Yadga, Kachur, Mugnoor, Surwar, Telkur Habal (T), Lohada, Hayyal, Sangavi(T), Yadhalli Satpatanhalli, Bibhalli, Bijjanhalli, Malkhed (J) Nrupathanga, Hoshalli, Batgera(B), Injepalli, Madkal Sompalli, Kontanpalli, Batgera(K), Kachwar Turkbommanhalli, Madhwar, Adki, Jawahar Nagar Nagasanpalli, Rajola(K), Ernapalli, Bomdepalli Indira Nagar, Imdapur, Ranjole, Biderched Chitkanpalli, Amarwadi, Jilladpalli, Gopanapalli(K) Gundepalli(K), Bannur, Lingampalli, Mallabad Anantapur, Benkanhalli, Udgi, Allhalli, Kalkhamb Hanmanhalli, Sindhanmadu, Kodla, Bhutpur, Rudrawaram Munkanpalli, Gundahalli(B), Mushthalli, Mailwar Turnur, Raghapur, Madna, Konapur, Devnoor Gudanhalli, Hulgoal, Handerki, Nachawar, Bilkal Dugnoor, Kolkunda, Malkapalli, Kadcharla, Mudhole Kadlapur, Khanderayanpalli, Ribbanpalli, Silarkot Nadepalli, Kadtal, Gajalapur, Medak, Shankerajpur Pakhal, Chandapur, Venkatapur, Motakpalli, Kishtapur Tolmamadi, Gangarawalpalli, Kanagadda, Shaklatpalli Itkal, Buragpalli, Yenagundi.

The villages having more than 50% ST population are None.

Sex ratio of Scheduled tribe population is 510.

Scheduled Tribes Literates and Illiterates by Sex:

	Persons	Males	Females
Literate	992	662	330
Illiterate	3,137	1,360	1,777
Literacy rate	29.8	40.9	19.3
Graduate	25	18	7

Scheduled Tribes (Dominant):

Naikda etc., Gond etc., Kadu Kuruba, Meda, Iruliga

For their cultural identity please see Appendix-II

Villages without Scheduled Tribes: There are 78 villages without any scheduled tribe population.

Literates and Illiterates by Sex (Total Population):

	Persons	Males	Females
Literate	50,911	32,583	18,328
Illiterate	105,115	44,625	60,490
Literacy rate	39	51	28
Graduate	1,924	1,468	456

Agriculture: ***Distribution of villages according to land use:***

Out of 117 villages, Total area (in hectare) is 98792, out of that 80.51 percent is cultivable and 2.54 percent of the cultivable area is irrigated.

Sources of Irrigation (Hectares): Government Canal 296.34, Private Canal 25.38, Well without Electricity 224.85, Well with Electricity 580.16, Tubewell without Electricity 1.62, Tubewell with Electricity 284.25, Tank 413.97, River 146.01, Lake 0, Waterfall 0, Others 50.65.

Villages with population of 5000 to 9999:
Kodla, Mudhole.

Villages with population of 10000 and above:
Malkhed (J).

Distribution of Workers:

	Persons	Males	Females	WPR
Cultivators	22,758	17,473	5,285	28.98
Agricultural Labour	34,866	10,615	24,251	44.39
Household Industry	1,838	952	886	2.34
Other Workers	19,074	13,310	5,764	24.29
Main Workers	55,529	36,905	18,624	70.71
Marginal Workers	23,007	5,445	17,562	29.29
Total Workers	78,536	42,350	36,186	

Religion: Major Religious Communities:

	Persons	Males	Females	Sex Ratio
Hindu (86.72%)	135,304	66,971	68,333	1,020
Muslim (10.45%)	16,305	8,035	8,270	1,029
Christian (0.29%)	460	240	220	917
Sikh (0.01%)	12	8	4	500
Buddhists (1.76%)	2,743	1,362	1,381	1,014
Jain (0.05%)	78	35	43	1,229

Agewise Data:

	Persons	Males	Females	Sex Ratio
All ages	156,026	77,208	78,818	1021
0-14	61,522	31,137	30,385	976
15-44	64,631	32,181	32,450	1008
45-79	28,552	13,291	15,261	1148
80+	1,156	508	648	1276
Age not stated	165	91	74	813

Languages (Dominant):
Kannada, Telugu, Urdu, Hindi, Marathi

Disabled Population:

	Persons	Males	Females	%
Total Disabled	2,886	1,558	1,328	
In Seeing	1,107	504	603	38.36
In Speech	297	161	136	10.29
In Hearing	168	85	83	5.82
In Movement	1,053	667	386	36.49
Mentally	261	141	120	9.04

SHAHPUR

Shahpur C.D. Block lies in the southern part of Gulbarga district. It is a part of Shahpur taluka. The Block is located at a distance of 78 kms. from district headquarters (Gulbarga). There are 154 villages in the block with the total population of 249,683 persons. Area of the C.D. Block is 1635.25 sq. kms. It is bounded by taluks Jevargi and Chitapur on north, district Raichur on south, taluk Yadgir oneast, taluks Shorapur and Jevargi on west, and it has common boundary with thestate of Andhra Pradesh on east.

Communications:

Roadways : S.H-15: Direction- Yadgir to Devdurga, Nearest Villages- Hattigudur, Gundhalli, Khanapur, Manginhal, Naikal, Gulsaram, Birnal, Gundgurthi, Hundekal, Tadibidi, Agastihal, Anwar, Bommanhalli, Munmutgi, Nandihalli Jagir, Beernur, Sawoor, Kollur, Tonnur. S.H-16: Direction-Sindgi to Bhimarayana-Gudi, Nearest Villages- Nadihal, Chamnal, Ukkinhal, Darshanapur, Rabbanhalli, Gogikona. S.H-19: Direction- Shorapur to Jevargi, Nearest Villages-Madkeri, Aralhalli, Sadyapur, Hulkal (K), Rajapur (K), Vibutihalli, .Rastapur, Mandgalli, Konganda, Hattigudur.

River: Krishna Nadi- Nearest Villages- Alkur, Hayyal (B), Ekchinti, Markal, Kollur, Tonnur, Chandral, Goudoor, Aneksugur, Gondenoor, Channur Jagir, Konkal, Tumkur, Itga Simt Wadgera, Habshihal, Rotnadgi, Kadrapur, Bendebembli, Kodal, Gonal, Shivepur, Sangam, Gundloor. Bhima Nadi- Nearest Villages- Anabi, Roza Simt Sirwal, Sirwal, Hursgundgi, Habballi, Ibrahimpur, Tangadgi, Chattanhalli, Maramkal, Balkal, Nalwadgi, Naikal, Gulsaram, Birnal, Bablad, Gaddesugur, Halgera, Godihal, Kumnoor, Arjungi, Kandhalli, Bilhar, Boodinhal, Machnoor, Benkanhalli Khalsa, Shivenoor, Joldhadgi, Konganda Simt Wadgera, Sangam, Gundloor, Agnihal, Sugoor. Anawar Nadi- Nearest Villages- Diggi, Benkanhalli Jagir, Kanne Kolur, Tippanhalli, Kadayapur, Anwar,Hayyal (K), Hayyal (B), Baswantpur, .Bommanhalli, Munmutgi,Ekchinti.

Reserved Forest: (Yadgir): Nearest Villages- Diggi, Saidapur, Vibutihalli, Ommerdoddi, Bantihal, Nagnatgi, Mahal Roza, Sagar, Rastapur.

Annual Rainfall: Normal Rianfall 777 mm.

Ground Water: Availability of the Ground Water in the Basin is 7859 H.A.M. and the utilization is 1381 H.A.M. It belongs to Over Exploited category. Depth to water level 2 to 10 meter below the ground. Most of the wells go down in summer months, according to the Ground Water Estimation Committee.

Soils: Deep Black, Medium Black Soil, Shallow Soil and Lateritic Soil.

Natural Division : It falls partly in the Gurmatkal Scrub by Upland,Lower Bhima Valley, Shorapur-Shahpur Upland and Middle Krishna Valley of the Northern Karnataka Plateau.

Administration:

Division: Gulbarga. Parliamentary Constituency: 6 Raichur

(ST).District: Gulbarga. Taluka: Shahpur. Assembly Constituency: 37 Shahpur, 38 Yadgir. Gram Panchayat: 36.
Regional Area Development Boards: The Hyderabad-Karnataka Area Development Board.
Border Villages: (State: Andhra Pradesh)- Joldhadgi, Konganda Simt Wadgera, Sangam, Gundloor, Agnihal, Sugoor.
Fairs: Hayyalappa Jatra: Hayyal Buzurg in Shahapur taluk of Gulbarga area is noted for a big temple of also called Hayyalappa shrine. About the month of January, a jatra takes place at this place. Shaik Sufi Sarmast Saheb Urs: Sagar, a place near Shahpur taluk of Gulbarga is noted for its Dargah of the saint Shaik Sufi Sarmast Saheb. a well-attended Urs takes place here annually.
Sangamnath Dev Jatra: Sangamnath Dev jatra, held at Diggi in the month of 30 Shravana (August). Diggi, situated on the outskirts of Shahpur town, is noted for its Sangamnath temple where a big jatra takes place about August every year. The nearest railway station to reach the place is Yadgir.
Villages: 154 **Inhabited:** 145 **Uninhabited:** 9

Ranking	District	State	National
Area	7	21	97
Population	4	38	239
Sex Ratio	3	57	1765
Child Sex Ratio	5	104	3250
Literacy Rate	9	174	6039
Density	5	79	5515
Work Participation Rate	3	124	1932

Gram Panchayats:
Chamnal, Ukkinhal, Madkeri, Mudbole, Anabi, Sirwal, Hothpet, Gogipeth, Gogikona, Kakkesgera, Wandurg, Hoskera, Nagnatgi, Doranahalli, Ibrahimpur, Chattanhalli, Kannekolur, Rastapur, Sagar, Hattigudur, Tewar Wadger, Tadibidi, Khanapur, Naikal, Gulsaram, Kadamgera(B), Hayyal (B), Kollur, Kurkunda, Ullesugar, Halgera, Wadgera, Honkal, Bilhar, Bendebembli, Gonal.
Amenities:
Education: Primary School in 143 villages, Middle school in 86 villages, Matriculation or Secondary School in 15 villages, namely Chamnal, Darshanapur, Gogipeth, Gogikona, Wandurg, Sirwal, Nagnatgi, Sagar, Rastapur, Doranahalli, Naikal, Hayyal (B), Wadgera, Konkal, Bendebembli.
Higher Secondary or Pre University Courses or Intermediate or Junior College in 3 villages of the CD Block,, namely Gogipeth, Gogikona, Wadgera.
College in 0 village, Adult Literacy Center in 27 villages.
Medical: Hospital in 2 villages, Dispensary in 4 villages, Health Center in 15 villages, Sub Center in 51 villages, Maternity and Child Welfare Center in 0 village, Community health workers in 98 villages.
The Villages having Hospital or Dispensary or Health Center are Hothpet, Wandurg, Aldhal, Tumkur.
Drinking Water: Tap water in 92 villages, Tank water in 30 villages, Well water in 122 villages, Tubewell in 61 villages and more than one source in 131 villages.
Bank: Banking facility in 14 villages, namely, Harangera, Singanhalli, Karkihalli, Aldhal Bevinhalli, Kanne Kolur, Ommerdoddi, Rastapur Hursgundgi, Gundhalli, Manginhal, Gulsaram, Wadgera Bendebembli.
Credit Society in 20 villages Agricultural Credit Society in 20 Non-Agricultural Credit Society in 0 village.
Others: Power supply in 140 villages, Cinema hall in 0 village, sport club in 14 villages, Stadium or Auditorium or Communit Hall in 145 villages, Post Office in 48 villages.
There are 118 villages having bus facilities.
Villages with most of facilities: Harangera Singanhalli, Aldhal, Rastapur, Hursgundgi, Gundhalli Gulsaram, Wadgera, Bendebembli.
Villages without amenities (Education):
Shanker Banda, Sangam..
Scheduled Castes: Out of the total population of 249819 persons, 61478 persons (24.61%) belong to Scheduled Castes.
The villages having less than 10% SC population are Gundapur, Gogipeth, Wandurg, Roza Simt Sirwal Hallisagar, Bantihal, Shanker Banda, Tewar Wadgera Sangam.
The villages having more than 50% SC population are Chandapur, Ukkinhal, Harangera, Karkihalli, Maktapur Hattigudur, Gundhalli, Sawoor.
Sex ratio of Scheduled Caste population is 496.
Scheduled Castes Literates and Illiterates by Sex:

	Persons	Males	Females
Literate	12,229	8,611	3,618
Illiterate	49,249	22,344	26,905
Literacy rate	25.3	35.6	15.0
Graduate	376	352	24

Scheduled Castes (Dominant):
Holaya etc., Madiga, Banjara etc., Bhambi etc. Generic Castes etc.
For their cultural identity please see Appendix-I
Villages without Scheduled Castes: There are 12 villages without any scheduled caste population.
Scheduled Tribes: Out of the total population of 249819 persons, 22615 persons (9.05%) belong to Scheduled Tribes.
The villages having less than 10% ST population are

Gundapur, Nadihal, Chamnal, Chandapur, Ukkinhal
Harangera, Darshanapur, Rabbanhalli, Gogipeth
Singanhalli, Madkeri, Hothpet, Aralhalli
Kodamanhalli, Hulkal (K), Kanchamkavi, Gogikona
Karkihalli, Bholkadamgera, Rajapur, Diggi, Saidapur
Maktapur, Saladpur, Anabi, Roza Simt Sirwal, Ingalgi
Shakapur, Madnal, Bevinhalli, Hallisagar
Benkanhalli Jagir, Kanne Kolur, Tippanhalli
Vibutihalli, Ommerdoddi, Dariyapur, Mahal Roza
Sagar, Rastapur, Mandgalli, Hattigudur, Hursgundgi
Habballi, Tangadgi, Maramkal, Balkal, Nalwadgi
Doranahalli , Gundhalli, Karangi, Khanapur
Manginhal, Naikal, Gulsaram, Bablad, Malhalli
Kurkunda, Tekural, Bolari, Gundgurthi, Hundekal
Tokapur, Tadibidi, Kyatnal, Tewar Wadgera, Agastihal
Hanchinal, Hayyal (B), Baswantpur, Munmutgi, Beernur
Sawoor, Aneksugur, Ullesugar, Hortoor, Halgera
Godihal, Arjungi, Konhalli, Kandhalli, Bilhar
Gondenoor, Tumkur, Habshihal, Rotnadgi, Kadrapur
Boodinhal, Machnoor, Benkanhalli Khalsa, Shivenoor
Bendebembli, Joldhadgi, Kodal, Gonal
Konganda Simt Wadgera, Shivepur, Sangam, Gundloor
Agnihal, Sugoor.

The villages having more than 50% ST population are None.

Sex ratio of Scheduled tribe population is 501.

Scheduled Tribes Literates and Illiterates by Sex:

	Persons	Males	Females
Literate	4,334	3,059	1,275
Illiterate	18,281	8,237	10,044
Literacy rate	24.0	34.0	14.0
Graduate	78	74	4

Scheduled Tribes (Dominant):

Naikda etc., Kadu Kuruba, Generic Tribes etc.
Iruliga, Koli Dhor etc.

For their cultural identity please see Appendix-II

Villages without Scheduled Tribes: There are 46 villages without any scheduled tribe population.

Literates and Illiterates by Sex (Total Population):

	Persons	Males	Females
Literate	69,355	46,128	23,227
Illiterate	180,464	79,649	100,815
Literacy rate	34	46	23
Graduate	2,153	1,925	228

Agriculture: ***Distribution of villages according to land use:*** Out of 154 villages, Total area (in hectare) is 163525, out of that 84.97 percent is cultivable and 22.35 percent of the cultivable area is irrigated.

Sources of Irrigation (Hectares): Government Canal 28522.53, Private Canal 0, Well without Electricity 220.68, Well with Electricity 1055.81, Tubewell without Electricity 10.11, Tubewell with Electricity 110.08, Tank 711.02, River 361.46, Lake 0, Waterfall 0, Others 64.77.

Villages with population of 5000 to 9999:
Gogipeth, Gogikona, Sirwal, Naikal, Wadgera.

Villages with population of 10000 and above:
Sagar, Doranahalli.

Distribution of Workers:

	Persons	Males	Females	WPR
Cultivators	42,788	33,140	9,648	36.26
Agricultural Labour	53,176	17,893	35,283	45.06
Household Industry	1,965	1,270	695	1.67
Other Workers	20,082	14,946	5,136	17.02
Main Workers	88,575	59,186	29,389	75.06
Marginal Workers	29,436	8,063	21,373	24.94
Total Workers	118,011	67,249	50,762	

Religion: Major Religious Communities:

	Persons	Males	Females	Sex Ratio
Hindu (80.13%)	200,177	101,010	99,167	982
Muslim (12.73%)	31,790	15,900	15,890	999
Christian (0.53%)	1,331	682	649	952
Sikh (0%)	5	3	2	667
Buddhists (6.33%)	15,820	7,834	7,986	1,019
Jain (0.04%)	107	51	56	1,098

Agewise Data:

	Persons	Males	Females	Sex Ratio
All ages	249,819	125,777	124,042	986
0-14	106,527	54,575	51,952	952
15-44	99,804	51,084	48,720	954
45-79	41,897	19,502	22,395	1148
80+	1,421	522	899	1722
Age not stated	170	94	76	809

Languages (Dominant):
Kannada, Urdu, Hindi, Telugu, Marathi

Disabled Population:

	Persons	Males	Females	%
Total Disabled	4,473	2,611	1,862	
In Seeing	2,131	1,218	913	47.64
In Speech	363	216	147	8.12
In Hearing	236	111	125	5.28
In Movement	1,472	915	557	32.91
Mentally	271	151	120	6.06

SHIGGAON

Shiggaon C.D. Block lies in the north-western part of Haveri district. It is a part of Shiggaon taluka. The Block is located at a distance of 31 kms. from district headquarters (Haveri). There are 92 villages in the block with the total population of 122,011 persons. Area of the C.D. Block is 565.80 sq. kms. It is bounded by district Dharwad on north, taluk Hangal on south, taluk Savanur and district Dharwad on east, and distric ts Uttar Kannada and Dharawad on west.

Communications:

Roadways : N.H-4: Direction- Hubli to Bankapura, Nearest Villages- Muthalli, Thimmapur, Adavisomapur, Neeralgi, Kadahalli, Shyadambi, Madli, Hulsogi, Gotagodi, Kamanah alli, Shiggaon (Rural), Khursapur, Chakapur, Bisanhalli, Munavalli, Ibrahimpur. S.H-1: Direction- Tadas to Hangal, Nearest Villages- Kamalanagar, Tadas, Adavisomapur, Kunnur, Dhundshi, Aratal, Bujruk Basapur, Sheelvant Somapur, Yattinahalli, Hosur, Konankeri, Chandapur, Jakkankatti, Torur, Kalkatti, Manchinkop, Muglikatti, Hanakanahalli, Hungund, Lakkikoppa. S.H-6: Direction- Mundgod to Savanur, Nearest Villages- Konankeri, Mulkeri, Neeralakatti, Chandapur, Muddinakoppa, Nidagundi, Baad, Shingapur, Narayanapura, Munavalli, Ibrahimpur. S.H-69: Direction- Kumta to Hubli, Nearest Villages- Kamalanagar, Muthalli, Tadas, Gudageri, Mamadapur, Kunnur.

Reserved Forest: Nearest Villages- Muthalli, Adavisomapur, Gudageri, Mamadapur, Kunnur, Dhundshi, Jondalgatti, Aratal, Bujruk Basapur, Hosur, Basavanakoppa, Bhadrapur, Konankeri, Mulkeri, Shyabala, Neeralakatti, Muddinakoppa, Torur, Kalkatti, Muglikatti, Andalagi, Shedagaravalli.

Annual Rainfall: Normal Rianfall 592 mm.

Ground Water: Availability of the Ground Water in the Basin is 52.73 MCM and the utilization is 17.62 MCM It belongs to Over Exploited category. Depth to water level 10 to 20 meter below the ground. Most of the wells go down in summer months, according to the Ground Water Estimation Committee.

Soils: Red Sandy Soil, Medium Soil, Deep Black Soil, Red Loamy Soil and Lateritic Soil.

Natural Division : It falls in Barada Basin of Central Karnataka Plateau.

Administration:

Division: Belgaum. Parliamentary Constituency: 10 Haveri. District: Haveri. Taluka: Shiggaon. Assembly Constituency: 83 Shiggaon, 84 Haveri (SC). Gram Panchayat: 20.

Regional Area Development Boards: The Maland Aera Development Board.

Villages: 92 **Inhabited:** 91 **Uninhabited:** 1

Ranking	District	State	National
Area	5	157	1277
Population	5	151	2811
Sex Ratio	5	164	4096
Child Sex Ratio	7	118	3485
Literacy Rate	5	67	2108
Density	1	50	4502
Work Participation Rate	6	64	1460

Gram Panchayats:

Tadas, N.M. Tadas, Hirebendigeri, Kyalkond, Basanal, Hulgur, Shisuvinal, Attigeri, Kabanur, Hiremanakatti, Madli, Kunnur, Dhundshi, Hosur, Wanahalli, Bannur, Hiremallur, Hanumarahalli, Narayanapura, Baad, Chandapur, Konankeri , Andalagi, Hotanahalli, Kundur.

Amenities:

Education: Primary School in 87 villages, Middle school in 59 villages, Matriculation or Secondary School in 7 villages, namely Kunnur, Hirebendigeri, Basanal, Attigeri, Hungund, Narayanapura, Hotanahalli.

Higher Secondary or Pre University Courses or Intermediate or Junior College in 1 village of the CD Block,, namely Narayanapura.

College in 0 village, Adult Literacy Center in 2 villages.

Medical: Hospital in 1 village, Dispensary in 3 villages, Health Center in 4 villages, Sub Center in 25 villages, Maternity and Child Welfare Center in 5 villages, Community health workers in 26 villages.

The Villages having Hospital or Dispensary or Health Center are Dhundshi, Shisuvinal, Mugali, Kundur.

Drinking Water: Tap water in 45 villages, Tank water in 34 villages, Well water in 32 villages, Tubewell in 12 villages and more than one source in 80 villages.

Bank: Banking facility in 6 villages, namely, Tadas, Dhundshi, Konankeri, Hirebendigeri, Hulgur Kabanur.

Credit Society in 24 villages Agricultural Credit Society in 23 Non-Agricultural Credit Society in 0 village.

Others: Power supply in 91 villages, Cinema hall in 2 villages, sport club in 0 village, Stadium or Auditorium or Community Hall in 0 village, Post Office in 23 villages.

There are 81 villages having bus facilities.

Villages with most of facilities: Tadas, Dhundshi Konankeri, Hirebendigeri, Hulgur, Kabanur.

Villages without amenities (Education):

Bujruk Basapur, Shiggaon (Rural), Manchinkop..

Scheduled Castes: Out of the total population of 122091 persons, 14716 persons (12.05%) belong to Scheduled Castes. The villages having less than 10% SC population are Adavisomapur, Kunnur, Kadahalli, Jondalgatti Hiremanakatti (Manakatti), Bisatikoppa, Gotagodi Sheelvant Somapur, Hosur, Konankeri, Mulkeri Shyabala, Chandapur, Chikbendigeri, Belwalakoppa Attigeri, Shisuvinal, Hulgur, Kyalkond, Surapgatti Chikmanakatti, Kabanur, Kengapur, Bannur, Bannikoppa Hiremallur, Ganjigatti, Shiggaon (Rural), Chikmallur Torur, Manchinkop, Nidagundi, Kalyan, Chakapur, Baad Shingapur, Muglikatti, Hanakanahalli, Hungund Shidlapur, Mallanaikankoppa, Mukabasarikatti Narayanapura, Munavalli, Ibrahimpur , Sadashivapeth Hale Bankapur, Hulikatti, Lakkikoppa, Kundur

Jalikatti.
The villages having more than 50% SC population are Kamalanagar, Mamadapur, Makapur, Neeralakatti Shivapur.
Sex ratio of Scheduled Caste population is 481.

Scheduled Castes Literates and Illiterates by Sex:

	Persons	Males	Females
Literate	5,603	3,668	1,935
Illiterate	9,113	3,973	5,140
Literacy rate	46.4	58.5	33.3
Graduate	98	90	8

Scheduled Castes (Dominant):
Bhambi etc., Banjara etc., Chalavadi etc., Madiga Bhovi

For their cultural identity please see Appendix-I

Villages without Scheduled Castes: There are 10 villages without any scheduled caste population.

Scheduled Tribes: Out of the total population of 122091 persons, 9484 persons (7.77%) belong to Scheduled Tribes.
The villages having less than 10% ST population are Kamalanagar, Muthalli, Tadas, Thimmapur, Mamadapur Kunnur, Neeralgi, Dhundshi, Jondalgatti, Aratal Bujruk Basapur, Hiremanakatti (Manakatti) Sheelvant Somapur, Wanahalli, Makapur, Yattinahalli Hosur, Konankeri, Mulkeri, Neeralakatti Hirebendigeri, Chikbendigeri, Belwalakoppa Panigatti, Shisuvinal, Hulgur, Surapgatti Chikmanakatti, Bannur, Mugali, Bannikoppa Ganjigatti, Shiggaon (Rural), Shivapur, Jakkankatti Kankanwad, Torur, Nidagundi, Hunshikatti, Kalyan Khursapur, Motalli, Bisanhalli, Baad, Muglikatti Andalagi, Hanakanahalli, Hungund, Mukabasarikatti Narayanapura, Munavalli, Sadashivapeth Hale Bankapur, Hulikatti, Lakkikoppa, Hotanahalli Guddadachannapur, Kundur, Jalikatti.
The villages having more than 50% ST population are None.
Sex ratio of Scheduled tribe population is 484.

Scheduled Tribes Literates and Illiterates by Sex:

	Persons	Males	Females
Literate	4,387	2,817	1,570
Illiterate	5,097	2,080	3,017
Literacy rate	54.6	68.0	40.3
Graduate	74	65	9

Scheduled Tribes (Dominant):
Naikda etc., Meda, Koraga, Kadu Kuruba, Bhil etc.

For their cultural identity please see Appendix-II

Villages without Scheduled Tribes: There are 20 villages without any scheduled tribe population.

Literates and Illiterates by Sex (Total Population):

	Persons	Males	Females
Literate	66,177	39,945	26,232
Illiterate	55,914	23,052	32,862
Literacy rate	64	75	52
Graduate	1,459	1,217	242

Agriculture: ***Distribution of villages according to land use:***
Out of 92 villages, Total area (in hectare) is 56580.24, out of that 69.4 percent is cultivable and 12.38 percent of the cultivable area is irrigated.

Sources of Irrigation (Hectares): Government Canal 0, Private Canal 0, Well without Electricity 19.3, Well with Electricity 339.25, Tubewell without Electricity 6, Tubewell with Electricity 1097.75, Tank 2318.7, River 0.52, Lake 0, Waterfall 1838.64, Others 303.91.

Villages with population of 5000 to 9999:
Tadas, Hulgur.

Villages with population of 10000 and above: None

Distribution of Workers:

	Persons	Males	Females	WPR
Cultivators	22,563	17,500	5,063	35.94
Agricultural Labour	30,489	13,733	16,756	48.56
Household Industry	1,664	981	683	2.65
Other Workers	8,072	6,711	1,361	12.86
Main Workers	46,837	34,198	12,639	74.6
Marginal Workers	15,951	4,727	11,224	25.4
Total Workers	62,788	38,925	23,863	

Religion: Major Religious Communities:

	Persons	Males	Females	Sex Ratio
Hindu (78.95%)	96,395	49,753	46,642	937
Muslim (17.53%)	21,406	11,041	10,365	939
Christian (0.07%)	91	46	45	978
Sikh (0%)	2	1	1	1,000
Buddhists (0%)	1	1	-	-
Jain (2.42%)	2,954	1,542	1,412	916

Agewise Data:

	Persons	Males	Females	Sex Ratio
All ages	122,091	62,997	59,094	938
0-14	41,436	21,221	20,215	953
15-44	58,550	30,687	27,863	908
45-79	21,011	10,594	10,417	983
80+	937	410	527	1285
Age not stated	157	85	72	847

Languages (Dominant):
Kannada, Urdu, Hindi, Telugu, Marathi

Disabled Population:

	Persons	Males	Females	%
Total Disabled	2,368	1,428	940	
In Seeing	857	484	373	36.19
In Speech	282	169	113	11.91
In Hearing	139	68	71	5.87

In Movement	832	556	276	35.14

Mentally	258	151	107	10.9

SHIKARPUR

Shikarpur C.D. Block lies in the eastern part of Shimoga district. It is a part of Shikarpur taluka. The Block is located at a distance of 50 kms. from district headqu arters (Shimoga). There are 176 villages in the block with the total population of 167,502 persons. Area of the C.D. Block is 885.98 sq. kms. It is bounded by taluk Sorab and district Haveri on north, taluk Shimoga and district Davanagere on south, districts Davanagere and Haveri on east, taluks Sagar and Sorab on west.

Communications:

Roadways : S.H-1: Direction- Tirthahalli to Hangal, Neare st Villages- Thandagunda, Thogarsi, Malooru, Idukinahosak oppa, Devikoppa, Belagavi, Kalenahalli, Ambligola, Hariha rapura, Saluru, Gama. S.H-48: Direction- Siralkoppa to Honnali, Nearest Villages- Thadagani, Udugani, Bhadrapura, Kutrahalli, Punedahalli, Jakkanahalli, Sanda, Kotta, Kalenahalli, Beguru Dodda Thanda, Balekoppa, Bhandibhyr anahalli, Huluginakatte, Baluru, Jakkinakoppa, Nallinakop pa, Hosuru.

River: Kumudvati Nadi- Nearest Villages- Guddada Thum minakatte, Kutrahalli, Ambaragoppa, Seelavanthanakoppa, Thumrihosuru, Kotta, Kalenahalli, Kappanahalli, Suragiha lli, Nimbegondi, Harnahalli, Mattikote, Mugalagere, Godda nakoppa, Puradahalu, Channahalli, Saluru, Gama, Issuru, Harigehalu, Arasinagere, Kalmane, Hithala, Sanyasikoppa, Churchugundi, Thattihalli, Anjanapura.

Canal: Nearest Villages- Kutrahalli, Ambaragoppa, Seelav anthanakoppa, Thumrihosuru, Punedahalli, Jakkanahalli, Sanda, Amtekoppa, Sadashivapura, Kappanahalli, Kotipura, Hirekalavathi, Mallapura, A. Annapura, Ambligola, Harih arapura, Bannuru, Ramapura, Hothanakatte, Suragihalli, Nimbegondi, Harnahalli, Mattikote, Mugalagere, Nelavagilu, Beguru Dodda, Thanda, Beguru , Baganakatte, Sanklapura, Dabbanabhyranahalli, Saluru, Gama, Bhadrapura, Chikkaj ogihalli, Issuru, Harigehalu, Arasinagere, Madravalli, Kalmane, Hunsekoppa, Hithala, Sanyasikoppa, Churchugundi, Doddajogihalli, Mathighatta, Thattihalli.

Reserved Forest: Nearest Villages- Adaganti, Bhakthanako ppa, Thirthahalu, Guddada Thumminakatte, Chikkajamburu, Kuskuru, Ujjanipura, Basavapura, Bhogi, Nagihalli, Kutrahalli, Ambaragoppa, Seelavanthanakoppa, Thumrihosuru, Punedahalli, Jakkanahalli, Suragihalli, Harnahalli, Kaginalli, Baluru.

Annual Rainfall: Normal Rianfall 1014.13 mm.

Ground Water: Availability of the Ground Water in the Basin is 88.55 MCM and the utilization is 52.67 MCM. It belongs to Safe category. Depth to water level 5 to 20 meter below the ground. Most of the wells go down in summer months, according to the Ground Water Estimati on Committee.

Soils: Reddish to Brownish Clayey Loam.

Natural Division : It falls partly in Sagar-Sorab-Shikarp ur Rolling Humid Region and Shimoga Forested Hills of the Central Karnataka Plateau.

Administration:

Division: Bangalore. Parliamentary Constituency: 14 Shimoga. District: Shimoga. Taluka: Shikarpur. Assembly Constituency: 115 Shikarpur. Gram Panchayat: 43.

Regional Area Development Boards: The Maland Aera Development Board.

Fairs: Banashankaramma Jatra: Banashankaramma jatra is held at Bandanlike in the month of January for three days. Bandalike (also called Bandanike) about 35 kms. to the north of Shikaripur town, is now an uninhabi ted village.

Huchcharaya Swamy Jatra: Huchcharaya Swamy temple jatra is held at Shikaripur near Shimoga in the month of April for seven days. Shikaripur is about 65 kms. north-west of Shimoga. It is situated on the right bank of the Chrodi or Kumudvati river and is the headqua rters town of the Shikaripur taluk.

Kedareshvara Car Festival: Kedareshvara Car festival is held at Belagavi near Shimoga in about the month of March every year. Belagavi also known as Belagami, is about 21 kms. north-west of Shikarpur town.

Mallikarjunaswamy Jatra: Mallikarjunaswamy jatra is held at Togarsi near Shimoga in about the month of March -April for one month every year. Togarsi is about 29 kms. north-west of Shikarpur and about ten kms. north -west of Shiralkoppa.

Teppotsava Festival: It is held at Madagadakere near Shimoga around the month of February every year. Madaga dakere also known as Masur-Madagadakere about 14 kms. north-east of Shikarpur on the border with Dharwar district and has a large tank. It has also a ruined fort.

Veerabhadra Temple Car Festival: It is held at Talagunda near Shimoga around the month of April every year. Talag unda is situated about five kms. north of Shiralkoppa and about 24 kms. north-west of Shikarpur. It was an ancient agrahara town called Sthanakudur from which the illustrious Kadambas of Banavasi hailed.

Villages: 176 **Inhabited:** 155 **Uninhabited:** 21

Ranking	District	State	National
Area	6	104	575
Population	4	115	1340
Sex Ratio	4	91	2400
Child Sex Ratio	2	24	1536

Literacy Rate	6	50	1781
Density	2	84	4894
Work Participation Rate	2	87	1984

Gram Panchayats:
Haragi, Thogarsi, Chikkamagadi, Inam Agrahara Muchadi, Malavalli, Narasapura, Bilaki, Koratigere, Sunnadakoppa, Thalagunda, Belagavi, Thadagani, Udugani, Hirejamburu, Manchikoppa, Chikkajamburu, Guddada Thumminakatte, Mattikote, Kittadahalli, Baganakatte, Maravalli, Kaginalli, Gogga, Beguru , Goddanakoppa, Nelavagilu, Ambaragoppa, Jakkanahalli, Amtekoppa, Kappanahalli, Muddanahalli, Hosuru, Jakkinakoppa, Tharalaghatta, Gama, Saluru, Mudubasiddapura, Arasinagere, Issuru, Churchugundi, Hithala, Kalmane, Harogoppa.

Amenities:

Education: Primary School in 133 villages, Middle school in 90 villages, Matriculation or Secondary School in 28 villages, namely Inam Agrahara Muchadi, Bilaki, Mayathammana Muchadi, Thogarsi, Haragi, Thalagunda, Belagavi, Huluginakoppa, Thadasanahalli, Chikkajamburu, Thadagani, Jamburuhosakoppa, Udugani, Ambaragoppa, Shettihalli, A. Annapura, Suragihalli, Mattikote, Nelavagilu, Beguru, Maravalli, Kaginalli, Hosuru, Saluru, Gama, Issuru, Hithala, Thattihalli.
Higher Secondary or Pre University Courses or Intermediate or Junior College in 1 village of the CD Block,, namely Hithala.
College in 0 village, Adult Literacy Center in 0 village.

Medical: Hospital in 2 villages, Dispensary in 11 villages, Health Center in 9 villages, Sub Center in 10 villages, Maternity and Child Welfare Center in 0 village, Community health workers in 0 village.
The Villages having Hospital or Dispensary or Health Center are Yelagere, Bilaki, Haragi, Thadasanahalli, Kadenandihalli, Kappanahalli, Hothanakatte, Maravalli, Hosuru, Chikkajogihalli, Hithala.

Drinking Water: Tap water in 2 villages, Tank water in 6 villages, Well water in 24 villages, Tubewell in 129 villages and more than one source in 110 villages.

Bank: Banking facility in 7 villages, namely, Bilaki, Thogarsi, Kappanahalli, Hosuru, Saluru Issuru, Harogoppa.
Credit Society in 41 villages Agricultural Credit Society in 34 Non-Agricultural Credit Society in 6 villages.

Others: Power supply in 151 villages, Cinema hall in 1 village, sport club in 155 villages, Stadium or Auditorium or Community Hall in 155 villages, Post Office in 58 villages.
There are 109 villages having bus facilities.

Villages with most of facilities: Bilaki, Thogarsi Kappanahalli, Hosuru, Saluru.

Villages without amenities (Education):
Channapura, Siddihalli, Donanagudde, Kadethinahalli, Sahasravalli, Guddadahosalli, Idukinahosakoppa, Vadagatte, Mayasettikoppa, Sadapura, Hakkali, Bhakthanakoppa, Dasanapura, Kutrahalli, Hariharapura, Ramapura, Channahalli, Bhandibhyranahalli, Anaginabylu, Sanyasikoppa, Yerekatte, Sidiginahalu..

Scheduled Castes: Out of the total population of 167573 persons, 43130 persons (25.74%) belong to Scheduled Castes.
The villages having less than 10% SC population are Inam Agrahara Muchadi, Narasapura, Shankrikoppa Kolagi, Thandagunda, Karnelli, Kawli, Kodihalli Haragi, Sahasravalli, Hunsekatte, Guddadahosalli Idukinahosakoppa, Devikoppa, Thadasanahalli Bhakthanakoppa, Thadagani, Jamburuhosakoppa Kyadigikoppa, Kutrahalli, Kaniya, Kotta, A. Annapura Hariharapura, Yarekoppa, Ramapura, Suragihalli Nimbegondi, Harnahalli, Mattikote, Mugalagere Nelavagilu, Kittadahalli, Dabbanabhyranahalli Kenchigondanakoppa, Thimlapura, Gogga, Kaginalli Jakkinakoppa, Aralehalli, Madravalli, Hunsekoppa Nandihalli, Yerekatte, Sidiginahalu.
The villages having more than 50% SC population are Inam Muthalli, Siddihalli, Mulakoppa, Ragikoppa Vadagatte, Shivapura, Thalagunda, Mayasettikoppa Bidarikoppa, Hakkali, Manchikoppa, Neralagi Bhadrapura, Dasanapura, Bhogi, Shettihalli Sadashivapura, Mallapura, Sanklapura, Guledahalli Baluru, Nallinakoppa, Hosuru, Sanyasikoppa Tharalaghatta, Thattihalli, Harogoppa, Athibylu Yalaneerakoppa.
Sex ratio of Scheduled Caste population is 493.

Scheduled Castes Literates and Illiterates by Sex:

	Persons	Males	Females
Literate	18,015	11,351	6,664
Illiterate	25,115	10,503	14,612
Literacy rate	49.3	61.2	37.1
Graduate	429	390	39

Scheduled Castes (Dominant):
Bhovi, Banjara etc., Adi Karnataka, Chalavadi etc. Madiga

For their cultural identity please see Appendix-I

Villages without Scheduled Castes: There are 28 villages without any scheduled caste population.

Scheduled Tribes: Out of the total population of 167573 persons, 10971 persons (6.55%) belong to Scheduled Tribes.
The villages having less than 10% ST population are Yelagere, Chikkamagadi, Inam Agrahara Muchadi Mallenahalli, Malavalli, Narasapura, Shankrikoppa

Channapura, Kolagi, Thandagunda, Siddihalli Kanas0Gi, Bilaki, Mulakoppa, Mayathammana Muchadi Koratigere, Donanagudde, Kanahalli, Kadethinahalli Thogarsi, Kodihalli, Haragi, Sahasravalli Hunsekatte, Malooru, Idukinahosakoppa, Devikoppa Vadagatte, Shivapura, Thalagunda, Malagondanakoppa Belagavi, Mayasettikoppa, Basavanandihalli Huluginakoppa, Thadasanahalli, Bidarikoppa Mugalikoppa, Hakkali, Belavanthanakoppa, Manchikoppa Bhakthanakoppa, Guddada Thumminakatte, Chikkajamburu Neralagi, Jamburuhosakoppa, Kyadigikoppa, Udugani Bhadrapura, Kuskuru, Dasanapura, Hirejamburu Kodikoppa, Bhogi, Kutrahalli, Thumrihosuru Punedahalli, Jakkanahalli, Sanda, Haraguvalli Kaniya, Chikkalavathi, Amtekoppa, Shettihalli, Kotta Sadashivapura, Kalenahalli, Kappanahalli, Mallapura Mudubasiddapura, A. Annapura, Ambligola Hariharapura, Yarekoppa, Bannuru, Ramapura Hothanakatte, Chunchinakoppa, Suragihalli Harnahalli, Mattikote, Mugalagere, Goddanakoppa Channahalli, Beguru Dodda Thanda, Beguru Kittadahalli, Kavaspura, Dindadahalli, Sanklapura Dabbanabhyranahalli, Kenchigondanakoppa Muddanahalli, Kengatti, Doopadahalli, Thimlapura Ittigehalli, Bhandibhyranahalli, Gogga, Kaginalli Baluru, Jakkinakoppa, Aralehalli, Nallinakoppa Saluru, Gama, Chikkajogihalli, Issuru, Arasinagere Madravalli, Hunsekoppa, Hithala, Sanyasikoppa Churchugundi, Doddajogihalli, Thattihalli Hirekoralahalli, Harogoppa, Sidiginahalu, Athibylu Yalaneerakoppa.

The villages having more than 50% ST population are None.

Sex ratio of Scheduled tribe population is 489.

Scheduled Tribes Literates and Illiterates by Sex:

	Persons	Males	Females
Literate	5,662	3,423	2,239
Illiterate	5,309	2,183	3,126
Literacy rate	60.3	71.1	48.9
Graduate	115	92	23

Scheduled Tribes (Dominant):

Naikda etc., Hasalaru, Meda, Kadu Kuruba Hakkipikki

For their cultural identity please see Appendix-II

Villages without Scheduled Tribes: There are 63 villages without any scheduled tribe population.

Literates and Illiterates by Sex (Total Population):

	Persons	Males	Females
Literate	94,882	54,968	39,914
Illiterate	72,691	30,017	42,674
Literacy rate	66	75	56
Graduate	2,454	2,046	408

Agriculture: ***Distribution of villages according to land use:*** Out of 176 villages, Total area (in hectare) is 88598, out of that 48.17 percent is cultivable and 52.19 percent of the cultivable area is irrigated.

Sources of Irrigation (Hectares): Government Canal 7355.79, Private Canal 39.12, Well without Electricity 5.99, Well with Electricity 13.76, Tubewell without Electricity 91.99, Tubewell with Electricity 4293.81, Tank 9866.77, River 210, Lake 0, Waterfall 0.2, Others 394.86.

Villages with population of 5000 to 9999: None

Villages with population of 10000 and above: None

Distribution of Workers:

	Persons	Males	Females	WPR
Cultivators	40,198	30,031	10,167	47.85
Agricultural Labour	34,390	13,700	20,690	40.93
Household Industry	1,423	967	456	1.69
Other Workers	8,003	6,333	1,670	9.53
Main Workers	63,437	46,488	16,949	75.51
Marginal Workers	20,577	4,543	16,034	24.49
Total Workers	84,014	51,031	32,983	

Religion: Major Religious Communities:

	Persons	Males	Females	Sex Ratio
Hindu (91.01%)	152,507	77,259	75,248	974
Muslim (8.39%)	14,062	7,213	6,849	950
Christian (0.13%)	215	111	104	937
Sikh (0%)	-	-	-	-
Buddhists (0.01%)	20	9	11	1,222
Jain (0.04%)	63	33	30	909

Agewise Data:

	Persons	Males	Females	Sex Ratio
All ages	167,573	84,985	82,588	972
0-14	54,804	27,830	26,974	969
15-44	81,906	41,477	40,429	975
45-79	29,530	15,024	14,506	966
80+	1,223	589	634	1076
Age not stated	110	65	45	692

Languages (Dominant):

Kannada, Urdu, Hindi, Telugu, Tamil

Disabled Population:

	Persons	Males	Females	%
Total Disabled	3,094	1,880	1,214	
In Seeing	1,361	810	551	43.99
In Speech	299	159	140	9.66
In Hearing	133	69	64	4.3
In Movement	1,008	674	334	32.58
Mentally	293	168	125	9.47

SHIMOGA

Shimoga C.D. Block lies in the southern part of Shimoga district. It is a part of Shimoga taluka. The Block is located at a distance of 00 kms. from district headqu arters (Shimoga). There are 214 villages in the block with the total population of 170,901 persons. Area of the C.D. Block is 1017.88 sq. kms. It is bounded by district Davanagere and taluk Shikarpur on north, distri ct Chikmagalur on south, taluk Bhadravati on east, taluks Sagar, Hosanagara and Tirthahalli on west.

Communications:

Roadways : N.H-13: Direction- Tirthahally to Channagiri, Nearest Villages- Kudli, Hoisana Halli, Pillangere, Javalli, Chikkudli, Taragana, Halli, Belagalu, Haro Bena valli, Gajanuru State Forest, Hosahalli, Lakshmi Pura, Honna Pura, Gajanuru, Veera Pura, Gajanuru Agrahara, Thimkapura, Holebenavalli, Hanumanthapura. N.H-206: Direction- Sagar to Bhadravati, Nearest Villages- Kone Hosuru, Thuppuru, Sannivasa, Choradi, Kumsi, Gudena Koppa, Channadevana Koppa, Chikkadanavandi, Hosakote, Ayanuru, Doddadanavandi, Ko Halli, Yalavalli, Veeragara na Bairana Koppa, Mudina Koppa, Tevara Koppa, Guddada Arakere, Shri Rampura. S.H-25: Direction- Shimoga to Honnali, Nearest Villages- Gondichatnahalli, Madike Chiluru, Holaluru, Hole Hatti, Melina, Hanasavadi, Hole Hanasavadi, Bedara Hosahalli, Goravina Katte, Bullapura, Suguru. S.H-26: Direction- Hosanagara to Nyamati, Neare st Villages- Galigekola, Chinna Mane, Mandagatta, Israpura, Mallapura, Kondajji, Rampura, Bhairana Koppa, Rama Nagara, Harana Halli, Sanke Devana Koppa, Nagarabavi, Ayanuru, Dagali Mane, Ko Halli, Adagadi, Chikkamathali, Suduru.

Railway Station: Nearest Villages- Shetti Kere, Somashet ti Koppa, Ragi Hosahalli, Konagavalli, Sevalal Nagara, Kote Ganguru.

River: Tunga Nadi- Nearest Villages- Gondichatnahalli, Madike Chiluru, Hadona Halli, Holaluru, Hole Hatti, Hole Hanasavadi, Bedara Hosahalli, Goravina Katte, Bullapura, Suguru, Kudli, Hoisana Halli, Pillangere, Gajanuru State Forest, Hosahalli, Lakshmi Pura, Mathuru, Honna Pura, Gajanuru, Gajanuru Agrahara, Thimkapura, Halalakka Valli, Kadekal, Kuskuru, Holebenavalli, Hanum anthapura, Nydile, Belagalu. Bhadra Nadi- Nearest Village s- Kudli, Chikkudli, Belagalu, Yankata P ura, Malena Halli, Kati Kere, Sakre Bylu. Kumudvati Nadi- Nearest Villages- Shetti Kere, Vaderakoppa, Gunduru, Choradi, Kumsi, Singana Halli, Made Koppa, Suduru. Tungabhadra Nadi- Nearest Villages- Madike Chiluru, Hadona Halli, Holaluru, Hole Hatti, Suguru.

Canal: Nearest Villages- Madike Chiluru, Holaluru, Hole Hatti, Lingapura, Mathodu, Berala Katte, Melina Hanasava di, Hole Hanasavadi, Bedara Hosahalli, Goravina Katte, Bullapura, Suguru, Kudli, Hoisana Halli, Pillangere, Javalli, Chikkudli, Haro Benavalli, Sadashiva Pura, Gajanuru State Forest, Hosahalli, Lakshmi Pura, Mathuru, Gajanuru, Veera Pura, Gajanuru Agrahara, Halalakka Valli, Kadekal, Kuskuru, Yaraganalu, Kachina Katte, Mandenakoppa, Santhe Kaduru, Dummalli, Bidare, Holebenavalli, Hanumanthapura, Honnavile, Machena Halli, Nidige, Sogane, Rampura, Korala Halli.

Annual Rainfall: Normal Rianfall 996.71 mm.

Ground Water: Availability of the Ground Water in the Basin is 135.12.14 MCM and the utilization is 40.50 MCM. It belongs to Safe category. Depth to water level 2 to 10 meter below the ground. Most of the wells go down in summer months, according to the Ground Water Estimation Committee.

Soils: Reddish to Brownish Clayey Loam.

Natural Division : It falls partly in Upper Tungabhadra Valley and Shimoga Forested Hills of the Central Karnata ka Plateau.

Administration:

Division: Bangalore. Parliamentary Constituency: 14 Shimoga. District: Shimoga. Taluka: Shimoga. Assembly Constituency: 111 Shimoga Rural (SC), 113 Shimoga, 114 Tirthalli. Gram Panchayat: 37.

Regional Area Development Boards: The Maland Aera Development Board.

Fairs: Bheemeshwara Jatra: It is held at Shimoga in around the month of May for one day, every year. Brahmeshwara Jatra and Chintamani Narasimha Jatra: The jatra is held annually at Kudli around the month of October for three days and Chintamani Narasimha jatra is held around the month of November for one day every year. Kudli, is at the confluence (kudali) of the Tunga and the Bhadra rivers. They unite here to form the Tunga bhadra at a distance of about 16 kms. north-east of Shimoga. Channakeshava Temple Car Festival: An annual car festival of the Channakeshava temple is heid at Hosahalli. Hosah alli is situated on the bank of river Tunga, about 6 kilometers south of Shimoga city. It is an ancient agrah ara town which was known for traditional Sanskrit learning. Guddekal Siddheshwara Car Festival: The cattle fair is held annually at Shimoga for fifteen days during about January-February. Shimoga, situated on the bank of the river Tunga about 274 kms. south-west of Bangalore city, is the headquarters town of the taluk, sub-division and district of the same name.

Kote-Anjaneya Festival: It is held at Shimoga in about the month of March-April for three days every year. Lakshami-Keshava Car Festival: A car festival of Lord Lakshami-Keshava is held at Mathur near Shimoga in the month of Phalguna (February-March) every year.

Mathur,situated on the bank of the river Tunga on the Shimoga Tirthahalli Road, is about nine kilometres south of Shimoga city.

Lakshminarayana Jatra: Lakshminarayana jatra is held at Shimoga in about the month of May for one day every year.

Rameshwara Jatra: Rameshwara jatra is held at Kudli near Shimoga around the month of March for one day every year.

Sangameshwara Car Festival: It is held at Kudli near near Shimoga during the month of March-April every year.

Syed Jatmalin Baba Urs: Hosahalli near Shimoga is situated on the bank of the river Tunga, about 16 kms. south of Shimoga city on Shimoga-Tirthahalli Road. It is an ancie nt agrahara town which was known for traditional Sanskrit learning. An annual car festival of the Channakeshava temple, and an annual Urs in memory of Syed Jatmalin Baba take place here.

Venkataramana Jatra: It is held at Kumsi near Shimoga around the month of May for one day every year. Kumsi, about 24 kms. north-west of Shimoga city on Bangalore-H onnavar Road, is a hobli headquarters.

Venkataramana Jatra: It is held at Pillangere near Shimo ga around the month of July for one day. Pillangere, about nine kilometres north-east of Shimoga city on Shimoga-Holehonour Road, is on the banks of the river Tunga. It has a temple on a hill-top, dedicated to Venkata ramana and Ranganatha. It is much frequented by devotees. The spot commands a panoramic view of the neighbouring area.

Villages: 214 **Inhabited:** 195 **Uninhabited:** 19

Ranking	District	State	National
Area	5	81	425
Population	3	113	1261
Sex Ratio	5	99	2507
Child Sex Ratio	3	29	1624
Literacy Rate	5	46	1683
Density	5	139	5268
Work Participation Rate	3	103	3273

Gram Panchayats:

Choradi, Kumsi, Bale Koppa, Harana Halli, Rama Nagara, Mallapura, Kunchena Halli, Kommanalu, Harama Ghatta, Hadona Halli, Holaluru, Suguru, Abbalagere, Kote Ganguru, Konagavalli, Ayanuru, Mandagatta, Thammadi Halli, Shirigere, Puradalu, Melina Hanasavadi, Pillangere, Kudli, Beeranahalli, Shetti Halli, Hosudi, Holebenavalli, Bidare, Nidige, Santhe Kaduru, Mathuru, Hosahalli, Agasavalli, Gajanuru, Kadekal, Korala Halli, Umble Bylu.

Amenities:

Education: Primary School in 136 villages, Middle school in 79 villages, Matriculation or Secondary School in 25 villages, namely Choradi, Kumsi, Mandagatta, Rama Nagara, Harana Halli, Konagavalli, Ayanuru, Thammadi Halli, Shirigere, Puradalu, Agasavalli, Harama Ghatta, Holaluru, Abbalagere, Suguru, Pillangere, Beerana Halli, Shetti Halli, Mathuru, Gajanuru, Kachina Katte, Santhe Kaduru, Yalavatti, Nidige, Umble Bylu.

Higher Secondary or Pre University Courses or Intermediate or Junior College in 2 villages of the CD Block,, namely Ayanuru, Holaluru.

College in 1 village, Adult Literacy Center in 2 villages., College is in village, namely Holaluru.

Medical: Hospital in 0 village, Dispensary in 16 villages, Health Center in 8 villages, Sub Center in 20 villages, Maternity and Child Welfare Center in 4 villages, Community health workers in 1 village.

The Villages having Hospital or Dispensary or Health Center Are Choradi, Kumsi, Mandagatta, Rampura, Harana Halli, Thyaja Valli, Ayanuru, Shirigere, Gondichatnahalli, Harama Ghatta, Hadona Halli, Holaluru, Kommanalu, Shetti Halli, Mathuru, Nidige, Umble Bylu.

Drinking Water: Tap water in 96 villages, Tank water in 76 villages, Well water in 124 villages, Tubewell in 88 villages and more than one source in 177 villages.

Bank: Banking facility in 13 villages, namely, Kumsi, Harana Halli, Ayanuru, Ko Halli, Shirigere Harama Ghatta, Holaluru, Mathuru, Gajanuru, Kadekal Machena Halli, Nidige, Umble Bylu.

Credit Society in 25 villages Agricultural Credit Society in 24 Non-Agricultural Credit Society in 2 villages.

Others: Power supply in 189 villages, Cinema hall in 3 villages sport club in 195 villages, Stadium or Auditorium or Communi Hall in 195 villages, Post Office in 55 villages.

There are 128 villages having bus facilities.

Villages with most of facilities: Kumsi Harana Halli, Ayanuru, Ko Halli, Shirigere Harama Ghatta, Holaluru, Mathuru, Nidige, Umble Bylu.

Villages without amenities (Education): Sannivasa, Gunduru, Kempena Koppa, Gopa Shettipura, Gudena Koppa, Made Koppa, Kesavina Katte, Rampura, Bhairana Koppa, Sanke Devana Koppa, Mysavalli, Valakeshava Pura, Sevalal Nagara, Somagoppa, Nagarabavi, Dagali Mane, Pugate Koppa, Veeragarana Bhairana Koppa, Muddina Koppa, Anesara, Adagadi, Thavare Koppa, Bilvadera Koppa, Maleshankara State Forest, Gejjenahalli, Kallaganguru, Bhairanakoppa, Guddada Arakere,

Aladevara Hosuru, Shetty Halli, Basavapura, Kalluru, Kalla Pura, Lingapura, Kommanalu, Hole Hanasavadi, Belagalu, B Beeranahalli, Sadashiva Pura, Gowdanaykana Halli, Buklapura, Sakre Bylu, Kudagala Mane, Gajanuru State Forest, Thatti Kere, Lakshmi Pura, Veera Pura, Gajanuru Mullakere, Gajanuru Agrahara, Sakre Bylu, Thimkapura, Mandenakoppa, Bekkina Kalmatha, Hanumanthapura, Rampura, Korala Halli, Sari Gere, Kydotlu, Belagalu..

Scheduled Castes: Out of the total population of 170840 persons, 43980 persons (25.74%) belong to Scheduled Castes.

The villages having less than 10% SC population are Thuppuru, Alkuni, Sannivasa, Horabylu, Koragi Shanthi Kere, Shetti Kere, Vaderakoppa Kempena Koppa, Gopa Shettipura, Gudena Koppa Chikkadanavandi, Rechi Koppa, Ragi Hosahalli Singana Halli, Made Koppa, Chinna Mane, Dyavanakere Vitagondana Koppa, Mallapura, Rampura, Harana Halli Sanke Devana Koppa, Somagoppa, Nagarabavi Dagali Mane, Pugate Koppa, Ittige Halli, Hosuru Malalakoppa, Adagadi, Chikkamathali, Suduru Doddamathali, Adina Kottige, Koodi , Thavare Koppa Male Shankara, Maleshankara State Forest Manjari Koppa, Bhairanakoppa, Virupina Koppa Thevara Koppa, Guddada Arakere, Puradalu Shetty Halli, Chitra Shetty Halli, Hole Hatti Lingapura, Alada Halli, Mojappana Hosuru Melina Hanasavadi, Taragana Halli, Beerana Halli Sakre Bylu, Kudagala Mane, Hosahalli, Mathuru Honna Pura, Veera Pura, Sakre Bylu, Thimkapura Kachina Katte, Rampura, Huruli Halli, Ganidalu Sari Gere, Siddamaji Hosuru, Kakana Hosudi.

The villages having more than 50% SC population are Narayana Pura, Suthu Kote, Ratti Halli, Mysavalli Valakeshava Pura, Sevalal Nagara, Yare Koppa Muddina Koppa, Anesara, Gejjenahalli, Kallaganguru Anupina Katte, Kalluru, Kunchena Halli, Boodi Gere Hunasodu, Channamumba Pura, Chikkudli, Gudra Koppa Buklapura, Lakshmi Pura, Mandenakoppa, Dummalli Bekkina Kalmatha, Hanumanthapura, Belagalu.

Sex ratio of Scheduled Caste population is 493.

Scheduled Castes Literates and Illiterates by Sex:

	Persons	Males	Females
Literate	18,696	11,473	7,223
Illiterate	25,284	10,823	14,461
Literacy rate	50.2	60.8	39.3
Graduate	309	267	42

Scheduled Castes (Dominant):

Banjara etc., Bhovi, Adi Karnataka, Adi Dravida Madiga

For their cultural identity please see Appendix-I

Villages without Scheduled Castes: There are 45 villages without any scheduled caste population.

Scheduled Tribes: Out of the total population of 170840 persons, 10366 persons (6.07%) belong to Scheduled Tribes.

The villages having less than 10% ST population are Kone Hosuru, Thuppuru, Alkuni, Sannivasa, Horabylu Shanthi Kere, Shetti Kere, Vaderakoppa, Gunduru Kumsi, Kempena Koppa, Gopa Shettipura, Chikka Marasa Bale Koppa, Hubbana Halli, Gudena Koppa Chikkadanavandi, Rechi Koppa, Ragi Hosahalli Singana Halli, Made Koppa, Mandagatta, Dyavanakere Vitagondana Koppa, Kesavina Katte, Hitturu Narayana Pura, Mallapura, Suthu Kote, Ratti Halli Rampura, Bhairana Koppa, Harana Halli, Arena Koppa Sanke Devana Koppa, Mysavalli, Valakeshava Pura Yadavala, Sevalal Nagara, Yare Koppa, Somagoppa Veerannana Benavalli, Nagarabavi, Doddadanavandi Dagali Mane, Ko Halli, Pugate Koppa Veeragarana Bhairana Koppa, Muddina Koppa, Anesara Channa Halli, Ittige Halli, Hosuru, Malalakoppa Kachi Koppa, Adagadi, Chikkamathali, Suduru Doddamathali, Adina Kottige, Koodi , Gavate Thevaru Bilguni, Thammadi Halli, Thavare Koppa Bilvadera Koppa, Shirigere, Male Shankara Maleshankara State Forest, Manjari Koppa, Sidlipura Gejjenahalli, Kallaganguru, Puradalu, Anupina Katte Hanumantha Pura, Govindapura, Agasavalli Shetty Halli, Chitra Shetty Halli, Basavapura Echavadi, Kalluru, Gondichatnahalli, Kunchena Halli Kalla Pura, Boodi Gere, Harama Ghatta Madike Chiluru, Hadona Halli, Holaluru, Lingapura Kyathina Koppa, Somina Koppa, Bikkona Halli Abbalagere, Hunasodu, Mojappana Hosuru Channamumba Pura, Belala Katte, Melina Hanasavadi Hole Hanasavadi, Bullapura, Suguru, Kudli Hoisana Halli, Pillangere, Javalli, Chikkudli Taragana Halli, Belagalu, Yankata Pura B Beeranahalli, Beerana Halli, Haro Benavalli Gudra Koppa, Malena Halli, Gowdanaykana Halli Buklapura, Kati Kere, Sakre Bylu, Kudagala Mane Gajanuru State Forest, Hosakoppa, Hosahalli Lakshmi Pura, Mathuru, Honna Pura, Gajanuru Veera Pura, Gajanuru Agrahara, Sakre Bylu, Kadekal Kuskuru, Yaraganalu, Kachina Katte, Mandenakoppa Santhe Kaduru, Dummalli, Bidare, Yalavatti Bekkina Kalmatha, Hanumanthapura, Hosudi, Honnavile Machena Halli, Nidige, Sogane, Rampura, Korala Halli Lakkinakoppa, Huruli Halli, Ganidalu, Sari Gere Kydotlu, Belagalu, Siddamaji Hosuru, Linga Pura

Kakana Hosudi, Umble Bylu.

The villages having more than 50% ST population are None.

Sex ratio of Scheduled tribe population is 491.

Scheduled Tribes Literates and Illiterates by Sex:

	Persons	Males	Females
Literate	4,672	2,742	1,930
Illiterate	5,694	2,539	3,155
Literacy rate	53.3	61.7	44.7
Graduate	103	79	24

Scheduled Tribes (Dominant):

Naikda etc., Hakkipikki, Meda, Kadu Kuruba Jenu Kuruba

For their cultural identity please see Appendix-II

Villages without Scheduled Tribes: There are 105 villages without any scheduled tribe population.

Literates and Illiterates by Sex (Total Population):

	Persons	Males	Females
Literate	97,595	55,556	42,039
Illiterate	73,245	31,148	42,097
Literacy rate	67	75	58
Graduate	3,230	2,435	795

Agriculture: ***Distribution of villages according to land use:*** Out of 214 villages, Total area (in hectare) is 101788, out of that 38.33 percent is cultivable and 52.48 percent of the cultivable area is irrigated.

Sources of Irrigation (Hectares): Government Canal 7959.68, Private Canal 57.8, Well without Electricity 192.25, Well with Electricity 1061.68, Tubewell without Electricity 61.5, Tubewell with Electricity 2226.1, Tank 6910.47, River 1064.6, Lake 0, Waterfall 0, Others 940.87.

Villages with population of 5000 to 9999: Kumsi, Harana Halli.

Villages with population of 10000 and above: None

Distribution of Workers:

	Persons	Males	Females	WPR
Cultivators	24,646	20,503	4,143	31.99
Agricultural Labour	34,648	16,916	17,732	44.97
Household Industry	1,402	909	493	1.82
Other Workers	16,354	13,069	3,285	21.23
Main Workers	61,124	45,303	15,821	79.33
Marginal Workers	15,926	6,094	9,832	20.67
Total Workers	77,050	51,397	25,653	

Religion: Major Religious Communities:

	Persons	Males	Females	Sex Ratio
Hindu (90.5%)	154,615	78,481	76,134	970
Muslim (8.83%)	15,078	7,640	7,438	974
Christian (0.45%)	761	378	383	1,013
Sikh (0%)	-	-	-	-
Buddhists (0%)	-	-	-	-
Jain (0.1%)	167	87	80	920

Agewise Data:

	Persons	Males	Females	Sex Ratio
All ages	170,840	86,704	84,136	970
0-14	54,847	27,721	27,126	979
15-44	84,980	43,211	41,769	967
45-79	29,514	15,074	14,440	958
80+	1,402	645	757	1174
Age not stated	97	53	44	830

Languages (Dominant):

Kannada, Hindi, Urdu, Tamil, Telugu

Disabled Population:

	Persons	Males	Females	%
Total Disabled	2,722	1,579	1,143	
In Seeing	950	485	465	34.9
In Speech	296	173	123	10.87
In Hearing	165	93	72	6.06
In Movement	986	627	359	36.22
Mentally	325	201	124	11.94

SHIRHATTI

Shirhatti C.D. Block lies in the south-western part of Gadag district. It is a part of Shirhatti taluka. The Block is located at a distance of 26 kms. from district headquarters (Gadag). There are 87 villages in the block with the total population of 133,511 persons. Area of the C.D. Block is 940.53 sq. kms. It is bounded by taluk Gadag and Mundargi, and district Dharwad on north, districts Haveri and Bellary on south, taluk Mundargi and district Bellary on east, and district Dharwad on west.

Communications:

Roadways : S.H-6: Direction- Savanur to Gadag, Nearest Villages- Holalapur, Magadi, Gojanur, Desai Ban, Lakshme shwar (Hireban) (Rural), Hulgeriban, Bastiban, Pethaban, Gulaganjikoppa, Govanal.

River: Tungabhadra Nadi- Nearest Villages- Tolali, Itagi, Sasarwad, Basapur, Kallaganur.

Reserved Forest: Nearest Villages- Akkigund, Shettikeri, Kundralli, Nadigatti, Adrahalli, Sogiwal, Suranagi, Yallapur, Balehosur, Parasapur Shirahatti (Rural), Varavi, Guddadapur, Jalligeri, Kadakol, Kusalapur, Majjur, Shivajinagar, Chabbi, Tegginabhavanur, Machenahalli, Ranatur, Devihal, Wadavi, Alagilawad, Govanakoppa, Koganur, Tangod, Itagi.

Annual Rainfall: Normal Rianfall 748.9 mm.

Ground Water: Availability of the Ground Water in the Basin is 4754 H.A.M. and the utilization is 584 H.A. M. It belongs to Over Exploited category. Depth to water level 5 to 20 meter below the ground. Most of the wells go down in summer months, according to the

Ground Water Estimation Committee.

Soils: Medium to deep black soils.

Natural Division : It falls partly in the Dharwad-Gadag Plateau, Kalghatgi-Lakshmeshwar Residual Hills and the Middle Tungabhadra Valley of the Central Karnataka Plateau.

Administration:

Division: Belgaum. Parliamentary Constituency: 10 Haveri. District: Gadag. Taluka: Shirhatti. Assembly Constituency: 65 Shirhatti (SC). Gram Panchayat: 24.

Regional Area Development Boards: The Bailu Seeme Area Development Board.

Villages: 87 **Inhabited:** 87 **Uninhabited:** 0

Ranking	District	State	National
Area	3	95	493
Population	3	142	2387
Sex Ratio	3	115	2823
Child Sex Ratio	4	112	3419
Literacy Rate	4	85	2746
Density	2	41	5669
Work Participation Rate	4	140	1292

Gram Panchayats:

Yalavatti, Magadi, Chabbi, Kadakol, Machenahalli, Ranatur, Adrahalli, Battur, Gojanur, Ramageri, Shigli, Haradagatti, Doddur, Futagao Badni, Bellatti, Bannikoppa, Tarikoppa, Wadavi, Konchigeri, Suranagi, Balehosur, Koganur, Itagi, Hebbal.

Amenities:

Education: Primary School in 78 villages, Middle school in 55 villages, Matriculation or Secondary School in 16 villages, namely Madhalli, Yalavatti, Magadi, Gojanur, Ramageri, Futagao Badni, Shigli, Suranagi, Balehosur, Kadakol, Bellatti, Bannikoppa, Wadavi, Koganur, Hebbal, Itagi.

Higher Secondary or Pre University Courses or Intermediate or Junior College in 4 villages of the CD Block,, namely Magadi, Bellatti, Bannikoppa, Hebbal.

College in 1 village, Adult Literacy Center in 0 village., College is in village, namely Bellatti.

Medical: Hospital in 1 village, Dispensary in 4 villages, Health Center in 5 villages, Sub Center in 32 villages, Maternity and Child Welfare Center in 8 villages, Community health workers in 19 villages.

The Villages having Hospital or Dispensary or Health Center are Magadi, Shigli, Suranagi, Balehosur.

Drinking Water: Tap water in 41 villages, Tank water in 13 villages, Well water in 42 villages, Tubewell in 15 villages and more than one source in 70 villages.

Bank: Banking facility in 7 villages, namely, Yalavatti, Shigli, Suranagi, Bellatti, Bannikoppa Hebbal, Itagi.

Credit Society in 21 villages Agricultural Credit Society in 19 Non-Agricultural Credit Society in 7 villages.

Others: Power supply in 84 villages, Cinema hall in 2 villages, sport club in 8 villages, Stadium or Auditorium or Community Hall in 0 village, Post Office in 30 villages.

There are 74 villages having bus facilities.

Villages with most of facilities: Yalavatti Shigli, Suranagi, Bellatti, Bannikoppa, Hebbal Itagi.

Villages without amenities (Education): Desai Ban, Lakshmeshwar (Hireban) (Rural), Hulgeriban, Pethaban, Suvarnagiri, Shirahatti (Rural), Tegginabhavanur, Hosur..

Scheduled Castes: Out of the total population of 133566 persons, 27945 persons (20.92%) belong to Scheduled Castes.

The villages having less than 10% SC population are Holalapur, Desai Ban, Bastiban, Pethaban Futagao Badni, Sogiwal, Hire Mallapur Wadeyar Mallapur, Gulaganjikoppa, Shigli, Shyabala Amarapur, Hullur, Khanapur, Kusalapur, Majjur Tegginabhavanur, Nave Bhavanur, Machenahalli Sugnalli, Hadagali, Bhavanur, Bannikoppa Narayanapura, Chikkasavanur, Hosur, Kerihalli Bijjur, Nagaramaduvu, Chavadal, Sasarwad, Basapur Kallaganur.

The villages having more than 50% SC population are Hulgeriban, Akkigund, Adrahalli, Haradagatti Ullatti, Doddur, Suvarnagiri, Guddadapur Shivajinagar, Sevanagar, Belaghatti.

Sex ratio of Scheduled Caste population is 490.

Scheduled Castes Literates and Illiterates by Sex:

	Persons	Males	Females
Literate	9,179	6,131	3,048
Illiterate	18,766	8,127	10,639
Literacy rate	39.6	52.0	26.8
Graduate	158	151	7

Scheduled Castes (Dominant):

Banjara etc., Bhambi etc., Bhovi, Dom etc., Korama

For their cultural identity please see Appendix-I

Villages without Scheduled Castes: There are 8 villages without any scheduled caste population.

Scheduled Tribes: Out of the total population of 133566 persons, 11644 persons (8.72%) belong to Scheduled Tribes.

The villages having less than 10% ST population are Madhalli, Yattinahalli, Yalavatti, Holalapur, Magadi Desai Ban, Hulgeriban, Akkigund, Shettikeri Kundralli, Battur, Bastiban, Pethaban, Adarakatti Futagao Badni, Sankadal, Nadigatti, Adrahalli Sogiwal, Haradagatti, Gulaganjikoppa, Govanal Shigli, Shyabala, Doddur, Amarapur, Hullur

Suvarnagiri, Yallapur, Khanapur, Parasapur Shirahatti (Rural), Varavi, Guddadapur, Kusalapur Shivajinagar, Chabbi, Tegginabhavanur, Ranatur Devihal, Bellatti, Narayanapura, Kokkargundi Tarikoppa, Sevanagar, Alagilawad, Govanakoppa Bijjur, Nagaramaduvu, Koganur, Tangod, Kanakawad Hebbal, Tolali, Sasarwad, Basapur.

The villages having more than 50% ST population are Kondikoppa, Wadeyar Mallapur, Nave Bhavanur Bhavanur.

Sex ratio of Scheduled tribe population is 492.

Scheduled Tribes Literates and Illiterates by Sex:

	Persons	Males	Females
Literate	5,460	3,497	1,963
Illiterate	6,184	2,413	3,771
Literacy rate	54.8	69.3	39.9
Graduate	125	109	16

Scheduled Tribes (Dominant):

Naikda etc., Kota, Jenu Kuruba, Iruliga Koli Dhor etc.

For their cultural identity please see Appendix-II

Villages without Scheduled Tribes: There are 17 villages without any scheduled tribe population.

Literates and Illiterates by Sex (Total Population):

	Persons	Males	Females
Literate	69,051	43,055	25,996
Illiterate	64,515	25,004	39,511
Literacy rate	60	74	46
Graduate	1,875	1,607	268

Agriculture: ***Distribution of villages according to land use:*** Out of 87 villages, Total area (in hectare) is 94053, out of that 78.92 percent is cultivable and 5.07 percent of the cultivable area is irrigated.

Sources of Irrigation (Hectares): Government Canal 129.1, Private Canal 0, Well without Electricity 11.51, Well with Electricity 744.72, Tubewell without Electricity 48.62, Tubewell with Electricity 2351.03, Tank 142.87, River 166.74, Lake 0, Waterfall 0, Others 169.3.

Villages with population of 5000 to 9999: Suranagi, Balehosur, Bellatti.

Villages with population of 10000 and above: Shigli.

Distribution of Workers:

	Persons	Males	Females	WPR
Cultivators	22,330	16,210	6,120	31.66
Agricultural Labour	37,528	16,108	21,420	53.22
Household Industry	2,429	1,704	725	3.44
Other Workers	8,234	6,807	1,427	11.68
Main Workers	60,129	38,382	21,747	85.26
Marginal Workers	10,392	2,447	7,945	14.74
Total Workers	70,521	40,829	29,692	

Religion: Major Religious Communities:

	Persons	Males	Females	Sex Ratio
Hindu (91.74%)	122,533	62,447	60,086	962
Muslim (6.81%)	9,095	4,619	4,476	969
Christian (0.03%)	40	18	22	1,222
Sikh (0%)	2	1	1	1,000
Buddhists (0%)	2	1	1	1,000
Jain (0.97%)	1,289	668	621	930

Agewise Data:

	Persons	Males	Females	Sex Ratio
All ages	133,566	68,059	65,507	963
0-14	45,388	23,019	22,369	972
15-44	62,419	32,698	29,721	909
45-79	24,632	11,907	12,725	1069
80+	1,072	397	675	1700
Age not stated	55	38	17	447

Languages (Dominant):

Kannada, Hindi, Urdu, Telugu, Marathi

Disabled Population:

	Persons	Males	Females	%
Total Disabled	2,343	1,315	1,028	
In Seeing	839	419	420	35.81
In Speech	203	112	91	8.66
In Hearing	140	71	69	5.98
In Movement	921	565	356	39.31
Mentally	240	148	92	10.24

SHORAPUR

Shorapur C.D. Block lies in the south-western part of Gulbarga district. It is a part of Shorapur taluka. The Block is located at a distance of 107 kms. From district headquarters (Gulbarga). There are 201 villages in the block with the total population of 293,098 persons. Area of the C.D. Block is 1816.63 sq. kms. It is bounded by taluk Jevargi on north, Raichur district on south, taluk Shahpur on east, and district Bijapur on west.

Communications:

Roadways : S.H-16: Direction- Sindgi to Shahpur, Nearest Villages- Hadnoor, Malla (K), Malla, Yevor, Dand Sholapur, Sevanagar. S.H-19: Direction- Lingsugur to Yadgir, Nearest Villages- Bapparga, Hullikera, Ammapur (S.K), Devapur, Kampapur, Aralhalli, Tinthni, Dadlapur, Bandoli, Devikera, Bijaspur, Arkera Khalsa, Kumbarpeth, Kaudimatti, Havinhal, Kagarhal.

River: Don Nadi- Nearest Villages- Bapparga, Hagratgi, Boodihal, Horatti, Uppaidinni, Bardevanhal, Kodekal, Hullikera, Ammapur (S.K), Tangadbail, Rayangola. Krishna Nadi- Nearest Villages- Geddalmari, Jamalpur, Dharampur, Ammapur (S.K),Tangadbail, Rayangola, Hanuman Nagar, Narayanpur Rural, Myalingaddi,

Jangangaddi, Devapur, Kampapur, Aralhalli, Tinthni, Dadlapur, Bandoli, Hunsiholi, Kekkera, Yedalbhavi, Benchigaddi,Lingadhalli, Shalgi, Hemnoor, Choudeshwarhal, Mushtalli, Bevinhal, Sugur, Hemwadgi, Adwadgi.

Reserved Forest: (Tangarbal): Nearest Villages-Tangadbail, Rayangola, Kotigud.

Annual Rainfall: Normal Rianfall 777 mm.

Ground Water: Availability of the Ground Water in the Basin is 10744 H.A.M. and the utilization is 2081 H.A.M. It belongs to Over Exploited category. Depth to water level 2 to 10 meter below the ground. Most of the wells go down in summer months, according to the Ground Water Estimation Committee.

Soils: Deep Black, Medium Black Soil, Shallow Soil and Lateritic Soil.

Natural Division : It falls in Sub-micro regions of the Shorapur-Shahpur Upland and the Middle Krishna Valley of the Northern Karnataka Plateau.

Administration:

Division: Gulbarga. Parliamentary Constituency: 6 Raichur (ST) District: Gulbarga. Taluka: Shorapur. Assembly Constituency:3 6 Shorapur (ST). Gram Panchayat: 42. Regional Area Development Boards: The Hyderabad-Karnataka Area Development Board.

Fairs: Channabasaveshwara Jatra: It is held at Kodekal near Gulbarga two times in a year, in the month of 15th Kartika (October-November) and 15th chaitra (March-April). Kodekal is a place of religious importance visited by pilgrims throughout the year. The Shri Channabasavesh wara temple situated in this place attracts a large number of devotees. During the Jatra, some ten thousand people congregate here. Kodekal is also noted for its Dargah which is venerated by the Hindus also. Kodekal is in the extreme south-west of Gulbarga area and lies some 16 kms. to the north of the Krishna river, in Shorapur taluk.

Chhaya Bhagavathi Festival: It is a place very near to Narayanapur on the banks of the Krishna river in Shorapur taluk.The river runs into a fall at this place. A portion of the river runs into a cave and emerges out. A festival is held here on Vaishakha Shuddha Tadige when thousands of pilgrims congregate to offer worship to Chhaya Bhagavathi, a wife of .the Sun-god

Gopalaswami Fair: It is held at Shorapur near Gulbarga in the month of 23 Shravana (August) for two days. Shorapur is the headquarters of the taluk of the same name. The nearest railway station is Yadgir which is about 40 kms. It was known in the old days by the name of Surapura. After the advent of Muslim rule, it began to be called as Shorapur. Not only Shorapur is historically famous but it is also a place of some religious importance. It was the capital of a line of rulers whose domain comprised the area which extended from the Bhima river to the Krishna. It became prominent during the first war of independence in 1857, when the Bedar Raja of Shorapur revolted against the British rule. Prior to this, the Bedar Rajas had battled hard against Emperor Aurangzeb.A Hindu shrine in the town dedicated to the god Gopalaswami devotees throughout the year. A big fair is held here during attracts Gokulashtand. Col. Meadows Taylor who is the author of several historical novels lived here for some time. The house that he built is called Taylor's Manzil and is visited by a number of people.Soon after the 1857 revolt when order was restored, Shorapur State was made over to the Nizam of Hyderabad.

Villages: 201 **Inhabited:** 190 **Uninhabited:** 11

Ranking	District	State	National
Area	1	9	68
Population	1	19	80
Sex Ratio	5	66	1979
Child Sex Ratio	4	99	3171
Literacy Rate	7	169	5687
Density	7	116	5384
Work Participation Rate	1	114	2678

Gram Panchayats:

Malla(B), Yevor, Nagnoor, Yalgi, Yektapur, Kembhavi, Parsanahalli, Malgatti, Kardakal, Mudnoor(K), Agni, Baichbal, Devargonal, Devikera, Arkerakhalsa, Wagingera, Pethammapur, Kachakanoor, Arkera(J), Kolihal, Khanapur, Hemnoor, Aldhal, Devatkal, Hebbal(B), Wajjal, Malnoor, Hunsgi, Devapur, Sugur, Tinthni, Kekkera, Kamnatgi, Rajankollur, Hagratgi, Bardevanhal, Kodekal, Bailkunti, Geddalmari, Marnal, Jogandabhavi, Narayanpurrural.

Amenities:

Education: Primary School in 187 villages, Middle school in 95 villages, Matriculation or Secondary School in 23 villages, namely Yalgi, Malla, Nagnoor, Kembhavi, Chincholi, Heggandoddi, Mudnoor (K), Baichbal, Kachaknoor, Gundalgare, Wajjal, Hunsgi, Rajankollur, Kodekal, Geddalmari, Narayanpur Rural, Benkanhalli, Devapur, Kekkera, Jalibenchi, Devargonal, Peth Ammapur, Bijaspur.

Higher Secondary or Pre University Courses or Intermediate or Junior College in 4 villages of the CD Block,, namely Nagnoor, Kembhavi, Hunsgi, Kodekal.

College in 1 village, Adult Literacy Center in 28 villages., College is in village, namely Kekkera.

Medical: Hospital in 0 village, Dispensary in 8 villages,

Health Center in 16 villages, Sub Center in 32 villages, Maternity and Child Welfare Center in 6 villages, Community health workers in 40 villages.

The Villages having Hospital or Dispensary or Health Center are Kembhavi, Hunsgi, Rajankollur, Rajwal, Geddalmari, Krishnanagar, Hebbal (B), Aldhal, Manjalapur (K), Kekkera, Rattal, Bijaspur.

Drinking Water: Tap water in 60 villages, Tank water in 36 villages, Well water in 164 villages, Tubewell in 35 villages and more than one source in 178 villages.

Bank: Banking facility in 14 villages, namely, Yevor, Khanapur (Sk), Nagnoor, Kembhavi, Wajjal Hunsgi, Rajankollur, Kodekal, Devatinagar Geddalmari, Krishnanagar, Narayanpur Rural, Devapur Kekkera.

Credit Society in 23 villages Agricultural Credit Society in 21 Non-Agricultural Credit Society in 1 village.

Others: Power supply in 186 villages, Cinema hall in 4 villages, sport club in 6 villages, Stadium or Auditorium or Community Hall in 190 villages, Post Office in 52 villages.

There are 115 villages having bus facilities.

Villages with most of facilities: Yevor, Nagnoor Kembhavi, Hunsgi, Rajankollur, Kodekal, Geddalmari Krishnanagar, Narayanpur Rural, Kekkera.

Villages without amenities (Education): Murakanal, Badlapur - Becharak, Kampapur..

Scheduled Castes: Out of the total population of 293133 persons, 56928 persons (19.42%) belong to Scheduled Castes.

The villages having less than 10% SC population are Yalgi, Gogaddihal, Malkapur, Fathepur, Murakanal Nadkoor, Jainapur, Heggandoddi, Tippanatgi, Amlihal Yediapur, Kanhalli, Badlapur - Becharak, Karibhavi Devapur Jagir, Banhatti, Bapparga, Hagratgi, Gulbal Horatti, Kurekanhal, Mudilinganhal, Bassapur Yenniwadgera, Rajwal, Bailkunti, Kamalpur, Kotigud Jangangaddi, Kampapur, Raigera, Siddapur, Bhailapur Manjalapur (K), Dadlapur, Bandoli, Kekkera Hombalkal, Benchigaddi, Lingadhalli, Mavinmatti Chigirhal, Machgundal, Siddapur (G), Kurbantalahalli Peth Ammapur, Godihal Jagir, Kupgal, Hemwadgi.

The villages having more than 50% SC population are Sevanagar, Shivaji Nagar, Bevinhal (S.K.), Ramnagar Bhagyanagar, Kangandanahalli, Mailapur, Rayanpala Devatinagar, Krishnanagar, Dharampur, Jogandabhavi Hanuman Nagar, Rajunagar, Hanmanhal, Jairamnagar Venkatapur.

Sex ratio of Scheduled Caste population is 497.

Scheduled Castes Literates and Illiterates by Sex:

	Persons	Males	Females
Literate	13,669	9,674	3,995
Illiterate	43,259	18,961	24,298
Literacy rate	30.0	42.4	17.5
Graduate	437	399	38

Scheduled Castes (Dominant):

Banjara etc., Holaya etc., Madiga, Bhambi etc. Bhovi

For their cultural identity please see Appendix-I

Villages without Scheduled Castes: There are 18 villages without any scheduled caste population.

Scheduled Tribes: Out of the total population of 293133 persons, 53738 persons (18.33%) belong to Scheduled Tribes.

The villages having less than 10% ST population are Wandgnoor, Yalgi, Malla (K), Malla, Sevanagar Khanapur (Sk), Kembhavi, Shivaji Nagar Bevinhal (S.K.), Chincholi, Dornahalli Muneerbommanhalli, Yektapur, Alhal, Huvinhalli Kachapur, Malhalli, Nadkoor, Jainapur, Heggandoddi Tippanatgi, Agni, Handral, Mudnoor (B), Mudnoor (K) Rampur, Yediapur, Teggihalli, Badlapur - Becharak Agthirth, Sadab, Baichbal, Gundalgare, Ramnagar Isampur, Bhagyanagar, Kaldevanhalli, Channur, Wajjal Devapur Jagir, Hunsgi, Balshattihal, Manjlapur Bapparga, Hagratgi, Rajankollur, Yenniwadgera Marnal, Mailapur, Devatinagar, Krishnanagar Dharampur, Jogandabhavi, Kamalpur, Hanuman Nagar Hebbal (B), Bachimatti, Konal, Handral, Gonal Aldhal, Nagaral, Kampapur, Rajunagar, Santpur Hunsiholi, Hanmanhal, Hombalkal, Jairamnagar Mavinmatti, Machgundal, Bahirimabdi, Rattal Devikera, Peth Ammapur, Venkatapur, Kaudimatti Havinhal, Mushtalli, Sugur, Hemwadgi.

The villages having more than 50% ST population are Gogaddihal, Goudgera, Shakhapur, Banhatti, Gulbal Bassapur, Yerkihal, Rajwal, Bailkunti, Tangadbail Aralhalli, Raigera, Siddapur, Bhailapur, Dadlapur Bandoli, Sonnapur, Benchigaddi, Lingadhalli, Kupgal Lingadhalli, Shakhapur, Karnal, Choudeshwarhal Adwadgi.

Sex ratio of Scheduled tribe population is 497.

Scheduled Tribes Literates and Illiterates by Sex:

	Persons	Males	Females
Literate	12,385	8,825	3,560
Illiterate	41,353	18,201	23,152
Literacy rate	28.6	40.7	16.5
Graduate	227	206	21

Scheduled Tribes (Dominant):

Naikda etc., Kadu Kuruba, Generic Tribes etc. Koli Dhor etc., Meda

For their cultural identity please see Appendix-II

Villages without Scheduled Tribes: There are

41 villages without any scheduled tribe population.

Literates and Illiterates by Sex (Total Population):

	Persons	Males	Females
Literate	96,411	64,265	32,146
Illiterate	196,722	83,744	112,978
Literacy rate	40	53	27
Graduate	3,391	2,980	411

Agriculture: ***Distribution of villages according to land use:*** Out of 201 villages, Total area (in hectare) is 181663, out of that 83.14 percent is cultivable and 41.91 percent of the cultivable area is irrigated.

Sources of Irrigation (Hectares): Government Canal 60223.44, Private Canal 943.11, Well without Electricity 195.99, Well with Electricity 538.95, Tubewell without Electricity 12.22, Tubewell with Electricity 126.06, Tank 242.83, River 774.05, Lake 26.2, Waterfall 0, Others 214.06.

Villages with population of 5000 to 9999:
Kodekal, Narayanpur Rural.

Villages with population of 10000 and above:
Kembhavi, Hunsgi, Kekkera.

Distribution of Workers:

	Persons	Males	Females	WPR
Cultivators	43,503	34,873	8,630	32.79
Agricultural Labour	61,517	21,433	40,084	46.37
Household Industry	2,841	1,745	1,096	2.14
Other Workers	24,809	18,543	6,266	18.7
Main Workers	98,089	67,546	30,543	73.93
Marginal Workers	34,581	9,048	25,533	26.07
Total Workers	132,670	76,594	56,076	

Religion: Major Religious Communities:

	Persons	Males	Females	Sex Ratio
Hindu (88.16%)	258,439	130,541	127,898	980
Muslim (9.09%)	26,655	13,443	13,212	983
Christian (0.09%)	260	143	117	818
Sikh (0%)	7	3	4	1,333
Buddhists (2.14%)	6,285	3,137	3,148	1,004
Jain (0.06%)	162	78	84	1,077

Agewise Data:

	Persons	Males	Females	Sex Ratio
All ages	293,133	148,009	145,124	981
0-14	124,493	63,688	60,805	955
15-44	120,429	61,563	58,866	956
45-79	46,230	22,009	24,221	1101
80+	1,788	629	1,159	1843
Age not stated	193	120	73	608

Languages (Dominant):
Kannada, Urdu, Hindi, Telugu, Marathi

Disabled Population:

	Persons	Males	Females	%
Total Disabled	4,505	2,467	2,038	
In Seeing	1,727	841	886	38.34
In Speech	481	247	234	10.68
In Hearing	313	172	141	6.95
In Movement	1,602	996	606	35.56
Mentally	382	211	171	8.48

SHRIRANGAPATTANA

Shrirangapattana C.D. Block lies in the southern part of Mandya district. It is a part of Shrirangapattana taluk. The Block is located at a distance of 28 kms. from district headquarters (Mandya). There are 96 villa ges in the block with the total population of 139,234 persons. Area of the C.D. Block is 341.97 sq. kms. It is bounded by taluks Pandavapura and Mandya on north, and district Mysore on south, east and west.

Communications:

Roadways : S.H.-7: Direction- Pandavapura to Pandavapura, Nearest Village- Kadathanalu. S.H.-17: Direction- Mysore to Mandya, Nearest Villages- Kirangur, Siddapura, Ganang ooru, Gowdahalli, T.M.Hosur, M.Shettihalli, Sabbanakuppe, K.Shettihalli, Palahalli, Karimanti, Bommur Agrahara, Brahmapura. S.H-19: Direction- Pandavapur to Kirangur, Nearest Villages- Kirangur, Darasaguppe.

Railway Station: Villages- Nelamane, Chindagirikoppalu, Madarahalli, Kuppedada.

River: Cauvery Nadi- Nearest Villages- Doddegowdanakoppa lu, Agrahara, Kirangur, Kallikoppalu, Chinnayakanahalli, Maralagala, Mundagadore,l Hangarahalli,l Arakere, Gande hosahalli, Belagola, Hongahalli, Yadathittu, Karekura, Belagola, Palahalli, Karimanti, Bommur Agrahara, Melapu ra, Mahadevapura, Bidarahalli. Lokpavani Nadi- Nearest Villages- Kirangur, Chindagirikoppalu, Chinnenahalli, M.Shettihalli, Sabbanakuppe, Ballenahalli, Kudalakuppe, K.Shettihalli, Kallikoppalu, Chinnayakanahalli.

Canal: Nearest Villages- Doddegowdanakoppalu, Agrahara, Kirangur, Darasaguppe, Nelamane, Chindagirikoppalu, Chinnenahalli, Neelana Koppalu, Nagaraghatta, M.Shettih alli, Sabbanakuppe, Ballenahalli, Kudalakuppe, K.Shettiha lli, Kallikoppalu, Chinnayakanahalli, Maralagala, Allapat na, Mundagadore, Hangarahalli, Vadiyandahalli, Hunasanaha lli, Kodiyala, Aladahalli, Peehalli, Ballekere, Arakere, Madarahalli, Gandehosahalli, Hongahalli, Majjigepura, Balamuri, Yadathittu, Karekura, Mogarahalli, Jakkanakup pe, Hosahalli, Kempalingapura, Palahalli, Karimanti, Bommur Agrahara, Brahmapura, Naguvanahalli, Belavadi, Hosur, Chandagalu, Melapura, Mahadevapura, Bidarahalli, Kemmannupura, Taripura, Hebbadi, Doddankanahalli, Chikkankanahalli.

Annual Rainfall: Normal Rianfall 655.8 mm.

Ground Water: Availability of the Ground Water in the Basin is 5209.19 H.A.M. and the utilization is 1699.

25 H.A.M. It belongs to Over Expoited category. Depth to water level 2 to 10 meter below the ground. Most of the wells go down in summer months, according to the Ground Water Estimation Committee.

Soils: Red Sandy Loams to Red Clay Loam.

Natural Division : It falls partly in Cauvery-Hemavati Valley and Shimsha Basin of the Southern Karnataka Plateau.

Administration:

Division: Mysore. Parliamentary Constituency: 20 Mandya. District: Mandya. Taluka: Shrirangapattana. Assembly Constituency: 190 Shrirangapattana. Gram Panchayat: 21.

Fairs: Ranganathaswamy Fair: It is held at Srirangapatna near Mandya in the month of Pushya (December-January). Sriran gapatna is situated at the western or upper end of an island in the Cauvery about 5 kms. in length from west to east and 1.65 kms. in breadth. The eastern end of the island is occupied by the suburb of Ganjam. Sriranga patna, the headquarters of the taluk of the same name, stands on the Mysore-Bangalore railway route and the Bangalore-Mysore road, 129 miles south-west from Bangalo re and 1.5 kms. north-east from Mysore city. The town derives its name from the presiding deity of local Ranga natha temple.

Venkataramanaswami Temple Jatra: Karighatta is a hill rising to 2,697 feet in the Srirangapatna taluk east of the point where the Lokapavani joins the Cauvery. There is a Venkataramanaswami temple on the top of the hill. A Kalyana Mantapa is also attached to the temple and marriages and other functions are celebrated there. The annual jatra held here about the month of magha (February-March) for seven days, attracts a large number of people.

Villages: 96 **Inhabited:** 90 **Uninhabited:** 6

Ranking	District	State	National
Area	7	172	2349
Population	7	139	2179
Sex Ratio	5	85	2294
Child Sex Ratio	5	169	4965
Literacy Rate	1	83	2683
Density	1	26	2696
Work Participation Rate	2	9	963

Gram Panchayats:

K. R. Sagara, Hulikere , Belagola, Hosahalli, Palahalli, Kirangur, K. Shettihalli, Darasaguppe, Ballenahalli, Sabbanakuppe, T. M. Hosur, Kodiyala, Tadagavadi, Gamanahalli, Arakere, Gandehosahalli, Mundagadore, Mahadevapura, Melapura, Naguvanahalli, Chikkankanahalli.

Amenities:

Education: Primary School in 72 villages, Middle school in 49 villages, Matriculation or Secondary School in 16 villages, namely T.M.Hosur, M.Shettihalli, Ballenahalli, Mundagadore, Alagud, Kodiyala, Gamanahalli, Neralekere, Arakere, Belagola, Mogarahalli, Palahalli, Naguvanahalli, Mahadevapura, Bidarahalli, Chikkankanahalli.

Higher Secondary or Pre University Courses or Intermediate or Junior College in 2 villages of the CD Block,, namely Alagud, Arakere.

College in 0 village, Adult Literacy Center in 5 villages.

Medical: Hospital in 2 villages, Dispensary in 6 villages, Health Center in 10 villages, Sub Center in 26 villages, Maternity and Child Welfare Center in 7 villages, Community health workers in 8 villages.

The Villages having Hospital or Dispensary or Health Center are T.M.Hosur, Ballenahalli, Mundagadore, Arakere, Hongahalli, Belagola, Palahalli.

Drinking Water: Tap water in 84 villages, Tank water in 32 villages, Well water in 72 villages, Tubewell in 67 villages and more than one source in 86 villages.

Bank: Banking facility in 18 villages, namely, Achappana Koppalu, Kirangur, Darasaguppe, Nelamane T.M.Hosur, Ballenahalli, K.Shettihalli Hunasanahalli, Kodiyala, Tadagavadi, Arakere Kuppedada, Belagola, Palahalli, Naguvanahalli Mahadevapura, Chikkankanahalli, Sugganahalli.

Credit Society in 17 villages Agricultural Credit Society in 13 Non-Agricultural Credit Society in 5 villages.

Others: Power supply in 89 villages, Cinema hall in 7 villages, sport club in 2 villages, Stadium or Auditorium or Community Hall in 1 village, Post Office in 32 villages.

There are 71 villages having bus facilities.

Villages with most of facilities: Achappana Koppalu Kirangur, Darasaguppe, T.M.Hosur, Ballenahalli K.Shettihalli, Hunasanahalli, Kodiyala, Tadagavadi Arakere, Belagola, Palahalli, Naguvanahalli Mahadevapura, Chikkankanahalli, Sugganahalli.

Villages without amenities (Education):

Makanakoppalu, Agrahara, Kallikoppalu, Vitalapura, Hongahalli, Avverahalli, Anagahalli, Yadathittu, Jakkanakuppe, Kempalingapura, Karimanti, Brahmapura, Kemmannupura, Doddankanahalli..

Scheduled Castes: Out of the total population of 139255 persons, 21601 persons (15.51%) belong to Scheduled Castes. The villages having less than 10% SC population are Makanakoppalu, Achappana Koppalu, Agrahara Darasaguppe, Chindagirikoppalu, Gowdahalli T.M.Hosur, Ballenahalli, Kallikoppalu Chinnayakanahalli, Mollenahalli, Chottahalli Bannahalli, Vitalapura, Neralekere, Ballekere

Bettahalli, Chikkaharohalli, Tadagavadi, Garakahalli Arakere, Hulikere, Beechanakuppe, Basthipura Majjigepura, Balamuri, Jakkanakuppe, Kempalingapura Palahalli, Karimanti, Brahmapura, Naguvanahalli Chandagalu, Bidarahalli, Kemmannupura, Taripura Sugganahalli.

The villages having more than 50% SC population are Kalenahalli, Neelana Koppalu, Hangarahalli Channanakere, Belavadi, Doddankanahalli.

Sex ratio of Scheduled Caste population is 502.

Scheduled Castes Literates and Illiterates by Sex:

	Persons	Males	Females
Literate	10,163	5,877	4,286
Illiterate	11,438	4,883	6,555
Literacy rate	54.1	62.8	45.4
Graduate	261	211	50

Scheduled Castes (Dominant):

Adi Karnataka, Bhovi, Madiga, Generic Castes etc.
Adi Dravida

For their cultural identity please see Appendix-I

Villages without Scheduled Castes: There are 20 villages without any scheduled caste population.

Scheduled Tribes: Out of the total population of 139255 persons, 1356 persons (0.97%) belong to Scheduled Tribes.

The villages having less than 10% ST population are Kadathanalu, Makanakoppalu, Achappana Koppalu Doddegowdanakoppalu, Agrahara, Rampura, Kirangur Darasaguppe, Nelamane, Chindagirikoppalu Chinnenahalli, Siddapura, Ganangooru, Gowdahalli T.M.Hosur, Kalenahalli, Neelana Koppalu M.Shettihalli, Sabbanakuppe, Ballenahalli Kudalakuppe, K.Shettihalli, Kallikoppalu Chinnayakanahalli, Maralagala, Allapatna Mundagadore, Hangarahalli, Gobbaragala, Hunjanakere Channanakere, Jakkanahalli, Alagud, Mollenahalli Chottahalli, Hunasanahalli, Kodiyala, Aladahalli Peehalli, Bannahalli, Gamanahalli, Vitalapura Neralekere, Ballekere, Bettahalli, Chikkaharohalli Doddaharohalli, Tadagavadi, Garakahalli, Arakere Madarahalli, Gandehosahalli, Hongahalli, Hulikere Beechanakuppe, Avverahalli, Basthipura, Anagahalli Majjigepura, Balamuri, Karekura, Belagola Mogarahalli, Jakkanakuppe, Hosahalli, Kempalingapura Palahalli, Karimanti, Bommur Agrahara, Brahmapura Naguvanahalli, Belavadi, Hosur, Chandagalu, Melapura Mahadevapura, Bidarahalli, Channahalli, Kemmannupura Taripura, Hebbadi, Hampapura, Huralikyathanahalli Doddankanahalli, Chikkankanahalli, Sugganahalli Bonthagahalli.

The villages having more than 50% ST population are None.

Sex ratio of Scheduled tribe population is 492.

Scheduled Tribes Literates and Illiterates by Sex:

	Persons	Males	Females
Literate	610	352	258
Illiterate	746	337	409
Literacy rate	52.2	59.2	45.0
Graduate	10	9	1

Scheduled Tribes (Dominant):

Naikda etc., Meda, Soligaru, Generic Tribes etc.
Kadu Kuruba

For their cultural identity please see Appendix-II

Villages without Scheduled Tribes: There are 60 villages without any scheduled tribe population.

Literates and Illiterates by Sex (Total Population):

	Persons	Males	Females
Literate	74,262	42,556	31,706
Illiterate	64,993	27,979	37,014
Literacy rate	60	69	52
Graduate	2,690	2,120	570

Agriculture: ***Distribution of villages according to land use:*** Out of 96 villages, Total area (in hectare) is 34197, out of that 68.95 percent is cultivable and 46.72 percent of the cultivable area is irrigated.

Sources of Irrigation (Hectares): Government Canal 10098.58, Private Canal 0, Well without Electricity 28, Well with Electricity 440.13, Tubewell without Electricity 0, Tubewell with Electricity 299.64, Tank 12.76, River 0, Lake 0, Waterfall 0, Others 137.46.

Villages with population of 5000 to 9999: Kirangur, Arakere, Belagola, Palahalli, Mahadevapura.

Villages with population of 10000 and above: None

Distribution of Workers:

	Persons	Males	Females	WPR
Cultivators	32,164	23,454	8,710	41.6
Agricultural Labour	27,742	12,771	14,971	35.88
Household Industry	1,257	708	549	1.63
Other Workers	16,150	11,945	4,205	20.89
Main Workers	55,727	41,684	14,043	72.08
Marginal Workers	21,586	7,194	14,392	27.92
Total Workers	77,313	48,878	28,435	

Religion: Major Religious Communities:

	Persons	Males	Females	Sex Ratio
Hindu (97.11%)	135,231	68,481	66,750	975
Muslim (1.99%)	2,776	1,428	1,348	944
Christian (0.63%)	873	436	437	1,002
Sikh (0.02%)	33	18	15	833
Buddhists (0.19%)	271	136	135	993
Jain (0.02%)	28	14	14	1,000

Agewise Data:

	Persons	Males	Females	Sex Ratio
All ages	139,255	70,535	68,720	974
0-14	38,462	19,590	18,872	963
15-44	71,845	36,449	35,396	971
45-79	27,409	13,803	13,606	986
80+	1,338	582	756	1299
Age not stated	201	111	90	811

Languages (Dominant):
Kannada, Tamil, Urdu, Telugu, Marathi

Disabled Population:

	Persons	Males	Females	%
Total Disabled	3,157	1,880	1,277	
In Seeing	2,005	1,199	806	63.51
In Speech	269	140	129	8.52
In Hearing	147	61	86	4.66
In Movement	527	350	177	16.69
Mentally	209	130	79	6.62

SIDDAPUR

Siddapur C.D. Block lies in the south-eastern part of Uttara Kannada district. It is a part of Siddapur taluka. The Block is located at a distance of 130 kms. from district headquarters (Karwar). There are 196 villages in the block with the total population of 86,725 persons. Area of the C.D. Block is 840.70 sq. kms. It is bounded by taluk Sirsi on north, district Shimoga and taluk Honavar on south, district Shimoga on east, taluks Honav ar, Kumta and Sirsi on west.

Communications:

Roadways : N.H-206: Direction- Honavar to Shimoga, Villages- Malemane, Hejani, Kodkani, Koralkai, Musavalli, Malavalli, Manmane. S.H-48: Direction- Kumta to Sorab, Nearest Villages- Gijagini, Bilegod, Dodmane, Uppingadde, Kalkai, Kibale, Gubbagod, Kyadgi, Lakkabbekeri, Balgod, Sashiguli, Huvinmane, Nirgar, Bilgi, Hosamanju, Kuravan te, Muttige (Gunjagod), Gunjagod, Bedkani, Tyarshi, Shira lgi. S.H-93: Direction- Khanapur to Manmane, Nearest Villages- Sampagod, Balekai, Hosakoppa, Tarehalli-Kansur, Kangod-Kansur, Ghattikai, Kalgadde, Tyagali, Hirekai (Tyagali), Kalen Halli, Padavanbail, Kallur, Hasavante, Man mane, Tumbargod, Nidgod, Mandlikoppa, Kunaji, Avargu ppa, Halagadikoppa, Kastur, Akkunji, Arendur, Kavanchur.

River: Sharavati Nadi- Nearest Villages- Malemane, Hejani, Kodkani. Tadri Nadi- Nearest Villages- Hukli (Nilkund), Shivalmane, Manigar, Sarkuli, Kelgin Sarkuli, Umbalmane, Unchalli, Harigar, Balekoppa (Kibballi), Hegnur, Kibballi, Keregadde, Hasargod, Balesar, Karkisa val, Muthalli, Shamemane, Karjagi, Bannige, Mutmurd, Adkalli, Yelugar, Gijagini, Naigar, Illimane, Honnekomb, Havinbil, Hadrimane, Musavalli, Malavalli. Bennihall Nadi- Nearest Village- Hallibail. Kansi Nadi- Nearest Villages- Musavalli, Heggekoppa, Kallur, Hasavante, Manmanel, Shiralgi, Balekoppa (Shiralgi), Bikkalse, Mugdur, Akkunji, Arendur, Kavanchur.

Annual Rainfall: Normal Rianfall 3038.6 mm.

Ground Water: Availability of the Ground Water in the Basin is 6177 H.A.M. and the utilization is 3014 H.A. M. It belongs to Safe category. Depth to water level 2 to 20 meter below the ground. Most of the wells go down in summer months, according to the Ground Water Estimation Committee.

Soils: Lateritic Soils

Natural Division : It falls partly in Sirsi-Siddapur Dissected Humid Tract of the Karnataka Coast (Western Coastal Region).

Administration:

Division: Belgaum. Parliamentary Constituency: 12 Uttara Kannada. District: Uttara Kannada. Taluka: Siddapur. Assembly Constituency: 80 Sirsi. Gram Panchayat: 21.

Regional Area Development Boards: The Maland Aera Development Board.

Fairs: Marikambadevi Jatra: Marikamba Devi jatra is held at Bilgi near Uttara Kannada for seven days around the month of March-April once a year. Bilgi, 13 kms. from Siddapur with rich antiquity was a taluk headquarters between 1799 and 1859, when the whole taluk was merged with Sirsi taluk. The name of the place has been mentio ned as Svetapura (Bilgi) in an inscription dated 1652 A.D. but, this appears to be Sankritisation of Billige.

Narasimha Car Festival: An annual Car festival of Narasi mha is held during the month of January at Shiralgi near Uttara Kannada. Shiralgi 16.5 kms. from Siddapur is found mentioned as Siruvalige in a copper plate inscritp ion at Halatkatta (Siddapur) dated 1770 of Bilagi Somashekara.

Rameshwara Jatra: It is held at Itgi near Uttara Kannada for one day in the month of March-April every year. Itgi nine kms. from Siddapur, has temples dedicated to Rameshwara, a Vithala Mandira and Kshetrapala. The Rameshwara temple is the earliest one with the stepped octagonal Kadambanagara shikhara, a garbhagriha and a small navaranga.

Shani Deva Jatra: It is held at Bedakani near Uttara Kannada for one day in the month of April. Bedkani about seven kms. from Siddapur is of rich antiquity. It has been mentioned as Bedkani in an inscription near the Maruti temple of 1437. It has remains of a fort and its moat (kani). There are temples dedicated to Shaneshw ara, Maruti, Ishwara, Kumara Rama, etc. The Shaneshwara temple appears to be locally popular as the annual jatra is held during April and it is one of the biggest in the taluk.

Villages: 196 **Inhabited:** 195 **Uninhabited:** 1

Ranking	District	State	National
Area	5	113	641
Population	5	162	3883
Sex Ratio	6	87	2285
Child Sex Ratio	11	172	5195
Literacy Rate	4	14	493
Density	1	6	6113
Work Participation Rate	6	164	305

Gram Panchayats:
Nilkund, Heggarani, Analebail, Hasargod, Tarehalli-Kansur, Tyagali, Harshikatta, Sovinkoppa, Kyadgi, Dodmane, Wajgod, Itagi, Bilgi, Bidarkan, Kolsirsi, Kangod, Shiralgi, Bedkani, Halgeri, Manmane, Kavanchur.

Amenities:
Education: Primary School in 128 villages, Middle school in 74 villages, Matriculation or Secondary School in 17 villages, namely Hallibail, Nirgan, Sarkuli, Heggarani, Kibballi, Harshikatta, Tarehalli-Kansur, Dodmane, Bilgi, Itagi, Halgeri, Husur, Bidarkan, Kolsirsi, Bedkani, Kangod, Kavanchur.

Higher Secondary or Pre University Courses or Intermediate or Junior College in 3 villages of the CD Block,, namely Tyagali, Bilgi, Halgeri.

College in 0 village, Adult Literacy Center in 0 village.

Medical: Hospital in 0 village, Dispensary in 2 villages, Health Center in 3 villages, Sub Center in 5 villages, Maternity and Child Welfare Center in 1 village, Community health workers in 24 villages.

The Villages having Hospital or Dispensary or Health Center are Heggarani, Bilgi.

Drinking Water: Tap water in 27 villages, Tank water in 14 villages, Well water in 184 villages, Tubewell in 8 villages and more than one source in 162 villages.

Bank: Banking facility in 27 villages, namely, Kanchikai, Murur, Heggarani, Analebail, Halegouri Hasargod, Balesar, Harshikatta, Kodsar-Halkani Tarehalli-Kansur, Kangod-Kansur, Dodmane, Gubbagod Wajgod, Bilgi, Itagi, Alavalli, Halgeri, Koralkai Manmane, Bidarkan, Heggadde, Gunjagod, Bedkani Avarguppa, Kangod, Shiralgi.

Credit Society in 19 villages Agricultural Credit Society in 19 Non-Agricultural Credit Society in 6 villages.

Others: Power supply in 186 villages, Cinema hall in 0 village, sport club in 0 village, Stadium or Auditorium or Community Hall in 0 village, Post Office in 60 villages.

There are 113 villages having bus facilities.

Villages with most of facilities: Kanchikai Heggarani, Analebail, Hasargod, Balesar, Harshikatta Tarehalli-Kansur, Dodmane, Bilgi, Alavalli, Halgeri Bedkani.

Villages without amenities (Education):
Tandagundi, Nandyane, Kelgin Sarkuli, Umbalmane, Halehalla, Harigar, Ainbail, Halegouri, Harshimane, Manikmane, Shamemane, Tagginbalgar, Malenhalli, Yelugar, Malubalgar, Bhandarkeri, Hangarkhanda, Balekai, Kalkatte Hunasekoppa, Hosakoppa, Madankal, Kodgadde, Haldot, Surgikoppa, Gijagini, Kodigadde, Kaunsale, Uppingadde, Kallole, Naigar, Kibale, Talekeri, Honnekomb, Ojagar, Chapparmane, Mavinkod, Lakkabbekeri, Masalemakki, Sangolimane, Nirgar, Kuravante, Malemane, Hejani, Hemagar, Kulibid, Padavanbail, Mattigar, Kilar, Koralkai, Kallur, Manmane, Malalavalli, Hingar, Kuppagar, Kodgibail, Tumbargod, Nidgod, Bandisara, Uppadaki, Hematemane, Heggadde, Maghegar, Bhankuli, Algod..

Scheduled Castes: Out of the total population of 86820 persons, 5573 persons (6.42%) belong to Scheduled Castes. The villages having less than 10% SC population are Hallibail, Kanchikai, Mulgunda, Hukli (Nilkund) Hutgar (Nilkund), Tandagundi, Handiyane Math Nandyane, Hullunde, Nirgan, Manigar, Sarkuli Kelgin Sarkuli, Umbalmane, Bidarmane, Taresar Heggarani, Halehalla, Hegge, Hostot, Harigar Balekoppa (Kibballi), Ainbail, Hegnur, Analebail Keregadde, Halegouri, Attimurd, Harshimane Harshikatta, Manikmane, Hutagar (Muthalli) Muthalli, Shamemane, Karjagi, Bannige, Mutmurd Tagginbalgar, Adkalli, Malenhalli, Yelugar Malubalgar, Hirekai (Kodsar Halkani) Kodsar (Muthalli), Bhandarkeri, Sampagod Matti Halli, Hangarkhanda, Balekai Kalkatte Hunasekoppa, Tarehalli-Kansur Kangod-Kansur, Ghattikai, Madankal, Devisar Shigehalli, Kodgadde, Shelur, Hirekai (Tyagali) Surgikoppa, Mudhalli, Gijagini , Bilegod, Nirgod Kodigadde, Kaunsale, Uppingadde, Kallole, Naigar Kalkai, Kibale, Begar, Illimane, Honnekomb, Havinbil Sovinkoppa, Ojagar, Hadrimane, Mavinkod Lakkabbekeri, Balgod, Danmav , Suttalmane Masalemakki, Wajgod, Sangolimane, Kelginmane, Nirgar Tarakhanda, Kattekai, Golikai, Bilgi, Hosamanju Kuravante, Itagi, Keremane, Hukali (Wajgod) Malemane, Hejani, Kudagund, Alavalli, Chandraghatgi Hemagar , Kodkani, Kulibid, Mensi, Nagarbhavi Padavanbail, Mattigar, Kilar, Malvajaddi, Koralkai Musavalli, Malavalli, Heggekoppa, Kallur, Hasavante Manmane, Malalavalli, Hingar, Muttige (Kaval Koppa)

Naligar, Kavalkoppa, Kodgibail, Golgod, Bandisara
Kolsirsi, Uppadaki, Hematemane, Heggadde, Balguli
Maghegar, Bhankuli, Muttige (Gunjagod), Algod
Bedkani, Avarguppa, Halagadikoppa, Wadageri, Kangod
Kolgi, Shiralgi, Bikkalse, Mugdur, Akkunji
Haralikoppa, Arendur, Kavanchur, Dugadikoppa, Nejjur.

The village having more than 50% SC population is None.

Sex ratio of Scheduled Caste population is 496.

Scheduled Castes Literates and Illiterates by Sex:

	Persons	Males	Females
Literate	2,511	1,432	1,079
Illiterate	3,062	1,376	1,686
Literacy rate	52.9	59.6	46.1
Graduate	25	18	7

Scheduled Castes (Dominant):

Chalavadi etc., Halsar etc., Bhovi, Banjara etc.
Mukri

For their cultural identity please see Appendix-I

Villages without Scheduled Castes: There are 88 villages without any scheduled caste population.

Scheduled Tribes: Out of the total population of 86820 persons, 791 persons (0.91%) belong to Scheduled Tribes.

The villages having less than 10% ST population are
Hallibail, Kanchikai, Mulgunda, Nilkund
Hukli (Nilkund), Shivalmane, Hutgar (Nilkund)
Tandagundi, Handiyane Math, Nandyane, Hullunde
Nirgan, Manigar, Sarkuli, Kelgin Sarkuli, Umbalmane
Bidarmane, Murur, Taresar, Heggarani, Halehalla
Hegge, Unchalli, Hostot, Harigar
Balekoppa (Kibballi), Ainbail, Hegnur, Kibballi
Analebail, Keregadde, Halegouri, Hasargod, Attimurd
Balesar, Karkisaval, Honnehadda, Harshimane
Harshikatta, Manikmane, Hutagar (Muthalli)
Muthalli, Shamemane, Karjagi, Bannige, Mutmurd
Tagginbalgar, Adkalli, Malenhalli, Yelugar, Halkani
Malubalgar, Gavingudde, Hirekai (Kodsar Halkani)
Kodsar (Muthalli), Bhandarkeri, Sampagod
Matti Halli, Hangarkhanda, Balekai
Kalkatte Hunasekoppa, Hosakoppa, Tarehalli-Kansur
Kangod-Kansur, Ghattikai, Madankal, Devisar
Girgadde, Arehalla, Shigehalli, Kodgadde, Kalgadde
Shelur, Haldot, Tyagali, Hirekai (Tyagali)
Kalen Halli, Surgikoppa, Mudhalli, Gijagini , Bilegod
Nirgod, Kaunsale, Dodmane, Uppingadde, Kallole
Kadavadi, Naigar, Kalkai, Kibale, Kudegod, Talekeri
Begar, Gubbagod, Illimane, Honnekomb, Havinbil
Sovinkoppa, Ojagar, Hadrimane, Chapparmane, Mavinkod
Kyadgi, Lakkabbekeri, Danmav , Suttalmane
Masalemakki, Wajgod, Sangolimane, Kelginmane
Sashiguli, Nirgar, Tarakhanda, Kattekai, Golikai
Bilgi, Hosamanju, Kuravante, Taragod, Itagi
Keremane, Hukali (Wajgod), Malemane, Hejani
Alavalli, Hemagar , Kodkani, Mensi, Halgeri
Nagarbhavi, Padavanbail, Mattigar, Husur, Kilar
Malvajaddi, Koralkai, Musavalli, Malavalli
Heggekoppa, Kallur, Hasavante, Manmane, Malalavalli
Godlabil, Hingar, Muttige (Kaval Koppa), Naligar
Kavalkoppa, Kuppagar, Kodgibail, Bidarkan, Golgod
Heggodmane, Tumbargod, Nidgod, Mandlikoppa, Kunaji
Bandisara, Kolsirsi, Uppadaki, Hematemane, Heggadde
Balguli, Maghegar, Bhankuli, Muttige (Gunjagod)
Gunjagod, Algod, Bedkani, Tyarshi, Avarguppa
Halagadikoppa, Aigod, Wadageri, Kastur, Ballatte
Kangod, Kolgi, Shiralgi, Balekoppa (Shiralgi)
Bikkalse, Mugdur, Akkunji, Haralikoppa, Arendur
Kavanchur, Dugadikoppa, Nejjur.

The villages having more than 50% ST population are None.

Sex ratio of Scheduled tribe population is 498.

Scheduled Tribes Literates and Illiterates by Sex:

	Persons	Males	Females
Literate	357	196	161
Illiterate	434	201	233
Literacy rate	55.4	60.7	50.0
Graduate	2	2	0

Scheduled Tribes (Dominant):

Hasalaru, Naikda etc., Kudiya etc., Meda, Bhil etc.

For their cultural identity please see Appendix-II

Villages without Scheduled Tribes: There are 151 villages without any scheduled tribe population.

Literates and Illiterates by Sex (Total Population):

	Persons	Males	Females
Literate	58,234	32,340	25,894
Illiterate	28,586	11,635	16,951
Literacy rate	77	85	69
Graduate	1,870	1,327	543

Agriculture: ***Distribution of villages according to land use:***
Out of 196 villages, Total area (in hectare) is 84070, out of that 14.57 percent is cultivable and 4.51 percent of the cultivable area is irrigated.

Sources of Irrigation (Hectares): Government Canal 226.74, Private Canal 2078.26, Well without Electricity 65.1, Well with Electricity 249.84, Tubewell without Electricity 0, Tubewell with Electricity 0, Tank 0, River 0, Lake 20.24, Waterfall 0, Others 0.08.

Villages with population of 5000 to 9999: None

Villages with population of 10000 and above: None

Distribution of Workers:

	Persons	Males	Females	WPR

Cultivators	13,478	7,908	5,570	26.53
Agricultural Labour	5,593	2,207	3,386	11.01
Household Industry	441	253	188	0.87
Other Workers	31,299	19,211	12,088	61.6
Main Workers	32,649	26,348	6,301	64.26
Marginal Workers	18,162	3,231	14,931	35.74
Total Workers	50,811	29,579	21,232	

Religion: Major Religious Communities:

	Persons	Males	Females	Sex Ratio
Hindu (96.22%)	83,534	42,271	41,263	976
Muslim (3.3%)	2,865	1,469	1,396	950
Christian (0.4%)	351	193	158	819
Sikh (0.01%)	7	5	2	400
Buddhists (0%)	3	2	1	500
Jain (0.05%)	45	25	20	800

Agewise Data:

	Persons	Males	Females	Sex Ratio
All ages	86,820	43,975	42,845	974
0-14	24,374	12,543	11,831	943
15-44	44,032	22,067	21,965	995
45-79	17,749	9,066	8,683	958
80+	645	286	359	1255
Age not stated	20	13	7	538

Languages (Dominant):
Kannada, Konkani, Urdu, Hindi, Marathi

Disabled Population:

	Persons	Males	Females	%
Total Disabled	1,798	992	806	
In Seeing	879	448	431	48.89
In Speech	149	85	64	8.29
In Hearing	115	61	54	6.4
In Movement	475	303	172	26.42
Mentally	180	95	85	10.01

SIDLAGHATTA

Sidlaghatta C.D. Block lies in the northern part of Kolar district. It is a part of Sidlaghatta taluka. The Block is located at a distance of 59 kms. from distr ict headquarters (Kolar). There are 290 villages in the block with the total population of 152,720 persons. Area of the C.D. Block is 661.24 sq. kms. It is bounded by taluks Bagepalli and Chintamani on north, district Bangalore Rural on south, taluks Chintamani and Kolar on east, taluks Gudibanda, Chikballapur and district Bangalore Rural on west.

Communications:

Roadways : S.H.-5: Direction- Bagepalli to Chintamani, Nearest Villages- Nallaguttahalli, Kotagal, Sonaganahal li, Sadali, Iragappanahalli, S.Gollahalli, Jarugahalli, Purabyrenahalli, Hiriyelachenahalli, Dibburahalli, Kudupakunte, Rayappanahalli, Thimmanayakanahalli, G. Kurubarahalli, Gorla Gummanahalli, Gonimaradahalli, Chokkanahalli, Gangahalli, Ganjigunte, Devaguttahalli. S.H.-35: Direction- Hosakote to Sidlaghatta, Nearest Villages- Sidlaghatta (Rural), Anur, Belluti, Hithalahal li, Bodaguru, Baktharahalli, Malamachanahalli, Thaduru, Thotliganahalli, Nagamangala, Nallenahalli, Yannangur, Hosahalli, Chokkandahalli, Sugatur, Kurabarahalli, Jangamakote, Ghatamaranahalli, Hosapete, Yedulathippenah alli, Devaganahalli. S.H.-58: Direction- Chikballapur to Chintamani, Nearest Villages- Yaramalliahna Hunaseha lli, Kadirinaikanahalli, Handiganala, Sidlaghatta (Rural), Budhala, Thaladummanahalli, Sonnenahalli, Bommanahalli, Pindipapanahalli, Channahalli, Ammanakere. S.H.-74: Diirection- Chikballapur to Kolar, Nearest Villages- Venkatapura, Jangamakote, Amani Balladakere, Ghatamaranahalli, Hosapete, Pakiranahosahalli, K.G.Chikkaballa, Haradi Plantation, Mallenahalli, Gambeeranahalli, Devenahalli, Haradi, Kumbiganahalli, Kariyanapura. S.H.-82: Direction- Bangalore to Chintamani, Nearest Villages- Kumbiganahalli, Kariyanapura.

Railway Station: Villages- Yaramalliahna Hunasehalli, Iddalodu, Budhala.

River: Papagni Nadi- Nearest Villages- Muchataladinne, Thalakayalabetta, Dimbarlahalli, Maralappanahalli, Vaddahalli, Kudupakunte, Rayappanahalli, Thimmanayakanahalli, Gorla Gummanahalli. Chitravati Nadi- Nearest Villages- Thimmasandra, Byraganahalli, Varasandra, Sadalavarahalli, Settikere.

Reserved Forest: Nearest Villages- Nadipinayakanahalli, Arikere, Athiganahalli, Jangamakote Plantation, Yannang ur, Chokkandahalli, Yedulathippenahalli, Devaganahalli, Gollahalli, Hireballa, Vallappanahalli, Thataparthi, Krishnahalli.

Annual Rainfall: Normal Rianfall 747.08 mm.

Ground Water: Availability of the Ground Water in the Basin is (Information not avablable) H.A.M. and the utilization is (Information not avablable) H.A.M. It belongs to (Information not avablable) category. Depth to water level 5 to 20 meter below the ground. Most of the wells go down in summer months, according to the Ground Water Estimation Committee.

Soils: Red Soils.

Natural Division : It falls in Sidlaghatta-Sriniwaspur Uplands of the Southern Karnataka Plateau.

Administration:

Division: Bangalore. Parliamentary Constituency: 28 Kolar (SC). District: Kolar. Taluka: Sidlaghatta. Assemb ly Constituency: 142 Sidlaghatta. Gram Panchayat: 27.

Regional Area Development Boards: The Bailu Seeme Area Development Board.

Fairs: Ganga Devi Jatra: It is held at Melur near Kolar about the month of April for eight days. Melur, in the Jangamkote hobli of the Sidlaghatta taluk is about 10 kms. south of Sidlaghatta. A fair, which attracts about 25,000 people takes place here in connection with the Gangadevi parishe, held for seven days in the month of Chaitra. A cattle fair is also held on the occassion in which about ten thousand cattle are brought for sale.

Villages: 290 **Inhabited:** 243 **Uninhabited:** 47

Ranking	District	State	National
Area	8	140	1011
Population	8	130	1782
Sex Ratio	2	74	2085
Child Sex Ratio	11	130	3770
Literacy Rate	5	103	3117
Density	1	7	4306
Work Participation Rate	7	56	343

Gram Panchayats:
S.Devaganahalli, Sadali , Thimmasandra, Dibburahalli, Basettihalli, Thimmanayakanahalli, Ganjigunte, Kundalagurki, Palicherlu, Doddathekahalli, Abbaludu, Handiganala, Devaramallur, Yaramalliahna Hunasehalli, Kothanur, Thummanahalli, Anur, Melur, Mallur, Baktharahalli, Malamachanahalli, Cheemangala, Nagamangala, Hosapete, Venkatapura, Jangamakote, Kumbiganahalli.

Amenities:

Education: Primary School in 197 villages, Middle school in 91 villages, Matriculation or Secondary School in 26 villages, namely Thimmasandra, Sadali, Chakappanahalli, Dibburahalli, Alagurki, Basettihalli, Rameswara, Doddathekahalli, Ganjigunte, Kundalagurki, Abbaludu, Yaramalliahna Hunasehalli, Kadirinaikanahalli, Hanumanthapura, Sidlaghatta (Rural), Muthur, Mallur, Melur, Baktharahalli, Thotliganahalli, Nadipinayakanahalli, Narayanadasarahalli, Cheemangala, Baluvanahalli, Jangamakote, Kumbiganahalli.

Higher Secondary or Pre University Courses or Intermediate or Junior College in 6 villages of the CD Block,, namely Sadali, Sidlaghatta (Rural), Mallur, Yannur, Jangamakote, Gambeeranahalli.

College in 1 village, Adult Literacy Center in 0 village., College is in village, namely Sidlaghatta (Rural).

Medical: Hospital in 1 village, Dispensary in 1 village, Health Center in 12 villages, Sub Center in 27 villages, Maternity and Child Welfare Center in 1 village, Community health workers in 3 villages.

The Villages having Hospital or Dispensary or Health Center are Thimmasandra, Abbaludu.

Drinking Water: Tap water in 187 villages, Tank water in 37 villages, Well water in 35 villages, Tubewell in 55 villages and more than one source in 190 villages.

Bank: Banking facility in 19 villages, namely, Dibburahalli, Basettihalli, Ganjigunte, Kundalagurki Abbaludu, Pindipapanahalli, Bodaguru, Japtihosahalli Chikkadasarahalli, Doddadasarahalli, Sorakayalahalli Melur, Malamachanahalli, Nagamangala, Arikere Cheemangala, Jangamakote, Hosapete, Thimmasandra.

Credit Society in 20 villages Agricultural Credit Society in 5 Non-Agricultural Credit Society in 2 villages.

Others: Power supply in 233 villages, Cinema hall in 5 villages sport club in 0 village, Stadium or Auditorium or Community Hall in 0 village, Post Office in 25 villages.

There are 161 villages having bus facilities.

Villages with most of facilities: Basettihalli Ganjigunte, Kundalagurki, Abbaludu, Bodaguru, Melur Nagamangala, Cheemangala, Jangamakote, Hosapete Thimmasandra.

Villages without amenities (Education):
Kanivenahalli, Eegaletihalli, S.Kurubarahalli, Venkatakrishnammanahalli, Hiriyelachenahalli, Muchataladinne, Atagollahalli, Ivarahalli, Balegowdanahalli, Nallarallahalli, Vaddahalli, Nakkalahalli, Yerabachanahalli, Maraganaparthi, Binnamangala, Doddagummanahalli, Dhanamittenahalli, Tharabahalli, Mallahalli, Vankamaradahalli, Ropparlahalli, Chikkapapanahalli, Gyaradi, Kurubachanapade, Pyayalahalli, Nellimaradahalli, Bommanahalli, Channahalli, Mallasettipura, Chinthudupi, Kuppenahalli, Halsurdinne, Patalammanahalli, Pura, Mithanahalli, Ghatamaranahalli, Devaganahalli, Gollahalli, Krishnahalli, Kariyanapura..

Scheduled Castes: Out of the total population of 152867 persons, 38759 persons (25.35%) belong to Scheduled Castes. The villages having less than 10% SC population are Uppakuntahalli, Kamanahalli, Venkatapura Byraganahalli, S.M.Kondarajanahalli, Halehalli Eegaletihalli, Bandahalli, S.Gundlahalli Venkatakrishnammanahalli, Muchataladinne Atagollahalli, Nakkalahalli, Ivarahalli Balegowdanahalli, Nallarallahalli, Dyavarahalli Bachanahalli, Hale Ganjigunte, Kachinayakanahalli Maraganaparthi, Ajjakadirenahalli, Garimillahalli Binnamangala, Chikkathekahalli, Maddenahalli Dhanamittenahalli, Kannappanahalli, Tharabahalli Devaguttahalli, Mallahalli, Vankamaradahalli Siddapura, Gangapura, Ropparlahalli Chikkapapanahalli, Basavanaparthi, Marappanahalli

Chikkadasenahalli, Kadirinaikanahalli
L Muthakadahalli, Kurubachanapade, Nellimaradahalli
Sidlaghatta (Rural), Kothanur, Keshavapura
Dabarganahalli, Kannamangala, Malamachanahalli
Mugiludupi, Hosahalli, Kurabarahalli
Ghatamaranahalli, Yedulathippenahalli
Krishnammanahosahalli, K.G.Chikkaballa, Sundrahalli.
The villages having more than 50% SC population are
Kanivenahalli, Mallasettyhalli, Neralemaradahalli
Nallappanahalli, Hiriyelachenahalli
Thurukachenahalli, Anur Thimmanahalli
Kondarajanahalli, G.Peddanahalli, G.Kurubarahalli
Gorla Gummanahalli, Byraganahalli, T.Peddanahalli
Gonimaradahalli, Nagireddihalli, Chyage, Gyaradi
Goramadagu, Sorakayalahalli, Mallasettipura
Halsurdinne, Patalammanahalli, Nallenahalli
Gollahalli, Thataparthi.
Sex ratio of Scheduled Caste population is 497.

Scheduled Castes Literates and Illiterates by Sex:

	Persons	Males	Females
Literate	14,450	9,100	5,350
Illiterate	24,309	10,411	13,898
Literacy rate	44.0	55.2	32.7
Graduate	295	267	28

Scheduled Castes (Dominant):

Adi Karnataka, Madiga, Adi Dravida, Bhovi
Holaya etc.

For their cultural identity please see Appendix-I

Villages without Scheduled Castes: There are 71 villages without any scheduled caste population.

Scheduled Tribes: Out of the total population of 152867 persons, 15646 persons (10.24%) belong to Scheduled Tribes.
The villages having less than 10% ST population are
Sonaganahalli, Venkatapura, Kanivenahalli
Sadalavarahalli, S.M.Kondarajanahalli
Mallasettyhalli, Eegaletihalli, Neralemaradahalli
Sadali , Nallappanahalli, S.Devaganahalli
S.Gundlahalli, S.Kurubarahalli, S.Gollahalli
Venkatakrishnammanahalli, Jarugahalli
Byyappanahalli, Dibburahalli, Muchataladinne
Atagollahalli, Thurukachenahalli, Ivarahalli
Dimbarlahalli, Madenahalli, Kumbarahalli
Anur Thimmanahalli, Ammagarahalli, Dyavarahalli
Seethahalli, Vaddahalli, Rayappanahalli
Thimmanayakanahalli, Nakkalahalli
Chikkabandaragatta, Kyasagere, Vemagallu
Kondarajanahalli, Lakkenahalli, G.Peddanahalli
Yerabachanahalli, Doddabandaragatta, G.Kurubarahalli
Gorla Gummanahalli, Anemadagu, Kachinayakanahalli
Basettihalli, Rameswara, Maraganaparthi
Ajjakadirenahalli, Byraganahalli, Sadahalli
Chikkathekahalli, Doddathekahalli, Gowdanahalli
Dhanamittenahalli, T.Peddanahalli, Tharabahalli
Somanahalli, Gonimaradahalli, Chokkanahalli
Gangahalli, Devaguttahalli, Nagireddihalli
Settihalli, Mallahalli, Kotahalli, Kempenahalli
Dogaranayakanahalli, Palicherlu, Gollahalli
Kachahalli, Donahalli, Basavanaparthi
Varahunasenhalli, Koothandahalli, Chyage, Abbaludu
Gudihalli, Haralahalli, Varadanayakanahalli
Cheemanahalli, Marappanahalli, Chikkadasenahalli
Doddadasenahalli, Gyaradi, Yaramalliahna Hunasehalli
Beerappanahalli, Devaramallur, L Muthakadahalli
Pyayalahalli, Handiganala, Nellimaradahalli
Sidlaghatta (Rural), Budhala, Thaladummanahalli
Sonnenahalli, Bommanahalli, Pindipapanahalli
Seegehalli, Goramadagu, Hujagur, Thippenahalli
Bachahalli, Anur, Chowdasandra, Ganganahalli
Kambadahalli, Japtihosahalli, Doddadasarahalli
Sorakayalahalli, Thummanahalli, Mallasettipura
Gudlanarasimhanahalli, Kuppenahalli
K.Muthakadahalli, Halsurdinne, Muthur, Mallur
Ragimakalahalli, Kachahalli, Baktharahalli
Thotliganahalli, Pura, Kakichokkandahalli
Ankathatti, Nagamangala, Nallenahalli
Nadipinayakanahalli, Arikere, Narayanadasarahalli
Yannur, Athiganahalli, Hosahalli, Chokkandahalli
Mithanahalli, Venkatapura, Baluvanahalli, Sugatur
Byarasandra, Kurabarahalli, Jangamakote
Ghatamaranahalli, Hosapete, Devaganahalli
Gollahalli, Hireballa, Krishnahalli, Pura K.G.
Hemarlahalli, Krishnammanahosahalli
Kalinayakanahalli, Pakiranahosahalli
K.G.Chikkaballa, Sundrahalli, Kalyapura
Mallenahalli, Gambeeranahalli, Ambiganahalli
Devenahalli, Haradi, Amaravathi, Thimmasandra.
The villages having more than 50% ST population are
Kamanahalli, Nakkalahalli, Balegowdanahalli
Hale Ganjigunte, Dadamagatta, Garimillahalli
Binnamangala, Maddenahalli, Vankamaradahalli
Thathahalli, Kurubachanapade, Anur Hunasenahalli
Byranaikanahalli, Keshavapura, Dabarganahalli
Kannamangala, Yedulathippenahalli.
Sex ratio of Scheduled tribe population is 493.

Scheduled Tribes Literates and Illiterates by Sex:

	Persons	Males	Females
Literate	5,821	3,621	2,200
Illiterate	9,825	4,307	5,518
Literacy rate	44.0	54.1	33.6
Graduate	82	70	12

Scheduled Tribes (Dominant):
Naikda etc., Meda, Hakkipikki, Kadu Kuruba Dubla etc.

For their cultural identity please see Appendix-II

Villages without Scheduled Tribes: There are 145 villages without any scheduled tribe population.

Literates and Illiterates by Sex (Total Population):

	Persons	Males	Females
Literate	76,981	46,496	30,485
Illiterate	75,886	30,780	45,106
Literacy rate	58	70	46
Graduate	2,326	1,976	350

Agriculture: ***Distribution of villages according to land use:*** Out of 290 villages, Total area (in hectare) is 66124, out of that 57.1 percent is cultivable and 25.65 percent of the cultivable area is irrigated.

Sources of Irrigation (Hectares): Government Canal 185.37, Private Canal 64.94, Well without Electricity 1291.34, Well with Electricity 714.66, Tubewell without Electricity 398.44, Tubewell with Electricity 3949.33, Tank 2385.96, River 31.94, Lake 0, Waterfall 0, Others 663.45.

Villages with population of 5000 to 9999: Jangamakote.

Villages with population of 10000 and above: None

Distribution of Workers:

	Persons	Males	Females	WPR
Cultivators	36,708	22,089	14,619	41.48
Agricultural Labour	27,010	11,719	15,291	30.52
Household Industry	2,632	1,531	1,101	2.97
Other Workers	22,137	13,265	8,872	25.02
Main Workers	69,409	43,269	26,140	78.44
Marginal Workers	19,078	5,335	13,743	21.56
Total Workers	88,487	48,604	39,883	

Religion: Major Religious Communities:

	Persons	Males	Females	Sex Ratio
Hindu (96.67%)	147,778	74,639	73,139	980
Muslim (3.19%)	4,869	2,522	2,347	931
Christian (0.06%)	92	49	43	878
Sikh (0%)	6	4	2	500
Buddhists (0.03%)	45	24	21	875
Jain (0.01%)	11	7	4	571

Agewise Data:

	Persons	Males	Females	Sex Ratio
All ages	152,867	77,276	75,591	978
0-14	48,589	24,704	23,885	967
15-44	71,537	35,753	35,784	1001
45-79	30,780	15,852	14,928	942
80+	1,845	896	949	1059
Age not stated	116	71	45	634

Languages (Dominant):
Kannada, Telugu, Urdu, Tamil, Marathi

Disabled Population:

	Persons	Males	Females	%
Total Disabled	2,759	1,534	1,225	
In Seeing	1,123	575	548	40.7
In Speech	293	165	128	10.62
In Hearing	203	99	104	7.36
In Movement	837	527	310	30.34
Mentally	303	168	135	10.98

SINDGI

Sindgi C.D. Block lies in the eastern part of Bijapur district. It is a part of Sindgi taluk. The Block is located at a distance of 60 kms. from district headquarters (Bijapur). There are 148 villages in the block with the total Pop. of 298,597 persons. Area of theC.D. Block is 2174.98 sq. kms. It is bounded by district Gulbarga on north and east, taluks Basavana Bagevadi and Muddebihal on south, taluks Bijapur and Indi on west.

Communications:

Roadways : S.H-12: Direction- Bijapur to Jevargi, Nearest Villages- Bisnal, Gabasavalgi, Moratgi, Hanchinal, Sindgi (Rural), Yargal (K.D), Yargal (B.K), Chikka-Sindgi, Bandal, Kanolli, Kokatnur, Padaganur, Nivalkhed, Devara Hippargi, Bommanjogi. S.H-16: Direction- Chikka-Sindgi to Shahpur, Nearest Villages-Sindgi (Rural), Yankanchi, Mannapur, Antargangi, Kerur, Sasabal, Golgeri, Dambal. S.H-41: Direction- Indi to Muddevihal, Nearest Villages- Chikkarugi, Kadlewad(P.C.H), Mulsavalgi, Nivalkhed,Ingalgi, Devara Hippargi.

River: Don Nadi- Nearest Villages- Devara Hippargi, Devoor, Mannur, Budihal Don, Kondguli, Hanchali, Nagaral Don, Bibi-Ingalgi, Ambalnur. Naole Nadi- Nearest Vill.- Kadani, Thontapur, Vibhutihalli, Guddalli, Ramanahalli, Balaganur, Chandkavathe, Somapur, Budihal (P.H), Othihal, Kannolli, Bommanjogi, Shantinagar, Ibrahimpur, Jalwad. Bhima Nadi- Nearest Villages- Kadani, Tavarkhed (Old), Tarapur (Old), Madanalli, Byadgihal (Old), Devangaon, Kadlewad (P.A), Shambewad, Kumashigi, Havalgi, Shirasgi, Bagalur, Kulekumatgi.

Annual Rainfall: Normal Rianfall 569 mm

Ground Water: Availability of the Ground Water in the Basin is 10695.33 H.A.M. and the utilization is 7083.61 H.A.M. It belongs to Over Exploited category. Depth to water level 5 to 10 meter belowthe ground. Most of the wells go down in summer months, according to the Ground Water Estimation Committee.

Soils: Black Soils.

Natural Division : It falls partly in the Lower Bhima Valley and the Bijapur-Basavana Bagewadi Upland of the Northern Karnataka Plateau.

Administration:

Division: Belgaum. Parliamentary Constituency: 4 Bijapur. District: Bijapur. Taluka: Sindgi. Assembly Constituency: 27 Devar Hippargi, 33 Sindgi. Gram Panchayat: 40. Regional Area Development Boards: The Bailu Seeme Area Development Board.

Fairs: Gollaleshvara Fair: Golageri is a place 20 kms. from Sindgi and 56 kms. from Indi Road railway station. There is a temple of Gollaleshvara said to be about six century old. According to a tradition, a shepherd boy named Balala installed the linga in this temple. The idols of Avamma and Malkamma found in the temple are also notable. The ratha of this temple is said to be the biggest in the area. An annual fair is held known as 'Gollaleshwara fair'. Hanumantha Car Festival: Korwar near Bijapur is a place about 20 kms. south of Sindgi. It has a well-known temple of god Hanumantha, which is looked upon as a jagruta sthana. According to a legend, the image was installed by sage Agastya. An annual car festival, which is held in the month of Chaitra (March-April), attracts a large number of people from the surrounding areas.

Villages: 148 **Inhabited:** 147 **Uninhabited:** 1

Ranking	District	State	National
Area	3	4	44
Population	3	17	70
Sex Ratio	3	138	3340
Child Sex Ratio	4	151	4222
Literacy Rate	5	143	4413
Density	5	163	5747
Work Participation Rate	3	143	3881

Gram Panchayats:

Kadani, Devangaon, Bommanahalli, Almel, Balaganur, Korhalli, Devaranavadgi, Bagalur, Malaghan, Gabasavalgi, Moratgi, Chattarki, Chandkavathe, Rampur(P.A), Yargal(B.K), Sungathan, Yankanchi, Byakod, Bandal, Kannolli, Kokatnur, Gubbewad, Handiganur, Golgeri, Honnalli, Hittinahalli, Chikkarugi, Mulsavalgi, Harnal, Devara Hippargi, Mannur, Jalwad, Korwar, Kondguli, Kerutagi, Yalgod, Hunshyal, Kalkeri, Bekinal, Aski.

Amenities:

Education: Primary School in 144 villages, Middle school in 124 villages, Matriculation or Secondary School in 38 villages, namely Kadani, Devangaon, Almel, Balaganur, Devaranavadgi, Bagalur, Kakkalameli, Malaghan, Gabasavalgi, Moratgi, Bhantnur, Chandkavathe, Yargal(B.K), Nagavi(B.K), Sungathan, Yankanchi, Kannolli, Kokatnur, Gubbewad, Golgeri, Honnalli, Chandnagar, Hittinahalli, Chikkarugi, Kadlewad(P.C.H), Mulsavalgi, Ingalgi, Devara Hippargi, Mannur, Jalwad, Korwar, Kondguli, Yalgod, Tilgul, Bibi-Ingalgi, Binjalbhavi, Kalkeri, Aski.

Higher Secondary or Pre University Courses or Intermediate or Junior College in 8 villages of the CD Block,, namely Almel, Malaghan, Moratgi, Golgeri, Hittinahalli, Devara Hippargi, Korwar, Kalkeri.

College in 2 villages, Adult Literacy Center in 0 village., Colleges are in villages, namely Almel, Hittinahalli.

Medical: Hospital in 0 village, Dispensary in 4 villages, Health Center in 11 villages, Sub Center in 57 villages, Maternity and Child Welfare Center in 0 village, Community health workers in 28 villages.

The Villages having Hospital or Dispensary or Health Center are Devangaon, Almel, Balaganur, Chikka-Sindgi, Kannolli, Kerutagi.

Drinking Water: Tap water in 73 villages, Tank water in 6 villages, Well water in 147 villages, Tubewell in 73 villages and more than one source in 147 villages.

Bank: Banking facility in 20 villages, namely, Devangaon, Almel, Balaganur, Devaranavadgi, Malaghan Gabasavalgi, Moratgi, Chandkavathe, Yargal(B.K) Sungathan, Yankanchi, Kannolli, Gubbewad, Golgeri Honnalli, Chikkarugi, Jalwad, Korwar, Kondguli, Aski. Credit Society in 47 villages Agricultural Credit Society in 47 Non-Agricultural Credit Society in 0 village.

Others: Power supply in 147 villages, Cinema hall in 4 villages sport club in 147 villages, Stadium or Auditorium or Communi Hall in 147 villages, Post Office in 78 villages.

There are 123 villages having bus facilities.

Villages with most of facilities: Devangaon, Almel Balaganur, Devaranavadgi, Malaghan, Gabasavalgi Moratgi, Chandkavathe, Yargal(B.K), Sungathan Yankanchi, Kannolli, Gubbewad, Golgeri, Honnalli Chikkarugi, Jalwad, Korwar, Kondguli, Aski.

Villages without amenities (Education):

Sindgi (Rural) *, Shantinagar, Tirupatinagar..

Scheduled Castes: Out of the total population of 298923 persons, 54298 persons (18.16%) belong to Scheduled Castes. The villages having less than 10% SC population are Guddalli, Gundgi, Havalgi, Kulekumatgi, Somajal Bisnal, Jatinal, Surgihalli, Chattarki, Hachyal Chandkavathe, Sindgi (Rural) *, Yargal(B.K) Goravagundagi, Nandgeri, Mannapur, Bandal, Borgi Hadaginal, Bastihal, Bramhadevanmadu, Khanapur Nivalkhed, Ibrahimpur, Budihal Don, Animadu Chattanahalli, Asantapur, Halagundaknal, Hunshyal Nagaral Don, Ambalnur, Turkangeri, Bannihatti(P.T) Aski.

The villages having more than 50% SC population are

Guthargi, Benakotgi, Chandnagar, Hittinahalli Shantinagar, Devoor, Indiranagar, Tirupatinagar Kadrapur.

Sex ratio of Scheduled Caste population is 487.

Scheduled Castes Literates and Illiterates by Sex:

	Persons	Males	Females
Literate	19,099	13,154	5,945
Illiterate	35,199	14,725	20,474
Literacy rate	42.9	57.7	27.4
Graduate	791	734	57

Scheduled Castes (Dominant):

Banjara etc., Holaya etc., Bhambi etc., Bhovi Madiga

For their cultural identity please see Appendix-I

Villages without Scheduled Castes: There are 7 villages without any scheduled caste population.

Scheduled Tribes: Out of the total population of 298923 persons, 4960 persons (1.66%) belong to Scheduled Tribes.

The villages having less than 10% ST population are Kadani, Tavarkhed (Old), Tarapur (Old), Madanalli Byadgihal (Old), Kadlewad(P.A), Shambewad, Kumashigi Bommanahalli, Kurabathalli, Almel, Thontapur Vibhutihalli, Guddalli, Ramanahalli, Balaganur Nagarhalli, Huvinahalli, Korhalli, Madari Uchitnavadgi, Alahalli, Gundgi, Devaranavadgi Havalgi, Shirasgi, Bagalur, Kulekumatgi, Kakkalameli Somajal, Asangihal, Malaghan, Mangalur, Aheri Bisnal, Gabasavalgi, Jatinal, Basavanagar, Moratgi Hanchinal, Kerur, Guthargi, Bhantnur, Surgihalli Chattarki, Hachyal, Chandkavathe, Hikkangutti Kalahalli, Rampur(P.A), Bableshwar, Benakotgi Sindgi (Rural) *, Yargal(K.D), Yargal(B.K) Bhankalgi, Nagavi(B.K), Nagavi(K.D), Goravagundagi Khainur, Muradi, Sungathan, Nandgeri, Yankanchi Byalihal, Mannapur, Antargangi, Madabal, Byakod Chikka-Sindgi, Bandal, Ganihar, Somapur Budihal(P.H), Othihal, Kokatnur, Puradol Banahatti(P.A), Gubbewad, Handiganur, Bastihal Kannaguddihal, Dhavalar, Sasabal, Golgeri Chikka-Allapur , Dambal, Karavinal, Bramhadevanmadu Khanapur, Honnalli, Ganganahalli, Chandnagar Hittinahalli, Chikkarugi, Mulsavalgi, Padaganur Nivalkhed, Harnal, Ingalgi, Devara Hippargi Bommanjogi, Shantinagar, Devoor, Mannur, Ibrahimpur Indiranagar, Jalwad, Budihal Don, Korwar Warkanhalli, Kondguli, Kerutagi, Tirupatinagar Yalgod, Wandal, Kadrapur, Saladhalli , Animadu Asantapur, Halagundaknal, Algur, Hunshyal, Kudargond Tilgul, Hanchali, Nagaral Don, Bibi-Ingalgi Ambalnur, Kesaratti, Binjalbhavi, Kalkeri Rampur(P.T), Turkangeri, Budihal(P.T), Wanakihal Bekinal, Bannihatti(P.T), Jalpur, Aski, Neeralgi.

The villages having more than 50% ST population are None.

Sex ratio of Scheduled tribe population is 487.

Scheduled Tribes Literates and Illiterates by Sex:

	Persons	Males	Females
Literate	1,757	1,189	568
Illiterate	3,203	1,355	1,848
Literacy rate	43.1	57.2	28.4
Graduate	63	56	7

Scheduled Tribes (Dominant):

Koli Dhor etc., Naikda etc., Generic Tribes etc. Pardhi etc., Kurumans

For their cultural identity please see Appendix-II

Villages without Scheduled Tribes: There are 82 villages without any scheduled tribe population.

Literates and Illiterates by Sex (Total Population):

	Persons	Males	Females
Literate	126,119	83,039	43,080
Illiterate	172,804	70,042	102,762
Literacy rate	51	65	35
Graduate	5,171	4,638	533

Agriculture: ***Distribution of villages according to land use:*** Out of 148 villages, Total area (in hectare) is 217498, out of that 95.17 percent is cultivable and 8.5 percent of the cultivable area is irrigated.

Sources of Irrigation (Hectares): Government Canal 812.25, Private Canal 48.56, Well without Electricity 747.55, Well with Electricity 13287.78, Tubewell without Electricity 22.3, Tubewell with Electricity 1901.88, Tank 326.8, River 445.02, Lake 0, Waterfall 0, Others 0.

Villages with population of 5000 to 9999: Devangaon, Balaganur, Moratgi, Chandkavathe Yankanchi, Kannolli, Jalwad, Korwar, Kalkeri.

Villages with population of 10000 and above: Almel, Devara Hippargi.

Distribution of Workers:

	Persons	Males	Females	WPR
Cultivators	44,112	35,762	8,350	35.95
Agricultural Labour	58,477	25,118	33,359	47.66
Household Industry	3,052	2,230	822	2.49
Other Workers	17,058	14,033	3,025	13.9
Main Workers	88,852	65,695	23,157	72.41
Marginal Workers	33,847	11,448	22,399	27.59
Total Workers	122,699	77,143	45,556	

Religion: Major Religious Communities:

	Persons	Males	Females	Sex Ratio
Hindu (83.85%)	250,633	128,579	122,054	949
Muslim (15.56%)	46,526	23,611	22,915	971

Christian (0.02%)	67	28	39	1,393
Sikh (0%)	5	2	3	1,500
Buddhists (0.2%)	610	308	302	981
Jain (0.23%)	681	342	339	991

Agewise Data:

	Persons	Males	Females	Sex Ratio
All ages	298,923	153,081	145,842	953
0-14	116,961	60,191	56,770	943
15-44	125,255	65,127	60,128	923
45-79	53,710	26,415	27,295	1033
80+	2,542	1,115	1,427	1280
Age not stated	455	233	222	953

Languages (Dominant):
Kannada, Urdu, Hindi, Telugu, Marathi

Disabled Population:

	Persons	Males	Females	%
Total Disabled	6,350	3,748	2,602	
In Seeing	3,270	1,915	1,355	51.5
In Speech	600	341	259	9.45
In Hearing	311	153	158	4.9
In Movement	1,719	1,087	632	27.07
Mentally	450	252	198	7.09

SINDHNUR

Sindhnur C.D. Block lies in the southern part of Raichur district. It is a part of Sindhnur taluka. The Block is located at a distance of 91 kms. from district headqu arters (Raichur). There are 173 villages in the block with the total population of 298,863 persons. Area of the C.D. Block is 1567.70 sq. kms. It is bounded by taluks Lingsugur and Manvi on north, district Koppal on south and west, and district Bellary on east.

Communications:

Roadways : S.H-19: Direction- Lingsugur to Bellary, Neare st Villages- Sunkanur, Hasamakal, Gudadur, Rangapur, Muddapur, Harapur, Yelekudalgi, Bassapur - (Ej), Kunnatgi, Pagadadinni, Mullur, Kallur, Butaldinni, Mallapur, Kannari, Maldinni, Yelragi, Hosshalli (Ej), Budiwal, Somlapur, Dhadesugur, Bassapur (D), Kengal, Sasalmari, Malakapur. S.H-23: Direction- Gangawati to Manvi, Neare st Villages- Hanchinhal (K), Sivajawalgera, Sultanpur, Jawalgera, Dibbanakhed, Turakatti (D), Ramathanhal, Banniganur, Yapalparvi, Konganhatti, Sindhnur (Rural), Hosshalli (Ej), Gorebal, Sasalmari. S.H-29: Nearest Villages- Mullur (U). S.H-30: Direction- Kushtagi to Sindhnur, Nearest Villages- Kardchalami, Gorloti, Umloti, Bukanhatti, Turvihal, Kalmangi, Gunjanalli, Virapapur, Arlihalli, Hosalapur.

River: Maski Nadi- Nearest Villages- Sunkanur, Chikkkad bur, Kyathanahatti, Udbal (Umli), Hullur, Shankerbandi - (D), Balganur, Goudanbhavi, Govindnaikandoddi, Belliga nur, Buddinni, Jalwadgi, Siranguddi, Diddigi, Ramathanhal, Banniganur, Yapalparvi, Walkamdinni, Ragalparvi, Mandah osur (D), Puldinni, Dumti, Gonwar, Hulgunchi, Ayyanur. Tungabhadra Nadi- Nearest Villages- Ayyanur, Chintamand oddi, Chitrali, Pulmeswardinni, Hedginhal, Walbellary, Uppal, Salgunda, Cincheri, Dhadesugur, Bassapur (D), Kengal, Mukunda, Kurtkota (D), Arlihalli (Simth Mukunda), Singapur.

Canal: Nearest Villages- Turvihal, Hosshalli (K), Jambun athanahalli, Bassapur (K), Hanchinhal (K), Boppur, Matur, Sunkanur, Chikkkadbur, Kyathanahatti, Parapura, Merinah al, Hanpanhal, Gudgaldinni, Hanchinhal (U), Hedigibal, Gonhal, Hullur, Shankerbandi - (D), Balganur, Goudanbha vi, Govindnaikandoddi, Belliganur, Buddinni, Jalwadgi, Siranguddi, Diddigi, Ramathanhal, Banniganur, Yapalparvi, Walkamdinni, Somlapur, Gorebal, Konthanur, Channahalli, Siddrampur, Roudkunda, Gobberkal, Turvihal, Hosshalli (K), Jambunathanahalli, Bassapur (K), Hanchinhal (K), Boppur, Matur, Sunkanur, Chikkkadbur, Kyathanahatti, Parapura, Merinahal, Hanpanhal, Gudgaldinni, Hanchinhal (U), Hedigibal, Gonhal, Hullur, Shankerbandi (D), Balganur, Goudanbhavi, Govindnaikandoddi, Belliganur, Buddinni, Jalwadgi, Siranguddi, Diddigi, Ramathanhal, Banniganur, Yapalparvi, Walkamdinni, Somlapur, Gorebal, Konthanur, Channahalli, Siddrampur, Roudkunda, Gobberkal.

Annual Rainfall: Normal Rianfall 582 mm.

Ground Water: Availability of the Ground Water in the Basin is 184.95 H.A.M. and the utilization is 17.79 H.A.M. It belongs to Over Exploited category. Depth to water level 2 to 10 meter below the ground. Most of the wells go down in summer months, according to the Ground Water Estimation Committee.

Soils: Mixed Red and Black Soils.

Natural Division : It falls partly in the Middle Tungabha dra Valley and the Arkera-Mudgal-Kanakgiri Upland of the Central Karnataka Plateau.

Administration:

Division: Gulbarga. Parliamentary Constituency: 8 Koppal. District: Raichur. Taluka: Sindhnur. Assembly Constituency: 58 Sindhnur, 59 Maski (ST). Gram Panchayat: 34. Regional Area Development Boards: The Hyderabad - Karnataka Area Development Board.

Fairs: Ambadevi Temple Fair: Somalapur in Sindhanur taluk about 20 kilometers from Sindhanur, is well known for its Ambadevi temple, situated at the foot of a hill, where annually a fair takes place in the month of Pushya (December-January) which is largely attended.

Gaddi-Khader Wali Urs: Mukkunda, in Sindhanur taluk of Roichar area is situated on the banks of the Tungabha dra, nearby a hill, about 26 kms. from Sindhanur. There is an old and large fort on the top of the hill. At the entrance to the Mukkunda, there is an old temple of Murari, built of stone. An island in the river has the dargah of Gaddikhader Wali, where an annual Urs is held which attracts a large number of people.

Villages: 173 **Inhabited:** 160 **Uninhabited:** 13

Ranking	District	State	National
Area	3	26	119
Population	1	18	71
Sex Ratio	1	23	955
Child Sex Ratio	3	34	1673
Literacy Rate	1	156	4784
Density	3	66	4874
Work Participation Rate	1	84	1654

Gram Panchayats:
Gunda, Umloti, Kalmangi, Turvihal, Bassapur (K), Jalihal, Hanchinhal (K), Gunjanalli, Virapapur, Devergudi, Tidgol, Baphur, Kholabal, Gudadur, Udbal (Umli), Balganur, Pagadadinni, Butaldinni, Sindhnur (Rural), Goudanbhavi, Jawalgera, Ramathanhal, Ragalparvi, Gonwar, Badarli, Dhadesugur, Alabanoor, Madsirwar, Salgunda, Somlapur, Hosshalli (Ej), Goreba, Roudkunda, Channahalli, Mukunda.

Amenities:
Education: Primary School in 71 villages, Middle school in 64 villages, Matriculation or Secondary School in 13 villages, namely Umloti, Turvihal, Tidgol, Gudadur, Balganur, Jawalgera, Gonwar, Kannari, Alabanoor, Gonniganoor, Sindhnur (Rural), Somlapur, Gorebal.
Higher Secondary or Pre University Courses or Intermediate or Junior College in 1 village of the CD Block,, namely Balganur.
College in 0 village, Adult Literacy Center in 0 village.
Medical: Hospital in 2 villages, Dispensary in 14 villages, Health Center in 12 villages, Sub Center in 39 villages, Maternity and Child Welfare Center in 2 villages, Community health workers in 10 villages.
The Villages having Hospital or Dispensary or Health Center are Turvihal, Kalmangi, Jalihal, Gunjanalli, Kanoor, Kunnatgi, Hullur, Balganur, Jawalgera , Ragalparvi, Hedginhal, Gonniganoor, Sindhnur (Rural), Salgunda, Dhadesugur.
Drinking Water: Tap water in 47 villages, Tank water in 51 villages, Well water in 71 villages, Tubewell in 9 villages and more than one source in 129 villages.
Bank: Banking facility in 18 villages, namely, Gunda, Umloti, Turvihal, Jalihal, Udbal (Umli) Kanoor, Kunnatgi, Mallapur, Balganur, Jawalgera Walbellary, Belgurki, Sindhnur (Rural), Somlapur Salgunda, Dhadesugur, Gorebal, Roudkunda.
Credit Society in 31 villages Agricultural Credit Society in 31 Non-Agricultural Credit Society in 8 villages.
Others: Power supply in 128 villages, Cinema hall in 6 villages sport club in 160 villages, Stadium or Auditorium or Communi Hall in 160 villages, Post Office in 54 villages.
There are 103 villages having bus facilities.
Villages with most of facilities: Gunda, Umloti Turvihal, Jalihal, Udbal (Umli), Mallapur, Balganur Jawalgera, Sindhnur (Rural), Somlapur, Salgunda Dhadesugur, Gorebal, Roudkunda.
Villages without amenities (Education): Mahampur, Bommanahal-U, Gudihal, Gadratigi, Hattigudda, Hirebhergi, Bhogapur, Virapur, Hosshalli (K), Jambunathanahalli, Gandhinagar, Hanumapur, Hokarani, Bagalapur, Boppur, Kaniganhalu, Matur, Nedigol, Sunkanur, Chikkkadbur, Kyathanahatti, Parapura, Merinahal, Nanjaldinni, Hanchinhal (U), Kanoor, Gonhal, Rangapur, Muddapur, Putkanhal (D), Chiratanal, Bommanhal - (Ej), Devergudi, Manganhal - (D), Bassapur - (Ej), Kunnatgi, Tippanhatti, Kallur, Hullur, Shankerbandi - (D), Goudanbhavi, Govindnaikandoddi, Belliganur, Konganaikandoddi, Maskihatti, Bendlhatti, Nagonagathi, Jujulapur, Locknaikandoddi, Konganaikandoddi, Sivajawalgera, Amarapur Khadehola - (D), Sultanpur, Dibbanakhed, Turakatti - (D), Maldinni Khadehola, Kanakraddi Khadehola, Banniganur, Yapalparvi, Mandahosur - (D), Hulgunchi, Chintamandoddi, Chitrali, Pulmeswardinni, Yeddaldoddi, Udbal (Jagir), Belgurki, Maldinni, Haretnur, Puldinni, Hosalapur, Siddapur - (D), Joladarasi, Sashalli, Hosshalli (Ej), Amarapur, Nandikal - (D), Kaggal - (D), Cincheri, Bassapur (D), Kengal, Hatti, Konthanur, Siddrampur, Mavinmadu, Simth Mavina Madu, Kurtkota (D), Singapur..
Scheduled Castes: Out of the total population of 298902 persons, 54117 persons (18.11%) belong to Scheduled Castes. The villages having less than 10% SC population are Mahampur, Bommanahal-U, Ratanapur, Gudihal Kardchalami, Gorloti, Jambunathanahalli Bassapur (K), Bagalapur, Boppur, Kaniganhalu Nedigol, Chikkkadbur, Rangapur, Putkanhal (D) Chiratanal, Manganhal - (D), Tippanhatti, Hullur Konganaikandoddi, Jujulapur, Diddigi Locknaikandoddi, Konganaikandoddi Amarapur Khadehola - (D), Dibbanakhed, Timmapur Mandahosur - (D), Chintamandoddi, Kannari, Maldinni Haretnur, Puldinni, Gonniganoor, Hosalapur Sindhnur (Rural), Siddapur - (D), Sashalli Nandikal - (D), Kaggal - (D), Cincheri, Dhadesugur

Bassapur (D), Hatti, Siddrampur, Simth Mavina Madu Kurtkota (D).

The village having more than 50% SC population is None.

Sex ratio of Scheduled Caste population is 505.

Scheduled Castes Literates and Illiterates by Sex:

	Persons	Males	Females
Literate	15,033	10,450	4,583
Illiterate	39,084	16,328	22,756
Literacy rate	34.8	49.3	20.9
Graduate	182	171	11

Scheduled Castes (Dominant):

Madiga, Chalavadi etc., Bhovi, Bhambi etc.
Banjara etc.

For their cultural identity please see Appendix-I

Villages without Scheduled Castes: There are 29 villages without any scheduled caste population.

Scheduled Tribes: Out of the total population of 298902 persons, 44526 persons (14.9%) belong to Scheduled Tribes.

The villages having less than 10% ST population are Sankanhal, Gudihal, Umloti, Jambunathanahalli Bassapur (K), Hanchinhal (K), Uppaldoddi (Umli) Tidgol, Virapapur, Arlihalli, Sunkanur, Chikkkadbur Hasamakal , Gudadur, Merinahal, Hedigibal, Gonhal Muddapur, Harapur, Yelekudalgi, Mullur, Kallur Mallapur, Hullur, Shankerbandi - (D), Balganur Buddinni, Jalwadgi, Konganaikandoddi, Bendlhatti Nagonagathi, Konganaikandoddi, Sivajawalgera Amarapur Khadehola - (D), Dibbanakhed Kanakraddi Khadehola, Giniwar, Udbal (Jagir) Gomarsi, Madsirwar, Hosalapur, Sindhnur (Rural) Siddapur - (D), Joladarasi, Sashalli, Hosshalli (Ej) Amarapur, Nandikal - (D), Kaggal - (D), Budiwal Somlapur, Salgunda, Cincheri, Dhadesugur Bassapur (D), Kengal, Gorebal, Siddrampur, Mavinmadu Roudkunda, Simth Mavina Madu, Huda, Mukunda Kurtkota (D), Singapur.

The villages having more than 50% ST population are Mahampur, Bhogapur, Virapur, Kardchalami, Gorloti Bagalapur, Putkanhal (D), Manganhal - (D) Locknaikandoddi, Yapalparvi, Mandahosur - (D) Puldinni, Hulgunchi, Chintamandoddi, Puldinni Gonniganoor.

Sex ratio of Scheduled tribe population is 503.

Scheduled Tribes Literates and Illiterates by Sex:

	Persons	Males	Females
Literate	11,793	8,561	3,232
Illiterate	32,733	13,554	19,179
Literacy rate	32.9	48.2	17.9
Graduate	81	78	3

Scheduled Tribes (Dominant):

Naikda etc., Kadu Kuruba, Meda, Iruliga
Konda Kapus

For their cultural identity please see Appendix-II

Villages without Scheduled Tribes: There are 28 villages without any scheduled tribe population.

Literates and Illiterates by Sex (Total Population):

	Persons	Males	Females
Literate	119,268	76,735	42,533
Illiterate	179,634	72,160	107,474
Literacy rate	48	63	34
Graduate	2,053	1,812	241

Agriculture: ***Distribution of villages according to land use:*** Out of 173 villages, Total area (in hectare) is 156770, out of that 88.58 percent is cultivable and 24.06 percent of the cultivable area is irrigated.

Sources of Irrigation (Hectares): Government Canal 33406.94, Private Canal 0, Well without Electricity 0, Well with Electricity 0, Tubewell without Electricity 0, Tubewell with Electricity 0, Tank 0, River 0, Lake 0, Waterfall 0, Others 0.

Villages with population of 5000 to 9999: Virapapur, Jawalgera , Somlapur, Salgunda, Sasalmari Roudkunda.

Villages with population of 10000 and above: Turvihal, Gandhinagar, Balganur, Sindhnur (Rural) Gorebal.

Distribution of Workers:

	Persons	Males	Females	WPR
Cultivators	54,529	40,387	14,142	36.96
Agricultural Labour	75,136	28,987	46,149	50.93
Household Industry	2,323	1,383	940	1.57
Other Workers	15,533	10,859	4,674	10.53
Main Workers	106,176	70,177	35,999	71.97
Marginal Workers	41,345	11,439	29,906	28.03
Total Workers	147,521	81,616	65,905	

Religion: Major Religious Communities:

	Persons	Males	Females	Sex Ratio
Hindu (90.4%)	270,216	134,627	135,589	1,007
Muslim (8.72%)	26,060	12,961	13,099	1,011
Christian (0.23%)	695	369	326	883
Sikh (0.01%)	19	11	8	727
Buddhists (0%)	1	-	1	-
Jain (0.02%)	73	38	35	921

Agewise Data:

	Persons	Males	Females	Sex Ratio
All ages	298,902	148,895	150,007	1007
0-14	119,643	60,504	59,139	977
15-44	131,777	65,989	65,788	997
45-79	45,870	21,784	24,086	1106

80+	1,451	531	920	1733
Age not stated	161	87	74	851

Languages (Dominant):

Kannada, Telugu, Urdu, Bengali, Hindi

Disabled Population:

	Persons	Males	Females	%
Total Disabled	3,552	1,939	1,613	
In Seeing	1,385	696	689	38.99
In Speech	373	214	159	10.5
In Hearing	178	86	92	5.01
In Movement	1,272	766	506	35.81
Mentally	344	177	167	9.68

SIRA

Sira C.D. Block lies in the north-western part of Tumkur district. It is a part of Sira taluka. The Block is located at a distance of 45 kms. from district headquart ers (Tumkur). There are 249 villages in the block with the total population of 251,199 persons. Area of the C.D. Block is 1538.07 sq. kms. It is bounded by district Chitradurga on north, taluks Gubbi and Tumkur on south, taluks Koratagere, Tumkur and Madhugiri on east, taluk Chiknayakanhalli and district Chitradurga on west. It has common boundary with the state of Andhra Pradesh on north and east.

Communications:

Roadways : N.H.-4: Direction- Belgaum to Bangalore, Nearest Villages- Pinnanahole, Ujjanakunte, Maranagere, Tavarikeri, Mosarakunte, Manangi, Panjiganahalli, Dwaralu, Bhuvanahalli, Kallukote, Gummanahalli, Yemmerahalli, Yaliyuru, Kadavigere, Chikkanahalli, Halenahalli, Bhupasa-ndra, Karejavanahalli, Kallambella, Kataveeranahalli, Kageli nganahalli, Vaddanahalli, Seebi Agrahara, Yaladabagi, Seebi. S.H.-58: Direction- Mudigere to Gauribidanur, Nearest Villages- Chikkasandra Kaval, Anthapura, Magodu, Borasandra, Guligenahalli, Muganahalli, Nyayagere, Ratnasandra, Thaggihalli, Halkur, Girinathanahalli, Sira (Rural), Halkur Kaval, Gummanahalli, Mekerahalli, Mudigere Kaval, Huildore, Honnenahalli, Kaniverampura, Bukkapatna, Balapura, Kilaradahalli, Budiggudda Kaval.

River: Suvarnamukhi Nadi- Nearest Villages- Dyagerahalli, Herur, Muddenahalli, Hosur, Narayanapura, Dandikere, Hunasehalli, Pinnanahole, Ujjanakunte, Maranagere, Tavarekere, Mosarakunte, Melekote, Ranganahalli, Devarah alli, Badakanahalli, Kaggaladu, Bhuthakatnahalli, Chikkan akote, Melukunte, Madalur, Kotta, Bidarakere, Dwaralu, Gajjarahalli.

Canal: Nearest Villages- Narayanapura, Dandikere, Hunase halli, Pinnanahole, Ujjanakunte, Maranagere, Tavarekere, Mosarakunte, Devarahalli, Madalur, Kotta, Bidarakere, Gajjarahalli, Lakshmisagar, Kallukote, Sira (Rural).

Annual Rainfall: Normal Rianfall 602.05 mm.

Ground Water: Availability of the Ground Water in the Basin is 11269.81 H.A.M. and the utilization is 12842. 69 H.A.M. It belongs to Over Exploited category. Depth to water level 2 to 20 meter below the ground. Most of the wells go down in summer months, according to the Ground Water Estimation Committee.

Soils: Red Sandy Soil.

Natural Division : It falls partly in Suvarnamukhi Basin, Madhugiri Hills and Chiknayakanhalli-Sira Scrubby Upland of the Southern Karnataka Plateau.

Administration:

Division: Bangalore. Parliamentary Constituency: 19 Tumkur, 18 Chitradurga (SC). District: Tumkur. Taluka: Sira. Assembly Constituency: 128 Chiknayakanhalli, 136 Sira. Gram Panchayat: 36.

Regional Area Development Boards: The Bailu Seeme Area Development Board.

Border Villages: (State: Andhra Pradesh)- Tadakalur, Chiratahalli, Hosakote, Vardapura, Doddabanagere, Narag ondanahalli, Baragur, Narasipura, Harogere, Badamaranahal li, Hariyajjanahalli, Kallahalli, Madalur, Koratakere, Honnagondanahalli, Magodu.

Fairs: Narasimhaswamy Car Festival: It is held at Seebi in the month of February for fifteen days. It is situated about 20 kms. north of the Tumkur town on the Tumkur-C hitradurga road. Formerly, it was known as 'Sibur' and Harihara-Rayapura and had been an agrahara town. It is noted for its temple of Narasimha, at which there takes place a large annual festival in the month of Magha (about February). The temple has architectural peculiarities of four periods.

Villages: 249 **Inhabited:** 235 **Uninhabited:** 14

Ranking	District	State	National
Area	1	29	126
Population	2	35	225
Sex Ratio	7	108	2679
Child Sex Ratio	7	127	3644
Literacy Rate	7	90	2831
Density	2	21	5344
Work Participation Rate	9	108	779

Gram Panchayats:

Dwaranakunte, Tadakalur, Hulikunte, Doddabanagere, Baragur, Handikunte, Hosahalli, Nadur, Hemdore, Bevinahalli, Hosur, Hunasehalli, Tavarekere, Gowdagere, Melukunte, Madalur, Honnagondanahalli, Kotta, Bhuvanahalli , Lakshmisagar, Nerlegudda, Bukkapatna, Ramalingapura, Huildore, Dodda Agrahara, Chikkanahalli, Yaliyuru, Magodu, Ratnasandra, Bhupasandra, Kallambella, Gopaladevarahalli, Tarur, Chinnenahalli, Seebi Agrahara, Seebi.

Amenities:

Education: Primary School in 193 villages, Middle school in 132 villages, Matriculation or Secondary School in 42 villages, namely Dwaranakunte, Tadakalur, Doddabanagere, Hulikunte, Musakaloti, Yanjalagere, Dasarahalli, Badenahalli, Baragur, Harogere, Rangapura, Hosur, Changavara, Bevinahalli, Hunasehalli, Tavarekere, Nadur, Bandakunte, Maddakkanahalli(Jodi), Melukunte, Madalur, Panjiganahalli, Gollahalli, Magodu, Guligenahalli, Ratnasandra, Ganadahunase, Bukkapatna, Sakshihalli, Dodda Agrahara, Benche, Sidlakona, Chikkanahalli, Kalapura, Talagunda, Tarur, Kallambella, Kataveeranahalli, Brammasandra, Seebi Agrahara, Hunjunalu, Seebi.

Higher Secondary or Pre University Courses or Intermediate or Junior College in 12 villages of the CD Block,, namely Tadakalur, Hulikunte, Baragur, Tavarekere, Nadur, Sira (Rural), Bukkapatna, Sidlakona, Chikkanahalli, Kallambella, Kataveeranahalli, Brammasandra.

College in 2 villages, Adult Literacy Center in 0 village., Colleges are in villages, namely Nadur, Sira (Rural).

Medical: Hospital in 1 village, Dispensary in 8 villages, Health Center in 8 villages, Sub Center in 25 villages, Maternity and Child Welfare Center in 2 villages, Community health workers in 4 villages.

The Villages having Hospital or Dispensary or Health Center are Hulikunte, Nadur, Panjiganahalli, Sira (Rural), Yaliyuru, Bukkapatna, Dodda Agrahara, Brammasandra.

Drinking Water: Tap water in 158 villages, Tank water in 52 villages, Well water in 65 villages, Tubewell in 43 villages and more than one source in 182 villages.

Bank: Banking facility in 13 villages, namely, Bevinahalli, Hunasehalli, Tavarekere, Ranganahalli Nadur, Madalur, Honnagondanahalli, Guligenahalli Sira (Rural), Chikkagula, Huildore, Bukkapatna Kallambella.

Credit Society in 27 villages Agricultural Credit Society in 24 Non-Agricultural Credit Society in 4 villages.

Others: Power supply in 234 villages, Cinema hall in 6 villages, sport club in 235 villages, Stadium or Auditorium or Community Hall in 235 villages, Post Office in 69 villages.

There are 171 villages having bus facilities.

Villages with most of facilities: Tavarekere Nadur, Madalur, Honnagondanahalli, Guligenahalli Sira (Rural), Bukkapatna.

Villages without amenities (Education): Hosakote, Vardapura, Sasamaru, Katanahalli, Hariyajjanahalli, Herur, Pinnanahole, Katanahalli, Cheelanahalli, Chikkasandra Kaval, Kusukunte Kaval, Halkur Kaval, Ramanahalli, Doddahaladamadu, Ranganahalli, Sadarakaranahalli, Lingasettihalli, Channenahalli, Chakkenahalli, Jadarahalli, Kumbarahalli, Punjihalli, Handimalku, Kalappanahalli, Salapura, Basavanahalli, Battiganahalli, Kallaobanahalli, Chikkagiriyanahalli, Devarahalli, Chikkathimmanahalli, Channenahalli, Hosaburju, Ranganahalli, Thoriyappanahalli, Chinnenahalli, Kalenahalli, Thippanahalli, Borasandra, Jodidevarahalli, Kappenahalli..

Scheduled Castes: Out of the total population of 251385 persons, 57381 persons (22.83%) belong to Scheduled Castes.

The villages having less than 10% SC population are Hosakote, Vardapura, Gandihalli, Katanahalli Badenahalli, Sankapura, Bevinahalli, Pinnanahole Maranagere, Katanahalli, Bandakunte, Balenahalli Bhuthakatnahalli, Cheelanahalli, Anthapura Kusukunte Kaval, Kusukunte, Koratakere, Ratnasandra Girinathanahalli, Ramanahalli, Ganadahunase Manganahalli, Guddadaranganahalli, Lingasettihalli Channenahalli, Thimmanahalli, Jadarahalli Thuppadakona, Basavanahalli, Obalihalli Yaramadanahalli, Basavanahalli, Kallaobanahalli Chikkagiriyanahalli, Sidlakona, Matanahalli Devarahalli, Honnenahalli, Muchaveeranahalli Chikkathimmanahalli, Bettanahalli, Channenahalli Hosaburju, Ranganahalli, Vaddanahalli, Chinnenahalli Kalenahalli, Javanahalli, Seebi Agrahara, Borasandra Kappenahalli, Dasarahalli, Saluparahalli Venkatapura.

The villages having more than 50% SC population are Maddakkanahalli(Jodi), Badakanahalli, Manangi Ranganahalli, Chikkasandra Kaval, Anupanahalli Padmapura, Sira (Rural), Yemmerahalli Mudigere Kaval, Gungarapente, Nerlegudda Doddahaladamadu, Hyaldore Kaval, Sadarakaranahalli Chakkenahalli, Handimalku, Kenchappanahalli Dodda Agrahara, Salapura, Doddachikkanahalli Thoriyappanahalli.

Sex ratio of Scheduled Caste population is 490.

Scheduled Castes Literates and Illiterates by Sex:

	Persons	Males	Females
Literate	24,927	15,602	9,325
Illiterate	32,454	13,668	18,786
Literacy rate	50.5	62.0	38.6
Graduate	550	498	52

Scheduled Castes (Dominant):

Madiga, Adi Karnataka, Bhovi, Banjara etc.

Adi Dravida

For their cultural identity please see Appendix-I

Villages without Scheduled Castes: There are 42 villages without any scheduled caste population.

Scheduled Tribes: Out of the total population of 251385 persons, 25401 persons (10.1%) belong to Scheduled Tribes.

The villages having less than 10% ST population are Nejanthi, Tadakalur, Bejjihalli, Hosakote Doddabanagere, Nidagatta, Musakaloti, Karehalli Sasamaru, Yanjalagere, Kotti, Kyadikunte, Yadaladaku Chikka Hulikunte, Chikkabanagere, Naragondanahalli Kaligonahalli, Dasarahalli, Gopikunte, Hosahalli Ramanahalli, Badenahalli, Agrahara, Kadarehalli Yalpenahalli, Harogere, Handikunte Karekyathanahalli, Pujarimuddanahalli, Ragalahalli Hariyajjanahalli, Kallahalli, Dyagerahalli, Herur Muddenahalli, Sankapura, Changavara, Bevinahalli Siddapura, Kaluverahalli, Narayanapura, Hunasehalli Pinnanahole, Maranagere, Ranganahalli, Katanahalli Kumbarahalli, Gomaranahalli, Hosahalli, Hemdore Kamagondanahalli, Nadur, Rangapura, Hanumanahalli Bandakunte, Honnenahalli, Balenahalli Maddakkanahalli(Jodi), Badakanahalli, Gowdagere Kaggaladu, Chikkanakote, Melukunte, Bhoppanadu Madalur, Kotta, Bidarakere, Manangi, Dwaralu Gajjarahalli, Lakshmisagar, Cheelanahalli Ranganahalli, Devarapura, Chikkasandra Kaval Kallukote, Vojukunte, Kusukunte Kaval, Kusukunte Anupanahalli, Gollahalli, Honnagondanahalli Borasandra, Guligenahalli, Muganahalli, Ratnasandra Arehalli, Padmapura, Thaggihalli, Girinathanahalli Channanakunte, Sira (Rural), Gummanahalli Yemmerahalli, Mudigere Kaval, Chikkagula Gungarapente, Ajjenahalli, Doddahaladamadu Yarradakatte, Kurubarahalli, Manganahalli, Huildore Honnenahalli, Nimbemaradahalli, Guddadaranganahalli Ranganahalli, Hyaldore Kaval, Sadarakaranahalli Lingasettihalli, Hunasekatte, Thimmanahalli Chakkenahalli, Jadarahalli, Balapura, Kilaradahalli Sakshihalli, Handimalku, Vaddanahalli Kenchappanahalli, Dodda Agrahara, Kanchiganahalli Kalappanahalli, Thuppadakona, Ramalingapura Salapura, Hosahalli, Halebijjanabella Hosabijjanabella, Benche, Gopaladevarahalli Kallaobanahalli, Chikkagiriyanahalli, Katamala Bhupasandra, Mayasandra, Matanahalli, Devarahalli Doddachikkanahalli, Honnenahalli, Chinnappanahalli Balanapalya, Bettanahalli, Channenahalli, Tarur Thoriyappanahalli, Karejavanahalli, Kallambella Kagelinganahalli, Vaddanahalli, Balabasavanahalli Neladimmanahalii, Chinnenahalli, Javanahalli Yaladabagi, Thippanahalli, Dasarahalli.

The villages having more than 50% ST population are Dandikere, Anthapura, Nyayagere, Channenahalli Kumbarahalli, Maragondanahalli, Battiganahalli Sidlakona, Hosaburju, Jodidevarahalli, Kappenahalli Saluparahalli.

Sex ratio of Scheduled tribe population is 493.

Scheduled Tribes Literates and Illiterates by Sex:

	Persons	Males	Females
Literate	12,818	7,779	5,039
Illiterate	12,583	5,088	7,495
Literacy rate	57.7	69.2	45.9
Graduate	277	243	34

Scheduled Tribes (Dominant):

Naikda etc., Hakkipikki, Kadu Kuruba Generic Tribes etc.

For their cultural identity please see Appendix-II

Villages without Scheduled Tribes: There are 69 villages without any scheduled tribe population.

Literates and Illiterates by Sex (Total Population):

	Persons	Males	Females
Literate	131,108	79,489	51,619
Illiterate	120,277	48,389	71,888
Literacy rate	60	71	48
Graduate	3,890	3,395	495

Agriculture: ***Distribution of villages according to land use:*** Out of 249 villages, Total area (in hectare) is 153807, out of that 68.15 percent is cultivable and 20.04 percent of the cultivable area is irrigated.

Sources of Irrigation (Hectares): Government Canal 723.03, Private Canal 0, Well without Electricity 141.43, Well with Electricity 2222.52, Tubewell without Electricity 272.57, Tubewell with Electricity 8964.09, Tank 6082.91, River 21, Lake 0, Waterfall 1112.83, Others 1467.4.

Villages with population of 5000 to 9999: Nadur, Madalur, Bukkapatna.

Villages with population of 10000 and above: None

Distribution of Workers:

	Persons	Males	Females	WPR
Cultivators	68,595	41,905	26,690	48.86
Agricultural Labour	40,785	16,342	24,443	29.05
Household Industry	8,063	2,688	5,375	5.74
Other Workers	22,950	16,535	6,415	16.35
Main Workers	110,183	69,855	40,328	78.48
Marginal Workers	30,210	7,615	22,595	21.52
Total Workers	140,393	77,470	62,923	

Religion: Major Religious Communities:

	Persons	Males	Females	Sex Ratio
Hindu (97.14%)	244,201	124,229	119,972	966
Muslim (2.64%)	6,646	3,376	3,270	969
Christian (0.1%)	247	123	124	1,008

Sikh (0.01%)	16	9	7	778
Buddhists (0%)	-	-	-	-
Jain (0.02%)	40	24	16	667

Agewise Data:

	Persons	Males	Females	Sex Ratio
All ages	251,385	127,878	123,507	966
0-14	79,509	40,796	38,713	949
15-44	116,942	58,937	58,005	984
45-79	51,959	26,716	25,243	945
80+	2,716	1,280	1,436	1122
Age not stated	259	149	110	738

Languages (Dominant):

Kannada, Urdu, Telugu, Hindi, Marathi

Disabled Population:

	Persons	Males	Females	%
Total Disabled	6,330	3,971	2,359	
In Seeing	3,350	2,148	1,202	52.92
In Speech	637	353	284	10.06
In Hearing	361	204	157	5.7
In Movement	1,523	998	525	24.06
Mentally	459	268	191	7.25

SIRSI

Sirsi C.D. Block lies in the central south-east part of Uttara Kannada district. It is a part of Sirsi taluka. The Block is located at a distance of 120 kms. from district headquarters (Karwar). There are 228 villages in the block with the total population of 110,194 persons. Area of the C.D. Block is 1287.52 sq. kms. It is bound ed by taluks Yellapur and Mundgod on north, district Shimoga and taluk Siddapur on south, districts Haveri and Shimoga on east, taluks Ankola and kumta on west.

Communications:

Roadways : S.H-2: Direction- Bislakoppa to Haveri, Nearest Villages- Bislakoppa, Malalgaon, Benagi, Hallikoppa, Danaganahalli, Badanagod, Kalangi. S.H-69: Direction- Kumta to Mundgod, Nearest Villages- Teppar, Hebre, Devimane, Hosur, Bandal, Khurse, Sampakhanda, Kugtemane, Janmane, Hanumanthi, Hostota, Mattigar, Neggu, Uratota, Isloor,Sannakeri, Huldevansar, Goudalli, Chipgi, Sankadmane, Heepnalli, Sirsimakki, Mundagesar, Wadgeri, Hudelkoppa,Bislakoppa, Yekkambi, Malalgaon, Benagi. S.H-93: Direction- Khanapur to Shimoga, Nearest Villages- Hulgol, Bhairumbe, Bommanalli, Agasal, Dasangadde, Sadashivalli, Chipgi, Mundagesar, Yadalli, Karsulli, Mashigadde , Kalkai, Kangod, Hannondugudde, Ajjibal, Jaganalli, Bislakoppa.

River: Varada Nadi- Nearest Villages- Kantraji, Ajjarni, Kadgod, Tigani, Banavasi, Bhasi, Mugvalli, Chikkadugli, Kalkoppa, Naroor. Sonda Nadi- Nearest Villages- Sonagin mane, Kodnagadde, Mogadde, Mathadeval, Hulgol, Malenalli. Patnada Halla Nadi- Nearest Villages- Kodnagadde, Mensi, Guruvalli, Audala, Mogadde, Bakkal, Muregar, Kudragod, Neelkani, Naigar, Jaddigadde, Manadur, Devanalli.

Annual Rainfall: Normal Rianfall 2457.7 mm.

Ground Water: Availability of the Ground Water in the Basin is 10578 H.A.M. and the utilization is 3666 H. A.M. It belongs to Safe category. Depth to water level 5 to 20 meter below the ground. Most of the wells go down in summer months, according to the Ground Water Estimation Committee.

Soils: Lateritic Soils.

Natural Division : It falls partly in Western Ghats, Yellapur Dandeli Forest and Sirsi-Siddapur Dissected Humid Tract of the Karnataka Coast (Western Coastal Region).

Administration:

Division: Belgaum. Parliamentary Constituency: 12 Uttara Kannada. District: Uttara Kannada. Taluka: Sirsi. Assembly Constituency: 80 Sirsi, 81 Yelllapur. Gram Panchayat: 27.

Regional Area Development Boards: The Maland Aera Development Board.

Fairs: Madhukeshwara Jatra: Madhukeshwara jatra is held at Banavasi for five days in the months of March-April-M ay every year. Banavasi a hobli centre 22 kms. from Sirsi, is one of the oldest towns in Karnataka, now existing in beautiful natural surroundings. It has many interesti ng monuments. The place name is found variedly used from time to time.

Marigudi Jatra: Marigudi jatra is held at Hulekal near Uttara Kannada in the month of Kartika (October-November). Hulekal or Hancharta a Hobli centre 14 kms. from Sirsi has been mentioned as Huliyakallu in the 16th century, a sati stone which records the death of one Birappa son of Hulivittaya Mallappa of Hullyakallu. The place has a Vyasaraya Matha founded by Madhwa saint, Vyasathir ta of Vijayanagar times who was also a contemporary of Vadiraja.

Marikamba Devi Jatra: Marikamba Devi jatra is held at Sirsi once in two years, for seven days in about March. Sirsi (taluk headquarters) the sub-divisional headquart ers (90 kilometres from Karwar) is the elevated place in the district and is normally compared with siror the head.

Sahasralinga Jatra: It is held at Sahasralinga near Uttara Kannada. Sahasralinga, which was originally known as Sahasrahalli, forms a beautiful valley where the river Shalmala flows. One has to take deviation at Hulgol (2.5 kms. from Sirsi) on Sirsi-Yellapur road and further walk in the interior forest (1.5 kms.) in order to reach this place. Several inscriptions mention this place as Sahasrahalli. But, it is clearly mentioned in the Jnana Deepika (a Samskrita work) that the Swarnav

alli Matha was earlier at the spot of Sahasrahalli and was later shifted due to frequent attacks by robbers.
Satyanatheshwara Temple Jatra: It is held at Bakkala near Uttara Kannada around the month of January-February. At Bakkala, 3 kms. from Hulekal, there is a Satyanathes hwara temple founded by Vyasaraya. There is an inscription and two hero-stones near this temple. During the annual jatra (January-February) the devotees specially make offerings with bakula (renje or pagade hoovu) flowers to the ratha and hence it is said the place is symbolica lly called Bakkala. There is a hero-stone (broken) which has a Hoysala inscription engraved on it. The outer walls of the garbhagriha have carvings in relief of Surya, Brahma, the Saptamatrikas and dakshinamurti. The Navaranga ceiling has sculptures of Vishnu, Subrahma nya, Umamaheshwara, Veerabhadra, etc.
Swarnavalli Matha Festival: A number of festivities including vratas, special poojas, car festivals, vardhan tis and aradhanas are celebrated with religious rites during every year at the Swaranavalli Matha in Sonda of Sirsi Taluk near Uttara Kannada. Vasantotsava for nine days from Chaitra Shudha Padyami to Navami is celeb rated at the matha with Srichakra Pooja, Rudrabhisheka and Vedaparayana twice a day.
Swarnavalli Matha Jatra: It is held at Swarnavalli near Uttara Kannada in the month of Vaishaka (March-April) every year. Swarnavalli 16 kms. from Sirsi is a place of religious importance.
Syed Mohammad Shariful Madani Urs: It is held once in five years at Ullal. Ullal Town is situated on the south bank of the Netravati river at a distance of eight kms. from Mangalore. A branch of the Chauta Royal family of Puttige ruled from Ullal. Somanatha of Ullal was their family deity.
Vadiraja Jatra: Vadiraja jatra is held at Sonda near Uttara Kannada for one day in the months of April-May every year. Sonda 19 kms. from Sirsi is a place of consi derable antiquity.
Venkataramana Jatra: Venkataramana jatra is held at Manjuguni near Uttara Kannada for one day in the month of April every year. Manjuguni 26 kilometres from Sirsi is a place of pilgrimage.

Villages: 222 **Inhabited:** 221 **Uninhabited:** 1

Ranking	District	State	National
Area	2	52	226
Population	3	155	3148
Sex Ratio	8	116	2841
Child Sex Ratio	10	168	4940
Literacy Rate	2	10	448
Density	4	100	6215
Work Participation Rate	8	167	2322

Gram Panchayats:
Vanalli , Kodnagadde , Harehulekal , Bhairumbe , Isloor , Bislakoppa , Badanagod , Andgi , Bankanal , Dodnalli , Hutgar , Itaguli , Salkani , Devanalli , Bandal , Shivalli , Janmane , Neggu , Hunsekoppa, Yadalli , Kangod , Kulve , Unchalli , Sugavi , Gudnapur, Banavasi , Bhasi .

Amenities:
Education: Primary School in 181 villages, Middle school in 112 villages, Matriculation or Secondary School in 21 villages, namely Vanalli, Hancharata, Bhairumbe, Salkani, Itaguli, Dasangadde, Shivagaon, Sampakhanda, Neggu, Chipgi, Yadalli, Baroor, Bislakoppa, Yekkambi, Badanagod, Bilur, Andgi, Bengle, Gudnapur, Banavasi, Naroor.
Higher Secondary or Pre University Courses or Intermediate or Junior College in 4 villages of the CD Block,, namely Hancharata, Sampakhanda, Mundagesar, Yadalli. College in 0 village, Adult Literacy Center in 0 village.
Medical: Hospital in 0 village, Dispensary in 5 villages, Health Center in 6 villages, Sub Center in 11 villages, Maternity and Child Welfare Center in 0 village, Community health workers in 163 villages.
The Villages having Hospital or Dispensary or Health Center are Mensi , Kakkalli , Bhairumbe , Balavalli , Mattigar.
Drinking Water: Tap water in 59 villages, Tank water in 7 villages, Well water in 217 villages, Tubewell in 29 villages and more than one source in 194 villages.
Bank: Banking facility in 20 villages, namely, Vanalli, Hancharata, Agasal, Salkani, Shivalli Shivagaon, Janmane, Isloor, Ajjibal, Yekkambi Benagi, Badanagod, Bellankeri, Kirwatti, Halgadde Unchalli, Bengle, Gudnapur, Umblekoppa, Banavasi.
Credit Society in 24 villages Agricultural Credit Society in 23 Non-Agricultural Credit Society in 1 village.
Others: Power supply in 218 villages, Cinema hall in 2 villages sport club in 0 village, Stadium or Auditorium or Community Hall in 0 village, Post Office in 73 villages.
There are 163 villages having bus facilities.
Villages with most of facilities: Vanalli Hancharata, Salkani, Shivalli, Shivagaon, Janmane Yekkambi, Badanagod, Bellankeri, Kirwatti, Halgadde Unchalli, Bengle, Gudnapur, Banavasi.
Villages without amenities (Education): Nakshe, Neelkani, Tattisar, Arasapur, Kelgin Onikeri, Modur, Karjigimane, Kalugar, Bugadi, Hakkigadde, Hallusargi, Heggar, Yachadi, Bommanalli, Hanagar, Kukri, Nurkalkoppa, Bilgalmane, Sankadmane, Kageri,

Karsulli, Amblihonda, Padageri, Hannondugudde, Angodkoppa, Wadgeri, Benagi, Kotekoppa, Fharsi, Kyadgikoppa, Kalgundikoppa, Gadgeri, Mugilkoppa, Hadalagi, Umblekoppa, Somanalli, Kalli, Kogod, Chikkadugli..

Scheduled Castes: Out of the total population of 110215 persons, 10463 persons (9.49%) belong to Scheduled Castes. The villages having less than 10% SC population are Dhoranagiri , Sonaginmane , Muski , Kakkalli Shirgani , Gonsar , Vanalli , Guruvalli , Audala Mogadde, Kodigar , Bakkal , Nakshe , Muregar Kudragod , Neelkani , Naigar , Jaddigadde , Manadur Tattisar , Singanalli , Hancharata , Sonda , Hulgol Malenalli , Arasapur , Golikoppa , Bommanalli Agasal , Kelgin Onikeri , Modur , Salkani Shigehalli , Balegadde , Karjigimane , Koppa Andolli , Devarkoppa , Harepal , Sadashivalli Mundganmane , Kelginkeri , Sarguppa , Devanmane Benagaon , Kallalli , Devanalli , Onigadde , Kalugar Manjaguni , Teppar , Hebre , Devimane, Bugadi , Hosur Bandal , Kambigar , Hakkigadde , Mudgar , Kotgehalli Shivagaon , Kanalli, Hostota , Sampakhanda Kugtemane , Badagi , Balavalli , Janmane , Kodgibail Heggar , Yachadi , Kalve , Sannalli , Janmane (H) Hunsekoppa, Hanumanthi , Hostota , Bommanalli Hanagar , Kukri , Adalli , Kondalgi , Neggu , Uratota Bappanalli , Tataguni , Tuduguni , Boppanalli , Pura Huldevansar , Somanalli , Chipgi, Dodnalli , Byagadde Husri , Bachagaon , Bilgalmane , Hedigemane Sankadmane , Heepnalli , Sirsimakki , Mundagesar Terkanalli , Kageri , Yadalli , Karsulli , Amblihonda Mashigadde , Padageri , Kangod , Hannondugudde Ajjibal , Karoor , Balgar , Jaganalli , Bislakoppa Baroor , Kulve , Gadihalli , Shivalli , Angodkoppa Mudebail , Wadgeri , Bislakoppa , Ullal , Adnalli Yekkambi , Hebballi , Malalgaon , Kotekoppa Mattihalli , Ummadi , Bilur , Kuppalli , Gongatta Kandraji , Malanji , Fharsi , Kyadgikoppa , Madankeri Kankoppa , Halsinkoppa , Kabbe , Kerekoppa, Unchalli Bidralli , Vaddinakoppa , Kalgundikoppa , Mugilkoppa Madralli , Gudnapur, Navanageri , Somanalli Uplekoppa , Koppa , Kalli , Kogod , Mundgehalli Kadgod , Mugvalli , Kalkoppa.

The village having more than 50% SC population is None.

Sex ratio of Scheduled Caste population is 490.

Scheduled Castes Literates and Illiterates by Sex:

	Persons	Males	Females
Literate	5,013	2,937	2,076
Illiterate	5,450	2,394	3,056
Literacy rate	56.2	65.1	47.1
Graduate	63	51	12

Scheduled Castes (Dominant):

Chalavadi etc., Bhovi, Bhambi etc., Moger Banjara etc.

For their cultural identity please see Appendix-I

Villages without Scheduled Castes: There are 67 villages without any scheduled caste population.

Scheduled Tribes: Out of the total population of 110215 persons, 977 persons (0.89%) belong to Scheduled Tribes. The villages having less than 10% ST population are Dhoranagiri , Kalgadde Kanchigadde , Sonaginmane Kodnagadde , Mensi , Balekaimane , Muski , Kakkalli Kanamuski , Shirgani , Gonsar , Vanalli , Guruvalli Audala , Mogadde, Mathadeval , Kodigar , Bakkal Nakshe , Koligar , Muregar , Kudragod , Neelkani Naigar , Jaddigadde , Manadur , Tattisar , Singanalli Hancharata , Sonda , Hulgol , Malenalli , Arasapur Belale , Golikoppa , Bhairumbe , Bommanalli , Agasal Harehulekal , Kelgin Onikeri , Melin Onikeri , Modur Salkani , Kadbal , Shigehalli , Balegadde Karjigimane , Itaguli , Koppa , Andolli , Devarkoppa Harepal , Dasangadde , Sadashivalli , Mundganmane Kelginkeri , Sarguppa , Devanmane , Benagaon Kallalli , Devanalli , Onigadde , Kalugar , Manjaguni Teppar , Hebre , Devimane, Bugadi , Hosur , Bandal Khurse , Kambigar , Hakkigadde , Mudgar , Kotgehalli Shivalli , Shivagaon , Kanalli, Hostota , Navilgar Sampakhanda , Kugtemane , Badagi , Balavalli Janmane , Kodgibail , Hallusargi , Yachadi , Kalve Sannalli , Janmane (H), Hunsekoppa, Hanumanthi Hostota , Bommanalli , Mattigar , Hanagar , Kukri Adalli , Kondalgi , Nerlavalli , Neggu , Uratota Bappanalli , Tataguni , Tuduguni , Boppanalli Isloor , Sannakeri , Achanalli , Pura , Huldevansar Goudalli , Somanalli , Chipgi, Narebail , Dodnalli Byagadde , Nurkalkoppa , Husri , Bachagaon , Kalgar Bilgalmane , Hedigemane , Sankadmane , Heepnalli Sirsimakki , Mundagesar , Terkanalli , Kageri Yadalli , Karsulli , Amblihonda , Mashigadde Betkoppa , Padageri , Kangod , Hannondugudde Ajjibal , Karoor , Balgar , Jaganalli , Bislakoppa Baroor , Kulve , Gadihalli , Shivalli , Angodkoppa Mudebail , Wadgeri , Hudelkoppa , Bislakoppa , Ullal Adnalli , Yekkambi , Hebballi , Malalgaon , Benagi Hallikoppa , Kotekoppa , Danaganahalli , Kalangi Bellankeri , Kuppagadde , Mattihalli , Ummadi , Bilur Kuppalli , Gongatta , Gonur , Kandraji , Bankanal Malanji , Fharsi , Kirwatti , Waddal, Santolli Hebbatti , Andgi , Margundi , Halgadde , Sugavi

Madankeri , Kankoppa , Halsinkoppa , Kabbe Kerekoppa, Unchalli , Bidralli , Vaddinakoppa Kalgundikoppa , Gadgeri , Bengle , Mugilkoppa Kalkardi , Hadalagi , Madralli , Gudnapur Navanageri , Golikatta , Umblekoppa , Somanalli Uplekoppa , Koppa , Kalli , Kogod , Sahasralli Mundgehalli , Kantraji , Ajjarni , Kadgod , Tigani Banavasi , Bhasi , Mugvalli , Chikkadugli , Naroor.

The villages having more than 50% ST population are None.

Sex ratio of Scheduled tribe population is 467.

Scheduled Tribes Literates and Illiterates by Sex:

	Persons	Males	Females
Literate	484	297	187
Illiterate	493	224	269
Literacy rate	58.6	68.0	48.1
Graduate	6	5	1

Scheduled Tribes (Dominant):

Naikda etc., Meda, Hasalaru, Koraga, Hakkipikki

For their cultural identity please see Appendix-II

Villages without Scheduled Tribes: There are 188 villages without any scheduled tribe population.

Literates and Illiterates by Sex (Total Population):

	Persons	Males	Females
Literate	74,708	41,004	33,704
Illiterate	35,507	15,149	20,358
Literacy rate	78	84	71
Graduate	2,929	2,090	839

Agriculture: ***Distribution of villages according to land use:*** Out of 222 villages, Total area (in hectare) is 128752, out of that 12.9 percent is cultivable and 11.19 percent of the cultivable area is irrigated.

Sources of Irrigation (Hectares): Government Canal 96.42, Private Canal 0, Well without Electricity 26.13, Well with Electricity 593.51, Tubewell without Electricity 3.47, Tubewell with Electricity 176.66, Tank 620.58, River 99.88, Lake 0, Waterfall 0, Others 268.6.

Villages with population of 5000 to 9999: Banavasi.

Villages with population of 10000 and above: None

Distribution of Workers:

	Persons	Males	Females	WPR
Cultivators	14,183	10,749	3,434	25.92
Agricultural Labour	9,750	5,112	4,638	17.82
Household Industry	832	528	304	1.52
Other Workers	29,960	19,913	10,047	54.75
Main Workers	46,454	34,191	12,263	84.89
Marginal Workers	8,271	2,111	6,160	15.11
Total Workers	54,725	36,302	18,423	

Religion: Major Religious Communities:

	Persons	Males	Females	Sex Ratio
Hindu (92.45%)	101,895	51,848	50,047	965
Muslim (6.67%)	7,354	3,790	3,564	940
Christian (0.62%)	688	369	319	864
Sikh (0%)	3	2	1	500
Buddhists (0%)	-	-	-	-
Jain (0.22%)	244	126	118	937

Agewise Data:

	Persons	Males	Females	Sex Ratio
All ages	110,215	56,153	54,062	963
0-14	30,946	15,890	15,056	948
15-44	55,344	27,885	27,459	985
45-79	22,944	11,925	11,019	924
80+	945	432	513	1188
Age not stated	36	21	15	714

Languages (Dominant):

Kannada, Urdu, Marathi, Konkani, Hindi

Disabled Population:

	Persons	Males	Females	%
Total Disabled	2,211	1,256	955	
In Seeing	965	512	453	43.65
In Speech	157	94	63	7.1
In Hearing	191	104	87	8.64
In Movement	646	413	233	29.22
Mentally	252	133	119	11.4

SIRUGUPPA

Siruguppa C.D. Block lies in the northern part of Bellary district. It is a part of Siruguppa taluka. The Block is located at a distance of 56 kms. from district headqu arters (Bellary). There are 84 villages in the block with the total population of 168,739 persons. Area of the C.D. Block is 969.95 sq. kms. It is bounded by taluks Bellary and Hospet on south, district Koppal and Raichur on west. It has common boundary with the state of Andhra Pradesh on north and east.

Communications:

Roadways : S.H-19: Direction- Sindhnur to Bellary, NearestVillages- Devalapura, Halekota, Dasanur, Ibrampura, Bhyrapura, Karur, Sanavasapura, Hagalur.

River: Tungabhadra Nadi- Nearest Villages- Herakal, Kenchanagudda, Nittur, Udegolam, Nadivi, Manursugur, Manur, Dasanur, Bagawady, Halekota, Honnarahalli, Chikka Bellary, Hatcholli, Matur, Tasalla Kudlur. Hagari Nadi- Nearest Villages- Araliganur, Manjinahal, Poppanahal, Bagawady, Kesarakoni, Halekota, Seedaragadda, Kududarah al, Nagalapura, Gajiginahal, Kuruvalli, T.Rampura, Karchi ganur, Chanakanur, Tondehal, Raravi, Boggur, Saliganur, Kotehal, Kotehalsugur, Uppara Hosahalli, Hirehal, Muden ur, Kenchagarabelagal, Balakundi, Mylapura, Kuriganur, Mota Sugur, Uttanur, Ulur, Talur.

Canal: Nearest Villages- Devalapura, Halekota, Udegolam, Nadivi, Manursugur, Manur, Muddatanur, Malapura, Havina hal, Sirigeri, Siddaramapura, Dasapura, Konchigeri, Bagaw ady, Kesarakoni, Kududarahal, Nagalapura, Gajiginahal, Karchiganur, Ibrampura, Raravi, Saliganur, Kotehal, Kotehalsugur, Bandrahal, Chikka Bellary, Halumuravani, Kottalachinta, Bommalapura, Agasanur, Nadanga, Uppara, Hosahalli, Kenchagarabelagal, Balakundi, Kuriganur, Buduguppa, Gosabalu, Bhyrapura, Karur, Mota Sugur, Uttanur, Darur, Sanavasapura, Hagalur, Ulur, Talur, Hagalur Hosahalli.

Annual Rainfall: Normal Rianfall 642.2 mm.

Ground Water: Availability of the Ground Water in the Basin is (Information not avablable) H.A.M. and the utilization is (Information not avablable) H.A.M.
It belongs to (Information not avablable) category.
Depth to water level 5 to 20 meter below the ground.
Most of the wells go down in summer months, according to the Ground Water Estimation Committee.

Soils: Black and Red Sandy Soils.

Natural Division : It falls partly in Middle Tungabhadra Valley and Lower Vedavati (Hagari) Basin of the Central Karnataka Plateau.

Administration:

Division: Gulbarga. Parliamentary Constituency: 10 Haveri.District: Bellary. Taluka: Siruguppa. Assembly Constituency: 82 Hangal. Gram Panchayat: 26.

Regional Area Development Boards: The Hyderabad - Karnataka Area Development Board.

Border Villages: (State: Andhra Pradesh)- Raravi, Bandra hal, Matur, Tasalla, Kudlur, Vattumuruvani, Beerahalli, Kallukuttiganahal, Basarahalli, Bhyragamadinne, Ravihal, Nagarahal, Nadanga, Alabanur, B.M.Sugur, Ittigihal, Kenchagarabelagal, Mylapura, Kuriganur, Mota Sugur, Uttanur, Ulur, Talur.

Villages: 84 **Inhabited:** 83 **Uninhabited:** 1

Ranking	District	State	National
Area	5	86	464
Population	3	114	1313
Sex Ratio	1	31	1095
Child Sex Ratio	5	100	3164
Literacy Rate	7	170	5690
Density	1	8	5160
Work Participation Rate	3	99	345

Gram Panchayats:
Kenchanagudda, Desanur, Bagawady, Kududarahal, Hatcholli, Beerahalli, Ravihal, B.M.Sugur, Raravi, Kuruvalli, Boggur, Halekota, Uppara Hosahalli, Kotehalsugur, Kenchagarabelagal, Balakundi, Karur, Uttanur, Talur, Hagalur Hosahalli, Sanavasapura, Konchigeri, Sirigeri, Muddatanur, Manursugur, Nadivi.

Amenities:

Education: Primary School in 50 villages, Middle school in 49 villages, Matriculation or Secondary School in 7 villages, namely Sirigeri, Raravi, Hatcholli, Ravihal, B.M.Sugur, Karur, Talur.
Higher Secondary or Pre University Courses or Intermediate or Junior College in 1 village of the CD Block,, namely Sirigeri.
College in 0 village, Adult Literacy Center in 0 village.

Medical: Hospital in 6 villages, Dispensary in 21 villages, Health Center in 8 villages, Sub Center in 31 villages, Maternity and Child Welfare Center in 0 village, Community health workers in 3 villages.
The Villages having Hospital or Dispensary or Health Center are Manursugur, Manur, Muddatanur, Malapura, Sirigeri, Dasanur, Bagawady, Seedaragadda, Kududarahal, Nagalapura, Kuruvalli, Raravi, Kotehalsugur, Hatcholli, Ravihal, B.M.Sugur, Kenchagarabelagal, Karur, Uttanur, Darur, Talur, Hagalur Hosahalli.

Drinking Water: Tap water in 80 villages, Tank water in 3 villages, Well water in 18 villages, Tubewell in 7 villages and more than one source in 82 villages.

Bank: Banking facility in 16 villages, namely, Manursugur, Muddatanur, Sirigeri, Dasanur Kududarahal, Raravi, Hatcholli, Agasanur, B.M.Sugur Uppara Hosahalli, Kenchagarabelagal, Buduguppa Bhyrapura, Karur, Talur, Hagalur Hosahalli.
Credit Society in 27 villages Agricultural Credit Society in 26 Non-Agricultural Credit Society in 17 villages.

Others: Power supply in 83 villages, Cinema hall in 2 villages, sport club in 83 villages, Stadium or Auditorium or Communit Hall in 83 villages, Post Office in 45 villages.
There are 73 villages having bus facilities.

Villages with most of facilities: Manursugur Muddatanur, Sirigeri, Dasanur, Kududarahal, Raravi Hatcholli, Agasanur, B.M.Sugur, Uppara Hosahalli Kenchagarabelagal, Buduguppa, Karur, Talur Hagalur Hosahalli.

Villages without amenities (Education):
Devalapura, Manjinahal, Poppanahal, Udegolam, Manur, Gundiganur, Siddaramapura, Dasapura, Kesarakoni, Halekota, Seedaragadda, T.Rampura, Saliganur, Kotehal, Honnarahalli, Matur, Kallukuttiganahal, Basarahalli, Akkatangirahal, Halumuravani, Bhyragamadinne, Gubbihal, Mitte Sugur, Venkatapur, Alabanur, Ittigihal, Hirehal, Mudenur, Kuriganur, Gosabalu, Bhyrapura, Hagalur, Ulur..

Scheduled Castes: Out of the total population of 168842

persons, 33970 persons (20.12%) belong to Scheduled Castes. The villages having less than 10% SC population are Manjinahal, Gundiganur, Dasapura, Halekota T.Rampura, Saliganur, Kotehal, Halumuravani Bhyragamadinne, Gubbihal, Mitte Sugur, Gosabalu Darur.

The village having more than 50% SC population is None.

Sex ratio of Scheduled Caste population is 504.

Scheduled Castes Literates and Illiterates by Sex:

	Persons	Males	Females
Literate	6,883	5,044	1,839
Illiterate	27,087	11,817	15,270
Literacy rate	25.4	37.9	13.4
Graduate	79	74	5

Scheduled Castes (Dominant):

Madiga, Chalavadi etc., Bhovi, Adi Karnataka Banjara etc.

For their cultural identity please see Appendix-I

Villages without Scheduled Castes: There are 5 villages without any scheduled caste population.

Scheduled Tribes: Out of the total population of 168842 persons, 32435 persons (19.21%) belong to Scheduled Tribes. The villages having less than 10% ST population are Araliganur, Manjinahal, Manursugur, Muddatanur Malapura, Gundiganur, Dasanur, Kesarakoni Seedaragadda, Gajiginahal, Kuruvalli, Ibrampura Chanakanur, Tondehal, Kotehal, Kotehalsugur Honnarahalli, Hatcholli, B.M.Sugur, Uppara Hosahalli Mudenur, Mylapura, Gosabalu, Karur, Mota Sugur Hagalur, Ulur.

The villages having more than 50% ST population are Halekota, Halekota, Saliganur, Akkatangirahal Mitte Sugur.

Sex ratio of Scheduled tribe population is 502.

Scheduled Tribes Literates and Illiterates by Sex:

	Persons	Males	Females
Literate	6,847	5,020	1,827
Illiterate	25,588	11,135	14,453
Literacy rate	26.3	38.9	13.9
Graduate	63	57	6

Scheduled Tribes (Dominant):

Naikda etc., Generic Tribes etc., Dubla etc. Konda Kapus, Bhil etc.

For their cultural identity please see Appendix-II

Villages without Scheduled Tribes: There are 6 villages without any scheduled tribe population.

Literates and Illiterates by Sex (Total Population):

	Persons	Males	Females
Literate	55,987	37,487	18,500
Illiterate	112,855	46,835	66,020
Literacy rate	40	54	26
Graduate	1,071	937	134

Agriculture: ***Distribution of villages according to land use:*** Out of 84 villages, Total area (in hectare) is 96995, out of that 86.94 percent is cultivable and 37.75 percent of the cultivable area is irrigated.

Sources of Irrigation (Hectares): Government Canal 22239.6, Private Canal 155.63, Well without Electricity 1.21, Well with Electricity 614.15, Tubewell without Electricity 0, Tubewell with Electricity 5443.35, Tank 0, River 3376.69, Lake 0, Waterfall 0, Others 0.

Villages with population of 5000 to 9999:

Halekota, Dasanur, Raravi, Karur.

Villages with population of 10000 and above:

Sirigeri.

Distribution of Workers:

	Persons	Males	Females	WPR
Cultivators	28,086	19,372	8,714	30.24
Agricultural Labour	55,956	23,579	32,377	60.26
Household Industry	1,453	804	649	1.56
Other Workers	7,369	5,484	1,885	7.94
Main Workers	85,677	47,262	38,415	92.26
Marginal Workers	7,187	1,977	5,210	7.74
Total Workers	92,864	49,239	43,625	

Religion: Major Religious Communities:

	Persons	Males	Females	Sex Ratio
Hindu (92.44%)	156,083	77,896	78,187	1,004
Muslim (7.2%)	12,160	6,111	6,049	990
Christian (0.16%)	272	142	130	915
Sikh (0.01%)	19	12	7	583
Buddhists (0%)	-	-	-	-
Jain (0.02%)	28	14	14	1,000

Agewise Data:

	Persons	Males	Females	Sex Ratio
All ages	168,842	84,322	84,520	1002
0-14	68,159	34,664	33,495	966
15-44	72,762	36,574	36,188	989
45-79	26,934	12,687	14,247	1123
80+	861	323	538	1666
Age not stated	126	74	52	703

Languages (Dominant):

Kannada, Urdu, Telugu, Hindi, Coorgi/Kodagu

Disabled Population:

	Persons	Males	Females	%
Total Disabled	3,056	1,698	1,358	
In Seeing	1,493	805	688	48.85
In Speech	246	138	108	8.05
In Hearing	117	55	62	3.83
In Movement	934	564	370	30.56

Mentally	266	136	130	8.7

SOMVARPET

Somvarpet C.D. Block lies in the north-eastern part of Kodagu district. It is a part of Somvarpet taluka. The Block is located at a distance of 40 kms. from district headquarters (Madikeri). There are 135 villages in the block with the total population of 185,501 persons. Area of the C.D. Block is 990.83 sq. kms. It is bounded by district Hassan on north, taluk Virajpet on south, districts Hassan, Mysore and taluk Virajpet on east, district Dakshina Kannada on west.

Communications:

Roadways : SH- 8: Direction- Mudravalli to Arkalgud, Nearest Villages- Mudravalli, Hulse, Bellarahalli, Nakalagodu, Hebbulse, Kitturu. SH- 27: Direction- Kufuba thur to Madikeri, Nearest Villages- Kasuru, Doddakodli, Kirikodli, Bydagotta, Sivaralli, Avaradalu, Mudravalli, Hulse, Nakalagodu, Gopalapura, Chowdena Halli, Hithluke ri, Nandigunda, Heggula, Gowdalli, Sunti, Honnahanakodu, Channapura, Choudlu, Balagunda, Kusubur, Aigur, Kumbur, Muvathoklu, Kandanakolli, Anjanageri Bettageri, Garagan dur. SH- 88: Direction- Madikeri to Piriyapatna, Nearest Villages- Kedakal Negadal, Ulugulli, Andagove, Kanbylu Baichanalli, Horur, 7 Th Hosakote, Anekad Forest, Mullus oge, Baichanalli, Basavana, Halli, Attur Forest. SH- 88 B: Direction- Madikeri to Virajpet, Nearest Villages- Irale Valamudi, Cherala Srimangala, Kudlurchettalli, Abyathamangala, Nelliyahadikeri.

River: Cauvery Nadi- Nearest Villages- Manajur, Siranga lal, Thorenur, Hebbale, Hulse, Kudige, Kudumangalore, Mullusoge, Baichanalli, Basavana Halli, Rasulpura, Attur Forest, Nanjarayapatna, Abyathamangala, Nelliyahad ikeri, Valnur Hyagathur, Rangasamudra. Hemavati Nadi- Nearest Villages- Kasuru, Kelakodli, Janardanahalli, Urugutti, Doddabilaha, Madre, Bembalur, Kattepura, Kattepura Forest, Agalli, Doddakolathur. Harangi Hole Nadi- Nearest Villages- Aigur, Gadinad Forest, Muvathok lu, Anjanageri Bettageri, Garagandur, Blockcut From.Jaink albetta, Yedavanadu Forest I Bit.

Reserved Forest: Nearest Village- Aigur. (Attur R.F.): Nearest Villages- Nakur Sirangala, Andagove, Attur Nallur, Cherala Srimangala, 7Th Hosakote , Kudumangalore, Bendebetta Forest, Anekad Forest, Mullusoge, Basavana Halli, Attur Forest, Nanjarayapatna, Kudlurchettalli, Valnur Hyagathur. (Malambi R.F.): Nearest Villages- Nandigunda, Heggula, Doddamolathe, Malambi Forest No. 2, Malambi Forest, Doddakanagalu, Alur , Malambi, Mullur, Harohalli, Gonimarur, Ganagur, Nidtha Forest I Bit, Nidtha Forest Ii Bit, Mavina Halla Forest. (Yedavanadu R.F.): Nearest Villages- Kusubur, Gadinad Forest, Belur Basavanalli, Negalale Karkalli, Nerugalale, Nidtha Forest Ii Bit, Yelakanur, Herur, Jainkalbetta Forest, Blockcut From.Jainkalbetta, Yedavanadu Forest I Bit, Kudige, Bendebetta Forest.

Annual Rainfall: Normal Rianfall 2099.9 mm.

Ground Water: Availability of the Ground Water in the Basin is 63.09 MCM and the utilization is 2335.67 MCM. It belongs to Safe category. Depth to water level 2 to 20 meter below the ground. Most of the wells go down in summer months, according to the Ground Water Estimati on Committee.

Soils: Reddish brown forest soil, Yellowish grey to greyish sandy loam soils and mixed soils

Natural Division : It falls partly in Patti-Brahmagiri Ghats and Somvarpet-Virajpet Rolling Humid Region of the Southern Karnataka Plateau.

Administration:

Division: Mysore. Parliamentary Constituency: 21 Mysore Paschim. District: Kodagu. Taluka: Somvarpet. Assembly Constituency: 208 Madikeri. Gram Panchayat: 40.

Regional Area Development Boards: The Maland Aera Development Board.

Fairs : Abbi Mata Fair: It is located in a pleasant valley surrounded by green hill which is six kilometers away from Somvarpet. Here lies a branch of the Muruga Rajendra Matha of Chitradurga. The structure of the Matha is built partly in stone and partly in brick and mortar with elaborately carved wooden doors and windows, but now it is in a dilapidated condition.

Basavanna Temple Fair: It is held at Nidtha in Kodagu area in the month of March-April every year. Nidtha was but originally known as 'Nidtha' evidenced by the Mulur inscription and is situated at a distance of 35 kms. from Somvarpet. The Mallikarjuna temple of this place referred to in the inscription is now extinct. Only the Basavanna temple which has been recently renovated is given historical antiquity.

Betegara Muttappa Jatra: It is held at Somvarpet in Kodagu area. The name obviously was derived from the regular fair conducted every Monday (Somavara). Hence, it came to be known as Somvarpet.

Ishwara Temple Festival: The Ishwara temple pujas are organised every year on the occasion of "Thula Sankrammana" at Kumarvalli near Coorg. The Pushpagiri or Subramanyahill, the celebrated mountain (5,626 feet), is in the north-west of Coorg, about 38 kms from Somvarpet and 1.65 kms from Kumaralli, which is amidst dense jungles.

Malang Shah Vali's Urs: An Urs in honour of Malang Shah Vali is held at his dargah at Somvarpet. Somavarpet, a prominent town in North Kodagu is about 40 kms. from Madikeri. The dargah of Malang Shah Vali is claimed to be a 300 years old structure. The urs at this dargah is celebrated in the shaban month which is accompanied by a Kawwali programme.

Nanjundeshwara Fair: It is held at Nanjarayapattana near Kodagu around the month of March-April every year. Nanjundeshwara or Nanjarayappattana is 17 kms. away from Kushalnagar. A historic place on the left bank of the river Cauvery, it was known as 'Holesalalli'. During the 16th century, Nanjundaraja of the Changalva dynasty built a palace and called this town after his name as 'Nanjarapattana'.

Suggidevara Festival: It is held at Yaduru near Kodagu around the months of January-February for twelve days every year. Yaduru is just five kms. away from Somvarpet. On the left side of the road from the Yaduru tank are some 1.5 Kolegallus (sacrificial stones). After a wedding, persons related to such families keep the (ede) sacrif icial offering (ede) at these stones.

Villages: 135 **Inhabited:** 130 **Uninhabited:** 5

Ranking	District	State	National
Area	3	82	442
Population	1	102	935
Sex Ratio	1	17	837
Child Sex Ratio	3	54	2362
Literacy Rate	2	15	524
Density	3	115	4923
Work Participation Rate	1	91	2676

Gram Panchayats:

Kodlipet, Besoru, Bydagotta, Dundalli, Handli, Sanivarasanthe, Nidtha, Gowdalli, Tholur Shettalli, Bettadalli, Santhalli, Hanagallu, Choudlu, Doddamolathe, Alur , Ganagur, Sirangala, Thorenur, Hebbale, Nerugalale, Belur (Balagunda), Kiragandur, Garvale, Madapur, Haradur, Nakur Sirangala , Aigur, Kudige, Kudumangalore, Mullusoge, Kushalnagar, Godde Hosur, 7 Th Hosakote , Kodagarahalli, Suntikoppa, Kedakal, Kambibani, Chettalli, Valnur Hyagathur, Nelliyahadikeri, Nanjarayapatna.

Amenities:

Education: Primary School in 110 villages, Middle school in 82 villages, Matriculation or Secondary School in 37 villages, namely Doddakodli, Niluvagilu, Bellarahalli, Bidarur, Gowdalli, Alur, Ankanalli, Bettadalli, Shanthalli, Tholur Shettalli, Hanagallu, Yedur, Kalakandur, Choudlu, Balagunda, Aigur*, Belur Basavanalli, Gonimarur, Surlabi, Garvale, Kumbur, Muvathoklu, Ulugulli, Garagandur, Andagove, Kanbylu Baichanalli, Cherala Srimangala, Sirangala, Thorenur, Hebbale, Kudige, Kudumangalore, Mullusoge, Basavana Halli, Nanjarayapatna, Abyathamangala, Nelliyahadikeri.
Higher Secondary or Pre University Courses or Intermediate or Junior College in 9 villages of the CD Block,, namely Doddakodli, Bidarur, Alur, Choudlu, Aigur*, Kumbur, Sirangala, Hebbale, Mullusoge.
College in 4 villages, Adult Literacy Center in 4 villages., Colleges are in villages, namely Doddakodli, Bidarur, Yedur, Mullusoge.

Medical: Hospital in 3 villages, Dispensary in 11 villages, Health Center in 16 villages, Sub Center in 33 villages, Maternity and Child Welfare Center in 3 villages, Community health workers in 0 village.
The Villages having Hospital or Dispensary or Health Center are Bidarur, Alur , Aigur*, Surlabi, Kumbur, Ulugulli, Cherala Srimangala, Sirangala, Kudige, Mullusoge, Nanjarayapatna.

Drinking Water: Tap water in 91 villages, Tank water in 36 villages, Well water in 114 villages, Tubewell in 43 villages and more than one source in 119 villages.

Bank: Banking facility in 32 villages, namely, Janardanahalli, Urugutti, Ist Kudlur, Doddabandara Koragallu, Avaradalu, Mudravalli, Bellarahalli Doddakolathur, Chowdena Halli, Shanthalli Doddatholur, Kalakandur, Aigur*, Masagodu, Yelakanur Surlabi, Sirangalli, Kandanakolli, Kedakal Negadal Ulugulli, Anjanageri Bettageri, Garagandur 7 Th Hosakote, Manajur, Thorenur, Hulse, Marur Kudige, Anekad Forest, Basavana Halli Nelliyahadikeri.
Credit Society in 19 villages Agricultural Credit Society in 18 Non-Agricultural Credit Society in 0 village.

Others: Power supply in 129 villages, Cinema hall in 7 villages sport club in 9 villages, Stadium or Auditorium or Community Hall in 1 village, Post Office in 84 villages.
There are 98 villages having bus facilities.

Villages with most of facilities: Shanthalli Aigur*, Surlabi, Ulugulli, Garagandur, 7 Th Hosakote Thorenur, Hulse, Kudige, Basavana Halli.

Villages without amenities (Education). Kasuru, Sivaralli, Honnekodi, Kattepura Forest, Koragallu, Avaradalu, Nakalagodu, Hebbulse, Cheekanalli, Sidigalale, Heggula, Malambi Forest, Mensa, Mylathpura, Nidtha Forest I Bit, Nakur Sirangala, Mavina Halla Forest, Jainkalbetta Forest, Bendebetta Forest, Anekad Forest..

Scheduled Castes: Out of the total population of 185515 persons, 29167 persons (15.72%) belong to Scheduled Castes. The villages having less than 10% SC population are Ist Kudlur, Kattepura Forest, Managali, Dundalli

Malambi Forest, Kundalli, Kumaralli, Kothanalli
Haraga, Koothi, Thalthare Shetalli, Thakeri
Gadinad Forest, Negalale Karkalli, Nerugalale
Nidtha Forest I Bit, Yedavanadu Forest Ii, Surlabi
Garvale, Herur, Andagove, 7 Th Hosakote
Mavina Halla Forest, Jainkalbetta Forest
Yedavanadu Forest I Bit, Bendebetta Forest
Anekad Forest, Mullusoge, Basavana Halli, Rasulpura
Attur Forest, Nanjarayapatna, Nelliyahadikeri
Valnur Hyagathur, Rangasamudra.

The village having more than 50% SC population is None.

Sex ratio of Scheduled Caste population is 504.

Scheduled Castes Literates and Illiterates by Sex:

	Persons	Males	Females
Literate	16,048	9,188	6,860
Illiterate	13,119	5,268	7,851
Literacy rate	63.4	73.3	53.7
Graduate	273	217	56

Scheduled Castes (Dominant):
Adi Karnataka, Pale, Bhovi, Moger, Adi Dravida

For their cultural identity please see Appendix-I

Villages without Scheduled Castes: There are 14 villages without any scheduled caste population.

Scheduled Tribes: Out of the total population of 185515 persons, 8878 persons (4.79%) belong to Scheduled Tribes.

The villages having less than 10% ST population are
Kasuru, Kelakodli, Doddakodli, Janardanahalli
Neergunda, Kirikodli, Bydagotta, Urugutti
Doddabilaha, Madre, Bembalur, Sivaralli, Kerekeri
Honnekodi, Kattepura Forest, Agalli, Niluvagilu
Doddabandara, Koragallu, Avaradalu, Mudravalli
Hulse, Bellarahalli, Nakalagodu, Hebbulse, Managali
Kitturu, Dundalli, Cheekanalli, Kajur, Bidarur
Doddakolathur, Gopalapura, Chowdena Halli
Sidigalale, Hithlukeri, Nandigunda, Heggula
Gowdalli, Sunti, Honnahanakodu, Doddamolathe
Channapura, Malambi Forest, Doddakanagalu, Alur
Mullur, Nidtha, Mensa, Ankanalli, Mylathpura
Harohalli, Kundalli, Kumaralli, Kothanalli
Bettadalli, Haraga, Shanthalli, Koothi
Tholur Shettalli, Chikka Tholur, Doddatholur
Abbimatta, Thalthare Shetalli, Thakeri, Biligeri
Kiragandur, Hanagallu, Yedur, Kalakandur, Choudlu
Balagunda, Kusubur, Aigur*, Belur Basavanalli
Masagodu, Nerugalale, Gonimarur, Ganagur, Yelakanur
Surlabi, Garvale, Sirangalli, Kumbur, Muvathoklu
Kandanakolli, Kedakal Negadal, Ulugulli
Anjanageri Bettageri, Garagandur, Nakur Sirangala
Andagove, Cherala Srimangala, 7 Th Hosakote , Manajur
Sirangala, Thorenur, Hebbale, Hulse, Marur
Mullusoge, Baichanalli, Rasulpura, Attur Forest
Abyathamangala, Nelliyahadikeri.

The villages having more than 50% ST population are
Gadinad Forest, Nidtha Forest I Bit
Mavina Halla Forest, Jainkalbetta Forest
Yedavanadu Forest I Bit, Bendebetta Forest
Anekad Forest.

Sex ratio of Scheduled tribe population is 498.

Scheduled Tribes Literates and Illiterates by Sex:

	Persons	Males	Females
Literate	4,109	2,352	1,757
Illiterate	4,769	2,101	2,668
Literacy rate	54.1	61.7	46.4
Graduate	47	38	9

Scheduled Tribes (Dominant):
Naikda etc., Jenu Kuruba, Yerava, Kuruba, Soligaru

For their cultural identity please see Appendix-II

Villages without Scheduled Tribes: There are 49 villages without any scheduled tribe population.

Literates and Illiterates by Sex (Total Population):

	Persons	Males	Females
Literate	124,818	67,757	57,061
Illiterate	60,697	24,426	36,271
Literacy rate	77	84	70
Graduate	5,445	3,583	1,862

Agriculture: ***Distribution of villages according to land use:*** Out of 135 villages, Total area (in hectare) is 99083, out of that 46.85 percent is cultivable and 3.21 percent of the cultivable area is irrigated.

Sources of Irrigation (Hectares): Government Canal 1186.72, Private Canal 0, Well without Electricity 0, Well with Electricity 59.36, Tubewell without Electricity 0, Tubewell with Electricity 26.18, Tank 0, River 16.19, Lake 0, Waterfall 189, Others 12.13.

Villages with population of 5000 to 9999:
Bidarur, Choudlu, Ulugulli, Kudige, Kudumangalore Mullusoge, Nelliyahadikeri.

Villages with population of 10000 and above: None

Distribution of Workers:

	Persons	Males	Females	WPR
Cultivators	11,386	8,282	3,104	12.62
Agricultural Labour	5,286	2,619	2,667	5.86
Household Industry	813	510	303	0.9
Other Workers	72,748	43,770	28,978	80.62
Main Workers	84,754	52,768	31,986	93.93
Marginal Workers	5,479	2,413	3,066	6.07
Total Workers	90,233	55,181	35,052	

Religion: Major Religious Communities:

	Persons	Males	Females	Sex Ratio

Hindu (85.18%)	158,022	78,518	79,504	1,013
Muslim (11.19%)	20,763	10,290	10,473	1,018
Christian (3.23%)	5,986	3,006	2,980	991
Sikh (0%)	2	1	1	1,000
Buddhists (0.32%)	597	297	300	1,010
Jain (0.02%)	40	19	21	1,105

Agewise Data:

	Persons	Males	Females	Sex Ratio
All ages	185,515	92,183	93,332	1012
0-14	53,400	27,027	26,373	976
15-44	94,166	46,171	47,995	1040
45-79	36,434	18,356	18,078	985
80+	1,391	564	827	1466
Age not stated	124	65	59	908

Languages (Dominant):
Kannada, Malayalam, Tulu, Tamil, Coorgi/Kodagu

Disabled Population:

	Persons	Males	Females	%
Total Disabled	2,979	1,567	1,412	
In Seeing	1,343	637	706	45.08
In Speech	276	170	106	9.26
In Hearing	272	124	148	9.13
In Movement	804	501	303	26.99
Mentally	284	135	149	9.53

SORAB

Sorab C.D. Block lies in the northern part of Shimoga district. It is a part of Sorab taluka. The Block is located at a distance of 88 kms. from district headquart ers (Shimoga). There are 306 villages in the block with the total population of 176,604 persons. Area of the C.D. Block is 1148.00 sq. kms. It is bounded by district Haveri on north, taluk Sagar on south, taluk Shikarpur and district Haveri on east, and district Uttara Kannada on west.

Communications:

Roadways : S.H-1: Direction- Siralkoppa to Hangal, Villages- Bommarsikoppa, Agasanahalli, Neralige, Mallap ura, Kubaturu, Anavatti, Devasthanadahakkalu (Kotipura), Thalluru, Hunsavalli, Chikkadagodu, Nellikoppa, Thathuru, Negavadi, Kanakoppa. S.H-48: Direction- Siddapur to Siralkoppa, Nearest Villages- Andavalli, Kadasuru, Thand ige, Yelasi, Halesoraba, Karadigere, Gunda Setti Koppa, Tirumalapura, Chikkashakuna, Kanukoppa, Kodakani, Andige, Channapura, Mavali, Bedavatti, Gerukoppa, Biluvani, Suthukote, Chatradahalli, Kolgunisi.

River: Varada Nadi-Villages- Shakunavalli, Sabara, Thuilikoppa, Mallasamudra, Telagadde, Kachavi, Bankasana, Kaliggeri, Jademadapura, Chagaturu, Varadikoppa, Hosakoppa, Tumarikoppa, Muguru, Dwarahalli, Bommarsi koppa, Agasanahalli, Thoravanda, Mudidoddikoppa (Mudi), Lakkavalli, Bennuru, Kathuvalli, Haralikoppa, Kerehalli, Hirekalagodu, Eduru, Kamaruru, Bennuru, Nyarshi, Pura, Hiremakoppa, Chikkamakoppa, Chandraguthi, Holemaruru, Andavalli, Heche, Kadasuru, Abasi, Hosuru, Gudavi, Gunjanur, Ankaravalli. Dandavati Nadi- Nearest Villages- Kubaturu, Lakkavalli, Bennuru, Kotekoppa, Haralikoppa, Samanavalli, Hosahalli, Siddihalli, Hasavi, Kathuru, Gendla, Malagikurli, Bilagi, Kummuru, Malekoppa, Korako du, Kuppagadde, Haya, Bettadakurli State Forest, Mathigha tta, Oturu, Halesoraba, Nadahalli, Maruru, Tirumalapura, Hire Shakuna, Chikkashakuna, Udri, Chilanuru, Kanagodu, Siravanthi, Avalagodu, Kuppe, Kappagalale, Malalagadde. Mavin Hole Nadi- Nearest Villages- Abasi, Haralige, Mutaguppe, Nadavadadodderi, Magadi, Ramagondanakoppa, Veeranapura, Nandigudde, Kyasanuru,, Halasinakoppa, Devagundikoppa, Holekoppa, Amachi.

Annual Rainfall: Normal Rianfall 1410 mm.

Ground Water: Availability of the Ground Water in the Basin is 103.37 MCM and the utilization is 65.00 MCM. It belongs to Safe category. Depth to water level 5 to 20 meter below the ground. Most of the wells go down in summer months, according to the Ground Water Estimati on Committee.

Soils: Reddish to Brownish Clayey Loam.

Natural Division : It falls in Sagar-Sorab-Shikarpur Rolling Humid Region of the Central Karnataka Plateau.

Administration:

Division: Bangalore. Parliamentary Constituency: 14 Shimoga. District: Shimoga. Taluka: Sorab. Assembly Constituency: 116 Sorab. Gram Panchayat: 39.

Regional Area Development Boards: The Maland Aera Development Board.

Fairs: Hole-Lingeshwara Jatra: Lord Hole-Lingeshwara Jatra is held at Bankasana in about the month of January every year. Bankasana is about 31 kms. to the north of Sorab town. It has what is called an udbhava-linga named Holelingeshvara at the confluence of the Varada river and the Dandavati stream. A well-known jatra is held about the month of January. A cattle fair also takes place on the occasion.

Renukamba Car Festival: It is held at Chandragutti near Shimoga for a period of fifteen days in about the month of March every year. Chandragutti, about 16 kms. north-west of Sorab town, is the headquarters of the hobli of the same name. It was formerly well-fortified in the old days, it was called Chandraguptapura, Chandra guttipura, Chandraguttipete and Guttidurga. The village is situated at the base of a high-peaked hill of the same name and is surrounded by a thickly-forested area. The summit is 848 metres high above the sea-level. Granite stone (locally called Chandragutti-Kallu) is found in abundance here.

Villages: 306 **Inhabited:** 279 **Uninhabited:** 27

Ranking	District	State	National
Area	4	65	309
Population	2	110	1091
Sex Ratio	7	103	2549
Child Sex Ratio	6	110	3412
Literacy Rate	4	30	1198
Density	3	85	5481
Work Participation Rate	4	122	1990

Gram Panchayats:

Jade, Thelagunda, Telagadde, Shakunavalli, Agasanahalli, Mudidoddikoppa (Mudi), Hurali, Anavatti, Kubaturu, Kathuvalli, Samanavalli, Thalluru, Yennekoppa, Bharangi, Hanchi, Thathuru, Gendla, Dyavanahalli, Harishi, Bennuru, Kuppagadde, Udri, Thavanandi, Gudavi, Nyarshi, Chandraguthi, Heche, Halesoraba , Kodakani , Mavali, Biluvani, Chittur, Shigga, Heggodu, Mutaguppe, Hosabale, Nisarani, Ulavi, Induvalli.

Amenities:

Education: Primary School in 200 villages, Middle school in 104 villages, Matriculation or Secondary School in 23 villages, namely Jade, Lakkavalli, Anavatti, Thalluru, Yennekoppa, Thathuru, Bharangi, Ginivala, Kerehalli, Thavanandi, Kuppagadde, Harishi, Hosabale, Chandraguthi, Kadasuru, Gudavi, Halesoraba, Chikkashakuna, Mavali, Biluvani, Hosabale, Malalagadde, Ulavi.

Higher Secondary or Pre University Courses or Intermediate or Junior College in 2 villages of the CD Block,, namely Jade, Anavatti.

College in 1 village, Adult Literacy Center in 1 village., College is in village, namely Anavatti.

Medical: Hospital in 0 village, Dispensary in 21 villages, Health Center in 10 villages, Sub Center in 36 villages, Maternity and Child Welfare Center in 1 village, Community health workers in 1 village.

The Villages having Hospital or Dispensary or Health Center are Alahalli, Jade, Kaliggeri, Mudidoddikoppa (Mudi), Mallapura, Kathuvalli, Anavatti, Yennekoppa, Thathuru, Bharangi, Kuppagadde, Harishi, Chandraguthi, Gudavi, Oturu, Udri, Nisarani, Hosabale, Heggodu, Ulavi, Shigga.

Drinking Water: Tap water in 24 villages, Tank water in 49 villages, Well water in 206 villages, Tubewell in 124 villages and more than one source in 247 villages.

Bank: Banking facility in 11 villages, namely, Jade, Thelagunda, Shakunavalli, Anavatti, Thathuru Kuppagadde, Harishi, Chandraguthi, Udri, Hosabale Ulavi.

Credit Society in 23 villages Agricultural Credit Society in 22 Non-Agricultural Credit Society in 3 villages.

Others: Power supply in 276 villages, Cinema hall in 4 villages sport club in 279 villages, Stadium or Auditorium or Communi Hall in 279 villages, Post Office in 40 villages.

There are 178 villages having bus facilities.

Villages with most of facilities: Jade Shakunavalli, Anavatti, Thathuru, Kuppagadde Harishi, Chandraguthi, Udri, Hosabale, Ulavi.

Villages without amenities (Education): Kalkoppa, Mangapura, Makoppa, Shanthapura, Arethelagadde, Devarahosakoppa, Kaliggeri, Jigarikoppa, Bommarsikoppa, Ujjanipura, Bennuru, Kodikoppa, Chikkachowti, Gummanalu, Haralikoppa, Hunsekoppa, Thekkuru, Siddihalli State Forest, Bilavagodu, Thotlagondanakoppa, Malagikurli, Bettadakurli State Forest, Badanakatte, Chikkalagodu, Kenchikoppa, Shindli, Horabylu, Sambapura, Mannathi, Kundagodu, Kamalapura, Thoragondanakoppa, Kakkarasi, Goggehalli, Hosuru, Kallambi, Kanthanahalli, Kuduregani, Maruru, Hire Shakuna, Uppalli, Kanukoppa, Kunaji, Channapura, Boppagondanakoppa, Kasaraguppe, Shanthakoppa, Kelaginakiragunasi, Halaghatta, Chilanuru, Melinakiragunasi, Hirale, Kodanakatte, Nadavadadodderi, Veeranapura, Nandigudde, Siravanthi, Avalagodu, Kappagalale, Halagalale, Chimanuru, Kondagalale, Kolisalu, Charanthihosakoppa, Dalavaihosakoppa, Brahmanavadadodderi, Sannamane, Horabailukoppa, Holekoppa, Amachi, Karjikoppa, Brahmanavadasagadde, Ammagondanakoppa, Kumbathi, Brahmanavadaholekatte, Nadavadaholekatte, Brahamanavadainduvalli, Hesarikoppa, Karekoppa..

Scheduled Castes: Out of the total population of 178145 persons, 34303 persons (19.26%) belong to Scheduled Castes. The villages having less than 10% SC population are Bankavalli, Alahalli, Kalkoppa, Mangapura, Makoppa Shankrikoppa, Telagadde, Kaliggeri, Halekoppa Bommarsikoppa, Thoravanda, Ujjanipura, Lakkavalli Kotekoppa, Hunsavalli, Nellikoppa, Bharangi Jogihalli, Gummanalu, Kerehalli, Jaddihalli Hunsekoppa, Sampagodu, Thekkuru, Kulaga Puttanahalli, Siddihalli State Forest, Bommanahalli Kerekoppa, Sarekoppa, Bilavagodu, Thavanandi Malagikurli, Bilagi, Kummuru, Malekoppa, Korakodu Kuppagadde, Bettadakurli State Forest, Badanakatte Telagundli, Chikkalagodu, Kenchikoppa, Eduru Kamaruru, Mangarshikoppa, Kuntagalale, Nalluru Narchi, Mangalore, Sambapura, Mannathi, Kundagodu Mavinaballikoppa, Kodambi, Nyarshi, Pura

Chikkamakoppa, Kathavai, Basthikoppa, Andavalli Heche, Kakkarasi, Abasi, Haralige, Goggehalli Hosuru, Kallambi, Chowdikoppa, Thyavagodu Kuduregani, Thandige, Yelasi, Thavarehalli Chitrahattihalli, Oturu, Gunda Setti Koppa, Maruru Hire Shakuna, Uppalli, Kanukoppa, Kunaji Shanthagere, Andige, Uraganahalli, Chikkavali Devathikoppa, Channapura, Thavarekoppa, Haruru Kaspadikoppa, Gerukoppa, Boppagondanakoppa Chatradahalli, Arekoppa, Manamane, Jiralekoppa Shanthakoppa, Kelaginakiragunasi, Halaghatta Chilanuru, Kanagodu, Nisarani, Melinakiragunasi Kodanakatte, Nadavadadodderi, Ramagondanakoppa Veeranapura, Nandigudde, Kyasanuru, Siravanthi Kuppe, Kappagalale, Halagalale, Chimanuru Kondagalale, Kolisalu, Malalagadde, Kerekoppa Brahmanavadadodderi, Sannamane, Horabailukoppa Halasinakoppa, Holekoppa, Bhadrapura, Duguru, Barige Karjikoppa, N.Sagadde, Brahmanavadasagadde Ammagondanakoppa, Kulavalli, Brahmanavadaholekatte Kannuru, Kanahalli, Kaisodi, Maisavi Nadavadaholekatte, Shigga, Hirekasavi, Induvalli Hesarikoppa, Hesari, Shadalakoppa.

The villages having more than 50% SC population are Kodikoppa, Devarahosakoppa, Sabara, Hosakoppa Hosahalli, Devasthanadahakkalu (Kotipura), Thalluru Yennekoppa, Belavantanakoppa, Thathuru, Hiremagadi Ginivala, Haralikoppa, Guddekoppa, Kanak0Ppa Guduginakoppa, Holemaruru, Bedavatti, Biluvani Suthukote, Thalakalakoppa.

Sex ratio of Scheduled Caste population is 486.

Scheduled Castes Literates and Illiterates by Sex:

	Persons	Males	Females
Literate	15,824	9,873	5,951
Illiterate	18,479	7,744	10,735
Literacy rate	54.1	65.8	41.8
Graduate	375	342	33

Scheduled Castes (Dominant):

Bhovi, Adi Karnataka, Chalavadi etc., Banjara etc. Korama

For their cultural identity please see Appendix-I

Villages without Scheduled Castes: There are 92 villages without any scheduled caste population.

Scheduled Tribes: Out of the total population of 178145 persons, 6618 persons (3.71%) belong to Scheduled Tribes.

The villages having less than 10% ST population are Alahalli, Kamaruru, Kalkoppa, Jade, Mangapura Makoppa, Thelagunda, Shanthapura, Kodikoppa Arethelagadde, Devarahosakoppa, Shakunavalli Shankrikoppa, Sabara, Thuilikoppa, Telagadde Kachavi, Shanuvalli, Bankasana, Salige, Kaliggeri Jigarikoppa, Halekoppa, Chagaturu, Hanaji, Hosakoppa Tumarikoppa, Muguru, Dwarahalli, Bommarsikoppa Thoravanda, Ujjanipura, Mallapura, Kubaturu Vittalapura, Lakkavalli, Bennuru, Kathuvalli Kotekoppa, Samanavalli, Hosahalli, Kodikoppa Anavatti, Devasthanadahakkalu (Kotipura), Hurali Thalluru, Hunsavalli, Yennekoppa, Kamanavalli Hirechowti, Chikkadagodu, Nellikoppa, Thathuru Gangavalli, Hiremagadi, Ginivala, Haralikoppa Kerehalli, Basuru, Jaddihalli, Hunsekoppa, Sampagodu Thekkuru, Kulaga, Dyavanahalli, Puttanahalli Thalaguppa, Siddihalli State Forest, Siddihalli Hasavi, Gendla, Nittakki, Bommanahalli, Kerekoppa Sarekoppa, Bilavagodu, Thavanandi Thotlagondanakoppa, Malagikurli, Bilagi, Kummuru Malekoppa, Korakodu, Kuppagadde Bettadakurli State Forest, Badanakatte, Bettadakurli Guddekoppa, Negavadi, Chikkabburu, Kanak0Ppa Guduginakoppa, Telagundli, Chikkalagodu Hirekalagodu, Kenchikoppa, Eduru, Kamaruru Mangarshikoppa, Harishi, Shindli, Kuntagalale Nalluru, Narchi, Horabylu, Mangalore, Bennuru Sambapura, Hosabale, Mannathi, Kundagodu Baragavalli, Mavinaballikoppa, Kodambi, Kamalapura Nyarshi, Pura, Chandraguthi, Kathavai, Basthikoppa Thoragondanakoppa, Holemaruru, Andavalli, Heche Kadasuru, Kakkarasi, Abasi, Haralige, Mutaguppe Goggehalli, Gudavi, Kallambi, Gunjanur, Ankaravalli Chowdikoppa, Kanthanahalli, Saremaruru, Thyavagodu Kuduregani, Jambehalli, Thandige, Yelasi Thavarehalli, Chitrahattihalli, Oturu, Halesoraba Karadigere, Gunda Setti Koppa, Nadahalli, Maruru Hire Shakuna, Chikkashakuna, Uppalli, Kanukoppa Kodakani, Kunaji, Andige, Uraganahalli, Hiriyavali Chikkavali, Udri, Devathikoppa, Channapura, Mavali Thavarekoppa, Haruru, Kaspadikoppa, Yalavalli Bedavatti, Gerukoppa, Boppagondanakoppa, Biluvani Suthukote, Chatradahalli, Kolgunisi, Arekoppa Manamane, Jiralekoppa, Kasaraguppe, Shanthakoppa Kelaginakiragunasi, Halaghatta, Chilanuru, Kanagodu Nisarani, Melinakiragunasi, Hirale, Hosabale Kodanakatte, Nadavadadodderi, Magadi, Mudagodu Ramagondanakoppa, Veeranapura, Nandigudde, Kyasanuru Thalakalakoppa, Banadakoppa, Siravanthi, Kuppe Byrekoppa, Kappagalale, Halagalale, Heggodu Chimanuru, Kondagalale, Pura, Kolisalu, Malalagadde Kerekoppa, Charanthihosakoppa, Dalavaihosakoppa Brahmanavadadodderi, Sannamane, Horabailukoppa Halasinakoppa, Holekoppa, Amachi, Bhadrapura, Duguru

Barige, Horabailu, Hodabatte, Ulavi, Karjikoppa N.Sagadde, Brahmanavadasagadde, Ammagondanakoppa Kumbathi, Talebylu, Brahmanavadaholekatte, Kannuru Kanahalli, Kaisodi, Maisavi, Hunavalli Nadavadaholekatte, Shigga, Kundagasavi, Induvalli Hesarikoppa, Hesari, Karekoppa, Chittur, Indihalli Shadalakoppa.

The villages having more than 50% ST population are None.

Sex ratio of Scheduled tribe population is 491.

Scheduled Tribes Literates and Illiterates by Sex:

	Persons	Males	Females
Literate	3,531	2,133	1,398
Illiterate	3,087	1,236	1,851
Literacy rate	61.9	73.6	49.8
Graduate	79	68	11

Scheduled Tribes (Dominant):

Naikda etc., Hasalaru, Meda, Koraga, Kadu Kuruba

For their cultural identity please see Appendix-II

Villages without Scheduled Tribes: There are 204 villages without any scheduled tribe population.

Literates and Illiterates by Sex (Total Population):

	Persons	Males	Females
Literate	107,959	62,353	45,606
Illiterate	70,186	28,103	42,083
Literacy rate	70	80	60
Graduate	3,226	2,573	653

Agriculture: ***Distribution of villages according to land use:*** Out of 306 villages, Total area (in hectare) is 114800, out of that 37.73 percent is cultivable and 52.84 percent of the cultivable area is irrigated.

Sources of Irrigation (Hectares): Government Canal 36.72, Private Canal 0, Well without Electricity 1.92, Well with Electricity 148.67, Tubewell without Electricity 26.45, Tubewell with Electricity 3067.35, Tank 18639.6, River 359.18, Lake 0, Waterfall 0, Others 605.88.

Villages with population of 5000 to 9999: Anavatti.

Villages with population of 10000 and above: None

Distribution of Workers:

	Persons	Males	Females	WPR
Cultivators	42,460	31,306	11,154	47.12
Agricultural Labour	34,779	14,256	20,523	38.6
Household Industry	2,030	1,463	567	2.25
Other Workers	10,838	8,328	2,510	12.03
Main Workers	67,501	49,627	17,874	74.91
Marginal Workers	22,606	5,726	16,880	25.09
Total Workers	90,107	55,353	34,754	

Religion: Major Religious Communities:

	Persons	Males	Females	Sex Ratio
Hindu (92.65%)	165,046	83,775	81,271	970
Muslim (6.36%)	11,324	5,803	5,521	951
Christian (0.36%)	650	314	336	1,070
Sikh (0%)	2	-	2	-
Buddhists (0%)	5	2	3	1,500
Jain (0.06%)	114	56	58	1,036

Agewise Data:

	Persons	Males	Females	Sex Ratio
All ages	178,145	90,456	87,689	969
0-14	53,290	27,292	25,998	953
15-44	90,397	45,815	44,582	973
45-79	32,572	16,485	16,087	976
80+	1,578	695	883	1271
Age not stated	308	169	139	822

Languages (Dominant):

Kannada, Urdu, Telugu, Konkani, Marathi

Disabled Population:

	Persons	Males	Females	%
Total Disabled	3,731	2,251	1,480	
In Seeing	1,695	993	702	45.43
In Speech	354	197	157	9.49
In Hearing	161	92	69	4.32
In Movement	1,118	736	382	29.97
Mentally	403	233	170	10.8

SRINGERI

Sringeri C.D. Block lies in the western part of Chikmaga lur district. It is a part of Sringeri taluka. The Block is located at a distance of 90 kms. from district headqu arters (Chikmagalur). There are 48 villages in the block with the total population of 32,679 persons. Area of the C.D. Block is 442.34 sq. kms. It is bounded by distr ict Shimoga and taluk Koppa on north, taluk Mudigere on south, taluk Koppa on east, districts Udupi and Shimo ga on west.

Communications:

Roadways : N.H.-13: Direction- Mangalore to Koppa, Nearest Vill.- Yadadalu, Karki Khan Estate, Sunkadamakki, Nemmaru, Nemmar, Estate, Gulaganjimane, Kere, Muduba, Kelakoppa, Addagadde, Kavadi, Belandur, Uluvalli, Sring eri (Rural), Vidyaranyapura. S.H.-66: Direction- Muduba to Mudigere, Nearest Villages- Muduba, Sheerlu.

River: Tunga Nadi- Nearest Villages- Yadadalu, Yedadalli, Balekadi, Karki Khan Estate, Sunkadamakki, Nemmaru, Nemmar Estate, Gulaganjimane, Addagadde, Kavadi, Belandur, Sringeri (Rural), Masige, Halandur, Menase, Vidyaranyapura, Kochavalli, Bettagere, Vykuntapura.

Annual Rainfall: Normal Rianfall 3773.2 mm.

Ground Water: Availability of the Ground Water in the Basin is 8317 H.A.M. and the utilization is 3798 H.A. M. It belongs to Safe category. Depth to water level 5 to 20 meter below the ground. Most of the wells go down in summer months, according to the Ground Water Estimation Committee.

Soils: Red Loamy and Sandy Soils.

Natural Division : It falls in Sringeri-Koppa Rolling Humid Tract of Central Karnataka Plateau.

Administration:

Division: Mysore. Parliamentary Constituency: 15 Udupi. District: Chikmagalur. Taluka: Sringeri. Assembly Const ituency: 123 Sringeri. Gram Panchayat: 9.

Regional Area Development Boards: The Maland Aera Development Board.

Fairs and Festivals: Bhoomi-Hunnime Festival: During the Deepavali "Bhoomi-Hunnime" festival is celebrated by the farmers of Sringeri, Mudigere, Koppa, Narasmharajapura and Chikmagalur taluks of Chikmagalur area. The cultivat ors go to their fields with members of their families, and there a temporary mantapa is set up and decorated with sugar canes, banana plants and mango leaves, and crops and worshipped. They return home carrying a portion of the yields of the field and hold a feast.

Shanta-Rishyashringapura Jatra: Rishyashringapura, also called Markal and popularly known as Kigga lies eight kms. west of Sringeri town. The ruins of an old fort can be seen in the village. Five epigraphs recording some grants, four of which are of about the 8th century A.D. and the fifth of about the eleventh century A.D. , refer to the deity Kilganeshvara of the place. Kilga seems to be an old name of this village which is of considerable antiquity.

Sringeri Matha Festivals: Sringeri near Chikmagalur, situated on the banks of the Tunga river, is 88 kms. west of Chikmagalur, 102 kms. south-west of Shimoga, 122 kms. south-west of Tarikere, and 334 kms. north-west of Bangalore city. It is the headquarter of the taluk of the same name. A legend associates the place with sage Vibhandaka and his son sage Rishyashringa who figur es in the Ramayana as the chief priest at a great sacrifi ce performed by king Dasharatha, father of Ramachandra. The place is said to have been named after Rishyashringa as Rishyashringagiri (mountain of Rishyashringa) which was shortened into Shringagiri and Shringeri. Sringeri is widely known for its Matha called Jagadguru Shankarac harya Mahasamsthanam Dakshinamnanaya Shri Sharada Peetham, which is of Adwaita school of Philosophy and Smarta tradition, various temples, enthralling natural scenery and salubrious climate.

Villages: 49 **Inhabited:** 48 **Uninhabited:** 1

Ranking	District	State	National
Area	7	167	1714
Population	7	175	5984
Sex Ratio	3	30	1085
Child Sex Ratio	4	73	2772
Literacy Rate	1	7	330
Density	7	152	6252
Work Participation Rate	7	173	3646

Gram Panchayats:

Begar, Darekoppa, Addagadde, Menase, Vidyaranyapura, Rushyashringapura, Nemmaru, Kuthagodu, Kere.

Amenities:

Education: Primary School in 28 villages, Middle school in 28 villages, Matriculation or Secondary School in 8 villages, namely Begar, Rushyashringapura (Markal), Nemmaru, Darekoppa, Addagadde, Sringeri (Rural), Menase, Vidyaranyapura.

Higher Secondary or Pre University Courses or Intermediate or Junior College in 1 village of the CD Block,, namely Sringeri (Rural).

College in 1 village, Adult Literacy Center in 0 village., College is in village, namely Sringeri (Rural).

Medical: Hospital in 0 village, Dispensary in 1 village, Health Center in 2 villages, Sub Center in 2 villages, Maternity and Child Welfare Center in 2 villages, Community health workers in 0 village.

The Village having Hospital or Dispensary or Health Center is Sringeri (Rural).

Drinking Water: Tap water in 27 villages, Tank water in 8 villages, Well water in 47 villages, Tubewell in 3 villages and more than one source in 47 villages.

Bank: Banking facility in 6 villages, namely, Begar, Rushyashringapura (Markal), Nemmaru Addagadde, Menase, Heruru.

Credit Society in 1 village Agricultural Credit Society in 1 Non-Agricultural Credit Society in 0 village.

Others: Power supply in 48 villages, Cinema hall in 2 villages, sport club in 48 villages, Stadium or Auditorium or Communit Hall in 48 villages, Post Office in 16 villages.

There are 30 villages having bus facilities.

Villages with most of facilities: Begar.

Villages without amenities (Education):

Kumbaragodu, K.Masige, Kogodu, Balekadi, Sunkadamakki, Nemmar Estate, Mathuvalli Estate, Gulaganjimane, Muduba, Sheerlu, Hadi, Hadikiruru, Balagere, Melukoppa, Halandur, Bettagere, Kunthur, Gundre, Kuthagodu, Ginikal..

Scheduled Castes: Out of the total population of 32681 persons, 3752 persons (11.48%) belong to Scheduled Castes. The villages having less than 10% SC population are Asanabalu, Begar, Kumbaragodu, Meega, K.Masige Rushyashringapura (Markal), Yedadalli, Balekadi Sunkadamakki, Mathuvalli Estate, Sheerlu, Malanadu

Hadikiruru, Balagere, Nallur, Darekoppa, Melukoppa Kelakoppa, Honnavalli, Masige, Kikkare (Kikkre) Kunthur, Kuthagodu.

The village having more than 50% SC population is None.

Sex ratio of Scheduled Caste population is 510.

Scheduled Castes Literates and Illiterates by Sex:

	Persons	Males	Females
Literate	2,023	1,092	931
Illiterate	1,729	748	981
Literacy rate	61.3	67.4	55.4
Graduate	33	18	15

Scheduled Castes (Dominant):

Adi Karnataka, Bhovi, Chalavadi etc., Banjara etc. Adi Dravida

For their cultural identity please see Appendix-I

Villages without Scheduled Castes: There are 6 villages without any scheduled caste population.

Scheduled Tribes: Out of the total population of 32681 persons, 2764 persons (8.46%) belong to Scheduled Tribes.

The villages having less than 10% ST population are Asanabalu, Begar, Kumbaragodu, Neelandur, Meega Rushyashringapura (Markal), Kogodu, Gandagatta Yadadalu, Yedadalli, Haruru (Harur), Kere, Nallur Darekoppa, Melukoppa, Kelakoppa, Addagadde, Kavadi Belandur, Honnavalli, Uluvalli, Sringeri (Rural) Masige, Menase, Vidyaranyapura, Kochavalli Bettagere, Vykuntapura, Kunthur, Heruru, Kuthagodu Ginikal.

The villages having more than 50% ST population are None.

Sex ratio of Scheduled tribe population is 508.

Scheduled Tribes Literates and Illiterates by Sex:

	Persons	Males	Females
Literate	1,565	835	730
Illiterate	1,199	524	675
Literacy rate	65.7	70.9	60.6
Graduate	25	20	5

Scheduled Tribes (Dominant):

Gowdalu, Hasalaru, Naikda etc., Maleru Generic Tribes etc.

For their cultural identity please see Appendix-II

Villages without Scheduled Tribes: There are 8 villages without any scheduled tribe population.

Literates and Illiterates by Sex (Total Population):

	Persons	Males	Females
Literate	23,085	12,381	10,704
Illiterate	9,596	3,931	5,665
Literacy rate	80	86	73
Graduate	1,186	737	449

Agriculture: ***Distribution of villages according to land use:*** Out of 49 villages, Total area (in hectare) is 44234, out of that 13.22 percent is cultivable and 2.55 percent of the cultivable area is irrigated.

Sources of Irrigation (Hectares): Government Canal 0, Private Canal 1, Well without Electricity 0, Well with Electricity 69.11, Tubewell without Electricity 0, Tubewell with Electricity 0, Tank 66.47, River 10.76, Lake 0, Waterfall 0, Others 2.7.

Villages with population of 5000 to 9999: None

Villages with population of 10000 and above: None

Distribution of Workers:

	Persons	Males	Females	WPR
Cultivators	5,021	4,135	886	34.21
Agricultural Labour	5,182	2,760	2,422	35.31
Household Industry	401	181	220	2.73
Other Workers	4,072	3,132	940	27.75
Main Workers	12,813	9,501	3,312	87.31
Marginal Workers	1,863	707	1,156	12.69
Total Workers	14,676	10,208	4,468	

Religion: Major Religious Communities:

	Persons	Males	Females	Sex Ratio
Hindu (95.6%)	31,242	15,575	15,667	1,006
Muslim (3.87%)	1,264	645	619	960
Christian (0.47%)	155	79	76	962
Sikh (0%)	-	-	-	-
Buddhists (0%)	1	1	-	-
Jain (0.04%)	14	9	5	556

Agewise Data:

	Persons	Males	Females	Sex Ratio
All ages	32,681	16,312	16,369	1003
0-14	8,359	4,157	4,202	1011
15-44	16,863	8,309	8,554	1029
45-79	7,040	3,614	3,426	948
80+	401	225	176	782
Age not stated	18	7	11	1571

Languages (Dominant):

Kannada, Tulu, Urdu, Marathi, Malayalam

Disabled Population:

	Persons	Males	Females	%
Total Disabled	1,062	705	357	
In Seeing	673	478	195	63.37
In Speech	65	37	28	6.12
In Hearing	77	41	36	7.25
In Movement	191	114	77	17.98
Mentally	56	35	21	5.27

SRINIVASPUR

Srinivaspur C.D. Block lies in the eastern part of Kolar district. It is a part of Srinivaspur taluka. The Block is located at a distance of 25 kms. from district headqu arters (Kolar). There are 347 villages in the block with the total population of 161,686 persons. Area of the C.D. Block is 858.60 sq. kms. It is bounded by taluks Kolar and Mulbagal on south, and taluks Chintamani and Kolar on west. It has common boundary with the state of Andhra Pradesh on north and east.

Communications:

Roadways : S.H.-58: Direction- Chintamani to Mulbagal, Nearest Villages- Alambagiri, Kollur, Boyinachapalli, Srinivaspur (Rural), Srinivaspur Amanikere, Hebbata, Ketheganahalli, Lingarajapura, Meesaganapalli, Arikere, Kattibissanahalli, Yadarur, Lakshmisagara. S.H.-82: Direction- Chintamani to Madanapalli, Nearest Villages- Rayalpad, Mandyala, Madarankapalli, Yendaguttapalli, Guntapalli, Manchineellakote, Thoopalli, Marimakalapalli, Sunnakal, Subbagundlapalli, Nelavanki, Chakapalli, Kothapalli, Doddabandarlahalli, Kasettipalli, Vyshnavar ipalli, Kamalavaripalli , Gundedu, Lakshmisagara, Nachaga dde, Thadigol, Seeglapalya, Rajapalli.

Railway Station: Villages- Panasamakalapalli, Dalasanur.

Annual Rainfall: Normal Rianfall 796.53 mm.

Ground Water: Availability of the Ground Water in the Basin is (Information not avablable) H.A.M. and the utilization is (Information not avablable) H.A.M. It belongs to (Information not avablable) category. Depth to water level 5 to 20 meter below the ground. Most of the wells go down in summer months, according to the Ground Water Estimation Committee.

Soils: Red Soils.

Natural Division : It falls in Sidlaghatta-Srinivaspur Uplands of the Southern Karnataka Plateau.

Administration:

Division: Bangalore. Parliamentary Constituency: 28 Kolar (SC). District: Kolar. Taluka: Srinivaspur. Assemb ly Constituency: 144 Srinivaspur. Gram Panchayat: 25.

Regional Area Development Boards: The Bailu Seeme Area Development Board.

Border Villages: (State: Andhra Pradesh)- Marasanapalli, Kothahudya, Gudipalli, Kurigepalli, Reddivaripalli (R), Vangasavaripalli, Kothapalli, Kottevaripalli, Chint amanipalli, Chikkevaripalli, Balevaripalli, Bodireddipalli, Mudimadugu, Guntapalli, Sunnakal, Jeedimakalapalli (S), Mulagollapalli, Kamatampalli, Banalapalli, Kannampa lli, Guttapalli, Koolagurki, Somayajilapalli, Raghunathap ura, Channaiahgaripalli, Matakansandra, Rajagundlapalli, Karangi, Kannampalli.

Villages: 347 **Inhabited:** 296 **Uninhabited:** 51

Ranking	District	State	National
Area	4	110	617
Population	7	118	1513
Sex Ratio	4	76	2153
Child Sex Ratio	1	13	1033
Literacy Rate	3	100	3074
Density	6	29	4907
Work Participation Rate	10	90	993

Gram Panchayats:

Byraganapalli, Kurigepalli, Mudimadugu, Rayalpad, Yeramvaripalli, Addagal, Gownipalli, Kodipalli, Thadigol, Nelavanki, Lakshmipura, Pulugurkote, Somayajilapalli, Ronur, Arikunte, J.Thimmasandra, Hodali, Muthakapalli, Yeldur, Chaldiganahalli, Nambihalli, Mastenahalli, Dalasanur, Lakshmisagara, Kolathur.

Amenities:

Education: Primary School in 233 villages, Middle school in 104 villages, Matriculation or Secondary School in 19 villages, namely Kurigepalli, Mudimadugu, Byraganapalli, Rayalpad, Gownipalli, Addagal, Lakshmipura, Pulugurkote, Mothakapalli, Arikunte, Ronur, Somayajilapalli, Alavatta, Pathapalli, Nambihalli, Dalasanur, Mastenahalli, Muthakapalli, Yeldur.

Higher Secondary or Pre University Courses or Intermediate or Junior College in 4 villages of the CD Block,, namely Rayalpad, Gownipalli, Dalasanur, Yeldur.

College in 0 village, Adult Literacy Center in 10 villages.

Medical: Hospital in 2 villages, Dispensary in 4 villages, Health Center in 12 villages, Sub Center in 32 villages, Maternity and Child Welfare Center in 15 villages, Community health workers in 0 village.

The Villages having Hospital or Dispensary or Health Center are Gownipalli, Lakshmipura, Doddapalli, Ronur, Somayajilapalli.

Drinking Water: Tap water in 185 villages, Tank water in 25 villages, Well water in 34 villages, Tubewell in 125 villages and more than one source in 232 villages.

Bank: Banking facility in 13 villages, namely, Kurigepalli, Rayalpad, Gownipalli, Bathalaguttapalli Addagal, Kasettipalli, Lakshmipura, Doddapalli Ronur, Somayajilapalli, Dalasanur, Yeldur Lakshmisagara.

Credit Society in 13 villages Agricultural Credit Society in 11 Non-Agricultural Credit Society in 1 village.

Others: Power supply in 281 villages, Cinema hall in 4 villages sport club in 1 village, Stadium or Auditorium or Community Hall in 1 village, Post Office in 37 villages.

There are 202 villages having bus facilities.

Villages with most of facilities: Kurigepalli Rayalpad, Gownipalli, Addagal, Lakshmipura, Ronur Somayajilapalli, Dalasanur, Yeldur, Lakshmisagara.

Villages without amenities (Education):

Katamguntapalli, Raghunathapura, Chikkevaripalli,

Bodireddipalli, Vyapalahalli, Hosahudya, Kotekallur, Upparapalli, M.Thummalapalli, Malamotakpalli, Dombarapalli, Jathavarthapalli, Manjevaripalli, Sanakamvaripalli, Thorlavaripalli, Diguvamarampalli, Bayapalli, Pathagownipalli, Agrahara, Yendaguttapalli, Chikkakondamari, Thammareddigaripalli, Thoopalli, Kurupalli (M), Sunnakal, Mulagollapalli, Gowdathatagadde, Sheshapura (K.G.), Sathanurapalli, Krishnapura, Chigarekunte, Lingapura, Bachuvaripalli, Kokkantivaripalli, Machuvaripalli, Kannampalli, Kamatampalli, Lakshmanapura, Chinnepalli, Brahmanapalli, Chikkathimmanahalli, Seegahalli, Nilaturu, Apparasanahalli, Ramapura, Katara Muddalahalli, Ganganahalli, Boyinachapalli, Lingarajapura, Kuppahalli, Anchiganahalli, Kurubarahalli, Kostenahalli, Venkatapura, Ganganatta, Kannampalli, Veerasandra..

Scheduled Castes: Out of the total population of 161762 persons, 47277 persons (29.23%) belong to Scheduled Castes. The villages having less than 10% SC population are Kothahudya, Katamguntapalli, Reddivaripalli (R) Chikkevaripalli, Balevaripalli, Bodireddipalli Vyapalahalli, Hosahudya, Kundathavaripalli Pathagownipalli, Bhimaguttapalli, Thummalavaripalli Jinkalavaripalli, Mulagollapalli, Sathanurapalli Bachuvaripalli, Chinnepalli, Mothakapalli Chakarlapalli, Dasara Thimmanahalli, Apparasanahalli Ramapura, Raghunathapura, Pathapalli, Chowdanahalli Ganganahalli, Byrapalli, Nallapalli (H), Noolapura Kostenahalli, Venkatapura, Narayanapura, Ganganatta Karangi, Kannampalli, Veerasandra, Vadigepalli (S) Harlakunte.

The villages having more than 50% SC population are Kothur (A), Raghunathapura, Chintamanipalli Upparapalli, Dombarapalli, Bhogamvaripalli Diguvachinthapalli, Thummalapalli (G) , Karipalli Diguvamarampalli, Kambalapalli, Kandlevaripalli Chikkakondamari, Koppavaripalli, Kothapet Gowdathatagadde, Marepalli, Sheshapura (K.G.) Muddepalli, Pandivaripalli, Jeedimakalapalli (P) Krishnapura, Chigarekunte, Kannampalli, Guttapalli Chokkareddipalli, Kanagamakalapalli, Pillakunte J.Thimmasandra, Chaldiganahalli, Lingarajapura Koneti Thimmanahalli, Kurubarahalli, Gowdahalli Attikunte, Arikere, Beerganahalli, Manjulanagara.

Sex ratio of Scheduled Caste population is 496.

Scheduled Castes Literates and Illiterates by Sex:

	Persons	Males	Females
Literate	18,837	12,117	6,720
Illiterate	28,440	11,725	16,715
Literacy rate	46.4	59.1	33.4
Graduate	441	399	42

Scheduled Castes (Dominant):

Adi Karnataka, Bhovi, Adi Dravida, Chenna Dasar etc. Madiga

For their cultural identity please see Appendix-I

Villages without Scheduled Castes: There are 70 villages without any scheduled caste population.

Scheduled Tribes: Out of the total population of 161762 persons, 18887 persons (11.68%) belong to Scheduled Tribes. The villages having less than 10% ST population are Kothahudya, Kothur (A), Gudipalli Reddivaripalli (R), Chintamanipalli, Balevaripalli Bodireddipalli, Balthmari, Pathur, Pedduru Hosahudya, Byraganapalli, Chillarpalli, Kotekallur Bykothuru, Yadaganapalli, Vempalli, Yeramvaripalli Upparapalli, Gudisivaripalli, Basavanapalli M.Thummalapalli, Malamotakpalli, Dombarapalli Jathavarthapalli, Manjevaripalli, Bhogamvaripalli Sanakamvaripalli, Diguvachinthapalli, Adirajapalli Thummalapalli (G) , Chilepalli, Avaganapalli Diguvamarampalli, Pathagownipalli Reddivaripalli (G), Kambalapalli, Yagavachinthapalli Kempareddigaripalli, Chirkorapalli, Madarankapalli Kandlevaripalli, Yendaguttapalli, Chikkakondamari Pathanelavanki, Koppavaripalli, Marimakalapalli Jinkalavaripalli, Gowdathatagadde Pacharamakalapalli, Subbagundlapalli, Chakapalli Kothapalli, Doddabandarlahalli, Kasettipalli Kamalavaripalli , Marepalli, Koosandra, Gundedu Lakshmisagara, Sheshapura (K.G.), Gollapalli . S Muddepalli, Pandivaripalli, Sathanurapalli Jeedimakalapalli (P), Krishnapura, Pathakote Gorivimakalapalli, Kondasandra, Reddimpalli Chigarekunte, Devareddipalli, Upparapalli Burakayalakote, Lingapura, Kotaballapalli, Iladoni Kokkantivaripalli, Pulugurkote, Kannampalli Bandapalli, Kamatampalli, Seeglapalya, Kappalli Lakshmanapura, Naruvamakalapalli, Purnapalli Adavichambakur, Guttapalli, Koolagurki, Mothakapalli Pegalapalli, Chokkareddipalli, Locheruvapalli Chikkathimmanahalli, Seegahalli, Kurumakalapalli Kanagamakalapalli, Arikunte, Maniganahalli, Kothur Kummakunte, Byapalli, Kambalapalli, Yachanapalli Nilaturu, Nagedepalli, Thimmasandra (R) Kaniganapalli, Doddapalli, Ronur, Dimbala, Champalli Kotraguli, Devalapalli, Hodali, Chokkanapalli Ramapura, Raghunathapura, Channaiahgaripalli Matakansandra, Alambagiri, J.Thimmasandra, Kiruvara

Alavatta , Thupalli, Doddamaladoddi, Pathapalli
Dwarasandra, Aramakalahalli, Sathandahalli
Katara Muddalahalli, Ganganahalli, Boyinachapalli
Byrapalli, Avalakuppa, Nallapalli (H)
Panasamakalapalli, Unikili, Mogilahalli, Nambihalli
Varatanahalli, Y.Hosakote, Yaluvakunte, Agrahara
C. Hosuru, Chiruvanahalli, Chaldiganahalli
Ketheganahalli, Lingarajapura, Obepalli
Meesaganapalli, Yaluvahalli, Hosahalli, Dalasanur
Koneti Thimmanahalli, Kuppahalli
Kaadu Devandlahalli, Bissanahalli, Bagalahalli
Mastenahalli, Kurubarahalli, Noolapura, Gandlahalli
Booraganahalli, Kostenahalli, Bangavadi, Gowdahalli
Valagernahalli, Hoohalli, Kodicheruvu
Padathimmanahalli, Thinnalli, Gijiganahalli
Pathamuthakapalli, Vadigepalli .K, Neelatur
Peddapalli, Achampalli, Seegehalli, Arikere
Veerasandra, Seethareddihalli, Kattibissanahalli
Beerganahalli, Yadarur, Chintamakalapalli, Shyagatur
Manjulanagara, Lakshmisagara, Sheshapura, Harlakunte
Pindiganagara.

The villages having more than 50% ST population are
Katamguntapalli, Baddipalli, Mudivaripalli
A.Vyapalapalli, Thummalavaripalli, Buragamakalapalli
Guntapalli, Thammareddigaripalli, Kurupalli (M)
Ammagaripet, Mulagollapalli, Nambuvaripalli
Thanterlapalli, Bachuvaripalli, Gangannagaripalli
Banalapalli, Machuvaripalli, Gullakunte
Pathaballapalli, Chinnepalli, Guntavaripalli
Chakarlapalli, Gopalapura, Veerthimmanahalli
Venkatapura, Narayanapura, Ganganatta, Karangi
Kannampalli, Yammanuru.

Sex ratio of Scheduled tribe population is 490.

Scheduled Tribes Literates and Illiterates by Sex:

	Persons	Males	Females
Literate	7,523	4,843	2,680
Illiterate	11,364	4,792	6,572
Literacy rate	46.4	58.8	33.6
Graduate	179	161	18

Scheduled Tribes (Dominant):

Naikda etc., Hakkipikki, Iruliga
Generic Tribes etc., Meda

For their cultural identity please see Appendix-II

Villages without Scheduled Tribes: There are 162 villages without any scheduled tribe population.

Literates and Illiterates by Sex (Total Population):

	Persons	Males	Females
Literate	82,182	50,530	31,652
Illiterate	79,580	31,303	48,277
Literacy rate	58	71	45
Graduate	3,023	2,572	451

Agriculture: ***Distribution of villages according to land use:*** Out of 347 villages, Total area (in hectare) is 85860, out of that 56.18 percent is cultivable and 23.29 percent of the cultivable area is irrigated.

Sources of Irrigation (Hectares): Government Canal 0, Private Canal 0, Well without Electricity 22.66, Well with Electricity 0, Tubewell without Electricity 136.71, Tubewell with Electricity 6847.47, Tank 4196.63, River 0, Lake 30.77, Waterfall 0, Others 0.

Villages with population of 5000 to 9999:
Gownipalli.

Villages with population of 10000 and above: None

Distribution of Workers:

	Persons	Males	Females	WPR
Cultivators	38,400	22,800	15,600	43.39
Agricultural Labour	23,938	9,707	14,231	27.05
Household Industry	1,377	887	490	1.56
Other Workers	24,787	16,233	8,554	28.01
Main Workers	72,288	45,622	26,666	81.68
Marginal Workers	16,214	4,005	12,209	18.32
Total Workers	88,502	49,627	38,875	

Religion: Major Religious Communities:

	Persons	Males	Females	Sex Ratio
Hindu (93.18%)	150,734	76,180	74,554	979
Muslim (6.68%)	10,809	5,541	5,268	951
Christian (0.09%)	148	76	72	947
Sikh (0%)	2	-	2	-
Buddhists (0%)	-	-	-	-
Jain (0%)	4	2	2	1,000

Agewise Data:

	Persons	Males	Females	Sex Ratio
All ages	161,762	81,833	79,929	977
0-14	49,627	25,205	24,422	969
15-44	75,011	38,013	36,998	973
45-79	34,999	17,616	17,383	987
80+	2,037	947	1,090	1151
Age not stated	88	52	36	692

Languages (Dominant):
Telugu, Kannada, Urdu, Hindi, Marathi

Disabled Population:

	Persons	Males	Females	%
Total Disabled	3,026	1,662	1,364	
In Seeing	1,168	583	585	38.6
In Speech	314	177	137	10.38
In Hearing	234	114	120	7.73
In Movement	991	622	369	32.75
Mentally	319	166	153	10.54

SULYA

Sulya C.D. Block lies in the south-eastern part of Dakshina Kannada district. It is a part of Sulya taluka. The

Block is located at a distance of 83 kms. from district headquarters (Mangalore). There are 40 villages in the block with the total population of 122,696 persons. Area of the C.D. Block is 809.44 sq. kms. It is bounded by taluk Puttur and district Hassan on north, district Kodagu on south and east, taluk Puttur on west. It has common boundary with the state of Kerala on south-west.

Communications:

Roadways : SH-37: Direction- Uppinamgadi to Subramanya, Nearest Village- Subramanya. SH- 88: Direction- Mangalo re to Madikeri, Nearest Villages- Jalsoor, Kanaka Majalu, Aletty, Aranthodu, Sampaje.

Railway Station: Yedamangala

River: Kallaji Nadi- Nearest Villages- Yenekallu, Inakidu, Balagodu, Hariharapallathadka. Payaswani Nadi- Nearest Villages- Jalsoor, Mandekolu, Ajjavara, Aletty, Thodikana, Aranthodu, Sampaje. Belanile Hole Nadi- Nearest Villages- Jalsoor, Kanaka Majalu, Aletty, Aranthodu, Sampaje.

Reserved Forest: (Aivarnad R.F.): Villages- Bellare, Kalanja, Aivarnadu, Amarapadnoor. (Jalsur R.F.): Nearest Villages- Aivarnadu, Jalsoor, Kanaka Majalu, Amarapadnoor. (Balpa R.F.): Nearest Villages- Balpa, Guthigaru, Nalkooru, Yenekallu. (Devachalla R.F.): Nearest Villages- Amaramu dnur, Guthigaru, Devachalla. (Yenekal R.F.): Nearest Villages- Madappady, Nalkooru, Yenekallu, Subramanya, Inakidu, Balagodu, Hariharapallathadka, Kollamogru, Kalmakaru. (Kallapattamale R.F.): Nearest Villages- Peruvaje, Kodiyala. (Mandekolu R.F.): Nearest Villages: Mandekolu, Ajjavara. (Alletty East R.F.): Nearest Villag es- Mandekolu, Aletty. (Medinadka West R.F.): Nearest Village- Ajjavara. (Pumale R.F.): Nearest Villages- Nellurkembraje, Ubaradka Mittur, Aletty, Aranthodu, Markanja. (Sampaji R.F.): Nearest Villages- Aranthodu, Markanja, Madappady, Sampaje. (Yenmuru R.F.): Nearest Villages- Yedamangala, Yenmooru, Aivathoklu, Kenya. (Thodikana R.F.): Nearest Villages- Thodikana, Sampaje.

Annual Rainfall: Normal Rianfall 3744 mm.

Ground Water: Availability of the Ground Water in the Basin is (Information not avablable) H.A.M. and the utilization is (Information not avablable) H.A.M. It belongs to (Information not avablable) category. Depth to water level 5 to 20 meter below the ground. Most of the wells go down in summer months, according to the Ground Water Estimation Committee.

Natural Division : It falls partly in Western Ghats (Daks hina Kannada) and Beltangadi Dissected zone of the Karnat aka Coast (Western Coastal Region).

Administration:

Division: Mysore. Parliamentary Constituency: 17 Dakshina Kannada. District: Dakshina Kannada. Taluka: Sulya. Assembly Constituency: 207 Sulya (SC). Gram Panchayat: 27.

Regional Area Development Boards: The Maland Aera Development Board.

Border Villages: (State: Kerala)- Kanaka Majalu, Mandek olu, Aletty.

Fairs: Kukkesubramanya Temple Car Festival: Kulkunda is a hamlet of Subramanya near Dakshina Kannada and is situated at the cross round junction of Uppinangady-Bisle ghat Road on one side and Uppinangady-Subramanya Road on the other. It is about three kilometres from Subraman ya proper, 48 kms. from the Sullia town and about 104 kms. from Mangalore. An annual cattle fair held on a large scale is well known. It begins on the full moon day of Kartika and runs for about fifteen days at the time of the annual car festival of the Kukke-Subramanya temple.

Subramanya Fair: It is held annually at Subramanya around the month of November-December. Subramanya below the western ghats, is a distance of 104 kms. from Mangalore, and 33 kms. from Puttur. It is also known as Kukke-Subr amanya and Pushpagiri. It is one of the seven places of pilgrimage in the region and lies in the midst of two mountains, namely, Kumara Parvata and Shesha Parvata. The place gained importance from about the eighth centu ry. Adi-Shankaracharya is said to have visited this place.

Villages: 40 **Inhabited:** 40 **Uninhabited:** 0

Ranking	**District**	**State**	**National**
Area	3	118	705
Population	5	149	2781
Sex Ratio	5	46	1523
Child Sex Ratio	5	162	4629
Literacy Rate	3	5	293
Density	3	39	5535
Work Participation Rate	5	127	1242

Gram Panchayats:

Bellare, Kodiyala, Yedamangala, Yenmooru, Balila, Kalanja, Aivarnadu, Jalsoor, Kanakamajalu, Mandekolu, Ajjavara, Amaramudnur, Kalmadka, Panja, Balpa, Guthigaru, Nellurkembraje, Ubaradkamittur, Aletty, Aranthodu, Markanja, Devachalla, Subramanya, Hariharapallathaaadka, Madappady, Sampaje, Kollamogru.

Amenities:

Education: Primary School in 40 villages, Middle school in 40 villages, Matriculation or Secondary School in 18 villages, namely Balila, Bellare, Aivarnadu, Jalsoor, Kanaka Majalu, Ajjavara, Amarapadnoor, Amaramudnur, Aletty, Aranthodu, Markanja, Yedamangala, Aivathoklu, Guthigaru, Yenekallu, Subramanya,

Hariharapallathadka, Kollamogru.

Higher Secondary or Pre University Courses or Intermediate or Junior College in 6 villages of the CD Block,, namely Bellare, Aivarnadu, Aranthodu, Aivathoklu, Guthigaru, Subramanya.

College in 2 villages, Adult Literacy Center in 14 villages., Colleges are in villages, namely Bellare, Subramanya.

Medical: Hospital in 2 villages, Dispensary in 14 villages, Health Center in 5 villages, Sub Center in 31 villages, Maternity and Child Welfare Center in 4 villages, Community health workers in 17 villages.

The Villages having Hospital or Dispensary or Health Center are Balila, Bellare, Mupperia, Aivarnadu, Ajjavara, Amaramudnur, Nellurkembraje, Sampaje, Murulya, Yenmooru, Aivathoklu, Kuthkunja, Balpa, Guthigaru, Subramanya, Kollamogru.

Drinking Water: Tap water in 36 villages, Tank water in 26 villages, Well water in 40 villages, Tubewell in 39 villages and more than one source in 40 villages.

Bank: Banking facility in 11 villages, namely, Bellare, Jalsoor, Amaramudnur, Aranthodu, Sampaje Yenmooru, Aivathoklu, Guthigaru, Yenekallu Subramanya, Kollamogru.

Credit Society in 21 villages Agricultural Credit Society in 20 Non-Agricultural Credit Society in 2 villages.

Others: Power supply in 40 villages, Cinema hall in 0 village, sport club in 1 village, Stadium or Auditorium or Community Hall in 0 village, Post Office in 38 villages.

There are 40 villages having bus facilities.

Villages with most of facilities: Bellare, Jalsoor Amaramudnur, Aranthodu, Sampaje, Yenmooru Aivathoklu, Guthigaru, Yenekallu, Subramanya Kollamogru.

Villages without Amenities (Education): None..

Scheduled Castes: Out of the total population of 122726 persons, 17621 persons (14.36%) belong to Scheduled Castes.

The villages having less than 10% SC population are Mupperia, Amarapadnoor, Aletty, Aranthodu, Madappady Aivathoklu, Pambethady, Kuthkunja, Yenekallu Hariharapallathadka, Kollamogru.

The village having more than 50% SC population is None.

Sex ratio of Scheduled Caste population is 497.

Scheduled Castes Literates and Illiterates by Sex:

	Persons	Males	Females
Literate	9,110	5,196	3,914
Illiterate	8,511	3,667	4,844
Literacy rate	59.8	68.0	51.5
Graduate	69	55	14

Scheduled Castes (Dominant):

Holaya etc., Moger, Maila, Ajila, Adi Dravida

For their cultural identity please see Appendix-I

Villages without Scheduled Castes: There are 0 village without any scheduled caste population.

Scheduled Tribes: Out of the total population of 122726 persons, 9870 persons (8.04%) belong to Scheduled Tribes.

The villages having less than 10% ST population are Peruvaje, Kodiyala, Balila, Bellare, Kalanja Aivarnadu, Jalsoor, Kanaka Majalu, Mandekolu Ajjavara, Ubaradka Mittur, Thodikana, Aranthodu Markanja, Madappady, Sampaje, Murulya, Yedamangala Yenmooru, Aivathoklu, Kenya, Balpa, Guthigaru Devachalla, Nalkooru, Yenekallu, Inakidu, Balagodu Kollamogru, Kalmakaru.

The villages having more than 50% ST population are None.

Sex ratio of Scheduled tribe population is 498.

Scheduled Tribes Literates and Illiterates by Sex:

	Persons	Males	Females
Literate	6,323	3,488	2,835
Illiterate	3,547	1,468	2,079
Literacy rate	72.4	80.4	64.5
Graduate	130	91	39

Scheduled Tribes (Dominant):

Marati, Naikda etc., Malaikudi, Koraga, Meda

For their cultural identity please see Appendix-II

Villages without Scheduled Tribes: There are 0 village without any scheduled tribe population.

Literates and Illiterates by Sex (Total Population):

	Persons	Males	Females
Literate	86,164	46,536	39,628
Illiterate	36,562	15,089	21,473
Literacy rate	80	87	74
Graduate	3,692	2,326	1,366

Agriculture: ***Distribution of villages according to land use:*** Out of 40 villages, Total area (in hectare) is 80944, out of that 27.29 percent is cultivable and 60.74 percent of the cultivable area is irrigated.

Sources of Irrigation (Hectares): Government Canal 0, Private Canal 21.05, Well without Electricity 3357.9, Well with Electricity 3391.75, Tubewell without Electricity 69.48, Tubewell with Electricity 1327.5, Tank 313.46, River 1561.13, Lake 416.63, Waterfall 596.56, Others 2363.14.

Villages with population of 5000 to 9999: Jalsoor, Mandekolu, Ajjavara, Aletty, Sampaje.

Villages with population of 10000 and above: None

Distribution of Workers:

	Persons	Males	Females	WPR
Cultivators	720	430	290	1.08
Agricultural Labour	461	220	241	0.69

Household Industry	7,418	546	6,872	11.17
Other Workers	57,813	37,661	20,152	87.05
Main Workers	55,786	35,589	20,197	84
Marginal Workers	10,626	3,268	7,358	16
Total Workers	66,412	38,857	27,555	

Religion: Major Religious Communities:

	Persons	Males	Females	Sex Ratio
Hindu (87.89%)	107,870	54,096	53,774	994
Muslim (10.79%)	13,239	6,675	6,564	983
Christian (1.26%)	1,546	815	731	897
Sikh (0%)	-	-	-	-
Buddhists (0%)	-	-	-	-
Jain (0.04%)	49	27	22	815

Agewise Data:

	Persons	Males	Females	Sex Ratio
All ages	122,726	61,625	61,101	991
0-14	34,457	17,864	16,593	929
15-44	61,283	29,988	31,295	1044
45-79	25,663	13,091	12,572	960
80+	1,254	637	617	969
Age not stated	69	45	24	533

Languages (Dominant):
Tulu, Kannada, Malayalam, Tamil, Marathi

Disabled Population:

	Persons	Males	Females	%
Total Disabled	2,869	1,644	1,225	
In Seeing	1,727	1,010	717	60.2
In Speech	256	147	109	8.92
In Hearing	115	59	56	4.01
In Movement	444	274	170	15.48
Mentally	327	154	173	11.4

SUPA

Supa C.D. Block lies in the north-western part of Uttara Kannada district. It is a part of Supa taluka. The Block is located at a distance of 100 kms. from district headq uarters (Karwar). There are 120 villages in the block with the total population of 48,901 persons. Area of the C.D. Block is 1783.23 sq. kms. It is bounded by district Belgaum on north, taluk Karwar on south, taluks Yellapur and Haliyal on east, and it has common boundary with the State of Goa on west.

Communications:

Roadways : N.H-4 A: Direction- Panji to Belgaum, Nearest Villages- Rangarook, Varlewadi, Akheti, Anamod, Atle, Kalambuli, Devulli (Tinai), Payaswadi, Ramnagar. S. H-28: Direction- Ambeli to Haliyal, Nearest Villages- Usoda, Pusheli, Aveda. S.H-95: Direction- Karwar to Belgaum, Nearest Villages- Ramnagar, Bori, Shindholi, Velif Kumbeli, Kumbral, Vaini, Bamanawadi, Jagalbet, Kurandi, Ambeli, Samjoida, Deriye, Katel, Kateli (Kumbar Wada), Nujji, Badpoli, Anashi, Nigundi, Godashet, Chapo li (Kalsai), Devulli (Joida), Joida.

Railway Station: Village- Kalambuli.

River: Kali Nadi- Nearest Villages- Aveda, Mavalinge, Badgund, Ambeli, Khodli, Birampali, Sannamaga, Kavale, Shevali, Yeramukh, Neturge, Birkhol. Nagi Nadi- Nearest Villages- Viral, Bazar Kunang, Asulli, Terali, Karanjoida, Panjeli, Ambeli. Pandhri Nadi- Nearest Villages- Akheti, Vatala, Kamra, Kasarle, Wada, Varande, Vaini, Kurandi, Aveda, Pisose, Viral, Anamod, Kalambuli, Devulli (Tinai), Konshet, Kunagini, Ivoli, Aveda Poppal Wadi, Iliye Dabe, Ghavane, Bandoda, Ambeli. Kaneri Nadi- Nearest Villages- Kalamkhand, Zalawali, Kateli (Kumbar Wada), Nujji, Nigundi, Kalasai, Godashet, Hudasa, Avurli, Gangoda, Ambolli, Gund, Chinchkhand, Bidoli, Shevali.

Annual Rainfall: Normal Rianfall 2323 mm.

Ground Water: Availability of the Ground Water in the Basin is 10835 H.A.M. and the utilization is 1237 H. A.M. It belongs to Safe category. Depth to water level 5 to 20 meter below the ground. Most of the wells go down in summer months, according to the Ground Water Estimation Committee.

Soils: Lateritic Soil.

Natural Division : It falls in Western Ghats (Uttara Kannada) of the Karnataka Coast (Western Coastal Region).

Administration:

Division: Belgaum. Parliamentary Constituency: 12 Uttara Kannada. District: Uttara Kannada. Taluka: Supa. Assembly Constituency: 76 Haliyal. Gram Panchayat: 15.

Regional Area Development Boards: The Maland Aera Development Board.

Border Villages: (State: Goa)- Viranjol, Palada, Karambal, Anamod, Atle, Kalambuli, Ivoli, Kuveshi, Diggi, Asulli, Kundal, Zalawali, Terali, Nujji.

Fairs: Channabasavanna Temple Jatra: At the Channaba-savanna temple at Ulvi Jatras are held during Shivaratri, Makara Sankranti and Basava Jayanti. The major festival is on Magha Poornima. It is for eight days, culminataing with Poornima and more than two lakh people visit this jatra. Once on every Poornima there will be the jatra when small car festival takes place, and huge car (dodda ratha) is taken out on the above mentioned jatras. Every Monday there will be the palaki utsava and in Shravana, on Monday utsava will have better attendance than in other months. Ulvi (Supa tq.), a separate revenue village (36 kms. from Joida and 90 kms. from Karwar) is an ancie nt Veerashaiva centre and a place of pilgrimage. The place name is mentioned differently as 'Uliva,' Ulidvi, or 'Ulivi', etc. Uli or Ulive means to stay or hide oneself. Channabasavanna's stay here or his using the place as a hide-out might have brought the name to the place.

Villages: 120 **Inhabited:** 114 **Uninhabited:** 6

Ranking	District	State	National
Area	1	12	74
Population	11	173	5341
Sex Ratio	4	52	1639
Child Sex Ratio	2	23	1452
Literacy Rate	10	57	1866
Density	6	141	6325
Work Participation Rate	11	175	3296

Gram Panchayats:

Akheti, Kalambuli, Bazar Kunang, Asu, Ramnagar , Shingargaon, Jagalbet, Aveda , Pradhani, Nagoda, Joida, Katel, Anashi, Ulavi, Nandigadde.

Amenities:

Education: Primary School in 81 villages, Middle school in 30 villages, Matriculation or Secondary School in 10 villages, namely Anamod, Kalambuli, Ramnagar, Jagalbet, Aveda, Birampali, Pradhani, Kateli (Kumbar Wada), Joida, Ulavi.

Higher Secondary or Pre University Courses or Intermediate or Junior College in 2 villages of the CD Block,, namely Ramnagar, Joida.

College in 0 village, Adult Literacy Center in 0 village.

Medical: Hospital in 2 villages, Dispensary in 4 villages, Health Center in 3 villages, Sub Center in 7 villages, Maternity and Child Welfare Center in 1 village, Community health workers in 0 village.

The Villages having Hospital or Dispensary or Health Center are Anamod, Ramnagar , Jagalbet, Gund, Ulavi.

Drinking Water: Tap water in 24 villages, Tank water in 22 villages, Well water in 63 villages, Tubewell in 11 villages and more than one source in 86 villages.

Bank: Banking facility in 12 villages, namely, Kalambuli, Ramnagar, Asu, Jagalbet, Aveda, Ambeli Pradhani, Kateli (Kumbar Wada), Joida, Nandigadde Yeramukh, Ulavi.

Credit Society in 11 villages Agricultural Credit Society in 11 Non-Agricultural Credit Society in 1 village.

Others: Power supply in 74 villages, Cinema hall in 0 village, sport club in 0 village, Stadium or Auditorium or Community Hall in 0 village, Post Office in 23 villages.

There are 37 villages having bus facilities.

Villages with most of facilities: Kalambuli Ramnagar, Asu, Jagalbet, Aveda, Kateli (Kumbar Wada) Joida, Ulavi.

Villages without amenities (Education): Payaswadi, Kunagini, Aveda Poppal Wadi, Durg, Bori, Varande, Kasarle, Bandoda, Pisose, Velif Kumbeli, Kumbral, Bamanawadi, Durgi, Kasarwadi, Donshet, Usoda, Pusheli, Kurandi, Konda (Haliyal), Badgund, Samjoida, Chapakhand, Amagaon, Katel, Devulli (Joida), Tinai Khand, Kumbeli, Chinchkhand, Tulasgeri, Vadkal, Bedasgadde, Neturge, Birkhol..

Scheduled Castes: Out of the total population of 48914 persons, 3127 persons (6.39%) belong to Scheduled Castes.

The villages having less than 10% SC population are Viranjol, Palada, Rangarook, Varlewadi, Vatala Karambal, Anamod, Devulli (Tinai), Payaswadi Chandawadi, Konshet, Kunagini, Ivoli Aveda Poppal Wadi, Iliye Dabe, Durg, Chapali , Asu Bori, Shindholi, Varande, Wada, Kasarle, Boregali Kamra, Bandoda, Pisose, Viral, Bazar Kunang Kuveshi, Diggi, Asulli, Velif Kumbeli, Miras Kumbeli Amshet, Malamba, Vaijagaon, Timbholi, Kumbral, Vaini Bamanawadi, Durgi, Kasarwadi, Shingargaon, Kudalgaon Donshet, Usoda, Pusheli, Jagalbet, Kurandi Konda (Haliyal), Badgund , Ambeli , Panjeli Karanjoida, Nagoda, Chapakhand, Amarde, Bapeli Khodli, Birampali, Pradhani, Sangave, Gavegali Phansoli, Virnoli, Amagaon, Kundal, Zalawali, Terali Deriye, Katel, Kateli (Kumbar Wada), Nujji, Badpoli Anashi, Nigundi, Kalasai, Godashet, Chapoli (Kalsai) Devulli (Joida), Tinai Khand, Hudasa, Kumbeli Avurli, Gangoda, Ambolli, Gund, Nandigadde Chinchkhand, Kariyadi, Chafer, Tulasgeri, Vadkal Bedasgadde, Shevali, Yeramukh, Shivapur, Hebbal Ulavi, Kodthalli, Neturge, Birkhol.

The village having more than 50% SC population is None.

Sex ratio of Scheduled Caste population is 493.

Scheduled Castes Literates and Illiterates by Sex:

	Persons	Males	Females
Literate	1,693	1,024	669
Illiterate	1,434	560	874
Literacy rate	64.3	76.3	51.8
Graduate	71	56	15

Scheduled Castes (Dominant):

Mahar etc., Bhambi etc., Holaya etc., Banjara etc. Bhovi

For their cultural identity please see Appendix-I

Villages without Scheduled Castes: There are 64 villages without any scheduled caste population.

Scheduled Tribes: Out of the total population of 48914 persons, 813 persons (1.66%) belong to Scheduled Tribes.

The villages having less than 10% ST population are Viranjol, Palada, Rangarook, Varlewadi, Akheti Vatala, Karambal, Anamod, Kalambuli, Devulli (Tinai) Payaswadi, Chandawadi, Konshet, Kunagini, Ivoli Aveda Poppal Wadi, Iliye Dabe, Durg, Chapali

Ramnagar , Asu, Bori, Shindholi, Varande, Wada Kasarle, Boregali, Kamra, Bandoda, Pisose, Viral Bazar Kunang, Kuveshi, Diggi, Asulli, Velif Kumbeli Miras Kumbeli, Amshet, Malamba, Vaijagaon, Timbholi Kumbral, Vaini, Bamanawadi, Durgi, Kasarwadi Shingargaon, Kudalgaon, Donshet, Pusheli, Jagalbet Kurandi, Aveda , Konda (Haliyal), Mavalinge, Badgund Panjeli, Karanjoida, Nagoda, Samjoida, Chapoli (A) Chapakhand, Amarde, Khodli, Birampali, Sangave Gavegali, Phansoli, Virnoli, Amagaon, Kundal Zalawali, Terali, Deriye, Katel Kateli (Kumbar Wada), Nujji, Badpoli, Anashi Nigundi, Kalasai, Godashet, Chapoli (Kalsai) Devulli (Joida), Tinai Khand, Joida, Nagari, Hudasa Kumbeli, Avurli, Gangoda, Ambolli, Gund, Nandigadde Chinchkhand, Kariyadi, Chafer, Bidoli, Tulasgeri Vadkal, Bedasgadde, Shevali, Yeramukh, Shivapur Hebbal, Ulavi, Kodthalli, Neturge, Birkhol.

The villages having more than 50% ST population are None.

Sex ratio of Scheduled tribe population is 487.

Scheduled Tribes Literates and Illiterates by Sex:

	Persons	Males	Females
Literate	365	228	137
Illiterate	448	189	259
Literacy rate	53.7	64.6	41.9
Graduate	14	13	1

Scheduled Tribes (Dominant):

Naikda etc., Kadu Kuruba, Gond etc., Koli Dhor etc. Palliyan

For their cultural identity please see Appendix-II

Villages without Scheduled Tribes: There are 95 villages without any scheduled tribe population.

Literates and Illiterates by Sex (Total Population):

	Persons	Males	Females
Literate	27,404	16,136	11,268
Illiterate	21,510	8,454	13,056
Literacy rate	65	77	54
Graduate	900	636	264

Agriculture: ***Distribution of villages according to land use:*** Out of 120 villages, Total area (in hectare) is 178322.96, out of that 4.08 percent is cultivable and 2.72 percent of the cultivable area is irrigated.

Sources of Irrigation (Hectares): Government Canal 0, Private Canal 0, Well without Electricity 0, Well with Electricity 0, Tubewell without Electricity 0, Tubewell with Electricity 0, Tank 8.09, River 10.52, Lake 1.62, Waterfall 0, Others 177.28.

Villages with population of 5000 to 9999: Ramnagar.

Villages with population of 10000 and above: None

Distribution of Workers:

	Persons	Males	Females	WPR
Cultivators	8,640	5,571	3,069	39.34
Agricultural Labour	3,785	1,692	2,093	17.24
Household Industry	406	239	167	1.85
Other Workers	9,129	6,808	2,321	41.57
Main Workers	17,202	12,705	4,497	78.33
Marginal Workers	4,758	1,605	3,153	21.67
Total Workers	21,960	14,310	7,650	

Religion: Major Religious Communities:

	Persons	Males	Females	Sex Ratio
Hindu (92.56%)	45,275	22,701	22,574	994
Muslim (4.3%)	2,104	1,096	1,008	920
Christian (2.95%)	1,442	741	701	946
Sikh (0.02%)	12	7	5	714
Buddhists (0.01%)	4	2	2	1,000
Jain (0.07%)	34	19	15	789

Agewise Data:

	Persons	Males	Females	Sex Ratio
All ages	48,914	24,590	24,324	989
0-14	15,581	7,885	7,696	976
15-44	24,094	12,043	12,051	1001
45-79	8,917	4,528	4,389	969
80+	301	124	177	1427
Age not stated	21	10	11	1100

Languages (Dominant):

Marathi, Konkani, Kannada, Urdu, Telugu

Disabled Population:

	Persons	Males	Females	%
Total Disabled	1,156	662	494	
In Seeing	624	321	303	53.98
In Speech	55	26	29	4.76
In Hearing	66	31	35	5.71
In Movement	323	231	92	27.94
Mentally	88	53	35	7.61

TARIKERE

Tarikere C.D. Block lies in the northern part of Chikmag alur district. It is a part of Tarikere taluka. The Block is located at a distance of 56 kms. from district headqu arters (Chikmagalur). There are 249 villages in the block with the total population of 190,020 persons. Area of the C.D. Block is 1212.11 sq. kms. It is bounded by districts Shimoga, Chitradurga and Davanagere on north, taluks Kadur and Chikmagalur on south, district Chitradurga on east, and taluk Narsimharajapura on west.

Communications:

Roadways : N.H.-206: Direction- Shimoga to Tumkur, Nearest Villages- Malalichannenahalli, H.Rangapura, Thimm apura, Belenahalli, Hurulihalli, Perumenahalli, Seethapura,

Shivagange, Seethapura (Kaval), Chakonahalli, Hosur, Geramaradi, Bettadahalli, Koranahalli, Rajanahalli, K.Chattanahalli, Jannapura, Shivapura, Kotebasavanahalli, Siddarahalli, Pundanahalli. S.H.-24: Direction- Hosur to Hosdurga, Nearest Villages- Chakonahalli, Hosur, Bettadahalli, Siddarahalli, Bettadavarekere, Savemardika val, Makanahalli, Vaderahalli, Doddabokikere, Belibasavan ahalli, Brahmanahalli, Katiganere, Gowrapura , Ajjampura, Sokke, Paravatharayanakere Kaval, Sollapur, Tamatadahal li, Mugali, Begur, Sriramapura, Southanahalli, Gondedahal li. S.H.-57: Direction- Chikmagalur to Tarikere, Nearest Villages- Channapura, Doranalu, Hosahalli, Kenchapura, Lingadahalli (Kaval), Lingadahalli, Kallahalu, Yaradahanklu, Marekallahalli, Pillebeeranahalli, Kamanadurga, Udeva.

Railway Station: Villages- Shivagange, Banoor, Hebbur, Bandre, Ajjampura.

River: Bhadra Nadi- Nearest Villages- Sevalal Nagar, Siddlipura, Gopala, Karkuchi, Sompura, Malikoppa, Lakka valli, Hunasanahalli, Kundurkaval.

Annual Rainfall: Normal Rianfall 857.4 mm.

Ground Water: Availability of the Ground Water in the Basin is 14816 H.A.M. and the utilization is 7315 H. A.M. It belongs to Safe category. Depth to water level 2 to 20 meter below the ground. Most of the wells go down in summer months, according to the Ground Water Estimation Committee.

Soils: Red Loamy and Sandy Soils.

Natural Division : It falls partly in Kudremukh-Bababudan Forested Hilly zone and Upper Vedavati Basin of the Central Karnataka Plateau.

Administration:

Division: Mysore. Parliamentary Constituency: 14 Shimoga.District: Chikmagalur. Taluka: Tarikere. Assembly Constituency: 126 Tarikere. Gram Panchayat: 46.

Regional Area Development Boards: The Maland Aera Development Board.

Fairs: Amriteshvara Temple Jatra: It is held at Amritapu ra in Chikmagalur area in the month of April every year. Amritapura eleven kilometers north-east of Tarikere town, is the headquarters of the hobli of the same name. It has an extensive and splendid temple of Amriteshvara, a Hoysala structure which is a monument protected by the Central Government.

Kendadamonappaswamy Temple Jatra: It is held at Giriyapu ra in about the month of February-March for four days. Giriyapura is situated at a distance of about 15 kms. north-east of Kadur town. It has old temples of Basave shvara and Kendada Monappaswami and also a guddige of Marula-Siddheshvara. A Shivayoga Mandira and an ashrama called Shantidhama Shri Guru Kumarashrama were founded here fifty years back by Sadashiva Shivacharya of Halusw amay Matha of Sakrepatna to commemorate the renowned saint Hanagal Kumaraswamy.

Keshava Deva Jatra: It is held at Tarikere near Chikmaga lur in about the month of November for three days. Tarik ere is situated at a distance of 56 kms. north of Chikmag alur town and 235 kms. north-west of Bangalore.

Karalamma Temple Jatra: Karalamma temple jatra is held at Ajjampura near Chikmagalur in about the month of April for six days every year. Ajjampura is 22 kms. east of Tarikere town, 62 kms. north-east of Chikmagal ur town.

Mayasha Kaliyan Urs: Kamanadurga near Chikmagalur, is situated on the eastern face of the Haba Budan mountains, 32 kms. south of Tarikere town, on the Chikmagalur-Tari kere road, about midway between those two places.

Nuliya Chandayya Jatra: It is held at Nandi near Chikmag alur around the month of October-November for about 7 days. Nandi is seven kms. south-east of Tarikere town, has the Gaddige in a shrine Nuliya Chandayya, an eminent Shiva-sharana of the 12th century A.D. who was an associate of Basaveshwara.

Obaleshvara Jatra: It is held at Gopala near Chikmagalur around the month of February-March every year. Gopala is situated by the side of the river Bhadra, about 12 kms. north-west of Tarikere town. There is a fine but mutilated figure of Veeranjaneya in high relief at the entrance to the locality where there was a fort.

Renukamba Jatra: It is held at Baggavalli near Chikmagal ur around the month of April for five days. Baggavalli, 24 kms. east of Tarikere town, is an ancient place.

Siddharameshwara Jatra: Sollapura near Chikmagalur 32 kms. east of Tarikere town, has a famous temple dedicated to Siddharameshvara. There is a pond, and a tank called Giriyammajikere near the temple.

Someshwara Jatra: It is held at Somapura near Chikmagalur around the month of January for three days. Somapura is 20 kms. west of Tarikere town. A legend relates, that the place had the hermitage of sage Jamadagni, the father of Parashurama and that latter washed here his axe which had the last drop of blood, after a campaign.

Veerbhadra Jatra: It is held at Kalhattipura near Chikma galur around the months of April-May for three days. Kalhattipura is 20 kms. south of Tarikere town. This is the nearest place to Kalhattigiri, a peak which is 1,877 metres (6,155 feet) in height. There is a shrine of Kattin Choudeshvari on Kalhattigiri. Near Kalhattipura, there is a waterfall known as Kalahasti Falls or Kalhatti Falls which is about 10 kms. from Kemmannugundi

Veerabhadra Jatra: Lingadahalli near Chikmagalur is 15 kms.

south of Tarikere town. It marks the transition from mainland to maidan. It has a temple of Veerabhadra and a shrine of Kariyamma. Some paleolithic tools were unear thed at this place. An annual jatra of the Veerabhadra temple is held around May for 10 days.

Zahiruddin Shah Urs: An annual Urs is held at Hadikere near Chikmagalur in honour of Zahiruddin Shah at his dargah for two days. Hadikere is about six kilometres north of Tarikore town.

Villages: 249 **Inhabited:** 206 **Uninhabited:** 43

Ranking	District	State	National
Area	3	61	275
Population	3	96	850
Sex Ratio	7	82	2264
Child Sex Ratio	6	80	2871
Literacy Rate	5	36	1329
Density	5	142	5464
Work Participation Rate	2	120	3323

Gram Panchayats:

Karkuchi, Gopala, Malalichannenahalli, Hadikere, Bukkambudi, Cheeranahalli, Kallenahalli, Thygadakatte, Shivane, Chikkanvangala, Amrutapura, Belenahalli, Bhavikere, Lakkavalli, Kenchikoppa, Halasur, Mudugodu, Nerlekere, Hunasaghatta, Javoor, Anuvanahalli, Gadihalli, Naranapura, Attimogge, Siddarahalli, Bargenahalli, Bettadahalli, Koranahalli, Sokke, Gowrapura , Mugali, Begur, Sollapur, Ajjampura , Baggavalli, Shanubhoganahalli, Doranalu, Gulladamane, Sunnadahalli, Kudlur, Koratikere, Nandi Battlu, Lingadahalli (Kaval), Thigada, Udeva, Kamanadurga.

Amenities:

Education: Primary School in 98 villages, Middle school in 89 villages, Matriculation or Secondary School in 31 villages, namely Karkuchi, Bhavikere, Lakkavalli, Upparabeeranahalli, Mudugodu, Malalichannenahalli, Doranalu, Bettadahalli, Hadikere, Kuntinamadu, Nerlekere, Hunasaghatta, Shanubhoganahalli, Kudlur, Bhaktana Katte, Dandoor, Bukkambudi, Shivane, Hirekanvangala, Naranapura, Hanne, Hebbur, Bandre, Gadihalli, Ajjampura, Sokke, Sollapur, Channapura, Mudigere, Lingadahalli, Kamanadurga.

Higher Secondary or Pre University Courses or Inter-mediate or Junior College in 5 villages of the CD Block,, namely Lakkavalli, Bukkambudi, Shivane, Ajjampura, Lingadahalli.

College in 1 village, Adult Literacy Center in 3 villages., College is in village, namely Ajjampura.

Medical: Hospital in 4 villages, Dispensary in 17 villages, Health Center in 11 villages, Sub Center in 22 villages, Maternity and Child Welfare Center in 11 villages, Community health workers in 9 villages.

The Villages having Hospital or Dispensary or Health Center are Arsikere, Lakkavalli, Mudugodu, A.Rangapura, Bettadahalli, Hadikere, Nerlekere, Hunasaghatta, Bukkambudi, Shivane, Gadihalli, Ajjampura, Nandi, Nandi Battlu, Manchethevaru, Thigada, Kamanadurga.

Drinking Water: Tap water in 123 villages, Tank water in 82 villages, Well water in 114 villages, Tubewell in 134 villages and more than one source in 180 villages.

Bank: Banking facility in 17 villages, namely, Ganjigere, Lakkavalli, Mudugodu, H.Rangapura Bettadahalli, Nerlekere, Hunasaghatta, Kudlur Bukkambudi, Shivane, Ajjampura, Sollapur, Begur Baggavalli, Lingadahalli (Kaval), Ballavara Kamanadurga.

Credit Society in 24 villages Agricultural Credit Society in 21 Non-Agricultural Credit Society in 5 villages.

Others: Power supply in 206 villages, Cinema hall in 6 villages sport club in 206 villages, Stadium or Auditorium or Communi Hall in 206 villages, Post Office in 49 villages.

There are 92 villages having bus facilities.

Villages with most of facilities: Lakkavalli Mudugodu, Bettadahalli, Nerlekere, Hunasaghatta Bukkambudi, Shivane, Ajjampura, Sollapur Kamanadurga.

Villages without amenities (Education):

Sevalal Nagar, Siddlipura, Ganjigere, Arsikere, Kesarakoppa, Sompura, Basavanahalli, Shanthipura, Sale Borna Halli, Vaddaradibba, Hirigapura, Haruvanahalli, Gurupura, Guddadabeeranahalli, H.Rangapura, Thimmapura, Hurulihalli, Gulladahatti, Jodikodihalli, Yerebylu, Hirekathur, A.Rangapura, Ramapura, Chikkathur, Seethapura (Kaval), Sidakanahalli, Govindapura, Chakonahalli, Hosur, Dyamapura, Byrapura, Geramaradi, Lakkenahalli, Mallenahalli, Mirlenahalli, Mudugundi, Medihalli, Soppinahalli, Bommenahalli, Samatala, Savemardikaval, Narasipura, Makanahalli, Vaderahalli, Rajanahalli, Bokikere, K.Gollarahalli, Shivapura, Siddarahalli, Pundanahalli, Billahalli, Nagabovanahalli, Nagenahalli, Karehalli, Jodijayapura, Attigatta, Siragalipura, Makanahalli, Koppadahalli, Hariyanahalli, Shivanekaval, Gijikatte, Rangapura, Banoor, Siddapura, Thimmapura, Hosahalli, Giriyapura, Thyarajjanahalli, Beernahalli, Asunde, Siraganahalli, Annapura, Garagadahalli, Arabala, Mylanahalli, Kallapura, Gowrapura, Attimogge, Thippagondanahalli, Kallasettihalli, Thimmapura, Karanaghatta,

Paravatharayanakere Kaval, Tamatadahalli, Heggadehalli, Southanahalli, Malenahalli, Mallenahalli, Gondedahalli, Baggavalli Kaval, Kurubarahalli, Somenahalli, Chinnapura, Tyagadabagi, Kenchenahalli, Hosahalli, Kenchapura, Ranganathapura, Hulithimmapura, Lingadahalli (Kaval), Shankaraghatta, Ballavara, Yaradahanklu, Marekallahalli, Gangur, Pillebeeranahalli..

Scheduled Castes: Out of the total population of 190104 persons, 44960 persons (23.65%) belong to Scheduled Castes. The villages having less than 10% SC population are Siddlipura, Gundenahalli, Ganjigere, Rangenahalli Sale Borna Halli, Doddakundur, Haruvanahalli Guddadabeeranahalli, Gulladahatti, Kerehosahalli Ramapura, Sidakanahalli, Govindapura, Attiganalu Dyamapura, Geramaradi, Yerehalli, Mallenahalli Lakshmisagara, Soppinahalli, Narasipura, Makanahalli Rajanahalli, Bokikere, K.Gollarahalli, Pundanahalli Kudlur, Billahalli, Nagabovanahalli, Nagenahalli Kallenahalli, Jodijayapura, Attigatta, Makanahalli Koppadahalli, Hariyanahalli, Gijikatte, Anuvanahalli Javoor, Siddapura, Hosahalli, Naranapura Abbinaholalu, Beernahalli, Asunde, Siraganahalli Bandre, Annapura, Arabala, Guddadahalli, Mylanahalli Kallapura, Gowrapura , Attimogge, Thippagondanahalli Kallasettihalli, Rangapura, Karanaghatta, Sollapur Tamatadahalli, Mugali, Southanahalli, Mallenahalli Baggavalli Kaval, Veerapura, Kurubarahalli Nagavangala, Somenahalli, Chinnapura, Kenchenahalli Gulladamane, Yaradahanklu, Marekallahalli, Gangur. The villages having more than 50% SC population are Sompura, Bargenahalli, Gurupura, H.Rangapura Perumenahalli, Seethapura (Kaval), Yalugere Hosahalli, Ramenahalli, Savemardikaval, Kenchapura Shivanekaval, Giriyapura, Thimmapura, Begur Hosahalli, Ranganathapura, Nandi Battlu Lingadahalli (Kaval), Pillebeeranahalli Kallathipura, Kamanadurga.

Sex ratio of Scheduled Caste population is 496.

Scheduled Castes Literates and Illiterates by Sex:

	Persons	Males	Females
Literate	20,308	12,151	8,157
Illiterate	24,652	10,522	14,130
Literacy rate	52.6	62.6	42.4
Graduate	466	387	79

Scheduled Castes (Dominant):

Banjara etc., Madiga, Bhovi, Adi Karnataka Adi Dravida

For their cultural identity please see Appendix-I

Villages without Scheduled Castes: There are 74 villages without any scheduled caste population.

Scheduled Tribes: Out of the total population of 190104 persons, 6581 persons (3.46%) belong to Scheduled Tribes. The villages having less than 10% ST population are Sevalal Nagar, Siddlipura, Gopala, Karkuchi Gundenahalli, Ganjigere, Bhavikere, Rangenahalli Sompura, Malikoppa, Lakkavalli, Kenchikoppa, Halasur Mudugodu, Basavanahalli, Shanthipura Sale Borna Halli, Vaddaradibba, Hirigapura Mandaravalli, Doddakundur, Hunasanahalli Haruvanahalli, Bargenahalli, Gurupura Guddadabeeranahalli, Malalichannenahalli H.Rangapura, Thimmapura, Belenahalli, Hurulihalli Gulladahatti, Yerebylu, Hirekathur, Perumenahalli Kerehosahalli, Chikkathur, Seethapura (Kaval) Siddarahalli, Sidakanahalli, Yalugere, Govindapura Hosur, Attiganalu, Dyamapura, Byrapura, Doranalu Geramaradi, Bettadahalli, Hadikere, Nagenahalli Hosahalli, Vittalapura, Ramenahalli, Lakkenahalli Yerehalli, Mallenahalli, Lakshmisagara, Mirlenahalli Amrutapura, Nerlekere, Mudugundi, Medihalli Soppinahalli, Bommenahalli, Samatala, Savemardikaval Hunasaghatta, Narasipura, Makanahalli Shanubhoganahalli, Vaderahalli, Doddabokikere Koranahalli, Rajanahalli, K.Chattanahalli, Bokikere Shivapura, Mundre, Siddarahalli, Pundanahalli Kudlur, Kenchapura, Billahalli, Nagabovanahalli Beeranahalli, Nagenahalli, Karehalli, Bhaktana Katte Kallenahalli, Bukkambudi, Attigatta, Siragalipura Makanahalli, Koppadahalli, Kanabagatte Hariyanahalli, Shivane, Shivanekaval, Thygadakatte Banoor, Anuvanahalli, Javoor, Danayakapura Chikkanvangala, Siddapura, Thimmapura Hirekanvangala, Hosahalli, Naranapura, Bankana Katte Abbinaholalu, Tadaga, Giriyapura, Basavapura Thyarajjanahalli, Beernahalli, Nandipura, Hanne Gejjegondanahalli, Hebbur, Asunde, Siraganahalli Bandre, Annapura, Garagadahalli, Guddadahalli Mylanahalli, Kallapura, Gadihalli, Katiganere Gowrapura , Ajjampura, Attimogge, Thippagondanahalli Kallasettihalli, Rangapura, Thimmapura, Karanaghatta Sokke, Sollapur, Tamatadahalli, Mugali, Begur Southanahalli, Malenahalli, Mallenahalli Gondedahalli, Baggavalli, Baggavalli Kaval Veerapura, Kurubarahalli, Nagavangala, Koratikere Somenahalli, Channapura, Chinnapura, Mudigere Tyagadabagi, Kenchenahalli, Hosahalli, Sunnadahalli Nandi, Kenchapura, Gulladamane, Mallenahalli Ranganathapura, Nandi Battlu, Hulithimmapura Lingadahalli (Kaval), Lingadahalli, Shankaraghatta

Ballavara, Manchethevaru, Tanigebylu, Thigada Gonagilakatte, Yaradahanklu, Marekallahalli, Gangur Pillebeeranahalli, Kallathipura, Kamanadurga.

The villages having more than 50% ST population are None.

Sex ratio of Scheduled tribe population is 481.

Scheduled Tribes Literates and Illiterates by Sex:

	Persons	Males	Females
Literate	3,461	2,028	1,433
Illiterate	3,120	1,385	1,735
Literacy rate	59.7	68.3	50.6
Graduate	66	55	11

Scheduled Tribes (Dominant):

Naikda etc., Meda, Gowdalu, Generic Tribes etc. Kadu Kuruba

For their cultural identity please see Appendix-II

Villages without Scheduled Tribes: There are 146 villages without any scheduled tribe population.

Literates and Illiterates by Sex (Total Population):

	Persons	Males	Females
Literate	115,328	65,892	49,436
Illiterate	74,776	30,342	44,434
Literacy rate	69	78	60
Graduate	4,704	3,732	972

Agriculture: ***Distribution of villages according to land use:*** Out of 249 villages, Total area (in hectare) is 121211, out of that 44.72 percent is cultivable and 22.1 percent of the cultivable area is irrigated.

Sources of Irrigation (Hectares): Government Canal 3590.87, Private Canal 263.06, Well without Electricity 120.63, Well with Electricity 665.79, Tubewell without Electricity 387.46, Tubewell with Electricity 5516.71, Tank 755.12, River 0.15, Lake 4.15, Waterfall 100.09, Others 575.13.

Villages with population of 5000 to 9999:
Lakkavalli, Lingadahalli.

Villages with population of 10000 and above:
Ajjampura.

Distribution of Workers:

	Persons	Males	Females	WPR
Cultivators	32,346	26,310	6,036	37.04
Agricultural Labour	33,667	15,932	17,735	38.55
Household Industry	2,733	1,650	1,083	3.13
Other Workers	18,592	13,205	5,387	21.29
Main Workers	67,477	50,662	16,815	77.26
Marginal Workers	19,861	6,435	13,426	22.74
Total Workers	87,338	57,097	30,241	

Religion: Major Religious Communities:

	Persons	Males	Females	Sex Ratio
Hindu (92.11%)	175,105	88,667	86,438	975
Muslim (5.31%)	10,087	5,072	5,015	989
Christian (1%)	1,904	975	929	953
Sikh (0%)	3	2	1	500
Buddhists (0%)	5	4	1	250
Jain (0.11%)	216	114	102	895

Agewise Data:

	Persons	Males	Females	Sex Ratio
All ages	190,104	96,234	93,870	975
0-14	54,297	27,704	26,593	960
15-44	94,481	47,076	47,405	1007
45-79	39,017	20,269	18,748	925
80+	2,054	1,035	1,019	985
Age not stated	255	150	105	700

Languages (Dominant):
Kannada, Tamil, Urdu, Telugu, Hindi

Disabled Population:

	Persons	Males	Females	%
Total Disabled	3,473	2,010	1,463	
In Seeing	1,730	958	772	49.81
In Speech	324	193	131	9.33
In Hearing	211	116	95	6.08
In Movement	906	572	334	26.09
Mentally	302	171	131	8.7

TIPTUR

Tiptur C.D. Block lies in the south-western part of Tumkur district. It is a part of Tiptur taluka. The Block is located at a distance of 72 kms. from district headquarters (Tumkur). There are 231 villages in the block with the total population of 163,783 persons. Area of the C.D. Block is 774.60 sq. kms. It is bounded by taluk Chiknayakanhalli on north, district Hassan on south and west, taluks Gubbi and Turuvekere on east.

Communications:

Roadways : N.H.-206: Direction- Shimoga to Tumkur, Nearest Villages- Chowdlapura, Siddanahalli, Thimmalapura, Biligere, Kibbanahalli Amanikere, Hatna, Kamagondanahalli, Rajathadripura, Yagachikatti, Hindiskere, Kibbanahalli, Shettihalli, Sidlehalli, Ramenahalli, Karadi, Madihalli, Bennaikanahalli, Bommenahalli, Kotanaikanahalli, Huchag ondanahalli, Tiptur [Rural], Koppa, Madenur, Mathihalli, Hirebidare, Siddapura, Karikere. S.H.-19: Direction- Chiknayakanhalli to Turavekere, Nearest Villages- Hatna, Badanekatte, Beerasandra, Katigenahalli, Kibbanahalli, Kundur.

S.H.-68 A: Direction- Hassan to Tiptur, Nearest Villages- Thimmalapura, Harachanahalli, Anagondanahalli, Maranagere Lingadahalli, Honnenahalli, Chatnahalli, Shankaranahal li, Thadasur, Melapura, Lakkihalli Kaval , S.Lakkihalli, Bannihalli.

Railway Station: Villages- Aralaguppe, Shettihalli, Karadi, Kuppalu, Konehalli.

Annual Rainfall: Normal Rianfall 736.13 mm.

Ground Water: Availability of the Ground Water in the Basin is 6696.86 H.A.M. and the utilization is 6842. 73 H.A.M. It belongs to Over Exploited category. Depth to water level 2 to 10 meter below the ground. Most of the wells go down in summer months, according to the Ground Water Estimation Committee.

Soils: Red Sandy Soil.

Natural Division : It falls in Tiptur-Turuvekere Plateau of the Southern Karnataka Plateau.

Administration:

Division: Bangalore. Parliamentary Constituency: 19 Tumkur. District: Tumkur. Taluka: Tiptur. Assembly Const ituency: 129 Tiptur. Gram Panchayat: 26.

Regional Area Development Boards: The Bailu Seeme Area Development Board.

Fairs: Gopalakrishnaswami Jatra: It is held at Nonavina kere near Tumkur around the month of April for four days. Nonavinakere is situated about 15 kms. south-east of Tiptur town.

Shankareshwaraswami Jatra: It is held at Keregodi near Tumkur about the month of March for three days. Keregodi is situated about 6 kms. from Tiptur. At the entrance, there are two lions well carved in black stone with an open mouth, which attract the visitors.

Villages: 231 **Inhabited:** 227 **Uninhabited:** 4

Ranking	District	State	National
Area	8	129	783
Population	8	116	1441
Sex Ratio	3	55	1659
Child Sex Ratio	5	65	2609
Literacy Rate	1	23	910
Density	7	53	4564
Work Participation Rate	4	70	1481

Gram Panchayats:

Gyaraghatta, Baluvaneralu, Halkurke, Manakikere, Sarathavalli, Honnavalli, Gudigondanahalli, Mathihalli, Huchagondanahalli, Karadi, Biligere, Hindiskere, Aralaguppe, Kuppalu, Eachanur, Rangapura, Thadasur, Gurugadahalli, Dasarighatta, Hunaseghatta, Masavanagatta, Gungaramale, Bajaguru, Nonavinakere, Nagaraghatta, Nallikere.

Amenities:

Education: Primary School in 196 villages, Middle school in 125 villages, Matriculation or Secondary School in 37 villages, namely Gowdanakatte, Halkurke, Bommenahalli, Baluvaneralu, Honnavalli, Patarehalli, Manakikere, Sarathavalli, Kagehallada Kaval, Biligere, Hindiskere, Aralaguppe, Kuppalu, Ballekatte, Karadalu, Kallushettihalli, Konehalli, Gudigondanahalli, Halepalya, Chikkamarapanahalli, Kotanaikanahalli, Hindiskere, Eachanur, Madenur, Gowdanakatte, Rangapura, Thadasur, Dasarighatta, Belagarahalli, Albur, Nonavinakere, Sugur, Hunaseghatta, Bajaguru, Vignasanthe, Masavanagatta, Bisalehalli.

Higher Secondary or Pre University Courses or Intermediate or Junior College in 7 villages of the CD Block,, namely Halkurke, Honnavalli, Biligere, Kuppalu, Rangapura, Nonavinakere, Hunaseghatta.

College in 0 village, Adult Literacy Center in 0 village.

Medical: Hospital in 0 village, Dispensary in 9 villages, Health Center in 9 villages, Sub Center in 27 villages, Maternity and Child Welfare Center in 0 village, Community health workers in 0 village.

The Villages having Hospital or Dispensary or Health Center are Baluvaneralu, Aralaguppe, Konehalli, Rangapura, Thadasur, Ramachandrapura, Burudeghatta, Ganganaghatta, Masavanagatta.

Drinking Water: Tap water in 39 villages, Tank water in 11 villages, Well water in 12 villages, Tubewell in 127 villages and more than one source in 150 villages.

Bank: Banking facility in 14 villages, namely, Rangapura, Halkurke, Baluvaneralu, Honnavalli Biligere, Aralaguppe, Karadi, Goragondanahalli Maranagere, Gurugadahalli, Rangapura, Nallikere Hunaseghatta, Kasavanahalli.

Credit Society in 28 villages Agricultural Credit Society in 27 Non-Agricultural Credit Society in 1 village.

Others: Power supply in 227 villages, Cinema hall in 6 villages sport club in 227 villages, Stadium or Auditorium or Communi Hall in 227 villages, Post Office in 48 villages.

There are 140 villages having bus facilities.

Villages with most of facilities: Halkurke Baluvaneralu, Honnavalli, Biligere, Aralaguppe Goragondanahalli, Rangapura, Nallikere, Hunaseghatta.

Villages without amenities (Education):

Vaderahalli, Halkurike A.M.Kaval, Kenchamaranahalli, Byadarahalli, Halkurke Amanikere, Hanumanthapura, Halugowdanakatte, Krishnapura, Thammadihalli, Badanekatte, Sidlehalli, Karadi, Kattehalli, Eranakall Kaval, Tiptur [Rural], Shanthanahalli, Eachanur Kaval, Shankaranahalli, Chikkakottigehalli, Ballekatte, Hogavanaghatta, Melapura, Lakkihalli Kaval, Voddaramallenahalli, Kurubaramallenahalli, Yadehalli, Agarahara, Nagaraghatta Kaval, Lingadevarahalli, Hullenahalli Kaval, Kabballi Kaval..

Scheduled Castes: Out of the total population of 164020 persons, 25406 persons (15.49%) belong to Scheduled Castes. The villages having less than 10% SC population are

Mallidevihalli, Vaderahalli, Rudrapura, Muddenahalli Halkurike A.M.Kaval, Doddikatte, Kenchamaranahalli Lakshmanapura, Byadarahalli, Halkurke Amanikere Mayagondanahalli, Hosahalli, Dasanakatte, Hulihalli Anivala, Chikkahonnavalli, Sooranahalli Hanumanthapura, Chowdenahalli, Ramanahalli Honnavalli, Krishnapura, Vittalapura, Thammadihalli Patarehalli, Ghatikinakere, Hurulihalli Sarathavalli, Paruvagondanahalli, Vasudevarahalli Kalkere, Gedlahalli, Byranaikanahalli Annamallenahalli, Kagehallada Kaval, Chowdlapura Thimmalapura, Badanekatte, Karekurchi (B) Hindiskere, Mallenahalli, Nyakenahalli, Ramenahalli Kattehalli, Uppinahalli, Shivapura, Ayarahalli K.Lakkihalli, Halepalya, Ramasettyhalli Bommenahalli, Kotanaikanahalli, Hindiskere Shanthanahalli, Kodihalli, Hullukatte, Timlapura Bennenahalli, Honnenahalli, Shankaranahalli Rangapura, Dasihalli, Hogavanaghatta, Melapura Shivara, Lakkihalli Kaval , S.Lakkihalli, Bannihalli Kallahalli, Ramachandrapura, Dasarighatta, Jayapura Hedagarahalli, Karikere, Yadehalli, Basthihalli Albur, Nonavinakere, Kuduvanaghatta, Chiggave Kaidala, Shakunagiri Gollarahatti, Kodihalli Nagaraghatta Kaval, N.Melanahalli, Ganganaghatta J.Mallenahalli, Bajaguru, Vignasanthe, Makanahalli Madihalli, Kasavanahalli, Kasavanahalli Kaval J.Mallenahalli, Hullenahalli, Hullenahalli Kaval Virupakshipura, Matanahalli, Jabaghatta Rayashettyhalli, Sannenahalli, Kallahalli Kabballi Kaval, Gungaramale.

The villages having more than 50% SC population are Thimmarayanahalli, Satheramanahalli, Ginikikere Eranakall Kaval, Bidarammanagudi Kaval Maragondanahalli, Peddihalli, Goragondanahalli Hirebidare, Chikkarangapura, Lingadevarahalli Bisalehalli.

Sex ratio of Scheduled Caste population is 503.

Scheduled Castes Literates and Illiterates by Sex:

	Persons	Males	Females
Literate	13,286	7,719	5,567
Illiterate	12,120	4,901	7,219
Literacy rate	59.7	69.9	49.6
Graduate	345	274	71

Scheduled Castes (Dominant):

Adi Karnataka, Madiga, Bhovi, Chalavadi etc.

Adi Dravida

For their cultural identity please see Appendix-I

Villages without Scheduled Castes: There are 43 villages without any scheduled caste population.

Scheduled Tribes: Out of the total population of 164020 persons, 6463 persons (3.94%) belong to Scheduled Tribes.

The villages having less than 10% ST population are Rattenahalli, Mallidevihalli, Vaderahalli, Rangapura Gowdanakatte, Kodagihalli, Doddikatte Kenchamaranahalli, Adinayakanahalli Thimmarayanahalli, Lakshmanapura, Byadarahalli Halenahalli, Halkurke Amanikere, Halkurke Mayagondanahalli, Baluvaneralu, Dasanakatte Hulihalli, Anivala, Chikkahonnavalli, Sooranahalli Chowdenahalli, Kodihalli, Gyaraghatta, Ramanahalli Honnavalli, Halugowdanakatte, Krishnapura Vittalapura, Thammadihalli, Patarehalli Nelagondanahalli, Satheramanahalli, Ghatikinakere Byrapura, Sarathavalli, Paruvagondanahalli Thimmalapura, Harachanahalli, Vasudevarahalli Harisamudra, Byranaikanahalli, Kagehallada Kaval Chowdlapura, Thimmalapura, Biligere, Badanekatte Karekurchi (B), Yagachikatti, Beerasandra Katigenahalli, Hindiskere, Kibbanahalli, Kundur Gadabanahalli, Aralaguppe, Madlehalli, Mallenahalli Byrapura, Shettihalli, Sidlehalli, Nyakenahalli Ramenahalli, Karadi, Mallipatna, Kattehalli Kondlighatta, Kuppalu, Ballekatte, Uppinahalli Kadushettihalli, Shivapura, Karadalu, Ginikikere Eranakall Kaval, Ayarahalli, Kotigehalli, Konehalli Bidarammanagudi Kaval, K.Lakkihalli, Nagathihalli Maragondanahalli, Gudigondanahalli, Bommalapura Madihalli, Kanchaghatta, Annapura, Halepalya Edenahalli, Ramasettyhalli, Doddamarapanahalli Chikkamarapanahalli, Bennaikanahalli, Bommenahalli Peddihalli, Kotanaikanahalli, Huchagondanahalli Koppa, Hindiskere, Shanthanahalli, Kodihalli Eachanur Kaval, Eachanur, Hullukatte Goragondanahalli, Havenahalli, Hosahalli Anagondanahalli, Maranagere, Lingadahalli, Madenur Mathihalli, Hirebidare, Siddapura, Karikere Chikkabidare, Gowdanakatte, Timlapura, Singenahalli Gurugadahalli, Bennenahalli, Honnenahalli Chatnahalli, Shankaranahalli, Keragodi, Rangapura Chikkarangapura, Chikkakottigehalli, Ballekatte Narasikatte, Dasihalli, Hogavanaghatta, Thadasur Melapura, Shivara, Lakkihalli Kaval , S.Lakkihalli Bannihalli, Kallahalli, Ramachandrapura Dasarighatta, Jayapura, Voddaramallenahalli Aladahalli, Hedagarahalli, Belagarahalli Kannughatta, Haroghatta, Kurubaramallenahalli Karikere, Nallikere, Burudeghatta, Yadehalli Basthihalli, Nonavinakere, Kuduvanaghatta Gopalapura, Chiggave, Agarahara, Muguthihalli

Kaidala, Nagaraghatta, Shakunagiri Gollarahatti Kodihalli, Honnenahalli, Bochihalli, Sugur Nagaraghatta Kaval, N.Melanahalli, Lingadevarahalli Kurubarahalli, Mattighatta, G.Melanahalli Ganganaghatta, J.Mallenahalli, Hunaseghatta Machaghatta, Ballekere, Bajaguru, Vignasanthe Makanahalli, Madihalli, Kasavanahalli Kasavanahalli Kaval, J.Mallenahalli Maragondanahalli, Bidarakere, Hullenahalli Hullenahalli Kaval, Virupakshipura, Matanahalli Jabaghatta, Rayashettyhalli, Ganjalaghatta Masavanagatta, Bisalehalli, Kallahalli Kabballi Kaval, Gungaramale.

The villages having more than 50% ST population are None.

Sex ratio of Scheduled tribe population is 493.

Scheduled Tribes Literates and Illiterates by Sex:

	Persons	Males	Females
Literate	3,723	2,136	1,587
Illiterate	2,740	1,139	1,601
Literacy rate	64.9	73.9	55.8
Graduate	75	60	15

Scheduled Tribes (Dominant):

Naikda etc., Meda, Hakkipikki, Soligaru, Gond etc.

For their cultural identity please see Appendix-II

Villages without Scheduled Tribes: There are 131 villages without any scheduled tribe population.

Literates and Illiterates by Sex (Total Population):

	Persons	Males	Females
Literate	106,015	60,473	45,542
Illiterate	58,005	22,025	35,980
Literacy rate	72	82	63
Graduate	3,607	2,842	765

Agriculture: ***Distribution of villages according to land use:*** Out of 231 villages, Total area (in hectare) is 77460, out of that 67.48 percent is cultivable and 22.06 percent of the cultivable area is irrigated.

Sources of Irrigation (Hectares): Government Canal 319.28, Private Canal 0, Well without Electricity 43.3, Well with Electricity 429.73, Tubewell without Electricity 53.01, Tubewell with Electricity 9388.2, Tank 1297.12, River 0, Lake 0, Waterfall 0, Others 0.

Villages with population of 5000 to 9999: Honnavalli.

Villages with population of 10000 and above: None

Distribution of Workers:

	Persons	Males	Females	WPR
Cultivators	42,174	30,134	12,040	47.55
Agricultural Labour	21,648	6,921	14,727	24.41
Household Industry	3,065	1,876	1,189	3.46
Other Workers	21,813	15,056	6,757	24.59
Main Workers	67,873	49,582	18,291	76.52
Marginal Workers	20,827	4,405	16,422	23.48
Total Workers	88,700	53,987	34,713	

Religion: Major Religious Communities:

	Persons	Males	Females	Sex Ratio
Hindu (96.59%)	158,430	79,641	78,789	989
Muslim (2.63%)	4,316	2,204	2,112	958
Christian (0.21%)	344	170	174	1,024
Sikh (0.04%)	65	40	25	625
Buddhists (0%)	6	3	3	1,000
Jain (0.04%)	67	34	33	971

Agewise Data:

	Persons	Males	Females	Sex Ratio
All ages	164,020	82,498	81,522	988
0-14	41,675	21,202	20,473	966
15-44	81,675	40,648	41,027	1009
45-79	38,352	19,538	18,814	963
80+	2,151	1,017	1,134	1115
Age not stated	167	93	74	796

Languages (Dominant):

Kannada, Telugu, Urdu, Marathi, Hindi

Disabled Population:

	Persons	Males	Females	%
Total Disabled	3,408	1,869	1,539	
In Seeing	1,415	706	709	41.52
In Speech	347	200	147	10.18
In Hearing	282	139	143	8.27
In Movement	1,032	650	382	30.28
Mentally	332	174	158	9.74

TIRTHAHALLI

Tirthahalli C.D. Block lies in the southern part of Shimoga district. It is a part of Tirthahalli taluka. The Block is located at a distance of 60 kms. from district headquarters (Shimoga). There are 247 villages in the block with the total population of 128,403 persons. Area of the C.D. Block is 1240.24 sq. kms. It is bound ed by taluks Hosangara and Shimoga on north, district Chikmagalur and Udupi on south, district Chikmagalur and taluk Shimoga on east, district Udupi and taluk Hosangara on west.

Communications:

Roadways : N.H-13: Direction- Tirthahally to Koppa & Shimoga, Nearest Villages- Talale, Bommanahalli, Melinap adaravalli, Kelanarasi, Bhandya, Kudumallige, Bekshikenji gudde, Bejjavalli, Nandagadde, Malur, Kasagaru, Kudige, Thuduru, Beguvalli, Jambuvalli, Kangalakoppa, Lingapura, Biluve, Odalamane, Bharathipura, Yadehalli, Melinakuruv alli, Theerthahalli (Rural), Buklapura (Rural), Melige, Balagatte, Devangi, Vatagaru, Bekkanur. S.H-1: Directio n- Tirthahally to Shikarpur, Nearest Villages- Muniyur,

Humchadakatte, Kesare, Mandaka, Karadiga, Hadigallu, Halavanahalli, Sannikoppa, Konandur, Halesara, Kolige, Jagatagaru, Jambetalluru, Guddekoppa. Malali, Tyarandoor, Araga, Nijagooru, Hiresara, Neraturu, Sarala, Shirupat hi, Yoginarasipura. S.H-25: Direction- Udupi to Tirthahal ly, Nearest Villages- Surali Bale Bailu, Bintala, Mulubag ilu, Hosahalli, Lakkunda, Kolagi, Megaravalli, Hosuru, Talluru.

River: Tunga Nadi- Nearest Villages- Bommanahalli, Bekshikenjigudde, Kudige, Thuduru, Beguvalli, Jambuvalli, Kangalakoppa, Lingapura, Aralapura, Biluve, Odalamane, Bharathipura, Surali Bale Bailu, Mulubagilu, Guddekoppa, Alageri, Hunasavalli, Melinakuruvalli, Theerthahalli (Rural), Buklapura (Rural), Kelakere, Halumahishi, Mahishi, Hedduru, Munduvalli, Kyadigere, Holekoppa, Dabbanagad de, Nambala, Harogolige, Hosaagrahara, Kulurum, Salgadi, Basavani, Bhandigadi.Malati Hole Nadi- Nearest Villag es- Mulubagilu, Hosahalli, Lakkunda, Alamanepalbasagere, Herabailu, Kodlu, Guddekoppa, Alageri, Megaravalli, Baggodige, Chakkodabylu, Shiruru, Changaru, Arehalli, Kesalur, Malalur, Kunda. Begar Halla Nadi- Nearest Villages- Malalur, Kunda, Bidaragodu.

Annual Rainfall: Normal Rianfall 2671.90 mm.

Ground Water: Availability of the Ground Water in the Basin is 107.08 MCM and the utilization is 16.11 MCM. It belongs to Safe category. Depth to water level 2 to 20 meter below the ground. Most of the wells go down in summer months, according to the Ground Water Estimati on Committee.

Soils: Reddish to Brownish Clayey Loam.

Natural Division : It falls partly in Tirthahalli Rolling Tract and Western Ghats (Shimoga) of the Central Karnata ka Plateau.

Administration:

Division: Bangalore. Parliamentary Constituency: 14 Shimoga. District: Shimoga. Taluka: Tirthahalli. Assembly Constituency: 114 Tirthalli. Gram Panchayat: 39.

Regional Area Development Boards: The Maland Aera Development Board.

Fairs: Antige-Pantige Festival: An intersting folk-custom called Antige-Pantige is observed during the Deepavali in parts of Chikmagalur adjoining the Tirthahalli taluk. After pooja in temples in the evening a flame is taken from the Nandadeepa of the temples and is carried from house to house by groups of men during three days of the festival. They joyously sing Antige-Pantige folk songs which express pious wishes for all-round prosperity of every family and humour, chivalry, compassion and the like in respect of various aspects of life.

Ashwathanarayana Car Festival: It is held in about the month of March-April at Mahishi every year. Mahishi about 16 kms. north-east of Tirthahalli on Tirthahalli-S himoga road, is situated in the midst of enchanting natur al scenery. There are several shrines dedicated to Ashwat hanarayana, Guddada-Venkataramana, Ishvara, Gopala-Krishna and Keshava.

Durga Devi Jatra: It is held at Basavapatna near Shimoga in about the month of March-April. Basavapatna, a hamlet of Hosakere, about 31 kilometers north-west of Channagiri town, is the hobli headquarters of Basavapatna I circle. The village is situated in a narrow valley enclosed with hills.

Gopalakrishna Jatra: It is held at Agumbe near Shimoga in about the month of January-February every year. Agumbe, a hamlet of Tallur, about 32 kms. to the south-west of Tirthahalli town, is the headquarters of the Agumbe hobli. It is situated atop a ghat-head and is about 60 kilometers away. It is a border village between Shimo ga and South Kanara area and the border of Chikmagalur district is also closeby.

Kartika-Deepotsava: It is held at Mrugavadhe near Shimoga in about the month of October-November every year. Mrugavadhe is situated about 26 kms. south-east of Tirthahalli town.

Kesaragutti Rameshvara Jatra: It is held at Balagar in about the month of April every year. Balagar is about 8 kms. north-east of Tirthahalli town on the Shimo ga-Tirthahalli Road, situated on the bank of the river Tunga.

Marikamba Jatra: It is held at Kavaledurga near Shimoga, once in three years for two days. Kavaledurga also called Bhuvanagiridurga is situated at a distance of about 20 kms. north-west of Tirthahalli town.

Marikamba Jatra: It is held at Tirthahalli near Shimoga, once in three years for two days. Tirthahalli, about 65 kms. south-west of Shimoga city, is a taluk headqua rters town which is also a commercial centre situated on both the banks of the Tunga river.

Sarigiro Makkan Urs: It is held at Basavapatna near Shimoga in the month of Safar for one day. Basavapatna, a hamlet of Hosakere village is about 31 kms. north-west of Channagiri town. The village is situated in a narrow valley enclosed with hills.

Shakatapura Samsthana Tengina Matha Festival: Handigadi near Chikmagalur is on the bank of the river Tunga, 12 kms. north-west of Koppa town. There is a matha here called Shakatapura Samsthana Tengina Matha. A sect of Brahmins known as Kotaḍavaru from Kota in Udipi taluk of Dakshina Kannada are its followers. Five epigraphs dating from 1381 to 1448 A.D. which record grants to this monastery, which has been called therein as Muniyur -matha, were found here.

Venkataramana Jatra: It is held at Melige around the month of March every year. Melige about ten kilometres to the south-east of Tirthahalli town, has a Jaina basadi dedicated to Anantanatha. An inscription stone standing here dated 1608 A.D. states that the temple was first erected by one Bommana Sreshthi and that it was rebuilt in stone by his grandsons in that year.

Villages: 247 **Inhabited:** 245 **Uninhabited:** 2

Ranking	District	State	National
Area	3	54	253
Population	6	145	2568
Sex Ratio	1	10	473
Child Sex Ratio	1	15	1120
Literacy Rate	1	16	526
Density	1	9	6112
Work Participation Rate	5	163	472

Gram Panchayats:

Humchadakatte, Aralasurali, Hadigallu, Demlapura, Hanagere, Singanabidare, Kannangi, Triyambakapura, Konandur, Nonaburu, Guddekoppa, Bhandya, Lingapura, Thuduru, Bejjavalli, Kudumallige, Aralapura, Araga, Saluru, Neraturu, Hedduru , Melige, Melinakuruvalli , Mulubagilu, Hosahalli, Megaravalli, Herabailu, Kolagi , Talluru, Bidaragodu, Honnetalu, Arehalli, Thirthamuthur, Basavani, Harogolige, Devangi, Salgadi, Shedgar.

Amenities:

Education: Primary School in 170 villages, Middle school in 103 villages, Matriculation or Secondary School in 24 villages, namely Muniyur,.Konandur, Nonaburu, Guddekoppa, Hallusale, Yogimalali, Aranalli, Kannangi, Kuchhalu, Kudumallige, Yadavathi, Nandagadde, Malur, Thuduru, Saluru, Araga, Mulubagilu, Kodlu, Melinakuruvalli, Theerthahalli (Rural), Melige, Basavani, Megaravalli, Talluru.

Higher Secondary or Pre University Courses or Intermediate or Junior College in 8 villages of the CD Block,, namely Konandur, Attigadde, Nandagadde, Malur, Theerthahalli (Rural), Kelakere, Basavani, Megaravalli.

College in 3 villages, Adult Literacy Center in 1 village., Colleges are in villages, namely Konandur, Theerthahalli (Rural), Kelakere.

Medical: Hospital in 3 villages, Dispensary in 23 villages, Health Center in 9 villages, Sub Center in 34 villages, Maternity and Child Welfare Center in 11 villages, Community health workers in 11 villages.

The Villages having Hospital or Dispensary or Health Center are Humchadakatte, Hodalakutra, Hallusale, Yogimalali, Garaga, Kannangi, Bettadasaravani, Bekshikenjigudde, Sheeke, Guthiyadehalli, Malur, Kudige, Lingapura, Saluru, Araga, Herabailu, Harogolige, Devangi, Katagaru, Basavani, Megaravalli, Honnetalu, Talluru.

Drinking Water: Tap water in 10 villages, Tank water in 23 villages, Well water in 232 villages, Tubewell in 57 villages and more than one source in 214 villages.

Bank: Banking facility in 23 villages, namely, Humchadakatte, Konandur, Aralasurali, Kannangi Bejjavalli, Malur, Thuduru, Lingapura, Saluru, Araga Hosahalli, Devangi, Salgadi, Katagaru, Basavani Kabase, Megaravalli, Honnetalu, Talluru, Balehalli Muthuvalli, Thirthamuthur, Kesalur.

Credit Society in 35 villages Agricultural Credit Society in 31 Non-Agricultural Credit Society in 3 villages.

Others: Power supply in 231 villages, Cinema hall in 2 villages sport club in 245 villages, Stadium or Auditorium or Communi Hall in 245 villages, Post Office in 66 villages.

There are 165 villages having bus facilities.

Villages with most of facilities: Humchadakatte Konandur, Aralasurali, Kannangi, Bejjavalli, Malur Saluru, Araga, Devangi, Katagaru, Basavani Megaravalli, Honnetalu, Talluru, Thirthamuthur.

Villages without amenities (Education): Kesare, Umblebailu, Beede, Hirekallahalli, Chikkallalli, Melinakadagodu, Mandaka, Hosakoppa, Suruli, Halavanahalli, Sannikoppa, Halesara, Kolige, Mavadi, Nandigodu, Agasadi, Udukere, Kittandur, Karakuchi, Shiranalli, Adinasara, Bommanahalli, Melinapadaravalli, Halaga, Jeerahalli, Kalavathi, Neralakoppa, Thotadakoppa, Bhandya, Hirethota, Yadehallipal, Guthiyadehalli, Kudige, Tyananduru, Hemmakki, Lingapura, Beesu, Kavaledurga, Boblihinchuvalli, Khabgal, Kalammana Gudi, Nijagooru, Muktihariharapura, Hosakoppa, Kesturu, Geruvalli, Aralapura, Odalamane, Yadagudde, Yoginarasipura, Bintala, Hosahalli, Kolagibylu, Bogarukoppa, Haralimutt, Hosaagrahara, Ingladi, Kuluru, Angalagodige, Munnurhalli, Hasandur, Manikoppa, Kolige, Shedgar, Thumbramane, Patlamane, Hadaginamakki, Vatagaru, Guruvalli, Kabase, Huruli, Baggodige, Yadamane, Kesalur..

Scheduled Castes: Out of the total population of 128399 persons, 12325 persons (9.6%) belong to Scheduled Castes. The villages having less than 10% SC population are Humchadakatte, Umblebailu, Huttalli, Vatagaru Thorebailu, Hirekallahalli, Chikkallalli Melinakadagodu, Karekoppa, Shankarahalli, Mallesara

Karadiga, Aklapura, Halesara, Kolige, Hullukodu
Kattekoppa, Nonaburu, Aralasurali, Balagodu
Shankarapura, Mavadi, Nandigodu, Jagatagaru
Maragalale, Jambetalluru, Hodalakutra, Tyarandoor
Hallusale, Udukere, Kittandur, Triyambakapura
Virupapura, Yogimalali, Alase, Aranalli, Karakuchi
Hanagere, Shiranalli, Hegalathi, Garaga, Kombinakai
Jogikoppa, Adinasara, Mallapura, Talale
Bommanahalli, Melinapadaravalli, Kelanarasi, Halaga
Jeerahalli, Attigadde, Kalavathi, Thotadakoppa
Bhandya, Kudumallige, Hirethota, Bejjavalli
Hosabeedu, Kuduvalli, Yadavathi, Bylubadagi
Yadehallipal, Shedgar, Guthiyadehalli, Kaveri
Nandagadde, Malur, Kudige, Tyananduru, Beguvalli
Jambuvalli, Shinduvadi, Halasavala, Lingapura
Neralamane, Beesu, Nekragodu, Hosakodige, Kimmane
Bobli, Boblihinchuvalli, Saluru, Mitla Godu, Khabgal
Kadegadde, Hiresara, Muktihariharapura, Beluru
Hosakoppa, Kokkodu, Kesturu, Horani, Geruvalli
Neraturu, Sarala, Aralapura, Biluvehariharapura
Kanaboor, Odalamane, Bharathipura, Nellisara
Yadehalli, Yoginarasipura, Bintala, Mulubagilu
Hosahalli, Shettigalakoppa, Kolagibylu, Lakkunda
Bogarukoppa, Kodlu, Guddekoppa, Hunasavalli
Theerthahalli (Rural), Kelakere, Halumahishi
Hedduru , Kyadigere, Holekoppa, Nambala, Haralimutt
Andagere, Devangi, Ingladi, Kuluru, Munnurhalli
Hasandur, Mrugavadhe, Manikoppa, Kolige, Shedgar
Thumbramane, Patlamane, Almane, Hadaginamakki
Vatagaru, Basavani, Bhandigadi, Guruvalli
Keeranakere, Shuntihaklu, Huruli, Hanasa, Bilumane
Shivalli, Dasanakodige, Kolagi , Megaravalli
Baggodige, Chakkodabylu, Honnetalu, Hosuru, Talluru
Balehalli, Nantur, Changaru, Holalurbetagere
Yadamane, Kasaravalli, Muthuvalli, Malalur, Kunda
Bidaragodu.

The village having more than 50% SC population is None.

Sex ratio of Scheduled Caste population is 502.

Scheduled Castes Literates and Illiterates by Sex:

	Persons	Males	Females
Literate	5,798	3,336	2,462
Illiterate	6,527	2,804	3,723
Literacy rate	54.8	63.3	46.4
Graduate	108	84	24

Scheduled Castes (Dominant):

Adi Karnataka, Bhovi, Halsar etc., Moger
Adi Dravida

For their cultural identity please see Appendix-I

Villages without Scheduled Castes: There are 58 villages without any scheduled caste population.

Scheduled Tribes: Out of the total population of 128399 persons, 2182 persons (1.7%) belong to Scheduled Tribes.

The villages having less than 10% ST population are
Muniyur, Humchadakatte, Kesare, Umblebailu, Huttalli
Alur, Vatagaru, Thorebailu, Beede, Hirekallahalli
Chikkallalli, Melinakadagodu, Karekoppa, Mandaka
Shankarahalli, Hosakoppa, Mallesara, Suruli
Karadiga, Hadigallu, Halavanahalli, Sannikoppa
Demlapura, Aklapura, Hullathi, Konandur, Halesara
Kolige, Hullukodu, Kattekoppa, Hosakere, Nonaburu
Shiragaru, Aralasurali, Shankarapura, Mavadi
Yamaravalli, Bandya, Nandigodu, Khandaka
Agalabagilu, Jagatagaru, Maragalale, Jambetalluru
Guddekoppa, Malali, Hodalakutra, Agasadi, Tyarandoor
Hallusale, Udukere, Kittandur, Triyambakapura
Virupapura, Yogimalali, Alase, Aranalli, Karakuchi
Hanagere, Shiranalli, Hegalathi, Garaga
Basavanagadde, Kombinakai, Jogikoppa, Adinasara
Mallapura, Salekoppa, Venkanahalli, Kannangi
Kikkeri, Singanabidare, Keegadi, Talale
Bommanahalli, Melinapadaravalli, Kelanarasi, Kulunde
Halaga, Ubburu, Attigadde, Kalavathi, Marahalli
Neralakoppa, Thotadakoppa, Bettadasaravani, Danasale
Bhandya, Kukke, Kudumallige, Bekshikenjigudde
Hirethota, Bejjavalli, Hosabeedu, Nayadavalli
Sheeke, Yadavathi, Bylubadagi, Yadehallipal, Shedgar
Kaveri, Nandagadde, Malur, Kasagaru, Kudige, Thuduru
Tyananduru, Beguvalli, Jambuvalli, Hemmakki
Shinduvadi, Halasavala, Kangalakoppa, Lingapura
Neralamane, Beesu, Nekragodu, Tenginakoppa
Tenkabylu, Kavaledurga, Bobli, Boblihinchuvalli
Saluru, Mitla Godu, Khabgal, Kadegadde
Kalammana Gudi, Araga, Nijagooru, Hire Gadde
Muktihariharapura, Beluru, Hosakoppa, Kokkodu
Kesturu, Horani, Geruvalli, Neraturu, Sarala
Shirupathi, Aralapura, Biluvehariharapura, Kanaboor
Biluve, Odalamane, Bharathipura, Nellisara
Yadagudde, Yoginarasipura, Surali Bale Bailu
Bintala, Mulubagilu, Hosahalli, Shettigalakoppa
Lakkunda, Herabailu, Bogarukoppa, Kodlu, Guddekoppa
Alageri, Hunasavalli, Melinakuruvalli
Theerthahalli (Rural), Buklapura (Rural), Kelakere
Halumahishi, Mahishi, Hedduru , Kyadigere, Holekoppa
Dabbanagadde, Nambala, Melige, Balagatte, Haralimutt
Harogolige, Hosaagrahara, Andagere, Devangi, Ingladi
Kuluru, Salgadi, Katagaru, Angalagodige, Munnurhalli
Hasandur, Mrugavadhe, Manikoppa, Kolige, Shedgar
Thumbramane, Patlamane, Honnekere, Almane
Hadaginamakki, Vatagaru, Haluvani, Basavani

Bhandigadi, Keeranakere, Herambapura, Bellangi Kabase, Huruli, Hanasa, Bilumane, Dasanakodige Kolagi , Megaravalli, Baggodige, Chakkodabylu Shiruru, Honnetalu, Hosuru, Talluru, Balehalli Nantur, Changaru, Arehalli, Holalurbetagere Yadamane, Kasaravalli, Muthuvalli, Thirthamuthur Chikkaluru, Kesalur, Malalur, Kunda, Bidaragodu.

The villages having more than 50% ST population are None.

Sex ratio of Scheduled tribe population is 505.

Scheduled Tribes Literates and Illiterates by Sex:

	Persons	Males	Females
Literate	1,128	637	491
Illiterate	1,054	444	610
Literacy rate	59.1	68.3	50.3
Graduate	32	26	6

Scheduled Tribes (Dominant):

Hasalaru, Naikda etc., Maleru , Koraga Generic Tribes etc.

For their cultural identity please see Appendix-II

Villages without Scheduled Tribes: There are 162 villages without any scheduled tribe population.

Literates and Illiterates by Sex (Total Population):

	Persons	Males	Females
Literate	87,260	47,195	40,065
Illiterate	41,139	16,033	25,106
Literacy rate	77	85	69
Graduate	4,363	2,970	1,393

Agriculture: ***Distribution of villages according to land use:*** Out of 247 villages, Total area (in hectare) is 124024, out of that 23.39 percent is cultivable and 47.75 percent of the cultivable area is irrigated.

Sources of Irrigation (Hectares): Government Canal 657.71, Private Canal 6.93, Well without Electricity 303.75, Well with Electricity 249.91, Tubewell without Electricity 0.81, Tubewell with Electricity 337.2, Tank 7187.51, River 319.53, Lake 414.28, Waterfall 47.24, Others 4323.86.

Villages with population of 5000 to 9999: None

Villages with population of 10000 and above: None

Distribution of Workers:

	Persons	Males	Females	WPR
Cultivators	31,309	19,882	11,427	41.72
Agricultural Labour	30,228	12,018	18,210	40.28
Household Industry	1,968	751	1,217	2.62
Other Workers	11,533	8,768	2,765	15.37
Main Workers	55,575	38,142	17,433	74.06
Marginal Workers	19,463	3,277	16,186	25.94
Total Workers	75,038	41,419	33,619	

Religion: Major Religious Communities:

	Persons	Males	Females	Sex Ratio
Hindu (93.79%)	120,431	59,276	61,155	1,032
Muslim (5.04%)	6,475	3,213	3,262	1,015
Christian (0.93%)	1,190	583	607	1,041
Sikh (0.01%)	13	5	8	1,600
Buddhists (0%)	-	-	-	-
Jain (0.02%)	28	14	14	1,000

Agewise Data:

	Persons	Males	Females	Sex Ratio
All ages	128,399	63,228	65,171	1031
0-14	32,577	16,598	15,979	963
15-44	65,369	31,482	33,887	1076
45-79	29,026	14,461	14,565	1007
80+	1,350	641	709	1106
Age not stated	77	46	31	674

Languages (Dominant):

Kannada, Urdu, Tulu, Konkani, Marathi

Disabled Population:

	Persons	Males	Females	%
Total Disabled	2,147	1,209	938	
In Seeing	788	400	388	36.7
In Speech	290	152	138	13.51
In Hearing	159	82	77	7.41
In Movement	639	412	227	29.76
Mentally	271	163	108	12.62

TIRUMAKUDAL - NARSIPUR

Tirumakudal-Narsipur C.D. Block lies in the eastern part of Mysore district. It is a part of Tirumakudal-Narsipur taluka. The Block is located at a distance of 32 kms. from district headquarters (Mysore). There are 132 villages in the block with the total population of 245, 036 persons. Area of the C.D. Block is 594.87 sq. kms. It is bounded by district Mandya on north, and on east with district Chamarajanagar, district Chamara janagar on south, taluks Mysore and Nanjangud on west.

Communications:

Roadways : NH-212: Direction- Mysore to Kollegal, Nearest Villages- S.K.P.Agrahara, Sosale, Binakanahalli, S.Megad ahalli, Bommanayakanahalli, Hosakote, Induvalu, Yadadore, Gargeswari, Algodu, Karohatti, Chowhalli, Nilasoge, Kuruburu, Madrahalli, Muguru. SH-86: Direction- Mysore to Malvalli, Nearest Villages- Hegguru, Bannur (Rural), Nanjapura, Basavanahalli, Maliyuru Chamanahalli, Ranganathapur.

River: Cauvery Nadi- Nearest Villages- Bannur (Rural), Senapathihalli, Jodi Bagore, Uddibagur, Somanathapura, Sosale, Binakanahalli, S.Megadahalli, Muthalavadi , Dodabagilu, Rangasamudra, Honnuru, Muthathi, Ramanatha pura Hundi, Yadadore, Gargeswari, Thirumakudalu, Algodu, Chowhalli, Nilasoge, Hosapura, Hiriyuru, Madapura, Maradipura, Akkur, Maranapura, T.Bettahalli, Madavadi, Holesalu (Kaveripura), Vadayandahalli, Hemmige, Mavinah alli, Talakadu, Kukkuru, Malangi, Kaliyuru. Kabbani Nadi- Nearest Villages- Channanjevadeyanapura, Hosakote, Induv alu, Yadadore, Gargeswari, Thirumakudalu, Byrapura, Hunsuru, Kiragasuru, Kudluru, Danayakanapura.

Canal: Nearest Villages- Aravattigekoppalu, B.Seehalli, Yach enahalli, Hegguru, Thuruganuru, Banagavadi, Hanuman alu, Bhugathagahalli, Madigahalli, Kodagahalli, Bannur (Rural), Beedanahalli, Yadahalli, Nanjapura, Basavanahal li, Maliyuru, Senapathihalli, Ganiganakoppalu, Bevinahalli, Kethupura, Somanathapura, Kolathuru, Hasuvatti, Chikka buhalli, S.K.P.Agrahara, Sosale, Binakanahalli, S.Megadah alli, Muthalavadi , Kayyambahalli, Kargahalli, Doddabagilu, Hunuganahalli, Ranganathapur, Rangasamudra, Basavanapu ra, Hittuvalli, Thumbala, Honnuru, Muthathi, Channanjevad eyanapura, Hosakote, Induvalu, Ramanathapura Hundi, Yadadore, Gargeswari, Danayakanapura, Koppalu (Kalihundi), Madavadi, Holesalu (Kaveripura), Vijayapura, Settahalli, Vadayandahalli, Talakadu, Kukkuru.

Annual Rainfall: Normal Rianfall 718 mm.

Ground Water: Availability of the Ground Water in the Basin is 3209.83 H.A.M. and the utilization is 2269. 92 H.A.M. It belongs to Over Exploited category. Depth to water level 2 to 20 meter below the ground. Most of the wells go down in summer months, according to the Ground Water Estimation Committee.

Soils: Red Sandy Soils, Red Loamy Soils and Deep Black Soils.

Natural Division : It falls in Kabbani-Cauvery Valley of the Southern Karnataka Plateau.

Administration:

Division: Mysore. Parliamentary Constituency: 22 Mysore Purab. District: Mysore. Taluka: Tirumakudal Assembly Constituency: 219 Varuna, 220 T. Narsipur (SC). Gram Panchayat: 36.

Border Villages: (State: Tamil Nadu)- Berambadi State Forest, Kaniyanapura, Bandipura State Forest, Bandipura District Forest.

Fairs: Hemadramma Jatra: The Jatra of the goddess Hemadramma is held at Bannur in the month of Magha (January-February) for five days. Among the temples here are the Kosalesvara, Hanumantesvara, Janamejaya and the Sarovaranjaneya. The first temple is in ruins. There is a Tamil inscription on its south wall.

Tibba Devi Jatra: It is held at Mugur near Mysore around the month of December-January every year. The Desesvara temple at this place is a large building with a fine gopura and lofty lamp pillar in front. The Pancha-linga shrines in the prakara has well-carved doorways and lintels. A number of modern inscriptions on brass-plated doorways, vehicles and bells are to be seen in the Tibba devi or Tripurasundari temple. The top parapet round the temple contains mortar figures of various forms of Parvati, Lakshmi and Saraswati, as also figures of the ashtadikpalakas or regents of the directions, the 10 avataras of Vishnu, the Saptamatrikah, etc. In front of the temple is a beautiful mantapa built in the Sarace nic style in brick and mortar.

Villages: 132 **Inhabited:** 121 **Uninhabited:** 11

Ranking	District	State	National
Area	7	154	1188
Population	2	42	262
Sex Ratio	5	121	2965
Child Sex Ratio	5	85	2885
Literacy Rate	5	139	4269
Density	7	175	2666
Work Participation Rate	1	8	4706

Gram Panchayats:

B. Seehalli, Thuruganuru, Ankanahalli, Hegguru, Hanumanalu, Kodagahalli, Beedanahalli, Maliyuru, Athahalli, Rangasamudra, Thumbala, Kethupura, Somanathapura, Ukkalagere, Chidravalli, Kolathuru, Doddabagilu, Muthalavadi, Binakanahalli, Sosale, Gargeswari, Hosakote, Kiragasuru, Byrapura, Algodu, Karohatti, Madapura, Hemmige, Holesalu (Kaveripura), Settahalli (B), Kaliyuru, Talakadu, T. Doddapura, Kotthegala, Vatalu, Muguru.

Amenities:

Education: Primary School in 121 villages, Middle school in 92 villages, Matriculation or Secondary School in 27 villages, namely B.Seehalli, Yachenahalli, Menasikyathanahalli, Doddamulagudu, Thuruganuru, Kodagahalli, Athahalli, Kethupura, Somanathapura, Chidravalli, Sosale, Binakanahalli, Muthalavadi, Doddabagilu, Madegowdanahundi, Yadadore, Gargeswari, Byrapura, Kiragasuru, Kuruburu, Vatalu, Muguru, Madapura, T.Bettahalli, Holesalu (Kaveripura), Talakadu, Malangi.

Higher Secondary or Pre University Courses or Intermediate or Junior College in 4 villages of the CD Block,, namely Gargeswari, Byrapura, Muguru, Talakadu.

College in 1 village, Adult Literacy Center in 0 village., College is in village, namely Byrapura.

Medical: Hospital in 5 villages, Dispensary in 15 villages, Health Center in 13 villages, Sub Center in 41 villages, Maternity and Child Welfare Center in 3 villages, Community health workers in 45 villages.

The Villages having Hospital or Dispensary or Health Center are Yachenahalli, Doddamulagudu, Hegguru, Thuruganuru, Kodagahalli, Somanathapura, Sosale, Muthalavadi , Kayyambahalli, Kuppaya, Gargeswari,

Byrapura, Muguru, Holesalu (Kaveripura), Malangi.
Drinking Water: Tap water in 105 villages, Tank water in 57 villages, Well water in 116 villages, Tubewell in 62 villages and more than one source in 121 villages.
Bank: Banking facility in 25 villages, namely, Doddamulagudu, Hegguru, Thuruganuru, Kodagahalli Kethupura, Somanathapura, Chidravalli Naragyathanahalli, Horalahalli, Sosale, Doddabagilu Rangasamudra, Thumbala, Gargeswari, Byrapura, Algodu Hiriyuru, Kuruburu, Muguru, T.Bettahalli Holesalu (Kaveripura), Vijayapura, Hemmige, Talakadu Kaliyuru.
Credit Society in 121 villages Agricultural Credit Society in 11 Non-Agricultural Credit Society in 57 villages.
Others: Power supply in 121 villages, Cinema hall in 7 villages, sport club in 0 village, Stadium or Auditorium or Community Hall in 0 village, Post Office in 52 villages.
There are 110 villages having bus facilities.
Villages with most of facilities: Doddamulagudu Hegguru, Thuruganuru, Kodagahalli, Kethupura Somanathapura, Chidravalli, Sosale, Doddabagilu Rangasamudra, Thumbala, Gargeswari, Byrapura, Algodu Kuruburu, Muguru, Holesalu (Kaveripura), Hemmige Talakadu, Kaliyuru.
Villages without Amenities (Education): None..
Scheduled Castes: Out of the total population of 245839 persons, 66278 persons (26.96%) belong to Scheduled Castes.
The villages having less than 10% SC population are B.Seehalli, Hunasagahalli, Maragowdanahalli Goravanahalli, Ankanahalli, Banagavadi, Hanumanalu Bhugathagahalli, Beedanahalli, Basavanahalli Kanchanahalli, Ganiganakoppalu, Chimili Mudukanapura, Seegodipura, S.K.P.Agrahara Pattehundi, Madegowdanahundi, Agasthapura Ramanathapura Hundi, Gargeswari, Thirumakudalu T.Megadahalli.
The villages having more than 50% SC population are Maliyuru, Kempanapura, Kallipura, Chikkalaxmipura Thammadipura, Hasuvatti, Naragyathanahalli, Sosale Kayyambahalli, Muthathi, Yadadore, Hunsuru Chowhalli, Hosapura, Madrahalli, Chandahalli Maranapura, T.Bettahalli, Vijayapura, Vadayandahalli.
Sex ratio of Scheduled Caste population is 492.

Scheduled Castes Literates and Illiterates by Sex:

	Persons	Males	Females
Literate	28,539	16,536	12,003
Illiterate	37,739	17,140	20,599
Literacy rate	49.3	56.0	42.2
Graduate	1,188	1,006	182

Scheduled Castes (Dominant):
Adi Karnataka, Madiga, Bhovi, Generic Castes etc. Bhambi etc.
For their cultural identity please see Appendix-I
Villages without Scheduled Castes: There are 20 villages without any scheduled caste population.
Scheduled Tribes: Out of the total population of 245839 persons, 31849 persons (12.96%) belong to Scheduled Tribes.
The villages having less than 10% ST population are Aravattigekoppalu, B.Seehalli, Hunasagahalli Maragowdanahalli, Goravanahalli, Yachenahalli Menasikyathanahalli, Doddamulagudu, Hegguru Thuruganuru, Banagavadi, Hanumanalu, Bhugathagahalli Madigahalli, Kodagahalli, Beedanahalli, Yadahalli Nanjapura, Basavanahalli, Maliyuru, Athahalli Kunthanahalli, B.Bettahalli, Kanchanahalli Bevinahalli, Chimili, Ramegowdanapura, Kempanapura S.Doddapura, Kallipura, Kethupura, Chikkalaxmipura Ukkalagere, Mudukanapura, Seegodipura, Kolathuru Halavara, Konagalli, Kannayakanahalli, Thammadipura Naragyathanahalli, Horalahalli, Chikkabuhalli Muthalavadi , Kayyambahalli, Kargahalli, Doddabagilu Hunuganahalli, Pattehundi, Madegowdanahundi Ranganathapur, Rangasamudra, Hittuvalli, Kuppaya Thumbala, Muthathi, Agasthapura, Bommanayakanahalli Hosakote, Gargeswari, Thirumakudalu, Kiragasuru Kudluru, Danayakanapura, Bannahalli, Yaraganahalli Karohatti, Chowhalli, Hiriyuru, Kotthegala, Kuruburu Vatalu, Sujjaluru, Hyakanuru, Adibettahalli Madrahalli, Kannahalli, Hosahalli, Madapura Chandahalli, Maranapura, T.Bettahalli, Madavadi Vijayapura, Vadayandahalli, T.Doddapura, Thottavadi Mavinahalli.
The villages having more than 50% ST population are Budahalli, Nagalagere, S.K.P.Agrahara, S.Megadahalli Ramanathapura Hundi, Algodu, Akkur, Kukkuru.
Sex ratio of Scheduled tribe population is 497.

Scheduled Tribes Literates and Illiterates by Sex:

	Persons	Males	Females
Literate	12,311	7,219	5,092
Illiterate	19,538	8,814	10,724
Literacy rate	44.4	51.8	36.9
Graduate	360	324	36

Scheduled Tribes (Dominant):
Naikda etc., Meda, Generic Tribes etc., Soligaru Kadu Kuruba
For their cultural identity please see Appendix-II
Villages without Scheduled Tribes: There are 64 villages without any scheduled tribe population.
Literates and Illiterates by Sex (Total Population):

	Persons	Males	Females

Literate	111,841	64,791	47,050
Illiterate	133,998	60,562	73,436
Literacy rate	52	59	44
Graduate	4,238	3,571	667

Agriculture: ***Distribution of villages according to land use:***
Out of 132 villages, Total area (in hectare) is 59487, out of that 74.51 percent is cultivable and 49.79 percent of the cultivable area is irrigated.

Sources of Irrigation (Hectares): Government Canal 21440.21, Private Canal 0, Well without Electricity 203.16, Well with Electricity 274.17, Tubewell without Electricity 12.14, Tubewell with Electricity 168.17, Tank 53.06, River 0, Lake 0, Waterfall 0, Others 0.

Villages with population of 5000 to 9999:
Sosale, Algodu, Muguru, Talakadu.

Villages with population of 10000 and above:
Byrapura.

Distribution of Workers:

	Persons	Males	Females	WPR
Cultivators	34,529	32,336	2,193	36.04
Agricultural Labour	42,310	27,363	14,947	44.16
Household Industry	1,095	455	640	1.14
Other Workers	17,874	15,182	2,692	18.66
Main Workers	71,101	61,232	9,869	74.21
Marginal Workers	24,707	14,104	10,603	25.79
Total Workers	95,808	75,336	20,472	

Religion: Major Religious Communities:

	Persons	Males	Females	Sex Ratio
Hindu (91.97%)	226,092	115,162	110,930	963
Muslim (3.22%)	7,920	4,131	3,789	917
Christian (0.19%)	461	210	251	1,195
Sikh (0%)	12	5	7	1,400
Buddhists (4.51%)	11,080	5,694	5,386	946
Jain (0.01%)	32	20	12	600

Agewise Data:

	Persons	Males	Females	Sex Ratio
All ages	245,839	125,353	120,486	961
0-14	71,209	36,352	34,857	959
15-44	121,846	62,222	59,624	958
45-79	50,019	25,585	24,434	955
80+	2,622	1,111	1,511	1360
Age not stated	143	83	60	723

Languages (Dominant):
Kannada, Urdu, Telugu, Tamil, Hindi

Disabled Population:

	Persons	Males	Females	%
Total Disabled	3,806	2,119	1,687	
In Seeing	1,849	979	870	48.58
In Speech	468	257	211	12.3
In Hearing	206	98	108	5.41
In Movement	908	570	338	23.86
Mentally	375	215	160	9.85

TUMKUR

Tumkur C.D. Block lies in the eastern part of Tumkur district. It is a part of Tumkur taluka. The Block is located at a distance of (00) kms. from district headqua rters (Tumkur). There are 373 villages in the block with the total population of 267,009 persons. Area of the C.D. Block is 961.24 sq. kms. It is bounded by taluks Sira and Koratagere on north, taluk Kunigal and district Bangalore Rural on south, taluk Koratagere and district Bangalore Rural on east, and taluk Gubbi on west.

Communications:
Roadways : N.H.-4: Direction- Chitradurga to Bangalore, Nearest Villages- Gowdihalli, Nelahal, Chikkaseebi, Devarahalli, Giriyanahalli, Lingenahalli, Thimmarajanah alli, Bommanahalli, Ajjagonahalli, G.Nagenahalli, Vasanth anarasapura, Chikkenahalli, Seebidasarahalli, Kora, Katti genahalli, Kora Amanikere, Hanchihalli, Siddaganga Matha, Basavapatna, Mydala, Chokkenahalli, Singanahalli, Manch akalkuppe, Pandithanahalli, Hirehalli, Chikkahalli, Nandi halli, Thimmalapura, Yellapura, Vaddarahalli, Belagumba, Kundur, Maranayakanapalya. N.H.-206: Direction- Shimoga to Tumkur, Nearest Villages- Kotnahalli, Peramanahalli, Vokkodi, Agalakote, Heggere, Gollahalli, Mallasandra, Hebbathanahalli. S.H.-3: Direction- Magadi to Koratagere, Nearest Villages- Bellibattalahalli, Urdigere, Dasachar ipalya, Byatha, Vitravuthanahalli, Kodagihalli, Hikkal, Kuruvelu, Kempohalli. S.H.-33: Direction- Kunigal to Koratagere, Nearest Villages- Gerahalli, Hosahalli, Lingapura, Chikkagundagal, Hanumanthagiri, M.Gollahalli, Beladhara, Appaiahnapalya, Hirekodathakal, Obalapura, Arakere, Amalapura, Yellapura, Maralur, Amanikere, Nagavalli, Nagavalli Amanikere, Lakkenahalli, Ballagere, Cholapura, Hebbur Amanikere, Kambalapura, Kalyanapura, Hebbur, Ramanahalli, Kalkere, Gulur Amanikere, Kaidala, Cholenahalli, Vaddarahatti, Banavara, Naruganahalli, Akkathangiyarakatte Kaval, Hosur, Gulur.

Railway Station: Villages- Hirehalli, Chikkahalli, Agala kote, Heggere, Mallasandra.

River: Shimsaha Nadi- Direction- Nearest Villages- Aregu jjanahalli, Madagondanahalli, Myadala Amanikere, Kesarama du, Bommanahalli, Singanahalli, Machanahalli, Manchakalku ppe, Pemmanahalli, Byatha, Kodagihalli, Hikkal, Kadagujja nahalli, Kempohalli, Heggere, Gollahalli, Mallasandra Valagere Kaval, Mallasandra, Hebbathanahalli, Mallasandra Amanikere, Kumkumanahalli, Amani Hosakere, Maralur Amanikere, Nagavalli, Gulur Amanikere, Sankapura, Gulur , Guleharavi, Mudalakod, K.Palasandra, Manchagondanahalli.

Annual Rainfall: Normal Rianfall 740.49 mm.

Ground Water: Availability of the Ground Water in the

Basin is 9341.42 H.A.M. and the utilization is 9987. 84 H.A.M. It belongs to Over Exploited category. Depth to water level 5 to 20 meter below the ground. Most of the wells go down in summer months, according to the Ground Water Estimation Committee.

Soils: Red Loamy Soil.

Natural Division : It falls partly in Madhugiri Hills, Upper Pennar Basin and Tumkur-Kunigal Plateau of the Southern Karnataka Plateau.

Administration:

Division: Bangalore. Parliamentary Constituency: 19 Tumkur. District: Tumkur. Taluka: Tumkur. Assembly Constituency: 133 Tumkur Rural. Gram Panchayat: 41.

Regional Area Development Boards: The Bailu Seeme Area Development Board.

Fairs: Anjaneyaswami Car Festival: Car festival of Anjan eyaswami, held at Settihalli in the month of March for three days. Settihalli is situated about 5 kms. south-east of the Tumkur town.

Kambada Ugra-Narasimha Jatra: Kambada Ugra - Narasimha jatra, is held at Hatyal near Tumkur in the month of March. Hatyal, a small hill near Rajatadripura on the Bangalo re-Shimoga road between Tumkur and Tiptur, a few kms from north of the Banasandra Railway Station, has a temple of Kambada Ugra-Narasimha.

Lakshmikanta Car Festival: Car Festival of Lakshmikanta is held at Tumkur in the month of January for one day. Tumkur is situated at the north-western base of the Devarayanadurga group of hills, on an elevated ground near a large tank.

Narasimhaswamy Jatra: It is held at Devarayawadurga near Tumkur in the month of March for three days. Devar ayawadurga, is situated at a fortified hill, about 15 kms. east at the Tumkur town.

Siddhalingeshwara Jatra: It is held at Siddhaganga near Tumkur in the month of February for three days. Siddhaga nga, situated about five kms. east of the Tumkur town, has now developed into a famous centre of pilgrimage.

Someshwara Car Festival: It is held at Bellave near Tumkur in the month of March for three days. Bellave situated about 15 kms. north-west of Tumkur, is an ancient place and seems to have been formerly an importa nt trade centre.

Villages: 373 **Inhabited:** 358 **Uninhabited:** 15

Ranking	District	State	National
Area	7	90	474
Population	1	30	150
Sex Ratio	10	172	4639
Child Sex Ratio	10	156	4342
Literacy Rate	4	45	1648
Density	5	32	3769
Work Participation Rate	1	31	1092

Gram Panchayats:

Nelahal, Kestur, Devalapura, Sorekunte, Thimmarajanahalli, Kora, Chikkathotlakere, Beladhara, Obalapura, Arakere, Oorukere, Bellavi, Doddanaravangala, Bugudanahalli, Heggere, Swandenahalli, Belagumba, Aregujjanahalli, Urdigere, Seethakal, Mydala, Mallasandra, Hethenahalli, Gulur, Kesaramadu, Hirehalli, K. Palasandra, Galigenahalli, Areyur, Sirivara, Gangonahalli, Nagavalli, Holakallu, Haralur, Maskal, Honnudike, Honasigere, Ballagere, Kanakuppe, Hebbur, Nidavalalu.

Amenities:

Education: Primary School in 269 villages, Middle school in 164 villages, Matriculation or Secondary School in 40 villages, namely Sorekunte, Bugudanahalli, Doddanaravangala, Hanumanthapura, Thippedasarahalli, Kestur, Brahmasandra, Kora, Hirethotlakere, Chikkathotlakere, Beladhara, Obalapura, Urdigere, Siddaganga Matha, Mydala, Kesaramadu, Hirehalli, Byatha, Hiredoddavadi, Seethakal, Oorukere, Yellapura, Mallasandra, Halanur, Swandenahalli, Belagumba, Areyur, Nagavalli, Sirivara, Honasigere, Ballagere, Kanakuppe, Honnenahalli, Hebbur, Doddasarangi, Gulur, Hullenahalli, Honnudike, Haralur, Maskal.

Higher Secondary or Pre University Courses or Intermediate or Junior College in 17 villages of the CD Block,, namely Bellavi, Bugudanahalli, Kestur, Melehalli, Chikkathotlakere, Urdigere, Hirehalli, Oorukere, Heggere, Mallasandra, Halanur, Nagavalli, Ballagere, Hebbur, Gulur, Honnudike, Maskal.

College in 1 village, Adult Literacy Center in 0 village., College is in village, namely Urdigere.

Medical: Hospital in 1 village, Dispensary in 4 villages, Health Center in 9 villages, Sub Center in 41 villages, Maternity and Child Welfare Center in 1 village, Community health workers in 2 villages.

The Villages having Hospital or Dispensary or Health Center are Hirehalli, Seethakal, Honasigere, Guleharavi.

Drinking Water: Tap water in 158 villages, Tank water in 48 villages, Well water in 58 villages, Tubewell in 123 villages and more than one source in 224 villages.

Bank: Banking facility in 22 villages, namely, Sorekunte, Giriyanahalli, Channenahalli, Bellavi Bugudanahalli, Kempanadodderi, Kora Chikkathotlakere, Lingapura, Beladhara, Urdigere Siddaganga Matha, Hirehalli, Mallasandra, Nagavalli Sirivara, Thavarakere, Hebbur, Nidavalalu

Kambathanahalli, Gulur, Honnudike.

Credit Society in 40 villages Agricultural Credit Society in 36 Non-Agricultural Credit Society in 6 villages.

Others: Power supply in 358 villages, Cinema hall in 5 villages, sport club in 358 villages, Stadium or Auditorium or Community Hall in 358 villages, Post Office in 55 villages.

There are 176 villages having bus facilities.

Villages with most of facilities: Bellavi Bugudanahalli, Kora, Chikkathotlakere, Beladhara Urdigere, Hirehalli, Mallasandra, Nagavalli Sirivara, Hebbur, Gulur, Honnudike.

Villages without amenities (Education): Nelahal, Giriyanahalli, Lingenahalli, Bommanahalli, Vaderahalli, Lakshmisagara, Harivanapura, Appinayakanahalli, Devarajanahalli, Bellavi Amanikere, Banavara, Echalakunte, Doddanaravangala Amanikere, Bugudanahalli Amanikere, Bhahujanahalli, Kodithimmanahalli, Sangenahalli, Kenchenahalli, Badachikkanahalli, Veeranapalya, Rampura, Sogenahalli, Kallanapalya, Kestur Amanikere, G.Nagenahalli, Vasanthanarasapura, Katenahalli, Singrihalli, Hanchihalli, Gerahalli, Chindagiripalya, Chikkakodathakal, Devarayanadurga State Forest, Kumbarahalli, Gollahalli, Kondanayakanahalli, Ramadevarabetta, Myadala Amanikere, Suragondanahalli, Ojenahalli, Harohalli, Linganahalli, Hebbaka Amanikere, Seegepalya, Mallenahalli, Thimmalapura, Thippanahalli, Amalapura, Mallasandra Valagere Kaval, Mallasandra Amanikere, Kothihalli Kaval, Amani Hosakere, Maralur Amanikere, Karadigere, Puradakatte Kaval, Gollahalli, Thimmasandra, Nagenahalli, Puradakatte, Honasigere Kaval, Hebbur Amanikere, Voderapura, Pogadamaranahalli Kaval, Pogadamaranahalli, Doddaguni, Thondagere Kaval, Nandihalli, Sarangipalya, Gulur Amanikere, Kallumata, Kondapura, Haluhosahalli, Cholenahalli, Vaddarahatti, Hosur, Manangi, Kithaganahalli, Mudalakod, K.Palasandra, Gangasandra, Honnenahalli, Anupanahalli, Gunigollahalli, Chikkahonnudike, Ramanahalli, Thammadihalli, Chikkakoratagere, Devara Amanikere, Pullasandra..

Scheduled Castes: Out of the total population of 267732 persons, 55414 persons (20.7%) belong to Scheduled Castes.

The villages having less than 10% SC population are Somasagara, Devarahalli, Giriyanahalli, Puradakunte Lingenahalli, Thimmarajanahalli, Vaderahalli Haralakatte, Lakshmisagara, Harivanapura Majjige Kempanahalli, Huchabasavanahalli Appinayakanahalli, Lingenahalli, Chikkabellavi Bellavi Amanikere, Thimmalapura, Echalakunte Gowdanahalli, Bugudanahalli Amanikere, Kannenahalli Hanumanthapura, Kempadalihalli, Kolalakunte Bhahujanahalli, Thippedasarahalli, Nandihalli Sangenahalli, Kenchenahalli, Badachikkanahalli Veeranapalya, Rampura, Kallanapalya Kestur Amanikere, G.Nagenahalli, Vasanthanarasapura Buradaghatta, Palasandra, Singrihalli, Muddenahalli Thirumalapalya, Gerahalli, Lingapura, Hanumanthagiri Chikkakodathakal, Channamuddenahalli Devarayanadurga State Forest, Kumbarahalli Durgadahalli, Devarayanadurga, Ramadevarabetta Siddaganga Matha, Myadala Amanikere, Bommanahalli Machanahalli, Manchakalkuppe, Sangapura Vitravuthanahalli, Hikkal, Kadagujjanahalli Suragondanahalli, Harohalli, Gidaganahalli Linganahalli, Hebbaka Amanikere, Seegepalya, Kuppur Mallasandra Valagere Kaval, Mallasandra Amanikere Lakshmanasandra, Amani Hosakere, Maralur Amanikere Samudranahalli, Channigappanapalya, Mallappanahalli Gollahalli, Pannasandra, Thimmasandra, Nagenahalli Kodimuddanahalli, Rayapura, Bommanahalli Ragimuddanahalli, Honasigere Kaval, Honasigere Singanapalya, Ramakrishnapura, Doddagollahalli Kuduvanakunte, Thimmasandara, Hebbur Amanikere Kalyanapura, Pogadamaranahalli, Chikkapura Karenahalli, Bannikuppe, Sangalapura, Narasapura Thimmanapalya, Huliyapura, Thondagere Kaval Gulur Amanikere, Kallumata, Cholenahalli Shettappanahalli, Hosur, Kithaganahalli, Sankapura Mudalakod, Gowripura, Gangasandra Gandhamachanahalli, Arehalli, Kothigegollahalli Gunigollahalli, Buchanahalli, Chikkahonnudike Varadanahalli, Jolumaranahalli, Thammadihalli Pullasandra.

The villages having more than 50% SC population are Nagarjunahalli, Devarajanahalli, Kodithimmanahalli Nayakanapalya, Sogenahalli, Kallasettigunte Obalapura, Thimmanayakanahalli, Janupanahalli Kondanayakanahalli, Ojenahalli, Dyapenahalli Pandithanahalli, Balagere Kaval, Doddaguni Honnenahalli, Bychapura, Siddapura.

Sex ratio of Scheduled Caste population is 490.

Scheduled Castes Literates and Illiterates by Sex:

	Persons	Males	Females
Literate	27,012	16,262	10,750
Illiterate	28,402	12,014	16,388
Literacy rate	56.4	66.6	45.7
Graduate	770	682	88

Scheduled Castes (Dominant):

Adi Karnataka, Madiga, Adi Dravida, Bhovi
Chalavadi etc.

For their cultural identity please see Appendix-I

Villages without Scheduled Castes: There are 75 villages without any scheduled caste population.

Scheduled Tribes: Out of the total population of 267732 persons, 19641 persons (7.34%) belong to Scheduled Tribes.

The villages having less than 10% ST population are Mallenahalli, Gowdihalli, Somasagara, Puradakunte Thimmarajanahalli, Kurikempanahalli, Bommanahalli Haralakatte, Lakshmisagara, Harivanapura Majjige Kempanahalli, Appinayakanahalli Devarajanahalli, Channenahalli, Lingenahalli Chikkabellavi, T.Gollahalli, Singipura, Aslipura Banavara, Thimmalapura, Echalakunte, Agalagunte Bugudanahalli, Gowdanahalli, Kaggere, Kotnahalli Doddanaravangala, Bugudanahalli Amanikere Kannenahalli, Hanumanthapura, Kodithimmanahalli Nandihalli, Shambonahalli, Sangenahalli Kenchenahalli, Kodihalli, Basappanapalya Badachikkanahalli, Veeranapalya, Gowragondanahalli Rampura, Konthihalli, Bittanakurike, Nayakanapalya Amruthagiri, Sogenahalli, Kestur Amanikere Vasanthanarasapura, Chikkenahalli, Buradaghatta Katenahalli, Palasandra, Kallasettigunte Honnenahalli, Karikere, Hariyappanahalli Kattigenahalli, Kora Amanikere, Hanchihalli Melehalli, Muddenahalli, Hirethotlakere Chikkathotlakere, Thirumalapalya, Hiregundagal Gerahalli, Lingapura, Chikkagundagal, Bommanahalli Narasipura, Chindagiripalya, Kenchanapalya Hanumanthagiri, M.Gollahalli, Beladhara Appaiahnapalya, Hirekodathakal, Obalapura Ahobala Agrahara, Channamuddenahalli Devarayanadurga State Forest, Anupanahalli Thimmanayakanahalli, Kumbarahalli, Devarayanadurga Urdigere, Aregujjanahalli, Madagondanahalli Gollahalli, Janupanahalli, Kondanayakanahalli Ramadevarabetta, Siddaganga Matha, Basavapatna Mydala, Myadala Amanikere, Chokkenahalli, Kallahalli Kesaramadu, Bommanahalli, Singanahalli, Machanahalli Pandithanahalli, Hirehalli, Kolihalli, Sangapura Chikkahalli, Nandihalli, Vadekal, Vitravuthanahalli Kodagihalli, Hikkal, Kuruvelu, Kadagujjanahalli Sathagatta, Hiredoddavadi, Suragondanahalli Ojenahalli, Kalenahalli, Harohalli, Dyapenahalli Gidaganahalli, Linganahalli, Narasapura, Hebbaka Hebbaka Amanikere, Kuchangi, Ramagondanahalli Mallenahalli, Thimmalapura, Arakere, Thippanahalli Ajjappanahalli, Yellapura, Hosahalli, Haronahalli Agalakote, Heggere, Gollahalli Mallasandra Valagere Kaval, Kothihalli Kaval Kumkumanahalli, Lakshmanasandra, Amani Hosakere Maralur Amanikere, Beeranakal, Mutsandra Pandithanahalli, Maranayakanapalya, Gulaganjihalli Samudranahalli, Channigappanapalya, Siddappanapalya Mallappanahalli, Karadigere Kaval, Karadigere Menasandra, Makanahalli, Govindarajapura Puradakatte Kaval, Gollahalli, Bidarakatte Dommanakuppe, Pannasandra, Sopanahalli, Thimmasandra Nagavalli, Nagenahalli, Gangonahalli Kodimuddanahalli, Sirivara, Rayapura, Bommanahalli Ragimuddanahalli, Lingapura, Lakkenahalli Honasigere Kaval, Honasigere, Singanapalya Yeladahalli, Ballagere, Cholapura, Kembalalu Kanakuppe, Ramakrishnapura, Doddagollahalli Kuduvanakunte, Bisalahalli, Garagadakuppe Thimmasandara, Rayavara, Hebbur Amanikere Kambalapura, Kalyanapura, Voderapura, Balagere Kaval Pogadamaranahalli Kaval, Chikkapura, Begur Thavarakere, Bidanagere, Honnenahalli, Karanakuppe Hebbur, Ramanahalli, Bychanahalli, Bannikuppe Kalkere, Sangalapura, Narasapura, Doddaguni Narayanakere, Thimmanapalya, Nidavalalu, Thondagere Huliyapura, Thondagere Kaval, Yellapura Chikkasarangi, Hosahalli, Kambathanahalli Gulur Amanikere, Hethenahalli, Kallumata, Kondapura Haluhosahalli, Cholenahalli, Shettappanahalli Vaddarahatti, Banavara, Akkathangiyarakatte Kaval Hosur, Kithaganahalli, Sankapura, Gulur , Guleharavi Mudalakod, K.Palasandra, Manchagondanahalli Gowripura, Gangasandra, Honnenahalli, Hullenahalli Virupasandra, Anupanahalli, Honnudike Veeranaikanahalli, Gandhamachanahalli, Arehalli Cholamballi, Kowthamaranahalli, Byrasandra, Haralur Gudipalasandra, Bychapura, Kethohalli, Inapura Gunigollahalli, Buchanahalli, Chikkahonnudike Kodihalli, Ramanahalli, Varadanahalli, Siddapura Bidarakatte, Thammadihalli, Bommanahalli.

The villages having more than 50% ST population are Devarahalli, Lingenahalli, Vaderahalli Doddaveeranahalli, Kempadalihalli, Bhahujanahalli Thippedasarahalli, Kallanapalya, G.Nagenahalli Kuppur.

Sex ratio of Scheduled tribe population is 485.

Scheduled Tribes Literates and Illiterates by Sex:

	Persons	Males	Females
Literate	10,837	6,536	4,301
Illiterate	8,804	3,580	5,224
Literacy rate	62.6	73.2	51.3

Graduate	289	232	57

Scheduled Tribes (Dominant):
Naikda etc., Chodhara, Generic Tribes etc., Meda Kadu Kuruba

For their cultural identity please see Appendix-II

Villages without Scheduled Tribes: There are 159 villages without any scheduled tribe population.

Literates and Illiterates by Sex (Total Population):

	Persons	Males	Females
Literate	157,558	94,266	63,292
Illiterate	110,174	44,802	65,372
Literacy rate	67	77	56
Graduate	5,423	4,392	1,031

Agriculture: *Distribution of villages according to land use:* Out of 373 villages, Total area (in hectare) is 96124, out of that 66.74 percent is cultivable and 24.39 percent of the cultivable area is irrigated.

Sources of Irrigation (Hectares): Government Canal 164.11, Private Canal 0, Well without Electricity 7.28, Well with Electricity 582.08, Tubewell without Electricity 172.26, Tubewell with Electricity 10168.06, Tank 3956.91, River 3.4, Lake 0.23, Waterfall 107.65, Others 485.58.

Villages with population of 5000 to 9999:
Siddaganga Matha, Hebbur.

Villages with population of 10000 and above: None

Distribution of Workers:

	Persons	Males	Females	WPR
Cultivators	76,100	46,058	30,042	51.68
Agricultural Labour	34,541	12,106	22,435	23.46
Household Industry	4,816	1,367	3,449	3.27
Other Workers	31,801	24,344	7,457	21.6
Main Workers	113,216	76,145	37,071	76.88
Marginal Workers	34,042	7,730	26,312	23.12
Total Workers	147,258	83,875	63,383	

Religion: Major Religious Communities:

	Persons	Males	Females	Sex Ratio
Hindu (91.63%)	245,313	127,546	117,767	923
Muslim (7.78%)	20,838	10,712	10,126	945
Christian (0.27%)	720	302	418	1,384
Sikh (0.01%)	30	21	9	429
Buddhists (0.04%)	95	47	48	1,021
Jain (0.07%)	182	115	67	583

Agewise Data:

	Persons	Males	Females	Sex Ratio
All ages	267,732	139,068	128,664	925
0-14	81,317	43,798	37,519	857
15-44	127,367	65,227	62,140	953
45-79	55,915	28,544	27,371	959
80+	2,946	1,382	1,564	1132
Age not stated	187	117	70	598

Languages (Dominant):
Kannada, Urdu, Telugu, Tamil, Marathi

Disabled Population:

	Persons	Males	Females	%
Total Disabled	4,597	2,663	1,934	
In Seeing	2,151	1,249	902	46.79
In Speech	518	282	236	11.27
In Hearing	237	114	123	5.16
In Movement	1,288	796	492	28.02
Mentally	403	222	181	8.77

TURUVEKERE

Turuvekere C.D. Block lies in the southern part of Tumkur district. It is a part of Turuvekere taluka. The Block is located at a distance of 72 kms. from district headqu arters (Tumkur). There are 243 villages in the block with the total population of 156,104 persons. Area of the C.D. Block is 772.88 sq. kms. It is bounded by taluks Gubbi and Tiptur on north, districts Hassan and Mandya on south, taluks Gubbi and Kunigal on east, and taluk Tiptur on west.

Communications:

Roadways : S.H.-19: Direction- Chiknayakanhalli to Shira ngapattana, Nearest Villages- Bommenahalli, Banasandra, Balamadihalli, Kunikenahalli, Neeragunda, N.Manchenahal li, Lokammanahalli, N.Ganganahalli, Chowdenahalli, Bedisw aste, Tavarekere, Turuvekere (Rural), Aralikere, Madihalli, Kallanakere, Sangalapura, Chikkonahalli, Kachihalli, Honakere, Bommenahalli, Chikkapura, Kerevalagerehalli , Kodinagasandra, Mayasandra, Chikkasettikere, Doddasett ikere, Dananayakanapura Kaval.

Railway Station: Villages- Bommenahalli, Banasandra, Hulisandra.

River: Shimsaha Nadi- Nearest Villages- Malladevanahalli, K.Dodderi, Chikkamalligere, Kodihalli, Doddamargonahalli, Sondemargonahalli, Mallur, Manichendur, Hitalakoppa, Guddenahalli, Kanakur, Dummanahalli, Thuyalahalli, Mallenahalli, Kamanahalli, Koppa, Muthsandra, Tharamanakote.

Canal: Nearest Villages- Sunkalapura, Turuvekere Amruth Maha Kaval, Arisinadahalli, Turuvekere Amanikere, Muniyur, Bediswaste, Tavarekere.

Annual Rainfall: Normal Rianfall 723.8 mm.

Ground Water: Availability of the Ground Water in the Basin is 6724.68 H.A.M. and the utilization is 6132. 26 H.A.M. It belongs to Over Exploited category. Depth to water level 5 to 20 meter below the ground. Most of the wells go down in summer months, according to the Ground Water Estimation Committee.

Soils: Red Sandy Soil.

Natural Division : It falls partly in Tumkur-Kunigal Plateau and Tiptur-Turuvekere Plateau of the Southern

Karnataka Plateau.

Administration:

Division: Bangalore. Parliamentary Constituency: 19 Tumkur. District: Tumkur. Taluka: Turuvekere. Assembly Constituency: 130 Turuvekere. Gram Panchayat: 26. Regional Area Development Boards: The Bailu Seeme Area Development Board.

Fairs: Udusalamma Jatra: It is held at Turuvekere near Tumkur in the month of March for seven days. It appears to have been founded as an agrahara or rent-free village given to priests about the middle of the thirteenth century under the name of Sarvajna - Srivijaya-Narasimha pura, after the Hoysala king Narasimha III, by his general Sovanna Dannayaka.

Villages: 243 **Inhabited:** 232 **Uninhabited:** 11

Ranking	District	State	National
Area	9	130	788
Population	9	125	1659
Sex Ratio	2	20	939
Child Sex Ratio	3	61	2522
Literacy Rate	2	32	1209
Density	10	102	4696
Work Participation Rate	6	76	2355

Gram Panchayats:

Banasandra, Dandinashivara, Ammasandra, Sampige, Sampigehosahalli, Kondajji, Hullekere, Muniyur, Lokammanahalli, Anekere, Kodigehalli, Madihalli, Talkere, Vadavanaghatta, Soravanahalli, Muthugadahalli, Gonitumkur, Thandaga, Kanathur, Aremallenahalli, Dabbeghatta, Mavinakere, Mayasandra, Bytharahosahalli, Manichendur, Settigondanahalli.

Amenities:

Education: Primary School in 192 villages, Middle school in 119 villages, Matriculation or Secondary School in 40 villages, namely Banasandra, Anekere, Lokammanahalli, Pura, Talkere, Muniyur, Turuvekere (Rural), Kodigehalli, Madihalli, Hadavanahalli, Masthigondanahalli, Sampige, Ammasandra, Dandinashivara, Hullekere, Machenahalli, Kondajji, Kurubarahalli, Sampigehosahalli, Dombaranahalli, Kalkere, Thandaga, Aladahalli, Goni Tumkur, Mavinakere, Aremallenahalli, Hulikal, Biganenahalli, Kadehalli, Dabbeghatta, Benakanakere, Byalahalli, Muthugadahalli, Kodinagasandra, Mayasandra, Seegehalli, Settigondanahalli, Manichendur, Bytharahosahalli, Hanchihall.

Higher Secondary or Pre University Courses or Intermediate or Junior College in 9 villages of the CD Block,, namely Banasandra, Hadavanahalli, Ammasandra, Dandinashivara, Hullekere, Mavinakere, Dabbeghatta, Kodinagasandra, Mayasandra.

College in 1 village, Adult Literacy Center in 1 village., College is in village, namely Chikkahalli Kaval.

Medical: Hospital in 0 village, Dispensary in 4 villages, Health Center in 11 villages, Sub Center in 1 village, Maternity and Child Welfare Center in 1 village, Community health workers in 1 village.

The Villages having Hospital or Dispensary or Health Center are Banasandra, T.Hosahalli, Kodigehalli, Sampige, Machenahalli, Thandaga, Bramhadevarahalli.

Drinking Water: Tap water in 73 villages, Tank water in 2 villages, Well water in 6 villages, Tubewell in 35 villages and more than one source in 109 villages.

Bank: Banking facility in 13 villages, namely, Banasandra, Kodigehalli, Sampige, Dandinashivara Hullekere, Kondajji, Thandaga, Goni Tumkur Mavinakere, Dabbeghatta, Mayasandra, Seegehalli Bytharahosahalli.

Credit Society in 28 villages Agricultural Credit Society in 24 Non-Agricultural Credit Society in 12 villages.

Others: Power supply in 232 villages, Cinema hall in 3 villages sport club in 232 villages, Stadium or Auditorium or Communi Hall in 232 villages, Post Office in 51 villages.

There are 146 villages having bus facilities.

Villages with most of facilities: Banasandra Kodigehalli, Sampige, Dandinashivara, Thandaga Goni Tumkur, Mavinakere, Dabbeghatta, Mayasandra Seegehalli.

Villages without amenities (Education):

Guladahalli, Lingapura, Kolaghatta Kaval, Pundareekanakallahalli, N.Ganganahalli, Pura Amanikere, Turuvekere Amanikere, Mallaghatta Amanikere, Gundi Kaval, Shivanehalli, Veerasagara Kere Kaval, Byadarahalli Kaval, Harigondanahalli, Sasalu, Sarigehalli, Basavasagara C Kaval, Bantarahalli, Donkihalli, Vaderahalli, Basavanahalli, Hunisemaradahalli, Chandrapura, Bramhadevarahalli, Vaderahalli Kaval, Devihalli, Abalakatte, Benkikere, Byadarahalli, Rajapura, Byadarakodigehalli, K.Ganganahalli, K.Bevinahalli, Illenahalli Kaval, Burudehosahalli, Kadalagidada Kaval, Doddabeeranakere, Kommaradevanahalli, Koppa..

Scheduled Castes: Out of the total population of 156780 persons, 20879 persons (13.32%) belong to Scheduled Castes. The villages having less than 10% SC population are Guladahalli, Lingapura, G.Manchenahalli Balamadihalli, Ajjenahalli, Kolaghatta Kaval Seegehalli, Lokammanahalli, N.Ganganahalli Kalanjihalli, Pura Amanikere, Turuvekere Amanikere

Tavarekere, Turuvekere (Rural), Madihalli
Dwaranahalli, Mangikuppe, Kallanakere, Sangalapura
Chakuvalli , Yeladabagi, Masthigondanahalli
Veerasagara Kere Kaval, Singasandra
Angarekhanahalli, Veerasagara, Halugondanahalli
Ammasandra, Ballekatte, Harigondanahalli
Sarigehalli, Hattihalli, Akkalasandra, Halesampige
Hosur, Kurubarahalli, Sampigehosahalli
Basavasagara C Kaval, Doddagoraghatta, D.Settihalli
Dombaranahalli , Bantarahalli, Vaderahalli
Ayarahalli, Chikkahalli Kaval, Marappanahalli
Hunisemaradahalli, Chandrapura, Aladahalli
Melnahalli, Muddanahalli, K.Mavinahalli, Kanathur
Bramhadevarahalli, Vaderahalli Kaval
Vittaladevarahalli, Kolala, Hedagihalli, Devihalli
Abalakatte, Nagalapura, Benkikere, Byadarahalli
Karadigere, Mavinakere, Rajapura, Kadesur
Devanayakanahalli, Badagarahalli, Byadarakodigehalli
K.Ganganahalli, K.Bevinahalli, Sopanahalli
Biganenahalli, Illenahalli Kaval, Burudehosahalli
Gottikere, Hindumaranahalli, Dabbeghatta
Benakanakere, Guralamata, Honakere, Mugalur
Byalahalli, Neralakatte, Malladevanahalli
Vadavanaghatta, Angadigere, Muthugadahalli
Kerevalagerehalli , Soravanahalli, K.Dodderi
Doddamalligerei, Kodihalli, Doddamargonahalli
Ajjanahalli, Seegehalli, Haralakere, Gainathapura
Narigehalli, Lenkanahalli, G.Dodderi
Settigondanahalli, Manichendur, Hitalakoppa
Guddenahalli, Kanakur, Dasihalli, Kallunagathihalli
Bytharahosahalli, Ambaladevanahalli
Kommaradevanahalli, Dummanahalli, Mallenahalli
Koppa, Vittalapura, Muthsandra, Tharamanakote.

The villages having more than 50% SC population are
Gundi Kaval, Shivanehalli, Basavanahalli
Kadehalli Kaval, Dananayakanapura Kaval, Ramasagara.

Sex ratio of Scheduled Caste population is 499.

Scheduled Castes Literates and Illiterates by Sex:

	Persons	Males	Females
Literate	10,922	6,409	4,513
Illiterate	9,957	4,054	5,903
Literacy rate	59.6	70.1	49.1
Graduate	263	221	42

Scheduled Castes (Dominant):
Madiga, Adi Karnataka, Adi Dravida, Bhovi
Chalavadi etc.

For their cultural identity please see Appendix-I

Villages without Scheduled Castes: There are 50 villages without any scheduled caste population.

Scheduled Tribes: Out of the total population of 156780 persons, 4056 persons (2.59%) belong to Scheduled Tribes.

The villages having less than 10% ST population are
Mudlapura, Somalapura, A.Hosahalli, Guladahalli
Bommenahalli, Banasandra, Hulisandra, Heggere
Lingapura, Dunda, Bugudanahalli, G.Manchenahalli
Balamadihalli, Kunikenahalli, Neeragunda
Ajjenahalli, Kolaghatta Kaval, Seegehalli
Pundareekanakallahalli, Kolaghatta, Anekere
N.Manchenahalli, Lokammanahalli, N.Ganganahalli
Chowdenahalli, Kalanjihalli, M.Bevinahalli
Srirampura, Pura, Chendur, Talkere, Sunkalapura
Arisinadahalli, Turuvekere Amanikere, Muniyur
Tavarekere, Toremavinahalli, Chikkaturuvekere
Mallaghatta, Mallaghatta Amanikere, Doddaghatta
Guddenahalli, Somenahalli, Kalkere, T.Hosahalli
Turuvekere (Rural), Kodigehalli, Sulekere, Aralikere
Madihalli, Dwaranahalli, Mangikuppe, Kallanakere
Hulikere, D.Hosahalli, Hadavanahalli, Honnenahalli
Gundi Kaval, Appasandra, Chakuvalli , Shivanehalli
Yeladabagi, Masthigondanahalli
Veerasagara Kere Kaval, Sampige, Veerasagara
Halugondanahalli, Dandinashivara, Siddapura
Byadarahalli Kaval, Ballekatte, Raghavadevanahalli
Harigondanahalli, Sasalu, Arakere, Ramadihalli
Machenahalli, Rayasandra, Koppa, Sarigehalli
Jakkanahalli, Hattihalli, Beechanahalli, Kondajji
Akkalasandra, Tovinakere, Halesampige, Hosur
Sampigehosahalli, Basavasagara C Kaval
Doddagoraghatta, Chikkagoraghatta, Chimmanahalli
Dombaranahalli , Bantarahalli, Karigondanahalli
Harikaranahalli, Donkihalli, Vaderahalli, Kalkere
Ayarahalli, Sadarahalli, Basavanahalli
Chikkahalli Kaval, Marappanahalli, Govindaghatta
Hunisemaradahalli, Thandaga, Chandrapura, Aladahalli
Melnahalli, Muddanahalli, K.Mavinahalli, Kanathur
Bramhadevarahalli, Vaderahalli Kaval, Kyamasandra
Vittaladevarahalli, Kolala, Hedagihalli, Devihalli
Abalakatte, Goni Tumkur, Nagalapura, Benkikere
Obbenagasandra, Mudigere, Byadarahalli, Karadigere
Mavinakere, Rajapura, Kadesur, Devanayakanahalli
Naduvanahalli, Badagarahalli, Aremallenahalli
K.Ganganahalli, Hulikal, Habakanahalli
K.Bevinahalli, Biganenahalli, Kadehalli
Kadehalli Kaval, Melinavalagerahalli
Halladahosahalli, Burudehosahalli, Gottikere
Hindumaranahalli, Dabbeghatta, Benakanakere
Beechanahalli, Guralamata, Chikkonahalli, Kachihalli
Honakere, Mugalur, Byalahalli, Neralakatte
Malladevanahalli, Vadavanaghatta, Angadigere
Haralahalli, Bommenahalli, Chikkapura

Muthugadahalli, Anadagu, Kerevalagerehalli Mayasandra, Soravanahalli, K.Dodderi Doddamalligerei, Kodihalli, Doddamargonahalli Ajjanahalli, Sondemargonahalli, Nagegowdana Byala Seegehalli, Kadalagidada Kaval, Haralakere Ittigehalli, Yaradahalli, Gainathapura, Narigehalli Lenkanahalli, G.Dodderi, Mallur, Manichendur Hitalakoppa, Guddenahalli, Kanakur, Dasihalli Jadiya, Doddasettikere, Kallunagathihalli Dananayakanapura Kaval, Doddabeeranakere Chikkabeeranakere, Ramasagara, Bytharahosahalli Varahasandra, Ambaladevanahalli, Kommaradevanahalli Dummanahalli, Thuyalahalli, Mallenahalli Kamanahalli, Koppa, Vittalapura, Hanchihall Muthsandra, Tharamanakote.

The villages having more than 50% ST population are None.

Sex ratio of Scheduled tribe population is 499.

Scheduled Tribes Literates and Illiterates by Sex:

	Persons	Males	Females
Literate	2,276	1,317	959
Illiterate	1,780	714	1,066
Literacy rate	63.1	72.7	53.3
Graduate	55	42	13

Scheduled Tribes (Dominant):

Naikda etc., Soligaru, Hakkipikki, Meda Generic Tribes etc.

For their cultural identity please see Appendix-II

Villages without Scheduled Tribes: There are 163 villages without any scheduled tribe population.

Literates and Illiterates by Sex (Total Population):

	Persons	Males	Females
Literate	97,400	55,847	41,553
Illiterate	59,380	22,213	37,167
Literacy rate	70	81	59
Graduate	3,327	2,713	614

Agriculture: ***Distribution of villages according to land use:*** Out of 243 villages, Total area (in hectare) is 77288, out of that 68.16 percent is cultivable and 22.31 percent of the cultivable area is irrigated.

Sources of Irrigation (Hectares): Government Canal 0, Private Canal 0, Well without Electricity 0, Well with Electricity 27.13, Tubewell without Electricity 125.65, Tubewell with Electricity 9336.2100000001, Tank 2040.1, River 9, Lake 0, Waterfall 0, Others 212.71.

Villages with population of 5000 to 9999: None

Villages with population of 10000 and above: None

Distribution of Workers:

	Persons	Males	Females	WPR
Cultivators	48,920	32,291	16,629	61.64
Agricultural Labour	14,254	5,625	8,629	17.96
Household Industry	1,542	937	605	1.94
Other Workers	14,648	10,452	4,196	18.46
Main Workers	60,870	45,743	15,127	76.7
Marginal Workers	18,494	3,562	14,932	23.3
Total Workers	79,364	49,305	30,059	

Religion: Major Religious Communities:

	Persons	Males	Females	Sex Ratio
Hindu (95.71%)	150,059	74,750	75,309	1,007
Muslim (3.89%)	6,097	2,997	3,100	1,034
Christian (0.04%)	58	29	29	1,000
Sikh (0%)	4	3	1	333
Buddhists (0%)	1	-	1	-
Jain (0.19%)	295	154	141	916

Agewise Data:

	Persons	Males	Females	Sex Ratio
All ages	156,780	78,060	78,720	1008
0-14	41,585	21,010	20,575	979
15-44	75,603	37,172	38,431	1034
45-79	37,509	18,915	18,594	983
80+	1,921	884	1,037	1173
Age not stated	162	79	83	1051

Languages (Dominant):

Kannada, Urdu, Telugu, Marathi, Coorgi/Kodagu

Disabled Population:

	Persons	Males	Females	%
Total Disabled	2,758	1,509	1,249	
In Seeing	1,297	696	601	47.03
In Speech	298	150	148	10.8
In Hearing	165	82	83	5.98
In Movement	709	425	284	25.71
Mentally	289	156	133	10.48

UDUPI

Udupi C.D. Block lies in the western part of Udupi distr ict. It is a part of Udupi taluka. The Block is located at a distance of 00 kms. from district headquarters (Udupi). There are 99 villages in the block with the total population of 374,943 persons. Area of the C.D. Block is 837.73 sq. kms. It is bounded by taluk Kundapu ra on north, district Dakshina Kannada on south, taluks Karkal and Kundapur on east, and Lakshadweep sea on west.

Communications:

Roadways : N.H.-17: Direction- Karkal to Mangalore, Villages- Manoor, Kotathattu, Giliyar, Balkudru, Irody, Pandeshwara, Hosala, Varamballi, Kumragod, Handady, Chanthar, 52 Heroor, Baikady, Tonse East, Uppoor, Kelar kalabettu, Udyavara, Kote, Moodabettu, Pangala, Uliargoli, Padu, Muloor, Bada, Tenka, Padebettu, Nadsal, Hejamadi. S.H.-25 A: Direction- Udupi to Hebri, Nearest Villages- Perdoor, Badagabettu (No.80), Athradi, Anjaru, Bommarab ettu. S.H.-37: Direction- Udupi to Karkal, Nearest Village s- Korangrapady, Manipura, Alevoor, Belle, Kattingere. S.H.-52: Direction- Hosanagara to Someshwara, Villages- Hiliyana. S.H.-66: Direction- Nadsol to Karkal, Villages- Yellur, Padebettu, Nadsal, Nandicoor, Santhoor.

River: Mulkir Nadi- Nearest Villages- Hejamadi, Palimar, Nandicoor, Santhoor. Swarna Nadi- Nearest Villages- Tonse West, Tonse East, Uppoor, Havanje, Bellampalli, Kukkehalli, Perdoor, Bellarpadi, 41 Shiroor, Athradi, Anjaru, Bommarabettu. Madisal Hole Nadi- Nearest Villag es- Haradi, 52 Heroor, Baikady, Uppoor, Havanje, Aroor, Cherkady, Bellampalli, Kukkehalli, Haluvalli, 38 Kalthur, Hosoor, Perdoor. Sita Nadi- Nearest Villages- Balkudru, Irody, Pandeshwara, Moodahadu, Hosala, Kachur, Hanehalli, Nadur, Avarse, 33 Shiroor, Kadur, Haradi, Varamballi, Kumragod, Handady, Matpady, Neelavar, Pejamangoor, 34 Kudi, Nanchar, Nalkur. Suda Hole Nadi- Nearest Villag es- Kurkalu, Belle, Kattingere, Shirva.

Reserved Forest: Nearest Village- Bommarabettu. (Varwadi R.F.): Nearest Villages- Kudi (82), Pernankila. (Pilarkan R.F.): Nearest Village- Pilar.

Annual Rainfall: Normal Rianfall 3406 mm.

Ground Water: Availability of the Ground Water in the Basin is 15073 H.A.M. and the utilization is 6645 H. A.M. It belongs to Safe category. Depth to water level 2 to 20 meter below the ground. Most of the wells go down in summer months, according to the Ground Water Estimation Committee.

Soils: Sandy Soil.

Natural Division : It falls partly in Kundapur-Mangalore Coast, Bainduru-Bantval Plain and Western Ghats (Dakshina Kannada) of the Karnataka Coast.

Coastal Villages: (Lakshadeep Sea)- Manoor, Kotathattu, Kodi, Balkudru, Irody, Tonse West, Haradi, Badanidiyur, Tenkanidyoor, Udyavara, Mattu, Kote, Pangala, Uliargoli, Padu, Muloor, Bada, Tenka, Nadsal, Hejamadi.

Administration:

Division: Mysore. Parliamentary Constituency: 15 Udupi. District: Udupi. Taluka: Udupi. Assembly Constituency: 119 Kundapura, 120 Udupi, 121 Kaup. Gram Panchayat: 61.

Regional Area Development Boards: The Maland Aera Development Board.

Fairs and Festivals: Krishna Temple Festival: Lord Krishna Temple festival is held at Udipi in about the month of January for seven days every year.

Kumbha Sankramana Festival: It is held at the temple of Durgaparameshwari at Mandarthi near Dakshina Kannada. Mandarthi, a hamlet attached to Heggunje, is at a dista nce of about 25 kms. north of Udipi.

Mahishasuramardini Temple Festival: Kunjary, a hamlet of Kurkal near Dakshina Kannada is about eleven kms. from Udipi. The hamlet consists of two small hills, one of which is about three hundred feet and the other of about two hundred feet in height. These two hills are called Kunjarugiri and Parashuramagiri respectively.

Mandarthi Duragaparameshwari Temple Festival: Durgapara meshwari temple festival is held at Mandarthi near Dakshina Kannada every year. Mandarthi, a hamlet attached to the Heggunje, is at a distance of about 25 kms. north of Udipi.

Villages: 99 **Inhabited:** 99 **Uninhabited:** 0

Ranking	District	State	National
Area	3	115	646
Population	1	4	11
Sex Ratio	3	3	55
Child Sex Ratio	1	51	2272
Literacy Rate	1	1	193
Density	2	153	2456
Work Participation Rate	1	4	3694

Gram Panchayats:

Kota, Kotathattu, Vaddarse, Shiriyara, Billadi, Yedthady, Pandeshwara, Kodi, Irody, Haradi, Varamballi, Chanthar, Handady, Barkur, Hanehalli, Heggunje, Avarse, Kadur, Kanjal, Kalyanapura, Tonse , Badanidiyur, Tenkanidyoor, Uppoor, Havanje, Cherkady, Kokkarne, Nalkur, Kenjoor, Karje, Perdoor, Kukkehalli, Ambalpady , Kadekar , Udyavara, Alevoor, Badagabettu (No.80), Athradi, Bommarabettu, Bairampalli, Kodibettu, Manipura, Kote, Katapadi, Kurkalu, Belle, Innanje, Uliargoli, Kaup, Majoor, Shirva, Mallar, Belpu, 108 Kalthur, Yellur, Bada, Tenka, Padubidre, Hejamadi, Palimar, Mudarangadi.

Amenities:

Education: Primary School in 99 villages, Middle school in 97 villages, Matriculation or Secondary School in 50 villages, namely Manoor, Kotathattu, Giliyar, Vaddarse, Kodi, Irody, Kavadi, Yedthady, Hanehalli, Nadur, Heggunje, Avarse, Hiliyana, Tonse West, Varamballi, Matpady, Chanthar, Tonse East, Uppoor, Aroor, Cherkady, Bellampalli, Pejamangoor, Nalkur, Hosoor, Perdoor, Kelarkalabettu, Udyavara, Alevoor, Badagabettu (No.80), Bommarabettu, Kudi (82), Marne, Mattu, Moodabettu, Belle, Shirva, Innanje, Pangala, Uliargoli, Padu, Muloor, Bada, 108 Kalthur, Yellur, Tenka, Nadsal, Hejamadi, Palimar, Santhoor.

Higher Secondary or Pre University Courses or Intermediate or Junior College in 19 villages of the CD Block,, namely Kotathattu, Hanehalli, Hiliyana, Tonse West, Varamballi, Chanthar, Tonse East, Pejamangoor,

Bommarabettu, Belle, Shirva, Innanje, Padu, Bada, Tenka, Nadsal, Hejamadi, Palimar, Santhoor.

College in 6 villages, Adult Literacy Center in 18 villages., Colleges are in villages, namely Varamballi, Chanthar, Tonse East, Shirva, Padu, Palimar.

Medical: Hospital in 4 villages, Dispensary in 53 villages, Health Center in 14 villages, Sub Center in 75 villages, Maternity and Child Welfare Center in 7 villages, Community health workers in 34 villages.

The Villages having Hospital or Dispensary or Health Center are Giliyar, Kodi, Balkudru, Irody, Pandeshwara, Hosala, Yedthady, Kachur, Hanehalli, Avarse, Tonse West, Haradi, Varamballi, Chanthar, 52 Heroor, Tonse East, Uppoor, Havanje, Aroor, Neelavar, Cherkady, Bellampalli, Kukkehalli, Nalkur, Hosoor, Perdoor, Udyavara, Korangrapady, Manipura, Alevoor, Athradi, Bommarabettu, Hirebettu, Pernankila, Mattu, Kote, Moodabettu, Kurkalu, Belle, Kattingere, Shirva, Majoor, Pangala, Uliargoli, Padu, Bada, Belpu, 108 Kalthur, Kuthyar, Yellur, Tenka, Nadsal, Hejamadi, Palimar.

Drinking Water: Tap water in 88 villages, Tank water in 3 villages, Well water in 99 villages, Tubewell in 26 villages and more than one source in 99 villages.

Bank: Banking facility in 59 villages, namely, Kotathattu, Giliyar, Vaddarse, Pandeshwara Moodahadu, Hosala, Kavadi, Achalady, Shiriyara Herady, Kachur, Hanehalli, Nadur, Heggunje, Hiliyana 33 Shiroor, Kadur, Varamballi, Handady, 52 Heroor Baikady, Tonse East, Uppoor, Havanje, Neelavar Cherkady, Bellampalli, Kukkehalli, Pejamangoor 34 Kudi, Nanchar, Kenjoor, Hosoor, 41 Shiroor Badanidiyur, Udyavara, Manipura, Alevoor Badagabettu (No.80), Anjaru, Bommarabettu, Kudi (82) Hirebettu, Marne, Pernankila, Mattu, Kote Moodabettu, Kurkalu, Belle, Shirva, 92 Heroor Pangala, Uliargoli, Kuthyar, Pilar, Yellur, Nadsal Santhoor.

Credit Society in 35 villages Agricultural Credit Society in 28 Non-Agricultural Credit Society in 8 villages.

Others: Power supply in 99 villages, Cinema hall in 5 villages, sport club in 2 villages, Stadium or Auditorium or Community Hall in 1 village, Post Office in 94 villages.

There are 96 villages having bus facilities.

Villages with most of facilities: Kotathattu Giliyar, Pandeshwara, Moodahadu, Hosala, Kavadi Achalady, Shiriyara, Kachur, Hanehalli, Heggunje Hiliyana, 33 Shiroor, Varamballi, Handady, 52 Heroor Baikady, Tonse East, Uppoor, Havanje, Neelavar Cherkady, Bellampalli, Kukkehalli, Pejamangoor 34 Kudi, Nanchar, Kenjoor, Hosoor, 41 Shiroor Badanidiyur, Udyavara, Manipura, Alevoor Badagabettu (No.80), Anjaru, Bommarabettu, Kudi (82) Hirebettu, Marne, Pernankila, Mattu, Kote Moodabettu, Kurkalu, Belle, Shirva, 92 Heroor Pangala, Uliargoli, Kuthyar, Pilar, Yellur, Nadsal Santhoor.

Villages without Amenities (Education): None..

Scheduled Castes: Out of the total population of 376579 persons, 21501 persons (5.71%) belong to Scheduled Castes.

The villages having less than 10% SC population are Manoor, Kotathattu, Giliyar, Bannady, Vaddarse, Kodi Irody, Pandeshwara, Moodahadu, Hosala, Kavadi Achalady, Shiriyara, Kakkunje, Billadi, Yedthady Herady, Kachur, Hanehalli, Nadur, Heggunje, Vandar Avarse, Hiliyana, 33 Shiroor, Kadur, Tonse West Varamballi, Kumragod, Matpady, Chanthar, 52 Heroor Baikady, Tonse East, Uppoor, Havanje, Aroor Neelavar, Cherkady, Bellampalli, Kukkehalli Haluvalli, Pejamangoor, 34 Kudi, Nanchar, Nalkur Kenjoor, 38 Kalthur, Hosoor, Perdoor, Bairampalli Bellarpadi, Badanidiyur, Tenkanidyoor, Udyavara Manipura, Alevoor, Badagabettu (No.80), Athradi Anjaru, Bommarabettu, Kudi (82), Hirebettu, Marne Pernankila, Mattu, Kote, Kurkalu, Kattingere, Shirva 92 Heroor, Padoor, Majoor, Innanje, Uliargoli, Padu Muloor, Bada, Belpu, 108 Kalthur, Kuthyar, Pilar Yellur, Padebettu, Nadsal, Hejamadi, Palimar Nandicoor, Santhoor.

The village having more than 50% SC population is None.

Sex ratio of Scheduled Caste population is 509.

Scheduled Castes Literates and Illiterates by Sex:

	Persons	Males	Females
Literate	14,416	7,769	6,647
Illiterate	7,085	2,794	4,291
Literacy rate	75.0	82.3	68.0
Graduate	567	341	226

Scheduled Castes (Dominant):

Adi Dravida, Mundala, Moger, Bathada, Bhovi

For their cultural identity please see Appendix-I

Villages without Scheduled Castes: There are 0 village without any scheduled caste population.

Scheduled Tribes: Out of the total population of 376579 persons, 15206 persons (4.04%) belong to Scheduled Tribes.

The villages having less than 10% ST population are Manoor, Kotathattu, Giliyar, Bannady, Vaddarse, Kodi Balkudru, Irody, Pandeshwara, Moodahadu, Hosala Kavadi, Achalady, Shiriyara, Kakkunje, Billadi Yedthady, Kachur, Hanehalli, Nadur, Heggunje, Vandar

Avarse, Hiliyana, 33 Shiroor, Kadur, Tonse West Haradi, Varamballi, Kumragod, Handady, Matpady 52 Heroor, Baikady, Tonse East, Uppoor, Havanje Neelavar, Pejamangoor, 34 Kudi, Nanchar, Nalkur Kenjoor, Perdoor, Bairampalli, Bellarpadi 41 Shiroor, Badanidiyur, Kelarkalabettu Tenkanidyoor, Udyavara, Korangrapady, Manipura Pernankila, Mattu, Kote, Moodabettu, Kurkalu, Belle Kattingere, Shirva, 92 Heroor, Padoor, Majoor Innanje, Pangala, Uliargoli, Padu, Muloor, Bada Belpu, 108 Kalthur, Kuthyar, Pilar, Yellur, Tenka Padebettu, Nadsal, Hejamadi, Palimar, Nandicoor Santhoor.

The villages having more than 50% ST population are None.

Sex ratio of Scheduled tribe population is 504.

Scheduled Tribes Literates and Illiterates by Sex:

	Persons	Males	Females
Literate	9,862	5,378	4,484
Illiterate	5,344	2,161	3,183
Literacy rate	72.6	79.9	65.4
Graduate	239	162	77

Scheduled Tribes (Dominant):

Marati, Koraga, Naikda etc., Hasalaru, Jenu Kuruba

For their cultural identity please see Appendix-II

Villages without Scheduled Tribes: There are 5 villages without any scheduled tribe population.

Literates and Illiterates by Sex (Total Population):

	Persons	Males	Females
Literate	282,852	141,805	141,047
Illiterate	93,727	34,646	59,081
Literacy rate	83	90	77
Graduate	16,600	9,669	6,931

Agriculture: *Distribution of villages according to land use:*

Out of 99 villages, Total area (in hectare) is 83773, out of that 39.36 percent is cultivable and 33.22 percent of the cultivable area is irrigated.

Sources of Irrigation (Hectares): Government Canal 0, Private Canal 0, Well without Electricity 1989.41, Well with Electricity 5258.38, Tubewell without Electricity 30.78, Tubewell with Electricity 75.4, Tank 500.65, River 982.36, Lake 0, Waterfall 0, Others 2117.6.

Villages with population of 5000 to 9999:

Manoor, Kotathattu, Tonse West, Varamballi Tonse East, Uppoor, Cherkady, Tenkanidyoor Badagabettu (No.80), Bommarabettu, Belle, Uliargoli Bada, Yellur, Hejamadi.

Villages with population of 10000 and above:

Perdoor, Udyavara, Shirva, Nadsal.

Distribution of Workers:

	Persons	Males	Females	WPR
Cultivators	33,574	18,496	15,078	19.63
Agricultural Labour	30,456	13,036	17,420	17.81
Household Industry	22,124	2,897	19,227	12.94
Other Workers	84,837	65,108	19,729	49.61
Main Workers	149,390	91,505	57,885	87.37
Marginal Workers	21,601	8,032	13,569	12.63
Total Workers	170,991	99,537	71,454	

Religion: Major Religious Communities:

	Persons	Males	Females	Sex Ratio
Hindu (84.21%)	317,102	148,495	168,607	1,135
Muslim (8.13%)	30,603	14,968	15,635	1,045
Christian (7.59%)	28,585	12,848	15,737	1,225
Sikh (0.01%)	25	16	9	563
Buddhists (0%)	17	10	7	700
Jain (0.04%)	161	75	86	1,147

Agewise Data:

	Persons	Males	Females	Sex Ratio
All ages	376,579	176,451	200,128	1134
0-14	93,249	47,367	45,882	969
15-44	185,274	84,906	100,368	1182
45-79	92,841	42,079	50,762	1206
80+	5,067	2,010	3,057	1521
Age not stated	148	89	59	663

Languages (Dominant):

Tulu, Kannada, Konkani, Marathi, Urdu

Disabled Population:

	Persons	Males	Females	%
Total Disabled	6,522	3,417	3,105	
In Seeing	2,584	1,220	1,364	39.62
In Speech	867	460	407	13.29
In Hearing	339	151	188	5.2
In Movement	1,571	953	618	24.09
Mentally	1,161	633	528	17.8

VIRAJPET

Virajpet C.D. Block lies in the south-eastern part of Kodagu district. It is a part of Virajpet taluka. The Block is located at a distance of 30 kms. from district headquarters (Madikeri). There are 94 villages in the block with the total population of 175,337 persons.

Area of the C.D. Block is 1640.38 sq. kms. It is bounded by taluk Somvarpet and district Mysore on north, district Mysore on east, and taluk Madikeri on west. It has common boundary with the state of Kerala on south.

Communications:

Roadways : SH- 21: Direction- Gonikopal to Manantavadi, Nearest Villages- Halligattu, Hysodlur, Hudikeri, Begur, Mugatageri, Bellur, T. Shettigeri, Kumtoor, Manchalli & Forest, Kutta. SH- 27: Direction- Madikeri to Virajpet, Nearest Villages- Nalkeri, Maithadi, Devan ageri, Arameri, Kadanur, Kuklur. SH- 88 A: Direction-

Virajpet to Hunsur, Nearest Villages- Nangala, Balugodu, Bittangala, Kolatodu Bygodu, Hathur, Kaikeri, Hebbale, Arekeri Forest - I, Nokya, Aruvath0Klu, Kunda. SH-88 B: Direction- Cannanore to Madikeri, Nearest Villages- Heggala, Aimangala, Maggula, Arji, Nangala, Guhya, Karadigodu, Siddapura, Puliyeri, Ammathi, Kavadi, Karma du, Nalvathoklu.

River: Cauvery Nadi- Nearest Villages- Nalkeri, Maithadi, Halugunda, Hachinad, Guhya, Karadigodu. Lakshmantirtha Nadi- Nearest Villages- Maldare, Channayan Kote, Hebbale, Devamachi Forest, Arekeri Forest - I, Arekeri Forest.

Reserved Forest: (Brahmagiri R.F.): Nearest Villages- Parakatageri, Theralu, Badagarakeri, Kurchi, Manchalli & Forest, Kutta. (Nalkeri R.F.): Nearest Villages- Kothur, Nalkeri Forest, Kutta, Badaga. (Devamachi R.F.): Nearest Villages- Channayan Kote, Badagabanangala, Hebbale, Devamachi Forest, Arekeri Forest - I, Nokya. (Dubari R.F.): Nearest Villages- Karadigodu, Maldare. (Hathugattu R.F.): Nearest Villages- Kanur, Nittur, Hathugattu Forest I. (Kerti R.F.): Nearest Villages- Palangala, Kedamullur, Heggala, Arji, Nangala. (Urti R.F.): Nearest Villages- V.Badaga, 1St Rudraguppe, Kuttandi.

Annual Rainfall: Normal Rianfall 2450 mm.

Ground Water: Availability of the Ground Water in the Basin is 119.53 MCM and the utilization is 3043.09 MCM. It belongs to Safe category. Depth to water level 2 to 20 meter below the ground. Most of the wells go down in summer months, according to the Ground Water Estimati on Committee.

Soils: Reddish brown forest soil, Yellowish grey to greyish sandy loam soils and mixed soils.

Natural Division : It falls partly in Patti-Brahmagiri Ghats, Somvarpet-Virajpet Rolling Humid Region and Yedav anad-Nalkari Forest Belt of the Southern Karnataka Plateau.

Administration:

Division: Mysore. Parliamentary Constituency: 21 Mysore Paschim. District: Kodagu. Taluka: Virajpet. Assembly Constituency: 209 Virajpet. Gram Panchayat: 36.

Regional Area Development Boards: The Maland Aera Development Board.

Border Villages: (State: Kerala)- Kedamullur, Heggala, V.Badaga, Parakatageri, Theralu, Kurchi, Manchalli & Forest, Kutta.

Fairs: Ayyappa Fair: It is held at Mattur in about the month of March every year. Mattur is located at a distan ce of 10 kms. from Ponnampet and is surrounded by coffee plantations. Among the temples of this place are those of Mahadeva Chamundi and Ayyappa. The Ayyappa temple also called Eshwara temple is built in the style of the Kodagu Rajas.

Bhagavathi Fair: It is held at Halugunda in Kodagu area in the month of Magha (February-March). Halugunda is two kms. away from Chembebellur which appears to be an old site with many temples which witness various folk practices.

Chamundi Fair: It is held at Bellur near Kodagu in around the month of May every year. Bellur is an ancient place which is 11 kms. away from Ponnampet and can be reached through Hudikeri.

Harihara Fair: Harihara situated at a distance of about four kms. from Bellur and 15 kms. from Ponnampet, is one of the prominent pilgrimage centres of Kodagu. The Subrahmanya temple which is now completely modernis ed is the chief attraction here. In the garbhagriha the image of Subrahmanya has a modern Shivalinga by its side. The shikhara over the garbhagriha is also recent.

Kuttadamma Fair: It is held at Kutta in about the month of March-April every year. Kutta is the border region of Kodagu opening into Kerala. It is 24 kms. away from Ponnampet through which runs the main road leading Viraj pet to Nagarahole.

Syed Sheik Mir Hazarat Urs: Hudikeri is close to Kalgude swara and lies seven kms. from Ponnampet. Five kms. from Hudikeri is Aivatte which comes under the Virajpet taluk. This is a very popular pilgrimage centre of the Muslims, who congregate at the dargah of Syed Sheik Mir Hazarat. An Urs is celebrated during every Rajjab month, which attracts people from different parts of the district.

Not far from Aivatte is Kondangeri which has a hundred-year old dargah of Abdul Shah Vali Shariff. It is believed that the Jamma Masjid nearby was constructed during Tipu's time.

Villages: 94 **Inhabited:** 94 **Uninhabited:** 0

Ranking	District	State	National
Area	1	19	94
Population	2	109	1090
Sex Ratio	3	49	1629
Child Sex Ratio	2	16	1140
Literacy Rate	3	25	945
Density	1	70	6064
Work Participation Rate	2	160	1699

Gram Panchayats:

Kadanga Marur, Halugunda, Kannangala, Siddapura, Maldare, Channayan Kote, Titimati, Devarapura, Palibetta, Ammathi, Karmadu, Chembe Belliyur, Kadanur, Kedamullur, Betoli , Bittangala, Bilugunda, Hosoor, Gonikoppal, Mayamudi, Balele, Ponappasante, Kirgur, Ponnampet, Aruvathoklu, Hathur, B.Shettigeri,

Birunani, Hudikeri, Balyamandur, T. Shettigeri, Srimangala, Kutta, Nalkeri, Kanur, Nittur.

Amenities:

Education: Primary School in 90 villages, Middle school in 67 villages, Matriculation or Secondary School in 22 villages, namely Nalkeri, Devanageri, Betoli, Kuklur, Halugunda, Guhya, Ammathi, Bettakeri, Mekur Hosakeri, Hathur, Hebbale, Nokya, Mayamudi, Kuttandi, Halligattu, Bekke Sodlur, Hudikeri, Mugatageri, T. Shettigeri, Kutta, Balele, Bilur.

Higher Secondary or Pre University Courses or Intermediate or Junior College in 6 villages of the CD Block,, namely Guhya, Kaikeri, Mayamudi, Halligattu, T. Shettigeri, Balele.

College in 4 villages, Adult Literacy Center in 1 village., Colleges are in villages, namely Betoli, Kaikeri, Halligattu, Kumtoor.

Medical: Hospital in 10 villages, Dispensary in 21 villages, Health Center in 16 villages, Sub Center in 51 villages, Maternity and Child Welfare Center in 2 villages, Community health workers in 17 villages.

The Villages having Hospital or Dispensary or Health Center are Kadanga Marur, Heggala, Betoli, Kannangala, Karadigodu, Maldare, Siddapura, Puliyeri, Ammathi, Mekur Hosakeri, Badagabanangala, Kaikeri, Nokya, Halligattu, Kanur, Parakatageri, T. Shettigeri, Kumtoor, Kutta, Balele, Devanur.

Drinking Water: Tap water in 51 villages, Tank water in 46 villages, Well water in 91 villages, Tubewell in 47 villages and more than one source in 89 villages.

Bank: Banking facility in 39 villages, namely, Kunjalageri, Kadanga Marur, Arameri, Betoli, Maggula V.Badaga, Balugodu, Bittangala, Halugunda, Hachinad Byrambada, Siddapura, Ammathi, Bettakeri Mekur Hosakeri, Badagabanangala, Kalathmadu, Hathur Kaikeri, Hebbale, Devamachi Forest Arekeri Forest - I, Arekeri Forest - Iii, Mayamudi Kunda, Matoor, Bekke Sodlur, Parakatageri, Hysodlur Bellur, T. Shettigeri, Kothur, Nalkeri Nemmale East And West, Kutta, Badaga, Dhanugala Balele, Nittur.

Credit Society in 45 villages Agricultural Credit Society in 38 Non-Agricultural Credit Society in 4 villages.

Others: Power supply in 90 villages, Cinema hall in 6 villages, sport club in 13 villages, Stadium or Auditorium or Community Hall in 2 villages, Post Office in 70 villages.

There are 83 villages having bus facilities.

Villages with most of facilities: Kadanga Marur Arameri, Betoli, Maggula, Bittangala, Halugunda Siddapura, Ammathi, Mekur Hosakeri, Badagabanangala Hathur, Hebbale, Arekeri Forest - Iii, Mayamudi Kunda, Matoor, Bekke Sodlur, Parakatageri, Kothur Nalkeri, Nemmale East And West, Kutta, Badaga Balele, Nittur.

Villages without amenities (Education): Aimangala, Yedur, Byrambada, Kavadi..

Scheduled Castes: Out of the total population of 178148 persons, 18713 persons (10.5%) belong to Scheduled Castes. The villages having less than 10% SC population are Nalkeri, Palangala, Kedamullur, Heggala, Aimangala Arji, V.Badaga, 1St Rudraguppe, Halugunda Kannangala, Karadigodu, Ammathi, Kavadi, Karmadu Nalvathoklu, Hosakote, Kalathmadu, Kolatodu Bygodu Hathur, Arekeri Forest - I, Arekeri Forest - Ii Arekeri Forest - Iii, Mayamudi, Kunda, B.Shettigeri Kuttandi, Halligattu, Kirgur, Matoor, Bekke Sodlur Parakatageri, Theralu, Badagarakeri, Hysodlur, Begur Mugatageri, Chikka Mandur, Balyamandur T. Shettigeri, Harihara, Kothur, Nalkeri Forest Nalkeri, Kumtoor, Kurchi, Manchalli & Forest, Badaga Dhanugala, Bilur, Nittur, Hathugattu Forest I.

The village having more than 50% SC population is None.

Sex ratio of Scheduled Caste population is 507.

Scheduled Castes Literates and Illiterates by Sex:

	Persons	Males	Females
Literate	10,465	5,807	4,658
Illiterate	8,248	3,422	4,826
Literacy rate	64.9	73.3	56.8
Graduate	141	100	41

Scheduled Castes (Dominant):

Adi Karnataka, Pale, Adi Dravida

Generic Castes etc., Madiga

For their cultural identity please see Appendix-I

Villages without Scheduled Castes: There are 4 villages without any scheduled caste population.

Scheduled Tribes: Out of the total population of 178148 persons, 29660 persons (16.65%) belong to Scheduled Tribes. The villages having less than 10% ST population are Kunjalageri, Nalkeri, Bellumadu, Kadanga Marur Maithadi, Devanageri, Arameri, Heggala, Betoli Kottoli, Kadanur, Kuklur, Chembe Belliyur, Aimangala Maggula, Arji, Nangala, Balugodu, Bittangala Halugunda, Kannangala, Guhya, Siddapura, Puliyeri Karmadu, Nalvathoklu, Bilugunda, Mekur Hosakeri Badagabanangala, Kalathmadu, B.Shettigeri Halligattu, Kirgur, Parakatageri, Mugatageri, Bellur Harihara.

The villages having more than 50% ST population are Devamachi Forest, Arekeri Forest - I

Arekeri Forest - Ii, Arekeri Forest - Iii
Nalkeri Forest, Hathugattu Forest I.
Sex ratio of Scheduled tribe population is 499.

Scheduled Tribes Literates and Illiterates by Sex:

	Persons	Males	Females
Literate	7,526	4,387	3,139
Illiterate	22,134	10,474	11,660
Literacy rate	30.3	35.4	25.2
Graduate	61	38	23

Scheduled Tribes (Dominant):
Yerava, Jenu Kuruba, Kuruba, Naikda etc., Paniyan
For their cultural identity please see Appendix-II

Village without Scheduled Tribes: There is 1 village without any scheduled tribe population.

Literates and Illiterates by Sex (Total Population):

	Persons	Males	Females
Literate	111,782	60,207	51,575
Illiterate	66,366	29,343	37,023
Literacy rate	72	77	67
Graduate	8,201	4,544	3,657

Agriculture: ***Distribution of villages according to land use:*** Out of 94 villages, Total area (in hectare) is 164038, out of that 44.83 percent is cultivable and 0.78 percent of the cultivable area is irrigated.

Sources of Irrigation (Hectares): Government Canal 0, Private Canal 0, Well without Electricity 0, Well with Electricity 0, Tubewell without Electricity 0, Tubewell with Electricity 0, Tank 13.14, River 24.63, Lake 0, Waterfall 0, Others 538.19.

Villages with population of 5000 to 9999:
Channayan Kote, Badagabanangala, Kaikeri, Halligattu Kutta.

Villages with population of 10000 and above: None

Distribution of Workers:

	Persons	Males	Females	WPR
Cultivators	4,515	3,221	1,294	4.88
Agricultural Labour	3,659	2,020	1,639	3.96
Household Industry	590	333	257	0.64
Other Workers	83,718	50,783	32,935	90.52
Main Workers	86,686	53,904	32,782	93.73
Marginal Workers	5,796	2,453	3,343	6.27
Total Workers	92,482	56,357	36,125	

Religion: Major Religious Communities:

	Persons	Males	Females	Sex Ratio
Hindu (84.21%)	150,024	75,243	74,781	994
Muslim (12.28%)	21,869	11,131	10,738	965
Christian (3.31%)	5,888	2,976	2,912	978
Sikh (0.03%)	47	34	13	382
Buddhists (0.01%)	25	22	3	136
Jain (0.01%)	17	9	8	889

Agewise Data:

	Persons	Males	Females	Sex Ratio
All ages	178,148	89,550	88,598	989
0-14	50,608	25,601	25,007	977
15-44	88,625	43,812	44,813	1023
45-79	37,415	19,442	17,973	924
80+	1,422	651	771	1184
Age not stated	78	44	34	773

Languages (Dominant):
Malayalam, Coorgi/Kodagu, Kannada, Tamil, Tulu

Disabled Population:

	Persons	Males	Females	%
Total Disabled	2,354	1,253	1,101	
In Seeing	1,158	564	594	49.19
In Speech	232	130	102	9.86
In Hearing	208	102	106	8.84
In Movement	520	339	181	22.09
Mentally	236	118	118	10.03

YADGIR

Yadgir C.D. Block lies in the south-eastern part of Gulbarga district. It is a part of Yadgir taluka. The Block is located at a distance of 76 kms. from district headquarters (Gulbarga). There are 164 villages in the block with the total population of 250,051 persons. Area of the C.D. Block is 1692.12 sq. kms. It is bounded by taluks Chitapur and Sedam on north, taluks Shahpur and Chitapur on west, and it has common boundary with the state of Andhra Pradesh on south and east.

Communications:

Roadways : S.H-15: Direction- Shorapur to Sedam, Nearest Villages- Yekkhalli, Bagalmadu, Motenhalli, Hattikuni, Chamenhalli, Bandhalli, Yedhalli, Dastrabad.

Railway Station: Villages- Viswaspur, Thangunda, Lingera, Kudlur, Saidapur, Kyathanhalli.

River: Bhima Nadi- Nearest Villages- Talak, Hedgimadra, Thangunda, Tumkur, Yadgir (B) (Rural), Mazra-Hosalli, Mustur, Koulur, Lingera, Malhar, Sawoor, Anur, Anur (K), Belgunda, Bhimenhalli, Gondadgi, Gudur. Pedda Vagu Nadi- Nearest Villages- Magdampur, Paspool, Chintenpalli, Yelahar, Ghanpur, Gopalpur, Totlur, Yelsathi, Nandepalli, Karengi, Holibet, Jaigram, Sanklapur, Edlur, Chaler.

Reserved Forest: Nearest Villages- Bagalmadu, Motenhalli, Kotgera, Patapur, Sutarhosalli, Katgi-Shahapur, Belgera, Ashinal, Rampur (G), Shivapur, Kamalanagar, Subashnagar, Yemphed, Tatelgera, Magdampur, Paspool, Kandkur, Chintenpalli, Indiranagar, Himalpur, Budur, Narayanpur, Borabanda, Nazrapur, Chanderki, Keshwar, Dantapur, Jawaharnagar, Putpak, Ramasamudra, Panchasheelanagar, Arkera (K), Gunjunur, Bettadhalli, Dharmapur, Minaspur, Anpur. (Yadgir R.F.): Nearest Villages- Wadenhalli, Yergol, Bachwar, Yekkhalli, Hattikuni, Samnapur,

Venkateshwarnagar, Alipur, Horencha.

Annual Rainfall: Normal Rianfall 777 mm.

Ground Water: Availability of the Ground Water in the Basin is 7249 H.A.M. and the utilization is 3909 H.A.M. It belongs to Over Exploited category. Depth to water level 5 to 20 meter below the ground. Most of the wells go summer months, according to the Ground Water Estimation Committee.

Soils: Deep Black, Medium Black Soil, Shallow Soil and Lateritic Soil.

Natural Division : It falls partly in the Kagna Basin, Gurmatkal Scrubby Upland and Lower Bhima Valley of the Northern Karnataka Plateau.

Administration:

Division: Gulbarga. Parliamentary Constituency: 6 Raichur (ST), 5 Gulbarga (SC). District: Gulbarga. Taluka: Yadgir. Assembly Constituency: 38 Yadgir, 39 Gurmitkal. Gram . Panchayat: 39

Regional Area Development Boards: The Hyderabad - Karnataka Area Development Board.

Border Villages: (State: Andhra Pradesh)- Chanderki, Madepalli, Dantapur, Putpak, Minaspur, Anpur, Kuntimari, Narsapur, Nasalwai, Gurnur, Karengi, Holibet, Jaigram, Sanklapur, Edlur, Azalapur, Chaler, Badepalli, Kadechur, Gudur, Badiyal, Mavinhalli, Bomraldoddi, Duppalli, Chandapur.

Fairs: Channabasaveshwara Jatra: It is held at Kodekal near Gulbarga two times in a year, in the month of 15th Kartika (October-November) and 15th chaitra (March-April). Kodekal is a place of religious importance visited by pilgrims throughout the year. The Shri Channabasaveshwara temple situated in this place attracts a large number of devotees. During the Jatra, some ten thousand people congregate here. Kodekal is also noted for its Dargah which is venerated by the Hindus also. Kodekal is in the extreme south-west of Gulbarga area and lies some 16 kms. to the north of the Krishna river, in Shorapur .taluk Mailaralinga Jatra: Mailaralinga jatra held annually at Yadgir near Gulbarga in the month of Chaitra (March-April) for two days.Yadgir is about 70 kms. from the district headquarters town at Gulbarga. Close to the town and towards the east of the railway station, there is a hill well-fortified by the Yadava kings. An inscription found on the Nizam Buruz gives an account of Nizam Ali Khan's visit to the Governor of the place. The town contains a Jama Masjid. Because of its location on the principal railway route and also of its proximity to Wadi Junction, Yadgir has assumed commercial importance with a sizeable import and export trade in foodgrains. The river Bhima flows closeby. Yadgir is also a religious centre and the famous Mailaralingam temple here attracts a large number of devotees.

Villages: 164 **Inhabited:** 152 **Uninhabited:** 12

Ranking	District	State	National
Area	4	16	85
Population	3	37	236
Sex Ratio	2	40	1467
Child Sex Ratio	1	28	1519
Literacy Rate	10	175	6221
Density	1	3	5590
Work Participation Rate	5	132	204

Gram Panchayats:

Yergol, Motenhalli, Gajarakot, Kakalwar, Chanderki, Chapetla, Hattikuni, Alipur, Arkera (B), Bandhalli, Hongera, Putpak, Minaspur, Chinakhar, Kandkur, Paspool, Munderga, Mudnal, Thangunda, Workenhalli, Ramasamudra, Arkera (K), Konkal, Anpur, Yelahar, Halgera, Koulur, Balichakkar, Yelsathi, Jaigram, Madhawar, Kale-Belgunda, Malhar, Kilenkera, Azalapur, Saidapur, Belgunda, Badiyal, Kadechur.

Amenities:

Education: Primary School in 149 villages, Middle school in 80 villages, Matriculation or Secondary School in 17 villages, namely Yergol, Hattikuni, Hongera, Gajarkot, Kakalwar, Kandkur, Chanderki, Putpak, Hedgimadra, Ramasamudra, Yelahar, Madhawar, Balichakkar, Malhar, Konkal, Saidapur, Kadechur.

Higher Secondary or Pre University Courses or Intermediate or Junior College in 2 villages of the CD Block,, namely Konkal, Saidapur.

College in 0 village, Adult Literacy Center in 8 villages.

Medical: Hospital in 0 village, Dispensary in 11 villages, Health Center in 13 villages, Sub Center in 38 villages, Maternity and Child Welfare Center in 1 village, Community health workers in 12 villages.

The Villages having Hospital or Dispensary or Health Center are Wadenhalli, Hattikuni, Samnapur, Gajarkot, Mudnal, Mailapur, Balichakkar, Konkal, Azalapur, Saidapur, Kadechur.

Drinking Water: Tap water in 136 villages, Tank water in 86 villages, Well water in 140 villages, Tubewell in 89 villages and more than one source in 149 villages.

Bank: Banking facility in 16 villages, namely, Yergol, Gajarkot, Kandkur, Chintenpalli, Himalpur Putpak, Ramasamudra, Yelahar, Ghanpur, Madhawar Balichakkar, Neelhalli, Konkal, Yelsathi, Saidapur Kadechur.

Credit Society in 26 villages Agricultural Credit Society in 24 Non-Agricultural Credit Society in 3 villages.

Others: Power supply in 151 villages, Cinema hall in 0 village, sport club in 3 villages, Stadium or Auditorium or Community Hall in 152 villages, Post Office in 65 villages.

There are 121 villages having bus facilities.

Villages with most of facilities: Yergol, Gajarkot Kandkur, Putpak, Ramasamudra, Yelahar, Ghanpur Madhawar, Balichakkar, Konkal, Yelsathi, Saidapur Kadechur.

Villages without amenities (Education): Balajinagar, Nawaburz, Holibet..

Scheduled Castes: Out of the total population of 250173 persons, 62567 persons (25.01%) belong to Scheduled Castes.

The villages having less than 10% SC population are Khanapur-Hosalli, Kotgera, Rampur(G), Shivapur Devarahalli, Siddapur(B), Madepalli, Bomshathalli Thangunda, Tumkur, Maskehhalli, Mailapur, Koulur Nagalapur, Ghanpur, Gopalpur, Gudalgunta, Nawaburz Nandepalli, Karengi, Holibet, Turkandoddi Sourashtrahalli, Belgunda, Badiyal, Mavinhalli Bomraldoddi, Chandapur.

The villages having more than 50% SC population are Siddarthnagar, Samnapur, Venkateshwarnagar Balajinagar, Kurkumbal, Kamalanagar, Subashnagar Indiranagar, Borabanda, Jawaharnagar, Mallapur Viswaspur, Mudnal, Bhimnagar, Ashoknagar Panchasheelanagar, Lingera, Bettadhalli.

Sex ratio of Scheduled Caste population is 497.

Scheduled Castes Literates and Illiterates by Sex:

	Persons	Males	Females
Literate	11,170	7,710	3,460
Illiterate	51,397	23,752	27,645
Literacy rate	22.5	31.0	14.0
Graduate	143	132	11

Scheduled Castes (Dominant):

Madiga, Banjara etc., Holaya etc., Bhovi Generic Castes etc.

For their cultural identity please see Appendix-I

Villages without Scheduled Castes: There are 16 villages without any scheduled caste population.

Scheduled Tribes: Out of the total population of 250173 persons, 19138 persons (7.65%) belong to Scheduled Tribes.

The villages having less than 10% ST population are Achola, Siddarthnagar, Arkera(B), Yergol Khanapur-Hosalli, Chintkunta, Sutarhosalli Katgi-Shahapur, Samnapur, Venkateshwarnagar Balajinagar, Alipur, Horencha, Chamenhalli Bandhalli, Hongera, Belgera, Ashinal, Kurkumbal Rampur(G), Gajarkot, Devarahalli, Siddapur(B) Mitha-Tipdampalli, Kakalwar, Chapetla, Yedlapur Kamalanagar, Subashnagar, Tatelgera, Paspool Kandkur, Chintenpalli, Indiranagar, Himalpur, Budur Borabanda, Nazrapur, Chanderki, Madepalli, Keshwar Dantapur, Jawaharnagar, Mallapur, Putpak, Viswaspur Tumkur, Bhimnagar, Ashoknagar, Panchasheelanagar Arkera(K), Mailapur, Koulur, Shettikera, Yelahar Ghanpur, Gopalpur, Totlur, Madhawar, Balichakkar Lingera, Sawoor, Kilenkera, Kanekal, Gudalgunta Wanksambar, Wadwat, Nawaburz, Bettadhalli, Dharmapur Chinakhar, Muslapalli, Anpur, Konkal, Yelsathi Nandepalli, Kuntimari, Nasalwai, Gurnur, Karengi Torentippa, Holibet, Jaigram, Sanklapur, Edlur Turkandoddi, Azalapur, Chaler, Anur, Anur(K) Saidapur, Rampur, Balched, Badepalli Sourashtrahalli, Kadechur, Dadal, Rachanhalli Mungal, Kyathanhalli, Belgunda, Bhimenhalli Gondadgi, Sangwar, Shattihalli, Kondapur, Gudur Badiyal, Mavinhalli, Bomraldoddi, Duppalli Chandapur.

The villages having more than 50% ST population are None.

Sex ratio of Scheduled tribe population is 495.

Scheduled Tribes Literates and Illiterates by Sex:

	Persons	Males	Females
Literate	3,193	2,242	951
Illiterate	15,945	7,416	8,529
Literacy rate	21.0	29.1	12.6
Graduate	36	35	1

Scheduled Tribes (Dominant):

Naikda etc., Meda, Chenchu etc. Generic Tribes etc., Gond etc.

For their cultural identity please see Appendix-II

Villages without Scheduled Tribes: There are 85 villages without any scheduled tribe population.

Literates and Illiterates by Sex (Total Population):

	Persons	Males	Females
Literate	58,394	39,463	18,931
Illiterate	191,779	86,107	105,672
Literacy rate	29	39	19
Graduate	1,386	1,206	180

Agriculture: ***Distribution of villages according to land use:*** Out of 164 villages, Total area (in hectare) is 169212, out of that 74.57 percent is cultivable and 10.01 percent of the cultivable area is irrigated.

Sources of Irrigation (Hectares): Government Canal 2114.95, Private Canal 0, Well without Electricity 600.82, Well with Electricity 1031.3, Tubewell without Electricity 95.89, Tubewell with Electricity 1955.03, Tank 6736, River 46.54, Lake 0, Waterfall 0, Others 46.4.

Villages with population of 5000 to 9999: Yergol, Hattikuni.

Villages with population of 10000 and above: None

Distribution of Workers:

	Persons	Males	Females	WPR
Cultivators	53,048	39,632	13,416	38.15
Agricultural Labour	59,497	16,023	43,474	42.79
Household Industry	3,257	1,881	1,376	2.34
Other Workers	23,248	15,958	7,290	16.72
Main Workers	95,061	62,302	32,759	68.36
Marginal Workers	43,989	11,192	32,797	31.64
Total Workers	139,050	73,494	65,556	

Religion: Major Religious Communities:

	Persons	Males	Females	Sex Ratio
Hindu (89.86%)	224,801	112,952	111,849	990
Muslim (7.62%)	19,057	9,463	9,594	1,014
Christian (2.09%)	5,234	2,592	2,642	1,019
Sikh (0%)	2	1	1	1,000
Buddhists (0.32%)	804	415	389	937
Jain (0.02%)	57	33	24	727

Agewise Data:

	Persons	Males	Females	Sex Ratio
All ages	250,173	125,570	124,603	992
0-14	104,164	53,450	50,714	949
15-44	96,682	48,902	47,780	977
45-79	47,247	22,267	24,980	1122
80+	1,654	715	939	1313
Age not stated	426	236	190	805

Languages (Dominant):

Kannada, Telugu, Hindi, Urdu, Marathi

Disabled Population:

	Persons	Males	Females	%
Total Disabled	5,967	3,327	2,640	
In Seeing	3,371	1,849	1,522	56.49
In Speech	425	243	182	7.12
In Hearing	369	171	198	6.18
In Movement	1,479	883	596	24.79
Mentally	323	181	142	5.41

YELANDUR

Yelandur C.D. Block lies in the eastern part of Chamarajanagar district. It is a part of Yelandur taluka. The Block is located at a distance of 18 kms. from district headquarters (Chamarajanagar). There are 28 villages in the block with the total population of 69,384 persons. Area of the C.D. Block is 264.65 sq. kms. It is bounded by taluk Kollegal on north and east, and taluk Chamarajanagar on south and west.

Communications:

Roadways : NH- 209: Direction- Chamrajanagar to Kollegal, Nearest Villages- Mamballi, Agara, Maddur, Jodimellahalli, Duggahatti, Yelandur, Rural, Yeriyur, Avalkandalli, Duyamkandalli.

River: Suvarnavati Nadi- Nearest Villages- Mamballi, Agara, Bannisarige, Alkereagrahara, Ganiganur, Yelandur Rural, Yeriyur, Duyamkandalli, Ambale, Shivakahalli, Maddur. Hebba Halla Nadi- Nearest Villages- Maddur, Alkereagrahara, Gowdahalli.

Reserved Forest: (Biligerirangaswamy R.F.): Nearest Villages-Maddur, Gowdahalli, Biligiriranganabetta, Gumballi, Yeragamballi, K.Devarahalli.

Annual Rainfall: Normal Rianfall 788.83 mm.

Ground Water: Availability of the Ground Water in the Basin is 2995 H.A.M. and the utilization is 1650 H.A.M. It belongs to Safe category. Depth to water level 2 to 10 meter below the ground. Most of the wells go down in summer months, according to the Ground Water Estimation Committee.

Soils: Red Soils, Black Soils and Mixed Soils.

Natural Division : It falls in Cauvery Forested Region of the Southern Karnataka Plateau.

Administration:

Division: Mysore. Parliamentary Constituency: 22 Mysore Purab. District: Chamarajanagar. Taluka: Yelandur. Assembly Constituency: 222 Kollegal (SC). Gram Panchayat: 11.

Fairs: Biligiri Rangasvami Temple Car Festival: It is held at Biligiri-Rangan Hills in the month of Vaisakha (March -April) every year.

Villages: 28 **Inhabited:** 28 **Uninhabited:** 0

Ranking	District	State	National
Area	4	174	3187
Population	4	169	4487
Sex Ratio	3	107	2660
Child Sex Ratio	3	72	2722
Literacy Rate	2	157	4862
Density	4	168	3941
Work Participation Rate	1	38	4247

Gram Panchayats:

Mamballi , Agara, Maddur, Kesthur, Honnur, Duggahatti, Yeriyur, Gowdahalli, Gumballi, Yeragamballi, Ambale .

Amenities:

Education: Primary School in 27 villages, Middle school in 23 villages, Matriculation or Secondary School in 7 villages, namely Kesthur, Mamballi, Maddur, Gowdahalli, Biligiriranganabetta, Honnur, Yeragamballi.

Higher Secondary or Pre University Courses or Intermediate or Junior College in 1 village of the CD Block,, namely Biligiriranganabetta.

College in 0 village, Adult Literacy Center in 1 village.

Medical: Hospital in 1 village, Dispensary in 4 villages, Health Center in 2 villages, Sub Center in 1 village, Maternity and Child Welfare Center in 2 villages,

Community health workers in 0 village.
The Villages having Hospital or Dispensary or Health Center are Mamballi, Agara, Gowdahalli, Biligiriranganabetta.
Drinking Water: Tap water in 27 villages, Tank water in 27 villages, Well water in 27 villages, Tubewell in 26 villages and more than one source in 28 villages.
Bank: Banking facility in 6 villages, namely, Kesthur, Mamballi, Agara, Gowdahalli Biligiriranganabetta, Yelandur Rural.
Credit Society in 12 villages Agricultural Credit Society in 5 Non-Agricultural Credit Society in 12 villages.
Others: Power supply in 28 villages, Cinema hall in 3 villages, sport club in 0 village, Stadium or Auditorium or Community Hall in 0 village, Post Office in 23 villages.
There are 27 villages having bus facilities.
Villages with most of facilities: Mamballi, Agara Gowdahalli, Biligiriranganabetta.
Villages without amenities (Education):
Duyamkandalli..
Scheduled Castes: Out of the total population of 69386 persons, 24543 persons (35.37%) belong to Scheduled Castes.
The villages having less than 10% SC population are Agara, A.Devarahalli, Biligiriranganabetta Uppinamole, Duyamkandalli, K.Devarahalli.
The village having more than 50% SC population is None.
Sex ratio of Scheduled Caste population is 491.

Scheduled Castes Literates and Illiterates by Sex:

	Persons	Males	Females
Literate	11,147	6,345	4,802
Illiterate	13,396	6,159	7,237
Literacy rate	51.7	57.8	45.4
Graduate	603	511	92

Scheduled Castes (Dominant):
Adi Karnataka, Madiga, Bhovi, Bhambi etc.
Adi Dravida
For their cultural identity please see Appendix-I
Villages without Scheduled Castes: There are 4 villages without any scheduled caste population.
Scheduled Tribes: Out of the total population of 69386 persons, 10668 persons (15.37%) belong to Scheduled Tribes.
The villages having less than 10% ST population are Kesthur, Katnavadi, Kinakahalli, Mamballi Shivakahalli, A.Devarahalli, Malarpalya, Gowdahalli Honnur, Duggahatti, Yelandur Rural, Uppinamole Komaranapura, Vadagere.
The villages having more than 50% ST population are None.
Sex ratio of Scheduled tribe population is 487.

Scheduled Tribes Literates and Illiterates by Sex:

	Persons	Males	Females
Literate	4,000	2,477	1,523
Illiterate	6,668	2,997	3,671
Literacy rate	42.7	51.6	33.3
Graduate	100	85	15

Scheduled Tribes (Dominant):
Naikda etc., Soligaru, Generic Tribes etc., Meda
Jenu Kuruba
For their cultural identity please see Appendix-II
Villages without Scheduled Tribes: There are 8 villages without any scheduled tribe population.

Literates and Illiterates by Sex (Total Population):

	Persons	Males	Females
Literate	29,158	17,066	12,092
Illiterate	40,228	18,201	22,027
Literacy rate	48	55	40
Graduate	1,169	1,008	161

Agriculture: *Distribution of villages according to land use:*
Out of 28 villages, Total area (in hectare) is 26465, out of that 40.91 percent is cultivable and 46.89 percent of the cultivable area is irrigated.
Sources of Irrigation (Hectares): Government Canal 3037.72, Private Canal 0, Well without Electricity 20.23, Well with Electricity 721.6, Tubewell without Electricity 0, Tubewell with Electricity 398.67, Tank 889.1, River 0, Lake 0, Waterfall 0, Others 10.25.
Villages with population of 5000 to 9999:
Kesthur, Mamballi, Maddur, Ambale, Yeragamballi.
Villages with population of 10000 and above: None

Distribution of Workers:

	Persons	Males	Females	WPR
Cultivators	5,059	4,786	273	17.6
Agricultural Labour	15,333	10,402	4,931	53.34
Household Industry	1,304	707	597	4.54
Other Workers	7,051	4,811	2,240	24.53
Main Workers	18,333	14,686	3,647	63.77
Marginal Workers	10,414	6,020	4,394	36.23
Total Workers	28,747	20,706	8,041	

Religion: Major Religious Communities:

	Persons	Males	Females	Sex Ratio
Hindu (88.09%)	61,119	30,997	30,122	972
Muslim (2.33%)	1,614	806	808	1,002
Christian (0.04%)	29	14	15	1,071
Sikh (0%)	-	-	-	-
Buddhists (7.36%)	5,109	2,639	2,470	936
Jain (0.03%)	19	9	10	1,111

Agewise Data:

	Persons	Males	Females	Sex Ratio
All ages	69,386	35,267	34,119	967

0-14	20,244	10,260	9,984	973
15-44	34,705	17,636	17,069	968
45-79	13,640	7,020	6,620	943
80+	695	302	393	1301
Age not stated	102	49	53	1082

Languages (Dominant):
Kannada, Urdu, Hindi, Telugu, Tamil

Disabled Population:

	Persons	Males	Females	%
Total Disabled	1,687	1,045	642	
In Seeing	1,053	657	396	62.42
In Speech	141	70	71	8.36
In Hearing	55	38	17	3.26
In Movement	324	219	105	19.21
Mentally	114	61	53	6.76

YELBARGA

Yelbarga C.D. Block lies in the western central part of Koppal district. It is a part of Yelbarga taluka. The Block is located at a distance of 40 kms. from district headquarters (Koppal). There are 144 villages in the block with the total population of 223,826 persons. Area of the C.D. Block is 1489.66 sq. kms. It is bound ed by district Gadag and taluk Kushtagi on north, taluk Koppal on south, taluks Koppal, Gangawati and Kushtagi on east, and district Gadag on west.

Communications:

Roadways : N.H-13: Direction- Kushtagi to Chitradurga, Nearest Villages- Yeddoni, Kalbhavi, Mataldinni, Chikwa nkal Kunta, Hire Wankal, Kunta, Uchalkunta, Bukkanhatti, Gunhalu, Kolihal. N.H-63: Direction- Hubli to Koppal, Nearest Villages- Bhanapur, Talbal, Bannikoppa, Tadkal, Lakmapur. S.H-6: Direction- Gadag to Kushtagi, Nearest Villages- Sankanur, Sirgumpi, Sompur. S.H-6 A: Direction- Kushtagi to Koppal, Nearest Villages- Hire Arlihalli, Budakunti, Hosur, Mandalmari, Taralkatti, Narsapur, Murdi, Guttur, Vangera, Bevoor, Nelgeri, Kudri Moti. S.H-30: Direction- Kushtagi to Gajendragarh, Nearest Village s- Katral, Bandi, Kadbalkatti.

Railway Station: Villages- Sompur.

River: Hire Halla Nadi- Nearest Villages- Sanganhal, Yelburga, Kallur, Budgumpi, Sirur, Bedwatti, Yadiapur, Balgera, Arkeri, Muthalu.

Annual Rainfall: Normal Rianfall 571.92 mm.

Ground Water: Availability of the Ground Water in the Basin is 15897 H.A.M. and the utilization is 13202 H. A.M. It belongs to Over Exploited category. Depth to water level 10 to 20 meter below the ground. Most of the wells go down in summer months, according to the Ground Water Estimation Committee.

Soils: Black Cotton Soil.

Natural Division : It falls partly in the Kustagi-Yelbarga Plateau and Arkera-Mudgal-Kanakgiri Upland of the Centr al Karnataka Plateau.

Administration:

Division: Gubarga. Parliamentary Constituency: 8 Koppal. District: Koppal. Taluka: Yelbarga. Assembly Constituen cy: 63 Yelbarga. Gram Panchayat: 33.

Regional Area Development Boards: The Hyderabad - Karnataka Area Development Board.

Villages: 144 **Inhabited:** 138 **Uninhabited:** 6

Ranking	District	State	National
Area	1	34	145
Population	3	65	422
Sex Ratio	3	65	1921
Child Sex Ratio	4	157	4376
Literacy Rate	2	134	4030
Density	1	17	5548
Work Participation Rate	4	128	688

Gram Panchayats:
Hiremyageri, Mudhol, Ballutgi, Bandi, Vajra Bandi, Hire Arlihalli, Mataldinni, Talkere, Gandhal, Hire Wankal Kunta, Gunhalu, Bevoor, Vangera, Murdi, Chikmyageri, Gedigera, Balgera, Kallur, Sanganhal, Karmudi, Rajoor, Yarihanchinal, Mandalgeri, Bannikoppa, Tadkal, Bhanapur, Itagi, Kuknoor, Benakal, Sirur, Hirebeedinhalu, Mangalore, Kudri Moti.

Amenities:

Education: Primary School in 135 villages, Middle school in 94 villages, Matriculation or Secondary School in 26 villages, namely Hiremyageri, Mudhol, Ballutgi, Bandi, Vajra Bandi, Bandihal, Hire Arlihalli, Hire Wankal Kunta, Talkere, Gandhal, Gunhalu, Chikmyageri, Bevoor, Mangalore, Sirur, Yadiapur, Yarihanchinal, Rajoor, Kuknoor, Mandalgeri, Itagi, Masabhanchinhal, Benakal, Sompur, Bannikoppa, Tadkal. Higher Secondary or Pre University Courses or Intermediate or Junior College in 6 villages of the CD Block,, namely Hire Wankal Kunta, Bevoor, Mangalore, Kuknoor, Itagi, Tadkal.

College in 1 village, Adult Literacy Center in 19 villages., College is in village, namely Kuknoor.

Medical: Hospital in 5 villages, Dispensary in 13 villages, Health Center in 13 villages, Sub Center in 34 villages, Maternity and Child Welfare Center in 32 villages, Community health workers in 26 villages.

The Villages having Hospital or Dispensary or Health Center are Hiremyageri, Mudhol, Ballutgi, Bandi, Konasagar, Kallur, Yeddoni, Taralkatti, Bevoor, Mangalore, Balgera, Rajoor, Kuknoor, Itagi, Tadkal.

Drinking Water: Tap water in 49 villages, Tank water in 76 villages, Well water in 36 villages, Tubewell in 26 villages and more than one source in 123 villages.

Bank: Banking facility in 11 villages, namely, Mudhol, Bandi, Hire Wankal Kunta, Talkere, Murdi Bevoor, Mangalore, Sirur, Kuknoor, Itagi, Tadkal.

Credit Society in 26 villages Agricultural Credit Society in 18 Non-Agricultural Credit Society in 4 villages.

Others: Power supply in 138 villages, Cinema hall in 7 villages, sport club in 138 villages, Stadium or Auditorium or Community Hall in 138 villages, Post Office in 52 villages.

There are 105 villages having bus facilities.

Villages with most of facilities: Mudhol, Bandi Hire Wankal Kunta, Talkere, Murdi, Bevoor, Mangalore Sirur, Kuknoor, Itagi, Tadkal.

Villages without amenities (Education): Sompur, G.Virapur, Putakmari..

Scheduled Castes: Out of the total population of 224931 persons, 33232 persons (14.77%) belong to Scheduled Castes.

The villages having less than 10% SC population are Sankanur, Katral, Sirgumpi, Sompur, Kadbalkatti Konasagar, Hagedhal, Boon Koppa, Makkahalli, Lagalur G.Jarkunti, Karmudi, Kallur, Kalak Bandi, Matrangi Hire Arlihalli, Budakunti, Putakmari, Yeddoni, Budur Guntamadu, Sidlabhavi, Chikka Mannapur, Vanjabhavi Choudapur, Hosur, Ningalbandi, Mandalmari Yapaldinni, Uppaldinni, Chikwankal Kunta, Tippanhal Gunhalu, Myadneri, Hulegudda, Guttur, Ryavanki Vangera, Bevoor, Tipparasanhalu, Muthalu, Chendinhal Binhal, Chanpanhalli, Konapur, Harishankerbandi Gorelekoppa, Bhatpanhalli, Mandalgeri, Benakal Bhanapur, Talbal, Bannikoppa, Advihalli, Chitapur Komlapur.

The village having more than 50% SC population is None.

Sex ratio of Scheduled Caste population is 496.

Scheduled Castes Literates and Illiterates by Sex:

	Persons	Males	Females
Literate	10,032	6,889	3,143
Illiterate	23,200	9,847	13,353
Literacy rate	38.1	52.3	23.9
Graduate	177	163	14

Scheduled Castes (Dominant):

Madiga, Bhambi etc., Banjara etc., Bhovi Chalavadi etc.

For their cultural identity please see Appendix-I

Villages without Scheduled Castes: There are 13 villages without any scheduled caste population.

Scheduled Tribes: Out of the total population of 224931 persons, 24677 persons (10.97%) belong to Scheduled Tribes.

The villages having less than 10% ST population are Sankanur, Sirgumpi, Sompur, Hiremyageri, Mudhol Chikoppa, Tumurguddi, Ballutgi, Bandi, Kadbalkatti Chikbannigol, Boon Koppa, Dammur, Madlur, G.Virapur Kudri Kotgi, Maranhal, Hosahalli, Karmudi, Bandihal Tondihal, Sanganhal, Malaksamudra, Kudgunti, Kallur Kalak Bandi, Budur, Vanjabhavi, Markat, Choudapur Mataldinni, Hosur, Nilogal, Uppaldinni Hire Wankal Kunta, Bukkanhatti, Hunsihal, Kolihal Hanmapur, Gedigera, Narsapur, Chikmyageri, Budgumpi Ryavanki, Vangera, Nelgeri, Bhairnaikanhalli Mangalore, Kavalkere, Sirur, Bedwatti, Yadiapur Balgera, Chendoor, Arkeri, Muthalu, Kadar Halli Hirebeedinhalu, Chendinhal, Binhal, Chiken Koppa Dyampur, Rajoor, Konapur, Kakkihalli Harishankerbandi, Kuknoor, Gorelekoppa, Bhatpanhalli Sidnekoppa, Mandalgeri, Itagi, Masabhanchinhal Nittali, Gavarhal, Benakal, Veerapur, Bhanapur Mannapur, Sompur, Tadkal, Lakmapur.

The villages having more than 50% ST population are Salbhavi, Guntamadu, N.Jarkunti, Biraldinni Chikwankal Kunta, Tippanhal, Tipparasanhalu Chikbeedinhalu.

Sex ratio of Scheduled tribe population is 491.

Scheduled Tribes Literates and Illiterates by Sex:

	Persons	Males	Females
Literate	8,578	5,912	2,666
Illiterate	16,099	6,655	9,444
Literacy rate	43.0	58.7	27.0
Graduate	136	123	13

Scheduled Tribes (Dominant):

Naikda etc., Generic Tribes etc., Koli Dhor etc. Chodhara, Dubla etc.

For their cultural identity please see Appendix-II

Villages without Scheduled Tribes: There are 14 villages without any scheduled tribe population.

Literates and Illiterates by Sex (Total Population):

	Persons	Males	Females
Literate	98,803	64,623	34,180
Illiterate	126,128	48,848	77,280
Literacy rate	53	69	37
Graduate	2,852	2,391	461

Agriculture: ***Distribution of villages according to land use:*** Out of 144 villages, Total area (in hectare) is 148966, out of that 83.98 percent is cultivable and 12.3 percent of the cultivable area is irrigated.

Sources of Irrigation (Hectares): Government Canal 48.93, Private Canal 0, Well without Electricity 95.15, Well with Electricity 1765.67, Tubewell without Electricity 477.69, Tubewell with Electricity 6811.43, Tank 103.09, River 0,

Lake 0, Waterfall 5415.97, Others 669.67.

Villages with population of 5000 to 9999:
Mudhol, Mangalore, Tadkal.

Villages with population of 10000 and above:
Kuknoor.

Distribution of Workers:

	Persons	Males	Females	WPR
Cultivators	44,001	30,842	13,159	36.58
Agricultural Labour	56,598	18,632	37,966	47.05
Household Industry	3,252	2,001	1,251	2.7
Other Workers	16,441	12,093	4,348	13.67
Main Workers	87,399	54,952	32,447	72.66
Marginal Workers	32,893	8,616	24,277	27.34
Total Workers	120,292	63,568	56,724	

Religion: Major Religious Communities:

	Persons	Males	Females	Sex Ratio
Hindu (91.71%)	206,273	104,125	102,148	981
Muslim (6.61%)	14,868	7,468	7,400	991
Christian (0.04%)	85	44	41	932
Sikh (0%)	5	4	1	250
Buddhists (0%)	6	1	5	5,000
Jain (0.17%)	393	183	210	1,148

Agewise Data:

	Persons	Males	Females	Sex Ratio
All ages	224,931	113,471	111,460	982
0-14	88,929	45,778	43,151	943
15-44	95,532	48,971	46,561	951
45-79	38,277	17,831	20,446	1147
80+	1,685	606	1,079	1781
Age not stated	508	285	223	782

Languages (Dominant):
Kannada, Hindi, Urdu, Coorgi/Kodagu, Telugu

Disabled Population:

	Persons	Males	Females	%
Total Disabled	4,054	2,290	1,764	
In Seeing	1,430	758	672	35.27
In Speech	375	215	160	9.25
In Hearing	272	127	145	6.71
In Movement	1,521	959	562	37.52
Mentally	456	231	225	11.25

YELLAPUR

Yellapur C.D. Block lies in the north central part of Uttara Kannada district. It is a part of Yellapur taluka. The Block is located at a distance of 96 kms. from district headquarters (Karwar). There are 127 villages in the block with the total population of 55,566 persons. Area of the C.D. Block is 1236.40 sq. kms. It is bounded by taluk Haliyal and District Dharwad on north, taluks Ankola and Sirsi on south, district Dharwad and taluk Mundgod on east, taluks Ankola, Karwar and Supa on west.

Communications:

Roadways : N.H-63: Direction- Ankola to Hubli, Nearest Villages- Kannadagal, Belegeri, Donagar, Gharwas, Gopadm ane, Jogadamane, Komadi, Idagundi, Chikkumane, Gullapur, Arbail, Dabaguli, Madnur, Kolikeri, Kiravatti, Hosalli. S.H-6: Direction- Karwar to Mundgod, Nearest Villages- Kalache, Bare, Mavinamane, Honagadde, Targar, Chimanalli, Idagundi, Telangar, Vajralli, Heggapur, Madnur. S.H-93: Direction- Khanapur to Shimoga, Nearest Villages- Lalguli, Kannigeri, Kannadagal, Belegeri, Chandguli, Malalgaon, Hutkhanda, Kanchanahalli, Chikkotti, Kampli, Kusguli, Hasanagi, Shigemaneummachagi, Hiresar, Bidralli, Chavat ti, Kanagod-Balehadda, Sankadagundi, Tarehalli.

River: Tallihalla Nadi- Nearest Villages- Lalguli, Kanni geri, Kanchanahalli. Kali Nadi - Nearest Villages- Kattige, Dehalli, Nagarakhan, Lalguli, Baraballi, Kodsalli, Kalache. Sonda Nadi- Nearest Villages- Harigadde, Ileha lli, Chavatti, Kannur - Heggaranii, Tarehalli. Bedti Nadi- Nearest Villages- Chikkumane, Gullapur, Arbail, Kelashi, Magod, Chandguli, Malalgaon, Hutkhanda, Kalasu ru, Madnur, Hosalli, Bankasalli, Somanalli, Chikkotti, Kampli, Harigadde.

Annual Rainfall: Normal Rianfall 2339.2 mm.

Ground Water: Availability of the Ground Water in the Basin is 10351 H.A.M. and the utilization is 1250 H. A.M. It belongs to Safe category. Depth to water level 5 to 20 meter below the ground. Most of the wells go down in summer months, according to the Ground Water Estimation Committee.

Soils: Lateritic Soil.

Natural Division : It falls partly in Western Ghats, Yellapur-Dandeli Forest and the Sirsi-Siddapur Dissected Humid Tract of the Karnataka Coast (Western Coastal Region).

Administration:

Division: Belgaum. Parliamentary Constituency: 12 Uttara Kannada. District: Uttara Kannada. Taluka: Yellapur. Assembly Constituency: 81 Yellapur. Gram Panchayat: 14.

Regional Area Development Boards: The Maland Aera Development Board.

Fairs: Horo Mangalavara: Grama Devi (Kalamma and Durgamma) of Yellapur are ancient deities. A jatra of Devi for nine days from the fourth Wednesday in February (Phalguna) (once in three years) is held at Yellapur. Acharis are the priests of the temple. Before jatra, people of Yellapur town and neighbouring villages stay out of their houses between 11 am to 4 pm on the first three Tuesdays and take their food outside. This traditi on is locally known as Horo Mangalavara. Ramalingeshwara Jatra: It is held at Idagundi in about the month of February. Idagundi, about 10 kms. from

Yellapur, is considered a holy place. The place name Idagundani mentioned in inscriptions found at Gunjavati (Mundgod taluk) and Baindur (Yellapur taluk) refer to Idagundi. The place also finds a mention in the Skandapu rana, where it is stated that Idagundi, Kavadikere and Analgar are together regarded as Srikshetras. The Ramali ngeshwara temple which is an ancient one is completely renovated. According to tradition the linga was installed by Sri Rama during his journey through South India.

Villages: 127 **Inhabited:** 127 **Uninhabited:** 0

Ranking	District	State	National
Area	3	55	257
Population	10	172	5031
Sex Ratio	10	158	3759
Child Sex Ratio	8	148	4229
Literacy Rate	7	27	1109
Density	7	145	6312
Work Participation Rate	10	174	3381

Gram Panchayats:

Kannigeri, Kiravatti, Madnur, Angod, Dehalli, Vajralli, Mavinamane, Idagundi, Nandolli, Kampli, Hasanagi, Hittlalli, Shigemaneummachagi, Kundargi.

Amenities:

Education: Primary School in 85 villages, Middle school in 51 villages, Matriculation or Secondary School in 12 villages, namely Bisgod, Kalache, Mavinamane, Idagundi, Vajralli, Gullapur, Nandolli, Kiravatti, Hosalli, Kampli, Hasanagi, Bharatanahalli.

Higher Secondary or Pre University Courses or Intermediate or Junior College in 2 villages of the CD Block,, namely Gullapur, Kampli.

College in 0 village, Adult Literacy Center in 0 village.

Medical: Hospital in 0 village, Dispensary in 4 villages, Health Center in 5 villages, Sub Center in 13 villages, Maternity and Child Welfare Center in 0 village, Community health workers in 0 village.

The Villages having Hospital or Dispensary or Health Center are Dehalli, Shigemaneummachagi, Hittlalli, Chavatti.

Drinking Water: Tap water in 23 villages, Tank water in 8 villages, Well water in 126 villages, Tubewell in 9 villages and more than one source in 111 villages.

Bank: Banking facility in 14 villages, namely, Bisgod, Angod, Kalache, Kanur, Idagundi, Vajralli Gullapur, Kiravatti, Kampli, Shigemaneummachagi Hittlalli, Chavatti, Bharatanahalli, Kundargi.

Credit Society in 12 villages Agricultural Credit Society in 11 Non-Agricultural Credit Society in 1 village.

Others: Power supply in 120 villages, Cinema hall in 0 village, Sport club in 0 village, Stadium or Auditorium or Community Hall in 0 village, Post Office in 36 villages.

There are 61 villages having bus facilities.

Villages with most of facilities: Kalache Idagundi, Vajralli, Kiravatti, Kampli Shigemaneummachagi, Hittlalli, Chavatti, Kundargi.

Villages without amenities (Education): Hukkali, Gotguli, Belegeri, Shistamudi, Shigepal, Baraballi, Kodsalli, Lingadabailu, Gopadmane, K0Madi, Jogalepal, Chikkumane, Kavadikere, Analgar, Hulagan, Holemadu, Chandguli, Kalasuru, Heggapur, Bankasalli, Bendigeri, Gadijogadmane, Somanalli, Harigadde, Yadalli, Devarakallalli, Aalwad, Puratbomnalli, Hotageri, Mudanagi, Halagod, Hitlasara, Sankadagundi, Totadakallalli, Hunasemane, Jaddigadde, Kannur - Heggaranii, Hasalmane, Bellambi, Sampekoppa, Beejanakoppa..

Scheduled Castes: Out of the total population of 55574 persons, 2558 persons (4.6%) belong to Scheduled Castes.

The villages having less than 10% SC population are Kattige, Dehalli, Bisgod, Nagarakhan, Hukkali Gotguli, Lalguli, Kannigeri, Kannadagal, Belegeri Angod, Savagadde, Baragadde, Shistamudi, Tatagar Shigepal, Hutakmane, Hiriyal, Baraballi, Kodsalli Kalache, Kanur, Bare, Marahalli, Benadaguli Mavinamane, Honagadde, Targar, Beegar, Baginkatta Chimanalli, Lingadabailu, Hamsana Gadde, Donagar Gharwas, Gopadmane, Jogadamane, K0Madi, Idagundi Telangar, Vajralli, Jogalepal, Ambagaon, Kodlagadde Chikkumane, Gullapur, Arbail, Dabaguli, Kelashi Hastakaragadde, Balekani, Nandolli, Kavadikere Belakanda, Analgar, Hulagan, Sulagar, Heggumbale Holemadu, Devaragadde, Magod , Hutkhanda, Madnur Kolikeri, Kanchanahalli, Kiravatti, Bankasalli Gadijogadmane, Bhomnalli, Somanalli, Chikkotti Kampli, Harigadde, Tolagod, Yadalli, Kundoor Malakoppa, Aalwad, Kerehosalli, Bilki, Puratbomnalli Hotageri, Mudanagi, Shiranala, Halagod, Hitlasara Baichgod, Halasinkoppa, Kanenalli, Hiresar, Bidralli Ilehalli, Kotemane, Hunasemane, Hullaramane Jakkolli, Jaddigadde, Savane, Uchageri, Bharanii Kannur - Heggaranii, Tarehalli, Hemmadi, Vanakemane Kundargi, Hasalmane, Bellambi, Sampekoppa Beejanakoppa.

The village having more than 50% SC population is None.

Sex ratio of Scheduled Caste population is 497.

Scheduled Castes Literates and Illiterates by Sex:

	Persons	Males	Females
Literate	1,220	706	514
Illiterate	1,338	580	758

Literacy rate	57.4	65.7	48.9
Graduate	31	26	5

Scheduled Castes (Dominant):

Bhovi, Moger, Bhambi etc., Chalavadi etc.
Mahar etc.

For their cultural identity please see Appendix-I

Villages without Scheduled Castes: There are 73 villages without any scheduled caste population.

Scheduled Tribes: Out of the total population of 55574 persons, 494 persons (0.89%) belong to Scheduled Tribes.

The villages having less than 10% ST population are Kattige, Dehalli, Bisgod, Nagarakhan, Hukkali Gotguli, Lalguli, Kannigeri, Kannadagal, Belegeri Angod, Savagadde, Baragadde, Geral, Shistamudi Tatagar, Shigepal, Hutakmane, Hiriyal, Balagar Baraballi, Kodsalli, Kalache, Kanur, Bare, Marahalli Benadaguli, Mavinamane, Honagadde, Targar, Beegar Baginkatta, Chimanalli, Lingadabailu, Hamsana Gadde Donagar, Gharwas, Gopadmane, Jogadamane, K0Madi Idagundi, Telangar, Vajralli, Jogalepal, Ambagaon Kodlagadde, Chikkumane, Gullapur, Arbail, Dabaguli Kelashi, Hastakaragadde, Balekani, Nandolli Kavadikere, Belakanda, Analgar, Hulagan, Sulagar Heggumbale, Holemadu, Devaragadde, Magod , Chandguli Malalgaon, Hutkhanda, Kalasuru, Heggapur, Madnur Kolikeri, Kanchanahalli, Kiravatti, Bankasalli Bendigeri, Gadijogadmane, Bhomnalli, Somanalli Chikkotti, Kampli, Harigadde, Tolagod, Yadalli Kundoor, Kusguli, Hasanagi, Devarakallalli Malakoppa, Aalwad, Kerehosalli, Bilki, Puratbomnalli Hotageri, Mudanagi, Shiranala, Halagod, Hitlasara Baichgod, Halasinkoppa, Kanenalli Shigemaneummachagi, Hiresar, Bidralli, Hittlalli Ilehalli, Chavatti, Kanagod-Balehadda, Sankadagundi Kotemane, Totadakallalli, Hunasemane, Hullaramane Jakkolli, Jaddigadde, Savane, Uchageri Bharatanahalli, Bharanii, Kannur - Heggaranii Tarehalli, Hemmadi, Vanakemane, Kundargi, Hasalmane Bellambi, Sampekoppa, Beejanakoppa.

The villages having more than 50% ST population are None.

Sex ratio of Scheduled tribe population is 457.

Scheduled Tribes Literates and Illiterates by Sex:

	Persons	Males	Females
Literate	206	145	61
Illiterate	288	123	165
Literacy rate	49.1	62.5	32.5
Graduate	3	3	0

Scheduled Tribes (Dominant):

Naikda etc., Meda, Irular, Generic Tribes etc.
Kadu Kuruba

For their cultural identity please see Appendix-II

Villages without Scheduled Tribes: There are 109 villages without any scheduled tribe population.

Literates and Illiterates by Sex (Total Population):

	Persons	Males	Females
Literate	33,864	19,285	14,579
Illiterate	21,710	9,281	12,429
Literacy rate	71	78	63
Graduate	1,028	753	275

Agriculture: ***Distribution of villages according to land use:*** Out of 127 villages, Total area (in hectare) is 123640.02, out of that 6.59 percent is cultivable and 9.35 percent of the cultivable area is irrigated.

Sources of Irrigation (Hectares): Government Canal 2.33, Private Canal 0, Well without Electricity 58.02, Well with Electricity 506.74, Tubewell without Electricity 0, Tubewell with Electricity 0, Tank 27.55, River 0, Lake 0, Waterfall 0, Others 168.38.

Villages with population of 5000 to 9999: None

Villages with population of 10000 and above: None

Distribution of Workers:

	Persons	Males	Females	WPR
Cultivators	7,857	6,359	1,498	31.59
Agricultural Labour	5,707	3,274	2,433	22.94
Household Industry	215	147	68	0.86
Other Workers	11,094	7,772	3,322	44.6
Main Workers	21,063	16,235	4,828	84.68
Marginal Workers	3,810	1,317	2,493	15.32
Total Workers	24,873	17,552	7,321	

Religion: Major Religious Communities:

	Persons	Males	Females	Sex Ratio
Hindu (91.66%)	50,938	26,163	24,775	947
Muslim (4.93%)	2,739	1,422	1,317	926
Christian (3.2%)	1,781	914	867	949
Sikh (0%)	2	2	-	-
Buddhists (0%)	-	-	-	-
Jain (0.03%)	16	8	8	1,000

Agewise Data:

	Persons	Males	Females	Sex Ratio
All ages	55,574	28,566	27,008	945
0-14	16,499	8,591	7,908	920
15-44	27,473	14,047	13,426	956
45-79	11,095	5,683	5,412	952
80+	482	233	249	1069
Age not stated	25	12	13	1083

Languages (Dominant):

Kannada, Marathi, Konkani, Urdu, Telugu

Disabled Population:

	Persons	Males	Females	%

Total Disabled	1,402	794	608		In Hearing	83	50	33	5.92
In Seeing	638	324	314	45.51	In Movement	416	261	155	29.67
In Speech	113	71	42	8.06	Mentally	152	88	64	10.84

APPENDICES

Appendix-I : Scheduled Castes

Adi Andhra

Birth: A pre-delivery ritual is performed during a woman's first pregnancy. The first child is delivered at the natal home of the mother and birth pollution is observed for ten days. The *Pushpavati* (puberty) ritual is observed for girls which is performed by the maternal uncle.

Marriage: *Marriage with one's maternal uncle's* or paternal *aunt's daughter* is common. Girls usually get married between 13 and 18 years of age after menarche, and boys marry between the age of 18 and 24 years. In many places, adult marriages are in vogue. Bride-price is paid both in cash and kind. Either of the spouses can seek divorce through social approval on the grounds of adultery, serious illness, etc. The incidence of divorce is, however, on the decline. After divorce, the children are usally looked after by the father. Remarriage on account of widowhood or divorce is permissible. *Marriages are solemnised at the bride's residence and marriage expenses are borne by the bride's parents.*

Death: Burial is the prevalent mode of disposal of the dead. Death pollution is observed for ten full days. The *pedda karma* (mortuary rites) is performed. Ancestor worship is observed annually.

Ornaments : *Thali* and toe-rings are main ornaments of married women.

Foods : The Adi Andhras are basically non-vegetarians. However, while in Andhra Pradesh and Karnataka they eat *pork and beef* in Tamil Nadu they avoid eating pork and buffalo meat. Rice, *ragi* and *jowar* are their staple cereals.

Traditional Occupation : The traditional occupation of Adi Andhras belonging to Madiga sub-group is to make or repair leather footwear and other works associated with skin and hide, whereas those belonging to Mala sub-group are engaged in weaving cotton cloth.

Adi Dravida

Birth: The *seemantham* (pre-delivery rituals) is performed in the sixth month of pregnancy. In Andhra Pradesh, the said ritual is observed during the seventh or ninth month of pregnancy of the woman. The first delivery takes place at the woman's natal home. Post-natal restrictions are enforced and birth pollution is observed for eleven days.

The child naming ceremony is performed for both male and female children as is the *mudi edikiradu* (tonsure) ceremony. The *mangoi neerattuvizha* (puberty rites) on the first menstruation of a girl is observed after the six days' pollution.

Marriage: Endogamy is practised at the caste level. Preferential types of marriages are arranged either with the maternal uncle's or paternal aunt's daughter. The common age at marriage for boys is 21 years and that for girls is 16 years. Marriage is arranged through negotiation. Dowry and bride-price are paid the amount of which varies from place to place and according to the economic status of the family. The marriage ceremony is performed at the bride's residence, followed by a feast hosted by the bride's parents. Monogamy is the norm. Divorce and remarriage are permitted for both the sexes. Adultery and maladjustment are the common reasons for divorce. Widower and widow remarriages are also permitted.

Death: Their dead are usually buried but the first-born is cremated. The cremation is also practised in the event of an unnatural death. In Karnataka, the dead are buried in the burial ground at a place earmarked for the community. In Tamil Nadu, the *periya karyam* (mortuary rites) are performed on the fifteenth day to mark the end of death pollution. However, the period of pollution varies from place to place or from one State to another. As indicated above, the pollution period is observed for fifteen days among the people of this caste in Tamil Nadu, while it is eleven days among them in Karnataka.

Ornaments : A marriage badge, *metti* (toe-rings) and glass *gajulu* (bangles) are the most common ornaments of a married woman of this caste.

Foods : Rice, *jowar* and *ragi* are the staple food of the Adi Dravidas. They are non-vegetarians, and chicken, mutton, fish, pork and beef are occasionally consumed. Carrion eating is discontinued in some areas, though it still persists elsewhere.

Traditional Occupation : Cultivation and wage labour are their traditional occupations. However, in the states namely Andhra Pradesh and Karnataka, their traditional occupations varied to some extent. In Andhra Pradesh while one of the groups is largely a land-owning agricultural community, another group (i.e. Savu Mala) is of grave-diggers who also attend to the burials. In Karnataka, the Adi Dravidas carried carcasses which were used to make leather-articles. Many of them were engaged as village messengers.

Adi Karnataka

Birth: Generally, a woman in her first pregnancy is invited to her father's house for confinement even when she stays in the same village. During the seventh month of her pregnancy, a function called *Sogalu Sastra* or *Basiruasige* is performed. On this occasion, the family presents the pregnant woman with a green *saree* and green bangles, and *Arathi* is performed in the evening. After this function, the pregnant woman is taken to her father's house during the seventh or ninth month but not during the sixth or eighth month. As soon as the child is born, the information is sent to her husband's family. Her husband has to see the child and mother as soon as he can make it convenient, but within 11 days from the day of birth, and that too with a few specified commodities. The visit with these items is called *Akki Enne Sastra*. He should take a little quantity of rice, jaggery, oil, pepper, cummin, turmeric, lime, etc. During the succeeding 10 days after the day of birth, the *Dayadis* (families of agnatic kinsmen) observe pollution and during this period they do not perform *puja* (prayer) either in their houses or in temples. Others also do not eat the food cooked by them.

Marriage: *Swakula* (within the clan) marriages are never contracted. Thus, before a marriage can be settled, factors like the *gotras* and sub-castes of the bride and bridegroom are verified, and it has to be confirmed that both the bride and the bridegroom belong to different *kulas*. Consanguineous marriages are very common in this caste. The common types are: marrying (1) sister's daughter, (2) paternal aunt's daughter and, (3) maternal uncle's daughter. The caste members prefer to marry among their own kith and kin who may be staying in distant villages.

Death: Generally, the dead are buried. If a person dies of certain diseases like leukoderma, leprosy, etc., the body is cremated. It is considered very inauspicious to bury dead persons who have leukoderma or leprosy, and the people believe that famine and drought will follow if they are buried. The agnatic relatives consider themselves to be polluted for the subsequent 11 days. During this period, *puja* is not performed either in the house or in the temple and the mourning persons do not mingle with others freely. On the eleventh day, a function called *halu-thuppa* is performed. *Hombale* (arecanut flowers), cooked rice, betel leaf, milk, *ghee*, jaggery, etc. are carried to the graveyard and the *hombale* is planted at the place of burial. To this, *puja* is performed, and milk and *ghee* are poured over by all those who are present. A *yede* is also placed nearby. The eldest son of the dead person carries on his right shoulder a pot full of water, and goes thrice round this planted *hombale*. Then, he breaks the pot by letting it fall behind him. The party then returns home, and a feast is arranged to which relatives and friends are invited. The *shraddha* (death rites) is not performed yearly.

Dwelling : The houses of Adi Karnatakas are generally located at a distance from the main settlement of others in the village, but there is an intimate social contact between them. Their visit to the village and that of others to their settlement is a matter of daily occurrence. They live in houses with mud walls and tiled roofs. A few reside in thatched huts. The most common type that is found is called *Thottimane*. *Thotti* is the rectangular portion within a house where the rain water falling over the inclined roofs is collected and drained out.

Dress : Generally, men wear knickers (shorts) and shirts. These have come into vogue during the last 50 years or so. Before that, the villagers used to wear *dhotis* of small sizes with *kache* covering only half the thighs. Knicker became popular among the working class because of its convenience as well as its cheapness. Men put on a towel or an upper cloth which is also used as a head dress while at work. *Kache panche* is worn only by a few, while all others wear *dhoti* as a *datti* which hangs right up to the ankle. *Lungis*, i.e. *dhotis* of two yards length are also used by a few young persons. The women use sarees and blouses. Handloom sarees of coarse variety of the size 8 yards × 45" are very common. Blouses are got stitched from coarse chint of plain colour or with designs of different colours.

Ornaments : Among the men, some wear ear-studs and a few who can afford put on finger-rings very frequently made of silver. Apart from this, men do not wear any other ornaments. A few boys put on ear-studs and no other ornaments.

Foods : *Ragi* is the staple food (cereal). Some households use rice as a staple food, while others use rice in small quantities every day in addition to *ragi*. Many households cook rice only on festivals and other important occasions. *Ragi* is converted into *aata* (flour) which i.e. is cooked well in water, with frequent stirring, until a thick paste is formed which is later rounded into a circular lump called *mudde*. This is eaten with *saru* (soup) prepared out of *arhar dal*, beans, *dal* of horse gram and a little green vegetables to which sufficient chillies, turmeric, coriander, etc.

Traditional Occupation : In Karnataka, the Adi Karnatakas had tradi-tionally been engaged as musicians during festivals and they also used to erect *pandals* for ceremonial occasions.

Adiya

Birth: During the seventh month of the first pregnancy, the *bayake mangal* (a pre-delivery ritual) is performed. Birth pollution is observed for five days in the case of a male child and seven days for a girl child. Post-natal food restrictions are enforced on the new mother. The *teranda mangal* (puberty) ceremony is performed on the first menstruation.

Marriage: The caste endogamy and clan exogamy are practised by the people of this caste. Marriage with one's maternal uncle's daughter or paternal aunt's daughter is preferred. Adult marriage is the rule and marriages are settled through negotiations. Bride-price is paid in cash. Marriages are solemnized at the bride's residence. Earlier, the bride's maternal uncle used to tie the *tali* (the marriage symbol of a small ornament tied in string) but, at present, the groom ties it. Marriage expenses are borne by the bride's family. The patrilocal rule of residence is followed after marriage. In cases of adultery, divorce with social approval is permissible; and compensation is paid to the aggrieved party. Widow, widower and divorcee are allowed to remarry.

Death: Cremation is the common method of disposal of the dead, and the mortal remains are immersed in the river. Death pollution is observed for sixteen days. Ancestor worship is performed.

Ornaments : The *tali* or *thali* (sacred pendant) is the symbol of a married woman.

Foods : The Adiyas are non-vegetarians who also eat pork. Rice is their staple cereal. Horse gram is the main pulse used, and groundnut oil is their cooking medium.

Traditional Occupation : Basket-making and playing music on ceremonial occasions have been their traditional occupations.

Ager

Birth: In the seventh or ninth month of the first pregnancy, a feast is arranged and, the pregnant woman is given a saree as a gift on this occasion. A woman in child-birth is unclean for twelve days. Pre-delivery and post-natal restrictions, as also observed locally, are prevalent among the Agers. Naming and *mundan* (tonsure) ceremonies are observed for male children. The ears of girl children are pierced within three years after the birth.

Marriage: Marriages are prohibited in the same *bali*. A man may marry his maternal uncle's daughter. Traditionally, he is not allowed to marry his paternal aunt's or maternal uncle's daughter. He may marry two sisters. Brothers may marry sisters of another family. In the past, girls were married at the age of six to eleven years and boys at six to twenty-five years but only adult marriages are practised at present. The negotiations for a marriage are commenced by the boy's father. When a match is settled, the boy's father treats the company present there to a rupee's worth of toddy. He has to pay the *hennateru* (a bridal portion of some money) to the girl. The marriage ceremonies last for four days. On the first day, the boy's parents go to the girl's father's house, and treat the girl's party to a dinner of rice and coconut juice. On the second day, the marriage takes place. On the third day, the bridegroom takes his bride to his house and a feast is given by his father. The festivities end on the fourth day with a feast by the girl's father. The binding portion of the ceremony consists of throwing sacred grains of rice on the bride and bridegroom.

Death: The dead are either burnt or buried with their head facing to the north. About two pounds of rice grains and a few coins are buried with the corpse. On every new moon day and holiday, cooked rice and fish, placed on a plantain leaf, are offered to the crows for the propitiation of the dead. They do not perform the *shraddha* (the death rites).

However, the above traditional practice of disposal of dead has undergone a considerable change. Now, the dead are cremated and the mortal remains are disposed off in water. After the death pollution, *shraddha* is performed on the twelfth day and a feast is given to the kinsmen.

Ornaments : The *thali* (sacred pendant), *daregundu* (sacred beads) and toe-rings are the marriage symbols for women.

Foods : They are non-vegetarians, and relish the meat of goats, hogs, fowls, rats and fish. Wheat, rice and *ragi* are their staple cereals eaten with different pulses.

Traditional Occupation : Their traditional callings is making salt and they also work as field labourers. They make palm-leaf umbrellas which are used in Kanara area throughout the year. Like the Buttál and other field labourers, they are generally indebted to land-owners and work off loans by serving on very low wages.

Ajila/Nalakeyava/Nalkadaya

Birth: Pre-delivery ritual is performed during the seventh month of pregnancy. Birth pollution is observed for fifteen days and on the sixteenth day, the naming ceremony is performed. The *karapattavani* (puberty ritual) is also observed.

Marriage: Marriage with one's maternal uncle's daughter or paternal aunt's daughter is allowed. Only adult marriages are practised which are settled through negotiation. Monogamy is the norm and some money is paid as the bride-price.

The marriage ceremony is concluded in a single day. The contracting couple are seated on planks, and the *gurikára* (caste headman) throws coloured rice over their heads and ties round their necks a turmeric-dyed string with beads strung on it. Those assembled then throw rice over them. The hands of the contracting couple are joined by the *Gurikára* or their respective fathers, and the *dhare* water specially procured for marriage is poured thereon. The *kai pattans* (divorced, widow or widower remarriages) are allowed. Junior sororate is practised.

Death: The dead are either buried or cremated. After burial or cremation, *dhupe* (a mound) is made over the spot. Round it, four posts are stuck in the ground and are decorated so as to resemble a small car. The *uttarakriyas* (final death ceremonies) are generally performed on the fifth or seventh day. On this day, cooked food is offered to the deceased by placing it near the *dhupe* or on the spot where he breathed his last. This is followed by a feast. If the ceremony is not performed on one of the recognized days, the permission of some Bants or Billavas must be obtained before it can be carried out.

Foods : Rice is their staple food. Being non-vegetarians, the Nalkadayas relish chicken, meat and fish. Men regularly take alcoholic drinks, whereas women consume alcohol occasionally.

Traditional Occupation : Traditional occupations of the Nalakeyavas/Nalkadayas are ritual-dancing, fortune-telling, exorcism and basket-making. Their women are skillful basket-weavers.

Anamuk

Foods : They are non-vegetarians. Rice is their staple cereal and, in addition, they take *jowar* and maize alongwith pulses.

Traditional Occupation : Information on traditional occupation of Anamuks is not available.

Aray Mala

Birth: Customs connected with pregnancy and child-birth are the same as in other corresponding castes in the respective areas of their habitation.

Puberty: When the girl comes of age, offerings of flowers and fruits are made to the family gods. She is bathed, dressed in a robe and decked with flowers. She is bathed on the fourth day, when her relatives and friends of the family are treated to a feast.

Marriage: The prohibitions of intermarriage prevailing among them are the same as those in the corresponding castes in the respective areas of their habitation. A young man may marry the daughter of his elder sister. Exchange of daughters between two families is generally allowed.

Death: The Aray Mala dead are either cremated or buried. The period of mourning is 10 days. On the 11th day, they are purified by a bath when they are free from pollution. The family priest gives them the sanctified water to drink and on the 12th day, the caste people are treated to a feast.

Dwelling : An Aray Mala house is generally a hall of 30 to 35 feet in length and fifteen to twenty feet in breadth. On one side is the hearth around which are the domestic utensils, a few earthen or copper pots and other vessels. At the other end are secured their bullocks. In another small enclosure are secured their chickens. In the space between the two extremities are kept *ragi,* in a large vessel of basketry, and the implements of husking rice. This space is used for the dual purpose of dining and sleeping.

Dress : The men wear a narrow waist cloth and shoulder cloth with a black blanket thrown over it, besides a scarf. Coats and shirts are also other additions on gala days. Their women wear a dark robe the lower end of which hangs like a petticoat to the knees and the upper end is drawn towards the head.

Ornaments : They wear cheap gold and silver ornaments on their heads, necks, fingers, wrists, noses and ears. They smear red marks made with vermilion powder on their foreheads. These women wear *bugudi* on the ear, *tali* round the neck, and bangles and rings on wrists and fingers. The *bugudi* and *tali* are made of gold, and the bangles and rings are either of gold or silver. They also wear glass or lac bangles.

Foods : The staple cereal of the Aray Malas is cheap rice, *ragi* and millet. They also eat fish, fowl, mutton and venison. They also drink liquor but not in excess.

Traditional Occupation : Most of the of this caste were engaged in the past in the primitive forms of tillage by forest clearing and raising crops of grains on the clearings. This form of tillage was known as *Kumri* tillage and *Hakkal Vala Kumri.*

Arundhatiya/Arunthathiyar

Birth: The first confinement takes place at the residence of parents of the pregnant woman. The subsequent deliveries are conducted at the husband's house. The parents of the woman visit her house during the fifth or seventh month, present her a saree and blouse, and take her to their place for delivery. A separate arrangement is made for delivery in the house. The area is enclosed either with wattle or with a cloth curtain and a cot is placed inside the enclosure where the pregnant woman rests. Generally, the caste *dai* (midwife) attends to the delivery and the remuneration paid to her differs from State to State. In addition to the little amount paid traditionally, which ofcourse is more in case of a male child, food is given to her on the days of her service. The *dai* cuts the umbilical cord immediately after birth and buries it in the earth outside the house..

Puberty: The normal age of puberty is between 13 and 16 years. The maternal uncle of the girl erects a small hut where she lives during the period of her pollution lasting for eight days. The girl is seated on a mat spread over palmyra leaves or that of *jowar.* She is given final bath on the last day and new clothes are presented to her. The castewomen are invited in the evening, and sweets, betel leaves and arecanuts are distributed to them. From that day onwards, the girl can enter the kitchen and touch the utensils. That hut meant for the girl's stay is burnt by the same person who erected it.

Marriage: Endogamy is practised at the caste level. A person is permitted to marry his maternal uncle's or paternal aunt's daughter. Maternal uncle-niece alliances are also permitted. Adult marriage is the practised norm. Negotiation is the mode of acquiring a spouse. The expenses for marriage feasts are shared by both the bride's and the groom's families. An elderly and educated person of the caste officiates the marriage for which a quantity of Talambralu rice, *dhoti* and some money are paid to him as remuneration. Payment of bride-price is prevalent, and its amount traditionally fixed less has increased at present. A few socially and economically better-off members of the caste also consult the Brahmin priest on various occasions relating to marriage ceremony in their family. Nowadays, at many places in Tamil Nadu, dowry is paid in kind. Widow remarriages are accepted but permission of the caste *Panchayat* is essential. Either spouses can secure divorce on the ground of adultery and compensation is payable to the aggrieved party. Sororate and levirate marriages are permissible.

Death: They bury their dead, and the death pollution is observed for ten days.

Dwelling : The dwelling of these people is locally known as *thata kujllu* or *gudise.* Usually, the clusters are located on the outskirts of the village. No special importance is attached to the selection of the house site. Whenever they build houses, they consult the Brahmin or a learned man to know whether the site is good for their family. If the site is considered to be good, a pole ending in 'V' shape is fixed at the north-east corner of the plot. The family god is worshipped and a coconut is offered. *Pandaram*—a mixture of coconut pieces, jaggery and *borugulu* (puffed rice) are distributed among the invitees. The ground plan of the *thata kujllus* is rectangular. Usually, these are built on high plinths..

Dress : The dress of a male consists of *chokka* (shirt)-the upper garment and *Puncha* (*dhoti*)-the lower garment. The dress of a female comprises a *cheera* (saree) and a *ravika* (blouse). Males put *kanduva* (a piece of cloth) of one yard length on their shoulders.

Ornaments : The marriage symbol for women is the *thali* (sacred pendant). The other ornaments that are used by women-folk are *kammalu* (ear ornaments), *vadanam* (ornament for waist) and *mattelu* (toe-rings).

Foods : The staple food of Arundhatiyas is *jowar*, *sajj* (spiked millet), *arikelu* (kodi millet), *ragi* (finger millet) and rice. They use *nukalu* (broken pieces of rice) as a supplement to rice. They take food thrice a day. The previous night's leftover (*saddi*) is taken as the first meal of the day in the early morning. In the afternoon, they take their second meal that consists of *ragi sankoti* (food prepared out of ragi flour and a little rice mixed with water) and *chutney*. The third meal consisting of rice and curry, made out of *dal* and some vegetables, is taken in the night. They are non-vegetarians as well and eat the flesh of fowl, goat and sheep. They eat beef and pork as well. All kinds of fish are taken. The flesh of the dead animals is also consumed.

Traditional Occupation : The traditional occupation of Arundhatiyas is to make leather goods. They get a fixed quantity of grain from the villagers for their services. Some of them are employed as field servants.

Arwa Mala

Birth: On the third day after the birth of a child, the *purud* ceremony is performed when a goat is killed and the head is placed on the rim of the pit in which the child's umbilical cord has been buried. The body of the killed goat is cooked, and a feast is provided to guests and friends. The head forms the perquisite of the midwife. On the twenty-first day, the mother goes to a well, offers *puja* (prayer) to its rim, marches three times round it and returns home with a jar filled with water. The water is sprinkled throughout the house and the mother is rendered ceremonially pure. The child is generally named on the fifth day after its birth. But there is change in this custom these days as many members of the caste do not practise it at all.

Marriage: A man is permitted to marry the daughter of his maternal uncle, paternal aunt and of elder sister. The marriageable age for boys is between 18 to 30 years, whereas for girls it is between 13 to 22 years. The earlier practice of *oli* (bride-price) has been replaced by *varakatnam* (dowry) at many places. Marriages are arranged through negotiations. Residence after marriage is patrilocal. A man can marry two sisters from a family but two brothers cannot marry two sisters from the same. Immediately after marriage, the girl is sent to her husband by the *vadibiyam* (send-off) ceremony. A widow is allowed to marry again but she cannot marry her late husband's brother. The ceremony in such marriages is very simple. A *saree* and a *choli* are presented to the bride and a *pusti* (marriage badge) is tied round her neck by the widows attending the ceremony.

Death: The dead are either buried or burnt, according to the pecuniary circumstances of the family of the deceased. In the case of burning, the ashes and bones are collected on the third day after death. The ashes are thrown into a river and the bones are buried under a platform. In the case of burial, the corpse is laid in the grave with its head pointing to the south. After burial, the bier bearers and other mourners bathe, and the meat of the cooked fowl and wine are distributed among them as a blessing from the *dasri* (the caste priest).

Dress : *Saree* and *choli* is the common dress of women. Men reportedly wear the dress generally used by other caste people of similar economic status in the area.

Ornaments : The *pusti* (marriage-pendant) and *metti* (toe-rings) are the ornaments worn by the married women.

Foods : They are non-vegetarians who relish mutton, beef and pork. Rice and *ragi* are their staple cereals, and they also consume pulses. Groundnut oil is used as the cooking medium.

Traditional Occupation : The traditional occupation of Arwa Malas includes sale of firewood and agricultural labour. Wage earners are paid both in cash and kind.

Baira

Birth: The pre-delivery ritual called *sreemantha*s performed. Birth pollution is observed for eleven days. Naming ceremony and *osage* (puberty rites) are also observed.

Marriage: Marriages with one's paternal aunt's daughter and maternal uncle's daughter are permitted. But the uncle-niece marriages are prohibited among them. Junior sororate is allowed. The *kaiwatta* (widow remarriage) takes place without any auspicious rituals. Bride-price is still prevalent with little amount and also a *saree* presented to the girl's mother. Dowry, although not practised earlier, has now become quite common with its amount running into hundreds of rupees. The marriage rituals/ceremonies are performed by *gurikara* or *yajamana* (their own caste leader). Adult marriages are common which are arranged through negotiation.

The marriage symbols are the *tali* (sacred pendant), toe-rings and the finger-ring.

Death: Their dead are generally buried. In case of unnatural deaths such as suicides, accidents, chronic diseases, expectant mothers and those women who die during delivery, cremation is resorted to. The purification ceremony takes place on the fifth day by sprinkling sacred water in the house. On the fifteenth day, the departed soul is offered *bojja* (food and other items) at the burial site.

Ornaments : The *Tali* or *thali* (sacred pendant), toe-rings and finger-rings are the main ornaments of married women as stated above.

Foods : Rice is their staple food which is supplemented with a variety of grams. They are occasional non-vegetarians, and eat chicken, mutton, pork and beef. Groundnut, coconut and sesamum oils are used for cooking.

Traditional Occupation : The traditional occupation of Bairas is basket making. Forests are their main natural resource, and hunting and gathering forest produces are their major occupations.

Bakad / Bant

Birth: Pre-delivery restrictions on a pregnant woman exist in this caste. The naming ceremony is observed after the birth pollution lasting for six days. The *colangi* (tonsure) and ear-piercing ceremonies are performed for both male and female children within three years of their birth.

Puberty: At a puberty ceremony among the Bants, the girl sits in the courtyard of her house on five unhusked coconuts covered with the bamboo cylinder which is used for storing paddy. Women place fourour pots, filled with water, betel leaves and nuts round the girl. They also place some contents over her head. She is then secluded in an outhouse. The women are entertained with a feast which must include fowl and fish curry. The coconuts are given to a washerman. On the fourth day, the girl is bathed and received back at the house. Beaten-rice and rice flour mixed with jaggery (crude sugar) are served to those assembled. Thus, the girl is kept in *gosha* (secluded) for the period of her menstruation and is fed with a generous diet.

Marriage: Marriage with cross-cousins as well as junior levirate are permitted. The post-marital rule of residence is patrilocal. Though the infant marriage is not prohibited, it is not commonally practised. There are two forms of marriages: one is called *kai dhare* (marriages between virgins and bachelors), and the other is called *budu dhare* (marriages of widows). After a match has been arranged, the *ponnapathera* or *nischaya tambula* (formal betrothal) takes place. The bridegroom's relatives and friends proceed on the appointed day to the bride's house and are entertained at a grand dinner hosted there to which the bride's relatives and friends are bidden. Subsequently, the *karnavans* (heads) of the two families formally engage to perform the marriage. The plates of betel leaves and arecanuts are exchanged, and the betel and nuts partaken of by the two parties.

Death: The Bants cremate their dead, except in the case of children under seven years of age and those who have died of leprosy or of epidemic diseases such as cholera or small pox. The funeral pyre consists at least partly of mango wood. Elaborate death ceremonies are performed only if the deceased was old or a respected member of the caste. The corpse is generally cremated in one of the rice fields belonging to the family. After the funeral, the male members of the family return home, and place a vessel containing water and light in a room. One or two women remain in this room and the light is kept burning until the *bojja* or final death ceremonies are over. The water in the vessel is renewed twice daily.

Dwelling : Well-to-do Bants usually occupy substantial houses on their estates. In many such houses, there is much fine wood-work; and, in some cases, the pillars of the porches and verandahs are also of the same. The doorways are artistically and elaborately carved. These houses have been described as being well built, thatched with palm, and generally prettily situated with beautiful scenic prospects stretching away on all sides.

Foods : The Bants are non-vegetarians but do not take beef. Yet, there are some families of position called Ballals amongst whom heads of families abstain from animal food. Fish and meat of the wild boar are relished. Their staple diet consists of boiled rice, *ragi*, and pulses like *tur*, *urad*, peas and beans. Roots and tubers are also consumed.

Traditional Occupation : The Bants were originally a military class corresponding to the Nayars of Malabar in Kerala. The term 'Nadava' instead of 'Bant' used for these people in the northern portion of South Canara (now Dakshin Kannad) points to a territorial organization of the Nads similar to the *tara* (territorial unit) of the Nayars prevailing in Malabar. Correspondingly, the Bants of the northern parts of Kanara (Kannad) still identify with the territorial name of Nad Bants or warriors of the *nad* or territory.

Anyway, the traditional occupation of Bakads or Bants is stated to be toddy-tapping.

Bakuda

Birth: The *bayake maduve* (desire-fulfilling ceremony) is observed during the first pregnancy of a woman. Birth pollution is observed for sixteen days.

Marriage: Clan exogamy is observed by the Bakudas. Marriage with one's paternal aunt's or maternal uncle's daughter is preferred. They prefer adult-marriages which are arranged through negotiation.

Ornaments : The *karimani* (pendant) and toe-rings are two important ornaments worn by the married women. Men do not wear any ornament.

Foods : Rice is the staple food of the Bakudas. Different pulses, and locally available vegetables and fruits are eaten. They are non-vegetarians and eat fowls, fish, mutton, etc. but avoid beef.

Traditional Occupation : Agricultural Labour has remained the traditional occupation of Bakudas in Karnataka. They have largely been landless. In Kerala also, they were bonded to dominant communities and worked as agricultural labourers on the locally known *mulada mani* (an annual contract). In Tamil Nadu, a large majority of them are the landless agricultural labourers and a few are employed in the low level of white collar jobs particularly in the urban areas.

Bandi

Birth: Pre-delivery rituals known as *bayake ootha* are performed during the seventh month of pregnancy. The *oothaka* (post-delivery pollution) is observed for ten days. Post-natal restrictions on the mother are enforced. The *jawala* (tonsure) ceremony is performed for both male and female children within one year after their birth.

Puberty: Puberty rites are performed and the related rituals are somewhat similar to those observed by local caste people.

Marriage: As pointed out by Enthoven (*op. cit.*), marriage among the Bandis in the past was rare as their girls used to become prostitutes. However, in the present time in marriages, the offer is made by the boy's father. Marriages are allowed with one's maternal uncle's and paternal uncle's daughter. In Tamil Nadu, uncle-niece marriages are also prevalent. Adult marriages are the norm and are arranged through negotiation. Earlier *thira* (bride-price) was paid but this custom is no longer in existence. After the marriage, patrilocal residence is common. The marriage ceremony is performed at the bride's residence and the marriage feast is hosted by her parents. Cases of divorce are rare. Widow and widower remarriages and junior sororate marriages are allowed.

Death: Traditionally, their dead used to be buried. Cremation is nowadays the common method for disposal of dead, and the mortal remains are immersed in a river or in the sea. Death pollution lasts for 14 days. Ancestor worship is observed every year during *Maga masa* (February-March).

Ornaments : The *tali* (sacred pendant) and toe-rings are the marriage symbols for women. At least these two ornaments are worn generally by the married women.

Foods : They are non-vegetarians and eat fowls, fish, mutton and pork but abstain from eating beef. However, their staple cereal is rice which is supplemented with varieties of pulses. Groundnut and coconut oils are used for cooking.

Traditional Occupation : Traditionally, the Bandis used to work as village servants and bonded labourers in Karnataka. They were employed as domestic servants by Brahmins and other high caste Hindus. They used to engage themselves in cleaning copper pots, pounding rice, cleaning the floor with cowdung paste, collecting fire wood, etc. In Tamil Nadu, their traditional occupations were agriculture and agricultural labour.

Banjara, Lambani

Birth: The confinement of a pregnant woman takes place in the husband's house. In fact, it was formerly the custom that when a Banjara woman was married and sent to her husband's house, she seldom or never returned to her father's house. But of late, the Banjaras have adopted the practice of bringing the woman to her parent's house for the delivery. During the wife's pregnancy, the husband observes the usual abstinence such as not killing an animal or carrying a corpse.

Marriage: Marriage of a man with his sister's or maternal uncle's or paternal aunt's daughter was not formerly allowed. But this rule of exclusion has gradually lost its vigour and such marriages have now become fairly common. A Banjara may not marry the daughter of a paternal uncle or maternal aunt being such connections considered as incest. Two sisters may be married by one man but not simultaneously; and two brothers may marry two sisters of a family. The rule of exclusion is not covered by the rule of exogamy which prohibits marriage between a man and a woman standing analogously towards each other as brother and sister, parent and child, etc.

Divorce: Divorce is very easy and may be obtained almost at will. The only necessary condition is the assent of the *Naik* or *Nayak* for which some fee is paid to him. If the woman is subsequently married to her paramour, the latter has to pay the marriage expenses to the husband in addition to the usual bride-price both in cash and kind (bullocks). A fine is also to be paid to the castemen. If, however, she marries one not responsible for the divorce, her new life-partner pays only the bride-price. It is said that if a woman is pregnant at the time of elopement, the child is claimed by the husband and is delivered to him.

Death: The Banjaras generally dispose-off their dead by cremation. Bodies of unmarried persons are, however, carried by hand and buried with heads placed towards the north. On the third day, a party of elderly persons goes to the graveyard, and places some milk and dry grain on the grave. All take bath that day and the pollution is completely removed. In the case of death of a married person, the body is washed thoroughly in warm water and is covered with a new cloth as shroud. *Ghee* and jaggery are mixed together and put into the mouth of the corpse.

Dress : The dress and ornaments of the women form a characteristic feature of the Banjaras. They wear a skirt or *lunga* made of stout coarse print of Karwar cloth embroidered in heavy patterns. The *kanchali* (bodice) is also elaborately embroidered and is open at the back where it is tied with coloured ribbons. The bodice has three flaps with profuse needlework, and is bordered with lead discs-styled *ghugra* and *phoonda* (tassels). Two of them-*thunthania* fall upon the breasts and the other *khaviya* is sewn on the upper arm of the shoulder. Their a *chatiya* (veil) is also made of the same coarse cloth measuring about five feet and has an elaborate worked border. One end of it, tucked to the *petia* or *lunga* at the left side, goes over the head and hangs loose on the right shoulder. To that part of the veil which covers the head, a thick border-styled *ghoomto* with leaden beads and discs is attached which hangs on the forehead. At the back on the veil are sewn *ladakis* (pendants) made of black thread and embedded in metal cups-styled *topli*. *Jhalaro* is the thick waistband worked into the *petia*..

Ornaments : Their jewels are numerous and include strings of glass and wooden beads, besides those of brass and other metals. The more important of them are: *amti* and *top* are attached to the hair and are always coveredby the veil passing over them.

Bathada

Birth: The a *bayake* (pre-delivery ritual) is observed during the seventh month of pregnancy. The baby is ceremonially named on the twelfth day. Pre-delivery and post-natal restrictions are enforced on the women. Post-natal pollution is observed for eleven days. The *chowra* (tonsure) ceremony is performed only in the case of male children. Puberty rite known as *shobhana* is observed on the fifth day after menarche.

Marriage: Cross-cousin marriages or marriages with one's maternal uncle's or paternal aunt's daughter are permitted and practised. Exchange of daughters in marriage between two families is also permitted. Adult marriages are in vogue and marriages are settled through negotiation. It is a traditional practice to pay *terawu* (bride-price) whose amount from family to family. The *badhi* (dowry) was not practised earlier but at present it is paid in cash. *Dhare* ceremony (pouring coconut water or cow's milk on the hands of the bride and bridegroom), *thali* (marriage-badge) tying, and *Akshat aropana* (putting sacred rice over the bridal couple) are the important and binding parts for completion of marriage. Their *gurikaras* (caste headmen) assist in performing the marriage ritual. Divorce can be sought by either spouses on grounds of adultery and maladjustment, but it has to be approved by the caste elders. Widows, widowers and divorcees can remarry.

Death: Burial is the traditional practice to dispose of the dead. In recent days, cremation is also resorted to dispose-off the dead. The corpse of the child is invariably buried. In the case of death of a pregnant woman, the corpse is buried with face downward. Death pollution is observed for ten days and the house is purified on the eleventh day by sprinkling *tirtha* (sacred water) brought from a temple or a Brahmin's house. On the twelfth day, the *bojja* (death rite) is performed.

Ornaments : *Tali* or *thati* and toe-rings are the main ornaments usually worn by the married women.

Foods : The Bathadas are non-vegetarians and relish pork. Rice is their staple cereal. Pulses such as red gram and *tur*, and vegetables are also consumed. Coconut oil is the cooking medium.

Traditional Occupation : The Bathadas were traditionally agricultural labourers. They worked as *moolade-okkalu* (bonded labourers) attached to land-owning castes like Brahmin, Bant and Bhillava. In return, the Bathadas used to get shelter, food and financial help at the time of marriages and illness. They are now free from bonded labour and generally work as casual or daily wage labourers. It is stated that the Bathadas used earlier to serve their master in disposal of the dead by digging the grave or arranging the funeral pyre. However, such practice is reported to be abandoned since the last few decades.

Beda Jangam, Budga Jangam

Birth: Pre-delivery rituals are observed. Like people of the other local castes/communities, the Beda Jangams, Budga Jangams enforce certain restrictions on women during the pre-and post-natal periods. In the fifth or sixth month, the child is given *annaprasana* (ritually fed with cereals). In the case of a male child, the *puttuventrukalu theeyuta* (tonsure ceremony) is performed. For a female child, the ears and nose are pierced before three years of age.

Marriage: The caste is endogamous and the caste men follow surname exogamy. Marriage with either one's maternal uncle's or paternal aunt's or elder sister's daughter is preferred. The common age at marriage for boys is 20 years and for girls it is 14 years. The custom of *oli* (bride-price) is still practised. Marriage rituals which last for a day only are usually performed in the bride's residence. The marriage expenses are generally borne by the groom's side. After marriage, patrilocal residence is the norm. Incompatibility or adultery may lead to divorce if either party seeks divorce, and it is granted after the approval of the *Kula peddalu* (caste elders). Compensation is mostly paid to the aggrieved party. Remarriage is permissible for widows, widowers and divorcees. Sororate is allowed.

Death: Burial is the common mode of disposal of the dead. On the third day, *dina karyamu* (mortuary rites) is performed. Ancestor worship is observed every year on the *Kottamavasya* (lumar conjunction of the fortnight) days.

Ornaments : *Thali* (marriage spendant) made of *nalla poosalu* (black beads), a nose-ring, toe-rings and nose-stud are the common ornaments for married women and these are usually worn by them.

Foods : The Beda Jangams are non-vegetarians and eat pork also, though they abstain from taking beef. Their staple cereal is rice, and it is eaten with pulses like red gram, black gram and green gram. Only occasionally, they consume roots and tubers. Groundnut and sunflower oils are used as the cooking medium.

Traditional Occupation : Traditional occupation of Beda Jangams, Budga Jangams was soothsaying and seeking alms. They were religious mendicants. Traditionally, they officiated as priests for people of the Holeya and Madiga castes and communities.

Bellara

Birth: In the seventh month of pregnancy, the *bayake* (a pre-delivery ritual) is performed. A woman is treated with a ceremonial feast during the period of birth pollution which lasts for eleven days. The naming ceremony is performed after the twelfth day of the child's birth.

Puberty: The puberty ritual is conducted on the fifth day after menarche.

Marriage: Marriage with the paternal aunt's or the maternal uncle's daughter is preferred, while uncle-niece marriages are prohibited. Adult marriages are arranged through negotiation. The age-old custom of *teravu* (paying bride-price) is still prevalent among them and its amount varies from case to case. Dowry, though was not practised earlier, has now been started recently and the amount varies from a few hundred to thousand rupees. Marriage rituals like *dhare* and *thali*-tying are performed at the bride's house but consummation takes place at the bridegroom's residence. Junior sororate is permitted. Unlike their customary practice, the bride now goes to stay with her husband after marriage. The *kaiwatta* (widow remarriage) takes place without any auspicious rituals. A man can divorce his wife, with the approval of elders, on charges of adultery, and in such cases the children stay with the mother.

Death: Their dead are buried. Death pollution is observed for ten days. The ancestors are worshipped once a year. At some places, the dead are disposed-off by cremation. On the eleventh day, the departed soul is offered food and other items at the site of the cremation. The relatives are fed with specially prepared food called *koti purmanna*.

Dwelling : The houses of Bellaras built in groups of three to four families in a single segment or cluster are generally found at the outskirts of the villages. They live in small huts which resemble those of other neighbouring communities.

Ornaments : *Karimani* (*tali*) and toe-rings are the most common ornaments worn by the married women.

Foods : The Bellaras are non-vegetarians and eat pork. But their staple food is rice and it is eaten with pulses like red grams. The caste people also eat tubers and roots that are available in the forest. Coconut oil is the cooking medium.

Traditional Occupation : The Bellara is a caste of basket-makers. The people of this caste used in past to make variety of baskets mainly from bamboo. These baskets were usedfor domestic and agricultural purposes, and also for storage of grains, apart from winnowing fans and cradles. The bamboo was freely collected from the nearby jungles.

Bhambi, Bhambhi, Asadaru...etc./

Chamar/Chambhar/Meghval/ Samagara

The customs followed by the Bhambis, Asadarus, in Karnataka State are briefly presented in the following paragraphs. These customs vary, to some extent, from one State to another, and also from Bhambis, Asadarus to Chamars, Mochis, and from Chambhars to Samgaras.

Birth: The *kupsa* (pre-delivery ritual) is observed during the seventh month of pregnancy. Birth pollution lasts for twenty days. Post-natal restrictions also the new mother exist.

Puberty: The *hosige* (puberty ceremony) is observed and the first menstrual pollution lasts for twelve days.

Marriage: Marriage with one's paternal aunt's or maternal uncle's daughter is permitted. Earlier, child marriages were practised but nowadays this practice has been replaced by adult marriages. Mates are acquired through negotiation. The *thiru* (bride-price) is payable in cash. Junior sororate is allowed. Men can seek divorce on ground of maladjustment, adultery and serious illness of their wives. The divorced woman is paid compensation and it is the father who takes over the responsibility of the children after divorce. Widowers and male divorcees are allowed to remarry. Marriages are solemnized at the bridegroom's residence and the marriage feasts are hosted by the groom's father.

Death: Their dead are buried and the *thithi* (observance of the twelfth day ritual) marks the end of the death pollution.

Dress : The dress of a male consists of a *chokka* (shirt)–an upper garment and a *dhoti* (*Pancha*)–a lower garment. A cloth is also put on the shoulders from the right to the left side. Women wear *saree* and blouse.

Ornaments : In Andhra Pradesh, the common ornaments worn by women include a *Murugulu* (bracelet) on the left hand, a *Sajjalu* on the right hand, and *addapusalu* and *Kadalu* (nose studs). In Karnataka, the *thali* (sacred pendant) and toe-rings are the ornaments worn by the married women.

Foods : The caste people are non-vegetarian. The staple cereals consumed are rice and *jowar*. The common pulse used is red gram.

Traditional Occupation : Leather work was the traditional occupation of the caste people.

Bharatar/Paravan

Birth: Among Bharatars, the first delivery generally takes place in the house of the parents of the mother. The delivery is attended to by a *kudimagal* (a woman belonging to the barber caste) who is traditionally paid about five rupees for her work. The placenta is usually buried in the backyard of the house where the mother takes her bath during the period of pollution. Birth pollution is observed for twenty-two days although, according to some reports, it is observed only for fifteenth days. During the first three days, no solid food is given to the mother. On the fifteenth or twenty-second day as the case may be, pollution is terminated by performing *Punyahava-chanam*. In this ceremony, water sanctified by a Brahmin is brought and sprinkled all over the house to remove the pollution completely

Puberty: When a Bharatar girl attains puberty, she is kept separately in a portion of the house. Puberty entails pollution for sixteen days. A few have reported that it lasts for 22 days. On the sixteenth or twenty-second day, *sadangu kazhithal* takes place wherein pollution is terminated. During this ceremony, a ceremonial bath is given to the girl and the maternal uncle presents her with a new *saree*, mirror, powder, snow, flowers, etc. A Brahmin is invited and asked to sprinkle water on the girl and in the house. The womenfolk observe pollution for three to four days when they attain menstruation. During the period of pollution, they are not allowed to touch the vessels used by other members of the household.

Marriage: The initiative for a marriage always comes from the groom's side. The groom's parents and maternal uncle go to the bride's place to see her. If both the parties agree to the alliance, the *vettrilai pakku kai mattral* takes place in which betel leaves and arecanuts are exchanged. The date for the *nichayatham-boolam* (betrothal) is also fixed immediately. On the betrothal day, the groom's party visit the house of the bride and present her with a *saree*, betel, flowers, etc. No bride-price is given by them. Then, the *muhurtham* (an auspicious day and timings) is fixed for celebration of the marriage after consulting the astrologers. Generally, eight or fifteen days after betrothal the marriage takes place.

Death: The Bharatars cremate the dead bodies of elders and in case of children, the bodies are buried. If the eldest son dies, he is, however, cremated and not buried. The last day, obsequies called *Kalleduppu* are performed on the sixteenth day. On this occasion, rice and pulses are cooked in the cremation ground and thrown to the crows. The relatives are invited for this and given a vegetarian feast. On the seventeenth day, the close relatives take oil bath and terminate the pollution completely. Then, they participate in a non-vegetarian dinner. This marks the end of pollution. The Bharatars perform death anniversaries in memory of the departed soul.

The Sunnambu Paravans dispose-off their dead either by cremation or burial. If they decide to bury the dead, they dig a pit in the north-south direction and place the head towards the south. On the sixteenth day, they perform the *karumanthiram* (last day obsequies). The Sunnambu Paravans have their own burial ground and other caste Hindu members do not make use of it.

Dwelling : The Bharatars' houses are not built on any specified layout. They form an irregular cluster. Some houses are separate but most of them touch each other so as to be contiguous. Most of the houses are mud-walled with thatched roofings. The material used for thatching is mostly palm leaf. The roofings are generally low probably to guard against strong winds. A few of the houses are brick-walled and for the roofing, they have used a type of country tiles which resemble the Mangalore tiles. These flat tiles are locally made by the potters. The roofings, whether thatched or tiled, are highly slanting so that during heavy rain water can drain-off quickly without causing any leak. Most of the houses have only one room with a verandah. The inner room is used both as kitchen and for keeping household articles. The outer verandah is used for sleeping during non-rainy days. The plastering in the houses is renewed every year in the month of *thai* (January-February) and the houses are white-washed.

Dress : Men wear short *dhoties*. They do not generally put on any cloth or towel over the upper body but wear shirts on important occasions. The women-folk wear *sarees* of eight yards' length, and the style of wearing is similar to that found among the Paravan women of Kanyakumari. In this style, the saree *palluv* put on the right side is thrown under the arm pit and brought round over the shoulder and then tied in the front into a knot. They also wear a loose jacket which is buttoned in the front at the top. The ends of the blouse at the front are tied into a knot below the breast. They prefer clothes of dark colours. Elderly widows wear white *sarees*. Older women do not generally wear blouses.

Ornaments : The Bharatar women wear a pair of *Kammals* (ear-studs) in the ear-lobes, one or two nose-screws and a couple of glass bangles. A few old women have dialated ear-lobes in which are worn ornaments called *pambadam, tandatti muduchu, asthuraban* and *meladu*. These ornaments form a bunch in the ear-lobes. They are similar to the ones worn by Nadar women in Ramanathapuram, Tirunelveli, Katta-bomman and Madurai districts of Tamil Nadu.

Foods : The staple diet of the Bharatars is rice. Cultivation of millet in the parts where they live is not extensive and as such it is taken occasionally. They take meals three times a day. The morning and mid-day meals are in the shape of rice gruel. The night meal is in a solid form with a sauce prepared with fish or vegetable. Their consumption of vegetables is inadequate but to compensate that they take plenty of fish. They are essentially non-vegetarians and have no objection to consume mutton, chicken, duck, etc. However, they are prohibited from eating beef and pork. They do not also eat the flesh of rat or bandicoot. They observe Fridays and Tuesdays as vegetarian days.

Traditional Occupation : The Bharatars engaged in fishing are freshwater fishermen. They are not very skilful in this line like the Mukkavans and Meena-Paravans. A few among them do fishing in shallow waters. The income earned by the Bharatars in fishing is meagre and is supplemented by other occupations. The mainstay of the Sunnambu Paravans is collection of shells from the sea and burning them for lime.

Bhovi

Birth: In the seventh or the eighth month of the first pregnancy, the *simant* ceremony is observed. Birth pollution lasts upto the tenth day and the naming ceremony is performed on the same day.

Puberty: When a girl attains puberty, she is confined in a special hut in which a piece of iron, margosa leaves (*melia Azadirachta)*, sticks of *Strychnos*

Nux-vomica and the arka plant (*Calotropis gigantea*) are placed to ward-off evil spirits. For fear of these spirits, she is not allowed to eat meat though eggs are permitted. On the seventh day, a fowl is killed, waved in front of the girl and thrown away. At the end of the period of pollution, the hut is burnt down. Sometimes when the girl bathes on the first day, a sieve is held over her head and water poured through it. In some places on the eleventh day, chicken broth mixed with arrack (liquor) is administered on the girl in order to make her back and waist strong. The hen from which the broth is made must be a black one, and she must have laid eggs for the first time.

Marriage: Marriage with one's maternal uncle's or paternal aunt's or elder sister's daughter is permitted. Both child and adult marriages were practised in the past but at present, adult marriage is the norm. The marriage ceremony, in its simplest form, is that the bride and bridegroom walk three times round a stake placed in the ground. In the more elaborate ritual on the betrothal day, the bride-price, etc. are fixed and an adjournment is made to the toddy shop. The marriage rituals include *aradhana* (prayer or worship), *dhare* (jointing hands together of bride and groom) and *muharta* (auspicious occasion for performing the actual marriage ritual). Junior sororate is allowed. Either spouse can seek divorce with social approval on the grounds of adultery, barrenness and maladjustment. A woman found guilty of immorality is to carry a basketful of earth from house to house before she is re-admitted to the caste. The remarriage of a widow, widower and divorcee is allowed.

Death: Their dead are generally buried. Among some Bhovis, the corpse wrapped up in a new thick coarse cloth and with a *dhubati* is carried by four men to the burial-ground. On the way to the grave, the corpse is laid on the ground and rice is thrown over its eyes. It is then washed and the *namam* (Vaishnavite sect mark) is painted or *vibuthi* (sacred ashes) is smeared on the forehead of a man and *kunkumam* (coloured powder) on that of a female. Earth is thrown into the grave before it is filled in by those assembled there. On the *karmandhiram* (last day of the death ceremonies), the relations proceed to a tank or well outside the village and take bath. An effigy is made with mud to which cooked rice, etc. are offered. Some rice is cooked and placed on an *arka* (*Calotropis*) leaf as an offering to the crows. The widow of the deceased man is taken to the water's edge and made to sit on a winnow. Her bangles are broken and the *bottu* (the vermilion mark) is snapped by her brother.

Dwelling : The Bhovis live in houses built with mud-terraced flat roof or with straw/grass roof. The walls of these houses are generally made up of mud.

Dress : The dress for males include shirt, *banian* and *'jubba'* for the upper garments, and knicker or *dhoti* of four yards for the lower garments. *Dhotis* are used occasionally in the form of *kache* by the elders and in the form of *'dhotti'* by the youngsters. The typical dress of the females is *saree* worn in the ordinary style without any form of *kache* and a blouse. The coarser varieties of *saree* of 40 counts are generally worn by them.

Ornaments : Ornaments used by the men are rings and ear-studs. The ear-rings, nose-studs and toe-rings are the most common ornaments used by women irrespective of the economic condition. Silver ornaments like *kalumuri* and chain for the ankles are also popular. Glass bangles and *kadagas* made of silver or brass are most common ornaments worn on hands by the women.

Foods : *Ragi* lumps form their main diet. A soup called *saru* prepared by using vegetables, pulses and spice forms the main side dish for the *ragi* lumps which are dipped in the soup and then swallowed. They are non-vegetarians and their chief non-vegetarian food comprises mutton got from sheep, goats and poultry.

Traditional Occupation : Earth-digging, stone-cutting and daily wage labour have been their traditional occupations.

Bindla/Kolupulvandlu

Birth: No ceremony is celebrated during the period of pregnancy, but the woman is fed with whatever she desires. However, she is served with *pulagam* (rice boiled with green gram *dal* and turmeric powder), *payasam* (preparation of rice and milk with sugar) and sometimes even intoxicating liquors. If in the past the delivery was found very difficult then one of the male members of the family used to secure a gun and shoot in the air so that immediately after hearing the sound the delivery could take place. Such a belief still continues among the people. Also at the time of delivery if the pregnant woman is suffering from severe pains, all the neighbouring women sit there and produce sounds by beating a brass vessel with a ladle. They utter the words *'Rama, Rama, Narayana, Narayana'* until the delivery takes place. With the utterance of *Rama Rama* along with the sounds, they believe that God blesses the pregnant woman with easy delivery. The pregnant woman is taken to her parents' place during the advanced stage of pregnancy for the first confinement. The other births take place at her husband's house only.

Puberty: The menstruating girl is made to rest in a separate shed raised for this purpose. The period of pollution is for nine days and the purificatory ceremony is performed on the tenth day. She is fed with delicious food on all the nine days. But bath is given on alternate days. As the girl is married before puberty in this caste or community and she happens to live at her husband's place, her parents are called for on the day of cessation of pollution. They bring new clothes for both the girl and her husband. If the girl is healthy enough, the consummation ceremony is performed on the third day after the completion of pollution otherwise it is postponed until the girl feels better. They strictly observe the pollution for five days for the subsequent menses and the woman is not allowed to touch any utensils during these days.

Marriage: Marriage through negotiation is the only type in practice. They take sufficient care to see that all marriages are performed before attainment of puberty by the girls. It would be very difficult to perform marriages after attainment of puberty by the girls. Usually, girls are married between nine and twelve years of age while the marriageable age for the boys is between 16 and 20 years. The preferential alliances for marriage are maternal uncle's daughter, paternal aunt's daughter, and own sister's daughter. Widow remarriage is permitted in this caste. If both parties agree, the acceptance is conveyed to the caste *Panchayat*. The children if any of the deceased husband may, however, be handed over to his relations.

Death: Their dead are cremated and dead infants are buried. On the third day, they celebrate the *chinna divasam* (the day of mortury rites). Some special dishes are prepared on that day and a fowl is sacrificed. The food is taken by the son to the funeral ground. The ashes at the crematory are collected and heaped below a tree. The bones that are burnt away are collected and covered in a pit along with the food taken there. Everyday, the place where the deceased breathed his last is cleaned and decorated with *muggulu* (camphor), flowers, etc. The eldest son or, in his absence, the wife of the deceased takes food in a leaf plate at the spot until the day of final obsequies and collects those leaf plates at a place. On the eleventh day, the final obsequies take place. A sheep is sacrificed on that day. Soon after the food is prepared, the son takes it to the funeral ground along with the used leaf plates, eats it and burns all the leaf plates. On that day, some stones are fixed on the spot where the bones of the dead were buried..

Dwelling : The dwellings of the people of this caste are always in a corner of the village. The usual house type is known as *purigudisa* (a hut roofed with locally available grass). A plot is selected for the house construction, and is cleaned and sprinkled with cowdung water at the central portion. An interesting test is conducted by head of the household to fix up the site. Nine *cowries* (*Cypro Arabica*) are taken and thrown nine times on the spot. The total number of *cowries* which are turned flat in each throw are counted. The total figure is divided by nine, if it exceeds nine. The remainder is noted and referred to a book named *Navagraha Chintamani* for the decision. Usually, the remainders 4, 5 and 6 are considered to be lucky. After selecting the plot, an auspicious day is fixed for the commencement of the house construction.

Dress : The dress of a male consists of a *dhoti* of four yards in length and a shirt requiring about three yards of cloth. People over 40 years of age wear headgear of three yards in length. The young ones alone wear *banians*. Coarse cloth is generally preferred as they work in fields, etc. The dress of a female consists of a handloom *saree* of seven to eight yards in length and a blouse stitched in a cloth of one yard. Excepting the young women, others generally do not use the bodice. The women of the above age group have become accustomed to wearing bodice only after noticing the higher caste people or getting exposed to the city life. Unmarried boys wear knickers and shirts. The girls use petticoats and blouses.

Ornaments : Men aged 40 years and above wear *kammalu* (ear ornaments). Women wear *kammalu*, *kalavarlu* (ear ornaments), *ontimutyam theegalu* and *besari* (nose ornaments) made either of gold or brass. They also wear an ornament known as *nanupatteda* round their neck. Both males and females have tattoo marks on their forehead and forearms. Sometimes, small dots are also found on the cheeks of the females. The tattoo marks seem to serve a decorative purpose.

Food : They consume all kinds of cereals but most often rice, wheat, *jonna* (great millet), *samulu* (little millet), maize and *ragi* (finger millet). They do not eat any wild roots. Everyday, food is taken thrice. In the morning, the leftovers of the previous night are taken. In the afternoon, gruel prepared out of *jowar* or *ragi* flour is taken with *chutney* (prepared with *dal*, chillis, salt and tamarind) which forms the second meal. The third meal is taken late in the evening when rice with curry (prepared out of vegetables) is consumed. Among the vegetables, *gummadi* (pumpkin) and *potla* (snakegourd) are prohibited as they are worshippers of *Amba* (goddess). The flesh of fowls, peacocks and *kanjulu* (partridges) among birds and that of sheep, goat, tortoise and pig among animals is eaten. Beef is prohibited by the people of this caste. They eat the flesh of scaly and scaleless fish and drink liquor. They eat the flesh of the dead animals only if the animals are domesticated by them. On festive days, sweets are prepared in addition to their daily menu.

Traditional Occupation : The traditional occupation of the people of this caste was to worship and appease the various goddesses. *Jamdika* was the musical instrument which played an important role at the time of worship and invocation of goddesses like *Mutyalamma*, *Mahishamma* and *Ellamma*. In the past, women of the caste were not accustomed to go out of the home and seek labour.Bindla/Kolupulvandlu

Byagara

Birth: A perpetuator of the family line is rated high and, hence, the joy is all the greater if the child born is a male. If a man fails to have issue from his wife within a reasonable period after marriage, he takes a second wife. Barrenness is considered a curse. Prayers for having a child are offered to such goddesses as *Yellamma*, *Huligemma* or even to the stone planted at the main entrance of the village. It was not uncommon in the past to take a vow that if a girl child was born, she would be dedicated to the service of the goddess. Such a dedicated child or woman would spend her entire life singing the glory of the goddess and leading the life of a *Basavi* (prostitute).

Puberty: When a girl menstruates for the first time, she is considered ritually impure. She is segregated and is confined to a corner of the house. If she is already married, the news is conveyed to her parents-in-law who send choice food articles to her. On the ninth (or the fifth) day, she is bathed and her clothes, dishes, etc. are all cleaned. The caste members are treated to a feast and in the evening a simple ceremony is held.

Marriage: Pre-puberty marriage is more in vogue among Byagaras. The marriageable age for girls is between 10 and 15 years. Marriage after the girl's attainment of puberty exposes one to social ridicule. But this increased nowadays, and girls are married after they attain puberty. Boys are married before the age of 23 or 24 years. A woman is entitled to undergo the *lagna* (marriage rite) only once during her life-time, while no such restrictions exist for a man. However, a widow or divorcee is permitted to join another man.

Death: Their dead are buried. The unmarried dead are buried in lying posture and the married ones in seated posture. The dead bodies of a pregnant woman, a woman dying soon after childbirth and of a leper are cremated. At some places, the corpse of a leper is usually thrown into the river. In several villages and towns, the Byagaras have a separate graveyard. The corpse is disposed-off during daytime and never after dusk.

Dwelling : The Byagaras generally live in the outskirts or at a little away from *gramtana* (village site). Their settlement is termed either *Byagara oni* or *Harijanwada*.

Ornaments : The more commonly used men's ornaments are finger-rings and ear-studs. A few men may also be seen wearing silver armlets or silver wristlets. A few relatively well-to-do wear the *Metimuruvu*—a crescent shaped gold ornament on the upper lobe of the right ear. Silver finger-ring (sometimes of copper, if poor) worn on the small finger of the right hand is called *honnugura* and is normally presented to a man by his in-laws on betrothal. Some men, more often boys, wear silver waist-strings.

Traditional Occupation : Settled cultivation, farm labour and 'begar' service such as grave digging, etc. were the traditional occupations of the Byagaras.

Chakkiliyan/Pagadai/Madari

Birth: The people of this caste observe pre-delivery rituals for pregnant women. The pregnant woman is taken to her parental home in the seventh month of her first pregnancy. The *Valaikappu* ceremony is held in which an elderly woman adorns the hands of the pregnant woman with glass bangles. A *maruthuvachi* (midwife) attends to the delivery. The confinement period is fifteen days. Immediately after birth, the baby is given three drops of the milk of the ass. The first child in a family is named after the family deity or an ancestor. The tonsuring and earboring ceremonies (only of girls) are conducted within three years of birth. These ceremonies are performed in the temples of family deities. Half of the expenses of each such ceremony is borne by the maternal uncle of the child.

Marriage: Maternal uncle-niece and cross-cousin marriages are practised. Adult marriage is the norm. Girls are usually married between the ages of 16 and 20 years, while boys marry between 20 and 26 years of age. Bride-price as well as dowry are prevalent. In Pondicherry, bride-price is not offered but in the name of *secrvarisai*, the parents of the bride offer the couple some clothes and household articles. The marriages are arranged, through negotiation, by the parents of the groom and the bride. The marriage rituals last for two days. Weddings are held at the residence of the bridegroom

Death: The dead are either cremated or buried. While the Saivite Chakkiliyans bury their dead, the others cremate them. The eldest son performs the last rites. A death entails pollution for 16 days. The *karumathi* (an expiatory ceremony) is performed on the last day.

Dress : Men and women have very simple attire-*dhoti* (a piece of cloth measuring two yards) and a towel or upper cloth constitute the typical dress of an adult male. Women wear only a coloured *saree* of eight yards. Only young women wear jackets with the *sarees*. Young boys wear a small 'Komanam' (a piece of cloth of three inches breadth suported by a waist-cord). Only when they are grown up (say five or six years), they use a towel in the form of a *dhoti* but without any shirt or upper cloth. Little girls upto the age of two or three years go naked but sometimes, they wear 'Arai-moodi' (a leaf shaped piece of silver suspended by a waist-cord). This has been so due to their poor economic condition, but some definite changes have taken place in their dress pattern in the recent years.

Ornaments : Ear-rings and nose-rings are very common; invariably all middle aged and young women wear these rings. *Kunukkus* (rings made of lead) are common among the girls. Even men wear *Kadukkan* (ear-rings).

Food : The diet of the Chakkiliyans/Pagadais/ Madaris is generally cereal. Rice as well as millet grains such as cumbu, cholam, varagu, etc. are taken. Almost all of their households take non-vegetarian food which includes even beef and pork.

Traditional Occupation : The Chakkiliyans are traditional leather workers. In the past, they used to remove dead cattle as well of the caste Hindus in the nearby villages.

Chalavadi

Birth: For the first delivery, a woman is taken to the house of her parents. On the fifth day after delivery, *purudu* (purification) ceremony is performed and the mother is given bath. The parents consult a Lingayat *Jangam* (caste priest) and name the child on that day. The common names are those of forefathers and of deities. Sometimes, father's name is also given to the child. The usual names are Anjappa, Barsappa, Hanumanthappa, Kedireppa, Nagamma, Narasimhulu, Rachappa, Rajappa, Timmappa, etc. They invite relatives and friends to attend the function. The invitees present clothes and ornaments to the child.

The maternal uncle of the child attends the tonsure ceremony which usually takes place in a temple. He cuts five locks of hair and then the barber completes the work. On this happy occasion, the barber receives some money, new clothes and sweets. All the relatives and friends present on the occasion dine together.

Puberty: When the girl attains maturity, she is made to sit in a separate room for ten days on a mat of palmyra leaves. On the eleventh day, she is given bath. Some relatives send her sweets and other eatables. In the evening, some of the relatives present her new clothes and the women assembled sing songs.

Marriage: Marriage through negotiation is the only system in practice. Marrying one's maternal uncle's daughter, paternal aunt's daughter and sister's daughter is common. The usual marriageable age for a girl is between 12 and 13 years, and for a boy between 18 and 25 years. The father sends some of his close relatives to locate a bride for his son. When a suitable girl is located, the father and mother of the boy negotiate the marriage. If they are satisfied, the bride's parents are invited to the boy's house. When both parties are satisfied, they go to a Lingayat *Jangam* who fixes an auspicious day for marriage. The marriage is usually celebrated at the bride's residence.

Death: The dead are usually buried in lying posture with the head to the south. Those dying of infectious diseases are cremated. After death, the corpse is given hot water bath. Vermilion is applied to the forehead and the family god is worshipped. On the way to the burial ground, the bier is placed on the ground for some time and the people shout the name of the dead. The body is buried in a grave dug by a man of the caste. On the third day, they pour some milk on the grave and construct a *samadhi* (raised plateform). They have given up the old practice of taking intoxicating liquors and meat during the ceremonies associated with death..

Dress : The pattern of dressing of the Chalavadis is very simple. Men wear either *dhoti* or a knicker and a shirt. Some old people wear turbans also. The dress of women consists of a *saree* and a blouse. Chiidren below the age of five years go naked in the streets. Sometimes, the boys wear shirts and the girls wear gowns. Elderly women generally tie their hair into a knot in the back, whereas young women wear plaits.

Ornaments : The ornaments of Chalavadis are few. Women wear *mattelu* made of silver and *ungaralu* (finger-rings) made of either gold or silver. Married women wear *puste* (marriage-locket). But there is no taboo attached to the wearing of other ornaments popular among the women of other castes in the village. *Mattetu* and *puste* cannot be worn by unmarried girls and widows as they are symbols of married status. Except these, they can wear any other ornaments.

Generally, most of the women get their body tattooed. But this practice is very rare among men. Tattooing is done by Koya (Scheduled Tribe) women. It serves only a decorative purpose.

Foods : They generally take *ragi sankati* (a liquid preparation with finger millet) with *karam* (chilly powder). Occasionally, they take *jowar roti* also. They have rice once in a week or on festive occasions with other items like vegetable *sambar* (a liquid preparation prepared with *dhal*, tamarind and vegetables), curry and *rasam* (a liquid preparation made out of tamarind juice). On festive occasions, they have *payasam* (a sweet preparation). They consume vegetables like brinjals, cucumbers, etc. which are commonly available. Being non-vegetarian, they take only the flesh of goat, sheep, chicken and hare. But they eat all types of fish. They do not relish the flesh of dead animals. Eating of beef is strictly prohibited.

Traditional Occupation : The traditional occupation of the people of this caste was that of blowing trumpets and other musical instruments during marriage and other festive occasions, apart from weaving in Andhra Pradesh. In Karnataka, their traditional occupation was stated to be carrying carcasses and working as village servants. Three decades ago, they were usually paid meagre wages in cash for their day's service in Andhra Pradesh. These people are very proficient in playing different kinds of musical instruments.

Chandala

Foods : The Chandalas are non-vegetarians. Rice and *ragi* are their staple cereals.

Traditional Occupation : Traditional occupation of the Chandalas is stated to be cultivation and weaving.

Chenna Dasar, Holaya Dasar/ Holeya Dasari

Birth: The *kupsa* (a pre-delivery ritual) is performed in the fifth month of pregnancy of a woman. Birth pollution is observed for one month. The naming ceremony is performed on the tenth day for boys and on the fifth day for girls. The *Jawala* (tonsure ceremony) is observed only for boys when they are five years of age.

The *neriyudu* (puberty rites) are performed for the girls after observing the first menstrual pollution for eleven days.

Marriage: Both cross-cousin as well as uncle-niece types of marriages are allowed. Marriages are settled through negotiations and adult marriages are the norm. A bride-price of Rs. 20 is paid before the marriage. This amount has increased in the recent years. Tying *tali* (marriage badge) around the bride's neck by the groom and offering *akshats* (sprinkling turmeric's coloured rice over the bridal couple by the people assembled at the time of marriage) are the essential marriage rites. An elderly person of their caste serves as the functionary in conducting marriage rituals. Divorce is allowed with social approval on grounds of adultery and maladjustment. The bride-price, *tali* and marriage expenses have to be returned before the dissolution of marriage. Widower, widow or divorcee remarriages are permitted. Such marriages are called *Udike*. Junior sororate is practised. The marriage ceremony and the consummation of marriage take place at the bridegroom's residence. dead is burial in which the dead body is buried in sitting position facing east. Children below ten years of age are buried in lying position. The corpse of the pregnant woman or one who died during or soon after delivery is cremated. Those who died due to cancer, tuberculosis, leprosy, etc. are also cremated. The mourning period is observed for nine days. On the third day after the disposal of dead body, milk is poured over the grave. On the ninth day, the house is cleaned by smearing the floor with cow-dung and sprinkling sacred water brought from the temple or well.

Dwelling : The Holeya Dasaris generally live, alongside the houses of Holayas, away from the main village settlement. These houses are found in separate hamlets at the fringe of the villages. Their locality or settlement is called *Holageri*.

Ornaments : *Tali* and toe-rings are the main ornaments of married women.

Foods : They are occasionally non-vegetarians. They eat chicken, mutton, etc. but not beef. Rice, *jowar* and wheat are their staple cereals, and gram, *tur* and *urad* are the pulses consumed by them.

Traditional Occupation : The Chenna Dasars/ Holeya Dasaris are traditionally Vaishnava mendicants who are dedicated to Lord Venkateshwara. They are engaged in singing devotional songs, narrating legendary and historic stories regarding kings, gods, etc. They also look after the cleanliness of the temple premises of Hanuman (Monkey-God), and sing devotional songs every morning and evening sitting near the *garudagamba* (lamp-post) of the temple as stated earlier. For this service, they are given a small piece of cultivable land as *inamibhoomi* (gift land). The Vaishnavite castes such as Beda, Walmiki, Wodda, Kabber, etc. invite them to perform the *pooja* (worship) sitting at the doorsteps of their houses, after they come back from the pilgrimage to Venkatara of Tirupathi. For this service, the Holeya Dasaris are given *Gopala tumbuwadu* (alms in cash and kind). They also serve as the functionaries at the time of marriage and other socio-religious ceremonies among the Holeyas.

Dakkal, Dokkalwar

Birth: The pregnancy of a woman is made known to her husband by the other female members of the family after two months. If the pregnant woman has her parents alive, then she is taken to her parents' house during the ninth month. She stays there till the completion of second month for the child after its birth. The subsequent births usually take place at her husband's place only. They do not go to hospital for delivery. A portion of the house is separated for the purpose of confinement which is enclosed by clothes or a cot. The delivery is attended to by a *dai* (midwife) who is usually an experienced woman of the caste. If the delivery is difficult, a woman from the barber community is invited to attend. Normally, a barber woman does not serve Dakkala community.

Puberty: The normal age of puberty among the girls in this caste is between 12 and 14 years. During the first menstruation, pollution is observed for 10 days and final bath is given on the 11th day. The girl is segregated on all these 10 days. A separate hut is erected by the maternal uncle and in his absence the parents themselves attend to this. The food served to her is very simple consisting of rice and curry (prepared out of *dal*). Sweets are also given to her. She takes bath every day during the period of pollution and changes the clothes. On the 11th day, she is given oil bath and is presented with a new *saree* and blouse. Relatives are treated with a feast on that day.

Marriage: Marriage through negotiation is common in this caste or community. The normal age at marriage for males is between 20 and 25 years, while for females it is between 12 and 18 years. The permissible partners for marriage are maternal uncle's daughter, paternal aunt's daughter and own sister's daughter. Marriage is endogamous with reference to caste and exogamous with reference to *intiperulu* or *gotramulu*. There is no practice of dowry payment among them. Marriage is celebrated at the residence of the groom. An elderly man of the caste officiates during the marriage.

Death: Their dead are usually buried, head facing south and upwards. Soon after the death, the corpse is given bath and wrapped in a new cloth. Turmeric is applied to the face and head. The corpse is placed on the bier and is carried by four persons to the burial ground. Only the nearest relatives follow the corpse. The eldest son holds the fire pot and leads the corpse. On the way, the corpse is brought down. Some *sambrani* powder is sprinkled in the fire pot and the smoke is made to pass over the corpse. The carriers of the bier change their places at this spot. The pit is dug by a Dakkal man and the corpse is placed in it. It is covered with mud and a stone is placed over it.

Dwelling : Their settlements are generally crowded and they live along with people of the other castes like. Mala and Madiga. Only two types of houses *Chapillu* or *Chapagudise* and *chuttillu* are prevalent among the Dakkalas. The *Chapillu* is an improvised hut temporarily erected since they wander from one village to the other. There are no regular walls as such for these huts. The ground plan is circular with about five feet radius and at the centre of it, a pole of five feet is fixed in the ground. There is a small entrance to this hut and one has to bend very low while entering it because it is so low roofed and unplastered. Cooking is not done inside except in the rainy season for fear of fire accidents. This is exclusively used for sleeping and living purpose.

Dress : A Dakkala male wears a *dhoti*, shirt and a head-gear. He can have moustaches and long hair on the head, and also a bag hanging down the shoulders containing some medicines and a bundle of palmyra leaf books. He also wears *gongali* (a woollen blanket) on the shoulders and keeps a staff in his hand. The dress of a female is comprised of a *saree* and a blouse only. The pattern of wearing *saree* is local. The girls wear frocks or a skirt and blouse. The dress of boys consists of knicker and a shirt.

Ornaments : There are no special ornaments for females except the usual ones like *pusthe*, bangles, ear ornaments and *mattelu*. A nose ornament called *mukku pogu* on the nostril is popular among female members of this caste. Both male and female have tattoo marks for decorative purpose.

Foods : The staple food of Dakkals, Dakkalwars/ Dakkaligas consists of rice, *jowar*, maize and *sajjalu* (bulrush millet). They also eat tubers like *alligaddalu*, *govinda gaddalu* and *seema pendalam* (yam) which are available in the forest and are obtained by digging to a depth of 3 to 4 feet in the surrounding places. Their routine food habit consists of two meals—one in the afternoon and the other in the night. The first meal consists of *jonna gataka* or *janna sankati* (solid food prepared out of *jowar flour*) and *karam* (chutney prepared out of chillis).

Traditional Occupation : Since they are traditional bards of Madigas, their main occupation is to give particulars relating to the genealogy of different families of Madigas. They tell some stories relating to their origin and charge some rupees from every Madiga household once in a year. Every Dakkala has a jurisdiction over 10 to 20 villages where he has a right to collect the amount from the household earmarked for him.

Devendrakulathan/Kudumban

Birth: Pre and post-delivery rituals are observed. Soon after birth, the new born is given *Cennai* (palm jaggery water) and pollution is observed for sixteen days. The tonsure ceremony is arranged in the family deity's temple.

Puberty: On attaining puberty, a girl is secluded for sixteen days in a hut made by her maternal uncle. This is followed by *cadanku* (a puberty ceremony) in which the maternal uncle presents a goat for the feast and a *saree* to the girl.

Marriage: Marriages are arranged by parents and a man can marry his cross-cousin or his elder sister's daughter. Adult marriage is practised. A *tali* (marriage locket) is the marriage symbol for a woman. Marriage rituals are performed at the bride's residence or in a *Kalyana mandapam* but nuptials are performed at the groom's residence. Divorce and widow remarriages are allowed. Levirate and sororate are also practised. Either spouse can seek divorce on grounds of adultery, barrenness, maladjustment, impotency, cruelty and insanity. But such cases are decided by the caste *Panchayat*.

Death: Their dead are either cremated or buried and death pollution is observed for sixteen days.

Dwelling : These caste people live in huts which are almost of the local pattern, but similar to that of Parayans/Paraiyans. Their huts are generally found, in a separate settlement, at a distance from the main village.

Ornaments : Women wear a *tali*, toe-rings and *bindi* as symbols of marriage.

Food : Rice and *ragi* are their staple food supplemented with different kinds of grams. They are non-vegetarians but they abstain from taking beef and pork.

Traditional Occupation : Cultivation is their traditional occupation and some of them own land. However, majority of them are landless. Therefore, they work as agricultural labourers and daily wage labourers.

Dhor

Birth: Birth of the first child generally takes place in the parental house of the woman. Subsequent deliveries take place at her husband's house. The expectant mother is brought to her natal house for the first delivery in the seventh or ninth month after performing the *Kuppasa Todisuvudu* ceremony in which the parents present her with a green *saree* and *choli*, and feed her with sweet dishes. During the pregnancy, the husband does not attend to a funeral or carry the bier and also abstains from killing a cobra or any live animals. The pregnant woman is denied chicken, banana and other items of food which are hard to digest.

Puberty: On attainment of puberty, a girl is considered impure for five days during which she is given bath daily. She is confined to a corner of the house to segregate her from the rest of the members. She may enter the house on the sixth day after being purified by a bath and sprinkling of cow's urine over her head. For 9 to 11 days, she is seated on *hase* (wooden plank or bench) when the married women wave *aarthi* (a lighted lamp with camphor circularty around her) and sing songs. Betel nuts and leaves, and sweet preparations are distributed to the invitees. The girl during this period is fed with nutritious food like milk, *ghee*, sweet cakes and other dishes. If she is married, the husband is also seated by her side on*hase* on the last day.

Marriage: The girls usually get married after puberty. The normal age for the girl to marry is 16 years and above, while the boys get married after 20 years of age.

The offer of marriage generally comes from the parents of the boy. Before the negotiations are started, the parents of the boy ascertain, through their caste people and friends, the social and economic status of the parents of the girl. Only after being satisfied of the desirability of the alliance and when both parties agree to this marriage, the parents of the boy with some elder castemen go to girl's place for making a formal proposal. After the confirmation, the bride-price is negotiated. Bride-price is not paid if the boy is educated and is in Government employment. Instead, the girl's parents pay dowry to the boy.

Death: Their dead are generally buried. Only the dead bodies of pregnant women and lepers are cremated. Generally, the dead body of the married persons are buried in the sitting posture, while of the unmarried persons are lowered down in the pit. It is said that in the district of Uttar Kannad and some parts of Belgaum, they cremate the dead body of a married person. They observe death pollution for three days. On the 9th or 11th or 12th day, an emblem of the deceased is embossed on a silver or copper plate and is worshipped with the household deity. On that day, they also feed their caste people. They perform the *Mhal* or *Shraddha* (annual death ceremony) on the Full-Moon day of *Bhadrapada* in the month of September, or in the month of *Chaitra* (March-April) when the images of all the deceased are worshipped and *Ede* (the mound of wet flour or cooked rice) is offered to crows in the names of all the deceased ancestors.

Dwelling : The Dhors reside in clusters of houses segregated from the residential quarters of people of the other high castes. Although the different Scheduled Castes live adjacent to each other, generally each caste has a separate *gally* (settlement) of its own. Dhors who thus have their own separate settlement have also their own drinking water well and a temple for offering worship.

Dress : The dress of men consists of a *dhotra*— the lower unsewn garment, *angi*-the upper sewn garment with half or full sleeves and *patka* oı *peta*—the headgear or a cap. The *dhotra* covers the body from waist to the knees and it is worn in *kachche* style. Formerly, the Dhors used to wear a red turban but nowadays they use only white turbans due to the increasing price of the former. When going to cities and neighbouring villages, the elderly men wear coats. Very few use footwear. The women's dress consists of *sarees* and blouses. They wear sarees measuring eight yards of a coarse variety and of deep colours. Women while working in the fields tuck one end of the saree at the back drawing it between their legs.Dhor

Ornaments : Only a few elderly men wear gold *kudike* (ear studs) and *mura* (rings). Some of the well-to-do Dhors wear silver waist strings. Women of course are fond of ornaments but their possession and use is limited by financial abilities. They are fond of necklaces made of glass beads. The ornaments commonly worn by women are *hoovu* (ear studs), *moogubattu* (nose screw), glass bangles, *gundudale* (necklace), *dabu* (waist belt), *kadaga* (wristlets), *kalandige* (anklets), *nagara* and *bille* (worn on the back of the head), *kalachainu* (worn at ankles), etc. Their ornaments are made of gold or silver. Married women invariably put on ear-rings, nose-ring, glass bangles, a neck ornament called *karemanisara* (strings of black beads) and toe-rings. They wear a *kumkum* mark on their forehead. Unmarried girls can also wear all these ornaments except *karemanisara* and toe-rings.

Foods : The staple food of Dhors is *jowar*. Wheat and rice are used on festive and other ceremonial occasions. The *jowar ki rotis* (baked cakes) are generally consumed with such side dishes as vegetable curry or *palya*. The consumption of vegetables is meagre except during the monsoon season when vegetables like brinjal, radish, gourds, etc. grown in the village would become available to them.

Traditional Occupation : Leather tanning has been the traditional occupation of the Dhors.

Occupational Distribution : The hereditary occupation of Dhors is leather tanning as mentioned above, though since four or five decades many of the households are seen to be pursuing cultivation and agricultural labour or general labour as their principal occupations. Substantial number of households are having agricultural lands and a majority of the cultivators depend on lands taken on lease. Most of their women work as agricultural labour in addition to assisting their men in leather tanning.

Dom, Dombara, Paidi, Pano/ Domban/Pamidi

Birth: As a precautionary step for an easy delivery, they pray to the Sun God on an auspicious day during the sixth month of pregnancy. From the seventh month onwards, the pregnant woman is forbidden from doing difficult duties like fetching water, pounding the grains and collecting firewood from the woods. There is a custom among the Dombs to send the pregnant woman to her parent's house for confinement during the ninth month. She stays there for about two to three months after delivery. But this custom is observed only for the first two deliveries and for subsequent deliveries, she stays at her husband's house only.

Puberty: The attainment of puberty is locally known as *minaru theeruta*. When the girl attains puberty, she is asked to sit in a separate hut erected by the maternal uncle's son with the branches of *rooda* tree. But in some cases, the girl is kept separately in the verandah. The pollution is observed for nine days, and on the tenth day the final bath is given. On this day, the *Desari* (caste priest) is invited to officiate the purificatory ceremony. For subsequent menses, pollution is observed for seven days. The woman during these days is not allowed to touch the utensils and is served food separately. On the eighth day, she takes bath and attends to the routine household duties. Similarly, when a Paidi girl reaches puberty, she is kept under pollution for a varying number of days. On the last day, a Madiga is summoned who cuts her finger and toe nails. After this she bathes and becomes pollution free.

Marriage: There are only two types of marriages in vogue in this community: marriage through negotiation and marriage by elopement. The admissible partners for the marriage are *menarikam* (one's maternal uncle's daughter), *eduru menarikam* (one's paternal aunt's daughter) and elder brother's widow. Also, girls belonging to the same *intiperu* are prohibited to become as marriage partners. Inter-caste marriages are never preferred. Very rarely, they marry sister's daughter. Polygamy is in practice. Usually, they prefer the marital alliances with the families of nearby villages. The normal age at marriage for a boy is between 18 and 25 years, while that for a girl is between 10 and 18 years. But in certain cases, the betrothal ceremony is celebrated for boys and girls during the fourth or fifth year after their birth, provided they have any one of the preferential mates. There is no spectacular ceremony attached to this occasion.

Death: Dombs cremate their dead. But the corpse is buried where the death is due to infectious diseases like cholera or plague and also where the deceased are children. They observe the pollution for eleven days. Initial obsequies are celebrated on the third day and the final obsequies on the twelfth day. On the third day, a pig is cut and cooked, and a feast is arranged. One of the legs of the pig is hung at the spot where the deceased was laid down before his death. But this custom has decreased in the present time. On the twelfth day, the ashes of the deceased are mixed in the river waters. In the case of burial, the grave is dug, and the bones of the deceased are collected and mixed in river waters. The bath on 12th day removes the pollution. On that day, a non-vegetarian feast is arranged for the people of the caste. There is no practice of constructing *samadhis* (tombs or graveyard) of the dead person in this community.

Dwelling : *Dombo Sai* is the usual name given to the Dombs' colony which would usually be in a corner of the village. The settlement pattern is composite and all these caste men live in one area.

While selecting the site for house construction, the owner marks the area with lime powder and places three grains of rice at each of the four corners. These three grains are placed in a particular way so as thetwo grains placed first should support the third one placed upon them. The arrangement is covered by stones and mud. After a week, they take out the covering of stones and mud, and if the top grain is still found to be on the two grains at all the four corners then the site is considered to be lucky. If not, they go in for some other site.

Dress : The dress of males generally consists of a narrow cloth bound round the loins with its ends hanging down in front and behind. A coarse long cloth is wrapped round the upper portion of the body when the weather is chill. But some of the males also use *dhotis* and shirts.

The female dress consists of a *saree* of seven or eight yards in length. They do not wear blouses. The girls wear petticoats and blouses. The boys wear a shirt to cover the upper portion of the body, while a cloth is bound round the loins. Almost all women of married status wear vermilion on the forehead. The *pachchabottu* (tattooing) is mostly found among all the women of this caste.

Ornaments : There are several ornaments for women. The important among them are *andelu* and *kadiyalu* (brass or silver anklets), *jamdar*, *nakupuda* and *bulaki* (brass ornaments of the nose), *khaddas* (German silver bangles), *khagadas* (a silver ornament worn around the neck), *nagulu* (a snake-shaped brass ornament for ear-lobe), *kamma* (a brass ornament for each ear-lobe) and copper rings worn on the fingers.

Food : The Dombs eat rice, wheat, *ragi* (finger millet), *sama* (little millet) and *korra* (Italian millet) as staple food. Generally, they take their meals thrice in a day. Usually, the leftovers of the previous night are eaten in the morning; in the afternoon they take the food prepared out of *ragi* flour; and in the night they take rice with some curry. All kinds of grains and vegetables are consumed by them. They also eat roots like *seemapendalam* (tapioca), etc. Among birds, the flesh of fowls and doves are consumed. Very often they take beef and pork, in addition to the flesh of goat and sheep. They very much relish all kinds of fish.

Traditional Occupation : The traditional occupation of the people of this caste is weaving and serving as musicians during the marriages of the people of various castes. It is recorded that they were generally weavers but in tracts of Jaipur (in Rajathan) they were employed as horse-keepers, tom-tom beaters and scavengers (Thurston 1909: 174). All this holds good even today. The Dombs, however, were forced to give up weaving because they could not invest the required amount for maintaining this cottage industry.

In the *Census Report of 1901*, the Panos are described as brokers, pedlars, sycophants and cheats. But at present, they are not engaged as sycophants and cheats though they are occupied as brokers and pedlars.

Ellamalawar, Yellammalawandlu

Traditional Occupation : Information on traditional occupation of Ellamalawars, Yellammalawandlus is not available.

Ganti Chores

Birth: Birth pollution is observed for twelve days when the mother and the new-born are confined to a room. The naming, and ear and nose-piercing ceremonies are observed for the child after a month of his or her birth.

Puberty: When a girl attains puberty, she is secluded for five days and a puberty rite known as *rutumati* is observed.

Marriage: Marriage with one's paternal aunt's, maternal uncle's or elder sister's daughter is permitted. Child marriage was their traditional practice but nowadays adult marriage is common. Marriage is arranged through negotiation. Bride-price is paid in cash. The marriage rituals are performed at the bride-groom's residence and the marriage feast is hosted by the bride's parents. The consummation of marriage also takes place at the bridegroom's house. A necklace of black beads and toe-rings are the marriage symbols for women. They admit men and women of all castes except Muhammadans and Pariahs into their community. Among some of these classes, there are no marriage ceremonies at all. The mere congregation of men and women around the bride and bridegroom, and a formal worship by the pair of a deity set up for the occasion constitute a marriage. They then treat themselves to a hearty meal and drink. The widows and divorced women can marry in the same or neighbouring group without any compunction.

Death: The Ganti Chores cremate their dead and dispose off the mortal remains in flowing water. Mortuary rituals are performed on the tenth day.

Ornaments : The *mangal sutra* (a necklace of black beads) and toe-rings are the marriage symbols for women.

Foods : *Jowar*, rice and wheat are their staple food, and red gram is the common pulse consumed. They are non-vegetarians who eat pork. Both men and women drink home-made alcoholic drinks but sometimes they purchase liquor from the market.

Traditional Occupation : According to Enthoven (1922), the Ganti Chores were known in the past for thefts, house-breaking, robberies and dacoities. Enthoven further says that they did not hesitate to commit murder, if necessary, to effect escape. Before starting on a predatory expedition, they used to select a convenient place and march straight to it in batches of 20 and 30 persons including women and children. While proceeding, they made themselves fully acquainted with the villages and different routes on the way in order to avoid making enquiries about them on their return journey. But this was only when they commited crimes. The boys were let loose to commit petty thefts of fowl, sheep, etc. The old men and women used to go to the villages during the day time and reconnoitre the houses at their leisure on the pretext of offering beads, needles, etc.

Garoda, Garo

Birth: A pre-delivery ritual is observed during the ninth month of pregnancy. Birth pollution is observed and the child is named within six years of birth.

Marriage: Child marriages were common in the past. But nowadays, adult marriages are preferred. Monogamy is the rule and the marriage is arranged through negotiations. Both bride-price and dowry are common among them. Divorce and remarriage are permitted with the approval of the caste elders. The pre-marriage rituals performed are *Ganeshsthapan* and *pithi*. The marriage is solemnized at the bride's house. Some of the marriage rituals are *chori* (theft), *havan* (offerings to fire), *hastmilapan* (hand shake) and *sathphera* (seven circal circumambulations).

Death: They cremate their dead and the death pollution is observed for twelve days. Crows are fed on the twelfth day.

Foods : They are vegetarians and rice is their staple cereals. Pulses like red gram and *tur*, and vegetables are also consumed.

Traditional Occupation : As observed by Thurston (op.cit.), the Garodas were a class of mendicants who were snake charmers. They also used to perform various juggling and mountebank tricks.

Godda

Birth: A ritual called *bayake madime* (fulfilling the desire of a pregnant woman) is observed during the seventh month of pregnancy. Pre-delivery and post-natal restrictions on the mother exist. The birth pollution period is observed for sixteen days and the naming ceremony is performed on that day.

Puberty: The *madimal madime* (puberty ritual) is performed at the time of first menarche of the girl.

Marriage: The cross-cousin marriages (with maternal uncle's daughter or paternal aunt's daughter) are prevalent. Two brothers of a family are permitted to marry two sisters of another family. Exchange of daughters in marriage between two families is also permitted. It is a common traditional practice to pay bride-price which is locally known as *terawu* or *warah kattuwadu*. The *gurikaras* (caste headmen) of both the parties of the spouses and the other caste elders assemble, and fix the bride-price. Earlier, the bride-price was paid in terms of a few *warahs* (one *Warah* was equivalent to Rs. 4).

Death: Their traditional practice is to bury their dead. However, these days they practise both cremation and burial to dispose off their dead. The Goddas have a separate burial ground away from that of the caste Hindus, and they dig the grave themselves for the disposal of the dead. The corpse is buried with the head facing towards south. After lowering the body in the grave, the waist thread is removed and a *tarula* plant is planted on the grave. The corpses of children are buried but the corpses of women died after delivery are cremated. The corpses of those died of diseases such as leprosy are cremated to avoid further spread of the disease. After a lapse of three *amavasyas* (with the complete absence of moon on the 15th day of the month), the *bojjas* (final rites) are performed.

Ornaments : *Tali* or *karimani* and toe-rings are the marriage symbols for women. These are worn by all the married women.

Foods : The Goddas are non-vegetarians and their staple food is rice, pulses, vegetables and *kenes* (roots). Earlier, they used to eat pork but of late, this has been discontinued.

Traditional Occupation : A few decades ago, the Goddas, worked as bonded agricultural labourers to caste Hindu landlords such as Brahmin, Bant, etc. Such workers were known as *okkalu*. It was customary and a traditional practice that these labourers dwelt in their master's land. They received every help in kind and cash for their needs such as in marriage, illness, etc. They are now free from bonded labour.

Gosangi

Birth: No ceremony is observed during the pregnancy of the woman. The usual prohibition against the pregnant woman's husband's doing such things as carrying a corpse, putting on the roof of the house, etc. prevails in this caste also. Pregnant women are not allowed to take certain harmful foods like papaya, jaggery and *nuvvulu*. When the women show signs of approaching delivery, they make a vow to their family god, and set apart a small coin in earnest of a larger offering to be made in case of safe delivery. On the birth of the child, it is washed and the navel cord is cut by the midwife who generally happens to be the elderly woman of the couple's own caste. The navel-string and the after birth are buried below the eves of the house. On the third day, a little milk is poured on the spot. Post-delivery pollution is observed for twenty-one days.

Puberty: When a girl attains puberty, she is kept outside for eleven days and is not allowed either to touch other persons or to enter the inner portion of the house. The *Pushpavathi* (puberty rites) ceremony is celebrated on the last day.

Marriage: Earlier, pre-puberty marriages were common but at present adult marriage is the norm. The marriageable age for boys and girls is around 20 and 18 years respectively. Cross-cousin and uncle-niece marriages are common. Marriages also take place between the groups with different surnames. Nowadays, a few cases of intercaste marriages with Madigas, and Shahukarlus Velamas can also be seen. Traditionally, marriages used to be celebrated for four days but nowadays marriage celebrations last only for one day.

Death: Their dead are buried, except in the case of pregnant women and lepers whose bodies are cremated. *Sutaka* (death pottution) is observed for three days for the death of any agnate. All except the parents merely bathe after the death of a child. On the third day, they go to the graveyard and put some fried grain, milk and *ghee* on the child's grave.

Ornaments : Bangles, *tali* or *thali* and toe-rings are the marriage symbols for women.

Foods : The *ghataka* (food prepared from *jowar* and maize) is their staple food. Some of them also eat rice; *tur* and *urad* are the common pulses. *Mullangi* (radish), carrot and *gochi* (cabbage) are some of the vegetables consumed by them. The Gosangis are non-vegetarians as well.

Traditional Occupation : As recorded by Hassan (op.cit.), the Gosangi is one of the castes of leather workers and rope makers. Many people of this caste are also engaged as village watchmen and musicians. The Gosangis were traditionally engaged as village servants especially for the maintenance of the *Sarkari pani* (water ponds and tanks) in the villages. They were paid remuneration in kind.

Halleer

Birth: By tradition, the first delivery of a woman takes place in her natal house. When his wife is pregnant, the husband is supposed to neither kill animals, fowls, snakes, etc., nor should he carry a bier.

The Halleers celebrate a small function called *Udi Thumbuvudu* or *Bayake Oota* during the seventh or ninth month of the first pregnancy.

Puberty: On her attaining first puberty, a girl is considered impure for five days. On the sixth day after taking ritual bath, a few married women fill her lap with betel leaves, nuts, rice, fruits, etc. *Sobana* (pleasantry with blessings) songs are sung for nine days while the girl is seated on *hase* (a low stool). If she is married, she is seated along with her husband.

Marriage: In the past, pre-puberty marriage of a girl was the rule. In case the girl was not married before her attaining puberty, her parents had to pay a fine to the caste *Panchayat*. Now, the boys are generally married between 18 and 25 years and girls between 14 and 20 years of age.

The negotiations for marriage are initiated from the boy's side. The boy's father, accompanied by a few relatives, goes to the girl's residence for settling the alliance.

Death: The Halleers either bury or burn their dead. The dead bodies of children and of persons suffering from *thonnu* (leucoderma) and small—pox are usually buried, and others are cremated. Whether buried or cremated, the head of the corpse is always directed towards the south with the face upwards. The chief mourner is the eldest son and in his absence any other close relative acts as mourner.

Dwelling : The Halleers reside in separate localities locally called *keri* in Kannada and *vados* in Konkani. Their settlements are at a little distance away from those of other caste Hindus. Their settlement is generally surrounded by green paddy fields and coconut gardens. The houses are usually spread in shapeless and dispersed clusters without streets and lanes.

Ornaments : The young men wear *muru* (ear-rings) made of gold or silver. A few of them also wear gold, silver or brass rings on their fingers. Some of them wear *ududar* (a silver girdle) round their waist. A necklace of black beads locally called *dharemani* or *karemanisara* denotes the married status of a woman. Widows and unmarried girls are forbidden from wearing it. They also wear ear-rings called *kudka*, *joda*, *bugudi* and *sarpali*. However, *bugudi* which is worn on the upper ear-lobe has lost its popularity among the women of the present generation. Nose-rings made of gold and the *moogutis* or *nattus* (toe-rings made of silver), are worn only by the married women. Among the women, glass bangles are common except for the widows.

Foods : Their staple diet consists of rice and fish. They generally take three meals a day. The first meal is taken in the morning and it consists of *ragi kanji* or rice *kanji* and fish or vegetable curry. Their lunch at noon and supper in the evening are similar. They eat all kinds of fish, both scaled and unscaled. They also eat fowls, goats, wild boar, deer, rabbits, hedgehog called *pisaya* or *barka*, etc., in addition to wild birds and wild fowl. But they do not eat beef, pork, flesh of peacocks and bisons. Condiments are used in large quantities while preparing fish and non-vegetarian curries. Coconuts are also used in good quantity.

Traditional Occupation : Halleers in the past were hereditary musicians. Very few of them are now engaged in this occupation. At present, they are principally agricultural labourers. But for some of them, music is a subsidiary occupation. They are engaged as musicians at the time of marriages of Holers, Mukris and other Scheduled Castes. They also head the processions of temple deities at the time of annual fairs. They do all kinds of agricultural work on daily wages. Several of them also work as forest labourers during the slack agricultural season. Many of them work as general labourers in the construction of roads and in laterite stone quarries. Though many Halleers are tenants cultivating small bits of land, they depend to a large extent on daily wages for their maintenance.

Halsar, Haslar, Hulasvar, Halasvar/ Hasla

Birth: A woman in childbirth is impure for twelve days and the cradling takes place on the fifteenth day. No other ceremonies are observed by the castemen.

Puberty: A girl attaining puberty is kept in a secluded place for twelve days. She is exhibited before the womenfolk every evening. She is given a bath on the fifth, seventh and twelfth day. After bath on the twelfth day, she is purified by drinking *tirtha* (holy water) brought from the *Dasayya's* (priest) house and keeping a *kalasa* (earthen pot with water, flowers, etc.) with her. If the girl is already married, she lives with her husband from the twelfth day onwards.

Marriage: Girls are married either before or after the attainment of their age. Parties belonging to the mother's *bali* are not allowed to contract marriages. But if one of the parties belongs to the father's *bali*, marriages are allowed. In some places, one's father's *bali* is also avoided. A man may marry his paternal aunt's or maternal uncle's daughter. They do not marry their sister's daughter. Girls for whom husbands cannot be procured are not dedicated as *Basavis* or Devadasi. Two families may exchange daughters in marriage but two sisters are not married to the same man at one time. The younger is married to her brother-in-law after the death of her elder sister. But some say that a man cannot marry his deceased wife's sister also.

Death: Their dead are either cremated or buried. Those who had worn Yellammana Devara *tali* or Guthammadevara beads during their life-time are cremated. A Holeya plays an important part in the funeral ceremonies of the Hasalars. He digs the pit for burial or supplies fuel for cremation and piles it up on the burning ground. He also leads the funeral procession by carrying fire in an earthen pot and is followed by Hasalars with torches in their hands. About halfway from the burial ground, the dead body is lowered on the ground.

Dwelling : They live in small isolated huts. These are, however, provided not only with the usual principal entrance through which one has to crawl in but also with a half-concealed hole in the rear. This hole is a kind of portern through which the shy inmates used to steal out in the past into the jungle at the merest suspicion of danger or on the approach of a stranger.

Dress : The men wear the long cloth, a country blanket across their shoulders and a head-scarf. The women wear a robe whose skirt is worn like a petticoat.

Ornaments : They wear the brass-hair ornament, some of these are nose-ring, necklets, glass bangles, brass wristlets and toe-rings. A widow removes her nose-ring, toe-rings and wristlets. Women who have become *Dasyyas* under a vow put on *kumkuma,* while the other women do not do so.

Foods : They eat mutton, fowls, wild pig and venison, and are fond of palm-spirit. Flesh is mostly eaten on the *Yugadi* (New Year's day) in April, on the *Dussehra* in October and on the *Dipawali* in November. The Hasalars do not eat beef but are very partial to toddy drinking and chewing betel leaves. It is said that they do not eat the flesh of milk-yielding creatures. They do not touch carcasses of cattle nor do they cook until they are removed from their houses. Their ordinary diet consists of rice-gruel for breakfast, *ragi*-gruel for dinner, and cooked rice and curry for supper.

Traditional Occupation : Many of the Hasalars have traditionally been agricultural serfs attached to their masters who were to support them, get them married and treat them whenever they were unwell. They were most like the agrestic serfs of Malabar, Cochin and Travancore, and worked as labourers in fields and gardens. They were engaged in cane work and also removed carcasses for which they were paid in kind.

Handi Jogis

Birth: The birth of a child is considered to be a divine or blessing of God for the people of this caste. Stillbirths and abortions or miscarriages are attributed to the wrath of God or other evil spirits. To prevent such occurrences, *pujas* (prayer for worship) are performed to the family deities and at various temples in their villages. Vows are also observed to various deities. Barrenness is likewise attributed to sins of the past life and they undertake pilgrimage to sacred places like Tirupathi, Vidurashwatha, Nandi, etc.

Puberty: On the attainment of puberty, the girl is considered to be polluted for 12 days. During the first three days, she stays in a separate hut in front of the house and is helped by some women. Generally, the hut is constructed by her maternal uncle with green leaves of the *neem* tree. She may enter the house on the third day but her movements are limited to only particular portions of the house. She cannot enter the kitchen. During this period, the girl has to pass sleepless nights as they believe that ghosts and evil spirits haunt her during her sleep. For 12 days, she is given some nourishing food like rice, *ghee*, fruits, and special dishes. The temporary hut prepared for her is burnt by the maternal uncle on the twelfth day.

Marriage: Boys and girls are generally married at the ages of 25 and 15 years respectively. In the past till about 40 years back, pre-puberty marriages were common among them. Marriages through payment are generally in vogue. Till about 60 years ago, marriages through elopement were also taking place. But this practice has disappeared due to their contact with the villagers and their settled habits. They have now started celebrating marriages, more or less, in a similar fashion as people of some other castes in the village do. The practice of paying *voli* (bride-price) is prevalent among them. Negotiations for the marriage are initiated by the parents of the boy.

Death: The Handi Jogis bury their dead. Only the dead bodies of lepers and of a few others are cremated. In the case of death of a pregnant woman, the corpse is seated in the burial ground and water in a new pot is placed in front of it. After the ceremonies, the body is washed. They do not carry the corpse on the bier but carry it on their hands, after wrapping it in a white cloth. All the relatives throw rice on the eyes of the corpse. Some cooked rice called *kulu* (food) carried in a pot by the eldest son in front of the corpse is strewn before it while it is taken to the burial ground. Midway, the corpse is laid on ground and the carriers exchange their positions. I

Dwelling : The Handi Jogis, formerly being nomads, have now begun to lead a settled life in rural and urban areas. They generally live at a little distance from the main village or town. Their settlements are more like tiny hamlets with less than 10 households in each hamlet. Each of their habitations is a collection of a few low-roofed huts in a cluster of irregular shapes. Invariably, there are low sheds to pen their pigs near the huts.

Dress : Men wear knickers and *angi* (shirts) with half sleeves. Old men wear *dhotis* as lower garments. About five or six decades ago, men used to wear only a loin cloth as their lower garment. But now with their increasing contact with other upper caste people, they have begun to wear knickers. The *peta* (headgear) worn by their elders is slowly being replaced by a towel hanging on the shoulders which at times is also tied round the head. In the olden times, the use of *chappals* (footwear) was limited to a very small number of people of this caste.

Ornaments : Due to their poverty-stricken conditions, they possess very few ornaments in spite of their inherent love for them. The ornaments now in use among them are: *kammalu* (ear-rings), *shempachainu* (ear-chains), *kalandiga* and *kaluchainu* (silver anklets and chains), *dabu* (silver waist-belts), (*moogu bottu*) (nose-rings), and *todu bale* (silver armlet). Married women wear strings of black beads with *mangalya* (marriage badge). The *Kadagas* (silver wristlets) are used by aged women only.

Foods : *Ragi* is their staple food which is very similar to that of the people of the other castes of this region. Generally, they consume *hittu*–(made of ragi flour boiled with water) and the use of rice is limited to only those who grow paddy. They take their meals thrice a day and the menu is common for all the meals. Their menu consists of *ragi* balls and *saru* (vegetable curry) prepared with pulses and chillies. They are non-vegetarians. They eat domesticated animals like sheep, goat, pig and poultry. They also eat parrot, *Shambar* crow (*pheasant* crow), fish and rabbit. But they abjure from eating beef and bison flesh. The *Payasa, holige, kajjaya, kadabu,* etc. are their popular festival sweet dishes. *Dosas* and *rotis* are occasionally prepared for breakfast. Non-vegetarian dishes are not prepared during festivals and religious ceremonies.

Traditional Occupation : Pig-rearing and begging have been their ancestral occupations.

Holeya

Birth: To ensure the safe delivery of a child, and elderly man with a reputation for magic gives some oil which is administered to the mother. Arrack is taken to allay pains in the belly after delivery. A *mantrasani* (literally a witch) or midwife cuts the umbilical cord and attends on the mother. The severed umbilical cord is tied to the cradle to act as a charm. The mother lives for nine days on rice only. Musk and *gorochanamo* are given to both the mother and the child.

Puberty: When a girl comes of age, she is kept aloof in a new shed formed with green *lakkali* leaves for the purpose. She remains in the shed for a period of three to seven days, when she is supposed to be in a state of pollution. This pollution among the Holaya's is observed with even more strictness than among the people of the higher castes. The washerwoman of the caste supplies her with washed clothes. She may enter the temple or her ordinary dwelling only after a bath on the fifth or the seventh day.

Marriage: Holeya girls are married either before or after puberty. When a girl is married, she is not sent to her husband's house immediately after the marriage. But she continues to live with her parents even after attainment of puberty until the marriage is consummated. If a girl remains unmarried due to the absence of a suitor, she is married to trees honge (*Bargamia glabra*), bevu (neem or margosa) and yakke (*calotropis gigantea*), or is dedicated to a shrine like those of Billigiri Ranga or Siddappaji. She may then live with any man of the caste without loss of status. She is known as *kulamaga* (son of the family) and inherits the rights and privileges of a son. She also discharges the son's duties by performing the funeral ceremonies and attending to obsequies in respect of death of her parents.

Death : Soon after death, the body is washed and shrouded in a new cloth. The marks of *nama* (symbol of god) with ashes are put on the forehead. The body is also smeared with ashes and sandal paste, and decked with flowers. It is then placed on a bier, of *Kalli* wood, in a sitting posture in the case of Vaishnavite or in a lying posture with the right flank down in the case of Saivite. Before starting to the burial ground, exchange of betel leaves takes place between the deceased and his surviving wife. As soon as the bier is lifted, an earthen pot is smashed at the place where it had been placed.

Dwelling : The Holeyas are a settled people. They usually live in groups of low lying huts built of mud and huddled close together. These are not provided with windows and have ventilators open to the sky. Their street is known as *Holageri* in Kannada. The *keri* means 'a street' or 'quarters' and *Holageri* (*Holeya* and *Keri*) means 'Holeya quarter' which is commonly located outside the main village. But near Mysore and other important urban centres, they have built fine tiled houses. and exhibited other signs of growing prosperity.

Dress : Males dress themselves with a loin cloth and a *kambli*. Women wear *sarees* of 8 yeards. They seem to have preference for dark colour and broad borders for the *sarees*. The fold of the *saree* is adjusted to the front. The "pallav" is thrown on the left shoulder. This is in contrast to the style of wearing *sarees* by women of Telugu-speaking Malas who throw the "pallav" over the right shoulder. The women wear loose jackets with arms extending up to the elbows. These jackets are buttoned up in the front. They are provided with pockets in which they keep *pan-supari*, etc. The widows are found to throw the "pallav" of the *saree* over the head to cover its (head) rear portion. Very young girls wear either gowns or *pavadai* (skirts) and jackets.

Ornaments : The women are fond of wearing too many glass bangles, beads and jewels of base-metal. In the wrists, they wear stout silver bangles which are rectangular in shape and not oval as usually found in other parts. These rectangular-shaped thick silver bangles are called by them as *Sollu*. In addition to *sollu*, married women wear a string of corals in their wrists. They call this ornament as *kaimani*. Black glass bangles are worn in large numbers by married women. Many girls are found to wear *sarigais* (wristlets made of silver). In the leg, they wear silver *kappus* circular in shape, and *golusus* (loose chains). Married women wear *minjis* (silver rings) in the second toes. In the ear lobes, they wear *kammals* which are stone-studded. They wear *kuppaitalukku* in the upper ear.

Foods : The staple cereal of the Holeyas is *ragi* as is the case with most people in these parts of the States. *Ragi* is cooked by converting it into flour and boiling it in water. They cook the meal into a thick paste. On rare occasions, they eat rice. The cooked meal is rolled into balls and served. They cook twice a day but eat three times on the same day. As a side dish, they prepare some sauce with tamarind and chillies. They add a few vegetables or greens in the sauce. This is sometimes made of pulses. As this is a hilly region with cold climate, they prefer their cooked *ragi* rather thicker and hotter than in a liquid form prepared in the plains.

Traditional Occupation : The Holeyas were traditionally agrestic serfs. They were chiefly employed as labourers in agriculture and hand-looms manufacturing the various kinds of coarse or homespun cloth which were worn extensively by the people of the poorer classes. In some parts of the Mysore district, considerable numbers of the Holeyas were engaged specially in betel and vine gardening. As labourers, they were employed in innumerable pursuits in which manual labour preponderated.

Jaggali

Birth: The first confinement always takes place at the residence of the parents of the pregnant woman. The ceremony concerning the expectant motherhood is not observed, except that during the fifth month they propitiate the deity *Balamma* or *Balagamma*. A pregnant sheep is sacrificed to the deity. The parents of the woman present her a *saree* and a blouse. In the seventh month, she is taken to her parents' house for delivery. They bring the woman and baby back on the twenty-seventh day after the childbirth. An experienced *dai* (acting as midwife) attends to the delivery and is given only food but no remuneration. She cuts the umbilical cord and deposits it in the earth outside the house. Birth pollution is observed for nine days. The new-born child is named on the twenty-seventh day.

Puberty: A girl on attaining puberty is unclean for five days. On the 5th day, she bathes, touches a green leaf and becomes ceremonially pure.

Marriage: The Jaggalis cannot marry outside their sub-caste nor within the same exogamous unit. This simple rule of exogamy is supplemented by allowing a man to marry the daughter of his elder sister or of maternal uncle or of paternal aunt. In other words, they practise cross-cousin marriages. Two sisters may also be married to the same man.

Death: Their dead are usually buried, except in the case of women in pregnancy and lepers who are burnt. Married agnates are mourned for ten days and unmarried for three days. No *sradha* (annual death rites) is performed but birds are fed with cooked flesh on the third day after death. During the period of mourning, the chief mourner may not eat flesh, molasses, oil or turmeric nor may he sleep on a bed. On the tenth day after death, a feast is given to the caste people and purification is obtained. It is said that the *Jaggalis* burn their dead in a lying posture with the head pointing to the south. They collect the ashes and bones on the third day after death, and either throw them into a sacred stream or bury them.

Dwelling : Their dwelling is known as *'puri-illu'*, while the local pattern is *penkutillu*. Importance is not at all attached to the selection of a house site. These people mostly suffer from lack of land for house construction. The ceremony concerning the commencement of house construction is not observed among the people of this caste. The reason for this may be their poor economic status. Both family and hired labour are used for house construction. Jaggalis live in dormitory type of houses.

Dress : *Pancha* (*dhoti*) and *lalchi* (loose shirt) are the lower and upper garments of males. *Banians* are also used by males.

The dress of a female consists of *koka* (saree) of seven or eight yards in length. They prefer mostly red and white colours. Women generally do not wear blouses after the first confinement which is an indication of elderliness.

Ornaments : The ornaments used by Jaggali women are *Kammalu* (ear ornaments), *Mukkupogu* (nose ornaments), *Kadiyalu* (leg ornaments) and *Mattelu* (toe-rings). These ornaments are also used by the Madiga, Arundhatiya and Jambuvulu women. These caste people have tattoo marks on different parts of their body. This is done by a class of people locally known as *Pachabottollu* or *Parikimuggulavallu*. The most favoured designs are *Sivuni padalu, Chandamana chukkalu, Terri, Banthi chettu* and *Mutyala Mukkupogu*.

Foods : The staple food of Jaggalis are rice, *chollu* (finger millet), *jowar, samalu* (little millet) and *udalu* (branyard millet). They also consume some of the roots such as *Seema pendalam* (yam), *chama dumpa* (elephant ear), *sari kanda* (elephant foot) and *sothi dumpa* (a kind of yam). The food is taken thrice a day. The Jaggalis take their breakfast in the morning, the items being *chaddi annam* (last night's left-overs) and *kanji* (gruel prepared out of rice). The second meal comprises of *chodi ambali* (the gruel prepared out of ragi flour) which is taken at noon, and the third meal is taken in the night with rice and *kura* (curry). Being non-vegetarian, they take meat at least once in fifteen days, and relish fish, egg, beef and carrion.

Traditional Occupation : The traditional occupations of Jaggalis were skinning of dead animals, leather dressing and the making of leather ropes. They also made leather buckets for hauling water from wells, and other leather articles used in husbandry. In addition to their traditional occupation, they were field servants and used to supply the above articles to the farmers for which they used to get a fixed quantity of grain for each plough. They also served as musicians at the marriage and other ceremonies of the caste Hindus.

Jambuvulu

Birth: The first confinement takes place at the residence of the parents of a pregnant woman. The parents of the woman present her a *saree* and a blouse on this occasion. During the seventh month, she is taken to her parents house for delivery. The husband or some boy from his family bring the woman and baby back from her parents' house after about two months from the date of delivery. An arrangement is made separately for delivery in the house. The area is enclosed either with wattle or with a cloth curtain and a cot is placed inside the enclosure where the pregnant woman rests. An experienced woman of the caste (*dai*) attends to the delivery.

Puberty: The observation of attainment of the first puberty of a girl is also an important occasion in the social life of Jambuvulus. The maternal uncle of the girl erects a small hut where she stays during the period of pollution. The girl is seated on a mat spread over palmyra leaves in some cases and over *jowar* leaves in other cases. The pollution period is observed for nine days. Immediately after the girl has attained puberty, all the neighbourly women of the caste are informed. They in turn bring some jaggery and rice, and give it to the family concerned. Some delicious items such as *Arisalu, Polelu,* etc. are prepared everyday and given to the girl. Bath is given to her on the first three days and then on alternative days till the completion of pollution.

Marriage: The marriages are contracted through negotiation. Marriage is preferred with one's maternal uncle's daughter, paternal aunt's daughter or elder sister's daughter. One can also marry one's brother's wife's younger sister. Marriage is exogamous wherein it is not contracted among the people of the same *intiperulu*. Though the custom of the child betrothal exists, it is observed rarely specially when the parents of the boy or of the girl fall ill seriously. At that time, the age of the girl or boy is not taken into account but to please the seriously ill persons, betrothal is performed with an assurance that the marriages will certainly be performed.

Death: Both cremation and burial are the prevalent practices for disposing of their dead. The initial obsequies are known as *chinna divasam,* while the final obsequies are known as *pedda divasam*. On the final day of the obsequies, widow of the deceased is taken to the nearby stream by women of the caste. Her bangles, *puste* and *mattelu* (toe-rings) are removed by a widow of the caste. The vermilion mark on the forehead of the widow is also rubbed off. She is presented a new *saree* and blouse by the nearest relatives after she returns home from the stream. Thus ends the ceremony.

Dwelling : The Jambuvulu houses are located usually on the outskirts of the village. The local names for their dwellings are *puripaka* or *puri-illu*. The house-site is selected in consultation with the stone cutter (oddara). A Brahmin is also consulted to fix up an auspicious day for beginning the construction. Usually, a Thursday is considered to be good for this purpose. On that day, the plot is cleaned and a pole is fixed at the centre of the site. *Vaddera* (caste head) is invited to officiate. A small pit is dug and nine cereals and pulses with a small piece of gold and some money are placed in it.

Dress : *Pancha* (*dhoti*) and *lalchi* (loose shirt) are the lower and upper garments respectively of males. *Banians* are also used by them. The dress of a female consists of *koka* (saree) of seven or eight yards in length. They prefer mostly red and white colours. Women generally do not wear blouses after the first confinement. Not wearing jackets is an indication of their elderliness.

Ornaments : The ornaments used by womenfolk are *kammalu* (ear-rings), *mukkupuduka* (nose ornament), *nagara* (ornament for plait), *kadiyalu* (leg ornaments) and *muttelu* (toe-rings).

All people of the caste have tattoo marks on different parts of their body. This is done by a class of people locally known as *pachabottollu* or *parikimuggu lavallu*. Their most favoured designs are *Sivuni padalu* (feet of Lord Siva), *chandamama chukkalu* (moon and stars), *jerri* (centipede), *banthi chettu* (tagetes or French marigold) and *mutyala mukkupogu* (nose ornament made with pearls).

Food : The Jambuvulus eat mostly *jowar* and rice. All people take food thrice a day. They also eat goat and sheep, flesh of fowl, beef and pork. Among birds they eat doves, geese, parrots, *kanjulu* (patridges), etc. All kinds of fish are taken. Some of them are *svada, marupu, gidisa, parigi* and *zella*. The flesh of the dead animals is also said to be consumed by them.

Traditional Occupation : The traditional occupation of Jambuvulus is tanning and leather work. In villages, each Jambuvulu household is attached to a fixed number of cultivating households. They are paid yearly in kind by these cultivators and, in turn, these Jambuvulus have to prepare leather buckets and *chappals* (foot wear) for them. The dead cattle are given to them by the cultivators on the condition that two pairs of *chappals* should be given in return. For the preparation of leather buckets, the farmers themselves supply the leather. Though their traditional occupation does not provide sufficient bread, hardly any Jambuvulu departs from his age-old occupation.

Kadaiyan

Birth: The post-delivery pollution is observed among the people of this caste and the period lasts for fifteen days in Karnataka and Kerala and sixteen days in Tamil Nadu. Ceremonies related to naming and feeding of the first cereals to the new born child are also performed.

Puberty: A puberty rite (called *Vayasariyunnadu* in Kerala and *cadanku* in Tamil Nadu) is performed on the first menstruation of a girl. On this occasion, fifteen days of pollution are observed.

Marriage: The Kadaiyans practise caste endogamy. Marriages are arranged by parents, and cross-cousin marriages (marriages with one's maternal uncle's daughter or paternal aunt's daughter) are preferred. Adult marriages are practised and monogamy is the norm. While in Kerala the bride-price is paid (both in cash and kind), in Tamil Nadu dowry is paid both in cash and kind. The situation is, more or less, the same among the people of this caste in Karnataka State. Divorce is permissible and a simple separation may lead to divorce. Divorce compensation is given to the wife, whereas the children, if any, may live with either parent. Widows are allowed to remarry and a widower can marry his deceased wife's younger sister.

Death: In Kerala, their dead are buried but in Karnataka and Tamil Nadu, they are either buried or cremated. The eldest son performs the *kolli* (death rite) for the mother and the youngest son performs it for the father. Ancestor worship is observed.

Foods : The Kadaiyans are non-vegetarians. While in Kerala they relish beef and pork, in Tamil Nadu they do not eat beef. Rice, millets and *ragi* are their staple cereals in Tamil Nadu. In Karnataka and Kerala also, rice is their staple cereal which is taken with pulses like red, green and black grams.

Traditional Occupation : In Kerala, the traditional occupations of Kadaiyans are the manufacturing of knives and agricultural implements made of iron, while in Karnataka and Tamil Nadu they are a fishing community. Generally, they sell fish to middlemen.

Kalladi

Birth: A pre-delivery ritual is performed in the seventh month of pregnancy. The post-delivery pollution is observed for fifteen days. The post-natal restrictions are also observed.

Puberty: The *therandu kalyanas* (puberty rites) for girls are observed among the people of this community.

Marriage: Caste endogamy and clan exogamy are practised. Adult marriage is the norm and marriages are settled through negotiations. The marriage with one's paternal aunt's daughter is allowed. Payment of *Achara panam* (bride-price) is prevalent and it is given in cash. The marriage ceremony is held at the bride's residence and the marriage feast is hosted by her parents. Either spouse can seek divorce but it has to be approved by the elders of the family or caste council. After the divorce, the responsibility of the children, if any, can be taken by either parent. Widow, widower and divorcee remarriages are permissible. Sororate and levirate forms of marriages also are allowed.

Death: Their dead are buried and pollution period lasts for fifteen days. Ancestor worship is observed every year.

Ornaments : The *tali* (marriage locket), bangles and ear-studs are the main ornaments of married women.

Foods : The Kalladis are non-vegetarians and relish pork. Rice is their staple cereal which is taken along with pulses like *tur*, peas and beans.

Traditional Occupation : The traditional occupation of the Kalladis is mat-making, and trapping of birds and animals.

Kepmari

Birth: Birth pollution lasts upto the tenth day, and the naming ceremony is performed on the same day.

Puberty: When a girl comes of age for the first time, her period of uncleanliness is for sixteen days. After that, she is bathed by a few married women of her family and neighbourhood. The members of the caste or community especially women are treated to a feast.

Marriage: Their marriage customs and ceremonies like the preliminary negotiations, formal engagement, the fixing of an auspicious day for marriage, ancestor worship before marriage, erection of the pandal with 12 poles, *tali*-tying (tying the marriage locket), marriage feast, etc. are all the same as among the people of the other corresponding castes. Their marriage is of both infant and adult children. In the former case the girls are between 12 and 14 years, while in the latter case the boys are between 16 and 25 years of age. The *mulakutipanam* (bride-price) is paid which they call price for mother suckling the girl during infancy.

Death: The Kepmaris bury their dead with the head pointing towards the south. Only the cloth in which the corpse has been rolled is buried along with the dead body. The party returns home, after bathing in a neighbouring river, tank or well. On both the third and fifth day after the death of a person, the spirit of the dead is fed at the burial ground after which the agnates assemble at the burial ground left the place. Then, they have their bath which sets them free from pollution. At the end of the month or before the expiry of the third month, all the castemen and relations are invited to a dinner when offerings of food are made to a *kalasa* (earthen pot) ritually set up in the name of the deceased. The ceremony ends with this funeral feast.

Dwelling : They are said to have had formed in the past their temporary settlements before setting on their thieving operations. But they now have their settled habitations in the regions or areas where they are found more in number.

Foods : They are non-vegetarians and eat even pork. Their staple cereals are *ragi*, rice and wheat.

Traditional Occupation : Cultivation was put forward as their ostensible means of livelihood in the past. Some members of the community possessed lands and paid taxes in their own names. This was said to be their only link with cultivation. But in reality, any crop that could be raised belonged to the actual worker in the field. It is said that thieving was the special occupation vocation of the castemen. In their thieving excursions, they were said to have formed themselves into small groups with one or two women and a trained boy or girl about seven years old in each group. Every group used to proceed to a particular village. In the villages, if they happened to see children playing around, the woman and the trained boy or girl used to strip them of their jewels.

Koosa

Birth: In the case of first pregnancy, the *Hoovu Mudisuvudu* or *Halanna Hakuvudu* ceremony is observed by the people of this caste during the fifth month. The *Bayake* ceremony performed at the woman's natal home is intended to mark the commencement of the ninth month. The pregnant woman receives the present of a new *saree* and a blouse from her parents-in-law. A feast is also held to which her affinal kins are invited. Later, decked with flowers and ornaments and dressed in new garments, the pregnant woman sits on a plank or a chair. In front of her a variety of choice dishes such as *ladu kajjaya, chakkuli, karjikai*, etc. are displayed. Those who wish, may offer her some presents. Then, two married women wave *arathi* (lamp) with comphor, etc. in front of her. Thereafter, a measure of rice and a coconut is placed in her robe.

Puberty: Girl menstruating for the first time is held impure for 5, 9 or 12 days. Soon after its occurrence, she is given *eaidu moge neeru* (a ritual bath). Five married women of the *Kudige* or Koodige (hamlet), each carrying a pot full of water, circumambulate five times and bathe the girl who sits on a plank. Though well-dressed and decked with areca and other flowers, the girl should remain outside the residential hut. She may use cattle-shed or else the *chavadi* (pial) of the hut. Elderly women of the caste try to engage and entertain her by singing songs and by making gossips as she should not attend to any outdoor work whatsoever. If already married, message is sent to her husband's kins and they are invited to attend the *thale neeru madume* or *hatu moge neeru huyyuvudus* (purificatory rite) performed, according to convenience, on either the fifth, ninth or the twelfth day.

Marriage: The Koosas have *balis* (exogamous divisions) which are traced through the females line. A man cannot marry his own or classificatory elder sister's daughter as that would amount to incest. So also, the parallel cousin-marriage is a taboo. But the cross-cousin marriages are allowed and practised though such marriages are of late on the decline. While contracting an alliance, the utmost care is taken to see that the *balis* of the marrying couple and of their fathers are different. An elder brother's wife is reckoned as equivalent to one's own mother.

Death: The Koosas generally bury their dead. A person on his death bed is removed to the *chavadi* (pial or open verandah) of the hut. His relatives pour water, sanctified by *Tulsi* (sweet basil), into his mouth when life is about to be extinct. The nearest and the dearest of the person are sent for to have a final look of him. Soon after death, a coconut is broken and in each half the coconut-oil-wick-lamps are lit. These are placed on grains of rice and paddy spread over the ground near the head and feet of the corpse. The burial takes place before dusk.

Dwelling : The settlements of Koosas are no exception to the general pattern of settlements in the area. Even within a village, they live in two or more distinct hamlets. Normally, their settlements are called *Koosalara gudi* or *Koosalara salu* and the hamlets where they reside are known by other names such as *Thoplu, Nagaramathad Darkast, Kambigara Kodlu Kotebagila*, etc. Their settlements do not conform to any established pattern but personal convenience seems to be its chief determinant. In keeping with the regional pattern, their houses are also independent units with open space all round and in some cases are encircled by hedgeroves.

Dress : Men's dress consists of an unsewn lower garment called either a *dhoti* or a loincloth and an upper sewn garment such as a banian or a shirt. Some of the younger men use underwear-knickers. While at work, they wear caps made out of *adike hale* sheaths covering the inflorescence of arecanuts. Head scarves are also used, though some leave their heads bare. Use of footwear is not very common. Boys wear knickers and shirts with or without banians.

Ornaments : The common ornaments worn by men are ear-studs of gold and finger-rings of silver. On the occasion of marriage, the women put on a pair of *kalminchu* (toe-rings) and also a black-bead necklace. They may even adorn their necks, on special occasion, with a borrowed gold necklace as only a few can afford to have of their own. Most of the women use gold ornaments in the ears and nose. All married women invariably wear a necklace of black-beads and only a few who are relatively affluent insert the *tali* (the gold marriage pendant) in it.

Foods : Rice is the staple cereal of the people of this caste. Like other indigenous people of the region, they also prefer parboiled rice to raw rice. It is consumed in the form of gruel and also as cooked rice with soup, vegetable or fish curry. Pulses such as *arhar* and gram are used only occasionally. Normally, they take food thrice a day. The breakfast consists of salted gruel (usually the stuff prepared on the previous evening and kept overnight) and the mid–day meal is of the freshly prepared gruel with *chutney* or salt to pep it. Little quantities of cooked rice, fish or vegetable curry and gruel constitute the menu for the night. Their food habits vary from season to season. However, during the bearing season of June and July jackfruits are consumed either raw or are used in preparing *dosas* (pancakes).

Traditional Occupation : According to their own version, they were immigrants, to their preent inhabitated areas not as conquerers but as people ready to take up servitude. Most of them were agrestic serfs of the indigenous land-owning castes such as Bunt or Nadavar, Jain, Brahmin, etc. A few of them were cultivating their master's lands as share-croppers. They did not have any rights on utilization of forest-wealth nor did they have any special association with forests. As labourers, they would gather leaves and twigs for their landlords but a few would, occasionally, gather faggots for sale.

Koracha/Korama

Birth: The people of both castes regard the birth of a child as a divine boon. Still-births, abortions or miscarriages and barrenness are attributed to sins committed in this or in the past life. Birth of the first child generally takes place in the parental house of the woman. During the fifth, seventh or ninth month of the pregnancy, the expectant mother is taken to her parents' house after performing the *Sogulu* ceremony. At that time, she is presented with a *saree*, a *choli* (blouse), and is also served with a sumptuous meal. During her pregnancy, she is given ordinary food and she continues to attend to all her normal work in the household as also in the fields. They generally prefer the birth of a male child. The delivery takes place in a screened-off corner of the residential house.

Puberty: On attainment of puberty, a girl is considered to be under pollution for five to nine days. For these days, she lives in a separate green hut specially constructed for the purpose. The girl is given bath daily. She may enter the house on the third day when she is purified by the bath and cow's urine sprinkled over her head. From the third or fifth day, she is seated on *hase* (wooden plank), and *arathi* (lighted wick) is waved around her and the womenfolk sing songs. The green hut is destroyed on the ninth day by the maternal uncle who had constructed it.

Marriage: Both Korachas and Koramas regard the cases of premarital and extra-marital relationships with horror. The male offender is publicly disgraced and fined or excommunicated. Extra-marital or premarital relationship of female with a person of the lower caste is also seriously viewed and punished with her excommunication from the caste.

Death: The Koramas and Korachas normally bury their dead, though in some parts of the State they cremate dead body of the aged person, the pregnant woman and those who had suffered from chronic diseases. The eldest son acts as the chief mourner in the case of his father's death and the youngest son in the case of mother's death. In their absence, brother or some other close relative from the male's side acts as the chief mourner. On the third day, the chief mourner, the carriers of the bier and other relatives go to the burial ground, and offer cooked rice and water to the deceased. Again, on the fifth day they similarly offer food at the grave. It is believed that the spirit of the deceased lingers about in the bodies of crows which should eat this food.

Dwelling : The residential houses of these people are found both in rural and urban areas. In towns, they invariably have a colony of their own which is a little away from the town proper. About five to six decades ago, the wandering Korachas used to stay outside the villages in temporary huts made of bent bamboo sticks in the ground. But these days, their houses in villages are found adjacent to the houses of the people of other castes like Vokkaliga, Beda, Kuruba, etc.

Dress : The traditional dress of both the Koracha and Korama females consists of a *saree* and a blouse. The males wear knickers, *dhoties* and shirts. However, there is some regional variation in the matter of their dress patterns. For instance, in the districts of Mysore, Bangalore and Kolar, men use knickers as the lower garment, whereas in the districts of Shimoga, Bellary and Chitradurga *dhoti* is used as the lower garment. It is not uncommon to see younger men in pyjamas/trousers and T-shirts particularly in the urban areas. Elderly men in the districts of Shimoga, Bellary, Chitradurga and Chikmagalur use *mundasu* (a headgear).

Ornaments : The ornaments worn by both males and females are usually made of gold, silver, brass, etc. The females have ornaments called *vali* or *bendoli* (ear-stud) for the ears, besides *bugudi* (ear ornament which is worn on the upper lobe of the ear), *kalandige* (silver anklets) and *kalachainu* (silver chains) for the ankles. They have also ornaments like glass bangles or *kadagas* (wristlet) for the wrists, *gejjedabu* (waistbelt) or *dabu* for the waist, and *nattu* or *besari* (nose-ring) for the nose. They have many types of necklaces made of glass, brass or silver. A few of them also wear finger-rings made of gold or silver.

Foods : The Koramas and Korachas are non-vegetarians. They eat mutton, fowl and pork but beef is prohibited. They also consume fish and eggs. Their daily menu consists of *ragi* balls and vegetable curry in the districts of Mysore, Bangalore, Kolar and Hassan. But in the districts of Chitradurga and Bellary, *rotti* (bread made of *jowar* flour) and pulses are consumed. Only on festival and ceremonial occasions, do they take rice and non-vegetarian food. They use groundnut oil as the medium for cooking. Spices and condiments are used in the preparation of special dishes and non-vegetarian food. They usually have three meals a day but many of them take food, according to convenience and not at a fixed hour.

Traditional Occupation : Basket-making was their principal household industry in the past and it was also their hereditary occupation. They prepared bamboo baskets of different sizes and shapes. Their work did not require much technical skill or capital. Women and children also worked in this industry. About one or two decades back, the basket-making was almost a preserve of the people of this caste and a few other castes like Medars, etc.

Kotegar, Metri

Birth: A woman in child-birth is considered impure for eleven days, and the cradling takes place on the fifteenth day. No other ceremony is observed by the people of this caste.

Puberty: A girl attaining her age is kept in a secluded place for twelve days. She is exhibited before the women-folk every evening. She is given bath on the fifth, seventh and twelfth day. After bath on the twelfth day, she is purified by drinking *tirtha* (holy water) brought from the *dasayya's* (caste priest) house and by keeping a *kalasa* (earthen pot) with her. If the girl is already married, she lives with her husband from the twelfth day onwards.

Marriage: Girls were traditionally married either before or after the attainment of their age. However, at present adult marriages are practised. The paternal aunt's daughter, maternal uncle's daughter or elder sister's daughter is generally preferred while negotiating marriage. Two families can exchange daughters in marriages. The two sisters of a family are not married to the same man at a time, but the younger is married after the death of the elder one. Marriage takes place in the boy's house.

Death: Their traditional practice to dispose-off the dead was burial. But since the last two decades or so, cremation is resorted to. The corpse of children, whose ear-piercing ceremony has taken place, are cremated. The pregnant women or those who died during or after delivery are also cremated. On the third day, the rice cooked in new earthen pots is taken to the burial or cremation site and is offered to the soul of the dead which is later eaten by crows. The death pollution is observed for twelve days. The *booja* (death rite) or removal of death pollution is performed on the twelfth day by cleaning and smearing the house with cowdung paste, washing the clothes and utensils, and sprinkling throughout the house, the holy water brought from the temple.

Dwelling : The Kotegars generally live in small clusters of four to five families and their houses are located at the outskirts of villages.

Ornaments : *Tali* and toe-rings are the main ornaments worn by the married women.

Foods : The people of this caste are non-vegetarians but do not eat beef. However, rice and *jowar* are their staple cereals.

Traditional Occupation : The traditional occupation of the Kotegars was basketry, as stated earlier. They used to prepare varieties of baskets of bamboo used for domestic and agricultural purposes. These people were also traditionally engaged in menial services such as lifting of dead cattle, skinning of dead animals and arranging pyres for the dead people of the other castes. They also used to sell wet skins to the Dhors for tanning.

Lingader

Foods : The Lingaders are strict vegetarians and abstain from all forms of liquor. Their staple cereals are rice, *jowar* and wheat.

Traditional Occupation : The Lingaders (probably the unclean caste attached to the Lingayat caste or community) used in the past to provide menial services to their patron families.

Machala

Foods : They are non-vegetarians, and eat chicken, mutton, pork and beef. However, rice, *jowar* and wheat are the staple cereals consumed along with pulses.

Traditional Occupation : Information about traditional occupation of Machalas is not available, except their being engaged in begging in the past.

Madiga

Birth: Normally, the first delivery of a woman takes place in her mother's house. The other confinements take place in the husband's house. They use the inner room of the house for delivery. During the period of pregnancy, the mother takes rich food but is asked to avoid fish, gingelly, pappaya, etc. whichare considered as abortifacients. Assistance for the delivering mother is provided by the elderly women of the caste or community. If any woman from outside her family takes up this job, she receives a token remuneration.

Puberty: Immediately on attainment of puberty, a thatched dormitory is constructed with coconut leaves and the girl stays in it. She remains in it for nine days. Each day, the hut is renewed by relations by putting more coconut thatches. On the ninth day, she is given a ceremonious bath and is taken to the house. A small ceremony is held on this occasion. Plantain fruits and puffed rice are tied to the end of the 'pallav' of her *saree* before she enters the house. The relations are fed on the occasion.

Marriage: The Madigas prefer marrying their elder sister's daughter and maternal and paternal cross-cousins. The initiative for a marriage alliance comes from the bridegroom's side. The boy's parents and relations along with a *oor ejamanan* (caste head) visit the bride's house taking along with them betel, arecanut, flowers, etc.

Death: Burial is the common method of disposal of their dead. Immediately on the death of a person, the body is taken out of the house and kept outside. After the relations arrive, a bath is given to the body and it is taken to the burial ground. On the third day, the place of burial is revisited. Tender coconuts, milk, etc. are placed near the place of burial. On the eleventh day, a purification ceremony is undergone by offering *pooja* (worship) to the departed soul. A feast is given on this day to the caste people and relatives.

Dwelling : The Madigas live in a separate locality called *cherry*. Their houses are constructed in a line on either side of the streets and are away from the houses of caste Hindus. There is not much difference between the general pattern of the houses of others and that of the Madigas. The roofing of all the houses is low. The walls of *pucca* houses are made of country bricks or stones in random rubble. The thatched houses have mud walls with no proper plastering.

Dress : Their men wear short *dhotis* at the waist. They put on half-shirts or coat over their body. Bare bodies are seldom seen in this part of the country. Their women wear coloured *sarees* of eight yards' length. Young girls are found either in their skirts or in gowns. Boys wear shorts and shirts.

Ornaments : The ornaments worn by the Madiga women are of typical characteristic of the Karnataka region. In the ear lobes, they wear *kammals* (stone-studded ear-rings). Stone-studded nose-screws are worn on the nose. They wear cheap chains or a string of glass beads or corals in the neck. Married women wear coin-shaped *pottu tali* (marriage badge) in a string of black beads. In the wrists, they wear a series of glass bangles, *kai mani* (a string of corals), *kappu,* etc. Some wear a *Sarigai* (silver bracelet) also. In the waist, they invariably wear *ottiyanam* (a silver or rolled-gold plated metallic belt) over the *saree.* Some of their men also wear ear-rings and *sarigai* on their wrists.

Foods : There is a local saying that the wants of most people would be met by *kali* and *puli* meaning *ragi* meal and tamarind. These two form the essential ingredients of the monotonous meal of the poor class people of this locality. The *kali* is made by cooking *ragi* flour into a pasty thick solid meal. This is generally eaten hot along with a sauce prepared with pulses and tamarind. Rice is taken as a luxury item during festive occasions. The Madigas cook their meals twice a day in the morning and evening, and eat the same thrice in a day.

Traditional Occupation : The Madigas' traditional economic way of life has well been brought out by Chatterton (1904). According to him, "they (Madigas) live in hamlets at a respectable distance from the villages of the caste people, by whom they are greatly despised. Their habits are squalid in the extreme, and the odour of a Madiga hamlet is revolting. They perform all the lowest kinds of service for the caste people, especially bearing burdens and working in leather. They take charge of the ox or buffalo as soon as it dies. They remove the skin and tan it, and eat the loathsome carcass, which makes them specially despised, and renders their touch polluting.

Mahar

Birth: During her first pregnancy, the woman receives greater care and attention. In some villages, a preliminary *Kupsa* (blouse) ceremony is performed during the fifth month to announce the glad news to their relatives. It is, however, more common to hold this ceremony during the seventh month at her husband's home and also at her parental home. With the commencement of the eighth month, she refrains from doing heavy and exhausting work, and also from eschewing certain items of food considered injurious for her health. Her husband, too, observes certain restrictions until the delivery occurs.

Puberty: A girl menstruating for the first time is considered impure for five days. Soon after the event, a few women gather together and ritually bathe the girl. She remains in a corner of the 'pial' which is in front of the house and her touch is considered to be defiling. She does not attend to any work whatsoever and, instead, is fed on a rich diet. Women of the neighbourhood keep her company and sing *Shobane* (pleasant) songs to keep her amused. On the fifth day, a final purificatory bath is given to her by married women and the girl is usually given a new *saree* by the parents or her in-laws in case she is already married.

Marriage: In former days, the custom of dedicating women for the service of some goddess or the other was said to be widespread among the Mahars. Such women (called *Basavi, Joguni* or *Jogti,* etc. in different regions) were ceremoniously wedded to some symbol representing the spouse of the patron goddess and, in their day-to-day life, were permitted to live with any paramour of their choice. This form of prostitution, it is said, was very common and their standards of morality were loose.

Dwelling : Their houses face either the north or the east. In large villages, several rows of houses abutting the street may be found. Being economically badly-off, they build their houses of cheap and locally available material. These are single-storeyed with no compound or fence around. Most of their settlements are overcrowded and usually no open space is allowed all round the house. The houses generally have only one entrance at the front leading to the hall or the main living room. Kitchen is another important element of the house. Other amenities such as separate bath and latrine are totally lacking. As their houses are overcroweded, they lack privacy too.

Dress : The man's lower garment in common use is *Dhoti.* In Uttar Kannad district of Karnataka State, the Mahars are more frequently seen in mere loinclothes covering the waist and thighs. In towns and large villages, use of underwear, knickers, shirts and pyjamas is also slowly coming into vogue among the educated and urban youth. The older generation uses *rumala* (headscarf). Women's dress consists of a *saree* and a blouse. Boys put on knickers and shirts, while girls dress themselves in frocks or skirts and blouses. Because of poverty, many Mahar men, women and children are often seen in tattered clothes. For want of sufficient spare clothing, it is difficult even to maintain their clothes clean.

Ornaments : It is a common practice among the Mahars to pierce the earlobes of their infant boys and adorn them with ear-rings or ear-studs of gold (sometimes copper is also used). Anklets of silver and silver waist-string are the other ornaments in use for boys of a tender age. Those men who can afford to do so put on finger-rings of either gold or silver. Women put on several ornaments such as ear-studs, nose-screw, necklaces, bangles, waist-belt and toe-rings. The names of these ornaments vary from region to region.

Foods : In some places, *jowar* happens to be their staple cereal while in Uttar Kannad and in some parts of Belgaum districts, rice is consumed in larger quantities. They also use pulses such as *tur*, gram, *masur* and *moong* besides other millets. Wheat is rarely consumed. The customary habit of taking food thrice a day is common among them. *Holige* and *payasa* are the two sweet dishes they prepare on festival days.

Traditional Occupation : Their main traditional source of livelihood was rendering service in various forms to the village community. In turn, many were enjoying *inam*-rights over small bits of Government-owned agricultural landbesides *baluta* or *aya*, a periodic payment in kind by their patron-cultivators. Enthoven (1922) provides some details about the traditional occupation of Mahars. He states, "The Mahars are hereditary village servants and are considered authorities in all boundary matters.

Mahyavanshi, Dhed, Vankar, Maru Vankar

Birth: Pre-delivery rituals are observed in the seventh month of the first pregnancy and the *chathi* or *Chhathi* is observed on the sixth day after child birth.

Marriage: Clan exogamy is strictly observed and marriages are arranged through negotiation. Earlier, the marriageable age was ten to fifteen years for both boys and girls, but now adult marriage is common. Bride-price is prevalent. Divorce has to be approved by the caste elders. Remarriage after widowhood or divorce is permitted.

Death: Their dead are either buried or cremated and death pollution is observed for twelve days.

Foods : They are non-vegetarians, and their staple cereals are rice and wheat.

Traditional Occupation : The traditional occupation of people of the caste was village service, including skinning of dead animals and weaving of coarse cloth.

Maila

Birth: The *huva mudisuva habbas* (pre-delivery rituals) are performed during the seventh month of the first pregnancy. Birth pollution lasts for eleven days. The naming ceremony is performed on the fifth day, and the first feeding of cereals ceremony is also observed.

Puberty: The *pile* or *nareda maduve* (puberty rite) is performed on the first menstruation of the girl.

Marriage: The caste endogamy and also clan exogamy are practised. Marriage with one's paternal aunt's daughter, maternal auncle's daughter or elder sister's daughter is preferred. Adult marriages are the norm and the marriages are settled through negotiation. Both bride-price and dowry are in practice. Marriages are solemnised at the bride's residence and the marriage feast is hosted by both the sides. Junior sororate and junior levirate types of marriage are permitted. Divorce is allowed with the approval of elders/caste council. Adultery and cruelty are the reasons for seeking divorce. Both men and women can seek divorce. The divorce compensation is given to the husband's parents, if the divorce is initiated by the wife. After divorce, the children, if any, are looked after by the father. Widow, widower or divorcee remarriages are allowed.

Death: Their dead are cremated. Death pollution lasts for sixteen days. Ancestor worship is observed every year.

Ornaments : The *belakallu* (a string of white beads), toe-rings and blue or red bangles are the main ornaments of married women. In Karnataka, *tali* (marriage locket) is considered the marriage symbol of a woman.

Foods : The Mailas are non-vegetarians, and are said to relish pork, beef and carrion. However, rice is their staple food, and is supplemented with yam and tapioca. Coconut oil and animal fat are said to be used for cooking.

Traditional Occupation : Traditional occupations of the people of this caste were hunting, gathering forest products, fishing, and trapping of birds and animals.

Mala Dasari/Mala Dasu

Birth: The ceremonies conducted at the time of birth by people of both of these castes resemble in many respects the ceremonies among other Hindu castes. During the fifth or seventh month of the first pregnancy, *seemantham* is performed. Five married women are seated along with the pregnant woman and new clothes, flowers, *laddu* (sweet meat), *ghee*, jaggery, etc. are presented to her. The family tries to satisfy all her desires before delivery. The delivery takes place in a dark room of the house and is assisted by an elderly woman of the caste who is paid fee with free food for five days. After delivery, she takes hot water bath on every alternate day from the seventh day onwards. Only after eleventh day, she is allowed to move freely.

Puberty: When a girl attains puberty, she is made to sit in a corner of the house on a *peetha* (wooden plank). In the evening, the neighbouring married ladies are invited. They apply vermilion to her forehead and offer *arathi* (flame of camphor). A feast is arranged in the night. Pollution is observed for nine days in the case of Mala Dasaris and eleven days in the case of Mala Dasus. During this period food, water, etc. are served to her in separate vessels. If the girl is married, pollution is observed for five weeks. Her food consists of rice, curry, *ghee*, milk, jaggery and coconut. In either case, new clothes are presented to the girl on this occasion by her parents. No one touches her during this period.

Marriage: Marriage through negotiation is the only type known to them. A man may marry his maternal uncle's daughter, paternal aunt's daughter, wife's sister or sister's daughter. Though they are a sub-section of Malas, they do not marry them. They marry within their own caste but only those not belonging to the same *intiperulu* (surname) as stated earlier. The marriageable age for males is between 12 and 25 years and for females between 9 and 16 years. Polygamy is also prevalent among them. Mala Dasari/Mala DasuMailaMahyavanshi, Dhed, Vankar, Maru Vankar

Death: Their dead are buried. Soon after death, the body is given hot water bath and *namam* (the sect sign) is marked on the forehead. Wet turmeric is applied to the feet and face of the dead body. A garland of *ganneru* (oleander) flowers is placed around the neck. Flowers are tied to the wrists also. The body is kept on a bier in lying posture and is completely covered with dry paddy straw. All the relatives throw *akshintalu* (rice mixed with turmeric) on the dead body. They turn round a few copper coins thrice over the head of the dead body and place them in a vessel before it (the dead body). These are later given to the *Dasari* who sings a devotional song. The body is raised by all the kith and kins, and is later carried by four persons to the burial ground.

Dwelling : The people of this caste or community live, on the outskirts of the village, away from the main habitation. Their huts are known as *puri gudiselu* or *kottamulu*. These usually consist of one or two rooms and are generally square or rectangular in shape with thatched roofs of palmyra or date palm leaves, paddy or *jowar* hay, *kandikampa* (stalks of red gram), or bamboo rafters, etc.

Dress : Adult males wear a *dhoti*, a shirt and an upper cloth. A few people who can afford wear *chappals*. Women wear a *saree* and *ravika* (blouse). Boys wear knickers and shirts, while girls wear *langalu* (skirts) and *cholilu* (blouse). There is no special dress for a bride or bridegroom except that the latter wears a turban at the time of marriage. Elderly women tie their hair into a knot at the back, whereas young women and girls wear plaits.

Foods : Rice and *jowar* constitute their staple food. They take *ambali* (gruel), *rotti*, chilli powder and *chintapandu karam* (preparation with tamarind and chillis), etc. They take *dhal* (pulse) in the form of *rasam* (a liquid food). *Paramannam* (rice cooked in milk and jaggery or sugar added) or *ariselu* and *garelu* form the items of a festival dinner. Non-vegetarian dishes like chicken or mutton are also taken on such occasions. Eating beef which was widely prevalent among them in the pre-Independence days is now on the wane due to the efforts of the Bapuji Sevak Sangh. Some of the younger members of the present generation are reportedly averse to the killing of domestic animals like fowl, sheep, etc.

Traditional Occupation : In the past, the Mala Dasaris/Mala Dasus used to earn their livelihood by organising street plays on festive occasions. Some of their favourite plays were Bobbili Katha, Mugguru Marateelu and Desingaraju.

Mala Jangam

Birth: There is no hard and fast rule regarding the place of delivery of a child. The expectant mother is, however, taken to her parents' house for the first confinement either in the fifth or seventh month of her pregnancy but no particular ceremony is observed on this occasion. Generally, the Mala Jangam women do not go to hospitals for cases of delivery. The woman is kept in a separate room in the house itself. A native nurse or an elderly caste woman called *manthrasani* attends to the delivery. Birth pollution is observed for eight days. The mother and child are given hot water bath on the fifth day. Another water bath, with the mixture of turmeric powder and oil, is given as a preliminary to the purificatory bath on the ninth day.

Puberty: Usually, girls attain puberty between the age of 12 to 14 years. When the girl attains puberty, she is made to sit in an enclosure erected specially for the purpose. Pollution is observed for a period of 12 days. The girl is forbidden to come out of the enclosure and is also not allowed to participate in domestic activities. During the period of pollution, bath is, however, given to the girl on the fifth, ninth, and the eleventh days.

Marriage: As a custom, the proposal of marriage comes from the boy's parents. Initially, the boy's father makes full enquiry regarding the surname, etc. of the girl's father. When he is satisfied about the respectability of the family, he goes with relatives and friends to the girl's father and pays him cash towards the bride-price. The amount depends on the financial position of the boy's father.

Death: As stated by Hassan (1920), their dead are buried even now in a sitting posture with their face to the north. A new pot is brought and water is boiled in it. The corpse is given a hot water bath and vermilion is applied on its forehead. It is dressed in new clothes and decorated with flowers. A framework of bamboos or country wood is prepared and, at the central portion of the framework, a cone-shaped shed is erected with the country wood. The corpse wraped in new clothes is placed in a sitting posture inside the shed and is carried by four people to the burial ground. Either the eldest or the youngest son carries a new pot with fire and leads the corpse to the burial ground. He should not look back. Friends and relatives follow the funeral procession.

Dwelling : The Mala Jangams generally live on the outskirts of the villages. The main entrance to their hut or houses is always towards the north. They could not give any reason for this except that it was a traditional practice. There are two types of houses which are locally known as *Middelu* and *Gudiselu*. The main difference between these two types of houses is in respect of the roof alone.

Dress : Men wear *pancha* or *dhotis* of four and half yards length and a *kamij* (shirt). They always keep a *gongadi* (country rug) on their shoulders and cover their heads with it in summer. Women wear *sarees* of eight yards' length and a *ravika* (blouse). The same dress is used on special occasions too.

Ornaments : Most of their women use ornaments made of silver and brass, and very few use gold ornaments. The married women wear *puste* placed amidst the threaded black beads and the *mattelu* (toe-rings). The other ornaments they wear are *kadialu* (big rings around the ankles) and *guntelu* (ear-rings). Different kinds of chains locally known as *chowkalu*, *gundlu* and *teegelu*, and necklaces are used which are made of silver and gold. The bangles made of glass and silver, and finger-rings of silver or brass are very popular among them.

Both women and men have tattoo marks on their bodies. The usual tattoo marks are *Saraswathi* (Goddess of learning), *Chandamama* (Moon), *chettu* (tree) and names of gods. Some people have it purely for decorative purposes and some others as a hereditary custom. A few others feel that tattooing has got some medicinal value in curing bodily pains.

Foods : The staple food of Mala Jangams consists of *jowar* and rice. Occasionally, they take *roti* (bread) made of wheat. They use all kinds of vegetables and fruits without any restriction. They take food twice a day. They eat the flesh of goat, sheep and fowl but do not eat beef or pork. They relish all kinds of fish. They do not eat wild roots. On festive occasions, they prepare a special dish of *payasam* (a sweet preparation with milk).

Traditional Occupation : The traditional occupations of most of Mala Jangams was to officiate as priests at ceremonies of the Saivite section of Malas. Others were engaged in wage-labour, manufacturing, cultivation, etc.

Mala Masti/Mashti

Birth: On the third day after the birth of the first child, the *purud* ceremony is performed when a goat is killed and the head is placed on the rim of the pit in which the child's umbilical cord has been buried. The head forms the perquisite of the midwife. On the twenty-first day, the mother goes to a well, offers *puja* (obtation) to its rim, marches three times around it and returns home with a jar filled with water. The water is sprinkled throughout the house and the mother is rendered ceremonially pure. The child is named generally on the fifth day after its birth. Generally, no such ceremony is performed for the subsequent child unless he is a male.

Marriage: Cross-cousin marriages are prevalent among them. The marriageable age for boys and girls has been around fifteen and ten years respectively. But it has increased during the recent decades. Immediately after marriage, the girl is sent to her husband by the *vadibiyam* ceremony. Cohabitation before puberty is tolerated. Divorce is permitted on the ground of the wife's adultery and is effected with a sanction of the caste council. As a symbol of separation, some salt is tied in the woman's garment and she is driven out of the house. A young and issueless or with small children widow is allowed to marry again but she cannot marry her late husband's brother.

Ornaments : *Tali* or *Thali* (marriage-locket), bangles and toe-rings are the marriage symbols for women. These ornaments are generally worn by them.

Foods : Maize and *jowar* or *ghataka* are their staple cereals. Some of them also take rice. Pulses like *tur* and *urad*, and all kinds of seasonal vegetables are eaten by them. Groundnut and palm oils are used for cooking.

Traditional Occupation : The Mala Mastis/Mashtis were landless, and seeking alms was their traditional occupation. They begged only from the Malas at the time of harvesting. After collecting one rupee or some paddy from each family, they used to entertain their patrons by performing epic and *puranic* folk-dramas and dances.

Mala Sale, Netkani

Birth: The *muttudu* (post-delivery pollution) is observed for twenty-one days and the naming ceremony of the child takes place on the twenty-first day. The tonsure ceremony called *puttentukulu theeyuta* is performed for both male and female children.

Puberty: The *pushpavathi* (puberty) ceremony is performed at menarche of the girls.

Marriage: Marriage with one's maternal uncle's daughter is preferred. Girls are married after they attain puberty. Marriages are arranged through negotiation. Dowry is paid both in cash and kind. Marriage rituals and consummation ceremony are performed at the groom's residence. Divorce and remarriage are allowed and either spouse can seek divorce.

Death: Their dead are buried in a sitting posture. Death pollution is observed for ten days. Ancestor worship called *peddalaku biyyamu ichuta* is observed every year on *pethiramavasya* day (the lunar conjunction day of a forthnight) in the month of July-August.

Ornaments : Toe-rings and *tali* (marriage-locket) are the main ornaments of married women.

Foods : The people of this caste are non-vegetarians but do not eat beef and pork. Rice and maize are the staple cereals which they eat with red and green grams.

Traditional Occupation : The Mala Sales, Netkanis are the Telugu weavers. Hence, weaving has been their traditional occupation.

Mala

Birth: The news of pregnancy of a woman is passed on to her parents. In case of the first pregnancy, the parents of the pregnant woman visit her at her in–laws' house in the ninth month to conduct *Soolvalavi*–a feast arranged in honour of her fertility. But her food habits are not changed during the pre-natal period. The delivery usually takes place in an inner room of the house, and is attended to by some experienced elderly woman of the village. If there is difficulty in childbirth, the services of a trained midwife or a doctor is sought. To ward-off evil spirits, a sickle and some *mim* (*Melia Azadirachta*) leaves are kept upon the place of delivery.

Puberty: The horror of pollution during puberty is recognised by the Malas. In former days, the menstruating girl was kept in a seclusion hut away from the dwelling place. She was allowed to join the family after 15 days and that too after a ritual purification ceremony. But nowadays, the menstruating girl is allowed to remain secluded in a portion of the house which is separated by bamboo and palmyra leaf screens or a piece of cloth. These screens are burnt during the time of her purification or the piece of cloth is cleaned. The girl, however, remains secluded for 15-16 days and is not expected to be seen by the menfolk. Food is served to her for all the 15 days in her enclosure and the vessels used by her are not used in the household. On the sixteenth day, '*Isoga*' (purification ceremony) is performed when the *Nalangu* (turmeric paste) is smeared on her body, and she is given a ceremonial bath and adorned with new clothes.

Marriage: Marriage of a girl either in the same lineage or in the same brother's clan is prohibited. Neither do the people of Malas take from nor give girls in marriage to other castes. Though they consider the Tamil Paraiyans as of the same social status, exchange food and water with them and invite one another in their social functions, yet intermarriage is a taboo. The marriageable age for the girls usually is after puberty and for the boys above 20 years. Child marriages are very rare. Monogamy is the usual practice, though polygamous marriages have also been reported in a few cases.

Death: The Malas dispose off their dead both by burial and by cremation, though the former is more common. Cremation is practised mostly by the affluent people of the caste as it entails more expenditure. There appears to be slight variation in the practices connected with death among the Vaishnavite and Saivite sections of people of this caste. The former allows the person to die inside the house while the latter, fearing pollution, removes the person outside the door as soon as it is realised that death is near.

Dwelling : In the rural areas, they are invariably settled in hamlets, on the outskirts of the village, away from the main habitation. In the urban areas, however, they are found to live intermingled with the people of other castes mostly of lower social status. The Malas, hamlet is locally known as *Cheri*. The *Cheri* is connected with the main village usually by a footpath or, in some cases, a cart road which may run through the hamlet. In the villages, they have water sources of their own which the caste Hindus would not use. In some urban areas, the Government has provided them the protected water supply and electricity connections.

Dress : The Mala males wear *lungis* of four cubit in length wrapped round the loin and reaching up to the ankles. Occasionally, they may wear a towel over the shoulders as an upper cloth. While they are at work, they wear only a small loin cloth. The youngsters wear shirts and *banians*, in addition to the loin cloth. The Mala women wear *chela* (*saree*) of six yards in length the *pallav* of which is thrown on the left shoulder. Somewomen throw the *pallav* on the right shoulder. When the women go out for work, they pull up the lower edge of their *saree* and tuck it in the waist so the portion below the knees becomes bare.

Ornaments : The Mala women do not appear to be very fond of ornaments. Yet, they wear *mukku pottuka* (nose-screws) on both the *alae* (sides) of the nose. At the lower end of the septum of the nose is worn *Bullakku*. These ornaments are mostly made of cheap metals but a few well-to-do may use silver or gold. In the lower ear-lobes are worn cheap stone-studded *kammal* and *mattal* (ear-studs) mostly made of cheap metals. Glass and plastic bangles known as *chai ghazlu* are used by young women. The unmarried women and girls use coloured *thanda* (yellow, black and red beads, strung on thread) as neck chains. Cheap factory-made aluminium or steel rings known as *'ungaram'* are also worn by them. Silver chain like *Kolusu* with ornamentation is also worn by them. *Bottu* (marriage-badge) and *Mettu* (toe-rings) are worn only by the married women.

Foods : Rice, *cholam* and *ragi* form the staple food of the Malas. But the latter two are more frequently used. These are cooked in solid or semi-solid forms, and are consumed along with some vegetable and occasionally with non-vegetarian dishes. They generally take meals thrice a day. The morning and mid-day meals are in the form of semi-solid gruel. At night, cooked rice along with some sauce or side dish is consumed. This is the principal meal for them. They eat fish, mutton, beef, pork and chicken. It is also reported that rats, rabbits and gauna are also occasionally consumed by them. Chewing betel-leaves, arecanut, tobacco and lime is much liked by them.

Traditional Occupation : The traditional occupation of Malas had been weaving coarse cloth and working as farm labourers for people of the backward castes. A few cultivated their own land. Those who could not weave, subsisted by day-labour. As a rule, they stuck to one masterand were engaged in cultivation throughout the year. According to their own traditional belief, they were once wealthy and prosperous people as long as goddess *Lakshmi* was gracious to them. They account thus for their present poverty and change of occupation.

Mang Garudi, Mang Garodi

Birth: Generally, the expectant mother stays at her husband's house for confinement. A ceremony is performed during the 7th month usually for the first delivery. Some do not celebrate it even for the first one due to their poverty. The parents of the girl give a new *saree* and a blouse piece on this occasion. Very few people go to hospitals for delivery. Usually, some experienced old lady of their own caste assists in all cases of delivery and no payment is made to her. Bath is given to the mother and the child on the fourth day after delivery. The *purudu* (purification) ceremony is performed on ninth or eleventh day after which pollution ceases. Naming ceremony for the child is usually performed on the 21st day after the delivery.

Puberty: A girl is treated as grown up when she is found in her first menstruation. The girl is segregated for nine days in a separate room or in a part of the house separated by a *thatti* or a screen. During this period, she is neither allowed to work nor touch anybody. On the tenth day, she is given bath which marks the end of pollution. In the evening, women are invited for *nalugu* (ritual purification) when gingelly oil or coconut oil is applied to the arms and face of the girl. Then, the flour of black or green gram and of the rice mixed with water is applied. The girl is given head-bath and is clad in new clothes. On this occasion, her parents present a new saree or a *patta* (half saree) to her. From the day of her first menstruation, she is not allowed to mingle with the other men of her caste.

Marriage: Among the Mang Garodis, there are two types of Marriages. In the first case, the parents take the initiative and in the other, the younger generation or the prospective life partners take the initiative. The first one called marriage by negotiation is preferred by the people of this caste. But in the case of widows and divorced women who are allowed to remarry, the first type of marriage is not applicable.

Death: Their dead are buried. The corpse is given

bath with warm water and is decorated with new clothes and *tilak* (vermilion mark) on the forehead. It is carried by four people on a bier to the burial ground. It is kept on the ground, just before they reach the burial ground, to remove the clothes on the body. The persons carrying it exchange sides and again carry it to the burial ground. A pit is dug by their own caste members and the corpse is kept in it in a lying posture with head pointing to the south, and the pit is covered with earth. Tombs are constructed with earth after two or three months. Mourning is observed for 7 to 9 days. The obsequies are observed for seven days and these are generally performed by the eldest son of the family. The final ceremony takes place on the seventh day.

Dwelling : The Mang Garodis live in small huts built on plain grounds with the mud walls. Sometimes, these are built in low lying areas with no erected platforms, and that too in the remote parts of the town. The walls do not exceed a height of four or four and a half feet. The doorways are low and while entering the hut the inmates have to bend their heads. The roofing is done with grass of paddy hay covered over bamboos, wooden sticks and rafters. In the centre, there is a strong round wooden rag and towards both ends the grass is covered in a slanting manner.

Dress : Men wear either a loin cloth *lungi* or *dhoti* (gochi pancha) and a shirt. Elderly people wear turban as headgear. Underwears or knickers and banians are also used. The elderly women wear their costumes in the Maharashtrian fashion. But the younger ones wear *sarees* and blouses in the Telugu fashion. Clothes are purchased normally once in a year for the entire family.

Ornaments : Generally, the married women wear *puste* (marriage-locket) and *mattelu* (toe-rings). They also wear chains and necklaces of black beads, threaded to a string, round their neck or hanging and *sandalu* (big silver bangle) in the wrist. The ordinary women wear brass bangles along with coloured glass bangles. They also wear rings of silver and brass on the fingers. They have the custom of tattooing the body which is done profusely on their arms, chest and forehead for both men and women.

Foods : The staple food of Mang Garodis is *jonna rots* (*jowar* bread) with onion or tamarind *chutney*. Rice is consumed occasionally along with some vegetable curry or *pappu* (dal). They relish all kinds of meat such as chicken, mutton, beef, pork, eggs and fish. In the past, they used to eat the leavings of the people of almost all castes except Dakkalwars. Their festival meal consists of a sweet dish and rice. They are also said to get indulged excessively in alcoholic drinks.

Traditional Occupation : The Mang Garudis or Mang Garodis have traditionally been snake-charmers, acrobats and mat-weavers.

Mang

Birth: By social custom, the parents, siblings and relatives of the expectant mother bring her during the fifth, seventh or ninth month of her first pregnancy to her natal home for the first delivery. Subsequent deliveries take place at her husband's house. She continues to do all her normal domestic duties. However, she does not perform fieldwork during her first pregnancy. During the period of pregnancy, she is fed, as far as their resources permit, with nutritious food. She is given easily digestible food. During his wife's pregnancy, the husband also has to observe certain restrictions. For instance, he must not carry a corpse and should not kill any animal such as sheep, goat, poultry, etc.

Puberty: A girl attaining puberty is considered impure for five, seven or ten days depending on the regional practices. The period of her impurity is prescribed by the *Bhat*, if the stellar conciliation at the time of her attaining puberty is not auspicious. The girl bathes daily during the period of her impurity. Everyday, she is seated on a plank when the women sing *Sobana* (auspicious or well-being) songs and wave *arathi* (a lighted lamp with camphor) about her. If she is married, the husband is seated by her side and consummation of marriage is also to take place within that month. Her husband is presented with a new *dhoti*, shawl and shirt by her father. Women are considered impure during their monthly sickness for three days.

Marriage: The boys are married around 20 years and the girls around 15 years of age. This has increased in the recent decades. The pre-marital and extra-marital relationships are considered grave crimes, and the offenders are publicly disgraced and even excommunicated by the caste council. Extra-marital relationship of a female with a lower caste man means loss of caste. The marriages are contracted only with the known members and in the known regions. There are no marriage-alliances between different sub-castes pursuing traditional and hereditary occupations. Marriage between members of the identical *Kula* or *Bali* (exogamous groups) is prohibited. Both post-puberty and pre-puberty marriages are prevalent.

Death: The Mangs bury their dead. Dead bodies of the pregnant women and the lepers are cremated. Deceased children and the unmarried dead are buried in lying posture.

The death pollution is observed for three days and the chief mourner is held impure till the funeral feast is held. During this period, performance of religious and auspicious ceremonies is forbidden. They perform annual *Shradha* (death ceremony) in the month of *Mhal* (*Navarathri*) or on the day of *Yugadi* (Hindu New Year's day) festival when they set up *'Kalasa'* (pitcher) and offer worship to images of all the deceased of the family. A few caste men are fed on the day.

Dwelling : The Mangs are predominantly living in rural areas though a small number of them have settled down in towns. The habitat where they live is called *Mangwada* or *Madarkeri*. Generally, the people of this community live on the outskirts of villages and towns. Their settlements are found to be just adjacent to those of other Scheduled Castes like Holers, Chalvadis and Mahars.

Dress : The common dress of a male now is a half-sleeved *Angi* or *jubba, dhoti* and a *rumal* (headgear). Today, the youth prefer Gandhi cap in place of *rumal*. In urban and semi-urban areas, the use of pants and slacks is also noticed among the youth. The common dress of a female consists of a *saree* and *kuppasa*. On festive and ceremonial occasions, they use cleaner and a little costlier sets of dresses. The mode of wearing the dress does not, in any way, differ from that of the people of other castes in the region. It is only during the busy agricultural seasons, women in the districts of Belgaum and North Kanara tuck up the ends of their *sarees* at the back while working in the fields. Boys wear knickers and half-sleeved shirts. Girls below the age of 10 years use frocks and jackets.

Ornaments : Both men and women wear ornaments made of gold, silver and brass. Generally, women wear ornaments on the ears, head, legs and neck. The *bendoli, bangarada hoovu, vali* (of gold), *jogera haralu* (of cheap metal), *hookuddi* (of silver) and *terapina sara* (of brass and silver) are different types of ear-rings worn by the women. *Bugudi,* an ornament on the upper ear-lobes, is going out of use among the younger generation. Waist-belt called *nadupatti* or *dabu* made of silver is worn by the older women. Nose ornaments like *muguti* and *moogubattu* made of gold are worn by all the married women. But *kalendige* and *kaluchanu* or anklets made of silver are worn by the young and old females.

Foods : The staple diet of Mangs consist of *jowar* bread *(roti)* or bread made of *sajje* (*bajra*) and pulses, rice, *ragi* and vegetables. Millets are also consumed considerably. The millets generally consumed are navane, *same* and *arka*. Their holiday dishes are *polies* (sweet cakes prepared with jaggery, *tur dhal* and wheat flour), *huggi* (sweet gruel), *kajjaya, kadubu,* etc. Cooked rice and soup are taken only on special festive occasions with holiday dishes.

By tradition, they are non-vegetarians. They formerly ate carrion but, of late, they have given it up. They eat beef, sheep, poultry and birds like *kaujugs*, parrots, etc. But they do not take pork. They eat all kinds of fish.

Traditional Occupation : The Mangs followed in the past a number of traditional and hereditary vocations. Some of these Mangwere making sandals, working as village watchmen, etc. However, they did not profess any single traditional occupation. In some places where it was not the monopoly of Holers and Chalvadis, they removed dead cattle of the village-folk. Many of them also served as Madaris and Gastes whose duty was to dig graves and also doing night-watching.

Manne

Birth: The rituals such as *pushpavathi* on menarche and *purudu* on delivery are observed by them.

Marriage: The Mannes are endogamous. Marriages with one's sister's daughter, maternal uncle's daughter or paternal aunt's daughter is preferred. Marriage through negotiation is the usual mode of acquiring a mate. Earlier, the custom of payment of *oli* (bride-price) was in practice, but now dowry is prevalent and it ranges from Rs. 5000 to Rs. 15000. A Brahmin priest is consulted for fixing an auspicious day and time for solemnising the marriage, but the *Satani* locally known as *ayyavaru* officiates at marriage rituals. After marriage, patrilocal residence is the norm. Divorce is secured on the grounds of incompatibility and adultery. Remarriage of widows and divorcees is permitted.

Death: Their dead are generally buried. The corpse is laid in the grave with its head pointing to the south. The *satani* officiates at the death rites also like that at marriage rituals.

Ornaments : The *thali* (marriage-locket) and *mettelu* (toe-rings) are the common ornaments worn by the married women among the people of this caste.

Foods : They are non-vegetarians. They eat the meat of sheep, goat, fowl, rabbit and fish. They also eat eggs but abstain from eating beef and pork. However, their staple cereals are rice, maize, *jowar* and *ragi*.

Traditional Occupation : The Mannes have

traditionally been agriculturists, agricultural labourers and village watchmen.

Mavilan

Birth: The *pungan* (pre-delivery ritual) and post-delivery restrictions on the mother are observed. Birth pollution lasts for seven to eleven days. The ceremonies connected with the naming of children, and the first feeding of cereals to the new-born child are observed.

Similarly, the ceremony related to the *tharatta kalayanam* or *therandu kuli* (puberty) of the girl is observed.

Marriage: The caste endogamy and *tharavadu* (clan or *gotra*) exogamy are the observed norms. Marriage with one's maternal uncle's or paternal aunt's daughter is allowed. Adult-marriages are practised and are settled though negotiation. Bride-price has been virtually replaced by dowry in Kerala, but in Tamil Nadu both the *purisapanam* (bride-price) and dowry are given in cash and kind. Marriage rituals are performed at the bride's residence and the marriage feast is hosted by her parents. Monogamy is the norm and junior sororate is permissible. Divorce and remarriage are also allowed for either sex.

Death: While in Kerala their dead are buried, in Karnataka and Tamil Nadu the corpse is either buried or cremated. In the case of cremation, the mortal remains are immersed in a river. The death pollution is observed for thirteen days. Ancestor worship is performed every year.

Dwelling : The Mavilans live in *Mapuras* (huts) which are constructed with mud walls and thatched roof.

Ornaments : The *tali* (marriage-locket) and toe-rings are the main ornaments of married Mavilan women.

Foods : They are occasional non-vegetarians and eat pork but abstain from eating beef. However, rice alongwith roots like *kachil* (tubers) and like *kappa* (tapioca) form their staple food.

Traditional Occupation : The traditional occupation of Mavilans was collection and selling of medicinal herbs, basket-making, farm labour and working as *mahouts* (the care-takers and riders of elephants).

Mehtar/Bhangi, Balmiki, Olgana, Rukhi, Malkana,...etc.

Birth: During the seventh month of pregnancy, the expectant mother is normally taken to her father's house for the first delivery. No particular function is observed to celebrate the occasion of expectant motherhood. No special food is prescribed for her in the prenatal period. But during the postnatal period, she is served with *gond* (an indigenous preparation) which is supposed to generate heat and produce milk in the mother. Delivery is attended to by the local *Dai* (midwife). They observe no pollution during the childbirth. The woman is given bath on the sixth day after delivery. No special ceremony is observed for naming the child who is named on the sixth day after the birth. Usually, the child is named after the grandparents.

Puberty: The attainment of puberty by girls is not an occasion for celebration among the Mehtars. This is perhaps extension of the general attitude of the people irrespective of caste or community background in north India. It is taken in a normal routine way. When informed by her daughter about the attainment of her (latter's) puberty, the mother pays some special attention to her. When convenient, the girl is given bath as no belief exists among the Mehtars that bath should be given on a particular day. Neither relatives nor the neighbours are informed about the attainment of puberty by the girl. No specified period of pollution is observed on the attainment of puberty. However, the *sobanes* (puberty rites) are performed for girls in Karnataka.

Marriage: The Marriages between members of the same exogamous *gotra* are prohibited. The rule of exogamy is so strictly observed that no male can marry a girl belonging to his mother's or grand-mother's side. Marriage with either maternal uncle or paternal aunt is also prohibited. That means, they cannot have marital relations with any *gotra* that falls under (1) the father's *gotra*, (2) maternal grandfather's *gotra*, and (3) maternal grandmother's (mother's mother or father's) *gotra*. However, the brother of the husband can marry sister of his sister-in-law.

Death: When a person dies, the dead body is given bath, tied on a bier and borne by four persons to the burial ground. In the past, the corpse used to be carried on a cot to the burial ground. No musical instruments are engaged on this occasion. On reaching the cremation ground, the bier is lowered. Ornaments, if any, on the dead body are removed and after applying *ghee* the body is cremated. The ashes are then collected and are mixed in the river. The eldest son is the chief mourner in case of a man's death, and in the case of a woman's death, the husband is the chief mourner. The period of mourning is for 12 days and on the thirteenth day, obsequies are performed in the presence of the *Pandit* (priest) of their caste who recites *mantras* (hymns) and receives *dakshina* (monetary gift).

Dwelling : In the past when their touch was considered to desecrate the people of the higher castes, they were forced to live on the outskirts of the village. Though even now this practice continues in the rural areas, they live alongwith people of the other castes yet in separate localities in the urban areas. For example, it has been found in the Hyderabad city that the Mehtars live in different localities considered by them to be convenient for their work, though the considerations of untouchability and defilement in this regard cannot be ruled out. Their houses are clustered.

Dress : The men's dress consists of *dhoti, lunghi, kamij* (shirt) and a *rumal* (head gear) of three to four yards in length, whereas women's dress consists of *kurta* and *pyajama*. They wear *salwar* over the *kurta* and a portion of it covers their head also. They observe *purdah* (veil) system to some extent in their houses. They hide their face behind the *salwar* in the presence of any male person except their husband, brother and father. But when they go out for work, many among them do not observe *purdah*. Even on occasion of wedding, neither the bride nor the bridegroom puts on any special dress. Nowadays, a few females wear *sarees* and blouses, and younger males put on pants and shirts like people of the upper castes. They wear footwear also.

Ornaments : The males do not wear any ornaments except finger rings. But their women wear neck ornaments like *teep* (necklace made of beads), *hasli* (made of gold or silver), *jhalri* (a chain with rupees) and *har* (gold or silver chain). Their nose ornament is *purli*, and *jhumki* and *bhujini* are ear ornaments. Generally, they wear a silver anklet which they call as chain. Married women wear *kante* (ear-ring), *chalkhade* and *ekade* (silver anklets), as stated earlier. All these ornaments are made of either gold or silver.

Foods : The staple diet of the people of this caste or community is wheat and *jowar*. Rice is rarely eaten. They consume freely all kinds of cereals, pulses andvegetables. They are not accustomed to use leafy green vegetables. Mutton and fish are considered edible by Mehtars. Among birds, they eat only fowls, and take pork. The consumption of beef as well as the flesh of animals that have died a natural death is taboo. They do not take meat and fish on Saturdays as they worship Lord Venkateswara on that day.

Traditional Occupation : As stated earlier, Thurston (1909: 59) has observed that Mehtar is a sweeper and his wife is Matranee or Mehatrani. That means, the Mehtar and his wife have traditionally been engaged in sweeping, scavenging, etc. Hunting in which a sizeabled number of Mehtars were said to have indulge prior to their migration from Marathwada region of Maharashtra is no longer practised by them. In the past, this community was regarded as an indispensable factor in the rural and urban life, and its people were entitled to certain allowances either in cash or in kind under the *Jajmani* system (the system of patron-client relationship).

Moger

Birth: Greater recognition and care are bestowed on an expectant mother during her first pregnancy. Their custom prescribes that she should reside at her husband's place subsequent to marriage. It also enjoins that she should be taken to her natal home for giving birth to her first child and the related confinement. During the seventh month of her pregnancy, the *bayake* or *sammana* (a feast comprising dishes she desires most) is arranged on an auspicious day at her husband's residence. Her own parents and siblings arrive with the dishes of her choice and a live hen to participate in the feast. She is given an oil bath, and decked with ornaments and flowers. It is also customary for her parents-in-law to give her a new *saree* on the occasion.

Puberty: When a girl menstruates for the first time, the headman's wife assisted by four other married women bathes her ceremonially. The girl spends her days of impurity for three, six or eight days (depending upon the local practices) in a nearby cattle shed or else in a secluded corner of the outer verandah of the dwelling. During this period, she is given *avalakki* (beaten rice), jaggery, copra and other nutrients. She also refrains from doing any work whatsoever. Womenfolk of the neighbourhood entertain her through folk songs, gossip, etc. Her ritual impurity is removed on the fourth, seventh or the ninth day by giving her another ceremonial bath and administering to her of *theertha* (consecrated water) obtained from a Brahmin or a temple. Her father (or her father-in-law, if she is already married) presents her a *saree* and blouse on this occasion.

Marriage: The Mogers are generally monogamous and resort to bigamy only under exceptional situations such as confirmed barrenness of wife or from some chronic ailment suffered by her. Their custom permits a man to marry his elder brother's widow but he does not inherit her as a matter of right. Nowadays, she exercises free choice while selecting a new spouse and may even prefer to remain a widow forever, specially if she has already children. The custom of marrying one's wife's sister is not in vogue among them. Marriage of persons belonging to the same *bali* as also that of persons begotten by men of common *bali* is strictly forbidden, as stated earlier.

Death: The dead among them are usually buried, though disposal by cremation is also allowed and resorted to occasionally. Corpses of pregnant women are also buried. In some places, a live hen is also interned with it. In some other places, it is customary to plant a sapling of banana at the grave of a pregnant woman and guard it carefully till it yields fruits. Only the family members consume these fruits. Anyway, the corpse is laid on its back in the grave with its head oriented to the south and the feet pointing to the north. They are not accustomed of erecting any tombs or shrines to commemorate their dead.

Dwelling : The Mogers mostly live in small groups in villages. There is not a single village wherein they are found in large numbers, say even 100 persons. Even within a village, the regional settlement pattern prevents any clustering of a large number of households in a particular area.

Dress : Men usually wear *thundu panje* (also called *mundu*) or a short *dhoti* as the lower garment for covering the body between the waist and the knees. The upper part of the body is covered by a *banian* or a shirt with a collar. Sometimes both are used. *Mundasa* (headscarf) is a sheet of cloth offering protection against the elements when wound round the head. While at work and especially during the rainy season, it is more common among them to puton caps called *hale toppi* made out of sheaths of arecanut bunch.

Ornaments : Men put on gold ear-studs and silver finger-rings. On the occasion of a man's marriage, he is decorated with a black-bead necklace, a gold chain if available, silver finger-rings and a pair of silver (or brass or aluminium) chains passed over his shoulders like cross belts. Women use gold ear-studs, gold nose-screws, bead necklaces (but occasionally gold or silver necklaces), glass and also brass or silver bangles, finger-rings and toe-rings of either silver or brass. Young girls usually wear tawdry pieces for ear-studs and glass bangles. Widows are not permitted to put on glass bangles, black-bead necklaces and toe-rings.

Foods : The staple cereal consumed by the Mogers is rice. They are non-vegetarians and also consume fish, either bought locally or caught from the nearby streams. Occasionally, they get some flesh of animals or birds. They may also consume the flesh of deers, wild boars, pigs, rabbits, porcupine, sheep and goats, besides poultry and a variety of birds. They keep poultry on a small scale. Beef eating is said to have always been a taboo among them. The Mogers are also said to be fond of taking toddy (the intoxicating liquor).

Traditional Occupation : It appears from the tradition of Mogers that their forefathers must have been hunters (armed with bows) and food gatherers. The bow-worship, occasional hunting expeditions and seasonal quest for edible roots are perhaps survival tactics of their long forgotten tradition. But with the advent of more powerful and culturally advanced communities, they seem to have taken kindly to settled life as agricultural labourers. According to Fuchs (1981: 96), "In the past they were palanquin bearers for the wealthy".

Mukri

Birth: Traditionally, the first delivery takes place in the girl's parents' house. Before leaving her husband's house for delivery, she is given by her parents *kajjaya* (a basketful of sweets) and a new *saree*. They also perform a ceremony called *udi thumbuvadu* when rice and a coconut are presented to her along with the *saree*. This ceremony is usually performed in the seventh month of the pregnancy. The following day, her husband's family also performs a similar ceremony, and it is only after this ceremony that she leaves for her parental home. The expectant mother is forbidden from eating fish such as mackarel and land shark, and also vegetables such as sweet-gourd, pumpkin and papaya.

Puberty: A girl attaining *dindu* (puberty) is considered impure for three days. On the fourth day, all her clothes are washed. The cowdung and cow's urine are sprinkled over her, and a little of it is also administered to her with *tulsi* leaf after her bath. In some families, the bath on the fourth day permits her to move about all over the house except the kitchen. She can enter the kitchen and attend to usual domestic duties only after the fifth day. In some families, the pollution lasts for five days. When a girl attains puberty, her sister gives her a bath on the fifth day and applies sandal paste to her forehead. Then, she is given the blossoms of coconut and arecanut trees in recognition of her having become fit to beer children.

Marriage: The Mukri girls are married both before or after puberty. About 50 years ago, they used to get married before attaining puberty. But in recent times, post-puberty marriages are more common among the Mukris. The girls are generally married between the age of twelve and sixteen years, and boys between eighteen and twenty-four years. The custom of paying *thiru* (bride-price) is said to be widely prevalent among them.

Death: The Mukris generally bury their dead. It is said that they cannot afford cremation. Only those who can afford it, cremate their dead. When a person is about to die, the inmates of the house shift him to the *jagali* (verandah in front of the house) and pour a few drops of coconut water or place a *tulsi* leaf into his mouth. After life is gone, the hands are folded on the chest and tied together with grass or some creeper. This is called *sankole* (hand cuffing). If a married woman dies and is survived by her husband, the body is decked with flowers, with *kum-kum* on the forehead and a little rice is placed in the folds of her *saree* by *muththaides* (married women).

Dwelling : The hamlets of the Mukris are found in separate settlements locally known as *keris*. Each settlement consists of a group of houses surrounded by a thorny hedge or low stone wall. Generally, their settlement is situated on an elevated land surrounded by paddy fields. The Gramvakkals, Halavakki Vakkals and Halleers are also found near their *keris* but at a little distance. The Mukris live in thatched huts having rectangular ground plans and sloping roofs. The height of the plinth is about one foot, built of mud and stones. The walls are generally of mud with low roofs of bamboo available from the nearby jungles. The roofs have either two or four sides sloping downwards to allow rainwater to run off easily.

Dress : The dress of their men consisted in the past of a loin cloth, a blanket to be thrown on the shoulder and red *rumal* (headscarf) which is now replaced by a white turban. Men use shirts and *dhotis* but quite a few even now use only a loin cloth as their lower garment. Many use *todapa* (a small piece of loose cloth) as an upper garment. Very few of the old persons wear *chappals* (footwear). Their women wear *sarees* in the conventional manner but tie the free end of the *pallav* round the neck. They do not wear any headgear. The use of a blouse is still uncommon in rural areas. The Mukri women do not usually wear bodice and, so, one end of the *saree* covers their bosom. Very few women wear footwear.

Ornaments : The Mukri women are fond of necklaces made of glass beads. Generally, the ornaments of a woman consist of *kudike* (ear-rings), *mugute* (nose-rings), *tali gundu* (marriage-locket), and a string of golden and glass beads. The bead necklace for married women has five rows with more of red and yellow beads. A married woman wears ear-rings, nose-ring, glass bangles, strings of black beads, toe-rings, brass armlets and *mungadaga* (silver wristlets). An unmarried woman wears all the above ornaments except the *karimanisara* (strings of black beads) and toe-rings. But a widow is precluded from wearing ear and nose-rings, bangles and strings of black beads.

Foods : The staple diet of the Mukris mainly consists of *kuchgi akki* (parboiled rice). It is said that in the past, the Mukris used to grow *ragi* in *kumri* (shifting cultivation) lands in forests. But nowadays, they have ceased to raise any crops in the forests and their consumption of *ragi* gruel is also very much reduced. About their dietary habits, Campbell (1884) writes, "Their food is *ragi* gruel eaten with dried fish, and boiled rice saturated with cheap fish curry. Both men and women drink liquor (toddy) and eat flesh except that they do not touch beef or pork. Most of their ceremonies are invariably associated with the drinking of toddy.

Traditional Occupation : Traditionally the Mukris have been agricultural labourers. Many of them work in arecanut gardens, while others take up any available petty work. A few of them own cultivable land, but many take land on lease for cultivation. Some of them work in the laterite quarries or as forest labourers. Their women also earn wages as agricultural labourers, besides attending to their domestic chores. The important agricultural operations needing larger female labour are weeding, transplanting and harvesting. In addition, they work in the gardens and in road construction.

Mundala

Birth: A pregnant woman is usually invited to her parental home for the first childbirth and confinement. The symptoms of pregnancy are widely known and the first one receives greater recognition. It is marked by holding a feast called *bayake* on a convenient day either during the fifth or the seventh or sometimes in the ninth month of her pregnancy. Her mother takes this opportunity to visit her. It is customary for her to present some cloth to her daughter's husband on this occasion.

Puberty: A girl's first menstruation *(tale neeru maduve)* brings happy news into her home. The fellow caste-women of the neighbourhood headed by the wife of their headman give her a ritual bath. Henceforth, the girl is segregated for five or more commonly nine days as any physical contact with her is supposed to be defiling. During this period, she lives in the cow shed or in a corner of the *chavadi* or open verandah. On the fifth, ninth, or sometimes, on the thirteenth day, the final purificatory rite is performed. After a ceremonial bath, the girl sips a few drops of *thirtha* (holy water) given to her by the caste headman.

Marriage: Generally, girls are married at the age of 15 years, although of late post-puberty marriages are becoming very common. Men get married while hey are in the age group of 24-30 years. Mundalas favour cross-cousin marriages but disallow the union of parallel-cousins as stated earlier. Marriage is almost arranged by negotiations and the parents and elders of a boy take the initiative in the selection of a bride.

Death: Their dead are buried. Though cremation is not forbidden, it is resorted to only by a few who can afford the requisite expenses. They perform elaborate rites for their ever-married and elderly dead. The corpses of children and the unmarried young are disposed of without much ado. The Mundalas do not erect any tomb or shrine in the memory of their dead. Though no death anniversaries are performed, their custom enjoins offering of food to the spirits of the dead on all important occasions and festivals celebrated by the family. During the month of *Paggu* (March-April), a feast is held especially for the propitiation of the spirits of the ancestors.

Dwelling : In villages, they live in huts built in a haphazard manner on lands owned by local landlords. Government has granted house-sites to several Mundalas. In all such cases though separated by compound or fence, their houses tend to be closer and linear. The rectangular or 'L'-shaped alignments may sometimes be discerned in such colonies.

Ornaments : Finger-rings of gold or silver and ear-studs of gold are the ornaments of their men. Interestingly, *gurikaras* (their leaders) are sometimes expected to put on gold bangles. On ceremonial occasions,the priest also wears a silver necklace. Their women put on ear-studs of gold, gold or silver necklace or a necklace of black beads with a gold pendant called *tali*, nose-ring, glass bangles and silver or brass toe-rings. Widows do not wear these ornaments. Tattooing is not much in vogue among the Mundalas.

Foods : Boiled rice is the staple cereal and *ganji* or gruel is the common dish in vogue among the Mundalas. In urban areas, the use of wheat and *jowar* flour, *soji*, etc. is slowly coming into vogue especially for preparing the light refreshments. They usually take fresh food. On the ordinary days, they do not prepare dishes out of unripe banana including the central core of the stem of banana plant and ash gourd as these are prescribed for the occasion of funeral feast. They prepare and consume *payasa*, *paramanna* (sweet dishes), *idli*, *kadubu* and *dosa* (pancakes) which are common among the people in the region.

Traditional Occupation : The agricultural labour especially as *moolada alu* or serfs seems to have had been their chief occupation in the former days. In that capacity, they were required to render certain essential services to upper caste landlords particularly at the time of disposal of their (the latter's) dead. For that, they used to receive some customary payment.

Nadia, Hadi

Birth: The pre-delivery ceremony is practised and birth pollution is observed for forty days.

Marriage: They practise endogamy among themselves. Child marriages have now been replaced by post-puberty marriages. Negotiation is the common mode of acquiring a mate. Monogamy is the norm. Bride-price is paid, but at the same time dowry is also demanded. Levirate is permitted. Before marriage, a *sagai* (betrothal) ceremony is arranged which is followed by the marriage rituals. These are performed at the bride's place. They allow remarriage of widows. **Death:** Their dead are buried and death pollution is observed for twelve days.

Food : The Nadias are non-vegetarians and eat mutton, fish, chicken, etc. But their staple cereals are wheat, rice and maize.

Traditional Occupation : Making leather strips, and dealing with bones and skins of dead animals were the traditional occupations of the Nadias, Hadis. They also use to deal with bones and skins of dead animals.

Nayadi

Birth: Interestingly, a pregnant woman is said to crave for the flesh of a monkey or a jungle squirrel during the sixth month of her first pregnancey. During the seventh month, the family members perform a ceremony of *ozhinnukalayuka* (exorcism) which supposedly relieves her from the influences of the demons, if any. Abortion and other kinds of illnesses are attributed to the malignant influences of evil spirits whom they always fear. To ward-off such calamities, they tie a magic thread around her neck invoking the aid and support of their hill deities so also the spirits of their ancestors.

Marriage: The parents arrange the match for their children. Marriage with maternal uncle's or paternal aunt's daughter is permissible. A suitable young woman is sought for and the conjugal contract is made by the parents of the young man with whose conduct the woman's parents are satisfied with. Bride-price is paid. The day for the marriage ceremony is chosen. The bridegroom is dressed in a small neat loin cloth and skull cap made of the bark of areca palm.

Death: Generally, the Nayadis have their separate burial grounds and they either cremate or bury their dead. When a person of their caste dies, the pollution lasts for ten days. On the tenth day, they collect a small quantity of rice, some grass, water in a coconut shell, and entire plantain leaf and a lighted wick. All the agnates assemble and go to a closeby river or water reservoir to bathe. A sand heap or a figure of earth to represent the deceased is made and the plantain leaf with the articles referred to above are placed near it. The eldest son performs the ceremony by standing before the leaf with his face towards the east.

Dwelling : The Nayadis live mostly in isolated huts on the tops of hills, as stated earlier. For constructing their huts, they generally select a shola or glade where there is a pond or a stream. Some families live on the land of their landlords. They keep a vigil on the crops of the landlords during night so as to guard them against the attacks of the wild beasts.

Dress : Their men wear a small dirty loin cloth extending above the knees and are seldom seen with a second one. Their women also wear a *kacha* (twice folded loin cloth) and are seldom seen with an upper cloth.

Ornaments : The men wear ear-rings of brass and also wear charms around the arms or loins to cure disease or protect themselves from the attack of the demons. The *karimani* (pendant) and toe-rings are two important ornaments worn by their married women. The ear-lobes of Nayadi women are dilated to contain wooden plugs which serve as *thodas* (ear-rings). Round their neck are several strings of beads with shells and pendants which are not removed even after the death of their husband. Girls or unmarried women do not wear any ornaments in particular.

Food : Their chief foods are *kanji* and boiled rice prepared by them early in the morning. Anything that remains out of the morning meal is given to the children during the day. They consume the roots of the nux vomica. These roots are cut into thin slices and are boiled with salt to form a vegetable curry. The vegetables consumed by them are tubers of yams (Dioscorea) and colocasia, jackfruits and pumpkins. They are also said to consume the flesh of monkeys, goats, wild squirrels, deer, rats, doves, quails, fowls, paddy birds, tortoises and crocodiles.

Traditional Occupation : Traditionally, the Nayadis were skilful hunters, as mentioned above. They collected wax of the honey bees and *mattipasa* (resin) from the *mattipal* tree (Aliyanthus malabarica) to be sold by them later. They prepared a type of rope from malanar plants and thebark of *kayul* trees. They also made slings of fibres with which they used to shoot birds. During the *Onam* and *Vishu* festivals, the Nayadis offered four ropes to every Nambudiri *illam* and two to every Nair house near their village. In return, they used to get some paddy, a few coins and a piece of cloth.

Paky, Moti, Thoti

Birth: They do not perform any ceremonies connected even with first pregnancy. The husband comes to know about his wife's pregnancy only when the other women of his family or neighbourhood inform him. The tonsure ceremony is, however, observed only for the first born child and not for the subsequent ones. The celebration takes place during the third or fifth year of birth of the child. As the barbers do not serve the Pakys, the maternal uncle of the child cuts the hair.

Marriage: The marriageable age for females is between 13 and 16 years, while that for males is between 20 and 25 years. The marriage is exogamous with regard to their *intiperu*. *Gotram* (clan) is not the criteria for fixing up the marriage as they have forgotten their *gotramulu*. So, *intiperu* is the deciding factor in contracting the marriages among them. Their marital relations are, therefore, prohibited between descendants of the same *intiperu*, as stated earlier. In other words, the permissible partners for a boy are maternal uncle's daughter, paternal aunt's daughter and his own sister's daughter. The custom of marrying the daughter of maternal uncle is locally known as *menarikam* and is mostly preferred.

Death: Their dead are usually cremated. But in the case of an unmarried deceased, the body is buried. In the case of burial, the dead body is lowered into the pit dug by the caste people in such a way that the face kept in southward direction is laid downwards. It is stripped-off all clothings and belongings. Instead, some copper coins, betel leaves and arecanuts are placed inside the pit alongwith the body. In the case of cremation, the eldest son lits the pyre. The ashes are collected and mixed in holy water on an auspicious day fixed by the Brahmin.

Dwelling : The Pakys usually live along with the Malas and Madigas in corners of the village or town. In some places, both Pakys and Saprus live side by side.

The two types of houses in existence among the people of this community are: *Palaka illu* and *Chuttillu*. They observe all the ceremonies connected with house construction and house warming just as in the case of the Saprus. The method of construction and materials used for these types of houses are all the same as those used by people of the Sapru caste. A well-to-do Paky possesses a *daba illu* (pucca house).

Dress : Their women wear *sarees* of seven or eight yards length and blouses. Those women who are employed as scavengers in municipality use footwear. The men use *dhoties*, trousers and knickers as lower garments while shirts and banians are used as upper garments. All these are of cotton only. They use the *dhoties* with red or black border. All children use clothes similar to those worn by children of the other castes. Girls use a *petticoat* (rounded lower garment) and blouse while boys wear knickers, shirts and occasionally banians too. Previously, the people of this caste used to wear *gochi* (a cloth taken between the loins and tied around the waist). But nowadays, most of them have given up this mode of dress.

Ornaments : There are no special ornaments used by the people of this caste. Usually, married women wear *puste*, ear-rings made of gold or silver, nose-rings and toe-rings of silver. The unmarried women and widows generally do not wear any ornament. Some men wear finger-rings made of silver or gold.

Foods : The staple foods of Pakys, Motis, Thotis are *ragi* (finger millet), *gantelu* (bulrush millet), rice and wheat. Preparing cakes out of wheat flour is very common among them. They are non-vegetarians. The flesh of fowls, *kamjulu* (partridges), sheep and goats is consumed. Eating beef and pork is not deprecated. All varieties of fish are eaten. Also, some wild roots like *matingi pendalam* (yam) and *ganatha dumpa* form a part of their food. The *Ganatha dumpa* is usually obtained by digging to a depth of 6 ft., while other roots can easily be obtained by digging to a depth of 2 ft. in the local forest.

Traditional Occupation : Scavenging has been the predominant occupation of the Pakys since the early time. Normally, the head of each household as well as his wife are employed as scavengers and earn their livelihood. In villages, they are employed in scavenging and agricultural labour. Thoti is, however, a caste of village servants traditionally engaged in the work for conveying messages and summon people to appear before the village council. The people of this caste used to serve in the past as *talaris* (assistants to the village officer). Many of them now work as scavengers in municipalities and other local bodies as mentioned above.

Pale

Birth: In the fifth month of the first pregnancy of a woman, a pre-delivery ritual is performed and she is given a feast. The birth pollution is observed for seven days. A month after the birth, the *Kunjige peru idikkal* (naming ceremony) is performed.

Marriage: Clan/*Kudvy* exogamy is observed. Marriage with one's paternal aunt's or maternal uncle's daughter is practised. Adult marriage is the norm now and it is arranged through negotiation. A notional bride-price of Rs. 15 or so is paid in cash. Marriage rituals called *dampatimadime* (the couple being tied together through marriage) are performed by the caste elders at the bride's residence. But the marriage is consummated at the bridegroom's house. Junior sororate is allowed. Divorce is permissible on the grounds of adultery and maladjustment but it requires approval of the caste elders. Both males and females are allowed to remarry after divorce or widowerhood and widowhood.

Death: Their dead are generally buried. The death pollution is observed for seven days. On the sixteenth day, *mada* (obsequies) is performed. The ancestors are worshipped once in a year.

Ornaments : The marriage symbols for women are *karimani*, and finger and toe-rings.

Foods : They are non-vegetarians and eat pork. However, their staple cereal is rice eaten with pulses.

Traditional Occupation : Their traditional occupation was to work in coffee plantations. But many others were engaged in agricultural labour.

Pallan/Pannadi

Birth: The *kachipothu* (pre-delivery ritual) is

performed in the seventh or ninth month of the first pregnancy of the woman. Delivery takes place in her natal home and the birth pollution is observed for 30 days. The *mundan* (tonsure) ceremony for both male and female children and the *kathu kuthu* (ear-boring) ceremony for female children are performed during the third month after their birth.

Puberty: When a Pallan girl attains puberty, she is bathed and dressed in a cloth brought by a washerwoman. She is also presented flowers and fruits by her relations. She is put in a hut constructed of coconut leaves, branches of *Pongamia glabra* and wild sugarcane (*Saccharum arundinaceum*). Her diet includes jaggery (crude sugar), milk and plantains. On the seventh day, she is again bathed and presented with another cloth. The hut is burnt down and, for three days, she lives in a corner of the pial of her home. On the eleventh day, she is once again bathed, presented with new clothes by her relations and permitted to enter the house.

Marriage: Cross-cousin marriages are prevalent among the Pallans. They prefer to marry their sister's daughter, maternal uncle's daughter or paternal aunt's daughter. Marriages are arranged by elders through negotiation. Monogamy is the norm. The *parisam* (bride-price) has to be given to the bride's father or the bride on the marriage day.

Death: There is a peculiar custom of disposing the dead body among the Konga Pallans. For instance, when a death occurs among them, the big toes and thumbs of the corpse are tied together. A lighted lamp and a metal vessel with raw rice, jaggery and a broken coconut are placed near its head. Three pieces of firewood, arranged in the form of a triangle, are lighted and a small pot is placed on them wherein some rice is cooked in turmeric water. The corpse is bathed, and placed in a pandal made of four plantain trees and four green leafy branches. The nearest relations place a new cloth over it.

Dwelling : The Pallans/Pannadis are found residing in most of the villages of Tamil Nadu but they are never permitted to dwell within the limits of a village *nattam* (inside the boundary of the main village). Their huts form the *Pallacheri* (a small detached hamlet) situated at a considerable distance from the houses of high caste Hindus. But these are barely separated from that of the *Parei-cheris* of the Paraiyas. Their huts are similar to that of Parayans/Paraiyans.

Foods : Their staple food are rice and *ragi* supplemented with pulses such as gram, beans, peas, *moong*, *tur* and *urad*. They are non-vegetarians but they abstain from taking beef and pork. However, the educated Pallans/Pallars rejoice both beef and pork in the urban areas.

Traditional Occupation : The Pallans/Pannadis are the traditional agricultural labourers, as mentioned above. Their other occupations include plantation work and that in animal husbandry.

Pambada, Pambanda

Birth: The pregnant woman is taken by her parents to their house, after three months of her first pregnancy, for the first confinement. Subsequent confinements take place at the husband's house only. There is no ceremony attached to pregnancy. When the woman concerned reaches an advanced stage of pregnancy, she is made to observe certain taboos like not going out after dusk or lifting heavy articles or drawing water from wells.

Puberty: The period of pollution of a girl's first menstruation is observed for 11 days. They also observe her segregation. An enclosure is erected by her maternal uncle of the girl in which she is made to sit. She does not take part in the household activities during the period of her pollution. But she is served different delicious edibles everyday. On the 12th day, she is given bath, and a new *saree* and a new blouse are given to her by her parents. A feast is also arranged for the relatives. The enclosure then is demolished and burnt by the maternal uncle.

Marriage: The premarital sex life is not allowed among the Pambadas; and it is viewed seriously, if it occurs. The parties involved in such activities are compelled to marry, if they belong to their own caste. No intercaste marriage is permitted. Excepting the permitted marital alliance with maternal uncle's daughter or paternal sister's daughter, own sister's daughter and wife's younger sister, they do not marry any other relation. Besides, marriages are not contracted between persons belonging to the same *gotra*. Marriages are arranged though negotiation. The boy's father accompanied by four or five caste people goes to the nearby villages to find a suitable girl.

Death: The dead among the Pambadas are now invariably buried, while about seven decades ago they were either cremated or buried. The corpse is buried with the head facing south. The same procedure of burial is followed even if the death occurs due to diseases like smallpox, cholera, etc.

Dwelling : The single roomed dwellings of Pambadas are locally known as *chuttagudise* or *bodaillu*. These are circular in shape. The walls of these houses are made of reeds plastered with mud and cowdung. These are also white washed on the inner side and plastered with red coloured mud on the outer side. The roof is thatched with grass or palmyra leaves and occasionally with crude tiles made by the village potter. There are neither windows nor ventilators for their houses. The floor is plastered with cowdung twice a week.

Dress : The male's dress consists of a *lungi* of two yards in length and a shirt made out of three yards of cloth. Some people wear drawers and others *langota* (a cloth which is used to cover the loins). They always carry a towel with them. Besides its usual function, wearing a towel on the shoulder is considered as a mark of respect and maturity. It is said that in the past, the males used to wear *dhotis* of four yards in length.

Ornaments : Males were once wearing *murugu pogulu, antu pogulu* (ear ornaments) and *kapulu* (bangles). But these are not used by them nowadays. Gold is used rarely. Brass and silver articles are purchased at weekly shandies. The following are the common ornaments used by the Pambada women:

1. *Addiga* (neck ornament), 2. *Jhumka* (ear ornament), 3. *Chainu* (neck ornament), and 4. *Mukkara* (nose ornament).

Foods : The staple food of Pambadas consists of rice, *sajja* (bulrush millet) and *ragi* (finger millet). Food is taken thrice a day. The first meal of the day consisting of the leftovers of the previous night and locally called *saddi* is taken in the morning. In the afternoon, they take *sangati (ragi* food). The third meal is taken in the night during which they take rice with some *dal* and curry. The flesh of goat, sheep, fowl and pig is also taken but they do not eat beef. There is no taboo in consuming the flesh of dead animals but it depends upon the taste of the person. All varieties of fish are taken. On festivals, they eat meat along with some sweet dishes.

Traditional Occupation : Spirit possession, divination, exorcism and the *bhuta kola* (ritual dance to appease the spirits) for earning livelihood have remained the traditional occupations of the people of this caste in Karnataka. Thurston (1909) describes the Pambada "as a small class of Canarese devil-dancers in South Canara". In Kerala, the traditional occupation of the Pambadas is folk-dancing. Similarly, in Andhra Pradesh also, they have traditionally been engaged as musicians at the time of worship of village gods and celebration of *jataras* (the religious procession). As their services are required only on a few occasions, they have taken up different occupations like agriculture, agricultural labour, etc.

Panchama

Birth: The pre-delivery and post-natal restrictions are observed particularly with regard to food and movement of the woman. For instance, papaya is avoided by pregnant women. Similarly, vegetables like angulas gourd, green plantain, pumpkin, and the non-vegetarian items like prawn and fish are not consumed by them in the first month after the delivery. During the post-natal period, a nursing mother is given meal once a day in the forenoon and milk at night for a month or so. The coffee made out of old jaggery is also given to her during this period. After childbirth, the mother and child are given *purudu* (ritual bath) on the seventh day. In the sixth month, the *palasari* ceremony (the first feeding of cereals to the child) is performed.

Puberty: The rituals related to puberty of the girls are observed among the people of this caste.

Marriage: Group endogamy and surname exogamy are the general marriage rules observed by the people of the Panchama caste. Marriage with one's maternal uncle's daughter, paternal aunt's daughter and elder sister's daughter is preferred. Marriages are arranged through negotiation and adult marriage is the norm. The marriage rituals are officiated by a Brahmin priest or by an elderly member of the community. The *sethamanam* tying a *thali or tali* (marriage-locket) around the bride's neck by the groom or *thalambralu posukonuta* (pouring turmeric-smeared rice on each other's head), *nakshatramu* (paying obeisance to Arundathi star) by the bridal couple, etc. are the important marriage rituals observed by the Panchamas. Dowry is given both in cash and kind but the custom of bride-price is not in vogue among them.

Death: Their dead are generally cremated. However, the poor among them bury their dead. Death pollution is observed for twelve days. The *chinnakaryamu* (mortuary rites) and *peddakaryamu* (the final death rites) are performed on the third and twelfth days respectively. The *samvatsarikamu* (first death anniversary) is performed just before the completion of the first year.

Foods : Since the Panchamas are non-vegetarians, they reportedly eat beef and pork also. Rice is their staple food which is taken with pulses like *Kandi pappu* (red gram) and *Pesara pappu* (green gram). Roots and tubers available in the market are also consumed by them.

Traditional Occupation : Traditionally, the Panchamas were agricultural labourers. They were largely landless and only a few of them owned cultivable land of small sizes.

Panniandi

Birth: The people of this caste observe the *Valaikappu* (a pre-delivery ritual). The first delivery takes place at the woman's natal home. The naming and *mundan* (tonsure) ceremonies are performed for both boys and girls.

Puberty: When a Panniandi girl attains puberty, the *chadanku* ceremony is observed for her ritual purification from the pollution of her menarche.

Marriage: The cross-cousin and uncle-niece marriages are common among them. But the marriages between brotherly clans are prohibited. Marriages are usually arranged through negotiations. Bride-price is said to be prevalent among them and is paid in cash. The marriage ceremony is performed either at the bride's house or at a public place. But the consummation ceremony takes place at the bride's mother's residence. Divorce is sanctioned through the approval of elders/ caste council. Remarriage of divorced and of widow or widower is also permitted among them.

Death: Their dead are generally buried. The death rites are supervised by their *pattakaran* (headman).

Foods : They are non-vegetarians, and reportedly take pork and beef. But their staple cereals are rice and *ragi*. Groundnut, mustard, coconut or sunflower oil are used for cooking their meals.

Traditional Occupation : Piggery has been the traditional occupation of the Panniandis both in Karnataka and Tamil Nadu.

Paraiyan/Samban

Birth: When a married young woman is pre-gnant, she is taken to her parents' house during the seventh or the eighth month. But during this period, no ceremony related to her pregnancy is performed. The woman after childbirth is secluded for two weeks in a temporary hut erected at a short distance from the main house or dwelling. During the time of her seclusion, she is also debarred from touching vessels and provisions, and has to be fed by another person. Her usual diet is *kanji* in the morning and other boiled rice at night. The only medicine administered to her during this period is a mixture of coriander seeds, and *uluva* (*Trigonella foenum grace*) prepared by bruising and boiling in water and mixed with *kanji*.

Marriage: Marriage among kinsfolk is prohibited particularly within four degrees on the mother's side and six degrees on the father's side. A marriage with the daughter of one's maternal uncle or of maternal aunt is permitted.

The girls are generally married between 12 and sixteen years of age. This has certainly increased during the recent decades.

Death: Their dead are buried. Relatives and other castemen carry the dead body on a bier to the burial ground which is dug either in the deceased's own compound or outside in the neighbourhood. A grave is dug, the floor made smooth, and the body covered with a mat is placed in it. A little rice is also put into the grave as food for the spirit or soul of the departed. The grave is then filled in with layers of earth. Those assembled return home after bathing. The chief mourner is either son or nephew of the deceased. He is also in-charge of the death ceremonies. The pollution lasts for 16 days.

Dwelling : The Paraiyans live in huts that barely provide them shelter in the odd seasons. The combination of mud walls and roofed with coconut and palmyra leavesis the most common type of hut among the Paraiyans. The floor is generally made of earth. There is no interior partition in the hut which is used as the kitchen, the dining room, store-room, sleeping apartment, etc. The huts are mostly small in size with less than 200 square feet in the floor area.

Ornaments : Few women are seen wearing ear-rings and nose-rings of some sort of metal. They are fond of tattooing. Their arms are elaborately tattooed with ornamental designs of beautiful flowers and figures. Men also tattoo the inner side of their arms with their names. For Christian Parayans, a cross is a favourite design of tattoo. Children also use simple lines drawn down from the forehead.

Food : All of them are non-vegetarians and they reportedly take beef, pork, etc. They are said to eat even the flesh of dead cattle. But their poverty restricts their meat or fish intake to once in a month. Their staple cereals are rice or millets like *ragi* supplemented with vegetables and pulses.

Traditional Occupation : Traditional occupation of the people of this caste includes manufacture of wickerwork (baskets), bamboo mats and umbrellas. They are also said to have been engaged in every kind of agricultural work. The Tamil inscriptions of the twelfth to fifteenth century A.D. have described their occupations as cultivation, mowing the grass for horse and weaving (Karashima 1997: 24). Anyway, they plough the ground but do not use the buffaloes which are regarded as unclean. They bathe at the mere touch of them, but have no objection to using bullocks. They skin the dead animals and reserve the hides for themselves.

Raneyar

Birth: The pre-delivery rituals are observed during the seventh month of the first pregnancy of their women. Birth pollution lasts for eleven days. Naming ceremony of the child is performed on the twelfth day after the completion of birth pollution.

Puberty: The puberty rites for the menstruating girls are also observed.

Marriage: Cross-cousin marriages such as marriage with one's maternal uncle's daughter and paternal aunt's daughter are preferred. Adult marriage is the norm among the people of this caste and it is settled through negotiation. The *terawu* (bride-price) is practised. Traditionally, the amount of bride-price was Rs. 12 but it varies from Rs. 50 to Rs. 100 at present days. The main marriage rituals among the Raneyars are *dhare ereyuwadu* (betrothal) and *tali* (marriage locket) tying. The marriage rituals are performed by the *budhivant* or *yajaman* (their caste headman).

Death: Their traditional practice to dispose of the dead is cremation. However, in recent years burial is also resorted to in many places to avoid expenses on cremation. The corpses of children below ten years of age are buried, placing their head towards the south. The dead bodies of the expectant mothers and those who die during delivery are cremated. On the eleventh day, the *tirtha* (sacred water) brought from a temple is sprinkled throughout the house to remove the death pollution. On the twelfth day, the soul of the dead is offered several varieties of food which is placed on the burial or cremation ground and is left to be eaten by crows.

Dwelling : The Raneyars live in hutments and in clusters of houses on the hillocks. These are away from the main village settlements.

Foods : They are non-vegetarians. They eat chicken, meat, beef and pork. However, rice is their staple food.

Traditional Occupation : The Raneyars traditionally carried carcasses and worked as agricultural wage labourers. Till a few decades ago, they used to work as bonded labourers for a certain period of time or were permanently attached to local landlords belonging to the Bant, Brahmin and other land owing castes or communities. Such agricultural labourers were known as *mooladawaru*. But now, this system is not in existence.

Sapari

Birth: They observe birth pollution and give a purificatory bath to the mother on the fifth, ninth or eleventh day after the birth of a child. The naming ceremony of the child takes place on the tenth day.

Puberty: The attainment of puberty among the Sapari girls has a social significance and a ceremony is observed on this occasion.

Marriage: Cross-cousin marriage like marrying the paternal aunt's daughter or the maternal aunt's daughter is preferred. The pre-puberty marriage was practised earlier. But nowadays, adult marriages are common among the members of this caste. Bride-price is prevalent in some places, though it is only symbolic. In the most areas, it has been replaced by dowry which is paid in kind. Both husband and wife have the right to divorce.

Death: Both cremation and burial o their dead are practised among the people of this caste. They perform initial obsequies on the third day and the final rites on the ninth or eleventh day after the death of a person.

Foods : They are non-vegetarians. But their staple cereals are rice, wheat and millet.

Traditional Occupation : Selling fruits and seeds have been the traditional occupation of Saparis.

Sillekyatha

Birth: The custom of inviting the woman to her parental home during her first pregnancy is not customary among the Sillekyathas. However, such a practice is slowly becoming popular among the families of the *Bambe* section of the caste. During the advanced stage of pregnancy, the woman refrains from exhausting and strenuous work. She is also careful about the food she eats.

Puberty: During her first menstruation, the girl is regarded impure and is segregated for five days. The Sillekyathas erect isolation huts called *hasiru gudisalu* (green hut) for use by such a girl and it is usually erected by her maternal uncle. The hut (or more appropriately the screen) is usually of twigs and leaves of *honge* (*Pongamia glabra*). For the first three days, the hut is burnt each day and a new one is erected in its place. Before the girl enters, a coconut is rolled into the hut. Sometimes, the *katte* (outer verandah) of the normal residence is itself used by the girl during these five days. Soon after the menstruation occurs for the first time, the girl is ceremonially bathed by the women of the caste.

Marriage: As stated above, the Sillekyathas are divided into two major endogamous groups on the basis of two characteristic professions of fishing and leather-puppet-shadow play. For generations, they have lost special contacts with each other and their knowledge about the supposed unity of both the groups in the remote past is based on hearsay. Each group is self-contained as the people in it are sub-divided into numerous exogamous clans bearing distinct names. Among both the groups, cross-cousin marriages are allowed and practised while the union of parallel-cousins is a taboo. However, a man may marry his own sister's daughter. Under certain circumstances (such as sterility of former wife), a man may marry his wife's younger sister.

Death: Among Sillekyathas, the dead are usually buried. Corpses of lepers and also those of pregnant women are, however, cremated. On the third or on fifth day after death, the house is cleaned and rendered pure by the sprinkling of *gomuthra* (cow's urine) or *thirtha* (holy water) obtained from their temple. At some places (e.g. Ambalagere, Bhaktana-katte), it is the *madivala* (washerman) who purifies the premises by sprinkling water or cow's urine. The mourners visit the burial ground and offer two *edes* (food served on plantain leaves)—one at the spot where the corpse was lowered on the way to the graveyard and the other on the grave.

Dwelling : Their houses have rectangular plans and are usually single-storeyed. In the Malnad region, they live in tiled houses with sloping roofs, while in the Maidan region they too dwell in houses with flat mud terraces. Huts, however, have sloping roofs irrespective of the region of their location. Their houses are usually small and contain a *jagali* or open verandah, a hall or living room and a kitchen. These are seldom provided with bathrooms and latrines as their use is not common at all among them. Those rearing pigs have a separate pigsty while those having cattle, sometimes, accommodate these animals also within their dwelling unit.

Dress : The Sillekyatha men usually dress themselves with *dhotis* or *lungis* and shirts. The *dhoti* may be worn with or without a *kache* (one end of it is passed between the thighs and tucked at the back). In the latter case, it covers the waist and hangs below down to the ankles like a petticoat. *Lungis* which cannot be worn in *kache* style are also in common use. Several young and middle aged men ordinarily put on knickers and preserve *dhotis* and *lungis* for special occasions. Boys and adolescents invariably put on knickers and shirts.

Ornaments : Gold ear-studs and finger-rings either of gold or silver are ornaments in use among some of their men. Young boys are adorned with silver anklets, silver waist-strings and gold ear-rings. Their women too are very fond of ornaments of gold and silver. *Chidi* (ear-studs) of gold, *bavuli* (crescent-shaped gold piece worn on the upper rim of the ears), *bugudi* and *eidara gadaga* (both ear-ornaments of gold), black bead necklace with *tali* (the gold pendant), *moogabattu* (nose-screw of gold), *sontapatti* (waist-band of silver), *bandi* (silver armlet), *sarige* (silver wristlet), glass bangles and silver toe-rings are common ornaments used by them.

Foods : Both the sections of Sillekyathas are non-vegetarians. They occasionally consume the meat of sheep, goats and poultry. Beef is a taboo among them and it has been so for generations. *Ragi*, *jowar* and maize are their staple cereals. A few who can afford eat cooked rice everyday at least in small quantities. For most of them, rice and wheat preparations are meant for festive or certain social occasions. *Mudde* (the round lump of cooked *ragi* or *jowar* meal or a combination of both) and *saru* (a soup of pulse or vegetables or both) or *roti* (unleavened cake made out of *ragi*, *jowar* or maize flour) and *chutney* (paste-like spiced side-dish) are the items of their everyday food.

Traditional Occupation : It seems that the ancestors of Sillekyathas were Mahratta Okkaligas and had followed the profession of agriculture (see Nanjundayya and Iyer 1931, Aiyar 1912, Campbell 1884, and Enthoven 1922). Subsequent to their exodus from Maharashtra, they seem to have exhibited a pronounced preference for a nomadic life and for earnestly practising the profession of fishing or leather-puppet-shadow-play or both, as stated earlier.

Sindhollu (Chindollu)

Birth: The attainment of first pregnancy of a woman is made known to her husband by other female members of the family. No ceremonies are connected with the pregnancy. Usually, the confinement of the woman takes place at her husband's place. There is no practice among them of going to hospital for delivery. However, in the complicated cases, they use the services of the local *dais* (mid-wife) or go to hospital. The arrangement for segregation of the expectant mother is made inside the house with the help of a cot or mats.

Puberty: Immediately after attainment of puberty, the girl is made to sit in an enclosure erected by her maternal uncle. She stays there for five days after which the pollution ceases automatically on her taking bath. She is fed with delicious items of food on all these five days and bath is given to her on alternate days. On the sixth day, she is given final bath and her parents present her a *saree* and a blouse.

Marriage: Marriage through negotiation is the only type of marriage prevalent among the Sindhollus. The normal age at marriage for a girl is between 12 and 15 years, while for a boy it is between 15 and 18 years. This has increased in the cases of both boys and girls during the recent decades. The preferential partners for a boy are maternal uncle's daughter or paternal aunt's daughter. Another type of allowed union for a man is to marry his deceased wife's younger sister.

Death: Their dead are buried with head to the south and face upwards. The corpse is bathed in cold water and wrapped in a new cloth. The turmeric paste of powder is applied to the forehead and also to other parts of the body. The dead body is carried on a bier by four nearest relatives to the burial ground. A procession also follows to the burial ground. However, there is no accompaniment of musical instruments while the corpse is taken to the burial ground. The obsequies are performed initially on the third day and finally on the ninth day. The death pollution is observed for eight days.

Dwelling : The Sindhollus live in *gudiselus* (small huts). These huts or houses are situated near about the Madiga locality. They consult the *vadrangi* (carpenter) for the house construction. After his approval, they fix up an auspicious day for the commencement of the house construction in consultation with *Mitha Ayyalwar*. On the day of commencement, they break coconut, worship God and start the work. The huts are erected on the ground itself without any raised platforms. The ground plan of a hut is rectangular. Four poles of six feet in height are also fixed on the four corners of the rectangular-shaped floor.

Dress : The dress of a Sindhollu male consists of *dhoti* and shirt, while that of a female is *saree* and blouse. They wear it in local fashion. Usually, males keep two *dhotis*, two shirts and a head gear, while females have two *sarees* and two blouses. Throughout the year, they adjust with these two pairs of clothes. As such, they spend only small amount of money on clothing. The dress of the boys generally consists of a knicker and shirt, and sometimes a small *dhoti*. The dress of the girls consists of a skirt and blouse.

Ornaments : Males do not wear any ornaments except the silver bangles on the forearms or shoulders. Married women wear only *puste gajjelu* (a chain with marriage locket made of gold) and *mattelu* (silver toe-rings). Both males and females have tattoo marks on their foreheads or forearms. These decorations are done by people locally called *Chukka botlollu* or *Eramushtollu*.

Foods : The Sindhollus are non-vegetarian but their staple food is rice, *jowar* and maize. They also eat wheat. Food is taken thrice a day. Early in the morning, they take leftovers of the previous night. In the afternoon, they make *ambali* (gruel) or *gatika* (soft semi-solid preparation made out of *ragi* flour) or cooked rice with some curry. In the night, they take *gatika* with some curry or, in some cases, whatever they receive as alms from the Madigas. The flesh of pigs, sheep, goats and fowls is consumed. The flesh of sparrows, crows and patridges is also said to be eaten by them.

Traditional Occupation : The traditional occupation of Sindhollus was performing dances and reciting the *Veedhi Bhagavatham* (narrating mythological and epic stories). They believed in having a right to beg from the Madigas and, in fact, they depended upon it. Even today, there is not any major change occurred in their traditional occupational pattern. Traditionally, the performances of either dance or *Veedhi Bhagavatham* were given between 12 noon and 6 p.m. on any day. These were arranged with the help of the Madigas.

Sudugadu Siddha

Birth: Generally, a woman in her first pregnancy is invited to her parents' house for her confinement. During the fifth month of her pregnancy, a function called *Kubura* or *Madi ikkuvadu* is performed. On this occasion, the family presents her with a *saree* and bangles. The other rituals observed by the people of this caste on different periods are *Namakarana* (naming ceremony) and the *Javala* or *Chowla* (tonsure) for the birth of the male child.

Puberty: The *hosige* (puberty) ceremony on the first menstruation of a girl is observed among the people of this caste.

Marriage: The cross-cousin marriages (marriges with one's maternal uncle's or paternal aunt's or elder sister's daughters) are preferred. Monogamy is the usual form of marriage among the Sudugadu Siddhas. The marriages are settled through negotiation. The marriage rituals are performed at the bridegroom's residence and the consummation ceremony takes place at the bride's residence.

Death: Their dead are generally buried. On the third day after burial, rice gruel and water are offered to the spirit of the dead either near the grave or by the side of a tank or river, if the dead body is cremated. The ceremony is sometimes repeated on the eleventh day. The period of pollution is for ten days. The castemen are fed on the twelfth day. An image of the deceased is made of gold or silver and worshipped along with the household gods. The deceased ancestors are propitiated with offerings once in a year either in the dark fortnight of the *Bhadrapada* (July-August) or the *Karthika* (November-December) month.

Dress : The ordinary dress of the castemen does not differ from that of the Okkaligas. But while going out for begging, they wear ochre-coloured breeches (an upper cloth) and a turban entwined with various coloured kerchiefs along with peacock feathers stuck into it. They suspend garlands of *rudraksha* beads from their neck, paint their foreheads with ashes and bracelets, and carry a wallet (a wooden or metal bell and a conch shell). There is nothing peculiar in the dress of their womenfolk. They get tattooed with the most common patterns of *jogi jade* (plaited hair), *madankaiyi* (hand of cupid), *yele thotta* (betel garden) and the moon.

Foods : They are reportedly flesh eaters but they abstain from eating the flesh of cow or monkey. Both men and women occasionally consume mutton, chicken and egg. But rice, *jowar* and *ragi* are their staple food.

Traditional Occupation : Their traditional occupation was begging for which they roamed about the nearby area. They were receiving the contribution of a fowl, one *hana* and a handful of rice from *Kulavadis* for allowing them to collect *Nela bhaga* for the use of the burial ground by the other castes, as stated earlier. On their part, the *Kulavadis* used to take the cloth of the corpse and a fee for every dead body burned or buried. They were, therefore, paying the members of this caste something in acknowledgement of the *Siddhas'* superior right.

Tirgar, Tirbanda

Birth: The Pre-delivery ritual known as *Simantha* is performed in the seventh month of the first pregnancy of the woman. On the sixth day after delivery, *chatri puja* (oblation to the female deity) is performed. The new-born child is also named on that day.

Marriage: Members of the same clan cannot intermarry. A member of the caste also cannot marry his paternal aunt's or maternal uncle's daughter. However, a man may marry two sisters, and two brothers may also marry two sisters. Polygamy is said to be permitted. A man can marry a second wife after the age of thirty, if the first wife is barren or is suffering from an incurable disease or he cannot live with her. Girls are generally married between the age of seven to twelve years. But this has been replaced by the adult marriages wherein girls are married at the age of 18 years or so.

Death: Their dead are either burnt or buried. Bachelors and spinsters are buried. In the burial pit, the corpse is laid with head towards the north. The bones and ashes of the burnt are thrown into the river. Where there is no river, these bones and ashes are mounded into a heap and water from a jar is poured over it. Funeral rites are performed on the tenth, eleventh and thirteenth days after death. On the thirteenth day, a feast is given to the people of the caste.

Foods : They are non-vegetarians. They eat the flesh of goats, sheep, cows, buffaloes, domestic fowls, hare and also fish. But their staple cereals are rice, *ragi*, and urad pulse.

Traditional Occupation : The traditional occupation of the people of this caste had been making *tirs* or arrows, as stated earlier. When the demand for arrows ceased, they took to working as field labourers.

Tiruvalluvar/Vallon/Valluvan

Birth: Delivery of the Valluvan woman usually takes place in the house of her husband. But in the case of first delivery, the expectant mother is taken to her parents' house during the 7th or 9th month of pregnancy. The people of the caste in the villages do not have any separate pollution shed for confining the pregnant woman and giving birth to a child. The delivery takes place in a room within the living house. It is normally attended to by an elderly woman of the caste who has some experience by constant practice. The placenta is buried in the backyard. The birth pollution is observed for 7 to 9 days.

Puberty: When a girl attains puberty, pollution is observed for fifteen days. During this period, she is kept in a partitioned enclosure within the house. During these fifteen days, the girl is given a rich diet consisting of eggs, sweetened rice flour, chicken, etc. On the sixteenth day, she is given a ceremonious bath after which she has free access to any part of the house. The temporary partitioned shed put up for the purpose of her seclusion is dismantled and burnt. On this day, the maternal uncle also presents her with new clothes, and the close relatives are invited and fed. During her subsequent menstruations, she is secluded till the period of her menarche is over.

Marriage: The cross-cousin as well as maternal uncle-niece marriages are practised by the people of this caste. Junior levirate and junior sororate forms of marriage are also allowed. The adult marriage through negotiation is the general norm nowadays, but in the past child marriages were also prevalent. The Valluvans follow patrilocal residence after marriage, i.e. the wife after marriage stays in her husband's house.

Death: Their dead are buried. In most places, the burial is done in a lying posture with head towards the south. In some places, it is said that the body is buried in a sitting posture. The eldest son pushes the first shod of earth into the pit in which the corpse is to be buried. The last day obsequies are performed on the 16th day. The relatives revisit the place of burial and perform *pooja* (oblation) to a *Lingam* (the image of phallic) moulded for the occasion with earth. Rice and edibles are offered in a leaf before the *Lingam,* and are left there to be eaten by crows. The party returns home and the members take oil bath which marks the end of the period of pollution. The *Tali* is then removed from the neck of the widow of the deceased.

Dwelling : The Valluvans live in a separate site adjoining the Paraiyar settlement which itself is isolated at about two furlongs from the main village. The general pattern of their housing follows the normal rural pattern in any other part of the States where they are located.

Dress : In Tamil Nadu and Pondicherry, the men wear only *lungis*. The Saivites put holy ash on their forehead, abdomen, shoulders and chest. They also wear a *rudraksha mala* (garland of beads) as well as the *Sivalingamala* (phallic symbol of Lord Shiva). The Vaishnavites also decorate their forehead with *Vaishnava namam* (symbol of Lord Vishnu). A few wear the *Poonool* (sacred thread).

Ornaments : A few ornaments worn by their women-folk are cheap ones made of silver or base metal. A *kammal* (ear-stud) in the ear and a few glass bangles are all that can be seen on a woman of ordinary means. A few young women are, however, found to wear neck chains, *kappu* (bangles), nose-screws and *mattal* (ear link). The *tali* to be worn by married women is rather peculiar shaped and no woman of other caste in these parts of the respective States is known to wear such a type of *tali*. Many women are found with tattoo marks on their arms and legs.

Foods : The staple diet of the Valluvans is rice and millets, depending upon the availability. If they have both rice and millets, they eat rice for the night meal, and keep the millet for the morning and the midday meals. Normally, they consume food thrice a day but cook only once and that is after dusk. The night meal is in a solid form but the morning and midday meals are generally in *koozh* (gruel). When they take their meal in a solid form, they always have a side-dish of some sauce prepared with vegetables or dried fish. Occasionally, they take mutton and chicken. But the Saivites are pure vegetarians.

Traditional Occupation : The traditional occupations of people of the caste was astrology, and officiating as priests in the marriage ceremonies of their own and of the Pallar caste. In Kerala, fishing and daily wage labour have been the traditional occupations of Valluvans. Their professional duties included writing charms for sick people, preparing horoscopes, making forecast of good or evil by means of cobalistic square marked on the ground and beating the tom-tom.

Statewise Distribution of Individual Scheduled Caste Population by Sex and Literacy Rate

Caste		*Population (Nos.)*	*Male (Nos.)*	*Female (Nos.)*	*Literacy Rate (%)*
All Scheduled	Total	8,563,930	4,339,745	4,224,185	52.87
Castes	Rural	6,417,243	3,245,315	3,171,928	47.25
	Urban	2,146,687	1,094,430	1,052,257	69.27
Adi Andhra	Total	25,938	13,226	12,712	73.91
	Rural	1,745	904	841	56.39
	Urban	24,193	12,322	11,871	75.17
Adi Dravida	Total	616,332	310,097	306,235	70.14
	Rural	229,248	114,735	114,513	57.75
	Urban	387,084	195,362	191,722	77.43
Adi Karnataka	Total	2,199,170	1,113,027	1,086,143	56.73
	Rural	1,675,495	844,319	831,176	51.57
	Urban	523,675	268,708	254,967	72.97

Caste		Population (Nos.)	Male (Nos.)	Female (Nos.)	Literacy Rate (%)
Adiya	Total	635	306	329	40.73
	Rural	629	303	326	40.45
	Urban	6	3	3	66.67
Ager	Total	6,233	3,106	3,127	68.29
	Rural	4,238	2,108	2,130	64.11
	Urban	1,995	998	997	76.86
Ajila	Total	2,138	1,081	1,057	66.06
	Rural	1,894	957	937	65.84
	Urban	244	124	120	67.77
Anamuk	Total	19	10	9	83.33
	Rural	-	-	-	0.00
	Urban	19	10	9	83.33
Aray Mala	Total	284	139	145	65.83
	Rural	139	64	75	46.90
	Urban	145	75	70	82.68
Arunthathiyar	Total	1,313	671	642	42.29
	Rural	831	430	401	34.05
	Urban	482	241	241	56.01
Arwa Mala	Total	20	10	10	57.89
	Rural	9	3	6	62.50
	Urban	11	7	4	54.55
Baira	Total	3,870	1,978	1,892	69.60
	Rural	3,463	1,758	1,705	68.69
	Urban	407	220	187	77.53
Bakad	Total	687	330	357	55.37
	Rural	608	290	318	50.97
	Urban	79	40	39	88.41
Bant	Total	1,605	781	824	86.38
	Rural	115	58	57	90.43
	Urban	1,490	723	767	86.10
Bakuda	Total	1,219	601	618	80.37
	Rural	528	256	272	70.46
	Urban	691	345	346	87.77
Balagai	Total	4,940	2,416	2,524	60.17
	Rural	3,705	1,804	1,901	53.32
	Urban	1,235	612	623	80.44

Caste		Population (Nos.)	Male (Nos.)	Female (Nos.)	Literacy Rate (%)
Bandi	Total	2,817	1,384	1,433	45.43
	Rural	1,886	943	943	37.91
	Urban	931	441	490	60.33
Banjara etc.	Total	997,338	514,491	482,847	42.98
	Rural	886,730	455,330	431,400	40.54
	Urban	110,608	59,161	51,447	62.15
Bathada	Total	2,103	1,018	1,085	66.49
	Rural	1,393	666	727	64.26
	Urban	710	352	358	70.95
Beda Jangam etc.	Total	54,873	27,958	26,915	75.24
	Rural	39,682	20,142	19,540	73.11
	Urban	15,191	7,816	7,375	80.78
Bellara	Total	1,251	600	651	56.21
	Rural	921	438	483	62.04
	Urban	330	162	168	37.55
Bhangi etc.	Total	8,879	4,431	4,448	50.91
	Rural	4,327	2,167	2,160	35.69
	Urban	4,552	2,264	2,288	64.51
Bhambi etc.	Total	564,599	283,377	281,222	46.76
	Rural	455,712	228,646	227,066	41.80
	Urban	108,887	54,731	54,156	66.65
Bhovi	Total	955,752	484,479	471,273	49.24
	Rural	715,488	362,566	352,922	45.61
	Urban	240,264	121,913	118,351	59.92
Bindla	Total	10	4	6	100.00
	Rural	1	1	-	100.00
	Urban	9	3	6	100.00
Byagara	Total	4,146	2,112	2,034	34.14
	Rural	3,679	1,877	1,802	32.68
	Urban	467	235	232	46.07
Chakkiliyan	Total	399	193	206	55.69
	Rural	192	103	89	48.75
	Urban	207	90	117	62.42
Chalavadi etc.	Total	256,920	129,432	127,488	54.00
	Rural	192,206	96,859	95,347	49.43
	Urban	64,714	32,573	32,141	67.34
Chandala	Total	101	50	51	55.68

Caste		Population (Nos.)	Male (Nos.)	Female (Nos.)	Literacy Rate (%)
	Rural	69	32	37	45.16
	Urban	32	18	14	80.77
Chenna	Total	44,551	22,516	22,035	48.26
Dasar etc.	Rural	36,949	18,666	18,283	46.51
	Urban	7,602	3,850	3,752	56.72
Dakkal etc.	Total	162	84	78	43.65
	Rural	122	66	56	35.87
	Urban	40	18	22	64.71
Dakkaliga	Total	244	119	125	28.50
	Rural	123	57	66	36.46
	Urban	121	62	59	20.62
Dhor etc.	Total	26,182	13,315	12,867	70.04
	Rural	13,247	6,716	6,531	60.40
	Urban	12,935	6,599	6,336	79.59
Dom etc.	Total	20,811	10,382	10,429	49.31
	Rural	15,597	7,762	7,835	46.84
	Urban	5,214	2,620	2,594	56.64
Ellamalwar etc.	Total	239	110	129	55.14
	Rural	200	92	108	53.63
	Urban	39	18	21	62.86
Ganti Chores	Total	3,877	1,921	1,956	63.09
	Rural	2,446	1,222	1,224	54.11
	Urban	1,431	699	732	77.83
Garoda etc.	Total	60	34	26	62.75
	Rural	11	7	4	54.55
	Urban	49	27	22	65.00
Godda	Total	2,011	1,034	977	66.59
	Rural	1,610	819	791	67.02
	Urban	401	215	186	64.86
Gosangi	Total	1,634	837	797	46.75
	Rural	474	218	256	49.49
	Urban	1,160	619	541	45.58
Halleer	Total	5,914	2,966	2,948	51.07
	Rural	5,561	2,789	2,772	49.82
	Urban	353	177	176	69.93
Halsar etc.	Total	10,275	5,057	5,218	63.62
	Rural	8,503	4,171	4,332	59.68
	Urban	1,772	886	886	81.72
Handi Jogis	Total	17,643	8,847	8,796	44.52
	Rural	12,601	6,282	6,319	42.58
	Urban	5,042	2,565	2,477	49.42
Hasla	Total	692	328	364	52.96
	Rural	673	316	357	52.33
	Urban	19	12	7	75.00
Holar etc.	Total	24,924	12,536	12,388	54.53
	Rural	21,092	10,600	10,492	50.60
	Urban	3,832	1,936	1,896	75.61
Holaya etc.	Total	641,472	325,756	315,716	51.75
	Rural	526,014	266,239	259,775	47.51
	Urban	115,458	59,517	55,941	70.59
HoleyaDasari	Total	1,077	529	548	49.24
	Rural	802	385	417	49.29
	Urban	275	144	131	49.07
Jaggali	Total	548	273	275	35.14
	Rural	404	198	206	30.14
	Urban	144	75	69	50.00
Jambuvulu	Total	5,739	2,914	2,825	50.66
	Rural	3,822	1,921	1,901	42.09
	Urban	1,917	993	924	67.63
Kadaiyan	Total	91	42	49	52.00
	Rural	41	21	20	13.33
	Urban	50	21	29	77.78
Kalladi	Total	1,070	528	542	43.93
	Rural	798	398	400	43.74
	Urban	272	130	142	44.50
Kepmaris	Total	12	8	4	80.00
	Rural	1	-	1	0.00
	Urban	11	8	3	88.89
Kolupulvandlu	Total	12	6	6	63.64
	Rural	7	3	4	85.71
	Urban	5	3	2	25.00
Koosa	Total	860	415	445	55.18
	Rural	839	405	434	54.41
	Urban	21	10	11	84.21

Caste		Population (Nos.)	Male (Nos.)	Female (Nos.)	Literacy Rate (%)
Koracha	Total	49,184	24,893	24,291	49.14
	Rural	35,759	17,992	17,767	46.90
	Urban	13,425	6,901	6,524	55.20
Koramà	Total	115,110	58,279	56,831	56.30
	Rural	77,425	39,330	38,095	52.44
	Urban	37,685	18,949	18,736	64.20
Kotegar etc.	Total	3,029	1,538	1,491	72.87
	Rural	1,659	843	816	58.83
	Urban	1,370	695	675	88.84
Kudumban	Total	161	83	78	72.11
	Rural	37	18	19	61.11
	Urban	124	65	59	75.68
Kuravan	Total	673	342	331	71.50
	Rural	261	136	125	65.73
	Urban	412	206	206	75.00
Lingader	Total	2,812	1,487	1,325	75.49
	Rural	1,268	670	598	67.63
	Urban	1,544	817	727	81.96
Machala	Total	175	83	92	77.22
	Rural	57	27	30	54.00
	Urban	118	56	62	87.96
Madari	Total	1,087	563	524	51.06
	Rural	557	301	256	39.78
	Urban	530	262	268	62.67
Madiga	Total	1,305,976	660,077	645,899	45.74
	Rural	1,048,066	529,195	518,871	42.12
	Urban	257,910	130,882	127,028	60.19
Mahar etc.	Total	64,578	32,544	32,034	63.34
	Rural	51,801	26,147	25,654	59.44
	Urban	12,777	6,397	6,380	78.88
Mahyavanshi etc.	Total	191	101	90	69.88
	Rural	67	38	29	54.24
	Urban	124	63	61	78.50
Maila	Total	1,290	638	652	44.03
	Rural	1,179	585	594	42.93
	Urban	111	53	58	55.79
Mala	Total	15,804	7,958	7,846	62.19
	Rural	6,485	3,240	3,245	37.08
	Urban	9,319	4,718	4,601	78.56
Mala Dasari	Total	3,921	1,967	1,954	54.84
	Rural	2,380	1,197	1,183	46.55
	Urban	1,541	770	771	67.15
Mala Hannai	Total	3	1	2	100.00
	Rural	1	-	1	100.00
	Urban	2	1	1	100.00
Mala Jangam	Total	96	58	38	46.15
	Rural	47	27	20	68.29
	Urban	49	31	18	21.62
Mala Masti	Total	27	11	16	6.25
	Rural	-	-	-	0.00
	Urban	27	11	16	6.25
Mala Sale etc.	Total	53	30	23	72.09
	Rural	27	15	12	60.87
	Urban	26	15	11	85.00
Mala Sanyasi	Total	623	309	314	35.96
	Rural	617	308	309	35.58
	Urban	6	1	5	66.67
Mang etc.	Total	23,824	12,045	11,779	50.27
	Rural	20,044	10,208	9,836	48.96
	Urban	3,780	1,837	1,943	57.24
Mang Garudi etc.	Total	2,252	1,107	1,145	40.85
	Rural	469	224	245	45.07
	Urban	1,783	883	900	39.69
Manne	Total	149	77	72	53.28
	Rural	24	14	10	33.33
	Urban	125	63	62	57.43
Masthi	Total	96	48	48	45.78
	Rural	76	38	38	34.92
	Urban	20	10	10	80.00
Mavilan	Total	50	26	24	68.89
	Rural	7	3	4	14.29
	Urban	43	23	20	78.95

Caste		Population (Nos.)	Male (Nos.)	Female (Nos.)	Literacy Rate (%)
Meghval etc.	Total	47	23	24	51.35
	Rural	19	7	12	36.36
	Urban	28	16	12	57.69
Moger	Total	75,304	37,674	37,630	63.40
	Rural	65,819	32,974	32,845	61.24
	Urban	9,485	4,700	4,785	78.05
Mukri	Total	10,470	5,301	5,169	61.53
	Rural	9,114	4,614	4,500	60.37
	Urban	1,356	687	669	69.23
Mundala	Total	25,842	12,607	13,235	76.15
	Rural	14,865	7,311	7,554	70.57
	Urban	10,977	5,296	5,681	83.61
Nadia etc.	Total	363	236	127	71.17
	Rural	178	138	40	56.80
	Urban	185	98	87	85.98
Nalkadaya	Total	1,811	925	886	69.91
	Rural	1,555	790	765	69.83
	Urban	256	135	121	70.42
Nalakeyava	Total	4,932	2,491	2,441	69.39
	Rural	4,569	2,315	2,254	69.06
	Urban	363	176	187	73.35
Nayadi	Total	827	428	399	71.15
	Rural	351	187	164	57.05
	Urban	476	241	235	81.42
Pale	Total	12,050	5,956	6,094	54.75
	Rural	11,789	5,813	5,976	54.22
	Urban	261	143	118	78.07
Pallan	Total	2,593	1,321	1,272	74.66
	Rural	2,074	1,040	1,034	71.00
	Urban	519	281	238	89.49
Pambada	Total	777	358	419	77.86
	Rural	458	213	245	75.18
	Urban	319	145	174	81.66
Panchama	Total	522	273	249	57.02
	Rural	454	234	220	55.53
	Urban	68	39	29	66.67
Panniandi	Total	62	26	36	56.00
	Rural	16	4	12	60.00
	Urban	46	22	24	54.29
Paraiyan etc.	Total	2,606	1,297	1,309	58.81
	Rural	1,701	863	838	66.16
	Urban	905	434	471	43.89
Paravan	Total	2,492	1,260	1,232	66.87
	Rural	2,139	1,074	1,065	65.88
	Urban	353	186	167	72.82
Raneyar	Total	3,111	1,492	1,619	70.35
	Rural	2,455	1,177	1,278	67.21
	Urban	656	315	341	82.01
Samagara	Total	82,861	42,333	40,528	66.92
	Rural	41,507	21,343	20,164	57.16
	Urban	41,354	20,990	20,364	76.55
Samban	Total	128	64	64	74.76
	Rural	74	37	37	61.67
	Urban	54	27	27	93.02
Sapari	Total	63	26	37	42.55
	Rural	46	20	26	24.24
	Urban	17	6	11	85.71
Sillekyathas	Total	23,480	11,884	11,596	42.15
	Rural	20,340	10,306	10,034	41.78
	Urban	3,140	1,578	1,562	44.53
Sindhollu etc.	Total	163	75	88	50.00
	Rural	121	54	67	50.98
	Urban	42	21	21	47.06
Sudugadu	Total	21,331	10,907	10,424	40.96
Siddha	Rural	16,283	8,280	8,003	44.02
	Urban	5,048	2,627	2,421	30.53
Thoti	Total	1,387	717	670	53.54
	Rural	1,181	610	571	52.44
	Urban	206	107	99	60.00
Tirgar etc.	Total	615	314	301	51.88
	Rural	463	240	223	43.21
	Urban	152	74	78	75.18
Valluvan	Total	802	407	395	87.34
	Rural	85	40	45	65.28
	Urban	717	367	350	89.83
Generic	Total	174,436	89,220	85,216	55.29
Castes etc.	Rural	94,404	47,963	46,441	42.82
	Urban	80,032	41,257	38,775	69.54

Distribution of Individual Scheduled Castes Population by Sex (State/District)

State/District	Population (Nos.)	Male (Nos.)	Female (Nos.)
KARNATAKA	**8,563,930**	**4,339,745**	**4,224,185**
Belgaum	462,020	233,431	228,589
Bagalkot *	250,604	124,009	126,595
Bijapur	334,254	171,108	163,146
Gulbarga	717,595	365,974	351,621
Bidar	298,812	153,649	145,163
Raichur	317,276	159,340	157,936
Koppal *	185,209	92,736	92,473
Gadag *	137,414	69,796	67,618
Dharwad	131,969	67,007	64,962
Uttara Kannada	101,896	51,309	50,587
Haveri *	175,360	90,108	85,252
Bellary	374,218	188,536	185,682
Chitradurga	336,487	172,092	164,395
Davanagere*	333,227	170,365	162,862
Shimoga	269,519	136,299	133,220
Udupi *	67,689	33,345	34,344
Chikmagalur	233,134	116,796	116,338
Tumkur	474,044	241,177	232,867
Kolar	671,692	338,459	333,233
Bangalore	851,047	435,162	415,885
Bangalore Rural	377,679	191,831	185,848
Mandya	247,213	123,695	123,518
Hassan	311,726	155,409	156,317
Dakshina Kannada	131,160	65,818	65,342
Kodagu	67,422	33,384	34,038
Mysore	467,640	237,476	230,164
Chamarajanagar*	237,624	121,434	116,190
Adi Andhra			
Karnataka	**25,938**	**13,226**	**12,712**
Belgaum	178	97	81
Bagalkot *	1	1	-
Bijapur	4	1	3
Bidar	51	29	22
Raichur	39	22	17
Koppal *	5	3	2
Gadag *	4	3	1
Dharwad	328	162	166
Uttara Kannada	17	11	6
Haveri *	9	4	5
Bellary	1,301	659	642
Chitradurga	19	11	8
Davanagere*	57	32	25
Shimoga	233	125	108
Udupi *	86	44	42
Chikmagalur	49	23	26
Tumkur	72	41	31
Kolar	3,369	1,668	1,701
Bangalore	18,872	9,660	9,212
Bangalore Rural	140	73	67
Mandya	113	57	56
Hassan	85	43	42
Dakshina Kannada	59	30	29
Kodagu	410	196	214
Mysore	188	88	100
Chamarajanagar*	249	143	106
Adi Dravida			
Karnataka	**616,332**	**310,097**	**306,235**
Belgaum	130	57	73
Bagalkot *	7	6	1
Bijapur	7	5	2
Gulbarga	86	41	45
Bidar	19	11	8
Raichur	1,455	730	725
Koppal *	651	320	331
Gadag *	70	38	32
Dharwad	2,059	1,014	1,045
Uttara Kannada	716	353	363
Haveri *	58	27	31
Bellary	7,521	3,734	3,787
Chitradurga	9,303	4,749	4,554
Davanagere*	8,455	4,281	4,174
Shimoga	14,408	7,259	7,149
Udupi *	38,447	18,796	19,651
Chikmagalur	16,371	8,188	8,183

State/District	Population (Nos.)	Male (Nos.)	Female (Nos.)
Tumkur	51,980	26,204	25,776
Kolar	129,160	64,262	64,898
Bangalore	247,655	125,963	121,692
Bangalore Rural	31,400	15,849	15,551
Mandya	10,046	5,013	5,033
Hassan	9,876	4,923	4,953
Dakshina Kannada	16,486	8,150	8,336
Kodagu	3,238	1,624	1,614
Mysore	14,618	7,436	7,182
Chamarajanagar*	2,110	1,064	1,046
Adi Karnataka			
Karnataka	**2,199,170**	**1,113,027**	**1,086,143**
Belgaum	152	92	60
Bagalkot *	63	36	27
Bijapur	53	34	19
Gulbarga	135	71	64
Bidar	184	103	81
Raichur	201	106	95
Koppal *	160	84	76
Gadag *	45	26	19
Dharwad	431	217	214
Uttara Kannada	592	323	269
Haveri *	318	175	143
Bellary	93,404	46,635	46,769
Chitradurga	45,519	23,531	21,988
Davanagere*	40,861	20,951	19,910
Shimoga	71,793	36,221	35,572
Udupi *	818	414	404
Chikmagalur	93,395	46,630	46,765
Tumkur	111,569	56,710	54,859
Kolar	269,119	136,127	132,992
Bangalore	343,453	175,468	167,985
Bangalore Rural	187,996	95,723	92,273
Mandya	172,297	86,053	86,244
Hassan	202,565	100,839	101,726
Dakshina	456	757	699
Kannada	1		
Kodagu	36,421	18,051	18,370
Mysore	342,533	174,119	168,414
Chamarajanagar*	183,637	93,531	90,106
Adiya			
Karnataka	**635**	**306**	**329**
Kodagu	635	306	329
Ager			
Karnataka	**6,233**	**3,106**	**3,127**
Belgaum	13	6	7
Bagalkot *	2	1	1
Bijapur	1	1	-
Gulbarga	1	1	-
Raichur	1	1	-
Dharwad	17	9	8
Uttara Kannada	6,139	3,059	3,080
Haveri *	1	-	1
Shimoga	8	4	4
Chikmagalur	5	3	2
Kolar	6	3	3
Bangalore	28	13	15
Hassan	3	1	2
Dakshina Kannada	5	3	2
Kodagu	3	1	2
Ajila			
Karnataka	**2,138**	**1,081**	**1,057**
Bidar	1	1	-
Dharwad	4	2	2
Haveri *	1	-	1
Davanagere*	6	3	3
Kolar	10	4	6
Bangalore	142	74	68
Hassan	4	1	3
Dakshina Kannada	620	832	788
Kodagu	349	164	185
Mysore	1	-	1
Anamuk			
Karnataka	**19**	**10**	**9**
Belgaum	6	3	3
Bijapur	1	1	-
Tumkur	5	3	2

State/District	Population (Nos.)	Male (Nos.)	Female (Nos.)
Kolar	5	2	3
Bangalore	2	1	1
Aray Mala			
Karnataka	**284**	**139**	**145**
Bagalkot *	8	2	6
Bijapur	3	1	2
Gulbarga	31	16	15
Bidar	35	14	21
Raichur	1	-	1
Gadag *	5	3	2
Davanagere*	44	24	20
Shimoga	8	5	3
Kolar	47	22	25
Bangalore	86	43	43
Bangalore Rural	6	4	2
Mandya	5	3	2
Dakshina Kannada	5	2	3
Arunthathiyar			
Karnataka	**1,313**	**671**	**642**
Belgaum	1	1	-
Bijapur	1	1	-
Gulbarga	2	1	1
Dharwad	3	1	2
Uttara Kannada	5	3	2
Bellary	4	2	2
Shimoga	576	276	300
Udupi *	4	2	2
Chikmagalur	57	33	24
Kolar	24	11	13
Bangalore	593	316	277
Dakshina Kannada	11	7	4
Kodagu	16	10	6
Mysore	8	4	4
Chamarajanagar*	8	3	5
Arwa Mala			
Karnataka	**20**	**10**	**10**
Belgaum	5	1	4
Bidar	1	1	-
Bellary	6	4	2
Kolar	4	2	2
Bangalore	4	2	2
Baira			
Karnataka	**3,870**	**1,978**	**1,892**
Belgaum	18	7	11
Gulbarga	22	9	13
Dharwad	1	-	1
Bellary	4	3	1
Chitradurga	1	1	-
Davanagere*	4	2	2
Chikmagalur	3	2	1
Kolar	31	17	14
Bangalore	134	73	61
Bangalore Rural	15	6	9
Hassan	21	12	9
Dakshina Kannada	3,436	1,754	1,682
Kodagu	169	87	82
Mysore	11	5	6
Bakad			
Karnataka	**687**	**330**	**357**
Gulbarga	7	4	3
Raichur	3	1	2
Uttara Kannada	585	276	309
Udupi *	3	2	1
Bangalore	11	7	4
Dakshina Kannada	74	38	36
Mysore	4	2	2
Bakuda			
Karnataka	**1,219**	**601**	**618**
Belgaum	6	3	3
Dharwad	1	1	-
Uttara Kannada	50	16	34
Bellary	6	2	4
Udupi *	64	28	36
Chikmagalur	10	5	5

State/District	Population (Nos.)	Male (Nos.)	Female (Nos.)
Kolar	2	-	2
Bangalore	17	10	7
Mandya	3	2	1
Hassan	5	4	1
Dakshina Kannada	985	495	490
Kodagu	70	35	35
Balagai			
Karnataka	**4,940**	**2,416**	**2,524**
Belgaum	4	1	3
Bagalkot *	2	1	1
Bidar	37	15	22
Raichur	30	18	12
Dharwad	16	8	8
Uttara Kannada	6	3	3
Haveri *	5	2	3
Bellary	18	11	7
Chitradurga	8	4	4
Shimoga	21	11	10
Udupi *	3	3	-
Chikmagalur	47	23	24
Tumkur	463	213	250
Kolar	1,593	767	826
Bangalore	1,221	633	588
Bangalore Rural	572	276	296
Mandya	148	76	72
Hassan	177	79	98
Dakshina Kannada	1	1	-
Kodagu	383	185	198
Mysore	146	69	77
Chamarajanagar*	39	17	22
Bandi			
Karnataka	**2,817**	**1,384**	**1,433**
Belgaum	529	261	268
Bagalkot *	435	210	225
Bijapur	503	257	246
Gulbarga	478	249	229
Bidar	16	9	7
Raichur	51	25	26
Koppal *	70	29	41

State/District	Population (Nos.)	Male (Nos.)	Female (Nos.)
Gadag *	24	9	15
Dharwad	67	31	36
Uttara Kannada	319	144	175
Haveri *	143	73	70
Bellary	12	5	7
Shimoga	10	5	5
Chikmagalur	3	2	1
Tumkur	4	2	2
Kolar	14	10	4
Bangalore	93	43	50
Hassan	10	5	5
Mysore	36	15	21
Banjara etc.			
Karnataka	**997,338**	**514,491**	**482,847**
Belgaum	22,315	11,605	10,710
Bagalkot *	39,329	20,171	19,158
Bijapur	117,466	61,457	56,009
Gulbarga	207,157	106,716	100,441
Bidar	47,022	24,320	22,702
Raichur	43,167	22,263	20,904
Koppal *	31,143	15,940	15,203
Gadag *	38,184	19,692	18,492
Dharwad	10,032	5,216	4,816
Uttara Kannada	7,132	3,690	3,442
Haveri *	43,558	22,653	20,905
Bellary	65,805	33,920	31,885
Chitradurga	46,743	23,754	22,989
Davanagere*	91,068	46,976	44,092
Shimoga	49,889	25,339	24,550
Udupi *	909	467	442
Chikmagalur	35,707	18,002	17,705
Tumkur	35,514	18,314	17,200
Kolar	8,624	4,370	4,254
Bangalore	8,797	4,776	4,021
Bangalore Rural	18,646	9,742	8,904
Mandya	1,024	521	503
Hassan	17,909	9,053	8,856
Dakshina Kannada	724	410	314
Kodagu	485	239	246

State/District	Population (Nos.)	Male (Nos.)	Female (Nos.)
Mysore	2,031	1,053	978
Chamarajanagar*	6,958	3,832	3,126
Bant			
Karnataka	**1,605**	**781**	**824**
Belgaum	91	44	47
Bagalkot *	19	9	10
Bijapur	13	7	6
Gadag *	5	3	2
Dharwad	136	75	61
Uttara Kannada	1,334	639	695
Haveri *	7	4	3
Bathada			
Karnataka	**2,103**	**1,018**	**1,085**
Belgaum	2	-	2
Bagalkot *	7	3	4
Gulbarga	8	4	4
Dharwad	10	5	5
Davanagere*	2	2	-
Shimoga	177	92	85
Udupi *	1,854	889	965
Chikmagalur	4	2	2
Tumkur	6	3	3
Bangalore	18	10	8
Hassan	1	-	1
Dakshina Kannada	5	4	1
Kodagu	9	4	5
Beda Jangam etc.			
Karnataka	**54,873**	**27,958**	**26,915**
Belgaum	2,101	1,053	1,048
Bagalkot *	344	179	165
Bijapur	720	382	338
Gulbarga	1,489	748	741
Bidar	7,677	3,872	3,805
Raichur	7,753	3,858	3,895
Koppal *	4,159	2,117	2,042
Gadag *	457	245	212
Dharwad	945	500	445
Uttara Kannada	197	112	85
Haveri *	2,560	1,323	1,237
Bellary	2,484	1,318	1,166
Chitradurga	3,008	1,529	1,479
Davanagere*	7,352	3,787	3,565
Shimoga	2,142	1,094	1,048
Udupi *	7	4	3
Chikmagalur	3,459	1,764	1,695
Tumkur	2,238	1,144	1,094
Kolar	2,358	1,179	1,179
Bangalore	1,143	585	558
Bangalore Rural	1,384	705	679
Mandya	79	43	36
Hassan	478	249	229
Dakshina Kannada	42	20	22
Kodagu	4	3	1
Mysore	283	140	143
Chamarajanagar*	10	5	5
Bellara			
Karnataka	**1,251**	**600**	**651**
Belgaum	28	13	15
Bijapur	13	5	8
Gulbarga	18	7	11
Bidar	7	3	4
Raichur	174	78	96
Koppal *	27	12	15
Gadag *	31	20	11
Dharwad	7	3	4
Uttara Kannada	5	2	3
Bellary	6	4	2
Davanagere*	3	1	2
Shimoga	5	3	2
Udupi *	694	337	357
Chikmagalur	37	17	20
Kolar	1	-	1
Bangalore	76	40	36
Bangalore Rural	3	-	3
Mandya	4	2	2
Hassan	58	25	33
Dakshina Kannada	12	5	7
Kodagu	6	3	3

State/District	Population (Nos.)	Male (Nos.)	Female (Nos.)
Mysore	6	3	3
Chamarajanagar*	30	17	13
Bhambi etc.			
Karnataka	**564,599**	**283,377**	**281,222**
Belgaum	117,672	59,217	58,455
Bagalkot *	90,496	43,907	46,589
Bijapur	62,248	31,244	31,004
Gulbarga	19,332	9,816	9,516
Bidar	6,267	3,232	3,035
Raichur	22,473	11,237	11,236
Koppal *	29,649	14,943	14,706
Gadag *	46,154	23,344	22,810
Dharwad	44,508	22,509	21,999
Uttara Kannada	11,019	5,568	5,451
Haveri *	60,608	30,953	29,655
Bellary	4,976	2,505	2,471
Chitradurga	5,488	2,786	2,702
Davanagere*	7,538	3,768	3,770
Shimoga	7,115	3,557	3,558
Udupi *	767	382	385
Chikmagalur	1,503	753	750
Tumkur	6,735	3,444	3,291
Kolar	4,262	2,157	2,105
Bangalore	5,659	2,964	2,695
Bangalore Rural	2,697	1,334	1,363
Mandya	1,189	570	619
Hassan	1,388	710	678
Dakshina Kannada	848	468	380
Kodagu	470	240	230
Mysore	3,119	1,547	1,572
Chamarajanagar*	419	222	197
Bhangi etc.			
Karnataka	**8,879**	**4,431**	**4,448**
Belgaum	1,452	735	717
Bagalkot *	449	243	206
Bijapur	225	115	110
Gulbarga	1,097	580	517
Bidar	930	472	458
Raichur	695	318	377
Koppal *	586	296	290
Gadag *	288	123	165
Dharwad	400	205	195
Uttara Kannada	1,056	495	561
Haveri *	89	44	45
Bellary	166	77	89
Chitradurga	8	3	5
Davanagere*	53	29	24
Shimoga	40	21	19
Udupi *	22	10	12
Chikmagalur	11	5	6
Tumkur	8	4	4
Kolar	8	3	5
Bangalore	701	353	348
Bangalore Rural	20	9	11
Mandya	150	78	72
Hassan	53	26	27
Dakshina Kannada	96	43	53
Kodagu	4	1	3
Mysore	257	138	119
Chamarajanagar*	15	5	10
Bhovi			
Karnataka	**955,752**	**484,479**	**471,273**
Belgaum	24,886	12,502	12,384
Bagalkot *	25,056	12,435	12,621
Bijapur	17,611	8,903	8,708
Gulbarga	47,081	23,818	23,263
Bidar	12,262	6,263	5,999
Raichur	36,375	18,083	18,292
Koppal *	24,009	12,079	11,930
Gadag *	18,974	9,541	9,433
Dharwad	17,648	8,923	8,725
Uttara Kannada	14,482	7,326	7,156
Haveri *	29,341	15,002	14,339
Bellary	53,386	27,035	26,351
Chitradurga	65,452	33,310	32,142
Davanagere*	57,637	29,452	28,185
Shimoga	76,230	38,709	37,521
Udupi *	2,643	1,384	1,259

State/District	Population (Nos.)	Male (Nos.)	Female (Nos.)
Chikmagalur	26,661	13,396	13,265
Tumkur	66,678	33,929	32,749
Kolar	121,658	61,653	60,005
Bangalore	90,632	46,420	44,212
Bangalore Rural	46,391	23,622	22,769
Mandya	18,352	9,210	9,142
Hassan	24,719	12,346	12,373
Dakshina Kannada	2,165	1,127	1,038
Kodagu	2,898	1,523	1,375
Mysore	25,451	12,884	12,567
Chamarajanagar*	7,074	3,604	3,470
Bindla			
Karnataka	**10**	**4**	**6**
Belgaum	1	-	1
Kolar	1	1	-
Bangalore	4	3	1
Kodagu	4	-	4
Byagara			
Karnataka	**4,146**	**2,112**	**2,034**
Belgaum	9	3	6
Bagalkot *	97	49	48
Bijapur	9	6	3
Gulbarga	998	516	482
Bidar	83	44	39
Raichur	1,736	866	870
Koppal *	176	87	89
Dharwad	21	8	13
Uttara Kannada	5	3	2
Bellary	298	157	141
Chitradurga	14	7	7
Davanagere*	21	9	12
Shimoga	21	14	7
Udupi *	6	3	3
Chikmagalur	13	7	6
Tumkur	5	3	2
Kolar	80	43	37
Bangalore	142	74	68
Bangalore Rural	61	32	29
Mandya	37	21	16

State/District	Population (Nos.)	Male (Nos.)	Female (Nos.)
Dakshina Kannada	300	151	149
Kodagu	14	9	5
Chakkiliyan			
Karnataka	**399**	**193**	**206**
Belgaum	14	8	6
Bagalkot *	29	12	17
Bidar	1	1	-
Raichur	15	9	6
Koppal *	17	8	9
Gadag *	21	12	9
Dharwad	113	47	66
Uttara Kannada	12	8	4
Haveri *	2	2	-
Bellary	7	5	2
Chitradurga	8	4	4
Davanagere*	2	-	2
Shimoga	10	2	8
Udupi *	1	-	1
Chikmagalur	1	1	-
Tumkur	5	3	2
Kolar	2	1	1
Bangalore	67	31	36
Bangalore Rural	2	2	-
Hassan	10	6	4
Dakshina Kannada	20	12	8
Kodagu	36	17	19
Chamarajanagar*	4	2	2
Chalavadi etc.			
Karnataka	**256,920**	**129,432**	**127,488**
Belgaum	11,110	5,577	5,533
Bagalkot *	13,866	6,889	6,977
Bijapur	3,461	1,699	1,762
Gulbarga	1,541	756	785
Bidar	94	44	50
Raichur	38,265	19,063	19,202
Koppal *	13,269	6,572	6,697
Gadag *	12,980	6,585	6,395
Dharwad	21,994	11,226	10,768
Uttara Kannada	11,767	6,045	5,722

State/District	Population (Nos.)	Male (Nos.)	Female (Nos.)
Haveri *	10,345	5,316	5,029
Bellary	25,090	12,495	12,595
Chitradurga	9,462	4,814	4,648
Davanagere*	9,409	4,737	4,672
Shimoga	12,902	6,618	6,284
Udupi *	19	12	7
Chikmagalur	2,833	1,403	1,430
Tumkur	18,832	9,527	9,305
Kolar	25,725	13,103	12,622
Bangalore	3,813	1,942	1,871
Bangalore Rural	7,676	3,788	3,888
Mandya	517	274	243
Hassan	1,734	840	894
Dakshina Kannada	96	49	47
Kodagu	19	6	13
Mysore	92	46	46
Chamarajanagar*	9	6	3
Chandala			
Karnataka	**101**	**50**	**51**
Bagalkot *	38	16	22
Bijapur	1	1	-
Raichur	17	8	9
Koppal *	7	3	4
Gadag *	7	4	3
Dharwad	6	4	2
Uttara Kannada	6	3	3
Haveri *	4	3	1
Shimoga	2	1	1
Udupi *	4	3	1
Bangalore	5	2	3
Mandya	4	2	2
Chenna Dasar etc.			
Karnataka	**44,551**	**22,516**	**22,035**
Belgaum	10,232	5,218	5,014
Bagalkot *	6,737	3,308	3,429
Bijapur	1,814	901	913
Gulbarga	1,703	839	864
Bidar	41	21	20
Raichur	2,024	1,014	1,010

State/District	Population (Nos.)	Male (Nos.)	Female (Nos.)
Koppal *	4,193	2,113	2,080
Gadag *	2,061	1,075	986
Dharwad	1,034	529	505
Uttara Kannada	125	70	55
Haveri *	961	488	473
Bellary	3,036	1,576	1,460
Chitradurga	690	365	325
Davanagere*	2,490	1,257	1,233
Shimoga	983	489	494
Udupi *	73	38	35
Chikmagalur	54	25	29
Tumkur	45	27	18
Kolar	5,544	2,803	2,741
Bangalore	248	121	127
Bangalore Rural	36	17	19
Hassan	63	29	34
Dakshina Kannada	351	183	168
Kodagu	3	2	1
Mysore	10	8	2
Dakkal etc.			
Karnataka	**162**	**84**	**78**
Belgaum	2	-	2
Bagalkot *	3	1	2
Gulbarga	7	6	1
Bidar	17	10	7
Raichur	5	2	3
Koppal *	9	4	5
Bellary	17	7	10
Chitradurga	17	9	8
Davanagere*	27	15	12
Chikmagalur	2	1	1
Tumkur	23	11	12
Kolar	3	1	2
Bangalore	6	3	3
Bangalore Rural	1	-	1
Hassan	6	4	2
Dakshina Kannada	6	3	3
Kodagu	5	4	1
Mysore	6	3	3

State/District	Population (Nos.)	Male (Nos.)	Female (Nos.)
Dakkaliga			
Karnataka	**244**	**119**	**125**
Belgaum	35	20	15
Bagalkot *	44	22	22
Gulbarga	7	3	4
Bidar	22	10	12
Raichur	18	8	10
Gadag *	3	-	3
Dharwad	15	5	10
Bellary	11	6	5
Chitradurga	25	13	12
Davanagere*	5	1	4
Chikmagalur	3	3	-
Tumkur	8	4	4
Kolar	23	9	14
Bangalore	8	6	2
Hassan	10	5	5
Mysore	7	4	3
Dhor etc.			
Karnataka	**26,182**	**13,315**	**12,867**
Belgaum	8,831	4,395	4,436
Bagalkot *	2,059	1,079	980
Bijapur	2,996	1,509	1,487
Gulbarga	4,737	2,413	2,324
Bidar	2,652	1,366	1,286
Raichur	233	127	106
Koppal *	96	43	53
Gadag *	612	324	288
Dharwad	2,632	1,365	1,267
Uttara Kannada	361	186	175
Haveri *	231	113	118
Bellary	56	32	24
Chitradurga	5	2	3
Davanagere*	122	65	57
Shimoga	23	13	10
Udupi *	15	7	8
Chikmagalur	6	3	3
Tumkur	4	1	3
Kolar	11	7	4

State/District	Population (Nos.)	Male (Nos.)	Female (Nos.)
Bangalore	464	245	219
Bangalore Rural	6	3	3
Mandya	5	4	1
Hassan	5	2	3
Dakshina Kannada	7	3	4
Mysore	13	8	5
Dom etc.			
Karnataka	**20,811**	**10,382**	**10,429**
Belgaum	3,545	1,740	1,805
Bagalkot *	457	229	228
Bijapur	298	145	153
Gulbarga	463	220	243
Bidar	21	11	10
Raichur	134	59	75
Koppal *	1,091	529	562
Gadag *	1,214	600	614
Dharwad	1,229	638	591
Uttara Kannada	29	16	13
Haveri *	341	176	165
Bellary	818	420	398
Chitradurga	120	61	59
Davanagere*	1,327	662	665
Shimoga	977	488	489
Udupi *	13	6	7
Chikmagalur	443	217	226
Tumkur	1,406	713	693
Kolar	3,841	1,895	1,946
Bangalore	416	215	201
Bangalore Rural	1,424	716	708
Mandya	109	51	58
Hassan	515	267	248
Dakshina Kannada	50	25	25
Kodagu	2	2	-
Mysore	500	266	234
Chamarajanagar*	28	15	13
Ellamalwar etc.			
Karnataka	**239**	**110**	**129**
Gulbarga	1	1	-
Bidar	30	15	15

State/District	Population (Nos.)	Male (Nos.)	Female (Nos.)
Uttara Kannada	4	2	2
Shimoga	3	2	1
Tumkur	40	21	19
Kolar	34	14	20
Bangalore	36	16	20
Bangalore Rural	2	1	1
Mandya	87	37	50
Kodagu	2	1	1
Ganti Chores			
Karnataka	**3,877**	**1,921**	**1,956**
Belgaum	2,264	1,113	1,151
Bagalkot *	130	68	62
Bijapur	101	46	55
Gadag *	774	394	380
Dharwad	436	217	219
Uttara Kannada	41	22	19
Haveri *	100	47	53
Bellary	4	1	3
Davanagere*	2	-	2
Shimoga	3	3	-
Chikmagalur	4	2	2
Bangalore	9	2	7
Hassan	5	3	2
Chamarajanagar*	4	3	1
Garoda etc.			
Karnataka	**60**	**34**	**26**
Bidar	1	1	-
Koppal *	6	3	3
Shimoga	11	7	4
Chikmagalur	2	2	-
Kolar	7	4	3
Bangalore	32	17	15
Mandya	1	-	1
Generic Castes etc.			
Karnataka	**174,436**	**89,220**	**85,216**
Belgaum	8,243	4,103	4,140
Bagalkot *	3,404	1,704	1,700
Bijapur	5,103	2,588	2,515
Gulbarga	17,801	9,068	8,733

State/District	Population (Nos.)	Male (Nos.)	Female (Nos.)
Bidar	9,023	4,701	4,322
Raichur	12,689	6,372	6,317
Koppal *	6,997	3,439	3,558
Gadag *	1,013	542	471
Dharwad	2,852	1,462	1,390
Uttara Kannada	1,265	648	617
Haveri *	3,625	1,851	1,774
Bellary	13,872	7,016	6,856
Chitradurga	665	350	315
Davanagere*	2,238	1,207	1,031
Shimoga	1,108	556	552
Udupi *	1,087	537	550
Chikmagalur	3,599	1,874	1,725
Tumkur	1,583	790	793
Kolar	3,438	1,717	1,721
Bangalore	42,045	21,869	20,176
Bangalore Rural	5,967	3,037	2,930
Mandya	5,309	2,701	2,608
Hassan	7,237	3,712	3,525
Dakshina Kannada	1,774	894	880
Kodagu	2,242	1,117	1,125
Mysore	7,496	3,923	3,573
Chamarajanagar*	2,761	1,442	1,319
Godda			
Karnataka	**2,011**	**1,034**	**977**
Belgaum	5	1	4
Bagalkot *	3	2	1
Bijapur	27	18	9
Gulbarga	22	11	11
Bidar	190	87	103
Raichur	11	7	4
Dharwad	7	4	3
Uttara Kannada	107	59	48
Davanagere*	11	6	5
Shimoga	5	3	2
Udupi *	605	308	297
Chikmagalur	5	4	1
Tumkur	9	5	4
Kolar	12	7	5

State/District	Population (Nos.)	Male (Nos.)	Female (Nos.)
Bangalore	221	119	102
Mandya	3	2	1
Hassan	10	6	4
Dakshina Kannada	749	382	367
Chamarajanagar*	9	3	6
Gosangi			
Karnataka	**1,634**	**837**	**797**
Belgaum	145	74	71
Bidar	36	19	17
Koppal *	18	9	9
Gadag *	21	12	9
Dharwad	462	250	212
Haveri *	47	24	23
Bellary	223	109	114
Davanagere*	104	53	51
Shimoga	213	108	105
Udupi *	20	11	9
Chikmagalur	201	97	104
Kolar	7	3	4
Bangalore	35	19	16
Bangalore Rural	5	2	3
Hassan	79	36	43
Dakshina Kannada	18	11	7
Halleer			
Karnataka	**5,914**	**2,966**	**2,948**
Belgaum	12	8	4
Bagalkot *	762	372	390
Bijapur	1,830	906	924
Gulbarga	182	90	92
Bidar	141	73	68
Dharwad	6	3	3
Uttara Kannada	2,917	1,478	1,439
Shimoga	7	5	2
Udupi *	1	-	1
Chikmagalur	2	2	-
Tumkur	1	1	-
Bangalore	14	7	7
Bangalore Rural	15	7	8
Hassan	6	3	3
Dakshina Kannada	18	11	7
Halsar etc.			
Karnataka	**10,275**	**5,057**	**5,218**
Belgaum	110	54	56
Bijapur	73	38	35
Gulbarga	14	7	7
Bidar	22	12	10
Raichur	5	3	2
Gadag *	10	3	7
Dharwad	728	357	371
Uttara Kannada	5,811	2,870	2,941
Haveri *	196	104	92
Bellary	42	22	20
Shimoga	1,280	621	659
Udupi *	120	55	65
Chikmagalur	1,607	786	821
Bangalore	21	9	12
Mandya	1	-	1
Hassan	231	115	116
Dakshina Kannada	4	1	3
Handi Jogis			
Karnataka	**17,643**	**8,847**	**8,796**
Bijapur	101	50	51
Gulbarga	38	19	19
Raichur	34	16	18
Koppal *	37	17	20
Dharwad	17	6	11
Uttara Kannada	45	22	23
Haveri *	621	322	299
Bellary	1,181	614	567
Chitradurga	65	32	33
Davanagere*	1,118	558	560
Shimoga	1,141	572	569
Chikmagalur	948	455	493
Tumkur	1,881	932	949
Kolar	3,216	1,630	1,586
Bangalore	2,076	1,051	1,025
Bangalore Rural	1,034	523	511
Mandya	568	282	286

State/District	Population (Nos.)	Male (Nos.)	Female (Nos.)
Hassan	1,734	851	883
Dakshina Kannada	172	97	75
Kodagu	50	28	22
Mysore	1,292	633	659
Chamarajanagar*	274	137	137
Hasla			
Karnataka	**692**	**328**	**364**
Uttara Kannada	71	35	36
Haveri *	4	3	1
Shimoga	170	76	94
Udupi *	429	204	225
Chikmagalur	8	4	4
Bangalore	5	3	2
Dakshina Kannada	4	2	2
Kodagu	1	1	-
Holar etc.			
Karnataka	**24,924**	**12,536**	**12,388**
Belgaum	11,310	5,751	5,559
Bagalkot *	1,765	868	897
Bijapur	10,622	5,295	5,327
Gulbarga	433	217	216
Bidar	74	42	32
Raichur	18	12	6
Koppal *	6	2	4
Gadag *	44	25	19
Dharwad	58	38	20
Uttara Kannada	102	54	48
Haveri *	5	3	2
Bellary	7	5	2
Davanagere*	4	1	3
Shimoga	19	8	11
Udupi *	3	1	2
Chikmagalur	20	12	8
Tumkur	16	8	8
Kolar	1	-	1
Bangalore	240	110	130
Bangalore Rural	49	26	23
Mandya	30	13	17
Hassan	59	25	34

State/District	Population (Nos.)	Male (Nos.)	Female (Nos.)
Dakshina Kannada	16	6	10
Kodagu	18	11	7
Mysore	5	3	2
Holaya etc.			
Karnataka	**641,472**	**325,756**	**315,716**
Belgaum	121,557	61,362	60,195
Bagalkot *	33,472	16,528	16,944
Bijapur	82,614	41,903	40,711
Gulbarga	238,545	121,414	117,131
Bidar	110,827	57,135	53,692
Raichur	615	309	306
Koppal *	131	70	61
Gadag *	97	54	43
Dharwad	691	395	296
Uttara Kannada	1,604	829	775
Haveri *	64	34	30
Bellary	138	69	69
Chitradurga	46	22	24
Davanagere*	65	35	30
Shimoga	370	197	173
Udupi *	1,144	587	557
Chikmagalur	780	402	378
Tumkur	1,595	796	799
Kolar	2,303	1,166	1,137
Bangalore	6,795	3,520	3,275
Bangalore Rural	5,337	2,690	2,647
Mandya	1,880	903	977
Hassan	863	431	432
Dakshina Kannada	27,390	13,683	13,707
Kodagu	1,742	828	914
Mysore	777	385	392
Chamarajanagar*	30	9	21
HoleyaDasari			
Karnataka	**1,077**	**529**	**548**
Belgaum	31	18	13
Bagalkot *	221	103	118
Bijapur	2	1	1
Gulbarga	482	233	249
Bidar	82	40	42

State/District	Population (Nos.)	Male (Nos.)	Female (Nos.)
Raichur	122	60	62
Koppal *	38	22	16
Gadag *	5	4	1
Dharwad	8	2	6
Uttara Kannada	6	2	4
Haveri *	9	4	5
Bellary	17	9	8
Shimoga	3	2	1
Tumkur	2	1	1
Kolar	2	-	2
Bangalore	29	18	11
Dakshina Kannada	10	5	5
Kodagu	8	5	3
Jaggali			
Karnataka	**548**	**273**	**275**
Belgaum	1	1	-
Raichur	6	2	4
Bellary	8	4	4
Chitradurga	133	63	70
Davanagere*	2	1	1
Shimoga	9	7	2
Chikmagalur	1	-	1
Tumkur	14	6	8
Kolar	170	81	89
Bangalore	94	50	44
Bangalore Rural	102	53	49
Mandya	1	1	-
Mysore	7	4	3
Jambuvulu			
Karnataka	**5,739**	**2,914**	**2,825**
Bagalkot *	4	2	2
Bijapur	6	3	3
Bidar	5	1	4
Raichur	5	1	4
Gadag *	1	1	-
Uttara Kannada	7	3	4
Bellary	15	10	5
Chitradurga	11	4	7
Davanagere*	15	8	7

State/District	Population (Nos.)	Male (Nos.)	Female (Nos.)
Shimoga	26	16	10
Udupi *	1	-	1
Chikmagalur	22	7	15
Tumkur	105	53	52
Kolar	10	4	6
Bangalore	486	246	240
Bangalore Rural	484	239	245
Mandya	1,278	666	612
Hassan	48	25	23
Dakshina Kannada	13	10	3
Kodagu	65	31	34
Mysore	2,318	1,176	1,142
Chamarajanagar*	814	408	406
Kadaiyan			
Karnataka	**91**	**42**	**49**
Belgaum	5	4	1
Gulbarga	5	2	3
Bidar	21	11	10
Shimoga	4	2	2
Chikmagalur	10	4	6
Bangalore	25	9	16
Bangalore Rural	3	1	2
Mandya	6	2	4
Dakshina Kannada	3	3	-
Mysore	9	4	5
Kalladi			
Karnataka	**1,070**	**528**	**542**
Belgaum	9	4	5
Bijapur	16	10	6
Gulbarga	93	50	43
Bidar	53	24	29
Raichur	4	2	2
Koppal *	10	3	7
Gadag *	8	7	1
Uttara Kannada	6	1	5
Haveri *	4	2	2
Bellary	1	1	-
Davanagere*	3	2	1
Shimoga	7	4	3

State/District	Population (Nos.)	Male (Nos.)	Female (Nos.)
Udupi *	16	3	13
Chikmagalur	709	347	362
Kolar	1	1	-
Bangalore	94	48	46
Mandya	6	3	3
Dakshina Kannada	21	11	10
Mysore	9	5	4
Kepmaris			
Karnataka	**12**	**8**	**4**
Gulbarga	1	-	1
Davanagere*	11	8	3
Kolupulvandlu			
Karnataka	**12**	**6**	**6**
Belgaum	1	-	1
Raichur	8	4	4
Udupi *	1	-	1
Bangalore	2	2	-
Koosa			
Karnataka	**860**	**415**	**445**
Bijapur	1	-	1
Gulbarga	1	1	-
Raichur	1	-	1
Uttara Kannada	6	4	2
Shimoga	10	5	5
Udupi *	762	367	395
Chikmagalur	65	31	34
Bangalore	13	6	7
Dakshina Kannada	1	1	-
Koracha			
Karnataka	**49,184**	**24,893**	**24,291**
Belgaum	140	67	73
Bagalkot *	16	6	10
Bijapur	56	29	27
Gulbarga	64	35	29
Bidar	24	11	13
Raichur	1,286	635	651
Koppal *	333	171	162
Gadag *	221	102	119
Dharwad	220	110	110
Uttara Kannada	163	67	96
Haveri *	1,281	658	623
Bellary	10,377	5,348	5,029
Chitradurga	4,204	2,133	2,071
Davanagere*	8,541	4,407	4,134
Shimoga	2,729	1,345	1,384
Udupi *	2	-	2
Chikmagalur	2,704	1,364	1,340
Tumkur	2,444	1,215	1,229
Kolar	11,113	5,559	5,554
Bangalore	1,217	604	613
Bangalore Rural	817	426	391
Mandya	31	13	18
Hassan	1,062	514	548
Dakshina Kannada	32	17	15
Kodagu	1	-	1
Mysore	105	57	48
Chamarajanagar*	1	-	1
Korama			
Karnataka	**115,110**	**58,279**	**56,831**
Belgaum	11,747	6,048	5,699
Bagalkot *	11,123	5,616	5,507
Bijapur	4,420	2,283	2,137
Gulbarga	2,820	1,391	1,429
Bidar	477	254	223
Raichur	2,838	1,393	1,445
Koppal *	3,276	1,675	1,601
Gadag *	4,815	2,445	2,370
Dharwad	3,808	1,898	1,910
Uttara Kannada	1,425	711	714
Haveri *	5,087	2,652	2,435
Bellary	2,047	1,052	995
Chitradurga	3,362	1,713	1,649
Davanagere*	4,531	2,313	2,218
Shimoga	6,941	3,472	3,469
Udupi *	16	7	9
Chikmagalur	5,297	2,648	2,649
Tumkur	7,412	3,750	3,662
Kolar	1,110	575	535

State/District	Population (Nos.)	Male (Nos.)	Female (Nos.)
Bangalore	10,593	5,259	5,334
Bangalore Rural	5,180	2,658	2,522
Mandya	5,065	2,526	2,539
Hassan	3,403	1,693	1,710
Dakshina Kannada	102	50	52
Kodagu	365	159	206
Mysore	4,742	2,401	2,341
Chamarajanagar*	3,108	1,637	1,471
Kotegar etc.			
Karnataka	**3,029**	**1,538**	**1,491**
Belgaum	103	47	56
Bagalkot *	15	9	6
Gulbarga	143	77	66
Bidar	15	9	6
Raichur	29	16	13
Gadag *	4	2	2
Dharwad	120	62	58
Uttara Kannada	1,030	522	508
Haveri *	41	17	24
Bellary	9	6	3
Davanagere*	10	5	5
Shimoga	1,078	553	525
Udupi *	21	9	12
Chikmagalur	36	19	17
Tumkur	8	4	4
Bangalore	120	62	58
Bangalore Rural	13	7	6
Mandya	1	1	-
Hassan	1	1	-
Dakshina Kannada	225	107	118
Mysore	7	3	4
Kudumban			
Karnataka	**161**	**83**	**78**
Gulbarga	1	1	-
Shimoga	3	2	1
Udupi *	3	1	2
Bangalore	32	20	12
Dakshina Kannada	91	44	47
Kodagu	31	15	16
Kuravan			
Karnataka	**673**	**342**	**331**
Belgaum	84	40	44
Bagalkot *	41	23	18
Bijapur	36	15	21
Gulbarga	32	19	13
Raichur	34	15	19
Koppal *	1	1	-
Gadag *	9	4	5
Dharwad	41	22	19
Uttara Kannada	2	1	1
Haveri *	3	3	-
Bellary	6	4	2
Chitradurga	32	17	15
Davanagere*	1	1	-
Shimoga	43	21	22
Udupi *	28	14	14
Chikmagalur	4	3	1
Bangalore	193	97	96
Bangalore Rural	11	4	7
Mandya	1	-	1
Hassan	1	1	-
Dakshina Kannada	44	23	21
Kodagu	25	13	12
Mysore	1	1	-
Lingader			
Karnataka	**2,812**	**1,487**	**1,325**
Belgaum	84	42	42
Bagalkot *	18	6	12
Bijapur	376	192	184
Gulbarga	430	225	205
Bidar	360	198	162
Raichur	54	28	26
Koppal *	13	8	5
Gadag *	13	7	6
Dharwad	61	32	29
Uttara Kannada	4	2	2
Haveri *	86	47	39
Bellary	38	22	16

State/District	Population (Nos.)	Male (Nos.)	Female (Nos.)
Chitradurga	83	45	38
Davanagere*	74	35	39
Shimoga	41	22	19
Chikmagalur	23	11	12
Tumkur	51	24	27
Kolar	20	6	14
Bangalore	699	391	308
Bangalore Rural	19	11	8
Mandya	44	20	24
Hassan	96	50	46
Dakshina Kannada	4	1	3
Kodagu	2	1	1
Mysore	81	40	41
Chamarajanagar*	38	21	17
Machala			
Karnataka	**175**	**83**	**92**
Belgaum	3	1	2
Bijapur	3	2	1
Raichur	15	6	9
Gadag *	15	9	6
Dharwad	25	9	16
Uttara Kannada	41	20	21
Davanagere*	4	2	2
Udupi *	8	4	4
Chikmagalur	1	-	1
Tumkur	1	1	-
Bangalore	44	22	22
Bangalore Rural	1	1	-
Hassan	1	1	-
Dakshina Kannada	13	5	8
Madari			
Karnataka	**1,087**	**563**	**524**
Belgaum	341	181	160
Bagalkot *	17	11	6
Bijapur	33	22	11
Gulbarga	32	15	17
Bidar	14	7	7
Raichur	2	1	1
Gadag *	3	2	1

State/District	Population (Nos.)	Male (Nos.)	Female (Nos.)
Dharwad	294	143	151
Uttara Kannada	34	17	17
Haveri *	1	1	-
Bellary	6	3	3
Davanagere*	3	3	-
Shimoga	12	5	7
Udupi *	9	7	2
Chikmagalur	27	13	14
Tumkur	13	8	5
Kolar	107	54	53
Bangalore	77	34	43
Mandya	7	5	2
Dakshina Kannada	23	15	8
Kodagu	7	3	4
Mysore	25	13	12
Madiga			
Karnataka	**1,305,976**	**660,077**	**645,899**
Belgaum	23,827	12,130	11,697
Bagalkot *	9,589	4,569	5,020
Bijapur	5,585	2,830	2,755
Gulbarga	147,990	75,003	72,987
Bidar	65,186	33,423	31,763
Raichur	134,329	67,385	66,944
Koppal *	61,145	30,181	30,964
Gadag *	4,683	2,327	2,356
Dharwad	4,181	2,130	2,051
Uttara Kannada	1,192	585	607
Haveri *	11,227	5,734	5,493
Bellary	82,450	40,853	41,597
Chitradurga	140,048	71,743	68,305
Davanagere*	86,541	43,895	42,646
Shimoga	9,134	4,577	4,557
Udupi *	19	13	6
Chikmagalur	26,570	13,397	13,173
Tumkur	159,807	81,518	78,289
Kolar	69,722	35,061	34,661
Bangalore	55,084	28,211	26,873
Bangalore Rural	58,610	29,473	29,137

State/District	Population (Nos.)	Male (Nos.)	Female (Nos.)
Mandya	27,497	13,815	13,682
Hassan	29,293	14,533	14,760
Dakshina Kannada	381	215	166
Kodagu	1,631	805	826
Mysore	61,232	30,874	30,358
Chamarajanagar*	29,023	14,797	14,226
Mahar etc.			
Karnataka	**64,578**	**32,544**	**32,034**
Belgaum	40,196	20,129	20,067
Bagalkot *	49	24	25
Bijapur	212	108	104
Gulbarga	2,991	1,509	1,482
Bidar	17,145	8,759	8,386
Raichur	74	39	35
Koppal *	42	27	15
Gadag *	32	16	16
Dharwad	887	430	457
Uttara Kannada	1,305	654	651
Haveri *	20	6	14
Bellary	43	26	17
Chitradurga	5	3	2
Davanagere*	13	7	6
Shimoga	43	19	24
Udupi *	99	45	54
Chikmagalur	7	5	2
Kolar	13	7	6
Bangalore	144	81	63
Bangalore Rural	5	1	4
Hassan	27	14	13
Dakshina Kannada	320	162	158
Kodagu	88	48	40
Mysore	29	16	13
Chamarajanagar*	789	409	380
Mahyavanshi etc.			
Karnataka	**191**	**101**	**90**
Belgaum	28	15	13
Gulbarga	4	1	3
Koppal *	12	7	5

State/District	Population (Nos.)	Male (Nos.)	Female (Nos.)
Uttara Kannada	5	4	1
Davanagere*	1	1	-
Shimoga	1	-	1
Udupi *	11	8	3
Bangalore	120	61	59
Bangalore Rural	8	4	4
Chamarajanagar*	1	-	1
Maila			
Karnataka	**1,290**	**638**	**652**
Belgaum	7	3	4
Gulbarga	2	1	1
Bidar	7	3	4
Koppal *	6	2	4
Uttara Kannada	5	3	2
Shimoga	2	2	-
Chikmagalur	12	6	6
Bangalore	21	13	8
Mandya	1	1	-
Hassan	14	8	6
Dakshina Kannada	1,179	579	600
Kodagu	34	17	17
Mala			
Karnataka	**15,804**	**7,958**	**7,846**
Belgaum	47	27	20
Bijapur	102	48	54
Gulbarga	3,365	1,679	1,686
Bidar	59	27	32
Raichur	3,696	1,863	1,833
Koppal *	785	386	399
Gadag *	32	16	16
Dharwad	2,840	1,395	1,445
Uttara Kannada	887	471	416
Haveri *	5	3	2
Bellary	362	178	184
Chitradurga	8	4	4
Davanagere*	3	3	-
Shimoga	64	38	26
Udupi *	4	1	3
Chikmagalur	65	35	30

State/District	Population (Nos.)	Male (Nos.)	Female (Nos.)
Tumkur	12	6	6
Kolar	1,390	699	691
Bangalore	1,407	743	664
Bangalore Rural	15	7	8
Mandya	32	18	14
Hassan	18	12	6
Dakshina Kannada	567	278	289
Kodagu	33	18	15
Mysore	6	3	3
Mala Dasari			
Karnataka	**3,921**	**1,967**	**1,954**
Belgaum	11	5	6
Bijapur	5	3	2
Gulbarga	392	190	202
Raichur	2,522	1,256	1,266
Koppal *	332	164	168
Gadag *	5	3	2
Dharwad	8	4	4
Bellary	543	285	258
Davanagere*	1	1	-
Tumkur	7	5	2
Kolar	19	12	7
Bangalore	65	33	32
Dakshina Kannada	2	2	-
Kodagu	4	1	3
Mysore	5	3	2
Mala Hannai			
Karnataka	**3**	**1**	**2**
Raichur	2	1	1
Bangalore	1	-	1
Mala Jangam			
Karnataka	**96**	**58**	**38**
Gulbarga	44	28	16
Bidar	18	11	7
Chikmagalur	29	16	13
Bangalore	5	3	2
Mala Masti			
Karnataka	27	11	16
Gadag *	27	11	16

State/District	Population (Nos.)	Male (Nos.)	Female (Nos.)
Mala Sale etc.			
Karnataka	53	30	23
Bidar	16	9	7
Uttara Kannada	4	2	2
Haveri *	1	1	-
Bellary	9	6	3
Shimoga	4	2	2
Kolar	3	2	1
Bangalore	10	6	4
Dakshina Kannada	6	2	4
Mala Sanyasi			
Karnataka	623	309	314
Kolar	550	274	276
Bangalore	20	9	11
Bangalore Rural	53	26	27
Mang etc.			
Karnataka	**23,824**	**12,045**	**11,779**
Belgaum	8,351	4,188	4,163
Bagalkot *	776	382	394
Bijapur	133	58	75
Gulbarga	2,511	1,253	1,258
Bidar	11,490	5,876	5,614
Raichur	5	4	1
Gadag *	13	7	6
Dharwad	201	103	98
Uttara Kannada	17	13	4
Haveri *	100	49	51
Bellary	5	3	2
Davanagere*	1	-	1
Shimoga	12	5	7
Udupi *	10	5	5
Chikmagalur	2	1	1
Tumkur	10	3	7
Kolar	93	44	49
Bangalore	56	30	26
Bangalore Rural	20	13	7
Hassan	5	1	4
Dakshina Kannada	13	7	6
Mang Garudi etc.			

State/District	Population (Nos.)	Male (Nos.)	Female (Nos.)
Karnataka	**2,252**	**1,107**	**1,145**
Belgaum	283	137	146
Bijapur	553	262	291
Gulbarga	490	252	238
Bidar	637	313	324
Uttara Kannada	4	3	1
Tumkur	9	3	6
Kolar	229	108	121
Bangalore	15	7	8
Bangalore Rural	32	22	10
Manne			
Karnataka	**149**	**77**	**72**
Belgaum	60	33	27
Bagalkot *	9	5	4
Gulbarga	5	3	2
Bidar	7	3	4
Gadag *	19	10	9
Uttara Kannada	5	1	4
Davanagere*	1	1	-
Kolar	14	6	8
Bangalore	8	3	5
Mandya	2	1	1
Dakshina Kannada	15	9	6
Kodagu	4	2	2
Masthi			
Karnataka	**96**	**48**	**48**
Belgaum	5	1	4
Bagalkot *	5	3	2
Gulbarga	44	21	23
Uttara Kannada	8	5	3
Haveri *	1	1	-
Bellary	6	4	2
Shimoga	1	-	1
Chikmagalur	19	10	9
Kolar	1	-	1
Dakshina Kannada	2	-	2
Mysore	4	3	1
Mavilan			
Karnataka	**50**	**26**	**24**
Bellary	2	1	1
Shimoga	6	2	4
Bangalore	29	18	11
Hassan	5	2	3
Dakshina Kannada	8	3	5
Meghval etc.			
Karnataka	**47**	**23**	**24**
Belgaum	2	1	1
Gulbarga	20	7	13
Chitradurga	1	1	-
Chikmagalur	4	1	3
Tumkur	1	1	-
Bangalore	15	10	5
Dakshina Kannada	1	1	-
Kodagu	3	1	2
Moger			
Karnataka	**75,304**	**37,674**	**37,630**
Belgaum	77	35	42
Bagalkot *	22	12	10
Bijapur	44	23	21
Gulbarga	160	81	79
Bidar	264	131	133
Raichur	9	4	5
Koppal *	105	51	54
Gadag *	9	4	5
Dharwad	58	31	27
Uttara Kannada	16,489	8,124	8,365
Haveri *	37	17	20
Bellary	11	8	3
Davanagere*	24	13	11
Shimoga	3,294	1,603	1,691
Udupi *	6,171	3,092	3,079
Chikmagalur	1,311	645	666
Tumkur	7	2	5
Kolar	1	1	-
Bangalore	138	71	67
Bangalore Rural	9	6	3
Hassan	3,411	1,682	1,729
Dakshina Kannada	41,140	20,817	20,323

State/District	Population (Nos.)	Male (Nos.)	Female (Nos.)
Kodagu	2,503	1,215	1,288
Mysore	10	6	4
Mukri			
Karnataka	**10,470**	**5,301**	**5,169**
Belgaum	4	2	2
Bagalkot *	18	10	8
Gulbarga	2	-	2
Bidar	25	10	15
Dharwad	12	8	4
Uttara Kannada	9,941	5,032	4,909
Haveri *	11	4	7
Bellary	4	1	3
Shimoga	8	3	5
Udupi *	152	70	82
Chikmagalur	2	1	1
Bangalore	17	12	5
Hassan	6	4	2
Dakshina Kannada	268	144	124
Mundala			
Karnataka	**25,842**	**12,607**	**13,235**
Belgaum	45	20	25
Bagalkot *	16	10	6
Bijapur	18	9	9
Gulbarga	32	23	9
Bidar	11	6	5
Raichur	47	26	21
Koppal *	5	4	1
Gadag *	24	13	11
Dharwad	180	87	93
Uttara Kannada	17	8	9
Haveri *	32	17	15
Bellary	6	5	1
Chitradurga	9	5	4
Davanagere*	4	1	3
Shimoga	29	13	16
Udupi *	4,689	2,312	2,377
Chikmagalur	4,159	1,989	2,170
Tumkur	11	4	7
Kolar	1,008	500	508

State/District	Population (Nos.)	Male (Nos.)	Female (Nos.)
Bangalore	155	93	62
Bangalore Rural	3	1	2
Hassan	140	72	68
Dakshina Kannada	15,030	7,303	7,727
Kodagu	154	76	78
Mysore	17	10	7
Chamarajanagar*	1	-	1
Nadia etc.			
Karnataka	**363**	**236**	**127**
Belgaum	6	3	3
Bagalkot *	5	2	3
Gulbarga	6	4	2
Bidar	13	8	5
Raichur	1	1	-
Koppal *	4	3	1
Gadag *	11	6	5
Dharwad	36	21	15
Uttara Kannada	5	3	2
Haveri *	3	2	1
Davanagere*	6	5	1
Shimoga	1	-	1
Chikmagalur	1	-	1
Tumkur	19	7	12
Kolar	3	2	1
Bangalore	111	57	54
Bangalore Rural	10	3	7
Mandya	105	101	4
Hassan	7	3	4
Dakshina Kannada	5	3	2
Mysore	1	-	1
Chamarajanagar*	4	2	2
Nalakeyava			
Karnataka	**4,932**	**2,491**	**2,441**
Gulbarga	6	4	2
Udupi *	1,147	560	587
Chikmagalur	65	36	29
Kolar	6	1	5
Bangalore	10	3	7
Dakshina Kannada	3,698	1,887	1,811

State/District	Population (Nos.)	Male (Nos.)	Female (Nos.)
Nalkadaya			
Karnataka	**1,811**	**925**	**886**
Raichur	1	-	1
Shimoga	5	3	2
Udupi *	471	242	229
Chikmagalur	16	7	9
Kolar	1	1	-
Bangalore	10	5	5
Bangalore Rural	5	2	3
Mandya	10	5	5
Dakshina Kannada	1,292	660	632
Nayadi			
Karnataka	**827**	**428**	**399**
Belgaum	35	18	17
Gulbarga	6	2	4
Bidar	6	3	3
Raichur	116	58	58
Koppal *	5	4	1
Gadag *	4	2	2
Dharwad	17	9	8
Uttara Kannada	23	12	11
Haveri *	15	7	8
Bellary	17	11	6
Chitradurga	6	4	2
Davanagere*	88	48	40
Shimoga	49	24	25
Udupi *	4	3	1
Chikmagalur	35	15	20
Tumkur	18	8	10
Kolar	16	11	5
Bangalore	287	142	145
Bangalore Rural	5	4	1
Mandya	8	5	3
Hassan	24	13	11
Dakshina Kannada	23	12	11
Kodagu	5	2	3
Mysore	5	3	2
Chamarajanagar*	10	8	2
Pale			
Karnataka	**12,050**	**5,956**	**6,094**
Belgaum	31	12	19
Bagalkot *	74	43	31
Bijapur	221	124	97
Gulbarga	14	9	5
Dharwad	1	-	1
Uttara Kannada	56	33	23
Shimoga	16	8	8
Chikmagalur	20	7	13
Tumkur	5	3	2
Kolar	39	19	20
Bangalore	58	38	20
Hassan	554	269	285
Dakshina Kannada	16	6	10
Kodagu	10,945	5,385	5,560
Pallan			
Karnataka	**2,593**	**1,321**	**1,272**
Bijapur	4	1	3
Gulbarga	8	5	3
Raichur	307	145	162
Dharwad	29	15	14
Uttara Kannada	15	7	8
Bellary	30	20	10
Chitradurga	17	8	9
Davanagere*	3	2	1
Shimoga	9	4	5
Chikmagalur	215	115	100
Kolar	30	18	12
Bangalore	324	183	141
Bangalore Rural	8	4	4
Mandya	9	5	4
Hassan	20	8	12
Dakshina Kannada	560	289	271
Kodagu	985	477	508
Mysore	20	15	5
Pambada			
Karnataka	**777**	**358**	**419**
Chitradurga	19	9	10
Udupi *	194	82	112
Kolar	33	17	16
Bangalore	45	20	25
Dakshina Kannada	486	230	256
Panchama			
Karnataka	**522**	**273**	**249**
Belgaum	29	17	12

State/District	Population (Nos.)	Male (Nos.)	Female (Nos.)
Bagalkot *	26	15	11
Bijapur	137	70	67
Gulbarga	2	1	1
Koppal *	87	43	44
Gadag *	4	2	2
Dharwad	72	39	33
Uttara Kannada	21	10	11
Haveri *	21	8	13
Davanagere*	8	5	3
Shimoga	84	43	41
Udupi *	4	2	2
Bangalore	22	16	6
Hassan	5	2	3
Panniandi			
Karnataka	**62**	**26**	**36**
Shimoga	22	11	11
Udupi *	2	-	2
Chikmagalur	2	1	1
Bangalore	24	11	13
Hassan	5	1	4
Kodagu	7	2	5
Paraiyan etc.			
Karnataka	**2,606**	**1,297**	**1,309**
Belgaum	39	23	16
Bagalkot *	20	8	12
Bijapur	1	1	-
Gulbarga	29	17	12
Raichur	70	29	41
Gadag *	1	-	1
Dharwad	29	15	14
Uttara Kannada	5	2	3
Shimoga	29	14	15
Udupi *	107	48	59
Chikmagalur	311	151	160
Tumkur	274	140	134
Kolar	10	5	5
Bangalore	418	196	222
Mandya	104	57	47
Hassan	66	35	31
Dakshina Kannada	596	303	293
Kodagu	367	182	185
Mysore	13	5	8

State/District	Population (Nos.)	Male (Nos.)	Female (Nos.)
Chamarajanagar*	117	66	51
Paravan			
Karnataka	**2,492**	**1,260**	**1,232**
Belgaum	2	1	1
Bagalkot *	4	2	2
Gulbarga	1	1	-
Bidar	5	2	3
Uttara Kannada	1	1	-
Davanagere*	3	1	2
Udupi *	913	453	460
Chikmagalur	31	19	12
Bangalore	101	57	44
Bangalore Rural	4	3	1
Dakshina Kannada	1,408	713	695
Kodagu	16	6	10
Mysore	3	1	2
Raneyar			
Karnataka	**3,111**	**1,492**	**1,619**
Gulbarga	14	8	6
Bidar	4	2	2
Dharwad	1	-	1
Haveri *	16	6	10
Bellary	2	1	1
Chitradurga	2	1	1
Shimoga	4	3	1
Udupi *	827	394	433
Chikmagalur	703	327	376
Mandya	26	15	11
Hassan	9	4	5
Dakshina Kannada	1,236	596	640
Kodagu	267	135	132
Samagara			
Karnataka	**82,861**	**42,333**	**40,528**
Belgaum	26,650	13,688	12,962
Bagalkot *	6,796	3,444	3,352
Bijapur	12,954	6,760	6,194
Gulbarga	10,325	5,355	4,970
Bidar	4,650	2,343	2,307
Raichur	672	352	320
Koppal *	485	247	238
Gadag *	2,822	1,341	1,481
Dharwad	7,484	3,756	3,728

State/District	Population (Nos.)	Male (Nos.)	Female (Nos.)
Uttara Kannada	948	470	478
Haveri *	1,341	672	669
Bellary	360	199	161
Chitradurga	39	23	16
Davanagere*	512	261	251
Shimoga	648	326	322
Udupi *	2,060	1,027	1,033
Chikmagalur	288	145	143
Tumkur	17	10	7
Kolar	4	2	2
Bangalore	420	226	194
Bangalore Rural	40	21	19
Mandya	7	3	4
Hassan	69	40	29
Dakshina Kannada	3,162	1,565	1,597
Kodagu	78	40	38
Mysore	30	17	13
Samban			
Karnataka	**128**	**64**	**64**
Belgaum	53	25	28
Bagalkot *	1	1	-
Bijapur	5	3	2
Koppal *	1	-	1
Dharwad	5	2	3
Kolar	1	1	-
Bangalore	45	22	23
Dakshina Kannada	1	1	-
Kodagu	16	9	7
Sapari			
Karnataka	**63**	**26**	**37**
Belgaum	7	2	5
Dharwad	1	-	1
Chikmagalur	6	4	2
Kolar	39	15	24
Bangalore	9	4	5
Dakshina Kannada	1	1	-
Sillekyathas			
Karnataka	**23,480**	**11,884**	**11,596**
Belgaum	865	430	435
Bagalkot *	1,168	584	584
Bijapur	764	392	372
Gulbarga	40	17	23
Raichur	1,767	896	871
Koppal *	356	165	191
Gadag *	709	346	363
Dharwad	1,032	517	515
Uttara Kannada	136	65	71
Haveri *	1,271	676	595
Bellary	2,148	1,088	1,060
Chitradurga	929	474	455
Davanagere*	2,192	1,115	1,077
Shimoga	1,824	923	901
Udupi *	63	35	28
Chikmagalur	1,036	521	515
Tumkur	2,645	1,336	1,309
Kolar	599	291	308
Bangalore	936	486	450
Bangalore Rural	881	437	444
Mandya	930	476	454
Hassan	1,054	543	511
Dakshina Kannada	82	43	39
Kodagu	33	20	13
Mysore	18	7	11
Chamarajanagar*	2	1	1
Sindhollu etc.			
Karnataka	**163**	**75**	**88**
Belgaum	6	2	4
Bidar	12	8	4
Raichur	10	5	5
Koppal *	2	1	1
Chikmagalur	28	9	19
Tumkur	1	1	-
Bangalore	31	15	16
Mandya	68	32	36
Dakshina Kannada	1	1	-
Mysore	4	1	3
Sudugadu Siddha			
Karnataka	**21,331**	**10,907**	**10,424**
Belgaum	1,733	876	857
Bagalkot *	1,374	705	669
Bijapur	624	328	296
Gulbarga	1,313	666	647
Bidar	411	214	197
Raichur	992	492	500

State/District	Population (Nos.)	Male (Nos.)	Female (Nos.)
Koppal *	1,652	848	804
Gadag *	795	416	379
Dharwad	1,381	720	661
Uttara Kannada	156	80	76
Haveri *	1,501	774	727
Bellary	1,767	922	845
Chitradurga	913	485	428
Davanagere*	602	304	298
Shimoga	1,408	709	699
Udupi *	7	4	3
Chikmagalur	1,417	724	693
Tumkur	390	197	193
Kolar	10	6	4
Bangalore	65	39	26
Bangalore Rural	345	165	180
Mandya	7	3	4
Hassan	2,453	1,222	1,231
Mysore	15	8	7
Thoti			
Karnataka	**1,387**	**717**	**670**
Belgaum	33	16	17
Bidar	4	1	3
Raichur	1	-	1
Dharwad	8	4	4
Haveri *	1	1	-
Bellary	2	1	1
Davanagere*	1	-	1
Shimoga	10	5	5
Chikmagalur	17	8	9
Tumkur	7	4	3
Kolar	753	402	351
Bangalore	402	204	198
Bangalore Rural	111	52	59
Mandya	4	2	2
Dakshina Kannada	21	10	11
Kodagu	11	6	5
Mysore	1	1	-
Tirgar etc.			
Karnataka	**615**	**314**	**301**
Belgaum	23	14	9
Bagalkot *	112	63	49
Bijapur	24	12	12
Gulbarga	239	124	115
Bidar	5	3	2
Raichur	13	6	7
Koppal *	1	-	1
Gadag *	18	8	10
Bellary	1	-	1
Davanagere*	2	2	-
Udupi *	4	2	2
Chikmagalur	3	2	1
Tumkur	20	10	10
Kolar	28	12	16
Bangalore	96	44	52
Hassan	4	2	2
Dakshina Kannada	5	3	2
Kodagu	9	5	4
Mysore	1	-	1
Chamarajanagar*	7	2	5
Valluvan			
Karnataka	**802**	**407**	**395**
Belgaum	2	-	2
Bagalkot *	1	-	1
Bidar	2	2	-
Raichur	1	-	1
Koppal *	1	1	-
Gadag *	14	8	6
Dharwad	15	8	7
Uttara Kannada	1	1	-
Haveri *	1	-	1
Bellary	27	17	10
Davanagere*	1	1	-
Shimoga	3	2	1
Udupi *	3	1	2
Chikmagalur	8	4	4
Tumkur	9	4	5
Kolar	1	1	-
Bangalore	566	284	282
Mandya	2	1	1
Hassan	6	3	3
Dakshina Kannada	48	22	26
Kodagu	17	7	10
Mysore	32	17	15
Chamarajanagar*	41	23	18

Appendix-II : Scheduled Tribes

Adiyan

The women wear a saree with a knot over the right shoulder (sindha kettu) and bear tattoo marks on their forearms. Regarding food habits they are non-vegetarians, and their staple diet is rice supplemented with pulses like gram, peace and beans. The cooking medium is coconut and palm oil. Men drink alcoholic beverages and smoke beedis. The mode of acquiring a mate is through mutual consent and negotiation but instances of marriage by elopement also exist. Monogamy is the norm. The dead are buried and death pollution is observed for a period of thirteen days. When a man dies, his wife observes pollution till the death ceremony (kaka pula) is over. Ancestor worship also takes place. Their traditional occupation is agricultural labour.

Barda

They are non-vegetarians who eat pork, fish egg and mutton. Their staple food is bajra, jawar, wheat and rice supplemented with tur, urad, moong, masur, moth, etc. They eat various local leafy and green vegetables. They drink black tea however the consumption of milk is very low. They are endogamous and adhere to clan exogamy. A male is allowed to marry his mother's brother's daughter. They select mates through negotiation (lagan), by elopement (pali lagan), by service (ghar-jawai) and by courtship (haski-khushi lagan). They normally practice monogamy but polygyny is also allowed. Levirate (junior) and sororate (junior) are reported. The expectant mother is not allowed to eat certain vegetables, fish or egg. The delivery is conducted by a woman of their community called dai. On the sixth day of birth, a ritual (chat) is performed by the mother of the newborn in which she worships the place where the child was born. Their traditional occupation was hunting and gathering but now they depend on wage labour. They works as agricultural and casual labourers.

Bavcha

The Bavcha are non-vegetarians; jawar and rice are their staple cereals. They eat pulses and vegetables. Milk and its products are consumed. Liquor, which is often purchased and sometimes brewed by them, is liberally consumed. Marriages are arranged through negotiation and marriage by elopement, an earlier practice, is no longer in vogue. In case of an intra-clan marriage, close kin are avoided. Consanguineous alliances are allowed. Monogamy is prevalent and polygyny is non-existent. Levirate is permitted. During a marriage, rituals like Ganapati puja and chakla puja are at times performed. The Bavcha observe a pre-delivery ritual (khoda-bharva) in the seventh month of a woman's first pregnancy. Regarding funeral practises they carry the dead body on a bier (thatidi) along with food articles and a few untensils to the burial ground. The death rite (shraddh) is performed on the third and twelfth day and thereafter annually. A majority of the Bavcha are landless. They were wood-cutters once, but nowadays they work mostly as agricultural and non-agricultural labourers.

Bhil etc.

They eat cereals like maize, banti, rice, kodra and wheat, and pulses like tur, urad, moong and chavali. They are non-vegetarians who eat mutton, chicken, egg and fish. They drink alcoholic liquor which they regularly prepare from the mahua flowers. They maintain clan exogamy. The marriage age is sixteen years and above for boys and fourteen years and above for girls. Most of their marriages take place by elopement. The marriage is solemnized at the bride's natal home. Polygyny is allowed but rarely practised. The sacred black bead necklace and the vermilion mark are the marriage symbols for a woman. The amount of bride price to be paid is decided on by the elders and is obligatory in a marriage contract. Remarriage is allowed for both the sexes. After the death of parents, ancestral property is shared equally by the sons. On the seventh day after childbirth they name the child worship their family deity. When a death occurs, the dead body is bathed and worshipped. They are cremated and the community members offer firewood. On the twelfth day, a feast is offered to the fellow members of the community. Agriculture, animal husbandry, wage labour and the gathering of forest produce are the main occupations. Children above ten years take part in agricultural operations.

Chaudhri

The Chenchu are non-vegetarians, their staple food comprises jowar, ragi and rice. The consumption of beedis, cigarettes and betel leaves is common among them and the men consume alcohol regularly. Marriages are arranged through negotiation and by elopement. Both men and women can initiate a divorce. The puberty ceremony is performed for girls. Each Chenchu clan has a separate burial ground. Death pollution lasts for three to fifteen days and its terminated by performing the peddadivasam ceremony. The traditional source of income for the Chenchu was from ferest produce; they formerly collected honey, tarmarind, roots and tubers.

Chodhara

The Chodhara tribal community is divided in five sub divisions. Chodhara tribal community carries on conversation in the famous Chodri language which is a Bhil language. In order to sustain their livelihood, maximum of this Chodhari tribal people have taken up the occupation of farming, thereby producing ample crops like cotton, vegetables, and rice. Hunting, finishing, and collecting produce from the woods accomplish additional foods. Societal structure of this Chodhari tribal community follows the customs and practices of that of all other tribal communities. Interestingly, these Chodhara tribes establish close links with all the Rajput clans. Marriage too has been held in high esteem by all the Chodhari tribal community. Generally, each and every members of this Chodhari tribal community marries with in the same class. As per the custom, the Chodhari tribal people marry within the individual group and also have the permission to get married outside their own clans. In that matter also, the rule of monogamy is widely prevalent.

Dubla

The Dubla are non-vegetaians and rice is their staple died. Wheat and jowar are also eaten along with pulses. They consume home-made liquor or liquor or mahua (Bassia latifolia). They are monogamous. While arranging a marriage alliance, they avoid relations from within four six generations of one's parents and prefer negotiated marriages; through marriages by mutual consent are also frequent. The marriage symbols for women are black necklace (kaliganthi) and a dot on the forehead (kunku and tikki). Bride price is paid. The rule of residence after marriage is patrilocal.

Gamit

The Gamit are non-vegetarians. Rice and jowar are the staple cereals eaten by them. They drink alcoholic beverages. They are monogamous, prefer adult marriage and generally acquire mates through negotiation. The symbols of marriage for the women are necklace (mangalsuttra) and silver anklets. Bride price is paid and the rule of residence after marriage is patrilocal. The Gamit observe a pre-delivery ritual (srimant) in the seventh month of the first pregnancy and a post-delivery purificatory rite (chhatti) is performed on the fifth and sixth day for a boy and girl child, respectively. A marriage is solemnized at the bride's parent's house and a Brahmnan priest officiates over it. The dead are cremated and the mortal remains are disposed off in water but children below two years of age are buried. Barwa (obsequies) is observed on the twelfth day and a feast is arranged for the kin and relatives.

Gond etc.

They are non-vegetarians who eat fish, chicken and mutton. Rice and jowar are staple cereals. The men drink alcohol occasionally. Junior sororate and cross-cousin marriages are permitted. The marriage symbols are ear-rings, nose-stud and toe-rings. Widowers and male divorcees can remarry. A pre-delivery ritual called seemant is observed. The naming ceremony is performed on the eleventh day. The dead are cremated and death pollution is observed for three days. Mat-weaving is a leisure activity.

Gowdalu

Rice is their staple cereal, occasionally supplemented with chicken, fish, mutton and meat of wild boar, but beef is taboo. Both the men and women take alcoholic drinks occasionally. They allow cross-cousin marriages and junior sororate is permitted. Adult marriage is the general practice. Marriages are settled through negotiation. A necklace (thali) and toe-rings are the symbols of a married women. They do not allow divorce but the remarriage of pre-delivery ritual (bayake) is observed in the seventh month of pregnancy and the naming ceremony is observed on the twelfth day after childbirth, which follows eleven days of birth pollution. Cremation is practised by community. Obsequies are performed on the twelfth day after eleven days of pollution. Ancestor worship is observed every year.

Hakkipikki

They are non-vegetarians and rice, ragi and jowar are their staple cereals. Alcoholic drinks are consumed regularly by both the men and women. Adult marriage is the rule among them and marriages are mostly arranged by negotiation though instances of marriage through exchange and elopement are also reported. Monogamy is the common form and some cases of polygyny have been reported. A necklace (thali) and toe-rings are the marriage symbols for women. Certain pre-delivery restrictions are observed; Chatti is observed on the sixth day as a mark of initial purification from birth pollution, with a major purification ceremony observed after three months. The dead are buried and death pollution is observed for twelve days. Ancestor worship is part of the death rituals.

Hasalaru

They are non-vegetarians and eat pork. Rice is their staple food. Monogamy is the form of marriage. The marriage symbols for women are a vermilion mark, a necklace (thali) and toe-rings. The remarriage of widows, widowers and divorcees is allowed. Pre-delivery rituals (bayake) are performed during the fifth month of pregnancy. Birth pollution is observed for ten days and the naming ceremony is performed on the eleventh day. They bury the dead, observe death pollution for twelve days and perform ancestor worship. Ugadi, Dussehra, Diwali and Sankranti are the festivals observed. Folk-songs are sung by women.

Hill Pulaya

They are non-vegetarians and their staple food is rice which is eaten with pulsed like gram, tur, moong , beans, roots and tubers. The cooking medium is coconut oil and nowadays palm oil is also being used. Men consume alcoholic drinks occasionally which they purchase from the market. Only the males smoke, while betel chewing is common to both the sexes. Marriages are arranged by elders through negotiation. They follow monogamy, but a few cases of polygyny are reported. The marriage symbol is a black bead necklace, and now a yellow thread is also used. Widow, widower and divorcee remarriages are permitted. They Karavazhi observe birth pollution for five or seven days. Puberty rites (thanni utharuthu) are observed. The dead are buried and three days of pollution are observed. Ancestral worship is observed after a death.

Iruliga

The Iruligas are a jungle tribe; they speak a dialect of their own among themselves, which is very close to Tamil and Kannada. The term Iruliga might have been derived from Irul (night), perhaps from their dark color. They are black or brownish black in complexion, thick lips and curly hair. The primary occupations are hunting, collection of honey, cultivation, basket making and agricultural labourers. They have their tribal organization, and their headman is Gouda. The descent of the family is patriarchal, patrilineal, and patrilocal type. Widow Remarriage is practiced. The dead are buried and sometimes cremated.

Irular

They eat rice, ragi and all kinds of pulses. Groundnut and palm oils are the cooking medium. They prefer marriage alliances between the maternal uncle and niece, and between cross-cousins. Marriage through negotiation, exchange and elopement are the common ways of acquiring mates. Monogamy is the common form, through polygyny is also permitted. Birth pollution is observed for seven days and the naming and tonsure ceremonies are also performed. The dead are either buried or cremated and a period of pollution is observed. The dead rites of Krichai are performed on the third day and that karmandaram in the third month. The Irular celebrate the festivals of Sivaratri, Pongal and Diwali. The community has its own oral traditions. Both men and women sing folk-songs. At present they are engaged in basket and mat making.

Jenu Kuruba

In the Kannada language, the term 'Jenu' signifies honey and 'Kuruba' standards for casts. Therefore their name suggests that these Jenu Kuruba tribes have adapted the profession of honey gathering. Moreover the Jenu Kuruba lead a carefree lifestyle of a typical nomad, adapting to various occupations like conventional food collectors, shifting cultivators. These Jenu Kuruba tribes also carry on cultivation as a supplementary profession. Instead of ploughing the field, these Jenu Kuruba tribes rub the surface with a sort of bamboo spear. Housing settlement of these Jenu Kuruba tribes too witnesses the style and excellence of the whole of the Jenu Kuruba tribal community. Most of these Jenu Kuruba tribal communities reside in some tiny houses, popularly known as Hadi or Hatti. Only very currently, this Jenu Kuruba tribal community has settled down in numerous of huge hamlets, with the sincere initiatives of the government and other well fare organizations. The Jenu Kuruba tribal community converse in their local language which is knows as Jenu Kuruba.

Kadu Kuruba

The term Kadu Kuruba has got an etymological importance. If one dissects the term, one can find that in the Kannada language, Kadu signifies forest and Kuruba stands for tribal community. Thus Kadu Kuruba constitutes of the people residing in forest areas, as a whole. These Kadu Kuruba tribes are one of the sub castes of the famous Kuruba tribal community, Cultural excellence is widely being depicted in all its aspects like dance, language, religion, festival etc. Just like many of the tribal communities of the whole of the Indian subcontinent, these Kadu Kuruba tribes also are the ardent followers of Hindusim. Over the years, this Kadu tribal community have adapted to diverse occupational activities. The common practice is that in all the famous temples like Beeralingeshwara and Milaralingeshwara, all the priests that are being duly appointed belong to this Kadu Kuruba tribal community. If one can go back to the golden pages of the history of the Indian subcontinent, one can find the names of these Kadu Kuruba tribes over there also.

Kammara/Ozulu

Their staple food is millet (chollu) and rice. They are non-vegetarians and eat chicken, mutton, fish and flesh of some wild animals. They have gotra groups among them, some of which are Kamba, Surya, Nagra, Payya and Hanumantha. Cross-cousion marriage are common among them. Levirate and sorotate are allowed in this community. Traditionally, marriage by service and marriage by elopement were common among them. Monogamy is the common form of marriage among them. They observe birth pollution for thirteen days. The dead are cremated and death pollutions is observed for seven days. Traditionally, the Kammara, Ozulu were blacksmiths. Now most of them are wage labourers and peasants. They accept food and water from the Bagatha, Kotiya, Goundu, Mukha Dora, Manne Dora and Konda Dora but not from the Valmiki, Ghasi, Paidi and Dombu.

Kaniyan etc.

Their staple food consists of ragi, rice and jowar. Adult marriage is the rule, and mates for marriage are acquired through negotiation. Consanguineous marriages between cross-cousins and the maternal uncle-niece are practiced. Monogamy is the general form. Divorce is not permissible among them. Remarriage is allowed for widowers but not for widows. Pollution caused by childbirth is observed for ten days. The naming and tonsure rites are performed. The dead are buried and death pollution is observed for ten days.

Kathodi etc.

The principal occupation of the people living here is agriculture, but since there is a dearth of land holdings, many of them are employed as farm labourers in the lands of others. They even or try to find service in other areas. Dance and music form an inseparable part of the culture of Kathodi tribe. They are shy and peace loving tribal people living a very simple life by following their culture and traditions. The Kathodi tribe lives in the forests and depends on the forests for their livelihood. Most of the people are involved in profession of making catechew or Katha.

Kattunaikan

They are non-vegetaians and pork. Rice and ragi are their staple cereals. They consume roots and tubers. Coconut oil is their medium of cooking. They consume milk and milk products. Men occasionally consume alcoholic drinks. Beedis, cigarettes and loose tobacco smoking, tobacco. They prefer adult marriage and acquire mates by capture, service, elopement, exchange and negotiation. Monogamy and sororal polygyny are the forms of marriage found among them. Widows; widowers and divorcees are allowed to remarry. The dead are cremated and the remains are disposed off in water. Death pollution and ancestor worship are observed.

Kokna

They are non-vegetarians but do not eat beef. Pork and goat meat are eaten occasionally. Rice is their staple cereals, supplemented with and jowar or nagu. Groundnut oil is their cooking medium. They are generally a monogamous people, through polygyny is allowed in the community. The Kokna are permitted to marry cross-cousins. Vermilion and anklets are the symbols of a married women. Bride price, known as pend, is very high among them and a good number of Kokna men, who are unable to pay it, remain unmarried. The women participate in social, ritual and economic activities along with the men. They also work as daily-wage labourers or agricultural labourers and contribute towards the family income. The Kokna cremate the dead. Their village council is headed by a mukhiya.

Koli Dhor etc.

They are non-vegetarians and also eat beef and carrion. They prefer to marry after attaining adulthood, and alliances are contracted through negotiation, service and other means. Both monogamy and polygyny are practice. The necklace (mangalsutra) is the marriage symbols for the Dhor Koli women. Bride price (pend) is paid by them in kind. Remarriage is permitted for widows, widowers and divorcees. The tonsure ceremony for the male child is performed after one year. The betrothal takes place at the home of the bride-to-be. The dead are either buried or cremated, depending upon the financial condition of the bereaved family, and a memorial stone is kept over the grave or the place of cremation. Daharo, a death rite, is performed after the completion of one month to remove pollution.

Konda Kapu

The Konda Kapu are non-vegetarians and eat beef. They often consume an indigenous alcoholic drink jeelugukallu (caryota palm toddy) and sara (distilled liquor). They prefer cross-cousin marriage and both sororate and levirate are permitted. The age at marriage for boys is above sixteen years, while for girls to older girls. Marriage by capture, elopement, exchange, negotiation and service are usual modes of acquiring spouses. Monogamy is the usual form but polygyny is also practiced. Vermillion, necklace and toe-rings are the symbols of marriage for the Konda Kapu women. Remarriage of the members of either sex is permitted. Most of their marriages are negotiated and the families are mainly nuclear.

Koraga

Rice is their staple food. Different pulses, milk, milk products, roots, pork, beef and meat of other animals are eaten. Coconut oil is the medium of cooking. Vegetable and fruit consumption is moderate. Alcoholic drinks like arrack and toddy are consumed. Smoking of beedis and chewing of betel leaves are common among them. Endogamy at the group level and exogamy at the clan level are observed. A man may marry his father's sister's daughter or his mother's brother's daughter. The symbols of marriage are a necklace (karimani), toe and finger-rings. Widows, widowers and divorcees are allowed to remarry. When a women becomes pregnant for the first time, a ceremony called bayake is observed. Birth pollution exists for seven days and after that, the naming ceremony is performed. The dead are buried and death pollution is observed for thirteen days. Afterwards the bones are kept in a heap and the spirit is appeased.

Kota

They are non-vegetairans. Cereals like rice, jowar and ragi and varieties of pulses and vegetables are the major constituents of their food. Groundnut and palm oil are used for cooking. They consume coffee, tea, milk and milk products. The Kota men regularly drink liquor. They practise exgamy at the village level also. Marriage to one's mother's brother's daughter and father's sister's daughter are common. Motes are acquired by elopement, exchange and negotiation. Monogamy is the form of marriage. Necklace, finger- and toe-rings are marriage symbols for the Kota women. Bride price is paid in cash and kind. Remarriage is permitted for widows, widowers and divorcees. Sororate and levirate are permitted. The dead are cremated and the bones are disposed off in water. Death pollution and annual ancestor worship are observed.

Koya

They are non-vegetarians and eat beef. The staple food is rice and they consume all kind of pulses. Food is cooked in coconut and palm oil. They smoke beedis, cigarettes and chew betel leaves along with tobacco. Marriages between cross-cousin are common, but the sister's brother's daughter is considered more suitable then the father's sister's daughter. Adult marriages are the norm. spouses are acquired by negotiation and exchange. Monogamy is the form of marriage and the paying of mehar, the guarantee money, to the bride by the bridegroom is obligatory. Marriage rituals are elaborate and continue for four to seven days, depending upon the economic solvency of families concerned. Death rites are performed by the qazi or his assistants, and the dead are buried.

Koya

They eat rice as their staple food, and this is supplemented by pulses, vegetables, roots and tubers. Consanguineous marriage between cross-cousin and between the maternal uncle and niece are in vogue. They prefer adult marriage and arrange alliances through negotiation. These people are monogamous. Symbols of marriage for the women are vermilion, necklace and toe-rings. Bride price in cash and residence after marriage is patrilocal. Post-delivery pollution is not observed by them, but the childhood rites of naming, tonsure and cereal-feeding are observed. Marriage rituals are performed at the bride's residence, while the nuptial ceremony takes place at the groom's house. Death pollution is observed, and ancestor worship is a part of the death rites.

Kudiya etc.

They are non-vegetarians and eat pork. Rice is their staple food. Though other form of alliance are allowed, adult marriage through negotiation is the norm and monogamy the prevalent form. Pre-delivery rituals are observed in the community during the seventh month of pregnancy. Birth pollution is observed for sixteen days and on the fortieth day, the naming ceremony takes place. The dead are cremated and the bones are immersed in the river Cauvery. Pollution caused by death lasts for eleven days. The Kudiya worship their ancestors.

Kuruba

They also show a very low incidence of the sickle cell trait. They are non-vegetarians. Ragi and rice are their staple food. Marriage with one's father's sister's daughter, the mother's brother's daughter and the elder sister's daughter is practised among them. A few cases of marriage by elopement have been reported. The people are monogamous. A marriage pendant (thali) and toe-rings are the marriage symbols for their women. The remarriage of widows, widowers and male or female divorcee is permissible. Among the Jenu Kuruba, post-delivery pollution lasts till the twelfth day. The naming ceremony is observed on the same day. The marriage rituals are performed at the bride's residence and the marriage feast is arranged by the bride's parents. The Jenu Kuruba bury the dead and observe pollution for twelve days. These people celebrate the festivals of Navaratri, Ugadi, Maha Shivrathri and a few others.

Kurumanas

They are non-vegetarians, beef and pork are not eaten. The men consume alcoholic drinks occasionally and purchase the same from the liquor shops. These days the Kuruman eat more pulses and vegetables than they did earlier. Smoking and chewing of betel leaves is common among them. Marriages between cross-cousins is the preferred norm, as also between the maternal uncle and niece. Girl get married after ataining puberty. Marriages are mostly arranged by the parents through negotiation; the village headman is also consulted. Monogamy is the general rule, but instances of polygyny do exist, specially when the first wife has no issue. A marriage pendant (thali) and toe-rings are the marriage symbols for women. Besides the bride price, the payment of dowry has recently been introduced. Women are not allowed to remarry after divorce or after the death of the husbands, while for a widower or a male divorcee, no such restriction exists. Traditionally, the Kuruman reared goats and sheep, but now they have switched over to an agricultural economy.

Maha Malasar

They once used to eat ragi, horse-gram, maize, cassava, wild roots and tubers. Now rice is a major component of their diet. They eat all types of meat except beef and poultry. The men consume alcoholic drinks purchased from the market occasionally. They prefer marriage between cross-cousin. The Maha Malasar girls marry one or two years after they attain puberry. Marriage alliance are generally arranged by the elders through negotiation. Monogamy is the norm among them. The marriage pendant (thali) is the symbols of a married women. Childbirth takes place in a separate hut built for the purpose and pollution is observed for six days. They bury the dead and observed death pollution for three to seven days. Hunting, gathering, trapping of birds and animals and shifting cultivation were the traditional occupations of the Maha Malasar. Now they derive their livelihood by collecting minor forest produce and as non-skilled labourers.

Malaikudi

They are fond of hunting and relish the meat of wild boar, rabbit, fowl, but they do not eat beef. Rice of a coarse variety is their staple food supplemented by tapioca and yam, at some places. Marriage to one's mother's brother's daughter and father's sister's daughter is allowed. Junior sororate is permitted. Adult marriage is the general practice among them. Matrimonial alliances are often settled through negotiation. Monogamy is the usual form of marriage. The marriage ritual of dhare or the pouring of sacred water is performed in the presence of the headman (gurikara) of the community council. The dead are cremated and a pollution period of eleven days is observed. Folk-songs are sung and drums are played on certain occasions. Only the men perform the traditional folk-dance.

Malayekandi

They are non-vegetarians who eat mutton, chicken, egg and fish. They drink alcoholic liquor which they regularly prepare from the mahua flowers. They maintain clan exogamy. The marriage age is sixteen years and above for boys and fourteen years and above for girls. Most of their marriages take place by elopement. The marriage is solemnized at the bride's natal home. Polygyny is allowed but rarely practised. The sacred black bead necklace and the vermilion mark are the marriage symbols for a woman. The amount of bride price to be paid is decided on by the elders and is obligatory in a marriage contract. Remarriage is allowed for both the sexes. After the death of parents, ancestral property is shared equally by the sons. On the seventh day after childbirth they name the child worship their family deity. When a death occurs, the dead body is bathed and worshipped. They are cremated and the community members offer firewood. On the twelfth day, a feast is offered to the fellow members of the community. Agriculture, animal husbandry, wage labour and the gathering of forest produce are the main occupations. Children above ten years take part in agricultural operations.

Maleru

They are non-vegetarians. Eat chicken, mutton, wild boar, and play a variety of game occasionally. Toddy and arrack are the alcoholic drinks consumed occasionally by the men. They prepare their own brew. Endogamy is practised at the group level. Marriage to one's mother's brother's daughter and father's sister's daughter is permitted. Sororate (jouior) is allowed. Adult marriage is the practice. Marriages are settled through negotiation. Monogamy is the usual form of marriage. Widow, widower and male and female divorcee remarriage is allowed. The dead are cremated and a pollution period of eleven days is observed. Income is earned by making baskets, mats, etc. from bamboo.

Marati

Rice is their staple food and gram, tur and urad are the pulses eaten. They rarely eat non-vegetarian food. Coconut oil is the cooking medium. The men drink alcoholic beverage occasionally, which they purchase from the market. They prefer adult marriage and arrange alliance through negotiation. Monogamy is the popular form. Marriage symbols for married Marati women are vermilion, the marriage pendant (thali) and toe-rings. The remarriage of widows, widowers and male and female divorcee is allowed. The dead are buried and death pollution is observed for eleven days. Ugadi, Dasara, Deepavali, Balasantu and Gondhel are the festivals observed by them.

Meda

The Meda are non-vegetarians and eat pork. Their staple food is rice while the commonly used pulse is tur. Men consume distilled liquor and toddy. They smoke beedis and chew betel leaves. Marriage to one's father's sister's daughter or mother's brother's daughter is allowed. Adult marriage is preferred and alliances are contracted through negotiation. Divorce is not permissible, but widows and widowers can remarry. The Meda observe birth, a naming ceremony is observed for a child. The dead are cremated and in some cases burial is also carried out. Death pollution is observed for seven days and on the thirteenth day obsequies are performed. The Meda are primarily basket-makers. The Meda festivals are Huttari and Kail Muhurta. The men sing folk-songs and perform dances. The musical instruments played during song and dance sessions, are percussion and wind types.

Mslasar

They are non-vegetarians, and eat all types of meat except carrion. Their staple food consists of ragi, samai (a kind of millet), maize and locally available roots and tubers. Marriage to one's mother's brother's daughter and the elder sister's daughter is common. Marriages are generally arranged by the elders through negotiation. Monogamy is the norm but polygyny also accurs. Divorce is permitted and widows, widowers and divorcees are allowed to remarry. A pre-delivery ritual is observed during the seventh month of pregnancy. Birth pollution lasts for five or seven days and certain post-natal restrictions are observed. The dead are buried and death pollution lasts for three months. Their traditional occupations include trapping of birds and animals, animal husbandry, and collection of minor forest produce. Now most of them are forest labourers or forest guards and some are tea plantation employees.

Naikda/ Nayaka

They are non-vegetarians and they mostly eat bajra rice, tur and gram. They are monogamous and usually seek alliances through negotiation. Bride price is paid in their marriage. They are patrilocal. The women use anklets, ear-rings and vermilion as the symbols of marriage. A widow can remarry her deceased husband's younger brother after six to twelve months. Certain rites are performed for a newborn baby on the fifth or sixth day after birth and purificatory rites are observed on the eleventh day. Marriage rituals continue for three days. The dead are usually performed on the ninth or tenth day. The primary occupations of the Nayaka are cultivation and agricultural labour. They are also engaged as carpenters while some are employed in timber industries.

Palliyan

They are non-vegetarians, but do not take beef and pork. Their staple food grains are rice and ragi. They consume all kinds of pulses and use groundnut oil and palm oil as cooking media. They also eat tubers, vegetables, fruits, milk and milk products, and drink black tea and black coffee. The men and women of this community consume alcoholic drinks regularly. Marriages between cross-cousin as well as acquired through negotiation or by elopement, and monogamy, but polygyny is also practised. The symbols of marriage for the women are badges and toe-rings. The customs of bride price and dowry exist in the community. In this community, pre-delivery rituals and restrictions, post-delivery pollution and restrictions, naming and tonsure ceremonies for both male and female children and puberty rites for girls are observed. This community of food gatherers has now taken up the vocation of agricultural and plantation labourers.

Paniyan

The women of this community can be identified by their particular way of wearing a saree, which is knows as cela. They are non-vegetarians and eat pork. Rice is their staple food, supplemented with ragi. They prefer to marry after attaining adulthood. Marriage to one's father's sister's daughter and mother's brother's daughter is preferred. Acquiring spouses through negotiation is common, but instances of marriage by service and elopement also exist. They are monogamous and follow both neolocal and patrilocl rules of residence. Marriage symbols for the Paniyan women are badges (thali), red waistbands and nose-rings. Bride price is paid as a custom. Delivery ritual and a period of post-delivery pollution, the ceremonies of naming and the first feeding of cereals are observed for a baby. There are some prescribed rites to be performed on the occasion of a girl attaining puberty. The dead are buried and a period of death pollution is observed. Ancestor worship is apart of their death rites.

Pardhi

They are non-vegetarians but do not eat beef. Alcoholic drinks like the country made gavti are consumed regularly. They marry at an early age. The custom of paying bride price is prevalent in this community. Consanguineous marriages are in vogue, including those between the maternal uncle and niece. Marriages are preferably arranged through negotiation. Divorce is allowed and the remarriage of divorcees and widowed persons is permitted. They bury the dead, keep some food on the grave on the second day, and observe a death rite on the twelfth day. Their traditional occupation is the hunting of animals and birds. Some of them are landowning agriculturists, but at the time of drought they switch over to their traditional occupation.

Patelia

They are non-vegetarians, and their staple cereals are maize and wheat. They brew liquor from mahua (Bassia laitifolia) in rural areas. They are monogamous and prefer adult marriage. Spouses are often acquired through negotiation. The symbols of marriage for the Patelia women are necklaces, toe-rings and a dot on the forehead. Bride price is paid by these people. The post-birth purificatory rites of chhatti is celebrated on the sixth day after birth. Another ritual, kuwa poojan, is held on the fortieth day. The tonsure ceremony is performed only for the first son. The dead are cremated and the bones are disposed off in the river. As part of the death rites, feasts are arranged by the bereaved family on the eleventh and twelfth day after death.

Rathawa

They are non-vegetarians, and eat meat, fish, poultry and eggs. The major part of their diet consists of home-made bread prepared of maize and wheat, and various pulses and vegetables. The girls and boys marry when they are between twelve and twenty years and twenty and twenty-fours years, respectively. The marriage alliances are usually negotiated by the parents. Monogamy is the common practice. Vermilion is the symbol of the married Rathawa women. Bride price is paid by these people. Widow, widower and divorcee remarriage is permissible. In this community, birth pollution is observed for forty or forty-five days. The dead are cremated, and certain death rites are observed on the eleventh, twelfth and thirteen day after the cremation.

Sholaga

They are non-vegetarians who take pork. Ragi is their staple food. women of this community play an important role in agricultural operations, animal husbandry, fishing and some other spheres. Basket making are their traditional as well as present day occupations.

Soligaru

They are non-vegetarians, and eat mainly tubers. Kulthi and beans are the pulses used, while groundnut and nigar seed oil are used for cooking. They consume only non-alcoholic beverages like milk, coffee and tea and smoke beedis and wild Indian hamp. They also chew betel leaves. Endogamy is practised by them at group level and exogamy at clan level. Marriage to one's mother's brother's daughter and father's sister's daughter is preferred. They practise adult marriage and generally arrange alliance through negotiation. Some cases of marriage by elopement have also taken place. The symbols of a married women are a pendant and toe-rings. The remarriage of widowes, widowers and divorcees is permitted. A widower is allowed to marry his deceased wife's younger sister. The traditional occupations of Soliga were shifting cultivation and the collection of minor forest produce. Now they have taken to forest and agricultural labour.

Toda

They are vegetarians. Their consumption of fruits and vegetables is moderate; roots and tubers are also eaten. The Toda men regularly consume alcoholic drinks. Endogamy and exogamy are practiced at both patri and matriclan levels. Marriage to one's mother's brother's or father's sister's daughter is preferred. Monogamy is an ideal norm. Polygynous unions are in existence, but adelphic polyandry has reportedly diet out. Mates are usually acquired through negotiation, otherwise marriage by elopement is permissible, but marriage by capture is no longer practised. Bride price is paid both in cash and kind. The Toda women take part in agricultural operations, tend cattle, collect fuel and fetch portable water. The Toda funeral rites are rather elaborate. The first of these rites is observed at the time of cremation, and the second one, now rarely observed, is performed at the time of cremating a relic of the deceased. At the time of these funeral rites, buffalo sacrifice is obligatory.

Varli

They are non-vegetarians but avoid beef and pork. Their staple food is rice, supplemented with jawar and wheat. Milk consumption is negligible. They are fond of alcoholic drinks prepared from molasses and of the kind available at local shops as well. The Varli practise polygyny occasionally. The first marriage is called lagan and the second and subsequent marriages are called nowli. Necklaces and toe-rings are the symbols of marriage for women. Bride price, is paid both in cash and kind. A divorced person may remarry. The marriage is solemnized at the bride's natal house. The dead are cremated, but infants are buried.

Vitolia etc

They are non-vegetarians, The men consume alcoholic drinks occasionally and purchase the same from the liquor shops. These days the Vitolia eat more pulses and vegetables than they did earlier. Smoking and chewing of betel leaves is common among them. Marriages between cross-cousins is the preferred norm, as also between the maternal uncle and niece. Girl get married after ataining puberty. Marriages are mostly arranged by the parents through negotiation; the village headman is also consulted. Monogamy is the general rule, but instances of polygyny do exist, specially when the first wife has no issue. A marriage pendant (thali) and toe-rings are the marriage symbols for women. Besides the bride price, the payment of dowry has recently been introduced. Women are not allowed to remarry after divorce or after the death of the husbands, while for a widower or a male divorcee, no such restriction exists. Traditionally, the Vitolia reared goats and sheep, but now they have switched over to an agricultural economy.

Yerava

They are non-vegetarians and eat pork, mutton, fish, and chicken. Jowar, rice and ragi are their staple cereals. They eat roots and tubers. Both their men and women consume alcoholic drinks regularly. Marriage to the father's sister's daughter or mother's brother's daughter is preferred by them. Monogamy is the common form of marriage. Widows, widowers, and male and female divorcee are allowed to remarry. The naming ceremony of a child is held on the fifth day after birth. The dead are buried and death pollution is observed. Ancestor worship is a part of their death rites.

Statewise Distribution of Individual Scheduled Tribes Population by Sex and Literacy Rate

Tribe		*Population (Nos.)*	*Male (Nos.)*	*Female (Nos.)*	*Literacy Rate (%)*
All Scheduled	Total	3463986	1756238	1707748	48.27
Tribes	Rural	2934530	1486073	1448457	45.26
	Urban	529456	270165	259291	64.57
Adiyan	Total	295	157	138	71.71
	Rural	72	43	29	63.33
	Urban	223	114	109	74.24
Barda	Total	149	81	68	62.40
	Rural	38	17	21	22.22
	Urban	111	64	47	73.47
Bavacha etc.	Total	454	219	235	68.85
	Rural	328	150	178	63.53
	Urban	126	69	57	81.03
Bhil etc.	Total	1633	869	764	44.40
	Rural	1098	586	512	29.56
	Urban	535	283	252	72.53
Chenchu etc.	Total	497	230	267	24.06
	Rural	465	213	252	20.86
	Urban	32	17	15	72.00
Chodhara	Total	359	206	153	67.09
	Rural	196	118	78	56.50
	Urban	163	88	75	80.58
Dubla etc.	Total	384	207	177	49.10
	Rural	214	111	103	29.57
	Urban	170	96	74	73.97
Gamit etc.	Total	288	157	131	75.00
	Rural	84	43	41	56.58
	Urban	204	114	90	83.14
Gond etc.	Total	136700	70123	66577	51.45
	Rural	125306	64151	61155	49.77
	Urban	11394	5972	5422	69.68
Gowdalu	Total	12507	6347	6160	66.06
	Rural	7780	3906	3874	62.73
	Urban	4727	2441	2286	71.58
Hakkipikki	Total	8414	4272	4142	24.55
	Rural	7362	3753	3609	24.74
	Urban	1052	519	533	23.17
Hasalaru	Total	20820	10237	10583	53.62
	Rural	20330	10006	10324	52.94
	Urban	490	231	259	79.78
Irular	Total	819	415	404	38.28
	Rural	692	345	347	32.28
	Urban	127	70	57	71.15
Iruliga	Total	8486	4392	4094	32.86
	Rural	8038	4157	3881	30.59
	Urban	448	235	213	71.43
Jenu Kuruba	Total	29828	15133	14695	40.83
	Rural	27226	13784	13442	37.34
	Urban	2602	1349	1253	75.55
Kadu Kuruba	Total	17112	8810	8302	53.38
	Rural	9725	4937	4788	35.90
Kammara	Total	38	20	18	61.29
	Rural	31	13	18	66.67
	Urban	7	7	0	42.86
Kaniyan etc.	Total	271	139	132	70.95
	Rural	77	42	35	78.26
	Urban	194	97	97	68.02
Kathodi etc.	Total	477	251	226	62.78
	Rural	184	105	79	57.86
	Urban	293	146	147	66.10
Kattunayakan	Total	144	70	74	76.69
	Rural	15	8	7	23.08
	Urban	129	62	67	82.50
Kokna etc.	Total	3182	1449	1733	85.26
	Rural	2463	1119	1344	84.08
	Urban	719	330	389	89.38

Tribe		Population (Nos.)	Male (Nos.)	Female (Nos.)	Literacy Rate (%)
Koli Dhor etc.	Total	80627	41465	39162	46.46
	Rural	74335	38182	36153	44.53
	Urban	6292	3283	3009	68.51
Konda Kapus	Total	279	145	134	68.75
	Rural	128	66	62	55.45
	Urban	151	79	72	80.00
Koraga	Total	16071	7951	8120	59.81
	Rural	11776	5862	5914	54.57
	Urban	4295	2089	2206	73.93
Kota	Total	221	113	108	72.25
	Rural	129	66	63	62.73
	Urban	92	47	45	85.19
Koya etc.	Total	1640	826	814	49.85
	Rural	1516	770	746	49.20
	Urban	124	56	68	57.84
Kudiya etc.	Total	2733	1342	1391	70.97
	Rural	2456	1212	1244	70.09
	Urban	277	130	147	78.84
Kuruba	Total	2540	1306	1234	39.57
	Rural	2399	1222	1177	37.98
	Urban	141	84	57	64.62
Kurumans	Total	798	405	393	65.36
	Rural	371	185	186	55.56
	Urban	427	220	207	74.04
Maha Malasar	Total	13	8	5	84.62
	Rural	6	3	3	66.67
	Urban	7	5	2	100.00
Malaikudi	Total	7979	3993	3986	71.51
	Rural	7861	3931	3930	71.30
	Urban	118	62	56	85.71
Malasar	Total	103	52	51	71.43
	Rural	69	35	34	75.81
	Urban	34	17	17	62.07
Malayekandi	Total	144	71	73	69.57
	Rural	114	59	55	64.29
	Urban	30	12	18	92.31
Maleru	Total	1360	679	681	85.13
	Rural	964	471	493	82.41
	Urban	396	208	188	91.67

Tribe		Population (Nos.)	Male (Nos.)	Female (Nos.)	Literacy Rate (%)
Maratha	Total	2657	1294	1363	74.85
	Rural	2471	1204	1267	73.37
	Urban	186	90	96	94.05
Marati	Total	63549	31567	31982	73.93
	Rural	57720	28653	29067	72.87
	Urban	5829	2914	2915	84.25
Meda	Total	37371	18778	18593	66.26
	Rural	14510	7323	7187	58.03
	Urban	22861	11455	11406	71.49
Naikda etc.	Total	2918649	1479569	1439080	47.25
	Rural	2484275	1258013	1226262	44.44
	Urban	434374	221556	212818	62.92
Palliyan	Total	536	266	270	66.60
	Rural	249	123	126	58.90
	Urban	287	143	144	73.39
Paniyan	Total	724	381	343	33.94
	Rural	680	357	323	31.44
	Urban	44	24	20	71.05
Pardhi etc.	Total	5403	2733	2670	29.74
	Rural	2752	1412	1340	21.98
	Urban	2651	1321	1330	37.47
Patelia	Total	193	107	86	79.75
	Rural	62	42	20	86.27
	Urban	131	65	66	76.79
Rathawa	Total	41	26	15	47.50
	Rural	21	13	8	35.00
	Urban	20	13	7	60.00
Sholaga	Total	124	65	59	46.36
	Rural	114	60	54	42.00
	Urban	10	5	5	90.00
Soligaru	Total	29908	15144	14764	38.70
	Rural	27502	13892	13610	35.87
	Urban	2406	1252	1154	70.02
Toda	Total	55	32	23	51.06
	Rural	24	14	10	45.00
	Urban	31	18	13	55.56
Varli	Total	85	43	42	78.95
	Rural	40	19	21	61.11
	Urban	45	24	21	95.00

State/District		Population (Nos.)	Male (Nos.)	Female	Rate (%)
Vitolia etc.	Total	154	78	76	65.41
	Rural	91	45	46	42.86
	Urban	63	33	30	96.43
Yerava	Total	21948	10971	10977	29.11
	Rural	21311	10658	10653	27.77
	Urban	637	313	324	71.05
Generic Tribes	Total	25224	13044	12180	65.35
	Rural	8860	4574	4286	46.94
	Urban	16364	8470	7894	75.16

Distribution of Individual Scheduled Tribes Population by Sex (State)

State/District	Population (Nos.)	Male (Nos.)	Female Rate (%)
KARNATAKA	**3,463,986**	**1,756,238**	**1,707,748**
Belgaum	243,451	122,979	120,472
Bagalkot *	80,181	40,171	40,010
Bijapur	30,051	15,455	14,596
Gulbarga	154,195	77,926	76,269
Bidar	182,219	93,455	88,764
Raichur	303,042	152,080	150,962
Koppal *	138,588	70,063	68,525
Gadag *	54,410	27,739	26,671
Dharwad	70,442	36,234	34,208
Uttara Kannada	23,781	11,978	11,803
Haveri *	127,163	65,498	61,665
Bellary	364,638	183,662	180,976
Chitradurga	266,235	136,194	130,041
Davanagere*	209,701	106,932	102,769
Shimoga	55,997	28,435	27,562
Udupi *	41,613	20,572	21,041
Chikmagalur	41,019	20,570	20,449
Tumkur	193,819	98,795	95,024
Kolar	205,711	104,278	101,433
Bangalore	86,018	44,971	41,047
Bangalore Rural	61,555	31,537	30,018
Mandya	17,193	8,693	8,500
Hassan	26,451	13,297	13,154
Dakshina Kannada	62,936	31,579	31,357
Kodagu	46,115	23,109	23,006
Mysore	271,351	136,831	134,520
Chamarajanagar*	106,111	53,205	52,906
Adiyan			
Karnataka	**295**	**157**	**138**
Belgaum	4	1	3
Gulbarga	4	2	2
Dharwad	5	2	3
Uttara Kannada	3	1	2
Shimoga	24	13	11
Chikmagalur	2	1	1
Kolar	17	6	11
Bangalore	175	93	82
Mandya	5	3	2
Hassan	16	7	9
Dakshina Kannada	9	7	2
Kodagu	24	16	8
Mysore	7	5	2
Barda			
Karnataka	**149**	**81**	**68**
Belgaum	12	7	5
Bagalkot *	3	1	2
Gulbarga	34	19	15
Raichur	19	12	7
Dharwad	1	1	-
Uttara Kannada	13	4	9
Bellary	1	1	-
Shimoga	13	5	8
Tumkur	1	1	-
Bangalore	27	17	10
Hassan	3	2	1
Dakshina Kannada	2	2	-
Kodagu	16	7	9
Mysore	4	2	2

State/District	Population (Nos.)	Male (Nos.)	Female Rate (%)
Bavacha etc.			
Karnataka	**454**	**219**	**235**
Belgaum	19	10	9
Bagalkot *	4	1	3
Raichur	5	3	2
Koppal *	1	-	1
Dharwad	5	3	2
Uttara Kannada	16	6	10
Bellary	1	1	-
Davanagere*	51	29	22
Shimoga	1	1	-
Chikmagalur	15	8	7
Tumkur	7	5	2
Bangalore	55	33	22
Bangalore Rural	258	111	147
Mandya	14	8	6
Hassan	2	-	2
Bhil etc.			
Karnataka	**1,633**	**869**	**764**
Belgaum	86	43	43
Bagalkot *	157	78	79
Bijapur	26	13	13
Gulbarga	27	17	10
Bidar	17	10	7
Raichur	15	12	3
Koppal *	16	10	6
Gadag *	12	7	5
Dharwad	17	8	9
Uttara Kannada	120	67	53
Haveri *	65	31	34
Bellary	31	18	13
Davanagere*	23	10	13
Shimoga	5	3	2
Udupi *	1	1	-
Chikmagalur	34	18	16
Tumkur	1	1	-
Kolar	25	11	14
Bangalore	169	91	78
Bangalore Rural	5	3	2

State/District	Population (Nos.)	Male (Nos.)	Female Rate (%)
Hassan	8	6	2
Kodagu	56	25	31
Mysore	656	351	305
Chamarajanagar*	61	35	26
Chenchu etc.			
Karnataka	**497**	**230**	**267**
Belgaum	2	2	-
Bijapur	33	17	16
Gulbarga	312	144	168
Raichur	9	3	6
Koppal *	7	1	6
Gadag *	3	1	2
Uttara Kannada	79	35	44
Chitradurga	2	-	2
Davanagere*	2	1	1
Shimoga	20	9	11
Udupi *	8	4	4
Chikmagalur	5	4	1
Tumkur	4	2	2
Kolar	6	3	3
Bangalore	5	4	1
Chodhara			
Karnataka	**359**	**206**	**153**
Belgaum	18	10	8
Bagalkot *	15	6	9
Bijapur	10	5	5
Gulbarga	18	12	6
Bidar	44	26	18
Raichur	51	27	24
Koppal *	22	10	12
Gadag *	13	6	7
Dharwad	19	11	8
Uttara Kannada	41	21	20
Haveri *	10	4	6
Bellary	4	1	3
Davanagere*	15	7	8
Shimoga	1	1	-
Tumkur	35	35	-
Bangalore	25	16	9
Mysore	18	8	10

State/District	Population (Nos.)	Male (Nos.)	Female Rate (%)
Dubla etc.			
Karnataka	**384**	**207**	**177**
Belgaum	21	11	10
Bagalkot *	19	9	10
Bijapur	36	20	16
Gulbarga	40	22	18
Bidar	4	3	1
Koppal *	13	8	5
Gadag *	33	17	16
Dharwad	58	31	27
Uttara Kannada	4	2	2
Haveri *	4	2	2
Bellary	8	4	4
Chitradurga	1	1	-
Davanagere*	62	36	26
Shimoga	19	11	8
Udupi *	4	2	2
Chikmagalur	7	3	4
Tumkur	3	-	3
Kolar	10	2	8
Bangalore	34	21	13
Bangalore Rural	4	2	2
Gamit etc.			
Karnataka	**288**	**157**	**131**
Belgaum	4	2	2
Bijapur	1	-	1
Gulbarga	31	13	18
Bidar	14	6	8
Koppal *	1	1	-
Gadag *	5	2	3
Dharwad	11	5	6
Uttara Kannada	8	2	6
Bellary	1	1	-
Shimoga	1	-	1
Chikmagalur	5	3	2
Kolar	1	-	1
Bangalore	184	112	72
Bangalore Rural	2	2	-
Hassan	2	1	1
Dakshina Kannada	7	3	4

State/District	Population (Nos.)	Male (Nos.)	Female Rate (%)
Kodagu	5	2	3
Mysore	5	2	3
Generic Tribes etc.			
Karnataka	**25,224**	**13,044**	**12,180**
Belgaum	255	125	130
Bagalkot *	111	79	32
Bijapur	144	77	67
Gulbarga	1,196	627	569
Bidar	2,346	1,180	1,166
Raichur	302	170	132
Koppal *	289	152	137
Gadag *	81	40	41
Dharwad	378	192	186
Uttara Kannada	80	53	27
Haveri *	98	56	42
Bellary	957	477	480
Chitradurga	89	48	41
Davanagere*	380	199	181
Shimoga	122	65	57
Udupi *	334	179	155
Chikmagalur	570	295	275
Tumkur	309	163	146
Kolar	1,016	515	501
Bangalore	12,473	6,432	6,041
Bangalore Rural	521	261	260
Mandya	507	261	246
Hassan	507	253	254
Dakshina Kannada	363	184	179
Kodagu	390	197	193
Mysore	824	447	377
Chamarajanagar*	582	317	265
Gond etc.			
Karnataka	**136,700**	**70,123**	**66,577**
Belgaum	30	16	14
Bagalkot *	22	13	9
Bijapur	20	14	6
Gulbarga	12,250	6,295	5,955
Bidar	111,858	57,443	54,415
Raichur	225	108	117
Koppal *	43	26	17

State/District	Population (Nos.)	Male (Nos.)	Female Rate (%)
Gadag *	9	6	3
Dharwad	174	85	89
Uttara Kannada	8,437	4,238	4,199
Haveri *	11	5	6
Bellary	63	35	28
Chitradurga	1	1	-
Davanagere*	375	182	193
Shimoga	471	230	241
Udupi *	371	196	175
Chikmagalur	115	55	60
Tumkur	15	7	8
Kolar	55	25	30
Bangalore	1,555	824	731
Bangalore Rural	9	4	5
Mandya	5	2	3
Hassan	224	118	106
Dakshina Kannada	115	66	49
Kodagu	45	26	19
Mysore	198	101	97
Chamarajanagar*	4	2	2
Gowdalu			
Karnataka	**12,507**	**6,347**	**6,160**
Belgaum	11	7	4
Bagalkot *	2	1	1
Bijapur	17	8	9
Gulbarga	17	9	8
Bidar	59	28	31
Raichur	12	7	5
Koppal *	4	3	1
Dharwad	1	1	-
Uttara Kannada	23	14	9
Bellary	64	33	31
Chitradurga	9	5	4
Davanagere*	13	8	5
Shimoga	136	65	71
Udupi *	58	29	29
Chikmagalur	7,067	3,520	3,547
Tumkur	11	6	5
Kolar	53	33	20
Bangalore	4,641	2,402	2,239
Bangalore Rural	30	19	11
Mandya	43	21	22
Hassan	26	15	11
Dakshina Kannada	65	36	29
Kodagu	46	28	18
Mysore	37	17	20
Chamarajanagar*	62	32	30
Hakkipikki			
Karnataka	**8,414**	**4,272**	**4,142**
Belgaum	19	8	11
Bagalkot *	9	5	4
Bidar	16	8	8
Dharwad	11	7	4
Uttara Kannada	40	21	19
Bellary	519	255	264
Davanagere*	691	337	354
Shimoga	898	443	455
Chikmagalur	216	115	101
Tumkur	513	286	227
Kolar	1,089	561	528
Bangalore	579	289	290
Bangalore Rural	900	452	448
Mandya	853	425	428
Hassan	799	413	386
Dakshina Kannada	47	27	20
Kodagu	25	14	11
Mysore	1,096	558	538
Chamarajanagar*	94	48	46
Hasalaru			
Karnataka	**20,820**	**10,237**	**10,583**
Belgaum	1	1	-
Bagalkot *	1	1	-
Bijapur	4	1	3
Gulbarga	23	12	11
Bidar	3	2	1
Raichur	1	-	1
Uttara Kannada	1,022	493	529
Davanagere*	5	2	3
Shimoga	6,754	3,378	3,376

State/District	Population (Nos.)	Male (Nos.)	Female Rate (%)
Udupi *	149	72	77
Chikmagalur	11,949	5,842	6,107
Bangalore	66	35	31
Bangalore Rural	2	-	2
Hassan	775	359	416
Dakshina Kannada	65	39	26
Irular			
Karnataka	**819**	**415**	**404**
Belgaum	1	-	1
Bijapur	1	-	1
Gulbarga	20	12	8
Bidar	22	6	16
Raichur	23	9	14
Gadag *	6	3	3
Dharwad	10	6	4
Uttara Kannada	12	6	6
Shimoga	38	16	22
Chikmagalur	10	4	6
Kolar	32	15	17
Bangalore	244	127	117
Bangalore Rural	356	181	175
Mandya	8	5	3
Hassan	27	20	7
Kodagu	3	2	1
Mysore	2	1	1
Chamarajanagar*	4	2	2
Iruliga			
Karnataka	**8,486**	**4,392**	**4,094**
Belgaum	84	44	40
Bagalkot *	30	15	15
Bijapur	11	3	8
Gulbarga	376	189	187
Bidar	175	90	85
Raichur	86	34	52
Koppal *	144	66	78
Gadag *	32	19	13
Dharwad	56	29	27
Uttara Kannada	10	2	8
Haveri *	81	40	41
Bellary	13	5	8

State/District	Population (Nos.)	Male (Nos.)	Female Rate (%)
Davanagere*	4	1	3
Shimoga	12	10	2
Udupi *	6	3	3
Chikmagalur	4	2	2
Tumkur	206	103	103
Kolar	86	43	43
Bangalore	1,389	738	651
Bangalore Rural	5,645	2,939	2,706
Mandya	14	7	7
Hassan	14	5	9
Kodagu	3	1	2
Mysore	5	4	1
Jenu Kuruba			
Karnataka	**29,828**	**15,133**	**14,695**
Belgaum	68	34	34
Bagalkot *	70	34	36
Bijapur	21	16	5
Gulbarga	73	39	34
Bidar	6	2	4
Raichur	109	59	50
Gadag *	28	15	13
Dharwad	58	31	27
Uttara Kannada	124	62	62
Haveri *	4	3	1
Bellary	27	14	13
Chitradurga	6	3	3
Davanagere*	94	47	47
Shimoga	199	102	97
Udupi *	84	51	33
Chikmagalur	30	15	15
Tumkur	50	30	20
Kolar	75	35	40
Bangalore	1,822	943	879
Bangalore Rural	123	66	57
Mandya	59	31	28
Hassan	58	34	24
Dakshina Kannada	64	39	25
Kodagu	10,037	5,088	4,949
Mysore	15,759	7,947	7,812
Chamarajanagar*	780	393	387

State/District	Population (Nos.)	Male (Nos.)	Female Rate (%)
Kadu Kuruba			
Karnataka	**17,112**	**8,810**	**8,302**
Belgaum	638	315	323
Bagalkot *	74	38	36
Bijapur	1,787	917	870
Gulbarga	4,134	2,126	2,008
Bidar	14	5	9
Raichur	275	143	132
Koppal *	57	27	30
Gadag *	109	45	64
Dharwad	1,117	575	542
Uttara Kannada	437	237	200
Haveri *	217	105	112
Bellary	182	100	82
Chitradurga	14	8	6
Davanagere*	131	61	70
Shimoga	383	195	188
Udupi *	79	43	36
Chikmagalur	89	48	41
Tumkur	160	82	78
Kolar	195	106	89
Bangalore	4,191	2,195	1,996
Bangalore Rural	416	208	208
Mandya	160	75	85
Hassan	52	25	27
Dakshina Kannada	74	52	22
Kodagu	472	233	239
Mysore	1,378	698	680
Chamarajanagar*	277	148	129
Kammara			
Karnataka	**38**	**20**	**18**
Dakshina Kannada	38	20	18
Kaniyan etc.			
Karnataka	**271**	**139**	**132**
Chamarajanagar*	271	139	132
Kathodi etc.			
Karnataka	**477**	**251**	**226**
Belgaum	64	36	28
Bijapur	13	5	8
Gulbarga	28	15	13
Bidar	8	2	6
Raichur	66	35	31
Koppal *	1	1	-
Dharwad	107	50	57
Uttara Kannada	11	11	-
Bellary	39	22	17
Davanagere*	35	19	16
Chikmagalur	2	1	1
Bangalore	74	38	36
Bangalore Rural	5	1	4
Dakshina Kannada	12	10	2
Mysore	12	5	7
Kattunayakan			
Karnataka	**144**	**70**	**74**
Shimoga	9	3	6
Kolar	36	18	18
Bangalore	93	44	49
Mysore	6	5	1
Kokna etc.			
Karnataka	**3,182**	**1,449**	**1,733**
Belgaum	40	17	23
Bagalkot *	4	3	1
Bijapur	3	1	2
Gulbarga	6	3	3
Bidar	43	19	24
Dharwad	11	4	7
Uttara Kannada	3,006	1,370	1,636
Udupi *	27	13	14
Tumkur	4	3	1
Bangalore	26	10	16
Hassan	4	1	3
Dakshina Kannada	8	5	3
Koli Dhor etc.			
Karnataka	**80,627**	**41,465**	**39,162**
Belgaum	2,596	1,326	1,270
Bagalkot *	2,609	1,304	1,305
Bijapur	6,951	3,583	3,368
Gulbarga	8,808	4,581	4,227

State/District	Population (Nos.)	Male (Nos.)	Female Rate (%)
Bidar	58,970	30,299	28,671
Raichur	45	23	22
Koppal *	79	45	34
Gadag *	83	44	39
Dharwad	226	123	103
Uttara Kannada	28	16	12
Haveri *	77	41	36
Bellary	1	1	-
Chitradurga	7	4	3
Davanagere*	18	8	10
Shimoga	5	3	2
Udupi *	1	-	1
Chikmagalur	20	9	11
Tumkur	7	3	4
Kolar	10	5	5
Bangalore	73	41	32
Bangalore Rural	9	5	4
Dakshina Kannada	2	1	1
Kodagu	1	-	1
Mysore	1	-	1
Konda Kapus			
Karnataka	**279**	**145**	**134**
Gulbarga	5	2	3
Bidar	4	2	2
Raichur	33	19	14
Dharwad	17	12	5
Bellary	23	10	13
Davanagere*	76	38	38
Shimoga	4	3	1
Bangalore	105	53	52
Chamarajanagar*	12	6	6
Koraga			
Karnataka	**16,071**	**7,951**	**8,120**
Belgaum	77	39	38
Bagalkot *	85	45	40
Bijapur	28	17	11
Gulbarga	75	39	36
Bidar	13	4	9
Raichur	49	20	29

State/District	Population (Nos.)	Male (Nos.)	Female Rate (%)
Gadag *	7	3	4
Dharwad	101	54	47
Uttara Kannada	361	181	180
Haveri *	799	415	384
Bellary	15	7	8
Davanagere*	3	2	1
Shimoga	354	170	184
Udupi *	8,966	4,400	4,566
Chikmagalur	175	92	83
Tumkur	2	-	2
Kolar	5	4	1
Bangalore	307	159	148
Bangalore Rural	32	14	18
Mandya	8	5	3
Hassan	12	6	6
Dakshina Kannada	4,542	2,252	2,290
Kodagu	48	20	28
Mysore	7	3	4
Kota			
Karnataka	**221**	**113**	**108**
Gadag *	40	20	20
Dharwad	8	5	3
Uttara Kannada	46	21	25
Haveri *	11	5	6
Shimoga	10	4	6
Udupi *	2	2	-
Kolar	28	14	14
Bangalore	14	7	7
Dakshina Kannada	47	26	21
Kodagu	4	2	2
Mysore	11	7	4
Koya etc.			
Karnataka	**1,640**	**826**	**814**
Gulbarga	980	500	480
Bidar	467	231	236
Raichur	19	11	8
Bellary	5	2	3
Davanagere*	62	33	29
Bangalore	98	44	54

State/District	Population (Nos.)	Male (Nos.)	Female Rate (%)
Mandya	2	1	1
Kodagu	7	4	3
Kudiya etc.			
Karnataka	**2,733**	**1,342**	**1,391**
Belgaum	8	5	3
Bagalkot *	9	4	5
Dharwad	11	7	4
Uttara Kannada	7	5	2
Bellary	8	4	4
Shimoga	7	5	2
Udupi *	22	13	9
Chikmagalur	35	19	16
Bangalore	114	53	61
Bangalore Rural	16	4	12
Mandya	1	1	-
Dakshina Kannada	547	273	274
Kodagu	1,946	948	998
Chamarajanagar*	2	1	1
Kuruba			
Karnataka	**2,540**	**1,306**	**1,234**
Kodagu	2,540	1,306	1,234
Kurumans			
Karnataka	**798**	**405**	**393**
Belgaum	3	1	2
Bagalkot *	48	19	29
Bijapur	13	6	7
Gulbarga	13	6	7
Raichur	2	1	1
Koppal *	8	4	4
Dharwad	6	4	2
Haveri *	15	9	6
Davanagere*	5	2	3
Shimoga	120	59	61
Udupi *	13	9	4
Chikmagalur	59	28	31
Kolar	7	3	4
Bangalore	274	146	128
Bangalore Rural	95	46	49
Dakshina Kannada	63	34	29
Kodagu	4	3	1
Mysore	50	25	25
Maha Malasar			
Karnataka	**13**	**8**	**5**
Belgaum	8	4	4
Chitradurga	5	4	1
Malaikudi			
Karnataka	**7,979**	**3,993**	**3,986**
Belgaum	4	2	2
Bijapur	5	3	2
Dharwad	6	1	5
Haveri *	1	-	1
Shimoga	11	6	5
Udupi *	1,508	748	760
Chikmagalur	457	232	225
Bangalore	41	21	20
Hassan	18	11	7
Dakshina Kannada	5,854	2,930	2,924
Kodagu	58	31	27
Mysore	3	2	1
Chamarajanagar*	13	6	7
Malasar			
Karnataka	**103**	**52**	**51**
Belgaum	5	3	2
Raichur	12	8	4
Uttara Kannada	65	32	33
Bellary	3	1	2
Udupi *	1	-	1
Bangalore	17	8	9
Malayekandi			
Karnataka	**144**	**71**	**73**
Belgaum	8	2	6
Bangalore	22	10	12
Dakshina Kannada	113	58	55
Kodagu	1	1	-
Maleru			
Karnataka	**1,360**	**679**	**681**
Gulbarga	10	6	4
Raichur	6	3	3

State/District	Population (Nos.)	Male (Nos.)	Female Rate (%)
Koppal *	6	2	4
Gadag *	3	1	2
Bellary	2	-	2
Shimoga	254	129	125
Udupi *	6	2	4
Chikmagalur	565	285	280
Tumkur	6	3	3
Kolar	4	3	1
Bangalore	232	119	113
Bangalore Rural	10	6	4
Mandya	4	1	3
Hassan	35	14	21
Dakshina Kannada	93	48	45
Kodagu	116	51	65
Mysore	8	6	2
Maratha			
Karnataka	**2,657**	**1,294**	**1,363**
Kodagu	2,657	1,294	1,363
Marati			
Karnataka	**63,549**	**31,567**	**31,982**
Udupi *	27,245	13,455	13,790
Dakshina Kannada	36,304	18,112	18,192
Meda			
Karnataka	**37,371**	**18,778**	**18,593**
Belgaum	1,885	923	962
Bagalkot *	344	174	170
Bijapur	81	42	39
Gulbarga	3,534	1,750	1,784
Bidar	447	230	217
Raichur	885	448	437
Koppal *	245	114	131
Gadag *	313	142	171
Dharwad	1,942	970	972
Uttara Kannada	333	158	175
Haveri *	923	471	452
Bellary	1,764	890	874
Chitradurga	912	448	464
Davanagere*	2,418	1,233	1,185
Shimoga	3,159	1,612	1,547

State/District	Population (Nos.)	Male (Nos.)	Female Rate (%)
Udupi *	81	38	43
Chikmagalur	1,753	903	850
Tumkur	1,131	545	586
Kolar	1,582	773	809
Bangalore	1,655	839	816
Bangalore Rural	2,691	1,374	1,317
Mandya	2,155	1,079	1,076
Hassan	1,798	926	872
Dakshina Kannada	286	133	153
Kodagu	803	401	402
Mysore	3,349	1,694	1,655
Chamarajanagar*	902	468	434
Naikda etc.			
Karnataka	2,918,649	1,479,569	1,439,080
Belgaum	237,340	119,915	117,425
Bagalkot *	75,158	37,635	37,523
Bijapur	20,173	10,378	9,795
Gulbarga	121,270	61,009	60,261
Bidar	7,333	3,688	3,645
Raichur	300,690	150,874	149,816
Koppal *	137,647	69,590	68,057
Gadag *	53,303	27,202	26,101
Dharwad	64,102	32,992	31,110
Uttara Kannada	9,424	4,901	4,523
Haveri *	124,843	64,310	60,533
Bellary	360,852	181,751	179,101
Chitradurga	265,188	135,671	129,517
Davanagere*	205,219	104,667	100,552
Shimoga	42,848	21,835	21,013
Udupi *	2,633	1,305	1,328
Chikmagalur	17,797	9,051	8,746
Tumkur	190,570	97,136	93,434
Kolar	200,457	101,620	98,837
Bangalore	53,240	27,996	25,244
Bangalore Rural	49,093	25,146	23,947
Mandya	11,246	5,704	5,542
Hassan	21,430	10,759	10,671
Dakshina Kannada	14,104	7,171	6,933
Kodagu	5,671	2,841	2,830

State/District	Population (Nos.)	Male (Nos.)	Female Rate (%)
Mysore	240,130	120,958	119,172
Chamarajanagar*	86,888	43,464	43,424
Palliyan			
Karnataka	**536**	**266**	**270**
Raichur	4	2	2
Gadag *	2	1	1
Dharwad	2	2	-
Uttara Kannada	8	3	5
Shimoga	17	8	9
Chikmagalur	15	6	9
Kolar	115	58	57
Bangalore	224	115	109
Bangalore Rural	2	1	1
Mandya	18	10	8
Hassan	12	6	6
Dakshina Kannada	55	24	31
Kodagu	53	24	29
Mysore	9	6	3
Paniyan			
Karnataka	**724**	**381**	**343**
Belgaum	1	1	-
Dharwad	3	2	1
Shimoga	6	4	2
Chikmagalur	12	6	6
Kolar	1	1	-
Bangalore	43	24	19
Mandya	18	11	7
Hassan	31	17	14
Dakshina Kannada	19	8	11
Kodagu	500	263	237
Mysore	90	44	46
Pardhi etc.			
Karnataka	**5,403**	**2,733**	**2,670**
Belgaum	85	41	44
Bagalkot *	1,400	700	700
Bijapur	659	321	338
Gulbarga	807	417	390
Bidar	240	115	125
Gadag *	311	155	156
Dharwad	1,795	929	866
Uttara Kannada	5	4	1
Shimoga	1	-	1
Kolar	6	3	3
Bangalore	94	48	46
Patelia			
Karnataka	**193**	**107**	**86**
Bagalkot *	4	3	1
Gulbarga	19	12	7
Bidar	3	2	1
Raichur	6	3	3
Gadag *	5	4	1
Dharwad	41	17	24
Bellary	1	1	-
Davanagere*	2	1	1
Kolar	7	4	3
Bangalore	81	42	39
Bangalore Rural	2	2	-
Hassan	7	6	1
Kodagu	15	10	5
Rathawa			
Karnataka	**41**	**26**	**15**
Belgaum	19	10	9
Bidar	2	2	-
Uttara Kannada	1	1	-
Bellary	4	2	2
Shimoga	4	3	1
Bangalore	10	7	3
Dakshina Kannada	1	1	-
Sholaga			
Karnataka	**124**	**65**	**59**
Belgaum	14	8	6
Gadag *	5	2	3
Bangalore	5	3	2
Kodagu	5	3	2
Mysore	11	6	5
Chamarajanagar*	84	43	41
Soligaru			
Karnataka	**29,908**	**15,144**	**14,764**
Belgaum	1	-	1

State/District	Population (Nos.)	Male (Nos.)	Female Rate (%)
Bagalkot *	2	2	-
Gulbarga	61	37	24
Bidar	39	18	21
Raichur	58	31	27
Gadag *	5	3	2
Dharwad	15	8	7
Uttara Kannada	7	5	2
Bellary	34	16	18
Davanagere*	8	5	3
Shimoga	83	41	42
Udupi *	12	6	6
Chikmagalur	6	3	3
Tumkur	697	337	360
Kolar	672	353	319
Bangalore	1,090	542	548
Bangalore Rural	1,087	565	522
Mandya	2,055	1,033	1,022
Hassan	568	284	284
Dakshina Kannada	10	5	5
Kodagu	1,080	537	543
Mysore	6,243	3,212	3,031
Chamarajanagar*	16,075	8,101	7,974
Toda			
Karnataka	**55**	**32**	**23**
Belgaum	7	3	4
Bagalkot *	1	1	-
Bidar	4	3	1
Bellary	2	1	1
Udupi *	1	1	-
Kolar	10	5	5
Bangalore	25	15	10
Hassan	1	-	1
Mysore	4	3	1
Varli			
Karnataka	**85**	**43**	**42**
Belgaum	1	1	-
Bidar	18	7	11
Raichur	2	1	1
Gadag *	2	1	1
Bangalore	60	32	28
Kodagu	2	1	1
Vitolia etc.			
Karnataka	**154**	**78**	**76**
Belgaum	6	3	3
Bidar	6	4	2
Koppal *	5	3	2
Dharwad	3	1	2
Shimoga	5	2	3
Tumkur	1	1	-
Bangalore	117	60	57
Bangalore Rural	1	-	1
Kodagu	2	1	1
Mysore	8	3	5
Yerava			
Karnataka	**21,948**	**10,971**	**10,977**
Belgaum	6	3	3
Bijapur	14	8	6
Gulbarga	24	11	13
Bidar	44	20	24
Raichur	33	14	19
Dharwad	125	66	59
Uttara Kannada	10	6	4
Haveri *	4	1	3
Bellary	14	9	5
Chitradurga	1	1	-
Davanagere*	9	4	5
Shimoga	3	1	2
Udupi *	1	-	1
Chikmagalur	5	2	3
Tumkur	86	46	40
Kolar	111	59	52
Bangalore	250	123	127
Bangalore Rural	241	125	116
Mandya	18	10	8
Hassan	22	9	13
Dakshina Kannada	27	13	14
Kodagu	19,480	9,729	9,751
Mysore	1,420	711	70

SURVEY OF RURAL INDIA

LIST OF VOLUMES

SOUTH ZONE

Vol. 1 : Andhra Pradesh (A-J)
Vol. 2 : Andhra Pradesh (K-P)
Vol. 3 : Andhra Pradesh (Q-Z)
Vol. 4 : Karnataka
Vol. 5 : Kerala, Lekshdweep
Vol. 6 : Tamil Nadu (A-P)
Vol. 7 : Tamil Nadu (Q-Z), Pondicherry, Andaman & Nicobar Islands.

WEST ZONE

Vol. 8 : Gujrat, Dadra & Nagara and Haveli, Daman & Diu
Vol. 9 : Maharashtra
Vol. 10 : Maharashtra, Goa
Vol. 11 : Rajasthan

CENTRAL ZONE

Vol. 12 : Chhattisgarh
Vol. 13 : Madhya Pradesh
Vol. 14 : Madhra Pradesh
Vol. 15 : Uttar Pradesh
Vol. 16 : Uttar Pradesh
Vol. 17 : Uttar Pradesh

NORTH ZONE

Vol. 18 : Haryana, Delhi.
Vol. 19 : Himachal Pradesh, Jammu & Kashmir Uttarakhand
Vol. 20 : Punjab, Chandigarh.

EAST ZONE

Vol. 21 : Bihar
Vol. 22 : Bihar
Vol. 23 : Jharkhand
Vol. 24 : Orrisa
Vol. 25 : West Bangal.

NORTH EAST ZONE

Vol. 26 : Assam, Sikkim
Vol. 27 : Arunachal Pradesh, Manipur, Meghalaya, Mizoram, Nagaland, Tripura.

SURVEY OF RURAL INDIA

A Comprehensive Study of Gram Panchayat and Community Development Block

In 27 Volumes

Volume 1

Andhra Pradesh

(A – J)

Editor

Dr. N. Seshagiri

GYAN

Survey of Rural India
Andhra Pradesh (A – J)

ISBN : 978-81-212-1100-0 (Set)
ISBN : 978-81-212-1101-7 [Vol. 1 Andhra Pradesh (A – J)]

Published in 2013 in India by
Gyan Publishing House
23, Main Ansari Road, Daryaganj,
New Delhi - 110002
Phones : 0091-011-23282060, 23261060
Fax : (011) 23285914
E-mail: books@gyanbooks.com
website: gyanbooks.com

Laser Type Setting : Rajender Vashist, Delhi
Printed at : G. Print Process, Delhi

Contents

Volume – 2 (K – P)

1. Coconut, C.D. Block : Allavaram (District : East Godavari)

2. Wheat, C.D.Block : Jeelugumilli (District : West Godavari)

Somasila Dam, C.D. Block : Ananthasagaram. District : Nellore.

4. Bheemunipatnam, C.D. Block : Bheemunipatnam (District : Visakhapatnam)

5. Kaigal Waterfall, C.D. Block : Baireddipalle (District : Chittoor)

6. Kailasakona Waterfall, C.D. Block : Chandragiri (District : Chittoor)

7. Krishna Wildlife Sanctuary, C.D. Block : Avanigadda (District : Krishna)

8. Kolleru Wildlife Sanctuary, C.D. Block : Eluru (District : West Godavari)

Volume – 3 (Q – Z)

List of Photographs (A – J)

1. Coconut, C.D.Block : Allavaram (District : East Godavari).
2. Wheat, C.D.Block : Jeelugumilli (District : West Godavari).
3. Somasila Dam, C.D.Block : Ananthasagaram (District : Nellore).
4. Bheemunipatnam, C.D.Block : Bheemunipatnam (District : Visakhapatnam).
5. Kaigal Waterfall, C.D.Block : Baireddipalle (District : Chittoor).
6. Kailasakona Waterfall, C.D.Block : Chandragiri (District : Chittoor).
7. Krishna Wildlife Sanctuary, C.D.Block : Avanigadda (District : Krishna).
8. Kolleru Wildlife Sanctuary, C.D.Block : Eluru (District : West Godavari).

Preface

The Community Development Block in India is a demarcated rural area for administration and development. The area is administered by a Block Development Officer. A Community Development block covers several gram panchayats, which are local administrative unit at the village level. It was launched on a pilot basis in 1952 to provide for substantial streamlining of the country's agricultural sector, and for sustained improvements in systems of rural health and hygiene, rural education and communication among others. By the end of the First Five Year Plan period, there were 248 blocks which rapidly increased to around 3,000 blocks covering about seventy percent of the rural population in the country by the end of the Second Five Year Plan period. By 1964 there were 6,312 blocks covering the entire country.

India has travelled a considerable distance on the road to development since independence and has made significant progress in various sectors. However, new challenging demands have emerged calling for more integrated rural information. Acute shortage of basic facilities such as drinking water, medical support, education infrastructure is still felt in the face of over 27 per cent of rural population who are still facing poverty and essential sustenance. The Block Development Offices face daunting job of having to accelerate the development process and correct imbalances in tune with the wishes and aspirations of the rural people. Progressive policies and huge investments are being inducted by the Ministry of Rural Development at the Centre towards this, while State Governments are continuously upgrading their implementation machinery.

In addition, new paradigms like rural marketing by a host of retail and manufacturing enterprises as well as expanding technological infrastructure for telecommunication, IT, Transport and Energy among others are posing demands of new types of information on rural India.

Agriculture is a mainstay of the Indian economy. Agriculture and allied sectors contribute nearly 18 per cent of Gross Domestic Product (GDP) of India. Total area coverage under food grains has been reported as 123.22 million hectares. Out of 328.7 million hectares of geographical area of India about 142 million hectares is the net cultivated area. Of this, about 57 million hectare (40%) is irrigated and the remaining is rain fed. This area poses numerous problems for bringing about intensive agricultural production. Information on the four main river systems of India, feeding much of the irrigation schemes- The Himalayan Rivers, The Brahmaputra–centric Rivers, The Deccan Rivers and The Inland Rivers – has to be accurate enough to facilitate efficient irrigation planning.

The government has started focusing on the development of rural heath infrastructure. In the rural areas, services are provided through a network of integrated health and family welfare delivery system. An extensive network of about 3,500 Community Health Centers, 25,000 Primary Health Centers and 1,37,311 Sub-Centers have been set up to provide primary health care at the grassroots level. One sub-centre manned by one female and one male multipurpose worker covers a population of 5000 in plain areas and 3,000 in hilly, tribal, backward and difficult terrain areas. One Primary Health Centre covers a population of 30,000 in the plain areas and 20,000 in tribal and terrain areas. One Community Health Centre covers 80,000 to 1,20,000 Population.

Universalisation of Elementary Education (UEE) has been accepted as a national goal. The Ninth Five year plan envisages UEE to mean universal access, universal retention and universal achievement. As a result of the efforts made by the central and state governments, 94 per cent of country's rural population has primary schools within 1 Km. At the upper primary stage, 84 per cent of the rural population have a school within a distance of three kilometers.

The social milieu of India is not only vast but also diverse. We have tried to capture a representative sample of this diversity. Economic and social development of Scheduled Castes and Scheduled Tribes, who together comprise 24 per cent of the population, and other disadvantaged sections of our society, has called for special efforts, as provided for in the Constitution, of an unprecedented magnitude not faced by any other country in the world.

With deep satisfaction and a sense of accomplishment the book 'SURVEY OF RURAL INDIA (A COMPREHENSIVE STUDY OF GRAM PANCHAYAT AND COMMUNITY DEVELOPMENT BLOCK)' is presented to the readers in 27 Volumes. Such a massive work on Rural India has been commissioned in support of rural-oriented initiatives, containing a wide spectrum of information brought out in a single coherent publication.

All facts and figures have been diligently collected and very little has been left to chance or conjecture by meticulously adhering to documentation and professional standards. We cherish the hope that the twenty-seven volumes presented here will prove to be an invaluable companion to all researchers, scholars, planners, administrators, corporate investors, libraries, NGOs and all those who want to know about any of our Community Development Blocks.

Every detail of the information collected, collated and formatted has gone through meticulous validation checks and rechecks. In line with the constant evolution of the rural scenario, this encyclopedia too will have to be updated and improved in successive editions. A country as vast and complex as India is, there will always be scope for improving the work through suggestions, omissions and additions pointed out. We request the beneficiaries of this encyclopedia to so participate in its evolution.

We sincerely thank the Ministries/Departments of Agriculture, Rural Development, Textiles, Mines, Energy, Finance, Railways, Labour, Human Resource Development, Health and Family Welfare, Culture, Environment and Forest, Minority Affairs, Panchayti Raj, Parliamentary Affairs, Rural Development, Statistics, Tribal affairs, Water Resources, Women and Child Development, University Grants Commission, Law, Justice and Company Affairs, Tourism, Information and Broadcasting, Road Transport and Highways, Home Affairs, Social Justice and Empowerment, Science and Technology, Publication Division, Meteorological Department, Census Commissioner, Backward Classes Commission, Election Commission, Central Statistical Organisation, National Sample Survey Organisation, Anthropological Survey of India, Directorate General of Health Services, Archaeological Survey of India, Central Board of Irrigation and Power, State Statistical Officers, State Editors and gazetteers, State Librarians, Directors of State Information Centers and other connected with the government for the valuable material they have made available to us. We have studied the contents of a large number of published works and drawn from them. We owe a debt of gratitude to all such publishers, authors, editors and compilers. The credit for producing and furnishing authentic data actually goes to them. We have only weaved, consolidated and formatted the content of the information collected by them.

Gyan Publishing House went far beyond the normal call of publishers to give background support to the preparation of these volumes.

DISCLAIMER

This publication contains the collected, collated, formatted and validated information on Community Development Blocks (CD Block) of India on a best and sincere effort basis for presentation in a single encyclopedic work. This work does not constitute an advisory for research, analysis or investment planning, nor, in general, any professional advice. The reader should seek the services of appropriate specialists for such advice.

The information presented here is to be regarded as a first information service on any CDB. The reader should make his/her own deeper investigation of the information on any particular CDB, or state before making any decision or investment of any kind. The Editorial Board or the Publishers cannot be held responsible for loss, if any, incurred as result of specific planning or decision or investments made by the reader in pursuance of this work.

Dr. N. Seshagiri

Introduction

Location

Andhra Pradesh is the fifth largest state in India and it forms the major link between the north and the south of India. It is the biggest and most populous state in the south of India. It falls into a draught in some years due to the south-west monsoon rain that arrives late.

It is bounded by Madhya Pradesh, Chhattisgarh and Orissa in the north, the Bay of Bengal in the east, Tamil Nadu and Karnataka in the south and Maharashtra in the west.

Area

Andhra Pradesh lies between 12°41' and 22°N latitude and 77° and 84°40'E longitude. It is spread over an area of 275,068 sq. km.

Physical Aspects

Physiography

The three main geomorphic provinces of Andhra Pradesh are:

1. The coastal plains, blessed with pleasant weather and rich alluvial plains.
2. The eastern ghats which consist of exotic forest and rivers running through rocky hills.
3. Coal beds, gneisse, granites and basaltic lava that constitute the peninsular plateau.

Climate

Andhra Pradesh receives rainfall from the south-west monsoon as well as the north-east monsoon. The first begins in the second week of June and lasts till September while the second occurs in October-November.

The state's coastal areas receive heavy rains during the north-east monsoon and are also subject to cyclonic conditions which cause enormous damage to residential accommodation and to standing crops. The rainfall decreases from north to south. The Nizamabad district in Telangana receives about 87.5 cm of rain while Anantpur in Rayalaseema receives only 31 cm.

The state has a really hot summer but after the rain begins in the middle of June, there is a decline in the heat when humidity takes over. There is a mild winter in December but the temperature does not go down below 16° Celsius. While the south-west monsoon is comparatively heavy in the northern parts of the state, the north-east monsoon brings more rain to the southern areas like Rayalaseema. The hot season causes the mercury to rise to troublesome proportions in the months of April and May when it could shoot upto 40 degrees and more.

Hills

The state is dotted with hill ranges from the north to the south, running erratically down the middle of the country dividing it into western and eastern or coastal Andhra. These hills form integral geographical entities of Andhra life and history.

In the north, there are Simhachalam and Annavaram hills, in the middle country there are the Srisailam hill ranges and in the south are the Tirumalai-Tirupati hills.

Rivers

The state has two great rivers, Godavari and Krishna which spring from the Western Ghats in Maharashtra and flow eastward and joins the Bay of Bengal.

The Godavari enters the state of Andhra Pradesh direct from Maharashtra, but the Krishna first goes to Karnataka where it flows for a considerable distance before entering Andhra Pradesh. Besides these two big rivers, there are the Tungabhadra, the Pennar and many other small rivers and rivulets. Pennar originates in the Karnataka plateau.

Like all the peninsular rivers and even those which arise in central India, like the Narmada, Sone and Chambal, all these are rain fed rivers as there is no snow below the Himalayas. Andhra Pradesh has considerable topographical variations with dense forest in the north east, flat paddy lands in the coastal plains, several noteworthy beaches along the Bay of Bengal and the stark boulder-strewn region around Hyderabad.

Soils

The state has red, black alluvial, lateric, and coastal sandy soil. With shale and limestone landscapes also present.

Annual Rainfall

It varies from 561 mm in Rayalaseema Region to about 1113 mm in the north-eastern part of the state. No. of rainy days varies from 52 in coastal Andhra to 41 days in Rayalaseema and Telangana regions.

Ground Water

Annual Replenishable Ground water Resource: 36.50 BCM, Net Annual Ground Water Availability: 32.95 BCM, Annual Ground Water Draft: 14.90 BCM, Stage of Ground Water Development: 45 %. Ground Water Development & Management: Over Exploited: 219 Mandals, Critical: 77 Mandals, Semi- critical: 175 Mandals.

Forest

Andhra pradesh State is bestowed with two mighty river systems of Krishna and Godavari. The State has wide and varied vegetation types enriched by a variety of flora and fauna. Andhra Pradesh being located strategically in the central region of the Indian sub-continent has representatives of the magnificent Indian plant and animal life. Its varied topography ranging from the hills of Eastern Ghats and Nallamallas to the shores of Bay of Bengal supports varied ecotypes, which in turn support a rich diversity of flora & fauna. The forest in the state can broadly be divided into four major biotic provinces, namely, Deccan Plateau - 53%, Central Plateau - 35%, Eastern Highland -11% and East Coastal Plains - 1%. The vegetation found in the state is largely of dry deciduous type with a mixture of Teak, and species of the genera *Terminalia, Dalbergias, Pterocarpus, Anogeissus* etc. The hills of Eastern Ghats add greatly to the Biological Diversity and provide centers of endemism for plants, birds and lesser forms of animal life. The varied habitat harbors a diversity of fauna which includes Tiger, Panther, Wolf, Wild Dog, Hyena, Sloth Bear, Gaur, Black Buck, Chinkara, Chowsingha, Nilgai, Cheetal, Sambar and a number of Birds and Reptiles. The long sea coast provides the nesting ground for sea turtles, the back water of Pulicat lake are the feeding grounds for Flamingo & Grey Pelican, the estuaries of river Godavari and Krishna support rich mangrove forests with Fishing Cat and Otters as key stone species. The State is a proud possessor of some rare and endemic plants like *Cycas beddomei, Pterocarpus santalinus, Terminalia pallida, Syzygium alternifolium, Shorea talura, Shorea tumburgia, Psilotum nudam* etc. Similarly the Double banded or the Jerdon's Courser, the Golden Gecko, the Slender Loris which are rare and endangered are endemic to the State.

Natural Division

Godavari Depression,
Telangana Plateau,
Krishna Piodmont Plain,
Royala Seema,
Southern Andhra Costal Plain,
Krishna Delta,
Godavari Delta,
Northern Andhra Costal Plain.

Communications

Transportation

The state has excellent rail, road and air connections to various parts of the country.

An expansive 1,45,000 km. network of roads is on the anvil. 1,400 kms. of major highways are presently being upgraded with aid from the World Bank.

A.P. has over 5,000 kms. of rail lines, with one third of the country's rail cargo passing through the Vijayawada rail terminal.

Roads

Roads form an important component of physical infrastructure to promote development and growth. An efficient transportation system is the lifeline of the economy. The status of roads therefore constitutes a significant index of the economic well-being of the society.

The road density in Andhra Pradesh is 0.70 kms. per One Square Kilometer and 293 kms. per One Lac Population against the all India's average of 1.00 kms. per One Square Kilometer and 389 kms. per Lac Population (as per 1991 census, Population of A.P. is 66.355 Millions and India is 844.324 Millions). While the foregoing figures show that the density and coverage of road network is marginally lower than the national average, however internationally, it is very low compared to the developed countries of the West and developing countries in South-East Asia. This indicates that the road network in Andhra Pradesh needs to be expanded and improved substantially to bring it on par with the best national and international levels.

The share of road transportation in the total goods has increased from 22% in 1956 to more than 81% in 2000 and the passenger traffic has increased from 28% in 1956 to more than 88% in 2000 and is expected to go up further by 2020. The number of vehicles on road has also registered a phenomenal growth. There has been an annual growth rate of 9%-16% p.a., which is one of the highest in the country. From a level of 24,500 in 1956, the number of vehicles has risen to 35,97,351 in 2000 and is expected to reach 83,00,000 by 2020. Against this proliferation of vehicular growth, the road network has increased from 26,762 kms. in 1956 to 1,91,175 kms. in 2000. As a result of the heavy growth in vehicles and non-corresponding increase in roads, there is a tremendous pressure for expanding and developing the road network of the State.

The State has different categories and classification of roads. The National Highways are maintained and developed by Government of India. The State Highways, Major District Roads and Other District Roads are maintained by Roads and Buildings Department, Government of Andhra Pradesh. The important rural roads are maintained by the Panchayati Raj Department of the State Government. Internal roads in villages, towns and municipalities are maintained by the Local Bodies. There are also certain roads, which are specific to projects and are maintained by the respective project agencies.

Railways

Andhra Pradesh is covered by a 5055 km. railway route. The older 1000 kms. of metre gauge are being converted into broad guage, to ensure smoother movement of goods. 35 million tonnes of cargo is handled annually by railways. Inland Container Freight Depots with customs clearance are available at Sanathnagar and Hyderabad, and an inland container station is set up at Guntur.

Administration

Andhra Pradesh has a Vidhan Sabha (legislative assembly, lower house) of 294 seats, and a Vidhan Parishad (legislative council, upper house) of 90 members. 31 members are elected from local bodies, 31 members are elected from the assembly, eight members are elected from teachers, eight members are elected from graduates, and 12 members are nominated by the Governor. In the Parliament of India Andhra Pradesh has 18 in the Rajya Sabha, the Upper House, and 42 in the Lok Sabha, the Lower House. Andhra Pradesh had a series of governments headed by Indian National Congress (INC) Party until 1982. N. Chandrababu Naidu held the record for the longest serving chief minister (1995 to 2004). P. V. Narasimha Rao served as the chief minister of the state from 1971 to 1973, and went on to become the Prime Minister of India in 1991. The first Chief Minister of Andhra Pradesh was Neelam Sanjiva Reddy, who later served as President of India. The Congress Chief Ministers of the state are Damodaram Sanjivayya, Kasu Brahmananda Reddy, P. V. Narasimha Rao, Jalagam Vengala Rao, Marri Chenna Reddy, Tanguturi Anjaiah, Bhavanam Venkatarami Reddy, Kotla Vijaya Bhaskara Reddy, Nadendla Bhaskara Rao, Nedurumalli Janardhana Reddy, Y. S. Rajasekhara Reddy, Konijeti Rosaiah and N. Kiran Kumar Reddy.

Gram Panchayat

Gram panchayats are local self-governments at the village or small town level in India. As of 2002 there were about 21,807 gram panchayats in India. The gram panchayat is the foundation of the Panchayat System. A gram panchayat can be set up in villages with minimum population of 300. Sometimes two or more villages are clubbed together to form group-gram panchayat when the population of the individual villages is less than 300.

Education

By 2020, Andhra Pradesh plans not just to be a literate but a knowledge society fully capable of meeting the challenges of the 21st century. With a progressive and well - managed education system and many institutions of learning and skill building, it aims to make an effective and complete transition into a knowledge society. To achieve this vision, the State plans to steadily increase literacy levels from the current 44% of the population to over 95% and increase the adult literacy from the current 55% for males and 33% for females to over 95% over all.

Medical

The Andhra Pradesh Rural Health Initiative (APRHI) Collaboration works to improve health status, prevent and manage non-communicable disease, prevent premature death, and enhance access to health services for the people of rural Andhra Pradesh. We aim to achieve this through the design, implementation and evaluation of affordable and sustainable interventions that can be incorporated in the existing primary health care infrastructure of rural areas.

Bank

The Andhra Pradesh State Cooperative Bank Limited (APCOB) is a Scheduled State Coopr ative Bank for the State of Andhra Pradesh. The Bank is committed to agricultural and rural development through the Cooperatives. The cooperative credit system in Andhra Pradesh with the APCOB at its apex level is a federal system consisting of a family of 22 affiliated District Cooperative Central Banks (DCCBs), which in turn, have 557 Branches and 2748 Primary Agricultural Cooperative Societies (PACS) through which developmental agricultural credit is provided, to serve a sizeable chunk of the total membership of the PACS of around 1.5 crores...

Scheduled Castes

The total population of Andhra Pradesh, as per the 2001 Census is 76,210,007. Of this, 12,339,496 (16.2 per cent) are Scheduled Castes (SCs). The SC population constitutes 7.4 per cent of the country's SC population. The Scheduled Castes and Scheduled Tribes Order (Amendment) Act, 1976, have notified 59 SCs in Andhra Pradesh. None of the SCs has been notified with an area restriction. Andhra Pradesh occupies 4th position in terms of SC population among 32 states/UTs having SC population.

The growth rate of SC population in the decade 1991-2001 at 16.5 per cent has been higher if compared to the overall growth rate of the state population (14.6 per cent) as a whole. Among the numerically major SCs, Mala have recorded the highest growth rate of 29.7 per cent, followed by Madiga (25.5 per cent). On the other hand, Adi Andhra caste, the fourth largest in the state have recorded a negative growth (-80.5 per cent). Adi Dravida have also recorded a low growth rate of 4 per cent. Due to the ethnic affinity, it is likely that a number of Adi Andhra and Adi Dravida have reported themselves as Mala and/or Madiga, resulting in such a large differential in growth rate.

Out of the 59 SCs, Mala, Madiga, Adi Dravida and Adi Andhra together constitute 93.6 per cent of the SC population of the state. Madiga are numerically the largest SCs with a population of 6,074,250, constituting 49.2 per cent of the state SC population. They are followed by Mala having a population of 5,139,305 (41.6 per cent), Adi Dravida with a population of 194,806 (1.6 per cent) and Adi Andhra (1.2 per cent). Nineteen (19) SCs have returned a population below one thousand each in 2001 census.

As per 2001 Census, 82.5 per cent of SCs are living in the rural areas of the state. Among the numerically major SCs, Adi Dravida has the highest (88.7 per cent) rural population, followed by Madiga (85.1 per cent), Mala (81.9 per cent) and Adi Andhra (76.8 per cent). Among the districts, Nellore has returned the highest (22 per cent) SC population to its total population, while Visakhapatnam has the lowest (7.6 per ent).

Sex ratio (SC)

The overall sex ratio of the SC population of Andhra Pradesh is 981 females per 1000 males, which is higher than 978 for SC population of the state in 2001. The sex ratio of SC population has registered an increase over 969 reported at 1991 Census. Among the districts, the highest sex ratio (1046) is recorded in Nizamabad and the lowest in Anantapur (956).

The Statement below shows sex ratio and child sex ratio (0-6) of the SC population at the national, state and the numerically largest four SCs at 2001 Census:

Age Groups	*All SCs (India)*	*All SCs (Andhra Pradesh)*	*Madiga (Andhra Pradesh)*	*Mala*	*Adi Dravida*	*Adi Andhra*
All Ages	936	981	975	979	938	973
0-6	938	973	975	969	944	969

As may be seen from the above statement, the overall as well as the child sex ratio (0-6) among SC population of Andhra Pradesh are significantly higher than the corresponding sex ratios aggregated for SC population at national level. Similar pattern is seen in respect of all the major SCs.

Literacy and educational level (SC)

Literacy and level of education are two basic indicators of the level of development achieved by a group/society. The literacy results in awareness besides contributing to the overall improvement of health, hygiene and other social conditions. According to 2001 Census, percentage of SC literates, (who can read and write with understanding) aged 7 years and above is 53.5 per cent, which is lower than 60.5 per cent reported for the state population as a whole. The literacy data show that the SC population of the state has made a significant improvement during the decade 1991- 2001. The literacy rate, which was 31.6 per cent in 1991, has increased by 21.9 percentage points in 2001.

Among the major SCs, Adi Andhra have been reported the highest literacy rate of 69.6 per cent, followed by Adi Dravida (65.4 per cent) and Mala (60 per cent). More than half of Madigas are illiterate with literacy rate of 47.5 per cent. The female literacy rate of 43.3 per cent among SC population is lower compared to the total females of the state (50.4 per cent) as well their male counterparts (63.5 per cent). The highest and lowest female literacy rate of 63 per cent and 36.9 per cent have been recorded among Adi Andhra and Madiga.

Educational levels attained by major SCs

Name of SC	Literate without educational level	Below primary	Primary	Middle	Matric/Secondary/Higher Secondary Intermediate etc.	Technical & Non-technical diploma	Graduate & above
All SCs	4.6	30.3	32.0	10.6	17.8	1.0	3.7
Madiga	5.1	34.3	31.7	9.8	15.7	0.7	2.7
Mala	4.2	26.9	32.2	11.3	19.6	1.2	4.6
Adi Dravida	4.7	24.6	37.3	12.7	17.5	0.8	2.4
Adi Andhra	3.2	25.0	32.2	11.9	19.9	1.5	6.3

Out of total literates, 34.9 per cent are literates having attained educational level below the Primary level. The literates, who have attained education up to Primary and Middle levels, constitute 32 per cent and 10.6 per cent respectively. 17.8 per cent are having educational level up to Matric/Higher Secondary etc. levels, implying that every 6th SC literate is a Matriculate. Literates with educational level of Graduation and above are 3.7 per cent. Individually, Adi Andhra (6.3 per cent) have highest percentage of Graduation and above educational levels.

The educational level table also shows that the drop out is conspicuous after the Primarily level and again after Matric/Secondary levels. This pattern is consistent among all the major SCs.

Population in the age group 5-14 years are the potential students. 72.8 per cent of the SC children of Andhra Pradesh in this age group have been attending various educational institutions. At the individual caste level, Adi Dravida, Adi Andhra and Mala have more percentage of school going children than the overall state SC population.

Economic activity (SC)

Work Participation Rate (WPR)

The work participation rate (WPR) is the percentage of workers to the total population. The WPR of the SC population is 50.5 per cent at 2001 Census, which is higher than 45.8 per cent recorded for state population as a whole. The WPR of SC population however, has declined marginally as compared to 51.8 per cent reported at 1991 Census. The male WPR has been 54.4 per cent and female WPR 45.6 per cent at 2001 Census.

At individual caste level, the WPR varies from the highest 52.2 per cent among Madiga to the lowest 45.9 per cent among Adi Andhra. Adi Andhra have also recorded the lowest female WPR of 36.5 per cent.

Category of Workers (SC)

There has been a decline in the SC main workers from 95.6 per cent at 1991 Census to 79.2 per cent at 2001 Census. This, in turn, has resulted in corresponding increase in the marginal workers from 4.4 per cent in 1991 to 20.8 per cent in 2001. Out of total workers, 'agricultural labourers' constitute 68.3 per cent, which is higher than 22.7 percentage points when compared to 45.6 per cent registered for SC population at the national level. 'Other workers' account for 20.1 per cent and only 9.7 per cent has been returned as 'cultivators'. Remaining 1.9 per cent are workers in the 'household industry'.

At the individual caste level, Adi Dravida have recorded the highest 72.7 per cent agricultural labourers, followed by Adi Andhra (71.4 per cent), Madiga (70.4 per cent) and Mala (68 per cent).

Marital status (SC)

Marital status is one of the important determinants of fertility and growth of a population. The 2001 Census data on marital status show that 46.6 per cent persons among the SCs of Andhra Pradesh are 'never married'. The 'currently married' constitute 47.7 per cent while 5.1 per cent are 'widowed'. Only 0.6 per cent are 'divorced and separated'.

Though a majority of girls and boys among SCs in Andhra Pradesh are getting married after attaining the legal age of marriage, the marriages of SC girls below 18 years (3 per cent) are higher than 2.8 per cent recorded among SC population at the national level. The incidences of marriage among boys below 21 years at 2.6 per cent are; however, lower than 3.1 per cent aggregated at the national level for SC population.

The mean number of children ever born per ever married SC women of all ages as well as 45-49 years age group are 2.6 and 3.4 respectively, which are lower than the corresponding figures of 3.2 and 4.2 for SC population at the national level.

Religion (SC)

Out of the 12,339,496 SC population of Andhra Pradesh, 26,507 are Buddhists, 1178 are Sikhs, and the remaining are Hindus, as per 2001 Census.

Scheduled Tribes

The total population of Andhra Pradesh, as per the 2001 Census, is 76,210,007. Of which, 5,024,104 (6.6 per cent) are Scheduled Tribes (STs). The ST population constitutes 6 per cent of the country's ST population. The Scheduled Castes and Scheduled Tribes Orders (Amendment) Act, 1976 have notified 33 STs in the state. Out of the 33 STs, five namely, Goudu, Malis, Nayaks, Thoti and Valmiki have been notified with an area restriction. Goudu, Nayaks and Valmiki have been notified in the Agency tracts area, which comprises Srikakulum, Vizianagaram, Visakhapatnam, East Godavari, West Godavari and Khammam districts. Malis have been notified in the state excluding Adilabad, Hyderabad, Karimnagar, Khammam, Mahbubnagar, Medak, Nalgonda, Nizamabad and Warangal districts. Thoti have been notified in the Adilabad, Hyderabad, Karimnagar, Khammam, Mahbubnagar, Medak, Nalgonda, Nizamabad and Warangal districts.

Twelve tribes namely, Bodo Gadaba, Gutob Gadaba, Bondo Poraja, Khond Poroja, Parangiperja, Chenchu, Dongaria Khonds, Kuttiya Kondhs, Kolam, Kondareddis, Konda Savaras, and Thoti have been recognized as Primitive Tribal Groups (PTGs). Except Kondareddis and Thoti, population on other PTGs are not available separately as these are notified as sub-groups/sections of main communities. The population of Kondareddis and Thoti is 83,096 and 2,074 respectively, as per the 2001 Census.

The growth rate of ST population in the decade 1991-2001 at 19.6 per cent has been higher if compared to the overall growth rate of 14.6 per cent of the state population as a whole. Among the numerically major STs, highest growth rate of 36 per cent has been recorded in the case of Sugalis, followed by Koya (24.4 per cent), Gond (18.9 per cent), Yenadis (16.8 per cent) and Yerukulas (12.8 per cent).

Out of the 33 STs, Sugalis are numerically the largest ST with a population of 2,077,947 constituting 41.4 per cent of the state's ST population. They are followed by Koya 568,019 (11.3 per cent), Yenadis 462,167 (9.2 per cent), Yerukulas 437,459 (8.7 per cent) and Gond 252,038 (5 per cent). These five (5) STs together account for 76 per cent of the ST population of the state.

Of the total ST population, 92.5 per cent are residing in rural areas. Among the major STs, Gond have the highest (97.6 per cent) rural population, followed by Koya (95.5 per cent), Sugalis (93.7 per cent), Yenadis (86.4 per cent) and Yerukulas (77.5 per cent). District-wise distribution of ST population shows that they are mainly concentrated in the districts of Khammam, Visakhapatnam, Warangal, Adilabad and Nalgonda. These five districts constitute 48.9 per cent of the total ST population of the state.

Sex ratio (ST)

The overall sex ratio of the ST population is 972 females per 1000 males, which is marginally lower than 978 reported for the state population as a whole at 2001 Census. The overall sex ratio of the ST population has registered an increase over 960 reported at the 1991 Census. The sex ratio of above 1000 among ST population in the five contiguous districts namely, Srikakulam (1009), Vizianagaram (1025), Visakhapatnam (1003), East Godavari (1011) and West Godavari (1018) have returned higher sex ratio among STs. In the remaining 18 districts it varies between 994 (Nizamabad) and 921 (Nalgonda). The Statement below shows the sex ratio and child sex ratio (0-6) at the national, state and numerically the largest five STs at 2001 Census:

Age Groups	*All STs (India)*	*All STs (Andhra Pradesh)*	*Sugalis*	*Koya*	*Gond*	*Yenadis*	*Yerukulas*
All Ages	978	972	939	1006	1013	957	984
0-6	973	972	944	1000	999	950	971

As shown in the statement, the child sex ratio (0-6) of ST population of Andhra Pradesh is equal to the child sex ratio of ST population at the national level. Among the numerically major STs, Sugalis and Yenadis have lower sex ratio both in overall and 0-6 age group populations than the state ST population and the other major STs.

Literacy and educational level (ST)

Literacy and level of education are two basic indicators of the level of development achieved by a group/society. The literacy results in a more awareness besides contributing to the overall improvement of health, hygiene and other social conditions. According to 2001 Census, percentage of literate persons (those who can read & write with understanding), aged 7 years and above, among ST population of Andhra Pradesh is 37 per cent, which is lower than 60.5 per cent reported for state population as a whole. The literacy data show that the ST population of the state has made significant improvement in literacy during the decade 1991-2001. The literacy rate, which was 17.1 per cent in 1991, has increased by 19.9 percentage points in 2001. But in comparison to other states/UTs, the position of ST population of Andhra Pradesh is not satisfactory. At the district level, the highest literacy rate has been recorded in Hyderabad (55.4 per cent) and the lowest in Mahbubnagar (25.8 per cent).

Educational levels attained by major STs

Name of ST	*Literate without educational level*	*Below primary*	*Primary*	*Middle*	*Matric/Secondary/Higher Secondary Intermediate etc.*	*Technical & Non-technical diploma*	*Graduate & above*
All STs	6.3	42.0	28.4	8.5	12.3	0.6	1.8
Sugalis	5.6	43.6	25.7	8.7	13.3	0.8	2.3
Koya	6.5	43.4	29.2	8.5	10.9	0.4	1.2
Gond	7.7	50.0	25.1	7.2	9.1	0.2	0.6
Yenadis	9.7	47.0	29.7	5.3	6.9	0.4	1.1
Yerukulas	4.4	32.2	30.8	10.3	17.7	1.3	3.3

Among the major STs, Yerukulas have reported the highest literacy rate (45.4 per cent), followed by Koya (41.8 per cent), Gond (36.4 per cent), Yenadis (35.3 per cent) and Sugalis (34.3 per cent). The female literacy rate of 26.1 per cent among the ST population is matter of concern as almost a fourth of ST females are illiterate in the state.

Out of total literates, 48.3 per cent are literates without any educational level or have attained below Primary level. The literates, who have attained education up to Primary level and Middle level, constitute 28.4 per cent and 8.5 per cent respectively.

12.3 per cent are having educational level up to Matric/Higher Secondary etc. levels, implying that every 8th ST literate is a Matriculate. Literates with educational level of Graduation & above are 1.8 per cent. Individually, Yerukulas (3.3 per cent) have the highest percentage of Graduate & above educational level.

The educational level table also shows that the drop out is conspicuous after the Primary level and again after Matric/Secondary levels. This pattern is consistent among all the major SCs.

Population in the age group 5-14 years are the potential students. Only 60.7 per cent of the ST population in this age group has been attending various educational institutions.

Economic activity (ST)

Work Participation Rate (WPR)

The work participation rate (WPR) is the percentage of workers to the total population. The WPR of the ST population is 53.9 per cent at 2001 Census, which is almost equal to 54.3 per cent recorded in 1991. The WPR among male 55.7 per cent and females 52 per cent more than half of male/female have been returned workers among ST at 2001 Census.

At the individual caste level by & large consistent pattern is noted in WPR. The highest WPR of 56.5 per cent is reported for Yenadis and lowest among Yerukulas (50.5 per cent). Yurukulas have also recorded the lowest female WPR of 45.2 per cent.

Category of Workers (ST)

There has been a decline in the main workers from 93.9 per cent at 1991 Census to 79.3 per cent at 2001 Census. This, in turn, has resulted in corresponding increase in the marginal workers from 6.1 per cent in 1991 to 20.7 per cent in 2001. Out of total workers, 'agricultural labourers' constitute 49.3 per cent, which is significantly higher when compared to 36.9 per cent recorded for ST population at the national level. 'Cultivators' accounts for 34.3 per cent and 13.5 per cent have been returned as 'other workers'. Remaining 3 per cent have been workers in 'household industry'.

At the individual caste level, among major STs, Yenadis have the maximum 76.2 per cent 'agricultural labourers'.

Marital status (ST)

Marital status is one of the important determinants of fertility and growth of a population. The 2001 Census data on marital status show that 48.7 per cent persons among the STs of Andhra Pradesh are 'never married'. The 'currently married' constitute 46.9 per cent while 4 per cent are 'widowed' and only 0.5 per cent are 'divorced and separated'.

A majority of girls and boys among STs in Andhra Pradesh are getting married after attaining the legal age of marriage. However, marriages of ST girls below 18 years (3.2 per cent) are higher than that recorded among ST population at national level (2.1 per cent). Similarly, the incidence of marriage among boys below 21 years at 3.6 per cent is also higher than 2.8 per cent aggregated for ST population at the national level.

The mean number of children ever born per

married ST woman of all ages as well as 45-49 years age group are 2.7 and 3.6 respectively, which are lower than corresponding figures of 3.2 and 4.1 for ST population at the national level.

Religion (ST)

The 2001 Census data show that Hindus constitute 98.9 per cent of ST population of Andhra Pradesh, followed by Christians 35,983 (0.7 per cent) and Muslims 4,643 (0.1 per cent).

Agriculture

Agriculture is the main occupation of about 62 per cent of the people in Andhra Pradesh. Rice is a major food crop and staple food of the State contributing about 77 per cent of the foodgrain production. Other important crops are jowar, bajra, maize, ragi, small millets, pulses, castor, tobacco, cotton and sugarcane. Forest covers 23 per cent of the states area. Important forest products are teak, eucalyptus, cashew, casurina, bamboo, softwood, etc. The production of food grains in the state for the first time since formation of the State is recorded at 204.04 lakhs tones in 2008-09 as against 199.17 lakh tones in 2007-08.

The Government is working with a mission of "Sustainable Agriculture Production with minimum cost of cultivation, eventually enhancing the return on income to the farmer ". In the process of making the mission a reality, the Government is implementing schemes for the welfare of farmers like 9 hours free power supply, subsidized seed, subsidized interst rate on crop loans, subsidized and quality agricultural inputs etc., Andhra Pradesh occupies the first position in respect of agricultural loans from commercial and cooperative banks.

The debt waiver scheme of Central Government and the incentive scheme of the State Government have helped about one crore farmers in the state to the tune of Rs.16,000 crore. The Government of Andhra Pradesh is also keen on introducing cooperative farming to set up farm yields.

Irrigation

A total of 86 project (44 Major+30 Medium+4 Flood Banks+8 Modernisation) have been taken up under jalayagnam programme, with the aim of completing the ongoing and new projects in a record time to provide immediate irrigation to water starved areas on top priority by mobilizing funds from all possible sources. Till now, 12 projects were completed and water released for 19 more projects creating partial irrigaion potential and the remaining projects are programmed to be completed in a time bound and planned manner, Andhra Pradesh Government has been making huge budgetary allocations for the execution of irrigation projects and it is the first state to involve in the management of irrigation sources.

Religion

Distribution of Religion by Sex with Percentage of Total Population (State)

Religion	*T/R/U*	*Persons*	*Males*	*Females*	*%age*
Total	Total	76,210,007	38,527,413	37,682,594	100.00
Population	Rural	55,401,067	27,937,204	27,463,863	100.00
	Urban	20,808,940	10,590,209	10,218,731	100.00
Hindu	Total	67,809,192	34,262,369	33,546,823	88.98
	Rural	51,722,451	26,084,321	25,638,130	93.36
	Urban	16,086,741	8,178,048	7,908,693	77.31
Muslim	Total	6,983,471	3,560,501	3,422,970	9.16
	Rural	2,927,745	1,480,009	1,447,736	5.28
	Urban	4,055,726	2,080,492	1,975,234	19.49
Christian	Total	1,180,445	579,638	600,807	1.55
	Rural	643,937	316,512	327,425	1.16
	Urban	536,508	263,126	273,382	2.58
Sikh	Total	55,012	31,115	23,897	0.07
	Rural	19,248	11,137	8,111	0.03
	Urban	35,764	19,978	15,786	0.17
Buddhist	Total	38,314	19,518	18,796	0.05
	Rural	24,443	12,340	12,103	0.04
	Urban	13,871	7,178	6,693	0.07
Jain	Total	44,266	22,858	21,408	0.06
	Rural	2,975	1,586	1,389	0.01
	Urban	41,291	21,272	20,019	0.20
Other	Total	4,765	2,448	2,317	0.01
Religions	Rural	1,329	685	644	0.00
	Urban	3,436	1,763	1,673	0.02
Religion	Total	94,542	48,966	45,576	0.12
Not Stated	Rural	58,939	30,614	28,325	0.11
	Urban	35,603	18,352	17,251	0.17

Language

The main languages spoken in Andhra Pradesh are Telugu, Urdu, Hindi, Banjara and English followed by Tamil, Kannada, Marathi and Oriya. Telugu is the principal and official language of the State. It was also referred to as 'Tenugu' in the past. 'Andhra' is the name given to it since the medieval times. Some argued that

'Telugu' was a corruption of 'Trilinga' (Sanskrit meaning three 'lingas'). A general description of the land of the Telugus was made in the medieval times as the land marked by three lingas of the three famous shrines of Draksharamam (East Godavari district), Kaleswaram (Karimnagar district) and Srisailam (Kurnool district).

Main Language : Telugu

Telugu is the most widely spoken language of the Dravidian family which consists of 24 languages spanning the entire South-Asia, from Baluchistan to Sri Lanka. In terms of population, Telugu ranks second to Hindi among the Indian languages. According to the 1981* Census, Telugu is spoken by over 45 million in Andhra Pradesh. It has also spread to the other parts of the globe, i.e., Burma, Indo-China, South-Africa and the U.S.A. Being a mellifluous language, it is called, by its admirers as the 'Italian of the East'.

Its vocabulary is very much influenced by Sanskrit. In the course of time, some Sanskrit expressions used in Telugu got so naturalised that people regarded them as pure Telugu words. Some Kannada and Tamil words were also taken into Telugu but they did not gain much currency.

With the advent of the Muslim rule, several Persian and Arabic words entered into the Telugu language. But they were confined to the spoken language and to the language of the judiciary and the executive.

The influence of Persian and Arabic is discernible to a considerable extent in the languages spoken in Telangana due to its long association with the Muslim rule. There is also a great element of English words in the vocabulary of Coastal Andhra and Rayalaseema because these regions were directly under the British rule for nearly a century and a half.

The evolution of Telugu can be traced through centuries in terms of its form as well as its function. Although culturally Telugu is close to its southern neighbours - Tamil and Kannada - genetically, it is closer to its northern neighbours - Gondi, Konda, Kui, Kuvi, Pengo and Manda. There is evidence to show that these languages were freely borrowed from Telugu even from the prehistoric period whereas borrowing between Telugu and Tamil and Kannada has been mostly during the historic period, i.e., post-5th century B.C.

It is possible to identify broadly four stages in the history of the Telugu language.

(1) B.C. 200 - A.D. 500

(2) A.D. 500 -A.D.1100

(3) A.D. 1100 -A.D.1400 and

(4) A.D. 1400 -A.D.1900.

During the first phase, we only come across names of places and personal names of Telugu in Prakrit and Sanskrit inscriptions found in the Telugu country. Telugu was exposed to the influence of Prakrit as early as the 3rd century B.C. From this we know that the language of the people was Telugu, although the language of the rulers was different. The first complete Telugu inscription belongs to the Renati Cholas, found in Erragudipadu, Kamalapuram taluk of Cuddapah district and assigned to about A.D. 575. Telugu was exposed to the influence of Sanskrit about this period. It appears that literature also existed in Telugu about the same time, because we find literary style in the inscriptions some three centuries even before Nannaya's (A.D. 1022) Mahabharatam. During the time of Nannaya, the popular language had considerably diverged from the literary language.

In the period A.D. 500-1100, the literary languages confined to the poetic works, flourished in the courts of kings and among scholars. Phonetic changes, which occurred in the popular language, are reflected in the literary language, although the two streams remained apart in grammar and vocabulary. During A.D. 1100-1400 the literary language got stylized and rigid, closing itself from the influence of contemporary spoken language. Ketana (13th century AD), a disciple of Tikkana prohibited the use of spoken words in the poetic works and quoted some spoken forms. During the period A.D. 1400-1900, many changes culminating in today's form of Telugu took place.

The prose language of the 19th century, as can be seen from the 'Kaifiyats', shows the educated speech as base with occasional influence of literary language. We also notice the influence of Urdu language on Telugu before the spread of English education.

From the foregoing overview of the history of the Telugu language, one can see that what we now use as modern standard Telugu, had its beginnings in the spoken variety, right from the 10th century A.D. The language was progressively enriched by contact with Sanskrit, Prakrit, Urdu and English from early times.

Four Areas of Use of Telugu Language

Until the advent of the printing press and the school system of education, Telugu was broadly used in four areas:

(1) inscriptions,

(2) poetry,

(3) folk literature,

(4) common speech (social and perhaps official).

The language of the inscriptions had always been based on the contemporary speech of the educated with an occasional admixture of literary and rustic expressions. Folk literature, which was in the form of songs, drew mainly on the speech of the common people among whom it circulated, basically rural in its character. Both in its appeal and form, the poetic language was confined to royal courts and the elite.

Care was taken to keep it insulated from the speech of even the scholars and poets, who used it in other areas of communication. Because of this restriction on the medium, prose never emerged as a form of classical literature in Telugu. Even the sparse scientific writing on prosody, arithmetic, medicine and grammar was cast either in Telugu verse or in Sanskrit slokas. The emergence of popular literary forms like the satakas devotional songs and the yaksha gana necessitated extensive reliance on contemporary spoken language in their appeal and expressiveness.

Early commentaries, historical accounts (like Rayavachakam), and the few prose works, which were written for instructional purposes in the first half of the 19th century, were all written in educated speech which was distinct from the language of the literary dialect. In 1853, Chinnayasuri, a Telugu pundit in the Presidency College, first experimented with a prose variety based on the classical poetic language in his book "Niti Chandrika".

In 1855, he published Bala Vyakaranamu, an excellent grammar of the poetic language, but it was intended for school study and as a guide to 'Correct Writing'. These works had, to some extent, given support to traditional pundits, who upheld the Kavya bhasha as primary and the spoken language as its degenerate form.

The influence of Chinnayasuri temporarily arrested the growth of creative prose by famous writers until Gurazada Appa Rao appeared on the scene and produced his social play Kanyasulkam in 1897 in a near modern language. The controversy that raged between the two schools, classical and modern subsided in 1919 with a victory for the classic writers to perpetuate the use of the so-called granthikam (or the poetic dialect) as the language of the text-book language and the medium of examination. However, teaching has all along been done only in the spoken variety of the teacher.

For about 90 years (1850-1940), Telugu prose had a stunted growth, although scholars like Kandukuri Viresalingam and Panuganti Lakshminarasimha Rao used a 'liberalized poetic variety' in their writings, which was neither fully classical nor fully modern.

Literature

Telugu literature is generally divided into six periods, viz.,

(1) the pre-Nannaya period (up to A.D. 1020),

(2) the Age of the Puranas (1020-1400),

(3) the Age of Srinatha (1400-1510),

(4) the Age of the Prabandhas (1510-1600),

(5) the Southern period (1600-1820), and

(6) the Modern Period (after 1820).

In the earliest period there were only inscriptions from A.D. 575 onwards. Nannaya's (1022-1063) translation of the Sanskrit Mahabharata into Telugu is the piece of Telugu literature as yet discovered. The diction is so masterly that historians think that there must have been earlier works in Telugu. After the death of Nannaya, there was a kind of social and religious revolution in the Telugu country.

Virasaivism propagated bhakti towards Siva as the only means of attaining salvation. Tikkana (13th century) and Yerrana (14th century) continued the translation of the Mahabharata started by Nannaya. Yerrana was also a devotee of Siva. Quite a few poets continued writing in Telugu and we come to the age of Srinatha.

During this period, some Telugu poets translated Sanskrit poems and dramas, while others attempted original narrative poems. The popular Telugu literary form called the Prabandha, was evolved during this period. Srinatha (1365-1441) was the foremost poet, who popularised this style of composition (a story in verse having a tight metrical scheme). Srinatha's, Sringara Naishadham is particularly well-known.

We may also refer to the Ramayana poets in this context. The earliest Ramayana in Telugu is generally known as the Ranganatha Ramayana, though authorised by the chief Gona Buddha Reddi. Then there were the great religious poets like Potana (1450-1510), Jakkana (second half of the 14th century) and Gaurana (first half of the 15th century).

Golden Period of Telugu Literature

The golden period of Telugu literature was the 16th and 17th centuries A.D., Krishnadevaraya's Amuktamalayada is regarded as a Mahakavya. Peddana's Manucharitra is another outstanding Mahakavya. Telugu literature flourished in the south in the Samsthanas like Madurai, Tanjavur etc., and that is why the age itself was called the 'Southern Period'.

We find a comparatively larger number of poets among the rulers, women and non-Brahmins who popularised the desi metres.

With the conquest of the Deccan by the Mughals in A.D.1687, there ensued a period of decadence (1750-1850) in literature. Then emerged a period of transition (1850-1910), following a long period of Renaissance. The Europeans like C.P.Brown played an important role in the development of Telugu language and literature. In common with the rest of India, Telugu literature of this period was increasingly influenced by the European literary forms like the novel, short story, prose, drama, belles-letters, etc.

The father of modern Telugu literature is Kandukuri Viresalingam Pantulu (1848-1919), who wrote a novel, Rajasekhara Charitamu, inspired by the Vicar of Wakefield. He was the first person in modern times to use literature to eradicate social evils. He was followed by Rayaprolu Subba Rao, Gurazada Appa Rao, Viswanatha Satyanarayana, Katuri Venkateswara Rao, Jashuva, Devulapalli Venkata Krishna Sastry, Sri Sri, Puttaparty Narayana Charyulu and others in the sphere of poetry. Viswanatha Satyanarayana had won the coveted Jnanapith Award. "Kanyasulkam" (Bride-Money), the first social play in Telugu by Gurazada Appa Rao was a thumping success.

We also find the progressive movement, free verse movement and Digambara style finding expression in Telugu verse. The well-known modern Telugu novelists were Unnava Lakshminarayana (of Malapalli fame), Viswanatha Satyanarayana (Veyi Padagalu), Kutumba Rao and Buchchi Babu. Telugu is specially known for its daring experiments in the field of poetry and drama.

Other Important Languages

Urdu, another important language of the State and spoken by the Muslims is Indian in origin. Though many words in it found their way from the Arabic and Persian, it has always been true to the idiom of the western Hindi dialect. It was "the language of the Exalted Court" at Delhi in the Mughal period. It acquired the shortened name `Urdu' and became the handmaid of the Persian culture in India.

The 1981 census recorded 41,69,179 Urdu-speaking persons in the State comprising 21,21,859 males and 20,47,320 females. Hyderabad City, the State's Capital accounted for 35 per cent of the Urdu-speaking people in Hyderabad district, forming over 8 per cent of the population, and came next to Telugu. Guntur, Anantapur and Cuddapah districts also accounted for a sizeable number of Urdu-speaking people. In the Telangana region, the overall proportion of Urdu-speaking people is very high.

Hindi speaking people, numbering 13,83,792, (7,10,313 males and 6,73,479 females) and forming about three per cent of the population, held the third place. None of the remaining languages was spoken by even 2 per cent of the population. Thus Tamil, Kannada and Marathi account for still smaller proportions. These individual languages, however, account for a fairly substantial proportion of speakers in some districts. There were 6,45,463 Tamil, 4,84,330 Kannada, 4,31,352 Marathi and 2,36,420 Oriya speaking people in the State.

People speaking Tamil are found concentrated in Chittoor district, which adjoins Tamil Nadu. They are also found to some extent in Nellore and Hyderabad districts. Kannada and Marathi speakers can be seen in districts like Anantapur and Kurnool, and Adilabad and Nizamabad respectively which have close proximity to the adjoining Kannada and Marathi areas of Karnataka and Maharashtra states.

Of the numerous other languages spoken in the State, the 1981 Census recorded 44,489 persons speaking Malayalam; 36,180 speaking Gujarati, 18,544 speaking Bengali, Punjabi -16,833, Sindhi - 9,521, Assami -248 and Kashmiri -121. Of the foreign languages spoken in the State, 414 speak Arabic and three, Tibetan.

The principal tribal languages spoken in the State are Banjara/Sugali/Lambadi (45,00,000) , Koya (1,58,097), Gondi (1,12,303), Savara (47,609), Jatapu (23,366), Kolami (13,395), Khondi/Kondh (11,890), Gadaba (11,291) and Donda (9,951).

Distribution of Language

		Persons	*Males*	*Females*
Assamese	Total	1,302	957	345
	Rural	56	37	19
	Urban	1,246	920	326
Bengali	Total	30,281	16,558	13,723
	Rural	12,786	6,682	6,104
	Urban	17,495	9,876	7,619
Gujarati	Total	43,844	22,701	21,143
	Rural	4,130	2,225	1,905
	Urban	39,714	20,476	19,238
Hindi	Total	1,841,290	960,685	880,605
	Rural	1,414,438	730,420	684,018
	Urban	426,852	230,265	196,587
Kannada	Total	519,507	261,528	257,979
	Rural	408,102	204,363	203,739
	Urban	111,405	57,165	54,240
Kashmiri	Total	612	332	280
	Rural	4	4	-
	Urban	608	328	280
Konkani	Total	3,794	1,874	1,920

		Persons	Males	Females
	Rural	202	107	95
	Urban	3,592	1,767	1,825
Malayalam	Total	66,409	37,228	29,181
	Rural	8,159	4,730	3,429
	Urban	58,250	32,498	25,752
Manipuri	Total	221	163	58
	Rural	2	-	2
	Urban	219	163	56
Marathi	Total	503,609	255,013	248,596
	Rural	336,296	168,730	167,566
	Urban	167,313	86,283	81,030
Nepali	Total	6,634	4,120	2,514
	Rural	1,945	1,243	702
	Urban	4,689	2,877	1,812
Oriya	Total	259,947	129,697	130,250
	Rural	200,160	98,958	101,202
	Urban	59,787	30,739	29,048
Punjabi	Total	24,773	13,669	11,104
	Rural	1,481	842	639
	Urban	23,292	12,827	10,465
Sanskrit	Total	199	119	80
	Rural	65	44	21
	Urban	134	75	59
Sindhi	Total	12,919	6,563	6,356
	Rural	102	61	41
	Urban	12,817	6,502	6,315
Tamil	Total	753,484	387,503	365,981
	Rural	466,151	237,871	228,280
	Urban	287,333	149,632	137,701
Telugu	Total	56,375,755	28,537,184	27,838,571
	Rural	43,083,713	21,775,794	21,307,919
	Urban	13,292,042	6,761,390	6,530,652
Urdu	Total	5,560,154	2,836,179	2,723,975
	Rural	2,205,054	1,120,395	1,084,659
	Urban	3,355,100	1,715,784	1,639,316
Adi	Total	18	7	11
	Rural	6	2	4
	Urban	12	5	7
Anal	Total	4	4	-
	Rural	-	-	-
	Urban	4	4	-
Arabic/Arbi	Total	295	162	133
	Rural	68	35	33
	Urban	227	127	100
Bhili/Bhilodi	Total	1,277	638	639
	Rural	191	90	101
	Urban	1,086	548	538
Bhumij	Total	443	225	218
	Rural	433	220	213
	Urban	10	5	5
Bishnupuriya	Total	2	2	-
	Rural	-	-	-
	Urban	2	2	-
Bodo/Boro	Total	74	71	3
	Rural	-	-	-
	Urban	74	71	3
Coorgi/Kodagu	Total	84	43	41
	Rural	3	2	1
	Urban	81	41	40
Dimasa	Total	21	8	13
	Rural	-	-	-
	Urban	21	8	13
Dogri	Total	596	397	199
	Rural	19	11	8
	Urban	577	386	191
English	Total	9,626	4,784	4,842
	Rural	458	248	210
	Urban	9,168	4,536	4,632
Gadaba	Total	9,197	4,598	4,599
	Rural	8,761	4,380	4,381
	Urban	436	218	218
Gangte	Total	2	1	1
	Rural	-	-	-
	Urban	2	1	1
Garo	Total	14	11	3
	Rural	1	-	1
	Urban	13	11	2
Gondi	Total	144,259	72,305	71,954
	Rural	141,442	70,830	70,612
	Urban	2,817	1,475	1,342
Halabi	Total	11	7	4
	Rural	11	7	4
	Urban	-	-	-
Hmar	Total	6	6	-
	Rural	-	-	-
	Urban	6	6	-
Ho	Total	1	1	-
	Rural	-	-	-
	Urban	1	1	-
Jatapu	Total	25,503	12,520	12,983
	Rural	25,492	12,514	12,978
	Urban	11	6	5
Karbi/Mikir	Total	5	2	3
	Rural	-	-	-
	Urban	5	2	3
Kharia	Total	22	13	9
	Rural	12	8	4
	Urban	10	5	5
Khasi	Total	21	16	5
	Rural	-	-	-
	Urban	21	16	5
Khond/Kondh	Total	26,814	13,699	13,115
	Rural	26,808	13,697	13,111
	Urban	6	2	4
Kinnauri	Total	11	5	6
	Rural	1	1	-
	Urban	10	4	6
Kolami	Total	23,910	12,074	11,836

		Persons	Males	Females
	Rural	23,785	11,979	11,806
	Urban	125	95	30
Konda	Total	16,852	8,408	8,444
	Rural	16,789	8,379	8,410
	Urban	63	29	34
Korku	Total	8	6	2
	Rural	-	-	-
	Urban	8	6	2
Korwa	Total	11	5	6
	Rural	2	-	2
	Urban	9	5	4
Koya	Total	168,828	84,520	84,308
	Rural	166,464	83,234	83,230
	Urban	2,364	1,286	1,078
Kui	Total	5,502	2,778	2,724
	Rural	5,502	2,778	2,724
	Urban	-	-	-
Kuki	Total	72	68	4
	Rural	-	-	-
	Urban	72	68	4
Kurukh/Oraon	Total	54	26	28
	Rural	46	24	22
	Urban	8	2	6
Lahnda	Total	2,432	1,235	1,197
	Rural	2,432	1,235	1,197
	Urban	-	-	-
Lushai/Mizo	Total	14	7	7
	Rural	1	-	1
	Urban	13	7	6
Malto	Total	3	1	2
	Rural	-	-	-
	Urban	3	1	2
Monpa	Total	4	4	-
	Rural	-	-	-
	Urban	4	4	-
Munda	Total	6	5	1
	Rural	2	2	-
	Urban	4	3	1
Mundari	Total	1,172	607	565
	Rural	1,160	597	563
	Urban	12	10	2
Nicobarese	Total	2	1	1
	Rural	-	-	-
	Urban	2	1	1
Nissi/Dafla	Total	1	1	-
	Rural	-	-	-
	Urban	1	1	.
Nocte	Total	7	7	-
	Rural	-	-	-
	Urban	7	7	-
Paite	Total	6	6	-
	Rural	-	-	-
	Urban	6	6	-
Parji	Total	1,302	660	642
	Rural	1,296	658	638
	Urban	6	2	4
Phom	Total	2	1	1

		Persons	Males	Females
	Rural	-	-	-
	Urban	2	1	1
Santali	Total	53	30	23
	Rural	7	6	1
	Urban	46	24	22
Savara	Total	52,824	26,254	26,570
	Rural	52,629	26,152	26,477
	Urban	195	102	93
Tangsa	Total	3	2	1
	Rural	-	-	-
	Urban	3	2	1
Thado	Total	8	6	2
	Rural	-	-	-
	Urban	8	6	2
Tibetan	Total	3	3	-
	Rural	2	2	-
	Urban	1	1	-
Total of Other	Total	11,114	5,870	5,244
Languages	Rural	4,112	2,227	1,885
	Urban	7,002	3,643	3,359
Tripuri	Total	7	6	1
	Rural	-	-	-
	Urban	7	6	1
Tulu	Total	763	387	376
	Rural	101	51	50
	Urban	662	336	326
Vaiphei	Total	3	3	-
	Rural	-	-	-
	Urban	3	3	-
Zou	Total	2	2	-
	Rural	-	-	-
	Urban	2	2	-

Age wise Data

According to the Population Reference Bureau's 2000 World Data Sheets, life expectancy at birth for Indians is between 60 and 61 years. This was also confirmed by the most recent Census of India in 2001. Only 4% of our population is over the age of 65%. In parts of the world with much better access to medicine and healthcare, these numbers are substantially higher.

Disabled

Distribution of Disabled Persons by Type of Disabilty and Residence (in %)

India/ States/ Union	*T/R/U*	*Total disabled popul-ation*	*In seeing*	*In speech*	*In hear-ing*	*In move-ment*	*Mental*
INDIA	T	21906769	48.5	7.5	5.8	27.9	10.3
	R	16388382	48.0	7.6	6.2	28.4	9.7
	U	5518387	50.0	7.2	4.3	26.3	12.1

India/ States/ Union	T/R/U	Total disabled population	In seeing	In speech	In hearing	In movement	Mental
ANDHRA PRADESH	T	1364981	42.6	10.2	5.4	30.5	11.4
	R	1050400	41.4	10.2	5.8	31.4	11.1
	U	314581	46.5	10.0	3.9	27.4	12.2
Adilabad	T	33722	40.5	11.3	4.5	31.5	12.2
	R	26550	40.8	11.2	4.8	31.6	11.6
	U	7172	39.0	11.7	3.5	31.2	14.6
Nizamabad	T	39939	45.6	8.9	4.1	30.4	11.0
	R	33874	45.2	8.9	4.3	31.0	10.6
	U	6065	47.9	8.7	3.2	26.8	13.4
Karimnagar	T	60650	48.8	9.7	4.8	25.2	11.6
	R	48876	46.6	9.9	5.0	26.7	11.8
	U	11774	57.8	9.1	3.8	18.7	10.6
Medak	T	47272	45.9	9.4	4.5	30.1	10.0
	R	42078	45.5	9.3	4.6	30.7	9.8
	U	5194	48.7	10.5	3.4	25.5	11.8
Hyderabad	T	52590	50.1	9.0	3.3	23.3	14.3
	R	0	0.0	0.0	0.0	0.0	0.0
	U	52590	50.1	9.0	3.3	23.3	14.3
Rangareddi	T	59075	48.7	8.7	3.9	27.9	10.8
	R	30641	46.8	8.5	4.6	30.9	9.2
	U	28434	50.7	8.9	3.2	24.7	12.5
Mahbubnagar	T	66015	44.9	8.6	5.2	32.0	9.3
	R	60318	44.7	8.6	5.3	32.2	9.1
	U	5697	46.7	8.8	3.0	29.9	11.5
Nalgonda	T	73616	46.7	8.2	4.6	30.2	10.3
	R	65774	46.3	8.3	4.8	30.5	10.2
	U	7842	50.3	7.9	2.8	27.4	11.6
Warangal	T	67121	48.1	9.7	4.3	28.3	9.5
	R	56430	46.7	9.8	4.7	29.4	9.4
	U	10691	55.7	9.0	2.4	22.7	10.3
Khammam	T	63695	49.9	8.9	4.3	26.7	10.3
	R	52641	49.6	8.7	4.4	26.9	10.4
	U	11054	51.1	9.8	3.5	25.8	9.8
Srikakulam	T	51608	43.6	10.2	6.1	29.5	10.6
	R	47248	44.2	10.1	6.2	29.2	10.4
	U	4360	36.5	11.3	5.7	33.4	13.1
Vizianagaram	T	49406	46.7	9.7	6.2	28.6	8.8
	R	41383	46.6	9.6	6.4	28.7	8.7
	U	8023	46.8	10.3	5.0	28.2	9.7
Visakhapatnam	T	67263	48.5	10.4	4.8	25.9	10.3
	R	40026	43.1	11.1	6.3	29.4	10.0
	U	27237	56.4	9.2	2.7	20.9	10.8
East Godavari	T	92680	48.7	9.9	4.1	27.5	9.8
	R	71364	47.6	10.1	4.3	28.1	10.0
	U	21316	52.4	9.6	3.4	25.5	9.1
West Godavari	T	61135	29.7	12.3	6.2	38.6	13.3
	R	49797	29.4	12.3	6.3	38.6	13.4
	U	11338	31.0	12.3	5.4	38.5	12.7
Krishna	T	71156	35.8	11.5	5.7	33.8	13.2
	R	53656	35.0	11.5	6.0	34.1	13.4
	U	17500	37.9	11.4	4.9	32.9	12.8
Guntur	T	76735	39.2	11.3	4.9	31.5	13.1
	R	54778	37.3	11.9	5.2	31.8	13.8
	U	21957	43.9	9.7	4.0	30.8	11.6
Prakasam	T	48931	34.3	12.3	5.5	35.3	12.6
	R	42510	34.2	12.0	5.6	35.6	12.6
	U	6421	35.0	14.0	4.5	33.5	12.9
Nellore	T	49653	36.0	11.4	7.8	32.4	12.4
	R	41697	35.7	11.4	8.1	32.4	12.3
	U	7956	37.3	10.9	6.3	32.4	13.1
Cuddapah	T	46029	36.0	11.3	8.2	31.8	12.7
	R	38103	36.0	11.2	8.5	31.9	12.4
	U	7926	35.8	11.9	6.7	31.4	14.2
Kurnool	T	65261	40.2	9.3	6.9	32.6	11.0
	R	53091	40.0	9.2	7.4	32.7	10.8
	U	12170	41.2	9.7	4.8	32.5	11.8
Anantapur	T	63895	33.6	10.6	8.0	35.2	12.6
	R	52750	33.6	10.6	8.6	35.1	12.2
	U	11145	33.9	10.7	5.4	35.7	14.3
Chittoor	T	57534	33.5	12.5	6.9	34.0	13.1
	R	46815	33.1	11.9	7.3	34.3	13.4
	U	10719	35.5	14.8	5.2	32.8	11.7

Drinking Water :

Distribution of Household by Sources of Drinking Water

		Total	Rural	Urban
INDIA				
Tap	Total	70,448,827	33,583,755	36,865,072
	Within Premises	39,966,085	13,289,645	26,676,440
	Near Premises	24,998,605	16,908,647	8,089,958
	Away	5,484,137	3,385,463	2,098,674
Hand-pump	Total	68,456,319	59,736,874	8,719,445
	Within Premises	21,332,741	16,899,373	4,433,368
	Near Premises	36,605,076	33,442,465	3,162,611
	Away	10,518,502	9,395,036	1,123,466
Tubewell	Total	10,676,594	7,930,488	2,746,106
	Within Premises	3,138,814	1,583,518	1,555,296
	Near Premises	4,794,142	4,065,129	729,013
	Away	2,743,638	2,281,841	461,797
Well	Total	34,873,103	30,732,819	4,140,284
	Within Premises	9,961,068	7,618,694	2,342,374
	Near Premises	15,650,450	14,555,796	1,094,654
	Away	9,261,585	8,558,329	703,256

		Total	Rural	Urban
Tank,	Total	1,936,671	1,769,496	167,175
Pond, etc.	Within Premises	268,380	233,258	35,122
	Near Premises	860,293	798,155	62,138
	Away	807,998	738,083	69,915
River,	Total	1,943,863	1,840,868	102,995
Canal	Within Premises	0	0	0
	Near Premises	829,904	778,200	51,704
	Away	1,113,959	1,062,668	51,291
Spring	Total	1,415,997	1,283,098	132,899
	Within Premises	0	0	0
	Near Premises	614,404	539,449	74,955
	Away	801,593	743,649	57,944
Any other	Total	2,212,561	1,394,161	818,400
	Within Premises	136,181	74,259	61,922
	Near Premises	759,396	472,891	286,505
	Away	1,316,984	847,011	469,973
ANDHRA PRADESH				
Tap	Total	8,105,960	5,104,676	3,001,284
	Within Premises	3,465,131	1,618,398	1,846,733
	Near Premises	3,685,087	2,829,246	855,841
	Away	955,742	657,032	298,710
Hand-pump	Total	4,399,109	3,910,729	488,380
	Within Premises	623,254	453,799	169,455
	Near Premises	2,790,361	2,570,531	219,830
	Away	985,494	886,399	99,095
Tubewell	Total	999,858	726,562	273,296
	Within Premises	337,946	156,797	181,149
	Near Premises	390,430	344,959	45,471
	Away	271,482	224,806	46,676
Well	Total	2,778,668	2,478,492	300,176
	Within Premises	828,803	645,324	183,479
	Near Premises	1,160,731	1,094,881	65,850
	Away	789,134	738,287	50,847
Tank,	Total	158,628	152,127	6,501
Pond, etc.	Within Premises	4,514	3,525	989
	Near Premises	72,180	69,703	2,477
	Away	81,934	78,899	3,035
River,	Total	136,935	131,689	5,246
Canal	Within Premises	0	0	0
	Near Premises	52,836	50,386	2,450
	Away	84,099	81,303	2,796
Spring	Total	70,660	68,810	1,850
	Within Premises	0	0	0
	Near Premises	26,944	25,646	1,298
	Away	43,716	43,164	552
Any other	Total	200,039	103,133	96,906
	Within Premises	12,063	5,521	6,542
	Near Premises	59,569	30,739	28,830
	Away	128,407	66,873	61,534

Electricity

Important power projects in the State are : the Nagarjunasagar and Neelam Sanjiva Reddy Sagar (Srisailam Hydel Project), Upper Sileru, Lower Sileru, Tungabhadra Hydel projects and Nellore, Ramagundam, Kothagudem, Vijayawada and Muddarnur thermal power projects. The Srisailam Hydro Electric project (Right Bank) with an installed capacity of 770 MW and the Srisailam Left Bank HES capacity of 900 MW and the Nagarjunasagar complex with 960 MW are the principal sources of hydel generation. Vijaya Dam Thermal Power station with an installed capacity of 1,260 MW and Kothagudem Thermal Power station with an installed capacity of 1,220 MW are the main sources of thermal power generation. The 1,000 coal-based Simhadri Thermal Power station aims at supplying the entire energy generated to the State.

Installed capacity of the State as on June, 2009 is 13,472.33 MW. The annual revenue from sale of power is Rs.13,945 crores (including non-tariff income). Government is particularly committed to the welfare of farmers by way of enhancing free power from seven hours to nine hours to all agriculture consumers. Govt. also waived to power consumption arrears amounting to Rs. 1,259 Crores relating to agricultural consumers. During the year 2008-09,81,036 new agricultural connections were released. 21 new projects are programmed by APGENCO, out of which, 2 projects Rayalaseema TPP State II and Dr. Narla Tata Rao TPS State II (VTPS) are already functioning.

Distribution of Workers

Total Population, Total Workers, Main Workers, Marginal Workers and Non-Workers–India, States and Union Territories :

*India/State/ Union territory**	*Total Rural Urban*	*Persons Males Females*	*Total population*	*Total workers*
INDIA	Total	Persons	1,025,251,059	402,512,190
		Males	530,422,415	275,463,736
		Females	494,828,644	127,048,454

*India/State/ Union territory**	*Total Rural Urban*	*Persons Males Females*	*Total population*	*Total workers*
	Rural	Persons	740,255,371	310,655,339
		Males	380,438,194	199,199,602
		Females	359,817,177	111,455,737
	Urban	Persons	284,995,688	91,856,851
		Males	149,984,221	76,264,134
		Females	135,011,467	15,592,717
Andhra Pradesh	Total	Persons	76,111,243	34,865,117
		Males	38,490,506	21,725,810
		Females	37,620,737	13,139,307
	Rural	Persons	55,296,875	28,159,160
		Males	27,890,340	16,309,047
		Females	27,406,535	11,850,113
	Urban	Persons	20,814,368	6,705,957
		Males	10,600,166	5,416,763
		Females	10,214,202	1,289,194

Main workers	*Marginal workers*	*Non-workers*
313,173,394	89,338,796	622,738,869
240,520,672	34,943,064	254,958,679
72,652,722	54,395,732	367,780,190
229,672,348	80,982,991	429,600,032
169,333,233	29,866,369	181,238,592
60,339,115	51,116,622	248,361,440
83,501,046	8,355,805	193,138,837
71,187,439	5,076,695	73,720,087
12,313,607	3,279,110	119,418,750
29,001,326	5,863,791	41,246,126
19,517,524	2,208,286	16,764,696
9,483,802	3,655,505	24,481,430
22,943,260	5,215,900	27,137,715
14,484,219	1,824,828	11,581,293
8,459,041	3,391,072	15,556,422
6,058,066	647,891	14,108,411
5,033,305	383,458	5,183,403
1,024,761	264,433	8,925,008

Total Workers (Main + Marginal) and their Categories–India, States and Union Territories :

*India/State / Union territory**	*Total Rural Urban*	*Persons Males Females*	*Total workers (Main+ Marginal)*	*Cultivators*
INDIA	Total	Persons	402,512,190	127,628,287
		Males	275,463,736	86,328,447
		Females	127,048,454	41,299,840
	Rural	Persons	310,655,339	124,682,055
		Males	199,199,602	84,046,644
		Females	111,455,737	40,635,411
	Urban	Persons	91,856,851	2,946,232
		Males	76,264,134	2,281,803
		Females	15,592,717	664,429
Andhra Pradesh	Total	Persons	34,865,117	7,903,635
		Males	21,725,810	5,287,272
		Females	13,139,307	2,616,363
	Rural	Persons	28,159,160	7,784,145
		Males	16,309,047	5,188,706
		Females	11,850,113	2,595,439
	Urban	Persons	6,705,957	119,490
		Males	5,416,763	98,566
		Females	1,289,194	20,924

Agricultural Labourers	*Household Industry*	*Other Workers workers*
107,447,725	16,395,870	151,040,308
57,354,281	8,312,191	123,468,817
50,093,444	8,083,679	27,571,491
103,122,189	11,709,533	71,141,562
54,749,291	5,642,112	54,761,555
48,372,898	6,067,421	16,380,007
4,325,536	4,686,337	79,898,746
2,604,990	2,670,079	68,707,262
1,720,546	2,016,258	11,191,484
13,818,754	1,569,699	11,573,029
6,431,834	666,358	9,340,346
7,386,920	903,341	2,232,683
13,379,667	1,198,770	5,796,578
6,188,479	481,882	4,449,980
7,191,188	716,888	1,346,598
439,087	370,929	5,776,451
243,355	184,476	4,890,366
195,732	186,453	886,085

Fairs and Festivals

Afzal Shah Biyabani Urs : It is celebrated for about one week from 21st to 28th of *Safar* (June-July) in memory of the saint Afzal Shah Biyabani at Kazipet near Warangal.

Baba Fakiruddin Saheb Urs : It is celebrated annually for three days from the thirteenth of *Jamadi-us-sani* (October-November) near his *samadhi* at Pallavolu near Cuddapah. *Gandhothsavam* is on the first day, *urs* on the second and the actual *janda uthsavam i.e.,* taking the flag in a procession and tying to the tree is on the third. Rams and goats are sacrificed in every house in the name of the saint, *palav* is prepared and is distributed to the poor, the neighbours and guests etc., on the second day. The festival has been celebrated for the past 150 years.

Chintalamma Teertham : It is celebrated on *Jaistha Sudha Vidiya,* (May-June) at the temple of Chintalamma at Pasarapudilanka a town situated on the right bank of river Vainateyam, a branch of Vasishta Godavari in East Godavari district.

Dasthagiriswamy Urs : It is celebrated for three days from *Phalghuna Suddha Chathurdasi* (February-March) at Korrapudu near Cuddapah. A week before the festival a long bamboo pole is brought from the forest and the flag is hoisted on *Chathurdasi,* the first day of the *urs* at the specified place.

Eswaramma Aradhana : It is celebrated at the temple of Eswaramma at Ayyavaripalle near Nellore.

The celebration takes place from *Margasira Bahula Navami* to *Ekadasi* (November-December) for 3 days, and the *uthsavam* is celebrated for two days on *Magha Bahula Triodasi* and *Chaturdasi* (January-February) during *Mahasivaratri.* Cocoanuts, fruits and flowers are offered to the deity. Oil bath, fasting and *jagarana* are the prescribed austerities and customs for the devotees.

Fathekhan Hajrath Urs : It is celebrated for three days during *Rajab* (November-December) at Sangareddy near Medak. On the first day the *darga* is decorated with dots of sandal paste and flowers and on the second day the flag of the saint is taken out on a horse back to the accompaniment of music. Devotees liquidate their vows on this day by worshipping the *darga* and offering fruits, flowers and cash. Display of fire works is done on a large scale. *Quavali* (singing in praise of the saint) is the main function on the third day.

Garagalamma Teertham : It is celebrated for three days from *Chaitra Suddha Padyami* (March-April) at Mummidiva-rappadu in East Godavari district.

Hazarat Khader Vali Urs : It is celebrated for three days during Margasiram or Pushyam (November-December) at Konakondla in Anantapur district. On the first day of the festival there is gandham, shamshir on the second day and jayarath on the third day. On the last day, the descendants of his family who commenced the Urs after the death of the sage are taken in procession.

Jamal Vali Urs : It is celebrated for two days from the full moon day in Phalgunam (February-March) at Kanagudur near Cuddapah. On the first day gandham is brought to Vennapusa house from the house of Syed of Proddatur and from there brought with music and kept on the tomb at 4 A.M., on Padyami. The next night i.e., on the night of Padyami, janda (flag) is taken out in procession with music in the village and installed at the darga. Devotees, Muslims as well as Hindus, fulfil their vows by naming their children after the saint and by observing tonsure ceremonies during the festival.

Kamelibaba Fair : There is an annual religious conference at the Kamelibaba Ashram on Ashijana hill which forms the northern end of the Kondapalle hill range in Krishna district Kamelibaba got this popular name as he invariably wore a blanket.

Lady Fatima Festival : It is the Christian annual festival observed at Kazipet near Warangal.

Madanagopalaswamy Festival : It is celebrated for a day on Karthika Suddha Dwadasi (October-November) at Sankaraguptam in East Godavari district. Abhishekams and sahasranama pujas are performed. This festival is being celebrated for the past many years but is of local significance.

Nagobha Jatra : It is celebrated for five days from *Pushya Bahula Amavasya* (December-January) at Keslapur Buzurg in Adilabad district. *Puja* is performed at the midnight of *Pushya Amavasya.*

Parasavedeeswaraswamy Festival : It is celebrated for two days from *Magha Bahula Triodasi* (February-March) at Ammapalle near Mahbubnagar. *Abhishekam, kalyanam* and *vratam* are the rituals observed during the festival.

Rangamma Perantalu : It is celebrated every year from *Chaitra Suddha Ekadasi* to *Purnima* (March-April) for five days at Telaprolu near Krishna district.

Sai Baba Abhishekam : It is done to the image of Shirdi Sai Baba on Vijaydasami day (September-October) at Puttaparthi near Anantapur district.

Vakulamma Teertham : It is celebrated during Sankranti for three days from 14th January, at Ryali in East Godavari area.

Yellamma Jatara : It is celebrated for five days on every Tuesday commencing from the second Tuesday in Magham (January-February). One notable practice, during the festival, is that a woman belonging to the family of the orginal *Pujari* who is of Ediga community covers completely her mouth with a silver wire which

Abbreviations

BCM : Billion Cubic Meter
C : Flood Control
C.D. Block : Community Development Block
CB : Buttress
ER : Rockfill
GP : Gram Panchayat
GDP : Gross Domestic Product
H : Hydro-electric
HAM : Hectare Meter
HQ : Headquarters
I : Irrigation
L : Uncontrolled Spillway
MCM : Million Cubic Meter
MM : Millimeter
MV : Multi Arch
N : Navigation
NA : Not Available
NH : National Highway
O.G : Outgrowth
PG : Gravity
R : Purposes
S : Water Supply Recreational
SC : Scheduled Caste
SH : State Highway
Sqs. Kms : Square Kilometers
ST : Scheduled Tribes
TE : Earth
U : C.-Under Construction
UE : Universalisation of Elementary Education
VA : Arch
V : Controlled Spillway
WRP : Work Participation Rate

A.KONDURU

A. Konduru C.D. Block lies in the northern part of Krishna district. The Block is located at a distance of 105 kms. from district headquarters (Machilipatnam). There are 13 villages in the block with the total population of 44,930 persons. Area of the C.D. Block is 207.61 sq. kms. It is bounded in the north by Mandal Tiruvuru, in the south by Mandals Mylavaram and Reddigu dem, in the east by Mandals Vissannapet and Reddigudem, and in the west by Mandals Gampalegudem and Mylavaram.

Communications:

Roadways : NH- 221: Direction- Tiruvuru to Mylavaram. Nearest Villages- Polisettipadu, Vallampatla, A.Konduru. State Highway (S.H.): Direction- A. Konduru to Nuzvid. Nearest Villages- A.Konduru, Kummarakuntla, Madhavaram (West), Repudi.

River: Ippala Vagu: Nearest Villages-Marepalle, Gollama ndala, Kambampadu, Atlapragada, Koduru, A.Konduru, Repud

Annaul Rainfall: Average Rainfall 1018 mm

Ground Water: Availability of the Ground Water in the Basin is (Information not avavible) H.A.M .and the utilization is (Information not avavible) H.A.M. It belongs to (Information not avavible) category. Depth to water level varies from 3 to 10 meter below the ground. Most of the wells go down in summer months.

Natural Division : Krishna Delta Region

Administration:

Division: Coastal Andhra. Parliamentary Constituency: 29 Vijayawada. District: Krishna. Mandal: A. Konduru. Assembly Constituency: 188 Tiruvuru (SC). Gram Panchay at: 16.

Villages: 13 **Inhabited:** 13 **Uninhabited:** 0

Ranking	District	State	National
Area	11	504	4047
Population	40	662	5512
Sex Ratio	42	933	3188
Child Sex Ratio	34	686	2813
Literacy Rate	49	784	4839
Density	4	354	4495
Work Participation Rate	47	656	883

Gram Panchayats:

A.Konduru, Cheemalapadu, Gollamandala, Gopalapuram Jeelakunta, Kambhampadu, Koduru, Krishnaraopalem Kummarikuntla, Madhavaram, Marepalli, Polisettipadu Ramachandrapuram, Repudi, Repudi Thanda, Vallampatla.

Amenities:

Education: Primary School in 13 villages, Middle school in 7 villages, Matriculation or Secondary School in 4 villages, namely Polisettipadu, Kambampadu, Koduru, Cheemalapadu.

Higher Secondary or Pre University Courses or Intermediate or Junior College in 0 village of the CD Block, College in 0 village, Adult Literacy Center in 4 villages.

Medical: Hospital in 0 village, Dispensary in 0 village, Health Center in 2 villages, Sub Center in 7 villages, Maternity and Child Welfare Center in 0 village, Community health workers in 0 village.

The Village having Hospital or Dispensary or Health Center is Cheemalapadu.

Drinking Water: Tap water in 7 villages, Tank water in 2 villages, Well water in 12 villages, Tubewell in 2 villages and more than one source in 12 villages.

Bank: Banking facility in 4 villages, namely, Polisettipadu, A.Konduru, Repudi, Cheemalapadu.

Credit Society in 9 villages Agricultural Credit Society in 7 Non-Agricultural Credit Society in 9 villages.

Others: Power supply in 13 villages, Cinema hall in 3 villages, sport club in 0 village, Stadium or Auditorium or Community Hall in 0 village, Post Office in 8 villages.

There are 12 villages having bus facilities.

Villages with most of facilities: Polisettipadu A.Konduru, Repudi, Cheemalapadu.

Villages without Amenities (Education): None..

Scheduled Castes: Out of the total population of 44930 persons, 11173 persons (24.87%) belong to Scheduled Castes.

The villages having less than 10% SC population are None..

The villages having more than 50% SC population are None.

Sex ratio of Scheduled Caste population is 484.

Scheduled Castes Literates and Illiterates by Sex:

	Persons	Males	Females
Literate	4,339	2,663	1,676
Illiterate	6,834	3,101	3,733
Literacy rate	45.0	53.5	35.9
Graduate	87	70	17

Scheduled Castes (Dominant):

Madiga, Mala, Beda Jangam etc., Mala Dasu Pambada etc.

For their cultural identity please see Appendix-I

Villages without Scheduled Castes: There are 2 villages without any scheduled caste population.

Scheduled Tribes: Out of the total population of 44930 persons, 10957 persons (24.39%) belong to Scheduled Tribes.

The villages having less than 10% ST population are Marepalle, Kambampadu, Koduru, Atlapragada Madhavaram (East).

The villages having more than 50% ST population are None.

Sex ratio of Scheduled tribe population is 478.

Scheduled Tribes Literates and Illiterates by Sex:

	Persons	Males	Females
Literate	3,304	2,390	914
Illiterate	7,653	3,326	4,327
Literacy rate	36.2	50.0	21.0
Graduate	40	38	2

Scheduled Tribes (Dominant):
Sugalis etc., Yerukulas, Yenadis, Kammara
For their cultural identity please see Appendix-II
Villages without Scheduled Tribes: There are 0 village without any scheduled tribe population.
Literates and Illiterates by Sex (Total Population):

	Persons	Males	Females
Literate	18,628	11,394	7,234
Illiterate	26,302	11,575	14,727
Literacy rate	48	57	38
Graduate	446	355	91

Agriculture: ***Distribution of villages according to land use:*** Out of 13 villages, Total area (in hectare) is 20761, out of that 49.81 percent is cultivable and 30.2 percent of the cultivable area is irrigated.
Sources of Irrigation (Hectares): Government Canal 944.52, Private Canal 0, Well without Electricity 0, Well with Electricity 0, Tubewell without Electricity 141.28, Tubewell with Electricity 696.35, Tank 1143.68, River 0, Lake 0, Waterfall 0, Others 196.76.
Villages with population of 5000 to 9999:
Kambampadu, A.Konduru.
Villages with population of 10000 and above:
Cheemalapadu.
Distribution of Workers:

	Persons	Males	Females	WPR
Cultivators	4,729	3,490	1,239	19.2
Agricultural Labour	16,400	7,479	8,921	66.6
Household Industry	477	274	203	1.94
Other Workers	3,020	2,507	513	12.26
Main Workers	21,226	12,680	8,546	86.19
Marginal Workers	3,400	1,070	2,330	13.81
Total Workers	24,626	13,750	10,876	

Religion: Major Religious Communities:

	Persons	Males	Females	Sex Ratio
Hindu (95.9%)	43,087	22,070	21,017	952
Muslim (2.78%)	1,248	639	609	953
Christian (1.27%)	572	249	323	1,297
Sikh (0%)	-	-	-	-
Buddhists (0%)	-	-	-	-
Jain (0%)	-	-	-	-

Agewise Data:

	Persons	Males	Females	Sex Ratio
All ages	44,930	22,969	21,961	956
0-14	15,114	7,750	7,364	950
15-44	21,645	11,104	10,541	949
45-79	7,883	3,971	3,912	985
80+	259	131	128	977
Age not stated	29	13	16	1231

Languages (Dominant):
Telugu, Hindi, Urdu, Gondi, Tamil
Disabled Population:

	Persons	Males	Females	%
Total Disabled	888	440	448	
In Seeing	297	136	161	33.45
In Speech	103	55	48	11.6
In Hearing	61	28	33	6.87
In Movement	322	162	160	36.26
Mentally	105	59	46	11.82

ACHAMPET

Achampet C.D. Block lies in the central east part of Mahbubnagar district. The Block is located at a distance of 85 kms. from district headquarters (Mahbubnagar). There are 22 villages in the block with the total population of 57,313 persons. Area of the C.D. Block is 372.42 sq. kms. It is bounded by Nalgonda district on northern and eastern side, Uppununthala Mandal on north western side, Balmoor Mandal on west, and Amrabad Mandal on south.

Communications:
Roadways : State Highway (S.H.): Direction- Balmoor to Srisailam. Nearest Villages- Nadimpalle, Achampet, Tangapur, Bolghatpalle, Rangapur, Brahmanapalle.
River: Dindi Nadi- Nearest Villages- Chandapur, Ainole, Singavaram, Bommenapalle, Siddapur, Mannavaripalle, Ghanapur, Akkavaram.
Backwards Region Grants Fund: It receives Backward Region Grants.

Integrated Child Development Scheme (ICDS) Project: Achampeta, Total Anganwadi Centres: 272
Annual Rainfall: Average Rainfall 709 mm
Ground Water: Availability of the Ground Water in the Basin is 3060 H.A.M. and the utilization is 1434 H. A.M. It belongs to Safe category. Depth to water level varies from 2 to 5 meter below the ground. Most of the wells go down in summer months. The well density in the entire block is 5 wells per sq. km. Total no. of the wells in the block are enumerated as 2459, according to the Ground Water Estimation Committee.
Natural Division : Telangana Plateau Region
Administration:
Division: Talangana. Parliamentary Constituency: 12 Nagarkurnool (SC). District: Mahbubnagar. Mandal: Acham pet. Assembly Constituency: 82 Achampet (SC). Gram Panch ayat: 21.
Villages: 22 **Inhabited:** 22 **Uninhabited:** 0

Ranking	District	State	National
Area	5	63	2111
Population	14	319	4953
Sex Ratio	55	994	3555
Child Sex Ratio	58	1035	4945
Literacy Rate	2	518	3919
Density	63	827	5499
Work Participation Rate	51	890	2559

Gram Panchayats:
Achampet, Akkaram, Bolgattupally, Bommanpally Chandapur, Chennaram(Pn), Choutapally, Devultanda Ganpur, Gumpanpally, Hazipur, Inole, Laxmapur(Pn) Lingotam, Mannevaripally, Nadimpally, Polkampally Pulazala, Rangapur, Siddapur, Singaram.

Amenities:

Education: Primary School in 22 villages, Middle school in 10 villages, Matriculation or Secondary School in 4 villages, namely Nadimpalle, Achampet, Tangapur, Ainole.

Higher Secondary or Pre University Courses or Intermediate or Junior College in 1 village of the CD Block,, namely Achampet.

College in 0 village, Adult Literacy Center in 21 villages.

Medical: Hospital in 1 village, Dispensary in 1 village, Health Center in 3 villages, Sub Center in 10 villages, Maternity and Child Welfare Center in 22 villages, Community health workers in 0 village.

The Villages having Hospital or Dispensary or Health Center are Achampet, Siddapur.

Drinking Water: Tap water in 22 villages, Tank water in 22 villages, Well water in 22 villages, Tubewell in 22 villages and more than one source in 22 villages.

Bank: Banking facility in 2 villages, namely, Achampet, Siddapur.

Credit Society in 13 villages Agricultural Credit Society in 2 Non-Agricultural Credit Society in 2 villages.

Others: Power supply in 22 villages, Cinema hall in 1 village, sport club in 1 village, Stadium or Auditorium or Community Hall in 1 village, Post Office in 13 villages.

There are 21 villages having bus facilities.

Villages with most of facilities: Achampet Siddapur.

Villages without Amenities (Education): None..

Scheduled Castes: Out of the total population of 57313 persons, 9367 persons (16.34%) belong to Scheduled Castes.

The villages having less than 10% SC population are Gumpampalle, Lakshmapur (P.N), Bolghatpalle Rangapur, Brahmanapalle, Ainole, Singavaram Siddapur, Akkavaram.

The villages having more than 50% SC population are None.

Sex ratio of Scheduled Caste population is 481.

Scheduled Castes Literates and Illiterates by Sex:

	Persons	Males	Females
Literate	4,063	2,735	1,328
Illiterate	5,304	2,130	3,174
Literacy rate	50.6	65.4	34.5
Graduate	140	109	31

Scheduled Castes (Dominant):

Madiga, Mala, Generic Castes etc., Beda Jangam etc. Dom etc.

For their cultural identity please see Appendix-I

Villages without Scheduled Castes: There is 1 village without any scheduled caste population.

Scheduled Tribes: Out of the total population of 57313 persons, 15652 persons (27.31%) belong to Scheduled Tribes.

The villages having less than 10% ST population are Palukapalle, Puljala, Chennaram (Sabak), Nadimpalle Achampet, Tangapur.

The villages having more than 50% ST population are Gumpampalle, Lakshmapur (P.N), Bolghatpalle Rangapur, Ainole, Singavaram, Siddapur, Ghanapur Akkavaram.

Sex ratio of Scheduled tribe population is 481.

Scheduled Tribes Literates and Illiterates by Sex:

	Persons	Males	Females
Literate	4,067	2,985	1,082
Illiterate	11,585	5,132	6,453
Literacy rate	32.3	46.1	17.7
Graduate	107	93	14

Scheduled Tribes (Dominant):

Sugalis etc., Yerukulas, Chenchu etc.
Generic Tribes etc., Kammara

For their cultural identity please see Appendix-II

Villages without Scheduled Tribes: There are 2 villages without any scheduled tribe population.

Literates and Illiterates by Sex (Total Population):

	Persons	Males	Females
Literate	25,887	16,271	9,616
Illiterate	31,426	13,140	18,286
Literacy rate	54	66	41
Graduate	1,626	1,291	335

Agriculture: ***Distribution of villages according to land use:*** Out of 22 villages, Total area (in hectare) is 37243, out of that 25.89 percent is cultivable and 23.53 percent of the cultivable area is irrigated.

Sources of Irrigation (Hectares): Government Canal 0, Private Canal 0, Well without Electricity 134.88, Well with Electricity 1246, Tubewell without Electricity 24, Tubewell with Electricity 526, Tank 338, River 0, Lake 0, Waterfall 0, Others 0.

Villages with population of 5000 to 9999: None

Villages with population of 10000 and above:

Achampet.

Distribution of Workers:

	Persons	Males	Females	WPR
Cultivators	10,191	5,947	4,244	37.64
Agricultural Labour	7,925	3,136	4,789	29.27
Household Industry	831	409	422	3.07
Other Workers	8,125	6,321	1,804	30.01
Main Workers	23,432	14,445	8,987	86.55
Marginal Workers	3,640	1,368	2,272	13.45
Total Workers	27,072	15,813	11,259	

Religion: Major Religious Communities:

	Persons	Males	Females	Sex Ratio
Hindu (90.46%)	51,846	26,642	25,204	946
Muslim (8.8%)	5,045	2,548	2,497	980
Christian (0.48%)	273	134	139	1,037
Sikh (0%)	1	1	-	-
Buddhists (0%)	-	-	-	-
Jain (0%)	-	-	-	-

Agewise Data:

	Persons	Males	Females	Sex Ratio
All ages	57,313	29,411	27,902	949
0-14	21,575	11,513	10,062	874
15-44	26,469	13,460	13,009	966
45-79	8,845	4,250	4,595	1081
80+	351	138	213	1543
Age not stated	73	50	23	460

Languages (Dominant):

Telugu, Hindi, Urdu, Tamil, Oriya

Disabled Population:

	Persons	Males	Females	%
Total Disabled	865	494	371	
In Seeing	309	190	119	35.72
In Speech	98	56	42	11.33
In Hearing	31	16	15	3.58
In Movement	347	195	152	40.12
Mentally	80	37	43	9.25

ACHANTA

Achanta C.D. Block lies in the south-eastern part of West Godavari district. The Block is located at a dista nce of 110 kms. from district headquarters (Eluru). There are 10 villages in the block with the total popul ation of 63,358 persons. Area of the C.D. Block is 73. 01 sq. kms. It is bounded in the north by Mandal Penugo nda, in the south by Mandals Poduru and Yelamanchili, in the east by river Vasista Godavari and district East Godavari, and in the west by Mandals Penumantra and Peduru.

Communications :

Roadways : Metalled Roads: Nearest Villages- Achanta, Kodamanchili, Koderu, Penumanchili, Achanta Vemavaram.

River: Vasista Godavari Nadi- Nearest Villages- Pedamal lam, Koderu, Karugorumilli, Valluru.

Backwards Region Grants Fund: It receives Backward Region Grants.

Annaul Rainfall: Average Rainfall 1496 mm

Ground Water: Availability of the Ground Water in the Basin is (Information not avavible) H.A.M .and the utilization is (Information not avavible) H.A.M. It belongs to (Information not avavible) category. Depth to water level varies from 3 to 10 meter below the ground. Most of the wells go down in summer months.

Natural Division : Godavari Delta Region

Administration:

Division: Coastal Andhra. Parliamentary Constituency: 26 Narsapuram. District: West Godavari. Mandal: Achanta. Assembly Constituency: 175 Achanta. Gram Panchayat: 12

Fairs and Festivals:

Venkateswaraswamy Festival : It is celebrated for six days from Magha Suddha Dasami to Purnima (January -Febr uary). Kalyanam on Dwadasi and Chakraatheertham on Purnima are the important rituals observed. The legends connected with the name of the Achanteswara Kshetram are narrated here under. The place was originally called Marthandapuram after protecting the deity of the place Marthandeswara. The deity was facing west towards the village and on account of the fierce looks of the deity, fire accidents were occuring frequently in the village and therefore, it was not prospering. In response to their prayers to save them from the severity of his sight, the Lord revealed in their dream that his divine spouse alone could counteract the effect of his sight. The villagers therefore installed in front of the shrine, facing the Lord, Mahishasuramardini (Parvati Devi, wife of Lord Siva assumed this form when she fought, against and killed Mahishasura, a demon) in another shirne. These two shrines can now be found in Sri Rameswaraswamy temple.

Villages: 10 **Inhabited:** 10 **Uninhabited:** 0

Ranking	**District**	**State**	**National**
Area	42	1076	5927
Population	34	225	4748
Sex Ratio	19	428	1670
Child Sex Ratio	43	979	4461
Literacy Rate	12	16	482
Density	18	882	1019
Work Participation Rate	5	20	2965

Gram Panchayats:

A Vemavaram, Achanta, Ayodyalanka, Bimalapuram

Kandharavalli, Karugoramilli, Kodamanchali, Koderu Pedamallam, Penumanchali, Seshamma Cheruvu, Valluru.

Amenities:

Education: Primary School in 10 villages, Middle school in 8 villages, Matriculation or Secondary School in 6 villages, namely Achanta, Kodamanchili, Penumanchili, Achanta Vemavaram, Valluru, Bhimalapuram.

Higher Secondary or Pre University Courses or Intermediate or Junior College in 1 village of the CD Block,, namely Achanta.

College in 0 village, Adult Literacy Center in 10 villages.

Medical: Hospital in 0 village, Dispensary in 2 villages, Health Center in 2 villages, Sub Center in 8 villages, Maternity and Child Welfare Center in 0 village, Community health workers in 0 village.

The Villages having Hospital or Dispensary or Health Center are Achanta, Valluru.

Drinking Water: Tap water in 10 villages, Tank water in 10 villages, Well water in 10 villages, Tubewell in 10 villages and more than one source in 10 villages.

Bank: Banking facility in 4 villages, namely, Achanta, Kodamanchili, Valluru, Bhimalapuram.

Credit Society in 5 villages Agricultural Credit Society in 4 Non-Agricultural Credit Society in 1 village.

Others: Power supply in 10 villages, Cinema hall in 2 villages, sport club in 0 village, Stadium or Auditorium or Community Hall in 0 village, Post Office in 9 villages.

There are 10 villages having bus facilities.

Villages with most of facilities: Achanta Kodamanchili, Valluru, Bhimalapuram.

Villages without Amenities (Education): None..

Scheduled Castes: Out of the total population of 63358 persons, 17209 persons (27.16%) belong to Scheduled Castes.

The villages having less than 10% SC population are None..

The villages having more than 50% SC population are None.

Sex ratio of Scheduled Caste population is 494.

Scheduled Castes Literates and Illiterates by Sex:

	Persons	Males	Females
Literate	11,312	6,111	5,201
Illiterate	5,897	2,596	3,301
Literacy rate	76.1	81.5	70.7
Graduate	262	202	60

Scheduled Castes (Dominant):

Mala, Madiga, Arundhatiya, Adi Andhra, Relli

For their cultural identity please see Appendix-I

Villages without Scheduled Castes: There are 0 village without any scheduled caste population.

Scheduled Tribes: Out of the total population of 63358 persons, 312 persons (0.49%) belong to Scheduled Tribes.

The villages having less than 10% ST population are Achanta, Kodamanchili, Pedamallam, Koderu Kandaravalli, Karugorumilli, Penumanchili Achanta Vemavaram, Valluru, Bhimalapuram.

The villages having more than 50% ST population are None.

Sex ratio of Scheduled tribe population is 516.

Scheduled Tribes Literates and Illiterates by Sex:

	Persons	Males	Females
Literate	123	62	61
Illiterate	189	89	100
Literacy rate	47.7	50.4	45.2
Graduate	4	3	1

Scheduled Tribes (Dominant):

Yerukulas, Chenchu etc., Koya etc.

Generic Tribes etc., Sugalis etc.

For their cultural identity please see Appendix-II

Villages without Scheduled Tribes: There are 2 villages without any scheduled tribe population.

Literates and Illiterates by Sex (Total Population):

	Persons	Males	Females
Literate	43,130	23,155	19,975
Illiterate	20,228	8,715	11,513
Literacy rate	77	83	72
Graduate	1,332	1,030	302

Agriculture: ***Distribution of villages according to land use:*** Out of 10 villages, Total area (in hectare) is 7301, out of that 79.81 percent is cultivable and 100 percent of the cultivable area is irrigated.

Sources of Irrigation (Hectares): Government Canal 5827.05, Private Canal 0, Well without Electricity 0, Well with Electricity 0, Tubewell without Electricity 0, Tubewell with Electricity 0, Tank 0, River 0, Lake 0, Waterfall 0, Others 0.

Villages with population of 5000 to 9999: Kodamanchili, Achanta Vemavaram, Valluru Bhimalapuram.

Villages with population of 10000 and above: Achanta.

Distribution of Workers:

	Persons	Males	Females	WPR
Cultivators	3,245	2,877	368	10.75
Agricultural Labour	20,589	12,155	8,434	68.18
Household Industry	2,190	832	1,358	7.25
Other Workers	4,175	3,345	830	13.82
Main Workers	20,596	15,497	5,099	68.2
Marginal Workers	9,603	3,712	5,891	31.8
Total Workers	30,199	19,209	10,990	

Religion: Major Religious Communities:

	Persons	Males	Females	Sex Ratio
Hindu (98.21%)	62,222	31,338	30,884	986
Muslim (0.39%)	249	124	125	1,008
Christian (1.34%)	851	393	458	1,165
Sikh (0.02%)	15	5	10	2,000
Buddhists (0%)	-	-	-	-
Jain (0.01%)	7	5	2	400

Agewise Data:

	Persons	Males	Females	Sex Ratio
All ages	63,358	31,870	31,488	988
0-14	19,130	9,663	9,467	980
15-44	31,448	15,929	15,519	974
45-79	12,332	6,047	6,285	1039
80+	390	191	199	1042
Age not stated	58	40	18	450

Languages (Dominant):

Telugu, Urdu, Gondi, Hindi, Oriya

Disabled Population:

	Persons	Males	Females	%
Total Disabled	1,335	729	606	
In Seeing	532	254	278	39.85
In Speech	157	79	78	11.76
In Hearing	73	35	38	5.47
In Movement	438	285	153	32.81
Mentally	135	76	59	10.11

ADDAKAL

Addakal C.D. Block lies in the central part of Mahbubnagar district. The Block is located at a distance of 35 kms. from district headquarters (Mahbubnagar). There are 21 villages in the block with the total population of 46,380 persons. Area of the C.D. Block is 191.28 sq. kms. It is bounded by Bhoothpur Mandal on north, Mahbubnagar Mandal on north-west, Devarkadra Mandal on west, Peddamandadi Mandal on south, and Ghanpur Mandal on east.

Communications:

Roadways : NH- 7: Direction- Kurnool to Hyderabad. Nearest Villages- Janampeta, Thunkinipur, Katavaram, Addakal, Sankalamaddi, Komireddipalle, Ponnakal, Gudibanda.

River: Pedda Vagu: Nearest Villages- Sankalamaddi, Komireddipalle, Ponnakal, Gudibanda, Nizalapur, Rachala, Shakhapur, Kandur.

Backwards Region Grants Fund: It receives Backward Region Grants.

Annual Rainfall: Average Rainfall 623 mm

Ground Water: Availability of the Ground Water in the Basin is 1301 H.A.M. and the utilization is 1140 H. A.M. It belongs to SC category. Depth to water level varies from 2 to 5 meter below the ground. Most of the wells go down in summer months. The well density in the entire block is 16 wells per sq. km. Total no. of the wells in the block are enumerated as 3146, according to the Ground Water Estimation Committee.

Natural Division : Telangana Plateau Region

Administration:

Division: Telangana. Parliamentary Constituency: 11 Mahbubnagar. District: Mahbubnagar. Mandal: Addakal. Assembly Constituency: 76 Devarkadra. Gram Panchayat: 20

Fairs and Festivals:

Sri Gumani Saheb Urs : It is observed for one day during the end of Safar (Muslim month—June-July) in memory of the saint. Every Thursday, the villagers worship the saint. Horses made of silver are offered in fulfilment of vows. This festival has been taking place since the year, 1332 AD. According to the legend about Gumani Saheb, long ago, a stranger was camping in the night under a margosa tree. He slept wrapping his body completely with his shawl. His horse was there tied to a side. Next day morning, the shawl was there intact but the man under it had disappeared. People realised that this was a miracle, constructed a tomb at that place and celebrated the Urs.

Villages: 21 **Inhabited:** 21 **Uninhabited:** 0

Ranking	District	State	National
Area	57	604	4333
Population	37	623	5450
Sex Ratio	43	802	2685
Child Sex Ratio	28	657	2630
Literacy Rate	32	987	5632
Density	48	464	4181
Work Participation Rate	10	567	1172

Gram Panchayats:

Addakal, Dasaripally, Gajulapet, Gudibanda, Janampet Kandur, Kataram, Kommreddypally, Nandipet, Nijalapur Polkampally, Ponnakal, Rachala, Sankalamaddi Shakapur, Shakrapoor, Thimmaipally, Thimmapoor Thunkinipur, Vemula.

Amenities:

Education: Primary School in 21 villages, Middle school in 13 villages, Matriculation or Secondary School in 10 villages, namely Vemula, Polkampalle, Janampeta, Sankalamaddi, Ponnakal, Rachala, Shakhapur, Katavaram, Addakal, Kandur.

Higher Secondary or Pre University Courses or Intermediate or Junior College in 0 village of the CD Block, College in 0 village, Adult Literacy Center in 20 villages.

Medical: Hospital in 0 village, Dispensary in 1 village, Health Center in 2 villages, Sub Center in 8 villages, Maternity and Child Welfare Center in 0 village,

Community health workers in 0 village.
The Village having Hospital or Dispensary or Health Center is Addakal.
Drinking Water: Tap water in 21 villages, Tank water in 21 villages, Well water in 21 villages, Tubewell in 21 villages and more than one source in 21 villages.
Bank: Banking facility in 2 villages, namely, Sankalamaddi, Addakal.
Credit Society in 8 villages Agricultural Credit Society in 2 Non-Agricultural Credit Society in 6 villages.
Others: Power supply in 21 villages, Cinema hall in 0 village, sport club in 0 village, Stadium or Auditorium or Community Hall in 0 village, Post Office in 11 villages.
There are 20 villages having bus facilities.
Villages with most of facilities: Sankalamaddi Addakal.
Villages without Amenities (Education): None..
Scheduled Castes: Out of the total population of 46380 persons, 5895 persons (12.71%) belong to Scheduled Castes.
The villages having less than 10% SC population are Nandipet, Gajulapeta, Janampeta, Kankapur, Nizalapur Katavaram, Thimmaipalle.
The villages having more than 50% SC population are None.
Sex ratio of Scheduled Caste population is 486.
Scheduled Castes Literates and Illiterates by Sex:

	Persons	Males	Females
Literate	1,312	951	361
Illiterate	4,583	2,078	2,505
Literacy rate	26.6	37.4	15.1
Graduate	22	19	3

Scheduled Castes (Dominant):
Madiga, Generic Castes etc., Mala, Beda Jangam etc. Mala Dasari
For their cultural identity please see Appendix-I
Villages without Scheduled Castes: There is 1 village without any scheduled caste population.
Scheduled Tribes: Out of the total population of 46380 persons, 1901 persons (4.1%) belong to Scheduled Tribes.
The villages having less than 10% ST population are Nandipet, Dasaripalle, Vemula, Gajulapeta Polkampalle, Thimmapur, Janampeta, Thunkinipur Sankalamaddi, Nizalapur, Komireddipalle, Ponnakal Rachala, Gudibanda, Shakhapur, Addakal, Kandur.
The villages having more than 50% ST population are None.
Sex ratio of Scheduled tribe population is 493.
Scheduled Tribes Literates and Illiterates by Sex:

	Persons	Males	Females
Literate	288	216	72
Illiterate	1,613	747	866
Literacy rate	19.1	28.4	9.6
Graduate	5	5	0

Scheduled Tribes (Dominant):
Sugalis etc., Yerukulas, Generic Tribes etc.
For their cultural identity please see Appendix-II
Villages without Scheduled Tribes: There are 3 villages without any scheduled tribe population.
Literates and Illiterates by Sex (Total Population):

	Persons	Males	Females
Literate	16,123	10,654	5,469
Illiterate	30,257	12,942	17,315
Literacy rate	41	53	28
Graduate	586	501	85

Agriculture: ***Distribution of villages according to land use:*** Out of 21 villages, Total area (in hectare) is 19129, out of that 72.21 percent is cultivable and 16.77 percent of the cultivable area is irrigated.
Sources of Irrigation (Hectares): Government Canal 0, Private Canal 0, Well without Electricity 0, Well with Electricity 52, Tubewell without Electricity 0, Tubewell with Electricity 1813, Tank 451, River 0, Lake 0, Waterfall 0, Others 0.
Villages with population of 5000 to 9999: None
Villages with population of 10000 and above: None
Distribution of Workers:

	Persons	Males	Females	WPR
Cultivators	6,185	4,156	2,029	25.36
Agricultural Labour	12,035	4,700	7,335	49.35
Household Industry	622	338	284	2.55
Other Workers	5,543	4,158	1,385	22.73
Main Workers	19,180	11,386	7,794	78.65
Marginal Workers	5,205	1,966	3,239	21.35
Total Workers	24,385	13,352	11,033	

Religion: Major Religious Communities:

	Persons	Males	Females	Sex Ratio
Hindu (94.08%)	43,634	22,222	21,412	964
Muslim (5.48%)	2,541	1,264	1,277	1,010
Christian (0.37%)	172	96	76	792
Sikh (0%)	-	-	-	-
Buddhists (0%)	-	-	-	-
Jain (0%)	-	-	-	-

Agewise Data:

	Persons	Males	Females	Sex Ratio
All ages	46,380	23,596	22,784	966
0-14	16,501	8,513	7,988	938
15-44	20,827	10,682	10,145	950
45-79	8,723	4,230	4,493	1062
80+	264	130	134	1031
Age not stated	65	41	24	585

Languages (Dominant):

Telugu, Urdu, Hindi, Tamil, Others

Disabled Population:

	Persons	Males	Females	%
Total Disabled	939	503	436	
In Seeing	362	178	184	38.55
In Speech	70	36	34	7.45
In Hearing	60	32	28	6.39
In Movement	362	211	151	38.55
Mentally	85	46	39	9.05

ADDANKI

Addanki C.D. Block lies in the northern part of Prakasam district. The Block is located at a distance of 36 kms. from district headquarters (Ongole). There are 19 villages in the block with the total population of 74,904 persons. Area of the C.D. Block is 252.15 sq. kms. It is bounded in the north by Mandal Ballikura va, in the south by Mandals Chimakurthi, Maddipadu and Korisapadu, in the east by Mandals Korisapdu and Janaka varam Panguluru, and in the west by Mandals Tallur and Mundlamuru.

Communications:

Roadways : State Highways (S.H.): Direction- Darsi to Addanki. and Guntur to Korisapadu. Nearest Villages- Chinakotha Palle, Kalavakuru, Chakraya Palem, Gopalapur am, Narasimha Puram, Addanki (North) (U), Ramayapalem (U), Mani Keswaram.

River: Gundlakamma Nadi- Nearest Villages- Vemparala, Kotikalapudi, Nannurupadu, Addanki (South) (U), Chakra ya Palem, Gopalapuram, Narasimha Puram, Addanki (North) (U), Ramayapalem (U), Mani Keswaram.

The Block is identified as a drought-prone area.

Annual Rainfall: Average Rainfall 829.0 mm

Ground Water: Availability of the Ground Water in the Basin is 17.71 MCM and the utilization is 8.88 MCM It belongs to Safe category. Depth to water level varies from 2 to 5 meter below the ground. Most of the wells go down in summer months., according to the Ground Water Estimation Committee.

Administration:

Division: Coastal Andhra. Parliamentary Constituency: 32 Baptala (SC). District: Prakasam. Mandal: Addanki. Assembly Constituency: 224 Addanki. Gram Panchayat: 27

Palces of Tourist Interest:

Addanki : Addanki lies 38 kms. to the north-west of Ongle on the Ongole-Narasaraopet road. The etymological explanation offered in respect of this village is that, it was named after Addadu and Anki, the two Voddes (stone cutters). The history of the place can be traced to the period of the Eastern Chalukya ruler Vijayaditya III, whose undated inscription registering, that the king appointed Panduranga as his general, has come to light at the place. The Manual refers to the old fort here (now in ruins) which is said to have been built about 300 years ago by Hari Palakudu, son of the renowned Pratapa Rudrudu (Pratapa Rudra). Eight inscriptions on the pillars of the Nagareswara-swamy temple are noticed. Yerrapragada, one of the Kavitrayam, lived in this village when Prolaya Vema Reddi ruled from Addanki. Addanki Nancharamma is the most famous deity known throughout Andhra which is one of the forms of goddess Durga of Parvathiconsort of Lord Siva. She is referred to along with Kanaka Durga of Vijayawada, Nookalamma of Anakappalle, etc., and temples to this deity viz, Addanki Nancharamma are found in several other areas also. Remnants of an old fort belonging to the Yadava Kings of Chakranarayana dynasty and of Reddy Kingdom can be traced here.

The Siva temple in the centre of the village tank and the Vinayaka temple are very ancient temples, said to have been in existence even prior to the advent of Christian era (B.C.), while the Chennakesava temple is said to have been constructed by the Rajas of Vijaya nagara empire.

Dharmavaram : Situated 48 kms. north of Ongole and 5 kms. east of the Addanki-Narasaraopet road, Dharma- varam derived its name from the Siva Linga established by Dharmaraja, the eldest of the Pandavas. Of the templ es of Dharmeswaraswamy, Bhimeswaraswamy Mallikarjunasv Chenna- kesavaswamy and Sitaramaswamy in the village, the first four are ancient ones. An inscription of 1522 (A.D. 1600) noted at the first threshold of Sitara maswamy temple mentions the terms of revenue settlement of Eklaskhanpuram, a village near Dharmavaram in Addanki sima was founded by Eklas Khan, the trusted General of Muhammad-Quil, son of Ibrahim Qutub Shah of Golkonda. Another undated inscription found in the southern compound wall of the same temple records the charitable endowments made for, the religious merit of one Khan Azyani Khan Abdul Saheb by the residents of the suburbs of Eklaskhanpuram and Balupuram.

Manikeswaram : Lying about 32 kms. north-west of Ongole, this villages was originally called Buddapundi, which was gifted for the worship of Mandu- keswaraswamy when the temple was constructed by a Chola King and was consequently named Mandukeswaram. It later came to be known as Manikeswaram. The temple of Mandukeswara- swamy (Malleswaraswamy) stands on the slope of a hill. Adjoining the temple and touching the hill on the north and the western sides flows the Gundlakamma river.

The stone steps from the temple leading to the Gundlak amma, the 'Prakaram' and the kitchen are said to have been constructed by one Manchiraiu. The landscape, viewed from the temple, is quite picturesque.

Villages: 19 **Inhabited:** 18 **Uninhabited:** 1

Ranking	District	State	National
Area	24	301	3352
Population	3	69	4288
Sex Ratio	22	625	2163
Child Sex Ratio	30	731	3106
Literacy Rate	14	286	2865
Density	36	643	3557
Work Participation Rate	10	376	1757

Gram Panchayats:

Addanki, Bommanampadu, Chakrayapalem Chinakothapalli, Dharmavaram, Dhenuvakonda Gopalapuram, Gowada, Jarlapalem, Kalavakuru Kotikalapudi, Kunkupadu, Manikeswaram, Modepalli Mylavaram, Nagulapadu, Perayapalem, Ramayapalem Sankavarappadu, Singarakondapalem, Timmayapalem Uppalapadu, Vangapadu, Velamuripadu, Vemparala Venkatapuram, Vipparlavaripalem.

Amenities:

Education: Primary School in 18 villages, Middle school in 9 villages, Matriculation or Secondary School in 3 villages, namely Addanki (North) (U), Ramayapalem (U), Dhenuva Konda.

Higher Secondary or Pre University Courses or Intermediate or Junior College in 0 village of the CD Block, College in 0 village, Adult Literacy Center in 17 villages.

Medical: Hospital in 0 village, Dispensary in 1 village, Health Center in 1 village, Sub Center in 13 villages, Maternity and Child Welfare Center in 0 village, Community health workers in 0 village.

The Villages having Hospital or Dispensary or Health Center are Dhenuva Konda.

Drinking Water: Tap water in 18 villages, Tank water in 18 villages, Well water in 18 villages, Tubewell in 18 villages and more than one source in 18 villages.

Bank: Banking facility in 1 villages, namely, Addanki (North) (U).

Credit Society in 9 villages Agricultural Credit Society in 7 Non-Agricultural Credit Society in 5 villages.

Others: Power supply in 18 villages, Cinema hall in 1 village, sport club in 0 village, Stadium or Auditorium or Community Hall in 0 village, Post Office in 14 villages.

There are 18 villages having bus facilities.

Village with most of facilities: Addanki (North) (U).

Villages without Amenities (Education): None..

Scheduled Castes: Out of the total population of 74904 persons, 18905 persons (25.24%) belong to Scheduled Castes.

The villages having less than 10% SC population are None..

The villages having more than 50% SC population are None.

Sex ratio of Scheduled Caste population is 491.

Scheduled Castes Literates and Illiterates by Sex:

	Persons	Males	Females
Literate	8,339	5,253	3,086
Illiterate	10,566	4,367	6,199
Literacy rate	51.6	63.9	38.9
Graduate	349	267	82

Scheduled Castes (Dominant):

Madiga, Mala, Beda Jangam etc., Jambuvulu Dakkal etc.

For their cultural identity please see Appendix-I

Villages without Scheduled Castes: There is 1 village without any scheduled caste population.

Scheduled Tribes: Out of the total population of 74904 persons, 2438 persons (3.25%) belong to Scheduled Tribes.

The villages having less than 10% ST population are Mylavaram, Uppalapadu, Vemparala, Chinakotha Palle Dharmavaram, Kalavakuru, Chakraya Palem Bommanampadu, Addanki (North) (U), Ramayapalem (U) Kotikalapudi, Kunkupadu, Modepalle, Dhenuva Konda Nannurupadu, Mani Keswaram, Addanki (South) (U).

The villages having more than 50% ST population are None.

Sex ratio of Scheduled tribe population is 495.

Scheduled Tribes Literates and Illiterates by Sex:

	Persons	Males	Females
Literate	763	484	279
Illiterate	1,675	747	928
Literacy rate	36.7	46.4	27.0
Graduate	17	16	1

Scheduled Tribes (Dominant):

Yenadis, Yerukulas, Chenchu etc., Sugalis etc. Kammara

For their cultural identity please see Appendix-II

Villages without Scheduled Tribes: There is 1 village without any scheduled tribe population.

Literates and Illiterates by Sex (Total Population):

	Persons	Males	Females
Literate	38,914	23,237	15,677
Illiterate	35,990	14,645	21,345
Literacy rate	60	70	48
Graduate	2,372	1,789	583

Agriculture: ***Distribution of villages according to land use:*** Out of 19 villages, Total area (in hectare) is 25215, out of that 71.24 percent is cultivable and 36.18 percent of the

cultivable area is irrigated.

Sources of Irrigation (Hectares): Government Canal 1152.75, Private Canal 0, Well without Electricity 1364.86, Well with Electricity 0, Tubewell without Electricity 0, Tubewell with Electricity 94.71, Tank 918.57, River 850, Lake 0, Waterfall 0, Others 2117.77.

Villages with population of 5000 to 9999:
Dharmavaram, Kalavakuru.

Villages with population of 10000 and above:
Addanki (North) (U), Addanki (South) (U).

Distribution of Workers:

	Persons	Males	Females	WPR
Cultivators	10,369	6,612	3,757	26.67
Agricultural Labour	17,340	7,737	9,603	44.6
Household Industry	712	370	342	1.83
Other Workers	10,460	8,182	2,278	26.9
Main Workers	34,916	21,653	13,263	89.8
Marginal Workers	3,965	1,248	2,717	10.2
Total Workers	38,881	22,901	15,980	

Religion: Major Religious Communities:

	Persons	Males	Females	Sex Ratio
Hindu (94.49%)	70,779	35,800	34,979	977
Muslim (4.79%)	3,586	1,831	1,755	958
Christian (0.6%)	448	209	239	1,144
Sikh (0.01%)	6	3	3	1,000
Buddhists (0%)	1	1	-	-
Jain (0%)	-	-	-	-

Agewise Data:

	Persons	Males	Females	Sex Ratio
All ages	74,904	37,882	37,022	977
0-14	22,235	11,319	10,916	964
15-44	36,431	18,473	17,958	972
45-79	15,464	7,741	7,723	998
80+	699	313	386	1233
Age not stated	75	36	39	1083

Languages (Dominant):
Telugu, Urdu, Tamil, Gondi, Marathi

Disabled Population:

	Persons	Males	Females	%
Total Disabled	894	475	419	
In Seeing	256	126	130	28.64
In Speech	118	59	59	13.2
In Hearing	51	29	22	5.7
In Movement	352	192	160	39.37
Mentally	117	69	48	13.09

ADDATEEGALA

Addateegala C.D. Block lies in the northern part of East Godavari district. The Block is located at a dista nce of 114 kms. from district headquarters (Kakinada). There are 99 villages in the block with the total population of 38,387 persons. Area of the C.D. Block is 168.54 sq. kms. It is bounded in the north by Mandals Y. Ramavaram and Vishakhapatnam, in the south by Mandal Yeleswaram, in the east by Mandals Yeleswaram and Rajavommangi, and in the west by Mandal Gangavaram.

Communications :

Roadways : State Highway (S.H.): Direction- Yeleswaram to Narsipatnam. Nearest Villages Kottampalem, Konalova, Kothurupadu.

River: Madieru Nadi- Nearest Villages- Kinaparti, Gavar ayyapeta, Kottampalem, Venkatanagaram, Gondolu, Atchiyya peta, Veerabhadrapuram, Rajanagaram, Sarampeta, Gangampa lem.

Backwards Region Grants Fund: It receives Backward Region Grants.

Integrated Child Development Scheme (ICDS) Project:
Annaul Rainfall: Average Rainfall 990 mm

Ground Water: Availability of the Ground Water in the Basin is (Information not avavible) H.A.M .and the utilization is (Information not avavible) H.A.M. It belongs to (Information not avavible) category. Depth to water level varies from 3 to 10 meter below the ground. Most of the wells go down in summer months.

Forest and Reserved **Forest:** Nearest Villages- Kalimamidi, Jalluru, Thungamadugula, Duppalapalem, Panasaloddi, Panukuratipalem, Kovelapalem, Bhimudupakalu, Kottampal em, Bodlanka, Venkatanagaram, Papampeta, Gondolu, Atchiy yapeta, Konalova, Rajanagaram, Sarampeta, Rajavaram, Gangampalem, Kothurupadu, Thimmapuram, D. Krishnavara Rayapalle, Somannapalem, Pedamunakanagedda, Mallavaram Mamillu, Paidiputtapadu, Mitlapalem, Kinaparti, Gavaray yapeta, Veerabhadrapuram, Yellavaram, Puligogulapadu, Uppalapadu, Gadichinnampalem.

Natural Division : Godavari Delta Region

Administration:

Division: Coastal Andhra. Parliamentary Constituency: 18 Araku (ST). District: East Godavari. Mandal: Addatee gala. Assembly Constituency: 172 Rampachodavarm (ST). Gram Panchayat: 22.

Villages: 99 **Inhabited:** 90 **Uninhabited:** 9

Ranking	District	State	National
Area	11	720	4730
Population	52	877	5808
Sex Ratio	34	469	1768
Child Sex Ratio	34	411	1523
Literacy Rate	38	355	3218
Density	9	781	4347
Work Participation Rate	55	614	2308

Gram Panchayats:

Addateegala, Bheemudupakalu, Bodlanka, D.Bheemavaram

D.Ramavaram, Dakodu, Dhanyampalem, Doramamidi Ducherthi, Gondolu, Gontuvanipalem, Kimmuru Konalova, Matlapadu, Puligogulapadu, Rayapalli Somannapalem, Thimmapuram, Thungamadugula Veeravaram, Vetamamidi, Yellavaram.

Amenities:

Education: Primary School in 82 villages, Middle school in 12 villages, Matriculation or Secondary School in 6 villages, namely Peddavadisakarra, Rayapalle, Addateegala, Kottampalem, Yellavaram, Gontuvanipalem.

Higher Secondary or Pre University Courses or Intermediate or Junior College in 1 village of the CD Block,, namely Addateegala.

College in 1 village, Adult Literacy Center in 19 villages., College is in village, namely Addateegala.

Medical: Hospital in 1 village, Dispensary in 2 villages, Health Center in 11 villages, Sub Center in 13 villages, Maternity and Child Welfare Center in 0 village, Community health workers in 0 village.

The Villages having Hospital or Dispensary or Health Center are Chinavadisakarra, Ducherthi, Rayapalle, Vedullakonda, Thungamadugula, Duppalapalem, Dhanayampalem, Bhimavaram, Addateegala, Papampeta, Konalova, Yellavaram, Thimmapuram.

Drinking Water: Tap water in 90 villages, Tank water in 90 villages, Well water in 90 villages, Tubewell in 90 villages and more than one source in 90 villages.

Bank: Banking facility in 3 villages, namely, Rayapalle, Addateegala, Veerabhadrapuram.

Credit Society in 9 villages Agricultural Credit Society in 3 Non-Agricultural Credit Society in 7 villages.

Others: Power supply in 90 villages, Cinema hall in 1 village, sport club in 1 village, Stadium or Auditorium or Community Hall in 0 village, Post Office in 25 villages.

There are 34 villages having bus facilities.

Villages with most of facilities: Rayapalle Addateegala.

Villages without amenities (Education):
Kalimamidi, Yellapuram, Ratnampalem, Panasaloddi, Bandakonda, Latchireddipalem, Gadichinnampalem, D. Krishnavaram..

Scheduled Castes: Out of the total population of 38387 persons, 2187 persons (5.7%) belong to Scheduled Castes.

The villages having less than 10% SC population are Chikkapugedda, Seetharam, Rollagedda, Bandamamillu Dabbapalem, Chakirevula, Makaram, Veeravaram Mulakayala Bhimavaram, Chodavaram, Peddavadisakarra Penikelapadu, Vangalamadugu, Chinavadisakarra Ducherthi, Tirumalawada, Jajipalem, Uligogula D. Ramavaram, Rayapalle, Vedullakonda, Vutlapalem D. Ammapeta, Kalimamidi, Yellapuram, Somannapalem Anukulapalem, Ravulapalem, Ravigudem, Settipalle Chaparatipalem, Jalluru, Thungamadugula, Ratnampalem Mamidipalem, Nukarai, Duppalapalem, Tiyyamamidi Dhanayampalem, Pedamunakanagedda, Panasaloddi Darsinuthula @ Regulapadu, Doramamidi, Bhimavaram Nimmalapalem, Mallavaram Mamillu, Paidiputtapadu Chinamunakanagedda, Mitlapalem, Panukuratipalem Bandakonda, Anigeru, Addateegala, Kovelapalem Languparti, Dokkapalem, Latchireddipalem, Vetamamidi Bhimudupakalu, Kinaparti, Gavarayyapeta, Kottampalem Bodlanka, Venkatanagaram, Papampeta Chinna Addateegala, D. Pinjarikonda, Konalova Veerabhadrapuram, Rajanagaram, Sarampeta Kottampalem, Badadam, Yellavaram, Matlapadu Kothurupadu, Thimmapuram, Gadichinnampalem D. Krishnavaram, Kimmuru, Doddivaka, Sarampetapadu Puligogulapadu.

The villages having more than 50% SC population are None.

Sex ratio of Scheduled Caste population is 479.

Scheduled Castes Literates and Illiterates by Sex:

	Persons	Males	Females
Literate	1,022	546	476
Illiterate	1,165	594	571
Literacy rate	53.9	55.5	52.2
Graduate	53	33	20

Scheduled Castes (Dominant):
Madiga, Mala, Relli, Adi Andhra, Manne

For their cultural identity please see Appendix-I

Villages without Scheduled Castes: There are 63 villages without any scheduled caste population.

Scheduled Tribes: Out of the total population of 38387 persons, 23537 persons (61.32%) belong to Scheduled Tribes.

The villages having less than 10% ST population are Dakodu, Ratnampalem, Panasaloddi, Gontuvanipalem Kimmuru.

The villages having more than 50% ST population are Chikkapugedda, Seetharam, Rollagedda, Dabbapalem Chakirevula, Makaram, Veeravaram Mulakayala Bhimavaram, Chodavaram, Peddavadisakarra Penikelapadu, Vangalamadugu, Chinavadisakarra Ducherthi, Tirumalawada, Jajipalem, Uligogula D. Kothuru, D. Ramavaram, Rayapalle, Vedullakonda Vutlapalem, D. Ammapeta, Kalimamidi, Yellapuram Somannapalem, Anukulapalem, Ravulapalem, Ravigudem Settipalle, Chaparatipalem, Jalluru, Thungamadugula Mamidipalem, Nukarai, Duppalapalem, Tiyyamamidi Dhanayampalem, Pedamunakanagedda Darsinuthula @ Regulapadu, Doramamidi, Bhimavaram

Nimmalapalem, Mallavaram Mamillu, Paidiputtapadu Chinamunakanagedda, Mitlapalem, Panukuratipalem Bandakonda, Anigeru, Kovelapalem, Languparti Dokkapalem, Latchireddipalem, Vetamamidi Bhimudupakalu, Kottampalem, Bodlanka, Venkatanagaram Chinna Addateegala, D. Pinjarikonda, Gondolu Atchiyyapeta, Rajanagaram, Sarampeta, Kottampalem Badadam, Matlapadu, Uppalapadu, Gadichinnampalem Doddivaka, Sarampetapadu, Puligogulapadu.

Sex ratio of Scheduled tribe population is 501.

Scheduled Tribes Literates and Illiterates by Sex:

	Persons	Males	Females
Literate	10,494	5,693	4,801
Illiterate	13,043	6,061	6,982
Literacy rate	51.8	56.3	47.3
Graduate	71	51	20

Scheduled Tribes (Dominant):

Kondareddis, Koya etc., Kammara, Valmiki Konda Dhoras

For their cultural identity please see Appendix-II

Villages without Scheduled Tribes: There are 11 villages without any scheduled tribe population.

Literates and Illiterates by Sex (Total Population):

	Persons	Males	Females
Literate	19,113	10,307	8,806
Illiterate	19,274	9,023	10,251
Literacy rate	58	62	53
Graduate	403	297	106

Agriculture: ***Distribution of villages according to land use:*** Out of 99 villages, Total area (in hectare) is 16854, out of that 59.26 percent is cultivable and 10.26 percent of the cultivable area is irrigated.

Sources of Irrigation (Hectares): Government Canal 298.2, Private Canal 0, Well without Electricity 0, Well with Electricity 0, Tubewell without Electricity 0, Tubewell with Electricity 0, Tank 726.44, River 0, Lake 0, Waterfall 0, Others 0.

Villages with population of 5000 to 9999: Addateegala.

Villages with population of 10000 and above: None

Distribution of Workers:

	Persons	Males	Females	WPR
Cultivators	7,411	4,753	2,658	39.15
Agricultural Labour	8,878	4,647	4,231	46.9
Household Industry	353	207	146	1.86
Other Workers	2,288	1,732	556	12.09
Main Workers	14,642	9,385	5,257	77.35
Marginal Workers	4,288	1,954	2,334	22.65
Total Workers	18,930	11,339	7,591	

Religion: Major Religious Communities:

	Persons	Males	Females	Sex Ratio
Hindu (97.51%)	37,430	18,880	18,550	983
Muslim (0.8%)	306	155	151	974
Christian (1.66%)	639	289	350	1,211
Sikh (0%)	-	-	-	-
Buddhists (0%)	1	1	-	-
Jain (0%)	-	-	-	-

Agewise Data:

	Persons	Males	Females	Sex Ratio
All ages	38,387	19,330	19,057	986
0-14	13,624	7,059	6,565	930
15-44	18,143	9,049	9,094	1005
45-79	6,443	3,142	3,301	1051
80+	111	55	56	1018
Age not stated	66	25	41	1640

Languages (Dominant):

Telugu, Urdu, Oriya, Gondi, Tamil

Disabled Population:

	Persons	Males	Females	%
Total Disabled	791	429	362	
In Seeing	386	189	197	48.8
In Speech	84	46	38	10.62
In Hearing	58	29	29	7.33
In Movement	180	116	64	22.76
Mentally	83	49	34	10.49

ADILABAD

Adilabad C.D. Block lies in the northern part of Adilab ad district. It is a part of Adilabad Mandal. The Block is located at a distance of 0 kms. from district headqu arters (Adilabad). There are 41 villages in the block with the total population of 39,451 persons. Area of the C.D. Block is 321.30 sq. kms. It is bounded by Jainad Mandal on north and east, Narnoor Mandal on south-east, Inderavelly Mandal on south and south-west, Talamadugu Mandal on south-west and west, and Tamsi Mandal from north-west.

Communications :

Roadways : NH- 7: Direction- Hyderabad to Nagpur. Nearest Villages- Bheemseri, Chanda, Mavala, Belluri, Battisaw argaon. State Highway (S.H): Direstion- Mudkhed to Adila bad. Nearest Villages- Rampoor (Royati), Battisawargaon.

Integrated Child Development Scheme (ICDS) Project: Adilabad, Total Anganwadi Centres: 312

Backwards Region Grants Fund: It receives Backward Region Grants.

Annual Rainfall: Average Rainfall 1207 mm

Ground Water: Availability of the ground water in the Basin is 4055 H.A.M. and the utilization is 1323 H. A.M. It belongs to Safe category. Depth to water level varies less than 5 meter below the ground. Most of the wells go down in summer months, according to the Ground Water Estimation Committee.

Natural Division : Telangana Plateau Region

Administration:

Division: Telangana. Parliamentary Constituency: 1 Adilabad (ST). District: Adilabad. Mandal: Adilabad. Assembly Constituency: 7 Adilabad. Gram Panchayat: 23

Fairs and Festivals:

Akadi Festival : It is observed by Gonds either on Sunday or Thursday before the Full Moon Day in the month of Akadi (June-July). This festival is performed in honour of Sri Polam Raju Devara who is the monarch of hills and forests and as such it is performed in the nearby forest. All the male members with their children and cattle go to the nearby forest where the Rajula Devara is propitiated. The premises are smeared with cow dung and decorated with jowar flour. Kheer or payasam (sweet rice) is cooked and the cattle are fed in the name of this deity. Afterwards two goats and two fowls are sacrificed to appease the Rajula Devara. A straight line of ten to fifteen meters is drawn with turmeric powder and the cattle are made to cross over it before they are driven away to the forest without any guard. In the meantime, the women prepare the feast with the meat of the sacrificed anima ls and it is consumed by all the persons present on the occasion. The Kheer is also served to all invitees. The cattle, thus driven to the forest for grazing, are brought back on the following day from the forest. If on return to the village all the cattle are found, it is believed that the Polam Raju has protected their cattle against the wild animals. In case one or two animals are lost, they will be alert all through the year to protect their cattle against wild animals. From this festive day the Dhandari dance is played till the end of Deepavali. Besides participating in this festival each household sacrifices a fowl to Pocha mma, invoking her blessing to protect its cattle against diseases.

Bheemana Festival : It perform Sanchi Bheemana festival on any Monday before the New Moon Day. The premises of God are cleaned with dung and decorated with designs of jowar flour. All the Rajgond households contribute equally for the purchase of a goat to be sacrificed to this deity housed in a rectangular shed, situated to the west of the village. A design with jowar flour, turmeric and charcoal powder locally known as pattu is drawn before this deity. The Devari or the Patel cleans the goat with water and decorates it with turmer ic and vermilion. Then the Devari of the Patel as the case may be offers it to this God by reciting some Gond verses. Afterwards the animal is sacrificed in the evening by any one of the participants. Then the meat of this sacrificed animal is cooked. Kudumulu with blackgram dal and rice are prepared. All the Rajgo nds enjoy this meat and kudumulu followed by heavy drink. The traditional musical instruments are played by Rajgonds on this occasion and Dhimsa dance is also played.

Villages: 41 **Inhabited:** 38 **Uninhabited:** 3

Ranking	**District**	**State**	**National**
Area	9	85	2335
Population	19	804	5709
Sex Ratio	10	82	563
Child Sex Ratio	16	251	788
Literacy Rate	20	725	4630
Density	15	211	5972
Work Participation Rate	29	1007	578

Gram Panchayats:

Ankoli, Anukunta, Arli(B), Battisawargoan, Bheemseri Chanda, Chinchughat, Jamdapur, Kachkanti Khanapur-Ch, Khandala, Kumbhajheri, Landasangvi Lokari, Mavala, Pippaldhari, Pochara, Ramai, Rampur Thantholi, Waghapur, Wanwat, Yapalguda.

Amenities:

Education: Primary School in 37 villages, Middle school in 15 villages, Matriculation or Secondary School in 7 villages, namely Pochara, Bheemseri, Chanda, Yapalguda, Ankoli, Waghapur, Wanwat.

Higher Secondary or Pre University Courses or Intermediate or Junior College in 0 village of the CD Block, College in 0 village, Adult Literacy Center in 32 villages.

Medical: Hospital in 0 village, Dispensary in 0 village, Health Center in 2 villages, Sub Center in 9 villages, Maternity and Child Welfare Center in 0 village, Community health workers in 0 village.

The Village having Hospital or Dispensary or Health Center is Mavala.

Drinking Water: Tap water in 31 villages, Tank water in 30 villages, Well water in 38 villages, Tubewell in 30 villages and more than one source in 38 villages.

Bank: Banking facility in 1 villages, namely, Ramai.

Credit Society in 15 villages Agricultural Credit Society in 13 Non-Agricultural Credit Society in 10 villages.

Others: Power supply in 38 villages, Cinema hall in 0 village, sport club in 0 village, Stadium or Auditorium or Community Hall in 0 village, Post Office in 16 villages.

There are 20 villages having bus facilities.

Village with most of facilities: Ramai.

Villages without amenities (Education):
Nishanghat..

Scheduled Castes: Out of the total population of 40687 persons, 6076 persons (14.93%) belong to Scheduled Castes.
The villages having less than 10% SC population are Landasangvi, Nishanghat, Arli (Buzurg), Takli Jamuldhari, Kachkanti, Tontoli, Kottur (Nevegaon) Borenur, Lokari, Ankoli, Maleborgaon, Chinchughat Ankapoor, Asodabhurki, Wanwat, Khandala, Hathigutta Tippa, Maregaon, Khanapoor.
The villages having more than 50% SC population are None.
Sex ratio of Scheduled Caste population is 508.

Scheduled Castes Literates and Illiterates by Sex:

	Persons	Males	Females
Literate	2,594	1,662	932
Illiterate	3,482	1,327	2,155
Literacy rate	49.6	64.7	35.0
Graduate	29	29	0

Scheduled Castes (Dominant):
Madiga, Mala, Mahar, Generic Castes etc.
Beda Jangam etc.

For their cultural identity please see Appendix-I

Villages without Scheduled Castes: There are 12 villages without any scheduled caste population.

Scheduled Tribes: Out of the total population of 40687 persons, 13191 persons (32.42%) belong to Scheduled Tribes.
The villages having less than 10% ST population are Jamdapur, Dimma, Pochara, Rampoor (Royati) Bheemseri, Chanda, Landasangvi, Battisawargaon Mavala, Belluri.
The villages having more than 50% ST population are Takli, Jamuldhari, Kottur (Nevegaon), Lokari Maleborgaon, Chinchughat, Ankapoor, Asodabhurki Wanwat, Khandala, Lohara, Hathigutta, Tippa Maregaon, Khanapoor, Chichadhari.
Sex ratio of Scheduled tribe population is 512.

Scheduled Tribes Literates and Illiterates by Sex:

	Persons	Males	Females
Literate	4,065	2,513	1,552
Illiterate	9,126	3,926	5,200
Literacy rate	38.2	48.5	28.5
Graduate	21	21	0

Scheduled Tribes (Dominant):
Gond etc., Kolam etc., Sugalis etc., Pardhan, Thoti

For their cultural identity please see Appendix-II

Villages without Scheduled Tribes: There are 8 villages without any scheduled tribe population.

Literates and Illiterates by Sex (Total Population):

	Persons	Males	Females
Literate	17,050	10,637	6,413
Illiterate	23,637	9,453	14,184
Literacy rate	49	63	37
Graduate	295	266	29

Agriculture: *Distribution of villages according to land use:*
Out of 41 villages, Total area (in hectare) is 34304, out of that 37.95 percent is cultivable and 4.03 percent of the cultivable area is irrigated.

Sources of Irrigation (Hectares): Government Canal 190.6, Private Canal 0, Well without Electricity 0, Well with Electricity 95.31, Tubewell without Electricity 0, Tubewell with Electricity 93.09, Tank 38.4, River 0, Lake 1, Waterfall 0, Others 106.11.

Villages with population of 5000 to 9999: None

Villages with population of 10000 and above: None

Distribution of Workers:

	Persons	Males	Females	WPR
Cultivators	8,940	4,866	4,074	39.69
Agricultural Labour	9,414	3,804	5,610	41.8
Household Industry	467	273	194	2.07
Other Workers	3,701	2,750	951	16.43
Main Workers	19,163	10,442	8,721	85.09
Marginal Workers	3,359	1,251	2,108	14.91
Total Workers	22,522	11,693	10,829	

Religion: Major Religious Communities:

	Persons	Males	Females	Sex Ratio
Hindu (96.1%)	39,101	19,267	19,834	1,029
Muslim (2.16%)	879	485	394	812
Christian (0.09%)	37	18	19	1,056
Sikh (0%)	1	-	1	-
Buddhists (1.55%)	632	307	325	1,059
Jain (0%)	1	-	1	-

Agewise Data:

	Persons	Males	Females	Sex Ratio
All ages	40,687	20,090	20,597	1025
0-14	15,186	7,629	7,557	991
15-44	18,671	9,319	9,352	1004
45-79	6,498	3,011	3,487	1158
80+	241	82	159	1939
Age not stated	91	49	42	857

Languages (Dominant):
Telugu, Gondi, Marathi, Kolami, Hindi

Disabled Population:

	Persons	Males	Females	%
Total Disabled	549	301	248	
In Seeing	223	115	108	40.62
In Speech	63	36	27	11.48
In Hearing	38	20	18	6.92
In Movement	177	105	72	32.24

Mentally	48	25	23	8.74

ADONI

Adoni C.D. Block lies in the western part of Kurnool district. It is a part of Adoni Mandal. The Block is located at a distance of 85 kms. from district headquarters (Kurnool). There are 42 villages in the block with the total population of 80,774 persons. Area of the C.D. Block is 502.48 sq. kms. It is bounded in the north by Mandals Kowthalam, Peddakadubur and Yemmiganur in the south by Mandals Holagunda, Alur and Aspari, in the east by Mandal Pattikonda, and in the west it touches the state of Karnataka.

Communications:

Roadways : State Highways (S.H.): Direction- Guntakal to Raichur. and Gooty. Nearest Villages- Ballekallu, Pesalabanda, Kapati, Sambagallu, Naranapuram, Chagi, Dhanapuram, Mandagiri (Rural), Dibbanakal, Gonabavi, Kadithota, Ganekal, Pandavagallu, Pedda Thumbalam, Isvi, Virupapuram, Kuppagal.

Railway Station: Kuppagal.

It is identified as a drought-prone area.

Integrated Child Development Scheme (ICDS) Project: Adoni, Total Anganwadi Centres: 188

Annual Rainfall: Average Rainfall 664 mm

Ground Water: Availability of the Ground Water in the Basin is 3985 H.A.M. and the utilization is 1566 H. A.M. It belongs to Safe category. Depth to water level varies from 2 to 10 meter below the ground. Most of the wells go down in summer months. The well density in the entire block is 4 wells per sq. km. Total no. of the wells in the block are enumerated as 1965, according to the Ground Water Estimation Committee.

Forest and Reserved **Forest:** Nearest Villages- Doddanakeri, Pesalabanda, S.Kondapuram, Isvi.

Natural Division : Rayalaseema Region

Administration:

Division: Rayala Seema. Parliamentary Constituency: 35 Kurnool. District: Kurnool. Mandal: Adoni. Assembly Constituency: 265 Adoni. Gram Panchayat: 37.

Border Villages: (Karnataka)- Nearest Villages- Hanavalu, Santhekudlur, Pedda Harivanam, Yadavalle.

Villages: 42 **Inhabited:** 41 **Uninhabited:** 1

Ranking	District	State	National
Area	1	8	1487
Population	4	34	4078
Sex Ratio	14	654	2230
Child Sex Ratio	34	711	2952
Literacy Rate	49	1071	6064
Density	6	16	5400
Work Participation Rate	35	867	114

Gram Panchayats:

104 Basapuram, Arekal Baladur, Basarakodu Billekallu, Bychigeri, Chinna Harivanam Chinnapendekal, Dhanapuram, Dibbanakal, Doddanakeri G.Hosalli, Ganekal, Gonabavi, Hanavalu, Isvi Jalibenchi, Kadithota, Kapati, Kuppagal, Madire Mandageri, Mantriki, Nagalapuram, Naganathana Halli Naranapuram, Nettekal, Pandavagallu, Pedda Harivanam Pedda Pendekal, Pedda Thumbalam, Pesalabanda Sadapuram, Salakalakonda, Sambagallu, Santhakudlur Virupapuram.

Amenities:

Education: Primary School in 40 villages, Middle school in 13 villages, Matriculation or Secondary School in 4 villages, namely Pedda Harivanam, Pedda Thumbalam, Arekal, Mandagiri (Rural).

Higher Secondary or Pre University Courses or Intermediate or Junior College in 0 village of the CD Block, College in 0 village, Adult Literacy Center in 30 villages.

Medical: Hospital in 1 village, Dispensary in 1 village, Health Center in 1 village, Sub Center in 16 villages, Maternity and Child Welfare Center in 0 village, Community health workers in 0 village.

The Villages having Hospital or Dispensary or Health Center are Pedda Harivanam.

Drinking Water: Tap water in 41 villages, Tank water in 41 villages, Well water in 41 villages, Tubewell in 41 villages and more than one source in 41 villages.

Bank: Banking facility in 3 villages, namely, Pedda Thumbalam, Arekal, Mandagiri (Rural).

Credit Society in 19 villages Agricultural Credit Society in 9 Non-Agricultural Credit Society in 17 villages.

Others: Power supply in 41 villages, Cinema hall in 2 villages, sport club in 0 village, Stadium or Auditorium or Community Hall in 1 village, Post Office in 32 villages.

There are 34 villages having bus facilities.

Villages with most of facilities: Pedda Thumbalam Mandagiri (Rural).

Villages without amenities (Education): S.Kondapuram..

Scheduled Castes: Out of the total population of 80789 persons, 14557 persons (18.02%) belong to Scheduled Castes. The villages having less than 10% SC population are Yadavalle, Baladur, Chinna Gonehal, Ganekal Pandavagallu, Mantriki, Sulthanapuram Chinnapendekal, V.Kondapuram.

The villages having more than 50% SC population are None.

Sex ratio of Scheduled Caste population is 497.

Scheduled Castes Literates and Illiterates by Sex:

	Persons	Males	Females
Literate	3,448	2,525	923
Illiterate	11,109	4,797	6,312
Literacy rate	29.9	43.7	16.0
Graduate	46	42	4

Scheduled Castes (Dominant):
Madiga, Mala, Mala Dasari, Chalavadi, Byagara
For their cultural identity please see Appendix-I
Villages without Scheduled Castes: There are 4 villages without any scheduled caste population.
Scheduled Tribes: Out of the total population of 80789 persons, 553 persons (0.68%) belong to Scheduled Tribes. The villages having less than 10% ST population are Hanavalu, Santhekudlur, Pedda Harivanam, Yadavalle Baladur, Chinna Gonehal, Chinna Harivanam, Madire Kadithota, G.Hosalli, Ganekal, Pandavagallu Kuppagal, Pedda Thumbalam, Ballekallu, Jalibenchi Doddanakeri, Mantriki, Sulthanapuram, Pesalabanda Kapati, Arekal, Chinnapendekal, Sambagallu Bychigeri, S.Kondapuram, Isvi, V.Kondapuram Basapuram, Naganathana Halli, Naranapuram, Chagi Dhanapuram, Mandagiri (Rural), Dibbanakal, Nettekal Salakalakonda, Basarakodu, Huvvanur, Gonabavi Virupapuram.
The villages having more than 50% ST population are None.
Sex ratio of Scheduled tribe population is 477.
Scheduled Tribes Literates and Illiterates by Sex:

	Persons	Males	Females
Literate	74	55	19
Illiterate	479	234	245
Literacy rate	17.0	24.6	9.0
Graduate	1	1	0

Scheduled Tribes (Dominant):
Koya etc., Yerukulas, Bagata
For their cultural identity please see Appendix-II
Villages without Scheduled Tribes: There are 28 villages without any scheduled tribe population.
Literates and Illiterates by Sex (Total Population):

	Persons	Males	Females
Literate	22,243	16,098	6,145
Illiterate	58,546	24,809	33,737
Literacy rate	34	49	19
Graduate	332	300	32

Agriculture: ***Distribution of villages according to land use:*** Out of 42 villages, Total area (in hectare) is 50248, out of that 74.62 percent is cultivable and 5.82 percent of the cultivable area is irrigated.
Sources of Irrigation (Hectares): Government Canal 1458, Private Canal 0, Well without Electricity 0, Well with Electricity 351.55, Tubewell without Electricity 0, Tubewell with Electricity 148.56, Tank 184, River 0, Lake 0, Waterfall 0, Others 41.
Villages with population of 5000 to 9999:
Pedda Harivanam, Pedda Thumbalam.
Villages with population of 10000 and above: None
Distribution of Workers:

	Persons	Males	Females	WPR
Cultivators	14,182	8,707	5,475	30.57
Agricultural Labour	27,100	11,772	15,328	58.42
Household Industry	616	317	299	1.33
Other Workers	4,488	3,430	1,058	9.68
Main Workers	39,386	21,852	17,534	84.91
Marginal Workers	7,000	2,374	4,626	15.09
Total Workers	46,386	24,226	22,160	

Religion: Major Religious Communities:

	Persons	Males	Females	Sex Ratio
Hindu (91.37%)	73,816	37,341	36,475	977
Muslim (8.01%)	6,474	3,319	3,155	951
Christian (0.58%)	469	231	238	1,030
Sikh (0%)	-	-	-	-
Buddhists (0%)	-	-	-	-
Jain (0%)	-	-	-	-

Agewise Data:

	Persons	Males	Females	Sex Ratio
All ages	80,789	40,907	39,882	975
0-14	34,541	17,802	16,739	940
15-44	33,562	17,101	16,461	963
45-79	12,213	5,791	6,422	1109
80+	343	131	212	1618
Age not stated	130	82	48	585

Languages (Dominant):
Telugu, Kannada, Urdu, Hindi, Marathi
Disabled Population:

	Persons	Males	Females	%
Total Disabled	1,236	674	562	
In Seeing	485	245	240	39.24
In Speech	117	68	49	9.47
In Hearing	60	24	36	4.85
In Movement	403	254	149	32.61
Mentally	171	83	88	13.83

AGALI

Agali C.D. Block lies in the south-western part of Anantapur district. The Block is located at a distance of 128 kms. from district headquarters (Anantapur). There are 09 villages in the block with the total population of 31,886 persons. Area of the C.D. Block is 123.43 sq. kms. It is bounded in the north and east by Mandal Rolla, and it has common boundary with the state of Karnataka in the south and west.

Communications:

Roadways : Metalled Roads: Nearest Villages- Ravudi, Inagalore,Narasambudi, Madhudi, Agali.

]It receives the backward Region Grants, and is identif ied as a drought-prone area as well.

Annual Rainfall: Average Rainfall 601 mm

Ground Water: Availability of the Ground Water in the Basin is 918 H.A.M. and the utilization is 1326 H.A. M. It belongs to OE category. Depth to water level varies from 10 to 20 meter below the ground. Most of the wells go down in summer months. The well density in the entire block is 13 wells per sq. km. Total no. of the wells in the block are enumerated as 1815, according to the Ground Water Estimation Committee.

Natural Division : Rayalaseema Region

Administration:

Division: Rayala Seema. Parliamentary Constituency: 37 Hindupur. District: Anantapur.

Mandal: Agali. Assembly Constituency: 275 Madakasira (SC). Gram Panchayat: 9.

Border Villages: (Karnataka)- Nearest Villages- Ravudi, P. Byadigera, Hulikeradevarahalli, Agali, Kodihalli.

Places of Tourist Interest:

Agali : This village is about 42 kms. south-west of Madakasira. A mantapam and a tank at the place are claimed to have been built by Sir Thomas Munro. There is also a Jain temple bearing the image of one of the thirthankaras. The Agali tank fed by the Swarnamukhi has a registered ayacut of 358 hectares.

Fairs and Festivals:

Sri Bhoothappa Panduga Festival : Sri Bhoothappa Panduga festival is held annually for two days commencing from Chaitra Suddha Ekadasi (March-April) at Madhudi near Madakasira in Anantapur. Karianna and Kenchanna, twin deities, are represented by two shield-like thick wooden discs coloured on the outside and with a handle on the inside at the centre, through which the left hand is thrust and the shield is held. The outside is painted to represent a human face. The shields repre senting Karianna (the dark) and Kenchanna (the red) can be distinguished by the conspicuous colour on it. The faces of the two wearers are also coloured. Anoth er person ordinarily dressed holds a bunch of bells in one hand and margosa leaves in the other facing the former two persons and sounding the bells in a particular way by the movement of the hand. The two follow him crying "Kalala la oh!" On the first day, Karianna (the person representing Karianna) holds in the mouth the bleeding throat of a lamb, which he is supposed to have bitten with his teeth and carries it round the temple of Anjaneya in which the stone and formless images of Bhoothappas are housed.

Villages: 9 **Inhabited:** 8 **Uninhabited:** 1

Ranking	District	State	National
Area	63	931	5420
Population	57	995	6007
Sex Ratio	9	747	2476
Child Sex Ratio	44	895	3961
Literacy Rate	13	471	3729
Density	20	305	3980
Work Participation Rate	4	508	771

Gram Panchayats:

Agali, Hullekeradevarahalli, Ingalore, Kodihalli Madhudi, Narasambudi, P.Byadigera, Ragelinganahalli Ravudi.

Amenities:

Education: Primary School in 8 villages, Middle school in 4 villages, Matriculation or Secondary School in 3 villages, namely Madhudi, Agali, Kodihalli.

Higher Secondary or Pre University Courses or Inter-mediate or Junior College in 1 village of the CD Block,, namely Agali.

College in 0 village, Adult Literacy Center in 0 village.

Medical: Hospital in 0 village, Dispensary in 1 village, Health Center in 1 village, Sub Center in 6 villages, Maternity and Child Welfare Center in 0 village, Community health workers in 0 village.

The Village having Hospital or Dispensary or Health Center is Madhudi.

Drinking Water: Tap water in 4 villages, Tank water in 3 villages, Well water in 8 villages, Tubewell in 0 village and more than one source in 8 villages.

Bank: Banking facility in 1 villages, namely, Agali.

Credit Society in 2 villages Agricultural Credit Society in 2 Non-Agricultural Credit Society in 0 village.

Others: Power supply in 8 villages, Cinema hall in 1 village, sport club in 0 village, Stadium or Auditorium or Community Hall in 0 village, Post Office in 8 villages.

There are 8 villages having bus facilities.

Village with most of facilities: Agali.

Villages without Amenities (Education): None..

Scheduled Castes: Out of the total population of 31886 persons, 6708 persons (21.04%) belong to Scheduled Castes.

The villages having less than 10% SC population are None..

The villages having more than 50% SC population are None.

Sex ratio of Scheduled Caste population is 486.

Scheduled Castes Literates and Illiterates by Sex:

	Persons	Males	Females
Literate	2,616	1,681	935
Illiterate	4,092	1,766	2,326
Literacy rate	45.0	56.0	33.3
Graduate	42	37	5

Scheduled Castes (Dominant):

Madiga, Mala, Dom etc., Dakkal etc., Adi Andhra

For their cultural identity please see Appendix-I

Villages without Scheduled Castes: There is 1 village without any scheduled caste population.

Scheduled Tribes: Out of the total population of 31886 persons, 199 persons (0.62%) belong to Scheduled Tribes. The villages having less than 10% ST population are Ravudi, Inagalore, Narasambudi, Madhudi P. Byadigera, Agali, Kodihalli.

The villages having more than 50% ST population are None.

Sex ratio of Scheduled tribe population is 447.

Scheduled Tribes Literates and Illiterates by Sex:

	Persons	Males	Females
Literate	86	57	29
Illiterate	113	53	60
Literacy rate	50.0	58.8	38.7
Graduate	10	7	3

Scheduled Tribes (Dominant):

Sugalis etc., Kammara, Yerukulas

For their cultural identity please see Appendix-II

Villages without Scheduled Tribes: There are 3 villages without any scheduled tribe population.

Literates and Illiterates by Sex (Total Population):

	Persons	Males	Females
Literate	15,204	9,445	5,759
Illiterate	16,682	6,742	9,940
Literacy rate	55	67	42
Graduate	317	260	57

Agriculture: ***Distribution of villages according to land use:*** Out of 9 villages, Total area (in hectare) is 12342, out of that 71.1 percent is cultivable and 15.72 percent of the cultivable area is irrigated.

Sources of Irrigation (Hectares): Government Canal 0, Private Canal 0, Well without Electricity 0, Well with Electricity 720, Tubewell without Electricity 180, Tubewell with Electricity 479, Tank 0, River 0, Lake 0, Waterfall 0, Others 0.

Villages with population of 5000 to 9999: Inagalore, Agali, Kodihalli.

Villages with population of 10000 and above: None

Distribution of Workers:

	Persons	Males	Females	WPR
Cultivators	6,367	4,761	1,606	35.75
Agricultural Labour	7,924	3,072	4,852	44.5
Household Industry	1,520	484	1,036	8.54
Other Workers	1,997	1,497	500	11.21
Main Workers	12,685	8,171	4,514	71.23
Marginal Workers	5,123	1,643	3,480	28.77
Total Workers	17,808	9,814	7,994	

Religion: Major Religious Communities:

	Persons	Males	Females	Sex Ratio
Hindu (98.11%)	31,282	15,872	15,410	971
Muslim (1.53%)	489	254	235	925
Christian (0.06%)	19	9	10	1,111
Sikh (0%)	-	-	-	-
Buddhists (0%)	-	-	-	-
Jain (0.12%)	39	22	17	773

Agewise Data:

	Persons	Males	Females	Sex Ratio
All ages	31,886	16,187	15,699	970
0-14	10,278	5,214	5,064	971
15-44	14,491	7,290	7,201	988
45-79	6,836	3,558	3,278	921
80+	265	118	147	1246
Age not stated	16	7	9	1286

Languages (Dominant):

Kannada, Telugu, Urdu, Hindi, Marathi

Disabled Population:

	Persons	Males	Females	%
Total Disabled	564	330	234	
In Seeing	231	113	118	40.96
In Speech	71	47	24	12.59
In Hearing	23	13	10	4.08
In Movement	179	118	61	31.74
Mentally	60	39	21	10.64

AGIRIPALLE

Agiripalle C.D. Block lies in the northern part of Krishna district. The Block is located at a distance of 95 kms. from district headquarters (Machilipatnam). There are 23 villages in the block with the total population of 57,900 persons. Area of the C.D. Block is 224.08 sq. kms. It is bounded in the north by Mandal Nuzvid, in the south by Mandal Gannavaram, in the east by Mandals Nuzvid and Bapulapadu, and in the west by Mandals Vijayawada Rural, G. Konduru and Mylavaram.

Communications:

Roadways : Metalled Roads: Nearest Villages- Vadlamanu, Vattigudipadu, Edulagudem, Kalaturu, Chopparametla, Agiripalle, Nugondapalle, Pothavarappadu, Adivinekkalam.

Annaul Rainfall: Average Rainfall 1512 mm

Ground Water: Availability of the Ground Water in the Basin is (Information not avavible) H.A.M .and the utilization is (Information not avavible) H.A.M. It belongs to (Information not avavible) category. Depth to water level varies from 3 to 10 meter below the ground. Most of the wells go down in summer months.

Natural Division : Krishna Delta Region

Administration:

Division: Coastal Andhra. Parliamentary Constituency: 27 Eluru. District: Krishna. Mandal: Agiripalle. Assemb ly Constituency: 189 Nuzvid. Gram Panchayat: 25.

Fairs and Festivals:

Maghothsavam Adhyanothsavam : It is celebrated for 12 days from Pushya Bahula Ekadasi to Magha Suddha Saptami (January-February) at Sri Sohanachalaswamy temple. The daily routine during this period is taking out a procession of the Lord in the town on one of the vahanams i.e., aswa, gaja, ponna, garuda, sesha etc. There are four mantapams at the four corners of the village. The Lord is taken down the hill from the southern side and the procession proceeds to the mantap ams situated in the south-east corner of the village. The residents of the locality offer worship and naived yam. Then the procession proceeds to the mantapam in the north-east corner which is the Kalyanamantapam, otherwise known as Kotayi. After the residents of the locality make offerings, the procession is taken to the other mantapams and finally to the temple. Santhi Kalyanams on Magha Suddha Ashatami (January-February) and the car festival with Pushapyagam on the next day are the rituals.

Villages: 23 **Inhabited:** 21 **Uninhabited:** 2

Ranking	District	State	National
Area	6	415	3765
Population	21	307	4928
Sex Ratio	43	953	3288
Child Sex Ratio	38	769	3350
Literacy Rate	38	264	2780
Density	27	823	3978
Work Participation Rate	39	506	2524

Gram Panchayats:

Adavinekkalam, Agiripalli, Ammavarigudem Boddanapalli, Chinnagiripalli, Chopparametla, Edara Edulagudem, Gollagudem, Kalaturu, Kanasanapalli Kommuru, Kotha Edara, Krishnavaram, Narasingapalem Nugondapalli, Pinnamareddipalli, Pothavarappadu S.A.Peta, Sagguru, Sitharampuram, Suravaram Thotapalli, Vadlamanu, Vattigudipadu.

Amenities:

Education: Primary School in 21 villages, Middle school in 10 villages, Matriculation or Secondary School in 4 villages, namely Edara, Edulagudem, Agiripalle, Adivinekkalam. Higher Secondary or Pre University Courses or Intermediate or Junior College in 1 village of the CD Block,, namely Agiripalle.

College in 0 village, Adult Literacy Center in 3 villages.

Medical: Hospital in 0 village, Dispensary in 1 village, Health Center in 3 villages, Sub Center in 7 villages, Maternity and Child Welfare Center in 0 village, Community health workers in 0 village.

The Village having Hospital or Dispensary or Health Center is Agiripalle.

Drinking Water: Tap water in 17 villages, Tank water in 0 villages, Well water in 3 villages, Tubewell in 2 villages and more than one source in 14 villages.

Bank: Banking facility in 3 villages, namely, Edara, Agiripalle, Adivinekkalam.

Credit Society in 13 villages Agricultural Credit Society in 11 Non-Agricultural Credit Society in 10 villages.

Others: Power supply in 21 villages, Cinema hall in 1 village, sport club in 0 village, Stadium or Auditorium or Community Hall in 0 village, Post Office in 14 villages.

There are 20 villages having bus facilities.

Villages with most of facilities: Edara Agiripalle, Adivinekkalam.

Villages without Amenities (Education): None..

Scheduled Castes: Out of the total population of 57900 persons, 14492 persons (25.03%) belong to Scheduled Castes.

The villages having less than 10% SC population are None..

The villages having more than 50% SC population are Malliboinapalle, Pinnamareddipalle, Pothavarappadu Narasingapalem.

Sex ratio of Scheduled Caste population is 485.

Scheduled Castes Literates and Illiterates by Sex:

	Persons	Males	Females
Literate	7,648	4,251	3,397
Illiterate	6,844	3,209	3,635
Literacy rate	60.6	65.5	55.4
Graduate	212	156	56

Scheduled Castes (Dominant):

Madiga, Mala, Madiga Dasu etc., Relli, Dakkal etc.

For their cultural identity please see Appendix-I

Villages without Scheduled Castes: There are 2 villages without any scheduled caste population.

Scheduled Tribes: Out of the total population of 57900 persons, 648 persons (1.12%) belong to Scheduled Tribes.

The villages having less than 10% ST population are Edara, Malliboinapalle, Vadlamanu, Tadepalle Vattigudipadu, Ananthasagaram, Edulagudem, Kalaturu Chopparametla, Agiripalle, Nugondapalle Pinnamareddipalle, Boddanapalle, Pothavarappadu Adivinekkalam, Kanasanapalle, Thotapalle Narasingapalem, Sagguru, Krishnavaram, Suravaram.

The villages having more than 50% ST population are None.

Sex ratio of Scheduled tribe population is 480.

Scheduled Tribes Literates and Illiterates by Sex:

	Persons	Males	Females
Literate	136	90	46
Illiterate	512	247	265
Literacy rate	25.5	33.0	17.7
Graduate	5	3	2

Scheduled Tribes (Dominant):

Yerukulas, Yenadis, Sugalis etc., Chenchu etc. Koya etc.

For their cultural identity please see Appendix-II

Villages without Scheduled Tribes: There are 6 villages without any scheduled tribe population.

Literates and Illiterates by Sex (Total Population):

	Persons	Males	Females
Literate	30,521	17,101	13,420
Illiterate	27,379	12,528	14,851
Literacy rate	60	66	54
Graduate	990	734	256

Agriculture: ***Distribution of villages according to land use:*** Out of 23 villages, Total area (in hectare) is 22408, out of that 42.3 percent is cultivable and 37.84 percent of the cultivable area is irrigated.

Sources of Irrigation (Hectares): Government Canal 587.59, Private Canal 0, Well without Electricity 29, Well with Electricity 535.43, Tubewell without Electricity 0, Tubewell with Electricity 186.25, Tank 2177.69, River 0, Lake 0, Waterfall 0, Others 70.66.

Villages with population of 5000 to 9999:

Edara, Adivinekkalam.

Villages with population of 10000 and above:

Agiripalle.

Distribution of Workers:

	Persons	Males	Females	WPR
Cultivators	5,013	4,336	677	17.56
Agricultural Labour	18,255	9,627	8,628	63.96
Household Industry	562	224	338	1.97
Other Workers	4,713	3,853	860	16.51
Main Workers	20,487	14,937	5,550	71.78
Marginal Workers	8,056	3,103	4,953	28.22
Total Workers	28,543	18,040	10,503	

Religion: Major Religious Communities:

	Persons	Males	Females	Sex Ratio
Hindu (93.59%)	54,187	27,846	26,341	946
Muslim (2.63%)	1,520	735	785	1,068
Christian (3.55%)	2,058	1,027	1,031	1,004
Sikh (0%)	-	-	-	-
Buddhists (0%)	-	-	-	-
Jain (0%)	-	-	-	-

Agewise Data:

	Persons	Males	Females	Sex Ratio
All ages	57,900	29,629	28,271	954
0-14	17,640	8,979	8,661	965
15-44	28,152	14,398	13,754	955
45-79	11,602	6,019	5,583	928
80+	449	208	241	1159
Age not stated	57	25	32	1280

Languages (Dominant):

Telugu, Urdu, Tamil, Gondi, Hindi

Disabled Population:

	Persons	Males	Females	%
Total Disabled	946	554	392	
In Seeing	252	140	112	26.64
In Speech	115	62	53	12.16
In Hearing	44	28	16	4.65
In Movement	372	236	136	39.32
Mentally	163	88	75	17.23

AINAVILLI

Ainavilli C.D. Block lies in the southern part of East Godavari district. The Block is located at a distance of 51 kms. from district headquarters (Kakinada). There are 17 villages in the block with the total population of 65,253 persons. Area of the C.D. Block is 91.34 sq. kms. It is bounded in the north by Mandal Pamarru and River Gowthami Godavari, in the south by Mandals Amalapuram and Mummidivaram, in the east by Mandal Mummidivaram, and in the west by Mandals Ambajipeta and Kapileswarapuram.

Communications :

Roadways : State Highway (S.H.): Direction- Amlapuram to Draksharama. Nearest Villages- Siripalle, Vilasa, Ainavilli, Totharamudi, Kotipalli Bhaga.

River: Gowthami Godavari: Nearest Villages- Madupalle, Veeravallipalem, Veluvalapalle, Kondukuduru, Sanapalli Lanka, Ainavilli, Totharamudi, Kotipalli Bhaga.

Backwards Region Grants Fund: It receives Backward Region Grants.

Annaul Rainfall: Average Rainfall 1108.6 mm

Ground Water: Availability of the Ground Water in the Basin is (Information not avavible) H.A.M .and the utilization is (Information not avavible) H.A.M. It belongs to (Information not avavible) category. Depth to water level varies from 3 to 10 meter below the ground. Most of the wells go down in summer months.

Natural Division : Godavari Delta Region

Administration:

Division: Coastal Andhra. Parliamentary Constituency: 24 Amalapuram (SC). District: East Godavari. Mandal:

Ainavilli. Assembly Constituency: 165 Gannavaram (SC). Gram Panchayat: 21.

Fairs and Festivals:

Alivelu Akkamma Jatara : It is celebrated for two days in Vaisakham (April-May) at the temple of Suleramanyas wamy at Kondukuduru. The old as well as young carry ganda deepamulu on their heads with shouts to the deity as offerings. The garagalu are taken in a procession. Fruits, palaharam and toddy are offered and goats and fowls are sacrificed to the deity. This Jatara is being celebrated from ancient times and it is of local significance. Kapus are the patrons. A large number of Hindus in the locality and from neighbouring areas, congregate. The pujari is an Asadi with heredita ry rights. The naivedyam offered by the devotees is taken by the pujaris.

Villages: 17 **Inhabited:** 16 **Uninhabited:** 1

Ranking	District	State	National
Area	40	1046	5791
Population	43	204	4680
Sex Ratio	24	379	1552
Child Sex Ratio	50	703	2946
Literacy Rate	7	27	704
Density	18	994	1447
Work Participation Rate	20	40	3742

Gram Panchayats:

Ainavilli, Ainavillilanka, Chintana Lanka, K.J.Puram Kondukuduru, Krapa, Madupalle, Magam, Nallacheruvu Nedunuru, Pedapalem, Pothukurru, Pottilanka S.Mulapalem, Sanapalli Lanka, Sankaraigudem Siripalle, Totharamudi, Veeravallipalem Veluvalapalle, Vilasa.

Amenities:

Education: Primary School in 16 villages, Middle school in 11 villages, Matriculation or Secondary School in 8 villages, namely Veeravallipalem, Chintana Lanka, Ainavilli, Kondukuduru, K. Jagannadhapuram, Siripalle, Nedunuru, Vilasa.

Higher Secondary or Pre University Courses or Intermediate or Junior College in 2 villages of the CD Block,, namely Ainavilli, Sanapalli Lanka.

College in 0 village, Adult Literacy Center in 13 villages.

Medical: Hospital in 1 village, Dispensary in 1 village, Health Center in 11 villages, Sub Center in 8 villages, Maternity and Child Welfare Center in 0 village, Community health workers in 0 village.

The Villages having Hospital or Dispensary or Health Center are Madupalle, Veeravallipalem, Chintana Lanka, Ainavilli, Totharamudi, Kondukuduru, Krapa, Sanapalli Lanka, K. Jagannadhapuram, Siripalle, Nedunuru.

Drinking Water: Tap water in 16 villages, Tank water in 15 villages, Well water in 16 villages, Tubewell in 15 villages and more than one source in 16 villages.

Bank: Banking facility in 3 villages, namely, Ainavilli, Totharamudi, Nedunuru.

Credit Society in 12 villages Agricultural Credit Society in 11 Non-Agricultural Credit Society in 5 villages.

Others: Power supply in 16 villages, Cinema hall in 3 villages, sport club in 1 village, Stadium or Auditorium or Community Hall in 1 village, Post Office in 13 villages.

There are 15 villages having bus facilities.

Villages with most of facilities: Ainavilli Nedunuru.

Villages without Amenities (Education): None..

Scheduled Castes: Out of the total population of 65253 persons, 20583 persons (31.54%) belong to Scheduled Castes.

The villages having less than 10% SC population are None..

The villages having more than 50% SC population are None.

Sex ratio of Scheduled Caste population is 493.

Scheduled Castes Literates and Illiterates by Sex:

	Persons	Males	Females
Literate	12,180	6,776	5,404
Illiterate	8,403	3,668	4,735
Literacy rate	67.7	74.4	60.9
Graduate	314	236	78

Scheduled Castes (Dominant):

Mala, Jambuvulu, Madiga, Adi Andhra Beda Jangam etc.

For their cultural identity please see Appendix-I

Villages without Scheduled Castes: There is 1 village without any scheduled caste population.

Scheduled Tribes: Out of the total population of 65253 persons, 348 persons (0.53%) belong to Scheduled Tribes.

The villages having less than 10% ST population are Madupalle, Veeravallipalem, Chintana Lanka Veluvalapalle, Ainavilli, Totharamudi, Kondukuduru Krapa, Sanapalli Lanka, K. Jagannadhapuram Siripalle, Sirasavalli Savaram, Nedunuru, Vilasa Magam, Pothukurru.

The villages having more than 50% ST population are None.

Sex ratio of Scheduled tribe population is 500.

Scheduled Tribes Literates and Illiterates by Sex:

	Persons	Males	Females
Literate	132	61	71
Illiterate	216	113	103
Literacy rate	43.9	42.4	45.2

Graduate	0	0	0

Scheduled Tribes (Dominant):

Yerukulas, Koya etc., Yenadis, Valmiki

For their cultural identity please see Appendix-II

Villages without Scheduled Tribes: There are 3 villages without any scheduled tribe population.

Literates and Illiterates by Sex (Total Population):

	Persons	Males	Females
Literate	43,027	23,267	19,760
Illiterate	22,226	9,508	12,718
Literacy rate	74	80	69
Graduate	1,298	1,009	289

Agriculture: ***Distribution of villages according to land use:*** Out of 17 villages, Total area (in hectare) is 9134, out of that 74.96 percent is cultivable and 79.14 percent of the cultivable area is irrigated.

Sources of Irrigation (Hectares): Government Canal 3590.83, Private Canal 0, Well without Electricity 0, Well with Electricity 0, Tubewell without Electricity 909, Tubewell with Electricity 918.73, Tank 0, River 0, Lake 0, Waterfall 0, Others 0.

Villages with population of 5000 to 9999:

Ainavilli, Totharamudi, Sanapalli Lanka, Nedunuru Vilasa.

Villages with population of 10000 and above: None

Distribution of Workers:

	Persons	Males	Females	WPR
Cultivators	3,339	3,059	280	11.54
Agricultural Labour	17,718	10,236	7,482	61.25
Household Industry	1,810	1,057	753	6.26
Other Workers	6,060	5,005	1,055	20.95
Main Workers	24,043	17,488	6,555	83.12
Marginal Workers	4,884	1,869	3,015	16.88
Total Workers	28,927	19,357	9,570	

Religion: Major Religious Communities:

	Persons	Males	Females	Sex Ratio
Hindu (98.56%)	64,313	32,364	31,949	987
Muslim (0.44%)	285	143	142	993
Christian (0.93%)	604	244	360	1,475
Sikh (0%)	-	-	-	-
Buddhists (0%)	-	-	-	-
Jain (0%)	-	-	-	-

Agewise Data:

	Persons	Males	Females	Sex Ratio
All ages	65,253	32,775	32,478	991
0-14	19,068	9,622	9,446	982
15-44	31,998	16,172	15,826	979
45-79	13,685	6,740	6,945	1030
80+	437	210	227	1081
Age not stated	65	31	34	1097

Languages (Dominant):

Telugu, Gondi, Urdu, Hindi, Malayalam

Disabled Population:

	Persons	Males	Females	%
Total Disabled	1,726	962	764	
In Seeing	958	511	447	55.5
In Speech	141	76	65	8.17
In Hearing	57	26	31	3.3
In Movement	422	270	152	24.45
Mentally	148	79	69	8.57

AKIVIDU

Akividu C.D. Block lies in the southern part of West Godavari district. The Block is located at a distance of 45 kms. from district headquarters (Eluru). There are 15 villages in the block with the total population of 74,766 persons. Area of the C.D. Block is 111.29 sq. kms. It is bounded in the north by Mandal Nidamarru, in the south by Mandal Kalla, in the east by Mandal Mandalundi, and in the west by district Krishna.

Communications :

Roadways : Metalled Roads: Nearest Villages- Dharmapuram, Madivada, Ajjamuru, Akividu, Dumpagadapa, A.I.Bheemava ram, Cherukumilli, Kuppanapudi.

Railway Station: Akividu.

River: Upputeru Nadi- Nearest Villages- Dumpagadapa, A.I.Bheemavaram, Cherukumilli.

Backwards Region Grants Fund: It receives Backward Region Grants.

Annaul Rainfall: Average Rainfall 1523 mm

Ground Water: Availability of the Ground Water in the Basin is (Information not avavible) H.A.M .and the utilization is (Information not avavible) H.A.M. It belongs to (Information not avavible) category. Depth to water level varies from 3 to 10 meter below the ground. Most of the wells go down in summer months.

Natural Division : Godavari Delta Region

Administration:

Division: Coastal Andhra. Parliamentary Constituency: 26 Narsapuram. District: West Godavari. Mandal: Akividu. Assembly Constituency: 179 Undi. Gram Panchayat: 16.

Villages: 15 **Inhabited:** 15 **Uninhabited:** 0

Ranking	District	State	National
Area	29	980	5586
Population	9	71	4296
Sex Ratio	17	424	1677
Child Sex Ratio	14	256	844
Literacy Rate	8	10	372
Density	44	1027	1569
Work Participation Rate	15	49	4066

Gram Panchayats:

A.I.Bheemavaram, Ajjamuru, Akiveedu, Apparaopeta

Cherukumilli, Chinakapavaram, Chinamillipadu Dumpagadapa, Gummuluru, Kollaparru, Kuppanapudi Mandapadu, Pedakapavaram, Rajulapet, Siddapuram Taratavau.

Amenities:

Education: Primary School in 14 villages, Middle school in 7 villages, Matriculation or Secondary School in 7 villages, namely Pedakapavaram, Chinakapavaram, Siddapuram, Akividu, Dumpagadapa, A.I.Bheemavaram, Cherukumilli. Higher Secondary or Pre University Courses or Intermediate or Junior College in 2 villages of the CD Block,, namely Akividu, Dumpagadapa.

College in 1 village, Adult Literacy Center in 12 villages., College is in village, namely Dumpagadapa.

Medical: Hospital in 1 village, Dispensary in 1 village, Health Center in 1 village, Sub Center in 11 villages, Maternity and Child Welfare Center in 0 village, Community health workers in 0 village.

The Village having Hospital or Dispensary or Health Center is Akividu.

Drinking Water: Tap water in 15 villages, Tank water in 15 villages, Well water in 15 villages, Tubewell in 15 villages and more than one source in 15 villages.

Bank: Banking facility in 4 villages, namely, Chinakapavaram, Siddapuram, Madivada, Akividu.

Credit Society in 1 village Agricultural Credit Society in 1 Non-Agricultural Credit Society in 0 village.

Others: Power supply in 15 villages, Cinema hall in 2 villages, sport club in 1 village, Stadium or Auditorium or Community Hall in 0 village, Post Office in 10 villages.

There are 14 villages having bus facilities.

Villages with most of facilities: Chinakapavaram Siddapuram, Madivada, Akividu.

Villages without amenities (Education): Kolleru..

Scheduled Castes: Out of the total population of 74766 persons, 4929 persons (6.59%) belong to Scheduled Castes.

The villages having less than 10% SC population are Kolleru, Pedakapavaram, Chinakapavaram, Taratava Kollaparru, Siddapuram, Madivada, Akividu Dumpagadapa, A.I.Bheemavaram, Cherukumilli.

The villages having more than 50% SC population are None.

Sex ratio of Scheduled Caste population is 502.

Scheduled Castes Literates and Illiterates by Sex:

	Persons	Males	Females
Literate	3,191	1,696	1,495
Illiterate	1,738	757	981
Literacy rate	75.1	79.1	70.9
Graduate	99	70	29

Scheduled Castes (Dominant):

Mala, Adi Andhra, Madiga, Generic Castes etc., Relli

For their cultural identity please see Appendix-I

Villages without Scheduled Castes: There are 0 village without any scheduled caste population.

Scheduled Tribes: Out of the total population of 74766 persons, 569 persons (0.76%) belong to Scheduled Tribes.

The villages having less than 10% ST population are Kolleru, Pedakapavaram, Chinakapavaram, Gummuluru Taratava, Kollaparru, Siddapuram, Dharmapuram Madivada, Ajjamuru, Akividu, Dumpagadapa A.I.Bheemavaram, Cherukumilli, Kuppanapudi.

The villages having more than 50% ST population are None.

Sex ratio of Scheduled tribe population is 522.

Scheduled Tribes Literates and Illiterates by Sex:

	Persons	Males	Females
Literate	293	154	139
Illiterate	276	118	158
Literacy rate	66.4	72.0	61.2
Graduate	2	2	0

Scheduled Tribes (Dominant):

Yerukulas, Chenchu etc., Yenadis, Konda Dhoras Koya etc.

For their cultural identity please see Appendix-II

Villages without Scheduled Tribes: There are 7 villages without any scheduled tribe population.

Literates and Illiterates by Sex (Total Population):

	Persons	Males	Females
Literate	51,834	27,496	24,338
Illiterate	22,932	10,105	12,827
Literacy rate	79	83	75
Graduate	2,152	1,552	600

Agriculture: ***Distribution of villages according to land use:***

Out of 15 villages, Total area (in hectare) is 11129, out of that 60.23 percent is cultivable and 100 percent of the cultivable area is irrigated.

Sources of Irrigation (Hectares): Government Canal 6703, Private Canal 0, Well without Electricity 0, Well with Electricity 0, Tubewell without Electricity 0, Tubewell with Electricity 0, Tank 0, River 0, Lake 0, Waterfall 0, Others 0.

Villages with population of 5000 to 9999:

Siddapuram, Madivada, Dumpagadapa.

Villages with population of 10000 and above:

Akividu.

Distribution of Workers:

	Persons	Males	Females	WPR
Cultivators	3,579	3,275	304	11.31
Agricultural Labour	18,847	11,513	7,334	59.54
Household Industry	616	386	230	1.95

Other Workers	8,611	7,338	1,273	27.2
Main Workers	25,959	20,353	5,606	82.01
Marginal Workers	5,694	2,159	3,535	17.99
Total Workers	31,653	22,512	9,141	

Religion: Major Religious Communities:

	Persons	Males	Female	Sex Ratio
Hindu (83.04%)	62,084	31,288	30,796	984
Muslim (3.79%)	2,836	1,418	1,418	1,000
Christian (13.12%)	9,807	4,878	4,929	1,010
Sikh (0%)	2	2	-	-
Buddhists (0%)	1	1	-	-
Jain (0%)	-	-	-	-

Agewise Data:

	Persons	Males	Females	Sex Ratio
All ages	74,766	37,601	37,165	988
0-14	22,519	11,372	11,147	980
15-44	37,057	18,799	18,258	971
45-79	14,480	7,072	7,408	1048
80+	548	259	289	1116
Age not stated	162	99	63	636

Languages (Dominant):

Telugu, Urdu, Gondi, Tamil, Hindi

Disabled Population:

	Persons	Males	Females	%
Total Disabled	1,269	677	592	
In Seeing	525	267	258	41.37
In Speech	125	59	66	9.85
In Hearing	52	27	25	4.1
In Movement	404	235	169	31.84
Mentally	163	89	74	12.84

ALAIR

Alair C.D. Block lies in the north part of Nalgonda district. The Block is located at a distance of 93 kms. from district headquarters (Nalgonda). There are 14 villages in the block with the total population of 50,242 persons. Area of the C.D. Block is 197.91 sq. kms. It is bounded by Warangal district on north and east, Gundala Mandal on south-east, Atmakur Mandal on south, Yadagirigutta on west, and Rajapet Mandal on north-west.

Communications:

Roadways : NH: Direction- Secunderabad to Cherial. and Alair to Purkal. Nearest Villages- Kolanupaka, Alair, Sharajpet, Kolluru, Golankonda.

Railway Station: Alair.

River: Alair Nadi- Nearest Villages- Ikkurthi, Kolluru. It receives Backward Region Grants, and is identified as a drought prone area, as well.

Annual Rainfall: Average Rainfall 784 mm

Ground Water: Availability of the Ground Water in the Basin is 2106 H.A.M. and the utilization is 1789 H. A.M. It belongs to SC category. Depth to water level varies from 10 to 20 meter below the ground. Most of the wells go down in summer months. The well density in the entire block is 14 wells per sq. km. Total no. of the wells in the block are enumerated as 3186, according to the Ground Water Estimation Committee.

Natural Division : Krishna Piedmont Plain Region

Administration:

Division: Telangana. Parliamentary Constituency: 14 Bhongir. District: Nalgonda. Mandal: Alair. Assembly Constituency: 97 Alair. Gram Panchayat: 18.

Fairs and Festivals:

Mahaveera Festival: It is celebrated at the Jain temple for three days from Chaitra Suddha Triodasi to Purnima (March-April). During all the three days as many devotees as possible perform puja to one or other of the idols in the temple. There is nobody called pujari. Someone incharge of the temple performs puja first in the morning. Afterwards any devotee can worship the idols. The following daily programme of puja is observed during the three days. All idols are first bathed in milk, next in water and later rubbed with clean cloth thrice. Then chandanam (sandal paste), kesari and flowers are applied particularly to the navangams (nine parts of the body-feet, knees, hands, shoulders, head, forehead, throat, umbilicus and heart). No naivedyam is offered, the belief of Jains being that after mukthi (salvation) there would be no hunger. But harathi is in practice. The temple car is taken round the temple in procession on the third day with an image of Jina (Mahaveera). It was used to be previously taken through the important streets of the village. This is a very ancient festival; its importance extending to the whole of the country. This is a Swethambar temple, wherein the idols are decorated with clothes and jewels, whereas Digambar sect of Jains worship nude idols.

Villages: 14 **Inhabited:** 14 **Uninhabited:** 0

Ranking	District	State	National
Area	37	570	4218
Population	20	503	5268
Sex Ratio	3	307	1353
Child Sex Ratio	41	856	3765
Literacy Rate	4	169	2028
Density	54	856	4032
Work Participation Rate	12	524	2772

Gram Panchayats:

Alair, Ammanabole, Bahadurpet, Dilwarpur, Golankonda Gundlagudem, Ikkurthy, Kolanpaka, Kollur Mandanpally, Manthapuri, Matoor, Patelgudem Raghavapur, Sharajipet, Sharbanapuram, Tangutoor

Turpugudem.

Amenities:

Education: Primary School in 14 villages, Middle school in 9 villages, Matriculation or Secondary School in 7 villages, namely Kolanupaka, Tangutoor, Sharajpet, Alair, Kolluru, Amman Bole, Golankonda.

Higher Secondary or Pre University Courses or Intermediate or Junior College in 1 village of the CD Block,, namely Alair.

College in 1 village, Adult Literacy Center in 9 villages., College is in village, namely Alair.

Medical: Hospital in 1 village, Dispensary in 2 villages, Health Center in 1 village, Sub Center in 6 villages, Maternity and Child Welfare Center in 1 village, Community health workers in 0 village.

The Villages having Hospital or Dispensary or Health Center are Kolanupaka, Alair.

Drinking Water: Tap water in 14 villages, Tank water in 14 villages, Well water in 14 villages, Tubewell in 14 villages and more than one source in 14 villages.

Bank: Banking facility in 1 villages, namely, Alair.

Credit Society in 5 villages Agricultural Credit Society in 5 Non-Agricultural Credit Society in 0 village.

Others: Power supply in 14 villages, Cinema hall in 1 village, sport club in 0 village, Stadium or Auditorium or Community Hall in 0 village, Post Office in 8 villages.

There are 13 villages having bus facilities.

Village with most of facilities: Alair.

Villages without Amenities (Education): None..

Scheduled Castes: Out of the total population of 50242 persons, 9802 persons (19.51%) belong to Scheduled Castes.

The villages having less than 10% SC population are None..

The villages having more than 50% SC population are None.

Sex ratio of Scheduled Caste population is 502.

Scheduled Castes Literates and Illiterates by Sex:

	Persons	Males	Females
Literate	4,804	2,880	1,924
Illiterate	4,998	2,005	2,993
Literacy rate	56.9	69.0	45.1
Graduate	107	92	15

Scheduled Castes (Dominant):

Madiga, Mala, Beda Jangam etc., Malajangam Chamar etc.

For their cultural identity please see Appendix-I

Villages without Scheduled Castes: There are 0 village without any scheduled caste population.

Scheduled Tribes: Out of the total population of 50242 persons, 1058 persons (2.11%) belong to Scheduled Tribes.

The villages having less than 10% ST population are Kolanupaka, Srinivasa Puram, Patelguda, Tangutoor Sharajpet, Alair, Bahadurpet, Manthapuri, Dilawarpur Ikkurthi, Kolluru, Matoor, Amman Bole, Golankonda.

The villages having more than 50% ST population are None.

Sex ratio of Scheduled tribe population is 456.

Scheduled Tribes Literates and Illiterates by Sex:

	Persons	Males	Females
Literate	432	300	132
Illiterate	626	276	350
Literacy rate	49.5	63.2	33.3
Graduate	9	9	0

Scheduled Tribes (Dominant):

Sugalis etc., Yerukulas, Koya etc., Kammara

For their cultural identity please see Appendix-II

Villages without Scheduled Tribes: There are 2 villages without any scheduled tribe population.

Literates and Illiterates by Sex (Total Population):

	Persons	Males	Females
Literate	28,102	16,708	11,394
Illiterate	22,140	8,477	13,663
Literacy rate	65	77	52
Graduate	1,156	928	228

Agriculture: ***Distribution of villages according to land use:*** Out of 14 villages, Total area (in hectare) is 19791, out of that 25.97 percent is cultivable and 35.23 percent of the cultivable area is irrigated.

Sources of Irrigation (Hectares): Government Canal 0, Private Canal 0, Well without Electricity 0, Well with Electricity 1205, Tubewell without Electricity 0, Tubewell with Electricity 606, Tank 0, River 0, Lake 0, Waterfall 0, Others 0.

Villages with population of 5000 to 9999:

Kolanupaka.

Villages with population of 10000 and above:

Alair.

Distribution of Workers:

	Persons	Males	Females	WPR
Cultivators	5,196	3,522	1,674	21.65
Agricultural Labour	8,786	3,031	5,755	36.6
Household Industry	2,011	934	1,077	8.38
Other Workers	8,012	6,254	1,758	33.38
Main Workers	18,393	11,880	6,513	76.62
Marginal Workers	5,612	1,861	3,751	23.38
Total Workers	24,005	13,741	10,264	

Religion: Major Religious Communities:

	Persons	Males	Females	Sex Ratio
Hindu (94.7%)	47,578	23,840	23,738	996

Muslim (3.84%)	1,930	970	960	990
Christian (1.3%)	651	330	321	973
Sikh (0%)	2	2	-	-
Buddhists (0%)	-	-	-	-
Jain (0.06%)	32	16	16	1,000

Agewise Data:

	Persons	Males	Females	Sex Ratio
All ages	50,242	25,185	25,057	995
0-14	16,221	8,186	8,035	982
15-44	22,478	11,348	11,130	981
45-79	10,880	5,334	5,546	1040
80+	547	261	286	1096
Age not stated	116	56	60	1071

Languages (Dominant):

Telugu, Urdu, Hindi, Gondi, Marathi

Disabled Population:

	Persons	Males	Females	%
Total Disabled	1,183	665	518	
In Seeing	580	308	272	49.03
In Speech	96	55	41	8.11
In Hearing	62	30	32	5.24
In Movement	334	210	124	28.23
Mentally	111	62	49	9.38

ALAMPUR

Alampur C.D. Block lies in the southern part of Mahbubn agar district. The Block is located at a distance of 130 kms. from district headquarters (Mahbubnagar). There are 26 villages in the block with the total popul ation of 41,224 persons. Area of the C.D. Block is 271. 21 sq. kms. It is bounded by Pebbair and Veepangandla Mandals on north and north-east, Kurnool district on south-east and south-west, Manopad Mandal on west.

Communications:

Roadways : Metalled Roads: Nearest Villages- Thakkasila, Maramunagala, Alampur, Bhairapur, Baswapur.

Railway Station: Bhairapur.

River: Krishna Nadi- Nearest Villages- Maramunagala, Pragatoor, Seripalle, Kyatur, Yapaladevipadu, Utkur, Gundimalla, Uppalapadu, Kudavelli. Tungabhadra Nadi- Nearest Villages- Gundimalla, Uppalapadu, Kudavelli, Chagatur, Bairampalle, Alampur, Singavaram, Ryalampadu, Sultanpur, Jillellapadu.

Backwards Region Grants Fund: It receives Backward Region Grants.

Annual Rainfall: Average Rainfall 588 mm

Ground Water: Availability of the Ground Water in the Basin is 3986 H.A.M. and the utilization is 1601 H. A.M. It belongs to Safe category. Depth to water level varies from 2 to 5 meter below the ground. Most of the wells go down in summer months. The well density in the entire block is 3 wells per sq. km. Total no. of the wells in the block are enumerated as 616, accor ding to the Ground Water Estimation Committee.

Natural Division : Telangana Plateau Region

Administration:

Division: Telangana. Parliamentary Constituency: 12 Nagakurnool (SC). District: Mahbubnagar. Mandal: Alampur. Assembly Constituency: 80 Alampur (SC). Gram Panchaya t: 19.

Places of Tourist Interest:

Alampur : Alampur is situated at a distance of 10 kms. from Alampur Road Railway Station on the Secunderabad-Dronachalam section of the South Central Railway. This place is located on the banks of Tungabhadra and a large number of antiquities belonging to, the Chalukyan period are found here. This place is also known as the western gateway to Srisailam temple and also as Dakshinakasi (Varanasi of the South). The two groups of temples—Brahmeswara and Papanatha have made Alampu a popular spot. The plans and decorations of these temples resemble the plans and carvings of some of the rock cut temples of Western India. In a temple called, Nava Brahmalaya, the idol of Bala Brahmeswara is resplendant and is supposed to be a Jyotirlinga. An interesting feature here is that any quantity of water used for Abhisheka goes inside and not a drop comes out. The other shrines of this place are those of Siva, Narasimha Surya, Mahishasura Mardhani, Venkate swara, Kamakshi and Virabhadra. The Hindu festivals that attract a large number of devotees are that of Bala Brahmeswara, Surya- narayana, Narasimha, Virabhadra, Sanga-meswara of Jogulamba. A Muslim fort and Shah Ali Dargah of seventh century are also in existence. Handloom weaving is an important industry of this place. Gadwal sarees are noted for their exquisite silk and 'Zari' work and command a good market througho ut India. The temple of Chennakesava is held in great veneration. Brahmotsavam celebrated in honour of the deity is attended by a large number of devotees.

Fairs and Festival:

Sri Balabrahmeswara Festival : It is celebrated for five days commencing from Mahasivaratri day, i.e., Magha Bahula Chathurdasi (Feburary-March). Alampur is located on the bank of the river Tungabhadra and it abounds in the antiquities of the Chalukyan times. The Chalukyas who ruled these parts in the 7th and 8th centuries are responsible for the construction of the temples at Alampur. The Rashtrakutas in the ninth century, the Kalyani Chalukyas in the tenth and eleventh centuries, their queens, subordinate kings, ministers and rich subjects made several gifts to the temple. The sixty-four ghattams (sacred spots for bath, etc.) all along the bank of the Tungabhadra down to Sangameswaram in Kurnool District about 33 kms. down the river where the Bhavanasi joins the Krishna river, were constructed during this period. The Kakatiy as inaugurated veerapuja (hero worship). Their stone statues and figures carved on stone slabs were placed in fort walls, temple walls and temples and were worshi pped.

Villages: 26 **Inhabited:** 21 **Uninhabited:** 5

Ranking	District	State	National
Area	24	234	3091
Population	54	786	5681
Sex Ratio	44	803	2684
Child Sex Ratio	61	1091	5614
Literacy Rate	4	610	4266
Density	46	448	5526
Work Participation Rate	52	897	1118

Gram Panchayats:
Alampur, Baswapur, Bhairapur, Bheemawaram, Bukkapur Gundimalla, Imampur, Kasipur, Konair, Kyathur Linganvai, Maramunagala, Pragatoor, Ryalampad Seripally, Singavaram, Sultanpur, Thakkasila, Utkoor.

Amenities:
Education: Primary School in 21 villages, Middle school in 11 villages, Matriculation or Secondary School in 6 villages, namely Thakkasila, Kyatur, Bukkapur, Alampur, Koneru, Linganavai.
Higher Secondary or Pre University Courses or Intermediate or Junior College in 0 village of the CD Block, College in 0 village, Adult Literacy Center in 18 villages.
Medical: Hospital in 1 village, Dispensary in 1 village, Health Center in 3 villages, Sub Center in 7 villages, Maternity and Child Welfare Center in 0 village, Community health workers in 0 village.
The Villages having Hospital or Dispensary or Health Center are Thakkasila, Kyatur, Alampur.
Drinking Water: Tap water in 21 villages, Tank water in 21 villages, Well water in 21 villages, Tubewell in 21 villages and more than one source in 21 villages.
Bank: Banking facility in 2 villages, namely, Kyatur, Alampur.
Credit Society in 13 villages Agricultural Credit Society in 3 Non-Agricultural Credit Society in 11 villages.
Others: Power supply in 21 villages, Cinema hall in 2 villages, sport club in 0 village, Stadium or Auditorium or Community Hall in 0 village, Post Office in 11 villages.
There are 20 villages having bus facilities.
Village with most of facilities: Kyatur, Alampur.

Villages without Amenities (Education): None..
Scheduled Castes: Out of the total population of 41224 persons, 9020 persons (21.88%) belong to Scheduled Castes.
The villages having less than 10% SC population are None..
The villages having more than 50% SC population are None.
Sex ratio of Scheduled Caste population is 495.
Scheduled Castes Literates and Illiterates by Sex:

	Persons	Males	Females
Literate	3,156	2,010	1,146
Illiterate	5,864	2,542	3,322
Literacy rate	41.2	52.2	30.0
Graduate	143	119	24

Scheduled Castes (Dominant):
Madiga, Mala, Generic Castes etc., Chamar etc.
Adi Dravida
For their cultural identity please see Appendix-I
Villages without Scheduled Castes: There are 7 villages without any scheduled caste population.
Scheduled Tribes: Out of the total population of 41224 persons, 192 persons (0.47%) belong to Scheduled Tribes.
The villages having less than 10% ST population are Thakkasila, Maramunagala, Pragatoor, Seripalle Kyatur, Utkur, Bheemavaram, Bukkapur, Gundimalla Bairampalle, Alampur, Imampur, Koneru, Linganavai Bhairapur, Baswapur, Kasipur, Singavaram, Ryalampadu Sultanpur.
The villages having more than 50% ST population are None.
Sex ratio of Scheduled tribe population is 484.
Scheduled Tribes Literates and Illiterates by Sex:

	Persons	Males	Females
Literate	83	54	29
Illiterate	109	45	64
Literacy rate	52.2	65.1	38.2
Graduate	0	0	0

Scheduled Tribes (Dominant):
Yerukulas, Sugalis etc., Generic Tribes etc.
For their cultural identity please see Appendix-II
Villages without Scheduled Tribes: There are 20 villages without any scheduled tribe population.
Literates and Illiterates by Sex (Total Population):

	Persons	Males	Females
Literate	18,319	11,549	6,770
Illiterate	22,905	9,423	13,482
Literacy rate	52	64	39
Graduate	768	630	138

Agriculture: ***Distribution of villages according to land use:***
Out of 26 villages, Total area (in hectare) is 27121, out of

that 59.99 percent is cultivable and 8.56 percent of the cultivable area is irrigated.

Sources of Irrigation (Hectares): Government Canal 576, Private Canal 0, Well without Electricity 0, Well with Electricity 347, Tubewell without Electricity 0, Tubewell with Electricity 374, Tank 0, River 0, Lake 0, Waterfall 0, Others 96.

Villages with population of 5000 to 9999: None

Villages with population of 10000 and above: Alampur.

Distribution of Workers:

	Persons	Males	Females	WPR
Cultivators	4,045	2,677	1,368	18.3
Agricultural Labour	13,430	5,786	7,644	60.76
Household Industry	536	269	267	2.42
Other Workers	4,094	3,103	991	18.52
Main Workers	17,981	10,167	7,814	81.34
Marginal Workers	4,124	1,668	2,456	18.66
Total Workers	22,105	11,835	10,270	

Religion: Major Religious Communities:

	Persons	Males	Females	Sex Ratio
Hindu (84.34%)	34,770	17,723	17,047	962
Muslim (15.4%)	6,348	3,191	3,157	989
Christian (0.12%)	50	26	24	923
Sikh (0%)	1	-	1	-
Buddhists (0%)	-	-	-	-
Jain (0%)	-	-	-	-

Agewise Data:

	Persons	Males	Females	Sex Ratio
All ages	41,224	20,972	20,252	966
0-14	14,744	7,742	7,002	904
15-44	18,369	9,464	8,905	941
45-79	7,756	3,644	4,112	1128
80+	300	95	205	2158
Age not stated	55	27	28	1037

Languages (Dominant):

Telugu, Urdu, Kannada, Hindi, Tamil

Disabled Population:

	Persons	Males	Females	%
Total Disabled	864	416	448	
In Seeing	355	153	202	41.09
In Speech	77	39	38	8.91
In Hearing	40	19	21	4.63
In Movement	299	155	144	34.61
Mentally	93	50	43	10.76

ALAMURU

Alamuru C.D. Block lies in the south-western part of East Godavari district. The Block is located at a dista nce of 70 kms. from district headquarters (Kakinada). There are 15 villages in the block with the total population of 71,472 persons. Area of the C.D. Block is 78.32 sq. kms. It is bounded in the north by Mandals Kadiam and Mandapeta, in the south and east by Mandal Kapileswarapuram, and in the west by Mandals Atreyapuram and Ravulapalem.

Communications :

Roadways : NH- 5: Direction- Tanuku to Rajahmundry. Nearest Villages- Madiki, Baduguvanilanka, Choppela, Jonnada.

River: Gowthami Nadi- Nearest Villages- Alamuru, Badugu vanilanka, Choppela, Jonnada.

Backwards Region Grants Fund: It receives Backward Region Grants.

Annaul Rainfall: Average Rainfall 1108.6 mm

Ground Water: Availability of the Ground Water in the Basin is (Information not avavible) H.A.M .and the utilization is (Information not avavible) H.A.M. It belongs to (Information not avavible) category. Depth to water level varies from 3 to 10 meter below the ground. Most of the wells go down in summer months.

Natural Division : Godavari Delta Region

Administration:

Division: Coastal Andhra. Parliamentary Constituency: 24 Amalapuram (SC). District: East Godavari. Mandal: Alamuru. Assembly Constituency: 166 Kothapeta. Gram Panchayat: 18.

Villages: 15 **Inhabited:** 15 **Uninhabited:** 0

Ranking	District	State	National
Area	47	1068	5887
Population	26	106	4404
Sex Ratio	37	499	1865
Child Sex Ratio	46	619	2533
Literacy Rate	26	208	2325
Density	45	1067	915
Work Participation Rate	10	14	4605

Gram Panchayats:

Alamuru, Baduguvanilanka, Chemudulanka, Chintaluru Choppela, Gummileru, Jonnada, Kalavacherla, Madiki Modukuru, Mulastanam, Narsipuddi, Navabupeta Pedapalle, Penikeru, Pinapalle, Sandhipudi Suryarao Peta.

Amenities:

Education: Primary School in 15 villages, Middle school in 11 villages, Matriculation or Secondary School in 3 villages, namely Choppela, Jonnada, Alamuru.

Higher Secondary or Pre University Courses or Intermediate or Junior College in 1 village of the CD Block,, namely Alamuru.

College in 0 village, Adult Literacy Center in 15 villages.

Medical: Hospital in 3 villages, Dispensary in 2 villages,

Health Center in 10 villages, Sub Center in 5 villages, Maternity and Child Welfare Center in 0 village, Community health workers in 0 village.

The Villages having Hospital or Dispensary or Health Center are Baduguvanilanka, Madiki, Choppela, Narsipudi, Gummileru, Pinapalle, Penikeru, Jonnada, Alamuru, Chintaluru.

Drinking Water: Tap water in 15 villages, Tank water in 15 villages, Well water in 15 villages, Tubewell in 15 villages and more than one source in 15 villages.

Bank: Banking facility in 7 villages, namely, Madiki, Choppela, Narsipudi, Modukuru, Pedapalle Jonnada, Alamuru.

Credit Society in 8 villages Agricultural Credit Society in 8 Non-Agricultural Credit Society in 8 villages.

Others: Power supply in 15 villages, Cinema hall in 2 villages, sport club in 0 village, Stadium or Auditorium or Community Hall in 0 village, Post Office in 14 villages.

There are 15 villages having bus facilities.

Villages with most of facilities: Madiki, Choppela Narsipudi, Modukuru, Jonnada, Alamuru.

Villages without Amenities (Education): None..

Scheduled Castes: Out of the total population of 71472 persons, 10661 persons (14.92%) belong to Scheduled Castes.

The villages having less than 10% SC population are None..

The villages having more than 50% SC population are None.

Sex ratio of Scheduled Caste population is 505.

Scheduled Castes Literates and Illiterates by Sex:

	Persons	Males	Females
Literate	5,844	3,130	2,714
Illiterate	4,817	2,152	2,665
Literacy rate	62.7	67.9	57.7
Graduate	165	114	51

Scheduled Castes (Dominant):

Mala, Madiga, Adi Andhra, Arundhatiya, Relli

For their cultural identity please see Appendix-I

Villages without Scheduled Castes: There are 0 village without any scheduled caste population.

Scheduled Tribes: Out of the total population of 71472 persons, 559 persons (0.78%) belong to Scheduled Tribes.

The villages having less than 10% ST population are Baduguvanilanka, Madiki, Choppela, Narsipudi Modukuru, Gummileru, Pinapalle, Pedapalle Kalavacherla, Penikeru, Navabpeta, Jonnada, Alamuru Chintaluru, Sandhipudi.

The villages having more than 50% ST population are None.

Sex ratio of Scheduled tribe population is 462.

Scheduled Tribes Literates and Illiterates by Sex:

	Persons	Males	Females
Literate	175	94	81
Illiterate	384	207	177
Literacy rate	36.8	37.6	36.0
Graduate	1	1	0

Scheduled Tribes (Dominant):

Yerukulas, Yenadis, Konda Dhoras, Kondareddis Chenchu etc.

For their cultural identity please see Appendix-II

Villages without Scheduled Tribes: There are 2 villages without any scheduled tribe population.

Literates and Illiterates by Sex (Total Population):

	Persons	Males	Females
Literate	39,222	20,618	18,604
Illiterate	32,250	15,401	16,849
Literacy rate	63	65	60
Graduate	1,177	902	275

Agriculture: ***Distribution of villages according to land use:*** Out of 15 villages, Total area (in hectare) is 7832, out of that 70.23 percent is cultivable and 94.92 percent of the cultivable area is irrigated.

Sources of Irrigation (Hectares): Government Canal 3749.19, Private Canal 0, Well without Electricity 0, Well with Electricity 0, Tubewell without Electricity 0, Tubewell with Electricity 1471.6, Tank 0, River 0, Lake 0, Waterfall 0, Others 0.

Villages with population of 5000 to 9999:
Madiki.

Villages with population of 10000 and above:
Choppela, Jonnada, Alamuru.

Distribution of Workers:

	Persons	Males	Females	WPR
Cultivators	3,544	3,393	151	12.58
Agricultural Labour	18,832	14,274	4,558	66.83
Household Industry	952	628	324	3.38
Other Workers	4,849	4,027	822	17.21
Main Workers	24,327	20,637	3,690	86.34
Marginal Workers	3,850	1,685	2,165	13.66
Total Workers	28,177	22,322	5,855	

Religion: Major Religious Communities:

	Persons	Males	Females	Sex Ratio
Hindu (98.83%)	70,633	35,598	35,035	984
Muslim (0.52%)	374	198	176	889
Christian (0.62%)	440	210	230	1,095
Sikh (0.02%)	12	7	5	714
Buddhists (0%)	-	-	-	-
Jain (0%)	-	-	-	-

Agewise Data:

	Persons	Males	Females	Sex Ratio

All ages	71,472	36,019	35,453	984
0-14	21,466	10,833	10,633	982
15-44	35,527	18,140	17,387	958
45-79	14,002	6,837	7,165	1048
80+	417	178	239	1343
Age not stated	60	31	29	935

Languages (Dominant):
Telugu, Gondi, Urdu, Hindi, Oriya

Disabled Population:

	Persons	Males	Females	%
Total Disabled	1,212	752	460	
In Seeing	531	349	182	43.81
In Speech	123	63	60	10.15
In Hearing	46	17	29	3.8
In Movement	393	261	132	32.43
Mentally	119	62	57	9.82

ALLADURG

Alladurg C.D. Block lies in the northern part of Medak district. The Block is located at a distance of 42 kms. from district headquarters (Sangareddy). There are 20 villages in the block with the total population of 42,856 persons. Area of the C.D. Block is 134.75 sq. kms. It is bounded by Shankarampet (A) Mandal on north, Tekmal Mandal on east, Andole Mandal on south-ea st, and Regode Mandal on south and west.

Communications :

Roadways : State Highway (S.H.): Direction- Shankarampet to Andole. Nearest Villages- Alladurg, Chilever, Musla pur, Peddapur..

Backwards Region Grants Fund: It receives Backward Region Grants.

Mahila Samakhya (Education for Women's Equality): It is decleared Socialy and Educationally Backward Block by the Government.

Annual Rainfall: Average Rainfall 943 mm

Ground Water: Availability of the Ground Water in the Basin is 1203 H.A.M. and the utilization is 903 H.A. M. It belongs to Semi Critical category. Depth to water level varies from 2 to 10 meter below the ground. Most of the wells go down in summer months. The well density in the entire block is 10 wells per sq. km. Total no. of the wells in the block are enumerated as 1521, according to the Ground Water Estimation Committee.

Natural Division : Telangana Plateau Region

Administration:

Division: Telangana. Parliamentary Constituency: 5 Zahirabad. District: Medak. Mandal: Alladurg. Assembly Constituency: 36 Andole (SC). Gram Panchayat: 22.

Villages: 20 **Inhabited:** 20 **Uninhabited:** 0

Ranking	District	State	National
Area	44	883	5258
Population	30	728	5609
Sex Ratio	24	616	2107
Child Sex Ratio	9	171	481
Literacy Rate	37	995	5666
Density	33	724	3369
Work Participation Rate	6	328	2053

Gram Panchayats:

Alladurg, Appajipalle, Bhahirandibba, Bijilipur Chevella, Chilever, Gadipeddapur, Gorrekal Kaidampally, Keroor, Mahammadapur, Marvelly Mupparam, Muslapur, Nagulapalle, Palvatla, Peddapur Pothulaboguda, Rampur, Reddipally, Venkatraopet Watpalle.

Amenities:

Education: Primary School in 20 villages, Middle school in 11 villages, Matriculation or Secondary School in 5 villages, namely Alladurg, Chilever, Muslapur, Peddapur, Marvelly.

Higher Secondary or Pre University Courses or Intermediate or Junior College in 0 village of the CD Block, College in 0 village, Adult Literacy Center in 7 villages.

Medical: Hospital in 0 village, Dispensary in 1 village, Health Center in 2 villages, Sub Center in 5 villages, Maternity and Child Welfare Center in 0 village, Community health workers in 0 village.

The Village having Hospital or Dispensary or Health Center is Mupparam.

Drinking Water: Tap water in 19 villages, Tank water in 19 villages, Well water in 20 villages, Tubewell in 19 villages and more than one source in 20 villages.

Bank: Banking facility in 3 villages, namely, Alladurg, Watpalle, Marvelly.

Credit Society in 10 villages Agricultural Credit Society in 4 Non-Agricultural Credit Society in 9 villages.

Others: Power supply in 20 villages, Cinema hall in 0 village, sport club in 0 village, Stadium or Auditorium or Community Hall in 0 village, Post Office in 7 villages.

There are 17 villages having bus facilities.

Villages with most of facilities: Alladurg Watpalle, Marvelly.

Villages without Amenities (Education): None..

Scheduled Castes: Out of the total population of 42856 persons, 9719 persons (22.68%) belong to Scheduled Castes.

The villages having less than 10% SC population are None..

The villages having more than 50% SC population are None.

Sex ratio of Scheduled Caste population is 489.

Scheduled Castes Literates and Illiterates by Sex:

	Persons	Males	Females

Literate	2,628	1,795	833
Illiterate	7,091	3,170	3,921
Literacy rate	31.8	42.2	20.7
Graduate	55	53	2

Scheduled Castes (Dominant):

Mala, Madiga, Beda Jangam etc., Byagara Generic Castes etc.

For their cultural identity please see Appendix-I

Villages without Scheduled Castes: There are 0 village without any scheduled caste population.

Scheduled Tribes: Out of the total population of 42856 persons, 1939 persons (4.52%) belong to Scheduled Tribes. The villages having less than 10% ST population are Alladurg, Appajipalle, Chilever, Muslapur Bhahirandibba, Chevella, Pothulaboguda, Gorrekal Watpalle, Shahednagar @ Ghatpalle, Gowtapoor Palvatla, Nagulapalle, Peddapur, Buddaipalle Bijilipur, Marvelly, Keroor.

The villages having more than 50% ST population are None.

Sex ratio of Scheduled tribe population is 469.

Scheduled Tribes Literates and Illiterates by Sex:

	Persons	Males	Females
Literate	392	326	66
Illiterate	1,547	703	844
Literacy rate	25.1	39.1	9.0
Graduate	7	7	0

Scheduled Tribes (Dominant):

Sugalis etc., Yerukulas

For their cultural identity please see Appendix-II

Villages without Scheduled Tribes: There are 13 villages without any scheduled tribe population.

Literates and Illiterates by Sex (Total Population):

	Persons	Males	Females
Literate	14,828	9,973	4,855
Illiterate	28,028	11,698	16,330
Literacy rate	41	54	27
Graduate	381	335	46

Agriculture: ***Distribution of villages according to land use:*** Out of 20 villages, Total area (in hectare) is 13474, out of that 51.81 percent is cultivable and 14.86 percent of the cultivable area is irrigated.

Sources of Irrigation (Hectares): Government Canal 0, Private Canal 0, Well without Electricity 0, Well with Electricity 5.2, Tubewell without Electricity 0, Tubewell with Electricity 8.09, Tank 1009.18, River 0, Lake 0, Waterfall 0, Others 14.65.

Villages with population of 5000 to 9999: None

Villages with population of 10000 and above: Alladurg.

Distribution of Workers:

	Persons	Males	Females	WPR
Cultivators	6,620	4,570	2,050	31.25
Agricultural Labour	10,891	4,483	6,408	51.41
Household Industry	753	432	321	3.55
Other Workers	2,921	2,395	526	13.79
Main Workers	16,444	10,228	6,216	77.62
Marginal Workers	4,741	1,652	3,089	22.38
Total Workers	21,185	11,880	9,305	

Religion: Major Religious Communities:

	Persons	Males	Females	Sex Ratio
Hindu (91.58%)	39,246	19,888	19,358	973
Muslim (8.22%)	3,522	1,737	1,785	1,028
Christian (0.11%)	48	29	19	655
Sikh (0%)	1	1	-	-
Buddhists (0%)	-	-	-	-
Jain (0%)	-	-	-	-

Agewise Data:

	Persons	Males	Females	Sex Ratio
All ages	42,856	21,671	21,185	978
0-14	15,257	7,814	7,443	953
15-44	18,778	9,546	9,232	967
45-79	8,434	4,144	4,290	1035
80+	341	142	199	1401
Age not stated	46	25	21	840

Languages (Dominant):

Telugu, Urdu, Hindi, Marathi, Kannada

Disabled Population:

	Persons	Males	Females	%
Total Disabled	1,032	589	443	
In Seeing	486	251	235	47.09
In Speech	63	40	23	6.1
In Hearing	57	28	29	5.52
In Movement	343	223	120	33.24
Mentally	83	47	36	8.04

ALLAGADDA

Allagadda C.D. Block lies in the south-eastern part of Kurnool district. The Block is located at a distance of 92 kms. from district headquarters (Kurnool). There are 20 villages in the block with the total population of 71,576 persons. Area of the C.D. Block is 280.04 sq. kms. It is bounded in the north by Mandals Sirvel and Rudravaram, in the south by Mandals Uyyalawada and Chagalamarri, and district Cuddapah, in the east by district Cuddapah, and in the west by Mandals Sirvel, Dornipadu and Uyyalawada.

Communications:

Roadways : NH: Direction- Koilkuntla to Proddatur. Neare st Villages- Devarayapuram, Allagadda, Patha Kandukur, G.Jambuladinne, Gubagundam, Peddachintakunta, Kotha

Kandukur, Chinta Kommadinne. State Highway (S.H.): Direction- Sirvel to Allagadda. Nearest Villages- G. Jambuladinne, Gubagundam, Peddachintakunta, Kotha Kandu kur, Bathalur, Nallagatla.

River: Vakrileru Nadi- Nearest Villages- Kotha Kandukur, Chinta Kommadinne.

It is identified as a drought-prone area.

Integrated Child Development Scheme (ICDS) Project: Allagadda, Total Anganwadi Centres: 227

Annual Rainfall: Average Rainfall 800 mm

Ground Water: Availability of the Ground Water in the Basin is 3268 H.A.M. and the utilization is 1780 H. A.M. It belongs to Safe category. Depth to water level varies from 5 meter to more than 10 meter below the ground. Most of the wells go down in summer months. The well density in the entire block is 0 wells per sq. km. Total no. of the wells in the block are enumera ted as 0, according to the Ground Water Estimation Commi ttee.

Forest and Reserved **Forest:** Nearest Villages- Yadawada, R.Krishnapuram, Mittalapalle, Ahobilam, Bachepalle.

Natural Division : Rayalaseema Region

Administration:

Division: Rayala Seema. Parliamentary Constituency: 34 Nandyal. District: Kurnool. Mandal: Allagadda. Assem bly Constituency: 253 Auagadda. Gram Panchayat: 20.

Villages: 20 **Inhabited:** 20 **Uninhabited:** 0

Ranking	District	State	National
Area	24	209	3003
Population	6	104	4402
Sex Ratio	9	569	2024
Child Sex Ratio	38	801	3464
Literacy Rate	15	475	3732
Density	43	590	4012
Work Participation Rate	10	518	1593

Gram Panchayats:

Ahobilam, Allagadda, Bachepalle, Bathalur
Chinta Kommadinne, G.Jambuladinne, Gopalapuram
Gubagundam, Kotha Kandukur, Marripalle, Mittapalle
Nallagatla, Obulampalle, Padakandla, Patha Kandukur
Peddachintakunta, Peraipalli, R.Krishnapuram
S.Lingamdinne, Yadawada.

Amenities:

Education: Primary School in 20 villages, Middle school in 10 villages, Matriculation or Secondary School in 3 villages, namely Padakandla, Allagadda, Ahobilam.

Higher Secondary or Pre University Courses or Intermediate or Junior College in 1 village of the CD Block,, namely Allagadda.

College in 1 village, Adult Literacy Center in 17 villages., Colleges is in village, namely Allagadda.

Medical: Hospital in 1 village, Dispensary in 2 villages, Health Center in 2 villages, Sub Center in 14 villages, Maternity and Child Welfare Center in 1 village, Community health workers in 0 village.

The Villages having Hospital or Dispensary or Health Center are Allagadda, Ahobilam.

Drinking Water: Tap water in 20 villages, Tank water in 20 villages, Well water in 20 villages, Tubewell in 20 villages and more than one source in 20 villages.

Bank: Banking facility in 2 villages, namely, Allagadda, Ahobilam.

Credit Society in 16 villages Agricultural Credit Society in 7 Non-Agricultural Credit Society in 15 villages.

Others: Power supply in 20 villages, Cinema hall in 1 village, sport club in 0 village, Stadium or Auditorium or Community Hall in 0 village, Post Office in 20 villages.

There are 19 villages having bus facilities.

Villages with most of facilities: Allagadda Ahobilam.

Villages without Amenities (Education): None..

Scheduled Castes: Out of the total population of 71576 persons, 14366 persons (20.07%) belong to Scheduled Castes.

The villages having less than 10% SC population are None..

The villages having more than 50% SC population are None.

Sex ratio of Scheduled Caste population is 495.

Scheduled Castes Literates and Illiterates by Sex:

	Persons	Males	Females
Literate	5,159	3,319	1,840
Illiterate	9,207	3,937	5,270
Literacy rate	42.2	53.9	30.3
Graduate	247	188	59

Scheduled Castes (Dominant):

Mala, Madiga, Mala Dasari, Dom etc.

Generic Castes etc.

For their cultural identity please see Appendix-I

Villages without Scheduled Castes: There are 0 village without any scheduled caste population.

Scheduled Tribes: Out of the total population of 71576 persons, 2353 persons (3.29%) belong to Scheduled Tribes.

The villages having less than 10% ST population are Bathalur, Nallagatla, Gopalapuram, G.Jambuladinne Gubagundam, Devarayapuram, Peddachintakunta Padakandla, Obulampalle, Yadawada, Palasagaram Allagadda, S.Lingamdinne, Patha Kandukur Chinta Kommadinne, Kotha Kandukur, R.Krishnapuram Mittalapalle.

The villages having more than 50% ST population are

None.

Sex ratio of Scheduled tribe population is 495.

Scheduled Tribes Literates and Illiterates by Sex:

	Persons	Males	Females
Literate	954	614	340
Illiterate	1,399	574	825
Literacy rate	48.7	62.5	34.8
Graduate	25	20	5

Scheduled Tribes (Dominant):

Yerukulas, Sugalis etc., Chenchu etc., Yenadis Kammara

For their cultural identity please see Appendix-II

Villages without Scheduled Tribes: There are 12 villages without any scheduled tribe population.

Literates and Illiterates by Sex (Total Population):

	Persons	Males	Females
Literate	33,649	21,127	12,522
Illiterate	37,927	15,030	22,897
Literacy rate	55	68	41
Graduate	2,371	1,898	473

Agriculture: ***Distribution of villages according to land use:***
Out of 20 villages, Total area (in hectare) is 28005, out of that 59.54 percent is cultivable and 29.39 percent of the cultivable area is irrigated.

Sources of Irrigation (Hectares): Government Canal 1791, Private Canal 0, Well without Electricity 29, Well with Electricity 549, Tubewell without Electricity 0, Tubewell with Electricity 2520, Tank 12, River 0, Lake 0, Waterfall 0, Others 0.

Villages with population of 5000 to 9999:
Peddachintakunta.

Villages with population of 10000 and above:
Allagadda.

Distribution of Workers:

	Persons	Males	Females	WPR
Cultivators	7,380	4,931	2,449	19.89
Agricultural Labour	18,793	7,901	10,892	50.65
Household Industry	1,726	892	834	4.65
Other Workers	9,205	7,455	1,750	24.81
Main Workers	31,556	19,348	12,208	85.05
Marginal Workers	5,548	1,831	3,717	14.95
Total Workers	37,104	21,179	15,925	

Religion: Major Religious Communities:

	Persons	Males	Females	Sex Ratio
Hindu (80.46%)	57,592	29,130	28,462	977
Muslim (17.77%)	12,717	6,383	6,334	992
Christian (1.36%)	972	486	486	1,000
Sikh (0.01%)	4	4	-	-
Buddhists (0%)	1	1	-	-
Jain (0%)	2	1	1	1,000

Agewise Data:

	Persons	Males	Females	Sex Ratio
All ages	71,576	36,157	35,419	980
0-14	24,024	12,234	11,790	964
15-44	34,462	17,640	16,822	954
45-79	12,568	6,044	6,524	1079
80+	373	164	209	1274
Age not stated	149	75	74	987

Languages (Dominant):
Telugu, Urdu, Hindi, Tamil, Gondi

Disabled Population:

	Persons	Males	Females	%
Total Disabled	1,132	656	476	
In Seeing	364	176	188	32.16
In Speech	168	93	75	14.84
In Hearing	82	54	28	7.24
In Movement	385	254	131	34.01
Mentally	133	79	54	11.75

ALLAVARAM

Allavaram C.D. Block lies in the southern part of East Godavari district. The Block is located at a distance of 102 kms. from district headquarters (Kakinada). There are 16 villages in the block with the total popul ation of 119.40 persons. Area of the C.D. Block is 694. 26 sq. kms. It is bounded in the north by Mandal Amalap uram, in the south by the Bay of Bengal, in the east by Mandal Uppalaguptam, and in the west by Mandal Mamid ikuduru and River Vainateyam Godavari.

Communications :

Roadways : Metalled Roads: Nearest Villages- Bodasakurru, Allavaram, Godilanka, Mogallamuru, Bendamurulanka, Komaragiripatnam.

River: Vainateyam Nadi- Nearest Villages- Bodasakurru, Godi, Mogallamuru, Bendamurulanka.

Note: Census figures (concerned) are not given.

Backwards Region Grants Fund: It receives Backward Region Grants.

Annaul Rainfall: Average Rainfall 1406.0 mm

Ground Water: Availability of the Ground Water in the Basin is (Information not avavible) H.A.M .and the utilization is (Information not avavible) H.A.M. It belongs to (Information not avavible) category. Depth to water level varies from 3 to 10 meter below the ground. Most of the wells go down in summer months.

Coastal Villages: Bendamurulanka, Komaragiripatnam, Samanthakuru.

Natural Division : Godavari Delta Region

Administration:

Division: Coastal Andhra. Parliamentary Constituency: 24 Amalapuram (SC). District: East Godavari. Mandal: Allavaram. Assembly Constituency: 163 Amalapuram (SC).

Gram Panchayat: 21.

Villages: 14 **Inhabited:** 14 **Uninhabited:** 0

Ranking	District	State	National
Area	22	951	5482
Population	35	163	4555
Sex Ratio	21	340	1457
Child Sex Ratio	28	335	1193
Literacy Rate	12	56	1074
Density	27	1037	1940
Work Participation Rate	35	75	4169

Gram Panchayats:

Allavaram, Bendamurlanka, Bodasakurru, Devaguptam Devaguptamravulapalem, Godi, Godilanka, Godithippa Gudala, Gundipudi, Kodurupadu, Komaragiripatnam Mogallamuru, Pallipalem, Rellugadda, Samanthakurru Tadikona, Thummalapalle, Thurpulanka, Vodalarevu Yentrikona.

Amenities:

Education: Primary School in 14 villages, Middle school in 8 villages, Matriculation or Secondary School in 5 villages, namely Allavaram, Devaguptam, Godilanka, Bendamurulanka, Komaragiripatnam.

Higher Secondary or Pre University Courses or Intermediate or Junior College in 0 village of the CD Block, College in 0 village, Adult Literacy Center in 10 villages.

Medical: Hospital in 0 village, Dispensary in 3 villages, Health Center in 1 village, Sub Center in 9 villages, Maternity and Child Welfare Center in 0 village, Community health workers in 0 village.

The Villages having Hospital or Dispensary or Health Center are Allavaram, Bendamurulanka, Komaragiripatnam.

Drinking Water: Tap water in 14 villages, Tank water in 14 villages, Well water in 14 villages, Tubewell in 14 villages and more than one source in 14 villages.

Bank: Banking facility in 3 villages, namely, Allavaram, Devaguptam, Komaragiripatnam.

Credit Society in 10 villages Agricultural Credit Society in 7 Non-Agricultural Credit Society in 7 villages.

Others: Power supply in 14 villages, Cinema hall in 3 villages, sport club in 0 village, Stadium or Auditorium or Community Hall in 0 village, Post Office in 11 villages.

There are 14 villages having bus facilities.

Villages with most of facilities: Allavaram Devaguptam, Komaragiripatnam.

Villages without Amenities (Education): None..

Scheduled Castes: Out of the total population of 68079 persons, 20749 persons (30.48%) belong to Scheduled Castes. The villages having less than 10% SC population are None..

The villages having more than 50% SC population are None.

Sex ratio of Scheduled Caste population is 497.

Scheduled Castes Literates and Illiterates by Sex:

	Persons	Males	Females
Literate	12,221	6,814	5,407
Illiterate	8,528	3,631	4,897
Literacy rate	67.5	74.6	60.2
Graduate	251	206	45

Scheduled Castes (Dominant):

Mala, Adi Andhra, Madiga, Jambuvulu, Panchama etc.

For their cultural identity please see Appendix-I

Villages without Scheduled Castes: There are 0 village without any scheduled caste population.

Scheduled Tribes: Out of the total population of 68079 persons, 394 persons (0.58%) belong to Scheduled Tribes.

The villages having less than 10% ST population are Bodasakurru, Allavaram, Gudala, Tadikona, Yentrikona Devaguptam, Rellugadda, Godilanka, Godi Thurupulanka, Mogallamuru, Bendamurulanka Komaragiripatnam, Samanthakuru.

The villages having more than 50% ST population are None.

Sex ratio of Scheduled tribe population is 449.

Scheduled Tribes Literates and Illiterates by Sex:

	Persons	Males	Females
Literate	160	99	61
Illiterate	234	118	116
Literacy rate	50.5	57.9	41.8
Graduate	4	4	0

Scheduled Tribes (Dominant):

Yerukulas, Koya etc., Sugalis etc., Yenadis Kondareddis

For their cultural identity please see Appendix-II

Villages without Scheduled Tribes: There are 2 villages without any scheduled tribe population.

Literates and Illiterates by Sex (Total Population):

	Persons	Males	Females
Literate	42,358	23,222	19,136
Illiterate	25,721	10,932	14,789
Literacy rate	71	78	64
Graduate	1,156	870	286

Agriculture: ***Distribution of villages according to land use:*** Out of 14 villages, Total area (in hectare) is 11940, out of that 66.15 percent is cultivable and 62.78 percent of the cultivable area is irrigated.

Sources of Irrigation (Hectares): Government Canal 4958.63, Private Canal 0, Well without Electricity 0, Well with Electricity 0, Tubewell without Electricity 0, Tubewell with Electricity 0, Tank 0, River 0, Lake 0,

Waterfall 0, Others 0.

Villages with population of 5000 to 9999:
Bodasakurru, Devaguptam, Bendamurulanka.

Villages with population of 10000 and above:
Allavaram, Komaragiripatnam.

Distribution of Workers:

	Persons	Males	Females	WPR
Cultivators	3,099	2,947	152	10.9
Agricultural Labour	17,061	9,786	7,275	59.98
Household Industry	849	432	417	2.98
Other Workers	7,434	6,278	1,156	26.14
Main Workers	22,873	17,600	5,273	80.42
Marginal Workers	5,570	1,843	3,727	19.58
Total Workers	28,443	19,443	9,000	

Religion: Major Religious Communities:

	Persons	Males	Females	Sex Ratio
Hindu (98.39%)	66,981	33,634	33,347	991
Muslim (0.38%)	260	126	134	1,063
Christian (1.19%)	810	377	433	1,149
Sikh (0.01%)	7	5	2	400
Buddhists (0%)	-	-	-	-
Jain (0%)	-	-	-	-

Agewise Data:

	Persons	Males	Females	Sex Ratio
All ages	68,079	34,154	33,925	993
0-14	20,847	10,566	10,281	973
15-44	33,039	16,635	16,404	986
45-79	13,665	6,689	6,976	1043
80+	464	241	223	925
Age not stated	64	23	41	1783

Languages (Dominant):
Telugu, Urdu, Gondi, Malayalam, Hindi

Disabled Population:

	Persons	Males	Females	%
Total Disabled	1,941	1,141	800	
In Seeing	1,148	669	479	59.14
In Speech	176	99	77	9.07
In Hearing	52	25	27	2.68
In Movement	402	259	143	20.71
Mentally	163	89	74	8.4

ALLUR

Allur C.D. Block lies in the north-eastern part of Nellore district. The Block is located at a distance of 32 kms. from district headquarters (Nellore). There are 15 villages in the block with the total population of 52,990 persons. Area of the C.D. Block is 177.74 sq. kms. It is bounded in the north by Mandal Bogole, in the south by Mandals Kodavalur and Vidavalur, in the east by the Bay of Bengal and Vidavalur Mandal, and in the west by Mandals Dagadarthi and Kodavalur.

Communications:

Roadways : NH- 5: Direction- Vijayawada to Nellore. Nearest Villages- Singapeta, Batrakagollu, North Amuluru.

Railway Station: Allur.

Annual Rainfall: Average Rainfall 1133 mm

Ground Water: Availability of the Ground Water in the Basin is 9633 H.A.M. and the utilization is 907 H.A. M. It belongs to Safe category. Depth to water level varies from less than 5 meter below the ground. Most of the wells go down in summer months, according to the Ground Water Estimation Committee.

Coastal Villages: Nearest Villages- Isakapalle, Gogulap alle, Allur.

Administration:

Division: Coastal Andhra. Parliamentary Constituency: 39 Nellore.District: Nellore.

Mandal: Allur.Assembly Constituency: 233 Kavali.Gram Panchayat: 13.

Villages: 15 **Inhabited:** 14 **Uninhabited:** 1

Ranking	District	State	National
Area	35	680	4571
Population	11	422	5140
Sex Ratio	18	400	1584
Child Sex Ratio	36	956	4319
Literacy Rate	21	245	2595
Density	19	771	3546
Work Participation Rate	7	373	2254

Gram Panchayats:
Allur, Batragagallu, Beerangunta, East Gogulapalli Graddgunta, Indupur, Iskapalli, North Amulur North Mopur, Purini, Singa Pet, Velicherla Westgogulapalli.

Amenities:

Education: Primary School in 13 villages, Middle school in 7 villages, Matriculation or Secondary School in 4 villages, namely Allurupeta, Isakapalle, Allur, North Mopuru. Higher Secondary or Pre University Courses or Intermediate or Junior College in 1 village of the CD Block,, namely Allur.

College in 1 village, Adult Literacy Center in 12 villages., College is in village, namely Allur.

Medical: Hospital in 1 village, Dispensary in 0 village, Health Center in 1 village, Sub Center in 10 villages, Maternity and Child Welfare Center in 1 village, Community health workers in 0 village.

The Village having Hospital or Dispensary or Health Center is Allur.

Drinking Water: Tap water in 13 villages, Tank water in 13 villages, Well water in 13 villages, Tubewell in 13 villages and more than one source in 13 villages.

Bank: Banking facility in 4 villages, namely,

Singapeta, Allurupeta, Isakapalle, Allur.
Credit Society in 10 villages Agricultural Credit Society in 4 Non-Agricultural Credit Society in 10 villages.
Others: Power supply in 14 villages, Cinema hall in 3 villages, sport club in 0 village, Stadium or Auditorium or Community Hall in 0 village, Post Office in 11 villages.
There are 12 villages having bus facilities.
Villages with most of facilities: Singapeta Allurupeta, Isakapalle, Allur.
Villages without amenities (Education):
Kalambotlavari Khandrika..
Scheduled Castes: Out of the total population of 52990 persons, 13570 persons (25.61%) belong to Scheduled Castes.
The villages having less than 10% SC population are None..
The villages having more than 50% SC population are None.
Sex ratio of Scheduled Caste population is 496.
Scheduled Castes Literates and Illiterates by Sex:

	Persons	Males	Females
Literate	7,290	4,132	3,158
Illiterate	6,280	2,702	3,578
Literacy rate	61.8	70.1	53.6
Graduate	168	121	47

Scheduled Castes (Dominant):
Mala, Samban, Madiga, Arundhatiya
Generic Castes etc.
For their cultural identity please see Appendix-I
Villages without Scheduled Castes: There is 1 village without any scheduled caste population.
Scheduled Tribes: Out of the total population of 52990 persons, 9615 persons (18.14%) belong to Scheduled Tribes.
The villages having less than 10% ST population are Isakapalle, Gogulapalle, Graddagunta, North Amuluru Kalambotlavari Khandrika.
The villages having more than 50% ST population are None.
Sex ratio of Scheduled tribe population is 494.
Scheduled Tribes Literates and Illiterates by Sex:

	Persons	Males	Females
Literate	3,668	2,013	1,655
Illiterate	5,947	2,854	3,093
Literacy rate	44.8	48.6	40.9
Graduate	8	5	3

Scheduled Tribes (Dominant):
Yenadis, Yerukulas, Kammara, Sugalis etc.
Konda Kapus
For their cultural identity please see Appendix-II
Villages without Scheduled Tribes: There are 2 villages without any scheduled tribe population.

Literates and Illiterates by Sex (Total Population):

	Persons	Males	Females
Literate	28,244	15,722	12,522
Illiterate	24,746	10,908	13,838
Literacy rate	61	68	54
Graduate	1,024	758	266

Agriculture: ***Distribution of villages according to land use:***
Out of 15 villages, Total area (in hectare) is 17773, out of that 41.01 percent is cultivable and 99.77 percent of the cultivable area is irrigated.
Sources of Irrigation (Hectares): Government Canal 6531.33, Private Canal 0, Well without Electricity 0, Well with Electricity 0, Tubewell without Electricity 0, Tubewell with Electricity 29, Tank 522, River 0, Lake 0, Waterfall 0, Others 190.
Villages with population of 5000 to 9999:
Allurupeta.
Villages with population of 10000 and above:
Isakapalle, Allur.
Distribution of Workers:

	Persons	Males	Females	WPR
Cultivators	3,038	2,565	473	11.47
Agricultural Labour	17,081	8,389	8,692	64.51
Household Industry	496	297	199	1.87
Other Workers	5,865	4,702	1,163	22.15
Main Workers	24,828	15,346	9,482	93.76
Marginal Workers	1,652	607	1,045	6.24
Total Workers	26,480	15,953	10,527	

Religion: Major Religious Communities:

	Persons	Males	Females	Sex Ratio
Hindu (90.88%)	48,158	24,246	23,912	986
Muslim (7.42%)	3,934	1,934	2,000	1,034
Christian (1.55%)	821	397	424	1,068
Sikh (0.02%)	11	11	-	-
Buddhists (0%)	-	-	-	-
Jain . (0.02%)	9	5	4	800

Agewise Data:

	Persons	Males	Females	Sex Ratio
All ages	52,990	26,630	26,360	990
0-14	15,950	8,210	7,740	943
15-44	25,242	12,597	12,645	1004
45-79	11,427	5,647	5,780	1024
80+	320	140	180	1286
Age not stated	51	36	15	417

Languages (Dominant):
Telugu, Tamil, Urdu, Gondi, Hindi
Disabled Population:

	Persons	Males	Females	%
Total Disabled	1,264	631	633	
In Seeing	644	297	347	50.95

In Speech	125	81	44	9.89
In Hearing	95	32	63	7.52

In Movement	290	161	129	22.94
Mentally	110	60	50	8.7

ALUR

Alur C.D. Block lies in the south-western part of Kurnool district. The Block is located at a distance of 97 kms. from district headquarters (Kurnool). There are 18 villages in the block with the total population of 49,066 persons. Area of the C.D. Block is 367.52 sq. kms. It is bounded in the north by Mandals Holagunda and Adoni, in the south by Mandals Chippagiri and Madikhera East, in the east by Mandals Aspari, Pattikonda and Maddikera, and in the west by Mandals Halaharvi and Holagunda.

Communications:

Roadways : State Highways (S.H.): Direction- Bellary to Kurnool. and Adoni to Gooty. Nearest Villages- Kammarachedu, Katriki, Manikurthi, Angaskal, Hulebeedu, Thumbalabeedu, Peddahottur, Alur, Kuruvalli, Hathi Belgal.

Railway Station: Molagavalli.

It is identified as a drought-prone area.

Integrated Child Development Scheme (ICDS) Project: Aluru, Total Anganwadi Centres: 201

Annual Rainfall: Average Rainfall 589 mm

Ground Water: Availability of the Ground Water in the Basin is 1883 H.A.M. and the utilization is 835 H.A.M. It belongs to Safe category. Depth to water level varies from 5 meter to more than 10 meter below the ground. Most of the wells go down in summer months. The well density in the entire block is 1 wells per sq. km. Total no. of the wells in the block are enumerated as 481, according to the Ground Water Estimation Committee.

Natural Division : Rayalaseema Region

Administration:

Division: Rayala Seema. Parliamentary Constituency: 35 Kurnool. District: Kurnool. Mandal: Alur. Assembly Constituency: 266 Alur. Gram Panchayat: 14.

Villages: 18 **Inhabited:** 18 **Uninhabited:** 0

Ranking	District	State	National
Area	10	66	2145
Population	26	546	5330
Sex Ratio	38	932	3194
Child Sex Ratio	24	570	2237
Literacy Rate	34	717	4618
Density	42	516	5794
Work Participation Rate	45	960	1338

Gram Panchayats:

Alur, Arikera, Hathi Belgal, Hulebeedu, Kammarachedu Kurukunda, Kuruvalli, Manikurthi, Marakattu Molagavalli, Muddanagiri, Musanahalli, Peddahothur Thumbalabeedu.

Amenities:

Education: Primary School in 18 villages, Middle school in 8 villages, Matriculation or Secondary School in 4 villages, namely Kammarachedu, Alur, Arikera, Molagavalli. Higher Secondary or Pre University Courses or Intermediate or Junior College in 1 village of the CD Block,, namely Alur.

College in 1 village, Adult Literacy Center in 17 villages., College is in village, namely Alur.

Medical: Hospital in 2 villages, Dispensary in 0 village, Health Center in 4 villages, Sub Center in 7 villages, Maternity and Child Welfare Center in 0 village, Community health workers in 0 village.

The Villages having Hospital or Dispensary or Health Center are Alur, Molagavalli.

Drinking Water: Tap water in 18 villages, Tank water in 18 villages, Well water in 18 villages, Tubewell in 18 villages and more than one source in 18 villages.

Bank: Banking facility in 2 villages, namely, Alur, Molagavalli.

Credit Society in 8 villages Agricultural Credit Society in 3 Non-Agricultural Credit Society in 7 villages.

Others: Power supply in 18 villages, Cinema hall in 2 villages, sport club in 0 village, Stadium or Auditorium or Community Hall in 0 village, Post Office in 14 villages.

There are 14 villages having bus facilities.

Villages with most of facilities: Alur Molagavalli.

Villages without Amenities (Education): None..

Scheduled Castes: Out of the total population of 49066 persons, 9827 persons (20.03%) belong to Scheduled Castes. The villages having less than 10% SC population are None..

The villages having more than 50% SC population are None.

Sex ratio of Scheduled Caste population is 470.

Scheduled Castes Literates and Illiterates by Sex:

	Persons	Males	Females
Literate	4,096	2,906	1,190
Illiterate	5,731	2,298	3,433
Literacy rate	50.1	66.5	31.3
Graduate	159	133	26

Scheduled Castes (Dominant):

Madiga, Mala, Bariki, Dom etc., Mala Dasari

For their cultural identity please see Appendix-I

Villages without Scheduled Castes: There are 0 village without any scheduled caste population.

Scheduled Tribes: Out of the total population of 49066

persons, 1025 persons (2.09%) belong to Scheduled Tribes.
The villages having less than 10% ST population are Kurukunda, A.Gonehal, Kammarachedu, Katriki Musanahalli, Marakattu, Manikurthi, Angaskal Muddanagiri, Karadiguddam, Hulebeedu, Thumbalabeedu Peddahottur, Alur, Kuruvalli, Hathi Belgal Molagavalli.
The villages having more than 50% ST population are None.
Sex ratio of Scheduled tribe population is 457.

Scheduled Tribes Literates and Illiterates by Sex:

	Persons	Males	Females
Literate	366	278	88
Illiterate	659	279	380
Literacy rate	44.8	59.5	25.1
Graduate	9	9	0

Scheduled Tribes (Dominant):
Sugalis etc., Yerukulas, Koya etc., Chenchu etc. Yenadis

For their cultural identity please see Appendix-II

Villages without Scheduled Tribes: There are 12 villages without any scheduled tribe population.

Literates and Illiterates by Sex (Total Population):

	Persons	Males	Females
Literate	20,457	13,607	6,850
Illiterate	28,609	11,475	17,134
Literacy rate	50	64	34
Graduate	828	669	159

Agriculture: ***Distribution of villages according to land use:*** Out of 18 villages, Total area (in hectare) is 36754, out of that 84.5 percent is cultivable and 2.89 percent of the cultivable area is irrigated.

Sources of Irrigation (Hectares): Government Canal 263.05, Private Canal 0, Well without Electricity 14.95, Well with Electricity 287.32, Tubewell without Electricity 0, Tubewell with Electricity 158.01, Tank 112.1, River 0, Lake 0, Waterfall 0, Others 62.88.

Villages with population of 5000 to 9999:
Molagavalli.

Villages with population of 10000 and above:
Alur.

Distribution of Workers:

	Persons	Males	Females	WPR
Cultivators	9,700	5,949	3,751	38.3
Agricultural Labour	11,251	4,839	6,412	44.43
Household Industry	380	204	176	1.5
Other Workers	3,993	2,895	1,098	15.77
Main Workers	21,105	12,496	8,609	83.34
Marginal Workers	4,219	1,391	2,828	16.66
Total Workers	25,324	13,887	11,437	

Religion: Major Religious Communities:

	Persons	Males	Females	Sex Ratio
Hindu (90.63%)	44,467	22,703	21,764	959
Muslim (8.51%)	4,174	2,164	2,010	929
Christian (0.71%)	347	172	175	1,017
Sikh (0%)	-	-	-	-
Buddhists (0%)	-	-	-	-
Jain (0.07%)	33	22	11	500

Agewise Data:

	Persons	Males	Females	Sex Ratio
All ages	49,066	25,082	23,984	956
0-14	19,130	9,972	9,158	918
15-44	21,313	10,983	10,330	941
45-79	8,249	3,962	4,287	1082
80+	324	138	186	1348
Age not stated	50	27	23	852

Languages (Dominant):
Telugu, Urdu, Kannada, Gondi, Marathi

Disabled Population:

	Persons	Males	Females	%
Total Disabled	1,089	585	504	
In Seeing	483	224	259	44.35
In Speech	108	64	44	9.92
In Hearing	99	49	50	9.09
In Movement	311	197	114	28.56
Mentally	88	51	37	8.08

AMADAGUR

Amadagur C.D. Block lies in the south-eastern part of Anantapur district. The Block is located at a distan ce of 110 kms. from district headquarters (Anantapur). There are 15 villages in the block with the total population of 26,093 persons. Area of the C.D. Block is 172.55 sq. kms. It is bounded in the north by Mandals Obuladevaracheruvu, Nallamada, Kadiri and Nallacheruvu, in the east by Mandal Tanakal, in the west by Mandal Obuladevaracheruvu, and it has common boundary with the state of Karnataka in the south and west.

Communications:

Roadways : NH, SH or Important Metalled Road is not available.

It receives the Backward Region Grants, and is identifi ed as a drought-prone area as well.

Annual Rainfall: Average Rainfall 622 mm

Ground Water: Availability of the Ground Water in the Basin is 838 H.A.M. and the utilization is 890 H.A. M. It belongs to OE category. Depth to water level varies from 10 to 20 meter below the ground. Most of the wells go down in summer months. The well density in the entire block is 7 wells per sq. km. Total no. of the wells in the block are enumerated as 1588, according to the Ground Water Estimation Committee.

Forest and Reserved **Forest:** Nearest Villages- Thummala, Pulikuntlapalle, Lokojipalle.

Natural Division : Rayalaseema Region

Administration:

Division: Rayala Seema. Parliamentary Constituency: 37 Hindupur. District: Anantapur.

Mandal: Amadagur. Assembly Constituency: 278 Puttaparthi. Gram Panchayat: 9.

Border Villages: (Karnataka)- Nearest Villages- Mohammadabad, Amadagur, Chinaganipalle, Ramanathapuram, Gadidamvaripalle, Thummala, Pulikuntlapalle, Lokojipalle, Edigavaripalle, Cheekirevulapalle, Karinireddipalle, Dademvaripalle.

Villages: 15 **Inhabited:** 13 **Uninhabited:** 2

Ranking	District	State	National
Area	56	704	4661
Population	62	1058	6126
Sex Ratio	1	173	926
Child Sex Ratio	1	9	44
Literacy Rate	48	712	4592
Density	2	120	5543
Work Participation Rate	34	903	364

Gram Panchayats:

Amadagur, Cheekirevulapalli, Chinaganipalli Gunduvaripalli, Jowkulakothapalli, Kassamudram Mohammadabad, Pulikuntapalli, Thummala.

Amenities:

Education: Primary School in 12 villages, Middle school in 5 villages, Matriculation or Secondary School in 3 villages, namely Jowkalakothapalle, Thummala, Amadagur.

Higher Secondary or Pre University Courses or Intermediate or Junior College in 0 village of the CD Block, College in 0 village, Adult Literacy Center in 0 village.

Medical: Hospital in 0 village, Dispensary in 2 villages, Health Center in 1 village, Sub Center in 6 villages, Maternity and Child Welfare Center in 0 village, Community health workers in 0 village.

The Villages having Hospital or Dispensary or Health Center are Mohammadabad, Thummala.

Drinking Water: Tap water in 0 village, Tank water in 9 villages, Well water in 12 villages, Tubewell in 2 villages and more than one source in 12 villages.

Bank: Banking facility in 1 villages, namely, Amadagur.

Credit Society in 3 villages Agricultural Credit Society in 3 Non-Agricultural Credit Society in 0 village.

Others: Power supply in 13 villages, Cinema hall in 1 village, sport club in 0 village, Stadium or Auditorium or Community Hall in 0 village, Post Office in 9 villages.

There are 9 villages having bus facilities.

Village with most of facilities: Amadagur.

Villages without amenities (Education):

Dademvaripalle..

Scheduled Castes: Out of the total population of 26093 persons, 3457 persons (13.25%) belong to Scheduled Castes.

The villages having less than 10% SC population are Jowkalakothapalle, Ramanathapuram, Edigavaripalle Cheekirevulapalle, Karinireddipalle, Dademvaripalle Lokojipalle.

The villages having more than 50% SC population are None.

Sex ratio of Scheduled Caste population is 494.

Scheduled Castes Literates and Illiterates by Sex:

	Persons	Males	Females
Literate	1,182	830	352
Illiterate	2,275	918	1,357
Literacy rate	39.5	55.0	23.8
Graduate	20	19	1

Scheduled Castes (Dominant):

Madiga, Mala

For their cultural identity please see Appendix-I

Villages without Scheduled Castes: There are 5 villages without any scheduled caste population.

Scheduled Tribes: Out of the total population of 26093 persons, 1053 persons (4.04%) belong to Scheduled Tribes.

The villages having less than 10% ST population are Jowkalakothapalle, Mohammadabad, Kassamudram Thummala, Amadagur, Chinaganipalle, Ramanathapuram Edigavaripalle, Cheekirevulapalle, Karinireddipalle Pulikuntlapalle.

The villages having more than 50% ST population are None.

Sex ratio of Scheduled tribe population is 499.

Scheduled Tribes Literates and Illiterates by Sex:

	Persons	Males	Females
Literate	291	205	86
Illiterate	762	323	439
Literacy rate	32.3	45.1	19.2
Graduate	5	5	0

Scheduled Tribes (Dominant):

Sugalis etc., Yerukulas

For their cultural identity please see Appendix-II

Villages without Scheduled Tribes: There are 6 villages without any scheduled tribe population.

Literates and Illiterates by Sex (Total Population):

	Persons	Males	Females
Literate	11,341	7,412	3,929
Illiterate	14,752	5,582	9,170
Literacy rate	50	65	34
Graduate	302	258	44

Agriculture: ***Distribution of villages according to land use:*** Out of 15 villages, Total area (in hectare) is 17256, out of that 64.66 percent is cultivable and 14.63 percent of the cultivable area is irrigated.

Sources of Irrigation (Hectares): Government Canal 0, Private Canal 0, Well without Electricity 0, Well with Electricity 1234.8, Tubewell without Electricity 0, Tubewell with Electricity 210.92, Tank 187.04, River 0, Lake 0, Waterfall 0, Others 0.

Villages with population of 5000 to 9999: Thummala, Amadagur.

Villages with population of 10000 and above: None

Distribution of Workers:

	Persons	Males	Females	WPR
Cultivators	6,196	3,762	2,434	40.6
Agricultural Labour	6,944	3,092	3,852	45.5
Household Industry	350	154	196	2.29
Other Workers	1,772	1,375	397	11.61
Main Workers	12,069	7,342	4,727	79.08
Marginal Workers	3,193	1,041	2,152	20.92
Total Workers	15,262	8,383	6,879	

Religion: Major Religious Communities:

	Persons	Males	Females	Sex Ratio
Hindu (93.49%)	24,395	12,142	12,253	1,009
Muslim (6.44%)	1,681	843	838	994
Christian (0.04%)	11	6	5	833
Sikh (0.01%)	3	1	2	2,000
Buddhists (0%)	1	1	-	-
Jain (0%)	-	-	-	-

Agewise Data:

	Persons	Males	Females	Sex Ratio
All ages	26,093	12,994	13,099	1008
0-14	7,784	3,878	3,906	1007
15-44	12,180	6,067	6,113	1008
45-79	5,897	2,951	2,946	998
80+	204	85	119	1400
Age not stated	28	13	15	1154

Languages (Dominant): Telugu, Urdu, Hindi, Kannada, Marathi

Disabled Population:

	Persons	Males	Females	%
Total Disabled	603	323	280	
In Seeing	199	96	103	33
In Speech	66	40	26	10.95
In Hearing	53	26	27	8.79
In Movement	218	129	89	36.15
Mentally	67	32	35	11.11

AMADALAVALASA

Amadalavalasa C.D. Block lies in the southern part of Srikakulam district. It is a part of Amadalavalsa Mandal. The Block is located at a distance of 13 kms. from district headquarters (Srikakulam). There are 38 villages in the block with the total population of 46,092 persons. Area of the C.D. Block is 90.54 sq. kms. It is bounded by in the north by Mandals Burja and Saubujjili, in the south by Mandals Etcherla and Srikakulam, in the east by Mandals Narasannapeta and Srikakulam, and in the west by Mandals Santhakaviti and Ponduru.

Communications:

Roadways : State Highway (S.H.): Direction- Palakonda to Amadalavalasa. Nearest Villages- Mandadi, Thallaval asa, Sylada, Peddajonnavalasa, Srinivasacharyulu Peta, villages.

Railway Station: Dusi.

River: Levyangulya Nadi- Nearest Villages- Garimellakot ha Valasa, Korapam, Marrikothavalasa, Nimmathorlavada, Korlakota, Kothavalasa, Thogaragam, Belamam, Thotada, Akkivaram, Kalivaram, Dusi.

Backwards Region Grants Fund: It receives Backward Region Grants.

Integrated Child Development Scheme (ICDS) Project: Amudalavalsa, Total Anganwadi Centres: 189

Annual Rainfall: Average Rainfall 938.0 mm

Ground Water: Availability of the Ground Water in the Basin is (Information not avavible) H.A.M .and the utilization is (Information not avavible) H.A.M. It belongs to (Information not avavible) category. Depth to water level varies from 3 to 10 meter below the ground. Most of the wells go down in summer months.

Administration:

Division: Coastal Andhra. Parliamentary Constituency: 19 Srikakulam. District: Srikakulam. Mandal: Amadalaval asa. Assembly Constituency: 125 Amadalavalasa. Gram Panchayat: 28.

Villages: 38 **Inhabited:** 36 **Uninhabited:** 2

Ranking	District	State	National
Area	35	1047	5795
Population	32	634	5467
Sex Ratio	25	326	1412
Child Sex Ratio	25	606	2452
Literacy Rate	6	296	2920
Density	34	959	2179
Work Participation Rate	8	103	3449

Gram Panchayats:

Akkulapeta, Belamam, Bobbilipeta, Cheemalavalasa Chinthalapeta, Chittivalasa, Dusi Garimella Kothavalasa, K.Munagavalasa, Kalivaram Kanugulavalasa, Katyacharyulapeta, Kollivalasa Korapam, Korlakota, Kothavalasa, Nelliparthi

Nimmathorlada, Ramachandrapuram, Srinivasacharyupeta Sylada, T.Jonnavalasa, Thogaram, Thotada, Turakapeta Vanjangi, Vanjangipeta, Vedullavalasa.

Amenities:

Education: Primary School in 35 villages, Middle school in 10 villages, Matriculation or Secondary School in 5 villages, namely Nimmathorlavada, Vedullavalasa, Korlakota, Thogaragam, Dusi.

Higher Secondary or Pre University Courses or Intermediate or Junior College in 1 village of the CD Block,, namely Thogaragam.

College in 1 village, Adult Literacy Center in 16 villages., College is in village, namely Thogaragam.

Medical: Hospital in 4 villages, Dispensary in 2 villages, Health Center in 5 villages, Sub Center in 8 villages, Maternity and Child Welfare Center in 1 village, Community health workers in 0 village.

The Villages having Hospital or Dispensary or Health Center are Akkulapeta, Korlakota, Thogaragam, Kalivaram, Dusi.

Drinking Water: Tap water in 36 villages, Tank water in 36 villages, Well water in 36 villages, Tubewell in 36 villages and more than one source in 36 villages.

Bank: Banking facility in 4 villages, namely, Chintalapeta, Akkulapeta, Thogaragam, Kalivaram.

Credit Society in 10 villages Agricultural Credit Society in 4 Non-Agricultural Credit Society in 7 villages.

Others: Power supply in 36 villages, Cinema hall in 1 village, sport club in 0 village, Stadium or Auditorium or Community Hall in 0 village, Post Office in 12 villages.

There are 26 villages having bus facilities.

Villages with most of facilities: Akkulapeta Thogaragam, Kalivaram.

Villages without amenities (Education):

Marrikothavalasa..

Scheduled Castes: Out of the total population of 46014 persons, 3970 persons (8.63%) belong to Scheduled Castes.

The villages having less than 10% SC population are Garimellakotha Valasa, Korapam, Nimmathorlavada Nelliparthi, Chintalapeta, Bobbilipeta, Chittivalasa Ramachandrapuram, Ponnampeta, Peddajonnavalasa Srinivasacharyulu Peta, Katyacharyulapeta, Korlakota Kothavalasa, Belamam, Dusi, Thotada, Akkivaram Vanjangipeta, Vanjangi, Kanugulavalasa.

The villages having more than 50% SC population are None.

Sex ratio of Scheduled Caste population is 493.

Scheduled Castes Literates and Illiterates by Sex:

	Persons	Males	Females
Literate	1,964	1,222	742
Illiterate	2,006	789	1,217
Literacy rate	56.9	69.4	43.8
Graduate	58	47	11

Scheduled Castes (Dominant):

Mala, Madiga, Adi Andhra, Relli, Generic Castes etc.

For their cultural identity please see Appendix-I

Villages without Scheduled Castes: There are 6 villages without any scheduled caste population.

Scheduled Tribes: Out of the total population of 46014 persons, 40 persons (0.09%) belong to Scheduled Tribes.

The villages having less than 10% ST population are Garimellakotha Valasa, Korapam, Marrikothavalasa Nimmathorlavada, Vedullavalasa, Turakapeta Dandemvalasa, Nelliparthi, Chintalapeta, Bobbilipeta Mandadi, Thallavalasa, Santha Kothavalasa Chinnajonnavalasa, Munagavalasa, Sylada Chittivalasa, Anandapuram, Ramachandrapuram Ponnampeta, Peddajonnavalasa, Srinivasacharyulu Peta Akkulapeta, Hanumanthapuram, Katyacharyulapeta Korlakota, Kothavalasa, Thogaragam, Kalivaram Belamam, Dusi, Thotada, Akkivaram, Vanjangipeta Vanjangi, Kanugulavalasa.

The villages having more than 50% ST population are None.

Sex ratio of Scheduled tribe population is 425.

Scheduled Tribes Literates and Illiterates by Sex:

	Persons	Males	Females
Literate	20	15	5
Illiterate	20	8	12
Literacy rate	52.6	65.2	33.3
Graduate	1	1	0

Scheduled Tribes (Dominant):

Yerukulas

For their cultural identity please see Appendix-II

Villages without Scheduled Tribes: There are 32 villages without any scheduled tribe population.

Literates and Illiterates by Sex (Total Population):

	Persons	Males	Females
Literate	23,999	14,798	9,201
Illiterate	22,015	8,283	13,732
Literacy rate	59	73	45
Graduate	1,316	1,155	161

Agriculture: ***Distribution of villages according to land use:*** Out of 38 villages, Total area (in hectare) is 9054, out of that 73.68 percent is cultivable and 73.72 percent of the cultivable area is irrigated.

Sources of Irrigation (Hectares): Government Canal 3055.16, Private Canal 453.45, Well without Electricity 0, Well with Electricity 0, Tubewell without Electricity 0, Tubewell with Electricity 0, Tank 1101.6, River 307.78, Lake 0,

Waterfall 0, Others 0.

Villages with population of 5000 to 9999:

Korlakota.

Villages with population of 10000 and above: None

Distribution of Workers:

	Persons	Males	Females	WPR
Cultivators	4,126	2,933	1,193	19.71
Agricultural Labour	11,533	5,931	5,602	55.08
Household Industry	1,014	554	460	4.84
Other Workers	4,265	3,596	669	20.37
Main Workers	14,874	10,681	4,193	71.04
Marginal Workers	6,064	2,333	3,731	28.96
Total Workers	20,938	13,014	7,924	

Religion: Major Religious Communities:

	Persons	Males	Females	Sex Ratio
Hindu (99.79%)	45,918	23,035	22,883	993
Muslim (0.04%)	19	10	9	900
Christian (0.1%)	48	23	25	1,087
Sikh (0%)	-	-	-	-
Buddhists (0%)	-	-	-	-
Jain (0%)	-	-	-	-

Agewise Data:

	Persons	Males	Females	Sex Ratio
All ages	46,014	23,081	22,933	994
0-14	13,404	6,856	6,548	955
15-44	22,372	11,304	11,068	979
45-79	9,910	4,741	5,169	1090
80+	233	116	117	1009
Age not stated	95	64	31	484

Languages (Dominant):

Telugu, Hindi, Urdu, Gondi, Oriya

Disabled Population:

	Persons	Males	Females	%
Total Disabled	989	561	428	
In Seeing	479	275	204	48.43
In Speech	105	54	51	10.62
In Hearing	44	25	19	4.45
In Movement	242	146	96	24.47
Mentally	119	61	58	12.03

AMALAPURAM

Amalapuram C.D. Block lies in the southern part of East Godavari district. It is a part of Amalapuram Mandal. The Block is located at a distance of 108 kms. from district headquarters (Kakinada). There are 16 villages in the block with the total population of 72,689 persons. Area of the C.D. Block is 75.32 sq. kms. It is bounded in the north by Mandal Ainavilli, in the south by River Godavari and Mandal Allavaram, in the east by Mandal Mummidivaram and Uppalaguptam, and in the west by Mandal Ambalajipeta.

Communications :

Roadways : State Highway (S.H): Direction- P. Gunnavaram to Drakshararam. Nearest Villages- A. Vemavaram, Janupa lle, Edarapalle, Indupalle, Gunnapalle Agraharam, Sakuru.

Backwards Region Grants Fund: It receives Backward Region Grants.

Integrated Child Development Scheme (ICDS) Project: Amalapuram, Total Anganwadi Centres: 260

Annaul Rainfall: Average Rainfall 1324.5 mm

Ground Water: Availability of the Ground Water in the Basin is (Information not avavible) H.A.M .and the utilization is (Information not avavible) H.A.M. It belongs to (Information not avavible) category. Depth to water level varies from 3 to 10 meter below the ground. Most of the wells go down in summer months.

Natural Division : Godavari Delta Region

Administration:

Division: Coastal Andhra. Parliamentary Constituency: 24 Amalapuram (SC). District: East Godavari. Mandal: Amalapuram. Assembly Constituency: 163 Amalapuram (SC). Gram Panchayat: 22.

Fairs and Festivals:

Jwalatoranothsavam : It is celebrated for one day on Kartika Suddha Purnima (October-November) at the temple of Mukteswara. On that day, according to mythology, Lord Siva took halahalam (poison), Parvati prayed to Agnideva (God of Fire) and made a vow that she would perform seva to Him along with Her husband annually. A toranam (festoon) is prepared with dried grass and is lit. The God and Goddess are placed in the palanquin. The people cross three times under the lighted toranam. The people take the unburnt grass of the toranam and feed their cattle with it. This custom came into vogue, as the villagers believe that, after eating that resid ual grass, their cattle would be safe and free from all diseases and ailments. Akasadeepalu are lit through out the month of Kartikam. Pujas are performed with one lakh leaves called lakshapathripuja and abhishekam is performed. All the people arrange dinners in the gardens. All the devotees who visit this place will go to Ainavilli village at a distance of a kilometre from here and have the darshan of Ganapati in the Vighs neswara temple there. Some devotees perform abhishekam with the water of one thousand, one hundred and sixteen cocoanuts there. They also have the darshan of Muleswara in Tottaramudi village at a distance of 2 kms. from here.

Prabhala Teertham : It is celebrated for a day on 15th January at the temple of Mukteswara. This festival is celebrated to please Rudra and Veerabhadra deities.

With their blessings, it is believed they are free from the visitation of the diseases in rainy and winter seasons. The procession images of the Gods of surround ing villages are brought with the prabhas into the compo und of Mukteswara temple. Vedas are read out and mantras are chanted with the attendance of beating drums and shrilling pipes. The people shout 'Sarabha, Sarabha, Jaisarabha' while following prabhas. Fruits and flowers are offered. This is really a fascinating and thrilling festival.

Villages: 16 **Inhabited:** 16 **Uninhabited:** 0

Ranking	District	State	National
Area	50	1071	5913
Population	25	102	4398
Sex Ratio	32	425	1679
Child Sex Ratio	27	318	1142
Literacy Rate	5	24	655
Density	46	1068	827
Work Participation Rate	7	11	4623

Gram Panchayats:
A.Vemavaram, A.Vemavarapadu, Bandarulanka Bhatnavilli, Chinthadagaruvu, Edarapalle G.Agraharam, Immidivarappadu, Indupalle, Janupalle Kamanagaruvu, Nadipudi, Nallamilli, Palagummi Peruru, Reddipalli, Rollapalem, Sakuru, Samanasa Savarappalem, Thandavapalle, V.Chintalapudi.

Amenities:

Education: Primary School in 16 villages, Middle school in 10 villages, Matriculation or Secondary School in 5 villages, namely Palagummi, A. Vemavaram, Amalapuram (Rural), Peruru, Vanne Chintalapudi.

Higher Secondary or Pre University Courses or Intermediate or Junior College in 2 villages of the CD Block,, namely Palagummi, Amalapuram (Rural).

College in 0 village, Adult Literacy Center in 14 villages.

Medical: Hospital in 1 village, Dispensary in 12 villages, Health Center in 0 village, Sub Center in 14 villages, Maternity and Child Welfare Center in 13 villages, Community health workers in 0 village.

The Villages having Hospital or Dispensary or Health Center are Palagummi, A. Vemavaram, Bhatnavilli, Janupalle, Edarapalle, Indupalle, Sakuru, Peruru, Immidivarappadu, Thandavapalle, Vanne Chintalapudi, Samanasa.

Drinking Water: Tap water in 16 villages, Tank water in 16 villages, Well water in 16 villages, Tubewell in 16 villages and more than one source in 16 villages.

Bank: Banking facility in 2 villages, namely, Peruru, Samanasa.

Credit Society in 12 villages Agricultural Credit Society in 12 Non-Agricultural Credit Society in 1 village.

Others: Power supply in 16 villages, Cinema hall in 2 villages, sport club in 0 village, Stadium or Auditorium or Community Hall in 0 village, Post Office in 16 villages.

There are 16 villages having bus facilities.

Village with most of facilities: Peruru, Samanasa.

Villages without Amenities (Education): None..

Scheduled Castes: Out of the total population of 71648 persons, 23092 persons (32.23%) belong to Scheduled Castes.

The villages having less than 10% SC population are None..

The villages having more than 50% SC population are None.

Sex ratio of Scheduled Caste population is 489.

Scheduled Castes Literates and Illiterates by Sex:

	Persons	Males	Females
Literate	13,719	7,733	5,986
Illiterate	9,373	4,078	5,295
Literacy rate	68.5	75.4	61.3
Graduate	351	256	95

Scheduled Castes (Dominant):
Mala, Jambuvulu, Madiga, Adi Andhra Beda Jangam etc.

For their cultural identity please see Appendix-I

Villages without Scheduled Castes: There are 0 village without any scheduled caste population.

Scheduled Tribes: Out of the total population of 71648 persons, 599 persons (0.84%) belong to Scheduled Tribes.

The villages having less than 10% ST population are Palagummi, Nadipudi, Nallamilli, A. Vemavaram Bhatnavilli, Amalapuram (Rural), Janupalle Edarapalle, Indupalle, Gunnapalle Agraharam, Sakuru Peruru, Immidivarappadu, Thandavapalle Vanne Chintalapudi, Samanasa.

The villages having more than 50% ST population are None.

Sex ratio of Scheduled tribe population is 464.

Scheduled Tribes Literates and Illiterates by Sex:

	Persons	Males	Females
Literate	176	99	77
Illiterate	423	222	201
Literacy rate	37.5	40.4	34.4
Graduate	1	1	0

Scheduled Tribes (Dominant):
Yerukulas, Chenchu etc., Koya etc.
Generic Tribes etc., Valmiki

For their cultural identity please see Appendix-II

Villages without Scheduled Tribes: There are 2 villages without any scheduled tribe population.

Literates and Illiterates by Sex (Total Population):

	Persons	Males	Females
Literate	47,274	25,674	21,600
Illiterate	24,374	10,374	14,000
Literacy rate	75	81	69
Graduate	1,889	1,420	469

Agriculture: ***Distribution of villages according to land use:*** Out of 16 villages, Total area (in hectare) is 7514, out of that 48.51 percent is cultivable and 100 percent of the cultivable area is irrigated.

Sources of Irrigation (Hectares): Government Canal 2958.28, Private Canal 0, Well without Electricity 0, Well with Electricity 0, Tubewell without Electricity 461.74, Tubewell with Electricity 225.18, Tank 0, River 0, Lake 0, Waterfall 0, Others 0.

Villages with population of 5000 to 9999:
Amalapuram (Rural), Edarapalle, Indupalle Vanne Chintalapudi.

Villages with population of 10000 and above:
Peruru.

Distribution of Workers:

	Persons	Males	Females	WPR
Cultivators	2,199	2,034	165	7.77
Agricultural Labour	15,755	9,734	6,021	55.7
Household Industry	695	343	352	2.46
Other Workers	9,634	8,289	1,345	34.06
Main Workers	23,424	18,498	4,926	82.82
Marginal Workers	4,859	1,902	2,957	17.18
Total Workers	28,283	20,400	7,883	

Religion: Major Religious Communities:

	Persons	Males	Females	Sex Ratio
Hindu (98.35%)	70,466	35,501	34,965	985
Muslim (0.76%)	543	258	285	1,105
Christian (0.85%)	608	274	334	1,219
Sikh (0%)	-	-	-	-
Buddhists (0%)	-	-	-	-
Jain (0%)	-	-	-	-

Agewise Data:

	Persons	Males	Females	Sex Ratio
All ages	71,648	36,048	35,600	988
0-14	21,513	11,068	10,445	944
15-44	35,668	17,961	17,707	986
45-79	13,966	6,792	7,174	1056
80+	432	205	227	1107
Age not stated	69	22	47	2136

Languages (Dominant):
Telugu, Urdu, Gondi, Hindi, Tamil

Disabled Population:

	Persons	Males	Females	%
Total Disabled	1,274	752	522	
In Seeing	518	305	213	40.66
In Speech	140	79	61	10.99
In Hearing	56	30	26	4.4
In Movement	373	231	142	29.28
Mentally	187	107	80	14.68

AMANGAL

Amangal C.D. Block lies in the north-east part of Mahbu bnagar district. The Block is located at a distance of 82 kms. from district headquarters (Mahbubnagar). There are 16 villages in the block with the total population of 54339 persons. Area of the C.D. Block is 201.78 sq. kms. It is bounded by Rangareddi district on north, Veldanda Mandal on south, Talakondapalle mandal on west, and Madgul mandal on east.

Communications:

Roadways : State Highway (S.H.): Direction- Hyderabad to Veldanda. Nearest Villages- Karkalpahad, Kadthal, Ekrajguda, Ramanuthula, Vithaipalle, Amangal..

Backwards Region Grants Fund: It receives Backward Region Grants.

Integrated Child Development Scheme (ICDS) Project: Amangal, Total Anganwadi Centres: 165

Annual Rainfall: Average Rainfall 607

Ground Water: Availability of the Ground Water in the Basin is 1270 H.A.M. and the utilization is 1296 H. A.M. It belongs to OE category. Depth to water level varies from 2 to 5 meter below the ground. Most of the wells go down in summer months. The well density in the entire block is 20 wells per sq. km. Total no. of the wells in the block are enumerated as 3631, according to the Ground Water Estimation Committe

Natural Division : Telangana Plateau Region

Administration:

Division: Telangana. Parliamentary Constituency: 12 Nagalkurnool (SC). District: Mahbubnagar. Mandal: Amang al. Assembly Constituency: 83 Kalwakurthy. Gram Panchaya t: 18.

Villages: 16 **Inhabited:** 16 **Uninhabited:** 0

Ranking	District	State	National
Area	53	538	4147
Population	22	390	5079
Sex Ratio	63	1088	4742
Child Sex Ratio	63	1094	5673
Literacy Rate	11	826	4976
Density	59	637	3868
Work Participation Rate	4	470	1732

Gram Panchayats:
Akuthotapalle, Amangal, Cherikonda, Ekwaipalle Kadthal, Kanapur, Karkalpahad, Maisigandi Mangalapalle, Meddigadda Thanda, Mudvin, Polepally Ramanuthula, Seetharam Nagar Tanda, Shettipally Singampally, Vasudevapur, Vithaipalle.

Amenities:

Education: Primary School in 15 villages, Middle school in 7 villages, Matriculation or Secondary School in 4 villages, namely Kadthal, Mudwin, Akuthotapalle, Amangal.

Higher Secondary or Pre University Courses or Intermediate or Junior College in 2 villages of the CD Block,, namely Kadthal, Amangal.

College in 2 villages, Adult Literacy Center in 15 villages., Colleges are in villages, namely Kadthal, Amangal.

Medical: Hospital in 1 village, Dispensary in 2 villages, Health Center in 1 village, Sub Center in 7 villages, Maternity and Child Welfare Center in 0 village, Community health workers in 0 village.

The Villages having Hospital or Dispensary or Health Center are Mudwin, Amangal.

Drinking Water: Tap water in 16 villages, Tank water in 16 villages, Well water in 16 villages, Tubewell in 16 villages and more than one source in 16 villages.

Bank: Banking facility in 4 villages, namely, Karkalpahad, Kadthal, Akuthotapalle, Amangal.

Credit Society in 5 villages Agricultural Credit Society in 2 Non-Agricultural Credit Society in 5 villages.

Others: Power supply in 16 villages, Cinema hall in 2 villages, sport club in 1 village, Stadium or Auditorium or Community Hall in 0 village, Post Office in 10 villages.

There are 13 villages having bus facilities.

Villages with most of facilities: Kadthal Akuthotapalle, Amangal.

Villages without amenities (Education): Ekrajguda..

Scheduled Castes: Out of the total population of 54339 persons, 8474 persons (15.59%) belong to Scheduled Castes.

The villages having less than 10% SC population are Vasudevapur, Ekrajguda, Cherikondapattipadkal Ramanuthula.

The villages having more than 50% SC population are None.

Sex ratio of Scheduled Caste population is 483.

Scheduled Castes Literates and Illiterates by Sex:

	Persons	Males	Females
Literate	2,735	1,934	801
Illiterate	5,739	2,450	3,289
Literacy rate	38.0	52.1	23.0
Graduate	47	45	2

Scheduled Castes (Dominant):

Madiga, Mala, Beda Jangam etc., Generic Castes etc. Bindla

For their cultural identity please see Appendix-I

Villages without Scheduled Castes: There are 2 villages without any scheduled caste population.

Scheduled Tribes: Out of the total population of 54339 persons, 14351 persons (26.41%) belong to Scheduled Tribes.

The villages having less than 10% ST population are Ekrajguda, Mudwin, Cherikonda Pattikalwakurthy Settipalle, Konapur, Chennampalle, Singam Palle.

The villages having more than 50% ST population are Vasudevapur, Karkalpahad, Cherikondapattipadkal Ramanuthula.

Sex ratio of Scheduled tribe population is 467.

Scheduled Tribes Literates and Illiterates by Sex:

	Persons	Males	Females
Literate	3,203	2,547	656
Illiterate	11,148	5,096	6,052
Literacy rate	27.6	41.6	11.9
Graduate	41	37	4

Scheduled Tribes (Dominant):

Sugalis etc., Chenchu etc., Yerukulas

For their cultural identity please see Appendix-II

Villages without Scheduled Tribes: There are 4 villages without any scheduled tribe population.

Literates and Illiterates by Sex (Total Population):

	Persons	Males	Females
Literate	21,544	14,355	7,189
Illiterate	32,795	13,910	18,885
Literacy rate	47	60	32
Graduate	822	680	142

Agriculture: ***Distribution of villages according to land use:*** Out of 16 villages, Total area (in hectare) is 20178, out of that 46.09 percent is cultivable and 11.33 percent of the cultivable area is irrigated.

Sources of Irrigation (Hectares): Government Canal 0, Private Canal 0, Well without Electricity 6.07, Well with Electricity 516.77, Tubewell without Electricity 0, Tubewell with Electricity 264.65, Tank 265.87, River 0, Lake 0, Waterfall 0, Others 0.

Villages with population of 5000 to 9999:

Kadthal, Mudwin.

Villages with population of 10000 and above:

Amangal.

Distribution of Workers:

	Persons	Males	Females	WPR
Cultivators	8,422	5,649	2,773	30.8
Agricultural Labour	9,395	3,094	6,301	34.36
Household Industry	1,519	863	656	5.56
Other Workers	8,007	5,981	2,026	29.28
Main Workers	22,412	14,067	8,345	81.97
Marginal Workers	4,931	1,520	3,411	18.03
Total Workers	27,343	15,587	11,756	

Religion: Major Religious Communities:

	Persons	Males	Females	Sex Ratio
Hindu (96.17%)	52,256	27,191	25,065	922

Muslim (3.45%)	1,872	967	905	936
Christian (0.31%)	168	85	83	976
Sikh (0.01%)	5	2	3	1,500
Buddhists (0%)	-	-	-	-
Jain (0%)	-	-	-	-

Agewise Data:

	Persons	Males	Females	Sex Ratio
All ages	54,339	28,265	26,074	922
0-14	19,918	10,630	9,288	874
15-44	24,742	12,793	11,949	934
45-79	9,137	4,566	4,571	1001
80+	448	220	228	1036
Age not stated	94	56	38	679

Languages (Dominant):
Telugu, Hindi, Urdu, Tamil, Oriya

Disabled Population:

	Persons	Males	Females	%
Total Disabled	780	422	358	
In Seeing	292	150	142	37.44
In Speech	70	31	39	8.97
In Hearing	59	26	33	7.56
In Movement	254	157	97	32.56
Mentally	105	58	47	13.46

AMARAPURAM

Amarapuram C.D. Block lies in the south-western part of Anantapur district. The Block is located at a distan ce of 104 kms. from district headquarters (Anantapur). There are 09 villages in the block with the total population of 52,717 persons. Area of the C.D. Block is 226.45 sq. kms. It has common boundary with the state of Karnataka in the north, east and west, and it is bounded by Mandal Gudibanda on south.

Communications:

Roadways : Metalled Roads: Nearest Villages- Amarapuram, Halukuru, Basavanahalli.

It receives the Backward Region Grants, and is identifi ed as a drought-prone area as well.

Annual Rainfall: Average Rainfall 546 mm

Ground Water: Availability of the Ground Water in the Basin is 1540 H.A.M. and the utilization is 2012 H. A.M. It belongs to OE category. Depth to water level varies from 10 to 20 meter below the ground. Most of the wells go down in summer months. The well density in the entire block is 8 wells per sq. km. Total no. of the wells in the block are enumerated as 2015, according to the Ground Water Estimation Committee.

Natural Division : Rayalaseema Region

Administration:

Division: Rayala Seema. Parliamentary Constituency: 37 Hindupur. District: Anantapur.

Mandal: Amarapuram. Assembly Constituency: 275 Madakasi ra (SC). Gram Panchayat: 9.

Border Villages: (Karnataka)- Nearest Villages- Valasa, Sivaram, Veerabommana Halli, Basavanahalli, Thammadeha lli, Amarapuram, Halukuru, Nidragatta, Hemavathi.

Places of Turist Interest:

Amarapuram

It is claimed that this place is associated with Amaras imha, the lexicographer and author of 'Amarakosa'. It is situated 42 kms. north-west of Madakasira. This place appears to have been a stronghold of Jains in the early centuries. Chandraka Bhattaraka, the disciple of Charukrithi Bhattaraka, a reputed Jain teacher, lies buried in Thama-dehalli Anjaneyaswamy temple, about 3 kms. from Amarapuram. On the elevated ground beyond the water spread of the Amarapuram tank, which commands an ayacut of over 365 kms. is the site of an old Jain 'Basadi' (monument to the dead) in a black stone 'Panavattam' (Pedestal). An inscription of 1278 A.D. by the side of the Panavattam records the gift of arecanut trees in Thamadehalli for the reconstruction of the temple of Prasanna-paraswadeva. There is also an incomplete Jain temple on the Thailagiri mound. The mosque in this village is the biggest in the taluk. Amarapuram is known for the cultivation of betel leaves and arecanuts.

Hemavathi : Located about 160 kms from Anantapur, Hemav athi once served as the capital of Pallavas. The place has a remarkable collection of Pallava and Chola archit ecture. It boasts of the ruins of an ancient fort, the Hemavathi Fort. Doddeswara Swamy Temple is another structure that was built during the Pallava reign. Some other renowned temples situated here are Siddeshwa ra Swamy, Mallikarjuna Swamy and Gorantla.

Fairs and Festivals:

Sri Ranganathaswamy Car Festival : It is celebrated for one day on Vaisakha Purnima (April-May). The uthsa va vigraham is kept in the house of Karnam of Sivaram and is taken out in a procession on a car on that day and is taken back to the Karnam's house after the procession is over. About 8 to 10 thousand Hindus, local and from the near by villages, irrespective of caste and creed congregate.

Villages: 9 **Inhabited:** 8 **Uninhabited:** 1

Ranking	District	State	National
Area	48	403	3719
Population	8	430	5153
Sex Ratio	16	839	2827
Child Sex Ratio	38	761	3265
Literacy Rate	38	655	4388

Density	47	571	4286
Work Participation Rate	7	600	1513

Gram Panchayats:
Aldahalli, Amarapuram, Basavanahalli, Halukuru Hemavathi, Nidragatta, Sivaram, Thammedahalli Valasa.

Amenities:
Education: Primary School in 8 villages, Middle school in 7 villages, Matriculation or Secondary School in 5 villages, namely Valasa, Amarapuram, Halukuru, Hemavathi, Basavanahalli.
Higher Secondary or Pre University Courses or Intermediate or Junior College in 1 village of the CD Block,, namely Amarapuram.
College in 0 village, Adult Literacy Center in 0 village.
Medical: Hospital in 0 village, Dispensary in 1 village, Health Center in 1 village, Sub Center in 8 villages, Maternity and Child Welfare Center in 0 village, Community health workers in 0 village.
The Village having Hospital or Dispensary or Health Center is Valasa.
Drinking Water: Tap water in 8 villages, Tank water in 0 villages, Well water in 0 village, Tubewell in 0 village and more than one source in 8 villages.
Bank: Banking facility in 2 villages, namely, Amarapuram, Hemavathi.
Credit Society in 2 villages Agricultural Credit Society in 2 Non-Agricultural Credit Society in 0 village.
Others: Power supply in 8 villages, Cinema hall in 3 villages, sport club in 0 village, Stadium or Auditorium or Community Hall in 0 village, Post Office in 8 villages.
There are 8 villages having bus facilities.
Villages with most of facilities: Amarapuram Hemavathi.
Villages without Amenities (Education): None..
Scheduled Castes: Out of the total population of 52717 persons, 11592 persons (21.99%) belong to Scheduled Castes.
The villages having less than 10% SC population are None..
The villages having more than 50% SC population are None.
Sex ratio of Scheduled Caste population is 494.

Scheduled Castes Literates and Illiterates by Sex:

	Persons	Males	Females
Literate	4,141	2,700	1,441
Illiterate	7,451	3,170	4,281
Literacy rate	42.4	54.5	29.9
Graduate	101	93	8

Scheduled Castes (Dominant):
Madiga, Mala, Chalavadi, Dom etc.
For their cultural identity please see Appendix-I
Villages without Scheduled Castes: There is 1 village without any scheduled caste population.
Scheduled Tribes: Out of the total population of 52717 persons, 441 persons (0.84%) belong to Scheduled Tribes.
The villages having less than 10% ST population are Valasa, Thammadehalli, Amarapuram, Halukuru Nidragatta, Hemavathi, Sivaram, Basavanahalli.
The villages having more than 50% ST population are None.
Sex ratio of Scheduled tribe population is 463.

Scheduled Tribes Literates and Illiterates by Sex:

	Persons	Males	Females
Literate	161	106	55
Illiterate	280	131	149
Literacy rate	43.5	52.5	32.7
Graduate	7	7	0

Scheduled Tribes (Dominant):
Sugalis etc., Yerukulas, Kammara, Yenadis
For their cultural identity please see Appendix-II
Villages without Scheduled Tribes: There are 2 villages without any scheduled tribe population.

Literates and Illiterates by Sex (Total Population):

	Persons	Males	Females
Literate	23,186	14,653	8,533
Illiterate	29,531	12,201	17,330
Literacy rate	51	63	38
Graduate	669	581	88

Agriculture: ***Distribution of villages according to land use:***
Out of 9 villages, Total area (in hectare) is 22645, out of that 71.93 percent is cultivable and 5.4 percent of the cultivable area is irrigated.
Sources of Irrigation (Hectares): Government Canal 0, Private Canal 0, Well without Electricity 0, Well with Electricity 364.39, Tubewell without Electricity 0, Tubewell with Electricity 514.77, Tank 0, River 0, Lake 0, Waterfall 0, Others 0.
Villages with population of 5000 to 9999:
Valasa, Thammadehalli, Halukuru, Hemavathi Basavanahalli.
Villages with population of 10000 and above:
Amarapuram.

Distribution of Workers:

	Persons	Males	Females	WPR
Cultivators	10,602	7,310	3,292	38.43
Agricultural Labour	11,547	4,874	6,673	41.86
Household Industry	1,789	693	1,096	6.49
Other Workers	3,648	2,892	756	13.22
Main Workers	20,776	13,569	7,207	75.31
Marginal Workers	6,810	2,200	4,610	24.69

Total Workers	27,586	15,769	11,817	

Religion: Major Religious Communities:

	Persons	Males	Females	Sex Ratio
Hindu (96.06%)	50,640	25,808	24,832	962
Muslim (3.55%)	1,871	939	932	993
Christian (0.17%)	90	42	48	1,143
Sikh (0.02%)	10	7	3	429
Buddhists (0%)	1	1	-	-
Jain (0.08%)	43	24	19	792

Agewise Data:

	Persons	Males	Females	Sex Ratio
All ages	52,717	26,854	25,863	963
0-14	17,429	8,864	8,565	966
15-44	23,679	11,971	11,708	978
45-79	11,035	5,723	5,312	928
80+	460	204	256	1255
Age not stated	114	92	22	239

Languages (Dominant):

Kannada, Telugu, Urdu, Hindi, Marathi

Disabled Population:

	Persons	Males	Females	%
Total Disabled	883	536	347	
In Seeing	337	195	142	38.17
In Speech	135	79	56	15.29
In Hearing	71	38	33	8.04
In Movement	248	175	73	28.09
Mentally	92	49	43	10.42

AMARAVATHI

Amravathi C.D. Block lies in the northern part of Guntur district. The Block is located at a distance of 27 kms. from district headquarters (Guntur). There are 17 villages in the block with the total population of 64,221 persons. Area of the C.D. Block is 202.79 sq. kms. It is bounded in the north by district Krishna, in the south by Mandals Pedakurapadu and Tadikonda, in the east by Mandal Thullur, and in the west by Mandals Khosuru and Atchampet.

Communications:

Roadways : Metalled Roads: Nearest Villages- Munugodu, Attalur, Jupudi, Pondugala, Malladi, Didugu, Lingapuram, Dharanikota, Amaravathi, Vykuntapuram, Pedda Madduru, Narukullapadu, Endroyi, Unguturu, Nemalikallu, Karlapu di.

River: Krishna Nadi- Nearset Villages- Puttipadu, Munug odu, Pondugala, Malladi, Didugu, Dharanikota, Amaravathi, Vykuntapuram.

Annual Rainfall: Average Rainfall 849 mm

Ground Water: Availability of the Ground Water in the Basin is 5113 H.A.M. and the utilization is 751 H.A. M. It belongs to Safe category. Depth to water level varies from 2 to 5 meter below the ground. Most of the wells go down in summer months.

Forest and Reserved **Forest:** Nearest Villages- Endroyi, Karlapudi.

Natural Division : Krishna Delta Region

Administration:

Division: Coastal Andhra . Parliamentary Constituency: 31 Narsaraopet. District: Guntur. Mandal: Amravathi. Assembly Constituency: 204 Pedakurapadu. Gram Panchaya t: 19.

Palaces of Tourist Interest:

Amaravathi: Some 30 kms. due west of Vijayawada, near the bank of the Krishna leiver, stands the ancient Buddhist centre of Amaravathi, the former capital of the Satvahanas, the successors to the Mauryas in this part of India. Here you can see the 2000 years old stupa with its intricately carved pillars and marble-su rfaced dome which itself is equally richly carved. The carvings depict the life of the Buddha as well as scenes from everyday life. It's not as large as that at Sanchi in Madhya Pradesh but it's worth a visit if you're interested in Buddhist relics of the Hinayana era. There's a museum on the site containing relics found in the area. Direct buses from Vijayawada to Amaravathi are few and far between, so it's better to take one of the hourly buses south to Guntur and then another bus from there. All up, 65 kms. trip takes two to three hours. The A.P.T.T.D.C. also organises bus tours as well as boat trips for return. Ask at the tourist infor mation at Vijayawada railway station or at the A.P.T. T.D.C.'s counter at the Krishnaveni Motel, Sitanagaram, in Vijayawada.

Amarawathi (Tadikonda): This village is the most import ant spot near Tadikonda along with the neighbouring village of Dharanikota. It is situated at a distance of 35 kms. to the north-west of Guntur. There is a world famous Buddhist Stupa depicting scenes from the life of Buddha, embodying various Buddhistic emblems, symbols and also inscriptions in Pali character. It has many tourist facilities and commands a vast stream of pilgrims all through the year. Among the famous shrines that are dedicated to Lord Shiva is the one at Amaravathi. A large congregation assembles on the Mahasivaratri day. (February-March).

Pondugala : Pondugala, is situated north of Gurazala on the bank of the Krishna river and is 11 kms. from Guntur, on the Guntur-Macherla highway. Of the temples at the place, the one dedicated to Gantala Ramalingesva ra Swamy is considered important and it contains some inscriptions on its pillars in pali. The temple of

Bobbanagi in Iyyagaripalem, a hamlet of Pondagala, on the bank of the Dandivagu, which was declared a protected monument, contains two inscriptions in Sanskr it.

Fairs and Festivals:

Sri Amareswaraswamy Rathothsavam : It is celebrated for 10 days from Magha Bahula Dasami to Phalguna Suddha Chavithi (January-February) at Amareswara Temple. Decoration of the Lord as a bridegroom on Dasami; ankur arpana and dhwajarohana on Ekadasi, gramothsavam and chiluka vahanam on Dwadasi, pulivahanam on Triodasi, kalyanam on Chathurdasi, keelugurrapu seva and rathot hsavam on Amavasya, choorna, avabrutha, vasanthothsavam and purnahuthi on Suddha Padyami, pavalimpu sevas from Vidiya to Chavithi are the rituals observed.

Villages: 17 **Inhabited:** 16 **Uninhabited:** 1

Ranking	District	State	National
Area	13	533	4131
Population	13	216	4718
Sex Ratio	45	717	2432
Child Sex Ratio	45	879	3882
Literacy Rate	23	250	2661
Density	23	270	3376
Work Participation Rate	36	332	692

Gram Panchayats:

Amaravathi, Attaluru, Dharanikota, Didugu, Endroy Enikapadu, Jupudi, Karlapudi, Lemalle, Lingapuram Malladi, Mandepudi, Munagodu, Muthyapalem Nemalikallu, Nurukullapadu, Pedamadduru, Unguturu Vykuntapuram.

Amenities:

Education: Primary School in 16 villages, Middle school in 9 villages, Matriculation or Secondary School in 5 villages, namely Munugodu, Attalur, Dharanikota, Amaravathi, Nemalikallu.

Higher Secondary or Pre University Courses or Intermediate or Junior College in 1 village of the CD Block,, namely Dharanikota.

College in 1 village, Adult Literacy Center in 0 village., College is in village, namely Dharanikota.

Medical: Hospital in 1 village, Dispensary in 3 villages, Health Center in 3 villages, Sub Center in 9 villages, Maternity and Child Welfare Center in 0 village, Community health workers in 0 village.

The Villages having Hospital or Dispensary or Health Center are Amaravathi, Narukullapadu, Karlapudi.

Drinking Water: Tap water in 16 villages, Tank water in 16 villages, Well water in 16 villages, Tubewell in 16 villages and more than one source in 16 villages.

Bank: Banking facility in 5 villages, namely, Attalur, Dharanikota, Amaravathi, Vykuntapuram Karlapudi.

Credit Society in 12 villages Agricultural Credit Society in 9 Non-Agricultural Credit Society in 1 village.

Others: Power supply in 16 villages, Cinema hall in 3 villages, sport club in 0 village, Stadium or Auditorium or Community Hall in 0 village, Post Office in 16 villages.

There are 15 villages having bus facilities.

Villages with most of facilities: Attalur Dharanikota, Amaravathi, Vykuntapuram, Karlapudi.

Villages without Amenities (Education): None..

Scheduled Castes: Out of the total population of 64221 persons, 16725 persons (26.04%) belong to Scheduled Castes.

The villages having less than 10% SC population are None..

The villages having more than 50% SC population are None.

Sex ratio of Scheduled Caste population is 491.

Scheduled Castes Literates and Illiterates by Sex:

	Persons	Males	Females
Literate	7,873	4,791	3,082
Illiterate	8,852	3,720	5,132
Literacy rate	55.0	65.7	43.8
Graduate	270	209	61

Scheduled Castes (Dominant):

Madiga, Mala, Mala Dasu, Generic Castes etc.

Dakkal etc.

For their cultural identity please see Appendix-I

Villages without Scheduled Castes: There is 1 village without any scheduled caste population.

Scheduled Tribes: Out of the total population of 64221 persons, 2661 persons (4.14%) belong to Scheduled Tribes.

The villages having less than 10% ST population are Munugodu, Attalur, Jupudi, Malladi, Didugu Lingapuram, Dharanikota, Amaravathi, Vykuntapuram Narukullapadu, Endroyi, Unguturu, Nemalikallu Karlapudi.

The villages having more than 50% ST population are None.

Sex ratio of Scheduled tribe population is 483.

Scheduled Tribes Literates and Illiterates by Sex:

	Persons	Males	Females
Literate	887	576	311
Illiterate	1,774	799	975
Literacy rate	38.5	49.2	27.5
Graduate	24	22	2

Scheduled Tribes (Dominant):

Yerukulas, Yenadis, Sugalis etc., Chenchu etc.

Koya etc.

For their cultural identity please see Appendix-II

Villages without Scheduled Tribes: There is 1 village without any scheduled tribe population.

Literates and Illiterates by Sex (Total Population):

	Persons	Males	Females
Literate	34,275	20,168	14,107
Illiterate	29,946	12,416	17,530
Literacy rate	61	70	51
Graduate	1,666	1,275	391

Agriculture: ***Distribution of villages according to land use:*** Out of 17 villages, Total area (in hectare) is 20279, out of that 65.79 percent is cultivable and 10.94 percent of the cultivable area is irrigated.

Sources of Irrigation (Hectares): Government Canal 258, Private Canal 0, Well without Electricity 152, Well with Electricity 105, Tubewell without Electricity 0, Tubewell with Electricity 10, Tank 35, River 0, Lake 0, Waterfall 0, Others 900.

Villages with population of 5000 to 9999: Dharanikota, Nemalikallu, Karlapudi.

Villages with population of 10000 and above: Amaravathi.

Distribution of Workers:

	Persons	Males	Females	WPR
Cultivators	7,706	5,311	2,395	21.12
Agricultural Labour	22,874	10,042	12,832	62.69
Household Industry	652	253	399	1.79
Other Workers	5,254	4,380	874	14.4
Main Workers	29,875	18,380	11,495	81.88
Marginal Workers	6,611	1,606	5,005	18.12
Total Workers	36,486	19,986	16,500	

Religion: Major Religious Communities:

	Persons	Males	Females	Sex Ratio
Hindu (87.8%)	56,389	28,586	27,803	973
Muslim (9.42%)	6,048	3,080	2,968	964
Christian (2.67%)	1,712	879	833	948
Sikh (0%)	3	1	2	2,000
Buddhists (0.01%)	7	3	4	1,333
Jain (0%)	1	-	1	-

Agewise Data:

	Persons	Males	Females	Sex Ratio
All ages	64,221	32,584	31,637	971
0-14	19,052	9,813	9,239	942
15-44	31,145	15,865	15,280	963
45-79	13,287	6,573	6,714	1021
80+	661	286	375	1311
Age not stated	76	47	29	617

Languages (Dominant): Telugu, Urdu, Tamil, Hindi, Gondi

Disabled Population:

	Persons	Males	Females	%
Total Disabled	1,154	642	512	
In Seeing	440	241	199	38.13
In Speech	143	71	72	12.39
In Hearing	64	34	30	5.55
In Movement	339	192	147	29.38
Mentally	168	104	64	14.56

AMBAJIPETA

Ambajipeta C.D. Block lies in the south-western part of East Godavari district. The Block is located at a distance of 90 kms. from district headquarters (Kakin ada). There are 13 villages in the block with the total population of 65,006 persons. Area of the C.D. Block is 53.90 sq. kms. It is bounded in the north by Mandal Kothapeta and Ainavilli, in the south by River Vainatey am Godavari and Mandal Mamidikuduru, in the east by Mandals Ainavilli and Amalapuram, and in the west by Mandal P. Gannavaram.

Communications :

Roadways : State Highway (S.H.): Direction- Kothapeta to Machavaram. Nearest Villages- Chiratapudi, Pulletiku rru, K. Pedapudi, Machavaram.

River: Vainateyam: Nearest Village- Thondavaram.

Backwards Region Grants Fund: It receives Backward Region Grants.

Annaul Rainfall: Average Rainfall 1108.6 mm

Ground Water: Availability of the Ground Water in the Basin is (Information not avavible) H.A.M .and the utilization is (Information not avavible) H.A.M. It belongs to (Information not avavible) category. Depth to water level varies from 3 to 10 meter below the ground. Most of the wells go down in summer months.

Natural Division : Godavari Delta Region

Administration:

Division: Coastal Andhra. Parliamentary Constituency: 24 Amalapuram (SC). District: East Godavari. Mandal: Ambajipeta. Assembly Constituency: 165 Gannavaram (SC). Gram Panchayat:16.

Places of Tourist Interest:

Ambajipeta : It is a hamlet in the village of Macharam situated at a distance of about 8 kms. from Amalapuram. Ambajipeta is noted for coconut gardens and coconut oil. Because of the commercial importance attached to coconuts and their by products, a Regional Coconut Research Station was established here, for improving the varieties and aiding the cultivators. Jack fruit is also an important produce of this place.

Villages: 13 **Inhabited:** 13 **Uninhabited:** 0

Ranking	District	State	National
Area	54	1088	6038
Population	44	207	4688
Sex Ratio	18	284	1321

Child Sex Ratio	52	739	3166
Literacy Rate	4	19	575
Density	31	1042	509
Work Participation Rate	1	1	4272

Gram Panchayats:

Chiratapudi, Gangalakurru, Gangalakurru Agraharam Irusumanda, Isukapudi, K. Pedapudi, Kamuzuvari Lanka Machavaram, Mosalipalli, Mukkamala, Nandampudi Pasupalli, Pulletikurru, Thondavaram, Vakkalagaruvu Vakkalanka.

Amenities:

Education: Primary School in 13 villages, Middle school in 9 villages, Matriculation or Secondary School in 5 villages, namely Pulletikurru, Mukkamala, Gangalakurru, Machavaram, Thondavaram.

Higher Secondary or Pre University Courses or Intermediate or Junior College in 2 villages of the CD Block,, namely Pulletikurru, Machavaram.

College in 2 villages, Adult Literacy Center in 11 villages., Colleges are in villages, namely Pulletikurru, Machavaram.

Medical: Hospital in 2 villages, Dispensary in 3 villages, Health Center in 1 village, Sub Center in 10 villages, Maternity and Child Welfare Center in 1 village, Community health workers in 0 village.

The Villages having Hospital or Dispensary or Health Center are Chiratapudi, Pulletikurru, Mukkamala, Machavaram.

Drinking Water: Tap water in 12 villages, Tank water in 12 villages, Well water in 13 villages, Tubewell in 12 villages and more than one source in 13 villages.

Bank: Banking facility in 3 villages, namely, Pulletikurru, Mukkamala, Machavaram.

Credit Society in 7 villages Agricultural Credit Society in 6 Non-Agricultural Credit Society in 3 villages.

Others: Power supply in 13 villages, Cinema hall in 4 villages, sport club in 0 village, Stadium or Auditorium or Community Hall in 0 village, Post Office in 13 villages.

There are 9 villages having bus facilities.

Villages with most of facilities: Pulletikurru Mukkamala, Machavaram.

Villages without Amenities (Education): None..

Scheduled Castes: Out of the total population of 65006 persons, 18938 persons (29.13%) belong to Scheduled Castes.

The villages having less than 10% SC population are None..

The villages having more than 50% SC population are None.

Sex ratio of Scheduled Caste population is 501.

Scheduled Castes Literates and Illiterates by Sex:

	Persons	Males	Females
Literate	11,057	6,035	5,022
Illiterate	7,881	3,410	4,471
Literacy rate	67.7	74.2	61.2
Graduate	318	249	69

Scheduled Castes (Dominant):

Mala, Jambuvulu, Adi Andhra, Madiga Beda Jangam etc.

For their cultural identity please see Appendix-I

Villages without Scheduled Castes: There are 0 village without any scheduled caste population.

Scheduled Tribes: Out of the total population of 65006 persons, 515 persons (0.79%) belong to Scheduled Tribes.

The villages having less than 10% ST population are Chiratapudi, Pulletikurru, Vakkalanka, Pasupalle Mukkamala, Irusumanda, Mosalipalle, Gangalakurru K. Pedapudi, Isukapudi, Machavaram, Nandampudi Thondavaram.

The villages having more than 50% ST population are None.

Sex ratio of Scheduled tribe population is 482.

Scheduled Tribes Literates and Illiterates by Sex:

	Persons	Males	Females
Literate	204	107	97
Illiterate	311	160	151
Literacy rate	48.6	50.5	46.6
Graduate	0	0	0

Scheduled Tribes (Dominant):

Yerukulas, Chenchu etc., Generic Tribes etc.

For their cultural identity please see Appendix-II

Villages without Scheduled Tribes: There are 2 villages without any scheduled tribe population.

Literates and Illiterates by Sex (Total Population):

	Persons	Males	Females
Literate	43,669	23,593	20,076
Illiterate	21,337	8,979	12,358
Literacy rate	76	82	70
Graduate	1,952	1,483	469

Agriculture: ***Distribution of villages according to land use:*** Out of 13 villages, Total area (in hectare) is 5390, out of that 69.07 percent is cultivable and 95.63 percent of the cultivable area is irrigated.

Sources of Irrigation (Hectares): Government Canal 1002.43, Private Canal 0, Well without Electricity 0, Well with Electricity 0, Tubewell without Electricity 34.82, Tubewell with Electricity 2522.92, Tank 0, River 0, Lake 0, Waterfall 0, Others 0.

Villages with population of 5000 to 9999:

Pulletikurru, Gangalakurru.

Villages with population of 10000 and above:

Machavaram.

Distribution of Workers:

	Persons	Males	Females	WPR
Cultivators	2,465	2,239	226	9.15
Agricultural Labour	14,955	8,723	6,232	55.49
Household Industry	1,867	1,050	817	6.93
Other Workers	7,665	6,635	1,030	28.44
Main Workers	21,787	16,943	4,844	80.84
Marginal Workers	5,165	1,704	3,461	19.16
Total Workers	26,952	18,647	8,305	

Religion: Major Religious Communities:

	Persons	Males	Females	Sex Ratio
Hindu (97.84%)	63,601	31,939	31,662	991
Muslim (0.78%)	507	242	265	1,095
Christian (1.32%)	860	374	486	1,299
Sikh (0%)	1	. -	1	-
Buddhists (0.01%)	5	2	3	1,500
Jain (0%)	-	-	-	-

Agewise Data:

	Persons	Males	Females	Sex Ratio
All ages	65,006	32,572	32,434	996
0-14	18,915	9,565	9,350	978
15-44	32,169	16,211	15,958	984
45-79	13,401	6,533	6,868	1051
80+	433	208	225	1082
Age not stated	88	55	33	600

Languages (Dominant):

Telugu, Urdu, Gondi, Hindi, Tamil

Disabled Population:

	Persons	Males	Females	%
Total Disabled	1,089	617	472	
In Seeing	434	229	205	39.85
In Speech	101	50	51	9.27
In Hearing	58	30	28	5.33
In Movement	367	224	143	33.7
Mentally	129	84	45	11.85

AMRABAD

Amrabad C.D. Block lies in the south eastern part of Mahbubnagar district. The Block is located at a distance of 109 kms. from district headquarters (Mahbubnagar). There are 17 villages in the block with the total population of 43,359 persons. Area of the C.D. Block is 1100 sq. kms. It is bounded by Achampet Mandal on north, Nalgonda and Guntur districts on east, Kurnool and Prakasam districts on south, and Kolapur and Lengal Mandals on west.

Communications :

Roadways : State Highway (S.H.): Direction- Achampet to Kurnool. Nearest Villages- Mannanur, Srisailam Project (L.F.C).

River: Dindi Nadi- Nearest Villages- Ippalapalle.

River Krishna Nadi- Nearest Villages- Srisailam Project (L.F.C).

Backwards Region Grants Fund: It receives Backward Region Grants.

Annual Rainfall: Average Rainfall 756 mm

Ground Water: Availability of the Ground Water in the Basin is 9238 H.A.M. and the utilization is 767 H.A.M. It belongs to Safe category. Depth to water level varies from 5 to 10 meter below the ground. Most of the wells go down in summer months. The well density in the entire block is 1 wells per sq. km. Total no. of the wells in the block are enumerated as 841, according to the Ground Water Estimation Committee.

Forest and Reserved **Forest:** (Amrabad R.F.)- Nearest Villages- Mannanur, Turkapalle, Macharam, Amrabad, Padra, Vankeshwaram, Udimilla, Gudur, Maredugu, Ippala palle, Gangupenta, Maddimadugu, Uppununthala (B.K), Lakshmapur (B.K), Thirumalapur (B.K), Vatwarlapalle, Srisailam Project (L.F.C).

Natural Division : Telangana Plateau Region

Administration:

Division: Telangana. Parliamentary Constituency: 12 Nagarkurnool (SC). District: Mahbubnagar. Mandal: Amrab ad. Assembly Constituency: 82 Achampet (SC) Gram Panchay at: 18.

Villages: 17 **Inhabited:** 17 **Uninhabited:** 0

Ranking	District	State	National
Area	1	1	353
Population	32	567	5367
Sex Ratio	47	824	2780
Child Sex Ratio	31	735	3117
Literacy Rate	6	727	4641
Density	57	606	6314
Work Participation Rate	64	1094	1632

Gram Panchayats:

Amrabad, Chitlamkunta, Ippalapally
Jangam Reddy Pally, Kalvanonipally, Kummaronipally
Laxmapoor (Bk), Macharam, Madhavanipally, Mannanoor
Maradugu, Padra, Thirumalapoor, Thurkapally
Udimilla, Vankeswaram, Vattavarlapally
Venkaswarla Bavi.

Amenities:

Education: Primary School in 15 villages, Middle school in 7 villages, Matriculation or Secondary School in 6 villages, namely Mannanur, Amrabad, Padra, Vankeshwaram, Vatwarlapalle, Srisailam Project (L.F.C).

Higher Secondary or Pre University Courses or Intermediate or Junior College in 1 village of the CD Block,, namely Srisailam Project (L.F.C).

College in 0 village, Adult Literacy Center in 14 villages.

Medical: Hospital in 2 villages, Dispensary in 2 villages, Health Center in 4 villages, Sub Center in 9 villages, Maternity and Child Welfare Center in 13 villages, Community health workers in 0 village.
The Villages having Hospital or Dispensary or Health Center are Mannanur, Turkapalle, Amrabad, Vatwarlapalle, Srisailam Project (L.F.C).
Drinking Water: Tap water in 17 villages, Tank water in 17 villages, Well water in 17 villages, Tubewell in 17 villages and more than one source in 17 villages.
Bank: Banking facility in 4 villages, namely, Mannanur, Amrabad, Padra, Srisailam Project (L.F.C).
Credit Society in 6 villages Agricultural Credit Society in 2 Non-Agricultural Credit Society in 3 villages.
Others: Power supply in 17 villages, Cinema hall in 0 village, sport club in 0 village, Stadium or Auditorium or Community Hall in 0 village, Post Office in 13 villages.
There are 15 villages having bus facilities.
Villages with most of facilities: Mannanur Amrabad, Padra, Srisailam Project (L.F.C).
Villages without amenities (Education): Gudur, Gangupenta..
Scheduled Castes: Out of the total population of 48359 persons, 15007 persons (31.03%) belong to Scheduled Castes.
The villages having less than 10% SC population are Gudur, Ippalapalle, Gangupenta, Maddimadugu Uppununthala (B.K).
The villages having more than 50% SC population are None.
Sex ratio of Scheduled Caste population is 504.
Scheduled Castes Literates and Illiterates by Sex:

	Persons	Males	Females
Literate	6,225	4,018	2,207
Illiterate	8,782	3,424	5,358
Literacy rate	48.6	63.5	34.1
Graduate	190	168	22

Scheduled Castes (Dominant):
Mala, Madiga, Generic Castes etc., Beda Jangam etc. Mala Dasari
For their cultural identity please see Appendix-I
Villages without Scheduled Castes: There is 1 village without any scheduled caste population.
Scheduled Tribes: Out of the total population of 48359 persons, 9100 persons (18.82%) belong to Scheduled Tribes.
The villages having less than 10% ST population are Turkapalle, Amrabad, Gudur, Thirumalapur (B.K) Srisailam Project (L.F.C).
The villages having more than 50% ST population are None.
Sex ratio of Scheduled tribe population is 478.

Scheduled Tribes Literates and Illiterates by Sex:

	Persons	Males	Females
Literate	2,937	2,067	870
Illiterate	6,163	2,680	3,483
Literacy rate	39.3	52.7	24.5
Graduate	60	55	5

Scheduled Tribes (Dominant):
Sugalis etc., Chenchu etc., Yerukulas, Kammara Generic Tribes etc.
For their cultural identity please see Appendix-II
Villages without Scheduled Tribes: There are 0 village without any scheduled tribe population.
Literates and Illiterates by Sex (Total Population):

	Persons	Males	Females
Literate	20,247	13,265	6,982
Illiterate	28,112	11,362	16,750
Literacy rate	49	64	35
Graduate	857	693	164

Agriculture: ***Distribution of villages according to land use:*** Out of 17 villages, Total area (in hectare) is 110045, out of that 30.46 percent is cultivable and 59.27 percent of the cultivable area is irrigated.
Sources of Irrigation (Hectares): Government Canal 18899, Private Canal 0, Well without Electricity 52.6, Well with Electricity 479.8, Tubewell without Electricity 38, Tubewell with Electricity 278, Tank 116, River 0, Lake 0, Waterfall 0, Others 0.
Villages with population of 5000 to 9999:
Mannanur, Padra, Vankeshwaram Srisailam Project (L.F.C).
Villages with population of 10000 and above:
Amrabad.
Distribution of Workers:

	Persons	Males	Females	WPR
Cultivators	9,391	5,522	3,869	38.17
Agricultural Labour	8,264	3,218	5,046	33.59
Household Industry	601	254	347	2.44
Other Workers	6,347	4,641	1,706	25.8
Main Workers	18,097	11,042	7,055	73.56
Marginal Workers	6,506	2,593	3,913	26.44
Total Workers	24,603	13,635	10,968	

Religion: Major Religious Communities:

	Persons	Males	Females	Sex Ratio
Hindu (92.38%)	44,673	22,700	21,973	968
Muslim (6.83%)	3,303	1,707	1,596	935
Christian (0.67%)	323	165	158	958
Sikh (0.01%)	7	5	2	400
Buddhists (0%)	-	-	-	-
Jain (0%)	-	-	-	-

Agewise Data:

	Persons	Males	Females	Sex Ratio
All ages	48,359	24,627	23,732	964
0-14	17,888	9,288	8,600	926
15-44	21,994	11,202	10,792	963
45-79	7,956	3,860	4,096	1061
80+	362	161	201	1248
Age not stated	159	116	43	371

Languages (Dominant):
Telugu, Hindi, Urdu, Kannada, Oriya

Disabled Population:

	Persons	Males	Females	%
Total Disabled	971	585	386	
In Seeing	472	307	165	48.61
In Speech	72	33	39	7.42
In Hearing	47	28	19	4.84
In Movement	300	178	122	30.9
Mentally	80	39	41	8.24

AMRUTHALUR

Amruthalur C.D. Block lies in the eastern part of Guntur district. The Block is located at a distance of 25 kms. from district headquarters (Guntur). There are 13 villages in the block with the total population of 46,960 persons. Area of the C.D. Block is 124.35 sq. kms. It is bounded in the north by Mandal Tenali, in the south by Mandals Pittalavanipadu and Churukupal le, in the east by Mandals Vemuru and Cherukupalle and in the west by Mandals Tsundur and Ponnur.

Communications:

Roadways : Metalled Roads: Nearest Villages- Kuchipudi, Mulpur, Peddapudi, Koditadiparru, Moparru, Thurumella, Amruthalur, Yelavarru, Intur, Govada.

Integrated Child Development Scheme (ICDS) Project: Amruthaluru, Total Anganwadi Centres: 179

Annual Rainfall: Average Rainfall 1037 mm

Ground Water: Availability of the Ground Water in the Basin is 5686 H.A.M. and the utilization is 506 H.A. M. It belongs to Safe category. Depth to water level varies from less than 2 meter below the ground. Most of the wells go down in summer months.

Natural Division : Krishna Delta Region

Administration:

Division: Coastal Andhra. Parliamentary Constituency: 32 Baptala (SC). District: Guntur. Mandal: Amruthalur. Assembly Constituency: 208 Vemuru (SC). Gram Panchayat: 15

Villages: 13 **Inhabited:** 13 **Uninhabited:** 0

Ranking	District	State	National
Area	42	925	5403
Population	42	602	5420
Sex Ratio	11	311	1351
Child Sex Ratio	7	178	525
Literacy Rate	1	48	954
Density	48	770	2897
Work Participation Rate	24	218	2253

Gram Panchayats:

Amruthalur, Bodapadu, Govada, Inturu, Korutadiparru Kuchipudi, Moparru, Mulpur, Panchalavaram, Pedapudi Pyaparru, Thurumella, Vamanagunta Palem, Yadavuru Yalavarru.

Amenities:

Education: Primary School in 13 villages, Middle school in 10 villages, Matriculation or Secondary School in 9 villages, namely Kuchipudi, Mulpur, Peddapudi, Moparru, Thurumella, Amruthalur, Pyaparru, Intur, Govada.
Higher Secondary or Pre University Courses or Intermediate or Junior College in 1 village of the CD Block,, namely Kuchipudi.
College in 0 village, Adult Literacy Center in 0 village.

Medical: Hospital in 0 village, Dispensary in 3 villages, Health Center in 5 villages, Sub Center in 10 villages, Maternity and Child Welfare Center in 0 village, Community health workers in 0 village.
The Villages having Hospital or Dispensary or Health Center are Kuchipudi, Moparru, Intur.

Drinking Water: Tap water in 13 villages, Tank water in 13 villages, Well water in 13 villages, Tubewell in 12 villages and more than one source in 13 villages.

Bank: Banking facility in 4 villages, namely, Kuchipudi, Amruthalur, Intur, Govada.
Credit Society in 7 villages Agricultural Credit Society in 5 Non-Agricultural Credit Society in 1 village.

Others: Power supply in 13 villages, Cinema hall in 3 villages, sport club in 0 village, Stadium or Auditorium or Community Hall in 0 village, Post Office in 13 villages.
There are 13 villages having bus facilities.

Villages with most of facilities: Kuchipudi Amruthalur, Intur, Govada.

Villages without Amenities (Education): None..

Scheduled Castes: Out of the total population of 46960 persons, 19828 persons (42.22%) belong to Scheduled Castes. The villages having less than 10% SC population are None..
The villages having more than 50% SC population are Mulpur, Peddapudi, Thurumella, Panchalavaram Yelavarru, Bodapadu.
Sex ratio of Scheduled Caste population is 494.

Scheduled Castes Literates and Illiterates by Sex:

	Persons	Males	Females
Literate	12,126	6,663	5,463
Illiterate	7,702	3,370	4,332

Literacy rate	69.0	75.0	62.9
Graduate	544	414	130

Scheduled Castes (Dominant):
Madiga, Mala, Relli, Generic Castes etc.
For their cultural identity please see Appendix-I
Villages without Scheduled Castes: There are 0 village without any scheduled caste population.
Scheduled Tribes: Out of the total population of 46960 persons, 1715 persons (3.65%) belong to Scheduled Tribes.
The villages having less than 10% ST population are Kuchipudi, Mulpur, Peddapudi, Koditadiparru, Moparru Thurumella, Amruthalur, Panchalavaram, Yelavarru Pyaparru, Bodapadu, Intur, Govada.
The villages having more than 50% ST population are None.
Sex ratio of Scheduled tribe population is 483.
Scheduled Tribes Literates and Illiterates by Sex:

	Persons	Males	Females
Literate	738	425	313
Illiterate	977	461	516
Literacy rate	49.9	55.7	43.7
Graduate	6	5	1

Scheduled Tribes (Dominant):
Yerukulas, Yenadis, Koya etc., Generic Tribes etc.
For their cultural identity please see Appendix-II
Villages without Scheduled Tribes: There are 0 village without any scheduled tribe population.
Literates and Illiterates by Sex (Total Population):

	Persons	Males	Females
Literate	30,427	16,418	14,009
Illiterate	16,533	7,119	9,414
Literacy rate	72	78	66
Graduate	1,644	1,203	441

Agriculture: ***Distribution of villages according to land use:***
Out of 13 villages, Total area (in hectare) is 12433, out of that 88.06 percent is cultivable and 99.75 percent of the cultivable area is irrigated.
Sources of Irrigation (Hectares): Government Canal 10702, Private Canal 94, Well without Electricity 9, Well with Electricity 0, Tubewell without Electricity 0, Tubewell with Electricity 117, Tank 0, River 0, Lake 0, Waterfall 0, Others 0.
Villages with population of 5000 to 9999:
Kuchipudi, Mulpur, Amruthalur, Intur.
Villages with population of 10000 and above: None
Distribution of Workers:

	Persons	Males	Females	WPR
Cultivators	3,982	3,427	555	16.46
Agricultural Labour	16,891	8,295	8,596	69.83
Household Industry	402	246	156	1.66
Other Workers	2,914	2,337	577	12.05
Main Workers	15,822	11,236	4,586	65.41
Marginal Workers	8,367	3,069	5,298	34.59
Total Workers	24,189	14,305	9,884	

Religion: Major Religious Communities:

	Persons	Males	Females	Sex Ratio
Hindu (93.84%)	44,066	22,111	21,955	993
Muslim (4.08%)	1,918	956	962	1,006
Christian (1.97%)	925	449	476	1,060
Sikh (0.02%)	11	4	7	1,750
Buddhists (0%)	-	-	-	-
Jain (0%)	-	-	-	-

Agewise Data:

	Persons	Males	Females	Sex Ratio
All ages	46,960	23,537	23,423	995
0-14	11,736	5,950	5,786	972
15-44	22,138	11,128	11,010	989
45-79	12,179	6,014	6,165	1025
80+	798	378	420	1111
Age not stated	109	67	42	627

Languages (Dominant):
Telugu, Urdu, Tamil, Gondi, Hindi
Disabled Population:

	Persons	Males	Females	%
Total Disabled	1,115	581	534	
In Seeing	457	210	247	40.99
In Speech	115	62	53	10.31
In Hearing	74	33	41	6.64
In Movement	316	192	124	28.34
Mentally	153	84	69	13.72

ANAKAPALLE

Anakapalle C.D. Block lies in the southern part of Vishakhapatnam district. It is a part of Anakapalle Mandal. The Block is located at a distance of 60 kms. from district headquarters (Vishakhapatnam). There are 32 villages in the block with the total population of 91,233 persons. Area of the C.D. Block is 161.46 sq. kms. It is bounded in the north by Mandals Chodavaram and Sabbavaram, in the south by Mandals Kasimkota and Munagapaka, in the east by Mandals Paravada and Sabbavaram, and in the west by Mandals Kasimkota, Butchayyapeta and a part of Chodavaram.

Communications :
Roadways : NH: Direction- Tuni to Vishakhapatnam. Nearest Villages- Pisinikada, Thummapala.
River: Sarada Nadi- Nearest Villages- Pisinikada, Thumm
Back
wards Region Grants Fund: It receives Backward Region Grants.
Annaul Rainfall: Average Rainfall 1219.0 mm
Ground Water: Availability of the Ground Water in the

Basin is (Information not avavible) H.A.M .and the utilization is (Information not avavible) H.A.M. It belongs to (Information not avavible) category. Depth to water level varies from 3 to 10 meter below the ground. Most of the wells go down in summer months.

Administration:

Division: Coastal Andhra. Parliamentary Constituency: 22 Anakapalle. District: Visakhapatnam. Mandal: Anakapa lle. Assembly Constituency: 149 Anakapalle. Gram Panchay at: 35.

Places of Tourist Interest:

Sankaram

Sankaram is a small village which is over 6 kms. from Anakapalle. There are two low contiguous rock hills running east and west, which are locally known as the Bojjanakonda. They contain some notable Buddhist remains. Three huge stupas at three different places, were cut with great difficulty from the rocks in these hills. The biggest of these is about nine metres in diameter. On the eastern side of the hills is a rock cut temple with numerous Buddhist sculptures and also a life size statue of Buddha. Sankaram is a place of archaeological importance.

Villages: 32 **Inhabited:** 32 **Uninhabited:** 0

Ranking	District	State	National
Area	21	769	4857
Population	1	11	3743
Sex Ratio	19	200	1058
Child Sex Ratio	32	607	2442
Literacy Rate	4	305	2966
Density	36	1060	1962
Work Participation Rate	4	76	4509

Gram Panchayats:

Akkireddipalem, Bhatlapudi, Bowluvada Ch.N.Agraharam, Dibbapalem, Golagam, Gopalapuram Koduru, Kondupalem, Koppaka, Kothuru, Kunchangi Kundram, Makavaram, Mamidipalem, Maredupudi, Marturu Mettapalem, P.S. Palem, Papayyapalem, Pisinikada R.V.Palem, Rajupalem, Rebaka, Sampathipuram Sankaram, Satyanarayanapuram, Seethanagaram Sundarayyapeta, Tagarampudi, Thummapala, V.J. Palem Valluru, Venkupalem, Vooderu.

Amenities:

Education: Primary School in 32 villages, Middle school in 17 villages, Matriculation or Secondary School in 8 villages, namely Allikhanudupalem, Mamidipalem, Kondupalem, Chintanippula Agraharam, Marturu, Seethanagaram, Thummapala, Koppaka.

Higher Secondary or Pre University Courses or Intermediate or Junior College in 0 village of the CD Block, College in 1 village, Adult Literacy Center in 13 villages., College is in village, namely Thummapala.

Medical: Hospital in 0 village, Dispensary in 1 village, Health Center in 11 villages, Sub Center in 3 villages, Maternity and Child Welfare Center in 0 village, Community health workers in 0 village.

The Village having Hospital or Dispensary or Health Center is Tagarampudi.

Drinking Water: Tap water in 32 villages, Tank water in 32 villages, Well water in 32 villages, Tubewell in 32 villages and more than one source in 32 villages.

Bank: Banking facility in 4 villages, namely, Kondupalem, Chintanippula Agraharam, Thummapala Rajupalem.

Credit Society in 3 villages Agricultural Credit Society in 1 Non-Agricultural Credit Society in 1 village.

Others: Power supply in 32 villages, Cinema hall in 0 village, sport club in 0 village, Stadium or Auditorium or Community Hall in 0 village, Post Office in 20 villages.

There are 24 villages having bus facilities.

Villages with most of facilities: Chintanippula Agraharam Rajupalem.

Villages without Amenities (Education): None..

Scheduled Castes: Out of the total population of 91336 persons, 5515 persons (6.04%) belong to Scheduled Castes. The villages having less than 10% SC population are Jagannadhapuram, Vooderu, Allikhanudupalem Mamidipalem, Papayya Santha Palem, Papayya Palem Kondupalem, Chintanippula Agraharam, Makavaram Marturu, Bowluvada, Seethanagaram, Kunchangi Kundram, Venkupalem, Sampathipuram, Pisinikada Thummapala, Rebaka, Koduru, Gopalapuram, Maredupudi Maredupudi Agraharam, Koppaka, Bhatlapudi, Golagam Valluru, Rajupalem.

The villages having more than 50% SC population are None.

Sex ratio of Scheduled Caste population is 513.

Scheduled Castes Literates and Illiterates by Sex:

	Persons	Males	Females
Literate	2,875	1,636	1,239
Illiterate	2,640	1,048	1,592
Literacy rate	59.9	69.9	50.5
Graduate	117	85	32

Scheduled Castes (Dominant):

Mala, Madiga, Relli, Adi Andhra, Generic Castes etc.

For their cultural identity please see Appendix-I

Villages without Scheduled Castes: There are 2 villages without any scheduled caste population.

Scheduled Tribes: Out of the total population of 91336 persons, 700 persons (0.77%) belong to Scheduled Tribes.

The villages having less than 10% ST population are Mettapalem, Jagannadhapuram, Tagarampudi, Vooderu Allikhanudupalem, Mamidipalem, Papayya Santha Palem Papayya Palem, Kondupalem, Chintanippula Agraharam Makavaram, Marturu, Bowluvada, Seethanagaram Kunchangi, Kundram, Venkupalem, Vetajangalapalem Sampathipuram, Pisinikada, Thummapala, Rebaka Koduru, Gopalapuram, Maredupudi Maredupudi Agraharam, Koppaka, Bhatlapudi, Golagam Sankaram, Valluru, Rajupalem.

The villages having more than 50% ST population are None.

Sex ratio of Scheduled tribe population is 489.

Scheduled Tribes Literates and Illiterates by Sex:

	Persons	Males	Females
Literate	274	167	107
Illiterate	426	191	235
Literacy rate	48.2	56.6	39.2
Graduate	6	6	0

Scheduled Tribes (Dominant):

Yerukulas, Manna Dhora, Gadabas, Bagata, Yenadis

For their cultural identity please see Appendix-II

Villages without Scheduled Tribes: There are 18 villages without any scheduled tribe population.

Literates and Illiterates by Sex (Total Population):

	Persons	Males	Females
Literate	47,134	28,178	18,956
Illiterate	44,202	17,395	26,807
Literacy rate	59	71	47
Graduate	2,341	1,760	581

Agriculture: ***Distribution of villages according to land use:*** Out of 32 villages, Total area (in hectare) is 16146, out of that 59.07 percent is cultivable and 46.63 percent of the cultivable area is irrigated.

Sources of Irrigation (Hectares): Government Canal 7, Private Canal 1133, Well without Electricity 0, Well with Electricity 910, Tubewell without Electricity 0, Tubewell with Electricity 266, Tank 2131, River 0, Lake 0, Waterfall 0, Others 0.

Villages with population of 5000 to 9999: None

Villages with population of 10000 and above: Thummapala.

Distribution of Workers:

	Persons	Males	Females	WPR
Cultivators	7,930	5,418	2,512	21.8
Agricultural Labour	8,625	4,329	4,296	23.71
Household Industry	1,354	854	500	3.72
Other Workers	18,474	14,576	3,898	50.78
Main Workers	29,287	22,244	7,043	80.5
Marginal Workers	7,096	2,933	4,163	19.5
Total Workers	36,383	25,177	11,206	

Religion: Major Religious Communities:

	Persons	Males	Females	Sex Ratio
Hindu (98.23%)	89,717	44,769	44,948	1,004
Muslim (1.04%)	947	470	477	1,015
Christian (0.62%)	569	286	283	990
Sikh (0.06%)	52	25	27	1,080
Buddhists (0%)	4	1	3	3,000
Jain (0%)	-	-	-	-

Agewise Data:

	Persons	Males	Females	Sex Ratio
All ages	91,336	45,573	45,763	1004
0-14	28,362	14,256	14,106	989
15-44	45,362	23,048	22,314	968
45-79	16,992	7,973	9,019	1131
80+	378	167	211	1263
Age not stated	242	129	113	876

Languages (Dominant):

Telugu, Urdu, Oriya, Gondi, Tamil

Disabled Population:

	Persons	Males	Females	%
Total Disabled	1,634	901	733	
In Seeing	792	396	396	48.47
In Speech	190	104	86	11.63
In Hearing	53	28	25	3.24
In Movement	444	293	151	27.17
Mentally	155	80	75	9.49

ANANDAPURAM

Anandapuram C.D. Block lies in the eastern part of Vishakhapatnam district. The Block is located at a distance of 37 kms. from district headquarters (Vishakh apatnam). There are 32 villages in the block with the total population of 55,525 persons. Area of the C.D. Block is 205.32 sq. kms. It is bounded in the north by Mandal Padmanabham, in the south by Mandals Vishakha patnam Rural and Bheemunipatnam, in the east by Mandal Bheemunipatnam, and in the west by district Vizianagaram and Mandal Pendurthi.

Communications :

Roadways : NH: Direction- Vishakhapatnam to Bheemunipatn am. Nearest Villages- Vemulavalasa, Vellanki, Gambheeram. State Highway (S.H.): Direction- Simhachalam to Bheemu nipatnam. Nearest Villages- Vemulavalasa, Gandigundam, Mamidilova, Gangasani Agraharam, Narayana Gajapathiraj upuram, Palavalasa, Anandapuram, Peddipalem, Sontyam, Gudilova, Vellanki, Tarluvada, Gambheeram.

River: Rain Fed- Nearest Villages- Bheemannadorapalem, Gorinta, Kanamam, Sontyam, Gudilova, Tarluvada, Gambhe eram, Gidijala.

Annaual Rainfall: Average Rainfall 975.0 mm

Ground Water: Availability of the Ground Water in the Basin is (Information not avavible) H.A.M .and the utilization is (Information not avavible) H.A.M. It belongs to (Information not avavible) category. Depth to water level varies from 3 to 10 meter below the ground. Most of the wells go down in summer months.

Administration:

Division: Coastal Andhra. Parliamentary Constituency: 21 Visakhapatnam. District: Visakhapatnam. Mandal: Anandapuram. Assembly Constituency: 139 Bhimili. Gram Panchayat: 26.

Villages: 32 **Inhabited:** 32 **Uninhabited:** 0

Ranking	District	State	National
Area	9	519	4092
Population	19	360	5035
Sex Ratio	31	558	1972
Child Sex Ratio	5	15	59
Literacy Rate	15	754	4735
Density	22	639	3858
Work Participation Rate	30	465	1745

Gram Panchayats:

Anandapuram, Bantupallivari Kallalu Bheemandorapalem, Boni, Chandaka, Gambheeram Gandigundam, Gidijala, Gottipalle, Kanamam Kolavanipalem, Kusulavada, Lodagalavanipalem Mamidilova, Mukundapuram, Mutcherla, Palavalasa Pandalapaka, Peddipalem, Pekeru, Ramavaram Sirlapalem, Sontyam, Tarluvada, Vellanki Vemulavalasa.

Amenities:

Education: Primary School in 30 villages, Middle school in 18 villages, Matriculation or Secondary School in 9 villages, namely Boni, Gottipalle, Gandigundam, Gidijala, Sontyam, Gudilova, Anandapuram, Vellanki, Gambheeram. Higher Secondary or Pre University Courses or Intermediate or Junior College in 0 village of the CD Block, College in 0 village, Adult Literacy Center in 31 villages.

Medical: Hospital in 0 village, Dispensary in 0 village, Health Center in 11 villages, Sub Center in 9 villages, Maternity and Child Welfare Center in 0 village, Community health workers in 0 village.

Drinking Water: Tap water in 32 villages, Tank water in 32 villages, Well water in 32 villages, Tubewell in 32 villages and more than one source in 32 villages.

Bank: Banking facility in 3 villages, namely, Gidijala, Sontyam, Anandapuram.

Credit Society in 3 villages Agricultural Credit Society in 3 Non-Agricultural Credit Society in 0 village.

Others: Power supply in 32 villages, Cinema hall in 1 village, sport club in 0 village, Stadium or Auditorium or Community Hall in 0 village, Post Office in 19 villages.

There are 24 villages having bus facilities.

Villages with most of facilities: Gidijala Sontyam, Anandapuram.

Villages without Amenities (Education): None..

Scheduled Castes: Out of the total population of 55525 persons, 4891 persons (8.81%) belong to Scheduled Castes. The villages having less than 10% SC population are Sirlapalem, Mukundapuram, Kusuluvada Jagannadhapuram, Bakurupalem, Mutcherla Tangudubilli, Kolavanipalem, Ramavaram, Mamidilova Gangasani Agraharam, Narayana Gajapathirajupuram Kanamam, Gorinta, Gidijala, Sontyam, Gudilova Palavalasa, Chandaka, Gambheeram.

The villages having more than 50% SC population are None.

Sex ratio of Scheduled Caste population is 499.

Scheduled Castes Literates and Illiterates by Sex:

	Persons	Males	Females
Literate	2,158	1,270	888
Illiterate	2,733	1,179	1,554
Literacy rate	51.6	61.2	42.2
Graduate	24	19	5

Scheduled Castes (Dominant):

Mala, Relli, Madiga, Generic Castes etc.

Beda Jangam etc.

For their cultural identity please see Appendix-I

Villages without Scheduled Castes: There are 2 villages without any scheduled caste population.

Scheduled Tribes: Out of the total population of 55525 persons, 832 persons (1.5%) belong to Scheduled Tribes. The villages having less than 10% ST population are Pekeru, Sirlapalem, Mukundapuram, Boni, Gottipalle Jagannadhapuram, Bakurupalem, Mutcherla Kolavanipalem, Bheemannadorapalem, Ramavaram Gandigundam, Dabbanda, Mamidilova Gangasani Agraharam, Kanamam, Gorinta, Gidijala Sontyam, Gudilova, Tarluvada, Palavalasa Pandalapaka, Chandaka, Anandapuram, Vemulavalasa Peddipalem, Vellanki, Gambheeram.

The villages having more than 50% ST population are None.

Sex ratio of Scheduled tribe population is 504.

Scheduled Tribes Literates and Illiterates by Sex:

	Persons	Males	Females
Literate	267	154	113
Illiterate	565	259	306
Literacy rate	38.7	44.4	32.9
Graduate	1	1	0

Scheduled Tribes (Dominant):

Manna Dhora, Yerukulas, Valmiki, Bagata

For their cultural identity please see Appendix-II

Villages without Scheduled Tribes: There are 20 villages without any scheduled tribe population.

Literates and Illiterates by Sex (Total Population):

	Persons	Males	Females
Literate	23,312	14,326	8,986
Illiterate	32,213	13,702	18,511
Literacy rate	49	59	38
Graduate	522	394	128

Agriculture: ***Distribution of villages according to land use:*** Out of 32 villages, Total area (in hectare) is 20532, out of that 44.61 percent is cultivable and 21.94 percent of the cultivable area is irrigated.

Sources of Irrigation (Hectares): Government Canal 111.3, Private Canal 0, Well without Electricity 244.87, Well with Electricity 132.16, Tubewell without Electricity 0, Tubewell with Electricity 179.9, Tank 899.64, River 0, Lake 0, Waterfall 0, Others 441.9.

Villages with population of 5000 to 9999: Anandapuram.

Villages with population of 10000 and above: None

Distribution of Workers:

	Persons	Males	Females	WPR
Cultivators	7,681	5,085	2,596	27.02
Agricultural Labour	12,923	5,904	7,019	45.46
Household Industry	872	587	285	3.07
Other Workers	6,951	5,505	1,446	24.45
Main Workers	23,087	15,174	7,913	81.22
Marginal Workers	5,340	1,907	3,433	18.78
Total Workers	28,427	17,081	11,346	

Religion: Major Religious Communities:

	Persons	Males	Females	Sex Ratio
Hindu (99.38%)	55,178	27,863	27,315	980
Muslim (0.35%)	192	89	103	1,157
Christian (0.17%)	95	48	47	979
Sikh (0.02%)	13	6	7	1,167
Buddhists (0%)	1	1	-	-
Jain (0%)	-	-	-	-

Agewise Data:

	Persons	Males	Females	Sex Ratio
All ages	55,525	28,028	27,497	981
0-14	18,349	9,263	9,086	981
15-44	26,472	13,469	13,003	965
45-79	10,310	5,113	5,197	1016
80+	226	96	130	1354
Age not stated	168	87	81	931

Languages (Dominant):

Telugu, Oriya, Urdu, Hindi, Bengali

Disabled Population:

	Persons	Males	Females	%
Total Disabled	1,049	630	419	
In Seeing	498	309	189	47.47
In Speech	118	55	63	11.25
In Hearing	33	22	11	3.15
In Movement	294	191	103	28.03
Mentally	106	53	53	10.1

ANANTAPUR

Anantapur C.D. Block lies in the central part of Ananta pur district. It is a part of Anantapur Mandal. The Block is located at a distance of (00) kms. from distri ct headquarters (Anantapur). There are 17 villages in the block with the total population of 55,818 persons. Area of the C.D. Block is 247.9 sq. kms. It is bounded in the north by Mandals Garladinne and Bukkarayasamudram, in the south by Mandals Raptadu and Dharmavarm, in the east by Mandals Bukkarayasamudram, Narpala and Bathalapalle, and in the west by Mandals Atmakur and Kudair.

Communications:

Roadways : NH- 7: Gooty to Bangalore. Nearest Village- Somanadoddi. NH- 205 Direction- Raptadu Mandal to Renig unta. Nearest Villages- Itikalapalle, Kandakur, Mannila. State Highway (S.H.): Direction- Kalyandurg to Papampe ta. and Bellary to Koilkuntla. Nearest Villages- Kodimi, Rachanapalle, Kurugunta, Gollapalle.

It receives the Backward Region Grants, and is identifi ed as a drought-prone area as well.

Annual Rainfall: Average Rainfall 581 mm

Ground Water: Availability of the Ground Water in the Basin is 2637 H.A.M. and the utilization is 2345 H. A.M. It belongs to SC category. Depth to water level varies from 10 to 20 meter below the ground. Most of the wells go down in summer months. The well density in the entire block is 12 wells per sq. km. Total no. of the wells in the block are enumerated as 3542, according to the Ground Water Estimation Committee.

Natural Division : Rayalaseema Region

Administration:

Division: Rayala Seema. Parliamentary Constituency: 37 Hindupur. District: Anantapur.

Mandal: Anantapur. Assembly Constituency: 273 Raptadu. Gram Panchayat: 25.

Fairs and Festivals:

Sri Brahmananda Eswaraswamy Festival : It is celebrated for three days from Phalguna Suddha Sapthami (February-March) in commemoration of the death anniversary of the saint at Katiganikalva. On Sapthami there is samar adhana and abhishekam to Sivalingam. Abhisheka theertham and prasadam are distributed to all. On the second day morning, there is navagrahajapam and in the night abhishekam and sahasranamarchana to Sita and Rama. Coconuts, flowers and fruits are offered. The devotees perform panchamrutha abhishekam. That day, the second day, Sri Achala Paripoornanandaswamy, the chief discip le of the departed guru, draws on the floor the thousa nd petalled lotus that is said to be at each individual's aperture in the crown and explains how mind is to be concentrated and salvation attained by controlling the mind and allowing the spirit to leave the body through that aperture. The festival concludes on the third day with the distribution of mahatheertham and mahaprasadam to all with the procession of Eswara and reading of puranams and lectures on Vedantham. Young and old engage themselves in kolatams singing in praise of gods and the saint Brahmananda Eswaraswamy. It is being celebrated for the past 106 years.

Sri Kati Koteswaraswamy Festival : Sri Kati Koteswarasw amy festival is celebrated for three days from Phalguna Purnima to Bahula Vidiya (February-March) at Mustoor in Anantapur district. On the evening of full moon day, the image of the deity is taken on a prabha to the hillock accompanied with music. During the night of Padyami, there is procession of the prabha and it is brought back to the village accompanied with music on the evening of the next day. Offerings are made in kind in fulfilment of vows. The festival is of ancient origin but of local significance. The chief patrons for the festival are Reddies (Kapus).

Villages: 17 **Inhabited:** 17 **Uninhabited:** 0

Ranking	District	State	National
Area	44	319	3405
Population	5	344	5006
Sex Ratio	62	1078	4469
Child Sex Ratio	61	1086	5439
Literacy Rate	8	412	3529
Density	62	879	4367
Work Participation Rate	8	622	2934

Gram Panchayats:

A.Narayanapuram, Akkampalli, Akuthotapalli, Alamuru Anantapur (Rural), Chinnampalli, Chiyyedu Itikalapalli, Kakkalapalli (Rural) Kakkalapalli Colony, Kamarupalli, Kandukur Katiganikalva, Kattakindapalli, Kodimi, Kurugunta Mannila, N.N.Kunta, Pulakunta, Rachanapalli Rajiv Colony, Rudrampeta, Somaladoddi, Thaticherla Upparapalli.

Amenities:

Education: Primary School in 16 villages, Middle school in 9 villages, Matriculation or Secondary School in 5 villages, namely Kurugunta, Kakkalapalle (Rural), Itikalapalle, Kandakur, Chiyyedu.

Higher Secondary or Pre University Courses or Intermediate or Junior College in 1 village of the CD Block,, namely Kurugunta.

College in 1 village, Adult Literacy Center in 5 villages., College is in village, namely Itikalapalle.

Medical: Hospital in 0 village, Dispensary in 2 villages, Health Center in 0 village, Sub Center in 7 villages, Maternity and Child Welfare Center in 0 village, Community health workers in 0 village.

The Villages having Hospital or Dispensary or Health Center are Itikalapalle, Kandakur.

Drinking Water: Tap water in 17 villages, Tank water in 0 villages, Well water in 0 village, Tubewell in 0 village and more than one source in 0 village.

Bank: Banking facility in 1 villages, namely, Chiyyedu.

Credit Society in 3 villages Agricultural Credit Society in 3 Non-Agricultural Credit Society in 0 village.

Others: Power supply in 17 villages, Cinema hall in 0 village, sport club in 1 village, Stadium or Auditorium or Community Hall in 1 village, Post Office in 13 villages.

There are 15 villages having bus facilities.

Village with most of facilities: Chiyyedu.

Villages without amenities (Education):

Gollapalle..

Scheduled Castes: Out of the total population of 55930 persons, 9675 persons (17.3%) belong to Scheduled Castes.

The villages having less than 10% SC population are None..

The villages having more than 50% SC population are None.

Sex ratio of Scheduled Caste population is 511.

Scheduled Castes Literates and Illiterates by Sex:

	Persons	Males	Females
Literate	4,001	2,300	1,701
Illiterate	5,674	2,434	3,240
Literacy rate	47.7	56.3	39.5
Graduate	388	336	52

Scheduled Castes (Dominant):

Madiga, Mala, Adi Andhra, Generic Castes etc.

Dom etc.

For their cultural identity please see Appendix-I

Villages without Scheduled Castes: There is 1 village without any scheduled caste population.

Scheduled Tribes: Out of the total population of 55930 persons, 1612 persons (2.88%) belong to Scheduled Tribes.

The villages having less than 10% ST population are Thaticherla, Somanadoddi, Rachanapalle, Sajjalakalva

Kurugunta, Gollapalle, Kamarupalle, Alamuru Katiganikalva, Kakkalapalle (Rural), Upparapalle Itikalapalle, Jangalapalle, Kandakur, Chiyyedu Mannila.

The villages having more than 50% ST population are None.

Sex ratio of Scheduled tribe population is 481.

Scheduled Tribes Literates and Illiterates by Sex:

	Persons	Males	Females
Literate	585	375	210
Illiterate	1,027	462	565
Literacy rate	42.8	52.9	32.0
Graduate	66	61	5

Scheduled Tribes (Dominant):

Sugalis etc., Yerukulas, Yenadis, Gond etc.

Generic Tribes etc.

For their cultural identity please see Appendix-II

Villages without Scheduled Tribes: There are 4 villages without any scheduled tribe population.

Literates and Illiterates by Sex (Total Population):

	Persons	Males	Females
Literate	27,176	17,031	10,145
Illiterate	28,754	11,954	16,800
Literacy rate	56	68	43
Graduate	2,506	2,035	471

Agriculture: ***Distribution of villages according to land use:***

Out of 17 villages, Total area (in hectare) is 24789, out of that 59.42 percent is cultivable and 9.64 percent of the cultivable area is irrigated.

Sources of Irrigation (Hectares): Government Canal 91.09, Private Canal 0, Well without Electricity 0, Well with Electricity 621.85, Tubewell without Electricity 0, Tubewell with Electricity 680.96, Tank 26.31, River 0, Lake 0, Waterfall 0, Others 0.

Villages with population of 5000 to 9999:

Itikalapalle, Kandakur.

Villages with population of 10000 and above:

Kakkalapalle (Rural).

Distribution of Workers:

	Persons	Males	Females	WPR
Cultivators	6,530	4,152	2,378	24.71
Agricultural Labour	8,601	3,562	5,039	32.55
Household Industry	1,541	1,092	449	5.83
Other Workers	9,754	7,271	2,483	36.91
Main Workers	23,640	15,263	8,377	89.46
Marginal Workers	2,786	814	1,972	10.54
Total Workers	26,426	16,077	10,349	

Religion: Major Religious Communities:

	Persons	Males	Females	Sex Ratio
Hindu (92.66%)	51,824	26,895	24,929	927
Muslim (6.6%)	3,694	1,886	1,808	959
Christian (0.62%)	349	167	182	1,090
Sikh (0.06%)	31	17	14	824
Buddhists (0%)	-	-	-	-
Jain (0%)	-	-	-	-

Agewise Data:

	Persons	Males	Females	Sex Ratio
All ages	55,930	28,985	26,945	930
0-14	17,978	9,184	8,794	958
15-44	28,621	15,008	13,613	907
45-79	8,932	4,604	4,328	940
80+	338	155	183	1181
Age not stated	61	34	27	794

Languages (Dominant):

Telugu, Urdu, Hindi, Tamil, Kannada

Disabled Population:

	Persons	Males	Females	%
Total Disabled	873	503	370	
In Seeing	245	136	109	28.06
In Speech	86	53	33	9.85
In Hearing	48	25	23	5.5
In Movement	382	223	159	43.76
Mentally	112	66	46	12.83

ANANTHAGIRI

Ananthagiri C.D. Block lies in the north-eastern part of Vishakhapatnam district. The Block is located at a distance of 108 kms. from district headquarters (Vish akhapatnam). There are 315 villages in the block with the total population of 44,192 persons. Area of the C.D. Block is 230.37 sq. kms. It is bounded in the north by Hukumpeta and Araku Valley Mandals, and distri ct Vizianagaram, in the south by Hukumpeta and Devarapal li Mandals, in the east by district Vizianagaram, and in the west by Mandal Hukumpeta.

Communications :

Roadways : State Highway (S.H.): Direction- Araku to K.Kotapadu. Nearest Villages- Bheesupuram, Talaripadu, Ananthagiri, Kottavalasa @ Verumulapuram, Diguva Kamba valasa, Damsarai, Bangarampeta, Chilakalagedda, Kasipatn am, Kotturu.

Railway Station: Borra, Sivalingapuram.

Integrated Child Development Scheme (ICDS) Project: Ananthagiri (Tribal), Total Anganwadi Centres: 123

Annaual Rainfall: Average Rainfall 975.0 mm

Ground Water: Availability of the Ground Water in the Basin is (Information not avavible) H.A.M .and the utilization is (Information not avavible) H.A.M. It belongs to (Information not avavible) category. Depth to water level varies from 3 to 10 meter below the ground. Most of the wells go down in summer months.

Forest and Reserved **Forest:** Nearest Villages- Bheemava ram, Sankuparti, Chippapalle.

Administration:

Division: Coastal Andhra. Parliamentary Constituency: 18 Araku (ST). District: Visakhapatnam. Mandal: Anantha giri. Assembly Constituency: 147 Araku Valley (ST). Gram Panchayat: 24.

Villages: 315 **Inhabited:** 274 **Uninhabited:** 41

Ranking	District	State	National
Area	6	383	3655
Population	38	688	5545
Sex Ratio	29	514	1826
Child Sex Ratio	2	2	19
Literacy Rate	37	1087	6198
Density	5	64	4851
Work Participation Rate	34	745	248

Gram Panchayats:

Ananthagiri, Bheemapolu, Borra, Chilakalagedda Garugubilli, Gumma, Gummakota, Jeenabadu, Kasipatnam Kivarla, Kondiba, Kotturu, Kunapuram, Lungaparti Narasimharajupuram, Pedabidda, Pedakota, Pinakota Pynampadu, Rampalle, Tokuru, Valasi, Vengada Yeguvasoba.

Amenities:

Education: Primary School in 195 villages, Middle school in 7 villages, Matriculation or Secondary School in 6 villages, namely Borra, Tokuru, Ananthagiri, Sivalingapuram, Chilakalagedda, Pinakota.

Higher Secondary or Pre University Courses or Intermediate or Junior College in 0 village of the CD Block, College in 0 village, Adult Literacy Center in 1 village.

Medical: Hospital in 0 village, Dispensary in 0 village, Health Center in 24 villages, Sub Center in 5 villages, Maternity and Child Welfare Center in 0 village, Community health workers in 0 village.

Drinking Water: Tap water in 262 villages, Tank water in 262 villages, Well water in 264 villages, Tubewell in 261 villages and more than one source in 266 villages.

Bank: Banking facility in 1 villages, namely, Kasipatnam.

Credit Society in 1 village Agricultural Credit Society in 1 Non-Agricultural Credit Society in 0 village.

Others: Power supply in 274 villages, Cinema hall in 0 village, sport club in 0 village, Stadium or Auditorium or Community Hall in 0 village, Post Office in 22 villages.

There are 22 villages having bus facilities.

Village with most of facilities: Kasipatnam.

Villages without amenities (Education):

Vatalamamidi, Bediliguda, Kummarivalasa, Gondiguda, Ranjaliguda @ Ranginiguda, Gottipadu, Rajupaka, Kotapartivalasa, China Rabha, Gadilalova, Gudem, Dabbalapadu, Katimanuvalasa, Katturu, Tattavalasa, Gadiguda, Tokavalasa, Jamuguda, Cheedivalasa, Nisaniguda, Limbaguda @ Nimmada, Heetaguda, Talaripadu, Nandigummi, Tenteliguda, Karakavalasa, Chittamvalasa, Kothavalasa, Samareddipalem, Diguva Kambavalasa, Damsarai, Marrimanuvalasa, Krishnapuram, Mirithidungada, Porlu, Vootamamidi, Palabandavalasa, Eguvamallelu, Diguvamallelu, Vanjalavalasa, Eetamanuvalasa, Nandulavalasa, Bhalluguda, Mangagumma, Chimiti, Kadarevu, Velagalapadu, Damukurai, Gangudivalasa, Zendagaruvu, Tumbarti, Taragam, Addategela, Buddigaruvu, Kannamgaruvu, Kottavalasa, Rallagaruvu, Tangellabanda, Cheedivalasa, Pandirimamidi, Gazzellagaruvu, Billakamba, Kudiya, Gummanti, Tunisebu, Bandakonda, Sariya, Valasala Garuvu, Gaddibanda, Ballagaruvu, Porlubanda, Borrapalem, Gulamalapalle, Chinaburuga, Chitrallapalem, Peda Buruga-I, Onukonda, Goppulapalem..

Scheduled Castes: Out of the total population of 44192 persons, 1097 persons (2.48%) belong to Scheduled Castes. The villages having less than 10% SC population are Karaiguda, Liddangi, Saraiguda, Bondyaguda Kunapuram, Kittalingi, Bonduguda, Karakavalasa Bheesupuram, Katika, Vatalamamidi, Chappadi Dekkapuram, Kontysimidi, Kotyaguda, Bediliguda Getuvalasa, Eguvamamidi, Pedduru, Borra Kummarivalasa, Tokuru, Boraborivalasa, Boringuvalasa Pooluguda, Kapativalasa, Baliyaguda, Gondiguda Ranjaliguda @ Ranginiguda, Sankuparti Chippapalle, Singavaram, Billakota, Gottipadu Rajupaka, Chittampadu, China Konela, Y.S.R.Puram Kotaparti, Bongija, Buruga, Rampalle, Sottadivalasa Kotapartivalasa, Peda Rabha, China Rabha, Gadilalova Gudem, R.T.Puram, Pedakonela, Dabbalapadu Katimanuvalasa, Boodi, Katturu, Mandaparti Seetampeta, Saravani Palem, Tattavalasa, Lanjilaguda Laxmipuram, Pandirimamidivalasa, Nandikota, Kondiba Gadiguda, Tokavalasa, Nadimivalasa, Dumbrivalasa Sada, Jakariguda, Jamuguda, Kosamamidi, Singarbha Ninnimamidi, Ballamamidi, Cheedivalasa, Nisaniguda Bodaguda, Seesaguda, Limbaguda @ Nimmada Diguvasobha, Sorasapodaru, Pooluguda, Eguvasobha Seesamanda, Kamalapuram, Heetaguda, Laxmipuram Baliaguda @ Cheedivalasa, Talaripadu, Regam Tenuputtu, Nandigummi, Patakota, Malingavalasa Tadiguda, Mondijanguda, Mardaguda, Ananthagiri Kottavalasa @ Verumulapuram, Gatuguda, Dandabadu Kambavalasa, Doraguda, Tenteliguda, Muvvamvalasa

Rayavalasa, Mulyaguda, Pooluguda, Pempuduvalasa
Kodamaguda, Karakavalasa, Cherukumadata
Chittamvalasa, Kantipuram, Kothavalasa, Kothavalasa
Samareddipalem, Sivalingapuram, Diguva Kambavalasa
Teegalamada, Panasamanuvalasa, Damsarai
Bangarampeta, Pallamvanivalasa, Marrimanuvalasa
Varakavadu, Dabbalapadu, Vantinivanipalem
Jeelugulapadu, Kittayyatota, Chilakalagedda
Venkayyapalem, Cheedivalasa, Kambavalasa, Gangavaram
Kotturu, Krishnapuram, Medaparti, Busipadu, Karivesu
Karakavalasa, Mirithidungada, Porlu, Vootamamidi
Maddipadu, Palabandavalasa, Cheedivalasa
Cherukubidda, Eguvamallelu, Diguvamallelu, Nelapalem
Karaiguda, Nimmavuta, Gumma, Vanjalavalasa
Eetamanuvalasa, Dhanukota, Nandulavalasa, Bhalluguda
Pedabidda, Mangagumma, Chimiti, Kadarevu
Mettavalasa, Yerrametta, Vanthanagaruvu
Velagalapadu, Pulusumamidi, Burugulapadu, Lungaparti
Rayipadu, Damukurai, Vootagedda, Gorregommu
Gangudivalasa, Kumburti, Patti, Damsalavalasa
Maddigaruvu, Zendagaruvu, Valasi, Nimmalapadu
Tumbarti, Diguvasonabha, Pynampadu, Moolapatnam
Banjoda, Mettavalasa, Mandruvalasa, Gommangipadu
Vengada, Cheedivalasa, Bandavalasa, Penamarti
Donkaiputtu, Nakkalamamidi, Pandirimamidi, Taragam
Addategela, Vantarbha, Jampaputtu, Buddigaruvu
Kannamgaruvu, Jalada, Voobalu, Tenkalavalasa
Kottavalasa, Kivarla, Rallagaruvu, Gangavaram
Tangellabanda, Bongija, Bonuru, Gaddibanda
Cheedivalasa, Pandirimamidi, Putikaputtu
Cheedigaruvu, Gazzellagaruvu, Billakamba, Kudiya
Pedabayalu, Boddaputtu, Gummanti, Velamamidi
Poderti, Tankota, Tunisebu, Bandakonda, Patipalle
Bembi, Madrebu, Dayarti, Sariya, Makanapalle
Rachakilam, Tamuta, Dibbapalem, Revallapalem
Pedagangavaram, Jeenapadu, Valasala Garuvu
Gaddibanda, Kotaparti, Velagalapadu, Mallampeta
Ballagaruvu, Gummanti, Kondemkota, Regulapalem
Pedakota, Porlubanda, Chatakamba, Borrapalem
Pinakota, Cheedimetta, Gulamalapalle, Chinaburuga
Chintapaka, Chitrallapalem, Peda Buruga-I
Kottamguda, Onukonda, Pedaburugu Ii, Chindugulapadu
Solabongu, Goppulapalem, Tattapudi.

The villages having more than 50% SC population are None.

Sex ratio of Scheduled Caste population is 504.

Scheduled Castes Literates and Illiterates by Sex:

	Persons	Males	Females
Literate	404	242	162
Illiterate	693	302	391
Literacy rate	43.4	53.1	34.2
Graduate	12	8	4

Scheduled Castes (Dominant):

Dom etc., Madiga, Mala, Relli, Generic Castes etc.

For their cultural identity please see Appendix-I

Villages without Scheduled Castes: There are 296 villages without any scheduled caste population.

Scheduled Tribes: Out of the total population of 44192 persons, 40057 persons (90.64%) belong to Scheduled Tribes.

The villages having less than 10% ST population are None..

The villages having more than 50% ST population are
Karaiguda, Liddangi, Saraiguda, Bondyaguda
Kunapuram, Kittalingi, Bonduguda, Karakavalasa
Bheesupuram, Katika, Vatalamamidi, Chappadi
Dekkapuram, Kontysimidi, Kotyaguda, Bediliguda
Getuvalasa, Eguvamamidi, Pedduru, Kummarivalasa
Tokuru, Boraborivalasa, Boringuvalasa, Pooluguda
Kapativalasa, Baliyaguda, Gondiguda
Ranjaliguda @ Ranginiguda, Sariapalle
Bheemavaram, Sankuparti, Chippapalle, Garugubilli
Singavaram, Billakota, Gottipadu, Rajupaka
Chittampadu, China Konela, Y.S.R.Puram, Kotaparti
Bongija, Buruga, Rampalle, Sottadivalasa
Kotapartivalasa, Peda Rabha, China Rabha, Gadilalova
Gudem, R.T.Puram, Pedakonela, Dabbalapadu
Katimanuvalasa, Boodi, Katturu, Mandaparti
Seetampeta, Saravani Palem, Tattavalasa, Lanjilaguda
Laxmipuram, Pandirimamidivalasa, Nandikota, Kondiba
Gadiguda, Tokavalasa, Nadimivalasa, Dumbrivalasa
Sada, Jakariguda, Jamuguda, Kosamamidi, Singarbha
Ninnimamidi, Ballamamidi, Cheedivalasa, Nisaniguda
Bodaguda, Seesaguda, Limbaguda @ Nimmada
Diguvasobha, Sorasapodaru, Pooluguda, Eguvasobha
Seesamanda, Kamalapuram, Heetaguda, Laxmipuram
Baliaguda @ Cheedivalasa, Talaripadu, Regam
Tenuputtu, Nandigummi, Patakota, Malingavalasa
Tadiguda, Mondijanguda, Mardaguda, Ananthagiri
Kottavalasa @ Verumulapuram, Gatuguda, Dandabadu
Kambavalasa, Doraguda, Tenteliguda, Muvvamvalasa
Rayavalasa, Mulyaguda, Pooluguda, Pempuduvalasa
Kodamaguda, Karakavalasa, Cherukumadata
Chittamvalasa, Kantipuram, Kothavalasa, Kothavalasa
Samareddipalem, Sivalingapuram, Diguva Kambavalasa
Teegalamada, Panasamanuvalasa, Damsarai
Bangarampeta, Pallamvanivalasa, Marrimanuvalasa
Tummanuvalasa, Varakavadu, Dabbalapadu
Vantinivanipalem, Jeelugulapadu, Kittayyatota
Chilakalagedda, Venkayyapalem, Cheedivalasa
Kambavalasa, Gangavaram, Kotturu, Krishnapuram

Medaparti, Busipadu, Karivesu, Karakavalasa Mirithidungada, Porlu, Vootamamidi, Maddipadu Palabandavalasa, Cheedivalasa, Cherukubidda Eguvamallelu, Diguvamallelu, Nelapalem, Karaiguda Nimmavuta, Gumma, Vanjalavalasa, Eetamanuvalasa Dhanukota, Nandulavalasa, Bhalluguda, Pedabidda Mangagumma, Chimiti, Kadarevu, Mettavalasa Yerrametta, Vanthanagaruvu, Velagalapadu Pulusumamidi, Burugulapadu, Lungaparti, Rayipadu Damukurai, Vootagedda, Gorregommu, Gangudivalasa Kumburti, Patti, Damsalavalasa, Maddigaruvu Zendagaruvu, Valasi, Nimmalapadu, Tumbarti Diguvasonabha, Pynampadu, Moolapatnam, Banjoda Mettavalasa, Mandruvalasa, Gommangipadu, Vengada Cheedivalasa, Bandavalasa, Penamarti, Donkaiputtu Nakkalamamidi, Taragam, Addategela, Vantarbha Jampaputtu, Buddigaruvu, Kannamgaruvu, Jalada Voobalu, Tenkalavalasa, Kottavalasa, Kivarla Rallagaruvu, Gangavaram, Tangellabanda, Bongija Bonuru, Gaddibanda, Cheedivalasa, Pandirimamidi Putikaputtu, Cheedigaruvu, Gazzellagaruvu Billakamba, Kudiya, Pedabayalu, Boddaputtu, Gummanti Velamamidi, Poderti, Tankota, Tunisebu, Bandakonda Patipalle, Bembi, Madrebu, Dayarti, Sariya Makanapalle, Tamuta, Dibbapalem, Revallapalem Jeenapadu, Valasala Garuvu, Gaddibanda, Kotaparti Velagalapadu, Mallampeta, Ballagaruvu, Gummanti Kondemkota, Regulapalem, Pedakota, Porlubanda Borrapalem, Pinakota, Cheedimetta, Gulamalapalle Chinaburuga, Chintapaka, Chitrallapalem Peda Buruga-I, Kottamguda, Onukonda, Pedaburugu Ii Chindugulapadu, Solabongu, Goppulapalem, Tattapudi.

Sex ratio of Scheduled tribe population is 497.

Scheduled Tribes Literates and Illiterates by Sex:

	Persons	Males	Females
Literate	9,237	6,365	2,872
Illiterate	30,820	13,766	17,054
Literacy rate	27.3	37.1	17.2
Graduate	85	79	6

Scheduled Tribes (Dominant):

Konda Dhoras, Bagata, Mukha Dhora etc., Valmiki Porja etc.

For their cultural identity please see Appendix-II

Villages without Scheduled Tribes: There are 42 villages without any scheduled tribe population.

Literates and Illiterates by Sex (Total Population):

	Persons	Males	Females
Literate	11,283	7,649	3,634
Illiterate	32,909	14,630	18,279
Literacy rate	30	40	20
Graduate	181	158	23

Agriculture: ***Distribution of villages according to land use:*** Out of 315 villages, Total area (in hectare) is 23038, out of that 53.83 percent is cultivable and 7.58 percent of the cultivable area is irrigated.

Sources of Irrigation (Hectares): Government Canal 58.94, Private Canal 0, Well without Electricity 0, Well with Electricity 0, Tubewell without Electricity 0, Tubewell with Electricity 0, Tank 0, River 0, Lake 0, Waterfall 14.58, Others 865.9.

Villages with population of 5000 to 9999: None

Villages with population of 10000 and above: None

Distribution of Workers:

	Persons	Males	Females	WPR
Cultivators	15,315	8,215	7,100	60.11
Agricultural Labour	8,155	3,610	4,545	32.01
Household Industry	280	128	152	1.1
Other Workers	1,729	1,232	497	6.79
Main Workers	19,271	10,474	8,797	75.63
Marginal Workers	6,208	2,711	3,497	24.37
Total Workers	25,479	13,185	12,294	

Religion: Major Religious Communities:

	Persons	Males	Females	Sex Ratio
Hindu (98.67%)	43,606	21,990	21,616	983
Muslim (0.15%)	68	33	35	1,061
Christian (1.16%)	513	253	260	1,028
Sikh (0%)	-	-	-	-
Buddhists (0.01%)	3	2	1	500
Jain (0%)	-	-	-	-

Agewise Data:

	Persons	Males	Females	Sex Ratio
All ages	44,192	22,279	21,913	984
0-14	16,426	8,573	7,853	916
15-44	20,448	9,892	10,556	1067
45-79	7,043	3,685	3,358	911
80+	91	44	47	1068
Age not stated	184	85	99	1165

Languages (Dominant):

Telugu, Oriya, Konda, Koda/Kora, Tamil

Disabled Population:

	Persons	Males	Females	%
Total Disabled	622	350	272	
In Seeing	248	141	107	39.87
In Speech	60	30	30	9.65
In Hearing	68	36	32	10.93
In Movement	139	88	51	22.35
Mentally	107	55	52	17.2

ANANTHASAGARAM

Ananthasagaram C.D. Block lies in the western part of Nellore district. The Block is located at a distance of 80 kms. from district headquarters (Nellore). There are 19 villages in the block with the total population of 39,908 persons. Area of the C.D. Block is 281.42 sq. kms. It is bounded in the north by Mandals Marripadu and Atmakur, in the south by Mandals Kaluvoya and Chejerla, and river Pennar, in the east by Mandal Atmakur, and in the west by district Cuddapah and Mandal Marripadu.

Communications:

Roadways : Metalled Roads: Nearest Villages- Chapurallap alle, Ananthasagaram, Padamati Kambhampadu, Somasila, Uppalapadu.

River: Pennar Nadi- Nearest Villages- Chapurallapalle, Ananthasagaram, Padamati Kambhampadu, Somasila, Vareku ntapadu, Bedusupalle, Devarayapalle Bit-Ii, Minagallu, Revuru.

Annual Rainfall: Average Rainfall 935 mm

Ground Water: Availability of the Ground Water in the Basin is 4424 H.A.M. and the utilization is 1559 H. A.M. It belongs to Safe category. Depth to water level varies from 5 to 10 meter below the ground. Most of the wells go down in summer months, according to the Ground Water Estimation Committee.

Administration:

Division: Coastal Andhra. Parliamentary Constituency: 39 Nellore.District: Nellore.

Mandal: Ananthasagaram. Assembly Constituency: 234 Atmakur. Gram Panchayat: 24.

Villages: 19 **Inhabited:** 18 **Uninhabited:** 1

Ranking	District	State	National
Area	17	202	2983
Population	28	825	5735
Sex Ratio	32	639	2180
Child Sex Ratio	41	987	4520
Literacy Rate	25	290	2899
Density	41	982	5675
Work Participation Rate	29	931	3671

Gram Panchayats:

Amanchiruvella, Anantasagaram, Bedusupalli Bommavaram, Chilakalamarri, Devarayapalli Bit-1 Devarayapalli Bit-Ii, Gowravaram, Gudigunta Inagaluru, Iskapalli, Kamireddypadu, Lingammagunta Manchalapalli, Mangupalli, Minagallu, Mustapuram Padamati Kambhampadu, Pathalapalli, Revuru, Somasila Uppalapadu, Variguntapadu, Vengampalli.

Amenities:

Education: Primary School in 17 villages, Middle school in 10 villages, Matriculation or Secondary School in 7 villages, namely Ananthasagaram, Kamireddipadu, Mangupalle, Somasila, Uppalapadu, Devarayapalle Bit-Ii, Revuru. Higher Secondary or Pre University Courses or Intermediate or Junior College in 1 village of the CD Block,, namely Ananthasagaram.

College in 0 village, Adult Literacy Center in 16 villages.

Medical: Hospital in 0 village, Dispensary in 2 villages, Health Center in 2 villages, Sub Center in 11 villages, Maternity and Child Welfare Center in 0 village, Community health workers in 0 village.

The Villages having Hospital or Dispensary or Health Center are Somasila, Revuru.

Drinking Water: Tap water in 18 villages, Tank water in 18 villages, Well water in 18 villages, Tubewell in 18 villages and more than one source in 18 villages.

Bank: Banking facility in 2 villages, namely, Ananthasagaram, Somasila.

Credit Society in 11 villages Agricultural Credit Society in 2 Non-Agricultural Credit Society in 11 villages.

Others: Power supply in 18 villages, Cinema hall in 1 village, sport club in 0 village, Stadium or Auditorium or Community Hall in 0 village, Post Office in 17 villages.

There are 16 villages having bus facilities.

Villages with most of facilities: Ananthasagaram Somasila.

Villages without amenities (Education): Chapurallapalle..

Scheduled Castes: Out of the total population of 39908 persons, 8994 persons (22.54%) belong to Scheduled Castes. The villages having less than 10% SC population are None..

The villages having more than 50% SC population are None.

Sex ratio of Scheduled Caste population is 499.

Scheduled Castes Literates and Illiterates by Sex:

	Persons	Males	Females
Literate	4,342	2,646	1,696
Illiterate	4,652	1,856	2,796
Literacy rate	55.3	67.8	42.9
Graduate	81	64	17

Scheduled Castes (Dominant):

Madiga, Mala, Arundhatiya

For their cultural identity please see Appendix-I

Villages without Scheduled Castes: There is 1 village without any scheduled caste population.

Scheduled Tribes: Out of the total population of 39908 persons, 2123 persons (5.32%) belong to Scheduled Tribes. The villages having less than 10% ST population are Chapurallapalle, Bommavaram, Gowravaram Amanichiruvella, Inagalur, Ananthasagaram Mangupalle, Pathalapalle, Padamati Kambhampadu Uppalapadu, Varekuntapadu, Bedusupalle

Devarayapalle Bit- I, Minagallu, Revuru.

The villages having more than 50% ST population are None.

Sex ratio of Scheduled tribe population is 441.

Scheduled Tribes Literates and Illiterates by Sex:

	Persons	Males	Females
Literate	637	447	190
Illiterate	1,486	740	746
Literacy rate	34.9	43.7	23.7
Graduate	3	3	0

Scheduled Tribes (Dominant):

Yenadis, Yerukulas, Sugalis etc.

For their cultural identity please see Appendix-II

Villages without Scheduled Tribes: There are 3 villages without any scheduled tribe population.

Literates and Illiterates by Sex (Total Population):

	Persons	Males	Females
Literate	20,870	12,785	8,085
Illiterate	19,038	7,401	11,637
Literacy rate	59	72	46
Graduate	801	655	146

Agriculture: ***Distribution of villages according to land use:*** Out of 19 villages, Total area (in hectare) is 28143, out of that 19.34 percent is cultivable and 70.31 percent of the cultivable area is irrigated.

Sources of Irrigation (Hectares): Government Canal 525, Private Canal 130, Well without Electricity 162, Well with Electricity 691, Tubewell without Electricity 195, Tubewell with Electricity 950, Tank 1143, River 0, Lake 0, Waterfall 0, Others 30.

Villages with population of 5000 to 9999: Ananthasagaram.

Villages with population of 10000 and above: None

Distribution of Workers:

	Persons	Males	Females	WPR
Cultivators	5,195	4,045	1,150	29.28
Agricultural Labour	8,448	4,009	4,439	47.62
Household Industry	335	217	118	1.89
Other Workers	3,764	3,164	600	21.22
Main Workers	13,975	10,290	3,685	78.77
Marginal Workers	3,767	1,145	2,622	21.23
Total Workers	17,742	11,435	6,307	

Religion: Major Religious Communities:

	Persons	Males	Females	Sex Ratio
Hindu (85.04%)	33,938	17,150	16,788	979
Muslim (14.63%)	5,840	2,978	2,862	961
Christian (0.24%)	97	41	56	1,366
Sikh (0%)	-	-	-	-
Buddhists (0.04%)	14	7	7	1,000
Jain (0%)	-	-	-	-

Agewise Data:

	Persons	Males	Females	Sex Ratio
All ages	39,908	20,186	19,722	977
0-14	12,307	6,466	5,841	903
15-44	18,121	9,093	9,028	993
45-79	9,170	4,496	4,674	1040
80+	289	122	167	1369
Age not stated	21	9	12	1333

Languages (Dominant):

Telugu, Urdu, Gondi, Tamil, Hindi

Disabled Population:

	Persons	Males	Females	%
Total Disabled	1,056	560	496	
In Seeing	365	157	208	34.56
In Speech	116	66	50	10.98
In Hearing	98	47	51	9.28
In Movement	354	226	128	33.52
Mentally	123	64	59	11.65

ANAPARTHY

Anaparthy C.D. Block lies in the south-western part of East Godavari district. The Block is located at a distance of 52 kms. from district headquarters (Kakin ada). There are 09 villages in the block with the total population of 68,519 persons. Area of the C.D. Block is 60.52 sq. kms. It is bounded in the north by Mandal Rajanagaram, in the south by Mandal Kapileswarapuram, in the east by Mandals Rayavaram and Biccavolu, and in the west by Mandals Mandapeta and Kapileswarapuram.

Communications :

Roadways : State Highway (S.H.): Direction- Rajahmundry to Samalkota. Nearest Villages- Anaparthy, Koppavaram.

Railway Station: Anaparthy.

Backwards Region Grants Fund: It receives Backward Region Grants.

Annaul Rainfall: Average Rainfall 990.4 mm

Ground Water: Availability of the Ground Water in the Basin is (Information not avavible) H.A.M .and the utilization is (Information not avavible) H.A.M. It belongs to (Information not avavible) category. Depth to water level varies from 3 to 10 meter below the ground. Most of the wells go down in summer months.

Natural Division : Godavari Delta Region

Administration:

Division: Coastal Andhra. Parliamentary Constituency: 25 Rajahmundry. District: East Godavari. Mandal: Anapar thy. Assembly Constituency: 159 Anaparthy. Gram Panchaya t: 11.

Villages: 9 **Inhabited:** 9 **Uninhabited:** 0

Ranking	District	State	National
Area	53	1086	6010
Population	33	151	4532

Sex Ratio	41	532	1950
Child Sex Ratio	10	81	214
Literacy Rate	18	101	1509
Density	51	1076	597
Work Participation Rate	2	3	4707

Gram Panchayats:
Anaparthy, Duppalapudi, Koppavaram, Kutukuluru Laxminarasa Puram, Mahendrawada, Pedaparthi Pera Ramachandrapuram, Polamuru, Pulagurtha Ramavaram.

Amenities:

Education: Primary School in 9 villages, Middle school in 8 villages, Matriculation or Secondary School in 6 villages, namely Anaparthy, Koppavaram, Mahendrawada, Polamuru, Ramavaram, Kutukuluru.

Higher Secondary or Pre University Courses or Intermediate or Junior College in 1 village of the CD Block,, namely Anaparthy.

College in 1 village, Adult Literacy Center in 9 villages., College is in village, namely Anaparthy.

Medical: Hospital in 1 village, Dispensary in 2 villages, Health Center in 1 village, Sub Center in 9 villages, Maternity and Child Welfare Center in 0 village, Community health workers in 0 village.

The Villages having Hospital or Dispensary or Health Center are Anaparthy, Ramavaram, Kutukuluru.

Drinking Water: Tap water in 9 villages, Tank water in 9 villages, Well water in 9 villages, Tubewell in 9 villages and more than one source in 9 villages.

Bank: Banking facility in 2 villages, namely, Anaparthy, Ramavaram.

Credit Society in 6 villages Agricultural Credit Society in 6 Non-Agricultural Credit Society in 3 villages.

Others: Power supply in 9 villages, Cinema hall in 1 village, sport club in 0 village, Stadium or Auditorium or Community Hall in 0 village, Post Office in 9 villages.

There are 8 villages having bus facilities.

Villages with most of facilities: Anaparthy Ramavaram.

Villages without Amenities (Education): None..

Scheduled Castes: Out of the total population of 68519 persons, 7872 persons (11.49%) belong to Scheduled Castes.

The villages having less than 10% SC population are None..

The villages having more than 50% SC population are None.

Sex ratio of Scheduled Caste population is 464.

Scheduled Castes Literates and Illiterates by Sex:

	Persons	Males	Females
Literate	4,124	2,487	1,637
Illiterate	3,748	1,731	2,017
Literacy rate	60.5	66.7	53.1
Graduate	108	76	32

Scheduled Castes (Dominant):
Madiga, Mala, Adi Andhra, Relli, Dom etc.

For their cultural identity please see Appendix-I

Villages without Scheduled Castes: There are 0 village without any scheduled caste population.

Scheduled Tribes: Out of the total population of 68519 persons, 370 persons (0.54%) belong to Scheduled Tribes.

The villages having less than 10% ST population are Duppalapudi, Anaparthy, Koppavaram, Mahendrawada Polamuru, Ramavaram, Kutukuluru, Pedaparthi Pulagurtha.

The villages having more than 50% ST population are None.

Sex ratio of Scheduled tribe population is 478.

Scheduled Tribes Literates and Illiterates by Sex:

	Persons	Males	Females
Literate	139	78	61
Illiterate	231	115	116
Literacy rate	45.0	49.1	40.7
Graduate	2	1	1

Scheduled Tribes (Dominant):
Yerukulas, Chenchu etc., Gadabas, Kondareddis Konda Kapus

For their cultural identity please see Appendix-II

Villages without Scheduled Tribes: There are 0 village without any scheduled tribe population.

Literates and Illiterates by Sex (Total Population):

	Persons	Males	Females
Literate	40,874	22,149	18,725
Illiterate	27,645	12,414	15,231
Literacy rate	68	73	63
Graduate	1,783	1,370	413

Agriculture: ***Distribution of villages according to land use:*** Out of 9 villages, Total area (in hectare) is 6052, out of that 81.81 percent is cultivable and 85.37 percent of the cultivable area is irrigated.

Sources of Irrigation (Hectares): Government Canal 3321.1, Private Canal 0, Well without Electricity 0, Well with Electricity 59.66, Tubewell without Electricity 0, Tubewell with Electricity 259.08, Tank 268.15, River 0, Lake 0, Waterfall 0, Others 318.8.

Villages with population of 5000 to 9999:
Koppavaram, Mahendrawada, Polamuru, Ramavaram Kutukuluru.

Villages with population of 10000 and above:
Anaparthy.

Distribution of Workers:

	Persons	Males	Females	WPR
Cultivators	4,201	3,973	228	15.74
Agricultural Labour	11,244	8,413	2,831	42.14
Household Industry	881	548	333	3.3
Other Workers	10,357	8,483	1,874	38.81
Main Workers	22,306	19,480	2,826	83.6
Marginal Workers	4,377	1,937	2,440	16.4
Total Workers	26,683	21,417	5,266	

Religion: Major Religious Communities:

	Persons	Males	Females	Sex Ratio
Hindu (97.77%)	66,989	33,800	33,189	982
Muslim (0.94%)	644	322	322	1,000
Christian (1.27%)	871	435	436	1,002
Sikh (0%)	-	-	-	-
Buddhists (0%)	-	-	-	-
Jain (0%)	-	-	-	-

Agewise Data:

	Persons	Males	Females	Sex Ratio
All ages	68,519	34,563	33,956	982
0-14	19,057	9,686	9,371	967
15-44	35,463	17,955	17,508	975
45-79	13,514	6,695	6,819	1019
80+	423	193	230	1192
Age not stated	62	34	28	824

Languages (Dominant):

Telugu, Urdu, Gondi, Gujarati, Hindi

Disabled Population:

	Persons	Males	Females	%
Total Disabled	1,448	902	546	
In Seeing	785	499	286	54.21
In Speech	118	64	54	8.15
In Hearing	55	23	32	3.8
In Movement	376	244	132	25.97
Mentally	114	72	42	7.87

ANDOLE

Andole C.D. Block lies in the eastern part of Medak district. The Block is located at a distance of 30 kms. from district headquarters (Sangareddy). There are 27 villages in the block with the total population of 59,325 persons. Area of the C.D. Block is 176.35 sq. kms. It is bounded by Tekmal Mandal on north, Kowdi palle Mandal on east, Hathnoora Mandal on south-east, Pulkal Mandal on south, Regode Mandal on west, and Alladurg Mandal on north-west.

Communications :

Roadways : State Highway (S.H.): Direction- Sangareddy to Alladurg. Nearest Villages- Ananthasagar, Almaipet, Ramsanpalle, Danampalle, Yerraram, Jogipet. Sangupet.

River: Manjira Nadi- Nearset Villages- Chintakunta, Rollapahad, Mansanpalle, Posanipet, Andole, Saibanpet, Ananthasagar, Almaipet.

Backwards Region Grants Fund: It receives Backward Region Grants.

Annual Rainfall: Average Rainfall 1031 mm

Ground Water: Availability of the Ground Water in the Basin is 1596 H.A.M. and the utilization is 1440 H. A.M. It belongs to Critical category. Depth to water level varies from 5 meter below the ground. Most of the wells go down in summer months. The well density in the entire block is 10 wells per sq. km. Total no. of the wells in the block are enumerated as 2051, according to the Ground Water Estimation Committee.

Natural Division : Telangana Plateau Region

Administration:

Division: Telangana. Parliamentary Constituency: 5 Zahirabad. District: Medak. Mandal: Andole. Assembly Constituency: 36 Andole (SC). Gram Panchayat: 23.

Fairs and Festival:

Joginathaswamy Uthsavam : It is celebrated for 11 days from Chaitra Suddha Panchami to Purnima (March-April). Rathothsavam is celebrated on Dasami. Lankadahanam on Purnima is an attractive function. Devotees offer cocoanuts and fruits. No devotee chooses to keep quiet without liquidating his vows as every one fears that a lapse in this respect would cause some mishap. An interesting story is that one issueless couple worshipp ed the Lord promising that they would deliver the child to the Lord if they begot one by his grace. Very soon they were blessed with a daughter whom they named as Jogamma. But later on they forgot about their vow. When she grew up, her parents fixed up her marriage. Mysteriously just before the marriage day a strong whirlwind swept the marriage pandal and the girl. It is believed that the wind carried her to the temple of Joginatha on the hill. Jogamma lived by begging and if on any day she had more than two days' ration, rats used to eat the excess by the power of the Lord. She spent the rest of her life in this manner in the temple. Later the devotees came to know about the fate of Jogamma and began to worship the Lord with sincerity. The devotees name their children after the Lord as Jogaiah, Jogamma, Jogireddy, Jogirao, Joginath etc. This is an ancient festival confined to Jogipeta and a few of its neighbouring villages. The Vaisyas conduct the festival and many thousands of Hindu devotees parti cipate in the festival. The peculiarity in the Joginatha temple is that both Siva and Parvati stand side by side in the form of Lingams without panivattam indicati ng, perhaps, that Siva is Ardhanareeswara (half Himself and half Parvati). The temple and the Lord face West. It is said that the cave in which Ramajogi did penance is still in existence. There is a small koneru on the hill, which used to have water during all seasons. But, owing to some contamination, it dries up now and then. Visitors sprinkle the sacred teertham of this koneru over their heads before they go for the darshan of the Lord.

Villages: 27 **Inhabited:** 27 **Uninhabited:** 0

Ranking	District	State	National
Area	35	688	4595
Population	10	283	4881
Sex Ratio	17	441	1711
Child Sex Ratio	2	85	212
Literacy Rate	17	742	4696
Density	32	723	3217
Work Participation Rate	3	295	2052

Gram Panchayats:

Aksanpalle, Almaipet, Andole, Annasagar, Chintakunta Dakoor, Jogipet, Kamsanpalle, Kichanapalle, Kodekal Mansanpalle, Masanpalle, Nadlapur, Neerdigunta Posanipet, Pothareddipalle, Ramsanpalle, Rollapahad Saibanpet, Sangaipet, Tadamanoor, Talelma, Yerraram.

Amenities:

Education: Primary School in 27 villages, Middle school in 11 villages, Matriculation or Secondary School in 5 villages, namely Neerdigunta, Tadamanoor, Dakoor, Jogipet, Andole.

Higher Secondary or Pre University Courses or Intermediate or Junior College in 1 village of the CD Block,, namely Jogipet.

College in 1 village, Adult Literacy Center in 6 villages., College is in village, namely Jogipet.

Medical: Hospital in 1 village, Dispensary in 2 villages, Health Center in 0 village, Sub Center in 10 villages, Maternity and Child Welfare Center in 2 villages, Community health workers in 0 village.

The Villages having Hospital or Dispensary or Health Center are Jogipet, Andole.

Drinking Water: Tap water in 27 villages, Tank water in 27 villages, Well water in 27 villages, Tubewell in 27 villages and more than one source in 27 villages.

Bank: Banking facility in 1 villages, namely, Jogipet.

Credit Society in 20 villages Agricultural Credit Society in 8 Non-Agricultural Credit Society in 18 villages.

Others: Power supply in 27 villages, Cinema hall in 1 village, sport club in 0 village, Stadium or Auditorium or Community Hall in 0 village, Post Office in 8 villages.

There are 17 villages having bus facilities.

Village with most of facilities: Jogipet.

Villages without Amenities (Education): None..

Scheduled Castes: Out of the total population of 59325 persons, 12755 persons (21.5%) belong to Scheduled Castes.

The villages having less than 10% SC population are None..

The villages having more than 50% SC population are None.

Sex ratio of Scheduled Caste population is 498.

Scheduled Castes Literates and Illiterates by Sex:

	Persons	Males	Females
Literate	3,716	2,447	1,269
Illiterate	9,039	3,958	5,081
Literacy rate	34.0	44.6	23.3
Graduate	72	62	10

Scheduled Castes (Dominant):

Madiga, Mala, Beda Jangam etc., Chamar etc., Byagara

For their cultural identity please see Appendix-I

Villages without Scheduled Castes: There is 1 village without any scheduled caste population.

Scheduled Tribes: Out of the total population of 59325 persons, 429 persons (0.72%) belong to Scheduled Tribes.

The villages having less than 10% ST population are Telelma, Serimallareddipalle, Kansanpalle Ramsanpalle, Kichanapalle, Chintakunta, Rollapahad Mansanpalle, Posanipet, Ananthasagar, Danampalle Yerraram, Neerdigunta, Brahmanpalle, Aksanpalle Tadamanoor, Kodekal, Nadlapur, Dakoor, Jogipet Mansanpalle, Pothareddipalle, Sangupet, Andole Saibanpet, Almaipet.

The villages having more than 50% ST population are None.

Sex ratio of Scheduled tribe population is 478.

Scheduled Tribes Literates and Illiterates by Sex:

	Persons	Males	Females
Literate	129	94	35
Illiterate	300	130	170
Literacy rate	37.2	51.4	21.3
Graduate	10	9	1

Scheduled Tribes (Dominant):

Sugalis etc., Yerukulas, Generic Tribes etc.

For their cultural identity please see Appendix-II

Villages without Scheduled Tribes: There are 20 villages without any scheduled tribe population.

Literates and Illiterates by Sex (Total Population):

	Persons	Males	Females
Literate	25,058	15,912	9,146
Illiterate	34,267	13,950	20,317
Literacy rate	49	62	36
Graduate	1,244	1,061	183

Agriculture: ***Distribution of villages according to land use:***

Out of 27 villages, Total area (in hectare) is 17635, out of

that 85.99 percent is cultivable and 32.57 percent of the cultivable area is irrigated.

Sources of Irrigation (Hectares): Government Canal 0, Private Canal 0, Well without Electricity 0, Well with Electricity 64.68, Tubewell without Electricity 0, Tubewell with Electricity 2179.33, Tank 2446.34, River 0, Lake 0, Waterfall 0, Others 248.95.

Villages with population of 5000 to 9999:
Andole.

Villages with population of 10000 and above:
Jogipet.

Distribution of Workers:

	Persons	Males	Females	WPR
Cultivators	6,844	4,687	2,157	23.11
Agricultural Labour	14,644	6,146	8,498	49.44
Household Industry	917	481	436	3.1
Other Workers	7,214	5,588	1,626	24.36
Main Workers	21,027	13,659	7,368	70.99
Marginal Workers	8,592	3,243	5,349	29.01
Total Workers	29,619	16,902	12,717	

Religion: Major Religious Communities:

	Persons	Males	Females	Sex Ratio
Hindu (87.95%)	52,176	26,285	25,891	985
Muslim (11.59%)	6,878	3,443	3,435	998
Christian (0.27%)	162	76	86	1,132
Sikh (0%)	1	1	-	-
Buddhists (0%)	-	-	-	-
Jain (0.08%)	48	23	25	1,087

Agewise Data:

	Persons	Males	Females	Sex Ratio
All ages	59,325	29,862	29,463	987
0-14	19,878	10,143	9,735	960
15-44	27,306	13,876	13,430	968
45-79	11,636	5,628	6,008	1068
80+	458	189	269	1423
Age not stated	47	26	21	808

Languages (Dominant):
Telugu, Urdu, Hindi, Marathi, Kannada

Disabled Population:

	Persons	Males	Females	%
Total Disabled	1,439	799	640	
In Seeing	725	357	368	50.38
In Speech	111	61	50	7.71
In Hearing	67	38	29	4.66
In Movement	437	296	141	30.37
Mentally	99	47	52	6.88

ANUMASAMUDRAMPETA

Anumasamudrampeta C.D. Block lies in the northern part of Nellore district. The Block is located at a distance of 54 kms. from district headquarters (Nellore). There are 23 villages in the block with the total population of 32,681 persons. Area of the C.D. Block is 290.77 sq. kms. It is bounded in the north by Mandal Kaligiri, in the south by Mandals Atmakur and Sangam, in the east by Mandals Kaligiri and Sangam, and in the west by Mandals vinjamur and Atmakur.

Communications:

Roadways : Metalled Roads: Nearest Villages- Gumparlapadu, Anumasamudrampeta, Kavali Yadavalli, Chiramana, Chand ulurupadu, Anumasamudram, Hasanapuram, Srikolanu.

Annual Rainfall: Average Rainfall 894 mm

Ground Water: Availability of the Ground Water in the Basin is 2679 H.A.M. and the utilization is 1872 H. A.M. It belongs to SC category. Depth to water level varies from 5 to 10 meter below the ground. Most of the wells go down in summer months, according to the Ground Water Estimation Committee.

Administration:

Division: Coastal Andhra. Parliamentary Constituency: 39 Nellore.District: Nellore. Mandal: Anumasamudrampeta. Assembly Constituency: 234 Atmakur. Gram Panchayat: 19

Villages: 23 **Inhabited:** 23 **Uninhabited:** 0

Ranking	District	State	National
Area	15	180	2884
Population	41	981	5983
Sex Ratio	21	471	1762
Child Sex Ratio	7	236	765
Literacy Rate	27	322	3062
Density	12	626	6035
Work Participation Rate	39	1023	1702

Gram Panchayats:
A.S.Peta, Akbarabad, Anumasamudram, Chiramana Chowtabheemavaram, Duba Gunta, Gudipadu Gumparlapadu, Hasanapuram, Jammavaram, K.Yadavalli Kondameeda Konduru, Kuppuru Pedu, Pandipadu Pedabbipuram, Ponugodu, Rajavolu, Sreekolanu Velpeligunta.

Amenities:

Education: Primary School in 23 villages, Middle school in 9 villages, Matriculation or Secondary School in 8 villages, namely Dubagunta, Gudipadu, Gumparlapadu, Anumasamudrampeta, Kavali Yadavalli, Chiramana, Kondameeda Konduru, Srikolanu.

Higher Secondary or Pre University Courses or Intermediate or Junior College in 0 village of the CD Block, College in 0 village, Adult Literacy Center in 22 villages.

Medical: Hospital in 0 village, Dispensary in 1 village, Health Center in 2 villages, Sub Center in 13 villages, Maternity and Child Welfare Center in 0 village, Community health workers in 0 village.

The Village having Hospital or Dispensary or Health Center is Chiramana.

Drinking Water: Tap water in 23 villages, Tank water in 23 villages, Well water in 23 villages, Tubewell in 23 villages and more than one source in 23 villages.

Bank: Banking facility in 2 villages, namely, Anumasamudrampeta, Kavali Yadavalli.

Credit Society in 16 villages Agricultural Credit Society in 3 Non-Agricultural Credit Society in 16 villages.

Others: Power supply in 23 villages, Cinema hall in 0 village, sport club in 0 village, Stadium or Auditorium or Community Hall in 0 village, Post Office in 23 villages.

There are 23 villages having bus facilities.

Villages with most of facilities: Anumasamudrampeta Kavali Yadavalli.

Villages without Amenities (Education): None..

Scheduled Castes: Out of the total population of 32681 persons, 4597 persons (14.07%) belong to Scheduled Castes.

The villages having less than 10% SC population are Chouta Bheemavaram, Gumparlapadu, Anumasamudrampeta Kunalammapadu, Akbarabad, Chandulurupadu Hasanapuram.

The villages having more than 50% SC population are None.

Sex ratio of Scheduled Caste population is 492.

Scheduled Castes Literates and Illiterates by Sex:

	Persons	Males	Females
Literate	2,194	1,337	857
Illiterate	2,403	998	1,405
Literacy rate	54.4	65.2	43.3
Graduate	36	31	5

Scheduled Castes (Dominant):

Madiga, Mala, Arundhatiya, Generic Castes etc. Adi Andhra

For their cultural identity please see Appendix-I

Villages without Scheduled Castes: There is 1 village without any scheduled caste population.

Scheduled Tribes: Out of the total population of 32681 persons, 1265 persons (3.87%) belong to Scheduled Tribes.

The villages having less than 10% ST population are Dubagunta, Chouta Bheemavaram, Gudipadu Gumparlapadu, Pandipadu, Pedabbipuram, Rajavolu Ponugodu, Anumasamudrampeta, Zammavaram Kavali Yadavalli, Velpulagunta, Kunalammapadu Akbarabad, Zuvvalaguntapalle, Chiramana Chandulurupadu, Anumasamudram, Kuppurupadu Kondameeda Konduru, Hasanapuram, Srikolanu.

The villages having more than 50% ST population are None.

Sex ratio of Scheduled tribe population is 493.

Scheduled Tribes Literates and Illiterates by Sex:

	Persons	Males	Females
Literate	226	126	100
Illiterate	1,039	515	524
Literacy rate	21.5	23.4	19.5
Graduate	1	0	1

Scheduled Tribes (Dominant):

Yenadis, Yerukulas, Koya etc., Sugalis etc.

For their cultural identity please see Appendix-II

Villages without Scheduled Tribes: There are 4 villages without any scheduled tribe population.

Literates and Illiterates by Sex (Total Population):

	Persons	Males	Females
Literate	16,725	10,282	6,443
Illiterate	15,956	6,173	9,783
Literacy rate	58	71	45
Graduate	518	425	93

Agriculture: ***Distribution of villages according to land use:*** Out of 23 villages, Total area (in hectare) is 29077, out of that 25.06 percent is cultivable and 41.78 percent of the cultivable area is irrigated.

Sources of Irrigation (Hectares): Government Canal 0, Private Canal 0, Well without Electricity 0, Well with Electricity 187, Tubewell without Electricity 0, Tubewell with Electricity 63, Tank 2795, River 0, Lake 0, Waterfall 0, Others 0.

Villages with population of 5000 to 9999: None

Villages with population of 10000 and above: None

Distribution of Workers:

	Persons	Males	Females	WPR
Cultivators	4,062	3,011	1,051	23.79
Agricultural Labour	7,590	3,242	4,348	44.45
Household Industry	2,183	965	1,218	12.78
Other Workers	3,242	2,530	712	18.98
Main Workers	11,918	7,982	3,936	69.79
Marginal Workers	5,159	1,766	3,393	30.21
Total Workers	17,077	9,748	7,329	

Religion: Major Religious Communities:

	Persons	Males	Females	Sex Ratio
Hindu (83.34%)	27,235	13,763	13,472	979
Muslim (16.38%)	5,352	2,648	2,704	1,021
Christian (0.15%)	49	19	30	1,579
Sikh (0%)	1	1	-	-
Buddhists (0%)	-	-	-	-
Jain (0%)	-	-	-	-

Agewise Data:

	Persons	Males	Females	Sex Ratio
All ages	32,681	16,455	16,226	986
0-14	9,757	4,990	4,767	955
15-44	15,484	7,803	7,681	984

45-79	7,151	3,524	3,627	1029
80+	267	123	144	1171
Age not stated	22	15	7	467

Languages (Dominant):

Telugu, Urdu, Gondi, Marathi, Hindi

Disabled Population:

	Persons	Males	Females	%
Total Disabled	888	486	402	
In Seeing	248	121	127	27.93
In Speech	92	54	38	10.36
In Hearing	71	32	39	8
In Movement	279	167	112	31.42
Mentally	198	112	86	22.3

ANUMULA

Anumula C.D. Block lies in the southern part of Nalgonda district. The Block is located at a distance of 38 kms. from district headquarters (Nalgonda). There are 27 villages in the block with the total population of 61,922 persons. Area of the C.D. Block is 329.32 sq. kms. It is bounded by Nidamanur Mandal on east, Peddavoora Mandal on west, Dameracherla Mandal on south, Gurrampode and Kangal Mandals on north.

Communications:

Roadways : Metalled Roads: Nearest Villages- Pulimamidi, Ambatpalle, Sreenadhapur, Ramadugu, Anumula, Palem, Ibrahim Peta.

River: Allai Nadi- Nearest Villages- Marepalle, Kummari kunta Kalva, Narayana Puram, Kupaspalle, Ambatpalle, Sreenadhapur, Ramadugu, Anumula, Palem, Ibrahim Peta, Rajavaram, Perur.

Backwards Region Grants Fund: It receives Backward Region Grants.

Ground Water: Availability of the Ground Water in the Basin is 5655 H.A.M. and the utilization is 1615 H. A.M. It belongs to Safe category. Depth to water level varies from 5 to 10 meter below the ground. Most of the wells go down in summer months. The well density in the entire block is 16 wells per sq. km. Total no. of the wells in the block are enumerated as 3707, according to the Ground Water Estimation Committee.

Natural Division : Krishna Piedmont Plain Region

Administration:

Division: Telangana. Parliamentary Constituency: 13 Nalgonda. District: Nalgonda. Mandal: Anumula. Assembly Constituency: 87 Nagarjuna Sagar. Gram Panchayat: 26.

Villages: 27 **Inhabited:** 25 **Uninhabited:** 2

Ranking	District	State	National
Area	4	103	2468
Population	5	248	4794
Sex Ratio	30	731	2492
Child Sex Ratio	33	759	3257
Literacy Rate	28	531	3970
Density	39	630	4913
Work Participation Rate	39	759	1713

Gram Panchayats:

Alwala, Annaram, Anumula, Boyagudem Chelmareddygudem, Garikeneti Thanda, Hazariguda Ibrahimpet, Kompally, Korvanigudem, Kothapally Marepally, Naidupalem, Palem, Peroor, Pulimamedi Rajavaram, Ramadugu, Rangundla, Silgapur, Srinathpur Srirampuram, Thimmapur, Tirmalagiri, Yacharam Yallapuram.

Amenities:

Education: Primary School in 24 villages, Middle school in 11 villages, Matriculation or Secondary School in 6 villages, namely Pulimamidi, Yacharam, Ramadugu, Anumula, Rajavaram, Tirumalagiri.

Higher Secondary or Pre University Courses or Intermediate or Junior College in 1 village of the CD Block,, namely Anumula.

College in 1 village, Adult Literacy Center in 2 villages., College is in village, namely Anumula.

Medical: Hospital in 0 village, Dispensary in 1 village, Health Center in 1 village, Sub Center in 9 villages, Maternity and Child Welfare Center in 1 village, Community health workers in 0 village.

The Village having Hospital or Dispensary or Health Center is Anumula.

Drinking Water: Tap water in 25 villages, Tank water in 25 villages, Well water in 25 villages, Tubewell in 25 villages and more than one source in 25 villages.

Bank: Banking facility in 3 villages, namely, Pulimamidi, Anumula, Tirumalagiri.

Credit Society in 13 villages Agricultural Credit Society in 9 Non-Agricultural Credit Society in 13 villages.

Others: Power supply in 25 villages, Cinema hall in 1 village, sport club in 0 village, Stadium or Auditorium or Community Hall in 0 village, Post Office in 10 villages.

There are 21 villages having bus facilities.

Villages with most of facilities: Anumula Tirumalagiri.

Villages without amenities (Education): Kosalamarri..

Scheduled Castes: Out of the total population of 61922 persons, 11026 persons (17.81%) belong to Scheduled Castes. The villages having less than 10% SC population are None..

The villages having more than 50% SC population are None.

Sex ratio of Scheduled Caste population is 488.

Scheduled Castes Literates and Illiterates by Sex:

	Persons	Males	Females
Literate	4,375	2,894	1,481
Illiterate	6,651	2,747	3,904
Literacy rate	48.0	61.9	33.3
Graduate	84	70	14

Scheduled Castes (Dominant):

Madiga, Mala, Beda Jangam etc., Bindla, Dom etc.

For their cultural identity please see Appendix-I

Villages without Scheduled Castes: There are 3 villages without any scheduled caste population.

Scheduled Tribes: Out of the total population of 61922 persons, 9822 persons (15.86%) belong to Scheduled Tribes. The villages having less than 10% ST population are Kosalamarri, Mukkamala, Venkatadri Palem, Annaram Marepalle, Kummarikunta Kalva, Pulimamidi, Yacharam Kupaspalle, Sreenadhapur, Ramadugu, Thimmapuram Anumula, Palem, Ibrahim Peta, Alwala, Kompalle Silgapur.

The villages having more than 50% ST population are None.

Sex ratio of Scheduled tribe population is 491.

Scheduled Tribes Literates and Illiterates by Sex:

	Persons	Males	Females
Literate	2,330	1,695	635
Illiterate	7,492	3,300	4,192
Literacy rate	29.7	43.0	16.3
Graduate	44	42	2

Scheduled Tribes (Dominant):

Sugalis etc., Yerukulas, Chenchu etc.

For their cultural identity please see Appendix-II

Villages without Scheduled Tribes: There are 13 villages without any scheduled tribe population.

Literates and Illiterates by Sex (Total Population):

	Persons	Males	Females
Literate	27,946	17,432	10,514
Illiterate	33,976	14,000	19,976
Literacy rate	53	66	41
Graduate	1,124	928	196

Agriculture: ***Distribution of villages according to land use:*** Out of 27 villages, Total area (in hectare) is 32934, out of that 79.87 percent is cultivable and 59.48 percent of the cultivable area is irrigated.

Sources of Irrigation (Hectares): Government Canal 4598.98, Private Canal 113.3, Well without Electricity 18.21, Well with Electricity 68.78, Tubewell without Electricity 60.69, Tubewell with Electricity 1120.9, Tank 1654.78, River 2707.72, Lake 0, Waterfall 116.14, Others 5185.97.

Villages with population of 5000 to 9999:

Rajavaram, Tirumalagiri, Perur.

Villages with population of 10000 and above:

Anumula.

Distribution of Workers:

	Persons	Males	Females	WPR
Cultivators	8,909	6,065	2,844	28.51
Agricultural Labour	16,190	6,495	9,695	51.81
Household Industry	682	420	262	2.18
Other Workers	5,470	4,343	1,127	17.5
Main Workers	24,751	15,163	9,588	79.2
Marginal Workers	6,500	2,160	4,340	20.8
Total Workers	31,251	17,323	13,928	

Religion: Major Religious Communities:

	Persons	Males	Females	Sex Ratio
Hindu (92.98%)	57,577	29,249	28,328	969
Muslim (5.96%)	3,688	1,898	1,790	943
Christian (0.72%)	443	182	261	1,434
Sikh (0%)	-	-	-	-
Buddhists (0.01%)	8	5	3	600
Jain (0%)	2	-	2	-

Agewise Data:

	Persons	Males	Females	Sex Ratio
All ages	61,922	31,432	30,490	970
0-14	22,321	11,449	10,872	950
15-44	28,308	14,217	14,091	991
45-79	10,719	5,494	5,225	951
80+	409	183	226	1235
Age not stated	165	89	76	854

Languages (Dominant):

Telugu, Hindi, Urdu, Tamil, Gondi

Disabled Population:

	Persons	Males	Females	%
Total Disabled	1,182	685	497	
In Seeing	465	254	211	39.34
In Speech	113	67	46	9.56
In Hearing	37	16	21	3.13
In Movement	426	269	157	36.04
Mentally	141	79	62	11.93

ARAKU VALLEY

Araku Valley C.D. Block lies in the northern part of Viskhapatnam district. It is a part of Araku Valley Mandal. The Block is located at a distance of 115 kms. from district headquarters (Visakhapatnam). There are 169 villages in the block with the total population of 42,191 persons. Area of the C.D. Block is 221.43 sq. kms. It is bounded in the north by district Viziana garam in the south by Mandals Dumbriguda, Hukumpeta and Anantagiri, in the east by Mandal Anantagiri and district Vizianagaram, in the west by Mandal Dubriguda, and it has common boundary with the state of Orissa on north.

Communications :

Roadways : Metalled Roads: Nearest Villages- Padmapuram, Yandapallivalasa, Bondaguda, Gattanaguda, Dingriputtu, Korraguda, Bosubeda, Boduguda, Gadyaguda, Kothaballugu da, Gandametta, Chinagangagudi, Pedagangagudi.

Railway Station: Yandapallivalasa, Gadyaguda, Gattaragu da.

Integrated Child Development Scheme (ICDS) Project: Araku (Tribal), Total Anganwadi Centres: 225

Annaual Rainfall: Average Rainfall 975.0 mm

Ground Water: Availability of the Ground Water in the Basin is (Information not avavible) H.A.M .and the utilization is (Information not avavible) H.A.M. It belongs to (Information not avavible) category. Depth to water level varies from 3 to 10 meter below the ground. Most of the wells go down in summer months.

Administration:

Division: Coastal Andhra. Parliamentary Constituency: 18 Araku (ST). District: Visakhapatnam. Mandal: Araku Valley. Assembly Constituency: 147 Araku Valley. Gram Panchayat: 14.

Border Villages: (Orissa)- Nearest Villages- Ranajilleda, Mala Singaram, Tudumu, Chittamgondi, Totavalasa, Dabuguda, Pedagaruvu, Domalajoru, Tungagedda, Kamalaban da, Mettapadu, Mettapadu, Chendrapodaru, Borrachinta.

Places of Turist Interest:

Araku Valley : Araku valley is about 115 kms. from Vishakhapatnam. The area of the valley is roughly, 36 sq. kms. and the altitude is between 600 and 900 metres above mean sea level. The entire area is inhabit ed by, aboriginal tribes and attracts visitors from all over the country. The journey to Araku Valley on the ghat road with thick forests on either side is in itself interesting and pleasant. The Ananthagiri hills on the way to Araku Valley are famous for coffee plantations. Araku Valley, has an Exploratory-cum-Demon stration Farm, which is about 20 hectares in extent, a Government Orchard and a Government Silk farm with mulbery gardens. Cocoons from the Silk farm are reeled in the farm, and the silk yarn and waste are sent to Hindupur (Anantapur area). The beautiful Araku Valley, with its bracing climate, orchards and the Ananthagiri Ghats, which present an enchanting view to the visitors, is attracting tourists not only from all parts of India but also from abroad, as there are good communica tion and halting facilities. The natural beauty of this valley is enhanced by the tribal people who abound here, with their own folklore and traditions. "Dhimsa dance" is a unique feature of the tribes of Araku Valley.

Villages: 169 **Inhabited:** 162 **Uninhabited:** 7

Ranking	District	State	National
Area	7	432	3833
Population	33	526	5301
Sex Ratio	18	182	991
Child Sex Ratio	4	7	37
Literacy Rate	26	915	5351
Density	24	681	4386
Work Participation Rate	33	628	1912

Gram Panchayats:

Baski, Bondam, Chinalabudu, Chompi, Gannela, Iragai Kothabhalluguda, Lotheru, Madagada, Madala Padmapuram, Pedalabudu, Siragam, Sunkarametta.

Amenities:

Education: Primary School in 142 villages, Middle school in 8 villages, Matriculation or Secondary School in 6 villages, namely Lotheru, Gannela, Padmapuram, Kothaballuguda, Pathaballuguda, Janamguda.

Higher Secondary or Pre University Courses or Inter-mediate or Junior College in 0 village of the CD Block, College in 0 village, Adult Literacy Center in 0 village.

Medical: Hospital in 0 village, Dispensary in 0 village, Health Center in 16 villages, Sub Center in 2 villages, Maternity and Child Welfare Center in 0 village, Community health workers in 0 village.

Drinking Water: Tap water in 160 villages, Tank water in 160 villages, Well water in 162 villages, Tubewell in 160 villages and more than one source in 162 villages.

Bank: Banking facility in 9 villages, namely, Totavalasa, Gangasanivalasa, Garudaguda Yandapallivalasa, Gugguda, Gadyaguda, Sunkarametta Pedagangagudi, Gattaraguda.

Credit Society in 0 village Agricultural Credit Society in 0 Non-Agricultural Credit Society in 0 village.

Others: Power supply in 162 villages, Cinema hall in 2 villages sport club in 0 village, Stadium or Auditorium or Community Hall in 0 village, Post Office in 21 villages.

There are 13 villages having bus facilities.

Villages with most of facilities: Yandapallivalasa Gadyaguda, Sunkarametta, Gattaraguda.

Villages without amenities (Education): Sabaka, Chendrapodaru, Borrachinta, Jarlangi, Jarimanuguda, Pedagaruvu, Dumbriguda, Chandrapoda, Gangasanivalasa, Musiriguda, Polliguda, Tokavalasa, Novvaguda, Bandapanuvalasa, Gandametta, Chinagangagudi, Pedageddavalasa..

Scheduled Castes: Out of the total population of 49619 persons, 461 persons (0.93%) belong to Scheduled Castes. The villages having less than 10% SC population are Ranajilleda, Mala Singaram, Tudumu, Chinalabudu Chittamgondi, Totavalasa, Cheedivalasa, Dabuguda

Raktakandi, Domalajoru, Tungagedda, Kamalabanda Sabaka, Kentubade, Kajjuruguda, Chellubadi Chendrapodaru, Borrachinta, Jarlangi, Jarimanuguda Pedagaruvu, Gatapadu, Dellipadu, Davadaguda Kundiguda, Dumbriguda, Chandrapoda, Landiguda Kikkatiguda, Totavalasa, Antiparthi, Sarubedda Peda Valasa, Gangasanivalasa, Duddikonda, Kaguvalasa Musiriguda, Addumanda, Morriguda, Iragai, Nanda Bonduguda, Baliyaguda, Urumulu, Tidiguda Validipanasa, Borrakaluvalasa, Lotheru, Tangulabedda Toradambuvalasa, Polliguda, Kandulaguddi, Tadaka Kaguvalasa, Pujaribanda, Kamalatota, Totavalasa Dappuguda, Gondiguda, Gannela, Tokavalasa, Polamguda Kosiguda, Ramakrishnanagar, Amalaguda, Kottavalasa Sarubedda, Pottangipadu, Madala, Battivalasa Musriguda, Borriguda, Lembaguda, Novvaguda Bishnuguda, Garudaguda, Pittamarriguda, Gatuguda Mulyagalugu, Ganjayavalasa, Peda Labudu, Panirangini Littiguda, Ravvalaguda, Sarabhaguda, Dolliguda Padmapuram, Yandapallivalasa, Pappuduvalasa Kottavalasa, Chompi, Tokavalasa, Kodipunjuvalasa Siragam, Bandapanuvalasa, Varra, Lamtampadu Jaginivalasa, Girliguda, Bamsuguda, Piripodaru Dungiyaputtu, Devarapalle, Bonduguda, Baski Todubanda, Gugguda, Doraguda, Manjuguda, Pitraguda Kusumguda, Vanthamuru, Kappalagondi, Bondaguda Gattanaguda, Nandiguda, Dingriputtu, Korraguda Pakanaguda, Danirangini, Madaguda, Dalapatiguda Bosubeda, Boduguda, Gadyaguda, Kothaballuguda Pathaballuguda, Hattaguda, Kinnamguda, Daburangini Korraguda, Limbaguda, Janamguda, Piribanda Sunkarametta, Gandametta, Chinagangagudi Pedagangagudi, Korraguda, Sukuruguda, Gattaraguda Ninnimamidivalasa, Kothavalasa, Bondam Rampuduvalasa, Ranginiguda, Boyiguda, Baliyaguda Rega, Koliyaguda, Majjivalasa, Gojara, Karakavalasa Kuruseela, Beddaguda, Vanthalaguda, Leddangi Sirasaguda, Adaru, Bairuguda, Pedageddavalasa Danasalavalasa.

The villages having more than 50% SC population are None.

Sex ratio of Scheduled Caste population is 471.

Scheduled Castes Literates and Illiterates by Sex:

	Persons	Males	Females
Literate	328	189	139
Illiterate	133	55	78
Literacy rate	82.6	90.9	73.5
Graduate	52	35	17

Scheduled Castes (Dominant):

Mala, Adi Andhra, Ghasi etc., Relli, Madiga

For their cultural identity please see Appendix-I

Villages without Scheduled Castes: There are 154 villages without any scheduled caste population.

Scheduled Tribes: Out of the total population of 49619 persons, 43429 persons (87.52%) belong to Scheduled Tribes. The villages having less than 10% ST population are None..

The villages having more than 50% ST population are Ranajilleda, Mala Singaram, Tudumu, Chinalabudu Totavalasa, Cheedivalasa, Dabuguda, Raktakandi Domalajoru, Kamalabanda, Sabaka, Kentubade Kajjuruguda, Chellubadi, Chendrapodaru, Borrachinta Jarlangi, Jarimanuguda, Pedagaruvu, Gatapadu Dellipadu, Davadaguda, Kundiguda, Dumbriguda Chandrapoda, Landiguda, Kikkatiguda, Totavalasa Antiparthi, Sarubedda, Peda Valasa, Gangasanivalasa Duddikonda, Kaguvalasa, Musiriguda, Morriguda Iragai, Nanda, Bonduguda, Baliyaguda, Urumulu Tidiguda, Validipanasa, Borrakaluvalasa, Lotheru Tangulabedda, Toradambuvalasa, Polliguda Kandulaguddi, Tadaka, Kaguvalasa, Pujaribanda Kamalatota, Totavalasa, Dappuguda, Gondiguda Gannela, Tokavalasa, Polamguda, Kosiguda Ramakrishnanagar, Amalaguda, Kottavalasa, Sarubedda Pottangipadu, Madala, Battivalasa, Musriguda Borriguda, Lembaguda, Novvaguda, Bishnuguda Garudaguda, Pittamarriguda, Gatuguda, Mulyagalugu Ganjayavalasa, Peda Labudu, Panirangini, Littiguda Sarabhaguda, Dolliguda, Padmapuram, Yandapallivalasa Pappuduvalasa, Kottavalasa, Chompi, Tokavalasa Kodipunjuvalasa, Siragam, Bandapanuvalasa, Varra Lamtampadu, Jaginivalasa, Girliguda, Bamsuguda Piripodaru, Dungiyaputtu, Devarapalle, Bonduguda Baski, Todubanda, Gugguda, Doraguda, Manjuguda Pitraguda, Kusumguda, Vanthamuru, Kappalagondi Bondaguda, Gattanaguda, Nandiguda, Dingriputtu Korraguda, Pakanaguda, Danirangini, Madaguda Dalapatiguda, Bosubeda, Boduguda, Gadyaguda Kothaballuguda, Pathaballuguda, Hattaguda Kinnamguda, Daburangini, Korraguda, Limbaguda Janamguda, Piribanda, Sunkarametta, Gandametta Chinagangagudi, Pedagangagudi, Korraguda, Sukuruguda Gattaraguda, Ninnimamidivalasa, Kothavalasa, Bondam Rampuduvalasa, Ranginiguda, Boyiguda, Baliyaguda Rega, Koliyaguda, Majjivalasa, Gojara, Karakavalasa Kuruseela, Beddaguda, Vanthalaguda, Leddangi Sirasaguda, Adaru, Bairuguda, Pedageddavalasa Danasalavalasa.

Sex ratio of Scheduled tribe population is 505.

Scheduled Tribes Literates and Illiterates by Sex:

	Persons	Males	Females
Literate	14,424	9,668	4,756
Illiterate	29,005	11,846	17,159
Literacy rate	39.4	53.0	25.9
Graduate	213	181	32

Scheduled Tribes (Dominant):
Konda Dhoras, Kotia etc., Valmiki, Porja etc.
Bagata

For their cultural identity please see Appendix-II

Villages without Scheduled Tribes: There are 9 villages without any scheduled tribe population.

Literates and Illiterates by Sex (Total Population):

	Persons	Males	Females
Literate	18,403	11,950	6,453
Illiterate	31,216	12,781	18,435
Literacy rate	44	57	31
Graduate	652	488	164

Agriculture: ***Distribution of villages according to land use:*** Out of 169 villages, Total area (in hectare) is 22143, out of that 64.69 percent is cultivable and 8.86 percent of the cultivable area is irrigated.

Sources of Irrigation (Hectares): Government Canal 404.28, Private Canal 0, Well without Electricity 7.76, Well with Electricity 0, Tubewell without Electricity 0, Tubewell with Electricity 2.02, Tank 212.38, River 0, Lake 0, Waterfall 0.23, Others 642.54.

Villages with population of 5000 to 9999:
Mala Singaram.

Villages with population of 10000 and above: None

Distribution of Workers:

	Persons	Males	Females	WPR
Cultivators	12,543	6,889	5,654	50.79
Agricultural Labour	7,133	3,028	4,105	28.88
Household Industry	1,011	358	653	4.09
Other Workers	4,009	2,652	1,357	16.23
Main Workers	17,169	9,878	7,291	69.52
Marginal Workers	7,527	3,049	4,478	30.48
Total Workers	24,696	12,927	11,769	

Religion: Major Religious Communities:

	Persons	Males	Females	Sex Ratio
Hindu (96.11%)	47,689	23,799	23,890	1,004
Muslim (0.55%)	275	150	125	833
Christian (3.05%)	1,514	703	811	1,154
Sikh (0.08%)	40	26	14	538
Buddhists (0.14%)	71	34	37	1,088
Jain (0%)	1	-	1	-

Agewise Data:

	Persons	Males	Females	Sex Ratio
All ages	49,619	24,731	24,888	1006
0-14	18,901	9,743	9,158	940
15-44	22,686	10,795	11,891	1102
45-79	7,663	4,003	3,660	914
80+	91	42	49	1167
Age not stated	278	148	130	878

Languages (Dominant):
Telugu, Oriya, Hindi, Konda, Others

Disabled Population:

	Persons	Males	Females	%
Total Disabled	669	370	299	
In Seeing	298	151	147	44.54
In Speech	72	39	33	10.76
In Hearing	58	31	27	8.67
In Movement	178	118	60	26.61
Mentally	63	31	32	9.42

ARDHAVEEDU

Ardhaveedu C.D. Block lies in the western part of Prakasam district. The Block is located at a distance of 140 kms. from district headquarters (Ongole). There are 13 villages in the block with the total population of 36,688 persons. Area of the C.D. Block is 253.03 sq. kms. It is bounded in the north by Mandal Dornala, in the south by Mandals Giddalur, Racherla and Cumbum, in the east by Mandal Markapur, and in the west by district Kurnool.

Communications:

Roadways : State Highway (S.H.): Direction- Cumbum to Markapur. Nearest Village- Kakarla village.

Hills: Nearest Villages- Gannepalle, Magutur, Potti Basavai Palle, Kakarla, Peda Kandukur, Ayyavari Palle.

The Block is identified as a drought-prone area.

Annual Rainfall: Average Rainfall 734.8 mm

Ground Water: Availability of the Ground Water in the Basin is 33.10 MCM and the utilization is 24.95 MCM It belongs to Semi Critical category. Depth to water level varies from 2 to 5 meter below the ground. Most of the wells go down in summer months., according to the Ground Water Estimation Committee.

Forest and Reserved **Forest:** Nearest Villages- Velagalapaya, Gannepalle, Magutur, Potti Basavai Palle, Peda Kandukur, Ayyavari Palle, Donakonda, Ardhaveedu, Bollu Palle, Papineni Palle, Bogolu, Yerraguntla,

Administration:

Division: Coastal Andhra. Parliamentary Constituency: 33 Ongole. District: Prakasam. Mandal: Ardhaveedu. Assembly Constituency: 231 Giddalur. Gram Panchayat: 15

Villages: 13 **Inhabited:** 12 **Uninhabited:** 1

Ranking	District	State	National
Area	23	298	3338
Population	43	905	5860
Sex Ratio	52	1067	4292

Child Sex Ratio	31	733	3142
Literacy Rate	30	537	4000
Density	43	779	5623
Work Participation Rate	44	916	2295

Gram Panchayats:

Ardhaveedu, Ayyavaripalli, Bogole, Bollupalli Donakonda, Gannepalli, Kakarla, Maguturu Mohiddinpuram, Nagulavaram, Papinenipalli Peddakandukuru, Rangapuram, Velagalapaya, Yachavaram.

Amenities:

Education: Primary School in 12 villages, Middle school in 7 villages, Matriculation or Secondary School in 6 villages, namely Gannepalle, Kakarla, Donakonda, Ardhaveedu, Papineni Palle, Bogolu.

Higher Secondary or Pre University Courses or Intermediate or Junior College in 1 village of the CD Block,, namely Ardhaveedu.

College in 0 village, Adult Literacy Center in 11 villages.

Medical: Hospital in 0 village, Dispensary in 2 villages, Health Center in 3 villages, Sub Center in 8 villages, Maternity and Child Welfare Center in 0 village, Community health workers in 0 village.

The Villages having Hospital or Dispensary or Health Center are Gannepalle, Ardhaveedu.

Drinking Water: Tap water in 12 villages, Tank water in 12 villages, Well water in 12 villages, Tubewell in 12 villages and more than one source in 12 villages.

Bank: Banking facility in 3 villages, namely, Gannepalle, Kakarla, Ardhaveedu.

Credit Society in 5 villages Agricultural Credit Society in 3 Non-Agricultural Credit Society in 2 villages.

Others: Power supply in 12 villages, Cinema hall in 1 village, sport club in 0 village, Stadium or Auditorium or Community Hall in 0 village, Post Office in 11 villages.

There are 12 villages having bus facilities.

Villages with most of facilities: Gannepalle Kakarla, Ardhaveedu.

Villages without Amenities (Education): None..

Scheduled Castes: Out of the total population of 36688 persons, 6090 persons (16.6%) belong to Scheduled Castes.

The villages having less than 10% SC population are None..

The villages having more than 50% SC population are None.

Sex ratio of Scheduled Caste population is 451.

Scheduled Castes Literates and Illiterates by Sex:

	Persons	Males	Females
Literate	3,082	2,170	912
Illiterate	3,008	1,172	1,836
Literacy rate	58.1	73.7	38.6
Graduate	68	57	11

Scheduled Castes (Dominant):

Madiga, Mala, Anamuk

For their cultural identity please see Appendix-I

Villages without Scheduled Castes: There are 3 villages without any scheduled caste population.

Scheduled Tribes: Out of the total population of 36688 persons, 2156 persons (5.88%) belong to Scheduled Tribes.

The villages having less than 10% ST population are Gannepalle, Potti Basavai Palle, Kakarla Ayyavari Palle, Donakonda, Ardhaveedu, Bollu Palle Papineni Palle, Bogolu.

The villages having more than 50% ST population are None.

Sex ratio of Scheduled tribe population is 480.

Scheduled Tribes Literates and Illiterates by Sex:

	Persons	Males	Females
Literate	765	551	214
Illiterate	1,391	571	820
Literacy rate	43.1	58.6	25.6
Graduate	14	12	2

Scheduled Tribes (Dominant):

Sugalis etc., Chenchu etc., Yerukulas, Yenadis

For their cultural identity please see Appendix-II

Villages without Scheduled Tribes: There are 4 villages without any scheduled tribe population.

Literates and Illiterates by Sex (Total Population):

	Persons	Males	Females
Literate	16,872	11,553	5,319
Illiterate	19,816	7,417	12,399
Literacy rate	53	70	35
Graduate	537	472	65

Agriculture: ***Distribution of villages according to land use:***

Out of 13 villages, Total area (in hectare) is 25303, out of that 59.44 percent is cultivable and 21.31 percent of the cultivable area is irrigated.

Sources of Irrigation (Hectares): Government Canal 0, Private Canal 0, Well without Electricity 0, Well with Electricity 0, Tubewell without Electricity 0, Tubewell with Electricity 2842.91, Tank 362.19, River 0, Lake 0, Waterfall 0, Others 0.

Villages with population of 5000 to 9999:

Gannepalle, Ardhaveedu.

Villages with population of 10000 and above: None

Distribution of Workers:

	Persons	Males	Females	WPR
Cultivators	7,052	4,120	2,932	38.91
Agricultural Labour	8,068	3,450	4,618	44.52
Household Industry	563	313	250	3.11
Other Workers	2,441	1,825	616	13.47

Main Workers	16,490	9,116	7,374	90.98
Marginal Workers	1,634	592	1,042	9.02
Total Workers	18,124	9,708	8,416	

Religion: Major Religious Communities:

	Persons	Males	Females	Sex Ratio
Hindu (88.54%)	32,484	16,818	15,666	932
Muslim (11.12%)	4,078	2,087	1,991	954
Christian (0.16%)	57	29	28	966
Sikh (0%)	-	-	-	-
Buddhists (0%)	-	-	-	-
Jain (0%)	-	-	-	-

Agewise Data:

	Persons	Males	Females	Sex Ratio
All ages	36,688	18,970	17,718	934
0-14	12,932	6,944	5,988	862
15-44	15,750	8,069	7,681	952
45-79	7,660	3,777	3,883	1028
80+	298	151	147	974
Age not stated	48	29	19	655

Languages (Dominant):

Telugu, Urdu, Hindi, Gondi, Nepali

Disabled Population:

	Persons	Males	Females	%
Total Disabled	628	371	257	
In Seeing	214	114	100	34.08
In Speech	69	50	19	10.99
In Hearing	58	34	24	9.24
In Movement	217	134	83	34.55
Mentally	70	39	31	11.15

ARMUR

Armur C.D. Block lies in the north-east part of Nizamab ad district. The Block is located at a distance of 28 kms. from district headquarters (Nizamabad). There are 23 villages in the block with the total population of 113,018 persons. Area of the C.D. Block is 210.10 sq. kms. It is bounded by Nandipet Mandal on west, north-west and north, Balkonda Mandal on north-east, Velpur Mandal on east and south-east, Jakranpalle Mandal on south-east, south and south-west, Makloor Mandal on south-west.

Communications :

Roadways : NH-7: Direction- Hyderabad to Adilabad Nearest Villages- Fathepur, Armur, Mamidipalle, Perkit. NH-16: Direction- Nizamabad to Metpalle Nearest Villages- Ankapur, Chepur, Armur, Mamidipalle, Perkit.

Backwards Region Grants Fund: It receives Backward Region Grants.

Integrated Child Development Scheme (ICDS) Project: Armoor, Total Anganwadi Centres: 320

Annual Rainfall: Average Rainfall 1072 mm

Ground Water: Availability of the Ground Water in the Basin is 2997 H.A.M. and the utilization is 2067 H. A.M. It belongs to Safe category. Depth to water level varies from 10 to 20 meter below the ground. Most of the wells go down in summer months, according to the Ground Water Estimation Committee.

Natural Division : Telangana Plateau Region

Administration:

Division: Telangana. Parliamentary Constituency: 4 Nizamabad. District: Nizamabad. Mandal: Armur. Assembly Constituency: 11 Armur. Gram Panchayat: 20.

Villages: 23 **Inhabited:** 22 **Uninhabited:** 1

Ranking	District	State	National
Area	18	492	4016
Population	1	2	3066
Sex Ratio	24	107	701
Child Sex Ratio	31	892	3943
Literacy Rate	1	338	3130
Density	26	604	2052
Work Participation Rate	1	85	1626

Gram Panchayats:

Aloor, Amdapoor, Ankapoor, Chepoor, Degaon, Fathepur Gaggupally, Govindpet, Issapally, Khanapur Komanpally, Macherla, Maggidi, Mamidipally, Manthani Mirdhapally, Perkit, Pipri, Rampoor, Surbiryal.

Amenities:

Education: Primary School in 22 villages, Middle school in 17 villages, Matriculation or Secondary School in 14 villages, namely Macherla, Degaon, Surbiriyal, Fathepur, Pipri, Merdepalle, Alur, Issapalle, Armur, Ankapur, Mamidipalle, Perkit, Chepur, Govindpet.

Higher Secondary or Pre University Courses or Intermediate or Junior College in 1 village of the CD Block,, namely Armur.

College in 1 village, Adult Literacy Center in 18 villages., College is in village, namely Armur.

Medical: Hospital in 1 village, Dispensary in 1 village, Health Center in 2 villages, Sub Center in 12 villages, Maternity and Child Welfare Center in 1 village, Community health workers in 15 villages.

The Village having Hospital or Dispensary or Health Center is Armur.

Drinking Water: Tap water in 21 villages, Tank water in 22 villages, Well water in 22 villages, Tubewell in 22 villages and more than one source in 22 villages.

Bank: Banking facility in 7 villages, namely, Surbiriyal, Fathepur, Pipri, Alur, Armur, Ankapur Perkit.

Credit Society in 14 villages Agricultural Credit Society in 12 Non-Agricultural Credit Society in 8 villages.

Others: Power supply in 22 villages, Cinema hall in 1 village, sport club in 1 village, Stadium or Auditorium or Community Hall in 1 village, Post Office in 20 villages.

There are 22 villages having bus facilities.

Villages with most of facilities: Surbiriyal Fathepur, Pipri, Alur, Armur, Ankapur, Perkit.

Villages without Amenities (Education): None..

Scheduled Castes: Out of the total population of 113018 persons, 17751 persons (15.71%) belong to Scheduled Castes.

The villages having less than 10% SC population are None..

The villages having more than 50% SC population are None.

Sex ratio of Scheduled Caste population is 508.

Scheduled Castes Literates and Illiterates by Sex:

	Persons	Males	Females
Literate	7,227	4,641	2,586
Illiterate	10,524	4,100	6,424
Literacy rate	47.2	62.1	33.0
Graduate	220	184	36

Scheduled Castes (Dominant):

Mala, Madiga, Gosangi, Beda Jangam etc., Chamar etc.

For their cultural identity please see Appendix-I

Villages without Scheduled Castes: There is 1 village without any scheduled caste population.

Scheduled Tribes: Out of the total population of 113018 persons, 3032 persons (2.68%) belong to Scheduled Tribes.

The villages having less than 10% ST population are Macherla, Degaon, Magdi, Fathepur, Pipri, Manthani Merdepalle, Alur, Gaggupalle, Rampur, Issapalle Armur, Ankapur, Mamidipalle, Perkit, Chepur Kotha Armur, Govindpet.

The villages having more than 50% ST population are None.

Sex ratio of Scheduled tribe population is 511.

Scheduled Tribes Literates and Illiterates by Sex:

	Persons	Males	Females
Literate	1,022	672	350
Illiterate	2,010	811	1,199
Literacy rate	39.5	54.2	26.0
Graduate	31	28	3

Scheduled Tribes (Dominant):

Gond etc., Sugalis etc., Yerukulas, Chenchu etc. Generic Tribes etc.

For their cultural identity please see Appendix-II

Villages without Scheduled Tribes: There are 2 villages without any scheduled tribe population.

Literates and Illiterates by Sex (Total Population):

	Persons	Males	Females
Literate	56,963	34,716	22,247
Illiterate	56,055	21,292	34,763
Literacy rate	58	72	45
Graduate	3,394	2,782	612

Agriculture: ***Distribution of villages according to land use:***

Out of 23 villages, Total area (in hectare) is 21008, out of that 73.58 percent is cultivable and 51.48 percent of the cultivable area is irrigated.

Sources of Irrigation (Hectares): Government Canal 2415.15, Private Canal 0, Well without Electricity 75.27, Well with Electricity 1765.64, Tubewell without Electricity 64.75, Tubewe with Electricity 1764.49, Tank 1301.85, River 0, Lake 0, Waterfall 0, Others 570.6.

Villages with population of 5000 to 9999:

Pipri, Alur, Ankapur, Mamidipalle, Perkit.

Villages with population of 10000 and above:

Armur.

Distribution of Workers:

	Persons	Males	Females	WPR
Cultivators	11,647	6,590	5,057	19.79
Agricultural Labour	12,938	6,781	6,157	21.99
Household Industry	15,843	1,970	13,873	26.92
Other Workers	18,416	14,788	3,628	31.3
Main Workers	54,005	28,508	25,497	91.78
Marginal Workers	4,839	1,621	3,218	8.22
Total Workers	58,844	30,129	28,715	

Religion: Major Religious Communities:

	Persons	Males	Females	Sex Ratio
Hindu (87.29%)	98,656	48,474	50,182	1,035
Muslim (11.52%)	13,022	6,642	6,380	961
Christian (0.71%)	797	390	407	1,044
Sikh (0.01%)	9	6	3	500
Buddhists (0%)	1	1	-	-
Jain (0%)	-	-	-	-

Agewise Data:

	Persons	Males	Females	Sex Ratio
All ages	113,018	56,008	57,010	1018
0-14	35,631	18,365	17,266	940
15-44	55,703	27,590	28,113	1019
45-79	20,977	9,781	11,196	1145
80+	604	205	399	1946
Age not stated	103	67	36	537

Languages (Dominant):

Telugu, Urdu, Others, Hindi, Marathi

Disabled Population:

	Persons	Males	Females	%
Total Disabled	1,763	967	796	
In Seeing	839	435	404	47.59
In Speech	161	89	72	9.13
In Hearing	77	31	46	4.37
In Movement	507	308	199	28.76

Mentally	179	104	75	10.15

ASIFABAD

Asifabad C.D. Block lies in the north-east part of Adilabad district. It is a part of Asifabad Mandal. The Block is located at a distance of 128 kms. from district headquarters (Adilabad). There are 60 villages in the block with the total population of 30,352 persons. Area of the C.D. Block is 300 sq. kms. It is bounded by Kerameri Mandal on north-west and north, Wankdi Mandal on north-east, Kagaznagar Mandal on north-east, Rebbana Mandal on north-east, east and south-east, Tiryani Mandal on south and south-west, Sirpur Mandal on west.

Communications :

Roadways : State Highway (S.H.): Direction- Rajura to Rebbana. Nearest Villages- Ippalnavegaon, Saleguda, Buruguda, Mothuguda, Appepalle.

River: Vatti Vagu: Nearest Villages- Ankusapur, Singar aopet, Chilatiguda, Chirrakunta, Padibonda, Danaboinapeta. Moaram Vagu Nadi- Nearest Villages- Nimbada, Kutoda, Babapur, Chilatiguda, Samela, Tumpalle, Dagleshwar, Kosara, Itukyal, Balegaon, Demmidiguda, Wavudham, Mankapur, Malan Gondi, Shakangondi, Ada – Dasnapur, Sirasgaon, Wadigondi, Mowad, Siryan Mowad, Balahanpur, Temrianmovad, Kowdianmovad, Suddha Ghat. Pedda Vagu- Nearest Villages- Danapur, Ippalnavegaon, Saleguda, Gudigudi, Govindapur, Gundi, Ada.

Backwards Region Grants Fund: It receives Backward Region Grants.

Mahila Samakhya (Education for Women's Equality): It is declared Socially and Educationally Backward Block by the Government.

Integrated Child Development Scheme (ICDS) Project: Asifabad (Tribal), Total Anganwadi Centres: 269

Annual Rainfall: Average Rainfall 1134 mm

Ground Water: Availability of the ground water in the Basin is 1880 H.A.M.and the utilization is 291 H.A. M. It belongs to Safe category. Depth to water level varies from 10 to 20 meter below the ground. Most of the wells go down in summer months, according to the Ground Water Estimation Committee.

Natural Division : Telangana Plateau Region

Administration:

Division: Telangana. Parliamentary Constituency: 1 Adilabad (ST). District: Adilabad. Mandal: Asifabad. Assembly Constituency: 5 Asifabad (ST). Gram Panchayat: 14

Villages: 60 **Inhabited:** 51 **Uninhabited:** 9

Ranking	District	State	National
Area	14	130	2614
Population	34	1020	6051
Sex Ratio	29	336	1389
Child Sex Ratio	11	168	450
Literacy Rate	50	1077	6105
Density	25	413	6162
Work Participation Rate	40	1065	1024

Gram Panchayats:

Ada, Ada Dasnapur, Asifabad, Babapur, Buruguda Chirrakunta, Edulawada, Gundi, Mowad, Rahapally Routsankepalle, Saleguda, Tumpalli, Yellaram.

Amenities:

Education: Primary School in 40 villages, Middle school in 6 villages, Matriculation or Secondary School in 1 village, namely Chirrakunta.

Higher Secondary or Pre University Courses or Intermediate or Junior College in 0 village of the CD Block, College in 0 village, Adult Literacy Center in 7 villages.

Medical: Hospital in 0 village, Dispensary in 1 village, Health Center in 1 village, Sub Center in 8 villages, Maternity and Child Welfare Center in 0 village, Community health workers in 0 village.

The Village having Hospital or Dispensary or Health Center is Chirrakunta.

Drinking Water: Tap water in 49 villages, Tank water in 49 villages, Well water in 50 villages, Tubewell in 49 villages and more than one source in 50 villages.

Bank: Banking facility in 1 villages, namely, Chirrakunta.

Credit Society in 3 villages Agricultural Credit Society in 1 Non-Agricultural Credit Society in 2 villages.

Others: Power supply in 51 villages, Cinema hall in 0 village, sport club in 0 village, Stadium or Auditorium or Community Hall in 0 village, Post Office in 11 villages.

There are 20 villages having bus facilities.

Village with most of facilities: Chirrakunta.

Villages without amenities (Education): Danapur, Kommuguda, Dagleshwar, Wadigondi, Siryan Mowad, Temrianmovad, Kowdianmovad, Suddha Ghat, Padibonda, Danaboinapeta, Mondepalle..

Scheduled Castes: Out of the total population of 30452 persons, 4252 persons (13.96%) belong to Scheduled Castes. The villages having less than 10% SC population are Wadiguda, Ada, Danapur, Ippalnavegaon, Nandupa Rajura, Kommuguda, Dadpapur, Khapri, Edulwada Chilatiguda, Samela, Dagleshwar, Kosara, Itukyal Balegaon, Demmidiguda, Wavudham, Mankapur, Kutoda Malan Gondi, Ada - Dasnapur, Wadigondi, Mowad Siryan Mowad, Temrianmovad, Kowdianmovad Suddha Ghat, Devadurgam, Padibonda, Danaboinapeta Mondepalle, Routsankepalle, Addaghat.

The villages having more than 50% SC population are None.

Sex ratio of Scheduled Caste population is 488.

Scheduled Castes Literates and Illiterates by Sex:

	Persons	Males	Females
Literate	1,609	1,083	526
Illiterate	2,643	1,095	1,548
Literacy rate	45.7	60.4	30.4
Graduate	25	25	0

Scheduled Castes (Dominant):

Mala, Madiga, Mahar, Mala Sale etc., Manne

For their cultural identity please see Appendix-I

Villages without Scheduled Castes: There are 34 villages without any scheduled caste population.

Scheduled Tribes: Out of the total population of 30452 persons, 7388 persons (24.26%) belong to Scheduled Tribes.

The villages having less than 10% ST population are Wadiguda, Danapur, Saleguda, Gundi, Cherpalle Nandupa, Rahapalle, Rajura, Yellaram, Kommuguda Ankusapur, Buruguda, Mothuguda, Appepalle, Kommuguda Edulwada, Singaraopet, Dagleshwar, Itukyal Perasnambal.

The villages having more than 50% ST population are Dadpapur, Khapri, Samela, Kosara, Wavudham, Mankapur Kutoda, Malan Gondi, Ada - Dasnapur, Wadigondi Mowad, Siryan Mowad, Balahanpur, Temrianmovad Kowdianmovad, Suddha Ghat, Devadurgam, Padibonda Danaboinapeta, Mondepalle, Routsankepalle, Addaghat.

Sex ratio of Scheduled tribe population is 506.

Scheduled Tribes Literates and Illiterates by Sex:

	Persons	Males	Females
Literate	1,457	993	464
Illiterate	5,931	2,659	3,272
Literacy rate	24.4	33.7	15.3
Graduate	10	10	0

Scheduled Tribes (Dominant):

Gond etc., Kolam etc., Sugalis etc., Pardhan Koya etc.

For their cultural identity please see Appendix-II

Villages without Scheduled Tribes: There are 22 villages without any scheduled tribe population.

Literates and Illiterates by Sex (Total Population):

	Persons	Males	Females
Literate	8,302	5,590	2,712
Illiterate	22,150	9,683	12,467
Literacy rate	33	45	22
Graduate	58	55	3

Agriculture: ***Distribution of villages according to land use:*** Out of 60 villages, Total area (in hectare) is 31596, out of that 50.47 percent is cultivable and 1.15 percent of the cultivable area is irrigated.

Sources of Irrigation (Hectares): Government Canal 136.8, Private Canal 0, Well without Electricity 0, Well with Electricity 1.2, Tubewell without Electricity 0, Tubewell with Electricity 0, Tank 38.47, River 0, Lake 0, Waterfall 0, Others 7.62.

Villages with population of 5000 to 9999: None

Villages with population of 10000 and above: None

Distribution of Workers:

	Persons	Males	Females	WPR
Cultivators	7,460	4,850	2,610	47.55
Agricultural Labour	5,055	1,827	3,228	32.22
Household Industry	713	352	361	4.54
Other Workers	2,462	1,781	681	15.69
Main Workers	11,896	7,782	4,114	75.82
Marginal Workers	3,794	1,028	2,766	24.18
Total Workers	15,690	8,810	6,880	

Religion: Major Religious Communities:

	Persons	Males	Females	Sex Ratio
Hindu (96.14%)	29,277	14,661	14,616	997
Muslim (1.82%)	553	292	261	894
Christian (0.03%)	8	2	6	3,000
Sikh (0.02%)	6	3	3	1,000
Buddhists (1.94%)	591	307	284	925
Jain (0%)	-	-	-	-

Agewise Data:

	Persons	Males	Females	Sex Ratio
All ages	30,452	15,273	15,179	994
0-14	11,867	5,958	5,909	992
15-44	13,290	6,713	6,577	980
45-79	5,090	2,496	2,594	1039
80+	183	91	92	1011
Age not stated	22	15	7	467

Languages (Dominant):

Marathi, Telugu, Gondi, Kolami, Hindi

Disabled Population:

	Persons	Males	Females	%
Total Disabled	569	296	273	
In Seeing	245	104	141	43.06
In Speech	65	34	31	11.42
In Hearing	23	11	12	4.04
In Movement	173	105	68	30.4
Mentally	63	42	21	11.07

ASPARI

Aspari C.D. Block lies in the western part of Kurnool district. The Block is located at a distance of 82 kms. from district headquarters (Kurnool). There are 20 villages in the block with the total population of 55,115 persons. Area of the C.D. Block is 429.69 sq. kms. It is bounded in the north by Mandals Yemmigan ur and Gonegandla, in the south by Mandals Alur and Pattikonda, in the east by Mandals Pattikonda and Devan akonda, and in the west by Mandals Alur and Adoni.

Communications:

Roadways : State Highways (S.H.): Direction- Alur to Kurnool. and Adoni to Pattikonda. Nearest Villages- Benigeri, Chiramandoddi, Chokkanahalli, Chinnahothur, Chigeli, Sankarabanda, Nagarur, Aspari, Muthkur, Bille kallu.

Railway Station: Nagarur, Aspari.

River: Handri Nadi- Nearest Villages- Muthkur, Chennam Vanka: Nearest Villages- Dudadudi Kotakonda, Karumanchi, Banavanur, Khyruppala, Yatakallu. Nallavagu Nadi- Nearest Villages- Khyruppala, Muthkur, Billekallu, Yatakallu.

It is identified as a drought-prone area.

Annual Rainfall: Average Rainfall 586 mm

Ground Water: Availability of the Ground Water in the Basin is 2585 H.A.M. and the utilization is 919 H.A. M. It belongs to Safe category. Depth to water level varies from 5 to 10 meter below the ground. Most of the wells go down in summer months. The well density in the entire block is 2 wells per sq. km. Total no. of the wells in the block are enumerated as 883, accor ding to the Ground Water Estimation Committee.

Forest and Reserved **Forest:** Nearest Villages- Mulugundam, Dudadudi Kotakonda, Karumanchi.

Natural Division : Rayalaseema Region

Administration:

Division: Rayala Seema. Parliamentary Constituency: 35 Kurnool. District: Kurnool. Mandal: Aspari. Assembly Constituency: 266 Alur. Gram Panchayat: 19.

Villages: 20 **Inhabited:** 20 **Uninhabited:** 0

Ranking	District	State	National
Area	3	24	1768
Population	19	368	5048
Sex Ratio	22	797	2673
Child Sex Ratio	50	998	4578
Literacy Rate	41	983	5615
Density	16	106	5858
Work Participation Rate	49	978	337

Gram Panchayats:

Aspari, Banavanur, Billekallu, Chigili, Chinnahothur Chiramandoddi, D. Kotakonda, Haligera, Joharapuram Karumanchi, Khyruppala, Mulugundam, Muthukur Nagarur, Putakalamarri, Sankarabanda, Tangaradona Thogalagallu, Yatakallu.

Amenities:

Education: Primary School in 20 villages, Middle school in 11 villages, Matriculation or Secondary School in 5 villages, namely Karumanchi, Nagarur, Chinnahothur, Aspari, Joharapuram.

Higher Secondary or Pre University Courses or Intermediate or Junior College in 0 village of the CD Block, College in 0 village, Adult Literacy Center in 20 villages.

Medical: Hospital in 0 village, Dispensary in 0 village, Health Center in 1 village, Sub Center in 11 villages, Maternity and Child Welfare Center in 0 village, Community health workers in 0 village.

Drinking Water: Tap water in 20 villages, Tank water in 20 villages, Well water in 20 villages, Tubewell in 20 villages and more than one source in 20 villages.

Bank: Banking facility in 2 villages, namely, Khyruppala, Aspari.

Credit Society in 11 villages Agricultural Credit Society in 3 Non-Agricultural Credit Society in 11 villages.

Others: Power supply in 20 villages, Cinema hall in 2 villages, sport club in 0 village, Stadium or Auditorium or Community Hall in 0 village, Post Office in 20 villages.

There are 16 villages having bus facilities.

Villages with most of facilities: Khyruppala Aspari.

Villages without Amenities (Education): None..

Scheduled Castes: Out of the total population of 55115 persons, 10758 persons (19.52%) belong to Scheduled Castes.

The villages having less than 10% SC population are None..

The villages having more than 50% SC population are None.

Sex ratio of Scheduled Caste population is 494.

Scheduled Castes Literates and Illiterates by Sex:

	Persons	Males	Females
Literate	3,429	2,458	971
Illiterate	7,329	2,988	4,341
Literacy rate	39.7	56.1	22.8
Graduate	71	58	13

Scheduled Castes (Dominant):

Madiga, Mala, Mala Dasari, Bariki Generic Castes etc.

For their cultural identity please see Appendix-I

Villages without Scheduled Castes: There is 1 village without any scheduled caste population.

Scheduled Tribes: Out of the total population of 55115 persons, 276 persons (0.5%) belong to Scheduled Tribes.

The villages having less than 10% ST population are Mulugundam, Dudadudi Kotakonda, Karumanchi Banavanur, Khyruppala, Muthkur, Billekallu Yatakallu, Thurvagal, Tangaradona, Haligera Benigeri, Nagarur, Chinnahothur, Chigeli Chiramandoddi, Sankarabanda, Chokkanahalli, Aspari

Joharapuram.

The villages having more than 50% ST population are None.

Sex ratio of Scheduled tribe population is 486.

Scheduled Tribes Literates and Illiterates by Sex:

	Persons	Males	Females
Literate	82	52	30
Illiterate	194	90	104
Literacy rate	37.6	47.3	27.8
Graduate	3	2	1

Scheduled Tribes (Dominant):

Yerukulas, Koya etc., Sugalis etc.

For their cultural identity please see Appendix-II

Villages without Scheduled Tribes: There are 9 villages without any scheduled tribe population.

Literates and Illiterates by Sex (Total Population):

	Persons	Males	Females
Literate	18,775	13,225	5,550
Illiterate	36,340	14,802	21,538
Literacy rate	41	57	25
Graduate	381	334	47

Agriculture: ***Distribution of villages according to land use:*** Out of 20 villages, Total area (in hectare) is 42968, out of that 84.92 percent is cultivable and 4.7 percent of the cultivable area is irrigated.

Sources of Irrigation (Hectares): Government Canal 0, Private Canal 0, Well without Electricity 0, Well with Electricity 701, Tubewell without Electricity 0, Tubewell with Electricity 856, Tank 157, River 0, Lake 0, Waterfall 0, Others 0.

Villages with population of 5000 to 9999: Aspari.

Villages with population of 10000 and above: None

Distribution of Workers:

	Persons	Males	Females	WPR
Cultivators	13,065	8,304	4,761	42.82
Agricultural Labour	14,569	5,514	9,055	47.75
Household Industry	360	227	133	1.18
Other Workers	2,518	1,860	658	8.25
Main Workers	25,107	14,591	10,516	82.29
Marginal Workers	5,405	1,314	4,091	17.71
Total Workers	30,512	15,905	14,607	

Religion: Major Religious Communities:

	Persons	Males	Females	Sex Ratio
Hindu (95.88%)	52,847	26,876	25,971	966
Muslim (4.03%)	2,222	1,129	1,093	968
Christian (0.05%)	28	12	16	1,333
Sikh (0%)	1	1	-	-
Buddhists (0%)	-	-	-	-
Jain (0.02%)	12	7	5	714

Agewise Data:

	Persons	Males	Females	Sex Ratio
All ages	55,115	28,027	27,088	966
0-14	22,829	11,823	11,006	931
15-44	23,078	11,922	11,156	936
45-79	8,844	4,128	4,716	1142
80+	303	124	179	1444
Age not stated	61	30	31	1033

Languages (Dominant):

Telugu, Urdu, Kannada, Marathi, Hindi

Disabled Population:

	Persons	Males	Females	%
Total Disabled	933	504	429	
In Seeing	283	138	145	30.33
In Speech	87	45	42	9.32
In Hearing	84	40	44	9
In Movement	390	237	153	41.8
Mentally	89	44	45	9.54

ASWAPURAM

Aswapuram C.D. Block lies in the northern part of Khamm am district. The Block is located at a distance of 140 kms. from district headquarters (Khammam). There are 11 villages in the block with the total population of 38,575 persons. Area of the C.D. Block is 328.44 sq. kms. It is bounded in the north by Mandals Manuguru and Dummugudem, in the south by Mandals Palwancha and Burgampahad, in the east by Mandals Dummugudem and Burgampahad, and in the west by Manuguru Mandal.

Communications:

Roadways : NH, SH or Important Metalled Road is not available.

River: Godavari Nadi- Nearest Villages- Kummarigudem, Amerla, Kesavapuram, Pamulapalle, Ammagaripalle, Chint riyala, Nellipaka.

Backwards Region Grants Fund: It receives Backward Region Grants.

Annual Rainfall: Average Rainfall 1141 mm

Ground Water: Availability of the Ground Water in the Basin is 2255 H.A.M.and the utilization is 119 H.A. M. It belongs to safe category. Depth to water level varies from 5 to 10 meter below the ground. Most of the wells go down in summer months. The well density in the entire block is 1 well per sq. km. Total no. of the wells in the block are enumerated as 288, accor ding to the Ground Water Estimation Committee.

Natural Division : Godavari Depression Region

Administration:

Division: Telangana. Parliamentary Constituency : 16 Mahbubabad . District: Khammam. Mandal: Aswapuram. Assembly Constituency: 110 Pinapaka (ST). Gram Panchaya t: 13.

Villages: 11 **Inhabited:** 10 **Uninhabited:** 1

Ranking	District	State	National
Area	10	106	2476
Population	29	866	5796
Sex Ratio	40	946	3252
Child Sex Ratio	45	858	3786
Literacy Rate	5	314	3021
Density	42	851	5987
Work Participation Rate	38	1014	2722

Gram Panchayats:
Amerda, Ammagaripalli, Anandapuram, Aswapuram Chin.riyala, Gollagudem, Gondigudem, Jaggaram Mallelamadugu, Mittagudem, Mondikunta, Nellipaka Thummalacheruvu.

Amenities:

Education: Primary School in 10 villages, Middle school in 4 villages, Matriculation or Secondary School in 3 villages, namely Aswapuram, Gandigudem, Nellipaka.

Higher Secondary or Pre University Courses or Intermediate or Junior College in 1 village of the CD Block,, namely Aswapuram.

College in 0 village, Adult Literacy Center in 10 villages.

Medical: Hospital in 0 village, Dispensary in 1 village, Health Center in 1 village, Sub Center in 7 villages, Maternity and Child Welfare Center in 0 village, Community health workers in 0 village.

The Village having Hospital or Dispensary or Health Center is Aswapuram.

Drinking Water: Tap water in 10 villages, Tank water in 10 villages, Well water in 10 villages, Tubewell in 10 villages and more than one source in 10 villages.

Bank: Banking facility in 2 villages, namely, Aswapuram, Nellipaka.

Credit Society in 4 villages Agricultural Credit Society in 3 Non-Agricultural Credit Society in 4 villages.

Others: Power supply in 10 villages, Cinema hall in 1 village, sport club in 0 village, Stadium or Auditorium or Community Hall in 0 village, Post Office in 5 villages.

There are 3 villages having bus facilities.

Villages with most of facilities: Aswapuram Nellipaka.

Villages without Amenities (Education): None..

Scheduled Castes: Out of the total population of 38643 persons, 4842 persons (12.53%) belong to Scheduled Castes.

The villages having less than 10% SC population are Kummarigudem, Ammagaripalle, Gandigudem, Mamillavai Thummalacheruvu.

The villages having more than 50% SC population are None.

Sex ratio of Scheduled Caste population is 496.

Scheduled Castes Literates and Illiterates by Sex:

	Persons	Males	Females
Literate	2,329	1,383	946
Illiterate	2,513	1,055	1,458
Literacy rate	56.3	66.0	46.4
Graduate	77	52	25

Scheduled Castes (Dominant):
Madiga, Mala, Beda Jangam etc., Adi Andhra Adi Dravida

For their cultural identity please see Appendix-I

Villages without Scheduled Castes: There are 2 villages without any scheduled caste population.

Scheduled Tribes: Out of the total population of 38643 persons, 12098 persons (31.31%) belong to Scheduled Tribes.

The villages having less than 10% ST population are None..

The villages having more than 50% ST population are Pamulapalle, Kummarigudem, Amerla, Gandigudem Mamillavai, Thummalacheruvu.

Sex ratio of Scheduled tribe population is 490.

Scheduled Tribes Literates and Illiterates by Sex:

	Persons	Males	Females
Literate	3,898	2,547	1,351
Illiterate	8,200	3,621	4,579
Literacy rate	38.4	49.2	27.2
Graduate	30	25	5

Scheduled Tribes (Dominant):
Koya etc., Sugalis etc., Yerukulas, Nayaks Konda Dhoras

For their cultural identity please see Appendix-II

Villages without Scheduled Tribes: There is 1 village without any scheduled tribe population.

Literates and Illiterates by Sex (Total Population):

	Persons	Males	Females
Literate	19,471	11,513	7,958
Illiterate	19,172	8,249	10,923
Literacy rate	59	68	49
Graduate	1,204	777	427

Agriculture: ***Distribution of villages according to land use:***
Out of 11 villages, Total area (in hectare) is 32843, out of that 23.07 percent is cultivable and 36.68 percent of the cultivable area is irrigated.

Sources of Irrigation (Hectares): Government Canal 0, Private Canal 0, Well without Electricity 68.39, Well with Electricity 0, Tubewell without Electricity 0, Tubewell with Electricity 131.52, Tank 2010.07, River 227.83, Lake 0, Waterfall 0, Others 341.15.

Villages with population of 5000 to 9999:
Nellipaka.

Villages with population of 10000 and above:

Aswapuram.

Distribution of Workers:

	Persons	Males	Females	WPR
Cultivators	3,573	2,808	765	19.48
Agricultural Labour	9,589	4,310	5,279	52.27
Household Industry	327	222	105	1.78
Other Workers	4,855	4,020	835	26.47
Main Workers	15,955	10,629	5,326	86.98
Marginal Workers	2,389	731	1,658	13.02
Total Workers	18,344	11,360	6,984	

Religion: Major Religious Communities:

	Persons	Males	Females	Sex Ratio
Hindu (94.33%)	36,451	18,633	17,818	956
Muslim (3.98%)	1,537	787	750	953
Christian (1.63%)	628	328	300	915
Sikh (0.03%)	12	7	5	714
Buddhists (0.01%)	4	1	3	3,000
Jain (0.01%)	4	2	2	1,000

Agewise Data:

	Persons	Males	Females	Sex Ratio
All ages	38,643	19,762	18,881	955
0-14	13,186	6,875	6,311	918
15-44	18,751	9,478	9,273	978
45-79	6,368	3,244	3,124	963
80+	272	128	144	1125
Age not stated	66	37	29	784

Languages (Dominant):

Telugu, Koya, Hindi, Urdu, Tamil

Disabled Population:

	Persons	Males	Females	%
Total Disabled	1,225	675	550	
In Seeing	690	394	296	56.33
In Speech	90	45	45	7.35
In Hearing	47	27	20	3.84
In Movement	321	166	155	26.2
Mentally	77	43	34	6.29

ASWARAOPETA

Aswaraopeta C.D. Block lies in the south-eastern part of Khammam district. The Block is located at a distance of 170 kms. from district headquarters (Khammam). There are 20 villages in the block with the total population of 51,756 persons. Area of the C.D. Block is 510.25 sq. kms. It is bounded in the north by Mandals Kukunoor and Velairpadu, in the south by Mandal Dammapeta and district West Godavari, in the east by district West Godavari, and in the west by Mandal Dammapeta.

Communications:

Roadways : State Highway (S.H.): Direction- Khammam to Rajahmundry. Nearest Villages- Achuthapuram, Naramuv arigudem, Aswaraopeta.

Integrated Child Development Scheme (ICDS) Project: Aswaraopet (Tribal), Total Anganwadi Centres: 300

Annual Rainfall: Average Rainfall 1163 mm

Ground Water: Availability of the Ground Water in the Basin is 6781 H.A.M.and the utilization is 1582 H.A. M. It belongs to safe category. Depth to water level varies from 5 to 10 meter below the ground. Most of the wells go down in summer months. The well density in the entire block is 1 well per sq. km. Total no. of the wells in the block are enumerated as 635, accor ding to the Ground Water Estimation Committee.

Natural Division : Godavari Depression Region

Administration:

Division: Telangana. Parliamentary Constituency: 17 Khammam. District: Khammam. Mandal: Aswaraopeta. Assemb ly Constituency: 118 Aswaraopeta (ST). Gram Panchayat: 16

Villages: 20 **Inhabited:** 19 **Uninhabited:** 1

Ranking	District	State	National
Area	3	7	1462
Population	16	458	5193
Sex Ratio	11	322	1396
Child Sex Ratio	1	10	51
Literacy Rate	21	642	4361
Density	34	609	6124
Work Participation Rate	42	1053	1639

Gram Panchayats:

Achuthapuram, Anantharam, Asupaka, Aswaraopeta Bachuvarigudem, Gummadavalli, Jammigudem Kannaigudem, Kavidigundla, Kotha Mamillavari Gudem Nandipadu, Naramvarigudem, Narayana Puram Ootlapalli, Peraigudem, Tirumalakunta.

Amenities:

Education: Primary School in 18 villages, Middle school in 6 villages, Matriculation or Secondary School in 3 villages, namely Tirumalakunta, Narayanapuram, Aswaraopeta. Higher Secondary or Pre University Courses or Intermediate or Junior College in 1 village of the CD Block,, namely Aswaraopeta.

College in 1 village, Adult Literacy Center in 17 villages., College is in village, namely Aswaraopeta.

Medical: Hospital in 0 village, Dispensary in 1 village, Health Center in 1 village, Sub Center in 10 villages, Maternity and Child Welfare Center in 0 village, Community health workers in 0 village.

The Village having Hospital or Dispensary or Health Center is Tirumalakunta.

Drinking Water: Tap water in 19 villages, Tank water in 19 villages, Well water in 19 villages, Tubewell in 19 villages and more than one source in 19 villages.

Bank: Banking facility in 3 villages, namely,

Narayanapuram, Asupaka, Aswaraopeta.
Credit Society in 17 villages Agricultural Credit Society in 2 Non-Agricultural Credit Society in 17 villages.

Others: Power supply in 19 villages, Cinema hall in 1 village, sport club in 0 village, Stadium or Auditorium or Community Hall in 0 village, Post Office in 7 villages.

There are 16 villages having bus facilities.

Villages with most of facilities: Narayanapuram Asupaka, Aswaraopeta.

Villages without Amenities (Education): None..

Scheduled Castes: Out of the total population of 51756 persons, 5376 persons (10.39%) belong to Scheduled Castes.
The villages having less than 10% SC population are Tirumalakunta, Durdapadu, Nandipadu, Gummadavalli Bachuvarigudem, Kavidigundla, Kannaigudem Anantharam, Khammampad, Guntimadugu, Ramannagudem Vedanthapuram, Jammigudem, Maddikonda Naramuvarigudem.
The villages having more than 50% SC population are None.
Sex ratio of Scheduled Caste population is 499.

Scheduled Castes Literates and Illiterates by Sex:

	Persons	Males	Females
Literate	2,225	1,226	999
Illiterate	3,151	1,469	1,682
Literacy rate	48.9	53.4	44.2
Graduate	78	53	25

Scheduled Castes (Dominant):
Madiga, Mala, Generic Castes etc., Mala Dasari Beda Jangam etc.

For their cultural identity please see Appendix-I

Villages without Scheduled Castes: There are 6 villages without any scheduled caste population.

Scheduled Tribes: Out of the total population of 51756 persons, 19688 persons (38.04%) belong to Scheduled Tribes.
The villages having less than 10% ST population are None..
The villages having more than 50% ST population are Durdapadu, Nandipadu, Bachuvarigudem, Kavidigundla Kannaigudem, Anantharam, Khammampad, Guntimadugu Ramannagudem, Vedanthapuram, Jammigudem, Maddikonda.
Sex ratio of Scheduled tribe population is 508.

Scheduled Tribes Literates and Illiterates by Sex:

	Persons	Males	Females
Literate	5,326	3,014	2,312
Illiterate	14,362	6,678	7,684
Literacy rate	32.6	37.4	28.0
Graduate	60	53	7

Scheduled Tribes (Dominant):
Koya etc., Gond etc., Sugalis etc., Nayaks Kondareddis

For their cultural identity please see Appendix-II

Villages without Scheduled Tribes: There is 1 village without any scheduled tribe population.

Literates and Illiterates by Sex (Total Population):

	Persons	Males	Females
Literate	22,494	12,629	9,865
Illiterate	29,262	13,327	15,935
Literacy rate	51	57	45
Graduate	871	675	196

Agriculture: ***Distribution of villages according to land use:***
Out of 20 villages, Total area (in hectare) is 51025, out of that 22.88 percent is cultivable and 40.07 percent of the cultivable area is irrigated.

Sources of Irrigation (Hectares): Government Canal 290.88, Private Canal 0, Well without Electricity 0, Well with Electricity 223, Tubewell without Electricity 0, Tubewell with Electricity 2812.18, Tank 1283.39, River 0, Lake 0, Waterfall 0, Others 69.08.

Villages with population of 5000 to 9999: None

Villages with population of 10000 and above: Aswaraopeta.

Distribution of Workers:

	Persons	Males	Females	WPR
Cultivators	7,025	4,925	2,100	26.6
Agricultural Labour	13,553	6,627	6,926	51.32
Household Industry	481	264	217	1.82
Other Workers	5,352	4,215	1,137	20.26
Main Workers	21,645	14,101	7,544	81.95
Marginal Workers	4,766	1,930	2,836	18.05
Total Workers	26,411	16,031	10,380	

Religion: Major Religious Communities:

	Persons	Males	Females	Sex Ratio
Hindu (94.02%)	48,663	24,402	24,261	994
Muslim (4.31%)	2,231	1,120	1,111	992
Christian (1.51%)	779	383	396	1,034
Sikh (0%)	2	2	-	-
Buddhists (0%)	-	-	-	-
Jain (0%)	-	-	-	-

Agewise Data:

	Persons	Males	Females	Sex Ratio
All ages	51,756	25,956	25,800	994
0-14	18,236	9,008	9,228	1024
15-44	25,645	12,913	12,732	986
45-79	7,499	3,867	3,632	939
80+	269	117	152	1299
Age not stated	107	51	56	1098

Languages (Dominant):
Telugu, Koya, Hindi, Urdu, Tamil

Disabled Population:

	Persons	Males	Females	%
Total Disabled	1,100	647	453	
In Seeing	535	304	231	48.64
In Speech	99	55	44	9
In Hearing	43	22	21	3.91
In Movement	277	177	100	25.18
Mentally	146	89	57	13.27

ATCHAMPET

Atchampet C.D. Block lies in the northern part of Guntur district. The Block is located at a distance of 43 kms. from district headquarters (Guntur). There are 18 villages in the block with the total population of 55,722 persons. Area of the C.D. Block is 191.17 sq. kms. It is bounded in the north by district Krishna, in the south by Mandals Krosuru and Amravathi, in the east by district Krishna and Mandal Amravathi, and in the west by Mandal Bellamkonda and district Nalgonda.

Communications:

Roadways : Metalled Roads: Nearest Villages- Madipadu Seri, Ginjupalle, Challagariga, Taduvoy, Chintapalle, Chamarru, Kogantivaripalem, Chigurupadu, Velpuru, Orvakallu.

River: Krishna Nadi- Nearest Villages- Madipadu Agrahar am, Madipadu Seri, Ginjupalle, Challagariga, Taduvoy, Chintapalle, Tallacheruvu, Kogantivaripalem, Ambadipudi, Konuru, Kastala Agraharam.

Annual Rainfall: Average Rainfall 818 mm

Ground Water: Availability of the Ground Water in the Basin is 5445 H.A.M. and the utilization is 724 H.A. M. It belongs to Safe category. Depth to water level varies from 2 to 5 meter below the ground. Most of the wells go down in summer months.

Natural Division : Krishna Delta Region

Administration:

Division: Coastal Andhra. Parliamentary Constituency: 31 Narsaraopet. District: Guntur.

Mandal: Atchampet. Assembly Constituency: 204 Pedakurap adu. Gram Panchayat: 19.

Villages: 18 **Inhabited:** 18 **Uninhabited:** 0

Ranking	District	State	National
Area	18	606	4335
Population	27	350	5020
Sex Ratio	51	852	2872
Child Sex Ratio	35	673	2723
Literacy Rate	49	769	4789
Density	4	47	3621
Work Participation Rate	38	391	200

Gram Panchayats:

Ambadipudi, Atchempet, Bangaru Thanda, Challagariga Chigurupadu, Chintapalli, Grandhasiri, Kastala Kogantivaripalem, Konduru, Konuru, Madipadu Mittapalem, Neeleswara Palem, Orvakallu, Pedapalem Rudravaram, Thallacheruvu, Velpuru.

Amenities:

Education: Primary School in 18 villages, Middle school in 7 villages, Matriculation or Secondary School in 3 villages, namely Tallacheruvu, Chamarru, Velpuru.

Higher Secondary or Pre University Courses or Intermediate or Junior College in 1 village of the CD Block,, namely Chamarru.

College in 0 village, Adult Literacy Center in 16 villages.

Medical: Hospital in 1 village, Dispensary in 0 village, Health Center in 1 village, Sub Center in 9 villages, Maternity and Child Welfare Center in 0 village, Community health workers in 0 village.

The Village having Hospital or Dispensary or Health Center is Chigurupadu.

Drinking Water: Tap water in 16 villages, Tank water in 16 villages, Well water in 17 villages, Tubewell in 16 villages and more than one source in 16 villages.

Bank: Banking facility in 3 villages, namely, Tallacheruvu, Chamarru, Pedapalem.

Credit Society in 6 villages Agricultural Credit Society in 4 Non-Agricultural Credit Society in 0 village.

Others: Power supply in 18 villages, Cinema hall in 0 village, sport club in 0 village, Stadium or Auditorium or Community Hall in 0 village, Post Office in 15 villages.

There are 17 villages having bus facilities.

Villages with most of facilities: Tallacheruvu Chamarru, Pedapalem.

Villages without Amenities (Education): None..

Scheduled Castes: Out of the total population of 55722 persons, 12539 persons (22.5%) belong to Scheduled Castes.

The villages having less than 10% SC population are None..

The villages having more than 50% SC population are None.

Sex ratio of Scheduled Caste population is 471.

Scheduled Castes Literates and Illiterates by Sex:

	Persons	Males	Females
Literate	4,499	3,080	1,419
Illiterate	8,040	3,559	4,481
Literacy rate	42.4	54.6	28.5
Graduate	121	96	25

Scheduled Castes (Dominant):

Madiga, Mala, Generic Castes etc.

For their cultural identity please see Appendix-I

Villages without Scheduled Castes: There are 0 village without any scheduled caste population.

Scheduled Tribes: Out of the total population of 55722 persons, 4874 persons (8.75%) belong to Scheduled Tribes. The villages having less than 10% ST population are Madipadu Agraharam, Challagariga, Chintapalle Tallacheruvu, Kogantivaripalem, Chigurupadu Pedapalem, Konduru, Mittapalem, Velpuru, Orvakallu Ambadipudi, Konuru, Kastala Agraharam.

The villages having more than 50% ST population are None.

Sex ratio of Scheduled tribe population is 487.

Scheduled Tribes Literates and Illiterates by Sex:

	Persons	Males	Females
Literate	1,334	951	383
Illiterate	3,540	1,549	1,991
Literacy rate	33.1	45.8	19.6
Graduate	19	18	1

Scheduled Tribes (Dominant):

Sugalis etc., Yerukulas, Yenadis, Chenchu etc.

Generic Tribes etc.

For their cultural identity please see Appendix-II

Villages without Scheduled Tribes: There are 2 villages without any scheduled tribe population.

Literates and Illiterates by Sex (Total Population):

	Persons	Males	Females
Literate	23,128	14,389	8,739
Illiterate	32,594	14,017	18,577
Literacy rate	48	59	37
Graduate	719	551	168

Agriculture: ***Distribution of villages according to land use:*** Out of 18 villages, Total area (in hectare) is 19117, out of that 55.22 percent is cultivable and 16.41 percent of the cultivable area is irrigated.

Sources of Irrigation (Hectares): Government Canal 1067, Private Canal 0, Well without Electricity 4, Well with Electricity 21, Tubewell without Electricity 0, Tubewell with Electricity 70, Tank 400, River 14, Lake 0, Waterfall 0, Others 156.

Villages with population of 5000 to 9999: Tallacheruvu, Velpuru, Orvakallu.

Villages with population of 10000 and above: Chamarru.

Distribution of Workers:

	Persons	Males	Females	WPR
Cultivators	7,264	4,690	2,574	22.07
Agricultural Labour	22,578	10,259	12,319	68.59
Household Industry	375	197	178	1.14
Other Workers	2,699	2,139	560	8.2
Main Workers	28,256	15,434	12,822	85.84
Marginal Workers	4,660	1,851	2,809	14.16
Total Workers	32,916	17,285	15,631	

Religion: Major Religious Communities:

	Persons	Males	Females	Sex Ratio
Hindu (89.21%)	49,711	25,379	24,332	959
Muslim (6.4%)	3,566	1,778	1,788	1,006
Christian (4.09%)	2,281	1,169	1,112	951
Sikh (0%)	1	1	-	-
Buddhists (0.01%)	3	-	3	-
Jain (0%)	-	-	-	-

Agewise Data:

	Persons	Males	Females	Sex Ratio
All ages	55,722	28,406	27,316	962
0-14	19,086	9,889	9,197	930
15-44	25,867	13,134	12,733	969
45-79	10,112	5,086	5,026	988
80+	490	214	276	1290
Age not stated	167	83	84	1012

Languages (Dominant):

Telugu, Urdu, Hindi, Tamil, Gondi

Disabled Population:

	Persons	Males	Females	%
Total Disabled	1,070	621	449	
In Seeing	477	291	186	44.58
In Speech	100	52	48	9.35
In Hearing	72	36	36	6.73
In Movement	325	196	129	30.37
Mentally	96	46	50	8.97

ATCHUTAPURAM

Atchuthapuram C.D. Block lies in the southern part of Vishakhapatnam district. The Block is located at a distance of 53 kms. from district headquarters (Visha khapatnam). There are 34 villages in the block with the total population of 58,898 persons. Area of the C.D. Block is 144.70 sq. kms. It is bounded in the north by Mandals Kasimkota, Munagapaka and Paravada, in the south by Mandal Rambilli and the Bay of Bengal, in the east by Mandal Paravada, and in the west by Mandals Yelamanchili and Rambilli.

Communications :

Roadways : Metalled Roads: Nearest Villages- Yerravaram, Thimmarajupeta, Haripalem, Kondakarla, Chodapalle, Veduruvada, Duppituru.

Backwards Region Grants Fund: It receives Backward Region Grants.

Annaul Rainfall: Average Rainfall 975.0 mm

Ground Water: Availability of the Ground Water in the Basin is (Information not avavible) H.A.M .and the utilization is (Information not avavible) H.A.M. It belongs to (Information not avavible) category. Depth to water level varies from 3 to 10 meter below the ground. Most of the wells go down in summer months.

Administration:

Division: Coastal Andhra. Parliamentary Constituency: 22 Anakapalle. District: Visakhapatnam. Mandal: Atchuta puram. Assembly Constituency: 151 Yelamanchili. Gram Panchayat: 27.

Villages: 34 **Inhabited:** 33 **Uninhabited:** 1

Ranking	District	State	National
Area	26	848	5124
Population	16	290	4892
Sex Ratio	24	429	1671
Child Sex Ratio	35	651	2610
Literacy Rate	16	756	4743
Density	27	911	2697
Work Participation Rate	11	181	3153

Gram Panchayats:
Atchuthapuram, Bhogapuram, Cheemalapalli, Chippada Chodapalli, Dibbapalem, Dopperla, Dosuru, Duppituru Haripalem, Iruvada, Jaggannapeta, Janguluru Khajipalem, Kondakarla, Maduthuru, Maruturu Melupakajagannadhapuram, Nunaparthi, Pedapadu Pudimadaka, Somavaram, Tantadi, Thimmarajupeta Uppavaram, Veduruvada, Yerravaram.

Amenities:

Education: Primary School in 32 villages, Middle school in 12 villages, Matriculation or Secondary School in 9 villages, namely Melupaka Jagannadhapuram, Haripalem, Kondakarla, Andalapalle, Dosuru, Maduthuru, Chodapalle, Duppituru, Pudimadaka.

Higher Secondary or Pre University Courses or Intermediate or Junior College in 0 village of the CD Block, College in 0 village, Adult Literacy Center in 11 villages.

Medical: Hospital in 0 village, Dispensary in 1 village, Health Center in 11 villages, Sub Center in 12 villages, Maternity and Child Welfare Center in 0 village, Community health workers in 0 village.

The Village having Hospital or Dispensary or Health Center is Kondakarla.

Drinking Water: Tap water in 33 villages, Tank water in 33 villages, Well water in 33 villages, Tubewell in 33 villages and more than one source in 33 villages.

Bank: Banking facility in 2 villages, namely, Duppituru, Pudimadaka.

Credit Society in 4 villages Agricultural Credit Society in 4 Non-Agricultural Credit Society in 0 village.

Others: Power supply in 33 villages, Cinema hall in 2 villages, sport club in 0 village, Stadium or Auditorium or Community Hall in 0 village, Post Office in 18 villages.

There are 23 villages having bus facilities.

Villages with most of facilities: Duppituru Pudimadaka.

Villages without amenities (Education): Gangamambapura Agraharam..

Scheduled Castes: Out of the total population of 58899 persons, 3487 persons (5.92%) belong to Scheduled Castes.

The villages having less than 10% SC population are Melupaka Jagannadhapuram, Uppavaram, Yerravaram Khajipalem, Thimmarajupeta, Andalapalle Cheemalapalle, Somavaram, Jagannadhapura Agraharam Dopperla, Iravada, Gangamambapura Agraharam Nunaparthi, Nadimpalle, Ravipalem, Janguluru Bhogapuram, Chodapalle, Veduruvada, Duppituru Uddlapalem, Pudimadaka, Chippada, Jogannapalem Tantadi.

The villages having more than 50% SC population are None.

Sex ratio of Scheduled Caste population is 490.

Scheduled Castes Literates and Illiterates by Sex:

	Persons	Males	Females
Literate	1,597	978	619
Illiterate	1,890	802	1,088
Literacy rate	52.7	63.5	41.5
Graduate	29	21	8

Scheduled Castes (Dominant):
Mala, Madiga, Relli, Beda Jangam etc.
Generic Castes etc.

For their cultural identity please see Appendix-I

Villages without Scheduled Castes: There are 4 villages without any scheduled caste population.

Scheduled Tribes: Out of the total population of 58899 persons, 70 persons (0.12%) belong to Scheduled Tribes.

The villages having less than 10% ST population are Melupaka Jagannadhapuram, Uppavaram, Yerravaram Jaggannapeta, Khajipalem, Pedapadu, Thimmarajupeta Haripalem, Kondakarla, Andalapalle, Cheemalapalle Somavaram, Jagannadhapura Agraharam, Dopperla Iravada, Gangamambapura Agraharam, Nunaparthi Nadimpalle, Ravipalem, Dosuru, Maduthuru, Janguluru Bhogapuram, Chodapalle, Veduruvada, Dibbapalem Maruturu, Duppituru, Uddlapalem, Pudimadaka Chippada, Jogannapalem, Tantadi.

The villages having more than 50% ST population are None.

Sex ratio of Scheduled tribe population is 457.

Scheduled Tribes Literates and Illiterates by Sex:

	Persons	Males	Females
Literate	33	19	14
Illiterate	37	19	18
Literacy rate	54.1	63.3	45.2
Graduate	1	1	0

Scheduled Tribes (Dominant):
Yerukulas, Chenchu etc., Bagata, Generic Tribes etc.

Konda Kapus

For their cultural identity please see Appendix-II

Villages without Scheduled Tribes: There are 27 villages without any scheduled tribe population.

Literates and Illiterates by Sex (Total Population):

	Persons	Males	Females
Literate	24,810	15,200	9,610
Illiterate	34,089	14,421	19,668
Literacy rate	49	59	38
Graduate	488	391	97

Agriculture: ***Distribution of villages according to land use:*** Out of 34 villages, Total area (in hectare) is 14473, out of that 70.42 percent is cultivable and 22.13 percent of the cultivable area is irrigated.

Sources of Irrigation (Hectares): Government Canal 1269.37, Private Canal 0, Well without Electricity 0, Well with Electricity 0, Tubewell without Electricity 0, Tubewell with Electricity 0, Tank 985.6, River 0, Lake 0, Waterfall 0, Others 0.

Villages with population of 5000 to 9999: Pudimadaka.

Villages with population of 10000 and above: None

Distribution of Workers:

	Persons	Males	Females	WPR
Cultivators	9,708	6,206	3,502	35.82
Agricultural Labour	8,362	4,242	4,120	30.86
Household Industry	1,013	657	356	3.74
Other Workers	8,016	6,251	1,765	29.58
Main Workers	22,370	15,949	6,421	82.55
Marginal Workers	4,729	1,407	3,322	17.45
Total Workers	27,099	17,356	9,743	

Religion: Major Religious Communities:

	Persons	Males	Females	Sex Ratio
Hindu (99.11%)	58,372	29,360	29,012	988
Muslim (0.44%)	258	129	129	1,000
Christian (0.33%)	195	91	104	1,143
Sikh (0.02%)	13	9	4	444
Buddhists (0.03%)	18	8	10	1,250
Jain (0%)	-	-	-	-

Agewise Data:

	Persons	Males	Females	Sex Ratio
All ages	58,899	29,621	29,278	988
0-14	18,675	9,692	8,983	927
15-44	28,102	14,125	13,977	990
45-79	11,772	5,637	6,135	1088
80+	255	115	140	1217
Age not stated	95	52	43	827

Languages (Dominant):

Telugu, Urdu, Tamil, Hindi, Gondi

Disabled Population:

	Persons	Males	Females	%
Total Disabled	911	538	373	
In Seeing	278	155	123	30.52
In Speech	109	61	48	11.96
In Hearing	46	24	22	5.05
In Movement	359	232	127	39.41
Mentally	119	66	53	13.06

ATLUR

Atlur C.D. Block lies in the eastern part of Cuddapah district. The Block is located at a distance of 74 kms. from district headquarters (Cuddapah). There are 23 villages in the block with the total population of 29,406 persons. Area of the C.D. Block is 192.46 sq. kms. It is bounded in the north by Mandal Badvel, in the south by Mandals Sidhout and Vontimitta, in the east by Mandal Gopavaram, and in the west by Mandals Khajipet, Chennur and Sidhout.

Communications:

Roadways : Metalled Roads: Nearest Villages- Yerraballe, Thamballagondi, Gujjalavaripalle, Shrotriya Venkatapur am, Kumbhagiri, Kondur, Atlur.

River: Penneru Nadi- Nearest Villages- Sivalapalle, Kokkarayapalle, Kanuparthi, Nazeerbegpalle, Gurrampadu, Ramanapalle, Chennur, Doulathapuram, Bayanapalle and River Sagileru southwardly to River Penneru, touch the following villages, respectively,

It receives Backward Region Grants, and is also identif ied as a drought-prone area as well.

Annual Rainfall: Average Rainfall 696 mm

Ground Water: Availability of the Ground Water in the Basin is 1354 H.A.M.and the utilization is 1134 H.A. M.It belongs to SC category. Depth to water level varies from 10 to 40 meter below the ground. Most of the wells go down in summer months, according to the Ground Water Estimation Committee.

Forest and Reserved **Forest:** (Velikonda R.F.)- Nearest Villages- Yerraballe, Thamballagondi, Gujjalavaripalle, Shrotriya Venkatapuram, Kondur, Atlur, Varikunta, Maddur, Thudur, Uppatur, Chenduvoy.

Natural Division : Rayalaseema Region

Administration:

Division: Rayala Seema. Parliamentary Constituency: 38 Kadapa. District: Cuddapah.

Mandal: Atlur. Assembly Constituency: 243 Badvel (SC).

Gram Panchayat: 12.

Villages: 23 **Inhabited:** 22 **Uninhabited:** 1

Ranking	District	State	National
Area	35	601	4318
Population	41	1029	6063
Sex Ratio	46	1037	3862

Child Sex Ratio	37	896	3976
Literacy Rate	46	506	3862
Density	29	839	5514
Work Participation Rate	31	896	2625

Gram Panchayats:

Atloor, Kamalakur, Kamasamudram, Konduru, Kumbagiri Madapur, Mannem Vari Palle, Mutukur, Reddy Palli Thamballagondi, Varikunta, Vemalur.

Amenities:

Education: Primary School in 21 villages, Middle school in 6 villages, Matriculation or Secondary School in 2 villages, namely Kamalakuru, Atlur.

Higher Secondary or Pre University Courses or Intermediate or Junior College in 0 village of the CD Block, College in 0 village, Adult Literacy Center in 2 villages.

Medical: Hospital in 0 village, Dispensary in 0 village, Health Center in 1 village, Sub Center in 5 villages, Maternity and Child Welfare Center in 0 village, Community health workers in 0 village.

Drinking Water: Tap water in 20 villages, Tank water in 21 villages, Well water in 22 villages, Tubewell in 21 villages and more than one source in 22 villages.

Bank: Banking facility in 1 villages, namely, Atlur.

Credit Society in 6 villages Agricultural Credit Society in 4 Non-Agricultural Credit Society in 3 villages.

Others: Power supply in 22 villages, Cinema hall in 0 village, sport club in 0 village, Stadium or Auditorium or Community Hall in 0 village, Post Office in 7 villages.

There are 14 villages having bus facilities.

Village with most of facilities: Atlur.

Villages without amenities (Education): Rangampalle..

Scheduled Castes: Out of the total population of 29406 persons, 7791 persons (26.49%) belong to Scheduled Castes.

The villages having less than 10% SC population are None..

The villages having more than 50% SC population are None.

Sex ratio of Scheduled Caste population is 489.

Scheduled Castes Literates and Illiterates by Sex:

	Persons	Males	Females
Literate	3,002	2,016	986
Illiterate	4,789	1,968	2,821
Literacy rate	44.4	58.6	29.7
Graduate	63	55	8

Scheduled Castes (Dominant):

Mala, Madiga, Generic Castes etc., Dakkal etc.

For their cultural identity please see Appendix-I

Villages without Scheduled Castes: There is 1 village without any scheduled caste population.

Scheduled Tribes: Out of the total population of 29406 persons, 586 persons (1.99%) belong to Scheduled Tribes.

The villages having less than 10% ST population are Yerraballe, Nallayapalle, Kamalakuru, Madapur Thamballagondi, Kumbhagiri, Kamasamudram, Vemalur Atlur, Muthukur, Jannavaram, Varikunta, Maddur Virur, Rangampalle, Thudur, Uppatur, Chenduvoy Malinenipatnam.

The villages having more than 50% ST population are None.

Sex ratio of Scheduled tribe population is 497.

Scheduled Tribes Literates and Illiterates by Sex:

	Persons	Males	Females
Literate	213	127	86
Illiterate	373	168	205
Literacy rate	43.7	51.2	36.0
Graduate	3	3	0

Scheduled Tribes (Dominant):

Yerukulas, Yenadis, Sugalis etc.

For their cultural identity please see Appendix-II

Villages without Scheduled Tribes: There are 13 villages without any scheduled tribe population.

Literates and Illiterates by Sex (Total Population):

	Persons	Males	Females
Literate	13,860	9,302	4,558
Illiterate	15,546	5,834	9,712
Literacy rate	54	70	36
Graduate	453	410	43

Agriculture: ***Distribution of villages according to land use:*** Out of 23 villages, Total area (in hectare) is 19246, out of that 32.53 percent is cultivable and 61.74 percent of the cultivable area is irrigated.

Sources of Irrigation (Hectares): Government Canal 0, Private Canal 0, Well without Electricity 0, Well with Electricity 1464.1, Tubewell without Electricity 0, Tubewell with Electricity 1735, Tank 546.7, River 0, Lake 0, Waterfall 0, Others 119.

Villages with population of 5000 to 9999: None

Villages with population of 10000 and above: None

Distribution of Workers:

	Persons	Males	Females	WPR
Cultivators	4,509	3,584	925	31.42
Agricultural Labour	7,261	3,564	3,697	50.6
Household Industry	680	357	323	4.74
Other Workers	1,899	1,464	435	13.23
Main Workers	10,482	7,571	2,911	73.05
Marginal Workers	3,867	1,398	2,469	26.95
Total Workers	14,349	8,969	5,380	

Religion: Major Religious Communities:

	Persons	Males	Females	Sex Ratio
Hindu (97.87%)	28,779	14,814	13,965	943
Muslim (2.07%)	610	310	300	968
Christian (0.03%)	10	7	3	429
Sikh (0.01%)	2	1	1	1,000
Buddhists (0%)	-	-	-	-
Jain (0%)	-	-	-	-

Agewise Data:

	Persons	Males	Females	Sex Ratio
All ages	29,406	15,136	14,270	943
0-14	8,840	4,557	4,283	940
15-44	14,382	7,505	6,877	916
45-79	5,948	2,957	2,991	1011
80+	172	80	92	1150
Age not stated	64	37	27	730

Languages (Dominant):

Telugu, Urdu, Hindi, Gondi

Disabled Population:

	Persons	Males	Females	%
Total Disabled	591	311	280	
In Seeing	222	86	136	37.56
In Speech	62	35	27	10.49
In Hearing	64	29	35	10.83
In Movement	178	123	55	30.12
Mentally	65	38	27	11

ATMAKUR

Atmakur C.D. Block lies in the central west part of Mahbubnagar district. The Block is located at a distance of 68 kms. from district headquarters (Mahbubnagar). There are 26 villages in the block with the total population of 55,686 persons. Area of the C.D. Block is 202.51 sq. kms. It is bounded by Chinnactantakunta Mandal on north, Kothakotha Mandal on east, Dharur and Godawari Mandals on south, and Narva Mandal on west.

Communications:

Roadways : Metalled Roads: Nearest Villages- Pamireddipa lle, Kankanvanipalle, Amarchinta, Khanapur, Pinamcherla, Gopanpeta, Balakistapur, Atmakur, Somsagar, Jurial, Guntipalle, Motlampalle.

Railway Station: Arepalle, Thippadampalle

River: Krishna Nadi- Nearest Villages- Nandimalla, Mulamalla, Jurial, Guntipalle, Motlampalle, Arepalle, Kathepalle, Thoompalle, Rechintala. Pedda Nadi- Nearest Villages- Karvena, Gopanpeta, Balakistapur, Medepalle, Devarapalle, Thippadampalle, Thoompalle, Veeraraghavap ur.

Backwards Region Grants Fund: It receives Backward Region Grants.

Integrated Child Development Scheme (ICDS) Project: Atmakur, Total Anganwadi Centres: 215

Annual Rainfall: Average Rainfall 583 mm

Ground Water: Availability of the Ground Water in the Basin is 6434 H.A.M. and the utilization is 2278 H. A.M. It belongs to Safe category. Depth to water level varies from 2 to 5 meter below the ground. Most of the wells go down in summer months. The well density in the entire block is 10 wells per sq. km. Total no. of the wells in the block are enumerated as 2124, according to the Ground Water Estimation Committee.

Natural Division : Telangana Plateau Region

Administration:

Division: Telangana. Parliamentary Constituency: 11 Mahbubnagar. District: Mahbubnagar. Mandal: Atmakur. Assembly Constituency: 77 Makthal. Gram Panchayat: 21

Villages: 26 **Inhabited:** 25 **Uninhabited:** 1

Ranking	**District**	**State**	**National**
Area	52	536	4137
Population	19	352	5022
Sex Ratio	21	538	1926
Child Sex Ratio	13	404	1457
Literacy Rate	22	957	5519
Density	45	394	3810
Work Participation Rate	3	451	962

Gram Panchayats:

Amarchinta, Arepalle, Atmakur, Devarapalle, Gopanpet Guntipalle, Jurial, Kankanvanipalle, Kathepalle Khanapur, Mastipur, Medepalle, Motlampalle, Mulmalla Nandimalla, Pamireddipalle, Pinamcherla, Rechintala Singampeta, Thippadampalle, Thoompalle.

Amenities:

Education: Primary School in 25 villages, Middle school in 8 villages, Matriculation or Secondary School in 3 villages, namely Amarchinta, Atmakur, Thippadampalle.

Higher Secondary or Pre University Courses or Intermediate or Junior College in 1 village of the CD Block,, namely Atmakur.

College in 0 village, Adult Literacy Center in 23 villages.

Medical: Hospital in 1 village, Dispensary in 1 village, Health Center in 0 village, Sub Center in 8 villages, Maternity and Child Welfare Center in 1 village, Community health workers in 0 village.

The Villages having Hospital or Dispensary or Health Center are Amarchinta, Atmakur.

Drinking Water: Tap water in 25 villages, Tank water in 25 villages, Well water in 25 villages, Tubewell in 25 villages and more than one source in 25 villages.

Bank: Banking facility in 2 villages, namely, Amarchinta, Atmakur.

Credit Society in 14 villages Agricultural Credit Society in 7 Non-Agricultural Credit Society in 9 villages.

Others: Power supply in 25 villages, Cinema hall in 2 villages, sport club in 1 village, Stadium or Auditorium or Community Hall in 0 village, Post Office in 12 villages.

There are 19 villages having bus facilities.

Villages with most of facilities: Amarchinta Atmakur.

Villages without Amenities (Education): None..

Scheduled Castes: Out of the total population of 55686 persons, 8025 persons (14.41%) belong to Scheduled Castes.

The villages having less than 10% SC population are Pamireddipalle, Kankanvanipalle, Amarchinta, Karvena Balakistapur, Guntipalle.

The villages having more than 50% SC population are None.

Sex ratio of Scheduled Caste population is 491.

Scheduled Castes Literates and Illiterates by Sex:

	Persons	Males	Females
Literate	2,287	1,589	698
Illiterate	5,738	2,498	3,240
Literacy rate	34.0	46.4	21.1
Graduate	69	60	9

Scheduled Castes (Dominant):

Madiga, Mala, Generic Castes etc., Beda Jangam etc. Bindla

For their cultural identity please see Appendix-I

Villages without Scheduled Castes: There are 5 villages without any scheduled caste population.

Scheduled Tribes: Out of the total population of 55686 persons, 1746 persons (3.14%) belong to Scheduled Tribes.

The villages having less than 10% ST population are Nandimalla, Mastipur, Pamireddipalle Kankanvanipalle, Amarchinta, Mulamalla, Singampeta Khanapur, Pinamcherla, Atmakur, Somsagar, Jurial Guntipalle, Medepalle, Devarapalle, Motlampalle Arepalle, Thippadampalle, Kathepalle, Thoompalle Veeraraghavapur, Rechintala.

The villages having more than 50% ST population are None.

Sex ratio of Scheduled tribe population is 511.

Scheduled Tribes Literates and Illiterates by Sex:

	Persons	Males	Females
Literate	215	164	51
Illiterate	1,531	689	842
Literacy rate	15.5	24.0	7.2
Graduate	4	1	3

Scheduled Tribes (Dominant):

Sugalis etc., Yerukulas, Gond etc. Generic Tribes etc.

For their cultural identity please see Appendix-II

Villages without Scheduled Tribes: There are 4 villages without any scheduled tribe population.

Literates and Illiterates by Sex (Total Population):

	Persons	Males	Females
Literate	19,963	12,798	7,165
Illiterate	35,723	15,291	20,432
Literacy rate	42	54	31
Graduate	1,107	906	201

Agriculture: ***Distribution of villages according to land use:*** Out of 26 villages, Total area (in hectare) is 20250, out of that 53.76 percent is cultivable and 23.96 percent of the cultivable area is irrigated.

Sources of Irrigation (Hectares): Government Canal 369, Private Canal 106, Well without Electricity 0, Well with Electricity 1552, Tubewell without Electricity 0, Tubewell with Electricity 125, Tank 274, River 82, Lake 0, Waterfall 0, Others 100.

Villages with population of 5000 to 9999: None

Villages with population of 10000 and above: Amarchinta, Atmakur.

Distribution of Workers:

	Persons	Males	Females	WPR
Cultivators	6,599	4,461	2,138	22.17
Agricultural Labour	11,582	4,424	7,158	38.91
Household Industry	4,041	1,343	2,698	13.58
Other Workers	7,545	5,864	1,681	25.35
Main Workers	23,834	13,846	9,988	80.07
Marginal Workers	5,933	2,246	3,687	19.93
Total Workers	29,767	16,092	13,675	

Religion: Major Religious Communities:

	Persons	Males	Females	Sex Ratio
Hindu (89.15%)	49,643	25,068	24,575	980
Muslim (8.73%)	4,863	2,448	2,415	987
Christian (1.98%)	1,105	529	576	1,089
Sikh (0%)	1	1	-	-
Buddhists (0%)	-	-	-	-
Jain (0%)	-	-	-	-

Agewise Data:

	Persons	Males	Females	Sex Ratio
All ages	55,686	28,089	27,597	982
0-14	20,267	10,406	9,861	948
15-44	25,867	13,021	12,846	987
45-79	9,223	4,506	4,717	1047
80+	264	124	140	1129
Age not stated	65	32	33	1031

Languages (Dominant):

Telugu, Urdu, Hindi, Marathi, Tamil

Disabled Population:

	Persons	Males	Females	%

Total Disabled	1,055	620	435	
In Seeing	550	317	233	52.13
In Speech	95	56	39	9

In Hearing	51	24	27	4.83
In Movement	269	168	101	25.5
Mentally	90	55	35	8.53

ATMAKUR

Atmakur C.D. Block lies in the northern part of Warangal district. The Block is located at a distance of 19 kms. from district headquarters (Warangal). There are 22 villages in the block with the total population of 57,419 persons. Area of the C.D. Block is 210.54 sq. kms. It is bounded in the north by Shayampet Mandal, in the south by Geesugonda Mandal, in the east by Mandals Shayampet and Duggondi, and in the west by Hasanparthy Mandal.

Communications:

Roadways : NH- 202: Direction- Warangal to Bijapur. Nearest Villages- Oorugonda, Oblapur, Penchikalpet, Atmakur, Brahamanpalle, Neerukulla.

Railway Station: Neerukulla.

Backwards Region Grants Fund: It receives Backward Region Grants.

Annual Rainfall: Avearge Rainfall 1092 mm

Ground Water: Availability of the Ground Water in the Basin is 4791 H.A.M.and the utilization is 1935 H.A. M. It belongs to Safe category. Depth to water level varies from 5 to 20 meter below the ground. Most of the wells go down in summer months. The well density in the entire block is 18 wells per sq. km. Total no. of the wells in the block are enumerated as 3762, according to the Ground Water Estimation Committee.

Natural Division : Godavari Depression Region

Administration:

Division: Telangana. Parliamentary Constituency. District: Warangal. Mandal: Atmakur.

Assembly Constituency: 104 Parkal. Gram Panchayat: 27

Villages: 22 **Inhabited:** 22 **Uninhabited:** 0

Ranking	District	State	National
Area	23	487	4006
Population	17	317	4951
Sex Ratio	27	631	2149
Child Sex Ratio	18	455	1695
Literacy Rate	21	535	3986
Density	18	357	3832
Work Participation Rate	23	455	887

Gram Panchayats:

Agrampahad, Akkampet, Atmakur, Choudlapalle, Damera Dammannapet, Durgampet, Gudepahad, House Buzurg Kamaram, Kogilvai, Kothagattu, Lyadalla, Malakpet Mustyalapalle, Nagaiahpally, Neerukulla, Oblapur Oorugonda, Pasaragonda, Peddapur, Penchikalapeta Pulkurthy, Singarajupalle, Takkallapahad Thirmalagiri, Venkatapur.

Amenities:

Education: Primary School in 22 villages, Middle school in 14 villages, Matriculation or Secondary School in 8 villages, namely Kogilvai, Pulkurthi, Oorugonda, Damera, Oblapur, Peddapur, Atmakur, Neerukulla.

Higher Secondary or Pre University Courses or Intermediate or Junior College in 1 village of the CD Block,, namely Atmakur.

College in 0 village, Adult Literacy Center in 12 villages.

Medical: Hospital in 2 villages, Dispensary in 0 village, Health Center in 4 villages, Sub Center in 9 villages, Maternity and Child Welfare Center in 1 village, Community health workers in 0 village.

The Villages having Hospital or Dispensary or Health Center are Damera, Atmakur.

Drinking Water: Tap water in 22 villages, Tank water in 22 villages, Well water in 22 villages, Tubewell in 22 villages and more than one source in 22 villages.

Bank: Banking facility in 6 villages, namely, Oorugonda, Damera, Peddapur, Penchikalpet, Atmakur Neerukulla.

Credit Society in 19 villages Agricultural Credit Society in 5 Non-Agricultural Credit Society in 18 villages.

Others: Power supply in 22 villages, Cinema hall in 1 village, sport club in 0 village, Stadium or Auditorium or Community Hall in 0 village, Post Office in 11 villages.

There are 21 villages having bus facilities.

Villages with most of facilities: Oorugonda Damera, Peddapur, Atmakur, Neerukulla.

Villages without Amenities (Education): None..

Scheduled Castes: Out of the total population of 57419 persons, 12584 persons (21.92%) belong to Scheduled Castes.

The villages having less than 10% SC population are None..

The villages having more than 50% SC population are None.

Sex ratio of Scheduled Caste population is 490.

Scheduled Castes Literates and Illiterates by Sex:

	Persons	Males	Females
Literate	5,107	3,226	1,881
Illiterate	7,477	3,190	4,287
Literacy rate	46.7	57.8	35.1
Graduate	98	89	9

Scheduled Castes (Dominant):

Madiga, Mala, Generic Castes etc., Beda Jangam etc. Gosangi

For their cultural identity please see Appendix-I

Villages without Scheduled Castes: There is 1 village without any scheduled caste population.

Scheduled Tribes: Out of the total population of 57419 persons, 598 persons (1.04%) belong to Scheduled Tribes. The villages having less than 10% ST population are Kogilvai, Pulkurthi, Singarajupalle, Venkatapur Ladalla, Pasargonda, Malakpet, Kothagattu, Oorugonda Damera, Oblapur, Mustyalpalle, Agrampahad, Peddapur Choudla Palle, Kamaram, Penchikalpet, Atmakur Brahamanpalle, House Buzurg, Neerukulla.

The villages having more than 50% ST population are None.

Sex ratio of Scheduled tribe population is 515.

Scheduled Tribes Literates and Illiterates by Sex:

	Persons	Males	Females
Literate	189	114	75
Illiterate	409	176	233
Literacy rate	38.4	48.3	29.3
Graduate	1	1	0

Scheduled Tribes (Dominant):

Yerukulas, Sugalis etc., Koya etc., Bhil

For their cultural identity please see Appendix-II

Villages without Scheduled Tribes: There are 9 villages without any scheduled tribe population.

Literates and Illiterates by Sex (Total Population):

	Persons	Males	Females
Literate	26,556	16,746	9,810
Illiterate	30,863	12,297	18,566
Literacy rate	53	66	40
Graduate	817	715	102

Agriculture: ***Distribution of villages according to land use:*** Out of 22 villages, Total area (in hectare) is 21053, out of that 81.24 percent is cultivable and 66.48 percent of the cultivable area is irrigated.

Sources of Irrigation (Hectares): Government Canal 0, Private Canal 0, Well without Electricity 0, Well with Electricity 9565.16, Tubewell without Electricity 0, Tubewell with Electricity 242.81, Tank 1562.69, River 0, Lake 0, Waterfall 0, Others 0.

Villages with population of 5000 to 9999:
Oorugonda, Peddapur, Atmakur.

Villages with population of 10000 and above: None

Distribution of Workers:

	Persons	Males	Females	WPR
Cultivators	8,947	5,451	3,496	28.3
Agricultural Labour	15,916	6,169	9,747	50.35
Household Industry	1,480	510	970	4.68
Other Workers	5,268	4,106	1,162	16.67
Main Workers	24,972	14,011	10,961	79
Marginal Workers	6,639	2,225	4,414	21
Total Workers	31,611	16,236	15,375	

Religion: Major Religious Communities:

	Persons	Males	Females	Sex Ratio
Hindu (96.31%)	55,302	27,992	27,310	976
Muslim (2.86%)	1,641	825	816	989
Christian (0.34%)	197	89	108	1,213
Sikh (0%)	-	-	-	-
Buddhists (0%)	1	-	1	-
Jain (0%)	-	-	-	-

Agewise Data:

	Persons	Males	Females	Sex Ratio
All ages	57,419	29,043	28,376	977
0-14	17,833	9,088	8,745	962
15-44	26,968	13,586	13,382	985
45-79	12,008	6,057	5,951	982
80+	516	262	254	969
Age not stated	94	50	44	880

Languages (Dominant):

Telugu, Urdu, Gondi, Marathi, Hindi

Disabled Population:

	Persons	Males	Females	%
Total Disabled	1,451	899	552	
In Seeing	811	526	285	55.89
In Speech	145	88	57	9.99
In Hearing	36	14	22	2.48
In Movement	360	218	142	24.81
Mentally	99	53	46	6.82

ATMAKUR

Atmakur C.D. Block lies in the northern part of Nellore district. The Block is located at a distance of 53 kms. from district headquarters (Nellore). There are 21 villages in the block with the total population of 59,242 persons. Area of the C.D. Block is 293.54 sq. kms. It is bounded in the north by Mandals Vinjamur and Anumasamudrampeta, in the south by Mandals Ananthas agaram and Chejerla, and river Pennar, in the east Mandal Sangam, and in the east by Mandals Ananthasagaram, Marripadu and Vinjamur.

Communications:

Roadways : State Highway (S.H.): Direction- Badvel to Nellore. Nearest Villages- Nellorepalem, Chiruvella Khandrika, Narampeta, Nagulapadu, Atmakur, Vasili, Karatampadu, Boyila Chiruvella.

River: Kaveru Nadi- Nearest Villages- Gandlavedu, Botikarlapadu, Padakandla, Aravedu, Boyila Chiruvella. Buggeru Nadi- Nearest Villages- Gandlavedu, Botikarlap adu, Aravedu, Karatampadu, Boyila Chiruvella. Pennar Nadi- Nearest Villages- Bandarupalle, Kanupurupalle, Battepadu.

Integrated Child Development Scheme (ICDS) Project:

Atmakur, Total Anganwadi Centres: 203

Annual Rainfall: Average Rainfall 919 mm

Ground Water: Availability of the Ground Water in the Basin is 3132 H.A.M. and the utilization is 1712 H. A.M. It belongs to Safe category. Depth to water level varies from 5 to 10 meter below the ground. Most of the wells go down in summer months, according to the Ground Water Estimation Committee.

Administration:

Division: Coastal Andhra. Parliamentary Constituency: 39 Nellore. District: Nellore.

Mandal: Maripadu. Assembly Constituency: 234 Atmakur. Gram Panchayat: 24.

Villages: 21 **Inhabited:** 21 **Uninhabited:** 0

Ranking	District	State	National
Area	14	173	2856
Population	7	285	4883
Sex Ratio	24	503	1854
Child Sex Ratio	25	677	2786
Literacy Rate	10	149	1895
Density	37	946	4711
Work Participation Rate	16	711	3384

Gram Panchayats:

Apparaopalem, Aravedu, Atmakur, Bandarupalli Battepadu, Boyalachiruvella, Cherlo Yadavalli, Depur Kanupurupalli, Karatampadu, Mahimalur, Murugalla Nagulapadu, Nallapareddipalli, Narampeta Nellorepalem, Nuvvurupadu, Padakandla, Pamidipadu Ramaswami Palli, Ravvalakollu, Vasili Venkata Raopalli, Vennawada.

Amenities:

Education: Primary School in 21 villages, Middle school in 9 villages, Matriculation or Secondary School in 6 villages, namely Karatampadu, Mahimalur, Bandarupalle, Atmakur, Vasili, Battepadu.

Higher Secondary or Pre University Courses or Intermediate or Junior College in 1 village of the CD Block,, namely Atmakur.

College in 1 village, Adult Literacy Center in 17 villages., College is in village, namely Atmakur.

Medical: Hospital in 1 village, Dispensary in 2 villages, Health Center in 2 villages, Sub Center in 9 villages, Maternity and Child Welfare Center in 0 village, Community health workers in 0 village.

The Villages having Hospital or Dispensary or Health Center are Atmakur, Battepadu.

Drinking Water: Tap water in 21 villages, Tank water in 20 villages, Well water in 21 villages, Tubewell in 21 villages and more than one source in 21 villages.

Bank: Banking facility in 2 villages, namely, Atmakur, Vasili.

Credit Society in 18 villages Agricultural Credit Society in 4 Non-Agricultural Credit Society in 18 villages.

Others: Power supply in 21 villages, Cinema hall in 1 village, sport club in 0 village, Stadium or Auditorium or Community Hall in 0 village, Post Office in 15 villages.

There are 21 villages having bus facilities.

Villages with most of facilities: Atmakur, Vasili.

Villages without Amenities (Education): None..

Scheduled Castes: Out of the total population of 59242 persons, 12200 persons (20.59%) belong to Scheduled Castes.

The villages having less than 10% SC population are None..

The villages having more than 50% SC population are None.

Sex ratio of Scheduled Caste population is 501.

Scheduled Castes Literates and Illiterates by Sex:

	Persons	Males	Females
Literate	6,519	3,812	2,707
Illiterate	5,681	2,277	3,404
Literacy rate	60.9	71.4	50.4
Graduate	230	179	51

Scheduled Castes (Dominant):

Madiga, Mala, Adi Andhra, Arundhatiya Generic Castes etc.

For their cultural identity please see Appendix-I

Villages without Scheduled Castes: There are 2 villages without any scheduled caste population.

Scheduled Tribes: Out of the total population of 59242 persons, 3833 persons (6.47%) belong to Scheduled Tribes.

The villages having less than 10% ST population are Gandlavedu, Botikarlapadu, Padakandla, Aravedu Karatampadu, Boyila Chiruvella, Nabbinagaram Pamidipadu, Nellorepalem, Chiruvella Khandrika Narampeta, Mahimalur, Nagulapadu, Jangalapalle Depuru, Bandarupalle, Kanupurupalle, Nuvvurupadu Vasili, Battepadu.

The villages having more than 50% ST population are None.

Sex ratio of Scheduled tribe population is 488.

Scheduled Tribes Literates and Illiterates by Sex:

	Persons	Males	Females
Literate	1,220	685	535
Illiterate	2,613	1,279	1,334
Literacy rate	38.3	42.3	34.1
Graduate	13	10	3

Scheduled Tribes (Dominant):

Yenadis, Yerukulas, Sugalis etc., Chenchu etc.

For their cultural identity please see Appendix-II

Villages without Scheduled Tribes: There are

4 villages without any scheduled tribe population.

Literates and Illiterates by Sex (Total Population):

	Persons	Males	Females
Literate	34,219	19,892	14,327
Illiterate	25,023	9,961	15,062
Literacy rate	65	75	55
Graduate	2,114	1,607	507

Agriculture: ***Distribution of villages according to land use:*** Out of 21 villages, Total area (in hectare) is 29355, out of that 54.65 percent is cultivable and 37.62 percent of the cultivable area is irrigated.

Sources of Irrigation (Hectares): Government Canal 1055.65, Private Canal 0, Well without Electricity 0, Well with Electricity 98, Tubewell without Electricity 0, Tubewell with Electricity 783.17, Tank 3912, River 0, Lake 0, Waterfall 0, Others 185.72.

Villages with population of 5000 to 9999: Mahimalur.

Villages with population of 10000 and above: Atmakur.

Distribution of Workers:

	Persons	Males	Females	WPR
Cultivators	6,175	4,529	1,646	22.7
Agricultural Labour	10,990	5,036	5,954	40.41
Household Industry	1,236	468	768	4.54
Other Workers	8,798	7,024	1,774	32.35
Main Workers	20,014	14,092	5,922	73.58
Marginal Workers	7,185	2,965	4,220	26.42
Total Workers	27,199	17,057	10,142	

Religion: Major Religious Communities:

	Persons	Males	Females	Sex Ratio
Hindu (82.5%)	48,876	24,598	24,278	987
Muslim (16.94%)	10,033	5,097	4,936	968
Christian (0.5%)	298	144	154	1,069
Sikh (0.01%)	5	3	2	667
Buddhists (0.01%)	5	2	3	1,500
Jain (0%)	-	-	-	-

Agewise Data:

	Persons	Males	Females	Sex Ratio
All ages	59,242	29,853	29,389	984
0-14	17,178	8,770	8,408	959
15-44	28,759	14,425	14,334	994
45-79	12,734	6,387	6,347	994
80+	493	227	266	1172
Age not stated	78	44	34	773

Languages (Dominant): Telugu, Urdu, Tamil, Hindi, Gondi

Disabled Population:

	Persons	Males	Females	%
Total Disabled	1,335	725	610	
In Seeing	447	207	240	33.48
In Speech	160	87	73	11.99
In Hearing	117	64	53	8.76
In Movement	434	268	166	32.51
Mentally	177	99	78	13.26

ATMAKUR

Atmakur C.D. Block lies in the north-eastern part of Kurnool district. The Block is located at a distance of 55 kms. from district headquarters (Kurnool). There are 14 villages in the block with the total population of 68,131 persons. Area of the C.D. Block is 187.27 sq. kms. It is bounded in the north by Mandal Srisailam, in the south by Mandal Bandi Atmakur, in the east by district Prakasam, and in the west by Mandals Kothap alle, Mulapadu and Velgode.

Communications:

Roadways : State Highways (S.H.): Direction- Atmakur to Nandikotur. Nandyal and Podili. Nearest Villages- Pinnapuram, Krishnapuram, Atmakur, Karivena, Siddepalle, Siddapuram.

It is identified as a drought-prone area.

Integrated Child Development Scheme (ICDS) Project: Atmakur, Total Anganwadi Centres: 176

Annual Rainfall: Average Rainfall 775 mm

Ground Water: Availability of the Ground Water in the Basin is 1690 H.A.M. and the utilization is 668 H.A. M. It belongs to Safe category. Depth to water level varies from 5 to 10 meter below the ground. Most of the wells go down in summer months. The well density in the entire block is 4 wells per sq. km. Total no. of the wells in the block are enumerated as 1091, according to the Ground Water Estimation Committee.

Forest and Reserved **Forest:** (Atmakur R.F.)- Nearest Villages- Pinnapuram, Siddepalle, Siddapuram, Bairlutyg udem, Nagalooty Gudum, Pothurajukunta, Pesurutlagudem.

Natural Division : Rayalaseema Region

Administration:

Division: Rayala Seema. Parliamentary Constituency: 34 Nandayal. District: Kurnool. Mandal: Atmakur. Assemb ly Constituency: 254 Srisailam. Gram Panchayat: 14.

Villages: 14 **Inhabited:** 12 **Uninhabited:** 2

Ranking	**District**	**State**	**National**
Area	46	641	4448
Population	8	161	4547
Sex Ratio	46	1012	3666
Child Sex Ratio	31	642	2646
Literacy Rate	3	310	3000
Density	53	999	2962
Work Participation Rate	2	234	3797

Gram Panchayats:

Amalapuram, Atmakur, Bapanthapuram, Indireswaram Karivena, Krishnapuram, Kurukunda, Mustapally Nallakalva, Pinnapuram, Siddapuram, Siddepalle Sreepathi Rao Peta, Vadla Ramapuram.

Amenities:

Education: Primary School in 11 villages, Middle school in 6 villages, Matriculation or Secondary School in 2 villages, namely Pinnapuram, Atmakur.

Higher Secondary or Pre University Courses or Intermediate or Junior College in 1 village of the CD Block,, namely Atmakur.

College in 1 village, Adult Literacy Center in 12 villages., College is in village, namely Atmakur.

Medical: Hospital in 1 village, Dispensary in 4 villages, Health Center in 3 villages, Sub Center in 6 villages, Maternity and Child Welfare Center in 9 villages, Community health workers in 0 village.

The Villages having Hospital or Dispensary or Health Center are Kurukunda, Indireswaram, Atmakur, Karivena.

Drinking Water: Tap water in 12 villages, Tank water in 12 villages, Well water in 12 villages, Tubewell in 12 villages and more than one source in 12 villages.

Bank: Banking facility in 1 villages, namely, Atmakur.

Credit Society in 7 villages Agricultural Credit Society in 2 Non-Agricultural Credit Society in 6 villages.

Others: Power supply in 12 villages, Cinema hall in 0 village, sport club in 0 village, Stadium or Auditorium or Community Hall in 0 village, Post Office in 10 villages.

There are 10 villages having bus facilities.

Village with most of facilities: Atmakur.

Villages without Amenities (Education): None..

Scheduled Castes: Out of the total population of 68131 persons, 10939 persons (16.06%) belong to Scheduled Castes.

The villages having less than 10% SC population are None..

The villages having more than 50% SC population are None.

Sex ratio of Scheduled Caste population is 482.

Scheduled Castes Literates and Illiterates by Sex:

	Persons	Males	Females
Literate	5,029	3,169	1,860
Illiterate	5,910	2,496	3,414
Literacy rate	54.3	65.8	41.9
Graduate	279	219	60

Scheduled Castes (Dominant):

Mala, Madiga, Beda Jangam etc., Adi Andhra, Relli

For their cultural identity please see Appendix-I

Villages without Scheduled Castes: There are 3 villages without any scheduled caste population.

Scheduled Tribes: Out of the total population of 68131 persons, 4316 persons (6.33%) belong to Scheduled Tribes.

The villages having less than 10% ST population are Vadla Ramapuram, Indireswaram, Pinnapuram Krishnapuram, Atmakur, Karivena.

The villages having more than 50% ST population are None.

Sex ratio of Scheduled tribe population is 504.

Scheduled Tribes Literates and Illiterates by Sex:

	Persons	Males	Females
Literate	1,725	1,083	642
Illiterate	2,591	1,059	1,532
Literacy rate	48.7	62.1	35.8
Graduate	36	29	7

Scheduled Tribes (Dominant):

Sugalis etc., Chenchu etc., Yerukulas, Yenadis Koya etc.

For their cultural identity please see Appendix-II

Villages without Scheduled Tribes: There are 3 villages without any scheduled tribe population.

Literates and Illiterates by Sex (Total Population):

	Persons	Males	Females
Literate	33,981	20,908	13,073
Illiterate	34,150	14,087	20,063
Literacy rate	59	70	47
Graduate	1,848	1,502	346

Agriculture: ***Distribution of villages according to land use:*** Out of 14 villages, Total area (in hectare) is 18468, out of that 66.63 percent is cultivable and 29.34 percent of the cultivable area is irrigated.

Sources of Irrigation (Hectares): Government Canal 0, Private Canal 0, Well without Electricity 0, Well with Electricity 1536.69, Tubewell without Electricity 0, Tubewell with Electricity 3.65, Tank 2070.24, River 0, Lake 0, Waterfall 0, Others 0.

Villages with population of 5000 to 9999: Kurukunda.

Villages with population of 10000 and above: Atmakur.

Distribution of Workers:

	Persons	Males	Females	WPR
Cultivators	4,563	3,278	1,285	15.86
Agricultural Labour	12,289	5,742	6,547	42.71
Household Industry	1,224	668	556	4.25
Other Workers	10,697	9,436	1,261	37.18
Main Workers	25,293	17,707	7,586	87.91
Marginal Workers	3,480	1,417	2,063	12.09
Total Workers	28,773	19,124	9,649	

Religion: Major Religious Communities:

	Persons	Males	Females	Sex Ratio
Hindu (63.33%)	43,144	22,030	21,114	958
Muslim (35.17%)	23,960	12,436	11,524	927
Christian (1.48%)	1,008	520	488	938
Sikh (0%)	-	-	-	-
Buddhists (0%)	-	-	-	-
Jain (0%)	-	-	-	-

Agewise Data:

	Persons	Males	Females	Sex Ratio
All ages	68,131	34,995	33,136	947
0-14	24,793	12,757	12,036	943
15-44	31,634	16,477	15,157	920
45-79	11,339	5,599	5,740	1025
80+	301	130	171	1315
Age not stated	64	32	32	1000

Languages (Dominant):

Telugu, Urdu, Hindi, Marathi, Tamil

Disabled Population:

	Persons	Males	Females	%
Total Disabled	1,007	591	416	
In Seeing	347	191	156	34.46
In Speech	130	76	54	12.91
In Hearing	60	30	30	5.96
In Movement	348	221	127	34.56
Mentally	122	73	49	12.12

ATMAKUR

Atmakur C.D. Block lies in the western part of Anantapur district. The Block is located at a distance of 27 kms. from district headquarters (Anantapur). There are 08 villages in the block with the total population of 35,995 persons. Area of the C.D. Block is 268.18 sq. kms. It is bounded in the north by Mandal Kudair, in the south by Mandals Kanaganapalle and Raptadu, in the east by Mandals Anantapur and Raptadu, and in the west by Mandals Beluguppa and Kalyandurg.

Communications:

Roadways : State Highway (S.H.): Direction- Kalyandurg to Anantapur. Nearest Villages- Padamatiyaleru, Talupu ru, Madigubba, Atmakur.

It receives Backward Region Grants, and is identified as a drought-prone area as well.

Annual Rainfall: Average Rainfall 339 mm

Ground Water: Availability of the Ground Water in the Basin is 1760 H.A.M. and the utilization is 1518 H. A.M. It belongs to SC category. Depth to water level varies from 5 to 10 meter below the ground. Most of the wells go down in summer months. The well density in the entire block is 6 wells per sq. km. Total no. of the wells in the block are enumerated as 1992, according to the Ground Water Estimation Committee.

Natural Division : Rayalaseema Region

Administration:

Division: Rayala Seema. Parliamentary Constituency: 37 Hindupur.District: Anantapur.

Mandal: Atmakur. Assembly Constituency: 274 Raptadu.

Gram Panchayat: 15.

Villages: 8 **Inhabited:** 8 **Uninhabited:** 0

Ranking	District	State	National
Area	35	248	3126
Population	48	917	5881
Sex Ratio	55	1049	3987
Child Sex Ratio	21	380	1414
Literacy Rate	9	413	3530
Density	28	375	5788
Work Participation Rate	41	957	915

Gram Panchayats:

Atmakur, B.Yaleru, Goridindla, Madigubba, Muttala P.Siddarampuram, P.Yaleru, Pampanur, Rangampeta Sanapa, Singampalli, Talupuru, Thopudurthi Vaddupalli, Vepacherla.

Amenities:

Education: Primary School in 8 villages, Middle school in 6 villages, Matriculation or Secondary School in 3 villages, namely Talupuru, Atmakur, Sanapa.

Higher Secondary or Pre University Courses or Intermediate or Junior College in 1 village of the CD Block,, namely Atmakur.

College in 0 village, Adult Literacy Center in 7 villages.

Medical: Hospital in 2 villages, Dispensary in 3 villages, Health Center in 1 village, Sub Center in 7 villages, Maternity and Child Welfare Center in 0 village, Community health workers in 0 village.

The Villages having Hospital or Dispensary or Health Center are Padamatiyaleru, Atmakur, Goridindla.

Drinking Water: Tap water in 8 villages, Tank water in 0 villages, Well water in 0 village, Tubewell in 1 village and more than one source in 8 villages.

Bank: Banking facility in 1 villages, namely, Atmakur.

Credit Society in 4 villages Agricultural Credit Society in 4 Non-Agricultural Credit Society in 0 village.

Others: Power supply in 8 villages, Cinema hall in 1 village, sport club in 0 village, Stadium or Auditorium or Community Hall in 0 village, Post Office in 8 villages.

There are 8 villages having bus facilities.

Village with most of facilities: Atmakur.

Villages without Amenities (Education): None..

Scheduled Castes: Out of the total population of 35995 persons, 5725 persons (15.9%) belong to Scheduled Castes. The villages having less than 10% SC population are

None..

The villages having more than 50% SC population are None.

Sex ratio of Scheduled Caste population is 495.

Scheduled Castes Literates and Illiterates by Sex:

	Persons	Males	Females
Literate	2,459	1,486	973
Illiterate	3,266	1,407	1,859
Literacy rate	49.9	59.5	40.0
Graduate	47	43	4

Scheduled Castes (Dominant):

Madiga, Mala, Mala Dasari, Adi Andhra Madasi Kuruva etc.

For their cultural identity please see Appendix-I

Villages without Scheduled Castes: There are 0 village without any scheduled caste population.

Scheduled Tribes: Out of the total population of 35995 persons, 3455 persons (9.6%) belong to Scheduled Tribes.

The villages having less than 10% ST population are Talupuru, Atmakur, Sanapa, Brahmana Yaleru Thopudurthi.

The villages having more than 50% ST population are None.

Sex ratio of Scheduled tribe population is 482.

Scheduled Tribes Literates and Illiterates by Sex:

	Persons	Males	Females
Literate	1,292	820	472
Illiterate	2,163	971	1,192
Literacy rate	44.8	55.2	33.8
Graduate	17	17	0

Scheduled Tribes (Dominant):

Sugalis etc., Yerukulas

For their cultural identity please see Appendix-II

Villages without Scheduled Tribes: There are 0 village without any scheduled tribe population.

Literates and Illiterates by Sex (Total Population):

	Persons	Males	Females
Literate	17,394	10,791	6,603
Illiterate	18,601	7,760	10,841
Literacy rate	56	67	44
Graduate	606	522	84

Agriculture: ***Distribution of villages according to land use:*** Out of 8 villages, Total area (in hectare) is 26819, out of that 58.49 percent is cultivable and 14.15 percent of the cultivable area is irrigated.

Sources of Irrigation (Hectares): Government Canal 0, Private Canal 0, Well without Electricity 0, Well with Electricity 1284.93, Tubewell without Electricity 0, Tubewell with Electricity 513.97, Tank 335.09, River 85.39, Lake 0, Waterfall 0, Others 0.

Villages with population of 5000 to 9999:

Padamatiyaleru, Atmakur, Goridindla.

Villages with population of 10000 and above: None

Distribution of Workers:

	Persons	Males	Females	WPR
Cultivators	7,644	4,849	2,795	38.82
Agricultural Labour	8,781	3,350	5,431	44.59
Household Industry	292	172	120	1.48
Other Workers	2,975	2,349	626	15.11
Main Workers	16,195	9,819	6,376	82.24
Marginal Workers	3,497	901	2,596	17.76
Total Workers	19,692	10,720	8,972	

Religion: Major Religious Communities:

	Persons	Males	Females	Sex Ratio
Hindu (96.94%)	34,895	17,967	16,928	942
Muslim (1.95%)	701	376	325	864
Christian (1.05%)	379	196	183	934
Sikh (0.01%)	2	1	1	1,000
Buddhists (0.01%)	2	1	1	1,000
Jain (0%)	-	-	-	-

Agewise Data:

	Persons	Males	Females	Sex Ratio
All ages	35,995	18,551	17,444	940
0-14	11,990	6,228	5,762	925
15-44	16,923	8,709	8,214	943
45-79	6,774	3,444	3,330	967
80+	230	124	106	855
Age not stated	78	46	32	696

Languages (Dominant):

Telugu, Hindi, Urdu, Gondi, Tamil

Disabled Population:

	Persons	Males	Females	%
Total Disabled	827	469	358	
In Seeing	267	133	134	32.29
In Speech	82	47	35	9.92
In Hearing	61	31	30	7.38
In Movement	299	188	111	36.15
Mentally	118	70	48	14.27

ATMAKUR (M)

Atmakur (M) C.D. Block lies in the northern part of Nalgonda district. The Block is located at a distance of 66 kms. from district headquarters (Nalgonda). There are 21 villages in the block with the total population of 38,813 persons. Area of the C.D. Block is 234.28 sq. kms. It is bounded by Alair Mandal on north, Gundala Mandal on north-east, Mothkur Mandal on east, Ramannap eta Mandal on south, Valigonda Mandal on west, Bhongir and Yadagirigutta Mandals on north-west.

Communications:

Roadways : Metalled Roads: Nearest Villages- Chada, Rahimkhanpet, Atmakur, Raipalle, Sarvepalle, Khaprai

Palle.

River: Alair Nadi- Nearest Villages- Kalwapalle, Morip irala, Koratikal, Rahimkhanpet, Atmakur, Raipalle, Khapr ai Palle. Musi Nadi- Nearest Village- Duppelli.

It receives Backward Region Grants, and is identified as a drought prone area as well.

Annual Rainfall: Average Rainfall 718 mm

Ground Water: Availability of the Ground Water in the Basin is 3047 H.A.M. and the utilization is 2465 H. A.M. It belongs to SC category. Depth to water level varies from 10 to 20 meter below the ground. Most of the wells go down in summer months. The well density in the entire block is 16 wells per sq. km. Total no. of the wells in the block are enumerated as 3707, according to the Ground Water Estimation Committee.

Natural Division : Krishna Piedmont Plain Region

Administration:

Division: Telangana. Parliamentary Constituency: 14 Bhongir. District: Nalgonda. Mandal: Atmakur (M). Assem bly Constituency: 97 Alair. Gram Panchayat: 27.

Villages: 21 **Inhabited:** 21 **Uninhabited:** 0

Ranking	District	State	National
Area	24	370	3592
Population	48	858	5786
Sex Ratio	15	527	1888
Child Sex Ratio	48	951	4265
Literacy Rate	35	638	4348
Density	42	661	5307
Work Participation Rate	49	850	1814

Gram Panchayats:

Athmakur, Chada, Chamapur, Chandepally, Duppelli Katepally, Khapuraipally, Kondapur, Koratikal Kurella, Lingarajpally, Modumaigudem, Moripirala Nancharipet, Narsapur, Pallerla, Pothireddypally Pullaigudem, Raghavapur, Rahimkhanpet, Raipally Sarvepally, Singaram, T Repaka, Thimmapur, Thukkapur Uppalaphad.

Amenities:

Education: Primary School in 19 villages, Middle school in 11 villages, Matriculation or Secondary School in 6 villages, namely Chada, Atmakur, Pallerla, Duppelli, Kurella, Khaprai Palle.

Higher Secondary or Pre University Courses or Intermediate or Junior College in 0 village of the CD Block, College in 0 village, Adult Literacy Center in 1 village.

Medical: Hospital in 0 village, Dispensary in 1 village, Health Center in 2 villages, Sub Center in 8 villages, Maternity and Child Welfare Center in 0 village, Community health workers in 0 village.

The Villages having Hospital or Dispensary or Health Center are Singaram (Patti) Chande Palle, Atmakur.

Drinking Water: Tap water in 21 villages, Tank water in 21 villages, Well water in 21 villages, Tubewell in 21 villages and more than one source in 21 villages.

Bank: Banking facility in 2 villages, namely, Chada, Atmakur.

Credit Society in 3 villages Agricultural Credit Society in 3 Non-Agricultural Credit Society in 1 village.

Others: Power supply in 21 villages, Cinema hall in 0 village, sport club in 1 village, Stadium or Auditorium or Community Hall in 0 village, Post Office in 12 villages.

There are 20 villages having bus facilities.

Villages with most of facilities: Chada, Atmakur.

Villages without amenities (Education):

Dursagani Palle, Dharmapur..

Scheduled Castes: Out of the total population of 38813 persons, 6902 persons (17.78%) belong to Scheduled Castes.

The villages having less than 10% SC population are None..

The villages having more than 50% SC population are None.

Sex ratio of Scheduled Caste population is 483.

Scheduled Castes Literates and Illiterates by Sex:

	Persons	Males	Females
Literate	2,355	1,557	798
Illiterate	4,547	2,012	2,535
Literacy rate	39.4	50.4	27.6
Graduate	35	31	4

Scheduled Castes (Dominant):

Madiga, Mala, Beda Jangam etc., Bindla, Mashti

For their cultural identity please see Appendix-I

Villages without Scheduled Castes: There are 2 villages without any scheduled caste population.

Scheduled Tribes: Out of the total population of 38813 persons, 352 persons (0.91%) belong to Scheduled Tribes.

The villages having less than 10% ST population are Chada, Dursagani Palle, Chande Palle, Chamapur Singaram (Patti) Chande Palle, Kalwapalle Moripirala, Koratikal, Rahimkhanpet, Atmakur Raipalle, Sarvepalle, Dharmapur, Thukkapur, Pallerla Lingaraj Palle, Narsapur, Duppelli, Raghavapur Kurella, Khaprai Palle.

The villages having more than 50% ST population are None.

Sex ratio of Scheduled tribe population is 491.

Scheduled Tribes Literates and Illiterates by Sex:

	Persons	Males	Females
Literate	129	85	44
Illiterate	223	94	129
Literacy rate	45.1	57.8	31.7

Graduate	15	14	1

Scheduled Tribes (Dominant):

Yerukulas, Sugalis etc.

For their cultural identity please see Appendix-II

Villages without Scheduled Tribes: There are 9 villages without any scheduled tribe population.

Literates and Illiterates by Sex (Total Population):

	Persons	Males	Females
Literate	17,188	10,675	6,513
Illiterate	21,625	8,897	12,728
Literacy rate	51	63	39
Graduate	401	349	52

Agriculture: ***Distribution of villages according to land use:*** Out of 21 villages, Total area (in hectare) is 23428, out of that 24.08 percent is cultivable and 27.51 percent of the cultivable area is irrigated.

Sources of Irrigation (Hectares): Government Canal 8, Private Canal 0, Well without Electricity 0, Well with Electricity 1062, Tubewell without Electricity 52, Tubewell with Electricity 354, Tank 76, River 0, Lake 0, Waterfall 0, Others 0.

Villages with population of 5000 to 9999:

Chada, Atmakur.

Villages with population of 10000 and above: None

Distribution of Workers:

	Persons	Males	Females	WPR
Cultivators	6,043	3,945	2,098	30.39
Agricultural Labour	8,158	2,671	5,487	41.02
Household Industry	966	578	388	4.86
Other Workers	4,721	3,616	1,105	23.74
Main Workers	16,084	9,758	6,326	80.87
Marginal Workers	3,804	1,052	2,752	19.13
Total Workers	19,888	10,810	9,078	

Religion: Major Religious Communities:

	Persons	Males	Females	Sex Ratio
Hindu (97.3%)	37,766	19,027	18,739	985
Muslim (2.45%)	950	499	451	904
Christian (0.23%)	90	43	47	1,093
Sikh (0.01%)	2	1	1	1,000
Buddhists (0%)	-	-	-	-
Jain (0%)	-	-	-	-

Agewise Data:

	Persons	Males	Females	Sex Ratio
All ages	38,813	19,572	19,241	983
0-14	12,476	6,393	6,083	952
15-44	16,668	8,316	8,352	1004
45-79	9,152	4,600	4,552	990
80+	467	233	234	1004
Age not stated	50	30	20	667

Languages (Dominant):

Telugu, Urdu, Gondi, Hindi, Marathi

Disabled Population:

	Persons	Males	Females	%
Total Disabled	1,139	681	458	
In Seeing	686	422	264	60.23
In Speech	59	36	23	5.18
In Hearing	42	21	21	3.69
In Movement	269	160	109	23.62
Mentally	83	42	41	7.29

ATMAKUR (S)

Atmakur C.D. Block lies in the north-east part of Nalgo nda district. The Block is located at a distance of 66 kms. from district headquarters (Nalgonda). There are 20 villages in the block with the total population of 49,419 persons. Area of the C.D. Block is 208.64 sq. kms. It is bounded by Jagireddigudem Mandal on north and north-west, Suryapet Mandal on west, Chivvemla Mandal on south, Mothey Mandal on west.

Communications:

Roadways : Metalled Roads: Nearest Villages- Patharla Pahad, Mukkudeu Devi Palle, Nammikal, Enubamla.

River: Paler Nadi- Nearest Village- Maktha Kotha Gudem.

Backwards Region Grants Fund: It receives Backward Region Grants.

Annual Rainfall: Average Rainfall 771 mm

Ground Water: Availability of the Ground Water in the Basin is 2652 H.A.M. and the utilization is 1659 H. A.M. It belongs to Safe category. Depth to water level varies from 10 to 20 meter below the ground. Most of the wells go down in summer months. The well density in the entire block is 16 wells per sq. km. Total no. of the wells in the block are enumerated as 3291, according to the Ground Water Estimation Committee.

Natural Division : Krishna Piedmont Plain Region

Administration:

Division: Telangana. Parliamentary Constituency: 13 Nalgonda. District: Nalgonda. Mandal: Atmakur (S). Assembly Constituency: 91 Suryapet. Gram Panchayat: 18

Villages: 20 **Inhabited:** 19 **Uninhabited:** 1

Ranking	District	State	National
Area	32	501	4033
Population	22	535	5314
Sex Ratio	41	823	2767
Child Sex Ratio	19	634	2548
Literacy Rate	53	900	5290
Density	5	146	4237
Work Participation Rate	21	585	427

Gram Panchayats:

Aipoor, Atmakur(S), Bopparam, Dacharam, Enubamula

Gattikal, Isthalapuram, Kandagatla, Kotapahad
Makta Kotta Gudem, Mukkudev Pally, Naseempet
Nemmikal, Patha Suryapet, Patherla Pahad
Ramanna Gudem, Settigudem, Thummala Penphad.

Amenities:

Education: Primary School in 17 villages, Middle school in 12 villages, Matriculation or Secondary School in 8 villages, namely Kandagatla, Patharla Pahad, Isthalapur, Aipur, Atmakur, Nammikal, Thummalapen Pahad, Kotapahad. Higher Secondary or Pre University Courses or Intermediate or Junior College in 0 village of the CD Block, College in 0 village, Adult Literacy Center in 1 village.

Medical: Hospital in 0 village, Dispensary in 1 village, Health Center in 1 village, Sub Center in 6 villages, Maternity and Child Welfare Center in 0 village, Community health workers in 0 village.

The Village having Hospital or Dispensary or Health Center is Atmakur.

Drinking Water: Tap water in 19 villages, Tank water in 19 villages, Well water in 19 villages, Tubewell in 19 villages and more than one source in 19 villages.

Bank: Banking facility in 3 villages, namely, Aipur, Atmakur, Nammikal.

Credit Society in 4 villages Agricultural Credit Society in 4 Non-Agricultural Credit Society in 0 village.

Others: Power supply in 19 villages, Cinema hall in 0 village, sport club in 0 village, Stadium or Auditorium or Community Hall in 0 village, Post Office in 12 villages.

There are 15 villages having bus facilities.

Villages with most of facilities: Aipur, Atmakur Nammikal.

Villages without amenities (Education):
Narayanappa Guda, Gollaguda..

Scheduled Castes: Out of the total population of 49419 persons, 9846 persons (19.92%) belong to Scheduled Castes.

The villages having less than 10% SC population are None..

The villages having more than 50% SC population are None.

Sex ratio of Scheduled Caste population is 486.

Scheduled Castes Literates and Illiterates by Sex:

	Persons	Males	Females
Literate	3,378	2,285	1,093
Illiterate	6,468	2,773	3,695
Literacy rate	40.5	53.4	26.9
Graduate	63	59	4

Scheduled Castes (Dominant):
Madiga, Mala, Mala Dasari, Sindhollu etc., Bindla

For their cultural identity please see Appendix-I

Villages without Scheduled Castes: There are 3 villages without any scheduled caste population.

Scheduled Tribes: Out of the total population of 49419 persons, 7529 persons (15.24%) belong to Scheduled Tribes.

The villages having less than 10% ST population are Isthalapur, Mukkudeu Devi Palle, Midthan Palle Maktha Kotha Gudem, Narayanappa Guda, Atmakur Gollaguda.

The villages having more than 50% ST population are None.

Sex ratio of Scheduled tribe population is 485.

Scheduled Tribes Literates and Illiterates by Sex:

	Persons	Males	Females
Literate	1,779	1,244	535
Illiterate	5,750	2,631	3,119
Literacy rate	28.4	38.4	17.7
Graduate	28	27	1

Scheduled Tribes (Dominant):
Sugalis etc., Yerukulas

For their cultural identity please see Appendix-II

Villages without Scheduled Tribes: There are 5 villages without any scheduled tribe population.

Literates and Illiterates by Sex (Total Population):

	Persons	Males	Females
Literate	18,751	12,034	6,717
Illiterate	30,668	13,133	17,535
Literacy rate	44	56	32
Graduate	530	476	54

Agriculture: ***Distribution of villages according to land use:*** Out of 20 villages, Total area (in hectare) is 20863, out of that 71.51 percent is cultivable and 28 percent of the cultivable area is irrigated.

Sources of Irrigation (Hectares): Government Canal 0, Private Canal 0, Well without Electricity 0, Well with Electricity 3557, Tubewell without Electricity 0, Tubewell with Electricity 346, Tank 275, River 0, Lake 0, Waterfall 0, Others 0.

Villages with population of 5000 to 9999:
Aipur, Nammikal.

Villages with population of 10000 and above: None

Distribution of Workers:

	Persons	Males	Females	WPR
Cultivators	8,758	5,145	3,613	31.24
Agricultural Labour	13,714	5,379	8,335	48.91
Household Industry	320	176	144	1.14
Other Workers	5,246	3,848	1,398	18.71
Main Workers	25,555	13,787	11,768	91.14
Marginal Workers	2,483	761	1,722	8.86
Total Workers	28,038	14,548	13,490	

Religion: Major Religious Communities:

	Persons	Males	Females	Sex Ratio

Hindu (96.13%)	47,508	24,210	23,298	962
Muslim (2.73%)	1,348	690	658	954
Christian (1.03%)	508	240	268	1,117
Sikh (0%)	-	-	-	-
Buddhists (0%)	-	-	-	-
Jain (0%)	-	-	-	-

Agewise Data:

	Persons	Males	Females	Sex Ratio
All ages	49,419	25,167	24,252	964
0-14	16,750	8,556	8,194	958
15-44	22,018	11,122	10,896	980
45-79	10,144	5,228	4,916	940
80+	479	244	235	963
Age not stated	28	17	11	647

Languages (Dominant):
Telugu, Hindi, Urdu, Gondi, Tamil

Disabled Population:

	Persons	Males	Females	%
Total Disabled	901	505	396	
In Seeing	270	139	131	29.97
In Speech	119	62	57	13.21
In Hearing	30	15	15	3.33
In Movement	384	227	157	42.62
Mentally	98	62	36	10.88

ATREYAPURAM

Atreyapuram C.D. Block lies in the south-western part of East Godavari district. The Block is located at a distance of 85 kms. from district headquarters (Kakin ada). There are 15 villages in the block with the total population of 63,059 persons. Area of the C.D. Block is 84.04 sq. kms. It is bounded in the north by Mandal Rajahmundry (Urban), in the south by Mandal Ravulapalem, in the east by Mandals Rajahmundry Rural, Kadiam and Alamuru, and in the west by district West Godavari.

Communications :

Roadways : State Highway (S.H.): Direction- Kothapeta to Rajahmundry. Nearesr Villages- Vaddiparru, Atreyapur am, Narkedimilli, Ryali.

River: Vasista Godavari Nadi- Nearest Villages- Perava ram, Rajavaram, Valicheru, Pulidindi, Vasanthawada, Kattunga, Lolla, Vadapalle, Merlapalem. Gowthami Godava ri Nadi- Nearest Villages- Peravaram, Rajavaram, Valiche ru, Vaddiparru, Atreyapuram, Narkedimilli, Ankampalem, Ryali.

Backwards Region Grants Fund: It receives Backward Region Grants.

Annaul Rainfall: Average Rainfall 990.4 mm

Ground Water: Availability of the Ground Water in the Basin is (Information not avavible) H.A.M .and the utilization is (Information not avavible) H.A.M. It belongs to (Information not avavible) category. Depth to water level varies from 3 to 10 meter below the ground. Most of the wells go down in summer months.

Natural Division : Godavari Delta Region

Administration:

Division: Coastal Andhra. Parliamentary Constituency: 24 Amlapuram (SC). District: East Godavari. Mandal: Atreyapuram. Assembly Constituency: 166 Kothapeta. Gram Panchayat: 17.

Places of Tourist Interest:

Ryali : This village lies at a distance of one and a half kms. from Ubalanka village on the Bobbarlanka-Am ala-puram bus route. Ryali is noted for the temple of Jaganmohini-Kesava Swami. The image of the Lord is an exquisite piece of sculpture, which is considered to be the only one of its kind in India. The figure in front is Kesava and on the reverse is the female attire with a hair-do representing Jaganmohini. The image, carved in black, is excellent. The image stands at a height of five feet and the front portion, besides the face of Kesava, contains sculptural representations of Dasavatara (ten incarnations of Lord Vishnu). At the feet of the image is the figure of the river Goddess Ganga, from which drops of water trickle down througho ut the day. This is considered a rare phenomenon. Much sanctity is attached to this temple and the congregation during Kalya-notsavam of the deity held during March-A pril, for five days is largely attended.

Fairs and Festivals:

Sri Gowthameswaraswamy Festival : It is celebrated for five days from Magha Bahula Ekadasi (January-Februa ry). Gowthameswaraswamy image is a stone Sivalingam of 0.3 meter height. This is a Swayambhu Sivalingam. This Lingam was found while ploughing a field and there was no pedestal for the Lingam. Lord is believed to have appeared in the dream of a devotee and told him that panuvattam (pedestal) of the Lingam was in the Godavari river. The devotees searched and found out the pedestal and installed it. The temple is in between Vasishta and Gowthami branches of the Godavari river. On the bank of the canal, there is a small temple of Veeranjaneyaswamy. Sri Adilakshmamma image of 0.3 meter height is in human form in sitting posture. There are the images of Sita, Rama, Lakshamana and Anjaneya in Sri Rama's Temple.

Sri Jaganmohini Kesavaswamy Kalyanamahoth-savam: It is celebrated for five days from Chaitra Suddha Navmi (March-April). In the distant past, Ryali was known as Rathnapuri as there were many traders dealing in gems and precious stones. They were going abroad for trade. One of the traders, on return from the foreign countries had rested on the seashore for the night. He heard very sweet music from the earth. That night Sri Jaganmohini Kesavaswamy appeared in his dream and ordained him to take him in a chariot and instal Him at the place where the pin of the chariot wheel slipsdown and the chariot stops. The trader woke up and dug where he heard the sound of musical instruments. He found an image of the Lord in that place and was bringing it in a chariot. It is believed that the chari ot stopped in this village and the pin fell down. The merchant enshrined the image of the Lord here and soon a village rose up. The place got the name 'Rali' (rali in vernacular means to fall down) and gradually it became Ryali.

Vakulamma Teertham : It is celebrated during Sankranti for three days from 14th January. Vfakulamma is housed in a temple. The idol which is of stone is awe-inspiri ng with a huge head and a long tongue. It is believed that she used to room and talk with the villagers. Vakulamma's original and correct name was Sarda, the Goddess of learning. Some Dravidian Brahmins from the south settled at Ryali. They were highly educated in Vedic and religious lore. When the local Brahmins made the place a hot bed for them, they left the place and while leaving it, they took with them the Sarada pitam (the main altar of Sarada) and left behind her stone image which fell into the hands of Saktheyas (worshippers of shakthi) who built a temple and began to offer fowls and goats according to their own custom and belief. The change from the gentle and divine appearance of Sarada to the present awe-inspiring look in the image also appears to have taken place at a subsequent date. Even pigs are immolated now. The name of the deity was also changed as Vakulamma (vakku means word or language or literature and Vakulam ma means the presiding deity of learning, namely, Sarada).

Villages: 15 **Inhabited:** 15 **Uninhabited:** 0

Ranking	District	State	National
Area	43	1057	5841
Population	45	229	4755
Sex Ratio	53	794	2706
Child Sex Ratio	55	797	3467
Literacy Rate	20	128	1736
Density	37	1052	1338
Work Participation Rate	17	33	4397

Gram Panchayats:

Ankampalem, Atreyapuram, Bobberlanka, Kattunga Lolla, Merlapalem, Narkedimilli, Peravaram Pulidindi, Rajavaram, Ryali, Tadipudi, Utchili Vadapalle, Vaddiparru, Vasanthawada, Velicheru.

Amenities:

Education: Primary School in 15 villages, Middle school in 8 villages, Matriculation or Secondary School in 5 villages, namely Peravaram, Atreyapuram, Lolla, Ankampalem, Ryali.

Higher Secondary or Pre University Courses or Intermediate or Junior College in 1 village of the CD Block,, namely Atreyapuram.

College in 1 village, Adult Literacy Center in 15 villages., College is in village, namely Atreyapuram.

Medical: Hospital in 0 village, Dispensary in 0 village, Health Center in 2 villages, Sub Center in 13 villages, Maternity and Child Welfare Center in 0 village, Community health workers in 0 village.

Drinking Water: Tap water in 15 villages, Tank water in 15 villages, Well water in 15 villages, Tubewell in 15 villages and more than one source in 15 villages.

Bank: Banking facility in 5 villages, namely, Rajavaram, Valicheru, Pulidindi, Atreyapuram, Ryali.

Credit Society in 13 villages Agricultural Credit Society in 11 Non-Agricultural Credit Society in 9 villages.

Others: Power supply in 15 villages, Cinema hall in 3 villages, sport club in 0 village, Stadium or Auditorium or Community Hall in 0 village, Post Office in 15 villages.

There are 15 villages having bus facilities.

Villages with most of facilities: Rajavaram Valicheru, Pulidindi, Atreyapuram, Ryali.

Villages without Amenities (Education): None..

Scheduled Castes: Out of the total population of 63059 persons, 13779 persons (21.85%) belong to Scheduled Castes.

The villages having less than 10% SC population are None..

The villages having more than 50% SC population are None.

Sex ratio of Scheduled Caste population is 500.

Scheduled Castes Literates and Illiterates by Sex:

	Persons	Males	Females
Literate	7,766	4,084	3,682
Illiterate	6,013	2,804	3,209
Literacy rate	64.8	68.5	61.1
Graduate	155	111	44

Scheduled Castes (Dominant):

Mala, Madiga, Beda Jangam etc., Relli, Adi Andhra

For their cultural identity please see Appendix-I

Villages without Scheduled Castes: There are 0 village without any scheduled caste population.

Scheduled Tribes: Out of the total population of 63059 persons, 197 persons (0.31%) belong to Scheduled Tribes.

The villages having less than 10% ST population are Peravaram, Rajavaram, Valicheru, Vaddiparru

Pulidindi, Vasanthawada, Utchili, Atreyapuram Kattunga, Lolla, Vadapalle, Narkedimilli, Ankampalem Ryali, Merlapalem.

The villages having more than 50% ST population are None.

Sex ratio of Scheduled tribe population is 497.

Scheduled Tribes Literates and Illiterates by Sex:

	Persons	Males	Females
Literate	54	29	25
Illiterate	143	70	73
Literacy rate	32.3	35.4	29.4
Graduate	2	1	1

Scheduled Tribes (Dominant):

Yerukulas, Chenchu etc., Koya etc., Valmiki

For their cultural identity please see Appendix-II

Villages without Scheduled Tribes: There are 2 villages without any scheduled tribe population.

Literates and Illiterates by Sex (Total Population):

	Persons	Males	Females
Literate	36,691	19,322	17,369
Illiterate	26,368	12,755	13,613
Literacy rate	66	69	64
Graduate	1,024	790	234

Agriculture: ***Distribution of villages according to land use:*** Out of 15 villages, Total area (in hectare) is 8405, out of that 70.4 percent is cultivable and 94.53 percent of the cultivable area is irrigated.

Sources of Irrigation (Hectares): Government Canal 4045.46, Private Canal 0, Well without Electricity 0, Well with Electricity 0, Tubewell without Electricity 398.67, Tubewell with Electricity 1149.67, Tank 0, River 0, Lake 0, Waterfall 0, Others 0.

Villages with population of 5000 to 9999:

Peravaram, Atreyapuram, Ankampalem.

Villages with population of 10000 and above:

Ryali.

Distribution of Workers:

	Persons	Males	Females	WPR
Cultivators	3,290	3,216	74	12.81
Agricultural Labour	17,735	12,694	5,041	69.08
Household Industry	694	438	256	2.7
Other Workers	3,955	3,270	685	15.4
Main Workers	23,545	18,853	4,692	91.71
Marginal Workers	2,129	765	1,364	8.29
Total Workers	25,674	19,618	6,056	

Religion: Major Religious Communities:

	Persons	Males	Females	Sex Ratio
Hindu (97.58%)	61,532	31,362	30,170	962
Muslim (0.65%)	412	200	212	1,060
Christian (1.69%)	1,066	489	577	1,180
Sikh (0%)	-	-	-	-
Buddhists (0%)	-	-	-	-
Jain (0%)	-	-	-	-

Agewise Data:

	Persons	Males	Females	Sex Ratio
All ages	63,059	32,077	30,982	966
0-14	18,875	9,637	9,238	959
15-44	31,251	16,090	15,161	942
45-79	12,518	6,143	6,375	1038
80+	366	183	183	1000
Age not stated	49	24	25	1042

Languages (Dominant):

Telugu, Urdu, Gondi, Hindi, Malayalam

Disabled Population:

	Persons	Males	Females	%
Total Disabled	1,163	709	454	
In Seeing	531	332	199	45.66
In Speech	109	64	45	9.37
In Hearing	50	28	22	4.3
In Movement	354	211	143	30.44
Mentally	119	74	45	10.23

ATTILI

Attili C.D. Block lies in the south-eastern part of West Godavari district. The Block is located at a dista nce of 54 kms. from district headquarters (Eluru). There are 14 villages in the block with the total population of 68,196 persons. Area of the C.D. Block is 85.86 sq. kms. It is bounded in the north by Mandal Tanuku, in the south by Mandal Pataoderu, in the east by Mandal Palacoderu, Veeravasaram, Penumantra, Iragavaram and Tanuk, and in the west by Mandals Undi, Ganapavaram and Pentapadu.

Communications :

Roadways : State Highway (S.H.): Direction- Tadepalligud em to Penumantra. Nearst Villages- Attili, Manchili.

Railway Station: Attili, Manchili, Unikili, Aravalli.

Backwards Region Grants Fund: It receives Backward Region Grants.

Annaul Rainfall: Average Rainfall 1523 mm

Ground Water: Availability of the Ground Water in the Basin is (Information not avavible) H.A.M .and the utilization is (Information not avavible) H.A.M. It belongs to (Information not avavible) category. Depth to water level varies from 3 to 10 meter below the ground. Most of the wells go down in summer months.

Natural Division : Godavari Delta Region

Administration:

Division: Coastal Andhra. Parliamentary Constituency: 26 Narsapuram. District: West Godavari. Mandal: Attili. Assembly Constituency: 180 Tanuku. Gram Panchayat:

18

Villages: 14 **Inhabited:** 14 **Uninhabited:** 0

Ranking	**District**	**State**	**National**
Area	37	1055	5831
Population	23	159	4544
Sex Ratio	18	426	1673
Child Sex Ratio	45	1031	4904
Literacy Rate	7	8	348
Density	30	953	1189
Work Participation Rate	9	27	3415

Gram Panchayats:
Aravalli, Attili, Ballipadu, Danthupalle, Eduru Gummampadu, K.Samudrapugattu, Kanchumarru, Kommara Lakshminarayanapuram, Manchili, Pali, Paluru Skinnerapuram, Tirupatipuram, Unikili Varadallapalem, Varighedu.

Amenities:
Education: Primary School in 14 villages, Middle school in 10 villages, Matriculation or Secondary School in 6 villages, namely Ballipadu, Attili, Pali, Manchili, Kommara, Skinnerapuram.
Higher Secondary or Pre University Courses or Intermediate or Junior College in 1 village of the CD Block,, namely Attili.
College in 1 village, Adult Literacy Center in 14 villages., College is in village, namely Attili.
Medical: Hospital in 2 villages, Dispensary in 1 village, Health Center in 2 villages, Sub Center in 7 villages, Maternity and Child Welfare Center in 1 village, Community health workers in 0 village.
The Villages having Hospital or Dispensary or Health Center are Attili, Manchili.
Drinking Water: Tap water in 14 villages, Tank water in 14 villages, Well water in 14 villages, Tubewell in 14 villages and more than one source in 14 villages.
Bank: Banking facility in 3 villages, namely, Tirupatipuram, Attili, Aravalli.
Credit Society in 7 villages Agricultural Credit Society in 7 Non-Agricultural Credit Society in 1 village.
Others: Power supply in 14 villages, Cinema hall in 2 villages, sport club in 0 village, Stadium or Auditorium or Community Hall in 0 village, Post Office in 14 villages.
There are 14 villages having bus facilities.
Villages with most of facilities: Tirupatipuram Attili, Aravalli.
Villages without Amenities (Education): None..
Scheduled Castes: Out of the total population of 68196 persons, 10575 persons (15.51%) belong to Scheduled Castes.
The villages having less than 10% SC population are None..
The villages having more than 50% SC population are None.
Sex ratio of Scheduled Caste population is 490.
Scheduled Castes Literates and Illiterates by Sex:

	Persons	Males	Females
Literate	7,182	3,878	3,304
Illiterate	3,393	1,515	1,878
Literacy rate	78.2	83.2	73.1
Graduate	202	143	59

Scheduled Castes (Dominant):
Mala, Madiga, Relli, Arundhatiya, Adi Andhra
For their cultural identity please see Appendix-I
Villages without Scheduled Castes: There are 0 village without any scheduled caste population.
Scheduled Tribes: Out of the total population of 68196 persons, 480 persons (0.7%) belong to Scheduled Tribes.
The villages having less than 10% ST population are Tirupatipuram, Varighedu, Gummampadu, Ballipadu Attili, Pali, Manchili, Paluru, Kommara, Eduru Kanchumarru, Skinnerapuram, Unikili, Aravalli.
The villages having more than 50% ST population are None.
Sex ratio of Scheduled tribe population is 477.
Scheduled Tribes Literates and Illiterates by Sex:

	Persons	Males	Females
Literate	208	114	94
Illiterate	272	137	135
Literacy rate	52.8	57.6	48.0
Graduate	3	3	0

Scheduled Tribes (Dominant):
Yerukulas, Yenadis, Chenchu etc., Kammara Sugalis etc.
For their cultural identity please see Appendix-II
Villages without Scheduled Tribes: There are 0 village without any scheduled tribe population.
Literates and Illiterates by Sex (Total Population):

	Persons	Males	Females
Literate	47,610	25,200	22,410
Illiterate	20,586	9,104	11,482
Literacy rate	79	84	75
Graduate	1,597	1,204	393

Agriculture: ***Distribution of villages according to land use:***
Out of 14 villages, Total area (in hectare) is 8586, out of that 83.94 percent is cultivable and 100 percent of the cultivable area is irrigated.
Sources of Irrigation (Hectares): Government Canal 7187, Private Canal 0, Well without Electricity 0, Well with Electricity 0, Tubewell without Electricity 0, Tubewell with Electricity 20, Tank 0, River 0, Lake 0, Waterfall 0, Others 0.

Villages with population of 5000 to 9999:
Manchili, Unikili, Aravalli.

Villages with population of 10000 and above:
Attili.

Distribution of Workers:

	Persons	Males	Females	WPR
Cultivators	4,107	3,698	409	13.2
Agricultural Labour	19,742	11,634	8,108	63.47
Household Industry	1,032	518	514	3.32
Other Workers	6,223	5,190	1,033	20.01
Main Workers	26,839	19,589	7,250	86.29
Marginal Workers	4,265	1,451	2,814	13.71
Total Workers	31,104	21,040	10,064	

Religion: Major Religious Communities:

	Persons	Males	Females	Sex Ratio
Hindu (97.36%)	66,395	33,456	32,939	985
Muslim (0.75%)	509	237	272	1,148
Christian (1.86%)	1,267	596	671	1,126
Sikh (0%)	-	-	-	-
Buddhists (0%)	-	-	-	-
Jain (0%)	-	-	-	-

Agewise Data:

	Persons	Males	Females	Sex Ratio
All ages	68,196	34,304	33,892	988
0-14	19,886	10,164	9,722	957
15-44	33,378	16,961	16,417	968
45-79	14,386	6,910	7,476	1082
80+	506	242	264	1091
Age not stated	40	27	13	481

Languages (Dominant):
Telugu, Urdu, Gondi, Hindi, Tamil

Disabled Population:

	Persons	Males	Females	%
Total Disabled	1,106	630	476	
In Seeing	270	124	146	24.41
In Speech	122	69	53	11.03
In Hearing	68	25	43	6.15
In Movement	517	344	173	46.75
Mentally	129	68	61	11.66

AVANIGADDA

Avanigadda C.D. Block lies in the southern part of Krishna district. The Block is located at a distance of 35 kms. from district headquarters (Machilipatnam). There are 07 villages in the block with the total population of 41,839 persons. Area of the C.D. Block is 80.08 sq. kms. It is bounded in the north by River Krishna and Mandal Mopidevi, in the south by Mandal Nagayalanka, in the east by Mandal Koduru, and in the west by district Guntur and River Krishna.

Communications:

Roadways : State Highway (S.H.): Direction- Gudivada to Divi. Nearest Villages- Aswaraopalem, Puligadda, Avanigadda, Vekanuru.

River: Krishna Nadi- Nearest Villages- Edlanka, Chiruvo lu Lanka, Puligadda, Avanigadda, Vekanuru.

Integrated Child Development Scheme (ICDS) Project: Avanigadda, Total Anganwadi Centres: 126

Annaul Rainfall: Average Rainfall 1071 mm

Ground Water: Availability of the Ground Water in the Basin is (Information not avavible) H.A.M .and the utilization is (Information not avavible) H.A.M. It belongs to (Information not avavible) category. Depth to water level varies from 3 to 10 meter below the ground. Most of the wells go down in summer months.

Natural Division Krishna Delta Region

Administration:

Division: Coastal Andhra . Parliamentary Constituency: 28 Machilipatnam. District: Krishna. Mandal: Avanigadda. Assembly Constituency: 195 Avanigadda. Gram Panchayat: 10

Villages: 7 **Inhabited:** 7 **Uninhabited:** 0

Ranking	**District**	**State**	**National**
Area	48	1063	5874
Population	43	767	5656
Sex Ratio	45	1010	3617
Child Sex Ratio	37	727	3130
Literacy Rate	9	59	1149
Density	47	1041	2106
Work Participation Rate	6	94	4260

Gram Panchayats:
Aswaraopalem, Avanigadda, Edlanka, Modumudi Puligadda, Ramachandrapuram, Ramakotipuram South Chiruvolulanka, Tungalavaripalem, Vekanuru.

Amenities:

Education: Primary School in 7 villages, Middle school in 5 villages, Matriculation or Secondary School in 3 villages, namely Puligadda, Avanigadda, Vekanuru.

Higher Secondary or Pre University Courses or Intermediate or Junior College in 1 village of the CD Block,, namely Avanigadda.

College in 1 village, Adult Literacy Center in 5 villages., College is in village, namely Avanigadda.

Medical: Hospital in 1 village, Dispensary in 0 village, Health Center in 1 village, Sub Center in 5 villages, Maternity and Child Welfare Center in 0 village, Community health workers in 0 village.

The Village having Hospital or Dispensary or Health Center is Avanigadda.

Drinking Water: Tap water in 4 villages, Tank water in 1 villages, Well water in 2 villages, Tubewell in 0

village and more than one source in 4 villages.
Bank: Banking facility in 1 villages, namely, Avanigadda.
Credit Society in 5 villages Agricultural Credit Society in 4 Non-Agricultural Credit Society in 5 villages.
Others: Power supply in 7 villages, Cinema hall in 1 village, sport club in 0 village, Stadium or Auditorium or Community Hall in 0 village, Post Office in 6 villages.
There are 6 villages having bus facilities.
Village with most of facilities: Avanigadda.
Villages without Amenities (Education): None..
Scheduled Castes: Out of the total population of 41839 persons, 6360 persons (15.2%) belong to Scheduled Castes.
The villages having less than 10% SC population are None..
The villages having more than 50% SC population are None.
Sex ratio of Scheduled Caste population is 491.

Scheduled Castes Literates and Illiterates by Sex:

	Persons	Males	Females
Literate	3,863	2,131	1,732
Illiterate	2,497	1,108	1,389
Literacy rate	68.6	73.9	63.1
Graduate	192	133	59

Scheduled Castes (Dominant):
Mala, Madiga, Relli, Generic Castes etc., Dom etc.
For their cultural identity please see Appendix-I
Villages without Scheduled Castes: There are 0 village without any scheduled caste population.
Scheduled Tribes: Out of the total population of 41839 persons, 1078 persons (2.58%) belong to Scheduled Tribes.
The villages having less than 10% ST population are Puligadda, Edlanka, Avanigadda, Chiruvolu Lanka Modumudi, Aswaraopalem, Vekanuru.
The villages having more than 50% ST population are None.
Sex ratio of Scheduled tribe population is 473.

Scheduled Tribes Literates and Illiterates by Sex:

	Persons	Males	Females
Literate	363	219	144
Illiterate	715	349	366
Literacy rate	41.2	47.2	34.5
Graduate	6	5	1

Scheduled Tribes (Dominant):
Yerukulas, Sugalis etc., Yenadis, Kammara, Koya etc.
For their cultural identity please see Appendix-II
Villages without Scheduled Tribes: There are 2 villages without any scheduled tribe population.

Literates and Illiterates by Sex (Total Population):

	Persons	Males	Females
Literate	26,163	14,400	11,763
Illiterate	15,676	7,079	8,597
Literacy rate	70	75	65
Graduate	1,908	1,373	535

Agriculture: ***Distribution of villages according to land use:*** Out of 7 villages, Total area (in hectare) is 8008, out of that 40.77 percent is cultivable and 73.54 percent of the cultivable area is irrigated.
Sources of Irrigation (Hectares): Government Canal 1927, Private Canal 0, Well without Electricity 0, Well with Electricity 0, Tubewell without Electricity 11, Tubewell with Electricity 463, Tank 0, River 1, Lake 0, Waterfall 0, Others 0.
Villages with population of 5000 to 9999:
Vekanuru.
Villages with population of 10000 and above:
Avanigadda.

Distribution of Workers:

	Persons	Males	Females	WPR
Cultivators	2,292	2,082	210	13.11
Agricultural Labour	9,122	5,017	4,105	52.17
Household Industry	478	207	271	2.73
Other Workers	5,593	4,609	984	31.99
Main Workers	12,676	9,898	2,778	72.5
Marginal Workers	4,809	2,017	2,792	27.5
Total Workers	17,485	11,915	5,570	

Religion: Major Religious Communities:

	Persons	Males	Females	Sex Ratio
Hindu (96.4%)	40,333	20,739	19,594	945
Muslim (2.05%)	857	438	419	957
Christian (1.43%)	600	274	326	1,190
Sikh (0%)	-	-	-	-
Buddhists (0%)	-	-	-	-
Jain (0%)	-	-	-	-

Agewise Data:

	Persons	Males	Females	Sex Ratio
All ages	41,839	21,479	20,360	948
0-14	12,228	6,591	5,637	855
15-44	20,548	10,525	10,023	952
45-79	8,676	4,190	4,486	1071
80+	301	125	176	1408
Age not stated	86	48	38	792

Languages (Dominant):
Telugu, Urdu, Hindi, Tamil, Malayalam

Disabled Population:

	Persons	Males	Females	%
Total Disabled	1,162	748	414	
In Seeing	559	376	183	48.11
In Speech	112	72	40	9.64
In Hearing	61	31	30	5.25

In Movement	313	206	107	26.94
Mentally	117	63	54	10.07

B.KODUR

B. Kodur C.D. Block lies in the north-eastern part of Cuddapah district. The Block is located at a distance of 68 kms. from district headquarters (Cuddapah). There are 19 villages in the block with the total popul ation of 19,450 persons. Area of the C.D. Block is 128. 99 sq. kms. It is bounded in the north by Mandal Poruma milla, in the south by Mandals Brahmamgarimattam and Badvel, in the east by Mandals Porumamilla and Gopavaram, and in the west by Mandals Brahmagarimattam and S. Mydukur.

Communications:

Roadways : State Highways (S.H.): Direction- S. Mydukur to Cumbum, and Porumamilla to Badvel. Nearest Villages- Madhavarayunipalle, Kamakunta, Peddullapalle, Kondampal le, Munnelli, Kodur.

River: Sagileru Nadi- Nearest Villages- Munnelli, Kodur, Channakesapuram, Papanapalle, Maratipalle, Ankanagodu Gunuru, Mekavaripalle, Prabhalaveedu, Thangedupalle. Receives Backward Region Grant, and is identified as a drought-prone area as well.

Annual Rainfall: Average Rainfall 687 mm

Ground Water: Availability of the Ground Water in the Basin is 980 H.A.M.and the utilization is 987 H.A.M. It belongs to OE category. Depth to water level varies from 5 to 20 meter below the ground. Most of the wells go down in summer months, according to the Ground Water Estimation Committee.

Natural Division : Rayalaseema Region

Administration:

Division: Rayala Seema. Parliamentary Constituency: 38 Kadapa. District: Cuddapah.
Mandal: B. Kodur. Assembly Constituency: 243 Badvel (SC). Gram Panchayat: 10.

Villages: 19 **Inhabited:** 15 **Uninhabited:** 4

Ranking	District	State	National
Area	48	905	5337
Population	50	1090	6217
Sex Ratio	26	701	2341
Child Sex Ratio	44	1002	4666
Literacy Rate	51	650	4384
Density	20	598	5550
Work Participation Rate	32	904	1611

Gram Panchayats:

B.Kodur, Itrampeta, Mekavaripalli, Munneli Payalakuntla, Pedullapalli, Prbhalaveedu S. Papanapalli, Thangedupalli, Thummalapalli.

Amenities:

Education: Primary School in 15 villages, Middle school in 6 villages, Matriculation or Secondary School in 2 villages, namely Munnelli, Kodur.
Higher Secondary or Pre University Courses or Intermediate or Junior College in 1 village of the CD Block,, namely Kodur.
College in 0 village, Adult Literacy Center in 6 villages.

Medical: Hospital in 1 village, Dispensary in 1 village, Health Center in 1 village, Sub Center in 0 village, Maternity and Child Welfare Center in 1 village, Community health workers in 0 village.
The Village having Hospital or Dispensary or Health Center is Kodur.

Drinking Water: Tap water in 13 villages, Tank water in 13 villages, Well water in 13 villages, Tubewell in 13 villages and more than one source in 13 villages.

Bank: Banking facility in 3 villages, namely, Munnelli, Kodur, Mekavaripalle.
Credit Society in 2 villages Agricultural Credit Society in 1 Non-Agricultural Credit Society in 2 villages.

Others: Power supply in 15 villages, Cinema hall in 0 village, sport club in 0 village, Stadium or Auditorium or Community Hall in 0 village, Post Office in 7 villages.
There are 11 villages having bus facilities.

Villages with most of facilities: Munnelli, Kodur.

Villages without Amenities (Education): None..

Scheduled Castes: Out of the total population of 19450 persons, 3202 persons (16.46%) belong to Scheduled Castes.
The villages having less than 10% SC population are Channakesapuram, Papanapalle, Maratipalle Madhavarayunipalle, Kamakunta, M.Narasimhapuram Kondampalle.
The villages having more than 50% SC population are None.
Sex ratio of Scheduled Caste population is 493.

Scheduled Castes Literates and Illiterates by Sex:

	Persons	Males	Females
Literate	1,249	817	432
Illiterate	1,953	808	1,145
Literacy rate	44.9	57.6	31.7
Graduate	25	24	1

Scheduled Castes (Dominant):
Madiga, Mala, Adi Andhra

For their cultural identity please see Appendix-I

Villages without Scheduled Castes: There are 10 villages without any scheduled caste population.

Scheduled Tribes: Out of the total population of 19450 persons, 241 persons (1.24%) belong to Scheduled Tribes.
The villages having less than 10% ST population are Munnelli, Kodur, Channakesapuram, Papanapalle Maratipalle, Ankanagodu Gunuru, Madhavarayunipalle

Kamakunta, M.Narasimhapuram, Mekavaripalle Peddullapalle, Kondampalle, Prabhalaveedu Thangedupalle, Thipparajupalle.

The villages having more than 50% ST population are None.

Sex ratio of Scheduled tribe population is 490.

Scheduled Tribes Literates and Illiterates by Sex:

	Persons	Males	Females
Literate	111	70	41
Illiterate	130	53	77
Literacy rate	51.6	66.0	37.6
Graduate	4	3	1

Scheduled Tribes (Dominant):

Yerukulas, Yenadis, Chenchu etc., Sugalis etc.

For their cultural identity please see Appendix-II

Villages without Scheduled Tribes: There are 11 villages without any scheduled tribe population.

Literates and Illiterates by Sex (Total Population):

	Persons	Males	Females
Literate	8,637	5,603	3,034
Illiterate	10,813	4,256	6,557
Literacy rate	51	65	36
Graduate	250	234	16

Agriculture: ***Distribution of villages according to land use:*** Out of 19 villages, Total area (in hectare) is 12897, out of that 58.85 percent is cultivable and 49.64 percent of the cultivable area is irrigated.

Sources of Irrigation (Hectares): Government Canal 116.99, Private Canal 0, Well without Electricity 12.52, Well with Electricity 146.56, Tubewell without Electricity 0, Tubewell with Electricity 1242.83, Tank 767.05, River 62.2, Lake 0, Waterfall 0, Others 1419.67.

Villages with population of 5000 to 9999:

Munnelli.

Villages with population of 10000 and above: None

Distribution of Workers:

	Persons	Males	Females	WPR
Cultivators	3,690	2,649	1,041	36.18
Agricultural Labour	4,734	2,059	2,675	46.42
Household Industry	491	221	270	4.81
Other Workers	1,284	849	435	12.59
Main Workers	7,626	4,913	2,713	74.77
Marginal Workers	2,573	865	1,708	25.23
Total Workers	10,199	5,778	4,421	

Religion: Major Religious Communities:

	Persons	Males	Females	Sex Ratio
Hindu (95.75%)	18,624	9,432	9,192	975
Muslim (1.7%)	331	170	161	947
Christian (2.49%)	484	250	234	936
Sikh (0%)	-	-	-	-
Buddhists (0%)	-	-	-	-
Jain (0%)	-	-	-	-

Agewise Data:

	Persons	Males	Females	Sex Ratio
All ages	19,450	9,859	9,591	973
0-14	6,251	3,160	3,091	978
15-44	9,087	4,620	4,467	967
45-79	3,994	2,012	1,982	985
80+	102	57	45	789
Age not stated	16	10	6	600

Languages (Dominant):

Telugu, Urdu, Gondi, Kannada

Disabled Population:

	Persons	Males	Females	%
Total Disabled	430	241	189	
In Seeing	117	62	55	27.21
In Speech	70	37	33	16.28
In Hearing	73	42	31	16.98
In Movement	128	79	49	29.77
Mentally	42	21	21	9.77

B.KOTHAKOTA

B. Kothakota C.D. Block lies in the north-western part of Chittoor district. The Block is located at a distance of 116 kms. from district headquarters (Chittoor). There are 09 villages in the block with the total population of 54,688 persons. Area of the C.D. Block is 229.19 sq. kms. It is bounded in the north by Mandals Pedda Thippasamudram, Mulakalacheruvu and Thambalapalle, in the south by Mandal Madanapalle, in the east by Mandal Kurabalakota, in the west by Mandal Pedda Thippa samudram, and it has common boundary with the state of Karnataka in the south.

Communications:

Roadways : State Highway (S.H.): Direction- Kadiri to Madanapalle. Nearest Villages- Bayyappagaripalle, Golla palle, Kotavooru, Thummanamgutta.

Railway Station: Thummanamgutta.

It receives the Backward Region Grants, and is identifi ed as a drought-prone area as well.

Annual Rainfall: Average Rainfall 613 mm

Ground Water: Availability of the Ground Water in the Basin is 1729 H.A.M.and the utilization is 1107 H.A. M. It belongs to Safe category. Depth to water level varies more than 10 meter below the ground. Most of the wells go down in summer months, according to the Ground Water Estimation Committee.

Forest and Reserved **Forest:** Nearest Villages- B.Kothako ta, Badikayalapalle, Gummasamudram, Gattu, Bayyappagarip alle, Gollapalle, Kotavooru.

Natural Division : Rayalaseema Region

Administration:

Division: Rayala Seema. Parliamentary Constituency: 41 Rajampet. District: Chittoor. Mandal: B. Kothakota. Assembly Constituency: 281 Thamballapalle. Gram Pancha yat: 11.

Border Villages- (Karnataka)- Nearest Villages- Gattu, Beerangi, Badikayalapalle.

Villages: 9 **Inhabited:** 9 **Uninhabited:** 0

Ranking	District	State	National
Area	11	387	3672
Population	12	379	5062
Sex Ratio	58	766	2599
Child Sex Ratio	28	564	2228
Literacy Rate	48	311	3006
Density	31	594	4223
Work Participation Rate	41	580	1602

Gram Panchayats:

B.Kothakota, Badikayalapalle, Bandaruvaripalle Beerangi, Boyyappagaripalle, Gattu, Gollapalle Gummasamudram, Kotavooru, Seelamvaripalle Thummanamgutta.

Amenities:

Education: Primary School in 9 villages, Middle school in 7 villages, Matriculation or Secondary School in 4 villages, namely B.Kothakota, Beerangi, Gattu, Gollapalle.

Higher Secondary or Pre University Courses or Intermediate or Junior College in 2 villages of the CD Block,, namely B.Kothakota, Beerangi.

College in 1 village, Adult Literacy Center in 5 villages., College is in village, namely B.Kothakota.

Medical: Hospital in 0 village, Dispensary in 1 village, Health Center in 1 village, Sub Center in 7 villages, Maternity and Child Welfare Center in 4 villages, Community health workers in 0 village.

The Village having Hospital or Dispensary or Health Center is Badikayalapalle.

Drinking Water: Tap water in 9 villages, Tank water in 9 villages, Well water in 9 villages, Tubewell in 9 villages and more than one source in 9 villages.

Bank: Banking facility in 4 villages, namely, B.Kothakota, Gattu, Bayyappagaripalie Thummanamgutta.

Credit Society in 3 villages Agricultural Credit Society in 3 Non-Agricultural Credit Society in 1 village.

Others: Power supply in 9 villages, Cinema hall in 1 village, sport club in 1 village, Stadium or Auditorium or Community Hall in 0 village, Post Office in 9 villages.

There are 9 villages having bus facilities.

Villages with most of facilities: B.Kothakota Gattu, Bayyappagaripalle, Thummanamgutta.

Villages without Amenities (Education): None..

Scheduled Castes: Out of the total population of 54688 persons, 5782 persons (10.57%) belong to Scheduled Castes.

The villages having less than 10% SC population are None..

The villages having more than 50% SC population are None.

Sex ratio of Scheduled Caste population is 466.

Scheduled Castes Literates and Illiterates by Sex:

	Persons	Males	Females
Literate	2,380	1,669	711
Illiterate	3,402	1,418	1,984
Literacy rate	47.4	61.9	30.5
Graduate	38	31	7

Scheduled Castes (Dominant):

Madiga, Mala, Generic Castes etc., Adi Andhra Adi Dravida

For their cultural identity please see Appendix-I

Villages without Scheduled Castes: There are 0 village without any scheduled caste population.

Scheduled Tribes: Out of the total population of 54688 persons, 1677 persons (3.07%) belong to Scheduled Tribes.

The villages having less than 10% ST population are B.Kothakota, Beerangi, Badikayalapalle Gummasamudram, Gattu, Bayyappagaripalle Thummanamgutta, Gollapalle, Kotavooru.

The villages having more than 50% ST population are None.

Sex ratio of Scheduled tribe population is 483.

Scheduled Tribes Literates and Illiterates by Sex:

	Persons	Males	Females
Literate	761	510	251
Illiterate	916	357	559
Literacy rate	51.8	67.6	35.1
Graduate	16	12	4

Scheduled Tribes (Dominant):

Yerukulas, Yenadis, Sugalis etc.

For their cultural identity please see Appendix-II

Villages without Scheduled Tribes: There are 0 village without any scheduled tribe population.

Literates and Illiterates by Sex (Total Population):

	Persons	Males	Females
Literate	28,004	17,278	10,726
Illiterate	26,684	10,508	16,176
Literacy rate	59	71	46
Graduate	1,066	847	219

Agriculture: ***Distribution of villages according to land use:*** Out of 9 villages, Total area (in hectare) is 22920, out of that 54.14 percent is cultivable and 12.18 percent of the cultivable area is irrigated.

Sources of Irrigation (Hectares): Government Canal 0,

Private Canal 0, Well without Electricity 0, Well with Electricity 494.39, Tubewell without Electricity 0, Tubewell with Electricity 372.82, Tank 626.15, River 0, Lake 0, Waterfall 0, Others 18.09.

Villages with population of 5000 to 9999:
Badikayalapalle, Gattu.

Villages with population of 10000 and above:
B.Kothakota.

Distribution of Workers:

	Persons	Males	Females	WPR
Cultivators	12,879	7,202	5,677	44.95
Agricultural Labour	7,774	3,839	3,935	27.13
Household Industry	844	542	302	2.95
Other Workers	7,156	5,391	1,765	24.97
Main Workers	25,123	15,466	9,657	87.68
Marginal Workers	3,530	1,508	2,022	12.32
Total Workers	28,653	16,974	11,679	

Religion: Major Religious Communities:

	Persons	Males	Females	Sex Ratio
Hindu (83.04%)	45,415	23,114	22,301	965
Muslim (16.66%)	9,110	4,587	4,523	986
Christian (0.25%)	137	72	65	903
Sikh (0%)	-	-	-	-
Buddhists (0%)	-	-	-	-
Jain (0%)	-	-	-	-

Agewise Data:

	Persons	Males	Females	Sex Ratio
All ages	54,688	27,786	26,902	968
0-14	16,524	8,605	7,919	920
15-44	26,635	13,334	13,301	998
45-79	11,104	5,660	5,444	962
80+	389	163	226	1387
Age not stated	36	24	12	500

Languages (Dominant):
Telugu, Urdu, Kannada, Tamil, Marathi

Disabled Population:

	Persons	Males	Females	%
Total Disabled	718	383	335	
In Seeing	188	79	109	26.18
In Speech	94	55	39	13.09
In Hearing	48	20	28	6.69
In Movement	258	161	97	35.93
Mentally	130	68	62	18.11

BACHANNAPET

Bachannapet C.D. Block lies in the south-western part of Warangal district. The Block is located at a distance of 70 kms. from district headquarters (Warangal). There are 23 villages in the block with the total popul ation of 43,521 persons. Area of the C.D. Block is 196. 46 sq. kms. It is bounded in the north by Cherial and Maddur Mandals, in the south by district Nalgonda, in the east by Mandals Jangaon and Narmetta, and in the west by district Medak.

Communications:

Roadways : State Highway (S.H.): Direction- Cherial to Alair. Nearest Villages- Alimpur, Katkoor, Bachannap et, Narayanapur, Pochannapet.

Backwards Region Grants Fund: It receives Backward Region Grants.

Annual Rainfail: Average Rainfall 869 mm

Ground Water: Availability of the Ground Water in the Basin is 2077 H.A.M.and the utilization is 2722 H.A. M. It belongs to OE category. Depth to water level varies from 10 to 20 meter below the ground. Most of the weils go down in summer months. The well density in the entire block is 25 wells per sq. km. Total no. of the wells in the block are enumerated as 4912, according to the Ground Water Estimation Committee.

Natural Division : Godavari Depression Region

Administration:

Division: Telangana. Parliamentary Constituency. Distri ct: Warangal. Mandal: Bachannapet. Assembly Constituency: 98 Jangaon. Gram Panchayat: 21.

Villages: 23 **Inhabited:** 23 **Uninhabited:** 0

Ranking	District	State	National
Area	28	578	4243
Population	34	710	5581
Sex Ratio	1	114	700
Child Sex Ratio	8	280	917
Literacy Rate	13	484	3775
Density	35	595	4428
Work Participation Rate	37	641	1603

Gram Panchayats:
Alimpur, Bachannapeta, Bandanagaram Chinnaramancherla, Dubbakuntapalle, Gangapur Itikalapalle, Katkoor, Kesireddipalle, Kodvatooru Konne, Lingampalli, Mansanpalle, Nagireddipalle Nakkavanigudem, Narayanapur, Padamati Keshavpur Pochannapet, Ramachandrapur, Salvapur, Tammadapalle.

Amenities:

Education: Primary School in 23 villages, Middle school in 13 villages, Matriculation or Secondary School in 6 villages, namely Konne, Katkoor, Kesireddipalle, Kodavatoor, Bachannapet, Pochannapet.

Higher Secondary or Pre University Courses or Intermediate or Junior College in 0 village of the CD Block, College in 0 village, Adult Literacy Center in 19 villages.

Medical: Hospital in 2 villages, Dispensary in 1 village, Health Center in 1 village, Sub Center in 8 villages, Maternity and Child Welfare Center in 0 village,

Community health workers in 0 village.
The Villages having Hospital or Dispensary or Health Center are Padamati Keshavapur, Bachannapet.
Drinking Water: Tap water in 23 villages, Tank water in 22 villages, Well water in 22 villages, Tubewell in 23 villages and more than one source in 23 villages.
Bank: Banking facility in 1 villages, namely, Bachannapet.
Credit Society in 20 villages Agricultural Credit Society in 4 Non-Agricultural Credit Society in 19 villages.
Others: Power supply in 23 villages, Cinema hall in 1 village, sport club in 0 village, Stadium or Auditorium or Community Hall in 0 village, Post Office in 22 villages.
There are 23 villages having bus facilities.
Village with most of facilities: Bachannapet.
Villages without Amenities (Education): None..
Scheduled Castes: Out of the total population of 43521 persons, 8427 persons (19.36%) belong to Scheduled Castes.
The villages having less than 10% SC population are None..
The villages having more than 50% SC population are None.
Sex ratio of Scheduled Caste population is 501.
Scheduled Castes Literates and Illiterates by Sex:

	Persons	Males	Females
Literate	3,429	2,165	1,264
Illiterate	4,998	2,041	2,957
Literacy rate	48.3	61.3	35.5
Graduate	56	53	3

Scheduled Castes (Dominant):
Madiga, Mala, Beda Jangam etc., Sindhollu etc. Pambada etc.
For their cultural identity please see Appendix-I
Villages without Scheduled Castes: There is 1 village without any scheduled caste population.
Scheduled Tribes: Out of the total population of 43521 persons, 279 persons (0.64%) belong to Scheduled Tribes.
The villages having less than 10% ST population are Salvapur, Mansanpalle, Padamati Keshavapur Lingampalle, Pullaguda, Dubbaguntapalle, Konne Nagireddipalle, Gangapur, Ramachandrapur Itikyalapalle, Alimpur, Katkoor, Bandanagaram Kesireddipalle, Lakshmapur, Kodavatoor Basireddipalle, Bachannapet, Tammadapalle Narayanapur, Pochannapet, Chinnaramancherla.
The villages having more than 50% ST population are None.
Sex ratio of Scheduled tribe population is 480.
Scheduled Tribes Literates and Illiterates by Sex:

	Persons	Males	Females
Literate	96	68	28
Illiterate	183	77	106
Literacy rate	41.9	58.1	25.0
Graduate	1	1	0

Scheduled Tribes (Dominant):
Yerukulas, Sugalis etc.
For their cultural identity please see Appendix-II
Villages without Scheduled Tribes: There are 9 villages without any scheduled tribe population.
Literates and Illiterates by Sex (Total Population):

	Persons	Males	Females
Literate	20,126	12,576	7,550
Illiterate	23,395	8,995	14,400
Literacy rate	54	69	40
Graduate	555	482	73

Agriculture: ***Distribution of villages according to land use:*** Out of 23 villages, Total area (in hectare) is 19647, out of that 83.22 percent is cultivable and 8.11 percent of the cultivable area is irrigated.
Sources of Irrigation (Hectares): Government Canal 0, Private Canal 0, Well without Electricity 12, Well with Electricity 981, Tubewell without Electricity 0, Tubewell with Electricity 333, Tank 0, River 0, Lake 0, Waterfall 0, Others 0.
Villages with population of 5000 to 9999: Bachannapet.
Villages with population of 10000 and above: None
Distribution of Workers:

	Persons	Males	Females	WPR
Cultivators	8,188	5,141	3,047	36.77
Agricultural Labour	6,818	2,510	4,308	30.62
Household Industry	3,191	948	2,243	14.33
Other Workers	4,070	3,207	863	18.28
Main Workers	18,838	10,832	8,006	84.6
Marginal Workers	3,429	974	2,455	15.4
Total Workers	22,267	11,806	10,461	

Religion: Major Religious Communities:

	Persons	Males	Females	Sex Ratio
Hindu (96.91%)	42,176	20,904	21,272	1,018
Muslim (2.56%)	1,115	563	552	980
Christian (0.48%)	210	90	120	1,333
Sikh (0%)	-	-	-	-
Buddhists (0%)	-	-	-	-
Jain (0%)	-	-	-	-

Agewise Data:

	Persons	Males	Females	Sex Ratio
All ages	43,521	21,571	21,950	1018
0-14	14,663	7,387	7,276	985
15-44	18,716	9,299	9,417	1013
45-79	9,678	4,662	5,016	1076

80+	445	212	233	1099
Age not stated	19	11	8	727

Languages (Dominant):

Telugu, Urdu, Gondi, Tamil, Marathi

Disabled Population:

	Persons	Males	Females	%
Total Disabled	1,022	589	433	
In Seeing	476	253	223	46.58
In Speech	68	37	31	6.65
In Hearing	48	24	24	4.7
In Movement	322	213	109	31.51
Mentally	108	62	46	10.57

BADANGI

Badangi C.D. Block lies in the central part of Vizianag aram district. The Block is located at a distance of 85 kms. from district headquarters (Vizianagaram). There are 29 villages in the block with the total popul ation of 48,219 persons. Area of the C.D. Block is 124. 93 sq. kms. It is bounded in the north by Mandals Bobbi li and Therlam, in the south by Dattarajeru and Merakamu ddiam, in the east by Mandals Therlam and Merakamudidam, and in the west by Mandal Ramabhadrapuram.

Communications :

Roadways : Metalled Roads: Nearest Villages- Gajarayuniv alasa, Tentuvalasa, Pedapalle, Veerasagaram, Koduru, Akulakatta, D.Venkayyapeta.

Railway Station: Donkinivalasa.

River: Vegavati Nadi- Butchampeta, Bheemavaram, Golladi, Paltheru, Anavaram, Pinapenki, Mugada.

Backwards Region Grants Fund: It receives Backward Region Grants.

Integrated Child Development Scheme (ICDS) Project: Badangi, Total Anganwadi Centres: 131.

Annaul Rainfall: Average Rainfall 886.7 mm

Ground Water: Availability of the Ground Water in the Basin is (Information not avavible) H.A.M .and the utilization is (Information not avavible) H.A.M. It belongs to (Information not avavible) category. Depth to water level varies from 3 to 10 meter below the ground. Most of the wells go down in summer months.

Administration:

Division: Coastal Andhra. Parliamentary Constituency: 20 Vizianagram. District: Vizianagram. Mandal: Badangi. Assembly Constituency: 133 Bobbili. Gram Panchayat: 25

Villages: 29 **Inhabited:** 27 **Uninhabited:** 2

Ranking	District	State	National
Area	26	922	5391
Population	27	574	5378
Sex Ratio	32	579	2011
Child Sex Ratio	7	77	192
Literacy Rate	17	849	5069
Density	12	128	2837
Work Participation Rate	13	208	387

Gram Panchayats:

Akulakatta, Anavaram, Badangi, Beemavaram Botchavanivalasa, Donkinivalasa, Gajarayunivalasa Golladhi, Gudepuvalasa, Koduru, Kotipalli Lakshmipuram, Mallampeta, Mugada, P.Venkampeta Paltheru, Pedapalli, Pinapenki, Pindrangivalasa Pinnavalasa, Pudivalasa, Rejeru, Thentuvalasa Vadada, Veerasagaram.

Amenities:

Education: Primary School in 27 villages, Middle school in 13 villages, Matriculation or Secondary School in 7 villages, namely Golladi, Paltheru, Rejeru, Vadada, Badangi, Koduru, D.Venkayyapeta.

Higher Secondary or Pre University Courses or Inter-mediate or Junior College in 1 village of the CD Block,, namely Badangi.

College in 1 village, Adult Literacy Center in 25 villages., College is in village, namely Badangi.

Medical: Hospital in 2 villages, Dispensary in 1 village, Health Center in 1 village, Sub Center in 12 villages, Maternity and Child Welfare Center in 0 village, Community health workers in 0 village.

The Villages having Hospital or Dispensary or Health Center are Vadada, Badangi.

Drinking Water: Tap water in 27 villages, Tank water in 27 villages, Well water in 27 villages, Tubewell in 27 villages and more than one source in 27 villages.

Bank: Banking facility in 5 villages, namely, Paltheru, Pinapenki, Badangi, Donkinivalasa Tentuvalasa.

Credit Society in 14 villages Agricultural Credit Society in 7 Non-Agricultural Credit Society in 12 villages.

Others: Power supply in 27 villages, Cinema hall in 2 villages, sport club in 0 village, Stadium or Auditorium or Community Hall in 0 village, Post Office in 15 villages.

There are 18 villages having bus facilities.

Villages with most of facilities: Paltheru Pinapenki, Badangi, Donkinivalasa.

Villages without Amenities (Education): None..

Scheduled Castes: Out of the total population of 48219 persons, 6037 persons (12.52%) belong to Scheduled Castes. The villages having less than 10% SC population are Golladi, Gopalakrishnarangarayapuram, P.Venkampeta Rejeru, Gudepuvalasa, Kamannavalasa, Lakshmipuram Gajarayunivalasa, Tentuvalasa, Pindrangivalasa Veerasagaram, Koduru, D.Venkayyapeta.

The villages having more than 50% SC population are

None.

Sex ratio of Scheduled Caste population is 459.

Scheduled Castes Literates and Illiterates by Sex:

	Persons	Males	Females
Literate	2,370	1,669	701
Illiterate	3,667	1,598	2,069
Literacy rate	44.5	57.2	29.1
Graduate	61	51	10

Scheduled Castes (Dominant):

Madiga, Mala, Relli, Dom etc., Generic Castes etc.

For their cultural identity please see Appendix-I

Villages without Scheduled Castes: There are 6 villages without any scheduled caste population.

Scheduled Tribes: Out of the total population of 48219 persons, 1699 persons (3.52%) belong to Scheduled Tribes. The villages having less than 10% ST population are Golladi, Bheemavaram, Paltheru, Anavaram, Pinapenki P.Venkampeta, Rejeru, Vadada, Kotipalle Gudepuvalasa, Mallampeta, Pudivalasa, Mugada Badangi, Donkinivalasa, Kamannavalasa Gajarayunivalasa, Tentuvalasa, Pedapalle Pindrangivalasa, Veerasagaram, Ramachandra Puram Koduru, D.Venkayyapeta.

The villages having more than 50% ST population are None.

Sex ratio of Scheduled tribe population is 490.

Scheduled Tribes Literates and Illiterates by Sex:

	Persons	Males	Females
Literate	529	343	186
Illiterate	1,170	523	647
Literacy rate	36.6	45.9	26.7
Graduate	3	3	0

Scheduled Tribes (Dominant):

Konda Dhoras, Yerukulas, Gadabas Generic Tribes etc., Sugalis etc.

For their cultural identity please see Appendix-II

Villages without Scheduled Tribes: There are 10 villages without any scheduled tribe population.

Literates and Illiterates by Sex (Total Population):

	Persons	Males	Females
Literate	19,575	12,796	6,779
Illiterate	28,644	11,561	17,083
Literacy rate	46	60	32
Graduate	836	706	130

Agriculture: ***Distribution of villages according to land use:*** Out of 29 villages, Total area (in hectare) is 12495, out of that 74.54 percent is cultivable and 43.39 percent of the cultivable area is irrigated.

Sources of Irrigation (Hectares): Government Canal 400.69, Private Canal 0, Well without Electricity 24.16, Well with Electricity 29.11, Tubewell without Electricity 0, Tubewell with Electricity 0, Tank 3278.75, River 3, Lake 38.75, Waterfall 0, Others 266.91.

Villages with population of 5000 to 9999:

Koduru.

Villages with population of 10000 and above: None

Distribution of Workers:

	Persons	Males	Females	WPR
Cultivators	10,948	5,805	5,143	38.8
Agricultural Labour	11,827	5,449	6,378	41.91
Household Industry	1,242	655	587	4.4
Other Workers	4,201	2,953	1,248	14.89
Main Workers	24,060	13,323	10,737	85.26
Marginal Workers	4,158	1,539	2,619	14.74
Total Workers	28,218	14,862	13,356	

Religion: Major Religious Communities:

	Persons	Males	Females	Sex Ratio
Hindu (98.88%)	47,681	24,092	23,589	979
Muslim (0.27%)	132	67	65	970
Christian (0.48%)	233	110	123	1,118
Sikh (0%)	-	-	-	-
Buddhists (0%)	-	-	-	-
Jain (0%)	1	-	1	-

Agewise Data:

	Persons	Males	Females	Sex Ratio
All ages	48,219	24,357	23,862	980
0-14	14,186	7,439	6,747	907
15-44	22,866	11,494	11,372	989
45-79	10,870	5,282	5,588	1058
80+	215	102	113	1108
Age not stated	82	40	42	1050

Languages (Dominant):

Telugu, Urdu, Gondi, Oriya, Hindi

Disabled Population:

	Persons	Males	Females	%
Total Disabled	921	516	405	
In Seeing	395	190	205	42.89
In Speech	93	52	41	10.1
In Hearing	48	31	17	5.21
In Movement	303	202	101	32.9
Mentally	82	41	41	8.9

BADVEL

Badvel C.D. Block lies in the eastern part of Cuddapah district. The Block is located at a distance of 50 kms. from district headquarters (Cuddapah). There are 24 villages in the block with the total population of 46,392 persons. Area of the C.D. Block is 210.06 sq. kms. It is bounded in the north by Mandals Brahmamg arimattam, B. Kodur and Gopavaram, in the south by Mandal Atlur, in the east by district. Nellore and Mandal

Gopavaram, and in the west by Mandals Khazipet and S. Myduku.

Communications:

Roadways : NH: Direction- Proddatur to Nellore. Nearest Villages- Gunthapalle, Gopalapuram,Chennampalle, Vanam pula. State Highway (S.H.): Direction- Jammalamadugu to Nellore. Nearest Villages- Gunthapalle, Gopalapuram, Chennampalle.

River: Sagileru Nadi- Nearest Villages- Chennampalle, Vanampula, Kondugaripalle, Kongalaveedu, Rajupalem, Godugunur, Puttayapalle.

Receives Backward Region Grant, and is identified as a drought-prone area as well.

Annual Rainfall: Average Rainfall 868 mm

Ground Water: Availability of the Ground Water in the Basin is 1353 H.A.M.and the utilization is 1258 H.A. M.It belongs to Cri category. Depth to water level varies from 10 to 20 meter below the ground. Most of the wells go down in summer months, according to the Ground Water Estimation Committee.

Forests and Reserved Forests: Nearest Villages- Vanampu la, Gopalapuram, Veerapalle, Thippanapalle.

Natural Division : Rayalaseema Region

Administration:

Division: Rayala Seema. Parliamentary Constituency: 38 Kadapa. District: Cuddapah.

Mandal: Badvel. Assembly Constituency: 243 Badvel (SC). Gram Panchayat: 10.

Villages: 24 **Inhabited:** 21 **Uninhabited:** 3

Ranking	District	State	National
Area	29	491	4015
Population	13	622	5449
Sex Ratio	12	449	1732
Child Sex Ratio	48	1050	5053
Literacy Rate	18	223	2404
Density	45	1050	4436
Work Participation Rate	17	644	4394

Gram Panchayats:

Anatha Rajupuram, Chinthala Cheruvu, Konasamudram Kongalaveedu, Puttayapalli, Rajupalem, Thippanapalli Tiruvengalapuram, Vanampula, Veerapalli.

Amenities:

Education: Primary School in 20 villages, Middle school in 9 villages, Matriculation or Secondary School in 3 villages, namely Badvel, Gunthapalle, Chennampalle.

Higher Secondary or Pre University Courses or Intermediate or Junior College in 1 village of the CD Block,, namely Badvel.

College in 2 villages, Adult Literacy Center in 7 villages., Colleges are in villages, namely Badvel, Gunthapalle.

Medical: Hospital in 1 village, Dispensary in 2 villages, Health Center in 3 villages, Sub Center in 5 villages, Maternity and Child Welfare Center in 2 villages, Community health workers in 0 village.

The Villages having Hospital or Dispensary or Health Center are Badvel, Chennampalle, Abbusahebpeta.

Drinking Water: Tap water in 7 villages, Tank water in 6 villages, Well water in 12 villages, Tubewell in 1 village and more than one source in 15 villages.

Bank: Banking facility in 4 villages, namely, Badvel, Gunthapalle, Chennampalle, Veerapalle.

Credit Society in 6 villages Agricultural Credit Society in 3 Non-Agricultural Credit Society in 4 villages.

Others: Power supply in 21 villages, Cinema hall in 2 villages, sport club in 0 village, Stadium or Auditorium or Community Hall in 0 village, Post Office in 12 villages.

There are 17 villages having bus facilities.

Villages with most of facilities: Badvel Gunthapalle, Chennampalle.

Villages without amenities (Education): Mohinuddinpuram..

Scheduled Castes: Out of the total population of 46392 persons, 9600 persons (20.69%) belong to Scheduled Castes.

The villages having less than 10% SC population are Chintalacheruvu, Mohinuddinpuram Imadapuram @ Pedakesampalle, Gopalapuram Venkatasettipalle, Godugunur, Puttayapalle.

The villages having more than 50% SC population are None.

Sex ratio of Scheduled Caste population is 507.

Scheduled Castes Literates and Illiterates by Sex:

	Persons	Males	Females
Literate	4,758	2,807	1,951
Illiterate	4,842	1,930	2,912
Literacy rate	57.7	69.6	46.3
Graduate	167	142	25

Scheduled Castes (Dominant):

Madiga, Mala

For their cultural identity please see Appendix-I

Villages without Scheduled Castes: There are 9 villages without any scheduled caste population.

Scheduled Tribes: Out of the total population of 46392 persons, 794 persons (1.71%) belong to Scheduled Tribes.

The villages having less than 10% ST population are Tiruvengalapuram, Ethirajupalle, Anantharajupuram Badvel, Gunthapalle, Chennampalle, Abbusahebpeta Chintalacheruvu, Bayanapalle, Mohinuddinpuram Vanampula, Gopalapuram, Konasamudram, Kongalaveedu Thippanapalle, Venkatasettipalle, Rajupalem Godugunur, Puttayapalle.

The villages having more than 50% ST population are None.

Sex ratio of Scheduled tribe population is 485.

Scheduled Tribes Literates and Illiterates by Sex:

	Persons	Males	Females
Literate	203	118	85
Illiterate	591	291	300
Literacy rate	32.1	36.5	27.5
Graduate	2	2	0

Scheduled Tribes (Dominant):

Yenadis, Yerukulas, Sugalis etc.

For their cultural identity please see Appendix-II

Villages without Scheduled Tribes: There are 11 villages without any scheduled tribe population.

Literates and Illiterates by Sex (Total Population):

	Persons	Males	Females
Literate	25,007	15,269	9,738
Illiterate	21,385	8,074	13,311
Literacy rate	62	76	48
Graduate	1,694	1,384	310

Agriculture: ***Distribution of villages according to land use:*** Out of 24 villages, Total area (in hectare) is 21009, out of that 26.16 percent is cultivable and 54.56 percent of the cultivable area is irrigated.

Sources of Irrigation (Hectares): Government Canal 0, Private Canal 0, Well without Electricity 10, Well with Electricity 533.8, Tubewell without Electricity 0, Tubewell with Electricity 706.68, Tank 1559.56, River 0, Lake 0, Waterfall 0, Others 188.5.

Villages with population of 5000 to 9999:

Gunthapalle.

Villages with population of 10000 and above:

Badvel.

Distribution of Workers:

	Persons	Males	Females	WPR
Cultivators	3,765	2,976	789	20.2
Agricultural Labour	8,061	4,319	3,742	43.24
Household Industry	831	373	458	4.46
Other Workers	5,984	5,095	889	32.1
Main Workers	15,156	11,286	3,870	81.3
Marginal Workers	3,485	1,477	2,008	18.7
Total Workers	18,641	12,763	5,878	

Religion: Major Religious Communities:

	Persons	Males	Females	Sex Ratio
Hindu (93.52%)	43,387	21,815	21,572	989
Muslim (6.1%)	2,829	1,436	1,393	970
Christian (0.29%)	134	71	63	887
Sikh (0%)	1	-	1	-
Buddhists (0%)	-	-	-	-
Jain (0%)	1	-	1	-

Agewise Data:

	Persons	Males	Females	Sex Ratio
All ages	46,392	23,343	23,049	987
0-14	14,502	7,176	7,326	1021
15-44	22,195	11,449	10,746	939
45-79	9,343	4,551	4,792	1053
80+	310	136	174	1279
Age not stated	42	31	11	355

Languages (Dominant):

Telugu, Urdu, Marathi, Gondi, Hindi

Disabled Population:

	Persons	Males	Females	%
Total Disabled	981	539	442	
In Seeing	364	184	180	37.1
In Speech	114	71	43	11.62
In Hearing	63	32	31	6.42
In Movement	314	191	123	32.01
Mentally	126	61	65	12.84

BAIREDDIPALLE

Baireddipalle C.D. Block lies in the south-western part of Chittoor district. The Block is located at a distance of 80 kms. from district headquarters (Chitt oor). There are 25 villages in the block with the total population of 50,094 persons. Area of the C.D. Block is 161.61 sq. kms. It is bounded in the north by Mandal Palamaneru, in the east by Mandal Palamaneru and in the west by Mandal Venkalagirikota, and it has common boundary with the state of Karnataka in the north and west, and with the state of Tamil Nadu in the east.

Communications:

Roadways : NH- 4: Direction- Bangalore to Chennai. Neare st Villages- Peddachellaragunta, Belupalle. NH- 219: Direction- Kuppam to Palamaneru. Nearest Villages- Peddachellaragunta, Belupalle, Kaigallu, Devadoddi, Pathurnatham, Baireddipalle, Kammanapalle, Belupalle.

It receives the Backward Region Grants, and is identifi ed as a drought-prone area as well.

Annual Rainfall: Average Rainfall 890 mm

Ground Water: Availability of the Ground Water in the Basin is 1452 H.A.M.and the utilization is 1538 H.A. M. It belongs to OE category. Depth to water level varies more than 10 meter below the ground. Most of the wells go down in summer months, according to the Ground Water Estimation Committee.

Forest and Reserved **Forest:** Nearest Villages- Alapalle, Gollachemana Palle, Belupalle, Lakkanapalle, Kambhampa lle, Theertham, Devadoddi, Gounithimmepalle, Meakalanagi reddi Palle, Donthirallapalle, Nellipatla, Raghunayakula Dinne, Thimmaiahgaripalle.

Natural Division : Rayalaseema Region

Administration:

Division: Rayala Seema. Parliamentary Constituency: 42 Chittoor (SC). District: Chittoor. Mandal: Baireddip alle. Assembly Constituency: 293 Palamner Gram Panchayat: 21

Border Villages: (Tamil Nadu)- Nearest Villages- Alapal le, Gollachemana Palle, Peddachellaragunta, Kambhampa lle, Theertham.

Villages: 25 **Inhabited:** 24 **Uninhabited:** 1

Ranking	**District**	**State**	**National**
Area	37	767	4853
Population	22	508	5275
Sex Ratio	15	261	1222
Child Sex Ratio	9	141	377
Literacy Rate	44	288	2877
Density	28	547	3434
Work Participation Rate	21	348	1453

Gram Panchayats:

Alapalle, Baireddipalle, Belupalle, Chappidipalle Devadoddi, Dharmapuri, Gadduru, Ganginayanipalle Gollachemanapalle, Gounithimmepalle, Kadapanatham Kambhampalle, Kammanapalle, Kothuru, Lakkanapalle Nellipatla, Pathapeta, Pathurunatham Peddachellaragunta, Theertham, Vengamvaripalle.

Amenities:

Education: Primary School in 22 villages, Middle school in 9 villages, Matriculation or Secondary School in 7 villages, namely Gollachemana Palle, Lakkanapalle, Theertham, Kadapanatham, Baireddipalle, Kammanapalle, Nellipatla.

Higher Secondary or Pre University Courses or Intermediate or Junior College in 0 village of the CD Block, College in 0 village, Adult Literacy Center in 12 villages.

Medical: Hospital in 0 village, Dispensary in 0 village, Health Center in 2 villages, Sub Center in 7 villages, Maternity and Child Welfare Center in 0 village, Community health workers in 0 village.

Drinking Water: Tap water in 24 villages, Tank water in 24 villages, Well water in 24 villages, Tubewell in 24 villages and more than one source in 24 villages.

Bank: Banking facility in 3 villages, namely, Settipalle, Theertham, Baireddipalle.

Credit Society in 2 villages Agricultural Credit Society in 1 Non-Agricultural Credit Society in 2 villages.

Others: Power supply in 24 villages, Cinema hall in 1 village, sport club in 0 village, Stadium or Auditorium or Community Hall in 0 village, Post Office in 11 villages.

There are 20 villages having bus facilities.

Villages with most of facilities: Theertham Baireddipalle.

Villages without amenities (Education): Donthirallapalle, Thimmaiahgaripalle..

Scheduled Castes: Out of the total population of 50094 persons, 10428 persons (20.82%) belong to Scheduled Castes. The villages having less than 10% SC population are Devadoddi, Kadapanatham, Mulathimmepalle Donthirallapalle, Raghunayakula Dinne.

The villages having more than 50% SC population are None.

Sex ratio of Scheduled Caste population is 497.

Scheduled Castes Literates and Illiterates by Sex:

	Persons	Males	Females
Literate	4,677	2,945	1,732
Illiterate	5,751	2,304	3,447
Literacy rate	53.0	66.1	39.6
Graduate	68	58	10

Scheduled Castes (Dominant):

Mala, Madiga, Adi Dravida, Adi Andhra, Arwa Mala

For their cultural identity please see Appendix-I

Villages without Scheduled Castes: There are 4 villages without any scheduled caste population.

Scheduled Tribes: Out of the total population of 50094 persons, 1333 persons (2.66%) belong to Scheduled Tribes. The villages having less than 10% ST population are Alapalle, Gollachemana Palle, Peddachellaragunta Belupalle, Settipalle, Lakkanapalle, Kambhampalle Theertham, Devadoddi, Pathurnatham, Kadapanatham Gounithimmepalle, Baireddipalle, Ganginayanipalle Kammanapalle, Dharmapuri, Mulathimmepalle Donthirallapalle, Chappidipalle, Nellipatla.

The villages having more than 50% ST population are None.

Sex ratio of Scheduled tribe population is 509.

Scheduled Tribes Literates and Illiterates by Sex:

	Persons	Males	Females
Literate	399	250	149
Illiterate	934	405	529
Literacy rate	36.9	46.0	27.6
Graduate	0	0	0

Scheduled Tribes (Dominant):

Yenadis, Yerukulas, Sugalis etc.

For their cultural identity please see Appendix-II

Villages without Scheduled Tribes: There are 7 villages without any scheduled tribe population.

Literates and Illiterates by Sex (Total Population):

	Persons	Males	Females
Literate	25,309	15,633	9,676
Illiterate	24,785	9,439	15,346
Literacy rate	59	73	45
Graduate	519	419	100

Agriculture: ***Distribution of villages according to land use:***

Out of 25 villages, Total area (in hectare) is 16162, out of that 56.22 percent is cultivable and 22.34 percent of the cultivable area is irrigated.

Sources of Irrigation (Hectares): Government Canal 0, Private Canal 0, Well without Electricity 0, Well with Electricity 1579.46, Tubewell without Electricity 0, Tubewell with Electricity 80.85, Tank 369.37, River 0, Lake 0, Waterfall 0, Others 0.

Villages with population of 5000 to 9999: Baireddipalle.

Villages with population of 10000 and above: None

Distribution of Workers:

	Persons	Males	Females	WPR
Cultivators	10,997	6,858	4,139	42.52
Agricultural Labour	10,492	5,182	5,310	40.57
Household Industry	828	416	412	3.2
Other Workers	3,547	2,663	884	13.71
Main Workers	20,703	13,254	7,449	80.05
Marginal Workers	5,161	1,865	3,296	19.95
Total Workers	25,864	15,119	10,745	

Religion: Major Religious Communities:

	Persons	Males	Females	Sex Ratio
Hindu (88.59%)	44,377	22,199	22,178	999
Muslim (11.28%)	5,650	2,838	2,812	991
Christian (0.12%)	59	31	28	903
Sikh (0%)	-	-	-	-
Buddhists (0%)	-	-	-	-
Jain (0%)	-	-	-	-

Agewise Data:

	Persons	Males	Females	Sex Ratio
All ages	50,094	25,072	25,022	998
0-14	17,552	8,768	8,784	1002
15-44	22,661	11,272	11,389	1010
45-79	9,460	4,835	4,625	957
80+	397	186	211	1134
Age not stated	24	11	13	1182

Languages (Dominant):

Telugu, Urdu, Tamil, Kannada, Marathi

Disabled Population:

	Persons	Males	Females	%
Total Disabled	699	387	312	
In Seeing	209	107	102	29.9
In Speech	86	48	38	12.3
In Hearing	83	39	44	11.87
In Movement	233	152	81	33.33
Mentally	88	41	47	12.59

BALANAGAR

Balanagar C.D. Block lies in the north-east part of Mahbubnagar district. The Block is located at a distance of 40 kms. from district headquarters (Mahbubnagar). There are 37 villages in the block with the total population of 61,592 persons. Area of the C.D. Block is 305.70 sq. kms. It is bounded by Farooqnagar Mandal on north, Keshampet Mandal on east, Jadcherla Mandal on south, and Nawabpet Mandal on west.

Communications:

Roadways : NH- 7: Direction- Jadcherla to Farooqnagar. Nearest Villages- Mothighanapur, Kethireddipalle, Peddayapalle, Seriguda, Gundlapotlapalle, Rajapur, Balanagar, Rangareddiguda.

Railway Station: Balanagar, Rajapur.

Backwards Region Grants Fund: It receives Backward Region Grants.

Annual Rainfall: Average Rainfall 596 mm

Ground Water: Availability of the Ground Water in the Basin is 1852 H.A.M. and the utilization is 2020 H. A.M. It belongs to OE category. Depth to water level varies from 2 meter below the ground. Most of the wells go down in summer months. The well density in the entire block is 19 wells per sq. km. Total no. of the wells in the block are enumerated as 5206, according to the Ground Water Estimation Committee.

Natural Division : Telangana Plateau Region

Administration:

Division: Telangana. Parliamentary Constituency: 11 Mahbubnagar. District: Mahbubnagar. Mandal: Balanagar. Assembly Constituency: 75 Jadcherla. Gram Panchayat: 31

Villages: 37 **Inhabited:** 37 **Uninhabited:** 0

Ranking	**District**	**State**	**National**
Area	13	151	2725
Population	9	257	4807
Sex Ratio	37	751	2536
Child Sex Ratio	22	556	2154
Literacy Rate	29	975	5586
Density	38	273	4716
Work Participation Rate	31	712	697

Gram Panchayats:

Agraharam Potlapally, Balanagar, Bodajanampet Chennavally, Chinnarevally, Dondlapalle Ediganipally, Gouthapoor, Gunded, Gundlapotlapally Hemajipoor, Kallepally, Kethireddipally, Khanapoor Kucherkal, Mallepally, Modampally, Mothighanapoor Mudireddypalli, Nandaram, Nerellapally, Peddaipally Peddarevally, Raipally, Rajapoor, Rangareddiguda Suraram, Thirumalagiri, Thirumalapur, Udithyal A Verannapally.

Amenities:

Education: Primary School in 37 villages, Middle school in 10 villages, Matriculation or Secondary School in 5 villages, namely Udithyal, Balanagar, Thirumalapur,

Peddarevelly, Rajapur.
Higher Secondary or Pre University Courses or Intermediate or Junior College in 0 village of the CD Block, College in 0 village, Adult Literacy Center in 33 villages.
Medical: Hospital in 0 village, Dispensary in 1 village, Health Center in 2 villages, Sub Center in 8 villages, Maternity and Child Welfare Center in 0 village, Community health workers in 0 village.
The Village having Hospital or Dispensary or Health Center is Rajapur.
Drinking Water: Tap water in 37 villages, Tank water in 37 villages, Well water in 37 villages, Tubewell in 37 villages and more than one source in 37 villages.
Bank: Banking facility in 2 villages, namely, Balanagar, Rajapur.
Credit Society in 14 villages Agricultural Credit Society in 1 Non-Agricultural Credit Society in 13 villages.
Others: Power supply in 37 villages, Cinema hall in 0 village, sport club in 0 village, Stadium or Auditorium or Community Hall in 0 village, Post Office in 12 villages.
There are 31 villages having bus facilities.
Villages with most of facilities: Balanagar Rajapur.
Villages without Amenities (Education): None..
Scheduled Castes: Out of the total population of 61592 persons, 9932 persons (16.13%) belong to Scheduled Castes.
The villages having less than 10% SC population are Kuthnepalle, Khanapur, Seriguda, Bibinagar Modampalle, Thirumalagiri.
The villages having more than 50% SC population are None.
Sex ratio of Scheduled Caste population is 496.
Scheduled Castes Literates and Illiterates by Sex:

	Persons	Males	Females
Literate	3,318	2,233	1,085
Illiterate	6,614	2,773	3,841
Literacy rate	39.5	52.7	26.0
Graduate	40	35	5

Scheduled Castes (Dominant):
Madiga, Mala, Byagara, Bindla, Generic Castes etc.
For their cultural identity please see Appendix-I
Villages without Scheduled Castes: There are 2 villages without any scheduled caste population.
Scheduled Tribes: Out of the total population of 61592 persons, 18383 persons (29.85%) belong to Scheduled Tribes.
The villages having less than 10% ST population are Balanagar, Nandaram, Dondlapalle, Seriguda Agraharam Potlapalle, Gundlapotlapalle, Chennavalli Raipalle.
The villages having more than 50% ST population are Nerellapalle, Raghvapur, Kuthnepalle, Appajipalle Bibinagar, Edganpalle, Kallepalle, Modampalle Thirumalagiri.
Sex ratio of Scheduled tribe population is 483.
Scheduled Tribes Literates and Illiterates by Sex:

	Persons	Males	Females
Literate	3,119	2,455	664
Illiterate	15,264	7,041	8,223
Literacy rate	21.4	32.5	9.4
Graduate	17	17	0

Scheduled Tribes (Dominant):
Sugalis etc., Yerukulas, Generic Tribes etc.
For their cultural identity please see Appendix-II
Villages without Scheduled Tribes: There are 2 villages without any scheduled tribe population.
Literates and Illiterates by Sex (Total Population):

	Persons	Males	Females
Literate	21,231	14,046	7,185
Illiterate	40,361	17,237	23,124
Literacy rate	42	54	29
Graduate	520	429	91

Agriculture: ***Distribution of villages according to land use:*** Out of 37 villages, Total area (in hectare) is 30568, out of that 83.22 percent is cultivable and 16.18 percent of the cultivable area is irrigated.
Sources of Irrigation (Hectares): Government Canal 0, Private Canal 0, Well without Electricity 0, Well with Electricity 294, Tubewell without Electricity 0, Tubewell with Electricity 3467, Tank 355, River 0, Lake 0, Waterfall 0, Others 0.
Villages with population of 5000 to 9999: Udithyal, Rajapur.
Villages with population of 10000 and above: None
Distribution of Workers:

	Persons	Males	Females	WPR
Cultivators	12,245	7,733	4,512	37.15
Agricultural Labour	13,453	4,705	8,748	40.82
Household Industry	998	490	508	3.03
Other Workers	6,261	4,748	1,513	19
Main Workers	26,600	15,473	11,127	80.71
Marginal Workers	6,357	2,203	4,154	19.29
Total Workers	32,957	17,676	15,281	

Religion: Major Religious Communities:

	Persons	Males	Females	Sex Ratio
Hindu (95.79%)	58,997	29,918	29,079	972
Muslim (3.96%)	2,442	1,289	1,153	894
Christian (0.22%)	138	68	70	1,029
Sikh (0.01%)	7	3	4	1,333
Buddhists (0%)	-	-	-	-
Jain (0%)	-	-	-	-

Agewise Data:

	Persons	Males	Females	Sex Ratio
All ages	61,592	31,283	30,309	969
0-14	23,941	12,288	11,653	948
15-44	26,765	13,617	13,148	966
45-79	10,330	5,114	5,216	1020
80+	489	229	260	1135
Age not stated	67	35	32	914

Languages (Dominant):
Telugu, Hindi, Urdu, Tamil, Oriya

Disabled Population:

	Persons	Males	Females	%
Total Disabled	965	544	421	
In Seeing	378	198	180	39.17
In Speech	94	61	33	9.74
In Hearing	48	22	26	4.97
In Movement	315	190	125	32.64
Mentally	130	73	57	13.47

BALAYAPALLE

Balayapalle C.D. Block lies in the southern part of Nellore district. The Block is located at a distance of 67 kms. from district headquarters (Nellore). There are 51 villages in the block with the total population of 32,653 persons. Area of the C.D. Block is 265.52 sq. kms. It is bounded in the north by Mandals Sydapuram and Gudur, in the south by district Chittoor and Mandal Venkatagiri, in the east by Mandals Gudur, Ojili and Pellakur, and in the west by Mandals Venkatagiri and Dakkili.

Communications:

Roadways : Metalled Roads: Nearest Villages- Venkataredd ipalle, Alimili, Ambalapudi, Chutti, Balayapalle, Mannuru, Pallipadu, Gottikadu, Subrahmanyam, Yachavaram, Venga mambapuram, Akkasamudram, Jayampu, Papireddipalle, Konai gunta, Gollagunta, Chilamanuru, Sangavaram, Kovurivarigu nta, Melchuru, Perimidi.

Railway Station: Jayampu, Nidigallu.

River: Alapalayeru Nadi- Nearest Village- Yachavaram.

Annual Rainfall: Average Rainfall 1103 mm

Ground Water: Availability of the Ground Water in the Basin is 2907 H.A.M. and the utilization is 1988 H. A.M. It belongs to Safe category. Depth to water level varies from 2 to 10 meter below the ground. Most of the wells go down in summer months, according to the Ground Water Estimation Committee.

Administration:

Division: Coastal Andhra. Parliamentary Constituency: 40 Tirupati (SC). District: Nellore. Mandal: Balayapalle. Assembly Constituency: 241 Venkatagiri. Gram Panchaya t: 24.

Villages: 51 **Inhabited:** 46 **Uninhabited:** 5

Ranking	District	State	National
Area	24	258	3176
Population	42	982	5985
Sex Ratio	29	584	2008
Child Sex Ratio	35	931	4146
Literacy Rate	38	435	3618
Density	1	50	5924
Work Participation Rate	37	995	203

Gram Panchayats:
Alimili, Balayapalli, Byaravaram, Chilamanuru Gottikadu, Hastakaveri, Jayampu, Kadagunta Kalaganda, Kamakuru, Katragunta, Kayyuru, Kotembedu Mannuru, Nidigallu, Nindali, Pakapudi, Pallipadu Pegilam, Perimidi, Sanagavaram, Siddagunta Uttapalli, Vengamambapuram.

Amenities:

Education: Primary School in 46 villages, Middle school in 8 villages, Matriculation or Secondary School in 5 villages, namely Balayapalle, Vengamambapuram, Jayampu, Pigilam, Nidigallu.
Higher Secondary or Pre University Courses or Intermediate or Junior College in 0 village of the CD Block, College in 0 village, Adult Literacy Center in 22 villages.

Medical: Hospital in 0 village, Dispensary in 0 village, Health Center in 1 village, Sub Center in 9 villages, Maternity and Child Welfare Center in 0 village, Community health workers in 0 village.

Drinking Water: Tap water in 46 villages, Tank water in 46 villages, Well water in 46 villages, Tubewell in 46 villages and more than one source in 46 villages.

Bank: Banking facility in 3 villages, namely, Balayapalle, Jayampu, Tikkavaram.
Credit Society in 18 villages Agricultural Credit Society in 5 Non-Agricultural Credit Society in 18 villages.

Others: Power supply in 46 villages, Cinema hall in 1 village, sport club in 0 village, Stadium or Auditorium or Community Hall in 0 village, Post Office in 18 villages.
There are 39 villages having bus facilities.

Villages with most of facilities: Balayapalle Jayampu.

Villages without Amenities (Education): None..

Scheduled Castes: Out of the total population of 32653 persons, 10159 persons (31.11%) belong to Scheduled Castes. The villages having less than 10% SC population are Arigepalle, Tikkavaram, Katragunta, Karimenagunta Konamgunta, Gollagunta, Muraharidondrao Khandrika.
The villages having more than 50% SC population are None.
Sex ratio of Scheduled Caste population is 499.

Scheduled Castes Literates and Illiterates by Sex:

	Persons	Males	Females
Literate	4,275	2,591	1,684
Illiterate	5,884	2,499	3,385
Literacy rate	48.6	58.8	38.3
Graduate	47	40	7

Scheduled Castes (Dominant):
Mala, Madiga, Arundhatiya, Generic Castes etc.
Adi Andhra

For their cultural identity please see Appendix-I

Villages without Scheduled Castes: There are 8 villages without any scheduled caste population.

Scheduled Tribes: Out of the total population of 32653 persons, 3685 persons (11.29%) belong to Scheduled Tribes. The villages having less than 10% ST population are Nindali, Venkatareddipalle, Chutti, Ramapuram Balayapalle, Pallipadu, Yachavaram, Vengamambapuram Akkasamudram, Pakapudi, Hastakaveri, Tikkavaram Tallapalle, Siddagunta, Nidigallu, Katragunta Kamakuru, Kotambedu, Kalaganda, Papireddipalle Gollagunta, Sangavaram, Mallemala Chakracharyulavari Khandrika.

The villages having more than 50% ST population are None.

Sex ratio of Scheduled tribe population is 483.

Scheduled Tribes Literates and Illiterates by Sex:

	Persons	Males	Females
Literate	845	489	356
Illiterate	2,840	1,417	1,423
Literacy rate	28.1	31.6	24.4
Graduate	1	1	0

Scheduled Tribes (Dominant):
Yenadis, Yerukulas, Generic Tribes etc.

For their cultural identity please see Appendix-II

Villages without Scheduled Tribes: There are 12 villages without any scheduled tribe population.

Literates and Illiterates by Sex (Total Population):

	Persons	Males	Females
Literate	15,749	9,312	6,437
Illiterate	16,904	7,182	9,722
Literacy rate	55	65	46
Graduate	387	318	69

Agriculture: ***Distribution of villages according to land use:*** Out of 51 villages, Total area (in hectare) is 26553, out of that 30.07 percent is cultivable and 78.17 percent of the cultivable area is irrigated.

Sources of Irrigation (Hectares): Government Canal 0, Private Canal 0, Well without Electricity 0, Well with Electricity 1988, Tubewell without Electricity 0, Tubewell with Electricity 65, Tank 3987, River 0, Lake 0, Waterfall 0, Others 202.

Villages with population of 5000 to 9999: None

Villages with population of 10000 and above: None

Distribution of Workers:

	Persons	Males	Females	WPR
Cultivators	6,932	4,442	2,490	35.39
Agricultural Labour	10,316	4,688	5,628	52.67
Household Industry	312	184	128	1.59
Other Workers	2,025	1,449	576	10.34
Main Workers	13,775	9,152	4,623	70.33
Marginal Workers	5,810	1,611	4,199	29.67
Total Workers	19,585	10,763	8,822	

Religion: Major Religious Communities:

	Persons	Males	Females	Sex Ratio
Hindu (98.12%)	32,039	16,201	15,838	978
Muslim (1.24%)	406	204	202	990
Christian (0.6%)	195	84	111	1,321
Sikh (0%)	1	-	1	-
Buddhists (0%)	-	-	-	-
Jain (0%)	-	-	-	-

Agewise Data:

	Persons	Males	Females	Sex Ratio
All ages	32,653	16,494	16,159	980
0-14	9,410	4,929	4,481	909
15-44	16,374	8,182	8,192	1001
45-79	6,668	3,291	3,377	1026
80+	173	74	99	1338
Age not stated	28	18	10	556

Languages (Dominant):
Telugu, Urdu, Gondi, Tamil, Others

Disabled Population:

	Persons	Males	Females	%
Total Disabled	762	389	373	
In Seeing	302	119	183	39.63
In Speech	75	45	30	9.84
In Hearing	75	39	36	9.84
In Movement	239	147	92	31.36
Mentally	71	39	32	9.32

BALIJIPETA

Balijipeta C.D. Block lies in the northern part of Vizianagaram district. The Block is located at a distan ce of 88 kms. from district headquarters (Vizianagaram). There are 34 villages in the block with the total population of 62,787 persons. Area of the C.D. Block is 182.85 sq. kms. It is bounded in the north by Mandal Garugubilli, in the south by Mandal Therlam, in the east by Mandal Srikakulam, and in the west by Mandals Bobbili and Seethanagaram.

Communications :

Roadways : Metalled Roads: Nearest Villages- Tumarada, Vengapuram, Palagara.

River: Suvarnamukhi Nadi- Nearest Villages- Ajjada, Muragadam, Chakarapalle, Gowripuram, Narayanapuram, Padamayavalasa, Arasada, Panukuvalasa (Near) Arasada, Palagara.

Backwards Region Grants Fund: It receives Backward Region Grants.

Annaul Rainfall: Average Rainfall 886.7 mm

Ground Water: Availability of the Ground Water in the Basin is (Information not avavible) H.A.M .and the utilization is (Information not avavible) H.A.M. It belongs to (Information not avavible) category. Depth to water level varies from 3 to 10 meter below the ground. Most of the wells go down in summer months.

Administration:

Division: Coastal Andhra. Parliamentary Constituency: 18 Araku (ST). District: Vizianagram. Mandal: Balijipeta. Assembly Constituency: 131 Parvathipuram (ST) Gram Panchayat: 24.

Villages: 34 **Inhabited:** 31 **Uninhabited:** 3

Ranking	District	State	National
Area	4	652	4486
Population	5	230	4760
Sex Ratio	16	154	851
Child Sex Ratio	19	264	836
Literacy Rate	18	878	5191
Density	17	171	3157
Work Participation Rate	25	280	500

Gram Panchayats:

Ajjada, Ampavalli, Arasada, Balijipeta, Barli Chakarapalli, Chilakalapalli, Galavalli, Gangada Mirthivalasa, Narannaiduvalasa, Narayanapuram Nookalawada, Padamayavalasa, Palagara, Panukuvalasa Pedapenki, Peddimpeta, Sivaramapuram, Subhadra Tumarada, Vantaram, Vengalarayapuram, Vengapuram.

Amenities:

Education: Primary School in 30 villages, Middle school in 14 villages, Matriculation or Secondary School in 7 villages, namely Ajjada, Arasada, Palagara, Chilkalapalle, Pedapenki, Vantaram, Narannaiduvalasa.

Higher Secondary or Pre University Courses or Intermediate or Junior College in 1 village of the CD Block,, namely Palagara.

College in 1 village, Adult Literacy Center in 25 villages., College is in village, namely Palagara.

Medical: Hospital in 0 village, Dispensary in 0 village, Health Center in 2 villages, Sub Center in 14 villages, Maternity and Child Welfare Center in 0 village, Community health workers in 0 village.

Drinking Water: Tap water in 31 villages, Tank water in 31 villages, Well water in 31 villages, Tubewell in 31 villages and more than one source in 31 villages.

Bank: Banking facility in 2 villages, namely, Palagara, Galavilli.

Credit Society in 11 villages Agricultural Credit Society in 7 Non-Agricultural Credit Society in 10 villages.

Others: Power supply in 31 villages, Cinema hall in 2 villages, sport club in 0 village, Stadium or Auditorium or Community Hall in 0 village, Post Office in 17 villages.

There are 25 villages having bus facilities.

Villages with most of facilities: Palagara Galavilli.

Villages without amenities (Education): Kondapuram..

Scheduled Castes: Out of the total population of 62787 persons, 8478 persons (13.5%) belong to Scheduled Castes.

The villages having less than 10% SC population are Muragadam, Peddimpeta, Gowripuram, Sivarampuram Subhadra, Badevalasa, Mirthivalasa, Chellimpeta Nookalavada, Janardhanapuram, Kondapuram Sri Rangaraja Puram, Galavilli.

The villages having more than 50% SC population are None.

Sex ratio of Scheduled Caste population is 497.

Scheduled Castes Literates and Illiterates by Sex:

	Persons	Males	Females
Literate	3,148	1,963	1,185
Illiterate	5,330	2,304	3,026
Literacy rate	42.4	52.4	32.2
Graduate	86	77	9

Scheduled Castes (Dominant):

Madiga, Mala, Relli, Dom etc.

For their cultural identity please see Appendix-I

Villages without Scheduled Castes: There are 7 villages without any scheduled caste population.

Scheduled Tribes: Out of the total population of 62787 persons, 1205 persons (1.92%) belong to Scheduled Tribes.

The villages having less than 10% ST population are Ajjada, Muragadam, Peddimpeta, Gowripuram Narayanapuram, Padamayavalasa, Arasada Panukuvalasa (Near) Arasada, Sivarampuram, Subhadra Badevalasa, Barli, Mirthivalasa, Chellimpeta Tumarada, Vengapuram, Palagara, Nookalavada Chilkalapalle, Pedapenki, Bhairipuram, Ampavilli Janardhanapuram, Vengalarayapuram, Kondapuram Vantaram, Gangada, Narannaiduvalasa Sri Rangaraja Puram, Galavilli.

The villages having more than 50% ST population are None.

Sex ratio of Scheduled tribe population is 489.

Scheduled Tribes Literates and Illiterates by Sex:

	Persons	Males	Females
Literate	351	224	127
Illiterate	854	392	462
Literacy rate	33.1	42.8	23.7
Graduate	3	3	0

Scheduled Tribes (Dominant):

Konda Dhoras, Gadabas, Yerukulas, Jatapus

For their cultural identity please see Appendix-II

Villages without Scheduled Tribes: There are 11 villages without any scheduled tribe population.

Literates and Illiterates by Sex (Total Population):

	Persons	Males	Females
Literate	24,845	15,898	8,947
Illiterate	37,942	15,318	22,624
Literacy rate	45	58	32
Graduate	1,012	863	149

Agriculture: ***Distribution of villages according to land use:*** Out of 34 villages, Total area (in hectare) is 18283, out of that 73.42 percent is cultivable and 35.96 percent of the cultivable area is irrigated.

Sources of Irrigation (Hectares): Government Canal 1669.81, Private Canal 0, Well without Electricity 43.57, Well with Electricity 4.77, Tubewell without Electricity 24.26, Tubewell with Electricity 40.46, Tank 3044.61, River 0, Lake 0, Waterfall 0, Others 0.

Villages with population of 5000 to 9999:

Palagara, Pedapenki.

Villages with population of 10000 and above: None

Distribution of Workers:

	Persons	Males	Females	WPR
Cultivators	12,460	7,099	5,361	34.45
Agricultural Labour	15,794	6,670	9,124	43.67
Household Industry	1,578	708	870	4.36
Other Workers	6,335	4,752	1,583	17.52
Main Workers	26,738	15,856	10,882	73.93
Marginal Workers	9,429	3,373	6,056	26.07
Total Workers	36,167	19,229	16,938	

Religion: Major Religious Communities:

	Persons	Males	Females	Sex Ratio
Hindu (99.76%)	62,635	31,144	31,491	1,011
Muslim (0.07%)	47	22	25	1,136
Christian (0.13%)	82	37	45	1,216
Sikh (0%)	-	-	-	-
Buddhists (0%)	-	-	-	-
Jain (0%)	-	-	-	-

Agewise Data:

	Persons	Males	Females	Sex Ratio
All ages	62,787	31,216	31,571	1011
0-14	18,633	9,451	9,182	972
15-44	29,495	14,674	14,821	1010
45-79	14,253	6,898	7,355	1066
80+	345	156	189	1212
Age not stated	61	37	24	649

Languages (Dominant):

Telugu, Urdu, Gondi, Oriya, Hindi

Disabled Population:

	Persons	Males	Females	%
Total Disabled	1,580	855	725	
In Seeing	693	339	354	43.86
In Speech	146	79	67	9.24
In Hearing	91	46	45	5.76
In Movement	530	333	197	33.54
Mentally	120	58	62	7.59

BALKONDA

Balkonda C.D. Block lies in the north-east part of Nizamabad district. The Block is located at a distance of 38 kms. from district headquarters (Nizamabad). There are 26 villages in the block with the total popul ation of 76,966 persons. Area of the C.D. Block is 204. 39 sq. kms. It is bounded by Adilabad district on north -west, north and north-east, Mortad Mandal on north-east, east and south-east, Velpur Mandal on south-east, Armur Mandal on south, south-west, west and north-west, Nandipet Mandal on north-west.

Communications :

Roadways : NH- 7: Direction- Hyderabad to Adilabad. Nearest Villages- Bussapur, Mukpal, Vempalle, Kisannagar, Balkonda, Chittapur, Doodgaon, Nallur.

River: Godavari Nadi- Nearest Villages- Soanpet, Chaker iyal, Kodecherla, Savel, Ratnapur, Keshapur, Kojan Kothur, Velgatur, Venchariyal, Doodgaon, Nallur.

Backwards Region Grants Fund: It receives Backward Region Grants.

Annual Rainfall: Average Rainfall 993 mm

Ground Water: Availability of the Ground Water in the Basin is 4981 H.A.M. and the utilization is 4233 H. A.M. It belongs to Semi Critical category. Depth to water level varies from 5 to 20 meter below the ground. Most of the wells go down in summer months, according to the Ground Water Estimation Committee.

Natural Division : Telangana Plateau Region

Administration:

Division: Telangana. Parliamentary Constituency: 4 Nizamabad. District: Nizamabad. Mandal: Balkonda. Assem bly Constituency: 19 Balkonda. Gram Panchayat: 25.

Villages: 26 **Inhabited:** 22 **Uninhabited:** 4

Ranking	District	State	National
Area	19	521	4103
Population	3	54	4212
Sex Ratio	8	31	288

Child Sex Ratio	22	645	2587
Literacy Rate	3	515	3915
Density	17	373	2904
Work Participation Rate	3	221	909

Gram Panchayats:

Balkonda, Baswapoor, Bodepally, Bussapur, Chakiryal Chittapur, Doodgaon, Ithwarpet, Jalalpur Kisan Nagar, Kodicherla, Kothapalli, Mendora, Mupkal Nagampet, Nagapoor, Nalloor, Renjarla, Savel Soanpet, Srirampoor, Vannel B, Velkatoor, Vempally Venchiryal.

Amenities:

Education: Primary School in 22 villages, Middle school in 17 villages, Matriculation or Secondary School in 11 villages, namely Soanpet, Doodgaon, Savel, Mendora, Mukpal, Velgatur, Renjarla, Kisannagar, Balkonda, Chittapur, Vannel Bashirabad.

Higher Secondary or Pre University Courses or Intermediate or Junior College in 1 village of the CD Block,, namely Balkonda.

College in 0 village, Adult Literacy Center in 13 villages.

Medical: Hospital in 3 villages, Dispensary in 3 villages, Health Center in 2 villages, Sub Center in 12 villages, Maternity and Child Welfare Center in 2 villages, Community health workers in 0 village.

The Villages having Hospital or Dispensary or Health Center are Soanpet, Doodgaon, Mukpal, Kisannagar, Balkonda.

Drinking Water: Tap water in 22 villages, Tank water in 21 villages, Well water in 21 villages, Tubewell in 21 villages and more than one source in 22 villages.

Bank: Banking facility in 7 villages, namely, Doodgaon, Mendora, Mukpal, Renjarla, Kisannagar Balkonda, Vannel Bashirabad.

Credit Society in 9 villages Agricultural Credit Society in 4 Non-Agricultural Credit Society in 1 village.

Others: Power supply in 22 villages, Cinema hall in 1 village, sport club in 0 village, Stadium or Auditorium or Community Hall in 0 village, Post Office in 19 villages.

There are 22 villages having bus facilities.

Villages with most of facilities: Doodgaon Mendora, Mukpal, Renjarla, Kisannagar, Balkonda Vannel Bashirabad.

Villages without Amenities (Education): None..

Scheduled Castes: Out of the total population of 76966 persons, 14019 persons (18.21%) belong to Scheduled Castes.

The villages having less than 10% SC population are None..

The villages having more than 50% SC population are None.

Sex ratio of Scheduled Caste population is 527.

Scheduled Castes Literates and Illiterates by Sex:

	Persons	Males	Females
Literate	5,921	3,622	2,299
Illiterate	8,098	3,012	5,086
Literacy rate	48.7	63.5	35.6
Graduate	105	95	10

Scheduled Castes (Dominant):

Mala, Madiga, Gosangi, Chamar etc., Mahar

For their cultural identity please see Appendix-I

Villages without Scheduled Castes: There are 4 villages without any scheduled caste population.

Scheduled Tribes: Out of the total population of 76966 persons, 4128 persons (5.36%) belong to Scheduled Tribes.

The villages having less than 10% ST population are Soanpet, Doodgaon, Chakeriyal, Kodecherla, Savel Mendora, Bussapur, Nallur, Jalalpur, Nagapur, Mukpal Venchariyal, Renjarla, Nagampet, Vempalle Kisannagar, Balkonda, Chittapur, Bodepalle Vannel Bashirabad.

The villages having more than 50% ST population are None.

Sex ratio of Scheduled tribe population is 513.

Scheduled Tribes Literates ınd Illiterates by Sex:

	Persons	Males	Females
Literate	1,336	886	450
Illiterate	2,792	1,124	1,668
Literacy rate	38.3	53.2	24.7
Graduate	12	10	2

Scheduled Tribes (Dominant):

Gond etc., Sugalis etc., Yerukulas, Yenadis Chenchu etc.

For their cultural identity please see Appendix-II

Villages without Scheduled Tribes: There are 4 villages without any scheduled tribe population.

Literates and Illiterates by Sex (Total Population):

	Persons	Males	Females
Literate	35,702	22,008	13,694
Illiterate	41,264	15,493	25,771
Literacy rate	54	68	40
Graduate	1,130	953	177

Agriculture: ***Distribution of villages according to land use:*** Out of 26 villages, Total area (in hectare) is 20440, out of that 47.35 percent is cultivable and 100 percent of the cultivable area is irrigated.

Sources of Irrigation (Hectares): Government Canal 2686.03, Private Canal 0, Well without Electricity 0, Well with Electricity 3269.73, Tubewell without Electricity 0, Tubewell with Electricity 3722, Tank 0, River 0, Lake 0, Waterfall 0, Others 0.

Villages with population of 5000 to 9999:
Soanpet, Mendora, Mukpal.

Villages with population of 10000 and above:
Balkonda.

Distribution of Workers:

	Persons	Males	Females	WPR
Cultivators	11,395	6,457	4,938	27.05
Agricultural Labour	9,978	5,381	4,597	23.69
Household Industry	6,637	854	5,783	15.76
Other Workers	14,116	8,161	5,955	33.51
Main Workers	39,268	19,574	19,694	93.22
Marginal Workers	2,858	1,279	1,579	6.78
Total Workers	42,126	20,853	21,273	

Religion: Major Religious Communities:

	Persons	Males	Females	Sex Ratio
Hindu (88.33%)	67,987	32,983	35,004	1,061
Muslim (10.47%)	8,056	4,076	3,980	976
Christian (1.02%)	786	375	411	1,096
Sikh (0.04%)	32	18	14	778
Buddhists (0.11%)	85	38	47	1,237
Jain (0.01%)	7	5	2	400

Agewise Data:

	Persons	Males	Females	Sex Ratio
All ages	76,966	37,501	39,465	1052
0-14	24,052	12,218	11,834	969
15-44	37,563	18,168	19,395	1068
45-79	14,862	6,933	7,929	1144
80+	437	161	276	1714
Age not stated	52	21	31	1476

Languages (Dominant):
Telugu, Urdu, Marathi, Hindi, Tamil

Disabled Population:

	Persons	Males	Females	%
Total Disabled	1,151	600	551	
In Seeing	472	222	250	41.01
In Speech	154	87	67	13.38
In Hearing	47	11	36	4.08
In Movement	350	215	135	30.41
Mentally	128	65	63	11.12

BALLIKURAVA

Ballikurava C.D. Block lies in the northern part of Prakasam district. The Block is located at a distance of 60 kms. from district headquarters (Ongole). There are 14 villages in the block with the total population of 49,713 persons. Area of the C.D. Block is 216.61 sq. kms. It is bounded in the north by Mandal Santhamag uluru and district Guntur, in the south by Mandals Mundl amuru and Addanki, in the east by district Guntur and Mandal Martur, and in the west by Mandals Santhamaguluru and Mundlamuru, and district Guntur.

Communications:

Roadways : State Highway (S.H.): Direction- Ongole to Guntur. Nearest Villages- Chennupalle, Sankaralingam Gudipadu, Vaidana, Koppera Padu.

River: Ramperu Nadi- Nearest Villages- Koppera Palem, Uppumaguluru, Ballikurava.

The block is identified as a drought-prone area.

Hills: Nearest Villages- Kukatla Palle, Gorre Padu, Vaidana, Koppera Padu, Sankaralingam Gudipadu.

Annual Rainfall: Average Rainfall 789.8 mm

Ground Water: Availability of the Ground Water in the Basin is 11.06 MCM and the utilization is 4.22 MCM It belongs to Safe category. Depth to water level varies from 2 to 5 meter below the ground. Most of the wells go down in summer months., according to the Ground Water Estimation Committee.

Forest and Reserved **Forest:** Nearest Villages- Koppera Palem, Uppumaguluru.

Administration:

Division: Coastal Andhra. Parliamentary Constituency: 32 Baptala (SC). District: Prakasam. Mandal: Ballikurava. Assembly Constituency: 224 Addanki. Gram Panchayat: 21

Villages: 14 **Inhabited:** 14 **Uninhabited:** 0

Ranking	District	State	National
Area	32	453	3901
Population	17	522	5297
Sex Ratio	33	883	2977
Child Sex Ratio	16	421	1545
Literacy Rate	42	733	4662
Density	5	68	4325
Work Participation Rate	24	606	261

Gram Panchayats:

Ambadipudi, Ballikurava, Chennupalli, Gorrepadu Guntupalli, K.Rajupalem, K.V.Palem, Konidena Kopperapadu, Kopperapalem, Kothuru, Kukatlapalli Mallayapalem, Mukteswaram, N.B.Padu, S.L.Gudipadu Uppumaguluru, Vallapalli, Velamavaripalem, Vemavaram Vydena.

Amenities:

Education: Primary School in 14 villages, Middle school in 9 villages, Matriculation or Secondary School in 6 villages, namely Uppumaguluru, Ballikurava, Guntupalle, Vaidana, Koppera Padu, Valla Palle.

Higher Secondary or Pre University Courses or Intermediate or Junior College in 1 village of the CD Block,, namely Ballikurava.

College in 0 village, Adult Literacy Center in 14 villages.

Medical: Hospital in 0 village, Dispensary in 1 village, Health Center in 1 village, Sub Center in 7 villages,

Maternity and Child Welfare Center in 0 village, Community health workers in 0 village.

The Villages having Hospital or Dispensary or Health Center are Konidena, Guntupalle.

Drinking Water: Tap water in 14 villages, Tank water in 14 villages, Well water in 14 villages, Tubewell in 14 villages and more than one source in 14 villages.

Bank: Banking facility in 3 villages, namely, Konidena, Ballikurava, Koppera Padu.

Credit Society in 9 villages Agricultural Credit Society in 7 Non-Agricultural Credit Society in 2 villages.

Others: Power supply in 14 villages, Cinema hall in 0 village, sport club in 0 village, Stadium or Auditorium or Community Hall in 0 village, Post Office in 13 villages.

There are 14 villages having bus facilities.

Villages with most of facilities: Konidena Ballikurava, Koppera Padu.

Villages without Amenities (Education): None..

Scheduled Castes: Out of the total population of 49713 persons, 12463 persons (25.07%) belong to Scheduled Castes.

The villages having less than 10% SC population are None..

The villages having more than 50% SC population are None.

Sex ratio of Scheduled Caste population is 485.

Scheduled Castes Literates and Illiterates by Sex:

	Persons	Males	Females
Literate	4,302	2,860	1,442
Illiterate	8,161	3,560	4,601
Literacy rate	40.6	51.9	28.3
Graduate	91	78	13

Scheduled Castes (Dominant):

Madiga, Mala, Dakkal etc.

For their cultural identity please see Appendix-I

Villages without Scheduled Castes: There are 0 village without any scheduled caste population.

Scheduled Tribes: Out of the total population of 49713 persons, 2675 persons (5.38%) belong to Scheduled Tribes.

The villages having less than 10% ST population are Koppera Palem, Uppumagûluru, Konidena, Ballikurava Chennupalle, Sankaralingam Gudipadu, Mukteswaram Guntupalle, Vaidana, Valla Palle.

The villages having more than 50% ST population are None.

Sex ratio of Scheduled tribe population is 477.

Scheduled Tribes Literates and Illiterates by Sex:

	Persons	Males	Females
Literate	756	525	231
Illiterate	1,919	874	1,045
Literacy rate	33.7	45.1	21.4
Graduate	14	12	2

Scheduled Tribes (Dominant):

Yenadis, Sugalis etc., Yerukulas,.Chenchu etc.

For their cultural identity please see Appendix-II

Villages without Scheduled Tribes: There are 0 village without any scheduled tribe population.

Literates and Illiterates by Sex (Total Population):

	Persons	Males	Females
Literate	21,338	13,386	7,952
Illiterate	28,375	11,975	16,400
Literacy rate	49	61	38
Graduate	693	573	120

Agriculture: ***Distribution of villages according to land use:*** Out of 14 villages, Total area (in hectare) is 21661, out of that 86.02 percent is cultivable and 54.88 percent of the cultivable area is irrigated.

Sources of Irrigation (Hectares): Government Canal 8823.53, Private Canal 0, Well without Electricity 10, Well with Electricity 134.9, Tubewell without Electricity 0, Tubewell with Electricity 0, Tank 1016, River 0, Lake 0, Waterfall 0, Others 242.

Villages with population of 5000 to 9999: Konidena, Valla Palle.

Villages with population of 10000 and above: None

Distribution of Workers:

	Persons	Males	Females	WPR
Cultivators	10,837	6,888	3,949	36.89
Agricultural Labour	13,877	5,964	7,913	47.24
Household Industry	285	142	143	0.97
Other Workers	4,374	2,639	1,735	14.89
Main Workers	26,840	15,220	11,620	91.38
Marginal Workers	2,533	413	2,120	8.62
Total Workers	29,373	15,633	13,740	

Religion: Major Religious Communities:

	Persons	Males	Females	Sex Ratio
Hindu (94.71%)	47,081	23,995	23,086	962
Muslim (4.84%)	2,405	1,235	1,170	947
Christian (0.43%)	216	124	92	742
Sikh (0%)	-	-	-	-
Buddhists (0%)	-	-	-	-
Jain (0%)	-	-	-	-

Agewise Data:

	Persons	Males	Females	Sex Ratio
All ages	49,713	25,361	24,352	960
0-14	15,455	7,924	7,531	950
15-44	23,416	11,968	11,448	957
45-79	10,328	5,234	5,094	973
80+	479	215	264	1228
Age not stated	35	20	15	750

Languages (Dominant):

Telugu, Urdu, Hindi, Gondi, Tamil

Disabled Population:

	Persons	Males	Females	%
Total Disabled	780	433	347	
In Seeing	286	137	149	36.67
In Speech	109	66	43	13.97
In Hearing	25	13	12	3.21
In Movement	243	152	91	31.15
Mentally	117	65	52	15

BALMOOR

Balmoor C.D. Block lies in the eastern part of Mahbubna gar district. The Block is located at a distance of 75 kms. from district headquarters (Mahbubnagar). There are 21 villages in the block with the total population of 31,240 persons. Area of the C.D. Block is 215.60 sq. kms. It is bounded by Uppununthala and Achampet Mandals on north, Amrabad and Lingal Mandal on south, Mandals Amrabad and Achampet on east, Telkapalle and Lingal Mandals on west.

Communications:

Roadways : State Highway (S.H.): Direction- Nagarkurnool to Achampet. Nearest Villages- Polepalle, Jinkunta, Gattuthumman, Mahadevpur, Polesettipalle.

Backwards Region Grants Fund: It receives Backward Region Grants.

Annual Rainfall: Average Rainfall 695 mm.

Ground Water: Availability of the Ground Water in the Basin is 1914 H.A.M. and the utilization is 1201 H. A.M. It belongs to Safe category. Depth to water level varies from 2 to 10 meter below the ground. Most of the wells go down in summer months. The well density in the entire block is 12 wells per sq. km. Total no. of the wells in the block are enumerated as 2535, according to the Ground Water Estimation Committee.

Forest and Reserved **Forest:** Nearest Villages- Bonala, Kondanagula, Ramagiri, Billakal.

Natural Division : Telangana Plateau Region

Administration:

Division: Telangana. Parliamentary Constituency: 12 Nagarkurnool (SC). District: Mahbubnagar. Mandal: Balmo or. Assembly Constituency: 82 Achampet (SC). Gram Pancha yat: 13.

Villages: 21 **Inhabited:** 19 **Uninhabited:** 2

Ranking	District	State	National
Area	47	463	3921
Population	62	1006	6027
Sex Ratio	48	829	2770
Child Sex Ratio	60	1085	5373
Literacy Rate	25	962	5535
Density	41	345	5625
Work Participation Rate	54	917	855

Gram Panchayats:

Ananthavaram, Balmoor, Banala, Chennaram Gattuthummen, Godal. Jinkunta, Kondanagula Kondareddypally, Laxmipally, Polisettypally Ramajipally, Thummanpet.

Amenities:

Education: Primary School in 19 villages, Middle school in 8 villages, Matriculation or Secondary School in 4 villages, namely Thummanpeta, Polesettipalle, Kondanagula, Balmoor.

Higher Secondary or Pre University Courses or Intermediate or Junior College in 1 village of the CD Block,, namely Kondanagula.

College in 1 village, Adult Literacy Center in 19 villages., College is in village, namely Kondanagula.

Medical: Hospital in 0 village, Dispensary in 1 village, Health Center in 1 village, Sub Center in 7 villages, Maternity and Child Welfare Center in 14 villages, Community health workers in 0 village.

The Village having Hospital or Dispensary or Health Center is Kondanagula.

Drinking Water: Tap water in 19 villages, Tank water in 19 villages, Well water in 19 villages, Tubewell in 19 villages and more than one source in 19 villages.

Bank: Banking facility in 2 villages, namely, Thummanpeta, Kondanagula.

Credit Society in 7 villages Agricultural Credit Society in 2 Non-Agricultural Credit Society in 7 villages.

Others: Power supply in 19 villages, Cinema hall in 0 village, sport club in 0 village, Stadium or Auditorium or Community Hall in 0 village, Post Office in 11 villages.

There are 17 villages having bus facilities.

Villages with most of facilities: Thummanpeta Kondanagula.

Villages without Amenities (Education): None..

Scheduled Castes: Out of the total population of 31240 persons, 7792 persons (24.94%) belong to Scheduled Castes. The villages having less than 10% SC population are None..

The villages having more than 50% SC population are None.

Sex ratio of Scheduled Caste population is 483.

Scheduled Castes Literates and Illiterates by Sex:

	Persons	Males	Females
Literate	2,049	1,479	570
Illiterate	5,743	2,549	3,194
Literacy rate	31.1	43.7	17.8
Graduate	52	48	4

Scheduled Castes (Dominant):

Madiga, Mala, Beda Jangam etc., Bindla, Mala Dasari

For their cultural identity please see Appendix-I

Villages without Scheduled Castes: There are 4 villages without any scheduled caste population.

Scheduled Tribes: Out of the total population of 31240 persons, 3783 persons (12.11%) belong to Scheduled Tribes. The villages having less than 10% ST population are Polepalle, Jinkunta, Thummanpeta, Gattuthumman Mahadevpur, Chennaram (P.G), Kondareddipalle, Godal Veeramrajupalle, Ramajipalle, Mylaram, Balmoor Ananthavaram.

The villages having more than 50% ST population are None.

Sex ratio of Scheduled tribe population is 466.

Scheduled Tribes Literates and Illiterates by Sex:

	Persons	Males	Females
Literate	1,196	848	348
Illiterate	2,587	1,173	1,414
Literacy rate	38.9	52.1	24.1
Graduate	18	17	1

Scheduled Tribes (Dominant):

Sugalis etc., Chenchu etc., Yerukulas, Koya etc.

For their cultural identity please see Appendix-II

Villages without Scheduled Tribes: There are 6 villages without any scheduled tribe population.

Literates and Illiterates by Sex (Total Population):

	Persons	Males	Females
Literate	11,193	7,369	3,824
Illiterate	20,047	8,534	11,513
Literacy rate	42	55	29
Graduate	337	286	51

Agriculture: ***Distribution of villages according to land use:*** Out of 21 villages, Total area (in hectare) is 21558, out of that 60.34 percent is cultivable and 17.61 percent of the cultivable area is irrigated.

Sources of Irrigation (Hectares): Government Canal 0, Private Canal 0, Well without Electricity 174, Well with Electricity 345, Tubewell without Electricity 0, Tubewell with Electricity 499, Tank 1213, River 0, Lake 0, Waterfall 0, Others 60.

Villages with population of 5000 to 9999: Kondanagula.

Villages with population of 10000 and above: None

Distribution of Workers:

	Persons	Males	Females	WPR
Cultivators	8,219	4,630	3,589	48.71
Agricultural Labour	5,705	2,145	3,560	33.81
Household Industry	392	200	192	2.32
Other Workers	2,556	1,881	675	15.15
Main Workers	14,408	7,892	6,516	85.4
Marginal Workers	2,464	964	1,500	14.6
Total Workers	16,872	8,856	8,016	

Religion: Major Religious Communities:

	Persons	Males	Females	Sex Ratio
Hindu (94.44%)	29,504	15,065	14,439	958
Muslim (5.32%)	1,661	803	858	1,068
Christian (0.16%)	50	16	34	2,125
Sikh (0.01%)	3	2	1	500
Buddhists (0%)	1	1	-	-
Jain (0%)	-	-	-	-

Agewise Data:

	Persons	Males	Females	Sex Ratio
All ages	31,240	15,903	15,337	964
0-14	11,375	5,998	5,377	896
15-44	13,552	6,882	6,670	969
45-79	6,017	2,882	3,135	1088
80+	263	128	135	1055
Age not stated	33	13	20	1538

Languages (Dominant):

Telugu, Hindi, Urdu, Gondi, Tamil

Disabled Population:

	Persons	Males	Females	%
Total Disabled	667	382	285	
In Seeing	288	179	109	43.18
In Speech	52	32	20	7.8
In Hearing	46	18	28	6.9
In Movement	227	124	103	34.03
Mentally	54	29	25	8.1

BANAGANAPALLE

Banaganapalle C.D. Block lies in the south-eastern part of Kurnool district. The Block is located at a distance of 60 kms. from district headquarters (Kurnool). There are 39 villages in the block with the total population of 89,030 persons. Area of the C.D. Block is 386.19 sq. kms. It is bounded in the north by Mandal Panyam, in the south by Mandals Peapalle, Owk and Sanja mala, in the east by Mandals Koilkutla, Gospadu and Panyam, and in the west by Mandals Peapalle, Dhone and Bethamcherla.

Communications:

Roadways : NH- 18: Direction- Kurnool to Koilkuntla. Nearest Villages- Kyapa, Kyapa, Kyapa, Kyapa, Kyapa, Kyapa, Banaganapalle, Banumukkala. State Highway (S. H.): Direction- Tadpetri to Nandyal. Nearest Villages- Banaganapalle, Banumukkala, Nandivargam, Thimmapuram, Nandavaram, Pandlapuram.

River: Jurreru Nadi- Nearest Villages- Kapulapaile, Banaganapalle, Banumukkala, Mittapalle.

It is identified as a drought-prone area.

Hills: Nearest Villages- Yerragudi, Kyapa, Kyapa, Beera volu, Namatheertham.

Integrated Child Development Scheme (ICDS) Project: Banaganapalli, Total Anganwadi Centres: 178

Annual Rainfall: Average Rainfall 624 mm

Ground Water: Availability of the Ground Water in the Basin is 2047 H.A.M. and the utilization is 2189 H. A.M. It belongs to OE category. Depth to water level varies from 5 to 10 meter below the ground. Most of the wells go down in summer months. The well density in the entire block is 4 wells per sq. km. Total no. of the wells in the block are enumerated as 1759, according to the Ground Water Estimation Committee.

Forest and Reserved **Forest:** Nearest Villages- Katikavan ikunta, Yerragudi, Hussainapuram, Enakandla, Gulamaliabad, Pasupula, Krishnagiri, Jwalapuram, Pathapadu, Meerapu ram, Yagantipalle.

Natural Division : Rayalaseema Region

Administration:

Division: Rayala Seema. Parliamentary Constituency: 34 Nandyal. District: Kurnool. Mandal: Banaganapalle. Assembly Constituency: 259 Banaganapalle. Gram Panchay at: 22.

Villages: 39 **Inhabited:** 38 **Uninhabited:** 1

Ranking	District	State	National
Area	6	54	2018
Population	2	15	3806
Sex Ratio	39	951	3287
Child Sex Ratio	42	844	3718
Literacy Rate	17	509	3872
Density	50	805	4315
Work Participation Rate	14	603	2411

Gram Panchayats:

Appalapuram, Banaganapalle, Beeravolu, Cheruvupalli Enakandla, Illurukothapeta, Krishnagiri, Kyapa Meerapuram, Mittapalle, Nandavaram, Nandivargam Palukur, Pasupula, Pathapadu, Ramatheertham Tangutoor, Thammadapalle, Thimmapuram, Venkatapuram Yagantipalle, Yerragudi.

Amenities:

Education: Primary School in 38 villages, Middle school in 10 villages, Matriculation or Secondary School in 7 villages, namely Palukur, Nandivargam, Nandavaram, Pasupula, Tangutoor, Banaganapalle, Illurukothapalle.

Higher Secondary or Pre University Courses or Intermediate or Junior College in 1 village of the CD Block,, namely Banaganapalle.

College in 1 village, Adult Literacy Center in 34 villages., College is in village, namely Banaganapalle.

Medical: Hospital in 1 village, Dispensary in 1 village, Health Center in 3 villages, Sub Center in 8 villages, Maternity and Child Welfare Center in 0 village, Community health workers in 0 village.

The Village having Hospital or Dispensary or Health Center is Banaganapalle.

Drinking Water: Tap water in 38 villages, Tank water in 38 villages, Well water in 38 villages, Tubewell in 38 villages and more than one source in 38 villages.

Bank: Banking facility in 5 villages, namely, Hussainapuram, Palukur, Nandivargam, Tangutoor Banaganapalle.

Credit Society in 21 villages Agricultural Credit Society in 7 Non-Agricultural Credit Society in 19 villages.

Others: Power supply in 38 villages, Cinema hall in 3 villages, sport club in 0 village, Stadium or Auditorium or Community Hall in 0 village, Post Office in 28 villages.

There are 33 villages having bus facilities.

Villages with most of facilities: Palukur Nandivargam, Tangutoor, Banaganapalle.

Villages without Amenities (Education): None..

Scheduled Castes: Out of the total population of 89030 persons, 14716 persons (16.53%) belong to Scheduled Castes.

The villages having less than 10% SC population are Hussainapuram, Thimmapuram, Meerapuram, Gulamaliabad Pasupula, Cherlokothuru, Bathulurupadu Banaganapalle, Banumukkala, Rallakothuru Jambuladinne, Gulam Nabipeta.

The villages having more than 50% SC population are None.

Sex ratio of Scheduled Caste population is 487.

Scheduled Castes Literates and Illiterates by Sex:

	Persons	Males	Females
Literate	5,292	3,642	1,650
Illiterate	9,424	3,906	5,518
Literacy rate	42.2	56.4	27.1
Graduate	182	150	32

Scheduled Castes (Dominant):

Mala, Madiga, Chamar etc., Generic Castes etc.

Adi Dravida

For their cultural identity please see Appendix-I

Villages without Scheduled Castes: There are 5 villages without any scheduled caste population.

Scheduled Tribes: Out of the total population of 89030 persons, 3231 persons (3.63%) belong to Scheduled Tribes.

The villages having less than 10% ST population are Katikavanikunta, Yerragudi, Hussainapuram Cherupalle, Palukur, Beeravolu, Nandivargam Jillella, Thimmapuram, Nandavaram, Venkatapuram Enakandla, Meerapuram, Krishnagiri, Cherlokothuru Jwalapuram, Pathapadu, Yagantipalle, Bathulurupadu Pandlapuram, Sankalapuram, Vittalapuram, Tangutoor Appalapuram, Kyapa, Kapulapalle, Mittapalle

Banaganapalle, Banumukkala, Thammadapalle Jambuladinne, Niluvugondla, Illurukothapalle Gulam Nabipeta.

The villages having more than 50% ST population are None.

Sex ratio of Scheduled tribe population is 483.

Scheduled Tribes Literates and Illiterates by Sex:

	Persons	Males	Females
Literate	1,045	757	288
Illiterate	2,186	915	1,271
Literacy rate	40.2	55.5	23.3
Graduate	30	27	3

Scheduled Tribes (Dominant):

Sugalis etc., Yerukulas, Yenadis, Savaras etc.

For their cultural identity please see Appendix-II

Villages without Scheduled Tribes: There are 21 villages without any scheduled tribe population.

Literates and Illiterates by Sex (Total Population):

	Persons	Males	Females
Literate	40,815	26,059	14,756
Illiterate	48,215	19,496	28,719
Literacy rate	54	67	40
Graduate	1,973	1,623	350

Agriculture: ***Distribution of villages according to land use:*** Out of 39 villages, Total area (in hectare) is 38619, out of that 75.62 percent is cultivable and 12.87 percent of the cultivable area is irrigated.

Sources of Irrigation (Hectares): Government Canal 46, Private Canal 0, Well without Electricity 0, Well with Electricity 6, Tubewell without Electricity 0, Tubewell with Electricity 3225, Tank 78, River 0, Lake 0, Waterfall 0, Others 403.

Villages with population of 5000 to 9999: Nandavaram.

Villages with population of 10000 and above: Palukur, Banaganapalle, Banumukkala.

Distribution of Workers:

	Persons	Males	Females	WPR
Cultivators	7,936	5,255	2,681	18.47
Agricultural Labour	14,555	5,744	8,811	33.88
Household Industry	882	456	426	2.05
Other Workers	19,587	14,148	5,439	45.59
Main Workers	35,021	22,712	12,309	81.52
Marginal Workers	7,939	2,891	5,048	18.48
Total Workers	42,960	25,603	17,357	

Religion: Major Religious Communities:

	Persons	Males	Females	Sex Ratio
Hindu (77.21%)	68,744	35,359	33,385	944
Muslim (22.22%)	19,786	9,955	9,831	988
Christian (0.49%)	437	211	226	1,071
Sikh (0.02%)	15	7	8	1,143
Buddhists (0%)	1	1	-	-
Jain (0%)	4	1	3	3,000

Agewise Data:

	Persons	Males	Females	Sex Ratio
All ages	89,030	45,555	43,475	954
0-14	31,786	16,509	15,277	925
15-44	42,130	21,892	20,238	924
45-79	14,546	6,926	7,620	1100
80+	446	160	286	1788
Age not stated	122	68	54	794

Languages (Dominant):

Telugu, Urdu, Hindi, Tamil, Marathi

Disabled Population:

	Persons	Males	Females	%
Total Disabled	1,606	858	748	
In Seeing	731	364	367	45.52
In Speech	144	79	65	8.97
In Hearing	88	45	43	5.48
In Movement	485	293	192	30.2
Mentally	158	77	81	9.84

BANDI ATMAKUR

Bandi Atmakur C.D. Block lies in the eastern part of Kurnool district. The Block is located at a distance of 57 kms. from district headquarters (Kurnool). There are 15 villages in the block with the total population of 43,988 persons. Area of the C.D. Block is 195.86 sq. kms. It is bounded in the north by Mandal Atmakur, in the south by Mandals Nandyal and Mahanandi, in the east by district Prakasam, and in the west by Manda ls Gadivemula and Nandyal.

Communications:

Roadways : State Highway (S.H.): Direction- Kolikuntla to Atmakur. Nearest Villages- Bhojanam, Paramatur, Santhajutur, Pedda Devalapuram, Bandi Atmakur, Parnapal le, Ayyavari Kodur.

River: Handri Nadi- Nearest Villages- Bhojanam, Paramat ur, Santhajutur, Bandi Atmakur, Yerraguntla, Kakanur. It is identified as a drought-prone area.

Annual Rainfall: Average Rainfall 825 mm

Ground Water: Availability of the Ground Water in the Basin is 1629 H.A.M. and the utilization is 744 H.A. M. It belongs to Safe category. Depth to water level varies from 5 to 10 meter below the ground. Most of the wells go down in summer months. The well density in the entire block is 1 wells per sq. km. Total no. of the wells in the block are enumerated as 690, accor ding to the Ground Water Estimation Committee.

Forest and Reserved **Forest:** (Atmakur R.F.)- Nearest Villages- Narayanapuram, Gali Chennaiah Palem, Ramapuram

Ernapadu, Kadamalakalva.

Natural Division : Rayalaseema Region

Administration:

Division: Rayala Seema. Parliamentary Constituency: 34 Nandayal. District: Kurnool. Mandal: Bandi Atmakur. Assembly Constituency: 254 Srisailam. Gram Panchayat: 19

Villages: 15 **Inhabited:** 15 **Uninhabited:** 0

Ranking	District	State	National
Area	44	582	4251
Population	32	697	5559
Sex Ratio	17	694	2331
Child Sex Ratio	43	864	3774
Literacy Rate	28	628	4314
Density	20	153	4380
Work Participation Rate	19	624	442

Gram Panchayats:

A. Kodur, B. Kodur, Bandi Atmakur, Bhojanam Chinnadevalapuram, Ernapadu, G.C. Palem G.Lingapuram, Kadamalakalva, Kakanur, Narayanapuram Paramatur, Parnapalle, Pedda Devalapuram, Ramapuram Santhajutur, Singavaram, Somayajulapalli Yerraguntla.

Amenities:

Education: Primary School in 15 villages, Middle school in 9 villages, Matriculation or Secondary School in 4 villages, namely Santhajutur, Narayanapuram, Bandi Atmakur, Ernapadu.

Higher Secondary or Pre University Courses or Intermediate or Junior College in 0 village of the CD Block, College in 0 village, Adult Literacy Center in 14 villages.

Medical: Hospital in 0 village, Dispensary in 1 village, Health Center in 1 village, Sub Center in 8 villages, Maternity and Child Welfare Center in 0 village, Community health workers in 0 village.

The Village having Hospital or Dispensary or Health Center is Ernapadu.

Drinking Water: Tap water in 15 villages, Tank water in 15 villages, Well water in 15 villages, Tubewell in 15 villages and more than one source in 15 villages.

Bank: Banking facility in 2 villages, namely, Bandi Atmakur, Ayyavari Kodur.

Credit Society in 13 villages Agricultural Credit Society in 5 Non-Agricultural Credit Society in 12 villages.

Others: Power supply in 15 villages, Cinema hall in 1 village, sport club in 0 village, Stadium or Auditorium or Community Hall in 0 village, Post Office in 15 villages.

There are 15 villages having bus facilities.

Villages with most of facilities: Bandi Atmakur Ayyavari Kodur.

Villages without Amenities (Education): None..

Scheduled Castes: Out of the total population of 43988 persons, 8903 persons (20.24%) belong to Scheduled Castes. The villages having less than 10% SC population are None..

The villages having more than 50% SC population are None.

Sex ratio of Scheduled Caste population is 488.

Scheduled Castes Literates and Illiterates by Sex:

	Persons	Males	Females
Literate	3,427	2,313	1,114
Illiterate	5,476	2,246	3,230
Literacy rate	45.0	59.3	30.0
Graduate	75	66	9

Scheduled Castes (Dominant):

Mala, Madiga, Mala Dasari

For their cultural identity please see Appendix-I

Villages without Scheduled Castes: There are 0 village without any scheduled caste population.

Scheduled Tribes: Out of the total population of 43988 persons, 2086 persons (4.74%) belong to Scheduled Tribes. The villages having less than 10% ST population are Bhojanam, Paramatur, Santhajutur, Narayanapuram Gali Chennaiah Palem, Ramapuram, Yerraguntla Parnapalle, Ernapadu, Ayyavari Kodur, Bayyapu Kodur Kadamalakalva.

The villages having more than 50% ST population are None.

Sex ratio of Scheduled tribe population is 499.

Scheduled Tribes Literates and Illiterates by Sex:

	Persons	Males	Females
Literate	699	449	250
Illiterate	1,387	597	790
Literacy rate	40.6	52.5	28.9
Graduate	10	9	1

Scheduled Tribes (Dominant):

Yerukulas, Chenchu etc., Sugalis etc., Yenadis Kammara

For their cultural identity please see Appendix-II

Villages without Scheduled Tribes: There are 3 villages without any scheduled tribe population.

Literates and Illiterates by Sex (Total Population):

	Persons	Males	Females
Literate	19,327	12,519	6,808
Illiterate	24,661	9,781	14,880
Literacy rate	51	66	37
Graduate	519	469	50

Agriculture: ***Distribution of villages according to land use:***

Out of 15 villages, Total area (in hectare) is 19586, out of that 73.8 percent is cultivable and 34.54 percent of the

cultivable area is irrigated.

Sources of Irrigation (Hectares): Government Canal 2985.24, Private Canal 1, Well without Electricity 13, Well with Electricity 91.36, Tubewell without Electricity 0, Tubewell with Electricity 663, Tank 960, River 0, Lake 0, Waterfall 0, Others 279.

Villages with population of 5000 to 9999:
Bandi Atmakur.

Villages with population of 10000 and above: None

Distribution of Workers:

	Persons	Males	Females	WPR
Cultivators	5,749	4,234	1,515	23.07
Agricultural Labour	14,448	5,862	8,586	57.98
Household Industry	1,460	729	731	5.86
Other Workers	3,262	2,475	787	13.09
Main Workers	18,933	11,296	7,637	75.98
Marginal Workers	5,986	2,004	3,982	24.02
Total Workers	24,919	13,300	11,619	

Religion: Major Religious Communities:

	Persons	Males	Females	Sex Ratio
Hindu (87.15%)	38,336	19,464	18,872	970
Muslim (11.97%)	5,266	2,646	2,620	990
Christian (0.85%)	375	182	193	1,060
Sikh (0%)	1	1	-	-
Buddhists (0%)	-	-	-	-
Jain (0%)	-	-	-	-

Agewise Data:

	Persons	Males	Females	Sex Ratio
All ages	43,988	22,300	21,688	973
0-14	14,659	7,617	7,042	925
15-44	20,708	10,533	10,175	966
45-79	8,328	4,023	4,305	1070
80+	236	100	136	1360
Age not stated	57	27	30	1111

Languages (Dominant):
Telugu, Urdu, Tamil, Gondi, Hindi

Disabled Population:

	Persons	Males	Females	%
Total Disabled	1,175	607	568	
In Seeing	610	283	327	51.91
In Speech	86	49	37	7.32
In Hearing	97	51	46	8.26
In Movement	274	160	114	23.32
Mentally	108	64	44	9.19

BANGARUPALEM

Bangarupalem C.D. Block lies in the southern part of Chittoor district. The Block is located at a distance of 21 kms. from district headquarters (Chittoor). There are 27 villages in the block with the total population of 69,253 persons. Area of the C.D. Block is 200.86 sq. kms. It is bounded in the north by Mandal Thavanamp alle, in the south by Mandal Yadamarri, in the east by Mandals Yadamarri and Thavanampalle, in the west by Mandals Palamaneru and Gangavaram, and it has common boundary with the state of Tamil Nadu in the south. Headquarters: Gollapalle.

Communications:

Roadways : NH- 4: Direction- Kolar to Chittoor. Nearest Villages- Thambuganipalle, Noonegundlapalle, Gundla Kattamanchi, Kallurupalle, Gollapalle, Palamakulapalle, Venkatagiri, Nalagampalle, Jambuvaripalle. Paleru, Mogili, Mahasamudram. State Highway (S.H.): Direction- Gollapalle to Chittoor. Nearest Villages- Sadakuppam, Venkatagiri, Nalagampalle, Jambuvaripalle.

River: Gajulapalle Eru- Nearest Villages- Thumba, Thumba Kuppam, Nallangadu, Sadakuppam Penruvulu Eru- Nearest Villages- Mahasamudram, Venkatagiri, Nalagampal le.

It receives the Backward Region Grants, and is identifi ed as a drought-prone area as well.

Integrated Child Development Scheme (ICDS) Project: Bangarupalem, Total Anganwadi Centres: 191

Annual Rainfall: Average Rainfall 988 mm

Ground Water: Availability of the Ground Water in the Basin is 3643 H.A.M.and the utilization is 2314 H.A. M. It belongs to Safe category. Depth to water level varies from 5 to 10 meter below the ground. Most of the wells go down in summer months, according to the Ground Water Estimation Committee.

Forest and Reserved **Forest:** Nearest Villages- Thumba, Thumba Kuppam, Setteri, Thoompayanapalle, Nallangadu, Mothagunta, Venkatagiri, Nalagampalle, Kurmaipalle, Kallurupalle, Bodabandla, Jambuvaripalle, Gollapalle, Palamakulapalle, Paleru, Mogili, Tekumanda, Keeramanda, Vepanapalle, Ragimanipenta, Kalvamogilappa Kandriga.

Natural Division : Rayalaseema Region

Administration:

Division: Rayala Seema. Parliamentary Constituency: 42 Chittoor (SC). District: Chittoor. Mandal: Bangarupa lem. Assembly Constituency: 292 Puthalapattu (SC). Gram Panchayat: 40.

Villages: 27 **Inhabited:** 27 **Uninhabited:** 0

Ranking	**District**	**State**	**National**
Area	17	546	4165
Population	5	135	4496
Sex Ratio	47	604	2110
Child Sex Ratio	10	150	398
Literacy Rate	14	74	1246
Density	42	778	3145
Work Participation Rate	11	275	2280

Gram Panchayats:

45.Gollapalli, Bangaru Palyam, Bodabandla
Bommaipalli, Cheekuru Palli, Chillagundlapalle
Echanerivaripalli, Gundlakattamanchi, Gunthur
Jambuvaripalle, Jilladupalli, K.M.Kandriga
Kallurupalle, Karidivaripalli, Katappagari Palli
Keeramanda, Kodalamadugu, Kurmaipalle, Mahasamudram
Mangalapalli, Mogili, Mogilivaripalli
Mogilivenkatagiri, Mungaramadugu, Nalagampalli
Nallangadu, Paleru, Perumallapalli, Ragimanipenta
Sadakuppam, Sankranthipalli, Setteri, Tekumanda
Thagguvaripalli, Thambuganipalle, Thimmojipalli
Thoompayanapalle, Thumba Kuppam, Tumba
Veluthuruchenu.

Amenities:

Education: Primary School in 25 villages, Middle school in 12 villages, Matriculation or Secondary School in 4 villages, namely Thambuganipalle, Gundla Kattamanchi, Gollapalle, Mogili.

Higher Secondary or Pre University Courses or Intermediate or Junior College in 1 village of the CD Block,, namely Gollapalle.

College in 0 village, Adult Literacy Center in 21 villages.

Medical: Hospital in 1 village, Dispensary in 1 village, Health Center in 2 villages, Sub Center in 13 villages, Maternity and Child Welfare Center in 0 village, Community health workers in 0 village.

The Villages having Hospital or Dispensary or Health Center are Thumba Kuppam, Gollapalle.

Drinking Water: Tap water in 27 villages, Tank water in 27 villages, Well water in 27 villages, Tubewell in 27 villages and more than one source in 27 villages.

Bank: Banking facility in 3 villages, namely, Mahasamudram, Gundla Kattamanchi, Gollapalle.

Credit Society in 14 villages Agricultural Credit Society in 10 Non-Agricultural Credit Society in 9 villages.

Others: Power supply in 27 villages, Cinema hall in 2 villages, sport club in 0 village, Stadium or Auditorium or Community Hall in 0 village, Post Office in 17 villages.

There are 26 villages having bus facilities.

Villages with most of facilities: Mahasamudram Gundla Kattamanchi, Gollapalle.

Villages without amenities (Education):
Mothagunta, Kalvamogilappa Kandriga..

Scheduled Castes: Out of the total population of 69253 persons, 19377 persons (27.98%) belong to Scheduled Castes. The villages having less than 10% SC population are Thoompayanapalle, Beripalle, Bodabandla, Tekumanda Kalvamogilappa Kandriga.

The villages having more than 50% SC population are None.

Sex ratio of Scheduled Caste population is 494.

Scheduled Castes Literates and Illiterates by Sex:

	Persons	Males	Females
Literate	11,241	6,515	4,726
Illiterate	8,136	3,286	4,850
Literacy rate	66.8	76.4	56.9
Graduate	272	236	36

Scheduled Castes (Dominant):
Mala, Madiga, Adi Dravida, Arwa Mala, Adi Andhra

For their cultural identity please see Appendix-I

Villages without Scheduled Castes: There are 0 village without any scheduled caste population.

Scheduled Tribes: Out of the total population of 69253 persons, 2787 persons (4.02%) belong to Scheduled Tribes. The villages having less than 10% ST population are Thumba, Thumba Kuppam, Setteri, Thoompayanapalle Sadakuppam, Nallangadu, Mothagunta, Venkatagiri Nalagampalle, Thambuganipalle, Noonegundlapalle Mahasamudram, Kurmaipalle, Beripalle Gundla Kattamanchi, Kallurupalle, Bodabandla Jambuvaripalle, Gollapalle, Paleru, Tekumanda Keeramanda, Vepanapalle, Ragimanipenta Kalvamogilappa Kandriga.

The villages having more than 50% ST population are None.

Sex ratio of Scheduled tribe population is 505.

Scheduled Tribes Literates and Illiterates by Sex:

	Persons	Males	Females
Literate	1,070	665	405
Illiterate	1,717	714	1,003
Literacy rate	46.9	58.2	35.6
Graduate	19	14	5

Scheduled Tribes (Dominant):
Yenadis, Yerukulas, Sugalis etc., Koya etc.

For their cultural identity please see Appendix-II

Villages without Scheduled Tribes: There are 5 villages without any scheduled tribe population.

Literates and Illiterates by Sex (Total Population):

	Persons	Males	Females
Literate	42,038	24,388	17,650
Illiterate	27,215	10,624	16,591
Literacy rate	70	80	59
Graduate	1,755	1,343	412

Agriculture: ***Distribution of villages according to land use:*** Out of 27 villages, Total area (in hectare) is 20085, out of that 69.17 percent is cultivable and 42.17 percent of the cultivable area is irrigated.

Sources of Irrigation (Hectares): Government Canal 0, Private Canal 0, Well without Electricity 0, Well with Electricity 4326.94, Tubewell without Electricity 5.02, Tubewell with Electricity 628.71, Tank 898.09, River 0, Lake 0, Waterfall 0, Others 0.

Villages with population of 5000 to 9999: Venkatagiri, Nalagampalle, Gollapalle.

Villages with population of 10000 and above: None

Distribution of Workers:

	Persons	Males	Females	WPR
Cultivators	12,401	7,778	4,623	35.89
Agricultural Labour	16,034	8,604	7,430	46.4
Household Industry	721	385	336	2.09
Other Workers	5,400	4,004	1,396	15.63
Main Workers	32,054	19,809	12,245	92.76
Marginal Workers	2,502	962	1,540	7.24
Total Workers	34,556	20,771	13,785	

Religion: Major Religious Communities:

	Persons	Males	Females	Sex Ratio
Hindu (94.86%)	65,696	33,247	32,449	976
Muslim (4.45%)	3,081	1,524	1,557	1,022
Christian (0.19%)	135	66	69	1,045
Sikh (0.01%)	5	2	3	1,500
Buddhists (0%)	1	1	-	-
Jain (0%)	-	-	-	-

Agewise Data:

	Persons	Males	Females	Sex Ratio
All ages	69,253	35,012	34,241	978
0-14	20,646	10,604	10,042	947
15-44	32,735	16,382	16,353	998
45-79	15,232	7,721	7,511	973
80+	564	265	299	1128
Age not stated	76	40	36	900

Languages (Dominant):

Telugu, Tamil, Urdu, Hindi, Kannada

Disabled Population:

	Persons	Males	Females	%
Total Disabled	1,080	617	463	
In Seeing	325	164	161	30.09
In Speech	111	62	49	10.28
In Hearing	50	27	23	4.63
In Movement	427	264	163	39.54
Mentally	167	100	67	15.46

BANSWADA

Banswada C.D. Block lies in the south-west part of Nizamabad district. The Block is located at a distance of 67 kms. from district headquarters (Nizamabad). There are 19 villages in the block with the total popul ation of 58,081 persons. Area of the C.D. Block is 112. 76 sq. kms. It is bounded by Birkoor Mandal on north-we st and north, Varni Mandal on north-east, Gandhari Mandal on east and south-east, Nizamsagar Mandal on south-east and south, Pitlam Mandal on south-west and west.

Communications :

Roadways : State Highway (S.H.): Direction- Bodhan to Yellreddy. Nearest Villages- Tadkole, Someshwar, Desaip et, Banswada, Tirmalapur.

River: Manjira Nadi- Nearest Villages- Chinna Nagaram, Chintal Nagaram, Budmi, Tadkole.

Backwards Region Grants Fund: It receives Backward Region Grants.

Integrated Child Development Scheme (ICDS) Project: Banswada, Total Anganwadi Centres: 183

Annual Rainfall: Average Rainfall 1220 mm

Ground Water: Availability of the Ground Water in the Basin is 1707 H.A.M. and the utilization is 933 H.A. M. It belongs to Safe category. Depth to water level varies from 5 to 10 meter below the ground. Most of the wells go down in summer months, according to the Ground Water Estimation Committee.

Natural Division : Telangana Plateau Region

Administration:

Division: Telangana. Parliamentary Constituency: 5 Zaheerabad. District: Nizamabad. Mandal: Banswada. Assembly Constituency: 14 Banswada. Gram Panchayat: 14

Villages: 19 **Inhabited:** 16 **Uninhabited:** 3

Ranking	District	State	National
Area	35	975	5571
Population	9	306	4925
Sex Ratio	19	77	554
Child Sex Ratio	5	260	834
Literacy Rate	6	614	4278
Density	36	908	2144
Work Participation Rate	2	99	3129

Gram Panchayats:

Banswada, Borlam, Budmi, Ch.Rampur, Desaipet Hanmajipet, Ibrahimpet, Kolloor, Konapur, Pocharam Sangojipet, Someshwar, Tadkole, Tirmalapur.

Amenities:

Education: Primary School in 16 villages, Middle school in 8 villages, Matriculation or Secondary School in 6 villages, namely Desaipet, Konapur, Ibrahimpet, Borlam, Banswada, Tadkole.

Higher Secondary or Pre University Courses or Intermediate or Junior College in 1 village of the CD Block,, namely Banswada.

College in 1 village, Adult Literacy Center in 2 villages., College is in village, namely Banswada.

Medical: Hospital in 1 village, Dispensary in 1 village, Health Center in 0 village, Sub Center in 6 villages, Maternity and Child Welfare Center in 1 village, Community health workers in 0 village.

The Village having Hospital or Dispensary or Health

Center is Banswada.

Drinking Water: Tap water in 16 villages, Tank water in 16 villages, Well water in 16 villages, Tubewell in 16 villages and more than one source in 16 villages.

Bank: Banking facility in 4 villages, namely, Chinna Rampur, Banswada, Tadkole, Tirmalapur.

Credit Society in 11 villages Agricultural Credit Society in 5 Non-Agricultural Credit Society in 6 villages.

Others: Power supply in 16 villages, Cinema hall in 1 village, sport club in 0 village, Stadium or Auditorium or Community Hall in 0 village, Post Office in 10 villages.

There are 13 villages having bus facilities.

Villages with most of facilities: Banswada Tadkole, Tirmalapur.

Villages without Amenities (Education): None..

Scheduled Castes: Out of the total population of 58081 persons, 6237 persons (10.74%) belong to Scheduled Castes.

The villages having less than 10% SC population are Someshwar, Chinna Rampur, Hanmajipet, Sangojipet Konapur, Ibrahimpet, Banswada, Tirmalapur.

The villages having more than 50% SC population are None.

Sex ratio of Scheduled Caste population is 522.

Scheduled Castes Literates and Illiterates by Sex:

	Persons	Males	Females
Literate	2,107	1,279	828
Illiterate	4,130	1,704	2,426
Literacy rate	38.6	49.4	28.9
Graduate	67	49	18

Scheduled Castes (Dominant):

Mala, Madiga, Chamar etc., Beda Jangam etc.

Generic Castes etc.

For their cultural identity please see Appendix-I

Villages without Scheduled Castes: There are 3 villages without any scheduled caste population.

Scheduled Tribes: Out of the total population of 58081 persons, 5500 persons (9.47%) belong to Scheduled Tribes.

The villages having less than 10% ST population are Kollur, Someshwar, Desaipet, Sangojipet, Ibrahimpet Banswada, Chinna Nagaram, Tadkole, Budmi.

The villages having more than 50% ST population are None.

Sex ratio of Scheduled tribe population is 498.

Scheduled Tribes Literates and Illiterates by Sex:

	Persons	Males	Females
Literate	1,512	1,144	368
Illiterate	3,988	1,619	2,369
Literacy rate:	34.4	51.5	16.9
Graduate	27	26	1

Scheduled Tribes (Dominant):

Sugalis etc., Yerukulas, Gond etc.

Generic Tribes etc., Yenadis

For their cultural identity please see Appendix-II

Villages without Scheduled Tribes: There are 7 villages without any scheduled tribe population.

Literates and Illiterates by Sex (Total Population):

	Persons	Males	Females
Literate	25,389	15,652	9,737
Illiterate	32,692	13,022	19,670
Literacy rate	52	65	39
Graduate	1,288	999	289

Agriculture: ***Distribution of villages according to land use:*** Out of 19 villages, Total area (in hectare) is 11275, out of that 65.33 percent is cultivable and 74.17 percent of the cultivable area is irrigated.

Sources of Irrigation (Hectares): Government Canal 2709.46, Private Canal 420.09, Well without Electricity 0, Well with Electricity 3.23, Tubewell without Electricity 43.43, Tubewell with Electricity 767.92, Tank 597.51, River 387.68, Lake 0, Waterfall 0, Others 533.8.

Villages with population of 5000 to 9999: Tadkole.

Villages with population of 10000 and above: Banswada.

Distribution of Workers:

	Persons	Males	Females	WPR
Cultivators	5,544	3,685	1,859	21.1
Agricultural Labour	10,443	4,456	5,987	39.75
Household Industry	1,868	695	1,173	7.11
Other Workers	8,420	6,631	1,789	32.05
Main Workers	18,950	12,458	6,492	72.12
Marginal Workers	7,325	3,009	4,316	27.88
Total Workers	26,275	15,467	10,808	

Religion: Major Religious Communities:

	Persons	Males	Females	Sex Ratio
Hindu (79.26%)	46,036	22,567	23,469	1,040
Muslim (20.23%)	11,748	5,945	5,803	976
Christian (0.35%)	204	115	89	774
Sikh (0.15%)	90	46	44	957
Buddhists (0%)	-	-	-	-
Jain (0%)	2	-	2	-

Agewise Data:

	Persons	Males	Females	Sex Ratio
All ages	58,081	28,674	29,407	1026
0-14	20,442	10,373	10,069	971
15-44	27,031	13,410	13,621	1016
45-79	10,184	4,722	5,462	1157
80+	360	131	229	1748
Age not stated	64	38	26	684

Languages (Dominant):

Telugu, Urdu, Hindi, Marathi, Kannada

Disabled Population:

	Persons	Males	Females	%
Total Disabled	1,010	614	396	
In Seeing	519	321	198	51.39
In Speech	103	55	48	10.2
In Hearing	39	17	22	3.86
In Movement	252	175	77	24.95
Mentally	97	46	51	9.6

BANTUMILLI

Bantumilli C.D. Block lies in the eastern part of Krish na district. The Block is located at a distance of 33 kms. from district headquarters (Machilipatnam). There are 19 villages in the block with the total population of 52,257 persons. Area of the C.D. Block is 125.30 sq. kms. It is bounded in the north by Mandals Mudinepa lle and Kalidindi, in the south by Mandal Pedana, in the east by Mandals Machilipatnam, Kruthivenu and Kalid indi, and in the west by Mandals Pedana and Mudinepalle.

Communications:

Roadways : Metalled Roads: Nearest Villages- Pedatummidi, Mulaparru, Maddetipalle, Munjuluru, Manimeswaram, Arthamuru, Pendurru, Bantumilli, Malleswaram, Narayanap uram.

Integrated Child Development Scheme (ICDS) Project: Bantumilli, Total Anganwadi Centres: 126

Annaul Rainfall: Average Rainfall 906 mm

Ground Water: Availability of the Ground Water in the Basin is (Information not avavible) H.A.M .and the utilization is (Information not avavible) H.A.M. It belongs to (Information not avavible) category. Depth to water level varies from 3 to 10 meter below the ground. Most of the wells go down in summer months.

Natural Division : Krishna Delta Region

Administration:

Division: Coastal Andhra. Parliamentary Constituency: 28 Machilipatnam. District: Krishna. Mandal: Bantumilli. Assembly Constituency: 193 Pedana. Gram Panchayat: 21

Villages: 19 **Inhabited:** 18 **Uninhabited:** 1

Ranking	District	State	National
Area	34	920	5385
Population	33	443	5172
Sex Ratio	21	509	1852
Child Sex Ratio	26	533	2070
Literacy Rate	19	124	1704
Density	40	926	2639
Work Participation Rate	14	172	3255

Gram Panchayats:

Amudalapalli, Arthamuru, Bantumilli, Barripadu Chinathummidi, Chorampudi, Kanchadam, Korlapadu Malaparajugudem, Mallampudi, Malleswaram Manimeswaram, Mulaparru, Munjuluru, Nagannacheruvu Nageswaraopeta, P.Ravigunta, Pedatummidi, Pendurru Ramavarapumodi, Sathuluru.

Amenities:

Education: Primary School in 18 villages, Middle school in 8 villages, Matriculation or Secondary School in 5 villages, namely Pedatummidi, Munjuluru, Arthamuru, Pendurru, Bantumilli.

Higher Secondary or Pre University Courses or Intermediate or Junior College in 1 village of the CD Block,, namely Bantumilli.

College in 1 village, Adult Literacy Center in 4 villages., College is in village, namely Bantumilli.

Medical: Hospital in 0 village, Dispensary in 0 village, Health Center in 1 village, Sub Center in 9 villages, Maternity and Child Welfare Center in 0 village, Community health workers in 0 village.

Drinking Water: Tap water in 8 villages, Tank water in 8 villages, Well water in 12 villages, Tubewell in 0 village and more than one source in 9 villages.

Bank: Banking facility in 3 villages, namely, Pedatummidi, Munjuluru, Bantumilli.

Credit Society in 13 villages Agricultural Credit Society in 5 Non-Agricultural Credit Society in 12 villages.

Others: Power supply in 18 villages, Cinema hall in 3 villages, sport club in 0 village, Stadium or Auditorium or Community Hall in 0 village, Post Office in 14 villages.

There are 14 villages having bus facilities.

Villages with most of facilities: Pedatummidi Munjuluru, Bantumilli.

Villages without Amenities (Education): None..

Scheduled Castes: Out of the total population of 52257 persons, 6250 persons (11.96%) belong to Scheduled Castes. The villages having less than 10% SC population are Chorampudi, Mulaparru, Chinatummidi, Munjuluru Arthamuru, Korlapadu, Pendurru, Bantumilli Malleswaram.

The villages having more than 50% SC population are None.

Sex ratio of Scheduled Caste population is 491.

Scheduled Castes Literates and Illiterates by Sex:

	Persons	Males	Females
Literate	3,569	1,959	1,610
Illiterate	2,681	1,225	1,456
Literacy rate	65.6	70.6	60.4
Graduate	119	82	37

Scheduled Castes (Dominant):

Mala, Madiga, Beda Jangam etc., Generic Castes etc.

Mala Dasu

For their cultural identity please see Appendix-I

Villages without Scheduled Castes: There are 2 villages without any scheduled caste population.

Scheduled Tribes: Out of the total population of 52257 persons, 971 persons (1.86%) belong to Scheduled Tribes. The villages having less than 10% ST population are Pedatummidi, Ramavarapumodi, Chorampudi, Mulaparru Maddetipalle, Amudalapalle, Satuluru, Kanchadam Barripadu, Munjuluru, Manimeswaram, Arthamuru Korlapadu, Pendurru, Bantumilli, Malleswaram Narayanapuram.

The villages having more than 50% ST population are None.

Sex ratio of Scheduled tribe population is 501.

Scheduled Tribes Literates and Illiterates by Sex:

	Persons	Males	Females
Literate	245	137	108
Illiterate	726	348	378
Literacy rate	30.7	34.5	26.9
Graduate	5	4	1

Scheduled Tribes (Dominant):

Yenadis, Yerukulas, Konda Dhoras, Sugalis etc. Savaras etc.

For their cultural identity please see Appendix-II

Villages without Scheduled Tribes: There are 4 villages without any scheduled tribe population.

Literates and Illiterates by Sex (Total Population):

	Persons	Males	Females
Literate	30,437	16,562	13,875
Illiterate	21,820	9,781	12,039
Literacy rate	66	72	61
Graduate	1,104	831	273

Agriculture: ***Distribution of villages according to land use:*** Out of 19 villages, Total area (in hectare) is 12531, out of that 83.75 percent is cultivable and 98.74 percent of the cultivable area is irrigated.

Sources of Irrigation (Hectares): Government Canal 10362.1, Private Canal 0, Well without Electricity 0, Well with Electricity 0, Tubewell without Electricity 0, Tubewell with Electricity 0, Tank 0, River 0, Lake 0, Waterfall 0, Others 0.

Villages with population of 5000 to 9999: Pedatummidi, Chorampudi, Mulaparru, Bantumilli.

Villages with population of 10000 and above: None

Distribution of Workers:

	Persons	Males	Females	WPR
Cultivators	5,364	4,602	762	22.24
Agricultural Labour	14,310	7,759	6,551	59.34
Household Industry	246	153	93	1.02
Other Workers	4,196	3,474	722	17.4
Main Workers	20,943	15,164	5,779	86.84
Marginal Workers	3,173	824	2,349	13.16
Total Workers	24,116	15,988	8,128	

Religion: Major Religious Communities:

	Persons	Males	Females	Sex Ratio
Hindu (91.66%)	47,900	24,144	23,756	984
Muslim (2.7%)	1,411	738	673	912
Christian (5.58%)	2,917	1,445	1,472	1,019
Sikh (0%)	1	-	1	-
Buddhists (0%)	1	-	1	-
Jain (0%)	-	-	-	-

Agewise Data:

	Persons	Males	Females	Sex Ratio
All ages	52,257	26,343	25,914	984
0-14	16,167	8,141	8,026	986
15-44	25,941	13,273	12,668	954
45-79	9,794	4,770	5,024	1053
80+	308	141	167	1184
Age not stated	47	18	29	1611

Languages (Dominant):

Telugu, Urdu, Gondi, Tamil, Hindi

Disabled Population:

	Persons	Males	Females	%
Total Disabled	915	506	409	
In Seeing	278	147	131	30.38
In Speech	119	69	50	13.01
In Hearing	70	34	36	7.65
In Movement	314	190	124	34.32
Mentally	134	66	68	14.64

BANTWARAM

Bantwaram C.D. Block lies in the north-west part of Rangareddy district. The Block is located at a distance of 110 kms. from district headquarters (Serilingampalle). There are 26 villages in the block with the total population of 34,121 persons. Area of the C.D. Block is 184.76 sq. kms. It is bounded by Marpalle and Mominp et Mandals on north-east, Vicarabad Mandal on east, Dharur Mandal on south, Peddumul Mandal on west, and it has common boundary with the state of Karnataka on north.

Communications :

Roadways : Metalled Roads: Nearest Villages- Bopanwaram, Madhvapur, Kothapalle, Sultanpur, Somaram. M, Mothkupa lle, Nagsanpalle, Kareempur, Yenkepalle, Rampur, Jinnaram. Backwards Region Grants Fund: It receives Backward Region Grants.

Annual Rainfall: Average Rainfall 799 mm

Ground Water: Availability of the Ground Water in the Basin is 1192 H.A.M. and the utilization is 592 H.A. M. It belongs to Safe category. Depth to water level varies from 10 to 20 meter below the ground. Most of the wells go down in summer months. The well density in the entire block is 7 wells per sq. km. Total no. of the wells in the block are enumerated as 1260, according to the Ground Water Estimation Committee.

Natural Division : Telangana Plateau Region

Administration:

Division: Telangana. Parliamentary Constituency: 10 Chevella. District: Rangareddy.

Mandal: Bantwaram. Assembly Constituency: 55 Vicarabad (SC). Gram Panchayat: 18.

Border Villages- (Karnataka)- Nearest Villages- Bopanwa ram, Turmamidi.

Villages: 26 **Inhabited:** 24 **Uninhabited:** 2

Ranking	District	State	National
Area	22	640	4446
Population	31	951	5938
Sex Ratio	7	334	1383
Child Sex Ratio	3	162	426
Literacy Rate	26	928	5396
Density	5	274	4962
Work Participation Rate	28	768	702

Gram Panchayats:

Bantaram, Barwad, Beerol, Boppanaram, Jinnaram Kankanalapalle, Kareempur, Kothapalle, Mala Somaram Mothukupalle, Nagsanpalle, Rampur, Rompalle Salbathapur, Turmamidi, Yacharam, Yenkepalle Yennaram.

Amenities:

Education: Primary School in 24 villages, Middle school in 8 villages, Matriculation or Secondary School in 3 villages, namely Turmamidi, Bantwaram, Mothkupalle.

Higher Secondary or Pre University Courses or Intermediate or Junior College in 0 village of the CD Block, College in 0 village, Adult Literacy Center in 8 villages.

Medical: Hospital in 0 village, Dispensary in 1 village, Health Center in 1 village, Sub Center in 5 villages, Maternity and Child Welfare Center in 0 village, Community health workers in 0 village.

The Village having Hospital or Dispensary or Health Center is Turmamidi.

Drinking Water: Tap water in 24 villages, Tank water in 24 villages, Well water in 24 villages, Tubewell in 24 villages and more than one source in 24 villages.

Bank: Banking facility in 24 villages, namely, Bopanwaram, Turmamidi, Bantwaram, Nagaram, Rompalle Mangraspalle, Salbathapur, Madhvapur, Kothapalle Sultanpur, Noorullapur, Yacharam, Somaram .M, Barwad Mothkupalle, Nagsanpalle, Beerol, Kareempur Yenkepalle, Yennaram, Rampur, Jinnaram Kankanalapalle, Malshetpalle.

Credit Society in 4 villages Agricultural Credit Society in 4 Non-Agricultural Credit Society in 0 village.

Others: Power supply in 24 villages, Cinema hall in 0 village, sport club in 0 village, Stadium or Auditorium or Community Hall in 0 village, Post Office in 10 villages.

There are 18 villages having bus facilities.

Villages with most of facilities: Turmamidi Bantwaram, Rompalle, Barwad, Mothkupalle, Yennaram.

Villages without Amenities (Education): None..

Scheduled Castes: Out of the total population of 34121 persons, 9358 persons (27.43%) belong to Scheduled Castes.

The villages having less than 10% SC population are None..

The villages having more than 50% SC population are None.

Sex ratio of Scheduled Caste population is 503.

Scheduled Castes Literates and Illiterates by Sex:

	Persons	Males	Females
Literate	2,675	1,736	939
Illiterate	6,683	2,912	3,771
Literacy rate	34.3	44.9	23.9
Graduate	42	37	5

Scheduled Castes (Dominant):

Madiga, Mala, Byagara, Beda Jangam etc., Mala Dasari

For their cultural identity please see Appendix-I

Villages without Scheduled Castes: There are 3 villages without any scheduled caste population.

Scheduled Tribes: Out of the total population of 34121 persons, 1361 persons (3.99%) belong to Scheduled Tribes.

The villages having less than 10% ST population are Bopanwaram, Turmamidi, Bantwaram, Rompalle Mangraspalle, Salbathapur, Madhvapur, Kothapalle Sultanpur, Noorullapur, Yacharam, Somaram .M Mothkupalle, Beerol, Kareempur, Yenkepalle, Yennaram Rampur, Jinnaram, Kankanalapalle.

The villages having more than 50% ST population are None.

Sex ratio of Scheduled tribe population is 475.

Scheduled Tribes Literates and Illiterates by Sex:

	Persons	Males	Females
Literate	364	268	96
Illiterate	997	446	551
Literacy rate	33.5	46.7	18.8
Graduate	9	7	2

Scheduled Tribes (Dominant):

Sugalis etc., Koya etc., Yerukulas, Kammara Chenchu etc.

For their cultural identity please see Appendix-II

Villages without Scheduled Tribes: There are

13 villages without any scheduled tribe population.

Literates and Illiterates by Sex (Total Population):

	Persons	Males	Females
Literate	12,410	7,920	4,490
Illiterate	21,711	9,196	12,515
Literacy rate	43	55	31
Graduate	240	208	32

Agriculture: ***Distribution of villages according to land use:*** Out of 26 villages, Total area (in hectare) is 18476, out of that 65.04 percent is cultivable and 13.47 percent of the cultivable area is irrigated.

Sources of Irrigation (Hectares): Government Canal 0, Private Canal 0, Well without Electricity 0, Well with Electricity 1618.78, Tubewell without Electricity 0, Tubewell with Electricity 0, Tank 0, River 0, Lake 0, Waterfall 0, Others 0.

Villages with population of 5000 to 9999: Turmamidi.

Villages with population of 10000 and above: None

Distribution of Workers:

	Persons	Males	Females	WPR
Cultivators	10,449	5,786	4,663	56.65
Agricultural Labour	6,495	2,720	3,775	35.21
Household Industry	144	72	72	0.78
Other Workers	1,358	1,084	274	7.36
Main Workers	17,173	9,253	7,920	93.1
Marginal Workers	1,273	409	864	6.9
Total Workers	18,446	9,662	8,784	

Religion: Major Religious Communities:

	Persons	Males	Females	Sex Ratio
Hindu (81.74%)	27,892	13,949	13,943	1,000
Muslim (15.84%)	5,405	2,752	2,653	964
Christian (2.4%)	819	413	406	983
Sikh (0%)	-	-	-	-
Buddhists (0%)	-	-	-	-
Jain (0%)	-	-	-	-

Agewise Data:

	Persons	Males	Females	Sex Ratio
All ages	34,121	17,116	17,005	994
0-14	12,814	6,486	6,328	976
15-44	14,810	7,530	7,280	967
45-79	6,184	2,954	3,230	1093
80+	295	137	158	1153
Age not stated	18	9	9	1000

Languages (Dominant):
Telugu, Urdu, Hindi, Marathi, Kannada

Disabled Population:

	Persons	Males	Females	%
Total Disabled	762	416	346	
In Seeing	435	220	215	57.09
In Speech	46	26	20	6.04
In Hearing	42	16	26	5.51
In Movement	204	135	69	26.77
Mentally	35	19	16	4.59

BAPATLA

Bapatla C.D. Block lies in the southern part of Guntur district. It is a part of Bapatla Mandal. The Block is located at a distance of 38 kms. from district headq uarters (Guntur). There are 20 villages in the block with the total population of 695,58 persons. Area of the C.D. Block is 233.91 sq. kms. It is bounded in the north by district Prakasam and Mandals Kakumanu and Ponnur, in the south by district Prakasam and the Bay of Bengal, in the east by Mandal Karlapalem, and in the west by district Prakasam.

Communications:

Roadways : State Highway (S.H.): Direction- Ongole to Ponnur. Nearest Villages- Etheru, Bharthipudi, Appikat la, Velicherla, Mulapalem, Murukondapadu, Bapatla West (Rural).

Railway Station: Bharthipudi, Appikatla, Murukondapadu, Bapatla West (Rural).

Integrated Child Development Scheme (ICDS) Project: Bapatala, Total Anganwadi Centres: 241

Annual Rainfall: Average Rainfall 880 mm

Ground Water: Availability of the Ground Water in the Basin is 9429 H.A.M. and the utilization is 1089 H. A.M. It belongs to Safe category. Depth to water level varies from 2 to 5 meter below the ground. Most of the wells go down in summer months.

Forest and Reserved **Forest:** (Mothyapalem R.F.)- Nearest Villages- Adivi, Maruproluvaripalem (Rural).

Natural Division : Krishna Delta Region

Administration:

Division: Coastal Andhra. Parliamentary Constituency: 32 Bapatla (SC). District: Guntur. Mandal: Bapatla. Assembly Constituency: 211 Bapatla. Gram Panchayat: 22

Fairs and Festivals:

Sri Bhavanarayanaswamy Festival : It is celebrated for 15 days from Vaisakha Suddha Padyami to Purnima (April-May). Everyday the Lord is taken in procession on one or the other vahanams such as hamsa, simha hanuman, enugu, sesha, ponnamanu etc., and the process ion on enugu and ponnamanu on Ekadasi and Chathurdasi are special. The marriage ceremony is inaugurated on Sapthami and the function concludes on Purnima with rathothsavam (car festival). The car starts from the temples and reaches the temple of Prapathyanjaneyas wamy through the intervening street called the car-stre et. Cocoanuts and pulihora are offered.

Villages: 20 **Inhabited:** 18 **Uninhabited:** 2

Ranking	District	State	National
Area	8	371	3598
Population	7	137	4502
Sex Ratio	9	300	1345
Child Sex Ratio	24	547	2130
Literacy Rate	32	377	3350
Density	39	610	3576
Work Participation Rate	37	381	1640

Gram Panchayats:

Appikatla, Asodivaripalem, Bethapudi, Bharthipudi East Bapatla, Etheru, Gopapuram, Gudipudi Jammulapalem, Jillellamudi, Kankatapalem, Marripudi Maruproluvaripalem, Mulapalem, Murukondapadu Muthayapalem, Narsayapalem, Pandurangapuram Pinnuboinavaripalem, Poondla, Tsundurupalli Vedullapalli.

Amenities:

Education: Primary School in 17 villages, Middle school in 11 villages, Matriculation or Secondary School in 9 villages, namely Poondla, Appikatla, Jammulapalem, Cheruvu, Narasayapalem, Murukondapadu, Bapatla West (Rural), Bapatla East (Rural), Adivi.

Higher Secondary or Pre University Courses or Intermediate or Junior College in 0 village of the CD Block, College in 0 village, Adult Literacy Center in 3 villages.

Medical: Hospital in 0 village, Dispensary in 2 villages, Health Center in 2 villages, Sub Center in 12 villages, Maternity and Child Welfare Center in 0 village, Community health workers in 0 village.

The Villages having Hospital or Dispensary or Health Center are Jillellamudi, Adivi.

Drinking Water: Tap water in 17 villages, Tank water in 17 villages, Well water in 18 villages, Tubewell in 16 villages and more than one source in 18 villages.

Bank: Banking facility in 7 villages, namely, Jillellamudi, Appikatla, Jammulapalem, Narasayapalem Kankatapalem, Bapatla West (Rural) Bapatla East (Rural).

Credit Society in 12 villages Agricultural Credit Society in 9 Non-Agricultural Credit Society in 1 village.

Others: Power supply in 18 villages, Cinema hall in 1 village, sport club in 0 village, Stadium or Auditorium or Community Hall in 0 village, Post Office in 15 villages.

There are 14 villages having bus facilities.

Villages with most of facilities: Jillellamudi Appikatla, Jammulapalem, Narasayapalem, Kankatapalem Bapatla West (Rural), Bapatla East (Rural).

Villages without amenities (Education):

Neredupalle..

Scheduled Castes: Out of the total population of 69125 persons, 13749 persons (19.89%) belong to Scheduled Castes.

The villages having less than 10% SC population are Jillellamudi, Neredupalle, Jammulapalem Murukondapadu, Bapatla West (Rural), Adivi.

The villages having more than 50% SC population are None.

Sex ratio of Scheduled Caste population is 491.

Scheduled Castes Literates and Illiterates by Sex:

	Persons	Males	Females
Literate	7,251	4,316	2,935
Illiterate	6,498	2,689	3,809
Literacy rate	59.7	69.4	49.5
Graduate	307	243	64

Scheduled Castes (Dominant):

Mala, Madiga, Mala Dasu, Mala Dasari Ellamalawar etc.

For their cultural identity please see Appendix-I

Villages without Scheduled Castes: There are 3 villages without any scheduled caste population.

Scheduled Tribes: Out of the total population of 69125 persons, 5847 persons (8.46%) belong to Scheduled Tribes.

The villages having less than 10% ST population are Jillellamudi, Gopapuram, Poondla, Etheru, Gudipudi Bharthipudi, Appikatla, Mulapalem, Jammulapalem Cheruvu, Narasayapalem, Kankatapalem Bapatla East (Rural), Maruproluvaripalem (Rural) Adivi.

The villages having more than 50% ST population are None.

Sex ratio of Scheduled tribe population is 511.

Scheduled Tribes Literates and Illiterates by Sex:

	Persons	Males	Females
Literate	2,636	1,485	1,151
Illiterate	3,211	1,374	1,837
Literacy rate	51.5	59.5	43.9
Graduate	131	104	27

Scheduled Tribes (Dominant):

Yerukulas, Yenadis, Kammara, Sugalis etc. Generic Tribes etc.

For their cultural identity please see Appendix-II

Villages without Scheduled Tribes: There are 4 villages without any scheduled tribe population.

Literates and Illiterates by Sex (Total Population):

	Persons	Males	Females
Literate	34,621	19,979	14,642
Illiterate	34,504	14,664	19,840
Literacy rate	57	66	48
Graduate	1,670	1,292	378

Agriculture: ***Distribution of villages according to land use:***

Out of 20 villages, Total area (in hectare) is 23391, out of that 72.26 percent is cultivable and 85.3 percent of the cultivable area is irrigated.

Sources of Irrigation (Hectares): Government Canal 14297.21, Private Canal 0, Well without Electricity 0, Well with Electricity 0, Tubewell without Electricity 0, Tubewell with Electricity 0, Tank 120, River 0, Lake 0, Waterfall 0, Others 0.

Villages with population of 5000 to 9999: Narasayapalem, Murukondapadu, Bapatla West (Rural) Bapatla East (Rural), Maruproluvaripalem (Rural) Adivi.

Villages with population of 10000 and above: None

Distribution of Workers:

	Persons	Males	Females	WPR
Cultivators	4,594	3,798	796	12.58
Agricultural Labour	26,016	12,639	13,377	71.26
Household Industry	513	231	282	1.41
Other Workers	5,385	4,193	1,192	14.75
Main Workers	29,521	18,443	11,078	80.86
Marginal Workers	6,987	2,418	4,569	19.14
Total Workers	36,508	20,861	15,647	

Religion: Major Religious Communities:

	Persons	Males	Females	Sex Ratio
Hindu (92.75%)	64,115	32,238	31,877	989
Muslim (2.81%)	1,941	957	984	1,028
Christian (4.13%)	2,852	1,389	1,463	1,053
Sikh (0%)	1	1	-	-
Buddhists (0%)	-	-	-	-
Jain (0%)	-	-	-	-

Agewise Data:

	Persons	Males	Females	Sex Ratio
All ages	69,125	34,643	34,482	995
0-14	19,873	10,074	9,799	973
15-44	33,782	17,002	16,780	987
45-79	14,748	7,217	7,531	1044
80+	656	309	347	1123
Age not stated	66	41	25	610

Languages (Dominant):
Telugu, Urdu, Tamil, Oriya, Gondi

Disabled Population:

	Persons	Males	Females	%
Total Disabled	1,079	572	507	
In Seeing	396	190	206	36.7
In Speech	124	67	57	11.49
In Hearing	62	25	37	5.75
In Movement	350	214	136	32.44
Mentally	147	76	71	13.62

BAPULAPADU

Bapulapadu C.D. Block lies in the eastern part of Krishna district. The Block is located at a distance of 70 kms. from district headquarters (Machilipatnam). There are 29 villages in the block with the total population of 83,286 persons. Area of the C.D. Block is 226.63 sq. kms. It is bounded in the north by Mandals Nuzvid and Musunuru, in the south by Mandals Unguturu and Nandivada, in the east by district West Godavari, and in the west by Mandals Agiripalle and Gannavaram.

Communications:

Roadways : NH- 9: Direction- Vijayawada to Eluru. Nearest Vilages- Bommuluru, Ampapuram, Kodurupadu,Veleru, Bapulapadu. State Highway (S.H.): Direction- Machilipatnam to Bapulapadu. Nearest Villages- Serinarasannapalem, Veleru, Bapulapadu, Kanumolu, Arugolanu.

Railway Station: Bapulapadu, Ampapuram, Veeravalli.

Annaul Rainfall: Average Rainfall 1512 mm

Ground Water: Availability of the Ground Water in the Basin is (Information not avavible) H.A.M .and the utilization is (Information not avavible) H.A.M. It belongs to (Information not avavible) category. Depth to water level varies from 3 to 10 meter below the ground. Most of the wells go down in summer months.

Natural Division : Krishna Delta Region

Administration:

Division: Coastal Andhra. Parliamentary Constituency: 28 Machilipatnam. District: Krishna. Mandal: Bapulapadu. Assembly Constituency: 190 Gannavaram. Gram Panchayat: 27

Villages: 29 **Inhabited:** 28 **Uninhabited:** 1

Ranking	**District**	**State**	**National**
Area	5	402	3713
Population	3	28	3995
Sex Ratio	24	550	1978
Child Sex Ratio	18	376	1388
Literacy Rate	26	159	1943
Density	29	833	2975
Work Participation Rate	23	238	2597

Gram Panchayats:
Ampapuram, Arugolanu, Bandarugudem, Bapulapadu Billampalli, Bommuluru, Chiriwada, Dantaguntla Kakulapadu, Kanumolu, Kodurupadu, Kothapalli Koyyuru, Madicherla, Mallavalli, Ogirala, Parikeedu R.A.Peta, Ramannagudem, Rangannagudem, Remalli S.N.Palem, Sitharampuram(A), Sitharampuram(K) Thippanagunta, Veeravalli, Veleru.

Amenities:

Education: Primary School in 26 villages, Middle school in 14 villages, Matriculation or Secondary School in 7 villages, namely Bapulapadu, Veleru, Remalle, Veeravalli, Kanumolu, Arugolanu, Ramannagudem.

Higher Secondary or Pre University Courses or Inter-

mediate or Junior College in 1 village of the CD Block,, namely Kanumolu.
College in 1 village, Adult Literacy Center in 5 villages., College is in village, namely Kanumolu.
Medical: Hospital in 0 village, Dispensary in 3 villages, Health Center in 2 villages, Sub Center in 13 villages, Maternity and Child Welfare Center in 0 village, Community health workers in 0 village.
The Villages having Hospital or Dispensary or Health Center are Veleru, Bandarugudem, Kanumolu.
Drinking Water: Tap water in 28 villages, Tank water in 11 villages, Well water in 9 villages, Tubewell in 13 villages and more than one source in 28 villages.
Bank: Banking facility in 4 villages, namely, Bapulapadu, Veeravalli, Kanumolu, Arugolanu.
Credit Society in 17 villages Agricultural Credit Society in 14 Non-Agricultural Credit Society in 9 villages.
Others: Power supply in 28 villages, Cinema hall in 2 villages, sport club in 0 village, Stadium or Auditorium or Community Hall in 0 village, Post Office in 23 villages.
There are 26 villages having bus facilities.
Villages with most of facilities: Bapulapadu Veeravalli, Kanumolu, Arugolanu.
Villages without amenities (Education): Venkatrajugudem, Kuripirala..
Scheduled Castes: Out of the total population of 83286 persons, 16465 persons (19.77%) belong to Scheduled Castes.
The villages having less than 10% SC population are Kothapalle, Rangannagudem, Ampapuram, Kodurupadu Dantaguntla.
The villages having more than 50% SC population are None.
Sex ratio of Scheduled Caste population is 492.

Scheduled Castes Literates and Illiterates by Sex:

	Persons	Males	Females
Literate	9,175	5,039	4,136
Illiterate	7,290	3,324	3,966
Literacy rate	64.2	69.5	58.8
Graduate	328	227	101

Scheduled Castes (Dominant):
Madiga, Mala, Relli, Madiga Dasu etc.
Beda Jangam etc.
For their cultural identity please see Appendix-I
Villages without Scheduled Castes: There is 1 village without any scheduled caste population.
Scheduled Tribes: Out of the total population of 83286 persons, 1765 persons (2.12%) belong to Scheduled Tribes.
The villages having less than 10% ST population are Mallavilli, Kothapalle, Billanapalle, Koyyuru Bommuluru, Bommuluru Khandrika, Bapulapadu, Veleru Remalle, Singannagudem, Rangannagudem Sobhanadripuram, Bandarugudem, Ampapuram, Kodurupadu Veeravalli, Serinarasannapalem, Kanumolu Dantaguntla, Kakulapadu, Tippanagunta Venkatrajugudem, Chirivada, Arugolanu, Kuripirala Ogirala, Ramannagudem.
The villages having more than 50% ST population are None.
Sex ratio of Scheduled tribe population is 481.

Scheduled Tribes Literates and Illiterates by Sex:

	Persons	Males	Females
Literate	501	323	178
Illiterate	1,264	593	671
Literacy rate	34.0	42.3	25.1
Graduate	12	9	3

Scheduled Tribes (Dominant):
Sugalis etc., Yerukulas, Yenadis, Chenchu etc.
Koya etc.
For their cultural identity please see Appendix-II
Villages without Scheduled Tribes: There are 9 villages without any scheduled tribe population.

Literates and Illiterates by Sex (Total Population):

	Persons	Males	Females
Literate	47,838	26,123	21,715
Illiterate	35,448	15,918	19,530
Literacy rate	65	70	60
Graduate	2,058	1,423	635

Agriculture: ***Distribution of villages according to land use:*** Out of 29 villages, Total area (in hectare) is 22663, out of that 72.59 percent is cultivable and 72.6 percent of the cultivable area is irrigated.
Sources of Irrigation (Hectares): Government Canal 6488.21, Private Canal 0, Well without Electricity 0, Well with Electricity 2088.23, Tubewell without Electricity 0, Tubewell with Electricity 1562.25, Tank 853.81, River 0, Lake 0, Waterfall 0, Others 950.13.
Villages with population of 5000 to 9999: Veeravalli, Kanumolu.
Villages with population of 10000 and above: Bapulapadu.

Distribution of Workers:

	Persons	Males	Females	WPR
Cultivators	4,973	4,251	722	12.09
Agricultural Labour	27,468	14,161	13,307	66.77
Household Industry	796	446	350	1.93
Other Workers	7,902	6,654	1,248	19.21
Main Workers	33,661	22,515	11,146	81.82
Marginal Workers	7,478	2,997	4,481	18.18
Total Workers	41,139	25,512	15,627	

Religion: Major Religious Communities:

	Persons	Males	Females	Sex Ratio
Hindu (89.64%)	74,658	37,744	36,914	978
Muslim (4.5%)	3,750	1,884	1,866	990
Christian (5.8%)	4,833	2,389	2,444	1,023
Sikh (0%)	2	2	-	-
Buddhists (0%)	-	-	-	-
Jain (0%)	-	-	-	-

Agewise Data:

	Persons	Males	Females	Sex Ratio
All ages	83,286	42,041	41,245	981
0-14	24,339	12,323	12,016	975
15-44	41,225	20,838	20,387	978
45-79	16,957	8,517	8,440	991
80+	667	310	357	1152
Age not stated	98	53	45	849

Languages (Dominant):

Telugu, Urdu, Hindi, Gondi, Oriya

Disabled Population:

	Persons	Males	Females	%
Total Disabled	2,023	1,052	971	
In Seeing	1,009	485	524	49.88
In Speech	187	95	92	9.24
In Hearing	95	51	44	4.7
In Movement	512	297	215	25.31
Mentally	220	124	96	10.87

BASHEERABAD

Basheerabad C.D. Block lies in the western part of Rangareddy district. The Block is located at a distance of 132 kms. from district headquarters (Serilingampalle). There are 31 villages in the block with the total population of 40,711 persons. Area of the C.D. Block is 209.06 sq. kms. It is bounded by Tandur Mandal on north, Yalal Mandal on east, Mahbubnagar district on south-east, and it has common boundary with the state of Karnataka from south and west.

Communications :

Roadways : Metalled Roads: Nearest Villages- connect the following villages, namely, Navandgi, Gangwar, Kyadgira, Jeevangi, Masanpalle (M), Korviched, Navalga, Allapur (Basheerabad), Manthangoud, Damerched, Parwath palle, Ekmai, Mailwar, Neelapalle, Jalalpur, Marpalle, Gotiga Khurd, Malkangiri, Khasimpur.

Railway Station: Reddighanapur.

River: Kagna Nadi- Nearest Villages- Inderched, Gangwar, Kyadgira, Jeevangi, Manthatti.

Backwards Region Grants Fund: It receives Backward Region Grants.

Annual Rainfall: Average Rainfall 740 mm

Ground Water: Availability of the Ground Water in the Basin is 1878 H.A.M. and the utilization is 615 H.A. M. It belongs to Safe category. Depth to water level varies from 5 to 10 meter below the ground. Most of the wells go down in summer months. The well density in the entire block is 3 wells per sq. km. Total no. of the wells in the block are enumerated as 713, accor ding to the Ground Water Estimation Committee.

Natural Division : Telangana Plateau Region

Administration:

Division: Telangana. Parliamentary Constituency: 10 Chevella. District: Rangareddy.

Mandal: Basheerabad. Assembly Constituency: 56 Tandur. Gram Panchayat: 16.

Border Villages: (Karnataka)- Nearest Villages- Inderch ed, Navandgi, Gangwar, Kyadgira, Jeevangi, Manthangoud, Ekmai, Kamsanpalle Buzurg, Mailwar, Ismailpur, Neelapa lle, Jalalpur.

Villages: 31 **Inhabited:** 29 **Uninhabited:** 2

Ranking	District	State	National
Area	19	498	4027
Population	25	802	5707
Sex Ratio	1	49	382
Child Sex Ratio	18	449	1582
Literacy Rate	30	967	5546
Density	20	647	4800
Work Participation Rate	26	735	1770

Gram Panchayats:

Basheerabad, Damarched, Ekmai, Gottiga Khurd Inderched, Jeevangi, Khasimpur, Korviched, Kyadgira Mailwar, Manthangoud, Manthatti, Navalga, Neelapalle Parvathpalle, Reddighanapur.

Amenities:

Education: Primary School in 29 villages, Middle school in 10 villages, Matriculation or Secondary School in 5 villages, namely Navandgi, Navalga, Ekmai, Mailwar, Gotiga Khurd.

Higher Secondary or Pre University Courses or Inter-mediate or Junior College in 0 village of the CD Block, College in 0 village, Adult Literacy Center in 2 villages.

Medical: Hospital in 1 village, Dispensary in 0 village, Health Center in 1 village, Sub Center in 7 villages, Maternity and Child Welfare Center in 0 village, Community health workers in 0 village.

The Villages having Hospital or Dispensary or Health Center are Navandgi, Korviched.

Drinking Water: Tap water in 29 villages, Tank water in 29 villages, Well water in 29 villages, Tubewell in 29 villages and more than one source in 29 villages.

Bank: Banking facility in 29 villages, namely, Inderched, Navandgi, Gangwar, Kyadgira, Jeevangi Manthatti, Reddighanapur, Kamsanpalle Maqta

Masanpalle (M), Korviched, Navalga
Allapur (Basheerabad), Manthangoud, Damerched
Parwathpalle, Kothlapur Buzurg, Ekmai
Kamsanpalle Buzurg, Mailwar, Ismailpur, Neelapalle
Jalalpur, Marpalle, Gotiga Kalan, Gotiga Khurd
Malkangiri, Khasimpur, Bahadurpur, Koppankote.
Credit Society in 10 villages Agricultural Credit Society in 6 Non-Agricultural Credit Society in 5 villages.

Others: Power supply in 29 villages, Cinema hall in 0 village, sport club in 0 village, Stadium or Auditorium or Community Hall in 0 village, Post Office in 12 villages.
There are 25 villages having bus facilities.

Villages with most of facilities: Navandgi
Manthatti, Reddighanapur, Korviched, Navalga
Manthangoud, Damerched, Mailwar, Neelapalle.

Villages without Amenities (Education): None..

Scheduled Castes: Out of the total population of 40711 persons, 7367 persons (18.1%) belong to Scheduled Castes.
The villages having less than 10% SC population are
Kyadgira, Masanpalle (M), Kothlapur Buzurg, Mailwar
Ismailpur, Koppankote.
The villages having more than 50% SC population are None.
Sex ratio of Scheduled Caste population is 507.

Scheduled Castes Literates and Illiterates by Sex:

	Persons	Males	Females
Literate	1,878	1,238	640
Illiterate	5,489	2,391	3,098
Literacy rate	30.7	41.3	20.5
Graduate	35	33	2

Scheduled Castes (Dominant):
Madiga, Mala, Beda Jangam etc., Mala Dasari, Mehtar

For their cultural identity please see Appendix-I

Villages without Scheduled Castes: There are
4 villages without any scheduled caste population.

Scheduled Tribes: Out of the total population of 40711 persons, 7681 persons (18.87%) belong to Scheduled Tribes.
The villages having less than 10% ST population are
Inderched, Gangwar, Kyadgira, Manthatti
Reddighanapur, Kamsanpalle Maqta
Allapur (Basheerabad), Parwathpalle, Ekmai
Kamsanpalle Buzurg, Mailwar, Marpalle, Gotiga Kalan
Gotiga Khurd, Malkangiri, Khasimpur.
The villages having more than 50% ST population are
Navalga, Manthangoud, Kothlapur Buzurg, Ismailpur
Koppankote.
Sex ratio of Scheduled tribe population is 499.

Scheduled Tribes Literates and Illiterates by Sex:

	Persons	Males	Females
Literate	1,543	1,107	436
Illiterate	6,138	2,740	3,398
Literacy rate	25.8	37.0	14.6
Graduate	8	8	0

Scheduled Tribes (Dominant):
Sugalis etc., Yerukulas, Chenchu etc., Kammara

For their cultural identity please see Appendix-II

Villages without Scheduled Tribes: There are
9 villages without any scheduled tribe population.

Literates and Illiterates by Sex (Total Population):

	Persons	Males	Females
Literate	14,135	8,869	5,266
Illiterate	26,576	11,102	15,474
Literacy rate	42	54	30
Graduate	316	258	58

Agriculture: ***Distribution of villages according to land use:***
Out of 31 villages, Total area (in hectare) is 20906, out of that 52.47 percent is cultivable and 9.84 percent of the cultivable area is irrigated.

Sources of Irrigation (Hectares): Government Canal 64.74, Private Canal 0, Well without Electricity 8.49, Well with Electricity 346.31, Tubewell without Electricity 0, Tubewell with Electricity 249.92, Tank 387.96, River 2.42, Lake 0, Waterfall 0, Others 19.01.

Villages with population of 5000 to 9999:
Navandgi.

Villages with population of 10000 and above: None

Distribution of Workers:

	Persons	Males	Females	WPR
Cultivators	5,764	4,070	1,694	28.82
Agricultural Labour	7,761	2,396	5,365	38.81
Household Industry	488	254	234	2.44
Other Workers	5,985	4,202	1,783	29.93
Main Workers	15,958	9,623	6,335	79.8
Marginal Workers	4,040	1,299	2,741	20.2
Total Workers	19,998	10,922	9,076	

Religion: Major Religious Communities:

	Persons	Males	Females	Sex Ratio
Hindu (90.28%)	36,754	18,074	18,680	1,034
Muslim (9.55%)	3,889	1,870	2,019	1,080
Christian (0.11%)	43	15	28	1,867
Sikh (0%)	-	-	-	-
Buddhists (0%)	-	-	-	-
Jain (0%)	-	-	-	-

Agewise Data:

	Persons	Males	Females	Sex Ratio
All ages	40,711	19,971	20,740	1039
0-14	15,846	7,939	7,907	996
15-44	17,427	8,638	8,789	1017
45-79	7,109	3,257	3,852	1183
80+	254	101	153	1515

Age not stated	75	36	39	1083

Languages (Dominant):

Telugu, Hindi, Urdu, Marathi, Kannada

Disabled Population:

	Persons	Males	Females	%
Total Disabled	861	469	392	
In Seeing	346	171	175	40.19
In Speech	82	44	38	9.52
In Hearing	58	31	27	6.74
In Movement	310	187	123	36
Mentally	65	36	29	7.55

BATHALAPALLE

Bathalapalle C.D. Block lies in the south-eastern part of Anantapur district. The Block is located at a distan ce of 32 kms. from district headquarters (Anantapur). There are 11 villages in the block with the total population of 35,318 persons. Area of the C.D. Block is 226.78 sq. kms. It is bounded in the north by Mandals Narpala and Tadimarri, in the south by Mandals Dharmav aram and Mudigubba, in the east by Mandal Mudigubba, and in the west by Mandals Anantapur and Dharmavarm.

Communications:

Roadways : NH- 205: Direction- Anantapur to Renigunta. Nearest Villages- Edula Mustur, Raghavampalle, Apparac heruvu, Sangala, Obulapuram, Dampetla, D.Cherlopalle, Bathalapalle. State Highway (S.H.): Direction- Dharmav aram to Narpala. Nearest Villages- Bathalapalle, Malyava ntham.

Railway Station: Obulapuram, D.Cherlopalle.

River: Chitravati Nadi- Nearest Villages- Chennarayapat nam, Gariselapalle, Apparacheruvu, Sangala, Obulapuram, Dampetla, D.Cherlopalle.

It receives the Backward Region Grants, and is identifi ed as a drought-prone area as well.

Annual Rainfall: Average l Rainfall 520 mm

Ground Water: Availability of the Ground Water in the Basin is 1394 H.A.M. and the utilization is 1814 H. A.M. It belongs to OE category. Depth to water level varies from 5 to 10 meter below the ground. Most of the wells go down in summer months. The well density in the entire block is 9 wells per sq. km. Total no. of the wells in the block are enumerated as 2106, according to the Ground Water Estimation Committee.

Natural Division : Rayalaseema Region

Administration:

Division: Rayala Seema. Parliamentary Constituency: 37 Hindupur. District: Anantapur.

Mandal: Bathalapalle. Assembly Constituency: 279 Dharma varam. Gram Panchayat: 12.

Villages: 11 **Inhabited:** 11 **Uninhabited:** 0

Ranking	**District**	**State**	**National**
Area	47	401	3712
Population	50	926	5900
Sex Ratio	35	964	3314
Child Sex Ratio	34	669	2731
Literacy Rate	31	608	4257
Density	31	393	5478
Work Participation Rate	31	887	959

Gram Panchayats:

Apparacheruvu, Bathalapalli, D.Cherlopalli, Dampetla Edula Mustur, Garisalapalli, Malyavantham Nallaboyanapalli, Obulapuram, Sangala, Sanjeevapuram Thambapuram.

Amenities:

Education: Primary School in 11 villages, Middle school in 4 villages, Matriculation or Secondary School in 2 villages, namely Bathalapalle, D.Cherlopalle.

Higher Secondary or Pre University Courses or Intermediate or Junior College in 1 village of the CD Block,, namely Bathalapalle.

College in 0 village, Adult Literacy Center in 11 villages.

Medical: Hospital in 0 village, Dispensary in 0 village, Health Center in 1 village, Sub Center in 7 villages, Maternity and Child Welfare Center in 0 village, Community health workers in .0 village.

Drinking Water: Tap water in 8 villages, Tank water in 0 villages, Well water in 0 village, Tubewell in 11 villages and more than one source in 11 villages.

Bank: Banking facility in 2 villages, namely, Bathalapalle, D.Cherlopalle.

Credit Society in 3 villages Agricultural Credit Society in 3 Non-Agricultural Credit Society in 0 village.

Others: Power supply in 11 villages, Cinema hall in 0 village, sport club in 0 village, Stadium or Auditorium or Community Hall in 0 village, Post Office in 10 villages.

There are 11 villages having bus facilities.

Villages with most of facilities: Bathalapalle D.Cherlopalle.

Villages without Amenities (Education): None..

Scheduled Castes: Out of the total population of 35318 persons, 4981 persons (14.1%) belong to Scheduled Castes.

The villages having less than 10% SC population are None..

The villages having more than 50% SC population are None.

Sex ratio of Scheduled Caste population is 498.

Scheduled Castes Literates and Illiterates by Sex:

	Persons	Males	Females
Literate	1,798	1,111	687
Illiterate	3,183	1,390	1,793

Literacy rate	41.1	50.8	31.4
Graduate	28	25	3

Scheduled Castes (Dominant):

Madiga, Mala, Matangi, Generic Castes etc.

For their cultural identity please see Appendix-I

Villages without Scheduled Castes: There is 1 village without any scheduled caste population.

Scheduled Tribes: Out of the total population of 35318 persons, 2208 persons (6.25%) belong to Scheduled Tribes. The villages having less than 10% ST population are Edula Mustur, Malyavantham, Raghavampalle Bathalapalle, Apparacheruvu, Obulapuram, Dampetla. The villages having more than 50% ST population are None.

Sex ratio of Scheduled tribe population is 490.

Scheduled Tribes Literates and Illiterates by Sex:

	Persons	Males	Females
Literate	777	527	250
Illiterate	1,431	598	833
Literacy rate	40.9	54.3	26.8
Graduate	17	14	3

Scheduled Tribes (Dominant):

Yerukulas, Sugalis etc.

For their cultural identity please see Appendix-II

Villages without Scheduled Tribes: There is 1 village without any scheduled tribe population.

Literates and Illiterates by Sex (Total Population):

	Persons	Males	Females
Literate	15,983	10,195	5,788
Illiterate	19,335	7,892	11,443
Literacy rate	52	64	38
Graduate	675	561	114

Agriculture: *Distribution of villages according to land use:* Out of 11 villages, Total area (in hectare) is 22678, out of that 77.58 percent is cultivable and 11.5 percent of the cultivable area is irrigated.

Sources of Irrigation (Hectares): Government Canal 0, Private Canal 0, Well without Electricity 0, Well with Electricity 1127.93, Tubewell without Electricity 0, Tubewell with Electricity 894.99, Tank 0, River 0, Lake 0, Waterfall 0, Others 0.

Villages with population of 5000 to 9999: Bathalapalle.

Villages with population of 10000 and above: None

Distribution of Workers:

	Persons	Males	Females	WPR
Cultivators	7,648	4,971	2,677	39.26
Agricultural Labour	7,763	2,923	4,840	39.85
Household Industry	643	416	227	3.3
Other Workers	3,428	2,662	766	17.6
Main Workers	16,561	9,910	6,651	85.01
Marginal Workers	2,921	1,062	1,859	14.99
Total Workers	19,482	10,972	8,510	

Religion: Major Religious Communities:

	Persons	Males	Females	Sex Ratio
Hindu (94.23%)	33,281	17,080	16,201	949
Muslim (5.23%)	1,848	912	936	1,026
Christian (0.2%)	70	37	33	892
Sikh (0.01%)	3	1	2	2,000
Buddhists (0%)	-	-	-	-
Jain (0%)	-	-	-	-

Agewise Data:

	Persons	Males	Females	Sex Ratio
All ages	35,318	18,087	17,231	953
0-14	11,171	5,770	5,401	936
15-44	17,082	8,798	8,284	942
45-79	6,815	3,407	3,408	1000
80+	223	99	124	1253
Age not stated	27	13	14	1077

Languages (Dominant):

Telugu, Urdu, Hindi, Kannada, Gondi

Disabled Population:

	Persons	Males	Females	%
Total Disabled	798	435	363	
In Seeing	251	114	137	31.45
In Speech	116	71	45	14.54
In Hearing	55	27	28	6.89
In Movement	271	172	99	33.96
Mentally	105	51	54	13.16

BAYYARAM

Bayyaram C.D. Block lies in the western part of Khammam district. The Block is located at a distance of 60 kms. from district headquarters (Khammam). There are 17 villages in the block with the total population of 42,326 persons. Area of the C.D. Block is 257.10 sq. kms. It is bounded in the north by district Warangal and Mandal Gundala, in the south by Mandals Garla and Singareni, in the east by Mandals Yellandu and Singareni, and in the west by district Warangal.

Communications:

Roadways : Metalled Roads: Nearest Villages- Kachanapalle, Lingagiri, Irsulapuram, Bayyaram.

River: Munneru Nadi- Nearest Villages- Uppalapadu, Bayyaram.

Backwards Region Grants Fund: It receives Backward Region Grants.

Annual Rainfall: Average Rainfall 1212 mm

Ground Water: Availability of the Ground Water in the Basin is 1556 H.A.M.and the utilization is 270 H.A. M. It belongs to safe category. Depth to water level varies from 5 to 10 meter below the ground. Most of the wells go down in summer months. The well density in the entire block is 1 wells per sq. km. Total no. of the wells in the block are enumerated as 635, accor ding to the Ground Water Estimation Committee.

Natural Division : Godavari Depression Region

Administration:

Division: Telangana. Parliamentary Constituency: 16 Mahbubabad (ST). District: Khammam. Mandal: Bayyaram. Assembly Constituency: 111 Yellandu (ST). Gram Panchay at:11.

Villages: 17 **Inhabited:** 17 **Uninhabited:** 0

Ranking	District	State	National
Area	19	284	3285
Population	27	750	5634
Sex Ratio	23	678	2297
Child Sex Ratio	17	229	728
Literacy Rate	37	854	5088
Density	30	526	5322
Work Participation Rate	26	852	1375

Gram Panchayats:

Balajipeta, Bayyaram, Gowraram, Irsulapuram Kambalapalli, Kothagudem, Kothapeta Ramachandrapuram, Uppalapadu, Venkatapuram Venkatrampuram.

Amenities:

Education: Primary School in 17 villages, Middle school in 5 villages, Matriculation or Secondary School in 3 villages, namely Irsulapuram, Bayyaram, Gandhampalle.

Higher Secondary or Pre University Courses or Intermediate or Junior College in 1 village of the CD Block,, namely Bayyaram.

College in 1 village, Adult Literacy Center in 13 villages., College is in village, namely Bayyaram.

Medical: Hospital in 0 village, Dispensary in 1 village, Health Center in 3 villages, Sub Center in 10 villages, Maternity and Child Welfare Center in 2 villages, Community health workers in 0 village.

The Villages having Hospital or Dispensary or Health Center are Uppalapadu, Bayyaram.

Drinking Water: Tap water in 17 villages, Tank water in 17 villages, Well water in 17 villages, Tubewell in 17 villages and more than one source in 17 villages.

Bank: Banking facility in 3 villages, namely, Venkatapuram, Bayyaram, Gandhampalle.

Credit Society in 5 villages Agricultural Credit Society in 2 Non-Agricultural Credit Society in 4 villages.

Others: Power supply in 17 villages, Cinema hall in 2 villages, sport club in 1 village, Stadium or Auditorium or Community Hall in 0 village, Post Office in 6 villages.

There are 13 villages having bus facilities.

Villages with most of facilities: Bayyaram Gandhampalle.

Villages without Amenities (Education): None..

Scheduled Castes: Out of the total population of 42326 persons, 3259 persons (7.7%) belong to Scheduled Castes.

The villages having less than 10% SC population are Gurimella, Motlathimma Puram, Jagathraopet Venkatapuram, Kommavaram, Kambalapalle, Kachanapalle Lingagiri, Irsulapuram, Ramachandra Puram Uppalapadu, Bayyaram, Dharmapuram.

The villages having more than 50% SC population are None.

Sex ratio of Scheduled Caste population is 491.

Scheduled Castes Literates and Illiterates by Sex:

	Persons	Males	Females
Literate	1,293	807	486
Illiterate	1,966	853	1,113
Literacy rate	45.7	55.9	35.2
Graduate	34	29	5

Scheduled Castes (Dominant):

Madiga, Mala, Beda Jangam etc., Bindla Generic Castes etc.

For their cultural identity please see Appendix-I

Villages without Scheduled Castes: There are 2 villages without any scheduled caste population.

Scheduled Tribes: Out of the total population of 42326 persons, 21363 persons (50.47%) belong to Scheduled Tribes.

The villages having less than 10% ST population are None..

The villages having more than 50% ST population are Gurimella, Motlathimma Puram, Jagathraopet Venkatapuram, Kommavaram, Kambalapalle, Kachanapalle Lingagiri, Ramachandra Puram, Singaram, Dharmapuram.

Sex ratio of Scheduled tribe population is 489.

Scheduled Tribes Literates and Illiterates by Sex:

	Persons	Males	Females
Literate	6,607	4,473	2,134
Illiterate	14,756	6,435	8,321
Literacy rate	36.8	48.6	24.3
Graduate	87	79	8

Scheduled Tribes (Dominant):

Sugalis etc., Koya etc., Yerukulas, Gond etc. Nayaks

For their cultural identity please see Appendix-II

Villages without Scheduled Tribes: There are 0 village without any scheduled tribe population.

Literates and Illiterates by Sex (Total Population):

	Persons	Males	Females
Literate	16,745	10,454	6,291

Illiterate	25,581	10,985	14,596
Literacy rate	46	57	35
Graduate	485	408	77

Agriculture: ***Distribution of villages according to land use:*** Out of 17 villages, Total area (in hectare) is 25711, out of that 36.08 percent is cultivable and 53.05 percent of the cultivable area is irrigated.

Sources of Irrigation (Hectares): Government Canal 171, Private Canal 0, Well without Electricity 63.02, Well with Electricity 743.85, Tubewell without Electricity 0, Tubewell with Electricity 10, Tank 2843.35, River 8, Lake 0, Waterfall 0, Others 1081.06.

Villages with population of 5000 to 9999: None

Villages with population of 10000 and above: Bayyaram.

Distribution of Workers:

	Persons	Males	Females	WPR
Cultivators	6,078	4,045	2,033	27.38
Agricultural Labour	12,099	5,369	6,730	54.5
Household Industry	570	319	251	2.57
Other Workers	3,454	2,529	925	15.56
Main Workers	14,456	9,119	5,337	65.11
Marginal Workers	7,745	3,143	4,602	34.89
Total Workers	22,201	12,262	9,939	

Religion: Major Religious Communities:

	Persons	Males	Females	Sex Ratio
Hindu (97.51%)	41,270	20,897	20,373	975
Muslim (1.85%)	784	403	381	945
Christian (0.39%)	165	85	80	941
Sikh (0.02%)	9	4	5	1,250
Buddhists (0%)	-	-	-	-
Jain (0%)	-	-	-	-

Agewise Data:

	Persons	Males	Females	Sex Ratio
All ages	42,326	21,439	20,887	974
0-14	14,705	7,648	7,057	923
15-44	19,824	9,912	9,912	1000
45-79	7,297	3,618	3,679	1017
80+	420	217	203	935
Age not stated	80	44	36	818

Languages (Dominant): Telugu, Hindi, Urdu, Tamil, Gondi

Disabled Population:

	Persons	Males	Females	%
Total Disabled	923	540	383	
In Seeing	334	176	158	36.19
In Speech	107	58	49	11.59
In Hearing	60	34	26	6.5
In Movement	322	215	107	34.89
Mentally	100	57	43	10.83

BAZARHATHNOOR

Bazarhathnoor C.D. Block lies in the north-west part of Adilabad district. The Block is located at a distance of 42 kms. from district headquarters (Adilabad). There are 31 villages in the block with the total popul ation of 23,657 persons. Area of the C.D. Block is 217. 80 sq. kms. It is bounded by Boath Mandal on south-west and south, Ichoda Mandal on south-west, Gudihathnoor Mandal on east and north-east, Talamadugu Mandal on north-east and north, and it has common boundary with the state of Maharashtra in the north-west, west and south-west.

Communications :

Roadways : State Highway (S.H.): Direction- Kinwat to Ichoda. Nearest Villages- Dehgaon, Bazarhatnur, Balanp ur, Kandli, Dignoor, Bhosra, Girnur, Pipri.

River: Kodam Nadi- Nearest Villages- Bhutai (Khurd), Dhabadi, Chintal Sangvi, Bandrev, Kankadurga, Mohada, Warthamanoor, Dehgaon, Bazarhatnur, Balanpur, Kandli.

Backwards Region Grants Fund: It receives Backward Region Grants.

Annual Rainfall: Average Rainfall 1134 mm

Ground Water: Availability of the ground water in the Basin is 1433 H.A.M.and the utilization is 623 H.A. M. It belongs to Safe category. Depth to water level varies from 5 to 10 meter below the ground. Most of the wells go down in summer months, according to the Ground Water Estimation Committee.

Forest and Reserved **Forest:** Nearest Villages- Waddur, Bondadi, Surdapur, Kishtapur, Shankarapur, Rolmanda, Buggaram, Kuntala (Khurd), Nagamalyal, Peechra, Boraga on,Bandemregad, Purushothampur, Rajura, Ispur, Dhonnora.

Natural Division : Telangana Plateau Region

Administration:

Division: Telangana. Parliamentary Constituency: 1 Adilabad (ST). District: Adilabad. Mandal: Bazarhathnoor. Assembly Constituency: 8 Boath (ST).Gram Panchayat: 13

Border Villages- (Maharashtra)- Nearest Villages- Manka pur (P), Jatarla, Bazarhatnur, Kolhari, Umarda (Buzurg).

Villages: 31 **Inhabited:** 28 **Uninhabited:** 3

Ranking	District	State	National
Area	42	451	3898
Population	46	1075	6170
Sex Ratio	46	903	3035
Child Sex Ratio	39	745	3189
Literacy Rate	6	462	3703
Density	29	487	6060
Work Participation Rate	34	1032	1250

Gram Panchayats:

Bazarhathnoor, Bhutai-B, Bhutai-K, Darampuri

Dehgaon, Girnur, Gokonda, Jatarla, Morkhandi, Pipri Rampur, Tembi, Warthamanoor.

Amenities:

Education: Primary School in 28 villages, Middle school in 7 villages, Matriculation or Secondary School in 2 villages, namely Jatarla, Bazarhatnur.

Higher Secondary or Pre University Courses or Intermediate or Junior College in 0 village of the CD Block, College in 0 village, Adult Literacy Center in 27 villages.

Medical: Hospital in 0 village, Dispensary in 1 village, Health Center in 1 village, Sub Center in 8 villages, Maternity and Child Welfare Center in 1 village, Community health workers in 0 village.

The Village having Hospital or Dispensary or Health Center is Dehgaon.

Drinking Water: Tap water in 27 villages, Tank water in 27 villages, Well water in 28 villages, Tubewell in 27 villages and more than one source in 28 villages.

Bank: Banking facility in 1 villages, namely, Bazarhatnur.

Credit Society in 5 villages Agricultural Credit Society in 4 Non-Agricultural Credit Society in 1 village.

Others: Power supply in 28 villages, Cinema hall in 0 village, sport club in 0 village, Stadium or Auditorium or Community Hall in 0 village, Post Office in 8 villages.

There are 16 villages having bus facilities.

Village with most of facilities: Bazarhatnur.

Villages without Amenities (Education): None..

Scheduled Castes: Out of the total population of 23657 persons, 3742 persons (15.82%) belong to Scheduled Castes.

The villages having less than 10% SC population are Umarda (Buzurg), Girjai, Bhutai (Khurd), Dhabadi Gokonda, Yesapur, Harkai, Ananthapur, Tembi Dharampuri, Chintal Sangvi, Bhutai (Buzurg) Mankapur (P), Jatarla, Kolhari, Balanpur, Mohada.

The villages having more than 50% SC population are None.

Sex ratio of Scheduled Caste population is 506.

Scheduled Castes Literates and Illiterates by Sex:

	Persons	Males	Females
Literate	1,846	1,143	703
Illiterate	1,896	704	1,192
Literacy rate	56.6	71.9	42.0
Graduate	37	35	2

Scheduled Castes (Dominant):

Madiga, Mahar, Mala, Mang, Mehtar

For their cultural identity please see Appendix-I

Villages without Scheduled Castes: There are 11 villages without any scheduled caste population.

Scheduled Tribes: Out of the total population of 23657 persons, 9903 persons (41.86%) belong to Scheduled Tribes.

The villages having less than 10% ST population are None..

The villages having more than 50% ST population are Umarda (Buzurg), Girjai, Bhutai (Khurd), Morekhandi Harkai, Ananthapur, Rampur, Dharampuri Chintal Sangvi, Mankapur (P), Jatarla, Kolhari Balanpur, Mohada.

Sex ratio of Scheduled tribe population is 481.

Scheduled Tribes Literates and Illiterates by Sex:

	Persons	Males	Females
Literate	4,266	2,907	1,359
Illiterate	5,637	2,229	3,408
Literacy rate	52.7	68.5	35.2
Graduate	36	36	0

Scheduled Tribes (Dominant):

Gond etc., Sugalis etc., Pardhan, Andh, Kolam etc.

For their cultural identity please see Appendix-II

Villages without Scheduled Tribes: There are 4 villages without any scheduled tribe population.

Literates and Illiterates by Sex (Total Population):

	Persons	Males	Females
Literate	10,855	7,124	3,731
Illiterate	12,802	4,955	7,847
Literacy rate	55	70	38
Graduate	186	177	9

Agriculture: ***Distribution of villages according to land use:*** Out of 31 villages, Total area (in hectare) is 21668, out of that 44.66 percent is cultivable and 4.97 percent of the cultivable area is irrigated.

Sources of Irrigation (Hectares): Government Canal 0, Private Canal 0, Well without Electricity 5.6, Well with Electricity 347, Tubewell without Electricity 0, Tubewell with Electricity 120, Tank 4, River 4, Lake 0, Waterfall 0, Others 0.

Villages with population of 5000 to 9999: None

Villages with population of 10000 and above: None

Distribution of Workers:

	Persons	Males	Females	WPR
Cultivators	5,234	3,100	2,134	42.79
Agricultural Labour	4,442	1,972	2,470	36.31
Household Industry	1,279	259	1,020	10.46
Other Workers	1,277	1,015	262	10.44
Main Workers	9,647	5,463	4,184	78.87
Marginal Workers	2,585	883	1,702	21.13
Total Workers	12,232	6,346	5,886	

Religion: Major Religious Communities:

	Persons	Males	Females	Sex Ratio
Hindu (96.58%)	22,847	11,659	11,188	960
Muslim (1.75%)	413	216	197	912

Christian (0.1%)	23	14	9	643
Sikh (0.03%)	7	3	4	1,333
Buddhists (1.52%)	359	184	175	951
Jain (0%)	1	-	1	-

Agewise Data:

	Persons	Males	Females	Sex Ratio
All ages	23,657	12,079	11,578	959
0-14	9,274	4,880	4,394	900
15-44	10,350	5,307	5,043	950
45-79	3,893	1,839	2,054	1117
80+	126	47	79	1681
Age not stated	14	6	8	1333

Languages (Dominant):

Telugu, Gondi, Marathi, Hindi, Urdu

Disabled Population:

	Persons	Males	Females	%
Total Disabled	311	174	137	
In Seeing	113	56	57	36.33
In Speech	27	16	11	8.68
In Hearing	18	12	6	5.79
In Movement	117	69	48	37.62
Mentally	36	21	15	11.58

BEJJANKI

Bejjanki C.D. Block lies in the south-west part of Karimnagar district. The Block is located at a distance of 38 kms. from district headquarters (Karimnagar). There are 25 villages in the block with the total population of 51,838 persons. Area of the C.D. Block is 251.85 sq. kms. It is bounded by Karimnagar Mandal on north, Timmapur Mandal on east, Koheda Mandal on south, Medal district on south-west, and Ellanthakunta Mandal on west.

Communications :

Roadways : State Highway (S.H.): Direction- Hyderabad to Karimnagar. Nearest Villages- Cherlapur, Muthannapet, Guggilla, Gagillapur, Dacharam, Thotapalle, Devakkapal le.

River: Manner Nadi- Nearest Villages- Gannervaram, Yaswada, Panthulu Kondapur, Cherlapur, Guggilla, Gagil lapur, Thotapalle, Devakkapalle.

Backwards Region Grants Fund: It receives Backward Region Grants.

Mahila Samakhya (Education for Women's Equality): It is decleared Socialy and Educationally Backward Block by the Government. .

Annual Rainfall: Average Rainfall 832 mm

Ground Water: Availability of the Ground Water in the Basin is 2758 H.A.M. and the utilization is 2971 H. A.M. It belongs to Over Exploited category. Depth to water level varies from more than 10 meter below the ground. Most of the wells go down in summer months. The well density in the entire block is 27 wells per sq. km. Total no. of the wells in the block are enumera ted as 6879, according to the Ground Water Estimation Committee.

Natural Division : Godavari Depression Region

Administration:

Division: Telangana. Parliamentary Constituency: 3 Karimnagar. District: Karimnagar. Mandal: Bejjanki. Assembly Constituency: 30 Manakondur (SC). Gram Pancha yat: 29.

Villages: 25 **Inhabited:** 23 **Uninhabited:** 2

Ranking	District	State	National
Area	9	303	3355
Population	18	454	5188
Sex Ratio	11	64	476
Child Sex Ratio	8	143	368
Literacy Rate	16	548	4034
Density	27	439	4650
Work Participation Rate	45	700	1084

Gram Panchayats:

Begumpet, Bejjanki, Cheelapoor, Cheemalakuntapally Chukkaraopally, Dacharam, Devakkapally, Gagillapur Ganneruvaram, Gopalpur, Gudem, Guggilla, Gundlapaly Gunkulkondapoor, Hanmajipally, Jangapally Kallepally, Kasimpeta, Laxmipoor, Madhapoor Muthannapeta, Mylaram, Parvella, Pechupally Potharam, Regulapalli, Thotapalli, Vadlur, Veerapur.

Amenities:

Education: Primary School in 23 villages, Middle school in 14 villages, Matriculation or Secondary School in 8 villages, namely Gannervaram, Vadlur-Begumpet, Jangapalle, Gunkulkondapur, Bejjanki, Gagillapur, Dacharam, Thotapalle.

Higher Secondary or Pre University Courses or Intermediate or Junior College in 1 village of the CD Block,, namely Bejjanki.

College in 0 village, Adult Literacy Center in 16 villages.

Medical: Hospital in 0 village, Dispensary in 1 village, Health Center in 2 villages, Sub Center in 10 villages, Maternity and Child Welfare Center in 2 villages, Community health workers in 0 village.

The Village having Hospital or Dispensary or Health Center is Gannervaram.

Drinking Water: Tap water in 23 villages, Tank water in 23 villages, Well water in 23 villages, Tubewell in 23 villages and more than one source in 23 villages.

Bank: Banking facility in 3 villages, namely, Gunkulkondapur, Bejjanki, Thotapalle.

Credit Society in 17 villages Agricultural Credit Society in 3 Non-Agricultural Credit Society in 17 villages.

Others: Power supply in 23 villages, Cinema hall in 1 village, sport club in 0 village, Stadium or Auditorium or Community Hall in 0 village, Post Office in 14 villages.
There are 21 villages having bus facilities.
Villages with most of facilities: Gunkulkondapur Bejjanki, Thotapalle.
Villages without Amenities (Education): None..
Scheduled Castes: Out of the total population of 51838 persons, 12564 persons (24.24%) belong to Scheduled Castes.
The villages having less than 10% SC population are None..
The villages having more than 50% SC population are None.
Sex ratio of Scheduled Caste population is 511.
Scheduled Castes Literates and Illiterates by Sex:

	Persons	Males	Females
Literate	4,826	2,971	1,855
Illiterate	7,738	3,170	4,568
Literacy rate	44.4	55.9	33.4
Graduate	56	54	2

Scheduled Castes (Dominant):
Madiga, Mala, Gosangi, Dakkal etc., Mashti
For their cultural identity please see Appendix-I
Villages without Scheduled Castes: There are 2 villages without any scheduled caste population.
Scheduled Tribes: Out of the total population of 51838 persons, 380 persons (0.73%) belong to Scheduled Tribes.
The villages having less than 10% ST population are Gannervaram, Yaswada, Gopalpur, Sangam, Mylaram Madhapur, Khasimpet, Parvella, Vadlur-Begumpet Jangapalle, Gunkulkondapur, Veerapur, Bejjanki Kallepalle, Cheelapur, Regulapalle, Potharam Muthannapet, Guggilla, Gagillapur, Dacharam Thotapalle, Devakkapalle.
The villages having more than 50% ST population are None.
Sex ratio of Scheduled tribe population is 505.
Scheduled Tribes Literates and Illiterates by Sex:

	Persons	Males	Females
Literate	129	76	53
Illiterate	251	112	139
Literacy rate	41.0	48.4	33.5
Graduate	0	0	0

Scheduled Tribes (Dominant):
Yerukulas, Chenchu etc., Sugalis etc.
For their cultural identity please see Appendix-II
Villages without Scheduled Tribes: There are 5 villages without any scheduled tribe population.
Literates and Illiterates by Sex (Total Population):

	Persons	Males	Females
Literate	24,024	14,819	9,205
Illiterate	27,814	10,709	17,105
Literacy rate	53	67	40
Graduate	595	503	92

Agriculture: ***Distribution of villages according to land use:***
Out of 25 villages, Total area (in hectare) is 25187, out of that 69.55 percent is cultivable and 32.67 percent of the cultivable area is irrigated.
Sources of Irrigation (Hectares): Government Canal 0, Private Canal 0, Well without Electricity 0, Well with Electricity 5508, Tubewell without Electricity 0, Tubewell with Electricity 214, Tank 0, River 0, Lake 0, Waterfall 0, Others 0.
Villages with population of 5000 to 9999:
Gannervaram, Bejjanki.
Villages with population of 10000 and above: None
Distribution of Workers:

	Persons	Males	Females	WPR
Cultivators	9,890	5,645	4,245	34.94
Agricultural Labour	11,833	4,347	7,486	41.81
Household Industry	1,918	982	936	6.78
Other Workers	4,664	3,514	1,150	16.48
Main Workers	23,687	13,118	10,569	83.68
Marginal Workers	4,618	1,370	3,248	16.32
Total Workers	28,305	14,488	13,817	

Religion: Major Religious Communities:

	Persons	Males	Females	Sex Ratio
Hindu (97.17%)	50,372	24,811	25,561	1,030
Muslim (1.49%)	773	388	385	992
Christian (0.94%)	488	223	265	1,188
Sikh (0%)	-	-	-	-
Buddhists (0%)	1	1	-	-
Jain (0%)	-	-	-	-

Agewise Data:

	Persons	Males	Females	Sex Ratio
All ages	51,838	25,528	26,310	1031
0-14	15,670	7,938	7,732	974
15-44	23,123	11,137	11,986	1076
45-79	12,464	6,163	6,301	1022
80+	554	280	274	979
Age not stated	27	10	17	1700

Languages (Dominant):
Telugu, Oriya, Urdu, Marathi, Tamil
Disabled Population:

	Persons	Males	Females	%
Total Disabled	1,193	675	518	
In Seeing	625	383	242	52.39
In Speech	109	52	57	9.14
In Hearing	86	33	53	7.21
In Movement	255	146	109	21.37

Mentally	118	61	57	9.89

BEJJUR

Bejjur C.D. Block lies in the eastern part of Adilabad district. The Block is located at a distance of 205 kms. from district headquarters (Adilabad). There are 46 villages in the block with the total population of 42,796 persons. Area of the C.D. Block is 584.70 sq. kms. It is bounded by Dahegaon Mandal on south-east, south and south-west, Kagaznagar Mandal on south-west, Sirpur Mandal on west, Kouthala Mandal on north-west, north and north-east, and it has common boundary with the state of Maharashtra in the north-west, north and north-east.

Communications :

Roadways : NH, SH or Important Metalled Road is not available.

River: Pranhita Nadi- Nearest Villages- Dimda, Chittam, Gudem, Buruguda, Koyapalle, Nagepalle, Mogavelly, Bombaiguda, Yelkapalle, Penchikalpet, Gannaram, Agargu da, Gundepalle, Somini, Talai, Telapalle, Muraliguda, Kammergaon, Nandigaon, Jilleda. Pedda Vagu: Nearest Villages- Bombaiguda, Yelkapalle, Penchikalpet, Gannaram, Agarguda.

Backwards Region Grants Fund: It receives Backward Region Grants.

Annual Rainfall: Average Rainfall 1266 mm

Ground Water: Availability of the ground water in the Basin is 5840 H.A.M. and the utilization is 314 H.A. M. It belongs to Safe category. Depth to water level varies from 5 to 10 meter below the ground. Most of the wells go down in summer months, according to the Ground Water Estimation Committee.

Natural Division : Telangana Plateau Region

Administration:

Division: Telangana. Parliamentary Constituency: 1 Adilabad (ST). District: Adilabad. Mandal: Bejjur. Assembly Constituency: 1 Sirpur. Gram Panchayat: 23.

Border Villages: (Maharashtra)- Nearest Villages- Dimda, Chittam, Gudem, Buruguda, Koyapalle, Nagepalle, Mogave lly, Somini, Talai, Telapalle, Muraliguda, Nandigaon.

Villages: 46 **Inhabited:** 43 **Uninhabited:** 3

Ranking	District	State	National
Area	1	4	1150
Population	15	731	5612
Sex Ratio	17	205	1037
Child Sex Ratio	5	87	205
Literacy Rate	52	1084	6157
Density	13	178	6265
Work Participation Rate	50	1088	511

Gram Panchayats:

Bejjur, Bombaiguda, Dimda, Gudem, Kamergaon Karjavelli, Kondapalle, Kukuda, Kushnepalle Lodpalle, Marthadi, Mogavelly, Munjampalle Muraliguda, Outsarangipalle, Papanpet, Penchikalpet Pothepally, Rebbena, Rudrapur, Somini, Yelkapalle Yellur.

Amenities:

Education: Primary School in 37 villages, Middle school in 6 villages, Matriculation or Secondary School in 3 villages, namely Bejjur, Outsarangipalle, Yelkapalle.

Higher Secondary or Pre University Courses or Intermediate or Junior College in 0 village of the CD Block, College in 0 village, Adult Literacy Center in 21 villages.

Medical: Hospital in 0 village, Dispensary in 2 villages, Health Center in 3 villages, Sub Center in 19 villages, Maternity and Child Welfare Center in 13 villages, Community health workers in 0 village.

The Villages having Hospital or Dispensary or Health Center are Ambhaghat, Bejjur, Agarguda.

Drinking Water: Tap water in 41 villages, Tank water in 41 villages, Well water in 43 villages, Tubewell in 41 villages and more than one source in 43 villages.

Bank: Banking facility in 2 villages, namely, Bejjur, Penchikalpet.

Credit Society in 6 villages Agricultural Credit Society in 3 Non-Agricultural Credit Society in 3 villages.

Others: Power supply in 43 villages, Cinema hall in 0 village, sport club in 0 village, Stadium or Auditorium or Community Hall in 0 village, Post Office in 14 villages.

There are 16 villages having bus facilities.

Village with most of facilities: Bejjur.

Villages without amenities (Education): Kethini, Rechini, Peddasiddapur, Tikkapalle, Talai..

Scheduled Castes: Out of the total population of 42796 persons, 8901 persons (20.8%) belong to Scheduled Castes. The villages having less than 10% SC population are Kethini, Buruguda, Nagepalle, Shivapalle, Ambhaghat Rechini, Kushnepalle, Chinnasiddapur, Peddasiddapur Agarguda, Gundepalle, Sushmeer, Tikkapalle.

The villages having more than 50% SC population are None.

Sex ratio of Scheduled Caste population is 506.

Scheduled Castes Literates and Illiterates by Sex:

	Persons	Males	Females
Literate	2,412	1,702	710
Illiterate	6,489	2,698	3,791
Literacy rate	33.0	47.2	19.2
Graduate	36	33	3

Scheduled Castes (Dominant):

Mala, Madiga, Manne, Mala Sale etc., Mahar

For their cultural identity please see Appendix-I

Villages without Scheduled Castes: There are 12 villages without any scheduled caste population.

Scheduled Tribes: Out of the total population of 42796 persons, 13447 persons (31.42%) belong to Scheduled Tribes.

The villages having less than 10% ST population are Rechini, Kushnepalle, Bejjur, Chinnasiddapur Lodpalle, Yelkapalle, Yellur, Penchikalpet.

The villages having more than 50% ST population are Kethini, Chittam, Koyapalle, Nagepalle, Mogavelly Shivapalle, Ambhaghat, Katepalle, Gabbai Peddasiddapur, Outsarangipalle, Koyachichal Gundepalle, Sushmeer, Somini, Tikkapalle, Muraliguda Kammergaon, Nandigaon.

Sex ratio of Scheduled tribe population is 502.

Scheduled Tribes Literates and Illiterates by Sex:

	Persons	Males	Females
Literate	3,050	2,141	909
Illiterate	10,397	4,559	5,838
Literacy rate	27.8	39.0	16.6
Graduate	15	15	0

Scheduled Tribes (Dominant):

Koya etc., Kolam etc., Manna Dhora, Sugalis etc. Gond etc.

For their cultural identity please see Appendix-II

Villages without Scheduled Tribes: There are 5 villages without any scheduled tribe population.

Literates and Illiterates by Sex (Total Population):

	Persons	Males	Females
Literate	11,240	7,818	3,422
Illiterate	31,556	13,538	18,018
Literacy rate	32	44	19
Graduate	113	106	7

Agriculture: ***Distribution of villages according to land use:*** Out of 46 villages, Total area (in hectare) is 60875, out of that 27.23 percent is cultivable and 4.93 percent of the cultivable area is irrigated.

Sources of Irrigation (Hectares): Government Canal 60, Private Canal 3.66, Well without Electricity 63.68, Well with Electricity 49.43, Tubewell without Electricity 0, Tubewell with Electricity 0, Tank 353.86, River 0, Lake 0, Waterfall 0, Others 286.44.

Villages with population of 5000 to 9999: None

Villages with population of 10000 and above: None

Distribution of Workers:

	Persons	Males	Females	WPR
Cultivators	9,505	7,381	2,124	41.02
Agricultural Labour	9,710	2,991	6,719	41.9
Household Industry	846	269	577	3.65
Other Workers	3,113	1,656	1,457	13.43
Main Workers	14,479	9,892	4,587	62.48
Marginal Workers	8,695	2,405	6,290	37.52
Total Workers	23,174	12,297	10,877	

Religion: Major Religious Communities:

	Persons	Males	Females	Sex Ratio
Hindu (95.7%)	40,955	20,442	20,513	1,003
Muslim (3.33%)	1,424	711	713	1,003
Christian (0.19%)	82	41	41	1,000
Sikh (0.01%)	3	3	-	-
Buddhists (0.74%)	317	153	164	1,072
Jain (0%)	-	-	-	-

Agewise Data:

	Persons	Males	Females	Sex Ratio
All ages	42,796	21,356	21,440	1004
0-14	16,413	8,305	8,108	976
15-44	19,051	9,414	9,637	1024
45-79	6,985	3,442	3,543	1029
80+	280	158	122	772
Age not stated	67	37	30	811

Languages (Dominant):

Telugu, Marathi, Koya, Urdu, Hindi

Disabled Population:

	Persons	Males	Females	%
Total Disabled	681	361	320	
In Seeing	350	174	176	51.4
In Speech	69	35	34	10.13
In Hearing	60	40	20	8.81
In Movement	148	79	69	21.73
Mentally	54	33	21	7.93

BELA

Bela C.D. Block lies in the north-east part of Adilabad district. The Block is located at a distance of 32 kms. from district headquarters (Adilabad). There are 47 villages in the block with the total population of 32,970 persons. Area of the C.D. Block is 254.60 sq. kms. It is bounded by Narnoor Mandal on south-east, Adilabad Mandal on south and south-west, Jainad Mandal on south-west, west and north-west, and it has common boundary with the state of Maharashtra in the north-west, north, north-east and east.

Communications :

Roadways : NH, SH or Important Metalled Road is not available.

River: Penganga Nadi- Nearest Villages- namely, Narayan pur, Sangdi, Bhedoda, Kamgarpur, Manyarpur, Khagdur, Mangrool.

Backwards Region Grants Fund: It receives Backward Region Grants.

Annual Rainfall: Average Rainfall 1219 mm

Ground Water: Availability of the ground water in the

Basin is 1807 H.A.M and the utilization is 844 H.A. M. It belongs to Safe category. Depth to water level varies from 5 to 10 meter below the ground. Most of the wells go down in summer months, according to the Ground Water Estimation Committee.

Natural Division : Telangana Plateau Region

Administration:

Division: Telangana. Parliamentary Constituency: 1 Adilabad (ST). District: Adilabad. Mandal: Bela. Assembly Constituency: 7 Adilabad. Gram Panchayat: 21.

Border Villages: (Maharashtra)- Nearest Villages- Kobhai, Ponnala, Narayanpur, Sangdi, Bhedoda, Kamgarpur, Manyarpur, Khagdur, Mangrool.

Villages: 47 **Inhabited:** 41 **Uninhabited:** 6

Ranking	District	State	National
Area	32	292	3325
Population	28	978	5978
Sex Ratio	36	670	2243
Child Sex Ratio	33	508	1919
Literacy Rate	3	414	3533
Density	22	367	5842
Work Participation Rate	25	970	902

Gram Panchayats:

Awalpur, Bela, Bhadi, Bhedoda, Bhodod (Kopsi) Chandpalle, Chaprala, Dehegoan, Dhoptala, Guda Junoni, Khogdur, Kobhai, Sadalpur, Sangdi, Sangvi Sirsanna, Sonkhos, Syedpur, Takli, Toyaguda.

Amenities:

Education: Primary School in 41 villages, Middle school in 10 villages, Matriculation or Secondary School in 5 villages, namely Sangdi, Sirsanna, Bela, Chandpalle, Syedpur. Higher Secondary or Pre University Courses or Intermediate or Junior College in 0 village of the CD Block, College in 0 village, Adult Literacy Center in 34 villages.

Medical: Hospital in 0 village, Dispensary in 1 village, Health Center in 1 village, Sub Center in 8 villages, Maternity and Child Welfare Center in 0 village, Community health workers in 0 village.

The Village having Hospital or Dispensary or Health Center is Sangvi.

Drinking Water: Tap water in 40 villages, Tank water in 40 villages, Well water in 41 villages, Tubewell in 40 villages and more than one source in 41 villages.

Bank: Banking facility in 2 villages, namely, Sirsanna, Bela.

Credit Society in 8 villages Agricultural Credit Society in 8 Non-Agricultural Credit Society in 1 village.

Others: Power supply in 41 villages, Cinema hall in 0 village, sport club in 0 village, Stadium or Auditorium or Community Hall in 0 village, Post Office in 6 villages.

There are 10 villages having bus facilities.

Villages with most of facilities: Sirsanna, Bela.

Villages without Amenities (Education): None..

Scheduled Castes: Out of the total population of 32970 persons, 1814 persons (5.5%) belong to Scheduled Castes. The villages having less than 10% SC population are Bhedoda, Guda, Mangrool, Kobhai, Dehegaon Bhodod (Kopsi), Shamshabad, Takli, Dhoptala, Patan Ramkam, Ponnala, Chandpalle, Chaprala, Warur, Junoni Karoni (K), Ekori, Masala (Buzurg), Bhadi Masala (Khurd), Syedpur, Sahej, Sangvi, Douna Boregaon, Pohar, Karoni (B), Sadarpur, Sonkhos Khadki, Pitgaon.

The villages having more than 50% SC population are None.

Sex ratio of Scheduled Caste population is 478.

Scheduled Castes Literates and Illiterates by Sex:

	Persons	Males	Females
Literate	764	473	291
Illiterate	1,050	474	576
Literacy rate	49.0	58.8	38.5
Graduate	11	11	0

Scheduled Castes (Dominant):

Madiga, Mahar, Beda Jangam etc., Mala, Chambhar

For their cultural identity please see Appendix-I

Villages without Scheduled Castes: There are 25 villages without any scheduled caste population.

Scheduled Tribes: Out of the total population of 32970 persons, 11317 persons (34.33%) belong to Scheduled Tribes. The villages having less than 10% ST population are Sangdi, Bhedoda, Guda, Manyarpur, Khagdur, Dehegaon Mohabatpur, Bhodod (Kopsi), Shamshabad, Dhoptala.

The villages having more than 50% ST population are Ramkam, Ponnala, Chandpalle, Warur, Karoni (K) Masala (Khurd), Syedpur, Toyaguda (Kora), Sahej Sangvi, Douna, Boregaon, Pohar, Karoni (B), Sadarpur Khadki, Pitgaon.

Sex ratio of Scheduled tribe population is 496.

Scheduled Tribes Literates and Illiterates by Sex:

	Persons	Males	Females
Literate	4,014	2,672	1,342
Illiterate	7,303	3,028	4,275
Literacy rate	43.9	57.9	29.6
Graduate	11	11	0

Scheduled Tribes (Dominant):

Gond etc., Kolam etc., Pardhan, Sugalis etc. Koya etc.

For their cultural identity please see Appendix-II

Villages without Scheduled Tribes: There are 7 villages without any scheduled tribe population.

Literates and Illiterates by Sex (Total Population):

	Persons	Males	Females
Literate	15,533	9,771	5,762
Illiterate	17,437	6,923	10,514
Literacy rate	56	69	42
Graduate	189	171	18

Agriculture: ***Distribution of villages according to land use:*** Out of 47 villages, Total area (in hectare) is 25451, out of that 57.45 percent is cultivable and 0 percent of the cultivable area is irrigated.

Sources of Irrigation (Hectares): Government Canal 0, Private Canal 0, Well without Electricity 0, Well with Electricity 0, Tubewell without Electricity 0, Tubewell with Electricity 0, Tank 0, River 0, Lake 0, Waterfall 0, Others 0.

Villages with population of 5000 to 9999: None

Villages with population of 10000 and above: None

Distribution of Workers:

	Persons	Males	Females	WPR
Cultivators	8,912	4,853	4,059	50.63
Agricultural Labour	6,482	2,616	3,866	36.83
Household Industry	373	246	127	2.12
Other Workers	1,834	1,480	354	10.42
Main Workers	14,617	8,041	6,576	83.05
Marginal Workers	2,984	1,154	1,830	16.95
Total Workers	17,601	9,195	8,406	

Religion: Major Religious Communities:

	Persons	Males	Females	Sex Ratio
Hindu (93.77%)	30,915	15,631	15,284	978
Muslim (5.38%)	1,774	908	866	954
Christian (0.09%)	30	20	10	500
Sikh (0.01%)	2	1	1	1,000
Buddhists (0.72%)	236	124	112	903
Jain (0%)	1	1	-	-

Agewise Data:

	Persons	Males	Females	Sex Ratio
All ages	32,970	16,694	16,276	975
0-14	12,424	6,424	6,000	934
15-44	14,730	7,474	7,256	971
45-79	5,566	2,693	2,873	1067
80+	224	85	139	1635
Age not stated	26	18	8	444

Languages (Dominant):

Marathi, Telugu, Gondi, Kolami, Hindi

Disabled Population:

	Persons	Males	Females	%
Total Disabled	450	270	180	
In Seeing	186	101	85	41.33
In Speech	37	26	11	8.22
In Hearing	12	10	2	2.67
In Movement	153	101	52	34
Mentally	62	32	30	13.78

BELLAMKONDA

Bellamkonda C.D. Block lies in the northern part of Guntur district. The Block is located at a distance of 45 kms. from district headquarters (Guntur). There are 13 villages in the block with the total population of 30,791 persons. Area of the C.D. Block is 108.73 sq. kms. It is bounded in the north by River Krishna, Mandal Atchampet and district Nalgonda, in the south by Mandal Rajupalem, in the east by Mandals Krosuru and Atchampet, and in the west by Mandals Machavaram and Piduguralla.

Communications:

Roadways : NH, SH or Important Metalled Road is not available.

River: Krishna Nadi- Nearest Villages- Pulichinta, Kolluru, Chityala, Kethavaram, Bodanam.

Railway Station: Bellamkonda.

Annual Rainfall: Average Rainfall 803 mm

Ground Water: Availability of the Ground Water in the Basin is 4306 H.A.M. and the utilization is 295 H.A. M. It belongs to Safe category. Depth to water level varies from 5 to 10 meter below the ground. Most of the wells go down in summer months.

Forest and Reserved **Forest:** Nearest Villages- Pulichinta, Kolluru, Chityala, Kethavaram, Venkatayapalem, Bodanam, Emmajigudem, Mannesultanpalem, Chandrajupalem.

Natural Division : Krishna Delta Region

Administration:

Division: Coastal Andhra . Parliamentary Constituency: 31 Narsaraopet. District: Guntur.

Mandal: Bellamkonda. Assembly Constituency: 204 Pedakur apadu. Gram Panchayat: 15.

Places of Tourist Interest:

Bellamkonda : The village is situated 19 kms. west of Sattenapalle, by the side of the Guntur Pondugala road, near Bellalmkonda railway station.There is hill fortress here. It consists of a single stone wall, connecting the principal elevated points of the hill and having tower bastions at the south-west and north-w est angles, which terminate the principal front. The entrance which is in this front, is gained by a winding pathway from the foot of the hill, near the village. In shape the fort is roughly an equilaterel triangle. It is believed to have been constructed by the Reddi kings of kondavidu.

Villages: 13 **Inhabited:** 13 **Uninhabited:** 0

Ranking	District	State	National
Area	50	993	5617
Population	57	1013	6038

Sex Ratio	42	682	2284
Child Sex Ratio	54	1062	5087
Literacy Rate	52	818	4953
Density	6	77	3712
Work Participation Rate	42	424	279

Gram Panchayats:
Bellamkonda, Bodanam, Chandrajupalem, Chityala Emmajigudem, Gangireddypalem, Kandipadu, Kollur Machayapalem, Mannesultanpalem, Nagireddypalem Nandirajupalem, Papayapalem, Vannayapalem Venkatayapalem.

Amenities:
Education: Primary School in 13 villages, Middle school in 4 villages, Matriculation or Secondary School in 2 villages, namely Papayapalem, Bellamkonda.
Higher Secondary or Pre University Courses or Intermediate or Junior College in 0 village of the CD Block, College in 0 village, Adult Literacy Center in 0 village.
Medical: Hospital in 0 village, Dispensary in 1 village, Health Center in 1 village, Sub Center in 6 villages, Maternity and Child Welfare Center in 0 village, Community health workers in 0 village.
The Village having Hospital or Dispensary or Health Center is Bellamkonda.
Drinking Water: Tap water in 13 villages, Tank water in 11 villages, Well water in 12 villages, Tubewell in 11 villages and more than one source in 13 villages.
Bank: Banking facility in 1 villages, namely, Bellamkonda.
Credit Society in 3 villages Agricultural Credit Society in 2 Non-Agricultural Credit Society in 0 village.
Others: Power supply in 13 villages, Cinema hall in 1 village, sport club in 0 village, Stadium or Auditorium or Community Hall in 0 village, Post Office in 10 villages.
There are 13 villages having bus facilities.
Village with most of facilities: Bellamkonda.
Villages without Amenities (Education): None..
Scheduled Castes: Out of the total population of 30791 persons, 4888 persons (15.87%) belong to Scheduled Castes.
The villages having less than 10% SC population are None..
The villages having more than 50% SC population are None.
Sex ratio of Scheduled Caste population is 491.

Scheduled Castes Literates and Illiterates by Sex:

	Persons	Males	Femaies
Literate	1,723	1,075	648
Illiterate	3,165	1,415	1,750
Literacy rate	42.2	52.4	32.0
Graduate	64	48	16

Scheduled Castes (Dominant):
Madiga, Mala, Mala Dasu, Mala Dasari
For their cultural identity please see Appendix-I
Villages without Scheduled Castes: There are 0 village without any scheduled caste population.
Scheduled Tribes: Out of the total population of 30791 persons, 4427 persons (14.38%) belong to Scheduled Tribes.
The villages having less than 10% ST population are Emmajigudem, Papayapalem, Chandrajupalem Vannayapalem, Machayapalem, Bellamkonda.
The villages having more than 50% ST population are None.
Sex ratio of Scheduled tribe population is 490.

Scheduled Tribes Literates and Illiterates by Sex:

	Persons	Males	Females
Literate	1,279	835	444
Illiterate	3,148	1,422	1,726
Literacy rate	34.7	45.2	24.2
Graduate	18	16	2

Scheduled Tribes (Dominant):
Sugalis etc., Chenchu etc., Yerukulas, Yenadis Kammara
For their cultural identity please see Appendix-II
Villages without Scheduled Tribes: There are 0 village without any scheduled tribe population.

Literates and Illiterates by Sex (Total Population):

	Persons	Males	Females
Literate	12,328	7,806	4,522
Illiterate	18,463	7,794	10,669
Literacy rate	47	59	35
Graduate	319	263	56

Agriculture: ***Distribution of villages according to land use:*** Out of 13 villages, Total area (in hectare) is 10873, out of that 64.42 percent is cultivable and 27.6 percent of the cultivable area is irrigated.
Sources of Irrigation (Hectares): Government Canal 1580, Private Canal 0, Well without Electricity 4, Well with Electricity 77, Tubewell without Electricity 12, Tubewell with Electricity 59, Tank 112, River 0, Lake 0, Waterfall 0, Others 89.
Villages with population of 5000 to 9999: Chandrajupalem, Bellamkonda.
Villages with population of 10000 and above: None

Distribution of Workers:

	Persons	Males	Females	WPR
Cultivators	4,570	2,772	1,798	25.79
Agricultural Labour	10,298	4,535	5,763	58.12
Household Industry	232	118	114	1.31
Other Workers	2,619	1,853	766	14.78
Main Workers	15,644	8,545	7,099	88.29

Marginal Workers	2,075	733	1,342	11.71
Total Workers	17,719	9,278	8,441	

Religion: Major Religious Communities:

	Persons	Males	Females	Sex Ratio
Hindu (91.89%)	28,295	14,366	13,929	970
Muslim (7.57%)	2,331	1,154	1,177	1,020
Christian (0.45%)	139	63	76	1,206
Sikh (0%)	-	-	-	-
Buddhists (0%)	-	-	-	-
Jain (0%)	-	-	-	-

Agewise Data:

	Persons	Males	Females	Sex Ratio
All ages	30,791	15,600	15,191	974
0-14	10,595	5,460	5,135	940
15-44	14,133	7,084	7,049	995
45-79	5,725	2,906	2,819	970
80+	278	117	161	1376
Age not stated	60	33	27	818

Languages (Dominant):

Telugu, Urdu, Hindi, Tamil, Gondi

Disabled Population:

	Persons	Males	Females	%
Total Disabled	653	351	302	
In Seeing	241	114	127	36.91
In Speech	91	52	39	13.94
In Hearing	39	14	25	5.97
In Movement	191	117	74	29.25
Mentally	91	54	37	13.94

BELLAMPALLE

Bellampalle C.D. Block lies in the south-eastern part of Adilabad district. It is a part of Bellampalle Mandal. The Block is located at a distance of 182 kms. from district headquarters (Adilabad). There are 12 villages in the block with the total population of 27,251 persons. Area of the C.D. Block is 143.16 sq. kms. It is bound ed by Tandur Mandal on north-west and north, Bhimini Mandal on north-east and east, Nennal Mandal on south-e ast, south and south-west, Mandamarri Mandal on south-we st and west.

Communications :

Roadways : State Highway (S.H.): Direction- Hyderabad to Tandur. Nearest Village- Kannal (Rural).

Backwards Region Grants Fund: It receives Backward Region Grants.

Annual Rainfall: Average Rainfall 1009 mm

Ground Water: Availability of the Ground Water in the Basin is 1575 H.A.M.and the utilization is 595 H.A. M. It belongs to Safe category. Depth to water level varies from 5 to 10 meter below the ground. Most of the wells go down in summer months, according to the Ground Water Estimation Committee.

Natural Division : Telangana Plateau Region

Administration:

Division: Telangana. Parliamentary Constituency: 2 Peddapalle (SC). District: Adilabad. Mandal: Bellampalle. Assembly Constituency: 3 Bellampalle (SC). Gram Panch ayat: 10.

Villages: 12 **Inhabited:** 12 **Uninhabited:** 0

Ranking	District	State	National
Area	48	789	4926
Population	40	1054	6106
Sex Ratio	40	830	2804
Child Sex Ratio	19	281	938
Literacy Rate	10	609	4263
Density	51	1092	5169
Work Participation Rate	6	821	5064

Gram Panchayats:

Akenipalle, Batwanpalle, Budha Kalan, Budha Khurd Chakepalle, Chandravelli, Gurjal, Kannal Patha Bellampalli, Perkapalle.

Amenities:

Education: Primary School in 12 villages, Middle school in 4 villages, Matriculation or Secondary School in 3 villages, namely Budha Khurd (Rural), Chandravelli, Akenipalle. Higher Secondary or Pre University Courses or Intermediate or Junior College in 1 village of the CD Block,, namely Akenipalle.

College in 1 village, Adult Literacy Center in 11 villages., College is in village, namely Akenipalle.

Medical: Hospital in 0 village, Dispensary in 1 village, Health Center in 0 village, Sub Center in 6 villages, Maternity and Child Welfare Center in 0 village, Community health workers in 0 village.

The Village having Hospital or Dispensary or Health Center is Akenipalle.

Drinking Water: Tap water in 12 villages, Tank water in 12 villages, Well water in 12 villages, Tubewell in 12 villages and more than one source in 12 villages.

Bank: None.

Credit Society in 6 villages Agricultural Credit Society in 2 Non-Agricultural Credit Society in 3 villages.

Others: Power supply in 12 villages, Cinema hall in 0 village, sport club in 0 village, Stadium or Auditorium or Community Hall in 0 village, Post Office in 1 village.

There are 5 villages having bus facilities.

Village with most of facilities: None.

Villages without Amenities (Education): None..

Scheduled Castes: Out of the total population of 27278 persons, 8049 persons (29.51%) belong to Scheduled Castes. The villages having less than 10% SC population are None..

The villages having more than 50% SC population are None.

Sex ratio of Scheduled Caste population is 491.

Scheduled Castes Literates and Illiterates by Sex:

	Persons	Males	Females
Literate	3,398	2,123	1,275
Illiterate	4,651	1,975	2,676
Literacy rate	49.1	60.0	37.7
Graduate	51	43	8

Scheduled Castes (Dominant):

Mala Sale etc., Madiga, Manne, Mala, Malajangam

For their cultural identity please see Appendix-I

Villages without Scheduled Castes: There are 0 village without any scheduled caste population.

Scheduled Tribes: Out of the total population of 27278 persons, 2247 persons (8.24%) belong to Scheduled Tribes.

The villages having less than 10% ST population are Kannal (Rural), Chakepalle, Budha Khurd (Rural) Chandravelli, Rangapet, Dugnepalle, Akenipalle.

The villages having more than 50% ST population are None.

Sex ratio of Scheduled tribe population is 498.

Scheduled Tribes Literates and Illiterates by Sex:

	Persons	Males	Females
Literate	564	372	192
Illiterate	1,683	756	927
Literacy rate	30.6	40.2	20.9
Graduate	3	3	0

Scheduled Tribes (Dominant):

Kolam etc., Sugalis etc., Koya etc., Gond etc. Manna Dhora

For their cultural identity please see Appendix-II

Villages without Scheduled Tribes: There are 4 villages without any scheduled tribe population.

Literates and Illiterates by Sex (Total Population):

	Persons	Males	Females
Literate	12,128	7,499	4,629
Illiterate	15,150	6,390	8,760
Literacy rate	52	63	40
Graduate	243	203	40

Agriculture: ***Distribution of villages according to land use:*** Out of 12 villages, Total area (in hectare) is 15702, out of that 42.56 percent is cultivable and 9.5 percent of the cultivable area is irrigated.

Sources of Irrigation (Hectares): Government Canal 0, Private Canal 0, Well without Electricity 0, Well with Electricity 112.1, Tubewell without Electricity 0, Tubewell with Electricity 5, Tank 517.94, River 0, Lake 0, Waterfall 0, Others 0.

Villages with population of 5000 to 9999: Akenipalle.

Villages with population of 10000 and above: None

Distribution of Workers:

	Persons	Males	Females	WPR
Cultivators	1,019	765	254	10.41
Agricultural Labour	3,288	1,573	1,715	33.58
Household Industry	241	153	88	2.46
Other Workers	5,243	4,335	908	53.55
Main Workers	5,721	4,800	921	58.43
Marginal Workers	4,070	2,026	2,044	41.57
Total Workers	9,791	6,826	2,965	

Religion: Major Religious Communities:

	Persons	Males	Females	Sex Ratio
Hindu (98.01%)	26,734	13,618	13,116	963
Muslim (1.2%)	328	171	157	918
Christian (0.7%)	191	89	102	1,146
Sikh (0%)	-	-	-	-
Buddhists (0%)	-	-	-	-
Jain (0%)	-	-	-	-

Agewise Data:

	Persons	Males	Females	Sex Ratio
All ages	27,278	13,889	13,389	964
0-14	9,808	5,089	4,719	927
15-44	12,627	6,364	6,263	984
45-79	4,582	2,299	2,283	993
80+	218	112	106	946
Age not stated	43	25	18	720

Languages (Dominant):

Telugu, Marathi, Hindi, Urdu, Gondi

Disabled Population:

	Persons	Males	Females	%
Total Disabled	452	247	205	
In Seeing	192	106	86	42.48
In Speech	61	27	34	13.5
In Hearing	15	10	5	3.32
In Movement	112	67	45	24.78
Mentally	72	37	35	15.93

BELUGUPPA

Beluguppa C.D. Block lies in the western part of Ananta pur district. The Block is located at a distance of 55 kms. from district headquarters (Anantapur). There are 14 villages in the block with the total population of 40,546 persons. Area of the C.D. Block is 338.39 sq. kms. It is bounded in the north by Mandals Kanekal and Uravakonda, in the south by Mandal Kalyandurg, in the east by Mandals Kalyandurg, Atmakur and Kudair, and in the west by Mandals Kanekal and Rayadurg.

Communications:

Roadways : State Highway (S.H.): Direction- Rayadurg to Anantapur. Nearest Villages- Narinjagundlapalle,

Narasapuram, Kalvapalle.

River: Pennar Nadi- Nearest Villages- Sreerangapuram, Budigumma, Ankampalle, Konampalle, Narinjagundlapalle, Narasapuram, Kalvapalle.

It receives Backward Region Grants, and is identified as a drought-prone area as well.

Annual Rainfall: Average Rainfall 489 mm

Ground Water: Availability of the Ground Water in the Basin is 1879 H.A.M. and the utilization is 1390 H. A.M. It belongs to SC category. Depth to water level varies from 10 to 20 meter below the ground. Most of the wells go down in summer months. The well density in the entire block is 6 wells per sq. km. Total no. of the wells in the block are enumerated as 1959, according to the Ground Water Estimation Committee.

Natural Division : Rayalaseema Region

Administration:

Division: Rayala Seema. Parliamentary Constituency: 36 Anantapur. District: Anantapur.

Mandal: Beluguppa. Assembly Constituency: 268 Uravakonda.

Gram Panchayat: 18.

Villages: 14 **Inhabited:** 14 **Uninhabited:** 0

Ranking	District	State	National
Area	12	90	2385
Population	38	811	5717
Sex Ratio	29	936	3198
Child Sex Ratio	17	279	942
Literacy Rate	12	456	3686
Density	57	720	5955
Work Participation Rate	52	1002	2044

Gram Panchayats:

Ankampalli, Avulenna, Beluguppa
Budigumma (Ramasagaram), Duddekunta, Gangavaram
Hanimireddipalli, Jeedipalli, Kalvapalli
N. Gundlapalli, Nakkalapalli, Narasapuram
Ramanepalli, Seerpi, Sreerangapuram, Thagguparthy
Virupapalli, Yerragudi.

Amenities:

Education: Primary School in 14 villages, Middle school in 10 villages, Matriculation or Secondary School in 7 villages, namely Beluguppa, Thagguparthy, Budigumma, Narasapuram, Seerpi, Gangavaram, Kalvapalle.

Higher Secondary or Pre University Courses or Intermediate or Junior College in 1 village of the CD Block,, namely Beluguppa.

College in 0 village, Adult Literacy Center in 0 village.

Medical: Hospital in 1 village, Dispensary in 2 villages, Health Center in 1 village, Sub Center in 7 villages, Maternity and Child Welfare Center in 1 village, Community health workers in 0 village.

The Villages having Hospital or Dispensary or Health Center are Beluguppa, Seerpi.

Drinking Water: Tap water in 14 villages, Tank water in 13 villages, Well water in 1 village, Tubewell in 0 village and more than one source in 14 villages.

Bank: Banking facility in 2 villages, namely, Beluguppa, Thagguparthy.

Credit Society in 4 villages Agricultural Credit Society in 0 Non-Agricultural Credit Society in 0 village.

Others: Power supply in 14 villages, Cinema hall in 2 villages, sport club in 0 village, Stadium or Auditorium or Community Hall in 0 village, Post Office in 13 villages.

There are 14 villages having bus facilities.

Villages with most of facilities: Beluguppa Thagguparthy.

Villages without Amenities (Education): None..

Scheduled Castes: Out of the total population of 40546 persons, 7492 persons (18.48%) belong to Scheduled Castes.

The villages having less than 10% SC population are None..

The villages having more than 50% SC population are None.

Sex ratio of Scheduled Caste population is 490.

Scheduled Castes Literates and Illiterates by Sex:

	Persons	Males	Females
Literate	2,666	1,640	1,026
Illiterate	4,826	2,178	2,648
Literacy rate	41.0	49.7	32.1
Graduate	35	29	6

Scheduled Castes (Dominant):

Madiga, Mala, Generic Castes etc., Mala Dasari

For their cultural identity please see Appendix-I

Villages without Scheduled Castes: There are 0 village without any scheduled caste population.

Scheduled Tribes: Out of the total population of 40546 persons, 3033 persons (7.48%) belong to Scheduled Tribes.

The villages having less than 10% ST population are Sreerangapuram, Narinjagundlapalle, Thagguparthy Budigumma, Ankampalle, Yerragudi, Avulenna, Seerpi Duddekunta, Konampalle, Gangavaram.

The villages having more than 50% ST population are None.

Sex ratio of Scheduled tribe population is 481.

Scheduled Tribes Literates and Illiterates by Sex:

	Persons	Males	Females
Literate	1,258	836	422
Illiterate	1,775	737	1,038
Literacy rate	49.6	63.7	34.5
Graduate	18	17	1

Scheduled Tribes (Dominant):

Sugalis etc., Yerukulas, Kammara

For their cultural identity please see Appendix-II

Villages without Scheduled Tribes: There are 5 villages without any scheduled tribe population.

Literates and Illiterates by Sex (Total Population):

	Persons	Males	Females
Literate	19,447	12,320	7,127
Illiterate	21,099	8,414	12,685
Literacy rate	55	68	41
Graduate	623	520	103

Agriculture: ***Distribution of villages according to land use:*** Out of 14 villages, Total area (in hectare) is 33838, out of that 78.31 percent is cultivable and 2.19 percent of the cultivable area is irrigated.

Sources of Irrigation (Hectares): Government Canal 0, Private Canal 0, Well without Electricity 0, Well with Electricity 211.56, Tubewell without Electricity 0, Tubewell with Electricity 367.53, Tank 0, River 0, Lake 0, Waterfall 0, Others 0.

Villages with population of 5000 to 9999: Beluguppa.

Villages with population of 10000 and above: None

Distribution of Workers:

	Persons	Males	Females	WPR
Cultivators	6,828	5,147	1,681	33.15
Agricultural Labour	10,608	4,560	6,048	51.51
Household Industry	369	207	162	1.79
Other Workers	2,790	2,164	626	13.55
Main Workers	13,438	9,170	4,268	65.25
Marginal Workers	7,157	2,908	4,249	34.75
Total Workers	20,595	12,078	8,517	

Religion: Major Religious Communities:

	Persons	Males	Females	Sex Ratio
Hindu (97.61%)	39,576	20,234	19,342	956
Muslim (2.06%)	835	436	399	915
Christian (0.15%)	59	26	33	1,269
Sikh (0%)	-	-	-	-
Buddhists (0.01%)	5	2	3	1,500
Jain (0%)	-	-	-	-

Agewise Data:

	Persons	Males	Females	Sex Ratio
All ages	40,546	20,734	19,812	956
0-14	13,444	6,959	6,485	932
15-44	18,472	9,453	9,019	954
45-79	8,212	4,131	4,081	988
80+	357	151	206	1364
Age not stated	61	40	21	525

Languages (Dominant):

Telugu, Hindi, Urdu, Kannada, Gondi

Disabled Population:

	Persons	Males	Females	%
Total Disabled	895	486	409	
In Seeing	327	176	151	36.54
In Speech	88	51	37	9.83
In Hearing	71	35	36	7.93
In Movement	304	174	130	33.97
Mentally	105	50	55	11.73

BESTAWARIPETA

Bestawaripeta C.D. Block lies in the south-western part of Prakasam district. It is a part of Bestawaripet Mandal. The Block is located at a distance of 110 kms. from district headquarters (Ongole). There are 20 villages in the block with the total population of 41,976 persons. Area of the C.D. Block is 230.95 sq. kms. It is bounded in the north by Mandals Cumbum and Tarlupadi, in the south by Mandals Komarolu and Chandrasekharapuram, in the east by Mandals Veligandla and Hanumanthunipadu, and in the west by mandals Racher la and Cumbum.

Communications:

Roadways : State Highway (S.H.): Direction- Mydukur to Cumbum. Nearest Villages- Ondutla, Papayapalle, Nekunambad, Salakalaveedu, Dathara Krishnapuram, China Obeneni Palle, Retla Palle, Peda Obeneni Palle, Moksha Gundum.

Railway Station: Jaggambotla Krishnapuram.

Hills: Nearest Villages- Pusalapadu, Salakalaveedu, Pitikayagulla, Moksha Gundum.

The Block is identified as a drought-prone area.

Integrated Child Development Scheme (ICDS) Project: Besthavaripet, Total Anganwadi Centres: 180

Annual Rainfall: Average Rainfall 763.1 mm

Ground Water: Availability of the Ground Water in the Basin is 20.51 MCM and the utilization is 22.13 MCM It belongs to Over Exploited category. Depth to water level varies from 2 to 5 meter below the ground. Most of the wells go down in summer months, according to the Ground Water Estimation Committee.

Forest and Reserved **Forest:** (Velikonda R.F.)- Salakalav eedu, China Obeneni Palle, Peda Obeneni Palle, Pothavaram, Pitikayagulla, Basine Palle, Pachala Venkata Puram, Galijerugulla, Kona Palle.

Administration:

Division: Coastal Andhra. Parliamentary Constituency: 33 Ongole. District: Prakasam. Mandal: Bestawaripeta. Assembly Constituency: 231 Giddalur. Gram Panchayat: 19

Villages: 20 **Inhabited:** 18 **Uninhabited:** 2

Ranking	**District**	**State**	**National**
Area	29	382	3648

Population	30	758	5645
Sex Ratio	49	1021	3695
Child Sex Ratio	40	843	3724
Literacy Rate	23	431	3597
Density	41	760	5005
Work Participation Rate	34	781	2213

Gram Panchayats:
Akkapalli, Basinepalli, Bestavaripeta
Ch.Obinenipalli, Chetticherla, Galijerugulla
J.B.K.Puram, J.C.Agrahram, Khajipuram, Konapalli
M.P.Cheruvu, Mokshagundam, Nekunambad, P.B.Puram
P.Obinenipalli, Pandillapalli, Pitikayagulla
Pusalapadu, Salakalaveedu.

Amenities:

Education: Primary School in 18 villages, Middle school in 7 villages, Matriculation or Secondary School in 6 villages, namely Pusalapadu, Papayapalle, Salakalaveedu, Pitikayagulla, Madhana Pullala Cheruvu, Galijerugulla.

Higher Secondary or Pre University Courses or Intermediate or Junior College in 0 village of the CD Block, College in 0 village, Adult Literacy Center in 18 villages.

Medical: Hospital in 0 village, Dispensary in 2 villages, Health Center in 3 villages, Sub Center in 7 villages Maternity and Child Welfare Center in 0 village, Community health workers in 0 village.

The Villages having Hospital or Dispensary or Health Center are Pitikayagulla, Moksha Gundum.

Drinking Water: Tap water in 18 villages, Tank water in 18 villages, Well water in 18 villages, Tubewell in 18 villages and more than one source in 18 villages.

Bank: Banking facility in 2 villages, namely, Pitikayagulla, Galijerugulla.

Credit Society in 7 villages Agricultural Credit Society in 1 Non-Agricultural Credit Society in 2 villages.

Others: Power supply in 18 villages, Cinema hall in 2 villages, sport club in 0 village, Stadium or Auditorium or Community Hall in 0 village, Post Office in 13 villages.

There are 15 villages having bus facilities.

Villages with most of facilities: Pitikayagulla Galijerugulla.

Villages without Amenities (Education): None..

Scheduled Castes: Out of the total population of 42089 persons, 8174 persons (19.42%) belong to Scheduled Castes.

The villages having less than 10% SC population are None..

The villages having more than 50% SC population are None.

Sex ratio of Scheduled Caste population is 469.

Scheduled Castes Literates and Illiterates by Sex:

	Persons	Males	Females
Literate	4,215	2,787	1,428
Illiterate	3,959	1,557	2,402
Literacy rate	59.9	74.4	43.3
Graduate	63	49	14

Scheduled Castes (Dominant):
Madiga, Mala, Adi Andhra, Beda Jangam etc.

For their cultural identity please see Appendix-I

Villages without Scheduled Castes: There are 4 villages without any scheduled caste population.

Scheduled Tribes: Out of the total population of 42089 persons, 187 persons (0.44%) belong to Scheduled Tribes.

The villages having less than 10% ST population are
Jaggambotla Krishnapuram, Ondutla, Pusalapadu
Papayapalle, Somavarapeta, Chinthala Palem
Nekunambad, Salakalaveedu, China Obeneni Palle
Retla Palle, Peda Obeneni Palle, Pitikayagulla
Basine Palle, Madhana Pullala Cheruvu, Moksha Gundum
Pachala Venkata Puram, Galijerugulla, Kona Palle.

The villages having more than 50% ST population are None.

Sex ratio of Scheduled tribe population is 487.

Scheduled Tribes Literates and Illiterates by Sex:

	Persons	Males	Females
Literate	66	44	22
Illiterate	121	52	69
Literacy rate	42.0	55.0	28.6
Graduate	1	1	0

Scheduled Tribes (Dominant):
Yerukulas, Yenadis, Sugalis etc.

For their cultural identity please see Appendix-II

Villages without Scheduled Tribes: There are 9 villages without any scheduled tribe population.

Literates and Illiterates by Sex (Total Population):

	Persons	Males	Females
Literate	20,128	13,388	6,740
Illiterate	21,961	8,235	13,726
Literacy rate	55	72	38
Graduate	694	608	86

Agriculture: ***Distribution of villages according to land use:*** Out of 20 villages, Total area (in hectare) is 23095, out of that 62.93 percent is cultivable and 35.14 percent of the cultivable area is irrigated.

Sources of Irrigation (Hectares): Government Canal 0, Private Canal 0, Well without Electricity 36, Well with Electricity 359, Tubewell without Electricity 0, Tubewell with Electricity 4100, Tank 612, River 0, Lake 0, Waterfall 0, Others 0.

Villages with population of 5000 to 9999:
Pusalapadu, Pitikayagulla.

Villages with population of 10000 and above: None

Distribution of Workers:

	Persons	Males	Females	WPR
Cultivators	7,166	4,642	2,524	34.37
Agricultural Labour	10,337	4,287	6,050	49.57
Household Industry	509	304	205	2.44
Other Workers	2,840	2,181	659	13.62
Main Workers	16,317	10,239	6,078	78.25
Marginal Workers	4,535	1,175	3,360	21.75
Total Workers	20,852	11,414	9,438	

Religion: Major Religious Communities:

	Persons	Males	Females	Sex Ratio
Hindu (95.4%)	40,152	20,639	19,513	945
Muslim (4.4%)	1,853	948	905	955
Christian (0.13%)	55	25	30	1,200
Sikh (0%)	-	-	-	-
Buddhists (0%)	-	-	-	-
Jain (0%)	-	-	-	-

Agewise Data:

	Persons	Males	Females	Sex Ratio
All ages	42,089	21,623	20,466	946
0-14	14,203	7,572	6,631	876
15-44	18,339	9,375	8,964	956
45-79	9,202	4,510	4,692	1040
80+	299	142	157	1106
Age not stated	46	24	22	917

Languages (Dominant):

Telugu, Urdu, Gondi, Tamil, Hindi

Disabled Population:

	Persons	Males	Females	%
Total Disabled	752	436	316	
In Seeing	218	119	99	28.99
In Speech	92	55	37	12.23
In Hearing	54	24	30	7.18
In Movement	276	178	98	36.7
Mentally	112	60	52	14.89

BETHAMCHERLA

Bethamcherla C.D. Block lies in the eastern part of Kurnool district. It is a part of Bethamcherla Mandal. The Block is located at a distance of 40 kms. from district headquarters (Kurnool). There are 09 villages in the block with the total population of 34,928 persons. Area of the C.D. Block is 223.43 sq. kms. It is bound ed in the north by Mandals Veldurthi, Orvakal and Panyam, in the south by Mandal Banaganapalle, in the east by Mandals Panyam and Banaganapalle, and in the west by Mandals Dhone and Veldurthi.

Communications:

Roadways : NH- 18: Direction- Orvakal to Banaganapalle. Nearest Villages- Gollagutta, Kolumulapalle.

Railway Station: Rangapuram.

It is identified as a drought-prone area.

Annual Rainfall: Average Rainfall 622 mm

Ground Water: Availability of the Ground Water in the Basin is 1305 H.A.M. and the utilization is 1413 H. A.M. It belongs to OE category. Depth to water level varies from 5 to 10 meter below the ground. Most of the wells go down in summer months. The well density in the entire block is 2 wells per sq. km. Total no. of the wells in the block are enumerated as 1126, according to the Ground Water Estimation Committee.

Forest and Reserved **Forest:** Nearest Villages- Muddavaram, Kolumulapalle, Gutupalle, Kothapalle, Rangapuram, Ambapuram, Gollagutta.

Natural Division : Rayalaseema Region

Administration:

Division: Rayala Seema. Parliamentary Constituency: 34 Nandayal. District: Kurnool. Mandal: Bethamcherla. Assembly Constituency: 260 Dhone. Gram Panchayat: 20

Villages: 9 **Inhabited:** 9 **Uninhabited:** 0

Ranking	**District**	**State**	**National**
Area	35	422	3784
Population	45	934	5912
Sex Ratio	29	846	2813
Child Sex Ratio	36	750	3182
Literacy Rate	36	770	4791
Density	12	38	5470
Work Participation Rate	36	885	175

Gram Panchayats:

Ambapuram, Bethamcherla, Bugganipalle, Ceement Nagar Emboy, Gollagutta, Gorumankonda, Gutupalle H Kottala, K K Kottala, Kolumulapalle, M.Pendakal Muddavaram, R.Bukkapuram, R.Kothapalle R.S.Rangapuram, Rahimanpuram, Sankalapuram Seetharamapuram, Thavisikonda.

Amenities:

Education: Primary School in 9 villages, Middle school in 7 villages, Matriculation or Secondary School in 1 village, namely Rangapuram.

Higher Secondary or Pre University Courses or Intermediate or Junior College in 0 village of the CD Block, College in 0 village, Adult Literacy Center in 9 villages.

Medical: Hospital in 0 village, Dispensary in 1 village, Health Center in 0 village, Sub Center in 6 villages, Maternity and Child Welfare Center in 0 village, Community health workers in 0 village.

The Village having Hospital or Dispensary or Health Center is Rangapuram.

Drinking Water: Tap water in 9 villages, Tank water in 9 villages, Well water in 9 villages, Tubewell in 9

villages and more than one source in 9 villages.
Bank: Banking facility in 1 villages, namely, Rangapuram.
Credit Society in 5 villages Agricultural Credit Society in 0 Non-Agricultural Credit Society in 5 villages.
Others: Power supply in 9 villages, Cinema hall in 1 village, sport club in 0 village, Stadium or Auditorium or Community Hall in 0 village, Post Office in 8 villages.
There are 9 villages having bus facilities.
Village with most of facilities: Rangapuram.
Villages without Amenities (Education): None..
Scheduled Castes: Out of the total population of 34927 persons, 8977 persons (25.7%) belong to Scheduled Castes.
The villages having less than 10% SC population are None..
The villages having more than 50% SC population are None.
Sex ratio of Scheduled Caste population is 495.

Scheduled Castes Literates and Illiterates by Sex:

	Persons	Males	Females
Literate	2,901	1,968	933
Illiterate	6,076	2,564	3,512
Literacy rate	38.7	52.1	25.1
Graduate	39	33	6

Scheduled Castes (Dominant):
Madiga, Mala
For their cultural identity please see Appendix-I
Villages without Scheduled Castes: There are 0 village without any scheduled caste population.
Scheduled Tribes: Out of the total population of 34927 persons, 98 persons (0.28%) belong to Scheduled Tribes.
The villages having less than 10% ST population are Pendakal, Muddavaram, Emboy, Kolumulapalle Gutupalle, Kothapalle, Rangapuram, Ambapuram Gollagutta.
The villages having more than 50% ST population are None.
Sex ratio of Scheduled tribe population is 582.

Scheduled Tribes Literates and Illiterates by Sex:

	Persons	Males	Females
Literate	33	20	13
Illiterate	65	21	44
Literacy rate	41.3	58.8	28.3
Graduate	3	2	1

Scheduled Tribes (Dominant):
Yerukulas, Kammara, Sugalis etc.
For their cultural identity please see Appendix-II
Villages without Scheduled Tribes: There are 2 villages without any scheduled tribe population.
Literates and Illiterates by Sex (Total Population):

	Persons	Males	Females
Literate	14,362	9,500	4,862
Illiterate	20,565	8,289	12,276
Literacy rate	48	63	33
Graduate	249	215	34

Agriculture: ***Distribution of villages according to land use:*** Out of 9 villages, Total area (in hectare) is 22343, out of that 54.59 percent is cultivable and 13.21 percent of the cultivable area is irrigated.
Sources of Irrigation (Hectares): Government Canal 0, Private Canal 0, Well without Electricity 0, Well with Electricity 4.04, Tubewell without Electricity 0, Tubewell with Electricity 1606.99, Tank 0, River 0, Lake 0, Waterfall 0, Others 0.
Villages with population of 5000 to 9999:
Kolumulapalle, Rangapuram.
Villages with population of 10000 and above: None
Distribution of Workers:

	Persons	Males	Females	WPR
Cultivators	7,268	4,231	3,037	35.26
Agricultural Labour	8,351	3,260	5,091	40.52
Household Industry	282	163	119	1.37
Other Workers	4,710	3,161	1,549	22.85
Main Workers	18,284	10,092	8,192	88.71
Marginal Workers	2,327	723	1,604	11.29
Total Workers	20,611	10,815	9,796	

Religion: Major Religious Communities:

	Persons	Males	Females	Sex Ratio
Hindu (95%)	33,179	16,878	16,301	966
Muslim (4.9%)	1,713	893	820	918
Christian (0.09%)	30	16	14	875
Sikh (0%)	1	1	-	-
Buddhists (0%)	-	-	-	-
Jain (0%)	-	-	-	-

Agewise Data:

	Persons	Males	Females	Sex Ratio
All ages	34,927	17,789	17,138	963
0-14	12,680	6,464	6,216	962
15-44	15,951	8,312	7,639	919
45-79	6,055	2,910	3,145	1081
80+	205	85	120	1412
Age not stated	36	18	18	1000

Languages (Dominant):
Telugu, Urdu, Gondi, Marathi, Tamil
Disabled Population:

	Persons	Males	Females	%
Total Disabled	971	482	489	
In Seeing	524	220	304	53.96
In Speech	51	22	29	5.25
In Hearing	65	25	40	6.69

In Movement	247	171	76	25.44

Mentally	84	44	40	8.65

BHADRACHALAM

Bhadrachalam C.D. Block lies in the northern part of Khammam district. It is a part of Bhadrachalam Mandal. The Block is located at a distance of 114 kms. from district headquarters (Khammam). There are 70 villages in the block with the total population of 35,355 persons. Area of the C.D. Block is 277.65 sq. kms. It is bound ed in the north by Dumugudem Mandal, in the south by Mandals Burgampahad and Kukunoor, in the east by Mandal Chintur, and in the west by Mandal Burgampur.

Communications:

Roadways : NH- 221: Direction- Palwancha to Konta. Neare st Villages- Lingalapalle, Ramagopalapuram, Buruguvai, Laxmipuram, Madhavaraopeta, Gollaguppa, Bandirevu, Narasingapeta, Purushothapatnam, K. Narayanapuram, Pandurangapuram, Yerragunta, Gundala, Pinapalle, Rayan apeta.

River: Godavari Nadi- Nearest Villages- Yetapaka, Madim eru, Seethampeta, Chinthalagudem, Kolanugudem, Chandramp alem, Seetapuram, Chowdavaram, Nellipaka, Devarapalle, Gogubaka, Gommu Koyagudem, Kapavaram, Gollagudem, Thotapalle, Rachagampalle, Mummadivaru, Gowridevi Peta, Nandigama, Murumoor, Gundala, Pinapalle, Rayanapeta.

Backwards Region Grants Fund: It receives Backward Region Grants.

Integrated Child Development Scheme (ICDS) Project:

Annual Rainfall: Average Rainfall 1159 mm

Ground Water: Availability of the Ground Water in the Basin is 2798 H.A.M.and the utilization is 239 H.A. M. It belongs to safe category. Depth to water level varies from 5 to 10 meter below the ground. Most of the wells go down in summer months. The well density in the entire block is 0.4 wells per sq. km. Total no. of the wells in the block are enumerated as 162, according to the Ground Water Estimation Committee.

Forest and Reserved **Forest:** (Ramachandra Puram R.F.)- Nearest Villages- Gottugudem, Fergusanpeta, Thunikic heruvu, Sreenivasapuram, Ramagopalapuram, Laxmipuram, Narasingapeta, Pitchikalapadu, Yetapaka, Lakshmidevipe ta, Purushothapatnam, Gundala, K. Narayanapuram, Penubal le, Pandurangapuram, Yerragunta, Chinna Nallakunta, Nallakunta, Devarapalle, Gogubaka, Gommu Koyagudem, Kapavaram, Boddugudem.

Natural Division : Godavari Depression Region

Administration:

Division: Telangana. Parliamentary Constituency: 16 Mahbubabad . District: Khammam. Mandal: Bhadrachalam . Assembly Constituency: 119 Bhadrachalam (ST). Gram Panchayat: 21.

Fairs and Festivals:

Sri Rama Navami Festival : It is celebrated for 10 days from Chaitra Suddha Sapthami to Bahula Padyami (March-April) at Sri Sitarama Chandraswamy temple. On Saptami day, the celebration is inaugurated with kalyanothsava ankurarpana in the morning and there is a procession in a palanquin in the evening. Dhwajaro hanam is on Ashtami morning. In the night, invocation of the thirty three crores of Devatas, bheripuja, ashta dik palakapuja, baliharanam, edurukolu and garudothsavam (procession on Garuda) are performed. The marriage ceremony is celebrated on the morning of Navami day. "On this day, small idols of Rama and Sita are bathed in sacred waters of the Godavari and decked with resple dent jewellery. They are placed in a small exquisitely decorated silver palanquin carried in processsion amidst scences of devotion and great enthusiasm to a huge Mantapam close by capable of accommodating thousands of pilgrims. The marriage ceremony is celebrated with due rites and great eclat to the chanting of Vedic hymns and the applause of the spectators".

Villages: 70 **Inhabited:** 62 **Uninhabited:** 8

Ranking	District	State	National
Area	16	214	3028
Population	33	927	5901
Sex Ratio	34	860	2884
Child Sex Ratio	20	326	1156
Literacy Rate	36	839	5017
Density	23	440	5874
Work Participation Rate	33	981	1093

Gram Panchayats:

Bhadrachalam, Chodavaram, G.Kothagudem, Gannavaram Gowridevipeta, Gundala, Kannaigudem, Krishnavaram Laxmipuram, Murumuru, Nallakunta, Nandigama Nellipaka, Pitchikalapadu, Purushothapatnam Ramagopalapuram, Rayanipeta, Thotapalli Tripura Penta Veedu, Venkatareddipeta, Vissapuram Yetapaka.

Amenities:

Education: Primary School in 54 villages, Middle school in 10 villages, Matriculation or Secondary School in 5 villages, namely K. Narayanapuram, Nellipaka, Tripura Penta Veedu, Gowridevi Peta, Nandigama. Higher Secondary or Pre University Courses or Inter-mediate or Junior College in 0 village of the CD Block, College in 0 village, Adult Literacy Center in 40 villages.

Medical: Hospital in 3 villages, Dispensary in 2 villages, Health Center in 2 villages, Sub Center in 6 villages, Maternity and Child Welfare Center in 0 village, Community health workers in 0 village.

The Villages having Hospital or Dispensary or Health Center are Nellipaka, Gogubaka, Gowridevi Peta.

Drinking Water: Tap water in 60 villages, Tank water in 60 villages, Well water in 62 villages, Tubewell in 60 villages and more than one source in 61 villages.

Bank: Banking facility in 5 villages, namely, Rangapuram, Seetapuram, Yerragunta Tripura Penta Veedu, Thotapalle.

Credit Society in 15 villages Agricultural Credit Society in 7 Non-Agricultural Credit Society in 9 villages.

Others: Power supply in 62 villages, Cinema hall in 2 villages, sport club in 0 village, Stadium or Auditorium or Community Hall in 0 village, Post Office in 15 villages.

There are 42 villages having bus facilities.

Villages with most of facilities: Tripura Penta Veedu Thotapalle.

Villages without amenities (Education):
Gottugudem, Gollaguppa, Yerraboru, Seethampeta, Seetapuram, Devarapalle..

Scheduled Castes: Out of the total population of 35311 persons, 6617 persons (18.74%) belong to Scheduled Castes.

The villages having less than 10% SC population are Gottugudem, Fergusanpeta, Thunikicheruvu Pattucheera, Buruguvai, Madhavaraopeta, Gollaguppa Bandirevu, Rangapuram, Kannapuram, Viswapuram Yerraboru, Kannapuram, Narasingapeta, Pitchikalapadu Seethampeta, Chandrampalem, Lakshmidevipeta Purushothapatnam, Seetapuram, K. Narayanapuram Pinapalle, Penuballe, Pandurangapuram, Yerragunta Chinna Nallakunta, Buttaigudem, Devarapalle Gommu Koyagudem, Kothagudem, Boddugudem Ayyavaripeta, Gollagudem, Thotapalle, Rachagampalle Rajupeta, Kistaram, Kusumanapalle, Achuthapuram Raghavapuram, Chelempalem, Nallakunta.

The villages having more than 50% SC population are None.

Sex ratio of Scheduled Caste population is 491.

Scheduled Castes Literates and Illiterates by Sex:

	Persons	Males	Females
Literate	2,876	1,750	1,126
Illiterate	3,741	1,615	2,126
Literacy rate	50.5	60.5	40.1
Graduate	54	49	5

Scheduled Castes (Dominant):
Mala, Madiga, Madiga Dasu etc., Mala Dasari Adi Andhra

For their cultural identity please see Appendix-I

Villages without Scheduled Castes: There are 43 villages without any scheduled caste population.

Scheduled Tribes: Out of the total population of 35311 persons, 17682 persons (50.08%) belong to Scheduled Tribes.

The villages having less than 10% ST population are Thallagudem, Seethampeta, Gundala, Kapavaram Tripura Penta Veedu, Gollagudem, Kapugampalle Gannavaram, Gowridevi Peta, Nandigama.

The villages having more than 50% ST population are Gottugudem, Fergusanpeta, Thunikicheruvu Lingalapalle, Ramagopalapuram, Pattucheera Buruguvai, Madhavaraopeta, Gollaguppa, Bandirevu Rangapuram, Kannapuram, Viswapuram, Yerraboru Kannapuram, Narasingapeta, Pitchikalapadu Chandrampalem, Lakshmidevipeta, K. Narayanapuram Pinapalle, Penuballe, Pandurangapuram, Yerragunta Chinna Nallakunta, Buttaigudem, Devarapalle Gogubaka, Gommu Koyagudem, Kothagudem, Boddugudem Ayyavaripeta, Thotapalle, Rajupeta, Kistaram Kusumanapalle, Achuthapuram, Raghavapuram Chelempalem, Nallakunta, Murumoor.

Sex ratio of Scheduled tribe population is 485.

Scheduled Tribes Literates and Illiterates by Sex:

	Persons	Males	Females
Literate	4,699	3,026	1,673
Illiterate	12,983	6,075	6,908
Literacy rate	31.5	39.3	23.2
Graduate	18	16	2

Scheduled Tribes (Dominant):
Koya etc., Sugalis etc., Nayaks, Valmiki Konda Kapus

For their cultural identity please see Appendix-II

Villages without Scheduled Tribes: There are 11 villages without any scheduled tribe population.

Literates and Illiterates by Sex (Total Population):

	Persons	Males	Females
Literate	14,095	8,449	5,646
Illiterate	21,216	9,551	11,665
Literacy rate	47	55	38
Graduate	294	234	60

Agriculture: ***Distribution of villages according to land use:*** Out of 70 villages, Total area (in hectare) is 27763, out of that 37.43 percent is cultivable and 35.56 percent of the cultivable area is irrigated.

Sources of Irrigation (Hectares): Government Canal 0, Private Canal 0, Well without Electricity 0, Well with Electricity 0, Tubewell without Electricity 0, Tubewell with Electricity 0, Tank 280.07, River 0, Lake 0, Waterfall 28.65, Others 3386.54.

Villages with population of 5000 to 9999: None

Villages with population of 10000 and above: None

Distribution of Workers:

	Persons	Males	Females	WPR

Cultivators	5,215	3,828	1,387	27.63
Agricultural Labour	10,744	4,805	5,939	56.93
Household Industry	219	151	68	1.16
Other Workers	2,695	1,990	705	14.28
Main Workers	16,758	9,926	6,832	88.79
Marginal Workers	2,115	848	1,267	11.21
Total Workers	18,873	10,774	8,099	

Religion: Major Religious Communities:

	Persons	Males	Females	Sex Ratio
Hindu (98.93%)	34,933	17,820	17,113	960
Muslim (0.52%)	182	82	100	1,220
Christian (0.49%)	172	85	87	1,024
Sikh (0%)	-	-	-	-
Buddhists (0%)	-	-	-	-
Jain (0%)	-	-	-	-

Agewise Data:

	Persons	Males	Females	Sex Ratio
All ages	35,311	18,000	17,311	962
0-14	11,604	5,954	5,650	949
15-44	17,279	8,922	8,357	937
45-79	6,105	2,954	3,151	1067
80+	210	107	103	963
Age not stated	113	63	50	794

Languages (Dominant):

Telugu, Koya, Hindi, Urdu, Tamil

Disabled Population:

	Persons	Males	Females	%
Total Disabled	800	461	339	
In Seeing	454	267	187	56.75
In Speech	67	36	31	8.38
In Hearing	37	18	19	4.62
In Movement	161	97	64	20.12
Mentally	81	43	38	10.12

BHAINSA

Bhainsa C.D. Block lies in the western part of Adilabad district. It is a part of Bhainsa Mandal. The Block is located at a distance of 127 kms. from district headquarters (Adilabad). There are 33 villages in the block with the total population of 34,442 persons. Area of the C.D. Block is 146.54 sq. kms. It is bounded by Kubeer Mandal on north-west, north and north-east, Kuntala Mandal on north-east, east and south-east, Lokeswaram Mandal on south-east, Mudhole Mandal on south and south-west, Tanoor Mandal on south-west, west and north-west.

Communications :

Roadways : NH- 222: Direction- Bhokar to Nirmal Nearest Villages- Thimmapur, Wanalpahad, Ekgaon, Pipri, Pangri, Badgaon, Dahegaon, Mategaon, Watoli, Pendapalle. State Highway (S.H.): Direction- Dharmaram to Bhainsa, Nearest Villages- Badgaon, Dahegaon

Backwards Region Grants Fund: It receives Backward Region Grants.

Annual Rainfall: Average Rainfall 1035 mm

Ground Water: Availability of the Ground Water in the Basin is 2708 H.A.M.and the utilization is 1833 H.A. M. It belongs to Safe category. Depth to water level varies from 10 to 20 meter below the ground. Most of the wells go down in summer months, according to the Ground Water Estimation Committee.

Natural Division : Telangana Plateau Region

Administration:

Division: Telangana. Parliamentary Constituency: 1 Adilabad (ST).District: Adilabad. Mandal: Bhainsa. Assembly Constituency: 10 Mudhole. Gram Panchayat: 19

Villages: 33 **Inhabited:** 33 **Uninhabited:** 0

Ranking	District	State	National
Area	44	522	4104
Population	24	943	5925
Sex Ratio	8	60	439
Child Sex Ratio	44	885	3867
Literacy Rate	30	859	5104
Density	8	55	5257
Work Participation Rate	11	841	224

Gram Panchayats:

Chichond, Chintalabori, Dahegaon, Ekgaon, Elegaon Hasgul, Kamol, Kotalgaon, Kumbhi, Mahagaon, Mategaon Mirzapur, Pangri, Pendapalle, Sunkli, Thimmapur Walegaon, Wanalpahad, Watoli.

Amenities:

Education: Primary School in 33 villages, Middle school in 8 villages, Matriculation or Secondary School in 3 villages, namely Thimmapur, Dahegaon, Kamol.

Higher Secondary or Pre University Courses or Intermediate or Junior College in 0 village of the CD Block, College in 0 village, Adult Literacy Center in 30 villages.

Medical: Hospital in 0 village, Dispensary in 1 village, Health Center in 0 village, Sub Center in 7 villages, Maternity and Child Welfare Center in 0 village, Community health workers in 0 village.

The Village having Hospital or Dispensary or Health Center is Dahegaon.

Drinking Water: Tap water in 33 villages, Tank water in 33 villages, Well water in 33 villages, Tubewell in 33 villages and more than one source in 33 villages.

Bank: Banking facility in 4 villages, namely, Mahagaon, Thimmapur, Wanalpahad, Dahegaon.

Credit Society in 7 villages Agricultural Credit Society in 4 Non-Agricultural Credit Society in 4 villages.

Others: Power supply in 33 villages, Cinema hall in 0 village, sport club in 0 village, Stadium or Auditorium or Community Hall in 0 village, Post Office in 10 villages.
There are 25 villages having bus facilities.
Villages with most of facilities: Mahagaon Thimmapur, Wanalpahad, Dahegaon.
Villages without Amenities (Education): None..
Scheduled Castes: Out of the total population of 34437 persons, 6827 persons (19.82%) belong to Scheduled Castes.
The villages having less than 10% SC population are None..
The villages having more than 50% SC population are None.
Sex ratio of Scheduled Caste population is 499.

Scheduled Castes Literates and Illiterates by Sex:

	Persons	Males	Females
Literate	2,162	1,472	690
Illiterate	4,665	1,945	2,720
Literacy rate	37.9	52.1	23.9
Graduate	22	18	4

Scheduled Castes (Dominant):
Mala, Madiga, Chamar etc., Mala Sale etc.
Dakkal etc.
For their cultural identity please see Appendix-I
Villages without Scheduled Castes: There are 0 village without any scheduled caste population.
Scheduled Tribes: Out of the total population of 34437 persons, 819 persons (2.38%) belong to Scheduled Tribes.
The villages having less than 10% ST population are Chichond, Kumbhi, Takli, Linga, Mirzapur, Siddur Gundagaon, Mahagaon, Chintalabori, Kotalgaon, Bijjur Sunkli, Thimmapur, Wanalpahad, Ekgaon, Pipri Babalgaon, Pangri, Manjri, Sirala, Badgaon, Dahegaon Walegaon, Kumsari, Khatgaon, Kamol, Hasgul, Mategaon Boregaon (Buzurg), Watoli, Pendapalle.
The villages having more than 50% ST population are None.
Sex ratio of Scheduled tribe population is 521.

Scheduled Tribes Literates and Illiterates by Sex:

	Persons	Males	Females
Literate	227	159	68
Illiterate	592	233	359
Literacy rate	33.2	47.3	19.6
Graduate	2	2	0

Scheduled Tribes (Dominant):
Gond etc., Yerukulas, Generic Tribes etc.
Sugalis etc., Chenchu etc.
For their cultural identity please see Appendix-II
Villages without Scheduled Tribes: There are 16 villages without any scheduled tribe population.

Literates and Illiterates by Sex (Total Population):

	Persons	Males	Females
Literate	13,395	8,877	4,518
Illiterate	21,042	8,059	12,983
Literacy rate	46	63	30
Graduate	211	197	14

Agriculture: ***Distribution of villages according to land use:*** Out of 33 villages, Total area (in hectare) is 20431, out of that 80.67 percent is cultivable and 11.06 percent of the cultivable area is irrigated.
Sources of Irrigation (Hectares): Government Canal 0, Private Canal 0, Well without Electricity 0, Well with Electricity 0, Tubewell without Electricity 29.54, Tubewell with Electricity 1138.78, Tank 655.17, River 0, Lake 0, Waterfall 0, Others 0.
Villages with population of 5000 to 9999: None
Villages with population of 10000 and above: None
Distribution of Workers:

	Persons	Males	Females	WPR
Cultivators	6,977	4,390	2,587	35.05
Agricultural Labour	6,857	3,326	3,531	34.45
Household Industry	3,752	384	3,368	18.85
Other Workers	2,321	1,785	536	11.66
Main Workers	17,448	8,809	8,639	87.65
Marginal Workers	2,459	1,076	1,383	12.35
Total Workers	19,907	9,885	10,022	

Religion: Major Religious Communities:

	Persons	Males	Females	Sex Ratio
Hindu (89.37%)	30,778	15,134	15,644	1,034
Muslim (7.09%)	2,440	1,201	1,239	1,032
Christian (0.07%)	24	11	13	1,182
Sikh (0%)	1	1	-	-
Buddhists (2.91%)	1,001	503	498	990
Jain (0%)	-	-	-	-

Agewise Data:

	Persons	Males	Females	Sex Ratio
All ages	34,437	16,936	17,501	1033
0-14	12,116	6,191	5,925	957
15-44	15,502	7,692	7,810	1015
45-79	6,546	2,923	3,623	1239
80+	214	87	127	1460
Age not stated	59	43	16	372

Languages (Dominant):
Telugu, Marathi, Urdu, Kannada, Hindi
Disabled Population:

	Persons	Males	Females	%
Total Disabled	654	378	276	
In Seeing	269	154	115	41.13
In Speech	58	34	24	8.87
In Hearing	44	24	20	6.73

In Movement	209	119	90	31.96

Mentally	74	47	27	11.31

BHAMINI

Bhamini C.D. Block lies in the north-western part of Srikakulam district. The Block is located at a distance of 70 kms. from district headquarters (Srikakulam). There are 22 villages in the block with the total population of 41,058 persons. Area of the C.D. Block is 107.07 sq. kms. It is bounded in the south by Mandals Seethampeta and Kothuru, in the east by Mandal Kothuru, and in the west by district Vizianagaram and Mandal Seethampeta. It has common boundary with the state of Orissa on north, east and west.

Communications:

Roadways : Metalled Roads: Nearest Villages- Battili, Gurandi, Nulakajodu, Singidi, Burujola, Bhamini, Liviri, Dimmidijola, Solikiri, Ghanasara, Kosali, Peddadimili, Chinnadimili.

River: Vamsadhara Nadi- Nearest Villages- Battili, Neradi, Nulakajodu, Singidi, Burujola, Bhamini, Liviri, Dimmidijola, Solikiri, Ghanasara, Kosali.

Hills: Nearest Villages- Vaddangi, Loharijola, Nulakajo du, Pasukudi, Maniga, Bhamini, Liviri, Dimmidijola, Solikiri.

Annual Rainfall: Average Rainfall 1085.6 mm

Ground Water: Availability of the Ground Water in the Basin is (Information not avavible) H.A.M .and the utilization is (Information not avavible) H.A.M. It belongs to (Information not avavible) category. Depth to water level varies from 3 to 10 meter below the ground. Most of the wells go down in summer months.

Administration:

Division: Coastal Andhra. Parliamentary Constituency: 18 Araku (ST). District: Srikakulam. Mandal: Bhamini. Assembly Constituency: 129 Palakonda (ST). Gram Pancha yat: 22.

Border Villages: (Orissa)- Nearest Villages- Battili, Gurandi, Neradi, Nulakajodu, Singidi, Pasukudi, Burujo la, Bhamini, Liviri, Dimmidijola, Palavalasa, Manumukonda, Vaddangi, Solikiri, Ghanasara, Kosali.

Villages: 22 **Inhabited:** 22 **Uninhabited:** 0

Ranking	District	State	National
Area	32	1004	5643
Population	35	793	5688
Sex Ratio	8	78	551
Child Sex Ratio	9	209	645
Literacy Rate	34	863	5113
Density	5	514	2856
Work Participation Rate	32	213	1336

Gram Panchayats:

Baleru, Battili, Bellumada, Bhamini, Burujola Chinnadimili, Dimmidijola, Ghanasara, Katragada Keesara, Korama, Kosali, Liviri, Maniga, Manumakonda Neradi, Nulakajodu, Pasukudi, Peddadimili, Sativada Thalada, Vaddangi.

Amenities:

Education: Primary School in 22 villages, Middle school in 7 villages, Matriculation or Secondary School in 4 villages, namely Battili, Bhamini, Solikiri, Peddadimili.

Higher Secondary or Pre University Courses or Intermediate or Junior College in 0 village of the CD Block, College in 0 village, Adult Literacy Center in 7 villages.

Medical: Hospital in 0 village, Dispensary in 1 village, Health Center in 2 villages, Sub Center in 9 villages, Maternity and Child Welfare Center in 1 village, Community health workers in 0 village.

The Village having Hospital or Dispensary or Health Center is Battili.

Drinking Water: Tap water in 22 villages, Tank water in 22 villages, Well water in 22 villages, Tubewell in 22 villages and more than one source in 22 villages.

Bank: Banking facility in 2 villages, namely, Battili, Bhamini.

Credit Society in 8 villages Agricultural Credit Society in 5 Non-Agricultural Credit Society in 5 villages.

Others: Power supply in 22 villages, Cinema hall in 1 village, sport club in 0 village, Stadium or Auditorium or Community Hall in 0 village, Post Office in 10 villages.

There are 19 villages having bus facilities.

Villages with most of facilities: Battili, Bhamini.

Villages without Amenities (Education): None..

Scheduled Castes: Out of the total population of 41058 persons, 7495 persons (18.25%) belong to Scheduled Castes.

The villages having less than 10% SC population are Palavalasa, Manumukonda, Bommika, Pasukudi, Burujola Maniga, Kosali.

The villages having more than 50% SC population are None.

Sex ratio of Scheduled Caste population is 515.

Scheduled Castes Literates and Illiterates by Sex:

	Persons	Males	Females
Literate	2,493	1,536	957
Illiterate	5,002	2,098	2,904
Literacy rate	39.3	50.1	29.2
Graduate	78	69	9

Scheduled Castes (Dominant):

Mala, Madiga, Dom etc., Relli, Pamidi

For their cultural identity please see Appendix-I

Villages without Scheduled Castes: There are 2 villages without any scheduled caste population.

Scheduled Tribes: Out of the total population of 41058

persons, 8178 persons (19.92%) belong to Scheduled Tribes. The villages having less than 10% ST population are Battili, Gurandi, Neradi, Nulakajodu, Singidi Chinnadimili.

The villages having more than 50% ST population are None.

Sex ratio of Scheduled tribe population is 503.

Scheduled Tribes Literates and Illiterates by Sex:

	Persons	Males	Females
Literate	2,304	1,505	799
Illiterate	5,874	2,559	3,315
Literacy rate	34.1	44.7	23.5
Graduate	34	29	5

Scheduled Tribes (Dominant):

Savaras etc., Jatapus, Porja etc., Kondhs etc. Konda Dhoras

For their cultural identity please see Appendix-II

Villages without Scheduled Tribes: There is 1 village without any scheduled tribe population.

Literates and Illiterates by Sex (Total Population):

	Persons	Males	Females
Literate	16,024	9,721	6,303
Illiterate	25,034	10,544	14,490
Literacy rate	46	57	36
Graduate	417	361	56

Agriculture: ***Distribution of villages according to land use:*** Out of 22 villages, Total area (in hectare) is 10708, out of that 77.61 percent is cultivable and 36.19 percent of the cultivable area is irrigated.

Sources of Irrigation (Hectares): Government Canal 0, Private Canal 0, Well without Electricity 131, Well with Electricity 55, Tubewell without Electricity 118, Tubewell with Electricity 192, Tank 2335, River 0, Lake 0, Waterfall 0, Others 176.

Villages with population of 5000 to 9999: Battili.

Villages with population of 10000 and above: None

Distribution of Workers:

	Persons	Males	Females	WPR
Cultivators	3,745	2,575	1,170	17.52
Agricultural Labour	13,936	7,097	6,839	65.19
Household Industry	701	387	314	3.28
Other Workers	2,994	2,107	887	14.01
Main Workers	15,372	9,595	5,777	71.91
Marginal Workers	6,004	2,571	3,433	28.09
Total Workers	21,376	12,166	9,210	

Religion: Major Religious Communities:

	Persons	Males	Females	Sex Ratio
Hindu (98.48%)	40,434	19,970	20,464	1,025
Muslim (0.05%)	20	8	12	1,500
Christian (1.39%)	570	269	301	1,119
Sikh (0%)	-	-	-	-
Buddhists (0%)	-	-	-	-
Jain (0%)	-	-	-	-

Agewise Data:

	Persons	Males	Females	Sex Ratio
All ages	41,058	20,265	20,793	1026
0-14	13,380	6,811	6,569	964
15-44	19,552	9,599	9,953	1037
45-79	7,808	3,699	4,109	1111
80+	274	127	147	1157
Age not stated	44	29	15	517

Languages (Dominant):

Telugu, Oriya, Savara, Others, Jatapu

Disabled Population:

	Persons	Males	Females	%
Total Disabled	802	418	384	
In Seeing	405	195	210	50.5
In Speech	79	41	38	9.85
In Hearing	50	23	27	6.23
In Movement	182	119	63	22.69
Mentally	86	40	46	10.72

BHATTIPROLU

Bhattiprolu C.D. Block lies in the south-eastern part of Guntur district. The Block is located at a distance of 35 kms. from district headquarters (Guntur). There are 12 villages in the block with the total population of 51,385 persons. Area of the C.D. Block is 97.80 sq. kms. It is bounded in the north by Mandals Vemuru and Kollur, and district Krishna in the south by Manda ls Nagaram and Repalle and district Krishna in the east by district Krishna and River Krishna, and in the west by Mandal Cherukupalle.

Communications:

Roadways : NH- 214 A: Direction- Madras to Machilipatnam. Nearest Villages- Sivangulapalem, Gorigapudi, Addepalli, Bhattiprolu, Surepalle, Konetipuram, Pedapulivarru.

Railway Station: Bhattiprolu, Pallekona.

River: Krishna Nadi- Nearest Villages- Pesarlanka, Pedalanka, Oleru.

Annual Rainfall: Average Rainfall 910 mm

Ground Water: Availability of the Ground Water in the Basin is 4954 H.A.M. and the utilization is 1304 H. A.M. It belongs to Safe category. Depth to water level varies from 2 to 5 meter below the ground. Most of the wells go down in summer months.

Natural Division Krishna Delta Region

Administration:

Division: Coastal Andhra. Parliamentary Constituency: 32 Bapatla (SC). District: Guntur. Mandal: Bhattiprolu. Assembly Constituency: 208 Vemuru (SC). Gram Panchayat:

16

Places of Tourist Interest:

Bhattiprolu : Bhattiprolu is situated at a distance of about 10 kms. to the north of Repalle town. It is connected by road and is a railway station on the Repal le Guntur broad gauge line of the South Central Railway. The town contains a damaged Buddhist Stupa and marble pillars. The Stupa according to the Archaeological department yielded three votive caskets.

Pedapulivarru : This ancient village lies 8 kms. to the north of Repalle town, on the right bank of the Krishna river and is connected by a road from Vellatura nd Bhattiprolu. The temples of Narendreswaraswamy and Varadarajaswamy existing here, are ancient and held in great veneration. The temple of Narendreswaraswamy is situated in the centre of the village and a white marble Sivalingam is installed in the main shrine and it is said that sun rays fall directly on it at sunrise on every Sankranthi day. There is also a huge bronze image of Nataraja called 'Tandaveswara' in this shrine. Facing the Narendreswaraswamy temple is the Varadaraja temple. The templehas a closed Mukhamantapam in front of the three Garbhalayams whichare provided with huge brass covering bearing highly decorative carvings. The brass covering on the doorway of the Central Garbha

Villages: 12 **Inhabited:** 12 **Uninhabited:** 0

Ranking	District	State	National
Area	47	973	5568
Population	33	467	5208
Sex Ratio	13	323	1402
Child Sex Ratio	30	600	2450
Literacy Rate	14	133	1782
Density	43	715	2424
Work Participation Rate	14	135	2031

Gram Panchayats:

Addapalli, Allamudi, Bhattiprolu, Chintamotu Gorigapudi, Ilavaram, Kannegantivaripalem Konetipuram, Oleru, Pallikona, Pedalanka Pedapulivarru, Pesaralanka, Rachuru, Sureepalle Vellaturu.

Amenities:

Education: Primary School in 12 villages, Middle school in 8 villages, Matriculation or Secondary School in 8 villages, namely Addepalli, Bhattiprolu, Surepalle, Pallekona, Pedapulivarru, Vellaturu, Pesarlanka, Oleru.

Higher Secondary or Pre University Courses or Intermediate or Junior College in 2 villages of the CD Block,, namely Bhattiprolu, Vellaturu.

College in 1 village, Adult Literacy Center in 0 village., College is in village, namely Bhattiprolu.

Medical: Hospital in 0 village, Dispensary in 1 village, Health Center in 2 villages, Sub Center in 8 villages, Maternity and Child Welfare Center in 0 village, Community health workers in 0 village.

The Village having Hospital or Dispensary or Health Center is Bhattiprolu.

Drinking Water: Tap water in 12 villages, Tank water in 12 villages, Well water in 12 villages, Tubewell in 12 villages and more than one source in 12 villages.

Bank: Banking facility in 2 villages, namely, Bhattiprolu, Pedapulivarru.

Credit Society in 6 villages Agricultural Credit Society in 3 Non-Agricultural Credit Society in 1 village.

Others: Power supply in 12 villages, Cinema hall in 2 villages, sport club in 0 village, Stadium or Auditorium or Community Hall in 0 village, Post Office in 10 villages.

There are 12 villages having bus facilities.

Villages with most of facilities: Bhattiprolu Pedapulivarru.

Villages without Amenities (Education): None..

Scheduled Castes: Out of the total population of 51385 persons, 13353 persons (25.99%) belong to Scheduled Castes.

The villages having less than 10% SC population are None..

The villages having more than 50% SC population are None.

Sex ratio of Scheduled Caste population is 495.

Scheduled Castes Literates and Illiterates by Sex:

	Persons	Males	Females
Literate	7,175	4,009	3,166
Illiterate	6,178	2,729	3,449
Literacy rate	61.1	67.8	54.3
Graduate	306	220	86

Scheduled Castes (Dominant):

Mala, Madiga, Generic Castes etc., Holeya Dasari Beda Jangam etc.

For their cultural identity please see Appendix-I

Villages without Scheduled Castes: There are 0 village without any scheduled caste population.

Scheduled Tribes: Out of the total population of 51385 persons, 2033 persons (3.96%) belong to Scheduled Tribes.

The villages having less than 10% ST population are Sivangulapalem, Addepalli, Bhattiprolu, Surepalle Konetipuram, Pallekona, Gorigapudi, Pedapulivarru Pesarlanka, Pedalanka, Oleru.

The villages having more than 50% ST population are None.

Sex ratio of Scheduled tribe population is 498.

Scheduled Tribes Literates and Illiterates by Sex:

	Persons	Males	Females

Literate	697	387	310
Illiterate	1,336	633	703
Literacy rate	39.8	44.1	35.5
Graduate	7	6	1

Scheduled Tribes (Dominant):

Yenadis, Yerukulas, Sugalis etc., Chenchu etc.

For their cultural identity please see Appendix-II

Villages without Scheduled Tribes: There is 1 village without any scheduled tribe population.

Literates and Illiterates by Sex (Total Population):

	Persons	Males	Females
Literate	30,243	16,673	13,570
Illiterate	21,142	9,099	12,043
Literacy rate	66	73	59
Graduate	1,693	1,235	458

Agriculture: ***Distribution of villages according to land use:*** Out of 12 villages, Total area (in hectare) is 11292, out of that 66.91 percent is cultivable and 99.37 percent of the cultivable area is irrigated.

Sources of Irrigation (Hectares): Government Canal 6966.71, Private Canal 0, Well without Electricity 0, Well with Electricity 0, Tubewell without Electricity 0, Tubewell with Electricity 1363.46, Tank 0, River 0, Lake 0, Waterfall 0, Others 0.

Villages with population of 5000 to 9999: Addepalli, Pedapulivarru, Vellaturu.

Villages with population of 10000 and above: Bhattiprolu.

Distribution of Workers:

	Persons	Males	Females	WPR
Cultivators	2,935	2,521	414	11
Agricultural Labour	15,244	7,522	7,722	57.12
Household Industry	3,598	1,747	1,851	13.48
Other Workers	4,913	3,892	1,021	18.41
Main Workers	23,454	14,518	8,936	87.88
Marginal Workers	3,236	1,164	2,072	12.12
Total Workers	26,690	15,682	11,008	

Religion: Major Religious Communities:

	Persons	Males	Females	Sex Ratio
Hindu (92.74%)	47,652	23,897	23,755	994
Muslim (4.33%)	2,223	1,112	1,111	999
Christian (2.76%)	1,416	717	699	975
Sikh (0%)	1	-	1	-
Buddhists (0.01%)	3	2	1	500
Jain (0%)	-	-	-	-

Agewise Data:

	Persons	Males	Females	Sex Ratio
All ages	51,385	25,772	25,613	994
0-14	13,958	7,146	6,812	953
15-44	24,405	12,301	12,104	984
45-79	12,408	6,023	6,385	1060
80+	552	275	277	1007
Age not stated	62	27	35	1296

Languages (Dominant):

Telugu, Urdu, Hindi, Tamil, Malayalam

Disabled Population:

	Persons	Males	Females	%
Total Disabled	949	515	434	
In Seeing	342	184	158	36.04
In Speech	141	62	79	14.86
In Hearing	41	20	21	4.32
In Movement	306	188	118	32.24
Mentally	119	61	58	12.54

BHEEMADEVARPALLE

Bheemadevarpalle C.D. Block lies in the southern part of Karimnagar district. The Block is located at a dista nce of 55 kms. from district headquarters (Karimnagar). There are 13 villages in the block with the total population of 39,657 persons. Area of the C.D. Block is 115.63 sq. kms. It is bounded by Huzurabad Mandal on north, Elkathuthi Mandal on east, Warangal district on south, Husnabad Mandal on west, and Saidapur Mandal on north-west.

Communications :

Roadways : State Highway (S.H.): Direction- Karimnagar to Warangal Nearest Villages- Gatlanarsingapur, Kothako nda.

Backwards Region Grants Fund: It receives Backward Region Grants.

Integrated Child Development Scheme (ICDS) Project: Bheemadevarpalle, Total Anganwadi Centres: 175

Annual Rainfall: Average Rainfall 832 mm

Ground Water: Availability of the Ground Water in the Basin is 1520 H.A.M. and the utilization is 1439 H. A.M. It belongs to Critical category. Depth to water level varies from more than 10 meter below the ground. Most of the wells go down in summer months. The well density in the entire block is 32 wells per sq. km. Total no. of the wells in the block are enumerated as 5737, according to the Ground Water Estimation Commi ttee.

Natural Division : Godavari Depression Region

Administration:

Division: Telangana. Parliamentary Constituency: 3 Karimnagar. District: Karimnagar. Mandal: Bheemadevarpa lle. Assembly Constituency: 32 Husnabad. Gram Panchayat: 20

Villages: 15 **Inhabited:** 15 **Uninhabited:** 0

Ranking	**District**	**State**	**National**
Area	31	677	4566

Population	17	388	5076
Sex Ratio	47	539	1933
Child Sex Ratio	17	299	1029
Literacy Rate	20	571	4114
Density	48	767	3476
Work Participation Rate	17	359	2238

Gram Panchayats:

Bheemdevarapalli, Bollonipalli, Chapaganithanda Dharmaram, Erabelli, Gatlanarsingapoor, Kannaram Katkur, Koppur, Kothakonda, Kothapalli, Mallaram Manikyapoor, Mulkanoor, Mustafapoor, Mutharam Ramnagar, Rangaiahpalli, Rathnagiri, Vangara.

Amenities:

Education: Primary School in 15 villages, Middle school in 14 villages, Matriculation or Secondary School in 9 villages, namely Vangara, Bheemadevarpalle, Manikyapur, Kothapalle, Mulkanoor, Gatlanarsingapur, Kothakonda, Mallaram, Katkur.

Higher Secondary or Pre University Courses or Intermediate or Junior College in 1 village of the CD Block,, namely Mulkanoor.

College in 0 village, Adult Literacy Center in 12 villages.

Medical: Hospital in 1 village, Dispensary in 1 village, Health Center in 2 villages, Sub Center in 9 villages, Maternity and Child Welfare Center in 0 village, Community health workers in 0 village.

The Villages having Hospital or Dispensary or Health Center are Vangara, Mulkanoor.

Drinking Water: Tap water in 15 villages, Tank water in 15 villages, Well water in 15 villages, Tubewell in 15 villages and more than one source in 15 villages.

Bank: Banking facility in 3 villages, namely, Vangara, Mulkanoor, Katkur.

Credit Society in 14 villages Agricultural Credit Society in 1 Non-Agricultural Credit Society in 14 villages.

Others: Power supply in 15 villages, Cinema hall in 2 villages, sport club in 0 village, Stadium or Auditorium or Community Hall in 0 village, Post Office in 15 villages.

There are 15 villages having bus facilities.

Villages with most of facilities: Vangara Mulkanoor, Katkur.

Villages without Amenities (Education): None..

Scheduled Castes: Out of the total population of 54379 persons, 11240 persons (20.67%) belong to Scheduled Castes.

The villages having less than 10% SC population are None..

The villages having more than 50% SC population are None.

Sex ratio of Scheduled Caste population is 501.

Scheduled Castes Literates and Illiterates by Sex:

	Persons	Males	Females
Literate	4,545	2,770	1,775
Illiterate	6,695	2,842	3,853
Literacy rate	46.6	56.7	36.5
Graduate	123	108	15

Scheduled Castes (Dominant):

Madiga, Mala, Gosangi, Beda Jangam etc., Dakkal etc.

For their cultural identity please see Appendix-I

Villages without Scheduled Castes: There are 0 village without any scheduled caste population.

Scheduled Tribes: Out of the total population of 54379 persons, 4051 persons (7.45%) belong to Scheduled Tribes.

The villages having less than 10% ST population are Vangara, Bheemadevarpalle, Ratnagiri, Manikyapur Koppur, Kothapalle, Mulkanoor, Mutharam (P.K) Gatlanarsingapur, Kothakonda, Kannaram.

The villages having more than 50% ST population are None.

Sex ratio of Scheduled tribe population is 489.

Scheduled Tribes Literates and Illiterates by Sex:

	Persons	Males	Females
Literate	1,294	864	430
Illiterate	2,757	1,206	1,551
Literacy rate	38.0	49.1	26.0
Graduate	19	19	0

Scheduled Tribes (Dominant):

Sugalis etc., Yerukulas, Thoti, Gond etc. Chenchu etc.

For their cultural identity please see Appendix-II

Villages without Scheduled Tribes: There is 1 village without any scheduled tribe population.

Literates and Illiterates by Sex (Total Population):

	Persons	Males	Females
Literate	24,856	15,532	9,324
Illiterate	29,523	11,906	17,617
Literacy rate	53	65	40
Graduate	866	760	106

Agriculture: ***Distribution of villages according to land use:*** Out of 15 villages, Total area (in hectare) is 17819, out of that 65.81 percent is cultivable and 50.51 percent of the cultivable area is irrigated.

Sources of Irrigation (Hectares): Government Canal 0, Private Canal 0, Well without Electricity 0, Well with Electricity 4020.83, Tubewell without Electricity 0, Tubewell with Electricity 13.75, Tank 1888.48, River 0, Lake 0, Waterfall 0, Others 0.

Villages with population of 5000 to 9999: Vangara, Mulkanoor.

Villages with population of 10000 and above: None

Distribution of Workers:

	Persons	Males	Females	WPR
Cultivators	9,712	6,051	3,661	35.79
Agricultural Labour	11,298	4,377	6,921	41.63
Household Industry	955	497	458	3.52
Other Workers	5,171	4,052	1,119	19.06
Main Workers	22,355	13,724	8,631	82.38
Marginal Workers	4,781	1,253	3,528	17.62
Total Workers	27,136	14,977	12,159	

Religion: Major Religious Communities:

	Persons	Males	Females	Sex Ratio
Hindu (97.07%)	52,784	26,621	26,163	983
Muslim (2.46%)	1,336	686	650	948
Christian (0.37%)	202	100	102	1,020
Sikh (0.03%)	17	9	8	889
Buddhists (0.01%)	4	2	2	1,000
Jain (0.01%)	4	2	2	1,000

Agewise Data:

	Persons	Males	Females	Sex Ratio
All ages	54,379	27,438	26,941	982
0-14	17,304	8,917	8,387	941
15-44	24,538	12,275	12,263	999
45-79	11,978	5,972	6,006	1006
80+	511	252	259	1028
Age not stated	48	22	26	1182

Languages (Dominant):

Telugu, Hindi, Urdu, Tamil, Marathi

Disabled Population:

	Persons	Males	Females	%
Total Disabled	1,164	719	445	
In Seeing	689	451	238	59.19
In Speech	96	50	46	8.25
In Hearing	43	17	26	3.69
In Movement	259	153	106	22.25
Mentally	77	48	29	6.62

BHEEMGAL

Bheemgal C.D. Block lies in the eastern part of Nizamab ad district. The Block is located at a distance of 55 kms. from district headquarters (Nizamabad). There are 24 villages in the block with the total population of 57,262 persons. Area of the C.D. Block is 222.62 sq. kms. It is bounded by Mortad Mandal on north, Kamma rpalle Mandal on north-east, east, south-east, south and south-west, Sirkonda Mandal on south-west, Jakranpa lle Mandal on south-west and west, Velpur Mandal on north-west.

Communications :

Roadways : Metalled Roads: Nearest Villages- Babapur, Kupkal, Mendhora, Babanagar, Bheemgal.

River: Phulang Nadi- Nearest Villages- Bheemgal, Bejjora, Sikandrapur, Gongappul, Salampur.

Backwards Region Grants Fund: It receives Backward Region Grants.

Integrated Child Development Scheme (ICDS) Project: Bheemgal, Total Anganwadi Centres: 247

Annual Rainfall: Average Rainfall 1040 mm

Ground Water: Availability of the Ground Water in the Basin is 2724 H.A.M. and the utilization is 3669 H. A.M. It belongs to Over Exploited category. Depth to water level varies from 10 to 20 meter below the ground. Most of the wells go down in summer months, according to the Ground Water Estimation Committee.

Natural Division : Telangana Plateau Region

Administration:

Division: Telangana Parliamentary Constituency: 4 Nizam abad. District: Nizamabad. Mandal: Bheemgal. Assembly Constituency: 19 Balkonda. Gram Panchayat: 18.

Villages: 24 **Inhabited:** 24 **Uninhabited:** 0

Ranking	District	State	National
Area	16	428	3809
Population	10	320	4955
Sex Ratio	10	33	299
Child Sex Ratio	16	440	1580
Literacy Rate	8	634	4335
Density	14	297	3995
Work Participation Rate	16	513	754

Gram Panchayats:

Baba Nagar, Babapoor, Bachanapally, Badabheemgal Bejjora, Bheemgal, Chengal, Devakkapet, Gongoppula Jagiryal, Kupkal, Mendora, Muchkoor, Pallikonda Pipri (J), Puranipet, Rahatnagar, Secundrapoor.

Amenities:

Education: Primary School in 24 villages, Middle school in 15 villages, Matriculation or Secondary School in 10 villages, namely Changal, Pedda Bheemgal, Babapur, Mendhora, Bheemgal, Bejjora, Sikandrapur, Gongappul, Muchkur, Pallikonda.

Higher Secondary or Pre University Courses or Intermediate or Junior College in 1 village of the CD Block,, namely Bheemgal.

College in 0 village, Adult Literacy Center in 16 villages.

Medical: Hospital in 1 village, Dispensary in 1 village, Health Center in 1 village, Sub Center in 11 villages, Maternity and Child Welfare Center in 0 village, Community health workers in 5 villages.

The Villages having Hospital or Dispensary or Health Center are Pedda Bheemgal, Bheemgal.

Drinking Water: Tap water in 24 villages, Tank water in 23 villages, Well water in 24 villages, Tubewell in 23 villages and more than one source in 24 villages.

Bank: Banking facility in 8 villages, namely, Babapur, Babanagar, Puranipet, Bheemgal, Sikandrapur

Gongappul, Muchkur, Pallikonda.
Credit Society in 6 villages Agricultural Credit Society in 2 Non-Agricultural Credit Society in 4 villages.
Others: Power supply in 24 villages, Cinema hall in 1 village, sport club in 0 village, Stadium or Auditorium or Community Hall in 0 village, Post Office in 16 villages.
There are 23 villages having bus facilities.
Villages with most of facilities: Babapur Babanagar, Puranipet, Bheemgal, Sikandrapur Gongappul, Muchkur, Pallikonda.
Villages without Amenities (Education): None..
Scheduled Castes: Out of the total population of 57262 persons, 7584 persons (13.24%) belong to Scheduled Castes.
The villages having less than 10% SC population are Babapur, Kupkal, Mendhora, Lingapurchouth Devan Palle, Karepalle, Rahathnagar, Gangarai Thallapalle.
The villages having more than 50% SC population are None.
Sex ratio of Scheduled Caste population is 518.

Scheduled Castes Literates and Illiterates by Sex:

	Persons	Males	Females
Literate	3,401	2,152	1,249
Illiterate	4,183	1,504	2,679
Literacy rate	51.8	68.4	36.5
Graduate	77	68	9

Scheduled Castes (Dominant):
Madiga, Mala, Gosangi, Chamar etc., Malajangam
For their cultural identity please see Appendix-I
Villages without Scheduled Castes: There are 4 villages without any scheduled caste population.
Scheduled Tribes: Out of the total population of 57262 persons, 5969 persons (10.42%) belong to Scheduled Tribes.
The villages having less than 10% ST population are Changal, Babapur, Jagriyal, Mendhora, Babanagar Puranipet, Bheemgal, Lingapurchouth, Bejjora Salampur, Muchkur, Pipri, Bachanpalle, Pallikonda.
The villages having more than 50% ST population are None.
Sex ratio of Scheduled tribe population is 498.

Scheduled Tribes Literates and Illiterates by Sex:

	Persons	Males	Females
Literate	1,357	1,025	332
Illiterate	4,612	1,973	2,639
Literacy rate	29.3	44.6	14.2
Graduate	5	5	0

Scheduled Tribes (Dominant):
Sugalis etc., Generic Tribes etc., Yerukulas Chenchu etc., Gond etc.
For their cultural identity please see Appendix-II

Villages without Scheduled Tribes: There are 5 villages without any scheduled tribe population.

Literates and Illiterates by Sex (Total Population):

	Persons	Males	Females
Literate	24,793	15,521	9,272
Illiterate	32,469	12,403	20,066
Literacy rate	51	66	37
Graduate	553	468	85

Agriculture: ***Distribution of villages according to land use:*** Out of 24 villages, Total area (in hectare) is 22264, out of that 53.96 percent is cultivable and 30.34 percent of the cultivable area is irrigated.
Sources of Irrigation (Hectares): Government Canal 28.33, Private Canal 0, Well without Electricity 0, Well with Electricity 779.63, Tubewell without Electricity 0, Tubewell with Electricity 1719.22, Tank 1117.68, River 0, Lake 0, Waterfall 0, Others 0.
Villages with population of 5000 to 9999:
Pedda Bheemgal.
Villages with population of 10000 and above:
Bheemgal.

Distribution of Workers:

	Persons	Males	Females	WPR
Cultivators	9,682	6,275	3,407	31.22
Agricultural Labour	4,403	2,376	2,027	14.2
Household Industry	8,993	1,059	7,934	29
Other Workers	7,930	5,489	2,441	25.57
Main Workers	26,904	13,528	13,376	86.76
Marginal Workers	4,104	1,671	2,433	13.24
Total Workers	31,008	15,199	15,809	

Religion: Major Religious Communities:

	Persons	Males	Females	Sex Ratio
Hindu (89.13%)	51,040	24,810	26,230	1,057
Muslim (9.88%)	5,657	2,856	2,801	981
Christian (0.96%)	548	250	298	1,192
Sikh (0%)	-	-	-	-
Buddhists (0%)	-	-	-	-
Jain (0%)	-	-	-	-

Agewise Data:

	Persons	Males	Females	Sex Ratio
All ages	57,262	27,924	29,338	1051
0-14	19,765	10,079	9,686	961
15-44	26,888	12,993	13,895	1069
45-79	10,266	4,708	5,558	1181
80+	250	95	155	1632
Age not stated	93	49	44	898

Languages (Dominant):
Telugu, Hindi, Urdu, Marathi, Gondi

Disabled Population:

	Persons	Males	Females	%

Total Disabled	819	467	352	
In Seeing	361	197	164	44.08
In Speech	70	37	33	8.55
In Hearing	28	12	16	3.42
In Movement	247	153	94	30.16
Mentally	113	68	45	13.8

BHEEMUNIPATNAM

Bheemunipatnam C.D. Block lies in the eastern part of Vishakhapatnam district. It is a part of Bheemunipat nam Mandal. The Block is located at a distance of 42 kms. from district headquarters (Vishakhapatnam). There are 19 villages in the block with the total population of 50,730 persons. Area of the C.D. Block is 110.80 sq. kms. It is bounded in the north by district Viziana garam, in the south by Mandal Vishakhapatnam Rural, in the east by the Bay of Bengal, and in the west by Mandals Padmanabham, Anandapuram and Vishakhapatnam.

Communications :

Roadways : NH- 5: Direction- Vishakhapatnam to Vizianaga ram. Nearest Villages- Bodametlapalem, Dakamarri, Kapul uppada, Nagarapalem, Tallavalasa, Kothavalasa. State Highway (S.H.): Direction- Bheemunipatnam to Anandapuram. Nearest Villages- Tallavalasa, Kothavalasa, Tatituru, Mulakuddu (Rural), Chippada.

River: Rain Fed- Nearest Villages- Nidigattu, Kapuluppa da, Chepalappada, Nerellavalasa (Rural), Tatituru, Nagar apalem, Mulakuddu (Rural), Chippada.

Annaul Rainfall: Average Rainfall 778 mm

Ground Water: Availability of the Ground Water in the Basin is (Information not avavible) H.A.M .and the utilization is (Information not avavible) H.A.M. It belongs to (Information not avavible) category. Depth to water level varies from 3 to 10 meter below the ground. Most of the wells go down in summer months. Coastel Villages: Nearest Villages- Mulakuddu (Rural), Chippada, Annavaram, Nidigattu, Kapuluppada, Chepalapp ada, Nerellavalasa (Rural).

Administration:

Division: Coastal Andhra. Parliamentary Constituency: 21 Visakhapatnam. District: Visakhapatnam. Mandal: Bheemunipatnam. Assembly Constituency: 139 Bhimili. Gram Panchayat: 21.

Places of Tourist Interest:

Bheemunipatnam : About 25 kms. north-east of Vizag is Bheemunipatnam, one of the safest beaches on this part of the coast. It's also the site of the ruins of the east coast's oldest Dutch settlement. A little way inland from here is Hollanders Green, the Dutch cemetery.

Some 90 kms. north of Vizag are the million year old limestone which are filled with fascinating stalagmite and stalactite formations. A further 30 kms. north is the Borra Caves, home to a number of isolated tribal communities.

Bheemunipatnam is situated at a distance of 34 kms. from Vishakhapatnam. The name Bheemunipatnam is said to have been derived after Bhima, the second of the Pandavas. During Bhima after killing the demon king Bakasura, installed the idol of Lord Narasimha the presiding deity of the place. The town is most pictures quely situated, at the mouth of the Chittivalasa, close to the big laterite topped Narasimha Hill, which is formed of deep red soil with brown and purple streaks of rocks. It is one of the oldest municipalities in the country, having been constituted as early as A. D. 1861. This place at first came, to prominence as a settlement of the Dutch, who built a fort and a facto ry in the 17th century A.D. The most important aspect of interest at the place, is the beach, which is perhaps, matchless for its beauty all along the east coast. It is a usual resort for seabathers as it is free from dangerous depths and sharks. Nearer the sea and facing the flagstaff, is a well equipped round bungalow, which, it is said, was originally, the Vizianagaram Raja's resort. The view of the seascape from the Verand ah of the bungalow is captivating. This place was an important port in olden days. It has a light house and it is a minor port, though it is seldom used now. Bheemuni- patnam is undoubtedly a place of holiday resort.

Villages: 19 **Inhabited:** 19 **Uninhabited:** 0

Ranking	District	State	National
Area	34	984	5592
Population	25	477	5228
Sex Ratio	37	799	2704
Child Sex Ratio	34	632	2545
Literacy Rate	18	815	4941
Density	32	1005	2407
Work Participation Rate	9	133	3861

Gram Panchayats:

Amanam, Annavaram, Bodamettapalem, Chepaluppada Chippada, Dakamarri, J.V. Agaraharam, K. Nagarapalem Kapuluppada, Laxmipuram, Majjipeta, Majjivalasa Mulakuddu, Nagarapalem, Narayanarajupeta, Nidigattu Pedanagamayyapalem, Rekhavanipalem, Singanabanda Tallavalasa, Tatituru.

Amenities:

Education: Primary School in 19 villages, Middle school in 9 villages, Matriculation or Secondary School in 4 villages, namely Tatituru, Tallavalasa, Jayanthivani Agraharam, Kapuluppada.

Higher Secondary or Pre University Courses or Intermediate or Junior College in 0 village of the CD Block, College in 0 village, Adult Literacy Center in 14 villages.
Medical: Hospital in 1 village, Dispensary in 2 villages, Health Center in 8 villages, Sub Center in 10 villages, Maternity and Child Welfare Center in 0 village, Community health workers in 0 village.
The Villages having Hospital or Dispensary or Health Center are Chippada, Kothavalasa.
Drinking Water: Tap water in 19 villages, Tank water in 17 villages, Well water in 19 villages, Tubewell in 17 villages and more than one source in 19 villages.
Bank: Banking facility in 1 villages, namely, Kapuluppada.
Credit Society in 1 village Agricultural Credit Society in 1 Non-Agricultural Credit Society in 0 village.
Others: Power supply in 19 villages, Cinema hall in 1 village, sport club in 0 village, Stadium or Auditorium or Community Hall in 0 village, Post Office in 13 villages.
There are 14 villages having bus facilities.
Village with most of facilities: Kapuluppada.
Villages without Amenities (Education): None..
Scheduled Castes: Out of the total population of 50956 persons, 3451 persons (6.77%) belong to Scheduled Castes.
The villages having less than 10% SC population are Bodametlapalem, Dakamarri, Singanabanda, Majjivalasa Tatituru, Nagarapalem, Chippada, Amanam, Annavaram Kothavalasa, Jayanthivani Agraharam, Kapuluppada Chepalappada.
The villages having more than 50% SC population are None.
Sex ratio of Scheduled Caste population is 487.
Scheduled Castes Literates and Illiterates by Sex:

	Persons	Males	Females
Literate	1,614	985	629
Illiterate	1,837	787	1,050
Literacy rate	54.6	65.4	43.5
Graduate	41	34	7

Scheduled Castes (Dominant):
Mala, Relli, Generic Castes etc., Madiga, Bariki
For their cultural identity please see Appendix-I
Villages without Scheduled Castes: There are 0 village without any scheduled caste population.
Scheduled Tribes: Out of the total population of 50956 persons, 13 persons (0.03%) belong to Scheduled Tribes.
The villages having less than 10% ST population are Bodametlapalem, Dakamarri, Narayanarajupeta Singanabanda, Majjivalasa, Tatituru, Nagarapalem Mulakuddu (Rural), Chippada, Amanam, Annavaram Tallavalasa, Kothavalasa, Jayanthivani Agraharam Ramayogi Agraharam, Nidigattu, Kapuluppada Chepalappada, Nerellavalasa (Rural).
The villages having more than 50% ST population are None.
Sex ratio of Scheduled tribe population is 462.
Scheduled Tribes Literates and Illiterates by Sex:

	Persons	Males	Females
Literate	7	4	3
Illiterate	6	3	3
Literacy rate	63.6	66.7	60.0
Graduate	0	0	0

Scheduled Tribes (Dominant):
Yerukulas, Bagata, Konda Dhoras, Generic Tribes etc.
For their cultural identity please see Appendix-II
Villages without Scheduled Tribes: There are 16 villages without any scheduled tribe population.
Literates and Illiterates by Sex (Total Population):

	Persons	Males	Females
Literate	20,552	12,912	7,640
Illiterate	30,404	13,013	17,391
Literacy rate	47	58	36
Graduate	398	311	87

Agriculture: ***Distribution of villages according to land use:*** Out of 19 villages, Total area (in hectare) is 11080, out of that 49.38 percent is cultivable and 24.51 percent of the cultivable area is irrigated.
Sources of Irrigation (Hectares): Government Canal 361.79, Private Canal 0, Well without Electricity 106.8, Well with Electricity 75.63, Tubewell without Electricity 30, Tubewell with Electricity 0, Tank 766.89, River 0, Lake 0, Waterfall 0, Others 0.
Villages with population of 5000 to 9999:
Dakamarri, Chippada, Kapuluppada.
Villages with population of 10000 and above: None
Distribution of Workers:

	Persons	Males	Females	WPR
Cultivators	2,573	1,890	683	11.94
Agricultural Labour	7,538	3,556	3,982	34.99
Household Industry	994	594	400	4.61
Other Workers	10,439	8,028	2,411	48.45
Main Workers	12,277	10,086	2,191	56.99
Marginal Workers	9,267	3,982	5,285	43.01
Total Workers	21,544	14,068	7,476	

Religion: Major Religious Communities:

	Persons	Males	Females	Sex Ratio
Hindu (98.77%)	50,329	25,577	24,752	968
Muslim (0.28%)	142	74	68	919
Christian (0.88%)	449	254	195	768
Sikh (0%)	1	1	-	-
Buddhists (0.02%)	9	6	3	500

Jain (0.01%)	3	3	-	-

Agewise Data:

	Persons	Males	Females	Sex Ratio
All ages	50,956	25,925	25,031	966
0-14	17,331	9,157	8,174	893
15-44	23,700	12,041	11,659	968
45-79	9,673	4,597	5,076	1104
80+	183	86	97	1128
Age not stated	69	44	25	568

Languages (Dominant):

Telugu, Hindi, Malayalam, Urdu, Oriya

Disabled Population:

	Persons	Males	Females	%
Total Disabled	1,131	646	485	
In Seeing	485	272	213	42.88
In Speech	134	70	64	11.85
In Hearing	68	38	30	6.01
In Movement	341	211	130	30.15
Mentally	103	55	48	9.11

BHIKNOOR

Bhiknoor C.D. Block lies in the south-east part of Nizamabad district. The Block is located at a distance of 72 kms. from district headquarters (Nizamabad). There are 19 villages in the block with the total popul ation of 59,645 persons. Area of the C.D. Block is 179. 88 sq. kms. It is bounded by Kamareddy Mandal on north-west and north, Domakonda Mandal on north-east and east, Medak district on south-west, south, south-west and west, and Tadwai Mandal on north-west.

Communications :

Roadways : NH- 7: Direction- Nizamabad to Hyderabad. Nearest Villages- Jangampalle, Anthampalle, Rameshwarp alle, Bhiknoor, Baswapur.

Railway Station: Talmadla, Bhiknoor

Backwards Region Grants Fund: It receives Backward Region Grants.

Annual Rainfall: Average Rainfall 984 mm

Ground Water: Availability of the Ground Water in the Basin is 2074 H.A.M. and the utilization is 2749 H. A.M. It belongs to Over Exploited category. Depth to water level varies from 10 to 20 meter and more than 20 meter below the ground. Most of the wells go down in summer months, according to the Ground Water Estimat ion Committee.

Natural Division : Telangana Plateau Region

Administration:

Division: Telangana. Parliamentary Constituency: 5 Zahirabad. District: Nizamabad. Mandal: Bhiknoor. Assem bly Constituency: 14 Banswada. Gram Panchayat: 18.

Villages: 19 **Inhabited:** 19 **Uninhabited:** 0

Ranking	District	State	National
Area	26	671	4540
Population	8	278	4868
Sex Ratio	32	416	1622
Child Sex Ratio	23	668	2711
Literacy Rate	4	544	4026
Density	19	431	3257
Work Participation Rate	7	306	1071

Gram Panchayats:

Anthampally, Baswapur, Bhagirthpally, Bhiknoor Gurjakunta, Issannapally, Jangampally, Kachapur Kancherla, Laxmidevanpally, Peddamallareddy Pondurthy, Rajampet, Rameshwerpally, Ryagatlapally Shivaipally, Talamadla, Thippapur.

Amenities:

Education: Primary School in 19 villages, Middle school in 10 villages, Matriculation or Secondary School in 8 villages, namely Rajampet, Jangampalle, Talmadla, Tippapur, Kachapur, Bhiknoor, Baswapur, Peddamallareddy.

Higher Secondary or Pre University Courses or Inter-mediate or Junior College in 1 village of the CD Block,, namely Bhiknoor.

College in 1 village, Adult Literacy Center in 16 villages., College is in village, namely Bhiknoor.

Medical: Hospital in 1 village, Dispensary in 1 village, Health Center in 2 villages, Sub Center in 9 villages, Maternity and Child Welfare Center in 0 village, Community health workers in 0 village.

The Village having Hospital or Dispensary or Health Center is Bhiknoor.

Drinking Water: Tap water in 19 villages, Tank water in 19 villages, Well water in 19 villages, Tubewell in 19 villages and more than one source in 19 villages.

Bank: Banking facility in 4 villages, namely, Rajampet, Jangampalle, Bhiknoor, Peddamallareddy.

Credit Society in 12 villages Agricultural Credit Society in 9 Non-Agricultural Credit Society in 2 villages.

Others: Power supply in 19 villages, Cinema hall in 1 village, sport club in 0 village, Stadium or Auditorium or Community Hall in 0 village, Post Office in 13 villages.

There are 18 villages having bus facilities.

Villages with most of facilities: Rajampet Jangampalle, Bhiknoor, Peddamallareddy.

Villages without Amenities (Education): None..

Scheduled Castes: Out of the total population of 59645 persons, 10249 persons (17.18%) belong to Scheduled Castes. The villages having less than 10% SC population are None..

The villages having more than 50% SC population are None.

Sex ratio of Scheduled Caste population is 481.

Scheduled Castes Literates and Illiterates by Sex:

	Persons	Males	Females
Literate	3,832	2,647	1,185
Illiterate	6,417	2,668	3,749
Literacy rate	43.3	57.7	27.9
Graduate	36	32	4

Scheduled Castes (Dominant):

Madiga, Mala, Malajangam, Generic Castes etc.
Gosangi

For their cultural identity please see Appendix-I

Villages without Scheduled Castes: There is 1 village without any scheduled caste population.

Scheduled Tribes: Out of the total population of 59645 persons, 1013 persons (1.7%) belong to Scheduled Tribes. The villages having less than 10% ST population are Peddapalle, Rajampet, Pondurthi, Jangampalle Talmadla, Tippapur, Rameshwarpalle, Anthampalle Laxmidevipalle, Kachapur, Bhiknoor, Gurjakunta Ryegatlapalle, Baswapur, Peddamallareddy, Kancherla Isannapalle, Bhagirathipalle.

The villages having more than 50% ST population are None.

Sex ratio of Scheduled tribe population is 462.

Scheduled Tribes Literates and Illiterates by Sex:

	Persons	Males	Females
Literate	266	206	60
Illiterate	747	339	408
Literacy rate	33.0	47.0	16.3
Graduate	3	3	0

Scheduled Tribes (Dominant):

Sugalis etc., Yerukulas, Generic Tribes etc.
Gond etc.

For their cultural identity please see Appendix-II

Villages without Scheduled Tribes: There are 6 villages without any scheduled tribe population.

Literates and Illiterates by Sex (Total Population):

	Persons	Males	Females
Literate	27,374	17,822	9,552
Illiterate	32,271	12,162	20,109
Literacy rate	53	69	37
Graduate	891	777	114

Agriculture: ***Distribution of villages according to land use:*** Out of 19 villages, Total area (in hectare) is 17988, out of that 67.32 percent is cultivable and 38.36 percent of the cultivable area is irrigated.

Sources of Irrigation (Hectares): Government Canal 0, Private Canal 0, Well without Electricity 0, Well with Electricity 7.32, Tubewell without Electricity 0, Tubewell with Electricity 4369.84, Tank 268.27, River 0, Lake 0, Waterfall 0, Others 0.

Villages with population of 5000 to 9999:

Rajampet, Jangampalle, Peddamallareddy.

Villages with population of 10000 and above:

Bhiknoor.

Distribution of Workers:

	Persons	Males	Females	WPR
Cultivators	11,454	7,054	4,400	35.52
Agricultural Labour	8,447	4,359	4,088	26.19
Household Industry	5,437	729	4,708	16.86
Other Workers	6,909	4,740	2,169	21.43
Main Workers	28,126	15,176	12,950	87.22
Marginal Workers	4,121	1,706	2,415	12.78
Total Workers	32,247	16,882	15,365	

Religion: Major Religious Communities:

	Persons	Males	Females	Sex Ratio
Hindu (95.08%)	56,709	28,508	28,201	989
Muslim (4.54%)	2,706	1,353	1,353	1,000
Christian (0.13%)	80	45	35	778
Sikh (0.03%)	20	11	9	818
Buddhists (0%)	-	-	-	-
Jain (0%)	-	-	-	-

Agewise Data:

	Persons	Males	Females	Sex Ratio
All ages	59,645	29,984	29,661	989
0-14	18,633	9,705	8,928	920
15-44	28,973	14,535	14,438	993
45-79	11,542	5,527	6,015	1088
80+	431	180	251	1394
Age not stated	66	37	29	784

Languages (Dominant):

Telugu, Urdu, Hindi, Tamil, Kannada

Disabled Population:

	Persons	Males	Females	%
Total Disabled	1,035	562	473	
In Seeing	392	193	199	37.87
In Speech	90	44	46	8.7
In Hearing	54	27	27	5.22
In Movement	358	214	144	34.59
Mentally	141	84	57	13.62

BHIMADOLE

Bhimadole C.D. Block lies in the southern part of West Godavari district. The Block is located at a distance of 22 kms. from district headquarters (Eluru). There are 11 villages in the block with the total population of 62,579 persons. Area of the C.D. Block is 211.94sq. kms. It is bounded in the north by Mandal Dwaraka Tirumala, in the south by district Krishna and Mandal Eluru, in the east by Mandals Ungutur and Nidamarru, and in the west by Mandals Eluru and Denduluru.

Communications :

Roadways : NH: Direction- Vijayawada to Tadepalligudem. Nearest Villages- Surappagudem, Bhimadole, Amberpeta, Pulla, Gundugolanu.
Lake: Kolleru- Nearest Villages- Agadallanka, Chettunna padu, Mallavaram, Pulla, Amberpeta.
Railway Station: Bhimadole, Pulla.
Backwards Region Grants Fund: It receives Backward Region Grants.
Integrated Child Development Scheme (ICDS) Project: Bheemadolu, Total Anganwadi Centres: 196
Annaul Rainfall: Average Rainfall 1292 mm
Ground Water: Availability of the Ground Water in the Basin is (Information not avavible) H.A.M .and the utilization is (Information not avavible) H.A.M. It belongs to (Information not avavible) category. Depth to water level varies from 3 to 10 meter below the ground. Most of the wells go down in summer months.
Natural Division : Godavari Delta Region
Administration:
Division: Coastal Andhra. Parliamentary Constituency: 27 Eluru. District: West Godavari. Mandal: Bhimadole. Assembly Constituency: 182 Ungutur. Gram Panchayat: 13
Villages: 11 **Inhabited:** 11 **Uninhabited:** 0

Ranking	District	State	National
Area	8	479	3983
Population	35	234	4767
Sex Ratio	6	203	1052
Child Sex Ratio	31	637	2596
Literacy Rate	14	20	588
Density	16	874	3580
Work Participation Rate	38	382	2873

Gram Panchayats:
Agadalanka, Amberpet, Bhimadole, Chettunnapadu Duddepudi, Gundugolanu, Kodurupadu, Korukollu Kurellagudem, Laxmipuram, Polasanipalli, Pulla Surappagudem.
Amenities:
Education: Primary School in 11 villages, Middle school in 8 villages, Matriculation or Secondary School in 6 villages, namely Polasanipalle, Bhimadole, Amberpeta, Pulla, Gundugolanu, Agadallanka.
Higher Secondary or Pre University Courses or Intermediate or Junior College in 2 villages of the CD Block,, namely Polasanipalle, Bhimadole.
College in 0 village, Adult Literacy Center in 10 villages.
Medical: Hospital in 0 village, Dispensary in 2 villages, Health Center in 2 villages, Sub Center in 8 villages, Maternity and Child Welfare Center in 0 village, Community health workers in 0 village.
The Villages having Hospital or Dispensary or Health Center are Bhimadole, Chettunnapadu.
Drinking Water: Tap water in 11 villages, Tank water in 11 villages, Well water in 11 villages, Tubewell in 11 villages and more than one source in 11 villages.
Bank: Banking facility in 5 villages, namely, Polasanipalle, Bhimadole, Pulla, Gundugolanu Agadallanka.
Credit Society in 2 villages Agricultural Credit Society in 2 Non-Agricultural Credit Society in 0 village.
Others: Power supply in 11 villages, Cinema hall in 3 villages, sport club in 0 village, Stadium or Auditorium or Community Hall in 0 village, Post Office in 8 villages.
There are 9 villages having bus facilities.
Villages with most of facilities: Bhimadole, Pulla Gundugolanu, Agadallanka.
Villages without Amenities (Education): None..
Scheduled Castes: Out of the total population of 62579 persons, 12051 persons (19.26%) belong to Scheduled Castes.
The villages having less than 10% SC population are None..
The villages having more than 50% SC population are None.
Sex ratio of Scheduled Caste population is 513.
Scheduled Castes Literates and Illiterates by Sex:

	Persons	Males	Females
Literate	7,846	3,980	3,866
Illiterate	4,205	1,894	2,311
Literacy rate	74.6	78.4	71.0
Graduate	198	143	55

Scheduled Castes (Dominant):
Mala, Madiga, Adi Andhra, Relli, Mala Dasu
For their cultural identity please see Appendix-I
Villages without Scheduled Castes: There are 2 villages without any scheduled caste population.
Scheduled Tribes: Out of the total population of 62579 persons, 392 persons (0.63%) belong to Scheduled Tribes.
The villages having less than 10% ST population are Polasanipalle, Surappagudem, Bhimadole, Amberpeta Duddepudi, Kodurupadu, Pulla, Gundugolanu Agadallanka, Chettunnapadu, Mallavaram.
The villages having more than 50% ST population are None.
Sex ratio of Scheduled tribe population is 500.
Scheduled Tribes Literates and Illiterates by Sex:

	Persons	Males	Females
Literate	220	115	105
Illiterate	172	81	91
Literacy rate	66.5	69.3	63.6
Graduate	1	1	0

Scheduled Tribes (Dominant):
Yerukulas, Yenadis, Sugalis etc., Kammara, Koya etc.
For their cultural identity please see Appendix-II
Villages without Scheduled Tribes: There are 5 villages without any scheduled tribe population.

Literates and Illiterates by Sex (Total Population):

	Persons	Males	Females
Literate	41,811	21,950	19,861
Illiterate	20,768	9,275	11,493
Literacy rate	76	80	72
Graduate	1,243	924	319

Agriculture: ***Distribution of villages according to land use:*** Out of 11 villages, Total area (in hectare) is 21194, out of that 53.71 percent is cultivable and 97.72 percent of the cultivable area is irrigated.

Sources of Irrigation (Hectares): Government Canal 8891, Private Canal 0, Well without Electricity 0, Well with Electricity 0, Tubewell without Electricity 0, Tubewell with Electricity 2125, Tank 108, River 0, Lake 0, Waterfall 0, Others 0.

Villages with population of 5000 to 9999:
Amberpeta, Agadallanka.

Villages with population of 10000 and above:
Bhimadole, Pulla, Gundugolanu.

Distribution of Workers:

	Persons	Males	Females	WPR
Cultivators	3,325	3,086	239	11.05
Agricultural Labour	22,139	12,413	9,726	73.58
Household Industry	448	184	264	1.49
Other Workers	4,178	3,498	680	13.89
Main Workers	22,409	15,921	6,488	74.47
Marginal Workers	7,681	3,260	4,421	25.53
Total Workers	30,090	19,181	10,909	

Religion: Major Religious Communities:

	Persons	Males	Females	Sex Ratio
Hindu (93.49%)	58,507	29,232	29,275	1,001
Muslim (1.06%)	666	330	336	1,018
Christian (5.34%)	3,339	1,627	1,712	1,052
Sikh (0.03%)	16	11	5	455
Buddhists (0%)	-	-	-	-
Jain (0%)	-	-	-	-

Agewise Data:

	Persons	Males	Females	Sex Ratio
All ages	62,579	31,225	31,354	1004
0-14	19,348	9,641	9,707	1007
15-44	30,589	15,327	15,262	996
45-79	12,199	6,035	6,164	1021
80+	393	191	202	1058
Age not stated	50	31	19	613

Languages (Dominant):
Telugu, Urdu, Hindi, Tamil, Gondi

Disabled Population:

	Persons	Males	Females	%
Total Disabled	850	483	367	
In Seeing	275	149	126	32.35
In Speech	104	61	43	12.24
In Hearing	47	20	27	5.53
In Movement	271	169	102	31.88
Mentally	153	84	69	18

BHIMAVARAM

Bhimavaram C.D. Block lies in the southern part of West Godavari district. It is a part of Bhimavaram Mandal. The Block is located at a distance of 65 kms. from district headquarters (Eluru). There are 14 villa ges in the block with the total population of 76,403 persons. Area of the C.D. Block is 158 sq. kms. It is bounded in the north by Mandals Undi and Palacoderu, in the south by district Krishna and Mandal Mogalthur, in the east by Mandals Narasapuram, Veeravasaram and Palacoderu, and in the west by Mandal Kalla.

Communications :
Roadways : Metalled Roads: Nearest Villages- Narasimhapu ram, Kovvada, Chinamiram (Rural), Taderu, Bethapudi, Tundurru.
River: Upputeru Nadi- Nearest Villages- Taderu, Yenamad urru, Komarada, Anakoderu, Losarigutlapadu, Dirusumarru, Bethapudi, Tundurru, Vempa.
Backwards Region Grants Fund: It receives Backward Region Grants.
Annaul Rainfall: Average Rainfall 1396 mm

Ground Water: Availability of the Ground Water in the Basin is (Information not avavible) H.A.M .and the utilization is (Information not avavible) H.A.M. It belongs to (Information not avavible) category. Depth to water level varies from 3 to 10 meter below the ground. Most of the wells go down in summer months.
Forest and Reserved **Forest:** Nearest Villages- Losarigut lapadu, Dirusumarru, Vempa.
Natural Division : Godavari Delta Region
Administration:
Division: Coastal Andhra. Parliamentary Constituency: 26 Narsapuram. District: West Godavari. Mandal: Bhimava ram. Assembly Constituency: 178 Bhimavaram. Gram Panchay at: 25.

Villages: 14 **Inhabited:** 14 **Uninhabited:** 0

Ranking	District	State	National
Area	19	785	4915
Population	7	52	4206
Sex Ratio	30	553	1984
Child Sex Ratio	28	518	1996

Literacy Rate	21	43	926
Density	24	914	2268
Work Participation Rate	24	117	3177

Gram Panchayats:
Anakoderu, Annavaram, Bethapudi, Chinamiram Deyyalatippa, Dirusumarru, Dongapindi Gollavanitippa, Gutlapadu, Jonnalagaruvu, Komarada Komatitippa (North), Kothapusalamarru, Losari Lvn Puram, Nagidipalem, Narasimhapuram, Pedagaruvu Rayalam, Sriramapuram, Taderu, Thokatippa, Tundurru Vempa, Yenamadurru.

Amenities:

Education: Primary School in 14 villages, Middle school in 11 villages, Matriculation or Secondary School in 7 villages, namely Chinamiram (Rural), Taderu, Anakoderu, Losarigutlapadu, Dirusumarru, Tundurru, Vempa.
Higher Secondary or Pre University Courses or Intermediate or Junior College in 0 village of the CD Block, College in 1 village, Adult Literacy Center in 14 villages., College is in village, namely Chinamiram (Rural).

Medical: Hospital in 0 village, Dispensary in 1 village, Health Center in 1 village, Sub Center in 11 villages, Maternity and Child Welfare Center in 0 village, Community health workers in 0 village.
The Village having Hospital or Dispensary or Health Center is Vempa.

Drinking Water: Tap water in 14 villages, Tank water in 14 villages, Well water in 14 villages, Tubewell in 14 villages and more than one source in 14 villages.

Bank: Banking facility in 5 villages, namely, Chinamiram (Rural), Losarigutlapadu, Dirusumarru Tundurru, Vempa.
Credit Society in 5 villages Agricultural Credit Society in 5 Non-Agricultural Credit Society in 0 village.

Others: Power supply in 14 villages, Cinema hall in 1 village, sport club in 1 village, Stadium or Auditorium or Community Hall in 0 village, Post Office in 12 villages.
There are 14 villages having bus facilities.

Villages with most of facilities: Chinamiram (Rural) Losarigutlapadu, Dirusumarru, Tundurru, Vempa.

Villages without Amenities (Education): None..

Scheduled Castes: Out of the total population of 77148 persons, 6637 persons (8.6%) belong to Scheduled Castes.
The villages having less than 10% SC population are Annavaram, Kovvada, Yenamadurru, Komarada, Anakoderu Losarigutlapadu, Dirusumarru, Tundurru.
The villages having more than 50% SC population are None.
Sex ratio of Scheduled Caste population is 501.

Scheduled Castes Literates and Illiterates by Sex:

	Persons	Males	Females
Literate	4,209	2,211	1,998
Illiterate	2,428	1,099	1,329
Literacy rate	72.9	76.8	68.9
Graduate	108	77	31

Scheduled Castes (Dominant):
Mala, Madiga, Adi Andhra, Arundhatiya, Relli

For their cultural identity please see Appendix-I

Villages without Scheduled Castes: There are 0 village without any scheduled caste population.

Scheduled Tribes: Out of the total population of 77148 persons, 456 persons (0.59%) belong to Scheduled Tribes.
The villages having less than 10% ST population are Annavaram, Narasimhapuram, Kovvada Chinamiram (Rural), Rayalam (Rural), Taderu Yenamadurru, Komarada, Anakoderu, Losarigutlapadu Dirusumarru, Bethapudi, Tundurru, Vempa.
The villages having more than 50% ST population are None.
Sex ratio of Scheduled tribe population is 485.

Scheduled Tribes Literates and Illiterates by Sex:

	Persons	Males	Females
Literate	147	89	58
Illiterate	309	146	163
Literacy rate	40.1	46.4	33.1
Graduate	4	3	1

Scheduled Tribes (Dominant):
Yerukulas, Yenadis, Savaras etc., Konda Dhoras Konda Kapus

For their cultural identity please see Appendix-II

Villages without Scheduled Tribes: There is 1 village without any scheduled tribe population.

Literates and Illiterates by Sex (Total Population):

	Persons	Males	Females
Literate	48,947	26,372	22,575
Illiterate	28,201	12,579	15,622
Literacy rate	72	77	67
Graduate	1,124	864	260

Agriculture: ***Distribution of villages according to land use:***
Out of 14 villages, Total area (in hectare) is 15801, out of that 55.37 percent is cultivable and 99.98 percent of the cultivable area is irrigated.

Sources of Irrigation (Hectares): Government Canal 8748.14, Private Canal 0, Well without Electricity 0, Well with Electricity 0, Tubewell without Electricity 0, Tubewell with Electricity 0, Tank 0, River 0, Lake 0, Waterfall 0, Others 0.

Villages with population of 5000 to 9999:
Anakoderu, Dirusumarru, Tundurru, Vempa.

Villages with population of 10000 and above:

Losarigutlapadu.

Distribution of Workers:

	Persons	Males	Females	WPR
Cultivators	5,986	5,496	490	16.68
Agricultural Labour	23,687	13,791	9,896	66.01
Household Industry	559	287	272	1.56
Other Workers	5,653	4,516	1,137	15.75
Main Workers	28,462	21,848	6,614	79.31
Marginal Workers	7,423	2,242	5,181	20.69
Total Workers	35,885	24,090	11,795	

Religion: Major Religious Communities:

	Persons	Males	Females	Sex Ratio
Hindu (82.83%)	63,905	32,369	31,536	974
Muslim (0.57%)	441	230	211	917
Christian (16.42%)	12,669	6,285	6,384	1,016
Sikh (0%)	-	-	-	-
Buddhists (0%)	1	1	-	-
Jain (0%)	-	-	-	-

Agewise Data:

	Persons	Males	Females	Sex Ratio
All ages	77,148	38,951	38,197	981
0-14	22,723	11,553	11,170	967
15-44	38,133	19,375	18,758	968
45-79	15,616	7,701	7,915	1028
80+	606	294	312	1061
Age not stated	70	28	42	1500

Languages (Dominant):

Telugu, Urdu, Gondi, Oriya, Hindi

Disabled Population:

	Persons	Males	Females	%
Total Disabled	1,401	739	662	
In Seeing	564	293	271	40.26
In Speech	150	81	69	10.71
In Hearing	78	37	41	5.57
In Movement	456	246	210	32.55
Mentally	153	82	71	10.92

BHIMINI

Bhimini C.D. Block lies in the south-east part of Adila bad district. The Block is located at a distance of 198 kms. from district headquarters (Adilabad). There are 35 villages in the block with the total population of 23,687 persons. Area of the C.D. Block is 242.80 sq. kms. It is bounded by Kagaznagar Mandal on north and north-east, Dahegaon Mandal on north-east, east and south-east, Vemanpalle Mandal on south-east, Nennal Mandal on south-east, south and south-west, Bellampalle Mandal on south-west, Tandur Mandal on south-west, west and north-west, Rebbana Mandal on north-west.

Communications :

Roadways : NH, SH or Important Metalled Road is not available.

River: Pedda Vagu: Nearest Village- Lingapur, Motkupalle, Gollaghat, Rebbena, Veerapur, Ankannapeta, Muthapur, Kannepalle, Metpalle.

Backwards Region Grants Fund: It receives Backward Region Grants.

Mahila Samakhya (Education for Women's Equality): It is decleared Socialy and Educationally Backward Block by the Government.

Annual Rainfall: Average Rainfall 1260 mm

Ground Water: Availability of the Ground Water in the Basin is 1610 H.A.M.and the utilization is 225 H.A. M. It belongs to Safe category. Depth to water level varies from 5 to 10 meter below the ground. Most of the wells go down in summer months, according to the Ground Water Estimation Committee.

Natural Division : Telangana Plateau Region

Administration:

Division: Telangana. Parliamentary Constituency: 3 Peddapalle (SC). District: Adilabad. Mandal: Bhimini. Assembly Constituency: 3 Bellampalle (ST). Gram Pancha yat: 13.

Villages: 35 **Inhabited:** 29 **Uninhabited:** 6

Ranking	District	State	National
Area	34	321	3410
Population	45	1074	6169
Sex Ratio	49	949	3245
Child Sex Ratio	52	1089	5497
Literacy Rate	46	1047	5930
Density	38	718	6166
Work Participation Rate	42	1067	2041

Gram Panchayats:

Bheemini, Jajjarvelly, Jankapur, Kannepalle Karjibheempur, Laxmipur, Mallidi, Metpalle Nayankanpet, Rebbena, Veegaon, Veerapur, Venkatapur.

Amenities:

Education: Primary School in 29 villages, Middle school in 7 villages, Matriculation or Secondary School in 2 villages, namely Bhimini, Kannepalle.

Higher Secondary or Pre University Courses or Intermediate or Junior College in 0 village of the CD Block, College in 0 village, Adult Literacy Center in 8 villages.

Medical: Hospital in 0 village, Dispensary in 1 village, Health Center in 1 village, Sub Center in 6 villages, Maternity and Child Welfare Center in 0 village, Community health workers in 0 village.

The Village having Hospital or Dispensary or Health Center is Kannepalle.

Drinking Water: Tap water in 28 villages, Tank water in 28 villages, Well water in 29 villages, Tubewell in 28 villages and more than one source in 29 villages.

Bank: Banking facility in 2 villages, namely, Bhimini, Jankapur.
Credit Society in 2 villages Agricultural Credit Society in 1 Non-Agricultural Credit Society in 1 village.
Others: Power supply in 29 villages, Cinema hall in 0 village, sport club in 0 village, Stadium or Auditorium or Community Hall in 0 village, Post Office in 9 villages.
There are 13 villages having bus facilities.
Villages with most of facilities: Bhimini Jankapur.
Villages without Amenities (Education): None..
Scheduled Castes: Out of the total population of 23687 persons, 6679 persons (28.2%) belong to Scheduled Castes.
The villages having less than 10% SC population are None..
The villages having more than 50% SC population are Akkalapalle, Rajaram, Rampur, Jankapur, Yellaram Kothapalle.
Sex ratio of Scheduled Caste population is 480.
Scheduled Castes Literates and Illiterates by Sex:

	Persons	Males	Females
Literate	2,093	1,371	722
Illiterate	4,586	2,102	2,484
Literacy rate	36.8	46.9	26.2
Graduate	21	18	3

Scheduled Castes (Dominant):
Mala Sale etc., Madiga, Mala, Manne, Mitha Ayyalvar
For their cultural identity please see Appendix-I
Villages without Scheduled Castes: There are 8 villages without any scheduled caste population.
Scheduled Tribes: Out of the total population of 23687 persons, 1695 persons (7.16%) belong to Scheduled Tribes.
The villages having less than 10% ST population are Karjibheempur, Akkalapalle, Laxmipur, Wadal Peddagudipet, Babapur, Peddapeta, Bhimini Bitturpalle, Mallidi, Venkatapur, Gollaghat, Veegaon Polampalle, Shiknam, Rampur, Tekulapalle, Jankapur Yellaram, Jajjarvelly, Kothapalle, Veerapur Metpalle.
The villages having more than 50% ST population are None.
Sex ratio of Scheduled tribe population is 498.
Scheduled Tribes Literates and Illiterates by Sex:

	Persons	Males	Females
Literate	335	251	84
Illiterate	1,360	600	760
Literacy rate	23.1	34.1	11.8
Graduate	1	1	0

Scheduled Tribes (Dominant):
Kolam etc., Koya etc., Manna Dhora, Pardhan Gond etc.
For their cultural identity please see Appendix-II
Villages without Scheduled Tribes: There are 19 villages without any scheduled tribe population.
Literates and Illiterates by Sex (Total Population):

	Persons	Males	Females
Literate	7,368	4,770	2,598
Illiterate	16,319	7,349	8,970
Literacy rate	36	46	26
Graduate	115	92	23

Agriculture: ***Distribution of villages according to land use:*** Out of 35 villages, Total area (in hectare) is 24764, out of that 59.71 percent is cultivable and 2.99 percent of the cultivable area is irrigated.
Sources of Irrigation (Hectares): Government Canal 0, Private Canal 0, Well without Electricity 0, Well with Electricity 0, Tubewell without Electricity 0, Tubewell with Electricity 9.89, Tank 420.43, River 12.11, Lake 0, Waterfall 0, Others 0.
Villages with population of 5000 to 9999: None
Villages with population of 10000 and above: None
Distribution of Workers:

	Persons	Males	Females	WPR
Cultivators	4,418	3,338	1,080	37.62
Agricultural Labour	4,687	1,694	2,993	39.91
Household Industry	319	238	81	2.72
Other Workers	2,321	1,810	511	19.76
Main Workers	7,171	5,625	1,546	61.06
Marginal Workers	4,574	1,455	3,119	38.94
Total Workers	11,745	7,080	4,665	

Religion: Major Religious Communities:

	Persons	Males	Females	Sex Ratio
Hindu (98.9%)	23,427	11,994	11,433	953
Muslim (0.92%)	219	110	109	991
Christian (0.08%)	19	7	12	1,714
Sikh (0%)	-	-	-	-
Buddhists (0.02%)	5	1	4	4,000
Jain (0%)	-	-	-	-

Agewise Data:

	Persons	Males	Females	Sex Ratio
All ages	23,687	12,119	11,568	955
0-14	8,349	4,378	3,971	907
15-44	10,634	5,375	5,259	978
45-79	4,487	2,256	2,231	989
80+	169	89	80	899
Age not stated	48	21	27	1286

Languages (Dominant):
Telugu, Marathi, Urdu, Hindi, Gondi
Disabled Population:

	Persons	Males	Females	%

Total Disabled	398	213	185	
In Seeing	144	73	71	36.18
In Speech	45	27	18	11.31

In Hearing	44	23	21	11.06
In Movement	119	64	55	29.9
Mentally	46	26	20	11.56

BHOGAPURAM

Bhogapuram C.D. Block lies in the southern part of Vizianagaram district. The Block is located at a distan ce of 20 kms. from district headquarters (Vizianagaram). There are 21 villages in the block with the total population of 52,572 persons. Area of the C.D. Block is 112.84 sq. kms. It is bounded in the north by Mandal Denkada and pusapatiregа, in the south by district Vishakhapatnam, in the east by the Bay of Bengal and Mandal Pusapatirega, and in the west by district Vishak hapatnam and Denkada Mandal.

Communications :

Roadways : NH-5: Direction- Rajapulova to Srikakulam. Nearest Villages- Amatam Ravivalasa, Savaravilli, Polipalle, Rajapulova, Ravada, Bhogapuram. NH- 43: Direction- Vishakhapatnam to Vizianagaram. Nearest Villages- Rajapulova, Cherakupalle, Gudivada.

River: Nellimarla Nadi- Nearest Villages- Kotabhogapuram, Nandigam, Subbannapeta @ Pilakavani Agraharam, Kongavanipalem,

Backwards Region Grants Fund: It receives Backward Region Grants.

Integrated Child Development Scheme (ICDS) Project: Bhogapuram, Total Anganwadi Centres: 208

Annaul Rainfall: Average Rainfall 886.7 mm

Ground Water: Availability of the Ground Water in the Basin is (Information not avavible) H.A.M .and the utilization is (Information not avavible) H.A.M. It belongs to (Information not avavible) category. Depth to water level varies from 3 to 10 meter below the ground. Most of the wells go down in summer months.

Coastel Villages: Nearest Villages- Kongavanipalem, Kancheru, Kancherupalem.

Administration:

Division: Coastal Andhra. Parliamentary Constituency: 20 Vizianagram. District: Vizianagram. Mandal: Bhogapur am. Assembly Constituency: 136 Nellimarla. Gram Panchayat.

Villages: 21 **Inhabited:** 19 **Uninhabited:** 2

Ranking	District	State	National
Area	32	974	5570
Population	16	433	5157
Sex Ratio	30	401	1582
Child Sex Ratio	33	793	3392
Literacy Rate	26	944	5462
Density	31	674	2370
Work Participation Rate	4	129	1879

Gram Panchayats:

A.Ravivalasa, Basavapalem(Thudem), Bhogapuram Byreddipalem, Chakivalasa, Chepala Kancheru Cherukupalli, Dallipeta, Gudepuvalasa, Gudivada Kancheru, Kavulavada, Kondrajupalem, Lingalavalasa Mukkam, Munjeru, Nandigam, Polipilli, Rajapulova Ramachandrapeta, Ravada, Savaravilli.

Amenities:

Education: Primary School in 18 villages, Middle school in 7 villages, Matriculation or Secondary School in 4 villages, namely Bhogapuram, Munjeru, Polipalle, Ravada.

Higher Secondary or Pre University Courses or Intermediate or Junior College in 1 village of the CD Block,, namely Bhogapuram.

College in 0 village, Adult Literacy Center in 17 villages.

Medical: Hospital in 1 village, Dispensary in 2 villages, Health Center in 1 village, Sub Center in 9 villages, Maternity and Child Welfare Center in 0 village, Community health workers in 0 village.

The Villages having Hospital or Dispensary or Health Center are Bhogapuram, Kongavanipalem.

Drinking Water: Tap water in 19 villages, Tank water in 19 villages, Well water in 19 villages, Tubewell in 19 villages and more than one source in 19 villages.

Bank: Banking facility in 2 villages, namely, Bhogapuram, Polipalle.

Credit Society in 9 villages Agricultural Credit Society in 2 Non-Agricultural Credit Society in 8 villages.

Others: Power supply in 19 villages, Cinema hall in 1 village, sport club in 0 village, Stadium or Auditorium or Community Hall in 0 village, Post Office in 12 villages.

There are 13 villages having bus facilities.

Villages with most of facilities: Bhogapuram Polipalle.

Villages without amenities (Education): Kancherupalem..

Scheduled Castes: Out of the total population of 52572 persons, 3914 persons (7.45%) belong to Scheduled Castes. The villages having less than 10% SC population are Kongavanipalem, Jaggayyapeta, Chakivalasa Amatam Ravivalasa, Savaravilli, Polipalle Rajapulova, Gudivada, Ravada, Basavapalem Kavulavada, Kancheru, Kancherupalem.

The villages having more than 50% SC population are None.

Sex ratio of Scheduled Caste population is 494.

Scheduled Castes Literates and Illiterates by Sex:

	Persons	Males	Females
Literate	1,739	1,007	732

Illiterate	2,175	973	1,202
Literacy rate	51.7	60.1	43.4
Graduate	41	31	10

Scheduled Castes (Dominant):

Mala, Relli, Madiga, Adi Andhra, Generic Castes etc.

For their cultural identity please see Appendix-I

Villages without Scheduled Castes: There are 3 villages without any scheduled caste population.

Scheduled Tribes: Out of the total population of 52572 persons, 77 persons (0.15%) belong to Scheduled Tribes. The villages having less than 10% ST population are Bhogapuram, Nandigam
Subbannapeta @ Pilakavani Agraharam
Kongavanipalem, Munjeru, Jaggayyapeta, Chakivalasa
Gudepuvalasa, Amatam Ravivalasa, Savaravilli
Polipalle, Rajapulova, Cherakupalle, Gudivada
Ravada, Basavapalem, Kavulavada, Kancheru
Kancherupalem.

The villages having more than 50% ST population are None.

Sex ratio of Scheduled tribe population is 597.

Scheduled Tribes Literates and Illiterates by Sex:

	Persons	Males	Females
Literate	31	15	16
Illiterate	46	16	30
Literacy rate	49.2	55.6	44.4
Graduate	0	0	0

Scheduled Tribes (Dominant):

Konda Dhoras, Yerukulas, Koya etc., Jatapus, Kammara

For their cultural identity please see Appendix-II

Villages without Scheduled Tribes: There are 17 villages without any scheduled tribe population.

Literates and Illiterates by Sex (Total Population):

	Persons	Males	Females
Literate	19,047	11,483	7,564
Illiterate	33,525	14,940	18,585
Literacy rate	43	51	34
Graduate	433	350	83

Agriculture: ***Distribution of villages according to land use:*** Out of 21 villages, Total area (in hectare) is 11282, out of that 65.06 percent is cultivable and 28.07 percent of the cultivable area is irrigated.

Sources of Irrigation (Hectares): Government Canal 1380.34, Private Canal 0, Well without Electricity 16.14, Well with Electricity 16.54, Tubewell without Electricity 0, Tubewell with Electricity 2.02, Tank 644.91, River 0, Lake 0, Waterfall 0, Others 0.

Villages with population of 5000 to 9999:

Bhogapuram, Kongavanipalem, Kancheru.

Villages with population of 10000 and above: None

Distribution of Workers:

	Persons	Males	Females	WPR
Cultivators	4,685	3,017	1,668	17.84
Agricultural Labour	9,732	3,867	5,865	37.07
Household Industry	773	363	410	2.94
Other Workers	11,065	8,413	2,652	42.14
Main Workers	16,527	12,545	3,982	62.95
Marginal Workers	9,728	3,115	6,613	37.05
Total Workers	26,255	15,660	10,595	

Religion: Major Religious Communities:

	Persons	Males	Females	Sex Ratio
Hindu (99.07%)	52,085	26,168	25,917	990
Muslim (0.24%)	125	65	60	923
Christian (0.54%)	282	149	133	893
Sikh (0%)	1	-	1	-
Buddhists (0%)	-	-	-	-
Jain (0%)	-	-	-	-

Agewise Data:

	Persons	Males	Females	Sex Ratio
All ages	52,572	26,423	26,149	990
0-14	18,380	9,515	8,865	932
15-44	24,422	12,271	12,151	990
45-79	9,543	4,535	5,008	1104
80+	177	74	103	1392
Age not stated	50	28	22	786

Languages (Dominant):

Telugu, Oriya, Gondi, Hindi, Urdu

Disabled Population:

	Persons	Males	Females	%
Total Disabled	1,271	651	620	
In Seeing	571	253	318	44.93
In Speech	162	88	74	12.75
In Hearing	57	25	32	4.48
In Movement	356	208	148	28.01
Mentally	125	77	48	9.83

BHONGIR

Bhongir C.D. Block lies in the north west part of Nalgo nda district. It is a part of Bhongir Mandal. The Block is located at a distance of 26 kms. from district headq uarters (Nalgonda). There are 26 villages in the block with the total population of 49,372. persons. Area of the C.D. Block is 239.35 sq. kms. It is bounded by Yadagirigutta Mandal on north, Atmakur (M) and Valig onda Mandals on east, Pochanpalle Mandal on south, Bibin agar Mandal on west, Bommalarmaram and M. Turkapalle Mandals on north-west.

Communications:

Roadways : NH- 9: Direction- Hyderabad to Warangal. Nearest Villages- Rayagiri (Rural), Anantharam (Rural), Pagidi Palle. State Highway (S.H.): Direction- Jagdevp

ur to Nadkudi. Nearest Villages- Timmapur, Anajipur, Nandanam, Hanmapur, Wadaparthy, Nagireddi Palle.
Railway Station: Rayagiri (Rurul), Pagidipalle, Bommaip alle, Nagireddipalle
River: Musi Nadi- Nearest Villages- Sure Palle. Shamee rpet Nadi- Nearset Villages- Tajpur, Hanmapur, Wadaparthy, Anantharam (Rural), Pagidi Palle, Bommai Palle, Anaji pur, Nandanam, Bolle Palle, Nagireddi Palle.
Backwards Region Grants Fund: It receives Backward Region Grants.
Annual Rainfall: Average Rainfall 818 mm
Ground Water: Availability of the Ground Water in the Basin is 2868 H.A.M. and the utilization is 2545 H. A.M. It belongs to SC category. Depth to water level varies from 10 to 20 meter below the ground. Most of the wells go down in summer months. The well density in the entire block is 20 wells per sq. km. Total no. of the wells in the block are enumerated as 5730, according to the Ground Water Estimation Committee.
Natural Division : Krishna Piedmont Plain Region
Administration:
Division: Telangana. Parliamentary Constituency: 14 Bhongir. District: Nalgonda. Mandal: Bhongir. Assembly Constituency: 94 Bhongir. Gram Panchayat: .
Villages: 26 **Inhabited:** 26 **Uninhabited:** 0

Ranking	District	State	National
Area	21	347	3512
Population	23	536	5316
Sex Ratio	19	663	2250
Child Sex Ratio	43	871	3826
Literacy Rate	17	321	3054
Density	37	614	4649
Work Participation Rate	32	699	1660

Gram Panchayats:
Anajipuram, Anantharam, Balampally, Banda Somaram Baswapur, Bn.Thimmapur, Bollepally, Bommaipally Chandupatla, Cheemalakondur, Gangasanipally Ghousenagar, Hanmapur, Jammapur, Kesaram, Kunoor Mannevaripampu, Muthireddigudem, Muthyalapally Nagireddipally, Namathpally, Nandanam Pacharlabodu Thanda, Pagidipally, Penchikalpahad Raigiri, Ramachandrapur, Reddinaikthanda, Surepally Tazpoor, Thukkapur, Veeravelly, Wadaigudem Wadaparthy, Yerrambelly.
Amenities:
Education: Primary School in 26 villages, Middle school in 18 villages, Matriculation or Secondary School in 5 villages, namely Rayagiri (Rural), Chandupatla, Anantharam (Rural), Anajipur, Bolle Palle.
Higher Secondary or Pre University Courses or Intermediate or Junior College in 0 village of the CD Block, College in 1 village, Adult Literacy Center in 0 village., College is in village, namely Rayagiri (Rural).
Medical: Hospital in 0 village, Dispensary in 2 villages, Health Center in 1 village, Sub Center in 8 villages, Maternity and Child Welfare Center in 1 village, Community health workers in 0 village.
The Villages having Hospital or Dispensary or Health Center are Rayagiri (Rural), Bolle Palle.
Drinking Water: Tap water in 26 villages, Tank water in 26 villages, Well water in 26 villages, Tubewell in 26 villages and more than one source in 26 villages.
Bank: Banking facility in 2 villages, namely, Gouse Nagar, Bolle Palle.
Credit Society in 1 village Agricultural Credit Society in 1 Non-Agricultural Credit Society in 0 village.
Others: Power supply in 26 villages, Cinema hall in 0 village, sport club in 0 village, Stadium or Auditorium or Community Hall in 0 village, Post Office in 12 villages.
There are 26 villages having bus facilities.
Village with most of facilities: Bolle Palle.
Villages without Amenities (Education): None..
Scheduled Castes: Out of the total population of 49308 persons, 8021 persons (16.27%) belong to Scheduled Castes.
The villages having less than 10% SC population are None..
The villages having more than 50% SC population are None.
Sex ratio of Scheduled Caste population is 497.
Scheduled Castes Literates and Illiterates by Sex:

	Persons	Males	Females
Literate	3,708	2,289	1,419
Illiterate	4,313	1,742	2,571
Literacy rate	54.2	67.1	41.4
Graduate	26	24	2

Scheduled Castes (Dominant):
Madiga, Mala, Beda Jangam etc., Mala Dasari Dom etc.
For their cultural identity please see Appendix-I
Villages without Scheduled Castes: There are 0 village without any scheduled caste population.
Scheduled Tribes: Out of the total population of 49308 persons, 2529 persons (5.13%) belong to Scheduled Tribes.
The villages having less than 10% ST population are Tajpur, Hanmapur, Wadaparthy, Timmapur, Baswapur Rayagiri (Rural), Kesaram, Kunoor, Chandupatla Cheemala Kondur, Mustyalapalle, Veera Vally Banda Somaram, Gouse Nagar, Yerram Balle, Tukkapur Ramachandrapur, Penchikala Pahad, Anantharam (Rural) Pagidi Palle, Bommai Palle, Anajipur, Nandanam

Nagireddi Palle.

The villages having more than 50% ST population are None.

Sex ratio of Scheduled tribe population is 487.

Scheduled Tribes Literates and Illiterates by Sex:

	Persons	Males	Females
Literate	710	489	221
Illiterate	1,819	809	1,010
Literacy rate	34.8	46.8	22.3
Graduate	9	9	0

Scheduled Tribes (Dominant):

Sugalis etc., Yerukulas, Savaras etc.

For their cultural identity please see Appendix-II

Villages without Scheduled Tribes: There are 10 villages without any scheduled tribe population.

Literates and Illiterates by Sex (Total Population):

	Persons	Males	Females
Literate	24,754	15,401	9,353
Illiterate	24,554	9,567	14,987
Literacy rate	58	72	45
Graduate	494	421	73

Agriculture: ***Distribution of villages according to land use:*** Out of 26 villages, Total area (in hectare) is 23934, out of that 74.6 percent is cultivable and 12.75 percent of the cultivable area is irrigated.

Sources of Irrigation (Hectares): Government Canal 0, Private Canal 0, Well without Electricity 0, Well with Electricity 560.09, Tubewell without Electricity 0, Tubewell with Electricity 1614.81, Tank 102, River 0, Lake 0, Waterfall 0, Others 0.

Villages with population of 5000 to 9999:

Rayagiri (Rural).

Villages with population of 10000 and above: None

Distribution of Workers:

	Persons	Males	Females	WPR
Cultivators	5,846	3,691	2,155	23.09
Agricultural Labour	9,744	2,948	6,796	38.48
Household Industry	972	474	498	3.84
Other Workers	8,761	7,010	1,751	34.6
Main Workers	20,162	13,035	7,127	79.62
Marginal Workers	5,161	1,088	4,073	20.38
Total Workers	25,323	14,123	11,200	

Religion: Major Religious Communities:

	Persons	Males	Females	Sex Ratio
Hindu (95.38%)	47,030	23,797	23,233	976
Muslim (2.14%)	1,056	530	526	992
Christian (2.32%)	1,144	596	548	919
Sikh (0.01%)	3	2	1	500
Buddhists (0%)	-	-	-	-
Jain (0%)	-	-	-	-

Agewise Data:

	Persons	Males	Females	Sex Ratio
All ages	49,308	24,968	24,340	975
0-14	16,263	8,248	8,015	972
15-44	22,497	11,396	11,101	974
45-79	9,993	5,059	4,934	975
80+	506	239	267	1117
Age not stated	49	26	23	885

Languages (Dominant):

Telugu, Hindi, Urdu, Gondi, Oriya

Disabled Population:

	Persons	Males	Females	%
Total Disabled	1,116	634	482	
In Seeing	591	330	261	52.96
In Speech	86	52	34	7.71
In Hearing	36	13	23	3.23
In Movement	306	184	122	27.42
Mentally	97	55	42	8.69

BHOOTHPUR

Bhoothpur C.D. Block lies in the central part of Mahbub nagar district. The Block is located at a distance of 10 kms. from district headquarters (Mahbubnagar). There are 17 villages in the block with the total population of 42,845 persons. Area of the C.D. Block is 182.05 sq. kms. It is bounded by Mahbubnagar and Jadecherla Mandals on north, Addakal Mandal on west, Ghanpur Mandal on south, and Thimmajipet Mandal on east.

Communications :

Roadways : NH- 7: Direction- Kurnool to Jadeherla. Neare st Villages- Hasnapur, Bhoothpur, Tadparthy, Gopalapur (Khurd), Annasagar, Tadikonda, Ravalpalle. State Highway (S.H.): Direction- Mahbubnagar to Bhoothpur Nearest Villages- Pothulamadugu, Bhoothpur, Amistapur.

Backwards Region Grants Fund: It receives Backward Region Grants.

Annual Rainfall: Average Rainfall 626 mm

Ground Water: Availability of the Ground Water in the Basin is 1074 H.A.M. and the utilization is 1162 H. A.M. It belongs to OE category. Depth to water level varies from 2 to 5 meter below the ground. Most of the wells go down in summer months. The well density in the entire block is 15 wells per sq. km. Total no. of the wells in the block are enumerated as 2808, according to the Ground Water Estimation Committee.

Natural Division : Telangana Plateau Region

Administration:

Division: Telangana. Parliamentary Constituency: 11 Mahbubnagar. District: Mahbubnagar. Mandal: Bhoothpur. Assembly Constituency: 76 Devarkadra. Gram Panchayat: 16

Villages: 17 **Inhabited:** 17 **Uninhabited:** 0

Ranking	District	State	National
Area	60	660	4505
Population	47	729	5610
Sex Ratio	26	581	2014
Child Sex Ratio	17	465	1691
Literacy Rate	27	971	5556
Density	37	263	4259
Work Participation Rate	13	591	677

Gram Panchayats:

Amisthapur, Annasagar, Bhattupally, Bhoothpur Elkicherla, Hasnapoor, Ippalapally, Kappeta Karivena, Kothamolgara, Kothur, Maddigatla Pathamolgara, Pothulamadugu, Thatikonda, Thatiparthy.

Amenities:

Education: Primary School in 17 villages, Middle school in 13 villages, Matriculation or Secondary School in 4 villages, namely Bhoothpur, Karvena, Tadikonda, Yelkicharla. Higher Secondary or Pre University Courses or Intermediate or Junior College in 0 village of the CD Block, College in 0 village, Adult Literacy Center in 16 villages.

Medical: Hospital in 0 village, Dispensary in 1 village, Health Center in 1 village, Sub Center in 7 villages, Maternity and Child Welfare Center in 0 village, Community health workers in 0 village.

The Village having Hospital or Dispensary or Health Center is Karvena.

Drinking Water: Tap water in 17 villages, Tank water in 17 villages, Well water in 17 villages, Tubewell in 17 villages and more than one source in 17 villages.

Bank: Banking facility in 3 villages, namely, Bhoothpur, Kothamolgara, Yelkicharla.

Credit Society in 9 villages Agricultural Credit Society in 1 Non-Agricultural Credit Society in 9 villages.

Others: Power supply in 17 villages, Cinema hall in 0 village, sport club in 0 village, Stadium or Auditorium or Community Hall in 0 village, Post Office in 11 villages.

There are 16 villages having bus facilities.

Villages with most of facilities: Bhoothpur Kothamolgara, Yelkicharla.

Villages without Amenities (Education): None..

Scheduled Castes: Out of the total population of 42845 persons, 6929 persons (16.17%) belong to Scheduled Castes.

The villages having less than 10% SC population are None..

The villages having more than 50% SC population are None.

Sex ratio of Scheduled Caste population is 509.

Scheduled Castes Literates and Illiterates by Sex:

	Persons	Males	Females
Literate	1,787	1,244	543
Illiterate	5,142	2,161	2,981
Literacy rate	31.0	44.2	18.4
Graduate	22	19	3

Scheduled Castes (Dominant):

Madiga, Mala, Generic Castes etc., Beda Jangam etc. Mala Dasari

For their cultural identity please see Appendix-I

Villages without Scheduled Castes: There are 0 village without any scheduled caste population.

Scheduled Tribes: Out of the total population of 42845 persons, 4216 persons (9.84%) belong to Scheduled Tribes.

The villages having less than 10% ST population are Ippalpalle, Hasnapur, Tadparthy, Kothamolgara Pothulamadugu, Annasagar, Tadikonda, Ravalpalle Kappeta, Pathamolgara, Maddigatla.

The villages having more than 50% ST population are None.

Sex ratio of Scheduled tribe population is 490.

Scheduled Tribes Literates and Illiterates by Sex:

	Persons	Males	Females
Literate	731	574	157
Illiterate	3,485	1,578	1,907
Literacy rate	21.9	33.8	9.6
Graduate	5	5	0

Scheduled Tribes (Dominant):

Sugalis etc., Yerukulas

For their cultural identity please see Appendix-II

Villages without Scheduled Tribes: There are 2 villages without any scheduled tribe population.

Literates and Illiterates by Sex (Total Population):

	Persons	Males	Females
Literate	14,968	10,057	4,911
Illiterate	27,877	11,577	16,300
Literacy rate	42	56	28
Graduate	392	333	59

Agriculture: ***Distribution of villages according to land use:***

Out of 17 villages, Total area (in hectare) is 18206, out of that 81.57 percent is cultivable and 9.04 percent of the cultivable area is irrigated.

Sources of Irrigation (Hectares): Government Canal 0, Private Canal 0, Well without Electricity 0, Well with Electricity 17.79, Tubewell without Electricity 0, Tubewell with Electricity 1325, Tank 0, River 0, Lake 0, Waterfall 0, Others 0.

Villages with population of 5000 to 9999:

Amistapur, Bhoothpur.

Villages with population of 10000 and above: None

Distribution of Workers:

	Persons	Males	Females	WPR
Cultivators	6,544	4,150	2,394	28.35

Agricultural Labour	10,700	3,860	6,840	46.35
Household Industry	687	312	375	2.98
Other Workers	5,155	4,037	1,118	22.33
Main Workers	19,309	10,995	8,314	83.64
Marginal Workers	3,777	1,364	2,413	16.36
Total Workers	23,086	12,359	10,727	

Religion: Major Religious Communities:

	Persons	Males	Females	Sex Ratio
Hindu (91.35%)	39,141	19,763	19,378	981
Muslim (8.58%)	3,674	1,858	1,816	977
Christian (0.05%)	23	10	13	1,300
Sikh (0%)	1	1	-	-
Buddhists (0%)	-	-	-	-
Jain (0%)	-	-	-	-

Agewise Data:

	Persons	Males	Females	Sex Ratio
All ages	42,845	21,634	21,211	980
0-14	16,131	8,267	7,864	951
15-44	19,105	9,710	9,395	968
45-79	7,305	3,517	3,788	1077
80+	272	121	151	1248
Age not stated	32	19	13	684

Languages (Dominant):

Telugu, Hindi, Urdu, Tamil, Malayalam

Disabled Population:

	Persons	Males	Females	%
Total Disabled	889	506	383	
In Seeing	352	202	150	39.6
In Speech	69	42	27	7.76
In Hearing	39	20	19	4.39
In Movement	343	201	142	38.58
Mentally	86	41	45	9.67

BHUPALPALLE

Bhupalpalle C.D. Block lies in the northern part of Warangal district. The Block is located at a distance of 66 kms. from district headquarters (Warangal). There are 20 villages in the block with the total population of 42,756 persons. Area of the C.D. Block is 225.60 sq. kms. It is bounded in the north by district Karim Nagar, in the south by Mandals Ghanpur (Mulung), Venkat apur and Tadvai, in the east by district Karim Nagar, and in the west by Mandals Chityal and Regonda.

Communications:

Roadways : Metalled Roads: Nearest Villages- Kothapalle, Gudadupalle, Kompalle, Jangedu, Bhupalpalle, Kamalapur, Rampur.

Backwards Region Grants Fund: It receives Backward Region Grants.

Annual Rainfall: Average Rainfall 1136 mm

Ground Water: Availability of the Ground Water in the Basin is 2879 H.A.M.and the utilization is 1229 H.A. M. It belongs to Safe category. Depth to water level varies from 5 to 20 meter below the ground. Most of the wells go down in summer months. The well density in the entire block is 8 wells per sq. km. Total no. of the wells in the block are enumerated as 1910, according to the Ground Water Estimation Committee.

Natural Division : Godavari Depression Region

Administration:

Division: Telangana. Parliamentary Constituency. Distri ct: Warangal. Mandal: Bhupalpalle. Assembly Constituency: 108 Bhupalpalle. Gram Panchayat: 20.

Villages: 20 **Inhabited:** 19 **Uninhabited:** 1

Ranking	District	State	National
Area	16	407	3736
Population	15	288	4889
Sex Ratio	15	484	1816
Child Sex Ratio	3	116	302
Literacy Rate	19	530	3965
Density	47	917	3952
Work Participation Rate	28	498	3206

Gram Panchayats:

Azamnagar, Bhupalpalle, Deekshakunta, Dudekulapalle Gollabudharam, Gorlaveedu, Gudadpalle, Jangedu Kamalapur, Khasimpalle, Kompalle, Kothapalle Moranchapalle, Nagaram, Nandigama, Neredpalle Pambapur, Pullururamaiahpalle, Rampur, Veshalapalle.

Amenities:

Education: Primary School in 19 villages, Middle school in 9 villages, Matriculation or Secondary School in 6 villages, namely Gorlavedu, Kothapalle, Kompalle, Jangedu, Bhupalpalle, Azamnagar.

Higher Secondary or Pre University Courses or Intermediate or Junior College in 1 village of the CD Block,, namely Bhupalpalle.

College in 0 village, Adult Literacy Center in 15 villages.

Medical: Hospital in 11 villages, Dispensary in 0 village, Health Center in 2 villages, Sub Center in 12 villages, Maternity and Child Welfare Center in 0 village, Community health workers in 0 village.

The Villages having Hospital or Dispensary or Health Center are Neredpalle, Gorlavedu, Kothapalle, Gudadupalle, Kompalle, Bhupalpalle, Kamalapur, Nagaram, Azamnagar, Budharam, Dudekulapalle.

Drinking Water: Tap water in 18 villages, Tank water in 18 villages, Well water in 19 villages, Tubewell in 18 villages and more than one source in 19 villages.

Bank: Banking facility in 4 villages, namely, Jangedu, Bhupalpalle, Kamalapur, Azamnagar.

Credit Society in 13 villages Agricultural Credit Society in 4 Non-Agricultural Credit Society in 12 villages.

Others: Power supply in 19 villages, Cinema hall in 2 villages, sport club in 0 village, Stadium or Auditorium or Community Hall in 0 village, Post Office in 10 villages.

There are 17 villages having bus facilities.

Villages with most of facilities: Jangedu Bhupalpalle, Kamalapur, Azamnagar.

Villages without Amenities (Education): None..

Scheduled Castes: Out of the total population of 58970 persons, 11518 persons (19.53%) belong to Scheduled Castes.

The villages having less than 10% SC population are None..

The villages having more than 50% SC population are None.

Sex ratio of Scheduled Caste population is 502.

Scheduled Castes Literates and Illiterates by Sex:

	Persons	Males	Females
Literate	4,327	2,615	1,712
Illiterate	7,191	3,125	4,066
Literacy rate	45.4	54.8	36.0
Graduate	69	63	6

Scheduled Castes (Dominant):

Madiga, Mala Sale etc., Mala, Manne Generic Castes etc.

For their cultural identity please see Appendix-I

Villages without Scheduled Castes: There is 1 village without any scheduled caste population.

Scheduled Tribes: Out of the total population of 58970 persons, 5349 persons (9.07%) belong to Scheduled Tribes.

The villages having less than 10% ST population are Neredpalle, Vajinepalle, Gorlavedu, Kothapalle Gudadupalle, Kompalle, Jangedu, Bhupalpalle Pambapur, Azamnagar, Nandigama, Deekshakunta.

The villages having more than 50% ST population are None.

Sex ratio of Scheduled tribe population is 502.

Scheduled Tribes Literates and Illiterates by Sex:

	Persons	Males	Females
Literate	1,633	1,064	569
Illiterate	3,716	1,600	2,116
Literacy rate	37.3	49.1	25.7
Graduate	27	26	1

Scheduled Tribes (Dominant):

Sugalis etc., Gond etc., Koya etc., Yerukulas Konda Dhoras

For their cultural identity please see Appendix-II

Villages without Scheduled Tribes: There are 4 villages without any scheduled tribe population.

Literates and Illiterates by Sex (Total Population):

	Persons	Males	Females
Literate	26,541	16,173	10,368
Illiterate	32,429	13,540	18,889
Literacy rate	53	64	42
Graduate	601	525	76

Agriculture: ***Distribution of villages according to land use:***

Out of 20 villages, Total area (in hectare) is 22560, out of that 48.88 percent is cultivable and 25.18 percent of the cultivable area is irrigated.

Sources of Irrigation (Hectares): Government Canal 0, Private Canal 0, Well without Electricity 0, Well with Electricity 229, Tubewell without Electricity 0, Tubewell with Electricity 0, Tank 2500, River 0, Lake 0, Waterfall 0, Others 48.

Villages with population of 5000 to 9999: None

Villages with population of 10000 and above: Jangedu, Bhupalpalle.

Distribution of Workers:

	Persons	Males	Females	WPR
Cultivators	6,972	4,385	2,587	26.51
Agricultural Labour	11,280	4,645	6,635	42.88
Household Industry	874	536	338	3.32
Other Workers	7,177	6,398	779	27.29
Main Workers	18,401	12,865	5,536	69.96
Marginal Workers	7,902	3,099	4,803	30.04
Total Workers	26,303	15,964	10,339	

Religion: Major Religious Communities:

	Persons	Males	Females	Sex Ratio
Hindu (95.83%)	56,511	28,473	28,038	985
Muslim (3.43%)	2,025	1,036	989	955
Christian (0.68%)	403	188	215	1,144
Sikh (0.01%)	3	2	1	500
Buddhists (0%)	-	-	-	-
Jain (0%)	-	-	-	-

Agewise Data:

	Persons	Males	Females	Sex Ratio
All ages	58,970	29,713	29,257	985
0-14	21,332	10,716	10,616	991
15-44	28,277	14,112	14,165	1004
45-79	8,927	4,674	4,253	910
80+	373	180	193	1072
Age not stated	61	31	30	968

Languages (Dominant):

Telugu, Hindi, Urdu, Gondi, Tamil

Disabled Population:

	Persons	Males	Females	%
Total Disabled	1,104	609	495	
In Seeing	517	290	227	46.83
In Speech	133	75	58	12.05
In Hearing	71	25	46	6.43
In Movement	281	176	105	25.45
Mentally	102	43	59	9.24

BIBINAGAR

Bibinagar C.D. Block lies in the western part of Nalgon da district. The Block is located at a distance of 81 kms. from district headquarters (Nalgonda). There are 25 villages in the block with the total population of 45,992 persons. Area of the C.D. Block is 166.40 sq. kms. It is bounded by Bammalaramaram Mandal on north, Bhongir Mandal on east, Pochampalle Mandal on south, and Rangareddy district on west.

Communications:

Roadways : State Highway (S.H.): Direction- Hyderabad to Kazipet. Nearest Villages- Kondamadugu, Gudur, Bibin agar, Rangapur, Nemarugomula.

Railway Station: Bibinagar.

River: Musi Nadi- Nearest Villages- Anantharam, Rudra Velly, Raghavapur, Annampatla, Maqdoom Palle, Ravi Pahad, Gurrala Dandi, Jam Palle, Madharam, Gudur, Bibin agar.

Backwards Region Grants Fund: It receives Backward Region Grants.

Annual Rainfall: Average Rainfall 786 mm

Ground Water: Availability of the Ground Water in the Basin is 2185 H.A.M. and the utilization is 1704 H. A.M. It belongs to SC category. Depth to water level varies from 10 to 20 meter below the ground. Most of the wells go down in summer months. The well density in the entire block is 10 wells per sq. km. Total no. of the wells in the block are enumerated as 2088, according to the Ground Water Estimation Committee.

Natural Division : Krishna Piedmont Plain Region

Administration:

Division: Telangana. Parliamentary Constituency: 14 Bhongir. District: Nalgonda. Mandal: Bibinagar. Assembly Constituency: 94 Bhongir. Gram Panchayat: 27.

Villages: 25 **Inhabited:** 25 **Uninhabited:** 0

Ranking	District	State	National
Area	52	734	4772
Population	27	635	5468
Sex Ratio	52	942	3253
Child Sex Ratio	40	815	3596
Literacy Rate	3	157	1937
Density	56	890	3786
Work Participation Rate	9	445	3022

Gram Panchayats:

Annampatla, Battugudem, Bibinagar, Brahamanapally Chinnaravula Pally, Gollagudem, Gudur, Gurraladandi Jainepally, Jameelapet, Jamepally, Jampally Kondamadugu, Laxmidevigudem, Madharam Maktha Anantharam, Mugdumpally, Nemergomula Padamati Somaram, Pallegudem, Raghavapur Raheemkhan Guda, Rairaopet, Ramunigundla Thanda Ravipadu, Rudravelly, Venkiryal.

Amenities:

Education: Primary School in 25 villages, Middle school in 15 villages, Matriculation or Secondary School in 6 villages, namely Jameelapet, Kondamadugu, Gudur, Bibinagar, Venkiryal, Chinaraval Palle.

Higher Secondary or Pre University Courses or Intermediate or Junior College in 0 village of the CD Block, College in 0 village, Adult Literacy Center in 6 villages.

Medical: Hospital in 0 village, Dispensary in 1 village, Health Center in 1 village, Sub Center in 6 villages, Maternity and Child Welfare Center in 0 village, Community health workers in 0 village.

The Village having Hospital or Dispensary or Health Center is Venkiryal.

Drinking Water: Tap water in 25 villages, Tank water in 25 villages, Well water in 25 villages, Tubewell in 25 villages and more than one source in 25 villages.

Bank: Banking facility in 1 villages, namely, Bibinagar.

Credit Society in 3 villages Agricultural Credit Society in 3 Non-Agricultural Credit Society in 2 villages.

Others: Power supply in 25 villages, Cinema hall in 1 village, sport club in 0 village, Stadium or Auditorium or Community Hall in 0 village, Post Office in 10 villages.

There are 22 villages having bus facilities.

Village with most of facilities: Bibinagar.

Villages without Amenities (Education): None..

Scheduled Castes: Out of the total population of 45992 persons, 7813 persons (16.99%) belong to Scheduled Castes.

The villages having less than 10% SC population are Jiya Palle, Bagdayara, Anantharam, Maqdoom Palle Ravi Pahad, Jam Palle.

The villages having more than 50% SC population are None.

Sex ratio of Scheduled Caste population is 493.

Scheduled Castes Literates and Illiterates by Sex:

	Persons	Males	Females
Literate	4,246	2,560	1,686
Illiterate	3,567	1,400	2,167
Literacy rate	63.8	76.4	51.0
Graduate	41	38	3

Scheduled Castes (Dominant):

Madiga, Mala, Generic Castes etc., Beda Jangam etc. Bindla

For their cultural identity please see Appendix-I

Villages without Scheduled Castes: There is 1 village without any scheduled caste population.

Scheduled Tribes: Out of the total population of 45992 persons, 4724 persons (10.27%) belong to Scheduled Tribes.

The villages having less than 10% ST population are Rayarao Pet, Jameelapet, Mahadevpur, Kondamadugu Jain Palle, Gudur, Bibinagar, Rangapur, Bagdayara Padamati Somaram, Venkiryal, Anantharam, Rudra Velly Raghavapur, Raheem Khan Guda, Annampatla Maqdoom Palle.

The villages having more than 50% ST population are None.

Sex ratio of Scheduled tribe population is 481.

Scheduled Tribes Literates and Illiterates by Sex:

	Persons	Males	Females
Literate	1,386	990	396
Illiterate	3,338	1,461	1,877
Literacy rate	35.6	48.9	21.2
Graduate	13	13	0

Scheduled Tribes (Dominant):

Sugalis etc., Yerukulas, Kammara, Gadabas, Koya etc.

For their cultural identity please see Appendix-II

Villages without Scheduled Tribes: There are 5 villages without any scheduled tribe population.

Literates and Illiterates by Sex (Total Population):

	Persons	Males	Females
Literate	25,658	15,473	10,185
Illiterate	20,334	8,056	12,278
Literacy rate	65	77	53
Graduate	678	565	113

Agriculture: ***Distribution of villages according to land use:*** Out of 25 villages, Total area (in hectare) is 16641, out of that 29.19 percent is cultivable and 33.03 percent of the cultivable area is irrigated.

Sources of Irrigation (Hectares): Government Canal 0, Private Canal 0, Well without Electricity 0, Well with Electricity 432.14, Tubewell without Electricity 0, Tubewell with Electricity 473.45, Tank 698.89, River 0, Lake 0, Waterfall 0, Others 0.

Villages with population of 5000 to 9999: Bibinagar.

Villages with population of 10000 and above: None

Distribution of Workers:

	Persons	Males	Females	WPR
Cultivators	4,512	2,899	1,613	21.22
Agricultural Labour	6,920	2,180	4,740	32.54
Household Industry	496	319	177	2.33
Other Workers	9,336	7,680	1,656	43.91
Main Workers	16,484	11,677	4,807	77.52
Marginal Workers	4,780	1,401	3,379	22.48
Total Workers	21,264	13,078	8,186	

Religion: Major Religious Communities:

	Persons	Males	Females	Sex Ratio
Hindu (96.37%)	44,323	22,684	21,639	954
Muslim (2.88%)	1,323	672	651	969
Christian (0.48%)	223	110	113	1,027
Sikh (0.01%)	5	2	3	1,500
Buddhists (0%)	-	-	-	-
Jain (0.01%)	6	2	4	2,000

Agewise Data:

	Persons	Males	Females	Sex Ratio
All ages	45,992	23,529	22,463	955
0-14	15,415	7,758	7,657	987
15-44	21,670	11,294	10,376	919
45-79	8,486	4,277	4,209	984
80+	385	179	206	1151
Age not stated	36	21	15	714

Languages (Dominant):

Telugu, Hindi, Urdu, Gondi, Tamil

Disabled Population:

	Persons	Males	Females	%
Total Disabled	797	462	335	
In Seeing	349	189	160	43.79
In Speech	52	28	24	6.52
In Hearing	32	14	18	4.02
In Movement	255	167	88	31.99
Mentally	109	64	45	13.68

BICCAVOLU

Biccavolu C.D. Block lies in the southern part of East Godavari district. The Block is located at a distance of 35 kms. from district headquarters (Kakinada). There are 14 villages in the block with the total population of 67,717 persons. Area of the C.D. Block is 102.22 sq. kms. It is bounded in the north by Mandals Rajanaga ram and Rangampeta, in the south by Mandals Rayavaram and Ramachandrapuram, in the east by Mandals Pedapudi and Samalkota, and in the west by Mandal Anaparthy.

Communications :

Roadways : State Highway (S.H.): Direction- Rajahmundry to Samalkota. Nearest Villages- Komaripalem, Biccavolu, Balabhadrapuram.

Railway Station: Biccavolu, Balabhadrapuram.

Backwards Region Grants Fund: It receives Backward Region Grants.

Annaul Rainfall: Average Rainfall 990.4 mm

Ground Water: Availability of the Ground Water in the Basin is (Information not avavible) H.A.M .and the utilization is (Information not avavible) H.A.M. It belongs to (Information not avavible) category. Depth to water level varies from 3 to 10 meter below the ground. Most of the wells go down in summer months.

Natural Division : Godavari Delta Region

Administration:

Division: Coastal Andhra. Parliamentary Constituency:

25 Rajahmundry. District: East Godavari. Mandal: Biccav olu. Assembly Constituency: 159 Anaparthy. Gram Panchaya t: 13.

Villages: 14 **Inhabited:** 14 **Uninhabited:** 0

Ranking	District	State	National
Area	33	1018	5698
Population	36	166	4570
Sex Ratio	7	141	821
Child Sex Ratio	26	307	1067
Literacy Rate	25	193	2238
Density	32	1044	1599
Work Participation Rate	26	52	4303

Gram Panchayats:

Arikarevula, Balabhadrapuram, Biccavolu, Illapalle Kapavaram, Komaripalem, Konkuduru, Melluru Pandalapaka, Railway Station Peta, Rangapuram Tossipudi, Voolapalle.

Amenities:

Education: Primary School in 13 villages, Middle school in 8 villages, Matriculation or Secondary School in 5 villages, namely Biccavolu, Balabhadrapuram, Pandalapaka, Voolapalle, Konkuduru.

Higher Secondary or Pre University Courses or Intermediate or Junior College in 0 village of the CD Block, College in 1 village, Adult Literacy Center in 10 villages., College is in village, namely Melluru.

Medical: Hospital in 0 village, Dispensary in 2 villages, Health Center in 1 village, Sub Center in 10 villages, Maternity and Child Welfare Center in 0 village, Community health workers in 0 village.

The Villages having Hospital or Dispensary or Health Center are Biccavolu, Pandalapaka.

Drinking Water: Tap water in 13 villages, Tank water in 13 villages, Well water in 14 villages, Tubewell in 13 villages and more than one source in 13 villages.

Bank: Banking facility in 2 villages, namely, Biccavolu, Pandalapaka.

Credit Society in 7 villages Agricultural Credit Society in 7 Non-Agricultural Credit Society in 1 village.

Others: Power supply in 14 villages, Cinema hall in 4 villages, sport club in 0 village, Stadium or Auditorium or Community Hall in 0 village, Post Office in 9 villages.

There are 9 villages having bus facilities.

Villages with most of facilities: Biccavolu Pandalapaka.

Villages without amenities (Education):

Rallakhandrika..

Scheduled Castes: Out of the total population of 67717 persons, 10233 persons (15.11%) belong to Scheduled Castes.

The villages having less than 10% SC population are None..

The villages having more than 50% SC population are None.

Sex ratio of Scheduled Caste population is 501.

Scheduled Castes Literates and Illiterates by Sex:

	Persons	Males	Females
Literate	4,950	2,676	2,274
Illiterate	5,283	2,428	2,855
Literacy rate	56.4	61.5	51.4
Graduate	106	76	30

Scheduled Castes (Dominant):

Mala, Madiga, Relli, Adi Andhra, Dom etc.

For their cultural identity please see Appendix-I

Villages without Scheduled Castes: There is 1 village without any scheduled caste population.

Scheduled Tribes: Out of the total population of 67717 persons, 476 persons (0.7%) belong to Scheduled Tribes.

The villages having less than 10% ST population are Rangapuram, Illapalle, Thummalapalle, Rallakhandrika Biccavolu, Balabhadrapuram, Kapavaram, Komaripalem Tossipudi, Pandalapaka, Voolapalle, Konkuduru Arikarevula, Melluru.

The villages having more than 50% ST population are None.

Sex ratio of Scheduled tribe population is 494.

Scheduled Tribes Literates and Illiterates by Sex:

	Persons	Males	Females
Literate	129	76	53
Illiterate	347	165	182
Literacy rate	33.5	40.2	27.0
Graduate	4	3	1

Scheduled Tribes (Dominant):

Yerukulas, Yenadis, Chenchu etc., Konda Dhoras Sugalis etc.

For their cultural identity please see Appendix-II

Villages without Scheduled Tribes: There are 2 villages without any scheduled tribe population.

Literates and Illiterates by Sex (Total Population):

	Persons	Males	Females
Literate	37,291	20,091	17,200
Illiterate	30,426	13,551	16,875
Literacy rate	63	69	58
Graduate	1,228	1,022	206

Agriculture: ***Distribution of villages according to land use:*** Out of 14 villages, Total area (in hectare) is 10222, out of that 80.25 percent is cultivable and 82.62 percent of the cultivable area is irrigated.

Sources of Irrigation (Hectares): Government Canal 4837.54, Private Canal 90, Well without Electricity 0, Well with Electricity 0, Tubewell without Electricity 0, Tubewell with Electricity 1031.55, Tank 802.01, River 0, Lake 0, Waterfall 0, Others 16.2.

Villages with population of 5000 to 9999:
Balabhadrapuram, Komaripalem, Pandalapaka Voolapalle, Konkuduru.

Villages with population of 10000 and above:
Biccavolu.

Distribution of Workers:

	Persons	Males	Females	WPR
Cultivators	3,219	3,072	147	11.65
Agricultural Labour	16,743	11,452	5,291	60.58
Household Industry	815	465	350	2.95
Other Workers	6,863	5,667	1,196	24.83
Main Workers	22,114	18,790	3,324	80.01
Marginal Workers	5,526	1,866	3,660	19.99
Total Workers	27,640	20,656	6,984	

Religion: Major Religious Communities:

	Persons	Males	Females	Sex Ratio
Hindu (97.51%)	66,033	32,800	33,233	1,013
Muslim (1.45%)	980	510	470	922
Christian (1%)	680	318	362	1,138
Sikh (0%)	-	-	-	-
Buddhists (0%)	3	2	1	500
Jain (0%)	-	-	-	-

Agewise Data:

	Persons	Males	Females	Sex Ratio
All ages	67,717	33,642	34,075	1013
0-14	19,865	9,998	9,867	987
15-44	33,739	16,856	16,883	1002
45-79	13,599	6,552	7,047	1076
80+	428	189	239	1265
Age not stated	86	47	39	830

Languages (Dominant):
Telugu, Urdu, Gondi, Tamil, Hindi

Disabled Population:

	Persons	Males	Females	%
Total Disabled	1,142	664	478	
In Seeing	589	336	253	51.58
In Speech	113	63	50	9.89
In Hearing	34	11	23	2.98
In Movement	308	201	107	26.97
Mentally	98	53	45	8.58

BICHKUNDA

Bichkunda C.D. Block lies in the western part of Nizama bad district. The Block is located at a distance of 75 kms. from district headquarters (Nizamabad). There are 38 villages in the block with the total population of 55,621 persons. Area of the C.D. Block is 252.84 sq. kms. It is bounded by Madnoor Mandal on north-west and north, Birkoor Mandal on north-east, Pitlon Mandal on east and south-east, district Medak on north and south-west, and Jukkal Mandal on south-west and west.

Communications :

Roadways : State Highway (S.H.): Direction- Madnoor to Pitlam. Nearest Villages- Rajola, Kandarpalle, Fathl apur, Jagannathapalle, Shantapur, Malkapur (Kodapgalpatt i), Pedda Kodapgal.

River: Manjari Nadi- Nearest Villages- Wajidnagar, Bandaranjal, Gundekalloor, Khatgaon, Shetloor, Hasgul, Pulkal, Gundenamali.

Backwards Region Grants Fund: It receives Backward Region Grants.

Annual Rainfall: Average Rainfall 928 mm

Ground Water: Availability of the Ground Water in the Basin is 2229 H.A.M. and the utilization is 1223 H. A.M. It belongs to Safe category. Depth to water level varies from 5 to 20 meter below the ground. Most of the wells go down in summer months, according to the Ground Water Estimation Committee.

Natural Division : Telangana Plateau Region

Administration:

Division: Telangana. Parliamentary Constituency: 5 Zahirabad. District: Nizamabad. Mandal: Bichkunda. Assembly Constituency: 13 Jukkal (SC). Gram Panchayat: 26

Villages: 38 **Inhabited:** 35 **Uninhabited:** 3

Ranking	District	State	National
Area	9	300	3341
Population	12	356	5027
Sex Ratio	34	486	1809
Child Sex Ratio	18	499	1833
Literacy Rate	30	977	5592
Density	32	798	4440
Work Participation Rate	26	645	2379

Gram Panchayats:
Bandarenjal, Begumpur, Bichkunda, Burugupalli Devada Big, Devada Small, Dhadgi Big, Dhadgi Small Fathlapur, Gopanpalli, Gundekolloor, Gundenamli Hasgul, Kaslabad, Khatgaon, Kodapgal Big Missionkallali, Pulkal, Rajula, Shantapur, Shetlur Sirsamunder, Takkadpalli(B), Wadlam, Wajidnagar Yellaram.

Amenities:

Education: Primary School in 34 villages, Middle school in 9 villages, Matriculation or Secondary School in 5 villages, namely Hasgul, Bichkunda, Pulkal, Shantapur, Pedda Kodapgal.

Higher Secondary or Pre University Courses or Intermediate or Junior College in 1 village of the CD Block,, namely Bichkunda.

College in 1 village, Adult Literacy Center in 13 villages.,

College is in village, namely Bichkunda.

Medical: Hospital in 1 village, Dispensary in 1 village, Health Center in 2 villages, Sub Center in 9 villages, Maternity and Child Welfare Center in 2 villages, Community health workers in 0 village.

The Villages having Hospital or Dispensary or Health Center are Bichkunda, Pulkal, Shantapur, Pedda Kodapgal.

Drinking Water: Tap water in 35 villages, Tank water in 34 villages, Well water in 35 villages, Tubewell in 34 villages and more than one source in 35 villages.

Bank: Banking facility in 5 villages, namely, Bichkunda, Pedda Dhadgi, Pulkal, Shantapur Pedda Kodapgal.

Credit Society in 15 villages Agricultural Credit Society in 3 Non-Agricultural Credit Society in 15 villages.

Others: Power supply in 35 villages, Cinema hall in 1 village, sport club in 0 village, Stadium or Auditorium or Community Hall in 0 village, Post Office in 11 villages.

There are 30 villages having bus facilities.

Villages with most of facilities: Bichkunda Pedda Dhadgi, Pulkal, Shantapur, Pedda Kodapgal.

Villages without amenities (Education):
Jagannathapalle..

Scheduled Castes: Out of the total population of 55621 persons, 9045 persons (16.26%) belong to Scheduled Castes.

The villages having less than 10% SC population are None..

The villages having more than 50% SC population are None.

Sex ratio of Scheduled Caste population is 498.

Scheduled Castes Literates and Illiterates by Sex:

	Persons	Males	Females
Literate	2,164	1,467	697
Illiterate	6,881	3,070	3,811
Literacy rate	28.4	38.5	18.4
Graduate	50	46	4

Scheduled Castes (Dominant):
Madiga, Mala, Generic Castes etc., Chamar etc.
Byagara

For their cultural identity please see Appendix-I

Villages without Scheduled Castes: There are 5 villages without any scheduled caste population.

Scheduled Tribes: Out of the total population of 55621 persons, 3062 persons (5.51%) belong to Scheduled Tribes.

The villages having less than 10% ST population are Rajola, Mishankallali, Gundekalloor, Khatgaon Shetloor, Meka, Hasgul, Sirsamundar, Gopanpalle Bichkunda, Kandarpalle, Fathlapur, Dowlatapur Chinna Dhadgi, Chinna Devada, Pedda Devada Pedda Dhadgi, Pulkal, Wajidnagar, Gundenamali Bandaranjal, Rajapur, Tupdal (Kowlasa) Pedda Takkadpalle, Jagannathapalle Chinna Takkadpalle, Manyapur, Seetarampalle Shantapur, Pedda Kodapgal, Kheslabad.

The villages having more than 50% ST population are None.

Sex ratio of Scheduled tribe population is 487.

Scheduled Tribes Literates and Illiterates by Sex:

	Persons	Males	Females
Literate	541	413	128
Illiterate	2,521	1,157	1,364
Literacy rate	23.1	34.5	11.2
Graduate	20	17	3

Scheduled Tribes (Dominant):
Sugalis etc., Yerukulas, Generic Tribes etc.
Gond etc.

For their cultural identity please see Appendix-II

Villages without Scheduled Tribes: There are 23 villages without any scheduled tribe population.

Literates and Illiterates by Sex (Total Population):

	Persons	Males	Females
Literate	19,337	12,561	6,776
Illiterate	36,284	15,465	20,819
Literacy rate	41	54	29
Graduate	619	541	78

Agriculture: ***Distribution of villages according to land use:***
Out of 38 villages, Total area (in hectare) is 25282, out of that 67.53 percent is cultivable and 17.54 percent of the cultivable area is irrigated.

Sources of Irrigation (Hectares): Government Canal 0, Private Canal 0, Well without Electricity 0, Well with Electricity 0, Tubewell without Electricity 0, Tubewell with Electricity 1631.44, Tank 1278, River 0, Lake 0, Waterfall 0, Others 84.99.

Villages with population of 5000 to 9999: None

Villages with population of 10000 and above:
Bichkunda.

Distribution of Workers:

	Persons	Males	Females	WPR
Cultivators	6,107	4,444	1,663	23.08
Agricultural Labour	14,569	6,139	8,430	55.06
Household Industry	728	440	288	2.75
Other Workers	5,054	4,171	883	19.1
Main Workers	17,191	11,335	5,856	64.97
Marginal Workers	9,267	3,859	5,408	35.03
Total Workers	26,458	15,194	11,264	

Religion: Major Religious Communities:

	Persons	Males	Females	Sex Ratio
Hindu (85.58%)	47,601	24,015	23,586	982

Muslim (13.37%)	7,439	3,717	3,722	1,001
Christian (0.06%)	35	19	16	842
Sikh (0.12%)	68	36	32	889
Buddhists (0.02%)	11	6	5	833
Jain (0%)	1	-	1	-

Agewise Data:

	Persons	Males	Females	Sex Ratio
All ages	55,621	28,026	27,595	985
0-14	20,208	10,383	9,825	946
15-44	24,649	12,528	12,121	968
45-79	10,280	4,892	5,388	1101
80+	411	183	228	1246
Age not stated	73	40	33	825

Languages (Dominant):
Telugu, Urdu, Kannada, Hindi, Marathi

Disabled Population:

	Persons	Males	Females	%
Total Disabled	1,361	737	624	
In Seeing	606	286	320	44.53
In Speech	128	67	61	9.4
In Hearing	82	37	45	6.02
In Movement	443	294	149	32.55
Mentally	102	53	49	7.49

BIJINAPALLE

Bijinapalle C.D. Block lies in the central part of Mahbubnagar district. The Block is located at a distance of 34 kms. from district headquarters (Mahbubnagar). There are 24 villages in the block with the total population of 61,989 persons. Area of the C.D. Block is 259.14 sq. kms. It is bounded by Thimmajipet Mandal on north, Tadoor and Nagarkurnool Mandals on east, Gopalapeta Mandal on south, and Ghanpur Mandal on west.

Communications:

Roadways : State Highway (S.H.): Direction- Mahbubnagar to Nagarkurnool. and Wanaparthy to Jadeherla. Nearest Villages- Manganur, Velgonda, Vattem, Lingasanipalle, Venkatapur, Palem, Bijinapalle, Mahadevpeta, Shainpalle, Mammaipalle, Boyapur.

Backwards Region Grants Fund: It receives Backward Region Grants.

Integrated Child Development Scheme (ICDS) Project: Bijinepalli, Total Anganwadi Centres: 147

Annual Rainfall: Average Rainfall 625 mm

Ground Water: Availability of the Ground Water in the Basin is 1677 H.A.M. and the utilization is 1425 H. A.M. It belongs to SC category. Depth to water level varies from 2 to 5 meter below the ground. Most of the wells go down in summer months. The well density in the entire block is 10 wells per sq. km. Total no. of the wells in the block are enumerated as 2696, according to the Ground Water Estimation Committee.

Natural Division : Telangana Plateau Region

Administration:

Division: Telangana. Parliamentary Constituency: 12 Nagarkurnool (SC). District: Mahbubnagar. Mandal: Bijinapalle. Assembly Constituency: 81 Nagarkurnool. Gram Panchayat: 20.

Villages: 24 **Inhabited:** 23 **Uninhabited:** 1

Ranking	District	State	National
Area	30	279	3260
Population	7	246	4789
Sex Ratio	50	880	2989
Child Sex Ratio	52	946	4217
Literacy Rate	34	998	5684
Density	54	539	4217
Work Participation Rate	11	579	1426

Gram Panchayats:
Allipur, Bijinepally, Gangaram, Gouraram, Gudlanarva Kanapur, Karkonda, Lattupally, Lingasanipally Mahadevpet, Manganoor, Mommaipally, Palem, Polepally Salkarpet, Shainpally, Vasanthapur, Vattem, Velgonda Waddeman.

Amenities:

Education: Primary School in 23 villages, Middle school in 13 villages, Matriculation or Secondary School in 7 villages, namely Manganur, Velgonda, Vattem, Palem, Bijinapalle, Gangaram, Vaddemanu.

Higher Secondary or Pre University Courses or Intermediate or Junior College in 0 village of the CD Block, College in 1 village, Adult Literacy Center in 21 villages., College is in village, namely Palem.

Medical: Hospital in 0 village, Dispensary in 1 village, Health Center in 2 villages, Sub Center in 10 villages, Maternity and Child Welfare Center in 18 villages, Community health workers in 0 village.

The Village having Hospital or Dispensary or Health Center is Bijinapalle.

Drinking Water: Tap water in 23 villages, Tank water in 23 villages, Well water in 23 villages, Tubewell in 23 villages and more than one source in 23 villages.

Bank: Banking facility in 2 villages, namely, Palem, Bijinapalle.

Credit Society in 12 villages Agricultural Credit Society in 4 Non-Agricultural Credit Society in 12 villages.

Others: Power supply in 23 villages, Cinema hall in 2 villages, sport club in 0 village, Stadium or Auditorium or Community Hall in 0 village, Post Office in 18 villages.

There are 19 villages having bus facilities.

Villages with most of facilities: Palem Bijinapalle.

Villages without Amenities (Education): None..

Scheduled Castes: Out of the total population of 61989 persons, 11018 persons (17.77%) belong to Scheduled Castes.

The villages having less than 10% SC population are None..

The villages having more than 50% SC population are None.

Sex ratio of Scheduled Caste population is 488.

Scheduled Castes Literates and Illiterates by Sex:

	Persons	Males	Females
Literate	2,804	2,029	775
Illiterate	8,214	3,613	4,601
Literacy rate	30.0	42.3	17.0
Graduate	62	55	7

Scheduled Castes (Dominant):

Madiga, Mala, Mashti, Bindla, Beda Jangam etc.

For their cultural identity please see Appendix-I

Villages without Scheduled Castes: There is 1 village without any scheduled caste population.

Scheduled Tribes: Out of the total population of 61989 persons, 5906 persons (9.53%) belong to Scheduled Tribes.

The villages having less than 10% ST population are Manganur, Velgonda, Vasanthapur, Lingasanipalle Palem, Gudlanarva, Bijinapalle, Mahadevpeta Shainpalle, Mammaipalle, Allipur, Salkarpet Vaddemanu, Boyapur, Khanapur.

The villages having more than 50% ST population are None.

Sex ratio of Scheduled tribe population is 492.

Scheduled Tribes Literates and Illiterates by Sex:

	Persons	Males	Females
Literate	746	529	217
Illiterate	5,160	2,472	2,688
Literacy rate	16.1	22.8	9.4
Graduate	9	8	1

Scheduled Tribes (Dominant):

Sugalis etc., Yerukulas, Chenchu etc.

For their cultural identity please see Appendix-II

Villages without Scheduled Tribes: There are 4 villages without any scheduled tribe population.

Literates and Illiterates by Sex (Total Population):

	Persons	Males	Females
Literate	21,228	14,091	7,137
Illiterate	40,761	17,538	23,223
Literacy rate	40	53	28
Graduate	1,112	866	246

Agriculture: ***Distribution of villages according to land use:***

Out of 24 villages, Total area (in hectare) is 25915, out of that 77.19 percent is cultivable and 12.74 percent of the cultivable area is irrigated.

Sources of Irrigation (Hectares): Government Canal 0, Private Canal 0, Well without Electricity 0, Well with Electricity 0, Tubewell without Electricity 0, Tubewell with Electricity 2154.48, Tank 393, River 0, Lake 0, Waterfall 0, Others 0.

Villages with population of 5000 to 9999: Manganur, Palem, Bijinapalle, Latpalle, Vaddemanu.

Villages with population of 10000 and above: None

Distribution of Workers:

	Persons	Males	Females	WPR
Cultivators	9,648	6,434	3,214	30.17
Agricultural Labour	15,178	5,555	9,623	47,47
Household Industry	910	485	425	2.85
Other Workers	6,238	4,810	1,428	19.51
Main Workers	23,688	14,300	9,388	74.09
Marginal Workers	8,286	2,984	5,302	25.91
Total Workers	31,974	17,284	14,690	

Religion: Major Religious Communities:

	Persons	Males	Females	Sex Ratio
Hindu (94.22%)	58,406	29,878	28,528	955
Muslim (4.96%)	3,075	1,495	1,580	1,057
Christian (0.65%)	400	198	202	1,020
Sikh (0%)	2	-	2	-
Buddhists (0%)	-	-	-	-
Jain (0%)	-	-	-	-

Agewise Data:

	Persons	Males	Females	Sex Ratio
All ages	61,989	31,629	30,360	960
0-14	22,112	11,650	10,462	898
15-44	28,144	14,278	13,866	971
45-79	11,198	5,460	5,738	1051
80+	421	186	235	1263
Age not stated	114	55	59	1073

Languages (Dominant):

Telugu, Hindi, Urdu, Tamil, Others

Disabled Population:

	Persons	Males	Females	%
Total Disabled	1,132	661	471	
In Seeing	471	288	183	41.61
In Speech	93	46	47	8.22
In Hearing	36	24	12	3.18
In Movement	404	229	175	35.69
Mentally	128	74	54	11.31

BIRKOOR

Birkoor C.D. Block lies in the western part of Nizamabad district. The Block is located at a distance of 45 kms. from district headquarters (Nizamabad). There are 31 villages in the block with the total population of 47,114 persons. Area of the C.D. Block is 177.49 sq. kms. It is bounded by Kotgiri Mandal on north,

Varni Mandal on north-east, Banswada Mandal on east and south, Bichkunda Mandal on south-west, west and north-west.

Communications :

Roadways : State Highway (S.H.): Direction- Bodha to Yellareda. Nearest Villages- Nasurullabad, Namli, Sangam, Kamshetpalle, Durki.

River: Manjira Nadi- Nearest Villages- Nagapur, Birkoor, Kishtapur, Chincholi, Chinna Damarancha, Pedda Damaran cha.

Backwards Region Grants Fund: It receives Backward Region Grants.

Annual Rainfall: Average Rainfall 1064 mm

Ground Water : Availability of the Ground Water in the Basin is 3117 H.A.M. and the utilization is 2186 H.A.M. It belongs to Semi Critical category. Depth to water level varies from 5 to 10 meter below the ground. Most of the wells go down in summer months, according to the Ground Water Estimation Committee.

Natural Division : Telangana Plateau Region

Administration:

Division: Telangana. Parliamentary Constituency: 5 Zahirabad. District: Nizamabad. Mandal: Birkoor. Assemb ly Constituency: 14 Banswada. Gram Panchayat.

Villages: 31 **Inhabited:** 24 **Uninhabited:** 7

Ranking	District	State	National
Area	27	682	4575
Population	21	598	5416
Sex Ratio	21	91	614
Child Sex Ratio	21	595	2357
Literacy Rate	29	954	5506
Density	22	531	3905
Work Participation Rate	15	483	1393

Gram Panchayats:

Ankole, Annaram, Barangedgi, B'Devpalli, Bhairapur Birkur, Boppaspalli, Damrancha, Durki, Kistapoor Mailaram, Mirzapoor, Nachupalli, Nasrullabad, Nemli Sangam, Thimmapur.

Amenities:

Education: Primary School in 24 villages, Middle school in 13 villages, Matriculation or Secondary School in 8 villages, namely Nasurullabad, Namli, Bommandevpalle, Mirzapur, Birkoor, Pedda Damarancha, Veerapur, Durki.

Higher Secondary or Pre University Courses or Intermediate or Junior College in 0 village of the CD Block, College in 1 village, Adult Literacy Center in 23 villages., College is in village, namely Durki.

Medical: Hospital in 0 village, Dispensary in 0 village, Health Center in 1 village, Sub Center in 8 villages, Maternity and Child Welfare Center in 0 village, Community health workers in 0 village.

Drinking Water: Tap water in 24 villages, Tank water in 24 villages, Well water in 24 villages, Tubewell in 24 villages and more than one source in 24 villages.

Bank: Banking facility in 5 villages, namely, Nasurullabad, Mirzapur, Birkoor, Chinna Annaram Durki.

Credit Society in 16 villages Agricultural Credit Society in 9 Non-Agricultural Credit Society in 3 villages.

Others: Power supply in 24 villages, Cinema hall in 1 village, sport club in 0 village, Stadium or Auditorium or Community Hall in 0 village, Post Office in 13 villages.

There are 24 villages having bus facilities.

Villages with most of facilities: Nasurullabad Mirzapur, Birkoor, Durki.

Villages without Amenities (Education): None..

Scheduled Castes: Out of the total population of 47114 persons, 6536 persons (13.87%) belong to Scheduled Castes.

The villages having less than 10% SC population are None..

The villages having more than 50% SC population are None.

Sex ratio of Scheduled Caste population is 514.

Scheduled Castes Literates and Illiterates by Sex:

	Persons	Males	Females
Literate	1,487	980	507
Illiterate	5,049	2,197	2,852
Literacy rate	26.5	35.9	17.6
Graduate	20	18	2

Scheduled Castes (Dominant):

Mala, Madiga, Gosangi, Generic Castes etc. Chamar etc.

For their cultural identity please see Appendix-I

Villages without Scheduled Castes: There are 7 villages without any scheduled caste population.

Scheduled Tribes: Out of the total population of 47114 persons, 5729 persons (12.16%) belong to Scheduled Tribes.

The villages having less than 10% ST population are Barangedgi, Mallapur, Bairapur, Nasurullabad, Namli Bommandevpalle, Baswaipalle, Kamshetpalle, Mirzapur Birkoor, Kishtapur, Chincholi, Pedda Damarancha Chinna Annaram, Veerapur, Durki.

The villages having more than 50% ST population are None.

Sex ratio of Scheduled tribe population is 500.

Scheduled Tribes Literates and Illiterates by Sex:

	Persons	Males	Females
Literate	1,473	1,104	369
Illiterate	4,256	1,762	2,494
Literacy rate	31.9	48.0	16.0

Graduate	35	32	3

Scheduled Tribes (Dominant):

Sugalis etc., Yerukulas, Generic Tribes etc.

Gond etc., Koya etc.

For their cultural identity please see Appendix-II

Villages without Scheduled Tribes: There are 15 villages without any scheduled tribe population.

Literates and Illiterates by Sex (Total Population):

	Persons	Males	Females
Literate	17,132	10,895	6,237
Illiterate	29,982	12,405	17,577
Literacy rate	42	55	30
Graduate	537	434	103

Agriculture: ***Distribution of villages according to land use:*** Out of 31 villages, Total area (in hectare) is 17748, out of that 57.18 percent is cultivable and 93.17 percent of the cultivable area is irrigated.

Sources of Irrigation (Hectares): Government Canal 3316.07, Private Canal 0, Well without Electricity 0, Well with Electricity 143.88, Tubewell without Electricity 0, Tubewell with Electricity 3622.17, Tank 1855.34, River 0, Lake 0, Waterfall 0, Others 518.19.

Villages with population of 5000 to 9999: Birkoor.

Villages with population of 10000 and above: None

Distribution of Workers:

	Persons	Males	Females	WPR
Cultivators	6,546	4,428	2,118	26.53
Agricultural Labour	13,367	5,573	7,794	54.17
Household Industry	815	370	445	3.3
Other Workers	3,948	3,000	948	16
Main Workers	14,724	9,218	5,506	59.67
Marginal Workers	9,952	4,153	5,799	40.33
Total Workers	24,676	13,371	11,305	

Religion: Major Religious Communities:

	Persons	Males	Females	Sex Ratio
Hindu (88.75%)	41,812	20,648	21,164	1,025
Muslim (10.92%)	5,147	2,575	2,572	999
Christian (0.27%)	128	60	68	1,133
Sikh (0.01%)	6	3	3	1,000
Buddhists (0%)	-	-	-	-
Jain (0%)	-	-	-	-

Agewise Data:

	Persons	Males	Females	Sex Ratio
All ages	47,114	23,300	23,814	1022
0-14	15,216	7,812	7,404	948
15-44	21,924	10,890	11,034	1013
45-79	9,364	4,313	5,051	1171
80+	407	176	231	1313
Age not stated	203	109	94	862

Languages (Dominant):

Telugu, Hindi, Urdu, Kannada, Marathi

Disabled Population:

	Persons	Males	Females	%
Total Disabled	827	449	378	
In Seeing	322	156	166	38.94
In Speech	90	51	39	10.88
In Hearing	39	18	21	4.72
In Movement	298	188	110	36.03
Mentally	78	36	42	9.43

BOATH

Boath C.D. Block lies in the north-west part of Adilabad district. The Block is located at a distance of 46 kms. from district headquarters (Adilabad). There are 39 villages in the block with the total population of 42,766 persons. Area of the C.D. Block is 271.60 sq. kms. It is bounded by Bazarhathanoor Mandal on north-east, Neradigonda Mandal on north-east, east and south-east, Sarangapur Mandal on south and south-we st, and it has common boundary with the state of Maharas htra in South-west, west, north-west and north.

Communications :

Roadways : State Highway (S.H.): Direction- Kinwat to Pochera. Nearest Villages- Ghanpur, Sonala, Kowtha (Buzurg), Sakhera, Kangutta, Pochera.

Backwards Region Grants Fund: It receives Backward Region Grants.

Integrated Child Development Scheme (ICDS) Project: Boath, Total Anganwadi Centres: 252

Annual Rainfall: Average Rainfall 1167 mm

Ground Water: Availability of the ground water in the Basin is 2244 H.A.M.and the utilization is 1591 H.A. M. It belongs to Semi Critical category. Depth to water level varies from 5 to 10 meter below the ground. Most of the wells go down in summer months, according to the Ground Water Estimation Committee.

Natural Division : Telangana Plateau Region

Administration:

Division: Telangana. Parliamentary Constituency: 1 Adilabad (ST).District: Adilabad. Mandal: Boath. Assemb ly Constituency: 8 Boath (ST).Gram Panchayat: 18.

Border Villages: (Maharashtra)- Nearest Villages- Wajar, Chintalabori, Ghanpur, Nigini.

Places of Turist Interest:

Pochera Waterfalls: Pochera Waterfalls presents a strik ing vista with gushing waters of Godavari River. Sited near National Highway No. 7, the cascade lies about 50 kms from Adilabad. The place attracts numerous touri sts and visitors throughout the year. During winters, the falls becomes all more attractive with heavy waters.

Villages: 39 **Inhabited:** 31 **Uninhabited:** 8

Ranking	District	State	National
Area	17	141	2662
Population	16	733	5614
Sex Ratio	19	217	1100
Child Sex Ratio	18	258	841
Literacy Rate	7	488	3784
Density	28	467	5748
Work Participation Rate	22	949	1182

Gram Panchayats:

Anduru, Babera, Boath (B), Chintalbori, Dhannur (B) Ghanpur, Kangutta, Karathwada, Kowtha, Kuchalapur Marlapalle, Nigini, Pardi (K), Patnapur, Pochera Sakhera, Sonala, Wajar.

Amenities:

Education: Primary School in 29 villages, Middle school in 10 villages, Matriculation or Secondary School in 6 villages, namely Sonala, Kowtha (Buzurg), Marlapalle, Boath (Buzurg), Dhannur (Buzurg), Patnapur.

Higher Secondary or Pre University Courses or Intermediate or Junior College in 1 village of the CD Block,, namely Boath (Buzurg).

College in 0 village, Adult Literacy Center in 0 village.

Medical: Hospital in 1 village, Dispensary in 1 village, Health Center in 14 villages, Sub Center in 10 villages, Maternity and Child Welfare Center in 1 village, Community health workers in 0 village.

The Villages having Hospital or Dispensary or Health Center are Ghanpur, Sonala, Kowtha (Buzurg), Tewiti, Pardi (Khurd), Gollapur, Kantegaon, Marlapalle, Boath (Buzurg), Pochera, Kuchalapur, Dhannur (Buzurg), Pippaladhari, Patnapur.

Drinking Water: Tap water in 28 villages, Tank water in 28 villages, Well water in 31 villages, Tubewell in 28 villages and more than one source in 29 villages.

Bank: Banking facility in 2 villages, namely, Sonala, Boath (Buzurg).

Credit Society in 16 villages Agricultural Credit Society in 16 Non-Agricultural Credit Society in 7 villages.

Others: Power supply in 31 villages, Cinema hall in 1 village, sport club in 1 village, Stadium or Auditorium or Community Hall in 0 village, Post Office in 10 villages.

There are 14 villages having bus facilities.

Villages with most of facilities: Sonala Boath (Buzurg).

Villages without amenities (Education): Suradapur, Birlagondi..

Scheduled Castes: Out of the total population of 42766 persons, 5481 persons (12.82%) belong to Scheduled Castes.

The villages having less than 10% SC population are Wajar, Chintalabori, Sangvi, Tewiti, Pardi (Buzurg) Pardi (Khurd), Gollapur, Babera, Kantegaon, Nigini Marlapalle, Nakkalawada, Pippaladhari, Patnapur Suradapur, Narayanpur, Anduru, Birlagondi Dhannur (Khurd), Nagapur.

The villages having more than 50% SC population are None.

Sex ratio of Scheduled Caste population is 491.

Scheduled Castes Literates and Illiterates by Sex:

	Persons	Males	Females
Literate	2,321	1,601	720
Illiterate	3,160	1,187	1,973
Literacy rate	49.1	67.0	30.8
Graduate	37	36	1

Scheduled Castes (Dominant):

Madiga, Mala, Mahar, Chamar etc., Beda Jangam etc.

For their cultural identity please see Appendix-I

Villages without Scheduled Castes: There are 19 villages without any scheduled caste population.

Scheduled Tribes: Out of the total population of 42766 persons, 13116 persons (30.67%) belong to Scheduled Tribes.

The villages having less than 10% ST population are Sonala, Marlapalle, Boath (Buzurg), Kangutta Pochera, Kuchalapur.

The villages having more than 50% ST population are Wajar, Chintalabori, Ghanpur, Kowtha (Khurd) Sakhera, Tewiti, Pardi (Buzurg), Gollapur, Babera Kantegaon, Nigini, Nakkalawada, Karathwada, Patnapur Suradapur, Narayanpur, Anduru, Birlagondi Dhannur (Khurd), Nagapur.

Sex ratio of Scheduled tribe population is 496.

Scheduled Tribes Literates and Illiterates by Sex:

	Persons	Males	Females
Literate	5,113	3,426	1,687
Illiterate	8,003	3,190	4,813
Literacy rate	48.4	64.3	32.2
Graduate	19	19	0

Scheduled Tribes (Dominant):

Gond etc., Sugalis etc., Koya etc., Andh, Pardhan

For their cultural identity please see Appendix-II

Villages without Scheduled Tribes: There are 9 villages without any scheduled tribe population.

Literates and Illiterates by Sex (Total Population):

	Persons	Males	Females
Literate	19,673	12,694	6,979
Illiterate	23,093	8,665	14,428
Literacy rate	54	70	38
Graduate	516	468	48

Agriculture: ***Distribution of villages according to land use:*** Out of 39 villages, Total area (in hectare) is 31122, out of that 44.65 percent is cultivable and 8.69 percent of the

cultivable area is irrigated.

Sources of Irrigation (Hectares): Government Canal 14.4, Private Canal 0, Well without Electricity 0, Well with Electricity 216.4, Tubewell without Electricity 20, Tubewell with Electricity 956.4, Tank 0, River 0, Lake 0, Waterfall 0, Others 0.

Villages with population of 5000 to 9999:
Sonala.

Villages with population of 10000 and above:
Boath (Buzurg).

Distribution of Workers:

	Persons	Males	Females	WPR
Cultivators	8,236	4,686	3,550	36.68
Agricultural Labour	6,481	3,328	3,153	28.87
Household Industry	4,217	403	3,814	18.78
Other Workers	3,517	2,802	715	15.67
Main Workers	20,705	10,658	10,047	92.22
Marginal Workers	1,746	561	1,185	7.78
Total Workers	22,451	11,219	11,232	

Religion: Major Religious Communities:

	Persons	Males	Females	Sex Ratio
Hindu (92.31%)	39,479	19,723	19,756	1,002
Muslim (7.46%)	3,191	1,590	1,601	1,007
Christian (0.05%)	21	9	12	1,333
Sikh (0%)	-	-	-	-
Buddhists (0.03%)	13	8	5	625
Jain (0%)	-	-	-	-

Agewise Data:

	Persons	Males	Females	Sex Ratio
All ages	42,766	21,359	21,407	1002
0-14	16,139	8,272	7,867	951
15-44	18,816	9,511	9,305	978
45-79	7,406	3,410	3,996	1172
80+	333	126	207	1643
Age not stated	72	40	32	800

Languages (Dominant):
Telugu, Hindi, Gondi, Urdu, Marathi

Disabled Population:

	Persons	Males	Females	%
Total Disabled	679	428	251	
In Seeing	258	168	90	38
In Speech	61	37	24	8.98
In Hearing	40	21	19	5.89
In Movement	244	159	85	35.94
Mentally	76	43	33	11.19

BOBBILI

Bobbili C.D. Block lies in the northern part of Viziana garam district. It is a part of Bobbili Mandal. The Block is located at a distance of 65 kms. from district headquarters (Vizianagaram). There are 42 villages in the block with the total population of 66,065 persons. Area of the C.D. Block is 167.94 sq. kms. It is bound ed in the north by Mandals Seethanagaram and Balijipeta, in the south by Mandal Badangi, in the east by Mandals Balijipeta and Therlam, and in the west by Mandals Ramabhadrapuram and Makkuva.

Communications :

Roadways : State Highway (S.H.): Direction- Ramabhadrapu ram to Parvathipuram. Nearest Villages- Komatipalle (Near) Bobbili, Kalavarai Agraharam, Vakadavalasa, Chintada, Pakki, Paradhi, Gorla Seetharampuram, Mettav alasa.

Railway Station: Kasidoravalasa, Narayanappavalasa.

Backwards Region Grants Fund: It receives Backward Region Grants.

Integrated Child Development Scheme (ICDS) Project: Bobbili, Total Anganwadi Centres: 252.

Annaul Rainfall: Average Rainfall 1122.6 mm

Ground Water: Availability of the Ground Water in the Basin is (Information not avavible) H.A.M .and the utilization is (Information not avavible) H.A.M. It belongs to (Information not avavible) category. Depth to water level varies from 3 to 10 meter below the ground. Most of the wells go down in summer months.

Administration:

Division: Coastal Andhra. Parliamentary Constituency: 20 Vizianagram. District: Vizianagram. Mandal: Bobbili. Assembly Constituency: 133 Bobbili. Gram Panchayat: 30

Places of Tourist Interest:

Bobbili : Bobbili is situated at a distance of 65 kms. from Vizianagaram. The earlier name of this town was Peddapuli (Tiger). Due to the efflux of time, it gradua lly changed to Pebbuli, Bebbuli and finally Bobbili. This place has an important Railway Junction on the Raipur-Vizianagaram line. Bobbili is associated with the historic battle between Zamindar of Vizianagaram and the French on one side and the Raja of Bobbili on the other. The Raja of Bobbili erected a war memorial at the place where the actual battle took place to, commemorate the tragic event and the memorial can be seen towards north-east on the outskirts of the town. Bobbili is famous for the manufacture of 'Vinas' and wellknown as one of the important towns where fine arts flourished. There is also a fine temple of Lord Venugopala.

Villages: 42 **Inhabited:** 38 **Uninhabited:** 4

Ranking	District	State	National
Area	9	724	4744
Population	4	193	4638

Sex Ratio	15	153	850
Child Sex Ratio	25	444	1594
Literacy Rate	11	760	4755
Density	15	148	2773
Work Participation Rate	12	194	431

Gram Panchayats:
Alajangi, Ch.Boddavalasa, Chintada, Dibbagudivalasa Gongada Valasa, Gopalarayudupeta Gorlasitarama Puram, J.Rangarayapuram@Kvpeta Jagannadhapuram, Kalavari, Kammavalasa, Karada Kasimdora Valasa, Kinthalavalasa, Komatipalli Kondadevupalli, Kotha Penta, Krishnapuram M.Boorjavalasa, Mettavalasa, Narayanappa Valasa Pakki, Paradhi, Penta, Piridi, Ramuduvalasa Rangaraya Puram, Seethayyapeta, Sivadavalasa Velagalavalasa.

Amenities:

Education: Primary School in 38 villages, Middle school in 15 villages, Matriculation or Secondary School in 8 villages, namely Kalavarai Agraharam, Chintada, Pakki, Piridi, Patha Bobbili (Rural), Paradhi, Gorla Seetharampuram, Alajangi.

Higher Secondary or Pre University Courses or Intermediate or Junior College in 0 village of the CD Block, College in 0 village, Adult Literacy Center in 32 villages.

Medical: Hospital in 0 village, Dispensary in 5 villages, Health Center in 2 villages, Sub Center in 18 villages, Maternity and Child Welfare Center in 0 village, Community health workers in 0 village.

The Villages having Hospital or Dispensary or Health Center are Velagavalasa (Near) Addumanda, Komatipalle (Near) Bobbili, Sivadavalasa, Piridi, Karada.

Drinking Water: Tap water in 38 villages, Tank water in 38 villages, Well water in 38 villages, Tubewell in 38 villages and more than one source in 38 villages.

Bank: Banking facility in 3 villages, namely, Chintada, Piridi, Paradhi.

Credit Society in 19 villages Agricultural Credit Society in 13 Non-Agricultural Credit Society in 14 villages.

Others: Power supply in 38 villages, Cinema hall in 0 village, sport club in 0 village, Stadium or Auditorium or Community Hall in 0 village, Post Office in 22 villages.

There are 23 villages having bus facilities.

Villages with most of facilities: Chintada, Piridi Paradhi.

Villages without Amenities (Education): None..

Scheduled Castes: Out of the total population of 66117 persons, 8634 persons (13.06%) belong to Scheduled Castes. The villages having less than 10% SC population are Nimmalapadu, Kalavarai Agraharam, Kondadevupalle Kammavalasa, Patha Bobbili (Rural), Donguruvalasa Kasidoravalasa, Narayanappavalasa, Paradhi Bankuruvalasa, Bhojarajapuram, Mettavalasa Panukuvalasa (Near) Mettavalasa Burjavalasa (Near) Mettavalasa, Penta Janardhanarangarayapuram @ Kunukuvanivalasa.

The villages having more than 50% SC population are None.

Sex ratio of Scheduled Caste population is 501.

Scheduled Castes Literates and Illiterates by Sex:

	Persons	Males	Females
Literate	3,405	2,141	1,264
Illiterate	5,229	2,166	3,063
Literacy rate	45.5	57.4	33.6
Graduate	79	68	11

Scheduled Castes (Dominant):
Madiga, Mala, Relli, Dom etc., Beda Jangam etc.

For their cultural identity please see Appendix-I

Villages without Scheduled Castes: There are 8 villages without any scheduled caste population.

Scheduled Tribes: Out of the total population of 66117 persons, 2508 persons (3.79%) belong to Scheduled Tribes. The villages having less than 10% ST population are Velagavalasa (Near) Addumanda, Gopalarayudupeta Rajupeta, Seethayyapeta Janardhana Ranga Rayapuram @ Kintalavanipeta Lingamvalasa, Komatipalle (Near) Bobbili Kalavarai Agraharam, Vakadavalasa, Chintada, Pakki Ramuduvalasa, Sivadavalasa, Kondadevupalle Kammavalasa, Muttavalasa, Piridi, Krishnapuram Jagannadhapuram (Near) Bobbili Chitrakota Boddavalasa, Narayanappavalasa, Paradhi Bankuruvalasa, Mettavalasa Burjavalasa (Near) Mettavalasa, Penta Rangarayapuram Janardhanarangarayapuram @ Kunukuvanivalasa Alajangi.

The villages having more than 50% ST population are None.

Sex ratio of Scheduled tribe population is 500.

Scheduled Tribes Literates and Illiterates by Sex:

	Persons	Males	Females
Literate	835	523	312
Illiterate	1,673	731	942
Literacy rate	39.2	49.3	29.2
Graduate	7	7	0

Scheduled Tribes (Dominant):
Konda Dhoras, Jatapus, Gadabas, Yerukulas Manna Dhora

For their cultural identity please see Appendix-II

Villages without Scheduled Tribes: There are 17 villages without any scheduled tribe population.

Literates and Illiterates by Sex (Total Population):

	Persons	Males	Females
Literate	28,047	18,027	10,020
Illiterate	38,070	14,850	23,220
Literacy rate	49	63	34
Graduate	931	824	107

Agriculture: ***Distribution of villages according to land use:*** Out of 42 villages, Total area (in hectare) is 16794, out of that 70.95 percent is cultivable and 51.42 percent of the cultivable area is irrigated.

Sources of Irrigation (Hectares): Government Canal 1138.02, Private Canal 0, Well without Electricity 143.72, Well with Electricity 65.59, Tubewell without Electricity 84.53, Tubewell with Electricity 203.22, Tank 4396.3, River 0, Lake 0, Waterfall 0, Others 94.73.

Villages with population of 5000 to 9999:
Chintada, Piridi, Alajangi.

Villages with population of 10000 and above: None

Distribution of Workers:

	Persons	Males	Females	WPR
Cultivators	11,467	6,752	4,715	29.99
Agricultural Labour	18,023	6,863	11,160	47.14
Household Industry	1,033	595	438	2.7
Other Workers	7,711	5,884	1,827	20.17
Main Workers	25,429	16,099	9,330	66.51
Marginal Workers	12,805	3,995	8,810	33.49
Total Workers	38,234	20,094	18,140	

Religion: Major Religious Communities:

	Persons	Males	Females	Sex Ratio
Hindu (99.71%)	65,923	32,790	33,133	1,010
Muslim (0.11%)	73	33	40	1,212
Christian (0.11%)	75	31	44	1,419
Sikh (0%)	2	1	1	1,000
Buddhists (0%)	-	-	-	-
Jain (0%)	-	-	-	-

Agewise Data:

	Persons	Males	Females	Sex Ratio
All ages	66,117	32,877	33,240	1011
0-14	19,433	9,937	9,496	956
15-44	31,606	15,677	15,929	1016
45-79	14,579	7,020	7,559	1077
80+	348	170	178	1047
Age not stated	151	73	78	1068

Languages (Dominant):
Telugu, Konda, Jatapu, Gondi, Oriya

Disabled Population:

	Persons	Males	Females	%
Total Disabled	1,811	969	842	
In Seeing	959	492	467	52.95
In Speech	140	82	58	7.73
In Hearing	127	63	64	7.01
In Movement	462	274	188	25.51
Mentally	123	58	65	6.79

BODHAN

Bodhan C.D. Block lies in the north-west part of Nizama bad district. It is a part of Bodhan Mandal. The Block is located at a distance of 32 kms. from district headq uarters (Nizamabad.). There are 39 villages in the block with the total population of 60,555 persons. Area of the C.D. Block is 269.97 sq. kms. It is bounded by Ranjal Mandal on north and north-east, Yedpalle Mandal on north-east and east, Varni Mandal on south-east, south and south-west, and Kotgiri Mandal on south-west.

Communications :

Roadways : State Highway (S.H.): Direction- Nanded to Banswada. Nearest Villages- Amdapur, Achampalle (Rural), Naganpalle, Ladmavandi, Minarpalle, Ootpalle, Bodhan (Rural), Saloora.

River: Manjira Nadi- Nearest Villages- Taggelli, Mandha rna, Hunsa, Khajapur, Saloora.

Backwards Region Grants Fund: It receives Backward Region Grants.

Integrated Child Development Scheme (ICDS) Project: Bodhan, Total Anganwadi Centres: 303

Annual Rainfall: Average Rainfall 1076 mm

Ground Water: Availability of the Ground Water in the Basin is 4686 H.A.M. and the utilization is 3781 H. A.M. It belongs to Semi Critical category. Depth to water level varies from 10 to 20 meter below the ground. Most of the wells go down in summer months, according to the Ground Water Estimation Committee.

Natural Division : Telangana Plateau Region

Administration:

Division: Telangana. Parliamentary Constituency: 4 Nizamabad. District: Nizamabad. Mandal: Bodhan. Assembly Constituency: 12 Bodhan. Gram Panchayat: 32.

Border Villages: (Maharashtra)- Nearest Villages- Bhikn alli, Khandgaon, Siddapur, Kaldurthi, Rampur, Mandharna, Hunsa, Hangarga, Taggelli, Saloora.

Fairs and Festivals:

Shivaratri Festival : It is celebrated for one day on Magha Bahula Chaturdasi (January-February). There are indications that the Bodhan had a historical past with great Saivite influence. Around what is known as the fort area, there appeared to have been a fort with holes in the walls through which the invaders and marauders were shot with guns. A moat around the fort filled with water provided security to the fort.

The fort had four gates on four sides. It is said that in the past the place went by the name Bahudhanyap uram (place of profuse grain and Bahudhanapuram (place of prosperity).

Villages: 39 **Inhabited:** 35 **Uninhabited:** 4

Ranking	District	State	National
Area	6	239	3106
Population	7	266	4837
Sex Ratio	22	96	658
Child Sex Ratio	12	383	1369
Literacy Rate	14	745	4706
Density	31	722	4382
Work Participation Rate	24	626	2048

Gram Panchayats:

Achanpally, Amdapur, Bardhipur, Bellalfarm Bhavanipet, Errajpally, Hangarga (V)_, Hunsa Jadi Jamalpur, Kaldurki, Khajapur, Khandgaon Kopparthy Camp, Kumanpally, Kupparga, Langdapur Mandarna, Mavandikalan, Mawandikurd, Minarpally Naganpally, Ootpally, Pegadapally, Pentakalan Pentakurd, Salampahad, Saloora, Saloora Camp, Sangam Siddapur (K), Srinivas Nagar, Taggelli.

Amenities:

Education: Primary School in 34 villages, Middle school in 14 villages, Matriculation or Secondary School in 7 villages, namely Kaldurthi, Mavandi (Khurd), Penta Kalan, Saloora, Amdapur, Penta Khurd, Sangam.

Higher Secondary or Pre University Courses or Intermediate or Junior College in 1 village of the CD Block,, namely Penta Khurd.

College in 0 village, Adult Literacy Center in 15 villages.

Medical: Hospital in 0 village, Dispensary in 0 village, Health Center in 1 village, Sub Center in 11 villages, Maternity and Child Welfare Center in 0 village, Community health workers in 0 village.

Drinking Water: Tap water in 34 villages, Tank water in 34 villages, Well water in 34 villages, Tubewell in 35 villages and more than one source in 35 villages.

Bank: Banking facility in 8 villages, namely, Kaldurthi, Penta Kalan, Saloora, Bodhan (Rural) Naganpalle, Salampad, Bhavanipet, Sangam.

Credit Society in 22 villages Agricultural Credit Society in 14 Non-Agricultural Credit Society in 5 villages.

Others: Power supply in 35 villages, Cinema hall in 0 village, sport club in 0 village, Stadium or Auditorium or Community Hall in 0 village, Post Office in 19 villages.

There are 31 villages having bus facilities.

Villages with most of facilities: Kaldurthi Penta Kalan, Saloora, Salampad, Bhavanipet, Sangam.

Villages without amenities (Education): Lakmapur..

Scheduled Castes: Out of the total population of 60600 persons, 12159 persons (20.06%) belong to Scheduled Castes.

The villages having less than 10% SC population are None..

The villages having more than 50% SC population are None.

Sex ratio of Scheduled Caste population is 513.

Scheduled Castes Literates and Illiterates by Sex:

	Persons	Males	Females
Literate	3,956	2,457	1,499
Illiterate	8,203	3,462	4,741
Literacy rate	37.9	48.7	27.8
Graduate	71	66	5

Scheduled Castes (Dominant):

Mala, Madiga, Gosangi, Chamar etc.

Generic Castes etc.

For their cultural identity please see Appendix-I

Villages without Scheduled Castes: There are 5 villages without any scheduled caste population.

Scheduled Tribes: Out of the total population of 60600 persons, 2764 persons (4.56%) belong to Scheduled Tribes.

The villages having less than 10% ST population are Bhiknalli, Hangarga, Kopperga, Khandgaon, Siddapur Kaldurthi, Mavandi (Khurd), Pegadpalle, Penta Kalan Langadapur, Mavandi (Kalan), Rampur, Fathepur Taggelli, Mandharna, Hunsa, Khajapur, Saloora Jadijamalpur, Bhandarpalle, Bardipur, Narsapur Erajpalle, Amdapur, Bodhan (Rural), Naganpalle Lakmapur, Komanpalle, Salampad, Penta Khurd Bhavanipet, Sangam.

The villages having more than 50% ST population are None.

Sex ratio of Scheduled tribe population is 506.

Scheduled Tribes Literates and Illiterates by Sex:

	Persons	Males	Females
Literate	793	549	244
Illiterate	1,971	817	1,154
Literacy rate	35.2	49.6	21.4
Graduate	23	21	2

Scheduled Tribes (Dominant):

Sugalis etc., Yerukulas, Gond etc., Chenchu etc. Koya etc.

For their cultural identity please see Appendix-II

Villages without Scheduled Tribes: There are 28 villages without any scheduled tribe population.

Literates and Illiterates by Sex (Total Population):

	Persons	Males	Females
Literate	25,635	15,524	10,111
Illiterate	34,965	14,479	20,486
Literacy rate	49	60	38

Graduate	821	669	152

Agriculture: ***Distribution of villages according to land use:*** Out of 39 villages, Total area (in hectare) is 26997, out of that 54.44 percent is cultivable and 67.56 percent of the cultivable area is irrigated.

Sources of Irrigation (Hectares): Government Canal 3299.43, Private Canal 0, Well without Electricity 0, Well with Electricity 6.87, Tubewell without Electricity 0, Tubewell with Electricity 6289.57, Tank 78.09, River 0, Lake 0, Waterfall 0, Others 256.53.

Villages with population of 5000 to 9999: Saloora.

Villages with population of 10000 and above: None

Distribution of Workers:

	Persons	Males	Females	WPR
Cultivators	7,450	5,622	1,828	24.55
Agricultural Labour	16,312	7,622	8,690	53.76
Household Industry	1,280	362	918	4.22
Other Workers	5,300	3,647	1,653	17.47
Main Workers	24,923	15,326	9,597	82.14
Marginal Workers	5,419	1,927	3,492	17.86
Total Workers	30,342	17,253	13,089	

Religion: Major Religious Communities:

	Persons	Males	Females	Sex Ratio
Hindu (84.39%)	51,139	25,272	25,867	1,024
Muslim (14.16%)	8,578	4,296	4,282	997
Christian (1.43%)	868	427	441	1,033
Sikh (0%)	-	-	-	-
Buddhists (0.02%)	12	7	5	714
Jain (0%)	-	-	-	-

Agewise Data:

	Persons	Males	Females	Sex Ratio
All ages	60,600	30,003	30,597	1020
0-14	20,194	10,161	10,033	987
15-44	28,305	14,176	14,129	997
45-79	11,676	5,485	6,191	1129
80+	366	150	216	1440
Age not stated	59	31	28	903

Languages (Dominant):

Telugu, Urdu, Kannada, Marathi, Hindi

Disabled Population:

	Persons	Males	Females	%
Total Disabled	1,018	573	445	
In Seeing	418	210	208	41.06
In Speech	106	54	52	10.41
In Hearing	50	29	21	4.91
In Movement	314	198	116	30.84
Mentally	130	82	48	12.77

BOGOLE

Bogole C.D. Block lies in the north-eastern part of Nellore district. It is a part of Kavurpalle Mandal. The Block is located at a distance of 36 kms. from district headquarters (Nellore). There are 11 villages in the block with the total population of 40,473 persons. Area of the C.D. Block is 167.76 sq. kms. It is bound ed in the north by Mandals Jaladanki and Kavali, in the south by Mandals Dagadarthi and Allur, in the east by the Bay of Bengal, and in the west by Mandals Jalada nki and Dagadarthi.

Headquarters: Kuvurpalle.

Communications:

Roadways : NH- 5: Direction- Nellore to Ongole. Nearest Village- Allimadugu, Bogole village.

Railway Station: Bogole, Bitragunta.

River: Bungala Kadav: Nearest Villages- Allimadugu village.

Annual Rainfall: Average Rainfall 1124 mm

Ground Water: Availability of the Ground Water in the Basin is 2127 H.A.M. and the utilization is 613 H.A. M. It belongs to Safe category. Depth to water level varies from 2 to 10 meter below the ground. Most of the wells go down in summer months, according to the Ground Water Estimation Committee.

Coastal Villages: Nearest Village- Juvvaladinne.

Administration:

Division: Coastal Andhra. Parliamentary Constituency: 39 Nellore. District: Nellore.

Mandal: Bogole. Assembly Constituency: 233 Kavali.

Gram Panchayat: 16.

Fairs and Festivals:

Sri Prasanna Venkateswaraswamy Brahmoth-savam : Sri Prasanna Venkateswaraswamy Brahmoth-savam takes place for seven days from Phalguna Suddha Dasami to Bahula Padyami (February-March) at Bitragunta near Nellore. Ankurarpana on the first day, dhwajarohana on the second day, Hanumanthaseva on the third, Garudaseva and Harikatha on the fourth, enugu vahanothsavam on the fifth day morning and theppa uthsavam in the night, akshatharohana on the sixth day morning' rathothsavam in the afternoon and aswavahanam and alakaladopu in the night and on the last day ekanthaseva are celebrated. With this the festival concludes. These rituals are celebrated by the devotees. Cocoanuts, pumpkins, rice, ghee, silver and gold coins are offered. It is of very ancient origin and a widely known one. The temples of Sri Prasanna Venkateswara-swamy on the hill with the stone images in human form are the places of worship.

Villages: 11 **Inhabited:** 11 **Uninhabited:** 0

Ranking	District	State	National
Area	38	725	4748

Population	27	814	5720
Sex Ratio	9	264	1230
Child Sex Ratio	30	837	3688
Literacy Rate	23	262	2763
Density	20	773	4196
Work Participation Rate	13	572	2257

Gram Panchayats:

A.B. Kandrika, Allimadugu, Bitragunta, Bogole Chenaraunipalem, J.P. Gudur, Juvvaladinne Kovurupalli, Mungamuru, Nagulavaram Sundaragirivari. Kandrika, Sv Palem, Thalluru Umamaheswarapuram, V.N.R Pet, Yenugula Bavi.

Amenities:

Education: Primary School in 11 villages, Middle school in 4 villages, Matriculation or Secondary School in 3 villages, namely Bogole, Bitragunta, Mungamur.

Higher Secondary or Pre University Courses or Intermediate or Junior College in 1 village of the CD Block,, namely Bitragunta.

College in 0 village, Adult Literacy Center in 9 villages.

Medical: Hospital in 0 village, Dispensary in 1 village, Health Center in 0 village, Sub Center in 8 villages, Maternity and Child Welfare Center in 0 village, Community health workers in 0 village.

The Village having Hospital or Dispensary or Health Center is Bogole.

Drinking Water: Tap water in 11 villages, Tank water in 11 villages, Well water in 11 villages, Tubewell in 11 villages and more than one source in 11 villages.

Bank: Banking facility in 2 villages, namely, Bogole, Bitragunta.

Credit Society in 8 villages Agricultural Credit Society in 3 Non-Agricultural Credit Society in 8 villages.

Others: Power supply in 11 villages, Cinema hall in 1 village, sport club in 0 village, Stadium or Auditorium or Community Hall in 0 village, Post Office in 9 villages.

There are 9 villages having bus facilities.

Villages with most of facilities: Bogole Bitragunta.

Villages without Amenities (Education): None..

Scheduled Castes: Out of the total population of 40406 persons, 8479 persons (20.98%) belong to Scheduled Castes.

The villages having less than 10% SC population are None..

The villages having more than 50% SC population are None.

Sex ratio of Scheduled Caste population is 509.

Scheduled Castes Literates and Illiterates by Sex:

	Persons	Males	Females
Literate	4,823	2,747	2,076
Illiterate	3,656	1,419	2,237
Literacy rate	65.0	75.2	55.1
Graduate	123	83	40

Scheduled Castes (Dominant):

Mala, Madiga, Arundhatiya, Samban, Beda Jangam etc.

For their cultural identity please see Appendix-I

Villages without Scheduled Castes: There is 1 village without any scheduled caste population.

Scheduled Tribes: Out of the total population of 40406 persons, 4529 persons (11.21%) belong to Scheduled Tribes.

The villages having less than 10% ST population are Thalluru, Jakkepalligudur, Umamaheswarapuram Sambasivapuram, Juvvaladinne Siddavarapu Venkatesupalem, Mallayapalem.

The villages having more than 50% ST population are None.

Sex ratio of Scheduled tribe population is 501.

Scheduled Tribes Literates and Illiterates by Sex:

	Persons	Males	Females
Literate	1,774	956	818
Illiterate	2,755	1,304	1,451
Literacy rate	46.0	49.8	42.3
Graduate	17	14	3

Scheduled Tribes (Dominant):

Yerukulas, Yenadis, Kammara, Sugalis etc., Jatapus

For their cultural identity please see Appendix-II

Villages without Scheduled Tribes: There are 2 villages without any scheduled tribe population.

Literates and Illiterates by Sex (Total Population):

	Persons	Males	Females
Literate	21,156	12,221	8,935
Illiterate	19,250	7,999	11,251
Literacy rate	60	70	51
Graduate	543	387	156

Agriculture: ***Distribution of villages according to land use:*** Out of 11 villages, Total area (in hectare) is 16776, out of that 40.48 percent is cultivable and 88.22 percent of the cultivable area is irrigated.

Sources of Irrigation (Hectares): Government Canal 4920, Private Canal 360, Well without Electricity 0, Well with Electricity 281, Tubewell without Electricity 0, Tubewell with Electricity 430, Tank 0, River 0, Lake 0, Waterfall 0, Others 0.

Villages with population of 5000 to 9999: Juvvaladinne.

Villages with population of 10000 and above: Bogole.

Distribution of Workers:

	Persons	Males	Females	WPR
Cultivators	4,455	3,059	1,396	22.12

Agricultural Labour	10,148	4,232	5,916	50.39
Household Industry	301	168	133	1.49
Other Workers	5,236	4,388	848	26
Main Workers	12,073	8,765	3,308	59.95
Marginal Workers	8,067	3,082	4,985	40.05
Total Workers	20,140	11,847	8,293	

Religion: Major Religious Communities:

	Persons	Males	Females	Sex Ratio
Hindu (89.07%)	35,989	17,996	17,993	1,000
Muslim (5.35%)	2,160	1,094	1,066	974
Christian (5.51%)	2,227	1,117	1,110	994
Sikh (0%)	-	-	-	-
Buddhists (0%)	-	-	-	-
Jain (0%)	-	-	-	-

Agewise Data:

	Persons	Males	Females	Sex Ratio
All ages	40,406	20,220	20,186	998
0-14	12,198	6,217	5,981	962
15-44	19,627	9,770	9,857	1009
45-79	8,315	4,104	4,211	1026
80+	236	112	124	1107
Age not stated	30	17	13	765

Languages (Dominant):
Telugu, Tamil, Urdu, Others, English

Disabled Population:

	Persons	Males	Females	%
Total Disabled	1,006	528	478	
In Seeing	430	219	211	42.74
In Speech	114	65	49	11.33
In Hearing	57	22	35	5.67
In Movement	296	167	129	29.42
Mentally	109	55	54	10.83

BOINPALLE

Boinpalle C.D. Block lies in the north-west part of Karimnagar district. The Block is located at a distance of 30 kms. from district headquarters (Karimnagar). There are 16 villages in the block with the total population of 37,564 persons. Area of the C.D. Block is 136.46 sq. kms. It is bounded by Kodimial Mandal on north, Gangadhara Mandal on east, Karimnagar Mandal on south-east, Ellanthakunta Mandal on south, Sircilla Mandal on south-west, and Vemulawada Mandal on west.

Communications :

Roadways : State Highway (S.H.): Direction- Gangadhara to Vardavelli. and Sircilla to Karimnagar. Nearest Villages- Shabashpalle, Kodurupaka, Thadagonda, Boinpal le, Vilasagar, Vardavelli, Narsingapur, Kothapeta.

River: Manner Nadi- Nearest Villages- Manwada, Mallapur, Shabashpalle, Kodurupaka.

Backwards Region Grants Fund: It receives Backward Region Grants.

Annual Rainfall: Average Rainfall 901 mm

Ground Water: Availability of the Ground Water in the Basin is 1053 H.A.M. and the utilization is 1344 H. A.M. It belongs to Over Exploited category. Depth to water level varies from more than 5 to 10 meter below the ground. Most of the wells go down in summer months. The well density in the entire block is 31 wells per sq. km. Total no. of the wells in the block are enumera ted as 4151, according to the Ground Water Estimation Committee.

Natural Division : Godavari Depression Region

Administration:

Division: Telangana. Parliamentary Constituency: 3 Karimnagar. District: Karimnagar. Mandal: Boinpalle. Assembly Constituency: 27 Choppadandi (SC). Gram Panch ayat: 24.

Villages: 16 **Inhabited:** 16 **Uninhabited:** 0

Ranking	District	State	National
Area	53	879	5241
Population	49	892	5836
Sex Ratio	18	106	673
Child Sex Ratio	10	193	578
Literacy Rate	22	618	4290
Density	22	319	3806
Work Participation Rate	28	450	794

Gram Panchayats:

Anathapally, Boinpalli, Buruguaplly, Desaipalli Dundrapally, Gundannapalli, Jaggaraopally Kodurupaka, Korem, Kothapeta, Malkapoor, Mallapoor Manwada, Marlapet, Narsigapoor, Neelojipally Ramannapet, Ratnampet, Shabaspalli, Stambampalli Thadakonda, Vardavelly, Venkatraopally, Vilasagar.

Amenities:

Education: Primary School in 16 villages, Middle school in 9 villages, Matriculation or Secondary School in 6 villages, namely Korem, Boinpalle, Vilasagar, Kodurupaka, Narsingapur, Mallapur.

Higher Secondary or Pre University Courses or Intermediate or Junior College in 0 village of the CD Block, College in 0 village, Adult Literacy Center in 9 villages.

Medical: Hospital in 0 village, Dispensary in 1 village, Health Center in 3 villages, Sub Center in 5 villages, Maternity and Child Welfare Center in 2 villages, Community health workers in 0 village.

The Villages having Hospital or Dispensary or Health Center are Boinpalle, Vilasagar, Kodurupaka.

Drinking Water: Tap water in 16 villages, Tank water in 16 villages, Well water in 16 villages, Tubewell in 16 villages and more than one source in 16 villages.

Bank: Banking facility in 3 villages, namely,

Boinpalle, Vilasagar, Kodurupaka.
Credit Society in 16 villages Agricultural Credit Society in 6 Non-Agricultural Credit Society in 16 villages.
Others: Power supply in 16 villages, Cinema hall in 0 village, sport club in 0 village, Stadium or Auditorium or Community Hall in 0 village, Post Office in 13 villages.
There are 16 villages having bus facilities.
Villages with most of facilities: Boinpalle Vilasagar, Kodurupaka.
Villages without Amenities (Education): None..
Scheduled Castes: Out of the total population of 37564 persons, 9908 persons (26.38%) belong to Scheduled Castes.
The villages having less than 10% SC population are None..
The villages having more than 50% SC population are None.
Sex ratio of Scheduled Caste population is 503.

Scheduled Castes Literates and Illiterates by Sex:

	Persons	Males	Females
Literate	3,834	2,400	1,434
Illiterate	6,074	2,521	3,553
Literacy rate	44.9	56.6	33.5
Graduate	66	60	6

Scheduled Castes (Dominant):
Madiga, Mala, Generic Castes etc., Beda Jangam etc. Bindla
For their cultural identity please see Appendix-I
Villages without Scheduled Castes: There are 0 village without any scheduled caste population.
Scheduled Tribes: Out of the total population of 37564 persons, 114 persons (0.3%) belong to Scheduled Tribes.
The villages having less than 10% ST population are Dundrapalle, Ananthapalle, Malkapur, Thadagonda Korem, Burgupalle, Sthambhampalle, Boinpalle Vilasagar, Vardavelli, Shabashpalle, Kodurupaka Narsingapur, Kothapeta, Manwada, Mallapur.
The villages having more than 50% ST population are None.
Sex ratio of Scheduled tribe population is 509.

Scheduled Tribes Literates and Illiterates by Sex:

	Persons	Males	Females
Literate	51	35	16
Illiterate	63	21	42
Literacy rate	51.5	68.6	33.3
Graduate	0	0	0

Scheduled Tribes (Dominant):
Yerukulas, Sugalis etc., Gond etc.
For their cultural identity please see Appendix-II
Villages without Scheduled Tribes: There are 9 villages without any scheduled tribe population.

Literates and Illiterates by Sex (Total Population):

	Persons	Males	Females
Literate	16,882	10,604	6,278
Illiterate	20,682	7,997	12,685
Literacy rate	51	65	38
Graduate	428	378	50

Agriculture: ***Distribution of villages according to land use:***
Out of 16 villages, Total area (in hectare) is 13647, out of that 84.36 percent is cultivable and 34.42 percent of the cultivable area is irrigated.
Sources of Irrigation (Hectares): Government Canal 0, Private Canal 0, Well without Electricity 0, Well with Electricity 3430, Tubewell without Electricity 0, Tubewell with Electricity 533, Tank 0, River 0, Lake 0, Waterfall 0, Others 0.
Villages with population of 5000 to 9999:
Vilasagar.
Villages with population of 10000 and above: None
Distribution of Workers:

	Persons	Males	Females	WPR
Cultivators	6,955	4,106	2,849	33.23
Agricultural Labour	7,613	3,239	4,374	36.37
Household Industry	3,318	902	2,416	15.85
Other Workers	3,046	2,365	681	14.55
Main Workers	19,662	10,224	9,438	93.93
Marginal Workers	1,270	388	882	6.07
Total Workers	20,932	10,612	10,320	

Religion: Major Religious Communities:

	Persons	Males	Females	Sex Ratio
Hindu (98.13%)	36,861	18,258	18,603	1,019
Muslim (1.54%)	577	282	295	1,046
Christian (0.28%)	105	51	54	1,059
Sikh (0%)	1	-	1	-
Buddhists (0%)	-	-	-	-
Jain (0%)	-	-	-	-

Agewise Data:

	Persons	Males	Females	Sex Ratio
All ages	37,564	18,601	18,963	1019
0-14	11,299	5,636	5,663	1005
15-44	17,136	8,411	8,725	1037
45-79	8,707	4,350	4,357	1002
80+	408	194	214	1103
Age not stated	14	10	4	400

Languages (Dominant):
Telugu, Urdu, Hindi, Marathi, Oriya
Disabled Population:

	Persons	Males	Females	%
Total Disabled	514	285	229	
In Seeing	223	127	96	43.39
In Speech	65	29	36	12.65

In Hearing	29	14	15	5.64
In Movement	143	87	56	27.82

Mentally	54	28	26	10.51

BOLLAPALLE

Bollapalle C.D. Block lies in the western part of Guntur district. The Block is located at a distance of 73 kms. from district headquarters (Guntur). There are 14 villages in the block with the total population of 55,378 persons. Area of the C.D. Block is 276.21 sq. kms. It is bounded in the north by Mandals Durgi, Karempudi and Piduguralla, in the south by Mandal Vinukonda, in the east by Mandals Ipur and Nekarikallu, and in the west by district Prakasam and Durgi.

Communications:

Roadways : State Highway (S.H.): Direction- Karempudi to Ipur. Nearest Village- Mellavagu.

Annual Rainfall: Average Rainfall 683 mm

Ground Water: Availability of the Ground Water in the Basin is 3759 H.A.M. and the utilization is 3150 H. A.M. It belongs to Semi Critical category. Depth to water level varies from 2 to 5 meter below the ground. Most of the wells go down in summer months.

Forest and Reserved **Forest:** Nearest Villages- Ayyannapa lem, Garikapadu, Mellavagu, Gummanampadu, Remidicherla, Gandiganumala, Ravulapuram, Gutlapalle, Kanumalacheruvu, Perurupadu, Vellatur, Bollapalle, Vaddemgunta, Sariko ndapalem.

Natural Division : Krishna Delta Region

Administration:

Division: Coastal Andhra. Parliamentary Constituency: 218 Virukunda. District: Guntur. Mandal: Bollapalle. Assembly Constituency: 31-Narasaraopet. Gram Panchayat: 22

Villages: 14 **Inhabited:** 14 **Uninhabited:** 0

Ranking	District	State	National
Area	5	218	3037
Population	29	364	5041
Sex Ratio	39	659	2232
Child Sex Ratio	10	255	808
Literacy Rate	57	1059	5974
Density	3	43	4730
Work Participation Rate	53	715	195

Gram Panchayats:

Ayyannapalem, Bandlamotu, Bollapalli, Domalagundam Gandiganumala, Garikapadu, Gummanampadu, Gutlapalli Jayanthiramapuram, Kanumalacheruvu, Lalipuram Mellavagu, Mugachintalapalem, Naidupalem, Palukuru Pamidipadu, Perurupadu, Ravulapuram, Remidicherla Sarikondayapalem, Vaddemgunta, Vellatur.

Amenities:

Education: Primary School in 14 villages, Middle school in 7 villages, Matriculation or Secondary School in 3 villages, namely Gummanampadu, Vellatur, Bollapalle.

Higher Secondary or Pre University Courses or Intermediate or Junior College in 0 village of the CD Block, College in 0 village, Adult Literacy Center in 0 village.

Medical: Hospital in 0 village, Dispensary in 0 village, Health Center in 1 village, Sub Center in 10 villages, Maternity and Child Welfare Center in 0 village, Community health workers in 0 village.

Drinking Water: Tap water in 14 villages, Tank water in 14 villages, Well water in 14 villages, Tubewell in 14 villages and more than one source in 14 villages.

Bank: Banking facility in 2 villages, namely, Gummanampadu, Vellatur.

Credit Society in 5 villages Agricultural Credit Society in 4 Non-Agricultural Credit Society in 0 village.

Others: Power supply in 14 villages, Cinema hall in 0 village, sport club in 0 village, Stadium or Auditorium or Community Hall in 0 village, Post Office in 12 villages.

There are 14 villages having bus facilities.

Villages with most of facilities: Gummanampadu Vellatur.

Villages without Amenities (Education): None..

Scheduled Castes: Out of the total population of 55378 persons, 8922 persons (16.11%) belong to Scheduled Castes.

The villages having less than 10% SC population are None..

The villages having more than 50% SC population are None.

Sex ratio of Scheduled Caste population is 497.

Scheduled Castes Literates and Illiterates by Sex:

	Persons	Males	Females
Literate	2,569	1,771	798
Illiterate	6,353	2,720	3,633
Literacy rate	34.9	47.4	22.0
Graduate	76	57	19

Scheduled Castes (Dominant):

Madiga, Mala, Madiga Dasu etc., Mala Dasu Mala Dasari

For their cultural identity please see Appendix-I

Villages without Scheduled Castes: There are 0 village without any scheduled caste population.

Scheduled Tribes: Out of the total population of 55378 persons, 14556 persons (26.28%) belong to Scheduled Tribes.

The villages having less than 10% ST population are None..

The villages having more than 50% ST population are None.

Sex ratio of Scheduled tribe population is 486.

Scheduled Tribes Literates and Illiterates by Sex:

	Persons	Males	Females
Literate	3,305	2,416	889
Illiterate	11,251	5,060	6,191
Literacy rate	28.1	39.9	15.6
Graduate	92	77	15

Scheduled Tribes (Dominant):

Sugalis etc., Yerukulas, Chenchu etc., Yenadis Koya etc.

For their cultural identity please see Appendix-II

Villages without Scheduled Tribes: There are 0 village without any scheduled tribe population.

Literates and Illiterates by Sex (Total Population):

	Persons	Males	Females
Literate	16,507	11,224	5,283
Illiterate	38,871	16,822	22,049
Literacy rate	36	48	23
Graduate	537	425	112

Agriculture: ***Distribution of villages according to land use:*** Out of 14 villages, Total area (in hectare) is 27621, out of that 50.43 percent is cultivable and 20.7 percent of the cultivable area is irrigated.

Sources of Irrigation (Hectares): Government Canal 2232.89, Private Canal 0, Well without Electricity 0, Well with Electricity 0, Tubewell without Electricity 0, Tubewell with Electricity 534.27, Tank 116.89, River 0, Lake 0, Waterfall 0, Others 0.

Villages with population of 5000 to 9999: Garikapadu, Gutlapalle, Vellatur, Bollapalle.

Villages with population of 10000 and above: None

Distribution of Workers:

	Persons	Males	Females	WPR
Cultivators	8,836	5,660	3,176	27.7
Agricultural Labour	20,211	8,878	11,333	63.36
Household Industry	452	197	255	1.42
Other Workers	2,401	1,854	547	7.53
Main Workers	23,578	13,790	9,788	73.91
Marginal Workers	8,322	2,799	5,523	26.09
Total Workers	31,900	16,589	15,311	

Religion: Major Religious Communities:

	Persons	Males	Females	Sex Ratio
Hindu (92.27%)	51,099	25,885	25,214	974
Muslim (5.61%)	3,109	1,568	1,541	983
Christian (2.02%)	1,121	572	549	960
Sikh (0%)	-	-	-	-
Buddhists (0%)	2	-	2	-
Jain (0%)	1	1	-	-

Agewise Data:

	Persons	Males	Females	Sex Ratio
All ages	55,378	28,046	27,332	975
0-14	20,348	10,276	10,072	980
15-44	24,809	12,652	12,157	961
45-79	9,717	4,876	4,841	993
80+	395	186	209	1124
Age not stated	109	56	53	946

Languages (Dominant):

Telugu, Hindi, Urdu, Tamil, Gondi

Disabled Population:

	Persons	Males	Females	%
Total Disabled	1,408	880	528	
In Seeing	793	543	250	56.32
In Speech	112	56	56	7.95
In Hearing	68	36	32	4.83
In Movement	305	178	127	21.66
Mentally	130	67	63	9.23

BOMMALARAMARAM

Bommalaramaram C.D. Block lies in the north-west part of Nalgonda district. The Block is located at a distance of 108 kms. from district headquarters (Nalgonda). There are 24 villages in the block with the total population of 34,114 persons. Area of the C.D. Block is 196.77 sq. kms. It is bounded by Medak district on north, M. Turkapalle Mandal on east, Bhongir Mandal on south-east, Bibinagar Mandal on south, and Rangareddi district on west.

Communications:

Roadways : NH, SH or Important Metalled Road is not available.

River: Musi Nadi- Nearest Villages- Muneerabad, Bandaki ndi Palle, Jalalpur, Solipeta, Cheekati Mamidi, Maryala, Malyala, Yavapur, Hazipur, Medi Palle, Mailaram.

Backwards Region Grants Fund: It receives Backward Region Grants.

Annual Rainfall: Average Rainfall 689 mm

Ground Water: Availability of the Ground Water in the Basin is 2293 H.A.M. and the utilization is 1891 H. A.M. It belongs to SC category. Depth to water level varies from 10 to 20 meter below the ground. Most of the wells go down in summer months. The well density in the entire block is 12 wells per sq. km. Total no. of the wells in the block are enumerated as 2017 accor ding to the Ground Water Estimation Committee.

Natural Division : Krishna Piedmont Plain Region

Administration:

Division: Telangana. Parliamentary Constituency: 14 Bhongir. District: Nalgonda. Mandal: Bommalaramaram. Assembly Constituency: 97 Alair. Gram Panchayat: 25.

Villages: 24 **Inhabited:** 23 **Uninhabited:** 1

Ranking	**District**	**State**	**National**
Area	51	727	4754

Population	58	952	5939
Sex Ratio	40	807	2690
Child Sex Ratio	16	527	2005
Literacy Rate	39	690	4508
Density	28	500	4686
Work Participation Rate	34	706	1295

Gram Panchayats:
B.Ramaram, Bandakadipally, Boinpally, Chikatimamidi Chouderpally, Hazipur, Jalalpur, Kanchalthanda Kandlakunta Thand, Laxmithanda, Machanpally, Malyala Mariyal, Medipally, Mylaram, Naginenipally Peddaparvathapur, Pilligundla Thanda, Pyararam Ramalingampally, Rangapur, Solipet, Thimmapur Thirumalagiri, Thumukunta.

Amenities:
Education: Primary School in 22 villages, Middle school in 9 villages, Matriculation or Secondary School in 5 villages, namely Jalalpur, Maryala, Pedda Parvathapur, Bommalaramaram, Medi Palle.
Higher Secondary or Pre University Courses or Intermediate or Junior College in 0 village of the CD Block, College in 0 village, Adult Literacy Center in 0 village.
Medical: Hospital in 0 village, Dispensary in 0 village, Health Center in 1 village, Sub Center in 6 villages, Maternity and Child Welfare Center in 0 village, Community health workers in 0 village.
Drinking Water: Tap water in 23 villages, Tank water in 23 villages, Well water in 23 villages, Tubewell in 23 villages and more than one source in 23 villages.
Bank: Banking facility in 2 villages, namely, Maryala, Bommalaramaram.
Credit Society in 5 villages Agricultural Credit Society in 5 Non-Agricultural Credit Society in 0 village.
Others: Power supply in 23 villages, Cinema hall in 0 village, sport club in 0 village, Stadium or Auditorium or Community Hall in 0 village, Post Office in 9 villages.
There are 21 villages having bus facilities.
Villages with most of facilities: Maryala Bommalaramaram.
Villages without amenities (Education):
Somaji Palle..
Scheduled Castes: Out of the total population of 34114 persons, 4712 persons (13.81%) belong to Scheduled Castes.
The villages having less than 10% SC population are Thimma Puram, Boin Palle, Somaji Palle Cheekati Mamidi, Yavapur, Tirumalagiri.
The villages having more than 50% SC population are None.
Sex ratio of Scheduled Caste population is 487.
Scheduled Castes Literates and Illiterates by Sex:

	Persons	Males	Females
Literate	1,868	1,213	655
Illiterate	2,844	1,202	1,642
Literacy rate	46.9	59.4	33.7
Graduate	12	7	5

Scheduled Castes (Dominant):
Madiga, Mala, Sindhollu etc., Generic Castes etc. Holeya Dasari
For their cultural identity please see Appendix-I
Villages without Scheduled Castes: There are 2 villages without any scheduled caste population.
Scheduled Tribes: Out of the total population of 34114 persons, 8031 persons (23.54%) belong to Scheduled Tribes.
The villages having less than 10% ST population are Muneerabad, Bandakindi Palle, Thumkunta, Jalalpur Solipeta, Malyala, Ranga Puram, Ramlingam Palle Pedda Parvathapur, Bommalaramaram, Nagineni Palle Maisi Reddy Palle, Hazipur, Medi Palle.
The villages having more than 50% ST population are Boin Palle, Somaji Palle, Cheekati Mamidi, Yavapur Tirumalagiri.
Sex ratio of Scheduled tribe population is 487.
Scheduled Tribes Literates and Illiterates by Sex:

	Persons	Males	Females
Literate	1,670	1,195	475
Illiterate	6,361	2,928	3,433
Literacy rate	25.9	36.1	15.2
Graduate	12	11	1

Scheduled Tribes (Dominant):
Sugalis etc., Yerukulas, Generic Tribes etc.
For their cultural identity please see Appendix-II
Villages without Scheduled Tribes: There are 6 villages without any scheduled tribe population.
Literates and Illiterates by Sex (Total Population):

	Persons	Males	Females
Literate	14,487	9,151	5,336
Illiterate	19,627	8,201	11,426
Literacy rate	50	62	38
Graduate	362	302	60

Agriculture: ***Distribution of villages according to land use:***
Out of 24 villages, Total area (in hectare) is 16751, out of that 52.3 percent is cultivable and 21.81 percent of the cultivable area is irrigated.
Sources of Irrigation (Hectares): Government Canal 0, Private Canal 0, Well without Electricity 0, Well with Electricity 726, Tubewell without Electricity 0, Tubewell with Electricity 1185, Tank 0, River 0, Lake 0, Waterfall 0, Others 0.
Villages with population of 5000 to 9999:
Maryala.

Villages with population of 10000 and above: None

Distribution of Workers:

	Persons	Males	Females	WPR
Cultivators	4,710	2,992	1,718	26.5
Agricultural Labour	5,918	1,852	4,066	33.3
Household Industry	814	304	510	4.58
Other Workers	6,331	4,832	1,499	35.62
Main Workers	13,386	8,661	4,725	75.32
Marginal Workers	4,387	1,319	3,068	24.68
Total Workers	17,773	9,980	7,793	

Religion: Major Religious Communities:

	Persons	Males	Females	Sex Ratio
Hindu (98.24%)	33,514	17,060	16,454	964
Muslim (1.41%)	482	232	250	1,078
Christian (0.22%)	76	38	38	1,000
Sikh (0.01%)	2	2	-	-
Buddhists (0%)	1	-	1	-
Jain (0%)	1	-	1	-

Agewise Data:

	Persons	Males	Females	Sex Ratio
All ages	34,114	17,352	16,762	966
0-14	11,796	5,979	5,817	973
15-44	14,900	7,694	7,206	937
45-79	7,075	3,500	3,575	1021
80+	309	163	146	896
Age not stated	34	16	18	1125

Languages (Dominant):

Telugu, Hindi, Oriya, Urdu, Gondi

Disabled Population:

	Persons	Males	Females	%
Total Disabled	599	373	226	
In Seeing	213	131	82	35.56
In Speech	52	36	16	8.68
In Hearing	34	26	8	5.68
In Movement	240	145	95	40.07
Mentally	60	35	25	10.02

BOMMANAHAL

Bommanahal C.D. Block lies in the north-western part of Anantapur district. It is a part of Bommanahal Mandal. The Block is located at a distance of 95 kms. from district headquarters (Anantapur). There are 16 villages in the block with the total population of 50,128 perso ns. Area of the C.D. Block is 283.66 sq. kms. It is bounded in the south by Mandals D. Hirehal and Kaneka, in the east by Mandals Vidapanakal and Uravakonda, in the west by Mandal D. Hirehal, and it has common boundary with the state of Karnataka on north.

Communications:

Roadways : State Highway (S.H.): Direction- Bellary to Kalyandurg. Nearest Villages- Untakal, Bommanahal, Uddehal, Kolaganahalli, Sreedharaghattu.

River: Chinna Hagari Nadi- Nearest Villages- Siddaramp uram, Haresamudram, Bandur, Uddehal, Kolaganahalli, Elanji, Sreedharaghattu. Vedavati Nadi- Nearest Village s- Kalludevanahalli, Sreedharaghattu, Singanahalli, Govindawada, D.Honnur.

It receives Backward Region Grants, and is identified as a drought-prone area as well.

Annual Rainfall: Average Rainfall 394 mm

Ground Water: Availability of the Ground Water in the Basin is 6143 H.A.M. and the utilization is 833 H.A. M. It belongs to safe category. Depth to water level varies from 5 to 10 meter below the ground. Most of the wells go down in summer months. The well density in the entire block is 6 wells per sq. km. Total no. of the wells in the block are enumerated as 1705, according to the Ground Water Estimation Committee.

Natural Division : Rayalaseema Region

Administration:

Division: Rayala Seema. Parliamentary Constituency: 36 Anantapur. District: Anantapur.

Mandal: Bommanahal. Assembly Constituency: 267 Rayadurg. Gram Panchayat: 19.

Border Villages: (Karnataka)- Nearest Villages- Nemakal lu, Bommanahal, Kuruvalli, Siddarampuram, Bollanaguddam

Fairs and Festivals:

Shabadivanu Urs : It is celebrated for three days from Vaisakha Bahula Tadiya to Panchami (May-June) at Bollan aguddam. Offerings are made to the sage in the form of sugar, cloth and cash. It is being celebrated for the past about 200 years. A story associated with Shaba divanu relates that once the English army camped in the forest at a distance of one and a half kilometers from Kalluhola. There was no water and the soldiers were thirsty. Then, Shabadivanu showed them a pond with water and saved them and their horses. Even now, the level of the water in the pond would never come down at any time.

Villages: 16 **Inhabited:** 16 **Uninhabited:** 0

Ranking	District	State	National
Area	31	196	2955
Population	13	506	5271
Sex Ratio	5	635	2142
Child Sex Ratio	8	80	193
Literacy Rate	62	980	5599
Density	4	142	5105
Work Participation Rate	20	806	413

Gram Panchayats:

Bandur, Bollanaguddam, Bommanahal, D.Honnur, Elanji Gonehal, Govindawada, Haresamudram, Kalluhola Kolaganahalli, Kuruvalli, Lingadahal, Nemakallu

Siddarampuram, Singanahalli, Sreedharaghatta Uddehal, Unthakal, Upparahal.

Amenities:

Education: Primary School in 16 villages, Middle school in 8 villages, Matriculation or Secondary School in 4 villages, namely Untakal, Bommanahal, Uddehal, D.Honnur. Higher Secondary or Pre University Courses or Intermediate or Junior College in 0 village of the CD Block, College in 0 village, Adult Literacy Center in 0 village.

Medical: Hospital in 0 village, Dispensary in 1 village, Health Center in 1 village, Sub Center in 7 villages, Maternity and Child Welfare Center in 16 villages, Community health workers in 0 village.

The Village having Hospital or Dispensary or Health Center is Sreedharaghattu.

Drinking Water: Tap water in 15 villages, Tank water in 0 villages, Well water in 0 village, Tubewell in 12 villages and more than one source in 16 villages.

Bank: Banking facility in 3 villages, namely, Bommanahal, Uddehal, D.Honnur.

Credit Society in 4 villages Agricultural Credit Society in 4 Non-Agricultural Credit Society in 0 village.

Others: Power supply in 16 villages, Cinema hall in 3 villages, sport club in 0 village, Stadium or Auditorium or Community Hall in 0 village, Post Office in 12 villages.

There are 16 villages having bus facilities.

Villages with most of facilities: Bommanahal Uddehal, D.Honnur.

Villages without Amenities (Education): None..

Scheduled Castes: Out of the total population of 50128 persons, 5731 persons (11.43%) belong to Scheduled Castes.

The villages having less than 10% SC population are None..

The villages having more than 50% SC population are None.

Sex ratio of Scheduled Caste population is 490.

Scheduled Castes Literates and Illiterates by Sex:

	Persons	Males	Females
Literate	1,318	887	431
Illiterate	4,413	2,037	2,376
Literacy rate	28.2	37.3	18.8
Graduate	16	13	3

Scheduled Castes (Dominant):

Madiga, Bariki, Adi Andhra, Mala Generic Castes etc.

For their cultural identity please see Appendix-I

Villages without Scheduled Castes: There are 0 village without any scheduled caste population.

Scheduled Tribes: Out of the total population of 50128 persons, 407 persons (0.81%) belong to Scheduled Tribes.

The villages having less than 10% ST population are Nemakallu, Untakal, Bommanahal, Kuruvalli Siddarampuram, Haresamudram, Bollanaguddam Kalludevanahalli, Bandur, Uddehal, Kolaganahalli Elanji, Sreedharaghattu, Singanahalli, Govindawada D.Honnur.

The villages having more than 50% ST population are None.

Sex ratio of Scheduled tribe population is 474.

Scheduled Tribes Literates and Illiterates by Sex:

	Persons	Males	Females
Literate	124	92	32
Illiterate	283	122	161
Literacy rate	37.5	52.9	20.4
Graduate	5	5	0

Scheduled Tribes (Dominant):

Yerukulas, Kammara, Sugalis etc.

For their cultural identity please see Appendix-II

Villages without Scheduled Tribes: There are 7 villages without any scheduled tribe population.

Literates and Illiterates by Sex (Total Population):

	Persons	Males	Females
Literate	17,399	11,401	5,998
Illiterate	32,729	13,958	18,771
Literacy rate	41	53	29
Graduate	435	342	93

Agriculture: ***Distribution of villages according to land use:*** Out of 16 villages, Total area (in hectare) is 28364, out of that 82.83 percent is cultivable and 32.62 percent of the cultivable area is irrigated.

Sources of Irrigation (Hectares): Government Canal 6214.17, Private Canal 0, Well without Electricity 20.24, Well with Electricity 36.44, Tubewell without Electricity 0, Tubewell with Electricity 769.63, Tank 100.81, River 0, Lake 0, Waterfall 0, Others 522.28.

Villages with population of 5000 to 9999: D.Honnur.

Villages with population of 10000 and above: None

Distribution of Workers:

	Persons	Males	Females	WPR
Cultivators	10,153	6,496	3,657	36.37
Agricultural Labour	14,557	6,363	8,194	52.14
Household Industry	278	154	124	1
Other Workers	2,931	2,104	827	10.5
Main Workers	25,165	14,557	10,608	90.14
Marginal Workers	2,754	560	2,194	9.86
Total Workers	27,919	15,117	12,802	

Religion: Major Religious Communities:

	Persons	Males	Females	Sex Ratio
Hindu (95.33%)	47,787	24,158	23,629	978

Muslim (3.81%)	1,909	987	922	934
Christian (0.15%)	77	44	33	750
Sikh (0%)	-	-	-	-
Buddhists (0%)	-	-	-	-
Jain (0%)	-	-	-	-

Agewise Data:

	Persons	Males	Females	Sex Ratio
All ages	50,128	25,359	24,769	977
0-14	18,929	9,607	9,322	970
15-44	22,615	11,631	10,984	944
45-79	8,243	3,968	4,275	1077
80+	295	126	169	1341
Age not stated	46	27	19	704

Languages (Dominant):

Telugu, Kannada, Urdu, Marathi, Hindi

Disabled Population:

	Persons	Males	Females	%
Total Disabled	568	333	235	
In Seeing	120	67	53	21.13
In Speech	83	51	32	14.61
In Hearing	45	17	28	7.92
In Movement	234	151	83	41.2
Mentally	86	47	39	15.14

BOMRASPET

Bomraspet C.D. Block lies in the northern part of Mahbu bnagar district. The Block is located at a distance of 74 kms. from district headquarters (Mahbubnagar). There are 27 villages in the block with the total population of 48,037 persons. Area of the C.D. Block is 244.32 sq. kms. It is bounded by Rangareddy district on north and east, Kosgi Mandal on south, and Kodangal Mandal on west.

Communications:

Roadways : State Highway (S.H.): Direction- Kodangal to Pargi. Nearest Villages- Kothur, Thunkumetla, Burha npur, Metlakunta, Nagireddipalle, Thirumalapur, Regadmai lwar.

Backwards Region Grants Fund: It receives Backward Region Grants.

Annual Rainfall: Annual Rainfall 576 mm

Ground Water : Availability of the Ground Water in the Basin is 1396 H.A.M. and the utilization is 807 H.A.M. It belongs to Safe category. Depth to water level varies from 2 to 5 meter below the ground. Most of the wells go down in summer months. The well density in the entire block is 9 wells per sq. km. Total no. of the wells in the block are enumerated as 2068, according to the Ground Water Estimation Committee.

Natural Division : Telangana Plateau Region

Administration:

Division: Telangana. Parliamentary Constituency: 11 Mahbubnagar. District: Mahbubnagar. Mandal: Bomraspet. Assembly Constituency: 72 Kodangal. Gram Panchayat: 26

Villages: 27 **Inhabited:** 25 **Uninhabited:** 2

Ranking	District	State	National
Area	33	331	3450
Population	34	578	5385
Sex Ratio	2	90	611
Child Sex Ratio	18	515	1900
Literacy Rate	52	1067	6033
Density	11	89	4774
Work Participation Rate	33	727	314

Gram Panchayats:

Amsanpalle, Bapally Tanda, Bomraspeta, Burhanpur Chilmalmailwar, Chowdapalle, Dudyal, Dupcherla Erlapally, Erpumalla, Goураram, Hakimpeta, Kothur Lagcherla, Lingampalle, Madanapally, Mahanthipur Metlakunta, Nagereddipalle, Namdapur, Polepalle Regadimailwar, Salimdapur, Thunkumetla, Wadcherla Yenkepally.

Amenities:

Education: Primary School in 25 villages, Middle school in 10 villages, Matriculation or Secondary School in 3 villages, namely Bomraspet, Dudyal, Hakimpeta.

Higher Secondary or Pre University Courses or Intermediate or Junior College in 0 village of the CD Block, College in 0 village, Adult Literacy Center in 22 villages.

Medical: Hospital in 0 village, Dispensary in 2 villages, Health Center in 2 villages, Sub Center in 9 villages, Maternity and Child Welfare Center in 0 village, Community health workers in 0 village.

The Villages having Hospital or Dispensary or Health Center are Bomraspet, Dudyal.

Drinking Water: Tap water in 25 villages, Tank water in 25 villages, Well water in 25 villages, Tubewell in 25 villages and more than one source in 25 villages.

Bank: Banking facility in 1 villages, namely, Bomraspet.

Credit Society in 12 villages Agricultural Credit Society in 1 Non-Agricultural Credit Society in 12 villages.

Others: Power supply in 25 villages, Cinema hall in 0 village, sport club in 0 village, Stadium or Auditorium or Community Hall in 0 village, Post Office in 19 villages.

There are 16 villages having bus facilities.

Village with most of facilities: Bomraspet.

Villages without Amenities (Education): None..

Scheduled Castes: Out of the total population of 48037 persons, 7267 persons (15.13%) belong to Scheduled Castes. The villages having less than 10% SC population are

None..

The villages having more than 50% SC population are None.

Sex ratio of Scheduled Caste population is 503.

Scheduled Castes Literates and Illiterates by Sex:

	Persons	Males	Females
Literate	1,699	1,154	545
Illiterate	5,568	2,458	3,110
Literacy rate	27.8	38.5	17.5
Graduate	22	20	2

Scheduled Castes (Dominant):

Madiga, Mala, Beda Jangam etc., Jambuvulu Generic Castes etc.

For their cultural identity please see Appendix-I

Villages without Scheduled Castes: There are 2 villages without any scheduled caste population.

Scheduled Tribes: Out of the total population of 48037 persons, 11880 persons (24.73%) belong to Scheduled Tribes.

The villages having less than 10% ST population are Yenkepalle, Dupcherla, Lingampalle, Nagireddipalle Nazkhanpalle, Chowdarpalle, Dudyal, Hakimpeta Polepalle.

The villages having more than 50% ST population are None.

Sex ratio of Scheduled tribe population is 510.

Scheduled Tribes Literates and Illiterates by Sex:

	Persons	Males	Females
Literate	1,272	983	289
Illiterate	10,608	4,841	5,767
Literacy rate	14.1	22.3	6.3
Graduate	12	12	0

Scheduled Tribes (Dominant):

Sugalis etc., Yerukulas, Chenchu etc.

For their cultural identity please see Appendix-II

Villages without Scheduled Tribes: There are 5 villages without any scheduled tribe population.

Literates and Illiterates by Sex (Total Population):

	Persons	Males	Females
Literate	13,577	9,061	4,516
Illiterate	34,460	14,701	19,759
Literacy rate	35	47	23
Graduate	304	263	41

Agriculture: ***Distribution of villages according to land use:*** Out of 27 villages, Total area (in hectare) is 24433, out of that 71.02 percent is cultivable and 13.43 percent of the cultivable area is irrigated.

Sources of Irrigation (Hectares): Government Canal 0, Private Canal 0, Well without Electricity 0, Well with Electricity 337.34, Tubewell without Electricity 0, Tubewell with Electricity 686.48, Tank 1194.65, River 0, Lake 0, Waterfall 0, Others 112.44.

Villages with population of 5000 to 9999: Bomraspet.

Villages with population of 10000 and above: None

Distribution of Workers:

	Persons	Males	Females	WPR
Cultivators	12,742	7,874	4,868	48.31
Agricultural Labour	9,966	3,002	6,964	37.79
Household Industry	739	368	371	2.8
Other Workers	2,927	2,199	728	11.1
Main Workers	21,491	11,972	9,519	81.49
Marginal Workers	4,883	1,471	3,412	18.51
Total Workers	26,374	13,443	12,931	

Religion: Major Religious Communities:

	Persons	Males	Females	Sex Ratio
Hindu (94%)	45,157	22,328	22,829	1,022
Muslim (5.83%)	2,802	1,400	1,402	1,001
Christian (0.13%)	61	25	36	1,440
Sikh (0%)	-	-	-	-
Buddhists (0%)	-	-	-	-
Jain (0%)	-	-	-	-

Agewise Data:

	Persons	Males	Females	Sex Ratio
All ages	48,037	23,762	24,275	1022
0-14	18,886	9,577	9,309	972
15-44	20,158	9,832	10,326	1050
45-79	8,654	4,171	4,483	1075
80+	282	153	129	843
Age not stated	57	29	28	966

Languages (Dominant):

Telugu, Hindi, Urdu, Tamil, Marathi

Disabled Population:

	Persons	Males	Females	%
Total Disabled	1,009	554	455	
In Seeing	549	294	255	54.41
In Speech	76	41	35	7.53
In Hearing	65	29	36	6.44
In Movement	263	159	104	26.07
Mentally	56	31	25	5.55

BONAKAL

Bonakal C.D. Block lies in the southern part of Khammam district. The Block is located at a distance of 28 kms. from district headquarters (Khammam). There are 18 villages in the block with the total population of 42,989 persons. Area of the C.D. Block is 158.64 sq. kms. It is bounded in the north by Mandals Chinthak ani and Wyra, in the south and east by Mandal Madhira, and in the west by district Krishna.

Communications:

Roadways : Metalled Roads: Nearest Villages- Chirunomula,

Ravinoothala, Peddabeeravalli, Chinna Beeravalli, Rapalle, Brahmanapalle (K), Kalakota, Narayanapuram, Bonakal.

Railway Station: Bonakal, Motamarri.

River: Wyra Nadi- Nearset Villages- Motamarri, Rapalle, Brahmanapalle (K), Kalakota.

Backwards Region Grants Fund: It receives Backward Region Grants.

Annual Rainfall: Average Rainfall 990 mm

Ground Water: Availability of the Ground Water in the Basin is 5270 H.A.M.and the utilization is 629 H.A. M. It belongs to safe category. Depth to water level varies from 5 to 10 meter below the ground. Most of the wells go down in summer months. The well density in the entire block is 4 wells per sq. km. Total no. of the wells in the block are enumerated as 646, accor ding to the Ground Water Estimation Committee.

Natural Division : Godavari Depression Region

Administration:

Division: Telangana. Parliamentary Constituency: 17 Khammam. District: Khammam. Mandal: Bonakal. Assembly Constituency: 114 Madhira (SC). Gram Panchayat: 20.

Villages: 18 **Inhabited:** 18 **Uninhabited:** 0

Ranking	District	State	National
Area	40	779	4899
Population	25	723	5600
Sex Ratio	24	712	2388
Child Sex Ratio	34	696	2874
Literacy Rate	16	538	4001
Density	15	259	3849
Work Participation Rate	10	461	664

Gram Panchayats:

Allapadu, Bonakal, Brahmanapalli, Chinna Beeravalli Chirunomula, Choppakatla Palem, Garlapadu Govindapuram, Janakipuram, Kalakota, Laxmipuram Motamarri, Mustikuntla, Narayanapuram Pedabeeravalli, Ramapuram, Rapalli, Ravinoothala Rayanipeta, Tutikuntla.

Amenities:

Education: Primary School in 18 villages, Middle school in 13 villages, Matriculation or Secondary School in 8 villages, namely Mustikuntla, Chirunomula, Ravinoothala, Peddabeeravalli, Kalakota, Bonakal, Govindapuram, Motamarri.

Higher Secondary or Pre University Courses or Intermediate or Junior College in 0 village of the CD Block, College in 0 village, Adult Literacy Center in 15 villages.

Medical: Hospital in 0 village, Dispensary in 1 village, Health Center in 1 village, Sub Center in 8 villages, Maternity and Child Welfare Center in 1 village, Community health workers in 0 village.

The Village having Hospital or Dispensary or Health Center is Bonakal.

Drinking Water: Tap water in 18 villages, Tank water in 18 villages, Well water in 18 villages, Tubewell in 18 villages and more than one source in 18 villages.

Bank: Banking facility in 2 villages, namely, Kalakota, Bonakal.

Credit Society in 17 villages Agricultural Credit Society in 8 Non-Agricultural Credit Society in 17 villages.

Others: Power supply in 18 villages, Cinema hall in 1 village, sport club in 0 village, Stadium or Auditorium or Community Hall in 0 village, Post Office in 14 villages.

There are 16 villages having bus facilities.

Villages with most of facilities: Kalakota Bonakal.

Villages without Amenities (Education): None..

Scheduled Castes: Out of the total population of 42989 persons, 12147 persons (28.26%) belong to Scheduled Castes.

The villages having less than 10% SC population are None..

The villages having more than 50% SC population are None.

Sex ratio of Scheduled Caste population is 494.

Scheduled Castes Literates and Illiterates by Sex:

	Persons	Males	Females
Literate	4,953	3,159	1,794
Illiterate	7,194	2,991	4,203
Literacy rate	47.4	59.6	34.9
Graduate	122	113	9

Scheduled Castes (Dominant):

Madiga, Mala, Dakkal etc., Beda Jangam etc.

For their cultural identity please see Appendix-I

Villages without Scheduled Castes: There are 0 village without any scheduled caste population.

Scheduled Tribes: Out of the total population of 42989 persons, 1712 persons (3.98%) belong to Scheduled Tribes.

The villages having less than 10% ST population are Tutikuntla, Laxmipuram, Garlapadu, Ramapuram Mustikuntla, Choppa Katlapalem, Chirunomula Peddabeeravalli, Chinna Beeravalli, Rapalle Brahmanapalle (K), Kalakota, Narayanapuram, Allapadu Govindapuram, Motamarri.

The villages having more than 50% ST population are None.

Sex ratio of Scheduled tribe population is 481.

Scheduled Tribes Literates and Illiterates by Sex:

	Persons	Males	Females
Literate	525	359	166
Illiterate	1,187	529	658

Literacy rate	35.6	46.7	23.5
Graduate	8	7	1

Scheduled Tribes (Dominant):
Sugalis etc., Yerukulas, Koya etc., Yenadis Generic Tribes etc.

For their cultural identity please see Appendix-II

Villages without Scheduled Tribes: There are 4 villages without any scheduled tribe population.

Literates and Illiterates by Sex (Total Population):

	Persons	Males	Females
Literate	19,908	12,087	7,821
Illiterate	23,081	9,711	13,370
Literacy rate	53	64	42
Graduate	691	582	109

Agriculture: *Distribution of villages according to land use:* Out of 18 villages, Total area (in hectare) is 15865, out of that 59.42 percent is cultivable and 57.48 percent of the cultivable area is irrigated.

Sources of Irrigation (Hectares): Government Canal 3530, Private Canal 2, Well without Electricity 159.62, Well with Electricity 39.8, Tubewell without Electricity 76, Tubewell with Electricity 0, Tank 1104, River 0, Lake 0, Waterfall 0, Others 506.62.

Villages with population of 5000 to 9999: None

Villages with population of 10000 and above: None

Distribution of Workers:

	Persons	Males	Females	WPR
Cultivators	4,889	3,373	1,516	20.18
Agricultural Labour	16,461	7,445	9,016	67.94
Household Industry	475	287	188	1.96
Other Workers	2,404	1,974	430	9.92
Main Workers	20,610	11,628	8,982	85.06
Marginal Workers	3,619	1,451	2,168	14.94
Total Workers	24,229	13,079	11,150	

Religion: Major Religious Communities:

	Persons	Males	Females	Sex Ratio
Hindu (92.13%)	39,604	20,097	19,507	971
Muslim (6.66%)	2,864	1,444	1,420	983
Christian (1.14%)	491	245	246	1,004
Sikh (0%)	-	-	-	-
Buddhists (0%)	2	-	2	-
Jain (0%)	-	-	-	-

Agewise Data:

	Persons	Males	Females	Sex Ratio
All ages	42,989	21,798	21,191	972
0-14	13,222	6,763	6,459	955
15-44	20,521	10,361	10,160	981
45-79	8,653	4,399	4,254	967
80+	496	237	259	1093
Age not stated	97	38	59	1553

Languages (Dominant):
Telugu, Urdu, Hindi, Tamil, Gondi

Disabled Population:

	Persons	Males	Females	%
Total Disabled	869	473	396	
In Seeing	275	140	135	31.65
In Speech	100	50	50	11.51
In Hearing	43	23	20	4.95
In Movement	343	203	140	39.47
Mentally	108	57	51	12.43

BONDAPALLE

Bondapalle C.D. Block lies in the southern part of Vizianagaram district. The Block is located at a distan ce of 16 kms. from district headquarters (Vizianagaram). There are 33 villages in the block with the total population of 50,531 persons. Area of the C.D. Block is 144.92 sq. kms. It is bounded in the north by Gajapa thinagaram Mandal, in the south by Mandals Gantyada and Vizianagaram, in the east by Mandals Nellimarla and Vizianagaram, and in the west by Mandal Gantyada and district Vishakhapatnam.

Communications :

Roadways : NH- 43: Direction- Salur to Vizianagaram. Nearest Villages- Nelivada, Garudabilli, Jiyyannavalasa, Ambativalasa, Gotlam, Bondapalle,

Railway Station: Bondapalle, Garudabilli, Gotlam.

Backwards Region Grants Fund: It receives Backward Region Grants.

Annaul Rainfall: Average Rainfall 886.7 mm

Ground Water: Availability of the Ground Water in the Basin is (Information not avavible) H.A.M .and the utilization is (Information not avavible) H.A.M. It belongs to (Information not avavible) category. Depth to water level varies from 3 to 10 meter below the ground. Most of the wells go down in summer months.

Forest and Reserved **Forest:** Nearest Villages- Veduruvada, Gumadam.

Administration:

Division: Coastal Andhra. Parliamentary Constituency: 20 Vizianagram. District: Vizianagram. Mandal: Bondapal le. Assembly Constituency: 135 Gajapathinagram. Gram Panchayat: 26.

Villages: 33 **Inhabited:** 31 **Uninhabited:** 2

Ranking	District	State	National
Area	18	847	5121
Population	21	495	5256
Sex Ratio	6	81	561
Child Sex Ratio	24	340	1187
Literacy Rate	24	929	5398
Density	16	164	3117
Work Participation Rate	24	270	480

Gram Panchayats:
Ambativalasa, Billalavalasa, Bondapalli Budatanapalli Rajeru, Chinatamarapalli, Devupalli Garudabilli, Gittupalli, Gollupalem, Gotlam Grahapathi Agraharam, J.Gumadam, Kanimeraka, Keratam Kindam Agraharam, Kondakindam, Kottapalem, Maruwada Maruwada Kothavalasa, Mudduru, Neliwada, Ompalli Rachakindam, Raindram, Veduruwada, Vendram.

Amenities:

Education: Primary School in 30 villages, Middle school in 7 villages, Matriculation or Secondary School in 4 villages, namely Devupalle, Rachakindam, Bondapalle, Nelivada. Higher Secondary or Pre University Courses or Intermediate or Junior College in 0 village of the CD Block, College in 0 village, Adult Literacy Center in 16 villages.

Medical: Hospital in 0 village, Dispensary in 1 village, Health Center in 1 village, Sub Center in 12 villages, Maternity and Child Welfare Center in 0 village, Community health workers in 0 village.
The Village having Hospital or Dispensary or Health Center is Gotlam.

Drinking Water: Tap water in 31 villages, Tank water in 31 villages, Well water in 31 villages, Tubewell in 31 villages and more than one source in 31 villages.

Bank: Banking facility in 2 villages, namely, Bondapalle, Gotlam.
Credit Society in 8 villages Agricultural Credit Society in 4 Non-Agricultural Credit Society in 5 villages.

Others: Power supply in 31 villages, Cinema hall in 1 village, sport club in 0 village, Stadium or Auditorium or Community Hall in 0 village, Post Office in 23 villages.
There are 18 villages having bus facilities.

Villages with most of facilities: Bondapalle Gotlam.

Villages without amenities (Education):
Mulapadu Karrivanipalem..

Scheduled Castes: Out of the total population of 50531 persons, 5712 persons (11.3%) belong to Scheduled Castes.
The villages having less than 10% SC population are Grahapati Agraharam, Kothapalem Mulapadu Karrivanipalem, Veduruvada, Gumadam Maruvada Kothavalasa, Kindam Agraharam, Tamatada Mudduru, Billalavalasa, Garudabilli, Kondakindam Ompilli, Vendram, Ayyanna Agraharam, Rollavaka Gotlam.
The villages having more than 50% SC population are None.
Sex ratio of Scheduled Caste population is 508.

Scheduled Castes Literates and Illiterates by Sex:

	Persons	Males	Females
Literate	2,106	1,265	841
Illiterate	3,606	1,543	2,063
Literacy rate	42.6	52.1	33.4
Graduate	44	38	6

Scheduled Castes (Dominant):
Mala, Relli, Madiga, Beda Jangam etc., Mahar

For their cultural identity please see Appendix-I

Villages without Scheduled Castes: There are 4 villages without any scheduled caste population.

Scheduled Tribes: Out of the total population of 50531 persons, 1445 persons (2.86%) belong to Scheduled Tribes.
The villages having less than 10% ST population are Devupalle, Gittupalle, Kanimeraka, Rayindram Chintamarapalle, Grahapati Agraharam, Maruvada Gumadam, Maruvada Kothavalasa, Budatanapalle Rajeru Kindam Agraharam, Rachakindam, Chamalavalasa Bondapalle, Tamatada, Mudduru, Billalavalasa Keratam, Nelivada, Garudabilli, Ompilli, Vendram Ayyanna Agraharam, Ambativalasa, Rollavaka, Gotlam Jiyyannavalasa.
The villages having more than 50% ST population are None.
Sex ratio of Scheduled tribe population is 499.

Scheduled Tribes Literates and Illiterates by Sex:

	Persons	Males	Females
Literate	332	199	133
Illiterate	1,113	525	588
Literacy rate	27.0	32.6	21.5
Graduate	0	0	0

Scheduled Tribes (Dominant):
Konda Dhoras, Yerukulas, Mukha Dhora etc., Gadabas Koya etc.

For their cultural identity please see Appendix-II

Villages without Scheduled Tribes: There are 16 villages without any scheduled tribe population.

Literates and Illiterates by Sex (Total Population):

	Persons	Males	Females
Literate	19,025	11,916	7,109
Illiterate	31,506	13,033	18,473
Literacy rate	43	55	32
Graduate	597	505	92

Agriculture: ***Distribution of villages according to land use:*** Out of 33 villages, Total area (in hectare) is 14492, out of that 82.85 percent is cultivable and 47.14 percent of the cultivable area is irrigated.

Sources of Irrigation (Hectares): Government Canal 1064.3, Private Canal 0, Well without Electricity 537.22, Well with Electricity 124.52, Tubewell without Electricity 2, Tubewell with Electricity 18.96, Tank 3912.27, River 0, Lake 0, Waterfall 0, Others 0.

Villages with population of 5000 to 9999:
Devupalle, Bondapalle.
Villages with population of 10000 and above: None
Distribution of Workers:

	Persons	Males	Females	WPR
Cultivators	9,163	5,331	3,832	31.66
Agricultural Labour	13,062	5,390	7,672	45.13
Household Industry	1,492	818	674	5.16
Other Workers	5,225	3,808	1,417	18.05
Main Workers	23,167	13,868	9,299	80.05
Marginal Workers	5,775	1,479	4,296	19.95
Total Workers	28,942	15,347	13,595	

Religion: Major Religious Communities:

	Persons	Males	Females	Sex Ratio
Hindu (99.16%)	50,109	24,748	25,361	1,025
Muslim (0.41%)	205	102	103	1,010
Christian (0.31%)	158	71	87	1,225
Sikh (0%)	-	-	-	-
Buddhists (0%)	-	-	-	-
Jain (0.01%)	6	3	3	1,000

Agewise Data:

	Persons	Males	Females	Sex Ratio
All ages	50,531	24,949	25,582	1025
0-14	15,396	7,781	7,615	979
15-44	23,077	11,465	11,612	1013
45-79	11,672	5,518	6,154	1115
80+	263	127	136	1071
Age not stated	123	58	65	1121

Languages (Dominant):
Telugu, Tamil, Hindi, Oriya, Urdu
Disabled Population:

	Persons	Males	Females	%
Total Disabled	1,178	628	550	
In Seeing	569	278	291	48.3
In Speech	105	51	54	8.91
In Hearing	83	37	46	7.05
In Movement	296	196	100	25.13
Mentally	125	66	59	10.61

BRAHMAMGARIMATTAM

Brahmamgarimattam C.D. Block lies in the north-eastern part of Cuddapah district. The Block is located at a distance of 83 kms. from district headquarters (Cuddapah). There are 20 villages in the block with the total population of 34,396 persons. Area of the C.D. Block is 395.50 sq. kms. It is bounded in the north by Mandal B. Kodur, in the south by Mandal Badvel, in the east by Mandals B. Kodur and Badvel, and in the west by Mandal S. Mydukur.

Communications:
Roadways : State Highway (S.H.): Direction- S. Mydukur to Badvel. Nearest Villages- Rekalakunta, Darbhavariagraharam, D.Lingampalle, Nagisettipalle.
River: Sagileru Nadi- Nearest Villages- Nagisettipalle, Mudumala, Godlaveedu, Gundapuram, Diguva Nelatur, Eguvanelatur, Dirasavancha.
Receives Backward Region Grant, and is identified as a drought prone area as well.
Annual Rainfall: Average Rainfall 755 mm
Ground Water: Availability of the Ground Water in the Basin is 1975 H.A.M.and the utilization is 1754 H.A.M.It belongs to SC category. Depth to water level varies from 20 to 40 meter below the ground. Most of the wells go down in summer months, according to the Ground Water Estimation Committee.
Forest and Reserved **Forest:** Nearest Villages- Mallepalle, Palugurallapalle (Part Iv), Somireddipalle, Jangamrajupalle, Rekalakunta.
Natural Division : Rayalaseema Region
Administration:
Division: Rayala Seema. Parliamentary Constituency: 38 Kadapa. District: Cuddapah.
Mandal: Brahmamgarimattam. Assembly Constituency: 252 Mydukur. Gram Panchayat: 11.
Fairs and Festivals:
Narmadeswaraswamy Brahmothsavam : It celebrated in Magham (January-February) from Magha Suddha Triodasi to Bahula Tadiya and from Magha Suddha Purnima to Padyami respectively. Offerings are made in the form of cocoa nuts, fruits and flowers. These festivals are celebrated for the past 200 years and are of local significance.
According to the legend about 200 years ago there lived a great philosopher, by the name of Govindaswamy who performed penance for a long time. He was the disciple of Garudadri Suraiah, a renowned teacher of Mudumala village. Death was at his control as blessed by God.
He was even able to postpone his death, when his devotees prayed him to live for 6 more days till his son was married. Before his death, he ordered his family to observe a festival on the day he had upadesam from his guru.
Siddaiahgari Festival : It is celebrated for two days from Chaitra Sudddha Padyami (March-April). Devotees offer incense and naivedyam. Sheep, goats and fowls are sacrificed in fulfilment of vows. This festival has been celebrated for the last 350 years and is widely known. Dudekulas patronise the festival. It attracts people of all communities in large numbers from distant places of the State. Venkatesamayyagari mutt and Siddaiahgari mutt with his idol on his jeevasamadhi are the places of worship in this village. Siddaiah was the chief disciple of Sri Pothuluri Veerabrahmendraswamy

of Kandimallayapalle. He was a seer who predicted the present and future happenings. He attained jeevasamadhi 350 years ago.

Villages: 20 **Inhabited:** 18 **Uninhabited:** 2

Ranking	District	State	National
Area	3	50	1956
Population	30	944	5926
Sex Ratio	51	1086	4684
Child Sex Ratio	14	489	1881
Literacy Rate	45	497	3829
Density	24	705	6208
Work Participation Rate	49	1080	1994

Gram Panchayats:

Diguva Nelatur, Dirasavancha, Godlaveedu, Mallepalli Mudumala, Nagisetti Palli, Paluguralla palli Rekalakunta, Somireddipalli, T. Chowdaravaripalli Thotlapalli.

Amenities:

Education: Primary School in 18 villages, Middle school in 6 villages, Matriculation or Secondary School in 2 villages, namely Paluguralla palle, Somireddipalle.

Higher Secondary or Pre University Courses or Intermediate or Junior College in 1 village of the CD Block,, namely Somireddipalle.

College in 0 village, Adult Literacy Center in 0 village.

Medical: Hospital in 0 village, Dispensary in 1 village, Health Center in 2 villages, Sub Center in 5 villages, Maternity and Child Welfare Center in 0 village, Community health workers in 0 village.

The Villages having Hospital or Dispensary or Health Center are Mallepalle, Dirasavancha.

Drinking Water: Tap water in 18 villages, Tank water in 18 villages, Well water in 18 villages, Tubewell in 18 villages and more than one source in 18 villages.

Bank: Banking facility in 1 villages, namely, Somireddipalle.

Credit Society in 4 villages Agricultural Credit Society in 2 Non-Agricultural Credit Society in 2 villages.

Others: Power supply in 18 villages, Cinema hall in 0 village, sport club in 0 village, Stadium or Auditorium or Community Hall in 0 village, Post Office in 11 villages.

There are 16 villages having bus facilities.

Village with most of facilities: Somireddipalle.

Villages without Amenities (Education): None..

Scheduled Castes: Out of the total population of 34396 persons, 8837 persons (25.69%) belong to Scheduled Castes.

The villages having less than 10% SC population are None..

The villages having more than 50% SC population are None.

Sex ratio of Scheduled Caste population is 470.

Scheduled Castes Literates and Illiterates by Sex:

	Persons	Males	Females
Literate	4,185	2,870	1,315
Illiterate	4,652	1,817	2,835
Literacy rate	55.3	70.5	37.6
Graduate	108	90	18

Scheduled Castes (Dominant):

Madiga, Mala, Adi Andhra, Mala Dasari Beda Jangam etc.

For their cultural identity please see Appendix-I

Villages without Scheduled Castes: There are 4 villages without any scheduled caste population.

Scheduled Tribes: Out of the total population of 34396 persons, 579 persons (1.68%) belong to Scheduled Tribes.

The villages having less than 10% ST population are Mallepalle, Mudumala, Paluguralla palle Papireddipalle, Paluguralla palle (Part Iv) Somireddipalle, T.Soudaravaripalle, Godlaveedu Gundapuram, G.Narasimhapuram, Diguva Nelatur Boodavada, Eguvanelatur, Jangamrajupalle Rekalakunta, Dirasavancha, Nagisettipalle.

The villages having more than 50% ST population are None.

Sex ratio of Scheduled tribe population is 446.

Scheduled Tribes Literates and Illiterates by Sex:

	Persons	Males	Females
Literate	170	121	49
Illiterate	409	200	209
Literacy rate	34.8	43.5	23.2
Graduate	3	3	0

Scheduled Tribes (Dominant):

Yenadis, Yerukulas, Sugalis etc., Kammara

For their cultural identity please see Appendix-II

Villages without Scheduled Tribes: There are 11 villages without any scheduled tribe population.

Literates and Illiterates by Sex (Total Population):

	Persons	Males	Females
Literate	16,056	10,895	5,161
Illiterate	18,340	6,978	11,362
Literacy rate	54	70	36
Graduate	593	495	98

Agriculture: ***Distribution of villages according to land use:*** Out of 20 villages, Total area (in hectare) is 39551, out of that 8.01 percent is cultivable and 60.91 percent of the cultivable area is irrigated.

Sources of Irrigation (Hectares): Government Canal 0, Private Canal 0, Well without Electricity 0, Well with Electricity 249.48, Tubewell without Electricity 0, Tubewell with Electricity 1319.6, Tank 361.51, River 0, Lake 0,

Waterfall 0, Others 0.

Villages with population of 5000 to 9999: Somireddipalle.

Villages with population of 10000 and above: None

Distribution of Workers:

	Persons	Males	Females	WPR
Cultivators	4,736	3,391	1,345	27.31
Agricultural Labour	8,941	3,865	5,076	51.57
Household Industry	386	211	175	2.23
Other Workers	3,276	2,491	785	18.89
Main Workers	12,046	8,172	3,874	69.47
Marginal Workers	5,293	1,786	3,507	30.53
Total Workers	17,339	9,958	7,381	

Religion: Major Religious Communities:

	Persons	Males	Females	Sex Ratio
Hindu (97.82%)	33,646	17,484	16,162	924
Muslim (1.14%)	391	200	191	955
Christian (0.94%)	324	174	150	862
Sikh (0%)	1	-	1	-
Buddhists (0%)	-	-	-	-
Jain (0%)	-	-	-	-

Agewise Data:

	Persons	Males	Females	Sex Ratio
All ages	34,396	17,873	16,523	924
0-14	11,626	6,127	5,499	898
15-44	16,223	8,552	7,671	897
45-79	6,283	3,062	3,221	1052
80+	179	85	94	1106
Age not stated	85	47	38	809

Languages (Dominant):

Telugu, Urdu, Gondi, Hindi, Tamil

Disabled Population:

	Persons	Males	Females	%
Total Disabled	689	383	306	
In Seeing	231	116	115	33.53
In Speech	74	40	34	10.74
In Hearing	63	32	31	9.14
In Movement	239	147	92	34.69
Mentally	82	48	34	11.9

BRAHMASAMUDRAM

Brahmasamudram C.D. Block lies in the western part of Anantapur district. The Block is located at a distan ce of 100 kms. from district headquarters (Anantapur). There are 13 villages in the block with the total population of 39,518 persons. Area of the C.D. Block is 284.3 sq. kms. It is bounded in the north by Mandals Gummagatta and Rayadurg, in the south by Mandal Settur, in the east by Mandals Settur, Kalyandurg and Beluguppa, and in the west and south it has common boundary with the state of Karnataka.

Communications:

Roadways : Metalled Roads: Nearest Villages- Eradikera, Vepalaparthy, Chelimenahalli, Brahmasamudram, Kannepal le, Theetakal, Pillalapalle, Santhekondapuram.

River: Hagari Nadi- Nearest Villages- Gundiganihalli, Bhyravanithippa, Vepalaparthy, Chelimenahalli, Bhairas amudram, Kannepalle, Theetakal.

It receives Backward Region Grants, and is identified as a drought-prone area as well.

Annual Rainfall: Average Rainfall 529 mm

Ground Water: Availability of the Ground Water in the Basin is 1644 H.A.M. and the utilization is 1074 H. A.M. It belongs to safe category. Depth to water level varies from 10 to 20 meter below the ground. Most of the wells go down in summer months. The well density in the entire block is 8 wells per sq. km. Total no. of the wells in the block are enumerated as 2441, according to the Ground Water Estimation Committee.

Natural Division : Rayalaseema Region

Administration:

Division: Rayala Seema. Parliamentary Constituency: 36 Anantapur. District: Anantapur.

Mandal: Brahmasamudram. Assembly Constituency: 273 Kalyandurg. Gram Panchayat: 16.

Border Villages: (Karnataka)- Nearest Villages- Bhyrava nithippa, West Kodipalle, Eradikera, Santhekondapuram.

Villages: 13 **Inhabited:** 13 **Uninhabited:** 0

Ranking	District	State	National
Area	30	195	2949
Population	40	838	5755
Sex Ratio	14	827	2769
Child Sex Ratio	24	424	1540
Literacy Rate	59	873	5168
Density	14	247	5718
Work Participation Rate	39	940	645

Gram Panchayats:

Bhairasamudram, Bhyravanithippa, Bommaganipalli Brahmasamudram, Eradikera, Gundiganihalli Kannepalli, Muppulakunta, Nagireddipalli Palavenkatapuram, Pillalapalli, Rayalappadoddi S. Kondapuram, Theetakal, Vepalaparthi West Kodipalli.

Amenities:

Education: Primary School in 13 villages, Middle school in 10 villages, Matriculation or Secondary School in 4 villages, namely Brahmasamudram, Yerrakondapuram, Theetakal, Santhekondapuram.

Higher Secondary or Pre University Courses or Intermediate or Junior College in 0 village of the CD Block, College in 0 village, Adult Literacy Center in 0 village.

Medical: Hospital in 0 village, Dispensary in 0 village, Health Center in 1 village, Sub Center in 7 villages, Maternity and Child Welfare Center in 0 village, Community health workers in 0 village.

Drinking Water: Tap water in 13 villages, Tank water in 0 villages, Well water in 0 village, Tubewell in 0 village and more than one source in 13 villages.

Bank: Banking facility in 2 villages, namely, Brahmasamudram, Pillalapalle.

Credit Society in 1 village Agricultural Credit Society in 1 Non-Agricultural Credit Society in 0 village.

Others: Power supply in 13 villages, Cinema hall in 0 village, sport club in 0 village, Stadium or Auditorium or Community Hall in 0 village, Post Office in 11 villages.

There are 12 villages having bus facilities.

Villages with most of facilities: Brahmasamudram Pillalapalle.

Villages without Amenities (Education): None..

Scheduled Castes: Out of the total population of 39518 persons, 6424 persons (16.26%) belong to Scheduled Castes.

The villages having less than 10% SC population are None..

The villages having more than 50% SC population are None.

Sex ratio of Scheduled Caste population is 496.

Scheduled Castes Literates and Illiterates by Sex:

	Persons	Males	Females
Literate	2,648	1,609	1,039
Illiterate	3,776	1,628	2,148
Literacy rate	48.5	59.0	38.0
Graduate	33	30	3

Scheduled Castes (Dominant):

Madiga, Mala

For their cultural identity please see Appendix-I

Villages without Scheduled Castes: There is 1 village without any scheduled caste population.

Scheduled Tribes: Out of the total population of 39518 persons, 1280 persons (3.24%) belong to Scheduled Tribes.

The villages having less than 10% ST population are Gundiganihalli, Bhyravanithippa, West Kodipalle Eradikera, Vepalaparthy, Chelimenahalli Brahmasamudram, Yerrakondapuram, Bhairasamudram Kannepalle, Theetakal, Santhekondapuram.

The villages having more than 50% ST population are None.

Sex ratio of Scheduled tribe population is 480.

Scheduled Tribes Literates and Illiterates by Sex:

	Persons	Males	Females
Literate	595	375	220
Illiterate	685	290	395
Literacy rate	53.3	64.7	41.0
Graduate	15	12	3

Scheduled Tribes (Dominant):

Sugalis etc., Yerukulas

For their cultural identity please see Appendix-II

Villages without Scheduled Tribes: There are 4 villages without any scheduled tribe population.

Literates and Illiterates by Sex (Total Population):

	Persons	Males	Females
Literate	15,164	9,879	5,285
Illiterate	24,354	10,241	14,113
Literacy rate	45	58	32
Graduate	237	208	29

Agriculture: ***Distribution of villages according to land use:*** Out of 13 villages, Total area (in hectare) is 28431, out of that 74.08 percent is cultivable and 14.01 percent of the cultivable area is irrigated.

Sources of Irrigation (Hectares): Government Canal 968.71, Private Canal 0, Well without Electricity 0, Well with Electricity 476.03, Tubewell without Electricity 1, Tubewell with Electricity 1448.27, Tank 56.58, River 0, Lake 0, Waterfall 0, Others 0.

Villages with population of 5000 to 9999: Pillalapalle, Santhekondapuram.

Villages with population of 10000 and above: None

Distribution of Workers:

	Persons	Males	Females	WPR
Cultivators	9,477	5,903	3,574	43.81
Agricultural Labour	8,708	3,448	5,260	40.26
Household Industry	1,350	634	716	6.24
Other Workers	2,096	1,489	607	9.69
Main Workers	17,915	10,115	7,800	82.82
Marginal Workers	3,716	1,359	2,357	17.18
Total Workers	21,631	11,474	10,157	

Religion: Major Religious Communities:

	Persons	Males	Females	Sex Ratio
Hindu (98.35%)	38,864	19,791	19,073	964
Muslim (1.16%)	458	231	227	983
Christian (0.48%)	191	95	96	1,011
Sikh (0%)	-	-	-	-
Buddhists (0%)	-	-	-	-
Jain (0%)	-	-	-	-

Agewise Data:

	Persons	Males	Females	Sex Ratio
All ages	39,518	20,120	19,398	964
0-14	15,221	7,729	7,492	969
15-44	17,502	8,868	8,634	974
45-79	6,470	3,349	3,121	932
80+	304	163	141	865
Age not stated	21	11	10	909

Languages (Dominant):
Telugu, Kannada, Urdu, Tamil, Hindi

Disabled Population:

	Persons	Males	Females	%
Total Disabled	948	575	373	
In Seeing	307	177	130	32.38
In Speech	103	60	43	10.86
In Hearing	99	65	34	10.44
In Movement	348	227	121	36.71
Mentally	91	46	45	9.6

BUCHINAIDU KANDRIGA

Buchinaidu Kandriga C.D. Block lies in the north-eastern part of Chittoor district. The Block is located at a distance of 112 kms. from district headquarters (Chittoor). There are 24 villages in the block with the total population of 30,885 persons. Area of the C.D. Block is 163.84 sq. kms. It is bounded in the north by Mandal Thottambedu and district Nellore, in the south by Mandals K.V.B. Puram and Varadaiahpalem, in the east by district Nellore and Mandal Varadaiahpalem, and in the west by Mandal Thottambedu.

Communications:

Roadways : State Highway (S.H.): Direction- Srikalahasti to Tada. Nearest Villages- Vijayagopalapuram, Chellamambapuram, Thimmabhupalapuram, Parlapalle, Pallamala, Katur, Kanamanambedu, Neerpakota, Kanchanaputtur, Nelavoy, Kumara Venkatapuram, Kallivettu, Talarivettu.

River: Kalangi Nadi- Nearest Villages- Therripadu, Putteri, Kothapalem.

It receives the Backward Region Grants, and is identified as a drought-prone area as well.

Annual Rainfall: Average Rainfall 1259 mm

Ground Water: Availability of the Ground Water in the Basin is 2473 H.A.M.and the utilization is 486 H.A.M. It belongs to Safe category. Depth to water level varies from 5 to 10 meter below the ground. Most of the wells go down in summer months, according to the Ground Water Estimation Committee.

Natural Division : Rayalaseema Region

Administration:

Division: Rayala Seema. Parliamentary Constituency: 40 Tirupati (SC). District: Chittur. Mandal: Buchinaidu Kandriga. Assembly Constituency: 288 Satyavedu (SC). Gram Panchayat: 24.

Villages: 24 **Inhabited:** 24 **Uninhabited:** 0

Ranking	**District**	**State**	**National**
Area	35	751	4812
Population	57	1011	6035
Sex Ratio	43	564	1963
Child Sex Ratio	2	35	95
Literacy Rate	53	396	3454
Density	13	267	4904
Work Participation Rate	51	756	685

Gram Panchayats:
Alathur, B.N.Kandriga, G.N.Khandriga, Gajulapellure Kallivettu, Kampalem, Kanamanambedu, Kanchanaputtur Karani, Katuru, Kothapalem, Kukkambakam, Neerpakota Nelavoy, P.V.Khandriga, Pallamala, Parlapalli Peddapalavedu, Putteri, R.Ananthapuram, Talarivettu V.S.Puram, Venugopalapuram, West Warathur.

Amenities:

Education: Primary School in 22 villages, Middle school in 7 villages, Matriculation or Secondary School in 2 villages, namely Pallamala, Kanamanambedu.

Higher Secondary or Pre University Courses or Intermediate or Junior College in 0 village of the CD Block, College in 0 village, Adult Literacy Center in 11 villages.

Medical: Hospital in 0 village, Dispensary in 1 village, Health Center in 1 village, Sub Center in 6 villages, Maternity and Child Welfare Center in 0 village, Community health workers in 0 village.

The Village having Hospital or Dispensary or Health Center is Alathur.

Drinking Water: Tap water in 24 villages, Tank water in 24 villages, Well water in 24 villages, Tubewell in 24 villages and more than one source in 24 villages.

Bank: None.

Credit Society in 9 villages Agricultural Credit Society in 9 Non-Agricultural Credit Society in 0 village.

Others: Power supply in 24 villages, Cinema hall in 1 village, sport club in 0 village, Stadium or Auditorium or Community Hall in 0 village, Post Office in 11 villages.

There are 19 villages having bus facilities.

Village with most of facilities: None.

Villages without amenities (Education):
Therripadu, Kumara Venkatapuram..

Scheduled Castes: Out of the total population of 30885 persons, 9813 persons (31.77%) belong to Scheduled Castes.

The villages having less than 10% SC population are Therripadu, Chellamambapuram, Thangellapuram Kumara Venkatapuram.

The villages having more than 50% SC population are None.

Sex ratio of Scheduled Caste population is 498.

Scheduled Castes Literates and Illiterates by Sex:

	Persons	Males	Females
Literate	4,202	2,616	1,586
Illiterate	5,611	2,313	3,298
Literacy rate	50.0	61.7	38.0
Graduate	65	52	13

Scheduled Castes (Dominant):

Mala, Madiga, Generic Castes etc.

For their cultural identity please see Appendix-I

Villages without Scheduled Castes: There are 3 villages without any scheduled caste population.

Scheduled Tribes: Out of the total population of 30885 persons, 4002 persons (12.96%) belong to Scheduled Tribes. The villages having less than 10% ST population are Bhavanisankarapuram, Therripadu, Chinnayyagunta Vijayagopalapuram, Kothapalem, Chellamambapuram Thimmabhupalapuram, Parlapalle, Kanamanambedu West Warathur, Nelavoy, Kumara Venkatapuram Talarivettu.

The villages having more than 50% ST population are None.

Sex ratio of Scheduled tribe population is 491.

Scheduled Tribes Literates and Illiterates by Sex:

	Persons	Males	Females
Literate	1,056	629	427
Illiterate	2,946	1,408	1,538
Literacy rate	31.8	36.8	26.6
Graduate	2	2	0

Scheduled Tribes (Dominant):

Yenadis, Yerukulas, Kammara

For their cultural identity please see Appendix-II

Villages without Scheduled Tribes: There are 2 villages without any scheduled tribe population.

Literates and Illiterates by Sex (Total Population):

	Persons	Males	Females
Literate	14,987	9,013	5,974
Illiterate	15,898	6,574	9,324
Literacy rate	56	67	45
Graduate	461	358	103

Agriculture: ***Distribution of villages according to land use:*** Out of 24 villages, Total area (in hectare) is 16385, out of that 59.9 percent is cultivable and 52.05 percent of the cultivable area is irrigated.

Sources of Irrigation (Hectares): Government Canal 127, Private Canal 0, Well without Electricity 0, Well with Electricity 852, Tubewell without Electricity 0, Tubewell with Electricity 1244, Tank 2861, River 0, Lake 0, Waterfall 0, Others 24.

Villages with population of 5000 to 9999: None

Villages with population of 10000 and above: None

Distribution of Workers:

	Persons	Males	Females	WPR
Cultivators	3,767	2,677	1,090	21.92
Agricultural Labour	10,583	5,210	5,373	61.59
Household Industry	675	402	273	3.93
Other Workers	2,158	1,627	531	12.56
Main Workers	13,465	8,486	4,979	78.36
Marginal Workers	3,718	1,430	2,288	21.64
Total Workers	17,183	9,916	7,267	

Religion: Major Religious Communities:

	Persons	Males	Females	Sex Ratio
Hindu (98.52%)	30,427	15,374	15,053	979
Muslim (1.24%)	384	178	206	1,157
Christian (0.21%)	65	31	34	1,097
Sikh (0.01%)	2	1	1	1,000
Buddhists (0%)	-	-	-	-
Jain (0%)	-	-	-	-

Agewise Data:

	Persons	Males	Females	Sex Ratio
All ages	30,885	15,587	15,298	981
0-14	9,367	4,789	4,578	956
15-44	15,518	7,784	7,734	994
45-79	5,823	2,940	2,883	981
80+	144	56	88	1571
Age not stated	33	18	15	833

Languages (Dominant):

Telugu, Tamil, Urdu, Nepali, Hindi

Disabled Population:

	Persons	Males	Females	%
Total Disabled	586	314	272	
In Seeing	230	102	128	39.25
In Speech	83	51	32	14.16
In Hearing	50	25	25	8.53
In Movement	167	105	62	28.5
Mentally	56	31	25	9.56

BUCHIREDDIPALEM

Buchireddipalem C.D. Block lies in the north-eastern part of Nellore district. The Block is located at a distance of 23 kms. from district headquarters (Nellore). There are 14 villages in the block with the total population of 72,566 persons. Area of the C.D. Block is 118.77 sq. kms. It is bounded in the north by Mandal Dagadarthi, in the south by Mandal Nellore and river Pennar, in the east by Mandals Dagadarthi, Kodavalur and Kovur, and in the west by Mandal Sangam.

Communications:

Roadways : State Highway (S.H.): Direction- Sangam to Nellore. Nearest Villages- Vavveru, Isakapalem.

River: Pennar Nadi- Nearest Villages- Panchedu, Minagal lu, Jonnawada, Penuballe, Sreerangaraja -Puram, Damarama dugu.

Integrated Child Development Scheme (ICDS) Project: Buchireddipalem, Total Anganwadi Centres: 233

Annual Rainfall: Average Rainfall 1091 mm

Ground Water: Availability of the Ground Water in the Basin is 5536 H.A.M. and the utilization is 4390 H. A.M. It belongs to SC category. Depth to water level varies from less than 5 meter below the ground. Most of the wells go down in summer months, according to the Ground Water Estimation Committee.

Administration:

Division: Coastal Andhra. Parliamentary Constituency: 39 Nellore.District: Nellore.

Mandal: Buchireddipalem. Assembly Constituency: 235 Kovur. Gram Panchayat: 15.

Fairs and Festivals:

Sri Kodanda Ramaswamy Brahmothsavam : It is celebrated for eleven days from Chaitra Suddha Navami to Bahula Chaviti (April-May). The function is inaugurated on the first day with ankurpana and the Lord coming out for darba. Dwajarohanam (flag hoisting), seshavahana uthsavam (procession on serpent) and navakalas aradhana (worship of the nine kalasams) are the functions on the second day. From the third to sixth, the functions are special pujas and offerings with procession on Suryaprabha, Vali, Hanuman and Guruda respectively. The marriage ceremony is on the seventh day when there is a procession on elephant during the night. The car festival, the pothsavam and ponnanmanu uthsavam in the night are the functions on the eighth day. Alakalad opu is on the ninth, theerthavari, dhwajavarohanam and purnahuti are the functions of the tenth day. It concl udes with ekanthaseva on the last day.

Sri Mallikarjunaswamy Kamakshikevi Brahmo-thsavam : It is celebrated for 10 days from Vaisakha Bahula Shash ti to Amavasya (April-May). Nandiseva (procession on Nandi vahanam), rathothsavam (car festival) and thalambralu (marriage ceremony) are the important funct ions which attract vast number of pilgrims. At dawn and dusk Mahanyasa Purvaka Rudrabhishekam is performed. The issueless, devil possessed and the sick observe fast, bathe in the river and perform pranacharam (prost rate) during Brahmothsavam and Saran navarathrothsavam in Asviyujam (September-October) hoping that the deity will grant His darsan in their dream. Some devotee observe pradakshinam (go round the temple) for the period of mandalam (40 days) or half a mandalam (20 days) or for several months. Devotees fulfil their vows. Sarees, blouses, money and ornaments are offered. This is of ancient origin and extends to the entire district and the neighbouring district as well and to parts of the Tamil Nadu State even.

Villages: 14 **Inhabited:** 14 **Uninhabited:** 0

Ranking	District	State	National
Area	44	955	5497
Population	3	94	4372
Sex Ratio	10	282	1315
Child Sex Ratio	39	972	4414
Literacy Rate	2	58	1147
Density	38	958	1782
Work Participation Rate	2	63	3446

Gram Panchayats:

Buchireddy Palem, Chellayapalem, Damaramadugu Isakapalem, Jonnawada, Kalayakagollu, Kattubadipalem Minagallu, Munulapudi, Nagaiah Gunta, Nagamambapuram Panchedu, Penuballi, Rebala, Vavveru.

Amenities:

Education: Primary School in 12 villages, Middle school in 10 villages, Matriculation or Secondary School in 5 villages, namely Vavveru, Rebala, Minagallu, Penuballe, Damaramadugu.

Higher Secondary or Pre University Courses or Intermediate or Junior College in 1 village of the CD Block,, namely Vavveru.

College in 1 village, Adult Literacy Center in 12 villages., College is in village, namely Vavveru.

Medical: Hospital in 1 village, Dispensary in 2 villages, Health Center in 3 villages, Sub Center in 8 villages, Maternity and Child Welfare Center in 1 village, Community health workers in 0 village.

The Villages having Hospital or Dispensary or Health Center are Vavveru, Rebala.

Drinking Water: Tap water in 13 villages, Tank water in 13 villages, Well water in 14 villages, Tubewell in 13 villages and more than one source in 13 villages.

Bank: Banking facility in 3 villages, namely, Vavveru, Jonnawada, Damaramadugu.

Credit Society in 12 villages Agricultural Credit Society in 1 Non-Agricultural Credit Society in 12 villages.

Others: Power supply in 14 villages, Cinema hall in 2 villages, sport club in 0 village, Stadium or Auditorium or Community Hall in 0 village, Post Office in 12 villages.

There are 10 villages having bus facilities.

Villages with most of facilities: Vavveru Jonnawada, Damaramadugu.

Villages without amenities (Education):

Kavetipalem, Sreerangaraja -Puram..

Scheduled Castes: Out of the total population of 72566 persons, 13206 persons (18.2%) belong to Scheduled Castes.

The villages having less than 10% SC population are None..

The villages having more than 50% SC population are None.

Sex ratio of Scheduled Caste population is 508.

Scheduled Castes Literates and Illiterates by Sex:

	Persons	Males	Females
Literate	8,283	4,444	3,839
Illiterate	4,923	2,057	2,866

Literacy rate	70.8	77.4	64.5
Graduate	329	234	95

Scheduled Castes (Dominant):
Mala, Madiga, Arundhatiya, Samban Generic Castes etc.

For their cultural identity please see Appendix-I

Villages without Scheduled Castes: There is 1 village without any scheduled caste population.

Scheduled Tribes: Out of the total population of 72566 persons, 7981 persons (11%) belong to Scheduled Tribes. The villages having less than 10% ST population are Munulapudi, Vavveru, Rebala, Minagallu Sreerangaraja -Puram.

The villages having more than 50% ST population are None.

Sex ratio of Scheduled tribe population is 496.

Scheduled Tribes Literates and Illiterates by Sex:

	Persons	Males	Females
Literate	2,483	1,371	1,112
Illiterate	5,498	2,654	2,844
Literacy rate	36.6	40.3	32.9
Graduate	22	15	7

Scheduled Tribes (Dominant):
Yenadis, Generic Tribes etc., Yerukulas Sugalis etc.

For their cultural identity please see Appendix-II

Villages without Scheduled Tribes: There are 0 village without any scheduled tribe population.

Literates and Illiterates by Sex (Total Population):

	Persons	Males	Females
Literate	44,906	24,844	20,062
Illiterate	27,660	11,514	16,146
Literacy rate	70	78	63
Graduate	2,518	1,848	670

Agriculture: ***Distribution of villages according to land use:*** Out of 14 villages, Total area (in hectare) is 11876, out of that 63.22 percent is cultivable and 71.44 percent of the cultivable area is irrigated.

Sources of Irrigation (Hectares): Government Canal 2338, Private Canal 0, Well without Electricity 0, Well with Electricity 0, Tubewell without Electricity 0, Tubewell with Electricity 2749, Tank 0, River 0, Lake 0, Waterfall 0, Others 277.

Villages with population of 5000 to 9999:
Rebala, Isakapalem, Damaramadugu.

Villages with population of 10000 and above:
Vavveru.

Distribution of Workers:

	Persons	Males	Females	WPR
Cultivators	3,832	3,283	549	11.62
Agricultural Labour	16,031	8,592	7,439	48.62
Household Industry	2,001	875	1,126	6.07
Other Workers	11,106	8,743	2,363	33.69
Main Workers	27,534	19,223	8,311	83.51
Marginal Workers	5,436	2,270	3,166	16.49
Total Workers	32,970	21,493	11,477	

Religion: Major Religious Communities:

	Persons	Males	Females	Sex Ratio
Hindu (82.44%)	59,827	30,001	29,826	994
Muslim (16.57%)	12,024	6,009	6,015	1,001
Christian (0.91%)	657	320	337	1,053
Sikh (0.03%)	21	8	13	1,625
Buddhists (0.01%)	6	3	3	1,000
Jain (0.01%)	4	3	1	333

Agewise Data:

	Persons	Males	Females	Sex Ratio
All ages	72,566	36,358	36,208	996
0-14	20,898	10,638	10,260	964
15-44	35,900	18,022	17,878	992
45-79	15,349	7,521	7,828	1041
80+	373	156	217	1391
Age not stated	46	21	25	1190

Languages (Dominant):
Telugu, Urdu, Tamil, Gondi, Hindi

Disabled Population:

	Persons	Males	Females	%
Total Disabled	1,048	594	454	
In Seeing	300	156	144	28.63
In Speech	135	81	54	12.88
In Hearing	60	29	31	5.73
In Movement	378	231	147	36.07
Mentally	175	97	78	16.7

BUKKAPATNAM

Bukkapatnam C.D. Block lies in the south-eastern part of Anantapur district. The Block is located at a distance of 65 kms. from district headquarters (Anantapur). There are 08 villages in the block with the total population of 40,701 persons. Area of the C.D. Block is 267.77 sq. kms. It is bounded in the north by Mandal Mudigubba, in the south by Mandal Puttaparthi, in the east by Mandals Nallamada and Mudigubba, and in the west by Mandals Kothacheruvu, Chennekothapalle and Dharmavaram.

Communications:

Roadways : Metalled Roads: Nearest Villages- Marala, Pamudurthi, Agraharam, Gunipalle, Siddarampuram, Bukkapatnam.

River: Chitravati Nadi- Nearest Village- Kothakota.

It receives the Backward Region Grants, and is identified as a drought-prone area as well.

Annual Rainfall: Average Rainfall 703 mm

Ground Water: Availability of the Ground Water in the Basin is 1049 H.A.M. and the utilization is 1080 H. A.M. It belongs to OE category. Depth to water level varies from 10 to 20 meter below the ground. Most of the wells go down in summer months. The well density in the entire block is 6 wells per sq. km. Total no. of the wells in the block are enumerated as 1701, according to the Ground Water Estimation Committee.

Forest and Reserved **Forest:** Nearest Villages- Agraharam, Gunipalle, Siddarampuram, Bukkapatnam, Kothakota.

Natural Division : Rayalaseema Region

Administration:

Division: Rayala Seema. Parliamentary Constituency: 37 Hindupur. District: Anantapur.

Mandal: Bukkapatnam. Assembly Constituency: 278 Puttapa rthi. Gram Panchayat: 11.

Villages: 8 **Inhabited:** 8 **Uninhabited:** 0

Ranking	**District**	**State**	**National**
Area	37	250	3133
Population	37	803	5708
Sex Ratio	43	985	3482
Child Sex Ratio	43	881	3893
Literacy Rate	17	489	3801
Density	43	542	5527
Work Participation Rate	32	898	1438

Gram Panchayats:

Agraharam, Bukkapatnam, Garikavaripalli, Gunipalli Kothakota, Krishnapuram, Marala, Narasimpalli Thanda Pamudurthi, Siddarampuram, Yadalankapalli.

Amenities:

Education: Primary School in 8 villages, Middle school in 6 villages, Matriculation or Secondary School in 5 villages, namely Krishnapuram, Marala, Pamudurthi, Siddarampuram, Bukkapatnam.

Higher Secondary or Pre University Courses or Intermediate or Junior College in 1 village of the CD Block,, namely Bukkapatnam.

College in 1 village, Adult Literacy Center in 8 villages., College is in village, namely Bukkapatnam.

Medical: Hospital in 0 village, Dispensary in 0 village, Health Center in 3 villages, Sub Center in 8 villages, Maternity and Child Welfare Center in 0 village, Community health workers in 0 village.

Drinking Water: Tap water in 8 villages, Tank water in 0 villages, Well water in 3 villages, Tubewell in 0 village and more than one source in 8 villages.

Bank: Banking facility in 3 villages, namely, Marala, Pamudurthi, Bukkapatnam.

Credit Society in 4 villages Agricultural Credit Society in 4 Non-Agricultural Credit Society in 0 village.

Others: Power supply in 8 villages, Cinema hall in 1 village, sport club in 0 village, Stadium or Auditorium or Community Hall in 0 village, Post Office in 8 villages.

There are 8 villages having bus facilities.

Villages with most of facilities: Marala Pamudurthi, Bukkapatnam.

Villages without Amenities (Education): None..

Scheduled Castes: Out of the total population of 40701 persons, 3870 persons (9.51%) belong to Scheduled Castes.

The villages having less than 10% SC population are Krishnapuram, Marala, Agraharam, Siddarampuram Kothakota.

The villages having more than 50% SC population are None.

Sex ratio of Scheduled Caste population is 480.

Scheduled Castes Literates and Illiterates by Sex:

	Persons	Males	Females
Literate	1,615	1,079	536
Illiterate	2,255	932	1,323
Literacy rate	47.4	60.5	33.0
Graduate	44	33	11

Scheduled Castes (Dominant):

Madiga, Mala, Adi Andhra, Generic Castes etc.

For their cultural identity please see Appendix-I

Villages without Scheduled Castes: There are 0 village without any scheduled caste population.

Scheduled Tribes: Out of the total population of 40701 persons, 3382 persons (8.31%) belong to Scheduled Tribes.

The villages having less than 10% ST population are Krishnapuram, Pamudurthi, Agraharam, Gunipalle Siddarampuram, Bukkapatnam.

The villages having more than 50% ST population are None.

Sex ratio of Scheduled tribe population is 470.

Scheduled Tribes Literates and Illiterates by Sex:

	Persons	Males	Females
Literate	1,334	941	393
Illiterate	2,048	850	1,198
Literacy rate	44.8	60.2	27.8
Graduate	53	49	4

Scheduled Tribes (Dominant):

Sugalis etc., Yerukulas

For their cultural identity please see Appendix-II

Villages without Scheduled Tribes: There are 0 village without any scheduled tribe population.

Literates and Illiterates by Sex (Total Population):

	Persons	Males	Females
Literate	19,405	12,432	6,973
Illiterate	21,296	8,441	12,855
Literacy rate	54	68	40

Graduate	966	817	149

Agriculture: ***Distribution of villages according to land use:*** Out of 8 villages, Total area (in hectare) is 26777, out of that 38.09 percent is cultivable and 8.38 percent of the cultivable area is irrigated.

Sources of Irrigation (Hectares): Government Canal 0, Private Canal 0, Well without Electricity 0, Well with Electricity 520.84, Tubewell without Electricity 0, Tubewell with Electricity 34.8, Tank 299.45, River 0, Lake 0, Waterfall 0, Others 0.

Villages with population of 5000 to 9999:
Pamudurthi.

Villages with population of 10000 and above:
Bukkapatnam.

Distribution of Workers:

	Persons	Males	Females	WPR
Cultivators	6,304	3,889	2,415	28.97
Agricultural Labour	10,734	4,780	5,954	49.33
Household Industry	590	378	212	2.71
Other Workers	4,132	3,334	798	18.99
Main Workers	16,390	10,231	6,159	75.32
Marginal Workers	5,370	2,150	3,220	24.68
Total Workers	21,760	12,381	9,379	

Religion: Major Religious Communities:

	Persons	Males	Females	Sex Ratio
Hindu (92.83%)	37,784	19,442	18,342	943
Muslim (7.06%)	2,872	1,406	1,466	1,043
Christian (0.09%)	37	20	17	850
Sikh (0%)	-	-	-	-
Buddhists (0%)	-	-	-	-
Jain (0%)	-	-	-	-

Agewise Data:

	Persons	Males	Females	Sex Ratio
All ages	40,701	20,873	19,828	950
0-14	11,803	6,105	5,698	933
15-44	19,795	10,327	9,468	917
45-79	8,832	4,312	4,520	1048
80+	248	116	132	1138
Age not stated	23	13	10	769

Languages (Dominant):
Telugu, Urdu, Hindi, Marathi, Gondi

Disabled Population:

	Persons	Males	Females	%
Total Disabled	1,010	538	472	
In Seeing	389	184	205	38.51
In Speech	76	45	31	7.52
In Hearing	69	31	38	6.83
In Movement	386	228	158	38.22
Mentally	90	50	40	8.91

BUKKARAYA SAMUDRAM

Bukkarayasamudram C.D. Block lies in the eastern part of Anantapur district. The Block is located at a distan ce of 05 kms. from district headquarters (Anantapur). There are 14 villages in the block with the total population of 52,985 persons. Area of the C.D. Block is 250.92 sq. kms. It is bounded in the north by Mandals Singanamala and Narpala, in the south by Mandals Anant apur and Narpala, in the east by Mandal Narpala, and in the west by Mandals Anantapur and Garladinne.

Communications:

Roadways : NH- 7: Direction- Kurnool to Bangalore Nearest Villages- Podaralla, Govindapalle, Bukkarayasamudram. State Highway (S.H.): Direction- Anantapur to Tadpatri. Nearest Villages- Bukkarayasamudram, Korrapadu, Bodiga nidoddi, Siddampeta, Reddipalle.

River: Pennar Nadi- Nearest Villages- Podaralla, Govind apalle, Bukkarayasamudram, Janthulur.

It receives the Backward Region Grant, and is identified as a drought-prone area as well.

Annual Rainfall: Average Rainfall 544 mm

Ground Water: Availability of the Ground Water in the Basin is 4397 H.A.M. and the utilization is 1651 H. A.M. It belongs to safe category. Depth to water level varies from 10 to 20 meter below the ground. Most of the wells go down in summer months. The well density in the entire block is 11 wells per sq. km. Total no. of the wells in the block are enumerated as 4102, according to the Ground Water Estimation Committee.

Natural Division : Rayalaseema Region

Administration:

Division: Rayala Seema. Parliamentary Constituency: 36 Anantapur. District: Anantapur.
Mandal: Bukkaraya Samudram. Assembly Constituency: 271 Sanganamala (SC). Gram Panchayat: 18.

Villages: 14 **Inhabited:** 14 **Uninhabited:** 0

Ranking	District	State	National
Area	42	310	3372
Population	6	423	5141
Sex Ratio	49	1040	3903
Child Sex Ratio	55	1014	4754
Literacy Rate	46	699	4545
Density	38	476	4571
Work Participation Rate	13	675	1207

Gram Panchayats:
B.K.Samudram, B.Kothapalli, Bommalatapalli, Chedulla Chennampalli, Danduvaripalli, Dayyalakuntapalli Govindapalli, Janthulur, K.K.Agraharam, Korrapadu Neelampalli, Pasalur, Podaralla, Reddipalli Regidikottur, Siddarampuram, Venkatapuram.

Amenities:

Education: Primary School in 12 villages, Middle school in 8 villages, Matriculation or Secondary School in 4 villages, namely Podaralla, Bodiganidoddi, Bukkarayasamudram, Kondakinda Agraharam.

Higher Secondary or Pre University Courses or Intermediate or Junior College in 1 village. of the CD Block,, namely Podaralla.

College in 0 village, Adult Literacy Center in 0 village.

Medical: Hospital in 0 village, Dispensary in 0 village, Health Center in 2 villages, Sub Center in 9 villages, Maternity and Child Welfare Center in 0 village, Community health workers in 0 village.

Drinking Water: Tap water in 9 villages, Tank water in 0 villages, Well water in 1 village, Tubewell in 12 villages and more than one source in 12 villages.

Bank: Banking facility in 1 villages, namely, Bukkarayasamudram.

Credit Society in 3 villages Agricultural Credit Society in 2 Non-Agricultural Credit Society in 0 village.

Others: Power supply in 14 villages, Cinema hall in 0 village, sport club in 0 village, Stadium or Auditorium or Community Hall in 0 village, Post Office in 10 villages.

There are 13 villages having bus facilities.

Village with most of facilities: Bukkarayasamudram.

Villages without amenities (Education):
Chennarayunipalle, Siddampeta..

Scheduled Castes: Out of the total population of 52985 persons, 9092 persons (17.16%) belong to Scheduled Castes.

The villages having less than 10% SC population are None..

The villages having more than 50% SC population are None.

Sex ratio of Scheduled Caste population is 487.

Scheduled Castes Literates and Illiterates by Sex:

	Persons	Males	Females
Literate	3,149	2,029	1,120
Illiterate	5,943	2,637	3,306
Literacy rate	40.5	50.6	29.7
Graduate	47	40	7

Scheduled Castes (Dominant):
Madiga, Mala, Generic Castes etc., Bariki

For their cultural identity please see Appendix-I

Villages without Scheduled Castes: There are 0 village without any scheduled caste population.

Scheduled Tribes: Out of the total population of 52985 persons, 2012 persons (3.8%) belong to Scheduled Tribes.

The villages having less than 10% ST population are Podaralla, Janthulur, Chedulla, Korrapadu Chennampalle, Bodiganidoddi, Chennarayunipalle Siddampeta, Govindapalle, Bukkarayasamudram Danduvaripalle, Kondakinda Agraharam.

The villages having more than 50% ST population are None.

Sex ratio of Scheduled tribe population is 478.

Scheduled Tribes Literates and Illiterates by Sex:

	Persons	Males	Females
Literate	690	453	237
Illiterate	1,322	598	724
Literacy rate	40.1	50.3	28.8
Graduate	14	13	1

Scheduled Tribes (Dominant):
Yerukulas, Sugalis etc., Kammara
Generic Tribes etc., Yenadis

For their cultural identity please see Appendix-II

Villages without Scheduled Tribes: There are 3 villages without any scheduled tribe population.

Literates and Illiterates by Sex (Total Population):

	Persons	Males	Females
Literate	22,846	14,390	8,456
Illiterate	30,139	12,896	17,243
Literacy rate	50	61	38
Graduate	811	666	145

Agriculture: ***Distribution of villages according to land use:*** Out of 14 villages, Total area (in hectare) is 25090, out of that 78.79 percent is cultivable and 31.72 percent of the cultivable area is irrigated.

Sources of Irrigation (Hectares): Government Canal 2465.29, Private Canal 0, Well without Electricity 0, Well with Electricity 2379.87, Tubewell without Electricity 0, Tubewell with Electricity 432.94, Tank 992.02, River 0, Lake 0, Waterfall 0, Others 0.

Villages with population of 5000 to 9999:
Podaralla, Chennampalle, Kondakinda Agraharam.

Villages with population of 10000 and above:
Bukkarayasamudram.

Distribution of Workers:

	Persons	Males	Females	WPR
Cultivators	7,484	5,073	2,411	26.41
Agricultural Labour	13,277	5,857	7,420	46.86
Household Industry	1,117	690	427	3.94
Other Workers	6,457	4,800	1,657	22.79
Main Workers	24,469	15,360	9,109	86.36
Marginal Workers	3,866	1,060	2,806	13.64
Total Workers	28,335	16,420	11,915	

Religion: Major Religious Communities:

	Persons	Males	Females	Sex Ratio
Hindu (94.96%)	50,313	25,928	24,385	940
Muslim (4.75%)	2,515	1,269	1,246	982
Christian (0.21%)	112	68	44	647
Sikh (0%)	1	-	1	-

Buddhists (0%)	-	-	-	-
Jain (0%)	-	-	-	-

Agewise Data:

	Persons	Males	Females	Sex Ratio
All ages	52,985	27,286	25,699	942
0-14	17,777	9,242	8,535	924
15-44	25,644	13,110	12,534	956
45-79	9,240	4,794	4,446	927
80+	253	104	149	1433
Age not stated	71	36	35	972

Languages (Dominant):
Telugu, Urdu, Gondi, Marathi, Hindi

Disabled Population:

	Persons	Males	Females	%
Total Disabled	875	493	382	
In Seeing	233	114	119	26.63
In Speech	99	56	43	11.31
In Hearing	69	28	41	7.89
In Movement	358	229	129	40.91
Mentally	116	66	50	13.26

BURGAMPAHAD

Burgampahad C.D. Block lies in the northern part of Khammam district. It is a part of Burgampahad Mandal. The Block is located at a distance of 115 kms. from district headquarters (Khammam). There are 17 villages in the block with the total population of 37,678 persons. Area of the C.D. Block is 320.11 sq. kms. It is bound ed in the north by Bhadrachalam Mandal, in the south by Palwancha Mandal, in the east by Kukunoor Mandal, and in the west by Aswapuram Mandal.

Communications:

Roadways : NH- 221: Direction- Nuzvid to Bhadrachalam. Nearest Villages- Pinapaka Pattinagar, Morampalle, Burgampahad, Sompalle, Seetharama Nagar.

River: Godavari Nadi- Nearset Villages- Nagineniprolu, Gumpanapalle, Ganapavaram, Ibrahimpeta, Ravigudem [Big], Irvendi, Mothepattinagar, Burgampahad, Sridhara, Burgampahad, Sompalle, Seetharama Nagar.

Integrated Child Development Scheme (ICDS) Project: Burgampahad (Tribal), Total Anganwadi Centres: 285

Annual Rainfall: Annual Rainfall 1201 mm

Ground Water: Availability of the Ground Water in the Basin is 2894 H.A.M.and the utilization is 254 H.A. M. It belongs to safe category. Depth to water level varies from 5 to 10 meter below the ground. Most of the wells go down in summer months. The well density in the entire block is 1 well per sq. km. Total no. of the wells in the block are enumerated as 213, accor ding to the Ground Water Estimation Committee.

Natural Division : Godavari Depression Region

Administration:

Division: Telangana. Parliamentary Constituency: 16 Mahbubabad (ST). District: Khammam. Mandal: Burgampahad. Assembly Constituency: 110 Pinapaka (ST). Gram Panchay at: 13.

Villages: 17 **Inhabited:** 16 **Uninhabited:** 1

Ranking	District	State	National
Area	12	124	2567
Population	31	888	5826
Sex Ratio	46	1084	4646
Child Sex Ratio	35	695	2917
Literacy Rate	13	490	3808
Density	41	766	5979
Work Participation Rate	36	1011	2237

Gram Panchayats:
Burgampahad, Ganapavaram, Iravendi, Lakshmipuram Morampalli, Musalimadugu, Nagineniprolu Peda Ravigudem, Pinapaka Pattinagar, Sarapaka Seetharama Nagar, Sridhara Velair, Tekulacheruvu.

Amenities:

Education: Primary School in 16 villages, Middle school in 9 villages, Matriculation or Secondary School in 4 villages, namely Nagineniprolu, Pinapaka Pattinagar, Morampalle, Burgampahad.

Higher Secondary or Pre University Courses or Intermediate or Junior College in 1 village of the CD Block,, namely Burgampahad.

College in 1 village, Adult Literacy Center in 15 villages., College is in village, namely Burgampahad.

Medical: Hospital in 1 village, Dispensary in 0 village, Health Center in 1 village, Sub Center in 8 villages, Maternity and Child Welfare Center in 0 village, Community health workers in 0 village.

The Village having Hospital or Dispensary or Health Center is Burgampahad.

Drinking Water: Tap water in 16 villages, Tank water in 16 villages, Well water in 16 villages, Tubewell in 16 villages and more than one source in 16 villages.

Bank: Banking facility in 1 villages, namely, Burgampahad.

Credit Society in 9 villages Agricultural Credit Society in 5 Non-Agricultural Credit Society in 8 villages.

Others: Power supply in 16 villages, Cinema hall in 1 village, sport club in 0 village, Stadium or Auditorium or Community Hall in 0 village, Post Office in 8 villages.

There are 15 villages having bus facilities.

Village with most of facilities: Burgampahad.

Villages without Amenities (Education): None..

Scheduled Castes: Out of the total population of 37884 persons, 8763 persons (23.13%) belong to Scheduled Castes. The villages having less than 10% SC population are

None..

The villages having more than 50% SC population are None.

Sex ratio of Scheduled Caste population is 487.

Scheduled Castes Literates and Illiterates by Sex:

	Persons	Males	Females
Literate	3,876	2,333	1,543
Illiterate	4,887	2,159	2,728
Literacy rate	52.3	61.6	42.5
Graduate	53	48	5

Scheduled Castes (Dominant):

Mala, Madiga, Generic Castes etc., Mala Dasari Beda Jangam etc.

For their cultural identity please see Appendix-I

Villages without Scheduled Castes: There are 2 villages without any scheduled caste population.

Scheduled Tribes: Out of the total population of 37884 persons, 9847 persons (25.99%) belong to Scheduled Tribes.

The villages having less than 10% ST population are Mothepattinagar, Burgampahad, Gumpanapalle Ganapavaram, Ibrahimpeta.

The villages having more than 50% ST population are None.

Sex ratio of Scheduled tribe population is 461.

Scheduled Tribes Literates and Illiterates by Sex:

	Persons	Males	Females
Literate	3,468	2,479	989
Illiterate	6,379	2,824	3,555
Literacy rate	42.1	55.4	26.3
Graduate	34	31	3

Scheduled Tribes (Dominant):

Koya etc., Sugalis etc., Nayaks, Generic Tribes etc. Yerukulas

For their cultural identity please see Appendix-II

Villages without Scheduled Tribes: There are 4 villages without any scheduled tribe population.

Literates and Illiterates by Sex (Total Population):

	Persons	Males	Females
Literate	17,532	10,881	6,651
Illiterate	20,352	8,804	11,548
Literacy rate	54	65	43
Graduate	397	320	77

Agriculture: ***Distribution of villages according to land use:*** Out of 17 villages, Total area (in hectare) is 32010, out of that 21.78 percent is cultivable and 35.76 percent of the cultivable area is irrigated.

Sources of Irrigation (Hectares): Government Canal 364.61, Private Canal 0, Well without Electricity 8.09, Well with Electricity 122.18, Tubewell without Electricity 3.2, Tubewell with Electricity 248.06, Tank 425.05, River 1321.68, Lake 0, Waterfall 0, Others 0.

Villages with population of 5000 to 9999:

Nagineniprolu, Morampalle, Burgampahad.

Villages with population of 10000 and above: None

Distribution of Workers:

	Persons	Males	Females	WPR
Cultivators	3,645	2,572	1,073	19.63
Agricultural Labour	11,109	5,423	5,686	59.82
Household Industry	784	310	474	4.22
Other Workers	3,032	2,447	585	16.33
Main Workers	14,164	8,995	5,169	76.27
Marginal Workers	4,406	1,757	2,649	23.73
Total Workers	18,570	10,752	7,818	

Religion: Major Religious Communities:

	Persons	Males	Females	Sex Ratio
Hindu (94.02%)	35,618	18,526	17,092	923
Muslim (5.21%)	1,972	998	974	976
Christian (0.69%)	262	130	132	1,015
Sikh (0%)	1	-	1	-
Buddhists (0%)	1	1	-	-
Jain (0%)	-	-	-	-

Agewise Data:

	Persons	Males	Females	Sex Ratio
All ages	37,884	19,685	18,199	925
0-14	13,062	6,895	6,167	894
15-44	18,306	9,482	8,824	931
45-79	6,146	3,094	3,052	986
80+	283	146	137	938
Age not stated	87	68	19	279

Languages (Dominant):

Telugu, Koya, Hindi, Urdu, Tamil

Disabled Population:

	Persons	Males	Females	%
Total Disabled	1,080	647	433	
In Seeing	606	370	236	56.11
In Speech	109	64	45	10.09
In Hearing	51	24	27	4.72
In Movement	215	134	81	19.91
Mentally	99	55	44	9.17

BURJA

Burja C.D. Block lies in the western part of Srikakulam district. The Block is located at a distance of 51 kms. from district headquarters (Srikakulam). There are 64 villages in the block with the total population of 41,852 persons. Area of the C.D. Block is 105.13 sq. kms. It is bounded in the north by Mandal Seethampe ta, in the south by Mandal Amadalavalasa, in the east by Mandal Sarubujjili, and in the west by Mandals Palak onda, Amadalavalasa and Santhakaviti.

Communications:

Roadways : Metalled Roads: Nearest Villages- Thuddali, Haripurampallapuram, Kothavalasa, Marripadu, Peddapeta, Paravasturamanna Peta, Jagannadhapuram, Appalapatnayak uni Peta, Gopidevipeta, Issadivalasa, Pendyalalakshimide vipeta, Korikanakurmiraja Puram, Sankurada, Turupuramabh adrarajupeta, Kollivalasa, Cheedivalasa, Thotavada, Narendrapuram, Jogipaduvenkata Puram, Adduripeta, Thima dam, Annampeta, Vykuntapuram, Ahobalacharyula Peta, Latchayyapeta, Uppinivalasa, Gudigeddavenkata Puram, Bodlapadu.

River: Nagavali Nadi- Nearest Villages- Yetivoddupartha, Vandra, Neelapuram, Gangabhagiradhi Puram, Allena, Burja, Vavam, Kakandyam, Lankam, Labham, Guttavalli.

Backwards Region Grants Fund: It receives Backward Region Grants.

Annual Rainfall: Average Rainfall 1085.6 mm

Ground Water: Availability of the Ground Water in the Basin is (Information not avavible) H.A.M .and the utilization is (Information not avavible) H.A.M. It belongs to (Information not avavible) category. Depth to water level varies from 3 to 10 meter below the ground. Most of the wells go down in summer months.

Forest and Reserved **Forest:** Nearest Villages- Boddapadu, Jangalapadu, Masenaputhi, Jogipaduvenkata Puram, Addur ipeta, Thimadam, Annampeta.

Administration:

Division: Coastal Andhra. Parliamentary Constituency: 19 Srikakulam. District: Srikakulam. Mandal: Burja. Assembly Constituency: 125 Amadalavalasa. Gram Panchay at: 27.

Villages: 64 **Inhabited:** 57 **Uninhabited:** 7

Ranking	District	State	National
Area	33	1008	5658
Population	34	766	5655
Sex Ratio	33	545	1930
Child Sex Ratio	13	278	931
Literacy Rate	12	392	3439
Density	13	654	2744
Work Participation Rate	27	190	1792

Gram Panchayats:

A.P.Peta, Allena, Annampeta, Burja, Ceedivalasa Chinalankam, Donkalapartha, Guttavelli, Kalaparthi Kantlam, Koaragam, Kollivalasa, Labham, Lakkupuram Mamidivalasa, Neeladevipuram, O.V.Peta, P.L.Devipeta Palavalasa, Pedalankam, Peddapeta, Singannapalem T.D.R.Rajupeta, Thotavada, Uppinivalasa, Vavam Vykuntapuram.

Amenities:

Education: Primary School in 49 villages, Middle school in 15 villages, Matriculation or Secondary School in 6 villages, namely Burja, Sankurada, Thotavada, Uppinivalasa, Vopivadavenkam Peta, Guttavalli.

Higher Secondary or Pre University Courses or Intermediate or Junior College in 0 village of the CD Block, College in 0 village, Adult Literacy Center in 27 villages.

Medical: Hospital in 1 village, Dispensary in 2 villages, Health Center in 2 villages, Sub Center in 11 villages, Maternity and Child Welfare Center in 1 village, Community health workers in 0 village.

The Villages having Hospital or Dispensary or Health Center are Burja, Thotavada, Gopalakrishnarangarayapuram.

Drinking Water: Tap water in 57 villages, Tank water in 57 villages, Well water in 57 villages, Tubewell in 57 villages and more than one source in 57 villages.

Bank: Banking facility in 5 villages, namely, Burja, Neeladevipuram, Sankurada, Thotavada Guttavalli.

Credit Society in 14 villages Agricultural Credit Society in 10 Non-Agricultural Credit Society in 8 villages.

Others: Power supply in 57 villages, Cinema hall in 0 village, sport club in 0 village, Stadium or Auditorium or Community Hall in 0 village, Post Office in 11 villages.

There are 38 villages having bus facilities.

Villages with most of facilities: Burja, Thotavada Guttavalli.

Villages without amenities (Education): Yetivoddupartha, Haripurampallapuram, Kothavalasa, Gangabhagiradhi Puram, Somidavalasa, Boddapadu, Adduripeta, Neelakantapuram..

Scheduled Castes: Out of the total population of 41852 persons, 5866 persons (14.02%) belong to Scheduled Castes.

The villages having less than 10% SC population are Yetivoddupartha, Haripurampallapuram, Kothavalasa Kilantra, Neelapuram, Allena, Paravasturamanna Peta Kondapeta, Jagannadhapuram, Appalapatnayakuni Peta Mamidivalasa, Sankurada, Gangampeta, Lankam Somidavalasa, Boddapadu, Jangalapadu, Masenaputhi Adduripeta, Vykuntapuram, Guttavalli, Chalikam Bodlapadu, Koragam.

The villages having more than 50% SC population are None.

Sex ratio of Scheduled Caste population is 468.

Scheduled Castes Literates and Illiterates by Sex:

	Persons	Males	Females
Literate	2,696	1,787	909
Illiterate	3,170	1,331	1,839
Literacy rate	52.8	65.4	38.3
Graduate	46	37	9

Scheduled Castes (Dominant):

Mala, Relli, Madiga, Adi Andhra, Generic Castes etc.

For their cultural identity please see Appendix-I

Villages without Scheduled Castes: There are 18 villages without any scheduled caste population.

Scheduled Tribes: Out of the total population of 41852 persons, 1288 persons (3.08%) belong to Scheduled Tribes. The villages having less than 10% ST population are Yetivoddupartha, Donkalapartha, Thuddali, Marripadu Palavalasa, Lakkupuram, Kilantra, Neelapuram Gangabhagiradhi Puram, Allena, Peddapeta Paravasturamanna Peta, Jagannadhapuram Appalapatnayakuni Peta, Pendyalalakshimidevipeta Korikanakurmiraja Puram, Burja, Vavam, Kakandyam Mamidivalasa, Neeladevipuram, Sankurada Turupuramabhadrarajupeta, Kollivalasa, Gangampeta Lankam, Labham, Cheedivalasa, Kantlam, Thotavada Narendrapuram, Thimadam, Annampeta T.V. Ramabhadra Raju Peta, Neelakantapuram Vykuntapuram, Ahobalacharyula Peta, Singannapalem Latchayyapeta, Uppinivalasa, Vopivadavenkam Peta Guttavalli, Kalaparthi, Gopalakrishnarangarayapuram Chalikam, Bodlapadu, Koragam, Boragavalasa.

The villages having more than 50% ST population are Haripurampallapuram, Kothavalasa, Gopidevipeta Somidavalasa, Boddapadu, Jangalapadu, Masenaputhi Adduripeta.

Sex ratio of Scheduled tribe population is 505.

Scheduled Tribes Literates and Illiterates by Sex:

	Persons	Males	Females
Literate	415	271	144
Illiterate	873	367	506
Literacy rate	37.5	48.9	26.0
Graduate	4	4	0

Scheduled Tribes (Dominant):

Jatapus, Savaras etc., Kotia etc., Yerukulas Konda Dhoras

For their cultural identity please see Appendix-II

Villages without Scheduled Tribes: There are 39 villages without any scheduled tribe population.

Literates and Illiterates by Sex (Total Population):

	Persons	Males	Females
Literate	20,690	12,825	7,865
Illiterate	21,162	8,288	12,874
Literacy rate	56	69	43
Graduate	706	609	97

Agriculture: ***Distribution of villages according to land use:***

Out of 64 villages, Total area (in hectare) is 10514, out of that 76.12 percent is cultivable and 64.13 percent of the cultivable area is irrigated.

Sources of Irrigation (Hectares): Government Canal 2617.69, Private Canal 0, Well without Electricity 4.2, Well with Electricity 15.62, Tubewell without Electricity 9.31, Tubewell with Electricity 90.91, Tank 2113.65, River 267.8, Lake 0, Waterfall 0, Others 13.6.

Villages with population of 5000 to 9999: None

Villages with population of 10000 and above: None

Distribution of Workers:

	Persons	Males	Females	WPR
Cultivators	5,770	3,687	2,083	26.53
Agricultural Labour	11,480	5,384	6,096	52.79
Household Industry	810	393	417	3.72
Other Workers	3,688	2,771	917	16.96
Main Workers	17,272	10,885	6,387	79.42
Marginal Workers	4,476	1,350	3,126	20.58
Total Workers	21,748	12,235	9,513	

Religion: Major Religious Communities:

	Persons	Males	Females	Sex Ratio
Hindu (99.52%)	41,653	21,007	20,646	983
Muslim (0.06%)	24	11	13	1,182
Christian (0.41%)	170	93	77	828
Sikh (0%)	-	-	-	-
Buddhists (0%)	-	-	-	-
Jain (0%)	-	-	-	-

Agewise Data:

	Persons	Males	Females	Sex Ratio
All ages	41,852	21,113	20,739	982
0-14	13,036	6,887	6,149	893
15-44	20,264	10,128	10,136	1001
45-79	8,330	3,995	4,335	1085
80+	186	84	102	1214
Age not stated	36	19	17	895

Languages (Dominant):

Telugu, Oriya, Savara, Gondi, Urdu

Disabled Population:

	Persons	Males	Females	%
Total Disabled	1,052	562	490	
In Seeing	482	237	245	45.82
In Speech	89	50	39	8.46
In Hearing	78	43	35	7.41
In Movement	295	175	120	28.04
Mentally	108	57	51	10.27

BUTCHAYYAPETA

Butchayyapeta C.D. Block lies in the eastern part of Vishakhapatnam district. The Block is located at a distance of 70 kms. from district headquarters (Vishakh apatnam). There are 40 villages in the block with the total population of 61,751 persons. Area of the C.D. Block is 176.40 sq. kms. It is bounded in the north by Mandals Ravikamatham, Madugula and Chodavaram, in the south by Mandal Kasimkota, in the east by Mandals

Chodavaram and Anakapalle, and in the west by Mandal Ravikamatham.

Communications :

Roadways : State Highway (S.H.): Direction- Narsipatnam to Chodavaram. Nearest Villages- Lopudi, Lingabhupala Puram Agraharam, Vijayaramarajupeta, Vaddadi, L.Singava ram, Pottidorapalem, Komallapudi.

Backwards Region Grants Fund: It receives Backward Region Grants.

Annaul Rainfall: Average Rainfall 975.0 mm

Ground Water: Availability of the Ground Water in the Basin is (Information not avavible) H.A.M .and the utilization is (Information not avavible) H.A.M. It belongs to (Information not avavible) category. Depth to water level varies from 3 to 10 meter below the ground. Most of the wells go down in summer months.

Forest and Reserved **Forest:** Nearest Villages- Pangidi, Pedapudi.

Administration:

Division: Coastal Andhra. Parliamentary Constituency: 22 Anakapalle. District: Visakhapatnam. Mandal: Butchay yapeta. Assembly Constituency: 145 Chodavaram. Gram Panchay: 32.

Villages: 40 **Inhabited:** 38 **Uninhabited:** 2

Ranking	District	State	National
Area	15	687	4594
Population	13	254	4803
Sex Ratio	8	70	497
Child Sex Ratio	18	185	517
Literacy Rate	28	943	5459
Density	19	444	3101
Work Participation Rate	22	268	1103

Gram Panchayats:

Butchayyapeta, Chinappannapalem, Chintapaka Chittiyyapalem, Dibbidi, Gantikorlam, Gunnempudi K.P. Agrahram, Kandipudi, Karaka, Komallapudi Kondapalem, Kondempudi, L. B. P. Agraharam L. Singavaram, Lopudi, Mallam, Mangalapuram Neelakantapuram, P. Bheemavaram, Peda Madina Pedapudi, Pedapudi Agraharam, Polepalle Pottidorapalem, R. Bheemavaram, R.Sivaramapuram Rajam, Turakalapudi, Typuram, Vaddadi Vijayaramarajupeta.

Amenities:

Education: Primary School in 37 villages, Middle school in 8 villages, Matriculation or Secondary School in 5 villages, namely Vaddadi, Dibbidi, Gunnempudi, Chintapaka, Turakalapudi.

Higher Secondary or Pre University Courses or Intermediate or Junior College in 1 village of the CD Block,, namely Vaddadi.

College in 0 village, Adult Literacy Center in 0 village.

Medical: Hospital in 1 village, Dispensary in 0 village, Health Center in 12 villages, Sub Center in 10 villages, Maternity and Child Welfare Center in 0 village, Community health workers in 0 village.

The Village having Hospital or Dispensary or Health Center is Vaddadi.

Drinking Water: Tap water in 38 villages, Tank water in 37 villages, Well water in 37 villages, Tubewell in 37 villages and more than one source in 38 villages.

Bank: Banking facility in 5 villages, namely, Vijayaramarajupeta, Vaddadi, Butchayyapeta, Rajam Chintapaka.

Credit Society in 6 villages Agricultural Credit Society in 6 Non-Agricultural Credit Society in 0 village.

Others: Power supply in 38 villages, Cinema hall in 1 village, sport club in 0 village, Stadium or Auditorium or Community Hall in 0 village, Post Office in 15 villages.

There are 34 villages having bus facilities.

Villages with most of facilities: Vijayaramarajupeta Vaddadi, Butchayyapeta, Rajam, Chintapaka.

Villages without amenities (Education): Bhatlova..

Scheduled Castes: Out of the total population of 61751 persons, 5350 persons (8.66%) belong to Scheduled Castes.

The villages having less than 10% SC population are Lingabhupala Puram Agraharam, Mangalapuram Vijayaramarajupeta, Chinappannapalem, Polepalle Dibbidi, P. Bheemavaram, Pottidorapalem, Gantikorlam Komallapudi, Kondempudi, Kondapalem Agraharam Gunnempudi, Kondapalem, Aithampudi, Butchayyapeta Kandipudi, Neelakantapuram, Rajam, Typuram China Madina, Peda Madina, Chintapaka Pedapudi Agraharam, Pangidi, Pedapudi, Karaka R. Sivarampuram, R. Bheemavaram, Appampalem Mallam Bhupathipalem, Mallam.

The villages having more than 50% SC population are None.

Sex ratio of Scheduled Caste population is 494.

Scheduled Castes Literates and Illiterates by Sex:

	Persons	Males	Females
Literate	2,321	1,452	869
Illiterate	3,029	1,256	1,773
Literacy rate	49.9	61.2	38.2
Graduate	43	36	7

Scheduled Castes (Dominant):

Mala, Madiga, Relli, Generic Castes etc.

Beda Jangam etc.

For their cultural identity please see Appendix-I

Villages without Scheduled Castes: There are

5 villages without any scheduled caste population.

Scheduled Tribes: Out of the total population of 61751 persons, 175 persons (0.28%) belong to Scheduled Tribes. The villages having less than 10% ST population are Lopudi, Lingabhupala Puram Agraharam, Mangalapuram Vijayaramarajupeta, Vaddadi, Chinappannapalem Polepalle, Dibbidi, P. Bheemavaram, L.Singavaram Pottidorapalem, Gantikorlam, Komallapudi, Kondempudi Kondapalem Agraharam, Gunnempudi, Kondapalem Aithampudi, Butchayyapeta, Kandipudi Neelakantapuram, Rajam, Typuram, Chittiyyapalem China Madina, Peda Madina, Chintapaka Pedapudi Agraharam, Pangidi, Pedapudi, Karaka Turakalapudi, R. Sivarampuram, R. Bheemavaram Appampalem, Mallam Bhupathipalem, Mallam.

The villages having more than 50% ST population are None.

Sex ratio of Scheduled tribe population is 514.

Scheduled Tribes Literates and Illiterates by Sex:

	Persons	Males	Females
Literate	70	49	21
Illiterate	105	36	69
Literacy rate	47.0	68.1	27.3
Graduate	2	2	0

Scheduled Tribes (Dominant):

Yerukulas, Bagata, Yenadis, Konda Dhoras, Porja etc.

For their cultural identity please see Appendix-II

Villages without Scheduled Tribes: There are 28 villages without any scheduled tribe population.

Literates and Illiterates by Sex (Total Population):

	Persons	Males	Females
Literate	22,865	14,197	8,668
Illiterate	38,886	16,228	22,658
Literacy rate	43	54	32
Graduate	505	395	110

Agriculture: ***Distribution of villages according to land use:*** Out of 40 villages, Total area (in hectare) is 17639, out of that 54.4 percent is cultivable and 48.02 percent of the cultivable area is irrigated.

Sources of Irrigation (Hectares): Government Canal 0, Private Canal 0, Well without Electricity 681.66, Well with Electricity 0, Tubewell without Electricity 60.18, Tubewell with Electricity 0, Tank 3866.49, River 0, Lake 0, Waterfall 0, Others 0.

Villages with population of 5000 to 9999: Vaddadi.

Villages with population of 10000 and above: None

Distribution of Workers:

	Persons	Males	Females	WPR
Cultivators	10,032	6,486	3,546	30.1
Agricultural Labour	17,100	8,162	8,938	51.3
Household Industry	996	496	500	2.99
Other Workers	5,203	3,445	1,758	15.61
Main Workers	23,826	15,279	8,547	71.48
Marginal Workers	9,505	3,310	6,195	28.52
Total Workers	33,331	18,589	14,742	

Religion: Major Religious Communities:

	Persons	Males	Females	Sex Ratio
Hindu (99.08%)	61,182	30,160	31,022	1,029
Muslim (0.26%)	162	70	92	1,314
Christian (0.46%)	282	131	151	1,153
Sikh (0.07%)	42	23	19	826
Buddhists (0.03%)	16	7	9	1,286
Jain (0%)	2	1	1	1,000

Agewise Data:

	Persons	Males	Females	Sex Ratio
All ages	61,751	30,425	31,326	1030
0-14	19,751	10,077	9,674	960
15-44	29,405	14,615	14,790	1012
45-79	12,241	5,590	6,651	1190
80+	213	87	126	1448
Age not stated	141	56	85	1518

Languages (Dominant):

Telugu, Oriya, Urdu, Gondi, Hindi

Disabled Population:

	Persons	Males	Females	%
Total Disabled	1,420	770	650	
In Seeing	780	430	350	54.93
In Speech	142	70	72	10
In Hearing	46	19	27	3.24
In Movement	326	184	142	22.96
Mentally	126	67	59	8.87

BUTTAYAGUDEM

Buttayagudem C.D. Block lies in the northern part of West Godavari district. The Block is located at a dista nce of 80 kms. from district headquarters (Eluru). There are 53 villages in the block with the total population of 51,878 persons. Area of the C.D. Block is 193.40 sq. kms. It is bounded in the north by district Khammam, in the south by Mandals Jangareddigudem and Koyyalagud em, in the east by Mandals Gopalapuram and Polavaram, and in the west by Mandal Jeelugumilli.

Communications :

Roadways : NH, SH or Important Metalled Road is not available.

Backwards Region Grants Fund: It receives Backward Region Grants.

Integrated Child Development Scheme (ICDS) Project: Buttaygudem (Tribal), Total Anganwadi Centres: 137

Annaul Rainfall: Average Rainfall 1005 mm

Ground Water: Availability of the Ground Water in the

Basin is (Information not avavible) H.A.M .and the utilization is (Information not avavible) H.A.M. It belongs to (Information not avavible) category. Depth to water level varies from 3 to 10 meter below the ground. Most of the wells go down in summer months.

Forest and Reserved **Forest:** Nearest Villages- Munjuluru, Gummuluru, Veeranna Palem, Upparilli, Dandipudi, Manga iah Palem, Chintalagudem, Puliramudugudem, Kannarappadu, Kopalle, Ravvarigudem, Itikalakunta, Palakunta, Ragapp agudem, Khandrikagudem, Cheemalavarigudem, Ammapalem, Merakagudem, Kurasakannappagudem, Kotaramachandrapuram Gunjavaram, Yerrayagudem, Pandugudem, Kamayyakunta.

Natural Division : Godavari Delta Region

Administration:

Division: Coastal Andhra. Parliamentary Constituency: 27 Eluru.District: West Godavari.

Mandal: Buttayagudem. Assembly Constituency: 186 Polava ram (ST). Gram Panchayat: 21.

Villages: 53 **Inhabited:** 50 **Uninhabited:** 3

Ranking	District	State	National
Area	15	599	4304
Population	42	453	5187
Sex Ratio	1	46	381
Child Sex Ratio	16	309	1060
Literacy Rate	46	238	2527
Density	2	462	3881
Work Participation Rate	42	476	1167

Gram Panchayats:

Achiyapalem, Aliveru, Anthervedigudem, Buttaigudem Doramamidi, Jainavarigudem, K.Nagavaram Kamayyakunta, Korsavarigudem, Kotaramachandrapuram Koyarajahmundry, Laxmudugudem, Mangaipalem Munjuluru, Nimmalagudem, Noothiramannapalem Puliramannagudem, R.Ganapavaram, Rajanagaram Ravvarigudem, Seethappagudem.

Amenities:

Education: Primary School in 50 villages, Middle school in 12 villages, Matriculation or Secondary School in 7 villages, namely Doramamidi, Puliramudugudem, Buttayagudem, Ganapavaram, Busarajupalle, Kotaramachandrapuram, Rajanagaram.

Higher Secondary or Pre University Courses or Intermediate or Junior College in 2 villages of the CD Block,, namely Buttayagudem, Kotaramachandrapuram.

College in 0 village, Adult Literacy Center in 16 villages.

Medical: Hospital in 1 village, Dispensary in 1 village, Health Center in 3 villages, Sub Center in 21 villages, Maternity and Child Welfare Center in 0 village, Community health workers in 0 village.

The Villages having Hospital or Dispensary or Health Center are Doramamidi, Rajanagaram.

Drinking Water: Tap water in 50 villages, Tank water in 50 villages, Well water in 50 villages, Tubewell in 50 villages and more than one source in 50 villages.

Bank: Banking facility in 5 villages, namely, Doramamidi, Puliramudugudem, Kopalle, Buttayagudem Ganapavaram.

Credit Society in 5 villages Agricultural Credit Society in 4 Non-Agricultural Credit Society in 1 village.

Others: Power supply in 50 villages, Cinema hall in 1 village, sport club in 0 village, Stadium or Auditorium or Community Hall in 0 village, Post Office in 22 villages.

There are 28 villages having bus facilities.

Villages with most of facilities: Doramamidi Puliramudugudem, Buttayagudem, Ganapavaram.

Villages without Amenities (Education): None..

Scheduled Castes: Out of the total population of 51878 persons, 4450 persons (8.58%) belong to Scheduled Castes. The villages having less than 10% SC population are Korsavarigudem, Aliveru, Antarvedigudem, Doramamidi Munjuluru, Urrinka, Gogumilli, Gummuluru Veeranna Palem, Upparilli, Dandipudi, Nagampalem Mangaiah Palem, Chintalagudem, Puliramudugudem Kannarappadu, Kopalle, Ravvarigudem, Itikalakunta Palakunta, Nimmalagudem, Ramannagudem Jaggisetti Gudem, Jainavarigudem, Koyarajahmundry Ramannapalem, Bothappagudem, Ragappagudem Khandrikagudem, Cheemalavarigudem, Ammapalem Merakagudem, Gunjavaram, Kurasakannappagudem Yerrayagudem, Pandugudem, Bandarlagudem Kamayyakunta, Lanka Palle, Lakshmipuram, Kovvada Rajanagaram, Muddappagudem.

The villages having more than 50% SC population are None.

Sex ratio of Scheduled Caste population is 507.

Scheduled Castes Literates and Illiterates by Sex:

	Persons	Males	Females
Literate	2,543	1,306	1,237
Illiterate	1,907	890	1,017
Literacy rate	66.0	69.3	62.9
Graduate	105	83	22

Scheduled Castes (Dominant):

Mala, Madiga, Arundhatiya, Adi Andhra Beda Jangam etc.

For their cultural identity please see Appendix-I

Villages without Scheduled Castes: There are 24 villages without any scheduled caste population.

Scheduled Tribes: Out of the total population of 51878 persons, 32768 persons (63.16%) belong to Scheduled Tribes. The villages having less than 10% ST population are

None..

The villages having more than 50% ST population are Korsavarigudem, Aliveru, Antarvedigudem, Doramamidi Munjuluru, Urrinka, Gogumilli, Gummuluru Veeranna Palem, Upparilli, Dandipudi, Nagampalem Mangaiah Palem, Chintalagudem, Puliramudugudem Kannarappadu, Kopalle, Ravvarigudem, Itikalakunta Palakunta, Jaggisetti Gudem, Jainavarigudem Marlagudem, Koyarajahmundry, Ramannapalem Bothappagudem, Ragappagudem, Khandrikagudem Cheemalavarigudem, Ammapalem, Merakagudem Gunjavaram, Kurasakannappagudem, Yerrayagudem Pandugudem, Bandarlagudem, Kamayyakunta, Lanka Palle Lakshmipuram, Kovvada, Rajanagaram, Muddappagudem.

Sex ratio of Scheduled tribe population is 515.

Scheduled Tribes Literates and Illiterates by Sex:

	Persons	Males	Females
Literate	15,581	8,116	7,465
Illiterate	17,187	7,772	9,415
Literacy rate	55.4	59.8	51.3
Graduate	116	93	23

Scheduled Tribes (Dominant):

Koya etc., Kondareddis, Sugalis etc., Nayaks Yerukulas

For their cultural identity please see Appendix-II

Villages without Scheduled Tribes: There are 3 villages without any scheduled tribe population.

Literates and Illiterates by Sex (Total Population):

	Persons	Males	Females
Literate	27,614	14,488	13,126
Illiterate	24,264	10,950	13,314
Literacy rate	61	66	57
Graduate	581	460	121

Agriculture: ***Distribution of villages according to land use:*** Out of 53 villages, Total area (in hectare) is 19341, out of that 62.31 percent is cultivable and 57.21 percent of the cultivable area is irrigated.

Sources of Irrigation (Hectares): Government Canal 12.14, Private Canal 0, Well without Electricity 0, Well with Electricity 0, Tubewell without Electricity 2511.77, Tubewell with Electricity 2017.23, Tank 2224.51, River 0, Lake 0, Waterfall 0, Others 128.73.

Villages with population of 5000 to 9999:

Doramamidi.

Villages with population of 10000 and above:

Buttayagudem.

Distribution of Workers:

	Persons	Males	Females	WPR
Cultivators	7,122	4,787	2,335	25.56
Agricultural Labour	17,153	7,969	9,184	61.56
Household Industry	467	296	171	1.68
Other Workers	3,121	2,258	863	11.2
Main Workers	22,942	13,360	9,582	82.34
Marginal Workers	4,921	1,950	2,971	17.66
Total Workers	27,863	15,310	12,553	

Religion: Major Religious Communities:

	Persons	Males	Females	Sex Ratio
Hindu (95.5%)	49,546	24,334	25,212	1,036
Muslim (2.26%)	1,170	586	584	997
Christian (2.12%)	1,098	488	610	1,250
Sikh (0%)	1	-	1	-
Buddhists (0%)	-	-	-	-
Jain (0%)	1	-	1	-

Agewise Data:

	Persons	Males	Females	Sex Ratio
All ages	51,878	25,438	26,440	1039
0-14	18,267	9,063	9,204	1016
15-44	24,512	11,874	12,638	1064
45-79	8,824	4,368	4,456	1020
80+	214	104	110	1058
Age not stated	61	29	32	1103

Languages (Dominant):

Koya, Telugu, Hindi, Urdu, Oriya

Disabled Population:

	Persons	Males	Females	%
Total Disabled	746	413	333	
In Seeing	157	91	66	21.05
In Speech	110	61	49	14.75
In Hearing	65	26	39	8.71
In Movement	295	168	127	39.54
Mentally	119	67	52	15.95

C.BELAGAL

C. Belagal C.D. Block lies in the northern part of Kurnool district. The Block is located at a distance of 42 kms. from district headquarters (Kurnool). There are 10 villages in the block with the total population of 48,139 persons. Area of the C.D. Block is 212.15 sq. kms. It is bounded in the north by River Tungabhadra and district Mahbubnagar, in the south by Mandals Yemmiganur, Gonegandla, Kodumur and Gudur, in the east by Mandals Kurnool and Gudur, and in the west by Mandal Nandavaram.

Communications:

Roadways : Metalled Roads: Nearest Villages- Gundrevula, Polakal, C.Belagal, Kambadahal.

River: Tungabhadra Nadi- Nearest Villages- Malasomapuram, Palukudoddi, Gundrevula, Kondapuram, Kothakota.

It is identified as a drought-prone area.

Annual Rainfall: Average Rainfall 629 mm

Ground Water: Availability of the Ground Water in the

Basin is 1785 H.A.M. and the utilization is 573 H.A. M. It belongs to Safe category. Depth to water level varies from 5 to 10 meter below the ground. Most of the wells go down in summer months. The well density in the entire block is 8 wells per sq. km. Total no. of the wells in the block are enumerated as 1732, according to the Ground Water Estimation Committee.

Natural Division : Rayalaseema Region

Administration:

Division: Rayala Seema. Parliamentary Constituency: 35 Kurnool. District: Kurnool. Mandal: C. Belagal. Assembly Constituency: 262 Kodumur (SC). Gram Panchayat: 12

Villages: 10 **Inhabited:** 9 **Uninhabited:** 1

Ranking	District	State	National
Area	39	478	3977
Population	28	576	5381
Sex Ratio	51	1064	4278
Child Sex Ratio	47	971	4395
Literacy Rate	50	1074	6077
Density	4	11	4351
Work Participation Rate	18	616	98

Gram Panchayats:

Brahmanadoddi, Burandoddi, C.Belagal, Gundrevula Kambadahal, Kondapuram, Kothakota, Mudumala Palukudoddi, Polakal, Sangala, Yanagandla.

Amenities:

Education: Primary School in 9 villages, Middle school in 8 villages, Matriculation or Secondary School in 3 villages, namely Kothakota, Polakal, C.Belagal.

Higher Secondary or Pre University Courses or Intermediate or Junior College in 1 village of the CD Block,, namely C.Belagal.

College in 0 village, Adult Literacy Center in 9 villages.

Medical: Hospital in 0 village, Dispensary in 1 village, Health Center in 2 villages, Sub Center in 7 villages, Maternity and Child Welfare Center in 0 village, Community health workers in 0 village.

The Village having Hospital or Dispensary or Health Center is Polakal.

Drinking Water: Tap water in 9 villages, Tank water in 9 villages, Well water in 9 villages, Tubewell in 9 villages and more than one source in 9 villages.

Bank: Banking facility in 3 villages, namely, Kothakota, Polakal, C.Belagal.

Credit Society in 8 villages Agricultural Credit Society in 3 Non-Agricultural Credit Society in 8 villages.

Others: Power supply in 9 villages, Cinema hall in 0 village, sport club in 0 village, Stadium or Auditorium or Community Hall in 0 village, Post Office in 9 villages.

There are 8 villages having bus facilities.

Villages with most of facilities: Kothakota Polakal, C.Belagal.

Villages without Amenities (Education): None..

Scheduled Castes: Out of the total population of 48139 persons, 12011 persons (24.95%) belong to Scheduled Castes.

The villages having less than 10% SC population are None..

The villages having more than 50% SC population are None.

Sex ratio of Scheduled Caste population is 464.

Scheduled Castes Literates and Illiterates by Sex:

	Persons	Males	Females
Literate	3,129	2,453	676
Illiterate	8,882	3,984	4,898
Literacy rate	32.0	46.5	15.0
Graduate	43	35	8

Scheduled Castes (Dominant):

Madiga, Mala, Mala Dasari

For their cultural identity please see Appendix-I

Villages without Scheduled Castes: There is 1 village without any scheduled caste population.

Scheduled Tribes: Out of the total population of 48139 persons, 202 persons (0.42%) belong to Scheduled Tribes.

The villages having less than 10% ST population are Palukudoddi, Gundrevula, Kondapuram, Kothakota Polakal, C.Belagal, Kambadahal, Burandoddi Brahmanadoddi.

The villages having more than 50% ST population are None.

Sex ratio of Scheduled tribe population is 436.

Scheduled Tribes Literates and Illiterates by Sex:

	Persons	Males	Females
Literate	61	50	11
Illiterate	141	64	77
Literacy rate	37.9	55.0	15.7
Graduate	2	1	1

Scheduled Tribes (Dominant):

Yerukulas, Sugalis etc.

For their cultural identity please see Appendix-II

Villages without Scheduled Tribes: There are 3 villages without any scheduled tribe population.

Literates and Illiterates by Sex (Total Population):

	Persons	Males	Females
Literate	13,335	9,604	3,731
Illiterate	34,804	15,289	19,515
Literacy rate	34	47	20
Graduate	306	256	50

Agriculture: ***Distribution of villages according to land use:*** Out of 10 villages, Total area (in hectare) is 21215, out of

that 71.92 percent is cultivable and 29.18 percent of the cultivable area is irrigated.

Sources of Irrigation (Hectares): Government Canal 1656, Private Canal 0, Well without Electricity 66, Well with Electricity 1154, Tubewell without Electricity 0, Tubewell with Electricity 0, Tank 413, River 1164, Lake 0, Waterfall 0, Others 0.

Villages with population of 5000 to 9999: Kondapuram, Kothakota, C.Belagal.

Villages with population of 10000 and above: Polakal.

Distribution of Workers:

	Persons	Males	Females	WPR
Cultivators	6,638	4,038	2,600	23.45
Agricultural Labour	19,400	8,879	10,521	68.54
Household Industry	449	231	218	1.59
Other Workers	1,818	1,285	533	6.42
Main Workers	25,708	13,289	12,419	90.82
Marginal Workers	2,597	1,144	1,453	9.18
Total Workers	28,305	14,433	13,872	

Religion: Major Religious Communities:

	Persons	Males	Females	Sex Ratio
Hindu (93.75%)	45,129	23,383	21,746	930
Muslim (5.1%)	2,455	1,230	1,225	996
Christian (0.95%)	456	226	230	1,018
Sikh (0%)	-	-	-	-
Buddhists (0%)	-	-	-	-
Jain (0%)	-	-	-	-

Agewise Data:

	Persons	Males	Females	Sex Ratio
All ages	48,139	24,893	23,246	934
0-14	19,578	10,428	9,150	877
15-44	21,001	10,845	10,156	936
45-79	7,250	3,485	3,765	1080
80+	233	95	138	1453
Age not stated	77	40	37	925

Languages (Dominant): Telugu, Urdu, Kannada, Hindi, Marathi

Disabled Population:

	Persons	Males	Females	%
Total Disabled	1,085	545	540	
In Seeing	537	222	315	49.49
In Speech	66	38	28	6.08
In Hearing	60	31	29	5.53
In Movement	347	212	135	31.98
Mentally	75	42	33	6.91

CHAGALAMARRI

Chagalamarri C.D. Block lies in the south-eastern part of Kurnool district. The Block is located at a distance of 102 kms. from district headquarters (Kurnool). There are 19 villages in the block with the total population of 47,076 persons. Area of the C.D. Block is 206.37 sq. kms. It is bounded in the north by Mandal Allagadda, and in the rest of directions by district Cuddapah.

Communications:

Roadways : NH- 18: Allagadda to Cuddapah. Nearest Villages- Chagalamarri, Pedda Bodhanam, Madduru, Chinna Bodhanam

River: Vakkileru Nadi- Nearest Villages- Rampalle, Pedda Bodhanam, Madduru, Brahmanapalle, Kalugotlapalle, Nallavemula. Havanasi Nadi- Nearest Villages- Muthyalapadu, Dantalavanipenta, Godiganuru, Madduru, Chagalamarri, Settiveedu.

It is identified as a drought prone area as well.

Annual Rainfall: Average Rainfall 798 mm

Ground Water: Availability of the Ground Water in the Basin is 2301 H.A.M. and the utilization is 2075 H.A.M. It belongs to Cri category. Depth to water level varies from 5 meter to more than 10 meter below the ground. Most of the wells go down in summer months. The well density in the entire block is 9 wells per sq. km. Total no. of the wells in the block are enumerated as 1925, according to the Ground Water Estimation Committee.

Forest and Reserved **Forest:** (Allagada R.F.)- Nearest Villages- Muthyalapadu, Dantalavanipenta, Godiganuru, Settiveedu, Chintala Cheruvu, Pedda Vangali, Chinna Vangali.

Natural Division : Rayalaseema Region

Administration:

Division: Rayala Seema. Parliamentary Constituency: 34 Nandyal. District: Kurnool. Mandal: Chagalamarri. Assembly Constituency: 253 Allagadda. Gram Panchayat: 18

Villages: 19 **Inhabited:** 19 **Uninhabited:** 0

Ranking	District	State	National
Area	40	515	4070
Population	30	600	5418
Sex Ratio	28	841	2822
Child Sex Ratio	41	846	3713
Literacy Rate	24	568	4099
Density	36	399	4344
Work Participation Rate	16	613	976

Gram Panchayats:

Brahmanapalle, Chagalamarri, Chinna Bodhanam Chinna Vangali, Chintala Cheruvu, D. Vanipenta Godiganuru, Gotlur, Kalugotlapalle, Madduru Mallavemula, Muthyalapadu, Nelampadu, Pedda Bodhanam Pedda Vangali, Rampalle, Settiveedu, Thodendlapalle.

Amenities:

Education: Primary School in 19 villages, Middle school in

7 villages, Matriculation or Secondary School in 4 villages, namely Muthyalapadu, Chagalamarri, Chintala Cheruvu, Chinna Vangali.

Higher Secondary or Pre University Courses or Intermediate or Junior College in 1 village of the CD Block,, namely Chagalamarri.

College in 1 village, Adult Literacy Center in 18 villages., College is in village, namely Chagalamarri.

Medical: Hospital in 0 village, Dispensary in 1 village, Health Center in 1 village, Sub Center in 8 villages, Maternity and Child Welfare Center in 0 village, Community health workers in 0 village.

The Villages having Hospital or Dispensary or Health Center are Muthyalapadu, Chagalamarri.

Drinking Water: Tap water in 19 villages, Tank water in 19 villages, Well water in 19 villages, Tubewell in 19 villages and more than one source in 19 villages.

Bank: Banking facility in 2 villages, namely, Pedda Bodhanam, Chagalamarri.

Credit Society in 7 villages Agricultural Credit Society in 2 Non-Agricultural Credit Society in 6 villages.

Others: Power supply in 19 villages, Cinema hall in 1 village, sport club in 0 village, Stadium or Auditorium or Community Hall in 0 village, Post Office in 12 villages.

There are 15 villages having bus facilities.

Villages with most of facilities: Pedda Bodhanam Chagalamarri.

Villages without Amenities (Education): None..

Scheduled Castes: Out of the total population of 47076 persons, 8389 persons (17.82%) belong to Scheduled Castes.

The villages having less than 10% SC population are None..

The villages having more than 50% SC population are None.

Sex ratio of Scheduled Caste population is 479.

Scheduled Castes Literates and Illiterates by Sex:

	Persons	Males	Females
Literate	3,020	2,094	926
Illiterate	5,369	2,280	3,089
Literacy rate	42.5	56.4	27.2
Graduate	119	96	23

Scheduled Castes (Dominant):

Mala, Madiga, Paky etc., Chamar etc.

Generic Castes etc.

For their cultural identity please see Appendix-I

Villages without Scheduled Castes: There is 1 village without any scheduled caste population.

Scheduled Tribes: Out of the total population of 47076 persons, 1974 persons (4.19%) belong to Scheduled Tribes.

The villages having less than 10% ST population are Chinna Bodhanam, Rampalle, Pedda Bodhanam Thodendlapalle, Muthyalapadu, Godiganuru, Madduru Nelampadu, Brahmanapalle, Kalugotlapalle, Gotlur Rajole, Nallavemula, Chagalamarri, Chintala Cheruvu Pedda Vangali, Chinna Vangali.

The villages having more than 50% ST population are None.

Sex ratio of Scheduled tribe population is 488.

Scheduled Tribes Literates and Illiterates by Sex:

	Persons	Males	Females
Literate	474	336	138
Illiterate	1,500	674	826
Literacy rate	31.0	42.9	18.6
Graduate	6	4	2

Scheduled Tribes (Dominant):

Sugalis etc., Yerukulas, Chenchu etc., Yenadis

For their cultural identity please see Appendix-II

Villages without Scheduled Tribes: There are 8 villages without any scheduled tribe population.

Literates and Illiterates by Sex (Total Population):

	Persons	Males	Females
Literate	21,067	13,630	7,437
Illiterate	26,009	10,355	15,654
Literacy rate	53	67	38
Graduate	1,225	1,015	210

Agriculture: ***Distribution of villages according to land use:*** Out of 19 villages, Total area (in hectare) is 20638, out of that 63.21 percent is cultivable and 38.09 percent of the cultivable area is irrigated.

Sources of Irrigation (Hectares): Government Canal 0, Private Canal 0, Well without Electricity 0, Well with Electricity 0, Tubewell without Electricity 0, Tubewell with Electricity 4739.19, Tank 87.04, River 0, Lake 0, Waterfall 0, Others 143.4.

Villages with population of 5000 to 9999: None

Villages with population of 10000 and above: Chagalamarri.

Distribution of Workers:

	Persons	Males	Females	WPR
Cultivators	5,461	3,686	1,775	21.68
Agricultural Labour	13,631	6,103	7,528	54.12
Household Industry	1,350	457	893	5.36
Other Workers	4,744	3,963	781	18.84
Main Workers	22,946	13,520	9,426	91.11
Marginal Workers	2,240	689	1,551	8.89
Total Workers	25,186	14,209	10,977	

Religion: Major Religious Communities:

	Persons	Males	Females	Sex Ratio
Hindu (68.83%)	32,401	16,535	15,866	960
Muslim (28.87%)	13,592	6,921	6,671	964

Christian (2.19%)	1,033	505	528	1,046
Sikh (0%)	-	-	-	-
Buddhists (0%)	-	-	-	-
Jain (0%)	-	-	-	-

Agewise Data:

	Persons	Males	Females	Sex Ratio
All ages	47,076	23,985	23,091	963
0-14	16,309	8,461	7,848	928
15-44	21,977	11,341	10,636	938
45-79	8,497	4,070	4,427	1088
80+	255	92	163	1772
Age not stated	38	21	17	810

Languages (Dominant):
Telugu, Urdu, Hindi, Gondi, Kannada

Disabled Population:

	Persons	Males	Females	%
Total Disabled	808	429	379	
In Seeing	348	169	179	43.07
In Speech	83	43	40	10.27
In Hearing	48	26	22	5.94
In Movement	251	160	91	31.06
Mentally	78	31	47	9.65

CHAGALLU

Chagallu C.D. Block lies in the eastern part of West Godavari district. The Block is located at a distance of 86 kms. from district headquarters (Eluru). There are 11 villages in the block with the total population of 64,371 persons. Area of the C.D. Block is 108.82 sq. kms. It is bounded in the north by Mandal Kovvur, in the south by Mandal Nidadavole, in the east by Mandal Kovvur, and in the west by Mandal Devarapalle.

Communications :

Roadways : Metalled Roads: Nearest Villages- Chagallu, Markondapadu, Unagatla, Singanamuppavaram, Brahmanagudem.

Railway Station: Chagallu, Nelaturu, Mallavaram, Markondapadu, Brahmanagudem, Daravaram.

Backwards Region Grants Fund: It receives Backward Region Grants.

Annaul Rainfall: Average Rainfall 1260 mm

Ground Water: Availability of the Ground Water in the Basin is (Information not avavible) H.A.M .and the utilization is (Information not avavible) H.A.M. It belongs to (Information not avavible) category. Depth to water level varies from 3 to 10 meter below the ground. Most of the wells go down in summer months.

Natural Division : Godavari Delta Region

Administration:

Division: Coastal Andhra. Parliamentary Constituency: 25 Rajahmundry. District: West Godavari. Mandal: Chagallu. Assembly Constituency: 173 Kovvur (SC). Gram Panchayat: 13.

Villages: 11 **Inhabited:** 11 **Uninhabited:** 0

Ranking	District	State	National
Area	30	992	5616
Population	31	214	4710
Sex Ratio	35	645	2213
Child Sex Ratio	22	391	1465
Literacy Rate	29	102	1511
Density	35	976	1861
Work Participation Rate	18	71	3623

Gram Panchayats:
Brahmanagudem, Chagallu, Chandravaram, Chikkala Dharavaram, Gowripalli, Kalavalapalli, Mallavaram Markundapadu, Nandigampadu, Nelaturu, S.Muppavaram Unagatla.

Amenities:

Education: Primary School in 11 villages, Middle school in 8 villages, Matriculation or Secondary School in 6 villages, namely Chagallu, Nelaturu, Mallavaram, Markondapadu, Unagatla, Brahmanagudem.

Higher Secondary or Pre University Courses or Intermediate or Junior College in 1 village of the CD Block,, namely Chagallu.

College in 0 village, Adult Literacy Center in 11 villages.

Medical: Hospital in 0 village, Dispensary in 1 village, Health Center in 1 village, Sub Center in 8 villages, Maternity and Child Welfare Center in 0 village, Community health workers in 0 village.

The Village having Hospital or Dispensary or Health Center is Markondapadu.

Drinking Water: Tap water in 11 villages, Tank water in 11 villages, Well water in 11 villages, Tubewell in 11 villages and more than one source in 11 villages.

Bank: Banking facility in 2 villages, namely, Chagallu, Mallavaram.

Credit Society in 6 villages Agricultural Credit Society in 4 Non-Agricultural Credit Society in 2 villages.

Others: Power supply in 11 villages, Cinema hall in 1 village, sport club in 1 village, Stadium or Auditorium or Community Hall in 1 village, Post Office in 8 villages.

There are 11 villages having bus facilities.

Villages with most of facilities: Chagallu Mallavaram.

Villages without Amenities (Education): None..

Scheduled Castes: Out of the total population of 64371 persons, 15444 persons (23.99%) belong to Scheduled Castes.

The villages having less than 10% SC population are None..

The villages having more than 50% SC population are None.

Sex ratio of Scheduled Caste population is 491.

Scheduled Castes Literates and Illiterates by Sex:

	Persons	Males	Females
Literate	8,648	4,707	3,941
Illiterate	6,796	3,147	3,649
Literacy rate	64.3	69.1	59.4
Graduate	234	171	63

Scheduled Castes (Dominant):

Mala, Madiga, Mala Dasari, Relli, Adi Andhra

For their cultural identity please see Appendix-I

Villages without Scheduled Castes: There are 0 village without any scheduled caste population.

Scheduled Tribes: Out of the total population of 64371 persons, 361 persons (0.56%) belong to Scheduled Tribes. The villages having less than 10% ST population are Chikkala, Chagallu, Nelaturu, Mallavaram Markondapadu, Nandigampadu, Unagatla, Kalavalapalle Singanamuppavaram, Brahmanagudem, Daravaram. The villages having more than 50% ST population are None.

Sex ratio of Scheduled tribe population is 504.

Scheduled Tribes Literates and Illiterates by Sex:

	Persons	Males	Females
Literate	119	64	55
Illiterate	242	115	127
Literacy rate	41.0	43.2	38.7
Graduate	2	2	0

Scheduled Tribes (Dominant):

Yerukulas, Chenchu etc., Sugalis etc., Koya etc. Kondareddis

For their cultural identity please see Appendix-II

Villages without Scheduled Tribes: There are 3 villages without any scheduled tribe population.

Literates and Illiterates by Sex (Total Population):

	Persons	Males	Females
Literate	38,198	20,615	17,583
Illiterate	26,173	11,958	14,215
Literacy rate	68	72	63
Graduate	1,387	1,043	344

Agriculture: ***Distribution of villages according to land use:*** Out of 11 villages, Total area (in hectare) is 10882, out of that 84.44 percent is cultivable and 64.74 percent of the cultivable area is irrigated.

Sources of Irrigation (Hectares): Government Canal 421.27, Private Canal 0, Well without Electricity 0, Well with Electricity 0, Tubewell without Electricity 0, Tubewell with Electricity 5527.68, Tank 0, River 0, Lake 0, Waterfall 0, Others 0.

Villages with population of 5000 to 9999:

Chikkala, Mallavaram, Unagatla, Kalavalapalle Brahmanagudem.

Villages with population of 10000 and above:

Chagallu.

Distribution of Workers:

	Persons	Males	Females	WPR
Cultivators	3,581	3,404	177	12.5
Agricultural Labour	17,803	10,841	6,962	62.13
Household Industry	419	262	157	1.46
Other Workers	6,853	5,426	1,427	23.91
Main Workers	25,704	18,642	7,062	89.7
Marginal Workers	2,952	1,291	1,661	10.3
Total Workers	28,656	19,933	8,723	

Religion: Major Religious Communities:

	Persons	Males	Females	Sex Ratio
Hindu (95.48%)	61,461	31,092	30,369	977
Muslim (2.87%)	1,850	956	894	935
Christian (1.63%)	1,052	520	532	1,023
Sikh (0%)	1	1	-	-
Buddhists (0%)	-	-	-	-
Jain (0%)	-	-	-	-

Agewise Data:

	Persons	Males	Females	Sex Ratio
All ages	64,371	32,573	31,798	976
0-14	19,590	9,964	9,626	966
15-44	31,878	16,255	15,623	961
45-79	12,433	6,128	6,305	1029
80+	404	190	214	1126
Age not stated	66	36	30	833

Languages (Dominant):

Telugu, Urdu, Hindi, Gondi, Tamil

Disabled Population:

	Persons	Males	Females	%
Total Disabled	1,123	598	525	
In Seeing	339	160	179	30.19
In Speech	178	93	85	15.85
In Hearing	81	31	50	7.21
In Movement	388	248	140	34.55
Mentally	137	66	71	12.2

CHAKRAYAPET

Chakrayapet C.D. Block lies in the south-western part of Cuddapah district. The Block is located at a distance of 47 kms. from district headquarters (Cuddapah). There are 17 villages in the block with the total popul ation of 30,682 persons. Area of the C.D. Block is 264. 94 sq. kms. It is bounded in the north by Mandals Vempa lle, Pendlimarri and Chintakommadinne, in the south by Mandal Galiveedu and district Anantapur, in the east by Mandals Galiveedu, Lakkireddipalle and Ramapuram, and in the west by district Anantapur and Mandal Vempalle.

Communications:

Roadways : Metalled Roads: Nearest Villages- Anjaneyapur am, Marellamadaka, Gandikovvur, Chakrayapet, Chilekampal le, Nersupalle, Surabhi.

River: Papaghni Nadi- Nearest Villages- Kumarakalva, Addalamarri, Anjaneyapuram, Marellamadaka, Gandikovvur, Errabommanapalle, Rajupalle, Kuppam, Chakrayapet.

It receives Backward Region Grants, and is also identif ied as a drought-prone area as well.

Annual Rainfall: Average Rainfall 627 mm

Ground Water: Availability of the Ground Water in the Basin is 2111 H.A.M.and the utilization is 1479 H.A. M.It belongs to SC category. Depth to water level varies from 5 to 20 meter below the ground. Most of the wells go down in summer months, according to the Ground Water Estimation Committee.

Forest and Reserved **Forest:** (Forest)- Nearest Villages- Kumarakalva, Kateneniyerragudi, Surabhi, Mahadevapalle, Gotlamitta. (Konamalopalle)- Nearest Villages- Marella madaka, Gandikovvur, Chakrayapet, Chilekampalle.

Natural Division : Rayalaseema Region

Administration:

Division: Rayala Seema. Parliamentary Constituency: 38 Kadapa. District: Cuddapah.

Mandal: Chakrayapet. Assembly Constituency:248 Pulivend la. Gram Panchayat: 16.

Villages: 17 **Inhabited:** 16 **Uninhabited:** 1

Ranking	District	State	National
Area	19	261	3184
Population	39	1015	6042
Sex Ratio	48	1056	4141
Child Sex Ratio	24	683	2824
Literacy Rate	50	649	4380
Density	4	111	6002
Work Participation Rate	38	1016	347

Gram Panchayats:

Addalamarri, Chakrayapet, Chilekampalli
Gaddamvaripalli, Gandikovvur, Gangarapuvandlapalli
K.Rajupalli, K.Yerragudi, Kallurupalli
Kumara Kaluva, Kuppam, Mahadevapalli, Marellamadaka
Nersupalli, Surabhi, Yrra Bommana Palli.

Amenities:

Education: Primary School in 16 villages, Middle school in 6 villages, Matriculation or Secondary School in 2 villages, namely Chakrayapet, Surabhi.

Higher Secondary or Pre University Courses or Intermediate or Junior College in 1 village of the CD Block,, namely Chakrayapet.

College in 1 village, Adult Literacy Center in 0 village., College is in village, namely Chakrayapet.

Medical: Hospital in 0 village, Dispensary in 0 village, Health Center in 2 villages, Sub Center in 3 villages, Maternity and Child Welfare Center in 0 village, Community health workers in 0 village.

The Village having Hospital or Dispensary or Health Center is Chakrayapet.

Drinking Water: Tap water in 16 villages, Tank water in 16 villages, Well water in 16 villages, Tubewell in 16 villages and more than one source in 16 villages.

Bank: Banking facility in 2 villages, namely, Chakrayapet, Surabhi.

Credit Society in 2 villages Agricultural Credit Society in 2 Non-Agricultural Credit Society in 0 village.

Others: Power supply in 16 villages, Cinema hall in 1 village, sport club in 0 village, Stadium or Auditorium or Community Hall in 0 village, Post Office in 12 villages.

There are 11 villages having bus facilities.

Villages with most of facilities: Chakrayapet Surabhi.

Villages without Amenities (Education): None..

Scheduled Castes: Out of the total population of 30682 persons, 3840 persons (12.52%) belong to Scheduled Castes.

The villages having less than 10% SC population are Addalamarri, Kateneniyerragudi, Kallurupalle, Kuppam Kondappagaripalle, Gotlamitta.

The villages having more than 50% SC population are None.

Sex ratio of Scheduled Caste population is 491.

Scheduled Castes Literates and Illiterates by Sex:

	Persons	Males	Females
Literate	1,307	922	385
Illiterate	2,533	1,032	1,501
Literacy rate	39.4	54.2	23.8
Graduate	33	27	6

Scheduled Castes (Dominant):

Mala, Madiga, Jambuvulu

For their cultural identity please see Appendix-I

Villages without Scheduled Castes: There are 3 villages without any scheduled caste population.

Scheduled Tribes: Out of the total population of 30682 persons, 1405 persons (4.58%) belong to Scheduled Tribes.

The villages having less than 10% ST population are Kumarakalva, Addalamarri, Marellamadaka, Gandikovvur Errabommanapalle, Rajupalle, Kuppam, Chakrayapet Chilekampalle, Nersupalle, Kondappagaripalle Surabhi, Mahadevapalle, Gotlamitta.

The villages having more than 50% ST population are None.

Sex ratio of Scheduled tribe population is 436.

Scheduled Tribes Literates and Illiterates by Sex:

	Persons	Males	Females

Literate	489	399	90
Illiterate	916	394	522
Literacy rate	39.7	57.0	16.9
Graduate	8	8	0

Scheduled Tribes (Dominant):
Sugalis etc., Yerukulas, Yenadis
For their cultural identity please see Appendix-II
Villages without Scheduled Tribes: There are 6 villages without any scheduled tribe population.
Literates and Illiterates by Sex (Total Population):

	Persons	Males	Females
Literate	13,568	9,096	4,472
Illiterate	17,114	6,740	10,374
Literacy rate	51	66	35
Graduate	478	424	54

Agriculture: ***Distribution of villages according to land use:*** Out of 17 villages, Total area (in hectare) is 26494, out of that 53.26 percent is cultivable and 28.23 percent of the cultivable area is irrigated.
Sources of Irrigation (Hectares): Government Canal 209.3, Private Canal 11.29, Well without Electricity 77.88, Well with Electricity 849.29, Tubewell without Electricity 0, Tubewell with Electricity 2163.47, Tank 171.53, River 0, Lake 222.11, Waterfall 0, Others 277.95.
Villages with population of 5000 to 9999: Surabhi.
Villages with population of 10000 and above: None
Distribution of Workers:

	Persons	Males	Females	WPR
Cultivators	7,002	4,363	2,639	39.31
Agricultural Labour	8,329	3,514	4,815	46.76
Household Industry	379	237	142	2.13
Other Workers	2,104	1,574	530	11.81
Main Workers	13,687	8,426	5,261	76.83
Marginal Workers	4,127	1,262	2,865	23.17
Total Workers	17,814	9,688	8,126	

Religion: Major Religious Communities:

	Persons	Males	Females	Sex Ratio
Hindu (91.6%)	28,104	14,528	13,576	934
Muslim (8.28%)	2,540	1,289	1,251	971
Christian (0.08%)	26	12	14	1,167
Sikh (0.01%)	4	2	2	1,000
Buddhists (0%)	-	-	-	-
Jain (0%)	-	-	-	-

Agewise Data:

	Persons	Males	Females	Sex Ratio
All ages	30,682	15,836	14,846	937
0-14	9,778	5,121	4,657	909
15-44	14,580	7,624	6,956	912
45-79	6,134	3,016	3,118	1034
80+	174	68	106	1559
Age not stated	16	7	9	1286

Languages (Dominant):
Telugu, Urdu, Hindi, Tamil, Marathi
Disabled Population:

	Persons	Males	Females	%
Total Disabled	511	275	236	
In Seeing	150	87	63	29.35
In Speech	84	41	43	16.44
In Hearing	50	26	24	9.78
In Movement	156	83	73	30.53
Mentally	71	38	33	13.89

CHALLAPALLE

Challapalle C.D. Block lies in the southern part of Krishna district. The Block is located at a distance of 26 kms. from district headquarters (Machilipatnam). There are 12 villages in the block with the total population of 53,813 persons. Area of the C.D. Block is 89.74 sq. kms. It is bounded in the north by Mandals Ghantasala and Machilipatnam, in the south by Mandals Mopidevi and Machilipatnam, in the east by Mandal Machi lipatnam, and in the west by River Krishna and district Guntur.
Communications:
Roadways : NH- 214 A: Direction- Mopidevi to Machilipatn am. Nearest Villages- Mangalapuram, Majeru. State Highw ay (S.H.): Direction- Gudivada to Mopidevi. Nearest Villages- Vakkalagadda, Challapalle.
River: Krishna Nadi- Nearest Villages- Cheedepudi, Velivolu, Nimmagadda, Nadakuduru.
Annaul Rainfall: Average Rainfall 1493 mm
Ground Water: Availability of the Ground Water in the Basin is (Information not avavible) H.A.M .and the utilization is (Information not avavible) H.A.M. It belongs to (Information not avavible) category. Depth to water level varies from 3 to 10 meter below the ground. Most of the wells go down in summer months.
Natural Division : Krishna Delta Region
Administration:
Division: Coastal Andhra. Parliamentary Constituency: 28 Machilipatnam. District: Krishna. Mandal: Challapalle. Assembly Constituency: 195 Avanigadda. Gram Panchayat: 11
Villages: 12 **Inhabited:** 11 **Uninhabited:** 1

Ranking	District	State	National
Area	47	1049	5802
Population	29	399	5099
Sex Ratio	6	214	1107
Child Sex Ratio	7	213	680
Literacy Rate	13	73	1239
Density	32	840	1831

Work Participation Rate	4	66	2641

Gram Panchayats:
Amudalalanka, Challapalli, Lakshmipuram, Majeru Mangalapuram, Nadakuduru, Pagolu, Puritigadda Vakkalagadda, Velivolu, Yarlagadda.

Amenities:
Education: Primary School in 11 villages, Middle school in 8 villages, Matriculation or Secondary School in 7 villages, namely Nadakuduru, Pagolu, Vakkalagadda, Challapalle, Lakshmipuram, Mangalapuram, Majeru.
Higher Secondary or Pre University Courses or Intermediate or Junior College in 2 villages of the CD Block,, namely Pagolu, Challapalle.
College in 1 village, Adult Literacy Center in 7 villages., College is in village, namely Challapalle.
Medical: Hospital in 1 village, Dispensary in 2 villages, Health Center in 2 villages, Sub Center in 7 villages, Maternity and Child Welfare Center in 2 villages, Community health workers in 0 village.
The Villages having Hospital or Dispensary or Health Center are Yarlagadda, Challapalle.
Drinking Water: Tap water in 6 villages, Tank water in 0 villages, Well water in 4 villages, Tubewell in 0 village and more than one source in 6 villages.
Bank: Banking facility in 4 villages, namely, Puritigadda, Challapalle, Lakshmipuram, Majeru.
Credit Society in 10 villages Agricultural Credit Society in 6 Non-Agricultural Credit Society in 10 villages.
Others: Power supply in 11 villages, Cinema hall in 2 villages, sport club in 0 village, Stadium or Auditorium or Community Hall in 0 village, Post Office in 9 villages.
There are 11 villages having bus facilities.
Villages with most of facilities: Puritigadda Challapalle, Lakshmipuram, Majeru.
Villages without Amenities (Education): None..
Scheduled Castes: Out of the total population of 53813 persons, 10830 persons (20.13%) belong to Scheduled Castes.
The villages having less than 10% SC population are None..
The villages having more than 50% SC population are None.
Sex ratio of Scheduled Caste population is 493.
Scheduled Castes Literates and Illiterates by Sex:

	Persons	Males	Females
Literate	6,072	3,339	2,733
Illiterate	4,758	2,156	2,602
Literacy rate	63.7	69.1	58.1
Graduate	168	118	50

Scheduled Castes (Dominant):
Madiga, Mala, Beda Jangam etc., Madiga Dasu etc. Mashti
For their cultural identity please see Appendix-I
Villages without Scheduled Castes: There is 1 village without any scheduled caste population.
Scheduled Tribes: Out of the total population of 53813 persons, 1333 persons (2.48%) belong to Scheduled Tribes.
The villages having less than 10% ST population are Velivolu, Nimmagadda, Nadakuduru, Puritigadda Yarlagadda, Pagolu, Vakkalagadda, Challapalle Lakshmipuram, Mangalapuram, Majeru.
The villages having more than 50% ST population are None.
Sex ratio of Scheduled tribe population is 489.
Scheduled Tribes Literates and Illiterates by Sex:

	Persons	Males	Females
Literate	503	284	219
Illiterate	830	397	433
Literacy rate	44.2	49.5	38.8
Graduate	4	4	0

Scheduled Tribes (Dominant):
Yerukulas, Yenadis, Sugalis etc., Koya etc. Chenchu etc.
For their cultural identity please see Appendix-II
Villages without Scheduled Tribes: There is 1 village without any scheduled tribe population.
Literates and Illiterates by Sex (Total Population):

	Persons	Males	Females
Literate	33,334	17,894	15,440
Illiterate	20,479	8,991	11,488
Literacy rate	70	75	64
Graduate	1,801	1,237	564

Agriculture: ***Distribution of villages according to land use:***
Out of 12 villages, Total area (in hectare) is 8973, out of that 63.29 percent is cultivable and 100 percent of the cultivable area is irrigated.
Sources of Irrigation (Hectares): Government Canal 5287.42, Private Canal 0, Well without Electricity 0, Well with Electricity 0, Tubewell without Electricity 0, Tubewell with Electricity 391.5, Tank 0, River 0, Lake 0, Waterfall 0, Others 0.
Villages with population of 5000 to 9999: None
Villages with population of 10000 and above:
Challapalle, Lakshmipuram.
Distribution of Workers:

	Persons	Males	Females	WPR
Cultivators	2,248	2,047	201	8.43
Agricultural Labour	15,310	7,557	7,753	57.44
Household Industry	1,450	731	719	5.44
Other Workers	7,644	6,027	1,617	28.68
Main Workers	23,675	15,674	8,001	88.83

Marginal Workers	2,977	688	2,289	11.17
Total Workers	26,652	16,362	10,290	

Religion: Major Religious Communities:

	Persons	Males	Females	Sex Ratio
Hindu (92.56%)	49,808	24,909	24,899	1,000
Muslim (4.22%)	2,270	1,144	1,126	984
Christian (3.16%)	1,703	820	883	1,077
Sikh (0%)	-	-	-	-
Buddhists (0%)	1	-	1	-
Jain (0%)	-	-	-	-

Agewise Data:

	Persons	Males	Females	Sex Ratio
All ages	53,813	26,885	26,928	1002
0-14	15,023	7,560	7,463	987
15-44	26,512	13,387	13,125	980
45-79	11,741	5,712	6,029	1055
80+	492	204	288	1412
Age not stated	45	22	23	1045

Languages (Dominant):

Telugu, Urdu, Tamil, Hindi, Malayalam

Disabled Population:

	Persons	Males	Females	%
Total Disabled	1,249	700	549	
In Seeing	533	272	261	42.67
In Speech	125	60	65	10.01
In Hearing	64	31	33	5.12
In Movement	377	253	124	30.18
Mentally	150	84	66	12.01

CHANDAM PET

Chandampet C.D. Block lies in the southern part of Nalgonda district. The Block is located at a distance of 75 kms. from district headquarters (Nalgonda). There are 23 villages in the block with the total population of 49,834 persons. Area of the C.D. Block is 480.36 sq. kms. It is bounded by Mahbubnagar district on south and south-west, Devarakonda Mandal on north-west and north, Pedda Adiserlapalle Mandal on north and east.

Communications:

Roadways : NH, SH or Important Metalled Road is not available.

River: Pedda Vagu: Nearest Villages- Pole Palle - Gannerlapalle, Neradugommu, Kotha Palle, Peddamunigal. Dindi Nadi- Nearest Villages- Achampet (P) Chandampet, Chandampet, Murpunuthala, Theldevarapalle, Bollaram Patti (Munagala), Rekulagadda, Yalmala Manda @ Bichya Thanda, Kambala Palle (Old), Rekula Valyam, Pogilla.

Backwards Region Grants Fund: It receives Backward Region Grants.

Annual Rainfall: Average Rainfall 600 mm

Ground Water: Availability of the Ground Water in the Basin is 3243 H.A.M. and the utilization is 2368 H. A.M. It belongs to SC category. Depth to water level varies from 2 to 20 meter below the ground. Most of the wells go down in summer months. The well density in the entire block is 6 wells per sq. km. Total no. of the wells in the block are enumerated as 2847, according to the Ground Water Estimation Committee.

Natural Division : Krishna Piedmont Plain Region

Administration:

Division: Telangana. Parliamentary Constituency: 13 Nalgonda. District: Nalgonda. Mandal: Chandam Pet. Assembly Constituency: 86 Devarakonda (ST). Gram Pancha yat: 19.

Villages: 23 **Inhabited:** 23 **Uninhabited:** 0

Ranking	District	State	National
Area	1	10	1574
Population	21	519	5292
Sex Ratio	59	1073	4371
Child Sex Ratio	58	1080	5287
Literacy Rate	59	1042	5906
Density	1	83	6111
Work Participation Rate	59	1050	302

Gram Panchayats:

Bachapuram, Chandempet, Chinamunagal, Chitryala Gagillapuram, Kambalapally, Kasharajupally Kothapally, Mududandla, Murpunutala, Neradugommu Peddamula, Peddamunagal, Pogilla Polepally Ramnagar), Rakulagadda, Teldevarapally Timmapuram, Yalmalamanda.

Amenities:

Education: Primary School in 22 villages, Middle school in 6 villages, Matriculation or Secondary School in 2 villages, namely Chandampet, Peddamunigal.

Higher Secondary or Pre University Courses or Intermediate or Junior College in 0 village of the CD Block, College in 0 village, Adult Literacy Center in 20 villages.

Medical: Hospital in 0 village, Dispensary in 0 village, Health Center in 1 village, Sub Center in 11 villages, Maternity and Child Welfare Center in 0 village, Community health workers in 0 village.

Drinking Water: Tap water in 23 villages, Tank water in 23 villages, Well water in 23 villages, Tubewell in 23 villages and more than one source in 23 villages.

Bank: Banking facility in 3 villages, namely, Chandampet, Neradugommu, Peddamunigal.

Credit Society in 3 villages Agricultural Credit Society in 2 Non-Agricultural Credit Society in 1 village.

Others: Power supply in 23 villages, Cinema hall in 0 village, sport club in 0 village, Stadium or Auditorium or Community Hall in 0 village, Post Office in 14 villages.

There are 20 villages having bus facilities.

Villages with most of facilities: Chandampet Neradugommu, Peddamunigal.

Villages without amenities (Education):
Dasarla Palle..

Scheduled Castes: Out of the total population of 49834 persons, 6779 persons (13.6%) belong to Scheduled Castes.
The villages having less than 10% SC population are
Achampet (P) Chandampet, Kethepalle, Kotha Palle
Batchapur, Bollaram Patti (Munagala), Rekulagadda
Dasarla Palle, Kacharaj Palle
Yalmala Manda @ Bichya Thanda, Pogilla.
The villages having more than 50% SC population are
None.
Sex ratio of Scheduled Caste population is 488.

Scheduled Castes Literates and Illiterates by Sex:

	Persons	Males	Females
Literate	2,221	1,546	675
Illiterate	4,558	1,923	2,635
Literacy rate	39.8	54.6	24.6
Graduate	17	16	1

Scheduled Castes (Dominant):
Madiga, Mala, Bindla, Generic Castes etc.
Dakkal etc.

For their cultural identity please see Appendix-I

Villages without Scheduled Castes: There are 4 villages without any scheduled caste population.

Scheduled Tribes: Out of the total population of 49834 persons, 24215 persons (48.59%) belong to Scheduled Tribes.
The villages having less than 10% ST population are
None..
The villages having more than 50% ST population are
Mududondla, Achampet (P) Chandampet, Neradugommu
Kethepalle, Kotha Palle, Batchapur, Theldevarapalle
Bollaram Patti (Munagala), Rekulagadda
Dasarla Palle, Kacharaj Palle
Yalmala Manda @ Bichya Thanda.
Sex ratio of Scheduled tribe population is 473.

Scheduled Tribes Literates and Illiterates by Sex:

	Persons	Males	Females
Literate	5,584	4,286	1,298
Illiterate	18,631	8,483	10,148
Literacy rate	29.0	42.4	14.2
Graduate	78	75	3

Scheduled Tribes (Dominant):
Sugalis etc., Chenchu etc., Yerukulas, Koya etc.

For their cultural identity please see Appendix-II

Villages without Scheduled Tribes: There is 1 village without any scheduled tribe population.

Literates and Illiterates by Sex (Total Population):

	Persons	Males	Females
Literate	14,965	10,417	4,548
Illiterate	34,869	15,378	19,491
Literacy rate	37	50	23
Graduate	292	258	34

Agriculture: ***Distribution of villages according to land use:***
Out of 23 villages, Total area (in hectare) is 48035, out of that 39.05 percent is cultivable and 8.17 percent of the cultivable area is irrigated.

Sources of Irrigation (Hectares): Government Canal 6, Private Canal 0, Well without Electricity 46, Well with Electricity 1084.9, Tubewell without Electricity 0, Tubewell with Electricity 354.15, Tank 41.27, River 0, Lake 0, Waterfall 0, Others 0.

Villages with population of 5000 to 9999:
Neradugommu, Kambala Palle (Old).

Villages with population of 10000 and above: None

Distribution of Workers:

	Persons	Males	Females	WPR
Cultivators	9,297	6,078	3,219	33.97
Agricultural Labour	13,655	5,334	8,321	49.89
Household Industry	479	293	186	1.75
Other Workers	3,941	3,014	927	14.4
Main Workers	21,948	12,903	9,045	80.18
Marginal Workers	5,424	1,816	3,608	19.82
Total Workers	27,372	14,719	12,653	

Religion: Major Religious Communities:

	Persons	Males	Females	Sex Ratio
Hindu (98.79%)	49,229	25,477	23,752	932
Muslim (0.9%)	447	233	214	918
Christian (0.29%)	143	80	63	788
Sikh (0%)	-	-	-	-
Buddhists (0%)	-	-	-	-
Jain (0%)	-	-	-	-

Agewise Data:

	Persons	Males	Females	Sex Ratio
All ages	49,834	25,795	24,039	932
0-14	20,716	10,848	9,868	910
15-44	21,445	11,117	10,328	929
45-79	7,365	3,680	3,685	1001
80+	268	133	135	1015
Age not stated	40	17	23	1353

Languages (Dominant):
Telugu, Hindi, Urdu, Tamil, Bengali

Disabled Population:

	Persons	Males	Females	%
Total Disabled	859	519	340	
In Seeing	385	241	144	44.82
In Speech	83	44	39	9.66
In Hearing	49	27	22	5.7
In Movement	281	171	110	32.71

Mentally	61	36	25	7.1

CHANDARLAPADU

Chandarlapadu C.D. Block lies in the north-western part of Krishna district. The Block is located at a distance of 130 kms. from district headquarters (Machil ipatnam). There are 23 villages in the block with the total population of 56,885 persons. Area of the C.D. Block is 223.02 sq. kms. It is bounded in the north by Mandals Jaggayapeta and Nandigama, in the south and west by district Guntur and river Krishna, and in the east by Mandals Nandigama and Kanchikacherla.

Communications:

Roadways : Metalled Roads: Nearest Villages- Muppalla, Bobbellapadu, Chandarlapadu, Kodavatikallu, Kasarabada, Pokkunuru.

River: Krishna Nadi- Nearest Villages- Katrenipalle, Gudimetla, Ustepalle, Kodavatikallu, Kasarabada, Pokkunuru, Punnavalli, Veladi, Popuru, Vibhareetapadu, Eturu.

Annaul Rainfall: Average Rainfall 1512 mm

Ground Water: Availability of the Ground Water in the Basin is (Information not avavible) H.A.M .and the utilization is (Information not avavible) H.A.M. It belongs to (Information not avavible) category. Depth to water level varies from 3 to 10 meter below the ground. Most of the wells go down in summer months.

Natural Division : Krishna Delta Region

Administration:

Division: Coastal Andhra. Parliamentary Constituency: 29 Vijayawada. District: Krishna. Mandal: Chandarlapadu. Assembly Constituency: 202 Nandigana (SC). Gram Pancha yat: 18.

Villages: 23 **Inhabited:** 20 **Uninhabited:** 3

Ranking	District	State	National
Area	8	424	3798
Population	22	325	4969
Sex Ratio	36	835	2815
Child Sex Ratio	46	1019	4783
Literacy Rate	41	315	3030
Density	1	73	4014
Work Participation Rate	41	520	273

Gram Panchayats:

Bobbillapadu, Chandarlapadu, Chintalapadu, Eturu Gudimetla, Kandrapadu, Kasarabada, Kodavatikallu Konayapalem, Munagalapalli, Muppalla, Pokkunuru Popuru, Punnavalli, Thotaravulapadu, Turlapadu Veladikothapalem, Vibhareetalapadu.

Amenities:

Education: Primary School in 20 villages, Middle school in 12 villages, Matriculation or Secondary School in 4 villages, namely Konayapalem, Muppalla, Chandarlapadu, Chintalapadu.

Higher Secondary or Pre University Courses or Intermediate or Junior College in 1 village of the CD Block,, namely Chintalapadu.

College in 0 village, Adult Literacy Center in 6 villages.

Medical: Hospital in 0 village, Dispensary in 1 village, Health Center in 1 village, Sub Center in 9 villages, Maternity and Child Welfare Center in 0 village, Community health workers in 0 village.

The Village having Hospital or Dispensary or Health Center is Eturu.

Drinking Water: Tap water in 10 villages, Tank water in 0 villages, Well water in 4 villages, Tubewell in 0 village and more than one source in 12 villages.

Bank: Banking facility in 4 villages, namely, Konayapalem, Muppalla, Chandarlapadu, Chintalapadu. Credit Society in 12 villages Agricultural Credit Society in 10 Non-Agricultural Credit Society in 9 villages.

Others: Power supply in 20 villages, Cinema hall in 1 village, sport club in 0 village, Stadium or Auditorium or Community Hall in 0 village, Post Office in 16 villages.

There are 19 villages having bus facilities.

Villages with most of facilities: Konayapalem Muppalla, Chandarlapadu, Chintalapadu.

Villages without Amenities (Education): None..

Scheduled Castes: Out of the total population of 56885 persons, 16073 persons (28.26%) belong to Scheduled Castes. The villages having less than 10% SC population are None..

The villages having more than 50% SC population are None.

Sex ratio of Scheduled Caste population is 490.

Scheduled Castes Literates and Illiterates by Sex:

	Persons	Males	Females
Literate	6,974	4,112	2,862
Illiterate	9,099	4,089	5,010
Literacy rate	51.0	59.2	42.6
Graduate	116	97	19

Scheduled Castes (Dominant):

Madiga, Mala, Mala Dasu

For their cultural identity please see Appendix-I

Villages without Scheduled Castes: There are 4 villages without any scheduled caste population.

Scheduled Tribes: Out of the total population of 56885 persons, 1575 persons (2.77%) belong to Scheduled Tribes. The villages having less than 10% ST population are Gudimetla, Konayapalem, Munagala Palle, Muppalla Bobbellapadu, Chandarlapadu, Thurlapadu Thotaravulapadu, Chintalapadu, Patempadu

Kodavatikallu, Kasarabada, Pokkunuru, Punnavalli Veladi, Popuru, Vibhareetapadu, Eturu.

The villages having more than 50% ST population are None.

Sex ratio of Scheduled tribe population is 487.

Scheduled Tribes Literates and Illiterates by Sex:

	Persons	Males	Females
Literate	576	319	257
Illiterate	999	489	510
Literacy rate	43.1	46.1	39.8
Graduate	3	3	0

Scheduled Tribes (Dominant):

Yenadis, Yerukulas, Sugalis etc.

For their cultural identity please see Appendix-II

Villages without Scheduled Tribes: There are 7 villages without any scheduled tribe population.

Literates and Illiterates by Sex (Total Population):

	Persons	Males	Females
Literate	29,178	16,819	12,359
Illiterate	27,707	12,160	15,547
Literacy rate	59	67	50
Graduate	620	499	121

Agriculture: ***Distribution of villages according to land use:*** Out of 23 villages, Total area (in hectare) is 22302, out of that 75.5 percent is cultivable and 18.88 percent of the cultivable area is irrigated.

Sources of Irrigation (Hectares): Government Canal 24.29, Private Canal 0, Well without Electricity 344.13, Well with Electricity 324.79, Tubewell without Electricity 0, Tubewell with Electricity 480.57, Tank 590.28, River 0, Lake 0, Waterfall 0, Others 1415.37.

Villages with population of 5000 to 9999:

Konayapalem, Muppalla.

Villages with population of 10000 and above:

Chandarlapadu.

Distribution of Workers:

	Persons	Males	Females	WPR
Cultivators	7,560	5,061	2,499	22.44
Agricultural Labour	22,684	10,630	12,054	67.33
Household Industry	394	289	105	1.17
Other Workers	3,051	2,521	530	9.06
Main Workers	31,412	17,898	13,514	93.24
Marginal Workers	2,277	603	1,674	6.76
Total Workers	33,689	18,501	15,188	

Religion: Major Religious Communities:

	Persons	Males	Females	Sex Ratio
Hindu (92.27%)	52,489	26,723	25,766	964
Muslim (6.96%)	3,957	2,041	1,916	939
Christian (0.56%)	319	159	160	1,006
Sikh (0%)	-	-	-	-
Buddhists (0%)	-	-	-	-
Jain (0%)	-	-	-	-

Agewise Data:

	Persons	Males	Females	Sex Ratio
All ages	56,885	28,979	27,906	963
0-14	17,407	8,937	8,470	948
15-44	27,243	13,865	13,378	965
45-79	11,615	5,876	5,739	977
80+	520	255	265	1039
Age not stated	100	46	54	1174

Languages (Dominant):

Telugu, Urdu, Gondi, Hindi, Tamil

Disabled Population:

	Persons	Males	Females	%
Total Disabled	993	543	450	
In Seeing	336	164	172	33.84
In Speech	120	65	55	12.08
In Hearing	89	41	48	8.96
In Movement	328	214	114	33.03
Mentally	120	59	61	12.08

CHANDRA SEKHARA PURAM

Chandrasekharapuram C.D. Block lies in the southern part of Prakasam district. The Block is located at a distance of 125 kms. from district headquarters (Ongo le). There are 38 villages in the block with the total population of 38,815 persons. Area of the C.D. Block is 300.14 sq. kms. It is bounded in the north by Mandals Bestavaripeta and Veligandla, in the south by district Nellore, in the east by Mandals Kanigiri and Lingasamud ram, and in the west by Mandals Bestavaripeta and Komaro lu, and district Cuddapah.

Communications:

Roadways : Metalled Roads: Nearest Villages- Pedagogulap alle, Mundlapadu, Chintala Palem, Arivemula, Yekunam Puram, Darsigunta Peta, Medanulu Vengana Palle, Bodavula Dinne, Kondabaina Palle, Ranganayuni Palle, Darsi Thimmakka Palle, Chandra Sekhara Puram, Musunoor, Komal igunta, Chinthapudi, Nagulavaram, Kovilam Padu, Regula Chilaka, Chennapanayuni Palle, Vatla Bayulu, Kotha Palle, Ambavaram, Pedaraju Palem, Nalajanam Padu, Kambh am Padu.

River: Dokkalavagu Nadi- Nearest Villages- Medanulu Vengana Palle, Kondabaina Palle, Kovilam Padu, Nallamad ugula, Uppalapadu, Guntachennam Palle, Regula Chilaka, Chennapanayuni Palle. Manneru Nadi- Nearest Villages- Mundlapadu, Chintala Palem, Arivemula, Yekunam Puram, Thummagunta, Darsigunta Peta, Ranganayuni Palle, Chand ra Sekhara Puram. Narellavagu Nadi- Nearest Village- Pedagogulapalle.

The Block is identified as a drought-prone area.

Annual Rainfall: Average Rainfall 777.1 mm

Ground Water: Availability of the Ground Water in the Basin is 23.26 MCM and the utilization is 13.97 MCM It belongs to Safe category. Depth to water level varies from 2 to 5 meter below the ground. Most of the wells go down in summer months, according to the Ground Water Estimation Committee.

Forest and Reserved **Forest:** (Velikonda R.F.)- Nearest Villages- Viranchi Puram, Pedagogulapalle, Mundlapadu, Chintala Palem, Arivemula, Yekunam Puram, Thummagunta, Bontha Vari Palle, Bodavula Dinne, Kondabaina Palle, Ranganayuni Palle, Darsi Thimmakka Palle, Nallamadugula, Uppalapadu, Guntachennam Palle, Chennapanayuni Palle, Vatla Bayulu, Malameedi Palle, Kotha Palle, Pedaraju Palem.

Administration:

Division: Coastal Andhra. Parliamentary Constituency: 33 Ongole. District: Prakasam. Mandal: Chandra Sekhara Puram. Assembly Constituency: 232 Kanigiri. Gram Pancha yat: 23.

Villages: 38 **Inhabited:** 36 **Uninhabited:** 2

Ranking	District	State	National
Area	11	162	2784
Population	39	857	5785
Sex Ratio	26	722	2449
Child Sex Ratio	18	438	1622
Literacy Rate	27	464	3706
Density	50	813	5845
Work Participation Rate	47	972	2458

Gram Panchayats:

Ambavaram, Ambavaram Kothapalli, Anikalapalli Arivemula, Ayyalurivaripalli, Boyamadugula Chandrasekhara Puram, Chennapanayunipalli Cherlopalli, Chintapudi, D.G.Peta, K.Agraharam Kambhampadu, Kovilampadu, Nallamadugula Pedarajupalem, Pedda Gollapalli, Pullagurapalli R.K.Palli, Regulachilaka, Uppalapadu, V.Bayalu Venganagunta.

Amenities:

Education: Primary School in 31 villages, Middle school in 9 villages, Matriculation or Secondary School in 4 villages, namely Chandra Sekhara Puram, Nallamadugula, Ambavaram, Pedaraju Palem.

Higher Secondary or Pre University Courses or Intermediate or Junior College in 1 village of the CD Block,, namely Chandra Sekhara Puram.

College in 1 village, Adult Literacy Center in 30 villages., College is in village, namely Chandra Sekhara Puram.

Medical: Hospital in 2 villages, Dispensary in 2 villages, Health Center in 1 village, Sub Center in 8 villages, Maternity and Child Welfare Center in 0 village, Community health workers in 0 village.

The Villages having Hospital or Dispensary or Health Center are Arivemula, Darsigunta Peta, Chandra Sekhara Puram.

Drinking Water: Tap water in 36 villages, Tank water in 36 villages, Well water in 36 villages, Tubewell in 36 villages and more than one source in 36 villages.

Bank: Banking facility in 4 villages, namely, Chandra Sekhara Puram, Nagulavaram, Uppalapadu Ambavaram.

Credit Society in 7 villages Agricultural Credit Society in 1 Non-Agricultural Credit Society in 7 villages.

Others: Power supply in 36 villages, Cinema hall in 1 village, sport club in 0 village, Stadium or Auditorium or Community Hall in 0 village, Post Office in 22 villages.

There are 32 villages having bus facilities.

Villages with most of facilities: Chandra Sekhara Puram Ambavaram.

Villages without amenities (Education):

Devaki Marri, Talaneelamala, Thummagunta, Ranganayuni Palle..

Scheduled Castes: Out of the total population of 38815 persons, 6385 persons (16.45%) belong to Scheduled Castes.

The villages having less than 10% SC population are Devaki Marri, Talaneelamala, Thummagunta Bontha Vari Palle, Medanulu Vengana Palle Ranganayuni Palle, Darsi Thimmakka Palle Chandra Sekhara Puram, Nagulavaram, Regula Chilaka Ambavaram.

The villages having more than 50% SC population are None.

Sex ratio of Scheduled Caste population is 495.

Scheduled Castes Literates and Illiterates by Sex:

	Persons	Males	Females
Literate	2,992	1,844	1,148
Illiterate	3,393	1,378	2,015
Literacy rate	54.8	67.1	42.3
Graduate	57	43	14

Scheduled Castes (Dominant):

Madiga, Mala, Generic Castes etc., Adi Andhra Mala Dasari

For their cultural identity please see Appendix-I

Villages without Scheduled Castes: There are 9 villages without any scheduled caste population.

Scheduled Tribes: Out of the total population of 38815 persons, 1047 persons (2.7%) belong to Scheduled Tribes.

The villages having less than 10% ST population are Devaki Marri, Venkataya Cheruvu, Boyamadugula Pedagogulapalle, Mundlapadu, Chintala Palem Arivemula, Yekunam Puram, Thummagunta

Darsigunta Peta, Bontha Vari Palle
Medanulu Vengana Palle, Bodavula Dinne
Kondabaina Palle, Ranganayuni Palle
Chandra Sekhara Puram, Musunoor, Komatigunta
Chinthapudi, Nagulavaram, Kovilam Padu
Anikalla Palle, Nallamadugula, Guntachennam Palle
Regula Chilaka, Chennapanayuni Palle, Vatla Bayulu
Kotha Palle, Ambavaram, Pedaraju Palem, Kambham Padu.

The villages having more than 50% ST population are None.

Sex ratio of Scheduled tribe population is 484.

Scheduled Tribes Literates and Illiterates by Sex:

	Persons	Males	Females
Literate	226	132	94
Illiterate	821	408	413
Literacy rate	27.7	31.9	23.3
Graduate	16	12	4

Scheduled Tribes (Dominant):

Yenadis, Yerukulas, Konda Dhoras, Kammara Chenchu etc.

For their cultural identity please see Appendix-II

Villages without Scheduled Tribes: There are 12 villages without any scheduled tribe population.

Literates and Illiterates by Sex (Total Population):

	Persons	Males	Females
Literate	18,326	11,927	6,399
Illiterate	20,489	7,769	12,720
Literacy rate	55	70	39
Graduate	434	372	62

Agriculture: ***Distribution of villages according to land use:***

Out of 38 villages, Total area (in hectare) is 30014, out of that 51.57 percent is cultivable and 8.78 percent of the cultivable area is irrigated.

Sources of Irrigation (Hectares): Government Canal 1358.63, Private Canal 0, Well without Electricity 0, Well with Electricity 0, Tubewell without Electricity 0, Tubewell with Electricity 0, Tank 0, River 0, Lake 0, Waterfall 0, Others 0.

Villages with population of 5000 to 9999:

Chandra Sekhara Puram.

Villages with population of 10000 and above: None

Distribution of Workers:

	Persons	Males	Females	WPR
Cultivators	4,955	3,535	1,420	26.22
Agricultural Labour	8,593	3,615	4,978	45.48
Household Industry	340	171	169	1.8
Other Workers	5,007	3,788	1,219	26.5
Main Workers	13,758	9,106	4,652	72.81
Marginal Workers	5,137	2,003	3,134	27.19
Total Workers	18,895	11,109	7,786	

Religion: Major Religious Communities:

	Persons	Males	Females	Sex Ratio
Hindu (93.53%)	36,304	18,390	17,914	974
Muslim (5.61%)	2,178	1,135	1,043	919
Christian (0.72%)	279	140	139	993
Sikh (0%)	-	-	-	-
Buddhists (0%)	-	-	-	-
Jain (0%)	-	-	-	-

Agewise Data:

	Persons	Males	Females	Sex Ratio
All ages	38,815	19,696	19,119	971
0-14	13,543	6,883	6,660	968
15-44	16,885	8,636	8,249	955
45-79	7,995	3,975	4,020	1011
80+	336	170	166	976
Age not stated	56	32	24	750

Languages (Dominant):

Telugu, Urdu, Gondi, Hindi, Tamil

Disabled Population:

	Persons	Males	Females	%
Total Disabled	692	414	278	
In Seeing	194	104	90	28.03
In Speech	86	57	29	12.43
In Hearing	31	19	12	4.48
In Movement	260	163	97	37.57
Mentally	121	71	50	17.49

CHANDRAGIRI

Chandragiri C.D. Block lies in the northern part of Chittoor district. The Block is located at a distance of 56 kms. from district headquarters (Chittoor). There are 23 villages in the block with the total population of 53,051 persons. Area of the C.D. Block is 95.89 sq. kms. It is bounded in the north by Mandals Chinnago ttigallu, Tirupati Urban and Tirupati Rural, in the south by Mandals Penumuru and Vedurukuppam, in the east by Mandals Tirupati Rural, Ramchandrapuram and Vedurukuppam, and in the west by Mandals Pakal and Pulicherla.

Communications:

Roadways : State Highway (S.H.): Direction- Chittoor to Renigunta. Nearest Villages- Agarala, Mamandur, Mungilipattukothapalle, Panapakam, Reddivaripalle, Narasinga Puram, Mittapalem.

Railway Station: Kotala, Narasinga Puram, Mungilipattuk othapalle, Panapakam.

River: Kalyani Nadi- Nearest Villages- Nagapatla, Ramir eddi Palle, Narasinga Puram, Reddivaripalle. Swarnamukhi Nadi- Nearest Villages- Thondawada, Chandragiri, Dornak ambala.

It receives the Backward Region Grants, and is identifi ed as a drought-prone area as well.

Integrated Child Development Scheme (ICDS) Project: Chandragiri, Total Anganwadi Centres: 127

Annual Rainfall: Average Rainfall 1020 mm

Ground Water: Availability of the Ground Water in the Basin is 4083 H.A.M.and the utilization is 1908 H.A. M. It belongs to Safe category. Depth to water level varies more than 10 meter below the ground. Most of the wells go down in summer months, according to the Ground Water Estimation Committee.

Forest and Reserved **Forest:** (Panapakkam R.F.)- Nearest Villages- Kondreddy Khandriga, Pullaiahgari Palle, Kotala, Thondawada, Sanambatla, Chandragiri, Agarala, Mamandur, Ithepalle, Mungilipattukothapalle, Kalroadpa lle, Dornakambala, Panapakam.

Natural Division : Rayalaseema Region

Administration:

Division: Rayala Seema. Parliamentary Constituency: . District: Chittoor. Mandal: Chandragiri. Assembly Constituency: 285 Chandragiri. Gram Panchayat: 33

Places of Tourist Interest:

Chandragiri : Chandragiri is at a distance of 11 kms. from Tirupati. It is a railway station on the Katpadi-Renigunta line. The river Swarnamukhi, flows to the south of the village. The fort and the Mahals (palaces) at the place are the attraction for tourists. The Raja Mahal is believed to have been built by Immadi Narasimha Yadavaraya in, A.D. 1000 and improved in later times, by the Vijayanagara kings. The fort stands on a huge granite rock which is about 183 meteres high. The south ern side of the hill is enclosed by strong walls, now in ruins, surrounded by a ditch, once fed by a natural spring, but now almost dry. The ramains at the lower fort contain the two Mahals, the lower portion of which is built in stone and the upper in brick. The Raja Mahal is majestic in appearance. The surrounding country is very fertile and the scenery charming. Archaeologic al remains consisting of desolate temples and finely carved mantapams, are found in the countryside. The Chandragiri Mahal is now maintained by the Archaeologic al department.

Villages: 23 **Inhabited:** 23 **Uninhabited:** 0

Ranking	District	State	National
Area	60	1033	5749
Population	14	417	5132
Sex Ratio	45	588	2077
Child Sex Ratio	46	867	3823
Literacy Rate	2	21	603
Density	60	996	2009
Work Participation Rate	3	82	3763

Gram Panchayats:

A.Gurrappagari Palle, Agarala, Arepalle Rangam Peta B.Kongaravari Palle, Bandarla Palle, Bheemavaram Buchinaidupalem, Chandragiri, Chinna Rama Puram Dornakambala, Gangudu Palle, Ithepalle, Kalroadpalle Kandulavari Palle, Kasipentla, Kondreddy Khandriga Kotala, M.Kongaravari Palle, Mamandur, Mittapalem Mungilipattu, Mungilipattukothapalle Narasinga Puram, Panapakam, Pichinaidupalle Pulithavari Palle, Pullaiahgari Palle Ramireddipalle, Rayal Puram, Reddivaripalle Sanambatla, Sesha Puram, Thondawada.

Amenities:

Education: Primary School in 22 villages, Middle school in 10 villages, Matriculation or Secondary School in 7 villages, namely Arepalle, Kotala, Thondawada, Chandragiri, Ithepalle, Mungilipattukothapalle, Panapakam.

Higher Secondary or Pre University Courses or Intermediate or Junior College in 3 villages of the CD Block,, namely Arepalle, Thondawada, Chandragiri.

College in 1 village, Adult Literacy Center in 20 villages., College is in village, namely Chandragiri.

Medical: Hospital in 1 village, Dispensary in 1 village, Health Center in 0 village, Sub Center in 9 villages, Maternity and Child Welfare Center in 0 village, Community health workers in 0 village.

The Village having Hospital or Dispensary or Health Center is Chandragiri.

Drinking Water: Tap water in 23 villages, Tank water in 23 villages, Well water in 23 villages, Tubewell in 23 villages and more than one source in 23 villages.

Bank: Banking facility in 3 villages, namely, Arepalle, Narasinga Puram, Chandragiri.

Credit Society in 8 villages Agricultural Credit Society in 5 Non-Agricultural Credit Society in 3 villages.

Others: Power supply in 23 villages, Cinema hall in 2 villages, sport club in 0 village, Stadium or Auditorium or Community Hall in 0 village, Post Office in 17 villages.

There are 20 villages having bus facilities.

Villages with most of facilities: Narasinga Puram Chandragiri.

Villages without amenities (Education):

Chintagunta..

Scheduled Castes: Out of the total population of 53051 persons, 11287 persons (21.28%) belong to Scheduled Castes.

The villages having less than 10% SC population are None..

The villages having more than 50% SC population are None.

Sex ratio of Scheduled Caste population is 504.

Scheduled Castes Literates and Illiterates by Sex:

	Persons	Males	Females
Literate	6,606	3,763	2,843
Illiterate	4,681	1,838	2,843
Literacy rate	66.9	77.0	57.0
Graduate	171	138	33

Scheduled Castes (Dominant):

Mala, Madiga, Generic Castes etc., Adi Andhra Bariki

For their cultural identity please see Appendix-I

Villages without Scheduled Castes: There is 1 village without any scheduled caste population.

Scheduled Tribes: Out of the total population of 53051 persons, 2851 persons (5.37%) belong to Scheduled Tribes. The villages having less than 10% ST population are Bheemavaram, Chinna Rama Puram, Sesha Puram Pullaiahgari Palle, Arepalle, Kotala Narasinga Puram, Mittapalem, Reddivaripalle Sanambatla, Chintagunta, Chandragiri, Agarala Mamandur, Ithepalle, Mungilipattukothapalle Panapakam, Dornakambala.

The villages having more than 50% ST population are None.

Sex ratio of Scheduled tribe population is 483.

Scheduled Tribes Literates and Illiterates by Sex:

	Persons	Males	Females
Literate	1,413	785	628
Illiterate	1,438	689	749
Literacy rate	59.9	64.7	54.9
Graduate	12	11	1

Scheduled Tribes (Dominant):

Yenadis, Yerukulas, Sugalis etc.

Generic Tribes etc., Chenchu etc.

For their cultural identity please see Appendix-II

Villages without Scheduled Tribes: There are 2 villages without any scheduled tribe population.

Literates and Illiterates by Sex (Total Population):

	Persons	Males	Females
Literate	35,566	19,846	15,720
Illiterate	17,485	6,961	10,524
Literacy rate	76	84	67
Graduate	2,655	1,945	710

Agriculture: ***Distribution of villages according to land use:*** Out of 23 villages, Total area (in hectare) is 9588, out of that 64.41 percent is cultivable and 53.03 percent of the cultivable area is irrigated.

Sources of Irrigation (Hectares): Government Canal 0, Private Canal 0, Well without Electricity 0, Well with Electricity 3005, Tubewell without Electricity 0, Tubewell with Electricity 270, Tank 0, River 0, Lake 0, Waterfall 0, Others 0.

Villages with population of 5000 to 9999: None

Villages with population of 10000 and above: Chandragiri.

Distribution of Workers:

	Persons	Males	Females	WPR
Cultivators	5,581	3,779	1,802	23.78
Agricultural Labour	9,091	4,782	4,309	38.74
Household Industry	895	495	400	3.81
Other Workers	7,901	6,121	1,780	33.67
Main Workers	19,482	13,489	5,993	83.02
Marginal Workers	3,986	1,688	2,298	16.98
Total Workers	23,468	15,177	8,291	

Religion: Major Religious Communities:

	Persons	Males	Females	Sex Ratio
Hindu (94.29%)	50,022	25,260	24,762	980
Muslim (5.26%)	2,788	1,425	1,363	956
Christian (0.33%)	174	83	91	1,096
Sikh (0.02%)	11	5	6	1,200
Buddhists (0%)	-	-	-	-
Jain (0.02%)	8	4	4	1,000

Agewise Data:

	Persons	Males	Females	Sex Ratio
All ages	53,051	26,807	26,244	979
0-14	14,118	7,324	6,794	928
15-44	25,902	13,090	12,812	979
45-79	12,460	6,125	6,335	1034
80+	465	198	267	1348
Age not stated	106	70	36	514

Languages (Dominant):

Telugu, Urdu, Tamil, Hindi, Kannada

Disabled Population:

	Persons	Males	Females	%
Total Disabled	826	449	377	
In Seeing	232	113	119	28.09
In Speech	82	47	35	9.93
In Hearing	78	36	42	9.44
In Movement	315	199	116	38.14
Mentally	119	54	65	14.41

CHANDRUGONDA

Chandrugonda C.D. Block lies in the southern part of Khammam district. The Block is located at a distance of 75 kms. from district headquarters (Khammam). There are 20 villages in the block with the total population of 47,517 persons. Area of the C.D. Block is 324.02 sq. kms. It is bounded in the north by Mandals Julurpad, Kothagudem and Mulkalapalle, in the south by Mandal Penuballi, in the east by Mandals Sathupalle, Dammapeta and Mulkalapalle, and in the west by Mandal Julurpad.

Communications:

Roadways : NH- 221: Direction- Tiruvuru to Kothagudem. Nearest Villages- Tippanapalle, Gumpena, Chandrugonda,

Maddukuru, Peddireddigudem.
Backwards Region Grants Fund: It receives Backward Region Grants.

Annual Rainfall: Average Rainfall 1058 mm

Ground Water: Availability of the Ground Water in the Basin is 3678 H.A.M.and the utilization is 528 H.A. M. It belongs to safe category. Depth to water level varies from 5 to 10 meter below the ground. Most of the wells go down in summer months. The well density in the entire block is 2 wells per sq. km. Total no. of the wells in the block are enumerated as 536, according to the Ground Water Estimation Committee.

Natural Division : Godavari Depression Region

Administration:

Division: Telangana. Parliamentary Constituency: 17 Khammam. District: Khammam. Mandal: Chandrugonda. Assembly Constituency: 118 Aswaraopeta (ST). Gram Panchayat: 17

Villages: 20 **Inhabited:** 20 **Uninhabited:** 0

Ranking	District	State	National
Area	11	116	2526
Population	21	590	5404
Sex Ratio	42	971	3370
Child Sex Ratio	25	529	2017
Literacy Rate	32	791	4857
Density	25	486	5605
Work Participation Rate	30	913	1245

Gram Panchayats:

Abbugudem, Annapureddipalli, Chandrugonda Dameracherla, Ganugapadu, Gumpena, Gurramgudem Maddukuru, Marrigudem, Narsapuram, Peddireddigudem Pentlam, Pokalagudem, Ravikampadu, Thungaram Tippanapalli, Vootupalli.

Amenities:

Education: Primary School in 20 villages, Middle school in 7 villages, Matriculation or Secondary School in 3 villages, namely Annapureddipalle, Chandrugonda, Peddireddigudem.

Higher Secondary or Pre University Courses or Intermediate or Junior College in 1 village of the CD Block,, namely Annapureddipalle.

College in 2 villages, Adult Literacy Center in 17 villages., Colleges are in villages, namely Annapureddipalle, Peddireddigudem.

Medical: Hospital in 0 village, Dispensary in 1 village, Health Center in 1 village, Sub Center in 11 villages, Maternity and Child Welfare Center in 0 village, Community health workers in 0 village.

The Village having Hospital or Dispensary or Health Center is Annapureddipalle.

Drinking Water: Tap water in 20 villages, Tank water in 20 villages, Well water in 20 villages, Tubewell in 20 villages and more than one source in 20 villages.

Bank: Banking facility in 3 villages, namely, Annadevam, Chandrugonda, Peddireddigudem.

Credit Society in 11 villages Agricultural Credit Society in 2 Non-Agricultural Credit Society in 10 villages.

Others: Power supply in 20 villages, Cinema hall in 3 villages, sport club in 0 village, Stadium or Auditorium or Community Hall in 0 village, Post Office in 12 villages.

There are 18 villages having bus facilities.

Villages with most of facilities: Chandrugonda Peddireddigudem.

Villages without Amenities (Education): None..

Scheduled Castes: Out of the total population of 47517 persons, 5856 persons (12.32%) belong to Scheduled Castes.

The villages having less than 10% SC population are Pokalagudem, Thungaram, Tippanapalle, Seethaigudem Teligerla, Annadevam, Pentlam, Namavaram, Narsapuram Dameracharla, Gurramgudem, Peddireddigudem Vootupalle.

The villages having more than 50% SC population are None.

Sex ratio of Scheduled Caste population is 455.

Scheduled Castes Literates and Illiterates by Sex:

	Persons	Males	Females
Literate	2,356	1,576	780
Illiterate	3,500	1,617	1,883
Literacy rate	46.9	57.5	34.2
Graduate	67	51	16

Scheduled Castes (Dominant):

Madiga, Mala, Mala Dasari, Generic Castes etc. Beda Jangam etc.

For their cultural identity please see Appendix-I

Villages without Scheduled Castes: There are 2 villages without any scheduled caste population.

Scheduled Tribes: Out of the total population of 47517 persons, 13965 persons (29.39%) belong to Scheduled Tribes.

The villages having less than 10% ST population are None..

The villages having more than 50% ST population are Pokalagudem, Thungaram, Seethaigudem, Annadevam Namavaram, Gurramgudem.

Sex ratio of Scheduled tribe population is 491.

Scheduled Tribes Literates and Illiterates by Sex:

	Persons	Males	Females
Literate	3,782	2,534	1,248
Illiterate	10,183	4,581	5,602
Literacy rate	32.6	42.7	22.0
Graduate	29	25	4

Scheduled Tribes (Dominant):
Sugalis etc., Koya etc., Gond etc., Nayaks Yerukulas

For their cultural identity please see Appendix-II

Villages without Scheduled Tribes: There are 0 village without any scheduled tribe population.

Literates and Illiterates by Sex (Total Population):

	Persons	Males	Females
Literate	19,511	11,924	7,587
Illiterate	28,006	12,423	15,583
Literacy rate	48	57	38
Graduate	500	395	105

Agriculture: ***Distribution of villages according to land use:*** Out of 20 villages, Total area (in hectare) is 32402, out of that 36.57 percent is cultivable and 34.06 percent of the cultivable area is irrigated.

Sources of Irrigation (Hectares): Government Canal 668.54, Private Canal 0, Well without Electricity 12.14, Well with Electricity 72.84, Tubewell without Electricity 0, Tubewell with Electricity 7.28, Tank 3013.4, River 0, Lake 0, Waterfall 0, Others 261.41.

Villages with population of 5000 to 9999: Chandrugonda, Peddireddigudem.

Villages with population of 10000 and above: None

Distribution of Workers:

	Persons	Males	Females	WPR
Cultivators	6,403	4,490	1,913	25.4
Agricultural Labour	14,855	6,812	8,043	58.93
Household Industry	392	238	154	1.56
Other Workers	3,556	2,936	620	14.11
Main Workers	22,405	13,564	8,841	88.89
Marginal Workers	2,801	912	1,889	11.11
Total Workers	25,206	14,476	10,730	

Religion: Major Religious Communities:

	Persons	Males	Females	Sex Ratio
Hindu (92.66%)	44,029	22,614	21,415	947
Muslim (6.7%)	3,185	1,594	1,591	998
Christian (0.62%)	296	136	160	1,176
Sikh (0%)	-	-	-	-
Buddhists (0%)	-	-	-	-
Jain (0%)	-	-	-	-

Agewise Data:

	Persons	Males	Females	Sex Ratio
All ages	47,517	24,347	23,170	952
0-14	16,434	8,520	7,914	929
15-44	22,297	11,427	10,870	951
45-79	8,358	4,179	4,179	1000
80+	375	192	183	953
Age not stated	53	29	24	828

Languages (Dominant):
Telugu, Hindi, Koya, Urdu, Tamil

Disabled Population:

	Persons	Males	Females	%
Total Disabled	863	511	352	
In Seeing	410	253	157	47.51
In Speech	103	57	46	11.94
In Hearing	25	8	17	2.9
In Movement	246	153	93	28.51
Mentally	79	40	39	9.15

CHANDUR

Chandur C.D. Block lies in the central west part of Nalgonda district. It is a part of Chandur Mandal. The Block is located at a distance of 32 kms. from district headquarters (Nalgonda). There are 16 villages in the block with the total population of 36,342 persons. Area of the C.D. Block is 189.75 sq. kms. It is bound ed by Munugode Mandal on north, Kangal Mandal on east, Gurampode Mandal on south-east, Nampalle Mandal on south, Mariguda and Narayanpur Mandals on west.

Communications:

Roadways : Metalled Roads: Nearest Villages- Sirdepalle, Gundrepalle.

Backwards Region Grants Fund: It receives Backward Region Grants.

Annual Rainfall: Average Rainfall 778 mm

Ground Water: Availability of the Ground Water in the Basin is 1739 H.A.M. and the utilization is 1712 H. A.M. It belongs to Cri category. Depth to water level varies from 10 to 20 meter below the ground. Most of the wells go down in summer months. The well density in the entire block is 15 wells per sq. km. Total no. of the wells in the block are enumerated as 3136, according to the Ground Water Estimation Committee.

Natural Division : Krishna Piedmont Plain Region

Administration:

Division: Telangana. Parliamentary Constituency: 14 Bhongir. District: Nalgonda. Mandal: Chandur. Assembly Constituency: 93 Munugode. Gram Panchayat: 16.

Villages: 16 **Inhabited:** 16 **Uninhabited:** 0

Ranking	**District**	**State**	**National**
Area	43	613	4354
Population	55	911	5871
Sex Ratio	29	724	2441
Child Sex Ratio	36	788	3410
Literacy Rate	41	708	4580
Density	33	560	4856
Work Participation Rate	37	746	1476

Gram Panchayats:
Angadipet, Bangarigadda, Bodangiparthy, Chandur Donipamla, Gatuppal, Gundrepally, Idikuda, Kastala

Kondapuram, Nermatta, Pullemla, Sirdepally Teratpally, Tummalapally, Udtalapally.

Amenities:

Education: Primary School in 16 villages, Middle school in 8 villages, Matriculation or Secondary School in 2 villages, namely Ghattuppal, Pullemla.

Higher Secondary or Pre University Courses or Intermediate or Junior College in 1 village of the CD Block,, namely Ghattuppal.

College in 0 village, Adult Literacy Center in 0 village.

Medical: Hospital in 0 village, Dispensary in 0 village, Health Center in 0 village, Sub Center in 6 villages, Maternity and Child Welfare Center in 0 village, Community health workers in 0 village.

Drinking Water: Tap water in 16 villages, Tank water in 16 villages, Well water in 16 villages, Tubewell in 16 villages and more than one source in 16 villages.

Bank: Banking facility in 1 villages, namely, Ghattuppal.

Credit Society in 7 villages Agricultural Credit Society in 4 Non-Agricultural Credit Society in 5 villages.

Others: Power supply in 16 villages, Cinema hall in 1 village, sport club in 0 village, Stadium or Auditorium or Community Hall in 0 village, Post Office in 12 villages.

There are 16 villages having bus facilities.

Village with most of facilities: Ghattuppal.

Villages without Amenities (Education): None..

Scheduled Castes: Out of the total population of 36330 persons, 6203 persons (17.07%) belong to Scheduled Castes.

The villages having less than 10% SC population are None..

The villages having more than 50% SC population are None.

Sex ratio of Scheduled Caste population is 499.

Scheduled Castes Literates and Illiterates by Sex:

	Persons	Males	Females
Literate	2,132	1,479	653
Illiterate	4,071	1,626	2,445
Literacy rate	40.9	56.8	25.0
Graduate	49	45	4

Scheduled Castes (Dominant):

Madiga, Mala, Beda Jangam etc., Bindla, Chamar etc.

For their cultural identity please see Appendix-I

Villages without Scheduled Castes: There are 0 village without any scheduled caste population.

Scheduled Tribes: Out of the total population of 36330 persons, 453 persons (1.25%) belong to Scheduled Tribes.

The villages having less than 10% ST population are Ghattuppal, Theratpalle, Kondapuram, Pullemla Bodangi Parthy, Kumandaniguda, Sirdepalle, Idikuda Nermata, Donipamula, Bangarigadda, Thummalapalle Gundrepalle, Angadipeta, Kasthala, Udathala Palle.

The villages having more than 50% ST population are None.

Sex ratio of Scheduled tribe population is 382.

Scheduled Tribes Literates and Illiterates by Sex:

	Persons	Males	Females
Literate	205	172	33
Illiterate	248	108	140
Literacy rate	53.1	72.0	22.5
Graduate	0	0	0

Scheduled Tribes (Dominant):

Sugalis etc., Yerukulas

For their cultural identity please see Appendix-II

Villages without Scheduled Tribes: There are 8 villages without any scheduled tribe population.

Literates and Illiterates by Sex (Total Population):

	Persons	Males	Females
Literate	15,369	10,125	5,244
Illiterate	20,961	8,306	12,655
Literacy rate	50	65	34
Graduate	400	355	45

Agriculture: ***Distribution of villages according to land use:*** Out of 16 villages, Total area (in hectare) is 18974, out of that 87.66 percent is cultivable and 15.87 percent of the cultivable area is irrigated.

Sources of Irrigation (Hectares): Government Canal 0, Private Canal 0, Well without Electricity 0, Well with Electricity 497.33, Tubewell without Electricity 0, Tubewell with Electricity 1278.78, Tank 863.17, River 0, Lake 0, Waterfall 0, Others 0.

Villages with population of 5000 to 9999: Ghattuppal.

Villages with population of 10000 and above: None

Distribution of Workers:

	Persons	Males	Females	WPR
Cultivators	3,885	2,772	1,113	20.71
Agricultural Labour	7,933	2,820	5,113	42.28
Household Industry	2,907	1,689	1,218	15.49
Other Workers	4,038	3,060	978	21.52
Main Workers	13,521	9,380	4,141	72.06
Marginal Workers	5,242	961	4,281	27.94
Total Workers	18,763	10,341	8,422	

Religion: Major Religious Communities:

	Persons	Males	Females	Sex Ratio
Hindu (96.98%)	35,232	17,841	17,391	975
Muslim (1.77%)	642	327	315	963
Christian (1.16%)	422	245	177	722
Sikh (0.02%)	8	2	6	3,000
Buddhists (0%)	1	1	-	-

Jain (0%)	-	-	-	-

Agewise Data:

	Persons	Males	Females	Sex Ratio
All ages	36,330	18,431	17,899	971
0-14	12,354	6,315	6,039	956
15-44	16,585	8,419	8,166	970
45-79	7,084	3,557	3,527	992
80+	282	127	155	1220
Age not stated	25	13	12	923

Languages (Dominant):

Telugu, Urdu, Hindi, Tamil, Gondi

Disabled Population:

	Persons	Males	Females	%
Total Disabled	798	422	376	
In Seeing	361	190	171	45.24
In Speech	76	38	38	9.52
In Hearing	43	22	21	5.39
In Movement	224	130	94	28.07
Mentally	94	42	52	11.78

CHANDURTHI

Chandurthi C.D. Block lies in the north-western part of Karimnagar district. The Block is located at a dista nce of 55 kms. from district headquarters (Karimnagar). There are 12 villages in the block with the total population of 40,558 persons. Area of the C.D. Block is 206.52 sq. kms. It is bounded by Kathlapur Mandal on north, Medipalle Mandal and Kodimial Mandal on north -east, Vemulawada Mandal on east, Konaraopet Mandal on south, and Nizamabad district on west.

Communications :

Roadways : Metalled Roads: Nearest Village- Sangula.

River: Mula Vagu- Nearest Villages- Sangula.

Backwards Region Grants Fund: It receives Backward Region Grants.

Annual Rainfall: Average Rainfall 1028 mm

Ground Water: Availability of the Ground Water in the Basin is 2050 H.A.M. and the utilization is 1904 H. A.M. It belongs to Critical category. Depth to water level varies from more than 10 meter below the ground. Most of the wells go down in summer months. The well density in the entire block is 23 wells per sq. km. Total no. of the wells in the block are enumerated as 4685, according to the Ground Water Estimation Commi ttee.

Natural Division : Godavari Depression Region

Administration:

Division: Telangana. Parliamentary Constituency: 3 Karimnagar. District: Karimnagar.

Mandal: Chandurthi. Assembly Constituency: 28 Vemulavada. Gram Panchayat: 18.

Villages: 12 **Inhabited:** 12 **Uninhabited:** 0

Ranking	District	State	National
Area	22	514	4068
Population	44	810	5715
Sex Ratio	16	100	648
Child Sex Ratio	15	253	791
Literacy Rate	41	872	5165
Density	14	187	4778
Work Participation Rate	47	728	535

Gram Panchayats:

Ananthapalli, Ashireddypally, Bandapally, Chandurthy Engal, Jogapur, Kattalingampet, Kistampet, Lingampet Mallial, Marrigadda, Moodapally, Narsingapur Ramannapet, Ramaraopally, Rudrangi, Sanugula Thimmapur.

Amenities:

Education: Primary School in 12 villages, Middle school in 10 villages, Matriculation or Secondary School in 7 villages, namely Rudrangi, Mallial, Chandurthi, Marrigadda, Sangula, Bandapalle, Moodepalle.

Higher Secondary or Pre University Courses or Inter-mediate or Junior College in 1 village of the CD Block,, namely Rudrangi.

College in 0 village, Adult Literacy Center in 11 villages.

Medical: Hospital in 0 village, Dispensary in 1 village, Health Center in 1 village, Sub Center in 7 villages, Maternity and Child Welfare Center in 0 village, Community health workers in 0 village.

The Village having Hospital or Dispensary or Health Center is Rudrangi.

Drinking Water: Tap water in 12 villages, Tank water in 12 villages, Well water in 12 villages, Tubewell in 12 villages and more than one source in 12 villages.

Bank: Banking facility in 1 villages, namely, Rudrangi.

Credit Society in 11 villages Agricultural Credit Society in 2 Non-Agricultural Credit Society in 10 villages.

Others: Power supply in 12 villages, Cinema hall in 1 village, sport club in 0 village, Stadium or Auditorium or Community Hall in 0 village, Post Office in 11 villages.

There are 12 villages having bus facilities.

Village with most of facilities: Rudrangi.

Villages without Amenities (Education): None..

Scheduled Castes: Out of the total population of 40558 persons, 7427 persons (18.31%) belong to Scheduled Castes. The villages having less than 10% SC population are None..

The villages having more than 50% SC population are None.

Sex ratio of Scheduled Caste population is 506.

Scheduled Castes Literates and Illiterates by Sex:

	Persons	Males	Females
Literate	2,848	1,805	1,043
Illiterate	4,579	1,867	2,712
Literacy rate	43.9	56.4	31.7
Graduate	47	43	4

Scheduled Castes (Dominant):
Madiga, Mala, Beda Jangam etc., Anamuk Ellamalawar etc.

For their cultural identity please see Appendix-I

Villages without Scheduled Castes: There are 0 village without any scheduled caste population.

Scheduled Tribes: Out of the total population of 40558 persons, 932 persons (2.3%) belong to Scheduled Tribes. The villages having less than 10% ST population are Rudrangi, Mallial, Chandurthi, Thimmapuram(Pn) Ananthapalle(Pk), Marrigadda, Jogapuram, Lingampeta Bandapalle, Yangal, Moodepalle.

The villages having more than 50% ST population are None.

Sex ratio of Scheduled tribe population is 456.

Scheduled Tribes Literates and Illiterates by Sex:

	Persons	Males	Females
Literate	251	197	54
Illiterate	681	310	371
Literacy rate	32.4	46.7	15.3
Graduate	0	0	0

Scheduled Tribes (Dominant):
Sugalis etc., Yerukulas

For their cultural identity please see Appendix-II

Villages without Scheduled Tribes: There are 3 villages without any scheduled tribe population.

Literates and Illiterates by Sex (Total Population):

	Persons	Males	Females
Literate	16,023	10,300	5,723
Illiterate	24,535	9,779	14,756
Literacy rate	45	59	32
Graduate	259	236	23

Agriculture: ***Distribution of villages according to land use:*** Out of 12 villages, Total area (in hectare) is 20652, out of that 52.86 percent is cultivable and 34 percent of the cultivable area is irrigated.

Sources of Irrigation (Hectares): Government Canal 0, Private Canal 0, Well without Electricity 0, Well with Electricity 3475.19, Tubewell without Electricity 0, Tubewell with Electricity 236.75, Tank 0, River 0, Lake 0, Waterfall 0, Others 0.

Villages with population of 5000 to 9999:
Rudrangi, Chandurthi.

Villages with population of 10000 and above: None

Distribution of Workers:

	Persons	Males	Females	WPR
Cultivators	7,412	4,504	2,908	32.1
Agricultural Labour	7,105	3,638	3,467	30.77
Household Industry	5,375	916	4,459	23.28
Other Workers	3,198	2,424	774	13.85
Main Workers	21,763	11,052	10,711	94.25
Marginal Workers	1,327	430	897	5.75
Total Workers	23,090	11,482	11,608	

Religion: Major Religious Communities:

	Persons	Males	Females	Sex Ratio
Hindu (96.86%)	39,285	19,454	19,831	1,019
Muslim (2.59%)	1,052	527	525	996
Christian (0.54%)	221	98	123	1,255
Sikh (0%)	-	-	-	-
Buddhists (0%)	-	-	-	-
Jain (0%)	-	-	-	-

Agewise Data:

	Persons	Males	Females	Sex Ratio
All ages	40,558	20,079	20,479	1020
0-14	12,686	6,443	6,243	969
15-44	18,935	9,126	9,809	1075
45-79	8,521	4,285	4,236	989
80+	376	193	183	948
Age not stated	40	32	8	250

Languages (Dominant):
Telugu, Urdu, Hindi, Tamil, Marathi

Disabled Population:

	Persons	Males	Females	%
Total Disabled	527	294	233	
In Seeing	274	155	119	51.99
In Speech	45	19	26	8.54
In Hearing	22	6	16	4.17
In Movement	132	85	47	25.05
Mentally	54	29	25	10.25

CHAPAD

Chapad C.D. Block lies in the north-western part of Cuddapah district. The Block is located at a distance of 50 kms. from district headquarters (Cuddapah). There are 19 villages in the block with the total population of 39,153 persons. Area of the C.D. Block is 126.26 sq. kms. It is bounded in the north by Mandal Duvvur, in the south by river Penneru and Mandal Kamalapuram, in the east by Mandals Khajipet and S. Mydukur, and in the west by Mandal Proddatur.

Communications:

Roadways : State Highway (S.H.): Direction- Proddatur to S. Mydukur. Nearest Villages- Bhadripalle, Pallavolu, Chapad, Alladupalle.

River: Penneru Nadi- Nearest Villages- Ananthapuram,

Vedurur. Kundu Nadi- Nearest Villages- Madur, Chiyyapadu, Kethavaram, Chapad, Alladupalle, Peddaguruvalur, Budidapadu, Vedurur, Kutchupapa, Chinnagurvalur. Receives Backward Region Grants, and is identified as a drought-prone area as well.

Annual Rainfall: Average Rainfall 682 mm

Ground Water: Availability of the Ground Water in the Basin is 2618 H.A.M.and the utilization is 1745 H.A. M.It belongs to Safe category. Depth to water level varies from 5 to 10 meter below the ground. Most of the wells go down in summer months, according to the Ground Water Estimation Committee.

Natural Division : Rayalaseema Region

Administration:

Division: Rayala Seema. Parliamentary Constituency: 38 Kadapa. District: Cuddapah.

Mandal: Chapad. Assembly Constituency: 252 Mydukur. Gram Panchayat: 22.

Fairs and Festivals:

Baba Fakiruddin Saheb Urs : It is celebrated annually for three days from the thirteenth of Jamadi-us-sani (October-November) near his samadhi. Gandhothsavam is on the first day, urs on the second and the actual janda uthsavam i.e., taking the flag in a procession and tying to the tree is on the third. Rams and goats are sacrificed in every house in the name of the saint, palav is prepared and is distributed to the poor, the neighbours and guests etc., on the second day. The festival has been celebrated for the past 150 years. About 120 years ago cholera broke out in the village (Khaderpalle) which took away many lives. Fakiruddin appeared to an elderly man of the place in his dream and told him that if he was worshipped cholera would subside. The villagers decided to worship Baba, brought a branch of varagogu tree from Penukonda in Anantapur district, planted it in the middle of their village and worshipped it. Cholera subsided. The faith of the villagers in Baba Fakiruddin increased and they constructed a pial round the varagogu tree.

Villages: 19 **Inhabited:** 17 **Uninhabited:** 2

Ranking	District	State	National
Area	49	917	5374
Population	20	847	5771
Sex Ratio	8	365	1487
Child Sex Ratio	12	471	1774
Literacy Rate	34	365	3296
Density	19	588	3431
Work Participation Rate	6	346	1582

Gram Panchayats:

Alladupalle, Annavaram, Ayyavaripalli, Badripalli Chapadu, Chinnaguruvalur, Chiyyapadu, Khaderpalli Kutchupapa, Lakshmipeta, Madur, N.Obayapalli Nagulapalli, Pallavolu, Peddaguravalur, Rajuvaripeta Seetharama Puram, Siddareddipalli, Somapuram T.Obayapalli, Vedururu, Viswanadhapuram.

Amenities:

Education: Primary School in 16 villages, Middle school in 10 villages, Matriculation or Secondary School in 7 villages, namely Madur, Chiyyapadu, Somapuram, Chapad, Alladupalle, Vedurur, Chinnagurvalur.

Higher Secondary or Pre University Courses or Intermediate or Junior College in 0 village of the CD Block, College in 1 village, Adult Literacy Center in 1 village., College is in village, namely Alladupalle.

Medical: Hospital in 0 village, Dispensary in 1 village, Health Center in 1 village, Sub Center in 8 villages, Maternity and Child Welfare Center in 0 village, Community health workers in 0 village.

The Village having Hospital or Dispensary or Health Center is Ananthapuram.

Drinking Water: Tap water in 17 villages, Tank water in 17 villages, Well water in 17 villages, Tubewell in 17 villages and more than one source in 17 villages.

Bank: Banking facility in 4 villages, namely, Madur, Chiyyapadu, Chapad, Chinnagurvalur.

Credit Society in 4 villages Agricultural Credit Society in 3 Non-Agricultural Credit Society in 2 villages.

Others: Power supply in 17 villages, Cinema hall in 0 village, sport club in 0 village, Stadium or Auditorium or Community Hall in 0 village, Post Office in 12 villages.

There are 15 villages having bus facilities.

Village with most of facilities: Madur Chiyyapadu, Chapad, Chinnagurvalur.

Villages without amenities (Education):

Budidapadu..

Scheduled Castes: Out of the total population of 39153 persons, 8288 persons (21.17%) belong to Scheduled Castes. The villages having less than 10% SC population are None..

The villages having more than 50% SC population are None.

Sex ratio of Scheduled Caste population is 500.

Scheduled Castes Literates and Illiterates by Sex:

	Persons	Males	Females
Literate	3,522	2,200	1,322
Illiterate	4,766	1,942	2,824
Literacy rate	50.4	62.9	37.8
Graduate	64	55	9

Scheduled Castes (Dominant):

Mala, Madiga, Madiga Dasu etc., Adi Andhra

Mala Dasu

For their cultural identity please see Appendix-I

Villages without Scheduled Castes: There are 5 villages without any scheduled caste population.

Scheduled Tribes: Out of the total population of 39153 persons, 516 persons (1.32%) belong to Scheduled Tribes. The villages having less than 10% ST population are Madur, Vengannagaripalle, Chiyyapadu, Morrayapalle Pitchapadu, Somapuram, Bhadripalle, Nerrawada Chapad, Pallavolu, Alladupalle, Peddaguruvalur Ananthapuram, Vedurur, Kutchupapa, Chinnagurvalur. The villages having more than 50% ST population are None.

Sex ratio of Scheduled tribe population is 510.

Scheduled Tribes Literates and Illiterates by Sex:

	Persons	Males	Females
Literate	188	114	74
Illiterate	328	139	189
Literacy rate	42.6	51.8	33.5
Graduate	5	5	0

Scheduled Tribes (Dominant):

Yerukulas, Yenadis, Sugalis etc.

For their cultural identity please see Appendix-II

Villages without Scheduled Tribes: There are 7 villages without any scheduled tribe population.

Literates and Illiterates by Sex (Total Population):

	Persons	Males	Females
Literate	19,299	12,004	7,295
Illiterate	19,854	7,649	12,205
Literacy rate	57	71	43
Graduate	725	642	83

Agriculture: ***Distribution of villages according to land use:*** Out of 19 villages, Total area (in hectare) is 12625, out of that 74.59 percent is cultivable and 87.31 percent of the cultivable area is irrigated.

Sources of Irrigation (Hectares): Government Canal 4575.97, Private Canal 0, Well without Electricity 0, Well with Electricity 113.51, Tubewell without Electricity 0, Tubewell with Electricity 3249.7, Tank 0, River 0, Lake 0, Waterfall 0, Others 283.18.

Villages with population of 5000 to 9999: None

Villages with population of 10000 and above: None

Distribution of Workers:

	Persons	Males	Females	WPR
Cultivators	5,875	4,315	1,560	28.9
Agricultural Labour	10,600	4,822	5,778	52.15
Household Industry	406	179	227	2
Other Workers	3,446	2,300	1,146	16.95
Main Workers	17,032	10,578	6,454	83.79
Marginal Workers	3,295	1,038	2,257	16.21
Total Workers	20,327	11,616	8,711	

Religion: Major Religious Communities:

	Persons	Males	Females	Sex Ratio
Hindu (88.18%)	34,527	17,363	17,164	989
Muslim (11.08%)	4,340	2,160	2,180	1,009
Christian (0.61%)	240	104	136	1,308
Sikh (0%)	-	-	-	-
Buddhists (0%)	-	-	-	-
Jain (0%)	-	-	-	-

Agewise Data:

	Persons	Males	Females	Sex Ratio
All ages	39,153	19,653	19,500	992
0-14	12,316	6,288	6,028	959
15-44	18,580	9,429	9,151	971
45-79	8,023	3,832	4,191	1094
80+	185	75	110	1467
Age not stated	49	29	20	690

Languages (Dominant):

Telugu, Urdu, Gondi, Others, Kannada

Disabled Population:

	Persons	Males	Females	%
Total Disabled	537	309	228	
In Seeing	169	94	75	31.47
In Speech	56	31	25	10.43
In Hearing	31	16	15	5.77
In Movement	196	120	76	36.5
Mentally	85	48	37	15.83

CHATRAI

Chatrai C.D. Block lies in the north-eastern part of Krishna district. The Block is located at a distance of 115 kms. from district headquarters (Machilipatnam). There are 16 villages in the block with the total population of 51,558 persons. Area of the C.D. Block is 242.08 sq. kms. It is bounded in the north by districts Khammam and West Godavari, in the south by Mandal Musunuru, in the east by district West Godavari, and in the west by Vissanapet Mandal.

Communications:

Roadways : Metalled Roads: Nearest Villages- Krishnaraopalem, Chanubanda.

River: Tammileru Nadi- Nearest Villages- Chinnampet, Kotapadu, Mankollu, Polavaram, Somavaram, Kothagudem.

Annaul Rainfall: Average Rainfall 1018 mm

Ground Water: Availability of the Ground Water in the Basin is (Information not avavible) H.A.M .and the utilization is (Information not avavible) H.A.M. It belongs to (Information not avavible) category. Depth to water level varies from 3 to 10 meter below the ground. Most of the wells go down in summer months.

Natural Division : Krishna Delta Region

Administration:

Division: Coastal Andhra. Parliamentary Constituency: 27 Eluru. District: Krishna. Mandal: Chatrai. Assembly Constituency: 189 Nuzvid. Gram Panchayat: 18.

Villages: 16 **Inhabited:** 16 **Uninhabited:** 0

Ranking	District	State	National
Area	2	339	3481
Population	34	462	5199
Sex Ratio	41	920	3153
Child Sex Ratio	31	609	2475
Literacy Rate	46	385	3394
Density	12	649	4548
Work Participation Rate	48	668	1774

Gram Panchayats:

Arugolanu Peta, Burugugudem, Chanubanda, Chatrai Cheepurugudem, Chinnampeta, Chittapur Janardhanavaram, Kotapadu, Kothagudem Krishnaraopalem, Marlapalem, Narasimharaopalem Parvathapuram, Polavaram, Pothanapalli, Somavaram Tummagudem.

Amenities:

Education: Primary School in 16 villages, Middle school in 12 villages, Matriculation or Secondary School in 6 villages, namely Chanubanda, Chinnampet, Chatrai, Chittapur, Polavaram, Somavaram.

Higher Secondary or Pre University Courses or Intermediate or Junior College in 0 village of the CD Block, College in 0 village, Adult Literacy Center in 9 villages.

Medical: Hospital in 1 village, Dispensary in 2 villages, Health Center in 1 village, Sub Center in 7 villages, Maternity and Child Welfare Center in 0 village, Community health workers in 0 village.

The Villages having Hospital or Dispensary or Health Center are Chanubanda, Chatrai, Chittapur.

Drinking Water: Tap water in 12 villages, Tank water in 2 villages, Well water in 16 villages, Tubewell in 7 villages and more than one source in 16 villages.

Bank: Banking facility in 5 villages, namely, Chanubanda, Chinnampet, Chatrai, Tummagudem Polavaram.

Credit Society in 10 villages Agricultural Credit Society in 6 Non-Agricultural Credit Society in 10 villages.

Others: Power supply in 16 villages, Cinema hall in 3 villages, sport club in 0 village, Stadium or Auditorium or Community Hall in 0 village, Post Office in 11 villages.

There are 16 villages having bus facilities.

Villages with most of facilities: Chanubanda Chinnampet, Chatrai, Tummagudem, Polavaram.

Villages without Amenities (Education): None..

Scheduled Castes: Out of the total population of 51558 persons, 14377 persons (27.89%) belong to Scheduled Castes.

The villages having less than 10% SC population are None..

The villages having more than 50% SC population are None.

Sex ratio of Scheduled Caste population is 487.

Scheduled Castes Literates and Illiterates by Sex:

	Persons	Males	Females
Literate	6,118	3,438	2,680
Illiterate	8,259	3,934	4,325
Literacy rate	49.2	53.7	44.3
Graduate	129	101	28

Scheduled Castes (Dominant):

Madiga, Mala, Mala Dasari, Generic Castes etc. Mala Dasu

For their cultural identity please see Appendix-I

Villages without Scheduled Castes: There are 0 village without any scheduled caste population.

Scheduled Tribes: Out of the total population of 51558 persons, 1943 persons (3.77%) belong to Scheduled Tribes.

The villages having less than 10% ST population are Krishnaraopalem, Chanubanda, Parvatapuram Chinnampet, Kotapadu, Mankollu, Burugugudem, Chatrai Arugolanupeta, Chittapur, Tummagudem Janardhanavaram, Polavaram, Somavaram, Kothagudem.

The villages having more than 50% ST population are None.

Sex ratio of Scheduled tribe population is 495.

Scheduled Tribes Literates and Illiterates by Sex:

	Persons	Males	Females
Literate	516	272	244
Illiterate	1,427	710	717
Literacy rate	32.4	33.9	30.9
Graduate	29	21	8

Scheduled Tribes (Dominant):

Sugalis etc., Yerukulas, Gond etc., Yenadis Kondareddis

For their cultural identity please see Appendix-II

Villages without Scheduled Tribes: There are 2 villages without any scheduled tribe population.

Literates and Illiterates by Sex (Total Population):

	Persons	Males	Females
Literate	25,619	14,425	11,194
Illiterate	25,939	11,925	14,014
Literacy rate	57	62	51
Graduate	626	489	137

Agriculture: ***Distribution of villages according to land use:*** Out of 16 villages, Total area (in hectare) is 24208, out of that 59.79 percent is cultivable and 52.21 percent of the cultivable area is irrigated.

Sources of Irrigation (Hectares): Government Canal 2169.48, Private Canal 0, Well without Electricity 0, Well with Electricity 726.52, Tubewell without Electricity 0, Tubewell with Electricity 1072, Tank 3269, River 0, Lake 0, Waterfall 0, Others 352.

Villages with population of 5000 to 9999: Chanubanda, Kotapadu.

Villages with population of 10000 and above: None

Distribution of Workers:

	Persons	Males	Females	WPR
Cultivators	5,305	4,366	939	19.76
Agricultural Labour	17,703	8,724	8,979	65.94
Household Industry	1,027	566	461	3.83
Other Workers	2,814	2,331	483	10.48
Main Workers	19,962	13,983	5,979	74.35
Marginal Workers	6,887	2,004	4,883	25.65
Total Workers	26,849	15,987	10,862	

Religion: Major Religious Communities:

	Persons	Males	Females	Sex Ratio
Hindu (95.01%)	48,983	25,065	23,918	954
Muslim (2.24%)	1,157	579	578	998
Christian (2.66%)	1,369	681	688	1,010
Sikh (0%)	-	-	-	-
Buddhists (0.02%)	10	5	5	1,000
Jain (0%)	-	-	-	-

Agewise Data:

	Persons	Males	Females	Sex Ratio
All ages	51,558	26,350	25,208	957
0-14	15,955	8,125	7,830	964
15-44	25,060	12,926	12,134	939
45-79	10,124	5,090	5,034	989
80+	366	181	185	1022
Age not stated	53	28	25	893

Languages (Dominant):
Telugu, Urdu, Hindi, Gondi, Tamil

Disabled Population:

	Persons	Males	Females	%
Total Disabled	984	533	451	
In Seeing	350	179	171	35.57
In Speech	106	58	48	10.77
In Hearing	64	30	34	6.5
In Movement	314	189	125	31.91
Mentally	150	77	73	15.24

CHEBROLU

Chebrolu C.D. Block lies in the eastern part of Guntur district.The Block is located at a distance of 13 kms. from district headquarters (Guntur). There are 11 villages in the block with the total population of 68,814 persons. Area of the C.D. Block is 134.19 sq. kms. It is bounded in the north by Mandal Pedakakani, in the south by Mandals Ponnur and Tsundur, in the east by Mandals Tsundur and Tenali, and in the west by Mandals Guntur and Vatticherukuru.

Communications:

Roadways : State Highway (S.H.): Direction- Guntur to Bapatla. Nearest Villages- Manchala, Narakodur, Vejendla, Chebrolu.

Railway Station: Vejendla.

Annual Rainfall: Average Rainfall 952 mm

Ground Water: Availability of the Ground Water in the Basin is 6686 H.A.M. and the utilization is 531 H.A. M. It belongs to Safe category. Depth to water level varies from 2 to 5 meter below the ground. Most of the wells go down in summer months.

Natural Division : Krishna Delta Region

Administration:

Division: Coastal Andhra. Parliamentary Constituency: 30 Guntur. District: Guntur. Mandal: Chebrolu. Assembly Constituency: 207 Ponnur. Gram Panchayat: 13.

Places of Tourist Interest:

Chebrolu: Chebrolu, a very ancient village with many historical remains, is situated on the Guntur-Bapatla road within a distance of 10 kms. from Guntur. The high mound, on which the village is situated, has yield ed some terra-cotta figurines, as well as some old coins, which reveal the existence of ancient civilisation at this place. Two gold coins pertaining to the period of the Roman Emperor Constantine, were unearthed at this place. A number of lead coins containing the figur es of ships animals and mosques were also unearted.

Villages: 11 **Inhabited:** 10 **Uninhabited:** 1

Ranking	**District**	**State**	**National**
Area	35	886	5263
Population	8	143	4517
Sex Ratio	57	1063	4293
Child Sex Ratio	16	409	1561
Literacy Rate	17	167	2000
Density	49	780	2152
Work Participation Rate	9	101	2306

Gram Panchayats:

Chebrolu, Godavarru, Gundavaram, Manchala Narakoduru, Salapadu, Sekuru, Srirangapuram Sudda Palli, Thotlapalem, V.N.Palem, Vadlamudi Vejendla.

Amenities:

Education: Primary School in 10 villages, Middle school in 6 villages, Matriculation or Secondary School in 5 villages, namely Narakodur, Vejendla, Vadlamudi, Chebrolu, Pathareddipalem.

Higher Secondary or Pre University Courses or Inter-

mediate or Junior College in 3 villages of the CD Block,, namely Narakodur, Vadlamudi, Chebrolu.
College in 2 villages, Adult Literacy Center in 9 villages., Colleges are in villages, namely Vadlamudi, Chebrolu.
Medical: Hospital in 0 village, Dispensary in 3 villages, Health Center in 4 villages, Sub Center in 10 villages, Maternity and Child Welfare Center in 0 village, Community health workers in 0 village.
The Villages having Hospital or Dispensary or Health Center are Vejendla, Suddapalle, Sekuru, Vadlamudi, Pathareddipalem.
Drinking Water: Tap water in 10 villages, Tank water in 10 villages, Well water in 10 villages, Tubewell in 10 villages and more than one source in 10 villages.
Bank: Banking facility in 4 villages, namely, Narakodur, Vejendla, Vadlamudi, Chebrolu.
Credit Society in 3 villages Agricultural Credit Society in 2 Non-Agricultural Credit Society in 1 village.
Others: Power supply in 10 villages, Cinema hall in 2 villages, sport club in 0 village, Stadium or Auditorium or Community Hall in 0 village, Post Office in 10 villages.
There are 10 villages having bus facilities.
Villages with most of facilities: Narakodur Vejendla, Vadlamudi, Chebrolu.
Villages without Amenities (Education): None..
Scheduled Castes: Out of the total population of 68814 persons, 12774 persons (18.56%) belong to Scheduled Castes.
The villages having less than 10% SC population are None..
The villages having more than 50% SC population are None.
Sex ratio of Scheduled Caste population is 494.

Scheduled Castes Literates and Illiterates by Sex:

	Persons	Males	Females
Literate	7,079	4,011	3,068
Illiterate	5,695	2,453	3,242
Literacy rate	63.4	70.8	55.7
Graduate	267	200	67

Scheduled Castes (Dominant):
Madiga, Mala, Beda Jangam etc., Mala Dasu, Dom etc.
For their cultural identity please see Appendix-I
Villages without Scheduled Castes: There are 2 villages without any scheduled caste population.
Scheduled Tribes: Out of the total population of 68814 persons, 1952 persons (2.84%) belong to Scheduled Tribes.
The villages having less than 10% ST population are Godavarru, Narakodur, Vejendla, Suddapalle, Sekuru Vadlamudi, Sreerangapuram, Chebrolu, Pathareddipalem.
The villages having more than 50% ST population are None.
Sex ratio of Scheduled tribe population is 483.

Scheduled Tribes Literates and Illiterates by Sex:

	Persons	Males	Females
Literate	741	455	286
Illiterate	1,211	555	656
Literacy rate	44.2	52.4	35.4
Graduate	9	9	0

Scheduled Tribes (Dominant):
Yenadis, Yerukulas, Sugalis etc., Koya etc.
Chenchu etc.
For their cultural identity please see Appendix-II
Villages without Scheduled Tribes: There are 2 villages without any scheduled tribe population.

Literates and Illiterates by Sex (Total Population):

	Persons	Males	Females
Literate	39,551	22,985	16,566
Illiterate	29,263	12,596	16,667
Literacy rate	65	73	56
Graduate	1,701	1,271	430

Agriculture: ***Distribution of villages according to land use:*** Out of 11 villages, Total area (in hectare) is 13418, out of that 82.59 percent is cultivable and 68.6 percent of the cultivable area is irrigated.
Sources of Irrigation (Hectares): Government Canal 6934, Private Canal 0, Well without Electricity 578, Well with Electricity 51, Tubewell without Electricity 8, Tubewell with Electricity 11, Tank 20, River 0, Lake 0, Waterfall 0, Others 0.
Villages with population of 5000 to 9999:
Narakodur, Vejendla, Vadlamudi.
Villages with population of 10000 and above:
Sekuru, Chebrolu, Pathareddipalem.

Distribution of Workers:

	Persons	Males	Females	WPR
Cultivators	5,673	4,305	1,368	16.25
Agricultural Labour	19,274	8,908	10,366	55.22
Household Industry	1,042	612	430	2.99
Other Workers	8,918	7,325	1,593	25.55
Main Workers	29,679	19,429	10,250	85.02
Marginal Workers	5,228	1,721	3,507	14.98
Total Workers	34,907	21,150	13,757	

Religion: Major Religious Communities:

	Persons	Males	Females	Sex Ratio
Hindu (85.46%)	58,811	30,431	28,380	933
Muslim (11.75%)	8,086	4,140	3,946	953
Christian (2.52%)	1,735	917	818	892
Sikh (0.08%)	54	28	26	929
Buddhists (0.03%)	20	11	9	818
Jain (0.02%)	15	9	6	667

Agewise Data:

	Persons	Males	Females	Sex Ratio
All ages	68,814	35,581	33,233	934
0-14	18,999	9,560	9,439	987
15-44	34,629	18,525	16,104	869
45-79	14,402	7,107	7,295	1026
80+	688	332	356	1072
Age not stated	96	57	39	684

Languages (Dominant):
Telugu, Urdu, Hindi, Tamil, Gondi

Disabled Population:

	Persons	Males	Females	%
Total Disabled	1,227	666	561	
In Seeing	410	206	204	33.41
In Speech	165	91	74	13.45
In Hearing	74	27	47	6.03
In Movement	381	237	144	31.05
Mentally	197	105	92	16.06

CHEEDIKADA

Cheedikada C.D. Block lies in the north-eastern part of Vishakhapatnam district. The Block is located at a distance of 108 kms. from district headquarters (Vish akhapatnam). There are 34 villages in the block with the total population of 45,630 persons. Area of the C.D. Block is 122.66 sq. kms. It is bounded in the north by Mandals Hukumpeta and Devarapalle, in the south by Mandals Madugula and Chodavaram, in the east by Mandal Devarapalle, and in the west by Mandals Madug ula and Paderu.

Communications :

Roadways : Metalled Roads: Nearest Village- Chukkapalle.

River: Budderu Nadi- Nearest Villages- Veerabhadrapeta, Konam, Manchala, Jaithavaram, Sirijam, Khandivara Agraharam, Lingabhupala Patnam, Appalarajupuram, Bylapu di Singavaram, Bylapudi, Dibbapalem, Kattuvari Agraharam, Dandi Suravaram.

Annaual Rainfall: Average Rainfall 975.0 mm

Ground Water: Availability of the Ground Water in the Basin is (Information not avavible) H.A.M .and the utilization is (Information not avavible) H.A.M. It belongs to (Information not avavible) category. Depth to water level varies from 3 to 10 meter below the ground. Most of the wells go down in summer months.

Administration:

Division: Coastal Andhra. Parliamentary Constituency: 22 Anakapalle. District: Visakhapatnam. Mandal: Cheedik ada. Assembly Constituency: 146 Maduguda Gram Panchayat: 23

Villages: 34 **Inhabited:** 30 **Uninhabited:** 4

Ranking	District	State	National
Area	33	935	5431
Population	35	641	5478
Sex Ratio	13	111	695
Child Sex Ratio	22	263	835
Literacy Rate	22	869	5148
Density	12	238	2939
Work Participation Rate	16	230	629

Gram Panchayats:

Adivi Agraharam, Appalarajupuram, Arjunagiri Bylapoudi Singavaram, Bylapudi, Cheedikada Cheedipalle, Chettupalle, Chukkapalle Dandi Suravaram, Dibbapalem, G. Kothapalle J.B. Puram, Jaithavaram, Khandivara, Konam Lingabhupala Patnam, Manchala, Pedagogada, Sirijam Tuni Valasa, Turuvolu, Veerabhadrapeta.

Amenities:

Education: Primary School in 30 villages, Middle school in 17 villages, Matriculation or Secondary School in 6 villages, namely Konam, Cheedikada, Turuvolu, Khandivara Agraharam, Lingabhupala Patnam, Appalarajupuram.

Higher Secondary or Pre University Courses or Inter-mediate or Junior College in 0 village of the CD Block, College in 0 village, Adult Literacy Center in 17 villages.

Medical: Hospital in 0 village, Dispensary in 1 village, Health Center in 11 villages, Sub Center in 10 villages, Maternity and Child Welfare Center in 0 village, Community health workers in 0 village.

The Village having Hospital or Dispensary or Health Center is Khandivara Agraharam.

Drinking Water: Tap water in 30 villages, Tank water in 30 villages, Well water in 30 villages, Tubewell in 30 villages and more than one source in 30 villages.

Bank: Banking facility in 1 villages, namely, Cheedikada.

Credit Society in 4 villages Agricultural Credit Society in 4 Non-Agricultural Credit Society in 0 village.

Others: Power supply in 30 villages, Cinema hall in 2 villages, sport club in 0 village, Stadium or Auditorium or Community Hall in 0 village, Post Office in 16 villages.

There are 15 villages having bus facilities.

Village with most of facilities: Cheedikada.

Villages without Amenities (Education): None..

Scheduled Castes: Out of the total population of 45630 persons, 2815 persons (6.17%) belong to Scheduled Castes. The villages having less than 10% SC population are Manchala, Cheedikada, Neelampeta Cheedipalle Agraharam, Arjunagiri Agraharam Turuvolu, Tangudubilli, G.Kothapalle, Jaithavaram Sirijam, Khandivara Agraharam, Bylapudi Singavaram Bylapudi, Dibbapalem, Kattuvari Agraharam

Dandi Suravaram, Tuni Valasa, Vintipalem
Advi Agraharam, Chinagogada, Pedagogada Agraharam
Chettupalle, Varahapura Agraharam, J.B.Puram
Chukkapalle.

The villages having more than 50% SC population are None.

Sex ratio of Scheduled Caste population is 528.

Scheduled Castes Literates and Illiterates by Sex:

	Persons	Males	Females
Literate	1,208	644	564
Illiterate	1,607	684	923
Literacy rate	48.4	55.3	42.3
Graduate	14	12	2

Scheduled Castes (Dominant):

Mala, Madiga, Relli, Adi Andhra, Generic Castes etc.

For their cultural identity please see Appendix-I

Villages without Scheduled Castes: There are 5 villages without any scheduled caste population.

Scheduled Tribes: Out of the total population of 45630 persons, 3115 persons (6.83%) belong to Scheduled Tribes.

The villages having less than 10% ST population are
Cheedikada, Vellanki, Neelampeta
Cheedipalle Agraharam, Arjunagiri Agraharam
Turuvolu, Tangudubilli, G.Kothapalle, Jaithavaram
Sirijam, Khandivara Agraharam, Lingabhupala Patnam
Appalarajupuram, Bylapudi Singavaram, Bylapudi
Dibbapalem, Kattuvari Agraharam, Dandi Suravaram
Tuni Valasa, Vintipalem, Advi Agraharam, Chinagogada
Pedagogada Agraharam, Chettupalle
Varahapura Agraharam, J.B.Puram, Chukkapalle.

The villages having more than 50% ST population are None.

Sex ratio of Scheduled tribe population is 488.

Scheduled Tribes Literates and Illiterates by Sex:

	Persons	Males	Females
Literate	963	618	345
Illiterate	2,152	978	1,174
Literacy rate	35.2	44.1	25.8
Graduate	5	4	1

Scheduled Tribes (Dominant):

Konda Dhoras, Gadabas, Bagata, Yerukulas
Reddi Dhoras

For their cultural identity please see Appendix-II

Villages without Scheduled Tribes: There are 20 villages without any scheduled tribe population.

Literates and Illiterates by Sex (Total Population):

	Persons	Males	Females
Literate	18,278	11,713	6,565
Illiterate	27,352	10,899	16,453
Literacy rate	46	59	32
Graduate	366	311	55

Agriculture: ***Distribution of villages according to land use:*** Out of 34 villages, Total area (in hectare) is 12266, out of that 70.15 percent is cultivable and 36.24 percent of the cultivable area is irrigated.

Sources of Irrigation (Hectares): Government Canal 399.98, Private Canal 0, Well without Electricity 0, Well with Electricity 0, Tubewell without Electricity 0, Tubewell with Electricity 10.52, Tank 2484.55, River 0, Lake 0, Waterfall 0, Others 223.25.

Villages with population of 5000 to 9999: None

Villages with population of 10000 and above: None

Distribution of Workers:

	Persons	Males	Females	WPR
Cultivators	11,238	6,726	4,512	43.12
Agricultural Labour	10,224	4,142	6,082	39.23
Household Industry	857	444	413	3.29
Other Workers	3,744	2,626	1,118	14.37
Main Workers	22,728	13,115	9,613	87.2
Marginal Workers	3,335	823	2,512	12.8
Total Workers	26,063	13,938	12,125	

Religion: Major Religious Communities:

	Persons	Males	Females	Sex Ratio
Hindu (99.13%)	45,233	22,423	22,810	1,017
Muslim (0.37%)	167	77	90	1,169
Christian (0.34%)	153	64	89	1,391
Sikh (0.02%)	9	4	5	1,250
Buddhists (0%)	1	1	-	-
Jain (0%)	-	-	-	-

Agewise Data:

	Persons	Males	Females	Sex Ratio
All ages	45,630	22,612	23,018	1018
0-14	13,788	7,145	6,643	930
15-44	21,301	10,530	10,771	1023
45-79	10,256	4,803	5,453	1135
80+	170	71	99	1394
Age not stated	115	63	52	825

Languages (Dominant):

Telugu, Gadaba, Tamil, Gondi, Oriya

Disabled Population:

	Persons	Males	Females	%
Total Disabled	839	453	386	
In Seeing	384	190	194	45.77
In Speech	102	62	40	12.16
In Hearing	43	17	26	5.13
In Movement	254	152	102	30.27
Mentally	56	32	24	6.67

CHEEPURUPALLE

Cheepurupalle C.D. Block lies in the southern part of Vizianagaram district. The Block is located at a distance of 30 kms. from district headquarters (Viziana garam). There are 32 villages in the block with the total population of 58,968 persons. Area of the C.D. Block is 122.02 sq. kms. It is bounded in the north and south by Mandal Garividi and district Srikakulam in the east by district Srikakulam, and in the west by Mandal Gadividi.

Communications :

Roadways : State Highway (S.H.): Direction- Cheepurupalle to Srikakulam. Nearest Villages- Anjaneyapuram, Gulivi ndada Agraharam, Cheepurupalle.

Ba

ckwards Region Grants Fund: It receives Backward Region Grants.

Integrated Child Development Scheme (ICDS) Project: Cheepurupalli, Total Anganwadi Centres: 210.

Annaul Rainfall: Average Rainfall 1154.8 mm

Ground Water: Availability of the Ground Water in the Basin is (Information not avavible) H.A.M .and the utilization is (Information not avavible) H.A.M. It belongs to (Information not avavible) category. Depth to water level varies from 3 to 10 meter below the ground. Most of the wells go down in summer months.

Administration:

Division: Coastal Andhra. Parliamentary Constituency: 20 Vizianagram. District: Vizianagram. Mandal: Cheepuru palle. Assembly Constituency: 134 Cheepurupalle. Gram Panchayat: 17.

Places of Tourist Interest:

Cheepurupalle : Cheepurupalle has a railway station on the Howrah Madras broad-guage line and is also well connected by road. There is an old ruined fort existing in the place. Three sets of copper-plate inscriptions were found in the place in 1867. A.D. and one of them records a grant made by the Eastern Chalukya ruler, Vishnuvardhana-I, who flourished from 615 A.D. to 633 A.D. Handloom weaving is an important industry of this place.

Villages: 32 **Inhabited:** 30 **Uninhabited:** 2

Ranking	District	State	National
Area	30	938	5437
Population	8	289	4890
Sex Ratio	7	97	662
Child Sex Ratio	15	183	518
Literacy Rate	6	636	4345
Density	34	844	2292
Work Participation Rate	3	118	2657

Gram Panchayats:

Alajangi, Cheepurupalli, Devarapodilam, G.Mulagam Gollalapalem, Itakarlapalli, Karakam, Karlam Mettapalli, Nimmavalasa, P.K Palavalasa, Parla Pathikayavalasa, Pedanadipalli, Peripi Ramalingapuram, Ravivalasa.

Amenities:

Education: Primary School in 30 villages, Middle school in 6 villages, Matriculation or Secondary School in 3 villages, namely Cheepurupalle, Mettapalle, Peddanadi Palle. Higher Secondary or Pre University Courses or Intermediate or Junior College in 1 village of the CD Block,, namely Cheepurupalle.

College in 0 village, Adult Literacy Center in 22 villages.

Medical: Hospital in 1 village, Dispensary in 0 village, Health Center in 2 villages, Sub Center in 9 villages, Maternity and Child Welfare Center in 0 village, Community health workers in 0 village.

The Village having Hospital or Dispensary or Health Center is Cheepurupalle.

Drinking Water: Tap water in 30 villages, Tank water in 30 villages, Well water in 30 villages, Tubewell in 30 villages and more than one source in 30 villages.

Bank: Banking facility in 5 villages, namely, Gulivindada Agraharam, Cheepurupalle, Mettapalle Anjaneyapuram, Karlam.

Credit Society in 8 villages Agricultural Credit Society in 3 Non-Agricultural Credit Society in 6 villages.

Others: Power supply in 30 villages, Cinema hall in 2 villages, sport club in 0 village, Stadium or Auditorium or Community Hall in 0 village, Post Office in 12 villages.

There are 22 villages having bus facilities.

Villages with most of facilities: Gulivindada Agraharam Cheepurupalle, Mettapalle, Anjaneyapuram, Karlam.

Villages without Amenities (Education): None..

Scheduled Castes: Out of the total population of 58968 persons, 6156 persons (10.44%) belong to Scheduled Castes. The villages having less than 10% SC population are Gulivindada Agraharam, Purreyavalasa, Anjaneyapuram Vijayarampuram, Aridivalasa, Peripi Purushothama Swamivari Lakshmipuram, Parla Sankupalem, Karlam, Palavalasa Bhoolokapathivarakattu.

The villages having more than 50% SC population are None.

Sex ratio of Scheduled Caste population is 547.

Scheduled Castes Literates and Illiterates by Sex:

	Persons	Males	Females
Literate	2,803	1,420	1,383
Illiterate	3,353	1,371	1,982
Literacy rate	53.2	59.5	48.0
Graduate	120	87	33

Scheduled Castes (Dominant):

Mala, Madiga, Relli, Dom etc., Generic Castes etc.
For their cultural identity please see Appendix-I
Villages without Scheduled Castes: There are 6 villages without any scheduled caste population.
Scheduled Tribes: Out of the total population of 58968 persons, 493 persons (0.84%) belong to Scheduled Tribes. The villages having less than 10% ST population are Gulivindada Agraharam, Cheepurupalle, Purreyavalasa Ramalingapuram, Viswanadhapuram, Mettapalle Alajangi, Ravivalasa, Anjaneyapuram, Vijayarampuram Aridivalasa, Peripi Purushothama Swamivari Lakshmipuram, Parla Pothayavalasa (Itakarlapalle), Itikarlapalle Gollalamulagam, Gollalapalem, Chinanadipalle Peddanadi Palle, Gatchalavalasa, Karakam, Sankupalem Karlam, Pathikayavalasa, Nimmalavalasa Devarapodilam, Gunidam, Palavalasa Bhoolokapathivarakattu.
The villages having more than 50% ST population are None.
Sex ratio of Scheduled tribe population is 509.
Scheduled Tribes Literates and Illiterates by Sex:

	Persons	Males	Females
Literate	197	97	100
Illiterate	296	145	151
Literacy rate	46.0	47.3	44.8
Graduate	4	3	1

Scheduled Tribes (Dominant):
Konda Dhoras, Yerukulas, Jatapus, Kondhs etc. Gadabas
For their cultural identity please see Appendix-II
Villages without Scheduled Tribes: There are 16 villages without any scheduled tribe population.
Literates and Illiterates by Sex (Total Population):

	Persons	Males	Females
Literate	26,098	15,435	10,663
Illiterate	32,870	13,756	19,114
Literacy rate	51	61	41
Graduate	1,597	1,232	365

Agriculture: ***Distribution of villages according to land use:*** Out of 32 villages, Total area (in hectare) is 12202, out of that 77.2 percent is cultivable and 14.48 percent of the cultivable area is irrigated.
Sources of Irrigation (Hectares): Government Canal 0, Private Canal 0, Well without Electricity 0, Well with Electricity 0, Tubewell without Electricity 0, Tubewell with Electricity 0, Tank 1364.12, River 0, Lake 0, Waterfall 0, Others 0.
Villages with population of 5000 to 9999:
Gulivindada Agraharam.
Villages with population of 10000 and above:
Cheepurupalle.
Distribution of Workers:

	Persons	Males	Females	WPR
Cultivators	6,006	4,377	1,629	21.18
Agricultural Labour	14,053	6,134	7,919	49.55
Household Industry	1,297	737	560	4.57
Other Workers	7,005	5,888	1,117	24.7
Main Workers	18,443	14,162	4,281	65.03
Marginal Workers	9,918	2,974	6,944	34.97
Total Workers	28,361	17,136	11,225	

Religion: Major Religious Communities:

	Persons	Males	Females	Sex Ratio
Hindu (98.69%)	58,196	28,826	29,370	1,019
Muslim (0.54%)	316	158	158	1,000
Christian (0.61%)	358	161	197	1,224
Sikh (0.01%)	6	4	2	500
Buddhists (0%)	-	-	-	-
Jain (0.01%)	4	2	2	1,000

Agewise Data:

	Persons	Males	Females	Sex Ratio
All ages	58,968	29,191	29,777	1020
0-14	19,231	9,624	9,607	998
15-44	27,904	13,797	14,107	1022
45-79	11,480	5,622	5,858	1042
80+	246	97	149	1536
Age not stated	107	51	56	1098

Languages (Dominant):
Telugu, Hindi, Oriya, Urdu, Tamil
Disabled Population:

	Persons	Males	Females	%
Total Disabled	1,599	876	723	
In Seeing	815	424	391	50.97
In Speech	140	76	64	8.76
In Hearing	106	52	54	6.63
In Movement	402	245	157	25.14
Mentally	136	79	57	8.51

CHEGUNTA

Chegunta C.D. Block lies in the north-east part of Medak district. The Block is located at a distance of 68 kms. from district headquarters (Sangareddy). There are 29 villages in the block with the total population of 530,85 persons. Area of the C.D. Block is 207.97 sq. kms. It is bounded by Ramayampet Mandal on north, Mirdoddi Mandal on north-east, Doultabad Mandal on east, Tupran Mandal on south, Veldurthy Mandal on south-west, and Shankarampet (R) Mandal on west.
Communications :
Roadways : NH- 7: Direction- Nizamabad to Hyderabad. Nearest Villages- Vallabhapur, Bheemraopalle, Ulli

Thimmaipalle, Reddipalle, Narsingi, Valloor, Chegunta, Wadiaram.

Railway Station: Chegunta.

Backwards Region Grants Fund: It receives Backward Region Grants.

Annual Rainfall: Average Rainfall 983 mm

Ground Water : Availability of the Ground Water in the Basin is 1986 H.A.M. and the utilization is 2105 H.A.M. It belongs to Over Exploited category. Depth to water level varies from 5 meter below the ground. Most of the wells go down in summer months. The well density in the entire block is 14 wells per sq. km. Total no. of the wells in the block are enumerated as 2850, according to the Ground Water Estimation Committee.

Natural Division : Telangana Plateau Region

Administration:

Division: Telangana. Parliamentary Constituency: 6 Medak. District: Medak. Mandal: Chegunta. Assembly Constituency: 41 Dubbak. Gram Panchayat: 29.

Villages: 29 **Inhabited:** 29 **Uninhabited:** 0

Ranking	District	State	National
Area	25	503	4042
Population	17	416	5129
Sex Ratio	12	224	1117
Child Sex Ratio	29	633	2524
Literacy Rate	26	877	5189
Density	20	473	4013
Work Participation Rate	19	519	1201

Gram Panchayats:

Ananthasagar, Bonala, Bonala Kondapur, Chandaipet Chegunta, Chetla Thimmaipalli, Chinna Shivnoor Chittojipalle, Gollapalle, Govindapur, Ibrahimpur Kamalpalle, Kasanpalle, Kondapur[Bonal], Makkarajpet Maldarajpally, Narsampalle, Narsingi, Peddashivnoor Polampalle, Pothanpalle, Pulamamidi, Rampur Reddipalle, Rukmapur, Ulli Thimmaipalle, Upperpalle Valloor, Wadiaram.

Amenities:

Education: Primary School in 29 villages, Middle school in 13 villages, Matriculation or Secondary School in 8 villages, namely Narsingi, Ibrahimpur, Reddipalle, Polampalle, Chegunta, Wadiaram, Makkarajpet, Chandaipet.

Higher Secondary or Pre University Courses or Intermediate or Junior College in 1 village of the CD Block,, namely Wadiaram.

College in 0 village, Adult Literacy Center in 16 villages.

Medical: Hospital in 0 village, Dispensary in 1 village, Health Center in 3 villages, Sub Center in 8 villages, Maternity and Child Welfare Center in 12 villages, Community health workers in 0 village.

The Villages having Hospital or Dispensary or Health Center are Narsingi, Ibrahimpur.

Drinking Water: Tap water in 29 villages, Tank water in 29 villages, Well water in 29 villages, Tubewell in 29 villages and more than one source in 29 villages.

Bank: Banking facility in 2 villages, namely, Narsingi, Chegunta.

Credit Society in 18 villages Agricultural Credit Society in 7 Non-Agricultural Credit Society in 18 villages.

Others: Power supply in 29 villages, Cinema hall in 1 village, sport club in 1 village, Stadium or Auditorium or Community Hall in 0 village, Post Office in 11 villages.

There are 23 villages having bus facilities.

Villages with most of facilities: Narsingi Chegunta.

Villages without Amenities (Education): None..

Scheduled Castes: Out of the total population of 53085 persons, 9017 persons (16.99%) belong to Scheduled Castes. The villages having less than 10% SC population are Gollapalle, Reddipalle, Chegunta, Chetlathimmaipalli Kasanpalle.

The villages having more than 50% SC population are None.

Sex ratio of Scheduled Caste population is 507.

Scheduled Castes Literates and Illiterates by Sex:

	Persons	Males	Females
Literate	2,545	1,690	855
Illiterate	6,472	2,755	3,717
Literacy rate	32.9	44.7	21.6
Graduate	17	14	3

Scheduled Castes (Dominant):

Madiga, Mala, Generic Castes etc., Beda Jangam etc. Byagara

For their cultural identity please see Appendix-I

Villages without Scheduled Castes: There is 1 village without any scheduled caste population.

Scheduled Tribes: Out of the total population of 53085 persons, 3635 persons (6.85%) belong to Scheduled Tribes. The villages having less than 10% ST population are Narsingi, Bheemraopalle, Rukmapur, Ibrahimpur Kistapur, Pulamamidi, Bonal, Kondapur [Bonal] Upperpalle, Govindapur, Ananthasagar Ulli Thimmaipalle, Reddipalle, Valloor, Polampalle Chegunta, Wadiaram, Chinna Shivnoor, Makkarajpet Chandaipet, Pothampalle.

The villages having more than 50% ST population are None.

Sex ratio of Scheduled tribe population is 494.

Scheduled Tribes Literates and Illiterates by Sex:

	Persons	Males	Females
Literate	613	452	161
Illiterate	3,022	1,389	1,633
Literacy rate	21.2	30.6	11.4
Graduate	0	0	0

Scheduled Tribes (Dominant):

Sugalis etc., Yerukulas, Generic Tribes etc.

For their cultural identity please see Appendix-II

Villages without Scheduled Tribes: There are 6 villages without any scheduled tribe population.

Literates and Illiterates by Sex (Total Population):

	Persons	Males	Females
Literate	20,485	13,347	7,138
Illiterate	32,600	13,182	19,418
Literacy rate	45	59	31
Graduate	562	474	88

Agriculture: ***Distribution of villages according to land use:*** Out of 29 villages, Total area (in hectare) is 20797, out of that 58.8 percent is cultivable and 61.78 percent of the cultivable area is irrigated.

Sources of Irrigation (Hectares): Government Canal 1203.58, Private Canal 0, Well without Electricity 0, Well with Electricity 0, Tubewell without Electricity 0, Tubewell with Electricity 2898.79, Tank 1198.92, River 0, Lake 0, Waterfall 2253.35, Others 0.

Villages with population of 5000 to 9999: Narsingi, Chegunta.

Villages with population of 10000 and above: None

Distribution of Workers:

	Persons	Males	Females	WPR
Cultivators	12,322	7,746	4,576	43.95
Agricultural Labour	7,676	3,045	4,631	27.38
Household Industry	2,551	480	2,071	9.1
Other Workers	5,490	3,873	1,617	19.58
Main Workers	23,886	13,703	10,183	85.19
Marginal Workers	4,153	1,441	2,712	14.81
Total Workers	28,039	15,144	12,895	

Religion: Major Religious Communities:

	Persons	Males	Females	Sex Ratio
Hindu (92.64%)	49,176	24,557	24,619	1,003
Muslim (6.8%)	3,610	1,821	1,789	982
Christian (0.4%)	212	102	110	1,078
Sikh (0.02%)	10	10	-	-
Buddhists (0%)	-	-	-	-
Jain (0.01%)	5	2	3	1,500

Agewise Data:

	Persons	Males	Females	Sex Ratio
All ages	53,085	26,529	26,556	1001
0-14	17,877	9,196	8,681	944
15-44	24,415	12,144	12,271	1010
45-79	10,352	5,014	5,338	1065
80+	392	148	244	1649
Age not stated	49	27	22	815

Languages (Dominant):

Telugu, Urdu, Hindi, Tamil, Oriya

Disabled Population:

	Persons	Males	Females	%
Total Disabled	907	527	380	
In Seeing	383	222	161	42.23
In Speech	114	62	52	12.57
In Hearing	48	22	26	5.29
In Movement	267	169	98	29.44
Mentally	95	52	43	10.47

CHEJERLA

Chejerla C.D. Block lies in the western part of Nellore district. The Block is located at a distance of 55 kms. from district headquarters (Nellore). There are 18 villages in the block with the total population of 33,755 persons. Area of the C.D. Block is 310.26 sq. kms. It is bounded in the north by River Pennar and Mandals Ananthasagaram, Atmakur and Sangam, in the south by Mandals Kaluvoya and Podalakur, in the east by Mandal Podalakur, and in the west by Mandal Kaluvoya.

Communications:

Roadways : Metalled Roads: Nearest Villages- Kotitheertham, Kakivaya, Nagulavellaturu, Chejerla, Thimmayapalem, Gollapalle, Perumallapadu, Pelleru, Mamuduru, Pathapadu, Paderu, Vavileru, Chittaluru, Nernoor, Yeturu.

River: Pennar Nadi- Nearest Villages- Kotitheertham, Chejerla, Thimmayapalem, Perumallapadu, Pelleru, Mamuduru.

Annual Rainfall: Average Rainfall 935 mm

Ground Water: Availability of the Ground Water in the Basin is 6016 H.A.M. and the utilization is 2501 H.A.M. It belongs to Safe category. Depth to water level varies from 5 to 10 meter below the ground. Most of the wells go down in summer months, according to the Ground Water Estimation Committee.

Administration:

Division: Coastal Andhra. Parliamentary Constituency: 39 Nellore.District: Nellore.

Mandal: Chejerla. Assembly Constituency:: 234 Atmakur.

Gram Panchayat: 22.

Places of Tourist Interest:

Chejerla : This village is situated 22 kms. north-east of Narasaraopet. It is reputed for its temple of Kapoteswara, one of the very earliest Hindu temples in the Andhra area, the origin of which dates back to the third or fourth century A.D.

Villages: 18 **Inhabited:** 18 **Uninhabited:** 0

Ranking	District	State	National
Area	11	143	2674
Population	38	960	5953
Sex Ratio	36	700	2353
Child Sex Ratio	45	1033	4906
Literacy Rate	16	203	2294
Density	24	818	6061
Work Participation Rate	40	1033	2499

Gram Panchayats:
Adurupalli, Bodipadu, Chejerla, Chithaluru
Gollapalli, Kakivaya, Kotitheertham, Madapalli
Mamuduru, Nagula Vellaturu, Nernuru
Nutakivari Kandriga, Obulayapalli, Paderu, Pathapadu
Pelleru, Perumallapadu, Thimmayapalem
Turpu Khambhampadu, Vavileru, Yanamadala, Yeturu.

Amenities:

Education: Primary School in 18 villages, Middle school in 8 villages, Matriculation or Secondary School in 4 villages, namely Kotitheertham, Nagulavellaturu, Pelleru, Mamuduru.

Higher Secondary or Pre University Courses or Intermediate or Junior College in 0 village of the CD Block, College in 0 village, Adult Literacy Center in 16 villages.

Medical: Hospital in 1 village, Dispensary in 3 villages, Health Center in 1 village, Sub Center in 10 villages, Maternity and Child Welfare Center in 0 village, Community health workers in 0 village.

The Villages having Hospital or Dispensary or Health Center are Kotitheertham, Pelleru, Chittaluru.

Drinking Water: Tap water in 18 villages, Tank water in 18 villages, Well water in 18 villages, Tubewell in 18 villages and more than one source in 18 villages.

Bank: Banking facility in 3 villages, namely, Chejerla, Mamuduru, Chittaluru.

Credit Society in 14 villages Agricultural Credit Society in 7 Non-Agricultural Credit Society in 14 villages.

Others: Power supply in 18 villages, Cinema hall in 0 village, sport club in 0 village, Stadium or Auditorium or Community Hall in 0 village, Post Office in 14 villages.

There are 17 villages having bus facilities.

Villages with most of facilities: Chejerla Mamuduru, Chittaluru.

Villages without Amenities (Education): None..

Scheduled Castes: Out of the total population of 33755 persons, 6927 persons (20.52%) belong to Scheduled Castes.

The villages having less than 10% SC population are None..

The villages having more than 50% SC population are None.

Sex ratio of Scheduled Caste population is 496.

Scheduled Castes Literates and Illiterates by Sex:

	Persons	Males	Females
Literate	3,494	2,057	1,437
Illiterate	3,433	1,434	1,999
Literacy rate	58.8	69.1	48.6
Graduate	36	25	11

Scheduled Castes (Dominant):
Madiga, Mala, Arundhatiya, Generic Castes etc.
Adi Andhra

For their cultural identity please see Appendix-I

Villages without Scheduled Castes: There is 1 village without any scheduled caste population.

Scheduled Tribes: Out of the total population of 33755 persons, 1955 persons (5.79%) belong to Scheduled Tribes.

The villages having less than 10% ST population are Kotitheertham, Billupadu, Kakivaya, Nagulavellaturu Chejerla, Thimmayapalem, Perumallapadu, Pelleru Mamuduru, Pathapadu, Paderu, Vavileru, Chittaluru Nernoor, Yeturu.

The villages having more than 50% ST population are None.

Sex ratio of Scheduled tribe population is 484.

Scheduled Tribes Literates and Illiterates by Sex:

	Persons	Males	Females
Literate	529	270	259
Illiterate	1,426	738	688
Literacy rate	33.0	33.3	32.7
Graduate	3	3	0

Scheduled Tribes (Dominant):
Yenadis, Yerukulas, Generic Tribes etc., Kammara

For their cultural identity please see Appendix-II

Villages without Scheduled Tribes: There are 0 village without any scheduled tribe population.

Literates and Illiterates by Sex (Total Population):

	Persons	Males	Females
Literate	18,685	10,936	7,749
Illiterate	15,070	6,176	8,894
Literacy rate	63	73	53
Graduate	500	406	94

Agriculture: ***Distribution of villages according to land use:*** Out of 18 villages, Total area (in hectare) is 31025, out of that 41.2 percent is cultivable and 35.8 percent of the cultivable area is irrigated.

Sources of Irrigation (Hectares): Government Canal 0, Private Canal 1009, Well without Electricity 0, Well with Electricity 1456, Tubewell without Electricity 0, Tubewell with Electricity 1150, Tank 727, River 0, Lake 0, Waterfall 0, Others 233.

Villages with population of 5000 to 9999:

Chejerla.

Villages with population of 10000 and above: None

Distribution of Workers:

	Persons	Males	Females	WPR
Cultivators	5,121	3,995	1,126	30.61
Agricultural Labour	7,240	3,380	3,860	43.28
Household Industry	459	228	231	2.74
Other Workers	3,910	2,681	1,229	23.37
Main Workers	12,851	9,166	3,685	76.81
Marginal Workers	3,879	1,118	2,761	23.19
Total Workers	16,730	10,284	6,446	

Religion: Major Religious Communities:

	Persons	Males	Females	Sex Ratio
Hindu (90.63%)	30,591	15,549	15,042	967
Muslim (9.29%)	3,135	1,552	1,583	1,020
Christian (0.07%)	25	8	17	2,125
Sikh (0%)	1	1	-	-
Buddhists (0.01%)	3	2	1	500
Jain (0%)	-	-	-	-

Agewise Data:

	Persons	Males	Females	Sex Ratio
All ages	33,755	17,112	16,643	973
0-14	9,889	5,144	4,745	922
15-44	15,970	8,028	7,942	989
45-79	7,534	3,762	3,772	1003
80+	307	141	166	1177
Age not stated	55	37	18	486

Languages (Dominant):

Telugu, Urdu, Gondi, Tamil, Hindi

Disabled Population:

	Persons	Males	Females	%
Total Disabled	831	462	369	
In Seeing	298	142	156	35.86
In Speech	95	59	36	11.43
In Hearing	70	29	41	8.42
In Movement	290	186	104	34.9
Mentally	78	46	32	9.39

CHENNARAOPET

Chennaraopet C.D. Block lies in the south-eastern part of Warangal district. The Block is located at a distance of 47 kms. from district headquarters (Warangal). There are 14 villages in the block with the total popul ation of 50,687 persons. Area of the C.D. Block is 129. 03 sq. kms. It is bounded in the north by Mandals Duggo ndi and Narsampet, in the south by Nekkonda and Gudur Mandals, in the east by Narsampet and Khanapur Mandals, and in the west by Sangam and Nekkonda Mandals.

Communications:

Roadways : Metalled Roads: Nearest Villages- Akkalchedu, Makdumpuram, Chennaraopet, Jhalli, Ameenabad, Lingagiri. Backwards Region Grants Fund: It receives Backward Region Grants.

Annual Rainfall: Average Rainfall 1064 mm

Ground Water: Availability of the Ground Water in the Basin is 3145. H.A.M.and the utilization is 1650 H. A.M. It belongs to Safe category. Depth to water level varies from 5 to 10 meter below the ground. Most of the wells go down in summer months. The well density in the entire block is 43 wells per sq. km. Total no. of the wells in the block are enumerated as 5589, according to the Ground Water Estimation Committee.

Natural Division : Godavari Depression Region

Administration:

Division: Telangana. Parliamentary Constituency. Distri ct: Warangal. Mandal: Chennaraopet. Assembly Constituenc y: 103 Narsampet. Gram Panchayat: 20.

Villages: 14 **Inhabited:** 14 **Uninhabited:** 0

Ranking	District	State	National
Area	43	904	5336
Population	28	488	5249
Sex Ratio	38	871	2929
Child Sex Ratio	44	1003	4667
Literacy Rate	46	902	5300
Density	4	190	2779
Work Participation Rate	5	196	539

Gram Panchayats:

Akkalchedu, Ameenabad, Ameenpet, Bapunagar, Bojervu Chennaraopeta, Gurijal, Jhalli, Khaderpet, Konapur Lingagiri, Lingapur, Makdumpur, Papaiahpeta Pata Maqdumpuram, Rajapalli, Surpalle Thimmarainipahad, Upparapalle, Yellaigudem.

Amenities:

Education: Primary School in 14 villages, Middle school in 12 villages, Matriculation or Secondary School in 7 villages, namely Gurijala, Makdumpuram, Chennaraopet, Upparapalle, Jhalli, Suripalle, Papaiahpeta.

Higher Secondary or Pre University Courses or Intermediate or Junior College in 0 village of the CD Block, College in 0 village, Adult Literacy Center in 8 villages.

Medical: Hospital in 0 village, Dispensary in 1 village, Health Center in 2 villages, Sub Center in 9 villages, Maternity and Child Welfare Center in 13 villages, Community health workers in 0 village.

The Village having Hospital or Dispensary or Health Center is Ameenabad.

Drinking Water: Tap water in 14 villages, Tank water in 14 villages, Well water in 14 villages, Tubewell in 14 villages and more than one source in 14 villages.

Bank: None.

Credit Society in 13 villages Agricultural Credit Society in 5

Non-Agricultural Credit Society in 13 villages.

Others: Power supply in 14 villages, Cinema hall in 1 village, sport club in 0 village, Stadium or Auditorium or Community Hall in 0 village, Post Office in 13 villages.

There are 14 villages having bus facilities.

Village with most of facilities: None.

Villages without Amenities (Education): None..

Scheduled Castes: Out of the total population of 50687 persons, 6330 persons (12.49%) belong to Scheduled Castes.

The villages having less than 10% SC population are None..

The villages having more than 50% SC population are None.

Sex ratio of Scheduled Caste population is 494.

Scheduled Castes Literates and Illiterates by Sex:

	Persons	Males	Females
Literate	2,144	1,426	718
Illiterate	4,186	1,778	2,408
Literacy rate	39.7	51.8	27.1
Graduate	21	18	3

Scheduled Castes (Dominant):

Madiga, Mala, Manne, Generic Castes etc., Bindla

For their cultural identity please see Appendix-I

Villages without Scheduled Castes: There are 0 village without any scheduled caste population.

Scheduled Tribes: Out of the total population of 50687 persons, 14266 persons (28.15%) belong to Scheduled Tribes.

The villages having less than 10% ST population are None..

The villages having more than 50% ST population are None.

Sex ratio of Scheduled tribe population is 487.

Scheduled Tribes Literates and Illiterates by Sex:

	Persons	Males	Females
Literate	2,996	2,167	829
Illiterate	11,270	5,146	6,124
Literacy rate	25.7	36.5	14.4
Graduate	41	40	1

Scheduled Tribes (Dominant):

Sugalis etc., Yerukulas, Yenadis, Koya etc.

Gond etc.

For their cultural identity please see Appendix-II

Villages without Scheduled Tribes: There are 0 village without any scheduled tribe population.

Literates and Illiterates by Sex (Total Population):

	Persons	Males	Females
Literate	19,133	12,580	6,553
Illiterate	31,554	13,265	18,289
Literacy rate	44	57	31
Graduate	457	391	66

Agriculture: ***Distribution of villages according to land use:***

Out of 14 villages, Total area (in hectare) is 12902, out of that 64.43 percent is cultivable and 38.84 percent of the cultivable area is irrigated.

Sources of Irrigation (Hectares): Government Canal 294.18, Private Canal 0, Well without Electricity 328.72, Well with Electricity 604.59, Tubewell without Electricity 36.42, Tubewell with Electricity 0, Tank 1458.65, River 0, Lake 0, Waterfall 0, Others 505.85.

Villages with population of 5000 to 9999:

Gurijala, Ameenabad, Papaiahpeta.

Villages with population of 10000 and above: None

Distribution of Workers:

	Persons	Males	Females	WPR
Cultivators	11,734	7,029	4,705	41.44
Agricultural Labour	12,080	4,096	7,984	42.66
Household Industry	614	378	236	2.17
Other Workers	3,889	3,149	740	13.73
Main Workers	24,475	13,733	10,742	86.43
Marginal Workers	3,842	919	2,923	13.57
Total Workers	28,317	14,652	13,665	

Religion: Major Religious Communities:

	Persons	Males	Females	Sex Ratio
Hindu (94.58%)	47,942	24,453	23,489	961
Muslim (2.23%)	1,130	581	549	945
Christian (2.11%)	1,067	530	537	1,013
Sikh (0.01%)	3	3	-	-
Buddhists (0%)	1	1	-	-
Jain (0%)	-	-	-	-

Agewise Data:

	Persons	Males	Females	Sex Ratio
All ages	50,687	25,845	24,842	961
0-14	17,213	9,159	8,054	879
15-44	23,109	11,594	11,515	993
45-79	9,946	4,894	5,052	1032
80+	379	182	197	1082
Age not stated	40	16	24	1500

Languages (Dominant):

Telugu, Hindi, Urdu, Tamil, Gondi

Disabled Population:

	Persons	Males	Females	%
Total Disabled	870	507	363	
In Seeing	387	230	157	44.48
In Speech	105	59	46	12.07
In Hearing	40	18	22	4.6
In Movement	244	138	106	28.05
Mentally	94	62	32	10.8

CHENNEKOTHAPALLE

Chennekothapalle C.D. Block lies in the southern part of Anantapur district. The Block is located at a distan ce of 48 kms. from district headquarters (Anantapur). There are 11 villages in the block with the total population of 42,308 persons. Area of the C.D. Block is 326.44 sq. kms. It is bounded in the north by Mandals Ramagiri, Kanaganapalle and Dharmavaram, in the south by Mandals Roddam, Penukonda and Kothacheruvu, in the east by Mandals Bukkapatnam, and in the west it has common boundary with the state of Karnataka.

Communications:

Roadways : NH- 7: Direction- Anantapur to Penukole. Nearest Villages- Chennekothapalle, Nagasamudram. State Highway (S.H.): Direction- Chennekothapalle to Dharmava ram. Nearest Villages- Chennekothapalle, Nagasamudram, Pyadindi.

Railway Station: Nagasamudram.

River: Chitravati Nadi- Nearest Villages- Kanumukkala, Veldurthi.

It receives the Backward Region Grants, and is identifi ed as a drought-prone area as well.

Integrated Child Development Scheme (ICDS) Project: Chinnakottapalli, Total Anganwadi Centres: 126

Annual Rainfall: Average Rainfall 354 mm

Ground Water: Availability of the Ground Water in the Basin is 2136 H.A.M. and the utilization is 2156 H. A.M. It belongs to OE category. Depth to water level varies from 10 to 20 meter below the ground. Most of the wells go down in summer months. The well density in the entire block is 6 wells per sq. km. Total no. of the wells in the block are enumerated as 2068, according to the Ground Water Estimation Committee.

Natural Division : Rayalaseema Region

Administration:

Division: Rayala Seema. Parliamentary Constituency: 37 Hindupur. District: Anantapur.

Mandal: Chennekothapalle. Assembly Constituency: 274 Raptadu. Gram Panchayat: 14.

Border Villages: (Karnataka)- Nearest Village- Mustikov ila.

Villages: 11 **Inhabited:** 11 **Uninhabited:** 0

Ranking	District	State	National
Area	16	111	2502
Population	30	751	5635
Sex Ratio	54	1048	3991
Child Sex Ratio	40	802	3484
Literacy Rate	24	553	4047
Density	53	631	5841
Work Participation Rate	45	969	1714

Gram Panchayats:

Basampalli, Basinepalli, Chennekothapalli Ganginepalli, Kanumukkala, Medapuram, Mustikovila Nagasamudram, Nyamaddala, Obulampalli, Poletipalli Pyadindi, Veldurthi, Venkatampalli.

Amenities:

Education: Primary School in 11 villages, Middle school in 9 villages, Matriculation or Secondary School in 6 villages, namely Nyamaddala, Chennekothapalle, Nagasamudram, Medapuram, Kanumukkala, Veldurthi.

Higher Secondary or Pre University Courses or Intermediate or Junior College in 1 village of the CD Block,, namely Chennekothapalle.

College in 0 village, Adult Literacy Center in 10 villages.

Medical: Hospital in 0 village, Dispensary in 1 village, Health Center in 1 village, Sub Center in 8 villages, Maternity and Child Welfare Center in 0 village, Community health workers in 0 village.

The Villages having Hospital or Dispensary or Health Center are Chennekothapalle, Medapuram.

Drinking Water: Tap water in 9 villages, Tank water in 10 villages, Well water in 11 villages, Tubewell in 11 villages and more than one source in 11 villages.

Bank: Banking facility in 4 villages, namely, Chennekothapalle, Medapuram, Kanumukkala Bramhanapalle.

Credit Society in 3 villages Agricultural Credit Society in 3 Non-Agricultural Credit Society in 0 village.

Others: Power supply in 11 villages, Cinema hall in 0 village, sport club in 0 village, Stadium or Auditorium or Community Hall in 0 village, Post Office in 10 villages.

There are 11 villages having bus facilities.

Villages with most of facilities: Chennekothapalle Medapuram, Kanumukkala.

Villages without Amenities (Education): None..

Scheduled Castes: Out of the total population of 42308 persons, 5761 persons (13.62%) belong to Scheduled Castes.

The villages having less than 10% SC population are None..

The villages having more than 50% SC population are None.

Sex ratio of Scheduled Caste population is 487.

Scheduled Castes Literates and Illiterates by Sex:

	Persons	Males	Females
Literate	1,985	1,290	695
Illiterate	3,776	1,666	2,110
Literacy rate	39.6	50.4	28.3
Graduate	65	59	6

Scheduled Castes (Dominant):

Madiga, Mala, Adi Andhra, Generic Castes etc.

For their cultural identity please see Appendix-I

Villages without Scheduled Castes: There are 0 village without any scheduled caste population.

Scheduled Tribes: Out of the total population of 42308 persons, 1354 persons (3.2%) belong to Scheduled Tribes. The villages having less than 10% ST population are Mustikovila, Nyamaddala, Chennekothapalle Nagasamudram, Pyadindi, Medapuram, Poletipalle Kanumukkala, Veldurthi, Bramhanapalle.

The villages having more than 50% ST population are None.

Sex ratio of Scheduled tribe population is 462.

Scheduled Tribes Literates and Illiterates by Sex:

	Persons	Males	Females
Literate	527	369	158
Illiterate	827	360	467
Literacy rate	44.1	57.0	28.9
Graduate	18	17	1

Scheduled Tribes (Dominant):

Sugalis etc., Yerukulas

For their cultural identity please see Appendix-II

Villages without Scheduled Tribes: There are 2 villages without any scheduled tribe population.

Literates and Illiterates by Sex (Total Population):

	Persons	Males	Females
Literate	19,645	12,577	7,068
Illiterate	22,663	9,226	13,437
Literacy rate	53	66	39
Graduate	766	662	104

Agriculture: ***Distribution of villages according to land use:*** Out of 11 villages, Total area (in hectare) is 32643, out of that 66.48 percent is cultivable and 6.54 percent of the cultivable area is irrigated.

Sources of Irrigation (Hectares): Government Canal 0, Private Canal 0, Well without Electricity 47.78, Well with Electricity 309.71, Tubewell without Electricity 0, Tubewell with Electricity 479.03, Tank 583, River 0, Lake 0, Waterfall 0, Others 0.

Villages with population of 5000 to 9999:

Nyamaddala, Chennekothapalle, Medapuram, Kanumukkala.

Villages with population of 10000 and above: None

Distribution of Workers:

	Persons	Males	Females	WPR
Cultivators	9,165	5,882	3,283	41.4
Agricultural Labour	7,738	2,833	4,905	34.95
Household Industry	1,725	1,152	573	7.79
Other Workers	3,511	2,630	881	15.86
Main Workers	17,853	11,231	6,622	80.64
Marginal Workers	4,286	1,266	3,020	19.36
Total Workers	22,139	12,497	9,642	

Religion: Major Religious Communities:

	Persons	Males	Females	Sex Ratio
Hindu (97.57%)	41,279	21,276	20,003	940
Muslim (2.24%)	947	488	459	941
Christian (0.08%)	32	15	17	1,133
Sikh (0%)	-	-	-	-
Buddhists (0%)	-	-	-	-
Jain (0%)	-	-	-	-

Agewise Data:

	Persons	Males	Females	Sex Ratio
All ages	42,308	21,803	20,505	940
0-14	13,805	7,134	6,671	935
15-44	19,924	10,328	9,596	929
45-79	8,228	4,167	4,061	975
80+	312	160	152	950
Age not stated	39	14	25	1786

Languages (Dominant):

Telugu, Urdu, Gondi, Hindi, Kannada

Disabled Population:

	Persons	Males	Females	%
Total Disabled	862	482	380	
In Seeing	304	166	138	35.27
In Speech	101	60	41	11.72
In Hearing	86	34	52	9.98
In Movement	249	149	100	28.89
Mentally	122	73	49	14.15

CHENNUR

Chennur C.D. Block lies in the southern part of Adilabad district. The Block is located at a distance of 257 kms. from district headquarters (Adilabad). There are 34 villages in the block with the total population of 51,365 persons. Area of the C.D. Block is 301.60 sq. kms. It is bounded by Nennal Mandal on north, Kotap alle Mandal on north-east and east, Karimnagar district on south-east and south, Jaipur Mandal on south-west, west and north-west.

Communications :

Roadways : NH- 16: Direction- Mancherial to Sironcha Nearest Villages- Akkapalle, Chintapalle, Chennur, Yellakkapet, Kistampet, Khambojipet, Lingampalle.

Backwards Region Grants Fund: It receives Backward Region Grants.

Integrated Child Development Scheme (ICDS) Project: Chennur, Total Anganwadi Centres: 231

Annual Rainfall: Average Rainfall 1162 mm

Ground Water: Availability of the Ground Water in the Basin is 2955 H.A.M.and the utilization is 1061 H.A. M. It belongs to Safe category. Depth to water level varies from 5 to 10 meter below the ground. Most of the wells go down in summer months, according to the Ground Water Estimation Committee.

Natural Division : Telangana Plateau Region

Administration:

Division: Telangana. Parliamentary Constituency: 2 Peddapalle. District: Adilabad. Mandal: Chennur. Assemb ly Constituency: 2 Chennur (SC). Gram Panchayat: 17.

Villages: 34 **Inhabited:** 30 **Uninhabited:** 4

Ranking	District	State	National
Area	19	158	2769
Population	3	468	5210
Sex Ratio	25	306	1357
Child Sex Ratio	24	354	1256
Literacy Rate	8	592	4206
Density	44	936	5226
Work Participation Rate	10	835	3337

Gram Panchayats:

Angarajpalle, Asnad, Buddaram, Chakepalle, Chennur Chintalpalle, Dugnepalle, Gangaram, Kachanpalle Kathersala, Kistampet, Kommera, Nagapur, Pokkur Somanpalle, Suddal, Sundersala.

Amenities:

Education: Primary School in 30 villages, Middle school in 8 villages, Matriculation or Secondary School in 1 village, namely Chennur.

Higher Secondary or Pre University Courses or Intermediate or Junior College in 1 village of the CD Block,, namely Chennur.

College in 1 village, Adult Literacy Center in 29 villages., College is in village, namely Chennur.

Medical: Hospital in 1 village, Dispensary in 1 village, Health Center in 2 villages, Sub Center in 8 villages, Maternity and Child Welfare Center in 0 village, Community health workers in 0 village.

The Village having Hospital or Dispensary or Health Center is Chennur.

Drinking Water: Tap water in 29 villages, Tank water in 29 villages, Well water in 30 villages, Tubewell in 29 villages and more than one source in 30 villages.

Bank: Banking facility in 1 villages, namely, Chennur.

Credit Society in 7 villages Agricultural Credit Society in 3 Non-Agricultural Credit Society in 6 villages.

Others: Power supply in 30 villages, Cinema hall in 1 village, sport club in 0 village, Stadium or Auditorium or Community Hall in 0 village, Post Office in 11 villages.

There are 16 villages having bus facilities.

Village with most of facilities: Chennur.

Villages without Amenities (Education): None..

Scheduled Castes: Out of the total population of 51365 persons, 13828 persons (26.92%) belong to Scheduled Castes. The villages having less than 10% SC population are Sankaram, Kannepalle, Akkapalle, Khambojipet Lingampalle, Kathersala.

The villages having more than 50% SC population are Narayanpur, Dugnepalle, Raipet, Angarajpalle Gangaram, Kommera, Narasakkapet, Chakepalle.

Sex ratio of Scheduled Caste population is 498.

Scheduled Castes Literates and Illiterates by Sex:

	Persons	Males	Females
Literate	4,367	2,825	1,542
Illiterate	9,461	4,123	5,338
Literacy rate	37.6	48.3	26.8
Graduate	49	45	4

Scheduled Castes (Dominant):

Mala Sale etc., Madiga, Mala, Manne Generic Castes etc.

For their cultural identity please see Appendix-I

Villages without Scheduled Castes: There are 8 villages without any scheduled caste population.

Scheduled Tribes: Out of the total population of 51365 persons, 2461 persons (4.79%) belong to Scheduled Tribes. The villages having less than 10% ST population are Kannepalle, Shivalingapur, Chennur, Kistampet Khambojipet, Kathersala, Narayanpur, Dugnepalle Raipet, Angarajpalle, Kachanpalle, Gangaram, Asnad Kommera, Sundersala, Narasakkapet, Pokkur Chakepalle, Ponnaram, Somanpalle, Nagapur, Beervelli.

The villages having more than 50% ST population are None.

Sex ratio of Scheduled tribe population is 490.

Scheduled Tribes Literates and Illiterates by Sex:

	Persons	Males	Females
Literate	823	539	284
Illiterate	1,638	717	921
Literacy rate	39.4	50.4	27.9
Graduate	8	6	2

Scheduled Tribes (Dominant):

Koya etc., Gond etc., Sugalis etc., Yerukulas Kammara

For their cultural identity please see Appendix-II

Villages without Scheduled Tribes: There are 16 villages without any scheduled tribe population.

Literates and Illiterates by Sex (Total Population):

	Persons	Males	Females
Literate	22,827	13,753	9,074
Illiterate	28,538	11,991	16,547
Literacy rate	52	63	41
Graduate	1,100	868	232

Agriculture: ***Distribution of villages according to land use:*** Out of 34 villages, Total area (in hectare) is 30164, out of that 46.63 percent is cultivable and 13.7 percent of the cultivable area is irrigated.

Sources of Irrigation (Hectares): Government Canal 0,

Private Canal 0, Well without Electricity 20, Well with Electricity 289.47, Tubewell without Electricity 0, Tubewell with Electricity 25, Tank 1588.5, River 4, Lake 0, Waterfall 0, Others 0.

Villages with population of 5000 to 9999: None

Villages with population of 10000 and above: Chennur.

Distribution of Workers:

	Persons	Males	Females	WPR
Cultivators	5,152	3,829	1,323	22.49
Agricultural Labour	9,903	4,002	5,901	43.24
Household Industry	640	412	228	2.79
Other Workers	7,208	5,866	1,342	31.47
Main Workers	16,880	11,926	4,954	73.7
Marginal Workers	6,023	2,183	3,840	26.3
Total Workers	22,903	14,109	8,794	

Religion: Major Religious Communities:

	Persons	Males	Females	Sex Ratio
Hindu (92.56%)	47,542	23,851	23,691	993
Muslim (6.53%)	3,353	1,656	1,697	1,025
Christian (0.46%)	234	114	120	1,053
Sikh (0.02%)	11	3	8	2,667
Buddhists (0.14%)	72	38	34	895
Jain (0%)	-	-	-	-

Agewise Data:

	Persons	Males	Females	Sex Ratio
All ages	51,365	25,744	25,621	995
0-14	17,511	8,925	8,586	962
15-44	24,273	12,208	12,065	988
45-79	9,095	4,375	4,720	1079
80+	387	177	210	1186
Age not stated	99	59	40	678

Languages (Dominant):
Telugu, Urdu, Hindi, Marathi, Gondi

Disabled Population:

	Persons	Males	Females	%
Total Disabled	669	387	282	
In Seeing	287	156	131	42.9
In Speech	79	45	34	11.81
In Hearing	40	23	17	5.98
In Movement	182	117	65	27.2
Mentally	81	46	35	12.11

CHENNUR

Chennur C.D. Block lies in the northern part of Cuddapah district. The Block is located at a distance of 10 kms. from district headquarters (Cuddapah). There are 15 villages in the block with the total population of 35,331 persons. Area of the C.D. Block is 94.65 sq. kms. It is bounded in the north by Mandals Vallur and Khajipet, in the south by Mandals Cuddapah and Atlur, in the east by Mandal Atlur, and in the west by Mandal Vallur.

Communications:

Roadways : State Highway (S.H.): Direction- Kurnool to Chittoor. Nearest Villages- Rudrabharathipeta, China machupalle, Chennur, Doulathapuram, Bayanapalle.

River: Penneru Nadi- Nearest Villages- Sivalapalle, Kokkarayapalle, Kanuparthi, Nazeerbegpalle, Gurrampadu, Ramanapalle, Chennur, Doulathapuram, Bayanapalle.

It receives Backward Region Grants, and is also identif ied as a drought-prone area as well.

Annual Rainfall: Average Rainfall 691 mm

Ground Water: Availability of the Ground Water in the Basin is 3194 H.A.M.and the utilization is 651 H.A. M.It belongs to Safe category. Depth to water level varies from 10 to 20 meter below the ground. Most of the wells go down in summer months, according to the Ground Water Estimation Committee.

Natural Division : Rayalaseema Region

Administration:

Division: Rayala Seema. Parliamentary Constituency: 38 Kadapa.District: Cuddapah. Mandal: Chennur. Assembly Constituency: 249 Kamalapuram. Gram Panchayat: 11.

Villages: 15 **Inhabited:** 14 **Uninhabited:** 1

Ranking	District	State	National
Area	50	1038	5760
Population	25	924	5898
Sex Ratio	27	726	2455
Child Sex Ratio	40	905	4027
Literacy Rate	5	137	1827
Density	36	918	2927
Work Participation Rate	4	227	3212

Gram Panchayats:
Balasinganapalli, Bayana Palli, Chennur Chinamachupalli, Gurrampadu, Kokkarayapalli Mundlapalli, Rachinnayapalli, Ramana Palli Sivalpalle, Upparapalli.

Amenities:

Education: Primary School in 14 villages, Middle school in 5 villages, Matriculation or Secondary School in 4 villages, namely Chennur, Bayanapalle, Ramanapalle, Chinamachupalle.

Higher Secondary or Pre University Courses or Intermediate or Junior College in 1 village of the CD Block,, namely Chennur.

College in 1 village, Adult Literacy Center in 0 village., College is in village, namely Chennur.

Medical: Hospital in 4 villages, Dispensary in 1 village, Health Center in 2 villages, Sub Center in 2 villages, Maternity and Child Welfare Center in 0 village,

Community health workers in 0 village.
The Villages having Hospital or Dispensary or Health Center are Chennur, Bayanapalle, Upparapalle, Chinamachupalle.
Drinking Water: Tap water in 14 villages, Tank water in 14 villages, Well water in 14 villages, Tubewell in 14 villages and more than one source in 14 villages.
Bank: Banking facility in 3 villages, namely, Sivalapalle, Chennur, Ramanapalle.
Credit Society in 2 villages Agricultural Credit Society in 1 Non-Agricultural Credit Society in 2 villages.
Others: Power supply in 14 villages, Cinema hall in 1 village, sport club in 0 village, Stadium or Auditorium or Community Hall in 0 village, Post Office in 13 villages.
There are 12 villages having bus facilities.
Village with most of facilities: Chennur.
Villages without Amenities (Education): None..
Scheduled Castes: Out of the total population of 35331 persons, 7049 persons (19.95%) belong to Scheduled Castes.
The villages having less than 10% SC population are None..
The villages having more than 50% SC population are None.
Sex ratio of Scheduled Caste population is 492.
Scheduled Castes Literates and Illiterates by Sex:

	Persons	Males	Females
Literate	3,496	2,146	1,350
Illiterate	3,553	1,438	2,115
Literacy rate	57.9	69.8	45.6
Graduate	62	52	10

Scheduled Castes (Dominant):
Mala, Madiga, Adi Andhra, Dom etc., Jambuvulu
For their cultural identity please see Appendix-I
Villages without Scheduled Castes: There is 1 village without any scheduled caste population.
Scheduled Tribes: Out of the total population of 35331 persons, 717 persons (2.03%) belong to Scheduled Tribes.
The villages having less than 10% ST population are Sivalapalle, Kokkarayapalle, Chennur, Bayanapalle Kanuparthi, Nazeerbegpalle, Gurrampadu, Ramanapalle Upparapalle, Dugganapalle, Chinamachupalle Mundlapalle, Rachinnayapalle.
The villages having more than 50% ST population are None.
Sex ratio of Scheduled tribe population is 509.
Scheduled Tribes Literates and Illiterates by Sex:

	Persons	Males	Females
Literate	195	120	75
Illiterate	522	232	290
Literacy rate	33.6	41.4	25.9
Graduate	4	3	1

Scheduled Tribes (Dominant):
Yenadis, Yerukulas, Sugalis etc.
For their cultural identity please see Appendix-II
Villages without Scheduled Tribes: There are 5 villages without any scheduled tribe population.
Literates and Illiterates by Sex (Total Population):

	Persons	Males	Females
Literate	20,330	12,188	8,142
Illiterate	15,001	5,735	9,266
Literacy rate	66	78	53
Graduate	1,053	873	180

Agriculture: ***Distribution of villages according to land use:*** Out of 15 villages, Total area (in hectare) is 9466, out of that 48.01 percent is cultivable and 82.89 percent of the cultivable area is irrigated.
Sources of Irrigation (Hectares): Government Canal 2570, Private Canal 0, Well without Electricity 0, Well with Electricity 686, Tubewell without Electricity 0, Tubewell with Electricity 511, Tank 0, River 0, Lake 0, Waterfall 0, Others 0.
Villages with population of 5000 to 9999: None
Villages with population of 10000 and above: Chennur.
Distribution of Workers:

	Persons	Males	Females	WPR
Cultivators	2,299	1,789	510	14.06
Agricultural Labour	10,006	5,327	4,679	61.19
Household Industry	924	508	416	5.65
Other Workers	3,123	2,408	715	19.1
Main Workers	12,887	8,395	4,492	78.81
Marginal Workers	3,465	1,637	1,828	21.19
Total Workers	16,352	10,032	6,320	

Religion: Major Religious Communities:

	Persons	Males	Females	Sex Ratio
Hindu (84.6%)	29,889	15,117	14,772	977
Muslim (14.73%)	5,204	2,693	2,511	932
Christian (0.51%)	180	86	94	1,093
Sikh (0.01%)	3	1	2	2,000
Buddhists (0%)	1	-	1	-
Jain (0%)	-	-	-	-

Agewise Data:

	Persons	Males	Females	Sex Ratio
All ages	35,331	17,923	17,408	971
0-14	10,912	5,695	5,217	916
15-44	16,583	8,405	8,178	973
45-79	7,566	3,696	3,870	1047
80+	200	92	108	1174
Age not stated	70	35	35	1000

Languages (Dominant):

Telugu, Urdu, Hindi, Gondi, Tamil

Disabled Population:

	Persons	Males	Females	%
Total Disabled	641	354	287	
In Seeing	216	104	112	33.7
In Speech	64	36	28	9.98
In Hearing	57	23	34	8.89
In Movement	214	133	81	33.39
Mentally	90	58	32	14.04

CHERIAL

Cherial C.D. Block lies in the western part of Warangal district. The Block is located at a distance of 104 kms. from district headquarters (Warangal). There are 21 villages in the block with the total population of 67,235 persons. Area of the C.D. Block is 272.01 sq. kms. It is bounded by Medak district on north and west, Bachannapet Mandal on south, and Maddur Mandal on east.

Communications:

Roadways : State Highway (S.H.): Direction- Siddipet to Jangaon. Nearest Villages- Cherial, Vechareni, Kista mpet, Marrimusthiayala, Musthiyala.

Backwards Region Grants Fund: It receives Backward Region Grants.

Integrated Child Development Scheme (ICDS) Project: Cheriyala, Total Anganwadi Centres: 263

Annual Rainfall: Average Rainfall 831 mm

Ground Water: Availability of the Ground Water in the Basin is 3273 H.A.M.and the utilization is 3294 H.A. M. It belongs to OE category. Depth to water level varies from 10 to 20 meter below the ground. Most of the wells go down in summer months. The well density in the entire block is 19 wells per sq. km. Total no. of the wells in the block are enumerated as 5179 accor ding to the Ground Water Estimation Committee.

Natural Division : Godavari Depression Region

Administration:

Division: Telangana. Parliamentary Constituency. Distri ct: Warangal. Mandal: Cherial.

Assembly Constituency: 98 Jangaon. Gram Panchayat: 25

Villages: 21 **Inhabited:** 21 **Uninhabited:** 0

Ranking	District	State	National
Area	6	229	3081
Population	8	175	4593
Sex Ratio	2	190	1020
Child Sex Ratio	20	491	1826
Literacy Rate	23	556	4060
Density	31	536	4115
Work Participation Rate	33	551	1416

Gram Panchayats:

Ainapur, Akunoor, Cheriyal, Chityal, Chunchankota Danampalle, Dommata, Gouraipalle, Gurijakunta Guruvannapeta, Kadavergu, Kistampeta, Komaravelly Marrimuchala, Musthyala, Nagapuri, Peddarajupeta Posanpalle, Pothireddipalle, Rampoor, Ramsagar Tadoor, Thapaspalle, Vechareni, Veerannapeta.

Amenities:

Education: Primary School in 21 villages, Middle school in 16 villages, Matriculation or Secondary School in 10 villages, namely Akunoor, Cherial, Vechareni, Marrimusthiayala, Komuravelle, Ainapur, Nagapuri, Kadavergu, Chunchankota, Musthiyala.

Higher Secondary or Pre University Courses or Intermediate or Junior College in 1 village of the CD Block,, namely Cherial.

College in 2 villages, Adult Literacy Center in 14 villages., Colleges are in villages, namely Cherial, Komuravelle.

Medical: Hospital in 2 villages, Dispensary in 1 village, Health Center in 1 village, Sub Center in 11 villages, Maternity and Child Welfare Center in 0 village, Community health workers in 0 village.

The Villages having Hospital or Dispensary or Health Center are Akunoor, Cherial.

Drinking Water: Tap water in 21 villages, Tank water in 20 villages, Well water in 20 villages, Tubewell in 20 villages and more than one source in 21 villages.

Bank: Banking facility in 2 villages, namely, Cherial, Komuravelle.

Credit Society in 19 villages Agricultural Credit Society in 3 Non-Agricultural Credit Society in 19 villages.

Others: Power supply in 21 villages, Cinema hall in 1 village, sport club in 0 village, Stadium or Auditorium or Community Hall in 0 village, Post Office in 18 villages.

There are 21 villages having bus facilities.

Villages with most of facilities: Cherial Komuravelle.

Villages without Amenities (Education): None..

Scheduled Castes: Out of the total population of 67235 persons, 13431 persons (19.98%) belong to Scheduled Castes.

The villages having less than 10% SC population are None..

The villages having more than 50% SC population are None.

Sex ratio of Scheduled Caste population is 501.

Scheduled Castes Literates and Illiterates by Sex:

	Persons	Males	Females
Literate	5,081	3,348	1,733
Illiterate	8,350	3,355	4,995

Literacy rate	44.6	59.1	30.2
Graduate	106	95	11

Scheduled Castes (Dominant):

Madiga, Mala, Beda Jangam etc., Byagara, Chamar etc.

For their cultural identity please see Appendix-I

Villages without Scheduled Castes: There are 0 village without any scheduled caste population.

Scheduled Tribes: Out of the total population of 67235 persons, 275 persons (0.41%) belong to Scheduled Tribes. The villages having less than 10% ST population are Tadoor, Chityal, Danampalle, Dommata, Akunoor Cherial, Vechareni, Kistampet, Marrimusthiayala Gouraipalle, Komuravelle, Ramsagar, Ainapur Tapaspalle, Guravannapet, Posanpalle, Nagapuri Pedarajupet, Kadavergu, Chunchankota, Musthiyala. The villages having more than 50% ST population are None.

Sex ratio of Scheduled tribe population is 491.

Scheduled Tribes Literates and Illiterates by Sex:

	Persons	Males	Females
Literate	91	68	23
Illiterate	184	72	112
Literacy rate	39.6	58.1	20.4
Graduate	5	5	0

Scheduled Tribes (Dominant):

Yerukulas, Sugalis etc., Generic Tribes etc. Chenchu etc.

For their cultural identity please see Appendix-II

Villages without Scheduled Tribes: There are 4 villages without any scheduled tribe population.

Literates and Illiterates by Sex (Total Population):

	Persons	Males	Females
Literate	30,461	19,175	11,286
Illiterate	36,774	14,353	22,421
Literacy rate	53	67	39
Graduate	1,189	1,026	163

Agriculture: ***Distribution of villages according to land use:*** Out of 21 villages, Total area (in hectare) is 27202, out of that 65.56 percent is cultivable and 16.9 percent of the cultivable area is irrigated.

Sources of Irrigation (Hectares): Government Canal 0, Private Canal 0, Well without Electricity 0, Well with Electricity 2545, Tubewell without Electricity 0, Tubewell with Electricity 469, Tank 0, River 0, Lake 0, Waterfall 0, Others 0.

Villages with population of 5000 to 9999:
Akunoor, Kadavergu, Musthiyala.

Villages with population of 10000 and above:
Cherial.

Distribution of Workers:

	Persons	Males	Females	WPR
Cultivators	12,317	7,639	4,678	35.06
Agricultural Labour	10,795	4,127	6,668	30.73
Household Industry	4,676	1,167	3,509	13.31
Other Workers	7,344	5,638	1,706	20.9
Main Workers	30,242	17,162	13,080	86.08
Marginal Workers	4,890	1,409	3,481	13.92
Total Workers	35,132	18,571	16,561	

Religion: Major Religious Communities:

	Persons	Males	Females	Sex Ratio
Hindu (95.02%)	63,884	31,833	32,051	1,007
Muslim (4.27%)	2,872	1,465	1,407	960
Christian (0.65%)	434	200	234	1,170
Sikh (0.01%)	5	4	1	250
Buddhists (0%)	-	-	-	-
Jain (0.01%)	4	2	2	1,000

Agewise Data:

	Persons	Males	Females	Sex Ratio
All ages	67,235	33,528	33,707	1005
0-14	22,478	11,324	11,154	985
15-44	29,336	14,604	14,732	1009
45-79	14,731	7,278	7,453	1024
80+	615	288	327	1135
Age not stated	75	34	41	1206

Languages (Dominant):

Telugu, Urdu, Gondi, Hindi, Kannada

Disabled Population:

	Persons	Males	Females	%
Total Disabled	1,571	848	723	
In Seeing	807	421	386	51.37
In Speech	125	66	59	7.96
In Hearing	75	39	36	4.77
In Movement	432	249	183	27.5
Mentally	132	73	59	8.4

CHERLA

Cherla C.D. Block lies in the northern part of Khammam district. The Block is located at a distance of 165 kms. from district headquarters (Khammam). There are 74 villages in the block with the total population of 38,540 persons. Area of the C.D. Block is 100.19 sq. kms. It is bounded in the south by Mandal Dummugudem, in the west by Mandals Venkatapuram, Pinapaka and Manuguru, and It has common boundary with the state of Chhattisgarh in the north and east.

Communications:

Roadways : State Highway (S.H.): Direction- Venkatapuram to Bhadrachalam. Nearest Villages- Koyyuru (Z), Regunta (G), Regunta (Z), Kothuru, Cherla(G), Ricepeta, Cherla (Z), Srinivasapuram (Z), Kaliveru (Z), R. Kothagudem, Mamidigudem Chalk, Subbampeta, Subbampeta (G), Chintak unta (Z), Puliboinapalle, Kudunuru (Z), Kudunuru (G),

Devarapalle (Z), Mamidigudem (Z), Gogubaka (Z), Rallag udem, Dandupeta (G), Dandupeta (Z), Kesavapuram, Tegada (Z).

River: Talperu Nadi- Nearest Villages- Kothapalle (G), Dandupeta (G), Dandupeta (Z), Kesavapuram, Bhumull anka, Dosillapalle, Unjupalle, Vaddipet (Z), Pusuguppa (Patch-Ii), Pusuguppa (Patch-I), Boinapalle, Uyyalamadu gu (G), Uyyalamadugu (Z), Chalamala (Z), Peda Midisileru Chalk-Iii, China Midisileru (G), China Midisileru (Z), Jangalapalle, Tegada (Z), Tegada (G), Gommugudem (Z). Godavari Nadi- Nearest Villages- Subbampeta, Subbampeta (G), Subbampeta (Z), Ramanujapuram, C. Kathigudem, Gommupulliboinapalle, Chintakunta (Z), Puliboinapalle, Gampalle (Z), Mogullapalle(G), Lingapuram(Z), Kothapa lle(Z), Kothapalle (G), Tegada (G), Gommugudem (Z), Lingala (Z), Mummidaram (Z), Jettigudem (Z), Kothagudem (Z), Katepalle, Sarangapani (G), Kudunuru (Z), Kudunuru (G), Devarapalle (Z), Mamidigudem (Z), Gogubaka (Z), Rallagudem.

Backwards Region Grants Fund: It receives Backward Region Grants.

Annual Rainfall: Average Rainfall 1438 mm

Ground Water: Availability of the Ground Water in the Basin is 5543 H.A.M.and the utilization is 138 H.A. M. It belongs to safe category. Depth to water level varies from 10 to 20 meter below the ground. Most of the wells go down in summer months. The well density in the entire block is 0.4 wells per sq. km. Total no. of the wells in the block are enumerated as 236, according to the Ground Water Estimation Committee.

Forest and Reserved **Forest:** (Cherla R.F.)- Nearest Villages- Subbampeta, Subbampeta (G), Subbampeta (Z), Ramanujapuram, Chimalapadu, Koyyuru (Z), Regunta (G), Regunta (Z), Singasamudram, Upperagudem, Cherla (Z), Dosillapalle, Unjupalle, Vaddipet (Z), Pusuguppa (Patc h-Iii), Pusuguppa (Patch-Ii), Pusuguppa (Patch-I), Boina palle, Chalamala (Z). (Pullgondala R.F.)- Nearest Villag es- Uyyalamadugu (G), Uyyalamadugu (Z), Tippapuram, Chalamala (Z), Peda Midisileru (Z), Peda Midisileru Chalk-Iii, Peda Midisileru Chalk-Ii, Peda Midisileru Chalk-I, China Midisileru (G), Jangalapalle, Srinivasap uram (Z), Kaliveru (Z), Tegada (Z), Kudunuru (Z), Kudunu ru (G), Devarapalle (Z), Mamidigudem (Z), Gogubaka (Z), Rallagudem, Mamidigudem Chalk.

Natural Division : Godavari Depression Region

Administration:

Division: Telangana. Parliamentary Constituency: 16 Mahbubabad (ST). District: Khammam. Mandal: Cherla. Assembly Constituency: 119 Bhadrachalam (ST). Gram Panchayat: 14.

Border Villages: (Chhattisgarh)- Nearest Villages- Subbampeta, Unjupalle, Vaddipet (Z), Pusuguppa (Patch-I ii), Pusuguppa, (Patch-Ii), Pusuguppa (Patch-I), Boinapa lle, Uyyalamadugu (G), Uyyalamadugu (Z), Tippapuram, Chalamala (Z), Bathinapalle, Kur, Napalle, Bodanalli (G), Bodanalli (Z), Chintaguppa, Puligundala.

Villages: 74 **Inhabited:** 59 **Uninhabited:** 15

Ranking	District	State	National
Area	45	1023	5717
Population	30	873	5803
Sex Ratio	6	147	807
Child Sex Ratio	15	226	709
Literacy Rate	23	679	4463
Density	31	544	2847
Work Participation Rate	1	211	1447

Gram Panchayats:

Cherla, Devarapalli, Gommugudem, Kudunuru Kurnapally, Mogallapally, Pedamidisileru, Peddipalli Pusuguppa, R.Kothagudem, Satyanarayanapuram Subbampeta, Tegada, Upparigudem.

Amenities:

Education: Primary School in 46 villages, Middle school in 11 villages, Matriculation or Secondary School in 3 villages, namely Cherla(G), Cherla (Z), R. Kothagudem.

Higher Secondary or Pre University Courses or Intermediate or Junior College in 1 village of the CD Block,, namely Cherla(G).

College in 0 village, Adult Literacy Center in 31 villages.

Medical: Hospital in 0 village, Dispensary in 1 village, Health Center in 3 villages, Sub Center in 11 villages, Maternity and Child Welfare Center in 9 villages, Community health workers in 0 village.

The Villages having Hospital or Dispensary or Health Center are Cherla(G), R. Kothagudem, Mamidigudem Chalk.

Drinking Water: Tap water in 53 villages, Tank water in 52 villages, Well water in 59 villages, Tubewell in 52 villages and more than one source in 55 villages.

Bank: Banking facility in 3 villages, namely, Cherla(G), Kurnapalle, R. Kothagudem.

Credit Society in 9 villages Agricultural Credit Society in 5 Non-Agricultural Credit Society in 6 villages.

Others: Power supply in 59 villages, Cinema hall in 2 villages, sport club in 0 village, Stadium or Auditorium or Community Hall in 0 village, Post Office in 12 villages.

There are 24 villages having bus facilities.

Villages with most of facilities: Cherla(G) R. Kothagudem.

Villages without amenities (Education):

Dandupeta (G), Bhumullanka, Uyyalamadugu (G),

Chalamala (Z), Peda Midisileru (Z),
Peda Midisileru Chalk-Iii, China Midisileru (Z),
Bodanalli (Z), Peddipalle, Mummidaram (Z),
Gogubaka (Z)..

Scheduled Castes: Out of the total population of 38540 persons, 4898 persons (12.71%) belong to Scheduled Castes.

The villages having less than 10% SC population are Subbampeta (G), Subbampeta (Z), Ramanujapuram C. Kathigudem, Chimalapadu, Koyyuru (Z), Regunta (G) Regunta (Z), Singasamudram, Upperagudem, Kothuru Chintakunta (Z), Puliboinapalle, Mogullapalle(G) Dandupeta (G), Kesavapuram, Bhumullanka Dosillapalle, Unjupalle, Vaddipet (Z) Pusuguppa (Patch-Ii), Uyyalamadugu (G), Tippapuram Chalamala (Z), Bathinapalle, Peda Midisileru (Z) Peda Midisileru Chalk-Iii, Peda Midisileru Chalk-I Kurnapalle, China Midisileru (G), Bodanalli (G) Bodanalli (Z), Chintaguppa, Kaliveru (Z) Lingala (Z), Peddipalle, Mummidaram (Z) Jettigudem (Z), Devarapalle (Z), Gogubaka (Z) Mamidigudem Chalk, Puligundala.

The villages having more than 50% SC population are Gommupulliboinapalle, Lingapuram(Z), Kudunuru (G) Rallagudem.

Sex ratio of Scheduled Caste population is 494.

Scheduled Castes Literates and Illiterates by Sex:

	Persons	Males	Females
Literate	2,353	1,396	957
Illiterate	2,545	1,082	1,463
Literacy rate	55.8	65.7	45.8
Graduate	50	43	7

Scheduled Castes (Dominant):

Mala, Madiga, Aray Mala, Mala Dasari, Mala Dasu

For their cultural identity please see Appendix-I

Villages without Scheduled Castes: There are 43 villages without any scheduled caste population.

Scheduled Tribes: Out of the total population of 38540 persons, 19554 persons (50.74%) belong to Scheduled Tribes.

The villages having less than 10% ST population are Chintakunta (Z), Puliboinapalle, Gampalle (Z) Lingapuram(Z), Kothapalle(Z), Dandupeta (G) Peda Midisileru Chalk-I, Tegada (G), Mummidaram (Z) Rallagudem.

The villages having more than 50% ST population are Subbampeta (G), Subbampeta (Z), Ramanujapuram C. Kathigudem, Chimalapadu, Koyyuru (Z), Regunta (G) Regunta (Z), Singasamudram, Upperagudem Gannavaram (Z), Kothuru, Bhumullanka, Dosillapalle Unjupalle, Vaddipet (Z), Pusuguppa (Patch-Ii) Uyyalamadugu (G), Tippapuram, Chalamala (Z) Bathinapalle, Peda Midisileru (Z) Peda Midisileru Chalk-Iii, Kurnapalle China Midisileru (G), China Midisileru (Z) Jangalapalle, Bodanalli (G), Bodanalli (Z) Chintaguppa, Kaliveru (Z), Peddipalle Jettigudem (Z), Devarapalle (Z), Mamidigudem Chalk Puligundala.

Sex ratio of Scheduled tribe population is 512.

Scheduled Tribes Literates and Illiterates by Sex:

	Persons	Males	Females
Literate	5,945	3,495	2,450
Illiterate	13,609	6,054	7,555
Literacy rate	36.6	44.3	29.3
Graduate	49	40	9

Scheduled Tribes (Dominant):

Koya etc., Nayaks, Yerukulas, Sugalis etc.
Gond etc.

For their cultural identity please see Appendix-II

Villages without Scheduled Tribes: There are 19 villages without any scheduled tribe population.

Literates and Illiterates by Sex (Total Population):

	Persons	Males	Females
Literate	16,547	9,525	7,022
Illiterate	21,993	9,625	12,368
Literacy rate	50	59	42
Graduate	473	366	107

Agriculture: ***Distribution of villages according to land use:*** Out of 74 villages, Total area (in hectare) is 10016, out of that 57.81 percent is cultivable and 69.11 percent of the cultivable area is irrigated.

Sources of Irrigation (Hectares): Government Canal 1017.22, Private Canal 0, Well without Electricity 267.6, Well with Electricity 79.12, Tubewell without Electricity 0, Tubewell with Electricity 129.91, Tank 804, River 44.58, Lake 0, Waterfall 1233.18, Others 426.46.

Villages with population of 5000 to 9999: None

Villages with population of 10000 and above: None

Distribution of Workers:

	Persons	Males	Females	WPR
Cultivators	5,309	3,833	1,476	26.63
Agricultural Labour	11,971	5,421	6,550	60.04
Household Industry	270	147	123	1.35
Other Workers	2,387	1,908	479	11.97
Main Workers	15,780	9,839	5,941	79.15
Marginal Workers	4,157	1,470	2,687	20.85
Total Workers	19,937	11,309	8,628	

Religion: Major Religious Communities:

	Persons	Males	Females	Sex Ratio
Hindu (97.71%)	37,656	18,690	18,966	1,015
Muslim (1.55%)	597	312	285	913

Christian (0.65%)	249	125	124	992
Sikh (0.02%)	9	5	4	800
Buddhists (0%)	1	1	-	-
Jain (0.01%)	2	1	1	1,000

Agewise Data:

	Persons	Males	Females	Sex Ratio
All ages	38,540	19,150	19,390	1013
0-14	13,285	6,649	6,636	998
15-44	18,652	9,170	9,482	1034
45-79	6,358	3,218	3,140	976
80+	204	92	112	1217
Age not stated	41	21	20	952

Languages (Dominant):
Telugu, Koya, Urdu, Tamil, Hindi

Disabled Population:

	Persons	Males	Females	%
Total Disabled	653	384	269	
In Seeing	302	186	116	46.25
In Speech	65	35	30	9.95
In Hearing	27	12	15	4.13
In Movement	174	105	69	26.65
Mentally	85	46	39	13.02

CHERUKUPALLE

Cherukupalle C.D. Block lies in the south-eastern part of Guntur district. The Block is located at a distance of 30 kms. from district headquarters (Guntur). There are 10 villages in the block with the total population of 58,484 persons. Area of the C.D. Block is 98.98 sq. kms. It is bounded in the north by Mandals Amruthal ur and Vemuru, in the south by Mandals Pittalavanipalem and Nagaram, in the east by Mandals Vemuru Bhattiprolu and Nagaram and in the west by Mandal Pittalavanipalem.

Communications:

Roadways : NH- 214: Direction- Madras to Machilipatnam. Nearest Villages- Rambhotlapalem, Kavuru, Arumbaka, Ponnapalle, Nadimpalle, Gudavalli, Kanagala.

Annual Rainfall: Average Rainfall 943 mm

Ground Water: Availability of the Ground Water in the Basin is 4030 H.A.M. and the utilization is 1091 H. A.M. It belongs to Safe category. Depth to water level varies from less than 2 meter below the ground. Most of the wells go down in summer months.

Natural Division : Krishna Delta Region

Administration:

Division: Coastal Andhra. Parliamentary Constituency: 32 Bapatla (SC). District: Guntur. Mandal: Cherukupalle. Assembly Constituency: 209 Repalle. Gram Panchayat: 16

Places of Tourist Interest:

Gudavalli : This village is situated at a distance of 15 kms. to the north-west of Repalle town and about 9 kms. away from the Bhattiprolu Railway Station. To the north of the village, there exists a mound known as 'Jathivadi Dibba' or foreigner's mound. This place is also important in the area for, cattle breeding and cattle trade.

Villages: 10 **Inhabited:** 10 **Uninhabited:** 0

Ranking	District	State	National
Area	55	1028	5731
Population	22	298	4907
Sex Ratio	3	136	779
Child Sex Ratio	14	362	1305
Literacy Rate	20	191	2209
Density	37	584	1865
Work Participation Rate	3	72	1570

Gram Panchayats:
Allavaripalem, Arepalli, Arumbaka, Balusulapalem Cherukupalli, Gudavalli, Gullapalli, Kanagala Kavuru, Kunchalavaripalem, Nadimpalli, Ponnapalli Rajavolu, Rambhotlapalem, Thummalapalem, Thurpupalem.

Amenities:

Education: Primary School in 10 villages, Middle school in 7 villages, Matriculation or Secondary School in 5 villages, namely Kavuru, Arumbaka, Gudavalli, Kanagala, Rajavolu.

Higher Secondary or Pre University Courses or Intermediate or Junior College in 2 villages of the CD Block,, namely Kavuru, Arumbaka.

College in 1 village, Adult Literacy Center in 0 village., College is in village, namely Arumbaka.

Medical: Hospital in 1 village, Dispensary in 2 villages, Health Center in 2 villages, Sub Center in 9 villages, Maternity and Child Welfare Center in 0 village, Community health workers in 0 village.

The Villages having Hospital or Dispensary or Health Center are Kavuru, Arumbaka.

Drinking Water: Tap water in 10 villages, Tank water in 10 villages, Well water in 10 villages, Tubewell in 10 villages and more than one source in 10 villages.

Bank: Banking facility in 3 villages, namely, Arumbaka, Gudavalli, Kanagala.

Credit Society in 6 villages Agricultural Credit Society in 4 Non-Agricultural Credit Society in 1 village.

Others: Power supply in 10 villages, Cinema hall in 3 villages, sport club in 0 village, Stadium or Auditorium or Community Hall in 0 village, Post Office in 10 villages.

There are 10 villages having bus facilities.

Villages with most of facilities: Arumbaka Gudavalli, Kanagala.

Villages without Amenities (Education): None..

Scheduled Castes: Out of the total population of 58484

persons, 5780 persons (9.88%) belong to Scheduled Castes. The villages having less than 10% SC population are None..

The villages having more than 50% SC population are None.

Sex ratio of Scheduled Caste population is 508.

Scheduled Castes Literates and Illiterates by Sex:

	Persons	Males	Females
Literate	3,369	1,838	1,531
Illiterate	2,411	1,003	1,408
Literacy rate	65.2	72.8	57.9
Graduate	194	139	55

Scheduled Castes (Dominant):

Mala, Madiga, Beda Jangam etc., Generic Castes etc.

For their cultural identity please see Appendix-I

Villages without Scheduled Castes: There are 0 village without any scheduled caste population.

Scheduled Tribes: Out of the total population of 58484 persons, 2249 persons (3.85%) belong to Scheduled Tribes. The villages having less than 10% ST population are Rambhotlapalem, Kavuru, Balusulapalem, Arumbaka Ponnapalle, Nadimpalle, Gudavalli, Kanagala Rajavolu, Arepalle.

The villages having more than 50% ST population are None.

Sex ratio of Scheduled tribe population is 506.

Scheduled Tribes Literates and Illiterates by Sex:

	Persons	Males	Females
Literate	680	373	307
Illiterate	1,569	737	832
Literacy rate	35.9	40.0	32.0
Graduate	10	10	0

Scheduled Tribes (Dominant):

Yenadis, Yerukulas, Sugalis etc., Koya etc.

For their cultural identity please see Appendix-II

Villages without Scheduled Tribes: There are 0 village without any scheduled tribe population.

Literates and Illiterates by Sex (Total Population):

	Persons	Males	Females
Literate	33,025	18,529	14,496
Illiterate	25,459	10,515	14,944
Literacy rate	63	72	55
Graduate	1,996	1,518	478

Agriculture: ***Distribution of villages according to land use:*** Out of 10 villages, Total area (in hectare) is 9897, out of that 79.76 percent is cultivable and 97.55 percent of the cultivable area is irrigated.

Sources of Irrigation (Hectares): Government Canal 7527.47, Private Canal 0, Well without Electricity 0, Well with Electricity 0, Tubewell without Electricity 0, Tubewell with Electricity 13.34, Tank 0, River 0, Lake 0, Waterfall 0, Others 159.84.

Villages with population of 5000 to 9999:

Rambhotlapalem, Kavuru, Kanagala, Arepalle.

Villages with population of 10000 and above:

Arumbaka.

Distribution of Workers:

	Persons	Males	Females	WPR
Cultivators	4,894	3,573	1,321	15.57
Agricultural Labour	19,078	8,710	10,368	60.71
Household Industry	1,487	780	707	4.73
Other Workers	5,968	4,660	1,308	18.99
Main Workers	27,688	16,751	10,937	88.1
Marginal Workers	3,739	972	2,767	11.9
Total Workers	31,427	17,723	13,704	

Religion: Major Religious Communities:

	Persons	Males	Females	Sex Ratio
Hindu (90.15%)	52,725	26,168	26,557	1,015
Muslim (8.24%)	4,817	2,419	2,398	991
Christian (1.54%)	898	434	464	1,069
Sikh (0%)	-	-	-	-
Buddhists (0%)	2	2	-	-
Jain (0%)	-	-	-	-

Agewise Data:

	Persons	Males	Females	Sex Ratio
All ages	58,484	29,044	29,440	1014
0-14	16,228	8,150	8,078	991
15-44	27,571	13,776	13,795	1001
45-79	13,874	6,722	7,152	1064
80+	721	353	368	1042
Age not stated	90	43	47	1093

Languages (Dominant):

Telugu, Urdu, Tamil, Hindi, Malayalam

Disabled Population:

	Persons	Males	Females	%
Total Disabled	990	575	415	
In Seeing	339	199	140	34.24
In Speech	152	82	70	15.35
In Hearing	44	24	20	4.44
In Movement	292	177	115	29.49
Mentally	163	93	70	16.46

CHEVELLA

Chevella C.D. Block lies in the north-west part of Rangareddy district. The Block is located at a distance of 42 kms. from district headquarters (Serilingampalle). There are 36 villages in the block with the total population of 55,784 persons. Area of the C.D. Block is 286.20 sq. kms. It is bounded by Shankarpalle Mandal on north, Moinabad Mandal on east, Shabad Mandal on south, Pudur Mandal on west, and Nawabpet Mandal on north-west.

Communications :

Roadways : Metalled Roads: Nearest Villages- Aloor Ii, Aloor Iii, Orella, Yenkepalle, Dearlapalle, Ibrahimpal le, Damergidda, Bastepur, Mirjaguda, Kistapur, Pamena, Allawada, Chevella, Kesavaram, Malkapur, Kanduwada.

Backwards Region Grants Fund: It receives Backward Region Grants.

Integrated Child Development Scheme (ICDS) Project: Chevella, Total Anganwadi Centres: 214

Annual Rainfall: Average Rainfall 813 mm

Ground Water: Availability of the Ground Water in the Basin is 2191 H.A.M. and the utilization is 1210 H. A.M. It belongs to Safe category. Depth to water level varies from 10 to 20 meter below the ground. Most of the wells go down in summer months. The well density in the entire block is 16 wells per sq. km. Total no. of the wells in the block are enumerated as 4405, according to the Ground Water Estimation Committee.

Natural Division : Telangana Plateau Region

Administration:

Division: Telangana. Parliamentary Constituency: 10 Chevella. District: Rangareddy.

Mandal: Chevella. Assembly Constituency: 53 Chevella (SC). Gram Panchayat: 30.

Place of Turist Interest:

Chevella : Chevella is situated at a distance of 42 kms. from Hyderabad city and 31 kms. from Vicarabad railway station. The temple of Venkateswara is the important place of worship here. The Natherlands Founda tion for Child Welfare has sponsored the establishment of an integrated child care project in India and it is gratifying to note that Chevella block has been selected for locating this project. This project came into being in April, 1969. The project aims at providing care to the expectant mothers and total care and welfa re to the child from birth to its adult age. The headqua rters of the Director, Indian Bureau, Indo-Dutch Project for Child Welfare, is however, located at Hyderabad.

Villages: 36 **Inhabited:** 36 **Uninhabited:** 0

Ranking	District	State	National
Area	4	189	2922
Population	9	348	5016
Sex Ratio	14	796	2689
Child Sex Ratio	1	71	183
Literacy Rate	12	469	3724
Density	12	490	4797
Work Participation Rate	25	733	1266

Gram Panchayats:

Allawada, Aloor, Antharam, Bastepur, Chanvelly Chevella, Damergidda, Devarampally, Devuniyerravally Gollapally, Gundal, Ibrahimpally, Kammeta, Kandawada Khanapur, Kowkuntla, Kummera, Malkapur, Mirjaguda Mudimiyal, Nyalata, Orella, Palgutta, Pamena Ramannaguda, Ravulapally(Khurd), Regadighanapur Tallaram, Tangadpally, Yenkepally.

Amenities:

Education: Primary School in 34 villages, Middle school in 18 villages, Matriculation or Secondary School in 9 villages, namely Aloor I, Kowkuntla, Tangedapalle, Orella, Chanvelli, Chevella, Malkapur, Kanduwada, Gundal. Higher Secondary or Pre University Courses or Inter- mediate or Junior College in 1 village of the CD Block,, namely Chevella.

College in 1 village, Adult Literacy Center in 1 village., College is in village, namely Chevella.

Medical: Hospital in 1 village, Dispensary in 1 village, Health Center in 1 village, Sub Center in 7 villages, Maternity and Child Welfare Center in 32 villages, Community health workers in 0 village.

The Villages having Hospital or Dispensary or Health Center are Aloor I, Chevella.

Drinking Water: Tap water in 36 villages, Tank water in 36 villages, Well water in 36 villages, Tubewell in 36 villages and more than one source in 36 villages.

Bank: Banking facility in 36 villages, namely, Hasthepur, Nowlaipalle, Anantawaram, Aloor I Aloor Ii, Aloor Iii, Kowkuntla, Tangedapalle Tallaram, Nyalata, Orella, Yenkepalle, Dearlapalle Kammeta, Gollapalle, Ravulapalle (Khurd), Mudimyal Kummera, Devuni Erravelly, Ibrahimpalle, Damergidda Bastepur, Mirjaguda, Kistapur, Naincheru, Khanapur Regadghanapur, Devarampalle, Chanvelli, Pamena Allawada, Chevella, Kesavaram, Malkapur, Kanduwada Gundal.

Credit Society in 9 villages Agricultural Credit Society in 7 Non-Agricultural Credit Society in 6 villages.

Others: Power supply in 36 villages, Cinema hall in 1 village, sport club in 0 village, Stadium or Auditorium or Community Hall in 0 village, Post Office in 9 villages.

There are 31 villages having bus facilities.

Villages with most of facilities: Anantawaram Aloor I, Kowkuntla, Tangedapalle, Nyalata, Orella Yenkepalle, Dearlapalle, Kammeta, Gollapalle Ravulapalle (Khurd), Mudimyal, Kummera Devuni Erravelly, Damergidda, Bastepur, Mirjaguda Khanapur, Regadghanapur, Devarampalle, Chanvelli Pamena, Allawada, Chevella, Kesavaram, Malkapur Kanduwada, Gundal.

Villages without Amenities (Education): None..

Scheduled Castes: Out of the total population of 55784 persons, 12552 persons (22.5%) belong to Scheduled Castes.

The villages having less than 10% SC population are None..

The villages having more than 50% SC population are None.

Sex ratio of Scheduled Caste population is 489.

Scheduled Castes Literates and Illiterates by Sex:

	Persons	Males	Females
Literate	4,971	3,145	1,826
Illiterate	7,581	3,275	4,306
Literacy rate	46.3	56.8	35.1
Graduate	78	67	11

Scheduled Castes (Dominant):

Madiga, Mala, Generic Castes etc., Bindla Beda Jangam etc.

For their cultural identity please see Appendix-I

Villages without Scheduled Castes: There are 2 villages without any scheduled caste population.

Scheduled Tribes: Out of the total population of 55784 persons, 496 persons (0.89%) belong to Scheduled Tribes.

The villages having less than 10% ST population are Hasthepur, Nowlaipalle, Anantawaram, Aloor I Aloor Ii, Aloor Iii, Kowkuntla, Tangedapalle Tallaram, Nyalata, Orella, Yenkepalle, Dearlapalle Kammeta, Gollapalle, Ravulapalle (Khurd), Mudimyal Kummera, Devuni Erravelly, Ibrahimpalle, Damergidda Bastepur, Mirjaguda, Kistapur, Naincheru, Khanapur Regadghanapur, Devarampalle, Chanvelli, Pamena Allawada, Chevella, Kesavaram, Malkapur, Kanduwada Gundal.

The villages having more than 50% ST population are None.

Sex ratio of Scheduled tribe population is 504.

Scheduled Tribes Literates and Illiterates by Sex:

	Persons	Males	Females
Literate	199	125	74
Illiterate	297	121	176
Literacy rate	47.2	60.4	34.4
Graduate	8	7	1

Scheduled Tribes (Dominant):

Yerukulas, Bagata, Chenchu etc., Sugalis etc. Koya etc.

For their cultural identity please see Appendix-II

Villages without Scheduled Tribes: There are 22 villages without any scheduled tribe population.

Literates and Illiterates by Sex (Total Population):

	Persons	Males	Females
Literate	26,273	16,568	9,705
Illiterate	29,511	11,812	17,699
Literacy rate	55	67	41
Graduate	664	552	112

Agriculture: ***Distribution of villages according to land use:*** Out of 36 villages, Total area (in hectare) is 28620, out of that 29.6 percent is cultivable and 14.48 percent of the cultivable area is irrigated.

Sources of Irrigation (Hectares): Government Canal 0, Private Canal 0, Well without Electricity 0, Well with Electricity 704.38, Tubewell without Electricity 0, Tubewell with Electricity 522.7, Tank 0, River 0, Lake 0, Waterfall 0, Others 0.

Villages with population of 5000 to 9999: Chevella.

Villages with population of 10000 and above: None

Distribution of Workers:

	Persons	Males	Females	WPR
Cultivators	17,661	9,531	8,130	59.57
Agricultural Labour	8,529	3,813	4,716	28.77
Household Industry	385	227	158	1.3
Other Workers	3,070	2,394	676	10.36
Main Workers	27,781	15,283	12,498	93.71
Marginal Workers	1,864	682	1,182	6.29
Total Workers	29,645	15,965	13,680	

Religion: Major Religious Communities:

	Persons	Males	Females	Sex Ratio
Hindu (90.85%)	50,682	25,731	24,951	970
Muslim (8.91%)	4,973	2,584	2,389	925
Christian (0.16%)	92	45	47	1,044
Sikh (0%)	-	-	-	-
Buddhists (0%)	-	-	-	-
Jain (0%)	-	-	-	-

Agewise Data:

	Persons	Males	Females	Sex Ratio
All ages	55,784	28,380	27,404	966
0-14	19,557	9,897	9,660	976
15-44	25,008	12,958	12,050	930
45-79	10,698	5,291	5,407	1022
80+	443	188	255	1356
Age not stated	78	46	32	696

Languages (Dominant):

Telugu, Urdu, Hindi, Kannada, Marathi

Disabled Population:

	Persons	Males	Females	%
Total Disabled	1,138	679	459	
In Seeing	616	360	256	54.13
In Speech	84	41	43	7.38
In Hearing	66	32	34	5.8
In Movement	296	198	98	26.01
Mentally	76	48	28	6.68

CHIGURUMAMIDI

Chigurumamidi C.D. Block lies in the southern part of Karimnagar district. The Block is located at a dista nce of 26 kms. from district headquarters (Karimnagar). There are 11 villages in the block with the total population of 41,019 persons. Area of the C.D. Block is 154.31 sq. kms. It is bounded by Timmapur Mandal on north, Saidapur Mandal on east, Husbabad Mandal on south, and Koheda Mandal on west.

Communications :

Roadways : NH, SH or Important Metalled Road is not available.

River: Manner Nadi- Nearest Villages- Mudimanikyam, Ramancha, Indurthi, Nawabpeta.

Backwards Region Grants Fund: It receives Backward Region Grants.

Mahila Samakhya (Education for Women's Equality): It is decleared Socialy and Educationally Backward Block by the Government.

Annual Rainfall: Average Rainfall 675 mm

Ground Water: Availability of the Ground Water in the Basin is 1831 H.A.M. and the utilization is 1074 H. A.M. It belongs to Safe category. Depth to water level varies from more than 10 meter below the ground. Most of the wells go down in summer months. The well density in the entire block is 30 wells per sq. km. Total no. of the wells in the block are enumerated as 4592, according to the Ground Water Estimation Committee.

Natural Division : Godavari Depression Region

Administration :

Division: Telangana. Parliamentary Constituency: 3 Karimnagar. District: Karimnagar. Mandal: Chigurumamidi. Assembly Constituency: 32 Husnabad. Gram Panchayat: 16

Villages: 11 **Inhabited:** 11 **Uninhabited:** 0

Ranking	District	State	National
Area	43	805	4975
Population	42	794	5692
Sex Ratio	51	667	2248
Child Sex Ratio	55	960	4328
Literacy Rate	17	562	4088
Density	38	570	3900
Work Participation Rate	32	480	1511

Gram Panchayats:

Bommanapalli, Chigurumamidi, Gagireddypally Indurthy, Kondapoor, Lambadipalli, Mudimanikyam Mulkanoor, Nawabpet, Ogulapoor, Pechupalli, Ramancha Rekonda, Seetharampoor, Sundaragiri, Ullampally.

Amenities:

Education: Primary School in 11 villages, Middle school in 10 villages, Matriculation or Secondary School in 10 villages, namely Mudimanikyam, Ramancha, Mulkanoor, Chigurumamidi, Rekonda, Bommanapalle, Sundaragiri, Indurthi, Nawabpeta, Ullampalle.

Higher Secondary or Pre University Courses or Intermediate or Junior College in 0 village of the CD Block, College in 0 village, Adult Literacy Center in 11 villages.

Medical: Hospital in 0 village, Dispensary in 0 village, Health Center in 1 village, Sub Center in 7 villages, Maternity and Child Welfare Center in 0 village, Community health workers in 0 village.

Drinking Water: Tap water in 11 villages, Tank water in 11 villages, Well water in 11 villages, Tubewell in 11 villages and more than one source in 11 villages.

Bank: Banking facility in 2 villages, namely, Chigurumamidi, Indurthi.

Credit Society in 11 villages Agricultural Credit Society in 3 Non-Agricultural Credit Society in 11 villages.

Others: Power supply in 11 villages, Cinema hall in 1 village, sport club in 0 village, Stadium or Auditorium or Community Hall in 0 village, Post Office in 10 villages.

There are 11 villages having bus facilities.

Villages with most of facilities: Chigurumamidi Indurthi.

Villages without Amenities (Education): None..

Scheduled Castes: Out of the total population of 41019 persons, 8346 persons (20.35%) belong to Scheduled Castes.

The villages having less than 10% SC population are None..

The villages having more than 50% SC population are None.

Sex ratio of Scheduled Caste population is 481.

Scheduled Castes Literates and Illiterates by Sex:

	Persons	Males	Females
Literate	3,513	2,261	1,252
Illiterate	4,833	2,072	2,761
Literacy rate	48.6	60.2	36.1
Graduate	34	29	5

Scheduled Castes (Dominant):

Madiga, Mala, Generic Castes etc., Gosangi, Mashti

For their cultural identity please see Appendix-I

Villages without Scheduled Castes: There are 0 village without any scheduled caste population.

Scheduled Tribes: Out of the total population of 41019 persons, 363 persons (0.88%) belong to Scheduled Tribes.

The villages having less than 10% ST population are Mudimanikyam, Ramancha, Mulkanoor, Chigurumamidi Rekonda, Bommanapalle, Sundaragiri, Indurthi Nawabpeta, Kondapur, Ullampalle.

The villages having more than 50% ST population are None.

Sex ratio of Scheduled tribe population is 512.

Scheduled Tribes Literates and Illiterates by Sex:

	Persons	Males	Females
Literate	142	88	54
Illiterate	221	89	132
Literacy rate	47.2	58.3	36.0
Graduate	0	0	0

Scheduled Tribes (Dominant):

Yerukulas, Sugalis etc.

For their cultural identity please see Appendix-II

Villages without Scheduled Tribes: There are 0 village without any scheduled tribe population.

Literates and Illiterates by Sex (Total Population):

	Persons	Males	Females
Literate	18,837	11,871	6,966
Illiterate	22,182	8,902	13,280
Literacy rate	53	66	39
Graduate	484	427	57

Agriculture: ***Distribution of villages according to land use:*** Out of 11 villages, Total area (in hectare) is 15430, out of that 62.54 percent is cultivable and 59.51 percent of the cultivable area is irrigated.

Sources of Irrigation (Hectares): Government Canal 0, Private Canal 0, Well without Electricity 0, Well with Electricity 5702, Tubewell without Electricity 0, Tubewell with Electricity 0, Tank 40, River 0, Lake 0, Waterfall 0, Others 0.

Villages with population of 5000 to 9999: Chigurumamidi, Indurthi.

Villages with population of 10000 and above: None

Distribution of Workers:

	Persons	Males	Females	WPR
Cultivators	7,273	4,361	2,912	33.62
Agricultural Labour	10,191	3,997	6,194	47.11
Household Industry	551	314	237	2.55
Other Workers	3,617	2,916	701	16.72
Main Workers	18,022	10,472	7,550	83.31
Marginal Workers	3,610	1,116	2,494	16.69
Total Workers	21,632	11,588	10,044	

Religion: Major Religious Communities:

	Persons	Males	Females	Sex Ratio
Hindu (97.44%)	39,970	20,255	19,715	973
Muslim (2.11%)	865	430	435	1,012
Christian (0.44%)	180	86	94	. 1,093
Sikh (0%)	-	-	-	-
Buddhists (0%)	-	-	-	-
Jain (0%)	-	-	-	-

Agewise Data:

	Persons	Males	Females	Sex Ratio
All ages	41,019	20,773	20,246	975
0-14	12,604	6,583	6,021	915
15-44	18,397	9,172	9,225	1006
45-79	9,571	4,802	4,769	993
80+	415	198	217	1096
Age not stated	32	18	14	778

Languages (Dominant):

Telugu, Urdu, Tamil, Hindi, Oriya

Disabled Population:

	Persons	Males	Females	%
Total Disabled	717	420	297	
In Seeing	320	181	139	44.63
In Speech	73	45	28	10.18
In Hearing	39	20	19	5.44
In Movement	198	137	61	27.62
Mentally	87	37	50	12.13

CHILAKALURIPET H/O.PURUSHOTHA PATNAM

Chilakaluripet C.D. Block lies in the southern part of Guntur district. It is a part of Chilakaluripet Mandal. The Block is located at a distance of 33 kms. from district headquarters (Guntur). There are 15 villages in the block with the total population of 60,237 persons. Area of the C.D. Block is 193.66 sq. kms. It is bounded in the north by Mandals Narasaraopet, Nadendla and Edlapadu, in the south and west by distr ict Prakasam, and in the west by Pedanandipadu and Edlap adu Mandals.

Communications:

Roadways : NH- 5: Direction- Ongole to Guntur. Nearest Villages- Murikipudi, Thatapudi, Chinna Pasumarru, Boppudi. State Highway (S.H.): Direction- Narasaraopet to Parchur, Nearest Villages- Govindapuram, Kavuru, Kanthetivari Khandrika, Gottipadu, Pasumarru (Rural). A stream, Vogaru Vagu, eastwardly, touches the following villages, Chinna Pasumarru, Boppudi, Gottipadu, Pasuma rru (Rural), Pothavaram, Manukondavaripalem, Kukkapallev aripalem, Rajapeta.

Annual Rainfall: Average Rainfall 806 mm

Ground Water: Availability of the Ground Water in the Basin is 5760 H.A.M. and the utilization is 629 H.A. M. It belongs to Safe category. Depth to water level varies from 2 to 5 meter below the ground. Most of the wells go down in summer months.

Natural Division : Krishna Delta Region

Administration:

Division: Coastal Andhra. Parliamentary Constituency: 31 Narsaraopet. District: Guntur. Mandal: Chilakaluripet. Assembly Constituency: 215 Chilakaluripet. Gram Panch ayat: 21.

Villages: 15 **Inhabited:** 13 **Uninhabited:** 2

Ranking	District	State	National

Area	17	597	4298
Population	28	361	5036
Sex Ratio	5	236	1153
Child Sex Ratio	43	841	3684
Literacy Rate	31	369	3305
Density	10	103	3672
Work Participation Rate	40	412	331

Gram Panchayats:
Boppudi, Dandamudi, Edavalli, Gangannapalem Gopalamvaripalem, Gottipadu, Govindapuram Kammavaripalem, Kattubadivaripalem, Kavuru Kukkapallivaripalem, Lingamguntla, Maddirala Manukondavaripalem, Murikipudi, Pasumarru Pothavaram, Rajapeta, Ramachandrapuram, Tatapudi Veluru.

Amenities:
Education: Primary School in 13 villages, Middle school in 10 villages, Matriculation or Secondary School in 7 villages, namely Govindapuram, Kavuru, Veluru, Pasumarru (Rural), Boppudi, Rajapeta, Murikipudi.
Higher Secondary or Pre University Courses or Intermediate or Junior College in 1 village of the CD Block,, namely Murikipudi.
College in 1 village, Adult Literacy Center in 0 village., College is in village, namely Rajapeta.
Medical: Hospital in 0 village, Dispensary in 2 villages, Health Center in 0 village, Sub Center in 9 villages, Maternity and Child Welfare Center in 1 village, Community health workers in 0 village.
The Villages having Hospital or Dispensary or Health Center are Govindapuram, Pasumarru (Rural).
Drinking Water: Tap water in 13 villages, Tank water in 13 villages, Well water in 13 villages, Tubewell in 13 villages and more than one source in 13 villages.
Bank: Banking facility in 3 villages, namely, Govindapuram, Pasumarru (Rural), Murikipudi.
Credit Society in 7 villages Agricultural Credit Society in 7 Non-Agricultural Credit Society in 0 village.
Others: Power supply in 13 villages, Cinema hall in 1 village, sport club in 0 village, Stadium or Auditorium or Community Hall in 0 village, Post Office in 12 villages.
There are 13 villages having bus facilities.
Villages with most of facilities: Govindapuram Pasumarru (Rural), Murikipudi.
Villages without Amenities (Education): None..
Scheduled Castes: Out of the total population of 55523 persons, 11144 persons (20.07%) belong to Scheduled Castes.
The villages having less than 10% SC population are None..
The villages having more than 50% SC population are None.
Sex ratio of Scheduled Caste population is 492.

Scheduled Castes Literates and Illiterates by Sex:

	Persons	Males	Females
Literate	4,683	2,952	1,731
Illiterate	6,461	2,704	3,757
Literacy rate	48.9	61.0	36.5
Graduate	141	104	37

Scheduled Castes (Dominant):
Madiga, Mala, Dakkal etc., Mala Dasari
For their cultural identity please see Appendix-I
Villages without Scheduled Castes: There are 3 villages without any scheduled caste population.
Scheduled Tribes: Out of the total population of 55523 persons, 2221 persons (4%) belong to Scheduled Tribes.
The villages having less than 10% ST population are Edavalli, Govindapuram, Kavuru, Pothavaram Manukondavaripalem, Veluru, Kukkapallevaripalem Gottipadu, Pasumarru (Rural), Boppudi, Rajapeta Murikipudi, Thatapudi.
The villages having more than 50% ST population are None.
Sex ratio of Scheduled tribe population is 498.

Scheduled Tribes Literates and Illiterates by Sex:

	Persons	Males	Females
Literate	628	390	238
Illiterate	1,593	726	867
Literacy rate	33.7	41.6	25.7
Graduate	9	8	1

Scheduled Tribes (Dominant):
Yerukulas, Yenadis, Sugalis etc., Chenchu etc.
For their cultural identity please see Appendix-II
Villages without Scheduled Tribes: There are 3 villages without any scheduled tribe population.

Literates and Illiterates by Sex (Total Population):

	Persons	Males	Females
Literate	28,087	16,654	11,433
Illiterate	27,436	11,111	16,325
Literacy rate	57	68	46
Graduate	1,426	1,114	312

Agriculture: *Distribution of villages according to land use:*
Out of 15 villages, Total area (in hectare) is 19366, out of that 76.52 percent is cultivable and 10.51 percent of the cultivable area is irrigated.
Sources of Irrigation (Hectares): Government Canal 0, Private Canal 0, Well without Electricity 38.82, Well with Electricity 295.44, Tubewell without Electricity 0, Tubewell with Electricity 0, Tank 32, River 57.02, Lake 0, Waterfall 0, Others 1134.57.
Villages with population of 5000 to 9999:

Govindapuram, Kavuru, Veluru, Pasumarru (Rural) Boppudi, Murikipudi.

Villages with population of 10000 and above: None

Distribution of Workers:

	Persons	Males	Females	WPR
Cultivators	9,034	5,277	3,757	27.4
Agricultural Labour	17,701	7,918	9,783	53.68
Household Industry	686	377	309	2.08
Other Workers	5,551	4,331	1,220	16.84
Main Workers	29,302	16,616	12,686	88.87
Marginal Workers	3,670	1,287	2,383	11.13
Total Workers	32,972	17,903	15,069	

Religion: Major Religious Communities:

	Persons	Males	Females	Sex Ratio
Hindu (84.03%)	46,658	23,328	23,330	1,000
Muslim (14.28%)	7,929	3,959	3,970	1,003
Christian (1.4%)	780	405	375	926
Sikh (0%)	-	-	-	-
Buddhists (0%)	2	1	1	1,000
Jain (0%)	-	-	-	-

Agewise Data:

	Persons	Males	Females	Sex Ratio
All ages	55,523	27,765	27,758	1000
0-14	15,223	7,663	7,560	987
15-44	27,115	13,598	13,517	994
45-79	12,434	6,106	6,328	1036
80+	552	265	287	1083
Age not stated	199	133	66	496

Languages (Dominant):
Telugu, Urdu, Tamil, Gondi, Hindi

Disabled Population:

	Persons	Males	Females	%
Total Disabled	885	493	392	
In Seeing	276	135	141	31.19
In Speech	108	57	51	12.2
In Hearing	46	21	25	5.2
In Movement	306	192	114	34.58
Mentally	149	88	61	16.84

CHILAMATHUR

Chilamathur C.D. Block lies in the southern part of Anantapur district. The Block is located at a distance of 108 kms. from district headquarters (Anantapur). There are 21 villages in the block with the total population of 46,399 persons. Area of the C.D. Block is 219.55 sq. kms. It is bounded in the north by Mandal Gorantla, in the west by Mandals Lepakshi and Hindupur, and it has common boundary with the state of Karnataka in the south and east.

Communications:

Roadways : NH- 7: Direction- Hyderabad to Bangalore. Nearest Villages- Kodur, Settipalle, Chilamathur.

River: Kushavati Nadi- Nearest Villages- Chilamathur, Kodur. Chitravati Nadi- Nearest Villages- Kodur, Chilamathur.

It receives the Backward Region Grants, and is identifi ed as a drought-prone area as well.

Annual Rainfall: Average Rainfall_ 514 mm

Ground Water: Availability of the Ground Water in the Basin is 1760 H.A.M. and the utilization is 1372 H. A.M. It belongs to SC category. Depth to water level varies from 10 to 20 meter below the ground. Most of the wells go down in summer months. The well density in the entire block is 9 wells per sq. km. Total no. of the wells in the block are enumerated as 2009, according to the Ground Water Estimation Committee.

Natural Division : Rayalaseema Region

Administration:

Division: Rayala Seema. Parliamentary Constituency: 37 Hindupur. District: Anantapur. Mandal: Lepakshi. Assembly Constituency: 276 Hindupur. Gram Panchayat: 11

Border Villages: (Karnataka)- Nearest Villages- Yagnise ttipalle, Hussainpuram, Chilamathur, Kodur, Chagaluru, Kambaladinne, Demakethepalle, Morasalapalle, Somaghatta, Veerapuram, Kodikonda.

Villages: 21 **Inhabited:** 15 **Uninhabited:** 6

Ranking	District	State	National
Area	50	442	3863
Population	24	621	5448
Sex Ratio	4	591	2060
Child Sex Ratio	19	364	1319
Literacy Rate	7	411	3525
Density	22	343	4570
Work Participation Rate	12	674	853

Gram Panchayats:
Chagaleru, Chilamathur, Demakethepalli, Kodi Konda Kodur, Morasalapalli, Palagala Palli, Settipalli Somaghatta, Tekulodu, Veera Puram.

Amenities:

Education: Primary School in 14 villages, Middle school in 7 villages, Matriculation or Secondary School in 5 villages, namely Demakethepalle, Chilamathur, Kodur, Muddireddipalle, Kodikonda.

Higher Secondary or Pre University Courses or Intermediate or Junior College in 1 village of the CD Block,, namely Chilamathur.

College in 0 village, Adult Literacy Center in 1 village.

Medical: Hospital in 0 village, Dispensary in 2 villages, Health Center in 1 village, Sub Center in 7 villages, Maternity and Child Welfare Center in 0 village, Community health workers in 0 village.

The Villages having Hospital or Dispensary or Health Center are Chilamathur, Kodur.

Drinking Water: Tap water in 11 villages, Tank water in 2 villages, Well water in 0 village, Tubewell in 13 villages and more than one source in 14 villages.

Bank: Banking facility in 3 villages, namely, Chilamathur, Settipalle, Kodikonda.

Credit Society in 3 villages Agricultural Credit Society in 3 Non-Agricultural Credit Society in 0 village.

Others: Power supply in 15 villages, Cinema hall in 1 village, sport club in 0 village, Stadium or Auditorium or Community Hall in 0 village, Post Office in 11 villages.

There are 11 villages having bus facilities.

Villages with most of facilities: Chilamathur Kodikonda.

Villages without amenities (Education):

Kanugamakulapalle..

Scheduled Castes: Out of the total population of 46399 persons, 5974 persons (12.88%) belong to Scheduled Castes. The villages having less than 10% SC population are Tekulodu, Hussainpuram, Subbaraopet, Muddireddipalle Morasalapalle.

The villages having more than 50% SC population are None.

Sex ratio of Scheduled Caste population is 486.

Scheduled Castes Literates and Illiterates by Sex:

	Persons	Males	Females
Literate	2,274	1,512	762
Illiterate	3,700	1,556	2,144
Literacy rate	44.5	57.2	30.9
Graduate	30	28	2

Scheduled Castes (Dominant):

Madiga, Mala, Generic Castes etc., Adi Andhra Adi Dravida

For their cultural identity please see Appendix-I

Villages without Scheduled Castes: There are 6 villages without any scheduled caste population.

Scheduled Tribes: Out of the total population of 46399 persons, 1094 persons (2.36%) belong to Scheduled Tribes. The villages having less than 10% ST population are Tekulodu, Demakethepalle, Yagnisettipalle Chilamathur, Kodur, Settipalle, Chagaluru Kanugamakulapalle, Subbaraopet, Muddireddipalle Somaghatta, Veerapuram, Morasalapalle, Kodikonda.

The villages having more than 50% ST population are None.

Sex ratio of Scheduled tribe population is 511.

Scheduled Tribes Literates and Illiterates by Sex:

	Persons	Males	Females
Literate	461	282	179
Illiterate	633	253	380
Literacy rate	49.8	62.5	37.8
Graduate	21	19	2

Scheduled Tribes (Dominant):

Sugalis etc., Yerukulas, Andh, Yenadis Generic Tribes etc.

For their cultural identity please see Appendix-II

Villages without Scheduled Tribes: There are 12 villages without any scheduled tribe population.

Literates and Illiterates by Sex (Total Population):

	Persons	Males	Females
Literate	22,580	14,072	8,508
Illiterate	23,819	9,370	14,449
Literacy rate	56	69	43
Graduate	513	406	107

Agriculture: ***Distribution of villages according to land use:*** Out of 21 villages, Total area (in hectare) is 21955, out of that 63.5 percent is cultivable and 8.83 percent of the cultivable area is irrigated.

Sources of Irrigation (Hectares): Government Canal 0, Private Canal 0, Well without Electricity 11.86, Well with Electricity 368.26, Tubewell without Electricity 0, Tubewell with Electricity 560.95, Tank 289.62, River 0, Lake 0, Waterfall 0, Others 0.

Villages with population of 5000 to 9999:

Kodur.

Villages with population of 10000 and above:

Chilamathur.

Distribution of Workers:

	Persons	Males	Females	WPR
Cultivators	10,976	7,314	3,662	42.78
Agricultural Labour	9,603	3,756	5,847	37.43
Household Industry	915	509	406	3.57
Other Workers	4,165	3,191	974	16.23
Main Workers	20,957	13,868	7,089	81.68
Marginal Workers	4,702	902	3,800	18.32
Total Workers	25,659	14,770	10,889	

Religion: Major Religious Communities:

	Persons	Males	Females	Sex Ratio
Hindu (89.78%)	41,659	21,030	20,629	981
Muslim (10.13%)	4,700	2,394	2,306	963
Christian (0.07%)	33	15	18	1,200
Sikh (0%)	-	-	-	-
Buddhists (0%)	-	-	-	-
Jain (0%)	1	-	1	-

Agewise Data:

	Persons	Males	Females	Sex Ratio
All ages	46,399	23,442	22,957	979
0-14	14,616	7,375	7,241	982
15-44	21,553	10,867	10,686	983

45-79	9,836	5,023	4,813	958
80+	334	149	185	1242
Age not stated	60	28	32	1143

Languages (Dominant):
Telugu, Urdu, Hindi, Kannada, Marathi

Disabled Population:

	Persons	Males	Females	%
Total Disabled	887	489	398	
In Seeing	328	162	166	36.98
In Speech	84	49	35	9.47
In Hearing	84	43	41	9.47
In Movement	264	164	100	29.76
Mentally	127	71	56	14.32

CHILKUR

Chilkur C.D. Block lies in the eastern part of Nalgonda district. The Block is located at a distance of 90 kms. from district headquarters (Nalgonda). There are 4 villages in the block with the total population of 37,770 persons. Area of the C.D. Block is 144.87 sq. kms. It is bounded by Munagala Mandal on north, Kodad Mandal on east, Huzurnagar Mandal on south, and Garidep alle Mandal on west.

Communications:
Roadways : Metalled Roads: Nearest Village- Chilkur. Backwards Region Grants Fund: It receives Backward Region Grants.

Annual Rainfall: Average Rainfall 796 mm

Ground Water: Availability of the Ground Water in the Basin is 4496 H.A.M. and the utilization is 138 H.A. M. It belongs to Safe category. Depth to water level varies from 5 to 10 meter below the ground. Most of the wells go down in summer months. The well density in the entire block is 2 wells per sq. km. Total no. of the wells in the block are enumerated as 243, accor ding to the Ground Water Estimation Committee.

Natural Division : Krishna Piedmont Plain Region

Administration:
Division: Telangana. Parliamentary Constituency: 13 Nalgonda. District: Nalgonda. Mandal: Chilkur. Assembly Constituency: 90 Kodad. Gram Panchayat: 13.

Villages: 4 **Inhabited:** 4 **Uninhabited:** 0

Ranking	District	State	National
Area	58	969	5549
Population	53	890	5830
Sex Ratio	21	669	2251
Child Sex Ratio	30	732	3111
Literacy Rate	15	317	3041
Density	40	644	3282
Work Participation Rate	4	310	1759

Gram Panchayats:
Acharlagudem, Arlagudem, Bethavole, Chennarigudem Chilkur, Janakinagar, Jerripotula Gudem, Kondapuram Narayanapuram, Polenigudem, Ramapuram, Sethalathanda Setharamapuram.

Amenities:
Education: Primary School in 4 villages, Middle school in 4 villages, Matriculation or Secondary School in 3 villages, namely Bethavole, Chilkur, Paleannaram.
Higher Secondary or Pre University Courses or Intermediate or Junior College in 0 village of the CD Block, College in 0 village, Adult Literacy Center in 0 village.
Medical: Hospital in 0 village, Dispensary in 1 village, Health Center in 1 village, Sub Center in 2 villages, Maternity and Child Welfare Center in 0 village, Community health workers in 0 village.
The Village having Hospital or Dispensary or Health Center is Bethavole.
Drinking Water: Tap water in 4 villages, Tank water in 4 villages, Well water in 4 villages, Tubewell in 4 villages and more than one source in 4 villages.
Bank: Banking facility in 2 villages, namely, Bethavole, Chilkur.
Credit Society in 3 villages Agricultural Credit Society in 3 Non-Agricultural Credit Society in 0 village.
Others: Power supply in 4 villages, Cinema hall in 0 village, sport club in 0 village, Stadium or Auditorium or Community Hall in 0 village, Post Office in 4 villages.
There are 4 villages having bus facilities.
Villages with most of facilities: Bethavole Chilkur.
Villages without Amenities (Education): None..
Scheduled Castes: Out of the total population of 37770 persons, 6039 persons (15.99%) belong to Scheduled Castes.
The villages having less than 10% SC population are None..
The villages having more than 50% SC population are None.
Sex ratio of Scheduled Caste population is 494.

Scheduled Castes Literates and Illiterates by Sex:

	Persons	Males	Females
Literate	2,569	1,579	990
Illiterate	3,470	1,477	1,993
Literacy rate	49.5	59.9	38.8
Graduate	47	45	2

Scheduled Castes (Dominant):
Madiga, Mala, Bindla, Madiga Dasu etc., Mala Dasari
For their cultural identity please see Appendix-I
Villages without Scheduled Castes: There are 0 village without any scheduled caste population.
Scheduled Tribes: Out of the total population of 37770

persons, 4198 persons (11.11%) belong to Scheduled Tribes.
The villages having less than 10% ST population are None..
The villages having more than 50% ST population are None.
Sex ratio of Scheduled tribe population is 487.

Scheduled Tribes Literates and Illiterates by Sex:

	Persons	Males	Females
Literate	1,669	1,114	555
Illiterate	2,529	1,040	1,489
Literacy rate	46.6	60.6	31.8
Graduate	61	58	3

Scheduled Tribes (Dominant):
Sugalis etc., Yerukulas, Yenadis

For their cultural identity please see Appendix-II

Villages without Scheduled Tribes: There is 1 village without any scheduled tribe population.

Literates and Illiterates by Sex (Total Population):

•	Persons	Males	Females
Literate	19,336	11,593	7,743
Illiterate	18,434	7,533	10,901
Literacy rate	59	69	47
Graduate	732	654	78

Agriculture: ***Distribution of villages according to land use:*** Out of 4 villages, Total area (in hectare) is 11488, out of that 80.96 percent is cultivable and 89.52 percent of the cultivable area is irrigated.

Sources of Irrigation (Hectares): Government Canal 6130, Private Canal 0, Well without Electricity 0, Well with Electricity 327, Tubewell without Electricity 0, Tubewell with Electricity 73, Tank 778, River 0, Lake 0, Waterfall 0, Others 1018.

Villages with population of 5000 to 9999: None

Villages with population of 10000 and above: Bethavole, Chilkur.

Distribution of Workers:

	Persons	Males	Females	WPR
Cultivators	5,003	3,370	1,633	25.5
Agricultural Labour	11,520	4,783	6,737	58.72
Household Industry	420	248	172	2.14
Other Workers	2,675	2,147	528	13.64
Main Workers	16,168	9,519	6,649	82.41
Marginal Workers	3,450	1,029	2,421	17.59
Total Workers	19,618	10,548	9,070	

Religion: Major Religious Communities:

	Persons	Males	Females	Sex Ratio
Hindu (94.03%)	35,516	17,971	17,545	976
Muslim (5.65%)	2,133	1,094	1,039	950
Christian (0.24%)	91	46	45	978
Sikh (0%)	-	-	-	-
Buddhists (0%)	-	-	-	-
Jain (0%)	-	-	-	-

Agewise Data:

	Persons	Males	Females	Sex Ratio
All ages	37,770	19,126	18,644	975
0-14	12,128	6,165	5,963	967
15-44	18,086	9,183	8,903	970
45-79	7,230	3,624	3,606	995
80+	294	132	162	1227
Age not stated	32	22	10	455

Languages (Dominant):
Telugu, Hindi, Urdu, Tamil, Gondi

Disabled Population:

	Persons	Males	Females	%
Total Disabled	1,107	658	449	
In Seeing	563	339	224	50.86
In Speech	83	49	34	7.5
In Hearing	26	9	17	2.35
In Movement	317	190	127	28.64
Mentally	118	71	47	10.66

CHILLAKUR

Chillakur C.D. Block lies in the south-eastern part of Nellore district. The Block is located at a distance of 40 kms. from district headquarters (Nellore). There are 30 villages in the block with the total population of 46,475 persons. Area of the C.D. Block is 323.25 sq. kms. It is bounded in the north by Mandals Gudur, Manubolu, Venkatachalam and Muthukur, in the south by Mandals Ojili and Kota, in the east by the Bay of Bengal and Mandal Kota, and in the west by Mandal Gudur.

Communications:

Roadways : NH- 5: Direction- Chennai to Nellore. Nearest Villages- Nakkalakalva Khandrika, Nelaballi, Budanam, Mutyalapadu (Rural), Chillakur, Kadivedu.

Railway Station: Oduru.

Annual Rainfall: Average Rainfall 1015 mm

Ground Water: Availability of the Ground Water in the Basin is 3093 H.A.M. and the utilization is 1158 H. A.M. It belongs to Safe category. Depth to water level varies from 2 to 10 meter below the ground. Most of the wells go down in summer months, according to the Ground Water Estimation Committee.

Coastal Villages: Nearest Village- Thamminapatnam.

Administration:

Division: Coastal Andhra. Parliamentary Constituency: 40 Tirupati (SC). District: Nellore. Mandal: Chillakur. Assembly Constituency: 239 Gudur (SC). Gram Panchayat: 31

Villages: 30 **Inhabited:** 28 **Uninhabited:** 2

Ranking	District	State	National
Area	10	118	2532

Population	17	618	5444
Sex Ratio	42	756	2560
Child Sex Ratio	6	225	730
Literacy Rate	39	455	3685
Density	34	876	5646
Work Participation Rate	25	923	2914

Gram Panchayats:

Annambaka, Ballavolu, Budanam, Chedimala, Chillakur Chinthavaram, East Kanupuru, Eguvarajupalem Kadivedu, Kalavakonda, Kammavari Palem, Lingavaram Manne Gunta, Momidi, Muthyalapadu Nelaballi-Retapalli, Oduru, Palicherlavaripalem Pallamala, Ponnavolu, Thammina Patnam, Theepanuru Thikkavaram, Thimmana Gaari Palem, Thippaguntapalem Thonukumala, Udathavaripalem, Vallipadu, Varagali Vellapalem, Yeruru.

Amenities:

Education: Primary School in 25 villages, Middle school in 12 villages, Matriculation or Secondary School in 5 villages, namely Chillakur, Thikkavaram, Chinthavaram, Momidi, Vallipadu.

Higher Secondary or Pre University Courses or Intermediate or Junior College in 1 village of the CD Block,, namely Chillakur.

College in 0 village, Adult Literacy Center in 21 villages.

Medical: Hospital in 0 village, Dispensary in 0 village, Health Center in 2 villages, Sub Center in 13 villages, Maternity and Child Welfare Center in 0 village, Community health workers in 0 village.

Drinking Water: Tap water in 27 villages, Tank water in 26 villages, Well water in 28 villages, Tubewell in 27 villages and more than one source in 27 villages.

Bank: Banking facility in 2 villages, namely, Thikkavaram, Chinthavaram.

Credit Society in 17 villages Agricultural Credit Society in 5 Non-Agricultural Credit Society in 17 villages.

Others: Power supply in 28 villages, Cinema hall in 0 village, sport club in 0 village, Stadium or Auditorium or Community Hall in 0 village, Post Office in 13 villages.

There are 25 villages having bus facilities.

Villages with most of facilities: Thikkavaram Chinthavaram.

Villages without amenities (Education):

Nakkalakalva Khandrika, Yogeswarunipalle..

Scheduled Castes: Out of the total population of 46475 persons, 15405 persons (33.15%) belong to Scheduled Castes.

The villages having less than 10% SC population are None..

The villages having more than 50% SC population are Budanam, Udathavariparlapalle, Yogeswarunipalle Ankulapaturu.

Sex ratio of Scheduled Caste population is 478.

Scheduled Castes Literates and Illiterates by Sex:

	Persons	Males	Females
Literate	7,125	4,452	2,673
Illiterate	8,280	3,586	4,694
Literacy rate	53.9	64.1	42.6
Graduate	139	105	34

Scheduled Castes (Dominant):

Mala, Madiga, Arundhatiya, Generic Castes etc.

Mala Dasari

For their cultural identity please see Appendix-I

Villages without Scheduled Castes: There are 5 villages without any scheduled caste population.

Scheduled Tribes: Out of the total population of 46475 persons, 6683 persons (14.38%) belong to Scheduled Tribes.

The villages having less than 10% ST population are Theepanur, Budanam, Udathavariparlapalle Thonukumala, Addepalle, Pallamala.

The villages having more than 50% ST population are None.

Sex ratio of Scheduled tribe population is 488.

Scheduled Tribes Literates and Illiterates by Sex:

	Persons	Males	Females
Literate	1,436	802	634
Illiterate	5,247	2,619	2,628
Literacy rate	26.0	28.2	23.6
Graduate	10	6	4

Scheduled Tribes (Dominant):

Yenadis, Yerukulas, Generic Tribes etc.

Sugalis etc., Chenchu etc.

For their cultural identity please see Appendix-II

Villages without Scheduled Tribes: There are 3 villages without any scheduled tribe population.

Literates and Illiterates by Sex (Total Population):

	Persons	Males	Females
Literate	21,878	12,759	9,119
Illiterate	24,597	10,847	13,750
Literacy rate	55	63	47
Graduate	647	483	164

Agriculture: ***Distribution of villages according to land use:*** Out of 30 villages, Total area (in hectare) is 32325, out of that 25.33 percent is cultivable and 73.62 percent of the cultivable area is irrigated.

Sources of Irrigation (Hectares): Government Canal 0, Private Canal 0, Well without Electricity 342.87, Well with Electricity 174.81, Tubewell without Electricity 0, Tubewell with Electricity 639.08, Tank 3517.65, River 0, Lake 0, Waterfall 0, Others 1353.42.

Villages with population of 5000 to 9999: None

Villages with population of 10000 and above: None

Distribution of Workers:

	Persons	Males	Females	WPR
Cultivators	2,661	2,377	284	12.26
Agricultural Labour	14,063	7,486	6,577	64.79
Household Industry	447	265	182	2.06
Other Workers	4,533	3,374	1,159	20.89
Main Workers	13,453	9,398	4,055	61.98
Marginal Workers	8,251	4,104	4,147	38.02
Total Workers	21,704	13,502	8,202	

Religion: Major Religious Communities:

	Persons	Males	Females	Sex Ratio
Hindu (93.81%)	43,600	22,141	21,459	969
Muslim (5.39%)	2,505	1,270	1,235	972
Christian (0.5%)	233	129	104	806
Sikh (0%)	-	-	-	-
Buddhists (0%)	-	-	-	-
Jain (0%)	-	-	-	-

Agewise Data:

	Persons	Males	Females	Sex Ratio
All ages	46,475	23,606	22,869	969
0-14	15,057	7,841	7,216	920
15-44	22,360	11,292	11,068	980
45-79	8,754	4,316	4,438	1028
80+	255	128	127	992
Age not stated	49	29	20	690

Languages (Dominant):

Telugu, Urdu, Tamil, Gondi, Hindi

Disabled Population:

	Persons	Males	Females	%
Total Disabled	1,167	614	553	
In Seeing	515	250	265	44.13
In Speech	112	51	61	9.6
In Hearing	125	54	71	10.71
In Movement	318	203	115	27.25
Mentally	97	56	41	8.31

CHIMAKURTHI

Chimakurthi C.D. Block lies in the eastern part of Prakasam district. The Block is located at a distance of 22 kms. from district headquarters (Ongole). There are 24 villages in the block with the total population of 64,590 persons. Area of the C.D. Block is 250.98 sq. kms. It is bounded in the north by Mandals Thallur and Addanki, in the south by Mandal Kondapi and River Musi, in the east by Mandals Maddipadu and Santhanuthal apadu, and in the west by Mandals Darsi, Podili and Marripudi, and River Musi.

Communications:

Roadways : State Highway (S.H.): Direction- Podili to Ongole. Nearest Villages- Yerragudipadu, Manchikalapadu, Chimakurthi, Rajupalem - Laxmipuram, Budavada.

River: Musi Nadi- Nearest Villages- Nippatlapadu, Mylav aram, Pulikonda, China Ravipadu, Bhusura Palle, Ramachan dra Puram, Pidathalapudi, Budavada.

The Block is identified as a drought-prone area.

Annual Rainfall: Average Rainfall 934.2 mm

Ground Water: Availability of the Ground Water in the Basin is 20.07 MCM and the utilization is 16.32 MCM It belongs to Semi Critical category. Depth to water level varies from 2 to 5 meter below the ground. Most of the wells go down in summer months, according to the Ground Water Estimation Committee.

Administration:

Division: Coastal Andhra. Parliamentary Constituency: 32 Baptala (SC). District: Prakasam. Mandal: Chimakurthi. Assembly Constituency: 226 Santhanuthalapadu (SC). Gram Panchayat: 24.

Villages: 24 **Inhabited:** 24 **Uninhabited:** 0

Ranking	District	State	National
Area	25	307	3368
Population	6	212	4706
Sex Ratio	27	729	2499
Child Sex Ratio	22	521	2002
Literacy Rate	18	326	3083
Density	48	795	3994
Work Participation Rate	19	512	2361

Gram Panchayats:

Bandlamudi, Budawada, Busarapalli, Chandrapadu Chimakurthy, Chinaravipadu, Devarapalem, E.V.Palem Gadiparthivaripalem, Gonugunta, Ilapavuluru K.V.Palem, M.V.Palem, Manchikalapadu, Nekunambadu Nippatlapadu, P.Nayudupalem, Pallamalli Pidathalapudi, Pulikonda, R.C.Puram, R.L.Puram Torragudipadu, Yarragudipadu.

Amenities:

Education: Primary School in 22 villages, Middle school in 11 villages, Matriculation or Secondary School in 3 villages, namely Bandlamudi, Chimakurthi, Rajupalem - Laxmipuram.

Higher Secondary or Pre University Courses or Intermediate or Junior College in 1 village of the CD Block,, namely Chimakurthi.

College in 1 village, Adult Literacy Center in 23 villages., College is in village, namely Chimakurthi.

Medical: Hospital in 1 village, Dispensary in 0 village, Health Center in 1 village, Sub Center in 8 villages, Maternity and Child Welfare Center in 0 village, Community health workers in 0 village.

The Village having Hospital or Dispensary or Health Center is Chimakurthi.

Drinking Water: Tap water in 24 villages, Tank water in

24 villages, Well water in 24 villages, Tubewell in 24 villages and more than one source in 24 villages.

Bank: Banking facility in 2 villages, namely, Chimakurthi, Gonugunta.

Credit Society in 11 villages Agricultural Credit Society in 4 Non-Agricultural Credit Society in 10 villages.

Others: Power supply in 24 villages, Cinema hall in 1 village, sport club in 0 village, Stadium or Auditorium or Community Hall in 0 village, Post Office in 16 villages.

There are 24 villages having bus facilities.

Villages with most of facilities: Chimakurthi Gonugunta.

Villages without Amenities (Education): None..

Scheduled Castes: Out of the total population of 64590 persons, 16884 persons (26.14%) belong to Scheduled Castes.

The villages having less than 10% SC population are None..

The villages having more than 50% SC population are None.

Sex ratio of Scheduled Caste population is 504.

Scheduled Castes Literates and Illiterates by Sex:

	Persons	Males	Females
Literate	7,487	4,540	2,947
Illiterate	9,397	3,840	5,557
Literacy rate	52.6	64.5	40.9
Graduate	181	141	40

Scheduled Castes (Dominant):

Mala, Madiga, Adi Andhra, Beda Jangam etc.

Generic Castes etc.

For their cultural identity please see Appendix-I

Villages without Scheduled Castes: There are 0 village without any scheduled caste population.

Scheduled Tribes: Out of the total population of 64590 persons, 1823 persons (2.82%) belong to Scheduled Tribes.

The villages having less than 10% ST population are

Devarapalem, Ilapavuluru, Rangasai Puram

Palla Malli, Nekunambadu, Chandrapadu, Yerragudipadu

Manchikalapadu, Torragudi Padu, Bandlamudi

Padamatinaidupalem, Kandurivari Agraharam

Chimakurthi, Nippatlapadu, Budavada

Rajupalem - Laxmipuram, Pulikonda, China Ravipadu

Bhusura Palle, Pidathalapudi, Gunduvari Laxmipuram

Gonugunta.

The villages having more than 50% ST population are None.

Sex ratio of Scheduled tribe population is 478.

Scheduled Tribes Literates and Illiterates by Sex:

	Persons	Males	Females
Literate	606	391	215
Illiterate	1,217	561	656
Literacy rate	40.0	50.0	29.4
Graduate	5	4	1

Scheduled Tribes (Dominant):

Yenadis, Yerukulas, Chenchu etc., Sugalis etc.

Kotia etc.

For their cultural identity please see Appendix-II

Villages without Scheduled Tribes: There are 4 villages without any scheduled tribe population.

Literates and Illiterates by Sex (Total Population):

	Persons	Males	Females
Literate	32,570	19,705	12,865
Illiterate	32,020	13,074	18,946
Literacy rate	58	70	47
Graduate	1,379	1,117	262

Agriculture: ***Distribution of villages according to land use:*** Out of 24 villages, Total area (in hectare) is 25098, out of that 61.36 percent is cultivable and 25.13 percent of the cultivable area is irrigated.

Sources of Irrigation (Hectares): Government Canal 2358, Private Canal 32, Well without Electricity 900, Well with Electricity 580, Tubewell without Electricity 0, Tubewell with Electricity 0, Tank 0, River 0, Lake 0, Waterfall 0, Others 0.

Villages with population of 5000 to 9999: Gonugunta.

Villages with population of 10000 and above: Chimakurthi.

Distribution of Workers:

	Persons	Males	Females	WPR
Cultivators	7,593	5,333	2,260	23.92
Agricultural Labour	15,195	7,048	8,147	47.86
Household Industry	792	402	390	2.49
Other Workers	8,168	6,833	1,335	25.73
Main Workers	30,013	19,104	10,909	94.54
Marginal Workers	1,735	512	1,223	5.46
Total Workers	31,748	19,616	12,132	

Religion: Major Religious Communities:

	Persons	Males	Females	Sex Ratio
Hindu (96.5%)	62,329	31,635	30,694	970
Muslim (2.9%)	1,872	951	921	968
Christian (0.58%)	375	184	191	1,038
Sikh (0%)	-	-	-	-
Buddhists (0.01%)	4	3	1	333
Jain (0%)	-	-	-	-

Agewise Data:

	Persons	Males	Females	Sex Ratio
All ages	64,590	32,779	31,811	970
0-14	20,903	10,471	10,432	996
15-44	30,833	15,896	14,937	940
45-79	12,387	6,201	6,186	998

80+	424	192	232	1208
Age not stated	43	19	24	1263

Languages (Dominant):
Telugu, Urdu, Tamil, Gondi, Hindi

Disabled Population:

	Persons	Males	Females	%
Total Disabled	880	497	383	
In Seeing	298	159	139	33.86
In Speech	124	72	52	14.09
In Hearing	48	20	28	5.45
In Movement	278	175	103	31.59
Mentally	132	71	61	15

CHINAGANJAM

Chinaganjam C.D. Block lies in the eastern part of Prakasam district. The Block is located at a distance of 40 kms. from district headquarters (Ongole). There are 07 villages in the block with the total population of 40,668 persons. Area of the C.D. Block is 120.90 sq. kms. It is bounded in the north by Mandal Karamchedu, in the south by Mandal Naguluppalapadu, in the east by Mandal Vetapalem and Bay of Bengal, and in the west by Mandals Naguluppalapadu and Inkollu.

Communications:

Roadways : NH- 214 A: Direction- Ongole to Guntur. Neare st Villages- Pedaganjam, Kadavakuduru, Motu Palle, China ganjam.

Railway Station: Kadavakuduru, Chinaganjam.

River: Ramperu Nadi- Nearest Villages- Kadavakuduru, Motu Palle, Chinaganjam.

The Block is identified as a drought-prone area.

Coastal Villages: Nearest Villages- Motu Palle, Pedagan jam.

Annual Rainfall: Average Rainfall 984.0 mm

Ground Water: Availability of the Ground Water in the Basin is 4.67 MCM and the utilization is 2.12 MCM It belongs to Safe category. Depth to water level varies from 2 to 5 meter below the ground. Most of the wells go down in summer months., according to the Ground Water Estimation Committee.

Annual Rainfall: Average Rainfall 936.8 mm

Administration:

Division: Coastal Andhra. Parliamentary Constituency: 32 Baptala (SC). District: Prakasam. Mandal: Chinganjam. Assembly Constituency: 223 Parchur. Gram Panchayat: 12

Places of Tourist Interest:

Motupalle : This village is situated 27 kms. to the south-west of Bapatla town. Motupalle is well-known as an ancient port, which flourished almost from the first century A.D. It was also referred to as Mohana-pu ri. It was in a very prosperous condition during the reign of the Satavahanas, Pallavas, Chalukyas and Cholas. Very near this port, a township known as Velapuri or Dvelapuri is referred to as having been constructed by the Buddhists. Traces of Buddhist stupas and sculptu re can be noticed at some places.

Villages: 7 **Inhabited:** 7 **Uninhabited:** 0

Ranking	District	State	National
Area	52	943	5460
Population	34	805	5710
Sex Ratio	11	277	1262
Child Sex Ratio	23	624	2528
Literacy Rate	21	395	3452
Density	38	738	3218
Work Participation Rate	6	296	2144

Gram Panchayats:

Chinnaganjam, Chinthagumpalli, Gonasapudi Kadavakuduru, Kothapalem, Motupalli, Munnamvaripalem Neelayapalem, Pallepalem, Pedaganjam, R.B.Palem Santharavuru.

Amenities:

Education: Primary School in 7 villages, Middle school in 5 villages, Matriculation or Secondary School in 3 villages, namely Kadavakuduru, Chinaganjam, Pedaganjam. Higher Secondary or Pre University Courses or Intermediate or Junior College in 1 village of the CD Block,, namely Chinaganjam.

College in 0 village, Adult Literacy Center in 7 villages.

Medical: Hospital in 0 village, Dispensary in 1 village, Health Center in 2 villages, Sub Center in 7 villages, Maternity and Child Welfare Center in 0 village, Community health workers in 0 village.

The Villages having Hospital or Dispensary or Health Center are Chinaganjam, Pedaganjam.

Drinking Water: Tap water in 7 villages, Tank water in 7 villages, Well water in 7 villages, Tubewell in 7 villages and more than one source in 7 villages.

Bank: Banking facility in 3 villages, namely, Santharavuru, Kadavakuduru, Chinaganjam.

Credit Society in 5 villages Agricultural Credit Society in 3 Non-Agricultural Credit Society in 4 villages.

Others: Power supply in 7 villages, Cinema hall in 1 village, sport club in 0 village, Stadium or Auditorium or Community Hall in 0 village, Post Office in 7 villages.

There are 7 villages having bus facilities.

Villages with most of facilities: Santharavuru Kadavakuduru, Chinaganjam.

Villages without Amenities (Education): None..

Scheduled Castes: Out of the total population of 40668 persons, 6316 persons (15.53%) belong to Scheduled Castes. The villages having less than 10% SC population are

None..

The villages having more than 50% SC population are None.

Sex ratio of Scheduled Caste population is 513.

Scheduled Castes Literates and Illiterates by Sex:

	Persons	Males	Females
Literate	3,549	2,085	1,464
Illiterate	2,767	993	1,774
Literacy rate	63.6	76.4	51.4
Graduate	149	118	31

Scheduled Castes (Dominant):

Mala, Madiga, Generic Castes etc.

For their cultural identity please see Appendix-I

Villages without Scheduled Castes: There are 0 village without any scheduled caste population.

Scheduled Tribes: Out of the total population of 40668 persons, 2208 persons (5.43%) belong to Scheduled Tribes.

The villages having less than 10% ST population are Santharavuru, Gonasapudi, Chinthagum Palle Motu Palle, Chinaganjam, Pedaganjam.

The villages having more than 50% ST population are None.

Sex ratio of Scheduled tribe population is 500.

Scheduled Tribes Literates and Illiterates by Sex:

	Persons	Males	Females
Literate	680	394	286
Illiterate	1,528	711	817
Literacy rate	36.6	42.6	30.6
Graduate	8	5	3

Scheduled Tribes (Dominant):

Yenadis, Yerukulas, Sugalis etc.

For their cultural identity please see Appendix-II

Villages without Scheduled Tribes: There are 0 village without any scheduled tribe population.

Literates and Illiterates by Sex (Total Population):

	Persons	Males	Females
Literate	20,088	12,076	8,012
Illiterate	20,580	8,289	12,291
Literacy rate	56	68	45
Graduate	937	741	196

Agriculture: ***Distribution of villages according to land use:*** Out of 7 villages, Total area (in hectare) is 12090, out of that 59.57 percent is cultivable and 71.28 percent of the cultivable area is irrigated.

Sources of Irrigation (Hectares): Government Canal 4911.4, Private Canal 0, Well without Electricity 0, Well with Electricity 0, Tubewell without Electricity 0, Tubewell with Electricity 0, Tank 0, River 0, Lake 0, Waterfall 0, Others 222.67.

Villages with population of 5000 to 9999:

Pedaganjam.

Villages with population of 10000 and above:

Chinaganjam.

Distribution of Workers:

	Persons	Males	Females	WPR
Cultivators	3,208	2,256	952	15.58
Agricultural Labour	11,082	5,288	5,794	53.81
Household Industry	221	112	109	1.07
Other Workers	6,085	4,239	1,846	29.54
Main Workers	17,439	10,796	6,643	84.67
Marginal Workers	3,157	1,099	2,058	15.33
Total Workers	20,596	11,895	8,701	

Religion: Major Religious Communities:

	Persons	Males	Females	Sex Ratio
Hindu (95.59%)	38,875	19,482	19,393	995
Muslim (2.71%)	1,103	553	550	995
Christian (1.6%)	650	312	338	1,083
Sikh (0%)	-	-	-	-
Buddhists (0%)	-	-	-	-
Jain (0%)	-	-	-	-

Agewise Data:

	Persons	Males	Females	Sex Ratio
All ages	40,668	20,365	20,303	997
0-14	12,247	6,136	6,111	996
15-44	19,683	9,991	9,692	970
45-79	8,294	4,024	4,270	1061
80+	397	189	208	1101
Age not stated	47	25	22	880

Languages (Dominant):

Telugu, Urdu, Gondi, Hindi, Tamil

Disabled Population:

	Persons	Males	Females	%
Total Disabled	724	388	336	
In Seeing	296	145	151	40.88
In Speech	77	37	40	10.64
In Hearing	50	23	27	6.91
In Movement	221	135	86	30.52
Mentally	80	48	32	11.05

CHINNACHINTAKUNTA

Chinnachintakunta C.D. Block lies in the central west part of Mahbubnagar district. The Block is located at a distance of 52 kms. from district headquarters (Mahbubnagar). There are 23 villages in the block with the total population of 45,548 persons. Area of the C.D. Block is 186 sq. kms. It is bounded by Dhanwada Mandal on north, Devarkadra and Kothakota Mandals on east, Atmakur Mandal on south, and Narva Mandal on west.

Communications:

Roadways : Metalled Roads: Nearest Villages- Thirumalapur, Undyala, Gudur, Ammapur, Kurumurthy, Maddur, Allipur,

Duppalle.

River: Krishna Nadi- Nearest Villages- Bandrepalle, Lalkota, Pallamarri, Mutchintala, Nellikondi, Waddemanu, Appampalle, Thirumalapur, Edulapur, Chinnachintakunta, Gudur, Kurumurthy, Maddur, Allipur, Duppalle, Kothapal le.

It receives Backward Region Grants, and is identified as a drought prone area as well.

Annual Rainfall: Average Rainfall 496 mm

Ground Water: Availability of the Ground Water in the Basin is 1120 H.A.M. and the utilization is 1102 H. A.M. It belongs to CRI category. Depth to water level varies from 2 to 5 meter below the ground. Most of the wells go down in summer months. The well density in the entire block is 11 wells per sq. km. Total no. of the wells in the block are enumerated as 2140, according to the Ground Water Estimation Committee.

Natural Division : Telangana Plateau Region

Administration:

Division: Telangana. Parliamentary Constituency: 11 Mahbubnagar. District: Mahbubnagar. Mandal: Chinnachint akunta. Assembly Constituency: 76 Devarkadra. Gram Panch ayat: 19.

Villages: 23 **Inhabited:** 23 **Uninhabited:** 0

Ranking	District	State	National
Area	58	607	4336
Population	42	678	5532
Sex Ratio	1	47	378
Child Sex Ratio	34	762	3234
Literacy Rate	36	1001	5692
Density	9	82	4285
Work Participation Rate	16	599	299

Gram Panchayats:

Allipur, Ammapur, Appampalle, Banderpalle Chinnachintakunta, Damganpur, Dasarapally, Duppalle Fareedpur, Gudur, Kurumurthy, Lalkota, Maddur Muchintala, Nellikondi, Pallamarri, Thirumalapur Undiyala, Waddemanu.

Amenities:

Education: Primary School in 23 villages, Middle school in 13 villages, Matriculation or Secondary School in 7 villages, namely Bandrepalle, Lalkota, Waddemanu, Appampalle, Undyala, Chinnachintakunta, Duppalle.

Higher Secondary or Pre University Courses or Intermediate or Junior College in 0 village of the CD Block, College in 0 village, Adult Literacy Center in 21 villages.

Medical: Hospital in 0 village, Dispensary in 1 village, Health Center in 1 village, Sub Center in 8 villages, Maternity and Child Welfare Center in 1 village, Community health workers in 0 village.

The Village having Hospital or Dispensary or Health Center is Undyala.

Drinking Water: Tap water in 23 villages, Tank water in 23 villages, Well water in 23 villages, Tubewell in 23 villages and more than one source in 23 villages.

Bank: Banking facility in 3 villages, namely, Lalkota, Undyala, Chinnachintakunta.

Credit Society in 11 villages Agricultural Credit Society in 6 Non-Agricultural Credit Society in 9 villages.

Others: Power supply in 23 villages, Cinema hall in 0 village, sport club in 0 village, Stadium or Auditorium or Community Hall in 0 village, Post Office in 16 villages.

There are 18 villages having bus facilities.

Villages with most of facilities: Lalkota, Undyala Chinnachintakunta.

Villages without Amenities (Education): None..

Scheduled Castes: Out of the total population of 44548 persons, 5743 persons (12.89%) belong to Scheduled Castes.

The villages having less than 10% SC population are Seetharampeta, Appampalle, Dasarpalle, Thirumalapur Chinnachintakunta, Ammapur, Duppalle.

The villages having more than 50% SC population are None.

Sex ratio of Scheduled Caste population is 526.

Scheduled Castes Literates and Illiterates by Sex:

	Persons	Males	Females
Literate	1,466	1,022	444
Illiterate	4,277	1,703	2,574
Literacy rate	29.9	44.4	17.0
Graduate	19	16	3

Scheduled Castes (Dominant):

Madiga, Mala, Beda Jangam etc., Generic Castes etc. Mala Dasari

For their cultural identity please see Appendix-I

Villages without Scheduled Castes: There are 0 village without any scheduled caste population.

Scheduled Tribes: Out of the total population of 44548 persons, 1305 persons (2.93%) belong to Scheduled Tribes.

The villages having less than 10% ST population are Bandrepalle, Lalkota, Pallamarri, Mutchintala Nellikondi, Seetharampeta, Damagnapur, Waddemanu Appampalle, Dasarpalle, Thirumalapur, Edulapur Lakshmidevipur, Undyala, Chinnachintakunta, Gudur Ammapur, Kurumurthy, Maddur, Allipur, Duppalle Kothapalle.

The villages having more than 50% ST population are None.

Sex ratio of Scheduled tribe population is 505.

Scheduled Tribes Literates and Illiterates by Sex:

	Persons	Males	Females

Literate	204	154	50
Illiterate	1,101	492	609
Literacy rate	20.2	32.0	9.4
Graduate	4	4	0

Scheduled Tribes (Dominant):
Sugalis etc., Yerukulas, Kattunayakan Generic Tribes etc.

For their cultural identity please see Appendix-II

Villages without Scheduled Tribes: There is 1 village without any scheduled tribe population.

Literates and Illiterates by Sex (Total Population):

	Persons	Males	Females
Literate	15,372	10,101	5,271
Illiterate	29,176	11,752	17,424
Literacy rate	40	54	27
Graduate	448	363	85

Agriculture: ***Distribution of villages according to land use:*** Out of 23 villages, Total area (in hectare) is 19110, out of that 50.68 percent is cultivable and 17.39 percent of the cultivable area is irrigated.

Sources of Irrigation (Hectares): Government Canal 220, Private Canal 0, Well without Electricity 0, Well with Electricity 490, Tubewell without Electricity 0, Tubewell with Electricity 750, Tank 224, River 0, Lake 0, Waterfall 0, Others 0.

Villages with population of 5000 to 9999: Chinnachintakunta.

Villages with population of 10000 and above: None

Distribution of Workers:

	Persons	Males	Females	WPR
Cultivators	5,225	3,447	1,778	20.31
Agricultural Labour	6,844	2,950	3,894	26.61
Household Industry	8,604	2,752	5,852	33.45
Other Workers	5,049	3,622	1,427	19.63
Main Workers	22,919	11,612	11,307	89.1
Marginal Workers	2,803	1,159	1,644	10.9
Total Workers	25,722	12,771	12,951	

Religion: Major Religious Communities:

	Persons	Males	Females	Sex Ratio
Hindu (87.12%)	38,808	19,044	19,764	1,038
Muslim (9.81%)	4,369	2,131	2,238	1,050
Christian (2.83%)	1,259	629	630	1,002
Sikh (0%)	2	1	1	1,000
Buddhists (0%)	-	-	-	-
Jain (0%)	-	-	-	-

Agewise Data:

	Persons	Males	Females	Sex Ratio
All ages	44,548	21,853	22,695	1039
0-14	15,078	7,698	7,380	959
15-44	20,687	10,020	10,667	1065
45-79	8,481	3,998	4,483	1121
80+	229	97	132	1361
Age not stated	73	40	33	825

Languages (Dominant):
Telugu, Urdu, Hindi, Tamil, Marathi

Disabled Population:

	Persons	Males	Females	%
Total Disabled	1,110	590	520	
In Seeing	559	293	266	50.36
In Speech	85	46	39	7.66
In Hearing	48	19	29	4.32
In Movement	339	195	144	30.54
Mentally	79	37	42	7.12

CHINNAGOTTIGALLU

Chinnagottigallu C.D. Block lies in the northern part of Chittoor district. The Block is located at a distance of 52 kms. from district headquarters (Chittoor). There are 10 villages in the block with the total popul ation of 24,910 persons. Area of the C.D. Block is 142. 42 sq. kms. It is bounded in the north by Mandal Yerrav aripalem, in the south by Mandals Pulicherla and Chandra giri, in the east by Mandals Tirupati Urban, Tirupati Rural and Chandragiri, and in the west by Mandal Rompic herla.

Communications:

Roadways : NH- 205: Direction- Madanapalle to Chandragiri. Nearest Villages- Chinnagotti Gallu, Thippireddigarip alle, Diguvuru, Chattevaripalem, Bhakarapet.

It receives the Backward Region Grants, and is identifi ed as a drought-prone area as well.

Integrated Child Development Scheme (ICDS) Project: Chinnagottigallu, Total Anganwadi Centres: 148

Annual Rainfall: Average Rainfall 770 mm

Ground Water: Availability of the Ground Water in the Basin is 1844 H.A.M.and the utilization is 1041 H.A. M. It belongs to Safe category. Depth to water level varies from 5 to 10 meter below the ground. Most of the wells go down in summer months, according to the Ground Water Estimation Committee.

Forest and Reserved **Forest:** Nearest Villages- Chitteche rla, Devarakonda, Bhakarapet, Yeguvuru.

Natural Division : Rayalaseema Region

Administration:

Division: Rayala Seema. Parliamentary Constituency: . District: Chittoor. Mandal: Chinnagottigallu. Assembly Constituency: 285 Chandragiri. Gram Panchayat: 14.

Villages: 10 **Inhabited:** 10 **Uninhabited:** 0

Ranking	**District**	**State**	**National**
Area	47	858	5152
Population	63	1066	6144

Sex Ratio	26	351	1441
Child Sex Ratio	21	431	1606
Literacy Rate	31	192	2212
Density	29	574	5148
Work Participation Rate	59	816	1530

Gram Panchayats:

Bhakarapet, Chinnagotti Gallu, Chittecherla Deendarlapalle, Devarakonda, Diguvuru Jangavandla Palle, Kotabylu, Nellutla Vari Palle Rangannagari Gadda, T.Settivaripalle Thippireddigaripalle, Yeguvuru.

Amenities:

Education: Primary School in 10 villages, Middle school in 5 villages, Matriculation or Secondary School in 2 villages, namely Chinnagotti Gallu, Bhakarapet.

Higher Secondary or Pre University Courses or Intermediate or Junior College in 1 village of the CD Block,, namely Chinnagotti Gallu.

College in 0 village, Adult Literacy Center in 6 villages.

Medical: Hospital in 1 village, Dispensary in 0 village, Health Center in 2 villages, Sub Center in 4 villages, Maternity and Child Welfare Center in 0 village, Community health workers in 0 village.

The Villages having Hospital or Dispensary or Health Center are Chinnagotti Gallu, Bhakarapet.

Drinking Water: Tap water in 10 villages, Tank water in 10 villages, Well water in 10 villages, Tubewell in 10 villages and more than one source in 10 villages.

Bank: Banking facility in 2 villages, namely, Chinnagotti Gallu, Bhakarapet.

Credit Society in 5 villages Agricultural Credit Society in 4 Non-Agricultural Credit Society in 5 villages.

Others: Power supply in 10 villages, Cinema hall in 2 villages, sport club in 0 village, Stadium or Auditorium or Community Hall in 0 village, Post Office in 9 villages.

There are 10 villages having bus facilities.

Villages with most of facilities: Chinnagotti Gallu Bhakarapet.

Villages without Amenities (Education): None..

Scheduled Castes: Out of the total population of 24910 persons, 4365 persons (17.52%) belong to Scheduled Castes.

The villages having less than 10% SC population are None..

The villages having more than 50% SC population are None.

Sex ratio of Scheduled Caste population is 497.

Scheduled Castes Literates and Illiterates by Sex:

	Persons	Males	Females
Literate	2,096	1,267	829
Illiterate	2,269	929	1,340
Literacy rate	55.2	66.9	43.5
Graduate	75	65	10

Scheduled Castes (Dominant):

Mala, Madiga, Generic Castes etc.

For their cultural identity please see Appendix-I

Villages without Scheduled Castes: There are 0 village without any scheduled caste population.

Scheduled Tribes: Out of the total population of 24910 persons, 656 persons (2.63%) belong to Scheduled Tribes.

The villages having less than 10% ST population are Kotabylu, Rangannagari Gadda, Chinnagotti Gallu Thippireddigaripalle, Diguvuru, Chattevaripalem Chittecherla, Devarakonda, Bhakarapet, Yeguvuru.

The villages having more than 50% ST population are None.

Sex ratio of Scheduled tribe population is 509.

Scheduled Tribes Literates and Illiterates by Sex:

	Persons	Males	Females
Literate	199	112	87
Illiterate	457	210	247
Literacy rate	35.5	40.0	31.1
Graduate	3	3	0

Scheduled Tribes (Dominant):

Yenadis, Yerukulas, Sugalis etc.

For their cultural identity please see Appendix-II

Villages without Scheduled Tribes: There is 1 village without any scheduled tribe population.

Literates and Illiterates by Sex (Total Population):

	Persons	Males	Females
Literate	13,934	8,329	5,605
Illiterate	10,976	4,171	6,805
Literacy rate	63	76	51
Graduate	756	599	157

Agriculture: ***Distribution of villages according to land use:***

Out of 10 villages, Total area (in hectare) is 14250, out of that 41.37 percent is cultivable and 19.91 percent of the cultivable area is irrigated.

Sources of Irrigation (Hectares): Government Canal 0, Private Canal 0, Well without Electricity 0, Well with Electricity 285.67, Tubewell without Electricity 0, Tubewell with Electricity 714.85, Tank 172.99, River 0, Lake 0, Waterfall 0, Others 0.

Villages with population of 5000 to 9999:

Chinnagotti Gallu.

Villages with population of 10000 and above: None

Distribution of Workers:

	Persons	Males	Females	WPR
Cultivators	5,790	3,336	2,454	43.52
Agricultural Labour	5,039	2,431	2,608	37.87
Household Industry	385	250	135	2.89

Other Workers	2,091	1,642	449	15.72
Main Workers	10,969	6,899	4,070	82.44
Marginal Workers	2,336	760	1,576	17.56
Total Workers	13,305	7,659	5,646	

Religion: Major Religious Communities:

	Persons	Males	Females	Sex Ratio
Hindu (86.7%)	21,597	10,820	10,777	996
Muslim (13.11%)	3,265	1,653	1,612	975
Christian (0.09%)	23	12	11	917
Sikh (0%)	1	1	-	-
Buddhists (0%)	-	-	-	-
Jain (0%)	-	-	-	-

Agewise Data:

	Persons	Males	Females	Sex Ratio
All ages	24,910	12,500	12,410	993
0-14	6,788	3,555	3,233	909
15-44	11,272	5,522	5,750	1041
45-79	6,557	3,300	3,257	987
80+	246	98	148	1510
Age not stated	47	25	22	880

Languages (Dominant):
Telugu, Urdu, Hindi, Tamil, Gondi

Disabled Population:

	Persons	Males	Females	%
Total Disabled	437	241	196	
In Seeing	144	79	65	32.95
In Speech	57	32	25	13.04
In Hearing	42	21	21	9.61
In Movement	137	76	61	31.35
Mentally	57	33	24	13.04

CHINNAKODUR

Chinnakodur C.D. Block lies in the north-east part of Medak district. The Block is located at a distance of 134 kms. from district headquarters (Sangareddy). There are 23 villages in the block with the total population of 56,294 persons. Area of the C.D. Block is 266.79 sq. kms. It is bounded by Karimnagar district on north and east, Nangoor Mandal on south-east, and Siddipet Mandal on south and west.

Communications :

Roadways : State Highway (S.H.): Direction- Siddipet to Karimnagar. Nearest Villages- Ananthasagar, Cherla Ankireddipalle, Mallaram, Peddakodur, Mandapalle, Ramuni Patta, Ibrahimpur.

Backwards Region Grants Fund: It receives Backward Region Grants.

Annual Rainfall: Average Rainfall 705 mm

Ground Water: Availability of the Ground Water in the Basin is 2609 H.A.M. and the utilization is 2405 H. A.M. It belongs to Critical category. Depth to water level varies from 5 to 10 meter below the ground. Most of the wells go down in summer months. The well density in the entire block is 37 wells per sq. km. Total no. of the wells in the block are enumerated as 9319, according to the Ground Water Estimation Committee.

Natural Division : Telangana Plateau Region

Administration:

Division: Telangana. Parliamentary Constituency: 6 Medak. District: Medak. Mandal: Chinnakodur. Assembly Constituency: 33 Siddipet. Gram Panchayat: 28.

Villages: 23 **Inhabited:** 23 **Uninhabited:** 0

Ranking	District	State	National
Area	5	253	3150
Population	12	337	4991
Sex Ratio	18	442	1693
Child Sex Ratio	1	72	181
Literacy Rate	15	658	4406
Density	8	215	4575
Work Participation Rate	33	677	585

Gram Panchayats:

Allipur, Ananthasagar, Chandlapur, Chelkalapally Cherlankireddipalle, Chinnakodur, Chowdaram Gangapur, Gonepalle, Gopulapur, Gurralagondi Ibrahimnagar, Jakkapur, Kasturipally, Kistapur Kothuripalle, Machapur, Mailaram, Malyal, Mandapalle Matendlu, Matindla, Medipalle, Peddakodur, Ramancha Ramuni Patla, Sikindlapur, Vittalpur.

Amenities:

Education: Primary School in 22 villages, Middle school in 20 villages, Matriculation or Secondary School in 9 villages, namely Gurralagondi, Allipur, Chinnakodur, Ramancha, Chandlapur, Peddakodur, Mandapalle, Gonepalle, Ibrahimpur.

Higher Secondary or Pre University Courses or Intermediate or Junior College in 0 village of the CD Block, College in 0 village, Adult Literacy Center in 10 villages.

Medical: Hospital in 0 village, Dispensary in 1 village, Health Center in 1 village, Sub Center in 8 villages, Maternity and Child Welfare Center in 0 village, Community health workers in 0 village.

The Village having Hospital or Dispensary or Health Center is Allipur.

Drinking Water: Tap water in 23 villages, Tank water in 23 villages, Well water in 23 villages, Tubewell in 23 villages and more than one source in 23 villages.

Bank: Banking facility in 2 villages, namely, Chinnakodur, Ibrahimpur.

Credit Society in 21 villages Agricultural Credit Society in 7 Non-Agricultural Credit Society in 21 villages.

Others: Power supply in 23 villages, Cinema hall in 0 village, sport club in 0 village, Stadium or Auditorium or Community

Hall in 0 village, Post Office in 19 villages.
There are 22 villages having bus facilities.
Villages with most of facilities: Chinnakodur Ibrahimpur.
Villages without amenities (Education): Sivampalle..
Scheduled Castes: Out of the total population of 56294 persons, 9911 persons (17.61%) belong to Scheduled Castes.
The villages having less than 10% SC population are None..
The villages having more than 50% SC population are None.
Sex ratio of Scheduled Caste population is 496.
Scheduled Castes Literates and Illiterates by Sex:

	Persons	Males	Females
Literate	3,709	2,459	1,250
Illiterate	6,202	2,540	3,662
Literacy rate	43.9	57.5	29.9
Graduate	41	39	2

Scheduled Castes (Dominant):
Madiga, Mala, Generic Castes etc., Beda Jangam etc. Chamar etc.
For their cultural identity please see Appendix-I
Villages without Scheduled Castes: There are 0 village without any scheduled caste population.
Scheduled Tribes: Out of the total population of 56294 persons, 597 persons (1.06%) belong to Scheduled Tribes.
The villages having less than 10% ST population are Malyal, Gurralagondi, Jakkapur, Vittalpur, Allipur Chowdaram, Ananthasagar, Cherla Ankireddipalle Mallaram, Medipalle, Chinnakodur, Machapur, Gangapur Ramancha, Chandlapur, Peddakodur, Mandapalle Gonepalle, Ramuni Patta, Ibrahimpur, Kothurpalle Sivampalle, Sikandlapur.
The villages having more than 50% ST population are None.
Sex ratio of Scheduled tribe population is 487.
Scheduled Tribes Literates and Illiterates by Sex:

	Persons	Males	Females
Literate	211	143	68
Illiterate	386	163	223
Literacy rate	41.5	54.2	27.8
Graduate	1	1	0

Scheduled Tribes (Dominant):
Yerukulas, Chenchu etc., Generic Tribes etc. Sugalis etc.
For their cultural identity please see Appendix-II
Villages without Scheduled Tribes: There are 3 villages without any scheduled tribe population.
Literates and Illiterates by Sex (Total Population):

	Persons	Males	Females
Literate	24,693	15,990	8,703
Illiterate	31,601	12,339	19,262
Literacy rate	51	65	36
Graduate	617	543	74

Agriculture: ***Distribution of villages according to land use:***
Out of 23 villages, Total area (in hectare) is 26679, out of that 69.31 percent is cultivable and 47.41 percent of the cultivable area is irrigated.
Sources of Irrigation (Hectares): Government Canal 0, Private Canal 0, Well without Electricity 0, Well with Electricity 6824.4, Tubewell without Electricity 0, Tubewell with Electricity 706, Tank 1236.03, River 0, Lake 0, Waterfall 0, Others 0.
Villages with population of 5000 to 9999: Jakkapur, Allipur, Chinnakodur.
Villages with population of 10000 and above: None
Distribution of Workers:

	Persons	Males	Females	WPR
Cultivators	13,214	7,660	5,554	41.63
Agricultural Labour	8,618	3,810	4,808	27.15
Household Industry	3,653	715	2,938	11.51
Other Workers	6,253	4,311	1,942	19.7
Main Workers	26,867	14,896	11,971	84.65
Marginal Workers	4,871	1,600	3,271	15.35
Total Workers	31,738	16,496	15,242	

Religion: Major Religious Communities:

	Persons	Males	Females	Sex Ratio
Hindu (98.03%)	55,184	27,773	27,411	987
Muslim (1.72%)	968	482	486	1,008
Christian (0.18%)	103	51	52	1,020
Sikh (0.01%)	7	5	2	400
Buddhists (0%)	-	-	-	-
Jain (0%)	-	-	-	-

Agewise Data:

	Persons	Males	Females	Sex Ratio
All ages	56,294	28,329	27,965	987
0-14	17,802	9,074	8,728	962
15-44	25,528	12,807	12,721	993
45-79	12,318	6,127	6,191	1010
80+	572	272	300	1103
Age not stated	74	49	25	510

Languages (Dominant):
Telugu, Urdu, Tamil, Hindi, Marathi
Disabled Population:

	Persons	Males	Females	%
Total Disabled	1,127	617	510	
In Seeing	536	280	256	47.56
In Speech	98	52	46	8.7
In Hearing	61	28	33	5.41

In Movement	296	186	110	26.26
Mentally	136	71	65	12.07

CHINNAMANDEM

Chinnamandem C.D. Block lies in the southern part of Cuddapah district. The Block is located at a distance of 68 kms. from district headquarters (Cuddapah). There are 09 villages in the block with the total population of 32,750 persons. Area of the C.D. Block is 146.58 sq. kms. It is bounded in the north by Mandal Rayachoti, in the south by district Chittoor, in the east by Mandal Sambepalle, and in the west by Mandal Galiveedu and district Chittoor.

Communications:

Roadways : Metalled Roads: Nearest Villages- Vandadi, Mallur, Devagudipalle, Chinnamandem.

Steam: Local stream touches the following villages, namely, Paramatikona, Vandadi, Mallur, Devagudipalle, Chinnamandem.

It receives Backward Region Grants, and is also identif ied as a drought-prone area as well.

Annual Rainfall: Average Rainfall 653 mm

Ground Water: Availability of the Ground Water in the Basin is 1268 H.A.M.and the utilization is 1463 H.A. M.It belongs to OE category. Depth to water level varies from 5 to 10 meter below the ground. Most of the wells go down in summer months, according to the Ground Water Estimation Committee.

Forest and Reserved **Forest:** Nearest Villages- Diguvagot tiveedu, Kalibanda, Paramatikona, T.Sakibanda, Chinnaman dem, Bonamala.

Natural Division : Rayalaseema Region

Administration:

Division: Rayala Seema. Parliamentary Constituency: 41 Rajampet.District: Cuddapah.

Mandal: Chinnamandem. Assembly Constituency: 247 Rayach oti.Gram Panchayat: 13.

Villages: 9 **Inhabited:** 9 **Uninhabited:** 0

Ranking	District	State	National
Area	44	833	5092
Population	32	980	5982
Sex Ratio	15	490	1796
Child Sex Ratio	3	181	528
Literacy Rate	29	336	3112
Density	12	457	4398
Work Participation Rate	16	630	1146

Gram Panchayats:

Bonamala, C.Polimerapalli, Chinnaerusupalli Chinnamandem, Devagudipalli, Diguva Gotti Veedu Kalibanda, Kesapuram, Kothapalli, Mallur Padamatikona, T. Sakibanda, Vandadi.

Amenities:

Education: Primary School in 9 villages, Middle school in 4 villages, Matriculation or Secondary School in 3 villages, namely T.Sakibanda, Mallur, Chinnamandem.

Higher Secondary or Pre University Courses or Intermediate or Junior College in 1 village of the CD Block,, namely Chinnamandem.

College in 1 village, Adult Literacy Center in 3 villages., College is in village, namely Chinnamandem.

Medical: Hospital in 0 village, Dispensary in 0 village, Health Center in 1 village, Sub Center in 3 villages, Maternity and Child Welfare Center in 1 village, Community health workers in 0 village.

Drinking Water: Tap water in 9 villages, Tank water in 9 villages, Well water in 9 villages, Tubewell in 9 villages and more than one source in 9 villages.

Bank: Banking facility in 2 villages, namely, T.Sakibanda, Chinnamandem.

Credit Society in 3 villages Agricultural Credit Society in 2 Non-Agricultural Credit Society in 2 villages.

Others: Power supply in 9 villages, Cinema hall in 2 villages, sport club in 0 village, Stadium or Auditorium or Community Hall in 0 village, Post Office in 9 villages.

There are 9 villages having bus facilities.

Villages with most of facilities: T.Sakibanda Chinnamandem.

Villages without Amenities (Education): None..

Scheduled Castes: Out of the total population of 32750 persons, 3456 persons (10.55%) belong to Scheduled Castes.

The villages having less than 10% SC population are None..

The villages having more than 50% SC population are None.

Sex ratio of Scheduled Caste population is 489.

Scheduled Castes Literates and Illiterates by Sex:

	Persons	Males	Females
Literate	1,417	976	441
Illiterate	2,039	790	1,249
Literacy rate	47.2	63.3	30.2
Graduate	28	27	1

Scheduled Castes (Dominant):

Madiga, Mala

For their cultural identity please see Appendix-I

Villages without Scheduled Castes: There are 0 village without any scheduled caste population.

Scheduled Tribes: Out of the total population of 32750 persons, 331 persons (1.01%) belong to Scheduled Tribes.

The villages having less than 10% ST population are Diguvagottiveedu, Kalibanda, Paramatikona T.Sakibanda, Vandadi, Mallur, Devagudipalle Chinnamandem, Bonamala.

The villages having more than 50% ST population are None.

Sex ratio of Scheduled tribe population is 480.

Scheduled Tribes Literates and Illiterates by Sex:

	Persons	Males	Females
Literate	135	88	47
Illiterate	196	84	112
Literacy rate	48.0	59.9	35.1
Graduate	4	4	0

Scheduled Tribes (Dominant):

Sugalis etc., Yenadis, Yerukulas

For their cultural identity please see Appendix-II

Villages without Scheduled Tribes: There are 4 villages without any scheduled tribe population.

Literates and Illiterates by Sex (Total Population):

	Persons	Males	Females
Literate	16,543	10,427	6,116
Illiterate	16,207	6,074	10,133
Literacy rate	58	73	43
Graduate	603	505	98

Agriculture: ***Distribution of villages according to land use:*** Out of 9 villages, Total area (in hectare) is 14658, out of that 60.16 percent is cultivable and 23.38 percent of the cultivable area is irrigated.

Sources of Irrigation (Hectares): Government Canal 60.91, Private Canal 0, Well without Electricity 97.12, Well with Electricity 1166.6, Tubewell without Electricity 0, Tubewell with Electricity 136.52, Tank 477.77, River 0, Lake 0, Waterfall 0, Others 122.97.

Villages with population of 5000 to 9999:

Paramatikona, Chinnamandem.

Villages with population of 10000 and above: None

Distribution of Workers:

	Persons	Males	Females	WPR
Cultivators	7,034	4,343	2,691	39.85
Agricultural Labour	6,700	2,766	3,934	37.96
Household Industry	499	260	239	2.83
Other Workers	3,416	2,701	715	19.36
Main Workers	14,891	9,202	5,689	84.37
Marginal Workers	2,758	868	1,890	15.63
Total Workers	17,649	10,070	7,579	

Religion: Major Religious Communities:

	Persons	Males	Females	Sex Ratio
Hindu (79.22%)	25,946	13,060	12,886	987
Muslim (20.48%)	6,706	3,394	3,312	976
Christian (0.22%)	72	38	34	895
Sikh (0%)	1	-	1	-
Buddhists (0%)	-	-	-	-
Jain (0%)	-	-	-	-

Agewise Data:

	Persons	Males	Females	Sex Ratio
All ages	32,750	16,501	16,249	985
0-14	10,188	5,255	4,933	939
15-44	14,884	7,511	7,373	982
45-79	7,348	3,597	3,751	1043
80+	272	109	163	1495
Age not stated	58	29	29	1000

Languages (Dominant):

Telugu, Urdu, Hindi, Tamil, Gondi

Disabled Population:

	Persons	Males	Females	%
Total Disabled	912	500	412	
In Seeing	378	199	179	41.45
In Speech	92	53	39	10.09
In Hearing	70	37	33	7.68
In Movement	262	154	108	28.73
Mentally	110	57	53	12.06

CHINTALAPUDI

Chintalapudi C.D. Block lies in the north west part of west Godavari district. The Block is located at a distance of 62 kms. from district headquarters (Eluru). There are 38 villages in the block with the total population of 83523 persons. Area of the C.D. Block is 348.81 sq. kms. It is bounded by Khammam district on north, in the east by Narasapuram mandal, in the south by Lungapalem mandal and the west by two districts namely, Khammam and Krishna.

Communications:

Roadways : State Highway (S.H.): Direction- Lingapalem to Aswaraopeta. Nearest Villages- Maddimethinagudem, Allipalle, Utasamudram, Erraguntapalle, Recharla, Chintalapudi, Urlagudem, Pragadavaram.

Backwards Region Grants Fund: It receives Backward Region Grants.

Annual Rainfall: Average Rainfall 1005 mm.

Ground Water: Availability of the Ground Water in the Basin is (Information not avavible) H.A.M .and the utilization is (Information not avavible) H.A.M. It belongs to (Information not avavible) category. Depth to water level varies from 3 to 10 meter below the ground. Most of the wells go down in summer months.

Natural Division : Godavari Delta Region.

Administration:

Division: Coastal Andhra, Parliamentary Constituency: 27 Eluru, District: West Godavari, Mandal: Chintalapudi, Assembly Constituency: 187 Chintalapudi (SC), Gram Panchayat: 20.

Villages: 38 **Inhabited:** 36 **Uninhabited:** 2

Ranking	District	State	National
Area	1	79	2292

Population	2	19	3930
Sex Ratio	13	372	1546
Child Sex Ratio	24	432	1610
Literacy Rate	45	230	2469
Density	11	849	4167
Work Participation Rate	44	563	2712

Gram Panchayats:
Chintalapudi, Chintapalli, Endapalli, Erraguntapalle Errampalle, Ganijerla, Lingagudem, Mallayagudem Namavaram, Pothunuru, Pragadavaram, Raghavapuram Recharla, Seethanagaram, Sivapuram, Thimmareddipalle Urlagudem, Utasamudram, Venkatadrigudem Venkatapuram.

Amenities:

Education: Primary School in 31 villages, Middle school in 12 villages, Matriculation or Secondary School in 6 villages, namely Raghavapuram, Venkatapuram, Seethanagaram, Erraguntapalle, Chintalapudi, Pragadavaram.

Higher Secondary or Pre University Courses or Intermediate or Junior College in 1 village of the CD Block,, namely Chintalapudi.

College in 1 village, Adult Literacy Center in 11 villages., College is in village, namely Chintalapudi.

Medical: Hospital in 2 villages, Dispensary in 1 village, Health Center in 2 villages, Sub Center in 10 villages, Maternity and Child Welfare Center in 2 villages, Community health workers in 0 village.

The Villages having Hospital or Dispensary or Health Center are Raghavapuram, Chintalapudi, Pragadavaram.

Drinking Water: Tap water in 36 villages, Tank water in 36 villages, Well water in 36 villages, Tubewell in 36 villages and more than one source in 36 villages.

Bank: Banking facility in 4 villages, namely, Raghavapuram, Erraguntapalle, Chintalapudi Pragadavaram.

Credit Society in 8 villages Agricultural Credit Society in 7 Non-Agricultural Credit Society in 1 village.

Others: Power supply in 36 villages, Cinema hall in 5 villages, sport club in 0 village, Stadium or Auditorium or Community Hall in 0 village, Post Office in 15 villages.

There are 30 villages having bus facilities.

Villages with most of facilities: Raghavapuram Erraguntapalle, Chintalapudi, Pragadavaram.

Villages without amenities (Education):
Gonnepalle, Maddimethinagudem, Lakshminarasimhapuram, Gopalapuram, Talarlapalle..

Scheduled Castes: Out of the total population of 84929 persons, 23477 persons (27.64%) belong to Scheduled Castes.

The villages having less than 10% SC population are Gurubhatlagudem, Lingagudem, Venkatadrigudem Namavaram, Chintampalle, Gonnepalle Rangapuram Khandrika, Maddimethinagudem Lakshminarasimhapuram, Gopalapuram, Urlagudem Talarlapalle.

The villages having more than 50% SC population are None.

Sex ratio of Scheduled Caste population is 499.

Scheduled Castes Literates and Illiterates by Sex:

	Persons	Males	Females
Literate	11,820	6,467	5,353
Illiterate	11,657	5,297	6,360
Literacy rate	58.2	63.6	52.8
Graduate	482	319	163

Scheduled Castes (Dominant):
Madiga, Mala, Beda Jangam etc., Adi Andhra, Relli

For their cultural identity please see Appendix-I

Villages without Scheduled Castes: There are 8 villages without any scheduled caste population.

Scheduled Tribes: Out of the total population of 84929 persons, 7038 persons (8.29%) belong to Scheduled Tribes.

The villages having less than 10% ST population are Gurubhatlagudem, Endapalle, Raghavapuram, Pothunuru Amudalachalaka, Mallayagudem, Ganijerla Venkatadrigudem, Pattayagudem, Seethanagaram Maddimethinagudem, Settivarigudem, Kantampalem Lakshminarasimhapuram, Gopalapuram, Chintalapudi Urlagudem, Kanupade, Venkammapalem, Ponukumadu Pragadavaram, Errampalle, Thimmareddipalle Sankuchakrapuram.

The villages having more than 50% ST population are None.

Sex ratio of Scheduled tribe population is 494.

Scheduled Tribes Literates and Illiterates by Sex:

	Persons	Males	Females
Literate	2,025	1,302	723
Illiterate	5,013	2,257	2,756
Literacy rate	34.8	44.4	25.0
Graduate	24	23	1

Scheduled Tribes (Dominant):
Sugalis etc., Gond etc., Yerukulas, Nayaks, Yenadis

For their cultural identity please see Appendix-II

Villages without Scheduled Tribes: There are 15 villages without any scheduled tribe population.

Literates and Illiterates by Sex (Total Population):

	Persons	Males	Females
Literate	45,789	25,339	20,450
Illiterate	39,140	17,321	21,819
Literacy rate	62	68	55
Graduate	1,992	1,424	568

Agriculture: ***Distribution of villages according to land use:***

Out of 38 villages, Total area (in hectare) is 34881, out of that 60.92 percent is cultivable and 62.09 percent of the cultivable area is irrigated.

Sources of Irrigation (Hectares): Government Canal 420.3, Private Canal 0, Well without Electricity 0, Well with Electricity 828.24, Tubewell without Electricity 0, Tubewell with Electricity 7947.5, Tank 3998.86, River 0, Lake 0, Waterfall 0, Others 0.

Villages with population of 5000 to 9999:
Raghavapuram, Erraguntapalle.

Villages with population of 10000 and above:
Chintalapudi, Pragadavaram.

Distribution of Workers:

	Persons	Males	Females	WPR
Cultivators	6,174	5,457	717	15.05
Agricultural Labour	25,625	12,870	12,755	62.46
Household Industry	820	453	367	2
Other Workers	8,409	6,582	1,827	20.5
Main Workers	32,846	21,856	10,990	80.06
Marginal Workers	8,182	3,506	4,676	19.94
Total Workers	41,028	25,362	15,666	

Religion: Major Religious Communities:

	Persons	Males	Females	Sex Ratio
Hindu (91.71%)	77,886	39,188	38,698	987
Muslim (2.65%)	2,252	1,110	1,142	1,029
Christian (5.43%)	4,615	2,276	2,339	1,028
Sikh (0.01%)	10	6	4	667
Buddhists (0%)	3	2	1	500
Jain (0%)	-	-	-	-

Agewise Data:

	Persons	Males	Females	Sex Ratio
All ages	84,929	42,660	42,269	991
0-14	27,794	14,008	13,786	984
15-44	40,227	20,097	20,130	1002
45-79	16,177	8,177	8,000	978
80+	583	295	288	976
Age not stated	148	83	65	783

Languages (Dominant):
Telugu, Hindi, Urdu, Gondi, Tamil

Disabled Population:

	Persons	Males	Females	%
Total Disabled	1,200	679	521	
In Seeing	304	152	152	25.33
In Speech	155	82	73	12.92
In Hearing	69	33	36	5.75
In Movement	468	300	168	39
Mentally	204	112	92	17

CHINTAPALLE

Chintapalle C.D. Block lies in the north-western part of Vishakhapatnam district. The Block is located at a distance of 140 kms. from district headquarters (Vish akhapatnam). There are 249 villages in the block with the total population of 64,404 persons. Area of the C.D. Block is 200.83 sq. kms. It is bounded in the north by Mandal Gangaraju Madugula, in the south by Mandals Koyyuru and Rolugunta, in the east by Mandal Gangaraju Madugula, and in the west by Mandal Gudemkoth avedhi.

Communications :

Roadways : Metalled Roads: Nearest Villages- Vedurupalle, Joharu, Vanthalapadu, Panasalapadu, Kolanubanda, Annav aram, Kummarivanchala, Meduru, Cherukumpakalu, Umrasigondi, Kinnerla, Gadapari, Antharla, Chintapalle, Balajipeta, Labbangi, Barikadorapakalu @ Rajupakalu, Krishnapur am, Terapalle, Kothaveedhi, Yernabili, Lammasingi, Ravim anupakalu.

Integrated Child Development Scheme (ICDS) Project:
Annaual Rainfall: Average Rainfall 975.0 mm

Ground Water: Availability of the Ground Water in the Basin is (Information not avavible) H.A.M .and the utilization is (Information not avavible) H.A.M. It belongs to (Information not avavible) category. Depth to water level varies from 3 to 10 meter below the ground. Most of the wells go down in summer months.

Forest and Reserved **Forest:** Nearest Villages- Lammadamp alle, Egajanaba, Digijanaba, Cheruvuru, Tadlapalle, Buradamamidi, Korukonda, Digavalasapalle, Burugubailu, Egavalasapalle, Kudumulu, Kappagondhi, Rallagedda Kothuru, Rallagedda, Kudumusari, Itikabedda, Velamjuvvi, Balapam, Tokapadu, Mandipalle, Karakapalle, Goppugudis elu, Merakalu, Donipolalu, Vanchuladurgam, Bokkellu, Bheemanupalle, Lumburu, Pusalapalem, Pedagondhi, Jadug uru, Varathanapalle, Somavaram, Lothugedda, Cherukumpakalu, Lingalagudi, Kothavuru, Junnulu, Pinapadu, Teegalame tta, Godugumamidi, Umrasigondi, Bheemasingi, Pedapakalu, Mamidipalle, Kinnerla, Vangasari, Vurisingi, Kolapari, Chinna Gedda, Kandulagodi, Mallavaram, Gerrilagadda, Chavatapadu, Vamigedda Kothuru, Pina Kothuru, Cherapal le, Bayalukinchangi, Vamigedda, Pandlimamidi, Chadalapadu Bourthy, Chowdupalle, Chadipeta, Chintapalle, Balajip eta, Ganugulapadu, Sallai, Sadika, Routhupayalu, Chintha luru, Korukonda, Vanajajulu, Barikadorapakalu @ Rajupa kalu, Madigunta, Krishnapuram, Terapalle, Yerrabommalu, Kommangi, Pamulachintabanda, Parikalu, Relangi, Korrab anda, Yerravaram, Samagiri, Kondavanchula, Chinnabarada, Pedabarada, Siripuram, Diguvapakalu, Gondipakalu, Baddimetta, Chitrallagoppu, Lammasingi, Bheemanapalle, Asirada, Gattumpakalu, Bowda, Kitumula, Rakota, Pakabu, Kurusingi, Turebongalu, Gummidipalem, Busulakota, Sanivaram, Veeravaram, Vandanapalle, Boddaputtu. Chinna yyapalem, Tamarapalle, Singavaram Kothuru, Anjalam, Kapasupadu.

Administration:

Division: Coastal Andhra. Parliamentary Constituency: 18 Araku (ST). District: Visakhapatnam. Mandal: Chintap alle. Assembly Constituency: 148 Paderu. Gram Panchayat: 17

Border Villages: (Orissa)- Nearest Villages- Lammadampa lle, Egajanaba, Digijanaba, Cheruvuru, Itikabedda, Velam juvvi, Balapam, Kitumula.

Places of Tourist Interest:

Lothugedda: This place is situated at about 42 kms. north-west of Narasapatnam, in a direct line of the Golugonda hills and roughly about 16 kms. north of Chintapalle. This village contains the ruins of three of four old granite temples of Siva, the largest of which has elaborate sculptural depictions. One odd group depicts, four men with long pointed beards and long pigtails carrying pickaxes on their shoulders, holding out their hands to receive a reward, which a king sitting on a throne with three ladies behind him, is in the act of bestowing. The villagers believe that the men, are the builders of the temple and that, barbers were probably rare on the hills in those days. Several inscriptions in Telugu are found in one of these temples.

Villages: 249 **Inhabited:** 242 **Uninhabited:** 7

Ranking	District	State	National
Area	11	547	4166
Population	10	213	4708
Sex Ratio	33	629	2151
Child Sex Ratio	7	20	72
Literacy Rate	33	1060	5985
Density	17	397	3347
Work Participation Rate	27	325	968

Gram Panchayats:

Annavaram, Balapam, Bennavaram, Chinthapalli Chowdupalle, Gondipakalu, Kitumula, Kommangi Kothapalem, Kudumsarai, Lothugedda, Lovasingi Pedabarada, Senivaram, Tajangi, Tammingulavalsa Yerrabommalu.

Amenities:

Education: Primary School in 114 villages, Middle school in 7 villages, Matriculation or Secondary School in 4 villages, namely Lothugedda, Chintapalle, Pedabarada, Lammasingi.

Higher Secondary or Pre University Courses or Intermediate or Junior College in 0 village of the CD Block, College in 1 village, Adult Literacy Center in 0 village., College is in village, namely Chintapalle.

Medical: Hospital in 1 village, Dispensary in 0 village, Health Center in 17 villages, Sub Center in 13 villages, Maternity and Child Welfare Center in 0 village, Community health workers in 0 village.

The Village having Hospital or Dispensary or Health Center is Chintapalle.

Drinking Water: Tap water in 212 villages, Tank water in 212 villages, Well water in 212 villages, Tubewell in 212 villages and more than one source in 217 villages.

Bank: None.

Credit Society in 0 village Agricultural Credit Society in 0 Non-Agricultural Credit Society in 0 village.

Others: Power supply in 242 villages, Cinema hall in 1 village, sport club in 0 village, Stadium or Auditorium or Community Hall in 0 village, Post Office in 17 villages.

There are 22 villages having bus facilities.

Village with most of facilities: None.

Villages without amenities (Education): Egajanaba, Cheruvuru, Tadlapalle, Buradamamidi, Digavalasapalle, Turamamidi, Veeravaram, Egavalasapalle, Kappagondhi, Goddibanda, Itikabedda, Velamjuvvi, Joheru, Tokapadu, Mandipalle, Karakapalle, Vandanapalle, Boddaputtu, Merakalu, Donipolalu, Vanchuladurgam, Sampangiputtu, Bokkellu, Bheemanupalle, Gorrelametta, Pullalamamidi, Lumburu, Chittamgaruvu, Kilimisingi Durgam, Pedagaruvu, Lakshmipuram, Pedagondhi, Gosaigondhi, Jaduguru, Boddajuvvi, Vedurupalle, Kuramanapakalu, Votti Busulu, Godugulametta, Jangampakalu, Lingalagudi, Junnulu, Pinapadu, Pinapadu, Pedakonda, Degalapalem, Godugumamidi, Bennavaram, Karakapalle, Gerrilagadda, Pina Kothuru, Genjigedda, Chadalapadu, Goyyalametta, Chadipeta, Balajipeta, Chilakalamamidi, Regubailu, Budidapadu, Bayapadu, Vanthamamidi, Rajubanda, Marrichettu Pakalu, Bangarugummi, Thallakota, Jangampakalu, Nagulagondi, Lubbagunta, Kikkisalabanda, Jangambanda, Relangi, Yernabili, Godugumamidi, Rolugunta, Thatibanda, Rachapanasa, Vanthamamidi, Borramamidi, Kagulabanda, Porlubanda, Thatipalem, Tappulamamidi, Boyalagudem, Seetharamapuram, Jerrigedda, Yerranabilli, Diguvapakalu, Chitrallagoppu, Nuthibanda, Ona Chakarayabanda, Ravimanupakalu, Gattumpakalu, Palada, Pathapadu, Kurusingi, Gummidipalem, Ubalagaruvu, Vookabanda, Singavaram, Singavaram Kothuru, Anjalam, Nimmalapalem, Gaddibanda, Sheekayabanda, Busibanda, Polamabanda, Cheemalabayalu, Vandlamamidi, Munthamamidi, Nagraharam, Bemudichatru, Lakkavaram, Nadimipalem, Kapasupadu, Dovarapalle, Palamamidi..

Scheduled Castes: Out of the total population of 64404

persons, 754 persons (1.17%) belong to Scheduled Castes.
The villages having less than 10% SC population are
Lammadampalle, Egajanaba, Digijanaba, Cheruvuru
Tadlapalle, Buradamamidi, Korukonda, Digavalasapalle
Turamamidi, Burugubailu, Veeravaram, Egavalasapalle
Kudumulu, Kappagondhi, Rallagedda Kothuru
Rallagedda, Kudumusari, Goddibanda, Kotagunnalu
Nimmalapadu, Itikabedda, Velamjuvvi, Joheru, Balapam
Tokapadu, Mandipalle, Karakapalle, Goppugudiselu
Vandanapalle, Turubongulu, Kitumula, Boddaputtu
Merakalu, Donipolalu, Vanchuladurgam, Sampangiputtu
Bokkellu, Bheemanupalle, Gorrelametta, Pullalamamidi
Lumburu, Pusalapalem, Chittamgaruvu
Kilimisingi Durgam, Tammingala, Puligondi
Pedagaruvu, Lakshmipuram, Pedagondhi, Gosaigondhi
Jaduguru, Varathanapalle, Somavaram, Suddagaruvu
Dongalega, Boddajuvvi, Vedurupalle, Joharu
Kattubanda, Vanthalapadu, Panasalapadu
Kuramanapakalu, Gochapalle, Votti Busulu
Godugulametta, Jangampakalu, Domalagondhi
Kolanubanda, Annavaram, Kummarivanchala, Lothugedda
Meduru, Cherukumpakalu, Lingalagudi, Bandabayalu
Kothavuru, Junnulu, Pinapadu, Pothurajugummalu
Bennavaram, Regallu, Pinapadu, Jeelugumetta
Pedakonda, Kadasilpa, Teegalametta, Godugumamidi
Kothapalem, Degalapalem, Godugumamidi, Kappalu
Bennavaram, Karakapalle, Umrasigondi, Bheemasingi
Pedapakalu, Mamidipalle, Debbagaruvu, Kinnerla
Vangasari, Vurisingi, Kolapari, Chinna Gedda
Kandulagodi, Mallavaram, Gadapari, Gerrilagadda
Chavatapadu, Vamigedda Kothuru, Pina Kothuru
Cherapalle, Genjigedda, Bayalukinchangi, Vamigedda
Pandlimamidi, Chadalapadu, Bourthy, Sathyavaram
Goyyalametta, Pasuvulabanda, Chowdupalle, Chadipeta
Antharla, Chintapalle, Balajipeta, Chilakalamamidi
Ganugulapadu, Sallai, Genjigedda, Sadika
Routhupayalu, Chinthaluru, Burisingi, Regubailu
Budidapadu, Korukonda, Vanajajulu, Bayapadu
Basangi Kothuru, Lambadampalle, Vanthamamidi
Rajubanda, Marrichettu Pakalu, Bangarugummi
Chinna Rajupakalu, Thallakota, Labbangikothaveedhi
Labbangi, Jangampakalu
Barikadorapakalu @ Rajupakalu, Madigunta
Krishnapuram, Terapalle, Yerrabommalu, Nagulagondi
Lubbagunta, Kikkisalabanda, Kudupusingi, Kommangi
Parikalu, Jangambanda, Relangi, Yerravaram, Samagiri
Yernabili, Godugumamidi, Rolugunta, Thatibanda
Rachapanasa, Vanthamamidi, Borramamidi, Kagulabanda
Pothurajugunnalu, Totamamidi, Porlubanda, Thatipalem
Tappulamamidi, Boyalagudem, Seetharamapuram
Yerrabanda, Jerrigedda, Yerranabilli, Kondavanchula
Chinnabarada, Pedabarada, Siripuram, Diguvapakalu
Gondipakalu, Rowrimthada, Baddimetta, Chitrallagoppu
Lammasingi, Nuthibanda, Ona Chakarayabanda
Ravimanupakalu, Bheemanapalle, Asirada, Gattumpakalu
Tajangi, Rachapanukulu, Palada, Bowda, Kitumula
Rakota, Balabadram, Pakabu, Pathapadu, Kurusingi
Turebongalu, Gummidipalem, Ubalagaruvu, Vookabanda
Busulakota, Sanivaram, Chinnayyapalem, Tamarapalle
Singavaram, Singavaram Kothuru, Anjalam, Usuruputtu
Nimmalapalem, Gaddibanda, Mulusubanda, Sheekayabanda
Busibanda, Polamabanda, Cheemalabayalu, Vandlamamidi
Jangambuddi, Munthamamidi, Nagraharam, Bemudichatru
Lakkavaram, Matchalamamidi, Gunnamamidi, Madimabanda
Rayipalem, Thatibanda, Nadimipalem, Kapasupadu
Dovarapalle, Palamamidi.

The villages having more than 50% SC population are
None.

Sex ratio of Scheduled Caste population is 504.

Scheduled Castes Literates and Illiterates by Sex:

	Persons	Males	Females
Literate	382	220	162
Illiterate	372	154	218
Literacy rate	61.4	70.1	52.6
Graduate	50	37	13

Scheduled Castes (Dominant):
Madiga, Mala, Relli, Adi Andhra, Dom etc.

For their cultural identity please see Appendix-I

Villages without Scheduled Castes: There are 224 villages without any scheduled caste population.

Scheduled Tribes: Out of the total population of 64404 persons, 55956 persons (86.88%) belong to Scheduled Tribes.
The villages having less than 10% ST population are
None..

The villages having more than 50% ST population are
Lammadampalle, Egajanaba, Digijanaba, Cheruvuru
Tadlapalle, Buradamamidi, Korukonda, Digavalasapalle
Turamamidi, Burugubailu, Veeravaram, Egavalasapalle
Kudumulu, Kappagondhi, Rallagedda Kothuru
Rallagedda, Kudumusari, Goddibanda, Kotagunnalu
Nimmalapadu, Itikabedda, Velamjuvvi, Joheru, Balapam
Tokapadu, Mandipalle, Karakapalle, Goppugudiselu
Vandanapalle, Turubongulu, Kitumula, Boddaputtu
Merakalu, Donipolalu, Vanchuladurgam, Sampangiputtu
Bokkellu, Bheemanupalle, Gorrelametta, Pullalamamidi
Lumburu, Pusalapalem, Chittamgaruvu
Kilimisingi Durgam, Tammingala, Puligondi
Pedagaruvu, Lakshmipuram, Pedagondhi, Gosaigondhi
Jaduguru, Varathanapalle, Somavaram, Suddagaruvu
Dongalega, Boddajuvvi, Vedurupalle, Joharu

Kattubanda, Vanthalapadu, Panasalapadu
Kuramanapakalu, Gochapalle, Votti Busulu
Godugulametta, Jangampakalu, Domalagondhi
Kolanubanda, Kummarivanchala, Lothugedda, Meduru
Cherukumpakalu, Lingalagudi, Bandabayalu, Kothavuru
Junnulu, Pinapadu, Pothurajugummalu, Bennavaram
Regallu, Pinapadu, Jeelugumetta, Pedakonda
Kadasilpa, Teegalametta, Godugumamidi, Kothapalem
Degalapalem, Godugumamidi, Kappalu, Bennavaram
Karakapalle, Umrasigondi, Bheemasingi, Pedapakalu
Mamidipalle, Debbagaruvu, Kinnerla, Vangasari
Vurisingi, Kolapari, Chinna Gedda, Kandulagodi
Mallavaram, Gadapari, Gerrilagadda, Chavatapadu
Vamigedda Kothuru, Pina Kothuru, Cherapalle
Genjigedda, Bayalukinchangi, Vamigedda, Pandlimamidi
Chadalapadu, Bourthy, Sathyavaram, Goyyalametta
Pasuvulabanda, Chowdupalle, Chadipeta, Antharla
Balajipeta, Chilakalamamidi, Ganugulapadu, Sallai
Genjigedda, Sadika, Routhupayalu, Chinthaluru
Burisingi, Regubailu, Budidapadu, Korukonda
Vanajajulu, Bayapadu, Basangi Kothuru, Lambadampalle
Vanthamamidi, Rajubanda, Marrichettu Pakalu
Bangarugummi, Chinna Rajupakalu, Thallakota
Labbangikothaveedhi, Labbangi, Jangampakalu
Barikadorapakalu @ Rajupakalu, Madigunta
Krishnapuram, Terapalle, Yerrabommalu, Nagulagondi
Lubbagunta, Kikkisalabanda, Kudupusingi, Kommangi
Parikalu, Jangambanda, Relangi, Yerravaram, Samagiri
Yernabili, Godugumamidi, Rolugunta, Thatibanda
Rachapanasa, Vanthamamidi, Borramamidi, Kagulabanda
Pothurajugunnalu, Totamamidi, Porlubanda, Thatipalem
Tappulamamidi, Boyalagudem, Seetharamapuram
Yerrabanda, Jerrigedda, Yerranabilli, Kondavanchula
Chinnabarada, Pedabarada, Siripuram, Diguvapakalu
Gondipakalu, Rowrimthada, Baddimetta, Lammasingi
Nuthibanda, Ona Chakarayabanda, Ravimanupakalu
Bheemanapalle, Asirada, Gattumpakalu, Tajangi
Rachapanukulu, Palada, Bowda, Kitumula, Rakota
Balabadram, Pakabu, Pathapadu, Kurusingi
Turebongalu, Gummidipalem, Ubalagaruvu, Vookabanda
Busulakota, Sanivaram, Chinnayyapalem, Tamarapalle
Singavaram, Singavaram Kothuru, Anjalam, Usuruputtu
Nimmalapalem, Gaddibanda, Mulusubanda, Sheekayabanda
Busibanda, Polamabanda, Cheemalabayalu, Vandlamamidi
Jangambuddi, Munthamamidi, Nagraharam, Bemudichatru
Lakkavaram, Matchalamamidi, Gunnamamidi, Madimabanda
Rayipalem, Thatibanda, Nadimipalem, Kapasupadu
Dovarapalle, Palamamidi.

Sex ratio of Scheduled tribe population is 495.

Scheduled Tribes Literates and Illiterates by Sex:

	Persons	Males	Females
Literate	14,678	10,296	4,382
Illiterate	41,278	17,976	23,302
Literacy rate	31.5	43.5	19.1
Graduate	113	97	16

Scheduled Tribes (Dominant):

Kondhs etc., Bagata, Konda Dhoras, Valmiki Mukha Dhora etc.

For their cultural identity please see Appendix-II

Villages without Scheduled Tribes: There are 7 villages without any scheduled tribe population.

Literates and Illiterates by Sex (Total Population):

	Persons	Males	Females
Literate	19,059	12,905	6,154
Illiterate	45,345	19,664	25,681
Literacy rate	35	47	23
Graduate	401	320	81

Agriculture: ***Distribution of villages according to land use:*** Out of 249 villages, Total area (in hectare) is 20083, out of that 62.71 percent is cultivable and 0.24 percent of the cultivable area is irrigated.

Sources of Irrigation (Hectares): Government Canal 30.6, Private Canal 0, Well without Electricity 0, Well with Electricity 0, Tubewell without Electricity 0, Tubewell with Electricity 0, Tank 4.05, River 0, Lake 0, Waterfall 0, Others 0.

Villages with population of 5000 to 9999: Chintapalle.

Villages with population of 10000 and above: None

Distribution of Workers:

	Persons	Males	Females	WPR
Cultivators	18,762	10,527	8,235	55.48
Agricultural Labour	11,111	5,003	6,108	32.86
Household Industry	383	191	192	1.13
Other Workers	3,560	2,394	1,166	10.53
Main Workers	27,744	16,032	11,712	82.04
Marginal Workers	6,072	2,083	3,989	17.96
Total Workers	33,816	18,115	15,701	

Religion: Major Religious Communities:

	Persons	Males	Females	Sex Ratio
Hindu (97.9%)	63,050	31,903	31,147	976
Muslim (0.55%)	356	177	179	1,011
Christian (1.38%)	890	411	479	1,165
Sikh (0%)	-	-	-	-
Buddhists (0%)	-	-	-	-
Jain (0%)	-	-	-	-

Agewise Data:

	Persons	Males	Females	Sex Ratio
All ages	64,404	32,569	31,835	977
0-14	24,463	12,874	11,589	900

15-44	30,797	15,114	15,683	1038
45-79	8,839	4,390	4,449	1013
80+	172	93	79	849
Age not stated	133	98	35	357

Languages (Dominant):

Telugu, Konda, Oriya, Khond/Kondh, Kui

Disabled Population:

	Persons	Males	Females	%
Total Disabled	632	372	260	
In Seeing	231	142	89	36.55
In Speech	94	55	39	14.87
In Hearing	34	18	16	5.38
In Movement	216	124	92	34.18
Mentally	57	33	24	9.02

CHINTHA PALLE

Chinthapalle C.D. Block lies in the south-western part of Nalgonda district. The Block is located at a distance of 50 kms. from district headquarters (Nalgonda). There are 22 villages in the block with the total popul ation of 44,053 persons. Area of the C.D. Block is 273. 16 sq. kms. It is bounded by Rangareddy district on north, Marriguda and Namapalle Mandals on east, Devarko nda Mandal on south, Mahbubnagar district on west.

Communications:

Roadways : State Highway (S.H.): Direction- Hyderabad to Guntur. Nearest Villages- Godkondla, Polepalle Ramna gar, Madnapur, Sakalsere Palle, Kurmaidu, Ummapur, Kurma Palle, Vinjamoor, Nasarla Palle, Chinthapalle, Mallared dipalle, Kokkirayala Gowraram.

Backwards Region Grants Fund: It receives Backward Region Grants.

Integrated Child Development Scheme (ICDS) Project: Chinthapalli, Total Anganwadi Centres: 216

Annual Rainfall: Average Rainfall 573 mm

Ground Water: Availability of the Ground Water in the Basin is 2219 H.A.M. and the utilization is 1454 H. A.M. It belongs to Safe category. Depth to water level varies from 10 to 20 meter below the ground. Most of the wells go down in summer months. The well density in the entire block is 10 wells per sq. km. Total no. of the wells in the block are enumerated as 2620, according to the Ground Water Estimation Committee.

Natural Division : Krishna Piedmont Plain Region

Administration:

Division: Telangana. Parliamentary Constituency: 13 Nalgonda. District: Nalgonda. Mandal: Chintha Palle. Assembly Constituency: 86 Devarakonda (ST). Gram Panch ayat: 20.

Villages: 22 **Inhabited:** 22 **Uninhabited:** 0

Ranking	District	State	National
Area	12	226	3065
Population	33	695	5556
Sex Ratio	34	758	2540
Child Sex Ratio	10	384	1394
Literacy Rate	45	789	4848
Density	14	330	5386
Work Participation Rate	51	864	817

Gram Panchayats:

Chakalisheripally, Chinthapally, Gadiya Gouraram Godakondla, Gollapally, Homanthalapally Kistrainaplly, Kurmapally, Kurmed, Madanapoor Mallareddypally, Modugulamallepally, Nasarlapally Nelvalapally, Pkmallepally, Polepally Ramnagar Thakkalapally, Theeded, Varkala, Vinjamoor.

Amenities:

Education: Primary School in 22 villages, Middle school in 8 villages, Matriculation or Secondary School in 7 villages, namely Godkondla, Kurmaidu, Kurma Palle, Vinjamoor, Gadya Gowraram, Chinthapalle, Teeded.

Higher Secondary or Pre University Courses or Inter-mediate or Junior College in 1 village of the CD Block,, namely Chinthapalle.

College in 0 village, Adult Literacy Center in 18 villages.

Medical: Hospital in 0 village, Dispensary in 2 villages, Health Center in 1 village, Sub Center in 8 villages, Maternity and Child Welfare Center in 1 village, Community health workers in 0 village.

The Villages having Hospital or Dispensary or Health Center are Godkondla, Chinthapalle.

Drinking Water: Tap water in 22 villages, Tank water in 22 villages, Well water in 22 villages, Tubewell in 22 villages and more than one source in 22 villages.

Bank: Banking facility in 2 villages, namely, Kurmaidu, Chinthapalle.

Credit Society in 9 villages Agricultural Credit Society in 7 Non-Agricultural Credit Society in 3 villages.

Others: Power supply in 22 villages, Cinema hall in 2 villages, sport club in 0 village, Stadium or Auditorium or Community Hall in 0 village, Post Office in 13 villages.

There are 21 villages having bus facilities.

Villages with most of facilities: Kurmaidu Chinthapalle.

Villages without Amenities (Education): None..

Scheduled Castes: Out of the total population of 44053 persons, 8445 persons (19.17%) belong to Scheduled Castes.

The villages having less than 10% SC population are Godkondla, Polepalle Ramnagar, Ummapur Kokkirayala Gowraram.

The villages having more than 50% SC population are None.

Sex ratio of Scheduled Caste population is 496.

Scheduled Castes Literates and Illiterates by Sex:

	Persons	Males	Females
Literate	3,011	2,056	955
Illiterate	5,434	2,198	3,236
Literacy rate	42.4	57.3	27.2
Graduate	45	36	9

Scheduled Castes (Dominant):

Madiga, Mala, Bindla, Mala Dasari, Samagara

For their cultural identity please see Appendix-I

Villages without Scheduled Castes: There are 0 village without any scheduled caste population.

Scheduled Tribes: Out of the total population of 44053 persons, 4747 persons (10.78%) belong to Scheduled Tribes. The villages having less than 10% ST population are Godkondla, Madnapur, Sakalsere Palle, Ummapur Kurma Palle, P.K. Mallepalle, Vinjamoor, Varkal Gadya Gowraram, Upparapalle, Nelvalapalle Tirumalapur, Nasarla Palle, Chinthapalle, Anajpur Mallareddipalle.

The villages having more than 50% ST population are None.

Sex ratio of Scheduled tribe population is 484.

Scheduled Tribes Literates and Illiterates by Sex:

	Persons	Males	Females
Literate	1,072	811	261
Illiterate	3,675	1,637	2,038
Literacy rate	28.3	42.0	14.1
Graduate	18	17	1

Scheduled Tribes (Dominant):

Sugalis etc., Yerukulas, Koya etc., Kammara

For their cultural identity please see Appendix-II

Villages without Scheduled Tribes: There are 6 villages without any scheduled tribe population.

Literates and Illiterates by Sex (Total Population):

	Persons	Males	Females
Literate	17,727	11,707	6,020
Illiterate	26,326	10,669	15,657
Literacy rate	48	62	33
Graduate	507	428	79

Agriculture: ***Distribution of villages according to land use:*** Out of 22 villages, Total area (in hectare) is 27317, out of that 85.54 percent is cultivable and 10.77 percent of the cultivable area is irrigated.

Sources of Irrigation (Hectares): Government Canal 0, Private Canal 0, Well without Electricity 0, Well with Electricity 675.09, Tubewell without Electricity 125.38, Tubewe with Electricity 742.19, Tank 973.65, River 0, Lake 0, Waterfall 0, Others 0.

Villages with population of 5000 to 9999:

Vinjamoor.

Villages with population of 10000 and above: None

Distribution of Workers:

	Persons	Males	Females	WPR
Cultivators	7,784	4,888	2,896	33
Agricultural Labour	10,054	3,856	6,198	42.62
Household Industry	983	583	400	4.17
Other Workers	4,770	3,637	1,133	20.22
Main Workers	21,183	12,181	9,002	89.79
Marginal Workers	2,408	783	1,625	10.21
Total Workers	23,591	12,964	10,627	

Religion: Major Religious Communities:

	Persons	Males	Females	Sex Ratio
Hindu (94.89%)	41,800	21,192	20,608	972
Muslim (4.82%)	2,124	1,119	1,005	898
Christian (0.2%)	90	47	43	915
Sikh (0.01%)	3	-	3	-
Buddhists (0%)	-	-	-	-
Jain (0%)	-	-	-	-

Agewise Data:

	Persons	Males	Females	Sex Ratio
All ages	44,053	22,376	21,677	969
0-14	15,543	7,911	7,632	965
15-44	20,347	10,364	9,983	963
45-79	7,731	3,884	3,847	990
80+	341	157	184	1172
Age not stated	91	60	31	517

Languages (Dominant):

Telugu, Hindi, Urdu, Gondi, Tamil

Disabled Population:

	Persons	Males	Females	%
Total Disabled	884	497	387	
In Seeing	381	219	162	43.1
In Speech	69	37	32	7.81
In Hearing	35	15	20	3.96
In Movement	310	183	127	35.07
Mentally	89	43	46	10.07

CHINTHAKANI

Chinthakani C.D. Block lies in the southern part of Khammam district. The Block is located at a distance of 23 kms. from district headquarters (Khammam). There are 16 villages in the block with the total population of 47,962 persons. Area of the C.D. Block is 182.10 sq. kms. It is bounded in the north by Mandals Khammam (U) and Nigerla, in the south by district Krishna, in the east by Mandals Bonakal and Wyra, and in the west by Mandal Mudigonda.

Communications:

Roadways : NH, SH or Important Metalled Road is not available.

Railway Station: Chinthakani, Nagula Vancha.

River: Munneru Nadi- Nearest Villages- Basvapuram,

Pandillapalle, Mathkepalle.

Backwards Region Grants Fund: It receives Backward Region Grants.

Annual Rainfall: Average Rainfall 988 mm

Ground Water: Availability of the Ground Water in the Basin is 3920 H.A.M.and the utilization is 1111 H.A. M. It belongs to safe category. Depth to water level varies from 5 to 10 meter below the ground. Most of the wells go down in summer months. The well density in the entire block is 0.1 wells per sq. km. Total no. of the wells in the block are enumerated as 63, according to the Ground Water Estimation Committee.

Natural Division : Godavari Depression Region

Administration:

Division: Telangana. Parliamentary Constituency: 17 Khammam. District: Khammam. Mandal: Chinthakani. Assembly Constituency: 114 Madhira (SC). Gram Panchayat: 20.

Villages: 16 **Inhabited:** 16 **Uninhabited:** 0

Ranking	District	State	National
Area	37	658	4502
Population	20	580	5388
Sex Ratio	20	648	2197
Child Sex Ratio	10	104	274
Literacy Rate	20	633	4333
Density	11	188	3924
Work Participation Rate	13	491	536

Gram Panchayats:

Ananthasagar, Basvapuram, Bopparam, Chinamandava Chinthakani, Jagannadhapuram, Kodumuru, Komatlagudem Latchagudem, Mathkepalli, Nagili Gonda Nagula Vancha, Nerada, Pandillapalli, Patharlapadu Proddutur, Ramakrishnapuram, Seethampeta Thimminenipalem, Vandanam.

Amenities:

Education: Primary School in 16 villages, Middle school in 12 villages, Matriculation or Secondary School in 5 villages, namely Kodumuru, Pandillapalle, Chinthakani, Nagula Vancha, Proddutur.

Higher Secondary or Pre University Courses or Intermediate or Junior College in 1 village of the CD Block,, namely Nagula Vancha.

College in 0 village, Adult Literacy Center in 15 villages.

Medical: Hospital in 0 village, Dispensary in 0 village, Health Center in 1 village, Sub Center in 10 villages, Maternity and Child Welfare Center in 2 villages, Community health workers in 0 village.

Drinking Water: Tap water in 16 villages, Tank water in 16 villages, Well water in 16 villages, Tubewell in 16 villages and more than one source in 16 villages.

Bank: Banking facility in 2 villages, namely, Chinthakani, Nagula Vancha.

Credit Society in 10 villages Agricultural Credit Society in 4 Non-Agricultural Credit Society in 10 villages.

Others: Power supply in 16 villages, Cinema hall in 0 village, sport club in 0 village, Stadium or Auditorium or Community Hall in 0 village, Post Office in 14 villages.

There are 13 villages having bus facilities.

Villages with most of facilities: Chinthakani Nagula Vancha.

Villages without Amenities (Education): None..

Scheduled Castes: Out of the total population of 47962 persons, 11102 persons (23.15%) belong to Scheduled Castes. The villages having less than 10% SC population are None..

The villages having more than 50% SC population are None.

Sex ratio of Scheduled Caste population is 489.

Scheduled Castes Literates and Illiterates by Sex:

	Persons	Males	Females
Literate	4,223	2,738	1,485
Illiterate	6,879	2,940	3,939
Literacy rate	44.2	55.8	32.0
Graduate	65	63	2

Scheduled Castes (Dominant):

Madiga, Mala, Mala Dasari, Dom etc.

Beda Jangam etc.

For their cultural identity please see Appendix-I

Villages without Scheduled Castes: There are 0 village without any scheduled caste population.

Scheduled Tribes: Out of the total population of 47962 persons, 972 persons (2.03%) belong to Scheduled Tribes. The villages having less than 10% ST population are Vandanam, Kodumuru, Nerada, Latchagudem, Basvapuram Ananthasagar, Pandillapalle, Chinthakani Mathkepalle, Thimminenipalem, Chinamandava Nagula Vancha, Patharlapadu, Proddutur, Nagili Konda.

The villages having more than 50% ST population are None.

Sex ratio of Scheduled tribe population is 492.

Scheduled Tribes Literates and Illiterates by Sex:

	Persons	Males	Females
Literate	311	195	116
Illiterate	661	299	362
Literacy rate	37.3	47.0	27.8
Graduate	2	2	0

Scheduled Tribes (Dominant):

Yerukulas, Sugalis etc., Koya etc., Yenadis

For their cultural identity please see Appendix-II

Villages without Scheduled Tribes: There are 0 village without any scheduled tribe population.

Literates and Illiterates by Sex (Total Population):

	Persons	Males	Females
Literate	21,483	13,079	8,404
Illiterate	26,479	11,192	15,287
Literacy rate	51	62	41
Graduate	554	501	53

Agriculture: ***Distribution of villages according to land use:*** Out of 16 villages, Total area (in hectare) is 18211, out of that 54.17 percent is cultivable and 53.15 percent of the cultivable area is irrigated.

Sources of Irrigation (Hectares): Government Canal 3002.8, Private Canal 53.2, Well without Electricity 462, Well with Electricity 252, Tubewell without Electricity 0, Tubewell with Electricity 0, Tank 1473.6, River 0, Lake 0, Waterfall 0, Others 0.

Villages with population of 5000 to 9999: None

Villages with population of 10000 and above: None

Distribution of Workers:

	Persons	Males	Females	WPR
Cultivators	6,321	4,045	2,276	23.01
Agricultural Labour	17,523	7,902	9,621	63.78
Household Industry	435	293	142	1.58
Other Workers	3,193	2,574	619	11.62
Main Workers	24,067	13,480	10,587	87.61
Marginal Workers	3,405	1,334	2,071	12.39
Total Workers	27,472	14,814	12,658	

Religion: Major Religious Communities:

	Persons	Males	Females	Sex Ratio
Hindu (92.96%)	44,586	22,570	22,016	975
Muslim (5.48%)	2,626	1,328	1,298	977
Christian (1.52%)	731	366	365	997
Sikh (0%)	-	-	-	-
Buddhists (0%)	-	-	-	-
Jain (0%)	-	-	-	-

Agewise Data:

	Persons	Males	Females	Sex Ratio
All ages	47,962	24,271	23,691	976
0-14	14,797	7,456	7,341	985
15-44	23,332	11,885	11,447	963
45-79	9,243	4,628	4,615	997
80+	525	266	259	974
Age not stated	65	36	29	806

Languages (Dominant):

Telugu, Urdu, Tamil, Gondi, Hindi

Disabled Population:

	Persons	Males	Females	%
Total Disabled	1,494	876	618	
In Seeing	783	472	311	52.41
In Speech	132	69	63	8.84
In Hearing	54	26	28	3.61
In Movement	395	248	147	26.44
Mentally	130	61	69	8.7

CHINTHAKOMMADINNE

Chintakommadinne C.D. Block lies in the central part of Cuddapah district. It is a part of Chintakommadinne Mandal. The Block is located at a distance of 08 kms. from district headquarters (Cuddapah). There are 24 villages in the block with the total population of 44,841 persons. Area of the C.D. Block is 336.42 sq. kms. It is bounded in the north by Mandal Valluru, in the south by Mandals Chakrayapet and Ramapuram, in the east by Mandals Cuddapah and Sidhout, and in the west by Mandal Pendlimarri.

Communications:

Roadways : State Highway (S.H.): Direction- Chinttoor to Cuddapah. Nearest Villages-Apparajupalle, Buggaletip alle, Kolumulapalle, Jamal Palle, Chinnakampalle, Utukur. Steam: Local stream touches the following villages, namely, Thadigotla, Krishnapuram, Kopparthi, K.Ramacha ndrapuram

It receives Backward Region Grants, and is also identif ied as a drought-prone area as well.

Annual Rainfall: Average Rainfall 589 mm

Ground Water: Availability of the Ground Water in the Basin is 3145 H.A.M.and the utilization is 2428 H.A. M.It belongs to SC category. Depth to water level varies from 5 to 10 meter below the ground. Most of the wells go down in summer months, according to the Ground Water Estimation Committee.

Natural Division : Rayalaseema Region

Administration:

Division: Rayala Seema. Parliamentary Constituency: 38 Kadapa. District: Cuddapah.

Mandal: Chinthakommadinne. Assembly Constituency: 249 Kamalapuram. Gram Panchayat: 14.

Villages: 24 **Inhabited:** 22 **Uninhabited:** 2

Ranking	District	State	National
Area	8	104	2470
Population	16	669	5520
Sex Ratio	42	934	3211
Child Sex Ratio	46	1042	4969
Literacy Rate	17	222	2403
Density	39	957	5764
Work Participation Rate	35	953	3443

Gram Panchayats:

Buggalapalli, Busireddi Palli, Chinta Komma Dinne Ippa Penta, Kammavari Palli, Kolumula Palli Kopparthi, Krishna Puram, Mamillapalli, Pabba Puram Papasaheb Pet, Rasoolpalli, Tadigotla, Utukur.

Amenities:

Education: Primary School in 20 villages, Middle school in

7 villages, Matriculation or Secondary School in 5 villages, namely Chinthakommadinne, Utukur, Viswanathapuram, Mamillapalle (Rural), Boggalapalle.

Higher Secondary or Pre University Courses or Intermediate or Junior College in 0 village of the CD Block, College in 1 village, Adult Literacy Center in 1 village., College is in village, namely Utukur.

Medical: Hospital in 1 village, Dispensary in 1 village, Health Center in 2 villages, Sub Center in 4 villages, Maternity and Child Welfare Center in 0 village, Community health workers in 0 village.

The Villages having Hospital or Dispensary or Health Center are Chinthakommadinne, Mamillapalle (Rural).

Drinking Water: Tap water in 20 villages, Tank water in 22 villages, Well water in 22 villages, Tubewell in 20 villages and more than one source in 22 villages.

Bank: Banking facility in 4 villages, namely, Chinthakommadinne, Viswanathapuram Mamillapalle (Rural), Boggalapalle.

Credit Society in 7 villages Agricultural Credit Society in 5 Non-Agricultural Credit Society in 3 villages.

Others: Power supply in 22 villages, Cinema hall in 0 village, sport club in 0 village, Stadium or Auditorium or Community Hall in 0 village, Post Office in 14 villages.

There are 19 villages having bus facilities.

Villages with most of facilities: Chinthakommadinne Viswanathapuram, Mamillapalle (Rural), Boggalapalle.

Villages without amenities (Education):
T.Ramachandrapuram, K.Ramachandrapuram..

Scheduled Castes: Out of the total population of 44787 persons, 6795 persons (15.17%) belong to Scheduled Castes.

The villages having less than 10% SC population are Rayalapanthulapalle, Papasahebpet, Balupalle K.Ramachandrapuram, Apparajupalle, Buggaletipalle Kolumulapalle, Chinnakampalle.

The villages having more than 50% SC population are None.

Sex ratio of Scheduled Caste population is 484.

Scheduled Castes Literates and Illiterates by Sex:

	Persons	Males	Females
Literate	3,346	2,118	1,228
Illiterate	3,449	1,387	2,062
Literacy rate	57.8	71.2	43.6
Graduate	110	82	28

Scheduled Castes (Dominant):

Mala, Madiga, Adi Andhra, Madiga Dasu etc., Dom etc.

For their cultural identity please see Appendix-I

Villages without Scheduled Castes: There are 6 villages without any scheduled caste population.

Scheduled Tribes: Out of the total population of 44787 persons, 2020 persons (4.51%) belong to Scheduled Tribes.

The villages having less than 10% ST population are Kopparthi, Thadigotla, Rayalapanthulapalle T.Ramachandrapuram, Krishnapuram, Pabbapuram Papasahebpet, Balupalle, K.Ramachandrapuram Kammavaripalle, Chinthakommadinne, Apparajupalle Utukur, Viswanathapuram, Mamillapalle (Rural) Boggalapalle, Buggaletipalle, Chinnakampalle Peddakampalle.

The villages having more than 50% ST population are None.

Sex ratio of Scheduled tribe population is 484.

Scheduled Tribes Literates and Illiterates by Sex:

	Persons	Males	Females
Literate	712	463	249
Illiterate	1,308	579	729
Literacy rate	42.0	53.2	30.2
Graduate	9	7	2

Scheduled Tribes (Dominant):

Sugalis etc., Yenadis, Yerukulas

For their cultural identity please see Appendix-II

Villages without Scheduled Tribes: There are 10 villages without any scheduled tribe population.

Literates and Illiterates by Sex (Total Population):

	Persons	Males	Females
Literate	23,945	14,732	9,213
Illiterate	20,842	8,170	12,672
Literacy rate	62	75	49
Graduate	913	739	174

Agriculture: ***Distribution of villages according to land use:*** Out of 24 villages, Total area (in hectare) is 32895, out of that 18.29 percent is cultivable and 51.88 percent of the cultivable area is irrigated.

Sources of Irrigation (Hectares): Government Canal 82, Private Canal 0, Well without Electricity 0, Well with Electricity 378, Tubewell without Electricity 0, Tubewell with Electricity 2534, Tank 127, River 0, Lake 0, Waterfall 0, Others 0.

Villages with population of 5000 to 9999: Chinthakommadinne, Utukur, Mamillapalle (Rural).

Villages with population of 10000 and above: None

Distribution of Workers:

	Persons	Males	Females	WPR
Cultivators	3,975	2,967	1,008	19.98
Agricultural Labour	9,550	4,918	4,632	48.01
Household Industry	559	310	249	2.81
Other Workers	5,806	4,566	1,240	29.19
Main Workers	16,815	11,507	5,308	84.54
Marginal Workers	3,075	1,254	1,821	15.46
Total Workers	19,890	12,761	7,129	

Religion: Major Religious Communities:

	Persons	Males	Females	Sex Ratio
Hindu (83.01%)	37,177	19,061	18,116	950
Muslim (15.82%)	7,085	3,591	3,494	973
Christian (0.97%)	436	209	227	1,086
Sikh (0.01%)	3	2	1	500
Buddhists (0%)	-	-	-	-
Jain (0%)	-	-	-	-

Agewise Data:

	Persons	Males	Females	Sex Ratio
All ages	44,787	22,902	21,885	956
0-14	15,072	7,918	7,154	904
15-44	21,336	10,916	10,420	955
45-79	8,094	3,951	4,143	1049
80+	202	70	132	1886
Age not stated	83	47	36	766

Languages (Dominant):

Telugu, Urdu, Hindi, Tamil, Gondi

Disabled Population:

	Persons	Males	Females	%
Total Disabled	564	322	242	
In Seeing	145	82	63	25.71
In Speech	81	46	35	14.36
In Hearing	45	23	22	7.98
In Movement	202	122	80	35.82
Mentally	91	49	42	16.13

CHINTUR

Chintur C.D. Block lies in the north-eastern part of Khammam district. The Block is located at a distance of 185 kms. from district headquarters (Khammam). There are 89 villages in the block with the total population of 36,763 persons. Area of the C.D. Block is 233.81 sq. kms. It is bounded in the south by Mandals Kunavaram and Vararamachandrapuram, in the east by district east Godavari, and in the west by Mandal Bhadrachalam, and it has common boundary with the states of chhattis garh and Orissa on north.

Communications:

Roadways : NH- 221: Direction- Palwancha to Konta. Neare st Villages- Narakonda, Katukapalle, Irkampeta, Pega, Venkagudem, Ahmmadalipeta. State Highway (S.H.): Direc tion- Chatti to Villarti. Nearest Villages- Yerrampeta, Pothanapalle, Ratnapuram, Gondigudem, Tulugonda, Chatti, Lakshmipuram.

River: Sabari Nadi- Nearest Villages- Palagudem, Chidu murum, Chatti, Kummuru, Mallethota, Ulumuru, Agraharapu Koderu, Pedda Seetanapalle, Mukkunuru, Lakshmipuram, Kuyuguru, Kalleru. Silaru Nadi- Nearest Villages- Kalleru, Madugur, Surannagandi, Guduru, Kothapalle, Vemulrai, Nelakota, Mothugudem.

Annual Rainfall: Average Rainfall 1314 mm

Ground Water: Availability of the Ground Water in the Basin is 4568 H.A.M.and the utilization is 175 H.A. M. It belongs to safe category. Depth to water level varies from 5 to 10 meter below the ground. Most of the wells go down in summer months. The well density in the entire block is 0.1 wells per sq. km. Total no. of the wells in the block are enumerated as 63, according to the Ground Water Estimation Committee.

Forest and Reserved **Forest:** (Bangarugudum R.F.)- Nearest Villages- Dongala Jaggaram, Narsingapeta, Mallampeta, Narakonda, Alligudem, Vinayakapuram, Surakunta, Katuka palle, Irkampeta, Balimela, Yedugurallapalle, Tatilanka, Uppanapalle, Uppanapalle Gattu, Vepala Padu, Maddigudem, Boddugudem, Pega, Venkagudem, Lachigudem, Ganganamett Sarivela, Venkatrampuram, Ahmmadalipeta, Burakanakota, Narayanapuram, Tummala, Narsimhapuram, Sigannagudem, Kannapuram, Palagudem, Suddagudem, Chidumurum, Chatti Lakshmipuram. (Kalleru R.F.)- Nearest Villages- Stafor dpeta, Ratnapuram, Kuyuguru, Kalleru, Madugur. (Lappavar am R.F.)- Nearest Villages- Kansuluru, Kannayagudem, Tatiyakulagudem, Pothanapalle, Stafordpeta, Surannagan di, Guduru, Devarapalle, Sirasanapalle, Kesaram, Gopanap alle, Yerrakondapakalu, Mittavada, Chowluru. (Maraiguda R.F.)- Nearest Villages- Kondapalle, Ramannapalem, Chinna Seethannapalle, Kothapalle, Mothugudem, Choppuma mide, Gondigudem, Tulugonda, Dondagudem, Yerrakondapal Thulasipakalu, Mittavada, Lakkagudem, Gamallakota, Tustigudem, Yeruvada, Jalliwada.

Natural Division : Godavari Depression Region

Administration:

Division: Telangana. Parliamentary Constituency: 16 Mahbubabad (ST). District: Khammam. Mandal: Chintur. Assembly Constituency: 119 Bhadrachalam (ST). Gram Panchayat: 15.

Border Villages: (Chhattisgarh)- Nearest Villages- Dongala Jaggaram, Narsingapeta, Mallampeta, Palagudem, Ahmmadalipeta, Burakanakota, Suddagudem, Chidumurum, (Orissa)- Nearest Villages- Kalleru, Madugur, Surannag andi, Guduru, Kothapalle, Vemulrai, Nelakota, Marrimaddi, Mothugudem.

Villages: 89 **Inhabited:** 80 **Uninhabited:** 9

Ranking	District	State	National
Area	23	373	3599
Population	32	904	5859
Sex Ratio	3	74	489
Child Sex Ratio	26	542	2046
Literacy Rate	46	1061	5998
Density	3	40	5457
Work Participation Rate	28	883	179

Gram Panchayats:

A.G.Koderu, Chadalavada, Chatti, Chidumuru, Chintoor Edugurallapalli, Guduru, Kalleru, Kothapalli Kummuru, Mothugudem, Mukkunuru, Pedda Seetanapalle Pega, Tummala.

Amenities:

Education: Primary School in 65 villages, Middle school in 6 villages, Matriculation or Secondary School in 4 villages, namely Yedugurallapalle, Narsimhapuram, Chintur, Mothugudem.

Higher Secondary or Pre University Courses or Intermediate or Junior College in 1 village of the CD Block,, namely Chintur.

College in 1 village, Adult Literacy Center in 27 villages., College is in village, namely Chintur.

Medical: Hospital in 2 villages, Dispensary in 1 village, Health Center in 4 villages, Sub Center in 16 villages, Maternity and Child Welfare Center in 29 villages, Community health workers in 0 village.

The Villages having Hospital or Dispensary or Health Center are Yedugurallapalle, Chintur, Guduru, Mothugudem.

Drinking Water: Tap water in 78 villages, Tank water in 78 villages, Well water in 78 villages, Tubewell in 78 villages and more than one source in 80 villages.

Bank: Banking facility in 2 villages, namely, Chintur, Yerrampeta.

Credit Society in 8 villages Agricultural Credit Society in 2 Non-Agricultural Credit Society in 8 villages.

Others: Power supply in 80 villages, Cinema hall in 2 villages, sport club in 0 village, Stadium or Auditorium or Community Hall in 0 village, Post Office in 14 villages.

There are 33 villages having bus facilities.

Villages with most of facilities: Chintur Yerrampeta.

Villages without amenities (Education):

Vinayakapuram, Balimela, Tatilanka, Uppanapalle, Venkatrampuram, Ahmmadalipeta, Kannapuram, Palagudem, Suddagudem, Stafordpeta, Dondagudem, Yerrakondapakalu, Lakkagudem, Chowluru..

Scheduled Castes: Out of the total population of 36763 persons, 1338 persons (3.64%) belong to Scheduled Castes.

The villages having less than 10% SC population are Dongala Jaggaram, Narsingapeta, Mallampeta Narakonda, Alligudem, Vinayakapuram, Surakunta Katukapalle, Irkampeta, Balimela, Yedugurallapalle Tatilanka, Uppanapalle, Uppanapalle Gattu Maddigudem, Boddugudem, Pega, Venkagudem, Lachigudem Ganganametta, Sarivela, Venkatrampuram Ahmmadalipeta, Burakanakota, Narayanapuram, Tummala Narsimhapuram, Sigannagudem, Kannapuram, Palagudem Suddagudem, Chidumurum, Chatti, Kummuru, Mallethota Ulumuru, Agraharapu Koderu, Thummargudem, Kondapalle Ramannapalem, Chinna Seethannapalle Pedda Seetanapalle, Narsingapeta, Mukkunuru, Chutur Vegithota, Kolthuru, Kansuluru, Kannayagudem Lakshmipuram, Yerrampeta, Pothanapalle, Stafordpeta Ratnapuram, Kuyuguru, Kalleru, Madugur, Surannagandi Guduru, Devarapalle, Kothapalle, Vemulrai, Nelakota Choppumamide, Gondigudem, Tulugonda, Dondagudem Sirasanapalle, Kesaram, Yerrakondapakalu, Lakkavaram Thulasipakalu, Mittavada, Lakkagudem, Chowluru Gamallakota, Chadalavada, Yeruvada.

The villages having more than 50% SC population are None.

Sex ratio of Scheduled Caste population is 525.

Scheduled Castes Literates and Illiterates by Sex:

	Persons	Males	Females
Literate	801	428	373
Illiterate	537	208	329
Literacy rate	69.5	79.7	60.7
Graduate	73	51	22

Scheduled Castes (Dominant):

Mala, Madiga, Dom etc., Generic Castes etc.

Adi Andhra

For their cultural identity please see Appendix-I

Villages without Scheduled Castes: There are 70 villages without any scheduled caste population.

Scheduled Tribes: Out of the total population of 36763 persons, 28681 persons (78.02%) belong to Scheduled Tribes.

The villages having less than 10% ST population are None..

The villages having more than 50% ST population are Dongala Jaggaram, Narsingapeta, Mallampeta Narakonda, Alligudem, Surakunta, Katukapalle Irkampeta, Balimela, Yedugurallapalle, Tatilanka Uppanapalle, Uppanapalle Gattu, Maddigudem Boddugudem, Pega, Venkagudem, Lachigudem Ganganametta, Sarivela, Venkatrampuram Ahmmadalipeta, Burakanakota, Narayanapuram, Tummala Narsimhapuram, Sigannagudem, Kannapuram, Palagudem Suddagudem, Chidumurum, Chatti, Kummuru, Mallethota Ulumuru, Agraharapu Koderu, Thummargudem, Kondapalle Ramannapalem, Chinna Seethannapalle Pedda Seetanapalle, Narsingapeta, Mukkunuru, Chutur Vegithota, Kolthuru, Kansuluru, Kannayagudem Lakshmipuram, Yerrampeta, Pothanapalle, Stafordpeta Ratnapuram, Kuyuguru, Kalleru, Madugur, Surannagandi Guduru, Devarapalle, Kothapalle, Vemulrai, Nelakota Choppumamide, Gondigudem, Tulugonda, Dondagudem Sirasanapalle, Kesaram, Yerrakondapakalu, Lakkavaram

Thulasipakalu, Mittavada, Lakkagudem, Chowluru Gamallakota, Chadalavada, Yeruvada.

Sex ratio of Scheduled tribe population is 509.

Scheduled Tribes Literates and Illiterates by Sex:

	Persons	Males	Females
Literate	5,962	3,583	2,379
Illiterate	22,719	10,488	12,231
Literacy rate	25.0	30.8	19.4
Graduate	66	58	8

Scheduled Tribes (Dominant):

Koya etc., Kondareddis, Sugalis etc., Valmiki Konda Kapus

For their cultural identity please see Appendix-II

Villages without Scheduled Tribes: There are 9 villages without any scheduled tribe population.

Literates and Illiterates by Sex (Total Population):

	Persons	Males	Females
Literate	10,867	6,333	4,534
Illiterate	25,896	11,775	14,121
Literacy rate	35	42	29
Graduate	417	324	93

Agriculture: ***Distribution of villages according to land use:*** Out of 89 villages, Total area (in hectare) is 23381, out of that 37.94 percent is cultivable and 1.94 percent of the cultivable area is irrigated.

Sources of Irrigation (Hectares): Government Canal 23.88, Private Canal 0, Well without Electricity 6.07, Well with Electricity 0, Tubewell without Electricity 0, Tubewell with Electricity 3.2, Tank 0, River 0, Lake 0, Waterfall 30.89, Others 108.4.

Villages with population of 5000 to 9999: None

Villages with population of 10000 and above: None

Distribution of Workers:

	Persons	Males	Females	WPR
Cultivators	11,363	6,438	4,925	53.13
Agricultural Labour	5,810	2,261	3,549	27.17
Household Industry	820	203	617	3.83
Other Workers	3,394	2,169	1,225	15.87
Main Workers	18,398	10,155	8,243	86.02
Marginal Workers	2,989	916	2,073	13.98
Total Workers	21,387	11,071	10,316	

Religion: Major Religious Communities:

	Persons	Males	Females	Sex Ratio
Hindu (96.97%)	35,649	17,551	18,098	1,031
Muslim (2%)	735	365	370	1,014
Christian (0.91%)	334	162	172	1,062
Sikh (0%)	1	1	-	-
Buddhists (0.01%)	4	2	2	1,000
Jain (0%)	-	-	-	-

Agewise Data:

	Persons	Males	Females	Sex Ratio
All ages	36,763	18,108	18,655	1030
0-14	12,960	6,470	6,490	1003
15-44	17,783	8,742	9,041	1034
45-79	5,875	2,837	3,038	1071
80+	94	26	68	2615
Age not stated	51	33	18	545

Languages (Dominant):

Koya, Telugu, Oriya, Urdu, Hindi

Disabled Population:

	Persons	Males	Females	%
Total Disabled	641	380	261	
In Seeing	280	152	128	43.68
In Speech	39	22	17	6.08
In Hearing	32	25	7	4.99
In Movement	207	131	76	32.29
Mentally	83	50	33	12.95

CHIPPAGIRI

Chippagiri C.D. Block lies in the south-western part of Kurnool district. The Block is located at a distance of 100 kms. from district headquarters (Kurnool). There are 14 villages in the block with the total population of 31,465 persons. Area of the C.D. Block is 300.14 sq. kms. It is bounded in the north by Mandal Alur, in the south by district Anantapur, in the east by Mandal Maddikera East, and in the west by Halaharvi Mandal.

Communications:

Roadways : State Highway (S.H.): Direction- Alur to Gooty. Nearest Villages- Nagaradona, Nemakal, Chippagiri, Kundanagurthi, Beldona, Bantanahal.

Railway Station: Gummanur, Bantanahal.

It is identified as a drought-prone area.

Annual Rainfall: Average Rainfall 517 mm

Ground Water: Availability of the Ground Water in the Basin is 2280 H.A.M. and the utilization is 158 H.A. M. It belongs to Safe category. Depth to water level varies from 10 meter below the ground. Most of the wells go down in summer months. The well density in the entire block is 1 wells per sq. km. Total no. of the wells in the block are enumerated as 130, according to the Ground Water Estimation Committee.

Natural Division : Rayalaseema Region

Administration:

Division: Rayala Seema. Parliamentary Constituency: 35 Kurnool. District: Kurnool. Mandal: Chippagiri. Assembly Constituency: 266 Alur. Gram Panchayat: 12.

Villages: 14 **Inhabited:** 14 **Uninhabited:** 0

Ranking	District	State	National
Area	18	163	2785

Population	50	1002	6021
Sex Ratio	26	817	2730
Child Sex Ratio	37	760	3261
Literacy Rate	22	561	4085
Density	38	430	6096
Work Participation Rate	52	1045	1070

Gram Panchayats:

Bantanahal, Beldona, Chippagiri, Degalahal Doulathapuram, Gummanur, Khajipuram, Kundanagurthi Nagaradona, Nemakal, Ramadurgam, Yerur.

Amenities:

Education: Primary School in 14 villages, Middle school in 7 villages, Matriculation or Secondary School in 3 villages, namely Nemakal, Chippagiri, Yerur.

Higher Secondary or Pre University Courses or Intermediate or Junior College in 0 village of the CD Block, College in 0 village, Adult Literacy Center in 14 villages.

Medical: Hospital in 0 village, Dispensary in 1 village, Health Center in 1 village, Sub Center in 6 villages, Maternity and Child Welfare Center in 0 village, Community health workers in 0 village.

The Village having Hospital or Dispensary or Health Center is Ramadurgam.

Drinking Water: Tap water in 14 villages, Tank water in 14 villages, Well water in 14 villages, Tubewell in 14 villages and more than one source in 14 villages.

Bank: Banking facility in 2 villages, namely, Nemakal, Chippagiri.

Credit Society in 6 villages Agricultural Credit Society in 3 Non-Agricultural Credit Society in 4 villages.

Others: Power supply in 14 villages, Cinema hall in 0 village, sport club in 0 village, Stadium or Auditorium or Community Hall in 0 village, Post Office in 10 villages.

There are 8 villages having bus facilities.

Villages with most of facilities: Nemakal Chippagiri.

Villages without Amenities (Education): None..

Scheduled Castes: Out of the total population of 31465 persons, 4128 persons (13.12%) belong to Scheduled Castes.

The villages having less than 10% SC population are Thimmapuram, Nemakal, Doulathapuram, Degalahal Gummanur, Bantanahal.

The villages having more than 50% SC population are None.

Sex ratio of Scheduled Caste population is 495.

Scheduled Castes Literates and Illiterates by Sex:

	Persons	Males	Females
Literate	1,616	1,112	504
Illiterate	2,512	973	1,539
Literacy rate	46.6	64.0	29.1
Graduate	23	23	0

Scheduled Castes (Dominant):

Madiga, Mala, Generic Castes etc., Mala Dasari

For their cultural identity please see Appendix-I

Villages without Scheduled Castes: There are 0 village without any scheduled caste population.

Scheduled Tribes: Out of the total population of 31465 persons, 67 persons (0.21%) belong to Scheduled Tribes.

The villages having less than 10% ST population are Ramadurgam, Thimmapuram, Nagaradona, Nemakal Nancharla, Doulathapuram, Chippagiri, Kundanagurthi Degalahal, Beldona, Yerur, Gummanur, Khajipuram Bantanahal.

The villages having more than 50% ST population are None.

Sex ratio of Scheduled tribe population is 373.

Scheduled Tribes Literates and Illiterates by Sex:

	Persons	Males	Females
Literate	40	35	5
Illiterate	27	7	20
Literacy rate	65.6	92.1	21.7
Graduate	3	3	0

Scheduled Tribes (Dominant):

Yerukulas, Sugalis etc.

For their cultural identity please see Appendix-II

Villages without Scheduled Tribes: There are 9 villages without any scheduled tribe population.

Literates and Illiterates by Sex (Total Population):

	Persons	Males	Females
Literate	14,218	9,369	4,849
Illiterate	17,247	6,643	10,604
Literacy rate	53	68	37
Graduate	402	348	54

Agriculture: ***Distribution of villages according to land use:*** Out of 14 villages, Total area (in hectare) is 30014, out of that 92.09 percent is cultivable and 7.34 percent of the cultivable area is irrigated.

Sources of Irrigation (Hectares): Government Canal 1828, Private Canal 0, Well without Electricity 0, Well with Electricity 61, Tubewell without Electricity 79, Tubewell with Electricity 0, Tank 20, River 0, Lake 0, Waterfall 0, Others 42.

Villages with population of 5000 to 9999: None

Villages with population of 10000 and above: None

Distribution of Workers:

	Persons	Males	Females	WPR
Cultivators	7,276	4,646	2,630	43.18
Agricultural Labour	7,153	2,885	4,268	42.45
Household Industry	495	205	290	2.94
Other Workers	1,928	1,426	502	11.44

Main Workers	12,538	8,328	4,210	74.4
Marginal Workers	4,314	834	3,480	25.6
Total Workers	16,852	9,162	7,690	

Religion: Major Religious Communities:

	Persons	Males	Females	Sex Ratio
Hindu (93.96%)	29,566	15,055	14,511	964
Muslim (5.11%)	1,609	826	783	948
Christian (0.72%)	228	101	127	1,257
Sikh (0%)	1	-	1	-
Buddhists (0%)	1	-	1	-
Jain (0%)	-	-	-	-

Agewise Data:

	Persons	Males	Females	Sex Ratio
All ages	31,465	16,012	15,453	965
0-14	11,306	5,892	5,414	919
15-44	13,999	7,159	6,840	955
45-79	5,883	2,839	3,044	1072
80+	240	104	136	1308
Age not stated	37	18	19	1056

Languages (Dominant):
Telugu, Urdu, Kannada, Marathi, Tamil

Disabled Population:

	Persons	Males	Females	%
Total Disabled	533	304	229	
In Seeing	191	96	95	35.83
In Speech	51	31	20	9.57
In Hearing	52	25	27	9.76
In Movement	168	114	54	31.52
Mentally	71	38	33	13.32

CHIRALA

Chirala C.D. Block lies in the north-eastern part of Prakasam district. It is a part of Chirala Mandal. The Block is located at a distance of 48 kms. from district headquarters (Ongole). There are 03 villages in the block with the total population of 36,526 persons. Area of the C.D. Block is 65.41 sq. kms. It is bounded in the north by district Guntur, in the south by Manda ls Karamchedu and Vetapalem, in the east by district Guntur and the Bay of Bengal, and in the west by Mandals Karamchedu and Parchur.

Communications:

Roadways : NH- 214 A: Direction- Ongole to Guntur. Neare st Villages- Ipuru Palem (Rural).

Railway Station: Ipuru Palem (Rural).

The Block is identified a drought-prone area.

Annual Rainfall: Average Rainfall 1016.1 mm

Ground Water: Availability of the Ground Water in the Basin is 41.97 MCM and the utilization is 4.02 MCM It belongs to Safe category. Depth to water level varies from 2 to 5 meter below the ground. Most of the wells go down in summer months., according to the Ground Water Estimation Committee.

Administration:

Division: Coastal Andhra. Parliamentary Constituency: 32 Bapatla (SC). District: Prakasam. Mandal: Chirala. Assembly Constituency: 225 Chirala. Gram Panchayat: 15

Villages: 3 **Inhabited:** 2 **Uninhabited:** 1

Ranking	District	State	National
Area	56	1085	5982
Population	44	908	5865
Sex Ratio	31	805	2678
Child Sex Ratio	39	845	3711
Literacy Rate	31	554	4055
Density	17	303	1983
Work Participation Rate	1	77	769

Gram Panchayats:
Burlavaripalem, Chirala Nagar, Devangapuri Devinuthala, Epurupalem, Gandhi Nagar Gavinivaripalem, Kavuruvaripalem, Kothapalem Pittuvanipalem, R.K.Puram, Salman Centre Thotavaripalem, Vijayanagar Colony, Vodarevu.

Amenities:

Education: Primary School in 2 villages, Middle school in 2 villages, Matriculation or Secondary School in 1 village, namely Ipuru Palem (Rural).

Higher Secondary or Pre University Courses or Intermediate or Junior College in 1 village of the CD Block,, namely Ipuru Palem (Rural).

College in 1 village, Adult Literacy Center in 2 villages., College is in village, namely Ipuru Palem (Rural).

Medical: Hospital in 0 village, Dispensary in 0 village, Health Center in 0 village, Sub Center in 2 villages, Maternity and Child Welfare Center in 0 village, Community health workers in 0 village.

Drinking Water: Tap water in 2 villages, Tank water in 2 villages, Well water in 2 villages, Tubewell in 2 villages and more than one source in 2 villages.

Bank: Banking facility in 2 villages, namely, Ipuru Palem (Rural), Gavinivari Palem.

Credit Society in 1 village Agricultural Credit Society in 0 Non-Agricultural Credit Society in 1 village.

Others: Power supply in 2 villages, Cinema hall in 0 village, sport club in 0 village, Stadium or Auditorium or Community Hall in 0 village, Post Office in 2 villages.

There are 2 villages having bus facilities.

Villages with most of facilities: Ipuru Palem (Rural) Gavinivari Palem.

Villages without Amenities (Education): None..

Scheduled Castes: Out of the total population of 36530

persons, 4750 persons (13%) belong to Scheduled Castes.
The villages having less than 10% SC population are None..
The villages having more than 50% SC population are None.
Sex ratio of Scheduled Caste population is 490.

Scheduled Castes Literates and Illiterates by Sex:

	Persons	Males	Females
Literate	2,536	1,477	1,059
Illiterate	2,214	945	1,269
Literacy rate	62.5	71.8	53.0
Graduate	76	62	14

Scheduled Castes (Dominant):
Mala, Madiga, Bindla

For their cultural identity please see Appendix-I

Villages without Scheduled Castes: There is 1 village without any scheduled caste population.

Scheduled Tribes: Out of the total population of 36530 persons, 1847 persons (5.06%) belong to Scheduled Tribes.
The villages having less than 10% ST population are None..
The villages having more than 50% ST population are None.
Sex ratio of Scheduled tribe population is 508.

Scheduled Tribes Literates and Illiterates by Sex:

	Persons	Males	Females
Literate	877	470	407
Illiterate	970	438	532
Literacy rate	55.7	60.7	50.8
Graduate	47	34	13

Scheduled Tribes (Dominant):
Yerukulas, Yenadis

For their cultural identity please see Appendix-II

Villages without Scheduled Tribes: There is 1 village without any scheduled tribe population.

Literates and Illiterates by Sex (Total Population):

	Persons	Males	Females
Literate	16,532	10,163	6,369
Illiterate	19,998	8,418	11,580
Literacy rate	53	64	41
Graduate	460	384	76

Agriculture: ***Distribution of villages according to land use:*** Out of 3 villages, Total area (in hectare) is 6541, out of that 59.13 percent is cultivable and 76.89 percent of the cultivable area is irrigated.

Sources of Irrigation (Hectares): Government Canal 1500, Private Canal 0, Well without Electricity 0, Well with Electricity 0, Tubewell without Electricity 0, Tubewell with Electricity 0, Tank 0, River 0, Lake 0, Waterfall 0, Others 1474.

Villages with population of 5000 to 9999: None

Villages with population of 10000 and above:
Ipuru Palem (Rural), Gavinivari Palem.

Distribution of Workers:

	Persons	Males	Females	WPR
Cultivators	3,678	2,898	780	18.38
Agricultural Labour	9,553	3,646	5,907	47.73
Household Industry	2,838	1,469	1,369	14.18
Other Workers	3,946	3,090	856	19.72
Main Workers	13,946	9,774	4,172	69.68
Marginal Workers	6,069	1,329	4,740	30.32
Total Workers	20,015	11,103	8,912	

Religion: Major Religious Communities:

	Persons	Males	Females	Sex Ratio
Hindu (98.53%)	35,994	18,331	17,663	964
Muslim (0.96%)	351	163	188	1,153
Christian (0.39%)	144	65	79	1,215
Sikh (0%)	-	-	-	-
Buddhists (0%)	1	1	-	-
Jain (0%)	-	-	-	-

Agewise Data:

	Persons	Males	Females	Sex Ratio
All ages	36,530	18,581	17,949	966
0-14	12,230	6,304	5,926	940
15-44	17,806	9,069	8,737	963
45-79	6,242	3,088	3,154	1021
80+	213	100	113	1130
Age not stated	39	20	19	950

Languages (Dominant):
Telugu, Urdu, Gondi, Tamil, Hindi

Disabled Population:

	Persons	Males	Females	%
Total Disabled	460	260	200	
In Seeing	141	80	61	30.65
In Speech	53	24	29	11.52
In Hearing	20	5	15	4.35
In Movement	181	116	65	39.35
Mentally	65	35	30	14.13

CHITTAMUR

Chittamur C.D. Block lies in the south-eastern part of Nellore district. The Block is located at a distance of 75 kms. from district headquarters (Nellore). There are 41 villages in the block with the total population of 37,246 persons. Area of the C.D. Block is 269.81 sq. kms. It is bounded in the north by Mandals Ojili, Kota and Vakadu, in the south by Mandals Sullurpeta and Deravarisatram, in the east by Mandal Vakadu, and in the west by Mandal Naidupet.

Communications:

Roadways : Metalled Roads: Nearest Villages- Chittamur, Somasamudram, Padarthivari- Khandrika, Pittivanipalle,

Mukkidipalem, Gangupalem, Mallam, Ranganathapuram, Kogili, Tadimedu, Mannemala, Yellasiri, Molakalapudi.

River: Swarnamukhi Nadi- Nearest Villages- Gunupadu, Mettu.

Annual Rainfall: Average Rainfall 1092 mm

Ground Water: Availability of the Ground Water in the Basin is 2965 H.A.M. and the utilization is 1599 H. A.M. It belongs to Safe category. Depth to water level varies from less than 5 meter below the ground. Most of the wells go down in summer months, according to the Ground Water Estimation Committee.

Administration:

Division: Coastal Andhra. Parliamentary Constituency: 40 Tirupati (SC). District: Nellore. Mandal: Chittamur. Assembly Constituency: 239 Gudur (SC). Gram Panchayat: 23

Villages: 41 **Inhabited:** 33 **Uninhabited:** 8

Ranking	District	State	National
Area	22	242	3109
Population	32	896	5842
Sex Ratio	38	713	2395
Child Sex Ratio	43	1012	4742
Literacy Rate	44	508	3871
Density	9	510	5738
Work Participation Rate	32	948	1328

Gram Panchayats:

Aletipadu, Aravapalem, Aruru, Buradagalikothapalem Chillamuru, Chittamur, Eswarawaka, Gunapadu Gunapatipalem, Jakkalavari Palle, Kogili, Mallam Mettu, Molakalapudi, North Varthuru, Pallam Parthi Pellakur, Ranganatha Puram, Tadimedu, Uppala Marthy Yakasiri, Yellasiri, Yellore.

Amenities:

Education: Primary School in 29 villages, Middle school in 8 villages, Matriculation or Secondary School in 4 villages, namely Gunupadu, Chittamur, Mallam, Yellasiri.

Higher Secondary or Pre University Courses or Intermediate or Junior College in 1 village of the CD Block,, namely Mallam.

College in 0 village, Adult Literacy Center in 20 villages.

Medical: Hospital in 0 village, Dispensary in 2 villages, Health Center in 2 villages, Sub Center in 9 villages, Maternity and Child Welfare Center in 0 village, Community health workers in 0 village.

The Villages having Hospital or Dispensary or Health Center are Gunupadu, Pellakuru.

Drinking Water: Tap water in 33 villages, Tank water in 33 villages, Well water in 33 villages, Tubewell in 33 villages and more than one source in 33 villages.

Bank: Banking facility in 3 villages, namely, Gunupadu, Chittamur, Mallam.

Credit Society in 13 villages Agricultural Credit Society in 8 Non-Agricultural Credit Society in 12 villages.

Others: Power supply in 33 villages, Cinema hall in 1 village, sport club in 0 village, Stadium or Auditorium or Community Hall in 0 village, Post Office in 13 villages.

There are 30 villages having bus facilities.

Villages with most of facilities: Gunupadu Chittamur, Mallam.

Villages without amenities (Education):

Putragunta, Mangalavaripalle, Gollapalem, Jalapeddipalem..

Scheduled Castes: Out of the total population of 37246 persons, 14466 persons (38.84%) belong to Scheduled Castes.

The villages having less than 10% SC population are Pittivanipalle, Mangalavaripalle, Gollapalem Jalapeddipalem.

The villages having more than 50% SC population are Somasamudram, Mukkidipalem, Tadimedu, Kokkupalem Palamparthy, Ellore, Veligajulapalle Buradagali Kothapalem.

Sex ratio of Scheduled Caste population is 488.

Scheduled Castes Literates and Illiterates by Sex:

	Persons	Males	Females
Literate	5,706	3,471	2,235
Illiterate	8,760	3,940	4,820
Literacy rate	45.7	54.6	36.5
Graduate	135	105	30

Scheduled Castes (Dominant):

Mala, Madiga, Generic Castes etc., Arundhatiya

For their cultural identity please see Appendix-I

Villages without Scheduled Castes: There are 12 villages without any scheduled caste population.

Scheduled Tribes: Out of the total population of 37246 persons, 4995 persons (13.41%) belong to Scheduled Tribes.

The villages having less than 10% ST population are Uppalamarthi, Addepudi, Chittamur, Somasamudram Pittivanipalle, Mukkidipalem, Kogili, Tadimedu Aruru, Kokkupalem, Palamparthy, Veligajulapalle Buradagali Kothapalem, Kalagurthipadu, Kummarapalem.

The villages having more than 50% ST population are None.

Sex ratio of Scheduled tribe population is 490.

Scheduled Tribes Literates and Illiterates by Sex:

	Persons	Males	Females
Literate	1,196	682	514
Illiterate	3,799	1,863	1,936
Literacy rate	28.5	31.9	24.9
Graduate	4	3	1

Scheduled Tribes (Dominant):

Yenadis, Yerukulas, Generic Tribes etc., Kammara

For their cultural identity please see Appendix-II

Villages without Scheduled Tribes: There are 14 villages without any scheduled tribe population.

Literates and Illiterates by Sex (Total Population):

	Persons	Males	Females
Literate	17,395	10,078	7,317
Illiterate	19,851	8,805	11,046
Literacy rate	54	62	46
Graduate	523	411	112

Agriculture: ***Distribution of villages according to land use:*** Out of 41 villages, Total area (in hectare) is 26984, out of that 46.29 percent is cultivable and 73.4 percent of the cultivable area is irrigated.

Sources of Irrigation (Hectares): Government Canal 0, Private Canal 0, Well without Electricity 0, Well with Electricity 101, Tubewell without Electricity 0, Tubewell with Electricity 2645, Tank 6423, River 0, Lake 0, Waterfall 0, Others 0.

Villages with population of 5000 to 9999: None

Villages with population of 10000 and above: None

Distribution of Workers:

	Persons	Males	Females	WPR
Cultivators	6,178	4,579	1,599	31.15
Agricultural Labour	11,374	5,431	5,943	57.35
Household Industry	189	139	50	0.95
Other Workers	2,091	1,501	590	10.54
Main Workers	16,889	10,698	6,191	85.16
Marginal Workers	2,943	952	1,991	14.84
Total Workers	19,832	11,650	8,182	

Religion: Major Religious Communities:

	Persons	Males	Females	Sex Ratio
Hindu (96.21%)	35,836	18,182	17,654	971
Muslim (3.23%)	1,202	598	604	1,010
Christian (0.52%)	195	95	100	1,053
Sikh (0%)	1	1	-	-
Buddhists (0.03%)	11	6	5	833
Jain (0%)	-	-	-	-

Agewise Data:

	Persons	Males	Females	Sex Ratio
All ages	37,246	18,883	18,363	972
0-14	11,139	5,953	5,186	871
15-44	18,354	9,181	9,173	999
45-79	7,546	3,647	3,899	1069
80+	187	93	94	1011
Age not stated	20	9	11	1222

Languages (Dominant):

Telugu, Urdu, Tamil, Gondi, Hindi

Disabled Population:

	Persons	Males	Females	%
Total Disabled	742	400	342	
In Seeing	252	123	129	33.96
In Speech	76	41	35	10.24
In Hearing	56	22	34	7.55
In Movement	266	168	98	35.85
Mentally	92	46	46	12.4

CHITTOOR

Chittoor C.D. Block lies in the southern part of Chitto or district. It is a part of Chittoor Mandal. The Block is located at a distance of (00) kms. from district headquarters (Chittoor). There are 35 villages in the block with the total population of 54,592 persons. Area of the C.D. Block is 188.78 sq. kms. It is bounded in the north by Mandals Thavanampalle, Puthalapattu, Penumuru and Gangadhara Nellore, in the south by Mandal Gudipala, in the east by Mandal Gangadhara Nellore, in the west by Mandals Thavanampalle and Yadamarri, and it has common boundary with the state of Tamil Nadu in the south and west.

Communications:

Roadways : NH- 4: Direction- Bangalore to Chennai. Neare st Villages- Anupalle, Anupalle, Siddampalle, Narigapal le. State Highway (S.H.): Direction- Chittoor to Chandra giri. Nearest Village- Murakambattu.

Railway Station: Siddampalle.

River: Ponnai Nadi- Nearest Villages- Muthukuru. Anagal lu, Paluru, Bakara Narasinga Rayani Peta, Pachanapalle, Settiappam Thangal.

It receives the Backward Region Grants, and is identifi ed as a drought-prone area as well.

Integrated Child Development Scheme (ICDS) Project: Chittoor, Total Anganwadi Centres: 206

Annual Rainfall: Average Rainfall 1048 mm

Ground Water: Availability of the Ground Water in the Basin is 2178 H.A.M.and the utilization is 2637 H.A. M. It belongs to OE category. Depth to water level varies more than 10 meter below the ground. Most of the wells go down in summer months, according to the Ground Water Estimation Committee.

Natural Division : Rayalaseema Region

Administration:

Division: Rayala Seema. Parliamentary Constituency: 42 Chittoor (SC). District: Chittoor. Mandal: Chittoor. Assembly Constituency: 291 Chittoor Gram Panchayat: 27

Border Villages: (Tamil Nadu)- Nearest Village- Thummin da.

Villages: 35 **Inhabited:** 34 **Uninhabited:** 1

Ranking	District	State	National
Area	24	620	4373
Population	11	378	5061

Sex Ratio	60	779	2656
Child Sex Ratio	58	1032	4908
Literacy Rate	13	71	1212
Density	62	1008	3637
Work Participation Rate	28	395	3905

Gram Panchayats:

Anagallu, Ananthapuram, Anupalle, Cherlopalle Chinthalagunta, Diguvamasapalle, Doddipalle Guvvakallu, Kurchivedu, Lakshmambapuram Mangasamudram, Mangasamudram Hcolyny, Mapakshi Murakambattu, Muthukoor, N.R.Peta, Narigapalli Nayanicheruvu, Pachanapalli, Paloor, Peddisettipalli Perumallakandiga, Thalambedu, Thenebanda Thimmasanipalle, Thoppatipalle, Thumminda.

Amenities:

Education: Primary School in 30 villages, Middle school in 10 villages, Matriculation or Secondary School in 7 villages, namely Mangasamudram (Rural), Murakambattu, Doddipalle, Bakara Narasinga Rayani Peta, Mapakshi, Thumminda, Thalambedu.

Higher Secondary or Pre University Courses or Intermediate or Junior College in 1 village of the CD Block,, namely Murakambattu.

College in 0 village, Adult Literacy Center in 12 villages.

Medical: Hospital in 0 village, Dispensary in 1 village, Health Center in 3 villages, Sub Center in 14 villages, Maternity and Child Welfare Center in 1 village, Community health workers in 0 village.

The Villages having Hospital or Dispensary or Health Center are Mangasamudram (Rural), Mapakshi.

Drinking Water: Tap water in 34 villages, Tank water in 34 villages, Well water in 34 villages, Tubewell in 34 villages and more than one source in 34 villages.

Bank: Banking facility in 3 villages, namely, Mangasamudram (Rural), Doddipalle Bakara Narasinga Rayani Peta.

Credit Society in 16 villages Agricultural Credit Society in 8 Non-Agricultural Credit Society in 10 villages.

Others: Power supply in 34 villages, Cinema hall in 1 village, sport club in 1 village, Stadium or Auditorium or Community Hall in 0 village, Post Office in 14 villages.

There are 32 villages having bus facilities.

Villages with most of facilities: Mangasamudram (Rural) Doddipalle.

Villages without amenities (Education):

Krishnapuram, Varadarajulapalle, Alukurupalle, Venkatapuram..

Scheduled Castes: Out of the total population of 54765 persons, 14552 persons (26.57%) belong to Scheduled Castes. The villages having less than 10% SC population are Doddipalle, Paluru, Arathala, Bandapalle, Gollapalle Mapakshi (Part), Peddisettipalle, Siddampalle Varadarajulapalle, Settiappam Thangal, Venkatapuram.

The villages having more than 50% SC population are Ayanavedu, Muthukuru, Anagallu, Guvvakallu Chinthalagunta, Ananthapuram, Pachanapalle Alukurupalle.

Sex ratio of Scheduled Caste population is 488.

Scheduled Castes Literates and Illiterates by Sex:

	Persons	Males	Females
Literate	8,288	4,777	3,511
Illiterate	6,264	2,675	3,589
Literacy rate	65.4	73.9	56.5
Graduate	97	77	20

Scheduled Castes (Dominant):

Adi Dravida, Adi Andhra, Madiga, Mala Generic Castes etc.

For their cultural identity please see Appendix-I

Villages without Scheduled Castes: There are 6 villages without any scheduled caste population.

Scheduled Tribes: Out of the total population of 54765 persons, 1128 persons (2.06%) belong to Scheduled Tribes. The villages having less than 10% ST population are Thenebanda, Mangasamudram (Rural), Murakambattu Doddipalle, Diguvamasapalle, Ayanavedu, Muthukuru Anagallu, Paluru, Bakara Narasinga Rayani Peta Arathala, Bandapalle, Krishnapuram, Gollapalle Guvvakallu, Anupalle, Mapakshi, Mapakshi (Part) Peddisettipalle, Thumminda, Siddampalle, Narigapalle Lakshmambapuram, Varadarajulapalle Perumalla Khandriga, Chinthalagunta, Thalambedu Ananthapuram, Pachanapalle, Settiappam Thangal S.Venkatapuram, Kurchivedu, Alukurupalle Venkatapuram.

The villages having more than 50% ST population are None.

Sex ratio of Scheduled tribe population is 486.

Scheduled Tribes Literates and Illiterates by Sex:

	Persons	Males	Females
Literate	388	235	153
Illiterate	740	345	395
Literacy rate	41.8	49.1	34.0
Graduate	2	2	0

Scheduled Tribes (Dominant):

Yenadis, Yerukulas, Generic Tribes etc., Kondareddis

For their cultural identity please see Appendix-II

Villages without Scheduled Tribes: There are 20 villages without any scheduled tribe population.

Literates and Illiterates by Sex (Total Population):

	Persons	Males	Females

Literate	33,477	19,478	13,999
Illiterate	21,288	8,367	12,921
Literacy rate	70	80	59
Graduate	1,079	814	265

Agriculture: ***Distribution of villages according to land use:*** Out of 35 villages, Total area (in hectare) is 18876, out of that 49.95 percent is cultivable and 38.75 percent of the cultivable area is irrigated.

Sources of Irrigation (Hectares): Government Canal 0, Private Canal 0, Well without Electricity 109.1, Well with Electricity 1810.22, Tubewell without Electricity 0, Tubewell with Electricity 1206.42, Tank 526.16, River 0, Lake 2, Waterfall 0, Others 0.

Villages with population of 5000 to 9999:
Thenebanda, Mangasamudram (Rural), Murakambattu.

Villages with population of 10000 and above: None

Distribution of Workers:

	Persons	Males	Females	WPR
Cultivators	6,142	4,559	1,583	26.03
Agricultural Labour	8,947	4,960	3,987	37.91
Household Industry	794	331	463	3.36
Other Workers	7,716	6,088	1,628	32.7
Main Workers	19,566	14,299	5,267	82.91
Marginal Workers	4,033	1,639	2,394	17.09
Total Workers	23,599	15,938	7,661	

Religion: Major Religious Communities:

	Persons	Males	Females	Sex Ratio
Hindu (93.74%)	51,337	26,116	25,221	966
Muslim (4.14%)	2,267	1,156	1,111	961
Christian (2.1%)	1,149	562	587	1,044
Sikh (0%)	-	-	-	-
Buddhists (0%)	-	-	-	-
Jain (0%)	-	-	-	-

Agewise Data:

	Persons	Males	Females	Sex Ratio
All ages	54,765	27,845	26,920	967
0-14	16,032	8,357	7,675	918
15-44	25,804	13,050	12,754	977
45-79	12,310	6,128	6,182	1009
80+	503	240	263	1096
Age not stated	116	70	46	657

Languages (Dominant):
Telugu, Tamil, Urdu, Hindi, Others

Disabled Population:

	Persons	Males	Females	%
Total Disabled	843	486	357	
In Seeing	248	126	122	29.42
In Speech	125	68	57	14.83
In Hearing	61	31	30	7.24
In Movement	306	205	101	36.3
Mentally	103	56	47	12.22

CHITVEL

Chitvel C.D. Block lies in the eastern part of Cuddapah district. The Block is located at a distance of 60 kms. from district headquarters (Cuddapah). There are 19 villages in the block with the total population of 43,042 persons. Area of the C.D. Block is 220.80 sq. kms. It is bounded in the north by Mandal Penagalur, in the south by Mandal Kodur, in the east by district Nellore, and in the west by Mandals Penagalur and Obula varipalle.

Communications:

Roadways : Metalled Roads: Nearest Villages- Malemarpuram, Mylapalle, Chitvel, Kampasamudram, K.S.Agraharam, Nagiripadu, Nethivaripalle, Maharajapuram @Siddareddip alle, K.V.R.R. Puram, Nagavaram.

Steam: Local stream touches the following villages, namely, Malemarpuram, Devamachupalle, Chitvel, Kampasa mudram, K.S.Agraharam, Nagiripadu, Nethivaripalle, Thumm akonda, Maharajapuram @Siddareddipalle, K.V.R.R. Puram, Kalvavarikandrika, Nagavaram.

It receives Backward Region Grants, and is also identif ied as a drought-prone area as well.

Annual Rainfall: Average Rainfall 924 mm

Ground Water: Availability of the Ground Water in the Basin is 1367 H.A.M.and the utilization is 1444 H.A. M.It belongs to OE category. Depth to water level varies from 10 to 20 meter below the ground. Most of the wells go down in summer months, according to the Ground Water Estimation Committee.

Forest and Reserved **Forest:** (Kalleti Kanama R.F.)- Nearest Villages- Malemarpuram, Mallemadugu, Chintala Chelika, Rajukunta, Cherlopalle, Nagiripadu, Nethivarip alle, Thummakonda, Maharajapuram @ Siddareddipalle.

Natural Division : Rayalaseema Region

Administration:

Division: Rayala Seema. Parliamentary Constituency: 41 Rajampet. District: Cuddapah.
Mandal: Chitvel. Assembly Constituency: 246 Kodur (SC).
Gram Panchayat: 20.

Villages: 19 **Inhabited:** 18 **Uninhabited:** 1

Ranking	District	State	National
Area	26	436	3843
Population	17	720	5596
Sex Ratio	18	515	1850
Child Sex Ratio	36	891	3949
Literacy Rate	28	324	3073
Density	35	906	4798
Work Participation Rate	21	734	3126

Gram Panchayats:

C.Kandulavaripalli, C.M.Rachapalli, Chitvel Devamachupalli, K.S.Agraharam, K.V.R.R.Puram Kampasamudram, Maharajupuram, Malemapuram Margopalli, Mylapalli, Nagavaram, Nagiripadu Nakkalapalli, Neethivaripalli, Pollopalli, Rajukunta Thimmaiahgaripalli, Thimmaiahpalem, Thummakonda.

Amenities:

Education: Primary School in 18 villages, Middle school in 7 villages, Matriculation or Secondary School in 5 villages, namely Malemarpuram, Chitvel, Kampasamudram, Nagiripadu, Nagavaram.

Higher Secondary or Pre University Courses or Intermediate or Junior College in 1 village of the CD Block,, namely Chitvel.

College in 1 village, Adult Literacy Center in 2 villages., College is in village, namely Chitvel.

Medical: Hospital in 1 village, Dispensary in 1 village, Health Center in 7 villages, Sub Center in 0 village, Maternity and Child Welfare Center in 0 village, Community health workers in 0 village.

The Villages having Hospital or Dispensary or Health Center are Malemarpuram, Devamachupalle, Chitvel, Kampasamudram, K.S.Agraharam, Nagiripadu, Nagavaram.

Drinking Water: Tap water in 18 villages, Tank water in 18 villages, Well water in 18 villages, Tubewell in 18 villages and more than one source in 18 villages.

Bank: Banking facility in 3 villages, namely, Chitvel, Nagiripadu, Nagavaram.

Credit Society in 6 villages Agricultural Credit Society in 2 Non-Agricultural Credit Society in 6 villages.

Others: Power supply in 18 villages, Cinema hall in 1 village, sport club in 0 village, Stadium or Auditorium or Community Hall in 0 village, Post Office in 10 villages.

There are 15 villages having bus facilities.

Villages with most of facilities: Chitvel Nagiripadu, Nagavaram.

Villages without Amenities (Education): None..

Scheduled Castes: Out of the total population of 43042 persons, 8407 persons (19.53%) belong to Scheduled Castes.

The villages having less than 10% SC population are Mallemadugu, Bhakrapuram, Thimmayapalem Maharajapuram @Siddareddipalle.

The villages having more than 50% SC population are None.

Sex ratio of Scheduled Caste population is 498.

Scheduled Castes Literates and Illiterates by Sex:

	Persons	Males	Females
Literate	3,558	2,276	1,282
Illiterate	4,849	1,945	2,904
Literacy rate	49.3	63.0	35.7
Graduate	94	83	11

Scheduled Castes (Dominant):

Mala, Madiga, Generic Castes etc., Mala Dasari

For their cultural identity please see Appendix-I

Villages without Scheduled Castes: There is 1 village without any scheduled caste population.

Scheduled Tribes: Out of the total population of 43042 persons, 2794 persons (6.49%) belong to Scheduled Tribes.

The villages having less than 10% ST population are Malemarpuram, Mylapalle, Devamachupalle, Chitvel Bhakrapuram, K.S.Agraharam, Nagiripadu K.V.R.R. Puram, Nagavaram.

The villages having more than 50% ST population are None.

Sex ratio of Scheduled tribe population is 495.

Scheduled Tribes Literates and Illiterates by Sex:

	Persons	Males	Females
Literate	796	492	304
Illiterate	1,998	919	1,079
Literacy rate	34.9	42.9	26.8
Graduate	17	13	4

Scheduled Tribes (Dominant):

Yenadis, Yerukulas, Sugalis etc., Chenchu etc.

For their cultural identity please see Appendix-II

Villages without Scheduled Tribes: There are 2 villages without any scheduled tribe population.

Literates and Illiterates by Sex (Total Population):

	Persons	Males	Females
Literate	21,798	13,427	8,371
Illiterate	21,244	8,267	12,977
Literacy rate	58	72	45
Graduate	790	672	118

Agriculture: ***Distribution of villages according to land use:***

Out of 19 villages, Total area (in hectare) is 22087, out of that 39.87 percent is cultivable and 91.89 percent of the cultivable area is irrigated.

Sources of Irrigation (Hectares): Government Canal 0, Private Canal 0, Well without Electricity 40, Well with Electricity 724, Tubewell without Electricity 0, Tubewell with Electricity 5810, Tank 1518.89, River 0, Lake 0, Waterfall 0, Others 0.

Villages with population of 5000 to 9999:

Malemarpuram, Chitvel, Nagiripadu.

Villages with population of 10000 and above: None

Distribution of Workers:

	Persons	Males	Females	WPR
Cultivators	7,084	5,156	1,928	35.56
Agricultural Labour	9,260	4,779	4,481	46.48
Household Industry	485	292	193	2.43
Other Workers	3,094	2,449	645	15.53

Main Workers	16,395	11,282	5,113	82.29
Marginal Workers	3,528	1,394	2,134	17.71
Total Workers	19,923	12,676	7,247	

Religion: Major Religious Communities:

	Persons	Males	Females	Sex Ratio
Hindu (95.36%)	41,046	20,703	20,343	983
Muslim (4.44%)	1,913	947	966	1,020
Christian (0.09%)	39	19	20	1,053
Sikh (0%)	2	1	1	1,000
Buddhists (0%)	-	-	-	-
Jain (0%)	-	-	-	-

Agewise Data:

	Persons	Males	Females	Sex Ratio
All ages	43,042	21,694	21,348	984
0-14	12,934	6,614	6,320	956
15-44	20,438	10,336	10,102	977
45-79	9,261	4,550	4,711	1035
80+	315	139	176	1266
Age not stated	94	55	39	709

Languages (Dominant):

Telugu, Urdu, Marathi, Gondi, Hindi

Disabled Population:

	Persons	Males	Females	%
Total Disabled	867	466	401	
In Seeing	353	155	198	40.72
In Speech	89	46	43	10.27
In Hearing	64	39	25	7.38
In Movement	237	157	80	27.34
Mentally	124	69	55	14.3

CHITYAL

Chityal C.D. Block lies in the north-western part of Warangal district. The Block is located at a distance of 64 kms. from district headquarters (Warangal). There are 32 villages in the block with the total population of 57,434 persons. Area of the C.D. Block is 300.81 sq. kms. It is bounded in the north by district Karim Nagar, in the south by Mandals Mogullapalle and Regonda, in the east by Mandal Bhupalpalle, and in the west by district Karim Nagar.

Communications:

Roadways : NH, SH or Important Metalled Road is not available.

River: Maner Nadi- Nearest Villages- Venkatraopalle, Kalikota, Kalvapalle, Vencherami, Boina Palle, Emped.

Backwards Region Grants Fund: It receives Backward Region Grants.

Mahila Samakhya (Education for Women's Equality): It is decleared Socialy and Educationally Backward Block by the Government.

Integrated Child Development Scheme (ICDS) Project: Chityal, Total Anganwadi Centres: 201

Annual Rainfall: Average Rainfall 1013 mm

Ground Water: Availability of the Ground Water in the Basin is 6029 H.A.M.and the utilization is 3115 H.A. M. It belongs to Safe category. Depth to water level varies from 10 to 20 and more than 20 meter below the ground. Most of the wells go down in summer months. The well density in the entire block is 18 wells per sq. km. Total no. of the wells in the block are enumera ted as 5556, according to the Ground Water Estimation Committee.

Natural Division : Godavari Depression Region

Administration:

Division: Telangana. Parliamentary Constituency. Distri ct: Warangal. Mandal: Chityal. Assembly Constituency: 108 Bhupalpalle. Gram Panchayat: 31

Villages: 32 **Inhabited:** 32 **Uninhabited:** 0

Ranking	District	State	National
Area	4	160	2778
Population	16	314	4947
Sex Ratio	11	399	1568
Child Sex Ratio	38	935	4142
Literacy Rate	39	787	4844
Density	2	159	4867
Work Participation Rate	43	749	460

Gram Panchayats:

Ankushapur, Ashireddipalle, Bhavusinghpalle Bornapalle, Chainpaka, Challagarige, Chityal Doothpalle, Dwarakapet, Empaid, Garmillapalle Giddemutharam, Gopalapur, Gummadavelli, Jadalpet Jookal, Kundanpalle, Muchiniparthy, Nawabpeta Ninepaka, Pangidipalle, Raghavapur Ramakishthapur(T), Ramakistapur (V), Subbakkapalle Tekumatla, Thirumalapur, Velchal, Vellampalle Venkatraopalle, Vodithal.

Amenities:

Education: Primary School in 32 villages, Middle school in 15 villages, Matriculation or Secondary School in 8 villages, namely Garimillapalle, Velchal, Kundanpalle, Tekumatta, Jadalapet, Chityal, Jookal, Challagarige. Higher Secondary or Pre University Courses or Inter-mediate or Junior College in 0 village of the CD Block, College in 0 village, Adult Literacy Center in 23 villages.

Medical: Hospital in 1 village, Dispensary in 3 villages, Health Center in 1 village, Sub Center in 11 villages, Maternity and Child Welfare Center in 1 village, Community health workers in 0 village.

The Villages having Hospital or Dispensary or Health Center are Navabpet, Chityal, Challagarige.

Drinking Water: Tap water in 31 villages, Tank water in 31 villages, Well water in 31 villages, Tubewell in 31 villages and more than one source in 31 villages.

Bank: Banking facility in 7 villages, namely, Tekumatta, Ramakistapur (T), Navabpet, Chityal Jookal, Challagarige, Gopalpur.

Credit Society in 28 villages Agricultural Credit Society in 8 Non-Agricultural Credit Society in 27 villages.

Others: Power supply in 32 villages, Cinema hall in 3 villages, sport club in 0 village, Stadium or Auditorium or Community Hall in 0 village, Post Office in 17 villages.

There are 29 villages having bus facilities.

Villages with most of facilities: Tekumatta Navabpet, Chityal, Jookal, Challagarige, Gopalpur.

Villages without Amenities (Education): None..

Scheduled Castes: Out of the total population of 57434 persons, 11844 persons (20.62%) belong to Scheduled Castes.

The villages having less than 10% SC population are Kalikota, Ramakistapur (V), Ankushapur, Kailapur Muchiniparthi.

The villages having more than 50% SC population are None.

Sex ratio of Scheduled Caste population is 498.

Scheduled Castes Literates and Illiterates by Sex:

	Persons	Males	Females
Literate	4,160	2,576	1,584
Illiterate	7,684	3,374	4,310
Literacy rate	41.3	51.0	31.5
Graduate	53	52	1

Scheduled Castes (Dominant):

Madiga, Mala, Generic Castes etc., Beda Jangam etc. Gosangi

For their cultural identity please see Appendix-I

Villages without Scheduled Castes: There is 1 village without any scheduled caste population.

Scheduled Tribes: Out of the total population of 57434 persons, 2665 persons (4.64%) belong to Scheduled Tribes.

The villages having less than 10% ST population are Venkatraopalle, Kalikota, Raghavapur, Garimillapalle Boina Palle, Emped, Vellampalle, Velchal Kundanpalle, Gummadavelli, Ramakistapur (V) Pangidipalle, Tekumatta, Ramakistapur (T) Ankushapur, Somanpalle, Navabpet, Kailapur Nain Paka, Jadalapet, Thirmalapur, Chityal, Jookal Challagarige, Muchiniparthi, Gopalpur, Doothpalle.

The villages having more than 50% ST population are None.

Sex ratio of Scheduled tribe population is 487.

Scheduled Tribes Literates and Illiterates by Sex:

	Persons	Males	Females
Literate	725	488	237
Illiterate	1,940	880	1,060
Literacy rate	33.1	43.2	22.4
Graduate	12	11	1

Scheduled Tribes (Dominant):

Sugalis etc., Gond etc., Yerukulas, Chenchu etc.

For their cultural identity please see Appendix-II

Villages without Scheduled Tribes: There are 9 villages without any scheduled tribe population.

Literates and Illiterates by Sex (Total Population):

	Persons	Males	Females
Literate	23,495	14,710	8,785
Illiterate	33,939	14,156	19,783
Literacy rate	48	60	36
Graduate	505	460	45

Agriculture: ***Distribution of villages according to land use:***

Out of 32 villages, Total area (in hectare) is 30081, out of that 67.43 percent is cultivable and 45.96 percent of the cultivable area is irrigated.

Sources of Irrigation (Hectares): Government Canal 0, Private Canal 0, Well without Electricity 0, Well with Electricity 7545, Tubewell without Electricity 0, Tubewell with Electricity 0, Tank 1779, River 0, Lake 0, Waterfall 0, Others 0.

Villages with population of 5000 to 9999: None

Villages with population of 10000 and above: None

Distribution of Workers:

	Persons	Males	Females	WPR
Cultivators	10,443	6,351	4,092	32.17
Agricultural Labour	17,479	6,870	10,609	53.84
Household Industry	837	554	283	2.58
Other Workers	3,706	3,081	625	11.42
Main Workers	28,327	15,338	12,989	87.25
Marginal Workers	4,138	1,518	2,620	12.75
Total Workers	32,465	16,856	15,609	

Religion: Major Religious Communities:

	Persons	Males	Females	Sex Ratio
Hindu (97.67%)	56,097	28,205	27,892	989
Muslim (1.67%)	961	476	485	1,019
Christian (0.08%)	45	24	21	875
Sikh (0.01%)	6	4	2	500
Buddhists (0%)	2	1	1	1,000
Jain (0%)	-	-	-	-

Agewise Data:

	Persons	Males	Females	Sex Ratio
All ages	57,434	28,866	28,568	990
0-14	18,554	9,356	9,198	983
15-44	26,173	13,210	12,963	981
45-79	12,002	5,953	6,049	1016
80+	543	267	276	1034

Age not stated	162	80	82	1025

Languages (Dominant):
Telugu, Hindi, Urdu, Tamil, Gondi
Disabled Population:

	Persons	Males	Females	%
Total Disabled	1,173	648	525	
In Seeing	438	240	198	37.34
In Speech	138	79	59	11.76
In Hearing	70	38	32	5.97
In Movement	398	217	181	33.93
Mentally	129	74	55	11

CHITYALA

Chityala C.D. Block lies in the central part of Nalgonda district. The Block is located at a distance of 25 kms. from district headquarters (Nalgonda). There are 16 villages in the block with the total population of 53,102 persons. Area of the C.D. Block is 237.68 sq. kms. It is bounded by Ramannapeta Mandal on north, Narkatpalle Mandal on east, Munugode Mandal on south, Choutupal and Narayanapuram Mandals on west.

Communications:
Roadways : NH- 9: Direction- Hyderabad to Chityala. Nearest Villages- Gundram Palle, Pittam Palle, Pedakapa rthy, Chityala.
Railway Station: Chityala.
Backwards Region Grants Fund: It receives Backward Region Grants.
Annual Rainfall: Average Rainfall 719 mm
Ground Water: Availability of the Ground Water in the Basin is 2189 H.A.M. and the utilization is 2422 H. A.M. It belongs to OE category. Depth to water level varies from 5 to 20 meter below the ground. Most of the wells go down in summer months. The well density in the entire block is 20 wells per sq. km. Total no. of the wells in the block are enumerated as 4838, according to the Ground Water Estimation Committee.
Natural Division : Krishna Piedmont Plain Region
Administration:
Division: Telangana. Parliamentary Constituency: 14 Bhongir. District: Nalgonda. Mandal: Chityala. Assembly Constituency: 95 Nekrakal (SC). Gram Panchayat: 16.
Villages: 16 **Inhabited:** 16 **Uninhabited:** 0

Ranking	District	State	National
Area	22	354	3547
Population	12	415	5128
Sex Ratio	27	707	2410
Child Sex Ratio	49	948	4267
Literacy Rate	7	227	2462
Density	58	928	4399
Work Participation Rate	24	631	3263

Gram Panchayats:
Aipoor, Chinakaparthy, Chityal, Ellikatte
Gundrampally, Nereda, Parepally, Pedakaparthy
Pittampally, Shivanenigudem, Sunkenpally
Thalla Vellemla, Urumadla, Vanipakala, Vattimarthy
Velminedu.

Amenities:
Education: Primary School in 16 villages, Middle school in 15 villages, Matriculation or Secondary School in 8 villages, namely Gundram Palle, Veliminedu, Pedakaparthy, Chinakaparthy, Urmadla, Chityala, Wattimarthy, Nerada.
Higher Secondary or Pre University Courses or Intermediate or Junior College in 1 village of the CD Block,, namely Chityala.
College in 1 village, Adult Literacy Center in 16 villages., College is in village, namely Chityala.
Medical: Hospital in 0 village, Dispensary in 1 village, Health Center in 2 villages, Sub Center in 8 villages, Maternity and Child Welfare Center in 0 village, Community health workers in 0 village.
The Village having Hospital or Dispensary or Health Center is Chityala.
Drinking Water: Tap water in 16 villages, Tank water in 16 villages, Well water in 16 villages, Tubewell in 16 villages and more than one source in 16 villages.
Bank: Banking facility in 3 villages, namely, Gundram Palle, Urmadla, Chityala.
Credit Society in 9 villages Agricultural Credit Society in 5 Non-Agricultural Credit Society in 7 villages.
Others: Power supply in 16 villages, Cinema hall in 1 village, sport club in 0 village, Stadium or Auditorium or Community Hall in 0 village, Post Office in 15 villages.
There are 16 villages having bus facilities.
Villages with most of facilities: Gundram Palle Urmadla, Chityala.
Villages without Amenities (Education): None..
Scheduled Castes: Out of the total population of 53102 persons, 8774 persons (16.52%) belong to Scheduled Castes.
The villages having less than 10% SC population are None..
The villages having more than 50% SC population are None.
Sex ratio of Scheduled Caste population is 494.
Scheduled Castes Literates and Illiterates by Sex:

	Persons	Males	Females
Literate	3,993	2,564	1,429
Illiterate	4,781	1,872	2,909
Literacy rate	53.8	68.6	38.8
Graduate	96	85	11

Scheduled Castes (Dominant):

Madiga, Mala, Generic Castes etc., Chamar etc.
Bindla

For their cultural identity please see Appendix-I

Villages without Scheduled Castes: There are 0 village without any scheduled caste population.

Scheduled Tribes: Out of the total population of 53102 persons, 367 persons (0.69%) belong to Scheduled Tribes. The villages having less than 10% ST population are Sunkene Palle, Gundram Palle, Aipoor, Pere Palle Pittam Palle, Veliminedu, Pedakaparthy Chinakaparthy, Talla Yellemla, Yelikatta, Urmadla Chityala, Shivaneni Gudem, Vanipakala, Wattimarthy Nerada.

The villages having more than 50% ST population are None.

Sex ratio of Scheduled tribe population is 439.

Scheduled Tribes Literates and Illiterates by Sex:

	Persons	Males	Females
Literate	153	116	37
Illiterate	214	90	124
Literacy rate	50.0	69.1	26.8
Graduate	1	1	0

Scheduled Tribes (Dominant):

Yerukulas, Sugalis etc., Generic Tribes etc.

For their cultural identity please see Appendix-II

Villages without Scheduled Tribes: There are 3 villages without any scheduled tribe population.

Literates and Illiterates by Sex (Total Population):

	Persons	Males	Females
Literate	28,318	17,319	10,999
Illiterate	24,784	9,604	15,180
Literacy rate	62	75	49
Graduate	1,409	1,163	246

Agriculture: ***Distribution of villages according to land use:*** Out of 16 villages, Total area (in hectare) is 23770, out of that 70.81 percent is cultivable and 14.53 percent of the cultivable area is irrigated.

Sources of Irrigation (Hectares): Government Canal 0, Private Canal 0, Well without Electricity 0, Well with Electricity 1546.3, Tubewell without Electricity 0, Tubewell with Electricity 900, Tank 0, River 0, Lake 0, Waterfall 0, Others 0.

Villages with population of 5000 to 9999:
Veliminedu.

Villages with population of 10000 and above:
Chityala.

Distribution of Workers:

	Persons	Males	Females	WPR
Cultivators	4,299	2,883	1,416	17.84
Agricultural Labour	7,845	2,218	5,627	32.56
Household Industry	2,526	1,570	956	10.48
Other Workers	9,423	7,684	1,739	39.11
Main Workers	19,744	13,277	6,467	81.95
Marginal Workers	4,349	1,078	3,271	18.05
Total Workers	24,093	14,355	9,738	

Religion: Major Religious Communities:

	Persons	Males	Females	Sex Ratio
Hindu (95.88%)	50,912	25,809	25,103	973
Muslim (3.56%)	1,893	961	932	970
Christian (0.4%)	210	108	102	944
Sikh (0.11%)	57	30	27	900
Buddhists (0%)	-	-	-	-
Jain (0%)	-	-	-	-

Agewise Data:

	Persons	Males	Females	Sex Ratio
All ages	53,102	26,923	26,179	972
0-14	17,469	8,918	8,551	959
15-44	24,532	12,489	12,043	964
45-79	10,612	5,274	5,338	1012
80+	448	219	229	1046
Age not stated	41	23	18	783

Languages (Dominant):

Telugu, Urdu, Gondi, Hindi, Marathi

Disabled Population:

	Persons	Males	Females	%
Total Disabled	1,020	606	414	
In Seeing	396	219	177	38.82
In Speech	88	48	40	8.63
In Hearing	47	20	27	4.61
In Movement	349	239	110	34.22
Mentally	140	80	60	13.73

CHIVVEMLA

Chivvemla C.D. Block lies in the eastern part of Nalgonda district. The Block is located at a distance of 57 kms. from district headquarters (Nalgonda). There are 15 villages in the block with the total population of 44,301 persons. Area of the C.D. Block is 148.22 sq. kms. It is bounded by Atmakur (S) Mandal on north, Mothay Mandal on east, Munagala Mandal on south-east, Penpahad Mandal on south, and Suryapet Mandal on west.

Communications:

Roadways : NH- 9: Direction- Suryapet to Vijaywada. Nearest Villages- Duraj Palle, Undrugonda, Vallabhapur, Gumpula, Thirumalagiri, Gunjaluru. State Highway (S. H.): Direction- Suryapet to Khammam. Nearset Villages- Beebiguda, Chendupatla, Chivvemla.

Backwards Region Grants Fund: It receives Backward Region Grants.

Annual Rainfall: Average Rainfall 843 mm

Ground Water: Availability of the Ground Water in the

Basin is 1771 H.A.M. and the utilization is 1272 H. A.M. It belongs to SC category. Depth to water level varies from 5 to 20 meter below the ground. Most of the wells go down in summer months. The well density in the entire block is 20 wells per sq. km. Total no. of the wells in the block are enumerated as 2967, according to the Ground Water Estimation Committee.

Natural Division : Krishna Piedmont Plain Region

Administration:

Division: Telangana. Parliamentary Constituency: 13 Nalgonda. District: Nalgonda. Mandal: Chivvemla. Assemb ly Constituency: 91 Suryapet. Gram Panchayat: 19.

Villages: 15 **Inhabited:** 15 **Uninhabited:** 0

Ranking	District	State	National
Area	57	831	5065
Population	32	685	5539
Sex Ratio	48	910	3096
Child Sex Ratio	14	419	1550
Literacy Rate	40	698	4542
Density	36	589	3534
Work Participation Rate	6	371	1585

Gram Panchayats:

Ailapuram, Beebi Gudem, Chandu Patla, Chivemla Duraj Palli, G.Thirumalagiri, Gayamvari Gudem Gunjalur, Kudakuda, Lakshminayakthanda Munyanaik Tanda, Pachyanayak Thanda Pandyanaik Tanda, Rollabandathanda, Thimma Puram Tuljaraopet, V.K .Pahad, Vallabhapur, Valyathanda.

Amenities:

Education: Primary School in 15 villages, Middle school in 7 villages, Matriculation or Secondary School in 5 villages, namely Kudakuda, Chendupatla, Chivvemla, Duraj Palle, Thirumalagiri.

Higher Secondary or Pre University Courses or Intermediate or Junior College in 0 village of the CD Block, College in 0 village, Adult Literacy Center in 0 village.

Medical: Hospital in 0 village, Dispensary in 1 village, Health Center in 1 village, Sub Center in 9 villages, Maternity and Child Welfare Center in 0 village, Community health workers in 0 village.

The Village having Hospital or Dispensary or Health Center is Vattikhammam Pahad.

Drinking Water: Tap water in 15 villages, Tank water in 15 villages, Well water in 15 villages, Tubewell in 15 villages and more than one source in 15 villages.

Bank: Banking facility in 2 villages, namely, Vattikhammam Pahad, Chivvemla.

Credit Society in 7 villages Agricultural Credit Society in 4 Non-Agricultural Credit Society in 4 villages.

Others: Power supply in 15 villages, Cinema hall in 0 village, sport club in 0 village, Stadium or Auditorium or Community Hall in 0 village, Post Office in 8 villages.

There are 15 villages having bus facilities.

Villages with most of facilities: Vattikhammam Pahad Chivvemla.

Villages without Amenities (Education): None..

Scheduled Castes: Out of the total population of 44301 persons, 8297 persons (18.73%) belong to Scheduled Castes.

The villages having less than 10% SC population are None..

The villages having more than 50% SC population are None.

Sex ratio of Scheduled Caste population is 487.

Scheduled Castes Literates and Illiterates by Sex:

	Persons	Males	Females
Literate	3,532	2,270	1,262
Illiterate	4,765	1,983	2,782
Literacy rate	50.2	62.6	36.9
Graduate	110	100	10

Scheduled Castes (Dominant):

Madiga, Mala, Beda Jangam etc., Mala Dasari, Jaggali

For their cultural identity please see Appendix-I

Villages without Scheduled Castes: There are 0 village without any scheduled caste population.

Scheduled Tribes: Out of the total population of 44301 persons, 15218 persons (34.35%) belong to Scheduled Tribes.

The villages having less than 10% ST population are Kudakuda, Undrugonda, Gumpula, Thirumalagiri Gunjaluru.

The villages having more than 50% ST population are Gayamvari Guda, Vattikhammam Pahad, Chivvemla Tuljarao Pet.

Sex ratio of Scheduled tribe population is 483.

Scheduled Tribes Literates and Illiterates by Sex:

	Persons	Males	Females
Literate	5,094	3,378	1,716
Illiterate	10,124	4,485	5,639
Literacy rate	40.0	51.2	28.0
Graduate	77	76	1

Scheduled Tribes (Dominant):

Sugalis etc., Yerukulas

For their cultural identity please see Appendix-II

Villages without Scheduled Tribes: There are 2 villages without any scheduled tribe population..

Literates and Illiterates by Sex (Total Population):

	Persons	Males	Females
Literate	18,742	11,881	6,861
Illiterate	25,559	10,749	14,810
Literacy rate	50	62	37
Graduate	559	488	71

Agriculture: ***Distribution of villages according to land use:*** Out of 15 villages, Total area (in hectare) is 14823, out of that 70.14 percent is cultivable and 24.05 percent of the cultivable area is irrigated.

Sources of Irrigation (Hectares): Government Canal 0, Private Canal 0, Well without Electricity 0, Well with Electricity 2072.41, Tubewell without Electricity 78.91, Tubewell with Electricity 0, Tank 349.22, River 0, Lake 0, Waterfall 0, Others 0.

Villages with population of 5000 to 9999: Kudakuda, Vattikhammam Pahad, Chivvemla.

Villages with population of 10000 and above: None

Distribution of Workers:

	Persons	Males	Females	WPR
Cultivators	6,103	3,823	2,280	27
Agricultural Labour	9,834	3,523	6,311	43.5
Household Industry	311	171	140	1.38
Other Workers	6,357	4,698	1,659	28.12
Main Workers	19,272	11,485	7,787	85.26
Marginal Workers	3,333	730	2,603	14.74
Total Workers	22,605	12,215	10,390	

Religion: Major Religious Communities:

	Persons	Males	Females	Sex Ratio
Hindu (95.13%)	42,143	21,521	20,622	958
Muslim (4.39%)	1,947	1,008	939	932
Christian (0.41%)	183	88	95	1,080
Sikh (0%)	-	-	-	-
Buddhists (0%)	-	-	-	-
Jain (0%)	-	-	-	-

Agewise Data:

	Persons	Males	Females	Sex Ratio
All ages	44,301	22,630	21,671	958
0-14	16,400	8,517	7,883	926
15-44	20,052	10,141	9,911	977
45-79	7,485	3,795	3,690	972
80+	295	135	160	1185
Age not stated	69	42	27	643

Languages (Dominant):
Telugu, Hindi, Urdu, Gondi, Tamil

Disabled Population:

	Persons	Males	Females	%
Total Disabled	1,015	590	425	
In Seeing	373	219	154	36.75
In Speech	106	73	33	10.44
In Hearing	48	20	28	4.73
In Movement	376	212	164	37.04
Mentally	112	66	46	11.03

CHODAVARAM

Chodavaram C.D. Block lies in the eastern part of Visha khapatnam district. The Block is located at a distance of 75 kms. from district headquarters (Vishakhapatnam). There are 31 villages in the block with the total population of 83,800 persons. Area of the C.D. Block is 165.20 sq. kms. It is bounded in the north by Mandals Cheedikada, Devarapalle and K. Kotapalle, in the south by Mandals Anakapalle and Sabbavaram, in the east by K. Kotapadu and Sabbavaram Mandals, and in the west by Butchayyapeta Mandal.

Communications :

Roadways : State Highway (S.H.): Direction- Narsipatnam to Sabbavaram. Nearest Villages- Laxmipuram, Adduru, Narasayyapeta, Ankupalem, Chodavaram, Duddupalem, Gajapathinagaram, Amberupuram, Rayapurajupeta, Venkanna palem, Govada.

River: Sarada Nadi- Nearest Villages- Gajapathinagaram, Amberupuram, Rayapurajupeta, Venkannapalem, Govada, Gavaravaram, Lakkavaram, Seemunapalle, Juttada, Bhoga puram, Muddurthi.

Backwards Region Grants Fund: It receives Backward Region Grants.

Annaul Rainfall: Average Rainfall 1040.7 mm

Ground Water: Availability of the Ground Water in the Basin is (Information not avavible) H.A.M .and the utilization is (Information not avavible) H.A.M. It belongs to (Information not avavible) category. Depth to water level varies from 3 to 10 meter below the ground. Most of the wells go down in summer months.

Forest and Reserved **Forest:** Nearest Villages- Adduru, Seemunapalle, Rayapurajupeta.

Administration:

Division: Coastal Andhra. Parliamentary Constituency: 22 Anakapalle. District: Visakhapatnam. Mandal: Chodava ram. Assembly Constituency: 145 Chodavaram. Gram Panchay at: 32.

Villages: 31 **Inhabited:** 31 **Uninhabited:** 0

Ranking	**District**	**State**	**National**
Area	17	743	4786
Population	2	24	3977
Sex Ratio	10	86	603
Child Sex Ratio	37	743	3157
Literacy Rate	6	389	3429
Density	26	907	2187
Work Participation Rate	7	105	3128

Gram Panchayats:
Adduru, Amberupuram, Ankupalem, Bennavolu Bhogapuram, Chakipalle, Chodavaram, Damunapalle Duddupalem, G.Jagannadhapuram, Gajapathinagaram Gandhavaram, Gandhigram, Gavaravaram, Govada Gowripatnam, Jannavaram, Juttada, Kannampalem Khandipalle, Lakkavaram, Laxmipuram, Muddurthi

Mycherlapalem, Narasayyapeta, Narsapuram Rayapurajupeta, Seemunapalle, Siimhadripuram Sreerampatnam, Thimmannapalem, Venkannapalem.

Amenities:

Education: Primary School in 31 villages, Middle school in 15 villages, Matriculation or Secondary School in 8 villages, namely Laxmipuram, Gavaravaram, Lakkavaram, Juttada, Chodavaram, Govada, Pakirsahebpeta, Chakipalle.

Higher Secondary or Pre University Courses or Intermediate or Junior College in 1 village of the CD Block,, namely Chodavaram.

College in 1 village, Adult Literacy Center in 3 villages., College is in village, namely Chodavaram.

Medical: Hospital in 1 village, Dispensary in 1 village, Health Center in 10 villages, Sub Center in 13 villages, Maternity and Child Welfare Center in 1 village, Community health workers in 0 village.

The Villages having Hospital or Dispensary or Health Center are Lakkavaram, Chodavaram.

Drinking Water: Tap water in 31 villages, Tank water in 31 villages, Well water in 31 villages, Tubewell in 31 villages and more than one source in 31 villages.

Bank: Banking facility in 3 villages, namely, Gavaravaram, Chodavaram, Govada.

Credit Society in 8 villages Agricultural Credit Society in 8 Non-Agricultural Credit Society in 0 village.

Others: Power supply in 31 villages, Cinema hall in 3 villages, sport club in 0 village, Stadium or Auditorium or Community Hall in 1 village, Post Office in 18 villages.

There are 24 villages having bus facilities.

Villages with most of facilities: Gavaravaram Chodavaram, Govada.

Villages without Amenities (Education): None..

Scheduled Castes: Out of the total population of 83801 persons, 6861 persons (8.19%) belong to Scheduled Castes.

The villages having less than 10% SC population are Laxmipuram, Damunapalle, Mycherlapalem, Gavaravaram Lakkavaram, Adduru, Juttada, Narasayyapeta Sreerampatnam, Chodavaram, Gajapathinagaram Rayapurajupeta, Duddupalem, Venkannapalem, Govada Bennavolu, Jannavaram, Thimmannapalem, Chakipalle Bhogapuram, Muddurthi, M.Kothapalle, Gandhavaram.

The villages having more than 50% SC population are None.

Sex ratio of Scheduled Caste population is 505.

Scheduled Castes Literates and Illiterates by Sex:

	Persons	Males	Females
Literate	3,505	2,064	1,441
Illiterate	3,356	1,329	2,027
Literacy rate	58.3	69.8	47.2
Graduate	170	138	32

Scheduled Castes (Dominant):

Mala, Relli, Madiga, Chachati, Adi Andhra

For their cultural identity please see Appendix-I

Villages without Scheduled Castes: There are 0 village without any scheduled caste population.

Scheduled Tribes: Out of the total population of 83801 persons, 392 persons (0.47%) belong to Scheduled Tribes.

The villages having less than 10% ST population are Laxmipuram, Damunapalle, Mycherlapalem, Khandipalle Gavaravaram, Lakkavaram, Adduru, Seemunapalle Juttada, Annavaram, Venkayyagaripeta, Narasayyapeta Gowripatnam, Sreerampatnam, Ankupalem, Chodavaram Gajapathinagaram, Amberupuram, Rayapurajupeta Duddupalem, Venkannapalem, Govada, Pakirsahebpeta Bennavolu, Jannavaram, Thimmannapalem, Chakipalle Bhogapuram, Muddurthi, M.Kothapalle, Gandhavaram.

The villages having more than 50% ST population are None.

Sex ratio of Scheduled tribe population is 464.

Scheduled Tribes Literates and Illiterates by Sex:

	Persons	Males	Females
Literate	214	137	77
Illiterate	178	73	105
Literacy rate	61.9	74.9	47.2
Graduate	10	10	0

Scheduled Tribes (Dominant):

Yerukulas, Bagata, Valmiki, Konda Dhoras Savaras etc.

For their cultural identity please see Appendix-II

Villages without Scheduled Tribes: There are 19 villages without any scheduled tribe population.

Literates and Illiterates by Sex (Total Population):

	Persons	Males	Females
Literate	41,361	24,935	16,426
Illiterate	42,440	16,498	25,942
Literacy rate	56	69	44
Graduate	2,548	1,918	630

Agriculture: ***Distribution of villages according to land use:*** Out of 31 villages, Total area (in hectare) is 16517, out of that 54.99 percent is cultivable and 56.73 percent of the cultivable area is irrigated.

Sources of Irrigation (Hectares): Government Canal 3483.81, Private Canal 0, Well without Electricity 37.41, Well with Electricity 70.48, Tubewell without Electricity 0, Tubewell with Electricity 216.39, Tank 1016.99, River 96.02, Lake 0, Waterfall 0, Others 231.52.

Villages with population of 5000 to 9999:

Ankupalem.

Villages with population of 10000 and above:

Chodavaram.

Distribution of Workers:

	Persons	Males	Females	WPR
Cultivators	13,491	8,048	5,443	34.5
Agricultural Labour	12,514	6,247	6,267	32
Household Industry	1,056	639	417	2.7
Other Workers	12,041	9,147	2,894	30.79
Main Workers	32,383	20,982	11,401	82.82
Marginal Workers	6,719	3,099	3,620	17.18
Total Workers	39,102	24,081	15,021	

Religion: Major Religious Communities:

	Persons	Males	Females	Sex Ratio
Hindu (98.79%)	82,790	40,942	41,848	1,022
Muslim (0.62%)	522	247	275	1,113
Christian (0.53%)	442	218	224	1,028
Sikh (0.01%)	12	8	4	500
Buddhists (0%)	1	1	-	-
Jain (0%)	-	-	-	-

Agewise Data:

	Persons	Males	Females	Sex Ratio
All ages	83,801	41,433	42,368	1023
0-14	25,105	12,721	12,384	974
15-44	40,661	20,263	20,398	1007
45-79	17,600	8,274	9,326	1127
80+	345	127	218	1717
Age not stated	90	48	42	875

Languages (Dominant):

Telugu, Urdu, Oriya, Gondi, Tamil

Disabled Population:

	Persons	Males	Females	%
Total Disabled	1,648	940	708	
In Seeing	854	478	376	51.82
In Speech	182	100	82	11.04
In Hearing	73	35	38	4.43
In Movement	395	246	149	23.97
Mentally	144	81	63	8.74

CHOPPADANDI

Choppadandi C.D. Block lies in the north-east part of Karimnagar district. The Block is located at a dista nce of 18 kms. from district headquarters (Karimnagar). There are 12 villages in the block with the total population of 48,659 persons. Area of the C.D. Block is 140.92 sq. kms. It is bounded by Pegadapalle Mandal on north, Dharmaram Mandal on north-east, Julapalle Mandal on east, Karimnagar Mandal on south, and Ramadugu Mandal on west.

Communications :

Roadways : Metalled Roads: Nearest Villages- Arnakonda, Choppadandi, Rukmapur, Kolimikunta.

Backwards Region Grants Fund: It receives Backward Region Grants.

Annual Rainfall: Average Rainfall 911 mm

Ground Water : Availability of the Ground Water in the Basin is 2579 H.A.M. and the utilization is 1698 H.A.M. It belongs to Safe category. Depth to water level varies from more than 5 to 10 meter below the ground. Most of the wells go down in summer months. The well density in the entire block is 27 wells per sq. km. Total no. of the wells in the block are enumera ted as 3824, according to the Ground Water Estimation Committee.

Natural Division : Godavari Depression Region

Administration:

Division: Telangana. Parliamentary Constituency: 3 Karimnagar. District: Karimnagar. Mandal: Choppandandi. Assembly Constituency: 27 Choppadandi (SC). Gram Panch ayat: 15.

Places of Tourist Interest:

Choppandandi : It is the largest populated village near Gangdhara. The place has some historical interest also. There is an inscription pertaining to the period of the Kakatiya ruler Prola, which mentions that a certain chief of the army, constructed the Sambhuswamy temple.

Villages: 12 **Inhabited:** 12 **Uninhabited:** 0

Ranking	District	State	National
Area	51	861	5177
Population	26	559	5353
Sex Ratio	55	770	2601
Child Sex Ratio	27	525	2003
Literacy Rate	18	565	4093
Density	43	662	3139
Work Participation Rate	9	273	1820

Gram Panchayats:

Arnakonda, Bhupalapatnam, Chakunta, Chityalapally Choppadandi, Desaipet, Gumlapur, Katnepalle Kolimikunta, Konerupally, Kurmapalli, Ragampeta Revelli, Rukmapur, Vedurugatta.

Amenities:

Education: Primary School in 12 villages, Middle school in 8 villages, Matriculation or Secondary School in 7 villages, namely Ragampeta, Arnakonda, Choppadandi, Gumlapur, Katnepalle, Rukmapur, Vedurughattu.

Higher Secondary or Pre University Courses or Intermediate or Junior College in 1 village of the CD Block,, namely Choppadandi.

College in 0 village, Adult Literacy Center in 10 villages.

Medical: Hospital in 1 village, Dispensary in 1 village, Health Center in 1 village, Sub Center in 7 villages, Maternity and Child Welfare Center in 0 village, Community health workers in 0 village.

The Village having Hospital or Dispensary or Health Center is Choppadandi.

Drinking Water: Tap water in 12 villages, Tank water in 12 villages, Well water in 12 villages, Tubewell in 12 villages and more than one source in 12 villages.

Bank: Banking facility in 2 villages, namely, Arnakonda, Choppadandi.

Credit Society in 11 villages Agricultural Credit Society in 2 Non-Agricultural Credit Society in 11 villages.

Others: Power supply in 12 villages, Cinema hall in 1 village, sport club in 0 village, Stadium or Auditorium or Community Hall in 0 village, Post Office in 11 villages.

There are 11 villages having bus facilities.

Villages with most of facilities: Arnakonda Choppadandi.

Villages without Amenities (Education): None..

Scheduled Castes: Out of the total population of 48659 persons, 12049 persons (24.76%) belong to Scheduled Castes.

The villages having less than 10% SC population are None..

The villages having more than 50% SC population are None.

Sex ratio of Scheduled Caste population is 479.

Scheduled Castes Literates and Illiterates by Sex:

	Persons	Males	Females
Literate	4,945	3,233	1,712
Illiterate	7,104	3,039	4,065
Literacy rate	47.5	59.5	34.4
Graduate	102	90	12

Scheduled Castes (Dominant):

Madiga, Mala, Mala Sale etc., Paky etc.

Generic Castes etc.

For their cultural identity please see Appendix-I

Villages without Scheduled Castes: There are 0 village without any scheduled caste population.

Scheduled Tribes: Out of the total population of 48659 persons, 665 persons (1.37%) belong to Scheduled Tribes.

The villages having less than 10% ST population are Ragampeta, Chityalpalle, Arnakonda, Bhupalapatnam Choppadandi, Gumlapur, Katnepalle, Konerupalle Rukmapur, Kolimikunta, Chakunta, Vedurughattu.

The villages having more than 50% ST population are None.

Sex ratio of Scheduled tribe population is 405.

Scheduled Tribes Literates and Illiterates by Sex:

	Persons	Males	Females
Literate	313	263	50
Illiterate	352	133	219
Literacy rate	55.8	74.3	24.2
Graduate	2	2	0

Scheduled Tribes (Dominant):

Yerukulas, Chenchu etc., Generic Tribes etc.

Mukha Dhora etc., Thoti

For their cultural identity please see Appendix-II

Villages without Scheduled Tribes: There are 3 villages without any scheduled tribe population.

Literates and Illiterates by Sex (Total Population):

	Persons	Males	Females
Literate	22,260	14,073	8,187
Illiterate	26,399	10,648	15,751
Literacy rate	53	66	39
Graduate	785	685	100

Agriculture: ***Distribution of villages according to land use:***

Out of 12 villages, Total area (in hectare) is 14092, out of that 78.16 percent is cultivable and 53.46 percent of the cultivable area is irrigated.

Sources of Irrigation (Hectares): Government Canal 1738, Private Canal 0, Well without Electricity 0, Well with Electricity 3558, Tubewell without Electricity 0, Tubewell with Electricity 18, Tank 575, River 0, Lake 0, Waterfall 0, Others 0.

Villages with population of 5000 to 9999:

Ragampeta, Arnakonda.

Villages with population of 10000 and above:

Choppadandi.

Distribution of Workers:

	Persons	Males	Females	WPR
Cultivators	5,995	3,704	2,291	23.99
Agricultural Labour	12,011	4,782	7,229	48.06
Household Industry	1,902	762	1,140	7.61
Other Workers	5,084	4,172	912	20.34
Main Workers	20,906	12,191	8,715	83.65
Marginal Workers	4,086	1,229	2,857	16.35
Total Workers	24,992	13,420	11,572	

Religion: Major Religious Communities:

	Persons	Males	Females	Sex Ratio
Hindu (97.4%)	47,395	24,091	23,304	967
Muslim (2.26%)	1,098	543	555	1,022
Christian (0.3%)	147	80	67	838
Sikh (0.03%)	13	6	7	1,167
Buddhists (0%)	-	-	-	-
Jain (0%)	-	-	-	-

Agewise Data:

	Persons	Males	Females	Sex Ratio
All ages	48,659	24,721	23,938	968
0-14	15,264	7,956	7,308	919
15-44	22,765	11,437	11,328	990
45-79	10,118	5,081	5,037	991
80+	480	231	249	1078
Age not stated	32	16	16	1000

Languages (Dominant):
Telugu, Urdu, Hindi, Tamil, Marathi

Disabled Population:

	Persons	Males	Females	%
Total Disabled	749	443	306	
In Seeing	314	192	122	41.92
In Speech	83	48	35	11.08
In Hearing	47	20	27	6.28
In Movement	205	127	78	27.37
Mentally	100	56	44	13.35

CHOUTUPPAL

Choutuppal C.D. Block lies in the central west part of Nalgonda district. It is a part of Choutuppal Mandal The Block is located at a distance of 50 kms. from district headquarters (Nalgonda). There are 16 villages in the block with the total population of 51,968 persons. Area of the C.D. Block is 250.61 sq. kms. It is bound ed by Pochampalle and Valigonda Mandal on north, Narayan apur Mandal on south, Rangareddy district on west, Chity ala and Ramannapeta Mandals on east.

Communications:

Roadways : NH- 9: Direction- Hyderabad to Vijayawada. Nearest Villages- Tupranpet, Malkapur, Devalamma Nagar am, Khairathpur, Yellagiri, Lakkaram, Tallasingaram, Lingoji Guda, Panthangi.

Backwards Region Grants Fund: It receives Backward Region Grants.

Annual Rainfall: Average Rainfall 693 mm

Ground Water: Availability of the Ground Water in the Basin is 2492 H.A.M. and the utilization is 2239 H. A.M. It belongs to SC category. Depth to water level varies from 10 to 20 meter below the ground. Most of the wells go down in summer months. The well density in the entire block is 13 wells per sq. km. Total no. of the wells in the block are enumerated as 3347, according to the Ground Water Estimation Committee.

Natural Division : Krishna Piedmont Plain Region

Administration:

Division: Telangana. Parliamentary Constituency: 14 Bhongir. District: Nalgonda. Mandal: Choutuppal. Assemb ly Constituency: 93 Munugode. Gram Panchayat: 25.

Villages: 16 **Inhabited:** 16 **Uninhabited:** 0

Ranking	District	State	National
Area	19	311	3378
Population	18	455	5189
Sex Ratio	58	1071	4378
Child Sex Ratio	47	940	4233
Literacy Rate	11	267	2792
Density	44	688	4631
Work Participation Rate	29	692	1929

Gram Panchayats:

Allapur, Ankireddigudem, Aregudem, Chinnakondur Choutuppal, D.Nagaram, Dharmojigudem, Gundlabavi Jaikesaram, Koyalagudem, Kuntlagudem, Lakkaram Lingojigudem, Malkapur, Mandollagudem, Masidgudem Nelapatla, Panthagi, Peddakondur, Peepalpahad S.Lingotam, Thalla Singaram, Thangedpally Toopranpet, Yellagiri.

Amenities:

Education: Primary School in 16 villages, Middle school in 10 villages, Matriculation or Secondary School in 9 villages, namely Malkapur, Devalamma Nagaram, Chinna Kondur, Nelapatla, Jai Kesaram, Swamulavari Lingotam, Tangad Palle, Lingoji Guda, Panthangi.

Higher Secondary or Pre University Courses or Intermediate or Junior College in 0 village of the CD Block, College in 0 village, Adult Literacy Center in 13 villages.

Medical: Hospital in 0 village, Dispensary in 1 village, Health Center in 1 village, Sub Center in 7 villages, Maternity and Child Welfare Center in 0 village, Community health workers in 0 village.

The Villages having Hospital or Dispensary or Health Center are Tangad Palle, Panthangi.

Drinking Water: Tap water in 16 villages, Tank water in 16 villages, Well water in 16 villages, Tubewell in 16 villages and more than one source in 16 villages.

Bank: Banking facility in 1 villages, namely, Devalamma Nagaram.

Credit Society in 2 villages Agricultural Credit Society in 1 Non-Agricultural Credit Society in 0 village.

Others: Power supply in 16 villages, Cinema hall in 0 village, sport club in 0 village, Stadium or Auditorium or Community Hall in 0 village, Post Office in 10 villages.

There are 16 villages having bus facilities.

Village with most of facilities: Devalamma Nagaram.

Villages without Amenities (Education): None..

Scheduled Castes: Out of the total population of 51824 persons, 8039 persons (15.51%) belong to Scheduled Castes.

The villages having less than 10% SC population are None..

The villages having more than 50% SC population are None.

Sex ratio of Scheduled Caste population is 498.

Scheduled Castes Literates and Illiterates by Sex:

	Persons	Males	Females
Literate	3,495	2,214	1,281
Illiterate	4,544	1,823	2,721
Literacy rate	51.2	64.6	37.7
Graduate	67	63	4

Scheduled Castes (Dominant):

Madiga, Mala, Generic Castes etc., Beda Jangam etc.

Bindla

For their cultural identity please see Appendix-I

Villages without Scheduled Castes: There are 0 village without any scheduled caste population.

Scheduled Tribes: Out of the total population of 51824 persons, 833 persons (1.61%) belong to Scheduled Tribes. The villages having less than 10% ST population are Tupranpet, Malkapur, Allapur, Devalamma Nagaram Khairathpur, Yellagiri, Lakkaram, Chinna Kondur Nelapatla, Jai Kesaram, Swamulavari Lingotam Tallasingaram, Tangad Palle, Lingoji Guda, Panthangi. The villages having more than 50% ST population are None.

Sex ratio of Scheduled tribe population is 495.

Scheduled Tribes Literates and Illiterates by Sex:

	Persons	Males	Females
Literate	198	137	61
Illiterate	635	284	351
Literacy rate	28.5	39.0	17.8
Graduate	0	0	0

Scheduled Tribes (Dominant):

Sugalis etc., Yerukulas, Konda Dhoras, Koya etc.

For their cultural identity please see Appendix-II

Villages without Scheduled Tribes: There are 3 villages without any scheduled tribe population.

Literates and Illiterates by Sex (Total Population):

	Persons	Males	Females
Literate	26,878	17,050	9,828
Illiterate	24,946	9,772	15,174
Literacy rate	60	73	45
Graduate	964	878	86

Agriculture: ***Distribution of villages according to land use:*** Out of 16 villages, Total area (in hectare) is 25062, out of that 70.39 percent is cultivable and 5.33 percent of the cultivable area is irrigated.

Sources of Irrigation (Hectares): Government Canal 0, Private Canal 0, Well without Electricity 0, Well with Electricity 699, Tubewell without Electricity 0, Tubewell with Electricity 242, Tank 0, River 0, Lake 0, Waterfall 0, Others 0.

Villages with population of 5000 to 9999:
Devalamma Nagaram, Chinna Kondur, Tangad Palle Panthangi.

Villages with population of 10000 and above: None

Distribution of Workers:

	Persons	Males	Females	WPR
Cultivators	5,206	3,164	2,042	19.79
Agricultural Labour	6,850	2,124	4,726	26.04
Household Industry	2,780	1,519	1,261	10.57
Other Workers	11,470	8,866	2,604	43.6
Main Workers	21,623	14,618	7,005	82.2
Marginal Workers	4,683	1,055	3,628	17.8
Total Workers	26,306	15,673	10,633	

Religion: Major Religious Communities:

	Persons	Males	Females	Sex Ratio
Hindu (97.21%)	50,376	26,058	24,318	933
Muslim (2.47%)	1,281	663	618	932
Christian (0.24%)	125	85	40	471
Sikh (0%)	-	-	-	-
Buddhists (0%)	-	-	-	-
Jain (0%)	-	-	-	-

Agewise Data:

	Persons	Males	Females	Sex Ratio
All ages	51,824	26,822	25,002	932
0-14	16,580	8,425	8,155	968
15-44	24,419	13,073	11,346	868
45-79	10,310	5,072	5,238	1033
80+	458	223	235	1054
Age not stated	57	29	28	966

Languages (Dominant):

Telugu, Urdu, Hindi, Gondi, Tamil

Disabled Population:

	Persons	Males	Females	%
Total Disabled	1,012	536	476	
In Seeing	469	227	242	46.34
In Speech	92	51	41	9.09
In Hearing	70	21	49	6.92
In Movement	280	180	100	27.67
Mentally	101	57	44	9.98

CHOWDEPALLE

Chowdepalle C.D. Block lies in the western part of Chittoor district. The Block is located at a distance of 52 kms. from district headquarters (Chittoor). There are 15 villages in the block with the total population of 40,410 persons. Area of the C.D. Block is 194.30 sq. kms. It is bounded in the north by Mandals Nimmanap alle and Somala, in the south by Mandals Punganur, Pedda panjani and Somala, in the east by Mandal Somala, and in the west by Mandals Nimmanapalle and Punganur.

Communications:

Roadways : State Highway (S.H.): Direction- Punganur to Sodam. Nearest Villages- Kondamarri, Gaddamvaripalle, Peddayallakuntla, Chowdepalle, Pudipatla, 29 -A. Chinta -Makulapalle, Laddigam.

It receives the Backward Region Grants, and is identifi ed as a drought-prone area as well.

Integrated Child Development Scheme (ICDS) Project: Chowdepalli, Total Anganwadi Centres: 113

Annual Rainfall: Average Rainfall 869 mm

Ground Water: Availability of the Ground Water in the

Basin is 2106 H.A.M.and the utilization is 1940 H.A. M. It belongs to Critical category. Depth to water level varies more than 10 meter below the ground. Most of the wells go down in summer months, according to the Ground Water Estimation Committee.

Natural Division : Rayalaseema Region

Administration:

Division: Rayala Seema. Parliamentary Constituency: 41 Rajampet. District: Chittoor. Mandal: Chowdepalle. Assembly Constituency: 284 Punganur. Gram Panchayat: 19

Villages: 15 **Inhabited:** 15 **Uninhabited:** 0

Ranking	District	State	National
Area	21	594	4281
Population	41	813	5719
Sex Ratio	19	331	1401
Child Sex Ratio	16	288	980
Literacy Rate	36	256	2698
Density	34	653	4619
Work Participation Rate	46	689	1788

Gram Panchayats:

29 A.Chintamakulapalle, A. Kothakota, Aminigunta Charala, Chowdepalle, Diguvapalle, Durgasamudram Gaddamvaripalle, Kagithi, Katiperi Kondaiahgari Palle, Kondamarri, Laddigam Pandillapalle, Parikidona, Peddayellakuntla Pudipatla, Settipeta, Vengalavaripalle.

Amenities:

Education: Primary School in 15 villages, Middle school in 10 villages, Matriculation or Secondary School in 6 villages, namely Kogathi, Chowdepalle, Settipeta, Pudipatla, A.Kothakota, Charala.

Higher Secondary or Pre University Courses or Intermediate or Junior College in 1 village of the CD Block,, namely Chowdepalle.

College in 0 village, Adult Literacy Center in 15 villages.

Medical: Hospital in 0 village, Dispensary in 2 villages, Health Center in 1 village, Sub Center in 8 villages, Maternity and Child Welfare Center in 1 village, Community health workers in 0 village.

The Villages having Hospital or Dispensary or Health Center are Kondamarri, Chowdepalle.

Drinking Water: Tap water in 15 villages, Tank water in 15 villages, Well water in 15 villages, Tubewell in 15 villages and more than one source in 15 villages.

Bank: Banking facility in 1 villages, namely, Chowdepalle.

Credit Society in 6 villages Agricultural Credit Society in 4 Non-Agricultural Credit Society in 5 villages.

Others: Power supply in 15 villages, Cinema hall in 1 village, sport club in 0 village, Stadium or Auditorium or Community Hall in 0 village, Post Office in 13 villages.

There are 15 villages having bus facilities.

Village with most of facilities: Chowdepalle.

Villages without Amenities (Education): None..

Scheduled Castes: Out of the total population of 40410 persons, 7535 persons (18.65%) belong to Scheduled Castes.

The villages having less than 10% SC population are None..

The villages having more than 50% SC population are None.

Sex ratio of Scheduled Caste population is 499.

Scheduled Castes Literates and Illiterates by Sex:

	Persons	Males	Females
Literate	3,407	2,106	1,301
Illiterate	4,128	1,667	2,461
Literacy rate	52.6	64.4	40.5
Graduate	58	49	9

Scheduled Castes (Dominant):

Mala, Madiga, Dom etc., Adi Andhra Generic Castes etc.

For their cultural identity please see Appendix-I

Villages without Scheduled Castes: There are 0 village without any scheduled caste population.

Scheduled Tribes. Out of the total population of 40410 persons, 470 persons (1.16%) belong to Scheduled Tribes.

The villages having less than 10% ST population are Diguvapalle, Kogathi, Kondamarri, Gaddamvaripalle Peddayallakuntla, Chowdepalle, Pandillapalle Settipeta, Pudipatla, 29 -A. Chinta -Makulapalle Katiperi, Laddigam, A.Kothakota, Durgasamudram Charala.

The villages having more than 50% ST population are None.

Sex ratio of Scheduled tribe population is 491.

Scheduled Tribes Literates and Illiterates by Sex:

	Persons	Males	Females
Literate	119	68	51
Illiterate	351	171	180
Literacy rate	32.2	36.8	27.6
Graduate	3	2	1

Scheduled Tribes (Dominant):

Yenadis, Yerukulas, Sugalis etc., Konda Dhoras

For their cultural identity please see Appendix-II

Villages without Scheduled Tribes: There are 6 villages without any scheduled tribe population.

Literates and Illiterates by Sex (Total Population):

	Persons	Males	Females
Literate	20,882	12,746	8,136
Illiterate	19,528	7,520	12,008

Literacy rate	60	74	47
Graduate	650	502	148

Agriculture: ***Distribution of villages according to land use:*** Out of 15 villages, Total area (in hectare) is 19429, out of that 46.35 percent is cultivable and 27.66 percent of the cultivable area is irrigated.

Sources of Irrigation (Hectares): Government Canal 0, Private Canal 0, Well without Electricity 12, Well with Electricity 646, Tubewell without Electricity 0, Tubewell with Electricity 989, Tank 844, River 0, Lake 0, Waterfall 0, Others 0.

Villages with population of 5000 to 9999: Chowdepalle.

Villages with population of 10000 and above: None

Distribution of Workers:

	Persons	Males	Females	WPR
Cultivators	9,231	5,633	3,598	45.08
Agricultural Labour	8,132	3,879	4,253	39.71
Household Industry	282	175	107	1.38
Other Workers	2,833	2,184	649	13.83
Main Workers	17,957	11,023	6,934	87.69
Marginal Workers	2,521	848	1,673	12.31
Total Workers	20,478	11,871	8,607	

Religion: Major Religious Communities:

	Persons	Males	Females	Sex Ratio
Hindu (89.57%)	36,196	18,175	18,021	992
Muslim (9.99%)	4,036	2,007	2,029	1,011
Christian (0.33%)	133	62	71	1,145
Sikh (0%)	-	-	-	-
Buddhists (0%)	1	1	-	-
Jain (0%)	-	-	-	-

Agewise Data:

	Persons	Males	Females	Sex Ratio
All ages	40,410	20,266	20,144	994
0-14	13,265	6,771	6,494	959
15-44	18,228	8,958	9,270	1035
45-79	8,450	4,297	4,153	966
80+	386	194	192	990
Age not stated	81	46	35	761

Languages (Dominant):
Telugu, Urdu, Others, Kannada, Tamil

Disabled Population:

	Persons	Males	Females	%
Total Disabled	669	390	279	
In Seeing	265	135	130	39.61
In Speech	66	40	26	9.87
In Hearing	35	16	19	5.23
In Movement	204	140	64	30.49
Mentally	99	59	40	14.8

CUDDAPAH

Cuddapah C.D. Block lies in the central part of Cuddapah district. It is a part of Cuddapah Mandal. The Block is located at a distance of (00) kms. from district headquarters (Cuddapah). There are 03 villages in the block with the total population of 7,376 persons. Area of the C.D. Block is 60.21 sq. kms. It is bounded in the north by Mandal Chennur, in the south and west by Mandal Chintakommadinne, and in the east by Mandals Chennur and Sidhout.

Communications:

Roadways : NH- 5: Direction- Chittoor to Kurnool. Nearest Villages- Pathacuddapah, Nagarajupet. State Highway (S.H.): Direction- Chittoor to Kurnool. and Renigunta. Nearest Villages- Nagarajupet, Puttampalli.

Railway Station: Pathacuddapah, Nagarajupet.

River: Penneru Nadi- Nearest Village- Pathacuddapah. Papaghni Nadi- Nearest Village- Pathacuddapah.

It receives Backward Region Grants, and is identified as a drough-prone area as well.

Integrated Child Development Scheme (ICDS) Project: Kadapa, Total Anganwadi Centres: 311

Hills: Nearest Village- Pathacuddapah.

Annual Rainfall: Average Rainfall 725 mm

Ground Water: Availability of the Ground Water in the Basin is 2504 H.A.M.and the utilization is 463 H.A. M.It belongs to Safe category. Depth to water level varies from 10 to 20 meter below the ground. Most of the wells go down in summer months.

Natural Division : Rayalaseema Region

Administration:

Division: Rayala Seema. Parliamentary Constituency: 39 Kadapa. District: Cuddapah.

Mandal: Cuddapah. Assembly Constituency: 245 Kadapa.

Gram Panchayat:

Fairs and Festivals:

Hussain Vali Urs : Hussain Vali Urs is celebrated for two days from the full moon day in Chaitram (March-April) in his memory at Chintakunta near Cuddapah. The descendants of Poli Subbi Reddy bring gandham on full moon day and Sri Bommi Reddy Gangi Reddy's family members bring the flag on the second day. Devotees fulfil their vows by offering umbrellas made of silver, hoisting flags and observing tonsure ceremonies. This urs has been celebrated for the last 100 years and is widely known in the area. The descendants of Poli Subbi Reddy and Bommi Reddy Gangi Reddy are the chief patrons of the festival. Some land had been endowed to the darga. A large number of devotees of the locality and from distant places belonging to all castes and communities congregate here. The descendants of Hussainaiah are the mujavars enjoying the lands and the house dedicated by Subbi Reddy.

Villages: 3 **Inhabited:** 3 **Uninhabited:** 0

Ranking	District	State	National
Area	51	1095	6107
Population	51	1095	6307
Sex Ratio	13	476	1783
Child Sex Ratio	1	6	34
Literacy Rate	4	118	1659
Density	51	1095	3759
Work Participation Rate	8	440	5243

Gram Panchayats:

Amenities:

Education: Primary School in 2 villages, Middle school in 1 village, Matriculation or Secondary School in 1 village, namely Pathacuddapah.

Higher Secondary or Pre University Courses or Intermediate or Junior College in 0 village of the CD Block, College in 0 village, Adult Literacy Center in 2 villages.

Medical: Hospital in 0 village, Dispensary in 0 village, Health Center in 0 village, Sub Center in 2 villages, Maternity and Child Welfare Center in 1 village, Community health workers in 0 village.

Drinking Water: Tap water in 3 villages, Tank water in 3 villages, Well water in 3 villages, Tubewell in 3 villages and more than one source in 3 villages.

Bank: None.

Credit Society in 1 village Agricultural Credit Society in 0 Non-Agricultural Credit Society in 0 village.

Others: Power supply in 3 villages, Cinema hall in 0 village, sport club in 0 village, Stadium or Auditorium or Community Hall in 0 village, Post Office in 1 village.

There are 2 villages having bus facilities.

Village with most of facilities: None.

Villages without Amenities (Education): None..

Scheduled Castes: Out of the total population of 7379 persons, 1911 persons (25.9%) belong to Scheduled Castes.

The villages having less than 10% SC population are None..

The villages having more than 50% SC population are None.

Sex ratio of Scheduled Caste population is 503.

Scheduled Castes Literates and Illiterates by Sex:

	Persons	Males	Females
Literate	1,119	670	449
Illiterate	792	279	513
Literacy rate	69.6	83.3	55.9
Graduate	20	19	1

Scheduled Castes (Dominant):

Mala, Madiga, Adi Andhra

For their cultural identity please see Appendix-I

Villages without Scheduled Castes: There are 0 village without any scheduled caste population.

Scheduled Tribes: Out of the total population of 7379 persons, 192 persons (2.6%) belong to Scheduled Tribes.

The villages having less than 10% ST population are None..

The villages having more than 50% ST population are None.

Sex ratio of Scheduled tribe population is 510.

Scheduled Tribes Literates and Illiterates by Sex:

	Persons	Males	Females
Literate	38	27	11
Illiterate	154	67	87
Literacy rate	26.0	35.5	15.7
Graduate	0	0	0

Scheduled Tribes (Dominant):

Yenadis, Sugalis etc., Yerukulas

For their cultural identity please see Appendix-II

Villages without Scheduled Tribes: There is 1 village without any scheduled tribe population.

Literates and Illiterates by Sex (Total Population):

	Persons	Males	Females
Literate	4,254	2,552	1,702
Illiterate	3,125	1,163	1,962
Literacy rate	67	79	54
Graduate	213	170	43

Agriculture: ***Distribution of villages according to land use:***
Out of 3 villages, Total area (in hectare) is 2641, out of that 31.64 percent is cultivable and 81.55 percent of the cultivable area is irrigated.

Sources of Irrigation (Hectares): Government Canal 418.72, Private Canal 0, Well without Electricity 0, Well with Electricity 9.72, Tubewell without Electricity 0, Tubewell with Electricity 218.88, Tank 0, River 34.04, Lake 0, Waterfall 0, Others 0.

Villages with population of 5000 to 9999: None

Villages with population of 10000 and above: None

Distribution of Workers:

	Persons	Males	Females	WPR
Cultivators	475	422	53	18.42
Agricultural Labour	898	592	306	34.82
Household Industry	33	19	14	1.28
Other Workers	1,173	997	176	45.48
Main Workers	2,178	1,805	373	84.45
Marginal Workers	401	225	176	15.55
Total Workers	2,579	2,030	549	

Religion: Major Religious Communities:

	Persons	Males	Females	Sex Ratio
Hindu (89.89%)	6,633	3,344	3,289	984
Muslim (8%)	590	292	298	1,021
Christian (1.9%)	140	72	68	944
Sikh (0%)	-	-	-	-
Buddhists (0%)	-	-	-	-
Jain (0%)	-	-	-	-

Agewise Data:

	Persons	Males	Females	Sex Ratio
All ages	7,379	3,715	3,664	986
0-14	2,317	1,162	1,155	994
15-44	3,582	1,828	1,754	960
45-79	1,424	706	718	1017
80+	51	18	33	1833
Age not stated	5	1	4	4000

Languages (Dominant):
Telugu, Urdu, Hindi, Malayalam, Tamil

Disabled Population:

	Persons	Males	Females	%
Total Disabled	79	43	36	
In Seeing	13	8	5	16.46
In Speech	16	5	11	20.25
In Hearing	3	2	1	3.8
In Movement	38	22	16	48.1
Mentally	9	6	3	11.39

CUMBUM

Cumbum C.D. Block lies in the western part of Prakasam district. The Block is located at a distance of 115 kms. from district headquarters (Ongole). There are 16 villages in the block with the total population of 45,131 persons. Area of the C.D. Block is 132.65 sq. kms. It is bounded in the north by Mandals Ardhavee du and Markapur, in the south by Mandals Racherla and Bestavaripeta, in the east by Mandals Bestavaripeta and Tarlupadu, and in the west by Mandals Ardhaveedu and Racherla.

Communications:

Roadways : State Highway (S.H.): Direction- Gidda to Tripuranthakam. Nearest Villages- Kagitalagudem, China Cumbum, Porumamilla Palle, Cumbum, Kandula Puram, Jangamguntla, Linga Puram, Yerrabalem, Anantha Palle, Thurimella.

Railway Station: Cumbum.

Rivers Gundlakamma Nadi- Nearest Villages- Linga Puram, Yerrabalem, Anantha Palle, Thurimella. Vemuleru Nadi- Nearest Villages- Auranga Bad, Ravipadu, Lanja Kota.

The Block is identified as a drought-prone area.

Annual Rainfall: Average Rainfall 733.3 mm

Ground Water: Availability of the Ground Water in the Basin is 10.28 MCM and the utilization is 10.02 MCM It belongs to Critical category. Depth to water level varies from 2 to 5 meter below the ground. Most of the wells go down in summer months., according to the Ground Water Estimation Committee.

Administration:

Division: Coastal Andhra. Parliamentary Constituency: 33 Ongole. District: Prakasam. Mandal: Cumbum. Assembly Constituency: 231 Gidalur. Gram Panchayat: 14.

Places of Tourist Interest:

Cumbum : Cumbum lies north of Giddalur on the Giddalur-Markapur road. It is a railway station on the Hubli-Mach ilipatnam line. A large tank was constructed in the town during the rule of Vijaya-nagar kings. The tank water spreads over 23 sq. kms. and it has registered ayacut of 2835 hectares. It irrigates about 4860 hectar es in 16 villages near about Cumbum. Nineteen inscriptio ns have been noted on the tank bund near the choultry in the Jami Masjid, the Gachirala Mosque and the Sailab -ka-katta.

Villages: 16 **Inhabited:** 14 **Uninhabited:** 2

Ranking	District	State	National
Area	51	894	5284
Population	25	654	5502
Sex Ratio	20	593	2081
Child Sex Ratio	44	920	4081
Literacy Rate	2	109	1557
Density	56	1062	3189
Work Participation Rate	5	288	4523

Gram Panchayats:

China Cumbum, Cumbum, Darga, H.,Gudem, Jangamguntla Kandulapuram, L.Kota, Lingapuram, Narsireddypalli Owrangabad, Peddanallakalva, Ravipadu, Turimella Yarrabalem.

Amenities:

Education: Primary School in 13 villages, Middle school in 10 villages, Matriculation or Secondary School in 7 villages, namely Linga Puram, Thurimella, Cumbum, Kandula Puram, Jangamguntla, Lanja Kota, Ravipadu. Higher Secondary or Pre University Courses or Inter-mediate or Junior College in 2 villages of the CD Block,, namely Thurimella, Cumbum.

College in 2 villages, Adult Literacy Center in 14 villages., Colleges are in villages, namely Cumbum, Kandula Puram.

Medical: Hospital in 1 village, Dispensary in 2 villages, Health Center in 2 villages, Sub Center in 7 villages, Maternity and Child Welfare Center in 0 village, Community health workers in 0 village.

The Villages having Hospital or Dispensary or Health Center are Thurimella, Cumbum.

Drinking Water: Tap water in 14 villages, Tank water in 14 villages, Well water in 14 villages, Tubewell in 14 villages and more than one source in 14 villages.

Bank: Banking facility in 2 villages, namely, Thurimella, Cumbum.

Credit Society in 5 villages Agricultural Credit Society in 3 Non-Agricultural Credit Society in 2 villages.

Others: Power supply in 14 villages, Cinema hall in 2 villages, sport club in 0 village, Stadium or Auditorium or Community Hall in 0 village, Post Office in 11 villages.

There are 11 villages having bus facilities.

Villages with most of facilities: Thurimella Cumbum.

Villages without Amenities (Education): None..

Scheduled Castes: Out of the total population of 45131 persons, 4722 persons (10.46%) belong to Scheduled Castes.

The villages having less than 10% SC population are Thurimella, Porumamilla Palle, Cumbum, Kagitalagudem Hazarat Gudem, Nadim Palle, Ravipadu.

The villages having more than 50% SC population are None.

Sex ratio of Scheduled Caste population is 498.

Scheduled Castes Literates and Illiterates by Sex:

	Persons	Males	Females
Literate	2,974	1,772	1,202
Illiterate	1,748	600	1,148
Literacy rate	71.1	84.2	57.8
Graduate	136	91	45

Scheduled Castes (Dominant):

Mala, Madiga, Generic Castes etc., Adi Andhra

For their cultural identity please see Appendix-I

Villages without Scheduled Castes: There are 6 villages without any scheduled caste population.

Scheduled Tribes: Out of the total population of 45131 persons, 499 persons (1.11%) belong to Scheduled Tribes.

The villages having less than 10% ST population are Linga Puram, Yerrabalem, Thurimella, China Cumbum Porumamilla Palle, Cumbum, Hazarat Gudem Kandula Puram, Jangamguntla, Lanja Kota, Nadim Palle Auranga Bad, Ravipadu.

The villages having more than 50% ST population are None.

Sex ratio of Scheduled tribe population is 479.

Scheduled Tribes Literates and Illiterates by Sex:

	Persons	Males	Females
Literate	207	130	77
Illiterate	292	130	162
Literacy rate	50.7	60.2	40.1
Graduate	11	10	1

Scheduled Tribes (Dominant):

Yerukulas, Yenadis, Sugalis etc., Koya etc. Chenchu etc.

For their cultural identity please see Appendix-II

Villages without Scheduled Tribes: There are 7 villages without any scheduled tribe population.

Literates and Illiterates by Sex (Total Population):

	Persons	Males	Females
Literate	26,594	16,477	10,117
Illiterate	18,537	6,324	12,213
Literacy rate	67	83	52
Graduate	1,702	1,395	307

Agriculture: ***Distribution of villages according to land use:*** Out of 16 villages, Total area (in hectare) is 13265, out of that 62.5 percent is cultivable and 24.69 percent of the cultivable area is irrigated.

Sources of Irrigation (Hectares): Government Canal 0, Private Canal 0, Well without Electricity 0, Well with Electricity 0, Tubewell without Electricity 0, Tubewell with Electricity 600.15, Tank 1446.77, River 0, Lake 0, Waterfall 0, Others 0.

Villages with population of 5000 to 9999: Thurimella, Kandula Puram.

Villages with population of 10000 and above: Cumbum.

Distribution of Workers:

	Persons	Males	Females	WPR
Cultivators	4,511	2,766	1,745	25.12
Agricultural Labour	6,629	2,804	3,825	36.92
Household Industry	322	183	139	1.79
Other Workers	6,494	5,304	1,190	36.17
Main Workers	15,661	10,124	5,537	87.22
Marginal Workers	2,295	933	1,362	12.78
Total Workers	17,956	11,057	6,899	

Religion: Major Religious Communities:

	Persons	Males	Females	Sex Ratio
Hindu (79.79%)	36,011	18,159	17,852	983
Muslim (18.78%)	8,475	4,326	4,149	959
Christian (1.15%)	519	258	261	1,012
Sikh (0%)	-	-	-	-
Buddhists (0%)	-	-	-	-
Jain (0%)	-	-	-	-

Agewise Data:

	Persons	Males	Females	Sex Ratio
All ages	45,131	22,801	22,330	979
0-14	13,954	7,194	6,760	940
15-44	20,652	10,591	10,061	950
45-79	10,159	4,859	5,300	1091
80+	313	131	182	1389
Age not stated	53	26	27	1038

Languages (Dominant):

Telugu, Urdu, Hindi, Tamil, Gondi

Disabled Population:

	Persons	Males	Females	%
Total Disabled	627	378	249	
In Seeing	131	70	61	20.89
In Speech	92	53	39	14.67
In Hearing	40	21	19	6.38
In Movement	244	160	84	38.92
Mentally	120	74	46	19.14

D.HIREHAL

D. Hirehal C.D. Block lies in the north-western part of Anantapur district. The Block is located at a distan ce of 108 kms. from district headquarters (Anantapur). There are 18 villages in the block with the total population of 39,394 persons. Area of the C.D. Block is 315.87 sq. kms. It is bounded in the south by Mandal Rayadurg, in the west by Mandals Bommanahal, Kanekal and Rayadurg, and it has common boundary with the state of Karnataka on north and west.

Communications:

Roadways : State Highway (S.H.): Direction- Molakalamuru to Bellary. Nearest Villages- Lingamanahalli, D.Hirehal, Jajarakal, Obulapuram.

Railway Station: Obulapuram, Somalapuram.

River: Chenna Hagari Nadi- Nearest Villages- Kudulur, Kadalur, Nagalapuram.

It receives Backward Region Grants, and is identified as a drought-prone area as well.

Annual Rainfall: Average Rainfall 409 mm

Ground Water: Availability of the Ground Water in the Basin is 1890 H.A.M. and the utilization is 1552 H. A.M. It belongs to SC category. Depth to water level varies from 5 to 10 meter below the ground. Most of the wells go down in summer months. The well density in the entire block is 6 wells per sq. km. Total no. of the wells in the block are enumerated as 1931, according to the Ground Water Estimation Committee.

Natural Division : Rayalaseema Region

Administration:

Division: Rayala Seema. Parliamentary Constituency: 36 Anantapur. District: Anantapur.

Mandal: D. Hirehal. Assembly Constituency: 267 Rayadurg. Gram Panchayat: 16.

Border Villages: (Karnataka)- Nearest Villages- Malapan agudi, H.Siddapuram, Obulapuram, D.Hirehal, H.Hossahalli, Pulakurthi, Lakshmipuram, Lingamanahalli, Jajarakal, Hirdehal, Somalapuram, Kudulur, Kadalur, Hulikal.

Villages: 18 **Inhabited:** 17 **Uninhabited:** 1

Ranking	District	State	National
Area	19	126	2591
Population	41	841	5759
Sex Ratio	44	986	3477
Child Sex Ratio	20	385	1410
Literacy Rate	60	932	5408
Density	32	395	5907
Work Participation Rate	51	992	966

Gram Panchayats:

Cherlopalli, D.Hirehal, Dodaghatta, Hulikal Jajarakal, Kadalur, Kudlur, M.Hanumapuram Madenahalli, Malapanagudi, Mallikethi, Muradi Nagalapuram, Obulapuram, Pulakurthi, Somalapuram.

Amenities:

Education: Primary School in 16 villages, Middle school in 5 villages, Matriculation or Secondary School in 3 villages, namely D.Hirehal, Somalapuram, Kudulur.

Higher Secondary or Pre University Courses or Intermediate or Junior College in 0 village of the CD Block, College in 0 village, Adult Literacy Center in 0 village.

Medical: Hospital in 0 village, Dispensary in 1 village, Health Center in 2 villages, Sub Center in 7 villages, Maternity and Child Welfare Center in 0 village, Community health workers in 0 village.

The Village having Hospital or Dispensary or Health Center is Muradi.

Drinking Water: Tap water in 17 villages, Tank water in 3 villages, Well water in 0 village, Tubewell in 17 villages and more than one source in 17 villages.

Bank: Banking facility in 2 villages, namely, D.Hirehal, Somalapuram.

Credit Society in 3 villages Agricultural Credit Society in 3 Non-Agricultural Credit Society in 0 village.

Others: Power supply in 17 villages, Cinema hall in 0 village, sport club in 0 village, Stadium or Auditorium or Community Hall in 0 village, Post Office in 9 villages.

There are 11 villages having bus facilities.

Villages with most of facilities: D.Hirehal Somalapuram.

Villages without amenities (Education): Lakshmipuram..

Scheduled Castes: Out of the total population of 39394 persons, 5726 persons (14.54%) belong to Scheduled Castes.

The villages having less than 10% SC population are None..

The villages having more than 50% SC population are None.

Sex ratio of Scheduled Caste population is 488.

Scheduled Castes Literates and Illiterates by Sex:

	Persons	Males	Females
Literate	1,421	1,002	419
Illiterate	4,305	1,930	2,375

Literacy rate	31.6	43.6	19.1
Graduate	3	3	0

Scheduled Castes (Dominant):
Madiga, Mala, Chalavadi, Generic Castes etc.
Mala Dasari

For their cultural identity please see Appendix-I

Villages without Scheduled Castes: There are 4 villages without any scheduled caste population.

Scheduled Tribes: Out of the total population of 39394 persons, 816 persons (2.07%) belong to Scheduled Tribes.
The villages having less than 10% ST population are Malapanagudi, Obulapuram, D.Hirehal, Lakshmipuram Madenahalli, Lingamanahalli, Jajarakal, Hirdehal Pulakurthi, Nagalapuram, Somalapuram, Kudulur Dodagatta, Kadalur, Hulikal, Muradi.
The villages having more than 50% ST population are None.
Sex ratio of Scheduled tribe population is 468.

Scheduled Tribes Literates and Illiterates by Sex:

	Persons	Males	Females
Literate	322	235	87
Illiterate	494	199	295
Literacy rate	49.5	68.3	28.3
Graduate	8	8	0

Scheduled Tribes (Dominant):
Sugalis etc., Yerukulas, Kammara, Bagata

For their cultural identity please see Appendix-II

Villages without Scheduled Tribes: There are 13 villages without any scheduled tribe population.

Literates and Illiterates by Sex (Total Population):

	Persons	Males	Females
Literate	14,065	9,476	4,589
Illiterate	25,329	10,721	14,608
Literacy rate	43	57	29
Graduate	297	253	44

Agriculture: ***Distribution of villages according to land use:*** Out of 18 villages, Total area (in hectare) is 31787, out of that 74.91 percent is cultivable and 11.84 percent of the cultivable area is irrigated.

Sources of Irrigation (Hectares): Government Canal 396.36, Private Canal 0, Well without Electricity 0, Well with Electricity 207.26, Tubewell without Electricity 0, Tubewell with Electricity 2215.76, Tank 0, River 0, Lake 0, Waterfall 0, Others 0.

Villages with population of 5000 to 9999:
D.Hirehal, Muradi.

Villages with population of 10000 and above: None

Distribution of Workers:

	Persons	Males	Females	WPR
Cultivators	9,236	5,822	3,414	45.12
Agricultural Labour	7,719	3,263	4,456	37.71
Household Industry	252	135	117	1.23
Other Workers	3,262	2,446	816	15.94
Main Workers	16,816	10,439	6,377	82.15
Marginal Workers	3,653	1,227	2,426	17.85
Total Workers	20,469	11,666	8,803	

Religion: Major Religious Communities:

	Persons	Males	Females	Sex Ratio
Hindu (96.86%)	38,158	19,548	18,610	952
Muslim (2.68%)	1,057	557	500	898
Christian (0.06%)	23	13	10	769
Sikh (0.03%)	11	7	4	571
Buddhists (0.01%)	4	2	2	1,000
Jain (0.03%)	10	4	6	1,500

Agewise Data:

	Persons	Males	Females	Sex Ratio
All ages	39,394	20,197	19,197	950
0-14	15,239	7,972	7,267	912
15-44	17,227	8,840	8,387	949
45-79	6,645	3,263	3,382	1036
80+	245	103	142	1379
Age not stated	38	19	19	1000

Languages (Dominant):
Telugu, Kannada, Urdu, Hindi, Tamil

Disabled Population:

	Persons	Males	Females	%
Total Disabled	605	359	246	
In Seeing	174	100	74	28.76
In Speech	78	39	39	12.89
In Hearing	30	15	15	4.96
In Movement	264	169	95	43.64
Mentally	59	36	23	9.75

DACHEPALLE

Dachepalle C.D. Block lies in the northern part of Guntur district. The Block is located at a distance of 72 kms. from district headquarters (Guntur). There are 12 villages in the block with the total population of 68,062 persons. Area of the C.D. Block is 261.27 sq. kms. It is bounded in the north by district Nalgonda and River Krishna, in the south and west by Mandal Gurazala, and in the east by Mandals Machavaram and Piduguralla.

Communications:

Roadways : State Highway (S.H.): Direction- Miryalaguda to Piduguralla. Nearest Villages- Gamalapadu, Dachepalle, Kesanapalle, Nadikudi, Pondugula, Amapuram.

Railway Station: Pondugula, Nadikudi.

River: Krishna Nadi- Nearest Villages- Bhatrupalem, Madinapadu, Dachepalle, Kesanapalle, Pondugula, Ramapu ram, Tangeda.

Annual Rainfall: Average Rainfall 761 mm

Ground Water: Availability of the Ground Water in the Basin is 10725 H.A.M. and the utilization is 1096 H. A.M. It belongs to Safe category. Depth to water level varies from 5 to 10 meter below the ground. Most of the wells go down in summer months.

Forest and Reserved **Forest:** Nearest Villages- Bhatrupal em, Gamalapadu, Madinapadu, Tangeda.

Natural Division : Krishna Delta Region

Administration:

Division: Coastal Andhra. Parliamentary Constituency: 31 Narsaraopet. District: Guntur. Mandal: Dachepalle. Assembly Constituency: 219 Gurajala. Gram Panchayat: 16

Places of Tourist Interest:

Dachepalle : This village on the Guntur-Macherla highway lies 11 kms. to the north-east of Gurazala town. The remains of the old fort can beseenin the neighbouring villages, especially at Ubbepalle near Gamalapadu where there is a small 'Sambhunigudi', containing a great deal of carved stone and four of five inscriptions ranging from A.D. 1300 to 1537. The temple of Ranganaya kaswamy which is an ancient one to the place, is noted for its architectural beauty.

Villages: 12 **Inhabited:** 12 **Uninhabited:** 0

Ranking	District	State	National
Area	6	271	3229
Population	9	164	4556
Sex Ratio	32	570	2017
Child Sex Ratio	22	509	1914
Literacy Rate	41	573	4118
Density	27	322	3962
Work Participation Rate	47	501	800

Gram Panchayats:

Bhatrupalem, Dachepalli, Gamalapadu, Katrapadu Kesanapalli, Kothuru, Madinapadu, Mutyalampadu Nadikudi, Pedagarlapadu, Pondugula, Ramapuram Sarangapalli, Srinagar, Takkellapadu, Tangeda.

Amenities:

Education: Primary School in 12 villages, Middle school in 8 villages, Matriculation or Secondary School in 5 villages, namely Ramapuram, Tangeda, Mutyalampadu, Dachepalle, Nadikudi.

Higher Secondary or Pre University Courses or Intermediate or Junior College in 1 village of the CD Block,, namely Dachepalle.

College in 0 village, Adult Literacy Center in 11 villages.

Medical: Hospital in 1 village, Dispensary in 2 villages, Health Center in 1 village, Sub Center in 10 villages, Maternity and Child Welfare Center in 1 village, Community health workers in 0 village.

The Villages having Hospital or Dispensary or Health Center are Mutyalampadu, Dachepalle, Nadikudi.

Drinking Water: Tap water in 12 villages, Tank water in 12 villages, Well water in 12 villages, Tubewell in 12 villages and more than one source in 12 villages.

Bank: Banking facility in 3 villages, namely, Mutyalampadu, Dachepalle, Nadikudi.

Credit Society in 6 villages Agricultural Credit Society in 6 Non-Agricultural Credit Society in 2 villages.

Others: Power supply in 12 villages, Cinema hall in 2 villages, sport club in 2 villages, Stadium or Auditorium or Community Hall in 2 villages, Post Office in 11 villages.

There are 12 villages having bus facilities.

Villages with most of facilities: Mutyalampadu Dachepalle, Nadikudi.

Villages without Amenities (Education): None..

Scheduled Castes: Out of the total population of 68062 persons, 9693 persons (14.24%) belong to Scheduled Castes.

The villages having less than 10% SC population are None..

The villages having more than 50% SC population are None.

Sex ratio of Scheduled Caste population is 490.

Scheduled Castes Literates and Illiterates by Sex:

	Persons	Males	Females
Literate	3,417	2,253	1,164
Illiterate	6,276	2,694	3,582
Literacy rate	41.5	53.4	29.0
Graduate	103	73	30

Scheduled Castes (Dominant):

Madiga, Mala, Mala Dasari, Bindla, Mala Dasu

For their cultural identity please see Appendix-I

Villages without Scheduled Castes: There are 0 village without any scheduled caste population.

Scheduled Tribes: Out of the total population of 68062 persons, 3724 persons (5.47%) belong to Scheduled Tribes.

The villages having less than 10% ST population are Pondugula, Ramapuram, Gamalapadu, Tangeda Mutyalampadu, Dachepalle, Nadikudi, Alugumallipadu Kesanapalle, Pedagarlapadu.

The villages having more than 50% ST population are None.

Sex ratio of Scheduled tribe population is 501.

Scheduled Tribes Literates and Illiterates by Sex:

	Persons	Males	Females
Literate	875	605	270
Illiterate	2,849	1,255	1,594
Literacy rate	28.9	40.1	17.8
Graduate	13	10	3

Scheduled Tribes (Dominant):

Sugalis etc., Yerukulas, Chenchu etc., Yenadis Kammara

For their cultural identity please see Appendix-II

Villages without Scheduled Tribes: There are 2 villages without any scheduled tribe population.

Literates and Illiterates by Sex (Total Population):

	Persons	Males	Females
Literate	30,785	19,129	11,656
Illiterate	37,277	15,249	22,028
Literacy rate	53	65	40
Graduate	1,160	911	249

Agriculture: ***Distribution of villages according to land use:*** Out of 12 villages, Total area (in hectare) is 26127, out of that 55.87 percent is cultivable and 35.54 percent of the cultivable area is irrigated.

Sources of Irrigation (Hectares): Government Canal 5162.59, Private Canal 0, Well without Electricity 0, Well with Electricity 0, Tubewell without Electricity 0, Tubewell with Electricity 0, Tank 0, River 0, Lake 0, Waterfall 0, Others 25.09.

Villages with population of 5000 to 9999:
Tangeda, Kesanapalle.

Villages with population of 10000 and above:
Dachepalle, Nadikudi.

Distribution of Workers:

	Persons	Males	Females	WPR
Cultivators	9,977	5,732	4,245	26.68
Agricultural Labour	19,455	8,335	11,120	52.02
Household Industry	500	259	241	1.34
Other Workers	7,468	6,117	1,351	19.97
Main Workers	33,922	19,234	14,688	90.7
Marginal Workers	3,478	1,209	2,269	9.3
Total Workers	37,400	20,443	16,957	

Religion: Major Religious Communities:

	Persons	Males	Females	Sex Ratio
Hindu (84.71%)	57,656	29,099	28,557	981
Muslim (13.35%)	9,086	4,622	4,464	966
Christian (1.74%)	1,184	594	590	993
Sikh (0.02%)	12	8	4	500
Buddhists (0%)	3	1	2	2,000
Jain (0%)	1	-	1	-

Agewise Data:

	Persons	Males	Females	Sex Ratio
All ages	68,062	34,378	33,684	980
0-14	22,810	11,617	11,193	964
15-44	32,857	16,579	16,278	982
45-79	11,850	5,922	5,928	1001
80+	465	214	251	1173
Age not stated	80	46	34	739

Languages (Dominant):
Telugu, Urdu, Hindi, Tamil, Gondi

Disabled Population:

	Persons	Males	Females	%
Total Disabled	896	520	376	
In Seeing	316	192	124	35.27
In Speech	96	48	48	10.71
In Hearing	42	19	23	4.69
In Movement	320	203	117	35.71
Mentally	122	58	64	13.62

DAGADARTHI

Dagadarthi C.D. Block lies in the north-eastern part of Nellore district. The Block is located at a distance of 34 kms. from district headquarters (Nellore). There are 22 villages in the block with the total population of 35,742 persons. Area of the C.D. Block is 252.94 sq. kms. It is bounded in the north by Mandals Kaligiri and Bogole, in the south by Mandals Sangam, Buchireddip alem and Kodavalur, in the east by Mandals Kodavur and Allur, and in the west by Mandals Anumasamudrampeta and Sangam.

Communications:

Roadways : NH- 5: Direction- Nellore to Ongole. Nearest Villages- Ananthavaram, Ulavapalle, Kothapalle Kowrugun ta.

Railway Station: Ananthavaram.

Annual Rainfall: Average Rainfall 1091 mm

Ground Water: Availability of the Ground Water in the Basin is 7930 H.A.M. and the utilization is 1245 H. A.M. It belongs to Safe category. Depth to water level varies from 5 to 10 meter below the ground. Most of the wells go down in summer months, according to the Ground Water Estimation Committee.

Administration:

Division: Coastal Andhra. Parliamentary Constituency: 39 Nellore.District: Nellore.

Mandal: Dagadarthi. Assembly Constituency: 233 Kavali. Gram Panchayat: 20.

Villages: 22 **Inhabited:** 22 **Uninhabited:** 0

Ranking	**District**	**State**	**National**
Area	27	299	3339
Population	35	921	5888
Sex Ratio	12	296	1298
Child Sex Ratio	34	908	4015
Literacy Rate	31	340	3143
Density	5	415	5682
Work Participation Rate	30	933	1030

Gram Panchayats:

Ananthavaram, Bodagudipadu, Chennur, Chowtaputhedu Dagadarthi, Damavaram, Dharamavaram, Dundigam K.K.Gunta, Katrayapadu, Manubolupadu, Pedaputhedu

Rangasamudram, Tadakalur, Thiruvedhipadu, Thurimerla Uchaguntapalem, Ulava Palla, Velipodu Yelamanchi Padu.

Amenities:

Education: Primary School in 22 villages, Middle school in 9 villages, Matriculation or Secondary School in 4 villages, namely Dundigam, Dagadarthi, Chennuru, Pedaputhedu. Higher Secondary or Pre University Courses or Intermediate or Junior College in 0 village of the CD Block, College in 0 village, Adult Literacy Center in 15 villages.

Medical: Hospital in 0 village, Dispensary in 1 village, Health Center in 2 villages, Sub Center in 7 villages, Maternity and Child Welfare Center in 0 village, Community health workers in 0 village.

The Village having Hospital or Dispensary or Health Center is Pedaputhedu.

Drinking Water: Tap water in 22 villages, Tank water in 22 villages, Well water in 22 villages, Tubewell in 22 villages and more than one source in 22 villages.

Bank: Banking facility in 3 villages, namely, Dagadarthi, Thurimerla, Pedaputhedu.

Credit Society in 14 villages Agricultural Credit Society in 2 Non-Agricultural Credit Society in 14 villages.

Others: Power supply in 22 villages, Cinema hall in 1 village, sport club in 0 village, Stadium or Auditorium or Community Hall in 0 village, Post Office in 16 villages.

There are 20 villages having bus facilities.

Villages with most of facilities: Dagadarthi Thurimerla, Pedaputhedu.

Villages without Amenities (Education): None..

Scheduled Castes: Out of the total population of 35742 persons, 9989 persons (27.95%) belong to Scheduled Castes.

The villages having less than 10% SC population are None..

The villages having more than 50% SC population are None.

Sex ratio of Scheduled Caste population is 500.

Scheduled Castes Literates and Illiterates by Sex:

	Persons	Males	Females
Literate	4,732	2,789	1,943
Illiterate	5,257	2,207	3,050
Literacy rate	54.8	65.1	44.6
Graduate	81	68	13

Scheduled Castes (Dominant):

Mala, Madiga, Arundhatiya, Mala Dasu Generic Castes etc.

For their cultural identity please see Appendix-I

Villages without Scheduled Castes: There are 0 village without any scheduled caste population.

Scheduled Tribes: Out of the total population of 35742 persons, 3082 persons (8.62%) belong to Scheduled Tribes.

The villages having less than 10% ST population are Bodagudipadu, Manubolupadu, Marellapadu, Dundigam Ithampadu, Rangasamudram, Lingalapadu, Katrayapadu Velupodu, Kaminenipalem, Damavaram, Ananthavaram Kothapalle Kowrugunta, Thiruveedhipadu Yelamanchipadu, Choutaputhedu.

The villages having more than 50% ST population are None.

Sex ratio of Scheduled tribe population is 490.

Scheduled Tribes Literates and Illiterates by Sex:

	Persons	Males	Females
Literate	931	563	368
Illiterate	2,151	1,008	1,143
Literacy rate	35.4	41.7	28.7
Graduate	8	6	2

Scheduled Tribes (Dominant):

Yenadis, Yerukulas, Sugalis etc., Chenchu etc. Koya etc.

For their cultural identity please see Appendix-II

Villages without Scheduled Tribes: There is 1 village without any scheduled tribe population.

Literates and Illiterates by Sex (Total Population):

	Persons	Males	Females
Literate	18,238	10,697	7,541
Illiterate	17,504	7,208	10,296
Literacy rate	58	68	48
Graduate	384	323	61

Agriculture: ***Distribution of villages according to land use:*** Out of 22 villages, Total area (in hectare) is 25292, out of that 35.04 percent is cultivable and 78.65 percent of the cultivable area is irrigated.

Sources of Irrigation (Hectares): Government Canal 4514.68, Private Canal 0, Well without Electricity 44.46, Well with Electricity 231.06, Tubewell without Electricity 0, Tubewell with Electricity 163.06, Tank 1503.8, River 0, Lake 0, Waterfall 0, Others 512.34.

Villages with population of 5000 to 9999: None

Villages with population of 10000 and above: None

Distribution of Workers:

	Persons	Males	Females	WPR
Cultivators	5,436	4,163	1,273	27.61
Agricultural Labour	10,854	4,664	6,190	55.12
Household Industry	407	241	166	2.07
Other Workers	2,993	2,042	951	15.2
Main Workers	16,671	10,151	6,520	84.67
Marginal Workers	3,019	959	2,060	15.33
Total Workers	19,690	11,110	8,580	

Religion: Major Religious Communities:

	Persons	Males	Females	Sex Ratio

Hindu (95.16%)	34,011	17,057	16,954	994
Muslim (4.01%)	1,433	694	739	1,065
Christian (0.71%)	252	129	123	953
Sikh (0%)	-	-	-	-
Buddhists (0.01%)	4	2	2	1,000
Jain (0%)	-	-	-	-

Agewise Data:

	Persons	Males	Females	Sex Ratio
All ages	35,742	17,905	17,837	996
0-14	10,506	5,344	5,162	966
15-44	16,742	8,387	8,355	996
45-79	8,180	4,014	4,166	1038
80+	284	138	146	1058
Age not stated	30	22	8	364

Languages (Dominant):

Telugu, Urdu, Hindi, Gondi, Tamil

Disabled Population:

	Persons	Males	Females	%
Total Disabled	795	396	399	
In Seeing	268	120	148	33.71
In Speech	76	38	38	9.56
In Hearing	69	29	40	8.68
In Movement	255	146	109	32.08
Mentally	127	63	64	15.97

DAHEGAON

Dahegaon C.D. Block lies in the south-east part of Adilabad district. The Block is located at a distance of 185 kms. from district headquarters (Adilabad). There are 39 villages in the block with the total popul ation of 30,596 persons. Area of the C.D. Block is 317. 80 sq. kms. It is bounded by Kagaznagar Mandal on west, north-west, north and north-east, Bejjur Mandal on north-west, Vemanpalle Mandal on south-east, south and south-west, Bhimini Mandal on south-west. It has common boundary with the state of Maharashtra on east.

Communications :

Roadways : NH, SH or Important Metalled Road is not available.

River: Pedda Vagu Nadi- Nearest Villages- Itial, Borla kunta, Kothmir, Beebra, Pesarkunta, Chedvai, Ainam, Saligaon, Laggaon, Vodduguda, Girvelli, Chinnaraspalle, Amargonda, Loha, Digida, Teepergaon, Motlaguda, Dubbag uda. Pranhita Nadi- Nearest Villages- Ravalpalle, Dubbag uda.

Backwards Region Grants Fund: It receives Backward Region Grants.

Annual Rainfall: Average Rainfall 1242 mm

Ground Water: Availability of the Ground Water in the Basin is 2856 H.A.M.and the utilization is 352 H.A. M. It belongs to Safe category. Depth to water level varies from 5 to 10 meter below the ground. Most of the wells go down in summer months, according to the Ground Water Estimation Committee.

Natural Division : Telangana Plateau Region

Administration:

Division: Telangana. Parliamentary Constituency: 1 Adilabad (ST). District: Adilabad. Mandal: Dahegaon. Assembly Constituency: 1 Sirpur. Gram Panchayat: 18.

Villages: 39 **Inhabited:** 38 **Uninhabited:** 1

Ranking	District	State	National
Area	11	96	2434
Population	33	1017	6046
Sex Ratio	11	120	718
Child Sex Ratio	1	13	53
Literacy Rate	51	1082	6137
Density	17	250	6186
Work Participation Rate	44	1071	654

Gram Panchayats:

Ainam, Beebra, Chandrapalle, Chedvai, Chinnagudipet Chinnaraspalle, Dahegaon, Girvelli, Hathni, Ityal Keslapur, Kothmir, Kunchavelli, Laggaon, Motleguda Rampur, Saligaon, Vodduguda.

Amenities:

Education: Primary School in 34 villages, Middle school in 8 villages, Matriculation or Secondary School in 3 villages, namely Beebra, Saligaon, Dahegaon.

Higher Secondary or Pre University Courses or Inter-mediate or Junior College in 0 village of the CD Block, College in 0 village, Adult Literacy Center in 0 village.

Medical: Hospital in 0 village, Dispensary in 1 village, Health Center in 1 village, Sub Center in 6 villages, Maternity and Child Welfare Center in 0 village, Community health workers in 0 village.

The Village having Hospital or Dispensary or Health Center is Dahegaon.

Drinking Water: Tap water in 37 villages, Tank water in 37 villages, Well water in 38 villages, Tubewell in 37 villages and more than one source in 37 villages.

Bank: Banking facility in 1 villages, namely, Dahegaon.

Credit Society in 1 village Agricultural Credit Society in 1 Non-Agricultural Credit Society in 1 village.

Others: Power supply in 38 villages, Cinema hall in 0 village, sport club in 0 village, Stadium or Auditorium or Community Hall in 0 village, Post Office in 11 villages.

There are 5 villages having bus facilities.

Village with most of facilities: Dahegaon.

Villages without amenities (Education): Bhogaram, Etapalle, Loha, Teepergaon..

Scheduled Castes: Out of the total population of 30596 persons, 9121 persons (29.81%) belong to Scheduled Castes.

The villages having less than 10% SC population are Borlakunta, Pedda Thimmapur, Etapalle, Amargonda Loha, Teepergaon, Ravalpalle.

The villages having more than 50% SC population are Keslapur, Pesarkunta, Chinna Thimmapur, Hathni Saligaon, Kammarpalle, Bhogaram, Bhamanagar Chandrapalle.

Sex ratio of Scheduled Caste population is 502.

Scheduled Castes Literates and Illiterates by Sex:

	Persons	Males	Females
Literate	2,403	1,628	775
Illiterate	6,718	2,913	3,805
Literacy rate	31.7	42.7	20.5
Graduate	24	23	1

Scheduled Castes (Dominant):

Manne, Mala, Mala Sale etc., Madiga, Mahar

For their cultural identity please see Appendix-I

Villages without Scheduled Castes: There are 6 villages without any scheduled caste population.

Scheduled Tribes: Out of the total population of 30596 persons, 3130 persons (10.23%) belong to Scheduled Tribes.

The villages having less than 10% ST population are Itial, Gorregutta, Borlakunta, Kothmir, Pesarkunta Chedvai, Ainam, Thangallapalle, Chinnagudipet Chinna Thimmapur, Pedda Thimmapur, Hathni, Madavelli Saligaon, Bhogaram, Vodduguda, Bhamanagar Kunchavelli, Girvelli, Chinnaraspalle, Amargonda Motlaguda.

The villages having more than 50% ST population are Polampalle, Etapalle, Loha, Digida, Teepergaon Ravalpalle.

Sex ratio of Scheduled tribe population is 512.

Scheduled Tribes Literates and Illiterates by Sex:

	Persons	Males	Females
Literate	695	452	243
Illiterate	2,435	1,075	1,360
Literacy rate	27.2	36.4	18.6
Graduate	7	6	1

Scheduled Tribes (Dominant):

Koya etc., Kolam etc., Sugalis etc., Gond etc. Manna Dhora

For their cultural identity please see Appendix-II

Villages without Scheduled Tribes: There are 11 villages without any scheduled tribe population.

Literates and Illiterates by Sex (Total Population):

	Persons	Males	Females
Literate	8,340	5,539	2,801
Illiterate	22,256	9,632	12,624
Literacy rate	33	44	22
Graduate	83	72	11

Agriculture: ***Distribution of villages according to land use:*** Out of 39 villages, Total area (in hectare) is 33309, out of that 53.33 percent is cultivable and 1.71 percent of the cultivable area is irrigated.

Sources of Irrigation (Hectares): Government Canal 0, Private Canal 0, Well without Electricity 8.49, Well with Electricity 42.5, Tubewell without Electricity 0, Tubewell with Electricity 23.06, Tank 220.16, River 0, Lake 8.5, Waterfall 0, Others 1.62.

Villages with population of 5000 to 9999: None

Villages with population of 10000 and above: None

Distribution of Workers:

	Persons	Males	Females	WPR
Cultivators	6,720	4,684	2,036	40.66
Agricultural Labour	6,940	2,446	4,494	41.99
Household Industry	794	270	524	4.8
Other Workers	2,073	1,495	578	12.54
Main Workers	10,942	7,506	3,436	66.21
Marginal Workers	5,585	1,389	4,196	33.79
Total Workers	16,527	8,895	7,632	

Religion: Major Religious Communities:

	Persons	Males	Females	Sex Ratio
Hindu (96.33%)	29,472	14,606	14,866	1,018
Muslim (1.73%)	528	255	273	1,071
Christian (0.1%)	30	15	15	1,000
Sikh (0%)	-	-	-	-
Buddhists (1.81%)	553	289	264	913
Jain (0%)	-	-	-	-

Agewise Data:

	Persons	Males	Females	Sex Ratio
All ages	30,596	15,171	15,425	1017
0-14	11,154	5,522	5,632	1020
15-44	13,796	6,848	6,948	1015
45-79	5,446	2,695	2,751	1021
80+	164	88	76	864
Age not stated	36	18	18	1000

Languages (Dominant):

Telugu, Marathi, Koya, Hindi, Urdu

Disabled Population:

	Persons	Males	Females	%
Total Disabled	396	212	184	
In Seeing	172	77	95	43.43
In Speech	53	23	30	13.38
In Hearing	20	10	10	5.05
In Movement	106	71	35	26.77
Mentally	45	31	14	11.36

DAKKILI

Dakkili C.D. Block lies in the south-western part of Nellore district. The Block is located at a distance of 74 kms. from district headquarters (Nellore). There are 50 villages in the block with the total population of 38,684 persons. Area of the C.D. Block is 277.14 sq. kms. It is bounded in the north by Mandals Rapur and Sydapuram, in the south by Mandal Venkatagiri, in the east by Mandals Balayapalle and Sydapuram, and in the west by district Guddapah.

Communications:

Roadways : Metalled Roads: Nearest Villages- Velikallu, Dakkili, Kandalavaripalle, Sanganapalle, Mopuru, Naidu palem, Lingasamudram, Surayapalem, Thimmayapalem, Palugodu, Pedayachasamudram, Nagavolu, Chennasamudram, Chapalpalle.

River: Alapalayeru Nadi- Nearest Villages- Dakkili, Pathanalapadu, Kothanalapadu, Bheemavaram, Daggavolu, Chakalapalle, Naidupalem, Lingasamudram, Noothalacheru vu, Althurupadu.

Annual Rainfall: Average Rainfall 1035 mm

Ground Water: Availability of the Ground Water in the Basin is 3195 H.A.M. and the utilization is 2671 H. A.M. It belongs to SC category. Depth to water level varies from 2 to 10 meter below the ground. Most of the wells go down in summer months, according to the Ground Water Estimation Committee.

Forest and Reserved **Forest:** Nearest Villages- Devulapal le, Madhavaiahpalem, Vembuluru, Attalasiddavaram, Nootha lacheruvu, Althurupadu, Pedayachasamudram, Cheekirenipal le, Theerthampadu, Dattanagaram, Mahasamudram.

Administration:

Division: Coastal Andhra. Parliamentary Constituency: 40 Tirupati (SC). District: Nellore. Mandal: Dakkili. Assembly Constituency: 241 Venkatagiri. Gram Panchayat: 26

Villages: 50 **Inhabited:** 43 **Uninhabited:** 7

Ranking	District	State	National
Area	18	217	3033
Population	30	864	5794
Sex Ratio	23	488	1804
Child Sex Ratio	10	365	1317
Literacy Rate	36	424	3574
Density	15	663	5707
Work Participation Rate	31	939	1826

Gram Panchayats:

Althurupadu, Amuduru, Chapalapalli, Dagga Volu
Dakkili, Danda Volu, Devulapalle
Koneswara Batla Palle, Linga Samudram
Madhavaiah Palem, Marla Gunta, Matmadugu, Mopuru
Nadimpalli, Nagavolu, Palugodu, Pathanalapadu
Sangana Palle, Sreepuram, Theertham Padu
Uppara Palli(D), V.Y.K.Samudram, Veli Kallu
Vellampalli(D), Vellampalli(M), Vembuluru.

Amenities:

Education: Primary School in 39 villages, Middle school in 6 villages, Matriculation or Secondary School in 4 villages, namely Dakkili, Pathanalapadu, Daggavolu, Mopuru. Higher Secondary or Pre University Courses or Intermediate or Junior College in 1 village of the CD Block,, namely Dakkili.

College in 0 village, Adult Literacy Center in 23 villages.

Medical: Hospital in 0 village, Dispensary in 0 village, Health Center in 1 village, Sub Center in 9 villages, Maternity and Child Welfare Center in 0 village, Community health workers in 0 village.

Drinking Water: Tap water in 42 villages, Tank water in 42 villages, Well water in 43 villages, Tubewell in 42 villages and more than one source in 43 villages.

Bank: Banking facility in 2 villages, namely, Dakkili, Mopuru.

Credit Society in 22 villages Agricultural Credit Society in 7 Non-Agricultural Credit Society in 21 villages.

Others: Power supply in 43 villages, Cinema hall in 1 village, sport club in 0 village, Stadium or Auditorium or Community Hall in 0 village, Post Office in 14 villages.

There are 43 villages having bus facilities.

Villages with most of facilities: Dakkili, Mopuru.

Villages without amenities (Education): Cherlopalle, Attalasiddavaram, Thimmanagunta..

Scheduled Castes: Out of the total population of 38684 persons, 11195 persons (28.94%) belong to Scheduled Castes. The villages having less than 10% SC population are Cherlopalle, Marlagunta, Velampalle Vempativaripalle, Kandalavaripalle Yellavajjulapalle, Attalasiddavaram, Surayapalem Thimmanagunta.

The villages having more than 50% SC population are Kothanalapadu, Dandavolu Upparapalle Vengamanaidupalle, Chakalapalle.

Sex ratio of Scheduled Caste population is 511.

Scheduled Castes Literates and Illiterates by Sex:

	Persons	Males	Females
Literate	5,005	2,847	2,158
Illiterate	6,190	2,622	3,568
Literacy rate	51.1	59.8	42.9
Graduate	65	47	18

Scheduled Castes (Dominant):

Mala, Madiga, Arundhatiya, Mala Dasu
Generic Castes etc.

For their cultural identity please see Appendix-I

Villages without Scheduled Castes: There are 14 villages without any scheduled caste population.

Scheduled Tribes: Out of the total population of 38684 persons, 3763 persons (9.73%) belong to Scheduled Tribes.

The villages having less than 10% ST population are Devulapalle, Marlagunta, Vembuluru, Kuppayapalem Vempativaripalle, Dakkili, Sanganapalle Yellavajjulapalle, Kothanalapadu, Daggavolu Dandavolu Upparapalle, Vengamanaidupalle, Sreepuram Nadimpalle, Mopuru, Chakalapalle, Naidupalem Surayapalem, Thimmayapalem, Pedayachasamudram Nagavolu, Theerthampadu, Thimmanagunta.

The villages having more than 50% ST population are None.

Sex ratio of Scheduled tribe population is 478.

Scheduled Tribes Literates and Illiterates by Sex:

	Persons	Males	Females
Literate	1,103	645	458
Illiterate	2,660	1,318	1,342
Literacy rate	34.9	39.3	30.1
Graduate	0	0	0

Scheduled Tribes (Dominant):

Yenadis, Generic Tribes etc., Yerukulas

For their cultural identity please see Appendix-II

Villages without Scheduled Tribes: There are 16 villages without any scheduled tribe population.

Literates and Illiterates by Sex (Total Population):

	Persons	Males	Females
Literate	18,785	11,201	7,584
Illiterate	19,899	8,283	11,616
Literacy rate	56	66	45
Graduate	382	311	71

Agriculture: ***Distribution of villages according to land use:*** Out of 50 villages, Total area (in hectare) is 27712, out of that 30.32 percent is cultivable and 52.73 percent of the cultivable area is irrigated.

Sources of Irrigation (Hectares): Government Canal 0, Private Canal 0, Well without Electricity 0, Well with Electricity 814, Tubewell without Electricity 55, Tubewell with Electricity 208, Tank 3093, River 0, Lake 0, Waterfall 0, Others 260.

Villages with population of 5000 to 9999: None

Villages with population of 10000 and above: None

Distribution of Workers:

	Persons	Males	Females	WPR
Cultivators	6,465	4,562	1,903	32.35
Agricultural Labour	11,091	5,780	5,311	55.49
Household Industry	1,014	587	427	5.07
Other Workers	1,416	1,021	395	7.08
Main Workers	15,211	10,015	5,196	76.11
Marginal Workers	4,775	1,935	2,840	23.89
Total Workers	19,986	11,950	8,036	

Religion: Major Religious Communities:

	Persons	Males	Females	Sex Ratio
Hindu (98.83%)	38,233	19,254	18,979	986
Muslim (0.9%)	348	178	170	955
Christian (0.24%)	93	45	48	1,067
Sikh (0%)	-	-	-	-
Buddhists (0%)	-	-	-	-
Jain (0%)	-	-	-	-

Agewise Data:

	Persons	Males	Females	Sex Ratio
All ages	38,684	19,484	19,200	985
0-14	11,910	6,001	5,909	985
15-44	18,727	9,462	9,265	979
45-79	7,773	3,889	3,884	999
80+	221	108	113	1046
Age not stated	53	24	29	1208

Languages (Dominant):

Telugu, Urdu, Gujarati, Hindi, Gondi

Disabled Population:

	Persons	Males	Females	%
Total Disabled	965	501	464	
In Seeing	366	173	193	37.93
In Speech	111	53	58	11.5
In Hearing	104	48	56	10.78
In Movement	296	185	111	30.67
Mentally	88	42	46	9.12

DAMARAGIDDA

Damaragidda C.D. Block lies in the north-west part of Mahbubnagar district. The Block is located at a distance of 78 kms. from district headquarters (Mahbubn agar). There are 28 villages in the block with the total population of 49,221 persons. Area of the C.D. Block is 215 sq. kms. It is bounded by Doulathabad Mandal on north-east, Maddur Mandal on east, Narayanpet Mandal on south, and it has common boundary with the state of Karnataka from west and north.

Communications:

Roadways : Metalled Roads: Nearest Village- Vathugundla. Backwards Region Grants Fund: It receives Backward Region Grants.

Annual Rainfall: Average Rainfall 556 mm

Ground Water: Availability of the Ground Water in the Basin is 1231 H.A.M. and the utilization is 859 H.A. M. It belongs to Safe category. Depth to water level varies from 2 to 5 meter below the ground. Most of the wells go down in summer months. The well density in the entire block is 11 wells per sq. km. Total no. of the wells in the block are enumerated as 2291, according to the Ground Water Estimation Committee.

Natural Division : Telangana Plateau Region

Administration:

Division: Telangana. Parliamentary Constituency: 11 Mahbubnagar. District: Mahbubnagar. Mandal: Damaragidda.

Assembly Constituency: 73 Narayanpet. Gram Panchayat: 23

Border Villages- (Karnataka)- Nearest Villages- Gadpa, Vithalapur, Ulligundam, Kanukurthy, Gadimunkanpalle, Udmalgidda, Sajnapur, Damaragidda.

Villages: 28 **Inhabited:** 28 **Uninhabited:** 0

Ranking	District	State	National
Area	48	466	3929
Population	29	540	5321
Sex Ratio	8	216	1094
Child Sex Ratio	45	888	3873
Literacy Rate	60	1086	6173
Density	16	107	4335
Work Participation Rate	19	610	339

Gram Panchayats:

Annasagar, Ashanpalli, Bapanpalle, Bommanpad Damaragidda, Desaipalle, Gadappa, Gadimunkanpalle Kamsanipalle, Kandanpalle, Kankurthy, Kyatanpalle Lokurthy, Maddelbeed, Malreddipalle, Mogala Madaka Narsapur, Pidampally, Sajnapur, Udmalgidda Ulligundam, Vathugundla, Vittalapoor.

Amenities:

Education: Primary School in 28 villages, Middle school in 7 villages, Matriculation or Secondary School in 3 villages, namely Mogalamadka, Kanukurthy, Damaragidda.

Higher Secondary or Pre University Courses or Intermediate or Junior College in 0 village of the CD Block, College in 0 village, Adult Literacy Center in 27 villages.

Medical: Hospital in 0 village, Dispensary in 1 village, Health Center in 2 villages, Sub Center in 8 villages, Maternity and Child Welfare Center in 1 village, Community health workers in 0 village.

The Village having Hospital or Dispensary or Health Center is Kanukurthy.

Drinking Water: Tap water in 28 villages, Tank water in 28 villages, Well water in 28 villages, Tubewell in 28 villages and more than one source in 28 villages.

Bank: Banking facility in 2 villages, namely, Kanukurthy, Damaragidda.

Credit Society in 7 villages Agricultural Credit Society in 1 Non-Agricultural Credit Society in 6 villages.

Others: Power supply in 28 villages, Cinema hall in 0 village, sport club in 0 village, Stadium or Auditorium or Community Hall in 0 village, Post Office in 16 villages.

There are 20 villages having bus facilities.

Villages with most of facilities: Kanukurthy Damaragidda.

Villages without Amenities (Education): None..

Scheduled Castes: Out of the total population of 49221 persons, 8843 persons (17.97%) belong to Scheduled Castes.

The villages having less than 10% SC population are Suddavanda, Laxmipur, Ashanpalle, Chakalavaripalle Yelsanpalle, Bapanpalle.

The villages having more than 50% SC population are None.

Sex ratio of Scheduled Caste population is 499.

Scheduled Castes Literates and Illiterates by Sex:

	Persons	Males	Females
Literate	1,656	1,210	446
Illiterate	7,187	3,216	3,971
Literacy rate	22.5	32.9	12.1
Graduate	35	31	4

Scheduled Castes (Dominant):

Madiga, Mala, Generic Castes etc., Mala Dasari Mashti

For their cultural identity please see Appendix-I

Villages without Scheduled Castes: There are 2 villages without any scheduled caste population.

Scheduled Tribes: Out of the total population of 49221 persons, 1947 persons (3.96%) belong to Scheduled Tribes.

The villages having less than 10% ST population are Gadpa, Vithalapur, Mogalamadka, Laxmipur, Narsapur Annasagar, Ulligundam, Kanukurthy, Malreddipalle Lokurthy, Ashanpalle, Ayyawaripalle, Desaipalle Chakalavaripalle, Yelsanpalle, Kandanpalle Piddampalle, Gadimunkanpalle, Udmalgidda, Sajnapur Damaragidda, Lingareddipalle, Bapanpalle Kyatanpalle, Kamsanipalle, Bommanpad.

The villages having more than 50% ST population are None.

Sex ratio of Scheduled tribe population is 490.

Scheduled Tribes Literates and Illiterates by Sex:

	Persons	Males	Females
Literate	357	264	93
Illiterate	1,590	729	861
Literacy rate	22.4	32.6	11.9
Graduate	2	2	0

Scheduled Tribes (Dominant):

Sugalis etc., Yerukulas, Chenchu etc., Kammara Generic Tribes etc.

For their cultural identity please see Appendix-II

Villages without Scheduled Tribes: There are 11 villages without any scheduled tribe population.

Literates and Illiterates by Sex (Total Population):

	Persons	Males	Females
Literate	12,829	8,832	3,997
Illiterate	36,392	15,758	20,634
Literacy rate	31	43	19
Graduate	384	331	53

Agriculture: ***Distribution of villages according to land use:***

Out of 28 villages, Total area (in hectare) is 21501, out of that 72.55 percent is cultivable and 11.83 percent of the cultivable area is irrigated.

Sources of Irrigation (Hectares): Government Canal 0, Private Canal 0, Well without Electricity 0, Well with Electricity 563, Tubewell without Electricity 0, Tubewell with Electricity 618, Tank 664, River 0, Lake 0, Waterfall 0, Others 0.

Villages with population of 5000 to 9999: Damaragidda.

Villages with population of 10000 and above: None

Distribution of Workers:

	Persons	Males	Females	WPR
Cultivators	9,025	6,510	2,515	32.74
Agricultural Labour	14,080	4,721	9,359	51.08
Household Industry	946	512	434	3.43
Other Workers	3,511	2,487	1,024	12.74
Main Workers	17,995	11,852	6,143	65.29
Marginal Workers	9,567	2,378	7,189	34.71
Total Workers	27,562	14,230	13,332	

Religion: Major Religious Communities:

	Persons	Males	Females	Sex Ratio
Hindu (95.8%)	47,152	23,564	23,588	1,001
Muslim (4.15%)	2,042	1,008	1,034	1,026
Christian (0.01%)	4	3	1	333
Sikh (0.01%)	6	5	1	200
Buddhists (0%)	-	-	-	-
Jain (0%)	-	-	-	-

Agewise Data:

	Persons	Males	Females	Sex Ratio
All ages	49,221	24,590	24,631	1002
0-14	18,601	9,668	8,933	924
15-44	21,265	10,458	10,807	1033
45-79	9,060	4,328	4,732	1093
80+	223	98	125	1276
Age not stated	72	38	34	895

Languages (Dominant):

Telugu, Urdu, Hindi, Kannada, Marathi

Disabled Population:

	Persons	Males	Females	%
Total Disabled	670	352	318	
In Seeing	278	144	134	41.49
In Speech	76	41	35	11.34
In Hearing	26	10	16	3.88
In Movement	246	134	112	36.72
Mentally	44	23	21	6.57

DAMERACHERLA

Dameracherla C.D. Block lies in the southern part of Nalgonda district. The Block is located at a distance of 59 kms. from district headquarters (Nalgonda). There are 18 villages in the block with the total population of 61,576 persons. Area of the C.D. Block is 340.95 sq. kms. It is bounded by Thripuraram and Miryalaguda Mandals on north, Neredcherla Mandal on east, Peddavoora and Anumula Mandals on west, Neredcherla Mandal on east, and Guntur district on south.

Communications:

Roadways : Metalled Roads: Nearest Villages- Kondrapolu, Dameracherla, Vadapalle.

Railway Station: Vadapalle.

River: Krishna Nadi- Nearest Villages- Vadapalle, Chity ala, Adavi Devula Palle, Mudimanikam, Kotha Palle, Irkig udem.

Backwards Region Grants Fund: It receives Backward Region Grants.

Annual Rainfall: Average Rainfall 737 mm

Ground Water: Availability of the Ground Water in the Basin is 4992 H.A.M. and the utilization is 786 H.A. M. It belongs to Safe category. Depth to water level varies from 5 to 10 meter below the ground. Most of the wells go down in summer months. The well density in the entire block is 3 wells per sq. km. Total no. of the wells in the block are enumerated as 1093, according to the Ground Water Estimation Committee.

Natural Division : Krishna Piedmont Plain Region

Administration: Division: Telangara. Parliamentary Constituency: 13 Nalgonda. District: Nalgonda. Mandal: Dameracherla. Assembly Constituency: 88 Miryalguda. Gram Panchayat: 24.

Villages: 18 **Inhabited:** 17 **Uninhabited:** 1

Ranking	**District**	**State**	**National**
Area	3	77	2285
Population	6	258	4810
Sex Ratio	47	906	3093
Child Sex Ratio	57	1057	5060
Literacy Rate	52	888	5252
Density	25	478	5117
Work Participation Rate	46	807	1220

Gram Panchayats:

Adavi Devulapally, Balaji Nagarthanda, Balnepally Bothalapalem, Champlathanda, Chityala, Damercherla Dilavarpur, Ganeshpahad Thanda, Irkiguda, Kallepally Keshvapur, Kjr Colony, Kondrapole, Mudimanikyam Muklacherla, Nadigadda, Narsapur Thalla Veerappa Gudem, Thimmapur, Ulsaipalem Veerlapalem, Wadapally, Watchya Thanda.

Amenities:

Education: Primary School in 17 villages, Middle school in 7 villages, Matriculation or Secondary School in 5 villages, namely Adavi Devula Palle, Dilawarpur, Kondrapolu, Dameracherla, Vadapalle.

Higher Secondary or Pre University Courses or Intermediate or Junior College in 0 village of the CD Block, College in 0 village, Adult Literacy Center in 17 villages.

Medical: Hospital in 0 village, Dispensary in 1 village, Health Center in 1 village, Sub Center in 11 villages, Maternity and Child Welfare Center in 0 village, Community health workers in 0 village.

The Village having Hospital or Dispensary or Health Center is Irkigudem.

Drinking Water: Tap water in 17 villages, Tank water in 17 villages, Well water in 17 villages, Tubewell in 17 villages and more than one source in 17 villages.

Bank: Banking facility in 3 villages, namely, Adavi Devula Palle, Dameracherla, Vadapalle.

Credit Society in 8 villages Agricultural Credit Society in 5 Non-Agricultural Credit Society in 6 villages.

Others: Power supply in 17 villages, Cinema hall in 1 village, sport club in 0 village, Stadium or Auditorium or Community Hall in 0 village, Post Office in 10 villages.

There are 17 villages having bus facilities.

Villages with most of facilities: Adavi Devula Palle Dameracherla, Vadapalle.

Villages without Amenities (Education): None..

Scheduled Castes: Out of the total population of 61576 persons, 7000 persons (11.37%) belong to Scheduled Castes.

The villages having less than 10% SC population are Baleenpalle, Chityala, Ulshayapalem, Timmapur Kalle Palle, Narsapur, Veerla Palem.

The villages having more than 50% SC population are None.

Sex ratio of Scheduled Caste population is 483.

Scheduled Castes Literates and Illiterates by Sex:

	Persons	Males	Females
Literate	2,565	1,740	825
Illiterate	4,435	1,879	2,556
Literacy rate	43.6	57.3	29.0
Graduate	47	44	3

Scheduled Castes (Dominant):

Mạdiga, Mala, Bindla, Malajangam, Dakkal etc.

For their cultural identity please see Appendix-I

Villages without Scheduled Castes: There is 1 village without any scheduled caste population.

Scheduled Tribes: Out of the total population of 61576 persons, 24517 persons (39.82%) belong to Scheduled Tribes.

The villages having less than 10% ST population are None..

The villages having more than 50% ST population are Mulkacharla, Baleenpalle, Ulshayapalem, Timmapur Kalle Palle, Dilawarpur, Kesawapur, Narsapur Veerla Palem.

Sex ratio of Scheduled tribe population is 490.

Scheduled Tribes Literates and Illiterates by Sex:

	Persons	Males	Females
Literate	6,135	4,651	1,484
Illiterate	18,382	7,843	10,539
Literacy rate	30.7	46.2	15.0
Graduate	86	83	3

Scheduled Tribes (Dominant):

Sugalis etc., Yerukulas, Koya etc., Gond etc.
Konda Kapus

For their cultural identity please see Appendix-II

Villages without Scheduled Tribes: There is 1 village without any scheduled tribe population.

Literates and Illiterates by Sex (Total Population):

	Persons	Males	Females
Literate	23,177	15,445	7,732
Illiterate	38,399	16,004	22,395
Literacy rate	45	59	30
Graduate	812	648	164

Agriculture: ***Distribution of villages according to land use:*** Out of 18 villages, Total area (in hectare) is 34995, out of that 38.62 percent is cultivable and 31.82 percent of the cultivable area is irrigated.

Sources of Irrigation (Hectares): Government Canal 2884, Private Canal 0, Well without Electricity 0, Well with Electricity 94.4, Tubewell without Electricity 30, Tubewell with Electricity 841.6, Tank 250.8, River 0, Lake 0, Waterfall 0, Others 200.8.

Villages with population of 5000 to 9999:
Adavi Devula Palle, Dilawarpur, Vadapalle.

Villages with population of 10000 and above:
Dameracherla.

Distribution of Workers:

	Persons	Males	Females	WPR
Cultivators	9,596	6,030	3,566	29.95
Agricultural Labour	14,536	5,147	9,389	45.36
Household Industry	297	184	113	0.93
Other Workers	7,616	5,967	1,649	23.77
Main Workers	26,101	15,662	10,439	81.45
Marginal Workers	5,944	1,666	4,278	18.55
Total Workers	32,045	17,328	14,717	

Religion: Major Religious Communities:

	Persons	Males	Females	Sex Ratio
Hindu (95.96%)	59,089	30,194	28,895	957
Muslim (3.19%)	1,962	995	967	972
Christian (0.71%)	439	218	221	1,014
Sikh (0.01%)	9	5	4	800
Buddhists (0%)	-	-	-	-
Jain (0%)	-	-	-	-

Agewise Data:

	Persons	Males	Females	Sex Ratio
All ages	61,576	31,449	30,127	958
0-14	22,750	11,908	10,842	910
15-44	28,291	14,215	14,076	990
45-79	10,046	5,080	4,966	978
80+	436	205	231	1127
Age not stated	53	41	12	293

Languages (Dominant):
Telugu, Hindi, Urdu, Gondi, Tamil

Disabled Population:

	Persons	Males	Females	%
Total Disabled	1,428	790	638	
In Seeing	700	372	328	49.02
In Speech	132	74	58	9.24
In Hearing	63	38	25	4.41
In Movement	379	217	162	26.54
Mentally	154	89	65	10.78

DAMMAPETA

Dammapeta C.D. Block lies in the eastern part of Khammam district. The Block is located at a distance of 100 kms. from district headquarters (Khammam). There are 22 villages in the block with the total population of 53,526 persons. Area of the C.D. Block is 449.80 sq. kms. It is bounded in the north by Mandal Kukunoor, in the south by Mandal Sathupalle and district West Godavari, in the east by Mandals Kukunoor and Aswaraope ta, and in the by west Mandals Mulkalapalle, Chandrugonda and Sathupalle.

Communications:

Roadways : State Highway (S.H.): Direction- Sathupalle to Aswaraopeta. Nearest Villages- Dammapeta, Ganeshpadu, Gunnepalle, Mustibanda, Sayanaraopalem, Mandalapalle, Akinepalle.

Backwards Region Grants Fund: It receives Backward Region Grants.

Annual Rainfall: Average Rainfall 1214 mm

Ground Water: Availability of the Ground Water in the Basin is 5691 H.A.M.and the utilization is 2229 H.A. M. It belongs to safe category. Depth to water level varies from 5 to 10 meter below the ground. Most of the wells go down in summer months. The well density in the entire block is 3 wells per sq. km. Total no. of the wells in the block are enumerated as 1264, according to the Ground Water Estimation Committee.

Natural Division : Godavari Depression Region

Administration:

Division: Telangana. Parliamentary Constituency: 17 Khammam. District: Khammam. Mandal: Dammapeta. Assembl Constituency: 118 Aswaraopeta (ST). Gram Panchayat: 18

Villages: 22 **Inhabited:** 21 **Uninhabited:** 1

Ranking	District	State	National
Area	5	18	1676
Population	14	405	5113
Sex Ratio	33	837	2834
Child Sex Ratio	24	475	1790
Literacy Rate	12	461	3698
Density	36	685	5966
Work Participation Rate	35	1006	1924

Gram Panchayats:

Akinepalli, Ankampalem, Dammapeta, Gandugulapalli Ganeshpadu, Jaggaram, Jamedarbanjar, Lingalapalli Malkaram, Mandalapalli, Moddulagudem, Mondivarre Mustibanda, Nacharam, Nagupalli, Patwarigudem Peddagollagudem, Tottipampu.

Amenities:

Education: Primary School in 19 villages, Middle school in 12 villages, Matriculation or Secondary School in 7 villages, namely Ankampalem, Patwarigudem, Malkaram, Dammapeta Nagupalle, Nacharam, Mandalapalle.

Higher Secondary or Pre University Courses or Intermediate or Junior College in 2 villages of the CD Block,, namely Dammapeta, Mandalapalle.

College in 0 village, Adult Literacy Center in 9 villages.

Medical: Hospital in 0 village, Dispensary in 6 villages, Health Center in 1 village, Sub Center in 10 villages, Maternity and Child Welfare Center in 1 village, Community health workers in 0 village.

The Villages having Hospital or Dispensary or Health Center are Nagupalle, Ganeshpadu, Gunnepalle, Naidupeta, Mustibanda, Mandalapalle.

Drinking Water: Tap water in 21 villages, Tank water in 21 villages, Well water in 21 villages, Tubewell in 21 villages and more than one source in 21 villages.

Bank: Banking facility in 3 villages, namely, Patwarigudem, Dammapeta, Nagupalle.

Credit Society in 9 villages Agricultural Credit Society in 3 Non-Agricultural Credit Society in 9 villages.

Others: Power supply in 21 villages, Cinema hall in 1 village, sport club in 0 village, Stadium or Auditorium or Community Hall in 0 village, Post Office in 10 villages.

There are 18 villages having bus facilities.

Villages with most of facilities: Patwarigudem Dammapeta, Nagupalle.

Villages without amenities (Education): Mallaram, Sayanaraopalem..

Scheduled Castes: Out of the total population of 53526 persons, 6152 persons (11.49%) belong to Scheduled Castes. The villages having less than 10% SC population are Katkuru, Ankampalem, Jaggaram, Balarajugudem

Peddagollagudem, Malkaram, Dammapeta, Nagupalle Naidupeta, Mallaram, Sayanaraopalem, Akinepalle.

The villages having more than 50% SC population are None.

Sex ratio of Scheduled Caste population is 478.

Scheduled Castes Literates and Illiterates by Sex:

	Persons	Males	Females
Literate	2,637	1,618	1,019
Illiterate	3,515	1,593	1,922
Literacy rate	50.4	58.8	41.1
Graduate	68	52	16

Scheduled Castes (Dominant):

Madiga, Mala, Beda Jangam etc., Madiga Dasu etc. Chamar etc.

For their cultural identity please see Appendix-I

Villages without Scheduled Castes: There are 4 villages without any scheduled caste population.

Scheduled Tribes: Out of the total population of 53526 persons, 23893 persons (44.64%) belong to Scheduled Tribes.

The villages having less than 10% ST population are None..

The villages having more than 50% ST population are Katkuru, Ankampalem, Jaggaram, Balarajugudem Patwarigudem, Peddagollagudem, Nagupalle, Gunnepalle Mallaram, Akinepalle.

Sex ratio of Scheduled tribe population is 495.

Scheduled Tribes Literates and Illiterates by Sex:

	Persons	Males	Females
Literate	8,725	5,295	3,430
Illiterate	15,168	6,776	8,392
Literacy rate	42.6	51.3	33.8
Graduate	49	43	6

Scheduled Tribes (Dominant):

Koya etc., Gond etc., Nayaks, Sugalis etc. Kondareddis

For their cultural identity please see Appendix-II

Villages without Scheduled Tribes: There are 2 villages without any scheduled tribe population.

Literates and Illiterates by Sex (Total Population):

	Persons	Males	Females
Literate	25,336	14,890	10,446
Illiterate	28,190	12,374	15,816
Literacy rate	55	63	46
Graduate	727	592	135

Agriculture: *Distribution of villages according to land use:* Out of 22 villages, Total area (in hectare) is 44979, out of that 36.27 percent is cultivable and 43.25 percent of the cultivable area is irrigated.

Sources of Irrigation (Hectares): Government Canal 0, Private Canal 0, Well without Electricity 0, Well with Electricity 0, Tubewell without Electricity 0, Tubewell with Electricity 4654.25, Tank 2401.68, River 0, Lake 0, Waterfall 0, Others 0.

Villages with population of 5000 to 9999:

Nagupalle.

Villages with population of 10000 and above:

Dammapeta.

Distribution of Workers:

	Persons	Males	Females	WPR
Cultivators	5,694	4,526	1,168	21
Agricultural Labour	16,468	8,098	8,370	60.72
Household Industry	473	275	198	1.74
Other Workers	4,484	3,248	1,236	16.53
Main Workers	23,720	15,013	8,707	87.47
Marginal Workers	3,399	1,134	2,265	12.53
Total Workers	27,119	16,147	10,972	

Religion: Major Religious Communities:

	Persons	Males	Females	Sex Ratio
Hindu (95.99%)	51,380	26,040	25,340	973
Muslim (2.17%)	1,161	573	588	1,026
Christian (1.77%)	945	630	315	500
Sikh (0%)	1	-	1	-
Buddhists (0%)	1	1	-	-
Jain (0%)	-	-	-	-

Agewise Data:

	Persons	Males	Females	Sex Ratio
All ages	53,526	27,264	26,262	963
0-14	18,239	9,522	8,717	915
15-44	25,577	12,873	12,704	987
45-79	9,267	4,645	4,622	995
80+	347	165	182	1103
Age not stated	96	59	37	627

Languages (Dominant):

Telugu, Koya, Urdu, Hindi, Tamil

Disabled Population:

	Persons	Males	Females	%
Total Disabled	1,204	691	513	
In Seeing	629	372	257	52.24
In Speech	95	45	50	7.89
In Hearing	61	27	34	5.07
In Movement	289	189	100	24
Mentally	130	58	72	10.8

DANDEPALLE

Dandepalle C.D. Block lies in the south-west part of Adilabad district. The Block is located at a distance of 168 kms. from district headquarters (Adilabad). There are 31 villages in the block with the total population of 46,824 persons. Area of the C.D. Block is 183. 30 sq. kms. It is bounded by Tiryani Mandal on north and north-east, Kasipet Mandal on north-east, Luxettipet Mandal from east, south-east and south, Karimnagar district on south-west and west, Jannaram Mandal on north-west.

Communications :

Roadways : State Highway (S.H.): Direction- Nirmal to Luxettipet. Nearest Villages- Allipur, Nagasamudram, Tallapet, Makulpet, Lingapur, Dandepalle, Medaripet, Narsapur, Venkatapur, Mutyampet, Rebbenpalle.

River: Godavari Nadi- Nearest Villages- namely, Gurrevu, Bikkanguda, Laxmikantapur, Dwaraka, Kondapur, Kasipet, Velganoor, Nambal, Gudam.

Backwards Region Grants Fund: It receives Backward Region Grants.

Annual Rainfall: Average Rainfall 1076 mm

Ground Water: Availability of the Ground Water in the Basin is 5697 H.A.M.and the utilization is 1953 H.A. M. It belongs to Safe category. Depth to water level varies from 5 to 10 meter below the ground. Most of the wells go down in summer months, according to the Ground Water Estimation Committee.

Natural Division : Telangana Plateau Region

Administration:

Division: Telangana. Parliamentary Constituency: 2 Peddapalle (SC). District: Adilabad. Mandal: Dandepalle. Assembly Constituency: 4 Mancherial. Gram Panchayat: 21

Villages: 31 **Inhabited:** 29 **Uninhabited:** 2

Ranking	District	State	National
Area	46	593	4280
Population	7	606	5427
Sex Ratio	21	238	1161
Child Sex Ratio	15	228	713
Literacy Rate	27	809	4916
Density	21	362	4198
Work Participation Rate	2	574	895

Gram Panchayats:

Chinthapalle, Dandepalle, Dharmaraopet, Dwaraka Gudem, Gudirevu, Kannepalli, Kasipet, Korvichelma Laxmikantapur, Lingapur, Mamidipalle, Medaripet Nagasamudram, Nambal, Narsapur, Nelkivenkatapur Peddapet, Rebbenpalle, Tallapet, Velganoor.

Amenities:

Education: Primary School in 28 villages, Middle school in 13 villages, Matriculation or Secondary School in 6 villages, namely Tallapet, Dandepalle, Medaripet, Dwaraka, Narsapur, Rebbenpalle.

Higher Secondary or Pre University Courses or Intermediate or Junior College in 0 village of the CD Block, College in 0 village, Adult Literacy Center in 24 villages.

Medical: Hospital in 0 village, Dispensary in 1 village, Health Center in 2 villages, Sub Center in 12 villages, Maternity and Child Welfare Center in 13 villages, Community health workers in 0 village.

The Villages having Hospital or Dispensary or Health Center are Lingapur, Kasipet.

Drinking Water: Tap water in 29 villages, Tank water in 29 villages, Well water in 29 villages, Tubewell in 29 villages and more than one source in 29 villages.

Bank: Banking facility in 3 villages, namely, Tallapet, Dandepalle, Mutyampet.

Credit Society in 13 villages Agricultural Credit Society in 10 Non-Agricultural Credit Society in 6 villages.

Others: Power supply in 29 villages, Cinema hall in 1 village, sport club in 0 village, Stadium or Auditorium or Community Hall in 0 village, Post Office in 12 villages.

There are 17 villages having bus facilities.

Villages with most of facilities: Tallapet Dandepalle, Mutyampet.

Villages without amenities (Education): Jaidapet..

Scheduled Castes: Out of the total population of 46824 persons, 9315 persons (19.89%) belong to Scheduled Castes.

The villages having less than 10% SC population are Makulpet, Kundelapahad, Laxmikantapur, Velganoor Jaidapet, Nambal.

The villages having more than 50% SC population are None.

Sex ratio of Scheduled Caste population is 499.

Scheduled Castes Literates and Illiterates by Sex:

	Persons	Males	Females
Literate	3,067	1,958	1,109
Illiterate	6,248	2,707	3,541
Literacy rate	38.6	49.0	28.1
Graduate	45	42	3

Scheduled Castes (Dominant):

Madiga, Mala, Mala Sale etc., Generic Castes etc. Paky etc.

For their cultural identity please see Appendix-I

Villages without Scheduled Castes: There are 5 villages without any scheduled caste population.

Scheduled Tribes: Out of the total population of 46824 persons, 3730 persons (7.97%) belong to Scheduled Tribes.

The villages having less than 10% ST population are Gurrevu, Nagasamudram, Dandepalle, Medaripet Laxmikantapur, Dwaraka, Peddapet, Dharmaraopet Narsapur, Venkatapur, Chintapalle, Karvichelma Mutyampet, Rebbenpalle, Kondapur, Kasipet, Velganoor Nambal, Gudam, Kamepalle.

The villages having more than 50% ST population are None.

Sex ratio of Scheduled tribe population is 503.

Scheduled Tribes Literates and Illiterates by Sex:

	Persons	Males	Females
Literate	1,155	733	422
Illiterate	2,575	1,122	1,453
Literacy rate	37.4	47.4	27.4
Graduate	38	33	5

Scheduled Tribes (Dominant):
Gond etc., Sugalis etc., Pardhan, Yerukulas Koya etc.

For their cultural identity please see Appendix-II

Villages without Scheduled Tribes: There are 11 villages without any scheduled tribe population.

Literates and Illiterates by Sex (Total Population):

	Persons	Males	Females
Literate	18,937	12,057	6,880
Illiterate	27,887	11,357	16,530
Literacy rate	47	60	34
Graduate	413	375	38

Agriculture: ***Distribution of villages according to land use:*** Out of 31 villages, Total area (in hectare) is 19448, out of that 65.56 percent is cultivable and 51.94 percent of the cultivable area is irrigated.

Sources of Irrigation (Hectares): Government Canal 4295.29, Private Canal 20.18, Well without Electricity 465.15, Well with Electricity 1461.69, Tubewell without Electricity 0, Tubewell with Electricity 10.11, Tank 129.6, River 0, Lake 0, Waterfall 0, Others 240.07.

Villages with population of 5000 to 9999: None

Villages with population of 10000 and above: None

Distribution of Workers:

	Persons	Males	Females	WPR
Cultivators	7,946	4,813	3,133	31.36
Agricultural Labour	11,833	5,073	6,760	46.69
Household Industry	1,163	553	610	4.59
Other Workers	4,400	3,203	1,197	17.36
Main Workers	19,862	11,765	8,097	78.38
Marginal Workers	5,480	1,877	3,603	21.62
Total Workers	25,342	13,642	11,700	

Religion: Major Religious Communities:

	Persons	Males	Females	Sex Ratio
Hindu (97.49%)	45,649	22,844	22,805	998
Muslim (1.91%)	893	438	455	1,039
Christian (0.52%)	243	113	130	1,150
Sikh (0%)	-	-	-	-
Buddhists (0%)	-	-	-	-
Jain (0%)	-	-	-	-

Agewise Data:

	Persons	Males	Females	Sex Ratio
All ages	46,824	23,414	23,410	1000
0-14	15,242	7,662	7,580	989
15-44	21,999	11,060	10,939	989
45-79	9,179	4,516	4,663	1033
80+	360	153	207	1353
Age not stated	44	23	21	913

Languages (Dominant):
Telugu, Gondi, Hindi, Urdu, Marathi

Disabled Population:

	Persons	Males	Females	%
Total Disabled	612	362	250	
In Seeing	235	137	98	38.4
In Speech	79	46	33	12.91
In Hearing	27	17	10	4.41
In Movement	213	128	85	34.8
Mentally	58	34	24	9.48

DARSI

Darsi C.D. Block lies in the northern part of Prakasam district. The Block is located at a distance of 70 kms. from district headquarters (Ongole). There are 38 villages in the block with the total population of 74,862 persons. Area of the C.D. Block is 408.87 sq. kms. It is bounded in the north by Mandal Kurichedu and district Guntur, in the south by Mandal Podili and river Musi, in the east by Mandals Chimakurthi, Tallur and Mundlamuru, and district Guntur, and in the west by Mandal Donakonda.

Communications:

Roadways : State Highway (S.H.): Direction- Kurichedu to Podili. Nearest Villages- Bandellapaya, Abbaya Palem, Chandaluru, Chalivendra, Venkatachalam Palle, Darsi, Bala Puram, Rajam Palle, Ramachandra Puram, Anna Varam.

River: Musi Nadi- Nearest Villages- Bandiveligandla, Yerrobana Palle, Ganeswara Puram, East Venkata Puram, Lakshmi Narayana Puram, Kothapalle, Korlamadugu, Thrip ura Sundari Puram, Krishna Puram, Pedauyyalawada, China Uyyalawada, Ramachandra Puram, Anna Varam.

The Block is identified as a drought-prone area.

Annual Rainfall: Average Rainfall 815.5 mm

Ground Water: Availability of the Ground Water in the Basin is 34.82 MCM and the utilization is 10.78 MCM It belongs to Safe category. Depth to water level varies from 2 to 5 meter below the ground. Most of the wells go down in summer months., according to the Ground Water Estimation Committee.

Administration:

Division: Coastal Andhra. Parliamentary Constituency: 33 Ongole. District: Prakasam. Mandal: Darsi. Assembly Constituency: 222 Darsi. Gram Panchayat: 26.

Villages: 38 **Inhabited:** 32 **Uninhabited:** 6

Ranking	District	State	National
Area	3	36	1880

Population	4	70	4292
Sex Ratio	30	790	2687
Child Sex Ratio	25	701	2878
Literacy Rate	39	701	4553
Density	27	471	4989
Work Participation Rate	33	778	1190

Gram Panchayats:

Bandiveligandla, Basireddypalli, Botlapalem Chandaluru, Darsi, Devavaram, East Chavatapalem East Veerayapalem, East Venkatapuram, Jamukuladinne Korlamadugu, Kothapalli, Lankojanapalli Mareddypalli, Papireddypalem, Peda Vuyyalawada Pothakamuru, Pothavaram, Rajampalli Ramachandrapuram, Samanthapudi, T.S.Puram Tanamchintala, Tummedalapadu, Venkatachalampalli Yarraobanapalli.

Amenities:

Education: Primary School in 32 villages, Middle school in 9 villages, Matriculation or Secondary School in 5 villages, namely Chandaluru, Darsi, Rajam Palle, Potha Kamuru, Kothapalle.

Higher Secondary or Pre University Courses or Intermediate or Junior College in 1 village of the CD Block,, namely Darsi.

College in 1 village, Adult Literacy Center in 29 villages., College is in village, namely Darsi.

Medical: Hospital in 1 village, Dispensary in 2 villages, Health Center in 2 villages, Sub Center in 20 villages, Maternity and Child Welfare Center in 1 village, Community health workers in 0 village.

The Villages having Hospital or Dispensary or Health Center are Chandaluru, Darsi, Potha Kamuru.

Drinking Water: Tap water in 32 villages, Tank water in 32 villages, Well water in 32 villages, Tubewell in 32 villages and more than one source in 32 villages.

Bank: Banking facility in 1 villages, namely, Darsi.

Credit Society in 5 villages Agricultural Credit Society in 2 Non-Agricultural Credit Society in 4 villages.

Others: Power supply in 32 villages, Cinema hall in 1 village, sport club in 0 village, Stadium or Auditorium or Community Hall in 0 village, Post Office in 19 villages.

There are 29 villages having bus facilities.

Village with most of facilities: Darsi.

Villages without Amenities (Education): None..

Scheduled Castes: Out of the total population of 74862 persons, 14041 persons (18.76%) belong to Scheduled Castes.

The villages having less than 10% SC population are Thummedalapadu, Yerrobana Palle, Jamukuladinne Thripura Sundari Puram.

The villages having more than 50% SC population are None.

Sex ratio of Scheduled Caste population is 500.

Scheduled Castes Literates and Illiterates by Sex:

	Persons	Males	Females
Literate	4,515	2,998	1,517
Illiterate	9,526	4,027	5,499
Literacy rate	38.6	51.0	26.0
Graduate	169	123	46

Scheduled Castes (Dominant):

Madiga, Mala, Adi Andhra, Beda Jangam etc.

Generic Castes etc.

For their cultural identity please see Appendix-I

Villages without Scheduled Castes: There are 6 villages without any scheduled caste population.

Scheduled Tribes: Out of the total population of 74862 persons, 2635 persons (3.52%) belong to Scheduled Tribes.

The villages having less than 10% ST population are Abbaya Palem, Thummedalapadu, Chandaluru Chalivendra, Venkatachalam Palle, Thanam Chinthala Potha Varam, Devavaram, Darsi, Lankojana Palle Jammigumpala @ K.S.Palem, Bandiveligandla Yerrobana Palle, Ganeswara Puram, East Venkata Puram Ramachandra Puram, Rajam Palle, East Choutapalem East Veeraya Palem, Cheruvu Komma Palem Samanthapudi, Jamukuladinne, Anna Varam Lakshmi Narayana Puram, Kothapalle, Korlamadugu Thripura Sundari Puram, Krishna Puram Pedauyyalawada, China Uyyalawada.

The villages having more than 50% ST population are None.

Sex ratio of Scheduled tribe population is 484.

Scheduled Tribes Literates and Illiterates by Sex:

	Persons	Males	Females
Literate	834	533	301
Illiterate	1,801	826	975
Literacy rate	38.7	48.5	28.5
Graduate	13	10	3

Scheduled Tribes (Dominant):

Yenadis, Yerukulas, Sugalis etc., Chenchu etc.

For their cultural identity please see Appendix-II

Villages without Scheduled Tribes: There are 16 villages without any scheduled tribe population.

Literates and Illiterates by Sex (Total Population):

	Persons	Males	Females
Literate	31,836	20,677	11,159
Illiterate	43,026	17,411	25,615
Literacy rate	50	64	36
Graduate	1,350	1,084	266

Agriculture: *Distribution of villages according to land use:*

Out of 38 villages, Total area (in hectare) is 40887, out of that 69.84 percent is cultivable and 31.35 percent of the cultivable area is irrigated.

Sources of Irrigation (Hectares): Government Canal 8045, Private Canal 0, Well without Electricity 0, Well with Electricity 0, Tubewell without Electricity 0, Tubewell with Electricity 0, Tank 339, River 0, Lake 0, Waterfall 0, Others 566.84.

Villages with population of 5000 to 9999:
Potha Kamuru.

Villages with population of 10000 and above:
Darsi.

Distribution of Workers:

	Persons	Males	Females	WPR
Cultivators	12,096	7,350	4,746	30.57
Agricultural Labour	17,355	7,752	9,603	43.87
Household Industry	1,050	419	631	2.65
Other Workers	9,063	6,759	2,304	22.91
Main Workers	34,494	20,475	14,019	87.19
Marginal Workers	5,070	1,805	3,265	12.81
Total Workers	39,564	22,280	17,284	

Religion: Major Religious Communities:

	Persons	Males	Females	Sex Ratio
Hindu (94.56%)	70,786	36,011	34,775	966
Muslim (3.72%)	2,785	1,436	1,349	939
Christian (1.61%)	1,208	593	615	1,037
Sikh (0.01%)	4	3	1	333
Buddhists (0%)	1	1	-	-
Jain (0%)	-	-	-	-

Agewise Data:

	Persons	Males	Females	Sex Ratio
All ages	74,862	38,088	36,774	966
0-14	25,837	13,140	12,697	966
15-44	35,385	18,043	17,342	961
45-79	13,069	6,642	6,427	968
80+	412	179	233	1302
Age not stated	159	84	75	893

Languages (Dominant):
Telugu, Urdu, Tamil, Hindi, Gondi

Disabled Population:

	Persons	Males	Females	%
Total Disabled	1,168	676	492	
In Seeing	435	240	195	37.24
In Speech	127	65	62	10.87
In Hearing	56	32	24	4.79
In Movement	403	257	146	34.5
Mentally	147	82	65	12.59

DATTIRAJERU

Dattirajeru C.D. Block lies in the southern part of Vizianagaram district. The Block is located at a distan ce of 79 kms. from district headquarters (Vizianagaram). There are 46 villages in the block with the total population of 54,786 persons. Area of the C.D. Block is 166.86 sq. kms. It is bounded in the north by Mandal Badangi, in the south by Mandals Mentada and Gajapathin agaram, in the east by Mandal Merakammudidam, and in the west by Mandals Mentada and Ramabhadrapura.

Communications :

Roadways : NH- 43: Direction- Salur to Vizianagaram. Nearest Villages- S. Burjavalasa, Marrivalasa, V. Krishnapuram, Komatipalle, Tadendoravalasa, Korapa Kothavalasa, Maradam, Pedamanapuram.

Railway Station: Maradam, Komatipalle.

Backwards Region Grants Fund: It receives Backward Region Grants.

Mahila Samakhya (Education for Women's Equality) : It is decleared Socialy and Educationally Backward Block by the Government.

Annaul Rainfall: Average Rainfall 886.7 mm

Ground Water: Availability of the Ground Water in the Basin is (Information not avavible) H.A.M .and the utilization is (Information not avavible) H.A.M. It belongs to (Information not avavible) category. Depth to water level varies from 3 to 10 meter below the ground. Most of the wells go down in summer months.

Administration:

Division: Coastal Andhra. Parliamentary Constituency: 20 Vizianagram. District: Vizianagram. Mandal: Dattiraj eru. Assembly Constituency: 135 Gajapathinagaram. Gram Panchayat: 35.

Villages: 46 **Inhabited:** 44 **Uninhabited:** 2

Ranking	District	State	National
Area	10	730	4761
Population	13	377	5060
Sex Ratio	9	110	697
Child Sex Ratio	1	31	85
Literacy Rate	28	1004	5700
Density	21	261	3287
Work Participation Rate	26	311	670

Gram Panchayats:

Bhoopalarajapuram, Chinachamalapalli, Chinakada Chowdantivalasa, Chukkapeta, Dasupeta, Datti Datti Rajeru, Gadasam, Gobhyam, Gutchimi Ingilapalli, K.Kothavalasa, K.Krishnapuram, Kannam Komatipalli, M.Lingalavalasa, Maradam P.Lingalavalasa, Patchalavalasa, Pedakada Pedamanapuram, Porali, Ramachandrapuram S.Boorjavalasa, S.Chintalavalasa, Saraivalasa Shikaruganji, T.Boorjavalasa, Tadendoravalasa V.Krishnapuram, Vangara, Vindhyavasi, Viziarampuram

Viziarampuram@Dasaripeta.

Amenities:

Education: Primary School in 42 villages, Middle school in 10 villages, Matriculation or Secondary School in 4 villages, namely Maradam, Datti, Datti Rajeru, Pedamanapuram. Higher Secondary or Pre University Courses or Intermediate or Junior College in 0 village of the CD Block, College in 0 village, Adult Literacy Center in 25 villages.

Medical: Hospital in 0 village, Dispensary in 0 village, Health Center in 2 villages, Sub Center in 15 villages, Maternity and Child Welfare Center in 0 village, Community health workers in 0 village.

Drinking Water: Tap water in 44 villages, Tank water in 44 villages, Well water in 44 villages, Tubewell in 44 villages and more than one source in 44 villages.

Bank: Banking facility in 2 villages, namely, Pedamanapuram, Porali.

Credit Society in 10 villages Agricultural Credit Society in 5 Non-Agricultural Credit Society in 5 villages.

Others: Power supply in 44 villages, Cinema hall in 2 villages, sport club in 0 village, Stadium or Auditorium or Community Hall in 0 village, Post Office in 25 villages.

There are 25 villages having bus facilities.

Villages with most of facilities: Pedamanapuram Porali.

Villages without amenities (Education):
Lakshmipuram, Viziarama Gajapathi Rajapuram..

Scheduled Castes: Out of the total population of 54786 persons, 6006 persons (10.96%) belong to Scheduled Castes.

The villages having less than 10% SC population are Korapakrishna Puram, Shikaruganji, Lingarajapuram S. Burjavalasa, Korapa Kothavalasa, Cherakupalle S.Chintalavalasa, Pachalavalasa, Bhojarajupuram Datti, Datti Venkatapuram, Timiteru Burjavalasa Timiteru, Bhupalarajapuram, Ingilapalle China Chamalapalle, Gadabavalasa, Lakshmipuram Viziaramapuram, Porali, Sarayyavalasa, Gadasam Dasupeta, Viziarama Gajapathi Rajapuram M.Lingalavalasa.

The villages having more than 50% SC population are None.

Sex ratio of Scheduled Caste population is 514.

Scheduled Castes Literates and Illiterates by Sex:

	Persons	Males	Females
Literate	1,946	1,224	722
Illiterate	4,060	1,695	2,365
Literacy rate	37.6	48.1	27.5
Graduate	36	31	5

Scheduled Castes (Dominant):
Mala, Madiga, Relli, Generic Castes etc.

For their cultural identity please see Appendix-I

Villages without Scheduled Castes: There are 11 villages without any scheduled caste population.

Scheduled Tribes: Out of the total population of 54786 persons, 762 persons (1.39%) belong to Scheduled Tribes.

The villages having less than 10% ST population are Chowdantivalasa, Korapakrishna Puram Pappala Lingalavalasa, Shikaruganji, Lingarajapuram Neelakanta Rajapuram, Korapa, Korapa Kothavalasa Cherakupalle, S.Chintalavalasa, Pachalavalasa Marrivalasa, Maradam, Bhojarajupuram, Datti Timiteru Burjavalasa, Timiteru, Bhupalarajapuram Datti Rajeru, Gutchimi, Vindhyavasi, V. Krishnapuram Komatipalle, Tadendoravalasa, China Chamalapalle Gadabavalasa, Viziaramapuram, Pedamanapuram, Vangara Gobhyam, Balabhadra Rajapuram, Porali, Sarayyavalasa Gadasam, Dasupeta, Kannam, Pedakada, Chinakada Viziarama Gajapathi Rajapuram, M.Lingalavalasa.

The villages having more than 50% ST population are None.

Sex ratio of Scheduled tribe population is 479.

Scheduled Tribes Literates and Illiterates by Sex:

	Persons	Males	Females
Literate	238	161	77
Illiterate	524	236	288
Literacy rate	35.7	46.4	24.1
Graduate	0	0	0

Scheduled Tribes (Dominant):
Konda Dhoras, Yerukulas, Manna Dhora Mukha Dhora etc., Gadabas

For their cultural identity please see Appendix-II

Villages without Scheduled Tribes: There are 22 villages without any scheduled tribe population.

Literates and Illiterates by Sex (Total Population):

	Persons	Males	Females
Literate	19,028	12,398	6,630
Illiterate	35,758	14,756	21,002
Literacy rate	40	53	28
Graduate	577	502	75

Agriculture: ***Distribution of villages according to land use:*** Out of 46 villages, Total area (in hectare) is 16685, out of that 69.17 percent is cultivable and 37.48 percent of the cultivable area is irrigated.

Sources of Irrigation (Hectares): Government Canal 0, Private Canal 0, Well without Electricity 0, Well with Electricity 0, Tubewell without Electricity 0, Tubewell with Electricity 0, Tank 4325.57, River 0, Lake 0, Waterfall 0, Others 0.

Villages with population of 5000 to 9999: None

Villages with population of 10000 and above: None

Distribution of Workers:

	Persons	Males	Females	WPR
Cultivators	12,641	7,444	5,197	41.3
Agricultural Labour	12,952	5,487	7,465	42.32
Household Industry	1,042	692	350	3.4
Other Workers	3,971	3,016	955	12.97
Main Workers	25,982	15,008	10,974	84.89
Marginal Workers	4,624	1,631	2,993	15.11
Total Workers	30,606	16,639	13,967	

Religion: Major Religious Communities:

	Persons	Males	Females	Sex Ratio
Hindu (99.4%)	54,460	26,999	27,461	1,017
Muslim (0.25%)	138	64	74	1,156
Christian (0.29%)	159	77	82	1,065
Sikh (0%)	-	-	-	-
Buddhists (0%)	-	-	-	-
Jain (0%)	-	-	-	-

Agewise Data:

	Persons	Males	Females	Sex Ratio
All ages	54,786	27,154	27,632	1018
0-14	16,891	8,616	8,275	960
15-44	25,559	12,624	12,935	1025
45-79	12,033	5,792	6,241	1078
80+	222	85	137	1612
Age not stated	81	37	44	1189

Languages (Dominant):

Telugu, Oriya, Urdu, Gondi, Hindi

Disabled Population:

	Persons	Males	Females	%
Total Disabled	1,255	693	562	
In Seeing	550	280	270	43.82
In Speech	139	81	58	11.08
In Hearing	91	48	43	7.25
In Movement	336	212	124	26.77
Mentally	139	72	67	11.08

DENDULURU

Denduluru C.D. Block lies in the south-western part of West Godavari district. The Block is located at a distance of 18 kms. from district headquarters (Eluru). There are 26 villages in the block with the total population of 65,768 persons. Area of the C.D. Block is 180.62 sq. kms. It is bounded in the north by Mandals Pedavegi and Dwaraka Tirumala, and in the south by Mandal Eluru, in the east by Mandals Bhimadole and Dwaraka Tirumala, and in the west by Mandals Eluru and Pedavegi.

Communications :

Roadways : NH-5: Direction- Eluru to Tadepallegudem. Nearest Villages- Komirepalle, Kovvali, Pothunuru, Denduluru. State Highway (S.H.): Direction- Eluru to Jangareddigudem. Nearest Villages- Gudigunta, Akkireddigudem, Naguladevunipadu, Galayagudem, Gopannapalem, Kothapalle, Challapalle, Somavarappadu, Vegavaram.

Railway Station: Kothagudem, Denduluru.

Backwards Region Grants Fund: It receives Backward Region Grants.

Annaul Rainfall: Average Rainfall 1005 mm

Ground Water: Availability of the Ground Water in the Basin is (Information not avavible) H.A.M .and the utilization is (Information not avavible) H.A.M. It belongs to (Information not avavible) category. Depth to water level varies from 3 to 10 meter below the ground. Most of the wells go down in summer months.

Natural Division : Godavari Delta Region

Administration:

Division: Coastal Andhra. Parliamentary Constituency: 27 Eluru. District: West Godavari. Mandal: Denduluru. Assembly Constituency: 183 Denduluru. Gram Panchayat: 17

Villages: 26 **Inhabited:** 26 **Uninhabited:** 0

Ranking	**District**	**State**	**National**
Area	17	669	4529
Population	29	198	4653
Sex Ratio	21	439	1703
Child Sex Ratio	36	807	3521
Literacy Rate	31	108	1549
Density	4	668	2995
Work Participation Rate	33	247	1851

Gram Panchayats:

Chalachintalapudi, Denduluru, Dosapadu, Galayagduem Gangannagudem, Gopannapalem, Joggannapalem Kothagudem, Kovvali, Medinaravupalem, Muppavaram Perugudem, Potunuru, Ramaraogudem, Sanigudem Somavarappadu, Sriramavaram.

Amenities:

Education: Primary School in 25 villages, Middle school in 12 villages, Matriculation or Secondary School in 5 villages, namely Gopannapalem, Challapalle, Denduluru, Kovvali, Pothunuru.

Higher Secondary or Pre University Courses or Intermediate or Junior College in 0 village of the CD Block, College in 0 village, Adult Literacy Center in 13 villages.

Medical: Hospital in 0 village, Dispensary in 4 villages, Health Center in 2 villages, Sub Center in 10 villages, Maternity and Child Welfare Center in 0 village, Community health workers in 0 village.

The Villages having Hospital or Dispensary or Health Center are Challachintalapudi, Denduluru, Kovvali, Pothunuru.

Drinking Water: Tap water in 26 villages, Tank water in

26 villages, Well water in 26 villages, Tubewell in 26 villages and more than one source in 26 villages.

Bank: Banking facility in 3 villages, namely, Gopannapalem, Denduluru, Kovvali.

Credit Society in 8 villages Agricultural Credit Society in 7 Non-Agricultural Credit Society in 1 village.

Others: Power supply in 26 villages, Cinema hall in 0 village, sport club in 0 village, Stadium or Auditorium or Community Hall in 0 village, Post Office in 12 villages.

There are 18 villages having bus facilities.

Villages with most of facilities: Gopannapalem Denduluru, Kovvali.

Villages without amenities (Education):
Kothagudem..

Scheduled Castes: Out of the total population of 65768 persons, 15661 persons (23.81%) belong to Scheduled Castes.

The villages having less than 10% SC population are Challachintalapudi, Thimmannagudem, Singavaram Saanigudem.

The villages having more than 50% SC population are Ramaraogudem, Narasimhapuram, Muppavaram Komirepalle, Challapalle.

Sex ratio of Scheduled Caste population is 491.

Scheduled Castes Literates and Illiterates by Sex:

	Persons	Males	Females
Literate	8,490	4,703	3,787
Illiterate	7,171	3,272	3,899
Literacy rate	63.5	69.2	57.6
Graduate	207	148	59

Scheduled Castes (Dominant):

Mala, Madiga, Adi Andhra, Beda Jangam etc.
Adi Dravida

For their cultural identity please see Appendix-I

Villages without Scheduled Castes: There is
1 village without any scheduled caste population.

Scheduled Tribes: Out of the total population of 65768 persons, 579 persons (0.88%) belong to Scheduled Tribes.

The villages having less than 10% ST population are Medinaraopalem, Challachintalapudi, Ramaraogudem Malakacherla, Thimmannagudem, Narasimhapuram Muppavaram, Komirepalle, Kothagudem, Sriramavaram Gudigunta, Akkireddigudem, Naguladevunipadu Saanigudem, Galayagudem, Gopannapalem, Kothapalle Challapalle, Somavarappadu, Vegavaram, Uppugudem Denduluru, Kovvali, Dosapadu, Pothunuru.

The villages having more than 50% ST population are None.

Sex ratio of Scheduled tribe population is 516.

Scheduled Tribes Literates and Illiterates by Sex:

	Persons	Males	Females
Literate	184	92	92
Illiterate	395	188	207
Literacy rate	38.6	41.3	36.2
Graduate	5	4	1

Scheduled Tribes (Dominant):

Yenadis, Yerukulas, Sugalis etc., Chenchu etc.
Konda Dhoras

For their cultural identity please see Appendix-II

Villages without Scheduled Tribes: There are
12 villages without any scheduled tribe population.

Literates and Illiterates by Sex (Total Population):

	Persons	Males	Females
Literate	38,768	20,959	17,809
Illiterate	27,000	12,139	14,861
Literacy rate	67	73	62
Graduate	1,194	861	333

Agriculture: ***Distribution of villages according to land use:***
Out of 26 villages, Total area (in hectare) is 18062, out of that 77.91 percent is cultivable and 98.6 percent of the cultivable area is irrigated.

Sources of Irrigation (Hectares): Government Canal 4614.76, Private Canal 190.54, Well without Electricity 760.81, Well wit[h] Electricity 0, Tubewell without Electricity 0, Tubewell with Electricity 5406.41, Tank 2295.38, River 184.16, Lake 0, Waterfall 0, Others 422.52.

Villages with population of 5000 to 9999:
Kovvali, Pothunuru.

Villages with population of 10000 and above:
Denduluru.

Distribution of Workers:

	Persons	Males	Females	WPR
Cultivators	5,016	4,477	539	14.76
Agricultural Labour	23,853	12,339	11,514	70.2
Household Industry	539	338	201	1.59
Other Workers	4,572	3,684	888	13.45
Main Workers	29,689	19,576	10,113	87.37
Marginal Workers	4,291	1,262	3,029	12.63
Total Workers	33,980	20,838	13,142	

Religion: Major Religious Communities:

	Persons	Males	Females	Sex Ratio
Hindu (92.18%)	60,622	30,563	30,059	984
Muslim (1.17%)	769	392	377	962
Christian (6.29%)	4,137	2,025	2,112	1,043
Sikh (0%)	1	-	1	-
Buddhists (0.01%)	4	2	2	1,000
Jain (0%)	-	-	-	-

Agewise Data:

	Persons	Males	Females	Sex Ratio
All ages	65,768	33,098	32,670	987
0-14	20,048	10,097	9,951	986

15-44	32,061	16,233	15,828	975
45-79	13,097	6,496	6,601	1016
80+	458	241	217	900
Age not stated	104	31	73	2355

Languages (Dominant):

Telugu, Urdu, Hindi, Gondi, Tamil

Disabled Population:

	Persons	Males	Females	%
Total Disabled	1,002	571	431	
In Seeing	245	145	100	24.45
In Speech	140	67	73	13.97
In Hearing	66	36	30	6.59
In Movement	406	250	156	40.52
Mentally	145	73	72	14.47

DENKADA

Denkada C.D. Block lies in the southern part of Viziana garam district. It is a part of Denkada Mandal. The Block is located at a distance of 5 kms. from district headquarters (Vizianagaram). There are 27 villages in the block with the total population of 46,409 persons. Area of the C.D. Block is 123.34 sq. kms. It is bound ed in the north by Mandals Vizianagaram (part) and Nelli merla, in the south by district Vishakhapatnam and Mandal Bhogapuram, in the east by Mandals Pusapathirega and Bhogapuram, and in the west by district Vishakhapatnam and Mandal Vizianagaram.

Communications :

Roadways : NH- 5: Direction- Bhogapuram to Srikakulam. Nearest Villages- Singavaram, Nathavalasa. NH- 43: Direction- Gajapathinagaram to Vishakhapatnam. Nearest Villages-Boddavalasa, Jonnada, Modavalasa, Singavaram, Nathavalasa. State Highway (S.H.): Direction- Vizianag aram to Singavaram. Nearest Villages- Pedatadivada, Gunupuru, Singavaram, Nathavalasa.

Railway Station: Nathavalasa, Denkada, Gantlam.

River: Nellimarla Nadi- Nearest Villages- Singavaram, Nathavalasa, Devunikollam, Munginapalle, Chollangipeta, Denkada, Gunupuru.

Annaul Rainfall: Average Rainfall 886.7 mm

Ground Water: Availability of the Ground Water in the Basin is (Information not avavible) H.A.M .and the utilization is (Information not avavible) H.A.M. It belongs to (Information not avavible) category. Depth to water level varies from 3 to 10 meter below the ground. Most of the wells go down in summer months.

Natural Division : Northern Andhra Coastal Plain Region.

Administration:

Division: Coastal Andhra. Parliamentary Constituency: 20 Vizianagram. District: Vizianagram. Mandal: Denkada. Assembly Constituency: 136 Nellimarla. Gram Panchayat: 26

Villages: 27 **Inhabited:** 27 **Uninhabited:** 0

Ranking	District	State	National
Area	28	932	5421
Population	32	617	5443
Sex Ratio	24	293	1290
Child Sex Ratio	12	147	378
Literacy Rate	19	880	5198
Density	4	20	2902
Work Participation Rate	15	220	130

Gram Panchayats:

Akkivaram, Akulapeta, Amakam, Bangarrajupeta Bantupalli, Boddavalasa, Chintalavalasa Chollangipeta Palem, D.Kollam, D.Tallavalasa Denkada, Gantlam, Golagam, Gunupuru, Gunupurupeta Jonnada, Kondarajupeta, Modavalasa, Mopada Natavalasa, Pedada, Pedatadivada, Pinatadivada Raghumanda, Singavaram, Vedullavalasa.

Amenities:

Education: Primary School in 27 villages, Middle school in 7 villages, Matriculation or Secondary School in 5 villages, namely Raghumanda, Pedatadivada, Denkada, Jonnada, Mopada.

Higher Secondary or Pre University Courses or Inter-mediate or Junior College in 0 village of the CD Block, College in 0 village, Adult Literacy Center in 20 villages.

Medical: Hospital in 0 village, Dispensary in 2 villages, Health Center in 2 villages, Sub Center in 10 villages, Maternity and Child Welfare Center in 0 village, Community health workers in 0 village.

The Villages having Hospital or Dispensary or Health Center are Pedatadivada, Boddavalasa.

Drinking Water: Tap water in 27 villages, Tank water in 27 villages, Well water in 27 villages, Tubewell in 27 villages and more than one source in 27 villages.

Bank: Banking facility in 1 villages, namely, Denkada.

Credit Society in 10 villages Agricultural Credit Society in 2 Non-Agricultural Credit Society in 8 villages.

Others: Power supply in 27 villages, Cinema hall in 1 village, sport club in 0 village, Stadium or Auditorium or Community Hall in 0 village, Post Office in 15 villages.

There are 15 villages having bus facilities.

Village with most of facilities: Denkada.

Villages without Amenities (Education): None..

Scheduled Castes: Out of the total population of 46486 persons, 4805 persons (10.34%) belong to Scheduled Castes. The villages having less than 10% SC population are Devunikollam, Nathavalasa, Pinatadivada Vedullavalasa, Amakam, Chittigunkalam, Boddavalasa Jonnada, Modavalasa, Bangarrajupeta, Mopada

D.Tallavalasa, Bellam, Akkivaram.

The villages having more than 50% SC population are None.

Sex ratio of Scheduled Caste population is 503.

Scheduled Castes Literates and Illiterates by Sex:

	Persons	Males	Females
Literate	1,986	1,180	806
Illiterate	2,819	1,208	1,611
Literacy rate	47.7	57.7	38.1
Graduate	27	20	7

Scheduled Castes (Dominant):

Mala, Madiga, Relli, Adi Andhra, Generic Castes etc.

For their cultural identity please see Appendix-I

Villages without Scheduled Castes: There are 0 village without any scheduled caste population.

Scheduled Tribes: Out of the total population of 46486 persons, 92 persons (0.2%) belong to Scheduled Tribes. The villages having less than 10% ST population are Raghumanda, Pedatadivada, Gunupuru, Devunikollam Munginapalle, Chollangipeta, Dwarapureddi Palem Singavaram, Nathavalasa, Denkada, Pinatadivada Vedullavalasa, Amakam, Chittigunkalam, Boddavalasa Jonnada, Modavalasa, Bangarrajupeta, Mopada, Golagam Gantlam, D.Tallavalasa, Bellam, Rajula Tammapuram Pedada, Bantupalle, Akkivaram.

The villages having more than 50% ST population are None.

Sex ratio of Scheduled tribe population is 500.

Scheduled Tribes Literates and Illiterates by Sex:

	Persons	Males	Females
Literate	30	22	8
Illiterate	62	24	38
Literacy rate	42.9	57.9	25.0
Graduate	0	0	0

Scheduled Tribes (Dominant):

Yerukulas, Savaras etc., Jatapus, Konda Dhoras

For their cultural identity please see Appendix-II

Villages without Scheduled Tribes: There are 19 villages without any scheduled tribe population.

Literates and Illiterates by Sex (Total Population):

	Persons	Males	Females
Literate	18,152	11,034	7,118
Illiterate	28,334	12,261	16,073
Literacy rate	45	55	35
Graduate	531	441	90

Agriculture: ***Distribution of villages according to land use:*** Out of 27 villages, Total area (in hectare) is 12335, out of that 71.25 percent is cultivable and 42.85 percent of the cultivable area is irrigated.

Sources of Irrigation (Hectares): Government Canal 1496.51, Private Canal 0, Well without Electricity 18.61, Well with Electricity 16.18, Tubewell without Electricity 3.64, Tubewell with Electricity 19.82, Tank 2061.88, River 0, Lake 0, Waterfall 0, Others 148.93.

Villages with population of 5000 to 9999: None

Villages with population of 10000 and above: None

Distribution of Workers:

	Persons	Males	Females	WPR
Cultivators	6,183	3,932	2,251	21.86
Agricultural Labour	12,919	4,599	8,320	45.68
Household Industry	919	508	411	3.25
Other Workers	8,258	6,329	1,929	29.2
Main Workers	20,254	13,455	6,799	71.62
Marginal Workers	8,025	1,913	6,112	28.38
Total Workers	28,279	15,368	12,911	

Religion: Major Religious Communities:

	Persons	Males	Females	Sex Ratio
Hindu (99.28%)	46,151	23,129	23,022	995
Muslim (0.33%)	154	74	80	1,081
Christian (0.29%)	134	67	67	1,000
Sikh (0%)	1	1	-	-
Buddhists (0%)	2	2	-	-
Jain (0%)	-	-	-	-

Agewise Data:

	Persons	Males	Females	Sex Ratio
All ages	46,486	23,295	23,191	996
0-14	14,893	7,498	7,395	986
15-44	21,817	11,076	10,741	970
45-79	9,527	4,593	4,934	1074
80+	179	87	92	1057
Age not stated	70	41	29	707

Languages (Dominant):

Telugu, Oriya, Urdu, Tamil, Gondi

Disabled Population:

	Persons	Males	Females	%
Total Disabled	1,388	710	678	
In Seeing	702	326	376	50.58
In Speech	121	67	54	8.72
In Hearing	69	28	41	4.97
In Movement	365	222	143	26.3
Mentally	131	67	64	9.44

DEVANAKONDA

Devanakonda C.D. Block lies in the western part of Kurnool district. The Block is located at a distance of 62 kms. from district headquarters (Kurnool). There are 15 villages in the block with the total population of 61,923 persons. Area of the C.D. Block is 479.56 sq. kms. It is bounded in the north by Gonegandla, in the south by Mandals Pattikonda and Tuggali, in the east by Mandals Gonegandla, Krishnagiri and Tuggali, and in the west by Mandals Gonegandla, Yemmiganur, Aspari and Pattikonda.

Communications:

Roadways : State Highway (S.H.): Direction- Alur to Kurnool. Nearest Villages- Kappatralla, Machapuram, Karivemula, Kunkanur, Velamakuru.

River: Handri Nadi- Nearest Villages- Potlapadu, Terne kal, Palakurthy, Kunkanur. Nalla Vagu: Nearest Villages- Velamakuru.

It is identified as a drought-prone area.

Annual Rainfall: Average Rainfall 612 mm

Ground Water: Availability of the Ground Water in the Basin is 3253 H.A.M. and the utilization is 1521 H. A.M. It belongs to Safe category. Depth to water level varies from 2 to 10 meter below the ground. Most of the wells go down in summer months. The well density in the entire block is 3 wells per sq. km. Total no. of the wells in the block are enumerated as 1383, according to the Ground Water Estimation Committee.

Forest and Reserved **Forest:** Nearest Villages- Kappatral la, S.Thimmapuram, Chellelichelimala, Jilledubudakala, Devanakonda, Nallachelimal, Gundlakonda.

Natural Division : Rayalaseema Region

Administration:

Division: Rayala Seema. Parliamentary Constituency: 35 Kurnool. District: Kurnool. Mandal: Devanakonda. Assembly Constituency: 266 Alur. Gram Panchayat: 20.

Villages: 15 **Inhabited:** 14 **Uninhabited:** 1

Ranking	District	State	National
Area	2	11	1575
Population	13	247	4793
Sex Ratio	23	810	2718
Child Sex Ratio	13	341	1214
Literacy Rate	43	994	5665
Density	5	12	5848
Work Participation Rate	47	973	101

Gram Panchayats:

Alarudinne, Chellelichelimala, Devanakonda Gundlakonda, Iranbanda, Jilledubudakala K.Venkatapuram, Kappatralla, Karivemula, Kunkanur Machapuram, Nallachelimala, Nelathalamarri Nellibanda, P.Kotakonda, Palakurthy, Palledoddi Potlapadu, Ternekal, Velamakuru.

Amenities:

Education: Primary School in 14 villages, Middle school in 8 villages, Matriculation or Secondary School in 3 villages, namely Ternekal, P.Kotakonda, Devanakonda.

Higher Secondary or Pre University Courses or Intermediate or Junior College in 0 village of the CD Block, College in 0 village, Adult Literacy Center in 14 villages.

Medical: Hospital in 0 village, Dispensary in 0 village, Health Center in 1 village, Sub Center in 7 villages, Maternity and Child Welfare Center in 0 village, Community health workers in 0 village.

Drinking Water: Tap water in 14 villages, Tank water in 14 villages, Well water in 14 villages, Tubewell in 14 villages and more than one source in 14 villages.

Bank: Banking facility in 2 villages, namely, Ternekal, Devanakonda.

Credit Society in 11 villages Agricultural Credit Society in 4 Non-Agricultural Credit Society in 10 villages.

Others: Power supply in 14 villages, Cinema hall in 1 village, sport club in 0 village, Stadium or Auditorium or Community Hall in 0 village, Post Office in 13 villages.

There are 11 villages having bus facilities.

Villages with most of facilities: Ternekal Devanakonda.

Villages without Amenities (Education): None..

Scheduled Castes: Out of the total population of 61923 persons, 10726 persons (17.32%) belong to Scheduled Castes.

The villages having less than 10% SC population are None..

The villages having more than 50% SC population are None.

Sex ratio of Scheduled Caste population is 491.

Scheduled Castes Literates and Illiterates by Sex:

	Persons	Males	Females
Literate	3,312	2,353	959
Illiterate	7,414	3,103	4,311
Literacy rate	38.3	53.1	22.8
Graduate	83	66	17

Scheduled Castes (Dominant):

Madiga, Mala, Mala Dasari, Madiga Dasu etc.

For their cultural identity please see Appendix-I

Villages without Scheduled Castes: There is 1 village without any scheduled caste population.

Scheduled Tribes: Out of the total population of 61923 persons, 647 persons (1.04%) belong to Scheduled Tribes.

The villages having less than 10% ST population are Potlapadu, Ternekal, Palakurthy, Kappatralla Machapuram, P.Kotakonda, Chellelichelimala Jilledubudakala, Karivemula, Kunkanur, Devanakonda Velamakuru, Nallachelimal, Gundlakonda.

The villages having more than 50% ST population are None.

Sex ratio of Scheduled tribe population is 464.

Scheduled Tribes Literates and Illiterates by Sex:

	Persons	Males	Females
Literate	201	148	53
Illiterate	446	199	247

Literacy rate	38.0	53.4	21.0
Graduate	8	6	2

Scheduled Tribes (Dominant):

Yerukulas, Sugalis etc., Koya etc., Kotia etc.

Kammara

For their cultural identity please see Appendix-II

Villages without Scheduled Tribes: There are 3 villages without any scheduled tribe population.

Literates and Illiterates by Sex (Total Population):

	Persons	Males	Females
Literate	20,574	14,317	6,257
Illiterate	41,349	17,188	24,161
Literacy rate	41	56	25
Graduate	522	439	83

Agriculture: ***Distribution of villages according to land use:*** Out of 15 villages, Total area (in hectare) is 47956, out of that 75.63 percent is cultivable and 6.47 percent of the cultivable area is irrigated.

Sources of Irrigation (Hectares): Government Canal 67.21, Private Canal 0, Well without Electricity 72.87, Well with Electricity 985, Tubewell without Electricity 0, Tubewell with Electricity 1046.12, Tank 174.09, River 0, Lake 0, Waterfall 0, Others 0.

Villages with population of 5000 to 9999: Ternekal, P.Kotakonda, Devanakonda, Gundlakonda.

Villages with population of 10000 and above: None

Distribution of Workers:

	Persons	Males	Females	WPR
Cultivators	13,962	8,456	5,506	38.69
Agricultural Labour	18,415	7,368	11,047	51.03
Household Industry	551	276	275	1.53
Other Workers	3,162	2,171	991	8.76
Main Workers	31,281	16,714	14,567	86.67
Marginal Workers	4,809	1,557	3,252	13.33
Total Workers	36,090	18,271	17,819	

Religion: Major Religious Communities:

	Persons	Males	Females	Sex Ratio
Hindu (91.65%)	56,752	28,863	27,889	966
Muslim (7.75%)	4,802	2,454	2,348	957
Christian (0.49%)	303	150	153	1,020
Sikh (0.01%)	5	3	2	667
Buddhists (0%)	-	-	-	-
Jain (0%)	-	-	-	-

Agewise Data:

	Persons	Males	Females	Sex Ratio
All ages	61,923	31,505	30,418	965
0-14	26,451	13,675	12,776	934
15-44	26,144	13,397	12,747	951
45-79	8,981	4,274	4,707	1101
80+	317	141	176	1248
Age not stated	30	18	12	667

Languages (Dominant):

Telugu, Urdu, Tamil, Kannada, Hindi

Disabled Population:

	Persons	Males	Females	%
Total Disabled	1,749	946	803	
In Seeing	895	433	462	51.17
In Speech	112	64	48	6.4
In Hearing	146	71	75	8.35
In Movement	455	301	154	26.01
Mentally	141	77	64	8.06

DEVARAKONDA

Devarakonda C.D. Block lies in the south west part of Nalgonda district. It is a part of Devarakonda Mandal. The Block is located at a distance of 63 kms. from district headquarters (Nalgonda). There are 28 villages in the block with the total population of 59,145 persons. Area of the C.D. Block is 322.59 sq. kms. It is bound ed by Chunthapalle and Nampalle Mandals on north, Gurram podem Mandal on north-east, Pedda Adiserlapalli Mandal on east, Chandampet Mandal on south, Gundlapalle Mandal on west, and Mahbubnagar district on north-west.

Communications:

Roadways : State Highway (S.H.): Direction- Hyderabad to Miryalaguda. Nearest Villages- Sere Palle, Chennaram, Kolmunthal Pahad, Kondamallapalle, Chinna Adiserla Palle,

River: Pedda Vagu: Nearest Villages- Komme Palle, Tatikole, Kacharam. Dindi Nadi- Nearest Villages- Mynam Palle, Madmadka, Shakavally, Pendli Pakala, Atchampet, Vardhamaniguda, Channamneni Palle.

Backwards Region Grants Fund: It receives Backward Region Grants.

Integrated Child Development Scheme (ICDS) Project: Devarakonda, Total Anganwadi Centres: 319

Annual Rainfall: Average Rainfall 639 mm

Ground Water: Availability of the Ground Water in the Basin is 3185 H.A.M. and the utilization is 2716 H. A.M. It belongs to SC category. Depth to water level varies from 2 to 20 meter below the ground. Most of the wells go down in summer months. The well density in the entire block is 9 wells per sq. km. Total no. of the wells in the block are enumerated as 3395, according to the Ground Water Estimation Committee.

Natural Division : Krishna Piedmont Plain Region

Administration:

Division: Telangana. Parliamentary Constituency: 13 Nalgonda. District: Nalgonda. Mandal: Devarakonda. Assembly Constituency: 86 Devarakonda (ST). Gram Pancha yat: 22.

Villages: 28 **Inhabited:** 27 **Uninhabited:** 1

Ranking	District	State	National
Area	6	119	2537
Population	7	286	4884
Sex Ratio	54	967	3365
Child Sex Ratio	44	877	3841
Literacy Rate	55	933	5416
Density	11	296	4983
Work Participation Rate	41	775	752

Gram Panchayats:
Chennamanenipally, Chennaram, Chinthakunta Deverkonda, Doniyal, Gajinagar, Gottimukkala Gummadavally, Iddampally, Kamepally, Kolmuntalapad Konda Bhemanapally, Konda Mallepally, Madmadaka Mudigonda, Mynampally, Padamatipally, Pendlipakala Sheripally, Tatikole, Telugupally, Turpupally.

Amenities:

Education: Primary School in 25 villages, Middle school in 9 villages, Matriculation or Secondary School in 4 villages, namely Padamati Palle, Kondabheemana Palle, Mudigonda, Kondamallapalle.

Higher Secondary or Pre University Courses or Intermediate or Junior College in 1 village of the CD Block,, namely Kondamallapalle.

College in 0 village, Adult Literacy Center in 19 villages.

Medical: Hospital in 0 village, Dispensary in 2 villages, Health Center in 0 village, Sub Center in 17 villages, Maternity and Child Welfare Center in 0 village, Community health workers in 0 village.

The Villages having Hospital or Dispensary or Health Center are Turupu Palle, Kondamallapalle.

Drinking Water: Tap water in 27 villages, Tank water in 27 villages, Well water in 27 villages, Tubewell in 27 villages and more than one source in 27 villages.

Bank: Banking facility in 2 villages, namely, Mudigonda, Kondamallapalle.

Credit Society in 5 villages Agricultural Credit Society in 3 Non-Agricultural Credit Society in 4 villages.

Others: Power supply in 27 villages, Cinema hall in 1 village, sport club in 0 village, Stadium or Auditorium or Community Hall in 0 village, Post Office in 14 villages.

There are 23 villages having bus facilities.

Villages with most of facilities: Mudigonda Kondamallapalle.

Villages without amenities (Education): Yepoor, Atchampet..

Scheduled Castes: Out of the total population of 59150 persons, 8733 persons (14.76%) belong to Scheduled Castes.

The villages having less than 10% SC population are Gottimukkala, Mudigonda, Sere Palle, Chennaram Yepoor, Kolmunthal Pahad, Madmadka, Atchampet Vardhamaniguda, Fakeerpoor.

The villages having more than 50% SC population are None.

Sex ratio of Scheduled Caste population is 494.

Scheduled Castes Literates and Illiterates by Sex:

	Persons	Males	Females
Literate	3,111	2,167	944
Illiterate	5,622	2,255	3,367
Literacy rate	43.1	59.6	26.4
Graduate	56	46	10

Scheduled Castes (Dominant):

Madiga, Mala, Beda Jangam etc., Bindla Sindhollu etc.

For their cultural identity please see Appendix-I

Villages without Scheduled Castes: There are 4 villages without any scheduled caste population.

Scheduled Tribes: Out of the total population of 59150 persons, 22618 persons (38.24%) belong to Scheduled Tribes.

The villages having less than 10% ST population are Iddam Palle, Tatikole, Kacharam, Shakavally Fakeerpoor.

The villages having more than 50% ST population are Mudigonda, Sere Palle, Chennaram, Yepoor Kolmunthal Pahad, Gazinagar, Mynam Palle, Madmadka Atchampet, Vardhamaniguda.

Sex ratio of Scheduled tribe population is 479.

Scheduled Tribes Literates and Illiterates by Sex:

	Persons	Males	Females
Literate	5,520	4,244	1,276
Illiterate	17,098	7,529	9,569
Literacy rate	30.5	45.1	14.7
Graduate	81	80	1

Scheduled Tribes (Dominant):

Sugalis etc., Yerukulas, Yenadis

For their cultural identity please see Appendix-II

Villages without Scheduled Tribes: There are 4 villages without any scheduled tribe population.

Literates and Illiterates by Sex (Total Population):

	Persons	Males	Females
Literate	21,106	14,324	6,782
Illiterate	38,044	15,973	22,071
Literacy rate	43	57	28
Graduate	593	492	101

Agriculture: ***Distribution of villages according to land use:***
Out of 28 villages, Total area (in hectare) is 32257, out of that 85 percent is cultivable and 8.4 percent of the cultivable area is irrigated.

Sources of Irrigation (Hectares): Government Canal 1304.8, Private Canal 0, Well without Electricity 0, Well with

Electricity 350, Tubewell without Electricity 0, Tubewell with Electricity 648, Tank 0, River 0, Lake 0, Waterfall 0, Others 0.

Villages with population of 5000 to 9999: Mudigonda, Kondamallapalle, Tatikole.

Villages with population of 10000 and above: None

Distribution of Workers:

	Persons	Males	Females	WPR
Cultivators	10,704	7,001	3,703	34.18
Agricultural Labour	13,702	5,193	8,509	43.76
Household Industry	949	496	453	3.03
Other Workers	5,959	4,378	1,581	19.03
Main Workers	23,807	14,845	8,962	76.03
Marginal Workers	7,507	2,223	5,284	23.97
Total Workers	31,314	17,068	14,246	

Religion: Major Religious Communities:

	Persons	Males	Females	Sex Ratio
Hindu (96.69%)	57,192	29,331	27,861	950
Muslim (2.6%)	1,535	763	772	1,012
Christian (0.55%)	324	151	173	1,146
Sikh (0.05%)	32	18	14	778
Buddhists (0.01%)	6	4	2	500
Jain (0.01%)	5	1	4	4,000

Agewise Data:

	Persons	Males	Females	Sex Ratio
All ages	59,150	30,297	28,853	952
0-14	22,957	11,933	11,024	924
15-44	26,497	13,479	13,018	966
45-79	9,301	4,710	4,591	975
80+	320	141	179	1270
Age not stated	75	34	41	1206

Languages (Dominant):

Telugu, Hindi, Urdu, Gondi, Tamil

Disabled Population:

	Persons	Males	Females	%
Total Disabled	1,560	875	685	
In Seeing	903	519	384	57.88
In Speech	95	49	46	6.09
In Hearing	60	28	32	3.85
In Movement	373	209	164	23.91
Mentally	129	70	59	8.27

DEVARAPALLE

Devarapalle C.D. Block lies in the north-eastern part of Vishakhapatnam district. The Block is located at a distance of 69 kms. from district headquarters (Visha khapatnam). There are 40 villages in the block with the total population of 57,536 persons. Area of the C.D. Block is 145.03 sq. kms. It is bounded in the north by Mandal Ananthagiri, in the south by Chodavaram Mandal, in the east by Mandals K. Kotapadu and Ananthag iri, and district Vizianagaram, and in the west by Manda ls Cheedikada and Hukumpeta.

Communications :

Roadways : Metalled Roads: Nearest Villages- Devarapalle, Kasipuram, Chinanandipalle, Kasipathirajupuram, Mushid ipalle, Alamandakothapalle.

River: Sarada Nadi- Nearest Villages- Sambuvanipalem, Devarapalle, Bethapudi, Raiwada, Gorupalem, Lovarayapu raju Peta, Lovamukundapuram, Sammeda, Chintalapudi, Pedasompuram, Marepalle, Tenugupudi, Venkatarajupuram, Vakapalle, Taruva, Vechalam, Mamidipalle, Thimiram, Kaligotla, Boilakintada.

Hills: Nearest Villages- Tenugupudi, Venkatarajupuram, Vakapalle, Chinagangavaram, Valabu.

Annaual Rainfall: Average Rainfall 975.0 mm

Ground Water: Availability of the Ground Water in the Basin is (Information not avavible) H.A.M .and the utilization is (Information not avavible) H.A.M. It belongs to (Information not avavible) category. Depth to water level varies from 3 to 10 meter below the ground. Most of the wells go down in summer months.

Administration:

Division: Coastal Andhra. Parliamentary Constituency: 22 Anakapalle. District: Visakhapatnam. Mandal: Devarap alle. Assembly Constituency: 146 Madugula. Gram Panchaya t: 27.

Villages: 40 **Inhabited:** 36 **Uninhabited:** 4

Ranking	District	State	National
Area	25	846	5119
Population	18	311	4944
Sex Ratio	23	398	1564
Child Sex Ratio	29	482	1775
Literacy Rate	20	867	5131
Density	3	36	2753
Work Participation Rate	12	193	171

Gram Panchayats:

Alamanda, Alamanda Kothapalle, Boila Kintada Chinanandipalle, Chintalapudi, Devarapalle Garisingi, K.Mutyalammapalem, Kaligotla, Kasipuram Kothapenta, Mamidipalle, Marepalle, Mulakala Palle Mushidi Palle, N.Gajapathinagaram, Nagayyapeta Pedanandipalle, Raiwada, Tamarabba, Taruva Tenugupudi, Thimiram, Vakapalle, Valabu, Vechalam Venkatarjupuram.

Amenities:

Education: Primary School in 35 villages, Middle school in 12 villages, Matriculation or Secondary School in 6 villages, namely Devarapalle, Kasipuram, Mushidipalle, Tenugupudi, Alamanda, Vechalam.

Higher Secondary or Pre University Courses or Inter-

mediate or Junior College in 1 village of the CD Block,, namely Devarapalle.

College in 0 village, Adult Literacy Center in 21 villages.

Medical: Hospital in 2 villages, Dispensary in 0 village, Health Center in 11 villages, Sub Center in 11 villages, Maternity and Child Welfare Center in 0 village, Community health workers in 0 village.

The Villages having Hospital or Dispensary or Health Center are Devarapalle, Vechalam.

Drinking Water: Tap water in 36 villages, Tank water in 36 villages, Well water in 36 villages, Tubewell in 36 villages and more than one source in 36 villages.

Bank: Banking facility in 2 villages, namely, Devarapalle, Alamanda.

Credit Society in 8 villages Agricultural Credit Society in 8 Non-Agricultural Credit Society in 0 village.

Others: Power supply in 36 villages, Cinema hall in 2 villages, sport club in 0 village, Stadium or Auditorium or Community Hall in 0 village, Post Office in 17 villages.

There are 20 villages having bus facilities.

Villages with most of facilities: Devarapalle Alamanda.

Villages without amenities (Education): Kasipathirajupuram..

Scheduled Castes: Out of the total population of 57536 persons, 3830 persons (6.66%) belong to Scheduled Castes.

The villages having less than 10% SC population are Valabu, Chinagangavaram, Sambuvanipalem, Devarapalle Bethapudi, Raiwada, Lovamukundapuram, Sammeda Chintalapudi, Kondakodabu, Chinasompuram Nagayyapeta, Chinanandipalle, Kasipathirajupuram Mushidipalle, Alamandakothapalle Pedanandipalle Agraharam, Sivaramachainulapalem Chainulapalem, Marepalle, Venkatarajupuram Vakapalle, Taruva, Alamanda, Vechalam, Mamidipalle Thimiram, Kaligotla, Boilakintada, Mulakalapalle Kothapenta.

The villages having more than 50% SC population are None.

Sex ratio of Scheduled Caste population is 433.

Scheduled Castes Literates and Illiterates by Sex:

	Persons	Males	Females
Literate	1,812	1,347	465
Illiterate	2,018	825	1,193
Literacy rate	52.5	67.9	31.7
Graduate	33	26	7

Scheduled Castes (Dominant):

Mala, Madiga, Relli, Manne, Chachati

For their cultural identity please see Appendix-I

Villages without Scheduled Castes: There are 7 villages without any scheduled caste population.

Scheduled Tribes: Out of the total population of 57536 persons, 4066 persons (7.07%) belong to Scheduled Tribes.

The villages having less than 10% ST population are Devarapalle, Raiwada, Nagayyapeta, Seetampeta Kasipuram, Chinanandipalle, Kasipathirajupuram Mushidipalle, Alamandakothapalle Pedanandipalle Agraharam, Sivaramachainulapalem Chainulapalem, Marepalle, Tenugupudi Venkatarajupuram, Vakapalle, Taruva, Alamanda Narasimha Gajapathinagaram, Vechalam, Mamidipalle Thimiram, Kaligotla, Boilakintada, Mulakalapalle Kothapenta.

The villages having more than 50% ST population are Valabu, Bethapudi, Lovamukundapuram, Sammeda Chintalapudi, Kondakodabu, Chinasompuram.

Sex ratio of Scheduled tribe population is 484.

Scheduled Tribes Literates and Illiterates by Sex:

	Persons	Males	Females
Literate	1,207	817	390
Illiterate	2,859	1,280	1,579
Literacy rate	34.4	45.0	23.0
Graduate	2	2	0

Scheduled Tribes (Dominant):

Konda Dhoras, Bagata, Manna Dhora, Yerukulas Valmiki

For their cultural identity please see Appendix-II

Villages without Scheduled Tribes: There are 18 villages without any scheduled tribe population.

Literates and Illiterates by Sex (Total Population):

	Persons	Males	Females
Literate	23,277	15,245	8,032
Illiterate	34,259	13,673	20,586
Literacy rate	46	60	32
Graduate	657	539	118

Agriculture: ***Distribution of villages according to land use:*** Out of 40 villages, Total area (in hectare) is 14503, out of that 63.5 percent is cultivable and 47.03 percent of the cultivable area is irrigated.

Sources of Irrigation (Hectares): Government Canal 2227.59, Private Canal 0, Well without Electricity 35, Well with Electricity 0, Tubewell without Electricity 0, Tubewell with Electricity 216.7, Tank 1841.73, River 0, Lake 0, Waterfall 0, Others 10.

Villages with population of 5000 to 9999: Devarapalle.

Villages with population of 10000 and above: None

Distribution of Workers:

	Persons	Males	Females	WPR
Cultivators	15,889	8,654	7,235	44.96

Agricultural Labour	13,593	5,995	7,598	38.46
Household Industry	1,618	1,029	589	4.58
Other Workers	4,244	3,000	1,244	12.01
Main Workers	31,699	17,732	13,967	89.69
Marginal Workers	3,645	946	2,699	10.31
Total Workers	35,344	18,678	16,666	

Religion: Major Religious Communities:

	Persons	Males	Females	Sex Ratio
Hindu (99.4%)	57,193	28,759	28,434	989
Muslim (0.22%)	127	63	64	1,016
Christian (0.28%)	160	72	88	1,222
Sikh (0%)	-	-	-	-
Buddhists (0%)	-	-	-	-
Jain (0%)	-	-	-	-

Agewise Data:

	Persons	Males	Females	Sex Ratio
All ages	57,536	28,918	28,618	990
0-14	16,524	8,746	7,778	889
15-44	27,296	13,748	13,548	985
45-79	13,358	6,277	7,081	1128
80+	233	80	153	1913
Age not stated	125	67	58	866

Languages (Dominant):

Telugu, Tamil, Gondi, Urdu, Hindi

Disabled Population:

	Persons	Males	Females	%
Total Disabled	1,074	611	463	
In Seeing	461	260	201	42.92
In Speech	150	86	64	13.97
In Hearing	49	25	24	4.56
In Movement	328	197	131	30.54
Mentally	86	43	43	8.01

DEVARAPALLE

Devarapalle C.D. Block lies in the north-east part of West Godavari district. The Block is located at a distance of 66 kms. from district headquarters (Eluru). There are 13 villages in the block with the total population of 72,324 persons. Area of the C.D. Block is 210.25 sq. kms. It is bounded in the north by Mandals Gopalapuram and Tallapudi, in the south by Mandals Tadepalligudem and Nidadavole, in the east by Mandals Chagallu and Kovvur, and in the west by Mandals Nallaje rla and Koyyalagudem.

Communications :

Roadways : Metalled Roads: Nearest Villages- Chinnayagud em, Yernagudem, Tyajampudi, Kurukuru, Dhumanthunigudem Devarapalle, Bandapuram, Duddukuru, Gowripatnam, Konda gudem.

Backwards Region Grants Fund: It receives Backward Region Grants.

Annaul Rainfall: Average Rainfall 1005 mm

Ground Water: Availability of the Ground Water in the Basin is (Information not avavible) H.A.M .and the utilization is (Information not avavible) H.A.M. It belongs to (Information not avavible) category. Depth to water level varies from 3 to 10 meter below the ground. Most of the wells go down in summer months.

Natural Division : Godavari Delta Region.

Administration:

Division: Coastal Andhra. Parliamentary Constituency: 25 Rajahmundry. District: West Godavari. Mandal: Devara palle. Assembly Constituency: 185 Gopalapuram (SC). Gram Panchayat: 15.

Villages: 13 **Inhabited:** 13 **Uninhabited:** 0

Ranking	District	State	National
Area	9	489	4012
Population	12	98	4383
Sex Ratio	37	656	2265
Child Sex Ratio	10	140	381
Literacy Rate	34	125	1706
Density	27	935	3153
Work Participation Rate	35	277	3328

Gram Panchayats:

Bandapuram, Chinnayagudem, Devarapalle Dhumanthunigudem, Duddukuru, Gowripatnam Krishnampalem, Kurukuru, Lakshmipuram, Pallantla Ramannapalem, Sangaigudem, Tyajampudi, Yadavolu Yernagudem.

Amenities:

Education: Primary School in 12 villages, Middle school in 9 villages, Matriculation or Secondary School in 6 villages, namely Chinnayagudem, Yernagudem, Pallantlai, Devarapalle, Duddukuru, Gowripatnam.

Higher Secondary or Pre University Courses or Intermediate or Junior College in 2 villages of the CD Block,, namely Devarapalle, Gowripatnam.

College in 2 villages, Adult Literacy Center in 12 villages., Colleges are in villages, namely Devarapalle, Gowripatnam.

Medical: Hospital in 0 village, Dispensary in 3 villages, Health Center in 3 villages, Sub Center in 8 villages, Maternity and Child Welfare Center in 0 village, Community health workers in 0 village.

The Villages having Hospital or Dispensary or Health Center are Yernagudem, Tyajampudi, Devarapalle.

Drinking Water: Tap water in 13 villages, Tank water in 13 villages, Well water in 13 villages, Tubewell in 13 villages and more than one source in 13 villages.

Bank: Banking facility in 5 villages, namely, Yadavole, Yernagudem, Devarapalle, Duddukuru Gowripatnam.

Credit Society in 9 villages Agricultural Credit Society in 8 Non-Agricultural Credit Society in 4 villages.

Others: Power supply in 13 villages, Cinema hall in 4 villages, sport club in 1 village, Stadium or Auditorium or Community Hall in 0 village, Post Office in 11 villages.

There are 13 villages having bus facilities.

Villages with most of facilities: Yadavole Yernagudem, Devarapalle, Duddukuru, Gowripatnam.

Villages without amenities (Education):
Kondagudem..

Scheduled Castes: Out of the total population of 72324 persons, 24361 persons (33.68%) belong to Scheduled Castes.

The villages having less than 10% SC population are None..

The villages having more than 50% SC population are None.

Sex ratio of Scheduled Caste population is 496.

Scheduled Castes Literates and Illiterates by Sex:

	Persons	Males	Females
Literate	12,408	6,709	5,699
Illiterate	11,953	5,564	6,389
Literacy rate	59.2	63.4	55.0
Graduate	330	274	56

Scheduled Castes (Dominant):
Mala, Madiga, Adi Andhra, Mala Dasari, Relli

For their cultural identity please see Appendix-I

Villages without Scheduled Castes: There are 0 village without any scheduled caste population.

Scheduled Tribes: Out of the total population of 72324 persons, 511 persons (0.71%) belong to Scheduled Tribes.

The villages having less than 10% ST population are Yadavole, Chinnayagudem, Yernagudem, Tyajampudi Kurukuru, Pallantlai, Dhumanthunigudem, Devarapalle Laxmipuram, Bandapuram, Duddukuru, Gowripatnam Kondagudem.

The villages having more than 50% ST population are None.

Sex ratio of Scheduled tribe population is 501.

Scheduled Tribes Literates and Illiterates by Sex:

	Persons	Males	Females
Literate	170	87	83
Illiterate	341	168	173
Literacy rate	41.0	41.4	40.5
Graduate	3	2	1

Scheduled Tribes (Dominant):
Yerukulas, Chenchu etc., Sugalis etc., Koya etc. Kondareddis

For their cultural identity please see Appendix-II

Villages without Scheduled Tribes: There are 2 villages without any scheduled tribe population.

Literates and Illiterates by Sex (Total Population):

	Persons	Males	Females
Literate	42,126	22,502	19,624
Illiterate	30,198	14,114	16,084
Literacy rate	66	70	63
Graduate	1,366	1,051	315

Agriculture: ***Distribution of villages according to land use:***
Out of 13 villages, Total area (in hectare) is 21025, out of that 84.29 percent is cultivable and 77.16 percent of the cultivable area is irrigated.

Sources of Irrigation (Hectares): Government Canal 0, Private Canal 0, Well without Electricity 0, Well with Electricity 5118, Tubewell without Electricity 0, Tubewell with Electricity 7570, Tank 935, River 0, Lake 0, Waterfall 0, Others 51.

Villages with population of 5000 to 9999:
Yadavole, Chinnayagudem, Tyajampudi, Duddukuru Gowripatnam.

Villages with population of 10000 and above:
Yernagudem, Devarapalle.

Distribution of Workers:

	Persons	Males	Females	WPR
Cultivators	4,979	4,692	287	15.02
Agricultural Labour	20,533	11,890	8,643	61.94
Household Industry	734	529	205	2.21
Other Workers	6,905	5,475	1,430	20.83
Main Workers	30,376	21,722	8,654	91.63
Marginal Workers	2,775	864	1,911	8.37
Total Workers	33,151	22,586	10,565	

Religion: Major Religious Communities:

	Persons	Males	Females	Sex Ratio
Hindu (96.67%)	69,919	35,364	34,555	977
Muslim (2.26%)	1,636	841	795	945
Christian (1.03%)	745	398	347	872
Sikh (0.01%)	6	4	2	500
Buddhists (0%)	-	-	-	-
Jain (0%)	-	-	-	-

Agewise Data:

	Persons	Males	Females	Sex Ratio
All ages	72,324	36,616	35,708	975
0-14	23,260	11,720	11,540	985
15-44	35,247	17,933	17,314	965
45-79	13,359	6,765	6,594	975
80+	400	167	233	1395
Age not stated	58	31	27	871

Languages (Dominant):
Telugu, Urdu, Malayalam, Gondi, Hindi

Disabled Population:

	Persons	Males	Females	%
Total Disabled	1,088	589	499	

In Seeing	309	150	159	28.4
In Speech	141	66	75	12.96
In Hearing	60	26	34	5.51
In Movement	434	279	155	39.89
Mentally	144	68	76	13.24

DEVARKADRA

Devarkadra C.D. Block lies in the central west part of Mahbubnagar district. The Block is located at a distance of 22 kms. from district headquarters (Mahbubn agar). There are 28 villages in the block with the total population of 52,041 persons. Area of the C.D. Block is 236.72 sq. kms. It is bounded by Koilkonda Mandal on north, Mahbubnagar Mandal on north east, Addakal and Peddamandedi Mandal on east, Kothakotamandal on south, and Chinnachintakunta Mandal on west.

Communications :

Roadways : State Highway (S.H.): Direction- Makthal to Jad Cherla. Nearest Villages- Venkataipalle, Chowdar palle.

Railway Station: Devarkadra, Puttapalle, Koukuntla

River: Pedda Vagu: Nearest Villages- Bollaram, Chinnara jmoor, Peddarajmoor, Baswapur, Gurakonda, Dokur, Gudiban da, Goplapurkalan.

Backwards Region Grants Fund: It receives Backward Region Grants.

Mahila Samakhya (Education for Women's Equality): It is decleared Socialy and Educationally Backward Block by the Government. .

Annual Rainfall: Average Rainfall 635 mm

Ground Water: Availability of the Ground Water in the Basin is 1766 H.A.M. and the utilization is 1525 H. A.M. It belongs to SC category. Depth to waier level varies from 2 to 5 meter below the ground. Most of the wells go down in summer months. The well density in the entire block is 0 wells per sq. km. Total no. of the wells in the block are enumerated as 0, accordi ng to the Ground Water Estimation Committee.

Natural Division : Telangana Plateau Region

Administration:

Division: Telangana. Parliamentary Constituency: 11 Mahbubnagar. District: Mahbubnagar. Mandal: Devarkadra. Assembly Constituency: 76 Devarkadra. Gram Panchayat: 23

Villages: 28 **Inhabited:** 28 **Uninhabited:** 0

Ranking	District	State	National
Area	39	357	3555
Population	26	446	5178
Sex Ratio	18	487	1798
Child Sex Ratio	49	914	4021
Literacy Rate	19	921	5371
Density	51	497	4442
Work Participation Rate	24	646	1290

Gram Panchayats:

Ajilapur, Baswaipalle, Baswapur, Bollaram Chinnarajamoor, Devarakadara, Dokur, Gaddegudem Gopanpalle, Gudibanda, Gurakonda, Hajilapur Isrampalle, Jeenugurala, Koukuntla, Laxmipalle Nagaram, Peddarajamoor, Perur, Puttapalle Rukulampalle, Varne, Venkataipalle.

Amenities:

Education: Primary School in 28 villages, Middle school in 11 villages, Matriculation or Secondary School in 4 villages, namely Devarkadra, Gopanpalle, Koukuntla, Perur. Higher Secondary or Pre University Courses or Intermediate or Junior College in 0 village of the CD Block, College in 0 village, Adult Literacy Center in 26 villages.

Medical: Hospital in 0 village, Dispensary in 2 villages, Health Center in 2 villages, Sub Center in 9 villages, Maternity and Child Welfare Center in 0 village, Community health workers in 0 village.

The Villages having Hospital or Dispensary or Health Center are Bollaram, Devarkadra.

Drinking Water: Tap water in 28 villages, Tank water in 28 villages, Well water in 28 villages, Tubewell in 28 villages and more than one source in 28 villages.

Bank: Banking facility in 3 villages, namely, Devarkadra, Koukuntla, Perur.

Credit Society in 17 villages Agricultural Credit Society in 4 Non-Agricultural Credit Society in 14 villages.

Others: Power supply in 28 villages, Cinema hall in 1 village, sport club in 0 village, Stadium or Auditorium or Community Hall in 0 village, Post Office in 16 villages.

There are 26 villages having bus facilities.

Villages with most of facilities: Devarkadra Koukuntla, Perur.

Villages without Amenities (Education): None..

Scheduled Castes: Out of the total population of 52041 persons, 7486 persons (14.38%) belong to Scheduled Castes. The villages having less than 10% SC population are None..

The villages having more than 50% SC population are None.

Sex ratio of Scheduled Caste population is 502.

Scheduled Castes Literates and Illiterates by Sex:

	Persons	Males	Females
Literate	1,992	1,351	641
Illiterate	5,494	2,376	3,118
Literacy rate	31.5	43.3	20.0
Graduate	26	26	0

Scheduled Castes (Dominant):

Madiga, Generic Castes etc., Mala, Beda Jangam etc. Mehtar

For their cultural identity please see Appendix-I

Villages without Scheduled Castes: There are 0 village without any scheduled caste population.

Scheduled Tribes: Out of the total population of 52041 persons, 998 persons (1.92%) belong to Scheduled Tribes. The villages having less than 10% ST population are Ajilapur, Chinnarajmoor, Peddarajmoor, Gaddeguda Venkataipalle, Balsupalle, Baswapur, Gurakonda Goplapurkalan, Devarkadra, Chowdarpalle, Hajilapur Baswaipalle, Laxmipalle, Jeenugurala, Dokur Meenuguvanipalle, Gudibanda, Gopanpalle, Puttapalle Koukuntla, Irampalle, Rekulampalle, Perur Muthyalampalle, Varne.

The villages having more than 50% ST population are None.

Sex ratio of Scheduled tribe population is 478.

Scheduled Tribes Literates and Illiterates by Sex:

	Persons	Males	Females
Literate	227	168	59
Illiterate	771	353	418
Literacy rate	28.8	40.3	15.9
Graduate	3	3	0

Scheduled Tribes (Dominant):

Sugalis etc., Yerukulas, Kammara, Savaras etc. Generic Tribes etc.

For their cultural identity please see Appendix-II

Villages without Scheduled Tribes: There are 4 villages without any scheduled tribe population.

Literates and Illiterates by Sex (Total Population):

	Persons	Males	Females
Literate	19,275	12,544	6,731
Illiterate	32,766	13,668	19,098
Literacy rate	44	57	31
Graduate	595	503	92

Agriculture: *Distribution of villages according to land use:* Out of 28 villages, Total area (in hectare) is 23671, out of that 78.14 percent is cultivable and 33.99 percent of the cultivable area is irrigated.

Sources of Irrigation (Hectares): Government Canal 1285.93, Private Canal 0, Well without Electricity 29.13, Well with Electricity 355.76, Tubewell without Electricity 0, Tubewell with Electricity 2236.5, Tank 1545.8, River 7.28, Lake 0, Waterfall 0, Others 827.09.

Villages with population of 5000 to 9999: Devarkadra.

Villages with population of 10000 and above: None

Distribution of Workers:

	Persons	Males	Females	WPR
Cultivators	7,103	4,921	2,182	26.12
Agricultural Labour	13,874	5,188	8,686	51.01
Household Industry	761	431	330	2.8
Other Workers	5,460	4,185	1,275	20.08
Main Workers	16,581	10,785	5,796	60.96
Marginal Workers	10,617	3,940	6,677	39.04
Total Workers	27,198	14,725	12,473	

Religion: Major Religious Communities:

	Persons	Males	Females	Sex Ratio
Hindu (93.84%)	48,835	24,598	24,237	985
Muslim (5.98%)	3,110	1,559	1,551	995
Christian (0.12%)	65	38	27	711
Sikh (0.03%)	18	9	9	1,000
Buddhists (0%)	2	2	-	-
Jain (0%)	2	1	1	1,000

Agewise Data:

	Persons	Males	Females	Sex Ratio
All ages	52,041	26,212	25,829	985
0-14	18,513	9,632	8,881	922
15-44	23,218	11,502	11,716	1019
45-79	9,904	4,903	5,001	1020
80+	343	139	204	1468
Age not stated	63	36	27	750

Languages (Dominant):

Telugu, Urdu, Hindi, Kannada, Tamil

Disabled Population:

	Persons	Males	Females	%
Total Disabled	909	494	415	
In Seeing	314	161	153	34.54
In Speech	71	37	34	7.81
In Hearing	54	29	25	5.94
In Movement	379	218	161	41.69
Mentally	91	49	42	10.01

DEVARUPPULA

Devaruppula C.D. Block lies in the southern part of Warangal district. The Block is located at a distance of 84 kms. from district headquarters (Warangal). There are 13 villages in the block with the total population of 41,058 persons. Area of the C.D. Block is 224.34 sq. kms. It is bounded in the north by Lingalaghanpur and Raghunathpalle Mandals, in the south and west by district Nalgonda, and in the east by Mandals Palakurthi and Kodakandla.

Communications:

Roadways : State Highway (S.H.): Direction- Jangaon to Suryapet. Nearest Villages- Ramrajpalle, Madoorkalan, Madoorkhurd, Kadavendi, Devaruppula, Gollapalle, Manpa had.

Backwards Region Grants Fund: It receives Backward Region Grants.

Annual Rainfall: Average Rainfall 749 mm

Ground Water: Availability of the Ground Water in the Basin is 1517 H.A.M.and the utilization is 1802 H.A. M. It belongs to OE category. Depth to water level varies from 5 to 20 meter below the ground. Most of the wells go down in summer months. The well density in the entire block is 14 wells per sq. km. Total no. of the wells in the block are enumerated as 3106, according to the Ground Water Estimation Committee.

Natural Division : Godavari Depression Region

Administration:

Division: Telangana. Parliamentary Constituency.District: Warangal. Mandal: Devaruppula. Assembly Constituency: 100 Palakurthi. Gram Panchayat: 18.

Villages: 13 **Inhabited:** 13 **Uninhabited:** 0

Ranking	District	State	National
Area	17	413	3762
Population	38	792	5689
Sex Ratio	32	741	2478
Child Sex Ratio	23	578	2310
Literacy Rate	27	600	4234
Density	19	368	4993
Work Participation Rate	44	779	904

Gram Panchayats:

Appireddi Palle, Chinnamadur, Chowdur, Devaruppula Dharamapuram, Dharavath Thanda, Gollapalle Kadavendi, Kamareddi Gudem, Kolkonda, Madhapuram Manpahad, Neermala, Padamati Thanda, Peddamadur Ramrajupalle, Seetharampur, Singarajupalle.

Amenities:

Education: Primary School in 13 villages, Middle school in 8 villages, Matriculation or Secondary School in 5 villages, namely Madoorkalan, Madoorkhurd, Kolkonda, Kadavendi, Devaruppula.

Higher Secondary or Pre University Courses or Intermediate or Junior College in 0 village of the CD Block, College in 0 village, Adult Literacy Center in 8 villages.

Medical: Hospital in 1 village, Dispensary in 1 village, Health Center in 1 village, Sub Center in 8 villages, Maternity and Child Welfare Center in 5 villages, Community health workers in 0 village.

The Villages having Hospital or Dispensary or Health Center are Madoorkalan, Madoorkhurd.

Drinking Water: Tap water in 13 villages, Tank water in 12 villages, Well water in 13 villages, Tubewell in 12 villages and more than one source in 13 villages.

Bank: Banking facility in 3 villages, namely, Madoorkhurd, Dharamapur, Devaruppula.

Credit Society in 13 villages Agricultural Credit Society in 2 Non-Agricultural Credit Society in 13 villages.

Others: Power supply in 13 villages, Cinema hall in 0 village, sport club in 0 village, Stadium or Auditorium or Community Hall in 0 village, Post Office in 11 villages.

There are 13 villages having bus facilities.

Villages with most of facilities: Madoorkhurd Dharamapur, Devaruppula.

Villages without Amenities (Education): None..

Scheduled Castes: Out of the total population of 41058 persons, 7274 persons (17.72%) belong to Scheduled Castes. The villages having less than 10% SC population are None..

The villages having more than 50% SC population are None.

Sex ratio of Scheduled Caste population is 485.

Scheduled Castes Literates and Illiterates by Sex:

	Persons	Males	Females
Literate	2,755	1,812	943
Illiterate	4,519	1,934	2,585
Literacy rate	44.0	55.9	31.3
Graduate	17	15	2

Scheduled Castes (Dominant):

Madiga, Generic Castes etc., Mala, Bindla, Mashti

For their cultural identity please see Appendix-I

Villages without Scheduled Castes: There are 0 village without any scheduled caste population.

Scheduled Tribes: Out of the total population of 41058 persons, 7807 persons (19.01%) belong to Scheduled Tribes. The villages having less than 10% ST population are Ramrajpalle, Neermiala, Singarajpalle, Madoorkhurd Chowdur, Kolkonda, Kadavendi, Devaruppula Gollapalle, Manpahad.

The villages having more than 50% ST population are None.

Sex ratio of Scheduled tribe population is 484.

Scheduled Tribes Literates and Illiterates by Sex:

	Persons	Males	Females
Literate	2,131	1,445	686
Illiterate	5,676	2,582	3,094
Literacy rate	33.2	43.6	22.1
Graduate	33	32	1

Scheduled Tribes (Dominant):

Sugalis etc., Yerukulas, Koya etc.

For their cultural identity please see Appendix-II

Villages without Scheduled Tribes: There are 3 villages without any scheduled tribe population.

Literates and Illiterates by Sex (Total Population):

	Persons	Males	Females
Literate	18,257	11,381	6,876
Illiterate	22,801	9,463	13,338
Literacy rate	52	64	40

Graduate	417	369	48

Agriculture: ***Distribution of villages according to land use:*** Out of 13 villages, Total area (in hectare) is 22435, out of that 70.2 percent is cultivable and 47.44 percent of the cultivable area is irrigated.

Sources of Irrigation (Hectares): Government Canal 0, Private Canal 0, Well without Electricity 0, Well with Electricity 3678, Tubewell without Electricity 0, Tubewell with Electricity 3216, Tank 577, River 0, Lake 0, Waterfall 0, Others 0.

Villages with population of 5000 to 9999: Madoorkhurd, Kadavendi, Devaruppula.

Villages with population of 10000 and above: None

Distribution of Workers:

	Persons	Males	Females	WPR
Cultivators	8,973	5,737	3,236	40.29
Agricultural Labour	9,576	3,433	6,143	43
Household Industry	1,040	663	377	4.67
Other Workers	2,681	2,078	603	12.04
Main Workers	17,451	10,537	6,914	78.36
Marginal Workers	4,819	1,374	3,445	21.64
Total Workers	22,270	11,911	10,359	

Religion: Major Religious Communities:

	Persons	Males	Females	Sex Ratio
Hindu (96.78%)	39,737	20,157	19,580	971
Muslim (2.12%)	872	449	423	942
Christian (1.05%)	431	229	202	882
Sikh (0%)	-	-	-	-
Buddhists (0%)	-	-	-	-
Jain (0%)	-	-	-	-

Agewise Data:

	Persons	Males	Females	Sex Ratio
All ages	41,058	20,844	20,214	970
0-14	13,668	7,058	6,610	937
15-44	17,923	8,951	8,972	1002
45-79	9,085	4,618	4,467	967
80+	353	202	151	748
Age not stated	29	15	14	933

Languages (Dominant):
Telugu, Hindi, Urdu, Marathi, Tamil

Disabled Population:

	Persons	Males	Females	%
Total Disabled	940	606	334	
In Seeing	443	306	137	47.13
In Speech	82	53	29	8.72
In Hearing	35	15	20	3.72
In Movement	285	178	107	30.32
Mentally	95	54	41	10.11

DEVIPATNAM

Devipatnam C.D. Block lies in the north western part of East Godavari district. The Block is located at a distance of 145 kms. from district headquarters (Kaki nada). There are 46 villages in the block with the total population of 27,898 persons. Area of the C.D. Block is 111.98 sq. kms. It is bounded in the north by distri ct Khammam and Mandal Rampachodavaram, in the south by Mandals Seethanagaram, Korukonda and Gokavaram, in the east by Gokavaram Mandal, and in the west by district West Godavari.

Communications :

Roadways : State Highway (S.H.): Direction- I. Polavaram to Rampachodavaram. Nearest Villages- Devipatnam, Daman apalle, Velagapalle, Rayavaram, A. Veeravaram, Dandangi.

River: Akhand Gowthani Godavari Nadi- Nearest Villages- Kondamodalu, Gonduru, Katchuluru, Manturu, Thoyyeru, Devipatnam.

Backwards Region Grants Fund: It receives Backward Region Grants.

Annaul Rainfall: Average Rainfall 990 mm

Ground Water: Availability of the Ground Water in the Basin is (Information not avavible) H.A.M .and the utilization is (Information not avavible) H.A.M. It belongs to (Information not avavible) category. Depth to water level varies from 3 to 10 meter below the ground. Most of the wells go down in summer months.

Forest and Reserved **Forest:** (Kondamudala R.F.)- Nearest Villages- Chintalagudem, Mamidivalasa, Thummuru, Gonduru Katchuluru, Peddanuthulu, Gangavaram, Mulagalagudem, Pamugandi, Donalanka, Maddirathigudem, Choppakonda, Yerrametla, Manturu, Kudakarayi, Damanapalle, Velagapa lle, Rayavaram, V. Ramannapalem, Lakshmipuram, Gumpana lle, Lingavaram, Thoyyeru, Devipatnam, Ganugulagondi, A. Veeravaram, China Ramanayyapeta, Pothavaram, Lothup alem, Kondamodalu, Kothapalle, Nereduvalasa, Nelakota, Devaram, Sarabhavaram, Indukuru.

Natural Division : Godavari Delta Region

Administration:

Division: Coastal Andhra. Parliamentary Constituency: 18 Araku (ST). District: East Godavari. Mandal: Devipat nam. Assembly Constituency: 172 Rampachodavaram (ST). Gram Panchayat: 14.

Villages: 46 **Inhabited:** 45 **Uninhabited:** 1

Ranking	**District**	**State**	**National**
Area	27	978	5581
Population	55	1050	6100
Sex Ratio	4	83	572
Child Sex Ratio	3	26	77
Literacy Rate	49	639	4352
Density	7	732	4089
Work Participation Rate	53	543	2100

Gram Panchayats:

Ch.Ramanayyapeta, Choppakonda, Devaram, Devipatnam Indukuru, Indukurupeta, Kondamodalu, Manturu, Palem Pamugandi, Pudipalli, Sarabhavaram, Thunnuru V.Ramannapalem.

Amenities:

Education: Primary School in 41 villages, Middle school in 7 villages, Matriculation or Secondary School in 3 villages, namely Devipatnam, Indukurupeta, Lothupalem.

Higher Secondary or Pre University Courses or Intermediate or Junior College in 0 village of the CD Block, College in 0 village, Adult Literacy Center in 19 villages.

Medical: Hospital in 0 village, Dispensary in 2 villages, Health Center in 2 villages, Sub Center in 12 villages, Maternity and Child Welfare Center in 0 village, Community health workers in 0 village.

The Villages having Hospital or Dispensary or Health Center are Kondamodalu, Indukurupeta.

Drinking Water: Tap water in 45 villages, Tank water in 45 villages, Well water in 45 villages, Tubewell in 45 villages and more than one source in 45 villages.

Bank: Banking facility in 2 villages, namely, Devipatnam, Indukurupeta.

Credit Society in 5 villages Agricultural Credit Society in 3 Non-Agricultural Credit Society in 3 villages.

Others: Power supply in 45 villages, Cinema hall in 3 villages, sport club in 0 village, Stadium or Auditorium or Community Hall in 0 village, Post Office in 15 villages.

There are 18 villages having bus facilities.

Villages with most of facilities: Devipatnam Indukurupeta.

Villages without amenities (Education):
Chintalagudem, Mamidivalasa, Nereduvalasa, Lingavaram..

Scheduled Castes: Out of the total population of 27898 persons, 1645 persons (5.9%) belong to Scheduled Castes.

The villages having less than 10% SC population are Kondamodalu, Chintalagudem, Mamidivalasa, Thummuru Gonduru, Katchuluru, Peddanuthulu, Gangavaram Mulagalagudem, Kothagudem, Thatiwada, Pedduru Pamugandi, Paluru, Donalanka, Maddirathigudem Choppakonda, Yerrametla, Manturu, Kudakarayi Damanapalle, Velagapalle, Rayavaram, V. Ramannapalem Lakshmipuram, Gumpanapalle, Nereduvalasa, Lingavaram Devipatnam, Ganugulagondi, A. Veeravaram China Ramanayyapeta, Dandangi, Pothavaram, Pudipalle Nelakota, Devaram, Sarabhavaram, Indukurupeta Ravilanka, Lothupalem.

The villages having more than 50% SC population are None.

Sex ratio of Scheduled Caste population is 512.

Scheduled Castes Literates and Illiterates by Sex:

	Persons	Males	Females
Literate	757	366	391
Illiterate	888	437	451
Literacy rate	54.6	54.6	54.5
Graduate	31	24	7

Scheduled Castes (Dominant):

Mala, Madiga, Adi Andhra, Generic Castes etc.
Mala Dasu

For their cultural identity please see Appendix-I

Villages without Scheduled Castes: There are 24 villages without any scheduled caste population.

Scheduled Tribes: Out of the total population of 27898 persons, 16198 persons (58.06%) belong to Scheduled Tribes.

The villages having less than 10% ST population are None..

The villages having more than 50% ST population are Kondamodalu, Chintalagudem, Mamidivalasa, Thummuru Gonduru, Katchuluru, Peddanuthulu, Gangavaram Mulagalagudem, Kothagudem, Thatiwada, Pedduru Pamugandi, Paluru, Donalanka, Maddirathigudem Choppakonda, Yerrametla, Manturu, Kudakarayi Damanapalle, Velagapalle, Rayavaram, V. Ramannapalem Lakshmipuram, Gumpanapalle, Nereduvalasa, Lingavaram Ganugulagondi, Dandangi, Pothavaram, Nelakota Ravilanka, Lothupalem, Indukuru.

Sex ratio of Scheduled tribe population is 510.

Scheduled Tribes Literates and Illiterates by Sex:

	Persons	Males	Females
Literate	6,065	3,437	2,628
Illiterate	10,133	4,506	5,627
Literacy rate	44.1	50.9	37.6
Graduate	39	32	7

Scheduled Tribes (Dominant):

Koya etc., Kondareddis, Kammara, Konda Dhoras
Valmiki

For their cultural identity please see Appendix-II

Villages without Scheduled Tribes: There is 1 village without any scheduled tribe population.

Literates and Illiterates by Sex (Total Population):

	Persons	Males	Females
Literate	12,178	6,596	5,582
Illiterate	15,720	7,182	8,538
Literacy rate	51	56	46
Graduate	229	190	39

Agriculture: ***Distribution of villages according to land use:*** Out of 46 villages, Total area (in hectare) is 11198, out of that 33.48 percent is cultivable and 13.53 percent of the cultivable area is irrigated.

Sources of Irrigation (Hectares): Government Canal 0,

Private Canal 0, Well without Electricity 0, Well with Electricity 0, Tubewell without Electricity 0, Tubewell with Electricity 0, Tank 507.2, River 0, Lake 0, Waterfall 0, Others 0.

Villages with population of 5000 to 9999: None

Villages with population of 10000 and above: None

Distribution of Workers:

	Persons	Males	Females	WPR
Cultivators	3,185	2,369	816	23.08
Agricultural Labour	9,133	4,750	4,383	66.19
Household Industry	181	97	84	1.31
Other Workers	1,300	899	401	9.42
Main Workers	10,718	7,016	3,702	77.67
Marginal Workers	3,081	1,099	1,982	22.33
Total Workers	13,799	8,115	5,684	

Religion: Major Religious Communities:

	Persons	Males	Females	Sex Ratio
Hindu (98.51%)	27,482	13,593	13,889	1,022
Muslim (0.5%)	139	66	73	1,106
Christian (0.91%)	253	106	147	1,387
Sikh (0%)	-	-	-	-
Buddhists (0%)	-	-	-	-
Jain (0%)	-	-	-	-

Agewise Data:

	Persons	Males	Females	Sex Ratio
All ages	27,898	13,778	14,120	1025
0-14	9,451	4,739	4,712	994
15-44	13,053	6,423	6,630	1032
45-79	5,216	2,524	2,692	1067
80+	107	55	52	945
Age not stated	71	37	34	919

Languages (Dominant):

Telugu, Koya, Gondi, Urdu, Tamil

Disabled Population:

	Persons	Males	Females	%
Total Disabled	411	244	167	
In Seeing	156	85	71	37.96
In Speech	39	25	14	9.49
In Hearing	21	13	8	5.11
In Movement	139	92	47	33.82
Mentally	56	29	27	13.63

DHANWADA

Dhanwado C.D. Block lies in the central west part of Mahbubnagar district. The Block is located at a distance of 42 kms. from district headquarters (Mahbubnagar). There are 18 villages in the block with the total population of 53,242 persons. Area of the C.D. Block is 248.57 sq. kms. It is bounded by Koilkonda Mandal on north, Narayanpet Mandal on west, Makthal, Narva and Chinna Chintakunta Mandals on south, and Devarkadra Mandal on east.

Communications :

Roadways : State Highway (S.H.): Direction- Narayanpet to Devarkandra. and Makthal to Chinna Chintakunta Mandal. Nearest Villages- Dhanwada, Mandipalle, Yamnanpalle, Yeligandla, Peddachintakunta, Teelair, Venkatapur.

River: Krishna Nadi- Nearest Villages- Gotur, Pasalpad, Rakonda.

Backwards Region Grants Fund: It receives Backward Region Grants.

Annual Rainfall: Average Rainfall 564 mm

Ground Water: Availability of the Ground Water in the Basin is 1493 H.A.M. and the utilization is 1113 H. A.M. It belongs to SC category. Depth to water level varies from 2 to 5 meter below the ground. Most of the wells go down in summer months. The well density in the entire block is 9 wells per sq. km. Total no. of the wells in the block are enumerated as 2220, according to the Ground Water Estimation Committee.

Natural Division : Telangana Plateau Region

Administration:

Division: Telangana. Parliamentary Constituency: 11 Mahbubnagar. District: Mahbubnagar. Mandal: Dhanwada. Assembly Constituency: 73 Narayanpet. Gram Panchayat: 19

Villages: 18 **Inhabited:** 18 **Uninhabited:** 0

Ranking	District	State	National
Area	32	317	3398
Population	24	411	5123
Sex Ratio	9	223	1112
Child Sex Ratio	51	928	4074
Literacy Rate	41	1019	5805
Density	33	202	4524
Work Participation Rate	26	665	559

Gram Panchayats:

Appampally, Cherlapally, Dhanwada, Gotur, Gunmukla Hanmanpalle, Kamsanpalle, Kistapur, Kondapur, Madwar Mandipalle, Marikal, Paspula, Peddachintakunta Poosalpad, Rakonda, Ramakistaiahpalle, Teelair Yeligandla.

Amenities:

Education: Primary School in 18 villages, Middle school in 10 villages, Matriculation or Secondary School in 5 villages, namely Dhanwada, Kondapur, Gotur, Gunmukla, Marikal. Higher Secondary or Pre University Courses or Intermediate or Junior College in 0 village of the CD Block, College in 0 village, Adult Literacy Center in 15 villages.

Medical: Hospital in 1 village, Dispensary in 1 village, Health Center in 2 villages, Sub Center in 8 villages, Maternity and Child Welfare Center in 0 village,

Community health workers in 0 village.
The Village having Hospital or Dispensary or Health Center is Marikal.

Drinking Water: Tap water in 18 villages, Tank water in 18 villages, Well water in 18 villages, Tubewell in 18 villages and more than one source in 18 villages.

Bank: Banking facility in 3 villages, namely, Dhanwada, Kondapur, Marikal.

Credit Society in 10 villages Agricultural Credit Society in 5 Non-Agricultural Credit Society in 10 villages.

Others: Power supply in 18 villages, Cinema hall in 2 villages, sport club in 0 village, Stadium or Auditorium or Community Hall in 0 village, Post Office in 15 villages.

There are 15 villages having bus facilities.

Villages with most of facilities: Dhanwada Kondapur, Marikal.

Villages without Amenities (Education): None..

Scheduled Castes: Out of the total population of 53242 persons, 8823 persons (16.57%) belong to Scheduled Castes.

The villages having less than 10% SC population are None..

The villages having more than 50% SC population are None.

Sex ratio of Scheduled Caste population is 506.

Scheduled Castes Literates and Illiterates by Sex:

	Persons	Males	Females
Literate	1,765	1,261	504
Illiterate	7,058	3,098	3,960
Literacy rate	23.6	34.4	13.3
Graduate	40	35	5

Scheduled Castes (Dominant):

Madiga, Mala, Generic Castes etc., Beda Jangam etc. Byagara

For their cultural identity please see Appendix-I

Villages without Scheduled Castes: There are 0 village without any scheduled caste population.

Scheduled Tribes: Out of the total population of 53242 persons, 3189 persons (5.99%) belong to Scheduled Tribes.

The villages having less than 10% ST population are Dhanwada, Gotur, Pasalpad, Madwar, Kamsanpalle Gunmukla, Yamnanpalle, Yeligandla, Paspul, Marikal Ibrahimpatnam, Peddachintakunta, Teelair, Venkatapur Rakonda.

The villages having more than 50% ST population are None.

Sex ratio of Scheduled tribe population is 481.

Scheduled Tribes Literates and Illiterates by Sex:

	Persons	Males	Females
Literate	390	323	67
Illiterate	2,799	1,332	1,467
Literacy rate	15.6	24.9	5.6
Graduate	5	5	0

Scheduled Tribes (Dominant):

Sugalis etc., Yerukulas, Chenchu etc.
Generic Tribes etc.

For their cultural identity please see Appendix-II

Villages without Scheduled Tribes: There are 8 villages without any scheduled tribe population.

Literates and Illiterates by Sex (Total Population):

	Persons	Males	Females
Literate	17,310	11,398	5,912
Illiterate	35,932	15,205	20,727
Literacy rate	39	51	26
Graduate	566	496	70

Agriculture: ***Distribution of villages according to land use:*** Out of 18 villages, Total area (in hectare) is 24856, out of that 72.28 percent is cultivable and 16.5 percent of the cultivable area is irrigated.

Sources of Irrigation (Hectares): Government Canal 813.4, Private Canal 0, Well without Electricity 0, Well with Electricity 1169.06, Tubewell without Electricity 0, Tubewell with Electricity 24.28, Tank 958.32, River 0, Lake 0, Waterfall 0, Others 0.

Villages with population of 5000 to 9999: Dhanwada, Kistapur, Kondapur, Marikal.

Villages with population of 10000 and above: None

Distribution of Workers:

	Persons	Males	Females	WPR
Cultivators	8,500	5,661	2,839	28.94
Agricultural Labour	12,603	4,268	8,335	42.91
Household Industry	3,451	1,409	2,042	11.75
Other Workers	4,817	3,779	1,038	16.4
Main Workers	21,742	12,526	9,216	74.03
Marginal Workers	7,629	2,591	5,038	25.97
Total Workers	29,371	15,117	14,254	

Religion: Major Religious Communities:

	Persons	Males	Females	Sex Ratio
Hindu (93.49%)	49,775	24,886	24,889	1,000
Muslim (6.22%)	3,309	1,638	1,671	1,020
Christian (0.23%)	124	64	60	938
Sikh (0%)	-	-	-	-
Buddhists (0%)	-	-	-	-
Jain (0%)	1	1	-	-

Agewise Data:

	Persons	Males	Females	Sex Ratio
All ages	53,242	26,603	26,639	1001
0-14	19,272	9,945	9,327	938
15-44	24,042	11,889	12,153	1022
45-79	9,570	4,595	4,975	1083
80+	319	152	167	1099

Age not stated	39	22	17	773

Languages (Dominant):

Telugu, Urdu, Hindi, Kannada, Marathi

Disabled Population:

	Persons	Males	Females	%
Total Disabled	1,108	628	480	
In Seeing	575	336	239	51.9
In Speech	65	35	30	5.87
In Hearing	44	21	23	3.97
In Movement	345	195	150	31.14
Mentally	79	41	38	7.13

DHARMAPURI

Dharampuri C.D. Block lies in the north-east part of Karimnagar district. The Block is located at a distance of 65 kms. from district headquarters (Karimnagar). There are 23 villages in the block with the total population of 73,230 persons. Area of the C.D. Block is 257.74 sq. kms. It is bounded by Adilabad district on north, east and south-east, Velgatoor Mandal on south-east, Gollapalle Mandal on south, Jagtial Mandal on south-west, and Sarangapur Mandal on west and north-west.

Communications :

Roadways : NH- 16: Direction- Jagtial to Luxettipet. Nearest Villages- Kamalapur, Velgonda, Chinnapur,Timma pur.

River: Godavari Nadi- Nearest villages- Arepalle, Maggi di, Jaina, Rajaram, Dharmapuri, Raipatnam, Stambampalle, Timmapur.

Backwards Region Grants Fund: It receives Backward Region Grants.

Annual Rainfall: Average Rainfall 1062 mm

Ground Water : Availability of the Ground Water in the Basin is 1486 H.A.M. and the utilization is 1594 H.A.M. It belongs to Safe category. Depth to water level varies from more than 10 meter below the ground. Most of the wells go down in summer months. The well density in the entire block is 16 wells per sq. km. Total no. of the wells in the block are enumerated as 3935, according to the Ground Water Estimation Commi ttee.

Natural Division : Godavari Depression Region

Administration:

Division: Telangana. Parliamentary Constituency: 2 Peddappalle (SC). District: Karimnagar. Mandal: Dharmap uri. Assembly Constituency: 22 Dharmapuri (SC). Gram Panchayat:27.

Places of Tourist Interest:

Dharmapuri : Dharmapuri is situated at a distance of about 48 kms. from Jagtial town and 51 kms. from Peddap alle railway station, on the Kazipet Balharshah Section of the South Central Railway. Dharmapuri attained relig ious importance, owing to the existence of the shrine dedicated to Narasimhaswamy, an incarnation of Lord Vishnu. Siva with Dakshinamurthy, Vinayaka, Saptha Mathrukas carved on a single slab of stone and Mahishas ura mardani, the sixty pillared temple, Mahalakshmi temple and Akkapalle Rajanna temple are the other templ es of importance that heighten the sanctity of the place to the Hindus. It is one of the places of tourist inter est in the State and the Kalyanot-savam of Lakshminarasi mhaswamy celebrated during February-March attracts nearly a lakh of pilgrims.

Fairs and Festivals:

Sri Lakshmi Narasimhaswamy Kalyanothsavam : It is celeb rated for 11 days from Phalguna Suddha Dasami to Bahula Panchami (February-March). The dolothsavam in Brahma Pushkarini on Purnima and the car festival on Bahula Panchami are very important. The chakra teertham funct ion in Godavari

River : is celebrated on similar lines as that held in Narasimhaswamy temple at Antarvedi (East Godavari) near the estuary of that great River :. This is an ancient festival extending to the whole district and to the neighbouring districts. About one lakh of Hindu devotees congregate. Dharmapuri Ramayanam states that the town was constructed by a king named Dharmavarma.

Villages: 23 **Inhabited:** 23 **Uninhabited:** 0

Ranking	District	State	National
Area	8	283	3279
Population	6	87	4347
Sex Ratio	15	76	534
Child Sex Ratio	12	243	757
Literacy Rate	53	991	5653
Density	21	315	3703
Work Participation Rate	23	423	788

Gram Panchayats:

Arepalli, Beersani, Buggaram, Chinnapoor Dammannapet, Dharmapuri, Donthapoor, Donur Gadepally, Gopalapoor, Jaina, Kamalapur, Maddunur Nagaram, Nerella, Pasigam, Pedda Nukkalapet, Rajaram Rayapatnam, Sandaiahpally, Sirikonda, Sthambampally Theegala Dharmaram, Thimmapoor, Thummenala, Velgonda Venkatapoor.

Amenities:

Education: Primary School in 22 villages, Middle school in 15 villages, Matriculation or Secondary School in 8 villages, namely Jaina, Rajaram, Donoor, Nerella, Dharmapuri, Velgonda, Buggaram, Madnoor.

Higher Secondary or Pre University Courses or Inter-

mediate or Junior College in 1 village of the CD Block,, namely Dharmapuri.
College in 1 village, Adult Literacy Center in 13 villages., College is in village, namely Dharmapuri.
Medical: Hospital in 0 village, Dispensary in 1 village, Health Center in 1 village, Sub Center in 12 villages, Maternity and Child Welfare Center in 1 village, Community health workers in 0 village.
The Village having Hospital or Dispensary or Health Center is Dharmapuri.
Drinking Water: Tap water in 21 villages, Tank water in 21 villages, Well water in 23 villages, Tubewell in 22 villages and more than one source in 23 villages.
Bank: Banking facility in 2 villages, namely, Nerella, Dharmapuri.
Credit Society in 18 villages Agricultural Credit Society in 5 Non-Agricultural Credit Society in 18 villages.
Others: Power supply in 23 villages, Cinema hall in 1 village, sport club in 0 village, Stadium or Auditorium or Community Hall in 0 village, Post Office in 16 villages.
There are 20 villages having bus facilities.
Villages with most of facilities: Nerella Dharmapuri.
Villages without amenities (Education): Maggidi..
Scheduled Castes: Out of the total population of 73230 persons, 15648 persons (21.37%) belong to Scheduled Castes.
The villages having less than 10% SC population are None..
The villages having more than 50% SC population are None.
Sex ratio of Scheduled Caste population is 507.
Scheduled Castes Literates and Illiterates by Sex:

	Persons	Males	Females
Literate	4,359	2,925	1,434
Illiterate	11,289	4,795	6,494
Literacy rate	32.3	44.1	20.9
Graduate	39	34	5

Scheduled Castes (Dominant):
Madiga, Mala, Mala Sale etc., Gosangi Mitha Ayyalvar
For their cultural identity please see Appendix-I
Villages without Scheduled Castes: There are 0 village without any scheduled caste population.
Scheduled Tribes: Out of the total population of 73230 persons, 588 persons (0.8%) belong to Scheduled Tribes.
The villages having less than 10% ST population are Arepalle, Donthapur, Maggidi, Theegala Dharmaram Jaina, Rajaram, Donoor, Nerella, Thummenala Dharmapuri, Timmapur, Kamalapur, Nagaram, Velgonda Chinnapur, Buggaram, Sirivanchakota, Gopulapur Sirikonda, Beersani, Madnoor, Raipatnam Stambampalle.
The villages having more than 50% ST population are None.
Sex ratio of Scheduled tribe population is 481.
Scheduled Tribes Literates and Illiterates by Sex:

	Persons	Males	Females
Literate	106	87	19
Illiterate	482	218	264
Literacy rate	20.5	31.4	8.0
Graduate	2	2	0

Scheduled Tribes (Dominant):
Gond etc., Sugalis etc., Yerukulas, Koya etc.
Generic Tribes etc.
For their cultural identity please see Appendix-II
Villages without Scheduled Tribes: There are 12 villages without any scheduled tribe population.
Literates and Illiterates by Sex (Total Population):

	Persons	Males	Females
Literate	25,644	16,516	9,128
Illiterate	47,586	19,608	27,978
Literacy rate	41	53	29
Graduate	835	684	151

Agriculture: ***Distribution of villages according to land use:*** Out of 23 villages, Total area (in hectare) is 25774, out of that 50.48 percent is cultivable and 61.05 percent of the cultivable area is irrigated.
Sources of Irrigation (Hectares): Government Canal 2685.38, Private Canal 0, Well without Electricity 1070.84, Well with Electricity 1477.45, Tubewell without Electricity 0, Tubewell with Electricity 41.28, Tank 2613.27, River 0, Lake 0, Waterfall 0, Others 54.6.
Villages with population of 5000 to 9999:
Rajaram.
Villages with population of 10000 and above:
Dharmapuri.
Distribution of Workers:

	Persons	Males	Females	WPR
Cultivators	11,271	6,967	4,304	28.03
Agricultural Labour	15,591	7,076	8,515	38.78
Household Industry	5,382	1,119	4,263	13.39
Other Workers	7,960	5,708	2,252	19.8
Main Workers	35,425	19,253	16,172	88.11
Marginal Workers	4,779	1,617	3,162	11.89
Total Workers	40,204	20,870	19,334	

Religion: Major Religious Communities:

	Persons	Males	Females	Sex Ratio
Hindu (96.97%)	71,012	35,030	35,982	1,027
Muslim (2.63%)	1,927	952	975	1,024
Christian (0.38%)	276	137	139	1,015

Sikh (0%)	3	1	2	2,000
Buddhists (0%)	-	-	-	-
Jain (0%)	-	-	-	-

Agewise Data:

	Persons	Males	Females	Sex Ratio
All ages	73,230	36,124	37,106	1027
0-14	23,665	11,916	11,749	986
15-44	34,519	16,845	17,674	1049
45-79	14,375	7,025	7,350	1046
80+	595	288	307	1066
Age not stated	76	50	26	520

Languages (Dominant):

Telugu, Urdu, Marathi, Oriya, Hindi

Disabled Population:

	Persons	Males	Females	%
Total Disabled	1,138	620	518	
In Seeing	464	238	226	40.77
In Speech	133	69	64	11.69
In Hearing	63	38	25	5.54
In Movement	303	186	117	26.63
Mentally	175	89	86	15.38

DHARMARAM

Dharamaram C.D. Block lies in the north-eastern part of Karimnagar district. The Block is located at a dista nce of 38 kms. from district headquarters (Karimnagar). There are 17 villages in the block with the total population of 49,636 persons. Area of the C.D. Block is 202.01 sq. kms. It is bounded by Velgatoor Mandal on north, Ramagundam Mandal on east, Julapalle Mandal on south, Choppadandi Mandal on south-west, and Pegadap alle Mandal on west.

Communications :

Roadways : Metalled Roads: Nearest Villages- Bommareddip alle, Mallapur.

Backwards Region Grants Fund: It receives Backward Region Grants.

Annual Rainfall: Average Rainfall 1038 mm

Ground Water: Availability of the Ground Water in the Basin is 3483 H.A.M. and the utilization is 1195 H. A.M. It belongs to Safe category. Depth to water level varies from more than 5 to 10 meter below the ground. Most of the wells go down in summer months. The well density in the entire block is 14 wells per sq. km. Total no. of the wells in the block are enumerated as 2796, according to the Ground Water Estimation Commi ttee.

Natural Division : Godavari Depression Region

Administration:

Division: Telangana. Parliamentary Constituency: 2 Peddapalle (SC). District: Karimnagar. Mandal: Dharmaram. Assembly Constituency: 22 Dharmapura (SC). Gram Panch ayat: 23.

Villages: 17 **Inhabited:** 17 **Uninhabited:** 0

Ranking	District	State	National
Area	24	537	4143
Population	22	523	5298
Sex Ratio	17	103	676
Child Sex Ratio	25	498	1825
Literacy Rate	48	927	5392
Density	29	443	4139
Work Participation Rate	36	559	1099

Gram Panchayats:

Abbapur, Banjerupalli, Bommareddipalli Botlavanaparthy, Chamanpally, Dharmaram Dongathurthy, Erraguntapalli, Gopalraopet Kammarikhanpet, Katekenapalli, Khanampalli Khilavanaparthy, Kothapalli, Kothur, Mallapur Myadaram, Narasimhlapalli, Narsingapur Paidichintalapalli, Pathipaka, Rachapally, Sayampet.

Amenities:

Education: Primary School in 17 villages, Middle school in 11 villages, Matriculation or Secondary School in 6 villages, namely Pathipaka, Bommareddipalle, Myadaram, Dongathurthy, Katkanpalle, Mallapur.

Higher Secondary or Pre University Courses or Inter-mediate or Junior College in 0 village of the CD Block, College in 1 village, Adult Literacy Center in 6 villages., College is in village, namely Mallapur.

Medical: Hospital in 1 village, Dispensary in 1 village, Health Center in 1 village, Sub Center in 7 villages, Maternity and Child Welfare Center in 0 village, Community health workers in 0 village.

The Village having Hospital or Dispensary or Health Center is Bommareddipalle.

Drinking Water: Tap water in 17 villages, Tank water in 17 villages, Well water in 17 villages, Tubewell in 17 villages and more than one source in 17 villages.

Bank: Banking facility in 3 villages, namely, Narsingapur, Bommareddipalle, Dongathurthy.

Credit Society in 17 villages Agricultural Credit Society in 2 Non-Agricultural Credit Society in 17 villages.

Others: Power supply in 17 villages, Cinema hall in 1 village, sport club in 0 village, Stadium or Auditorium or Community Hall in 0 village, Post Office in 10 villages.

There are 16 villages having bus facilities.

Villages with most of facilities: Bommareddipalle Dongathurthy.

Villages without Amenities (Education): None..

Scheduled Castes: Out of the total population of 49636 persons, 10432 persons (21.02%) belong to Scheduled Castes.

The villages having less than 10% SC population are None..

The villages having more than 50% SC population are None.

Sex ratio of Scheduled Caste population is 516.

Scheduled Castes Literates and Illiterates by Sex:

	Persons	Males	Females
Literate	3,689	2,037	1,652
Illiterate	6,743	3,013	3,730
Literacy rate	41.1	47.4	35.3
Graduate	57	51	6

Scheduled Castes (Dominant):

Madiga, Mala, Mala Sale etc., Beda Jangam etc. Sindhollu etc.

For their cultural identity please see Appendix-I

Villages without Scheduled Castes: There are 0 village without any scheduled caste population.

Scheduled Tribes: Out of the total population of 49636 persons, 2755 persons (5.55%) belong to Scheduled Tribes.

The villages having less than 10% ST population are Narsingapur, Pathipaka, Bommareddipalle, Myadaram Sayampeta, Khanampalle, Paidichinthala Palle Rachapalle, Dongathurthy, Botlavanaparthy Khilavanaparthy, Chamanpalle, Mallapur, Abbapuram.

The villages having more than 50% ST population are None.

Sex ratio of Scheduled tribe population is 490.

Scheduled Tribes Literates and Illiterates by Sex:

	Persons	Males	Females
Literate	730	455	275
Illiterate	2,025	951	1,074
Literacy rate	32.4	40.4	24.4
Graduate	6	6	0

Scheduled Tribes (Dominant):

Sugalis etc., Yerukulas, Chenchu etc., Thoti Gond etc.

For their cultural identity please see Appendix-II

Villages without Scheduled Tribes: There are 3 villages without any scheduled tribe population.

Literates and Illiterates by Sex (Total Population):

	Persons	Males	Females
Literate	18,443	11,311	7,132
Illiterate	31,193	13,279	17,914
Literacy rate	43	54	33
Graduate	385	323	62

Agriculture: ***Distribution of villages according to land use:***

Out of 17 villages, Total area (in hectare) is 20200, out of that 68.18 percent is cultivable and 64.09 percent of the cultivable area is irrigated.

Sources of Irrigation (Hectares): Government Canal 3445.2, Private Canal 0, Well without Electricity 0, Well with Electricity 3002.24, Tubewell without Electricity 82, Tubewell with Electricity 0, Tank 2297, River 0, Lake 0, Waterfall 0, Others 0.

Villages with population of 5000 to 9999:

Bommareddipalle, Myadaram.

Villages with population of 10000 and above: None

Distribution of Workers:

	Persons	Males	Females	WPR
Cultivators	7,335	4,687	2,648	27.66
Agricultural Labour	12,939	5,049	7,890	48.8
Household Industry	1,096	506	590	4.13
Other Workers	5,147	3,896	1,251	19.41
Main Workers	21,595	12,461	9,134	81.44
Marginal Workers	4,922	1,677	3,245	18.56
Total Workers	26,517	14,138	12,379	

Religion: Major Religious Communities:

	Persons	Males	Females	Sex Ratio
Hindu (98.38%)	48,831	24,183	24,648	1,019
Muslim (1.31%)	651	329	322	979
Christian (0.2%)	97	46	51	1,109
Sikh (0.03%)	16	9	7	778
Buddhists (0%)	-	-	-	-
Jain (0%)	-	-	-	-

Agewise Data:

	Persons	Males	Females	Sex Ratio
All ages	49,636	24,590	25,046	1019
0-14	16,011	8,031	7,980	994
15-44	22,647	11,118	11,529	1037
45-79	10,336	5,142	5,194	1010
80+	585	268	317	1183
Age not stated	57	31	26	839

Languages (Dominant):

Telugu, Hindi, Urdu, Tamil, Oriya

Disabled Population:

	Persons	Males	Females	%
Total Disabled	904	472	432	
In Seeing	417	200	217	46.13
In Speech	96	59	37	10.62
In Hearing	47	19	28	5.2
In Movement	222	128	94	24.56
Mentally	122	66	56	13.5

DHARMASAGAR

Dharmasagar C.D. Block lies in the western part of Warangal district. The Block is located at a distance of 22 kms. from district headquarters (Warangal). There are 19 villages in the block with the total population of 87,619 persons. Area of the C.D. Block is 259.90 sq. kms. It is bounded in the north district by Karim Nagar, in the south by Mandals Ghanpur (station) and Zaffergadh, in the east by Mandals Hasanparthy, Hanamko nda and Zaffergadh, and in the west by Ghanpur (station) Mandal.

Communications:

Roadways : NH- 202: Direction- Hyderabad to Warangal. Nearest Villages- Peddapendyala, Rampur.

Railway Station: Peddapendyala, Rampur.

Backwards Region Grants Fund: It receives Backward Region Grants.

Annual Rainfall: Average Rainfall 754 mm

Ground Water: Availability of the Ground Water in the Basin is 2860 H.A.M.and the utilization is 3161 H.A. M. It belongs to OE category. Depth to water level varies from 10 to 20 meter below the ground. Most of the wells go down in summer months. The well density in the entire block is 21 wells per sq. km. Total no. of the wells in the block are enumerated as 5385, according to the Ground Water Estimation Committee.

Natural Division : Godavari Depression Region

Administration:

Division: Telangana. Parliamentary Constituency. Distri ct: Warangal. Mandal: Dharmasagar. Assembly Constituency: 99 Ghanpur (Station) (SC). Gram Panchayat: 24.

Villages: 19 **Inhabited:** 19 **Uninhabited:** 0

Ranking	District	State	National
Area	7	277	3250
Population	6	138	4507
Sex Ratio	28	673	2302
Child Sex Ratio	27	721	3026
Literacy Rate	12	457	3693
Density	39	708	3903
Work Participation Rate	27	481	2003

Gram Panchayats:

Devunoor, Dharmapur, Dharmasagar, Gundlasagar Janakipur, Kammaripeta, Kyathampalle, Maddelagudem Malakapalle, Mallikudurla, Mupparam, Narayanagiri Peddapendyala, Peechara, Rampur, Rayagudem, Saipeta Shalapalli, Sodeshapalle, Somadevarapalle Thatikayala, Unikecherla, Velair, Yelkurthi.

Amenities:

Education: Primary School in 19 villages, Middle school in 13 villages, Matriculation or Secondary School in 9 villages, namely Velair, Peechera, Mallikudurla, Narayanagiri, Dharmasagar, Kyathampalle, Peddapendyala, Rampur, Malakpalle.

Higher Secondary or Pre University Courses or Intermediate or Junior College in 1 village of the CD Block,, namely Velair.

College in 1 village, Adult Literacy Center in 11 villages., College is in village, namely Peddapendyala.

Medical: Hospital in 0 village, Dispensary in 0 village, Health Center in 2 villages, Sub Center in 16 villages, Maternity and Child Welfare Center in 2 villages, Community health workers in 0 village.

Drinking Water: Tap water in 19 villages, Tank water in 19 villages, Well water in 19 villages, Tubewell in 19 villages and more than one source in 19 villages.

Bank: Banking facility in 3 villages, namely, Velair, Dharmasagar, Peddapendyala.

Credit Society in 19 villages Agricultural Credit Society in 7 Non-Agricultural Credit Society in 19 villages.

Others: Power supply in 19 villages, Cinema hall in 2 villages, sport club in 0 village, Stadium or Auditorium or Community Hall in 0 village, Post Office in 18 villages.

There are 19 villages having bus facilities.

Villages with most of facilities: Velair Dharmasagar, Peddapendyala.

Villages without Amenities (Education): None..

Scheduled Castes: Out of the total population of 69043 persons, 15101 persons (21.87%) belong to Scheduled Castes.

The villages having less than 10% SC population are None..

The villages having more than 50% SC population are None.

Sex ratio of Scheduled Caste population is 485.

Scheduled Castes Literates and Illiterates by Sex:

	Persons	Males	Females
Literate	7,060	4,305	2,755
Illiterate	8,041	3,472	4,569
Literacy rate	54.7	64.5	44.3
Graduate	178	140	38

Scheduled Castes (Dominant):

Madiga, Mala, Generic Castes etc., Gosangi Beda Jangam etc.

For their cultural identity please see Appendix-I

Villages without Scheduled Castes: There are 0 village without any scheduled caste population.

Scheduled Tribes: Out of the total population of 69043 persons, 3083 persons (4.47%) belong to Scheduled Tribes.

The villages having less than 10% ST population are Peechera, Gundlasagar, Sodeshapalle, Mallikudurla Narayanagiri, Mupparam, Devunoor, Somadevarapalle Unikicherla, Dharmasagar, Elkurthi (P.D), Janakipur Kyathampalle, Thatikayala, Peddapendyala, Rampur Dharmapur, Malakpalle.

The villages having more than 50% ST population are None.

Sex ratio of Scheduled tribe population is 482.

Scheduled Tribes Literates and Illiterates by Sex:

	Persons	Males	Females
Literate	868	572	296

Illiterate	2,215	1,025	1,190
Literacy rate	33.7	42.7	23.9
Graduate	14	13	1

Scheduled Tribes (Dominant):

Sugalis etc., Yerukulas, Koya etc.

Generic Tribes etc., Kulia

For their cultural identity please see Appendix-II

Villages without Scheduled Tribes: There is 1 village without any scheduled tribe population.

Literates and Illiterates by Sex (Total Population):

	Persons	Males	Females
Literate	32,639	20,062	12,577
Illiterate	36,404	14,914	21,490
Literacy rate	55	67	43
Graduate	1,051	811	240

Agriculture: ***Distribution of villages according to land use:*** Out of 19 villages, Total area (in hectare) is 25990, out of that 57.77 percent is cultivable and 39.94 percent of the cultivable area is irrigated.

Sources of Irrigation (Hectares): Government Canal 0, Private Canal 0, Well without Electricity 0, Well with Electricity 5151, Tubewell without Electricity 0, Tubewell with Electricity 0, Tank 846, River 0, Lake 0, Waterfall 0, Others 0.

Villages with population of 5000 to 9999:

Velair, Dharmasagar, Peddapendyala.

Villages with population of 10000 and above: None

Distribution of Workers:

	Persons	Males	Females	WPR
Cultivators	10,781	7,378	3,403	31.08
Agricultural Labour	15,159	5,579	9,580	43.71
Household Industry	1,304	726	578	3.76
Other Workers	7,439	5,699	1,740	21.45
Main Workers	26,355	16,649	9,706	75.99
Marginal Workers	8,328	2,733	5,595	24.01
Total Workers	34,683	19,382	15,301	

Religion: Major Religious Communities:

	Persons	Males	Females	Sex Ratio
Hindu (95.77%)	66,123	33,533	32,590	972
Muslim (2.47%)	1,705	879	826	940
Christian (1.6%)	1,108	514	594	1,156
Sikh (0.01%)	10	6	4	667
Buddhists (0%)	2	1	1	1,000
Jain (0%)	1	-	1	-

Agewise Data:

	Persons	Males	Females	Sex Ratio
All ages	69,043	34,976	34,067	974
0-14	21,929	11,278	10,651	944
15-44	31,228	15,677	15,551	992
45-79	15,128	7,628	7,500	983
80+	651	333	318	955
Age not stated	107	60	47	783

Languages (Dominant):

Telugu, Hindi, Urdu, Marathi, Gondi

Disabled Population:

	Persons	Males	Females	%
Total Disabled	1,455	804	651	
In Seeing	664	357	307	45.64
In Speech	154	72	82	10.58
In Hearing	51	21	30	3.51
In Movement	440	268	172	30.24
Mentally	146	86	60	10.03

DHARMAVARAM

Dharmavaram C.D. Block lies in the southern part of Anantapur district. It is a part of Dharmavaram Mandal. The Block is located at a distance of 25 kms. from district headquarters (Anantapur). There are 13 villages in the block with the total population of 43842 persons. Area of the C.D. Block is 368.33 sq. kms. It is bound ed in the north by Mandals Raptadu, Bukkarayasamudram and Bathalapalle, in the south by Mandals Kanaganapalle, Chennekothapalle and Bukkapatnam, in the east by Manda ls Mudigubba and Bukkapatnam, and in the west by Mandals Kamaganapalle and Raptadu.

Communications:

Roadways : NH- 7: Direction- Anantapur to Bangalore. Nearest Villages- Kunuthuru (Rural), Regatipalle, Pothulanagepalle, Mallakalva. State Highways (S.H.): Direction- Kananganapalle to Palasamudra. and Bathapalle to Bangalore. Nearest Villages- Kunuthuru (Rural), Regatipalle, Pothulanagepalle, Mallakalva, Gotlur, Thummala.

River Chitravati, north-eastwardly, touches the followi ng villages, namely, Subbaraopeta, Ravulacheruvu, Thumma la.

It receives the Backward Region Grant, and is identified as a drought-prone area as well.

Integrated Child Development Scheme (ICDS) Project: Dharmavaram, Total Anganwadi Centres: 165

Annual Rainfall: Average Rainfall 567 mm

Ground Water: Availability of the Ground Water in the Basin is 2707 H.A.M. and the utilization is 2994 H. A.M. It belongs to OE category. Depth to water level varies from 5 to 10 meter below the ground. Most of the wells go down in summer months. The well density in the entire block is 7 wells per sq. km. Total no. of the wells in the block are enumerated as 2634, according to the Ground Water Estimation Committee.

Forest and Reserved **Forest:** (Nalakota R.F.)- Nearest Villages- Pothulanagepalle, Mallakalva, Darsimala, Nelakota, Elukuntla.

Natural Division : Rayalaseema Region
Administration:
Division: Rayala Seema. Parliamentary Constituency: 37 Hindupur. District: Anantapur.
Mandal: Dharmavaram. Assembly Constituency: 279 Dharmav aram. Gram Panchayat: 18.

Places of Tourist Interest:
Dharmavaram : Dharmavaram is 34 kms. from Anantapur. It is a railway junction on the Bangalore-Guntakal line and is the terminus of the Pakala-Dharmavaram section. The important local temple is, the Lakshmi Chennakesava Swamy shrine. It has a storeyed tower, extensive enclosures and an entrance carved in the Vijayanagar style. The Ramalingeswara temple at the place is exquisite in its architecture and has a perenn ial water sprout (bugga). At dusk this Saikatha linga (an idol made of sand) looks as if it is imposed from above. Another Linga, which is nearby, is believed to have been installed by Hanuman. The seven small independent pillars in the temple when struck, produce 'Saptasvara' (the seven musical notes). The inhabitants are mostly weavers engaged in cotton and silk weaving. Dharmavaram silks are well known almost all over the country.

Sri Mohammad Shah Khader Vali Urs : It is celebrated for three days in November in his memory with gandhampu ja. His life history is read on the last day. Sugar is offered. The festival is widely known. About 25, 000 people from the town and from distant places belon ging to all communities congregate. It is reported that Tippu Sultan (1776-77) deputed Mohammad Ashroff Sahib to be in charge of Dharmavaram and the post of a kothwal for Dharmavaram was also created. Kothwal Abdul Nabi Sahib (1798-99) brought his guru Mohammad Shah Khader Vali Sahib from Chippagiri of Alur Taluk, Kurnool and kept him in his house. When the Vali died, his samaddhi (tomb) was constructed bebind the Chinna Upparige.

Villages: 13 **Inhabited:** 12 **Uninhabited:** 1

Ranking	District	State	National
Area	15	109	2482
Population	28	707	5575
Sex Ratio	46	998	3540
Child Sex Ratio	47	923	4094
Literacy Rate	49	724	4629
Density	48	573	5792
Work Participation Rate	42	959	1517

Gram Panchayats:
C.C.Kothakota, Chingicherla, Chintalapalli Darsimala, Dharmapuri, Elukuntla, Gotluru, Kunuthuru Mallakalva, Nelakota, Pothukunta, Pothulanagepalli Ravulacheruvu, Regatipalli, Subbaraopeta, Thummala Uppunesinapalli, Venkata Thimmapuram.

Amenities:
Education: Primary School in 12 villages, Middle school in 7 villages, Matriculation or Secondary School in 2 villages, namely Chigicherla, Kunuthuru (Rural).
Higher Secondary or Pre University Courses or Intermediate or Junior College in 0 village of the CD Block, College in 0 village, Adult Literacy Center in 0 village.
Medical: Hospital in 0 village, Dispensary in 1 village, Health Center in 1 village, Sub Center in 8 villages, Maternity and Child Welfare Center in 0 village, Community health workers in 0 village.
The Village having Hospital or Dispensary or Health Center is Gotlur.
Drinking Water: Tap water in 12 villages, Tank water in 0 villages, Well water in 0 village, Tubewell in 0 village and more than one source in 12 villages.
Bank: None.
Credit Society in 3 villages Agricultural Credit Society in 3 Non-Agricultural Credit Society in 0 village.
Others: Power supply in 12 villages, Cinema hall in 0 village, sport club in 0 village, Stadium or Auditorium or Community Hall in 0 village, Post Office in 12 villages.
There are 12 villages having bus facilities.
Village with most of facilities: None.
Villages without Amenities (Education): None..
Scheduled Castes: Out of the total population of 43819 persons, 6358 persons (14.51%) belong to Scheduled Castes.
The villages having less than 10% SC population are None..
The villages having more than 50% SC population are None.
Sex ratio of Scheduled Caste population is 490.

Scheduled Castes Literates and Illiterates by Sex:

	Persons	Males	Females
Literate	2,239	1,498	741
Illiterate	4,119	1,746	2,373
Literacy rate	40.1	52.6	27.1
Graduate	35	32	3

Scheduled Castes (Dominant):
Madiga, Mala, Adi Andhra, Generic Castes etc. Chalavadi
For their cultural identity please see Appendix-I
Villages without Scheduled Castes: There is 1 village without any scheduled caste population.
Scheduled Tribes: Out of the total population of 43819 persons, 3411 persons (7.78%) belong to Scheduled Tribes.
The villages having less than 10% ST population are Chigicherla, Gotlur, Subbaraopeta, Thummala

Kunuthuru (Rural), Regatipalle, Pothulanagepalle Elukuntla.

The villages having more than 50% ST population are None.

Sex ratio of Scheduled tribe population is 486.

Scheduled Tribes Literates and Illiterates by Sex:

	Persons	Males	Females
Literate	1,205	795	410
Illiterate	2,206	958	1,248
Literacy rate	40.9	52.5	28.6
Graduate	26	26	0

Scheduled Tribes (Dominant):

Sugalis etc., Yerukulas, Kammara

For their cultural identity please see Appendix-II

Villages without Scheduled Tribes: There are 2 villages without any scheduled tribe population.

Literates and Illiterates by Sex (Total Population):

	Persons	Males	Females
Literate	18,976	12,188	6,788
Illiterate	24,843	10,292	14,551
Literacy rate	49	62	36
Graduate	575	506	69

Agriculture: ***Distribution of villages according to land use:*** Out of 13 villages, Total area (in hectare) is 32786, out of that 68.97 percent is cultivable and 7.36 percent of the cultivable area is irrigated.

Sources of Irrigation (Hectares): Government Canal 0, Private Canal 0, Well without Electricity 0, Well with Electricity 1130.28, Tubewell without Electricity 0, Tubewell with Electricity 177.65, Tank 355.3, River 0, Lake 0, Waterfall 0, Others 0.

Villages with population of 5000 to 9999:

Gotlur, Ravulacheruvu, Kunuthuru (Rural).

Villages with population of 10000 and above: None

Distribution of Workers:

	Persons	Males	Females	WPR
Cultivators	8,479	5,252	3,227	36.53
Agricultural Labour	9,099	3,696	5,403	39.21
Household Industry	1,535	1,161	374	6.61
Other Workers	4,095	3,009	1,086	17.64
Main Workers	17,554	11,102	6,452	75.64
Marginal Workers	5,654	2,016	3,638	24.36
Total Workers	23,208	13,118	10,090	

Religion: Major Religious Communities:

	Persons	Males	Females	Sex Ratio
Hindu (97.11%)	42,554	21,834	20,720	949
Muslim (2.58%)	1,131	571	560	981
Christian (0.19%)	84	49	35	714
Sikh (0%)	-	-	-	-
Buddhists (0%)	-	-	-	-
Jain (0%)	-	-	-	-

Agewise Data:

	Persons	Males	Females	Sex Ratio
All ages	43,819	22,480	21,339	949
0-14	13,963	7,252	6,711	925
15-44	21,063	10,896	10,167	933
45-79	8,506	4,198	4,308	1026
80+	249	113	136	1204
Age not stated	38	21	17	810

Languages (Dominant):

Telugu, Urdu, Hindi, Marathi, Gondi

Disabled Population:

	Persons	Males	Females	%
Total Disabled	580	328	252	
In Seeing	141	80	61	24.31
In Speech	51	29	22	8.79
In Hearing	44	23	21	7.59
In Movement	250	147	103	43.1
Mentally	94	49	45	16.21

DHARPALLE

Dharpalle C.D. Block lies in the eastern part of Nizama bad district. The Block is located at a distance of 40 kms. from district headquarters (Nizamabad). There are 15 villages in the block with the total population of 44,152 persons. Area of the C.D. Block is 226.67 sq. kms. It is bounded by Jakranpalle Mandal on north and north-east, Bheemgal Mandal on north-east, Sirkonda Mandal on north-east, east and south-east, Sadasivanagar Mandal on south-east, south and south-west, and Dichpa lle Mandal on south-west, west and north-west.

Communications :

Roadways : NH, SH or Important Metalled Road is not available.

River: Phulang Nadi- Nearest Villages- Mailaram, Kesaram, Ramadugu, Lolam, Gouraram, Vengalpad, Nallavalle.

Backwards Region Grants Fund: It receives Backward Region Grants.

Annual Rainfall: Average Rainfall 1081 mm

Ground Water: Availability of the Ground Water in the Basin is 3001 H.A.M. and the utilization is 3179 H. A.M. It belongs to Over Exploited category. Depth to water level varies from 5 to 20 meter below the ground. Most of the wells go down in summer months, according to the Ground Water Estimation Committee.

Natural Division : Telangana Plateau Region

Administration:

Division: Telangana. Parliamentary Constituency: 4 Nizamabad. District: Nizamabad.. Mandal: Dharpalle. Assembly Constituency: 18 Nizamaba. Gram Panchayat: 18

Villages: 15 **Inhabited:** 14 **Uninhabited:** 1

Ranking	District	State	National
Area	15	419	3777
Population	26	690	5548
Sex Ratio	2	11	185
Child Sex Ratio	1	89	222
Literacy Rate	25	886	5225
Density	9	200	4764
Work Participation Rate	29	724	555

Gram Panchayats:
Ansanpally, Challagarga, Dammannapet, Danambanda (T) Dharpally, Donkal, Dubbaka, Gouraram, Govindpally Kesharam, Lolam, Mailaram, Nallavelli, Ramadugu Seethaipet, Sirnapally, Vengalpad, Yellareddypally.

Amenities:
Education: Primary School in 14 villages, Middle school in 8 villages, Matriculation or Secondary School in 6 villages, namely Mailaram, Dubbak, Ramadugu, Lolam, Dharpalle, Sirnapalle.
Higher Secondary or Pre University Courses or Intermediate or Junior College in 1 village of the CD Block,, namely Dharpalle.
College in 0 village, Adult Literacy Center in 12 villages.
Medical: Hospital in 1 village, Dispensary in 1 village, Health Center in 1 village, Sub Center in 9 villages, Maternity and Child Welfare Center in 5 villages, Community health workers in 0 village.
The Villages having Hospital or Dispensary or Health Center are Lolam, Dharpalle.
Drinking Water: Tap water in 13 villages, Tank water in 14 villages, Well water in 14 villages, Tubewell in 14 villages and more than one source in 14 villages.
Bank: Banking facility in 5 villages, namely, Dubbak, Ramadugu, Lolam, Dharpalle, Sirnapalle.
Credit Society in 5 villages Agricultural Credit Society in 3 Non-Agricultural Credit Society in 1 village.
Others: Power supply in 14 villages, Cinema hall in 1 village, sport club in 1 village, Stadium or Auditorium or Community Hall in 0 village, Post Office in 8 villages.
There are 14 villages having bus facilities.
Villages with most of facilities: Dubbak, Ramadugu Lolam, Dharpalle, Sirnapalle.
Villages without Amenities (Education): None..
Scheduled Castes: Out of the total population of 44152 persons, 5762 persons (13.05%) belong to Scheduled Castes.
The villages having less than 10% SC population are None..
The villages having more than 50% SC population are None.
Sex ratio of Scheduled Caste population is 516.

Scheduled Castes Literates and Illiterates by Sex:

	Persons	Males	Females
Literate	1,981	1,277	704
Illiterate	3,781	1,510	2,271
Literacy rate	39.4	53.1	26.9
Graduate	11	10	1

Scheduled Castes (Dominant):
Madiga, Mala, Gosangi, Malajangam
Generic Castes etc.
For their cultural identity please see Appendix-I
Villages without Scheduled Castes: There are 2 villages without any scheduled caste population.
Scheduled Tribes: Out of the total population of 44152 persons, 6136 persons (13.9%) belong to Scheduled Tribes.
The villages having less than 10% ST population are Mailaram, Challagarga, Kesaram, Ramadugu, Lolam Dharpalle, Sirnapalle.
The villages having more than 50% ST population are None.
Sex ratio of Scheduled tribe population is 511.

Scheduled Tribes Literates and Illiterates by Sex:

	Persons	Males	Females
Literate	1,307	1,009	298
Illiterate	4,829	1,992	2,837
Literacy rate	26.5	42.0	11.8
Graduate	11	11	0

Scheduled Tribes (Dominant):
Sugalis etc., Yerukulas, Gond etc., Koya etc.
Chenchu etc.
For their cultural identity please see Appendix-II
Villages without Scheduled Tribes: There are 3 villages without any scheduled tribe population.
Literates and Illiterates by Sex (Total Population):

	Persons	Males	Females
Literate	16,925	10,813	6,112
Illiterate	27,227	10,507	16,720
Literacy rate	45	60	31
Graduate	234	199	35

Agriculture: ***Distribution of villages according to land use:***
Out of 15 villages, Total area (in hectare) is 22368, out of that 29.19 percent is cultivable and 54.18 percent of the cultivable area is irrigated.
Sources of Irrigation (Hectares): Government Canal 535.97, Private Canal 0, Well without Electricity 0, Well with Electricity 1166.27, Tubewell without Electricity 0, Tubewell with Electricity 747.85, Tank 966.52, River 121.44, Lake 0, Waterfall 0, Others 0.
Villages with population of 5000 to 9999:
Dubbak, Lolam.
Villages with population of 10000 and above:

Dharpalle.

Distribution of Workers:

	Persons	Males	Females	WPR
Cultivators	9,036	5,483	3,553	36.65
Agricultural Labour	4,502	2,424	2,078	18.26
Household Industry	6,383	777	5,606	25.89
Other Workers	4,736	3,079	1,657	19.21
Main Workers	22,002	10,556	11,446	89.23
Marginal Workers	2,655	1,207	1,448	10.77
Total Workers	24,657	11,763	12,894	

Religion: Major Religious Communities:

	Persons	Males	Females	Sex Ratio
Hindu (93.18%)	41,139	19,828	21,311	1,075
Muslim (6.39%)	2,820	1,392	1,428	1,026
Christian (0.38%)	168	89	79	888
Sikh (0%)	-	-	-	-
Buddhists (0%)	1	1	-	-
Jain (0%)	-	-	-	-

Agewise Data:

	Persons	Males	Females	Sex Ratio
All ages	44,152	21,320	22,832	1071
0-14	15,115	7,736	7,379	954
15-44	20,304	9,588	10,716	1118
45-79	8,363	3,837	4,526	1180
80+	317	128	189	1477
Age not stated	53	31	22	710

Languages (Dominant):

Telugu, Hindi, Urdu, Tamil, Marathi

Disabled Population:

	Persons	Males	Females	%
Total Disabled	808	433	375	
In Seeing	400	219	181	49.5
In Speech	56	28	28	6.93
In Hearing	38	17	21	4.7
In Movement	227	126	101	28.09
Mentally	87	43	44	10.77

DHARUR

Dharur C.D. Block lies in the north-west part of Rangareddy district. The Block is located at a distance of 88 kms from district headquarters (Serilingampalle). There are 38 villages in the block with the total population of 73,200 persons. Area of the C.D. Block is 224.31 sq. kms. It is bounded by Bantwaram Mandal on north, Vicarabad Mandal on east, Pargi Mandal on south, Yalan Mandal on south-west, and Peddemul Mandal on west.

Communications :

Roadways : Metalled Roads: Nearest Villages- Gangaram, Ousapalle, Burugadda, Rampur, Ghattepalle, Rudraram, Dharur, Kerelly, Bacharam, Haridaspalle, Chintakunta, Dornal.

Railway Station: Dharur, Mailaram, Godamguda.

Backwards Region Grants Fund: It receives Backward Region Grants.

Annual Rainfall: Average Rainfall 870 mm

Ground Water: Availability of the Ground Water in the Basin is 1680 H.A.M. and the utilization is 1176 H. A.M. It belongs to Semi Critical category. Depth to water level varies from 5 to 20 meter below the ground. Most of the wells go down in summer months. The well density in the entire block is 6 wells per sq. km. Total no. of the wells in the block are enumerated as 1400, according to the Ground Water Estimation Committee.

Natural Division : Telangana Plateau Region

Administration:

Division: Telangana. Parliamentary Constituency: 10 Chevella. District: Rangareddy.

Mandal: Dharur. Assembly Constituency: 55 Vicarabad (SC). Gram Panchayat: 25.

Villages: 38 **Inhabited:** 37 **Uninhabited:** 1

Ranking	District	State	National
Area	13	414	3763
Population	21	738	5619
Sex Ratio	9	433	1652
Child Sex Ratio	14	329	1141
Literacy Rate	29	945	5469
Density	7	338	4886
Work Participation Rate	27	752	836

Gram Panchayats:

Allipur, Antharam, Chinthakunta, Dharur Dharur Station, Dornal, Ebbanur, Gaddameedigangaram Ghattepally, Godamguda, Gurudotla, Haridaspally Kerelly, Kondapur Kalan, Kukkinda, Mominkalan Munnurusomaram, Mylaram, Nagaram, Nagasamunder Rallachittempally, Rudraram, Sarpanpally Tharigopula, Zaidupally.

Amenities:

Education: Primary School in 37 villages, Middle school in 10 villages, Matriculation or Secondary School in 4 villages, namely Dharur, Kerelly, Tharigopul, Nagaram.

Higher Secondary or Pre University Courses or Intermediate or Junior College in 0 village of the CD Block, College in 0 village, Adult Literacy Center in 10 villages.

Medical: Hospital in 1 village, Dispensary in 0 village, Health Center in 1 village, Sub Center in 6 villages, Maternity and Child Welfare Center in 1 village, Community health workers in 0 village.

The Village having Hospital or Dispensary or Health Center is Dharur.

Drinking Water: Tap water in 37 villages, Tank water in

37 villages, Well water in 37 villages, Tubewell in 37 villages and more than one source in 37 villages.

Bank: Banking facility in 37 villages, namely, Nagasamundar, Gangaram, Narsapur, Dharmapur Chiltampalle, Somaram, Kacharam, Kondapur Khurd Kukinda, Ousapalle, Allapur, Rampur, Ghattepalle Rudraram, Dharur, Allipur, Ebbanoor, Kerelly Bacharam, Haridaspalle, Chintakunta, Dornal Kummar Palle, Mailaram, Tharigopul, Nagaram, Ampalle Gurudotla, Mominkhurd, Rajapur, Mominkalan, Antharam Nagsanpalle, Kondapur Kalan, Zaidupalle Surpanpalle, Godamguda.

Credit Society in 8 villages Agricultural Credit Society in 7 Non-Agricultural Credit Society in 2 villages.

Others: Power supply in 37 villages, Cinema hall in 0 village, sport club in 0 village, Stadium or Auditorium or Community Hall in 0 village, Post Office in 11 villages.

There are 28 villages having bus facilities.

Villages with most of facilities: Nagasamundar Dharur, Kerelly, Kummar Palle, Nagaram, Mominkalan.

Villages without Amenities (Education): None..

Scheduled Castes: Out of the total population of 42585 persons, 8133 persons (19.1%) belong to Scheduled Castes.

The villages having less than 10% SC population are Gangaram, Kacharam, Allapur, Rampur, Dornal Kummar Palle, Gurudotla, Nagsanpalle Kondapur Kalan.

The villages having more than 50% SC population are None.

Sex ratio of Scheduled Caste population is 507.

Scheduled Castes Literates and Illiterates by Sex:

	Persons	Males	Females
Literate	2,492	1,554	938
Illiterate	5,641	2,452	3,189
Literacy rate	36.7	46.6	27.1
Graduate	33	25	8

Scheduled Castes (Dominant):

Madiga, Mala, Byagara, Beda Jangam etc., Bindla

For their cultural identity please see Appendix-I

Villages without Scheduled Castes: There are 5 villages without any scheduled caste population.

Scheduled Tribes: Out of the total population of 42585 persons, 4946 persons (11.61%) belong to Scheduled Tribes.

The villages having less than 10% ST population are Nagasamundar, Gangaram, Narsapur, Dharmapur Chiltampalle, Somaram, Kacharam, Kondapur Khurd Kukinda, Ousapalle, Allapur, Rudraram, Allipur Ebbanoor, Kerelly, Bacharam, Haridaspalle Chintakunta, Tharigopul, Nagaram, Mominkhurd Rajapur, Mominkalan, Antharam, Nagsanpalle Kondapur Kalan, Zaidupalle, Surpanpalle, Godamguda.

The villages having more than 50% ST population are None.

Sex ratio of Scheduled tribe population is 490.

Scheduled Tribes Literates and Illiterates by Sex:

	Persons	Males	Females
Literate	844	621	223
Illiterate	4,102	1,899	2,203
Literacy rate	21.5	31.3	11.5
Graduate	14	13	1

Scheduled Tribes (Dominant):

Sugalis etc., Yerukulas, Chenchu etc.

Generic Tribes etc.

For their cultural identity please see Appendix-II

Villages without Scheduled Tribes: There are 23 villages without any scheduled tribe population.

Literates and Illiterates by Sex (Total Population):

	Persons	Males	Females
Literate	15,166	9,728	5,438
Illiterate	27,419	11,696	15,723
Literacy rate	43	54	31
Graduate	338	281	57

Agriculture: ***Distribution of villages according to land use:*** Out of 38 villages, Total area (in hectare) is 22431, out of that 52.15 percent is cultivable and 16.53 percent of the cultivable area is irrigated.

Sources of Irrigation (Hectares): Government Canal 778.15, Private Canal 0, Well without Electricity 52.61, Well with Electricity 235.05, Tubewell without Electricity 0, Tubewell with Electricity 677.86, Tank 163.41, River 0, Lake 0, Waterfall 0, Others 26.3.

Villages with population of 5000 to 9999: Dharur.

Villages with population of 10000 and above: None

Distribution of Workers:

	Persons	Males	Females	WPR
Cultivators	10,417	6,088	4,329	46.09
Agricultural Labour	8,929	3,633	5,296	39.51
Household Industry	415	219	196	1.84
Other Workers	2,840	2,164	676	12.57
Main Workers	19,841	11,248	8,593	87.79
Marginal Workers	2,760	856	1,904	12.21
Total Workers	22,601	12,104	10,497	

Religion: Major Religious Communities:

	Persons	Males	Females	Sex Ratio
Hindu (86.73%)	36,936	18,578	18,358	988
Muslim (12.82%)	5,458	2,748	2,710	986
Christian (0.34%)	144	74	70	946
Sikh (0%)	-	-	-	-
Buddhists (0%)	-	-	-	-

Jain (0%)	-	-	-	-

Agewise Data:

	Persons	Males	Females	Sex Ratio
All ages	42,585	21,424	21,161	988
0-14	16,305	8,230	8,075	981
15-44	18,392	9,412	8,980	954
45-79	7,513	3,644	3,869	1062
80+	334	120	214	1783
Age not stated	41	18	23	1278

Languages (Dominant):

Telugu, Urdu, Hindi, Marathi, Tamil

Disabled Population:

	Persons	Males	Females	%
Total Disabled	681	389	292	
In Seeing	298	154	144	43.76
In Speech	79	39	40	11.6
In Hearing	20	12	8	2.94
In Movement	219	145	74	32.16
Mentally	65	39	26	9.54

DHARUR

Dharur C.D. Block lies in the central west part of Mahbubnagar district. The Block is located at a distance of 120 kms. from district headquarters (Mahbubnagar). There are 25 villages in the block with the total population of 55,679 persons. Area of the C.D. Block is 320.35 sq. kms. It is bounded by Makthal, Narva and Atmakur Mandals on north, Gadwal Mandal on east, Maldakal Mandal on south-east, Chattu Mandal on south, and it has common border with the state of Karnataka on east.

Communications:

Roadways : State Highway (S.H.): Direction- Raichur to Gadwal. Nearest Villages- Alwalpad, Guvvaladinne, Kondapur, Umithyala, Kothulagidda, Marlabeedu.

River: Krishna Nadi- Nearest Villages- Nettempadu, Nagardoddi, Garlapadu, Upperu, Chintharevula.

Backwards Region Grants Fund : It receives Backward Region Grants.

Annual Rainfall: Average Rainfall 559 mm

Ground Water: Availability of the Ground Water in the Basin is 2113 H.A.M. and the utilization is 1543 H. A.M. It belongs to Semi Critical category. Depth to water level varies from 2 to 5 meter below the ground. Most of the wells go down in summer months. The well density in the entire block is 10 wells per sq. km. Total no. of the wells in the block are enumerated as 3241, according to the Ground Water Estimation Commi ttee.

Natural Division : Telangana Plateau Region

Administration:

Division: Telangana. Parliamentary Constituency: 11 Mahbubnagar. District: Mahbubnagar. Mandal: Dharur. Assembly Constituency: 79 Gadwal. Gram Panchayat: 26

Border Villages: (Karnataka)- Nearest Villages- Neelaha lli, Nettempadu, Erlabanda, Pagunta, Musaldoddi,Irkichedu, Guvvaladinne.

Villages: 25 **Inhabited:** 25 **Uninhabited:** 0

Ranking	**District**	**State**	**National**
Area	11	123	2562
Population	20	353	5023
Sex Ratio	25	576	2004
Child Sex Ratio	25	618	2461
Literacy Rate	63	1094	6288
Density	1	1	5168
Work Participation Rate	42	820	33

Gram Panchayats:

Alwalpad, Bureddypally, Chintarevula, Dharur Dyagadoddy, Earlabanda, Ganganpally, Garlapad Guddamdoddi, Guvvaladinne, Irkiched, Jampally Kondapur, Kothapalem, Kothulagidda, Manapur Marlabeedu, Neelahalli, Nettempad, Pagunta Palcherla, Pathapalem, Ryalampad, Uminthyala, Uppair Venkatapur.

Amenities:

Education: Primary School in 24 villages, Middle school in 8 villages, Matriculation or Secondary School in 3 villages, namely Upperu, Puranapalem, Dharur.

Higher Secondary or Pre University Courses or Inter-mediate or Junior College in 0 village of the CD Block, College in 0 village, Adult Literacy Center in 21 villages.

Medical: Hospital in 0 village, Dispensary in 1 village, Health Center in 2 villages, Sub Center in 7 villages, Maternity and Child Welfare Center in 0 village, Community health workers in 0 village.

The Village having Hospital or Dispensary or Health Center is Chintharevula.

Drinking Water: Tap water in 25 villages, Tank water in 25 villages, Well water in 25 villages, Tubewell in 25 villages and more than one source in 25 villages.

Bank: Banking facility in 2 villages, namely, Upperu, Dharur.

Credit Society in 13 villages Agricultural Credit Society in 2 Non-Agricultural Credit Society in 13 villages.

Others: Power supply in 25 villages, Cinema hall in 0 village, sport club in 0 village, Stadium or Auditorium or Community Hall in 0 village, Post Office in 12 villages.

There are 22 villages having bus facilities.

Villages with most of facilities: Upperu, Dharur.

Villages without amenities (Education):

Musaldoddi..

Scheduled Castes: Out of the total population of 55679 persons, 10492 persons (18.84%) belong to Scheduled Castes.

The villages having less than 10% SC population are None..

The villages having more than 50% SC population are None.

Sex ratio of Scheduled Caste population is 495.

Scheduled Castes Literates and Illiterates by Sex:

	Persons	Males	Females
Literate	1,492	1,141	351
Illiterate	9,000	4,159	4,841
Literacy rate	17.0	25.6	8.1
Graduate	26	25	1

Scheduled Castes (Dominant):

Madiga, Mala, Mala Dasari, Bindla

Generic Castes etc.

For their cultural identity please see Appendix-I

Villages without Scheduled Castes: There is 1 village without any scheduled caste population.

Scheduled Tribes: Out of the total population of 55679 persons, 2601 persons (4.67%) belong to Scheduled Tribes.

The villages having less than 10% ST population are Neelahalli, Mirzapuram, Nettempadu, Nagardoddi Garlapadu, Upperu, Chintharevula, Palcherla Mannapur, Dornala, Alwalpad, Ganganapalle Puranapalem, Erlabanda, Pagunta, Musaldoddi Venkatapuram, Kondapur, Kothulagidda, Marlabeedu Ryalampad, Dharur.

The villages having more than 50% ST population are None.

Sex ratio of Scheduled tribe population is 496.

Scheduled Tribes Literates and Illiterates by Sex:

	Persons	Males	Females
Literate	243	193	50
Illiterate	2,358	1,117	1,241
Literacy rate	11.9	18.8	5.0
Graduate	5	4	1

Scheduled Tribes (Dominant):

Sugalis etc., Yerukulas

For their cultural identity please see Appendix-II

Villages without Scheduled Tribes: There are 9 villages without any scheduled tribe population.

Literates and Illiterates by Sex (Total Population):

	Persons	Males	Females
Literate	11,957	8,524	3,433
Illiterate	43,722	19,600	24,122
Literacy rate	26	37	15
Graduate	270	236	34

Agriculture: ***Distribution of villages according to land use:*** Out of 25 villages, Total area (in hectare) is 32035, out of that 88.23 percent is cultivable and 26.2 percent of the cultivable area is irrigated.

Sources of Irrigation (Hectares): Government Canal 130, Private Canal 0, Well without Electricity 0, Well with Electricity 5753, Tubewell without Electricity 0, Tubewell with Electricity 565, Tank 871, River 85, Lake 0, Waterfall 0, Others 0.

Villages with population of 5000 to 9999: Upperu, Chintharevula, Dharur.

Villages with population of 10000 and above: None

Distribution of Workers:

	Persons	Males	Females	WPR
Cultivators	14,508	9,117	5,391	42.15
Agricultural Labour	16,719	6,180	10,539	48.57
Household Industry	408	216	192	1.19
Other Workers	2,787	2,094	693	8.1
Main Workers	28,340	15,710	12,630	82.33
Marginal Workers	6,082	1,897	4,185	17.67
Total Workers	34,422	17,607	16,815	

Religion: Major Religious Communities:

	Persons	Males	Females	Sex Ratio
Hindu (95.31%)	53,070	26,832	26,238	978
Muslim (4.53%)	2,525	1,248	1,277	1,023
Christian (0.1%)	55	27	28	1,037
Sikh (0%)	-	-	-	-
Buddhists (0%)	-	-	-	-
Jain (0%)	-	-	-	-

Agewise Data:

	Persons	Males	Females	Sex Ratio
All ages	55,679	28,124	27,555	980
0-14	21,514	11,064	10,450	945
15-44	24,950	12,511	12,439	994
45-79	9,004	4,459	4,545	1019
80+	176	72	104	1444
Age not stated	35	18	17	944

Languages (Dominant):

Telugu, Hindi, Urdu, Tamil, Kannada

Disabled Population:

	Persons	Males	Females	%
Total Disabled	950	551	399	
In Seeing	398	229	169	41.89
In Speech	95	46	49	10
In Hearing	56	22	34	5.89
In Movement	338	223	115	35.58
Mentally	63	31	32	6.63

DHONE

Dhone C.D. Block lies in the southern part of Kurnool district. The Block is located at a distance of 52 kms. from district headquarters (Kurnool). There are 16 villages in the block with the total population of 102,005 persons. Area of the C.D. Block is 419.87 sq. kms. It is bounded in the north by Mandals Krishnag iri and Veldurthi, in the south by Mandals Peapalle and Banaganapalle, in the east by Mandal Bethamcherla, and in the west by Mandal Tuggeli.

Communications:

Roadways : NH- 7: Direction- Gooty to Kurnool. Nearest Villages- Ungaranigundla, Dhone @ Dronachalam, Udumula padu, Kamaganikuntla.

Railway Station: Yapadinne, Dhone @ Dronachalam, Udumul apadu, Malkapuram.

It is identified as a drought-prone area.

Hills: Nearest Village- Venkatapuram.

Integrated Child Development Scheme (ICDS) Project: Dhone, Total Anganwadi Centres: 270

Annual Rainfall: Average Rainfall 544 mm

Ground Water: Availability of the Ground Water in the Basin is 2940 H.A.M. and the utilization is 1386 H. A.M. It belongs to Safe category. Depth to water level varies from 5 to 10 meter below the ground. Most of the wells go down in summer months. The well density in the entire block is 3 wells per sq. km. Total no. of the wells in the block are enumerated as 1215, according to the Ground Water Estimation Committee.

Forest and Reserved **Forest:** Nearest Villages- Yapadinne, Eddupenta, Shotrium Gundala, Kotha Buruju, Kothakota, Devarabanda, Kocheruvu, Ungaranigundla, Dhone @ Dronac halam, Kamaganikuntla, Malkapuram, Shotrium Valasala,

Natural Division : Rayalaseema Region

Administration:

Division: Rayala Seema. Parliamentary Constituency: 34 Nandyal. District: Kurnool. Mandal: Dhone. Assembly Constituency: 260 Dhone. Gram Panchayat: 25.

Villages: 16 **Inhabited:** 16 **Uninhabited:** 0

Ranking	District	State	National
Area	4	29	1823
Population	1	4	3405
Sex Ratio	20	777	2651
Child Sex Ratio	35	742	3178
Literacy Rate	6	371	3315
Density	52	897	4173
Work Participation Rate	13	565	3056

Gram Panchayats:

Avuladoddi, Chanugondla, Chinna Malkapuram Devarabanda, Dharmavaram, Dorapalli, Eddupenta Gosanipalli, Gummakonda, Jagadurthi, Kamaganikuntla Kamalapuram, Kannepukunta, Kocheruvu, Kotha Buruju Kothakota, Kotral, Mallempalli, U. Kothapalli Udumulapadu, Ungaranigundla, Venkatanayunipalli Venkatapuram, Yapadinne, Yerraguntla.

Amenities:

Education: Primary School in 16 villages, Middle school in 10 villages, Matriculation or Secondary School in 2 villages, namely Dhone @ Dronachalam, Malkapuram.

Higher Secondary or Pre University Courses or Intermediate or Junior College in 1 village of the CD Block,, namely Dhone @ Dronachalam.

College in 1 village, Adult Literacy Center in 16 villages., College is in village, namely Dhone @ Dronachalam.

Medical: Hospital in 1 village, Dispensary in 1 village, Health Center in 1 village, Sub Center in 11 villages, Maternity and Child Welfare Center in 14 villages, Community health workers in 0 village.

The Villages having Hospital or Dispensary or Health Center are Dhone @ Dronachalam.

Drinking Water: Tap water in 16 villages, Tank water in 16 villages, Well water in 16 villages, Tubewell in 16 villages and more than one source in 16 villages.

Bank: Banking facility in 3 villages, namely, Kothakota, Dhone @ Dronachalam, Malkapuram.

Credit Society in 9 villages Agricultural Credit Society in 4 Non-Agricultural Credit Society in 9 villages.

Others: Power supply in 16 villages, Cinema hall in 1 village, sport club in 0 village, Stadium or Auditorium or Community Hall in 0 village, Post Office in 13 villages.

There are 15 villages having bus facilities.

Villages with most of facilities: Kothakota Dhone @ Dronachalam, Malkapuram.

Villages without Amenities (Education): None..

Scheduled Castes: Out of the total population of 102005 persons, 14313 persons (14.03%) belong to Scheduled Castes. The villages having less than 10% SC population are None..

The villages having more than 50% SC population are None.

Sex ratio of Scheduled Caste population is 499.

Scheduled Castes Literates and Illiterates by Sex:

	Persons	Males	Females
Literate	5,637	3,488	2,149
Illiterate	8,676	3,685	4,991
Literacy rate	46.2	57.6	35.0
Graduate	243	173	70

Scheduled Castes (Dominant):

Madiga, Mala, Generic Castes etc., Adi Andhra Mala Dasari

For their cultural identity please see Appendix-I

Villages without Scheduled Castes: There are 0 village without any scheduled caste population.

Scheduled Tribes: Out of the total population of 102005 persons, 2291 persons (2.25%) belong to Scheduled Tribes.

The villages having less than 10% ST population are Yapadinne, Eddupenta, Chanugondla, Shotrium Gundala Kothakota, Devarabanda, Kocheruvu, Ungaranigundla Dhone @ Dronachalam, Venkatapuram, Udumulapadu Kamaganikuntla, Shotrium Valasala, Malkapuram.

The villages having more than 50% ST population are None.

Sex ratio of Scheduled tribe population is 495.

Scheduled Tribes Literates and Illiterates by Sex:

	Persons	Males	Females
Literate	915	602	313
Illiterate	1,376	556	820
Literacy rate	48.1	61.6	33.8
Graduate	38	33	5

Scheduled Tribes (Dominant):

Yerukulas, Sugalis etc., Kammara

For their cultural identity please see Appendix-II

Villages without Scheduled Tribes: There are 4 villages without any scheduled tribe population.

Literates and Illiterates by Sex (Total Population):

	Persons	Males	Females
Literate	49,695	30,950	18,745
Illiterate	52,310	20,909	31,401
Literacy rate	57	70	44
Graduate	3,000	2,297	703

Agriculture: ***Distribution of villages according to land use:*** Out of 16 villages, Total area (in hectare) is 41988, out of that 68.95 percent is cultivable and 6.85 percent of the cultivable area is irrigated.

Sources of Irrigation (Hectares): Government Canal 0, Private Canal 0, Well without Electricity 17, Well with Electricity 735, Tubewell without Electricity 0, Tubewell with Electricity 514, Tank 683, River 0, Lake 0, Waterfall 0, Others 108.86.

Villages with population of 5000 to 9999: Kocheruvu, Venkatapuram, Malkapuram.

Villages with population of 10000 and above: Dhone @ Dronachalam.

Distribution of Workers:

	Persons	Males	Females	WPR
Cultivators	12,942	7,674	5,268	27.63
Agricultural Labour	13,197	5,460	7,737	28.18
Household Industry	1,113	609	504	2.38
Other Workers	19,586	15,187	4,399	41.82
Main Workers	42,061	27,253	14,808	89.8
Marginal Workers	4,777	1,677	3,100	10.2
Total Workers	46,838	28,930	17,908	

Religion: Major Religious Communities:

	Persons	Males	Females	Sex Ratio
Hindu (87.23%)	88,974	45,303	43,671	964
Muslim (11.76%)	11,998	6,046	5,952	984
Christian (0.94%)	960	472	488	1,034
Sikh (0%)	3	1	2	2,000
Buddhists (0%)	-	-	-	-
Jain (0%)	-	-	-	-

Agewise Data:

	Persons	Males	Females	Sex Ratio
All ages	102,005	51,859	50,146	967
0-14	36,283	18,511	17,772	960
15-44	48,431	25,038	23,393	934
45-79	16,714	8,066	8,648	1072
80+	495	200	295	1475
Age not stated	82	44	38	864

Languages (Dominant):

Telugu, Urdu, Marathi, Hindi, Tamil

Disabled Population:

	Persons	Males	Females	%
Total Disabled	1,668	893	775	
In Seeing	577	260	317	34.59
In Speech	183	102	81	10.97
In Hearing	133	69	64	7.97
In Movement	580	354	226	34.77
Mentally	195	108	87	11.69

DICHPALLE

Dichpalle C.D. Block lies in the eastern part of Nizama bad district. The Block is located at a distance of 15 kms. from district headquarters (Nizamabad). There are 20 villages in the block with the total population of 71,091 persons. Area of the C.D. Block is 225.43 sq. kms. It is bounded by Jakranpalle Mandal on north-w est and north, Dharpalle on north-east, east and south-e ast, Sadasivanagar on south and south-west, Nizamabad Mandal on south-west, west and north-west, and Makloor Mandal on north-west.

Communications :

Roadways : NH- 7: Direction- Jakranpalle to Sadasivanagar. Nearest Villages- Mentrajpalle, Dichpalle, Indalwai, Gannaram, Ghanpur. State Highway (S.H.): Direction- Bodhan to Hyderabad. Nearest Villages- Bardipur, Amruth apur, Nadepalle, Ghanpur.

Railway Station : Nadepalle, Dichpalle, Ghanpur, Indalw ai, Nallavalle, Sirnapalle.

River: Godavari Nadi- Nearest Villages- Yanampalle, Suddulam, Koratpalle, Rampur.

Backwards Region Grants Fund: It receives Backward Region Grants.

Annual Rainfall: Average Rainfall 1062 mm

Ground Water: Availability of the Ground Water in the Basin is 3409 H.A.M. and the utilization is 3852 H. A.M. It belongs to Over Exploited category. Depth to

water level varies from 5 to 20 meter below the ground. Most of the wells go down in summer months, according to the Ground Water Estimation Committee.

Natural Division : Telangana Plateau Region

Administration:

Division: Telangana. Parliamentary Constituency: 4 Nizamabad. District: Nizamabad. Mandal: Nizamabad. Assembly Constituency: 18 Nizamabad (Rural). Gram Panch ayat: 23

Villages: 20 **Inhabited:** 20 **Uninhabited:** 0

Ranking	District	State	National
Area	14	408	3738
Population	4	112	4416
Sex Ratio	12	41	346
Child Sex Ratio	8	272	869
Literacy Rate	11	687	4490
Density	21	499	3391
Work Participation Rate	9	335	1294

Gram Panchayats:

Amruthapur, Bardipoor, Bibipur, Chandranpally Dharmaram (B), Dichpally, Doosgaon, Gannaram Gollapally, Indalwai, Kamalapur, Koratpally Mallapur, Mentrajpally, Mittapally, Nadpally Narsingpoor, Rampoor, Sampally, Suddapally, Suddulam Thirmanpally, Yanampally.

Amenities:

Education: Primary School in 20 villages, Middle school in 13 villages, Matriculation or Secondary School in 11 villages, namely Bardipur, Mentrajpalle, Suddepalle, Yanampalle, Suddulam, Mittapalle, Rampur, Dichpalle, Ghanpur, Indalwai, Gannaram.

Higher Secondary or Pre University Courses or Intermediate or Junior College in 0 village of the CD Block, College in 0 village, Adult Literacy Center in 15 villages.

Medical: Hospital in 1 village, Dispensary in 2 villages, Health Center in 3 villages, Sub Center in 11 villages, Maternity and Child Welfare Center in 0 village, Community health workers in 0 village.

The Villages having Hospital or Dispensary or Health Center are Bardipur, Dichpalle.

Drinking Water: Tap water in 19 villages, Tank water in 19 villages, Well water in 20 villages, Tubewell in 19 villages and more than one source in 20 villages.

Bank: Banking facility in 8 villages, namely, Bardipur, Mentrajpalle, Nadepalle, Mittapalle Rampur, Dichpalle, Ghanpur, Indalwai.

Credit Society in 11 villages Agricultural Credit Society in 5 Non-Agricultural Credit Society in 7 villages.

Others: Power supply in 20 villages, Cinema hall in 0 village, sport club in 0 village, Stadium or Auditorium or Community Hall in 0 village, Post Office in 14 villages.

There are 18 villages having bus facilities.

Villages with most of facilities: Bardipur Mentrajpalle, Nadepalle, Mittapalle, Rampur Dichpalle, Ghanpur, Indalwai.

Villages without Amenities (Education): None..

Scheduled Castes: Out of the total population of 71091 persons, 10217 persons (14.37%) belong to Scheduled Castes.

The villages having less than 10% SC population are None..

The villages having more than 50% SC population are None.

Sex ratio of Scheduled Caste population is 529.

Scheduled Castes Literates and Illiterates by Sex:

	Persons	Males	Females
Literate	4,133	2,321	1,812
Illiterate	6,084	2,490	3,594
Literacy rate	46.6	56.6	37.9
Graduate	65	51	14

Scheduled Castes (Dominant):

Mala, Madiga, Gosangi, Chamar etc., Malajangam

For their cultural identity please see Appendix-I

Villages without Scheduled Castes: There is 1 village without any scheduled caste population.

Scheduled Tribes: Out of the total population of 71091 persons, 10648 persons (14.98%) belong to Scheduled Tribes.

The villages having less than 10% ST population are Arepalle, Bardipur, Amruthapur, Suddepalle, Suddulam Rampur, Ghanpur, Mallapur.

The villages having more than 50% ST population are None.

Sex ratio of Scheduled tribe population is 500.

Scheduled Tribes Literates and Illiterates by Sex:

	Persons	Males	Females
Literate	2,878	2,108	770
Illiterate	7,770	3,211	4,559
Literacy rate	33.0	48.9	17.5
Graduate	31	29	2

Scheduled Tribes (Dominant):

Sugalis etc., Gond etc., Yerukulas, Chenchu etc. Koya etc.

For their cultural identity please see Appendix-II

Villages without Scheduled Tribes: There are 2 villages without any scheduled tribe population.

Literates and Illiterates by Sex (Total Population):

	Persons	Males	Females
Literate	30,734	18,960	11,774
Illiterate	40,357	15,841	24,516
Literacy rate	50	64	38
Graduate	782	630	152

Agriculture: ***Distribution of villages according to land use:*** Out of 20 villages, Total area (in hectare) is 22542, out of that 56.73 percent is cultivable and 76.17 percent of the cultivable area is irrigated.

Sources of Irrigation (Hectares): Government Canal 2058.49, Private Canal 0, Well without Electricity 81.82, Well with Electricity 739.32, Tubewell without Electricity 0, Tubewell with Electricity 4932.72, Tank 1495.13, River 88.16, Lake 0, Waterfall 202.42, Others 142.3.

Villages with population of 5000 to 9999:
Bardipur, Mentrajpalle, Nadepalle, Ghanpur, Indalwai Gannaram.

Villages with population of 10000 and above: None

Distribution of Workers:

	Persons	Males	Females	WPR
Cultivators	11,388	7,285	4,103	30.3
Agricultural Labour	11,014	5,838	5,176	29.3
Household Industry	6,883	972	5,911	18.31
Other Workers	8,305	5,412	2,893	22.09
Main Workers	32,552	17,605	14,947	86.6
Marginal Workers	5,038	1,902	3,136	13.4
Total Workers	37,590	19,507	18,083	

Religion: Major Religious Communities:

	Persons	Males	Females	Sex Ratio
Hindu (89.99%)	63,978	31,262	32,716	1,047
Muslim (8.42%)	5,985	2,995	2,990	998
Christian (1.48%)	1,054	507	547	1,079
Sikh (0.06%)	45	23	22	957
Buddhists (0.01%)	6	2	4	2,000
Jain (0.01%)	4	2	2	1,000

Agewise Data:

	Persons	Males	Females	Sex Ratio
All ages	71,091	34,801	36,290	1043
0-14	23,468	11,901	11,567	972
15-44	34,581	16,810	17,771	1057
45-79	12,440	5,855	6,585	1125
80+	497	186	311	1672
Age not stated	105	49	56	1143

Languages (Dominant):
Telugu, Hindi, Urdu, Marathi, Others

Disabled Population:

	Persons	Males	Females	%
Total Disabled	1,329	737	592	
In Seeing	708	375	333	53.27
In Speech	84	40	44	6.32
In Hearing	34	14	20	2.56
In Movement	387	238	149	29.12
Mentally	116	70	46	8.73

DILAWARPUR

Dilawarpur C.D. Block lies in the south-west part of Adilabad district. The Block is located at a distance of 127 kms. from district headquarters (Adilabad). There are 31 villages in the block with the total popul ation of 33,026 persons. Area of the C.D. Block is 211. 10 sq. kms. It is bounded by Sarangapur Mandal on north and north-east, Nirmal Mandal on east, south-east and south, Nizamabad district on south-west, Lokeshwaram Mandal on south-west and west, Kuntala Mandal on north-west.

Communications :

Roadways : NH- 222: Direction- Bhainsa to Nirmal Nearest Villages- Kalva, Daryapur, Shakapur, Sirgapur, Narsapur, New Lolam (R.C.), Rampur, Naseerabad.

River: Godavari Nadi- Nearest Villages- Temborni, Arli (Buzurg), Samanderpalle, Mujgi, Siddankunta, Ratna pur (K), Sangvi, Velmel, Narsapur. Pedda Vagu- Nearest Villages- Naseerabad, Arli (Buzurg), Samanderpalle, Chintalkunta, Gundampalle, Lingampalle, Mujgi, Siddank unta, Velmel.

Backwards Region Grants Fund: It receives Backward Region Grants.

Annual Rainfall: Average Rainfall 1133 mm

Ground Water: Availability of the Ground Water in the Basin is 2554 H.A.M.and the utilization is 1756 H.A. M. It belongs to Safe category. Depth to water level varies from 10 to 20 meter below the ground. Most of the wells go down in summer months, according to the Ground Water Estimation Committee.

Natural Division : Telangana Plateau Region

Administration:

Division: Telangana. Parliamentary Constituency: 1 Adilabad (ST). District: Adilabad. Mandal: Dilawarpur. Assembly Constituency: 9 Nirmal. Gram Panchayat: 15.

Villages: 31 **Inhabited:** 24 **Uninhabited:** 7

Ranking	**District**	**State**	**National**
Area	41	445	3880
Population	27	977	5977
Sex Ratio	2	9	175
Child Sex Ratio	47	989	4509
Literacy Rate	35	934	5421
Density	5	44	5540
Work Participation Rate	18	902	196

Gram Panchayats:
Dilawarpur, Gundampally, Kalwa, Kanjar, Kusli Lingampally, Lolam New, Madegaon, Narsapur(G) Rampur, Samandarpally, Sangvi, Sirgapur, Temborni Velmel.

Amenities:

Education: Primary School in 24 villages, Middle school in 9 villages, Matriculation or Secondary School in 5 villages, namely Narsapur, Gundampalle, Dilawarpur, Banaspalle,

Lingampalle.

Higher Secondary or Pre University Courses or Intermediate or Junior College in 0 village of the CD Block, College in 0 village, Adult Literacy Center in 23 villages.

Medical: Hospital in 0 village, Dispensary in 1 village, Health Center in 1 village, Sub Center in 10 villages, Maternity and Child Welfare Center in 0 village, Community health workers in 0 village.

The Village having Hospital or Dispensary or Health Center is Gundampalle.

Drinking Water: Tap water in 24 villages, Tank water in 24 villages, Well water in 24 villages, Tubewell in 24 villages and more than one source in 24 villages.

Bank: Banking facility in 1 villages, namely, Dilawarpur.

Credit Society in 8 villages Agricultural Credit Society in 3 Non-Agricultural Credit Society in 7 villages.

Others: Power supply in 24 villages, Cinema hall in 0 village, sport club in 0 village, Stadium or Auditorium or Community Hall in 0 village, Post Office in 6 villages.

There are 18 villages having bus facilities.

Village with most of facilities: Dilawarpur.

Villages without Amenities (Education): None..

Scheduled Castes: Out of the total population of 33026 persons, 5764 persons (17.45%) belong to Scheduled Castes.

The villages having less than 10% SC population are None..

The villages having more than 50% SC population are None.

Sex ratio of Scheduled Caste population is 538.

Scheduled Castes Literates and Illiterates by Sex:

	Persons	Males	Females
Literate	1,725	1,118	607
Illiterate	4,039	1,547	2,492
Literacy rate	34.2	48.7	22.1
Graduate	33	32	1

Scheduled Castes (Dominant):

Mala, Madiga, Generic Castes etc., Chamar etc.

Beda Jangam etc.

For their cultural identity please see Appendix-I

Villages without Scheduled Castes: There are 10 villages without any scheduled caste population.

Scheduled Tribes: Out of the total population of 33026 persons, 3373 persons (10.21%) belong to Scheduled Tribes.

The villages having less than 10% ST population are Kurli, Narsapur, Naseerabad, Rampur, Temborni Samanderpalle, Gundampalle, Dilawarpur, Sirgapur Banaspalle, Lingampalle, Kanjar, Ratnapur (K) Sangvi, Mallapur.

The villages having more than 50% ST population are None.

Sex ratio of Scheduled tribe population is 516.

Scheduled Tribes Literates and Illiterates by Sex:

	Persons	Males	Females
Literate	807	577	230
Illiterate	2,566	1,056	1,510
Literacy rate	28.6	42.6	15.7
Graduate	4	4	0

Scheduled Tribes (Dominant):

Sugalis etc., Gond etc., Generic Tribes etc.

Yerukulas, Andh

For their cultural identity please see Appendix-II

Villages without Scheduled Tribes: There are 12 villages without any scheduled tribe population.

Literates and Illiterates by Sex (Total Population):

	Persons	Males	Females
Literate	12,362	7,945	4,417
Illiterate	20,664	7,975	12,689
Literacy rate	43	58	29
Graduate	336	309	27

Agriculture: ***Distribution of villages according to land use:***

Out of 31 villages, Total area (in hectare) is 21820, out of that 54.04 percent is cultivable and 23.43 percent of the cultivable area is irrigated.

Sources of Irrigation (Hectares): Government Canal 170.86, Private Canal 0, Well without Electricity 0, Well with Electricity 347.03, Tubewell without Electricity 0, Tubewell with Electricity 1613.02, Tank 631.36, River 0, Lake 0, Waterfall 0, Others 0.

Villages with population of 5000 to 9999:

Narsapur, Dilawarpur.

Villages with population of 10000 and above: None

Distribution of Workers:

	Persons	Males	Females	WPR
Cultivators	4,699	3,164	1,535	23.8
Agricultural Labour	4,795	2,743	2,052	24.29
Household Industry	5,803	520	5,283	29.4
Other Workers	4,444	2,994	1,450	22.51
Main Workers	18,411	8,846	9,565	93.26
Marginal Workers	1,330	575	755	6.74
Total Workers	19,741	9,421	10,320	

Religion: Major Religious Communities:

	Persons	Males	Females	Sex Ratio
Hindu (88.4%)	29,196	14,020	15,176	1,082
Muslim (11.48%)	3,792	1,882	1,910	1,015
Christian (0.11%)	36	17	19	1,118
Sikh (0%)	-	-	-	-
Buddhists (0%)	-	-	-	-
Jain (0%)	-	-	-	-

Agewise Data:

	Persons	Males	Females	Sex Ratio
All ages	33,026	15,920	17,106	1074
0-14	10,671	5,415	5,256	971
15-44	15,621	7,427	8,194	1103
45-79	6,520	2,991	3,529	1180
80+	176	63	113	1794
Age not stated	38	24	14	583

Languages (Dominant):
Telugu, Urdu, Hindi, Marathi, Gondi

Disabled Population:

	Persons	Males	Females	%
Total Disabled	537	291	246	
In Seeing	248	125	123	46.18
In Speech	55	27	28	10.24
In Hearing	16	9	7	2.98
In Movement	154	93	61	28.68
Mentally	64	37	27	11.92

DOMA

Doma C.D. Block lies in the south-west part of Rangared dy district. The Block is located at a distance of 110 kms. from district headquarters (Serilingampalle). There are 28 villages in the block with the total popul ation of 42,571 persons. Area of the C.D. Block is 168. 22 sq. kms. It is bounded by Pargi Mandal on north, Kulkacharla Mandal on east, Gandeed Mandal on south, and Mahbubnagar district on west.

Communications :

Roadways : Metalled Roads: Nearest Villages- Sivareddipa lle, Dornalpalle, Bachpalle, Mothkur.

Backwards Region Grants Fund: It receives Backward Region Grants.

Annual Rainfall: Average Rainfall 742 mm

Ground Water: Availability of the Ground Water in the Basin is 1829 H.A.M. and the utilization is 1837 H. A.M. It belongs to Over Exploited category. Depth to water level varies from 10 to 20 meter below the ground. Most of the wells go down in summer months. The well density in the entire block is 12 wells per sq. km. Total no. of the wells in the block are enumerated as 2140, according to the Ground Water Estimation Commi ttee.

Natural Division : Telangana Plateau Region

Administration:

Division: Telangana. Parliamentary Constituency: 10 Chevella. District: Rangareddy.

Mandal: Doma. Assembly Constituency: 54 Pargi. Gram Panchayat: 21.

Villages: 28 **Inhabited:** 28 **Uninhabited:** 0

Ranking	District	State	National
Area	26	723	4739
Population	22	739	5620
Sex Ratio	6	275	1252
Child Sex Ratio	29	658	2598
Literacy Rate	32	996	5674
Density	4	266	4040
Work Participation Rate	15	528	684

Gram Panchayats:

Ainapur, Bachpally, Badampally, Bompally Brahmanpally, Budlapur, Dadapur, Dirsampally, Doma Dongayenkepally, Dornalpally, Gudur, Gumdal Kistapur, Mailaram, Mallepally, Mothukur, Ootpally Palepally, Rakonda, Sivareddypally.

Amenities:

Education: Primary School in 28 villages, Middle school in 12 villages, Matriculation or Secondary School in 6 villages, namely Kishtapur, Bompalle, Doma, Dirsampalle, Dadapur, Mothkur.

Higher Secondary or Pre University Courses or Intermediate or Junior College in 0 village of the CD Block, College in 0 village, Adult Literacy Center in 5 villages.

Medical: Hospital in 1 village, Dispensary in 1 village, Health Center in 1 village, Sub Center in 5 villages, Maternity and Child Welfare Center in 0 village, Community health workers in 0 village.

The Village having Hospital or Dispensary or Health Center is Mothkur.

Drinking Water: Tap water in 28 villages, Tank water in 28 villages, Well water in 28 villages, Tubewell in 28 villages and more than one source in 28 villages.

Bank: Banking facility in 28 villages, namely, Budlapur, Kishtapur, Pothreddypalle, Ootpalle Bompalle, Sivareddipalle, Gudur, Dongayankepalle Dornalpalle, Bachpalle, Doma, Timmaipalle, Rakonda Linganpalle, Dirsampalle, Brahmanpalle, Ganjipalle Badampalle, Kondaipalle, Gumdal, Dadapur Khammam Nacharam, Mallepalle, Batla Chandraram Ananthareddipalle, Ainapur, Palepalle, Mothkur.

Credit Society in 6 villages Agricultural Credit Society in 6 Non-Agricultural Credit Society in 0 village.

Others: Power supply in 28 villages, Cinema hall in 1 village, sport club in 0 village, Stadium or Auditorium or Community Hall in 0 village, Post Office in 9 villages.

There are 16 villages having bus facilities.

Villages with most of facilities: Kishtapur, Doma Dirsampalle, Mothkur.

Villages without Amenities (Education): None..

Scheduled Castes: Out of the total population of 42571 persons, 7758 persons (18.22%) belong to Scheduled Castes. The villages having less than 10% SC population are Timmaipalle, Linganpalle, Brahmanpalle, Ganjipalle

Batla Chandraram, Ananthareddipalle.
The villages having more than 50% SC population are None.
Sex ratio of Scheduled Caste population is 507.

Scheduled Castes Literates and Illiterates by Sex:

	Persons	Males	Females
Literate	1,782	1,176	606
Illiterate	5,976	2,645	3,331
Literacy rate	27.3	36.4	18.4
Graduate	19	18	1

Scheduled Castes (Dominant):
Madiga, Mala, Beda Jangam etc., Generic Castes etc. Bindla
For their cultural identity please see Appendix-I
Villages without Scheduled Castes: There are 4 villages without any scheduled caste population.
Scheduled Tribes: Out of the total population of 42571 persons, 5765 persons (13.54%) belong to Scheduled Tribes. The villages having less than 10% ST population are Gudur, Bachpalle, Doma, Rakonda, Linganpalle Kondaipalle, Gumdal, Dadapur, Khammam Nacharam Mallepalle, Batla Chandraram, Ananthareddipalle Ainapur, Palepalle.
The villages having more than 50% ST population are None.
Sex ratio of Scheduled tribe population is 497.

Scheduled Tribes Literates and Illiterates by Sex:

	Persons	Males	Females
Literate	972	695	277
Illiterate	4,793	2,205	2,588
Literacy rate	21.3	30.6	12.1
Graduate	5	5	0

Scheduled Tribes (Dominant):
Sugalis etc., Yerukulas, Chenchu etc.
For their cultural identity please see Appendix-II
Villages without Scheduled Tribes: There are 6 villages without any scheduled tribe population.

Literates and Illiterates by Sex (Total Population):

	Persons	Males	Females
Literate	14,421	9,309	5,112
Illiterate	28,150	12,011	16,139
Literacy rate	40	52	29
Graduate	317	264	53

Agriculture: ***Distribution of villages according to land use:***
Out of 28 villages, Total area (in hectare) is 16822, out of that 42.96 percent is cultivable and 62.95 percent of the cultivable area is irrigated.
Sources of Irrigation (Hectares): Government Canal 748.48, Private Canal 0, Well without Electricity 1.2, Well with Electricity 1662.56, Tubewell without Electricity 0, Tubewell with Electricity 285.34, Tank 1851.22, River 0, Lake 0, Waterfall 0, Others 0.
Villages with population of 5000 to 9999: None
Villages with population of 10000 and above: None

Distribution of Workers:

	Persons	Males	Females	WPR
Cultivators	11,851	7,611	4,240	51.56
Agricultural Labour	7,937	2,225	5,712	34.53
Household Industry	472	262	210	2.05
Other Workers	2,727	2,006	721	11.86
Main Workers	19,033	10,880	8,153	82.8
Marginal Workers	3,954	1,224	2,730	17.2
Total Workers	22,987	12,104	10,883	

Religion: Major Religious Communities:

	Persons	Males	Females	Sex Ratio
Hindu (91.14%)	38,800	19,408	19,392	999
Muslim (8.73%)	3,717	1,883	1,834	974
Christian (0.06%)	24	15	9	600
Sikh (0%)	1	1	-	-
Buddhists (0%)	-	-	-	-
Jain (0%)	-	-	-	-

Agewise Data:

	Persons	Males	Females	Sex Ratio
All ages	42,571	21,320	21,251	997
0-14	16,248	8,324	7,924	952
15-44	18,402	9,122	9,280	1017
45-79	7,628	3,741	3,887	1039
80+	257	113	144	1274
Age not stated	36	20	16	800

Languages (Dominant):
Telugu, Hindi, Urdu, Tamil, Marathi

Disabled Population:

	Persons	Males	Females	%
Total Disabled	729	399	330	
In Seeing	383	185	198	52.54
In Speech	68	44	24	9.33
In Hearing	30	19	11	4.12
In Movement	190	122	68	26.06
Mentally	58	29	29	7.96

DOMAKONDA

Domakonda C.D. Block lies in the south-east part of Nizamabad district. The Block is located at a distance of 72 kms. from district headquarters (Nizamabad). There are 21 villages in the block with the total popul ation of 55,189 persons. Area of the C.D. Block is 167. 50 sq. kms. It is bounded by Kamreddy Mandal on north, Machareddy Mandal on north-east, Karimnagar district on east, Medak district on south-east and south, Bhikno or Mandal on south-west, west and north-west.

Communications :

Roadways : Metalled Roads: Nearest Villages- Ambarpet, Jangaon, Bibipet, Siribibipet, Tujalpur.
River: Yedla katta Vagu: Nearest Villages- Ambarpet, Konapur, Ramreddipalle, Yadaram, Malkapur, Tujalpur.
Backwards Region Grants Fund: It receives Backward Region Grants.
Integrated Child Development Scheme (ICDS) Project : Domakonda, Total Anganwadi Centres: 226
Annual Rainfall: Average Rainfall 941 mm
Ground Water: Availability of the Ground Water in the Basin is 1690 H.A.M. and the utilization is 2382 H. A.M. It belongs to Over Exploited category. Depth to water level varies from more than 20 meter below the ground. Most of the wells go down in summer months, according to the Ground Water Estimation Committee.
Natural Division : Telangana Plateau Region
Administration:
Division: Telangana. Parliamentary Constituency: 5 Zahirabad. District: Nizamabad. Mandal: Domakonda. Assembly Constituency: 16 Kamareddy. Gram Panchayat: 17
Villages: 21 **Inhabited:** 20 **Uninhabited:** 1

Ranking	District	State	National
Area	28	710	4689
Population	13	367	5046
Sex Ratio	26	155	852
Child Sex Ratio	19	568	2207
Literacy Rate	9	652	4387
Density	15	320	3321
Work Participation Rate	8	323	796

Gram Panchayats:
Ambaripet, Anchanoor, Beebipet, Chitamanpally Domakonda, Gottumukla, Issanagar, Janagaon, Konapur Lingupally, Malkapur, Mamdapur, Muthyampet Sangameshwer, Tujalpur, Upparpally, Yadaram.
Amenities:
Education: Primary School in 20 villages, Middle school in 10 villages, Matriculation or Secondary School in 6 villages, namely Mutyampet, Domakonda, Ambarpet, Mohammadapur, Bibipet, Tujalpur.
Higher Secondary or Pre University Courses or Intermediate or Junior College in 1 village of the CD Block,, namely Domakonda.
College in 0 village, Adult Literacy Center in 20 villages.
Medical: Hospital in 0 village, Dispensary in 1 village, Health Center in 2 villages, Sub Center in 7 villages, Maternity and Child Welfare Center in 0 village, Community health workers in 0 village.
The Village having Hospital or Dispensary or Health Center is Domakonda.

Drinking Water: Tap water in 20 villages, Tank water in 20 villages, Well water in 20 villages, Tubewell in 20 villages and more than one source in 20 villages.
Bank: Banking facility in 3 villages, namely, Mutyampet, Domakonda, Bibipet.
Credit Society in 3 villages Agricultural Credit Society in 3 Non-Agricultural Credit Society in 0 village.
Others: Power supply in 20 villages, Cinema hall in 2 villages, sport club in 0 village, Stadium or Auditorium or Community Hall in 0 village, Post Office in 12 villages.
There are 19 villages having bus facilities.
Villages with most of facilities: Mutyampet Domakonda, Bibipet.
Villages without Amenities (Education): None..
Scheduled Castes: Out of the total population of 55189 persons, 10289 persons (18.64%) belong to Scheduled Castes. The villages having less than 10% SC population are None..
The villages having more than 50% SC population are None.
Sex ratio of Scheduled Caste population is 498.
Scheduled Castes Literates and Illiterates by Sex:

	Persons	Males	Females
Literate	3,329	2,294	1,035
Illiterate	6,960	2,874	4,086
Literacy rate	37.6	51.5	23.5
Graduate	44	39	5

Scheduled Castes (Dominant):
Madiga, Mala, Gosangi, Byagara, Chamar etc.
For their cultural identity please see Appendix-I
Villages without Scheduled Castes: There are 2 villages without any scheduled caste population.
Scheduled Tribes: Out of the total population of 55189 persons, 322 persons (0.58%) belong to Scheduled Tribes. The villages having less than 10% ST population are Chintamanpalle, Mutyampet, Domakonda, Lingupalle Sitarampur, Sangameshwar, Anchanur, Ambarpet Konapur, Ramreddipalle, Yadaram, Jangaon Sitarampalle, Mohammadapur, Bibipet, Malkapur Siribibipet, Issanagar, Ramchandrapur, Tujalpur.
The villages having more than 50% ST population are None.
Sex ratio of Scheduled tribe population is 506.
Scheduled Tribes Literates and Illiterates by Sex:

	Persons	Males	Females
Literate	116	72	44
Illiterate	206	87	119
Literacy rate	43.0	52.9	32.8
Graduate	6	5	1

Scheduled Tribes (Dominant):

Yerukulas, Sugalis etc.

For their cultural identity please see Appendix-II

Villages without Scheduled Tribes: There are 9 villages without any scheduled tribe population.

Literates and Illiterates by Sex (Total Population):

	Persons	Males	Females
Literate	24,220	15,633	8,587
Illiterate	30,969	11,817	19,152
Literacy rate	51	66	36
Graduate	760	664	96

Agriculture: ***Distribution of villages according to land use:*** Out of 21 villages, Total area (in hectare) is 17049, out of that 59.08 percent is cultivable and 56.28 percent of the cultivable area is irrigated.

Sources of Irrigation (Hectares): Government Canal 0, Private Canal 0, Well without Electricity 0, Well with Electricity 129.2, Tubewell without Electricity 94.4, Tubewell with Electricity 3397.61, Tank 1987.8, River 0, Lake 60.47, Waterfall 0, Others 0.

Villages with population of 5000 to 9999:
Bibipet.

Villages with population of 10000 and above:
Domakonda.

Distribution of Workers:

	Persons	Males	Females	WPR
Cultivators	8,945	5,975	2,970	29.44
Agricultural Labour	7,583	3,818	3,765	24.96
Household Industry	5,273	891	4,382	17.36
Other Workers	8,581	4,870	3,711	28.24
Main Workers	26,663	14,121	12,542	87.76
Marginal Workers	3,719	1,433	2,286	12.24
Total Workers	30,382	15,554	14,828	

Religion: Major Religious Communities:

	Persons	Males	Females	Sex Ratio
Hindu (95.91%)	52,933	26,323	26,610	1,011
Muslim (3.53%)	1,946	972	974	1,002
Christian (0.46%)	256	131	125	954
Sikh (0.01%)	6	2	4	2,000
Buddhists (0%)	-	-	-	-
Jain (0%)	-	-	-	-

Agewise Data:

	Persons	Males	Females	Sex Ratio
All ages	55,189	27,450	27,739	1011
0-14	17,449	8,964	8,485	947
15-44	26,200	13,042	13,158	1009
45-79	11,055	5,248	5,807	1107
80+	441	168	273	1625
Age not stated	44	28	16	571

Languages (Dominant):
Telugu, Urdu, Tamil, Marathi, Hindi

Disabled Population:

	Persons	Males	Females	%
Total Disabled	950	536	414	
In Seeing	386	202	184	40.63
In Speech	108	61	47	11.37
In Hearing	32	15	17	3.37
In Movement	341	208	133	35.89
Mentally	83	50	33	8.74

DONAKONDA

Donakonda C.D. Block lies in the northern part of Praka sam district. The Block is located at a distance of 93 kms. from district headquarters (Ongole). There are 30 villages in the block with the total population of 42,002 persons. Area of the C.D. Block is 387.37 sq. kms. It is bounded in the north by Mandals Tripuran thakam and Kurichedu, in the south by Mandals Markapur and Konakanamitla, in the east by Mandals Kurichedu and Darsi, and in the west by Peda Araveedu Mandal. River Gundlakamma binds on west.

Communications:

Roadways : State Highway (S.H.): Direction- Darsi to Kanigiri. Nearest Villages- Vabbapuram, Narasimhanayuni Palem, Manginapudi, Lakshmi Narayana Puram, Gudipadu, Aravallipadu, Vaddipadu, West Kambhampadu.

River: Gundlakamma Nadi- Nearest Villages- Battepadu, Padamara Lakshmipuram, Ramapuram, Kotcherla Kota, Siddayapalem. Musi Nadi- Nearest Villages- Vaddipadu, Kalavala Palle, Sangapuram, Tella Padu, West Kambhampa du.

Railway Station: Bada Puram.

The Block is identified as a drought-prone area.

Mahila Samakhya (Education for Women's Equality): It is decleared Socialy and Educationally Backward Block by the Government.

Ground Water: Availability of the Ground Water in the Basin is 23.41 MCM and the utilization is 24.77 MCM It belongs to Over Exploited category. Depth to water level varies from 2 to 5 meter below the ground. Most of the wells go down in summer months.

Administration:

Division: Coastal Andhra. Parliamentary Constituency: 33 Ongole. District: Prakasam. Mandal: Donakonda. Assem bly Constituency: 222 Darsi. Gram Panchayat: 18.

Villages: 30 **Inhabited:** 27 **Uninhabited:** 3

Ranking	District	State	National
Area	4	53	2007
Population	31	763	5651
Sex Ratio	40	935	3193
Child Sex Ratio	21	514	1938
Literacy Rate	53	950	5491
Density	30	502	6069

Work Participation Rate	51	1036	1305

Gram Panchayats:
Aravallipadu, Bhumanapalli, Chandavaram, Donakonda Gangadevipalli, Indlacheruvu, Kocherlakota Mallampeta, Manginapudi, P.Venkatapuram Peddannapalem, Polepalli, Ramapuram, Rudrasamudram Sangapuram, Tellabadu, Vaddipadu, West Lakshmipuram.

Amenities:

Education: Primary School in 26 villages, Middle school in 10 villages, Matriculation or Secondary School in 5 villages, namely Bada Puram, Vabbapuram, Narasimhanayuni Palem, Mallam Peta, Tella Padu.

Higher Secondary or Pre University Courses or Intermediate or Junior College in 1 village of the CD Block,, namely Bada Puram.

College in 1 village, Adult Literacy Center in 25 villages., College is in village, namely Bada Puram.

Medical: Hospital in 0 village, Dispensary in 0 village, Health Center in 0 village, Sub Center in 7 villages, Maternity and Child Welfare Center in 0 village, Community health workers in 0 village.

Drinking Water: Tap water in 27 villages, Tank water in 27 villages, Well water in 27 villages, Tubewell in 27 villages and more than one source in 27 villages.

Bank: Banking facility in 1 villages, namely, Bada Puram.

Credit Society in 5 villages Agricultural Credit Society in 2 Non-Agricultural Credit Society in 3 villages.

Others: Power supply in 27 villages, Cinema hall in 0 village, sport club in 0 village, Stadium or Auditorium or Community Hall in 0 village, Post Office in 19 villages.

There are 23 villages having bus facilities.

Village with most of facilities: Bada Puram.

Villages without amenities (Education):
West Kambhampadu..

Scheduled Castes: Out of the total population of 42002 persons, 10906 persons (25.97%) belong to Scheduled Castes.
The villages having less than 10% SC population are None..
The villages having more than 50% SC population are None.
Sex ratio of Scheduled Caste population is 485.

Scheduled Castes Literates and Illiterates by Sex:

	Persons	Males	Females
Literate	4,112	2,743	1,369
Illiterate	6,794	2,872	3,922
Literacy rate	44.7	57.5	30.8
Graduate	109	80	29

Scheduled Castes (Dominant):
Madiga, Mala, Adi Andhra, Mala Dasu, Relli

For their cultural identity please see Appendix-I

Villages without Scheduled Castes: There are 5 villages without any scheduled caste population.

Scheduled Tribes: Out of the total population of 42002 persons, 329 persons (0.78%) belong to Scheduled Tribes.
The villages having less than 10% ST population are Battepadu, Chandavaram, Pole Palle Padamara Lakshmipuram, Ramapuram, Rudra Samudram Bada Puram, Veera Venkata Puram, Yerrabalem Vabbapuram, Narasimhanayuni Palem, Indla Cheruvu Ragamakka Palle, Bhumanapalle, Mallam Peta Kotcherla Kota, Siddayapalem, Ananthavaram Manginapudi, Padamati Venkata Puram, Peddanna Palem Gudipadu, Aravallipadu, Vaddipadu, Sangapuram Tella Padu, West Kambhampadu.
The villages having more than 50% ST population are None.
Sex ratio of Scheduled tribe population is 486.

Scheduled Tribes Literates and Illiterates by Sex:

	Persons	Males	Females
Literate	102	81	21
Illiterate	227	88	139
Literacy rate	37.8	58.3	16.0
Graduate	4	4	0

Scheduled Tribes (Dominant):
Yerukulas, Sugalis etc., Yenadis

For their cultural identity please see Appendix-II

Villages without Scheduled Tribes: There are 17 villages without any scheduled tribe population.

Literates and Illiterates by Sex (Total Population):

	Persons	Males	Females
Literate	15,227	10,190	5,037
Illiterate	26,775	11,284	15,491
Literacy rate	43	56	29
Graduate	552	409	143

Agriculture: ***Distribution of villages according to land use:***
Out of 30 villages, Total area (in hectare) is 38737, out of that 64.83 percent is cultivable and 7.36 percent of the cultivable area is irrigated.

Sources of Irrigation (Hectares): Government Canal 279, Private Canal 0, Well without Electricity 0, Well with Electricity 857.18, Tubewell without Electricity 0, Tubewell with Electricity 305.7, Tank 178.37, River 0, Lake 0, Waterfall 228.68, Others 0.

Villages with population of 5000 to 9999: None

Villages with population of 10000 and above: None

Distribution of Workers:

	Persons	Males	Females	WPR
Cultivators	7,485	4,751	2,734	34.01
Agricultural Labour	9,466	3,818	5,648	43.01

Household Industry	419	217	202	1.9
Other Workers	4,641	3,351	1,290	21.08
Main Workers	17,149	10,168	6,981	77.91
Marginal Workers	4,862	1,969	2,893	22.09
Total Workers	22,011	12,137	9,874	

Religion: Major Religious Communities:

	Persons	Males	Females	Sex Ratio
Hindu (90.88%)	38,171	19,544	18,627	953
Muslim (4.92%)	2,066	1,027	1,039	1,012
Christian (4.17%)	1,753	897	856	954
Sikh (0%)	-	-	-	-
Buddhists (0%)	-	-	-	-
Jain (0%)	-	-	-	-

Agewise Data:

	Persons	Males	Females	Sex Ratio
All ages	42,002	21,474	20,528	956
0-14	15,133	7,858	7,275	926
15-44	18,415	9,458	8,957	947
45-79	8,098	4,002	4,096	1023
80+	323	135	188	1393
Age not stated	33	21	12	571

Languages (Dominant):

Telugu, Urdu, Gondi, Tamil, Hindi

Disabled Population:

	Persons	Males	Females	%
Total Disabled	1,382	755	627	
In Seeing	677	343	334	48.99
In Speech	98	61	37	7.09
In Hearing	103	50	53	7.45
In Movement	415	259	156	30.03
Mentally	89	42	47	6.44

DORAVARISATRAM

Doravaisatram C.D. Block lies in the southern part of Nellore district. The Block is located at a distance of 81 kms. from district headquarters (Nellore). There are 45 villages in the block with the total population of 32,243 persons. Area of the C.D. Block is 268.91 sq. kms. It is bounded in the north by Mandals Naidupet and Chittamur, in the south and east by Mandal Sullurpe ta, and in the west by Mandal, Naidupet and Pellakur, and district Chittoor.

Communications:

Roadways : NH- 5: Gudur to Chennai. Nearest Villages- Nelaballi, Nelapattu, Vengamambapuram, Akkarapaka, Melupaka, Ayyapalem, Minamanamudi, Lingampadu, Yekollu, Mavillapadu.

Railway Station: Yekollu, Akkarapaka.

A local stream touches the following villages, namely, Lingampadu, Yekollu, Mavillapadu, Venumbaka, Thaneyali, Buduru, Vetagiripalem, Buradamadugu, Modugulapalem.

Annual Rainfall: Average Rainfall 1131 mm

Ground Water: Availability of the Ground Water in the Basin is 3269 H.A.M. and the utilization is 1189 H. A.M. It belongs to Safe category. Depth to water level varies from 2 to 10 meter below the ground. Most of the wells go down in summer months, according to the Ground Water Estimation Committee.

Administration:

Division: Coastal Andhra. Parliamentary Constituency: 40 Tirupati (SC). District: Nellore. Mandal: Doravarist ram. Assembly Constituency: 240 Sullurpeta (SC). Gram Panchayat: 22.

Villages: 45 **Inhabited:** 42 **Uninhabited:** 3

Ranking	**District**	**State**	**National**
Area	23	244	3117
Population	43	988	5995
Sex Ratio	4	187	986
Child Sex Ratio	2	102	268
Literacy Rate	45	563	4089
Density	10	537	5953
Work Participation Rate	38	1001	1418

Gram Panchayats:

Akkarapaka, Anepudi, Budur, Kalluru, Kotha Palli Meezuru, Minamana Mudi, Modugulapalem, Nela Bali Nelapattu, Nellore Palli, Polireddy Palem Poolathota, Singanalthur, Sridhanamalli, Tanayali Thallam Padu, Thogaramudi, Utchuru, Vedurupattu Venumbaka, Yekollu.

Amenities:

Education: Primary School in 37 villages, Middle school in 5 villages, Matriculation or Secondary School in 2 villages, namely Poolathota, Tallampadu.

Higher Secondary or Pre University Courses or Intermediate or Junior College in 0 village of the CD Block, College in 0 village, Adult Literacy Center in 21 villages.

Medical: Hospital in 0 village, Dispensary in 0 village, Health Center in 2 villages, Sub Center in 8 villages, Maternity and Child Welfare Center in 0 village, Community health workers in 0 village.

Drinking Water: Tap water in 41 villages, Tank water in 41 villages, Well water in 42 villages, Tubewell in 41 villages and more than one source in 41 villages.

Bank: Banking facility in 2 villages, namely, Poolathota, Yekollu.

Credit Society in 8 villages Agricultural Credit Society in 4 Non-Agricultural Credit Society in 5 villages.

Others: Power supply in 42 villages, Cinema hall in 0 village, sport club in 0 village, Stadium or Auditorium or Community Hall in 0 village, Post Office in 13 villages.

There are 27 villages having bus facilities.

Village with most of facilities: Poolathota.

Villages without amenities (Education):
Suragunta Tagelu, Adapamudi, Buradamadugu, Lingampadu, Mallayapalem..

Scheduled Castes: Out of the total population of 32243 persons, 12323 persons (38.22%) belong to Scheduled Castes. The villages having less than 10% SC population are Muchalagunta, Anegottam, P.Khandrika (Arigundram) Anepudi (Nadimi Khandrika), Kalluru Suragunta Tagelu, Adapamudi, Lingampadu, Maneri Mallayapalem.

The villages having more than 50% SC population are Kothapalle, Kattuvapalle, Karikadu, Karatamudi Nelapattu, Yekollu, Kalluru Khandrika, Melupaka Mavillapadu, Modugulapalem, Ayyapalem, Chandanamudi Meezuru.

Sex ratio of Scheduled Caste population is 504.

Scheduled Castes Literates and Illiterates by Sex:

	Persons	Males	Females
Literate	4,894	2,970	1,924
Illiterate	7,429	3,143	4,286
Literacy rate	46.6	56.9	36.4
Graduate	88	69	19

Scheduled Castes (Dominant):
Mala, Madiga, Arundhatiya, Adi Andhra

For their cultural identity please see Appendix-I

Villages without Scheduled Castes: There are 10 villages without any scheduled caste population.

Scheduled Tribes: Out of the total population of 32243 persons, 3314 persons (10.28%) belong to Scheduled Tribes. The villages having less than 10% ST population are Muchalagunta, Singanalathuru, Kattuvapalle, Karikadu Anegottam, Karatamudi, P.Khandrika (Arigundram) Mylangam, Yekollu, Kalluru, Kalluru Khandrika Velukadu, Suragunta Tagelu, Adapamudi Surapu Agraharam, Melupaka, Mavillapadu, Thaneyali Utchuru, Vetagiripalem, Buradamadugu, Modugulapalem Lingampadu, Ayyapalem, Chandanamudi, Thogaramudi Meezuru.

The villages having more than 50% ST population are None.

Sex ratio of Scheduled tribe population is 498.

Scheduled Tribes Literates and Illiterates by Sex:

	Persons	Males	Females
Literate	883	530	353
Illiterate	2,431	1,132	1,299
Literacy rate	31.9	37.8	25.9
Graduate	4	3	1

Scheduled Tribes (Dominant):
Yenadis, Yerukulas, Generic Tribes etc.

For their cultural identity please see Appendix-II

Villages without Scheduled Tribes: There are 17 villages without any scheduled tribe population.

Literates and Illiterates by Sex (Total Population):

	Persons	Males	Females
Literate	14,639	8,643	5,996
Illiterate	17,604	7,427	10,177
Literacy rate	53	62	43
Graduate	324	268	56

Agriculture: ***Distribution of villages according to land use:*** Out of 45 villages, Total area (in hectare) is 26891, out of that 40.82 percent is cultivable and 73.36 percent of the cultivable area is irrigated.

Sources of Irrigation (Hectares): Government Canal 83, Private Canal 0, Well without Electricity 85, Well with Electricity 633, Tubewell without Electricity 23, Tubewell with Electricity 1651, Tank 5578, River 0, Lake 0, Waterfall 0, Others 0.

Villages with population of 5000 to 9999: None

Villages with population of 10000 and above: None

Distribution of Workers:

	Persons	Males	Females	WPR
Cultivators	4,334	3,498	836	25.62
Agricultural Labour	10,597	4,791	5,806	62.63
Household Industry	134	70	64	0.79
Other Workers	1,854	1,453	401	10.96
Main Workers	13,351	8,888	4,463	78.91
Marginal Workers	3,568	924	2,644	21.09
Total Workers	16,919	9,812	7,107	

Religion: Major Religious Communities:

	Persons	Males	Females	Sex Ratio
Hindu (94.51%)	30,474	15,185	15,289	1,007
Muslim (3.78%)	1,219	613	606	989
Christian (1.67%)	540	266	274	1,030
Sikh (0%)	-	-	-	-
Buddhists (0.01%)	2	1	1	1,000
Jain (0%)	-	-	-	-

Agewise Data:

	Persons	Males	Females	Sex Ratio
All ages	32,243	16,070	16,173	1006
0-14	9,832	4,966	4,866	980
15-44	15,665	7,811	7,854	1006
45-79	6,564	3,204	3,360	1049
80+	155	71	84	1183
Age not stated	27	18	9	500

Languages (Dominant):
Telugu, Urdu, Tamil, Gondi, Malayalam

Disabled Population:

	Persons	Males	Females	%
Total Disabled	696	361	335	

In Seeing	250	113	137	35.92
In Speech	56	33	23	8.05
In Hearing	82	37	45	11.78

In Movement	237	138	99	34.05
Mentally	71	40	31	10.2

DORNAKAL

Dornakal C.D. Block lies in the south-eastern part of Warangal district. The Block is located at a distance of 90 kms. from district headquarters (Warangal). There are 13 villages in the block with the total popul ation of 55,194 persons. Area of the C.D. Block is 161. 68 sq. kms. It is bounded in the north by Mandal Kuravi and district Khammam, in the south and east by district Khammam, and in the west by Mandal Kuravi.

Communications:

Roadways : Metalled Roads: Nearest Villages- Gollacherla, Dornakal, Uyyalawada.

Railway Station: Dornakal.

River: Maner Nadi- Nearest Villages- Ammapalem, Dornakal.

Backwards Region Grants Fund: It receives Backward Region Grants.

Annual Rainfall: Average Rainfall 949 mm

Ground Water: Availability of the Ground Water in the Basin is 3273 H.A.M.and the utilization is 2298 H.A. M. It belongs to SC category. Depth to water level varies from 5 to 10 meter below the ground. Most of the wells go down in summer months. The well density in the entire block is 23 wells per sq. km. Total no. of the wells in the block are enumerated as 3753, according to the Ground Water Estimation Committee.

Natural Division : Godavari Depression Region

Administration:

Division: Telangana. Parliamentary Constituency. Distri ct: Warangal. Mandal: Dornakal. Assembly Constituency: 101 Dornakal (ST). Gram Panchayat: 15.

Villages: 13 **Inhabited:** 13 **Uninhabited:** 0

Ranking	District	State	National
Area	38	766	4852
Population	20	366	5045
Sex Ratio	13	443	1713
Child Sex Ratio	9	292	982
Literacy Rate	33	705	4566
Density	42	740	3177
Work Participation Rate	8	287	2147

Gram Panchayats:

Adanalapadu, Ammapalem, Banjara, Burgupahad Chilkodu, Chilukoyala Padu, Dornakal, Gollacherla Kannegundla, Manneegudm, Mulkalapalli Perumandlasankeesa, Ravigudem, Uyyalawada, Vennaram.

Amenities:

Education: Primary School in 13 villages, Middle school in 7 villages, Matriculation or Secondary School in 4 villages, namely Dornakal, Perumandla -Sankesa, Mulkalapalle, Kannegundla.

Higher Secondary or Pre University Courses or Intermediate or Junior College in 2 villages of the CD Block,, namely Dornakal, Gurralakunta.

College in 0 village, Adult Literacy Center in 11 villages.

Medical: Hospital in 1 village, Dispensary in 1 village, Health Center in 2 villages, Sub Center in 10 villages, Maternity and Child Welfare Center in 0 village, Community health workers in 0 village.

The Villages having Hospital or Dispensary or Health Center are Chilkodu, Dornakal, Mannegudem.

Drinking Water: Tap water in 13 villages, Tank water in 13 villages, Well water in 13 villages, Tubewell in 13 villages and more than one source in 13 villages.

Bank: Banking facility in 1 villages, namely, Dornakal.

Credit Society in 12 villages Agricultural Credit Society in 2 Non-Agricultural Credit Society in 12 villages.

Others: Power supply in 13 villages, Cinema hall in 1 village, sport club in 1 village, Stadium or Auditorium or Community Hall in 0 village, Post Office in 10 villages.

There are 9 villages having bus facilities.

Village with most of facilities: Dornakal.

Villages without Amenities (Education): None..

Scheduled Castes: Out of the total population of 55194 persons, 6835 persons (12.38%) belong to Scheduled Castes. The villages having less than 10% SC population are Chilkodu, Gollacherla, Uyyalawada, Burgupahad Mannegudem, Vennaram, Gurralakunta.

The villages having more than 50% SC population are None.

Sex ratio of Scheduled Caste population is 503.

Scheduled Castes Literates and Illiterates by Sex:

	Persons	Males	Females
Literate	3,535	2,012	1,523
Illiterate	3,300	1,383	1,917
Literacy rate	59.2	68.3	50.4
Graduate	206	150	56

Scheduled Castes (Dominant):

Madiga, Mala, Generic Castes etc., Bindla, Paky etc.

For their cultural identity please see Appendix-I

Villages without Scheduled Castes: There is 1 village without any scheduled caste population.

Scheduled Tribes: Out of the total population of 55194 persons, 20659 persons (37.43%) belong to Scheduled Tribes. The villages having less than 10% ST population are None..

The villages having more than 50% ST population are Chilkodu, Gollacherla, Ravigudem, Vennaram Gurralakunta.

Sex ratio of Scheduled tribe population is 490.

Scheduled Tribes Literates and Illiterates by Sex:

	Persons	Males	Females
Literate	5,147	3,533	1,614
Illiterate	15,512	7,002	8,510
Literacy rate	30.1	40.5	19.2
Graduate	50	46	4

Scheduled Tribes (Dominant):

Sugalis etc., Yerukulas, Koya etc.

Generic Tribes etc., Gond etc.

For their cultural identity please see Appendix-II

Villages without Scheduled Tribes: There are 0 village without any scheduled tribe population.

Literates and Illiterates by Sex (Total Population):

	Persons	Males	Females
Literate	23,571	14,224	9,347
Illiterate	31,623	13,551	18,072
Literacy rate	50	60	40
Graduate	1,057	781	276

Agriculture: ***Distribution of villages according to land use:*** Out of 13 villages, Total area (in hectare) is 16166, out of that 73.88 percent is cultivable and 26.84 percent of the cultivable area is irrigated.

Sources of Irrigation (Hectares): Government Canal 0, Private Canal 0, Well without Electricity 0, Well with Electricity 1572, Tubewell without Electricity 0, Tubewell with Electricity 0, Tank 1341, River 0, Lake 0, Waterfall 0, Others 293.

Villages with population of 5000 to 9999:

Gollacherla, Mannegudem.

Villages with population of 10000 and above:

Dornakal.

Distribution of Workers:

	Persons	Males	Females	WPR
Cultivators	8,092	5,100	2,992	29.6
Agricultural Labour	12,860	5,500	7,360	47.04
Household Industry	691	343	348	2.53
Other Workers	5,695	4,542	1,153	20.83
Main Workers	22,479	13,576	8,903	82.23
Marginal Workers	4,859	1,909	2,950	17.77
Total Workers	27,338	15,485	11,853	

Religion: Major Religious Communities:

	Persons	Males	Females	Sex Ratio
Hindu (92.37%)	50,983	25,707	25,276	983
Muslim (4.82%)	2,662	1,324	1,338	1,011
Christian (2.19%)	1,207	558	649	1,163
Sikh (0%)	1	-	1	-
Buddhists (0%)	2	2	-	-
Jain (0.26%)	143	72	71	986

Agewise Data:

	Persons	Males	Females	Sex Ratio
All ages	55,194	27,775	27,419	987
0-14	18,905	9,491	9,414	992
15-44	25,824	13,114	12,710	969
45-79	9,823	4,840	4,983	1030
80+	542	264	278	1053
Age not stated	100	66	34	515

Languages (Dominant):

Telugu, Hindi, Urdu, Gondi, Tamil

Disabled Population:

	Persons	Males	Females	%
Total Disabled	1,398	793	605	
In Seeing	525	293	232	37.55
In Speech	204	109	95	14.59
In Hearing	63	34	29	4.51
In Movement	481	295	186	34.41
Mentally	125	62	63	8.94

DORNALA

Dornala C.D. Block lies in the western part of Prakasam district. The Block is located at a distance of 122 kms. from district headquarters (Ongole). There are 19 villages in the block with the total population of 39,149 persons. Area of the C.D. Block is 182.35 sq. kms. It is bounded in the north by Mandal Yerragond apalem, in the south by Mandal Ardhaveedu, in the east by Mandals Pedaaraveedu and Markapur, and in the west by district Kurnool.

Communications:

Roadways : State Highway (S.H.): Direction- Srisailam to Dornala. and Kurnool to Narasaraopet. Nearest Villag es- China Arutla, Thummala Bayalu, Chinthala, Dornala, Yadavalli, Pedamanthanala, Nallaguntla, Yeguva Cherlo Palle, Ayinamukkala, China Dornala.

The block is identified as a drought-prone area.

Forest and Reserved **Forest:** (Markapur Cumbum R.F.)- Nearest Villages- China Arutla, Peda Arutla, Chinthala, Marripalem, Peda Bommala Puram, Dornala, Yadavalli, Pedachama, Rolla Penta, Pedamanthanala, China Manthana la, Nallaguntla, Nalla Guntla Gudem, Yeguva Cherlo Palle, Chilaka Cherla Gudem, Ayinamukkala, China Dornala.

Annual Rainfall: Average Rainfall 859.9 mm

Ground Water: Availability of the Ground Water in the Basin is 15.74 MCM and the utilization is 17.75 MCM It belongs to Over Exploited category. Depth to water level varies from 2 to 5 meter below the ground. Most of the wells go down in summer months., according to the Ground Water Estimation Committee.

Administration:

Division: Coastal Andhra. Parliamentary Constituency: 33 Ongole. District: Prakasam. Mandal: Dornala. Assembly Constituency: 221 Yerragondapalem (SC). Gram Panchayat: 19

Villages: 19 **Inhabited:** 19 **Uninhabited:** 0

Ranking	District	State	National
Area	42	655	4494
Population	38	849	5773
Sex Ratio	44	987	3475
Child Sex Ratio	3	112	292
Literacy Rate	35	664	4425
Density	14	260	4513
Work Participation Rate	27	661	665

Gram Panchayats:

Chinna Dornala, Chinna Gudipadu, Dornala Jammidornala, Katakanipalli, Nallaguntla P.Bommalapuram, Y.Cherlopalli, Yadavalli.

Amenities:

Education: Primary School in 14 villages, Middle school in 7 villages, Matriculation or Secondary School in 4 villages, namely Peda Bommala Puram, Dornala, Ayinamukkala, Kata Kani Palle.

Higher Secondary or Pre University Courses or Intermediate or Junior College in 1 village of the CD Block,, namely Dornala.

College in 0 village, Adult Literacy Center in 9 villages.

Medical: Hospital in 0 village, Dispensary in 1 village, Health Center in 2 villages, Sub Center in 7 villages, Maternity and Child Welfare Center in 3 villages, Community health workers in 0 village.

The Villages having Hospital or Dispensary or Health Center are Peda Bommala Puram, Dornala.

Drinking Water: Tap water in 19 villages, Tank water in 19 villages, Well water in 19 villages, Tubewell in 19 villages and more than one source in 19 villages.

Bank: Banking facility in 4 villages, namely, Dornala, Rolla Penta, Pedamanthanala Yeguva Cherlo Palle.

Credit Society in 7 villages Agricultural Credit Society in 2 Non-Agricultural Credit Society in 3 villages.

Others: Power supply in 19 villages, Cinema hall in 1 village, sport club in 0 village, Stadium or Auditorium or Community Hall in 0 village, Post Office in 9 villages.

There are 14 villages having bus facilities.

Villages with most of facilities: Dornala Yeguva Cherlo Palle.

Villages without amenities (Education):

Peda Arutla, Rolla Penta, Pedamanthanala, China Manthanala, Nalla Guntla Gudem..

Scheduled Castes: Out of the total population of 39149 persons, 8578 persons (21.91%) belong to Scheduled Castes.

The villages having less than 10% SC population are China Arutla, Peda Arutla, Thummala Bayalu Chinthala, Marripalem, Pedachama, Rolla Penta Pedamanthanala, China Manthanala, Nalla Guntla Gudem.

The villages having more than 50% SC population are None.

Sex ratio of Scheduled Caste population is 494.

Scheduled Castes Literates and Illiterates by Sex:

	Persons	Males	Females
Literate	3,344	2,180	1,164
Illiterate	5,234	2,162	3,072
Literacy rate	47.3	60.3	33.6
Graduate	101	73	28

Scheduled Castes (Dominant):

Madiga, Mala, Generic Castes etc., Madiga Dasu etc. Adi Andhra

For their cultural identity please see Appendix-I

Villages without Scheduled Castes: There are 9 villages without any scheduled caste population.

Scheduled Tribes: Out of the total population of 39149 persons, 5457 persons (13.94%) belong to Scheduled Tribes.

The villages having less than 10% ST population are Dornala, Nallaguntla, Yeguva Cherlo Palle Ayinamukkala, China Dornala, Kata Kani Palle.

The villages having more than 50% ST population are China Arutla, Peda Arutla, Thummala Bayalu Chinthala, Marripalem, Pedachama, Rolla Penta Pedamanthanala, China Manthanala, Nalla Guntla Gudem Chilaka Cherla Gudem.

Sex ratio of Scheduled tribe population is 496.

Scheduled Tribes Literates and Illiterates by Sex:

	Persons	Males	Females
Literate	2,077	1,329	748
Illiterate	3,380	1,421	1,959
Literacy rate	48.0	60.4	35.2
Graduate	25	25	0

Scheduled Tribes (Dominant):

Chenchu etc., Sugalis etc., Yerukulas Generic Tribes etc., Bagata

For their cultural identity please see Appendix-II

Villages without Scheduled Tribes: There are 0 village without any scheduled tribe population.

Literates and Illiterates by Sex (Total Population):

	Persons	Males	Females
Literate	16,657	11,037	5,620
Illiterate	22,492	9,044	13,448
Literacy rate	51	65	35
Graduate	553	444	109

Agriculture: ***Distribution of villages according to land use:***

Out of 19 villages, Total area (in hectare) is 18235, out of that 56.3 percent is cultivable and 38.53 percent of the cultivable area is irrigated.

Sources of Irrigation (Hectares): Government Canal 0, Private Canal 0, Well without Electricity 80.65, Well with Electricity 100, Tubewell without Electricity 158, Tubewell with Electricity 1804.65, Tank 1611.94, River 0, Lake 0, Waterfall 200, Others 0.

Villages with population of 5000 to 9999:
Dornala, Ayinamukkala.

Villages with population of 10000 and above: None

Distribution of Workers:

	Persons	Males	Females	WPR
Cultivators	6,242	3,661	2,581	29.34
Agricultural Labour	10,209	4,239	5,970	47.99
Household Industry	577	198	379	2.71
Other Workers	4,246	3,164	1,082	19.96
Main Workers	14,177	8,472	5,705	66.64
Marginal Workers	7,097	2,790	4,307	33.36
Total Workers	21,274	11,262	10,012	

Religion: Major Religious Communities:

	Persons	Males	Females	Sex Ratio
Hindu (91.93%)	35,990	18,502	17,488	945
Muslim (6.98%)	2,731	1,383	1,348	975
Christian (0.88%)	346	161	185	1,149
Sikh (0%)	1	1	-	-
Buddhists (0%)	-	-	-	-
Jain (0%)	-	-	-	-

Agewise Data:

	Persons	Males	Females	Sex Ratio
All ages	39,149	20,081	19,068	950
0-14	14,935	7,702	7,233	939
15-44	17,683	9,043	8,640	955
45-79	6,266	3,190	3,076	964
80+	224	120	104	867
Age not stated	41	26	15	577

Languages (Dominant):
Telugu, Urdu, Hindi, Tamil, Others

Disabled Population:

	Persons	Males	Females	%
Total Disabled	811	459	352	
In Seeing	315	169	146	38.84
In Speech	107	56	51	13.19
In Hearing	37	18	19	4.56
In Movement	282	172	110	34.77
Mentally	70	44	26	8.63

DORNIPADU

Dornipadu C.D. Block lies in the south-eastern part of Kurnool district. The Block is located at a distance of 98 kms. from district headquarters (Kurnool). There are 09 villages in the block with the total population of 25,447 persons. Area of the C.D. Block is 118.37 sq. kms. It is bounded in the north by Mandal Gospadu, in the south by Mandals Uyyalawada and Allagadda, in the east by Mandals Allagadda, Sirvel and Gospadu, and in the west by Mandal Koilkuntla.

Communications:

Roadways : NH- 18: Direction- Banaganapalle to Allagadda. Nearest Villages- Chakarajuvemula, Arjunapuram, Kondap uram, Dornipadu, Ramachandrapuram.

River: Kunderu Nadi- Nearest Villages- Krislipadu village.

It is identified as a drought-prone area.

Annual Rainfall: Average Rainfall 695 mm

Ground Water: Availability of the Ground Water in the Basin is 3416 H.A.M. and the utilization is 58 H.A. M. It belongs to Safe category. Depth to water level varies from 5 to 10 meter below the ground. Most of the wells go down in summer months. The well density in the entire block is 0 wells per sq. km. Total no. of the wells in the block are enumerated as 45, accord ing to the Ground Water Estimation Committee.

Natural Division : Rayalaseema Region

Administration:

Division: Rayala Seema. Parliamentary Constituency: 34 Nandyal. District: Kurnool. Mandal: Dornipadu. Assem bly Constituency: 253 Allagadda. Gram Panchayat: 11.

Villages: 9 **Inhabited:** 9 **Uninhabited:** 0

Ranking	District	State	National
Area	52	957	5507
Population	53	1063	6137
Sex Ratio	8	565	1961
Child Sex Ratio	46	943	4208
Literacy Rate	10	380	3368
Density	22	209	4512
Work Participation Rate	21	660	574

Gram Panchayats:
Ammireddinagaram, Arjunapuram, Burrareddipalle Chakarajuvemula, Dornipadu, Gundupapala, Kondapuram Kristipadu, Ramachandrapuram, W.Govindinne W.Kothapalli.

Amenities:

Education: Primary School in 9 villages, Middle school in 5 villages, Matriculation or Secondary School in 3 villages, namely W.Govindinne, Kondapuram, Dornipadu.
Higher Secondary or Pre University Courses or Inter-mediate or Junior College in 0 village of the CD Block, College in 0 village, Adult Literacy Center in 9 villages.

Medical: Hospital in 0 village, Dispensary in 1 village, Health Center in 1 village, Sub Center in 4 villages, Maternity and Child Welfare Center in 0 village,

Community health workers in 0 village.

The Village having Hospital or Dispensary or Health Center is Chakarajuvemula.

Drinking Water: Tap water in 9 villages, Tank water in 9 villages, Well water in 9 villages, Tubewell in 9 villages and more than one source in 9 villages.

Bank: Banking facility in 1 villages, namely, Dornipadu.

Credit Society in 5 villages Agricultural Credit Society in 3 Non-Agricultural Credit Society in 4 villages.

Others: Power supply in 9 villages, Cinema hall in 1 village, sport club in 0 village, Stadium or Auditorium or Community Hall in 0 village, Post Office in 7 villages.

There are 9 villages having bus facilities.

Village with most of facilities: Dornipadu.

Villages without Amenities (Education): None..

Scheduled Castes: Out of the total population of 25447 persons, 5492 persons (21.58%) belong to Scheduled Castes.

The villages having less than 10% SC population are None..

The villages having more than 50% SC population are None.

Sex ratio of Scheduled Caste population is 490.

Scheduled Castes Literates and Illiterates by Sex:

	Persons	Males	Females
Literate	2,154	1,429	725
Illiterate	3,338	1,370	1,968
Literacy rate	46.1	59.8	31.7
Graduate	46	45	1

Scheduled Castes (Dominant):

Mala, Madiga, Beda Jangam etc., Adi Andhra

For their cultural identity please see Appendix-I

Villages without Scheduled Castes: There are 0 village without any scheduled caste population.

Scheduled Tribes: Out of the total population of 25447 persons, 159 persons (0.62%) belong to Scheduled Tribes.

The villages having less than 10% ST population are Gundupapala, W.Govindinne, Chakarajuvemula Burrareddipalle, Arjunapuram, Kondapuram, Dornipadu Krislipadu, Ramachandrapuram.

The villages having more than 50% ST population are None.

Sex ratio of Scheduled tribe population is 522.

Scheduled Tribes Literates and Illiterates by Sex:

	Persons	Males	Females
Literate	68	41	27
Illiterate	91	35	56
Literacy rate	49.3	61.2	38.0
Graduate	3	3	0

Scheduled Tribes (Dominant):

Yerukulas, Yenadis, Sugalis etc., Chenchu etc. Kammara

For their cultural identity please see Appendix-II

Villages without Scheduled Tribes: There are 3 villages without any scheduled tribe population.

Literates and Illiterates by Sex (Total Population):

	Persons	Males	Females
Literate	12,359	7,803	4,556
Illiterate	13,088	5,041	8,047
Literacy rate	57	71	42
Graduate	427	375	52

Agriculture: ***Distribution of villages according to land use:*** Out of 9 villages, Total area (in hectare) is 11838, out of that 88.39 percent is cultivable and 29.32 percent of the cultivable area is irrigated.

Sources of Irrigation (Hectares): Government Canal 3012.94, Private Canal 0, Well without Electricity 0, Well with Electricity 0, Tubewell without Electricity 0, Tubewell with Electricity 0, Tank 0, River 0, Lake 0, Waterfall 0, Others 54.58.

Villages with population of 5000 to 9999: Dornipadu.

Villages with population of 10000 and above: None

Distribution of Workers:

	Persons	Males	Females	WPR
Cultivators	3,359	2,562	797	23.62
Agricultural Labour	8,963	3,874	5,089	63.02
Household Industry	352	115	237	2.48
Other Workers	1,548	1,073	475	10.88
Main Workers	10,720	6,574	4,146	75.38
Marginal Workers	3,502	1,050	2,452	24.62
Total Workers	14,222	7,624	6,598	

Religion: Major Religious Communities:

	Persons	Males	Females	Sex Ratio
Hindu (84.17%)	21,420	10,806	10,614	982
Muslim (15.14%)	3,852	1,956	1,896	969
Christian (0.49%)	125	59	66	1,119
Sikh (0%)	-	-	-	-
Buddhists (0%)	-	-	-	-
Jain (0%)	-	-	-	-

Agewise Data:

	Persons	Males	Females	Sex Ratio
All ages	25,447	12,844	12,603	981
0-14	8,390	4,304	4,086	949
15-44	11,854	6,049	5,805	960
45-79	4,992	2,412	2,580	1070
80+	172	61	111	1820
Age not stated	39	18	21	1167

Languages (Dominant):

Telugu, Urdu, Gondi, Tamil, Oriya

Disabled Population:

	Persons	Males	Females	%
Total Disabled	411	228	183	
In Seeing	144	76	68	35.04
In Speech	28	16	12	6.81
In Hearing	31	14	17	7.54
In Movement	161	93	68	39.17
Mentally	47	29	18	11.44

DOULATHABAD

Doulathabad C.D. Block lies in the north-west part of Mahbubnagar district. The Block is located at a distance of 52 kms. from district headquarters (Mahbubn agar). There are 26 villages in the block with the total population of 42,550 persons. Area of the C.D. Block is 209.38 sq. kms. It is bounded by Kodangal Mandal on north, Kosgi Mandal on east, Maddur Mandal on south-east, Damaragidda Mandal on south, and it has common boundary with the state of Karnataka on west.

Communications:

Roadways : State Highway (S.H.): Direction- Yadgir to Kodangal. Nearest Villages- Chandrakal, Matoor, Anthwar, Bichal.

Backwards Region Grants Fund: It receives Backward Region Grants.

Annual Rainfall: Average Rainfall 661 mm

Ground Water: Availability of the Ground Water in the Basin is 1295 H.A.M. and the utilization is 1053 H. A.M. It belongs to SC category. Depth to water level varies from 2 to 5 meter below the ground. Most of the wells go down in summer months. The well density in the entire block is 12 wells per sq. km. Total no. of the wells in the block are enumerated as 2590, according to the Ground Water Estimation Committee.

Natural Division : Telangana Plateau Region.

Administration:

Division: Telangala. Parliamentary Constituency: 11 Mahbubnagar. District Mahbubnagar. Mandal: Doulathabad. Assembly Constituency: 72 Kodangal Gram Panchayat: 20

Border Villages: (Karnataka)- Nearest Villages- Chandra kal, Bichal, Anthwar.

Villages: 26 **Inhabited:** 26 **Uninhabited:** 0

Ranking	District	State	National
Area	50	495	4024
Population	49	740	5622
Sex Ratio	7	184	975
Child Sex Ratio	3	124	316
Literacy Rate	49	1049	5939
Density	20	127	4691
Work Participation Rate	29	707	384

Gram Panchayats:

Anthwar, Balampeta, Bichal, Challapur, Chandrakal Devarfaslawad, Doulatabad, Gokajasalawad, Gumdal Gundepalle, Imdapur, Kudrimalla, Matoor, Nandaram Netoor, Polkampalle, Sultanpur, Suraipalle Thimmareddipalle, Yamki.

Amenities:

Education: Primary School in 26 villages, Middle school in 8 villages, Matriculation or Secondary School in 4 villages, namely Chandrakal, Doulathabad, Balampeta, Gokafasalwad.

Higher Secondary or Pre University Courses or Inter-mediate or Junior College in 0 village of the CD Block, College in 0 village, Adult Literacy Center in 25 villages.

Medical: Hospital in 0 village, Dispensary in 1 village, Health Center in 1 village, Sub Center in 7 villages, Maternity and Child Welfare Center in 1 village, Community health workers in 0 village.

The Village having Hospital or Dispensary or Health Center is Gokafasalwad.

Drinking Water: Tap water in 26 villages, Tank water in 26 villages, Well water in 26 villages, Tubewell in 26 villages and more than one source in 26 villages.

Bank: Banking facility in 2 villages, namely, Doulathabad, Balampeta.

Credit Society in 10 villages Agricultural Credit Society in 2 Non-Agricultural Credit Society in 9 villages.

Others: Power supply in 26 villages, Cinema hall in 1 village, sport club in 0 village, Stadium or Auditorium or Community Hall in 0 village, Post Office in 11 villages.

There are 16 villages having bus facilities.

Villages with most of facilities: Doulathabad Balampeta.

Villages without Amenities (Education): None..

Scheduled Castes: Out of the total population of 42550 persons, 7025 persons (16.51%) belong to Scheduled Castes.

The villages having less than 10% SC population are None..

The villages having more than 50% SC population are None.

Sex ratio of Scheduled Caste population is 499.

Scheduled Castes Literates and Illiterates by Sex:

	Persons	Males	Females
Literate	1,300	915	385
Illiterate	5,725	2,604	3,121
Literacy rate	22.0	30.9	13.0
Graduate	13	10	3

Scheduled Castes (Dominant):

Madiga, Mala, Generic Castes etc., Byagara, Dandasi

For their cultural identity please see Appendix-I

Villages without Scheduled Castes: There are

0 village without any scheduled caste population.

Scheduled Tribes: Out of the total population of 42550 persons, 3335 persons (7.84%) belong to Scheduled Tribes. The villages having less than 10% ST population are Chandrakal, Kuppagiri, Matoor, Neetur, Kowdeed Nandaram, Kudrimalla, Saleempur, Suraipalle, Yamki Doulathabad, Bichal, Anthwar, Balampeta, Gundepalle Allapur, Sultanpur, Thirumalapur, Erlapalle Challapur.

The villages having more than 50% ST population are None.

Sex ratio of Scheduled tribe population is 489.

Scheduled Tribes Literates and Illiterates by Sex:

	Persons	Males	Females
Literate	669	537	132
Illiterate	2,666	1,167	1,499
Literacy rate	25.4	39.3	10.4
Graduate	14	14	0

Scheduled Tribes (Dominant):

Sugalis etc., Yerukulas, Porja etc.

For their cultural identity please see Appendix-II

Villages without Scheduled Tribes: There are 9 villages without any scheduled tribe population.

Literates and Illiterates by Sex (Total Population):

	Persons	Males	Females
Literate	13,013	8,737	4,276
Illiterate	29,537	12,472	17,065
Literacy rate	36	49	24
Graduate	276	233	43

Agriculture: ***Distribution of villages according to land use:*** Out of 26 villages, Total area (in hectare) is 20939, out of that 75.71 percent is cultivable and 15.75 percent of the cultivable area is irrigated.

Sources of Irrigation (Hectares): Government Canal 86, Private Canal 0, Well without Electricity 137.52, Well with Electricity 422.36, Tubewell without Electricity 35.4, Tubewell with Electricity 719.3, Tank 1012.72, River 0, Lake 0, Waterfall 0, Others 84.11.

Villages with population of 5000 to 9999: Doulathabad.

Villages with population of 10000 and above: None

Distribution of Workers:

	Persons	Males	Females	WPR
Cultivators	10,790	7,740	3,050	45.24
Agricultural Labour	9,705	2,420	7,285	40.69
Household Industry	626	290	336	2.62
Other Workers	2,732	1,905	827	11.45
Main Workers	18,074	10,823	7,251	75.77
Marginal Workers	5,779	1,532	4,247	24.23
Total Workers	23,853	12,355	11,498	

Religion: Major Religious Communities:

	Persons	Males	Females	Sex Ratio
Hindu (94.15%)	40,059	19,969	20,090	1,006
Muslim (5.52%)	2,348	1,173	1,175	1,002
Christian (0.25%)	108	49	59	1,204
Sikh (0%)	-	-	-	-
Buddhists (0%)	-	-	-	-
Jain (0%)	-	-	-	-

Agewise Data:

	Persons	Males	Females	Sex Ratio
All ages	42,550	21,209	21,341	1006
0-14	15,682	8,097	7,585	937
15-44	18,333	9,064	9,269	1023
45-79	8,218	3,908	4,310	1103
80+	269	110	159	1445
Age not stated	48	30	18	600

Languages (Dominant):

Telugu, Hindi, Urdu, Kannada, Marathi

Disabled Population:

	Persons	Males	Females	%
Total Disabled	807	445	362	
In Seeing	378	196	182	46.84
In Speech	65	36	29	8.05
In Hearing	58	25	33	7.19
In Movement	241	159	82	29.86
Mentally	65	29	36	8.05

DOULTABAD

Doultabad C.D. Block lies in the eastern part of Medak district. The Block is located at a distance of 80 kms. from district headquarters (Sangareddy). There are 32 villages in the block with the total population of 50,502 persons. Area of the C.D. Block is 241.84 sq. kms. It is bounded by Mirdoddi Mandal on north, Gajwel Mandal on east, Wargal Mandal on south, Tupran Mandal on south-west, and Chegunta Mandal on west.

Communications :

Roadways : Metalled Roads: Nearest Viullages- Godugupalle, Mohamadshapur, Ramaram, Tirmalapur, Chandampalle, Kothapalle, Lingareddipalle, Arepalle (Sivar Jaligaon).

Backwards Region Grants Fund: It receives Backward Region Grants.

Annual Rainfall: Average Rainfall 844 mm

Ground Water: Availability of the Ground Water in the Basin is 2399 H.A.M. and the utilization is 2535 H. A.M. It belongs to Over Exploited category. Depth to water level varies from 5 meter below the ground. Most of the wells go down in summer months. The well density in the entire block is 19 wells per sq. km. Total no. of the wells in the block are enumerated as 4394, according to the Ground Water Estimation Committee.

Natural Division : Telangana Plateau Region

Administration:

Division: Telangana. Parliamentary Constituency: 6 Medak. District: Medak. Mandal: Doultabad. Assembly Constituency: 41 Dubbak. Gram Panchayat: 28.

Villages: 32 **Inhabited:** 29 **Uninhabited:** 3

Ranking	District	State	National
Area	12	340	3485
Population	22	496	5257
Sex Ratio	28	734	2468
Child Sex Ratio	37	902	3960
Literacy Rate	36	989	5641
Density	1	99	4611
Work Participation Rate	35	687	327

Gram Panchayats:

Anajpur, Ankireddipalli, Arepalle Csj, Arepalle Sb Begumpeta, Chinnamasanpalle, Dommat, Doultabad Gajulapally, Godugupalle, Gollapally, Indupriyal Kothapalle, Lingarajpalle, Lingareddipalli Machanpalle, Mantoor, Mohamadshapur, Mubaraspur Ramaram, Ramsagar, Rayapole, Seripallibandaram Surampalle, Timmakkapalli, Tirumalapur, Waddepalle Yelkal.

Amenities:

Education: Primary School in 29 villages, Middle school in 14 villages, Matriculation or Secondary School in 5 villages, namely Doultabad, Dommat, Rayapole, Begumpet, Ramasagar.

Higher Secondary or Pre University Courses or Intermediate or Junior College in 0 village of the CD Block, College in 0 village, Adult Literacy Center in 9 villages.

Medical: Hospital in 0 village, Dispensary in 1 village, Health Center in 2 villages, Sub Center in 8 villages, Maternity and Child Welfare Center in 0 village, Community health workers in 0 village.

The Village having Hospital or Dispensary or Health Center is Rayapole.

Drinking Water: Tap water in 29 villages, Tank water in 29 villages, Well water in 29 villages, Tubewell in 29 villages and more than one source in 29 villages.

Bank: Banking facility in 3 villages, namely, Doultabad, Dommat, Rayapole.

Credit Society in 16 villages Agricultural Credit Society in 4 Non-Agricultural Credit Society in 16 villages.

Others: Power supply in 29 villages, Cinema hall in 1 village, sport club in 0 village, Stadium or Auditorium or Community Hall in 0 village, Post Office in 11 villages.

There are 25 villages having bus facilities.

Villages with most of facilities: Doultabad Dommat, Rayapole.

Villages without Amenities (Education): None..

Scheduled Castes: Out of the total population of 50502 persons, 10014 persons (19.83%) belong to Scheduled Castes.

The villages having less than 10% SC population are Lingarajpalle, Deepayampalle, Appaipalle Arepalle (Sivar Bejgaon).

The villages having more than 50% SC population are None.

Sex ratio of Scheduled Caste population is 483.

Scheduled Castes Literates and Illiterates by Sex:

	Persons	Males	Females
Literate	2,671	1,915	756
Illiterate	7,343	3,259	4,084
Literacy rate	31.9	44.5	18.5
Graduate	14	14	0

Scheduled Castes (Dominant):

Madiga, Mala, Bindla, Byagara, Generic Castes etc.

For their cultural identity please see Appendix-I

Villages without Scheduled Castes: There are 6 villages without any scheduled caste population.

Scheduled Tribes: Out of the total population of 50502 persons, 896 persons (1.77%) belong to Scheduled Tribes.

The villages having less than 10% ST population are Doultabad, Lingarajpalle, Dommat, Surampalle Mantoor, Anajpur, Rayapole, Mubarakpur Seripalle Bandaram, Konapur, Deepayampalle Godugupalle, Narasampalle (Patti Dommat) Indupiriyal, Machanpalle, Yelkal, Begumpet Appaipalle, Waddepalle, Ankireddipalli, Ramasagar Ramaram, Tirmalapur, Kothapalle, Chinna Masanpalle Arepalle (Sivar Bejgaon), Lingareddipalle Arepalle (Sivar Jaligaon).

The villages having more than 50% ST population are None.

Sex ratio of Scheduled tribe population is 458.

Scheduled Tribes Literates and Illiterates by Sex:

	Persons	Males	Females
Literate	224	169	55
Illiterate	672	317	355
Literacy rate	31.4	44.4	16.5
Graduate	0	0	0

Scheduled Tribes (Dominant):

Sugalis etc., Yerukulas, Generic Tribes etc.

For their cultural identity please see Appendix-II

Villages without Scheduled Tribes: There are 10 villages without any scheduled tribe population.

Literates and Illiterates by Sex (Total Population):

	Persons	Males	Females
Literate	17,357	11,959	5,398
Illiterate	33,145	13,678	19,467
Literacy rate	41	56	26

Graduate	228	200	28

Agriculture: ***Distribution of villages according to land use:*** Out of 32 villages, Total area (in hectare) is 24185, out of that 66.41 percent is cultivable and 21.01 percent of the cultivable area is irrigated.

Sources of Irrigation (Hectares): Government Canal 0, Private Canal 0, Well without Electricity 0, Well with Electricity 14.4, Tubewell without Electricity 0, Tubewell with Electricity 1413.32, Tank 1947.29, River 0, Lake 0, Waterfall 0, Others 0.

Villages with population of 5000 to 9999: None

Villages with population of 10000 and above: None

Distribution of Workers:

	Persons	Males	Females	WPR
Cultivators	13,500	8,001	5,499	47.32
Agricultural Labour	8,624	3,368	5,256	30.23
Household Industry	1,266	488	778	4.44
Other Workers	5,139	2,854	2,285	18.01
Main Workers	22,833	12,523	10,310	80.03
Marginal Workers	5,696	2,188	3,508	19.97
Total Workers	28,529	14,711	13,818	

Religion: Major Religious Communities:

	Persons	Males	Females	Sex Ratio
Hindu (93.87%)	47,407	24,055	23,352	971
Muslim (4.82%)	2,433	1,238	1,195	965
Christian (1.26%)	636	331	305	921
Sikh (0.02%)	9	4	5	1,250
Buddhists (0%)	-	-	-	-
Jain (0%)	-	-	-	-

Agewise Data:

	Persons	Males	Females	Sex Ratio
All ages	50,502	25,637	24,865	970
0-14	17,815	9,289	8,526	918
15-44	22,138	11,199	10,939	977
45-79	10,077	4,919	5,158	1049
80+	426	201	225	1119
Age not stated	46	29	17	586

Languages (Dominant):

Telugu, Urdu, Hindi, Gondi, Tamil

Disabled Population:

	Persons	Males	Females	%
Total Disabled	1,096	622	474	
In Seeing	534	289	245	48.72
In Speech	100	59	41	9.12
In Hearing	32	16	16	2.92
In Movement	327	198	129	29.84
Mentally	103	60	43	9.4

DUBBAK

Dubbak C.D. Block lies in the north-east part of Medak district. The Block is located at a distance of 135 kms. from district headquarters (Sangareddy). There are 26 villages in the block with the total population of 70,594 persons. Area of the C.D. Block is 244.01 sq. kms. It is bounded by Karimnagar district on north, Siddipet Mandal on east, Mirdoddi Mandal on south, Ramayampet Mandal on west, and Nizamabad district on north-west.

Communications :

Roadways : Metalled Roads: Nearest Villages- Pothareddipet, Chittapur, Dharmajipet, Habshipur, Pedda Gundavelly.

River: Kundaliar Nadi- Nearest Vil;lages- Akaram, Boppapur, Shivrampur, Engurthi, Pothareddipet, Chittapur.

Backwards Region Grants Fund: It receives Backward Region Grants.

Integrated Child Development Scheme (ICDS) Project: Dubbaka, Total Anganwadi Centres: 125

Annual Rainfall: Average Rainfall 860 mm

Ground Water: Availability of the Ground Water in the Basin is 2406 H.A.M. and the utilization is 2467 H. A.M. It belongs to Over Exploited category. Depth to water level varies from 5 meter below the ground. Most of the wells go down in summer months. The well density in the entire block is 32 wells per sq. km. Total no. of the wells in the block are enumerated as 6280, according to the Ground Water Estimation Committee.

Natural Division : Telangana Plateau Region

Administration:

Division: Telangana. Parliamentary Constituency: 6 Medak. District: Medak. Mandal: Dubbak. Assembly Constituency: 41 Dubbak. Gram Panchayat: 32.

Villages: 26 **Inhabited:** 25 **Uninhabited:** 1

Ranking	District	State	National
Area	11	334	3457
Population	3	120	4443
Sex Ratio	6	157	880
Child Sex Ratio	34	786	3382
Literacy Rate	11	557	4070
Density	12	314	3649
Work Participation Rate	9	399	786

Gram Panchayats:

Akaram, Appanpalle, Arepalle, Balwanthapur, Boppapur Cheekode, Chellapur, Chervapur, Chinna Nizampet Chittapur, Chowdarpalle, Dharmajipet, Dubbak Dumpalapalle, Enagurthi, Gambheerpur, Gosanpalli Habshipur, Hasanmirapur, Kammarpalle, Lachapet Mallaipalle, Padmanabhapally, Peddagundavelly Potharam, Pothareddipet, Raghottampalli, Rajakkapet Ramakkapet, Rameshampalli, Shivajinagar, Thimmapur.

Amenities:

Education: Primary School in 25 villages, Middle school in

17 villages, Matriculation or Secondary School in 13 villages, namely Akaram, Gambheerpur, Cheekode, Dubbak, Chillapur, Dumpalpalle, Lachapet, Ramakkapet, Pothareddipet, Chittapur, Dharmajipet, Pedda Gundavelly, Thimmapur.

Higher Secondary or Pre University Courses or Intermediate or Junior College in 1 village of the CD Block,, namely Dubbak.

College in 0 village, Adult Literacy Center in 7 villages.

Medical: Hospital in 1 village, Dispensary in 1 village, Health Center in 1 village, Sub Center in 10 villages, Maternity and Child Welfare Center in 1 village, Community health workers in 0 village.

The Villages having Hospital or Dispensary or Health Center are Dubbak, Pothareddipet.

Drinking Water: Tap water in 25 villages, Tank water in 23 villages, Well water in 23 villages, Tubewell in 25 villages and more than one source in 25 villages.

Bank: Banking facility in 3 villages, namely, Dubbak, Chittapur, Thimmapur.

Credit Society in 19 villages Agricultural Credit Society in 5 Non-Agricultural Credit Society in 19 villages.

Others: Power supply in 25 villages, Cinema hall in 1 village, sport club in 0 village, Stadium or Auditorium or Community Hall in 0 village, Post Office in 17 villages.

There are 24 villages having bus facilities.

Villages with most of facilities: Dubbak Chittapur, Thimmapur.

Villages without Amenities (Education): None..

Scheduled Castes: Out of the total population of 70594 persons, 13537 persons (19.18%) belong to Scheduled Castes.

The villages having less than 10% SC population are None..

The villages having more than 50% SC population are None.

Sex ratio of Scheduled Caste population is 506.

Scheduled Castes Literates and Illiterates by Sex:

	Persons	Males	Females
Literate	4,960	3,212	1,748
Illiterate	8,577	3,479	5,098
Literacy rate	42.4	55.9	29.4
Graduate	83	73	10

Scheduled Castes (Dominant):

Madiga, Mala, Generic Castes etc., Chamar etc. Malajangam

For their cultural identity please see Appendix-I

Villages without Scheduled Castes: There is 1 village without any scheduled caste population.

Scheduled Tribes: Out of the total population of 70594 persons, 1108 persons (1.57%) belong to Scheduled Tribes.

The villages having less than 10% ST population are Akaram, Potharam, Arepalle, Cheekode, Dubbak Mallaipalle, Rajakkapet, Yellapur, Chillapur Dumpalpalle, Chervapur, Lachapet, Ramakkapet Boppapur, Engurthi, Pothareddipet, Chittapur Chowdarpalle, Dharmajipet, Habshipur Pedda Gundavelly, Hasan Mirapur, Appanpalle Thimmapur.

The villages having more than 50% ST population are None.

Sex ratio of Scheduled tribe population is 485.

Scheduled Tribes Literates and Illiterates by Sex:

	Persons	Males	Females
Literate	376	262	114
Illiterate	732	309	423
Literacy rate	40.7	55.7	25.1
Graduate	7	6	1

Scheduled Tribes (Dominant):

Yerukulas, Sugalis etc., Generic Tribes etc. Chenchu etc., Koya etc.

For their cultural identity please see Appendix-II

Villages without Scheduled Tribes: There are 4 villages without any scheduled tribe population.

Literates and Illiterates by Sex (Total Population):

	Persons	Males	Females
Literate	32,290	20,836	11,454
Illiterate	38,304	14,284	24,020
Literacy rate	53	69	37
Graduate	1,026	888	138

Agriculture: ***Distribution of villages according to land use:*** Out of 26 villages, Total area (in hectare) is 24401, out of that 71.7 percent is cultivable and 42.23 percent of the cultivable area is irrigated.

Sources of Irrigation (Hectares): Government Canal 0, Private Canal 0, Well without Electricity 0, Well with Electricity 764, Tubewell without Electricity 0, Tubewell with Electricity 3719, Tank 2906, River 0, Lake 0, Waterfall 0, Others 0.

Villages with population of 5000 to 9999: Cheekode, Pothareddipet.

Villages with population of 10000 and above: Dubbak.

Distribution of Workers:

	Persons	Males	Females	WPR
Cultivators	10,773	7,113	3,660	27.55
Agricultural Labour	8,661	4,535	4,126	22.15
Household Industry	2,424	753	1,671	6.2
Other Workers	17,242	7,589	9,653	44.1
Main Workers	33,144	17,650	15,494	84.77
Marginal Workers	5,956	2,340	3,616	15.23

Total Workers	39,100	19,990	19,110	

Religion: Major Religious Communities:

	Persons	Males	Females	Sex Ratio
Hindu (95.5%)	67,419	33,540	33,879	1,010
Muslim (4.18%)	2,953	1,468	1,485	1,012
Christian (0.28%)	199	103	96	932
Sikh (0%)	2	1	1	1,000
Buddhists (0%)	-	-	-	-
Jain (0%)	-	-	-	-

Agewise Data:

	Persons	Males	Females	Sex Ratio
All ages	70,594	35,120	35,474	1010
0-14	22,212	11,165	11,047	989
15-44	33,064	16,508	16,556	1003
45-79	14,532	7,054	7,478	1060
80+	588	235	353	1502
Age not stated	198	158	40	253

Languages (Dominant):

Telugu, Urdu, Hindi, Tamil, Marathi

Disabled Population:

	Persons	Males	Females	%
Total Disabled	1,221	708	513	
In Seeing	545	307	238	44.64
In Speech	119	69	50	9.75
In Hearing	44	25	19	3.6
In Movement	375	227	148	30.71
Mentally	138	80	58	11.3

DUGGIRALA

Duggirala C.D. Block lies in the eastern part of Guntur district. The Block is located at a distance of 17 kms. from district headquarters (Guntur). There are 14 villages in the block with the total population of 60,420 persons. Area of the C.D. Block is 133.63 sq. kms. It is bounded in the north by Mandal Mangalagi ri and district Krishna, in the south by Mandals Pedakak ani and Tenali, in the east by Mandal Kollipara and district Krishna and in the west by Mandals Mangalagiri and Pedakakani. River Krishna binds on north-east.

Communications:

Roadways : Metalled Roads: Nearest Villages- conect the following villages, namely, Chiluvuru, Tummapudi, Morampudi, Duggirala, Chintalapudi.

River: Krishna Nadi- Nearest Villages- Pedakondur, Godavarru.

Railway Station: Chiluvuru, Duggirala.

Annual Rainfall: Average Rainfall 989 mm

Ground Water: Availability of the Ground Water in the Basin is 4743 H.A.M. and the utilization is 1178 H. A.M. It belongs to Safe category. Depth to water level varies from 5 to 10 meter below the ground. Most of the wells go down in summer months.

Natural Division : Krishna Delta Region

Administration:

Division: Coastal Andhra. Parliamentary Constituency: 30 Guntur. District: Guntur. Mandal: Duggirala. Assembly Constituency: 206 Mangalagiri. Gram Panchayat: 19.

Villages: 14 **Inhabited:** 14 **Uninhabited:** 0

Ranking	District	State	National
Area	36	891	5272
Population	20	268	4841
Sex Ratio	18	381	1536
Child Sex Ratio	46	918	4078
Literacy Rate	2	62	1165
Density	50	782	2442
Work Participation Rate	15	138	2309

Gram Panchayats:

Bikkasanivaripalem, Chiluvuru, Chinapalem Chintala Pudi, Chukkapallivari Palem, D.P.Agraharam Emani, Gandhi Nagar, Godavarru, K.R.Konduru Kazavaripalem, Manchikalapudi, Morampudi Pedakonduru, Pedapalem, Penumuli, Revendrapadu Srungarapuram,, Tummapudi.

Amenities:

Education: Primary School in 14 villages, Middle school in 9 villages, Matriculation or Secondary School in 6 villages, namely Chiluvuru, Tummapudi, Chinapalem, Kantamraju Konduru, Duggirala, Emani.

Higher Secondary or Pre University Courses or Intermediate or Junior College in 1 village of the CD Block,, namely Duggirala.

College in 1 village, Adult Literacy Center in 6 villages., College is in village, namely Duggirala.

Medical: Hospital in 0 village, Dispensary in 1 village, Health Center in 2 villages, Sub Center in 9 villages, Maternity and Child Welfare Center in 2 villages, Community health workers in 0 village.

The Villages having Hospital or Dispensary or Health Center are Perakalapudi, Morampudi.

Drinking Water: Tap water in 14 villages, Tank water in 14 villages, Well water in 14 villages, Tubewell in 14 villages and more than one source in 14 villages.

Bank: Banking facility in 3 villages, namely, Chiluvuru, Duggirala, Emani.

Credit Society in 7 villages Agricultural Credit Society in 5 Non-Agricultural Credit Society in 1 village.

Others: Power supply in 14 villages, Cinema hall in 3 villages, sport club in 0 village, Stadium or Auditorium or Community Hall in 0 village, Post Office in 10 villages.

There are 12 villages having bus facilities.

Villages with most of facilities: Chiluvuru

Duggirala, Emani.

Villages without Amenities (Education): None..

Scheduled Castes: Out of the total population of 60420 persons, 17795 persons (29.45%) belong to Scheduled Castes.

The villages having less than 10% SC population are None..

The villages having more than 50% SC population are None.

Sex ratio of Scheduled Caste population is 494.

Scheduled Castes Literates and Illiterates by Sex:

	Persons	Males	Females
Literate	11,141	6,116	5,025
Illiterate	6,654	2,896	3,758
Literacy rate	71.2	77.4	64.9
Graduate	445	315	130

Scheduled Castes (Dominant):

Madiga, Mala, Madiga Dasu etc., Mala Dasu, Relli

For their cultural identity please see Appendix-I

Villages without Scheduled Castes: There are 0 village without any scheduled caste population.

Scheduled Tribes: Out of the total population of 60420 persons, 1549 persons (2.56%) belong to Scheduled Tribes.

The villages having less than 10% ST population are Chiluvuru, Tummapudi, Srungarapuram, Pedakondur Godavarru, Chinapalem, Perakalapudi, Morampudi Kantamraju Konduru, Penumudi, Duggirala, Emani Chintalapudi, Devarapalle Agraharam.

The villages having more than 50% ST population are None.

Sex ratio of Scheduled tribe population is 487.

Scheduled Tribes Literates and Illiterates by Sex:

	Persons	Males	Females
Literate	701	417	284
Illiterate	848	377	471
Literacy rate	53.2	60.5	45.1
Graduate	14	13	1

Scheduled Tribes (Dominant):

Yerukulas, Sugalis etc., Yenadis, Chenchu etc. Kammara

For their cultural identity please see Appendix-II

Villages without Scheduled Tribes: There are 2 villages without any scheduled tribe population.

Literates and Illiterates by Sex (Total Population):

	Persons	Males	Females
Literate	37,899	20,560	17,339
Illiterate	22,521	9,786	12,735
Literacy rate	70	76	64
Graduate	1,816	1,279	537

Agriculture: ***Distribution of villages according to land use:***

Out of 14 villages, Total area (in hectare) is 13363, out of that 83.29 percent is cultivable and 96.36 percent of the cultivable area is irrigated.

Sources of Irrigation (Hectares): Government Canal 8708.79, Private Canal 0, Well without Electricity 0, Well with Electricity 0, Tubewell without Electricity 334.27, Tubewell with Electricity 1681.91, Tank 0, River 0, Lake 0, Waterfall 0, Others 0.

Villages with population of 5000 to 9999:

Chiluvuru, Tummapudi, Emani.

Villages with population of 10000 and above:

Duggirala.

Distribution of Workers:

	Persons	Males	Females	WPR
Cultivators	4,059	3,403	656	13.18
Agricultural Labour	20,120	10,068	10,052	65.33
Household Industry	392	196	196	1.27
Other Workers	6,227	4,861	1,366	20.22
Main Workers	26,329	17,074	9,255	85.49
Marginal Workers	4,469	1,454	3,015	14.51
Total Workers	30,798	18,528	12,270	

Religion: Major Religious Communities:

	Persons	Males	Females	Sex Ratio
Hindu (88.71%)	53,597	26,958	26,639	988
Muslim (9.29%)	5,611	2,808	2,803	998
Christian (1.91%)	1,152	548	604	1,102
Sikh (0%)	-	-	-	-
Buddhists (0%)	-	-	-	-
Jain (0.01%)	7	3	4	1,333

Agewise Data:

	Persons	Males	Females	Sex Ratio
All ages	60,420	30,346	30,074	991
0-14	16,566	8,465	8,101	957
15-44	29,485	14,909	14,576	978
45-79	13,625	6,625	7,000	1057
80+	662	303	359	1185
Age not stated	82	44	38	864

Languages (Dominant):

Telugu, Urdu, Hindi, Tamil, Marathi

Disabled Population:

	Persons	Males	Females	%
Total Disabled	1,401	714	687	
In Seeing	656	306	350	46.82
In Speech	160	82	78	11.42
In Hearing	103	51	52	7.35
In Movement	331	191	140	23.63
Mentally	151	84	67	10.78

DUGGONDI

Duggondi C.D. Block lies in the north-eastern part of Warangal district. The Block is located at a distance of 34 kms. from district headquarters (Warangal). There are 18 villages in the block with the total popul ation of 42,505 persons. Area of the C.D. Block is 117. 86 sq. kms. It is bounded in the north by Mandal Atmakur, in the south by Mandals Chennaraopet and Narsampet, in the east by Mandals Narsampet and Nallabelly, and in the west by Mandals Geesugonda and Sangam.

Communications:

Roadways : Metalled Roads: Nearest Villages- Nachinapalle, Mandapalle, Togarrai, Chalparthi.

Backwards Region Grants Fund: It receives Backward Region Grants.

Annual Rainfall: Avearge Rainfall 1070 mm

Ground Water: Availability of the Ground Water in the Basin is 2231 H.A.M.and the utilization is 2039 H.A. M. It belongs to Cri category. Depth to water level varies from 5 to 20 meter below the ground. Most of the wells go down in summer months. The well density in the entire block is 32 wells per sq. km. Total no. of the wells in the block are enumerated as 3804, according to the Ground Water Estimation Committee.

Natural Division : Godavari Depression Region

Administration:

Division: Telangana. Parliamentary Constituency. Distri ct: Warangal. Mandal: Duggondi. Assembly Constituency: 103 Narsampet. Gram Panchayat: 23.

Villages: 18 **Inhabited:** 18 **Uninhabited:** 0

Ranking	District	State	National
Area	47	958	5514
Population	36	741	5623
Sex Ratio	47	1016	3644
Child Sex Ratio	45	1013	4753
Literacy Rate	25	574	4121
Density	1	129	3010
Work Participation Rate	6	252	388

Gram Panchayats:

Advi Rangapoor, Babburonipally, Bandampally Chalaparthi, Chapala Banda, Deshaipally, Duggondi Gollapally, Keshwapur, Laxmipur, Mahammadapur Mallampally, Mandapalle, Maripally, Muddunoor Mysampally, Nachinepalle, Ponakal, Reballe Rekampalle, Thimmampet, Thogarrai, Venkatapur.

Amenities:

Education: Primary School in 17 villages, Middle school in 13 villages, Matriculation or Secondary School in 6 villages, namely Laxmipur, Duggondi, Mallampalle, Mahammadapur, Nachinapalle, Timmampet.

Higher Secondary or Pre University Courses or Intermediate or Junior College in 0 village of the CD Block, College in 0 village, Adult Literacy Center in 10 villages.

Medical: Hospital in 1 village, Dispensary in 2 villages, Health Center in 2 villages, Sub Center in 8 villages, Maternity and Child Welfare Center in 0 village, Community health workers in 0 village.

The Villages having Hospital or Dispensary or Health Center are Laxmipur, Duggondi.

Drinking Water: Tap water in 18 villages, Tank water in 18 villages, Well water in 18 villages, Tubewell in 18 villages and more than one source in 18 villages.

Bank: Banking facility in 4 villages, namely, Keshwapur, Duggondi, Mallampalle, Mandapalle.

Credit Society in 17 villages Agricultural Credit Society in 6 Non-Agricultural Credit Society in 17 villages.

Others: Power supply in 18 villages, Cinema hall in 0 village, sport club in 1 village, Stadium or Auditorium or Community Hall in 0 village, Post Office in 10 villages.

There are 18 villages having bus facilities.

Villages with most of facilities: Duggondi Mallampalle, Mandapalle.

Villages without amenities (Education): Polaram..

Scheduled Castes: Out of the total population of 42505 persons, 6934 persons (16.31%) belong to Scheduled Castes.

The villages having less than 10% SC population are None..

The villages having more than 50% SC population are None.

Sex ratio of Scheduled Caste population is 482.

Scheduled Castes Literates and Illiterates by Sex:

	Persons	Males	Females
Literate	2,537	1,689	848
Illiterate	4,397	1,901	2,496
Literacy rate	42.6	54.3	29.8
Graduate	29	27	2

Scheduled Castes (Dominant):

Madiga, Mala, Generic Castes etc., Manne Beda Jangam etc.

For their cultural identity please see Appendix-I

Villages without Scheduled Castes: There are 2 villages without any scheduled caste population.

Scheduled Tribes: Out of the total population of 42505 persons, 1759 persons (4.14%) belong to Scheduled Tribes.

The villages having less than 10% ST population are Laxmipur, Keshwapur, Polaram, Muddunoor, Duggondi Mallampalle, Mahammadapur, Venkatapur, Reballe Ponakal, Nachinapalle, Madhira Mandapalle, Togarrai Rekampalle, Chalparthi.

The villages having more than 50% ST population are None.

Sex ratio of Scheduled tribe population is 485.

Scheduled Tribes Literates and Illiterates by Sex:

	Persons	Males	Females
Literate	504	363	141

Illiterate	1,255	543	712
Literacy rate	34.2	48.2	19.6
Graduate	18	18	0

Scheduled Tribes (Dominant):

Sugalis etc., Yerukulas, Koya etc., Kammara

For their cultural identity please see Appendix-II

Villages without Scheduled Tribes: There are 3 villages without any scheduled tribe population.

Literates and Illiterates by Sex (Total Population):

	Persons	Males	Females
Literate	19,371	12,468	6,903
Illiterate	23,134	9,359	13,775
Literacy rate	52	66	38
Graduate	511	469	42

Agriculture: ***Distribution of villages according to land use:*** Out of 18 villages, Total area (in hectare) is 11787, out of that 75.39 percent is cultivable and 75.68 percent of the cultivable area is irrigated.

Sources of Irrigation (Hectares): Government Canal 0, Private Canal 0, Well without Electricity 0, Well with Electricity 5257, Tubewell without Electricity 0, Tubewell with Electricity 4, Tank 1464, River 0, Lake 0, Waterfall 0, Others 0.

Villages with population of 5000 to 9999: None

Villages with population of 10000 and above: None

Distribution of Workers:

	Persons	Males	Females	WPR
Cultivators	9,302	5,149	4,153	37.87
Agricultural Labour	11,417	4,487	6,930	46.48
Household Industry	940	539	401	3.83
Other Workers	2,902	2,315	587	11.82
Main Workers	19,038	10,423	8,615	77.51
Marginal Workers	5,523	2,067	3,456	22.49
Total Workers	24,561	12,490	12,071	

Religion: Major Religious Communities:

	Persons	Males	Females	Sex Ratio
Hindu (98.28%)	41,774	21,448	20,326	948
Muslim (1.21%)	516	264	252	955
Christian (0.43%)	183	100	83	830
Sikh (0%)	-	-	-	-
Buddhists (0%)	-	-	-	-
Jain (0%)	-	-	-	-

Agewise Data:

	Persons	Males	Females	Sex Ratio
All ages	42,505	21,827	20,678	947
0-14	13,034	6,929	6,105	881
15-44	19,886	10,045	9,841	980
45-79	9,128	4,593	4,535	987
80+	345	179	166	927
Age not stated	112	81	31	383

Languages (Dominant):

Telugu, Hindi, Marathi, Urdu, Tamil

Disabled Population:

	Persons	Males	Females	%
Total Disabled	1,197	654	543	
In Seeing	645	325	320	53.88
In Speech	108	63	45	9.02
In Hearing	60	27	33	5.01
In Movement	283	177	106	23.64
Mentally	101	62	39	8.44

DUMBRIGUDA

Dumbriguda C.D. Block lies in the northern part of Vishakhapatnam district. The Block is located at a distance of 149 kms. from district headquarters (Visakh apatnam). There are 87 villages in the block with the total population of 44,873 persons. Area of the C.D. Block is 464.10 sq. kms. It is bounded in south by Mandal Hukumpeta, and in the east by Mandals Hukumpeta and Arakuvalley, and it has common boundary with the state of Orissa on north, west and east.

Communications :

Roadways : Metalled Roads: Nearest Villages- Bitragonda, Korrai, Gatharagilleda, Gasaba, Logili, Kuda, Gorapur, Sagara, Anjoda, Araku, Kuridi, Nimmagedda, Rangilisingi, Thutangi, Lyganda, Guntaseema, Bodimela, Chelimarival asa, Jamguda, Pothangi, Livitiputtu, Vantharla, Arama, Billaputtu, Kinchumanda, Kusumavalasa, Uyyalaputtu, Kosangi, Dondalavalasa, Korra, Mamidivalasa, Pariseela, Padi, Borrapalem, Boddaputtu.

Annaual Rainfall: Average Rainfall 975.0 mm

Ground Water: Availability of the Ground Water in the Basin is (Information not avavible) H.A.M .and the utilization is (Information not avavible) H.A.M. It belongs to (Information not avavible) category. Depth to water level varies from 3 to 10 meter below the ground. Most of the wells go down in summer months.

Administration:

Division: Coastal Andhra. Parliamentary Constituency: 18 Araku (ST). District: Visakhapatnam. Mandal: Dumbrig uda. Assembly Constituency: 147 Araku Valley (ST). Gram Panchayat: 18.

Border Villages: (Orissa)- Nearest Villages- Kiridivala sa, Mallivalasa, Ranginivalasa, Chinakaguvalasa, Panasav alasa, Chamadapadu, Kollaputtu, Malinguvalasa, Sagirival asa, Kuda, Koranjiguda, Vasabanda, Gorapur, Nimmagedda, Sarai, Ujjangi, Ombi Kinjeru, Kujabangi, Rangilisingi, Kutti, Dathuru, Thutangi, Guntaseema.

Villages: 87 **Inhabited:** 87 **Uninhabited:** 0

Ranking	District	State	National
Area	2	15	1630
Population	37	667	5517

Sex Ratio	4	57	414
Child Sex Ratio	16	138	350
Literacy Rate	35	1083	6150
Density	10	222	6159
Work Participation Rate	38	1064	597

Gram Panchayats:

Araku, Arma, Gasaba, Guntagennela, Guntaseema Kandrum, Kinchumanda, Kithalangi, Kollaputtu, Korra Korrai, Kuridi, Lygonda, Pothangi, Rangilisingi Sagara, Sovva, Thutangi.

Amenities:

Education: Primary School in 84 villages, Middle school in 9 villages, Matriculation or Secondary School in 5 villages, namely Sagara, Guntaseema, Jamguda, Dumbriguda, Kinchumanda.

Higher Secondary or Pre University Courses or Intermediate or Junior College in 0 village of the CD Block, College in 0 village, Adult Literacy Center in 0 village.

Medical: Hospital in 1 village, Dispensary in 2 villages, Health Center in 17 villages, Sub Center in 2 villages, Maternity and Child Welfare Center in 0 village, Community health workers in 0 village.

The Villages having Hospital or Dispensary or Health Center are Gandha, Korra, Pariseela.

Drinking Water: Tap water in 87 villages, Tank water in 87 villages, Well water in 87 villages, Tubewell in 87 villages and more than one source in 87 villages.

Bank: None.

Credit Society in 1 village Agricultural Credit Society in 1 Non-Agricultural Credit Society in 0 village.

Others: Power supply in 87 villages, Cinema hall in 0 village, sport club in 0 village, Stadium or Auditorium or Community Hall in 0 village, Post Office in 25 villages.

There are 15 villages having bus facilities.

Village with most of facilities: None.

Villages without amenities (Education): Godasortu, Ranginiguda, Dondalavalasa..

Scheduled Castes: Out of the total population of 44873 persons, 267 persons (0.6%) belong to Scheduled Castes.

The villages having less than 10% SC population are Kiridivalasa, Mallivalasa, Ranginivalasa Chinakaguvalasa, Kotragondi, Goppilivalasa Chamadapadu, Kollaputtu, Bitragonda, Thotavalasa Korrai, Gatharagilleda, Gasaba, Logili, Demuduvalasa Badiyapadu, Sovva, Karakavalasa Vadiyavalasa @ Vaddevalasa, Malinguvalasa Sagirivalasa, Kamalabanda, Kuda, Koranjiguda Vasabanda, Gorapur, Sagara, Anjoda, Araku, Kuridi Nimmagedda, Sarai, Gadabagolugu, Ujjangi, Ombi Kinjeru, Kujabangi, Rangilisingi, Kutti, Dathuru Thutangi, Lyganda, Guntaseema, Lakka, Bodimela Chelimarivalasa, Musiri, Jamguda Sornayakguda @ Surusyaguda, Kandram, Paridi Pothangi, Pantalachinta, Pedapadu, Antriguda Dumbriguda, Livitiputtu, Vantharla, Arama, Godasortu Ranginiguda, Gondiguda, Billaputtu, Jurripadu Kinchumanda, Kusumavalasa, Uyyalaputtu, Kosangi Champaputtu, Seelamgondi, Nandiguda, Kithalangi Vayya, Morriguda, Gandha, Bairaguda, Sangamvalasa Dondalavalasa, Korra, Mamidivalasa, Pariseela, Padi Borrapalem, Boddaputtu, Gondivalasa, Guntagannela.

The villages having more than 50% SC population are None.

Sex ratio of Scheduled Caste population is 453.

Scheduled Castes Literates and Illiterates by Sex:

	Persons	Males	Females
Literate	133	85	48
Illiterate	134	61	73
Literacy rate	57.3	66.4	46.2
Graduate	13	10	3

Scheduled Castes (Dominant):

Relli, Mala, Adi Andhra, Dhor, Beda Jangam etc.

For their cultural identity please see Appendix-I

Villages without Scheduled Castes: There are 73 villages without any scheduled caste population.

Scheduled Tribes: Out of the total population of 44873 persons, 41928 persons (93.44%) belong to Scheduled Tribes.

The villages having less than 10% ST population are None..

The villages having more than 50% ST population are Kiridivalasa, Mallivalasa, Ranginivalasa Chinakaguvalasa, Kotragondi, Goppilivalasa Panasavalasa, Chamadapadu, Kollaputtu, Bitragonda Thotavalasa, Korrai, Gatharagilleda, Gasaba, Logili Demuduvalasa, Badiyapadu, Sovva, Karakavalasa Vadiyavalasa @ Vaddevalasa, Malinguvalasa Sagirivalasa, Kamalabanda, Kuda, Koranjiguda Vasabanda, Gorapur, Sagara, Anjoda, Araku, Kuridi Nimmagedda, Sarai, Gadabagolugu, Ujjangi, Ombi Kinjeru, Kujabangi, Rangilisingi, Kutti, Dathuru Thutangi, Lyganda, Guntaseema, Lakka, Bodimela Chelimarivalasa, Musiri, Jamguda Sornayakguda @ Surusyaguda, Kandram, Paridi Pothangi, Pantalachinta, Pedapadu, Antriguda Dumbriguda, Livitiputtu, Vantharla, Arama, Godasortu Ranginiguda, Gondiguda, Billaputtu, Jurripadu Kinchumanda, Kusumavalasa, Uyyalaputtu, Kosangi Champaputtu, Seelamgondi, Nandiguda, Kithalangi Vayya, Morriguda, Gandha, Bairaguda, Sangamvalasa Dondalavalasa, Korra, Mamidivalasa, Pariseela, Padi

Borrapalem, Boddaputtu, Gondivalasa, Guntagannela.
Sex ratio of Scheduled tribe population is 504.

Scheduled Tribes Literates and Illiterates by Sex:

	Persons	Males	Females
Literate	10,299	7,369	2,930
Illiterate	31,629	13,418	18,211
Literacy rate	29.7	42.9	16.7
Graduate	102	98	4

Scheduled Tribes (Dominant):

Kotia etc., Konda Dhoras, Valmiki, Mukha Dhora etc. Kondhs etc.

For their cultural identity please see Appendix-II

Villages without Scheduled Tribes: There are 0 village without any scheduled tribe population.

Literates and Illiterates by Sex (Total Population):

	Persons	Males	Females
Literate	12,003	8,107	3,896
Illiterate	32,870	13,944	18,926
Literacy rate	32	44	20
Graduate	208	177	31

Agriculture: ***Distribution of villages according to land use:*** Out of 87 villages, Total area (in hectare) is 46413, out of that 91.69 percent is cultivable and 0.36 percent of the cultivable area is irrigated.

Sources of Irrigation (Hectares): Government Canal 0, Private Canal 0, Well without Electricity 0, Well with Electricity 0, Tubewell without Electricity 0, Tubewell with Electricity 0, Tank 0, River 0, Lake 0, Waterfall 0, Others 154.22.

Villages with population of 5000 to 9999: None

Villages with population of 10000 and above: None

Distribution of Workers:

	Persons	Males	Females	WPR
Cultivators	16,175	9,139	7,036	66.54
Agricultural Labour	4,860	1,843	3,017	19.99
Household Industry	1,067	272	795	4.39
Other Workers	2,205	1,169	1,036	9.07
Main Workers	18,184	10,376	7,808	74.81
Marginal Workers	6,123	2,047	4,076	25.19
Total Workers	24,307	12,423	11,884	

Religion: Major Religious Communities:

	Persons	Males	Females	Sex Ratio
Hindu (98.41%)	44,160	21,664	22,496	1,038
Muslim (0.11%)	48	26	22	846
Christian (1.13%)	508	242	266	1,099
Sikh (0%)	-	-	-	-
Buddhists (0.13%)	57	29	28	966
Jain (0%)	-	-	-	-

Agewise Data:

	Persons	Males	Females	Sex Ratio
All ages	44,873	22,051	22,822	1035
0-14	16,742	8,439	8,303	984
15-44	20,420	9,498	10,922	1150
45-79	7,427	3,915	3,512	897
80+	74	41	33	805
Age not stated	210	158	52	329

Languages (Dominant):

Telugu, Oriya, Konda, Others, Hindi

Disabled Population:

	Persons	Males	Females	%
Total Disabled	642	374	268	
In Seeing	310	.182	128	48.29
In Speech	52	34	18	8.1
In Hearing	60	34	26	9.35
In Movement	169	97	72	26.32
Mentally	51	27	24	7.94

DUMMUGUDEM

Dummugudem C.D. Block lies in the northern part of Khammam district. The Block is located at a distance of 146 kms. from district headquarters (Khammam). There are 83 villages in the block with the total population of 44,393 persons. Area of the C.D. Block is 375.62 sq. kms. It is bounded in the north by Mandal Cherla, in the south by Mandal Bhadrachalam, in the east by Mandals Chintur and Bhadrachalam, and in the west by Mandal Aswapuram, and it has common boundary with the state of Chhattisgarh on east.

Communications:

Roadways : State Highway (S.H.): Direction- Kothagudem to Venkatapuram. Nearest Villages- Sitanagaram, Chinnab andirevu, Kotipallepadu, Pedanallaballi, Tailorpeta, Ramachandrapuram, Manguvai, Anjubaka, Katayagudem, Achuthapuram, Narayanapuram, Lakshmi Narasimharao Peta, Suravaram, Kasinagaram, Kesavapatnam, Byragulapadu, Dummugudem, Lakshminagaram, Kannapuram, Burra Vemul Kotha Dummugudem, Work Land Reguballe, Zamandari Regı alle, Seetharampuram, Narsapuram, Turubaka.

River: Godavari Nadi- Nearest Villages- Parnasala, Kothagudem, Pragallapalle, Nadikudi, Venkata Amapuram, Narayanapuram, Lakshmi Narasimharao Peta, Suravaram, Kasinagaram, Kesavapatnam, Byragulapadu, Dummugudem, Lakshminagaram, Kannapuram, Burra Vemula, Kotha Dummı udem, Work Land Reguballe, Zamandari Reguballe, Seetha rampuram, Narsapuram, Turubaka.

Backwards Region Grants Fund: It receives Backward Region Grants.

Annual Rainfall: Average Rainfall 1356 mm

Ground Water: Availability of the Ground Water in the Basin is 5729 H.A.M.and the utilization is 143 H.A. M. It belongs to sate category. Depth to water level varies from 5 to 20 meter below the ground. Most of the wells go down in summer months. The well density in the entire block is 0.2 wells per sq. km. Total no. of the wells in the block are enumerated as 88, according to the Ground Water Estimation Committee.

Forest and Reserved **Forest:** Nearest Villages- Ramachand runi Peta, Bojjiguppa, Koya Narsapuram, Cherupalle, Marayagudem, Jinnegattu, Kothapalle, Kommanapalle, Pedabandirevu, Mulakanapalle, Lingapuram, Paidagudem, Gouravaram, Sangam, Chinnabandirevu, Sughnapuram, Chintaguppa, Pata Jinnalagudem, Z. Veerabhadrapuram, Ramachandrapuram, Manguvai, Anjubaka, Achuthapuram, Mahadevapuram, Dabbanuthula, Kothuru, Yerraboru, Adavi Ramavaram, Arlagudem, Dharmapuram, Ramarao Peta, Patha Maredubaka, Maredubaka (Z), White Nagaram, Singavaram, Gangavaram, Fowlerpeta, Narayanarao Peta, Gurralabayalu, Lachigudem.

Natural Division : Godavari Depression Region

Administration:

Division: Telangana. Parliamentary Constituency: 16 Mahbubabad . District: Khammam. Mandal: Dummugudem. Assembly Constituency: 119 Bhadrachalam (ST). Gram Panchayat: 21.

Border Villages: (Chhattisgarh)- Nearest Villages- Mulakanapalle, Lingapuram, Paidagudem, Sughnapuram, Chintaguppa, Kothuru, Yerraboru, Bheemavaram, Kommanap alle, Pedda Kamalapuram, Adavi Ramavaram, Cherupalle, Marayagudem, Jinnegattu.

Villages: 83 **Inhabited:** 80 **Uninhabited:** 3

Ranking	District	State	National
Area	9	61	2092
Population	23	682	5536
Sex Ratio	4	112	696
Child Sex Ratio	3	17	66
Literacy Rate	43	955	5509
Density	13	243	5981
Work Participation Rate	37	1012	639

Gram Panchayats:

Anjipaka, Arlagudem, China Nallaballi, Dummugudem Gangolu, Gowraram, Kasinagaram, Kothapalli Laxminagaram, Mahadevapuram, Maraigudem, Nadikudi Narsapuram, Paidigudem, Parnasala, Pedakamalapuram Pedanallaballi, Pragallapalli, Ramaraopeta Singavaram, Turubaka.

Amenities:

Education: Primary School in 65 villages, Middle school in 11 villages, Matriculation or Secondary School in 6 villages, namely Parnasala, Dummugudem, Arlagudem, Khalsa Reguballe, Narsapuram, Kothapalle.

Higher Secondary or Pre University Courses or Intermediate or Junior College in 0 village of the CD Block, College in 0 village, Adult Literacy Center in 44 villages.

Medical: Hospital in 1 village, Dispensary in 1 village, Health Center in 2 villages, Sub Center in 13 villages, Maternity and Child Welfare Center in 0 village, Community health workers in 0 village.

The Villages having Hospital or Dispensary or Health Center are Dummugudem, Arlagudem.

Drinking Water: Tap water in 79 villages, Tank water in 79 villages, Well water in 79 villages, Tubewell in 79 villages and more than one source in 79 villages.

Bank: Banking facility in 4 villages, namely, Dummugudem, Lakshminagaram, Narsapuram, Bandarugude Credit Society in 9 villages Agricultural Credit Society in 3 Non-Agricultural Credit Society in 8 villages.

Others: Power supply in 80 villages, Cinema hall in 2 villages, sport club in 0 village, Stadium or Auditorium or Community Hall in 0 village, Post Office in 14 villages.

There are 29 villages having bus facilities.

Villages with most of facilities: Dummugudem Lakshminagaram, Narsapuram.

Villages without amenities (Education):

Lingapuram, Sangam, Tailorpeta, Kannapuram, Burra Vemula, Venkata Ramapuram, Kothagudem, Laxmipuram, Gangavaram, Bojjiguppa..

Scheduled Castes: Out of the total population of 44393 persons, 4874 persons (10.98%) belong to Scheduled Castes.

The villages having less than 10% SC population are Parnasala, Govindapuram, Pedabandirevu Mulakanapalle, Lingapuram, Paidagudem, Gouravaram Sangam, Lakshmi Narasimharao Peta, Suravaram Pedanallaballi, Lakshmipuram, Paidakulamadugu Kothajinnalagudem, Sughnapuram, Chintaguppa Pata Jinnalagudem, Khalsa Veerabhadrapuram Z. Veerabhadrapuram, Tailorpeta, Kesavapatnam Ramachandrapuram, Pragallapalle, Manguvai, Anjubaka Katayagudem, Lakshminagaram, Achuthapuram Mahadevapuram, Dabbanuthula, Kothuru, Rajupeta Chinna Kamalapuram, Pedda Kamalapuram, Yerraboru Adavi Ramavaram, Arlagudem, Dharmapuram Subbaraopeta, Nadikudi, Khalsa Reguballe Ramarao Peta, Patha Maredubaka, Venkata Ramapuram Bandarugudem, Kothagudem, Maredubaka (Z) White Nagaram, Singavaram, Laxmipuram, Gangavaram Fowlerpeta, Narayanarao Peta, Gurralabayalu Lachigudem, Ramachandruni Peta, Bojjiguppa Koya Narsapuram, Bheemavaram, Cherupalle Marayagudem, Jinnegattu, Kothapalle, Kommanapalle.

The villages having more than 50% SC population are Kotha Dummugudem, Work Land Reguballe Zamandari Reguballe, Narsapuram, Turubaka.

Sex ratio of Scheduled Caste population is 486.

Scheduled Castes Literates and Illiterates by Sex:

	Persons	Males	Females
Literate	2,265	1,340	925
Illiterate	2,609	1,166	1,443
Literacy rate	53.7	61.4	45.4
Graduate	46	33	13

Scheduled Castes (Dominant):

Mala, Madiga, Adi Andhra, Relli, Manne

For their cultural identity please see Appendix-I

Villages without Scheduled Castes: There are 50 villages without any scheduled caste population.

Scheduled Tribes: Out of the total population of 44393 persons, 29810 persons (67.15%) belong to Scheduled Tribes. The villages having less than 10% ST population are Parnasala, Lakshmi Narasimharao Peta, Kesavapatnam Pragallapalle, Burra Vemula, Kotha Dummugudem Work Land Reguballe, Zamandari Reguballe Seetharampuram, Narsapuram, Turubaka.

The villages having more than 50% ST population are Sitanagaram, Govindapuram, Pedabandirevu Mulakanapalle, Lingapuram, Paidagudem, Gouravaram Sangam, Lakshmipuram, Paidakulamadugu Kothajinnalagudem, Sughnapuram, Chintaguppa Pata Jinnalagudem, Khalsa Veerabhadrapuram Z. Veerabhadrapuram, Chinna Nallaballi, Tailorpeta Ramachandrapuram, Manguvai, Anjubaka, Katayagudem Achuthapuram, Mahadevapuram, Dabbanuthula, Kothuru Rajupeta, Chinna Kamalapuram, Pedda Kamalapuram Yerraboru, Adavi Ramavaram, Arlagudem, Dharmapuram Subbaraopeta, Nadikudi, Khalsa Reguballe Ramarao Peta, Patha Maredubaka, Venkata Ramapuram Kothagudem, Maredubaka (Z), White Nagaram Singavaram, Laxmipuram, Gangavaram, Fowlerpeta Narayanarao Peta, Gurralabayalu, Lachigudem Ramachandruni Peta, Bojjiguppa, Koya Narsapuram Bheemavaram, Cherupalle, Marayagudem, Jinnegattu Kothapalle, Kommanapalle.

Sex ratio of Scheduled tribe population is 506.

Scheduled Tribes Literates and Illiterates by Sex:

	Persons	Males	Females
Literate	8,024	4,775	3,249
Illiterate	21,786	9,957	11,829
Literacy rate	32.1	38.7	25.7
Graduate	61	54	7

Scheduled Tribes (Dominant):

Koya etc., Sugalis etc., Nayaks, Yerukulas Gond etc.

For their cultural identity please see Appendix-II

Villages without Scheduled Tribes: There are 9 villages without any scheduled tribe population.

Literates and Illiterates by Sex (Total Population):

	Persons	Males	Females
Literate	15,975	9,178	6,797
Illiterate	28,418	12,820	15,598
Literacy rate	42	49	36
Graduate	310	243	67

Agriculture: ***Distribution of villages according to land use:*** Out of 83 villages, Total area (in hectare) is 37565, out of that 27.37 percent is cultivable and 29.22 percent of the cultivable area is irrigated.

Sources of Irrigation (Hectares): Government Canal 2123.33, Private Canal 0, Well without Electricity 4.85, Well with Electricity 5.67, Tubewell without Electricity 0, Tubewell with Electricity 2.43, Tank 437.4, River 0, Lake 0, Waterfall 0, Others 430.13.

Villages with population of 5000 to 9999: None

Villages with population of 10000 and above: None

Distribution of Workers:

	Persons	Males	Females	WPR
Cultivators	7,233	5,434	1,799	29.54
Agricultural Labour	14,508	5,794	8,714	59.26
Household Industry	471	237	234	1.92
Other Workers	2,271	1,648	623	9.28
Main Workers	17,557	10,958	6,599	71.71
Marginal Workers	6,926	2,155	4,771	28.29
Total Workers	24,483	13,113	11,370	

Religion: Major Religious Communities:

	Persons	Males	Females	Sex Ratio
Hindu (97.41%)	43,244	21,432	21,812	1,018
Muslim (0.62%)	274	152	122	803
Christian (1.89%)	837	399	438	1,098
Sikh (0%)	-	-	-	-
Buddhists (0%)	-	-	-	-
Jain (0%)	-	-	-	-

Agewise Data:

	Persons	Males	Females	Sex Ratio
All ages	44,393	21,998	22,395	1018
0-14	16,232	8,150	8,082	992
15-44	20,992	10,417	10,575	1015
45-79	6,880	3,304	3,576	1082
80+	226	96	130	1354
Age not stated	63	31	32	1032

Languages (Dominant):

Koya, Telugu, Hindi, Urdu, Tamil

Disabled Population:

	Persons	Males	Females	%
Total Disabled	1,080	555	525	
In Seeing	543	276	267	50.28
In Speech	87	42	45	8.06

In Hearing	73	39	34	6.76
In Movement	271	150	121	25.09
Mentally	106	48	58	9.81

DURGI

Durgi C.D. Block lies in the western part of Guntur district. The Block is located at a distance of 88 kms. from district headquarters (Guntur). There are 10 villages in the block with the total population of 44,640 persons. Area of the C.D. Block is 405.27 sq. kms. It is bounded in the north by Mandals Veldurthi, Macherla, Gurazala and Karempudi (part), in the south by Prakasam district and Mandal Bollapalle, in the east by Mandal Karempudi, and in the west by Mandal Veldurthi.

Communications:

Roadways : State Highway (S.H.): Direction- Macherla to Karempudi Nearest Villages-Durgi, Dharmavaram, Obule sunipalle, Adigoppula, Atmakur.

River: Chandravanka Nadi- Nearest Villages-Polepalle, Mutukuru, Atmakur.

Hills: Nearest Villages- Durgi, Obulesunipalle, Adigopp ula, Nidanampadu.

Annual Rainfall: Average Rainfall 666 mm

Ground Water: Availability of the Ground Water in the Basin is 3801 H.A.M. and the utilization is 1292 H. A.M. It belongs to Safe category. Depth to water level varies from 2 to 5 meter below the ground. Most of the wells go down in summer months.

Forest and Reserved **Forest:** Nearest Villages- Polepalle, Mutukuru, Kolagutla.

Natural Division : Krishna Delta Region

Administration:

Division: Coastal Andhra Parliamentary Constituency: 31 Narsaraopet District: Guntur Mandal: Durgi Assembly Constituency: 220 Macherla Gram Panchayat: 14

Places of Tourist Interest:

Durgi : This village derived its name from the existence of a temple of Goddess Durga on the eastern side of the village. It is at a distance of 19 kms. to the South-west of Gurazala town. It is connected by a metal road from Gurazala, Macherla and Veldurthi) (Veludurthi). On the southern side of the village there are hill ranges, with reserved forests, while on the western side is the Buggavagu reservoir. The ruins of fortifica tions in the heart of the village, bear testimony to the existence of a fort in the bygone days. The village is full of interesting remains, among which nine inscri ptions throw light on the Kakatiya dynasty. This village is famous for the carving of stone idols and hence the Government of India has started a stone carving industry at this place, for imparting training in this art.

Villages: 10 **Inhabited:** 10 **Uninhabited:** 0

Ranking	District	State	National
Area	2	42	1900
Population	47	676	5529
Sex Ratio	47	773	2584
Child Sex Ratio	48	934	4150
Literacy Rate	50	773	4803
Density	2	31	6051
Work Participation Rate	57	1029	155

Gram Panchayats:

Adigoppula, Atmakur, Dharivemula, Dharmavaram, Durgi Jm Padu, Kakirala, Kancharagunta, Kolagutla, Mutukur Nidanampadu, Obulesunipalli, Polepalli, Terala.

Amenities:

Education: Primary School in 10 villages, Middle school in 5 villages, Matriculation or Secondary School in 4 villages, namely Mutukuru, Durgi, Obulesunipalle, Adigoppula. Higher Secondary or Pre University Courses or Intermediate or Junior College in 0 village of the CD Block, College in 0 village, Adult Literacy Center in 0 village.

Medical: Hospital in 1 village, Dispensary in 1 village, Health Center in 2 villages, Sub Center in 7 villages, Maternity and Child Welfare Center in 0 village, Community health workers in 0 village.

The Villages having Hospital or Dispensary or Health Center are Durgi, Adigoppula.

Drinking Water: Tap water in 10 villages, Tank water in 10 villages, Well water in 10 villages, Tubewell in 10 villages and more than one source in 10 villages.

Bank: Banking facility in 3 villages, namely, Mutukuru, Durgi, Adigoppula.

Credit Society in 4 villages Agricultural Credit Society in 4 Non-Agricultural Credit Society in 0 village.

Others: Power supply in 10 villages, Cinema hall in 1 village, sport club in 0 village, Stadium or Auditorium or Community Hall in 0 village, Post Office in 9 villages.

There are 9 villages having bus facilities.

Villages with most of facilities: Mutukuru, Durgi Adigoppula.

Villages without Amenities (Education): None..

Scheduled Castes: Out of the total population of 44640 persons, 7278 persons (16.3%) belong to Scheduled Castes.

The villages having less than 10% SC population are None..

The villages having more than 50% SC population are None.

Sex ratio of Scheduled Caste population is 490.

Scheduled Castes Literates and Illiterates by Sex:

	Persons	Males	Females
Literate	2,663	1,732	931
Illiterate	4,615	1,977	2,638
Literacy rate	43.4	55.7	30.7
Graduate	81	64	17

Scheduled Castes (Dominant):
Madiga, Mala, Beda Jangam etc., Mala Dasu Generic Castes etc.

For their cultural identity please see Appendix-I

Villages without Scheduled Castes: There is 1 village without any scheduled caste population.

Scheduled Tribes: Out of the total population of 44640 persons, 3810 persons (8.53%) belong to Scheduled Tribes. The villages having less than 10% ST population are Polepalle, Atmakur, Darivemula, Durgi, Dharmavaram Adigoppula.

The villages having more than 50% ST population are None.

Sex ratio of Scheduled tribe population is 492.

Scheduled Tribes Literates and Illiterates by Sex:

	Persons	Males	Females
Literate	1,110	731	379
Illiterate	2,700	1,206	1,494
Literacy rate	35.9	45.9	25.2
Graduate	17	14	3

Scheduled Tribes (Dominant):
Sugalis etc., Yerukulas, Chenchu etc., Yenadis Kammara

For their cultural identity please see Appendix-II

Villages without Scheduled Tribes: There is 1 village without any scheduled tribe population.

Literates and Illiterates by Sex (Total Population):

	Persons	Males	Females
Literate	18,494	11,688	6,806
Illiterate	26,146	10,994	15,152
Literacy rate	48	60	36
Graduate	574	490	84

Agriculture: ***Distribution of villages according to land use:*** Out of 10 villages, Total area (in hectare) is 40528, out of that 36.22 percent is cultivable and 22.87 percent of the cultivable area is irrigated.

Sources of Irrigation (Hectares): Government Canal 728, Private Canal 0, Well without Electricity 0, Well with Electricity 0, Tubewell without Electricity 0, Tubewell with Electricity 2328, Tank 302, River 0, Lake 0, Waterfall 0, Others 0.

Villages with population of 5000 to 9999: Mutukuru, Durgi, Adigoppula.

Villages with population of 10000 and above: None

Distribution of Workers:

	Persons	Males	Females	WPR
Cultivators	8,106	4,972	3,134	30.25
Agricultural Labour	14,263	5,683	8,580	53.23
Household Industry	430	230	200	1.6
Other Workers	3,997	3,063	934	14.92
Main Workers	23,289	13,068	10,221	86.91
Marginal Workers	3,507	880	2,627	13.09
Total Workers	26,796	13,948	12,848	

Religion: Major Religious Communities:

	Persons	Males	Females	Sex Ratio
Hindu (94.58%)	42,221	21,467	20,754	967
Muslim (3.52%)	1,573	790	783	991
Christian (1.72%)	770	385	385	1,000
Sikh (0%)	2	2	-	-
Buddhists (0%)	1	-	1	-
Jain (0%)	-	-	-	-

Agewise Data:

	Persons	Males	Females	Sex Ratio
All ages	44,640	22,682	21,958	968
0-14	14,897	7,639	7,258	950
15-44	21,136	10,760	10,376	964
45-79	8,237	4,102	4,135	1008
80+	341	166	175	1054
Age not stated	29	15	14	933

Languages (Dominant):
Telugu, Hindi, Urdu, Tamil, Gondi

Disabled Population:

	Persons	Males	Females	%
Total Disabled	751	412	339	
In Seeing	249	117	132	33.16
In Speech	82	41	41	10.92
In Hearing	40	22	18	5.33
In Movement	275	172	103	36.62
Mentally	105	60	45	13.98

DUTTALUR

Duttalur C.D. Block lies in the northern part of Nellore district. The Block is located at a distance of 94 kms. from district headquarters (Nellore). There are 16 villages in the block with the total population of 23,633 persons. Area of the C.D. Block is 272.09 sq. kms. It is bounded in the north by Mandals Varikunt apadu and Vinjamur, in the south by Mandal Marripadu, in the east by Mandal Vinjamur, and in the west by Mandal Udayagiri.

Communications:

Roadways : State Highway (S.H.): Direction- Badvel to Kanigiri. Nearest Villages- Theddupadu, Narrawada, Mandallanaidupalle, Duttalur, Papampalle, Nandipadu.

Annual Rainfall: Average Rainfall 1025 mm

Ground Water: Availability of the Ground Water in the Basin is 2706 H.A.M. and the utilization is 1315 H.

A.M. It belongs to Safe category. Depth to water level varies from more than 10 meter below the ground. Most of the wells go down in summer months, according to the Ground Water Estimation Committee.

Administration:

Division: Coastal Andhra. Parliamentary Constituency: 39 Nellore. District: Nellore.

Mandal: Duttalur. Assembly Constituency: 242 Udayagiri. Gram Panchayat: 17.

Fairs and Festivals:

Vengamamba, Tirunala : It takes place for 5 days from the Sunday following Jaishta Suddha Purnima (May-June) in commemoration of Vengamamba, a chaste Kamma woman who performed sati with her husband. For the thirst three days, uthsavams are celebrated ordinarily. But, on the fourth and fifth days uthsavams are celebarated with much pomp and ceremony, displaying fire works. Devotees fulfil their vows. Ornaments, money, coconuts and hair are offered to the deity. Carts load of pongal li is brought from the neighbouring two or three distric ts. Members of the 'Vemuri' familly are the patrons. Several thousands of devotees of all communities local and from the neighbouring places congregte there. Pujari is a Kamma of patchava family. Nitya naivedyam (daily offering) is offered and akhanda deeparadhana (contin uous burning of lamps) is maintained. On the last two days, there is free feeling irrespective of caste and creed.

Villages: 16 **Inhabited:** 15 **Uninhabited:** 1

Ranking	District	State	National
Area	20	228	3079
Population	45	1076	6171
Sex Ratio	2	93	619
Child Sex Ratio	1	14	58
Literacy Rate	26	308	2991
Density	27	842	6209
Work Participation Rate	45	1081	2647

Gram Panchayats:

Bandakinda Palli, Bodavaripalli, Bramheswaram Byravaram, Duttalur, Kotha Peta, Nandi Padu Narrawada, Papampalle, Rachavari Palli, Redla Dinne Somala Regada, Teddu Padu, Thimma Purm Venganna Palem, Venkatam Peta, Yerukollu.

Amenities:

Education: Primary School in 15 villages, Middle school in 10 villages, Matriculation or Secondary School in 3 villages, namely Narrawada, Duttalur, Nandipadu.

Higher Secondary or Pre University Courses or Intermediate or Junior College in 0 village of the CD Block, College in 0 village, Adult Literacy Center in 14 villages.

Medical: Hospital in 0 village, Dispensary in 0 village, Health Center in 2 villages, Sub Center in 7 villages, Maternity and Child Welfare Center in 0 village, Community health workers in 0 village.

Drinking Water: Tap water in 15 villages, Tank water in 15 villages, Well water in 15 villages, Tubewell in 15 villages and more than one source in 15 villages.

Bank: Banking facility in 3 villages, namely, Narrawada, Duttalur, Nandipadu.

Credit Society in 11 villages Agricultural Credit Society in 4 Non-Agricultural Credit Society in 11 villages.

Others: Power supply in 15 villages, Cinema hall in 1 village, sport club in 0 village, Stadium or Auditorium or Community Hall in 0 village, Post Office in 10 villages.

There are 14 villages having bus facilities.

Villages with most of facilities: Narrawada Duttalur, Nandipadu.

Villages without Amenities (Education): None..

Scheduled Castes: Out of the total population of 23633 persons, 4470 persons (18.91%) belong to Scheduled Castes.

The villages having less than 10% SC population are None..

The villages having more than 50% SC population are None.

Sex ratio of Scheduled Caste population is 516.

Scheduled Castes Literates and Illiterates by Sex:

	Persons	Males	Females
Literate	2,113	1,269	844
Illiterate	2,357	893	1,464
Literacy rate	54.2	67.2	42.0
Graduate	50	42	8

Scheduled Castes (Dominant):

Madiga, Mala, Adi Andhra, Dakkal etc.

Beda Jangam etc.

For their cultural identity please see Appendix-I

Villages without Scheduled Castes: There is 1 village without any scheduled caste population.

Scheduled Tribes: Out of the total population of 23633 persons, 414 persons (1.75%) belong to Scheduled Tribes.

The villages having less than 10% ST population are Theddupadu, Thimmapuram, Kothapeta, Narrawada Mandallanaidupalle, Somalaregada, Duttalur Brahmeswaram, Yerukollu, Rachavaripalle, Papampalle Venkatampeta, Nandipadu, Bhyravaram.

The villages having more than 50% ST population are None.

Sex ratio of Scheduled tribe population is 490.

Scheduled Tribes Literates and Illiterates by Sex:

	Persons	Males	Females
Literate	111	76	35

Illiterate	303	135	168
Literacy rate	32.5	43.4	21.0
Graduate	2	1	1

Scheduled Tribes (Dominant):
Yenadis, Yerukulas

For their cultural identity please see Appendix-II

Villages without Scheduled Tribes: There are 4 villages without any scheduled tribe population.

Literates and Illiterates by Sex (Total Population):

	Persons	Males	Females
Literate	12,283	7,645	4,638
Illiterate	11,350	4,041	7,309
Literacy rate	59	74	44
Graduate	394	349	45

Agriculture: ***Distribution of villages according to land use:*** Out of 16 villages, Total area (in hectare) is 27208, out of that 15.09 percent is cultivable and 48.1 percent of the cultivable area is irrigated.

Sources of Irrigation (Hectares): Government Canal 0, Private Canal 0, Well without Electricity 63.97, Well with Electricity 1131.97, Tubewell without Electricity 0, Tubewell with Electricity 261.53, Tank 337.67, River 0, Lake 0, Waterfall 0, Others 179.76.

Villages with population of 5000 to 9999:
Duttalur.

Villages with population of 10000 and above: None

Distribution of Workers:

	Persons	Males	Females	WPR
Cultivators	3,097	2,284	813	26.68
Agricultural Labour	3,387	1,212	2,175	29.18
Household Industry	407	254	153	3.51
Other Workers	4,718	3,025	1,693	40.64
Main Workers	8,160	5,591	2,569	70.29
Marginal Workers	3,449	1,184	2,265	29.71
Total Workers	11,609	6,775	4,834	

Religion: Major Religious Communities:

	Persons	Males	Females	Sex Ratio
Hindu (92.98%)	21,975	10,859	11,116	1,024
Muslim (6.03%)	1,424	705	719	1,020
Christian (0.87%)	206	110	96	873
Sikh (0.01%)	3	1	2	2,000
Buddhists (0.01%)	2	2	-	-
Jain (0%)	-	-	-	-

Agewise Data:

	Persons	Males	Females	Sex Ratio
All ages	23,633	11,686	11,947	1022
0-14	7,193	3,641	3,552	976
15-44	10,841	5,356	5,485	1024
45-79	5,338	2,575	2,763	1073
80+	238	103	135	1311
Age not stated	23	11	12	1091

Languages (Dominant):
Telugu, Urdu, Tamil, Hindi, Oriya

Disabled Population:

	Persons	Males	Females	%
Total Disabled	623	336	287	
In Seeing	222	100	122	35.63
In Speech	70	33	37	11.24
In Hearing	61	29	32	9.79
In Movement	199	131	68	31.94
Mentally	71	43	28	11.4

DUVVUR

Duvvur C.D. Block lies in the northern part of Cuddapah district. The Block is located at a distance of 68 kms. from district headquarters (Cuddapah). There are 20 villages in the block with the total population of 49,983 persons. Area of the C.D. Block is 220.78 sq. kms. It is bounded in the north by district Kurnool, in the south by Mandal Chapad, in the east by Mandal S. Mydukur, and in the west by Mandals Rajupalem and Proddatur, and River Kundu.

Communications:

Roadways : NH- 18: Direction- Kurnool to Chapad. Nearest Villages- Duvvur, Rajupalem, Gudipadu, Chintakunta, Idamadaka, Kanagudur, Jillela.

River: Kundu Nadi- Nearest Villages- Pedda Jonnavaram, Nelaturu, Idamadaka, Kanagudur, Jillela.

Receives Backward Region Grant, and is identified as a drought-prone area as well.

Annual Rainfall: Average Rainfall 706 mm

Ground Water: Availability of the Ground Water in the Basin is 3572 H.A.M.and the utilization is 2311 H.A. M.It belongs to Safe category. Depth to water level varies from 5 to 10 meter below the ground. Most of the wells go down in summer months, according to the Ground Water Estimation Committee.

Natural Division : Rayalaseema Region

Administration:

Division: Rayala Seema. Parliamentary Constituency: 38 Kadapa. District: Cuddapah.

Mandal: Duvvur. Assembly Constituency: 252 Mydukur. Gram Panchayat: 23.

Places of Tourist Interest:

Gudipadu : Gudipadu village is situated on the Cuddapah -Kurnool highway, about 11 kms. north-west of Mydukur. The temples dedicated to Chennakesava and Siva are noted for their beautiful sculptures.

Fairs and Festivals:

Jamal Vali Urs: It is celebrated for two days from the full moon day in Phalgunam (February-March). On the first day gandham is brought to Vennapusa house from the house of Syed of Proddatur and from there brought with music and kept on the tomb at 4 A.M., on Padyami. The next night i.e., on the night of Padyami, janda (flag) is taken out in procession with music in the village and installed at the darga. Devotees, Muslims as well as Hindus, fulfil their vows by naming their children after the saint and by observing tonsure ceremonies during the festival. Sadhus and fakirs sing songs relating to Jamaliah during the festival. Copra, sugar and cloth are also offered in filfilment of vows to cover the tomb. This festival is being celebrat ed for the past 240 years and is widely known. The chief patrons are Hindus of Vennapusa family. A congregation of 20 to 25 thousands of people belonged to all communi ties of the Kanagudur and those of other places of Cudda pah and Kurnool districts participate in the celebrations without any distinction. The mujavar is a Muslim appoi nted by the chief patron. Prasadam is distributed to all.

Villages: 20 **Inhabited:** 19 **Uninhabited:** 1

Ranking	District	State	National
Area	27	437	3845
Population	8	515	5285
Sex Ratio	28	735	2486
Child Sex Ratio	49	1073	5196
Literacy Rate	30	343	3147
Density	13	480	4355
Work Participation Rate	14	618	1229

Gram Panchayats:

Annapu Sastrula Palli, Bayanapalli, Bheemunipadu Bukkayapalli, Chinnasinganapalli, Chintha Kunta Duvvur, Gudipadu, Idamadaka, Kanagudur Krishnampalli, M. Yerraballi, Machanapalli Madirepalli, Moodindlapalli, Narayanapalli Neelapuram, Nelaturu, Pedda Jonnavaram Sanjeevareddy Palli, T. Sallabasayapalli, Venkupalli Zillella.

Amenities:

Education: Primary School in 19 villages, Middle school in 8 villages, Matriculation or Secondary School in 3 villages, namely Kanagudur, Duvvur, Gudipadu.

Higher Secondary or Pre University Courses or Intermediate or Junior College in 1 village of the CD Block,, namely Duvvur.

College in 1 village, Adult Literacy Center in 3 villages., College is in village, namely Duvvur.

Medical: Hospital in 0 village, Dispensary in 1 village, Health Center in 1 village, Sub Center in 6 villages, Maternity and Child Welfare Center in 0 village, Community health workers in 0 village.

The Village having Hospital or Dispensary or Health Center is Chintakunta.

Drinking Water: Tap water in 19 villages, Tank water in 19 villages, Well water in 19 villages, Tubewell in 19 villages and more than one source in 19 villages.

Bank: Banking facility in 3 villages, namely, Kanagudur, Duvvur, Chintakunta.

Credit Society in 6 villages Agricultural Credit Society in 5 Non-Agricultural Credit Society in 3 villages.

Others: Power supply in 19 villages, Cinema hall in 1 village, sport club in 0 village, Stadium or Auditorium or Community Hall in 0 village, Post Office in 15 villages.

There are 16 villages having bus facilities.

Villages with most of facilities: Kanagudur Duvvur, Chintakunta.

Villages without Amenities (Education): None..

Scheduled Castes: Out of the total population of 49983 persons, 8236 persons (16.48%) belong to Scheduled Castes.

The villages having less than 10% SC population are None..

The villages having more than 50% SC population are None.

Sex ratio of Scheduled Caste population is 492.

Scheduled Castes Literates and Illiterates by Sex:

	Persons	Males	Females
Literate	3,805	2,375	1,430
Illiterate	4,431	1,806	2,625
Literacy rate	53.9	66.6	41.0
Graduate	95	80	15

Scheduled Castes (Dominant):

Mala, Madiga, Adi Andhra, Generic Castes etc. Dakkal etc.

For their cultural identity please see Appendix-I

Villages without Scheduled Castes: There are 3 villages without any scheduled caste population.

Scheduled Tribes: Out of the total population of 49983 persons, 228 persons (0.46%) belong to Scheduled Tribes.

The villages having less than 10% ST population are Idamadaka, Kanagudur, Dasaripalle, Neelapuram Jillela, Pedda Jonnavaram, Duvvur, Madirepalle Chinna Singanapalle, T.Sallabasayapalle, Gollapalle Manerampalle, Rajupalem, Gudipadu, Nelaturu Ballakkivaripalle, Machanapalle Annapusastrula Palle, Chintakunta.

The villages having more than 50% ST population are None.

Sex ratio of Scheduled tribe population is 478.

Scheduled Tribes Literates and Illiterates by Sex:

	Persons	Males	Females

Literate	67	43	24
Illiterate	161	76	85
Literacy rate	34.0	42.2	25.3
Graduate	2	2	0

Scheduled Tribes (Dominant):
Yerukulas, Yenadis, Sugalis etc.
For their cultural identity please see Appendix-II
Villages without Scheduled Tribes: There are 11 villages without any scheduled tribe population.
Literates and Illiterates by Sex (Total Population):

	Persons	Males	Females
Literate	25,003	15,853	9,150
Illiterate	24,980	9,524	15,456
Literacy rate	58	73	43
Graduate	1,046	925	121

Agriculture: ***Distribution of villages according to land use:*** Out of 20 villages, Total area (in hectare) is 22078, out of that 52.07 percent is cultivable and 59.93 percent of the cultivable area is irrigated.
Sources of Irrigation (Hectares): Government Canal 3532.2, Private Canal 0, Well without Electricity 0, Well with Electricity 0, Tubewell without Electricity 0, Tubewell with Electricity 3151.51, Tank 205.5, River 0, Lake 0, Waterfall 0, Others 0.
Villages with population of 5000 to 9999:
Gudipadu, Chintakunta.
Villages with population of 10000 and above:
Duvvur.
Distribution of Workers:

	Persons	Males	Females	WPR
Cultivators	7,245	5,048	2,197	27.2
Agricultural Labour	14,960	6,348	8,612	56.16
Household Industry	489	230	259	1.84
Other Workers	3,942	3,091	851	14.8
Main Workers	19,589	12,315	7,274	73.54
Marginal Workers	7,047	2,402	4,645	26.46
Total Workers	26,636	14,717	11,919	

Religion: Major Religious Communities:

	Persons	Males	Females	Sex Ratio
Hindu (84.52%)	42,245	21,517	20,728	963
Muslim (15.19%)	7,594	3,794	3,800	1,002
Christian (0.23%)	116	54	62	1,148
Sikh (0%)	1	-	1	-
Buddhists (0%)	1	1	-	-
Jain (0%)	1	-	1	-

Agewise Data:

	Persons	Males	Females	Sex Ratio
All ages	49,983	25,377	24,606	970
0-14	16,437	8,602	7,835	911
15-44	23,160	11,833	11,327	957
45-79	10,015	4,798	5,217	1087
80+	272	103	169	1641
Age not stated	99	41	58	1415

Languages (Dominant):
Telugu, Urdu, Gondi, Tamil, Hindi
Disabled Population:

	Persons	Males	Females	%
Total Disabled	786	439	347	
In Seeing	273	153	120	34.73
In Speech	80	41	39	10.18
In Hearing	78	33	45	9.92
In Movement	258	155	103	32.82
Mentally	97	57	40	12.34

DWARAKATIRUMALA

Dwarka Tirumala C.D. Block lies in the western part of West Godavari district. The Block is located at a distance of 45 kms. from district headquarters (Eluru). There are 34 villages in the block with the total population of 63,399 persons. Area of the C.D. Block is 250.36 sq. kms. It is bounded in the north by Mandals Jangareddigudem and Koyyalagudem, in the south by Mandals Pedavegi, Denduluru and Bhimadole, in the east by Mandals Ungutur and Nallajerla, and in the west by Mandals Pedavegi and Kamaravapukota.
Communications :
Roadways : Metalled Roads: Nearest Villages- Chelikaniva nipothepalle, Dorasanipadu, Malleswaram, Dwarakatirumala, Kommugudem, Thimmapuram, Lingaraopalem, Tirumalampale Krishnapuram, Pangidigudem, M.Nagulapalle, Narayanapur am, Gunnampalle.
Backwards Region Grants Fund: It receives Backward Region Grants.

Annaul Rainfall: Average Rainfall 1005 mm
Ground Water: Availability of the Ground Water in the Basin is (Information not avavible) H.A.M .and the utilization is (Information not avavible) H.A.M. It belongs to (Information not avavible) category. Depth to water level varies from 3 to 10 meter below the ground. Most of the wells go down in summer months.
Natural Division : Godavari Delta Region
Administration:
Division: Coastal Andhra. Parliamentary Constituency: 25 Rajahmundry. District: West Godavari. Mandal: Dwarak atirumala. Assembly Constituency: 185 Gopalapuram (SC). Gram Panchayat: 24.
Villages: 34 **Inhabited:** 31 **Uninhabited:** 3

Ranking	**District**	**State**	**National**
Area	4	312	3382
Population	33	224	4747
Sex Ratio	46	993	3548

Child Sex Ratio	40	939	4225
Literacy Rate	41	166	1988
Density	8	764	4038
Work Participation Rate	43	526	2233

Gram Panchayats:

Ch.Pothapalli, Dorasanipadu, Dwaraka Tirumala G.Kothapalli, Gundugolanukunta, Gunnampalle I.S.Raghavapuram, Jajulakunta, Kodigudem, Komara M.Nagulapalli, Maddulagudem, Marampalle Narayanapuram, P.Kannapuram, Pangidigudem, Rajupalem Rallakunta, Ramannagudem, Ramasingaaram, Thimmapuram Thirumalampalem, Vempadu, Venkata Krishnapuram.

Amenities:

Education: Primary School in 29 villages, Middle school in 8 villages, Matriculation or Secondary School in 6 villages, namely G.Kothapalle, Dwarakatirumala, Tirumalampalem, Pangidigudem, M.Nagulapalle, Gunnampalle.

Higher Secondary or Pre University Courses or Intermediate or Junior College in 0 village of the CD Block, College in 0 village, Adult Literacy Center in 19 villages.

Medical: Hospital in 0 village, Dispensary in 1 village, Health Center in 2 villages, Sub Center in 11 villages, Maternity and Child Welfare Center in 0 village, Community health workers in 0 village.

The Villages having Hospital or Dispensary or Health Center are Chelikanivanipothepalle, Dwarakatirumala.

Drinking Water: Tap water in 31 villages, Tank water in 31 villages, Well water in 31 villages, Tubewell in 31 villages and more than one source in 31 villages.

Bank: Banking facility in 3 villages, namely, G.Kothapalle, Dwarakatirumala, Tirumalampalem.

Credit Society in 5 villages Agricultural Credit Society in 5 Non-Agricultural Credit Society in 0 village.

Others: Power supply in 31 villages, Cinema hall in 3 villages, sport club in 0 village, Stadium or Auditorium or Community Hall in 0 village, Post Office in 18 villages.

There are 30 villages having bus facilities.

Villages with most of facilities: G.Kothapalle Dwarakatirumala, Tirumalampalem.

Villages without amenities (Education):

Malleswaram, Krishnapuram..

Scheduled Castes: Out of the total population of 63399 persons, 21988 persons (34.68%) belong to Scheduled Castes.

The villages having less than 10% SC population are Malleswaram, Rallakunta, Kommugudem, Krishnapuram Havelilingapalem, Dadavalli.

The villages having more than 50% SC population are Kodigudem, G.Kothapalle, Kommara(North) Kommara(South), Sathenagudem, Sarabhapuram, Sattala.

Sex ratio of Scheduled Caste population is 485.

Scheduled Castes Literates and Illiterates by Sex:

	Persons	Males	Females
Literate	10,992	6,060	4,932
Illiterate	10,996	5,259	5,737
Literacy rate	58.0	62.3	53.5
Graduate	186	144	42

Scheduled Castes (Dominant):

Mala, Madiga, Adi Andhra, Mala Dasu Madiga Dasu etc.

For their cultural identity please see Appendix-I

Villages without Scheduled Castes: There are 6 villages without any scheduled caste population.

Scheduled Tribes: Out of the total population of 63399 persons, 766 persons (1.21%) belong to Scheduled Tribes.

The villages having less than 10% ST population are Chelikanivanipothepalle, Kodigudem, G.Kothapalle I.S.Raghavapuram, I.S.Jagannadhapuram Kommara(North), Kommara(South), Dorasanipadu Gundugolanukunta, Malleswaram, Dwarakatirumala Rallakunta, Sathenagudem, Kommugudem Venkatakrishnapuram, Ramannagudem, Thimmapuram Malasanikunta, Tirumalampalem, Krishnapuram Havelilingapalem, Vempadu, Pangidigudem M.Nagulapalle, Narayanapuram, Jajulakunta Gunnampalle, Sarabhapuram, P.Kannapuram, Sattala Dadavalli.

The villages having more than 50% ST population are None.

Sex ratio of Scheduled tribe population is 503.

Scheduled Tribes Literates and Illiterates by Sex:

	Persons	Males	Females
Literate	244	143	101
Illiterate	522	238	284
Literacy rate	38.5	45.0	32.0
Graduate	7	5	2

Scheduled Tribes (Dominant):

Sugalis etc., Yerukulas, Yenadis, Nayaks, Koya etc.

For their cultural identity please see Appendix-II

Villages without Scheduled Tribes: There are 19 villages without any scheduled tribe population.

Literates and Illiterates by Sex (Total Population):

	Persons	Males	Females
Literate	35,909	19,455	16,454
Illiterate	27,490	13,076	14,414
Literacy rate	65	68	61
Graduate	919	700	219

Agriculture: ***Distribution of villages according to land use:*** Out of 34 villages, Total area (in hectare) is 25035, out of that 82.96 percent is cultivable and 0 percent of the cultivable area is irrigated.

Sources of Irrigation (Hectares): Government Canal 0, Private Canal 0, Well without Electricity 0, Well with Electricity 0, Tubewell without Electricity 0, Tubewell with Electricity 0, Tank 0, River 0, Lake 0, Waterfall 0, Others 0.

Villages with population of 5000 to 9999: Tirumalampalem, Pangidigudem.

Villages with population of 10000 and above: None

Distribution of Workers:

	Persons	Males	Females	WPR
Cultivators	6,135	5,338	797	19.27
Agricultural Labour	20,495	11,019	9,476	64.39
Household Industry	551	366	185	1.73
Other Workers	4,648	3,742	906	14.6
Main Workers	27,756	18,900	8,856	87.2
Marginal Workers	4,073	1,565	2,508	12.8
Total Workers	31,829	20,465	11,364	

Religion: Major Religious Communities:

	Persons	Males	Females	Sex Ratio
Hindu (97.08%)	61,547	31,580	29,967	949
Muslim (1.64%)	1,040	539	501	929
Christian (1.18%)	750	377	373	989
Sikh (0%)	-	-	-	-
Buddhists (0.01%)	4	2	2	1,000
Jain (0%)	-	-	-	-

Agewise Data:

	Persons	Males	Females	Sex Ratio
All ages	63,399	32,531	30,868	949
0-14	20,196	10,371	9,825	947
15-44	30,861	15,902	14,959	941
45-79	11,959	6,074	5,885	969
80+	318	157	161	1025
Age not stated	65	27	38	1407

Languages (Dominant):

Telugu, Urdu, Hindi, Gondi, Tamil

Disabled Population:

	Persons	Males	Females	%
Total Disabled	997	570	427	
In Seeing	280	139	141	28.08
In Speech	126	71	55	12.64
In Hearing	81	34	47	8.12
In Movement	381	257	124	38.21
Mentally	129	69	60	12.94

EDLAPADU

Edlapadu C.D. Block lies in the southern part of Guntur district. The Block is located at a distance of 27 kms. from district headquarters (Guntur). There are 13 villages in the block with the total population of 49,492 persons. Area of the C.D. Block is 128.43 sq. kms. It is bounded in the north by Mandals Phirangi puram and Medikonduru, in the south Chilakaluripet and Pedanandipadu, in the east by Mandals Pedanandipadu (part), Prathipadu, Guntur and Medikonduru and in the west by Mandals Madendla and Phirangipuram.

Communications:

Roadways : NH- 5: Direrction- Ongole to Guntur. Nearest Villages- Vankayalapadu, Marripalem, Viswanadhuni Khand rika, Edlapadu, Thimmapuram. State Highway (S.H.): Neare st Village- Thimmapuram.

Annual Rainfall: Average Rainfall 899 mm

Ground Water: Availability of the Ground Water in the Basin is 6007 H.A.M. and the utilization is 329 H.A. M. It belongs to Safe category. Depth to water level varies from 2 to 5 meter below the ground. Most of the wells go down in summer months.

Forest and Reserved **Forest:** Nearest Villages- Kondaveedu, Solasa, Vankayalapadu, Marripalem.

Natural Division : Krishna Delta Region

Administration:

Division: Coastal Andhra. Parliamentary Constituency: 31 Narsaraopet. District: Guntur. Mandal: Edlapadu. Assembly Constituency: 215 Chilakaluripet. Gram Panchayat: 18.

Villages: 13 **Inhabited:** 12 **Uninhabited:** 1

Ranking	District	State	National
Area	41	907	5347
Population	36	530	5307
Sex Ratio	30	542	1917
Child Sex Ratio	51	1001	4663
Literacy Rate	28	333	3107
Density	7	78	2841
Work Participation Rate	23	209	282

Gram Panchayats:

Chengheeskhanpet, Dintenapadu, Edlapadu Guthavaripalem, Jaggapuram, Jaladi, Karuchola Kondaveedu, Kota, Kothapalem, Lingaraopalem Mydavolu, Sandepudi, Solasa, Thimmapuram, Turlapadu Unnava, Vankayalapadu.

Amenities:

Education: Primary School in 12 villages, Middle school in 9 villages, Matriculation or Secondary School in 6 villages, namely Solasa, Mydavolu, Unnava, Edlapadu, Jaladi, Sandepudi.

Higher Secondary or Pre University Courses or Intermediate or Junior College in 1 village of the CD Block,, namely Edlapadu.

College in 1 village, Adult Literacy Center in 8 villages., College is in village, namely Edlapadu.

Medical: Hospital in 1 village, Dispensary in 1 village, Health Center in 2 villages, Sub Center in 9 villages,

Maternity and Child Welfare Center in 0 village, Community health workers in 0 village.

The Villages having Hospital or Dispensary or Health Center are Unnava, Edlapadu.

Drinking Water: Tap water in 12 villages, Tank water in 12 villages, Well water in 12 villages, Tubewell in 12 villages and more than one source in 12 villages.

Bank: Banking facility in 3 villages, namely, Kondaveedu, Solasa, Edlapadu.

Credit Society in 4 villages Agricultural Credit Society in 4 Non-Agricultural Credit Society in 1 village.

Others: Power supply in 12 villages, Cinema hall in 1 village, sport club in 0 village, Stadium or Auditorium or Community Hall in 0 village, Post Office in 11 villages.

There are 11 villages having bus facilities.

Villages with most of facilities: Kondaveedu Solasa, Edlapadu.

Villages without Amenities (Education): None..

Scheduled Castes: Out of the total population of 49492 persons, 11394 persons (23.02%) belong to Scheduled Castes. The villages having less than 10% SC population are None..

The villages having more than 50% SC population are None.

Sex ratio of Scheduled Caste population is 492.

Scheduled Castes Literates and Illiterates by Sex:

	Persons	Males	Females
Literate	5,174	3,166	2,008
Illiterate	6,220	2,619	3,601
Literacy rate	53.4	64.2	42.2
Graduate	146	115	31

Scheduled Castes (Dominant):

Mala, Madiga, Beda Jangam etc., Jaggali, Adi Andhra

For their cultural identity please see Appendix-I

Villages without Scheduled Castes: There is 1 village without any scheduled caste population.

Scheduled Tribes: Out of the total population of 49492 persons, 1979 persons (4%) belong to Scheduled Tribes. The villages having less than 10% ST population are Kondaveedu, Solasa, Mydavolu, Vankayalapadu Marripalem, Unnava, Karuchola, Edlapadu, Thimmapuram Jaladi, Sandepudi, Thurlapadu.

The villages having more than 50% ST population are None.

Sex ratio of Scheduled tribe population is 473.

Scheduled Tribes Literates and Illiterates by Sex:

	Persons	Males	Females
Literate	597	402	195
Illiterate	1,382	640	742
Literacy rate	35.5	46.2	24.1
Graduate	12	11	1

Scheduled Tribes (Dominant):

Yerukulas, Yenadis, Sugalis etc., Chenchu etc. Generic Tribes etc.

For their cultural identity please see Appendix-II

Villages without Scheduled Tribes: There are 2 villages without any scheduled tribe population.

Literates and Illiterates by Sex (Total Population):

	Persons	Males	Females
Literate	25,181	14,823	10,358
Illiterate	24,311	10,154	14,157
Literacy rate	58	68	48
Graduate	1,085	864	221

Agriculture: ***Distribution of villages according to land use:*** Out of 13 villages, Total area (in hectare) is 12842, out of that 67.86 percent is cultivable and 26 percent of the cultivable area is irrigated.

Sources of Irrigation (Hectares): Government Canal 1828.5, Private Canal 0, Well without Electricity 2.02, Well with Electricity 79.71, Tubewell without Electricity 0, Tubewell with Electricity 165.91, Tank 50.63, River 0, Lake 0, Waterfall 0, Others 138.78.

Villages with population of 5000 to 9999: Kondaveedu, Edlapadu, Thimmapuram.

Villages with population of 10000 and above: None

Distribution of Workers:

	Persons	Males	Females	WPR
Cultivators	7,365	4,392	2,973	25.19
Agricultural Labour	16,155	6,993	9,162	55.26
Household Industry	623	257	366	2.13
Other Workers	5,092	4,012	1,080	17.42
Main Workers	24,313	14,237	10,076	83.16
Marginal Workers	4,922	1,417	3,505	16.84
Total Workers	29,235	15,654	13,581	

Religion: Major Religious Communities:

	Persons	Males	Females	Sex Ratio
Hindu (84.4%)	41,769	21,117	20,652	978
Muslim (10.63%)	5,259	2,602	2,657	1,021
Christian (4.87%)	2,408	1,227	1,181	963
Sikh (0.03%)	13	8	5	625
Buddhists (0.01%)	3	2	1	500
Jain (0.04%)	20	11	9	818

Agewise Data:

	Persons	Males	Females	Sex Ratio
All ages	49,492	24,977	24,515	982
0-14	14,223	7,286	6,937	952
15-44	24,259	12,226	12,033	984
45-79	10,463	5,188	5,275	1017
80+	479	240	239	996
Age not stated	68	37	31	838

Languages (Dominant):
Telugu, Urdu, Tamil, Hindi, Gondi

Disabled Population:

	Persons	Males	Females	%
Total Disabled	1,007	570	437	
In Seeing	411	202	209	40.81
In Speech	91	54	37	9.04
In Hearing	65	37	28	6.45
In Movement	338	216	122	33.57
Mentally	102	61	41	10.13

ELKATHURTHI

Elkathurthi C.D. Block lies in the south-east part of Karimnagar district. The Block is located at a dista nce of 55 kms. from district headquarters (Karimnagar). There are 13 villages in the block with the total population of 39,657 persons. Area of the C.D. Block is 115,63 sq. kms. It is bounded by Kamalapur Mandal on north, Warangal district on east, Bheemadevarapalle Mandal on south and west, and Huzurabad mandal on north -west.

Communications :

Roadways : Metalled Roads: Nearest Villages- Penchakalpe ta, Elkathurthi, Suraram, Vallabhapur, Kothulnaduma.

Backwards Region Grants Fund : It receives Backward Region Grants.

Annual Rainfall: Average Rainfall 895 mm

Ground Water: Availability of the Ground Water in the Basin is 1812 H.A.M. and the utilization is 1492 H. A.M. It belongs to Semi Critical category. Depth to water level varies from more than 10 meter below the ground. Most of the wells go down in summer months. The well density in the entire block is 32 wells per sq. km. Total no. of the wells in the block are enumera ted as 3568, according to the Ground Water Estimation Committee.

Natural Division : Godavari Depression Region

Administration:

Division: Telangana. Parliamentary Constituency: 3 Karimnagar. District: Karimnagar. Mandal: Elkathurthi. Assembly Constituency: 32 Husnabad. Gram Panchayat: 15

Villages: 13 **Inhabited:** 13 **Uninhabited:** 0

Ranking	District	State	National
Area	56	966	5541
Population	46	832	5746
Sex Ratio	56	804	2693
Child Sex Ratio	36	646	2631
Literacy Rate	11	528	3959
Density	40	583	3163
Work Participation Rate	11	282	1569

Gram Panchayats:

Baopeta, Chinthalapally, Damera, Dandepally Elkathurthy, Gopalpur, Jagannathapur, Jeelugula Keshavapur, Kothulanaduma, Penchikalpet, Suraram Thimmapur, Valbhapur, Veeranarayanapur.

Amenities:

Education: Primary School in 13 villages, Middle school in 12 villages, Matriculation or Secondary School in 8 villages, namely Jeelgul, Gopalpur, Damera, Elkathurthi, Suraram, Vallabhapur, Dandepalle, Baopet.

Higher Secondary or Pre University Courses or Intermediate or Junior College in 0 village of the CD Block, College in 0 village, Adult Literacy Center in 9 villages.

Medical: Hospital in 0 village, Dispensary in 0 village, Health Center in 2 villages, Sub Center in 7 villages, Maternity and Child Welfare Center in 0 village, Community health workers in 0 village.

Drinking Water: Tap water in 13 villages, Tank water in 12 villages, Well water in 12 villages, Tubewell in 12 villages and more than one source in 13 villages.

Bank: Banking facility in 2 villages, namely, Gopalpur, Elkathurthi.

Credit Society in 13 villages Agricultural Credit Society in 2 Non-Agricultural Credit Society in 13 villages.

Others: Power supply in 13 villages, Cinema hall in 1 village, sport club in 0 village, Stadium or Auditorium or Community Hall in 0 village, Post Office in 12 villages.

There are 13 villages having bus facilities.

Villages with most of facilities: Gopalpur Elkathurthi.

Villages without Amenities (Education): None..

Scheduled Castes: Out of the total population of 39657 persons, 11639 persons (29.35%) belong to Scheduled Castes. The villages having less than 10% SC population are None..

The villages having more than 50% SC population are None.

Sex ratio of Scheduled Caste population is 486.

Scheduled Castes Literates and Illiterates by Sex:

	Persons	Males	Females
Literate	4,608	2,927	1,681
Illiterate	7,031	3,053	3,978
Literacy rate	46.2	57.3	34.6
Graduate	124	111	13

Scheduled Castes (Dominant):

Madiga, Mala, Beda Jangam etc., Mala Sale etc. Generic Castes etc.

For their cultural identity please see Appendix-I

Villages without Scheduled Castes: There are 0 village without any scheduled caste population.

Scheduled Tribes: Out of the total population of 39657

persons, 414 persons (1.04%) belong to Scheduled Tribes. The villages having less than 10% ST population are Penchakalpeta, Jeelgul, Gopalpur, Damera Elkathurthi, Suraram, Vallabhapur, Kothulnaduma Veeranarayanapur, Dandepalle, Baopet, Thimmapur Keshwapur.

The villages having more than 50% ST population are None.

Sex ratio of Scheduled tribe population is 505.

Scheduled Tribes Literates and Illiterates by Sex:

	Persons	Males	Females
Literate	159	96	63
Illiterate	255	109	146
Literacy rate	43.8	53.9	34.1
Graduate	3	3	0

Scheduled Tribes (Dominant):

Yerukulas, Koya etc., Sugalis etc., Thoti Chenchu etc.

For their cultural identity please see Appendix-II

Villages without Scheduled Tribes: There is 1 village without any scheduled tribe population.

Literates and Illiterates by Sex (Total Population):

	Persons	Males	Females
Literate	18,327	11,437	6,890
Illiterate	21,330	8,731	12,599
Literacy rate	53	66	41
Graduate	648	569	79

Agriculture: ***Distribution of villages according to land use:*** Out of 13 villages, Total area (in hectare) is 11565, out of that 79.56 percent is cultivable and 73.44 percent of the cultivable area is irrigated.

Sources of Irrigation (Hectares): Government Canal 2588.75, Private Canal 0, Well without Electricity 0, Well with Electricity 2328.09, Tubewell without Electricity 0, Tubewell with Electricity 78.09, Tank 1762.59, River 0, Lake 0, Waterfall 0, Others 0.

Villages with population of 5000 to 9999: Damera, Elkathurthi.

Villages with population of 10000 and above: None

Distribution of Workers:

	Persons	Males	Females	WPR
Cultivators	5,767	3,876	1,891	27.86
Agricultural Labour	10,401	4,003	6,398	50.25
Household Industry	1,163	645	518	5.62
Other Workers	3,368	2,754	614	16.27
Main Workers	14,611	9,457	5,154	70.59
Marginal Workers	6,088	1,821	4,267	29.41
Total Workers	20,699	11,278	9,421	

Religion: Major Religious Communities:

	Persons	Males	Females	Sex Ratio
Hindu (96.68%)	38,340	19,507	18,833	965
Muslim (2.53%)	1,003	505	498	986
Christian (0.77%)	305	154	151	981
Sikh (0%)	-	-	-	-
Buddhists (0%)	-	-	-	-
Jain (0%)	-	-	-	-

Agewise Data:

	Persons	Males	Females	Sex Ratio
All ages	39,657	20,168	19,489	966
0-14	12,066	6,178	5,888	953
15-44	18,474	9,372	9,102	971
45-79	8,629	4,375	4,254	972
80+	411	193	218	1130
Age not stated	77	50	27	540

Languages (Dominant):

Telugu, Urdu, Marathi, Tamil, Hindi

Disabled Population:

	Persons	Males	Females	%
Total Disabled	846	491	355	
In Seeing	407	226	181	48.11
In Speech	82	40	42	9.69
In Hearing	41	20	21	4.85
In Movement	206	131	75	24.35
Mentally	110	74	36	13

ELLANTHAKUNTA

Ellanthakunta C.D. Block lies in the south-west part of Karimnagar district. The Block is located at a dista nce of 58 kms. from district headquarters (Karimnagar). There are 22 villages in the block with the total population of 48,990 persons. Area of the C.D. Block is 231.97 sq. kms. It is bounded by Boinpalle Mandal on north, Karimnagar Mandal on north-east, Bejjanki Mandal on east, Medak district on south, and Sircilla Mandal on west.

Communications :

Roadways : NH, SH or Important Metalled Road is not available.

River: Manner Nadi- Nearest Villages- Kandikatkoor, Pottur.

Backwards Region Grants Fund: It receives Backward Region Grants.

Mahila Samakhya (Education for Women's Equality): It is decleared Socialy and Educationally Backward Block by the Government.

Annual Rainfall: Average Rainfall 850 mm

Ground Water: Availability of the Ground Water in the Basin is 1984 H.A.M. and the utilization is 1926 H. A.M. It belongs to Critical category. Depth to water level varies from more than 10 meter below the ground. Most of the wells go down in summer months. The well density in the entire block is 35 wells per sq. km.

Total no. of the wells in the block are enumerated as 5562, according to the Ground Water Estimation Commi ttee.

Natural Division : Godavari Depression Region

Administration:

Division: Telangana. Parliamentary Constituency: 3 Karimnagar. District: Karimnagar. Mandal: Ellanthakunta. Assembly Constituency: 30 Manakondur (SC). Gram Pancha yat: 26.

Villages: 22 **Inhabited:** 22 **Uninhabited:** 0

Ranking	District	State	National
Area	12	378	3627
Population	25	550	5337
Sex Ratio	13	72	495
Child Sex Ratio	34	648	2590
Literacy Rate	21	589	4184
Density	23	328	4572
Work Participation Rate	43	676	812

Gram Panchayats:

Ananthagiri, Anantharam, Arepally, Dacharam Ellanthakunta, Galipally, Gollapally (G.P.) Gundaram, Jangamreddypally, Jawaharpet, Kandikatkoor Muskanipet, Narsakkapet, Obulapuram, Peddalingapuram Pottur, Raheemkhanpet, Repaka, Sirikonda Somarampet (G.P.), Thallapally, Theniguvaripally Thippapuram, Vallampatla, Vanthadupula, Veljipuram.

Amenities:

Education: Primary School in 22 villages, Middle school in 16 villages, Matriculation or Secondary School in 8 villages, namely Vallampatla, Kandikatkoor, Galipalle, Ellanthakunta, Peddalingapuram, Dacharam, Repaka, Gundaram(P.S.).

Higher Secondary or Pre University Courses or Intermediate or Junior College in 0 village of the CD Block, College in 0 village, Adult Literacy Center in 14 villages.

Medical: Hospital in 0 village, Dispensary in 1 village, Health Center in 1 village, Sub Center in 9 villages, Maternity and Child Welfare Center in 0 village, Community health workers in 0 village.

The Village having Hospital or Dispensary or Health Center id Peddalingapuram.

Drinking Water: Tap water in 22 villages, Tank water in 22 villages, Well water in 22 villages, Tubewell in 22 villages and more than one source in 22 villages.

Bank: Banking facility in 2 villages, namely, Ellanthakunta, Peddalingapuram.

Credit Society in 18 villages Agricultural Credit Society in 6 Non-Agricultural Credit Society in 18 villages.

Others: Power supply in 22 villages, Cinema hall in 1 village, sport club in 0 village, Stadium or Auditorium or Community Hall in 0 village, Post Office in 18 villages.

There are 21 villages having bus facilities.

Villages with most of facilities: Ellanthakunta Peddalingapuram.

Villages without Amenities (Education): None..

Scheduled Castes: Out of the total population of 48990 persons, 10905 persons (22.26%) belong to Scheduled Castes.

The villages having less than 10% SC population are None..

The villages having more than 50% SC population are None.

Sex ratio of Scheduled Caste population is 504.

Scheduled Castes Literates and Illiterates by Sex:

	Persons	Males	Females
Literate	4,341	2,688	1,653
Illiterate	6,564	2,722	3,842
Literacy rate	45.8	57.8	34.3
Graduate	51	48	3

Scheduled Castes (Dominant):

Madiga, Mala, Chamar etc., Generic Castes etc. Godari

For their cultural identity please see Appendix-I

Villages without Scheduled Castes: There are 0 village without any scheduled caste population.

Scheduled Tribes: Out of the total population of 48990 persons, 232 persons (0.47%) belong to Scheduled Tribes.

The villages having less than 10% ST population are Obulapuram (P.A), Veljipuram, Rahimkhanpet Vallampatla, Kandikatkoor, Pottur, Jawaharpet Galipalle, Vanthadupula, Thallapalle, Muskanipet Ellanthakunta, Jangamreddipalle, Anantharam Ramajipeta, Peddalingapuram, Dacharam, Sirikonda Ananthagiri, Thippapuram (P.A), Repaka Gundaram(P.S.).

The villages having more than 50% ST population are None.

Sex ratio of Scheduled tribe population is 483.

Scheduled Tribes Literates and Illiterates by Sex:

	Persons	Males	Females
Literate	72	46	26
Illiterate	160	74	86
Literacy rate	37.3	46.9	27.4
Graduate	3	2	1

Scheduled Tribes (Dominant):

Yerukulas, Sugalis etc., Koya etc., Thoti

For their cultural identity please see Appendix-II

Villages without Scheduled Tribes: There are 6 villages without any scheduled tribe population.

Literates and Illiterates by Sex (Total Population):

	Persons	Males	Females

Literate	22,386	13,975	8,411
Illiterate	26,604	10,155	16,449
Literacy rate	52	66	38
Graduate	524	480	44

Agriculture: ***Distribution of villages according to land use:*** Out of 22 villages, Total area (in hectare) is 23199, out of that 28.54 percent is cultivable and 40.89 percent of the cultivable area is irrigated.

Sources of Irrigation (Hectares): Government Canal 0, Private Canal 0, Well without Electricity 0, Well with Electricity 2464.8, Tubewell without Electricity 234.4, Tubewell with Electricity 8, Tank 0, River 0, Lake 0, Waterfall 0, Others 0.

Villages with population of 5000 to 9999: Repaka.

Villages with population of 10000 and above: None

Distribution of Workers:

	Persons	Males	Females	WPR
Cultivators	10,204	6,085	4,119	37.33
Agricultural Labour	10,024	3,623	6,401	36.68
Household Industry	2,235	769	1,466	8.18
Other Workers	4,868	3,433	1,435	17.81
Main Workers	22,760	12,464	10,296	83.28
Marginal Workers	4,571	1,446	3,125	16.72
Total Workers	27,331	13,910	13,421	

Religion: Major Religious Communities:

	Persons	Males	Females	Sex Ratio
Hindu (97.34%)	47,689	23,488	24,201	1,030
Muslim (2.23%)	1,093	539	554	1,028
Christian (0.35%)	171	85	86	1,012
Sikh (0%)	-	-	-	-
Buddhists (0%)	-	-	-	-
Jain (0%)	-	-	-	-

Agewise Data:

	Persons	Males	Females	Sex Ratio
All ages	48,990	24,130	24,860	1030
0-14	14,690	7,448	7,242	972
15-44	21,691	10,379	11,312	1090
45-79	11,969	5,996	5,973	996
80+	589	283	306	1081
Age not stated	51	24	27	1125

Languages (Dominant):
Telugu, Urdu, Hindi, Tamil, Oriya

Disabled Population:

	Persons	Males	Females	%
Total Disabled	963	551	412	
In Seeing	472	274	198	49.01
In Speech	107	65	42	11.11
In Hearing	59	32	27	6.13
In Movement	218	126	92	22.64
Mentally	107	54	53	11.11

ELURU

Eluru C.D. Block lies in the south-western part of West Godavari district. It is a part of Eluru Mandal. The Block is located at a distance of (00) kms. from district headquarters (Eluru). There are 18 villages in the block with the total population of 69,863 persons. Area of the C.D. Block is 208.38 sq. kms. It is bound ed in the north by Mandals Pedavegi, Denduluru and Bhima dale, in the south by district Krishna, in the east by district Krishna and Mandal Bhimadole, and in the west by Mandal Pedapadu and Pedavegi.

Communications :

Roadways : NH- 5: Direction- Vijayawada to Tadepalligudem. Nearest Villages- Eluru (Rural), Komadavole (Rural), Malkapuram.

Lake: Koleru- Nearest Villages- Ponangi, Manuru, Sreepa rru, Kalakurru, Chataparru, Jalipudi, Gudivakalanka, Kokkirailanka, Pydichintapadu, Prathikollanka, Komatil anka.

Backwards Region Grants Fund: It receives Backward Region Grants.

Annaul Rainfall: Average Rainfall 1005 mm

Ground Water: Availability of the Ground Water in the Basin is (Information not avavible) H.A.M .and the utilization is (Information not avavible) H.A.M. It belongs to (Information not avavible) category. Depth to water level varies from 3 to 10 meter below the ground. Most of the wells go down in summer months.

Natural Division : Godavari Delta Region

Administration:

Division: Coastal Andhra. Parliamentary Constituency: 27 Eluru. District: West Godavari. Mandal: Eluru. Assem bly Constituency: 184 Eluru. Gram Panchayat: 21.

Places of Tourist Interest:

Eluru : Eluru is situated on the border of the swamps round the Koler or Kolleru lake. There are two railway stations, namely, Powerpet and Eluru, situated on the Madras-Calcutta line, at about 57 and 59 kms. respectiv ely to the north of Vijayawada division. The ruins of an old fort reminds us of its glorious past. The woollen pile carpet industry, is an important industry, of this place. Among the temples at this place, the shrines of Janardhana and Jalapaharesvara are famous.

Villages: 18 **Inhabited:** 18 **Uninhabited:** 0

Ranking	**District**	**State**	**National**
Area	12	548	4167
Population	16	124	4460
Sex Ratio	33	627	2174
Child Sex Ratio	19	317	1150

Literacy Rate	10	13	416
Density	23	910	3113
Work Participation Rate	34	269	3150

Gram Panchayats:
Chataparru, Chodimella, Gudivakalanka, Jalipudi Kalakurru, Katlampudi, Kokkirailanka, Komadavole Komatilanka, Koteswara Durga Puram, Madepalli Malkapuram, Mondikodu, Ponangi, Prathikollalanka Pydichintapadu, Sanivarapupeta, Satrampadu Sreeparru, Tangellamudi, Venkatapuram.

Amenities:

Education: Primary School in 18 villages, Middle school in 11 villages, Matriculation or Secondary School in 4 villages, namely Sanivarapupeta, Eluru (Rural), Chataparru, Gudivakalanka.
Higher Secondary or Pre University Courses or Intermediate or Junior College in 0 village of the CD Block, College in 0 village, Adult Literacy Center in 14 villages.

Medical: Hospital in 0 village, Dispensary in 0 village, Health Center in 0 village, Sub Center in 10 villages, Maternity and Child Welfare Center in 0 village, Community health workers in 0 village.

Drinking Water: Tap water in 18 villages, Tank water in 18 villages, Well water in 18 villages, Tubewell in 18 villages and more than one source in 18 villages.

Bank: Banking facility in 3 villages, namely, Chataparru, Ponangi, Sreeparru.
Credit Society in 5 villages Agricultural Credit Society in 4 Non-Agricultural Credit Society in 1 village.

Others: Power supply in 18 villages, Cinema hall in 0 village, sport club in 1 village, Stadium or Auditorium or Community Hall in 0 village, Post Office in 15 villages.
There are 17 villages having bus facilities.

Villages with most of facilities: Chataparru Ponangi, Sreeparru.

Villages without Amenities (Education): None..

Scheduled Castes: Out of the total population of 70096 persons, 13134 persons (18.74%) belong to Scheduled Castes.
The villages having less than 10% SC population are Eluru (Rural), Sreeparru, Gudivakalanka Prathikollanka.
The villages having more than 50% SC population are None.
Sex ratio of Scheduled Caste population is 496.

Scheduled Castes Literates and Illiterates by Sex:

	Persons	Males	Females
Literate	8,770	4,709	4,061
Illiterate	4,364	1,909	2,455
Literacy rate	77.7	82.6	72.8
Graduate	202	143	59

Scheduled Castes (Dominant):
Mala, Madiga, Adi Andhra, Beda Jangam etc.
Generic Castes etc.

For their cultural identity please see Appendix-I

Villages without Scheduled Castes: There are 0 village without any scheduled caste population.

Scheduled Tribes: Out of the total population of 70096 persons, 459 persons (0.65%) belong to Scheduled Tribes.
The villages having less than 10% ST population are Chodimella, Sanivarapupeta, Eluru (Rural) Komadavole (Rural), Malkapuram, Chataparru, Jalipudi Katlampudi, Madepalle, Ponangi, Manuru, Sreeparru Kalakurru, Komatilanka, Gudivakalanka, Kokkirailanka Pydichintapadu, Prathikollanka.
The villages having more than 50% ST population are None.
Sex ratio of Scheduled tribe population is 497.

Scheduled Tribes Literates and Illiterates by Sex:

	Persons	Males	Females
Literate	246	134	112
Illiterate	213	97	116
Literacy rate	64.4	71.3	57.7
Graduate	2	2	0

Scheduled Tribes (Dominant):
Yerukulas, Chenchu etc., Sugalis etc., Koya etc. Konda Dhoras

For their cultural identity please see Appendix-II

Villages without Scheduled Tribes: There are 3 villages without any scheduled tribe population.

Literates and Illiterates by Sex (Total Population):

	Persons	Males	Females
Literate	47,804	25,809	21,995
Illiterate	22,292	9,639	12,653
Literacy rate	78	84	73
Graduate	1,286	921	365

Agriculture: ***Distribution of villages according to land use:*** Out of 18 villages, Total area (in hectare) is 20074, out of that 44.14 percent is cultivable and 99.4 percent of the cultivable area is irrigated.

Sources of Irrigation (Hectares): Government Canal 8294, Private Canal 0, Well without Electricity 0, Well with Electricity 0, Tubewell without Electricity 0, Tubewell with Electricity 513, Tank 0, River 0, Lake 0, Waterfall 0, Others 0.

Villages with population of 5000 to 9999:
Sanivarapupeta, Chataparru, Madepalle, Gudivakalanka.

Villages with population of 10000 and above:
Eluru (Rural).

Distribution of Workers:

	Persons	Males	Females	WPR

Cultivators	1,746	1,508	238	5.37
Agricultural Labour	21,102	12,029	9,073	64.93
Household Industry	1,186	517	669	3.65
Other Workers	8,464	7,010	1,454	26.04
Main Workers	26,586	18,417	8,169	81.81
Marginal Workers	5,912	2,647	3,265	18.19
Total Workers	32,498	21,064	11,434	

Religion: Major Religious Communities:

	Persons	Males	Females	Sex Ratio
Hindu (93.01%)	65,193	32,962	32,231	978
Muslim (2.52%)	1,768	904	864	956
Christian (4.35%)	3,051	1,537	1,514	985
Sikh (0.01%)	4	2	2	1,000
Buddhists (0.05%)	34	17	17	1,000
Jain (0%)	-	-	-	-

Agewise Data:

	Persons	Males	Females	Sex Ratio
All ages	70,096	35,448	34,648	977
0-14	22,113	11,223	10,890	970
15-44	35,216	17,866	17,350	971
45-79	12,182	6,076	6,106	1005
80+	421	185	236	1276
Age not stated	164	98	66	673

Languages (Dominant):

Telugu, Urdu, Gondi, Marathi, Hindi

Disabled Population:

	Persons	Males	Females	%
Total Disabled	980	517	463	
In Seeing	333	180	153	33.98
In Speech	113	62	51	11.53
In Hearing	53	15	38	5.41
In Movement	342	196	146	34.9
Mentally	139	64	75	14.18

ENKURU

Enkuru C.D. Block lies in the south western part of Khammam district. The Block is located at a distance of 44 kms. from district headquarters (Khammam). There are 11 villages in the block with the total population of 33,151 persons. Area of the C.D. Block is 183.82 sq. kms. It is bounded in the north by Mandals Kamepalle, Singareni and Julurpahad, in the south by Mandals Tallada and Kallur, in the east by Mandal Julurpahad, and in the west by Mandals Khammam Urban and Konijerla.

Communications:

Roadways : State Highway (S.H.): Direction- Tallada to Julupahad. Nearest Villages- Kesupalle, Nacharam, Medepalle, Enkuru, Thuthaka Lingampeta, Jannaram.

Annual Rainfall: Average Rainfall 1160 mm

Ground Water: Availability of the Ground Water in the Basin is 5213 H.A.M.and the utilization is 1007 H.A. M. It belongs to safe category. Depth to water level varies from 10 to 20 meter below the ground. Most of the wells go down in summer months. The well density in the entire block is 6 wells per sq. km. Total no. of the wells in the block are enumerated as 1109, according to the Ground Water Estimation Committee.

Natural Division : Godavari Depression Region

Administration:

Division: Telangana. Parliamentary Constituency: 17 Khammam. District: Khammam. Mandal: Enkuru. Assembly Constituency: 115Wyra (ST). Gram Panchayat:14.

Villages: 11 **Inhabited:** 11 **Uninhabited:** 0

Ranking	District	State	National
Area	35	648	4469
Population	35	972	5970
Sex Ratio	44	1053	4094
Child Sex Ratio	33	670	2737
Literacy Rate	19	627	4313
Density	14	251	5041
Work Participation Rate	23	791	655

Gram Panchayats:

Arikayalapadu, Bhagavan Nayak Thanda Burda Raghavapuram, Enkuru, Jannaram, Kesupalli Nacharam, Nukalampadu, Raimadaram, Raja Lingala Repallewada, Sriramgiri, Timmaraopeta Tutakalinganna Peta.

Amenities:

Education: Primary School in 11 villages, Middle school in 7 villages, Matriculation or Secondary School in 3 villages, namely Thimmaraopeta, Burda Raghavapuram, Enkuru. Higher Secondary or Pre University Courses or Intermediate or Junior College in 1 village of the CD Block,, namely Enkuru.

College in 0 village, Adult Literacy Center in 10 villages.

Medical: Hospital in 0 village, Dispensary in 1 village, Health Center in 1 village, Sub Center in 8 villages, Maternity and Child Welfare Center in 0 village, Community health workers in 0 village.

The Villages having Hospital or Dispensary or Health Center are Thuthaka Lingampeta.

Drinking Water: Tap water in 11 villages, Tank water in 11 villages, Well water in 11 villages, Tubewell in 11 villages and more than one source in 11 villages.

Bank: Banking facility in 2 villages, namely, Thimmaraopeta, Enkuru.

Credit Society in 8 villages Agricultural Credit Society in 5 Non-Agricultural Credit Society in 6 villages.

Others: Power supply in 11 villages, Cinema hall in 1 village, sport club in 0 village, Stadium or Auditorium or Community Hall in 0 village, Post Office in 9 villages.

There are 9 villages having bus facilities.

Villages with most of facilities: Thimmaraopeta Enkuru.

Villages without Amenities (Education): None..

Scheduled Castes: Out of the total population of 33151 persons, 4112 persons (12.4%) belong to Scheduled Castes. The villages having less than 10% SC population are Raimadaram, Burda Raghavapuram, Kesupalle, Medepalle Jannaram.

The villages having more than 50% SC population are None.

Sex ratio of Scheduled Caste population is 482.

Scheduled Castes Literates and Illiterates by Sex:

	Persons	Males	Females
Literate	1,634	1,033	601
Illiterate	2,478	1,097	1,381
Literacy rate	46.2	56.3	35.3
Graduate	40	31	9

Scheduled Castes (Dominant):

Madiga, Mala, Mala Dasari, Madiga Dasu etc.
Mala Dasu

For their cultural identity please see Appendix-I

Villages without Scheduled Castes: There are 0 village without any scheduled caste population.

Scheduled Tribes: Out of the total population of 33151 persons, 11708 persons (35.32%) belong to Scheduled Tribes. The villages having less than 10% ST population are None..

The villages having more than 50% ST population are None.

Sex ratio of Scheduled tribe population is 486.

Scheduled Tribes Literates and Illiterates by Sex:

	Persons	Males	Females
Literate	3,715	2,559	1,156
Illiterate	7,993	3,456	4,537
Literacy rate	37.9	50.7	24.3
Graduate	40	39	1

Scheduled Tribes (Dominant):

Sugalis etc., Koya etc., Yerukulas, Gond etc.
Nayaks

For their cultural identity please see Appendix-II

Villages without Scheduled Tribes: There is 1 village without any scheduled tribe population.

Literates and Illiterates by Sex (Total Population):

	Persons	Males	Females
Literate	14,638	9,177	5,461
Illiterate	18,513	7,926	10,587
Literacy rate	51	62	40
Graduate	412	324	88

Agriculture: ***Distribution of villages according to land use:*** Out of 11 villages, Total area (in hectare) is 18383, out of that 67.44 percent is cultivable and 24.98 percent of the cultivable area is irrigated.

Sources of Irrigation (Hectares): Government Canal 1598.63, Private Canal 0, Well without Electricity 197.48, Well with Electricity 807.72, Tubewell without Electricity 0, Tubewell with Electricity 48.55, Tank 196.65, River 0, Lake 0, Waterfall 0, Others 247.65.

Villages with population of 5000 to 9999: Burda Raghavapuram, Nacharam, Enkuru Thuthaka Lingampeta.

Villages with population of 10000 and above: None

Distribution of Workers:

	Persons	Males	Females	WPR
Cultivators	5,752	3,635	2,117	31.17
Agricultural Labour	10,141	4,231	5,910	54.96
Household Industry	315	194	121	1.71
Other Workers	2,243	1,841	402	12.16
Main Workers	15,876	9,109	6,767	86.04
Marginal Workers	2,575	792	1,783	13.96
Total Workers	18,451	9,901	8,550	

Religion: Major Religious Communities:

	Persons	Males	Females	Sex Ratio
Hindu (95.44%)	31,640	16,372	15,268	933
Muslim (3.45%)	1,144	553	591	1,069
Christian (1.08%)	358	174	184	1,057
Sikh (0%)	-	-	-	-
Buddhists (0%)	-	-	-	-
Jain (0%)	-	-	-	-

Agewise Data:

	Persons	Males	Females	Sex Ratio
All ages	33,151	17,103	16,048	938
0-14	11,490	6,087	5,403	888
15-44	15,729	8,048	7,681	954
45-79	5,536	2,760	2,776	1006
80+	312	157	155	987
Age not stated	84	51	33	647

Languages (Dominant):

Telugu, Hindi, Urdu, Others, Marathi

Disabled Population:

	Persons	Males	Females	%
Total Disabled	773	474	299	
In Seeing	342	225	117	44.24
In Speech	61	28	33	7.89
In Hearing	38	20	18	4.92
In Movement	247	159	88	31.95
Mentally	85	42	43	11

ETCHERLA

Etcherla C.D. Block lies in the southern part of Srikakulam district. It is a part of Etcherla Mandal. The

Block is located at a distance of 07 kms. from district headquarters (Srikakulam). There are 31 villages in the block with the total population of 82,051 persons. Area of the C.D. Block is 162.16 sq. kms. It is bounded in the north by Mandals Ponduru and Amadalavalasa, in the south by the Bay of Bengal, in the east by Mandal Srikakulam, and in the west by Mandals Ranasthan am and Laveru.

Communications:

Roadways : NH- 5: Direction- Ranasthanam to Srikakulam. Nearest Villages- Shermahammadpuram, Kusalapuram, Etcherla, Chilakalapalem, Arinam Akkivalasa.

River: Levyangulya Nadi- Nearest Villages- Ponnada, Bontalakoduru.

Backwards Region Grants Fund: It receives Backward Region Grants.

Annual Rainfall: Average Rainfall 1085.6 mm

Ground Water: Availability of the Ground Water in the Basin is (Information not avavible) H.A.M .and the utilization is (Information not avavible) H.A.M. It belongs to (Information not avavible) category. Depth to water level varies from 3 to 10 meter below the ground. Most of the wells go down in summer months.

Coastal Villages: Nearest Villages- Kuppili, Koyyam, Dharmavaram, Bontalakoduru.

Natural Division : Northern Andhra Coastal Plain Region.

Administration:

Division: Coastal Andhra, Parliamentary Constituency: 20 Viziangaram, District: Srikakulam, Mandal: Etcherla, Assembly Constituency: 126 Etcherla, Gram Panchayat: 28, Villages: 31.

Villages: 31 **Inhabited:** 27 **Uninhabited:** 4

Ranking	District	State	National
Area	5	760	4841
Population	1	31	4040
Sex Ratio	37	748	2548
Child Sex Ratio	18	417	1538
Literacy Rate	27	662	4419
Density	15	670	2195
Work Participation Rate	9	106	1858

Gram Panchayats:

A.A.Valasa, Ajjaram, Allinagaram, Badevanipeta Bhagiradhi Puram, Bontala Koduru, Budagatla Palem Chilakapalem, D.Matchelesam, Dharmavaram, Domam Etcherla, Fareedpeta, Ibrahimbad, Jarajam Kesavarao Peta, Kongaram, Kotha Peta, Koyyam Kuppili, Kusalapuram, Muddada, Ponnada, Pudivalasa S.M.Puram, S.S.R.Puram, Thamminaidu Peta, Thotapalem.

Amenities:

Education: Primary School in 27 villages, Middle school in 11 villages, Matriculation or Secondary School in 9 villages, namely Arinam Akkivalasa, Shermahammadpuram, Ibrahimbad, Duppalavalasa, Muddada, Etcherla, Chilakalapalem, Kuppili, Bontalakoduru.

Higher Secondary or Pre University Courses or Intermediate or Junior College in 2 villages of the CD Block,, namely Duppalavalasa, Etcherla.

College in 1 village, Adult Literacy Center in 12 villages., College is in village, namely Etcherla.

Medical: Hospital in 1 village, Dispensary in 1 village, Health Center in 2 villages, Sub Center in 15 villages, Maternity and Child Welfare Center in 0 village, Community health workers in 0 village.

The Villages having Hospital or Dispensary or Health Center is Shermahammadpuram.

Drinking Water: Tap water in 27 villages, Tank water in 27 villages, Well water in 27 villages, Tubewell in 27 villages and more than one source in 27 villages.

Bank: Banking facility in 2 villages, namely, Etcherla, Dharmavaram.

Credit Society in 15 villages Agricultural Credit Society in 3 Non-Agricultural Credit Society in 14 villages.

Others: Power supply in 27 villages, Cinema hall in 0 village, sport club in 0 village, Stadium or Auditorium or Community Hall in 0 village, Post Office in 11 villages.

There are 24 villages having bus facilities.

Villages with most of facilities: Etcherla Dharmavaram.

Villages without Amenities (Education): None..

Scheduled Castes: Out of the total population of 82051 persons, 7529 persons (9.18%) belong to Scheduled Castes.

The villages having less than 10% SC population are Ibrahimbad, Kusalapuram, Shermahammadpurampeta Domam, Thotapalem, Ponnada, Kongaram, Jarajam Chinaraopalle, Chilakalapalem, Nandigam, Ajjaram Kuppili, Koyyam, Bhagiradhipuram Voleti Atchanna Agraharam, Dharmavaram.

The villages having more than 50% SC population are None.

Sex ratio of Scheduled Caste population is 498.

Scheduled Castes Literates and Illiterates by Sex:

	Persons	Males	Females
Literate	4,143	2,353	1,790
Illiterate	3,386	1,430	1,956
Literacy rate	62.2	70.3	53.9
Graduate	104	91	13

Scheduled Castes (Dominant):

Mala, Madiga, Relli, Dom etc., Adi Andhra

For their cultural identity please see Appendix-I

Villages without Scheduled Castes: There are

8 villages without any scheduled caste population.

Scheduled Tribes: Out of the total population of 82051 persons, 372 persons (0.45%) belong to Scheduled Tribes.

The villages having less than 10% ST population are Arinam Akkivalasa, Shermahammadpuram, Ibrahimbad Thammunaidupeta, Jarapinaidupeta, Pudivalasa Kusalapuram, Duppalavalasa, Shermahammadpurampeta Domam, Thotapalem, Ponnada, Kongaram, Muddada Jarajam, Etcherla, Chinaraopalle, Chilakalapalem Nandigam, Santhaseetharampuram, Ajjaram, Kuppili Koyyam, Bhagiradhipuram, Voleti Atchanna Agraharam Dharmavaram, Bontalakoduru.

The villages having more than 50% ST population are None.

Sex ratio of Scheduled tribe population is 513.

Scheduled Tribes Literates and Illiterates by Sex:

	Persons	Males	Females
Literate	190	119	71
Illiterate	182	62	120
Literacy rate	60.7	76.8	44.9
Graduate	1	1	0

Scheduled Tribes (Dominant):

Yerukulas, Savaras etc., Jatapus, Konda Dhoras Kotia etc.

For their cultural identity please see Appendix-II

Villages without Scheduled Tribes: There are 18 villages without any scheduled tribe population.

Literates and Illiterates by Sex (Total Population):

	Persons	Males	Females
Literate	36,012	21,851	14,161
Illiterate	46,039	19,814	26,225
Literacy rate	51	61	40
Graduate	1,400	1,207	193

Agriculture: ***Distribution of villages according to land use:***

Out of 31 villages, Total area (in hectare) is 16218, out of that 76.28 percent is cultivable and 24.69 percent of the cultivable area is irrigated.

Sources of Irrigation (Hectares): Government Canal 1937.65, Private Canal 0, Well without Electricity 0, Well with Electricity 0, Tubewell without Electricity 140.42, Tubewell with Electricity 30.73, Tank 946.05, River 0, Lake 0, Waterfall 0, Others 0.

Villages with population of 5000 to 9999:

Ponnada, Muddada, Chilakalapalem, Kuppili, Koyyam Dharmavaram.

Villages with population of 10000 and above:

Shermahammadpuram.

Distribution of Workers:

	Persons	Males	Females	WPR
Cultivators	8,172	5,240	2,932	19.48
Agricultural Labour	20,368	8,444	11,924	48.54
Household Industry	1,144	555	589	2.73
Other Workers	12,274	10,007	2,267	29.25
Main Workers	28,133	19,827	8,306	67.05
Marginal Workers	13,825	4,419	9,406	32.95
Total Workers	41,958	24,246	17,712	

Religion: Major Religious Communities:

	Persons	Males	Females	Sex Ratio
Hindu (99.66%)	81,772	41,508	40,264	970
Muslim (0.17%)	139	76	63	829
Christian (0.09%)	76	42	34	810
Sikh (0.01%)	6	5	1	200
Buddhists (0%)	1	-	1	-
Jain (0%)	-	-	-	-

Agewise Data:

	Persons	Males	Females	Sex Ratio
All ages	82,051	41,665	40,386	969
0-14	27,512	14,159	13,353	943
15-44	39,175	19,948	19,227	964
45-79	14,894	7,340	7,554	1029
80+	338	151	187	1238
Age not stated	132	67	65	970

Languages (Dominant):

Telugu, Oriya, Urdu, Hindi, Gondi

Disabled Population:

	Persons	Males	Females	%
Total Disabled	2,020	1,130	890	
In Seeing	1,117	619	498	55.3
In Speech	150	73	77	7.43
In Hearing	72	42	30	3.56
In Movement	531	305	226	26.29
Mentally	150	91	59	7.43

ETURNAGARAM

Eturnagaram C.D. Block lies in the north-eastern part of Warangal district. The Block is located at a distance of 122 kms. from district headquarters (Warangal). There are 64 villages in the block with the total population of 37,153 persons. Area of the C.D. Block is 249.10 sq. kms. It is bounded in the north by district Karim Nagar in the south by Tadvai Mandal, in the east by district Khammam and Mandal Mangapet, and in the west Tadvai Mandal and district Karim Nagar. It has common boundary with state of Chhatisgarh on north.

Communications:

Roadways : NH- 202: Direction- Warangal to Bijapur. Nearest Villages- Akulavari Ghanpur, Papkapuram, Alugu belle, Medaram, Chirragudem, Chinaboinapalle, Shivapuram, Eturnagaram.

River Godavari Nadi- Nearest Villages- Gangaram(Guttala), Thupakulagudem, Devadhumula, Laxmipuram, Kothur, Gurrevula, Kannaigudem, Buttaigudem, Chinthagudem,

Singaram (Pattigorrevula), Etur, Kanthanpalle, Rampurag rahar, Mullakatta, Shankarajpalle, Roheer, Manasapalle, Ramannagudem, Ramnagar (Koyagudem), Yellapuram, Eturna garam.

Backwards Region Grants Fund: It receives Backward Region Grants.

Integrated Child Development Scheme (ICDS) Project: Eturunagaram, Total Anganwadi Centres: 267

Annual Rainfall: Average Rainfall 1265 mm

Ground Water: Availability of the Ground Water in the Basin is 6090 H.A.M.and the utilization is 637 H.A. M. It belongs to Safe category. Depth to water level varies less than 5 meter below the ground. Most of the wells go down in summer months. The well density in the entire block is 1 wells per sq. km. Total no. of the wells in the block are enumerated as 338, accor ding to the Ground Water Estimation Committee.

Forest and Reserved **Forest:** (Nagaram R.F.)- Nearest Villages- Marepalle, Bhupathipuram, Paredu, Rajannapet, Malkapalle, Chityala, Muppanapalle, Buttaigudem, Sarvai, Chinthagudem, Singaram (Pattigorrevula), Etur, Kantha npalle, Rampuragrahar, Mullakatta, Shankarajpalle, Roheer, Allamvari Ghanapuram, Maredupaka, Chalpaka, Banaji Bandham, Elishettipalle, Kondred, Kondai, Mallyala, Dodla, Gundenguvai, Chintagudem, Shapalle, Koratpalle (D), Chirragudem, Chinaboinapalle, Pedda Venkatapur, Chinavenkata Puram, Lingapuram.

Natural Division : Godavari Depression Region

Administration:

Division: Telangana. Parliamentary Constituency. District: Warangal.

Mandal: Eturnagaram. Assembly Constituency: 109 Mulug (ST). Gram Panchayat: 19.

Villages: 64 **Inhabited:** 41 **Uninhabited:** 23

Ranking	District	State	National
Area	11	314	3394
Population	43	897	5843
Sex Ratio	45	959	3281
Child Sex Ratio	4	114	306
Literacy Rate	9	425	3576
Density	37	624	5570
Work Participation Rate	47	907	1698

Gram Panchayats:

Ailapur, Buttaigudem, Chalpaka, Chinnaboinapally Etur, Eturnagaram, Gurrevula, Kondai, Koyaguda Mullakatta, Muppanapalle, Rajannapeta, Ramannagudem Roheer, Sarvai, Shankarajpalle, Shapalle, Shivapur Thupakulagudem.

Amenities:

Education: Primary School in 41 villages, Middle school in 14 villages, Matriculation or Secondary School in 3 villages, namely Akulavari Ghanpur, Eturnagaram, Chinaboinapalle.

Higher Secondary or Pre University Courses or Intermediate or Junior College in 2 villages of the CD Block,, namely Eturnagaram, Shivapuram.

College in 2 villages, Adult Literacy Center in 15 villages., Colleges are in villages, namely Ramnagar (Koyagudem), Pedda Venkatapur.

Medical: Hospital in 1 village, Dispensary in 2 villages, Health Center in 5 villages, Sub Center in 12 villages, Maternity and Child Welfare Center in 0 village, Community health workers in 0 village.

The Villages having Hospital or Dispensary or Health Center is Rajannapet, Akulavari Ghanpur, Eturnagaram.

Drinking Water: Tap water in 40 villages, Tank water in 40 villages, Well water in 40 villages, Tubewell in 40 villages and more than one source in 41 villages.

Bank: Banking facility in 7 villages, namely, Kannaigudem, Etur, Kanthanpalle, Rampuragrahar Akulavari Ghanpur, Eturnagaram, Ramannagudem.

Credit Society in 21 villages Agricultural Credit Society in 12 Non-Agricultural Credit Society in 17 villages.

Others: Power supply in 41 villages, Cinema hall in 7 villages, sport club in 0 village, Stadium or Auditorium or Community Hall in 0 village, Post Office in 22 villages.

There are 24 villages having bus facilities.

Villages with most of facilities: Etur Kanthanpalle, Akulavari Ghanpur, Eturnagaram Ramannagudem.

Villages without Amenities (Education): None..

Scheduled Castes: Out of the total population of 37153 persons, 8618 persons (23.2%) belong to Scheduled Castes. The villages having less than 10% SC population are Bhupathipuram, Rajannapet, Gangaram(Guttala) Laxmipuram, Chityala, Sarvai, Kanthanpalle Rampuragrahar, Allamvari Ghanapuram, Banaji Bandham Elishettipalle, Mallyala, Dodla, Buttaram, Ekkela Ramnagar (Koyagudem), Chinaboinapalle, Shivapuram.

The villages having more than 50% SC population are None.

Sex ratio of Scheduled Caste population is 489.

Scheduled Castes Literates and Illiterates by Sex:

	Persons	Males	Females
Literate	2,815	1,885	930
Illiterate	5,803	2,518	3,285
Literacy rate	39.8	51.9	27.0
Graduate	39	37	2

Scheduled Castes (Dominant):

Mala Sale etc., Madiga, Mala, Generic Castes etc. Kolupulvandlu

For their cultural identity please see Appendix-I

Villages without Scheduled Castes: There are 35 villages without any scheduled caste population.

Scheduled Tribes: Out of the total population of 37153 persons, 9323 persons (25.09%) belong to Scheduled Tribes. The villages having less than 10% ST population are Devadhumula, Laxmipuram, Gurrevula, Muppanapalle Buttaigudem, Roheer, Allamvari Ghanapuram Eturnagaram, Ramannagudem, Ramnagar (Koyagudem). The villages having more than 50% ST population are Bhupathipuram, Rajannapet, Gangaram(Guttala) Thupakulagudem, Gangugudem, Chityala, Kannaigudem Sarvai, Kanthanpalle, Rampuragrahar, Mullakatta Banaji Bandham, Elishettipalle, Ailapur, Mallyala Dodla, Buttaram, Ekkela.

Sex ratio of Scheduled tribe population is 466.

Scheduled Tribes Literates and Illiterates by Sex:

	Persons	Males	Females
Literate	4,770	3,161	1,609
Illiterate	4,553	1,819	2,734
Literacy rate	60.0	73.6	44.1
Graduate	53	44	9

Scheduled Tribes (Dominant):

Koya etc., Sugalis etc., Gond etc., Yerukulas Generic Tribes etc.

For their cultural identity please see Appendix-II

Villages without Scheduled Tribes: There are 25 villages without any scheduled tribe population.

Literates and Illiterates by Sex (Total Population):

	Persons	Males	Females
Literate	17,447	11,036	6,411
Illiterate	19,706	7,979	11,727
Literacy rate	56	68	42
Graduate	397	328	69

Agriculture: ***Distribution of villages according to land use:*** Out of 64 villages, Total area (in hectare) is 24907, out of that 54.76 percent is cultivable and 4.51 percent of the cultivable area is irrigated.

Sources of Irrigation (Hectares): Government Canal 0, Private Canal 0, Well without Electricity 0, Well with Electricity 31.44, Tubewell without Electricity 0, Tubewell with Electricity 0, Tank 465.38, River 0, Lake 0, Waterfall 0, Others 118.57.

Villages with population of 5000 to 9999: Eturnagaram.

Villages with population of 10000 and above: None

Distribution of Workers:

	Persons	Males	Females	WPR
Cultivators	5,026	3,582	1,444	26.82
Agricultural Labour	10,363	4,144	6,219	55.3
Household Industry	658	383	275	3.51
Other Workers	2,692	1,971	721	14.37
Main Workers	13,430	8,096	5,334	71.67
Marginal Workers	5,309	1,984	3,325	28.33
Total Workers	18,739	10,080	8,659	

Religion: Major Religious Communities:

	Persons	Males	Females	Sex Ratio
Hindu (93.89%)	34,883	17,844	17,039	955
Muslim (5.68%)	2,110	1,094	1,016	929
Christian (0.34%)	127	60	67	1,117
Sikh (0%)	1	1	-	-
Buddhists (0%)	-	-	-	-
Jain (0%)	-	-	-	-

Agewise Data:

	Persons	Males	Females	Sex Ratio
All ages	37,153	19,015	18,138	954
0-14	13,975	7,296	6,679	915
15-44	16,962	8,572	8,390	979
45-79	5,882	2,972	2,910	979
80+	226	111	115	1036
Age not stated	108	64	44	688

Languages (Dominant):

Telugu, Urdu, Gondi, Hindi, Koya

Disabled Population:

	Persons	Males	Females	%
Total Disabled	988	575	413	
In Seeing	586	344	242	59.31
In Speech	78	42	36	7.89
In Hearing	42	20	22	4.25
In Movement	196	120	76	19.84
Mentally	86	49	37	8.7

FAROOQNAGAR

Farooqnagar C.D. Block lies in the north-east part of Mahbubnagar district. It is a part of Farooqnagar Mandal. The Block is located at a distance of 52 kms. from district headquarters (Mahbubnagar). There are 35 villages in the block with the total population of 62,069 persons. Area of the C.D. Block is 266.08 sq. kms. It is bounded by Kothur Mandal on north, Kesha mpet Mandal on east, Balanagar Mandal on south, Kondur Mandal on west, and Rangareddy district on north-west.

Communications:

Roadways : NH- 7: Direction- Mahbubnagar to Hyderabad. Nearest Villages- Gantlavelli, Allisabguda, Chattanpal le, Solipur, Annaram, Ramakrishnapur, Raikal. A State Highway passes through this C.D. Block from Kondurg to Farooqnagar.

Railway Station: Burgul.

Backwards Region Grants Fund: It receives Backward Region Grants.

Annual Rainfall:

Ground Water: Availability of the Ground Water in the Basin is (Fig. not available) H.A.M. and the utilization is (Fig. not available) H.A.M. It belongs to (Not available) category. Depth to water level varies from less than 2 meter below the ground. Most of the wells go down in summer months. The well density in the entire block is (Fig. not available) wells per sq. km. Total no. of the wells in the block are enumerated as (Not available), according to the Ground Water Estimation Committee.

Natural Division : Telangana Plateau Region

Administration:

Division: Telangana. Parliamentary Constituency: 11 Mahbubnagar. District: Mahbubnagar. Mandal: Farooqnagar. Assembly Constituency: 84 Shadnagar Gram Panchayat: 29

Places of Tourist Interest:

Jogammaguda: Jogammagudem is situated at a distance of 5 kms. from Raikol (Rawikol) on the Hyderabad. Mahbu bnagar bus route. This village is considered as 'Uttara Rameswaram, on account of a big pond occupying an area of about 1674 sq. metres and a huge Sivalingam, believed to be the biggest in India.

Villages: 35 **Inhabited:** 29 **Uninhabited:** 6

Ranking	District	State	National
Area	26	254	3161
Population	4	233	4765
Sex Ratio	46	821	2775
Child Sex Ratio	21	528	2007
Literacy Rate	7	788	4849
Density	49	482	4263
Work Participation Rate	14	592	1233

Gram Panchayats:

Annaram, Ayyawari Palle, Bheemaram, Buchiguda Burgul, Chattanpalle, Chilkamarri, Chinchod Chintaguda, Chowlapally, Devuni Palle, Dooskal Elkatta, Farooqnagar, Gantlavelli, Hajipalle Kammadanam, Kamsanpalle, Kandivanam, Kishan Nagar Kondannaguda, Lingareddyguda, Madhurapur Mogalagidda, Nagula Palle, Raikal, Solipur, Veljerla Vittyal.

Amenities:

Education: Primary School in 28 villages, Middle school in 12 villages, Matriculation or Secondary School in 7 villages, namely Mogalgidda, Veljerla-Ii, Kishannagar, Chinchode, Kammadanam, Raikal, Burgul.

Higher Secondary or Pre University Courses or Intermediate or Junior College in 0 village of the CD Block, College in 0 village, Adult Literacy Center in 21 villages.

Medical: Hospital in 0 village, Dispensary in 1 village, Health Center in 4 villages, Sub Center in 12 villages, Maternity and Child Welfare Center in 0 village, Community health workers in 0 village.

The Villages having Hospital or Dispensary or Health Center are Mogalgidda, Elkatta, Chattanpalle.

Drinking Water: Tap water in 29 villages, Tank water in 29 villages, Well water in 29 villages, Tubewell in 29 villages and more than one source in 29 villages.

Bank: Banking facility in 1 villages, namely, Veljerla-Ii.

Credit Society in 9 villages Agricultural Credit Society in 1 Non-Agricultural Credit Society in 8 villages.

Others: Power supply in 29 villages, Cinema hall in 2 villages, sport club in 0 village, Stadium or Auditorium or Community Hall in 0 village, Post Office in 23 villages.

There are 27 villages having bus facilities.

Village with most of facilities: Veljerla-Ii.

Villages without amenities (Education): Thimmajipalle..

Scheduled Castes: Out of the total population of 62593 persons, 12072 persons (19.29%) belong to Scheduled Castes.

The villages having less than 10% SC population are None..

The villages having more than 50% SC population are None.

Sex ratio of Scheduled Caste population is 503.

Scheduled Castes Literates and Illiterates by Sex:

	Persons	Males	Females
Literate	4,138	2,656	1,482
Illiterate	7,934	3,345	4,589
Literacy rate	40.1	51.9	28.5
Graduate	44	37	7

Scheduled Castes (Dominant):

Madiga, Mala, Byagara, Generic Castes etc., Bindla

For their cultural identity please see Appendix-I

Villages without Scheduled Castes: There are 8 villages without any scheduled caste population.

Scheduled Tribes: Out of the total population of 62593 persons, 9396 persons (15.01%) belong to Scheduled Tribes.

The villages having less than 10% ST population are Rangasamudram (Yellampalle), Mogalgidda, Elkatta Nagulapalle, Chattanpalle, Kondannaguda, Buchchiguda Hajipalle, Chilkamarri (Chelka), Kammadanam Seriguda Madhurapur.

The villages having more than 50% ST population are None.

Sex ratio of Scheduled tribe population is 486.

Scheduled Tribes Literates and Illiterates by Sex:

	Persons	Males	Females
Literate	1,893	1,431	462
Illiterate	7,503	3,397	4,106
Literacy rate	25.5	37.8	12.8
Graduate	15	15	0

Scheduled Tribes (Dominant):

Sugalis etc., Yerukulas, Generic Tribes etc.

Yenadis

For their cultural identity please see Appendix-II

Villages without Scheduled Tribes: There are 10 villages without any scheduled tribe population.

Literates and Illiterates by Sex (Total Population):

	Persons	Males	Females
Literate	25,328	16,338	8,990
Illiterate	37,265	15,532	21,733
Literacy rate	48	61	35
Graduate	774	621	153

Agriculture: ***Distribution of villages according to land use:*** Out of 35 villages, Total area (in hectare) is 26610, out of that 84.1 percent is cultivable and 16.19 percent of the cultivable area is irrigated.

Sources of Irrigation (Hectares): Government Canal 0, Private Canal 0, Well without Electricity 0, Well with Electricity 390.01, Tubewell without Electricity 0, Tubewell with Electricity 2848.73, Tank 182.37, River 0, Lake 0, Waterfall 0, Others 202.34.

Villages with population of 5000 to 9999: Mogalgidda, Burgul.

Villages with population of 10000 and above: None

Distribution of Workers:

	Persons	Males	Females	WPR
Cultivators	11,295	7,351	3,944	34.52
Agricultural Labour	14,197	5,294	8,903	43.39
Household Industry	763	457	306	2.33
Other Workers	6,466	5,040	1,426	19.76
Main Workers	26,937	16,093	10,844	82.32
Marginal Workers	5,784	2,049	3,735	17.68
Total Workers	32,721	18,142	14,579	

Religion: Major Religious Communities:

	Persons	Males	Females	Sex Ratio
Hindu (92.56%)	57,939	29,441	28,498	968
Muslim (7.05%)	4,414	2,280	2,134	936
Christian (0.26%)	164	106	58	547
Sikh (0.02%)	12	9	3	333
Buddhists (0.01%)	6	3	3	1,000
Jain (0%)	-	-	-	-

Agewise Data:

	Persons	Males	Females	Sex Ratio
All ages	62,593	31,870	30,723	964
0-14	23,086	11,797	11,289	957
15-44	28,090	14,417	13,673	948
45-79	10,882	5,392	5,490	1018
80+	450	215	235	1093
Age not stated	85	49	36	735

Languages (Dominant):

Telugu, Hindi, Urdu, Oriya, Tamil

Disabled Population:

	Persons	Males	Females	%
Total Disabled	1,027	600	427	
In Seeing	518	289	229	50.44
In Speech	103	64	39	10.03
In Hearing	36	16	20	3.51
In Movement	263	169	94	25.61
Mentally	107	62	45	10.42

G.KONDURU

G. Konduru C.D. Block lies in the northern part of Krishna district. The Block is located at a distance of 97 kms. from district headquarters (Machilipatnam). There are 27 villages in the block with the total population of 53,499 persons. Area of the C.D. Block is 196.25 sq. kms. It is bounded in the north by distri ct Khammam and Mandal Mylaparem, in the south by Mandals Ibrahimpatnam and Vijayawada Rural, in the east by Mandals Agiripalle and Vijayawada (Rural), and in the west by Mandals Veerullapadu and Ibrahimpatnam.

Communications:

Roadways : Metalled Roads: Nearest Villages- Konduru, Chevuturu, Venkatapuram, Kuntamukkala, Pinapaka, Kavul uru.

Railway Station: Ganginenipalem, Cheruvu Madhavaram.

River: Krishna Nadi- Nearest Villages- Munagapadu, Cheruvu Madhavaram, Gaddamanugu, Konduru, Pinapaka, Narasayagudem, Velagaleru. Budameru Nadi- Nearest Villages- Kuntamukkala, Nandigama, Bhimavarappadu, Vellaturu, Velagaleru, Haveli Mutyalampadu, Kandulapadu.

Annaul Rainfall: Average Rainfall 1512 mm

Ground Water: Availability of the Ground Water in the Basin is (Information not avavible) H.A.M .and the utilization is (Information not avavible) H.A.M. It belongs to (Information not avavible) category. Depth to water level varies from 3 to 10 meter below the ground. Most of the wells go down in summer months.

Forest and Reserved **Forest:** (Kondapalle R.F.)- Nearest Villages- Petrampadu, Ganginenipalem, Telladevarapadu, Munagapadu, Cheruvu Madhavaram, Gaddamanugu, Kondu Chevuturu, Venkatapuram, Gurrajupalem, Kuntamukkala.

Natural Division : Krishna Delta Region

Administration:

Division: Coastal Andhra. Parliamentary Constituency:

29 Vijayawada. District: Krishna. Mandal: G. Konduru. Assembly Constituency: 201 Mylavaram. Gram Panchayat: 21

Villages: 27 **Inhabited:** 23 **Uninhabited:** 4

Ranking	**District**	**State**	**National**
Area	18	579	4245
Population	30	406	5114
Sex Ratio	18	464	1763
Child Sex Ratio	29	604	2458
Literacy Rate	28	194	2240
Density	16	667	3835
Work Participation Rate	37	456	1850

Gram Panchayats:

Atkuru, Ch Madhavaram, Chevuturu, China Nandigama Duggiralapadu, G Konduru, Gaddamanugu Ganginenipalem, Gurrajupalem, H Mutyalampadu Kandulapadu, Kattubadipalem, Koduru, Kowluru Kuntamukkala, Pinapaka, Sunnampadu, Telladevarapadu Velagaleru, Vellaturu, Venkatapuram.

Amenities:

Education: Primary School in 23 villages, Middle school in 9 villages, Matriculation or Secondary School in 6 villages, namely Ganginenipalem, Konduru, Kuntamukkala, Koduru, Kavuluru, Velagaleru.

Higher Secondary or Pre University Courses or Intermediate or Junior College in 1 village of the CD Block,, namely Kuntamukkala.

College in 0 village, Adult Literacy Center in 1 village.

Medical: Hospital in 0 village, Dispensary in 1 village, Health Center in 3 villages, Sub Center in 11 villages, Maternity and Child Welfare Center in 0 village, Community health workers in 0 village.

The Village having Hospital or Dispensary or Health Center is Vellaturu.

Drinking Water: Tap water in 17 villages, Tank water in 0 villages, Well water in 2 villages, Tubewell in 5 villages and more than one source in 2 villages.

Bank: Banking facility in 4 villages, namely, Ganginenipalem, Konduru, Vellaturu, Velagaleru.

Credit Society in 13 villages Agricultural Credit Society in 8 Non-Agricultural Credit Society in 11 villages.

Others: Power supply in 23 villages, Cinema hall in 1 village, sport club in 0 village, Stadium or Auditorium or Community Hall in 0 village, Post Office in 17 villages.

There are 23 villages having bus facilities.

Villages with most of facilities: Ganginenipalem Konduru, Vellaturu, Velagaleru.

Villages without Amenities (Education): None..

Scheduled Castes: Out of the total population of 53499 persons, 17247 persons (32.24%) belong to Scheduled Castes.

The villages having less than 10% SC population are None..

The villages having more than 50% SC population are Bhimavarappadu, Pinapaka, Haveli Mutyalampadu Chegireddipadu.

Sex ratio of Scheduled Caste population is 500.

Scheduled Castes Literates and Illiterates by Sex:

	Persons	Males	Females
Literate	9,419	4,905	4,514
Illiterate	7,828	3,719	4,109
Literacy rate	63.3	66.4	60.3
Graduate	173	128	45

Scheduled Castes (Dominant):

Madiga, Mala, Bindla, Madiga Dasu etc.

Holeya Dasari

For their cultural identity please see Appendix-I

Villages without Scheduled Castes: There are 5 villages without any scheduled caste population.

Scheduled Tribes: Out of the total population of 53499 persons, 2493 persons (4.66%) belong to Scheduled Tribes.

The villages having less than 10% ST population are Duggiralapadu, Ganginenipalem, Telladevarapadu Sunnampadu, Gaddamanugu, Konduru, Chevuturu Venkatapuram, Gurrajupalem, Kuntamukkala, Nandigama Koduru, Bhimavarappadu, Vellaturu, Atukuru, Pinapaka Kavuluru, Velagaleru, Haveli Mutyalampadu Kandulapadu, Chegireddipadu.

The villages having more than 50% ST population are None.

Sex ratio of Scheduled tribe population is 504.

Scheduled Tribes Literates and Illiterates by Sex:

	Persons	Males	Females
Literate	893	521	372
Illiterate	1,600	716	884
Literacy rate	42.9	50.2	35.7
Graduate	9	7	2

Scheduled Tribes (Dominant):

Sugalis etc., Yerukulas, Yenadis, Savaras etc.

For their cultural identity please see Appendix-II

Villages without Scheduled Tribes: There are 11 villages without any scheduled tribe population.

Literates and Illiterates by Sex (Total Population):

	Persons	Males	Females
Literate	29,456	15,718	13,738
Illiterate	24,043	11,216	12,827
Literacy rate	63	67	59
Graduate	785	579	206

Agriculture: ***Distribution of villages according to land use:*** Out of 27 villages, Total area (in hectare) is 19625, out of that 29.04 percent is cultivable and 56.22 percent of the

cultivable area is irrigated.

Sources of Irrigation (Hectares): Government Canal 11.33, Private Canal 0, Well without Electricity 20.23, Well with Electricity 20, Tubewell without Electricity 1109.23, Tubewell with Electricity 14, Tank 2029, River 0, Lake 0, Waterfall 0, Others 0.

Villages with population of 5000 to 9999: Konduru, Kavuluru.

Villages with population of 10000 and above: None

Distribution of Workers:

	Persons	Males	Females	WPR
Cultivators	4,499	3,690	809	16.33
Agricultural Labour	17,236	8,326	8,910	62.56
Household Industry	669	423	246	2.43
Other Workers	5,145	4,128	1,017	18.68
Main Workers	21,253	14,177	7,076	77.15
Marginal Workers	6,296	2,390	3,906	22.85
Total Workers	27,549	16,567	10,982	

Religion: Major Religious Communities:

	Persons	Males	Females	Sex Ratio
Hindu (95.77%)	51,236	25,825	25,411	984
Muslim (3.15%)	1,684	844	840	995
Christian (0.82%)	441	194	247	1,273
Sikh (0.01%)	3	2	1	500
Buddhists (0%)	-	-	-	-
Jain (0%)	-	-	-	-

Agewise Data:

	Persons	Males	Females	Sex Ratio
All ages	53,499	26,934	26,565	986
0-14	16,499	8,176	8,323	1018
15-44	26,019	13,160	12,859	977
45-79	10,443	5,335	5,108	957
80+	495	241	254	1054
Age not stated	43	22	21	955

Languages (Dominant):

Telugu, Hindi, Urdu, Gondi, Tamil

Disabled Population:

	Persons	Males	Females	%
Total Disabled	874	494	380	
In Seeing	248	140	108	28.38
In Speech	120	68	52	13.73
In Hearing	48	24	24	5.49
In Movement	341	206	135	39.02
Mentally	117	56	61	13.39

G.MADUGULA

Gangarajamadugula C.D. Block lies in the north-western part of Visakhapatnam district. The Block is located at a distance of 171 kms. from district headquarters (Vishakhapatnam). There are 328 villages in the block with the total population of 50,685 persons. Area of the C.D. Block is 200.86 sq. kms. It is bounded in the north by Pedabayalu Mandal, in the south by Mandals Chintapalle and Madugula, in the east by Mandals Madugu la and Paderu, and in the west by Mandal Chintapalle. It has common boundary with the state of Orissa on west.

Communications :

Roadways : Metalled Roads: Nearest Villages- Singam Valasa, Maddigaruvu, Pulusumamidi, Kumburla, Vandrangula, Gadigunta, Vakapalle, Nugumamidi, Nurmathi, Maddiveed hi, A.Bandaveedhi, Palamamidi, Sirlabanda, Vanchebu, Boddaputtu, Beeram, Thadiveedhi, Anarbha, Sadeku, Rolangiputtu, Agampadu, Vemarajukodapalle, Thummedala, Neredu, Jannera, Vennela, Buruguveedhi, Lakkulu, Kokki rapalle, Kulupadu, Chinnaurumu, Pedalanka, Pedaurumu, Rolangiputtu, Matchyapuram, Sangam, Bandaveedhi, K. Kodapalle, Ganneruputtu, G.M.Kothuru, Kumbidisingi.

Railway Station: K.G.Madugula.

Integrated Child Development Scheme (ICDS) Project: G. Madugula (Tribal), Total Anganwadi Centres: 96

Annaual Rainfall: Average Rainfall 975.0 mm

Ground Water: Availability of the Ground Water in the Basin is (Information not avavible) H.A.M .and the utilization is (Information not avavible) H.A.M. It belongs to (Information not avavible) category. Depth to water level varies from 3 to 10 meter below the ground. Most of the wells go down in summer months.

Administration :

Division: Coastal Andhra. Parliamentary Constituency: 18 Araku (ST). District: Visakhapatnam. Mandal: G. Madugula. Assembly Constituency: 148 Paderu (ST). Gram Panchayat: 17.

Border Villages: (Orissa)- Nearest Villages- Chilakapan asa, Garisingi, Valasapanasa, Vandrangipadu, Manepalle.

Villages: 328 **Inhabited:** 294 **Uninhabited:** 34

Ranking	District	State	National
Area	10	545	4164
Population	28	489	5250
Sex Ratio	34	634	2138
Child Sex Ratio	31	596	2380
Literacy Rate	38	1090	6214
Density	1	7	4049
Work Participation Rate	31	532	81

Gram Panchayats:

Bheeram, Boithala, G.Madugula, Gaduthuru, Gemmeli K.Kodapalli, Killamkota, Korapalli, Kumbidisingi Nurmathi, Palamamidi, Pedalochili, Pedaluvvasingi P Singarbha, Solabham, Vanjari, Vanthala.

Amenities:

Education: Primary School in 176 villages, Middle school in 16 villages, Matriculation or Secondary School in 7 villages,

namely Vallangula, Vennelakota, Bandaveedhi, G.M.Kothuru, K.G.Madugula, Boddagondi, Chittampadu.
Higher Secondary or Pre University Courses or Intermediate or Junior College in 0 village of the CD Block, College in 0 village, Adult Literacy Center in 0 village.
Medical: Hospital in 0 village, Dispensary in 0 village, Health Center in 26 villages, Sub Center in 12 villages, Maternity and Child Welfare Center in 1 village, Community health workers in 0 village.
Drinking Water: Tap water in 286 villages, Tank water in 287 villages, Well water in 288 villages, Tubewell in 287 villages and more than one source in 288 villages.
Bank: Banking facility in 1 villages, namely, K.G.Madugula.
Credit Society in 1 village Agricultural Credit Society in 1 Non-Agricultural Credit Society in 0 village.
Others: Power supply in 289 villages, Cinema hall in 0 village, sport club in 0 village, Stadium or Auditorium or Community Hall in 0 village, Post Office in 11 villages.
There are 29 villages having bus facilities.
Village with most of facilities: K.G.Madugula.
Villages without amenities (Education):
Chilakapanasa, Garisingi, Reyyalagedda, Madathakonda, Kappalu, Kodimamidi, Kuridilu, Sankulamaddi, Valasapanasa, Vandrangipadu, Manepalle, Busipalle, Chilakalapalem, Killupalle, Tartalu, Porlugunta, Sopalu, Sirasapalle, Jeelugulagoyya, Singarbagondi, Putikametta, Gondipalle, Subbulu, Chapagedda, Busulakota, Vandrangula, Varadamamidi, Nugumamidi, Thiyyagundam, Vayyampalle, Tarabusingi, Regadi, Chittugummi, Thaggimetta, Pulagondi, Pedakonda, Thummedala Neredu, Madhuramamidi, Lakkulu, Sariya, Busipalle, Korrapadu, Pedda Kiltaru, Mittalapadu, Thatipalem, Cheemakurapalem, Pedalanka, Darlamgondi, Gadderai, Busipalle, Pedapadu, Mulakaiputtu, Andanapalle, Ullikallalabanda, Mulagaruvu, Chinnakothuru, Kolambora, Chinthakota, Bobbampadu, Golagonda, Singarajupeta, Thotalagondi, Gondipadu, Vanjangipadu, Pedakantavaram, Bheemaloya, Kondabheemapalem, Chinaporlu, Tiyyamamidi, Vedurupalle, Panasalagedda, Barisingi, Vantalamamidi, Kajjapalle, Dabbagaruvu, Vanabharangipadu, Ganjigedda, Peddapinapalem, Ganugurolu, Bondulapanuku, Seetabanda, Goddalikarra, Gurralagummi, Mondikota, Porlu, Chuttukota, Kothakundalu, Mettapadu, Gorrilaputtu, Boddapadu, Akuthota, Jerrai, Rolugunta, Sadangi, Labbarla, Pittagullu @ Pittagudlu, Nittamamidi, Neyyalabanda, Pedagedda, Talabarusingi, Boddumamidi, Thallimamidi, Palamamidi, Chilakala Mamidi, Roppulu, Goradalu, Guntapalle, Bagarugudi, Thoka Chilaka, Karebanda, Gummadigondi, Olimamidi, Pinnapolam..
Scheduled Castes: Out of the total population of 50685 persons, 80 persons (0.16%) belong to Scheduled Castes.
The villages having less than 10% SC population are Chilakapanasa, Garisingi, Surtipalle, Reyyalagedda Madathakonda, Buradaveedhi, Kappalu, Kodimamidi Kuridilu, K.Bandaveedhi, Sankulamaddi, Vanukuru Killamkota, Sariyapalle, Valasapanasa, Vandrangipadu Manepalle, Busipalle, Chilakalapalem, Surimetta Alagam, Yesthala, Killupalle, Tartalu, Porlugunta Sopalu, Sirasapalle, Jamulaveedhi, Jeelugulagoyya Singarbagondi, Putikametta, Rachaveedhi, Gondipalle Mandibha, Subbulu, Boithela @ Bonkatili, Chapagedda Peddagaruvu, Singam Valasa, Maddigaruvu, Busulakota Yegarapalle, Panasapalle, Pulusumamidi, Digarapalle Pinajageeru, Kumburla, Vandrangula, Gadigunta Vakapalle, Dippalagondi, Vantalamamidi, Varadamamidi Yerragoppu, Nugumamidi, Nurmathi Mosaidipanuku Kothuru, Maddiveedhi, Boddagondi Thiyyagundam, Vayyampalle, Pinaluvvasingi, Sanguloya Aragadapalle, Peda Luvvasingi, Tarabusingi Kandulagade, A.Bandaveedhi, Palamamidi, Sirlabanda Vanchebu, Karakapalle, Bondapalle, Boddaputtu Mulagaruvu, Chittamputtu, Regadi, Chittugummi Valasamamidi, Surtipalle, Boddaputtu, Thaggimetta Mandivanam, Beeram, Salimerangi, Thadiveedhi Anarbha, Pedajageeru, Kitumulu, Korapalle Rudibayalu, Baram, Sadeku, Rolangiputtu M.Nittaputtu, Palakonda, Pulagondi, Pedakonda Gannelba, Vannelabha, Agampadu, Vemarajukodapalle Ubalagaruvu, Thummedala Neredu, Jannera, Vennela Buruguveedhi, Chepalle, G.Nittaputtu, Karnikalanka Singarbha, Rachapalle, Yegaratchapalle, Reemali Madhuramamidi, Vallangula, Lakkulu, Kokkirapalle Cheekumbanda, Vanabhampadu, Vennelakota, Devarapalle Yeduchavallu, Marripalem, Thoka Rai, Padmapuram Borramamidi, Busipalle, Goyyigunta, Balijipeta Gedalabanda, Ullivarapadu, Pina Kiltharu, Suvvapadu Krishnapuram, Sangambanda, Kinagari, Kuntalam Galipadu, Korrapadu, Pedda Kiltaru, Vanjari Porlubanda, Mittalapadu, Thatipalem, Luvvapalle Cheemakurapalem, Kimudupalle, Terlamamidi, Kulupadu Maddulabanda, Chinnaurumu, Pedalanka, Pedaurumu Darlamgondi, Goddubusulu, P.G.Madugula, Rolangiputtu Matchyapuram, Sangam, Bandaveedhi, K.Kodapalle Ganneruputtu, Chintalagondi, Gadderai, Urlumetta Andangisingi, G.M.Kothuru, K.G.Madugula, Jogulaputtu Busipalle, Balamanusanka, Varigelapalem, Kothurupadu Pedapadu, Udapalam, Mulakaiputtu, Andanapalle

Ullikallalabanda, Gondimelaka, Mulagaruvu, Gemmeli Chinnakothuru, Boddagondi, Chittampadu, G.Kothuru Varlamamidi, Ramachandrapalem, Kolambora Chinthakota, Sampangi Puttu, Bobbampadu, Kuneti Vattivagisa, Golagonda, Yenugugondi, Singarajupeta Degalarai, Thotalagondi, China Kantavaram, Gondipadu Vanjangipadu, Gonduru@ Y.B.Gonduru, Gurrayi Kumbidisingi, Chinnalochali, Mandigaruvu Pedakantavaram, Solabham, Bheemaloya, Godugumamidi S.Kothuru, Rallaputtu, Kondabheemapalem Barsingimetta, Gompam, Gadrayi, Chinaporlu Mangathapalem, Gaduthuru, Pachinapalle, Godda Kothapalle, Peddalochale, Rachapanuku, Vanthala Tiyyamamidi, Jarrai, Kuddangi, Chinna Pinapalem Gangadevigudi, Vedurupalle, Panasalagedda, Barisingi Goddukuralabanda, Vantalamamidi, Kothagaruvu, Addulu Pedavalasa, Pisumamidi, Kajjapalle, Pacheli Dabbagaruvu, Bangarumamidi, Vanabharangipadu Ganjigedda, Peddapinapalem, Ganugurolu, Vasamamidi Bondulapanuku, Seetabanda, Goddalikarra Gurralagummi, Peddabayalu, Jolamputtu, Mondikota Valasapadu, Porlu, Indugula, Kummaragunta Chuttukota, Kothakundalu, Mettapadu, Gorrilaputtu Lakkapadu, Pedaporlu, Ambalamamidi, Gemmelibaru Boddapadu, Akuthota, Jerrai, Rolugunta, Sadangi Labbarla, Pittagullu @ Pittagudlu, Nittamamidi Neyyalabanda, Pedagedda, Talabarusingi, Boddumamidi Thallimamidi, Palamamidi, Chilakala Mamidi, Roppulu Goradalu, Guntapalle, Bagarugudi, Mallipadu Thoka Chilaka, Karebanda, Gummadigondi, Olimamidi Pinnapolam.

The villages having more than 50% SC population are None.

Sex ratio of Scheduled Caste population is 538.

Scheduled Castes Literates and Illiterates by Sex:

	Persons	Males	Females
Literate	26	16	10
Illiterate	54	21	33
Literacy rate	38.8	51.6	27.8
Graduate	4	4	0

Scheduled Castes (Dominant):

Mala, Manne, Generic Castes etc., Madiga, Relli

For their cultural identity please see Appendix-I

Villages without Scheduled Castes: There are 318 villages without any scheduled caste population.

Scheduled Tribes: Out of the total population of 50685 persons, 47625 persons (93.96%) belong to Scheduled Tribes.

The villages having less than 10% ST population are None..

The villages having more than 50% ST population are Chilakapanasa, Garisingi, Surtipalle, Reyyalagedda Madathakonda, Buradaveedhi, Kappalu, Kodimamidi Kuridilu, K.Bandaveedhi, Sankulamaddi, Vanukuru Killamkota, Sariyapalle, Valasapanasa, Vandrangipadu Manepalle, Busipalle, Chilakalapalem, Surimetta Alagam, Yesthala, Killupalle, Tartalu, Porlugunta Sopalu, Sirasapalle, Jamulaveedhi, Jeelugulagoyya Singarbagondi, Putikametta, Rachaveedhi, Gondipalle Mandibha, Subbulu, Boithela @ Bonkatili, Chapagedda Peddagaruvu, Singam Valasa, Busulakota, Yegarapalle Panasapalle, Pulusumamidi, Digarapalle, Pinajageeru Kumburla, Vandrangula, Gadigunta, Vakapalle Dippalagondi, Vantalamamidi, Varadamamidi Yerragoppu, Nugumamidi, Nurmathi Mosaidipanuku Kothuru, Maddiveedhi, Boddagondi Thiyyagundam, Vayyampalle, Pinaluvvasingi, Sanguloya Aragadapalle, Peda Luvvasingi, Tarabusingi Kandulagade, A.Bandaveedhi, Palamamidi, Sirlabanda Vanchebu, Karakapalle, Bondapalle, Boddaputtu Mulagaruvu, Chittamputtu, Regadi, Chittugummi Valasamamidi, Surtipalle, Boddaputtu, Thaggimetta Mandivanam, Beeram, Salimerangi, Thadiveedhi Anarbha, Pedajageeru, Kitumulu, Korapalle Rudibayalu, Baram, Sadeku, Rolangiputtu M.Nittaputtu, Palakonda, Pulagondi, Pedakonda Gannelba, Vannelabha, Agampadu, Vemarajukodapalle Ubalagaruvu, Thummedala Neredu, Jannera, Vennela Chepalle, G.Nittaputtu, Karnikalanka, Singarbha Rachapalle, Yegaratchapalle, Reemali, Madhuramamidi Vallangula, Lakkulu, Kokkirapalle, Cheekumbanda Vanabhampadu, Vennelakota, Devarapalle, Yeduchavallu Marripalem, Thoka Rai, Padmapuram, Sariya Borramamidi, Goyyigunta, Balijipeta, Gedalabanda Ullivarapadu, Pina Kiltharu, Suvvapadu, Krishnapuram Sangambanda, Kinagari, Kuntalam, Galipadu, Korrapadu Pedda Kiltaru, Vanjari, Porlubanda, Mittalapadu Thatipalem, Luvvapalle, Cheemakurapalem, Kimudupalle Terlamamidi, Kulupadu, Maddulabanda, Chinnaurumu Pedalanka, Pedaurumu, Darlamgondi, Goddubusulu P.G.Madugula, Rolangiputtu, Matchyapuram, Sangam Bandaveedhi, K.Kodapalle, Ganneruputtu Chintalagondi, Urlumetta, Andangisingi, G.M.Kothuru K.G.Madugula, Jogulaputtu, Busipalle, Balamanusanka Varigelapalem, Kothurupadu, Pedapadu, Udapalam Mulakaiputtu, Andanapalle, Ullikallalabanda Gondimelaka, Mulagaruvu, Gemmeli, Chinnakothuru Boddagondi, Chittampadu, G.Kothuru, Varlamamidi Ramachandrapalem, Kolambora, Chinthakota Sampangi Puttu, Bobbampadu, Kuneti, Vattivagisa Golagonda, Yenugugondi, Singarajupeta, Degalarai

Thotalagondi, China Kantavaram, Gondipadu Vanjangipadu, Gonduru@ Y.B.Gonduru, Gurrayi Kumbidisingi, Chinnalochali, Mandigaruvu Pedakantavaram, Solabham, Bheemaloya, Godugumamidi S.Kothuru, Rallaputtu, Kondabheemapalem Barsingimetta, Gompam, Gadrayi, Chinaporlu Mangathapalem, Gaduthuru, Pachinapalle, Godda Kothapalle, Peddalochale, Rachapanuku, Vanthala Tiyyamamidi, Jarrai, Kuddangi, Chinna Pinapalem Gangadevigudi, Vedurupalle, Panasalagedda, Barisingi Goddukuralabanda, Vantalamamidi, Kothagaruvu, Addulu Pedavalasa, Kajjapalle, Pacheli, Dabbagaruvu Bangarumamidi, Vanabharangipadu, Ganjigedda Peddapinapalem, Ganugurolu, Vasamamidi Bondulapanuku, Seetabanda, Goddalikarra Gurralagummi, Peddabayalu, Jolamputtu, Mondikota Valasapadu, Porlu, Indugula, Kummaragunta Chuttukota, Kothakundalu, Mettapadu, Gorrilaputtu Lakkapadu, Pedaporlu, Ambalamamidi, Gemmelibaru Boddapadu, Akuthota, Jerrai, Rolugunta, Sadangi Labbarla, Pittagullu @ Pittagudlu, Nittamamidi Neyyalabanda, Pedagedda, Talabarusingi, Boddumamidi Thallimamidi, Palamamidi, Chilakala Mamidi, Roppulu Goradalu, Guntapalle, Bagarugudi, Mallipadu Thoka Chilaka, Karebanda, Gummadigondi, Olimamidi Pinnapolam.

Sex ratio of Scheduled tribe population is 494.

Scheduled Tribes Literates and Illiterates by Sex:

	Persons	Males	Females
Literate	11,209	8,033	3,176
Illiterate	36,416	16,044	20,372
Literacy rate	28.4	40.3	16.2
Graduate	43	41	2

Scheduled Tribes (Dominant):

Konda Dhoras, Kondhs etc., Bagata, Kammara, Valmiki

For their cultural identity please see Appendix-II

Villages without Scheduled Tribes: There are 35 villages without any scheduled tribe population.

Literates and Illiterates by Sex (Total Population):

	Persons	Males	Females
Literate	12,326	8,752	3,574
Illiterate	38,359	16,889	21,470
Literacy rate	29	41	17
Graduate	113	105	8

Agriculture: ***Distribution of villages according to land use:*** Out of 328 villages, Total area (in hectare) is 20088, out of that 48.71 percent is cultivable and 21.9 percent of the cultivable area is irrigated.

Sources of Irrigation (Hectares): Government Canal 0.02, Private Canal 0, Well without Electricity 0, Well with Electricity 0, Tubewell without Electricity 0, Tubewell with Electricity 0, Tank 0, River 0, Lake 0, Waterfall 0, Others 2142.83.

Villages with population of 5000 to 9999: None

Villages with population of 10000 and above: None

Distribution of Workers:

	Persons	Males	Females	WPR
Cultivators	22,899	11,755	11,144	75.58
Agricultural Labour	5,956	2,551	3,405	19.66
Household Industry	284	140	144	0.94
Other Workers	1,160	768	392	3.83
Main Workers	27,872	14,366	13,506	91.99
Marginal Workers	2,427	848	1,579	8.01
Total Workers	30,299	15,214	15,085	

Religion: Major Religious Communities:

	Persons	Males	Females	Sex Ratio
Hindu (96.72%)	49,021	24,813	24,208	976
Muslim (0.31%)	158	81	77	951
Christian (2.96%)	1,500	743	757	1,019
Sikh (0%)	-	-	-	-
Buddhists (0%)	-	-	-	-
Jain (0%)	-	-	-	-

Agewise Data:

	Persons	Males	Females	Sex Ratio
All ages	50,685	25,641	25,044	977
0-14	19,213	9,944	9,269	932
15-44	23,636	11,500	12,136	1055
45-79	7,304	3,756	3,548	945
80+	109	54	55	1019
Age not stated	423	387	36	93

Languages (Dominant):

Telugu, Konda, Oriya, Khond/Kondh, Koya

Disabled Population:

	Persons	Males	Females	%
Total Disabled	953	537	416	
In Seeing	562	322	240	58.97
In Speech	77	40	37	8.08
In Hearing	69	29	40	7.24
In Movement	189	110	79	19.83
Mentally	56	36	20	5.88

GADIVEMULA

Gadivemula C.D. Block lies in the eastern part of Kurno ol district. The Block is located at a distance of 43 kms. from district headquarters (Kurnool). There are 14 villages in the block with the total population of 39,337 persons. Area of the C.D. Block is 243.88 sq. kms. It is bounded in the north by Mandals Midthur and Pamulapadu, in the south by Mandals Panyam and Nandyal, in the east by Mandals Velgode and Bandi Atmak ur, and in the west by Orvakal Mandal.

Communications:

Roadways : Metalled Roads: Nearest Villages- Gani, Chenn akkapalle, Manchalakatta, Gadivemula, Korrapolur, Bilaka la Gudur.

River: Kunderu Nadi- Nearest Villages- Gadivemula, Korrapolur, Bilakala Gudur, Bujanur, Chindukuru, Gadiga revula, Thirupadu, Koratamaddi, Durvesi.

It is identified as a drought-prone area.

Annual Rainfall: Average Rainfall 692 mm

Ground Water: Availability of the Ground Water in the Basin is 3761 H.A.M. and the utilization is 885 H.A. M. It belongs to Safe category. Depth to water level varies from less than 5 meter below the ground. Most of the wells go down in summer months. The well density in the entire block is 2 wells per sq. km. Total no. of the wells in the block are enumerated as 800, accor ding to the Ground Water Estimation Committee.

Forest and Reserved **Forest:** Nearest Villages- Gani, Chennakkapalle, Gadigarevula, Durvesi.

Natural Division : Rayalaseema Region

Administration:

Division: Rayala Seema. Parliamentary Constituency: 34 Nandayal. District: Kurnool. Mandal: Gadivemula. Assembly Constituency: 257 Panyam. Gram Panchayat: 16

Villages: 14 **Inhabited:** 14 **Uninhabited:** 0

Ranking	District	State	National
Area	28	335	3460
Population	40	844	5765
Sex Ratio	35	900	3031
Child Sex Ratio	51	994	4580
Literacy Rate	18	523	3935
Density	31	358	5385
Work Participation Rate	34	863	888

Gram Panchayats:

Bilakala Gudur, Bujanur, Chindukuru, Durvesi Gadigarevula, Gadivemula, Gani, K.Bollavaram Karimaddala, Koratamaddi, Korrapolur Laxmaiahkunta Thanda, Manchalakatta, Ondutla Pesaravayi, Thirupadu.

Amenities:

Education: Primary School in 14 villages, Middle school in 6 villages, Matriculation or Secondary School in 3 villages, namely Gani, Gadivemula, Gadigarevula.

Higher Secondary or Pre University Courses or Intermediate or Junior College in 1 village of the CD Block,, namely Gadivemula.

College in 1 village, Adult Literacy Center in 14 villages., College is in village, namely Gadivemula.

Medical: Hospital in 0 village, Dispensary in 0 village, Health Center in 1 village, Sub Center in 8 villages, Maternity and Child Welfare Center in 0 village, Community health workers in 0 village.

Drinking Water: Tap water in 14 villages, Tank water in 14 villages, Well water in 14 villages, Tubewell in 14 villages and more than one source in 14 villages.

Bank: Banking facility in 2 villages, namely, Gani, Gadivemula.

Credit Society in 13 villages Agricultural Credit Society in 5 Non-Agricultural Credit Society in 13 villages.

Others: Power supply in 14 villages, Cinema hall in 1 village, sport club in 0 village, Stadium or Auditorium or Community Hall in 0 village, Post Office in 13 villages.

There are 13 villages having bus facilities.

Villages with most of facilities: Gani, Gadivemula.

Villages without Amenities (Education): None..

Scheduled Castes: Out of the total population of 39337 persons, 7447 persons (18.93%) belong to Scheduled Castes.

The villages having less than 10% SC population are None..

The villages having more than 50% SC population are None.

Sex ratio of Scheduled Caste population is 479.

Scheduled Castes Literates and Illiterates by Sex:

	Persons	Males	Females
Literate	3,099	2,074	1,025
Illiterate	4,348	1,809	2,539
Literacy rate	49.5	63.6	34.2
Graduate	103	90	13

Scheduled Castes (Dominant):

Madiga, Mala, Beda Jangam etc.

For their cultural identity please see Appendix-I

Villages without Scheduled Castes: There are 0 village without any scheduled caste population.

Scheduled Tribes: Out of the total population of 39337 persons, 1060 persons (2.69%) belong to Scheduled Tribes.

The villages having less than 10% ST population are Gani, Manchalakatta, Gadivemula, Korrapolur Bilakala Gudur, Bujanur, Pesaravayi, Chindukuru Gadigarevula, Thirupadu, Koratamaddi, Durvesi Karimaddala.

The villages having more than 50% ST population are None.

Sex ratio of Scheduled tribe population is 479.

Scheduled Tribes Literates and Illiterates by Sex:

	Persons	Males	Females
Literate	219	171	48
Illiterate	841	381	460
Literacy rate	25.6	38.3	11.7
Graduate	6	6	0

Scheduled Tribes (Dominant):

Sugalis etc., Yerukulas, Kammara, Koya etc.
Chenchu etc.

For their cultural identity please see Appendix-II

Villages without Scheduled Tribes: There are 4 villages without any scheduled tribe population.

Literates and Illiterates by Sex (Total Population):

	Persons	Males	Females
Literate	18,030	11,512	6,518
Illiterate	21,307	8,566	12,741
Literacy rate	54	67	39
Graduate	636	537	99

Agriculture: ***Distribution of villages according to land use:*** Out of 14 villages, Total area (in hectare) is 24389, out of that 64.29 percent is cultivable and 32.18 percent of the cultivable area is irrigated.

Sources of Irrigation (Hectares): Government Canal 2923, Private Canal 0, Well without Electricity 0, Well with Electricity 658, Tubewell without Electricity 0, Tubewell with Electricity 1356, Tank 108, River 0, Lake 0, Waterfall 0, Others 0.

Villages with population of 5000 to 9999: Gadivemula.

Villages with population of 10000 and above: None

Distribution of Workers:

	Persons	Males	Females	WPR
Cultivators	5,736	3,852	1,884	26.89
Agricultural Labour	12,249	5,377	6,872	57.42
Household Industry	320	190	130	1.5
Other Workers	3,027	2,327	700	14.19
Main Workers	18,415	10,816	7,599	86.33
Marginal Workers	2,917	930	1,987	13.67
Total Workers	21,332	11,746	9,586	

Religion: Major Religious Communities:

	Persons	Males	Females	Sex Ratio
Hindu (86.69%)	34,102	17,421	16,681	958
Muslim (13%)	5,112	2,595	2,517	970
Christian (0.24%)	96	50	46	920
Sikh (0%)	-	-	-	-
Buddhists (0%)	-	-	-	-
Jain (0%)	-	-	-	-

Agewise Data:

	Persons	Males	Females	Sex Ratio
All ages	39,337	20,078	19,259	959
0-14	13,057	6,778	6,279	926
15-44	18,360	9,474	8,886	938
45-79	7,573	3,668	3,905	1065
80+	268	111	157	1414
Age not stated	79	47	32	681

Languages (Dominant):
Telugu, Urdu, Hindi, Gondi, Marathi

Disabled Population:

	Persons	Males	Females	%
Total Disabled	1,026	538	488	
In Seeing	489	232	257	47.66
In Speech	104	52	52	10.14
In Hearing	77	36	41	7.5
In Movement	269	172	97	26.22
Mentally	87	46	41	8.48

GADWAL

Gadwal C.D. Block lies in the central west part of Mahbubnagar district. It is a part of Gadwal Mandal. The Block is located at a distance of 52 kms. from district headquarters (Mahbubnagar). There are 18 villa ges in the block with the total population of 42,817 persons. Area of the C.D. Block is 271.28 sq. kms. It is bounded by Atmakur Mandal on north and east, Pebbair Mandal on south-east, Itikyal Mandal on south, Dharur and Mandakal Mandals on west.

Communications:

Roadways : Metalled Roads: Nearest Villages- Yenkampeta, Gonpad, Sangala, Kakulavaram, Paramala.

Railway Station: Gadwal (Rural), Pudur.

River: Krishna Nadi- Nearest Villages- Yenkampeta, Rekulapalle, Kothapalle, Mulkalapalle, Gadwal (Rural), Beerole, Basapur, Gurramgadda.

Backwards Region Grants Fund: It receives Backward Region Grants.

Integrated Child Development Scheme (ICDS) Project: Gadwal, Total Anganwadi Centres: 265

Annual Rainfall: Average Rainfall 642 mm

Ground Water: Availability of the Ground Water in the Basin is 5258 H.A.M. and the utilization is 1306 H. A.M. It belongs to Safe category. Depth to water level varies from 2 to 5 meter below the ground. Most of the wells go down in summer months. The well density in the entire block is 5 wells per sq. km. Total no. of the wells in the block are enumerated as 1290, according to the Ground Water Estimation Committee.

Natural Division : Telangana Plateau Region

Administration:

Division: Telangana. Parliamentary Constituency: 12 Nagarkurnool (SC). District: Mahbubnagar. Mandal: Gadwal. Assembly Constituency: 79 Gadwal. Gram Panchayat: 24

Villages: 18 **Inhabited:** 18 **Uninhabited:** 0

Ranking	District	State	National
Area	23	233	3090
Population	48	730	5611
Sex Ratio	31	677	2281
Child Sex Ratio	4	125	320
Literacy Rate	61	1088	6201

Density	4	15	5444
Work Participation Rate	48	878	112

Gram Panchayats:
Ananthapur, Atmakur, Baswacheru, Beerole Chengonipally, Douderpally, Gonpad, Guntipally Gurramgadda, Jammiched, Kakulavaram, Kondapally Kothapally, Lathipur, Madanpally, Mailacheruvu Molkalpally, Parmala, Pudur, Rekulapally, Repally Sangala, Veerapur, Yenkampet.

Amenities:

Education: Primary School in 18 villages, Middle school in 9 villages, Matriculation or Secondary School in 3 villages, namely Gadwal (Rural), Pudur, Anantapur.
Higher Secondary or Pre University Courses or Intermediate or Junior College in 0 village of the CD Block, College in 0 village, Adult Literacy Center in 14 villages.

Medical: Hospital in 0 village, Dispensary in 1 village, Health Center in 0 village, Sub Center in 5 villages, Maternity and Child Welfare Center in 1 village, Community health workers in 0 village.
The Village having Hospital or Dispensary or Health Center is Jammiched.

Drinking Water: Tap water in 18 villages, Tank water in 18 villages, Well water in 18 villages, Tubewell in 18 villages and more than one source in 18 villages.

Bank: Banking facility in 1 villages, namely, Gadwal (Rural).
Credit Society in 13 villages Agricultural Credit Society in 3 Non-Agricultural Credit Society in 12 villages.

Others: Power supply in 18 villages, Cinema hall in 1 village, sport club in 1 village, Stadium or Auditorium or Community Hall in 1 village, Post Office in 10 villages.
There are 14 villages having bus facilities.

Village with most of facilities: Gadwal (Rural).

Villages without Amenities (Education): None..

Scheduled Castes: Out of the total population of 42815 persons, 7038 persons (16.44%) belong to Scheduled Castes.
The villages having less than 10% SC population are None..
The villages having more than 50% SC population are None.
Sex ratio of Scheduled Caste population is 488.

Scheduled Castes Literates and Illiterates by Sex:

	Persons	Males	Females
Literate	1,538	1,124	414
Illiterate	5,500	2,478	3,022
Literacy rate	26.5	37.5	14.7
Graduate	43	37	6

Scheduled Castes (Dominant):
Madiga, Generic Castes etc., Mala, Mala Dasari Dom etc.

For their cultural identity please see Appendix-I

Villages without Scheduled Castes: There is 1 village without any scheduled caste population.

Scheduled Tribes: Out of the total population of 42815 persons, 332 persons (0.78%) belong to Scheduled Tribes.
The villages having less than 10% ST population are Rekulapalle, Kothapalle, Yenkampeta, Mulkalapalle Gadwal (Rural), Atmakur, Gonpad, Sangala Jilladabanda, Kakulavaram, Paramala, Mellacheruvu Jammiched, Pudur, Anantapur, Beerole, Basapur Gurramgadda.
The villages having more than 50% ST population are None.
Sex ratio of Scheduled tribe population is 500.

Scheduled Tribes Literates and Illiterates by Sex:

	Persons	Males	Females
Literate	50	41	9
Illiterate	282	125	157
Literacy rate	18.7	29.7	7.0
Graduate	0	0	0

Scheduled Tribes (Dominant):
Yerukulas, Sugalis etc.

For their cultural identity please see Appendix-II

Villages without Scheduled Tribes: There are 5 villages without any scheduled tribe population.

Literates and Illiterates by Sex (Total Population):

	Persons	Males	Females
Literate	10,661	7,445	3,216
Illiterate	32,154	14,245	17,909
Literacy rate	30	41	18
Graduate	293	260	33

Agriculture: ***Distribution of villages according to land use:***
Out of 18 villages, Total area (in hectare) is 27127, out of that 75.31 percent is cultivable and 22.06 percent of the cultivable area is irrigated.

Sources of Irrigation (Hectares): Government Canal 1431.43, Private Canal 2.02, Well without Electricity 156.46, Well with Electricity 1336.28, Tubewell without Electricity 0, Tubewell with Electricity 385.48, Tank 831.38, River 362.89, Lake 0, Waterfall 0, Others 0.81.

Villages with population of 5000 to 9999:
Pudur.

Villages with population of 10000 and above: None

Distribution of Workers:

	Persons	Males	Females	WPR
Cultivators	6,998	4,833	2,165	27.68
Agricultural Labour	14,652	5,364	9,288	57.95
Household Industry	462	226	236	1.83
Other Workers	3,173	2,516	657	12.55

Main Workers	21,607	11,925	9,682	85.45
Marginal Workers	3,678	1,014	2,664	14.55
Total Workers	25,285	12,939	12,346	

Religion: Major Religious Communities:

	Persons	Males	Females	Sex Ratio
Hindu (92.97%)	39,803	20,210	19,593	969
Muslim (6.93%)	2,965	1,453	1,512	1,041
Christian (0.05%)	22	12	10	833
Sikh (0%)	1	1	-	-
Buddhists (0%)	-	-	-	-
Jain (0%)	-	-	-	-

Agewise Data:

	Persons	Males	Females	Sex Ratio
All ages	42,815	21,690	21,125	974
0-14	16,556	8,403	8,153	970
15-44	19,268	9,933	9,335	940
45-79	6,749	3,245	3,504	1080
80+	207	90	117	1300
Age not stated	35	19	16	842

Languages (Dominant):

Telugu, Urdu, Tamil, Gondi, Hindi

Disabled Population:

	Persons	Males	Females	%
Total Disabled	834	453	381	
In Seeing	396	218	178	47.48
In Speech	62	27	35	7.43
In Hearing	36	15	21	4.32
In Movement	280	163	117	33.57
Mentally	60	30	30	7.19

GAJAPATHINAGARAM

Gajapathinagaram C.D. Block lies in the southern part of Vizianagaram district. It is a part of Gajapathinaga ram Mandal. The Block is located at a distance of 20 kms. from district headquarters (Vizianagaram). There are 34 villages in the block with the total population of 50,772 persons. Area of the C.D. Block is 122.56 sq. kms. It is bounded in the north by Mandals Mentada and Dattirajeru, in the south by district Vishakhapatnam, and Mandals Bondapalle, Nellimarla and Gurla, in the east by Mandals Merakamudidam and Gurla, and in the west by Mandals Mentada.

Communications :

Roadways : NH- 43: Direction- Vizianagaram to Pottangi. Nearest Villages- Gudivada, Marupalle, Madhupada, Davalapeta, Dola Palem.

Railway Station: Narayana Gajapathi Rajapuram.

River: Champavathi Nadi- Nearest Villages- Kothabaggam, Chittayyavalasa, Konisa, Patruvada, Puritipenta, Kalam rajupeta, Pidiseela, Seetharamapuram,Davalapeta, Dola Palem.

Backwards Region Grants Fund: It receives Backward Region Grants.

Mahila, Samakhya (Education for Women's Equality): It is decleared Socialy and Educationally Backward Block by the Government.

Integrated Child Development Scheme (ICDS) Project: Gajapathinagaram, Total Anganwadi Centres: 158.

Annaul Rainfall: Average Rainfall 886.7 mm

Ground Water: Availability of the Ground Water in the Basin is (Information not avavible) H.A.M .and the utilization is (Information not avavible) H.A.M. It belongs to (Information not avavible) category. Depth to water level varies from 3 to 10 meter below the ground. Most of the wells go down in summer months.

Administration:

Division: Coastal Andhra. Parliamentary Constituency: 20 Vizianagram. District: Vizianagram. Mandal: Gajapath inagaram. Assembly Constituency: 135 Gajapathinagram. Gram Panchayat: 28.

Villages: 34 **Inhabited:** 33 **Uninhabited:** 1

Ranking	District	State	National
Area	29	936	5433
Population	18	484	5240
Sex Ratio	14	130	756
Child Sex Ratio	18	254	794
Literacy Rate	27	966	5542
Density	19	248	2649
Work Participation Rate	8	173	648

Gram Panchayats:

Bangarampeta, Bhudevipeta, Davalapeta Gajapatinagaram, Gangacholapenta, Gudivada Kalamrajupeta, Kenguva, Konisa, Kothabaggam Lingalavalasa, Logisa, M.Gumadam, M.Kothavalasa Madhupada, Marrivalasa, Marupally, Mutcherla Pathabaggam, Pidiseela, Puritipenta, Ramannapeta Salipeta, Seetharampuram, Srirangarajupuram Thummikapalli, Vemali, Zinnam.

Amenities:

Education: Primary School in 32 villages, Middle school in 8 villages, Matriculation or Secondary School in 3 villages, namely Marupalle, Puritipenta, Logisa.

Higher Secondary or Pre University Courses or Intermediate or Junior College in 0 village of the CD Block, College in 1 village, Adult Literacy Center in 27 villages., College is in village, namely Puritipenta.

Medical: Hospital in 0 village, Dispensary in 1 village, Health Center in 1 village, Sub Center in 9 villages, Maternity and Child Welfare Center in 0 village, Community health workers in 0 village.

The Village having Hospital or Dispensary or Health

Center is Marupalle.

Drinking Water: Tap water in 33 villages, Tank water in 33 villages, Well water in 33 villages, Tubewell in 33 villages and more than one source in 33 villages.

Bank: Banking facility in 2 villages, namely, Sriranga Rajapuram, Jinnam.

Credit Society in 8 villages Agricultural Credit Society in 4 Non-Agricultural Credit Society in 6 villages.

Others: Power supply in 33 villages, Cinema hall in 1 village, sport club in 0 village, Stadium or Auditorium or Community Hall in 0 village, Post Office in 17 villages.

There are 17 villages having bus facilities.

Village with most of facilities: Jinnam.

Villages without Amenities (Education): None..

Scheduled Castes: Out of the total population of 50812 persons, 4408 persons (8.68%) belong to Scheduled Castes.

The villages having less than 10% SC population are Bangarammapeta, Marupalle, Madhupada, Salipeta Chittayyavalasa, Konisa, Puritipenta, Davalapeta Dola Palem, M.Venkatapuram, Kalamrajupeta, Pidiseela Seetharamapuram, Thummikapalle, Sriranga Rajapuram Narayana Gajapathi Rajapuram, T.K.Seetharama Puram Lingalavalasa, Vemali, Rangupuram, M.Kothavalasa Logisa.

The villages having more than 50% SC population are None.

Sex ratio of Scheduled Caste population is 503.

Scheduled Castes Literates and Illiterates by Sex:

	Persons	Males	Females
Literate	1,473	903	570
Illiterate	2,935	1,289	1,646
Literacy rate	38.4	47.7	29.4
Graduate	55	42	13

Scheduled Castes (Dominant):

Mala, Madiga, Relli, Dom etc., Generic Castes etc.

For their cultural identity please see Appendix-I

Villages without Scheduled Castes: There are 4 villages without any scheduled caste population.

Scheduled Tribes: Out of the total population of 50812 persons, 598 persons (1.18%) belong to Scheduled Tribes.

The villages having less than 10% ST population are Bangarammapeta, Bhudevipeta, Gudivada, Marupalle Madhupada, Gangachollapenta, Salipeta, Pathabaggam Kothabaggam, Chittayyavalasa, Konisa, Patruvada Puritipenta, Davalapeta, Dola Palem, M.Venkatapuram Kalamrajupeta, Pidiseela, Seetharamapuram Thummikapalle, Sriranga Rajapuram Narayana Gajapathi Rajapuram, Mulakalagumadam T.K.Seetharama Puram, Lingalavalasa, Jinnam Ramannapeta, Vemali, Rangupuram, M.Kothavalasa Mutcherla, Logisa, Kenguva.

The villages having more than 50% ST population are None.

Sex ratio of Scheduled tribe population is 495.

Scheduled Tribes Literates and Illiterates by Sex:

	Persons	Males	Females
Literate	149	94	55
Illiterate	449	208	241
Literacy rate	30.1	37.3	22.6
Graduate	6	4	2

Scheduled Tribes (Dominant):

Konda Dhoras, Yerukulas, Gadabas, Jatapus Kondhs etc.

For their cultural identity please see Appendix-II

Villages without Scheduled Tribes: There are 18 villages without any scheduled tribe population.

Literates and Illiterates by Sex (Total Population):

	Persons	Males	Females
Literate	18,475	11,587	6,888
Illiterate	32,337	13,626	18,711
Literacy rate	42	53	31
Graduate	1,014	814	200

Agriculture: ***Distribution of villages according to land use:*** Out of 34 villages, Total area (in hectare) is 12232, out of that 72.31 percent is cultivable and 51.7 percent of the cultivable area is irrigated.

Sources of Irrigation (Hectares): Government Canal 153.33, Private Canal 0, Well without Electricity 115.56, Well with Electricity 174.12, Tubewell without Electricity 0, Tubewell with Electricity 118.37, Tank 4011.22, River 0, Lake 0, Waterfall 0, Others 0.

Villages with population of 5000 to 9999: Puritipenta.

Villages with population of 10000 and above: None

Distribution of Workers:

	Persons	Males	Females	WPR
Cultivators	9,873	5,753	4,120	34.67
Agricultural Labour	13,045	5,714	7,331	45.8
Household Industry	677	437	240	2.38
Other Workers	4,886	3,679	1,207	17.16
Main Workers	21,920	13,180	8,740	76.96
Marginal Workers	6,561	2,403	4,158	23.04
Total Workers	28,481	15,583	12,898	

Religion: Major Religious Communities:

	Persons	Males	Females	Sex Ratio
Hindu (99.31%)	50,460	25,022	25,438	1,017
Muslim (0.31%)	158	80	78	975
Christian (0.32%)	163	92	71	772
Sikh (0.01%)	5	4	1	250
Buddhists (0%)	1	1	-	-

Jain (0%)	-	-	-	-

Agewise Data:

	Persons	Males	Females	Sex Ratio
All ages	50,812	25,213	25,599	1015
0-14	15,483	7,929	7,554	953
15-44	23,944	11,840	12,104	1022
45-79	11,063	5,281	5,782	1095
80+	194	86	108	1256
Age not stated	128	77	51	662

Languages (Dominant):

Telugu, Tamil, Urdu, Gadaba, Gondi

Disabled Population:

	Persons	Males	Females	%
Total Disabled	1,136	591	545	
In Seeing	529	270	259	46.57
In Speech	126	68	58	11.09
In Hearing	66	29	37	5.81
In Movement	294	166	128	25.88
Mentally	121	58	63	10.65

GAJWEL

Gajwel C.D. Block lies in the South Eastern part of Medak district. The Block is located at a distance of 82 kms. from district headquarters (Medak). There are 26 villages in the block with the total population of 67,465 persons. Area of the C.D. Block is 206.60 sq. kms. It is bounded by Mandal Mirdoddi on north, Mandals Warangal and Jagdevpur on south, Mandals Konda pak and Jagdevpur on east, and Mandal Doulatabad on west.

Communications :

Roadways : State Highways (S.H.): Direction- Medak to Jagdevpur. and Hyderabad to Karimnagar. Nearest Village s- Jaligaon, Gajwel, Pragnapur, Akkaram, Rimmanguda, Kodakondla.

River: Kundaliar Nadi- Nearest Villages- Kolgur, Ahmadi pur, Singatam, Burugupalle, Havaiguda, Datarpalle, Rimma nguda, Kodakondla.

Backwards Region Grants Fund: It receives Backward Region Grants.

Annual Rainfall : Annual Rainfall 814 mm

Ground Water : Availability of the Ground Water in the Basin is 1787 H.A.M. and the utilization is 1921 H.A.M. It belongs to Over Exploited category. Depth to water level varies from 5 to 10 meter below the ground. Most of the wells go down in summer months, according to the Ground Water Estimation Committee.

Natural Division : Telangana Plateau Region

Administration:

Division: Telangana. Parliamentary Constituency: 6 Medak. District: Medak. Mandal: Gajwel. Assembly Consti tuency: 42 Gajwel. Gram Panchayat: 26.

Villages: 26 **Inhabited:** 25 **Uninhabited:** 1

Ranking	District	State	National
Area	26	513	4067
Population	6	172	4585
Sex Ratio	23	555	1970
Child Sex Ratio	43	980	4463
Literacy Rate	5	399	3471
Density	27	613	3298
Work Participation Rate	5	316	1655

Gram Panchayats:

Ahmedipur, Akkaram, Anantharaopally Bangla Venkatapur, Bayyaram, Bejgaon, Burugupalle Dacharam, Datarpalle, Dharmareddipalle, Dilalpur Gajwel, Giripally, Jaligaon, Kodakandla, Kolgur Komati Banda, Kyasaram, Makta Masanpalle Mutrajpalle, Pedched, Pragnapur, Rimmanaguda Serigiripalle, Singatam, Srigiripalle.

Amenities:

Education: Primary School in 25 villages, Middle school in 18 villages, Matriculation or Secondary School in 5 villages, namely Ahmadipur, Gajwel, Pragnapur, Rimmanguda, Kodakondla.

Higher Secondary or Pre University Courses or Intermediate or Junior College in 1 village of the CD Block,, namely Gajwel.

College in 1 village, Adult Literacy Center in 10 villages., College is in village, namely Gajwel.

Medical: Hospital in 1 village, Dispensary in 2 villages, Health Center in 2 villages, Sub Center in 10 villages, Maternity and Child Welfare Center in 2 villages, Community health workers in 0 village.

The Villages having Hospital or Dispensary or Health Center are Gajwel, Pragnapur.

Drinking Water: Tap water in 25 villages, Tank water in 25 villages, Well water in 24 villages, Tubewell in 25 villages and more than one source in 25 villages.

Bank: Banking facility in 3 villages, namely, Ahmadipur, Gajwel, Kodakondla.

Credit Society in 15 villages Agricultural Credit Society in 9 Non-Agricultural Credit Society in 14 villages.

Others: Power supply in 25 villages, Cinema hall in 2 villages, sport club in 1 village, Stadium or Auditorium or Community Hall in 1 village, Post Office in 17 villages.

There are 22 villages having bus facilities.

Villages with most of facilities: Ahmadipur Gajwel, Kodakondla.

Villages without Amenities (Education): None..

Scheduled Castes: Out of the total population of 67465 persons, 13062 persons (19.36%) belong to Scheduled Castes.

The villages having less than 10% SC population are None..

The villages having more than 50% SC population are None.

Sex ratio of Scheduled Caste population is 500.

Scheduled Castes Literates and Illiterates by Sex:

	Persons	Males	Females
Literate	4,296	2,898	1,398
Illiterate	8,766	3,629	5,137
Literacy rate	39.5	53.4	25.6
Graduate	54	46	8

Scheduled Castes (Dominant):

Madiga, Mala, Generic Castes etc., Manne, Bindla

For their cultural identity please see Appendix-I

Villages without Scheduled Castes: There is 1 village without any scheduled caste population.

Scheduled Tribes: Out of the total population of 67465 persons, 587 persons (0.87%) belong to Scheduled Tribes.

The villages having less than 10% ST population are Dilalpur, Seripalle, Kolgur, Ahmadipur, Singatam Burugupalle, Dacharam, Pedched, Bejgaon, Bayyaram Jaligaon, Dharmareddipalle, Bangla Venkatapur Maqta Masanpalle, Komatibanda, Gajwel, Sangapur Mutrajpalle, Pragnapur, Srigiripalle, Akkaram Datarpalle, Kyasaram, Rimmanguda, Kodakondla.

The villages having more than 50% ST population are None.

Sex ratio of Scheduled tribe population is 453.

Scheduled Tribes Literates and Illiterates by Sex:

	Persons	Males	Females
Literate	199	129	70
Illiterate	388	192	196
Literacy rate	46.7	60.3	33.0
Graduate	9	7	2

Scheduled Tribes (Dominant):

Yerukulas, Sugalis etc., Generic Tribes etc. Gond etc., Chenchu etc.

For their cultural identity please see Appendix-II

Villages without Scheduled Tribes: There are 6 villages without any scheduled tribe population.

Literates and Illiterates by Sex (Total Population):

	Persons	Males	Females
Literate	32,149	20,064	12,085
Illiterate	35,316	13,986	21,330
Literacy rate	56	70	42
Graduate	1,400	1,118	282

Agriculture: ***Distribution of villages according to land use:***

Out of 26 villages, Total area (in hectare) is 20659, out of that 75.78 percent is cultivable and 21.06 percent of the cultivable area is irrigated.

Sources of Irrigation (Hectares): Government Canal 474.87, Private Canal 0, Well without Electricity 0, Well with Electricity 0, Tubewell without Electricity 1.2, Tubewell with Electricity 564, Tank 2257.5, River 0, Lake 0, Waterfall 0, Others 0.

Villages with population of 5000 to 9999:

Pragnapur.

Villages with population of 10000 and above:

Gajwel.

Distribution of Workers:

	Persons	Males	Females	WPR
Cultivators	10,867	6,639	4,228	31.72
Agricultural Labour	10,620	3,730	6,890	30.99
Household Industry	3,263	846	2,417	9.52
Other Workers	9,514	7,568	1,946	27.77
Main Workers	28,719	17,329	11,390	83.82
Marginal Workers	5,545	1,454	4,091	16.18
Total Workers	34,264	18,783	15,481	

Religion: Major Religious Communities:

	Persons	Males	Females	Sex Ratio
Hindu (89.71%)	60,525	30,550	29,975	981
Muslim (9.23%)	6,229	3,167	3,062	967
Christian (0.92%)	623	292	331	1,134
Sikh (0.01%)	4	1	3	3,000
Buddhists (0.01%)	6	5	1	200
Jain (0%)	-	-	-	-

Agewise Data:

	Persons	Males	Females	Sex Ratio
All ages	67,465	34,050	33,415	981
0-14	23,427	12,069	11,358	941
15-44	30,462	15,329	15,133	987
45-79	12,992	6,386	6,606	1034
80+	490	214	276	1290
Age not stated	94	52	42	808

Languages (Dominant):

Telugu, Urdu, Hindi, Tamil, Gondi

Disabled Population:

	Persons	Males	Females	%
Total Disabled	958	558	400	
In Seeing	359	198	161	37.47
In Speech	102	53	49	10.65
In Hearing	38	17	21	3.97
In Movement	329	210	119	34.34
Mentally	130	80	50	13.57

GALIVEEDU

Galiveedu C.D. Block lies in the south-western part of Cuddapah district. The Block is located at a distance of 81 kms. from district headquarters (Cuddapah).

There are 14 villages in the block with the total popul ation of 46,168 persons. Area of the C.D. Block is 316. 06 sq. kms. It is bounded in the north by Mandal Galive edu, in the south and west by district Anantapur, and in the east by Mandals Lakkireddipalle, Rayachoti and Chinnamandem.

Communications:

Roadways : State Highway (S.H.): Direction- Kadiri to Rayachoti. Nearest Villages- Veligallu, Eguvagottiveedu, Galiveedu.

River: Papaghni Nadi- Nearest Villages- Talamudipi, Pandikunta, Thumukunta, Garugupalle, Pyarampalle, Araveedu, Galiveedu.

It receives Backward Region Grants, and is also identif ied as a drought-prone area as well.

Annual Rainfall: Average Rainfall 730 mm

Ground Water: Availability of the Ground Water in the Basin is 2672 H.A.M.and the utilization is 1927 H.A. M.It belongs to SC category. Depth to water level varies from 5 to 10 meter below the ground. Most of the wells go down in summer months, according to the Ground Water Estimation Committee.

Forest and Reserved **Forest:** Nearest Villages- Nooliveedu, Gundlacheruvu, Gopanapalle, Eguvagottiveedu.

Natural Division : Rayalaseema Region

Administration:

Division: Rayala Seema. Parliamentary Constituency: 41 Rajampet.District: Cuddapah.

Mandal: Galiveedu. Assembly Constituency: 247 Rayachoti.

Gram Panchayat: 17.

Villages: 14 **Inhabited:** 14 **Uninhabited:** 0

Ranking	District	State	National
Area	9	129	2613
Population	14	628	5459
Sex Ratio	32	783	2642
Child Sex Ratio	34	880	3883
Literacy Rate	44	483	3750
Density	15	501	5610
Work Participation Rate	34	915	1298

Gram Panchayats:

Araveedu, Boreddigaripalli, Cheemala Cheruvu Palli Eguva Gottiveedu, Galiveedu, Garugupalli Gopanapalli, Gorancheruvu, Gundlacheruvu, Korlakunta Nooleeveedu, Pandikunta, Poolia Kunta, Pyarampalli Talamudipi, Thummukunta, Veligallu.

Amenities:

Education: Primary School in 14 villages, Middle school in 6 villages, Matriculation or Secondary School in 4 villages, namely Nooliveedu, Galiveedu, Araveedu, Eguvagottiveedu.

Higher Secondary or Pre University Courses or Intermediate or Junior College in 1 village of the CD Block,, namely Galiveedu.

College in 1 village, Adult Literacy Center in 3 villages., College is in village, namely Galiveedu.

Medical: Hospital in 0 village, Dispensary in 2 villages, Health Center in 4 villages, Sub Center in 5 villages, Maternity and Child Welfare Center in 0 village, Community health workers in 0 village.

The Villages having Hospital or Dispensary or Health Center are Nooliveedu, Galiveedu.

Drinking Water: Tap water in 14 villages, Tank water in 14 villages, Well water in 14 villages, Tubewell in 14 villages and more than one source in 14 villages.

Bank: Banking facility in 2 villages, namely, Nooliveedu, Galiveedu.

Credit Society in 4 villages Agricultural Credit Society in 3 Non-Agricultural Credit Society in 3 villages.

Others: Power supply in 14 villages, Cinema hall in 2 villages, sport club in 0 village, Stadium or Auditorium or Community Hall in 0 village, Post Office in 13 villages.

There are 13 villages having bus facilities.

Villages with most of facilities: Nooliveedu Galiveedu.

Villages without Amenities (Education): None..

Scheduled Castes: Out of the total population of 46168 persons, 3813 persons (8.26%) belong to Scheduled Castes.

The villages having less than 10% SC population are Korlakunta, Pulikunta, Thumukunta, Garugupalle Gundlacheruvu, Pyarampalle, Veligallu, Galiveedu Eguvagottiveedu.

The villages having more than 50% SC population are None.

Sex ratio of Scheduled Caste population is 489.

Scheduled Castes Literates and Illiterates by Sex:

	Persons	Males	Females
Literate	1,346	911	435
Illiterate	2,467	1,037	1,430
Literacy rate	41.2	54.6	27.2
Graduate	23	18	5

Scheduled Castes (Dominant):

Madiga, Mala

For their cultural identity please see Appendix-I

Villages without Scheduled Castes: There are 0 village without any scheduled caste population.

Scheduled Tribes: Out of the total population of 46168 persons, 2038 persons (4.41%) belong to Scheduled Tribes.

The villages having less than 10% ST population are Talamudipi, Korlakunta, Pulikunta, Nooliveedu Thumukunta, Garugupalle, Gundlacheruvu, Gopanapalle Pyarampalle, Galiveedu, Araveedu, Eguvagottiveedu.

The villages having more than 50% ST population are None.

Sex ratio of Scheduled tribe population is 474.

Scheduled Tribes Literates and Illiterates by Sex:

	Persons	Males	Females
Literate	854	581	273
Illiterate	1,184	490	694
Literacy rate	48.1	63.1	32.0
Graduate	15	15	0

Scheduled Tribes (Dominant):

Sugalis etc., Yerukulas, Yenadis

For their cultural identity please see Appendix-II

Villages without Scheduled Tribes: There are 2 villages without any scheduled tribe population.

Literates and Illiterates by Sex (Total Population):

	Persons	Males	Females
Literate	21,786	14,330	7,456
Illiterate	24,382	9,146	15,236
Literacy rate	54	71	38
Graduate	735	627	108

Agriculture: ***Distribution of villages according to land use:*** Out of 14 villages, Total area (in hectare) is 31608, out of that 46.91 percent is cultivable and 12.05 percent of the cultivable area is irrigated.

Sources of Irrigation (Hectares): Government Canal 0, Private Canal 0, Well without Electricity 283.24, Well with Electricity 441.92, Tubewell without Electricity 0, Tubewell with Electricity 281.51, Tank 780.04, River 0, Lake 0, Waterfall 0, Others 0.

Villages with population of 5000 to 9999:

Nooliveedu.

Villages with population of 10000 and above:

Galiveedu.

Distribution of Workers:

	Persons	Males	Females	WPR
Cultivators	8,869	6,083	2,786	36.06
Agricultural Labour	11,091	4,666	6,425	45.09
Household Industry	707	330	377	2.87
Other Workers	3,929	3,017	912	15.97
Main Workers	16,182	11,453	4,729	65.79
Marginal Workers	8,414	2,643	5,771	34.21
Total Workers	24,596	14,096	10,500	

Religion: Major Religious Communities:

	Persons	Males	Females	Sex Ratio
Hindu (80.37%)	37,107	18,826	18,281	971
Muslim (19.56%)	9,029	4,632	4,397	949
Christian (0.05%)	22	12	10	833
Sikh (0%)	-	-	-	-
Buddhists (0%)	-	-	-	-
Jain (0.01%)	6	3	3	1,000

Agewise Data:

	Persons	Males	Females	Sex Ratio
All ages	46,168	23,476	22,692	967
0-14	14,704	7,628	7,076	928
15-44	21,231	10,960	10,271	937
45-79	9,790	4,700	5,090	1083
80+	412	171	241	1409
Age not stated	31	17	14	824

Languages (Dominant):

Telugu, Urdu, Hindi, Tamil, Gondi

Disabled Population:

	Persons	Males	Females	%
Total Disabled	1,091	585	506	
In Seeing	424	211	213	38.86
In Speech	113	64	49	10.36
In Hearing	84	41	43	7.7
In Movement	352	204	148	32.26
Mentally	118	65	53	10.82

GAMBHIRAOPET

Gambhiraopet C.D. Block lies in the western part of Karimnagar district. The Block is located at a distance of 81 kms. from district headquarters (Karimnagar). There are 18 villages in the block with the total population of 44,186 persons. Area of the C.D. Block is 156.92 sq. kms. It is bounded by Yellareddipet Mandal on north and east, Mustabad Mandal on south-east, Medal district on south, Nizamabad district on west.

Communications :

Roadways : State Highway (S.H.): Direction- Kamareddy to Karimnagar. Nearest Villages- Gajasingaram, Gorantial, Samudralingapuram, Dammannapet.

River: Manner Nadi- Nearest Villages- Laxmipuram, Raman ujapuram, Mallareddipet, Srinivasapuram, Gambhiraopet, Narmala, Desaipet, Kollamaddi, Kothapalle, Lingannapet, Mucherla.

Backwards Region Grants Fund: It receives Backward Region Grants.

Annual Rainfall: Average Rainfall 855 mm

Ground Water: Availability of the Ground Water in the Basin is 1499 H.A.M. and the utilization is 1363 H. A.M. It belongs to Critical category. Depth to water level varies from more than 10 meter below the ground. Most of the wells go down in summer months. The well density in the entire block is 13 wells per sq. km. Total no. of the wells in the block are enumerated as 2063, according to the Ground Water Estimation Commi ttee.

Natural Division : Godavari Depression Region

Administration:

Division: Telangana. Parliamentary Constituency: 3 Karimnagar. District: Karimnagar. Mandal: Gambhiraopet. Assembly Constituency: 29 Sircilla. Gram Panchayat: 15

Villages: 18 **Inhabited:** 17 **Uninhabited:** 1

Ranking	District	State	National
Area	42	790	4928
Population	36	689	5546
Sex Ratio	12	68	475
Child Sex Ratio	29	580	2281
Literacy Rate	32	779	4816
Density	26	437	3732
Work Participation Rate	24	426	1082

Gram Panchayats:

Dammannapet, Desaipet, Gajasingavaram, Gambhiraopet Gorantala, Kollamaddi, Kothapally, Lingannapet Mallareddypet, Mucherla, Mustafanager, Nagampet Narmal, Samudralingapur, Srigadha.

Amenities:

Education: Primary School in 16 villages, Middle school in 11 villages, Matriculation or Secondary School in 6 villages, namely Gorantial, Dammannapet, Mallareddipet, Gambhiraopet, Kothapalle, Lingannapet.

Higher Secondary or Pre University Courses or Intermediate or Junior College in 1 village of the CD Block,, namely Gambhiraopet.

College in 1 village, Adult Literacy Center in 5 villages., College is in village, namely Gambhiraopet.

Medical: Hospital in 1 village, Dispensary in 1 village, Health Center in 1 village, Sub Center in 7 villages, Maternity and Child Welfare Center in 0 village, Community health workers in 0 village.

The Village having Hospital or Dispensary or Health Center is Gambhiraopet.

Drinking Water: Tap water in 17 villages, Tank water in 17 villages, Well water in 17 villages, Tubewell in 17 villages and more than one source in 17 villages.

Bank: Banking facility in 2 villages, namely, Gambhiraopet, Lingannapet.

Credit Society in 11 villages Agricultural Credit Society in 2 Non-Agricultural Credit Society in 11 villages.

Others: Power supply in 17 villages, Cinema hall in 1 village, sport club in 0 village, Stadium or Auditorium or Community Hall in 0 village, Post Office in 12 villages.

There are 15 villages having bus facilities.

Villages with most of facilities: Gambhiraopet Lingannapet.

Villages without amenities (Education):

Ramanujapuram..

Scheduled Castes: Out of the total population of 44186 persons, 8590 persons (19.44%) belong to Scheduled Castes. The villages having less than 10% SC population are None..

The villages having more than 50% SC population are None.

Sex ratio of Scheduled Caste population is 509.

Scheduled Castes Literates and Illiterates by Sex:

	Persons	Males	Females
Literate	3,033	1,933	1,100
Illiterate	5,557	2,287	3,270
Literacy rate	40.6	52.9	28.9
Graduate	50	46	4

Scheduled Castes (Dominant):

Mala, Madiga, Chamar etc., Generic Castes etc. Bindla

For their cultural identity please see Appendix-I

Villages without Scheduled Castes: There are 3 villages without any scheduled caste population.

Scheduled Tribes: Out of the total population of 44186 persons, 1854 persons (4.2%) belong to Scheduled Tribes. The villages having less than 10% ST population are Gajasingaram, Gorantial, Samudralingapuram Lingampallekhurdu, Ramanujapuram, Mallareddipet Gambhiraopet, Mustafanagar, Narmala, Desaipet Kollamaddi, Srigadha, Kothapalle, Lingannapet.

The villages having more than 50% ST population are None.

Sex ratio of Scheduled tribe population is 508.

Scheduled Tribes Literates and Illiterates by Sex:

	Persons	Males	Females
Literate	442	286	156
Illiterate	1,412	626	786
Literacy rate	29.4	38.3	20.6
Graduate	5	5	0

Scheduled Tribes (Dominant):

Sugalis etc., Yerukulas, Generic Tribes etc., Andh

For their cultural identity please see Appendix-II

Villages without Scheduled Tribes: There are 7 villages without any scheduled tribe population.

Literates and Illiterates by Sex (Total Population):

	Persons	Males	Females
Literate	18,457	11,693	6,764
Illiterate	25,729	10,064	15,665
Literacy rate	48	62	35
Graduate	495	431	64

Agriculture: ***Distribution of villages according to land use:*** Out of 18 villages, Total area (in hectare) is 15691, out of that 61.57 percent is cultivable and 29.55 percent of the cultivable area is irrigated.

Sources of Irrigation (Hectares): Government Canal 845.71, Private Canal 40.46, Well without Electricity 0, Well with Electricity 1554.48, Tubewell without Electricity 0, Tubewell with Electricity 11.74, Tank 0, River 0, Lake 0, Waterfall 402.26, Others 0.

Villages with population of 5000 to 9999: None

Villages with population of 10000 and above:

Gambhiraopet.

Distribution of Workers:

	Persons	Males	Females	WPR
Cultivators	7,865	5,020	2,845	32.84
Agricultural Labour	5,580	2,896	2,684	23.3
Household Industry	4,770	579	4,191	19.92
Other Workers	5,734	3,797	1,937	23.94
Main Workers	21,625	11,269	10,356	90.3
Marginal Workers	2,324	1,023	1,301	9.7
Total Workers	23,949	12,292	11,657	

Religion: Major Religious Communities:

	Persons	Males	Females	Sex Ratio
Hindu (93.43%)	41,284	20,323	20,961	1,031
Muslim (5.88%)	2,600	1,297	1,303	1,005
Christian (0.67%)	296	134	162	1,209
Sikh (0%)	-	-	-	-
Buddhists (0%)	-	-	-	-
Jain (0%)	-	-	-	-

Agewise Data:

	Persons	Males	Females	Sex Ratio
All ages	44,186	21,757	22,429	1031
0-14	13,709	6,886	6,823	991
15-44	20,756	10,224	10,532	1030
45-79	9,262	4,441	4,821	1086
80+	437	197	240	1218
Age not stated	22	9	13	1444

Languages (Dominant):

Telugu, Urdu, Hindi, Tamil, Oriya

Disabled Population:

	Persons	Males	Females	%
Total Disabled	850	520	330	
In Seeing	397	249	148	46.71
In Speech	80	46	34	9.41
In Hearing	32	9	23	3.76
In Movement	257	168	89	30.24
Mentally	84	48	36	9.88

GAMPALAGUDEM

Gampalagudem C.D. Block lies in the northern part of Krishna district. The Block is located at a distance of 145 kms. from district headquarters (Machilipatnam). There are 21 villages in the block with the total population of 68,108 persons. Area of the C.D. Block is 209.65 sq. kms. It is bounded in the north, south and west by district Khammam, and in the east by Mandals Tiruvuru and A. Konduru.

Communications:

Roadways : Metalled Roads: Nearest Villages- Rajavaram, Penugolanu, Peda Komira, Chennavaram, Gampalagudem, Kanumuru, Kothapalle.

River: Kattaleru Nadi- Nearest Villages- Gosaveedu, Peda Komira, Gampalagudem, Kanumuru, Anumollanka, Kothapalle, Vinagadapa.

Annaul Rainfall: Average Rainfall 1048 mm

Ground Water: Availability of the Ground Water in the Basin is (Information not avavible) H.A.M .and the utilization is (Information not avavible) H.A.M. It belongs to (Information not avavible) category. Depth to water level varies from 3 to 10 meter below the ground. Most of the wells go down in summer months.

Natural Division : Krishna Delta Region

Administration:

Division: Coastal Andhra. Parliamentary Constituency: 29 Vijayawada. District: Krishna. Mandal: Gampalagudem. Assembly Constituency: 188 Tiruvuru (SC). Gram Panchay at: 24.

Villages: 21 **Inhabited:** 21 **Uninhabited:** 0

Ranking	District	State	National
Area	9	493	4021
Population	13	162	4550
Sex Ratio	47	1033	3793
Child Sex Ratio	44	899	3972
Literacy Rate	47	587	4179
Density	7	452	3314
Work Participation Rate	28	320	1134

Gram Panchayats:

Ambireddigudem, Amudala Lanka, Arlapadu Chintalanarva, Dundiralapadu, Gadevarigudem Gampalagudem, Gosaveedu, Gullapudi, Kanumuru Konijerla, Kothapalli, Lingala, Meduru, Nemali Peda Komera, Penugolanu, Rajavaram, Satyalapadu Sobbala, Tunikipadu, Ummadidevarapalli, Utukuru Vinagadapa.

Amenities:

Education: Primary School in 21 villages, Middle school in 12 villages, Matriculation or Secondary School in 5 villages, namely Nemali, Utukuru, Penugolanu, Gampalagudem, Kothapalle.

Higher Secondary or Pre University Courses or Intermediate or Junior College in 1 village of the CD Block,, namely Gampalagudem.

College in 0 village, Adult Literacy Center in 4 villages.

Medical: Hospital in 0 village, Dispensary in 1 village, Health Center in 2 villages, Sub Center in 10 villages, Maternity and Child Welfare Center in 2 villages, Community health workers in 0 village.

The Village having Hospital or Dispensary or Health Center is Penugolanu.

Drinking Water: Tap water in 8 villages, Tank water in 5 villages, Well water in 18 villages, Tubewell in 5

villages and more than one source in 19 villages.
Bank: Banking facility in 9 villages, namely, Ummadidevarapalle, Nemali, Konijerla, Utukuru Penugolanu, Gosaveedu, Meduru, Gampalagudem Vinagadapa.
Credit Society in 16 villages Agricultural Credit Society in 12 Non-Agricultural Credit Society in 13 villages.
Others: Power supply in 21 villages, Cinema hall in 4 villages, sport club in 0 village, Stadium or Auditorium or Community Hall in 0 village, Post Office in 14 villages.
There are 20 villages having bus facilities.
Villages with most of facilities: Nemali, Utukuru Penugolanu, Gosaveedu, Meduru, Gampalagudem Vinagadapa.
Villages without Amenities (Education): None..
Scheduled Castes: Out of the total population of 68108 persons, 21839 persons (32.07%) belong to Scheduled Castes.
The villages having less than 10% SC population are None..
The villages having more than 50% SC population are None.
Sex ratio of Scheduled Caste population is 479.

Scheduled Castes Literates and Illiterates by Sex:

	Persons	Males	Females
Literate	7,975	5,104	2,871
Illiterate	13,864	6,270	7,594
Literacy rate	42.3	52.1	31.7
Graduate	243	192	51

Scheduled Castes (Dominant):
Madiga, Mala, Beda Jangam etc., Mala Dasu Madiga Dasu etc.
For their cultural identity please see Appendix-I
Villages without Scheduled Castes: There are 0 village without any scheduled caste population.
Scheduled Tribes: Out of the total population of 68108 persons, 1155 persons (1.7%) belong to Scheduled Tribes.
The villages having less than 10% ST population are Ummadidevarapalle, Nemali, Konijerla, Utukuru Dundiralapadu, Tunikipadu, Rajavaram, Penugolanu Gosaveedu, Peda Komira, Chennavaram, Meduru Arlapadu, Gullapudi, Lingala, Gampalagudem, Kanumuru Anumollanka, Kothapalle, Narikampadu.
The villages having more than 50% ST population are None.
Sex ratio of Scheduled tribe population is 480.

Scheduled Tribes Literates and Illiterates by Sex:

	Persons	Males	Females
Literate	402	270	132
Illiterate	753	331	422
Literacy rate	40.7	52.2	28.0
Graduate	22	21	1

Scheduled Tribes (Dominant):
Sugalis etc., Yerukulas, Kammara Generic Tribes etc., Koya etc.
For their cultural identity please see Appendix-II
Villages without Scheduled Tribes: There is 1 village without any scheduled tribe population.

Literates and Illiterates by Sex (Total Population):

	Persons	Males	Females
Literate	31,131	18,727	12,404
Illiterate	36,977	16,302	20,675
Literacy rate	52	61	43
Graduate	1,156	943	213

Agriculture: ***Distribution of villages according to land use:*** Out of 21 villages, Total area (in hectare) is 20965, out of that 78.35 percent is cultivable and 29.2 percent of the cultivable area is irrigated.
Sources of Irrigation (Hectares): Government Canal 2519.34, Private Canal 32.3, Well without Electricity 91.87, Well with Electricity 192.51, Tubewell without Electricity 40.4, Tubewell with Electricity 93.7, Tank 866.3, River 0, Lake 0, Waterfall 161.9, Others 797.56.
Villages with population of 5000 to 9999: Utukuru, Penugolanu, Gampalagudem.
Villages with population of 10000 and above: None

Distribution of Workers:

	Persons	Males	Females	WPR
Cultivators	5,986	4,382	1,604	16.15
Agricultural Labour	24,507	10,970	13,537	66.12
Household Industry	491	335	156	1.32
Other Workers	6,082	5,109	973	16.41
Main Workers	34,844	20,176	14,668	94.01
Marginal Workers	2,222	620	1,602	5.99
Total Workers	37,066	20,796	16,270	

Religion: Major Religious Communities:

	Persons	Males	Females	Sex Ratio
Hindu (95.53%)	65,062	33,496	31,566	942
Muslim (3.66%)	2,491	1,270	1,221	961
Christian (0.79%)	536	251	285	1,135
Sikh (0%)	1	1	-	-
Buddhists (0%)	-	-	-	-
Jain (0%)	-	-	-	-

Agewise Data:

	Persons	Males	Females	Sex Ratio
All ages	68,108	35,029	33,079	944
0-14	21,465	11,085	10,380	936
15-44	33,263	17,086	16,177	947
45-79	12,771	6,538	6,233	953
80+	553	297	256	862
Age not stated	56	23	33	1435

Languages (Dominant):
Telugu, Urdu, Hindi, Tamil, Gondi

Disabled Population:

	Persons	Males	Females	%
Total Disabled	1,500	841	659	
In Seeing	423	234	189	28.2
In Speech	164	78	86	10.93
In Hearing	92	47	45	6.13
In Movement	604	375	229	40.27
Mentally	217	107	110	14.47

GANAPAVARAM

Ganapavaram C.D. Block lies in the southern part of West Godavari district. The Block is located at a dista nce of 60 kms. from district headquarters (Eluru). There are 25 villages in the block with the total population of 66,656 persons. Area of the C.D. Block is 99.85 sq. kms. It is bounded in the north by Mandal Pentapadu, in the south by Mandal Undi, in the east by Mandal Attili, and in the west by Mandal Nidamarru.

Communications :

Roadways : Metalled Roads: Nearest Villages- Jagannadhap uram, Chinaramachandrapuram, Saripalle, Ganapavaram, Kommara, Velagapalle, Varadarajapuram, Valluru, Veeres warapuram, Cherukuganuma Agraharam, Pippara, Moyyeru, Venkatrajapuram, Agraharagopavaram, Kesavaram, Seethal amkonde Padu.

Backwards Region Grants Fund: It receives Backward Region Grants.

Integrated Child Development Scheme (ICDS) Project: Ganapavaram, Total Anganwadi Centres: 175

Annaul Rainfall: Average Rainfall 1523 mm

Ground Water: Availability of the Ground Water in the Basin is (Information not avavible) H.A.M .and the utilization is (Information not avavible) H.A.M. It belongs to (Information not avavible) category. Depth to water level varies from 3 to 10 meter below the ground. Most of the wells go down in summer months.

Natural Division : Godavari Delta Region

Administration:

Division: Coastal Andhra. Parliamentary Constituency: 27 Eluru.District: West Godavari.

Mandal: Ganapavaram. Assembly Constituency: 182 Ungutur. Gram Panchayat: 25.

Villages: 25 **Inhabited:** 25 **Uninhabited:** 0

Ranking	District	State	National
Area	32	1024	5720
Population	25	183	4614
Sex Ratio	14	377	1555
Child Sex Ratio	6	100	273
Literacy Rate	11	14	420
Density	41	1007	1582
Work Participation Rate	16	51	3893

Gram Panchayats:

Agraharagopavaram, Ardhavaram
Cherukuganuma Agraharam, D.Appannapeta
Dasulakumudavalli, Ganapavaram, Jalli Kakinada
Jalli Kommara, Kasipadu, Kesavaram, Komarru
Komatlapalem, Kothapalli, Moyyeru, Muggalla
Mupparthipadu, Pippara, Saripalli
Seethalamkondepadu, Vakapalli, Valluru
Varadharajapuram, Veereswarapuram, Velagapalli
Venkatrajapuram.

Amenities:

Education: Primary School in 25 villages, Middle school in 12 villages, Matriculation or Secondary School in 7 villages, namely Saripalle, Ganapavaram, Ardhavaram, Kasipadu, Pippara, Dasulakumudavalli, Kesavaram.

Higher Secondary or Pre University Courses or Inter-mediate or Junior College in 1 village of the CD Block,, namely Ganapavaram.

College in 1 village, Adult Literacy Center in 20 villages., College is in village, namely Ganapavaram.

Medical: Hospital in 1 village, Dispensary in 2 villages, Health Center in 1 village, Sub Center in 11 villages, Maternity and Child Welfare Center in 0 village, Community health workers in 0 village.

The Villages having Hospital or Dispensary or Health Center are Ganapavaram, Ardhavaram, Pippara.

Drinking Water: Tap water in 25 villages, Tank water in 25 villages, Well water in 25 villages, Tubewell in 25 villages and more than one source in 25 villages.

Bank: Banking facility in 6 villages, namely, Saripalle, Ganapavaram, Kommara, Ardhavaram, Pippara Kesavaram.

Credit Society in 9 villages Agricultural Credit Society in 8 Non-Agricultural Credit Society in 1 village.

Others: Power supply in 25 villages, Cinema hall in 2 villages, sport club in 0 village, Stadium or Auditorium or Community Hall in 0 village, Post Office in 22 villages.

There are 25 villages having bus facilities.

Villages with most of facilities: Saripalle Ganapavaram, Kommara, Ardhavaram, Pippara, Kesavaram.

Villages without Amenities (Education): None..

Scheduled Castes: Out of the total population of 66656 persons, 11282 persons (16.93%) belong to Scheduled Castes.

The villages having less than 10% SC population are Chinaramachandrapuram, Saripalle, Kommara Cherukuganuma Agraharam.

The villages having more than 50% SC population are None.

Sex ratio of Scheduled Caste population is 494.

Scheduled Castes Literates and Illiterates by Sex:

	Persons	Males	Females
Literate	7,212	3,944	3,268
Illiterate	4,070	1,765	2,305
Literacy rate	74.5	79.6	69.2
Graduate	179	146	33

Scheduled Castes (Dominant):

Mala, Adi Andhra, Madiga, Relli, Beda Jangam etc.

For their cultural identity please see Appendix-I

Villages without Scheduled Castes: There are 0 village without any scheduled caste population.

Scheduled Tribes: Out of the total population of 66656 persons, 586 persons (0.88%) belong to Scheduled Tribes. The villages having less than 10% ST population are Jagannadhapuram, Chinaramachandrapuram, Saripalle Ganapavaram, Kommara, Velagapalle, Varadarajapuram Kothapalle, Ardhavaram, Jallikakinada, Muggula Valluru, Veereswarapuram, Vakapalle Cherukuganuma Agraharam, Kasipadu, Pippara, Komarru Dasulakumudavalli, Moyyeru, Mupparthipadu Venkatrajapuram, Agraharagopavaram, Kesavaram Seethalamkonde Padu.

The villages having more than 50% ST population are None.

Sex ratio of Scheduled tribe population is 447.

Scheduled Tribes Literates and Illiterates by Sex:

	Persons	Males	Females
Literate	256	155	101
Illiterate	330	169	161
Literacy rate	51.5	56.0	45.9
Graduate	5	4	1

Scheduled Tribes (Dominant):

Yerukulas, Yenadis, Sugalis etc., Chenchu etc. Koya etc.

For their cultural identity please see Appendix-II

Villages without Scheduled Tribes: There are 3 villages without any scheduled tribe population.

Literates and Illiterates by Sex (Total Population):

	Persons	Males	Females
Literate	45,831	24,306	21,525
Illiterate	20,825	9,172	11,653
Literacy rate	78	82	74
Graduate	1,669	1,254	415

Agriculture: ***Distribution of villages according to land use:*** Out of 25 villages, Total area (in hectare) is 9985, out of that 77.36 percent is cultivable and 100 percent of the cultivable area is irrigated.

Sources of Irrigation (Hectares): Government Canal 7724.52, Private Canal 0, Well without Electricity 0, Well with Electricity 0, Tubewell without Electricity 0, Tubewell with Electricity 0, Tank 0, River 0, Lake 0, Waterfall 0, Others 0.

Villages with population of 5000 to 9999:

Pippara.

Villages with population of 10000 and above:

Ganapavaram.

Distribution of Workers:

	Persons	Males	Females	WPR
Cultivators	4,356	4,154	202	15.08
Agricultural Labour	17,527	10,757	6,770	60.68
Household Industry	762	432	330	2.64
Other Workers	6,237	5,149	1,088	21.59
Main Workers	21,513	17,437	4,076	74.49
Marginal Workers	7,369	3,055	4,314	25.51
Total Workers	28,882	20,492	8,390	

Religion: Major Religious Communities:

	Persons	Males	Females	Sex Ratio
Hindu (94.15%)	62,758	31,562	31,196	988
Muslim (1.01%)	670	337	333	988
Christian (4.81%)	3,209	1,570	1,639	1,044
Sikh (0%)	1	-	1	-
Buddhists (0%)	1	1	-	-
Jain (0%)	-	-	-	-

Agewise Data:

	Persons	Males	Females	Sex Ratio
All ages	66,656	33,478	33,178	991
0-14	19,226	9,839	9,387	954
15-44	32,516	16,413	16,103	981
45-79	14,324	6,949	7,375	1061
80+	551	257	294	1144
Age not stated	39	20	19	950

Languages (Dominant):

Telugu, Urdu, Gondi, Hindi, Marathi

Disabled Population:

	Persons	Males	Females	%
Total Disabled	1,041	592	449	
In Seeing	341	161	180	32.76
In Speech	142	86	56	13.64
In Hearing	57	25	32	5.48
In Movement	363	230	133	34.87
Mentally	138	90	48	13.26

GANDEED

Gandeed C.D. Block lies in the southern part of Rangare ddy district. The Block is located at a distance of 90 kms. from district headquarters (Serilingampalle). There are 29 villages in the block with the total population of 61,683 persons. Area of the C.D. Block is 241.13 sq. kms. It is bounded by Doma Mandal on north, Kulacherla Mandal on east, and Mahbubnagar distr ict on south and west.

Communications :

Roadways : State Highway (S.H.): Direction- Kodangal to Mahbubnagar. Nearest Villages- Kaplapur, Vennached, Gandeed, Baispalle, Reddipalle, Salkerpet, Varahagirip alle, Komreddipalle, Nancherla, Mukarlabad, Annareddipal le, Lingaipalle, Mohammadabad.

Backwards Region Grants Fund: It receives Backward Region Grants.

Annual Rainfall: Average Rainfall 703 mm

Ground Water: Availability of the Ground Water in the Basin is 2593 H.A.M. and the utilization is 2480 H. A.M. It belongs to Critical category. Depth to water level varies from 10 to 20 meter below the ground. Most of the wells go down in summer months. The well density in the entire block is 13 wells per sq. km. Total no. of the wells in the block are enumerated as 3058, according to the Ground Water Estimation Commi ttee.

Natural Division : Telangana Plateau Region

Administration:

Division: Telangana. Parliamentary Constituency: 10 Chevella. District: Rangareddy.

Mandal: Gandeed. Assembly Constituency: 54 Pargi. Gram Panchayat: 24.

Villages: 29 **Inhabited:** 28 **Uninhabited:** 1

Ranking	District	State	National
Area	8	344	3493
Population	6	255	4804
Sex Ratio	3	158	877
Child Sex Ratio	13	328	1128
Literacy Rate	27	930	5399
Density	1	150	4007
Work Participation Rate	14	516	437

Gram Panchayats:

Balsulgonda, Chinnawarval, Chowderpally, Gadriyal Gandeed, Jakkalapalle, Janampally, Jannaram Julapally, Komreddipalle, Kondapur, Mangampet Mohammadabad, Mukarlabad, Nancherla, Pagadiyal Peddavarval, Rangareddy Palle, Reddipalle Rusumpally, Salkerpet, Shaikpally, Venkatreddy Pally Vennached.

Amenities:

Education: Primary School in 28 villages, Middle school in 13 villages, Matriculation or Secondary School in 8 villages, namely Vennached, Gandeed, Salkerpet, Balsulgonda, Komreddipalle, Nancherla, Julapalle, Mohammadabad. Higher Secondary or Pre University Courses or Intermediate or Junior College in 1 village of the CD Block,, namely Gandeed.

College in 0 village, Adult Literacy Center in 13 villages.

Medical: Hospital in 0 village, Dispensary in 2 villages, Health Center in 2 villages, Sub Center in 8 villages, Maternity and Child Welfare Center in 0 village, Community health workers in 0 village.

The Villages having Hospital or Dispensary or Health Center are Gandeed, Mohammadabad.

Drinking Water: Tap water in 28 villages, Tank water in 28 villages, Well water in 28 villages, Tubewell in 28 villages and more than one source in 28 villages.

Bank: Banking facility in 28 villages, namely, Kaplapur, Vennached, Jinnaram, Chelmilla, Salarnagar Peddavarval, Chinnavarval, Rusumpalle, Gandeed Baispalle, Reddipalle, Salkerpet, Govindapalle Pagdiyal, Balsulgonda, Kondapur, Mansoorpalle Komreddipalle, Nancherla, Gadrial, Chowderpalle Mangampet, Mukarlabad, Julapalle, Annareddipalle Lingaipalle, Mohammadabad, Sangaipalle.

Credit Society in 11 villages Agricultural Credit Society in 6 Non-Agricultural Credit Society in 8 villages.

Others: Power supply in 28 villages, Cinema hall in 2 villages, sport club in 0 village, Stadium or Auditorium or Community Hall in 0 village, Post Office in 10 villages.

There are 21 villages having bus facilities.

Villages with most of facilities: Vennached Rusumpalle, Gandeed, Salkerpet, Pagdiyal, Nancherla Gadrial, Chowderpalle, Mangampet, Mohammadabad.

Villages without Amenities (Education): None..

Scheduled Castes: Out of the total population of 61683 persons, 9292 persons (15.06%) belong to Scheduled Castes. The villages having less than 10% SC population are Jinnaram, Baispalle, Reddipalle, Pagdiyal Chowderpalle, Annareddipalle, Lingaipalle Mohammadabad, Sangaipalle.

The villages having more than 50% SC population are None.

Sex ratio of Scheduled Caste population is 502.

Scheduled Castes Literates and Illiterates by Sex:

	Persons	Males	Females
Literate	2,472	1,731	741
Illiterate	6,820	2,901	3,919
Literacy rate	32.0	44.6	19.2
Graduate	62	55	7

Scheduled Castes (Dominant):

Madiga, Mala, Generic Castes etc., Bindla Beda Jangam etc.

For their cultural identity please see Appendix-I

Villages without Scheduled Castes: There are 5 villages without any scheduled caste population.

Scheduled Tribes: Out of the total population of 61683 persons, 10121 persons (16.41%) belong to Scheduled Tribes.

The villages having less than 10% ST population are Kaplapur, Vennached, Chelmilla, Salarnagar Peddavarval, Chinnavarval, Rusumpalle, Gandeed Baispalle, Salkerpet, Kondapur, Komreddipalle.
The villages having more than 50% ST population are Govindapalle, Chowderpalle, Annareddipalle Lingaipalle, Sangaipalle.
Sex ratio of Scheduled tribe population is 499.

Scheduled Tribes Literates and Illiterates by Sex:

	Persons	Males	Females
Literate	2,262	1,608	654
Illiterate	7,859	3,462	4,397
Literacy rate	28.3	40.2	16.3
Graduate	34	32	2

Scheduled Tribes (Dominant):
Sugalis etc., Chenchu etc., Yerukulas, Koya etc. Kotia etc.
For their cultural identity please see Appendix-II
Villages without Scheduled Tribes: There are 6 villages without any scheduled tribe population.

Literates and Illiterates by Sex (Total Population):

	Persons	Males	Females
Literate	22,371	14,473	7,898
Illiterate	39,312	16,221	23,091
Literacy rate	43	57	30
Graduate	982	805	177

Agriculture: ***Distribution of villages according to land use:***
Out of 29 villages, Total area (in hectare) is 24113, out of that 39.64 percent is cultivable and 62.31 percent of the cultivable area is irrigated.
Sources of Irrigation (Hectares): Government Canal 0, Private Canal 0, Well without Electricity 0, Well with Electricity 143.98, Tubewell without Electricity 145.42, Tubewell with Electricity 1526.35, Tank 1635.92, River 0, Lake 8.09, Waterfall 0, Others 2495.75.
Villages with population of 5000 to 9999:
Vennached, Nancherla.
Villages with population of 10000 and above:
Mohammadabad.

Distribution of Workers:

	Persons	Males	Females	WPR
Cultivators	15,557	9,320	6,237	45.48
Agricultural Labour	13,891	4,679	9,212	40.61
Household Industry	1,066	506	560	3.12
Other Workers	3,692	2,667	1,025	10.79
Main Workers	27,935	15,423	12,512	81.67
Marginal Workers	6,271	1,749	4,522	18.33
Total Workers	34,206	17,172	17,034	

Religion: Major Religious Communities:

	Persons	Males	Females	Sex Ratio
Hindu (94.07%)	58,023	28,885	29,138	1,009
Muslim (5.86%)	3,614	1,789	1,825	1,020
Christian (0.05%)	33	15	18	1,200
Sikh (0%)	1	-	1	-
Buddhists (0%)	-	-	-	-
Jain (0%)	-	-	-	-

Agewise Data:

	Persons	Males	Females	Sex Ratio
All ages	61,683	30,694	30,989	1010
0-14	23,005	11,719	11,286	963
15-44	27,132	13,381	13,751	1028
45-79	11,010	5,306	5,704	1075
80+	366	178	188	1056
Age not stated	170	110	60	545

Languages (Dominant):
Telugu, Hindi, Urdu, Tamil, Kannada

Disabled Population:

	Persons	Males	Females	%
Total Disabled	985	538	447	
In Seeing	463	224	239	47.01
In Speech	95	60	35	9.64
In Hearing	47	25	22	4.77
In Movement	302	187	115	30.66
Mentally	78	42	36	7.92

GANDEPALLE

Gandepalle C.D. Block lies in the southern part of East Godavari district. The Block is located at a dista nce of 48 kms. from district headquarters (Kakinada). There are 13 villages in the block with the total population of 52.462 persons. Area of the C.D. Block is 165.95 sq. kms. It is bounded in the north by Mandal Jaggampeta, in the south by Mandals Rangampeta and Peddapuram, in the east by Mandals Peddapuram and Jagga mpeta, and in the west by Mandals Rajanagaram and Koruko nda.

Communications :
Roadways : NH- 5: Direction- Rajahmundry to Vishakhapatn am. Nearest Villages- Murari, Gandepalle, Mallepalle, Uppalapadu, Talluru, Pro. Ragampeta, Borrampalem.
Backwards Region Grants Fund: It receives Backward Region Grants.
Annaul Rainfall: Average Rainfall 1023.2 mm
Ground Water: Availability of the Ground Water in the Basin is (Information not avavible) H.A.M .and the utilization is (Information not avavible) H.A.M. It belongs to (Information not avavible) category. Depth to water level varies from 3 to 10 meter below the ground. Most of the wells go down in summer months.
Forest and Reserved **Forest:** Nearest Villages- Singaramp alem, Murari, North Tirupathi Rajapuram, Mallepalle.
Natural Division : Godavari Delta Region

Administration:

Division: Coastal Andhra. Parliamentary Constituency: 23 Kakinada. District: East Godavari. Mandal: Gandepalle. Assembly Constituency: 171 Jaggampeta. Gram Panchayat: 18

Villages: 13 **Inhabited:** 13 **Uninhabited:** 0

Ranking	District	State	National
Area	13	738	4777
Population	49	434	5161
Sex Ratio	14	272	1277
Child Sex Ratio	15	158	425
Literacy Rate	47	605	4248
Density	15	974	3380
Work Participation Rate	51	333	3594

Gram Panchayats:

Borrampalem, Gandepalle, K. Nayakampalle
K.Gopalapuram, Mallepalli, Murari, N.T.Rajapuram
Neeladriraopeta, P. Nayakampalle, P.Surampalem
Ramayyapalem, Singarampalem, Subbayamma Peta
Talluru, Uppalapadu, Yellamilli, Yerrampalem
Z.Ragampeta.

Amenities:

Education: Primary School in 13 villages, Middle school in 7 villages, Matriculation or Secondary School in 5 villages, namely Murari, Gandepalle, Mallepalle, Talluru, P.Nayakampalle.

Higher Secondary or Pre University Courses or Intermediate or Junior College in 1 village of the CD Block,, namely Gandepalle.

College in 0 village, Adult Literacy Center in 11 villages.

Medical: Hospital in 0 village, Dispensary in 0 village, Health Center in 1 village, Sub Center in 7 villages, Maternity and Child Welfare Center in 0 village, Community health workers in 0 village.

Drinking Water: Tap water in 13 villages, Tank water in 13 villages, Well water in 13 villages, Tubewell in 13 villages and more than one source in 13 villages.

Bank: Banking facility in 2 villages, namely, Gandepalle, Pro. Ragampeta.

Credit Society in 6 villages Agricultural Credit Society in 6 Non-Agricultural Credit Society in 1 village.

Others: Power supply in 13 villages, Cinema hall in 1 village, sport club in 0 village, Stadium or Auditorium or Community Hall in 0 village, Post Office in 12 villages.

There are 13 villages having bus facilities.

Villages with most of facilities: Gandepalle
Pro. Ragampeta.

Villages without Amenities (Education): None..

Scheduled Castes: Out of the total population of 52462 persons, 10062 persons (19.18%) belong to Scheduled Castes.

The villages having less than 10% SC population are None..

The villages having more than 50% SC population are None.

Sex ratio of Scheduled Caste population is 502.

Scheduled Castes Literates and Illiterates by Sex:

	Persons	Males	Females
Literate	3,225	1,688	1,537
Illiterate	6,837	3,325	3,512
Literacy rate	38.0	40.1	36.0
Graduate	58	44	14

Scheduled Castes (Dominant):

Mala, Madiga, Arundhatiya, Adi Andhra, Mala Dasari

For their cultural identity please see Appendix-I

Villages without Scheduled Castes: There are 0 village without any scheduled caste population.

Scheduled Tribes: Out of the total population of 52462 persons, 461 persons (0.88%) belong to Scheduled Tribes.

The villages having less than 10% ST population are Singarampalem, Murari, Gandepalle
North Tirupathi Rajapuram, Mallepalle, Uppalapadu
Talluru, Pro. Ragampeta, Borrampalem, Yellamilli
P.Nayakampalle, Yerrampalem, Surampalem.

The villages having more than 50% ST population are None.

Sex ratio of Scheduled tribe population is 514.

Scheduled Tribes Literates and Illiterates by Sex:

	Persons	Males	Females
Literate	158	84	74
Illiterate	303	140	163
Literacy rate	39.5	42.9	36.3
Graduate	2	2	0

Scheduled Tribes (Dominant):

Konda Dhoras, Yerukulas, Kammara, Yenadis
Kondareddis

For their cultural identity please see Appendix-II

Villages without Scheduled Tribes: There are 5 villages without any scheduled tribe population.

Literates and Illiterates by Sex (Total Population):

	Persons	Males	Females
Literate	23,642	12,400	11,242
Illiterate	28,820	13,869	14,951
Literacy rate	52	54	49
Graduate	541	425	116

Agriculture: ***Distribution of villages according to land use:*** Out of 13 villages, Total area (in hectare) is 16595, out of that 87.79 percent is cultivable and 36.71 percent of the cultivable area is irrigated.

Sources of Irrigation (Hectares): Government Canal 0, Private Canal 0, Well without Electricity 0, Well with

Electricity 0, Tubewell without Electricity 0, Tubewell with Electricity 3056.47, Tank 2291.61, River 0, Lake 0, Waterfall 0, Others 0.

Villages with population of 5000 to 9999:
Murari, Gandepalle, Mallepalle, Pro. Ragampeta.

Villages with population of 10000 and above: None

Distribution of Workers:

	Persons	Males	Females	WPR
Cultivators	3,546	3,386	160	15.25
Agricultural Labour	15,200	9,892	5,308	65.37
Household Industry	723	459	264	3.11
Other Workers	3,783	2,964	819	16.27
Main Workers	19,853	14,989	4,864	85.38
Marginal Workers	3,399	1,712	1,687	14.62
Total Workers	23,252	16,701	6,551	

Religion: Major Religious Communities:

	Persons	Males	Females	Sex Ratio
Hindu (98.91%)	51,892	25,970	25,922	998
Muslim (0.48%)	250	142	108	761
Christian (0.51%)	266	128	138	1,078
Sikh (0%)	1	-	1	-
Buddhists (0%)	-	-	-	-
Jain (0%)	-	-	-	-

Agewise Data:

	Persons	Males	Females	Sex Ratio
All ages	52,462	26,269	26,193	997
0-14	16,496	8,269	8,227	995
15-44	25,858	13,039	12,819	983
45-79	9,830	4,834	4,996	1034
80+	246	107	139	1299
Age not stated	32	20	12	600

Languages (Dominant):
Telugu, Gondi, Urdu, Tamil, Oriya

Disabled Population:

	Persons	Males	Females	%
Total Disabled	1,174	760	414	
In Seeing	619	441	178	52.73
In Speech	107	53	54	9.11
In Hearing	42	27	15	3.58
In Movement	291	178	113	24.79
Mentally	115	61	54	9.8

GANDHARI

Gandhari C.D. Block lies in the southern part of Nizama bad district. The Block is located at a distance of 52 kms. from district headquarters (Nizamabad). There are 37 villages in the block with the total population of 49,951 persons. Area of the C.D. Block is 365.40 sq. kms. It is bounded by Nizamabad Mandal on north-west, north and north-east, Dichpalle Mandal on north-east, Sadasivanagar Mandal on north-east, east and south-east, Tadwai Mandal on south-east, Lingampet Mandal on south-east, south and south-west, Yellareddy Mandal and Nizamsagar Mandal on south-west, Banswada Mandal on west and north-west, and Varni Mandal on north-west.

Communications :

Roadways : Metalled Roads: Nearest Villages- Pedda Goura ram, Venkatapur, Narsapur (Mudholi), Madholi, Sarvapur, Pothangal (Kalan), Pothangal (Khurd), Thimmapuram, Gandhari, Juvvadi.

Backwards Region Grants Fund: It receives Backward Region Grants.

Mahila Samakhya (Education for Women's Equality): It is decleared Socialy and Educationally Backward Block by the Government. .

Annual Rainfall: Average Rainfall 1220 mm

Ground Water: Availability of the Ground Water in the Basin is 4059 H.A.M. and the utilization is 2137 H. A.M. It belongs to Safe category. Depth to water level varies from 5 to 10 meter below the ground. Most of the wells go down in summer months, according to the Ground Water Estimation Committee.

Natural Division : Telangana Plateau Region

Administration:

Division: Telangana. Parliamentary Constituency: 5 Zahirabad. District: Nizamabad. Mandal: Gandhari. Assem bly Constituency: 15 Yellareaddy. Gram Panchayat: 19.

Villages: 37 **Inhabited:** 34 **Uninhabited:** 3

Ranking	District	State	National
Area	1	68	2166
Population	20	516	5286
Sex Ratio	33	447	1686
Child Sex Ratio	9	344	1198
Literacy Rate	36	1064	6028
Density	1	57	5761
Work Participation Rate	36	952	227

Gram Panchayats:
Burgul, Chadmal, Durgam, Gandhari, Gandivet Gourarm Kalan, Gurjal, Juvvadi, Mathusangam, Mudholi Nagloor, Neeral, Petsangam, Pothangal Kl Seethaipally, Uthnoor, Vajjapally Kl, Venkatapur Yacharam.

Amenities:

Education: Primary School in 33 villages, Middle school in 10 villages, Matriculation or Secondary School in 3 villages, namely Utnur, Gandivet, Gandhari.

Higher Secondary or Pre University Courses or Inter-mediate or Junior College in 0 village of the CD Block, College in 0 village, Adult Literacy Center in 12 villages.

Medical: Hospital in 1 village, Dispensary in 1 village, Health Center in 2 villages, Sub Center in 8 villages,

Maternity and Child Welfare Center in 1 village, Community health workers in 0 village.

The Village having Hospital or Dispensary or Health Center is Gandhari.

Drinking Water: Tap water in 32 villages, Tank water in 34 villages, Well water in 34 villages, Tubewell in 32 villages and more than one source in 34 villages.

Bank: Banking facility in 5 villages, namely, Utnur, Sithaipalle, Gandivet, Pothangal (Kalan) Gandhari.

Credit Society in 11 villages Agricultural Credit Society in 5 Non-Agricultural Credit Society in 5 villages.

Others: Power supply in 34 villages, Cinema hall in 1 village, sport club in 0 village, Stadium or Auditorium or Community Hall in 0 village, Post Office in 9 villages.

There are 28 villages having bus facilities.

Villages with most of facilities: Utnur, Gandivet Pothangal (Kalan), Gandhari.

Villages without amenities (Education):
Boppajiwadi..

Scheduled Castes: Out of the total population of 49951 persons, 5560 persons (11.13%) belong to Scheduled Castes.

The villages having less than 10% SC population are Chedmal, Durgam, Somaram, Yacharam, Boppajiwadi Gujjul, Neral, Katewadi, Pedda Gouraram, Venkatapur Narsapur (Mudholi), Madholi, Sithaipalle, Chinnapur Medpalle, Petasangam, Vandrikal.

The villages having more than 50% SC population are None.

Sex ratio of Scheduled Caste population is 504.

Scheduled Castes Literates and Illiterates by Sex:

	Persons	Males	Females
Literate	1,078	757	321
Illiterate	4,482	2,002	2,480
Literacy rate	23.1	33.0	13.5
Graduate	20	19	1

Scheduled Castes (Dominant):

Madiga, Mala, Gosangi, Beda Jangam etc., Byagara

For their cultural identity please see Appendix-I

Villages without Scheduled Castes: There are 8 villages without any scheduled caste population.

Scheduled Tribes: Out of the total population of 49951 persons, 13489 persons (27%) belong to Scheduled Tribes.

The villages having less than 10% ST population are Utnur, Karakwadi, Boppajiwadi, Pedda Gouraram Narsapur (Mudholi), Madholi, Sarvapur, Sithaipalle Chinnapur, Pothangal (Khurd), Thimmapuram, Juvvadi Vandrikal.

The villages having more than 50% ST population are Somaram, Yacharam, Gujjul, Neral, Katewadi Venkatapur.

Sex ratio of Scheduled tribe population is 486.

Scheduled Tribes Literates and Illiterates by Sex:

	Persons	Males	Females
Literate	2,346	1,937	409
Illiterate	11,143	4,994	6,149
Literacy rate	22.8	36.3	8.3
Graduate	51	48	3

Scheduled Tribes (Dominant):

Sugalis etc., Gond etc., Kammara, Kondhs etc. Koya etc.

For their cultural identity please see Appendix-II

Villages without Scheduled Tribes: There are 13 villages without any scheduled tribe population.

Literates and Illiterates by Sex (Total Population):

	Persons	Males	Females
Literate	14,111	9,692	4,419
Illiterate	35,840	15,444	20,396
Literacy rate	35	47	22
Graduate	297	256	41

Agriculture: ***Distribution of villages according to land use:*** Out of 37 villages, Total area (in hectare) is 36543, out of that 27.73 percent is cultivable and 26.43 percent of the cultivable area is irrigated.

Sources of Irrigation (Hectares): Government Canal 0, Private Canal 0, Well without Electricity 0, Well with Electricity 311.66, Tubewell without Electricity 0, Tubewell with Electricity 1204.32, Tank 1161.82, River 0, Lake 0, Waterfall 0, Others 0.

Villages with population of 5000 to 9999:
Gandhari.

Villages with population of 10000 and above: None

Distribution of Workers:

	Persons	Males	Females	WPR
Cultivators	16,740	9,232	7,508	60.26
Agricultural Labour	6,320	2,632	3,688	22.75
Household Industry	2,016	440	1,576	7.26
Other Workers	2,705	1,918	787	9.74
Main Workers	24,452	13,009	11,443	88.02
Marginal Workers	3,329	1,213	2,116	11.98
Total Workers	27,781	14,222	13,559	

Religion: Major Religious Communities:

	Persons	Males	Females	Sex Ratio
Hindu (93.6%)	46,752	23,532	23,220	987
Muslim (5.8%)	2,895	1,449	1,446	998
Christian (0.29%)	147	73	74	1,014
Sikh (0.07%)	34	20	14	700
Buddhists (0%)	1	1	-	-
Jain (0%)	1	-	1	-

Agewise Data:

	Persons	Males	Females	Sex Ratio
All ages	49,951	25,136	24,815	987
0-14	19,434	10,086	9,348	927
15-44	22,255	11,066	11,189	1011
45-79	7,881	3,802	4,079	1073
80+	311	145	166	1145
Age not stated	70	37	33	892

Languages (Dominant):
Telugu, Hindi, Urdu, Marathi, Gujarati

Disabled Population:

	Persons	Males	Females	%
Total Disabled	772	470	302	
In Seeing	361	220	141	46.76
In Speech	63	36	27	8.16
In Hearing	32	16	16	4.15
In Movement	240	153	87	31.09
Mentally	76	45	31	9.84

GANDLAPENTA

Gandlapenta C.D. Block lies in the south-eastern part of Anantapur district. The Block is located at a distance of 110 kms. from district headquarters (Anantapur). There are 13 villages in the block with the total population of 24,118 persons. Area of the C.D. Block is 149.7 sq. kms. It is bounded in the north by Mandals Kadiri and Talupula, in the south by Mandal Tanakal, in the east by Mandals Tanakal, Nambulipulikunta and Talupula, and in the west by Mandals Kadiri and Nallacheruvu.

Communications:

Roadways : Metalled Road: Nearest Villages- Maddivarigondi, Gandlapenta, Veparala, Kurumamidi, Chamalagondi. It receives the Backward Region Grants, and is identified as a drought-prone area as well.

Annual Rainfall: Average Rainfall 594 mm

Ground Water: Availability of the Ground Water in the Basin is 1036 H.A.M. and the utilization is 1016 H. A.M. It belongs to CRI category. Depth to water level varies from 10 to 20 meter below the ground. Most of the wells go down in summer months. The well density in the entire block is 7 wells per sq. km. Total no. of the wells in the block are enumerated as 1077, according to the Ground Water Estimation Committee.

Forest and Reserved **Forest:** Nearest Villages- Godduvelagala, Kamathampalle, Maddivarigondi, Thummalabylu, Gandlapenta, Jeenulakunta, Veparala, Kurumamidi, Chamalagondi, Malameedapalle.

Natural Division : Rayalaseema Region

Administration:

Division: Rayala Seema. Parliamentary Constituency: 37 Hindupur. District: Anantapur.
Mandal: Gandlapenta. Assembly Constituency: 280 Kadiri. Gram Panchayat: 12.

Villages: 13 **Inhabited:** 12 **Uninhabited:** 1

Ranking	District	State	National
Area	60	823	5045
Population	63	1071	6159
Sex Ratio	2	352	1433
Child Sex Ratio	4	39	97
Literacy Rate	26	572	4113
Density	23	347	5391
Work Participation Rate	26	866	862

Gram Panchayats:
Chamalagondi, Gandlapenta, Godduvelagala Jeenulakunta, Katarupalli, Kurumamidi Maddivarigondi, Malameedapalli, Somayajulapalli Thoopalli, Thummalabylu, Veparala.

Amenities:

Education: Primary School in 12 villages, Middle school in 3 villages, Matriculation or Secondary School in 1 village, namely Gandlapenta.
Higher Secondary or Pre University Courses or Intermediate or Junior College in 1 village of the CD Block,, namely Gandlapenta.
College in 0 village, Adult Literacy Center in 0 village.

Medical: Hospital in 0 village, Dispensary in 1 village, Health Center in 1 village, Sub Center in 5 villages, Maternity and Child Welfare Center in 0 village, Community health workers in 0 village.
The Village having Hospital or Dispensary or Health Center is Gandlapenta.

Drinking Water: Tap water in 4 villages, Tank water in 0 villages, Well water in 1 village, Tubewell in 6 villages and more than one source in 9 villages.

Bank: Banking facility in 1 villages, namely, Gandlapenta.
Credit Society in 2 villages Agricultural Credit Society in 2 Non-Agricultural Credit Society in 0 village.

Others: Power supply in 12 villages, Cinema hall in 0 village, sport club in 0 village, Stadium or Auditorium or Community Hall in 0 village, Post Office in 7 villages.
There are 11 villages having bus facilities.

Village with most of facilities: Gandlapenta.

Villages without Amenities (Education): None..

Scheduled Castes: Out of the total population of 24118 persons, 2498 persons (10.36%) belong to Scheduled Castes.
The villages having less than 10% SC population are Godduvelagala, Thummalabylu, Jeenulakunta, Veparala Kurumamidi, Malameedapalle.
The villages having more than 50% SC population are None.

Sex ratio of Scheduled Caste population is 505.

Scheduled Castes Literates and Illiterates by Sex:

	Persons	Males	Females
Literate	879	595	284
Illiterate	1,619	641	978
Literacy rate	40.1	54.8	25.7
Graduate	21	15	6

Scheduled Castes (Dominant):

Madiga, Mala, Generic Castes etc.

For their cultural identity please see Appendix-I

Villages without Scheduled Castes: There is 1 village without any scheduled caste population.

Scheduled Tribes: Out of the total population of 24118 persons, 2144 persons (8.89%) belong to Scheduled Tribes. The villages having less than 10% ST population are Godduvelagala, Kamathampalle, Maddivarigondi Gandlapenta, Jeenulakunta, Somayajulapalle Chamachenubylu, Malameedapalle.

The villages having more than 50% ST population are None.

Sex ratio of Scheduled tribe population is 491.

Scheduled Tribes Literates and Illiterates by Sex:

	Persons	Males	Females
Literate	667	494	173
Illiterate	1,477	598	879
Literacy rate	36.8	53.1	19.6
Graduate	5	5	0

Scheduled Tribes (Dominant):

Sugalis etc., Yerukulas, Yenadis

For their cultural identity please see Appendix-II

Villages without Scheduled Tribes: There are 4 villages without any scheduled tribe population.

Literates and Illiterates by Sex (Total Population):

	Persons	Males	Females
Literate	11,038	7,368	3,670
Illiterate	13,080	4,735	8,345
Literacy rate	53	70	35
Graduate	368	312	56

Agriculture: ***Distribution of villages according to land use:*** Out of 13 villages, Total area (in hectare) is 14972, out of that 55.86 percent is cultivable and 6.03 percent of the cultivable area is irrigated.

Sources of Irrigation (Hectares): Government Canal 0, Private Canal 0, Well without Electricity 0, Well with Electricity 405, Tubewell without Electricity 0, Tubewell with Electricity 54, Tank 45, River 0, Lake 0, Waterfall 0, Others 0.

Villages with population of 5000 to 9999: Gandlapenta.

Villages with population of 10000 and above: None

Distribution of Workers:

	Persons	Males	Females	WPR
Cultivators	5,039	3,415	1,624	37.79
Agricultural Labour	6,003	2,193	3,810	45.02
Household Industry	187	89	98	1.4
Other Workers	2,105	1,666	439	15.79
Main Workers	8,552	6,168	2,384	64.14
Marginal Workers	4,782	1,195	3,587	35.86
Total Workers	13,334	7,363	5,971	

Religion: Major Religious Communities:

	Persons	Males	Females	Sex Ratio
Hindu (80.56%)	19,430	9,738	9,692	995
Muslim (19.3%)	4,654	2,346	2,308	984
Christian (0.09%)	22	13	9	692
Sikh (0%)	-	-	-	-
Buddhists (0%)	-	-	-	-
Jain (0%)	-	-	-	-

Agewise Data:

	Persons	Males	Females	Sex Ratio
All ages	24,118	12,103	12,015	993
0-14	7,358	3,684	3,674	997
15-44	11,542	5,906	5,636	954
45-79	5,034	2,435	2,599	1067
80+	161	62	99	1597
Age not stated	23	16	7	438

Languages (Dominant):

Telugu, Urdu, Hindi, Gondi, Tamil

Disabled Population:

	Persons	Males	Females	%
Total Disabled	555	325	230	
In Seeing	176	96	80	31.71
In Speech	62	34	28	11.17
In Hearing	63	38	25	11.35
In Movement	196	126	70	35.32
Mentally	58	31	27	10.45

GANGADHARA

Gangadhara C.D. Block lies in the north-west part of Karimnagar district. The Block is located at a distance of 23 kms. from district headquarters (Karimnagar). There are 19 villages in the block with the total population of 46,879 persons. Area of the C.D. Block is 164.53 sq. kms. It is bounded by Mallial Mandal on north, Pegadapalle Mandal on north-east, Ramadugu Mandal on east, Karimnagar Mandal on south-east, Boinpa lle Mandal on south and west, and Kodimial Mandal on north-west.

Communications :

Roadways : Metalled Roads: Nearest Villages- Gangadhara, Uppara Mallial, Kurikial, Nayalakonda Palle, Garsekurt hi, Vaddyaram.

Backwards Region Grants Fund: It receives Backward Region Grants.

Mahila Samakhya (Education for Women's Equality): It is decleared Socialy and Educationally Backward Block by the Government.

Integrated Child Development Scheme (ICDS) Project: Gangadhara, Total Anganwadi Centres: 145

Annual Rainfall: Average Rainfall 915 mm

Ground Water: Availability of the Ground Water in the Basin is 1245 H.A.M. and the utilization is 1765 H. A.M. It belongs to Over Exploited category. Depth to water level varies from more than 5 to 10 meter below the ground. Most of the wells go down in summer months. The well density in the entire block is 34 wells per sq. km. Total no. of the wells in the block are enumera ted as 5287, according to the Ground Water Estimation Committee.

Natural Division : Godavari Depression Region

Administration:

Division: Telangana. Parliamentary Constituency: 3 Karimnagar. District: Karimnagar. Mandal: Gangadhara. Assembly Constituency: 27 Choppadandi (SC). Gram Panch ayat: 23.

Villages: 19 **Inhabited:** 19 **Uninhabited:** 0

Ranking	District	State	National
Area	37	746	4796
Population	30	605	5424
Sex Ratio	22	167	907
Child Sex Ratio	52	944	4201
Literacy Rate	23	619	4293
Density	20	310	3695
Work Participation Rate	22	421	782

Gram Panchayats:

Achampally, Burugupally, Gangadhara, Garshakurthy Gattubuthukur, Gopalraopally, Himmathnagar, Kacharam Kachireddypally, Kondannapally, Kondiapally Kurikyala, Laxmidevipally, Mallapur, Nagireddypoor Narayanpoor, Oddyaram, Rangaiahpally, Ryalapally Sarvareddypally, Tadijerry, Uppermallial Venkataipally.

Amenities:

Education: Primary School in 19 villages, Middle school in 13 villages, Matriculation or Secondary School in 8 villages, namely Burgupalle, Gangadhara, Mallapur, Uppara Mallial, Kurikial, Gattuboothkur, Garsekurthi, Vaddyaram.

Higher Secondary or Pre University Courses or Intermediate or Junior College in 0 village of the CD Block, College in 0 village, Adult Literacy Center in 13 villages.

Medical: Hospital in 1 village, Dispensary in 1 village, Health Center in 1 village, Sub Center in 9 villages, Maternity and Child Welfare Center in 0 village, Community health workers in 0 village.

The Village having Hospital or Dispensary or Health Center is Gangadhara.

Drinking Water: Tap water in 19 villages, Tank water in 19 villages, Well water in 19 villages, Tubewell in 19 villages and more than one source in 19 villages.

Bank: Banking facility in 3 villages, namely, Burgupalle, Gangadhara, Garsekurthi.

Credit Society in 14 villages Agricultural Credit Society in 4 Non-Agricultural Credit Society in 14 villages.

Others: Power supply in 19 villages, Cinema hall in 0 village, sport club in 0 village, Stadium or Auditorium or Community Hall in 0 village, Post Office in 12 villages.

There are 18 villages having bus facilities.

Villages with most of facilities: Burgupalle Gangadhara, Garsekurthi.

Villages without Amenities (Education): None..

Scheduled Castes: Out of the total population of 46879 persons, 9551 persons (20.37%) belong to Scheduled Castes.

The villages having less than 10% SC population are None..

The villages having more than 50% SC population are None.

Sex ratio of Scheduled Caste population is 493.

Scheduled Castes Literates and Illiterates by Sex:

	Persons	Males	Females
Literate	3,816	2,402	1,414
Illiterate	5,735	2,443	3,292
Literacy rate	46.0	57.3	34.4
Graduate	45	40	5

Scheduled Castes (Dominant):

Madiga, Mala, Gosangi, Manne, Bavuri

For their cultural identity please see Appendix-I

Villages without Scheduled Castes: There are 0 village without any scheduled caste population.

Scheduled Tribes: Out of the total population of 46879 persons, 284 persons (0.61%) belong to Scheduled Tribes.

The villages having less than 10% ST population are Venkataipalle, Ryalapalle, Kachireddipalle Kondaipalle, Burgupalle, Narasimhulapalle Sarvareddipalle, Nagireddipur, Gangadhara Narayanpur, Islampur, Mallapur, Uppara Mallial Kurikial, Nayalakonda Palle, Gattuboothkur Garsekurthi, Achampalle, Vaddyaram.

The villages having more than 50% ST population are None.

Sex ratio of Scheduled tribe population is 507.

Scheduled Tribes Literates and Illiterates by Sex:

	Persons	Males	Females
Literate	59	40	19
Illiterate	225	100	125
Literacy rate	27.1	36.4	17.6
Graduate	1	1	0

Scheduled Tribes (Dominant):
Yerukulas, Generic Tribes etc., Gond etc.
Sugalis etc., Savaras etc.
For their cultural identity please see Appendix-II
Villages without Scheduled Tribes: There are 8 villages without any scheduled tribe population.

Literates and Illiterates by Sex (Total Population):

	Persons	Males	Females
Literate	21,000	13,234	7,766
Illiterate	25,879	10,104	15,775
Literacy rate	51	66	38
Graduate	428	383	45

Agriculture: ***Distribution of villages according to land use:*** Out of 19 villages, Total area (in hectare) is 16454, out of that 67.81 percent is cultivable and 48.72 percent of the cultivable area is irrigated.

Sources of Irrigation (Hectares): Government Canal 0, Private Canal 0, Well without Electricity 0, Well with Electricity 4784, Tubewell without Electricity 0, Tubewell with Electricity 0, Tank 652, River 0, Lake 0, Waterfall 0, Others 0.

Villages with population of 5000 to 9999:
Gangadhara, Garsekurthi.

Villages with population of 10000 and above: None

Distribution of Workers:

	Persons	Males	Females	WPR
Cultivators	7,733	4,721	3,012	29.63
Agricultural Labour	8,724	3,707	5,017	33.43
Household Industry	4,928	1,139	3,789	18.88
Other Workers	4,710	3,550	1,160	18.05
Main Workers	22,805	12,002	10,803	87.39
Marginal Workers	3,290	1,115	2,175	12.61
Total Workers	26,095	13,117	12,978	

Religion: Major Religious Communities:

	Persons	Males	Females	Sex Ratio
Hindu (97.49%)	45,702	22,752	22,950	1,009
Muslim (1.76%)	826	412	414	1,005
Christian (0.66%)	308	151	157	1,040
Sikh (0%)	-	-	-	-
Buddhists (0%)	-	-	-	-
Jain (0%)	-	-	-	-

Agewise Data:

	Persons	Males	Females	Sex Ratio
All ages	46,879	23,338	23,541	1009
0-14	14,448	7,377	7,071	959
15-44	21,661	10,598	11,063	1044
45-79	10,289	5,131	5,158	1005
80+	456	222	234	1054
Age not stated	25	10	15	1500

Languages (Dominant):
Telugu, Urdu, Oriya, Hindi, Tamil

Disabled Population:

	Persons	Males	Females	%
Total Disabled	737	395	342	
In Seeing	332	171	161	45.05
In Speech	52	26	26	7.06
In Hearing	31	15	16	4.21
In Movement	197	116	81	26.73
Mentally	125	67	58	16.96

GANGADHARA NELLORE

Gangadhara Nellore C.D. Block lies in the north West part of west Godavari district. The Block is located at a distance of 10 kms. from district headquarters (Eluru). There are 35 villages in the block with the total population of 64799 persons. Area of the C.D. Block is 200.07 sq. kms. It is bounded by Penumuru, Vedurukuppam mandals in the north, Sri Rangarajapuram mandal in the east, Palasamudram mandal in the south east, Chittoor mandal in the west. It has common boundary with the state of Tamil Nadu from south.

Communications:
Roadways : State Highway (S.H.): Direction- Chittoor to Sri Rangarajapuram. Nearest Villages- Nellipalle, Kondepalle, Veerakanellore, Kotagaram, Peddakalva, Kalijavedu, Gangadharanellore, Gollapalle, Velkur.
River: Ponnal Nadi- Nearest Villages- Nandanoor, Kotrakona, Nallarallapalle, Mukkelathuru, Atmakur, Murthinayanipalle, Ellapalle, Bojjinayanipalle, B.C.Khandriga, Garigalapalle.

Annual Rainfall: Average Rainfall 909 mm.

Ground Water: Availability of the ground water in the Basin is 2208 H.A.M. and the utilization is 2062 H.A.M. It belongs to Critical category. Depth to water level varies more than 10 meter below the ground. Most of the wells go down in summer months, according to the Ground Water Estimation Committee.

Natural Division : Rayalaseema Region.

Administration:
Division: Rayala Seema, Parliamentary Constituency: 42 Chittoor (SC), District: Chittoor, Mandal: Gangadhara Nellore, Assembly Constituency: 290 Gangadhara Nellore (SC), Gram Panchayat: 32.

Villages: 35 **Inhabited:** 33 **Uninhabited:** 2

Ranking	District	State	National
Area	18	556	4180
Population	6	210	4695

Sex Ratio	61	793	2702
Child Sex Ratio	54	1017	4782
Literacy Rate	7	46	947
Density	56	956	3319
Work Participation Rate	15	322	3436

Gram Panchayats:
Agaramangalam, Ambodharapalle, Atmakur Balaganganapalle, Bangareddipalle, Bukkapatnam Chinnavepanjeri, Ellapalle, Gangadharanellore Kadapagunta, Kalijavedu, Kondepalle, Kotagaram Kothavenkatapuram, Kotrakona, Mahadevamangalam Mukkalathuru, Nallepalle, Nandanoor, Pachigunta Papireddipalle, Pathapalem, Pathavenkatapuram Peddakalva, Tiruveedhikuppam, Tungundram, Varathuru Veerakanellore, Velkuru, Vepanjeri, Vezzupalle Vinjam.

Amenities:
Education: Primary School in 32 villages, Middle school in 16 villages, Matriculation or Secondary School in 8 villages, namely Nellipalle, Vinjam, Veerakanellore, Gangadharanellore, Vepanjeri, Varathuru, Mukkelathuru, Tungundram.
Higher Secondary or Pre University Courses or Intermediate or Junior College in 0 village of the CD Block, College in 0 village, Adult Literacy Center in 18 villages.
Medical: Hospital in 0 village, Dispensary in 0 village, Health Center in 2 villages, Sub Center in 10 villages, Maternity and Child Welfare Center in 0 village, Community health workers in 0 village.
Drinking Water: Tap water in 33 villages, Tank water in 33 villages, Well water in 33 villages, Tubewell in 33 villages and more than one source in 33 villages.
Bank: Banking facility in 3 villages, namely, Vinjam, Gangadharanellore, Tungundram.
Credit Society in 13 villages Agricultural Credit Society in 11 Non-Agricultural Credit Society in 5 villages.
Others: Power supply in 33 villages, Cinema hall in 3 villages, sport club in 0 village, Stadium or Auditorium or Community Hall in 0 village, Post Office in 19 villages.
There are 27 villages having bus facilities.
Villages with most of facilities: Vinjam Gangadharanellore, Tungundram.
Villages without amenities (Education):
Errabodireddipalle..
Scheduled Castes: Out of the total population of 64831 persons, 22641 persons (34.92%) belong to Scheduled Castes.
The villages having less than 10% SC population are None..
The villages having more than 50% SC population are Mukkelathuru, Kadapagunta, Atmakur Murthinayanipalle, Pathavenkatapuram Bojjinayanipalle.
Sex ratio of Scheduled Caste population is 487.
Scheduled Castes Literates and Illiterates by Sex:

	Persons	Males	Females
Literate	12,943	7,693	5,250
Illiterate	9,698	3,917	5,781
Literacy rate	66.7	77.5	55.3
Graduate	130	115	15

Scheduled Castes (Dominant):
Adi Dravida, Adi Andhra, Mala, Madiga Generic Castes etc.
For their cultural identity please see Appendix-I
Villages without Scheduled Castes: There are 2 villages without any scheduled caste population.
Scheduled Tribes: Out of the total population of 64831 persons, 562 persons (0.87%) belong to Scheduled Tribes.
The villages having less than 10% ST population are Vezzupalle, Nellipalle, Kondepalle, Vinjam Veerakanellore, Kotagaram, Nandanoor, Kotrakona Peddakalva, Kalijavedu, Gangadharanellore Gollapalle, Agaramangalam, Vepanjeri, Varathuru Pachigunta, Bukkapatnam, Chinnavepanjeri, Velkur Mukkelathuru, Mahadevamangalam, Tungundram Kadapagunta, Atmakur, Errabodireddipalle Murthinayanipalle, Ambodharapalle, Pathapalem Pathavenkatapuram, Ellapalle, Bojjinayanipalle Garigalapalle, Kothavenkatapuram.
The villages having more than 50% ST population are None.
Sex ratio of Scheduled tribe population is 509.
Scheduled Tribes Literates and Illiterates by Sex:

	Persons	Males	Females
Literate	230	124	106
Illiterate	332	152	180
Literacy rate	50.0	54.2	45.9
Graduate	3	3	0

Scheduled Tribes (Dominant):
Yenadis, Yerukulas
For their cultural identity please see Appendix-II
Villages without Scheduled Tribes: There are 14 villages without any scheduled tribe population.
Literates and Illiterates by Sex (Total Population):

	Persons	Males	Females
Literate	40,721	23,745	16,976
Illiterate	24,110	9,233	14,877
Literacy rate	72	83	61
Graduate	1,119	852	267

Agriculture: ***Distribution of villages according to land use:***
Out of 35 villages, Total area (in hectare) is 20007, out of

that 54.18 percent is cultivable and 32.42 percent of the cultivable area is irrigated.

Sources of Irrigation (Hectares): Government Canal 0, Private Canal 0, Well without Electricity 0, Well with Electricity 3010.26, Tubewell without Electricity 0, Tubewell with Electricity 369.05, Tank 134.34, River 0, Lake 0, Waterfall 0, Others 0.

Villages with population of 5000 to 9999: Vinjam.

Villages with population of 10000 and above: None

Distribution of Workers:

	Persons	Males	Females	WPR
Cultivators	8,651	6,458	2,193	29.63
Agricultural Labour	13,189	7,609	5,580	45.18
Household Industry	1,025	594	431	3.51
Other Workers	6,328	4,138	2,190	21.68
Main Workers	26,146	17,602	8,544	89.56
Marginal Workers	3,047	1,197	1,850	10.44
Total Workers	29,193	18,799	10,394	

Religion: Major Religious Communities:

	Persons	Males	Females	Sex Ratio
Hindu (94.7%)	61,393	31,199	30,194	968
Muslim (3.93%)	2,547	1,330	1,217	915
Christian (1.24%)	805	401	404	1,007
Sikh (0%)	-	-	-	-
Buddhists (0%)	-	-	-	-
Jain (0%)	-	-	-	-

Agewise Data:

	Persons	Males	Females	Sex Ratio
All ages	64,831	32,978	31,853	966
0-14	20,167	10,499	9,668	921
15-44	29,704	14,976	14,728	983
45-79	14,304	7,197	7,107	987
80+	552	253	299	1182
Age not stated	104	53	51	962

Languages (Dominant):

Telugu, Tamil, Urdu, Gondi, Hindi

Disabled Population:

	Persons	Males	Females	%
Total Disabled	981	573	408	
In Seeing	286	165	121	29.15
In Speech	140	82	58	14.27
In Hearing	52	28	24	5.3
In Movement	368	227	141	37.51
Mentally	135	71	64	13.76

GANGAVARAM

Gangavaram C.D. Block lies in the northern part of East Godavari district. The Block is located at a dista nce of 100 kms. from district headquarters (Kakinada). There are 60 villages in the block with the total population of 25,938 persons. Area of the C.D. Block is 189.67 sq. kms. It is bounded in the north by Y. Ramavaram Mandal, in the south by Mandals Gokavaram, Jaggampeta and Yeleswaram, in the east by Mandals Addateegala and Yeleswaram, and in the west by Mandal Rampachodavaram.

Communications :

Roadways : State Highway (S.H.): Direction- Gokavaram to Jagampeta. Nearest Villages- Peda Addapalle, Jaggamp alem, Neeladonelapadu, Kotharamavaram, Chodavaram, Rajup etaloddi, Yamanapalle, Patharamavaram.

River: Uppudukalava Nadi- Nearest Villages- Kusumarai, Amudalabanda, Yerrampalem, Kothada, Surampalem, Donela palle, Rajupetaloddi, Yamanapalle, Patharamavaram. Eluru Nadi- Nearest Villages- Lingavaram, Kattumilli.

Backwards Region Grants Fund: It receives Backward Region Grants.

Annaul Rainfall: Average Rainfall 990 mm

Ground Water: Availability of the Ground Water in the Basin is (Information not avavible) H.A.M .and the utilization is (Information not avavible) H.A.M. It belongs to (Information not avavible) category. Depth to water level varies from 3 to 10 meter below the ground. Most of the wells go down in summer months.

Forest and Reserved **Forest:** Nearest Villages- Yetipalle, China Addapalle, Sarabhavaram, Cheedipalem, Goragommi, Vuyyalamadugu, Padagarlapadu, Chinagarlapadu, Vemulova, Pidathamamidi, Nellipudi, Bayyanapalle, Kotharamavaram, Chodavaram, Ummetha, Molleru, B.Sivaramapatnam, Loddip alem, Ramuldevapuram, Lingavaram.

Natural Division : Godavari Delta Region

Administration:

Division: Coastal Andhra. Parliamentary Constituency: 18 Araku (ST). District: East Godavari. Mandal: Gangava ram. Assembly Constituency: 172 Rampachodavaram (ST). Gram Panchayat: 17.

Villages: 60 **Inhabited:** 55 **Uninhabited:** 5

Ranking	**District**	**State**	**National**
Area	7	616	4357
Population	56	1059	6129
Sex Ratio	2	37	307
Child Sex Ratio	7	58	137
Literacy Rate	56	951	5495
Density	1	115	5760
Work Participation Rate	57	951	356

Gram Panchayats:

Amudalabanda, Bayyanapalli, Doramamidi, Gangavaram Jaggampalem, Jiyyampalem, Kothada, Lakkonda Marripalem, Mohanapuram, Molleru, Nellipudi Pandraprolu, Pidathamamidi, Surampalem, Yendapalli

Zaderu.

Amenities:

Education: Primary School in 52 villages, Middle school in 4 villages, Matriculation or Secondary School in 4 villages, namely Mohanapuram, Gangavaram, Kothada, Vemulova. Higher Secondary or Pre University Courses or Intermediate or Junior College in 0 village of the CD Block, College in 0 village, Adult Literacy Center in 14 villages.

Medical: Hospital in 0 village, Dispensary in 0 village, Health Center in 1 village, Sub Center in 10 villages, Maternity and Child Welfare Center in 0 village, Community health workers in 0 village.

Drinking Water: Tap water in 52 villages, Tank water in 52 villages, Well water in 52 villages, Tubewell in 52 villages and more than one source in 55 villages.

Bank: Banking facility in 3 villages, namely, Zaderu, Gangavaram, Nellipudi.

Credit Society in 12 villages Agricultural Credit Society in 9 Non-Agricultural Credit Society in 5 villages.

Others: Power supply in 55 villages, Cinema hall in 1 village, sport club in 0 village, Stadium or Auditorium or Community Hall in 0 village, Post Office in 16 villages.

There are 15 villages having bus facilities.

Villages with most of facilities: Zaderu Gangavaram, Nellipudi.

Villages without amenities (Education):

Vuyyalamadugu, Kamavarappadu, Kattumilli..

Scheduled Castes: Out of the total population of 25938 persons, 2002 persons (7.72%) belong to Scheduled Castes.

The villages having less than 10% SC population are Neelavaram, Lakshmipuram, Nuvvumamidi, Mohanapuram Pandraprolu, Barrimamidi, Karakapadu Pothandorapalem, Yellapuram, Marripalem, Yendapalle Zaderu, Kuramgondi, Yetipalle, Peda Addapalle E. Ramavaram, Komaravaram, China Addapalle Sarabhavaram, Cheedipalem, Pandrapottipalem Rajampalem, Gangavaram, Lakkonda, Goragommi Vuyyalamadugu, Padagarlapadu, Doramamidi Amudalabanda, Yerrampalem, Kothada, Chinagarlapadu Vemulova, Surampalem, Donelapalle, Kamavarappadu Kondalampalem, Ojubanda, Jaggampalem, Jiyyampalem Rajavaram, Rajupetaloddi, Yamanapalle Patharamavaram, Bayyanapalle, Kotharamavaram Ummetha, Loddipalem, Molleru, B.Sivaramapatnam Ramuldevapuram.

The villages having more than 50% SC population are None.

Sex ratio of Scheduled Caste population is 520.

Scheduled Castes Literates and Illiterates by Sex:

	Persons	Males	Females
Literate	674	346	328
Illiterate	1,328	615	713
Literacy rate	40.8	43.1	38.5
Graduate	27	24	3

Scheduled Castes (Dominant):

Mala, Madiga, Panchama etc., Adi Andhra Beda Jangam etc.

For their cultural identity please see Appendix-I

Villages without Scheduled Castes: There are 33 villages without any scheduled caste population.

Scheduled Tribes: Out of the total population of 25938 persons, 16652 persons (64.2%) belong to Scheduled Tribes.

The villages having less than 10% ST population are None..

The villages having more than 50% ST population are Neelavaram, Lakshmipuram, Nuvvumamidi, Mohanapuram Pandraprolu, Barrimamidi, Karakapadu Pothandorapalem, Yellapuram, Marripalem, Yendapalle Kuramgondi, Yetipalle, Peda Addapalle, E. Ramavaram Komaravaram, China Addapalle, Sarabhavaram Cheedipalem, Pandrapottipalem, Kusumarai, Rajampalem Gangavaram, Lakkonda, Goragommi, Vuyyalamadugu Padagarlapadu, Doramamidi, Amudalabanda, Yerrampalem Kothada, Chinagarlapadu, Vemulova, Surampalem Donelapalle, Kamavarappadu, Kondalampalem, Ojubanda Jaggampalem, Rajavaram, Rajupetaloddi, Yamanapalle Patharamavaram, Bayyanapalle, Ummetha, Loddipalem B.Sivaramapatnam.

Sex ratio of Scheduled tribe population is 514.

Scheduled Tribes Literates and Illiterates by Sex:

	Persons	Males	Females
Literate	5,938	3,082	2,856
Illiterate	10,714	5,014	5,700
Literacy rate	41.9	44.8	39.1
Graduate	46	35	11

Scheduled Tribes (Dominant):

Koya etc., Kondareddis, Kammara, Valmiki Konda Dhoras

For their cultural identity please see Appendix-II

Villages without Scheduled Tribes: There are 6 villages without any scheduled tribe population.

Literates and Illiterates by Sex (Total Population):

	Persons	Males	Females
Literate	9,353	4,878	4,475
Illiterate	16,585	7,779	8,806
Literacy rate	42	46	40
Graduate	136	108	28

Agriculture: ***Distribution of villages according to land use:*** Out of 60 villages, Total area (in hectare) is 18966, out of that 52.87 percent is cultivable and 4.45 percent of the

cultivable area is irrigated.

Sources of Irrigation (Hectares): Government Canal 434.37, Private Canal 0, Well without Electricity 0, Well with Electricity 0, Tubewell without Electricity 0, Tubewell with Electricity 0, Tank 11.72, River 0, Lake 0, Waterfall 0, Others 0.

Villages with population of 5000 to 9999: None

Villages with population of 10000 and above: None

Distribution of Workers:

	Persons	Males	Females	WPR
Cultivators	6,497	3,787	2,710	44.17
Agricultural Labour	6,902	3,270	3,632	46.92
Household Industry	208	113	95	1.41
Other Workers	1,102	736	366	7.49
Main Workers	11,822	6,897	4,925	80.37
Marginal Workers	2,887	1,009	1,878	19.63
Total Workers	14,709	7,906	6,803	

Religion: Major Religious Communities:

	Persons	Males	Females	Sex Ratio
Hindu (97.75%)	25,354	12,408	12,946	1,043
Muslim (0.37%)	97	44	53	1,205
Christian (1.81%)	470	197	273	1,386
Sikh (0%)	-	-	-	-
Buddhists (0%)	-	-	-	-
Jain (0%)	-	-	-	-

Agewise Data:

	Persons	Males	Females	Sex Ratio
All ages	25,938	12,657	13,281	1049
0-14	8,941	4,379	4,562	1042
15-44	12,168	5,868	6,300	1074
45-79	4,549	2,263	2,286	1010
80+	78	42	36	857
Age not stated	202	105	97	924

Languages (Dominant):
Telugu, Gondi, Urdu, Tamil

Disabled Population:

	Persons	Males	Females	%
Total Disabled	488	256	232	
In Seeing	218	116	102	44.67
In Speech	53	29	24	10.86
In Hearing	30	16	14	6.15
In Movement	134	70	64	27.46
Mentally	53	25	28	10.86

GANGAVARAM

Gangavaram C.D. Block lies in the south-western part of Chittoor district. The Block is located at a distance of 40 kms. from district headquarters (Chittoor). There are 16 villages in the block with the total popul ation of 48,879 persons. Area of the C.D. Block is 154. 72 sq. kms. It is bounded in the north by Mandal Peddap anjani, in the south by Mandals Bairaddipalle, Palamaner and Bangarupalem, in the east by Mandal Bangarupalem, and in the west it has common boundary with the state of Karnataka.

Communications:

Roadways : NH- 4: Direction- Bangalore to Chennai. Nerae st Villages- Gandrajupalle, Keelapalle, Pathikonda, Jeedimakulapalle, Gangavaram. NH- 205: Direction- Punga nur to Palamaner. Nearest Villages- Gandrajupalle, Keela palle, Pathikonda, Jeedimakulapalle, Gangavaram, Gunduga llu, Kallupalle, Melumoy, Gangavaram.

It receives the Backward Region Grants, and is identifi ed as a drought-prone area as well.

Annual Rainfall: Average Rainfall 863 mm

Ground Water: Availability of the Ground Water in the Basin is 1835 H.A.M.and the utilization is 1908 H.A. M. It belongs to OE category. Depth to water level varies more than 10 meter below the ground. Most of the wells go down in summer months, according to the Ground Water Estimation Committee.

Forest and Reserved **Forest:** (Peddoru R.F.)- Nearest Villages- Keelapalle, Pathikonda, Mamadugu, Jeedimakula palle, Kallupalle, Melumoy, Kothapalle, Keelapatla, Mogilpalle.

Natural Division : Rayalaseema Region

Administration:

Division: Rayala Seema. Parliamentary Constituency: 42 Chittoor (SC). District: Chittoor. Mandal: Gangavaram. Assembly Constituency: 293 Palamner. Gram Panchayat: 16

Border Villages: (Karnataka)- Nearest Villages- Gunduga llu, Pasupathur, Gandrajupalle.

Villages: 16 **Inhabited:** 16 **Uninhabited:** 0

Ranking	District	State	National
Area	42	800	4964
Population	26	552	5343
Sex Ratio	10	226	1116
Child Sex Ratio	42	818	3575
Literacy Rate	46	297	2921
Density	20	424	3384
Work Participation Rate	18	334	1051

Gram Panchayats:

Chowdireddipalle, Dandapalle, Gandrajupalle Gangavaram, Gundugallu, Jeedimakulapalle, Kalagatoor Kallupalle, Keelapalle, Keelapatla, Kothapalle Mamadugu, Melumoy, Pasupathuru, Pathikonda Thallapalle.

Amenities:

Education: Primary School in 16 villages, Middle school in 12 villages, Matriculation or Secondary School in 6 villages,

namely Gundugallu, Keelapalle, Jeedimakulapalle, Dandapalle, Kallupalle, Keelapatla.

Higher Secondary or Pre University Courses or Intermediate or Junior College in 0 village of the CD Block, College in 0 village, Adult Literacy Center in 11 villages.

Medical: Hospital in 0 village, Dispensary in 1 village, Health Center in 2 villages, Sub Center in 9 villages, Maternity and Child Welfare Center in 11 villages, Community health workers in 0 village.

The Village having Hospital or Dispensary or Health Center is Gangavaram.

Drinking Water: Tap water in 16 villages, Tank water in 16 villages, Well water in 16 villages, Tubewell in 16 villages and more than one source in 16 villages.

Bank: Banking facility in 2 villages, namely, Pathikonda, Kallupalle.

Credit Society in 6 villages Agricultural Credit Society in 6 Non-Agricultural Credit Society in 5 villages.

Others: Power supply in 16 villages, Cinema hall in 0 village, sport club in 0 village, Stadium or Auditorium or Community Hall in 0 village, Post Office in 10 villages.

There are 14 villages having bus facilities.

Villages with most of facilities: Pathikonda Kallupalle.

Villages without Amenities (Education): None..

Scheduled Castes: Out of the total population of 48879 persons, 9658 persons (19.76%) belong to Scheduled Castes.

The villages having less than 10% SC population are None..

The villages having more than 50% SC population are None.

Sex ratio of Scheduled Caste population is 510.

Scheduled Castes Literates and Illiterates by Sex:

	Persons	Males	Females
Literate	4,434	2,629	1,805
Illiterate	5,224	2,101	3,123
Literacy rate	53.6	65.4	42.5
Graduate	34	31	3

Scheduled Castes (Dominant):

Mala, Madiga, Adi Dravida, Adi Andhra

Generic Castes etc.

For their cultural identity please see Appendix-I

Villages without Scheduled Castes: There are 0 village without any scheduled caste population.

Scheduled Tribes: Out of the total population of 48879 persons, 804 persons (1.64%) belong to Scheduled Tribes.

The villages having less than 10% ST population are Gundugallu, Pasupathur, Gandrajupalle, Keelapalle Pathikonda, Mamadugu, Jeedimakulapalle, Maredupalle Dandapalle, Kalagatoor, Kallupalle, Melumoy Kothapalle, Gangavaram, Keelapatla, Mogilpalle.

The villages having more than 50% ST population are None.

Sex ratio of Scheduled tribe population is 511.

Scheduled Tribes Literates and Illiterates by Sex:

	Persons	Males	Females
Literate	278	156	122
Illiterate	526	237	289
Literacy rate	42.3	49.4	35.7
Graduate	3	3	0

Scheduled Tribes (Dominant):

Yerukulas, Yenadis, Sugalis etc.

Generic Tribes etc., Chenchu etc.

For their cultural identity please see Appendix-II

Villages without Scheduled Tribes: There are 3 villages without any scheduled tribe population.

Literates and Illiterates by Sex (Total Population):

	Persons	Males	Females
Literate	24,722	15,068	9,654
Illiterate	24,157	9,361	14,796
Literacy rate	59	73	46
Graduate	458	370	88

Agriculture: ***Distribution of villages according to land use:*** Out of 16 villages, Total area (in hectare) is 15474, out of that 71.03 percent is cultivable and 26.6 percent of the cultivable area is irrigated.

Sources of Irrigation (Hectares): Government Canal 0, Private Canal 86.64, Well without Electricity 0, Well with Electricity 1242.9, Tubewell without Electricity 0, Tubewell with Electricity 415.36, Tank 974.87, River 0, Lake 0, Waterfall 0, Others 204.45.

Villages with population of 5000 to 9999: Gandrajupalle, Gangavaram.

Villages with population of 10000 and above: None

Distribution of Workers:

	Persons	Males	Females	WPR
Cultivators	9,454	5,852	3,602	36.16
Agricultural Labour	11,286	5,138	6,148	43.16
Household Industry	504	173	331	1.93
Other Workers	4,903	3,558	1,345	18.75
Main Workers	21,656	13,043	8,613	82.82
Marginal Workers	4,491	1,678	2,813	17.18
Total Workers	26,147	14,721	11,426	

Religion: Major Religious Communities:

	Persons	Males	Females	Sex Ratio
Hindu (90.81%)	44,387	22,104	22,283	1,008
Muslim (8.98%)	4,391	2,274	2,117	931
Christian (0.09%)	43	24	19	792
Sikh (0%)	-	-	-	-
Buddhists (0%)	-	-	-	-

Jain (0%)	-	-	-	-

Agewise Data:

	Persons	Males	Females	Sex Ratio
All ages	48,879	24,429	24,450	1001
0-14	16,384	8,182	8,202	1002
15-44	22,520	11,261	11,259	1000
45-79	9,532	4,795	4,737	988
80+	388	175	213	1217
Age not stated	55	16	39	2438

Languages (Dominant):
Telugu, Urdu, Tamil, Kannada, Marathi

Disabled Population:

	Persons	Males	Females	%
Total Disabled	747	424	323	
In Seeing	221	112	109	29.59
In Speech	99	51	48	13.25
In Hearing	42	24	18	5.62
In Movement	272	175	97	36.41
Mentally	113	62	51	15.13

GANGUVARISIGADAM

Ganguvarisigadam C.D. Block lies in the south-western part of Srikakulam district. The Block is located at a distance of 52 kms. from district headquarters (Srika kulam). There are 43 villages in the block with the total population of 55,087 persons. Area of the C.D. Block is 138.34 sq. kms. It is bounded in the north by Mandals Rajam and Santhakaviti, in the south by district Vizianagaram and Mandal Ponduru, in the east by Mandals Santhakaviti and Ponduru, and in the west by district Vizianagaram.

Communications:

Roadways : State Highway (S.H.): Direction- Rajam to Ponduru. Nearest Villages- Mettavalasa, Palakhandyam, Jagannadhapuram, Santhavurity, Anandapuram, Abothulape ta, Vandrangi.

Railway Station: Bathuva, Ganguvarisigadam.

Backwards Region Grants Fund: It receives Backward Region Grants.

Mahila Samakhya (Education for Women's Equality): It is decleared Socialy and Educationally Backward Block by the Government.

Annual Rainfall: Average Rainfall 1085.6 mm

Ground Water: Availability of the Ground Water in the Basin is (Information not avavible) H.A.M .and the utilization is (Information not avavible) H.A.M. It belongs to (Information not avavible) category. Depth to water level varies from 3 to 10 meter below the ground. Most of the wells go down in summer months.

Administration:

Division: Coastal Andhra. Parliamentary Constituency: 20 Vizianagram. District: Srikakulam. Mandal: Ganguvari sigadam. Assembly Constituency: 126 Etcherla. Gram Panch ayat: 31.

Villages: 43 **Inhabited:** 42 **Uninhabited:** 1

Ranking	District	State	National
Area	18	868	5209
Population	25	370	5050
Sex Ratio	35	632	2162
Child Sex Ratio	21	512	1916
Literacy Rate	32	806	4901
Density	10	641	2742
Work Participation Rate	26	189	1753

Gram Panchayats:

Anandhapurm, Batuva, Chettupodilam, Dalemrajuvalasa Devaravalasa, Dhavalapeta, G.Sigadam, Geddakancharam Gobburu, Jada, Jagannadhavalasa, Kapparam, Madhupam Marrivalasa, Mettavalasa, Musinivalasa, Nadimivalasa Nagulavalasa, Niddam, Palakhandym, Penta, Punnam S.P.R.Purm, Santhavurity, Seetampeta Sethubheemavaram, T.D.Valasa, Vandrangi, Velagada Venkayyapeta, Yenduva.

Amenities:

Education: Primary School in 41 villages, Middle school in 10 villages, Matriculation or Secondary School in 5 villages, namely Dalemrajuvalasa, Ganguvarisigadam, Santhavurity, Yenduva, Devaravalasa.

Higher Secondary or Pre University Courses or Inter-mediate or Junior College in 0 village of the CD Block, College in 0 village, Adult Literacy Center in 21 villages.

Medical: Hospital in 0 village, Dispensary in 1 village, Health Center in 1 village, Sub Center in 10 villages, Maternity and Child Welfare Center in 27 villages, Community health workers in 0 village.

The Village having Hospital or Dispensary or Health Center is Santhavurity.

Drinking Water: Tap water in 42 villages, Tank water in 42 villages, Well water in 42 villages, Tubewell in 42 villages and more than one source in 42 villages.

Bank: Banking facility in 3 villages, namely, Bathuva, Ganguvarisigadam, Vandrangi.

Credit Society in 9 villages Agricultural Credit Society in 7 Non-Agricultural Credit Society in 4 villages.

Others: Power supply in 42 villages, Cinema hall in 2 villages, sport club in 0 village, Stadium or Auditorium or Community Hall in 0 village, Post Office in 16 villages.

There are 15 villages having bus facilities.

Villages with most of facilities: Ganguvarisigadam Vandrangi.

Villages without amenities (Education):
Naiduvalasa..

Scheduled Castes: Out of the total population of 55087 persons, 6656 persons (12.08%) belong to Scheduled Castes. The villages having less than 10% SC population are Dalemrajuvalasa, Naiduvalasa, Bathuva, Yenduvapeta Mettavalasa, Palakhandyam, Gedelapeta, Nakkapeta Seetharampuram, Anandapuram, S.P. Ramachandra Puram Yenduva, Narasimhapuram, Geddakancharam Seethubhimavaram, Penasam, Kapparam, Devaravalasa. The villages having more than 50% SC population are None.

Sex ratio of Scheduled Caste population is 487.

Scheduled Castes Literates and Illiterates by Sex:

	Persons	Males	Females
Literate	2,823	1,832	991
Illiterate	3,833	1,585	2,248
Literacy rate	48.5	60.8	35.2
Graduate	49	42	7

Scheduled Castes (Dominant):

Mala, Madiga, Relli, Beda Jangam etc., Bavuri

For their cultural identity please see Appendix-I

Villages without Scheduled Castes: There are 9 villages without any scheduled caste population.

Scheduled Tribes: Out of the total population of 55087 persons, 450 persons (0.82%) belong to Scheduled Tribes. The villages having less than 10% ST population are Sarveswarapuram, Mushinivalasa, Dalemrajuvalasa Naiduvalasa, Ullivalasa, Punnam, Bathuva, Jada Jagannadhavalasa, Yenduvapeta, Venkayyapeta Ganguvarisigadam, Gobburu, Mettavalasa, Palakhandyam Gedelapeta, Marrivalasa, Nagulavalasa, Penta Nakkapeta, Tankaladuggivalasa, Jagannadhapuram Seetharampuram, Santhavurity, Anandapuram Abothulapeta, Vandrangi, Niddam, Madhupam Chettupodilam, Chandrayyapeta, Nadimivalasa S.P. Ramachandra Puram, Yenduva, Narasimhapuram Geddakancharam, Seethubhimavaram, Gangannadora Palem Velagada, Kapparam, Devaravalasa.

The villages having more than 50% ST population are None.

Sex ratio of Scheduled tribe population is 484.

Scheduled Tribes Literates and Illiterates by Sex:

	Persons	Males	Females
Literate	167	120	47
Illiterate	283	112	171
Literacy rate	44.8	63.2	25.7
Graduate	1	1	0

Scheduled Tribes (Dominant):

Yerukulas, Gadabas, Konda Dhoras

For their cultural identity please see Appendix-II

Villages without Scheduled Tribes: There are 25 villages without any scheduled tribe population.

Literates and Illiterates by Sex (Total Population):

	Persons	Males	Females
Literate	22,648	14,368	8,280
Illiterate	32,439	13,492	18,947
Literacy rate	47	60	35
Graduate	591	515	76

Agriculture: ***Distribution of villages according to land use:*** Out of 43 villages, Total area (in hectare) is 13835, out of that 81.53 percent is cultivable and 36.32 percent of the cultivable area is irrigated.

Sources of Irrigation (Hectares): Government Canal 0, Private Canal 0, Well without Electricity 0, Well with Electricity 0, Tubewell without Electricity 65.74, Tubewell with Electricity 0, Tank 4031.35, River 0, Lake 0, Waterfall 0, Others 0.

Villages with population of 5000 to 9999: None

Villages with population of 10000 and above: None

Distribution of Workers:

	Persons	Males	Females	WPR
Cultivators	8,259	5,749	2,510	29.07
Agricultural Labour	14,179	6,487	7,692	49.91
Household Industry	1,314	745	569	4.63
Other Workers	4,656	3,654	1,002	16.39
Main Workers	19,558	14,208	5,350	68.85
Marginal Workers	8,850	2,427	6,423	31.15
Total Workers	28,408	16,635	11,773	

Religion: Major Religious Communities:

	Persons	Males	Females	Sex Ratio
Hindu (99.26%)	54,679	27,658	27,021	977
Muslim (0.24%)	134	72	62	861
Christian (0.44%)	245	115	130	1,130
Sikh (0%)	1	1	-	-
Buddhists (0%)	-	-	-	-
Jain (0%)	-	-	-	-

Agewise Data:

	Persons	Males	Females	Sex Ratio
All ages	55,087	27,860	27,227	977
0-14	18,319	9,565	8,754	915
15-44	25,250	12,776	12,474	976
45-79	11,162	5,366	5,796	1080
80+	302	123	179	1455
Age not stated	54	30	24	800

Languages (Dominant):

Telugu, Urdu, Gondi, Tamil, Hindi

Disabled Population:

	Persons	Males	Females	%
Total Disabled	1,452	764	688	
In Seeing	653	336	317	44.97
In Speech	124	61	63	8.54

In Hearing	127	64	63	8.75
In Movement	409	240	169	28.17

Mentally	139	63	76	9.57

GANNAVARAM

Gannavaram C.D. Block lies in the northern part of Krishna district. The Block is located at a distance of 94 kms. from district headquarters (Machilipatnam). There are 25 villages in the block with the total population of 80,404 persons. Area of the C.D. Block is 196.56 sq. kms. It is bounded in the north by Mandals Agiripalle and Bapulapadu, in the south by Mandals Vijayawada Rural and Unguturu, in the east by Mandals Unguturu and Bapulapadu, and in the west by Mandal Vijayawada Rural.

Communications:

Roadways : NH- 5: Direction- Vijayawada to Eluru. Nearest Villages- Kesarapalle, Allapuram, Buddavaram, China Avutapalle, Gannavaram.

Railway Station: Vedurupavuluru, Gannavaram.

Integrated Child Development Scheme (ICDS) Project: Gannavaram, Total Anganwadi Centres: 212

Annaul Rainfall: Average Rainfall 1620 mm

Ground Water: Availability of the Ground Water in the Basin is (Information not avavible) H.A.M .and the utilization is (Information not avavible) H.A.M. It belongs to (Information not avavible) category. Depth to water level varies from 3 to 10 meter below the ground. Most of the wells go down in summer months.

Natural Division : Krishna Delta Region

Administration:

Division: Coastal Andhra. Parliamentary Constituency: 28 Machilipatnam. District: Krishna. Mandal: Gannavaram. Assembly Constituency: 190 Gannavaram. Gram Panchayat: 21

Villages: 25 **Inhabited:** 23 **Uninhabited:** 2

Ranking	District	State	National
Area	17	577	4241
Population	4	37	4093
Sex Ratio	19	496	1855
Child Sex Ratio	30	598	2460
Literacy Rate	15	105	1518
Density	42	949	2686
Work Participation Rate	16	177	3395

Gram Panchayats:

Ajjampudi, Allapuram, B.B.Gudem, Buddavaram Buthumillipadu, Chikkavaram, Chinaavutapalli Gannavaram, Gollanapalli, Gopavarapugudem Jakkulanekkalam, Kesarapalli, Kondapavuluru Kothagudem, Maadalavarigudem, Mustabad Purushottapatnam, Savaragudem, Surampalli, Tempalli Veerapanenigudem.

Amenities:

Education: Primary School in 22 villages, Middle school in 12 villages, Matriculation or Secondary School in 5 villages, namely Gollanapalle, Veerapanenigudem, Vedurupavuluru, Gannavaram, Buddavaram.

Higher Secondary or Pre University Courses or Intermediate or Junior College in 2 villages of the CD Block,, namely Gannavaram, Buddavaram.

College in 2 villages, Adult Literacy Center in 6 villages., Colleges are in villages, namely Gannavaram, Buddavaram.

Medical: Hospital in 2 villages, Dispensary in 3 villages, Health Center in 2 villages, Sub Center in 8 villages, Maternity and Child Welfare Center in 0 village, Community health workers in 0 village.

The Villages having Hospital or Dispensary or Health Center are Gollanapalle, Kesarapalle, Gannavaram, Buthumillipadu.

Drinking Water: Tap water in 22 villages, Tank water in 0 villages, Well water in 0 village, Tubewell in 0 village and more than one source in 22 villages.

Bank: Banking facility in 3 villages, namely, Surampalle, Veerapanenigudem, Gannavaram.

Credit Society in 14 villages Agricultural Credit Society in 10 Non-Agricultural Credit Society in 13 villages.

Others: Power supply in 23 villages, Cinema hall in 1 village, sport club in 0 village, Stadium or Auditorium or Community Hall in 1 village, Post Office in 17 villages.

There are 20 villages having bus facilities.

Villages with most of facilities: Surampalle Veerapanenigudem, Gannavaram.

Villages without amenities (Education): Venkatanarasimhapuram..

Scheduled Castes: Out of the total population of 80404 persons, 17331 persons (21.55%) belong to Scheduled Castes. The villages having less than 10% SC population are Tempalle, Veerapanenigudem, Savarigudem Venkatanarasimhapuram.

The villages having more than 50% SC population are None.

Sex ratio of Scheduled Caste population is 499.

Scheduled Castes Literates and Illiterates by Sex:

	Persons	Males	Females
Literate	10,488	5,588	4,900
Illiterate	6,843	3,096	3,747
Literacy rate	68.8	73.4	64.2
Graduate	407	268	139

Scheduled Castes (Dominant):

Madiga, Mala, Mala Dasu, Beda Jangam etc., Relli

For their cultural identity please see Appendix-I

Villages without Scheduled Castes: There are 4 villages without any scheduled caste population.

Scheduled Tribes: Out of the total population of 80404 persons, 1716 persons (2.13%) belong to Scheduled Tribes. The villages having less than 10% ST population are Ramachandrapuram, Surampalle, Kondapavuluru Gopavarapugudem, Gollanapalle, Chikkavaram Metlapalle, Balliparru, Tempalle Bahubalendrunigudem, Purushottapatnam Vedurupavuluru, Savarigudem, Jakkulanekkalam Kesarapalle, Venkatanarasimhapuram, Gannavaram China Avutapalle, Allapuram, Buddavaram, Ajjampudi Buthumillipadu.

The villages having more than 50% ST population are None.

Sex ratio of Scheduled tribe population is 483.

Scheduled Tribes Literates and Illiterates by Sex:

	Persons	Males	Females
Literate	594	367	227
Illiterate	1,122	521	601
Literacy rate	40.2	47.9	31.8
Graduate	19	14	5

Scheduled Tribes (Dominant):

Sugalis etc., Yerukulas, Chenchu etc., Yenadis Konda Dhoras

For their cultural identity please see Appendix-II

Villages without Scheduled Tribes: There are 7 villages without any scheduled tribe population.

Literates and Illiterates by Sex (Total Population):

	Persons	Males	Females
Literate	48,065	26,195	21,870
Illiterate	32,339	14,325	18,014
Literacy rate	68	73	62
Graduate	2,952	2,000	952

Agriculture: ***Distribution of villages according to land use:*** Out of 25 villages, Total area (in hectare) is 19656, out of that 69.59 percent is cultivable and 62.37 percent of the cultivable area is irrigated.

Sources of Irrigation (Hectares): Government Canal 3684.03, Private Canal 0, Well without Electricity 0, Well with Electricity 86, Tubewell without Electricity 0, Tubewell with Electricity 825, Tank 3008, River 0, Lake 0, Waterfall 0, Others 1261.

Villages with population of 5000 to 9999: Surampalle, Vedurupavuluru, Kesarapalle, Buddavaram.

Villages with population of 10000 and above: Gannavaram.

Distribution of Workers:

	Persons	Males	Females	WPR
Cultivators	4,611	3,979	632	12.5
Agricultural Labour	21,440	10,791	10,649	58.14
Household Industry	645	405	240	1.75
Other Workers	10,181	8,233	1,948	27.61
Main Workers	34,055	22,372	11,683	92.35
Marginal Workers	2,822	1,036	1,786	7.65
Total Workers	36,877	23,408	13,469	

Religion: Major Religious Communities:

	Persons	Males	Females	Sex Ratio
Hindu (85.83%)	69,010	34,869	34,141	979
Muslim (5.85%)	4,706	2,385	2,321	973
Christian (8.19%)	6,589	3,211	3,378	1,052
Sikh (0.03%)	22	16	6	375
Buddhists (0%)	3	1	2	2,000
Jain (0%)	3	2	1	500

Agewise Data:

	Persons	Males	Females	Sex Ratio
All ages	80,404	40,520	39,884	984
0-14	25,034	12,694	12,340	972
15-44	38,054	19,209	18,845	981
45-79	16,546	8,224	8,322	1012
80+	706	350	356	1017
Age not stated	64	43	21	488

Languages (Dominant):

Telugu, Urdu, Hindi, Tamil, Oriya

Disabled Population:

	Persons	Males	Females	%
Total Disabled	1,295	699	596	
In Seeing	347	178	169	26.8
In Speech	149	74	75	11.51
In Hearing	63	28	35	4.86
In Movement	500	294	206	38.61
Mentally	236	125	111	18.22

GANTYADA

Gantyada C.D. Block lies in the southern part of Vizian agaram district. The Block is located at a distance of 12 kms. from district headquarters (Vizianagaram). There are 45 villages in the block with the total population of 67,546 persons. Area of the C.D. Block is 170.17 sq. kms. It is bounded in the north by distri ct Vishakhapatnam and Mandal Bondapalle, in the south by Mandal Jami, in the east by Mandal Vizianagaram, and in the west by district Vishakhapatnam and Mandal Srungavarapukota.

Communications :

Roadways : State Highway (S.H.): Direction- Srungavarapu kota to Vizianagaram. Nearest Villages- Kothavelagada, Vasadi, Kondathamarapalle, Buradapadu, Korlam, Gantyada, Kotarubilli, Narava, Ramavaram, Karakavalasa, Jadderu.

River: Gostani Nadi- Nearest Villages- Bheemavaram,

Jadderu, Thatipudi.

Backwards Region Grants Fund: It receives Backward Region Grants.

Integrated Child Development Scheme (ICDS) Project: Gantyada, Total Anganwadi Centres: 204

Annaul Rainfall: Average Rainfall 886.7 mm

Ground Water: Availability of the Ground Water in the Basin is (Information not avavible) H.A.M .and the utilization is (Information not avavible) H.A.M. It belongs to (Information not avavible) category. Depth to water level varies from 3 to 10 meter below the ground. Most of the wells go down in summer months.

Administration:

Division: Coastal Andhra. Parliamentary Constituency: 20 Vizianagram. District: Vizianagram. Mandal: Gantyada. Assembly Constituency: 135 Gajapathinagram. Gram Panch ayat: 35.

Villages: 45 **Inhabited:** 45 **Uninhabited:** 0

Ranking	District	State	National
Area	7	714	4700
Population	3	171	4580
Sex Ratio	29	355	1466
Child Sex Ratio	13	144	379
Literacy Rate	4	577	4133
Density	2	13	2751
Work Participation Rate	11	192	104

Gram Panchayats:

Bonangi, Budatanapalli, Buradapadu, Chandrampeta Chnamanapuram, Diguvakondaparti, Gantyada, Ginjeru Godiyada, Jaggapuram, Kirthubarthi, Kondatamarapalli Korlam, Kotaribilli, Kottavelagada, Lakkidam Madanapuram, Madupada, Mokalapadu, Murapaka, Narava Neelawathi, Pedamajipalem, Pedavemali, Penasam Pentasriramapuram, Pollanki, R.Vasantha Ramabhadrapuram, Ramavaram, Ravivalasa, Regubelli Siripuram, Tatipudi, Vasadi.

Amenities:

Education: Primary School in 41 villages, Middle school in 13 villages, Matriculation or Secondary School in 8 villages, namely Bonangi, Vasadi, Pedamajjipalem, Pentasrirampuram, Budatanapalle, Gantyada, Vasantha, Pedavemali.

Higher Secondary or Pre University Courses or Intermediate or Junior College in 0 village of the CD Block, College in 1 village, Adult Literacy Center in 26 villages., College is in village, namely Gantyada.

Medical: Hospital in 7 villages, Dispensary in 0 village, Health Center in 2 villages, Sub Center in 17 villages, Maternity and Child Welfare Center in 0 village, Community health workers in 0 village.

The Villages having Hospital or Dispensary or Health Center are Donkada, Vasadi, Kondathamarapalle, Pedamajjipalem, Buradapadu, Regubilli, Pentasrirampuram.

Drinking Water: Tap water in 45 villages, Tank water in 45 villages, Well water in 45 villages, Tubewell in 45 villages and more than one source in 45 villages.

Bank: Banking facility in 10 villages, namely, Thatipudi, Bonangi, Pedamajjipalem, Pentasrirampuram Budatanapalle, Gantyada, Lakhidam, Vasantha Pedavemali, Ravivalasa.

Credit Society in 14 villages Agricultural Credit Society in 8 Non-Agricultural Credit Society in 13 villages.

Others: Power supply in 45 villages, Cinema hall in 2 villages, sport club in 0 village, Stadium or Auditorium or Community Hall in 0 village, Post Office in 34 villages.

There are 37 villages having bus facilities.

Villages with most of facilities: Thatipudi Bonangi, Pedamajjipalem, Pentasrirampuram Budatanapalle, Gantyada, Lakhidam, Vasantha Pedavemali, Ravivalasa.

Villages without amenities (Education): Eguvakondaparthi, Mosalikandi, Alaparthi, Jadderu..

Scheduled Castes: Out of the total population of 67546 persons, 7903 persons (11.7%) belong to Scheduled Castes. The villages having less than 10% SC population are Eguvakondaparthi, Addateega, Diguvakondaparthi Mosalikandi, Alaparthi, Bheemavaram, Jadderu Madhupada, Vasadi, Kondathamarapalle, Ginjeru Buradapadu, Regubilli, Korlam Yerakannamdora Seetharamapuram, Kirtubarthi Budatanapalle, Penasam, Lakhidam, Pedavemali Murapaka, Jaggapuram, Nandam.

The villages having more than 50% SC population are None.

Sex ratio of Scheduled Caste population is 484.

Scheduled Castes Literates and Illiterates by Sex:

	Persons	Males	Females
Literate	3,568	2,231	1,337
Illiterate	4,335	1,843	2,492
Literacy rate	51.7	61.9	40.6
Graduate	63	47	16

Scheduled Castes (Dominant):

Mala, Madiga, Relli, Godagali, Generic Castes etc.

For their cultural identity please see Appendix-I

Villages without Scheduled Castes: There are 7 villages without any scheduled caste population.

Scheduled Tribes: Out of the total population of 67546 persons, 2224 persons (3.29%) belong to Scheduled Tribes. The villages having less than 10% ST population are

Madhupada, Thatipudi, Madhanapuram, Bonangi Kothavelagada, Ramabhadrapuram, Mokalapadu, Donkada Vasadi, Kondathamarapalle, Pedamajjipalem, Ginjeru Buradapadu, Regubilli, Pentasrirampuram, Pollanki Korlam, Yerakannamdora Seetharamapuram, Godiyada Kirtubarthi, Chinamanapuram, Budatanapalle, Penasam Neelavathi, Gantyada, Lakhidam, Vasantha Chandrampeta, Pedavemali, Murapaka, Siripuram Ravivalasa, Kotarubilli, Jaggapuram, Nandam, Narava Ramavaram.

The villages having more than 50% ST population are Eguvakondaparthi, Addateega, Diguvakondaparthi Mosalikandi, Alaparthi, Bheemavaram, Jadderu.

Sex ratio of Scheduled tribe population is 475.

Scheduled Tribes Literates and Illiterates by Sex:

	Persons	Males	Females
Literate	525	343	182
Illiterate	1,699	825	874
Literacy rate	27.7	34.2	20.4
Graduate	1	1	0

Scheduled Tribes (Dominant):

Konda Dhoras, Yerukulas, Valmiki, Bagata, Gadabas

For their cultural identity please see Appendix-II

Villages without Scheduled Tribes: There are 14 villages without any scheduled tribe population.

Literates and Illiterates by Sex (Total Population):

	Persons	Males	Females
Literate	31,243	19,232	12,011
Illiterate	36,303	14,676	21,627
Literacy rate	52	64	40
Graduate	1,202	1,005	197

Agriculture: ***Distribution of villages according to land use:*** Out of 45 villages, Total area (in hectare) is 17017, out of that 82.26 percent is cultivable and 51.88 percent of the cultivable area is irrigated.

Sources of Irrigation (Hectares): Government Canal 3380.1, Private Canal 0, Well without Electricity 6.48, Well with Electricity 0, Tubewell without Electricity 0, Tubewell with Electricity 147.3, Tank 3729.2, River 0, Lake 0, Waterfall 0, Others 0.

Villages with population of 5000 to 9999: None

Villages with population of 10000 and above: None

Distribution of Workers:

	Persons	Males	Females	WPR
Cultivators	14,469	8,766	5,703	34.09
Agricultural Labour	18,670	6,529	12,141	43.99
Household Industry	1,275	707	568	3
Other Workers	8,028	6,112	1,916	18.92
Main Workers	28,807	18,889	9,918	67.87
Marginal Workers	13,635	3,225	10,410	32.13
Total Workers	42,442	22,114	20,328	

Religion: Major Religious Communities:

	Persons	Males	Females	Sex Ratio
Hindu (99.19%)	66,999	33,639	33,360	992
Muslim (0.6%)	405	203	202	995
Christian (0.1%)	70	30	40	1,333
Sikh (0.01%)	6	3	3	1,000
Buddhists (0%)	-	-	-	-
Jain (0%)	-	-	-	-

Agewise Data:

	Persons	Males	Females	Sex Ratio
All ages	67,546	33,908	33,638	992
0-14	19,513	10,015	9,498	948
15-44	31,908	16,216	15,692	968
45-79	15,722	7,483	8,239	1101
80+	304	143	161	1126
Age not stated	99	51	48	941

Languages (Dominant):

Telugu, Urdu, Gondi, Oriya, Tamil

Disabled Population:

	Persons	Males	Females	%
Total Disabled	1,342	734	608	
In Seeing	484	244	240	36.07
In Speech	208	112	96	15.5
In Hearing	94	50	44	7
In Movement	419	254	165	31.22
Mentally	137	74	63	10.21

GARA

Gara C.D. Block lies in the southern part of Srikakulam district. The Block is located at a distance of 18 kms. from district headquarters (Srikakulam). There are 25 villages in the block with the total population of 75,017 persons. Area of the C.D. Block is 158.47 sq. kms. It is bounded in the north by Mandals Narasann apeta and Polaki, in the south and east by the Bay of Bengal, and in the west by Srikakulam Mandal.

Communications:

Roadways : Metalled Roads: Nearest Villages Buravalli, Ambalavalasa, Salihundam, Gara, Vomaravalli, Calingapa tnam, Jalluvalasa, Thulugu, Nizamabad, Sativada, Ampolu, Ramachandra Puram, Deepavali, Srikurmam, Jafrabad.

River: Vamsadhara Nadi- Nearest Villages- Buravalli, Ambalavalasa, Salihundam, Gara, Vomaravalli, Calingapa tnam.

Backwards Region Grants Fund: It receives Backward Region Grants.

Mahila Samakhya (Education for Women's Equality): It is decleared Socialy and Educationally Backward Block by the Government.

Integrated Child Development Scheme (ICDS) Project:

Gara, Total Anganwadi Centres: 170

Annual Rainfall: Average Rainfall 1085.6 mm

Ground Water: Availability of the Ground Water in the Basin is (Information not avavible) H.A.M .and the utilization is (Information not avavible) H.A.M. It belongs to (Information not avavible) category. Depth to water level varies from 3 to 10 meter below the ground. Most of the wells go down in summer months.

Coastel Villages: Nearest Villages- Thonangi, Srikurmam, Korlam, Vatsavalasa.

Administration:

Division: Coastal Andhra. Parliamentary Constituency: 19 Srikakulam. District: Srikakulam. Mandal: Gara. Assembly Constituency: 124 Srikakulam. Gram Panchayat: 24

Places of Turist Interest:

Srikurmam: Srikurmam Village is situated at a distance of 14.5. Kms to the South-East of Srikakulam town. The village was named after the temple, the presiding diety of which is Lord Vishnu in Kurmavatara. Srikurmam is a famous place of piligrimage and the temple here is the only one of its kind in the whole of India. The temple is noted for its architectural beauty and contains many inscriptions ranging from the Eleventh Century to the Ninteenth Century A.D. These inscriptions throw light on the different dynasties which have held sway over this region. Dolostavam is the important festival and more than 40, 000 piligrims congregate on this occasion.

Sailhundam: Salihundam is situated at a distance of 18 Kms. from Srikakulam town. The village assumed arche ological importance due to the excavation of Buddist Stupas. The Archeology Department had taken all precaut ionary measures to preserve these monuments.

Calingapatnam: It is situated at a distance of 25 Kms, fromSrikakulam.

It is an important coastal village. Dargha Shariff(Tomb of religious persons)

Shaik Madeena Acquiline is situated at this place.

Once it was a minor port and some Europeon merchants resided during East India Company regime.

There is one light house functioning here focusing to a distance of 23Kms.

The river vamsadhara joins the Bay of Bengal in this village.

Villages: 25 **Inhabited:** 24 **Uninhabited:** 1

Ranking	District	State	National
Area	8	781	4902
Population	4	67	4284
Sex Ratio	21	174	962
Child Sex Ratio	36	893	3944
Literacy Rate	11	370	3316
Density	30	912	2334
Work Participation Rate	14	125	3161

Gram Panchayats:

Amballavalasa, Ampolu, Balarampuram, Bandaruvanipeta Boravanipeta, Buravalli, Calingapatnam(U.I.), Gara Gonti, K.Sairagam, Korlam, Korni, Matchelesam Nizambad, Poosarlapadu, Ramachandrapuram, Salihundam Sathivada, Srikurmam, Thonangi, Tulugu @K.N.Puram Vadada, Vatchavalasa, Vomaravalli.

Amenities:

Education: Primary School in 23 villages, Middle school in 12 villages, Matriculation or Secondary School in 7 villages, namely Gara, Vomaravalli, Calingapatnam, Thonangi, Korni, Ampolu, Srikurmam.

Higher Secondary or Pre University Courses or Inter-mediate or Junior College in 1 village of the CD Block,, namely Calingapatnam.

College in 2 villages, Adult Literacy Center in 12 villages., Colleges are in villages, namely Calingapatnam, Srikurmam.

Medical: Hospital in 1 village, Dispensary in 2 villages, Health Center in 3 villages, Sub Center in 11 villages, Maternity and Child Welfare Center in 0 village, Community health workers in 0 village.

The Villages having Hospital or Dispensary or Health Center are Calingapatnam, Korlam.

Drinking Water: Tap water in 24 villages, Tank water in 24 villages, Well water in 24 villages, Tubewell in 24 villages and more than one source in 24 villages.

Bank: Banking facility in 3 villages, namely, Gara, Calingapatnam, Srikurmam.

Credit Society in 20 villages Agricultural Credit Society in 8 Non-Agricultural Credit Society in 19 villages.

Others: Power supply in 24 villages, Cinema hall in 3 villages, sport club in 0 village, Stadium or Auditorium or Community Hall in 0 village, Post Office in 13 villages.

There are 17 villages having bus facilities.

Villages with most of facilities: Gara Calingapatnam, Srikurmam.

Villages without amenities (Education):

Fakeertakya..

Scheduled Castes: Out of the total population of 75017 persons, 4302 persons (5.73%) belong to Scheduled Castes. The villages having less than 10% SC population are Gara, Vomaravalli, Calingapatnam, Thonangi, Korni Thulugu, Nizamabad, Fakeertakya, Sativada Kothurusyrigam, Ampolu, Ramachandra Puram, Vadada

Deepavali, Srikurmam, Jafrabad, Korlam, Vatsavalasa.
The villages having more than 50% SC population are None.

Sex ratio of Scheduled Caste population is 489.

Scheduled Castes Literates and Illiterates by Sex:

	Persons	Males	Females
Literate	2,268	1,336	932
Illiterate	2,034	861	1,173
Literacy rate	60.0	69.6	50.1
Graduate	55	46	9

Scheduled Castes (Dominant):

Mala, Adi Andhra, Madiga, Relli, Beda Jangam etc.

For their cultural identity please see Appendix-I

Villages without Scheduled Castes: There are 4 villages without any scheduled caste population.

Scheduled Tribes: Out of the total population of 75017 persons, 237 persons (0.32%) belong to Scheduled Tribes. The villages having less than 10% ST population are Buravalli, Ambalavalasa, Salihundam, Gara Vomaravalli, Calingapatnam, Thonangi, Korni Jalluvalasa, Thulugu, Nizamabad, Fakeertakya Sativada, Raghavapuram, Kothurusyrigam, Ampolu Ramachandra Puram, Vadada, Gonti, Deepavali Srikurmam, Jafrabad, Korlam, Vatsavalasa.

The villages having more than 50% ST population are None.

Sex ratio of Scheduled tribe population is 523.

Scheduled Tribes Literates and Illiterates by Sex:

	Persons	Males	Females
Literate	107	62	45
Illiterate	130	51	79
Literacy rate	55.7	67.4	45.0
Graduate	2	2	0

Scheduled Tribes (Dominant):

Yerukulas, Yenadis, Konda Dhoras, Konda Kapus Savaras etc.

For their cultural identity please see Appendix-II

Villages without Scheduled Tribes: There are 15 villages without any scheduled tribe population.

Literates and Illiterates by Sex (Total Population):

	Persons	Males	Females
Literate	37,048	21,945	15,103
Illiterate	37,969	15,428	22,541
Literacy rate	57	68	46
Graduate	1,011	837	174

Agriculture: ***Distribution of villages according to land use:*** Out of 25 villages, Total area (in hectare) is 15849, out of that 76.53 percent is cultivable and 51.42 percent of the cultivable area is irrigated.

Sources of Irrigation (Hectares): Government Canal 6068.23, Private Canal 0, Well without Electricity 0, Well with Electricity 0, Tubewell without Electricity 0, Tubewell with Electricity 163, Tank 5.49, River 0, Lake 0, Waterfall 0, Others 0.

Villages with population of 5000 to 9999:

Calingapatnam, Thonangi, Ampolu.

Villages with population of 10000 and above:

Srikurmam.

Distribution of Workers:

	Persons	Males	Females	WPR
Cultivators	5,401	3,961	1,440	15.64
Agricultural Labour	17,675	8,045	9,630	51.18
Household Industry	1,377	720	657	3.99
Other Workers	10,082	8,480	1,602	29.19
Main Workers	24,207	17,380	6,827	70.09
Marginal Workers	10,328	3,826	6,502	29.91
Total Workers	34,535	21,206	13,329	

Religion: Major Religious Communities:

	Persons	Males	Females	Sex Ratio
Hindu (99.63%)	74,736	37,230	37,506	1,007
Muslim (0.15%)	113	57	56	982
Christian (0.16%)	121	61	60	984
Sikh (0%)	-	-	-	-
Buddhists (0%)	1	-	1	-
Jain (0%)	-	-	-	-

Agewise Data:

	Persons	Males	Females	Sex Ratio
All ages	75,017	37,373	37,644	1007
0-14	24,980	12,764	12,216	957
15-44	34,915	17,524	17,391	992
45-79	14,602	6,856	7,746	1130
80+	444	188	256	1362
Age not stated	76	41	35	854

Languages (Dominant):

Telugu, Oriya, Others, Gondi, Urdu

Disabled Population:

	Persons	Males	Females	%
Total Disabled	1,520	839	681	
In Seeing	599	290	309	39.41
In Speech	173	94	79	11.38
In Hearing	88	46	42	5.79
In Movement	447	290	157	29.41
Mentally	213	119	94	14.01

GARIDE PALLE

Garidepalle C.D. Block lies in the central east part of Nalgonda district. The Block is located at a distance of 63 kms. from district headquarters (Nalgonda). There are 11 villages in the block with the total popul ation of 54,515 persons. Area of the C.D. Block is 190. 54 sq. kms. It is bounded by Neredcherla Mandal on south and west, Penpahad Mandal on north, Chilkur Mandal on north-east, Huzurnagar Mandal on west, and Mattepal le Mandal on south-west.

Communications:

Roadways : Metalled Roads: Nearest Villages- Ponugodu, Tallamalkapuram, Raini Gudem, Garidepalle.

Backwards Region Grants Fund: It receives Backward Region Grants.

Annual Rainfall: Average Rainfall 723 mm

Ground Water: Availability of the Ground Water in the Basin is 8711 H.A.M. and the utilization is 781 H.A. M. It belongs to Safe category. Depth to water level varies from 5 to 10 meter below the ground. Most of the wells go down in summer months. The well density in the entire block is 5 wells per sq. km. Total no. of the wells in the block are enumerated as 1009, according to the Ground Water Estimation Committee.

Natural Division : Krishna Piedmont Plain Region

Administration:

Division: Telangana. Parliamentary Constituency: 13 Nalgonda. District: Nalgonda. Mandal: Garide Palle. Assembly Constituency: 89 Huzurnagar. Gram Panchayat: 18

Villages: 11 **Inhabited:** 11 **Uninhabited:** 0

Ranking	District	State	National
Area	41	608	4341
Population	11	383	5070
Sex Ratio	36	780	2640
Child Sex Ratio	13	414	1539
Literacy Rate	25	494	3823
Density	26	479	3679
Work Participation Rate	7	415	1228

Gram Panchayats:

Abbireddygudem, Appannapeta, Gaddipally, Ganugubanda Garidepally, Kachavarigudem, Kalmalchervu Kalwapally, Keetavarigudem, Kondarampuram Kothagudem, L.B.Nagar, Ponugode, Qutubshahpuram Rayanigudem, Sarvaram, Tallamalkapuram, Velidanda.

Amenities:

Education: Primary School in 11 villages, Middle school in 10 villages, Matriculation or Secondary School in 5 villages, namely Gaddipalle, Ponugodu, Raini Gudem, Garidepalle, Kalmala Chervu.

Higher Secondary or Pre University Courses or Intermediate or Junior College in 1 village of the CD Block,, namely Garidepalle.

College in 0 village, Adult Literacy Center in 11 villages.

Medical: Hospital in 0 village, Dispensary in 2 villages, Health Center in 2 villages, Sub Center in 8 villages, Maternity and Child Welfare Center in 0 village, Community health workers in 0 village.

The Villages having Hospital or Dispensary or Health Center are Ponugodu, Garidepalle.

Drinking Water: Tap water in 11 villages, Tank water in 11 villages, Well water in 11 villages, Tubewell in 11 villages and more than one source in 11 villages.

Bank: Banking facility in 2 villages, namely, Gaddipalle, Kalmala Chervu.

Credit Society in 10 villages Agricultural Credit Society in 10 Non-Agricultural Credit Society in 6 villages.

Others: Power supply in 11 villages, Cinema hall in 2 villages, sport club in 0 village, Stadium or Auditorium or Community Hall in 0 village, Post Office in 9 villages.

There are 9 villages having bus facilities.

Villages with most of facilities: Gaddipalle Kalmala Chervu.

Villages without Amenities (Education): None..

Scheduled Castes: Out of the total population of 54515 persons, 10500 persons (19.26%) belong to Scheduled Castes.

The villages having less than 10% SC population are None..

The villages having more than 50% SC population are None.

Sex ratio of Scheduled Caste population is 496.

Scheduled Castes Literates and Illiterates by Sex:

	Persons	Males	Females
Literate	4,205	2,704	1,501
Illiterate	6,295	2,593	3,702
Literacy rate	46.4	58.9	33.6
Graduate	74	64	10

Scheduled Castes (Dominant):

Madiga, Mala, Beda Jangam etc., Bindla, Dom etc.

For their cultural identity please see Appendix-I

Villages without Scheduled Castes: There are 0 village without any scheduled caste population.

Scheduled Tribes: Out of the total population of 54515 persons, 4758 persons (8.73%) belong to Scheduled Tribes.

The villages having less than 10% ST population are Gaddipalle, Ponugodu, Raini Gudem, Kaluvapalle Sarvaram, Garidepalle, Ganugabanda.

The villages having more than 50% ST population are None.

Sex ratio of Scheduled tribe population is 479.

Scheduled Tribes Literates and Illiterates by Sex:

	Persons	Males	Females
Literate	1,604	1,151	453
Illiterate	3,154	1,330	1,824
Literacy rate	40.0	54.9	23.7
Graduate	31	30	1

Scheduled Tribes (Dominant):

Sugalis etc., Yerukulas, Yenadis, Bagata, Koya etc.

For their cultural identity please see Appendix-II

Villages without Scheduled Tribes: There are 0 village without any scheduled tribe population.

Literates and Illiterates by Sex (Total Population):

	Persons	Males	Females
Literate	25,643	15,844	9,799
Illiterate	28,872	11,864	17,008
Literacy rate	54	66	42
Graduate	948	847	101

Agriculture: ***Distribution of villages according to land use:*** Out of 11 villages, Total area (in hectare) is 19053, out of that 80.07 percent is cultivable and 71.56 percent of the cultivable area is irrigated.

Sources of Irrigation (Hectares): Government Canal 7787.32, Private Canal 0, Well without Electricity 0, Well with Electricity 376.71, Tubewell without Electricity 0, Tubewell with Electricity 227.83, Tank 974.04, River 0, Lake 0, Waterfall 0, Others 1551.51.

Villages with population of 5000 to 9999: Ponugodu, Raini Gudem, Kalmala Chervu.

Villages with population of 10000 and above: Garidepalle.

Distribution of Workers:

	Persons	Males	Females	WPR
Cultivators	8,037	5,534	2,503	27.4
Agricultural Labour	16,221	6,370	9,851	55.3
Household Industry	556	305	251	1.9
Other Workers	4,517	3,515	1,002	15.4
Main Workers	25,375	14,634	10,741	86.51
Marginal Workers	3,956	1,090	2,866	13.49
Total Workers	29,331	15,724	13,607	

Religion: Major Religious Communities:

	Persons	Males	Females	Sex Ratio
Hindu (96.56%)	52,642	26,764	25,878	967
Muslim (2.79%)	1,522	770	752	977
Christian (0.56%)	304	148	156	1,054
Sikh (0%)	-	-	-	-
Buddhists (0%)	-	-	-	-
Jain (0%)	-	-	-	-

Agewise Data:

	Persons	Males	Females	Sex Ratio
All ages	54,515	27,708	26,807	967
0-14	17,411	8,909	8,502	954
15-44	25,977	13,119	12,858	980
45-79	10,626	5,422	5,204	960
80+	452	231	221	957
Age not stated	49	27	22	815

Languages (Dominant): Telugu, Hindi, Urdu, Gondi, Tamil

Disabled Population:

	Persons	Males	Females	%
Total Disabled	1,379	779	600	
In Seeing	587	340	247	42.57
In Speech	89	51	38	6.45
In Hearing	69	34	35	5
In Movement	482	280	202	34.95
Mentally	152	74	78	11.02

GARIVIDI

Garividi C.D. Block lies in the southern part of Vizianagaram district. It is a part of Garividi Mandal. The Block is located at a distance of 30 kms. from district headquarters (Vizianagaram). There are 34 villages in the block with the total population of 64,718 persons. Area of the C.D. Block is 126.97 sq. kms. It is bounded in the north by Mandals Merakamudidam and district Srikakulam, in the south by Mandals Gurla, and Nellimarla, in the east by Mandal Cheepurupalle and district Srikakulam, and in the west by Mandals Gurla and Merakamudidam.

Communications :

Roadways : State Highway (S.H.): Nearest Villages- Vizianagaram to Rajam. Nearest Villages- Appannavalasa, Kapusambham, Burravarigollala Palem.

Backwards Region Grants Fund: It receives Backward Region Grants.

Annaul Rainfall: Average Rainfall 886.7 mm

Ground Water: Availability of the Ground Water in the Basin is (Information not avavible) H.A.M .and the utilization is (Information not avavible) H.A.M. It belongs to (Information not avavible) category. Depth to water level varies from 3 to 10 meter below the ground. Most of the wells go down in summer months.

Administration:

Division: Coastal Andhra. Parliamentary Constituency: 20 Vizianagram. District: Vizianagram. Mandal: Garividi. Assembly Constituency: 134 Cheepurupalle. Gram Panchayat: 28.

Villages: 34 **Inhabited:** 34 **Uninhabited:** 0

Ranking	**District**	**State**	**National**
Area	25	914	5365
Population	33	650	5495
Sex Ratio	8	99	645
Child Sex Ratio	20	331	1125
Literacy Rate	29	1013	5761
Density	1	5	3051
Work Participation Rate	22	257	65

Gram Panchayats:

Arthamuru, Bondapalli, Chukkavalasa, Devada, Dummeda Duvvam, Gadabavalasa, Geddapuvalsa, Gotnandi K..L.Puram, K.Palavalasa, Kapusambham, Koduru

Kondadadi, Kondapalem, Kondasambham, Konuru, Kumaram M.Duggivalasa, Mandiravalasa, Regati, Seripeta Sivaram, Tatigudaa, Thondrangi, V.P.Rega Vedurlavalasa, Yenuguvalasa.

Amenities:

Education: Primary School in 32 villages, Middle school in 8 villages, Matriculation or Secondary School in 2 villages, namely Thondrangi, Konuru.

Higher Secondary or Pre University Courses or Intermediate or Junior College in 0 village of the CD Block, College in 0 village, Adult Literacy Center in 32 villages.

Medical: Hospital in 0 village, Dispensary in 0 village, Health Center in 0 village, Sub Center in 8 villages, Maternity and Child Welfare Center in 0 village, Community health workers in 0 village.

Drinking Water: Tap water in 34 villages, Tank water in 34 villages, Well water in 34 villages, Tubewell in 34 villages and more than one source in 34 villages.

Bank: Banking facility in 1 villages, namely, Vedullavalasa.

Credit Society in 13 villages Agricultural Credit Society in 4 Non-Agricultural Credit Society in 10 villages.

Others: Power supply in 34 villages, Cinema hall in 0 village, sport club in 0 village, Stadium or Auditorium or Community Hall in 0 village, Post Office in 12 villages.

There are 15 villages having bus facilities.

Village with most of facilities: Vedullavalasa.

Villages without Amenities (Education): None..

Scheduled Castes: Out of the total population of 45194 persons, 4438 persons (9.82%) belong to Scheduled Castes.

The villages having less than 10% SC population are Kondadadi, Avagudem, Itamvalasa, Gadabavalasa Chukkavalasa, Kondasambham, Burravarigollala Palem Mandiravalasa, Baguvalasa

Neeladripuram @ Surammapeta, Chandapuram Jagannadhapuram, Regatiagraharam, Yenuguvalasa Thatiguda, Vijayarampuram (Near) Kumaram Gaddapuvalasa, Thondrangi, Sivaram, Devada.

The villages having more than 50% SC population are None.

Sex ratio of Scheduled Caste population is 499.

Scheduled Castes Literates and Illiterates by Sex:

	Persons	Males	Females
Literate	1,478	951	527
Illiterate	2,960	1,271	1,689
Literacy rate	38.7	49.8	27.6
Graduate	21	20	1

Scheduled Castes (Dominant):

Mala, Madiga, Relli, Dom etc., Godagali

For their cultural identity please see Appendix-I

Villages without Scheduled Castes: There are 9 villages without any scheduled caste population.

Scheduled Tribes: Out of the total population of 45194 persons, 604 persons (1.34%) belong to Scheduled Tribes.

The villages having less than 10% ST population are Kondadadi, Vedullavalasa, Avagudem, Gotnandi Bondapalle, Gadabavalasa, Mokhasaduggi Valasa Appannavalasa, Chukkavalasa, Kondasambham Kapusambham, Burravarigollala Palem, Mandiravalasa Baguvalasa, Neeladripuram @ Surammapeta Chandapuram, Jagannadhapuram, Regatiagraharam K. Palavalasa, Venkupatrunirega, Kumaram Yenuguvalasa, Konda Lakshmipuram, Thatiguda Vijayarampuram (Near) Kumaram, Gaddapuvalasa Seripeta, Thondrangi, Sivaram, Devada, Dummeda Konuru, Arthamuru.

The villages having more than 50% ST population are None.

Sex ratio of Scheduled tribe population is 545.

Scheduled Tribes Literates and Illiterates by Sex:

	Persons	Males	Females
Literate	214	113	101
Illiterate	390	162	228
Literacy rate	41.9	48.1	36.6
Graduate	0	0	0

Scheduled Tribes (Dominant):

Gadabas, Konda Dhoras, Yerukulas

Generic Tribes etc.

For their cultural identity please see Appendix-II

Villages without Scheduled Tribes: There are 20 villages without any scheduled tribe population.

Literates and Illiterates by Sex (Total Population):

	Persons	Males	Females
Literate	15,180	9,666	5,514
Illiterate	30,014	12,707	17,307
Literacy rate	39	51	28
Graduate	298	272	26

Agriculture: ***Distribution of villages according to land use:*** Out of 34 villages, Total area (in hectare) is 12697, out of that 72.27 percent is cultivable and 25.43 percent of the cultivable area is irrigated.

Sources of Irrigation (Hectares): Government Canal 0, Private Canal 0, Well without Electricity 21, Well with Electricity 44.89, Tubewell without Electricity 0, Tubewell with Electricity 16.19, Tank 2234.22, River 0, Lake 0, Waterfall 0, Others 17.

Villages with population of 5000 to 9999: None

Villages with population of 10000 and above: None

Distribution of Workers:

	Persons	Males	Females	WPR

Cultivators	8,585	4,863	3,722	30.44
Agricultural Labour	12,597	4,882	7,715	44.67
Household Industry	846	554	292	3
Other Workers	6,173	4,568	1,605	21.89
Main Workers	21,269	13,394	7,875	75.42
Marginal Workers	6,932	1,473	5,459	24.58
Total Workers	28,201	14,867	13,334	

Religion: Major Religious Communities:

	Persons	Males	Females	Sex Ratio
Hindu (99.6%)	45,014	22,295	22,719	1,019
Muslim (0.07%)	31	15	16	1,067
Christian (0.29%)	129	56	73	1,304
Sikh (0%)	-	-	-	-
Buddhists (0%)	-	-	-	-
Jain (0%)	-	-	-	-

Agewise Data:

	Persons	Males	Females	Sex Ratio
All ages	45,194	22,373	22,821	1020
0-14	15,052	7,567	7,485	989
15-44	21,003	10,362	10,641	1027
45-79	8,961	4,357	4,604	1057
80+	147	65	82	1262
Age not stated	31	22	9	409

Languages (Dominant):
Telugu, Gadaba, Oriya, Tamil, Gondi

Disabled Population:

	Persons	Males	Females	%
Total Disabled	1,322	704	618	
In Seeing	667	320	347	50.45
In Speech	89	42	47	6.73
In Hearing	100	61	39	7.56
In Movement	388	240	148	29.35
Mentally	78	41	37	5.9

GARLA

Gorla C.D. Block lies in the western part of Khammam district. The Block is located at a distance of 35 kms. from district headquarters (Khammam). There are 11 villages in the block with the total population of 34,936 persons. Area of the C.D. Block is 126.67 sq. kms. It is bounded in the north by Mandal Bayyaram, in the south by Mandal Kamepalle, in the east by Manda ls Bayyaram, Singareni and Kamepalle, and in the west by district Warangal.

Communications:

Roadways : Metalled Roads: Nearest Village- Kannaigudem.
Railway Station: Garla, Gopalapuram, Pocharam.
River: Munneru Nadi- Nearest Villages- Maddi Vancha, Rampuram, Mulkanoor.
Annual Rainfall: Average Rainfall 1006 mm
Ground Water: Availability of the Ground Water in the Basin is 944 H.A.M.and the utilization is 453 H.A.M. It belongs to safe category. Depth to water level varies from 5 to 10 meter below the ground. Most of the wells go down in summer months. The well density in the entire block is 8 wells per sq. km. Total no. of the wells in the block are enumerated as 1787, according to the Ground Water Estimation Committee.
Natural Division : Godavari Depression Region
Administration:
Division: Telangana. Parliamentary Constituency: 16 Mahbubabad (ST). District: Khammam. Mandal: Garla. Assembly Constituency: 111 Yellandu (ST). Gram Panchaya t: 10.
Villages: 11 **Inhabited:** 10 **Uninhabited:** 1

Ranking	District	State	National
Area	44	915	5369
Population	34	933	5911
Sex Ratio	18	619	2098
Child Sex Ratio	37	736	3104
Literacy Rate	30	774	4806
Density	26	488	3798
Work Participation Rate	9	448	1255

Gram Panchayats:
Buddharam, Garla, Gopalapuram, Marrigudem, Mulkanoor Pocharam, Pulluru, Rampuram, Seethampeta, Seripuram.

Amenities:
Education: Primary School in 10 villages, Middle school in 5 villages, Matriculation or Secondary School in 3 villages, namely Mulkanoor, Garla, Pulluru.
Higher Secondary or Pre University Courses or Intermediate or Junior College in 1 village of the CD Block,, namely Garla.
College in 0 village, Adult Literacy Center in 10 villages.
Medical: Hospital in 1 village, Dispensary in 2 villages, Health Center in 1 village, Sub Center in 5 villages, Maternity and Child Welfare Center in 1 village, Community health workers in 0 village.
The Villages having Hospital or Dispensary or Health Center are Mulkanoor, Garla.
Drinking Water: Tap water in 10 villages, Tank water in 10 villages, Well water in 10 villages, Tubewell in 10 villages and more than one source in 10 villages.
Bank: Banking facility in 3 villages, namely, Mulkanoor, Garla, Gopalapuram.
Credit Society in 6 villages Agricultural Credit Society in 3 Non-Agricultural Credit Society in 5 villages.
Others: Power supply in 10 villages, Cinema hall in 2 villages, sport club in 0 village, Stadium or Auditorium or Community Hall in 0 village, Post Office in 7 villages.
There are 6 villages having bus facilities.

Villages with most of facilities: Mulkanoor, Garla Gopalapuram.

Villages without Amenities (Education): None..

Scheduled Castes: Out of the total population of 34936 persons, 3761 persons (10.77%) belong to Scheduled Castes.

The villages having less than 10% SC population are None..

The villages having more than 50% SC population are None.

Sex ratio of Scheduled Caste population is 496.

Scheduled Castes Literates and Illiterates by Sex:

	Persons	Males	Females
Literate	1,777	1,072	705
Illiterate	1,984	825	1,159
Literacy rate	54.3	65.6	43.0
Graduate	52	41	11

Scheduled Castes (Dominant):

Madiga, Mala, Beda Jangam etc., Bindla, Dakkal etc.

For their cultural identity please see Appendix-I

Villages without Scheduled Castes: There are 2 villages without any scheduled caste population.

Scheduled Tribes: Out of the total population of 34936 persons, 16438 persons (47.05%) belong to Scheduled Tribes.

The villages having less than 10% ST population are None..

The villages having more than 50% ST population are Mulkanoor, Chandragiri, Buddharam, Seripuram Pulluru.

Sex ratio of Scheduled tribe population is 492.

Scheduled Tribes Literates and Illiterates by Sex:

	Persons	Males	Females
Literate	5,150	3,504	1,646
Illiterate	11,288	4,844	6,444
Literacy rate	37.4	49.9	24.3
Graduate	115	107	8

Scheduled Tribes (Dominant):

Sugalis etc., Koya etc., Yerukulas, Nayaks Generic Tribes etc.

For their cultural identity please see Appendix-II

Villages without Scheduled Tribes: There are 2 villages without any scheduled tribe population.

Literates and Illiterates by Sex (Total Population):

	Persons	Males	Females
Literate	14,448	8,982	5,466
Illiterate	20,488	8,678	11,810
Literacy rate	48	59	37
Graduate	526	435	91

Agriculture: ***Distribution of villages according to land use:***

Out of 11 villages, Total area (in hectare) is 12667, out of that 65.13 percent is cultivable and 39.14 percent of the cultivable area is irrigated.

Sources of Irrigation (Hectares): Government Canal 90.83, Private Canal 0, Well without Electricity 223.96, Well with Electricity 705.18, Tubewell without Electricity 0, Tubewell with Electricity 34, Tank 2074.42, River 40.4, Lake 0, Waterfall 0, Others 60.

Villages with population of 5000 to 9999: Mulkanoor.

Villages with population of 10000 and above: Garla.

Distribution of Workers:

	Persons	Males	Females	WPR
Cultivators	4,223	2,701	1,522	22.81
Agricultural Labour	11,413	5,262	6,151	61.66
Household Industry	378	198	180	2.04
Other Workers	2,496	1,891	605	13.48
Main Workers	11,916	7,252	4,664	64.38
Marginal Workers	6,594	2,800	3,794	35.62
Total Workers	18,510	10,052	8,458	

Religion: Major Religious Communities:

	Persons	Males	Females	Sex Ratio
Hindu (94.96%)	33,176	16,795	16,381	975
Muslim (3.9%)	1,363	661	702	1,062
Christian (0.52%)	182	89	93	1,045
Sikh (0%)	-	-	-	-
Buddhists (0%)	-	-	-	-
Jain (0.3%)	104	61	43	705

Agewise Data:

	Persons	Males	Females	Sex Ratio
All ages	34,936	17,660	17,276	978
0-14	11,834	6,165	5,669	920
15-44	15,898	8,038	7,860	978
45-79	6,909	3,325	3,584	1078
80+	260	113	147	1301
Age not stated	35	19	16	842

Languages (Dominant):

Telugu, Hindi, Urdu, Tamil, Marathi

Disabled Population:

	Persons	Males	Females	%
Total Disabled	994	555	439	
In Seeing	494	269	225	49.7
In Speech	83	40	43	8.35
In Hearing	41	21	20	4.12
In Movement	282	174	108	28.37
Mentally	94	51	43	9.46

GARLADINNE

Garladinne C.D. Block lies in the northern part of Anantapur district. The Block is located at a distance of 17 kms. from district headquarters (Anantapur). There are 18 villages in the block with the total popul ation of 49,140 persons. Area of the C.D. Block is 270. 22 sq. kms. It is bounded in the north by Mandal Pamidi, in the south by Mandals Kudair, Anantapur and Bukkaray asamudram, in the east by Mandal Singanamala, and in the west by Mandal Kudair. River Pennar binds on north.

Communications:

Roadways : NH-7: Direction- Kurnool to Anantapur. Nearest Villages- Kanampalle, Jambuladinne, Sirivaram, Muntima dugu, Kalluru Agraharam, Garladinne.

Railway Station: Kalluru Agraharam, Garladinne.

River: Pennar Nadi- Nearest Villages- Muntimadugu, Kalluru Agraharam, Kesavapuram, Kalluru, Illuru, Krishn apuram, Yerraguntla.

It receives Backward Region Grants, and is identified as a drought-prone area as well.

Annual Rainfall: Average Rainfall 568 mm

Ground Water: Availability of the Ground Water in the Basin is 4581 H.A.M. and the utilization is 2432 H. A.M. It belongs to safe category. Depth to water level varies from 5 to 10 meter below the ground. Most of the wells go down in summer months. The well density in the entire block is 13 wells per sq. km. Total no. of the wells in the block are enumerated as 3977, according to the Ground Water Estimation Committee.

Natural Division : Rayalaseema Region

Administration:

Division: Rayala Seema. Parliamentary Constituency: 36 Anantapur. District: Anantapur.

Mandal: Garladinne. Assembly Constituency: 271 Singanam ala (S)C. Gram Panchayat: 18.

Fairs and Festivals:

Sri Chithambaraswamy Car Festival : It is celebrated for three days from Magha Bahula Triodasi to Amavasya (February-March) at Penakacherla. This festival is being celebrated in commemoration of the birthday of Sri Chithambaraswamy. Silver and gold ornaments are offered to the Swamiji. The devotees name their children after the Swamiji in fulfilment of their vows. It is being celebrated for the past 130 years and is widely known. Reddys and Gollas of the village organise the festival on a grand scale. The devotees, local and from the neighbouring areas like Kurnool and Bellary, gather. All communities take part in the festival.

Villages: 18 **Inhabited:** 18 **Uninhabited:** 0

Ranking	District	State	National
Area	34	238	3104
Population	17	543	5325
Sex Ratio	8	736	2490
Child Sex Ratio	29	592	2389
Literacy Rate	23	552	4046
Density	49	578	5015
Work Participation Rate	18	782	1555

Gram Panchayats:

Budedu, Garladinne, Illuru, Kalluru, Kamalapuram Kanampalli, Kesavapuram, Koppalakonda, Kotanka Krishnapuram, M.P.R. Dam, Marthadu, Mukundapuram Muntimadugu, Penakacherla, Sirivaram, Thimmampeta Yerraguntla.

Amenities:

Education: Primary School in 17 villages, Middle school in 10 villages, Matriculation or Secondary School in 7 villages, namely Penakacherla, Koppalakonda, Kalluru Agraharam, Kalluru, Illuru, Marthadu, Garladinne.

Higher Secondary or Pre University Courses or Intermediate or Junior College in 1 village of the CD Block,, namely Garladinne.

College in 0 village, Adult Literacy Center in 11 villages.

Medical: Hospital in 0 village, Dispensary in 3 villages, Health Center in 2 villages, Sub Center in 9 villages, Maternity and Child Welfare Center in 0 village, Community health workers in 0 village.

The Villages having Hospital or Dispensary or Health Center are Penakacherla, Kalluru Agraharam, Illuru.

Drinking Water: Tap water in 12 villages, Tank water in 0 villages, Well water in 5 villages, Tubewell in 0 village and more than one source in 13 villages.

Bank: Banking facility in 4 villages, namely, Penakacherla, Kalluru Agraharam, Kalluru, Garladinne.

Credit Society in 5 villages Agricultural Credit Society in 5 Non-Agricultural Credit Society in 0 village.

Others: Power supply in 18 villages, Cinema hall in 3 villages, sport club in 0 village, Stadium or Auditorium or Community Hall in 0 village, Post Office in 12 villages.

There are 15 villages having bus facilities.

Villages with most of facilities: Penakacherla Kalluru Agraharam, Kalluru, Garladinne.

Villages without amenities (Education):

Obulapuram..

Scheduled Castes: Out of the total population of 49140 persons, 8799 persons (17.91%) belong to Scheduled Castes.

The villages having less than 10% SC population are None..

The villages having more than 50% SC population are None.

Sex ratio of Scheduled Caste population is 492.

Scheduled Castes Literates and Illiterates by Sex:

	Persons	Males	Females
Literate	2,926	1,833	1,093
Illiterate	5,873	2,633	3,240
Literacy rate	39.1	48.0	29.8

Graduate	50	39	11

Scheduled Castes (Dominant):

Madiga, Mala, Generic Castes etc.

For their cultural identity please see Appendix-I

Villages without Scheduled Castes: There are 2 villages without any scheduled caste population.

Scheduled Tribes: Out of the total population of 49140 persons, 1252 persons (2.55%) belong to Scheduled Tribes. The villages having less than 10% ST population are Penakacherla, Koppalakonda, Kesavapuram, Muntimadugu Kalluru Agraharam, Kalluru, Illuru, Kanampalle Ankampeta, Sirivaram, Yerraguntla, Kotanka, Marthadu Budedu, Garladinne, Jambuladinne.

The villages having more than 50% ST population are None.

Sex ratio of Scheduled tribe population is 491.

Scheduled Tribes Literates and Illiterates by Sex:

	Persons	Males	Females
Literate	386	240	146
Illiterate	866	397	469
Literacy rate	37.2	46.2	28.2
Graduate	2	2	0

Scheduled Tribes (Dominant):

Yerukulas, Sugalis etc., Kammara

For their cultural identity please see Appendix-II

Villages without Scheduled Tribes: There are 4 villages without any scheduled tribe population.

Literates and Illiterates by Sex (Total Population):

	Persons	Males	Females
Literate	22,529	14,016	8,513
Illiterate	26,611	10,928	15,683
Literacy rate	53	65	41
Graduate	732	586	146

Agriculture: ***Distribution of villages according to land use:*** Out of 18 villages, Total area (in hectare) is 27025, out of that 65.41 percent is cultivable and 29.61 percent of the cultivable area is irrigated.

Sources of Irrigation (Hectares): Government Canal 2562.85, Private Canal 87.01, Well without Electricity 0, Well with Electricity 1135.15, Tubewell without Electricity 0, Tubewell with Electricity 851.44, Tank 60.7, River 0, Lake 0, Waterfall 0, Others 537.82.

Villages with population of 5000 to 9999: Kalluru Agraharam, Marthadu, Garladinne.

Villages with population of 10000 and above: None

Distribution of Workers:

	Persons	Males	Females	WPR
Cultivators	7,803	5,547	2,256	30.38
Agricultural Labour	12,057	5,240	6,817	46.94
Household Industry	978	686	292	3.81
Other Workers	4,846	3,509	1,337	18.87
Main Workers	20,281	13,195	7,086	78.96
Marginal Workers	5,403	1,787	3,616	21.04
Total Workers	25,684	14,982	10,702	

Religion: Major Religious Communities:

	Persons	Males	Females	Sex Ratio
Hindu (92.32%)	45,367	23,042	22,325	969
Muslim (7.18%)	3,528	1,771	1,757	992
Christian (0.43%)	213	116	97	836
Sikh (0.01%)	6	3	3	1,000
Buddhists (0%)	-	-	-	-
Jain (0%)	-	-	-	-

Agewise Data:

	Persons	Males	Females	Sex Ratio
All ages	49,140	24,944	24,196	970
0-14	16,479	8,354	8,125	973
15-44	23,585	12,036	11,549	960
45-79	8,757	4,413	4,344	984
80+	263	112	151	1348
Age not stated	56	29	27	931

Languages (Dominant):

Telugu, Urdu, Hindi, Tamil, Marathi

Disabled Population:

	Persons	Males	Females	%
Total Disabled	978	527	451	
In Seeing	318	160	158	32.52
In Speech	92	49	43	9.41
In Hearing	59	29	30	6.03
In Movement	376	221	155	38.45
Mentally	133	68	65	13.6

GARUGUBILLI

Gargubilli C.D. Block lies in the north-east part of Vizianagaram district. It is a part of Garugubilli Mandal. The Block is located at a distance of 108 kms. from district headquarters (Vizianagaram). There are 34 villages in the block with the total population of 50,833 persons. Area of the C.D. Block is 138.36 sq. kms. It is bounded in the north by Mandals Komarada, Jiyyammavalasa and Komarada, in the south by Balajipeta and Seethanagaram, in the east by Mandals Balajipeta and Srikakulam, in the west by Mandals Komarada, Parvathipuram and Seethanagaram.

Communications:

Roadways : State Highway (SH): Direction- Parvathipuram to Palakonda. Nearest Villages- Naviri, Thotapalle, Gadabavalasa Gangarajapuram, Santhoshapuram, Sunki, Naguru, Chilakam.

River: Nagavali Nadi- Nearest Villages- Seetharampuram (Near) Sivvam, Kothuru, Chilakam, Sivvam, Marupenta, Sambannavalasa, Markondaputti, Gijaba, Naviri, Thotapa lle, Gadabavalasa Gangarajapuram, Santhoshapuram, Sunki.

Backwards Region Grants Fund: It receives Backward Region Grants.

Annual Rainfall: Average Rainfall 794.6 mm

Ground Water: Availability of the Ground Water in the Basin is (Information not avavible) H.A.M .and the utilization is (Information not avavible) H.A.M. It belongs to (Information not avavible) category. Depth to water level varies from 3 to 10 meter below the ground. Most of the wells go down in summer months.

Natural Division : Northern Andhra Coastal Plain Region.

Administration:

Division: Coastal Andhra, Parliamentary Constituency: 18 Araku (ST), District: Vizianagram, Mandal: Garugubil li, Assembly Constituency: 130 Kurupam (ST), Gram Pancha yat: 28.

Villages: 34 **Inhabited:** 31 **Uninhabited:** 3

Ranking	District	State	National
Area	20	867	5208
Population	17	482	5238
Sex Ratio	28	324	1386
Child Sex Ratio	34	1009	4694
Literacy Rate	3	549	4038
Density	25	398	2977
Work Participation Rate	18	239	972

Gram Panchayats:

B.V.Puram, Chilakam, Chinagudaba, Dalaivalasa Garugubilli, Gijaba, Gottivalasa, Konkadavaram Kotavanivalasa, Kothapalli, Kothuru, Lakhanapuram Markondaputti, Marupenta, Naguru, Naviri, Pedagadaba Pedduru, Rainderavalasa, Raopalli, Ravivalasa Santoshapuram, Sivvam, Sunki, Thotapalli, Uddavolu Ullibadra, Vallarigudaba.

Amenities:

Education: Primary School in 30 villages, Middle school in 15 villages, Matriculation or Secondary School in 7 villages, namely Markondaputti, Thotapalle, Ullibhadra, Naguru, Lakhanapuram, Garugubilli, Kothuru.

Higher Secondary or Pre University Courses or Intermediate or Junior College in 0 village of the CD Block, College in 0 village, Adult Literacy Center in 27 villages.

Medical: Hospital in 1 village, Dispensary in 3 villages, Health Center in 1 village, Sub Center in 12 villages, Maternity and Child Welfare Center in 4 villages, Community health workers in 0 village.

The Villages having Hospital or Dispensary or Health Center are Thotapalle, Hikkimvalasa, Garugubilli.

Drinking Water: Tap water in 31 villages, Tank water in 31 villages, Well water in 31 villages, Tubewell in 31 villages and more than one source in 31 villages.

Bank: Banking facility in 5 villages, namely, Thotapalle, Dalaivalasa, Lakhanapuram, Uddavolu Garugubilli.

Credit Society in 15 villages Agricultural Credit Society in 5 Non-Agricultural Credit Society in 14 villages.

Others: Power supply in 31 villages, Cinema hall in 0 village, sport club in 0 village, Stadium or Auditorium or Community Hall in 0 village, Post Office in 24 villages.

There are 25 villages having bus facilities.

Villages with most of facilities: Thotapalle Dalaivalasa, Lakhanapuram, Uddavolu, Garugubilli.

Villages without amenities (Education): Polinaiduvalasa..

Scheduled Castes: Out of the total population of 50833 persons, 6145 persons (12.09%) belong to Scheduled Castes.

The villages having less than 10% SC population are Gijaba, Naviri, Santhoshapuram, Sunki Sivarampuram (Near) Dalaivalasa, Gottivalasa Marupenta, Sambannavalasa, Naguru, Polinaiduvalasa Hikkimvalasa, Uddavolu, Burada Venkatapuram Garugubilli, Pedduru.

The villages having more than 50% SC population are None.

Sex ratio of Scheduled Caste population is 489.

Scheduled Castes Literates and Illiterates by Sex:

	Persons	Males	Females
Literate	2,369	1,490	879
Illiterate	3,776	1,649	2,127
Literacy rate	45.3	56.6	33.8
Graduate	55	50	5

Scheduled Castes (Dominant):

Mala, Madiga, Dom etc., Relli, Adi Andhra

For their cultural identity please see Appendix-I

Villages without Scheduled Castes: There are 4 villages without any scheduled caste population.

Scheduled Tribes: Out of the total population of 50833 persons, 1299 persons (2.56%) belong to Scheduled Tribes.

The villages having less than 10% ST population are Markondaputti, Gijaba, Naviri, Thotapalle Santhoshapuram, Sunki, Ullibhadra, Seetharampuram Konkadivaram, Sivarampuram (Near) Dalaivalasa Dalaivalasa, Gottivalasa, Marupenta, Sambannavalasa Naguru, Lakhanapuram, Chilakam, Hikkimvalasa Uddavolu, Chinagudaba, Pedagudaba, Rayandoravalasa Vallarigudaba, Burada Venkatapuram, Garugubilli Pedduru, Kothuru, Ravupalle, Kothapalle.

The villages having more than 50% ST population are None.

Sex ratio of Scheduled tribe population is 494.

Scheduled Tribes Literates and Illiterates by Sex:

	Persons	Males	Females

Literate	490	305	185
Illiterate	809	352	457
Literacy rate	43.8	54.1	33.3
Graduate	6	6	0

Scheduled Tribes (Dominant):
Konda Dhoras, Gadabas, Jatapus, Yerukulas Generic Tribes etc.

For their cultural identity please see Appendix-II

Villages without Scheduled Tribes: There are 11 villages without any scheduled tribe population.

Literates and Illiterates by Sex (Total Population):

	Persons	Males	Females
Literate	23,307	14,826	8,481
Illiterate	27,526	10,667	16,859
Literacy rate	53	68	38
Graduate	926	821	105

Agriculture: ***Distribution of villages according to land use:***
Out of 34 villages, Total area (in hectare) is 13838, out of that 73.73 percent is cultivable and 53 percent of the cultivable area is irrigated.

Sources of Irrigation (Hectares): Government Canal 2062.81, Private Canal 0, Well without Electricity 2.1, Well with Electricity 22.26, Tubewell without Electricity 11.82, Tubewell with Electricity 169.6, Tank 3138.59, River 0, Lake 0, Waterfall 0, Others 0.

Villages with population of 5000 to 9999:
Lakhanapuram.

Villages with population of 10000 and above: None

Distribution of Workers:

	Persons	Males	Females	WPR
Cultivators	10,770	6,328	4,442	38.86
Agricultural Labour	11,153	4,511	6,642	40.24
Household Industry	691	334	357	2.49
Other Workers	5,103	3,807	1,296	18.41
Main Workers	21,830	13,380	8,450	78.76
Marginal Workers	5,887	1,600	4,287	21.24
Total Workers	27,717	14,980	12,737	

Religion: Major Religious Communities:

	Persons	Males	Females	Sex Ratio
Hindu (99.35%)	50,502	25,346	25,156	993
Muslim (0.26%)	130	67	63	940
Christian (0.34%)	174	70	104	1,486
Sikh (0%)	1	-	1	-
Buddhists (0%)	-	-	-	-
Jain (0%)	-	-	-	-

Agewise Data:

	Persons	Males	Females	Sex Ratio
All ages	50,833	25,493	25,340	994
0-14	15,234	7,961	7,273	914
15-44	24,275	11,988	12,287	1025
45-79	11,052	5,383	5,669	1053
80+	230	132	98	742
Age not stated	42	29	13	448

Languages (Dominant):
Telugu, Oriya, Urdu, Hindi, Tamil

Disabled Population:

	Persons	Males	Females	%
Total Disabled	1,330	738	592	
In Seeing	675	348	327	50.75
In Speech	100	54	46	7.52
In Hearing	69	38	31	5.19
In Movement	378	243	135	28.42
Mentally	108	55	53	8.12

GEESUGONDA

Geesugonda C.D. Block lies in the central part of Waran gal district. It is a part of Geesugonda Mandal. The Block is located at a distance of 6 kms. from district headquarters (Warangal). There are 17 villages in the block with the total population of 49,950 persons. Area of the C.D. Block is 156.09 sq. kms. It is bounded in the north by Mandals Warangal, Atmakur and Duggondi, in the south by Mandals Sangam and Duggondi, in the east by Mandal Duggondi, and in the west by Warangal Mandal.

Communications:

Roadways : Metalled Roads: Nearest Villages- Geesugonda, Dharmaram, Machapur, Viswanathpur, Kommala.

Railway Station: Shayampet.

Backwards Region Grants Fund: It receives Backward Region Grants.

Annual Rainfall: Average Rainfall 1013 mm

Ground Water: Availability of the Ground Water in the Basin is 2536 H.A.M.and the utilization is 2203 H.A. M. It belongs to SC category. Depth to water level varies from 10 to 20 meter below the ground. Most of the wells go down in summer months. The well density in the entire block is 26 wells per sq. km. Total no. of the wells in the block are enumerated as 4077, according to the Ground Water Estimation Committee.

Natural Division : Godavari Depression Region

Administration:

Division: Telangana. Parliamentary Constituency Distric t: Warangal.Mandal: Geesugonda. Assembly Constituency: 104 Parkal. Gram Panchayat: 25.

Fair and Festival:

Sri Mallikarjunaswamy Festival : Sri Mallikarajunaswamy festival is celebrated from Pushya Suddha Purnima (Dece mber-January) to Chaitra Suddha Padyami (March-April) for four months at Gorrekunta near Warangal. The devote es chant Shiva mantras. Pujas are performed on every

Wednesday and Sunday. Patnam bonam, puttuvendrukalu (tonsure), kadapameedakanuka, sthbhanakodelu (steers), coconuts, fruits and sugar are offered in fulfilment of vows. This festival is being celebrated for the past 150 years and is widely known. Sri Katta Mallikarj unaswamy temple with His earthen image in human form is the place of worship. The legend about the deity Mallikarjunaswamy is givern hereunder. Several decades ago there lived a happy couple Yadi Reddy and Neelama Devi who having no children used to give away everything in charity, with the fond hope that God will some day fulfil their long cherished desire. Fortune smiled on the couple. Lord Brahma came in disguise, received charity and blessed them with six children. Yadi Reddy became so prosperous and rich that he constructed a great city with enclosure and called it Kollapuram. Giving up his past benevolent attitude, he became filled with arrogance and ordered his servants not to allow beggars into the city. He did not heed anybody 's advice. To mend Yadi Reddy, Lord Brahma once again came in disguise and requested for alms. The servants, though they did not allow him to enter into the city, informed Yadi Reddy about this. Yadi Reddy was so insolent that he ordered his men to snatch away the bowl and turn out the beggar. Lord Brahma became enraged and cursed-Yadi Reddy who consequently lost the city to his enemies and with it the pleasure and pomp, and had to dwell in the forests with his family for 12 years struggling for existence. Lord Siva who was then doing penance at Srisailam took pity on the couple and desired to alleviate their sufferings. He himself was born as their seventh son by name Mallanna or Malli karjuna. He regained the city that was lost and married a lovely Yadava maid Kethamma and ruled it in peace and plenty. The people worshipped him in reverence. But the legend differs from place to place and in a few parts of the district Lord Siva is known by diffe rent names as Mallikarjuna or Mylaru Devudu, etc.

Villages: 17 **Inhabited:** 17 **Uninhabited:** 0

Ranking	District	State	National
Area	40	799	4962
Population	27	472	5218
Sex Ratio	20	577	2022
Child Sex Ratio	30	799	3463
Literacy Rate	4	325	3076
Density	32	540	3278
Work Participation Rate	10	309	1427

Gram Panchayats:

Anantharam, Arepalle, Bodduchintalpalle Chandraipalle, Dharmaram, Dupakunta, Elkurthy Gangadevarapalle, Geesgonda, Gorrekunta, Janpaka Kommala, Konaimakula, Machapur, Manugonda Mariapuram, Mogilicherla, Nandanaikthanda, Ookal(H) Potharajupalle, Shayampet(H), Stambampalle Vanchangiri, Vasanthapur, Viswanathpur.

Amenities:

Education: Primary School in 16 villages, Middle school in 13 villages, Matriculation or Secondary School in 10 villages, namely Mogilicherla, Elkurthy, Geesugonda, Gorrekunta (Rural), Dharmaram, Shayampet, Ookal (H), Machapur, Viswanathpur, Kommala.

Higher Secondary or Pre University Courses or Intermediate or Junior College in 1 village of the CD Block,, namely Dharmaram.

College in 2 villages, Adult Literacy Center in 12 villages., Colleges are in villages, namely Geesugonda, Gorrekunta (Rural).

Medical: Hospital in 1 village, Dispensary in 2 villages, Health Center in 6 villages, Sub Center in 10 villages, Maternity and Child Welfare Center in 7 villages, Community health workers in 0 village.

The Villages having Hospital or Dispensary or Health Center are Elkurthy, Geesugonda, Ookal (H), Viswanathpur, Kommala.

Drinking Water: Tap water in 17 villages, Tank water in 17 villages, Well water in 17 villages, Tubewell in 17 villages and more than one source in 17 villages.

Bank: Banking facility in 4 villages, namely, Geesugonda, Gorrekunta (Rural), Dharmaram, Ookal (H).

Credit Society in 14 villages Agricultural Credit Society in 6 Non-Agricultural Credit Society in 14 villages.

Others: Power supply in 17 villages, Cinema hall in 0 village, sport club in 0 village, Stadium or Auditorium or Community Hall in 0 village, Post Office in 10 villages.

There are 16 villages having bus facilities.

Villages with most of facilities: Geesugonda Gorrekunta (Rural), Dharmaram, Ookal (H).

Villages without Amenities (Education): None..

Scheduled Castes: Out of the total population of 51090 persons, 11437 persons (22.39%) belong to Scheduled Castes.

The villages having less than 10% SC population are None..

The villages having more than 50% SC population are None.

Sex ratio of Scheduled Caste population is 493.

Scheduled Castes Literates and Illiterates by Sex:

	Persons	Males	Females
Literate	5,702	3,455	2,247
Illiterate	5,735	2,346	3,389
Literacy rate	57.5	68.6	46.1

Graduate	141	129	12

Scheduled Castes (Dominant):
Madiga, Mala, Generic Castes etc., Dom etc., Gosangi
For their cultural identity please see Appendix-I
Villages without Scheduled Castes: There is 1 village without any scheduled caste population.
Scheduled Tribes: Out of the total population of 51090 persons, 4173 persons (8.17%) belong to Scheduled Tribes. The villages having less than 10% ST population are Mogilicherla, Bodduchintalapalle, Manugonda Elkurthy, Ramachandrapur, Anantharam, Geesugonda Potharajpalle, Gorrekunta (Rural), Dharmaram Vasanthapur, Vanchangiri, Shayampet, Ookal (H). The villages having more than 50% ST population are None.
Sex ratio of Scheduled tribe population is 490.
Scheduled Tribes Literates and Illiterates by Sex:

	Persons	Males	Females
Literate	1,132	789	343
Illiterate	3,041	1,339	1,702
Literacy rate	32.9	44.9	20.3
Graduate	20	20	0

Scheduled Tribes (Dominant):
Sugalis etc., Yerukulas, Thoti, Gond etc., Pardhan
For their cultural identity please see Appendix-II
Villages without Scheduled Tribes: There are 3 villages without any scheduled tribe population.
Literates and Illiterates by Sex (Total Population):

	Persons	Males	Females
Literate	25,828	15,836	9,992
Illiterate	25,262	9,972	15,290
Literacy rate	58	71	46
Graduate	788	660	128

Agriculture: ***Distribution of villages according to land use:*** Out of 17 villages, Total area (in hectare) is 15500, out of that 80.88 percent is cultivable and 48.92 percent of the cultivable area is irrigated.
Sources of Irrigation (Hectares): Government Canal 0, Private Canal 0, Well without Electricity 12, Well with Electricity 4006, Tubewell without Electricity 0, Tubewell with Electricity 106.05, Tank 693.1, River 0, Lake 0, Waterfall 0, Others 1315.32.
Villages with population of 5000 to 9999:
Mogilicherla, Gorrekunta (Rural), Dharmaram.
Villages with population of 10000 and above: None
Distribution of Workers:

	Persons	Males	Females	WPR
Cultivators	7,809	4,314	3,495	29
Agricultural Labour	11,750	4,819	6,931	43.64
Household Industry	1,403	646	757	5.21
Other Workers	5,962	4,589	1,373	22.14
Main Workers	22,643	12,723	9,920	84.1
Marginal Workers	4,281	1,645	2,636	15.9
Total Workers	26,924	14,368	12,556	

Religion: Major Religious Communities:

	Persons	Males	Females	Sex Ratio
Hindu (94.54%)	48,299	24,379	23,920	981
Muslim (3.14%)	1,606	842	764	907
Christian (2.19%)	1,119	552	567	1,027
Sikh (0%)	-	-	-	-
Buddhists (0.01%)	5	3	2	667
Jain (0%)	-	-	-	-

Agewise Data:

	Persons	Males	Females	Sex Ratio
All ages	51,090	25,808	25,282	980
0-14	15,950	8,195	7,755	946
15-44	24,516	12,317	12,199	990
45-79	10,087	5,029	5,058	1006
80+	409	203	206	1015
Age not stated	128	64	64	1000

Languages (Dominant):
Telugu, Hindi, Marathi, Urdu, Gondi
Disabled Population:

	Persons	Males	Females	%
Total Disabled	865	483	382	
In Seeing	325	172	153	37.57
In Speech	109	61	48	12.6
In Hearing	48	24	24	5.55
In Movement	286	175	111	33.06
Mentally	97	51	46	11.21

GHANPUR

Ghanpur C.D. Block lies in the central part of Mahbubna gar district. The Block is located at a distance of 25 kms. from district headquarters (Mahbubnagar). There are 23 villages in the block with the total population of 42,049 persons. Area of the C.D. Block is 186.19 sq. kms. It is bounded by Bhoothpur Mandal on north, Bijnapalle and Gopalpeta Mandals on east, Wanaparthy Mandal on south-east, Peddamandai Mandal on south, and Addakal Mandal on west.
Communications:
Roadways : Metalled Roads: Nearest Village- Jangamaipalle.
Backwards Region Grants Fund: It receives Backward Region Grants.
Annual Rainfall: Average Rainfall 607 mm
Ground Water: Availability of the Ground Water in the Basin is 1233 H.A.M. and the utilization is 1188 H. A.M. It belongs to Cri category. Depth to water level varies from 2 to 5 meter below the ground. Most of the wells go down in summer months. The well density in the entire block is 14 wells per sq. km. Total no.

of the wells in the block are enumerated as 2628, according to the Ground Water Estimation Committee.

Natural Division : Telangana Plateau Region

Administration:

Division: Telangana. Parliamentary Constituency: 12 Nagarkurnool (SC). District: Mahbubnagar. Mandal: Ghanp ur. Assembly Constituency: 78 Wanaparthy. Gram Panchayat: 19

Villages: 23 **Inhabited:** 21 **Uninhabited:** 2

Ranking	District	State	National
Area	59	628	4417
Population	52	759	5647
Sex Ratio	38	760	2539
Child Sex Ratio	50	916	4028
Literacy Rate	38	1006	5708
Density	40	324	4361
Work Participation Rate	20	620	806

Gram Panchayats:

Agaram, Almaipally, Anthaipally, Appareddipally Ghanpur, Jangamaipally, Kamaluddinpur, Malkapur Mamidimada, Manajipet, Md.Hussainpally, Parvathapur Rukkannapally, Salkalapur, Shapur, Solipur Thirumalaipally, Upperpally, Venkatampally.

Amenities:

Education: Primary School in 21 villages, Middle school in 14 villages, Matriculation or Secondary School in 7 villages, namely Thirumalaipalle, Ghanpur, Mamidimada, Manajipet, Solipur, Balijapalle, Jangamaipalle.

Higher Secondary or Pre University Courses or Intermediate or Junior College in 0 village of the CD Block, College in 0 village, Adult Literacy Center in 20 villages.

Medical: Hospital in 0 village, Dispensary in 1 village, Health Center in 1 village, Sub Center in 6 villages, Maternity and Child Welfare Center in 1 village, Community health workers in 0 village.

The Village having Hospital or Dispensary or Health Center is Ghanpur.

Drinking Water: Tap water in 21 villages, Tank water in 21 villages, Well water in 21 villages, Tubewell in 21 villages and more than one source in 21 villages.

Bank: Banking facility in 1 villages, namely, Ghanpur.

Credit Society in 7 villages Agricultural Credit Society in 2 Non-Agricultural Credit Society in 6 villages.

Others: Power supply in 21 villages, Cinema hall in 1 village, sport club in 0 village, Stadium or Auditorium or Community Hall in 0 village, Post Office in 7 villages.

There are 20 villages having bus facilities.

Village with most of facilities: Ghanpur.

Villages without Amenities (Education): None..

Scheduled Castes: Out of the total population of 42049 persons, 6353 persons (15.11%) belong to Scheduled Castes.

The villages having less than 10% SC population are Anthaipalle, Malkimianpalle, Appareddipalle Mamidimada, Shapur, Upparapalle.

The villages having more than 50% SC population are None.

Sex ratio of Scheduled Caste population is 493.

Scheduled Castes Literates and Illiterates by Sex:

	Persons	Males	Females
Literate	1,399	1,004	395
Illiterate	4,954	2,216	2,738
Literacy rate	27.2	38.0	15.7
Graduate	14	12	2

Scheduled Castes (Dominant):

Madiga, Generic Castes etc., Mala, Beda Jangam etc. Bindla

For their cultural identity please see Appendix-I

Villages without Scheduled Castes: There are 3 villages without any scheduled caste population.

Scheduled Tribes: Out of the total population of 42049 persons, 6102 persons (14.51%) belong to Scheduled Tribes.

The villages having less than 10% ST population are Anthaipalle, Kamaluddinpur, Venkatampalle, Agaram Mohammed Hussainpalle, Ghanpur, Appareddipalle Salkalapur, Parwathapur, Suraipalle, Upparapalle Jangamaipalle.

The villages having more than 50% ST population are None.

Sex ratio of Scheduled tribe population is 486.

Scheduled Tribes Literates and Illiterates by Sex:

	Persons	Males	Females
Literate	1,042	783	259
Illiterate	5,060	2,353	2,707
Literacy rate	21.7	32.0	11.0
Graduate	2	2	0

Scheduled Tribes (Dominant):

Sugalis etc., Generic Tribes etc., Yerukulas Chenchu etc.

For their cultural identity please see Appendix-II

Villages without Scheduled Tribes: There are 6 villages without any scheduled tribe population.

Literates and Illiterates by Sex (Total Population):

	Persons	Males	Females
Literate	14,021	9,258	4,763
Illiterate	28,028	12,098	15,930
Literacy rate	40	52	28
Graduate	453	358	95

Agriculture: ***Distribution of villages according to land use:*** Out of 23 villages, Total area (in hectare) is 18616, out of

that 80.7 percent is cultivable and 20.42 percent of the cultivable area is irrigated.

Sources of Irrigation (Hectares): Government Canal 0, Private Canal 0, Well without Electricity 69, Well with Electricity 1155, Tubewell without Electricity 17, Tubewell with Electricity 1655, Tank 171, River 0, Lake 0, Waterfall 0, Others 0.

Villages with population of 5000 to 9999: Ghanpur, Manajipet.

Villages with population of 10000 and above: None

Distribution of Workers:

	Persons	Males	Females	WPR
Cultivators	5,343	3,429	1,914	23.96
Agricultural Labour	10,948	4,333	6,615	49.1
Household Industry	574	330	244	2.57
Other Workers	5,434	3,992	1,442	24.37
Main Workers	17,841	10,387	7,454	80.01
Marginal Workers	4,458	1,697	2,761	19.99
Total Workers	22,299	12,084	10,215	

Religion: Major Religious Communities:

	Persons	Males	Females	Sex Ratio
Hindu (96.46%)	40,562	20,613	19,949	968
Muslim (3.33%)	1,402	695	707	1,017
Christian (0.03%)	11	5	6	1,200
Sikh (0%)	1	-	1	-
Buddhists (0%)	-	-	-	-
Jain (0%)	-	-	-	-

Agewise Data:

	Persons	Males	Females	Sex Ratio
All ages	42,049	21,356	20,693	969
0-14	15,807	8,164	7,643	936
15-44	18,691	9,498	9,193	968
45-79	7,235	3,541	3,694	1043
80+	254	118	136	1153
Age not stated	62	35	27	771

Languages (Dominant):
Telugu, Hindi, Urdu, Tamil, Gondi

Disabled Population:

	Persons	Males	Females	%
Total Disabled	950	576	374	
In Seeing	435	270	165	45.79
In Speech	71	41	30	7.47
In Hearing	41	26	15	4.32
In Movement	326	195	131	34.32
Mentally	77	44	33	8.11

GHANPUR (MULUG)

Ghanpur (Mulung) C.D. Block lies in the northern part of Warangal district. The Block is located at a distance of 63 kms. from district headquarters (Warangal). There are 09 villages in the block with the total popul ation of 33,102 persons. Area of the C.D. Block is 119. 00 sq. kms. It is bounded in the north by Bhupalpalle Mandal, in the south by Mandals Regonda and Venkatapur, in the east by Venkatapur Mandal, and in the west by Bhupalpalle Mandal.

Communications:

Roadways : Metalled Roads: Nearest Villages- Chelpur, Karkapalle, Burrakayalagudem, Mylaram, Ghanpur.

Backwards Region Grants Fund: It receives Backward Region Grants.

Integrated Child Development Scheme (ICDS) Project: Ghanapur, Total Anganwadi Centres: 246

Annual Rainfall: Annual Rainfall 851 mm

Ground Water: Availability of the Ground Water in the Basin is 1337 H.A.M.and the utilization is 841 H.A. M. It belongs to Safe category. Depth to water level varies from 5 to 10 meter below the ground. Most of the wells go down in summer months. The well density in the entire block is 12 wells per sq. km. Total no. of the wells in the block are enumerated as 1399, according to the Ground Water Estimation Committee.

Natural Division : Godavari Depression Region

Administration:

Division: Telangana. Parliamentary Constituency. Distri ct: Warangal. Mandal: Ghanpur (Mulug). Assembly Constitu ency: 108 Bhupalpalle. Gram Panchayat: 10.

Villages: 9 **Inhabited:** 8 **Uninhabited:** 1

Ranking	District	State	National
Area	46	953	5491
Population	47	973	5973
Sex Ratio	8	370	1488
Child Sex Ratio	15	441	1608
Literacy Rate	30	696	4535
Density	36	605	3772
Work Participation Rate	20	443	1627

Gram Panchayats:

Baswarajpalle, Budharam, Chelpur, Dharmaraopet Gandhinagar, Ghanpur, Karkapalle, Kondapur, Mylaram Nagarampalle.

Amenities:

Education: Primary School in 8 villages, Middle school in 7 villages, Matriculation or Secondary School in 4 villages, namely Chelpur, Mylaram, Budharam, Ghanpur.

Higher Secondary or Pre University Courses or Inter-mediate or Junior College in 1 village of the CD Block,, namely Ghanpur.

College in 0 village, Adult Literacy Center in 4 villages.

Medical: Hospital in 0 village, Dispensary in 1 village, Health Center in 2 villages, Sub Center in 7 villages, Maternity and Child Welfare Center in 0 village,

Community health workers in 0 village.
The Village having Hospital or Dispensary or Health Center is Dharmaraopet.
Drinking Water: Tap water in 8 villages, Tank water in 8 villages, Well water in 8 villages, Tubewell in 8 villages and more than one source in 8 villages.
Bank: Banking facility in 2 villages, namely, Chelpur, Ghanpur.
Credit Society in 7 villages Agricultural Credit Society in 3 Non-Agricultural Credit Society in 7 villages.
Others: Power supply in 8 villages, Cinema hall in 2 villages, sport club in 0 village, Stadium or Auditorium or Community Hall in 0 village, Post Office in 7 villages.
There are 8 villages having bus facilities.
Villages with most of facilities: Chelpur, Ghanpur.
Villages without Amenities (Education): None..
Scheduled Castes: Out of the total population of 33102 persons, 6595 persons (19.92%) belong to Scheduled Castes.
The villages having less than 10% SC population are None..
The villages having more than 50% SC population are None.
Sex ratio of Scheduled Caste population is 492.

Scheduled Castes Literates and Illiterates by Sex:

	Persons	Males	Females
Literate	2,068	1,390	678
Illiterate	4,527	1,957	2,570
Literacy rate	37.3	49.6	24.7
Graduate	20	20	0

Scheduled Castes (Dominant):
Madiga, Mala, Mala Sale etc., Generic Castes etc. Beda Jangam etc.
For their cultural identity please see Appendix-I
Villages without Scheduled Castes: There is 1 village without any scheduled caste population.
Scheduled Tribes: Out of the total population of 33102 persons, 1624 persons (4.91%) belong to Scheduled Tribes.
The villages having less than 10% ST population are Chelpur, Dharmaraopet, Karkapalle, Mylaram, Budharam Ghanpur, Kondapur.
The villages having more than 50% ST population are None.
Sex ratio of Scheduled tribe population is 496.

Scheduled Tribes Literates and Illiterates by Sex:

	Persons	Males	Females
Literate	448	290	158
Illiterate	1,176	529	647
Literacy rate	33.1	42.9	23.4
Graduate	7	7	0

Scheduled Tribes (Dominant):
Sugalis etc., Gond etc., Chenchu etc., Yerukulas Koya etc.
For their cultural identity please see Appendix-II
Villages without Scheduled Tribes: There is 1 village without any scheduled tribe population.

Literates and Illiterates by Sex (Total Population):

	Persons	Males	Females
Literate	14,131	8,904	5,227
Illiterate	18,971	7,715	11,256
Literacy rate	50	63	37
Graduate	359	310	49

Agriculture: ***Distribution of villages according to land use:***
Out of 9 villages, Total area (in hectare) is 11901, out of that 67.78 percent is cultivable and 57.51 percent of the cultivable area is irrigated.
Sources of Irrigation (Hectares): Government Canal 0, Private Canal 0, Well without Electricity 0, Well with Electricity 1058, Tubewell without Electricity 0, Tubewell with Electricity 585, Tank 2996, River 0, Lake 0, Waterfall 0, Others 0.
Villages with population of 5000 to 9999:
Chelpur, Dharmaraopet, Ghanpur.
Villages with population of 10000 and above: None

Distribution of Workers:

	Persons	Males	Females	WPR
Cultivators	4,231	2,757	1,474	24.91
Agricultural Labour	8,815	3,505	5,310	51.9
Household Industry	1,038	926	112	6.11
Other Workers	2,902	2,319	583	17.08
Main Workers	13,952	8,512	5,440	82.14
Marginal Workers	3,034	995	2,039	17.86
Total Workers	16,986	9,507	7,479	

Religion: Major Religious Communities:

	Persons	Males	Females	Sex Ratio
Hindu (96.06%)	31,799	15,948	15,851	994
Muslim (3.63%)	1,203	620	583	940
Christian (0.27%)	90	47	43	915
Sikh (0%)	-	-	-	-
Buddhists (0%)	-	-	-	-
Jain (0%)	-	-	-	-

Agewise Data:

	Persons	Males	Females	Sex Ratio
All ages	33,102	16,619	16,483	992
0-14	11,022	5,604	5,418	967
15-44	15,287	7,661	7,626	995
45-79	6,548	3,237	3,311	1023
80+	232	110	122	1109
Age not stated	13	7	6	857

Languages (Dominant):
Telugu, Urdu, Hindi, Gondi, Tamil

Disabled Population:

	Persons	Males	Females	%
Total Disabled	762	458	304	
In Seeing	437	264	173	57.35
In Speech	72	38	34	9.45
In Hearing	13	9	4	1.71
In Movement	169	104	65	22.18
Mentally	71	43	28	9.32

GHANPUR (STATION)

Ghanpur (station) C.D. Block lies in the western part of Warangal district. The Block is located at a distance of 34 kms. from district headquarters (Warangal). There are 25 villages in the block with the total popul ation of 87,619 persons. Area of the C.D. Block is 328. 64 sq. kms. It is bounded in the north by district Karim Nagar and Dharmasagar Mandal, in the south by Mandals Raghunath Palle and Palakurthi, in the east by Mandals Dharmasagar, Zaffergadh and Palakurthi, and in the west by Mandals Narmetta and Raghunathpalle.

Communications:

Roadways : NH- 202: Direction- Hyderabad to Warangal. Nearest Villages- Chinnapendyal, Nashkal, Ghanpur (Station), Raghavapur, Chagal, Shivunipalle.

Railway Station: Nashkal Ghanpur (Station) Ippagudem.

Backwards Region Grants Fund: It receives Backward Region Grants.

Annual Rainfall: Average Rainfall 1181 mm

Ground Water: Availability of the Ground Water in the Basin is 3697 H.A.M.and the utilization is 5071 H.A. M. It belongs to OE category. Depth to water level varies from 10 to 20 meter below the ground. Most of the wells go down in summer months. The well density in the entire block is 25 wells per sq. km. Total no. of the wells in the block are enumerated as 8098, according to the Ground Water Estimation Committee.

Natural Division : Godavari Depression Region

Administration:

Division: Telangana. Parliamentary Constituency. Distri ct: Warangal. Mandal: Ghanpur (Station). Assembly Consti tuency: 99 Ghanpur (Station) (SC). Gram Panchayat: 28.

Villages: 25 **Inhabited:** 25 **Uninhabited:** 0

Ranking	District	State	National
Area	2	105	2475
Population	2	16	3861
Sex Ratio	21	585	2066
Child Sex Ratio	14	415	1530
Literacy Rate	16	501	3841
Density	38	684	3890
Work Participation Rate	25	478	1923

Gram Panchayats:

Chagal, Chilpur, Chinnapendyala, Deshai Thanda Fathepur, Ghanpur (Stn), Ippagudem, Kistajigudem Komatigudem, Kondapur, Kothapalle, Lingampalle Malkapur, Meedikonda, Namiligonda, Nashkal Pallagutta, Pamnoor, Raghavapur, Rajavaram Samudrala, Shivunipalle, Sreepathipalle Thanedarpalle, Thatikonda, Vangalapalle Venkatadripeta, Vishwanathpur.

Amenities:

Education: Primary School in 25 villages, Middle school in 18 villages, Matriculation or Secondary School in 11 villages, namely Sreepathipalle, Lingam Palle, Malkapur, Chilpur, Tatikonda, Pallagutta, Chinnapendyal, Ghanpur (Station), Chagal, Shivunipalle, Ippagudem. Higher Secondary or Pre University Courses or Inter-mediate or Junior College in 1 village of the CD Block,, namely Ghanpur (Station).

College in 1 village, Adult Literacy Center in 18 villages., College is in village, namely Ghanpur (Station).

Medical: Hospital in 1 village, Dispensary in 4 villages, Health Center in 2 villages, Sub Center in 14 villages, Maternity and Child Welfare Center in 0 village, Community health workers in 0 village.

The Villages having Hospital or Dispensary or Health Center are Tatikonda, Nashkal, Ghanpur (Station), Chagal, Ippagudem.

Drinking Water: Tap water in 25 villages, Tank water in 25 villages, Well water in 25 villages, Tubewell in 25 villages and more than one source in 25 villages.

Bank: Banking facility in 5 villages, namely, Kondapur, Malkapur, Ghanpur (Station), Shivunipalle Ippagudem.

Credit Society in 24 villages Agricultural Credit Society in 5 Non-Agricultural Credit Society in 24 villages.

Others: Power supply in 25 villages, Cinema hall in 2 villages, sport club in 0 village, Stadium or Auditorium or Community Hall in 0 village, Post Office in 25 villages.

There are 23 villages having bus facilities.

Villages with most of facilities: Kondapur Malkapur, Ghanpur (Station), Shivunipalle, Ippagudem.

Villages without Amenities (Education): None..

Scheduled Castes: Out of the total population of 87619 persons, 20800 persons (23.74%) belong to Scheduled Castes. The villages having less than 10% SC population are None..

The villages having more than 50% SC population are None.

Sex ratio of Scheduled Caste population is 490.

Scheduled Castes Literates and Illiterates by Sex:

	Persons	Males	Females
Literate	9,071	5,629	3,442

Illiterate	11,729	4,978	6,751
Literacy rate	51.5	62.5	39.9
Graduate	144	124	20

Scheduled Castes (Dominant):
Madiga, Mala, Beda Jangam etc., Generic Castes etc. Mala Dasari

For their cultural identity please see Appendix-I

Villages without Scheduled Castes: There are 0 village without any scheduled caste population.

Scheduled Tribes: Out of the total population of 87619 persons, 6997 persons (7.99%) belong to Scheduled Tribes. The villages having less than 10% ST population are Sreepathipalle, Malkapur, Venkatadripeta, Chilpur Krishnajigudem, Pallagutta, Chinnapendyal, Nashkal Pamnoor, Ghanpur (Station), Kothapalle, Meedikonda Raghavapur, Chagal, Shivunipalle, Namilligonda Ippagudem, Samudrala.

The villages having more than 50% ST population are None.

Sex ratio of Scheduled tribe population is 483.

Scheduled Tribes Literates and Illiterates by Sex:

	Persons	Males	Females
Literate	1,900	1,328	572
Illiterate	5,097	2,292	2,805
Literacy rate	33.2	44.5	20.9
Graduate	20	20	0

Scheduled Tribes (Dominant):
Sugalis etc., Yerukulas, Koya etc., Kammara Kattunayakan

For their cultural identity please see Appendix-II

Villages without Scheduled Tribes: There are 0 village without any scheduled tribe population.

Literates and Illiterates by Sex (Total Population):

	Persons	Males	Females
Literate	40,427	24,930	15,497
Illiterate	47,192	19,334	27,858
Literacy rate	54	66	42
Graduate	1,236	1,008	228

Agriculture: ***Distribution of villages according to land use:*** Out of 25 villages, Total area (in hectare) is 32861, out of that 71.25 percent is cultivable and 25 percent of the cultivable area is irrigated.

Sources of Irrigation (Hectares): Government Canal 0, Private Canal 0, Well without Electricity 0, Well with Electricity 5390.38, Tubewell without Electricity 0, Tubewell with Electricity 240.78, Tank 222.58, River 0, Lake 0, Waterfall 0, Others 0.

Villages with population of 5000 to 9999:
Tatikonda, Shivunipalle, Ippagudem.

Villages with population of 10000 and above:
Ghanpur (Station).

Distribution of Workers:

	Persons	Males	Females	WPR
Cultivators	12,945	8,514	4,431	29.44
Agricultural Labour	17,800	6,445	11,355	40.48
Household Industry	2,876	1,617	1,259	6.54
Other Workers	10,346	7,899	2,447	23.53
Main Workers	33,845	21,437	12,408	76.98
Marginal Workers	10,122	3,038	7,084	23.02
Total Workers	43,967	24,475	19,492	

Religion: Major Religious Communities:

	Persons	Males	Females	Sex Ratio
Hindu (96.44%)	84,504	42,675	41,829	980
Muslim (2.57%)	2,248	1,136	1,112	979
Christian (0.77%)	676	321	355	1,106
Sikh (0.03%)	22	8	14	1,750
Buddhists (0%)	-	-	-	-
Jain (0%)	-	-	-	-

Agewise Data:

	Persons	Males	Females	Sex Ratio
All ages	87,619	44,264	43,355	979
0-14	29,738	15,120	14,618	967
15-44	38,615	19,303	19,312	1000
45-79	18,188	9,187	9,001	980
80+	800	418	382	914
Age not stated	278	236	42	178

Languages (Dominant):
Telugu, Hindi, Urdu, Gondi, Tamil

Disabled Population:

	Persons	Males	Females	%
Total Disabled	1,950	1,086	864	
In Seeing	1,012	551	461	51.9
In Speech	188	101	87	9.64
In Hearing	80	34	46	4.1
In Movement	488	309	179	25.03
Mentally	182	91	91	9.33

GHANTASALA

Ghantasala C.D. Block lies in the southern part of Krishna district. The Block is located at a distance of 35 kms. from district headquarters (Machilipatnam). There are 21 villages in the block with the total population of 43,869 persons. Area of the C.D. Block is 118.54 sq. kms. It is bounded in the north by Mandals Pamidimukkala and Movva, in the south by Mandal Challa palle, in the east by Mandals Guduru and Challapalle, and in the west by River Krishna and district Guntur.

Communications:

Roadways : State Highway (S.H.): Direction- Mopidevi to Movva. Nearest Villages- Kodali, Tadepalle, Chitturpu.

River: Krishna Nadi- Nearest Village- Srikakulam.

Annaul Rainfall: Average Rainfall 955 mm

Ground Water: Availability of the Ground Water in the Basin is (Information not avavible) H.A.M .and the utilization is (Information not avavible) H.A.M. It belongs to (Information not avavible) category. Depth to water level varies from 3 to 10 meter below the ground. Most of the wells go down in summer months.

Natural Division : Krishna Delta Region

Administration:

Division: Coastal Andhra. Parliamentary Constituency: 28 Machilipatnam. District: Krishna. Mandal: Ghantasala. Assembly Constituency: 195 Avanigadda. Gram Panchayat: 22

Villages: 21 **Inhabited:** 20 **Uninhabited:** 1

Ranking	District	State	National
Area	38	956	5502
Population	41	705	5572
Sex Ratio	3	124	742
Child Sex Ratio	42	853	3762
Literacy Rate	12	70	1211
Density	10	611	2950
Work Participation Rate	22	232	1646

Gram Panchayats:

Atchampalem, Chilakalapudi, Chinakallepalli Chitturu, Chiturpu, Daliparru, Devarakota Ghantasala, Ghantasalapalem, Goginenipalem, Kodali Kothapalli, Lankapalli, Mallampalli, Papavinasanam Pushadam, Srikakulam, Tadepalli, Teluguraopalem V.Rudravaram, Vemulapalli, Yendakuduru.

Amenities:

Education: Primary School in 20 villages, Middle school in 12 villages, Matriculation or Secondary School in 5 villages, namely Srikakulam, Kodali, Mallampalle, Ghantasala, China Kallepalle.

Higher Secondary or Pre University Courses or Intermediate or Junior College in 0 village of the CD Block, College in 0 village, Adult Literacy Center in 3 villages.

Medical: Hospital in 0 village, Dispensary in 2 villages, Health Center in 2 villages, Sub Center in 9 villages, Maternity and Child Welfare Center in 0 village, Community health workers in 0 village.

The Villages having Hospital or Dispensary or Health Center are Srikakulam, Ghantasala.

Drinking Water: Tap water in 8 villages, Tank water in 6 villages, Well water in 19 villages, Tubewell in 4 villages and more than one source in 16 villages.

Bank: Banking facility in 4 villages, namely, Srikakulam, Kodali, Ghantasala, Lankapalle.

Credit Society in 14 villages Agricultural Credit Society in 7 Non-Agricultural Credit Society in 14 villages.

Others: Power supply in 20 villages, Cinema hall in 1 village, sport club in 0 village, Stadium or Auditorium or Community Hall in 0 village, Post Office in 14 villages.

There are 16 villages having bus facilities.

Villages with most of facilities: Srikakulam Kodali, Ghantasala, Lankapalle.

Villages without Amenities (Education): None..

Scheduled Castes: Out of the total population of 43869 persons, 14439 persons (32.91%) belong to Scheduled Castes.

The villages having less than 10% SC population are None..

The villages having more than 50% SC population are None.

Sex ratio of Scheduled Caste population is 498.

Scheduled Castes Literates and Illiterates by Sex:

	Persons	Males	Females
Literate	8,355	4,495	3,860
Illiterate	6,084	2,756	3,328
Literacy rate	65.8	70.5	61.0
Graduate	148	112	36

Scheduled Castes (Dominant):

Madiga, Mala, Holeya Dasari, Mala Dasari Generic Castes etc.

For their cultural identity please see Appendix-I

Villages without Scheduled Castes: There are 2 villages without any scheduled caste population.

Scheduled Tribes: Out of the total population of 43869 persons, 1218 persons (2.78%) belong to Scheduled Tribes.

The villages having less than 10% ST population are Srikakulam, Kodali, Kothapalle, V.Rudravaram Chilakalapudi, Mallampalle, Chitturu, Bollapadu Ghantasala, Tadepalle, China Kallepalle, Vemulapalle Chitturpu, Devarakota, Birudugadda, Daliparru Lankapalle, Pushadam, Endakuduru.

The villages having more than 50% ST population are None.

Sex ratio of Scheduled tribe population is 469.

Scheduled Tribes Literates and Illiterates by Sex:

	Persons	Males	Females
Literate	500	305	195
Illiterate	718	342	376
Literacy rate	48.7	56.8	39.8
Graduate	4	3	1

Scheduled Tribes (Dominant):

Yerukulas, Sugalis etc., Yenadis, Konda Dhoras Chenchu etc.

For their cultural identity please see Appendix-II

Villages without Scheduled Tribes: There are 5 villages without any scheduled tribe population.

Literates and Illiterates by Sex (Total Population):

	Persons	Males	Females

Literate	27,377	14,333	13,044
Illiterate	16,492	7,428	9,064
Literacy rate	70	74	66
Graduate	922	631	291

Agriculture: *Distribution of villages according to land use:* Out of 21 villages, Total area (in hectare) is 11853, out of that 78.78 percent is cultivable and 92.28 percent of the cultivable area is irrigated.

Sources of Irrigation (Hectares): Government Canal 8104.49, Private Canal 0, Well without Electricity 0, Well with Electricity 0, Tubewell without Electricity 0, Tubewell with Electricity 0, Tank 0, River 0, Lake 0, Waterfall 0, Others 0.

Villages with population of 5000 to 9999: Srikakulam.

Villages with population of 10000 and above: Ghantasala.

Distribution of Workers:

	Persons	Males	Females	WPR
Cultivators	3,246	3,023	223	13.81
Agricultural Labour	15,391	7,513	7,878	65.48
Household Industry	1,405	642	763	5.98
Other Workers	3,462	2,607	855	14.73
Main Workers	17,954	11,784	6,170	76.39
Marginal Workers	5,550	2,001	3,549	23.61
Total Workers	23,504	13,785	9,719	

Religion: Major Religious Communities:

	Persons	Males	Females	Sex Ratio
Hindu (94.46%)	41,438	20,617	20,821	1,010
Muslim (0.94%)	414	208	206	990
Christian (4.54%)	1,992	925	1,067	1,154
Sikh (0%)	-	-	-	-
Buddhists (0%)	1	1	-	-
Jain (0%)	-	-	-	-

Agewise Data:

	Persons	Males	Females	Sex Ratio
All ages	43,869	21,761	22,108	1016
0-14	11,539	5,851	5,688	972
15-44	20,742	10,292	10,450	1015
45-79	11,046	5,357	5,689	1062
80+	478	211	267	1265
Age not stated	64	50	14	280

Languages (Dominant): Telugu, Urdu, Hindi, Tamil, Gondi

Disabled Population:

	Persons	Males	Females	%
Total Disabled	894	471	423	
In Seeing	257	131	126	28.75
In Speech	114	55	59	12.75
In Hearing	69	24	45	7.72
In Movement	321	184	137	35.91
Mentally	133	77	56	14.88

GHATKESAR

Ghatkesar C.D. Block lies in the north-east part of Rangareddy district. It is a part of Ghatkesar Mandal. The Block is located at a distance of 23 kms. from district headquarters (Serilingampalle). There are 24 villages in the block with the total population of 70,229 persons. Area of the C.D. Block is 127.61 sq. kms. It is bounded by Keesara Mandal on north, Nalgonda district on east, Hayathnagar Mandal on south, and Uppal Mandal on west.

Communications :

Roadways : Metalled Roads: Nearest Villages- Annojiguda, Majarguda, Narepalle, Medipalle, Kondapur, Aushapur.

River: Musi Nadi- Nearest Villages- Peerzadguda, Parvathapur, Gulam Aliguda, Kachwanisingaram, Muthawalliguda, Prathapsingaram, Korremul, Edulabad.

Backwards Region Grants Fund: It receives Backward Region Grants.

Annual Rainfall: Average Rainfall 758 mm

Ground Water: Availability of the Ground Water in the Basin is 1647 H.A.M. and the utilization is 862 H.A.M. It belongs to Safe category. Depth to water level varies from 10 to 20 meter below the ground. Most of the wells go down in summer months. The well density in the entire block is 5 wells per sq. km. Total no. of the wells in the block are enumerated as 845, according to the Ground Water Estimation Committee.

Natural Division : Telangana Plateau Region

Administration:

Division: Telangana. Parliamentary Constituency: 7 Malkajgiri. District: Rangareddy.

Mandal: Ghatkesar. Assembly Constituency: 43 Medchal.

Gram Panchayat: 21.

Villages: 24 **Inhabited:** 21 **Uninhabited:** 3

Ranking	District	State	National
Area	29	911	5357
Population	2	119	4439
Sex Ratio	28	1059	4261
Child Sex Ratio	8	232	778
Literacy Rate	1	84	1348
Density	33	1083	2002
Work Participation Rate	1	80	4824

Gram Panchayats:

Ankushapur, Aushapur, Boduppal, Chengicherla Chowderguda, Edulabad, Ghanpur, Ghatkesar Ismailkhanguda, Kachivanisingaram, Kondapur Korremul, Medipally, N.F.C.Nagar, Narepally Parvathapur, Peerzadiguda, Pocharam, Pratapsingaram Venkatapur, Yamnampet.

Amenities:

Education: Primary School in 20 villages, Middle school in 15 villages, Matriculation or Secondary School in 10 villages, namely Annojiguda, Boduppal, Peerzadguda, Parvathapur, Prathapsingaram, Korremul, Kondapur, Aushapur, Ankushapur, Edulabad.

Higher Secondary or Pre University Courses or Intermediate or Junior College in 0 village of the CD Block, College in 0 village, Adult Literacy Center in 8 villages.

Medical: Hospital in 2 villages, Dispensary in 3 villages, Health Center in 3 villages, Sub Center in 5 villages, Maternity and Child Welfare Center in 5 villages, Community health workers in 0 village.

The Villages having Hospital or Dispensary or Health Center are Annojiguda, Korremul, Kondapur, Aushapur, Edulabad.

Drinking Water: Tap water in 21 villages, Tank water in 21 villages, Well water in 21 villages, Tubewell in 21 villages and more than one source in 21 villages.

Bank: Banking facility in 21 villages, namely, Changicherla, Pocharam, Ismailkhanguda Padamatisaiguda, Yamnampet, Annojiguda, Narepalle Medipalle, Boduppal, Miyapur, Peerzadguda Parvathapur, Kachwanisingaram, Muthawalliguda Prathapsingaram, Korremul, Kondapur, Aushapur Ankushapur, Madharam, Edulabad.

Credit Society in 7 villages Agricultural Credit Society in 1 Non-Agricultural Credit Society in 5 villages.

Others: Power supply in 21 villages, Cinema hall in 0 village, sport club in 0 village, Stadium or Auditorium or Community Hall in 0 village, Post Office in 8 villages.

There are 20 villages having bus facilities.

Villages with most of facilities: Annojiguda Boduppal, Kachwanisingaram, Muthawalliguda Prathapsingaram, Korremul, Kondapur, Aushapur Edulabad.

Villages without amenities (Education): Miyapur..

Scheduled Castes: Out of the total population of 70657 persons, 11792 persons (16.69%) belong to Scheduled Castes.

The villages having less than 10% SC population are None..

The villages having more than 50% SC population are None.

Sex ratio of Scheduled Caste population is 485.

Scheduled Castes Literates and Illiterates by Sex:

	Persons	Males	Females
Literate	5,971	3,742	2,229
Illiterate	5,821	2,334	3,487
Literacy rate	59.2	71.8	45.7
Graduate	162	121	41

Scheduled Castes (Dominant):

Madiga, Mala, Beda Jangam etc., Mahar Generic Castes etc.

For their cultural identity please see Appendix-I

Villages without Scheduled Castes: There are 5 villages without any scheduled caste population.

Scheduled Tribes: Out of the total population of 70657 persons, 2541 persons (3.6%) belong to Scheduled Tribes.

The villages having less than 10% ST population are Changicherla, Pocharam, Ismailkhanguda Padamatisaiguda, Yamnampet, Narepalle, Medipalle Boduppal, Miyapur, Peerzadguda, Parvathapur Kachwanisingaram, Muthawalliguda, Prathapsingaram Korremul, Kondapur, Aushapur, Ankushapur, Edulabad.

The villages having more than 50% ST population are None.

Sex ratio of Scheduled tribe population is 482.

Scheduled Tribes Literates and Illiterates by Sex:

	Persons	Males	Females
Literate	1,084	709	375
Illiterate	1,457	608	849
Literacy rate	51.9	64.3	38.0
Graduate	32	32	0

Scheduled Tribes (Dominant):

Sugalis etc., Yerukulas, Koya etc., Gond etc. Savaras etc.

For their cultural identity please see Appendix-II

Villages without Scheduled Tribes: There are 7 villages without any scheduled tribe population.

Literates and Illiterates by Sex (Total Population):

	Persons	Males	Females
Literate	41,966	24,935	17,031
Illiterate	28,691	11,577	17,114
Literacy rate	69	79	58
Graduate	3,082	2,208	874

Agriculture: ***Distribution of villages according to land use:*** Out of 24 villages, Total area (in hectare) is 12761, out of that 21.86 percent is cultivable and 73.43 percent of the cultivable area is irrigated.

Sources of Irrigation (Hectares): Government Canal 34.4, Private Canal 0, Well without Electricity 606.36, Well with Electricity 331.33, Tubewell without Electricity 0, Tubewell with Electricity 8, Tank 251.35, River 0, Lake 0, Waterfall 554.85, Others 262.16.

Villages with population of 5000 to 9999: Korremul, Edulabad.

Villages with population of 10000 and above: Boduppal, Peerzadguda.

Distribution of Workers:

	Persons	Males	Females	WPR

Cultivators	2,425	1,730	695	9.18
Agricultural Labour	5,667	2,371	3,296	21.45
Household Industry	804	489	315	3.04
Other Workers	17,527	14,589	2,938	66.33
Main Workers	22,180	17,103	5,077	83.94
Marginal Workers	4,243	2,076	2,167	16.06
Total Workers	26,423	19,179	7,244	

Religion: Major Religious Communities:

	Persons	Males	Females	Sex Ratio
Hindu (90.7%)	64,088	33,161	30,927	933
Muslim (6.57%)	4,644	2,403	2,241	933
Christian (2.19%)	1,545	757	788	1,041
Sikh (0.03%)	20	10	10	1,000
Buddhists (0.4%)	284	146	138	945
Jain (0.02%)	13	6	7	1,167

Agewise Data:

	Persons	Males	Females	Sex Ratio
All ages	70,657	36,512	34,145	935
0-14	23,852	12,337	11,515	933
15-44	35,513	18,318	17,195	939
45-79	10,748	5,610	5,138	916
80+	464	202	262	1297
Age not stated	80	45	35	778

Languages (Dominant):

Telugu, Urdu, Hindi, Marathi, Oriya

Disabled Population:

	Persons	Males	Females	%
Total Disabled	1,325	889	436	
In Seeing	645	447	198	48.68
In Speech	104	64	40	7.85
In Hearing	27	15	12	2.04
In Movement	405	277	128	30.57
Mentally	144	86	58	10.87

GHATTU

Ghattu C.D. Block lies in the south west part of Mahbub nagar district. The Block is located at a distance of 131 kms. from district headquarters (Mahbubnagar). There are 24 villages in the block with the total popul ation of 59,792 persons. Area of the C.D. Block is 342. 78 sq. kms. It is bounded by Dharur Mandal on north, Maldakal Mandal on east, Ieej Mandal on south, the block has common border with the state of Karnataka on west.

Communications:

Roadways : Metalled Roads: Nearest Villagse- Naudinne, Kaloor Timmanadoddi, Gorlakhandoddi, Apkondanhalli, Macherla, Muslimpalle, Mittadoddi.

It receives Backward Region Grants, and is identified as a drought prone area as well.

Annual Rainfall: Average Rainfall 404 mm

Ground Water: Availability of the Ground Water in the Basin is 1770 H.A.M. and the utilization is 994 H.A. M. It belongs to Safe category. Depth to water level varies from 2 to 5 meter below the ground. Most of the wells go down in summer months. The well density in the entire block is 9 wells per sq. km. Total no. of the wells in the block are enumerated as 3288, according to the Ground Water Estimation Committee.

Natural Division : Telangana Plateau Region

Administration:

Division: Telangana. Parliamentary Constituency: 12 Nagarkurnool (SC). District: Mahbubnagar. Mandal: Ghattu. Assembly Constituency: 79 Gadwal. Gram Panchayat: 24

Border Villages: (Karnataka)- Nearest Villages- Naudinne, Kuchinerla, Chintalakunta, Apkondanhalli, Muslimpalle, Chamankhandoddi, Induvasi, Boyalagudem.

Villages: 24 **Inhabited:** 21 **Uninhabited:** 3

Ranking	District	State	National
Area	9	86	2337
Population	11	275	4861
Sex Ratio	24	574	2005
Child Sex Ratio	16	468	1690
Literacy Rate	64	1095	6320
Density	2	4	5154
Work Participation Rate	41	818	58

Gram Panchayats:

Aloor, Aragidda, Balgera, Boyalagudem, Chagadona Chintalakunta, Ersandoddi, Ghattu, Gorlakhandoddi Induvasi, Kaloorthimmandoddi, Kuchinerla, Lingapoor Macherla, Mallampally, Mallapuram, Mittadoddi Nandinne, Penchikalpahad, Rayapuram, Thappetlamorsu Thummalapally, Thummalcheruvu, Yellamdoddi.

Amenities:

Education: Primary School in 21 villages, Middle school in 10 villages, Matriculation or Secondary School in 4 villages, namely Naudinne, Ghattu, Macherla, Chagadona.

Higher Secondary or Pre University Courses or Intermediate or Junior College in 0 village of the CD Block, College in 0 village, Adult Literacy Center in 21 villages.

Medical: Hospital in 0 village, Dispensary in 1 village, Health Center in 1 village, Sub Center in 9 villages, Maternity and Child Welfare Center in 0 village, Community health workers in 0 village.

The Village having Hospital or Dispensary or Health Center is Ghattu.

Drinking Water: Tap water in 21 villages, Tank water in 21 villages, Well water in 21 villages, Tubewell in 21 villages and more than one source in 21 villages.

Bank: Banking facility in 2 villages, namely,

Ghattu, Macherla.

Credit Society in 18 villages Agricultural Credit Society in 4 Non-Agricultural Credit Society in 18 villages.

Others: Power supply in 21 villages, Cinema hall in 1 village, sport club in 0 village, Stadium or Auditorium or Community Hall in 0 village, Post Office in 14 villages.

There are 21 villages having bus facilities.

Villages with most of facilities: Ghattu, Macherla.

Villages without Amenities (Education): None..

Scheduled Castes: Out of the total population of 59792 persons, 10417 persons (17.42%) belong to Scheduled Castes.

The villages having less than 10% SC population are Thummalacheruvu, Balgera, Chamankhandoddi Mallampalle.

The villages having more than 50% SC population are None.

Sex ratio of Scheduled Caste population is 495.

Scheduled Castes Literates and Illiterates by Sex:

	Persons	Males	Females
Literate	1,045	859	186
Illiterate	9,372	4,404	4,968
Literacy rate	12.4	20.2	4.4
Graduate	35	29	6

Scheduled Castes (Dominant):

Madiga, Mala, Mala Dasari, Generic Castes etc.

Byagara

For their cultural identity please see Appendix-I

Villages without Scheduled Castes: There are 5 villages without any scheduled caste population.

Scheduled Tribes: Out of the total population of 59792 persons, 1433 persons (2.4%) belong to Scheduled Tribes.

The villages having less than 10% ST population are Naudinne, Kaloor Timmanadoddi, Thummalacheruvu Kuchinerla, Chintalakunta, Rayapuram, Penchikapadu Aragidda, Thappetlamorsu, Gorlakhandoddi, Ghattu Yellamdoddi, Macherla, Balgera, Chamankhandoddi Mallampalle, Induvasi, Boyalagudem, Chagadona Mittadoddi.

The villages having more than 50% ST population are None.

Sex ratio of Scheduled tribe population is 491.

Scheduled Tribes Literates and Illiterates by Sex:

	Persons	Males	Females
Literate	146	119	27
Illiterate	1,287	611	676
Literacy rate	13.0	20.5	5.0
Graduate	4	4	0

Scheduled Tribes (Dominant):

Sugalis etc., Yerukulas

For their cultural identity please see Appendix-II

Villages without Scheduled Tribes: There are 13 villages without any scheduled tribe population.

Literates and Illiterates by Sex (Total Population):

	Persons	Males	Females
Literate	10,765	7,767	2,998
Illiterate	49,027	22,429	26,598
Literacy rate	22	32	13
Graduate	163	143	20

Agriculture: ***Distribution of villages according to land use:*** Out of 24 villages, Total area (in hectare) is 34279, out of that 46.22 percent is cultivable and 18.94 percent of the cultivable area is irrigated.

Sources of Irrigation (Hectares): Government Canal 0, Private Canal 0, Well without Electricity 1235, Well with Electricity 866, Tubewell without Electricity 268, Tubewell with Electricity 324, Tank 307, River 0, Lake 0, Waterfall 0, Others 0.

Villages with population of 5000 to 9999: Kuchinerla.

Villages with population of 10000 and above: None

Distribution of Workers:

	Persons	Males	Females	WPR
Cultivators	10,337	6,790	3,547	29.28
Agricultural Labour	21,325	9,151	12,174	60.4
Household Industry	1,338	706	632	3.79
Other Workers	2,308	1,676	632	6.54
Main Workers	28,883	15,911	12,972	81.8
Marginal Workers	6,425	2,412	4,013	18.2
Total Workers	35,308	18,323	16,985	

Religion: Major Religious Communities:

	Persons	Males	Females	Sex Ratio
Hindu (97.08%)	58,049	29,363	28,686	977
Muslim (2.79%)	1,671	801	870	1,086
Christian (0.05%)	29	14	15	1,071
Sikh (0%)	1	-	1	-
Buddhists (0%)	-	-	-	-
Jain (0%)	-	-	-	-

Agewise Data:

	Persons	Males	Females	Sex Ratio
All ages	59,792	30,196	29,596	980
0-14	25,037	12,728	12,309	967
15-44	25,875	13,192	12,683	961
45-79	8,547	4,119	4,428	1075
80+	296	140	156	1114
Age not stated	37	17	20	1176

Languages (Dominant):

Telugu, Urdu, Hindi, Kannada, Others

Disabled Population:

	Persons	Males	Females	%
Total Disabled	1,050	531	519	

In Seeing	393	165	228	37.43
In Speech	136	80	56	12.95
In Hearing	78	37	41	7.43
In Movement	346	206	140	32.95
Mentally	97	43	54	9.24

GIDDALUR

Giddalur C.D. Block lies in the south-western part of Prakasam district. The Block is located at a distance of 145 kms. from district headquarters (Ongole). There are 22 villages in the block with the total population of 78,462 persons. Area of the C.D. Block is 263.77 sq. kms. It is bounded in the north by Mandal Ardhaveedu, in the south by district Cuddapah, in the east by Mandals Racherla and Komarolu, and in the west by distr ict Kurnool.

Communications:

Roadways : State Highway (S.H.): Direction- Kurnool to Taticherla. Nearest Villages- Kongala Veedu, Chatti Reddy Palle, Gadikota, Uyyala Wada, Modam Palle, Giddal uru, Kristam Setti Palle, Mundla Padu, Kotha Kota, Kommu nuru, Sanjeevarao Peta.

Railway Station: Giddaluru, Kristam Setti Palle.

River: Gundlakamma Nadi- Nearest Villages- (Forest Area Only). Enumaleru Nadi- Nearest Villages- Mundla Padu, Kotha Kota, Kommunuru, Sanjeevarao Peta.

The Block is identified as a drought-prone area.

Integrated Child Development Scheme (ICDS) Project: Giddalur, Total Anganwadi Centres: 171

Annual Rainfall: Average Rainfall 636.2 mm

Ground Water: Availability of the Ground Water in the Basin is 24.51 MCM and the utilization is 69.73 MCM It belongs to Over Exploited category. Depth to water level varies from 2 to 5 meter below the ground. Most of the wells go down in summer months, according to the Ground Water Estimation Committee.

Forest and Reserved **Forest:** (Somidevapalle R.F.)- Neare st Villages- Ambavaram, Thimma Puram, Giddaluru, Kristam Setti Palle, Kanchi Palle, Mundla Padu, Kotha Kota, Sanjeevarao Peta, Gadikota, Uyyala Wada.

Administration:

Division: Coastal Andhra. Parliamentary Constituency: 33 Ongole. District: Prakasam. Mandal: Giddalur. Assemb ly Constituency: 231 Giddalur. Gram Panchayat:19.

Villages: 22 **Inhabited:** 18 **Uninhabited:** 4

Ranking	District	State	National
Area	19	265	3199
Population	2	44	4156
Sex Ratio	36	915	3175
Child Sex Ratio	48	1005	4701
Literacy Rate	7	175	2092
Density	55	984	3554
Work Participation Rate	9	375	3686

Gram Panchayats:

Adimurthipalli, Ambavaram, Ghadikota, Giddaluru Jayarampuram, K.S.Palli, Kanchipalli, Kommunuru Kongalaveedu, Kothakota, Mundlapadu, Narava Obulapuram, Podalakondapalli, Sanjevaraopeta Tamballapalli, Timmapuram, Vuyyalawada, Yellupalli.

Amenities:

Education: Primary School in 18 villages, Middle school in 8 villages, Matriculation or Secondary School in 7 villages, namely Ambavaram, Podili Konda Palle, Giddaluru, Kristam Setti Palle, Mundla Padu, Sanjeevarao Peta, Uyyala Wada.

Higher Secondary or Pre University Courses or Intermediate or Junior College in 2 villages of the CD Block,, namely Giddaluru, Gadikota.

College in 2 villages, Adult Literacy Center in 16 villages., Colleges are in villages, namely Giddaluru, Gadikota.

Medical: Hospital in 1 village, Dispensary in 1 village, Health Center in 1 village, Sub Center in 9 villages, Maternity and Child Welfare Center in 0 village, Community health workers in 0 village.

The Village having Hospital or Dispensary or Health Center is Giddaluru.

Drinking Water: Tap water in 18 villages, Tank water in 18 villages, Well water in 18 villages, Tubewell in 18 villages and more than one source in 18 villages.

Bank: Banking facility in 2 villages, namely, Giddaluru, Mundla Padu.

Credit Society in 10 villages Agricultural Credit Society in 4 Non-Agricultural Credit Society in 5 villages.

Others: Power supply in 18 villages, Cinema hall in 1 village, sport club in 1 village, Stadium or Auditorium or Community Hall in 0 village, Post Office in 13 villages.

There are 16 villages having bus facilities.

Villages with most of facilities: Giddaluru Mundla Padu.

Villages without Amenities (Education): None..

Scheduled Castes: Out of the total population of 78462 persons, 10771 persons (13.73%) belong to Scheduled Castes.

The villages having less than 10% SC population are Tripura Puram, Thamballa Palle, Kongala Veedu Giddaluru, Modam Palle.

The villages having more than 50% SC population are None.

Sex ratio of Scheduled Caste population is 500.

Scheduled Castes Literates and Illiterates by Sex:

	Persons	Males	Females
Literate	6,221	3,795	2,426

Illiterate	4,550	1,595	2,955
Literacy rate	66.7	81.3	52.1
Graduate	221	166	55

Scheduled Castes (Dominant):

Madiga, Mala, Chamar etc., Dom etc.

Generic Castes etc.

For their cultural identity please see Appendix-I

Villages without Scheduled Castes: There are 5 villages without any scheduled caste population.

Scheduled Tribes: Out of the total population of 78462 persons, 3204 persons (4.08%) belong to Scheduled Tribes.

The villages having less than 10% ST population are Ambavaram, Thimma Puram, Tripura Puram Thamballa Palle, Podili Konda Palle, Narava Giddaluru, Chatti Reddy Palle, Kanchi Palle Mundla Padu, Kotha Kota, Kommunuru, Sanjeevarao Peta Gadikota, Uyyala Wada.

The villages having more than 50% ST population are None.

Sex ratio of Scheduled tribe population is 498.

Scheduled Tribes Literates and Illiterates by Sex:

	Persons	Males	Females
Literate	1,199	792	407
Illiterate	2,005	817	1,188
Literacy rate	46.1	61.3	31.1
Graduate	16	14	2

Scheduled Tribes (Dominant):

Sugalis etc., Yerukulas, Yenadis, Chenchu etc.

Koya etc.

For their cultural identity please see Appendix-II

Villages without Scheduled Tribes: There are 10 villages without any scheduled tribe population.

Literates and Illiterates by Sex (Total Population):

	Persons	Males	Females
Literate	43,738	27,680	16,058
Illiterate	34,724	12,413	22,311
Literacy rate	64	80	48
Graduate	3,097	2,486	611

Agriculture: ***Distribution of villages according to land use:*** Out of 22 villages, Total area (in hectare) is 26377, out of that 60.96 percent is cultivable and 23.67 percent of the cultivable area is irrigated.

Sources of Irrigation (Hectares): Government Canal 0, Private Canal 0, Well without Electricity 0, Well with Electricity 0, Tubewell without Electricity 0, Tubewell with Electricity 3565.36, Tank 233.93, River 7.29, Lake 0, Waterfall 0, Others 0.

Villages with population of 5000 to 9999:

Ambavaram, Kristam Setti Palle, Mundla Padu.

Villages with population of 10000 and above:

Giddaluru.

Distribution of Workers:

	Persons	Males	Females	WPR
Cultivators	7,955	5,476	2,479	23.15
Agricultural Labour	13,601	5,597	8,004	39.58
Household Industry	1,354	498	856	3.94
Other Workers	11,452	9,245	2,207	33.33
Main Workers	29,163	18,927	10,236	84.87
Marginal Workers	5,199	1,889	3,310	15.13
Total Workers	34,362	20,816	13,546	

Religion: Major Religious Communities:

	Persons	Males	Females	Sex Ratio
Hindu (86.18%)	67,621	34,578	33,043	956
Muslim (11.92%)	9,356	4,763	4,593	964
Christian (1.61%)	1,263	600	663	1,105
Sikh (0.03%)	24	10	14	1,400
Buddhists (0.01%)	9	6	3	500
Jain (0%)	2	-	2	-

Agewise Data:

	Persons	Males	Females	Sex Ratio
All ages	78,462	40,093	38,369	957
0-14	25,223	12,985	12,238	942
15-44	37,265	19,122	18,143	949
45-79	15,368	7,742	7,626	985
80+	499	193	306	1585
Age not stated	107	51	56	1098

Languages (Dominant):

Telugu, Urdu, Hindi, Tamil, Kannada

Disabled Population:

	Persons	Males	Females	%
Total Disabled	1,157	652	505	
In Seeing	322	155	167	27.83
In Speech	131	72	59	11.32
In Hearing	103	51	52	8.9
In [illegible]ent	481	296	185	41.57
M[illegible]	120	78	42	10.37

GOKAVARAM

Gokavaram C.D. Block lies in the north-western part of East Godavari district. The Block is located at a distance of 68 kms. from district headquarters (Kakin ada). There are 15 villages in the block with the total population of 67,557 persons. Area of the C.D. Block is 166.34 sq. kms. It is bounded in the north by Mandals Gangavaram and Rampachodavaram, in the south by Mandals Korukonda and Jaggampe1rta, in the east by Mandal Gangavaram1, and in the west by Mandals Korukonda1, Devipatnam and Rampachodavaram.

Communications :

Roadways : State Highway (S.H.): Direction- Gokavaram to Pithapuram. Nearest Villages- Krishnunipalem, Atchut apuram, Gummalladuddi, Sivaramapatnam. (S.H.): Direction-

Rajahmundry to Rampaehoda Varan. Nearest Villages- Atchutapuram, Gummalladuddi, Krishnunipalem, Kothapalle, Gokavaram.

River: Uppudukalva Nadi- Nearest Villages- Kothapalle, Gokavaram.

Backwards Region Grants Fund: It receives Backward Region Grants.

Annaul Rainfall: Average Rainfall 1228.1 mm

Ground Water: Availability of the Ground Water in the Basin is (Information not avavible) H.A.M .and the utilization is (Information not avavible) H.A.M. It belongs to (Information not avavible) category. Depth to water level varies from 3 to 10 meter below the ground. Most of the wells go down in summer months.

Forest and Reserved **Forest:** (Tirumalaya Palem R.F.)- Nearest Villages- Kothapalle, Gummalladuddi, Rampa Yerrampalem, Takurupalem, Sudikonda, Sivaramapatnam, Mallavaram, Kalijolla, Bhupatipalem, Tirumalayapalem.

Natural Division : Godavari Delta Region

Administration:

Division: Coastal Andhra. Parliamentary Constituency: 18 Araku (ST). District: East Godavari. Mandal: Seethan agaram. Assembly Constituency: 171 Jaggampeta. Gram Panchayat: 14.

Villages: 15 **Inhabited:** 14 **Uninhabited:** 1

Ranking	District	State	National
Area	12	735	4773
Population	37	169	4578
Sex Ratio	12	246	1208
Child Sex Ratio	29	351	1254
Literacy Rate	36	328	3089
Density	25	1033	2699
Work Participation Rate	45	182	4105

Gram Panchayats:

Atchutapuram, Gadelapalem, Gangampalem, Gokavaram Gummalladuddi, Itikayala Palle, Kamarajupeta Kothapalle, Krishnuni Palem, Mallavaram Rampa Yerrampalem, Thanti Konda, Tirumalayapalem Vedurupaka.

Amenities:

Education: Primary School in 14 villages, Middle school in 9 villages, Matriculation or Secondary School in 6 v[illegible] namely Kothapalle, Gokavaram, Gummalladuddi, [illegible] Rampa Yerrampalem, Mallavaram, Bhupatipalem. Higher Secondary or Pre University Courses or [illegible] mediate or Junior College in 1 village of the CD Block,, namely Gokavaram.

College in 1 village, Adult Literacy Center in 8 villages., College is in village, namely Gokavaram.

Medical: Hospital in 0 village, Dispensary in 7 villages, Health Center in 1 village, Sub Center in 1 village, Maternity and Child Welfare Center in 12 villages, Community health workers in 0 village.

The Villages having Hospital or Dispensary or Health Center are Kothapalle, Gokavaram, Thantikonda, Gadelapalem, Rampa Yerrampalem, Sudikonda, Mallavaram.

Drinking Water: Tap water in 12 villages, Tank water in 14 villages, Well water in 14 villages, Tubewell in 12 villages and more than one source in 14 villages.

Bank: Banking facility in 5 villages, namely, Kothapalle, Gokavaram, Rampa Yerrampalem Sivaramapatnam, Mallavaram.

Credit Society in 6 villages Agricultural Credit Society in 6 Non-Agricultural Credit Society in 5 villages.

Others: Power supply in 14 villages, Cinema hall in 3 villages, sport club in 2 villages, Stadium or Auditorium or Community Hall in 0 village, Post Office in 12 villages.

There are 13 villages having bus facilities.

Villages with most of facilities: Kothapalle Gokavaram, Rampa Yerrampalem, Sivaramapatnam Mallavaram.

Villages without Amenities (Education): None..

Scheduled Castes: Out of the total population of 67557 persons, 11688 persons (17.3%) belong to Scheduled Castes.

The villages having less than 10% SC population are None..

The villages having more than 50% SC population are None.

Sex ratio of Scheduled Caste population is 504.

Scheduled Castes Literates and Illiterates by Sex:

	Persons	Males	Females
Literate	4,929	2,679	2,250
Illiterate	6,759	3,120	3,639
Literacy rate	49.4	53.8	45.0
Graduate	183	138	45

Scheduled Castes (Dominant):

Mala, Madiga, Relli, Adi Andhra, Beda Jangam etc.

For their cultural identity please see Appendix-I

Villages without Scheduled Castes: There are 2 villages without any scheduled caste population.

Scheduled Tribes: Out of the total population of 67557 persons, 2833 persons (4.19%) belong to Scheduled Tribes.

The villages having less than 10% ST population are Kothapalle, Gokavaram, Thantikonda, Gadelapalem Atchutapuram, Gummalladuddi, Rampa Yerrampalem Mallavaram, Bhupatipalem, Tirumalayapalem.

The villages having more than 50% ST population are None.

Sex ratio of Scheduled tribe population is 514.

Scheduled Tribes Literates and Illiterates by Sex:

	Persons	Males	Females
Literate	1,057	570	487
Illiterate	1,776	808	968
Literacy rate	44.8	50.0	39.9
Graduate	15	11	4

Scheduled Tribes (Dominant):
Konda Dhoras, Koya etc., Kammara, Yerukulas, Yenadis
For their cultural identity please see Appendix-II
Villages without Scheduled Tribes: There are 2 villages without any scheduled tribe population.

Literates and Illiterates by Sex (Total Population):

	Persons	Males	Females
Literate	34,153	18,305	15,848
Illiterate	33,404	15,493	17,911
Literacy rate	58	63	54
Graduate	1,060	856	204

Agriculture: ***Distribution of villages according to land use:***
Out of 15 villages, Total area (in hectare) is 16634, out of that 66.62 percent is cultivable and 37.61 percent of the cultivable area is irrigated.

Sources of Irrigation (Hectares): Government Canal 0, Private Canal 0, Well without Electricity 0, Well with Electricity 0, Tubewell without Electricity 0, Tubewell with Electricity 130, Tank 4038.3, River 0, Lake 0, Waterfall 0, Others 0.

Villages with population of 5000 to 9999:
Gummalladuddi, Rampa Yerrampalem, Mallavaram Tirumalayapalem.

Villages with population of 10000 and above:
Kothapalle, Gokavaram.

Distribution of Workers:

	Persons	Males	Females	WPR
Cultivators	3,523	3,231	292	12.52
Agricultural Labour	18,452	11,679	6,773	65.58
Household Industry	827	460	367	2.94
Other Workers	5,333	4,616	717	18.96
Main Workers	17,429	14,024	3,405	61.95
Marginal Workers	10,706	5,962	4,744	38.05
Total Workers	28,135	19,986	8,149	

Religion: Major Religious Communities:

	Persons	Males	Females	Sex Ratio
Hindu (97.97%)	66,186	33,126	33,060	998
Muslim (0.93%)	625	309	316	1,023
Christian (1.05%)	710	346	364	1,052
Sikh (0%)	-	-	-	-
Buddhists (0%)	1	1	-	-
Jain (0%)	-	-	-	-

Agewise Data:

	Persons	Males	Females	Sex Ratio
All ages	67,557	33,798	33,759	999
0-14	22,305	11,373	10,932	961
15-44	32,824	16,376	16,448	1004
45-79	12,044	5,863	6,181	1054
80+	306	141	165	1170
Age not stated	78	45	33	733

Languages (Dominant):
Telugu, Urdu, Gondi, Tamil, Hindi

Disabled Population:

	Persons	Males	Females	%
Total Disabled	1,075	621	454	
In Seeing	393	222	171	36.56
In Speech	102	52	50	9.49
In Hearing	56	25	31	5.21
In Movement	410	259	151	38.14
Mentally	114	63	51	10.6

GOLLAPALLE

Gollapalle C.D. Block lies in the northern part of Karimnagar district. The Block is located at a distance of 64 kms. from district headquarters (Karimnagar). There are 22 villages in the block with the total population of 41,648 persons. Area of the C.D. Block is 154.19 sq. kms. It is bounded by Dharmapuri Mandal on north, Velgatoor Mandal on east, Pegadapalle Mandal on south, Mallial Mandal on south-west, and Jagtial Mandal on west.

Communications :
Roadways : Metalled Roads: Nearest Villages- Datnur, Chilwakodur, Aggimalla, Gunjapadugu.
Backwards Region Grants Fund: It receives Backward Region Grants.
Annual Rainfall: Average Rainfall 1099 mm
Ground Water: Availability of the Ground Water in the Basin is 2405 H.A.M. and the utilization is 1168 H.A.M. It belongs to Safe category. Depth to water level varies from more than 5 to 10 meter below the ground. Most of the wells go down in summer months. The well density in the entire block is 13 wells per sq. km. Total no. of the wells in the block are enumerated as 3342 according to the Ground Water Estimation Commit tee.
Natural Division : Godavari Depression Region
Administration:
Division: Telangana. Parliamentary Constituency: 2 Peddapalle (SC). District: Karimnagar. Mandal: Gollapal le.. Assembly Constituency: 22 Dharmapuri (SC). Gram Panchayat: 25.
Villages: 22 **Inhabited:** 22 **Uninhabited:** 0

Ranking	District	State	National
Area	44	807	4977
Population	40	776	5667

Sex Ratio	14	73	490
Child Sex Ratio	5	65	153
Literacy Rate	49	935	5422
Density	7	67	3861
Work Participation Rate	31	466	257

Gram Panchayats:

Abbapur, Aggimalla, Atmakur, B.B.Raj Pally Bheemrajpally, Bonkur, Chandoli, Chilvakodur Dathnur, Gangapur, Gollapally, Govindpally Gunjapadugu, Ibrahimnagar, Israjpally, Lothunur Nandipally, Raghavapatnam, Rapalli, Shankaraopet Shekalla, Thirumalapur(M), Vengalapur, Venugumatla Yeshwantharaopet.

Amenities:

Education: Primary School in 22 villages, Middle school in 12 villages, Matriculation or Secondary School in 5 villages, namely Vengumatla, Chilwakodur, Gollapalle, Thirmalapuram, Ibrahim Nagar.

Higher Secondary or Pre University Courses or Intermediate or Junior College in 0 village of the CD Block, College in 0 village, Adult Literacy Center in 14 villages.

Medical: Hospital in 0 village, Dispensary in 5 villages, Health Center in 1 village, Sub Center in 7 villages, Maternity and Child Welfare Center in 0 village, Community health workers in 0 village.

The Villages having Hospital or Dispensary or Health Center are Chilwakodur, Gollapalle, Ibrahim Nagar, Aggimalla, Gunjapadugu.

Drinking Water: Tap water in 21 villages, Tank water in 22 villages, Well water in 22 villages, Tubewell in 21 villages and more than one source in 22 villages.

Bank: Banking facility in 2 villages, namely, Chilwakodur, Gollapalle.

Credit Society in 20 villages Agricultural Credit Society in 10 Non-Agricultural Credit Society in 17 villages.

Others: Power supply in 22 villages, Cinema hall in 2 villages, sport club in 0 village, Stadium or Auditorium or Community Hall in 0 village, Post Office in 11 villages.

There are 21 villages having bus facilities.

Villages with most of facilities: Chilwakodur Gollapalle.

Villages without Amenities (Education): None..

Scheduled Castes: Out of the total population of 41648 persons, 8738 persons (20.98%) belong to Scheduled Castes.

The villages having less than 10% SC population are None..

The villages having more than 50% SC population are None.

Sex ratio of Scheduled Caste population is 507.

Scheduled Castes Literates and Illiterates by Sex:

	Persons	Males	Females
Literate	2,580	1,692	888
Illiterate	6,158	2,616	3,542
Literacy rate	35.1	46.7	23.9
Graduate	22	19	3

Scheduled Castes (Dominant):

Madiga, Mala, Beda Jangam etc., Generic Castes etc. Sindhollu etc.

For their cultural identity please see Appendix-I

Villages without Scheduled Castes: There are 0 village without any scheduled caste population.

Scheduled Tribes: Out of the total population of 41648 persons, 311 persons (0.75%) belong to Scheduled Tribes.

The villages having less than 10% ST population are Gangapuram, Yeshwanthraopet, Israjpalle, Shakalla Vengumatla, Bonkur, Lothunur, Datnur, Abbapuram Chilwakodur, Gollapalle, Rapalle, Vengalapuram Thirmalapuram, Ibrahim Nagar, Raghavapatnam Aggimalla, Gunjapadugu, Bheemraj Palle, Chendoli Athmakur.

The villages having more than 50% ST population are None.

Sex ratio of Scheduled tribe population is 527.

Scheduled Tribes Literates and Illiterates by Sex:

	Persons	Males	Females
Literate	45	31	14
Illiterate	266	116	150
Literacy rate	19.1	27.7	11.3
Graduate	0	0	0

Scheduled Tribes (Dominant):

Sugalis etc., Yerukulas, Kammara

For their cultural identity please see Appendix-II

Villages without Scheduled Tribes: There are 9 villages without any scheduled tribe population.

Literates and Illiterates by Sex (Total Population):

	Persons	Males	Females
Literate	15,415	9,961	5,454
Illiterate	26,233	10,553	15,680
Literacy rate	43	57	30
Graduate	244	213	31

Agriculture: ***Distribution of villages according to land use:*** Out of 22 villages, Total area (in hectare) is 15418, out of that 75.77 percent is cultivable and 57.69 percent of the cultivable area is irrigated.

Sources of Irrigation (Hectares): Government Canal 1607.28, Private Canal 49.3, Well without Electricity 0, Well with Electricity 901.75, Tubewell without Electricity 0, Tubewell with Electricity 0, Tank 833.2, River 457.35, Lake 0, Waterfall 0, Others 2890.93.

Villages with population of 5000 to 9999: None

Villages with population of 10000 and above: None

Distribution of Workers:

	Persons	Males	Females	WPR
Cultivators	8,783	5,338	3,445	36.19
Agricultural Labour	9,431	3,755	5,676	38.86
Household Industry	2,629	688	1,941	10.83
Other Workers	3,425	2,442	983	14.11
Main Workers	21,401	11,382	10,019	88.19
Marginal Workers	2,867	841	2,026	11.81
Total Workers	24,268	12,223	12,045	

Religion: Major Religious Communities:

	Persons	Males	Females	Sex Ratio
Hindu (97.64%)	40,664	20,033	20,631	1,030
Muslim (1.85%)	772	378	394	1,042
Christian (0.44%)	182	86	96	1,116
Sikh (0.02%)	7	4	3	750
Buddhists (0%)	1	-	1	-
Jain (0%)	-	-	-	-

Agewise Data:

	Persons	Males	Females	Sex Ratio
All ages	41,648	20,514	21,134	1030
0-14	13,081	6,624	6,457	975
15-44	19,002	9,211	9,791	1063
45-79	9,016	4,413	4,603	1043
80+	403	194	209	1077
Age not stated	146	72	74	1028

Languages (Dominant):

Telugu, Urdu, Hindi, Gondi, Oriya

Disabled Population:

	Persons	Males	Females	%
Total Disabled	524	325	199	
In Seeing	196	115	81	37.4
In Speech	54	33	21	10.31
In Hearing	26	16	10	4.96
In Movement	171	111	60	32.63
Mentally	77	50	27	14.69

GOLLAPROLU

Gollaprolu C.D. Block lies in the eastern part of East Godavari district. The Block is located at a distance of 41 kms. from district headquarters (Kakinada). There are 12 villages in the block with the total population of 76,352 persons. Area of the C.D. Block is 124.15 sq. kms. It is bounded in the north by Mandals Prathipa du and Sankhavaram, in the south by Mandals Pithapuram and Kothapalle, in the east by Mandal Thondangi, and in the west by Mandals Prathipadu and Pithapuram.

Communications :

Roadways : NH- 5: Direction- Rajahmundry to Tuni. Nearest Village- Kodavali. State Highway (S.H.): Direction- Samalkota to Tuni. Nearest Villages- Durgada, Chebrolu, Gollaprolu.

Railway Station: Durgada, Gollaprolu.

Backwards Region Grants Fund: It receives Backward Region Grants.

Annaul Rainfall: Average Rainfall 1228.1 mm

Ground Water: Availability of the Ground Water in the Basin is (Information not avavible) H.A.M .and the utilization is (Information not avavible) H.A.M. It belongs to (Information not avavible) category. Depth to water level varies from 3 to 10 meter below the ground. Most of the wells go down in summer months.

Natural Division : Godavari Delta Region

Administration:

Division: Coastal Andhra. Parliamentary Constituency: 23 Kakinada. District: East Godavari. Mandal: Gollaprolu. Assembly Constituency: 156 Pithapuram. Gram Panchayat: 11

Villages: 12 **Inhabited:** 10 **Uninhabited:** 2

Ranking	District	State	National
Area	19	928	5410
Population	13	60	4235
Sex Ratio	48	624	2184
Child Sex Ratio	13	97	258
Literacy Rate	41	485	3774
Density	40	1055	1768
Work Participation Rate	33	62	4421

Gram Panchayats:

Chebrolu, Chendurthi, China Jaggampeta, Durgada Gollaprolu, K. Mallavaram, Kodavali, P. Mallavaram Tatiparthi, Vannepudi, Vijayanagaram.

Amenities:

Education: Primary School in 10 villages, Middle school in 8 villages, Matriculation or Secondary School in 5 villages, namely Durgada, Chebrolu, Tatiparthi, Gollaprolu, Mallavaram.

Higher Secondary or Pre University Courses or Intermediate or Junior College in 0 village of the CD Block, College in 0 village, Adult Literacy Center in 9 villages.

Medical: Hospital in 1 village, Dispensary in 2 villages, Health Center in 1 village, Sub Center in 6 villages, Maternity and Child Welfare Center in 0 village, Community health workers in 0 village.

The Villages having Hospital or Dispensary or Health Center are Chebrolu, Gollaprolu.

Drinking Water: Tap water in 10 villages, Tank water in 10 villages, Well water in 10 villages, Tubewell in 10 villages and more than one source in 10 villages.

Bank: Banking facility in 2 villages, namely, Chebrolu, Gollaprolu.

Credit Society in 4 villages Agricultural Credit Society in 4 Non-Agricultural Credit Society in 3 villages.

Others: Power supply in 10 villages, Cinema hall in 1 village, sport club in 0 village, Stadium or Auditorium or Community Hall in 0 village, Post Office in 9 villages.
There are 10 villages having bus facilities.

Villages with most of facilities: Chebrolu Gollaprolu.

Villages without Amenities (Education): None..

Scheduled Castes: Out of the total population of 76352 persons, 11694 persons (15.32%) belong to Scheduled Castes.
The villages having less than 10% SC population are None..
The villages having more than 50% SC population are None.
Sex ratio of Scheduled Caste population is 501.

Scheduled Castes Literates and Illiterates by Sex:

	Persons	Males	Females
Literate	4,387	2,334	2,053
Illiterate	7,307	3,497	3,810
Literacy rate	44.2	47.0	41.4
Graduate	121	95	26

Scheduled Castes (Dominant):
Mala, Madiga, Panchama etc., Adi Andhra, Relli

For their cultural identity please see Appendix-I

Villages without Scheduled Castes: There are 2 villages without any scheduled caste population.

Scheduled Tribes: Out of the total population of 76352 persons, 124 persons (0.16%) belong to Scheduled Tribes.
The villages having less than 10% ST population are Kodavali, Chendurthi, Durgada, Vijayanagaram Chebrolu, Vannepudi, China Jaggampeta, Tatiparthi Gollaprolu, Mallavaram.
The villages having more than 50% ST population are None.
Sex ratio of Scheduled tribe population is 516.

Scheduled Tribes Literates and Illiterates by Sex:

	Persons	Males	Females
Literate	57	29	28
Illiterate	67	31	36
Literacy rate	51.4	58.0	45.9
Graduate	1	1	0

Scheduled Tribes (Dominant):
Yerukulas, Yenadis, Kulia, Sugalis etc.

For their cultural identity please see Appendix-II

Villages without Scheduled Tribes: There are 5 villages without any scheduled tribe population.

Literates and Illiterates by Sex (Total Population):

	Persons	Males	Females
Literate	36,047	19,911	16,136
Illiterate	40,305	18,712	21,593
Literacy rate	54	59	49
Graduate	905	719	186

Agriculture: ***Distribution of villages according to land use:***
Out of 12 villages, Total area (in hectare) is 12415, out of that 77.12 percent is cultivable and 63.05 percent of the cultivable area is irrigated.

Sources of Irrigation (Hectares): Government Canal 2458, Private Canal 0, Well without Electricity 0, Well with Electricity 0, Tubewell without Electricity 541, Tubewell with Electricity 1337, Tank 1701, River 0, Lake 0, Waterfall 0, Others 0.

Villages with population of 5000 to 9999:
Tatiparthi.

Villages with population of 10000 and above:
Durgada, Chebrolu, Gollaprolu.

Distribution of Workers:

	Persons	Males	Females	WPR
Cultivators	3,585	3,416	169	11.71
Agricultural Labour	20,538	15,806	4,732	67.09
Household Industry	2,261	1,400	861	7.39
Other Workers	4,230	3,557	673	13.82
Main Workers	25,526	21,902	3,624	83.38
Marginal Workers	5,088	2,277	2,811	16.62
Total Workers	30,614	24,179	6,435	

Religion: Major Religious Communities:

	Persons	Males	Females	Sex Ratio
Hindu (98.69%)	75,348	38,123	37,225	976
Muslim (0.41%)	313	157	156	994
Christian (0.86%)	659	323	336	1,040
Sikh (0%)	3	3	-	-
Buddhists (0%)	1	1	-	-
Jain (0.02%)	17	10	7	700

Agewise Data:

	Persons	Males	Females	Sex Ratio
All ages	76,352	38,623	37,729	977
0-14	24,421	12,189	12,232	1004
15-44	38,026	19,561	18,465	944
45-79	13,464	6,665	6,799	1020
80+	347	155	192	1239
Age not stated	94	53	41	774

Languages (Dominant):
Telugu, Gondi, Urdu, Hindi, Oriya

Disabled Population:

	Persons	Males	Females	%
Total Disabled	1,428	872	556	
In Seeing	653	388	265	45.73
In Speech	162	85	77	11.34
In Hearing	64	34	30	4.48
In Movement	428	289	139	29.97
Mentally	121	76	45	8.47

GOLUGONDA

Golugonda C.D. Block lies in the south-western part of Vishakhapatnam district. The Block is located at a distance of 115 kms. from district headquarters (Vish akhapatnam). There are 36 villages in the block with the total population of 50,949 persons. Area of the C.D. Block is 140.10 sq. kms. It is bounded in the north by Mandals Koyyuru and Rolugunta, in the south by Mandal Nathavaram, in the east by Mandals Narsipatnam and Rolugunta, and in the west by Mandal Koyyuru.

Communications :

Roadways : State Highway (S.H.): Direction- Koyyuru to Narsipatnam. Nearest Villages- Pappusettipalem, Yarravaram, Pakalapadu, Cheedigummala.

River: Rain Fed- Nearest Villages- Krishnadevipeta, Thallacheedikada, Chodyam, Gadampalem, Komira, Pakalap adu, Polavaram, Cheedigummala, Yarakampeta, Gundupala.

Annaual Rainfall: Average Rainfall 975.0 mm

Ground Water: Availability of the Ground Water in the Basin is (Information not avavible) H.A.M .and the utilization is (Information not avavible) H.A.M. It belongs to (Information not avavible) category. Depth to water level varies from 3 to 10 meter below the ground. Most of the wells go down in summer months.

Forest and Reserved **Forest:** Nearest Villages- Agency Laxmipuram, Krishnadevipeta, Thallacheedikada, Kothamal lempeta, Lingamdora Palem, Golugonda, Darapalem, Pathama llempeta, Nagannadorapalem, Pappusettipalem, Yarravaram, Nallanki, Cheedigummala, Yarakampeta, Kotha Yellavaram, Jammadevipeta, Gadampalem, Gopalapatnam, Pogachetlapal em, Vadaparthi, Jammavaram, Kasimi.

Administration:

Division: Coastal Andhra. Parliamentary Constituency: 22 Anakapalle. District: Visakhapatnam. Mandal: Golugon da. Assembly Constituency: 153 Narsipatnam.

Gram Panchayat: 24.

Villages: 36 **Inhabited:** 34 **Uninhabited:** 2

Ranking	District	State	National
Area	27	863	5189
Population	26	479	5230
Sex Ratio	32	608	2089
Child Sex Ratio	26	442	1618
Literacy Rate	13	714	4607
Density	15	327	2998
Work Participation Rate	18	249	811

Gram Panchayats:

Agency Laxmipuram, Ammapeta, Cheedigummala Cheedikada, Chodyam, Gadampalem, Golugonda Gundupala, Jogampeta, K.D. Peta, Kasimi, Komira Konkasingi, Kotha Yellavaram, Kothamallempeta Lingamdora Palem, Lingampeta, Pakalapadu Pappusettipalem, Patha Mallempeta, Puttadigowrampeta Ravanapalli, Salika Mallavaram, Yetigairampeta.

Amenities:

Education: Primary School in 34 villages, Middle school in 7 villages, Matriculation or Secondary School in 2 villages, namely Agency Laxmipuram, Golugonda.

Higher Secondary or Pre University Courses or Intermediate or Junior College in 0 village of the CD Block, College in 0 village, Adult Literacy Center in 26 villages.

Medical: Hospital in 1 village, Dispensary in 1 village, Health Center in 8 villages, Sub Center in 10 villages, Maternity and Child Welfare Center in 0 village, Community health workers in 0 village.

The Village having Hospital or Dispensary or Health Center is Agency Laxmipuram.

Drinking Water: Tap water in 34 villages, Tank water in 34 villages, Well water in 34 villages, Tubewell in 34 villages and more than one source in 34 villages.

Bank: Banking facility in 4 villages, namely, Agency Laxmipuram, Chodyam, Kothamallempeta Cheedigummala.

Credit Society in 0 village Agricultural Credit Society in 0 Non-Agricultural Credit Society in 0 village.

Others: Power supply in 34 villages, Cinema hall in 2 villages, sport club in 0 village, Stadium or Auditorium or Community Hall in 0 village, Post Office in 13 villages.

There are 14 villages having bus facilities.

Villages with most of facilities: Agency Laxmipuram Chodyam, Kothamallempeta, Cheedigummala.

Villages without Amenities (Education): None..

Scheduled Castes: Out of the total population of 50949 persons, 7198 persons (14.13%) belong to Scheduled Castes. The villages having less than 10% SC population are Konkasingi, Kothamallempeta, Kothapalem Nagannadorapalem, Yarravaram, Nallanki Pallapu Nagannadora Palem, Seethakandi Mungerlapalem, Komira, Pakalapadu, Polavaram Yarakampeta, Gundupala, Kotha Yellavaram, Karaka Jammadevipeta, Pogachetlapalem, Vadaparthi Jammavaram, Kasimi.

The villages having more than 50% SC population are None.

Sex ratio of Scheduled Caste population is 453.

Scheduled Castes Literates and Illiterates by Sex:

	Persons	Males	Females
Literate	3,153	2,071	1,082
Illiterate	4,045	1,863	2,182
Literacy rate	50.3	60.0	38.4
Graduate	47	33	14

Scheduled Castes (Dominant):

Mala, Madiga, Relli, Godagali, Adi Andhra

For their cultural identity please see Appendix-I

Villages without Scheduled Castes: There are 10 villages without any scheduled caste population.

Scheduled Tribes: Out of the total population of 50949 persons, 5852 persons (11.49%) belong to Scheduled Tribes. The villages having less than 10% ST population are Cheedikada, Kumarapuram, Konkasingi Agency Laxmipuram, Krishnadevipeta, Thallacheedikada Kothamallempeta, Golugonda, Nagannadorapalem Pakalapadu, Polavaram, Cheedigummala, Yarakampeta Gundupala, Kotha Yellavaram, Ammapeta.

The villages having more than 50% ST population are Kothapalem, Nallanki, Pallapu Nagannadora Palem Seethakandi, Karaka, Pogachetlapalem, Vadaparthi Jammavaram, Kasimi.

Sex ratio of Scheduled tribe population is 498.

Scheduled Tribes Literates and Illiterates by Sex:

	Persons	Males	Females
Literate	2,014	1,220	794
Illiterate	3,838	1,719	2,119
Literacy rate	39.9	48.5	31.3
Graduate	16	14	2

Scheduled Tribes (Dominant):

Konda Dhoras, Gadabas, Bagata, Kammara, Manna Dhora

For their cultural identity please see Appendix-II

Villages without Scheduled Tribes: There are 8 villages without any scheduled tribe population.

Literates and Illiterates by Sex (Total Population):

	Persons	Males	Females
Literate	21,948	13,589	8,359
Illiterate	29,001	12,163	16,838
Literacy rate	50	61	38
Graduate	459	401	58

Agriculture: ***Distribution of villages according to land use:*** Out of 36 villages, Total area (in hectare) is 14010, out of that 61.37 percent is cultivable and 29.37 percent of the cultivable area is irrigated.

Sources of Irrigation (Hectares): Government Canal 1186.09, Private Canal 0, Well without Electricity 87.47, Well with Electricity 140.48, Tubewell without Electricity 18.6, Tubewell with Electricity 221.82, Tank 792.54, River 0, Lake 0, Waterfall 2.6, Others 76.15.

Villages with population of 5000 to 9999: Agency Laxmipuram, Golugonda.

Villages with population of 10000 and above: None

Distribution of Workers:

	Persons	Males	Females	WPR
Cultivators	8,232	5,085	3,147	29.17
Agricultural Labour	14,687	7,572	7,115	52.04
Household Industry	1,243	490	753	4.4
Other Workers	4,060	2,826	1,234	14.39
Main Workers	24,868	14,982	9,886	88.12
Marginal Workers	3,354	991	2,363	11.88
Total Workers	28,222	15,973	12,249	

Religion: Major Religious Communities:

	Persons	Males	Females	Sex Ratio
Hindu (99.07%)	50,475	25,508	24,967	979
Muslim (0.43%)	221	114	107	939
Christian (0.36%)	185	93	92	989
Sikh (0.01%)	6	5	1	200
Buddhists (0%)	-	-	-	-
Jain (0%)	-	-	-	-

Agewise Data:

	Persons	Males	Females	Sex Ratio
All ages	50,949	25,752	25,197	978
0-14	15,595	8,186	7,409	905
15-44	24,927	12,510	12,417	993
45-79	10,186	4,941	5,245	1062
80+	168	71	97	1366
Age not stated	73	44	29	659

Languages (Dominant):

Telugu, Gadaba, Urdu, Oriya, Tamil

Disabled Population:

	Persons	Males	Females	%
Total Disabled	748	406	342	
In Seeing	302	150	152	40.37
In Speech	96	55	41	12.83
In Hearing	47	21	26	6.28
In Movement	223	133	90	29.81
Mentally	80	47	33	10.7

GONEGANDLA

Gonegandla C.D. Block lies in the northern part of Kurnool district. The Block is located at a distance of 50 kms. from district headquarters (Kurnool). There are 16 villages in the block with the total population of 63,584 persons. Area of the C.D. Block is 277.43 sq. kms. It is bounded in the north by Mandals Yemmigan ur and C. Belagal, in the south by Mandals Aspari and Devanakonda, in the east by Mandals Kodumur and Krishna giri, and in the west by Mandals Aspari and Yemmiganur.

Communications:

Roadways : State Highway (S.H.): Direction- Alur to Kurnool. Nearest Villages- Thippanur, Lingamdinne

River: Handri Nadi- Nearest Villages- Ganjihalli, Banda meedi Agraharam, Byluppala, Iranbanda, Neruduppala, Handri Khairawadi, Errabadu, Vemugodu, Thippanur, Linga mdinne.

It is identified as a drought-prone area.

Annual Rainfall: Average Rainfall 612 mm

Ground Water: Availability of the Ground Water in the Basin is 3001 H.A.M. and the utilization is 1426 H. A.M. It belongs to Safe category. Depth to water level varies from 2 to 10 meter below the ground. Most of the wells go down in summer months. The well density in the entire block is 14 wells per sq. km. Total no. of the wells in the block are enumerated as 4001, according to the Ground Water Estimation Committee.

Natural Division : Rayalaseema Region

Administration:

Division: Rayala Seema. Parliamentary Constituency: 35 Kurnool. District: Kurnool. Mandal: Gonegandla. Assembly Constituency: 263 Yemmiganur. Gram Panchayat: 20

Villages: 16 **Inhabited:** 16 **Uninhabited:** 0

Ranking	District	State	National
Area	25	216	3031
Population	12	223	4741
Sex Ratio	15	658	2229
Child Sex Ratio	40	851	3703
Literacy Rate	45	1021	5807
Density	3	10	4331
Work Participation Rate	15	607	95

Gram Panchayats:

Alwala, B. Agraharam, Byluppala, Chinnamarriveedu Errabadu, Gajuladinne, Ganjihalli, Gonegandla Handri Khairawadi, Iranbanda, Kulumala, Kurnur Lingamdinne, Neruduppala, Ontedudinne Pedda Marriveedu, Pedda Nelatur, Puttapasam Thippanur, Vemugodu.

Amenities:

Education: Primary School in 16 villages, Middle school in 5 villages, Matriculation or Secondary School in 1 village, namely Gonegandla.

Higher Secondary or Pre University Courses or Intermediate or Junior College in 0 village of the CD Block, College in 0 village, Adult Literacy Center in 16 villages.

Medical: Hospital in 1 village, Dispensary in 0 village, Health Center in 1 village, Sub Center in 7 villages, Maternity and Child Welfare Center in 0 village, Community health workers in 0 village.

The Village having Hospital or Dispensary or Health Center is Gonegandla.

Drinking Water: Tap water in 16 villages, Tank water in 16 villages, Well water in 16 villages, Tubewell in 16 villages and more than one source in 16 villages.

Bank: Banking facility in 2 villages, namely, Gonegandla, Handri Khairawadi.

Credit Society in 12 villages Agricultural Credit Society in 5 Non-Agricultural Credit Society in 11 villages.

Others: Power supply in 16 villages, Cinema hall in 1 village, sport club in 0 village, Stadium or Auditorium or Community Hall in 0 village, Post Office in 14 villages.

There are 14 villages having bus facilities.

Villages with most of facilities: Gonegandla Handri Khairawadi.

Villages without Amenities (Education): None..

Scheduled Castes: Out of the total population of 63584 persons, 13354 persons (21%) belong to Scheduled Castes.

The villages having less than 10% SC population are None..

The villages having more than 50% SC population are None.

Sex ratio of Scheduled Caste population is 489.

Scheduled Castes Literates and Illiterates by Sex:

	Persons	Males	Females
Literate	3,778	2,638	1,140
Illiterate	9,576	4,181	5,395
Literacy rate	35.0	48.3	21.4
Graduate	105	91	14

Scheduled Castes (Dominant):

Madiga, Mala, Mala Dasari, Madiga Dasu etc., Byagara

For their cultural identity please see Appendix-I

Villages without Scheduled Castes: There are 0 village without any scheduled caste population.

Scheduled Tribes: Out of the total population of 63584 persons, 416 persons (0.65%) belong to Scheduled Tribes.

The villages having less than 10% ST population are Pedda Marriveedu, Alwala, Pedda Nelatur, Kulumala Gonegandla, Ganjihalli, Bandameedi Agraharam Byluppala, Iranbanda, Neruduppala, Handri Khairawadi Errabadu, Vemugodu, Thippanur, Lingamdinne, Kurnur.

The villages having more than 50% ST population are None.

Sex ratio of Scheduled tribe population is 490.

Scheduled Tribes Literates and Illiterates by Sex:

	Persons	Males	Females
Literate	99	64	35
Illiterate	317	148	169
Literacy rate	31.0	40.3	21.9
Graduate	0	0	0

Scheduled Tribes (Dominant):

Yerukulas, Koya etc., Sugalis etc., Kammara Generic Tribes etc.

For their cultural identity please see Appendix-II

Villages without Scheduled Tribes: There are 7 villages without any scheduled tribe population.

Literates and Illiterates by Sex (Total Population):

	Persons	Males	Females
Literate	20,032	13,876	6,156

Illiterate	43,552	18,320	25,232
Literacy rate	39	53	24
Graduate	492	430	62

Agriculture: ***Distribution of villages according to land use:*** Out of 16 villages, Total area (in hectare) is 27742, out of that 84.69 percent is cultivable and 27.53 percent of the cultivable area is irrigated.

Sources of Irrigation (Hectares): Government Canal 3736, Private Canal 16, Well without Electricity 135, Well with Electricity 1111, Tubewell without Electricity 484, Tubewell with Electricity 943, Tank 43, River 0, Lake 0, Waterfall 0, Others 0.

Villages with population of 5000 to 9999:
Alwala, Pedda Nelatur.

Villages with population of 10000 and above:
Gonegandla.

Distribution of Workers:

	Persons	Males	Females	WPR
Cultivators	11,260	6,407	4,853	30.26
Agricultural Labour	22,309	10,022	12,287	59.95
Household Industry	722	420	302	1.94
Other Workers	2,921	2,154	767	7.85
Main Workers	33,579	17,611	15,968	90.24
Marginal Workers	3,633	1,392	2,241	9.76
Total Workers	37,212	19,003	18,209	

Religion: Major Religious Communities:

	Persons	Males	Females	Sex Ratio
Hindu (87.13%)	55,401	28,097	27,304	972
Muslim (12.15%)	7,724	3,867	3,857	997
Christian (0.51%)	324	161	163	1,012
Sikh (0%)	-	-	-	-
Buddhists (0%)	-	-	-	-
Jain (0%)	-	-	-	-

Agewise Data:

	Persons	Males	Females	Sex Ratio
All ages	63,584	32,196	31,388	975
0-14	26,576	13,686	12,890	942
15-44	27,103	13,819	13,284	961
45-79	9,462	4,514	4,948	1096
80+	337	113	224	1982
Age not stated	106	64	42	656

Languages (Dominant):
Telugu, Urdu, Kannada, Hindi, Gondi

Disabled Population:

	Persons	Males	Females	%
Total Disabled	1,206	626	580	
In Seeing	459	216	243	38.06
In Speech	94	52	42	7.79
In Hearing	67	32	35	5.56
In Movement	453	260	193	37.56
Mentally	133	66	67	11.03

GOOTY

Gooty C.D. Block lies in the northern part of Anantapur district. It is a part of Gooty Mandal. The Block is located at a distance of 68 kms. from district headquar ters (Anantapur). There are 22 villages in the block with the total population of 34,749 persons. Area of the C.D. Block is 265.44 sq. kms. It is bounded in the north by Mandal Guntakal and district Kurnool, in the south by Mandals Pamidi and Peddavadngur, in the east by district Kurnool, and in the west by Mandal Guntakal.

Communications:

Roadways : NH- 7: Direction- Anantapur to Kurnool. Neare st Villages- Ubicherla, Karadikonda, Dharmapuram, Kothap eta. NH- 63: Direction- Bellary to Gooty. Nearest Villag es- Rajapuram, Marnepalle, Gooty (Rural). State Highway (S.H.): Direction- Pattikonda to Tadpatri. Nearest Villages- Kothapeta, Engilibanda, Basinepalle, Thondapa du, Jakkalacheruvu.

Railway Station: Jakkalacheruvu.

It receives Backward Region Grants, and is identified as a drought-prone area as well.

Integrated Child Development Scheme (ICDS) Project: Gooty, Total Anganwadi Centres: 271

Annual Rainfall: Average Rainfall 597 mm

Ground Water: Availability of the Ground Water in the Basin is 2730 H.A.M. and the utilization is 1556 H. A.M. It belongs to safe category. Depth to water level varies from 5 to 10 meter below the ground. Most of the wells go down in summer months. The well density in the entire block is 4 wells per sq. km. Total no. of the wells in the block are enumerated as 1275, according to the Ground Water Estimation Committee.

Natural Division : Rayalaseema Region

Administration:

Division: Rayala Seema. Parliamentary Constituency: 36 Anantapur. District: Anantapur. Mandal: Gooty. Assembly Constituency: 269 Guntakal. Gram Panchayat: 25.

Fairs and Festivals:

Hazrat Syed Basha Vali Urs : It is celebrated in these two dargahs simultaneously in memory of the great saint for two days from the 8th day after Milad-un-Nabi at Gooty. Urs and gandham are celebrated magnificently on the first and second days respectively. After the day of gandham, the devotees go to the hill in large numbers and pay homage in the dargah there. Sri Hazrat Syed Basha Vali was a Moulvi. When the Gooty fort was occupied by the Muslims, he is believed to have died in that battle. After the battle ended, in the fort, on the top of the hill, his tomb was constructed. His head was lying on the road outside the village at a distance of 1.25 kms. There also, a samadhi was built.

Sri Kalvagadda Anjaneyaswamy Rathothsavam : Sri Kalvaga dda Anjaneyaswamy Rathothsavam is celebrated for nine days from Chaitra Suddha Padyani (March-April) at Gooty in Anantapur. The car festival taking place on Navami extends from this temple to the Rama temple at the foot of the hill to the east of the village. After the close of the celebrations, the car is drawn back to its original place. Panakam and panyaram are distrib uted to all present. This festival is beeing celebrated from 1954. The temple of Kalvagadda Anjaneyaswamy situa ted at a distance of 0.5 km. to the west of the town was constructed about 120 years ago. Because this temple is on the bank of a small canal, it is known as Kalvag adda Anjaneyaswamy temple (In Telugu kalva means canal and gadda means bank).

Sri Kona Ranganathaswamy Festival : Sri Kona Ranganatha swamy festival is celebrated for 9 days from Chaitra Suddha Navami to Bahula Vidiya (March-April) at Alur in Gooty Taluk of Anantapur. On Chaitra Suddha Navami, the procession images of the deity are taken from Alur to the Ranganathaswamy temple, homam is performed by Brahmins in the night and the images given a bath in the tank. On the next day the procession images are brought back to the village in a palanquin and in the night, the images are taken out in a procession on simhavahanam, throughout the village, Seshavahanam on Ekadasi, hanumanthavahanam on Dwadasi, garudavahanam on Triodasi yenugavahanam on Chaturdasi, rathothsavam on Purnima, Aswavahanam on Bahula Padyami are the other rituals observed. On the morning of Vidiya, the images of the deities are taken in a palanquin to the hill, the homam is completed and prasadam is then distributed. This day is called thirthavadi day. The images are brought back in a palanquin on that night and the festi val terminates with the performance of chiluka vahanoths avam.

Villages: 22 **Inhabited:** 22 **Uninhabited:** 0

Ranking	District	State	National
Area	39	259	3178
Population	52	939	5917
Sex Ratio	61	1075	4374
Child Sex Ratio	32	613	2491
Literacy Rate	42	682	4472
Density	34	418	5827
Work Participation Rate	44	966	1038

Gram Panchayats:

Abbedoddi, Basinepalli, Bethapalli, Bramhanapalli Cherlopalli, Chetnepalli, Dharmapuram, Erragudi Gooty, Issurarallapalli, Jakkalacheruvu, Karidikonda Kojjepalli, Kothapeta, Lachenapalli, Mamadur Peddoddi, Rajapuram, T.Kothapalli, Thondapadu Turakapalli, Ubicherla, Utakallu, Vannedoddi Yangannapalli.

Amenities:

Education: Primary School in 22 villages, Middle school in 3 villages, Matriculation or Secondary School in 1 village, namely Jakkalacheruvu.

Higher Secondary or Pre University Courses or Intermediate or Junior College in 0 village of the CD Block, College in 1 village, Adult Literacy Center in 0 village., College is in village, namely Gooty (Rural).

Medical: Hospital in 0 village, Dispensary in 0 village, Health Center in 3 villages, Sub Center in 7 villages, Maternity and Child Welfare Center in 0 village, Community health workers in 0 village.

The Villages having Hospital or Dispensary or Health Center are Mamadur, Gooty (Rural).

Drinking Water: Tap water in 1 village, Tank water in 12 villages, Well water in 5 villages, Tubewell in 0 village and more than one source in 15 villages.

Bank: Banking facility in 1 villages, namely, Thondapadu.

Credit Society in 4 villages Agricultural Credit Society in 4 Non-Agricultural Credit Society in 0 village.

Others: Power supply in 22 villages, Cinema hall in 0 village, sport club in 0 village, Stadium or Auditorium or Community Hall in 0 village, Post Office in 12 villages.

There are 19 villages having bus facilities.

Village with most of facilities: None.

Villages without Amenities (Education): None..

Scheduled Castes: Out of the total population of 34710 persons, 5283 persons (15.22%) belong to Scheduled Castes. The villages having less than 10% SC population are None..

The villages having more than 50% SC population are None.

Sex ratio of Scheduled Caste population is 483.

Scheduled Castes Literates and Illiterates by Sex:

	Persons	Males	Females
Literate	1,743	1,119	624
Illiterate	3,540	1,611	1,929
Literacy rate	38.8	48.1	28.8
Graduate	24	22	2

Scheduled Castes (Dominant):

Madiga, Mala, Generic Castes etc.

For their cultural identity please see Appendix-I

Villages without Scheduled Castes: There are 0 village without any scheduled caste population.

Scheduled Tribes: Out of the total population of 34710 persons, 1542 persons (4.44%) belong to Scheduled Tribes. The villages having less than 10% ST population are Bethapalle, Utakallu, Ubicherla, Karadikonda Dharmapuram, Kojjepalle, Rajapuram, Marnepalle Peddoddi, Brahmanapalle, Eswarapalle, Mamadur Aniganidoddi, Abbedoddi, Turakapalle, Gooty (Rural) Kothapeta, Engilibanda, Thondapadu, Jakkalacheruvu. The villages having more than 50% ST population are None.

Sex ratio of Scheduled tribe population is 471.

Scheduled Tribes Literates and Illiterates by Sex:

	Persons	Males	Females
Literate	592	404	188
Illiterate	950	411	539
Literacy rate	45.2	58.2	30.5
Graduate	2	2	0

Scheduled Tribes (Dominant):

Yerukulas, Sugalis etc., Yenadis, Chenchu etc. Kammara

For their cultural identity please see Appendix-II

Villages without Scheduled Tribes: There are 9 villages without any scheduled tribe population.

Literates and Illiterates by Sex (Total Population):

	Persons	Males	Females
Literate	14,980	9,843	5,137
Illiterate	19,730	8,121	11,609
Literacy rate	50	64	36
Graduate	317	268	49

Agriculture: ***Distribution of villages according to land use:*** Out of 22 villages, Total area (in hectare) is 26546, out of that 60.85 percent is cultivable and 12.49 percent of the cultivable area is irrigated.

Sources of Irrigation (Hectares): Government Canal 114.58, Private Canal 0, Well without Electricity 16.19, Well with Electricity 522.25, Tubewell without Electricity 0, Tubewell with Electricity 929.51, Tank 435.63, River 0, Lake 0, Waterfall 0, Others 0.

Villages with population of 5000 to 9999: None

Villages with population of 10000 and above: None

Distribution of Workers:

	Persons	Males	Females	WPR
Cultivators	6,369	4,112	2,257	34.2
Agricultural Labour	8,903	4,048	4,855	47.81
Household Industry	421	251	170	2.26
Other Workers	2,930	2,138	792	15.73
Main Workers	12,939	8,287	4,652	69.48
Marginal Workers	5,684	2,262	3,422	30.52
Total Workers	18,623	10,549	8,074	

Religion: Major Religious Communities:

	Persons	Males	Females	Sex Ratio
Hindu (94.98%)	32,968	17,077	15,891	931
Muslim (4.71%)	1,635	836	799	956
Christian (0.21%)	72	36	36	1,000
Sikh (0%)	-	-	-	-
Buddhists (0%)	-	-	-	-
Jain (0%)	-	-	-	-

Agewise Data:

	Persons	Males	Females	Sex Ratio
All ages	34,710	17,964	16,746	932
0-14	12,214	6,385	5,829	913
15-44	16,389	8,568	7,821	913
45-79	5,920	2,925	2,995	1024
80+	172	75	97	1293
Age not stated	15	11	4	364

Languages (Dominant):

Telugu, Urdu, Hindi, Gondi, Tamil

Disabled Population:

	Persons	Males	Females	%
Total Disabled	734	390	344	
In Seeing	260	127	133	35.42
In Speech	70	37	33	9.54
In Hearing	42	19	23	5.72
In Movement	269	160	109	36.65
Mentally	93	47	46	12.67

GOPALAPURAM

Gopalapuram C.D. Block lies in the north-eastern part of West Godavari district. The Block is located at a distance of 82 kms. from district headquarters (Eluru). There are 19 villages in the block with the total population of 59,728 persons. Area of the C.D. Block is 212.88 sq. kms. It is bounded in the north by Mandal Polavaram, in the south by Mandal Devarapalle, in the east by Mandals Tallapudi, and in the west by Mandals Koyyalagudem and Buttayagudem.

Communications :

Roadways : Metalled Roads: Nearest Villages- Karicharlagudem, Jagannadhapuram, Komatigunta, Gopalapuram, Vellacl intalagudem, Chityala.

Backwards Region Grants Fund: It receives Backward Region Grants.

Integrated Child Development Scheme (ICDS) Project: Gopalapuram, Total Anganwadi Centres: 129

Annaul Rainfall: Average Rainfall 1005 mm

Ground Water: Availability of the Ground Water in the Basin is (Information not avavible) H.A.M .and the utilization is (Information not avavible) H.A.M. It belongs to (Information not avavible) category. Depth to water level varies from 3 to 10 meter below the ground. Most of the wells go down in summer months.

Natural Division : Godavari Delta Region

Administration:

Division: Coastal Andhra. Parliamentary Constituency: 25 Rajahmundry. District: West Godawari. Mandal: Gopala puram.Assembly Constituency: 185 Gopalapuram (SC).Gram Panchayat: 18.

Villages: 19 **Inhabited:** 18 **Uninhabited:** 1

Ranking	District	State	National
Area	7	476	3965
Population	37	276	4864
Sex Ratio	11	320	1407
Child Sex Ratio	11	179	526
Literacy Rate	40	164	1979
Density	12	852	3745
Work Participation Rate	39	434	2730

Gram Panchayats:

Bhimolu, Cherukumilli, Chityala, Dondapudi, Gangolu Gopalapuram, Guddigudem, Jagannadhapuram, Karagapadu Karicherlagudem, Komatikunta, Kovvurupadu Nandigudem, Rajampalem, Saggonda, Vadalakunta Vellachintalagudem, Venkatayapalem.

Amenities:

Education: Primary School in 17 villages, Middle school in 8 villages, Matriculation or Secondary School in 6 villages, namely Gangolu, Kovvurupadu, Vadalakunta, Gopalapuram, Vellachintalagudem, Chityala.

Higher Secondary or Pre University Courses or Intermediate or Junior College in 1 village of the CD Block,, namely Gopalapuram.

College in 0 village, Adult Literacy Center in 11 villages.

Medical: Hospital in 0 village, Dispensary in 1 village, Health Center in 2 villages, Sub Center in 9 villages, Maternity and Child Welfare Center in 0 village, Community health workers in 0 village.

The Village having Hospital or Dispensary or Health Center is Gangolu.

Drinking Water: Tap water in 18 villages, Tank water in 18 villages, Well water in 18 villages, Tubewell in 18 villages and more than one source in 18 villages.

Bank: Banking facility in 3 villages, namely, Dondapudi, Gopalapuram, Chityala.

Credit Society in 7 villages Agricultural Credit Society in 7 Non-Agricultural Credit Society in 1 village.

Others: Power supply in 18 villages, Cinema hall in 2 villages, sport club in 0 village, Stadium or Auditorium or Community Hall in 1 village, Post Office in 15 villages.

There are 15 villages having bus facilities.

Villages with most of facilities: Dondapudi Gopalapuram, Chityala.

Villages without amenities (Education): Saggonda..

Scheduled Castes: Out of the total population of 59728 persons, 19814 persons (33.17%) belong to Scheduled Castes.

The villages having less than 10% SC population are None..

The villages having more than 50% SC population are None.

Sex ratio of Scheduled Caste population is 502.

Scheduled Castes Literates and Illiterates by Sex:

	Persons	Males	Females
Literate	9,793	5,085	4,708
Illiterate	10,021	4,786	5,235
Literacy rate	57.7	60.3	55.1
Graduate	267	203	64

Scheduled Castes (Dominant):

Madiga, Mala, Adi Andhra, Mala Dasari, Relli

For their cultural identity please see Appendix-I

Villages without Scheduled Castes: There are 2 villages without any scheduled caste population.

Scheduled Tribes: Out of the total population of 59728 persons, 1059 persons (1.77%) belong to Scheduled Tribes.

The villages having less than 10% ST population are Karagapadu, Sagipadu, Dondapudi, Gangolu, Saggonda Bhimolu, Kovvurupadu, Guddigudem, Karicharlagudem Jagannadhapuram, Komatigunta, Vadalakunta Gopalapuram, Vellachintalagudem, Chityala Venkatayapalem, Cherukumilli.

The villages having more than 50% ST population are None.

Sex ratio of Scheduled tribe population is 508.

Scheduled Tribes Literates and Illiterates by Sex:

	Persons	Males	Females
Literate	417	203	214
Illiterate	642	318	324
Literacy rate	46.6	47.2	46.1
Graduate	4	4	0

Scheduled Tribes (Dominant):

Koya etc., Yerukulas, Yenadis, Chenchu etc. Sugalis etc.

For their cultural identity please see Appendix-II

Villages without Scheduled Tribes: There are 7 villages without any scheduled tribe population.

Literates and Illiterates by Sex (Total Population):

	Persons	Males	Females
Literate	33,841	17,712	16,129
Illiterate	25,887	12,245	13,642
Literacy rate	65	68	62
Graduate	976	757	219

Agriculture: ***Distribution of villages according to land use:***

Out of 19 villages, Total area (in hectare) is 21288, out of that 67.03 percent is cultivable and 49.12 percent of the cultivable area is irrigated.

Sources of Irrigation (Hectares): Government Canal 0, Private Canal 0, Well without Electricity 0, Well with Electricity 2898, Tubewell without Electricity 0, Tubewell with Electricity 2212, Tank 1900, River 0, Lake 0, Waterfall 0, Others 0.

Villages with population of 5000 to 9999: None

Villages with population of 10000 and above: Gangolu, Gopalapuram.

Distribution of Workers:

	Persons	Males	Females	WPR
Cultivators	4,617	4,314	303	15.99
Agricultural Labour	19,291	10,691	8,600	66.82
Household Industry	707	484	223	2.45
Other Workers	4,254	3,354	900	14.74
Main Workers	26,098	17,862	8,236	90.4
Marginal Workers	2,771	981	1,790	9.6
Total Workers	28,869	18,843	10,026	

Religion: Major Religious Communities:

	Persons	Males	Females	Sex Ratio
Hindu (96.16%)	57,432	28,856	28,576	990
Muslim (2.84%)	1,696	833	863	1,036
Christian (0.8%)	477	214	263	1,229
Sikh (0%)	1	1	-	-
Buddhists (0%)	-	-	-	-
Jain (0%)	-	-	-	-

Agewise Data:

	Persons	Males	Females	Sex Ratio
All ages	59,728	29,957	29,771	994
0-14	18,857	9,433	9,424	999
15-44	28,850	14,523	14,327	987
45-79	11,541	5,787	5,754	994
80+	391	185	206	1114
Age not stated	89	29	60	2069

Languages (Dominant):

Telugu, Urdu, Koya, Gondi, Tamil

Disabled Population:

	Persons	Males	Females	%
Total Disabled	929	512	417	
In Seeing	231	110	121	24.87
In Speech	104	60	44	11.19
In Hearing	93	48	45	10.01
In Movement	373	240	133	40.15
Mentally	128	54	74	13.78

GOPALPETA

Gopalpeta C.D. Block lies in the central part of Mahbubnagar district. The Block is located at a distance of 53 kms. from district headquarters (Mahbubnagar). There are 20 villages in the block with the total population of 55,907 persons. Area of the C.D. Block is 244.13 sq. kms. It is bounded by Bijinapalle and Nagarkurnool Mandals on north, Peddakothapalle Mandal on east, Pangal and Kodair Mandals on south, and Wanaparthy Mandal on west.

Communications:

Roadways : State Highway (S.H.): Direction- Wanaparthy to Bijinapalle. Nearest Villages- Buddharam, Polkepahad. Backwards Region Grants Fund: It receives Backward Region Grants.

Annual Rainfall: Average Rainfall 630 mm

Ground Water: Availability of the Ground Water in the Basin is 1625 H.A.M. and the utilization is 1544 H.A.M. It belongs to Cri category. Depth to water level varies from 2 to 5 meter below the ground. Most of the wells go down in summer months. The well density in the entire block is 21 wells per sq. km. Total no. of the wells in the block are enumerated as 5143, according to the Ground Water Estimation Committee.

Natural Division : Telangana Plateau Region

Administration:

Division: Telangana. Parliamentary Constituency: 12 Nagarkurnool (SC). District: Mahbubnagar. Mandal: Gopalpeta. Assembly Constituency: 78 Wanaparthy. Gram Panchayat: 17.

Villages: 20 **Inhabited:** 19 **Uninhabited:** 1

Ranking	District	State	National
Area	34	333	3453
Population	18	345	5007
Sex Ratio	41	778	2631
Child Sex Ratio	1	52	130
Literacy Rate	51	1054	5959
Density	35	216	4333
Work Participation Rate	18	608	588

Gram Panchayats:

Bandaraipakula, Buddaram, Chakalapally, Cheerkapally Chennaram, Chennur, Gopalpet, Jainthirmalapur Keshampet, Munnanoor, Nagapur, Polkepad, Revally Tadiparthy, Talpunur, Yedula, Yedutla.

Amenities:

Education: Primary School in 19 villages, Middle school in 12 villages, Matriculation or Secondary School in 6 villages, namely Buddharam, Revally, Gopalpeta, Yedutla, Chennaram, Yedula.

Higher Secondary or Pre University Courses or Intermediate or Junior College in 0 village of the CD Block, College in 0 village, Adult Literacy Center in 19 villages.

Medical: Hospital in 0 village, Dispensary in 1 village, Health Center in 2 villages, Sub Center in 9 villages, Maternity and Child Welfare Center in 0 village,

Community health workers in 0 village.
The Villages having Hospital or Dispensary or Health Center are Revally, Yedula.
Drinking Water: Tap water in 19 villages, Tank water in 19 villages, Well water in 19 villages, Tubewell in 19 villages and more than one source in 19 villages.
Bank: Banking facility in 1 villages, namely, Gopalpeta.
Credit Society in 12 villages Agricultural Credit Society in 3 Non-Agricultural Credit Society in 12 villages.
Others: Power supply in 19 villages, Cinema hall in 0 village, sport club in 0 village, Stadium or Auditorium or Community Hall in 0 village, Post Office in 14 villages.
There are 19 villages having bus facilities.
Village with most of facilities: Gopalpeta.
Villages without Amenities (Education): None..
Scheduled Castes: Out of the total population of 55907 persons, 12114 persons (21.67%) belong to Scheduled Castes.
The villages having less than 10% SC population are None..
The villages having more than 50% SC population are None.
Sex ratio of Scheduled Caste population is 486.
Scheduled Castes Literates and Illiterates by Sex:

	Persons	Males	Females
Literate	2,739	2,065	674
Illiterate	9,375	4,165	5,210
Literacy rate	27.2	39.5	14.0
Graduate	26	23	3

Scheduled Castes (Dominant):
Madiga, Mala, Beda Jangam etc., Generic Castes etc. Bindla
For their cultural identity please see Appendix-I
Villages without Scheduled Castes: There is 1 village without any scheduled caste population.
Scheduled Tribes: Out of the total population of 55907 persons, 4737 persons (8.47%) belong to Scheduled Tribes.
The villages having less than 10% ST population are Thadparthy, Thalpunur, Shanaipalle, Nagapur, Revally Gopalpeta, Munnanur, Jain Thirumalapur, Yedutla Chennaram, Cheerkapalle, Yedula, Konkalapalle Bandaraipakula.
The villages having more than 50% ST population are None.
Sex ratio of Scheduled tribe population is 497.
Scheduled Tribes Literates and Illiterates by Sex:

	Persons	Males	Females
Literate	684	531	153
Illiterate	4,053	1,853	2,200
Literacy rate	18.4	28.4	8.3
Graduate	3	2	1

Scheduled Tribes (Dominant):
Sugalis etc., Yerukulas
For their cultural identity please see Appendix-II
Villages without Scheduled Tribes: There is 1 village without any scheduled tribe population.
Literates and Illiterates by Sex (Total Population):

	Persons	Males	Females
Literate	16,903	11,520	5,383
Illiterate	39,004	16,898	22,106
Literacy rate	36	48	23
Graduate	592	484	108

Agriculture: ***Distribution of villages according to land use:*** Out of 20 villages, Total area (in hectare) is 24411, out of that 83.94 percent is cultivable and 17.34 percent of the cultivable area is irrigated.
Sources of Irrigation (Hectares): Government Canal 0, Private Canal 0, Well without Electricity 164, Well with Electricity 1122, Tubewell without Electricity 0, Tubewell with Electricity 1515, Tank 752, River 0, Lake 0, Waterfall 0, Others 0.
Villages with population of 5000 to 9999:
Buddharam, Gopalpeta, Yedula.
Villages with population of 10000 and above: None
Distribution of Workers:

	Persons	Males	Females	WPR
Cultivators	9,154	5,917	3,237	29.85
Agricultural Labour	12,433	4,573	7,860	40.54
Household Industry	449	267	182	1.46
Other Workers	8,631	5,910	2,721	28.14
Main Workers	25,251	15,031	10,220	82.34
Marginal Workers	5,416	1,636	3,780	17.66
Total Workers	30,667	16,667	14,000	

Religion: Major Religious Communities:

	Persons	Males	Females	Sex Ratio
Hindu (96.53%)	53,967	27,462	26,505	965
Muslim (3.34%)	1,866	922	944	1,024
Christian (0.1%)	55	24	31	1,292
Sikh (0%)	-	-	-	-
Buddhists (0%)	-	-	-	-
Jain (0%)	-	-	-	-

Agewise Data:

	Persons	Males	Females	Sex Ratio
All ages	55,907	28,418	27,489	967
0-14	19,618	10,113	9,505	940
15-44	25,171	12,957	12,214	943
45-79	10,659	5,135	5,524	1076
80+	392	185	207	1119
Age not stated	67	28	39	1393

Languages (Dominant):

Telugu, Hindi, Urdu, Tamil, Oriya

Disabled Population:

	Persons	Males	Females	%
Total Disabled	1,103	642	461	
In Seeing	505	291	214	45.78
In Speech	83	53	30	7.52
In Hearing	54	27	27	4.9
In Movement	370	218	152	33.54
Mentally	91	53	38	8.25

GOPAVARAM

Gopavaram C.D. Block lies in the eastern part of Cuddap ah district. The Block is located at a distance of 57 kms. from district headquarters (Cuddapah). There are 12 villages in the block with the total population of 45,330 persons. Area of the C.D. Block is 181.29 sq. kms. It is bounded in the north by Mandal Parumamil la, in the south by Mandals Vontimitta and Penagalur, in the east by district Nellore, and in the west by Mandals B. Kodur, Badvel, Atloor and Vontimitta.

Communications:

Roadways : State Highway (S.H.): Direction- Badvel to Atmakur. Nearest Villages-Madakalavaripalle, Gopavaram.

River: Penneru Nadi- Nearest Village- Obulam.

Receives Backward Region Grants, and is identified as a drought prone area as well.

Annual Rainfall: Average Rainfall 826 mm

Ground Water: Availability of the Ground Water in the Basin is 865 H.A.M.and the utilization is 350 H.A.M. It belongs to Safe category. Depth to water level varies from 10 to 40 meter below the ground. Most of the wells go down in summer months, according to the Ground Water Estimation Committee.

Forest and Reserved **Forest:** (Forest)- Nearest Villages- Kalvapalle, Lakkavaripalle, Ramapuram, Madakalavaripalle, Gopavaram. (Kokiletipanamma)- Nearest Villages- North Ramapuram, South Ramapuram, Brahmanapalle, Rekalakunta, Obulam.

Natural Division : Rayalaseema Region

Administration:

Division: Rayala Seema. Parliamentary Constituency: 38 Kadapa. District: Cuddapah.

Mandal: Gopavaram. Assembly Constituency: 243 Badvel (SC). Gram Panchayat: 8.

Villages: 12 **Inhabited:** 12 **Uninhabited:** 0

Ranking	District	State	National
Area	38	665	4519
Population	15	648	5490
Sex Ratio	45	1027	3771
Child Sex Ratio	31	808	3545
Literacy Rate	19	225	2450
Density	47	1071	4079
Work Participation Rate	11	539	4637

Gram Panchayats:

Bethayapalli, Bodecherla, Brahmanapalli, Gopavaram Kalvapalli, Rachayapet, S. Ramapuram, T. Sandrapalli.

Amenities:

Education: Primary School in 10 villages, Middle school in 4 villages, Matriculation or Secondary School in 4 villages, namely Madakalavaripalle, Gopavaram, North Ramapuram, Brahmanapalle.

Higher Secondary or Pre University Courses or Intermediate or Junior College in 1 village of the CD Block,, namely Madakalavaripalle.

College in 1 village, Adult Literacy Center in 7 villages., College is in village, namely Madakalavaripalle.

Medical: Hospital in 1 village, Dispensary in 2 villages, Health Center in 1 village, Sub Center in 3 villages, Maternity and Child Welfare Center in 1 village, Community health workers in 0 village.

The Villages having Hospital or Dispensary or Health Center are Madakalavaripalle, South Ramapuram.

Drinking Water: Tap water in 8 villages, Tank water in 9 villages, Well water in 11 villages, Tubewell in 8 villages and more than one source in 11 villages.

Bank: Banking facility in 4 villages, namely, Madakalavaripalle, Gopavaram, North Ramapuram South Ramapuram.

Credit Society in 4 villages Agricultural Credit Society in 1 Non-Agricultural Credit Society in 3 villages.

Others: Power supply in 11 villages, Cinema hall in 1 village, sport club in 0 village, Stadium or Auditorium or Community Hall in 0 village, Post Office in 4 villages.

There are 8 villages having bus facilities.

Villages with most of facilities: Madakalavaripalle Gopavaram, South Ramapuram.

Villages without amenities (Education):

Viswanathapuram, Obulam..

Scheduled Castes: Out of the total population of 45330 persons, 10011 persons (22.08%) belong to Scheduled Castes.

The villages having less than 10% SC population are None..

The villages having more than 50% SC population are None.

Sex ratio of Scheduled Caste population is 479.

Scheduled Castes Literates and Illiterates by Sex:

	Persons	Males	Females
Literate	5,013	3,280	1,733
Illiterate	4,998	1,931	3,067
Literacy rate	57.9	72.7	41.8
Graduate	309	230	79

Scheduled Castes (Dominant):

Mala, Madiga, Mala Dasari, Beda Jangam etc.

Dom etc.

For their cultural identity please see Appendix-I

Villages without Scheduled Castes: There is 1 village without any scheduled caste population.

Scheduled Tribes: Out of the total population of 45330 persons, 986 persons (2.18%) belong to Scheduled Tribes. The villages having less than 10% ST population are Kalvapalle, Lakkavaripalle, Ramapuram Madakalavaripalle, Gopavaram, North Ramapuram South Ramapuram, Brahmanapalle, Boddecherla Rekalakunta, Viswanathapuram, Obulam.

The villages having more than 50% ST population are None.

Sex ratio of Scheduled tribe population is 508.

Scheduled Tribes Literates and Illiterates by Sex:

	Persons	Males	Females
Literate	292	187	105
Illiterate	694	298	396
Literacy rate	37.5	47.7	27.1
Graduate	10	7	3

Scheduled Tribes (Dominant):

Yenadis, Yerukulas, Sugalis etc.

For their cultural identity please see Appendix-II

Villages without Scheduled Tribes: There are 5 villages without any scheduled tribe population.

Literates and Illiterates by Sex (Total Population):

	Persons	Males	Females
Literate	24,199	15,289	8,910
Illiterate	21,131	8,018	13,113
Literacy rate	62	76	47
Graduate	1,700	1,331	369

Agriculture: ***Distribution of villages according to land use:*** Out of 12 villages, Total area (in hectare) is 18130, out of that 25.68 percent is cultivable and 39.27 percent of the cultivable area is irrigated.

Sources of Irrigation (Hectares): Government Canal 0, Private Canal 0, Well without Electricity 0, Well with Electricity 494.9, Tubewell without Electricity 0, Tubewell with Electricity 123.3, Tank 1142.6, River 0, Lake 0, Waterfall 0, Others 67.5.

Villages with population of 5000 to 9999:

Gopavaram.

Villages with population of 10000 and above:

Madakalavaripalle.

Distribution of Workers:

	Persons	Males	Females	WPR
Cultivators	3,353	2,663	690	19.16
Agricultural Labour	5,644	2,985	2,659	32.25
Household Industry	1,148	554	594	6.56
Other Workers	7,356	5,992	1,364	42.03
Main Workers	13,038	10,322	2,716	74.5
Marginal Workers	4,463	1,872	2,591	25.5
Total Workers	17,501	12,194	5,307	

Religion: Major Religious Communities:

	Persons	Males	Females	Sex Ratio
Hindu (86.82%)	39,355	20,305	19,050	938
Muslim (11.34%)	5,141	2,596	2,545	980
Christian (1.82%)	824	401	423	1,055
Sikh (0%)	-	-	-	-
Buddhists (0%)	-	-	-	-
Jain (0%)	-	-	-	-

Agewise Data:

	Persons	Males	Females	Sex Ratio
All ages	45,330	23,307	22,023	945
0-14	15,040	8,010	7,030	878
15-44	21,797	11,042	10,755	974
45-79	8,162	4,099	4,063	991
80+	281	132	149	1129
Age not stated	50	24	26	1083

Languages (Dominant):

Telugu, Urdu, Tamil, Hindi, Marathi

Disabled Population:

	Persons	Males	Females	%
Total Disabled	871	483	388	
In Seeing	370	183	187	42.48
In Speech	96	51	45	11.02
In Hearing	66	32	34	7.58
In Movement	226	148	78	25.95
Mentally	113	69	44	12.97

GORANTLA

Gorantla C.D. Block lies in the southern part of Ananta pur district. The Block is located at a distance of 90 kms. from district headquarters (Anantapur). There are 21 villages in the block with the total population of 69,719 persons. Area of the C.D. Block is 314.54 sq. kms. It is bounded in the north by Mandals Penukonda and Puttaparthi, in the south by Mandal Chilamaltur, in the east by Mandal Obuladevaracheruvu, in the west by Mandals Hindupur and Somandepalle, and it has common boundary with the state of Karnataka in the south.

Communications:

Roadways : NH- 7: Direction- Anantapur to Bangalore. Nearest Villages- Vadigepalle, Budili, Palasamudram. State Highway (S.H.): Direction- Hindupur to Kadiri, and Gorantla to Puttaparthi. Nearest Villages- Palasam udram, Jowkuledudinne, Buganipalle, Mallapalle, Ragimaku lapalle, Katepalle, Devulacheruvu, Gowrivaripalle, Manda lapalle, Gorantla.

River: Chitravati Nadi- Nearest Villages- Gangampalle, Budili, Mandalapalle, Gorantla.

It receives the Backward Region Grants, and is identifi ed as a drought-prone area as well.

Annual Rainfall: Average Rainfall 595 mm

Ground Water: Availability of the Ground Water in the Basin is 1748 H.A.M. and the utilization is 1548 H. A.M. It belongs to SC category. Depth to water level varies from 5 to 10 meter below the ground. Most of the wells go down in summer months. The well density in the entire block is 9 wells per sq. km. Total no. of the wells in the block are enumerated as 2543, according to the Ground Water Estimation Committee.

Natural Division : Rayalaseema Region

Administration:

Division: Rayala Seema. Parliamentary Constituency: 37 Hindupur. District: Anantapur.

Mandal: Gorantla. Assembly Constituency: 277 Penukonda. Gram Panchayat: 16.

Border Villages: (Karnataka)- Nearest Villages- Puleru, Gowrivaripalle.

Villages: 21 **Inhabited:** 18 **Uninhabited:** 3

Ranking	District	State	National
Area	21	133	2633
Population	2	130	4476
Sex Ratio	30	937	3241
Child Sex Ratio	45	911	4034
Literacy Rate	27	582	4151
Density	45	564	4424
Work Participation Rate	9	640	1491

Gram Panchayats:

Budili, Gangampalli, Gorantla, Gownivaripalli Kammavaripalli, Kondapuram, Malasamudram, Mallapalli Mandalapalli, Narsimpalli, Palasamudram, Puleru Reddicheruvupalli, Vadigepalli, Vanavolu Venkataramanapalli.

Amenities:

Education: Primary School in 17 villages, Middle school in 7 villages, Matriculation or Secondary School in 6 villages, namely Vanavolu, Gorantla, Palasamudram, Devulacheruvu, Budili, Puleru.

Higher Secondary or Pre University Courses or Intermediate or Junior College in 1 village of the CD Block,, namely Gorantla.

College in 1 village, Adult Literacy Center in 0 village., College is in village, namely Gorantla.

Medical: Hospital in 0 village, Dispensary in 1 village, Health Center in 1 village, Sub Center in 10 villages, Maternity and Child Welfare Center in 0 village, Community health workers in 0 village.

The Village having Hospital or Dispensary or Health Center is Budili.

Drinking Water: Tap water in 9 villages, Tank water in 0 villages, Well water in 0 village, Tubewell in 2 villages and more than one source in 10 villages.

Bank: Banking facility in 4 villages, namely, Gorantla, Palasamudram, Budili, Gowrivaripalle.

Credit Society in 5 villages Agricultural Credit Society in 5 Non-Agricultural Credit Society in 0 village.

Others: Power supply in 18 villages, Cinema hall in 1 village, sport club in 0 village, Stadium or Auditorium or Community Hall in 0 village, Post Office in 12 villages.

There are 15 villages having bus facilities.

Villages with most of facilities: Gorantla Palasamudram, Budili, Gowrivaripalle.

Villages without amenities (Education): Jowkuledudinne..

Scheduled Castes: Out of the total population of 69714 persons, 7508 persons (10.77%) belong to Scheduled Castes.

The villages having less than 10% SC population are Jowkuledudinne, Vanavolu, Gorantla, Buganipalle Ragimakulapalle, Devulacheruvu, Puleru Jakkasamudram.

The villages having more than 50% SC population are None.

Sex ratio of Scheduled Caste population is 487.

Scheduled Castes Literates and Illiterates by Sex:

	Persons	Males	Females
Literate	2,467	1,695	772
Illiterate	5,041	2,154	2,887
Literacy rate	38.0	50.9	24.4
Graduate	70	59	11

Scheduled Castes (Dominant):

Madiga, Mala, Adi Andhra, Dom etc.

Generic Castes etc.

For their cultural identity please see Appendix-I

Villages without Scheduled Castes: There are 5 villages without any scheduled caste population.

Scheduled Tribes: Out of the total population of 69714 persons, 6179 persons (8.86%) belong to Scheduled Tribes.

The villages having less than 10% ST population are Jowkuledudinne, Kammavaripalle, Gorantla, Mallapalle Ragimakulapalle, Katepalle, Devulacheruvu, Budili Puleru, Maredipalle, Jakkasamudram, Gowrivaripalle.

The villages having more than 50% ST population are None.

Sex ratio of Scheduled tribe population is 482.

Scheduled Tribes Literates and Illiterates by Sex:

	Persons	Males	Females
Literate	2,319	1,544	775

Illiterate	3,860	1,655	2,205
Literacy rate	42.8	55.0	29.7
Graduate	71	67	4

Scheduled Tribes (Dominant):
Sugalis etc., Yerukulas, Chenchu etc.
For their cultural identity please see Appendix-II
Villages without Scheduled Tribes: There are 8 villages without any scheduled tribe population.
Literates and Illiterates by Sex (Total Population):

	Persons	Males	Females
Literate	31,838	20,469	11,369
Illiterate	37,876	15,183	22,693
Literacy rate	52	66	38
Graduate	1,273	1,031	242

Agriculture: ***Distribution of villages according to land use:*** Out of 21 villages, Total area (in hectare) is 31454, out of that 60.58 percent is cultivable and 6.4 percent of the cultivable area is irrigated.
Sources of Irrigation (Hectares): Government Canal 0, Private Canal 0, Well without Electricity 0, Well with Electricity 427.04, Tubewell without Electricity 12.95, Tubewell with Electricity 615.1, Tank 163.91, River 0, Lake 0, Waterfall 0, Others 0.
Villages with population of 5000 to 9999:
Mandalapalle, Vanavolu, Budili, Gowrivaripalle.
Villages with population of 10000 and above:
Gorantla.
Distribution of Workers:

	Persons	Males	Females	WPR
Cultivators	13,326	8,676	4,650	36.15
Agricultural Labour	14,741	6,211	8,530	39.99
Household Industry	1,414	992	422	3.84
Other Workers	7,384	5,934	1,450	20.03
Main Workers	29,298	19,513	9,785	79.47
Marginal Workers	7,567	2,300	5,267	20.53
Total Workers	36,865	21,813	15,052	

Religion: Major Religious Communities:

	Persons	Males	Females	Sex Ratio
Hindu (89.35%)	62,286	31,876	30,410	954
Muslim (10.46%)	7,290	3,709	3,581	965
Christian (0.16%)	112	51	61	1,196
Sikh (0.02%)	11	6	5	833
Buddhists (0%)	3	3	-	-
Jain (0%)	2	1	1	1,000

Agewise Data:

	Persons	Males	Females	Sex Ratio
All ages	69,714	35,652	34,062	955
0-14	22,037	11,502	10,535	916
15-44	32,573	16,634	15,939	958
45-79	14,604	7,289	7,315	1004
80+	472	208	264	1269
Age not stated	28	19	9	474

Languages (Dominant):
Telugu, Urdu, Hindi, Kannada, Marathi
Disabled Population:

	Persons	Males	Females	%
Total Disabled	1,107	628	479	
In Seeing	358	188	170	32.34
In Speech	121	60	61	10.93
In Hearing	89	43	46	8.04
In Movement	394	257	137	35.59
Mentally	145	80	65	13.1

GOSPADU

Gospadu C.D. Block lies in the eastern part of Kurnool district. The Block is located at a distance of 66 kms. from district headquarters (Kurnool). There are 15 villages in the block with the total population of 38,614 persons. Area of the C.D. Block is 134.05 sq. kms. It is bounded in the north by Mandal Nandyal, in the south by Mandals Darnipadu and Sirvel, in the east by Mandals Mahanandi and Sirvel, and in the west by Mandals Banaganapalle and Koilkuntla.
Communications:
Roadways : State Highway (S.H.): Direction- Allagaddu to Nandyal. Nearest Villages- Sambavaram, Deebaguntla, Kanalapalle.
River: Kunderu Nadi- Nearest Villages- Tellapuri, Rayapadu, S.Kuluru.
It is identified as a drought-prone area.
Annual Rainfall: Average Rainfall 741 mm
Ground Water: Availability of the Ground Water in the Basin is 2393 H.A.M. and the utilization is 393 H.A.M. It belongs to Safe category. Depth to water level varies from 5 to 10 meter below the ground. Most of the wells go down in summer months. The well density in the entire block is 2 wells per sq. km. Total no. of the wells in the block are enumerated as 328, according to the Ground Water Estimation Committee.
Natural Division : Rayalaseema Region
Administration:
Division: Rayala Seema. Parliamentary Constituency: 34 Nandayal. District: Kurnool. Mandal: Gospadu. Assembly Constituency: 258 Nandyal Gram Panchayat: 15.
Villages: 15 **Inhabited:** 15 **Uninhabited:** 0

Ranking	District	State	National
Area	51	887	5265
Population	42	868	5798
Sex Ratio	24	814	2721
Child Sex Ratio	22	546	2158
Literacy Rate	7	373	3327
Density	17	114	3659

Work Participation Rate	6	404	351

Gram Panchayats:
Deebaguntla, Gospadu, Jillela, Julepalle Kanalapalle, M.Chintakunta, M.Krishnapuram Nehru Nagar, Pasurapadu, Rayapadu, S.Nagulavaram Sambavaram, Tellapuri, Vantivelagala, Yalluru.

Amenities:

Education: Primary School in 15 villages, Middle school in 8 villages, Matriculation or Secondary School in 4 villages, namely Deebaguntla, Jillela, Gospadu, Yalluru.
Higher Secondary or Pre University Courses or Intermediate or Junior College in 0 village of the CD Block, College in 0 village, Adult Literacy Center in 15 villages.

Medical: Hospital in 0 village, Dispensary in 2 villages, Health Center in 3 villages, Sub Center in 7 villages, Maternity and Child Welfare Center in 0 village, Community health workers in 0 village.
The Villages having Hospital or Dispensary or Health Center are Deebaguntla, Jillela.

Drinking Water: Tap water in 15 villages, Tank water in 15 villages, Well water in 15 villages, Tubewell in 15 villages and more than one source in 15 villages.

Bank: Banking facility in 3 villages, namely, Deebaguntla, Gospadu, Yalluru.
Credit Society in 11 villages Agricultural Credit Society in 6 Non-Agricultural Credit Society in 11 villages.

Others: Power supply in 15 villages, Cinema hall in 3 villages, sport club in 0 village, Stadium or Auditorium or Community Hall in 0 village, Post Office in 12 villages.
There are 14 villages having bus facilities.

Villages with most of facilities: Deebaguntla Gospadu, Yalluru.

Villages without Amenities (Education): None..

Scheduled Castes: Out of the total population of 38614 persons, 10682 persons (27.66%) belong to Scheduled Castes.
The villages having less than 10% SC population are None..
The villages having more than 50% SC population are None.
Sex ratio of Scheduled Caste population is 489.

Scheduled Castes Literates and Illiterates by Sex:

	Persons	Males	Females
Literate	4,356	2,923	1,433
Illiterate	6,326	2,532	3,794
Literacy rate	47.9	62.8	32.2
Graduate	122	104	18

Scheduled Castes (Dominant):
Mala, Madiga

For their cultural identity please see Appendix-I

Villages without Scheduled Castes: There are 0 village without any scheduled caste population.

Scheduled Tribes: Out of the total population of 38614 persons, 235 persons (0.61%) belong to Scheduled Tribes.
The villages having less than 10% ST population are Pasurapadu, Julepalle, M.Chintakunta, S.Nagulavaram Sambavaram, Deebaguntla, Kanalapalle, Jillela Gospadu, Tellapuri, Rayapadu, S.Kuluru Vantivelagala, M.Krishnapuram, Yalluru.
The villages having more than 50% ST population are None.
Sex ratio of Scheduled tribe population is 506.

Scheduled Tribes Literates and Illiterates by Sex:

	Persons	Males	Females
Literate	118	78	40
Illiterate	117	38	79
Literacy rate	59.6	79.6	40.0
Graduate	7	5	2

Scheduled Tribes (Dominant):
Yerukulas, Sugalis etc., Yenadis, Kammara

For their cultural identity please see Appendix-II

Villages without Scheduled Tribes: There are 7 villages without any scheduled tribe population.

Literates and Illiterates by Sex (Total Population):

	Persons	Males	Females
Literate	19,004	12,102	6,902
Illiterate	19,610	7,544	12,066
Literacy rate	57	71	42
Graduate	737	631	106

Agriculture: ***Distribution of villages according to land use:***
Out of 15 villages, Total area (in hectare) is 13406, out of that 92.8 percent is cultivable and 53.84 percent of the cultivable area is irrigated.

Sources of Irrigation (Hectares): Government Canal 5973, Private Canal 254, Well without Electricity 0, Well with Electricity 310, Tubewell without Electricity 6, Tubewell with Electricity 29, Tank 0, River 0, Lake 0, Waterfall 0, Others 126.

Villages with population of 5000 to 9999:
Yalluru.

Villages with population of 10000 and above: None

Distribution of Workers:

	Persons	Males	Females	WPR
Cultivators	4,502	3,187	1,315	20.19
Agricultural Labour	14,581	6,601	7,980	65.39
Household Industry	289	145	144	1.3
Other Workers	2,925	1,952	973	13.12
Main Workers	19,938	11,147	8,791	89.42
Marginal Workers	2,359	738	1,621	10.58
Total Workers	22,297	11,885	10,412	

Religion: Major Religious Communities:

	Persons	Males	Females	Sex Ratio
Hindu (89.72%)	34,643	17,602	17,041	968
Muslim (9.38%)	3,622	1,855	1,767	953
Christian (0.16%)	63	33	30	909
Sikh (0%)	-	-	-	-
Buddhists (0%)	-	-	-	-
Jain (0%)	-	-	-	-

Agewise Data:

	Persons	Males	Females	Sex Ratio
All ages	38,614	19,646	18,968	965
0-14	12,548	6,488	6,060	934
15-44	18,258	9,411	8,847	940
45-79	7,523	3,626	3,897	1075
80+	244	96	148	1542
Age not stated	41	25	16	640

Languages (Dominant):

Telugu, Urdu, Marathi, Gondi, Tamil

Disabled Population:

	Persons	Males	Females	%
Total Disabled	832	429	403	
In Seeing	348	164	184	41.83
In Speech	90	44	46	10.82
In Hearing	69	27	42	8.29
In Movement	239	139	100	28.73
Mentally	86	55	31	10.34

GOVINDARAOPET

Govindraopet C.D. Block lies in the north-eastern part of Warangal district. The Block is located at a distance of 34 kms. from district headquarters (Warangal). There are 14 villages in the block with the total popul ation of 29,265 persons. Area of the C.D. Block is 88. 56 sq. kms. It is bounded in the north by Venkatapur Mandal, in the south by Mulug and Kothagudem Mandals, in the east by Tadvai Mandal, and in the west by Mulug Mandal. Headquarters: Loknavaram.

Communications:

Roadways : NH- 202: Direction- Warangal to Bijapur. Nearest Villages- Machchapur, Laknavaram, Chalwai, Rangapur, Kannaigudem, Pasranagaram, Rampur.

River: Vagu: Nearest Villages- Chalwai, Rangapur, Kanna igudem, Pasranagaram, Rampur, Ammakkapalle, Bussapur, Motlagudem, Medaram (Patti Chelva), Muthapur, Karlapal le.

Loknavaram Tank: Nearest Villages- Dammakkapalle, Bussa pur.

Backwards Region Grants Fund: It receives Backward Region Grants.

Annual Rainfall: Average Rainfall 1238 mm

Ground Water: Availability of the Ground Water in the Basin is 3488 H.A.M.and the utilization is 614 H.A. M. It belongs to Safe category. Depth to water level varies from 5 to 20 meter below the ground. Most of the wells go down in summer months. The well density in the entire block is 2 wells per sq. km. Total no. of the wells in the block are enumerated as 141, accor ding to the Ground Water Estimation Committee.

Natural Division : Godavari Depression Region

Administration:

Division: Telangana. Parliamentary Constituency. Distri ct: Warangal. Mandal: Govindaraopet. Assembly Constituen cy: 109 Mulug (ST). Gram Panchayat: 8.

Villages: 14 **Inhabited:** 10 **Uninhabited:** 4

Ranking	**District**	**State**	**National**
Area	50	1050	5809
Population	49	1032	6069
Sex Ratio	16	493	1805
Child Sex Ratio	39	941	4207
Literacy Rate	7	363	3289
Density	41	713	3266
Work Participation Rate	9	307	2028

Gram Panchayats:

Bussapur, Chalvai, Dumpillagudem, Govindaraopeta Karlapalle, Machapur, Motlagudem, Pasra(Nagaram).

Amenities:

Education: Primary School in 10 villages, Middle school in 6 villages, Matriculation or Secondary School in 3 villages, namely Chalwai, Pasranagaram, Laknavaram.

Higher Secondary or Pre University Courses or Intermediate or Junior College in 1 village of the CD Block,, namely Laknavaram.

College in 0 village, Adult Literacy Center in 8 villages.

Medical: Hospital in 2 villages, Dispensary in 0 village, Health Center in 2 villages, Sub Center in 6 villages, Maternity and Child Welfare Center in 0 village, Community health workers in 0 village.

The Villages having Hospital or Dispensary or Health Center are Pasranagaram, Laknavaram.

Drinking Water: Tap water in 10 villages, Tank water in 10 villages, Well water in 10 villages, Tubewell in 10 villages and more than one source in 10 villages.

Bank: Banking facility in 4 villages, namely, Chalwai, Rangapur, Pasranagaram, Laknavaram.

Credit Society in 9 villages Agricultural Credit Society in 4 Non-Agricultural Credit Society in 9 villages.

Others: Power supply in 10 villages, Cinema hall in 3 villages, sport club in 0 village, Stadium or Auditorium or Community Hall in 0 village, Post Office in 8 villages.

There are 9 villages having bus facilities.

Villages with most of facilities: Chalwai Rangapur, Pasranagaram, Laknavaram.

Villages without Amenities (Education): None..

Scheduled Castes: Out of the total population of 29265 persons, 4056 persons (13.86%) belong to Scheduled Castes.

The villages having less than 10% SC population are None..

The villages having more than 50% SC population are None.

Sex ratio of Scheduled Caste population is 493.

Scheduled Castes Literates and Illiterates by Sex:

	Persons	Males	Females
Literate	1,633	1,044	589
Illiterate	2,423	1,013	1,410
Literacy rate	47.9	60.3	35.0
Graduate	36	30	6

Scheduled Castes (Dominant):

Madiga, Mala, Mala Sale etc., Gosangi

Mitha Ayyalvar

For their cultural identity please see Appendix-I

Villages without Scheduled Castes: There are 4 villages without any scheduled caste population.

Scheduled Tribes: Out of the total population of 29265 persons, 6885 persons (23.53%) belong to Scheduled Tribes.

The villages having less than 10% ST population are None..

The villages having more than 50% ST population are None.

Sex ratio of Scheduled tribe population is 490.

Scheduled Tribes Literates and Illiterates by Sex:

	Persons	Males	Females
Literate	2,783	1,818	965
Illiterate	4,102	1,690	2,412
Literacy rate	48.1	62.7	33.4
Graduate	52	51	1

Scheduled Tribes (Dominant):

Sugalis etc., Koya etc., Gond etc., Yerukulas

Yenadis

For their cultural identity please see Appendix-II

Villages without Scheduled Tribes: There are 4 villages without any scheduled tribe population.

Literates and Illiterates by Sex (Total Population):

	Persons	Males	Females
Literate	14,417	8,709	5,708
Illiterate	14,848	6,031	8,817
Literacy rate	57	69	45
Graduate	426	367	59

Agriculture: *Distribution of villages according to land use:*

Out of 14 villages, Total area (in hectare) is 8854, out of that 36.22 percent is cultivable and 69.7 percent of the cultivable area is irrigated.

Sources of Irrigation (Hectares): Government Canal 0, Private Canal 0, Well without Electricity 24.28, Well with Electricity 133.54, Tubewell without Electricity 0, Tubewell with Electricity 30.35, Tank 1573.37, River 0, Lake 282.8, Waterfall 0, Others 190.99.

Villages with population of 5000 to 9999:

Chalwai.

Villages with population of 10000 and above: None

Distribution of Workers:

	Persons	Males	Females	WPR
Cultivators	4,642	3,422	1,220	31.65
Agricultural Labour	7,215	2,809	4,406	49.19
Household Industry	463	297	166	3.16
Other Workers	2,348	1,815	533	16.01
Main Workers	10,405	7,011	3,394	70.94
Marginal Workers	4,263	1,332	2,931	29.06
Total Workers	14,668	8,343	6,325	

Religion: Major Religious Communities:

	Persons	Males	Females	Sex Ratio
Hindu (95.67%)	27,997	14,116	13,881	983
Muslim (3.91%)	1,144	562	582	1,036
Christian (0.35%)	103	51	52	1,020
Sikh (0%)	-	-	-	-
Buddhists (0%)	-	-	-	-
Jain (0%)	-	-	-	-

Agewise Data:

	Persons	Males	Females	Sex Ratio
All ages	29,265	14,740	14,525	985
0-14	9,693	4,970	4,723	950
15-44	13,703	6,846	6,857	1002
45-79	5,602	2,784	2,818	1012
80+	229	122	107	877
Age not stated	38	18	20	1111

Languages (Dominant):

Telugu, Hindi, Urdu, Tamil, Oriya

Disabled Population:

	Persons	Males	Females	%
Total Disabled	886	538	348	
In Seeing	512	322	190	57.79
In Speech	58	33	25	6.55
In Hearing	46	20	26	5.19
In Movement	191	119	72	21.56
Mentally	79	44	35	8.92

GUDEM KOTHA VEEDHI

Gudemkothaveedhi C.D. Block lies in the western part of Vishakhapatnam district. It is a part of Gudemokotha veedhi Mandal. The Block is located at a distance of 211 kms. from district headquarters (Vishakhapatnam).

There are 173 villages in the block with the total population of 52,730 persons. Area of the C.D. Block is 131.07 sq. kms. It is bounded in the north by Mandal Koyyuru, in the south by Mandal Chintapalle, in the east by Mandals Chintapalle and Koyyuru, and in the west by district East Godavari, and it has common bound ary with the state of Orissa on north.

Communications :

Roadways : Metalled Roads: Nearest Villages- Busikonda, Jonnamamidi, Challanisilpa, Rosaiguda, Duppalawada, Chekkalamaddi, Dabbagedda, Gorrelova, Kothapalle, Gudem Patha Veedhi, Teemulabanda, Pujaripakalu, Asurodda, Rinthada, Ducharapalem, Neelavaram, Bonampalle, Gudem Colony.

River: Sileru Nadi- Nearest Village- Valasagedda.

Annaual Rainfall: Average Rainfall 975.0 mm

Ground Water: Availability of the Ground Water in the Basin is (Information not avavible) H.A.M .and the utilization is (Information not avavible) H.A.M. It belongs to (Information not avavible) category. Depth to water level varies from 3 to 10 meter below the ground. Most of the wells go down in summer months.

Forest and Reserved **Forest:** Nearest Villages- Valasaged da, Busikonda, Pilligedda, Katragedda, Santha Neredupalle, Jonnamamidi, Challanisilpa, Duppalawada, Kommarapalle, Neredupalle, Rallagedda, Agraharam, Petrai, Gangavaram, Naramamidi Gondi, Nimmachettu, Pilligondi, Gollapalle, Chintalawada, Peddammagondi, Rallagedda, Kondrupalle, Boddalalagondi, Gudimamidi, Gilligondi, Masangilli, Gunkurolu, Dabbagondi, Nadimiveedhi, Pebbampalle, Tadakapalle, Durgam, Godichinta, Chamagedda, Reyyalaged da, Ammavaridharakonda, Chelakaveedhi, Jajipakalu, Yenug ugondi, Kakulagedda, Chekkalamaddi, Darakonda, Kotturu, Yenugubayalu, Kongapakalu, Dabbagedda, Gorrelova, Cheedigunta, Chodirai, Tokarai, Chintagoppu, Madimalla, Kothurukota, Annavaram, Gummirevulu, Paramasingavaram, Kondajartha, Bathunuru, Galikonda, Muddula Busikonda, Jampalova, S.Kothuru, Saprla, Lankapakalu, Panasapalle, Siribala, Adagarapalle, Jerrilakothuru, Jerrila, Gudiw ada, Mondigedda, Burugupakalu, Ginjangi, Gaigampalle, Kondakichangi, Lubbagunta, Panasapalle, Nittamamidi Palem, Veeravaram, Kothapalem, Vanchula, Kothapalle, Gudem Patha Veedhi, Agraharam, Vadamamidi, Gummalagond Kampamanupakalu, Etarobbulu, Busulu, Sagulu, Lakkavar am, Yerracheruvulu, Kommalawada, Vanabalingam, Chintalap adu, Kondawada, Boddamanupakalu, Boddamamidi, Kunkkum Teemulabanda, Gudem Kotha Veedhi, Nelajaratha, Kakanu ru, Badasallu.

Administration:

Division: Coastal Andhra. Parliamentary Constituency: 18 Araku (ST). District: Visakhapatnam. Mandal: Gudem Kotha Veedhi. Assembly Constituency: 148 Paderu (ST). Gram Panchayat: 16.

Border Villages: (Orissa)- Nearest Villages- Valasagedda, Pilligedda, Katragedda, Neredupalle, Rallagedda, Petrai, Busikonda, Gangavaram, Naramamidi Gondi, Nimmac hettu, Pilligondi, Gollapalle.

Villages: 173 **Inhabited:** 170 **Uninhabited:** 3

Ranking	District	State	National
Area	31	878	5237
Population	24	465	5206
Sex Ratio	5	65	472
Child Sex Ratio	10	53	126
Literacy Rate	39	1091	6225
Density	7	108	2910
Work Participation Rate	15	223	341

Gram Panchayats:

A.Darakonda, Damanapalle, Darakonda, Devarapalli Duppalawada, G.K.Veedhi, Galikonda, Gummerevulu Jerrila, Lakkavarapupeta, Mondigedda, Peddavalasa Rinthada, Sankada, Sileru, Vanchula.

Amenities:

Education: Primary School in 122 villages, Middle school in 8 villages, Matriculation or Secondary School in 7 villages, namely Darakonda, Gudem Patha Veedhi, Pujaripakalu, Gudem Kotha Veedhi, Peddavalasa, R.V.Nagar, Yerravaram.

Higher Secondary or Pre University Courses or Inter-mediate or Junior College in 0 village of the CD Block, College in 0 village, Adult Literacy Center in 0 village.

Medical: Hospital in 0 village, Dispensary in 2 villages, Health Center in 17 villages, Sub Center in 5 villages, Maternity and Child Welfare Center in 1 village, Community health workers in 0 village.

The Villages having Hospital or Dispensary or Health Center are Peddavalasa, R.V.Nagar.

Drinking Water: Tap water in 162 villages, Tank water in 162 villages, Well water in 162 villages, Tubewell in 163 villages and more than one source in 166 villages.

Bank: Banking facility in 1 villages, namely, Peddavalasa.

Credit Society in 0 village Agricultural Credit Society in 0 Non-Agricultural Credit Society in 0 village.

Others: Power supply in 170 villages, Cinema hall in 0 village, sport club in 0 village, Stadium or Auditorium or Community Hall in 1 village, Post Office in 13 villages.

There are 31 villages having bus facilities.

Village with most of facilities: Peddavalasa.

Villages without amenities (Education):

Jonnamamidi, Challanisilpa, Petrai, Nimmachettu, Chintalawada, Peddammagondi, Kondrupalle, Boddalalagondi, Gilligondi, Gunkurolu, Dabbagondi, Durgam, Godichinta, Chelakaveedhi, Jajipakalu, Yenugugondi, Kakulagedda, Chodirai, Chintagoppu,

Kondajartha, Bathunuru, Muddula Busikonda, Jampalova, Marripalem, Kothawada, Gaigampalle, Chintalapadu, Kondawada, Boddamanupakalu, Boddamamidi, Kampamanupakalu, Pedapadu, Patha Yerragedda, Badasallu, Boyalapalem, Gomuvada, Chittamamidi, Dengurai, Jangampadu, Gunalanka, Kothagudem, Chapagedda, Rajumanupakalu, Kimulabanda..

Scheduled Castes: Out of the total population of 51404 persons, 811 persons (1.58%) belong to Scheduled Castes.

The villages having less than 10% SC population are Valasagedda, Busikonda, Pilligedda, Katragedda Santha Neredupalle, Jonnamamidi, Challanisilpa Rosaiguda, Duppalawada, Kommarapalle, Neredupalle Rallagedda, Agraharam, Petrai, Gangavaram Naramamidi Gondi, Nimmachettu, Gollapalle Chintalawada, Peddammagondi, Rallagedda, Kondrupalle Boddalalagondi, Gudimamidi, Gilligondi, Masangilli Gunkurolu, Dabbagondi, Nadimiveedhi, Pebbampalle Tadakapalle, Durgam, Godichinta, Chamagedda Reyyalagedda, Ammavaridharakonda, Chelakaveedhi Jajipakalu, Yenugugondi, Kakulagedda, Darakonda Kotturu, Yenugubayalu, Kongapakalu, Dabbagedda Kommalawada, Gorrelova, Cheedigunta, Chodirai Tokarai, Chintagoppu, Madimalla, Kothurukota Annavaram, Nelajaratha, Kakanuru, Gummirevulu Paramasingavaram, Kondajartha, Bathunuru, Galikonda Muddula Busikonda, Jampalova, S.Kothuru, Saprla Lankapakalu, Panasapalle, Marripalem, Munagarapalle Siribala, Adagarapalle, Jerrilakothuru, Jerrila Gudiwada, Mondigedda, Nemmathotapalem, Burugupakalu Kothawada, Ginjangi, Vanabalingam, Gaigampalle Kondakichangi, Lubbagunta, Panasapalle Nittamamidi Palem, Chintalapadu, Vanthadapalle Veeravaram, Kothapalem, Vanchula, Kondawada Korapalle, Cherapalle, Gondipalle, Boddamanupakalu Gudem Patha Veedhi, Agraharam, Vadamamidi Boddamamidi, Kunkkumpudi, Gummalagondi, Teemulabanda Pujaripakalu, Gudem Kotha Veedhi, Kampamanupakalu Etarobbulu, Busulu, Pedapadu, Sagulu, Lakkavaram Patha Yerragedda, Yerracheruvulu, Badasallu Dokuluru, Kokkitapadu, Rampulu, Chaparathipalem Thurumamidi, Nerudubanda, Lakkavarapupeta Boyalapalem, Garikibanda, Peddavalasa, Jadumuru Gomuvada, Vasuwada, Chittamamidi, Chinnajadumuru Dengurai, Gandepalle, Sankadakothuru, Nimmalapalem Suravaram, Kodisingi, Mangalapalem, Devarapalle Jangampadu, Gunalanka, Vusurugudem, Yernabilli Kotnabilli, Sankada, Asurodda, Rinthada Ducharapalem, Yebulu, Ramagedda, Neelavaram Bonampalle, Gudem Colony, Kothagudem, R.V.Nagar Kadugulu, Parikala, Rajumanupakalu, Pedakothuru Kodisingi, Doddikonda, Kattupalle, Lingavaram, Madem Damanapalle, Pippaladoddi, Signapalle, Annavaram.

The villages having more than 50% SC population are None.

Sex ratio of Scheduled Caste population is 475.

Scheduled Castes Literates and Illiterates by Sex:

	Persons	Males	Females
Literate	306	204	102
Illiterate	505	222	283
Literacy rate	45.6	58.1	31.9
Graduate	21	18	3

Scheduled Castes (Dominant):

Mala, Madiga, Generic Castes etc., Relli, Adi Andhra

For their cultural identity please see Appendix-I

Villages without Scheduled Castes: There are 142 villages without any scheduled caste population.

Scheduled Tribes: Out of the total population of 51404 persons, 47852 persons (93.09%) belong to Scheduled Tribes.

The villages having less than 10% ST population are None..

The villages having more than 50% ST population are Valasagedda, Busikonda, Pilligedda, Katragedda Santha Neredupalle, Jonnamamidi, Challanisilpa Rosaiguda, Duppalawada, Kommarapalle, Neredupalle Rallagedda, Agraharam, Petrai, Gangavaram Naramamidi Gondi, Nimmachettu, Gollapalle Chintalawada, Peddammagondi, Rallagedda, Kondrupalle Boddalalagondi, Gudimamidi, Gilligondi, Masangilli Gunkurolu, Dabbagondi, Nadimiveedhi, Pebbampalle Tadakapalle, Durgam, Godichinta, Chamagedda Reyyalagedda, Ammavaridharakonda, Chelakaveedhi Jajipakalu, Yenugugondi, Kakulagedda, Chekkalamaddi Darakonda, Kotturu, Yenugubayalu, Kongapakalu Dabbagedda, Kommalawada, Gorrelova, Cheedigunta Chodirai, Tokarai, Chintagoppu, Madimalla Kothurukota, Annavaram, Nelajaratha, Kakanuru Gummirevulu, Paramasingavaram, Kondajartha Bathunuru, Galikonda, Muddula Busikonda, Jampalova S.Kothuru, Saprla, Lankapakalu, Panasapalle Marripalem, Munagarapalle, Siribala, Adagarapalle Jerrilakothuru, Jerrila, Gudiwada, Mondigedda Nemmathotapalem, Burugupakalu, Kothawada, Ginjangi Vanabalingam, Gaigampalle, Kondakichangi, Lubbagunta Panasapalle, Nittamamidi Palem, Chintalapadu Vanthadapalle, Veeravaram, Kothapalem, Vanchula Kondawada, Korapalle, Cherapalle, Gondipalle Kothapalle, Boddamanupakalu, Gudem Patha Veedhi Agraharam, Vadamamidi, Boddamamidi, Kunkkumpudi Gummalagondi, Teemulabanda, Pujaripakalu

Gudem Kotha Veedhi, Kampamanupakalu, Etarobbulu Busulu, Pedapadu, Sagulu, Lakkavaram Patha Yerragedda, Yerracheruvulu, Badasallu Dokuluru, Kokkitapadu, Rampulu, Chaparathipalem Thurumamidi, Nerudubanda, Lakkavarapupeta Boyalapalem, Peddavalasa, Jadumuru, Gomuvada Vasuwada, Chittamamidi, Chinnajadumuru, Dengurai Gandepalle, Sankadakothuru, Nimmalapalem, Suravaram Kodisingi, Mangalapalem, Devarapalle, Jangampadu Gunalanka, Vusurugudem, Yernabilli, Kotnabilli Sankada, Asurodda, Rinthada, Ducharapalem, Yebulu Ramagedda, Neelavaram, Bonampalle, Gudem Colony Kothagudem, R.V.Nagar, Yerravaram, Chapagedda Kadugulu, Parikala, Rajumanupakalu, Kimulabanda Pedakothuru, Kodisingi, Doddikonda, Kattupalle Lingavaram, Madem, Damanapalle, Pippaladoddi Signapalle, Annavaram.

Sex ratio of Scheduled tribe population is 509.

Scheduled Tribes Literates and Illiterates by Sex:

	Persons	Males	Females
Literate	10,455	6,892	3,563
Illiterate	37,397	16,599	20,798
Literacy rate	26.9	36.1	18.0
Graduate	70	62	8

Scheduled Tribes (Dominant):

Bagata, Kondhs etc., Valmiki, Konda Dhoras Mukha Dhora etc.

For their cultural identity please see Appendix-II

Villages without Scheduled Tribes: There are 3 villages without any scheduled tribe population.

Literates and Illiterates by Sex (Total Population):

	Persons	Males	Females
Literate	12,052	7,884	4,168
Illiterate	39,352	17,424	21,928
Literacy rate	29	38	20
Graduate	154	133	21

Agriculture: ***Distribution of villages according to land use:*** Out of 173 villages, Total area (in hectare) is 13679, out of that 59.23 percent is cultivable and 8.93 percent of the cultivable area is irrigated.

Sources of Irrigation (Hectares): Government Canal 0, Private Canal 0, Well without Electricity 0, Well with Electricity 0, Tubewell without Electricity 0, Tubewell with Electricity 0, Tank 7.2, River 7.82, Lake 0, Waterfall 0, Others 723.3.

Villages with population of 5000 to 9999: None

Villages with population of 10000 and above: None

Distribution of Workers:

	Persons	Males	Females	WPR
Cultivators	17,408	9,700	7,708	62.07
Agricultural Labour	8,628	3,906	4,722	30.76
Household Industry	230	133	97	0.82
Other Workers	1,781	1,112	669	6.35
Main Workers	22,779	13,594	9,185	81.22
Marginal Workers	5,268	1,257	4,011	18.78
Total Workers	28,047	14,851	13,196	

Religion: Major Religious Communities:

	Persons	Males	Females	Sex Ratio
Hindu (97.84%)	50,295	24,742	25,553	1,033
Muslim (0.4%)	205	115	90	783
Christian (1.67%)	861	424	437	1,031
Sikh (0.04%)	22	16	6	375
Buddhists (0%)	1	-	1	-
Jain (0%)	-	-	-	-

Agewise Data:

	Persons	Males	Females	Sex Ratio
All ages	51,404	25,308	26,096	1031
0-14	19,481	9,661	9,820	1016
15-44	24,373	11,764	12,609	1072
45-79	7,299	3,743	3,556	950
80+	161	86	75	872
Age not stated	90	54	36	667

Languages (Dominant):

Telugu, Oriya, Konda, Gadaba, Khond/Kondh

Disabled Population:

	Persons	Males	Females	%
Total Disabled	725	414	311	
In Seeing	411	233	178	56.69
In Speech	55	35	20	7.59
In Hearing	28	20	8	3.86
In Movement	168	91	77	23.17
Mentally	63	35	28	8.69

GUDIBANDA

Gudibanda C.D. Block lies in the south-western part of Anantapur district. The Block is located at a distance of 115 kms. from district headquarters (Anantapur). There are 13 villages in the block with the total population of 47,838 persons. Area of the C.D. Block is 199.57 sq. kms. It is bounded in the north by Mandal Amarapuram, in the south by Mandal Rolla, in the east by Mandal Madakasira, and it has common boundary with the state of Karnataka in the north, east and west.

Communications:

Roadways : Metalled Roads: Nearest Villages- Kumbaranagehalli, Karikera, Kekathi, Gudibanda.

It receives the Backward Region Grants, and is identified as a drought-prone area as well.

Annual Rainfall: Average Rainfall 506 mm

Ground Water: Availability of the Ground Water in the Basin is 1034 H.A.M. and the utilization is 1431 H.A.M. It belongs to OE category. Depth to water level varies from 10 to 20 meter below the ground. Most of the wells go down in summer months. The well density in the entire block is 8 wells per sq. km. Total no. of the wells in the block are enumerated as 1827, according to the Ground Water Estimation Committee.

Natural Division : Rayalaseema Region

Administration:

Division: Rayala Seema. Parliamentary Constituency: 37 Hindupur. District: Anantapur.

Mandal: Gudibanda. Assembly Constituency: 275 Madakasira (SC). Gram Panchayat: 12.

Border Villages: (Karnataka)- Nearest Villages- Karikera, Rallahalli, Morubagal, Gunimorubagal, Muthukur, Kekat hi, Konkallu.

Villages: 13 **Inhabited:** 13 **Uninhabited:** 0

Ranking	District	State	National
Area	55	559	4189
Population	21	585	5396
Sex Ratio	37	970	3372
Child Sex Ratio	26	460	1711
Literacy Rate	53	790	4851
Density	42	541	4205
Work Participation Rate	6	575	1435

Gram Panchayats:

Chigathurpi, Gudibanda, Gunemorubagal, Jambulabanda Karikera, Konkallu, Kumbaranagehalli, Mandalahalli Morubagal, Muthukur, Rallahalli, S.Rayapuram.

Amenities:

Education: Primary School in 12 villages, Middle school in 8 villages, Matriculation or Secondary School in 6 villages, namely Kumbaranagehalli, Rallahalli, Kekathi, Gudibanda, Morubagal, Mandalahalli.

Higher Secondary or Pre University Courses or Intermediate or Junior College in 0 village of the CD Block, College in 0 village, Adult Literacy Center in 0 village.

Medical: Hospital in 0 village, Dispensary in 1 village, Health Center in 1 village, Sub Center in 7 villages, Maternity and Child Welfare Center in 0 village, Community health workers in 0 village.

The Village having Hospital or Dispensary or Health Center is Morubagal.

Drinking Water: Tap water in 12 villages, Tank water in 0 villages, Well water in 0 village, Tubewell in 1 village and more than one source in 10 villages.

Bank: Banking facility in 1 villages, namely, Gudibanda.

Credit Society in 3 villages Agricultural Credit Society in 3 Non-Agricultural Credit Society in 0 village.

Others: Power supply in 13 villages, Cinema hall in 3 villages, sport club in 0 village, Stadium or Auditorium or Community Hall in 0 village, Post Office in 11 villages.

There are 13 villages having bus facilities.

Village with most of facilities: Gudibanda.

Villages without amenities (Education): Pillenahalli..

Scheduled Castes: Out of the total population of 47838 persons, 11300 persons (23.62%) belong to Scheduled Castes.

The villages having less than 10% SC population are None..

The villages having more than 50% SC population are None.

Sex ratio of Scheduled Caste population is 488.

Scheduled Castes Literates and Illiterates by Sex:

	Persons	Males	Females
Literate	3,709	2,510	1,199
Illiterate	7,591	3,277	4,314
Literacy rate	38.6	50.7	25.7
Graduate	71	63	8

Scheduled Castes (Dominant):

Madiga, Mala, Dom etc., Beda Jangam etc., Chalavadi

For their cultural identity please see Appendix-I

Villages without Scheduled Castes: There is 1 village without any scheduled caste population.

Scheduled Tribes: Out of the total population of 47838 persons, 953 persons (1.99%) belong to Scheduled Tribes.

The villages having less than 10% ST population are Kumbaranagehalli, Karikera, Rallahalli, Pillenahalli Kekathi, Gudibanda, Chigathurpi, Morubagal Gunimorubagal, Muthukur, Mandalahalli, Konkallu S.Rayapuram.

The villages having more than 50% ST population are None.

Sex ratio of Scheduled tribe population is 461.

Scheduled Tribes Literates and Illiterates by Sex:

	Persons	Males	Females
Literate	319	243	76
Illiterate	634	271	363
Literacy rate	39.2	53.9	20.9
Graduate	24	22	2

Scheduled Tribes (Dominant):

Sugalis etc., Kammara, Yerukulas

For their cultural identity please see Appendix-II

Villages without Scheduled Tribes: There are 7 villages without any scheduled tribe population.

Literates and Illiterates by Sex (Total Population):

	Persons	Males	Females
Literate	19,792	12,852	6,940
Illiterate	28,046	11,657	16,389
Literacy rate	48	61	34
Graduate	476	427	49

Agriculture: ***Distribution of villages according to land use:*** Out of 13 villages, Total area (in hectare) is 19956, out of that 61.62 percent is cultivable and 5.83 percent of the cultivable area is irrigated.

Sources of Irrigation (Hectares): Government Canal 0, Private Canal 0, Well without Electricity 0, Well with Electricity 286.11, Tubewell without Electricity 0, Tubewell with Electricity 431.38, Tank 0, River 0, Lake 0, Waterfall 0, Others 0.

Villages with population of 5000 to 9999:
Rallahalli, Gudibanda, Morubagal, Mandalahalli.

Villages with population of 10000 and above: None

Distribution of Workers:

	Persons	Males	Females	WPR
Cultivators	10,623	7,100	3,523	42.23
Agricultural Labour	10,564	4,239	6,325	41.99
Household Industry	579	214	365	2.3
Other Workers	3,391	2,583	808	13.48
Main Workers	18,231	11,903	6,328	72.47
Marginal Workers	6,926	2,233	4,693	27.53
Total Workers	25,157	14,136	11,021	

Religion: Major Religious Communities:

	Persons	Males	Females	Sex Ratio
Hindu (97.58%)	46,678	23,907	22,771	952
Muslim (2.38%)	1,139	593	546	921
Christian (0.03%)	15	8	7	875
Sikh (0%)	-	-	-	-
Buddhists (0%)	-	-	-	-
Jain (0%)	-	-	-	-

Agewise Data:

	Persons	Males	Females	Sex Ratio
All ages	47,838	24,509	23,329	952
0-14	15,817	8,112	7,705	950
15-44	21,228	10,851	10,377	956
45-79	10,252	5,284	4,968	940
80+	502	241	261	1083
Age not stated	39	21	18	857

Languages (Dominant):
Kannada, Telugu, Urdu, Hindi, Marathi

Disabled Population:

	Persons	Males	Females	%
Total Disabled	1,111	615	496	
In Seeing	489	239	250	44.01
In Speech	118	63	55	10.62
In Hearing	58	37	21	5.22
In Movement	322	214	108	28.98
Mentally	124	62	62	11.16

GUDIHATHNOOR

Gudihathnoor C.D. Block lies in the north-west part of Adilabad district. The Block is located at a distance of 20 kms. from district headquarters (Adilabad). There are 21 villages in the block with the total popul ation of 25,704 persons. Area of the C.D. Block is 142. 60 sq. kms. It is bounded by Adilabad Mandal on north and north-east, Inderavelly Mandal on east and south-ea st, Ichoda Mandal on south and south-west, Bazarhathnoor Mandal on south-west and west, Talamudugu Mandal on north- west.

Communications :

Roadways : NH- 7: Direction- Nirmal to Adilabad. Nearest Villages- Kamalapur, Seetagondi, Gudihathinur, Mannur, Dongargaon.

Backwards Region Grants Fund: It receives Backward Region Grants.

Annual Rainfall: Average Rainfall 1102 mm

Ground Water: Availability of the ground water in the Basin is 1472 H.A.M. and the utilization is 579 H.A. M. It belongs to Safe category. Depth to water level varies from 5 to 10 meter below the ground. Most of the wells go down in summer months, according to the Ground Water Estimation Committee.

Natural Division : Telangana Plateau Region

Administration:

Division: Telangana. Parliamentary Constituency: 1 Adilabad (ST). District: Adilabad. Mandal: Gudihathnoor. Assembly Constituency: 8 Boath (ST). Gram Panchayat: 11

Villages: 21 **Inhabited:** 21 **Uninhabited:** 0

Ranking	District	State	National
Area	50	844	5116
Population	42	1061	6132
Sex Ratio	22	243	1167
Child Sex Ratio	9	142	375
Literacy Rate	5	450	3672
Density	34	602	5098
Work Participation Rate	5	802	1622

Gram Panchayats:
Gudihathinur, Kamala Pur, Kolhari, Lingapur Machapur, Mannur, Muthnur, Seetagondi, Shantapur Tosham, Umri B.

Amenities:

Education: Primary School in 20 villages, Middle school in 7 villages, Matriculation or Secondary School in 4 villages, namely Seetagondi, Tosham, Gudihathinur, Mannur. Higher Secondary or Pre University Courses or Intermediate or Junior College in 0 village of the CD Block, College in 0 village, Adult Literacy Center in 18 villages.

Medical: Hospital in 0 village, Dispensary in 1 village, Health Center in 1 village, Sub Center in 6 villages, Maternity and Child Welfare Center in 0 village,

Community health workers in 0 village.
The Village having Hospital or Dispensary or Health Center is Mannur.
Drinking Water: Tap water in 21 villages, Tank water in 21 villages, Well water in 21 villages, Tubewell in 21 villages and more than one source in 21 villages.
Bank: Banking facility in 3 villages, namely, Seetagondi, Lingapur, Gudihathinur.
Credit Society in 6 villages Agricultural Credit Society in 6 Non-Agricultural Credit Society in 4 villages.
Others: Power supply in 21 villages, Cinema hall in 0 village, sport club in 0 village, Stadium or Auditorium or Community Hall in 0 village, Post Office in 7 villages.
There are 9 villages having bus facilities.
Villages with most of facilities: Seetagondi Gudihathinur.
Villages without amenities (Education):
Rendlabori..
Scheduled Castes: Out of the total population of 25704 persons, 4980 persons (19.37%) belong to Scheduled Castes.
The villages having less than 10% SC population are Machapur, Neradigonda, Gondharkapur, Rendlabori Belluri, Tejapur.
The villages having more than 50% SC population are None.
Sex ratio of Scheduled Caste population is 495.
Scheduled Castes Literates and Illiterates by Sex:

	Persons	Males	Females
Literate	2,411	1,523	888
Illiterate	2,569	993	1,576
Literacy rate	57.6	72.7	42.4
Graduate	16	15	1

Scheduled Castes (Dominant):
Mahar, Madiga, Mala Sale etc., Mang, Mala
For their cultural identity please see Appendix-I
Villages without Scheduled Castes: There are 5 villages without any scheduled caste population.
Scheduled Tribes: Out of the total population of 25704 persons, 9372 persons (36.46%) belong to Scheduled Tribes.
The villages having less than 10% ST population are None..
The villages having more than 50% ST population are Vaijapur, Malkapur, Machapur, Neradigonda, Umri(B) Guruj, Gondharkapur, Rendlabori, Belluri, Tejapur.
Sex ratio of Scheduled tribe population is 503.
Scheduled Tribes Literates and Illiterates by Sex:

	Persons	Males	Females
Literate	3,258	2,182	1,076
Illiterate	6,114	2,477	3,637
Literacy rate	43.9	59.0	28.9
Graduate	18	17	1

Scheduled Tribes (Dominant):
Gond etc., Sugalis etc., Kolam etc., Pardhan, Thoti
For their cultural identity please see Appendix-II
Villages without Scheduled Tribes: There are 4 villages without any scheduled tribe population.
Literates and Illiterates by Sex (Total Population):

	Persons	Males	Females
Literate	11,553	7,338	4,215
Illiterate	14,151	5,513	8,638
Literacy rate	55	70	40
Graduate	131	121	10

Agriculture: ***Distribution of villages according to land use:***
Out of 21 villages, Total area (in hectare) is 14516, out of that 62.99 percent is cultivable and 1.86 percent of the cultivable area is irrigated.
Sources of Irrigation (Hectares): Government Canal 0, Private Canal 0, Well without Electricity 78.91, Well with Electricity 79.24, Tubewell without Electricity 2.02, Tubewell with Electricity 10.05, Tank 0, River 0, Lake 0, Waterfall 0, Others 0.
Villages with population of 5000 to 9999: None
Villages with population of 10000 and above: None
Distribution of Workers:

	Persons	Males	Females	WPR
Cultivators	6,001	3,194	2,807	47.53
Agricultural Labour	4,251	1,813	2,438	33.67
Household Industry	230	141	89	1.82
Other Workers	2,145	1,632	513	16.99
Main Workers	10,481	5,908	4,573	83
Marginal Workers	2,146	872	1,274	17
Total Workers	12,627	6,780	5,847	

Religion: Major Religious Communities:

	Persons	Males	Females	Sex Ratio
Hindu (89.73%)	23,063	11,533	11,530	1,000
Muslim (8.95%)	2,300	1,156	1,144	990
Christian (0.25%)	64	27	37	1,370
Sikh (0%)	-	-	-	-
Buddhists (1.02%)	261	125	136	1,088
Jain (0%)	-	-	-	-

Agewise Data:

	Persons	Males	Females	Sex Ratio
All ages	25,704	12,851	12,853	1000
0-14	10,585	5,371	5,214	971
15-44	11,282	5,674	5,608	988
45-79	3,640	1,724	1,916	1111
80+	164	71	93	1310
Age not stated	33	11	22	2000

Languages (Dominant):
Marathi, Gondi, Telugu, Hindi, Urdu

Disabled Population:

	Persons	Males	Females	%
Total Disabled	381	237	144	
In Seeing	155	97	58	40.68
In Speech	36	18	18	9.45
In Hearing	16	14	2	4.2
In Movement	126	80	46	33.07
Mentally	48	28	20	12.6

GUDIPALA

Gudipala C.D. Block lies in the southern part of Chitto or district. The Block is located at a distance of 14 kms. from district headquarters (Chittoor). There are 32 villages in the block with the total population of 42,387 persons. Area of the C.D. Block is 144.66 sq. kms. It is bounded in the north by Mandal Chittoor, i in the east by Mandal Gangadhara Nallore, in the west by Mandal Chittoor, and it has common boundary with the state of Tamil Nadu in the south, east and west.

Communications:

Roadways : NH- 4: Direction- Cuddapah to Chennai. Nearest Villages- Ramapuram, Muthukurpalle, Vasanthapuram, Basavapalle, Marakalakuppam, Kothapalle, Nangamangalam, Gudipala, Bomma Samudram. State Highway (S.H.): Gudipa la to Vellore. Nearest Villages- Gudipala, Bomma Samudram.

Railway Station: Mogaralapalle, Venkata Lakshmamba Puram, Nangamangalam.

It receives the Backward Region Grants, and is identifi ed as a drought-prone area as well.

Annual Rainfall: Average Rainfall 951 mm

Ground Water: Availability of the Ground Water in the Basin is 2101 H.A.M.and the utilization is 1767 H.A. M. It belongs to SC category. Depth to water level varies from 5 to 10 meter below the ground. Most of the wells go down in summer months, according to the Ground Water Estimation Committee.

Forest and Reserved **Forest:** Nearest Villages- Papasamud ram, Bandapalle, Chittapara, Bomma Samudram, Mandi Krish napuram.

Natural Division : Rayalaseema Region

Administration:

Division: Rayala Seema. Parliamentary Constituency: 42 Chittoor (SC). District: Chittoor. Mandal: Gudipala. Assembly Constituency: 291 Chittoor Gram Panchayat: 28

Border Villages: (Tamil Nadu)- Nearest Villages- Naraga llu, Ramapuram, Chittapara, Ragimanupatteda, Dakshina Brahmana Palle, Thimmaiahpalle, Venkata Lakshmamba Puram, Bomma Samudram, Nangamangalam, Mandi Krishnapu

Villages: 32 **Inhabited:** 30 **Uninhabited:** 2

Ranking	**District**	**State**	**National**
Area	45	849	5127
Population	36	745	5628
Sex Ratio	1	95	642
Child Sex Ratio	59	1039	4960
Literacy Rate	4	39	855
Density	58	993	3603
Work Participation Rate	26	387	3737

Gram Panchayats:

190 Ramapuram, 197 Ramapuram, Adilakshmambapuram Bandapalle, Basavapalle, Bommasamudram, Cheelapalle Chittapara, Getralamitta, Gollamadugu, Gudipala Kothapalle, Krishna Jammapuram, Kuppiganipalle Mandikrishnapuram, Marakalakuppam, Mogaralapalle Nangamangalam, Naragallu, Panaturu, Papasamudram Peyanapalle, Ramabhadrapuram, Srirangampalle Thimmaiahpalle, Vasanthapuram, Vengamambapuram Veppalamanuchenu.

Amenities:

Education: Primary School in 26 villages, Middle school in 12 villages, Matriculation or Secondary School in 5 villages, namely Adilakshmamba Puram, Srirangampalle, Vasanthapuram, Thimmaiahpalle, Bomma Samudram. Higher Secondary or Pre University Courses or Intermediate or Junior College in 1 village of the CD Block,, namely Bomma Samudram.

College in 0 village, Adult Literacy Center in 14 villages.

Medical: Hospital in 0 village, Dispensary in 0 village, Health Center in 4 villages, Sub Center in 9 villages, Maternity and Child Welfare Center in 0 village, Community health workers in 0 village.

The Village having Hospital or Dispensary or Health Center is Vasanthapuram.

Drinking Water: Tap water in 30 villages, Tank water in 30 villages, Well water in 30 villages, Tubewell in 30 villages and more than one source in 30 villages.

Bank: Banking facility in 3 villages, namely, Ramapuram, Bomma Samudram, Nangamangalam.

Credit Society in 10 villages Agricultural Credit Society in 8 Non-Agricultural Credit Society in 4 villages.

Others: Power supply in 30 villages, Cinema hall in 0 village, sport club in 0 village, Stadium or Auditorium or Community Hall in 0 village, Post Office in 12 villages.

There are 25 villages having bus facilities.

Villages with most of facilities: Ramapuram Bomma Samudram, Nangamangalam.

Villages without amenities (Education):

Gollapalle, Ragimanupatteda, Venkata Lakshmamba Puram, Bandarlapalle..

Scheduled Castes: Out of the total population of 42387 persons, 14660 persons (34.59%) belong to Scheduled Castes.

The villages having less than 10% SC population are Gollapalle, Adilakshmamba Puram
Cheruvu Mundara Khandriga, Krishna Jammapuram
Muthukurpalle, Bandapalle, Ragimanupatteda
Venkata Lakshmamba Puram, Bandarlapalle.

The villages having more than 50% SC population are Kaidugani Khandriga, Srirangampalle, Kothapalle
Basavapalle, Pasumanda, Marakalakuppam
Mandi Krishnapuram.

Sex ratio of Scheduled Caste population is 503.

Scheduled Castes Literates and Illiterates by Sex:

	Persons	Males	Females
Literate	9,495	5,197	4,298
Illiterate	5,165	2,083	3,082
Literacy rate	73.8	82.3	65.7
Graduate	153	112	41

Scheduled Castes (Dominant):

Adi Dravida, Adi Andhra, Madiga, Mala
Generic Castes etc.

For their cultural identity please see Appendix-I

Villages without Scheduled Castes: There are 8 villages without any scheduled caste population.

Scheduled Tribes: Out of the total population of 42387 persons, 719 persons (1.7%) belong to Scheduled Tribes.

The villages having less than 10% ST population are Ramapuram, Mogaralapalle, Cheelapalle, Gollapalle
Naragallu, Adilakshmamba Puram
Cheruvu Mundara Khandriga, Kaidugani Khandriga
Ramapuram, Krishna Janmapuram, Srirangampalle
Muthukurpalle, Kothapalle, Papasamudram, Bandapalle
Chittapara, Gudipala, Vasanthapuram, Basavapalle
Thimmaiahpalle, Ragimanupatteda
Venkata Lakshmamba Puram, Kuppiganipalle
Dakshina Brahmana Palle, Marakalakuppam
Bomma Samudram, Nangamangalam, Mandi Krishnapuram.

The villages having more than 50% ST population are None.

Sex ratio of Scheduled tribe population is 515.

Scheduled Tribes Literates and Illiterates by Sex:

	Persons	Males	Females
Literate	266	160	106
Illiterate	453	189	264
Literacy rate	44.5	54.6	34.8
Graduate	1	0	1

Scheduled Tribes (Dominant):

Yenadis, Yerukulas, Koya etc., Sugalis etc.

For their cultural identity please see Appendix-II

Villages without Scheduled Tribes: There are 12 villages without any scheduled tribe population.

Literates and Illiterates by Sex (Total Population):

	Persons	Males	Females
Literate	27,291	15,190	12,101
Illiterate	15,096	5,788	9,308
Literacy rate	73	83	64
Graduate	849	615	234

Agriculture: ***Distribution of villages according to land use:*** Out of 32 villages, Total area (in hectare) is 14467, out of that 50.31 percent is cultivable and 44.83 percent of the cultivable area is irrigated.

Sources of Irrigation (Hectares): Government Canal 0, Private Canal 0, Well without Electricity 0, Well with Electricity 2553.56, Tubewell without Electricity 0, Tubewell with Electricity 663.45, Tank 46.13, River 0, Lake 0, Waterfall 0, Others 0.

Villages with population of 5000 to 9999: None

Villages with population of 10000 and above: None

Distribution of Workers:

	Persons	Males	Females	WPR
Cultivators	6,234	4,324	1,910	33.27
Agricultural Labour	8,358	4,580	3,778	44.61
Household Industry	567	300	267	3.03
Other Workers	3,576	2,520	1,056	19.09
Main Workers	16,530	10,812	5,718	88.23
Marginal Workers	2,205	912	1,293	11.77
Total Workers	18,735	11,724	7,011	

Religion: Major Religious Communities:

	Persons	Males	Females	Sex Ratio
Hindu (94.87%)	40,212	19,904	20,308	1,020
Muslim (1.2%)	510	261	249	954
Christian (3.83%)	1,623	788	835	1,060
Sikh (0.01%)	5	4	1	250
Buddhists (0.01%)	3	2	1	500
Jain (0%)	-	-	-	-

Agewise Data:

	Persons	Males	Females	Sex Ratio
All ages	42,387	20,978	21,409	1021
0-14	12,037	6,125	5,912	965
15-44	19,047	9,303	9,744	1047
45-79	10,723	5,272	5,451	1034
80+	504	241	263	1091
Age not stated	76	37	39	1054

Languages (Dominant):

Telugu, Tamil, Urdu, Hindi, Kannada

Disabled Population:

	Persons	Males	Females	%
Total Disabled	604	364	240	
In Seeing	170	95	75	28.15
In Speech	101	59	42	16.72
In Hearing	29	20	9	4.8
In Movement	229	152	77	37.91

Mentally	75	38	37	12.42

GUDIVADA

Gudivada C.D. Block lies in the southern part of Krishna district. It is a part of Gudivada Mandal. The Block is located at a distance of 12 kms. from district headq uarters (Machilipatnam). There are 29 villages in the block with the total population of 55,576 persons.
Area of the C.D. Block is 107.5 sq. kms. It is bounded in the north by Mandal Nandivada, in the south by Manda ls Pamarru and Gudlavalleru, in the east by Mandal Mudin epalle, and in the west by Mandal Pedaparupudi.

Communications:

Roadways : State Highways (S.H.): Direction- Eluru to Machilipatnam. and Pamarru to Kaikalur. Nearest Village s- Lingavaram, Siddhantam, Ramanapudi, Valivarthipadu (Rural), Gangadharapuram, Seri Velpur, Bommuluru, China Yerukapadu, Ramachandrapuram, Moturu.

Railway Station: Guntakoduru, Moturu.

Integrated Child Development Scheme (ICDS) Project: Gudiwada, Total Anganwadi Centres: 172

Annaul Rainfall: Average Rainfall 1140 mm

Ground Water: Availability of the Ground Water in the Basin is (Information not avavible) H.A.M .and the utilization is (Information not avavible) H.A.M. It belongs to (Information not avavible) category. Depth to water level varies from 3 to 10 meter below the ground. Most of the wells go down in summer months.

Natural Division : Krishna Delta Region

Administration:

Division: Coastal Andhra. Parliamentary Constituency: 28 Machilipatnam. District: Krishna. Mandal: Gudivada. Assembly Constituency: 191 Gudivada. Gram Panchayat: 21

Villages: 29 **Inhabited:** 28 **Uninhabited:** 1

Ranking	District	State	National
Area	42	1002	5637
Population	46	846	5770
Sex Ratio	26	561	1976
Child Sex Ratio	16	334	1203
Literacy Rate	6	49	967
Density	22	775	2991
Work Participation Rate	24	245	2272

Gram Panchayats:

Billapadu, Bommuluru, Chirichintala, Chowtapalli Dondapadu, Guntakoduru, Kalvapudiagraharam Lingavaram, Mallayapalem, Moturu, Nuzella, Parnasa Ramannapudi, Seepudi, Seridintakurru, Serigolvepalli Serivelpuru, Siddantham, Sydepudi, Tattivarru Valivarthipadu.

Amenities:

Education: Primary School in 28 villages, Middle school in 11 villages, Matriculation or Secondary School in 6 villages, namely Moturu, Gudivada (Rural), Bethavolu (Rural), Gangadharapuram, Chowtapalle, Bommuluru.
Higher Secondary or Pre University Courses or Intermediate or Junior College in 1 village of the CD Block,, namely Bommuluru.
College in 0 village, Adult Literacy Center in 9 villages.

Medical: Hospital in 1 village, Dispensary in 0 village, Health Center in 1 village, Sub Center in 6 villages, Maternity and Child Welfare Center in 0 village, Community health workers in 0 village.
The Village having Hospital or Dispensary or Health Center is Moturu.

Drinking Water: Tap water in 21 villages, Tank water in 14 villages, Well water in 17 villages, Tubewell in 4 villages and more than one source in 23 villages.

Bank: Banking facility in 2 villages, namely, Dondapadu, Moturu.
Credit Society in 16 villages Agricultural Credit Society in 8 Non-Agricultural Credit Society in 15 villages.

Others: Power supply in 28 villages, Cinema hall in 0 village, sport club in 0 village, Stadium or Auditorium or Community Hall in 0 village, Post Office in 12 villages.
There are 25 villages having bus facilities.

Villages with most of facilities: Dondapadu Moturu.

Villages without Amenities (Education): None..

Scheduled Castes: Out of the total population of 39231 persons, 12463 persons (31.77%) belong to Scheduled Castes.
The villages having less than 10% SC population are Merakagudem, Gudivada (Rural), Bethavolu (Rural) Siddhantam, China Yerukapadu.
The villages having more than 50% SC population are Guntakoduru, Mandapadu (Rural), Gangadharapuram Tativarru, Kasipudi, Chirichintala.
Sex ratio of Scheduled Caste population is 492.

Scheduled Castes Literates and Illiterates by Sex:

	Persons	Males	Females
Literate	7,724	4,235	3,489
Illiterate	4,739	2,100	2,639
Literacy rate	71.7	77.3	65.9
Graduate	216	156	60

Scheduled Castes (Dominant):

Mala, Madiga, Generic Castes etc., Mala Dasari Madiga Dasu etc.

For their cultural identity please see Appendix-I

Villages without Scheduled Castes: There are 2 villages without any scheduled caste population.

Scheduled Tribes: Out of the total population of 39231

persons, 473 persons (1.21%) belong to Scheduled Tribes. The villages having less than 10% ST population are Lingavaram, Merakagudem, Valivarthipadu (Rural) Dondapadu, Saidepudi, Seri Golvepalle, Guntakoduru Moturu, Chilakamudi, Gudivada (Rural) Bethavolu (Rural), Pedayerukapadu (Rural) Mandapadu (Rural), Billapadu (Rural) Gangadharapuram, Siddhantam, Chowtapalle Kalvapudi Agraharam, Seri Dintakurru, Seri Velpur Bommuluru, China Yerukapadu, Tativarru, Seepudi Kasipudi, Ramanapudi, Chirichintala Ramachandrapuram.

The villages having more than 50% ST population are None.

Sex ratio of Scheduled tribe population is 471.

Scheduled Tribes Literates and Illiterates by Sex:

	Persons	Males	Females
Literate	120	78	42
Illiterate	353	172	181
Literacy rate	30.8	38.2	22.6
Graduate	3	3	0

Scheduled Tribes (Dominant):

Yerukulas, Sugalis etc., Yenadis, Jatapus Chenchu etc.

For their cultural identity please see Appendix-II

Villages without Scheduled Tribes: There are 12 villages without any scheduled tribe population.

Literates and Illiterates by Sex (Total Population):

	Persons	Males	Females
Literate	24,688	13,361	11,327
Illiterate	14,543	6,446	8,097
Literacy rate	72	77	67
Graduate	758	541	217

Agriculture: ***Distribution of villages according to land use:*** Out of 29 villages, Total area (in hectare) is 10751, out of that 73.45 percent is cultivable and 98.96 percent of the cultivable area is irrigated.

Sources of Irrigation (Hectares): Government Canal 7815.03, Private Canal 0, Well without Electricity 0, Well with Electricity 0, Tubewell without Electricity 0, Tubewell with Electricity 0, Tank 0, River 0, Lake 0, Waterfall 0, Others 0.

Villages with population of 5000 to 9999: None

Villages with population of 10000 and above: None

Distribution of Workers:

	Persons	Males	Females	WPR
Cultivators	1,857	1,617	240	9.46
Agricultural Labour	12,446	6,466	5,980	63.39
Household Industry	723	358	365	3.68
Other Workers	4,609	3,900	709	23.47
Main Workers	13,987	10,409	3,578	71.24
Marginal Workers	5,648	1,932	3,716	28.76
Total Workers	19,635	12,341	7,294	

Religion: Major Religious Communities:

	Persons	Males	Females	Sex Ratio
Hindu (89.14%)	34,969	17,698	17,271	976
Muslim (4.01%)	1,574	749	825	1,101
Christian (6.73%)	2,641	1,338	1,303	974
Sikh (0.05%)	18	10	8	800
Buddhists (0%)	1	-	1	-
Jain (0%)	-	-	-	-

Agewise Data:

	Persons	Males	Females	Sex Ratio
All ages	39,231	19,807	19,424	981
0-14	11,572	5,875	5,697	970
15-44	19,371	9,848	9,523	967
45-79	7,983	3,941	4,042	1026
80+	261	120	141	1175
Age not stated	44	23	21	913

Languages (Dominant):

Telugu, Urdu, Hindi, Tamil, Gondi

Disabled Population:

	Persons	Males	Females	%
Total Disabled	736	394	342	
In Seeing	225	108	117	30.57
In Speech	103	49	54	13.99
In Hearing	39	15	24	5.3
In Movement	253	154	99	34.38
Mentally	116	68	48	15.76

GUDLAVALLERU

Gudlavalleru C.D. Block lies in the south-eastern part of Krishna district. The Block is located at a distance of 24 kms. from district headquarters (Machilipatnam). There are 24 villages in the block with the total population of 55,592 persons. Area of the C.D. Block is 124.63 sq. kms. It is bounded in the north by Mandals Gudivada and Mudinepalle, in the south by Mandal Guduru, in the east by Mandal Pedana, and in the west by Mandal Pamarru.

Communications:

Roadways : State Highway (S.H.): Direction- Gudivada to Machilipatnam. Nearest Villages- Angaluru, Vemavarap palem, Vemavaram, Gudlavalleru, Kowtaram, Vadlamannadu

Railway Station: Gudlavalleru, Kowtaram, Vadlamannadu.

Annaul Rainfall: Average Rainfall 1153 mm

Ground Water: Availability of the Ground Water in the Basin is (Information not avavible) H.A.M .and the utilization is (Information not avavible) H.A.M. It belongs to (Information not avavible) category. Depth to water level varies from 3 to 10 meter below the ground. Most of the wells go down in summer months.

Natural Division : Krishna Delta Region

Administration:

Division: Coastal Andhra. Parliamentary Constituency: 28 Machilipatnam. District: Krishna. Mandal: Gudlavalle ru. Assembly Constituency: 191 Gudivada. Gram Panchayat: 22

Villages: 24 **Inhabited:** 22 **Uninhabited:** 2

Ranking	District	State	National
Area	36	924	5398
Population	26	357	5028
Sex Ratio	25	557	1982
Child Sex Ratio	24	429	1616
Literacy Rate	10	64	1180
Density	38	894	2473
Work Participation Rate	12	146	3041

Gram Panchayats:

Angaluru, Chandrala, Chinagonnuru, Chitram Dokiparru, Gadepudi, Gudlavalleru, Kattavanicheruvu Kowthavaram, Kuchikayalapudi, Kurada, Mamidikolla Penjendra, Polimetla, Puritipadu, Seridaggumilli Serikalvapudi, Vadlamannadu, Vemavaram Venuthurumilli, Vinnakota, Vulavalapudi.

Amenities:

Education: Primary School in 22 villages, Middle school in 10 villages, Matriculation or Secondary School in 7 villages, namely Angaluru, Vinnakota, Gudlavalleru, Penjendra, Dokiparru, Kowtaram, Vadlamannadu.

Higher Secondary or Pre University Courses or Intermediate or Junior College in 1 village of the CD Block,, namely Gudlavalleru.

College in 1 village, Adult Literacy Center in 4 villages., College is in village, namely Gudlavalleru.

Medical: Hospital in 1 village, Dispensary in 2 villages, Health Center in 1 village, Sub Center in 9 villages, Maternity and Child Welfare Center in 1 village, Community health workers in 0 village.

The Villages having Hospital or Dispensary or Health Center are Gudlavalleru, Dokiparru, Kowtaram.

Drinking Water: Tap water in 5 villages, Tank water in 4 villages, Well water in 22 villages, Tubewell in 1 village and more than one source in 6 villages.

Bank: Banking facility in 5 villages, namely, Angaluru, Gudlavalleru, Dokiparru, Kowtaram Vadlamannadu.

Credit Society in 16 villages Agricultural Credit Society in 8 Non-Agricultural Credit Society in 16 villages.

Others: Power supply in 22 villages, Cinema hall in 3 villages, sport club in 0 village, Stadium or Auditorium or Community Hall in 0 village, Post Office in 16 villages.

There are 17 villages having bus facilities.

Villages with most of facilities: Angaluru Gudlavalleru, Dokiparru, Kowtaram, Vadlamannadu.

Villages without Amenities (Education): None..

Scheduled Castes: Out of the total population of 55592 persons, 13557 persons (24.39%) belong to Scheduled Castes.

The villages having less than 10% SC population are None..

The villages having more than 50% SC population are None.

Sex ratio of Scheduled Caste population is 491.

Scheduled Castes Literates and Illiterates by Sex:

	Persons	Males	Females
Literate	7,813	4,345	3,468
Illiterate	5,744	2,561	3,183
Literacy rate	66.0	71.9	59.8
Graduate	181	131	50

Scheduled Castes (Dominant):

Mala, Madiga, Relli, Adi Andhra, Mala Dasari

For their cultural identity please see Appendix-I

Villages without Scheduled Castes: There are 3 villages without any scheduled caste population.

Scheduled Tribes: Out of the total population of 55592 persons, 1038 persons (1.87%) belong to Scheduled Tribes.

The villages having less than 10% ST population are Seri Kalavapudi, Angaluru, Vinnakota, Puritipadu Chinagonnuru, Seridaggumilli, Kurada, Chandrala Gudlavalleru, Penjendra, Chitram, Mamidikolla Dokiparru, Pesaramilli, Kowtaram, Vemavarappalem Vemavaram, Venuturumilli, Nagavaram, Ulavalapudi Gadepudi, Vadlamannadu.

The villages having more than 50% ST population are None.

Sex ratio of Scheduled tribe population is 476.

Scheduled Tribes Literates and Illiterates by Sex:

	Persons	Males	Females
Literate	371	227	144
Illiterate	667	317	350
Literacy rate	42.5	48.9	35.2
Graduate	5	4	1

Scheduled Tribes (Dominant):

Yerukulas, Yenadis, Sugalis etc., Chenchu etc. Koya etc.

For their cultural identity please see Appendix-II

Villages without Scheduled Tribes: There are 12 villages without any scheduled tribe population.

Literates and Illiterates by Sex (Total Population):

	Persons	Males	Females
Literate	34,613	18,961	15,652
Illiterate	20,979	9,098	11,881

Literacy rate	70	76	64
Graduate	1,376	943	433

Agriculture: ***Distribution of villages according to land use:*** Out of 24 villages, Total area (in hectare) is 12466, out of that 83.28 percent is cultivable and 99.25 percent of the cultivable area is irrigated.

Sources of Irrigation (Hectares): Government Canal 10303.23, Private Canal 0, Well without Electricity 0, Well with Electricity 0, Tubewell without Electricity 0, Tubewell with Electricity 0, Tank 0, River 0, Lake 0, Waterfall 0, Others 0.

Villages with population of 5000 to 9999: Dokiparru, Kowtaram.

Villages with population of 10000 and above: Gudlavalleru.

Distribution of Workers:

	Persons	Males	Females	WPR
Cultivators	3,413	3,089	324	12.85
Agricultural Labour	16,998	8,671	8,327	63.98
Household Industry	569	297	272	2.14
Other Workers	5,589	4,440	1,149	21.04
Main Workers	21,999	14,848	7,151	82.8
Marginal Workers	4,570	1,649	2,921	17.2
Total Workers	26,569	16,497	10,072	

Religion: Major Religious Communities:

	Persons	Males	Females	Sex Ratio
Hindu (88.77%)	49,347	24,966	24,381	977
Muslim (6.81%)	3,785	1,886	1,899	1,007
Christian (4.3%)	2,388	1,170	1,218	1,041
Sikh (0.02%)	12	5	7	1,400
Buddhists (0.01%)	3	1	2	2,000
Jain (0%)	1	1	-	-

Agewise Data:

	Persons	Males	Females	Sex Ratio
All ages	55,592	28,059	27,533	981
0-14	16,072	8,081	7,991	989
15-44	27,154	13,922	13,232	950
45-79	11,872	5,824	6,048	1038
80+	433	204	229	1123
Age not stated	61	28	33	1179

Languages (Dominant):
Telugu, Urdu, Hindi, Tamil, Oriya

Disabled Population:

	Persons	Males	Females	%
Total Disabled	963	501	462	
In Seeing	334	158	176	34.68
In Speech	117	70	47	12.15
In Hearing	57	23	34	5.92
In Movement	334	192	142	34.68
Mentally	121	58	63	12.56

GUDLURU

Gudluru C.D. Block lies in the south-eastern part of Prakasam district. The Block is located at a distance of 66 kms. from district headquarters (Ongole). There are 18 villages in the block with the total population of 42,382 persons. Area of the C.D. Block is 257.80 sq. kms. It is bounded in the north by Mandals Kandukur and Ulavapadu, in the south by district Nellore, in the east by the Bay of Bengal, and in the west by Manda ls Lingasamudram and Voletivaripalem.

Communications:

Roadways : NH- 5: Direction- Nellore to Ongole. Nearest Villages- Mocherla, Chevuru.

Railway Station: Mocherla.

Rivers Upputeru Nadi- Nearest Villages- Gundlapalem, Kothapeta, Gudluru, Basireddy Palem, Venkam Peta, Chinala Trapi. Manneru Nadi- Nearest Villages- Parakond apadu, Dappalampadu, Gundlapalem, Kothapeta, Basireddy Palem, Darakanipadu, Puretipalle.

The Block is identified as a drought-prone area.

Coastal Villages: Nearest Village- Ravur.

Annual Rainfall: Average Rainfall 1109.0 mm

Ground Water: Availability of the Ground Water in the Basin is 21.61 MCM and the utilization is 10.61 MCM It belongs to Safe category. Depth to water level varies from 2 to 5 meter below the ground. Most of the wells go down in summer months, according to the Ground Water Estimation Committee.

Administration:

Division: Coastal Andhra. Parliamentary Constituency: 39 Nellore. District: Prakasam. Mandal: Gudluru. Assemb ly Constituency: 228 Kandukur. Gram Panchayat: 23.

Villages: 18 **Inhabited:** 18 **Uninhabited:** 0

Ranking	District	State	National
Area	20	282	3277
Population	29	746	5629
Sex Ratio	21	617	2095
Child Sex Ratio	12	282	932
Literacy Rate	44	758	4751
Density	24	428	5327
Work Participation Rate	39	855	1063

Gram Panchayats:
Adavirajupalem, Ammavaripalem, Basireddypalem Chevuru, Chimidithapadu, Chinalatarapi, Dappalampadu Darakanipadu, Gudepalem, Gudluru, Kothapeta Mocherla, Mogalluru, Nayudupalem, Pajarla Parakondapadu, Potluru, Puretipalli, Ravuru Salipeta, Swarnajipuram, Venkampeta, Yelurupadu.

Amenities:

Education: Primary School in 17 villages, Middle school in 4 villages, Matriculation or Secondary School in 2 villages,

namely Gudluru, Ravur.
Higher Secondary or Pre University Courses or Intermediate or Junior College in 1 village of the CD Block,, namely Gudluru.
College in 0 village, Adult Literacy Center in 16 villages.
Medical: Hospital in 0 village, Dispensary in 2 villages, Health Center in 1 village, Sub Center in 9 villages, Maternity and Child Welfare Center in 0 village, Community health workers in 0 village.
The Villages having Hospital or Dispensary or Health Center are Gundlapalem, Gudluru.
Drinking Water: Tap water in 18 villages, Tank water in 18 villages, Well water in 18 villages, Tubewell in 18 villages and more than one source in 18 villages.
Bank: Banking facility in 2 villages, namely, Gudluru, Mocherla.
Credit Society in 10 villages Agricultural Credit Society in 2 Non-Agricultural Credit Society in 9 villages.
Others: Power supply in 18 villages, Cinema hall in 2 villages, sport club in 0 village, Stadium or Auditorium or Community Hall in 0 village, Post Office in 14 villages.
There are 17 villages having bus facilities.
Villages with most of facilities: Gudluru Mocherla.
Villages without amenities (Education):
Parakonda Paduagraharam..
Scheduled Castes: Out of the total population of 42382 persons, 11190 persons (26.4%) belong to Scheduled Castes.
The villages having less than 10% SC population are None..
The villages having more than 50% SC population are None.
Sex ratio of Scheduled Caste population is 496.
Scheduled Castes Literates and Illiterates by Sex:

	Persons	Males	Females
Literate	4,401	2,714	1,687
Illiterate	6,789	2,926	3,863
Literacy rate	45.5	55.9	35.0
Graduate	136	112	24

Scheduled Castes (Dominant):
Madiga, Mala, Adi Andhra, Dakkal etc.
Generic Castes etc.
For their cultural identity please see Appendix-I
Villages without Scheduled Castes: There is 1 village without any scheduled caste population.
Scheduled Tribes: Out of the total population of 42382 persons, 4155 persons (9.8%) belong to Scheduled Tribes.
The villages having less than 10% ST population are Parakonda Paduagraharam, Parakondapadu, Dappalampadu Gundlapalem, Kothapeta, Basireddy Palem Darakanipadu, Venkam Peta, Ammavari Palem, Ravur.
The villages having more than 50% ST population are None.
Sex ratio of Scheduled tribe population is 484.
Scheduled Tribes Literates and Illiterates by Sex:

	Persons	Males	Females
Literate	920	575	345
Illiterate	3,235	1,570	1,665
Literacy rate	26.3	31.8	20.4
Graduate	8	8	0

Scheduled Tribes (Dominant):
Yenadis, Yerukulas, Kammara
For their cultural identity please see Appendix-II
Villages without Scheduled Tribes: There are 2 villages without any scheduled tribe population.
Literates and Illiterates by Sex (Total Population):

	Persons	Males	Females
Literate	18,094	11,004	7,090
Illiterate	24,288	10,424	13,864
Literacy rate	49	59	39
Graduate	662	555	107

Agriculture: ***Distribution of villages according to land use:***
Out of 18 villages, Total area (in hectare) is 25780, out of that 41.51 percent is cultivable and 47.54 percent of the cultivable area is irrigated.
Sources of Irrigation (Hectares): Government Canal 0, Private Canal 95, Well without Electricity 0, Well with Electricity 350, Tubewell without Electricity 0, Tubewell with Electricity 2400, Tank 1733, River 0, Lake 0, Waterfall 0, Others 509.
Villages with population of 5000 to 9999:
Gudluru.
Villages with population of 10000 and above: None
Distribution of Workers:

	Persons	Males	Females	WPR
Cultivators	5,338	3,611	1,727	22.97
Agricultural Labour	13,202	6,005	7,197	56.81
Household Industry	578	270	308	2.49
Other Workers	4,121	3,122	999	17.73
Main Workers	17,667	11,081	6,586	76.02
Marginal Workers	5,572	1,927	3,645	23.98
Total Workers	23,239	13,008	10,231	

Religion: Major Religious Communities:

	Persons	Males	Females	Sex Ratio
Hindu (95.63%)	40,532	20,497	20,035	977
Muslim (3.01%)	1,274	652	622	954
Christian (1.14%)	485	234	251	1,073
Sikh (0%)	2	2	-	-
Buddhists (0.01%)	4	2	2	1,000
Jain (0%)	-	-	-	-

Agewise Data:

	Persons	Males	Females	Sex Ratio
All ages	42,382	21,428	20,954	978
0-14	12,906	6,516	6,390	981
15-44	19,695	10,025	9,670	965
45-79	9,108	4,545	4,563	1004
80+	320	163	157	963
Age not stated	353	179	174	972

Languages (Dominant):

Telugu, Urdu, Tamil, Gondi, Hindi

Disabled Population:

	Persons	Males	Females	%
Total Disabled	719	404	315	
In Seeing	208	115	93	28.93
In Speech	83	40	43	11.54
In Hearing	31	19	12	4.31
In Movement	249	139	110	34.63
Mentally	148	91	57	20.58

GUDUPALLE

Gudupalle C.D. Block lies in the south-western part of Chittoor district. The Block is located at a distance of 16 kms. from district headquarters (Chittoor). There are 48 villages in the block with the total popul ation of 38,480 persons. Area of the C.D. Block is 145. 13 sq. kms. It is bounded in the north by Mandal Santhi puram, in the east by Mandals Santhipuram and Kuppam, and it has common boundary with the state of Karnataka in the north and west, and with the state of Tamil Nadu in the south and west.

Communications:

Roadways : NH, SH or Important Metalled Road is not available.

Railway Station: Pogurupalle, Kotachembagiri, Ontipalle, Gudupalle.

It receives the Backward Region Grants, and is identifi ed as a drought-prone area as well.

Annual Rainfall: Average Rainfall 856 mm

Ground Water: Availability of the Ground Water in the Basin is 2101 H.A.M.and the utilization is 1767 H.A. M. It belongs to SC category. Depth to water level varies more than 10 meter below the ground. Most of the wells go down in summer months, according to the Ground Water Estimation Committee.

Natural Division : Rayalaseema Region

Administration:

Division: Rayala Seema. Parliamentary Constituency: 42 Chittoor (SC). District: Chittoor. Mandal: Gudupalle. Assembly Constituency: 294 Kuppam Gram Panchayat: 18

Border Villages: (Karnataka)- Nearest Villages- Bisanat ham, Athinatham, Avulathimmanapalle, Pogurupalle, Lingap uram Dinne, Peddagollapalle, Chinnagollapalle, Kodiganip alle, Burugulapalle, Sanganapalle, Chinnaparthikunta, (Tamil Nadu)- Thalai Agraharam, Kotamakanepalle, Onnap anayani Kothur, Jarugukonda.

Villages: 48 **Inhabited:** 47 **Uninhabited:** 1

Ranking	District	State	National
Area	44	845	5117
Population	47	874	5805
Sex Ratio	7	210	1069
Child Sex Ratio	6	107	269
Literacy Rate	65	890	5261
Density	17	389	3911
Work Participation Rate	36	486	949

Gram Panchayats:

Agaram, Beggilapalle, Cheekatipalle Chinnagollapalle, Dasimanipalle, Gudupalle Gundlasagaram, Kanamanapalle, Kanchibandarlapalle Kodathanapalle, Kuppiganipalle, Onnappanayanikothur Peddabadaniwada, Pogurupalle, Sanganapalle Settipalle, Sodiganipalle, Yamaganipalle.

Amenities:

Education: Primary School in 42 villages, Middle school in 8 villages, Matriculation or Secondary School in 2 villages, namely Gudupalle, Settipalle.

Higher Secondary or Pre University Courses or Intermediate or Junior College in 0 village of the CD Block, College in 0 village, Adult Literacy Center in 11 villages.

Medical: Hospital in 0 village, Dispensary in 1 village, Health Center in 0 village, Sub Center in 7 villages, Maternity and Child Welfare Center in 2 villages, Community health workers in 0 village.

The Village having Hospital or Dispensary or Health Center is Yamaganipalle.

Drinking Water: Tap water in 47 villages, Tank water in 47 villages, Well water in 47 villages, Tubewell in 47 villages and more than one source in 47 villages.

Bank: Banking facility in 3 villages, namely, Kotachembagiri, Gudupalle, Bijiganipalle.

Credit Society in 6 villages Agricultural Credit Society in 6 Non-Agricultural Credit Society in 3 villages.

Others: Power supply in 47 villages, Cinema hall in 4 villages, sport club in 0 village, Stadium or Auditorium or Community Hall in 0 village, Post Office in 9 villages.

There are 28 villages having bus facilities.

Village with most of facilities: Gudupalle.

Villages without amenities (Education):

Lingapuram Dinne, Anganamalakothuru, Gokarlapalle, Anagarlapalle, Vengepalle..

Scheduled Castes: Out of the total population of 38480 persons, 4740 persons (12.32%) belong to Scheduled Castes.

The villages having less than 10% SC population are Bisanatham, Lingapuram Dinne, Anganamalakothuru Kuppiganipalle, Ontipalle, Peddagollapalle Sirigiripalle, Agaram, Yamaganipalle, Nalagampalle Gokarlapalle, Settipalle @ K.Bandarlapalle Kanamanapalle, Gundlasagaram, Nakkanapalle Kotapalle, Anagarlapalle, Malavanikothur Kodiganipalle, Burugulapalle, Boyanapalle Chinnaparthikunta, Peddaparthikunta Thalai Agraharam, Alugumanipalle, Sonnarasanapalle Thimmanayanipalle, Dinnepalle, Maldepalle.

The villages having more than 50% SC population are None.

Sex ratio of Scheduled Caste population is 503.

Scheduled Castes Literates and Illiterates by Sex:

	Persons	Males	Females
Literate	1,846	1,223	623
Illiterate	2,894	1,133	1,761
Literacy rate	46.5	61.6	31.3
Graduate	22	17	5

Scheduled Castes (Dominant):

Adi Dravida, Mala, Adi Andhra, Madiga Generic Castes etc.

For their cultural identity please see Appendix-I

Villages without Scheduled Castes: There are 19 villages without any scheduled caste population.

Scheduled Tribes: Out of the total population of 38480 persons, 306 persons (0.8%) belong to Scheduled Tribes.

The villages having less than 10% ST population are Bisanatham, Athinatham, Avulathimmanapalle Pogurupalle, Lingapuram Dinne, Dasimanipalle Anganamalakothuru, Kuppiganipalle, Kotachembagiri Ontipalle, Peddagollapalle, Chinnagollapalle Sirigiripalle, Gudupalle, Agaram, Yamaganipalle Nalagampalle, Beggilipalle, Gokarlapalle, Settipalle Settipalle @ K.Bandarlapalle, Kanamanapalle Gundlasagaram, Nakkanapalle, Kotapalle Kakinayanichigurla Palle, Anagarlapalle Cheekatipalle, Bijiganipalle, Vengepalle Irisiganipalle, Malavanikothur, Kodiganipalle Burugulapalle, Sanganapalle, Boyanapalle Chinnaparthikunta, Peddaparthikunta Thalai Agraharam, Kotamakanepalle Onnapanayani Kothur, Alugumanipalle Sonnarasanapalle, Sodiganipalle, Thimmanayanipalle Dinnepalle, Maldepalle.

The villages having more than 50% ST population are None.

Sex ratio of Scheduled tribe population is 542.

Scheduled Tribes Literates and Illiterates by Sex:

	Persons	Males	Females
Literate	99	59	40
Illiterate	207	81	126
Literacy rate	37.2	50.9	26.7
Graduate	0	0	0

Scheduled Tribes (Dominant):

Yerukulas, Yenadis

For their cultural identity please see Appendix-II

Villages without Scheduled Tribes: There are 38 villages without any scheduled tribe population.

Literates and Illiterates by Sex (Total Population):

	Persons	Males	Females
Literate	14,385	9,532	4,853
Illiterate	24,095	9,675	14,420
Literacy rate	45	59	30
Graduate	161	125	36

Agriculture: ***Distribution of villages according to land use:*** Out of 48 villages, Total area (in hectare) is 14515, out of that 48.85 percent is cultivable and 20.21 percent of the cultivable area is irrigated.

Sources of Irrigation (Hectares): Government Canal 0, Private Canal 0, Well without Electricity 9.2, Well with Electricity 572.29, Tubewell without Electricity 0, Tubewell with Electricity 84.31, Tank 767.05, River 0, Lake 0, Waterfall 0, Others 0.

Villages with population of 5000 to 9999: None

Villages with population of 10000 and above: None

Distribution of Workers:

	Persons	Males	Females	WPR
Cultivators	8,856	5,414	3,442	43.58
Agricultural Labour	6,696	2,632	4,064	32.95
Household Industry	297	144	153	1.46
Other Workers	4,472	3,118	1,354	22.01
Main Workers	14,511	9,295	5,216	71.41
Marginal Workers	5,810	2,013	3,797	28.59
Total Workers	20,321	11,308	9,013	

Religion: Major Religious Communities:

	Persons	Males	Females	Sex Ratio
Hindu (98.12%)	37,756	18,816	18,940	1,007
Muslim (1.78%)	684	367	317	864
Christian (0.05%)	21	13	8	615
Sikh (0.01%)	3	3	-	-
Buddhists (0.01%)	2	1	1	1,000
Jain (0%)	-	-	-	-

Agewise Data:

	Persons	Males	Females	Sex Ratio
All ages	38,480	19,207	19,273	1003
0-14	14,253	7,117	7,136	1003
15-44	16,638	8,211	8,427	1026
45-79	7,192	3,695	3,497	946

80+	355	163	192	1178
Age not stated	42	21	21	1000

Languages (Dominant):
Telugu, Tamil, Kannada, Urdu, Hindi
Disabled Population:

	Persons	Males	Females	%
Total Disabled	600	328	272	
In Seeing	173	82	91	28.83
In Speech	79	40	39	13.17
In Hearing	45	24	21	7.5
In Movement	221	138	83	36.83
Mentally	82	44	38	13.67

GUDUR

Gudur C.D. Block lies in the south-eastern part of Warangal district. The Block is located at a distance of 74 kms. from district headquarters (Warangal). There are 28 villages in the block with the total population of 53,884 persons. Area of the C.D. Block is 245.42 sq. kms. It is bounded in the north by Mandals Chennara opet, Khanapur and Kothagudem, in the south by Mandals Kesamudram and Mahabubabad, and district Khammam distri ct, in the east by Mandal Kothagudem, and in the west by Mandals Chennaraopet, Nekkonda and Kesamudram.

Communications:
Roadways : Metalled Roads: Nearest Villages- Gajulagattu, Ayodhyapur, Gudur, Bollepalle, Teegalveni, Damaravancha.
River: Maner Nadi- Nearest Villages- Ponugodu, Gudur, Teegalveni, Govindapur, Damaravancha.
Backwards Region Grants Fund: It receives Backward Region Grants.
Mahila Samakhya (Education for Women's Equality): It is decleared Socialy and Educationally Backward Block by the Government.
Integrated Child Development Scheme (ICDS) Project: Gudur, Total Anganwadi Centres: 230
Annual Rainfall: Average Rainfall 1148 mm
Ground Water: Availability of the Ground Water in the Basin is 4572 H.A.M.and the utilization is 1875 H.A. M. It belongs to Safe category. Depth to water level varies from 5 to 20 meter below the ground. Most of the wells go down in summer months. The well density in the entire block is 13 wells per sq. km. Total no. of the wells in the block are enumerated as 3074, according to the Ground Water Estimation Committee.
Natural Division : Godavari Depression Region
Administration:
Division: Telangana. Parliamentary Constituency. Distri ct: Warangal. Mandal: Gudur.
Assembly Constituency: 102 Mahbubabad. Gram Panchayat: 21
Places of Tourist Interested:
Pakhal : Situated in the revenue village of Pakhal near Gudur it was also constructed during the period of Kakatiyas about the year 1213 A.D. There is a wild life sanctuary being developed by the forest department.
Villages: 28 **Inhabited:** 28 **Uninhabited:** 0

Ranking	**District**	**State**	**National**
Area	13	326	3436
Population	23	396	5095
Sex Ratio	48	1043	3937
Child Sex Ratio	32	806	3483
Literacy Rate	49	956	5517
Density	6	217	4444
Work Participation Rate	38	647	589

Gram Panchayats:
Apparajpally, Ayodhyapur, Bhupathipet, Boddugonda Bollepally, Chinnayellapur, Dameravancha, Gajulaghat Govindapur, Gudur, Gundenga, Kollapur, Macharla Madanapur, Matwada, Naikpallyy, Ponugodu, Rajanpally Ramulathanda, Seethanagaram, Theegalaveni.
Amenities:
Education: Primary School in 27 villages, Middle school in 16 villages, Matriculation or Secondary School in 3 villages, namely Seetanagar, Gudur, Matwada.
Higher Secondary or Pre University Courses or Inter-mediate or Junior College in 1 village of the CD Block,, namely Matwada.
College in 0 village, Adult Literacy Center in 15 villages.
Medical: Hospital in 3 villages, Dispensary in 0 village, Health Center in 2 villages, Sub Center in 14 villages, Maternity and Child Welfare Center in 1 village, Community health workers in 0 village.
The Villages having Hospital or Dispensary or Health Center are Gudur, Teegalveni, Matwada.
Drinking Water: Tap water in 26 villages, Tank water in 26 villages, Well water in 28 villages, Tubewell in 26 villages and more than one source in 28 villages.
Bank: Banking facility in 2 villages, namely, Gudur, Apparajpalle.
Credit Society in 18 villages Agricultural Credit Society in 3 Non-Agricultural Credit Society in 18 villages.
Others: Power supply in 28 villages, Cinema hall in 1 village, sport club in 0 village, Stadium or Auditorium or Community Hall in 0 village, Post Office in 18 villages.
There are 22 villages having bus facilities.
Villages with most of facilities: Gudur Apparajpalle.
Villages without amenities (Education):
Keshavapatnam..
Scheduled Castes: Out of the total population of 53884 persons, 3736 persons (6.93%) belong to Scheduled Castes.

The villages having less than 10% SC population are Gundenga, Gajulagattu, Ayodhyapur, Ponugodu Keshavapatnam, Vengapet, Bhupathipet, Adivarampet Chinnayellapur, Seetanagar, Veerampet, Ootla Macherla, Bollepalle, Teegalveni, Govindapur Damaravancha, Apparajpalle, Boddugonda, Kolhapuram Kongaragidda, Matwada, Neelavancha, Thimmapur.
The villages having more than 50% SC population are None.
Sex ratio of Scheduled Caste population is 490.

Scheduled Castes Literates and Illiterates by Sex:

	Persons	Males	Females
Literate	1,629	1,009	620
Illiterate	2,107	897	1,210
Literacy rate	50.4	61.3	39.1
Graduate	29	25	4

Scheduled Castes (Dominant):
Madiga, Mala, Chamar etc., Generic Castes etc. Gosangi

For their cultural identity please see Appendix-I

Villages without Scheduled Castes: There are 6 villages without any scheduled caste population.

Scheduled Tribes: Out of the total population of 53884 persons, 29252 persons (54.29%) belong to Scheduled Tribes.
The villages having less than 10% ST population are None..
The villages having more than 50% ST population are Gundenga, Ponugodu, Keshavapatnam, Adivarampet Veerampet, Ootla, Macherla, Teegalveni, Govindapur Damaravancha, Boddugonda, Kongaragidda, Matwada Neelavancha, Thimmapur.
Sex ratio of Scheduled tribe population is 479.

Scheduled Tribes Literates and Illiterates by Sex:

	Persons	Males	Females
Literate	7,451	5,392	2,059
Illiterate	21,801	9,837	11,964
Literacy rate	30.4	42.3	17.5
Graduate	76	76	0

Scheduled Tribes (Dominant):
Sugalis etc., Koya etc., Yerukulas, Chenchù etc. Kotia etc.

For their cultural identity please see Appendix-II

Villages without Scheduled Tribes: There are 0 village without any scheduled tribe population.

Literates and Illiterates by Sex (Total Population):

	Persons	Males	Females
Literate	19,354	12,761	6,593
Illiterate	34,530	14,999	19,531
Literacy rate	42	54	30
Graduate	421	381	40

Agriculture: ***Distribution of villages according to land use:*** Out of 28 villages, Total area (in hectare) is 24543, out of that 36.47 percent is cultivable and 78.74 percent of the cultivable area is irrigated.

Sources of Irrigation (Hectares): Government Canal 0, Private Canal 0, Well without Electricity 43, Well with Electricity 4880, Tubewell without Electricity 0, Tubewell with Electricity 0, Tank 2126, River 0, Lake 0, Waterfall 0, Others 0.

Villages with population of 5000 to 9999: None

Villages with population of 10000 and above: Gudur.

Distribution of Workers:

	Persons	Males	Females	WPR
Cultivators	12,429	7,669	4,760	41.64
Agricultural Labour	13,080	4,633	8,447	43.82
Household Industry	613	403	210	2.05
Other Workers	3,725	2,956	769	12.48
Main Workers	23,736	14,052	9,684	79.53
Marginal Workers	6,111	1,609	4,502	20.47
Total Workers	29,847	15,661	14,186	

Religion: Major Religious Communities:

	Persons	Males	Females	Sex Ratio
Hindu (96.89%)	52,207	26,899	25,308	941
Muslim (2.85%)	1,536	786	750	954
Christian (0.17%)	92	49	43	878
Sikh (0%)	2	2	-	-
Buddhists (0%)	-	-	-	-
Jain (0%)	-	-	-	-

Agewise Data:

	Persons	Males	Females	Sex Ratio
All ages	53,884	27,760	26,124	941
0-14	19,719	10,474	9,245	883
15-44	24,492	12,516	11,976	957
45-79	9,217	4,537	4,680	1032
80+	400	203	197	970
Age not stated	56	30	26	867

Languages (Dominant):
Telugu, Hindi, Urdu, Tamil, Gondi

Disabled Population:

	Persons	Males	Females	%
Total Disabled	1,109	648	461	
In Seeing	550	314	236	49.59
In Speech	116	68	48	10.46
In Hearing	30	13	17	2.71
In Movement	331	207	124	29.85
Mentally	82	46	36	7.39

GUDUR

Gudur C.D. Block lies in the southern part of Nellore district. It is a part of Gudur Mandal. The Block is located at a distance of 41 kms. from district headquarters (Nellore). There are 24 villages in the block with the total population of 45,576 persons. Area of the C.D. Block is 253.84 sq. kms. It is bounded in the north by Mandals Sydapuram and Manubolu, in the south by Mandals Balayapalle, Ojili and Chillakur, in the east by Mandals Manubolu and Chillakur, and in the west by Mandals Sydapuram and Balayapalle.

Communications:

Roadways : State Highway (S.H.): Rapur to Gudur. Nearest Villages- Chennuru - I, Chennuru – II.

Railway Station: East Gudur (Rural), Kondagunta.

Integrated Child Development Scheme (ICDS) Project: Gudur, Total Anganwadi Centres: 166

Annual Rainfall: Average Rainfall 995 mm

Ground Water: Availability of the Ground Water in the Basin is 1288 H.A.M. and the utilization is 598 H.A.M. It belongs to Safe category. Depth to water level varies from 5 meter to more than 10 meter below the ground. Most of the wells go down in summer months according to the Ground Water Estimation Committee.

Administration:

Division: Coastal Andhra. Parliamentary Constituency: 4o Tirupati (SC). District: Nellore. Mandal: Gudur. Assembly Constituency: 239 Gudur (SC). Gram Panchayat: 23

Villages: 24 **Inhabited:** 23 **Uninhabited:** 1

Ranking	District	State	National
Area	26	295	3330
Population	18	642	5479
Sex Ratio	34	693	2349
Child Sex Ratio	20	575	2306
Literacy Rate	41	474	3731
Density	21	774	5060
Work Participation Rate	21	795	2264

Gram Panchayats:

Ayyavari Palem, Chennur, Divipalem, Kandali, Kandra Kommanetur, Kondagunta, Kundakur, Mangalapur Mekanur, Mittathmakur, Nellatur, Nernoor Pagadalapalli, Palicherla, Potupalem, Ramalingapuram Santhadasu Palli, Thimmasamudram, Thippavarappadu Vedicherla, Vendodu, Vinduru.

Amenities:

Education: Primary School in 23 villages, Middle school in 8 villages, Matriculation or Secondary School in 6 villages, namely Chennuru - I, Vinduru, Nellatur (Rural), East Gudur (Rural), Kondagunta, Ayyavaripalem.

Higher Secondary or Pre University Courses or Intermediate or Junior College in 0 village of the CD Block, College in 0 village, Adult Literacy Center in 18 villages.

Medical: Hospital in 1 village, Dispensary in 2 villages, Health Center in 1 village, Sub Center in 8 villages, Maternity and Child Welfare Center in 0 village, Community health workers in 0 village.

The Villages having Hospital or Dispensary or Health Center are Chennuru - I, Chennuru - Ii.

Drinking Water: Tap water in 22 villages, Tank water in 22 villages, Well water in 22 villages, Tubewell in 23 villages and more than one source in 23 villages.

Bank: Banking facility in 1 villages, namely, Chennuru - Ii.

Credit Society in 11 villages Agricultural Credit Society in 4 Non-Agricultural Credit Society in 9 villages.

Others: Power supply in 23 villages, Cinema hall in 1 village, sport club in 0 village, Stadium or Auditorium or Community Hall in 0 village, Post Office in 13 villages.

There are 23 villages having bus facilities.

Village with most of facilities: Chennuru - Ii.

Villages without Amenities (Education): None..

Scheduled Castes: Out of the total population of 45574 persons, 13715 persons (30.09%) belong to Scheduled Castes.

The villages having less than 10% SC population are None..

The villages having more than 50% SC population are None.

Sex ratio of Scheduled Caste population is 484.

Scheduled Castes Literates and Illiterates by Sex:

	Persons	Males	Females
Literate	5,600	3,518	2,082
Illiterate	8,115	3,554	4,561
Literacy rate	47.0	57.0	36.3
Graduate	87	69	18

Scheduled Castes (Dominant):

Mala, Madiga, Arundhatiya, Arwa Mala Generic Castes etc.

For their cultural identity please see Appendix-I

Villages without Scheduled Castes: There are 3 villages without any scheduled caste population.

Scheduled Tribes: Out of the total population of 45574 persons, 7708 persons (16.91%) belong to Scheduled Tribes.

The villages having less than 10% ST population are Kandali, Vinduru, Palicherla, Chemidthi, Kommaneturu Gollapalle, Mekanur.

The villages having more than 50% ST population are None.

Sex ratio of Scheduled tribe population is 479.

Scheduled Tribes Literates and Illiterates by Sex:

	Persons	Males	Females
Literate	1,958	1,154	804
Illiterate	5,750	2,865	2,885

Literacy rate	29.8	34.1	25.3
Graduate	10	8	2

Scheduled Tribes (Dominant):

Yenadis, Yerukulas, Kammara, Generic Tribes etc.

For their cultural identity please see Appendix-II

Villages without Scheduled Tribes: There is 1 village without any scheduled tribe population.

Literates and Illiterates by Sex (Total Population):

	Persons	Males	Females
Literate	21,761	12,640	9,121
Illiterate	23,813	10,455	13,358
Literacy rate	55	63	46
Graduate	677	522	155

Agriculture: ***Distribution of villages according to land use:*** Out of 24 villages, Total area (in hectare) is 25384, out of that 29.47 percent is cultivable and 78.78 percent of the cultivable area is irrigated.

Sources of Irrigation (Hectares): Government Canal 0, Private Canal 0, Well without Electricity 0, Well with Electricity 1834.1, Tubewell without Electricity 0, Tubewell with Electricity 1485.24, Tank 2573.96, River 0, Lake 0, Waterfall 0, Others 0.

Villages with population of 5000 to 9999: Vinduru.

Villages with population of 10000 and above: Chennuru – II.

Distribution of Workers:

	Persons	Males	Females	WPR
Cultivators	4,025	3,308	717	17.64
Agricultural Labour	12,545	6,682	5,863	54.97
Household Industry	1,472	918	554	6.45
Other Workers	4,780	3,506	1,274	20.94
Main Workers	18,070	12,976	5,094	79.18
Marginal Workers	4,752	1,438	3,314	20.82
Total Workers	22,822	14,414	8,408	

Religion: Major Religious Communities:

	Persons	Males	Females	Sex Ratio
Hindu (95.81%)	43,665	22,173	21,492	969
Muslim (3.83%)	1,746	846	900	1,064
Christian (0.26%)	117	51	66	1,294
Sikh (0%)	1	-	1	-
Buddhists (0%)	-	-	-	-
Jain (0%)	-	-	-	-

Agewise Data:

	Persons	Males	Females	Sex Ratio
All ages	45,574	23,095	22,479	973
0-14	13,433	7,053	6,380	905
15-44	22,517	11,376	11,141	979
45-79	9,376	4,556	4,820	1058
80+	222	95	127	1337
Age not stated	26	15	11	733

Languages (Dominant):

Telugu, Urdu, Tamil, Gondi, Nepali

Disabled Population:

	Persons	Males	Females	%
Total Disabled	916	486	430	
In Seeing	331	151	180	36.14
In Speech	114	64	50	12.45
In Hearing	76	29	47	8.3
In Movement	294	188	106	32.1
Mentally	101	54	47	11.03

GUDUR

Gudur C.D. Block lies in the northern part of Kurnool district. The Block is located at a distance of 22 kms. from district headquarters (Kurnool). There are 11 villages in the block with the total population of 41,228 persons. Area of the C.D. Block is 162.85 sq. kms. It is bounded in the north by Mandals C. Belag al and Kurnool, in the south by Mandal Kodumur, in the east by Mandal Kallur, and in the west by Mandals C. Belagal and Kodumur.

Communications:

Roadways : State Highway (S.H.): Direction- Alur to Kurnool. Nearest Villages- Chanugondla, Penchikalapadu, Kuruvanagalapuram.

It is identified as a drought-prone area.

Annual Rainfall: Average Rainfall 629 mm

Ground Water: Availability of the Ground Water in the Basin is 1288 H.A.M. and the utilization is 598 H.A. M. It belongs to Safe category. Depth to water level varies from 5 meter to more than 10 meter below the ground. Most of the wells go down in summer months. The well density in the entire block is 5 wells per sq. km. Total no. of the wells in the block are enumera ted as 453, according to the Ground Water Estimation Committee.

Natural Division : Rayalaseema Region

Administration:

Division: Rayala Seema. Parliamentary Constituency: 35 Kurnool. District: Kurnool. Mandal: Gudur. Assembly Constituency: 262 Kodumur (SC). Gram Panchayat: 10.

Villages: 11 **Inhabited:** 11 **Uninhabited:** 0

Ranking	**District**	**State**	**National**
Area	49	757	4833
Population	37	785	5679
Sex Ratio	21	785	2635
Child Sex Ratio	44	900	3963
Literacy Rate	38	800	4883
Density	29	349	4039
Work Participation Rate	11	527	868

Gram Panchayats:

Budidapadu, Chanugondla, Gudipadu, Gudur, Julakallu K.Nagalapuram, Mallapuram, Munagala, Penchikalapadu Regadi Khanapuram.

Amenities:

Education: Primary School in 11 villages, Middle school in 3 villages, Matriculation or Secondary School in 2 villages, namely Gudur, Chanugondla.

Higher Secondary or Pre University Courses or Intermediate or Junior College in 1 village of the CD Block,, namely Gudur.

College in 1 village, Adult Literacy Center in 11 villages., College is in village, namely Gudur.

Medical: Hospital in 0 village, Dispensary in 2 villages, Health Center in 1 village, Sub Center in 4 villages, Maternity and Child Welfare Center in 0 village, Community health workers in 0 village.

The Villages having Hospital or Dispensary or Health Center are Gudur, Chanugondla.

Drinking Water: Tap water in 11 villages, Tank water in 11 villages, Well water in 11 villages, Tubewell in 11 villages and more than one source in 11 villages.

Bank: Banking facility in 1 villages, namely, Gudur.

Credit Society in 9 villages Agricultural Credit Society in 2 Non-Agricultural Credit Society in 9 villages.

Others: Power supply in 11 villages, Cinema hall in 2 villages, sport club in 0 village, Stadium or Auditorium or Community Hall in 0 village, Post Office in 10 villages.

There are 10 villages having bus facilities.

Village with most of facilities: Gudur.

Villages without Amenities (Education): None..

Scheduled Castes: Out of the total population of 41228 persons, 9768 persons (23.69%) belong to Scheduled Castes.

The villages having less than 10% SC population are None..

The villages having more than 50% SC population are None.

Sex ratio of Scheduled Caste population is 492.

Scheduled Castes Literates and Illiterates by Sex:

	Persons	Males	Females
Literate	3,788	2,451	1,337
Illiterate	5,980	2,511	3,469
Literacy rate	46.4	59.1	33.3
Graduate	139	102	37

Scheduled Castes (Dominant):

Madiga, Mala, Mala Dasari, Beda Jangam etc.

For their cultural identity please see Appendix-I

Villages without Scheduled Castes: There are 2 villages without any scheduled caste population.

Scheduled Tribes: Out of the total population of 41228 persons, 159 persons (0.39%) belong to Scheduled Tribes.

The villages having less than 10% ST population are Munagala, Julakallu, Ponnakallu, Mallapuram Regadi Khanapuram, Gudur, Chanugondla, Gudipadu Penchikalapadu, Kuruvanagalapuram, Budidapadu.

The villages having more than 50% ST population are None.

Sex ratio of Scheduled tribe population is 516.

Scheduled Tribes Literates and Illiterates by Sex:

	Persons	Males	Females
Literate	47	29	18
Illiterate	112	48	64
Literacy rate	37.0	47.5	27.3
Graduate	5	4	1

Scheduled Tribes (Dominant):

Yerukulas, Sugalis etc., Kammara, Chenchu etc.

For their cultural identity please see Appendix-II

Villages without Scheduled Tribes: There are 7 villages without any scheduled tribe population.

Literates and Illiterates by Sex (Total Population):

	Persons	Males	Females
Literate	16,440	10,692	5,748
Illiterate	24,788	10,263	14,525
Literacy rate	48	61	34
Graduate	609	494	115

Agriculture: ***Distribution of villages according to land use:***

Out of 11 villages, Total area (in hectare) is 16285, out of that 76.34 percent is cultivable and 18.46 percent of the cultivable area is irrigated.

Sources of Irrigation (Hectares): Government Canal 435.45, Private Canal 0, Well without Electricity 0, Well with Electricity 1568, Tubewell without Electricity 0, Tubewell with Electricity 135, Tank 157, River 0, Lake 0, Waterfall 0, Others 0.

Villages with population of 5000 to 9999:

Chanugondla.

Villages with population of 10000 and above:

Gudur.

Distribution of Workers:

	Persons	Males	Females	WPR
Cultivators	5,018	3,138	1,880	22.89
Agricultural Labour	13,022	5,895	7,127	59.41
Household Industry	644	335	309	2.94
Other Workers	3,235	2,541	694	14.76
Main Workers	20,755	11,467	9,288	94.69
Marginal Workers	1,164	442	722	5.31
Total Workers	21,919	11,909	10,010	

Religion: Major Religious Communities:

	Persons	Males	Females	Sex Ratio

Hindu (86.39%)	35,617	18,145	17,472	963
Muslim (13.28%)	5,476	2,741	2,735	998
Christian (0.27%)	110	58	52	897
Sikh (0%)	-	-	-	-
Buddhists (0%)	-	-	-	-
Jain (0%)	-	-	-	-

Agewise Data:

	Persons	Males	Females	Sex Ratio
All ages	41,228	20,955	20,273	967
0-14	16,126	8,316	7,810	939
15-44	17,899	9,262	8,637	933
45-79	6,962	3,267	3,695	1131
80+	203	87	116	1333
Age not stated	38	23	15	652

Languages (Dominant):

Telugu, Urdu, Hindi, Kannada, Marathi

Disabled Population:

	Persons	Males	Females	%
Total Disabled	954	456	498	
In Seeing	353	149	204	37
In Speech	79	38	41	8.28
In Hearing	58	18	40	6.08
In Movement	359	200	159	37.63
Mentally	105	51	54	11.01

GUDURU

Guduru C.D. Block lies in the southern part of Krishna district. The Block is located at a distance of 12 kms. from district headquarters (Machilipatnam). There are 25 villages in the block with the total population of 53,250 persons. Area of the C.D. Block is 124.70 sq. kms. It is bounded in the north by Mandals Gudlaval luru and Pedana, in the south by Mandals Ghantasala, Challapalle and Machilipatnam, in the east by Mandal Machilipatnam, and in the west by Mandal Pamarru, Movva and Ghantasala.

Communications:

Roadways : State Highway (S.H.): Direction- Vijayawada to Machilipatnam. Nearest Villages- Tarakaturu, Kanchak odur, Rayavaram, Mallavolu, Ramarajupalem, Chittiguduru, Guduru.

Annaul Rainfall: Average Rainfall 955 mm

Ground Water: Availability of the Ground Water in the Basin is (Information not avavible) H.A.M .and the utilization is (Information not avavible) H.A.M. It belongs to (Information not avavible) category. Depth to water level varies from 3 to 10 meter below the ground. Most of the wells go down in summer months.

Natural Division : Krishna Delta Region

Administration:

Division: Coastal Andhra. Parliamentary Constituency: 28 Machilipatnam. District: Krishna. Mandal: Guduru. Assembly Constituency: 193 Pedana. Gram Panchayat: 27

Fairs and Festivals:

Narayanamma Perantalu Uthsavam : It is celebrated in Gudur. Srimathi Narayanamma was a Kapu lady of Palacher la village which is at a distance of about 5 kms. from Gudur. Gudur was her husband's village. Her husband used to do business in cattle in Rayalaseema and in Golkonda. Once, when he went for trade he fell sick on his way back to Gudur and died. At that time, Naraya namma was in her puttillu (parent's house). Some people came and told her the incident. Narayanamma then took her bath, anointed her body with saffron, wore saffron coloured clothes and followed the people to Gudur. When they came about a kilometre to the South of Gudur, her 'mattelu' (silver rings worn only by married women to their toes) slipped off. She marked the spot and asked the people accompanying her to prepare chithi (pyre). Without going to her husband's house she direct ly went to the elders of the village and asked their permission to perform satee along with her husband. At that time, the heads of the village were Munubolu Peda Ramana Reddy and Karanam Rangasayi. The Palegars were Muslims who were in Chittivelu village of Cuddapah district. So the village headmen sent some servants to the Palegars to obtain permission for Narayanamma's satee. The servants took rest at Sydapuram, 9 kms. to the west of Gudur as night fell by that time. They chanced to meet some strangers already carrying the permission for Narayanamma's satee. It was realised that it was all due to the power of Narayanamma and they all went to Gudur. A big fire pit was arranged at the spot where her mattelu slipped off and along with her husband's dead body, Srimati Narayanamma perfo rmed satee. Every year, Narayanamma festival is celebrat ed on the fourth day after Makara Sankramana, i.e., (17th January). The villagers bring their daughters to the deity, Narayanamma and give them new blouse pieces and sarees. Jaggery, sarees, jacket pieces and Bengalgram are offered to the deity. When cattle are lost by people, they pray to her and offer naivedyam having to get back their cattle. The local devotees participate in the festival irrespective of caste or creed.

Villages: 25 **Inhabited:** 25 **Uninhabited:** 0

Ranking	District	State	National
Area	35	923	5397
Population	31	410	5122
Sex Ratio	5	208	1078
Child Sex Ratio	1	22	79

Literacy Rate	16	111	1578
Density	23	786	2576
Work Participation Rate	13	159	2319

Gram Panchayats:

Akulamannadu, Akumarru, Chittiguduru, Gandram Guduru, Gurijepalli, Idugullapalli, Jakkamcherla Kalapatam, Kanchakoduru, Kankatava, Kappaladoddi Kokanarayanapalem, Lellagaruvu, Maddipatla Mallavolu, Mukkollu, Narikedalavaripalem Pinaguduru Lanka, Polavaram, Posinavaripalem Ramannapeta, Ramanujavartharlpalli, Ramarajupalem Rayavaram, Tarakaturu, Tummalapalem.

Amenities:

Education: Primary School in 25 villages, Middle school in 8 villages, Matriculation or Secondary School in 3 villages, namely Kankatava, Mallavolu, Guduru.

Higher Secondary or Pre. University Courses or Intermediate or Junior College in 0 village of the CD Block, College in 0 village, Adult Literacy Center in 6 villages.

Medical: Hospital in 0 village, Dispensary in 1 village, Health Center in 1 village, Sub Center in 11 villages, Maternity and Child Welfare Center in 0 village, Community health workers in 0 village.

The Village having Hospital or Dispensary or Health Center is Mallavolu.

Drinking Water: Tap water in 7 villages, Tank water in 0 villages, Well water in 25 villages; Tubewell in 0 village and more than one source in 7 villages.

Bank: Banking facility in 3 villages, namely, Tarakaturu, Polavaram, Guduru.

Credit Society in 17 villages Agricultural Credit Society in 11 Non-Agricultural Credit Society in 14 villages.

Others: Power supply in 25 villages, Cinema hall in 1 village, sport club in 0 village, Stadium or Auditorium or Community Hall in 0 village, Post Office in 18 villages.

There are 23 villages having bus facilities.

Villages with most of facilities: Tarakaturu Polavaram, Guduru.

Villages without Amenities (Education): None..

Scheduled Castes: Out of the total population of 53250 persons, 7500 persons (14.08%) belong to Scheduled Castes.

The villages having less than 10% SC population are Lellagaruvu, Kappaladoddi, Akulamannadu Pinagudurulanka, Rayavaram, Polavaram, Mallavolu Ramarajupalem, Kokanarayanapalem.

The villages having more than 50% SC population are None.

Sex ratio of Scheduled Caste population is 493.

Scheduled Castes Literates and Illiterates by Sex:

	Persons	Males	Females
Literate	4,452	2,488	1,964
Illiterate	3,048	1,313	1,735
Literacy rate	67.2	73.9	60.2
Graduate	81	65	16

Scheduled Castes (Dominant):

Mala, Madiga, Adi Andhra, Beda Jangam etc., Relli

For their cultural identity please see Appendix-I

Villages without Scheduled Castes: There is 1 village without any scheduled caste population.

Scheduled Tribes: Out of the total population of 53250 persons, 583 persons (1.09%) belong to Scheduled Tribes.

The villages having less than 10% ST population are Jakkamcherla, Mukkollu, Gandram, Lellagaruvu Ramanuja Varthalapalle, Kappaladoddi, Akulamannadu Kankatava, Gurjepalle, Kalapatam, Pinagudurulanka Tarakaturu, Maddipatla, Kanchakodur, Rayavaram Polavaram, Ramannapeta, Idugullapalle, Mallavolu Akumarru, Ramarajupalem, Chittiguduru, Guduru Narikedalapalem, Kokanarayanapalem.

The villages having more than 50% ST population are None.

Sex ratio of Scheduled tribe population is 506.

Scheduled Tribes Literates and Illiterates by Sex:

	Persons	Males	Females
Literate	152	86	66
Illiterate	431	202	229
Literacy rate	31.5	36.3	26.8
Graduate	1	0	1

Scheduled Tribes (Dominant):

Yerukulas, Yenadis, Sugalis etc., Konda Kapus

For their cultural identity please see Appendix-II

Villages without Scheduled Tribes: There are 6 villages without any scheduled tribe population.

Literates and Illiterates by Sex (Total Population):

	Persons	Males	Females
Literate	31,787	17,423	14,364
Illiterate	21,463	9,160	12,303
Literacy rate	67	74	61
Graduate	758	603	155

Agriculture: *Distribution of villages according to land use:* Out of 25 villages, Total area (in hectare) is 12470, out of that 83.78 percent is cultivable and 99.18 percent of the cultivable area is irrigated.

Sources of Irrigation (Hectares): Government Canal 10361.16, Private Canal 0, Well without Electricity 0, Well with Electricity 0, Tubewell without Electricity 0, Tubewell with Electricity 0, Tank 0, River 0, Lake 0, Waterfall 0, Others 0.

Villages with population of 5000 to 9999:

Akulamannadu, Mallavolu, Guduru.

Villages with population of 10000 and above: None

Distribution of Workers:

	Persons	Males	Females	WPR
Cultivators	4,326	3,765	561	16.04
Agricultural Labour	14,679	7,724	6,955	54.44
Household Industry	4,465	2,283	2,182	16.56
Other Workers	3,496	2,921	575	12.96
Main Workers	24,166	16,348	7,818	89.62
Marginal Workers	2,800	345	2,455	10.38
Total Workers	26,966	16,693	10,273	

Religion: Major Religious Communities:

	Persons	Males	Females	Sex Ratio
Hindu (93.75%)	49,923	24,976	24,947	999
Muslim (5.8%)	3,090	1,488	1,602	1,077
Christian (0.39%)	208	103	105	1,019
Sikh (0%)	-	-	-	-
Buddhists (0%)	-	-	-	-
Jain (0%)	-	-	-	-

Agewise Data:

	Persons	Males	Females	Sex Ratio
All ages	53,250	26,583	26,667	1003
0-14	15,484	7,735	7,749	1002
15-44	25,983	13,171	12,812	973
45-79	11,407	5,502	5,905	1073
80+	317	146	171	1171
Age not stated	59	29	30	1034

Languages (Dominant):

Telugu, Urdu, Tamil, Marathi, Gondi

Disabled Population:

	Persons	Males	Females	%
Total Disabled	904	516	388	
In Seeing	315	152	163	34.85
In Speech	117	72	45	12.94
In Hearing	40	21	19	4.42
In Movement	297	195	102	32.85
Mentally	135	76	59	14.93

GUMMAGATTA

Gummagatta C.D. Block lies in the western part of Anant apur district. The Block is located at a distance of 118 kms. from district headquarters (Anantapur). There are 11 villages in the block with the total population of 42,266 persons. Area of the C.D. Block is 238.65 sq. kms. It is bounded in the north by Mandal Rayadurg, in the south by River Hagari and Mandal Brahmasamudram, in the east by Mandal Rayadurg, and in the west it has common boundary with the state of Karnataka.

Communications:

Roadways : State Highway (S.H.): Direction- Rayadurg to Anantapur. Nearest Village- Bhupasamudram.

River: Hagari Nadi- Nearest Villages- Kalugodu, Gummaga tta, Bhupasamudram.

It receieves Backward, Region Grants, and is identified as a drought-prone area as well.

Annual Rainfall: Average Rainfall 488 mm

Ground Water: Availability of the Ground Water in the Basin is 2417 H.A.M. and the utilization is 1801 H. A.M. It belongs to SC category. Depth to water level varies from 10 to 20 meter below the ground. Most of the wells go down in summer months. The well density in the entire block is 9 wells per sq. km. Total no. of the wells in the block are enumerated as 2275, according to the Ground Water Estimation Committee.

Natural Division : Rayalaseema Region

Administration:

Division: Rayala Seema. Parliamentary Constituency: 36 Anantapur. District: Anantapur.

Mandal: Gummagatta. Assembly Constituency: 267 Rayadurg. Gram Panchayat: 15.

Border Villages: (Karnataka)- Nearest Villages- Galagala, Rangasamudram, Gollapalle, Tallakera.

Villages: 11 **Inhabited:** 11 **Uninhabited:** 0

Ranking	District	State	National
Area	45	350	3526
Population	31	752	5636
Sex Ratio	39	974	3362
Child Sex Ratio	13	203	634
Literacy Rate	61	939	5442
Density	13	244	5096
Work Participation Rate	19	800	640

Gram Panchayats:

75.Veerapuram, Belodu, Bhupasamudram, Galagala Gollapalli, Gonabhavi, Gummagatta, K.P. Doddi Kalugodu, Marem Palli, Netrapalli, Pulakunta Rangasamudram, Sirige Doddi, Tallakera.

Amenities:

Education: Primary School in 11 villages, Middle school in 7 villages, Matriculation or Secondary School in 4 villages, namely Galagala, Gollapalle, Belodu, Gummagatta. Higher Secondary or Pre University Courses or Intermediate or Junior College in 0 village of the CD Block, College in 0 village, Adult Literacy Center in 0 village.

Medical: Hospital in 0 village, Dispensary in 1 village, Health Center in 1 village, Sub Center in 5 villages, Maternity and Child Welfare Center in 0 village, Community health workers in 0 village.

The Village having Hospital or Dispensary or Health Center is Kalugodu.

Drinking Water: Tap water in 10 villages, Tank water in 1 villages, Well water in 1 village, Tubewell in 10 villages and more than one source in 11 villages.

Bank: Banking facility in 3 villages, namely,

Bhupasamudram, Tallakera, Gummagatta.
Credit Society in 3 villages Agricultural Credit Society in 2 Non-Agricultural Credit Society in 1 village.
Others: Power supply in 11 villages, Cinema hall in 3 villages, sport club in 0 village, Stadium or Auditorium or Community Hall in 0 village, Post Office in 9 villages.
There are 10 villages having bus facilities.
Villages with most of facilities: Bhupasamudram Tallakera, Gummagatta.
Villages without Amenities (Education): None..
Scheduled Castes: Out of the total population of 42266 persons, 7742 persons (18.32%) belong to Scheduled Castes.
The villages having less than 10% SC population are None..
The villages having more than 50% SC population are None.
Sex ratio of Scheduled Caste population is 487.
Scheduled Castes Literates and Illiterates by Sex:

	Persons	Males	Females
Literate	2,237	1,497	740
Illiterate	5,505	2,471	3,034
Literacy rate	35.4	45.8	24.2
Graduate	16	14	2

Scheduled Castes (Dominant):
Madiga, Mala, Chalavadi, Chandala
Generic Castes etc.
For their cultural identity please see Appendix-I
Villages without Scheduled Castes: There are 0 village without any scheduled caste population.
Scheduled Tribes: Out of the total population of 42266 persons, 490 persons (1.16%) belong to Scheduled Tribes.
The villages having less than 10% ST population are Galagala, Gollapalle, Belodu, S.Hosahalli Bhupasamudram, Kalugodu, Pulakunta, Rangasamudram Tallakera, Gummagatta.
The villages having more than 50% ST population are None.
Sex ratio of Scheduled tribe population is 482.
Scheduled Tribes Literates and Illiterates by Sex:

	Persons	Males	Females
Literate	199	132	67
Illiterate	291	122	169
Literacy rate	49.5	62.0	35.5
Graduate	3	3	0

Scheduled Tribes (Dominant):
Sugalis etc., Yerukulas, Rona etc., Kammara, Yenadis
For their cultural identity please see Appendix-II
Villages without Scheduled Tribes: There are 3 villages without any scheduled tribe population.
Literates and Illiterates by Sex (Total Population):

	Persons	Males	Females
Literate	15,054	10,155	4,899
Illiterate	27,212	11,501	15,711
Literacy rate	43	56	29
Graduate	190	161	29

Agriculture: ***Distribution of villages according to land use:*** Out of 11 villages, Total area (in hectare) is 23866, out of that 63.49 percent is cultivable and 18.07 percent of the cultivable area is irrigated.
Sources of Irrigation (Hectares): Government Canal 941.05, Private Canal 0, Well without Electricity 0, Well with Electricity 508.96, Tubewell without Electricity 0, Tubewell with Electricity 1287.71, Tank 0, River 0, Lake 0, Waterfall 0, Others 0.
Villages with population of 5000 to 9999:
Gollapalle, Kalugodu, Tallakera, Gummagatta.
Villages with population of 10000 and above: None
Distribution of Workers:

	Persons	Males	Females	WPR
Cultivators	9,386	5,797	3,589	41.24
Agricultural Labour	10,242	4,571	5,671	45.01
Household Industry	539	255	284	2.37
Other Workers	2,590	1,849	741	11.38
Main Workers	20,840	11,946	8,894	91.58
Marginal Workers	1,917	526	1,391	8.42
Total Workers	22,757	12,472	10,285	

Religion: Major Religious Communities:

	Persons	Males	Females	Sex Ratio
Hindu (96.44%)	40,761	20,883	19,878	952
Muslim (3.39%)	1,432	738	694	940
Christian (0.12%)	49	23	26	1,130
Sikh (0%)	-	-	-	-
Buddhists (0%)	-	-	-	-
Jain (0%)	-	-	-	-

Agewise Data:

	Persons	Males	Females	Sex Ratio
All ages	42,266	21,656	20,610	952
0-14	16,751	8,679	8,072	930
15-44	18,133	9,255	8,878	959
45-79	7,125	3,588	3,537	986
80+	247	128	119	930
Age not stated	10	6	4	667

Languages (Dominant):
Telugu, Kannada, Urdu, Hindi, Marathi
Disabled Population:

	Persons	Males	Females	%
Total Disabled	680	396	284	
In Seeing	205	96	109	30.15
In Speech	88	55	33	12.94
In Hearing	37	22	15	5.44

In Movement	269	176	93	39.56

Mentally	81	47	34	11.91

GUMMALAKSHMIPURAM

Gummalakshmipuram C.D. Block lies in the northern part of Vizianagaram district. The Block is located at a distance of 135 kms. from district headquarters (Vizian agaram). There are 124 villages in the block with the total population of 47,265 persons. Area of the C.D. Block is 110.89 sq. kms. It is bounded east Mandal Kurupam in the south by by Mandals Kamarada and Kurupam, and it has common boundary in the with the state of Orissa on north, west and east.

Communications :

Roadways : State Highways (S.H.): Direction- Kurupam to Gunupur. Nearest Villages- Thatiseela, Kaligottu, Regulapadu, Pirthani @ Elwinpeta, Gummalakshmipuram, Sadunuguda, Yeguvamanda. (S.H.): Direction- Gummalaksh mipuram to Bissamcuttack. Nearest Villages- Pirthani @ Elwinpeta, Lakkaguda, Savarakotapadu, Gummalakshmipu ram, Kothalikkidi, Kukkidi, Boddidi, Dummangi, Tenkasingi, Rella, Gunada, Kedaripuram.

Backwards Region Grants Fund: It receives Backward Region Grants.

Annaul Rainfall: Average Rainfall 886.7 mm

Ground Water: Availability of the Ground Water in the Basin is (Information not avavible) H.A.M .and the utilization is (Information not avavible) H.A.M. It belongs to (Information not avavible) category. Depth to water level varies from 3 to 10 meter below the ground. Most of the wells go down in summer months.

Forest and Reserved **Forest:** Nearest Villages- Addangija ngidi Bhadra, Thota, Japai, Kalliti, Kaligottu, Keesari, Dolukona, Vangara, Jamitipadu, Kedaripuram, Nondrukona, Rella, Dummangi, Boddidi, Chappaguda, Rayaganda, Gorati, Kothalikkidi, Iridi, Tholukharja, Gowduguda, Lumbesu, Lappiti, Vadabai, Chaparayibinnidi, Kanasingi, Kondruk uppa, Kondagudaba, Mantrajola, Gadivankadhara, Kondabinn idi, Mulajammu, Kurasingi, Alavadda, Vappangi, Kondavada, Kudda, Ranasingi, Lakkaguda, Savarakotapadu, Amiti, Puthikavalasa, Kuddapalavalasa, Yeguvamanda, Manda @ Diguva Manda, Karlaguda, Balesu, Tummiguda, Diguvad eruvada, Geesada (Pamula), Babbidi, Chorupalle, Vadaputti, Nellikikkuva, Dongurukikkuva, Jogipuram, Gedrajola, Vanakabadi (L.M.), Vandidi, Duddukhallu, Lovalakshmipu ram, Chintalapadu.

Administration:

Division: Coastal Andhra. Parliamentary Constituency: 18 Araku (ST). District: Viziangram. Mandal: Gummalaksh mipuram. Assembly Constituency: 130 Kurupam (ST). Gram Panchayat: 27.

Border Villages: (Orissa)- Nearest Villages- Kappakallu, Japai, Kaligottu, Keesari, Dolukona, Vangara, Jamitipa du, Gunada, Kedaripuram, Tenkasingi, Rella, Kosangibhadra, Dummangi, Kothaguda @ Dabbaliguda, Nigaram, Chapara yi Jangidibhadra, Sikharapai, Sivada Near Kukkidi, Sikal abai, Chemuduguda, Kanasingi, Kondrukuppa, Muliguda, Kukkidi, Kithalamba, Jarna, Kondagudaba, Mantrajola, Pedaravikona, Nondrukona, Sambuguda, Pusabadi, Goipaka, Gullalanka, Vadajangi, Ijjakai, Srirangapadu, Lada, Beerupadu, Kontesu, Tanku, Chinavankadhara, Thatiseela, Uriti.

Villages: 124 **Inhabited:** 119 **Uninhabited:** 5

Ranking	District	State	National
Area	33	983	5591
Population	29	595	5411
Sex Ratio	2	27	265
Child Sex Ratio	2	33	91
Literacy Rate	23	923	5375
Density	10	93	2583
Work Participation Rate	6	161	320

Gram Panchayats:

Balesu, Beerupadu, Chaparaibimmidi, Chemuduguda Chinageesada, Duddu Khallu, Dummangi, Elwinpeta G.L.Puram, Goipaka, Iridi, Jarna, Kedaripuram Kondawada, Kukkidi, Lakkaguda, Lumbesu, Manda Nelli Kikkuva, Nondrukona, P.Amity, Pedakarja Rayagada Jammu, Rella, Tadikonda, Vanakabadi Vangara.

Amenities:

Education: Primary School in 113 villages, Middle school in 12 villages, Matriculation or Secondary School in 6 villages, namely Pirthani @ Elwinpeta, Gummalakshmipuram, Regidi, Vandidi, Duddukhallu, Tikkabai.

Higher Secondary or Pre University Courses or Intermediate or Junior College in 2 villages of the CD Block,, namely Gummalakshmipuram, Regidi.

College in 1 village, Adult Literacy Center in 41 villages., College is in village, namely Pirthani @ Elwinpeta.

Medical: Hospital in 1 village, Dispensary in 1 village, Health Center in 5 villages, Sub Center in 21 villages, Maternity and Child Welfare Center in 36 villages, Community health workers in 0 village.

The Villages having Hospital or Dispensary or Health Center are Tenkasingi, Dummangi, Gummalakshmipuram, Regidi.

Drinking Water: Tap water in 119 villages, Tank water in 119 villages, Well water in 119 villages, Tubewell in 119 villages and more than one source in 119 villages.

Bank: Banking facility in 5 villages, namely, Keesari, Kedaripuram, Pirthani @ Elwinpeta Gummalakshmipuram, Regidi.

Credit Society in 12 villages Agricultural Credit Society in 1 Non-Agricultural Credit Society in 7 villages.

Others: Power supply in 119 villages, Cinema hall in 0 village, sport club in 0 village, Stadium or Auditorium or Community Hall in 0 village, Post Office in 31 villages.

There are 36 villages having bus facilities.

Villages with most of facilities: Kedaripuram Pirthani @ Elwinpeta, Gummalakshmipuram, Regidi.

Villages without amenities (Education): Kaligottu, Kondabinnidi, Srirangapadu, Boddidi, Regulapadu, Karlaguda..

Scheduled Castes: Out of the total population of 47265 persons, 2889 persons (6.11%) belong to Scheduled Castes.

The villages having less than 10% SC population are Kappakallu, Addangijangidi Bhadra, Thota, Japai Kalliti, Kaligottu, Keesari, Dolukona, Vangara Gunada, Nondrukona, Tenkasingi, Kosangibhadra Dummangi, Kothaguda @ Dabbaliguda, Nigaram Kukkidi, Boddidi, Chappaguda, Gorati Chaparayi Jangidibhadra, Sikharapai, Vamasi Tadikonda, Mangalapuram, Batugudaba Sivada Near Kukkidi, Sikalabai, Murada Mulabinnidi @ Mulalikkidi, Kothalikkidi, Iridi Tholukharja, Gowduguda, Lumbesu, Lappiti, Vadabai Vondrubhangi, Chaparayibinnidi, Kanasingi, Muliguda Mantrajola, Gadivankadhara, Kondabinnidi, Mulajammu Kurasingi, Alavadda, Vappangi, Kondavada Rayaghadajammu, Penguva, Chinageesada, Pedaravikona Nondrukona, Sambuguda, Pusabadi, Kithalamba Gullalanka, Vadajangi, Ijjakai, Dabbaliguda Srirangapadu, Lada, Beerupadu, Kontesu, Tanku Chinavankadhara, Boddidi, Atchaba Kusa @ Yadakhallu, Chinaravikona, Vallada, Gorada Kudda, Ranasingi, Vathada, Savarakotapadu Puttajammu, Thatiseela, Kaligottu, Regulapadu Sadunuguda, Amiti, Puthikavalasa, Yeguvamanda Karlaguda, Regidi, Bayyada, Gandra, Balesu Tummiguda, Diguvaderuvada, Geesada (Pamula), Babbidi Uriti, Jarna, Chorupalle, Kondakuneru, Vadaputti Nellikikkuva, Dongurukikkuva, Jogipuram, Gedrajola Vanakabadi (L.M.), Vandidi, Duddukhallu Chintalapadu, Tikkabai.

The villages having more than 50% SC population are None.

Sex ratio of Scheduled Caste population is 483.

Scheduled Castes Literates and Illiterates by Sex:

	Persons	Males	Females
Literate	1,424	928	496
Illiterate	1,465	567	898
Literacy rate	59.0	74.4	42.6
Graduate	53	46	7

Scheduled Castes (Dominant):

Dom etc., Mala, Madiga, Generic Castes etc., Relli

For their cultural identity please see Appendix-I

Villages without Scheduled Castes: There are 98 villages without any scheduled caste population.

Scheduled Tribes: Out of the total population of 47265 persons, 40265 persons (85.19%) belong to Scheduled Tribes.

The villages having less than 10% ST population are None..

The villages having more than 50% ST population are Kappakallu, Addangijangidi Bhadra, Thota, Japai Kalliti, Kaligottu, Keesari, Dolukona, Vangara Gunada, Kedaripuram, Nondrukona, Tenkasingi, Rella Kosangibhadra, Dummangi, Kothaguda @ Dabbaliguda Nigaram, Kukkidi, Boddidi, Chappaguda, Gorati Chaparayi Jangidibhadra, Sikharapai, Vamasi Tadikonda, Mangalapuram, Pedakharja, Batugudaba Sivada Near Kukkidi, Sikalabai, Chemuduguda, Murada Mulabinnidi @ Mulalikkidi, Kothalikkidi, Iridi Tholukharja, Gowduguda, Lumbesu, Lappiti, Vadabai Vondrubhangi, Chaparayibinnidi, Kanasingi, Muliguda Mantrajola, Gadivankadhara, Kondabinnidi, Mulajammu Kurasingi, Alavadda, Vappangi, Kondavada Rayaghadajammu, Penguva, Chinageesada, Pedaravikona Nondrukona, Sambuguda, Pusabadi, Kithalamba Gullalanka, Vadajangi, Ijjakai, Dabbaliguda Srirangapadu, Lada, Beerupadu, Kontesu, Tanku Chinavankadhara, Boddidi, Atchaba Kusa @ Yadakhallu, Chinaravikona, Vallada, Gorada Kudda, Ranasingi, Vathada, Lakkaguda, Savarakotapadu Puttajammu, Thatiseela, Kaligottu, Regulapadu Pirthani @ Elwinpeta, Sadunuguda, Amiti Puthikavalasa, Yeguvamanda, Manda @ Diguva Manda Karlaguda, Regidi, Bayyada, Gandra, Balesu Tummiguda, Diguvaderuvada, Geesada (Pamula), Babbidi Uriti, Jarna, Chorupalle, Kondakuneru, Vadaputti Nellikikkuva, Dongurukikkuva, Jogipuram, Gedrajola Vanakabadi (L.M.), Vandidi, Duddukhallu Lovalakshmipuram, Chintalapadu, Tikkabai.

Sex ratio of Scheduled tribe population is 520.

Scheduled Tribes Literates and Illiterates by Sex:

	Persons	Males	Females
Literate	12,897	7,930	4,967
Illiterate	27,368	11,401	15,967
Literacy rate	38.3	49.3	28.3
Graduate	75	69	6

Scheduled Tribes (Dominant):

Jatapus, Savaras etc., Konda Dhoras, Koya etc. Gadabas

For their cultural identity please see Appendix-II

Villages without Scheduled Tribes: There are 5 villages without any scheduled tribe population.

Literates and Illiterates by Sex (Total Population):

	Persons	Males	Females
Literate	17,285	10,606	6,679
Illiterate	29,980	12,398	17,582
Literacy rate	44	55	33
Graduate	394	340	54

Agriculture: ***Distribution of villages according to land use:*** Out of 124 villages, Total area (in hectare) is 11086, out of that 61.56 percent is cultivable and 5.66 percent of the cultivable area is irrigated.

Sources of Irrigation (Hectares): Government Canal 10, Private Canal 0, Well without Electricity 0, Well with Electricity 0, Tubewell without Electricity 0, Tubewell with Electricity 0, Tank 207.85, River 0, Lake 0, Waterfall 0, Others 168.57.

Villages with population of 5000 to 9999: None

Villages with population of 10000 and above: None

Distribution of Workers:

	Persons	Males	Females	WPR
Cultivators	11,071	5,848	5,223	41.51
Agricultural Labour	13,103	5,736	7,367	49.13
Household Industry	168	82	86	0.63
Other Workers	2,330	1,646	684	8.74
Main Workers	21,860	11,657	10,203	81.96
Marginal Workers	4,812	1,655	3,157	18.04
Total Workers	26,672	13,312	13,360	

Religion: Major Religious Communities:

	Persons	Males	Females	Sex Ratio
Hindu (99.13%)	46,852	22,791	24,061	1,056
Muslim (0.06%)	30	15	15	1,000
Christian (0.75%)	353	176	177	1,006
Sikh (0%)	-	-	-	-
Buddhists (0%)	-	-	-	-
Jain (0%)	-	-	-	-

Agewise Data:

	Persons	Males	Females	Sex Ratio
All ages	47,265	23,004	24,261	1055
0-14	18,837	9,510	9,327	981
15-44	20,559	9,803	10,756	1097
45-79	7,680	3,582	4,098	1144
80+	98	52	46	885
Age not stated	91	57	34	596

Languages (Dominant):

Telugu, Jatapu, Savara, Oriya, Konda

Disabled Population:

	Persons	Males	Females	%
Total Disabled	684	424	260	
In Seeing	332	206	126	48.54
In Speech	67	38	29	9.8
In Hearing	41	26	15	5.99
In Movement	187	122	65	27.34
Mentally	57	32	25	8.33

GUNDALA

Gundla C.D. Block lies in the north part of Nalgonda district. The Block is located at a distance of 60 kms. from district headquarters (Nalgonda. There are 20 villages in the block with the total population of 36,279 persons. Area of the C.D. Block is 204.28 sq. kms. It is bounded by Warangal district on north and east, Alair Mandal on west, Atmakur (M) Mandal on south-west, Mothkur Mandal on south, and Thirumalgiri Mandal on east.

Communications:

Roadways : Metalled Roads: Nearest Villages- Gundala.

River: Alair Nadi- Nearset Villages- Komme Palle, Anantaram, Brahman Palle, Suddala, Teryala, Palle Pahad, Paru Palle, Ambala, Vangala, Pedda Padishala, Bandakot ha Palle, Vastha Kondur.

Backwards Region Grants Fund: It receives Backward Region Grants.

Annual Rainfall: Average Rainfall 788 mm

Ground Water: Availability of the Ground Water in the Basin is 2651 H.A.M. and the utilization is 2263 H. A.M. It belongs to SC category. Depth to water level varies from 10 to 20 meter below the ground. Most of the wells go down in summer months. The well density in the entire block is 19 wells per sq. km. Total no. of the wells in the block are enumerated as 3940, according to the Ground Water Estimation Committee.

Natural Division : Krishna Piedmont Plain Region

Administration:

Division: Telangana. Parliamentary Constituency: 14 Bhongir. District: Nalgonda. Mandal: Gundala. Assembly Constituency: 97 Alair Gram Panchayat: 20.

Villages: 20 **Inhabited:** 20 **Uninhabited:** 0

Ranking	**District**	**State**	**National**
Area	35	523	4105
Population	56	913	5874
Sex Ratio	7	367	1476
Child Sex Ratio	50	967	4370
Literacy Rate	22	473	3733
Density	20	404	5086
Work Participation Rate	45	799	992

Gram Panchayats:

Ambala, Anantharam, Bandakothapally, Brahmanpally Gangapur, Gundala, Kommaipally, Marripadaga Masanpally, Nunegudem, Pallepahad, Parupally

Pedda Padishala, Ramaram, Seetharampur, Suddala Theriyala, Thurkalashapur, Vastakondur, Velmajala.

Amenities:

Education: Primary School in 20 villages, Middle school in 12 villages, Matriculation or Secondary School in 5 villages, namely Velmajala, Seetarampur, Suddala, Gundala, Pedda Padishala.

Higher Secondary or Pre University Courses or Intermediate or Junior College in 0 village of the CD Block, College in 0 village, Adult Literacy Center in 0 village.

Medical: Hospital in 0 village, Dispensary in 1 village, Health Center in 1 village, Sub Center in 8 villages, Maternity and Child Welfare Center in 0 village, Community health workers in 0 village.

The Village having Hospital or Dispensary or Health Center is Velmajala.

Drinking Water: Tap water in 20 villages, Tank water in 20 villages, Well water in 20 villages, Tubewell in 20 villages and more than one source in 20 villages.

Bank: Banking facility in 1 villages, namely, Gundala.

Credit Society in 2 villages Agricultural Credit Society in 2 Non-Agricultural Credit Society in 0 village.

Others: Power supply in 20 villages, Cinema hall in 0 village, sport club in 0 village, Stadium or Auditorium or Community Hall in 0 village, Post Office in 16 villages.

There are 17 villages having bus facilities.

Village with most of facilities: Gundala.

Villages without Amenities (Education): None..

Scheduled Castes: Out of the total population of 36279 persons, 7495 persons (20.66%) belong to Scheduled Castes.

The villages having less than 10% SC population are None..

The villages having more than 50% SC population are None.

Sex ratio of Scheduled Caste population is 489.

Scheduled Castes Literates and Illiterates by Sex:

	Persons	Males	Females
Literate	3,040	1,942	1,098
Illiterate	4,455	1,890	2,565
Literacy rate	48.4	60.7	35.7
Graduate	26	24	2

Scheduled Castes (Dominant):

Madiga, Mala, Beda Jangam etc., Madiga Dasu etc. Bindla

For their cultural identity please see Appendix-I

Villages without Scheduled Castes: There are 0 village without any scheduled caste population.

Scheduled Tribes: Out of the total population of 36279 persons, 462 persons (1.27%) belong to Scheduled Tribes.

The villages having less than 10% ST population are Komme Palle, Anantaram, Velmajala, Seetarampur Marpadaga, Gangapur, Masan Palle, Ramaram Brahman Palle, Suddala, Teryala, Palle Pahad Paru Palle, Ambala, Gundala, Turkala Shapur, Vangala Pedda Padishala, Bandakotha Palle, Vastha Kondur.

The villages having more than 50% ST population are None.

Sex ratio of Scheduled tribe population is 498.

Scheduled Tribes Literates and Illiterates by Sex:

	Persons	Males	Females
Literate	154	108	46
Illiterate	308	124	184
Literacy rate	39.3	53.5	24.2
Graduate	8	7	1

Scheduled Tribes (Dominant):

Yerukulas, Sugalis etc., Koya etc.

For their cultural identity please see Appendix-II

Villages without Scheduled Tribes: There are 7 villages without any scheduled tribe population.

Literates and Illiterates by Sex (Total Population):

	Persons	Males	Females
Literate	17,024	10,441	6,583
Illiterate	19,255	7,767	11,488
Literacy rate	55	67	42
Graduate	319	275	44

Agriculture: ***Distribution of villages according to land use:*** Out of 20 villages, Total area (in hectare) is 20429, out of that 35.89 percent is cultivable and 23.75 percent of the cultivable area is irrigated.

Sources of Irrigation (Hectares): Government Canal 0, Private Canal 0, Well without Electricity 0, Well with Electricity 816.51, Tubewell without Electricity 0, Tubewell with Electricity 880.06, Tank 44.53, River 0, Lake 0, Waterfall 0, Others 0.

Villages with population of 5000 to 9999: None

Villages with population of 10000 and above: None

Distribution of Workers:

	Persons	Males	Females	WPR
Cultivators	7,235	4,883	2,352	36.9
Agricultural Labour	8,863	2,910	5,953	45.2
Household Industry	694	394	300	3.54
Other Workers	2,816	2,171	645	14.36
Main Workers	16,024	9,427	6,597	81.72
Marginal Workers	3,584	931	2,653	18.28
Total Workers	19,608	10,358	9,250	

Religion: Major Religious Communities:

	Persons	Males	Females	Sex Ratio
Hindu (96.59%)	35,042	17,571	17,471	994
Muslim (2.27%)	823	419	404	964

Christian (0.47%)	170	92	78	848
Sikh (0%)	1	1	-	-
Buddhists (0%)	-	-	-	-
Jain (0%)	-	-	-	-

Agewise Data:

	Persons	Males	Females	Sex Ratio
All ages	36,279	18,208	18,071	992
0-14	11,789	6,065	5,724	944
15-44	15,473	7,632	7,841	1027
45-79	8,551	4,276	4,275	1000
80+	413	203	210	1034
Age not stated	53	32	21	656

Languages (Dominant):

Telugu, Urdu, Gondi, Tamil, Hindi

Disabled Population:

	Persons	Males	Females	%
Total Disabled	1,280	702	578	
In Seeing	813	451	362	63.52
In Speech	53	28	25	4.14
In Hearing	74	36	38	5.78
In Movement	261	151	110	20.39
Mentally	79	36	43	6.17

GUNDALA

Gundala C.D. Block lies in the north-western part of Khammam district. The Block is located at a distance of 105 kms. from district headquarters (Khammam). There are 21 villages in the block with the total population of 23,817 persons. Area of the C.D. Block is 898.97 sq. kms. It is bounded in the north by district Warangal and Mandal Pinapaka, in the south by Mandals Bayyaram, Yellandu and Tekulapalle, in the east by Mandals Kotha gudem, Palwancha and Manuguru, and in the west by distri ct Warangal.

Communications:

Roadways : Metalled Roads: Nearest Villages- Gundala, Galaba, Settipalle.

River: Kinnerasani Nadi- Nearest Villages- Allapalle, Ananthogu.

Backwards Region Grants Fund: It receives Backward Region Grants.

Annual Rainfall: Average Rainfall 1067 mm

Ground Water: Availability of the Ground Water in the Basin is 9563 H.A.M.and the utilization is 102 H.A. M. It belongs to safe category. Depth to water level varies from 5 to 10 meter below the ground. Most of the wells go down in summer months. The well density in the entire block is 0.1 wells per sq. km. Total no. of the wells in the block are enumerated as 114, according to the Ground Water Estimation Committee.

Natural Division : Godavari Depression Region

Administration:

Division: Telangana. Parliamentary Constituency: 16 Mahbubabad (ST). District: Khammam. Mandal: Gundala. Assembly Constituency: 110 Pinapaka (ST). Gram Panchay at: 6.

Villages: 21 **Inhabited:** 17 **Uninhabited:** 4

Ranking	District	State	National
Area	1	2	549
Population	43	1073	6168
Sex Ratio	13	475	1753
Child Sex Ratio	14	218	686
Literacy Rate	41	926	5389
Density	22	412	6327
Work Participation Rate	46	1095	1023

Gram Panchayats:

Allapalli, Ananthogu, Gundala, Markodu, Sayannapalli Settipalli.

Amenities:

Education: Primary School in 16 villages, Middle school in 6 villages, Matriculation or Secondary School in 1 village, namely Gundala.

Higher Secondary or Pre University Courses or Intermediate or Junior College in 0 village of the CD Block, College in 0 village, Adult Literacy Center in 15 villages.

Medical: Hospital in 1 village, Dispensary in 2 villages, Health Center in 1 village, Sub Center in 6 villages, Maternity and Child Welfare Center in 0 village, Community health workers in 0 village.

The Villages having Hospital or Dispensary or Health Center are Allapalle, Gundala.

Drinking Water: Tap water in 16 villages, Tank water in 16 villages, Well water in 16 villages, Tubewell in 16 villages and more than one source in 16 villages.

Bank: Banking facility in 1 villages, namely, Kachanapalle.

Credit Society in 7 villages Agricultural Credit Society in 1 Non-Agricultural Credit Society in 7 villages.

Others: Power supply in 17 villages, Cinema hall in 0 village, sport club in 0 village, Stadium or Auditorium or Community Hall in 0 village, Post Office in 8 villages.

There are 11 villages having bus facilities.

Village with most of facilities: Kachanapalle.

Villages without amenities (Education):

Konavarigudem..

Scheduled Castes: Out of the total population of 23817 persons, 1655 persons (6.95%) belong to Scheduled Castes. The villages having less than 10% SC population are Lingagudem, Sayanapalle, Chinna Venkatapuram Adavi Ramavaram, Pedda Venkatapuram, Ramanujagudem Mamakannu, Muthapuram, Konavarigudem, Gundala Galaba, Settipalle, Kachanapalle, Ananthogu.

The villages having more than 50% SC population are None.

Sex ratio of Scheduled Caste population is 482.

Scheduled Castes Literates and Illiterates by Sex:

	Persons	Males	Females
Literate	575	377	198
Illiterate	1,080	481	599
Literacy rate	43.1	54.6	30.8
Graduate	7	6	1

Scheduled Castes (Dominant):

Mala, Madiga, Mala Sale etc., Mala Dasari, Mala Dasu

For their cultural identity please see Appendix-I

Villages without Scheduled Castes: There are 8 villages without any scheduled caste population.

Scheduled Tribes: Out of the total population of 23817 persons, 18364 persons (77.1%) belong to Scheduled Tribes.

The villages having less than 10% ST population are None..

The villages having more than 50% ST population are Lingagudem, Sayanapalle, Chinna Venkatapuram Damarathogu, Adavi Ramavaram, Markode Pedda Venkatapuram, Ramanujagudem, Mamakannu Muthapuram, Konavarigudem, Gundala, Galaba Settipalle, Kachanapalle, Ananthogu.

Sex ratio of Scheduled tribe population is 501.

Scheduled Tribes Literates and Illiterates by Sex:

	Persons	Males	Females
Literate	5,718	3,743	1,975
Illiterate	12,646	5,426	7,220
Literacy rate	38.7	50.7	26.7
Graduate	26	23	3

Scheduled Tribes (Dominant):

Koya etc., Sugalis etc., Yerukulas, Nayaks

For their cultural identity please see Appendix-II

Villages without Scheduled Tribes: There are 4 villages without any scheduled tribe population.

Literates and Illiterates by Sex (Total Population):

	Persons	Males	Females
Literate	8,365	5,340	3,025
Illiterate	15,452	6,651	8,801
Literacy rate	43	55	32
Graduate	93	79	14

Agriculture: ***Distribution of villages according to land use:*** Out of 21 villages, Total area (in hectare) is 89896, out of that 4.55 percent is cultivable and 18.68 percent of the cultivable area is irrigated.

Sources of Irrigation (Hectares): Government Canal 0, Private Canal 0, Well without Electricity 94, Well with Electricity 131, Tubewell without Electricity 0, Tubewell with Electricity 0, Tank 316, River 0, Lake 0, Waterfall 0, Others 223.

Villages with population of 5000 to 9999: None

Villages with population of 10000 and above: None

Distribution of Workers:

	Persons	Males	Females	WPR
Cultivators	8,644	4,941	3,703	71.47
Agricultural Labour	2,359	799	1,560	19.51
Household Industry	250	186	64	2.07
Other Workers	841	609	232	6.95
Main Workers	10,230	6,009	4,221	84.59
Marginal Workers	1,864	526	1,338	15.41
Total Workers	12,094	6,535	5,559	

Religion: Major Religious Communities:

	Persons	Males	Females	Sex Ratio
Hindu (97.09%)	23,123	11,641	11,482	986
Muslim (2.06%)	491	246	245	996
Christian (0.84%)	200	103	97	942
Sikh (0%)	-	-	-	-
Buddhists (0%)	-	-	-	-
Jain (0%)	-	-	-	-

Agewise Data:

	Persons	Males	Females	Sex Ratio
All ages	23,817	11,991	11,826	986
0-14	9,893	5,023	4,870	970
15-44	10,465	5,275	5,190	984
45-79	3,301	1,611	1,690	1049
80+	110	55	55	1000
Age not stated	48	27	21	778

Languages (Dominant):

Telugu, Hindi, Urdu, Gondi, Koya

Disabled Population:

	Persons	Males	Females	%
Total Disabled	573	327	246	
In Seeing	339	196	143	59.16
In Speech	48	25	23	8.38
In Hearing	27	15	12	4.71
In Movement	127	74	53	22.16
Mentally	32	17	15	5.58

GUNDLA PALLE

Gundlapalle C.D. Block lies in the south-western part of Nalgonda district. The Block is located at a distance of 99 kms. from district headquarters (Nalgonda). There are 22 villages in the block with the total popul ation of 41,677 persons. Area of the C.D. Block is 264. 87 sq. kms. It is bounded by Devarakonda Mandal on north and north-east, Chandampet Mandal on east, and Mahbubnagar district on south and west.

Communications:

Roadways : Metalled Roads: Nearest Villages- Polepalle Ramnagar, Teeded, Yerraram, T.Gowararam, Khanapur, Bollana Palle, Cherkupalle, Gundla Palle.

River: Pedda Vagu: Nearest Villages- Brahmana Palle, Vavilkole, Rahmatpur, Kandukur, Dasarinemalipur, Kame Palle. Dindi Nadi- Nearest Villages- Gundla Palle, Gonakole, Bogguladona, Gonaboina Palle.

Backwards Region Grants Fund: It receives Backward Region Grants.

Annual Rainfall: Average Rainfall 738 mm

Ground Water: Availability of the Ground Water in the Basin is 2488 H.A.M. and the utilization is 1973 H. A.M. It belongs to SC category. Depth to water level varies from 10 to 20 meter below the ground. Most of the wells go down in summer months. The well density in the entire block is 9 wells per sq. km. Total no. of the wells in the block are enumerated as 2496, according to the Ground Water Estimation Committee.

Natural Division : Krishna Piedmont Plain Region

Administration:

Division: Telangana. Parliamentary Constituency: 13 Nalgonda. District: Nalgonda. Mandal: Gundla Palle. Assembly Constituency: 86 Devarakonda (ST).Gram Pancha yat: 16.

Villages: 22 **Inhabited:** 20 **Uninhabited:** 2

Ranking	District	State	National
Area	16	263	3186
Population	39	772	5663
Sex Ratio	50	925	3141
Child Sex Ratio	15	513	1937
Literacy Rate	54	901	5298
Density	16	333	5454
Work Participation Rate	54	882	825

Gram Panchayats:

Bogguladonna, Bolnepally, Cherkupally Dasarinemalipur, Gonaboinapally, Gundlapally Kamepally, Kandukur, Khanapur, Rahmanthpur Singarajpally, T Gouraram, Toukalapur, Vavikole Veeraboinapally, Yarraram.

Amenities:

Education: Primary School in 20 villages, Middle school in 9 villages, Matriculation or Secondary School in 4 villages, namely Kandukur, Kame Palle, Cherkupalle, Gundla Palle.

Higher Secondary or Pre University Courses or Intermediate or Junior College in 0 village of the CD Block, College in 0 village, Adult Literacy Center in 19 villages.

Medical: Hospital in 0 village, Dispensary in 0 village, Health Center in 1 village, Sub Center in 10 villages, Maternity and Child Welfare Center in 1 village, Community health workers in 0 village.

The Village having Hospital or Dispensary or Health Center is Gundla Palle.

Drinking Water: Tap water in 20 villages, Tank water in 20 villages, Well water in 20 villages, Tubewell in 20 villages and more than one source in 20 villages.

Bank: Banking facility in 2 villages, namely, Cherkupalle, Gundla Palle.

Credit Society in 8 villages Agricultural Credit Society in 7 Non-Agricultural Credit Society in 3 villages.

Others: Power supply in 20 villages, Cinema hall in 1 village, sport club in 0 village, Stadium or Auditorium or Community Hall in 0 village, Post Office in 13 villages.

There are 19 villages having bus facilities.

Villages with most of facilities: Cherkupalle Gundla Palle.

Villages without Amenities (Education): None..

Scheduled Castes: Out of the total population of 41677 persons, 8542 persons (20.5%) belong to Scheduled Castes.

The villages having less than 10% SC population are None..

The villages having more than 50% SC population are None.

Sex ratio of Scheduled Caste population is 493.

Scheduled Castes Literates and Illiterates by Sex:

	Persons	Males	Females
Literate	3,001	2,165	836
Illiterate	5,541	2,167	3,374
Literacy rate	41.5	59.1	23.4
Graduate	50	42	8

Scheduled Castes (Dominant):

Madiga, Mala, Beda Jangam etc., Mala Dasari, Mashti

For their cultural identity please see Appendix-I

Villages without Scheduled Castes: There are 3 villages without any scheduled caste population.

Scheduled Tribes: Out of the total population of 41677 persons, 10630 persons (25.51%) belong to Scheduled Tribes.

The villages having less than 10% ST population are Vavilkole, Rahmatpur, Kandukur, Dasarinemalipur T.Gowararam, Khanapur, Gundla Palle, Gonakole.

The villages having more than 50% ST population are Veeraboina Palle, Bollana Palle, Burhanpur Bogguladona, Kamadenigowararam.

Sex ratio of Scheduled tribe population is 477.

Scheduled Tribes Literates and Illiterates by Sex:

	Persons	Males	Females
Literate	2,454	1,947	507
Illiterate	8,176	3,609	4,567
Literacy rate	28.5	42.9	12.4
Graduate	43	42	1

Scheduled Tribes (Dominant):

Sugalis etc., Yerukulas, Chenchu etc., Kammara

For their cultural identity please see Appendix-II

Villages without Scheduled Tribes: There are 4 villages without any scheduled tribe population.

Literates and Illiterates by Sex (Total Population):

	Persons	Males	Females
Literate	15,605	10,682	4,923
Illiterate	26,072	10,618	15,454
Literacy rate	44	59	29
Graduate	366	308	58

Agriculture: ***Distribution of villages according to land use:*** Out of 22 villages, Total area (in hectare) is 26490, out of that 65.07 percent is cultivable and 9.73 percent of the cultivable area is irrigated.

Sources of Irrigation (Hectares): Government Canal 0, Private Canal 0, Well without Electricity 0, Well with Electricity 936, Tubewell without Electricity 0, Tubewell with Electricity 685, Tank 37, River 0, Lake 0, Waterfall 0, Others 20.

Villages with population of 5000 to 9999: None

Villages with population of 10000 and above: None

Distribution of Workers:

	Persons	Males	Females	WPR
Cultivators	8,315	5,678	2,637	37.09
Agricultural Labour	9,099	2,975	6,124	40.58
Household Industry	587	359	228	2.62
Other Workers	4,420	3,300	1,120	19.71
Main Workers	17,020	10,714	6,306	75.91
Marginal Workers	5,401	1,598	3,803	24.09
Total Workers	22,421	12,312	10,109	

Religion: Major Religious Communities:

	Persons	Males	Females	Sex Ratio
Hindu (94.87%)	39,539	20,240	19,299	954
Muslim (4.5%)	1,875	919	956	1,040
Christian (0.54%)	225	123	102	829
Sikh (0%)	1	1	-	-
Buddhists (0%)	-	-	-	-
Jain (0%)	-	-	-	-

Agewise Data:

	Persons	Males	Females	Sex Ratio
All ages	41,677	21,300	20,377	957
0-14	15,246	7,989	7,257	908
15-44	18,917	9,590	9,327	973
45-79	7,200	3,580	3,620	1011
80+	294	133	161	1211
Age not stated	20	8	12	1500

Languages (Dominant):

Telugu, Hindi, Urdu, Tamil, Gondi

Disabled Population:

	Persons	Males	Females	%
Total Disabled	975	508	467	
In Seeing	450	214	236	46.15
In Speech	82	45	37	8.41
In Hearing	57	25	32	5.85
In Movement	288	172	116	29.54
Mentally	98	52	46	10.05

GUNTAKAL

Guntakal C.D. Block lies in the northern part of Ananta pur district. It is a part of Guntakal Mandal. The Block is located at a distance of 75 kms. from district headq uarters (Anantapur). There are 18 villages in the block with the total population of 42,417 persons. Area of the C.D. Block is 357.95 sq. kms. It is bounded in the north by district Kurnool, in the south by Mandal Pamidi, in the east by Mandals Pamidi and Gooty, and in the west by district Kurnool, and Mandals Vidapanakal and Vajrakarur.

Communications:

Roadways : NH- 63: Direction- Bellary to Gooty. Nearest Villages- Guntakal (Rural), Dancherla, Yerrathimmarayac hervu, Patha Kothachervu, Nakkanadoddi, Thimmapuram.

Railway Station: Patha Kothachervu, Nakkanadoddi. It receives Backward Region Grants, and is identified as a drought-prone area as well.

Annual Rainfall: Average Rainfall 515 mm

Ground Water: Availability of the Ground Water in the Basin is 3836 H.A.M. and the utilization is 1874 H. A.M. It belongs to safe category. Depth to water level varies from 5 to 10 meter below the ground. Most of the wells go down in summer months. The well density in the entire block is 4 wells per sq. km. Total no. of the wells in the block are enumerated as 1663, according to the Ground Water Estimation Committee.

Natural Division : Rayalaseema Region

Administration:

Division: Rayala Seema. Parliamentary Constituency: 36 Anantapur. District: Anantapur.

Mandal: Guntakal. Assembly Constituency: 269 Guntakal. Gram Panchayat: 24.

Places of Tourist Interest:

Kasapuram : This place is about 4 kms. north of Guntakal and is known for the temple of Nettekanti Anjaneyaswami. There are a number of choultries built for the conven ience of devotees. Pilgrims from several parts congregate in large numbers, specially on Saturdays. The temple is richly endowed with landed property. Local tradition associates the installation of the deity with Sri Vyasa rayaswamy of Seshahali in Mysore. Muslims also make offerings to this deity. A huge procession is taken out once a year on the day next to Ugadi.

Fairs and Festival:

Sri Nettekani Anjaneyaswamy Aradhana : It takes place for three days from Chaitra Suddha Padyami (March-April), at Kasapuram. It is a widely known festival and more than 20,000 of devotees from the neighbouring places of Kurnool, Bellary and Anantapur area and a few hundreds from distant places of Tamil Nadu, and Maharashtra States. Even Christians and Muslims take part in the festival and some of them are also accustom ed to break coconuts before the Lord.

Villages: 18 **Inhabited:** 18 **Uninhabited:** 0

Ranking	District	State	National
Area	10	71	2215
Population	29	743	5626
Sex Ratio	24	896	3028
Child Sex Ratio	23	401	1479
Literacy Rate	55	823	4967
Density	12	239	5973
Work Participation Rate	55	1008	630

Gram Panchayats:

Ayyavaripalli, Chintalampalli, Dancherla Donimukkala, Dosaludiki, G.Kottala, Gundala Gundala Thanda, Gurrabadu, Imampuram, Kadiripalli Kasapuram, Konganapalli, Molakalpenta, N.Timmapuram N.Venkatampalli, Nagasamudram, Nakkanadoddi Nalladasarapalli, Nelagonda, Obulapuram Pathakotha Cheruvu, Puliguttapalli, Y.T.Cheruvu.

Amenities:

Education: Primary School in 18 villages, Middle school in 5 villages, Matriculation or Secondary School in 3 villages, namely Kasapuram, Patha Kothachervu, Nagasamudram. Higher Secondary or Pre University Courses or Intermediate or Junior College in 0 village of the CD Block, College in 0 village, Adult Literacy Center in 18 villages.

Medical: Hospital in 0 village, Dispensary in 2 villages, Health Center in 1 village, Sub Center in 5 villages, Maternity and Child Welfare Center in 0 village, Community health workers in 0 village.

The Villages having Hospital or Dispensary or Health Center are Yerrathimmarayachervu, Nagasamudram.

Drinking Water: Tap water in 15 villages, Tank water in 0 villages, Well water in 13 villages, Tubewell in 0 village and more than one source in 18 villages.

Bank: Banking facility in 1 villages, namely, Patha Kothachervu.

Credit Society in 4 villages Agricultural Credit Society in 4 Non-Agricultural Credit Society in 0 village.

Others: Power supply in 18 villages, Cinema hall in 0 village, sport club in 0 village, Stadium or Auditorium or Community Hall in 0 village, Post Office in 12 villages.

There are 18 villages having bus facilities.

Village with most of facilities: Patha Kothachervu.

Villages without Amenities (Education): None..

Scheduled Castes: Out of the total population of 42432 persons, 5079 persons (11.97%) belong to Scheduled Castes.

The villages having less than 10% SC population are Sangala, Ameenpalle, Konganapalle, Obulapuram Nakkanadoddi, Dancherla, Nagasamudram.

The villages having more than 50% SC population are None.

Sex ratio of Scheduled Caste population is 495.

Scheduled Castes Literates and Illiterates by Sex:

	Persons	Males	Females
Literate	1,588	1,020	568
Illiterate	3,491	1,546	1,945
Literacy rate	36.8	46.7	26.7
Graduate	12	10	2

Scheduled Castes (Dominant):

Madiga, Mala, Mala Dasari, Generic Castes etc. Madiga Dasu etc.

For their cultural identity please see Appendix-I

Villages without Scheduled Castes: There are 0 village without any scheduled caste population.

Scheduled Tribes: Out of the total population of 42432 persons, 3583 persons (8.44%) belong to Scheduled Tribes.

The villages having less than 10% ST population are Kasapuram, Sangala, Dosaludiki, Ameenpalle Konganapalle, Sankarabanda, Obulapuram Yerrathimmarayachervu, Patha Kothachervu Thimmapuram, Guntakal (Rural), Donimukkala Dancherla, Ayyavaripalle.

The villages having more than 50% ST population are None.

Sex ratio of Scheduled tribe population is 498.

Scheduled Tribes Literates and Illiterates by Sex:

	Persons	Males	Females
Literate	945	646	299
Illiterate	2,638	1,154	1,484
Literacy rate	32.3	44.0	20.5
Graduate	4	4	0

Scheduled Tribes (Dominant):

Sugalis etc., Yerukulas, Kammara

For their cultural identity please see Appendix-II

Villages without Scheduled Tribes: There are 4 villages without any scheduled tribe population.

Literates and Illiterates by Sex (Total Population):

	Persons	Males	Females
Literate	17,058	11,105	5,953
Illiterate	25,374	10,551	14,823
Literacy rate	47	60	34
Graduate	302	259	43

Agriculture: ***Distribution of villages according to land use:***

Out of 18 villages, Total area (in hectare) is 35797, out of

that 70.72 percent is cultivable and 8.46 percent of the cultivable area is irrigated.

Sources of Irrigation (Hectares): Government Canal 359.86, Private Canal 0, Well without Electricity 0, Well with Electricity 176.49, Tubewell without Electricity 0, Tubewell with Electricity 1145.55, Tank 448.15, River 0, Lake 0, Waterfall 0, Others 10.62.

Villages with population of 5000 to 9999: Nagasamudram.

Villages with population of 10000 and above: None

Distribution of Workers:

	Persons	Males	Females	WPR
Cultivators	8,501	5,390	3,111	36.02
Agricultural Labour	11,765	5,092	6,673	49.85
Household Industry	694	361	333	2.94
Other Workers	2,642	1,937	705	11.19
Main Workers	20,327	12,215	8,112	86.12
Marginal Workers	3,275	565	2,710	13.88
Total Workers	23,602	12,780	10,822	

Religion: Major Religious Communities:

	Persons	Males	Females	Sex Ratio
Hindu (94.77%)	40,214	20,530	19,684	959
Muslim (4.99%)	2,119	1,083	1,036	957
Christian (0.1%)	43	19	24	1,263
Sikh (0%)	-	-	-	-
Buddhists (0%)	-	-	-	-
Jain (0%)	-	-	-	-

Agewise Data:

	Persons	Males	Females	Sex Ratio
All ages	42,432	21,656	20,776	959
0-14	15,948	8,218	7,730	941
15-44	19,378	9,975	9,403	943
45-79	6,823	3,349	3,474	1037
80+	237	93	144	1548
Age not stated	46	21	25	1190

Languages (Dominant):

Telugu, Hindi, Urdu, Gondi, Marathi

Disabled Population:

	Persons	Males	Females	%
Total Disabled	730	398	332	
In Seeing	197	105	92	26.99
In Speech	76	42	34	10.41
In Hearing	50	25	25	6.85
In Movement	259	160	99	35.48
Mentally	148	66	82	20.27

GUNTUR

Guntur C.D. Block lies in the eastern part of Guntur district. It is a part of Guntur Mandal. The Block is located at a distance of (00) kms. from district headquarters (Guntur). There are 11 villages in the block with the total population of 86,804 persons. Area of the C.D. Block is 177.35 sq. kms. It is bounded in the north by Mandal Tadikonda, in the south by Manda ls Prathipadu, Vatticherukuru and Chebrolu, in the east by Mandals Pedakakani and Chebrolu and in the west by Mandals Medkenduru and Edlapadu.

Communications:

Roadways : NH- 5: Direction- Prathipadu to Pedakakani. Nearest Villages- Pothur, Chowdavaram. State Highway (S.H.): Direction- Edlapadu to Ongole and Chebrolu. Nearest Villages- Ankireddipalem (Rural), Nallapadu (Rural).

Railway Station: Nallapadu (Rural)

Annual Rainfall: Average Rainfall 890 mm

Ground Water: Availability of the Ground Water in the Basin is 6305 H.A.M. and the utilization is 230 H.A. M. It belongs to Safe category. Depth to water level varies from 2 to 5 meter below the ground. Most of the wells go down in summer months.

Natural Division : Krishna Delta Region

Administration:

Division: Coastal Andhra. Parliamentary Constituency: 30 Guntur. District: Guntur. Mandal: Guntur. Assembly Constituency: 212 Prathipadu (SC). Gram Panchayat: 22

Places of Tourist Interest:

Nallapadu: It is situated at a distance of 5 kms. South -West of Guntur and is referred to as Narasinga- puram, after the temple of Narasimhaswamy, on a hillock about 1.6 kms. away. Nallapadu is a place known for some ancient temples. The Agasthes- waraswamy temple, with its decorated Dhvajas- tambham and carvings of five hooded 'nagas' (Serpents), enshrining Siva and Bramaram ba and with the temple of Sankaracharya situated in the same compound is known for its antiquity. This temple is situated on an elevated platform, with a big gateway at the entrace and a huge rectangular slab, on which two pairs of feet are carved.

Fairs and Festivals:

Sri Bugga Malleswaraswamy Aradhanothsavam : It is celeb rated for one day on Magha Bahula Chathurdasi (January-February) during Mahasivaratri. Devotees fulfil their vows. Cocoanuts and fruits are offered. Bath in a well near the temple, fasting and jagaram are the domestic observances. This festival is being celebrated for the past about 150 years.

Sri Narasimhaswamy Kalyanothsavam : Sri Narasimhaswamy Kalyanothsavam is celebrated annually from Chaitra Suddha Saptami (March-April) for 16 days at the temple of Sri Lakshmi Narasimhaswamy. Ankurarpana (inauguratio

n) is on the first day, dhwajarohana (flag hoisting) is on the second day with procession on chilukavahanam in the night. Suryachandravahanam is on the third, simhavahanam on the fourth, yali (a kind of tree) vahan am on the fifth, Hanumanthavahanam on the sixth and ponnavahanam on the seventh. Kalyanamahothsavam is celebrated in the morning of the eighth day, i.e., on Chaturdasi followed by Enugavahanam (procession on an elephant vehicle) in the night. There is processi on on Garuda vahanam (on the morning of Purnima). The important function is the car festival during the night of Purnima. On Bahula Padyami, Paravathi vasanthothsavam, avabruthasnanam and procession on horse are the funct ions. On the night of Vidiya, pushpayagam is the function. This is to take the procession image of the Lord round the temple twelve times each time accompanied by a particular type of musical instruments and 12 naivedyams are offered. The festival is considered to be closed and the Lord is given rest for five days which in itself is a festival. This is called pavalimpu seva.On the first day, the Lord is decorated as Vennamu dda Gopala, on the second day as Kaliyamardana, on the third day as Sri Ranganayaka, on the fourth day as Parthasarathi and finally on the fifth day pattabhishek am (coronation) ceremony is performed.

Sri Raghunayakaswamy Kalyanamahothsavam : It is celebra ted for nine days from Chaitra Suddha Dasami to Bahula Tadiya (March-April) at Lingodhbhavaswamy temple. Prepa rations are made by Navami. Ankurarpana and garuda dhwaj am (hoisting a flag with the emblem of garuda, the sacred kite) on Dasami, seshathalpa mahothsavam (serpent bed) on Ekadasi, hamsa vahana mahothsavam (procession on swan) on Dwadasi, simhavahana mahothsavam (procession on lion) on Triodasi, Hanumantha vahanothsavam on Chaturdasi, Mohiniuthsavam and garuda vahanothsavam (procession on the sacred kite) in the night of Purnima, procession on Surya (Sun), Chandra (Moon), Enugu (elep hant) vananothsavams in the night on Bahula Padyami, Kalyanam (marriage) and rathothsavam in the evening of Vidiya and gurrapu (horse) vahanothsavam and donga la dopidi (a function in which the jewels of the deity are stolen by the robbers and restored back after a search) are the chief rituals that are observed during the festival. The noteworthy incident during the kalyan othsavam of the Lord is that the sacred kite, garuda is perambulated in the air from left to right every year. Rathothsavam attracts a large congregation and the huge car is dragged by about 1,000 devotees. Meluko lupu (waking up the Lord from sleep) with recitation of Suprabhatham, binde theertham with music and offering deepam, dhupam and naivedyam at dawn and offering naivedyam with music at dusk are the daily performances. In summer, the deity is richly decorated with jasmines. Devotees celebrate marriages in the temple. The akhan da jyoti (lamp) in the crypt is watched carefully to prevent it from extinguishing as it is believed to be a bad omen. Coconuts, fruits, flowers, jewellery and cloths are offered to the deity in fulfilment of vows. Jagarana on Purnima, bath in the Gundalakamma and darsan of alaya sikhara are observed by all. For the past seven or eight centuries this festival is being celebrated and devotees from the neighbouring places of Nellore and Kurnool also participate. A fair is held in connection with this festival for 12 days.

Sri Ramakoti Mahothsavam : Sri Ramakoti Mahothsavam is a great annual celebration. Sri Ramanama Kshetram is a very great religious centre of worship in Agraharam area of Guntur. The chief architect of this centre was a great devotee of Lord Rama, Sri Ragam Anjaneyulu. Sri Ragam Anjaneyulu was the son of Ragam Pichaiah Dasu and Sundaramma. In 1908 Sri Dasu was a Range Offic er at Vinukonda. Sundaramma used to worship Anjaneyaswar of the place. She named her son as Anjaneyulu. Even from his boyhood days, Anjaneyula used to sing in praise of lord name of Lord Rama. In 1916, when the boy was 8 years old, his father then working as Range Officer at Pecheruvu (on the way to Srisailam from Atmakur) got an earthen image of Lord Rama. He housed it in a toy-temple constructed with three tiles he could get and began to worship the same with wild flowers and offer wood -apples that are available in the forest area. It is this toy -temple that is the origin of the present Mandiram developing into a very great relig ious centre in India. The worship that was commenced that day is continuing unbroken till today. When his father came to Guntur, he kept it in a small nitche in the wall of their humble house in Singadipeta. He transferred the image of Rama to the small wooden temple which he made and commenced festivals on holy days. The boy was encouraged by his parents and relatives. He began to assemble the school-children of his age and perform bhajans on Saturdays in primary school in Agraharam. Sri Vasireddi Suryanarayana was his good companion and a bachelor who dedicated his life to the services of Lord Rama. In 1926, Anjaneyulu took one more stride and began daily Rama bhajana through the streets of the town. Kartika Sudha Purnima has been chosen as the day for establishing Sree Seetha Ramanama Sankeerthana Sangham. After the modest schooli ng, Anjayulu accompanied by Vasireddi Suryanarayana visited Bhadrachalam in 1926, Tirupathi in 1927 and Pandaripuram in 1928. The visits to these renowned religious centres and other sacred places and his exper iences there increased his belief in the efficacy of namasankeerthana (repetition of the name of the Lord). After visiting the above religious centres, he started a school on a pial in the spacious compouned of Lord Narasimha swamy temple for self-maintenance and called it as Sri Seetha Rama Vidyalayam. He had to accept marriage on 20-3-1930. On 19th September 1927 he had established with the co-operation of the other teachers of his school, 'Sri Seetha Ramanama Sankeerthana Mandir am' in the school building which he had taken on rent, opposite to Narasimhaswamy temple. He held bhanjan for a particular period thrice a day and for a longer period on Saturdays. In order to popularise the Bhajan and Ramanama Samkeerthana, Ramanama publication branch was started and the sankeerthanas were printed in bookl ets and distributed among the public. For ensuring the proper pronunciation of the several namamas, ekahams (one day conferences) and sapthahams (seven day confern ces) were held in several places of Guntur District and at times outside the district. Thus, the third branch of propaganda was added to the Shankeerthana (Bhajana) and Prachurana (Publication) Branches. The fourth branch of Annadanam (feeding the blind, lame and sick) with the raw rice etc; collected from door to door was opened in 1931. The fifth was the Sadhana branch established in 1932 for observing a code of daily practice and conduct for the attainment of spiri tual life. The sixth was the inauguration of Ramakoti Mahothsavam (worship of the books in which the sacred name 'Sree Rama' was written by one individual one crore times).

Villages: 11 **Inhabited:** 11 **Uninhabited:** 0

Ranking	District	State	National
Area	25	683	4579
Population	2	17	3879
Sex Ratio	31	568	2030
Child Sex Ratio	40	779	3401
Literacy Rate	19	190	2200
Density	46	761	2255
Work Participation Rate	10	114	2220

Gram Panchayats:

Adavitakkellapadu, Ankireddypalem, Budampadu Challavaripalem, Chinapalakaluru, Chowdavaram Dasupalem, Etukuru, Gorantla, Gorlavaripalem Jonnalagadda, Lalpuram, Laxmi Narasimhapuram Mallavaram, Nallapadu, Obulunaidupalem Pedapalakaluru, Pothuru, Reddypalem, Sivareddypalem Thokavaripalem, Thurakapalem.

Amenities:

Education: Primary School in 11 villages, Middle school in 10 villages, Matriculation or Secondary School in 7 villages, namely Peda Palakaluru, Jonnalagadda, Gorantla, Nallapadu (Rural), Guntur (Rural), Ankireddipalem (Rural), Etukur.

Higher Secondary or Pre University Courses or Intermediate or Junior College in 4 villages of the CD Block,, namely Peda Palakaluru, Jonnalagadda, Gorantla, Nallapadu (Rural).

College in 1 village, Adult Literacy Center in 10 villages., College is in village, namely Nallapadu (Rural).

Medical: Hospital in 1 village, Dispensary in 1 village, Health Center in 0 village, Sub Center in 8 villages, Maternity and Child Welfare Center in 0 village, Community health workers in 0 village.

The Village having Hospital or Dispensary or Health Center is Guntur (Rural).

Drinking Water: Tap water in 11 villages, Tank water in 10 villages, Well water in 11 villages, Tubewell in 10 villages and more than one source in 11 villages.

Bank: Banking facility in 4 villages, namely, Jonnalagadda, Gorantla, Nallapadu (Rural), Etukur.

Credit Society in 7 villages Agricultural Credit Society in 5 Non-Agricultural Credit Society in 0 village.

Others: Power supply in 11 villages, Cinema hall in 2 villages, sport club in 0 village, Stadium or Auditorium or Community Hall in 0 village, Post Office in 10 villages.

There are 11 villages having bus facilities.

Villages with most of facilities: Jonnalagadda Gorantla, Nallapadu (Rural), Etukur.

Villages without Amenities (Education): None..

Scheduled Castes: Out of the total population of 87082 persons, 16401 persons (18.83%) belong to Scheduled Castes.

The villages having less than 10% SC population are None..

The villages having more than 50% SC population are None.

Sex ratio of Scheduled Caste population is 492.

Scheduled Castes Literates and Illiterates by Sex:

	Persons	Males	Females
Literate	9,012	5,313	3,699
Illiterate	7,389	3,014	4,375
Literacy rate	63.5	73.9	52.8
Graduate	257	192	65

Scheduled Castes (Dominant):

Mala, Madiga, Mala Dasu, Arundhatiya Generic Castes etc.

For their cultural identity please see Appendix-I

Villages without Scheduled Castes: There are 0 village without any scheduled caste population.

Scheduled Tribes: Out of the total population of 87082 persons, 2197 persons (2.52%) belong to Scheduled Tribes. The villages having less than 10% ST population are China Palakaluru, Peda Palakaluru, Jonnalagadda Gorantla, Nallapadu (Rural), Guntur (Rural) Ankireddipalem (Rural), Pothur, Chowdavaram, Etukur Budampadu.

The villages having more than 50% ST population are None.

Sex ratio of Scheduled tribe population is 510.

Scheduled Tribes Literates and Illiterates by Sex:

	Persons	Males	Females
Literate	736	443	293
Illiterate	1,461	633	828
Literacy rate	39.6	48.0	31.3
Graduate	22	16	6

Scheduled Tribes (Dominant):

Yerukulas, Yenadis, Sugalis etc., Chenchu etc. Koya etc.

For their cultural identity please see Appendix-II

Villages without Scheduled Tribes: There are 0 village without any scheduled tribe population.

Literates and Illiterates by Sex (Total Population):

	Persons	Males	Females
Literate	48,521	27,990	20,531
Illiterate	38,561	15,988	22,573
Literacy rate	63	73	54
Graduate	2,622	1,911	711

Agriculture: ***Distribution of villages according to land use:*** Out of 11 villages, Total area (in hectare) is 17735, out of that 48.79 percent is cultivable and 15.35 percent of the cultivable area is irrigated.

Sources of Irrigation (Hectares): Government Canal 1101, Private Canal 0, Well without Electricity 1.8, Well with Electricity 49, Tubewell without Electricity 2, Tubewell with Electricity 60.2, Tank 114, River 0, Lake 0, Waterfall 0, Others 0.

Villages with population of 5000 to 9999:

Nallapadu (Rural), Guntur (Rural), Pothur, Etukur.

Villages with population of 10000 and above:

Peda Palakaluru, Gorantla, Ankireddipalem (Rural).

Distribution of Workers:

	Persons	Males	Females	WPR
Cultivators	3,934	2,742	1,192	8.95
Agricultural Labour	21,823	10,112	11,711	49.68
Household Industry	910	437	473	2.07
Other Workers	17,264	13,474	3,790	39.3
Main Workers	38,401	24,809	13,592	87.41
Marginal Workers	5,530	1,956	3,574	12.59
Total Workers	43,931	26,765	17,166	

Religion: Major Religious Communities:

	Persons	Males	Females	Sex Ratio
Hindu (91.17%)	79,394	40,092	39,302	980
Muslim (5.29%)	4,607	2,356	2,251	955
Christian (3.16%)	2,752	1,358	1,394	1,027
Sikh (0.04%)	32	16	16	1,000
Buddhists (0.01%)	13	7	6	857
Jain (0.01%)	6	4	2	500

Agewise Data:

	Persons	Males	Females	Sex Ratio
All ages	87,082	43,978	43,104	980
0-14	25,334	12,881	12,453	967
15-44	44,398	22,332	22,066	988
45-79	16,421	8,311	8,110	976
80+	757	364	393	1080
Age not stated	172	90	82	911

Languages (Dominant):

Telugu, Urdu, Hindi, Tamil, Others

Disabled Population:

	Persons	Males	Females	%
Total Disabled	1,121	649	472	
In Seeing	445	266	179	39.7
In Speech	142	77	65	12.67
In Hearing	46	20	26	4.1
In Movement	331	199	132	29.53
Mentally	157	87	70	14.01

GURAZALA

Gurazala C.D. Block lies in the northern part of Guntur district. The Block is located at a distance of 80 kms. from district headquarters (Guntur). There are 10 villages in the block with the total population of 62,246 persons. Area of the C.D. Block is 250.94 sq. kms. It is bounded in the north by district Nalgonda, in the south by Mandals Macherla, Durgi and Karempudi, in the east by Mandals Dachepalle and Karempudi, and in the west by Mandal Rentachintala. River Krishna binds on north.

Communications:

Roadways : Metalled Roads: Nearest Villages- Gangavaram, Pallegunta, Gurazala, Cherlagudi Padu.

Railway Station: Gurazala.

River: Krishna Nadi- Nearest Villages- Gottimukkala, Daida.

Integrated Child Development Scheme (ICDS) Project: Gurajala, Total Anganwadi Centres: 142

Annual Rainfall: Average Rainfall 719 mm

Ground Water: Availability of the Ground Water in the Basin is 12945 H.A.M. and the utilization is 628 H. A.M. It belongs to Safe category. Depth to water level varies from 2 to 5 meter below the ground. Most of the wells go down in summer months.

Forest and Reserved **Forest:** Nearest Villages- Gottimukk ala, Daida, Madugula.

Natural Division : Krishna Delta Region

Administration:

Division: Coastal Andhra. Parliamentary Constituency: 31 Narsaraopet. District: Guntur. Mandal: Gurazala. Assembly Constituency: 219 Gurajala. Gram Panchayat: 13

Villages: 10 **Inhabited:** 10 **Uninhabited:** 0

Ranking	**District**	**State**	**National**
Area	7	309	3371
Population	14	240	4778
Sex Ratio	26	482	1791
Child Sex Ratio	2	145	380
Literacy Rate	42	596	4213
Density	20	249	4099
Work Participation Rate	48	546	650

Gram Panchayats:

Ambapuram, Bodawada, Cherlagudipadu, Daida Gangavaram, Gogulapadu, Gottimukkala, Gurazala Kothaambapuram, Madugula, Palligunta, Pulipadu Telukutla.

Amenities:

Education: Primary School in 10 villages, Middle school in 6 villages, Matriculation or Secondary School in 2 villages, namely Pulipadu, Gurazala.

Higher Secondary or Pre University Courses or Intermediate or Junior College in 1 village of the CD Block,, namely Gurazala.

College in 1 village, Adult Literacy Center in 0 village., College is in village, namely Gurazala.

Medical: Hospital in 1 village, Dispensary in 0 village, Health Center in 3 villages, Sub Center in 8 villages, Maternity and Child Welfare Center in 1 village, Community health workers in 0 village.

The Villages having Hospital or Dispensary or Health Center are Gurazala, Cherlagudi Padu.

Drinking Water: Tap water in 10 villages, Tank water in 10 villages, Well water in 10 villages, Tubewell in 10 villages and more than one source in 10 villages.

Bank: Banking facility in 2 villages, namely, Pulipadu, Gurazala.

Credit Society in 7 villages Agricultural Credit Society in 7 Non-Agricultural Credit Society in 1 village.

Others: Power supply in 10 villages, Cinema hall in 1 village, sport club in 0 village, Stadium or Auditorium or Community Hall in 0 village, Post Office in 9 villages.

There are 10 villages having bus facilities.

Villages with most of facilities: Pulipadu Gurazala.

Villages without Amenities (Education): None..

Scheduled Castes: Out of the total population of 62246 persons, 9348 persons (15.02%) belong to Scheduled Castes.

The villages having less than 10% SC population are None..

The villages having more than 50% SC population are None.

Sex ratio of Scheduled Caste population is 495.

Scheduled Castes Literates and Illiterates by Sex:

	Persons	Males	Females
Literate	3,424	2,251	1,173
Illiterate	5,924	2,468	3,456
Literacy rate	42.7	55.4	29.6
Graduate	97	81	16

Scheduled Castes (Dominant):

Madiga, Mala, Beda Jangam etc., Generic Castes etc. Paky etc.

For their cultural identity please see Appendix-I

Villages without Scheduled Castes: There are 0 village without any scheduled caste population.

Scheduled Tribes: Out of the total population of 62246 persons, 2409 persons (3.87%) belong to Scheduled Tribes.

The villages having less than 10% ST population are Pulipadu, Gangavaram, Gogulapadu, Pallegunta Gurazala, Madugula, Cherlagudi Padu.

The villages having more than 50% ST population are None.

Sex ratio of Scheduled tribe population is 510.

Scheduled Tribes Literates and Illiterates by Sex:

	Persons	Males	Females
Literate	606	418	188
Illiterate	1,803	763	1,040
Literacy rate	30.3	42.4	18.5
Graduate	15	14	1

Scheduled Tribes (Dominant):

Sugalis etc., Yerukulas, Yenadis, Chenchu etc. Generic Tribes etc.

For their cultural identity please see Appendix-II

Villages without Scheduled Tribes: There are 0 village without any scheduled tribe population.

Literates and Illiterates by Sex (Total Population):

	Persons	Males	Females
Literate	28,229	17,634	10,595
Illiterate	34,017	13,722	20,295
Literacy rate	52	64	39
Graduate	1,229	995	234

Agriculture: ***Distribution of villages according to land use:*** Out of 10 villages, Total area (in hectare) is 25093, out of

that 69.31 percent is cultivable and 64.64 percent of the cultivable area is irrigated.

Sources of Irrigation (Hectares): Government Canal 11238.54, Private Canal 0, Well without Electricity 0, Well with Electricity 0, Tubewell without Electricity 0, Tubewell with Electricity 4.05, Tank 0, River 0, Lake 0, Waterfall 0, Others 0.

Villages with population of 5000 to 9999:
Pulipadu, Madugula, Cherlagudi Padu.

Villages with population of 10000 and above:
Gurazala.

Distribution of Workers:

	Persons	Males	Females	WPR
Cultivators	11,185	6,258	4,927	31.82
Agricultural Labour	18,771	8,664	10,107	53.4
Household Industry	401	215	186	1.14
Other Workers	4,796	3,838	958	13.64
Main Workers	30,795	17,124	13,671	87.6
Marginal Workers	4,358	1,851	2,507	12.4
Total Workers	35,153	18,975	16,178	

Religion: Major Religious Communities:

	Persons	Males	Females	Sex Ratio
Hindu (92.52%)	57,593	28,994	28,599	986
Muslim (5.37%)	3,344	1,680	1,664	990
Christian (1.88%)	1,171	582	589	1,012
Sikh (0.01%)	5	3	2	667
Buddhists (0%)	-	-	-	-
Jain (0%)	-	-	-	-

Agewise Data:

	Persons	Males	Females	Sex Ratio
All ages	62,246	31,356	30,890	985
0-14	19,285	9,644	9,641	1000
15-44	30,529	15,464	15,065	974
45-79	11,552	5,717	5,835	1021
80+	470	213	257	1207
Age not stated	410	318	92	289

Languages (Dominant):
Telugu, Urdu, Hindi, Gondi, Tamil

Disabled Population:

	Persons	Males	Females	%
Total Disabled	1,063	574	489	
In Seeing	407	203	204	38.29
In Speech	102	56	46	9.6
In Hearing	75	33	42	7.06
In Movement	323	195	128	30.39
Mentally	156	87	69	14.68

GURLA

Gurla C.D. Block lies in the southern part of Vizianaga ram district. The Block is located at a distance of 14 kms. from district headquarters (Vizianagaram). There are 39 villages in the block with the total popul ation of 62,251 persons. Area of the C.D. Block is 163. 60 sq. kms. It is bounded in the north by Mandals Merak ammudidam and Garividi, in the south by Mandal Nellimarla, in the east by Mandal Garividi, in the west by Mandals Gajjapathinagaram and Nellimarla.

Communications :

Roadways : State Highway (S.H.): Direction- Nellimarla to Cheepurupalle. Nearest Villages- Penubharthi, Chinth apallipeta, Polayavalasa, Gudem, Goshada, Gujjangivalasa, Garida,Chodavaram, Kella, Gurla.

Railway Station: Chinthapallipeta, Solipisomarajupeta, Gujjangivalasa.

River: Champavati Nadi- Nearest Villages-Anandapuram, Chinthalapeta, Kalavacherla, Gurla.

Backwards Region Grants Fund It receives Backward Region Grants.

Mahila Samakhya (Education for Women's Equality): It is decleared Socialy and Educationally Backward Block by the Government.

Annaul Rainfall: Average Rainfall 886.7 mm

Ground Water: Availability of the Ground Water in the Basin is (Information not avavible) H.A.M .and the utilization is (Information not avavible) H.A.M. It belongs to (Information not avavible) category. Depth to water level varies from 3 to 10 meter below the ground. Most of the wells go down in summer months.

Forest and Reserved **Forest:** Nearest Villages- Gurla, Solipisomarajupeta, Manyapuripeta, Kella, Damarasingi.

Administration:

Division: Coastal Andhra. Parliamentary Constituency: 20 Vizianagram. District: Vizianagram. Mandal: Gurla. Assembly Constituency: 134 Cheepurupalle. Gram Panchay at: 37.

Villages: 39 **Inhabited:** 39 **Uninhabited:** 0

Ranking	District	State	National
Area	12	752	4814
Population	6	239	4777
Sex Ratio	25	302	1338
Child Sex Ratio	22	332	1136
Literacy Rate	32	1025	5829
Density	24	326	2875
Work Participation Rate	14	216	810

Gram Panchayats:
Anandapuram, Atchutapuram, Bhupalapuram Chintalapeta, Chintapallipeta, Chodavaram Damarasingi, Devunikanapaka, Garida, Garikivalasa Goshada, Gudem, Gujjangivalasa, Gurla, Jammu Jammupeta, Kal;Avachrla, Kella, Kondagandredu Kotagandredu, Lavidam, Manyapuripeta, Nadupuru Nagallavalasa, Pakeerukittali, Palavalasa

Palligandredu, Pedabantupalli, Penubarti
Polayavalasa, Punnapureddipeta, Ragolu, S.S.R.Peta
Tatavarikittali, Tatipudi, Tettangi, Vallapuram.

Amenities:

Education: Primary School in 38 villages, Middle school in 11 villages, Matriculation or Secondary School in 6 villages, namely Pedabantupalle, Polayavalasa, Thettangi, Palavalasa, Kalavacherla, Kella.

Higher Secondary or Pre University Courses or Intermediate or Junior College in 1 village of the CD Block,, namely Thatipudi.

College in 0 village, Adult Literacy Center in 19 villages.

Medical: Hospital in 0 village, Dispensary in 2 villages, Health Center in 1 village, Sub Center in 13 villages, Maternity and Child Welfare Center in 0 village, Community health workers in 0 village.

The Villages having Hospital or Dispensary or Health Center are Gudem, Kotagandredu.

Drinking Water: Tap water in 39 villages, Tank water in 39 villages, Well water in 39 villages, Tubewell in 39 villages and more than one source in 39 villages.

Bank: Banking facility in 3 villages, namely, Gurla, Gujjangivalasa, Thatipudi.

Credit Society in 11 villages Agricultural Credit Society in 4 Non-Agricultural Credit Society in 10 villages.

Others: Power supply in 39 villages, Cinema hall in 0 village, sport club in 0 village, Stadium or Auditorium or Community Hall in 0 village, Post Office in 32 villages.

There are 26 villages having bus facilities.

Villages with most of facilities: Gurla Gujjangivalasa.

Villages without amenities (Education):
Gorlapeta Jagannadhapuram..

Scheduled Castes: Out of the total population of 62251 persons, 5584 persons (8.97%) belong to Scheduled Castes.

The villages having less than 10% SC population are
Kondagandredu, Pedabantupalle, Lavidam
Thathavarikittali, Penubharthi, Chinthapallipeta
Polayavalasa, Thettangi, Pakeerukittali
Nallacheruvu, Gudem, Palavalasa, Garikavalasa
Anandapuram, Chinthalapeta, Nakkalapeta
Kalavacherla, Gurla, Manyapuripeta
Gorlapeta Jagannadhapuram, Meesalapeta, Jammu
Nagallavalasa, Sadanandapuram, Golagam, Thatipudi.

The villages having more than 50% SC population are None.

Sex ratio of Scheduled Caste population is 497.

Scheduled Castes Literates and Illiterates by Sex:

	Persons	Males	Females
Literate	1,698	1,089	609
Illiterate	3,886	1,719	2,167
Literacy rate	35.7	45.6	25.7
Graduate	23	18	5

Scheduled Castes (Dominant):
Mala, Relli, Madiga, Bariki, Adi Andhra

For their cultural identity please see Appendix-I

Villages without Scheduled Castes: There are 6 villages without any scheduled caste population.

Scheduled Tribes: Out of the total population of 62251 persons, 701 persons (1.13%) belong to Scheduled Tribes.

The villages having less than 10% ST population are
Kondagandredu, Pedabantupalle, Lavidam
Thathavarikittali, Penubharthi, Chinthapallipeta
Chodavaram, Polayavalasa, Thettangi, Pakeerukittali
Palligantredu, Nallacheruvu, Gudem, Palavalasa
Garikavalasa, Nadupuru, Anandapuram, Chinthalapeta
Nakkalapeta, Kotagandredu, Kalavacherla, Goshada
Gurla, Solipisomarajupeta, Manyapuripeta, Kella
Gorlapeta Jagannadhapuram, Gujjangivalasa
Meesalapeta, Garida, Jammu, Nagallavalasa
Sadanandapuram, Ragolu, Golagam, Thatipudi
Vallapuram, Damarasingi.

The villages having more than 50% ST population are None.

Sex ratio of Scheduled tribe population is 505.

Scheduled Tribes Literates and Illiterates by Sex:

	Persons	Males	Females
Literate	166	107	59
Illiterate	535	240	295
Literacy rate	29.9	39.9	20.6
Graduate	1	1	0

Scheduled Tribes (Dominant):
Konda Dhoras, Yerukulas, Chenchu etc., Kotia etc.

For their cultural identity please see Appendix-II

Villages without Scheduled Tribes: There are 25 villages without any scheduled tribe population.

Literates and Illiterates by Sex (Total Population):

	Persons	Males	Females
Literate	20,403	13,404	6,999
Illiterate	41,848	17,797	24,051
Literacy rate	38	50	26
Graduate	497	448	49

Agriculture: ***Distribution of villages according to land use:*** Out of 39 villages, Total area (in hectare) is 16360, out of that 66.34 percent is cultivable and 35.08 percent of the cultivable area is irrigated.

Sources of Irrigation (Hectares): Government Canal 0, Private Canal 0, Well without Electricity 0, Well with Electricity 0, Tubewell without Electricity 0, Tubewell with Electricity 0, Tank 3807.47, River 0, Lake 0,

Waterfall 0, Others 0.

Villages with population of 5000 to 9999: None

Villages with population of 10000 and above: None

Distribution of Workers:

	Persons	Males	Females	WPR
Cultivators	10,206	6,619	3,587	29.95
Agricultural Labour	14,955	6,178	8,777	43.89
Household Industry	2,002	1,119	883	5.87
Other Workers	6,914	5,534	1,380	20.29
Main Workers	22,582	15,461	7,121	66.27
Marginal Workers	11,495	3,989	7,506	33.73
Total Workers	34,077	19,450	14,627	

Religion: Major Religious Communities:

	Persons	Males	Females	Sex Ratio
Hindu (99.52%)	61,955	31,058	30,897	995
Muslim (0.27%)	170	82	88	1,073
Christian (0.14%)	88	43	45	1,047
Sikh (0%)	-	-	-	-
Buddhists (0%)	-	-	-	-
Jain (0%)	-	-	-	-

Agewise Data:

	Persons	Males	Females	Sex Ratio
All ages	62,251	31,201	31,050	995
0-14	20,508	10,499	10,009	953
15-44	29,195	14,661	14,534	991
45-79	12,300	5,912	6,388	1081
80+	189	101	88	871
Age not stated	59	28	31	1107

Languages (Dominant):

Telugu, Oriya, Urdu, Gondi, Hindi

Disabled Population:

	Persons	Males	Females	%
Total Disabled	1,369	744	625	
In Seeing	556	275	281	40.61
In Speech	125	65	60	9.13
In Hearing	110	57	53	8.04
In Movement	476	289	187	34.77
Mentally	102	58	44	7.45

GURRAMKONDA

Gurramkonda C.D. Block lies in the north-western part of Chittoor district. The Block is located at a distance of 88 kms. from district headquarters (Chittoor). There are 17 villages in the block with the total popul ation of 41,769 persons. Area of the C.D. Block is 199. 83 sq. kms. It is bounded in the north by Mandals Kalak ada and Vayalpad, and district Cuddapah, in the south by Mandal Vayalpad, in the east, by Mandals Kalakada and Vayalpad and in the west by Mandals Madanapalle, Kurabalakota, Thambalapalle and Pedda Mandyam.

Communications:

Roadways : State Highway (S.H.): Direction- Kurabalakota to Rayachoti. Nearest Villages- Cherlopalle, Nadimikhan driga, Chittiboyanapalle, Gurramkonda, Khandriga,

It receives the Backward Region Grants, and is identifi ed as a drought-prone area as well.

Annual Rainfall: Average Rainfall 822 mm

Ground Water: Availability of the Ground Water in the Basin is 2069 H.A.M.and the utilization is 1467 H.A. M. It belongs to SC category. Depth to water level varies more than 10 meter below the ground. Most of the wells go down in summer months, according to the Ground Water Estimation Committee.

Forest and Reserved **Forest:** Nearest Villages- Pasalavan dla Palle, Yellutla, Cherlopalle, Chittiboyanapalle, Gurramkonda, Sangasamudram, Setlivaripalle, Tharigonda.

Natural Division : Rayalaseema Region

Administration:

Division: Rayala Seema. Parliamentary Constituency: 41 Rajampet. District: Chittoor. Mandal: Gurramkonda. Assembly Constituency: 282 Pileru. Gram Panchayat: 15

Villages: 17 **Inhabited:** 17 **Uninhabited:** 0

Ranking	District	State	National
Area	19	558	4185
Population	37	770	5660
Sex Ratio	34	434	1665
Child Sex Ratio	20	395	1454
Literacy Rate	47	298	2925
Density	40	736	4608
Work Participation Rate	45	684	2128

Gram Panchayats:

Amilepalle, Cherlopalle, Gurramkonda, Khandriga Marrimakulapalle, Marripadu, Nadimikandriga Ramapuram, Sangasamudram, Sarimadugu, Setlivaripalle T.Pasalavandlapalle, Tharigonda Tharigondarachapalle, Yellutla.

Amenities:

Education: Primary School in 16 villages, Middle school in 8 villages, Matriculation or Secondary School in 4 villages, namely Cherlopalle, Gurramkonda, Tharigonda, Marripadu.

Higher Secondary or Pre University Courses or Intermediate or Junior College in 1 village of the CD Block,, namely Gurramkonda.

College in 0 village, Adult Literacy Center in 16 villages.

Medical: Hospital in 0 village, Dispensary in 2 villages, Health Center in 1 village, Sub Center in 10 villages, Maternity and Child Welfare Center in 1 village, Community health workers in 0 village.

The Villages having Hospital or Dispensary or Health Center are Cherlopalle, Tharigonda.

Drinking Water: Tap water in 17 villages, Tank water in 17 villages, Well water in 17 villages, Tubewell in 17 villages and more than one source in 17 villages.
Bank: Banking facility in 3 villages, namely, Gurramkonda, Tharigonda, Marripadu.
Credit Society in 6 villages Agricultural Credit Society in 4 Non-Agricultural Credit Society in 5 villages.
Others: Power supply in 17 villages, Cinema hall in 2 villages, sport club in 0 village, Stadium or Auditorium or Community Hall in 0 village, Post Office in 15 villages.
There are 15 villages having bus facilities.
Villages with most of facilities: Gurramkonda Tharigonda, Marripadu.
Villages without Amenities (Education): None..
Scheduled Castes: Out of the total population of 41769 persons, 3789 persons (9.07%) belong to Scheduled Castes.
The villages having less than 10% SC population are Pasalavandla Palle, Cherlopalle, Nadimikhandriga Sarimadugu, Gurramkonda, Sangasamudram, Khandriga Amilepalle, Marripadu.
The villages having more than 50% SC population are None.
Sex ratio of Scheduled Caste population is 500.
Scheduled Castes Literates and Illiterates by Sex:

	Persons	Males	Females
Literate	1,360	877	483
Illiterate	2,429	1,017	1,412
Literacy rate	41.9	54.2	29.6
Graduate	31	25	6

Scheduled Castes (Dominant):
Madiga, Mala, Generic Castes etc.
For their cultural identity please see Appendix-I
Villages without Scheduled Castes: There is 1 village without any scheduled caste population.
Scheduled Tribes: Out of the total population of 41769 persons, 806 persons (1.93%) belong to Scheduled Tribes.
The villages having less than 10% ST population are Pasalavandla Palle, Yellutla, Cherlopalle Nadimikhandriga, Chittiboyanapalle, Gurramkonda Sangasamudram, Khandriga, Marrimakulapalle Amilepalle, Arigalavaripalle, Setlivaripalle Tharigonda, Ramapuram, Tharigondarajupalle Marripadu.
The villages having more than 50% ST population are None.
Sex ratio of Scheduled tribe population is 493.
Scheduled Tribes Literates and Illiterates by Sex:

	Persons	Males	Females
Literate	263	180	83
Illiterate	543	229	314
Literacy rate	38.9	52.3	24.9
Graduate	3	3	0

Scheduled Tribes (Dominant):
Sugalis etc., Yerukulas, Yenadis
For their cultural identity please see Appendix-II
Villages without Scheduled Tribes: There are 5 villages without any scheduled tribe population.
Literates and Illiterates by Sex (Total Population):

	Persons	Males	Females
Literate	21,314	13,001	8,313
Illiterate	20,455	8,005	12,450
Literacy rate	59	72	46
Graduate	797	647	150

Agriculture: ***Distribution of villages according to land use:*** Out of 17 villages, Total area (in hectare) is 19984, out of that 54.85 percent is cultivable and 8.45 percent of the cultivable area is irrigated.
Sources of Irrigation (Hectares): Government Canal 0, Private Canal 0, Well without Electricity 56.25, Well with Electricity 496.58, Tubewell without Electricity 8.91, Tubewell with Electricity 170.66, Tank 193.49, River 0, Lake 0, Waterfall 0, Others 0.
Villages with population of 5000 to 9999: Gurramkonda.
Villages with population of 10000 and above: None
Distribution of Workers:

	Persons	Males	Females	WPR
Cultivators	8,535	5,323	3,212	41.02
Agricultural Labour	7,459	3,172	4,287	35.85
Household Industry	485	274	211	2.33
Other Workers	4,327	3,539	788	20.8
Main Workers	16,904	10,978	5,926	81.25
Marginal Workers	3,902	1,330	2,572	18.75
Total Workers	20,806	12,308	8,498	

Religion: Major Religious Communities:

	Persons	Males	Females	Sex Ratio
Hindu (75.81%)	31,663	15,931	15,732	988
Muslim (23.94%)	9,999	5,029	4,970	988
Christian (0.05%)	20	10	10	1,000
Sikh (0%)	-	-	-	-
Buddhists (0%)	-	-	-	-
Jain (0%)	-	-	-	-

Agewise Data:

	Persons	Males	Females	Sex Ratio
All ages	41,769	21,006	20,763	988
0-14	13,138	6,609	6,529	988
15-44	18,755	9,488	9,267	977
45-79	9,412	4,700	4,712	1003
80+	380	171	209	1222
Age not stated	84	38	46	1211

Languages (Dominant):
Telugu, Urdu, Hindi, Tamil, Malayalam

Disabled Population:

	Persons	Males	Females	%
Total Disabled	747	411	336	
In Seeing	244	112	132	32.66
In Speech	97	52	45	12.99
In Hearing	60	30	30	8.03
In Movement	237	156	81	31.73
Mentally	109	61	48	14.59

GURRAMPODE

Gurrampode C.D. Block lies in the central south part of Nalgonda district. The Block is located at a distance of 30 kms. from district headquarters (Nalgonda). There are 27 villages in the block with the total popul ation of 39,667 persons. Area of the C.D. Block is 307. 37 sq. kms. It is bounded by Kangal Mandal on north, Anumula and Peddavoora Mandals on east, Pedda Adisolap alle Mandal on east, Devarakonda Mandal on south-west, and Nampalle and Chandur Mandals on west.

Communications:

Roadways : Metalled Roads: Nearest Villages- Chamled, Koppole, Amlur, Gurram Pode, Palwai, Parla Palle, Mailapur, Junuthla, Thanedar Palle, Chepur.

Backwards Region Grants Fund: It receives Backward Region Grants.

Mahila Samakhya (Education for Women's Equality): It is decleared Socialy and Educationally Backward Block by the Government.

Annual Rainfall: Average Rainfall 553 mm

Ground Water: Availability of the Ground Water in the Basin is 2976 H.A.M. and the utilization is 1875 H. A.M. It belongs to Safe category. Depth to water level varies from 5 to 20 meter below the ground. Most of the wells go down in summer months. The well density in the entire block is 8 wells per sq. km. Total no. of the wells in the block are enumerated as 2401, according to the Ground Water Estimation Committee.

Natural Division : Krishna Piedmont Plain Region

Administration:

Division: Telangana. Parliamentary Constituency: 13 Nalgonda. District: Nalgonda. Mandal: Gurrampode. Assem bly Constituency: 87 Nagarjuna Sagar. Gram Panchayat: 19

Villages: 27 **Inhabited:** 27 **Uninhabited:** 0

Ranking	District	State	National
Area	9	148	2705
Population	46	831	5745
Sex Ratio	38	786	2632
Child Sex Ratio	21	653	2629
Literacy Rate	47	831	4992
Density	8	225	5849
Work Participation Rate	57	974	600

Gram Panchayats:

Bollaram, Chamaled, Chepur, Chinthagudem, Gurrampode Junutthala, Kalwapally, Koppole, Makkapally, Mosangi Nadikuda, Pallepahad, Palwai, Pochampally Sulthanpur, Tenepally, Thanedharpally, Utlapally Vatticode.

Amenities:

Education: Primary School in 26 villages, Middle school in 10 villages, Matriculation or Secondary School in 6 villages, namely Pochampalle, Chamled, Koppole, Gurram Pode, Palwai, Chepur.

Higher Secondary or Pre University Courses or Intermediate or Junior College in 0 village of the CD Block, College in 0 village, Adult Literacy Center in 0 village.

Medical: Hospital in 0 village, Dispensary in 1 village, Health Center in 1 village, Sub Center in 10 villages, Maternity and Child Welfare Center in 0 village, Community health workers in 0 village.

The Village having Hospital or Dispensary or Health Center is Koppole.

Drinking Water: Tap water in 27 villages, Tank water in 27 villages, Well water in 27 villages, Tubewell in 27 villages and more than one source in 27 villages.

Bank: Banking facility in 2 villages, namely, Koppole, Gurram Pode.

Credit Society in 4 villages Agricultural Credit Society in 4 Non-Agricultural Credit Society in 2 villages.

Others: Power supply in 27 villages, Cinema hall in 1 village, sport club in 0 village, Stadium or Auditorium or Community Hall in 0 village, Post Office in 12 villages.

There are 23 villages having bus facilities.

Villages with most of facilities: Koppole Gurram Pode.

Villages without amenities (Education): Kondapur..

Scheduled Castes: Out of the total population of 39667 persons, 8007 persons (20.19%) belong to Scheduled Castes. The villages having less than 10% SC population are None..

The villages having more than 50% SC population are None.

Sex ratio of Scheduled Caste population is 493.

Scheduled Castes Literates and Illiterates by Sex:

	Persons	Males	Females
Literate	2,958	2,041	917
Illiterate	5,049	2,019	3,030
Literacy rate	43.9	59.3	27.8
Graduate	55	52	3

Scheduled Castes (Dominant):

Madiga, Mala, Beda Jangam etc., Chamar etc., Bindla

For their cultural identity please see Appendix-I

Villages without Scheduled Castes: There are 0 village without any scheduled caste population.

Scheduled Tribes: Out of the total population of 39667 persons, 1254 persons (3.16%) belong to Scheduled Tribes. The villages having less than 10% ST population are Pochampalle, Mulkala Palle, Kondapur, Chamled Vattikode, Koppole, Nadikuda, Bollaram (P) Koppole Amlur, Gurram Pode, Ootlapalle, Sulthanpur Chinthagudam, Shagazipur, Kalwapalle, Palwai Parla Palle, Makka Palle, Mailapur, Thanedar Palle Kacharam (P) Koppole, Palle Pahad, Chepur, Kothlapur Mosangi.

The villages having more than 50% ST population are None.

Sex ratio of Scheduled tribe population is 486.

Scheduled Tribes Literates and Illiterates by Sex:

	Persons	Males	Females
Literate	257	197	60
Illiterate	997	448	549
Literacy rate	25.4	38.5	12.0
Graduate	7	6	1

Scheduled Tribes (Dominant):

Sugalis etc., Yerukulas, Koya etc.

For their cultural identity please see Appendix-II

Villages without Scheduled Tribes: There are 15 villages without any scheduled tribe population.

Literates and Illiterates by Sex (Total Population):

	Persons	Males	Females
Literate	15,804	10,414	5,390
Illiterate	23,863	9,751	14,112
Literacy rate	47	61	32
Graduate	373	333	40

Agriculture: *Distribution of villages according to land use:* Out of 27 villages, Total area (in hectare) is 30736, out of that 77.12 percent is cultivable and 5 percent of the cultivable area is irrigated.

Sources of Irrigation (Hectares): Government Canal 0, Private Canal 0, Well without Electricity 0, Well with Electricity 242.09, Tubewell without Electricity 8, Tubewell with Electricity 773.97, Tank 160, River 0, Lake 0, Waterfall 0, Others 0.

Villages with population of 5000 to 9999: Koppole.

Villages with population of 10000 and above: None

Distribution of Workers:

	Persons	Males	Females	WPR
Cultivators	7,792	4,885	2,907	35.38
Agricultural Labour	10,386	4,248	6,138	47.16
Household Industry	501	245	256	2.27
Other Workers	3,345	2,404	941	15.19
Main Workers	19,258	11,127	8,131	87.44
Marginal Workers	2,766	655	2,111	12.56
Total Workers	22,024	11,782	10,242	

Religion: Major Religious Communities:

	Persons	Males	Females	Sex Ratio
Hindu (95.06%)	37,707	19,188	18,519	965
Muslim (4.67%)	1,854	920	934	1,015
Christian (0.16%)	64	36	28	778
Sikh (0%)	-	-	-	-
Buddhists (0%)	-	-	-	-
Jain (0%)	-	-	-	-

Agewise Data:

	Persons	Males	Females	Sex Ratio
All ages	39,667	20,165	19,502	967
0-14	13,865	7,249	6,616	913
15-44	18,145	9,126	9,019	988
45-79	7,348	3,643	3,705	1017
80+	250	117	133	1137
Age not stated	59	30	29	967

Languages (Dominant):

Telugu, Urdu, Hindi, Gondi, Tamil

Disabled Population:

	Persons	Males	Females	%
Total Disabled	909	512	397	
In Seeing	462	261	201	50.83
In Speech	105	64	41	11.55
In Hearing	48	29	19	5.28
In Movement	207	111	96	22.77
Mentally	87	47	40	9.57

HALAHARVI

Halaharvi C.D. Block lies in the south-western part of Kurnool district. The Block is located at a distance of 110 kms. from district headquarters (Kurnool). There are 24 villages in the block with the total population of 37,024 persons. Area of the C.D. Block is 285.19 sq. kms. It is bounded in the north by Mandal Holagunda, in the south by district Anantpur, in the east by Mandals Alur and Chippagiri, in the west by River Hagari, and it has common boundary with the state of Karnataka on west.

Communications:

Roadways : State Highways (S.H.): Direction- Bellary to Kurnool. and Bellary to Halaharvi. Nearest Villages- Halaharvi, Medehal, Chinthakunta.

Railway Station: Chakibanda, Bevinhal.

River: Hagari Nadi- Nearest Villages- Ballur, Siddapuram, Amruthapuram, Gulyam, J.Hosahalli.

It is identified as a drought-prone area.

Annual Rainfall: Average Rainfall 502 mm

Ground Water: Availability of the Ground Water in the Basin is 3105 H.A.M. and the utilization is 356 H.A. M. It belongs to Safe category. Depth to water level varies from more than 10 meter below the ground. Most of the wells go down in summer months. The well density in the entire block is 1 wells per sq. km. Total no. of the wells in the block are enumerated as 156, accor ding to the Ground Water Estimation Committee.

Natural Division : Rayalaseema Region

Administration:

Division: Rayala Seema. Parliamentary Constituency: 35 Kurnool. District: Kurnool. Mandal: Halaharvi. Assem bly Constituency: 266 Alur. Gram Panchayat: 15.

Border Villages: (Karnataka)- Nearest Villages- Ballur, Siddapuram, Amruthapuram, Gulyam, J.Hosahalli, Bapuram, Patcharahalli, Halaharvi, Medehal, Chinthakunta, Sirug apuram, Sreedarahal, Chakibanda.

Villages: 24 **Inhabited:** 24 **Uninhabited:** 0

Ranking	District	State	National
Area	23	193	2938
Population	43	898	5847
Sex Ratio	33	859	2870
Child Sex Ratio	4	195	596
Literacy Rate	33	716	4614
Density	10	32	5838
Work Participation Rate	46	968	156

Gram Panchayats:

Bapuram, Bevinahal, Bilehal, Chinthakunta, Gulyam Halaharvi, Hardagiri, Kaminhal, Kokkarachedu Mallikarjunapally, Medehal, Nitravatti, Siddapuram Tsakibanda, Virupapuram.

Amenities:

Education: Primary School in 23 villages, Middle school in 5 villages, Matriculation or Secondary School in 5 villages, namely Gulyam, Halaharvi, Hardagiri, Chinthakunta, Kokkarachedu.

Higher Secondary or Pre University Courses or Intermediate or Junior College in 0 village of the CD Block, College in 0 village, Adult Literacy Center in 22 villages.

Medical: Hospital in 0 village, Dispensary in 0 village, Health Center in 2 villages, Sub Center in 7 villages, Maternity and Child Welfare Center in 0 village, Community health workers in 0 village.

Drinking Water: Tap water in 24 villages, Tank water in 24 villages, Well water in 24 villages, Tubewell in 24 villages and more than one source in 24 villages.

Bank: Banking facility in 1 villages, namely, Halaharvi.

Credit Society in 2 villages Agricultural Credit Society in 2 Non-Agricultural Credit Society in 2 villages.

Others: Power supply in 24 villages, Cinema hall in 2 villages, sport club in 0 village, Stadium or Auditorium or Community Hall in 0 village, Post Office in 15 villages.

There are 10 villages having bus facilities.

Village with most of facilities: Halaharvi.

Villages without Amenities (Education): None..

Scheduled Castes: Out of the total population of 37024 persons, 5354 persons (14.46%) belong to Scheduled Castes. The villages having less than 10% SC population are Ballur, Siddapuram, Kurulehalli, Virupapuram Nitravatti, Machanur, Sirugapuram.

The villages having more than 50% SC population are None.

Sex ratio of Scheduled Caste population is 498.

Scheduled Castes Literates and Illiterates by Sex:

	Persons	Males	Females
Literate	1,886	1,313	573
Illiterate	3,468	1,376	2,092
Literacy rate	43.1	59.1	26.6
Graduate	36	32	4

Scheduled Castes (Dominant):

Madiga, Mala, Bariki, Generic Castes etc.

For their cultural identity please see Appendix-I

Villages without Scheduled Castes: There is 1 village without any scheduled caste population.

Scheduled Tribes: Out of the total population of 37024 persons, 207 persons (0.56%) belong to Scheduled Tribes. The villages having less than 10% ST population are Ballur, Siddapuram, Amruthapuram, Kurulehalli Bolugota, Virupapuram, Bilehal, Nitravatti, Gulyam J.Hosahalli, Bapuram, Patcharahalli, Halaharvi Machanur, Hardagiri, Medehal, Kaminahal Chinthakunta, Mallikarjunahalli, Sirugapuram Kokkarachedu, Sreedarahal, Chakibanda, Bevinhal.

The villages having more than 50% ST population are None.

Sex ratio of Scheduled tribe population is 430.

Scheduled Tribes Literates and Illiterates by Sex:

	Persons	Males	Females
Literate	71	57	14
Illiterate	136	61	75
Literacy rate	41.5	58.8	18.9
Graduate	1	1	0

Scheduled Tribes (Dominant):

Yerukulas, Sugalis etc.

For their cultural identity please see Appendix-II

Villages without Scheduled Tribes: There are 18 villages without any scheduled tribe population.

Literates and Illiterates by Sex (Total Population):

	Persons	Males	Females
Literate	15,300	10,366	4,934
Illiterate	21,724	8,507	13,217
Literacy rate	50	66	33
Graduate	304	266	38

Agriculture: ***Distribution of villages according to land use:*** Out of 24 villages, Total area (in hectare) is 28520, out of that 91.49 percent is cultivable and 16.05 percent of the cultivable area is irrigated.

Sources of Irrigation (Hectares): Government Canal 3896.38, Private Canal 0, Well without Electricity 0, Well with Electricity 16.58, Tubewell without Electricity 0, Tubewell with Electricity 14.97, Tank 233.76, River 0, Lake 0, Waterfall 6, Others 20.23.

Villages with population of 5000 to 9999:
Gulyam.

Villages with population of 10000 and above: None

Distribution of Workers:

	Persons	Males	Females	WPR
Cultivators	7,978	5,307	2,671	37.01
Agricultural Labour	11,408	4,755	6,653	52.92
Household Industry	436	195	241	2.02
Other Workers	1,735	1,287	448	8.05
Main Workers	16,811	9,825	6,986	77.98
Marginal Workers	4,746	1,719	3,027	22.02
Total Workers	21,557	11,544	10,013	

Religion: Major Religious Communities:

	Persons	Males	Females	Sex Ratio
Hindu (94.75%)	35,080	17,916	17,164	958
Muslim (5%)	1,853	914	939	1,027
Christian (0.19%)	69	29	40	1,379
Sikh (0%)	-	-	-	-
Buddhists (0%)	-	-	-	-
Jain (0%)	-	-	-	-

Agewise Data:

	Persons	Males	Females	Sex Ratio
All ages	37,024	18,873	18,151	962
0-14	14,516	7,452	7,064	948
15-44	15,819	8,162	7,657	938
45-79	6,405	3,135	3,270	1043
80+	231	86	145	1686
Age not stated	53	38	15	395

Languages (Dominant):
Telugu, Kannada, Urdu, Marathi, Hindi

Disabled Population:

	Persons	Males	Females	%
Total Disabled	694	385	309	
In Seeing	234	113	121	33.72
In Speech	78	41	37	11.24
In Hearing	45	25	20	6.48
In Movement	253	157	96	36.46
Mentally	84	49	35	12.1

HANAMKONDA

Hanamkonda C.D. Block lies in the western part of Waran gal district. It is a part of Hanamkonda Mandal. The Block is located at a distance of 0 kms. from district headquarters (Warangal). There are 16 villages in the block with the total population of 54,567 persons.
Area of the C.D. Block is 182,27 sq. kms. It is bounded in the north by Mandals Dharmasagar, Hasanparthy and Atmakur, in the south by Zaffergadh, Wardhannapet and Sangam Mandals, in the east by Mandals Sangam, Warangal, Geesugonda and Atmakur, and in the west by Dharmasagar Mandal.

Communications:

Roadways : NH- 202: Direction- Hyderabad to Bijapur. Nearest Villages- Waddepalle (Rural), Madikonda (Rural). Backwards Region Grants Fund: It receives Backward Region Grants.

Integrated Child Development Scheme (ICDS) Project: Hanumakonda, Total Anganwadi Centres: 273

Annual Rainfall: Average Rainfall 980 mm

Ground Water: Availability of the Ground Water in the Basin is 3958 H.A.M.and the utilization is 2583 H.A. M. It belongs to Safe category. Depth to water level varies from 5 to 10 meter below the ground. Most of the wells go down in summer months. The well density in the entire block is 15 wells per sq. km. Total no. of the wells in the block are enumerated as 3726, according to the Ground Water Estimation Committee.

Natural Division : Godavari Depression Region

Administration:

Division: Telangana. Parliamentary Constituency.Distric t: Warangal. Mandal: Hanamkonda Assembly Constituency: 107 Waradhanapet (SC) Gram Panchayat: 23.

Villages: 16 **Inhabited:** 16 **Uninhabited:** 0

Ranking	District	State	National
Area	32	656	4498
Population	21	380	5063
Sex Ratio	50	1085	4693
Child Sex Ratio	46	1027	4872
Literacy Rate	1	99	1507
Density	50	969	3523
Work Participation Rate	15	367	3565

Gram Panchayats:

Allipur, Arepalle, Ayedyapur, Bhattupalle, Enumamula Gopalpur, Gundla Singaram, Kadipikonda, Kondaparthy Kothapalle, Kothapet, Kummarigudem, Madikonda Mamnoor, Mulkalagudem, Nakkalapalle, Narsimulagudem Paidipalle, Palvelpula, Tekulagudem, Tharalapalle Thimmapur, Vanamalakanaparthi.

Amenities:

Education: Primary School in 16 villages, Middle school in 11 villages, Matriculation or Secondary School in 6 villages, namely Madikonda (Rural), Paidipalle, Tharalapalle, Kondaparthy, Thimmapur (Haveli) (Rural), Mamnoor. Higher Secondary or Pre University Courses or Intermediate or Junior College in 1 village of the CD Block,, namely Waddepalle (Rural).

College in 0 village, Adult Literacy Center in 0 village.

Medical: Hospital in 5 villages, Dispensary in 3 villages, Health Center in 4 villages, Sub Center in 7 villages, Maternity and Child Welfare Center in 1 village, Community health workers in 0 village.

The Villages having Hospital or Dispensary or Health Center are Madikonda (Rural), Waddepalle (Rural), Palvelpula (Rural), Kumarapalle (Rural), Paidipalle, Kondaparthy, Thimmapur (Haveli) (Rural), Nakkalapalle.

Drinking Water: Tap water in 16 villages, Tank water in 16 villages, Well water in 16 villages, Tubewell in 16 villages and more than one source in 16 villages.

Bank: Banking facility in 1 villages, namely, Madikonda (Rural).

Credit Society in 13 villages Agricultural Credit Society in 2 Non-Agricultural Credit Society in 13 villages.

Others: Power supply in 16 villages, Cinema hall in 2 villages, sport club in 1 village, Stadium or Auditorium or Community Hall in 0 village, Post Office in 7 villages.

There are 15 villages having bus facilities.

Village with most of facilities: Madikonda (Rural).

Villages without Amenities (Education): None..

Scheduled Castes: Out of the total population of 54686 persons, 18558 persons (33.94%) belong to Scheduled Castes.

The villages having less than 10% SC population are None..

The villages having more than 50% SC population are None.

Sex ratio of Scheduled Caste population is 487.

Scheduled Castes Literates and Illiterates by Sex:

	Persons	Males	Females
Literate	9,958	6,010	3,948
Illiterate	8,600	3,505	5,095
Literacy rate	62.7	73.9	50.9
Graduate	233	207	26

Scheduled Castes (Dominant):

Madiga, Mala, Manne, Beda Jangam etc., Adi Dravida

For their cultural identity please see Appendix-I

Villages without Scheduled Castes: There are 0 village without any scheduled caste population.

Scheduled Tribes: Out of the total population of 54686 persons, 1971 persons (3.6%) belong to Scheduled Tribes.

The villages having less than 10% ST population are Madikonda (Rural), Palvelpula (Rural), Paidipalle Kothapet, Bhathipalle, Kothapalle (H), Tharalapalle Vanamalakanaparthi, Kondaparthy, Ammavaripet Thimmapur (Haveli) (Rural), Allipur, Mamnoor Nakkalapalle.

The villages having more than 50% ST population are None.

Sex ratio of Scheduled tribe population is 464.

Scheduled Tribes Literates and Illiterates by Sex:

	Persons	Males	Females
Literate	892	586	306
Illiterate	1,079	470	609
Literacy rate	55.8	68.3	41.3
Graduate	32	30	2

Scheduled Tribes (Dominant):

Sugalis etc., Yerukulas, Koya etc., Gond etc. Generic Tribes etc.

For their cultural identity please see Appendix-II

Villages without Scheduled Tribes: There is 1 village without any scheduled tribe population.

Literates and Illiterates by Sex (Total Population):

	Persons	Males	Females
Literate	32,092	19,543	12,549
Illiterate	22,594	8,885	13,709
Literacy rate	68	79	55
Graduate	1,274	1,055	219

Agriculture: ***Distribution of villages according to land use:*** Out of 16 villages, Total area (in hectare) is 18227, out of that 55.73 percent is cultivable and 22.15 percent of the cultivable area is irrigated.

Sources of Irrigation (Hectares): Government Canal 115, Private Canal 0, Well without Electricity 238, Well with Electricity 1317, Tubewell without Electricity 4, Tubewell with Electricity 68, Tank 508, River 0, Lake 0, Waterfall 0, Others 0.

Villages with population of 5000 to 9999: Kondaparthy, Thimmapur (Haveli) (Rural), Mamnoor.

Villages with population of 10000 and above: Paidipalle.

Distribution of Workers:

	Persons	Males	Females	WPR
Cultivators	4,714	2,626	2,088	19.47
Agricultural Labour	8,890	3,447	5,443	36.71
Household Industry	911	420	491	3.76
Other Workers	9,700	7,995	1,705	40.06
Main Workers	19,853	12,708	7,145	81.99
Marginal Workers	4,362	1,780	2,582	18.01
Total Workers	24,215	14,488	9,727	

Religion: Major Religious Communities:

	Persons	Males	Females	Sex Ratio
Hindu (92.46%)	50,562	26,348	24,214	919
Muslim (6.49%)	3,551	1,808	1,743	964
Christian (1%)	549	257	292	1,136
Sikh (0.01%)	3	3	-	-
Buddhists (0%)	1	1	-	-
Jain (0%)	-	-	-	-

Agewise Data:

	Persons	Males	Females	Sex Ratio
All ages	54,686	28,428	26,258	924
0-14	18,012	9,680	8,332	861
15-44	26,285	13,446	12,839	955
45-79	9,921	5,055	4,866	963
80+	390	203	187	921
Age not stated	78	44	34	773

Languages (Dominant):
Telugu, Urdu, Hindi, Gondi, Tamil

Disabled Population:

	Persons	Males	Females	%
Total Disabled	1,063	671	392	
In Seeing	451	316	135	42.43
In Speech	123	71	52	11.57
In Hearing	34	15	19	3.2
In Movement	318	189	129	29.92
Mentally	137	80	57	12.89

HANUMANTHUNI PADU

Hanumanthunipadu C.D. Block lies in the southern part of Prakasam district. The Block is located at a distance of 102 kms. from district headquarters (Ongole). There are 27 villages in the block with the total population of 30,436 persons. Area of the C.D. Block is 346.28 sq. kms. It is bounded in the north by Mandals Tarlupadu and Konkanamitla, in the south by Mandal Veligandla, in the east by Mandal Kanigiri, and in the west by Mandal Bestavaripeta.

Communications:

***Roadways*:** State Highway (S.H.): Direction- Guntakal to Kandukur. Nearest Villages- Vemula Padu, Mohammada Puram, Thimmareddi Palle, Neelakanta Puram, Pedagola Palle, Hanumanthunipadu, Hazee Puram.

River: Dumaleru Nadi- Nearest Villages- Kutagundla, Doddi Chintala, Masaya Peta, Upendra Puram.

The Block is identified as a drought-prone area. Mohammada Puram, Nandanavanam.

Annual Rainfall: Average Rainfall 753.3 mm

Ground Water: Availability of the Ground Water in the Basin is 16.11 MCM and the utilization is 10.32 MCM It belongs to Safe category. Depth to water level varies from 2 to 5 meter below the ground. Most of the wells go down in summer months, according to the Ground Water Estimation Committee.

Forest and Reserved **Forest:** (Velikonda R.F.)- Nearest Villages- Peddivenkataya Palle, Annada Puram, Ummana Palle, Vemula Padu,

Administration:

Division: Coastal Andhra . Parliamentary Constituency: 33 Ongole. District: Prakasam. Mandal: Hanumanthuni Padu. Assembly Constituency: 232 Kanigiri. Gram Panchay at: 23.

Villages: 27 **Inhabited:** 25 **Uninhabited:** 2

Ranking	District	State	National
Area	8	83	2312
Population	53	1021	6052
Sex Ratio	48	1011	3595
Child Sex Ratio	17	418	1556
Literacy Rate	38	689	4494
Density	22	402	6204
Work Participation Rate	56	1079	983

Gram Panchayats:
Dasallapalli, Dasaripalli, Doddichinthala Gayamvaripalli, H.M.Padu, Hanumathapuram, Hazeepuram Kistampalli, Kondareddypalli, Kutagundla Lingamgunta, Mahammadapuram, Mittapalem Muppallapadu, Nallagandla, Nandanavanam Peda Gollapalli, Seetharampuram, Timmareddypalli Ummanapalli, Valicherla, Veeraramapuram, Vemulapadu.

Amenities:

Education: Primary School in 24 villages, Middle school in 7 villages, Matriculation or Secondary School in 6 villages, namely Mohammada Puram, Thimmareddi Palle, Pedagola Palle, Valicherla, Doddi Chintala, Hanumanthunipadu.

Higher Secondary or Pre University Courses or Intermediate or Junior College in 0 village of the CD Block, College in 0 village, Adult Literacy Center in 24 villages.

Medical: Hospital in 0 village, Dispensary in 1 village, Health Center in 1 village, Sub Center in 5 villages, Maternity and Child Welfare Center in 0 village, Community health workers in 0 village.

The Village having Hospital or Dispensary or Health Center is Annada Puram.

Drinking Water: Tap water in 25 villages, Tank water in 25 villages, Well water in 25 villages, Tubewell in 25 villages and more than one source in 25 villages.

Bank: Banking facility in 3 villages, namely, Vemula Padu, Thimmareddi Palle, Hanumanthunipadu.

Credit Society in 3 villages Agricultural Credit Society in 1 Non-Agricultural Credit Society in 3 villages.

Others: Power supply in 25 villages, Cinema hall in 0 village, sport club in 0 village, Stadium or Auditorium or Community

Hall in 0 village, Post Office in 8 villages.

There are 25 villages having bus facilities.

Villages with most of facilities: Vemula Padu Thimmareddi Palle, Hanumanthunipadu.

Villages without amenities (Education): Chinagolla Palle..

Scheduled Castes: Out of the total population of 30436 persons, 9188 persons (30.19%) belong to Scheduled Castes.

The villages having less than 10% SC population are Neelakanta Puram, Chinagolla Palle Veeragareddi Palle.

The villages having more than 50% SC population are None.

Sex ratio of Scheduled Caste population is 492.

Scheduled Castes Literates and Illiterates by Sex:

	Persons	Males	Females
Literate	3,953	2,500	1,453
Illiterate	5,235	2,168	3,067
Literacy rate	51.3	63.7	38.4
Graduate	79	64	15

Scheduled Castes (Dominant):

Madiga, Mala, Adi Andhra, Mala Dasu Generic Castes etc.

For their cultural identity please see Appendix-I

Villages without Scheduled Castes: There are 5 villages without any scheduled caste population.

Scheduled Tribes: Out of the total population of 30436 persons, 93 persons (0.31%) belong to Scheduled Tribes.

The villages having less than 10% ST population are Annada Puram, Ummana Palle, Hanumantha Puram Vemula Padu, Mohammada Puram, Thimmareddi Palle Raseedu Puram, Kotathippala, Kondareddi Palle Neelakanta Puram, Nallagandla, Pedagola Palle Valicherla, Nandanavanam, Veerarama Puram Ramaya Palle, Muppala Padu, Veeragareddi Palle Dasalla Palle, Kutagundla, Doddi Chintala Hanumanthunipadu, Hazee Puram, Masaya Peta.

The villages having more than 50% ST population are None.

Sex ratio of Scheduled tribe population is 495.

Scheduled Tribes Literates and Illiterates by Sex:

	Persons	Males	Females
Literate	43	29	14
Illiterate	50	18	32
Literacy rate	51.2	64.4	35.9
Graduate	7	7	0

Scheduled Tribes (Dominant):

Yerukulas, Sugalis etc., Yenadis

For their cultural identity please see Appendix-II

Villages without Scheduled Tribes: There are 17 villages without any scheduled tribe population.

Literates and Illiterates by Sex (Total Population):

	Persons	Males	Females
Literate	13,236	8,667	4,569
Illiterate	17,200	6,955	10,245
Literacy rate	50	64	36
Graduate	563	468	95

Agriculture: ***Distribution of villages according to land use:***

Out of 27 villages, Total area (in hectare) is 34628, out of that 34.08 percent is cultivable and 11.51 percent of the cultivable area is irrigated.

Sources of Irrigation (Hectares): Government Canal 0, Private Canal 0, Well without Electricity 0, Well with Electricity 1358, Tubewell without Electricity 0, Tubewell with Electricity 0, Tank 0, River 0, Lake 0, Waterfall 0, Others 0.

Villages with population of 5000 to 9999: None

Villages with population of 10000 and above: None

Distribution of Workers:

	Persons	Males	Females	WPR
Cultivators	4,628	2,728	1,900	27.96
Agricultural Labour	9,212	4,195	5,017	55.66
Household Industry	437	171	266	2.64
Other Workers	2,274	1,673	601	13.74
Main Workers	11,719	6,710	5,009	70.81
Marginal Workers	4,832	2,057	2,775	29.19
Total Workers	16,551	8,767	7,784	

Religion: Major Religious Communities:

	Persons	Males	Females	Sex Ratio
Hindu (96.29%)	29,306	15,042	14,264	948
Muslim (2.6%)	791	414	377	911
Christian (0.67%)	203	100	103	1,030
Sikh (0%)	-	-	-	-
Buddhists (0%)	-	-	-	-
Jain (0%)	-	-	-	-

Agewise Data:

	Persons	Males	Females	Sex Ratio
All ages	30,436	15,622	14,814	948
0-14	10,482	5,391	5,091	944
15-44	13,312	6,941	6,371	918
45-79	6,345	3,118	3,227	1035
80+	197	106	91	858
Age not stated	100	66	34	515

Languages (Dominant):

Telugu, Urdu, Gondi, Hindi, Oriya

Disabled Population:

	Persons	Males	Females	%
Total Disabled	583	327	256	
In Seeing	198	105	93	33.96
In Speech	69	40	29	11.84

In Hearing	29	17	12	4.97
In Movement	207	120	87	35.51
Mentally	80	45	35	13.72

HANWADA

Hanwada C.D. Block lies in the northern part of Mahbubn agar district. The Block is located at a distance of 10 kms. from district headquarters (Mahbubnagar). There are 20 villages in the block with the total population of 44,545 persons. Area of the C.D. Block is 170.93 sq. kms. It is bounded by Rangareddy district on north, Nawabpet Mandal on east, Mahbubnagar Mandal on south, and Koilkonda Mandal on west.

Communications:

Roadways : State Highway (S.H.): Direction- Kodangal to Mahbubnagar. Nearest Villages- Naginonipalle, Hanwada, Peddadharpalle, Chinnadharpalle, Kothapeta, Ibrahimbad.

Backwards Region Grants Fund: It receives Backward Region Grants.

Mahila Samakhya (Education for Women's Equality): It is decleared Socialy and Educationally Backward Block by the Government. .

Annual Rainfall: Average Rainfall 669 mm

Ground Water: Availability of the Ground Water in the Basin is 1474 H.A.M. and the utilization is 1153 H. A.M. It belongs to SC category. Depth to water level varies from 2 to 5 meter below the ground. Most of the wells go down in summer months. The well density in the entire block is 18 wells per sq. km. Total no. of the wells in the block are enumerated as 3107, according to the Ground Water Estimation Committee.

Natural Division : Telangana Plateau Region

Administration:

Division: Telangana. Parliamentary Constituency: 11 Mahbubnagar. District: Mahbubnagar. Mandal: Hanwada. Assembly Constituency: 74 Mahbubnagar. Gram Panchayat: 20

Villages: 20 **Inhabited:** 18 **Uninhabited:** 2

Ranking	District	State	National
Area	64	708	4686
Population	43	679	5533
Sex Ratio	22	559	1962
Child Sex Ratio	9	333	1148
Literacy Rate	47	1037	5888
Density	36	233	3960
Work Participation Rate	6	500	619

Gram Panchayats:

Ayodhyanagar, Buddaram, Chinnadarpally, Dachakpally Gudimalakapur, Gundyala, Hanwada, Ibrahimbad Kistampally, Kohtapeta, Kongatpally, Madharam Munimoksham, Naginonipally, Peddadarpally Sallonipally, Shaik Pally, Tankara, Thirumalagiri Vepur.

Amenities:

Education: Primary School in 18 villages, Middle school in 8 villages, Matriculation or Secondary School in 2 villages, namely Vepoor, Hanwada.

Higher Secondary or Pre University Courses or Intermediate or Junior College in 0 village of the CD Block, College in 0 village, Adult Literacy Center in 18 villages.

Medical: Hospital in 0 village, Dispensary in 1 village, Health Center in 1 village, Sub Center in 7 villages, Maternity and Child Welfare Center in 0 village, Community health workers in 0 village.

The Village having Hospital or Dispensary or Health Center is Vepoor.

Drinking Water: Tap water in 18 villages, Tank water in 18 villages, Well water in 18 villages, Tubewell in 18 villages and more than one source in 18 villages.

Bank: Banking facility in 2 villages, namely, Vepoor, Hanwada.

Credit Society in 12 villages Agricultural Credit Society in 1 Non-Agricultural Credit Society in 11 villages.

Others: Power supply in 18 villages, Cinema hall in 0 village, sport club in 0 village, Stadium or Auditorium or Community Hall in 0 village, Post Office in 11 villages.

There are 17 villages having bus facilities.

Villages with most of facilities: Vepoor, Hanwada.

Villages without Amenities (Education): None..

Scheduled Castes: Out of the total population of 44545 persons, 6630 persons (14.88%) belong to Scheduled Castes.

The villages having less than 10% SC population are Ayodhyanagar, Shaikpalle, Yarenpalle, Ammapur Chinnadharpalle.

The villages having more than 50% SC population are None.

Sex ratio of Scheduled Caste population is 501.

Scheduled Castes Literates and Illiterates by Sex:

	Persons	Males	Females
Literate	1,626	1,160	466
Illiterate	5,004	2,151	2,853
Literacy rate	29.8	42.5	17.0
Graduate	18	16	2

Scheduled Castes (Dominant):

Madiga, Mala, Mala Dasari, Beda Jangam etc.

Generic Castes etc.

For their cultural identity please see Appendix-I

Villages without Scheduled Castes: There are 5 villages without any scheduled caste population.

Scheduled Tribes: Out of the total population of 44545 persons, 7346 persons (16.49%) belong to Scheduled Tribes.

The villages having less than 10% ST population are Vepoor, Munimokesham, Yarenpalle, Madharam Naginonipalle, Hanwada, Peddadharpalle, Tankara Ibrahimbad.

The villages having more than 50% ST population are None.

Sex ratio of Scheduled tribe population is 494.

Scheduled Tribes Literates and Illiterates by Sex:

	Persons	Males	Females
Literate	1,805	1,254	551
Illiterate	5,541	2,462	3,079
Literacy rate	30.7	42.2	18.9
Graduate	27	27	0

Scheduled Tribes (Dominant):

Sugalis etc., Chenchu etc., Yerukulas

For their cultural identity please see Appendix-II

Villages without Scheduled Tribes: There are 3 villages without any scheduled tribe population.

Literates and Illiterates by Sex (Total Population):

	Persons	Males	Females
Literate	13,761	9,355	4,406
Illiterate	30,784	13,128	17,656
Literacy rate	37	50	24
Graduate	227	212	15

Agriculture: ***Distribution of villages according to land use:*** Out of 20 villages, Total area (in hectare) is 17091, out of that 64.38 percent is cultivable and 19.19 percent of the cultivable area is irrigated.

Sources of Irrigation (Hectares): Government Canal 0, Private Canal 0, Well without Electricity 0, Well with Electricity 883.85, Tubewell without Electricity 0, Tubewell with Electricity 1005.2, Tank 222.58, River 0, Lake 0, Waterfall 0, Others 0.

Villages with population of 5000 to 9999:

Gundiyal, Hanwada.

Villages with population of 10000 and above: None

Distribution of Workers:

	Persons	Males	Females	WPR
Cultivators	9,313	6,137	3,176	38.66
Agricultural Labour	9,840	2,738	7,102	40.85
Household Industry	500	234	266	2.08
Other Workers	4,436	3,398	1,038	18.42
Main Workers	20,755	11,747	9,008	86.16
Marginal Workers	3,334	760	2,574	13.84
Total Workers	24,089	12,507	11,582	

Religion: Major Religious Communities:

	Persons	Males	Females	Sex Ratio
Hindu (95.69%)	42,624	21,519	21,105	981
Muslim (4.26%)	1,897	947	950	1,003
Christian (0.02%)	9	6	3	500
Sikh (0%)	1	1	-	-
Buddhists (0%)	2	1	1	1,000
Jain (0%)	-	-	-	-

Agewise Data:

	Persons	Males	Females	Sex Ratio
All ages	44,545	22,483	22,062	981
0-14	17,532	9,046	8,486	938
15-44	18,661	9,332	9,329	1000
45-79	7,987	3,918	4,069	1039
80+	328	163	165	1012
Age not stated	37	24	13	542

Languages (Dominant):

Telugu, Hindi, Urdu, Tamil, Gondi

Disabled Population:

	Persons	Males	Females	%
Total Disabled	1,007	597	410	
In Seeing	510	301	209	50.65
In Speech	81	47	34	8.04
In Hearing	46	20	26	4.57
In Movement	282	171	111	28
Mentally	88	58	30	8.74

HASANPARTHY

Hasanparthy C.D. Block lies in the western part of Warangal district. It is a part of Hasanparthy Mandal. The Block is located at a distance of 18 kms. from district headquarters (Warangal). There are 18 villages in the block with the total population of 66,615 persons. Area of the C.D. Block is 156.56 sq. kms. It is bound ed in the north by district Karim Nagar, in the south by Warangal Mandals in the east by Atmakur Mandal, and in the west by Dharmasagar Mandal.

Communications:

Roadways : NH- 202: Direction- Warangal to Bijapur. Nearest Village- Vangapahad. State Highway (S.H.): Direction- Karim Nagar to Warangal. Nearest Villages- Ananthasagar, Yellapur, Bhimaram (Rural), Hasanparthy.

Railway Station: Yellapur, Hasanparthy.

Backwards Region Grants Fund: It receives Backward Region Grants.

Annual Rainfall: Average Rainfall 950 mm

Ground Water: Availability of the Ground Water in the Basin is 3884 H.A.M.and the utilization is 2528 H.A. M. It belongs to Safe category. Depth to water level varies from 10 to 20 meter below the ground. Most of the wells go down in summer months. The well density in the entire block is 21 wells per sq. km. Total no. of the wells in the block are enumerated as 3361, according to the Ground Water Estimation Committee.

Natural Division : Godavari Depression Region

Administration:

Division: Telangana. Parliamentary Constituency. District: Warangal. Mandal: Hasanparthy. Assembly Constituency: 107 Wardhanapet (SC). Gram Panchayat: 23.

Villages: 18 **Inhabited:** 17 **Uninhabited:** 1

Ranking	District	State	National
Area	39	795	4933
Population	9	182	4604
Sex Ratio	12	438	1710
Child Sex Ratio	13	363	1315
Literacy Rate	8	388	3421
Density	40	712	2575
Work Participation Rate	4	158	2027

Gram Panchayats:

Ananthasagar, Arvapalle, Bhimaram, Bironpally Chinthagattu, Devannapet, Gunturpally, Hasanparthy Jaigiri, Komatipalli, Madipalle, Mallareddypalle Mucherla, Munipally, Nagaram, Pegadapalle, Pembarthy Seethampeta, Seethanagaram, Siddapur, Sudanpalle Vangapahad, Yellapur.

Amenities:

Education: Primary School in 17 villages, Middle school in 13 villages, Matriculation or Secondary School in 10 villages, namely Yellapur, Bhimaram (Rural), Chinthagattu, Hasanparthy, Mutcherla, Nagaram, Mallareddipalle, Siddhapoor, Pegadapalle, Vangapahad.

Higher Secondary or Pre University Courses or Intermediate or Junior College in 2 villages of the CD Block,, namely Bhimaram (Rural), Hasanparthy.

College in 1 village, Adult Literacy Center in 12 villages., College is in village, namely Bhimaram (Rural).

Medical: Hospital in 1 village, Dispensary in 1 village, Health Center in 1 village, Sub Center in 16 villages, Maternity and Child Welfare Center in 0 village, Community health workers in 0 village.

The Village having Hospital or Dispensary or Health Center is Hasanparthy.

Drinking Water: Tap water in 17 villages, Tank water in 17 villages, Well water in 17 villages, Tubewell in 17 villages and more than one source in 17 villages.

Bank: Banking facility in 5 villages, namely, Yellapur, Bhimaram (Rural), Hasanparthy, Mutcherla Mallareddipalle.

Credit Society in 17 villages Agricultural Credit Society in 7 Non-Agricultural Credit Society in 17 villages.

Others: Power supply in 17 villages, Cinema hall in 2 villages, sport club in 0 village, Stadium or Auditorium or Community Hall in 0 village, Post Office in 17 villages.

There are 17 villages having bus facilities.

Villages with most of facilities: Yellapur Bhimaram (Rural), Hasanparthy, Mutcherla Mallareddipalle.

Villages without Amenities (Education): None..

Scheduled Castes: Out of the total population of 66879 persons, 17838 persons (26.67%) belong to Scheduled Castes.

The villages having less than 10% SC population are None..

The villages having more than 50% SC population are None.

Sex ratio of Scheduled Caste population is 492.

Scheduled Castes Literates and Illiterates by Sex:

	Persons	Males	Females
Literate	7,959	4,885	3,074
Illiterate	9,879	4,176	5,703
Literacy rate	52.3	62.9	41.3
Graduate	138	128	10

Scheduled Castes (Dominant):

Madiga, Mala, Mala Sale etc., Gosangi Beda Jangam etc.

For their cultural identity please see Appendix-I

Villages without Scheduled Castes: There is 1 village without any scheduled caste population.

Scheduled Tribes: Out of the total population of 66879 persons, 3028 persons (4.53%) belong to Scheduled Tribes.

The villages having less than 10% ST population are Ananthasagar, Madipalle, Yellapur, Jaigiri Devannapet, Chinthagattu, Hasanparthy, Pembarthy Mutcherla, Nagaram, Sudanpalle, Mallareddipalle Arvapalle, Pegadapalle, Vangapahad.

The villages having more than 50% ST population are None.

Sex ratio of Scheduled tribe population is 489.

Scheduled Tribes Literates and Illiterates by Sex:

	Persons	Males	Females
Literate	822	557	265
Illiterate	2,206	990	1,216
Literacy rate	34.5	46.4	22.4
Graduate	13	13	0

Scheduled Tribes (Dominant):

Sugalis etc., Yerukulas, Kammara, Koya etc., Yenadis

For their cultural identity please see Appendix-II

Villages without Scheduled Tribes: There are 4 villages without any scheduled tribe population.

Literates and Illiterates by Sex (Total Population):

	Persons	Males	Females
Literate	32,620	20,029	12,591
Illiterate	34,259	13,631	20,628
Literacy rate	56	69	44
Graduate	1,370	1,145	225

Agriculture: ***Distribution of villages according to land use:*** Out of 18 villages, Total area (in hectare) is 15658, out of

that 85.78 percent is cultivable and 66.61 percent of the cultivable area is irrigated.

Sources of Irrigation (Hectares): Government Canal 0, Private Canal 0, Well without Electricity 0, Well with Electricity 6621, Tubewell without Electricity 302, Tubewell with Electricity 0, Tank 2024, River 0, Lake 0, Waterfall 0, Others 0.

Villages with population of 5000 to 9999:
Pegadapalle, Vangapahad.

Villages with population of 10000 and above:
Hasanparthy.

Distribution of Workers:

	Persons	Males	Females	WPR
Cultivators	7,255	4,428	2,827	21.58
Agricultural Labour	14,317	5,092	9,225	42.59
Household Industry	1,762	696	1,066	5.24
Other Workers	10,285	8,473	1,812	30.59
Main Workers	27,399	16,685	10,714	81.5
Marginal Workers	6,220	2,004	4,216	18.5
Total Workers	33,619	18,689	14,930	

Religion: Major Religious Communities:

	Persons	Males	Females	Sex Ratio
Hindu (97.51%)	65,213	32,829	32,384	986
Muslim (1.95%)	1,302	649	653	1,006
Christian (0.45%)	298	146	152	1,041
Sikh (0%)	-	-	-	-
Buddhists (0.01%)	8	5	3	600
Jain (0%)	-	-	-	-

Agewise Data:

	Persons	Males	Females	Sex Ratio
All ages	66,879	33,660	33,219	987
0-14	21,123	10,695	10,428	975
15-44	31,512	15,836	15,676	990
45-79	13,518	6,774	6,744	996
80+	519	245	274	1118
Age not stated	207	110	97	882

Languages (Dominant):
Telugu, Hindi, Urdu, Gondi, Tamil

Disabled Population:

	Persons	Males	Females	%
Total Disabled	1,375	819	556	
In Seeing	737	463	274	53.6
In Speech	141	71	70	10.25
In Hearing	65	35	30	4.73
In Movement	298	180	118	21.67
Mentally	134	70	64	9.75

HATHNOORA

Hathnoora C.D. Block lies in the south-eastern part of Medak district. The Block is located at a distance of 32 kms. from district headquarters (Sangareddy). There are 33 villages in the block with the total population of 49,016 persons. Area of the C.D. Block is 221.05 sq. kms. It is bounded by Kowdipalle Mandal on north, Narsapur Mandal on east, Jinnaram Mandal on south-east, Sangareddy Mandal on south, Pulkal Mandal on west, and Andole Mandal on north-west.

Communications :

Roadways : State Highway (S.H.): Direction- Patancheru to Medak. Nearest Villages- Sirpuram, Lingapur, Madhura, Devalpalle, Taherkhanpet, Malkapur, Chandapur, Turkal Khanapur, Sadullanagar, Chintalcheru,Seri Sirpura, Hathnoora, Kasal.

River: Manjira Nadi- Nearest Villages- Cheekumaddur, Koniyal, Panyal, Reddikhanapur, Borpatla, Palapnoor, Seri Sirpura, Hathnoora, Kasal.

Backwards Region Grants Fund: It receives Backward Region Grants.

Annual Rainfall: Average Rainfall 933 mm

Ground Water: Availability of the Ground Water in the Basin is 1972 H.A.M. and the utilization is 1996 H. A.M. It belongs to Over Exploited category. Depth to water level varies from 5 meter below the ground. Most of the wells go down in summer months. The well density in the entire block is 12 wells per sq. km. Total no. of the wells in the block are enumerated as 2633, according to the Ground Water Estimation Committee.

Natural Division : Telangana Plateau Region

Administration:

Division: Telangana. Parliamentary Constituency: 6 Medak. District: Medak. Mandal: Hathnoora. Assembly Constituency: 37 Narsapur. Gram Panchayat: 23.

Villages: 33 **Inhabited:** 32 **Uninhabited:** 1

Ranking	**District**	**State**	**National**
Area	18	434	3838
Population	23	547	5333
Sex Ratio	16	405	1578
Child Sex Ratio	42	985	4460
Literacy Rate	23	853	5082
Density	21	495	4421
Work Participation Rate	25	638	1284

Gram Panchayats:
Borpatla, Chandapur, Cheekmaddur, Chintalcheru Doultabad, Govindarajpalle, Gundla Machanur Hathnoora, Kasala, Koniyal, Lingapur, Nagaram Naguldevpalle, Nastipur, Nawabpet, Palpanoor, Ponyal Reddikhanapur, Sadullapur, Sikandrapur, Sirpura Turkal Khanapur, Yellammaguda.

Amenities:

Education: Primary School in 32 villages, Middle school in 13 villages, Matriculation or Secondary School in 7 villages, namely Sirpuram, Hathnoora, Kasal, Doultabad,

Borpatla, Turkal Khanapur, Chintalcheru.
Higher Secondary or Pre University Courses or Intermediate or Junior College in 1 village of the CD Block,, namely Hathnoora.
College in 0 village, Adult Literacy Center in 15 villages.
Medical: Hospital in 0 village, Dispensary in 3 villages, Health Center in 2 villages, Sub Center in 9 villages, Maternity and Child Welfare Center in 2 villages, Community health workers in 0 village.
The Villages having Hospital or Dispensary or Health Center are Sirpuram, Hathnoora, Chintalcheru.
Drinking Water: Tap water in 32 villages, Tank water in 31 villages, Well water in 31 villages, Tubewell in 31 villages and more than one source in 31 villages.
Bank: Banking facility in 1 villages, namely, Hathnoora.
Credit Society in 15 villages Agricultural Credit Society in 7 Non-Agricultural Credit Society in 15 villages.
Others: Power supply in 32 villages, Cinema hall in 1 village, sport club in 0 village, Stadium or Auditorium or Community Hall in 0 village, Post Office in 11 villages.
There are 26 villages having bus facilities.
Village with most of facilities: Hathnoora.
Villages without Amenities (Education): None..
Scheduled Castes: Out of the total population of 49016 persons, 9718 persons (19.83%) belong to Scheduled Castes.
The villages having less than 10% SC population are Sirpuram, Lingapur, Madhura, Taherkhanpet, Kodapak Shairkhanpalle.
The villages having more than 50% SC population are None.
Sex ratio of Scheduled Caste population is 503.
Scheduled Castes Literates and Illiterates by Sex:

	Persons	Males	Females
Literate	2,743	1,811	932
Illiterate	6,975	3,023	3,952
Literacy rate	33.8	45.4	22.6
Graduate	21	19	2

Scheduled Castes (Dominant):
Madiga, Mala, Beda Jangam etc., Generic Castes etc. Byagara
For their cultural identity please see Appendix-I
Villages without Scheduled Castes: There are 3 villages without any scheduled caste population.
Scheduled Tribes: Out of the total population of 49016 persons, 2473 persons (5.05%) belong to Scheduled Tribes.
The villages having less than 10% ST population are Lingapur, Cheekumaddur, Koniyal, Panyal, Madhura Govindarajupalle, Naguldevpalle, Hathnoora, Kasal Devalpalle, Doultabad, Mangapur, Nastipur, Macherla Taherkhanpet, Malkapur, Reddikhanapur, Borpatla Palapnoor, Gundla Machanur, Chandapur Turkal Khanapur, Sadullanagar, Yellammaguda, Kodapak Nagaram, Shairkhanpalle, Royyapalle, Akwanchaguda.
The villages having more than 50% ST population are None.
Sex ratio of Scheduled tribe population is 485.
Scheduled Tribes Literates and Illiterates by Sex:

	Persons	Males	Females
Literate	630	463	167
Illiterate	1,843	811	1,032
Literacy rate	32.2	46.7	17.3
Graduate	1	1	0

Scheduled Tribes (Dominant):
Sugalis etc., Yerukulas, Koya etc.
Generic Tribes etc., Thoti
For their cultural identity please see Appendix-II
Villages without Scheduled Tribes: There are 16 villages without any scheduled tribe population.
Literates and Illiterates by Sex (Total Population):

	Persons	Males	Females
Literate	19,000	12,393	6,607
Illiterate	30,016	12,232	17,784
Literacy rate	46	60	32
Graduate	360	311	49

Agriculture: ***Distribution of villages according to land use:*** Out of 33 villages, Total area (in hectare) is 22105, out of that 79.64 percent is cultivable and 39.67 percent of the cultivable area is irrigated.
Sources of Irrigation (Hectares): Government Canal 159, Private Canal 0, Well without Electricity 0, Well with Electricity 0, Tubewell without Electricity 0, Tubewell with Electricity 3467.29, Tank 3330.83, River 0.2, Lake 0, Waterfall 0, Others 26.
Villages with population of 5000 to 9999: None
Villages with population of 10000 and above: None
Distribution of Workers:

	Persons	Males	Females	WPR
Cultivators	8,313	5,658	2,655	32.8
Agricultural Labour	11,798	4,446	7,352	46.54
Household Industry	1,076	518	558	4.24
Other Workers	4,161	3,291	870	16.42
Main Workers	17,616	11,135	6,481	69.5
Marginal Workers	7,732	2,778	4,954	30.5
Total Workers	25,348	13,913	11,435	

Religion: Major Religious Communities:

	Persons	Males	Females	Sex Ratio
Hindu (89.39%)	43,817	21,967	21,850	995
Muslim (9.2%)	4,511	2,313	2,198	950
Christian (1.15%)	566	282	284	1,007

Sikh (0.01%)	5	3	2	667
Buddhists (0.03%)	16	8	8	1,000
Jain (0.06%)	27	18	9	500

Agewise Data:

	Persons	Males	Females	Sex Ratio
All ages	49,016	24,625	24,391	990
0-14	17,089	8,813	8,276	939
15-44	22,037	11,041	10,996	996
45-79	9,475	4,563	4,912	1076
80+	355	171	184	1076
Age not stated	60	37	23	622

Languages (Dominant):

Telugu, Urdu, Hindi, Gujarati, Tamil

Disabled Population:

	Persons	Males	Females	%
Total Disabled	767	420	347	
In Seeing	364	188	176	47.46
In Speech	84	45	39	10.95
In Hearing	38	20	18	4.95
In Movement	196	117	79	25.55
Mentally	85	50	35	11.08

HAYATHNAGAR

Hayathnagar C.D. Block lies in the north-east part of Rangareddy district. It is a part of Hayathnagar Mandal. The Block is located at a distance of 26 kms. from district headquarters (Serilingampalle). There are 33 villages in the block with the total population of 98,181 persons. Area of the C.D. Block is 226.30 sq. kms. It is bounded by Ghatkesar Mandal on north, Nalgonda district on east, Ibrahamipatnam Mandal on south, Saroornagar Mandal on west, and Uppal Mandal on north-west.

Communications :

Roadways : NH- 9: Direction- Hyderabad to Nalgonda. Nearest Villages- Hathiguda, Kalvancha, Pedda Amberpet (Kalan), Laskerguda, Inamguda, Abdullapur, Batasingaram, Sagarpump, Mazidpur.

River: Musi Nadi- Nearest Villages- Marripalle, Qutubul lapur, Thimmaiguda, Gowrelli, Bacharam, Daira, Bandaravi ryal, Guntapalle, Piglipur, Batasingaram, Sagarpump, Mazidpur.

Integrated Child Development Scheme (ICDS) Project: Hayathnagar, Total Anganwadi Centres: 215

Backwards Region Grants Fund: It receives Backward Region Grants.

Annual Rainfall: Average Rainfall 730 mm

Ground Water: Availability of the Ground Water in the Basin is 2283 H.A.M. and the utilization is 1609 H. A.M. It belongs to Semi Critical category. Depth to water level varies from 2 to 20 meter below the ground. Most of the wells go down in summer months. The well density in the entire block is 5 wells per sq. km. Total no. of the wells in the block are enumerated as 1234, according to the Ground Water Estimation Commi ttee.

Natural Division : Telangana Plateau Region

Administration:

Division: Telangana. Parliamentary Constituency: 4 Bhongir. District: Rangareddy.

Mandal: Hayathnagar. Assembly Constituency: 48 Ibrahimp atnam. Gram Panchayat: 27.

Villages: 33 **Inhabited:** 28 **Uninhabited:** 5

Ranking	District	State	National
Area	12	404	3721
Population	4	158	4543
Sex Ratio	32	1081	4515
Child Sex Ratio	10	247	822
Literacy Rate	5	217	2389
Density	29	1004	3505
Work Participation Rate	9	365	3837

Gram Panchayats:

Abdullapur, Anajpur, Bacharam, Balijaguda Bandaraviryal, Batasingaram, Brahamanpally Chinnaraviryal, Gandicheruvu, Gowrelli, Injapur Kammaguda, Kawadipally, Koheda, Kuntloor, Laskerguda Mazidpur, Munganoor, Omarkhandaira, Pasmamla Pedda Amberpet, Qutbullapur, Ragannaguda Tattiannaram, Tharamatipet, Thorur, Thurkayamjal.

Amenities:

Education: Primary School in 27 villages, Middle school in 15 villages, Matriculation or Secondary School in 11 villages, namely Qutubullapur, Bacharam, Tharamathipet, Turkayamjal, Toroor (Faroor), Pedda Amberpet (Kalan), Koheda, Anajpur, Abdullapur, Kawadipalle, Batasingaram.

Higher Secondary or Pre University Courses or Intermediate or Junior College in 0 village of the CD Block, College in 1 village, Adult Literacy Center in 4 villages., College is in village, namely Pedda Amberpet (Kalan).

Medical: Hospital in 2 villages, Dispensary in 3 villages, Health Center in 2 villages, Sub Center in 7 villages, Maternity and Child Welfare Center in 1 village, Community health workers in 0 village.

The Villages having Hospital or Dispensary or Health Center are Qutubullapur, Bandaraviryal, Pasmamla, Koheda, Batasingaram.

Drinking Water: Tap water in 28 villages, Tank water in 28 villages, Well water in 28 villages, Tubewell in 28 villages and more than one source in 28 villages.

Bank: Banking facility in 28 villages, namely,

Tatti Annaram, Tatti Khana, Marripalle, Qutubullapur Thimmaiguda, Gowrelli, Bacharam, Bandaraviryal Tharamathipet, Baljaguda, Pasmamla, Kalvancha Turkayamjal, Manneguda, Toroor (Faroor), Munganoor Pedda Amberpet (Kalan), Koheda, Anajpur, Guntapalle Surmaiguda, Laskerguda, Inamguda, Abdullapur Kawadipalle, Batasingaram, Piglipur, Mazidpur.

Credit Society in 9 villages Agricultural Credit Society in 3 Non-Agricultural Credit Society in 8 villages.

Others: Power supply in 28 villages, Cinema hall in 0 village, sport club in 0 village, Stadium or Auditorium or Community Hall in 0 village, Post Office in 14 villages.

There are 28 villages having bus facilities.

Villages with most of facilities: Tatti Annaram Qutubullapur, Bandaraviryal, Tharamathipet, Pasmamla Turkayamjal, Toroor (Faroor), Pedda Amberpet (Kalan) Koheda, Anajpur, Guntapalle, Abdullapur Batasingaram, Mazidpur.

Villages without amenities (Education): Manneguda..

Scheduled Castes: Out of the total population of 68200 persons, 12917 persons (18.94%) belong to Scheduled Castes.

The villages having less than 10% SC population are Tatti Khana, Thimmaiguda, Kalvancha, Inamguda Mazidpur.

The villages having more than 50% SC population are None.

Sex ratio of Scheduled Caste population is 483.

Scheduled Castes Literates and Illiterates by Sex:

	Persons	Males	Females
Literate	5,502	3,538	1,964
Illiterate	7,415	3,142	4,273
Literacy rate	50.6	62.6	37.7
Graduate	60	50	10

Scheduled Castes (Dominant):

Madiga, Mala, Beda Jangam etc., Generic Castes etc. Bindla

For their cultural identity please see Appendix-I

Villages without Scheduled Castes: There are 7 villages without any scheduled caste population.

Scheduled Tribes: Out of the total population of 68200 persons, 638 persons (0.94%) belong to Scheduled Tribes.

The villages having less than 10% ST population are Tatti Annaram, Marripalle, Qutubullapur, Thimmaiguda Gowrelli, Bacharam, Bandaraviryal, Tharamathipet Baljaguda, Pasmamla, Kalvancha, Turkayamjal Manneguda, Toroor (Faroor), Munganoor Pedda Amberpet (Kalan), Koheda, Anajpur, Guntapalle Surmaiguda, Laskerguda, Inamguda, Abdullapur Kawadipalle, Batasingaram, Piglipur, Mazidpur.

The villages having more than 50% ST population are None.

Sex ratio of Scheduled tribe population is 475.

Scheduled Tribes Literates and Illiterates by Sex:

	Persons	Males	Females
Literate	267	178	89
Illiterate	371	157	214
Literacy rate	50.5	63.1	36.0
Graduate	7	7	0

Scheduled Tribes (Dominant):

Yerukulas, Sugalis etc., Koya etc., Chenchu etc. Yenadis

For their cultural identity please see Appendix-II

Villages without Scheduled Tribes: There are 12 villages without any scheduled tribe population.

Literates and Illiterates by Sex (Total Population):

	Persons	Males	Females
Literate	36,298	22,160	14,138
Illiterate	31,902	13,186	18,716
Literacy rate	62	73	51
Graduate	1,521	1,160	361

Agriculture: ***Distribution of villages according to land use:*** Out of 33 villages, Total area (in hectare) is 22630, out of that 10.37 percent is cultivable and 55.46 percent of the cultivable area is irrigated.

Sources of Irrigation (Hectares): Government Canal 378.61, Private Canal 0, Well without Electricity 0, Well with Electricity 174.82, Tubewell without Electricity 15.53, Tubewell with Electricity 398.05, Tank 332.25, River 0, Lake 0, Waterfall 0, Others 2.83.

Villages with population of 5000 to 9999: Turkayamjal, Pedda Amberpet (Kalan), Koheda.

Villages with population of 10000 and above: None

Distribution of Workers:

	Persons	Males	Females	WPR
Cultivators	3,153	2,135	1,018	10.91
Agricultural Labour	6,743	2,674	4,069	23.33
Household Industry	1,240	713	527	4.29
Other Workers	17,762	14,074	3,688	61.46
Main Workers	22,848	16,974	5,874	79.06
Marginal Workers	6,050	2,622	3,428	20.94
Total Workers	28,898	19,596	9,302	

Religion: Major Religious Communities:

	Persons	Males	Females	Sex Ratio
Hindu (92.55%)	63,121	32,755	30,366	927
Muslim (4.64%)	3,167	1,627	1,540	947
Christian (2.65%)	1,809	917	892	973
Sikh (0.04%)	29	12	17	1,417
Buddhists (0%)	-	-	-	-
Jain (0%)	-	-	-	-

Agewise Data:

	Persons	Males	Females	Sex Ratio
All ages	68,200	35,346	32,854	929
0-14	22,849	11,455	11,394	995
15-44	33,880	17,948	15,932	888
45-79	10,867	5,650	5,217	923
80+	511	243	268	1103
Age not stated	93	50	43	860

Languages (Dominant):

Telugu, Urdu, Tamil, Hindi, Marathi

Disabled Population:

	Persons	Males	Females	%
Total Disabled	1,111	678	433	
In Seeing	348	215	133	31.32
In Speech	96	49	47	8.64
In Hearing	80	52	28	7.2
In Movement	439	279	160	39.51
Mentally	148	83	65	13.32

HINDUPUR

Hindupur C.D. Block lies in the southern part of Ananta pur district. It is a part of Hindupur Mandal. The Block is located at a distance of 112 kms. from district headquarters (Anantapur). There are 14 villages in the block with the total population of 45,646 persons. Area of the C.D. Block is 158.69 sq. kms. It is bounded in the north by Mandal Somandepalle, in the east by Mandals Gorantla, Chilamathur, Lepakshi, in the west by Mandal Parigi, and it has common boundary with the state of Karnataka in the east and west.

Communications:

Roadways : State Highway (S.H.): Direction- Bangalore to Penukonda. Nearest Villages- Manesamudram, Kirikera, Devarapalle, Thumukunta.

Railway Station: Maluguru.

River: Pennar Nadi- Nearest Villages- Bevina Halli, Nakkalapalle, Santhebidanur, Chowlur, Kirikera, Devara palle, Thumukunta..

It receives the Backward Region Grants, and is identifi ed as a drought-prone area as well.

Integrated Child Development Scheme (ICDS) Project: Hindupur, Total Anganwadi Centres: 375

Annual Rainfall: Average Rainfall 667 mm

Ground Water: Availability of the Ground Water in the Basin is 2039 H.A.M. and the utilization is 2093 H. A.M. It belongs to OE category. Depth to water level varies from 10 to 20 meter below the ground. Most of the wells go down in summer months. The well density in the entire block is 9 wells per sq. km. Total no. of the wells in the block are enumerated as 2369, according to the Ground Water Estimation Committee.

Natural Division : Rayalaseema Region

Administration:

Division: Rayala Seema. Parliamentary Constituency: 37 Hindupur. District: Anantapur.

Mandal: Hindupur. Assembly Constituency: 276 Hindupur. Gram Panchayat: 14.

Border Villages: (Karnataka)- Nearest Villages- Bevina Halli, Nakkalapalle, Kotipi, Santhebidanur, Thungepalle, Chowlur, Thumukunta, Gollapuram.

Places of Tourist Interest:

Hindupur : Hindupur is situated at a distance of 105 kms. from Anantapur and it is an important commercial centre in the area. It is a railway station on the Guntakal-Bangalore line. An ancient Anjaneya- swamy temple, the Guddam-Ranga-swamy temple and the PetaVenka ta Ramaswamy temple deserve mention.

Villages: 14 **Inhabited:** 14 **Uninhabited:** 0

Ranking	District	State	National
Area	57	777	4896
Population	26	643	5480
Sex Ratio	45	997	3551
Child Sex Ratio	9	93	243
Literacy Rate	3	361	3255
Density	59	788	3666
Work Participation Rate	2	408	2333

Gram Panchayats:

Balampalli, Beerepalli, Bevina Halli, Chalivendala Chowlur, Gollapuram, Kaggallu, Kirikera, Kotipi Maluguru, Manesamudram, Pulakunta, Santhebidanur Thumukunta.

Amenities:

Education: Primary School in 14 villages, Middle school in 8 villages, Matriculation or Secondary School in 5 villages, namely Maluguru, Chalivendala, Kirikera, Santhebidanur, Chowlur.

Higher Secondary or Pre University Courses or Inter-mediate or Junior College in 1 village of the CD Block,, namely Maluguru.

College in 0 village, Adult Literacy Center in 6 villages.

Medical: Hospital in 0 village, Dispensary in 3 villages, Health Center in 2 villages, Sub Center in 8 villages, Maternity and Child Welfare Center in 0 village, Community health workers in 0 village.

The Villages having Hospital or Dispensary or Health Center are Sreekanthapuram (Rural), Kirikera, Santhebidanur.

Drinking Water: Tap water in 14 villages, Tank water in 0 villages, Well water in 0 village, Tubewell in 12 villages and more than one source in 14 villages.

Bank: Banking facility in 1 villages, namely, Kirikera.

Credit Society in 4 villages Agricultural Credit Society in 4 Non-Agricultural Credit Society in 0 village.

Others: Power supply in 14 villages, Cinema hall in 0 village, sport club in 0 village, Stadium or Auditorium or Community Hall in 0 village, Post Office in 13 villages.

There are 14 villages having bus facilities.

Village with most of facilities: Kirikera.

Villages without Amenities (Education): None..

Scheduled Castes: Out of the total population of 45569 persons, 8476 persons (18.6%) belong to Scheduled Castes.

The villages having less than 10% SC population are None..

The villages having more than 50% SC population are None.

Sex ratio of Scheduled Caste population is 469.

Scheduled Castes Literates and Illiterates by Sex:

	Persons	Males	Females
Literate	3,522	2,420	1,102
Illiterate	4,954	2,077	2,877
Literacy rate	48.3	62.0	32.5
Graduate	36	33	3

Scheduled Castes (Dominant):

Madiga, Mala

For their cultural identity please see Appendix-I

Villages without Scheduled Castes: There is 1 village without any scheduled caste population.

Scheduled Tribes: Out of the total population of 45569 persons, 263 persons (0.58%) belong to Scheduled Tribes.

The villages having less than 10% ST population are Manesamudram, Maluguru, Chalivendala Sreekanthapuram (Rural), Bevina Halli, Nakkalapalle Kirikera, Kotipi, Devarapalle, Santhebidanur Thungepalle, Chowlur, Thumukunta, Gollapuram.

The villages having more than 50% ST population are None.

Sex ratio of Scheduled tribe population is 479.

Scheduled Tribes Literates and Illiterates by Sex:

	Persons	Males	Females
Literate	139	88	51
Illiterate	124	49	75
Literacy rate	62.9	74.6	49.5
Graduate	4	3	1

Scheduled Tribes (Dominant):

Yerukulas, Sugalis etc., Generic Tribes etc.

For their cultural identity please see Appendix-II

Villages without Scheduled Tribes: There are 8 villages without any scheduled tribe population.

Literates and Illiterates by Sex (Total Population):

	Persons	Males	Females
Literate	22,528	14,113	8,415
Illiterate	23,041	9,264	13,777
Literacy rate	57	70	44
Graduate	472	366	106

Agriculture: *Distribution of villages according to land use:* Out of 14 villages, Total area (in hectare) is 15868, out of that 66.58 percent is cultivable and 21.71 percent of the cultivable area is irrigated.

Sources of Irrigation (Hectares): Government Canal 0, Private Canal 0, Well without Electricity 0, Well with Electricity 601.12, Tubewell without Electricity 0, Tubewell with Electricity 1615.93, Tank 77.09, River 0, Lake 0, Waterfall 0, Others 0.

Villages with population of 5000 to 9999: Maluguru, Chalivendala, Kirikera, Chowlur.

Villages with population of 10000 and above: None

Distribution of Workers:

	Persons	Males	Females	WPR
Cultivators	5,940	4,239	1,701	26.57
Agricultural Labour	9,207	4,376	4,831	41.19
Household Industry	1,452	941	511	6.5
Other Workers	5,754	4,433	1,321	25.74
Main Workers	19,202	12,826	6,376	85.9
Marginal Workers	3,151	1,163	1,988	14.1
Total Workers	22,353	13,989	8,364	

Religion: Major Religious Communities:

	Persons	Males	Females	Sex Ratio
Hindu (90.67%)	41,317	21,211	20,106	948
Muslim (9.18%)	4,181	2,127	2,054	966
Christian (0.12%)	53	28	25	893
Sikh (0%)	1	1	-	-
Buddhists (0%)	-	-	-	-
Jain (0.04%)	16	9	7	778

Agewise Data:

	Persons	Males	Females	Sex Ratio
All ages	45,569	23,377	22,192	949
0-14	14,838	7,626	7,212	946
15-44	21,608	11,096	10,512	947
45-79	8,777	4,487	4,290	956
80+	317	148	169	1142
Age not stated	29	20	9	450

Languages (Dominant):

Telugu, Urdu, Kannada, Marathi, Tamil

Disabled Population:

	Persons	Males	Females	%
Total Disabled	701	393	308	
In Seeing	226	112	114	32.24
In Speech	92	52	40	13.12
In Hearing	44	21	23	6.28
In Movement	244	155	89	34.81
Mentally	95	53	42	13.55

HIRAMANDALAM

Hiramandalam C.D. Block lies in the northern part of Srikakulam district. The Block is located at a distance of 43 kms. from district headquarters (Srikakulam). There are 40 villages in the block with the total population of 46,204 persons. Area of the C.D. Block is 103,13 sq. kms. It is bounded in the north by Mandals Kothuru and Pathapatnam, in the south by Mandals Seeth ampeta, Sarubujjili, Jalumuru and Saravakota, in the east by Mandals Pathapatnam and Saravakota, and in the west by Mandals Kothuru and Seethampeta.

Communications:

Roadways : Metalled Roads: Nearest Villages- Peddasankili, Korada, Kondakorada, Hiramandalam.

River: Vamsadhara Nadi- Nearest Villages- Komanapalle, Gulumuru, Durbalapuram, Tungatampara, Chorlangi, Gotta, Godiapadu, Korada, Hiramandalam, Mahalakshimipuram, Bhagiradhipuram, Pindruvada, Ambavalli, Majjigudem, Rellivalasa. Mahendravaram Nadi- Nearset Villages- Komanapalle, Mokhasa Avalangi, Kallata, Tampa.

Backwards Region Grants Fund: It receives Backward Region Grants.

Annual Rainfall: Average Rainfall 1085.6 mm

Ground Water: Availability of the Ground Water in the Basin is (Information not avavible) H.A.M .and the utilization is (Information not avavible) H.A.M. It belongs to (Information not avavible) category. Depth to water level varies from 3 to 10 meter below the ground. Most of the wells go down in summer months.

Forest and Reserved **Forest:** Nearest Villages- Majjigudem, Seedhi, Satyajagannadha Puram, Kittalapadu, Anthakapa lle.

Administration:

Division: Coastal Andhra. Parliamentary Constituency: 19 Srikakulam. District: Srikakulam. Mandal: Hiramandal am. Assembly Constituency: 123 Pathapatnam. Gram Panchay at: 23.

Villages: 40 **Inhabited:** 36 **Uninhabited:** 4

Ranking	District	State	National
Area	34	1017	5683
Population	31	627	5458
Sex Ratio	18	144	812
Child Sex Ratio	2	84	204
Literacy Rate	10	366	3300
Density	20	756	2464
Work Participation Rate	19	143	2208

Gram Panchayats:

Akkarapalli, Ambavellia, B R Puram
Chinnakollivalasa, Chorlangi, Dhanupuram, Duggupuram
Garlapadu, Gotta, Gulumuru, Hiramandalam, Kallata
Kittalapadu, Komanapalli, Kondaragolu
Mahalaximi Puram, Padali, Peddasankili, Pindruvada
Rugada, Tampa, Thungathampara, Tulagam.

Amenities:

Education: Primary School in 34 villages, Middle school in 13 villages, Matriculation or Secondary School in 3 villages, namely Tulagam, Hiramandalam, Bhagiradhipuram. Higher Secondary or Pre University Courses or Intermediate or Junior College in 1 village of the CD Block,, namely Hiramandalam.

College in 1 village, Adult Literacy Center in 19 villages., College is in village, namely Hiramandalam.

Medical: Hospital in 2 villages, Dispensary in 2 villages, Health Center in 1 village, Sub Center in 11 villages, Maternity and Child Welfare Center in 0 village, Community health workers in 0 village.

The Villages having Hospital or Dispensary or Health Center are Gulumuru, Korada, Hiramandalam.

Drinking Water: Tap water in 36 villages, Tank water in 36 villages, Well water in 36 villages, Tubewell in 36 villages and more than one source in 36 villages.

Bank: Banking facility in 2 villages, namely, Korada, Hiramandalam.

Credit Society in 8 villages Agricultural Credit Society in 5 Non-Agricultural Credit Society in 4 villages.

Others: Power supply in 36 villages, Cinema hall in 2 villages, sport club in 0 village, Stadium or Auditorium or Community Hall in 0 village, Post Office in 15 villages.

There are 24 villages having bus facilities.

Villages with most of facilities: Korada Hiramandalam.

Villages without amenities (Education): Tallapadu, Lingupuram..

Scheduled Castes: Out of the total population of 46204 persons, 6281 persons (13.59%) belong to Scheduled Castes. The villages having less than 10% SC population are Jagannadhapuram, Kondaragolu, Durbalapuram Tungatampara, Chorlangi, Mokhasa Avalangi, Tampa Lokonda, Anthili, Mahalakshimipuram, Bhagiradhipuram Mamidijola, Tallapadu, Lingupuram, Neeladevipuram Seedhi, Satyajagannadha Puram, Kittalapadu Anthakapalle.

The villages having more than 50% SC population are None.

Sex ratio of Scheduled Caste population is 500.

Scheduled Castes Literates and Illiterates by Sex:

	Persons	Males	Females
Literate	2,658	1,625	1,033
Illiterate	3,623	1,516	2,107
Literacy rate	49.0	59.9	38.1
Graduate	64	55	9

Scheduled Castes (Dominant):

Mala, Madiga, Relli, Dom etc., Pamidi

For their cultural identity please see Appendix-I

Villages without Scheduled Castes: There are 16 villages without any scheduled caste population.

Scheduled Tribes: Out of the total population of 46204 persons, 4382 persons (9.48%) belong to Scheduled Tribes. The villages having less than 10% ST population are Komanapalle, Gulumuru, Kondaragolu, Duggupuram Durbalapuram, Tungatampara, Kallata, Tampa, Gotta Korada, Padali, Garlapadu, Chinnakollivalasa Tulagam, Hiramandalam, Mahalakshimipuram Bhagiradhipuram, Lingupuram, Neeladevipuram Pindruvada, Ambavalli, Rellivalasa.

The villages having more than 50% ST population are Lokonda, Anthili, Mamidijola, Satyajagannadha Puram Anthakapalle.

Sex ratio of Scheduled tribe population is 510.

Scheduled Tribes Literates and Illiterates by Sex:

	Persons	Males	Females
Literate	1,840	1,067	773
Illiterate	2,542	1,081	1,461
Literacy rate	49.6	58.5	41.0
Graduate	11	9	2

Scheduled Tribes (Dominant):

Savaras etc., Jatapus, Konda Dhoras, Gadabas Yenadis

For their cultural identity please see Appendix-II

Villages without Scheduled Tribes: There are 14 villages without any scheduled tribe population.

Literates and Illiterates by Sex (Total Population):

	Persons	Males	Females
Literate	22,780	13,584	9,196
Illiterate	23,424	9,370	14,054
Literacy rate	57	69	46
Graduate	723	636	87

Agriculture: ***Distribution of villages according to land use:*** Out of 40 villages, Total area (in hectare) is 10310, out of that 69.43 percent is cultivable and 51.6 percent of the cultivable area is irrigated.

Sources of Irrigation (Hectares): Government Canal 501.13, Private Canal 0, Well without Electricity 0, Well with Electricity 0, Tubewell without Electricity 0, Tubewell with Electricity 0, Tank 3136.77, River 55.74, Lake 0, Waterfall 0, Others 0.

Villages with population of 5000 to 9999: Korada, Hiramandalam.

Villages with population of 10000 and above: None

Distribution of Workers:

	Persons	Males	Females	WPR
Cultivators	5,406	3,471	1,935	23.61
Agricultural Labour	12,019	5,795	6,224	52.48
Household Industry	888	472	416	3.88
Other Workers	4,588	3,738	850	20.03
Main Workers	17,111	11,720	5,391	74.72
Marginal Workers	5,790	1,756	4,034	25.28
Total Workers	22,901	13,476	9,425	

Religion: Major Religious Communities:

	Persons	Males	Females	Sex Ratio
Hindu (99.22%)	45,842	22,781	23,061	1,012
Muslim (0.17%)	77	31	46	1,484
Christian (0.52%)	240	117	123	1,051
Sikh (0%)	-	-	-	-
Buddhists (0%)	-	-	-	-
Jain (0%)	-	-	-	-

Agewise Data:

	Persons	Males	Females	Sex Ratio
All ages	46,204	22,954	23,250	1013
0-14	14,643	7,487	7,156	956
15-44	21,940	10,907	11,033	1012
45-79	9,263	4,394	4,869	1108
80+	304	141	163	1156
Age not stated	54	25	29	1160

Languages (Dominant):

Telugu, Oriya, Savara, Urdu, Gondi

Disabled Population:

	Persons	Males	Females	%
Total Disabled	925	523	402	
In Seeing	413	224	189	44.65
In Speech	82	40	42	8.86
In Hearing	79	42	37	8.54
In Movement	265	162	103	28.65
Mentally	86	55	31	9.3

HOLAGUNDA

Holagonda C.D. Block lies in the western part of Kurnool district. The Block is located at a distance of 115 kms. from district headquarters (Kurnool). There are 20 villages in the block with the total population of 46,359 persons. Area of the C.D. Block is 327.32 sq. kms. It is bounded in the north by Mandal Adoni, in the south by Mandal Halaharvi, in the east by Manda ls Adoni and Dalalur, in the west by River Hagari, and it has boundary with the state of Karnataka in the west.

Communications:

Roadways : Metalled Roads: Nearest Villages- Vandavagali, Hebbatam, Lingadahalli, Neraniki, Yellarthy, Chinnahyta, Holagunda, Marlamadiki, Peddahyta.

River: Hagari Nadi- Nearest Villages- Honnur, Nagarakan vi, Marlamadiki, Muddatamagi, Kogilathota.

It is identified as a drought-prone area.
Annual Rainfall: Average Rainfall 569 mm
Ground Water: Availability of the Ground Water in the Basin is 3250 H.A.M. and the utilization is 696 H.A. M. It belongs to Safe category. Depth to water level varies from 5 to 10 meter below the ground. Most of the wells go down in summer months. The well density in the entire block is 2 wells per sq. km. Total no. of the wells in the block are enumerated as 494, according to the Ground Water Estimation Committee.
Forest and Reserved **Forest:** Nearest Villages- Neraniki, Yellarthy, Holagunda, Peddahyta, Mugumangondi, Suluvoy.
Natural Division : Rayalaseema Region
Administration: Division: Rayala Seema
Parliamentary Constituency: 35 Kurnool. District: Kurnool. Mandal: Holagunda. Assembly Constituency: 266 Alur. Gram Panchayat: 17.
Border Villages: (Karnataka)- Nearest Villages- Gajjehalli, Holagunda, Honnur, Nagarakanvi, Marlamadiki, Muddatamagi, Kogilathota.
Fairs and Festivals:
Sri Honnurswamy Urs : It is celebrated for four days from Kartika Bahula Vidiya (November-December) at Honnur. On Vidiya, there is gandham puja, on Tadiya and Chaviti, there is deeparadhana and on Panchami, there is procession. On the urs day, the sword used by the Swamy is decorated with flowers and is taken in procession on horseback. On gandhothsavam day, gandham is distributed to all. The devotees name the horses, cows and bullocks after him and leave them free in fulfilment of vows. On the next day of the urs, goats and sheep are sacrified to the Swamy. It is being celebrated for the past two and a half centuries. There are the tombs of Sri Honnurswamy and of Gomata, and a dargah at Honnur.

Villages: 20 **Inhabited:** 20 **Uninhabited:** 0

Ranking	District	State	National
Area	16	110	2488
Population	31	624	5452
Sex Ratio	16	665	2237
Child Sex Ratio	21	559	2147
Literacy Rate	46	1026	5844
Density	18	144	5677
Work Participation Rate	39	932	419

Gram Panchayats:
Chinnahyta, Gajjehalli, Hebbatam, Holagunda, Honnur
Ingaladahal, Kogilathota, Lingadahalli
Maddi Lingadahalli, Marlamadiki, Neraniki
Neraniki Thanda, Pedda Gonehal, Sammathagiri
Suluvoy, Vandavagali, Yellarthy.

Amenities:
Education: Primary School in 20 villages, Middle school in 3 villages, Matriculation or Secondary School in 2 villages, namely Ingaladahal, Holagunda.
Higher Secondary or Pre University Courses or Intermediate or Junior College in 0 village of the CD Block, College in 0 village, Adult Literacy Center in 17 villages.
Medical: Hospital in 0 village, Dispensary in 1 village, Health Center in 1 village, Sub Center in 5 villages, Maternity and Child Welfare Center in 0 village, Community health workers in 0 village.
The Village having Hospital or Dispensary or Health Center is Ingaladahal.
Drinking Water: Tap water in 20 villages, Tank water in 20 villages, Well water in 20 villages, Tubewell in 20 villages and more than one source in 20 villages.
Bank: Banking facility in 2 villages, namely, Hebbatam, Holagunda.
Credit Society in 5 villages Agricultural Credit Society in 5 Non-Agricultural Credit Society in 3 villages.
Others: Power supply in 20 villages, Cinema hall in 1 village, sport club in 0 village, Stadium or Auditorium or Community Hall in 0 village, Post Office in 14 villages.
There are 18 villages having bus facilities.
Villages with most of facilities: Hebbatam Holagunda.
Villages without Amenities (Education): None..
Scheduled Castes: Out of the total population of 46359 persons, 6781 persons (14.63%) belong to Scheduled Castes.
The villages having less than 10% SC population are None..
The villages having more than 50% SC population are None.
Sex ratio of Scheduled Caste population is 494.
Scheduled Castes Literates and Illiterates by Sex:

	Persons	Males	Females
Literate	1,543	1,089	454
Illiterate	5,238	2,343	2,895
Literacy rate	27.7	39.0	16.3
Graduate	26	26	0

Scheduled Castes (Dominant):
Madiga, Mala, Bariki, Byagara, Mala Dasari
For their cultural identity please see Appendix-I
Villages without Scheduled Castes: There is 1 village without any scheduled caste population.
Scheduled Tribes: Out of the total population of 46359 persons, 1580 persons (3.41%) belong to Scheduled Tribes.
The villages having less than 10% ST population are
Gajjehalli, Vandavagali, Ingaladahal
Maddi Lingadahalli, Pedda Gonehal, Hebbatam

Lingadahalli, Yellarthy, Chinnahyta, Holagunda Honnur, Nagarakanvi, Marlamadiki, Muddatamagi Kogilathota, Peddahyta, Sammathagiri, Mugumangondi Suluvoy.

The villages having more than 50% ST population are None.

Sex ratio of Scheduled tribe population is 496.

Scheduled Tribes Literates and Illiterates by Sex:

	Persons	Males	Females
Literate	394	296	98
Illiterate	1,186	501	685
Literacy rate	31.2	46.3	15.7
Graduate	17	16	1

Scheduled Tribes (Dominant):

Sugalis etc., Yerukulas, Kammara

For their cultural identity please see Appendix-II

Villages without Scheduled Tribes: There are 8 villages without any scheduled tribe population.

Literates and Illiterates by Sex (Total Population):

	Persons	Males	Females
Literate	14,460	9,816	4,644
Illiterate	31,899	13,660	18,239
Literacy rate	38	51	25
Graduate	348	305	43

Agriculture: ***Distribution of villages according to land use:*** Out of 20 villages, Total area (in hectare) is 32732, out of that 76.63 percent is cultivable and 15.15 percent of the cultivable area is irrigated.

Sources of Irrigation (Hectares): Government Canal 2219, Private Canal 0, Well without Electricity 0, Well with Electricity 91, Tubewell without Electricity 0, Tubewell with Electricity 559, Tank 183, River 0, Lake 0, Waterfall 0, Others 747.

Villages with population of 5000 to 9999: None

Villages with population of 10000 and above: Holagunda.

Distribution of Workers:

	Persons	Males	Females	WPR
Cultivators	9,742	6,172	3,570	38.42
Agricultural Labour	12,958	5,606	7,352	51.1
Household Industry	393	202	191	1.55
Other Workers	2,263	1,703	560	8.92
Main Workers	21,185	12,258	8,927	83.55
Marginal Workers	4,171	1,425	2,746	16.45
Total Workers	25,356	13,683	11,673	

Religion: Major Religious Communities:

	Persons	Males	Females	Sex Ratio
Hindu (86.31%)	40,014	20,271	19,743	974
Muslim (13.31%)	6,171	3,119	3,052	979
Christian (0.3%)	140	70	70	1,000
Sikh (0%)	-	-	-	-
Buddhists (0%)	-	-	-	-
Jain (0%)	-	-	-	-

Agewise Data:

	Persons	Males	Females	Sex Ratio
All ages	46,359	23,476	22,883	975
0-14	19,059	9,759	9,300	953
15-44	19,757	10,083	9,674	959
45-79	7,268	3,529	3,739	1060
80+	253	92	161	1750
Age not stated	22	13	9	692

Languages (Dominant):

Kannada, Telugu, Urdu, Hindi, Tamil

Disabled Population:

	Persons	Males	Females	%
Total Disabled	869	439	430	
In Seeing	384	162	222	44.19
In Speech	59	41	18	6.79
In Hearing	49	21	28	5.64
In Movement	305	176	129	35.1
Mentally	72	39	33	8.29

HUKUMPETA

Hukumpeta C.D. Block lies in the northern part of Visak hapatnam district. The Block is located at a distance of 136 kms. from district headquarters (Visakhapatnam). There are 168 villages in the block with the total population of 50,115 persons. Area of the C.D. Block is 213.20 sq. kms. It is bounded in the north by Mandals Dumbriguda, Araku Valley and Ananthagiri, in the south by Mandals Paderu, Cheedikada and Davarapalle, in the east by Mandal Ananthagiri, and in the west by Mandal Pedabayalu.

Communications :

Roadways : Metalled Roads: Nearest Villages- Garudapalle, D.Chintalaveedhi, Teegalavalasa, Bijjapalle, Nakkalapu ttu, Patimamidi, Burmanguda, Konthili, Hukumpeta, Gadiki nchumanda, Sanyasammapalem, Addumanda, Neelamputtu, Dalemputtu, Marrivalasa, Mulusobha.

Annaual Rainfall: Average Rainfall 975.0 mm

Ground Water: Availability of the Ground Water in the Basin is (Information not avavible) H.A.M .and the utilization is (Information not avavible) H.A.M. It belongs to (Information not avavible) category. Depth to water level varies from 3 to 10 meter below the ground. Most of the wells go down in summer months.

Administration:

Division: Coastal Andhra. Parliamentary Constituency: 18 Araku (ST). District: Visakhapatnam. Mandal: Hukumpe ta. Assembly Constituency: 147 Araku Valley (ST). Gram Panchayat: 33.

Villages: 168 **Inhabited:** 168 **Uninhabited:** 0

Ranking	District	State	National
Area	8	475	3962
Population	30	507	5273
Sex Ratio	6	66	469
Child Sex Ratio	8	41	100
Literacy Rate	34	1069	6046
Density	2	26	4264
Work Participation Rate	32	593	147

Gram Panchayats:
Addumanda, Andiba, Bakuru, Baramasi, Bheemavaram Boddaputtu, Boorja, Cheekumaddula, Durgam Gadikinchumanda, Ganneruputtu, Gattum, Guda Hukumpeta, Jarrakonda, Konthili, Kotnapalli, Mattam Matyapuram, Merakachinta, Mettujoru, Muliaputtu Olda, Pathakota, Pattam, Rangaseela, Rapa, Santhari Sobakota, Sukuru, Tadigiri, Teegalavalasa Thadiputtu.

Amenities:
Education: Primary School in 124 villages, Middle school in 7 villages, Matriculation or Secondary School in 4 villages, namely Hukumpeta, Pedagaruvu, Sanyasammapalem, Bakuru.
Higher Secondary or Pre University Courses or Intermediate or Junior College in 0 village of the CD Block, College in 0 village, Adult Literacy Center in 0 village.
Medical: Hospital in 1 village, Dispensary in 0 village, Health Center in 19 villages, Sub Center in 0 village, Maternity and Child Welfare Center in 0 village, Community health workers in 0 village.
The Village having Hospital or Dispensary or Health Center is Hukumpeta.
Drinking Water: Tap water in 168 villages, Tank water in 168 villages, Well water in 168 villages, Tubewell in 168 villages and more than one source in 168 villages.
Bank: Banking facility in 2 villages, namely, Hukumpeta, Bakuru.
Credit Society in 0 village Agricultural Credit Society in 0 Non-Agricultural Credit Society in 0 village.
Others: Power supply in 168 villages, Cinema hall in 0 village, sport club in 0 village, Stadium or Auditorium or Community Hall in 0 village, Post Office in 17 villages.
There are 31 villages having bus facilities.
Village with most of facilities: Bakuru.
Villages without amenities (Education):
Tokaduggam, Edulagondi, Kangaruputtu, Patimamidi, Vallangiputtu, Lakeyaputtu, Patrimetta, Marripalem, Kokkisa, Sariyapolam, Dalamputtu, Vachanarangini, Sullipakoni, Kondayyapadu, Patakadavada, Degasalthangi, Egasalthangi, Dumbriguda, Billaputtu, Maddiputtu, Koditala, Pedirai, Totakurapadu, Turakalametta, Dalemputtu, Reedabanda, Gondipeta, Bilaiputtu, Tiyyaniputtu, Dalemputtu, Marrivalasa, Veerendla, Ranamkota, Kethampalem, Mulakayiputtu, Chittampadu, Palamamidi, Peesumamidi, Jarrakonda, Bangarubuddi, Dirrapalle, Kothavuru, Cheedigaruvu..
Scheduled Castes: Out of the total population of 50115 persons, 74 persons (0.15%) belong to Scheduled Castes. The villages having less than 10% SC population are Garudapalle, Rathulaputtu, Tokaduggam, Duggam Cheediputtu, Pandimetta, Besaiputtu, Baluroda Ontipaka, Rangaseela, Masada, Matchyapuram, Tadigiri D.Chintalaveedhi, Vukkurba, Allangiputtu Teegalavalasa, Bijjapalle, Kamayyapeta, Pamurai Amuru, Nakkalaputtu, Rangapalle, Kunturla Edulagondi, Arlada, Chilakalaputtu, Sampangiputtu Sobakota, Sundruputtu, M.Kothavuru, Matham M.Boddaputtu, Kodeli, Gotchari, Marriputtu Jogulaputtu, Kangaruputtu, Patimamidi, Burmanguda Kulapadu, Vallangiputtu, Lakeyaputtu, Malaguda Beeram, Muliaputtu, Konthili, Hukumpeta Chatraiputtu, Gadugupalle, Urrada, Kotnapalle Pedagaruvu, Marela, Patrimetta, Marripalem Chintalaveedhi, Rudi @ Degarudi, Pathakota Boddaputtu, Mangalamamidi, Kokkisa, Liviti, Irukurai Sariyapolam, Dalamputtu, Jeelugulaputtu, Mandiputtu Cheekatiputtu, Jangamputtu, Gatham, Kimiduputtu Vachanarangini, Sullipakoni, Boorja, Thumbaguda Kondayyapadu, Patakadavada, Degasalthangi Egasalthangi, Dumbriguda, Majjivalasa, Billaputtu Maddiputtu, Koditala, Panasaputtu, Pattam Nimmalapadu, Bairodivalasa @ Uppa, Pedirai Totakurapadu, Olda, Nittaputtu, Jakaramputtu Kanguputtu, Pusalagaruvu, Peddapadu, Turakalametta Dalemputtu, Rapa, Reedabanda, Gondirapa, Gondipeta Santhari, Chinaburuguputtu, Bilaiputtu, Nimmalapadu Boddaputtu, Tiyyaniputtu, Birisingi, Sukuru Barapalle, Gadikinchumanda, Sanyasammapalem Addumanda, Neelamputtu, Dalemputtu, Marrivalasa Mulusobha, Ramachandrapuram, Gummadiganduva Gangarajuputtu, Locheliputtu, Kutangi Tadiputtu Kuthangi, Buradagummi, Vakapalle, Veerendla, Sembi Sarasapadu, Allamputtu, Sampangiputtu, Durgam Bangarugaruvu, Ranamkota, Daragedda, Kethampalem Nurupanuku, Mulakayiputtu, Dabbagaruvu, Boddaputtu Mebha, Kotagummam, Bakuru, Chittampadu, Bheemavaram Maddiputtu, Andiba, Gangudi, Gummadigunta Donkinavalasa, Gillibaddu, Cheekumaddula Goppulapalem, Merakachinta, Gasarapalle, Palamamidi Patiguruvu, Gedelapadu, Sesaipanuku, Peesumamidi

Jarrakonda, Peda Nandiputtu, Bangarubuddi Dirrapalle, Ganika, Kothavuru, Cheedigaruvu.

The villages having more than 50% SC population are None.

Sex ratio of Scheduled Caste population is 622.

Scheduled Castes Literates and Illiterates by Sex:

	Persons	Males	Females
Literate	32	17	15
Illiterate	42	11	31
Literacy rate	49.2	63.0	39.5
Graduate	4	2	2

Scheduled Castes (Dominant):

Madiga, Chachati, Mala

For their cultural identity please see Appendix-I

Villages without Scheduled Castes: There are 164 villages without any scheduled caste population.

Scheduled Tribes: Out of the total population of 50115 persons, 47750 persons (95.28%) belong to Scheduled Tribes.

The villages having less than 10% ST population are None..

The villages having more than 50% ST population are Garudapalle, Rathulaputtu, Tokaduggam, Duggam Cheediputtu, Pandimetta, Besaiputtu, Baluroda Ontipaka, Rangaseela, Masada, Matchyapuram, Tadigiri D.Chintalaveedhi, Vukkurba, Allangiputtu Teegalavalasa, Bijjapalle, Kamayyapeta, Pamurai Amuru, Nakkalaputtu, Rangapalle, Kunturla Edulagondi, Arlada, Chilakalaputtu, Sampangiputtu Sobakota, Sundruputtu, Matham, M.Boddaputtu, Kodeli Gotchari, Marriputtu, Jogulaputtu, Kangaruputtu Patimamidi, Burmanguda, Kulapadu, Vallangiputtu Lakeyaputtu, Malaguda, Beeram, Muliaputtu, Konthili Hukumpeta, Chatraiputtu, Gadugupalle, Urrada Kotnapalle, Pedagaruvu, Marela, Patrimetta Marripalem, Chintalaveedhi, Rudi @ Degarudi Pathakota, Boddaputtu, Mangalamamidi, Kokkisa Liviti, Irukurai, Sariyapolam, Dalamputtu Jeelugulaputtu, Mandiputtu, Cheekatiputtu Jangamputtu, Gatham, Kimiduputtu, Vachanarangini Sullipakoni, Boorja, Thumbaguda, Kondayyapadu Patakadavada, Degasalthangi, Egasalthangi Dumbriguda, Majjivalasa, Billaputtu, Maddiputtu Koditala, Panasaputtu, Pattam, Nimmalapadu Bairodivalasa @ Uppa, Pedirai, Totakurapadu, Olda Nittaputtu, Jakaramputtu, Kanguputtu, Pusalagaruvu Peddapadu, Turakalametta, Dalemputtu, Rapa Reedabanda, Gondirapa, Gondipeta, Santhari Chinaburuguputtu, Bilaiputtu, Nimmalapadu Boddaputtu, Tiyyaniputtu, Birisingi, Sukuru Barapalle, Gadikinchumanda, Sanyasammapalem Addumanda, Neelamputtu, Dalemputtu, Marrivalasa Mulusobha, Ramachandrapuram, Gummadiganduva Gangarajuputtu, Locheliputtu, Kutangi Tadiputtu Kuthangi, Buradagummi, Vakapalle, Veerendla, Sembi Sarasapadu, Allamputtu, Sampangiputtu, Durgam Bangarugaruvu, Ranamkota, Daragedda, Kethampalem Nurupanuku, Mulakayiputtu, Dabbagaruvu, Boddaputtu Mebha, Kotagummam, Bakuru, Chittampadu, Bheemavaram Maddiputtu, Andiba, Gangudi, Gummadigunta Donkinavalasa, Gillibaddu, Cheekumaddula Goppulapalem, Merakachinta, Gasarapalle, Palamamidi Patiguruvu, Gedelapadu, Sesaipanuku, Peesumamidi Jarrakonda, Peda Nandiputtu, Bangarubuddi Dirrapalle, Ganika, Kothavuru, Cheedigaruvu.

Sex ratio of Scheduled tribe population is 508.

Scheduled Tribes Literates and Illiterates by Sex:

	Persons	Males	Females
Literate	13,263	9,000	4,263
Illiterate	34,487	14,477	20,010
Literacy rate	33.3	46.0	21.0
Graduate	137	128	9

Scheduled Tribes (Dominant):

Konda Dhoras, Bagata, Kondhs etc., Mukha Dhora etc. Valmiki

For their cultural identity please see Appendix-II

Villages without Scheduled Tribes: There is 1 village without any scheduled tribe population.

Literates and Illiterates by Sex (Total Population):

	Persons	Males	Females
Literate	14,350	9,684	4,666
Illiterate	35,765	14,996	20,769
Literacy rate	34	47	22
Graduate	248	226	22

Agriculture: ***Distribution of villages according to land use:*** Out of 168 villages, Total area (in hectare) is 21316, out of that 56.79 percent is cultivable and 27.86 percent of the cultivable area is irrigated.

Sources of Irrigation (Hectares): Government Canal 0, Private Canal 0, Well without Electricity 22, Well with Electricity 5, Tubewell without Electricity 27, Tubewell with Electricity 0, Tank 569, River 0, Lake 0, Waterfall 0, Others 2749.

Villages with population of 5000 to 9999: None

Villages with population of 10000 and above: None

Distribution of Workers:

	Persons	Males	Females	WPR
Cultivators	21,795	11,073	10,722	74.4
Agricultural Labour	6,323	2,641	3,682	21.58
Household Industry	117	64	53	0.4
Other Workers	1,060	709	351	3.62

Main Workers	25,661	13,300	12,361	87.6
Marginal Workers	3,634	1,187	2,447	12.4
Total Workers	29,295	14,487	14,808	

Religion: Major Religious Communities:

	Persons	Males	Females	Sex Ratio
Hindu (97.72%)	48,973	24,181	24,792	1,025
Muslim (0.29%)	143	68	75	1,103
Christian (1.42%)	712	305	407	1,334
Sikh (0.03%)	16	10	6	600
Buddhists (0.47%)	238	103	135	1,311
Jain (0%)	-	-	-	-

Agewise Data:

	Persons	Males	Females	Sex Ratio
All ages	50,115	24,680	25,435	1031
0-14	18,014	9,137	8,877	972
15-44	23,434	11,122	12,312	1107
45-79	8,255	4,284	3,971	927
80+	96	53	43	811
Age not stated	316	84	232	2762

Languages (Dominant):

Telugu, Konda, Oriya, Others, Khond/Kondh

Disabled Population:

	Persons	Males	Females	%
Total Disabled	716	397	319	
In Seeing	358	205	153	50
In Speech	65	36	29	9.08
In Hearing	61	32	29	8.52
In Movement	165	84	81	23.04
Mentally	67	40	27	9.36

HUSNABAD

Husnabad C.D. Block lies in the southern part of Karimn agar district. The Block is located at a distance of 39 kms. from district headquarters (Karimnagar). There are 24 villages in the block with the total population of 75,401 persons. Area of the C.D. Block is 258.55 sq. kms. It is bounded by Chigurumamidi Mandal on north, Saidapur Mandal on north-east, Bheemadevarpalle Mandal on east, Warangal district on south, Medal district on south-west, and Koheda Mandal on west.

Communications :

Roadways : Metalled Roads: Nearest Villages- Potlapalle, Husnabad, Mirzapur, Potharam (S), Thotapalle (S), Kuchanpalle, Pandilla, Regonda, Gandipalle, Jangaon, Akkannapeta.

Backwards Region Grants Fund: It receives Backward Region Grants.

Mahila Samakhya (Education for Women's Equality): It is decleared Socialy and Educationally Backward Block by the Government.

Integrated Child Development Scheme (ICDS) Project: Husnabad, Total Anganwadi Centres: 166

Annual Rainfall: Average Rainfall 834 mm

Ground Water: Availability of the Ground Water in the Basin is 2245 H.A.M. and the utilization is 2048 H. A.M. It belongs to Critical category. Depth to water level varies from more than 10 meter below the ground. Most of the wells go down in summer months. The well density in the entire block is 59 wells per sq. km. Total no. of the wells in the block are enumerated as 7941, according to the Ground Water Estimation Commi ttee.

Natural Division : Godavari Depression Region

Administration:

Division: Telangana. Parliamentary Constituency: 3 Karimnagar. District: Karimnagar. Mandal: Husnabad. Assembly Constituency: 32 Husnabad. Gram Panchayat: 32

Villages: 24 **Inhabited:** 24 **Uninhabited:** 0

Ranking	District	State	National
Area	7	281	3269
Population	4	64	4270
Sex Ratio	52	672	2305
Child Sex Ratio	41	707	2954
Literacy Rate	13	534	3989
Density	47	765	3617
Work Participation Rate	20	390	2235

Gram Panchayats:

Akkannapet, Anthakpet, Banjerupalli, Choutapally Dhrmaram, Gandhinagar, Gandipalli, Gouravelli Govardhanagiri, Gudatipalli, Husnabad, Janagan Jilleligada, Keshvapoor, Kuchanpalli Kundanivanipalli, Madatha, Mahamadappor, Malapalli Mallampalli, Merjapoor, Mothkulapalli, Nagaram Nandaram, Pandilla, Potharam (S), Pothatram (J) Potlapalli, Ramavaram, Regonda, Thotapalli, Ummapoor.

Amenities:

Education: Primary School in 24 villages, Middle school in 16 villages, Matriculation or Secondary School in 7 villages, namely Potlapalle, Husnabad, Potharam (S), Ramavaram, Anthakkapeta, Choutapalle, Mallampalle.

Higher Secondary or Pre University Courses or Intermediate or Junior College in 1 village of the CD Block,, namely Husnabad.

College in 0 village, Adult Literacy Center in 18 villages.

Medical: Hospital in 1 village, Dispensary in 2 villages, Health Center in 1 village, Sub Center in 11 villages, Maternity and Child Welfare Center in 1 village, Community health workers in 0 village.

The Villages having Hospital or Dispensary or Health Center are Husnabad, Akkannapeta.

Drinking Water: Tap water in 24 villages, Tank water in 24 villages, Well water in 24 villages, Tubewell in 24 villages and more than one source in 24 villages.

Bank: Banking facility in 2 villages, namely, Husnabad, Ramavaram.

Credit Society in 21 villages Agricultural Credit Society in 4 Non-Agricultural Credit Society in 21 villages.

Others: Power supply in 24 villages, Cinema hall in 1 village, sport club in 1 village, Stadium or Auditorium or Community Hall in 0 village, Post Office in 20 villages.

There are 24 villages having bus facilities.

Villages with most of facilities: Husnabad Ramavaram.

Villages without Amenities (Education): None..

Scheduled Castes: Out of the total population of 75401 persons, 12085 persons (16.03%) belong to Scheduled Castes.

The villages having less than 10% SC population are None..

The villages having more than 50% SC population are None.

Sex ratio of Scheduled Caste population is 484.

Scheduled Castes Literates and Illiterates by Sex:

	Persons	Males	Females
Literate	5,211	3,269	1,942
Illiterate	6,874	2,969	3,905
Literacy rate	49.7	60.1	38.5
Graduate	109	93	16

Scheduled Castes (Dominant):

Madiga, Mala, Beda Jangam etc., Generic Castes etc. Gosangi

For their cultural identity please see Appendix-I

Villages without Scheduled Castes: There are 0 village without any scheduled caste population.

Scheduled Tribes: Out of the total population of 75401 persons, 8260 persons (10.95%) belong to Scheduled Tribes.

The villages having less than 10% ST population are Potlapalle, Husnabad, Madudha, Mohammadapur, Nagaram Potharam (S), Thotapalle (S), Kuchanpalle, Pandilla Potharam (J), Ramavaram, Jangaon, Anthakkapeta Choutapalle, Kesavapur.

The villages having more than 50% ST population are None.

Sex ratio of Scheduled tribe population is 481.

Scheduled Tribes Literates and Illiterates by Sex:

	Persons	Males	Females
Literate	2,288	1,586	702
Illiterate	5,972	2,701	3,271
Literacy rate	33.9	45.2	21.7
Graduate	28	27	1

Scheduled Tribes (Dominant):

Sugalis etc., Yerukulas, Chenchu etc.
Generic Tribes etc., Thoti

For their cultural identity please see Appendix-II

Villages without Scheduled Tribes: There are 0 village without any scheduled tribe population.

Literates and Illiterates by Sex (Total Population):

	Persons	Males	Females
Literate	34,563	21,360	13,203
Illiterate	40,838	16,832	24,006
Literacy rate	53	65	41
Graduate	1,418	1,192	226

Agriculture: ***Distribution of villages according to land use:*** Out of 24 villages, Total area (in hectare) is 25855, out of that 72.59 percent is cultivable and 50.22 percent of the cultivable area is irrigated.

Sources of Irrigation (Hectares): Government Canal 0, Private Canal 0, Well without Electricity 0, Well with Electricity 6664, Tubewell without Electricity 0, Tubewell with Electricity 0, Tank 2762.2, River 0, Lake 0, Waterfall 0, Others 0.

Villages with population of 5000 to 9999: None

Villages with population of 10000 and above: Husnabad.

Distribution of Workers:

	Persons	Males	Females	WPR
Cultivators	14,347	8,770	5,577	38.52
Agricultural Labour	13,963	5,182	8,781	37.49
Household Industry	1,473	844	629	3.95
Other Workers	7,466	5,962	1,504	20.04
Main Workers	29,494	18,161	11,333	79.18
Marginal Workers	7,755	2,597	5,158	20.82
Total Workers	37,249	20,758	16,491	

Religion: Major Religious Communities:

	Persons	Males	Females	Sex Ratio
Hindu (95.82%)	72,246	36,620	35,626	973
Muslim (2.9%)	2,183	1,034	1,149	1,111
Christian (0.31%)	231	117	114	974
Sikh (0.02%)	16	9	7	778
Buddhists (0%)	-	-	-	-
Jain (0%)	-	-	-	-

Agewise Data:

	Persons	Males	Females	Sex Ratio
All ages	75,401	38,192	37,209	974
0-14	24,692	12,752	11,940	936
15-44	34,398	17,176	17,222	1003
45-79	15,553	7,874	7,679	975
80+	679	352	327	929
Age not stated	79	38	41	1079

Languages (Dominant):

Telugu, Hindi, Urdu, Tamil, Oriya

Disabled Population:

	Persons	Males	Females	%
Total Disabled	1,065	630	435	
In Seeing	434	251	183	40.75
In Speech	129	61	68	12.11
In Hearing	42	18	24	3.94
In Movement	327	220	107	30.7
Mentally	133	80	53	12.49

HUZURABAD

Huzurabad C.D. Block lies in the south-east part of Karimnagar district. The Block is located at a distance of 40 kms. from district headquarters (Karimnagar). There are 12 villages in the block with the total population of 71,201 persons. Area of the C.D. Block is 137.56 sq. kms. It is bounded by Veenavanka Mandal on north, Jammikunta Mandal on east, Kamalapur and Elkathurthi Mandals on south-east, Bheemadevarapalle Mandal on south, Saidapur Mandal on west, Shankarapatnam Mandal on north-west.

Communications :

Roadways : State Highway (S.H.): Direction- Karimnagar to Warangal Nearest Villages- Singapur, Huzurabad, Thummanapalle, Bornapalle, Katrepalle, Kandugula.

Backwards Region Grants Fund: It receives Backward Region Grants.

Integrated Child Development Scheme (ICDS) Project: Huzurabad, Total Anganwadi Centres: 206

Annual Rainfall: Average Rainfall 929 mm

Ground Water: Availability of the Ground Water in the Basin is 3430 H.A.M. and the utilization is 1946 H. A.M. It belongs to Safe category. Depth to water level varies from more than 10 meter below the ground. Most of the wells go down in summer months. The well density in the entire block is 29 wells per sq. km. Total no. of the wells in the block are enumerated as 5032, according to the Ground Water Estimation Committee.

Natural Division : Godavari Depression Region

Administration:

Division: Telangana. Parliamentary Constituency: 3 Karimnagar. District: Karimnagar. Mandal: Huzurabad. Assembly Constituency: 31 Huzurabad. Gram Panchayat: 20

Villages: 12 **Inhabited:** 12 **Uninhabited:** 0

Ranking	District	State	National
Area	52	873	5222
Population	7	109	4410
Sex Ratio	45	531	1943
Child Sex Ratio	48	889	3952
Literacy Rate	1	214	2371
Density	53	930	2127
Work Participation Rate	1	97	3267

Gram Panchayats:

Bornapally, Chelpur, Chinnapapaiahpalli Dhammakkapet, Dharmarajpalli, Huzurabad Ippalanarsingapur, Jupaka, Kandugula, Kankulagidda Katrapalli, Kothapalli, Peddapapaiahpalli Pothireddipet, Rampur, Rangapur, Singapur Sirsapalli, Thummanapalli, Venkatraopalli.

Amenities:

Education: Primary School in 12 villages, Middle school in 11 villages, Matriculation or Secondary School in 3 villages, namely Singapur, Chelpur, Huzurabad.

Higher Secondary or Pre University Courses or Intermediate or Junior College in 1 village of the CD Block,, namely Huzurabad.

College in 2 villages, Adult Literacy Center in 12 villages., Colleges are in villages, namely Singapur, Huzurabad.

Medical: Hospital in 1 village, Dispensary in 2 villages, Health Center in 1 village, Sub Center in 8 villages, Maternity and Child Welfare Center in 1 village, Community health workers in 0 village.

The Villages having Hospital or Dispensary or Health Center are Huzurabad, Bornapalle.

Drinking Water: Tap water in 12 villages, Tank water in 12 villages, Well water in 12 villages, Tubewell in 12 villages and more than one source in 12 villages.

Bank: Banking facility in 2 villages, namely, Singapur, Huzurabad.

Credit Society in 11 villages Agricultural Credit Society in 3 Non-Agricultural Credit Society in 10 villages.

Others: Power supply in 12 villages, Cinema hall in 1 village, sport club in 1 village, Stadium or Auditorium or Community Hall in 1 village, Post Office in 12 villages.

There are 12 villages having bus facilities.

Villages with most of facilities: Singapur Huzurabad.

Villages without Amenities (Education): None..

Scheduled Castes: Out of the total population of 71201 persons, 14105 persons (19.81%) belong to Scheduled Castes.

The villages having less than 10% SC population are None..

The villages having more than 50% SC population are None.

Sex ratio of Scheduled Caste population is 499.

Scheduled Castes Literates and Illiterates by Sex:

	Persons	Males	Females
Literate	6,643	3,948	2,695
Illiterate	7,462	3,125	4,337
Literacy rate	54.6	64.7	44.5
Graduate	226	191	35

Scheduled Castes (Dominant):

Madiga, Mala, Beda Jangam etc., Gosangi, Manne

For their cultural identity please see Appendix-I

Villages without Scheduled Castes: There are 0 village without any scheduled caste population.

Scheduled Tribes: Out of the total population of 71201 persons, 527 persons (0.74%) belong to Scheduled Tribes. The villages having less than 10% ST population are Singapur, Sirsapalle, Pothareddipeta, Chelpur, Jupak Huzurabad, Thummanapalle, Bornapalle, Katrepalle Kandugula, Kanukulagidda, Dharmaraju Palle.

The villages having more than 50% ST population are None.

Sex ratio of Scheduled tribe population is 499.

Scheduled Tribes Literates and Illiterates by Sex:

	Persons	Males	Females
Literate	171	113	58
Illiterate	356	151	205
Literacy rate	39.9	52.1	27.4
Graduate	4	4	0

Scheduled Tribes (Dominant):

Yerukulas, Thoti, Sugalis etc., Koya etc. Generic Tribes etc.

For their cultural identity please see Appendix-II

Villages without Scheduled Tribes: There are 2 villages without any scheduled tribe population.

Literates and Illiterates by Sex (Total Population):

	Persons	Males	Females
Literate	38,545	23,011	15,534
Illiterate	32,656	12,916	19,740
Literacy rate	62	74	51
Graduate	2,854	2,324	530

Agriculture: ***Distribution of villages according to land use:*** Out of 12 villages, Total area (in hectare) is 13755, out of that 76.07 percent is cultivable and 71.24 percent of the cultivable area is irrigated.

Sources of Irrigation (Hectares): Government Canal 2532.12, Private Canal 0, Well without Electricity 0, Well with Electricity 3821.07, Tubewell without Electricity 0, Tubewell with Electricity 0, Tank 1100.34, River 0, Lake 0, Waterfall 0, Others 0.

Villages with population of 5000 to 9999:

Chelpur.

Villages with population of 10000 and above:

Huzurabad.

Distribution of Workers:

	Persons	Males	Females	WPR
Cultivators	6,945	4,250	2,695	21.36
Agricultural Labour	13,623	5,385	8,238	41.9
Household Industry	1,671	966	705	5.14
Other Workers	10,271	8,592	1,679	31.59
Main Workers	28,288	17,969	10,319	87.01
Marginal Workers	4,222	1,224	2,998	12.99
Total Workers	32,510	19,193	13,317	

Religion: Major Religious Communities:

	Persons	Males	Females	Sex Ratio
Hindu (94.42%)	67,228	33,931	33,297	981
Muslim (5.2%)	3,699	1,857	1,842	992
Christian (0.27%)	191	95	96	1,011
Sikh (0.03%)	24	15	9	600
Buddhists (0%)	1	1	-	-
Jain (0%)	-	-	-	-

Agewise Data:

	Persons	Males	Females	Sex Ratio
All ages	71,201	35,927	35,274	982
0-14	21,996	11,193	10,803	965
15-44	34,339	17,334	17,005	981
45-79	14,123	7,048	7,075	1004
80+	596	260	336	1292
Age not stated	147	92	55	598

Languages (Dominant):

Telugu, Urdu, Hindi, Tamil, Marathi

Disabled Population:

	Persons	Males	Females	%
Total Disabled	1,022	612	410	
In Seeing	428	255	173	41.88
In Speech	121	69	52	11.84
In Hearing	32	13	19	3.13
In Movement	314	197	117	30.72
Mentally	127	78	49	12.43

HUZURNAGAR

Huzurnagar C.D. Block lies in the eastern part of Nalgo nda district. The Block is located at a distance of 65 kms. from district headquarters (Nalgonda). There are 7 villages in the block with the total population of 57,433 persons. Area of the C.D. Block is 110.48 sq. kms. It is bounded by Chilkur Mandal on north and north-east, Mellacheruvu Mandal on east, Matampalle Mandal on south, and Garidepalle Mandal on west.

Communications:

Roadways : Metalled Roads: Nearest Villages- Burugadda, Lingagiri, Amaravaram, Lakkavaram, Huzurnagar.

Backwards Region Grants Fund: It receives Backward Region Grants.

Integrated Child Development Scheme (ICDS) Project: Huzurnagar, Total Anganwadi Centres: 254

Annual Rainfall: Average Rainfall 789 mm

Ground Water: Availability of the Ground Water in the Basin is 5745 H.A.M. and the utilization is 302 H.A. M. It belongs to Safe category. Depth to water level varies from 2 to 10 meter below the ground. Most of the wells go down in summer months. The well density in the entire block is 5 wells per sq. km. Total no. of the wells in the block are enumerated as 582, according to the Ground Water Estimation Committee.

Natural Division : Krishna Piedmont Plain Region

Administration:

Division: Telangana. Parliamentary Constituency: 13 Nalgonda. District: Nalgonda. Mandal: Huzurnagar. Assembly Constituency: 89 Huzurnagar. Gram Panchayat: 10.

Villages: 7 **Inhabited:** 7 **Uninhabited:** 0

Ranking	District	State	National
Area	59	986	5601
Population	8	315	4948
Sex Ratio	42	834	2844
Child Sex Ratio	31	740	3185
Literacy Rate	6	226	2454
Density	55	885	2116
Work Participation Rate	1	95	2980

Gram Panchayats:

Amaravaram, Anjalipuram, Burugadda, Gopalapuram Huzurnagar, Karakayalagudem, Lakkavaram, Lingagiri Srinivaspuram, Vepalasingaram.

Amenities:

Education: Primary School in 7 villages, Middle school in 7 villages, Matriculation or Secondary School in 5 villages, namely Machavaram, Lingagiri, Amaravaram, Huzurnagar, Yepalasingaram.

Higher Secondary or Pre University Courses or Intermediate or Junior College in 1 village of the CD Block,, namely Huzurnagar.

College in 1 village, Adult Literacy Center in 5 villages., College is in village, namely Huzurnagar.

Medical: Hospital in 0 village, Dispensary in 1 village, Health Center in 0 village, Sub Center in 5 villages, Maternity and Child Welfare Center in 1 village, Community health workers in 0 village.

The Village having Hospital or Dispensary or Health Center is Lingagiri.

Drinking Water: Tap water in 7 villages, Tank water in 7 villages, Well water in 7 villages, Tubewell in 7 villages and more than one source in 7 villages.

Bank: Banking facility in 1 villages, namely, Huzurnagar.

Credit Society in 6 villages Agricultural Credit Society in 6 Non-Agricultural Credit Society in 3 villages.

Others: Power supply in 7 villages, Cinema hall in 1 village, sport club in 0 village, Stadium or Auditorium or Community Hall in 0 village, Post Office in 7 villages.

There are 7 villages having bus facilities.

Village with most of facilities: Huzurnagar.

Villages without Amenities (Education): None..

Scheduled Castes: Out of the total population of 57433 persons, 10325 persons (17.98%) belong to Scheduled Castes.

The villages having less than 10% SC population are None..

The villages having more than 50% SC population are None.

Sex ratio of Scheduled Caste population is 491.

Scheduled Castes Literates and Illiterates by Sex:

	Persons	Males	Females
Literate	4,752	3,000	1,752
Illiterate	5,573	2,255	3,318
Literacy rate	53.7	66.3	40.5
Graduate	188	146	42

Scheduled Castes (Dominant):

Madiga, Mala, Beda Jangam etc., Mala Dasari Generic Castes etc.

For their cultural identity please see Appendix-I

Villages without Scheduled Castes: There are 0 village without any scheduled caste population.

Scheduled Tribes: Out of the total population of 57433 persons, 1114 persons (1.94%) belong to Scheduled Tribes.

The villages having less than 10% ST population are Machavaram, Burugadda, Lingagiri, Amaravaram Lakkavaram, Huzurnagar, Yepalasingaram.

The villages having more than 50% ST population are None.

Sex ratio of Scheduled tribe population is 460.

Scheduled Tribes Literates and Illiterates by Sex:

	Persons	Males	Females
Literate	458	310	148
Illiterate	656	292	364
Literacy rate	48.0	59.1	34.5
Graduate	9	8	1

Scheduled Tribes (Dominant):

Sugalis etc., Yerukulas, Yenadis, Koya etc., Bagata

For their cultural identity please see Appendix-II

Villages without Scheduled Tribes: There are 2 villages without any scheduled tribe population.

Literates and Illiterates by Sex (Total Population):

	Persons	Males	Females
Literate	30,880	18,508	12,372
Illiterate	26,553	10,749	15,804
Literacy rate	62	73	51
Graduate	1,990	1,551	439

Agriculture: ***Distribution of villages according to land use:*** Out of 7 villages, Total area (in hectare) is 11048, out of that 53.83 percent is cultivable and 69.73 percent of the cultivable area is irrigated.

Sources of Irrigation (Hectares): Government Canal 3014,

Private Canal 0, Well without Electricity 0, Well with Electricity 0, Tubewell without Electricity 0, Tubewell with Electricity 0, Tank 933, River 0, Lake 0, Waterfall 0, Others 200.

Villages with population of 5000 to 9999:
Lingagiri.

Villages with population of 10000 and above:
Huzurnagar.

Distribution of Workers:

	Persons	Males	Females	WPR
Cultivators	4,279	3,072	1,207	15.85
Agricultural Labour	13,133	5,183	7,950	48.66
Household Industry	350	208	142	1.3
Other Workers	9,229	7,649	1,580	34.19
Main Workers	20,940	14,116	6,824	77.58
Marginal Workers	6,051	1,996	4,055	22.42
Total Workers	26,991	16,112	10,879	

Religion: Major Religious Communities:

	Persons	Males	Females	Sex Ratio
Hindu (90.83%)	52,166	26,616	25,550	960
Muslim (7.57%)	4,347	2,197	2,150	979
Christian (1.52%)	875	418	457	1,093
Sikh (0.03%)	20	11	9	818
Buddhists (0%)	1	-	1	-
Jain (0%)	-	-	-	-

Agewise Data:

	Persons	Males	Females	Sex Ratio
All ages	57,433	29,257	28,176	963
0-14	19,081	9,895	9,186	928
15-44	28,172	14,344	13,828	964
45-79	9,810	4,846	4,964	1024
80+	338	153	185	1209
Age not stated	32	19	13	684

Languages (Dominant):
Telugu, Urdu, Hindi, Gondi, Tamil

Disabled Population:

	Persons	Males	Females	%
Total Disabled	1,988	1,193	795	
In Seeing	1,177	726	451	59.21
In Speech	127	69	58	6.39
In Hearing	54	25	29	2.72
In Movement	478	290	188	24.04
Mentally	152	83	69	7.65

I. POLAVARAM

I.Polavaram C.D. Block lies in the south-eastern part of East Godavari district. The Block is located at a distance of 33 kms. from district headquarters (Kakin ada). There are 11 villages in the block with the total population of 67,454 persons. Area of the C.D. Block is 128.19 sq. kms. It is bounded in the north by River Gowthami Godavari and Mandals Pamarru and Tallarevu, in the south and east by River Vasista Godavari and Gowthami Godavari respectively, and Mandal Katrenikona, and in the west by River Vasista Godavari and Mandal Mummidivaram.

Communications :

Roadways : Metalled Roads: Nearest Villages- Pasuvullanka, Komaragiri, Patha Injaram, Yedurulanka, I. Polavaram, Muramalla.

River: Gowthami Godavari: Nearest Villages- Pasuvullan ka,, Komaragiri, Patha Injaram, Yedurulanka, Guthinadeevi, G. Vemavaram. Vasista Godavari: Nearest Villages- Pasuvullanka, G. Vemavaram, T. Kothapalle, Muramalla, Kesanakurru.

Backwards Region Grants Fund: It receives Backward Region Grants.

Annaul Rainfall: Average Rainfall 1108.6 mm

Ground Water: Availability of the Ground Water in the Basin is (Information not avavible) H.A.M .and the utilization is (Information not avavible) H.A.M. It belongs to (Information not avavible) category. Depth to water level varies from 3 to 10 meter below the ground. Most of the wells go down in summer months.

Natural Division : Godavari Delta Region

Administration:

Division: Coastal Andhra. Parliamentary Constituency: 24 Amalapuram (SC). District: East Godavari. Mandal: I Polavaram. Assembly Constituency: 162 Mummidivaram. Gram Panchayat: 14.

Villages: 11 **Inhabited:** 11 **Uninhabited:** 0

Ranking	District	State	National
Area	18	909	5350
Population	38	173	4586
Sex Ratio	31	414	1645
Child Sex Ratio	21	234	763
Literacy Rate	27	218	2388
Density	35	1048	2090
Work Participation Rate	37	89	4361

Gram Panchayats:
Bhiravapalem, G.Moolapalem, G.Vemavaram, Gogulanka Guthinadeevi, I.Polavaram, Kesanakurru, Komaragiri Muramalla, Pasuvullanka, Patha Injaram, T.Kothapalle Thillakkuppa, Yedurulanka.

Amenities:

Education: Primary School in 11 villages, Middle school in 9 villages, Matriculation or Secondary School in 4 villages, namely G. Vemavaram, I. Polavaram, Muramalla, Kesanakurru.

Higher Secondary or Pre University Courses or Intermediate or Junior College in 1 village of the CD Block,, namely I. Polavaram.

College in 0 village, Adult Literacy Center in 10 villages.

Medical: Hospital in 0 village, Dispensary in 1 village, Health Center in 1 village, Sub Center in 4 villages, Maternity and Child Welfare Center in 0 village, Community health workers in 0 village.

The Village having Hospital or Dispensary or Health Center is Kesanakurru.

Drinking Water: Tap water in 11 villages, Tank water in 11 villages, Well water in 11 villages, Tubewell in 11 villages and more than one source in 11 villages.

Bank: Banking facility in 4 villages, namely, Guthinadeevi, I. Polavaram, Muramalla, Kesanakurru.

Credit Society in 9 villages Agricultural Credit Society in 9 Non-Agricultural Credit Society in 5 villages.

Others: Power supply in 11 villages, Cinema hall in 2 villages, sport club in 0 village, Stadium or Auditorium or Community Hall in 0 village, Post Office in 10 villages.

There are 11 villages having bus facilities.

Villages with most of facilities: Guthinadeevi I. Polavaram, Muramalla, Kesanakurru.

Villages without Amenities (Education): None..

Scheduled Castes: Out of the total population of 67454 persons, 17237 persons (25.55%) belong to Scheduled Castes.

The villages having less than 10% SC population are None..

The villages having more than 50% SC population are None.

Sex ratio of Scheduled Caste population is 495.

Scheduled Castes Literates and Illiterates by Sex:

	Persons	Males	Females
Literate	9,215	5,123	4,092
Illiterate	8,022	3,584	4,438
Literacy rate	60.8	67.0	54.4
Graduate	242	182	60

Scheduled Castes (Dominant):

Mala, Jambuvulu, Adi Andhra, Madiga, Panchama etc.

For their cultural identity please see Appendix-I

Villages without Scheduled Castes: There are 0 village without any scheduled caste population.

Scheduled Tribes: Out of the total population of 67454 persons, 299 persons (0.44%) belong to Scheduled Tribes.

The villages having less than 10% ST population are Pasuvullanka, Komaragiri, Patha Injaram, Yedurulanka Guthinadeevi, G. Vemavaram, T. Kothapalle I. Polavaram, Muramalla, Kesanakurru, Thillakkuppa.

The villages having more than 50% ST population are None.

Sex ratio of Scheduled tribe population is 508.

Scheduled Tribes Literates and Illiterates by Sex:

	Persons	Males	Females
Literate	107	51	56
Illiterate	192	96	96
Literacy rate	43.5	42.9	44.1
Graduate	8	8	0

Scheduled Tribes (Dominant):

Yerukulas, Koya etc., Valmiki, Konda Dhoras Konda Kapus

For their cultural identity please see Appendix-II

Villages without Scheduled Tribes: There are 0 village without any scheduled tribe population.

Literates and Illiterates by Sex (Total Population):

	Persons	Males	Females
Literate	36,754	19,852	16,902
Illiterate	30,700	14,062	16,638
Literacy rate	62	67	58
Graduate	914	727	187

Agriculture: ***Distribution of villages according to land use:***

Out of 11 villages, Total area (in hectare) is 12819, out of that 68.22 percent is cultivable and 53.55 percent of the cultivable area is irrigated.

Sources of Irrigation (Hectares): Government Canal 4682.93, Private Canal 0, Well without Electricity 0, Well with Electricity 0, Tubewell without Electricity 0, Tubewell with Electricity 0, Tank 0, River 0, Lake 0, Waterfall 0, Others 0.

Villages with population of 5000 to 9999: Guthinadeevi, T. Kothapalle, I. Polavaram.

Villages with population of 10000 and above: G. Vemavaram, Kesanakurru.

Distribution of Workers:

	Persons	Males	Females	WPR
Cultivators	3,732	3,525	207	13.58
Agricultural Labour	17,148	10,711	6,437	62.39
Household Industry	516	339	177	1.88
Other Workers	6,089	5,356	733	22.15
Main Workers	21,996	17,562	4,434	80.03
Marginal Workers	5,489	2,369	3,120	19.97
Total Workers	27,485	19,931	7,554	

Religion: Major Religious Communities:

	Persons	Males	Females	Sex Ratio
Hindu (98.9%)	66,713	33,580	33,133	987
Muslim (0.36%)	240	125	115	920
Christian (0.7%)	469	193	276	1,430
Sikh (0%)	-	-	-	-
Buddhists (0.01%)	7	5	2	400
Jain (0%)	-	-	-	-

Agewise Data:

	Persons	Males	Females	Sex Ratio
All ages	67,454	33,914	33,540	989

0-14	20,842	10,447	10,395	995
15-44	33,441	16,949	16,492	973
45-79	12,718	6,299	6,419	1019
80+	423	204	219	1074
Age not stated	30	15	15	1000

Languages (Dominant):
Telugu, Urdu, Gondi, Hindi, Oriya

Disabled Population:

	Persons	Males	Females	%
Total Disabled	1,593	900	693	
In Seeing	956	535	421	60.01
In Speech	130	63	67	8.16
In Hearing	45	22	23	2.82
In Movement	352	224	128	22.1
Mentally	110	56	54	6.91

IBRAHIMPATNAM

Ibrahimpatnam C.D. Block lies in the north-west part of Karimnagar district. The Block is located at a dista nce of 95 kms. from district headquarters (Karimnagar). There are 18 villages in the block with the total population of 50,845 persons. Area of the C.D. Block is 184.20 sq. kms. It is bounded by Adilabad district on north-west, north and north-east, Mallapur Mandal on north-east and east, Metpalle Mandal on south-east and south, and Nizamabad district on south-west, west and north-west.

Communications :

Roadways : NH- 16: Direction- Nizamabad to Koratla. Nearest Villages- Errapur, Rajeswara Rao Pet. State Highway (S.H.): Direction- Nizamabad to Jagtial. Neare st Villages- Bandalingapur, Maidpalle (W).

River: Godavari Nadi- Nearest Villages- Komatikondapur, Erdandi, Mularampur, Vemulakurthi, Kamala Nagar.

Backwards Region Grants Fund: It receives Backward Region Grants.

Annual Rainfall: Average Rainfall 1010 mm

Ground Water: Availability of the Ground Water in the Basin is 2982 H.A.M. and the utilization is 1340 H. A.M. It belongs to Safe category. Depth to water level varies from more than 5 to 10 meter below the ground. Most of the wells go down in summer months. The well density in the entire block is 17 wells per sq. km. Total no. of the wells in the block are enumerated as 3911, according to the Ground Water Estimation Commi ttee.

Natural Division : Godavari Depression Region

Administration:

Division: Telangana. Parliamentary Constituency: 4 Nizamabad. District: Karimnagar. Mandal: Ibrahimpatnam. Assembly Constituency: 20 Koratla. Gram Panchayat: 20

Places of Tourist Interest:

Ibrahimpatnam : Ibrahimpatnam is situated at a distance of 32 kms. from Hyderabad city on the Hyderabad Nagarj unasagar Road. The place derived its name from Ibrahim Qutb Shah who ruled over the Golconda Kingdom from A.D. 1550 to 1580. The temples of Hanuman, Chennakesava, Narasimha, the Dargah of Ibrahim Qutub Shah, the chilla (building on the tankbund) raised in memory of the Muslim preacher Hazrat Ali and the 46 metres high mosque constitute the places of worship of the Hindus and Muslims. Among the works of public utility executed at the place during the reign of Ibrahim Qutb Shah, the tank of Ibrahimpatnam was the most important and it irrigates over 480 hectares. The Rangapur observatory, an important link in the chain of astronomical observ atories in India is, situated near Rangapur village about 56 kms. from Hyderabad City. It is reported to contain the largest telescope in South East Asia.

Fairs and Festivals:

Visweswaraswamy Temple Kalyanothsavam It is celebrated from margasira Suddha Ekadasi to margasisa Bahula Vidiya. Dhwajarohanam (flag hoisting) and the inauguration of the function take place on the first day, kalyanoths avam is celebrated on the fourth day night after ankurar panam, seva etc., during the intervening period. The car festival is held on Purnima. After vasanthothsavam on Bahula Padyami, the celebrations terminate with pavalimpuseva on Bahula Vidiya. Kondapalle with its ancient hill fort was under the yoke of Western Chalukya Kings during the reign of Thribhuvanamalla.

Villages: 18 **Inhabited:** 18 **Uninhabited:** 0

Ranking	District	State	National
Area	29	645	4461
Population	19	481	5236
Sex Ratio	6	26	264
Child Sex Ratio	31	614	2428
Literacy Rate	52	969	5550
Density	4	30	3789
Work Participation Rate	27	446	154

Gram Panchayats:

Ammakkapet, Bandalingapur, Bardipur, Dabba, Eradandi Errapur, Fakir Kondapur, Gudur, Ibrahimpatnam Keshavapur, Kojan Kothur, Komatikondapur, Maidpally Mularampur, Rajeshwar Raopet, Shathakkapally Thimmapur, Varshakonda, Vemulakurthy, Yamapur.

Amenities:

Education: Primary School in 18 villages, Middle school in 11 villages, Matriculation or Secondary School in 6 villages, namely Vemulakurthi, Godur, Ibrahimpatnam,

Varshakonda, Bandalingapur, Maidpalle (W).

Higher Secondary or Pre University Courses or Intermediate or Junior College in 0 village of the CD Block, College in 0 village, Adult Literacy Center in 16 villages.

Medical: Hospital in 0 village, Dispensary in 1 village, Health Center in 1 village, Sub Center in 8 villages, Maternity and Child Welfare Center in 0 village, Community health workers in 0 village.

The Village having Hospital or Dispensary or Health Center is Bandalingapur.

Drinking Water: Tap water in 18 villages, Tank water in 18 villages, Well water in 18 villages, Tubewell in 18 villages and more than one source in 18 villages.

Bank: Banking facility in 1 villages, namely, Ibrahimpatnam.

Credit Society in 17 villages Agricultural Credit Society in 5 Non-Agricultural Credit Society in 17 villages.

Others: Power supply in 18 villages, Cinema hall in 0 village, sport club in 0 village, Stadium or Auditorium or Community Hall in 0 village, Post Office in 11 villages.

There are 18 villages having bus facilities.

Village with most of facilities: Ibrahimpatnam.

Villages without Amenities (Education): None..

Scheduled Castes: Out of the total population of 50845 persons, 7509 persons (14.77%) belong to Scheduled Castes.

The villages having less than 10% SC population are None..

The villages having more than 50% SC population are None.

Sex ratio of Scheduled Caste population is 516.

Scheduled Castes Literates and Illiterates by Sex:

	Persons	Males	Females
Literate	2,625	1,692	933
Illiterate	4,884	1,946	2,938
Literacy rate	40.3	53.9	27.6
Graduate	23	23	0

Scheduled Castes (Dominant):

Mala, Madiga, Gosangi, Madiga Dasu etc., Malajangam

For their cultural identity please see Appendix-I

Villages without Scheduled Castes: There are 0 village without any scheduled caste population.

Scheduled Tribes: Out of the total population of 50845 persons, 1684 persons (3.31%) belong to Scheduled Tribes.

The villages having less than 10% ST population are Komatikondapur, Erdandi, Bardipur, Mularampur Vemulakurthi, Kamala Nagar, Yamapur, Fakir Kondapur Godur, Ibrahimpatnam, Varshakonda, Ammakkapet Rajeswara Rao Pet, Bandalingapur, Maidpalle (W).

The villages having more than 50% ST population are None.

Sex ratio of Scheduled tribe population is 489.

Scheduled Tribes Literates and Illiterates by Sex:

	Persons	Males	Females
Literate	419	305	114
Illiterate	1,265	555	710
Literacy rate	29.5	43.3	15.9
Graduate	5	5	0

Scheduled Tribes (Dominant):

Sugalis etc., Gond etc., Yerukulas, Chenchu etc. Bagata

For their cultural identity please see Appendix-II

Villages without Scheduled Tribes: There are 2 villages without any scheduled tribe population.

Literates and Illiterates by Sex (Total Population):

	Persons	Males	Females
Literate	18,347	11,770	6,577
Illiterate	32,498	12,967	19,531
Literacy rate	42	56	29
Graduate	245	226	19

Agriculture: ***Distribution of villages according to land use:***

Out of 18 villages, Total area (in hectare) is 18421, out of that 68.2 percent is cultivable and 51.98 percent of the cultivable area is irrigated.

Sources of Irrigation (Hectares): Government Canal 2287.6, Private Canal 0, Well without Electricity 500, Well with Electricity 3027.85, Tubewell without Electricity 0, Tubewell with Electricity 0, Tank 713.8, River 0, Lake 0, Waterfall 0, Others 0.

Villages with population of 5000 to 9999: Ibrahimpatnam, Bandalingapur.

Villages with population of 10000 and above: None

Distribution of Workers:

	Persons	Males	Females	WPR
Cultivators	9,384	5,398	3,986	30.72
Agricultural Labour	7,841	4,305	3,536	25.67
Household Industry	7,998	735	7,263	26.19
Other Workers	5,320	4,195	1,125	17.42
Main Workers	28,878	14,019	14,859	94.55
Marginal Workers	1,665	614	1,051	5.45
Total Workers	30,543	14,633	15,910	

Religion: Major Religious Communities:

	Persons	Males	Females	Sex Ratio
Hindu (96.76%)	49,197	23,926	25,271	1,056
Muslim (2.42%)	1,229	604	625	1,035
Christian (0.76%)	386	187	199	1,064
Sikh (0.03%)	15	11	4	364
Buddhists (0%)	-	-	-	-
Jain (0%)	-	-	-	-

Agewise Data:

	Persons	Males	Females	Sex Ratio

All ages	50,845	24,737	26,108	1055
0-14	15,930	8,105	7,825	965
15-44	24,750	11,869	12,881	1085
45-79	9,725	4,578	5,147	1124
80+	310	110	200	1818
Age not stated	130	75	55	733

Languages (Dominant):
Telugu, Hindi, Urdu, Oriya, Tamil

Disabled Population:

	Persons	Males	Females	%
Total Disabled	767	449	318	
In Seeing	323	205	118	42.11
In Speech	57	25	32	7.43
In Hearing	32	14	18	4.17
In Movement	241	142	99	31.42
Mentally	114	63	51	14.86

IBRAHIMPATNAM

Ibrahimpatnam C.D. Block lies in the eastern part of Rangareddy district. The Block is located at a distance of 30 kms. from district headquarters (Serilingampalle). There are 28 villages in the block with the total population of 67,198 persons. Area of the C.D. Block is 239.82 sq. kms. It is bounded by Hayathnagar Mandal on north, Nalgonda district on east, Manchal Mandal on south-east, Yacharam Mandal on south, Kandukur Mandal on south-west, Maheswaram Mandal on west, and Saroorna gar Mandal on north-west.

Communications :

Roadways : State Highway (S.H.): Direction- Hyderabad to Yacharam. Nearest Villages- Bongloor, Chintapalleguda, Ibrahimpatnam (Bagath), Mangalpalle.

Backwards Region Grants Fund: It receives Backward Region Grants.

Integrated Child Development Scheme (ICDS) Project: Ibrahimpatnam, Total Anganwadi Centres: 139

Annual Rainfall: Average Rainfall 721 mm

Ground Water: Availability of the Ground Water in the Basin is 2345 H.A.M. and the utilization is 2591 H. A.M. It belongs to Over Exploited category. Depth to water level varies from 5 to 20 meter below the ground. Most of the wells go down in summer months. The well density in the entire block is 9 wells per sq. km. Total no. of the wells in the block are enumerated as 2679, according to the Ground Water Estimation Commi ttee.

Natural Division : Telangana Plateau Region

Administration:

Division: Telangana. Parliamentary Constituency: 14 Bhongir. District: Rangareddy.

Mandal: Ibrahimpatnam. Assembly Constituency: 48 Ibrahi mpatnam. Gram Panchayat: 22.

Villages: 28 **Inhabited:** 22 **Uninhabited:** 6

Ranking	District	State	National
Area	9	346	3508
Population	5	177	4595
Sex Ratio	17	905	3106
Child Sex Ratio	16	397	1480
Literacy Rate	9	351	3200
Density	25	896	3748
Work Participation Rate	11	435	3046

Gram Panchayats:
Adibatla, Bongloor, Cherlapatelguda, Dandumailaram Ibrahimpatnam, Kappapahad, Kongarakalan, Mangalpalle Mukunoor, Naganpally, Nerrepally, Patelguda Pocharam, Polkampally, Raipole, Ramdaspally Seetharampet, Seriguda, Thurkaguda, Tulekalan Uppariguda, Yeliminedu.

Amenities:

Education: Primary School in 21 villages, Middle school in 14 villages, Matriculation or Secondary School in 10 villages, namely Kongara Kalan, Adibatla, Ibrahimpatnam (Khalsa), Polkampalle, Dandumailaram, Raipole, Ibrahimpatnam (Bagath), Mangalpalle, Pocharam, Yeliminedu.

Higher Secondary or Pre University Courses or Intermediate or Junior College in 1 village of the CD Block,, namely Ibrahimpatnam (Bagath).

College in 2 villages, Adult Literacy Center in 0 village., Colleges are in villages, namely Ibrahimpatnam (Khalsa), Ibrahimpatnam (Bagath).

Medical: Hospital in 1 village, Dispensary in 1 village, Health Center in 2 villages, Sub Center in 8 villages, Maternity and Child Welfare Center in 0 village, Community health workers in 0 village.

The Villages having Hospital or Dispensary or Health Center are Ibrahimpatnam (Khalsa), Dandumailaram, Ibrahimpatnam (Bagath).

Drinking Water: Tap water in 22 villages, Tank water in 22 villages, Well water in 22 villages, Tubewell in 22 villages and more than one source in 22 villages.

Bank: Banking facility in 22 villages, namely, Kongara Kalan, Adibatla, Bongloor, Chintapalleguda Ramdaspalle, Ibrahimpatnam (Khalsa), Naganpalle Polkampalle, Narrepalle, Dandumailaram, Muknoor Yengalaguda, Raipole, Ibrahimpatnam (Bagath) Mangalpalle, Ramreddiguda, Pocharam, Yeliminedu Yerrakunta, Turkaguda, Kappapahad, Toolekalan.

Credit Society in 9 villages Agricultural Credit Society in 5 Non-Agricultural Credit Society in 8 villages.

Others: Power supply in 22 villages, Cinema hall in 1 village, sport club in 0 village, Stadium or Auditorium or Community

Hall in 0 village, Post Office in 11 villages.
There are 21 villages having bus facilities.
Villages with most of facilities: Kongara Kalan Ibrahimpatnam (Khalsa), Polkampalle, Dandumailaram Raipole, Ibrahimpatnam (Bagath), Yeliminedu Toolekalan.
Villages without amenities (Education):
Yerrakunta..
Scheduled Castes: Out of the total population of 67198 persons, 15488 persons (23.05%) belong to Scheduled Castes.
The villages having less than 10% SC population are None..
The villages having more than 50% SC population are None.
Sex ratio of Scheduled Caste population is 496.
Scheduled Castes Literates and Illiterates by Sex:

	Persons	Males	Females
Literate	6,842	4,397	2,445
Illiterate	8,646	3,402	5,244
Literacy rate	51.5	65.6	37.2
Graduate	103	91	12

Scheduled Castes (Dominant):
Madiga, Mala, Beda Jangam etc., Bindla Generic Castes etc.
For their cultural identity please see Appendix-I
Villages without Scheduled Castes: There are 6 villages without any scheduled caste population.
Scheduled Tribes: Out of the total population of 67198 persons, 1941 persons (2.89%) belong to Scheduled Tribes.
The villages having less than 10% ST population are Bongloor, Chintapalleguda, Ramdaspalle Ibrahimpatnam (Khalsa), Naganpalle, Polkampalle Narrepalle, Dandumailaram, Muknoor, Yengalaguda Raipole, Ibrahimpatnam (Bagath), Mangalpalle Ramreddiguda, Pocharam, Yeliminedu, Yerrakunta Turkaguda, Kappapahad, Toolekalan.
The villages having more than 50% ST population are None.
Sex ratio of Scheduled tribe population is 522.
Scheduled Tribes Literates and Illiterates by Sex:

	Persons	Males	Females
Literate	611	342	269
Illiterate	1,330	586	744
Literacy rate	37.8	44.2	31.8
Graduate	15	14	1

Scheduled Tribes (Dominant):
Sugalis etc., Koya etc., Gond etc., Yerukulas Generic Tribes etc.
For their cultural identity please see Appendix-II
Villages without Scheduled Tribes: There are 14 villages without any scheduled tribe population.
Literates and Illiterates by Sex (Total Population):

	Persons	Males	Females
Literate	33,293	20,641	12,652
Illiterate	33,905	13,687	20,218
Literacy rate	58	70	45
Graduate	1,145	915	230

Agriculture: ***Distribution of villages according to land use:***
Out of 28 villages, Total area (in hectare) is 23982, out of that 46.49 percent is cultivable and 36.57 percent of the cultivable area is irrigated.
Sources of Irrigation (Hectares): Government Canal 0, Private Canal 0, Well without Electricity 213, Well with Electricity 2796.76, Tubewell without Electricity 213, Tubewell with Electricity 439.87, Tank 414.69, River 0, Lake 0, Waterfall 0, Others 0.
Villages with population of 5000 to 9999:
Kongara Kalan, Ibrahimpatnam (Khalsa), Dandumailaram.
Villages with population of 10000 and above:
Ibrahimpatnam (Bagath).
Distribution of Workers:

	Persons	Males	Females	WPR
Cultivators	5,428	3,707	1,721	17.5
Agricultural Labour	9,963	3,897	6,066	32.12
Household Industry	648	368	280	2.09
Other Workers	14,975	11,299	3,676	48.28
Main Workers	25,281	17,157	8,124	81.51
Marginal Workers	5,733	2,114	3,619	18.49
Total Workers	31,014	19,271	11,743	

Religion: Major Religious Communities:

	Persons	Males	Females	Sex Ratio
Hindu (93.62%)	62,908	32,117	30,791	959
Muslim (5.82%)	3,911	2,009	1,902	947
Christian (0.43%)	288	158	130	823
Sikh (0.04%)	24	16	8	500
Buddhists (0.02%)	14	4	10	2,500
Jain (0%)	-	-	-	-

Agewise Data:

	Persons	Males	Females	Sex Ratio
All ages	67,198	34,328	32,870	958
0-14	22,597	11,142	11,455	1028
15-44	32,272	16,960	15,312	903
45-79	11,618	5,861	5,757	982
80+	616	331	285	861
Age not stated	95	34	61	1794

Languages (Dominant):
Telugu, Urdu, Oriya, Hindi, Marathi
Disabled Population:

	Persons	Males	Females	%
Total Disabled	1,261	748	513	

In Seeing	398	212	186	31.56
In Speech	133	68	65	10.55
In Hearing	54	27	27	4.28

In Movement	499	340	159	39.57
Mentally	177	101	76	14.04

IBRAHIMPATNAM

Ibrahimpatnam C.D. Block lies in the north-western part of Krishna district. The Block is located at a distance of 90 kms. from district headquarters (Machili patnam). There are 18 villages in the block with the total population of 91,254 persons. Area of the C.D. Block is 104.81 sq. kms. It is bounded in the north by Mandal G. Konduru, in the south by district Guntur and River Krishna, in the east by Mandals Konduru and Vijayawada Rural, and in the west by Mandals Kanchikach erla, Veerullapadu and G. Konduru.

Communications:

Roadways : NH- 9: Direction- Secunderabad to Vijayawada. Nearest Villages- Zami Machavaram, Kethanakonda, Kacha varam, Guntupalle, Trilochanapuram, Mulapadu, Jupudi, Ibrahimpatnam, Tummalapalem.

Railway Station: Kondapalle.

River: Krishna Nadi- Nearest Villages- Damuluru, Kotika lapudi, Guntupalle, Trilochanapuram, Mulapadu, Jupudi, Ibrahimpatnam, Tummalapalem.

Annaul Rainfall: Average Rainfall 1512 mm

Ground Water: Availability of the Ground Water in the Basin is (Information not avavible) H.A.M .and the utilization is (Information not avavible) H.A.M. It belongs to (Information not avavible) category. Depth to water level varies from 3 to 10 meter below the ground. Most of the wells go down in summer months.

Forest and Reserved **Forest:** (Kondapalli R.F.)- Nearest Villages- Zami Navi Pothavaram, N.Pothavaram, Trilochan apuram, Jupudi, Ibrahimpatnam, Malkapuram, Kondapalle.

Natural Division : Krishna Delta Region

Administration:

Division: Coastal Andhra. Parliamentary Constituency: 29 Vijayawada. District: Krishna. Mandal: Ibrahimpatnam. Assembly Constituency: 201 Mylavaram. Gram Panchayat: 12

Fairs and Festivals:

Khilla Hazarath Gale Shahid Urs : It is an annual funct ion. Hazarath Gale Shahib, a valiant commander was behea ded on his horse back while fighting. His head fell on the Kondapalle hill while the trunk was seated firm on the horse back till it fell down after the horse has galloped a distance of over 12 kms. A Dargah was constructed at the spot where the trunk had fallen. The Dargah that was constructed at the place where the head rolled down is distinguished as Kondapalle Khilla Dargah. Urs is celebrated for two days from 27th of Ramzan (January-February). A procession starts at 7 a.m. on that day, many thousands of Muslims taking gilaf (saffron coloured cloth) and poola duppati (a cloth (chadar) covered with flowers designs) on a horse back. The tomb of Gale Shahib is covered with gilaf. Sweets are then offered to the tomb and later distribu ted among the congregation. The next day is a day of feasts when members of Muslim families are entertained at a dinner. A few poor people are also fed.

Villages: 18 **Inhabited:** 15 **Uninhabited:** 3

Ranking	District	State	National
Area	43	1010	5665
Population	1	12	3746
Sex Ratio	44	976	3464
Child Sex Ratio	19	373	1409
Literacy Rate	7	54	1062
Density	49	1069	1011
Work Participation Rate	2	19	4627

Gram Panchayats:

Chilukuru, Damuluru, Elaprolu, Guntupalli Ibrahimpatnam, Jupudi, Kachavaram, Ketanakonda Kondapalli, Kotikalapudi, Mulapadu, Thummalapalem.

Amenities:

Education: Primary School in 13 villages, Middle school in 6 villages, Matriculation or Secondary School in 4 villages, namely Mulapadu, Ibrahimpatnam, Kondapalle, Guntupalle.

Higher Secondary or Pre University Courses or Intermediate or Junior College in 2 villages of the CD Block,, namely Ibrahimpatnam, Kondapalle.

College in 2 villages, Adult Literacy Center in 5 villages., Colleges are in villages, namely Jupudi, Ibrahimpatnam.

Medical: Hospital in 2 villages, Dispensary in 1 village, Health Center in 1 village, Sub Center in 9 villages, Maternity and Child Welfare Center in 2 villages, Community health workers in 0 village.

The Villages having Hospital or Dispensary or Health Center are Ibrahimpatnam, Kondapalle.

Drinking Water: Tap water in 14 villages, Tank water in 0 villages, Well water in 5 villages, Tubewell in 0 village and more than one source in 12 villages.

Bank: Banking facility in 7 villages, namely, Damuluru, Kotikalapudi, Mulapadu, Ibrahimpatnam Kondapalle, Elaprolu, Guntupalle.

Credit Society in 9 villages Agricultural Credit Society in 6 Non-Agricultural Credit Society in 9 villages.

Others: Power supply in 15 villages, Cinema hall in 4 villages,

sport club in 2 villages, Stadium or Auditorium or Community Hall in 1 village, Post Office in 11 villages.

There are 15 villages having bus facilities.

Villages with most of facilities: Damuluru Kotikalapudi, Mulapadu, Ibrahimpatnam, Kondapalle Elaprolu, Guntupalle.

Villages without amenities (Education):
Zami Machavaram, Malkapuram..

Scheduled Castes: Out of the total population of 91254 persons, 19529 persons (21.4%) belong to Scheduled Castes.

The villages having less than 10% SC population are None..

The villages having more than 50% SC population are None.

Sex ratio of Scheduled Caste population is 483.

Scheduled Castes Literates and Illiterates by Sex:

	Persons	Males	Females
Literate	12,083	7,024	5,059
Illiterate	7,446	3,078	4,368
Literacy rate	71.2	79.8	62.0
Graduate	642	438	204

Scheduled Castes (Dominant):
Mala, Madiga, Relli, Beda Jangam etc.
Madiga Dasu etc.

For their cultural identity please see Appendix-I

Villages without Scheduled Castes: There are 3 villages without any scheduled caste population.

Scheduled Tribes: Out of the total population of 91254 persons, 4628 persons (5.07%) belong to Scheduled Tribes.

The villages having less than 10% ST population are Trilochanapuram, Zami Machavaram, Kethanakonda Kachavaram, Chilukuru, Damuluru, Kotikalapudi Mulapadu, Ibrahimpatnam, Malkapuram, Kondapalle Elaprolu, Tummalapalem, Guntupalle.

The villages having more than 50% ST population are None.

Sex ratio of Scheduled tribe population is 480.

Scheduled Tribes Literates and Illiterates by Sex:

	Persons	Males	Females
Literate	2,403	1,469	934
Illiterate	2,225	938	1,287
Literacy rate	59.6	69.5	48.7
Graduate	91	79	12

Scheduled Tribes (Dominant):
Sugalis etc., Yerukulas, Yenadis, Konda Dhoras
Koya etc.

For their cultural identity please see Appendix-II

Villages without Scheduled Tribes: There are 5 villages without any scheduled tribe population.

Literates and Illiterates by Sex (Total Population):

	Persons	Males	Females
Literate	57,014	32,093	24,921
Illiterate	34,240	14,679	19,561
Literacy rate	71	78	64
Graduate	4,059	2,654	1,405

Agriculture: ***Distribution of villages according to land use:***
Out of 18 villages, Total area (in hectare) is 10481, out of that 54.74 percent is cultivable and 57.16 percent of the cultivable area is irrigated.

Sources of Irrigation (Hectares): Government Canal 0, Private Canal 0, Well without Electricity 0, Well with Electricity 132.28, Tubewell without Electricity 3.24, Tubewell with Electricity 987.11, Tank 682.88, River 0, Lake 0, Waterfall 0, Others 1474.08.

Villages with population of 5000 to 9999: None

Villages with population of 10000 and above:
Ibrahimpatnam, Kondapalle, Guntupalle.

Distribution of Workers:

	Persons	Males	Females	WPR
Cultivators	1,735	1,530	205	4.83
Agricultural Labour	10,626	5,525	5,101	29.55
Household Industry	808	472	336	2.25
Other Workers	22,785	18,304	4,481	63.37
Main Workers	29,226	22,701	6,525	81.29
Marginal Workers	6,728	3,130	3,598	18.71
Total Workers	35,954	25,831	10,123	

Religion: Major Religious Communities:

	Persons	Males	Females	Sex Ratio
Hindu (87.98%)	80,284	41,173	39,111	950
Muslim (7.6%)	6,933	3,584	3,349	934
Christian (4.33%)	3,954	1,969	1,985	1,008
Sikh (0.01%)	5	3	2	667
Buddhists (0.01%)	7	4	3	750
Jain (0%)	4	2	2	1,000

Agewise Data:

	Persons	Males	Females	Sex Ratio
All ages	91,254	46,772	44,482	951
0-14	28,184	14,610	13,574	929
15-44	47,943	24,143	23,800	986
45-79	14,534	7,752	6,782	875
80+	483	214	269	1257
Age not stated	110	53	57	1075

Languages (Dominant):
Telugu, Urdu, Hindi, Tamil, Oriya

Disabled Population:

	Persons	Males	Females	%
Total Disabled	1,129	639	490	
In Seeing	261	149	112	23.12
In Speech	155	81	74	13.73
In Hearing	39	17	22	3.45

In Movement	479	280	199	42.43	Mentally	195	112	83	17.27

ICHCHAPURAM

Ichchapuram C.D. Block lies in the north-eastern part of Srikakulam district. It is a part of Ichchapuram Mandal. The Block is located at a distance of 134 kms. from district headquarters (Srikakulam). There are 24 villages in the block with the total population of 44,042 persons. Area of the C.D. Block is 99.28 sq. kms. It is bounded in the south by Mandal Kaviti, in the east by Bay of Bengal, and it has common bounda ry with the state of Orissa on north, east and west.

Communications:

Roadways : NH- 5: Direction- Waltair to Chitrapur. Neare st Village- Loddaputti.

River: Nearest Villages- Paitharikeerthipuram, Koligam, Boddabada, Arakabhadra, Sasanam, Takatlabarampuram, Birlangi, Masakapuram, Loddaputti, Dharmapuram, Kotari, Edupuram, Kesapuram, Burjapadu.

Backwards Region Grants Fund: It receives Backward Region Grants.

Integrated Child Development Scheme (ICDS) Project: Ichapuram, Total Anganwadi Centres: 269

Annual Rainfall: Average Rainfall 1036.5 mm

Ground Water: Availability of the Ground Water in the Basin is (Information not avavible) H.A.M .and the utilization is (Information not avavible) H.A.M. It belongs to (Information not avavible) category. Depth to water level varies from 3 to 10 meter below the ground. Most of the wells go down in summer months.

Coastal Villages: Nearest Village- Burjapadu

Administration:

Division: Coastal Andhra. Parliamentary Constituency: 19 Srikakulam. District: Srikakulam. Mandal: Ichchapuram. Assembly Constituency: 120 Ichachapuram. Gram Panchay at: 21.

Border Villages: (Orissa)- Nearest Villages- Muchindra, Kedaripuram, Balakrishnapuram, Munibhadra, Mandapalle, Telukunchi, Haripuram, Boddakali, Paitharikeerthipuram, Koligam, Boddabada, Arakabhadra, Birlangi, Masakapuram, Loddaputti, Sasanam, Takatlabarampuram, Tulasigam.

Villages: 24 **Inhabited:** 24 **Uninhabited:** 0

Ranking	**District**	**State**	**National**
Area	37	1075	5921
Population	33	692	5551
Sex Ratio	1	1	27
Child Sex Ratio	3	117	296
Literacy Rate	23	595	4212
Density	25	821	1847
Work Participation Rate	4	69	2511

Gram Panchayats:

Arakabadra, Balakrishnapuram, Birlangi, Boddabada Burjapadu, Dharmapuram, Edupuram, Haripuram Kedaripuram, Keerthipuram, Kesupuram, Koligam Kothari, Loddaputti, Mandapalli, Masakhapuram Mutchindra, Paitari, T.Berhampuram, Telukunchi Tulasigam.

Amenities:

Education: Primary School in 24 villages, Middle school in 7 villages, Matriculation or Secondary School in 5 villages, namely Koligam, Birlangi, Loddaputti, Dharmapuram, Edupuram.

Higher Secondary or Pre University Courses or Intermediate or Junior College in 0 village of the CD Block, College in 0 village, Adult Literacy Center in 12 villages.

Medical: Hospital in 0 village, Dispensary in 2 villages, Health Center in 1 village, Sub Center in 7 villages, Maternity and Child Welfare Center in 0 village, Community health workers in 0 village.

The Villages having Hospital or Dispensary or Health Center are Birlangi, Edupuram.

Drinking Water: Tap water in 24 villages, Tank water in 24 villages, Well water in 24 villages, Tubewell in 24 villages and more than one source in 24 villages.

Bank: None.

Credit Society in 1 village Agricultural Credit Society in 1 Non-Agricultural Credit Society in 0 village.

Others: Power supply in 24 villages, Cinema hall in 0 village, sport club in 0 village, Stadium or Auditorium or Community Hall in 0 village, Post Office in 10 villages.

There are 24 villages having bus facilities.

Village with most of facilities: None.

Villages without Amenities (Education): None..

Scheduled Castes: Out of the total population of 44085 persons, 1426 persons (3.23%) belong to Scheduled Castes. The villages having less than 10% SC population are Muchindra, Kedaripuram, Balakrishnapuram, Munibhadra Mandapalle, Telukunchi, Paitharikeerthipuram Koligam, Boddabada, Arakabhadra, Birlangi Masakapuram, Loddaputti, Tulasigam, Dharmapuram Purnatakam, Kotari, Edupuram, Kesapuram, Burjapadu.

The villages having more than 50% SC population are None.

Sex ratio of Scheduled Caste population is 546.

Scheduled Castes Literates and Illiterates by Sex:

	Persons	Males	Females
Literate	799	422	377
Illiterate	627	225	402
Literacy rate	65.9	79.9	55.1
Graduate	20	16	4

Scheduled Castes (Dominant):

Mala, Dandasi, Madiga, Bavuri, Mala Dasari

For their cultural identity please see Appendix-I

Villages without Scheduled Castes: There are 3 villages without any scheduled caste population.

Scheduled Tribes: Out of the total population of 44085 persons, 625 persons (1.42%) belong to Scheduled Tribes. The villages having less than 10% ST population are Muchindra, Kedaripuram, Balakrishnapuram, Munibhadra Mandapalle, Telukunchi, Haripuram, Boddakali Paitharikeerthipuram, Koligam, Boddabada Arakabhadra, Sasanam, Takatlabarampuram, Birlangi Masakapuram, Loddaputti, Tulasigam, Dharmapuram Purnatakam, Kotari, Edupuram, Kesapuram, Burjapadu. The villages having more than 50% ST population are None.

Sex ratio of Scheduled tribe population is 547.

Scheduled Tribes Literates and Illiterates by Sex:

	Persons	Males	Females
Literate	307	176	131
Illiterate	318	107	211
Literacy rate	55.3	70.1	43.1
Graduate	6	6	0

Scheduled Tribes (Dominant):

Kotia etc., Yerukulas, Savaras etc., Sugalis etc.

For their cultural identity please see Appendix-II

Villages without Scheduled Tribes: There are 19 villages without any scheduled tribe population.

Literates and Illiterates by Sex (Total Population):

	Persons	Males	Females
Literate	19,352	11,685	7,667
Illiterate	24,733	8,544	16,189
Literacy rate	52	70	38
Graduate	284	250	34

Agriculture: ***Distribution of villages according to land use:*** Out of 24 villages, Total area (in hectare) is 7403, out of that 72.69 percent is cultivable and 53.34 percent of the cultivable area is irrigated.

Sources of Irrigation (Hectares): Government Canal 762.79, Private Canal 0, Well without Electricity 0, Well with Electricity 0, Tubewell without Electricity 98.24, Tubewell with Electricity 52.14, Tank 751.18, River 0, Lake 0, Waterfall 0, Others 1205.77.

Villages with population of 5000 to 9999: Edupuram.

Villages with population of 10000 and above: None

Distribution of Workers:

	Persons	Males	Females	WPR
Cultivators	5,027	3,026	2,001	24.02
Agricultural Labour	9,733	3,557	6,176	46.5
Household Industry	897	366	531	4.29
Other Workers	5,274	3,628	1,646	25.2
Main Workers	12,768	8,019	4,749	61
Marginal Workers	8,163	2,558	5,605	39
Total Workers	20,931	10,577	10,354	

Religion: Major Religious Communities:

	Persons	Males	Females	Sex Ratio
Hindu (99.6%)	43,910	20,162	23,748	1,178
Muslim (0.08%)	37	17	20	1,176
Christian (0.1%)	42	19	23	1,211
Sikh (0%)	-	-	-	-
Buddhists (0%)	-	-	-	-
Jain (0%)	-	-	-	-

Agewise Data:

	Persons	Males	Females	Sex Ratio
All ages	44,085	20,229	23,856	1179
0-14	15,606	7,632	7,974	1045
15-44	19,555	8,756	10,799	1233
45-79	8,551	3,709	4,842	1305
80+	318	108	210	1944
Age not stated	55	24	31	1292

Languages (Dominant):

Telugu, Oriya, Urdu, Gondi, Marathi

Disabled Population:

	Persons	Males	Females	%
Total Disabled	915	487	428	
In Seeing	450	234	216	49.18
In Speech	84	48	36	9.18
In Hearing	35	15	20	3.83
In Movement	262	158	104	28.63
Mentally	84	32	52	9.18

ICHODA

Ichoda C.D. Block lies in the north-west part of Adilab ad district. The Block is located at a distance of 34 kms. from district headquarters (Adilabad). There are 42 villages in the block with the total population of 43,179 persons. Area of the C.D. Block is 245.10 sq. kms. It is bounded by Gudihathnoor Mandal on north and north-east, Utnoor Mandal on east and south-east, Khanapur Mandal on south-east, Neradigonda Mandal on south and south and south-west, Bazarhathnoor Mandal on west and north-west.

Communications :

Roadways : NH- 7: Direction- Nirmal to Adilabad Nearest Villages- Gubbam Junni, Babuldhole, Boregaon, Jamidi, Adegaon (Buzurg), Kokasmannar, Makhra, (Buzurg), Ichoda.

State Highway (S.H.): Direction- Kinwat to Ichoda, Nearest Villages- Ichoda, Adegaon (Khurd).

River: Kadam Nadi- Nearest Village- Babjepet village.

Backwards Region Grants Fund: It receives Backward Region Grants.

Annual Rainfall: Average Rainfall 1174 mm

Ground Water: Availability of the ground water in the Basin is 1868 H.A.M.and the utilization is 1032 H.A. M. It belongs to Safe category. Depth to water level varies from 5 to 10 meter below the ground. Most of the wells go down in summer months, according to the Ground Water Estimation Committee.

Forest and Reserved **Forest:** Nearest Villages- Neradigonda, Babjepet, Jogipet, Sirichalma, Narayanapur, Neradigonda (K).

Natural Division : Telangana Plateau Region

Administration:

Division: Telangana. Parliamentary Constituency: 1 Adilabad (ST). District: Adilabad. Mandal: Ichoda. Assembly Constituency: 8 Boath (ST). Gram Panchayat: 19

Villages: 42 **Inhabited:** 42 **Uninhabited:** 0

Ranking	District	State	National
Area	30	269	3217
Population	14	717	5593
Sex Ratio	43	857	2893
Child Sex Ratio	26	355	1271
Literacy Rate	9	602	4243
Density	39	754	5323
Work Participation Rate	13	853	2204

Gram Panchayats:

Adegaon K, Boregaon, Dhabha K, Dharampuri, Girjam Gundala, Ichoda, Keshavpatnam, Kokasmannur, Malyal Mankapur, Mokhra- B, Narsapur, Neredigonda-G, Ponna Sirichalma, Sirikonda, Soanpalle, Talamadri.

Amenities:

Education: Primary School in 40 villages, Middle school in 11 villages, Matriculation or Secondary School in 3 villages, namely Boregaon, Ponna, Ichoda.

Higher Secondary or Pre University Courses or Intermediate or Junior College in 1 village of the CD Block,, namely Ichoda.

College in 0 village, Adult Literacy Center in 0 village.

Medical: Hospital in 0 village, Dispensary in 2 villages, Health Center in 2 villages, Sub Center in 12 villages, Maternity and Child Welfare Center in 0 village, Community health workers in 0 village.

The Villages having Hospital or Dispensary or Health Center are Sirikonda, Ichoda, Narsapur.

Drinking Water: Tap water in 40 villages, Tank water in 40 villages, Well water in 42 villages, Tubewell in 40 villages and more than one source in 40 villages.

Bank: Banking facility in 3 villages, namely, Talamadri, Ichoda, Narsapur.

Credit Society in 12 villages Agricultural Credit Society in 10 Non-Agricultural Credit Society in 3 villages.

Others: Power supply in 42 villages, Cinema hall in 1 village, sport club in 0 village, Stadium or Auditorium or Community Hall in 0 village, Post Office in 1 village.

There are 17 villages having bus facilities.

Village with most of facilities: Ichoda.

Villages without amenities (Education):

Babuldhole, Lingapur..

Scheduled Castes: Out of the total population of 43179 persons, 7201 persons (16.68%) belong to Scheduled Castes.

The villages having less than 10% SC population are Gubba, Babuldhole, Sunkidi, Sirikonda, Heerapur Dhoba (Buzurg), Madapur, Girjam, Chincholi, Navagaon Salyada, Mankapur, Jalda, Makhra (Buzurg) Keshapatnam, Gundala, Neradigonda, Lingapur Gaidpalle, Gandiwagu, Babjepet, Jogipet, Narayanapur Neradigonda (K).

The villages having more than 50% SC population are None.

Sex ratio of Scheduled Caste population is 491.

Scheduled Castes Literates and Illiterates by Sex:

	Persons	Males	Females
Literate	3,206	2,118	1,088
Illiterate	3,995	1,546	2,449
Literacy rate	51.9	67.7	35.7
Graduate	80	71	9

Scheduled Castes (Dominant):

Madiga, Mahar, Mala, Paky etc., Beda Jangam etc.

For their cultural identity please see Appendix-I

Villages without Scheduled Castes: There are 13 villages without any scheduled caste population.

Scheduled Tribes: Out of the total population of 43179 persons, 12160 persons (28.16%) belong to Scheduled Tribes.

The villages having less than 10% ST population are Adegaon (Khurd), Junni, Adegaon (Buzurg), Navagaon Makhra (Khurd), Gundi, Keshapatnam, Narsapur.

The villages having more than 50% ST population are Gubba, Sunkidi, Heerapur, Girjam, Dhaba Khurd Salyada, Malyal, Mankapur, Neradigonda, Lingapur Gaidpalle, Gandiwagu, Babjepet, Narayanapur Neradigonda (K).

Sex ratio of Scheduled tribe population is 483.

Scheduled Tribes Literates and Illiterates by Sex:

	Persons	Males	Females
Literate	4,305	3,042	1,263
Illiterate	7,855	3,242	4,613
Literacy rate	43.7	59.3	26.8
Graduate	49	45	4

Scheduled Tribes (Dominant):

Gond etc., Sugalis etc., Andh, Pardhan, Kolam etc.

For their cultural identity please see Appendix-II

Villages without Scheduled Tribes: There is 1 village without any scheduled tribe population.

Literates and Illiterates by Sex (Total Population):

	Persons	Males	Females
Literate	18,381	12,053	6,328
Illiterate	24,798	9,953	14,845
Literacy rate	52	67	36
Graduate	419	359	60

Agriculture: ***Distribution of villages according to land use:*** Out of 42 villages, Total area (in hectare) is 26232, out of that 54.14 percent is cultivable and 4.49 percent of the cultivable area is irrigated.

Sources of Irrigation (Hectares): Government Canal 274.41, Private Canal 0, Well without Electricity 8.09, Well with Electricity 0, Tubewell without Electricity 7.2, Tubewell with Electricity 344, Tank 4, River 0, Lake 0, Waterfall 0, Others 0.

Villages with population of 5000 to 9999: Ichoda.

Villages with population of 10000 and above: None

Distribution of Workers:

	Persons	Males	Females	WPR
Cultivators	9,362	5,196	4,166	45.87
Agricultural Labour	6,585	2,935	3,650	32.26
Household Industry	1,036	355	681	5.08
Other Workers	3,428	2,883	545	16.79
Main Workers	18,577	10,701	7,876	91.01
Marginal Workers	1,834	668	1,166	8.99
Total Workers	20,411	11,369	9,042	

Religion: Major Religious Communities:

	Persons	Males	Females	Sex Ratio
Hindu (80.06%)	34,570	17,655	16,915	958
Muslim (19.12%)	8,255	4,171	4,084	979
Christian (0.17%)	72	34	38	1,118
Sikh (0.09%)	41	21	20	952
Buddhists (0.52%)	224	118	106	898
Jain (0%)	-	-	-	-

Agewise Data:

	Persons	Males	Females	Sex Ratio
All ages	43,179	22,006	21,173	962
0-14	17,662	9,238	8,424	912
15-44	19,031	9,679	9,352	966
45-79	6,187	2,950	3,237	1097
80+	230	101	129	1277
Age not stated	69	38	31	816

Languages (Dominant):

Marathi, Telugu, Gondi, Urdu, Lahnda

Disabled Population:

	Persons	Males	Females	%
Total Disabled	560	334	226	
In Seeing	218	111	107	38.93
In Speech	64	35	29	11.43
In Hearing	28	16	12	5
In Movement	183	129	54	32.68
Mentally	67	43	24	11.96

IEEJ

Ieej C.D. Block lies in the south western part of Mahbu bnagar district. The Block is located at a distance of 110 kms. from district headquarters (Mahbubnagar). There are 19 villages in the block with the total population of 70,689 persons. Area of the C.D. Block is 277.91 sq. kms. It is bounded by Maldakal Mandal on north, Itikyal Mandal on east, Waddipalle Mandal on south and south-east, Kurnool district on south and south-west, Ghattu Mandal on north-west, and It has common border with Karnataka on west.

Communications:

Roadways : Metalled Roads: Nearest Villages- B.Timmapur, Eklaspur, Venkatapur, Ieej.

River: Tungabhadra Nadi- Nearest Villages- Kudakanoor, Pullikal, Kesavapuram, Venisampur.

Backwards Region Grants Fund: It receives Backward Region Grants.

Annual Rainfall: Average Rainfall 510 mm

Ground Water: Availability of the Ground Water in the Basin is 1374 H.A.M. and the utilization is 3637 H. A.M. It belongs to Safe category. Depth to water level varies from 2 to 5 meter below the ground. Most of the wells go down in summer months. The well density in the entire block is 8 wells per sq. km. Total no. of the wells in the block are enumerated as 2223, according to the Ground Water Estimation Committee.

Natural Division : Telangana Plateau Region

Administration:

Division: Telangana. Parliamentary Constituency: 12 Nagarkurnool (SC). District: Mahbubnagar. Mandal: Ieej. Assembly Constituency: 80 Alampur (SC). Gram Panchayat: 19

Border Villages: (Karnataka)- Nearest Villages- Thothin onidoddi, Sindhanoor, Kudakanoor.

Fairs and Festivals:

Sri Beechupalleswamy Rathothsavam : It is celebrated for five days from Vaisakha Suddha Triodasi to Bahula Vidiya (April- May). The rituals observed during the festival are ankurapanam and dhwajarohanam (inaugurati on) in the morning and pallakiseva (procession) in the night of the first day, on the second upanayanamuhurth am in the morning and prabhavali in the night, on the third Vyas puja and vasanta puja in the morning and rathothsavam (car festival) in the night, on the fourth pallakiseva in the morning and prabhavali and paruveta in the night, and on the last day avabru thasnanam in the morning and pallakiseva and dhwajavaro hana visarjanam (conclusion) in the night. Rathothsavam forms an important part of the ritual. Besides the offerings of fruits, flowers, sweets, etc., cash and kind are also offered to the deity in fulfilment of vows.

Villages: 19 **Inhabited:** 18 **Uninhabited:** 1

Ranking	District	State	National
Area	18	213	3026
Population	1	118	4437
Sex Ratio	36	750	2530
Child Sex Ratio	19	516	1923
Literacy Rate	58	1079	6117
Density	18	113	4027
Work Participation Rate	8	521	350

Gram Panchayats:

Bhoompur, Bingidoddy, Chinnatandrapad, Eklaspur Gudidodi, Ieez, Jadadoddy, Kesavaram, Kutkanoor Medikonda, Pullikal, Sindhanoor, Thathinonidoddy Thoomkunta, Uppal, Uthanur, Venisompur, Venkatapuram Yapadinne.

Amenities:

Education: Primary School in 18 villages, Middle school in 14 villages, Matriculation or Secondary School in 8 villages, namely Uthanur, Yapadinne, Ieej, Medikonda, Sindhanoor, Pullikal, Chinna Tandrapadu, Uppal.

Higher Secondary or Pre University Courses or Intermediate or Junior College in 1 village of the CD Block,, namely Ieej.

College in 0 village, Adult Literacy Center in 17 villages.

Medical: Hospital in 0 village, Dispensary in 1 village, Health Center in 2 villages, Sub Center in 10 villages, Maternity and Child Welfare Center in 0 village, Community health workers in 0 village.

The Village having Hospital or Dispensary or Health Center is Medikonda.

Drinking Water: Tap water in 18 villages, Tank water in 18 villages, Well water in 18 villages, Tubewell in 18 villages and more than one source in 18 villages.

Bank: Banking facility in 2 villages, namely, Ieej, Sindhanoor.

Credit Society in 14 villages Agricultural Credit Society in 6 Non-Agricultural Credit Society in 13 villages.

Others: Power supply in 18 villages, Cinema hall in 1 village, sport club in 0 village, Stadium or Auditorium or Community Hall in 0 village, Post Office in 11 villages.

There are 15 villages having **bus** facilities.

Villages with most of facilities: Ieej, Sindhanoor.

Villages without Amenities (Education): None..

Scheduled Castes: Out of the total population of 70689 persons, 14934 persons (21.13%) belong to Scheduled Castes.

The villages having less than 10% SC population are None..

The villages having more than 50% SC population are None.

Sex ratio of Scheduled Caste population is 481.

Scheduled Castes Literates and Illiterates by Sex:

	Persons	Males	Females
Literate	2,840	2,123	717
Illiterate	12,094	5,629	6,465
Literacy rate	23.1	33.3	12.1
Graduate	86	68	18

Scheduled Castes (Dominant):

Madiga, Mala, Mala Dasari, Holeya Dasari Dakkal etc.

For their cultural identity please see Appendix-I

Villages without Scheduled Castes: There are 3 villages without any scheduled caste population.

Scheduled Tribes: Out of the total population of 70689 persons, 242 persons (0.34%) belong to Scheduled Tribes.

The villages having less than 10% ST population are Uthanur, Eklaspur, Devabanda, Bingidoddi, Thoomkunta Jadadoddi, Yapadinne, Venkatapur, Ieej, Medikonda Thothinonidoddi, Sindhanoor, Kudakanoor, Pullikal Kesavapuram, Venisampur, Chinna Tandrapadu, Uppal.

The villages having more than 50% ST population are None.

Sex ratio of Scheduled tribe population is 517.

Scheduled Tribes Literates and Illiterates by Sex:

	Persons	Males	Females
Literate	21	19	2
Illiterate	221	98	123
Literacy rate	11.0	20.4	2.0
Graduate	0	0	0

Scheduled Tribes (Dominant):

Yerukulas, Sugalis etc.

For their cultural identity please see Appendix-II

Villages without Scheduled Tribes: There are 10 villages without any scheduled tribe population.

Literates and Illiterates by Sex (Total Population):

	Persons	Males	Females
Literate	19,165	13,070	6,095
Illiterate	51,524	22,825	28,699
Literacy rate	33	44	21
Graduate	630	516	114

Agriculture: ***Distribution of villages according to land use:*** Out of 19 villages, Total area (in hectare) is 27791, out of that 89.95 percent is cultivable and 22.69 percent of the

cultivable area is irrigated.

Sources of Irrigation (Hectares): Government Canal 2713, Private Canal 72, Well without Electricity 602, Well with Electricity 1019, Tubewell without Electricity 162, Tubewell with Electricity 185, Tank 410, River 0, Lake 0, Waterfall 0, Others 509.

Villages with population of 5000 to 9999:
Medikonda, Pullikal, Uppal.

Villages with population of 10000 and above:
Ieej.

Distribution of Workers:

	Persons	Males	Females	WPR
Cultivators	9,297	6,166	3,131	23.91
Agricultural Labour	23,246	10,352	12,894	59.77
Household Industry	1,303	674	629	3.35
Other Workers	5,045	3,803	1,242	12.97
Main Workers	33,028	18,904	14,124	84.92
Marginal Workers	5,863	2,091	3,772	15.08
Total Workers	38,891	20,995	17,896	

Religion: Major Religious Communities:

	Persons	Males	Females	Sex Ratio
Hindu (92.73%)	65,553	33,304	32,249	968
Muslim (6.95%)	4,913	2,484	2,429	978
Christian (0.23%)	164	77	87	1,130
Sikh (0%)	-	-	-	-
Buddhists (0%)	1	1	-	-
Jain (0%)	-	-	-	-

Agewise Data:

	Persons	Males	Females	Sex Ratio
All ages	70,689	35,895	34,794	969
0-14	28,695	14,782	13,913	941
15-44	30,823	15,724	15,099	960
45-79	10,643	5,155	5,488	1065
80+	375	142	233	1641
Age not stated	153	92	61	663

Languages (Dominant):
Telugu, Urdu, Kannada, Marathi, Tamil

Disabled Population:

	Persons	Males	Females	%
Total Disabled	1,397	800	597	
In Seeing	625	372	253	44.74
In Speech	100	57	43	7.16
In Hearing	52	26	26	3.72
In Movement	501	290	211	35.86
Mentally	119	55	64	8.52

INDERAVELLY

Inderavelly C.D. Block lies in the north-west part of Adilabad district. The Block is located at a distance of 46 kms. from district headquarters (Adilabad). There are 34 villages in the block with the total popul ation of 38,642 persons. Area of the C.D. Block is 306. 50 sq. kms. It is bounded by Adilabad Mandal on north-w est, north and north-east, Narnoor Mandal on east, Utnoor Mandal on south-east, south and south-west, Gudihathno or Mandal on south-west, west and north-west.

Communications :

Roadways : Metalled Road: Nearest Villages- Ginnera, Indervelly (B), Yamaikunta, Muthnur, Dhannura (B), Dhannura (K), Keslapur.

Backwards Region Grants Fund: It receives Backward Region Grants.

Annual Rainfall: Average Rainfall 1348 mm

Ground Water: Availability of the ground water in the Basin is 3356 H.A.M. and the utilization is 723 H.A. M. It belongs to Safe category. Depth to water level varies from 5 to 10 meter below the ground. Most of the wells go down in summer months, according to the Ground Water Estimation Committee.

Natural Division : Telangana Plateau Region

Administration:

Division: Telangana. Parliamentary Constituency: 1 Adilabad (ST). District: Adilabad. Mandal: Inderavelly. Assembly Constituency: 6 Khanapur (ST). Gram Panchayat: 16

Places of Turist Interest:

Nagoba Temple : Dedicated to Sheshanag (The Serpent God), Nagoba Temple is a unique shrine in the whole world. It is located in Keslapur, which is about 32 Kms from Adilabad. During the month of Pushya (December -January), the temple attracts a large number of devotees from within and outside the state.

Fairs and Festival:

Nagobha jatra: It is celebrated for five days from Pushya Bahula Amavasya (December-January). Puja is performed at the midnight of Pushya Amavasya. A day before the main puja, all the people of the Mesram clan gather under a huge banyan tree near the shrine and do not enter houses till the worship is completed. Nagoda temple with the stone image of one deity is the only place of worship. The Mesram clan people of Edwen Saga of Adilabad District worship Seshnag (Serpen t-God) with great pomp. It has got an interesting myth about seven brothers. It is said that in the distant past there lived a Raja of Jajkial, with his wife Rukde vi and their son, Wordev, and daughter-in-law, Sondevi. Wordev and Sondevi were blessed with seven sons and their state was very prosperous. When these seven sons were yet small boys, a dreadful disease revaged the land and devoured all the inhabitants except the seven children. These seven children decided to desert the desolate village and to set out to some other place to eke out their livelihood. Late in the evening, they reached a village where there were seven cattle sheds. As it was growing dark, they took shelter in one of the cattle sheds. There was a menace from a tigress. Every night the tigress was breaking into one of the cattle sheds and killing the bulls and cows. But myster iously, nothing happened on that night when the seven children had slept in the cattle shed. The owners of the cattle sheds, pleased to see their cattle alive on the following morning, adopted the children.The seven brothers lived in the village for twelve years learning to herd the cattle. Later, they returned to their sweet home Keslapur with their cattle.

Villages: 34 **Inhabited:** 34 **Uninhabited:** 0

Ranking	District	State	National
Area	18	149	2714
Population	20	867	5797
Sex Ratio	9	75	513
Child Sex Ratio	6	121	311
Literacy Rate	18	721	4624
Density	31	545	5887
Work Participation Rate	26	985	1450

Gram Panchayats:
Dasnapur, Devapur, Dhannura (B), Dodanda, Ginnera Gourapur, Indervelly B, Keslapur, Muthnur Pochampalle, Rampur B, Tejapur, Wadagaon, Waipet Walganda Heerapur, Ymaikunta.

Amenities:

Education: Primary School in 34 villages, Middle school in 9 villages, Matriculation or Secondary School in 4 villages, namely Indervelly (B), Muthnur, Keslapur, Dasnapur. Higher Secondary or Pre University Courses or Inter-mediate or Junior College in 1 village of the CD Block,, namely Indervelly (B).
College in 0 village, Adult Literacy Center in 33 villages.

Medical: Hospital in 1 village, Dispensary in 1 village, Health Center in 3 villages, Sub Center in 8 villages, Maternity and Child Welfare Center in 2 villages, Community health workers in 0 village.
The Villages having Hospital or Dispensary or Health Center are Indervelly (B), Dhannura (B), Dasnapur.

Drinking Water: Tap water in 32 villages, Tank water in 33 villages, Well water in 34 villages, Tubewell in 33 villages and more than one source in 33 villages.

Bank: Banking facility in 2 villages, namely, Indervelly (K), Indervelly (B).
Credit Society in 7 villages Agricultural Credit Society in 6 Non-Agricultural Credit Society in 2 villages.

Others: Power supply in 34 villages, Cinema hall in 2 villages, sport club in 0 village, Stadium or Auditorium or Community Hall in 0 village, Post Office in 8 villages.
There are 9 villages having bus facilities.

Village with most of facilities: Indervelly (B).

Villages without Amenities (Education): None..

Scheduled Castes: Out of the total population of 38642 persons, 4666 persons (12.07%) belong to Scheduled Castes.
The villages having less than 10% SC population are Pipri, Ginnera, Indervelly (K), Gattepalle, Dodanda Dhannura (K), Goureepur, Keslapur, Harkapur, Anji Mamidiguda, Dasnapur, Mallapur, Tejapur, Lakampur Kondapur, Pochampalle, Lachimpur (K), Waipet Lachimpur (B), Walganda Heerapur, Dongargaon Wadagaon.
The villages having more than 50% SC population are None.
Sex ratio of Scheduled Caste population is 497.

Scheduled Castes Literates and Illiterates by Sex:

	Persons	Males	Females
Literate	2,194	1,381	813
Illiterate	2,472	965	1,507
Literacy rate	57.2	71.7	42.6
Graduate	28	24	4

Scheduled Castes (Dominant):
Mahar, Madiga, Mang, Mala Sale etc., Mala

For their cultural identity please see Appendix-I

Villages without Scheduled Castes: There are 9 villages without any scheduled caste population.

Scheduled Tribes: Out of the total population of 38642 persons, 23361 persons (60.45%) belong to Scheduled Tribes.
The villages having less than 10% ST population are None..
The villages having more than 50% ST population are Pipri, Ginnera, Indervelly (K), Gattepalle, Dodanda Goureepur, Keslapur, Harkapur, Anji, Mamidiguda Dasnapur, Keslaguda, Mallapur, Tejapur, Lakampur Kondapur, Pochampalle, Lachimpur (K), Waipet Lachimpur (B), Walganda Heerapur, Dongargaon Wadagaon.
Sex ratio of Scheduled tribe population is 516.

Scheduled Tribes Literates and Illiterates by Sex:

	Persons	Males	Females
Literate	7,968	5,053	2,915
Illiterate	15,393	6,254	9,139
Literacy rate	42.7	56.5	30.0
Graduate	38	36	2

Scheduled Tribes (Dominant):
Gond etc., Sugalis etc., Andh, Kolam etc., Pardhan

For their cultural identity please see Appendix-II

Villages without Scheduled Tribes: There are

0 village without any scheduled tribe population.

Literates and Illiterates by Sex (Total Population):

	Persons	Males	Females
Literate	15,404	9,771	5,633
Illiterate	23,238	9,274	13,964
Literacy rate	49	64	36
Graduate	148	126	22

Agriculture: ***Distribution of villages according to land use:*** Out of 34 villages, Total area (in hectare) is 30650, out of that 43.1 percent is cultivable and 0.83 percent of the cultivable area is irrigated.

Sources of Irrigation (Hectares): Government Canal 22.7, Private Canal 8, Well without Electricity 1.21, Well with Electricity 46.82, Tubewell without Electricity 0, Tubewell with Electricity 4.04, Tank 0, River 25.21, Lake 0, Waterfall 1.21, Others 0.

Villages with population of 5000 to 9999: Indervelly (B).

Villages with population of 10000 and above: None

Distribution of Workers:

	Persons	Males	Females	WPR
Cultivators	10,631	5,602	5,029	56.19
Agricultural Labour	6,019	2,575	3,444	31.81
Household Industry	258	132	126	1.36
Other Workers	2,012	1,643	369	10.63
Main Workers	16,121	8,946	7,175	85.21
Marginal Workers	2,799	1,006	1,793	14.79
Total Workers	18,920	9,952	8,968	

Religion: Major Religious Communities:

	Persons	Males	Females	Sex Ratio
Hindu (94.78%)	36,626	18,024	18,602	1,032
Muslim (3.2%)	1,238	624	614	984
Christian (0.16%)	62	25	37	1,480
Sikh (0.01%)	2	1	1	1,000
Buddhists (1.8%)	694	360	334	928
Jain (0%)	-	-	-	-

Agewise Data:

	Persons	Males	Females	Sex Ratio
All ages	38,642	19,045	19,597	1029
0-14	16,916	8,385	8,531	1017
15-44	16,153	8,057	8,096	1005
45-79	5,204	2,443	2,761	1130
80+	282	106	176	1660
Age not stated	87	54	33	611

Languages (Dominant):

Gondi, Marathi, Hindi, Telugu, Kolami

Disabled Population:

	Persons	Males	Females	%
Total Disabled	567	325	242	
In Seeing	240	131	109	42.33
In Speech	57	31	26	10.05
In Hearing	27	17	10	4.76
In Movement	175	103	72	30.86
Mentally	68	43	25	11.99

INDUKURPET

Indukurpet C.D. Block lies in the eastern part of Nello re district. The Block is located at a distance of 15 kms. from district headquarters (Nellore). There are 16 villages in the block with the total population of 57,460 persons. Area of the C.D. Block is 137.45 sq. kms. It is bounded in the north by river Pennar, and Mandals Kovur and Vidavalur, in the south by Mandal Thotapalligudur, in the east by the Bay of Bengal, and in the west by Mandals Kovur and Nellore.

Communications:

Roadways : State Highway (S.H.): Direction- Nellore to Mypadu. Nearest Villages- Mypadu, Somarajupalle, Komarika, Punnur, Lebur Bit - Ii, Jangamvani Doruvu.

River: Pennar Nadi- Nearest Villages- Pallipadu, Lebur Bit - I, Nidumusali, Mudivarthi Palem, Kudithipalem.

Integrated Child Development Scheme (ICDS) Project: Indukurupet, Total Anganwadi Centres: 201

Annual Rainfall: Average Rainfall 1143 mm

Ground Water: Availability of the Ground Water in the Basin is 6485 H.A.M. and the utilization is 8629 H. A.M. It belongs to OE category. Depth to water level varies from less than 5 meter below the ground. Most of the wells go down in summer months, according to the Ground Water Estimation Committee.

Coastal Villages: Nearest Villages- Kudithipalem, Ganga patnam, Mypadu, Koruturu.

Administration:

Division: Coastal Andhra. Parliamentary Constituency: 39 Nellore.District: Nellore.

Mandal: Indukurpet. Assembly Constituency: 235 Kovur. Gram Panchayat: 20.

Villages: 16 **Inhabited:** 16 **Uninhabited:** 0

Ranking	District	State	National
Area	42	876	5227
Population	8	313	4946
Sex Ratio	22	485	1812
Child Sex Ratio	21	599	2459
Literacy Rate	6	112	1595
Density	31	860	2634
Work Participation Rate	4	170	2791

Gram Panchayats:

Devis Pet, Gangapatnam, Indukurpet Bit2, Indukurpet1 Janagamvaridoryu, Komarika, Korutur Kothuru Chinthopu, Kudithi Palem, Lebur Bit 1 Leburu Bit-Ii, Mudivarthi Palem, Mypadu, Narasapuram Nidimusali, Pallipadu, Punnur, Ramudu Palem, Ravour

Somaraju Palli.

Amenities:

Education: Primary School in 16 villages, Middle school in 11 villages, Matriculation or Secondary School in 7 villages, namely Pallipadu, Mudivarthi Palem, Mypadu, Somarajupalle, Lebur Bit - Ii, Indukurpet Bit - Ii, Indukurpet Bit - I.

Higher Secondary or Pre University Courses or Intermediate or Junior College in 1 village of the CD Block,, namely Indukurpet Bit - Ii.

College in 0 village, Adult Literacy Center in 15 villages.

Medical: Hospital in 1 village, Dispensary in 2 villages, Health Center in 2 villages, Sub Center in 11 villages, Maternity and Child Welfare Center in 0 village, Community health workers in 0 village.

The Villages having Hospital or Dispensary or Health Center are Mudivarthi Palem, Lebur Bit - Ii.

Drinking Water: Tap water in 16 villages, Tank water in 16 villages, Well water in 16 villages, Tubewell in 16 villages and more than one source in 16 villages.

Bank: Banking facility in 5 villages, namely, Gangapatnam, Mypadu, Lebur Bit - Ii Indukurpet Bit - Ii, Indukurpet Bit - I.

Credit Society in 12 villages Agricultural Credit Society in 1 Non-Agricultural Credit Society in 12 villages.

Others: Power supply in 16 villages, Cinema hall in 3 villages, sport club in 0 village, Stadium or Auditorium or Community Hall in 0 village, Post Office in 13 villages.

There are 16 villages having bus facilities.

Villages with most of facilities: Gangapatnam Mypadu, Lebur Bit - Ii, Indukurpet Bit - Ii Indukurpet Bit - I.

Villages without Amenities (Education): None..

Scheduled Castes: Out of the total population of 57460 persons, 10772 persons (18.75%) belong to Scheduled Castes.

The villages having less than 10% SC population are None..

The villages having more than 50% SC population are None.

Sex ratio of Scheduled Caste population is 493.

Scheduled Castes Literates and Illiterates by Sex:

	Persons	Males	Females
Literate	6,517	3,581	2,936
Illiterate	4,255	1,885	2,370
Literacy rate	68.5	74.4	62.4
Graduate	112	80	32

Scheduled Castes (Dominant):

Mala, Madiga, Arundhatiya, Samban Generic Castes etc.

For their cultural identity please see Appendix-I

Villages without Scheduled Castes: There is 1 village without any scheduled caste population.

Scheduled Tribes: Out of the total population of 57460 persons, 6899 persons (12.01%) belong to Scheduled Tribes.

The villages having less than 10% ST population are Pallipadu, Mudivarthi Palem, Mypadu Indukurpet Bit - Ii, Indukurpet Bit - I Jangamvani Doruvu.

The villages having more than 50% ST population are None.

Sex ratio of Scheduled tribe population is 496.

Scheduled Tribes Literates and Illiterates by Sex:

	Persons	Males	Females
Literate	2,339	1,310	1,029
Illiterate	4,560	2,169	2,391
Literacy rate	39.9	44.1	35.6
Graduate	13	11	2

Scheduled Tribes (Dominant):

Yenadis, Yerukulas, Sugalis etc., Konda Kapus Konda Dhoras

For their cultural identity please see Appendix-II

Villages without Scheduled Tribes: There is 1 village without any scheduled tribe population.

Literates and Illiterates by Sex (Total Population):

	Persons	Males	Females
Literate	33,869	18,746	15,123
Illiterate	23,591	10,197	13,394
Literacy rate	67	74	60
Graduate	883	669	214

Agriculture: ***Distribution of villages according to land use:*** Out of 16 villages, Total area (in hectare) is 13745, out of that 72.72 percent is cultivable and 76.73 percent of the cultivable area is irrigated.

Sources of Irrigation (Hectares): Government Canal 4006, Private Canal 0, Well without Electricity 0, Well with Electricity 0, Tubewell without Electricity 0, Tubewell with Electricity 3663, Tank 0, River 0, Lake 0, Waterfall 0, Others 0.

Villages with population of 5000 to 9999: Gangapatnam, Mypadu, Lebur Bit - II Indukurpet Bit - II, Indukurpet Bit - I.

Villages with population of 10000 and above: None

Distribution of Workers:

	Persons	Males	Females	WPR
Cultivators	4,004	3,458	546	14.43
Agricultural Labour	18,022	9,896	8,126	64.96
Household Industry	469	298	171	1.69
Other Workers	5,249	4,272	977	18.92
Main Workers	23,545	16,182	7,363	84.87
Marginal Workers	4,199	1,742	2,457	15.13

Total Workers	27,744	17,924	9,820	

Religion: Major Religious Communities:

	Persons	Males	Females	Sex Ratio
Hindu (89.31%)	51,317	25,873	25,444	983
Muslim (9.99%)	5,741	2,867	2,874	1,002
Christian (0.57%)	328	168	160	952
Sikh (0.01%)	4	2	2	1,000
Buddhists (0%)	-	-	-	-
Jain (0.01%)	3	2	1	500

Agewise Data:

	Persons	Males	Females	Sex Ratio
All ages	57,460	28,943	28,517	985
0-14	16,821	8,631	8,190	949
15-44	28,175	14,090	14,085	1000
45-79	12,069	6,020	6,049	1005
80+	297	140	157	1121
Age not stated	98	62	36	581

Languages (Dominant):

Telugu, Urdu, Tamil, Gondi, Hindi

Disabled Population:

	Persons	Males	Females	%
Total Disabled	874	500	374	
In Seeing	275	149	126	31.46
In Speech	97	56	41	11.1
In Hearing	63	29	34	7.21
In Movement	318	200	118	36.38
Mentally	121	66	55	13.84

INKOLLU

Inkollu C.D. Block lies in the north-easern part of Prakasam district. The Block is located at a distance of 49 kms. from district headquarters (Ongole). There are 09 villages in the block with the total population of 48,565 persons. Area of the C.D. Block is 144.49 sq. kms. It is bounded in the north by Mandals Martur, Yeddanapudi and Parchur, in the south by Mandals Koris apadu and Naguluppalapadu, in the east by Mandals Karamc hedu, Chinaganjam and Naguluppalapadu, and in the west by Mandal Janakavaram Panguluru.

Communications:

Roadways : Metalled Roads: Nearest Villages- Pusapadu, Inkollu, Koniki, Duddukur, Bhimavaram.

The Block is identified as a drought-prone area.

Annual Rainfall: Average Rainfall 898.5 mm

Ground Water: Availability of the Ground Water in the Basin is 4.31 MCM and the utilization is 0.99 MCM It belongs to Safe category. Depth to water level varies from 2 to 5 meter below the ground. Most of the wells go down in summer months., according to the Ground Water Estimation Committee.

Administration:

Division: Coastal Andhra. Parliamentary Constituency: 32 Baptala (SC). District: Prakasam. Mandal: Inkollu. Assembly Constituency: 223 Parchur. Gram Panchayat: 13

Places of Tourist Interest:

Pavulur : This village 21 kms. to the west of Chirala town and 6 kms. from Inkollu, is connected by bus. There are four temples dedicated to Agasthes- waraswamy. Chennakesavaswamy, Sitaramaswamy and Anjaneyaswamy. The icon of Agastheswara- swamy resembles a huge white marble pillar and attracts many visitors, as a place of interest. The Anjaneya Swamy Temple is visited by people of far away places and offerings are made in fulfilment of vows.

Villages: 9 **Inhabited:** 9 **Uninhabited:** 0

Ranking	**District**	**State**	**National**
Area	50	851	5129
Population	19	562	5360
Sex Ratio	19	590	2059
Child Sex Ratio	53	1049	5054
Literacy Rate	1	80	1303
Density	15	301	3221
Work Participation Rate	7	299	762

Gram Panchayats:

Bheemavaram, Duddukuru, Gangavaram, Idupulapadu Inkollu, Koniki, Nagandla, Nakkalapalem, Pavulur Pusapadu, Subbareddypalem, Sudivaripalem Vankayalapadu.

Amenities:

Education: Primary School in 9 villages, Middle school in 8 villages, Matriculation or Secondary School in 7 villages, namely Idupulapadu, Pusapadu, Pavulur, Inkollu, Ganga Varam, Koniki, Duddukur.

Higher Secondary or Pre University Courses or Inter- mediate or Junior College in 1 village of the CD Block,, namely Inkollu.

College in 1 village, Adult Literacy Center in 9 villages., College is in village, namely Inkollu.

Medical: Hospital in 0 village, Dispensary in 2 villages, Health Center in 1 village, Sub Center in 7 villages, Maternity and Child Welfare Center in 0 village, Community health workers in 0 village.

The Villages having Hospital or Dispensary or Health Center are Idupulapadu, Duddukur.

Drinking Water: Tap water in 9 villages, Tank water in 9 villages, Well water in 9 villages, Tubewell in 9 villages and more than one source in 9 villages.

Bank: Banking facility in 2 villages, namely, Idupulapadu, Inkollu.

Credit Society in 6 villages Agricultural Credit Society in 6

Non-Agricultural Credit Society in 3 villages.

Others: Power supply in 9 villages, Cinema hall in 2 villages, sport club in 0 village, Stadium or Auditorium or Community Hall in 0 village, Post Office in 9 villages.

There are 9 villages having bus facilities.

Villages with most of facilities: Idupulapadu Inkollu.

Villages without Amenities (Education): None..

Scheduled Castes: Out of the total population of 48565 persons, 12694 persons (26.14%) belong to Scheduled Castes.

The villages having less than 10% SC population are None..

The villages having more than 50% SC population are None.

Sex ratio of Scheduled Caste population is 485.

Scheduled Castes Literates and Illiterates by Sex:

	Persons	Males	Females
Literate	7,136	4,403	2,733
Illiterate	5,558	2,132	3,426
Literacy rate	64.2	77.2	50.5
Graduate	244	205	39

Scheduled Castes (Dominant):

Mala, Madiga, Mala Dasu, Generic Castes etc.

Mala Dasari

For their cultural identity please see Appendix-I

Villages without Scheduled Castes: There are 0 village without any scheduled caste population.

Scheduled Tribes: Out of the total population of 48565 persons, 1656 persons (3.41%) belong to Scheduled Tribes.

The villages having less than 10% ST population are Nagandla, Idupulapadu, Pusapadu, Pavulur, Inkollu Ganga Varam, Koniki, Duddukur, Bhimavaram.

The villages having more than 50% ST population are None.

Sex ratio of Scheduled tribe population is 503.

Scheduled Tribes Literates and Illiterates by Sex:

	Persons	Males	Females
Literate	567	340	227
Illiterate	1,089	483	606
Literacy rate	40.4	49.0	32.0
Graduate	8	8	0

Scheduled Tribes (Dominant):

Yenadis, Yerukulas, Koya etc., Chenchu etc.

Sugalis etc.

For their cultural identity please see Appendix-II

Villages without Scheduled Tribes: There are 0 village without any scheduled tribe population.

Literates and Illiterates by Sex (Total Population):

	Persons	Males	Females
Literate	30,030	17,499	12,531
Illiterate	18,535	7,043	11,492
Literacy rate	69	80	58
Graduate	1,705	1,328	377

Agriculture: ***Distribution of villages according to land use:*** Out of 9 villages, Total area (in hectare) is 14450, out of that 85.41 percent is cultivable and 36.08 percent of the cultivable area is irrigated.

Sources of Irrigation (Hectares): Government Canal 4063.67, Private Canal 0, Well without Electricity 0, Well with Electricity 0, Tubewell without Electricity 0, Tubewell with Electricity 0, Tank 0, River 0, Lake 0, Waterfall 0, Others 388.81.

Villages with population of 5000 to 9999: Idupulapadu, Pusapadu, Pavulur.

Villages with population of 10000 and above: Inkollu.

Distribution of Workers:

	Persons	Males	Females	WPR
Cultivators	8,629	5,029	3,600	31.05
Agricultural Labour	13,879	6,107	7,772	49.94
Household Industry	229	149	80	0.82
Other Workers	5,053	4,015	1,038	18.18
Main Workers	25,000	14,432	10,568	89.96
Marginal Workers	2,790	868	1,922	10.04
Total Workers	27,790	15,300	12,490	

Religion: Major Religious Communities:

	Persons	Males	Females	Sex Ratio
Hindu (92.97%)	45,153	22,795	22,358	981
Muslim (6.59%)	3,199	1,640	1,559	951
Christian (0.35%)	170	85	85	1,000
Sikh (0%)	1	-	1	-
Buddhists (0%)	-	-	-	-
Jain (0%)	-	-	-	-

Agewise Data:

	Persons	Males	Females	Sex Ratio
All ages	48,565	24,542	24,023	979
0-14	12,439	6,451	5,988	928
15-44	23,610	11,896	11,714	985
45-79	11,774	5,836	5,938	1017
80+	625	281	344	1224
Age not stated	117	78	39	500

Languages (Dominant):

Telugu, Urdu, Tamil, Gondi, Oriya

Disabled Population:

	Persons	Males	Females	%
Total Disabled	810	468	342	
In Seeing	281	159	122	34.69
In Speech	112	63	49	13.83
In Hearing	37	19	18	4.57
In Movement	264	161	103	32.59

Mentally	116	66	50	14.32

IPUR

Ipur C.D. Block lies in the south-western part of Guntur district. The Block is located at a distance of 62 kms. from district headquarters (Guntur). There are 13 villages in the block with the total population of 43,453 persons. Area of the C.D. Block is 189.78 sq. kms. It is bounded in the north by Mandals Bollapal le and Nekarikallu, in the south by Mandals Bollapalle and Vinukonda, in the east by Mandals Savalyapuram and Rompicherla, and in the west by Mandal Bollapalle.

Communications:

Roadways : State Highway (S.H.): Direction- Vinukonda to Macherla. Nearest Villages- Bommarajupalle, Inumella, Ipur, Vanikunta, Angalur, Kondramutla, Kotcherla..

River: Koneru Nadi- Nearest Villages- Kondayapalem, Gundepalle, Kondramutla, Kotcherla.

Part of Rompicherla Mandal, falls in the Block.

Integrated Child Development Scheme (ICDS) Project: Ipur, Total Anganwadi Centres: 130

Annual Rainfall: Average Rainfall 706 mm

Ground Water: Availability of the Ground Water in the Basin is 4672 H.A.M. and the utilization is 628 H.A. M. It belongs to Safe category. Depth to water level varies from 2 to 5 meter below the ground. Most of the wells go down in summer months.

Forest and Reserved **Forest:** Nearest Villages- Bommaraju palle, Inumella, Muppalla, Chittapuram, Ipur, Vanikunta, Angalur, Agnigundala, Dasullapalle, Kondramutla, Kotch erla.

Natural Division : Krishna Delta Region

Administration:

Division: Coastal Andhra. Parliamentary Constituency: 31 Narsaraopet. District: Guntur. Mandal: Ipur. Assembly Constituency: 218 Vinukonda. Gram Panchayat: 15.

Places of Tourist Interest:

Agnigundala: This upland village, situated 16 kms. to the north of Vinukonda which is its nearest railway station, is 5 kms. away from, the Vinukonda-Gurazala road. The village seems to have derived its name from the Agnigundam into which the widows of the copper mine workers of the village plunged after the disastero us death of their husbands, due to the collapse of a tunnel over them in the course of excavation. On the south-western side of the village, the ruin of a fort can be seen. About 3 kms. to the west of the village, there exists a big rock with nine wells known as Thomm idi Donalu with perennial water supply. There are some old temples here, one of which is said to be beautifully sculptured.

Ipur : Ipur is situated 22 kms. to the north of Vinukon da, its nearest railway station, on the Vinukonda-Guraza la line. This village is of much antiquarian interest. There are seven deserted temples, with numerous inscri ptions, one of which has a date equivalent to A.D. 1278. There are nine inscriptions relating to the Kakatiya period at the place, recording the gifts of lands, money and goats as offerings to the temple. About a kms. to the east of the village, is a pillar of 2.42 metres height with Negendrudu, popularly known as 'Nagu- lamma,' carved on it and is declared a protected monum ent. The villagers pay their homage to this pillar on the Nagulachaviti day.

Villages: 13 **Inhabited:** 13 **Uninhabited:** 0

Ranking	District	State	National
Area	20	612	4353
Population	51	713	5584
Sex Ratio	25	451	1697
Child Sex Ratio	8	210	656
Literacy Rate	53	870	5157
Density	28	323	4334
Work Participation Rate	51	609	805

Gram Panchayats:

Agnigundala, Angalur, Bodipudivaripalem, Boggaram Bommarajupalli, Chittapuram, Gopuvaripalem, Inumella Ipur, Kondayapalem, Kondramutla, Kotcherla, Muppala Upparapalem, Vanikunta.

Amenities:

Education: Primary School in 12 villages, Middle school in 7 villages, Matriculation or Secondary School in 5 villages, namely Inumella, Muppalla, Ipur, Kondayapalem, Kotcherla.

Higher Secondary or Pre University Courses or Inter- mediate or Junior College in 1 village of the CD Block,, namely Muppalla.

College in 0 village, Adult Literacy Center in 2 villages.

Medical: Hospital in 1 village, Dispensary in 3 villages, Health Center in 1 village, Sub Center in 8 villages, Maternity and Child Welfare Center in 0 village, Community health workers in 0 village.

The Villages having Hospital or Dispensary or Health Center are Inumella, Muppalla, Ipur, Kotcherla.

Drinking Water: Tap water in 13 villages, Tank water in 13 villages, Well water in 13 villages, Tubewell in 13 villages and more than one source in 13 villages.

Bank: Banking facility in 3 villages, namely, Muppalla, Ipur, Kotcherla.

Credit Society in 5 villages Agricultural Credit Society in 5 Non-Agricultural Credit Society in 1 village.

Others: Power supply in 13 villages, Cinema hall in 2 villages,

sport club in 0 village, Stadium or Auditorium or Community Hall in 0 village, Post Office in 12 villages.

There are 13 villages having bus facilities.

Villages with most of facilities: Muppalla, Ipur Kotcherla.

Villages without amenities (Education): Dasullapalle..

Scheduled Castes: Out of the total population of 43453 persons, 8043 persons (18.51%) belong to Scheduled Castes.

The villages having less than 10% SC population are None..

The villages having more than 50% SC population are None.

Sex ratio of Scheduled Caste population is 484.

Scheduled Castes Literates and Illiterates by Sex:

	Persons	Males	Females
Literate	2,592	1,820	772
Illiterate	5,451	2,331	3,120
Literacy rate	38.1	51.7	23.5
Graduate	59	47	12

Scheduled Castes (Dominant):

Madiga, Mala, Mala Dasu, Mala Dasari Beda Jangam etc.

For their cultural identity please see Appendix-I

Villages without Scheduled Castes: There are 0 village without any scheduled caste population.

Scheduled Tribes: Out of the total population of 43453 persons, 2675 persons (6.16%) belong to Scheduled Tribes.

The villages having less than 10% ST population are Inumella, Muppalla, Chittapuram, Ipur, Vanikunta Kondayapalem, Angalur, Dasullapalle, Kotcherla.

The villages having more than 50% ST population are None.

Sex ratio of Scheduled tribe population is 488.

Scheduled Tribes Literates and Illiterates by Sex:

	Persons	Males	Females
Literate	674	487	187
Illiterate	2,001	883	1,118
Literacy rate	30.1	42.5	17.1
Graduate	11	9	2

Scheduled Tribes (Dominant):

Sugalis etc., Yerukulas, Yenadis, Chenchu etc. Gond etc.

For their cultural identity please see Appendix-II

Villages without Scheduled Tribes: There is 1 village without any scheduled tribe population.

Literates and Illiterates by Sex (Total Population):

	Persons	Males	Females
Literate	16,894	10,876	6,018
Illiterate	26,559	10,993	15,566
Literacy rate	46	58	33
Graduate	519	422	97

Agriculture: ***Distribution of villages according to land use:*** Out of 13 villages, Total area (in hectare) is 18979, out of that 50.79 percent is cultivable and 63.95 percent of the cultivable area is irrigated.

Sources of Irrigation (Hectares): Government Canal 5247.97, Private Canal 489.06, Well without Electricity 2.83, Well with Electricity 211.33, Tubewell without Electricity 0, Tubewell with Electricity 31.17, Tank 181.66, River 0, Lake 0, Waterfall 0, Others 0.

Villages with population of 5000 to 9999: Muppalla, Ipur, Kondramutla, Kotcherla.

Villages with population of 10000 and above: None

Distribution of Workers:

	Persons	Males	Females	WPR
Cultivators	8,523	5,597	2,926	36.02
Agricultural Labour	11,869	5,083	6,786	50.16
Household Industry	522	341	181	2.21
Other Workers	2,749	2,013	736	11.62
Main Workers	20,708	12,277	8,431	87.51
Marginal Workers	2,955	757	2,198	12.49
Total Workers	23,663	13,034	10,629	

Religion: Major Religious Communities:

	Persons	Males	Females	Sex Ratio
Hindu (95.69%)	41,582	20,944	20,638	985
Muslim (3.53%)	1,536	768	768	1,000
Christian (0.46%)	202	92	110	1,196
Sikh (0%)	-	-	-	-
Buddhists (0%)	-	-	-	-
Jain (0%)	-	-	-	-

Agewise Data:

	Persons	Males	Females	Sex Ratio
All ages	43,453	21,869	21,584	987
0-14	14,477	7,425	7,052	950
15-44	19,998	10,102	9,896	980
45-79	8,634	4,188	4,446	1062
80+	290	124	166	1339
Age not stated	54	30	24	800

Languages (Dominant):

Telugu, Hindi, Urdu, Gondi, Tamil

Disabled Population:

	Persons	Males	Females	%
Total Disabled	662	392	270	
In Seeing	108	57	51	16.31
In Speech	98	58	40	14.8
In Hearing	37	22	15	5.59
In Movement	298	178	120	45.02
Mentally	121	77	44	18.28

IRAGAVARAM

Iragavaram C.D. Block lies in the south-eastern part of West Godavari district. The Block is located at a distance of 83 kms. from district headquarters (Eluru). There are 21 villages in the block with the total population of 66,292 persons. Area of the C.D. Block is 81.19 sq. kms. It is bounded in the north by Mandals Attili, Tanuka and Peravali, in the south by Mandals Attili, Penumantra and Penugonda, in the east by Mandal Peravali, and in the west by Mandal Attili.

Communications :

Roadways : Metalled Roads: Nearest Villages- Relangi, Kakulaillindalaparru, Rapaka, Thurupuvipparru, Pekeru, Itempudi, Garuvuguntakhandrika.

Railway Station: Relangi.

Backwards Region Grants Fund: It receives Backward Region Grants.

Annaul Rainfall: Average Rainfall 1523 mm

Ground Water: Availability of the Ground Water in the Basin is (Information not avavible) H.A.M .and the utilization is (Information not avavible) H.A.M. It belongs to (Information not avavible) category. Depth to water level varies from 3 to 10 meter below the ground. Most of the wells go down in summer months.

Natural Division : Godavari Delta Region

Administration:

Division: Coastal Andhra. Parliamentary Constituency: 26 Narsapuram.District: West Godavari. Mandal: Iragavar am. Assembly Constituency: 180 Tanuku. Gram Panchayat: 21

Villages: 21 **Inhabited:** 21 **Uninhabited:** 0

Ranking	District	State	National
Area	41	1062	5867
Population	27	189	4629
Sex Ratio	31	556	1986
Child Sex Ratio	32	636	2621
Literacy Rate	13	18	544
Density	32	955	1147
Work Participation Rate	8	26	3432

Gram Panchayats:

Arjunudupalem, East Vipparru, Eletipadu, Goteru Inaparru, Iragavaram, Itempudi, K.Illindalaparru K.Kumudavalli, Kakileru, Kanteru, Kathavapadu Kavalipuram, Kothapadu, Ogidi, Pekeru, Podalada Rapaka, Relangi, Surampudi, Yerraicheruvu.

Amenities:

Education: Primary School in 21 villages, Middle school in 9 villages, Matriculation or Secondary School in 7 villages, namely Relangi, Kakulaillindalaparru, Surampudi, Thurupuvipparru, Eletipadu, Iragavaram, Kantheru. Higher Secondary or Pre University Courses or Intermediate or Junior College in 1 village of the CD Block,, namely Relangi.

College in 1 village, Adult Literacy Center in 13 villages., College is in village, namely Relangi.

Medical: Hospital in 0 village, Dispensary in 0 village, Health Center in 2 villages, Sub Center in 13 villages, Maternity and Child Welfare Center in 0 village, Community health workers in 0 village.

Drinking Water: Tap water in 21 villages, Tank water in 21 villages, Well water in 21 villages, Tubewell in 21 villages and more than one source in 21 villages.

Bank: Banking facility in 4 villages, namely, Relangi, Thurupuvipparru, Eletipadu, Iragavaram.

Credit Society in 10 villages Agricultural Credit Society in 10 Non-Agricultural Credit Society in 1 village.

Others: Power supply in 21 villages, Cinema hall in 1 village, sport club in 0 village, Stadium or Auditorium or Community Hall in 0 village, Post Office in 18 villages.

There are 18 villages having bus facilities.

Villages with most of facilities: Relangi Thurupuvipparru, Iragavaram.

Villages without Amenities (Education): None..

Scheduled Castes: Out of the total population of 66292 persons, 10695 persons (16.13%) belong to Scheduled Castes. The villages having less than 10% SC population are Thurupuvipparru, Repakakhandrika, Itempudi Eletipadu.

The villages having more than 50% SC population are None.

Sex ratio of Scheduled Caste population is 494.

Scheduled Castes Literates and Illiterates by Sex:

	Persons	Males	Females
Literate	6,775	3,705	3,070
Illiterate	3,920	1,706	2,214
Literacy rate	73.7	79.8	67.6
Graduate	144	111	33

Scheduled Castes (Dominant):

Mala, Madiga, Relli, Adi Andhra, Mala Dasari

For their cultural identity please see Appendix-I

Villages without Scheduled Castes: There is 1 village without any scheduled caste population.

Scheduled Tribes: Out of the total population of 66292 persons, 398 persons (0.6%) belong to Scheduled Tribes. The villages having less than 10% ST population are Relangi, Kavalipuram, Goteru, Kakulaillindalaparru Surampudi, Rapaka, Thurupuvipparru Kannayakumudavalli, Repakakhandrika, Pekeru Itempudi, Eletipadu, Garuvuguntakhandrika Iragavaram, Kothapadu, Ogidi, Inaparru, Kantheru Podalada, Kathavapadu, Kakileru.

The villages having more than 50% ST population are None.

Sex ratio of Scheduled tribe population is 465.

Scheduled Tribes Literates and Illiterates by Sex:

	Persons	Males	Females
Literate	171	92	79
Illiterate	227	121	106
Literacy rate	50.2	52.3	47.9
Graduate	2	2	0

Scheduled Tribes (Dominant):

Yerukulas, Yenadis, Chenchu etc., Koya etc. Sugalis etc.

For their cultural identity please see Appendix-II

Villages without Scheduled Tribes: There are 5 villages without any scheduled tribe population.

Literates and Illiterates by Sex (Total Population):

	Persons	Males	Females
Literate	44,595	23,954	20,641
Illiterate	21,697	9,505	12,192
Literacy rate	77	82	71
Graduate	1,259	991	268

Agriculture: ***Distribution of villages according to land use:*** Out of 21 villages, Total area (in hectare) is 8119, out of that 81.6 percent is cultivable and 100 percent of the cultivable area is irrigated.

Sources of Irrigation (Hectares): Government Canal 6604.45, Private Canal 0, Well without Electricity 0, Well with Electricity 0, Tubewell without Electricity 6.07, Tubewell with Electricity 14.57, Tank 0, River 0, Lake 0, Waterfall 0, Others 0.

Villages with population of 5000 to 9999:

Thurupuvipparru, Iragavaram.

Villages with population of 10000 and above:

Relangi.

Distribution of Workers:

	Persons	Males	Females	WPR
Cultivators	4,185	3,981	204	13.89
Agricultural Labour	19,157	11,805	7,352	63.59
Household Industry	1,275	513	762	4.23
Other Workers	5,511	4,366	1,145	18.29
Main Workers	26,299	19,571	6,728	87.29
Marginal Workers	3,829	1,094	2,735	12.71
Total Workers	30,128	20,665	9,463	

Religion: Major Religious Communities:

	Persons	Males	Females	Sex Ratio
Hindu (97.77%)	64,817	32,770	32,047	978
Muslim (0.44%)	294	143	151	1,056
Christian (1.72%)	1,138	526	612	1,163
Sikh (0.02%)	13	6	7	1,167
Buddhists (0%)	1	1	-	-
Jain (0%)	1	1	-	-

Agewise Data:

	Persons	Males	Females	Sex Ratio
All ages	66,292	33,459	32,833	981
0-14	19,325	9,846	9,479	963
15-44	32,847	16,854	15,993	949
45-79	13,647	6,536	7,111	1088
80+	439	203	236	1163
Age not stated	34	20	14	700

Languages (Dominant):

Telugu, Urdu, Gondi, Hindi, Oriya

Disabled Population:

	Persons	Males	Females	%
Total Disabled	1,138	627	511	
In Seeing	255	118	137	22.41
In Speech	133	76	57	11.69
In Hearing	104	47	57	9.14
In Movement	519	314	205	45.61
Mentally	127	72	55	11.16

IRALA

Irala C.D. Block lies in the southern part of Chittoor district. The Block is located at a distance of 26 kms. from district headquarters (Chittoor). There are 18 villages in the block with the total population of 48,891 persons. Area of the C.D. Block is 157.59 sq. kms. It is bounded in the north by Mandal Pakala, in the south by Mandal Thavanampalle, in the east by Mandals Puttalapattu and Pakala, and in the west by Mandal Somala.

Communications:

Roadways : State Highway (S.H.): Direction- Pileru to Chittoor. Nearest Villages- Polakala, Gundlapalle, Peddasamireddipalle.

River: Gajulapalla Eru- Nearest Villages- Puthramaddi, Kothapalle, Chigarapalle, Kanipakam.

It receives the Backward Region Grants, and is identifi ed as a drought-prone area as well.

Annual Rainfall: Average Rainfall 863 mm

Ground Water: Availability of the Ground Water in the Basin is 2604 H.A.M.and the utilization is 2465 H.A. M. It belongs to Critical category. Depth to water level varies more than meter below the ground. Most of the wells go down in summer months., according to the Ground Water Estimation Committee.

Forest and Reserved **Forest:** Nearest Villages- Ayyala Krishna Reddipalle, Nampalle, Polakala, Gundlapalle, Morampalle, Irala, Erlampalle, Sanganapalle, Kollapalle, Kaminayanipalle, Puthramaddi.

Natural Division : Rayalaseema Region

Administration:

Division: Rayala Seema. Parliamentary Constituency: 42 Chittoor (SC). District: Chittoor. Mandal: Irala. Assembly Constituency: 292 Puthalapattu (SC). Gram Panchayat: 28.

Places of Tourist Interest:

Kanipakam : The village is situated on the northern bank of the Bahuda river, at a distance of over 11 kms. north-west of Chittoor on the Chittoor-Irala road. The shrine of varasiddhi vinayaka, the deity of which is believed to be self-manifest (Swayambhu) is very famous. The brahmotsavam celebrated on the vinayaka chaviti day (Aug.-Sept.), attracts about thousands of devotees from all over the area.

Villages: 18 **Inhabited:** 18 **Uninhabited:** 0

Ranking	District	State	National
Area	39	786	4918
Population	25	551	5342
Sex Ratio	39	512	1847
Child Sex Ratio	61	1058	5084
Literacy Rate	9	53	1042
Density	51	857	3430
Work Participation Rate	20	345	2777

Gram Panchayats:

45.Kothapalle, Bheeminenivaripalle, Bommasamudram Chigarapalle, Chinakampalle, Eguvachavatapalle Erlampalle, Errepalle, Gundlapalle, Irala Iruvarampalle, Kaminayanipalle, Kanipakam Kollapalle, M.Paipalle, Maddipatlapalle, Mittoor Morampalle, Mudigolam, Nagamvandlapalle, Nampalle Pathapalem, Perraiahgaripalle, Polakala, Pulluru Puthramaddi, Vadrampalle, Vedagirivaripalle.

Amenities:

Education: Primary School in 17 villages, Middle school in 9 villages, Matriculation or Secondary School in 7 villages, namely Nampalle, Gundlapalle, Peddasamireddipalle, Irala, Puthramaddi, Mudigolam, Kanipakam.

Higher Secondary or Pre University Courses or Intermediate or Junior College in 3 villages of the CD Block,, namely Irala, Puthramaddi, Kanipakam.

College in 0 village, Adult Literacy Center in 8 villages.

Medical: Hospital in 0 village, Dispensary in 1 village, Health Center in 1 village, Sub Center in 14 villages, Maternity and Child Welfare Center in 1 village, Community health workers in 0 village.

The Village having Hospital or Dispensary or Health Center is Irala.

Drinking Water: Tap water in 18 villages, Tank water in 18 villages, Well water in 18 villages, Tubewell in 18 villages and more than one source in 18 villages.

Bank: Banking facility in 3 villages, namely, Polakala, Irala, Kanipakam.

Credit Society in 9 villages Agricultural Credit Society in 8 Non-Agricultural Credit Society in 2 villages.

Others: Power supply in 18 villages, Cinema hall in 4 villages, sport club in 0 village, Stadium or Auditorium or Community Hall in 0 village, Post Office in 15 villages.

There are 17 villages having bus facilities.

Villages with most of facilities: Polakala, Irala Kanipakam.

Villages without amenities (Education):

Venkata Samudra Agraharam..

Scheduled Castes: Out of the total population of 48891 persons, 12965 persons (26.52%) belong to Scheduled Castes.

The villages having less than 10% SC population are Ayyala Krishna Reddipalle, Peddasamireddipalle Puthramaddi.

The villages having more than 50% SC population are None.

Sex ratio of Scheduled Caste population is 495.

Scheduled Castes Literates and Illiterates by Sex:

	Persons	Males	Females
Literate	7,481	4,426	3,055
Illiterate	5,484	2,116	3,368
Literacy rate	65.2	76.5	53.8
Graduate	158	138	20

Scheduled Castes (Dominant):

Adi Dravida, Mala, Adi Andhra, Madiga, Arwa Mala

For their cultural identity please see Appendix-I

Villages without Scheduled Castes: There is 1 village without any scheduled caste population.

Scheduled Tribes: Out of the total population of 48891 persons, 1424 persons (2.91%) belong to Scheduled Tribes.

The villages having less than 10% ST population are Ayyala Krishna Reddipalle, Nampalle, Polakala Peddasamireddipalle, Morampalle, Irala Venkata Samudra Agraharam, Erlampalle, Sanganapalle Kollapalle, Pulluru, Kaminayanipalle, Mudigolam Kothapalle, Chigarapalle, Kanipakam.

The villages having more than 50% ST population are None.

Sex ratio of Scheduled tribe population is 478.

Scheduled Tribes Literates and Illiterates by Sex:

	Persons	Males	Females
Literate	514	321	193
Illiterate	910	423	487
Literacy rate	43.6	52.2	34.2
Graduate	0	0	0

Scheduled Tribes (Dominant):

Yenadis, Yerukulas

For their cultural identity please see Appendix-II

Villages without Scheduled Tribes: There are 4 villages without any scheduled tribe population.

Literates and Illiterates by Sex (Total Population):

	Persons	Males	Females
Literate	31,005	17,935	13,070
Illiterate	17,886	6,705	11,181
Literacy rate	71	82	60
Graduate	1,378	1,055	323

Agriculture: ***Distribution of villages according to land use:*** Out of 18 villages, Total area (in hectare) is 15761, out of that 57.69 percent is cultivable and 24.19 percent of the cultivable area is irrigated.

Sources of Irrigation (Hectares): Government Canal 0, Private Canal 0, Well without Electricity 0, Well with Electricity 1649.73, Tubewell without Electricity 0, Tubewell with Electricity 549.97, Tank 0, River 0, Lake 0, Waterfall 0, Others 0.

Villages with population of 5000 to 9999: Polakala, Mudigolam.

Villages with population of 10000 and above: None

Distribution of Workers:

	Persons	Males	Females	WPR
Cultivators	8,115	5,768	2,347	33.84
Agricultural Labour	9,713	5,085	4,628	40.51
Household Industry	1,017	623	394	4.24
Other Workers	5,133	3,557	1,576	21.41
Main Workers	20,806	13,875	6,931	86.77
Marginal Workers	3,172	1,158	2,014	13.23
Total Workers	23,978	15,033	8,945	

Religion: Major Religious Communities:

	Persons	Males	Females	Sex Ratio
Hindu (97.35%)	47,596	23,987	23,609	984
Muslim (2.47%)	1,206	604	602	997
Christian (0.08%)	41	21	20	952
Sikh (0%)	-	-	-	-
Buddhists (0%)	-	-	-	-
Jain (0%)	-	-	-	-

Agewise Data:

	Persons	Males	Females	Sex Ratio
All ages	48,891	24,640	24,251	984
0-14	12,733	6,676	6,057	907
15-44	22,846	11,321	11,525	1018
45-79	12,662	6,338	6,324	998
80+	543	256	287	1121
Age not stated	107	49	58	1184

Languages (Dominant):
Telugu, Tamil, Urdu, Kannada, Hindi

Disabled Population:

	Persons	Males	Females	%
Total Disabled	713	375	338	
In Seeing	188	88	100	26.37
In Speech	87	38	49	12.2
In Hearing	36	25	11	5.05
In Movement	285	161	124	39.97
Mentally	117	63	54	16.41

ITIKYAL

Itikyal C.D. Block lies in the southern part of Mahbubn agar district. The Block is located at a distance of 110 kms. from district headquarters (Mahbubnagar). There are 21 villages in the block with the total popul ation of 42,095 persons. Area of the C.D. Block is 304 sq. kms. It is bounded by Gadwal Mandal on north, Pebba ir Mandal on east, Manopad Mandal on south-east, Waddepa lle Mandal on south, Ieej Mandal on south-east, and Maldakal Mandal on west.

Communications:

Roadways : NH- 7: Direction- Hyderabad to Manopad Nearest Villages- Kondair, Thimmapur, Sasnool, Putandoddi, Munagala, Itikyal, Vemula, Vallur, Dharmavaram.

Railway Station: Itikyal, Peddadinne.

River: Krishna Nadi- Nearest Villages- Rajsrigarlapad, Bochuveerapur, Karpakula, Thimmapur, Sasnool.

Backwards Region Grants Fund: It receives Backward Region Grants.

Annual Rainfall: Average Rainfall 531 mm

Ground Water: Availability of the Ground Water in the Basin is 4609 H.A.M. and the utilization is 1486 H. A.M. It belongs to Safe category. Depth to water level varies from 2 to 5 meter below the ground. Most of the wells go down in summer months. The well density in the entire block is 6 wells per sq. km. Total no. of the wells in the block are enumerated as 1876, according to the Ground Water Estimation Committee.

Natural Division : Telangana Plateau Region

Administration:

Division: Telangana. Parliamentary Constituency: 12 Nagarkurnool (SC). District: Mahbubnagar. Mandal: Itiky al. Assembly Constituency: 80 Alampur (SC). Gram Panchay at: 22.

Villages: 21 **Inhabited:** 21 **Uninhabited:** 0

Ranking	District	State	National
Area	14	153	2740
Population	51	757	5644
Sex Ratio	57	1009	3592
Child Sex Ratio	47	886	3894
Literacy Rate	31	984	5620
Density	8	75	5725
Work Participation Rate	56	943	276

Gram Panchayats:
Batladinne, Beechupally, Chagapoor, Darmavaram

Gopaldinne, Itikyal, Kodandapuram, Kondair, Munagala Nakkalapally, Peddadinne, Putandoddy Rajasri Garlapad, Sasanool, Saterla, Shabad Shaikpally, Thimmapur, Udandapuram, Vallur, Vavilala Vemula.

Amenities:

Education: Primary School in 21 villages, Middle school in 13 villages, Matriculation or Secondary School in 7 villages, namely Thimmapur, Itikyal, Udandapur, Chagapur, Vemula, Vallur, Dharmavaram.

Higher Secondary or Pre University Courses or Intermediate or Junior College in 0 village of the CD Block, College in 0 village, Adult Literacy Center in 17 villages.

Medical: Hospital in 0 village, Dispensary in 1 village, Health Center in 1 village, Sub Center in 7 villages, Maternity and Child Welfare Center in 0 village, Community health workers in 0 village.

The Village having Hospital or Dispensary or Health Center is Chagapur.

Drinking Water: Tap water in 21 villages, Tank water in 21 villages, Well water in 21 villages, Tubewell in 21 villages and more than one source in 21 villages.

Bank: Banking facility in 2 villages, namely, Itikyal, Dharmavaram.

Credit Society in 10 villages Agricultural Credit Society in 4 Non-Agricultural Credit Society in 5 villages.

Others: Power supply in 21 villages, Cinema hall in 0 village, sport club in 0 village, Stadium or Auditorium or Community Hall in 0 village, Post Office in 11 villages.

There are 18 villages having bus facilities.

Villages with most of facilities: Itikyal Dharmavaram.

Villages without Amenities (Education): None..

Scheduled Castes: Out of the total population of 42095 persons, 8668 persons (20.59%) belong to Scheduled Castes.

The villages having less than 10% SC population are Dharmavaram, Bochuveerapur, Karpakula Rajsrigarlapad.

The villages having more than 50% SC population are None.

Sex ratio of Scheduled Caste population is 483.

Scheduled Castes Literates and Illiterates by Sex:

	Persons	Males	Females
Literate	2,472	1,853	619
Illiterate	6,196	2,627	3,569
Literacy rate	33.9	49.4	17.5
Graduate	61	53	8

Scheduled Castes (Dominant):

Madiga, Mala, Beda Jangam etc., Mala Dasari Ellamalawar etc.

For their cultural identity please see Appendix-I

Villages without Scheduled Castes: There are 2 villages without any scheduled caste population.

Scheduled Tribes: Out of the total population of 42095 persons, 259 persons (0.62%) belong to Scheduled Tribes.

The villages having less than 10% ST population are Gopaldinne, Mogilravalcheruvu, Kondair, Thimmapur Sasnool, Putandoddi, Munagala, Itikyal, Peddadinne Udandapur, Saterla, Vavilala, Shabad, Chagapur Vemula, Batladinne, Vallur, Dharmavaram Bochuveerapur, Karpakula, Rajsrigarlapad.

The villages having more than 50% ST population are None.

Sex ratio of Scheduled tribe population is 409.

Scheduled Tribes Literates and Illiterates by Sex:

	Persons	Males	Females
Literate	77	69	8
Illiterate	182	84	98
Literacy rate	35.7	52.7	9.4
Graduate	1	1	0

Scheduled Tribes (Dominant):

Yerukulas, Sugalis etc., Chenchu etc.

For their cultural identity please see Appendix-II

Villages without Scheduled Tribes: There are 10 villages without any scheduled tribe population.

Literates and Illiterates by Sex (Total Population):

	Persons	Males	Females
Literate	14,563	10,101	4,462
Illiterate	27,532	11,504	16,028
Literacy rate	41	56	26
Graduate	377	318	59

Agriculture: ***Distribution of villages according to land use:*** Out of 21 villages, Total area (in hectare) is 30409, out of that 71.29 percent is cultivable and 9.93 percent of the cultivable area is irrigated.

Sources of Irrigation (Hectares): Government Canal 645, Private Canal 82, Well without Electricity 0, Well with Electricity 753, Tubewell without Electricity 0, Tubewell with Electricity 439, Tank 194, River 0, Lake 0, Waterfall 0, Others 40.

Villages with population of 5000 to 9999: None

Villages with population of 10000 and above: None

Distribution of Workers:

	Persons	Males	Females	WPR
Cultivators	7,261	4,778	2,483	30.29
Agricultural Labour	13,850	5,667	8,183	57.77
Household Industry	273	150	123	1.14
Other Workers	2,589	2,024	565	10.8
Main Workers	22,044	12,082	9,962	91.95
Marginal Workers	1,929	537	1,392	8.05

Total Workers	23,973	12,619	11,354	

Religion: Major Religious Communities:

	Persons	Males	Females	Sex Ratio
Hindu (94.36%)	39,719	20,393	19,326	948
Muslim (5.39%)	2,271	1,157	1,114	963
Christian (0.08%)	35	18	17	944
Sikh (0%)	-	-	-	-
Buddhists (0%)	-	-	-	-
Jain (0%)	-	-	-	-

Agewise Data:

	Persons	Males	Females	Sex Ratio
All ages	42,095	21,605	20,490	948
0-14	15,509	8,107	7,402	913
15-44	19,062	9,872	9,190	931
45-79	7,222	3,497	3,725	1065
80+	267	104	163	1567
Age not stated	35	25	10	400

Languages (Dominant):

Telugu, Urdu, Tamil, Hindi, Gondi

Disabled Population:

	Persons	Males	Females	%
Total Disabled	816	488	328	
In Seeing	316	188	128	38.73
In Speech	54	32	22	6.62
In Hearing	45	23	22	5.51
In Movement	321	202	119	39.34
Mentally	80	43	37	9.8

JADCHERLA

Jadcherla C.D. Block lies in the central part of Mahbub nagar district. It is a part of Jadcherla Mandal. The Block is located at a distance of 16 kms. from district headquarters (Mahbubnagar). There are 29 villages in the block with the total population of 62,307 persons. Area of the C.D. Block is 271.47 sq. kms. It is bounded by Balanagar Mandal on north, Bhoothpur and Themmajipet Mandals on south, Mahbubnagar and Nawabpet Mandals on west, Midjil and Talakondapalle Mandals on east.

Communications:

Roadways : NH- 7: Direction- Kurnool to Farooqnagar. Nearest Villages- Bureddipalle, Malleboinpalle, Machar am, Polepalle, Aloor, Chintaboinpalle, Jadcherla. State Highway (S.H.): Direction- Badepalle to Kalwakurthy Mandal Nearest Villages- Ammapalle, Koduparthy, Alwanpa lle, Gangapur, Bureddipalle, Malleboinpalle, Shankarayap alle, Jadcherla, Kistaram, Nagasala.

Railway Station: Gollapalle.

Backwards Region Grants Fund: It receives Backward Region Grants.

Integrated Child Development Scheme (ICDS) Project: Jedcherla, Total Anganwadi Centres: 371

Annual Rainfall: Average Rainfall 628 mm

Ground Water: Availability of the Ground Water in the Basin is 1990 H.A.M. and the utilization is 1716 H. A.M. It belongs to SC category. Depth to water level varies from 2 to 5 meter below the ground. Most of the wells go down in summer months. The well density in the entire block is 14 wells per sq. km. Total no. of the wells in the block are enumerated as 4083, according to the Ground Water Estimation Committee.

Natural Division : Telangana Plateau Region

Administration:

Division: Telangana. Parliamentary Constituency: 11 Mahbubnagar. District: Mahbubnagar. Mandal: Jadcherla. Assembly Constituency: 75 Jadcherla. Gram Panchayat: 26

Fairs and Festival:

Parasavedeeswaraswamy Festival : It is celebrated for two days from Magha Bahula Triodasi (February-March). Abhishekam, kalyanam and vratam are the rituals observ ed during the festival. The festival is being celebrated from the past 100 years and is of local significance. The chief patrons of the festival are Vaisyas and Lingayats of the village. Thousands of Hindu devotees local and from neighbouring places congregate. The pujari is a Jangam without any hereditary rights. Prasa dam is distributed to all.

A fair is held for two days in connection with this festival near the temple.

The image of the deity Parasavedeeswaraswamy is a Sival ingam made of black stone. A peculiar feature in this temple is the absence of Nandi (bull) facing the Sivali ngam. There are a kalyanamantapam and rooms for pilgrims in the temple and the place where the temple is situated is known as Meenambaram. There is a story which says that once a passenger was cooking fish near the temple. Some persons who saw that incident asked him not to cook there; but the passenger turned a deaf ear to their words and when he was still attending to the cooking, all the fish flew into the sky and the place came to be called Meenambaram (meenu means fish and ambaram means sky) since then.

Villages: 29 **Inhabited:** 28 **Uninhabited:** 1

Ranking	District	State	National
Area	22	230	3085
Population	5	237	4775
Sex Ratio	35	730	2494
Child Sex Ratio	14	398	1468
Literacy Rate	5	694	4520
Density	60	671	4323
Work Participation Rate	17	605	1862

Gram Panchayats:

Aloor, Alwanpally, Badepally, Bureddipally Burugupally, Cherlpally, Chinna Adirala, Earlapally Gangapoor, Gollapally, Gopulapoor, Jadcherla Kishtaram, Kodgal, Konded, Lingampet, Macharam Malleboinpally, Nagasala, Narsurullabad, Nekkonda Pedda Adiryala, Peddapally, Polepally, Udandapur Vallur.

Amenities:

Education: Primary School in 26 villages, Middle school in 10 villages, Matriculation or Secondary School in 6 villages, namely Gollapalle, Kodgal, Pedda Adiryal, Gangapur, Polepalle, Jadcherla.

Higher Secondary or Pre University Courses or Intermediate or Junior College in 0 village of the CD Block, College in 0 village, Adult Literacy Center in 25 villages.

Medical: Hospital in 1 village, Dispensary in 1 village, Health Center in 0 village, Sub Center in 9 villages, Maternity and Child Welfare Center in 1 village, Community health workers in 0 village.

The Village having Hospital or Dispensary or Health Center is Jadcherla.

Drinking Water: Tap water in 28 villages, Tank water in 28 villages, Well water in 28 villages, Tubewell in 28 villages and more than one source in 28 villages.

Bank: Banking facility in 3 villages, namely, Pedda Adiryal, Gangapur, Jadcherla.

Credit Society in 12 villages Agricultural Credit Society in 1 Non-Agricultural Credit Society in 12 villages.

Others: Power supply in 28 villages, Cinema hall in 0 village, sport club in 0 village, Stadium or Auditorium or Community Hall in 0 village, Post Office in 9 villages.

There are 23 villages having bus facilities.

Villages with most of facilities: Pedda Adiryal Gangapur, Jadcherla.

Villages without amenities (Education): Koduparthy..

Scheduled Castes: Out of the total population of 62347 persons, 10694 persons (17.15%) belong to Scheduled Castes.

The villages having less than 10% SC population are Ammapalle, Koduparthy, Shankarayapalle Chintaboinpalle.

The villages having more than 50% SC population are None.

Sex ratio of Scheduled Caste population is 503.

Scheduled Castes Literates and Illiterates by Sex:

	Persons	Males	Females
Literate	3,262	2,200	1,062
Illiterate	7,432	3,116	4,316
Literacy rate	36.5	49.2	23.7
Graduate	63	54	9

Scheduled Castes (Dominant):

Madiga, Mala, Beda Jangam etc., Generic Castes etc. Bindla

For their cultural identity please see Appendix-I

Villages without Scheduled Castes: There are 4 villages without any scheduled caste population.

Scheduled Tribes: Out of the total population of 62347 persons, 9224 persons (14.79%) belong to Scheduled Tribes.

The villages having less than 10% ST population are Kishtaram, Ambatapur, Konded, Goplapur (Kalan) Nekkonda, Ammapalle, Koduparthy, Gangapur Uddandapur, Shankarayapalle, Jadcherla, Kistaram Nasrullabad, Alwanpalle.

The villages having more than 50% ST population are None.

Sex ratio of Scheduled tribe population is 480.

Scheduled Tribes Literates and Illiterates by Sex:

	Persons	Males	Females
Literate	2,495	1,844	651
Illiterate	6,729	2,956	3,773
Literacy rate	33.6	47.8	18.3
Graduate	60	50	10

Scheduled Tribes (Dominant):

Sugalis etc., Yerukulas, Generic Tribes etc. Savaras etc., Koya etc.

For their cultural identity please see Appendix-II

Villages without Scheduled Tribes: There are 10 villages without any scheduled tribe population.

Literates and Illiterates by Sex (Total Population):

	Persons	Males	Females
Literate	26,250	16,584	9,666
Illiterate	36,097	15,061	21,036
Literacy rate	50	62	37
Graduate	1,050	819	231

Agriculture: ***Distribution of villages according to land use:*** Out of 29 villages, Total area (in hectare) is 27147, out of that 89.79 percent is cultivable and 15.88 percent of the cultivable area is irrigated.

Sources of Irrigation (Hectares): Government Canal 0, Private Canal 0, Well without Electricity 0, Well with Electricity 87.6, Tubewell without Electricity 0, Tubewell with Electricity 3733.6, Tank 49.6, River 0, Lake 0, Waterfall 0, Others 0.

Villages with population of 5000 to 9999: None

Villages with population of 10000 and above: Jadcherla.

Distribution of Workers:

	Persons	Males	Females	WPR
Cultivators	10,311	6,315	3,996	33.33

Agricultural Labour	12,417	4,482	7,935	40.14
Household Industry	565	294	271	1.83
Other Workers	7,644	6,189	1,455	24.71
Main Workers	28,952	16,611	12,341	93.58
Marginal Workers	1,985	669	1,316	6.42
Total Workers	30,937	17,280	13,657	

Religion: Major Religious Communities:

	Persons	Males	Females	Sex Ratio
Hindu (87.24%)	54,394	27,579	26,815	972
Muslim (10.68%)	6,661	3,429	3,232	943
Christian (1.97%)	1,230	605	625	1,033
Sikh (0%)	-	-	-	-
Buddhists (0%)	-	-	-	-
Jain (0%)	-	-	-	-

Agewise Data:

	Persons	Males	Females	Sex Ratio
All ages	62,347	31,645	30,702	970
0-14	23,061	11,820	11,241	951
15-44	27,706	14,231	13,475	947
45-79	11,078	5,364	5,714	1065
80+	417	181	236	1304
Age not stated	85	49	36	735

Languages (Dominant):

Telugu, Hindi, Urdu, Marathi, Tamil

Disabled Population:

	Persons	Males	Females	%
Total Disabled	978	574	404	
In Seeing	364	204	160	37.22
In Speech	107	67	40	10.94
In Hearing	37	17	20	3.78
In Movement	364	219	145	37.22
Mentally	106	67	39	10.84

JAGDEVPUR

Jagdevpur C.D. Block lies in the south-eastern part of Medak district. The Block is located at a distance of 140 kms. from district headquarters (Sangareddy). There are 28 villages in the block with the total population of 44,520 persons. Area of the C.D. Block is 224.73 sq. kms. It is bounded by Kondapak Mandal on north, Warangal district on north-east, Nalgonda district on east and south, Mulug Mandal on south-west, Wargal Mandal on west, and Gajwel Mandal on north-west.

Communications :

Roadways : State Highway (S.H.): Direction- Hyderabad to Karimnagar. Nearest Villages- Ramachandrapur, Chinna Kistapur.

Backwards Region Grants Fund: It receives Backward Region Grants.

Annual Rainfall: Average Rainfall 759 mm

Ground Water: Availability of the Ground Water in the Basin is 1771 H.A.M. and the utilization is 1624 H. A.M. It belongs to Critical category. Depth to water level varies from 5 to 10 meter below the ground. Most of the wells go down in summer months. The well density in the entire block is 18.2 wells per sq. km. Total no. of the wells in the block are enumerated as 3424, according to the Ground Water Estimation Committee.

Natural Division : Telangana Plateau Region

Administration:

Division: Telangana. Parliamentary Constituency: 6 Medak. District: Medak. Mandal: Jagdevpur. Assembly Constituency: 42 Gajwel. Gram Panchayat: 23.

Villages: 28 **Inhabited:** 28 **Uninhabited:** 0

Ranking	District	State	National
Area	14	411	3749
Population	29	680	5534
Sex Ratio	4	145	804
Child Sex Ratio	14	252	795
Literacy Rate	25	864	5115
Density	2	123	4754
Work Participation Rate	38	721	369

Gram Panchayats:

Alirajpet, Angadi Kistapur, Baswapur, Chatlapalle Cheberthy, Chinna Kistapur, Dharmaram, Doulapur Gollapalle, Itikyal, Jagdevpur, Lingareddypalli Munigadapa, Peerlapalle, Rayavaram, Sivar Venkatapur Teegul, Teegul Narsapur, Thimmapur, Vardarajpur Venkatapur (B.G), Wattipalle, Yerravalle.

Amenities:

Education: Primary School in 28 villages, Middle school in 13 villages, Matriculation or Secondary School in 4 villages, namely Teegul, Itikyal, Jagdevpur, Munigadapa.

Higher Secondary or Pre University Courses or Intermediate or Junior College in 1 village of the CD Block,, namely Jagdevpur.

College in 0 village, Adult Literacy Center in 10 villages.

Medical: Hospital in 0 village, Dispensary in 2 villages, Health Center in 1 village, Sub Center in 8 villages, Maternity and Child Welfare Center in 13 villages, Community health workers in 0 village.

The Villages having Hospital or Dispensary or Health Center are Itikyal, Jagdevpur.

Drinking Water: Tap water in 28 villages, Tank water in 28 villages, Well water in 28 villages, Tubewell in 28 villages and more than one source in 28 villages.

Bank: Banking facility in 2 villages, namely, Teegul, Jagdevpur.

Credit Society in 16 villages Agricultural Credit Society in 6 Non-Agricultural Credit Society in 16 villages.

Others: Power supply in 28 villages, Cinema hall in 1 village, sport club in 0 village, Stadium or Auditorium or Community

Hall in 0 village, Post Office in 19 villages.
There are 23 villages having bus facilities.

Villages with most of facilities: Teegul
Jagdevpur.

Villages without Amenities (Education): None..

Scheduled Castes: Out of the total population of 44520 persons, 8334 persons (18.72%) belong to Scheduled Castes. The villages having less than 10% SC population are Ananthsagar, Sivar Venkatapur, Vardarajpur Jagdevpur, Kondapur.
The villages having more than 50% SC population are None.
Sex ratio of Scheduled Caste population is 504.

Scheduled Castes Literates and Illiterates by Sex:

	Persons	Males	Females
Literate	2,557	1,696	861
Illiterate	5,777	2,440	3,337
Literacy rate	36.1	48.4	24.1
Graduate	18	15	3

Scheduled Castes (Dominant):
Madiga, Mala, Paky etc., Manne, Bindla

For their cultural identity please see Appendix-I

Villages without Scheduled Castes: There is 1 village without any scheduled caste population.

Scheduled Tribes: Out of the total population of 44520 persons, 307 persons (0.69%) belong to Scheduled Tribes. The villages having less than 10% ST population are Ramachandrapur, Venkatapur, Chinna Kistapur Yellaiguda, Teegul Narsapur, Chatlapalle, Wattipalle Baswapur, Gopalpur, Thimmapur, Ananthsagar Rayavaram, Teegul, Angadi Kistapur, Cheberthy Alirajapet, Erravalle, Sivar Venkatapur, Vardarajpur Dharmaram, Itikyal, Peerlapalle, Jagdevpur Gollapalle, Venkatapur (Bg), Munigadapa, Kondapur Doulapur.
The villages having more than 50% ST population are None.
Sex ratio of Scheduled tribe population is 521.

Scheduled Tribes Literates and Illiterates by Sex:

	Persons	Males	Females
Literate	73	50	23
Illiterate	234	97	137
Literacy rate	31.3	44.6	19.0
Graduate	1	1	0

Scheduled Tribes (Dominant):
Yerukulas, Sugalis etc., Thoti, Generic Tribes etc.

For their cultural identity please see Appendix-II

Villages without Scheduled Tribes: There are 11 villages without any scheduled tribe population.

Literates and Illiterates by Sex (Total Population):

	Persons	Males	Females
Literate	17,445	11,223	6,222
Illiterate	27,075	10,890	16,185
Literacy rate	46	60	32
Graduate	365	319	46

Agriculture: ***Distribution of villages according to land use:*** Out of 28 villages, Total area (in hectare) is 22473, out of that 76.3 percent is cultivable and 19.41 percent of the cultivable area is irrigated.

Sources of Irrigation (Hectares): Government Canal 0, Private Canal 0, Well without Electricity 0, Well with Electricity 1310.45, Tubewell without Electricity 0, Tubewell with Electricity 1150.78, Tank 840.33, River 12, Lake 14.07, Waterfall 0, Others 0.

Villages with population of 5000 to 9999:
Jagdevpur.

Villages with population of 10000 and above: None

Distribution of Workers:

	Persons	Males	Females	WPR
Cultivators	9,104	5,896	3,208	35.91
Agricultural Labour	10,389	3,568	6,821	40.98
Household Industry	1,278	297	981	5.04
Other Workers	4,581	3,173	1,408	18.07
Main Workers	19,473	11,159	8,314	76.81
Marginal Workers	5,879	1,775	4,104	23.19
Total Workers	25,352	12,934	12,418	

Religion: Major Religious Communities:

	Persons	Males	Females	Sex Ratio
Hindu (95.21%)	42,387	21,059	21,328	1,013
Muslim (3.09%)	1,375	671	704	1,049
Christian (1.57%)	701	352	349	991
Sikh (0.02%)	10	6	4	667
Buddhists (0%)	2	2	-	-
Jain (0%)	-	-	-	-

Agewise Data:

	Persons	Males	Females	Sex Ratio
All ages	44,520	22,113	22,407	1013
0-14	15,147	7,601	7,546	993
15-44	19,275	9,587	9,688	1011
45-79	9,640	4,723	4,917	1041
80+	422	185	237	1281
Age not stated	36	17	19	1118

Languages (Dominant):
Telugu, Urdu, Tamil, Hindi, Gondi

Disabled Population:

	Persons	Males	Females	%
Total Disabled	1,071	596	475	
In Seeing	518	258	260	48.37
In Speech	100	52	48	9.34
In Hearing	56	31	25	5.23

In Movement	297	195	102	27.73

Mentally	100	60	40	9.34

JAGGAMPETA

Jaggampeta C.D. Block lies in the central part of East Godavari district. The Block is located at a distance of 45 kms. from district headquarters (Kakinada). There are 19 villages in the block with the total population of 74,239 persons. Area of the C.D. Block is 185.64 sq. kms. It is bounded in the north by Mandals Gokavaram, Gangavaram and Yeleswaram, in the south by Mandal Gandepalle, in the east by Mandals Peddapuram, Kirlampu di and Yeleswaram, and in the west by Mandal Gokavaram.

Communications :

Roadways : NH- 5: Direction- Rajahmundry to Vishakhapatn am. Nearest Villages- Marripaka, Jaggampeta, Ramavaram. State Highway (S.H.): Direction- Gokavaram to Pithapur am. Nearest Villages- Jaggampeta, Ramavaram, Manyanvarip alem, Govindapuram, Balabhadrapuram, Gurrappalem, Katrav ulapalle.

River: Eluru Nadi- Nearst Villages- Mamidada, Irripaka.

Backwards Region Grants Fund: It receives Backward Region Grants.

Annaul Rainfall: Average Rainfall 1228.1 mm

Ground Water: Availability of the Ground Water in the Basin is (Information not avavible) H.A.M .and the utilization is (Information not avavible) H.A.M. It belongs to (Information not avavible) category. Depth to water level varies from 3 to 10 meter below the ground. Most of the wells go down in summer months.

Natural Division : Godavari Delta Region

Administration:

Division: Coastal Andhra. Parliamentary Constituency: 23 Kakinada. District: East Godavari. Mandal: Jaggampeta. Assembly Constituency: 171 Jaggampeta. Gram Panchayat: 16

Villages: 19 **Inhabited:** 18 **Uninhabited:** 1

Ranking	District	State	National
Area	8	630	4423
Population	16	74	4313
Sex Ratio	26	391	1603
Child Sex Ratio	8	57	139
Literacy Rate	48	616	4288
Density	36	1051	2727
Work Participation Rate	46	186	4396

Gram Panchayats:

Gollalagunta, Govindapuram, Gurrappalem, Irripaka J.Kothuru, Jaggampeta, Kandregula, Katravulapalle Mallisala, Mamidada, Manyanvari Palem, Marripaka Narendrapatnam, Rajapudi, Ramavaram Vengayamma Puram.

Amenities:

Education: Primary School in 18 villages, Middle school in 8 villages, Matriculation or Secondary School in 5 villages, namely Mallisala, Rajapudi, Gollalagunta, Jaggampeta, Katravulapalle.

Higher Secondary or Pre University Courses or Intermediate or Junior College in 1 village of the CD Block,, namely Jaggampeta.

College in 1 village, Adult Literacy Center in 14 villages., College is in village, namely Jaggampeta.

Medical: Hospital in 1 village, Dispensary in 2 villages, Health Center in 2 villages, Sub Center in 11 villages, Maternity and Child Welfare Center in 0 village, Community health workers in 0 village.

The Villages having Hospital or Dispensary or Health Center are Gollalagunta, Jaggampeta, Katravulapalle.

Drinking Water: Tap water in 18 villages, Tank water in 18 villages, Well water in 18 villages, Tubewell in 18 villages and more than one source in 18 villages.

Bank: Banking facility in 3 villages, namely, Mallisala, Jaggampeta, Katravulapalle.

Credit Society in 8 villages Agricultural Credit Society in 4 Non-Agricultural Credit Society in 5 villages.

Others: Power supply in 18 villages, Cinema hall in 3 villages, sport club in 0 village, Stadium or Auditorium or Community Hall in 0 village, Post Office in 9 villages.

There are 16 villages having bus facilities.

Villages with most of facilities: Mallisala Jaggampeta, Katravulapalle.

Villages without Amenities (Education): None..

Scheduled Castes: Out of the total population of 74239 persons, 10200 persons (13.74%) belong to Scheduled Castes. The villages having less than 10% SC population are Manyanvaripalem, Rajapudi, Balabhadrapuram Seethanagaram.

The villages having more than 50% SC population are None.

Sex ratio of Scheduled Caste population is 496.

Scheduled Castes Literates and Illiterates by Sex:

	Persons	Males	Females
Literate	3,485	1,918	1,567
Illiterate	6,715	3,226	3,489
Literacy rate	40.3	43.6	36.9
Graduate	88	67	21

Scheduled Castes (Dominant):

Mala, Madiga, Adi Andhra, Generic Castes etc. Beda Jangam etc.

For their cultural identity please see Appendix-I

Villages without Scheduled Castes: There is 1 village without any scheduled caste population.

Scheduled Tribes: Out of the total population of 74239

persons, 1116 persons (1.5%) belong to Scheduled Tribes. The villages having less than 10% ST population are Narendrapatnam, Mamidada, Irripaka, Seethampeta Kandregula, Manyanvaripalem, Mallisala, Rajapudi Balabhadrapuram, Gollalagunta, Marripaka Gurrappalem, J. Kothuru, Jaggampeta, Seethanagaram Katravulapalle, Ramavaram.

The villages having more than 50% ST population are None.

Sex ratio of Scheduled tribe population is 475.

Scheduled Tribes Literates and Illiterates by Sex:

	Persons	Males	Females
Literate	401	233	168
Illiterate	715	353	362
Literacy rate	42.2	47.2	36.8
Graduate	3	2	1

Scheduled Tribes (Dominant):

Konda Dhoras, Yerukulas, Yenadis, Koya etc. Generic Tribes etc.

For their cultural identity please see Appendix-II

Villages without Scheduled Tribes: There are 10 villages without any scheduled tribe population.

Literates and Illiterates by Sex (Total Population):

	Persons	Males	Females
Literate	32,965	17,548	15,417
Illiterate	41,274	19,749	21,525
Literacy rate	51	54	48
Graduate	959	738	221

Agriculture: ***Distribution of villages according to land use:*** Out of 19 villages, Total area (in hectare) is 18564, out of that 80.85 percent is cultivable and 42.36 percent of the cultivable area is irrigated.

Sources of Irrigation (Hectares): Government Canal 2397.09, Private Canal 0, Well without Electricity 20, Well with Electricity 4.04, Tubewell without Electricity 4.08, Tubewell with Electricity 267.7, Tank 3664.07, River 0, Lake 0, Waterfall 0, Others 0.

Villages with population of 5000 to 9999: Mallisala, Rajapudi.

Villages with population of 10000 and above: Jaggampeta, Katravulapalle.

Distribution of Workers:

	Persons	Males	Females	WPR
Cultivators	4,013	3,756	257	13.52
Agricultural Labour	19,771	14,236	5,535	66.63
Household Industry	730	465	265	2.46
Other Workers	5,160	4,211	949	17.39
Main Workers	24,681	19,796	4,885	83.17
Marginal Workers	4,993	2,872	2,121	16.83
Total Workers	29,674	22,668	7,006	

Religion: Major Religious Communities:

	Persons	Males	Females	Sex Ratio
Hindu (98.65%)	73,237	36,805	36,432	990
Muslim (0.64%)	476	251	225	896
Christian (0.63%)	465	209	256	1,225
Sikh (0%)	1	-	1	-
Buddhists (0%)	-	-	-	-
Jain (0%)	-	-	-	-

Agewise Data:

	Persons	Males	Females	Sex Ratio
All ages	74,239	37,297	36,942	990
0-14	24,900	12,483	12,417	995
15-44	36,241	18,347	17,894	975
45-79	12,672	6,262	6,410	1024
80+	326	151	175	1159
Age not stated	100	54	46	852

Languages (Dominant):

Telugu, Urdu, Gondi, Hindi, Tamil

Disabled Population:

	Persons	Males	Females	%
Total Disabled	1,279	732	547	
In Seeing	562	326	236	43.94
In Speech	116	66	50	9.07
In Hearing	71	22	49	5.55
In Movement	397	248	149	31.04
Mentally	133	70	63	10.4

JAGGAYYAPETA

Jaggayyapeta C.D. Block lies in the north-western part of Krishna district. It is a part of Jaggayyapeta Mandal. The Block is located at a distance of 155 kms. from district headquarters (Machilipatnam). There are 26 villages in the block with the total population of 66,950 persons. Area of the C.D. Block is 223.17 sq. kms. It is bounded in the north by district Khammam, in the south by district Guntur and mandal Chandaralap adu, in the east by Mandal Nandigama, Penuganchiprolu and Vatsavai, and in the west by district Nalgonda.

Communications:

Roadways : NH- 9: Direction- Secunderabad to Vijayawada. Nearest Villages- Tirumalagiri, Shermohammedpet, Anumanchipalle, Garikapadu, Torraguntapalem, Chillakallu, Gowravaram.

River: Muniyeru Nadi- Nearest Villages- Malkapuram. Krishna Nadi- Nearest Villages- Mukteswarapuram, Ravir ala, Vedadri. Paleru Nadi- Nearest Villages- Balusupadu, Annavaram, Budawada, Tripuravaram, Jayanthipuram, Kowthavari Agraharam, Mukteswarapuram, Ravirala.

Hills: Nearest Villages- Ravirala, Vedadri.

Annaul Rainfall: Average Rainfall 1452 mm

Ground Water: Availability of the Ground Water in the Basin is (Information not avavible) H.A.M .and the

utilization is (Information not avavible) H.A.M. It belongs to (Information not avavible) category. Depth to water level varies from 3 to 10 meter below the ground. Most of the wells go down in summer months.
Forest and Reserved **Forest:** (Bodavada R.F.)- Nearest Villages- Takkellapadu, Ramachandrunipeta, Gandrai, Budawada, Tripuravaram, Chillakallu, Gowravaram, Pocha mpalle, Jayanthipuram, Kowthavari Agraharam, Mukteswarap uram, Ravirala, Vedadri, Bandipalem.

Natural Division : Krishna Delta Region

Administration:

Division: Coastal Andhra. Parliamentary Constituency: 29 Vijayawada. District: Krishna.
Mandal: Jaggayyapeta. Assembly Constituency: 203 Jaggay yapeta. Gram Panchayat: 17.

Villages: 24 **Inhabited:** 23 **Uninhabited:** 1

Ranking	District	State	National
Area	7	423	3791
Population	15	180	4601
Sex Ratio	28	605	2099
Child Sex Ratio	35	718	3024
Literacy Rate	22	145	1880
Density	8	525	3524
Work Participation Rate	31	368	1371

Gram Panchayats:

Annavaram, Anumanchipalli, Balusupadu, Bandipalem Budawada, Chillakallu, D. P. Thanda, Gandrai Gowravaram, Jayanthipuram, K. Agraharam, Malkapuram Mukteswarapuram, Pochampalli, Sher Mohammad Pet Takkellapadu, Vedadri.

Amenities:

Education: Primary School in 21 villages, Middle school in 10 villages, Matriculation or Secondary School in 4 villages, namely Gandrai, Chillakallu, Gowravaram, Mukteswarapuram.
Higher Secondary or Pre University Courses or Intermediate or Junior College in 0 village of the CD Block, College in 0 village, Adult Literacy Center in 11 villages.

Medical: Hospital in 0 village, Dispensary in 2 villages, Health Center in 1 village, Sub Center in 12 villages, Maternity and Child Welfare Center in 0 village, Community health workers in 0 village.
The Villages having Hospital or Dispensary or Health Center are Balusupadu, Vedadri.

Drinking Water: Tap water in 17 villages, Tank water in 0 villages, Well water in 22 villages, Tubewell in 0 village and more than one source in 23 villages.

Bank: Banking facility in 2 villages, namely, Gandrai, Jayanthipuram.
Credit Society in 11 villages Agricultural Credit Society in 6 Non-Agricultural Credit Society in 11 villages.

Others: Power supply in 23 villages, Cinema hall in 1 village, sport club in 0 village, Stadium or Auditorium or Community Hall in 0 village, Post Office in 18 villages.
There are 22 villages having bus facilities.

Villages with most of facilities: Gandrai Jayanthipuram.

Villages without amenities (Education):
Tripuravaram..

Scheduled Castes: Out of the total population of 66917 persons, 13604 persons (20.33%) belong to Scheduled Castes.
The villages having less than 10% SC population are None..
The villages having more than 50% SC population are None.
Sex ratio of Scheduled Caste population is 491.

Scheduled Castes Literates and Illiterates by Sex:

	Persons	Males	Females
Literate	7,080	3,636	3,444
Illiterate	6,524	3,293	3,231
Literacy rate	61.2	61.5	60.8
Graduate	137	107	30

Scheduled Castes (Dominant):
Madiga, Mala, Beda Jangam etc., Mala Dasari Panchama etc.

For their cultural identity please see Appendix-I

Villages without Scheduled Castes: There are 2 villages without any scheduled caste population.

Scheduled Tribes: Out of the total population of 66917 persons, 7491 persons (11.19%) belong to Scheduled Tribes.
The villages having less than 10% ST population are Ramachandrunipeta, Gandrai, Buchavaram, Malkapuram Tirumalagiri, Shermohammedpet, Anumanchipalle Garikapadu, Balusupadu, Annavaram, Torraguntapalem Gowravaram, Pochampalle, Kowthavari Agraharam Ravirala, Bandipalem.
The villages having more than 50% ST population are None.
Sex ratio of Scheduled tribe population is 489.

Scheduled Tribes Literates and Illiterates by Sex:

	Persons	Males	Females
Literate	3,042	1,587	1,455
Illiterate	4,449	2,242	2,207
Literacy rate	49.2	50.5	47.9
Graduate	24	22	2

Scheduled Tribes (Dominant):
Sugalis etc., Yerukulas, Yenadis, Koya etc. Kondareddis

For their cultural identity please see Appendix-II

Villages without Scheduled Tribes: There are

3 villages without any scheduled tribe population.

Literates and Illiterates by Sex (Total Population):

	Persons	Males	Females
Literate	37,642	19,263	18,379
Illiterate	29,275	14,563	14,712
Literacy rate	65	66	64
Graduate	1,154	835	319

Agriculture: ***Distribution of villages according to land use:*** Out of 24 villages, Total area (in hectare) is 22317, out of that 53.1 percent is cultivable and 57.27 percent of the cultivable area is irrigated.

Sources of Irrigation (Hectares): Government Canal 4389.19, Private Canal 0, Well without Electricity 34.82, Well with Electricity 1080.88, Tubewell without Electricity 0, Tubewell with Electricity 0, Tank 576.2, River 0, Lake 0, Waterfall 0, Others 442.11.

Villages with population of 5000 to 9999: Gandrai, Shermohammedpet, Chillakallu.

Villages with population of 10000 and above: None

Distribution of Workers:

	Persons	Males	Females	WPR
Cultivators	5,631	4,014	1,617	16
Agricultural Labour	21,293	9,560	11,733	60.51
Household Industry	480	236	244	1.36
Other Workers	7,787	6,420	1,367	22.13
Main Workers	27,795	17,163	10,632	78.98
Marginal Workers	7,396	3,067	4,329	21.02
Total Workers	35,191	20,230	14,961	

Religion: Major Religious Communities:

	Persons	Males	Females	Sex Ratio
Hindu (92.52%)	61,914	31,333	30,581	976
Muslim (6.63%)	4,438	2,216	2,222	1,003
Christian (0.81%)	542	267	275	1,030
Sikh (0.01%)	4	2	2	1,000
Buddhists (0%)	3	1	2	2,000
Jain (0%)	-	-	-	-

Agewise Data:

	Persons	Males	Females	Sex Ratio
All ages	66,917	33,826	33,091	978
0-14	22,375	11,465	10,910	952
15-44	32,884	16,607	16,277	980
45-79	11,164	5,525	5,639	1021
80+	425	192	233	1214
Age not stated	69	37	32	865

Languages (Dominant): Telugu, Urdu, Hindi, Tamil, Gondi

Disabled Population:

	Persons	Males	Females	%
Total Disabled	1,303	710	593	
In Seeing	449	219	230	34.46
In Speech	124	68	56	9.52
In Hearing	58	32	26	4.45
In Movement	486	281	205	37.3
Mentally	186	110	76	14.27

JAGTIAL

Jagtial C.D. Block lies in the north-western part of Karimnagar district. It is a part of Jagtial Mandal. The Block is located at a distance of 50 kms. from district headquarters (Karimnagar). There are 24 villag es in the block with the total population of 64,927. persons. Area of the C.D. Block is 215.53 sq. kms. It is bounded by Sarangapur Mandal on north, Dharmapuri Mandal on north-east, Gollapalle Mandal on east, Malli al Mandal on south, Medipalle Mandal on west, and Raikal Mandal on north-west.

Communications :

Roadways : State Highway (S.H.): Direction- Karimnagar to Nizamabad. Nearest Villages- Jagtial (Rural), Chelg al, Tatipalle, Dharur, Narsingapur.

Backwards Region Grants Fund: It receives Backward Region Grants.

Integrated Child Development Scheme (ICDS) Project: Jagityal, Total Anganwadi Centres: 367

Annual Rainfall: Average Rainfall 1160 mm

Ground Water: Availability of the Ground Water in the Basin is 3983 H.A.M. and the utilization is 1905 H. A.M. It belongs to Safe category. Depth to water level varies from more than 5 to 10 meter below the ground. Most of the wells go down in summer months. The well density in the entire block is 26 wells per sq. km. Total no. of the wells in the block are enumerated as 5385, according to the Ground Water Estimation Commi ttee.

Natural Division : Godavari Depression Region

Administration:

Division: Telangana. Parliamentary Constituency: 4 Nizamabad. District: Karimnagar. Mandal: Jagtial. Assem bly Constituency: 21 Jagtial. Gram Panchayat: 29.

Villages: 24 **Inhabited:** 24 **Uninhabited:** 0

Ranking	District	State	National
Area	17	464	3922
Population	9	206	4687
Sex Ratio	10	62	470
Child Sex Ratio	45	790	3377
Literacy Rate	34	794	4873
Density	6	66	3503
Work Participation Rate	18	364	256

Gram Panchayats:

Ambaripet, Anantharam, Anthargom, Balapally, Chelgal Dharmaram, Dharur, Gullapet, Habsipur, Hasnabad Hyderpally, Jabithapur, Kalleda, Kandalapally

Kannapur, Laxmipur, Lingampet, Morapalli, Mothe Narsingapur, Polasa, Porandla, Somanpalli Tarakaramanagar, Thakkalapally, Thatipally Thimmapur, Thippannapet, Veldurthy.

Amenities:

Education: Primary School in 24 villages, Middle school in 23 villages, Matriculation or Secondary School in 15 villages, namely Porandla, Thippannapet, Polasa, Gullapeta, Kalleda, Anantharam, Lakshmipuram, Jagtial (Rural), Chelgal, Morapalle, Anthargaon, Dharur, Narsingapur, Mothe (Rural), Jabithapur.

Higher Secondary or Pre University Courses or Intermediate or Junior College in 0 village of the CD Block, College in 1 village, Adult Literacy Center in 19 villages., College is in village, namely Thippannapet.

Medical: Hospital in 0 village, Dispensary in 3 villages, Health Center in 1 village, Sub Center in 8 villages, Maternity and Child Welfare Center in 1 village, Community health workers in 0 village.

The Villages having Hospital or Dispensary or Health Center are Kalleda, Lakshmipuram, Jagtial (Rural), Dharmaram.

Drinking Water: Tap water in 24 villages, Tank water in 24 villages, Well water in 24 villages, Tubewell in 24 villages and more than one source in 24 villages.

Bank: Banking facility in 3 villages, namely, Porandla, Kalleda, Lakshmipuram.

Credit Society in 24 villages Agricultural Credit Society in 3 Non-Agricultural Credit Society in 24 villages.

Others: Power supply in 24 villages, Cinema hall in 1 village, sport club in 1 village, Stadium or Auditorium or Community Hall in 1 village, Post Office in 21 villages.

There are 22 villages having bus facilities.

Villages with most of facilities: Porandla Kalleda, Lakshmipuram.

Villages without Amenities (Education): None..

Scheduled Castes: Out of the total population of 65044 persons, 11821 persons (18.17%) belong to Scheduled Castes.

The villages having less than 10% SC population are None..

The villages having more than 50% SC population are None.

Sex ratio of Scheduled Caste population is 507.

Scheduled Castes Literates and Illiterates by Sex:

	Persons	Males	Females
Literate	4,158	2,657	1,501
Illiterate	7,663	3,167	4,496
Literacy rate	40.8	53.4	28.8
Graduate	38	38	0

Scheduled Castes (Dominant):

Madiga, Mala, Malajangam, Beda Jangam etc. Sindhollu etc.

For their cultural identity please see Appendix-I

Villages without Scheduled Castes: There are 0 village without any scheduled caste population.

Scheduled Tribes: Out of the total population of 65044 persons, 613 persons (0.94%) belong to Scheduled Tribes.

The villages having less than 10% ST population are Kannapur, Porandla, Thippannapet, Polasa, Gullapeta Thakkallapalle, Habsipur, Somanpalle, Kalleda Anantharam, Lakshmipuram, Thimmapur Jagtial (Rural), Kandlapalle, Chelgal, Morapalle Tatipalle, Anthargaon, Dharur, Narsingapur, Eldurthi Jabithapur, Dharmaram.

The villages having more than 50% ST population are None.

Sex ratio of Scheduled tribe population is 509.

Scheduled Tribes Literates and Illiterates by Sex:

	Persons	Males	Females
Literate	200	143	57
Illiterate	413	158	255
Literacy rate	41.7	60.6	23.4
Graduate	3	3	0

Scheduled Tribes (Dominant):

Yerukulas, Sugalis etc., Gond etc., Koya etc., Thoti

For their cultural identity please see Appendix-II

Villages without Scheduled Tribes: There are 12 villages without any scheduled tribe population.

Literates and Illiterates by Sex (Total Population):

	Persons	Males	Females
Literate	26,789	17,081	9,708
Illiterate	38,255	14,944	23,311
Literacy rate	48	62	34
Graduate	484	426	58

Agriculture: ***Distribution of villages according to land use:*** Out of 24 villages, Total area (in hectare) is 21553, out of that 68.71 percent is cultivable and 85.23 percent of the cultivable area is irrigated.

Sources of Irrigation (Hectares): Government Canal 3604.81, Private Canal 26, Well without Electricity 1371.58, Well with Electricity 4551, Tubewell without Electricity 0, Tubewell with Electricity 30, Tank 2620.15, River 18, Lake 0, Waterfall 0, Others 400.

Villages with population of 5000 to 9999: Chelgal.

Villages with population of 10000 and above: None

Distribution of Workers:

	Persons	Males	Females	WPR
Cultivators	13,145	7,251	5,894	34.41
Agricultural Labour	10,371	4,871	5,500	27.15

Household Industry	7,221	1,168	6,053	18.9
Other Workers	7,466	5,508	1,958	19.54
Main Workers	34,294	17,521	16,773	89.77
Marginal Workers	3,909	1,277	2,632	10.23
Total Workers	38,203	18,798	19,405	

Religion: Major Religious Communities:

	Persons	Males	Females	Sex Ratio
Hindu (94.34%)	61,363	30,180	31,183	1,033
Muslim (4.98%)	3,239	1,642	1,597	973
Christian (0.49%)	319	142	177	1,246
Sikh (0.08%)	55	32	23	719
Buddhists (0%)	1	-	1	-
Jain (0%)	1	-	1	-

Agewise Data:

	Persons	Males	Females	Sex Ratio
All ages	65,044	32,025	33,019	1031
0-14	20,233	10,361	9,872	953
15-44	30,840	14,854	15,986	1076
45-79	13,375	6,535	6,840	1047
80+	540	239	301	1259
Age not stated	56	36	20	556

Languages (Dominant):

Telugu, Urdu, Hindi, Oriya, Gondi

Disabled Population:

	Persons	Males	Females	%
Total Disabled	826	472	354	
In Seeing	348	196	152	42.13
In Speech	93	50	43	11.26
In Hearing	34	14	20	4.12
In Movement	234	145	89	28.33
Mentally	117	67	50	14.16

JAINAD

Jainad C.D. Block lies in the north-east part of Adilabad district. The Block is located at a distance of 18 kms. from district headquarters (Adilabad). There are 55 villages in the block with the total population of 44,805 persons. Area of the C.D. Block is 283 sq. kms. It is bounded by Bela Mandal on east and south-east, Adilabad Mandal on south-east, south, west, and Tamsi Mandal on north-west, it has common boundary with the state of Maharashtra in the north-west, north and north-east.

Communications :

Roadways : NH- 7: Direction- Adilabad to Nagpur. Nearest Villages- Gimma (Khurd), Sirsonna, Mirzapur, Moudagada, Akoli, Kamai.

River: Penganga Nadi- Nearest Villages- Akoli, Kamai, Hathighat, Korta, Kedarpur, Dollara, Pendalwada, Sangvi (K), Hariyali, Kowtha, Kodekotha, Karanji

Backwards Region Grants Fund: It receives Backward Region Grants.

Annual Rainfall: Average Rainfall 1218 mm

Ground Water: Availability of the ground water in the Basin is 4128 H.A.M. and the utilization is 1049 H.A.M. It belongs to Safe category. Depth to water level varies from 5 to 10 meter below the ground. Most of the wells go down in summer months, according to the Ground Water Estimation Committee.

Natural Division : Telangana Plateau Region

Administration:

Division: Telangana. Parliamentary Constituency: 1 Adilabad (ST). District: Adilabad. Mandal: Jainad. Assembly Constituency: 7 Adilabad. Gram Panchayat: 29

Border Villages: (Maharashtra)- Nearest Villages- Hathighat, Korta, Kedarpur, Akoli, Kamai, Dollara, Pendalwada, Sangvi (K), Kowtha, Hariyali, Kodekotha, Karanji.

Places of Tourist Interest :

Jainad: Jainad is (around Puttaparthi) distance of 21 kms. from Adilabad. A Prakrit stone inscription with 20 shlokas in a temple have mentions that it was built by a Pallava chief. The temple has all the features of the Jain school of temple architecture and this perhaps accounts for the name of the village. The Lakshminarayanaswami Brahmotsavam is celebrated during the Karthika Suddha Astami—Bahula Saptami period, attracting a large number of devotees.

Villages: 55 **Inhabited:** 46 **Uninhabited:** 9

Ranking	District	State	National
Area	22	198	2960
Population	12	668	5519
Sex Ratio	15	183	979
Child Sex Ratio	48	996	4563
Literacy Rate	16	668	4440
Density	18	275	5436
Work Participation Rate	16	876	705

Gram Panchayats:

Ada, Akoli, Bahadurpur, Balapur, Belluri, Bhoraj Deepaiguda, Gimma(K), Guda, Jainad, Jamini, Kamai Kamta, Kanpamediguda, Karanji, Khapri, Korta, Kowtha Kura, Laxmipur, Mandagada, Mangurla, Nirala, Pardi B Pendalwada, Pipparawada, Sangvi(K), Sawapoor Taroda B.

Amenities:

Education: Primary School in 43 villages, Middle school in 12 villages, Matriculation or Secondary School in 4 villages, namely Gimma (Khurd), Pendalwada, Deepaiguda, Jainad. Higher Secondary or Pre University Courses or Intermediate or Junior College in 0 village of the CD Block, College in 0 village, Adult Literacy Center in 42 villages.

Medical: Hospital in 0 village, Dispensary in 1 village, Health Center in 1 village, Sub Center in 10 villages, Maternity and Child Welfare Center in 0 village, Community health workers in 0 village.
The Village having Hospital or Dispensary or Health Center is Jainad.
Drinking Water: Tap water in 45 villages, Tank water in 45 villages, Well water in 45 villages, Tubewell in 45 villages and more than one source in 45 villages.
Bank: Banking facility in 5 villages, namely, Gimma (Khurd), Pendalwada, Karanji, Jainad, Ada.
Credit Society in 6 villages Agricultural Credit Society in 6 Non-Agricultural Credit Society in 0 village.
Others: Power supply in 46 villages, Cinema hall in 0 village, sport club in 0 village, Stadium or Auditorium or Community Hall in 0 village, Post Office in 14 villages.
There are 34 villages having bus facilities.
Villages with most of facilities: Gimma (Khurd) Pendalwada, Jainad.
Villages without amenities (Education): Hathighat..
Scheduled Castes: Out of the total population of 44805 persons, 7266 persons (16.22%) belong to Scheduled Castes.
The villages having less than 10% SC population are Hathighat, Kedarpur, Dollara, Hashampur Tarada (Buzurg), Nirala, Balapur, Akurla, Kowtha Umri, Belgaon, Ballori, Muktapur, Pardi (Buzurg) Jamini, Kanpa (Mediguda), Mangurla.
The villages having more than 50% SC population are None.
Sex ratio of Scheduled Caste population is 498.

Scheduled Castes Literates and Illiterates by Sex:

	Persons	Males	Females
Literate	2,690	1,749	941
Illiterate	4,576	1,898	2,678
Literacy rate	42.8	55.8	29.9
Graduate	26	26	0

Scheduled Castes (Dominant):
Madiga, Mala, Mahar, Mehtar, Beda Jangam etc.
For their cultural identity please see Appendix-I
Villages without Scheduled Castes: There are 13 villages without any scheduled caste population.
Scheduled Tribes: Out of the total population of 44805 persons, 5038 persons (11.24%) belong to Scheduled Tribes.
The villages having less than 10% ST population are Guda, Gimma (Khurd), Sirsonna, Bhoraj, Fouzpur Poosai, Pipparwada, Kamai, Savapur, Hashampur Tarada (Buzurg), Nizampur, Nirala, Balapur, Akurla Deepaiguda, Kowtha, Bahadurpur, Khapri, Jainad Muktapur, Ada, Kamtha, Laxmipur (Uligan).
The villages having more than 50% ST population are None.
Sex ratio of Scheduled tribe population is 500.

Scheduled Tribes Literates and Illiterates by Sex:

	Persons	Males	Females
Literate	1,857	1,191	666
Illiterate	3,181	1,329	1,852
Literacy rate	44.2	57.1	31.4
Graduate	8	8	0

Scheduled Tribes (Dominant):
Pardhan, Gond etc., Kolam etc., Koya etc., Andh
For their cultural identity please see Appendix-II
Villages without Scheduled Tribes: There are 14 villages without any scheduled tribe population.

Literates and Illiterates by Sex (Total Population):

	Persons	Males	Females
Literate	19,596	12,459	7,137
Illiterate	25,209	9,880	15,329
Literacy rate	51	65	36
Graduate	263	244	19

Agriculture: ***Distribution of villages according to land use:*** Out of 55 villages, Total area (in hectare) is 28313, out of that 75.25 percent is cultivable and 4.09 percent of the cultivable area is irrigated.
Sources of Irrigation (Hectares): Government Canal 391.5, Private Canal 96, Well without Electricity 18, Well with Electricity 106.12, Tubewell without Electricity 24, Tubewell with Electricity 177.53, Tank 0, River 59.1, Lake 0, Waterfall 0, Others 0.
Villages with population of 5000 to 9999: None
Villages with population of 10000 and above: None

Distribution of Workers:

	Persons	Males	Females	WPR
Cultivators	10,823	6,246	4,577	43.36
Agricultural Labour	11,082	4,424	6,658	44.4
Household Industry	444	283	161	1.78
Other Workers	2,613	2,125	488	10.47
Main Workers	20,881	11,769	9,112	83.65
Marginal Workers	4,081	1,309	2,772	16.35
Total Workers	24,962	13,078	11,884	

Religion: Major Religious Communities:

	Persons	Males	Females	Sex Ratio
Hindu (94.84%)	42,494	21,179	21,315	1,006
Muslim (3.93%)	1,760	868	892	1,028
Christian (0.08%)	35	21	14	667
Sikh (0%)	-	-	-	-
Buddhists (1.15%)	515	270	245	907
Jain (0%)	1	1	-	-

Agewise Data:

	Persons	Males	Females	Sex Ratio
All ages	44,805	22,339	22,466	1006

0-14	15,102	7,740	7,362	951
15-44	20,693	10,452	10,241	980
45-79	8,680	4,012	4,668	1164
80+	296	111	185	1667
Age not stated	34	24	10	417

Languages (Dominant):
Telugu, Marathi, Gondi, Urdu, Hindi
Disabled Population:

	Persons	Males	Females	%
Total Disabled	689	387	302	
In Seeing	277	145	132	40.2
In Speech	71	44	27	10.3
In Hearing	47	28	19	6.82
In Movement	226	131	95	32.8
Mentally	68	39	29	9.87

JAINOOR

Jainoor C.D. Block lies in the north-east part of Adila bad district. The Block is located at a distance of 69 kms. from district headquarters (Adilabad). There are 16 villages in the block with the total population of 23,487 persons. Area of the C.D. Block is 226.60 sq. kms. It is bounded by Narnoor Mandal on north-west, north and north-east, Asifabad Mandal on north-east and east, Sirpur Mandal on south-east and south, Utnoor Mandal on south-west and west.

Communications :

Roadways : State Highway (S.H.): Direction- Utnoor to Asifabad. Nearest Villages- Bhusimatta, Daboli, Lendiguda, Ushegaon, Jainoor, Powerguda.

Backwards Region Grants Fund: It receives Backward Region Grants.

Mahila Samakhya (Education for Women's Equality): It is decleared Socialy and Educationally Backward Block by the Government.

Annual Rainfall: Average Rainfall 1343 mm

Ground Water: Availability of the ground water in the Basin is 1644 H.A.M.and the utilization is 309 H.A. M. It belongs to Safe category. Depth to water level varies from 10 to 20 meter below the ground. Most of the wells go down in summer months, according to the Ground Water Estimation Committee.

Natural Division : Telangana Plateau Region

Administration:

Division: Telangana. Parliamentary Constituency: 1 Adilabad (ST). District: Adilabad. Mandal: Jainoor. Assembly Constituency: 5 Asifabad (ST). Gram Panchayat: 12

Villages: 16 **Inhabited:** 16 **Uninhabited:** 0

Ranking	District	State	National
Area	38	412	3753
Population	47	1078	6173
Sex Ratio	42	847	2824
Child Sex Ratio	10	148	384
Literacy Rate	32	904	5310
Density	30	506	6100
Work Participation Rate	38	1046	1321

Gram Panchayats:

Addesara, Ashapalle, Daboli, Gudamamda, Jainoor Jamgaon, Jamni, Jandaguda, Marlawai, Patnapur Rasimatta, Ushegaon.

Amenities:

Education: Primary School in 16 villages, Middle school in 6 villages, Matriculation or Secondary School in 2 villages, namely Ushegaon, Marlawai.

Higher Secondary or Pre University Courses or Intermediate or Junior College in 1 village of the CD Block,, namely Ushegaon.

College in 0 village, Adult Literacy Center in 6 villages.

Medical: Hospital in 0 village, Dispensary in 2 villages, Health Center in 1 village, Sub Center in 7 villages, Maternity and Child Welfare Center in 0 village, Community health workers in 0 village.

The Villages having Hospital or Dispensary or Health Center are Ushegaon, Jainoor.

Drinking Water: Tap water in 16 villages, Tank water in 16 villages, Well water in 16 villages, Tubewell in 16 villages and more than one source in 16 villages.

Bank: Banking facility in 1 villages, namely, Jainoor.

Credit Society in 2 villages Agricultural Credit Society in 2 Non-Agricultural Credit Society in 2 villages.

Others: Power supply in 16 villages, Cinema hall in 0 village, sport club in 0 village, Stadium or Auditorium or Community Hall in 0 village, Post Office in 9 villages.

There are 8 villages having bus facilities.

Village with most of facilities: Jainoor.

Villages without Amenities (Education): None..

Scheduled Castes: Out of the total population of 23487 persons, 1745 persons (7.43%) belong to Scheduled Castes. The villages having less than 10% SC population are Patnapur, Bhusimatta, Rasimatta, Daboli, Lendiguda Ushegaon, Shivanur, Marlawai, Dubbaguda, Powerguda Jamni, Polasa.

The villages having more than 50% SC population are None.

Sex ratio of Scheduled Caste population is 492.

Scheduled Castes Literates and Illiterates by Sex:

	Persons	Males	Females
Literate	528	333	195
Illiterate	1,217	554	663

Literacy rate	38.9	48.9	28.8
Graduate	11	8	3

Scheduled Castes (Dominant):

Mang, Mala, Mahar, Madiga, Mala Sale etc.

For their cultural identity please see Appendix-I

Villages without Scheduled Castes: There are 5 villages without any scheduled caste population.

Scheduled Tribes: Out of the total population of 23487 persons, 14516 persons (61.8%) belong to Scheduled Tribes.

The villages having less than 10% ST population are None..

The villages having more than 50% ST population are Ashapalle, Gudamamda, Addesar, Bhusimatta, Rasimatta Daboli, Lendiguda, Ushegaon, Shivanur, Marlawai Dubbaguda, Powerguda, Polasa.

Sex ratio of Scheduled tribe population is 496.

Scheduled Tribes Literates and Illiterates by Sex:

	Persons	Males	Females
Literate	4,832	3,218	1,614
Illiterate	9,684	4,097	5,587
Literacy rate	41.9	55.1	28.4
Graduate	29	28	1

Scheduled Tribes (Dominant):

Gond etc., Sugalis etc., Kolam etc., Andh, Pardhan

For their cultural identity please see Appendix-II

Villages without Scheduled Tribes: There are 0 village without any scheduled tribe population.

Literates and Illiterates by Sex (Total Population):

	Persons	Males	Females
Literate	8,217	5,421	2,796
Illiterate	15,270	6,543	8,727
Literacy rate	44	57	31
Graduate	85	73	12

Agriculture: ***Distribution of villages according to land use:*** Out of 16 villages, Total area (in hectare) is 22465, out of that 36.38 percent is cultivable and 0.05 percent of the cultivable area is irrigated.

Sources of Irrigation (Hectares): Government Canal 0, Private Canal 0, Well without Electricity 4.04, Well with Electricity 0, Tubewell without Electricity 0, Tubewell with Electricity 0.4, Tank 0, River 0, Lake 0, Waterfall 0, Others 0.

Villages with population of 5000 to 9999: None

Villages with population of 10000 and above: None

Distribution of Workers:

	Persons	Males	Females	WPR
Cultivators	6,142	3,469	2,673	53.85
Agricultural Labour	3,160	1,175	1,985	27.71
Household Industry	379	171	208	3.32
Other Workers	1,724	1,301	423	15.12
Main Workers	8,376	5,027	3,349	73.44
Marginal Workers	3,029	1,089	1,940	26.56
Total Workers	11,405	6,116	5,289	

Religion: Major Religious Communities:

	Persons	Males	Females	Sex Ratio
Hindu (83.02%)	19,498	9,871	9,627	975
Muslim (16.27%)	3,821	2,005	1,816	906
Christian (0.13%)	30	13	17	1,308
Sikh (0%)	-	-	-	-
Buddhists (0.49%)	115	64	51	797
Jain (0%)	-	-	-	-

Agewise Data:

	Persons	Males	Females	Sex Ratio
All ages	23,487	11,964	11,523	963
0-14	10,602	5,512	5,090	923
15-44	9,673	4,987	4,686	940
45-79	3,018	1,377	1,641	1192
80+	153	64	89	1391
Age not stated	41	24	17	708

Languages (Dominant):

Gondi, Marathi, Hindi, Urdu, Kolami

Disabled Population:

	Persons	Males	Females	%
Total Disabled	441	258	183	
In Seeing	165	91	74	37.41
In Speech	56	28	28	12.7
In Hearing	41	23	18	9.3
In Movement	143	91	52	32.43
Mentally	36	25	11	8.16

JAIPUR

Jaipur C.D. Block lies in the southern part of Adilabad district. The Block is located at a distance of 206 kms. from district headquarters (Adilabad). There are 35 villages in the block with the total population of 46,786 persons. Area of the C.D. Block is 389.40 sq. kms. It is bounded by Nennal Mandal on north-west and north, Chennur Mandal on north-east, east and south -east, Karimnagar district on south and south-west, Mancherial Mandal on west and north-west, Mandamarri Mandal on north-west.

Communications :

Roadways : NH- 16: Direction- Mancherial to Chennur. Nearest Villages- Ramaraopet, Indaram, Bhimaram, Ankus hapur, Polampalle, Jaipur, Narva, Maddikunta, Pegadapalle.

River: Godavari Nadi- Nearest Villages- Kachanpalle, Tekumatla, Shetpalle, Bejjal, Kundaram, Rommipur, Kistapur, Velal, Gopalpur, Pownur, Shivvaram, Ramaraopet, Indaram.

Backwards Region Grants Fund: It receives Backward

Region Grants.

Annual Rainfall: Average Rainfall 1266 mm

Ground Water: Availability of the Ground Water in the Basin is 3559 H.A.M.and the utilization is 1332 H.A. M. It belongs to Safe category. Depth to water level varies from 5 to 10 meter below the ground. Most of the wells go down in summer months, according to the Ground Water Estimation Committee.

Natural Division : Telangana Plateau Region

Administration:

Division: Telangana. Parliamentary Constituency: 2 Peddapalle (SC). District: Adilabad. Mandal: Jaipur. Assembly Constituency: 2 Chennur (SC). Gram Panchayat: 24

Villages: 35 **Inhabited:** 32 **Uninhabited:** 3

Ranking	District	State	National
Area	8	52	1999
Population	8	609	5429
Sex Ratio	38	801	2701
Child Sex Ratio	38	737	3116
Literacy Rate	26	786	4843
Density	45	948	5949
Work Participation Rate	28	999	3393

Gram Panchayats:

Arepalle, Bejjal, Bhimaram, Burugupalle, Dampur Gangipallee, Indaram, Jaipur, Kistapur, Kothapalle Kundaram, Maddikal, Mittapally, Mudigunta Narasingapuram, Pegadapalle, Polampalle, Pownoor Ramaraopet, Shetpalle, Sivvaram, Tekumatla, Velal Yelkanti.

Amenities:

Education: Primary School in 32 villages, Middle school in 15 villages, Matriculation or Secondary School in 3 villages, namely Bhimaram, Jaipur, Indaram.

Higher Secondary or Pre University Courses or Intermediate or Junior College in 0 village of the CD Block, College in 0 village, Adult Literacy Center in 29 villages.

Medical: Hospital in 0 village, Dispensary in 0 village, Health Center in 2 villages, Sub Center in 10 villages, Maternity and Child Welfare Center in 0 village, Community health workers in 0 village.

The Village having Hospital or Dispensary or Health Center is Kundaram.

Drinking Water: Tap water in 31 villages, Tank water in 31 villages, Well water in 32 villages, Tubewell in 31 villages and more than one source in 31 villages.

Bank: Banking facility in 4 villages, namely, Bhimaram, Jaipur, Indaram, Kundaram.

Credit Society in 12 villages Agricultural Credit Society in 8 Non-Agricultural Credit Society in 7 villages.

Others: Power supply in 32 villages, Cinema hall in 0 village, sport club in 0 village, Stadium or Auditorium or Community Hall in 0 village, Post Office in 18 villages.

There are 13 villages having bus facilities.

Villages with most of facilities: Bhimaram, Jaipur Indaram, Kundaram.

Villages without Amenities (Education): None..

Scheduled Castes: Out of the total population of 46786 persons, 16044 persons (34.29%) belong to Scheduled Castes.

The villages having less than 10% SC population are None..

The villages having more than 50% SC population are Ankushapur, Polampalle, Narva, Arepalle, Kothapalle Gopalpur.

Sex ratio of Scheduled Caste population is 482.

Scheduled Castes Literates and Illiterates by Sex:

	Persons	Males	Females
Literate	5,557	3,627	1,930
Illiterate	10,487	4,681	5,806
Literacy rate	41.0	51.8	29.5
Graduate	29	28	1

Scheduled Castes (Dominant):

Mala Sale etc., Madiga, Manne, Mala Generic Castes etc.

For their cultural identity please see Appendix-I

Villages without Scheduled Castes: There are 3 villages without any scheduled caste population.

Scheduled Tribes: Out of the total population of 46786 persons, 3690 persons (7.89%) belong to Scheduled Tribes.

The villages having less than 10% ST population are Kankur, Mittapalle, Ankushapur, Polampalle, Jaipur Narva, Ramaraopet, Indaram, Tekumatla, Shetpalle Yelkanti, Gangipalle, Narasingapuram, Bejjal Maddulapalle, Kundaram, Rommipur, Kistapur Kothapalle, Velal, Gopalpur, Pownur, Shivvaram.

The villages having more than 50% ST population are None.

Sex ratio of Scheduled tribe population is 488.

Scheduled Tribes Literates and Illiterates by Sex:

	Persons	Males	Females
Literate	1,146	752	394
Illiterate	2,544	1,137	1,407
Literacy rate	36.5	47.2	25.5
Graduate	4	3	1

Scheduled Tribes (Dominant):

Koya etc., Gond etc., Sugalis etc., Yerukulas, Thoti

For their cultural identity please see Appendix-II

Villages without Scheduled Tribes: There are 12 villages without any scheduled tribe population.

Literates and Illiterates by Sex (Total Population):

	Persons	Males	Females
Literate	19,106	11,967	7,139
Illiterate	27,680	11,833	15,847
Literacy rate	48	59	36
Graduate	244	200	44

Agriculture: ***Distribution of villages according to land use:*** Out of 35 villages, Total area (in hectare) is 38937, out of that 46.87 percent is cultivable and 10.44 percent of the cultivable area is irrigated.

Sources of Irrigation (Hectares): Government Canal 12, Private Canal 0, Well without Electricity 5, Well with Electricity 84, Tubewell without Electricity 14, Tubewell with Electricity 25, Tank 1764.34, River 0, Lake 1, Waterfall 0, Others 0.

Villages with population of 5000 to 9999: Bhimaram, Indaram.

Villages with population of 10000 and above: None

Distribution of Workers:

	Persons	Males	Females	WPR
Cultivators	4,325	3,142	1,183	20.88
Agricultural Labour	10,010	4,523	5,487	48.33
Household Industry	553	320	233	2.67
Other Workers	5,823	5,002	821	28.12
Main Workers	14,711	10,402	4,309	71.03
Marginal Workers	6,000	2,585	3,415	28.97
Total Workers	20,711	12,987	7,724	

Religion: Major Religious Communities:

	Persons	Males	Females	Sex Ratio
Hindu (97.11%)	45,436	23,113	22,323	966
Muslim (2.32%)	1,085	550	535	973
Christian (0.54%)	252	132	120	909
Sikh (0%)	-	-	-	-
Buddhists (0%)	-	-	-	-
Jain (0%)	-	-	-	-

Agewise Data:

	Persons	Males	Females	Sex Ratio
All ages	46,786	23,800	22,986	966
0-14	16,085	8,305	7,780	937
15-44	21,308	10,876	10,432	959
45-79	8,990	4,420	4,570	1034
80+	363	178	185	1039
Age not stated	40	21	19	905

Languages (Dominant):

Telugu, Urdu, Hindi, Marathi, Tamil

Disabled Population:

	Persons	Males	Females	%
Total Disabled	655	343	312	
In Seeing	238	121	117	36.34
In Speech	85	38	47	12.98
In Hearing	32	14	18	4.89
In Movement	203	119	84	30.99
Mentally	97	51	46	14.81

JAJI REDDI GUDEM

Jajireddigudem C.D. Block lies in the north east part of Nalgonda district. The Block is located at a distance of 47 kms. from district headquarters (Nalgonda). There are 15 villages in the block with the total popul ation of 40,878 persons. Area of the C.D. Block is 194. 61 sq. kms. It is bounded by Thirumalgiri Mandal on north, Thungathurthi Nulhankal Mandal on east, Suryapet and Atmakur Mandals on south, Othkur and Saligouram Mandals on west.

Communications:

Roadways : Metalled Roads: Nearest Villages- Wardhamanu Kota, Devaraneni Kotha Palle, Parsai Palle, Jajireddi Gudem, Thimmapuram, Adivemula, Velpu Cherla.

River: Alair Nadi- Nearest Villages- Wardhamanu Kota, Jajireddi Gudem, Kesaram, Uyyalawada.

Backwards Region Grants Fund: It receives Backward Region Grants.

Annual Rainfall: Average Rainfall 870 mm

Ground Water: Availability of the Ground Water in the Basin is 2682 H.A.M. and the utilization is 1748 H. A.M. It belongs to Safe category. Depth to water level varies from 5 to 20 meter below the ground. Most of the wells go down in summer months.

Natural Division : Krishna Piedmont Plain Region

Administration:

Division: Telangana. Parliamentary Constituency: 14 Bhongir. District: Nalgonda. Mandal: Jaji Reddi Gudem. Assembly Constituency: 96 Thungathurthi (SC). Gram Panchayat: 13.

Villages: 15 **Inhabited:** 14 **Uninhabited:** 1

Ranking	**District**	**State**	**National**
Area	39	590	4275
Population	43	798	5698
Sex Ratio	26	698	2334
Child Sex Ratio	38	803	3465
Literacy Rate	38	681	4473
Density	17	350	4589
Work Participation Rate	26	679	869

Gram Panchayats:

Adivemla, D.Kothapally, Jaji Reddy Gudem Kesarla Pahad, Kodur, Kommala, Kunchamarthy Loya Pally, Machireddy Pally, Nagaram, Persaipally Thimmapur, Vardhamanukota.

Amenities:

Education: Primary School in 14 villages, Middle school in 10 villages, Matriculation or Secondary School in 4 villages, namely Wardhamanu Kota, Nagaram, Jajireddi Gudem, Thimmapuram.

Higher Secondary or Pre University Courses or Intermediate or Junior College in 1 village of the CD Block,, namely Jajireddi Gudem.

College in 0 village, Adult Literacy Center in 13 villages.

Medical: Hospital in 0 village, Dispensary in 1 village, Health Center in 4 villages, Sub Center in 8 villages, Maternity and Child Welfare Center in 0 village, Community health workers in 0 village.

The Villages having Hospital or Dispensary or Health Center are Wardhamanu Kota, Nagaram.

Drinking Water: Tap water in 14 villages, Tank water in 14 villages, Well water in 14 villages, Tubewell in 14 villages and more than one source in 14 villages.

Bank: Banking facility in 2 villages, namely, Nagaram, Jajireddi Gudem.

Credit Society in 3 villages Agricultural Credit Society in 3 Non-Agricultural Credit Society in 0 village.

Others: Power supply in 14 villages, Cinema hall in 1 village, sport club in 0 village, Stadium or Auditorium or Community Hall in 0 village, Post Office in 11 villages.

There are 11 villages having bus facilities.

Villages with most of facilities: Nagaram Jajireddi Gudem.

Villages without Amenities (Education): None..

Scheduled Castes: Out of the total population of 40878 persons, 7229 persons (17.68%) belong to Scheduled Castes.

The villages having less than 10% SC population are None..

The villages having more than 50% SC population are None.

Sex ratio of Scheduled Caste population is 498.

Scheduled Castes Literates and Illiterates by Sex:

	Persons	Males	Females
Literate	2,850	1,854	996
Illiterate	4,379	1,777	2,602
Literacy rate	46.4	60.2	32.5
Graduate	87	83	4

Scheduled Castes (Dominant):

Madiga, Mala, Generic Castes etc., Bindla Dakkal etc.

For their cultural identity please see Appendix-I

Villages without Scheduled Castes: There are 2 villages without any scheduled caste population.

Scheduled Tribes: Out of the total population of 40878 persons, 2747 persons (6.72%) belong to Scheduled Tribes.

The villages having less than 10% ST population are Wardhamanu Kota, Nagaram, Devaraneni Kotha Palle Bollam Palle, Jajireddi Gudem, Uyyalawada Kunchamarthi, Thimmapuram, Adivemula, Velpu Cherla Kasarla Pahad.

The villages having more than 50% ST population are None.

Sex ratio of Scheduled tribe population is 484.

Scheduled Tribes Literates and Illiterates by Sex:

	Persons	Males	Females
Literate	812	587	225
Illiterate	1,935	830	1,105
Literacy rate	35.2	49.2	20.3
Graduate	12	12	0

Scheduled Tribes (Dominant):

Sugalis etc., Yerukulas, Yenadis

For their cultural identity please see Appendix-II

Villages without Scheduled Tribes: There are 5 villages without any scheduled tribe population.

Literates and Illiterates by Sex (Total Population):

	Persons	Males	Females
Literate	17,603	11,266	6,337
Illiterate	23,275	9,449	13,826
Literacy rate	50	64	37
Graduate	594	537	57

Agriculture: ***Distribution of villages according to land use:*** Out of 15 villages, Total area (in hectare) is 19461, out of that 69.02 percent is cultivable and 32.76 percent of the cultivable area is irrigated.

Sources of Irrigation (Hectares): Government Canal 0, Private Canal 0, Well without Electricity 0, Well with Electricity 2890, Tubewell without Electricity 420, Tubewell with Electricity 1090, Tank 0, River 0, Lake 0, Waterfall 0, Others 0.

Villages with population of 5000 to 9999: Wardhamanu Kota, Jajireddi Gudem.

Villages with population of 10000 and above: None

Distribution of Workers:

	Persons	Males	Females	WPR
Cultivators	7,322	4,836	2,486	33.05
Agricultural Labour	10,894	4,061	6,833	49.17
Household Industry	782	344	438	3.53
Other Workers	3,156	2,449	707	14.25
Main Workers	17,192	10,279	6,913	77.6
Marginal Workers	4,962	1,411	3,551	22.4
Total Workers	22,154	11,690	10,464	

Religion: Major Religious Communities:

	Persons	Males	Females	Sex Ratio
Hindu (97.33%)	39,788	20,163	19,625	973
Muslim (2.17%)	889	450	439	976
Christian (0.37%)	153	76	77	1,013
Sikh (0%)	1	1	-	-
Buddhists (0%)	-	-	-	-
Jain (0%)	-	-	-	-

Agewise Data:

	Persons	Males	Females	Sex Ratio
All ages	40,878	20,715	20,163	973
0-14	13,624	7,047	6,577	933
15-44	18,057	8,942	9,115	1019
45-79	8,697	4,450	4,247	954
80+	429	232	197	849
Age not stated	71	44	27	614

Languages (Dominant):
Telugu, Hindi, Urdu, Gondi, Tamil

Disabled Population:

	Persons	Males	Females	%
Total Disabled	927	511	416	
In Seeing	476	275	201	51.35
In Speech	98	48	50	10.57
In Hearing	49	20	29	5.29
In Movement	239	140	99	25.78
Mentally	65	28	37	7.01

JAKRANPALLE

Jakranpalle C.D. Block lies in the north-eastern part of Nizamabad district. The Block is located at a distan ce of 25 kms. from district headquarters (Nizamabad). There are 15 villages in the block with the total population of 43,636 persons. Area of the C.D. Block is 151.48 sq. kms. It is bounded by Armur mandal on north and north-east, Velpur mandal on north-east, and east Bheemgal Mandal on south-east, Dichpalle Mandal on south-east, south and south-west, Makloor Mandal on south-west, west and north-west.

Communications :

Roadways : NH- 7: Direction- Hyderabad to Adilabad. Nearest Villages- Argul, Brahmanpalle, Jakranpalle, Poppalpalle, Sikindrapur, Padkal.

Backwards Region Grants Fund: It receives Backward Region Grants.

Annual Rainfall: Average Rainfall 878 mm

Ground Water: Availability of the Ground Water in the Basin is 2143 H.A.M. and the utilization is 3525 H. A.M. It belongs to Over Exploited category. Depth to water level varies from 10 to 20 meter below the ground. Most of the wells go down in summer months, according to the Ground Water Estimation Committee.

Natural Division : Telangana Plateau Region

Administration:

Division: Telangana. Parliamentary Constituency: 4 Nizamabad. District: Nizamabad Mandal: Jakranpalle. Assembly Constituency: 18 Nizamabad (Rural). Gram Panchayat: 15

Villages: 15 **Inhabited:** 15 **Uninhabited:** 0

Ranking	District	State	National
Area	30	818	5026
Population	28	709	5579
Sex Ratio	1	4	109
Child Sex Ratio	6	273	866
Literacy Rate	19	808	4910
Density	7	185	3658
Work Participation Rate	13	403	529

Gram Panchayats:

Argul, Brahmanpally, Chinthaloor, Jakranpally Kaligote, Keshpally, Kolipyak, Laxmapoor Manoharabad, Munipally, Narayanpet, Padkal Puppalapally, Secundrapoor, Thorlikonda.

Amenities:

Education: Primary School in 15 villages, Middle school in 12 villages, Matriculation or Secondary School in 8 villages, namely Munpalle, Argul, Brahmanpalle, Thorlikonda, Kolipaka, Jakranpalle, Padkal, Kaligote.

Higher Secondary or Pre University Courses or Intermediate or Junior College in 0 village of the CD Block, College in 0 village, Adult Literacy Center in 11 villages.

Medical: Hospital in 0 village, Dispensary in 1 village, Health Center in 1 village, Sub Center in 7 villages, Maternity and Child Welfare Center in 0 village, Community health workers in 0 village.

The Village having Hospital or Dispensary or Health Center is Padkal.

Drinking Water: Tap water in 15 villages, Tank water in 15 villages, Well water in 15 villages, Tubewell in 15 villages and more than one source in 15 villages.

Bank: Banking facility in 5 villages, namely, Munpalle, Argul, Thorlikonda, Jakranpalle, Padkal.

Credit Society in 7 villages Agricultural Credit Society in 4 Non-Agricultural Credit Society in 1 village.

Others: Power supply in 15 villages, Cinema hall in 0 village, sport club in 0 village, Stadium or Auditorium or Community Hall in 0 village, Post Office in 8 villages.

There are 15 villages having bus facilities.

Villages with most of facilities: Munpalle, Argul Thorlikonda, Jakranpalle, Padkal.

Villages without Amenities (Education): None..

Scheduled Castes: Out of the total population of 43636 persons, 7877 persons (18.05%) belong to Scheduled Castes.

The villages having less than 10% SC population are None..

The villages having more than 50% SC population are None.

Sex ratio of Scheduled Caste population is 530.

Scheduled Castes Literates and Illiterates by Sex:

	Persons	Males	Females
Literate	2,945	1,842	1,103
Illiterate	4,932	1,859	3,073

Literacy rate	43.5	58.9	30.3
Graduate	65	64	1

Scheduled Castes (Dominant):
Mala, Madiga, Gosangi, Generic Castes etc.
Mitha Ayyalvar

For their cultural identity please see Appendix-I

Villages without Scheduled Castes: There are 0 village without any scheduled caste population.

Scheduled Tribes: Out of the total population of 43636 persons, 3268 persons (7.49%) belong to Scheduled Tribes. The villages having less than 10% ST population are Narayanpet, Argul, Brahmanpalle, Thorlikonda Kolipaka, Jakranpalle, Sikindrapur, Padkal Manoharabad, Kaligote, Chintalur.
The villages having more than 50% ST population are None.
Sex ratio of Scheduled tribe population is 511.

Scheduled Tribes Literates and Illiterates by Sex:

	Persons	Males	Females
Literate	1,090	803	287
Illiterate	2,178	796	1,382
Literacy rate	41.1	62.5	20.9
Graduate	16	15	1

Scheduled Tribes (Dominant):
Sugalis etc., Gond etc., Yerukulas, Chenchu etc.
Thoti

For their cultural identity please see Appendix-II

Villages without Scheduled Tribes: There are 2 villages without any scheduled tribe population.

Literates and Illiterates by Sex (Total Population):

	Persons	Males	Females
Literate	17,669	11,030	6,639
Illiterate	25,967	9,706	16,261
Literacy rate	47	63	34
Graduate	479	433	46

Agriculture: ***Distribution of villages according to land use:*** Out of 15 villages, Total area (in hectare) is 15148, out of that 27.49 percent is cultivable and 82.86 percent of the cultivable area is irrigated.

Sources of Irrigation (Hectares): Government Canal 0, Private Canal 0, Well without Electricity 0, Well with Electricity 34.39, Tubewell without Electricity 0, Tubewell with Electricity 3197.59, Tank 184.97, River 0, Lake 33.99, Waterfall 0, Others 0.

Villages with population of 5000 to 9999:
Jakranpalle, Padkal.

Villages with population of 10000 and above: None

Distribution of Workers:

	Persons	Males	Females	WPR
Cultivators	6,710	3,673	3,037	27.41
Agricultural Labour	5,775	3,029	2,746	23.59
Household Industry	6,335	1,039	5,296	25.88
Other Workers	5,657	3,736	1,921	23.11
Main Workers	20,658	10,143	10,515	84.4
Marginal Workers	3,819	1,334	2,485	15.6
Total Workers	24,477	11,477	13,000	

Religion: Major Religious Communities:

	Persons	Males	Females	Sex Ratio
Hindu (95.04%)	41,473	19,675	21,798	1,108
Muslim (4.16%)	1,815	885	930	1,051
Christian (0.74%)	323	167	156	934
Sikh (0%)	-	-	-	-
Buddhists (0%)	-	-	-	-
Jain (0%)	-	-	-	-

Agewise Data:

	Persons	Males	Females	Sex Ratio
All ages	43,636	20,736	22,900	1104
0-14	14,046	6,967	7,079	1016
15-44	20,741	9,782	10,959	1120
45-79	8,520	3,852	4,668	1212
80+	291	115	176	1530
Age not stated	38	20	18	900

Languages (Dominant):
Telugu, Hindi, Urdu, Tamil, Marathi

Disabled Population:

	Persons	Males	Females	%
Total Disabled	684	370	314	
In Seeing	283	140	143	41.37
In Speech	76	36	40	11.11
In Hearing	32	11	21	4.68
In Movement	210	134	76	30.7
Mentally	83	49	34	12.13

JALADANKI

Jaladanki C.D. Block lies in the northern part of Nellore district. The Block is located at a distance of 62 kms. from district headquarters (Nellore). There are 12 villages in the block with the total population of 44,059 persons. Area of the C.D. Block is 307.49 sq. kms. It is bounded in the north by district Prakasam and Mandal Kavali, in the south by Mandals Dagadarthi and Bogole, in the east by Mandals Bogole and Kavali, and in the west by Mandal Kondapuram and Kaligiri.

Communications:

Roadways : Metalled Roads: Nearest Villages- Jaladanki, China Kraka, Brahmanakraka.

Annual Rainfall: Average Rainfall 1234 mm

Ground Water: Availability of the Ground Water in the Basin is 6352 H.A.M. and the utilization is 878 H.A. M. It belongs to Safe category. Depth to water level varies from 5 to 10 meter and more than 10 meter below the ground. Most of the wells go down in summer months, according to the Ground Water Estimation Committee.

Administration:

Division: Coastal Andhra. Parliamentary Constituency: 39 Nellore. District: Nellore.

Mandal: Jaladanki. Assembly Constituency: 242 Udayagiri.

Gram Panchayat: 16.

Villages: 12 **Inhabited:** 12 **Uninhabited:** 0

Ranking	District	State	National
Area	12	147	2703
Population	20	694	5555
Sex Ratio	40	740	2471
Child Sex Ratio	46	1070	5143
Literacy Rate	35	417	3542
Density	3	229	5656
Work Participation Rate	27	927	610

Gram Panchayats:

Annavaram, Brahmanakraka, Chamadala, Chinakraka Chowdavaram, Gattupalle, Gopannapalem, Jaladanki Jamallapalem, Kammavaripalem, Kesavaram, Kothapalem Krishnampadu, L.R.Agraharam, Samavarapadu Vemulapadu.

Amenities:

Education: Primary School in 12 villages, Middle school in 8 villages, Matriculation or Secondary School in 4 villages, namely Gattupalle, Jaladanki, Brahmanakraka, Somavarappadu.

Higher Secondary or Pre University Courses or Intermediate or Junior College in 0 village of the CD Block, College in 0 village, Adult Literacy Center in 11 villages.

Medical: Hospital in 0 village, Dispensary in 1 village, Health Center in 2 villages, Sub Center in 9 villages, Maternity and Child Welfare Center in 0 village, Community health workers in 0 village.

The Village having Hospital or Dispensary or Health Center is Jaladanki.

Drinking Water: Tap water in 12 villages, Tank water in 12 villages, Well water in 12 villages, Tubewell in 12 villages and more than one source in 12 villages.

Bank: Banking facility in 2 villages, namely, Jaladanki, Brahmanakraka.

Credit Society in 10 villages Agricultural Credit Society in 5 Non-Agricultural Credit Society in 10 villages.

Others: Power supply in 12 villages, Cinema hall in 1 village, sport club in 0 village, Stadium or Auditorium or Community Hall in 0 village, Post Office in 11 villages.

There are 12 villages having bus facilities.

Villages with most of facilities: Jaladanki Brahmanakraka.

Villages without Amenities (Education): None..

Scheduled Castes: Out of the total population of 44059 persons, 11164 persons (25.34%) belong to Scheduled Castes.

The villages having less than 10% SC population are None..

The villages having more than 50% SC population are None.

Sex ratio of Scheduled Caste population is 491.

Scheduled Castes Literates and Illiterates by Sex:

	Persons	Males	Females
Literate	5,020	3,027	1,993
Illiterate	6,144	2,658	3,486
Literacy rate	52.5	62.2	42.4
Graduate	79	75	4

Scheduled Castes (Dominant):

Mala, Madiga, Arundhatiya, Generic Castes etc.

For their cultural identity please see Appendix-I

Villages without Scheduled Castes: There are 0 village without any scheduled caste population.

Scheduled Tribes: Out of the total population of 44059 persons, 4150 persons (9.42%) belong to Scheduled Tribes.

The villages having less than 10% ST population are Chodavaram, Gattupalle, Jammalapalem, China Kraka Kodandaramapuram, Brahmanakraka, Somavarappadu Chamadala.

The villages having more than 50% ST population are None.

Sex ratio of Scheduled tribe population is 478.

Scheduled Tribes Literates and Illiterates by Sex:

	Persons	Males	Females
Literate	1,096	637	459
Illiterate	3,054	1,528	1,526
Literacy rate	31.5	35.6	27.2
Graduate	4	4	0

Scheduled Tribes (Dominant):

Yenadis, Yerukulas, Sugalis etc.

For their cultural identity please see Appendix-II

Villages without Scheduled Tribes: There is 1 village without any scheduled tribe population.

Literates and Illiterates by Sex (Total Population):

	Persons	Males	Females
Literate	21,424	12,717	8,707
Illiterate	22,635	9,652	12,983
Literacy rate	56	66	46
Graduate	545	467	78

Agriculture: ***Distribution of villages according to land use:*** Out of 12 villages, Total area (in hectare) is 30749, out of that 35.11 percent is cultivable and 66.87 percent of the cultivable area is irrigated.

Sources of Irrigation (Hectares): Government Canal 5743, Private Canal 0, Well without Electricity 0, Well with Electricity 198, Tubewell without Electricity 55, Tubewell with Electricity 28, Tank 1148, River 0, Lake 0, Waterfall 0, Others 47.

Villages with population of 5000 to 9999:
Jaladanki, Brahmanakraka.

Villages with population of 10000 and above: None

Distribution of Workers:

	Persons	Males	Females	WPR
Cultivators	8,294	5,439	2,855	33.18
Agricultural Labour	12,398	5,342	7,056	49.59
Household Industry	509	282	227	2.04
Other Workers	3,798	2,788	1,010	15.19
Main Workers	19,151	12,174	6,977	76.61
Marginal Workers	5,848	1,677	4,171	23.39
Total Workers	24,999	13,851	11,148	

Religion: Major Religious Communities:

	Persons	Males	Females	Sex Ratio
Hindu (94.5%)	41,637	21,158	20,479	968
Muslim (5.01%)	2,208	1,103	1,105	1,002
Christian (0.44%)	194	100	94	940
Sikh (0%)	-	-	-	-
Buddhists (0%)	1	-	1	-
Jain (0%)	-	-	-	-

Agewise Data:

	Persons	Males	Females	Sex Ratio
All ages	44,059	22,369	21,690	970
0-14	13,299	6,839	6,460	945
15-44	20,983	10,674	10,309	966
45-79	9,430	4,678	4,752	1016
80+	320	164	156	951
Age not stated	27	14	13	929

Languages (Dominant):
Telugu, Urdu, Tamil, Gondi, Hindi

Disabled Population:

	Persons	Males	Females	%
Total Disabled	800	448	352	
In Seeing	287	156	131	35.88
In Speech	112	69	43	14
In Hearing	50	26	24	6.25
In Movement	244	148	96	30.5
Mentally	107	49	58	13.38

JALUMURU

Jalumuru C.D. Block lies in the eastern part of Srikaku lam district. The Block is located at a distance of 38 kms. from district headquarters (Srikakulam). There are 54 villages in the block with the total population of 60,200 persons. Area of the C.D. Block is 136.10 sq. kms. It is bounded in the north by Mandals Sarubuji li and Saravakota, in the south by Mandal Narasannapeta, in the east by Mandal Kotabommali, and in the west by Sarubujjili Mandal.

Communications:

Roadways : Metalled Roads: Nearest Villages- Komanapalle, Boddapadu, Kondapolavalasa, Suravaram, Yelamanchili, Jalumuru, Jonanki, Lingalavalasa, Rana, Chinadugam, Tekkalipadu, Ravipadu.

Railway Station: Ravipadu.

River: Vamsadhara Nadi- Nearest Villages- Karakavalasa, Mukhalingam, Nagarikatakam, Atchutapuram, Komanapalle, Suravaram, Dompaka, Timadam, Syrigam, Makivalasa, Parlam, Andhavaram.

Annual Rainfall: Average Rainfall 1085.6 mm

Ground Water: Availability of the Ground Water in the Basin is (Information not avavible) H.A.M .and the utilization is (Information not avavible) H.A.M. It belongs to (Information not avavible) category. Depth to water level varies from 3 to 10 meter below the ground. Most of the wells go down in summer months.

Administration:

Division: Coastal Andhra . Parliamentary Constituency: 19 Srikakulam. District: Srikakulam. Mandal: Jalumuru. Assembly Constituency: 127 Narasannapeta. Gram Panchay at: 40.

Places of Turist Interest:

Srimukhalingam: Srimukhalingam is situated on the left bank of the river Vamsadara at a distance of about 48 Kms. from Srikakulam. It is famous for the temple of Srimukhalingeswara (Siva) belived to have been built in 9th Century. The sculpture in this temple is remarka bly elegant and precise and represents the Indo-Aryan style of architecture. The Mahasivarathri festival celebrated every year is attended by about 35, 000 pilgrims.

Villages: 54 **Inhabited:** 53 **Uninhabited:** 1

Ranking	**District**	**State**	**National**
Area	20	880	5247
Population	20	271	4849
Sex Ratio	9	80	569
Child Sex Ratio	33	863	3760
Literacy Rate	24	606	4251
Density	6	551	2491
Work Participation Rate	22	150	1458

Gram Panchayats:

Akkurada, Allada, Alladapea, Andhavaram
Atchyuthapuram, Basivada, Bodapadu, Challavanipeta
Chennaiahvalasa, Chinadugam, Darivada, Gotivada
Guggili, Hussainpuram, Jalumuru, Jonanki
Karakavalasa, Karavanja, Komanapalle
Kondapolavalasa, Kurmanadhapuram, Lingalavalasa
Makivalasa(P.), Marrivalasa, Nagarakatakam, Pagodu
Parlam, Peddadugam, Ramaiahvalasa, Rana, Ravipadu
Sri Mukhalingam, Subrahmanyapuram, Suravaram

Syrigam, Talatariya, Tekkalipadu, Timadam Venkatapuram, Yelamanchili.

Amenities:

Education: Primary School in 50 villages, Middle school in 16 villages, Matriculation or Secondary School in 6 villages, namely Mukhalingam, Timadam, Jalumuru, Lingalavalasa, Karavanja, Allada.

Higher Secondary or Pre University Courses or Intermediate or Junior College in 1 village of the CD Block,, namely Jalumuru.

College in 0 village, Adult Literacy Center in 23 villages.

Medical: Hospital in 0 village, Dispensary in 1 village, Health Center in 2 villages, Sub Center in 13 villages, Maternity and Child Welfare Center in 0 village, Community health workers in 0 village.

The Village having Hospital or Dispensary or Health Center is Timadam.

Drinking Water: Tap water in 53 villages, Tank water in 53 villages, Well water in 53 villages, Tubewell in 53 villages and more than one source in 53 villages.

Bank: Banking facility in 3 villages, namely, Mukhalingam, Allada, Ravipadu.

Credit Society in 12 villages Agricultural Credit Society in 7 Non-Agricultural Credit Society in 9 villages.

Others: Power supply in 53 villages, Cinema hall in 1 village, sport club in 0 village, Stadium or Auditorium or Community Hall in 0 village, Post Office in 16 villages.

There are 36 villages having bus facilities.

Villages with most of facilities: Mukhalingam Allada.

Villages without amenities (Education): Annupuram, Garinivalasa, Edulavalasa..

Scheduled Castes: Out of the total population of 60200 persons, 4455 persons (7.4%) belong to Scheduled Castes.

The villages having less than 10% SC population are Karakavalasa, Annupuram, Mukhalingam, Domalapalle Makivalasa, Jaminivalasa, Srimannarayana Puram Marrivalasa, Atchutapuram, Boddapadu Kondapolavalasa, Suravaram, Dompaka, Timadam Yelamanchili, Chennayavalasa, Subrahamanya Puram Venkatapuram, Jonanki, Talatariya, Darivada Lingalavalasa, Goliyaputti, Karavanja, Pagodu Syrigam, Alladapeta, Ramayyavalasa, Tallavalasa Edulavalasa, Basivada, Peddadugam, Chinadugam Tekkalipadu, Ravipadu, Yenetikothuru.

The villages having more than 50% SC population are None.

Sex ratio of Scheduled Caste population is 514.

Scheduled Castes Literates and Illiterates by Sex:

	Persons	Males	Females
Literate	1,767	1,079	688
Illiterate	2,688	1,085	1,603
Literacy rate	45.3	57.6	34.0
Graduate	30	27	3

Scheduled Castes (Dominant):

Mala, Madiga, Relli, Jaggali, Chandala

For their cultural identity please see Appendix-I

Villages without Scheduled Castes: There are 10 villages without any scheduled caste population.

Scheduled Tribes: Out of the total population of 60200 persons, 391 persons (0.65%) belong to Scheduled Tribes.

The villages having less than 10% ST population are Karakavalasa, Annupuram, Mukhalingam, Domalapalle Garinivalasa, Srimannarayana Puram, Marrivalasa Nagarikatakam, Atchutapuram, Komanapalle, Boddapadu Kondapolavalasa, Suravaram, Dompaka, Timadam Akkurada, Yelamanchili, Chennayavalasa, Jalumuru Subrahamanya Puram, Venkatapuram, Jonanki Talatariya, Darivada, Lingalavalasa, Rana Goliyaputti, Karavanja, Velusoda, Pagodu Mahammadpuram, Syrigam, Makivalasa, Parlam Andhavaram, Allada, Alladapeta, Gotivada Ramayyavalasa, Kotturu, Kurmanadhapuram, Tallavalasa Gunduvalasa, Guggili, Edulavalasa, Basivada Peddadugam, Chinadugam, Tekkalipadu, Ravipadu Yenetikothuru.

The villages having more than 50% ST population are None.

Sex ratio of Scheduled tribe population is 522.

Scheduled Tribes Literates and Illiterates by Sex:

	Persons	Males	Females
Literate	159	96	63
Illiterate	232	91	141
Literacy rate	49.2	62.8	37.1
Graduate	1	1	0

Scheduled Tribes (Dominant):

Savaras etc., Yerukulas, Kondhs etc., Konda Dhoras Yenadis

For their cultural identity please see Appendix-II

Villages without Scheduled Tribes: There are 42 villages without any scheduled tribe population.

Literates and Illiterates by Sex (Total Population):

	Persons	Males	Females
Literate	27,223	16,586	10,637
Illiterate	32,977	13,148	19,829
Literacy rate	52	64	40
Graduate	1,045	883	162

Agriculture: ***Distribution of villages according to land use:*** Out of 54 villages, Total area (in hectare) is 13607, out of that 76.91 percent is cultivable and 70.89 percent of the

cultivable area is irrigated.

Sources of Irrigation (Hectares): Government Canal 5609, Private Canal 0, Well without Electricity 0, Well with Electricity 0, Tubewell without Electricity 0, Tubewell with Electricity 0, Tank 1810, River 0, Lake 0, Waterfall 0, Others 0.

Villages with population of 5000 to 9999: None

Villages with population of 10000 and above: None

Distribution of Workers:

	Persons	Males	Females	WPR
Cultivators	7,891	5,082	2,809	24.69
Agricultural Labour	18,755	8,281	10,474	58.68
Household Industry	1,018	542	476	3.19
Other Workers	4,296	3,462	834	13.44
Main Workers	23,371	14,353	9,018	73.13
Marginal Workers	8,589	3,014	5,575	26.87
Total Workers	31,960	17,367	14,593	

Religion: Major Religious Communities:

	Persons	Males	Females	Sex Ratio
Hindu (99.64%)	59,986	29,636	30,350	1,024
Muslim (0.03%)	21	6	15	2,500
Christian (0.19%)	115	49	66	1,347
Sikh (0%)	2	2	-	-
Buddhists (0%)	1	-	1	-
Jain (0%)	-	-	-	-

Agewise Data:

	Persons	Males	Females	Sex Ratio
All ages	60,200	29,734	30,466	1025
0-14	18,452	9,449	9,003	953
15-44	28,381	13,978	14,403	1030
45-79	12,957	6,126	6,831	1115
80+	355	149	206	1383
Age not stated	55	32	23	719

Languages (Dominant):

Telugu, Oriya, Gondi, Urdu, Marathi

Disabled Population:

	Persons	Males	Females	%
Total Disabled	1,115	624	491	
In Seeing	395	188	207	35.43
In Speech	147	80	67	13.18
In Hearing	74	39	35	6.64
In Movement	382	253	129	34.26
Mentally	117	64	53	10.49

JAMI

Jami C.D. Block lies in the southern part of Vizianagar am district. The Block is located at a distance of 22 kms. from district headquarters (Vizianagaram). There are 28 villages in the block with the total population of 58,191 persons. Area of the C.D. Block is 141.47 sq. kms. It is bounded in the north by Mandals Srungava rapukota and Gantyada, in the south by Mandal Kothavalasa and district Vishakhapatnam, in the east by Mandal Vizianagaram and district Vishakhapatnam, and in the west by Mandals Lakkavarapukota and Srungavarapukota.

Communications :

Roadways : Metalled Roads: Nearest Villages- Chintada, Pavada, Jagaram, Vizinigiri, Jami, Alamanda, Godikommu, Godikommu Singavaram, Lotlapalle, Jamiagraharam, Bheem asingi, Attada, Kumaram, Mokhasa Kothavalasa.

Railway Station: Lotlapalle, Kumaram.

River: Rain Fed Nadi- Nearest Villages- Thanavaram, Vizinigiri, Thandrangi, Jagjamiagraharam, Bheemasingi, Somayajulapalem, Attada, Mokhasa Kothavalasa, Aram, Sasanapalle, Jami, Lakshmipuram.

Backwards Region Grants Fund: It receives Backward Region Grants.

Annaul Rainfall: Average Rainfall 886.7 mm

Ground Water: Availability of the Ground Water in the Basin is (Information not avavible) H.A.M .and the utilization is (Information not avavible) H.A.M. It belongs to (Information not avavible) category. Depth to water level varies from 3 to 10 meter below the ground. Most of the wells go down in summer months.

Administration:

Division: Coastal Andhra. Parliamentary Constituency: 21 Visakhapatnam. District: Vizianagram. Mandal: Jami. Assembly Constituency: 138 Srungavarapukota. Gram Panchayat: 25.

Villages: 28 **Inhabited:** 27 **Uninhabited:** 1

Ranking	District	State	National
Area	19	859	5168
Population	10	305	4920
Sex Ratio	26	304	1337
Child Sex Ratio	17	206	651
Literacy Rate	8	677	4461
Density	23	284	2676
Work Participation Rate	9	174	724

Gram Panchayats:

Alamanda, Annamrajupeta, Attada, Bheemasingi Chintada, Godukommu, Jaddetivalasa, Jagaram, Jami Jannivalasa, Kalagada, Kumaram, Lakshmipuram Lotlapalli, Mokhasa Kothavalasa, Pavada Ramabhadrapuram, Ramayyapalem, Sasanapalli Sirikipalem, Thanavaram, Thandrangi, V.R.Palem Venne, Vizinigiri.

Amenities:

Education: Primary School in 27 villages, Middle school in 10 villages, Matriculation or Secondary School in 4 villages, namely Vizinigiri, Jami, Alamanda, Kumaram.

Higher Secondary or Pre University Courses or Inter-

mediate or Junior College in 0 village of the CD Block, College in 1 village, Adult Literacy Center in 20 villages., College is in village, namely Jami.

Medical: Hospital in 0 village, Dispensary in 1 village, Health Center in 2 villages, Sub Center in 9 villages, Maternity and Child Welfare Center in 0 village, Community health workers in 0 village.

The Village having Hospital or Dispensary or Health Center is Annamrajupeta.

Drinking Water: Tap water in 27 villages, Tank water in 27 villages, Well water in 27 villages, Tubewell in 27 villages and more than one source in 27 villages.

Bank: Banking facility in 2 villages, namely, Jami, Alamanda.

Credit Society in 10 villages Agricultural Credit Society in 5 Non-Agricultural Credit Society in 9 villages.

Others: Power supply in 27 villages, Cinema hall in 3 villages, sport club in 0 village, Stadium or Auditorium or Community Hall in 0 village, Post Office in 16 villages.

There are 19 villages having bus facilities.

Villages with most of facilities: Jami, Alamanda.

Villages without Amenities (Education): None..

Scheduled Castes: Out of the total population of 58191 persons, 6966 persons (11.97%) belong to Scheduled Castes.

The villages having less than 10% SC population are Thandrangi, Venne, Sasanapalle, Ramabhadrapuram Kalagada, Lotlapalle, Bheemasingi, Attada Annamrajupeta.

The villages having more than 50% SC population are None.

Sex ratio of Scheduled Caste population is 495.

Scheduled Castes Literates and Illiterates by Sex:

	Persons	Males	Females
Literate	2,895	1,778	1,117
Illiterate	4,071	1,740	2,331
Literacy rate	47.6	58.0	37.1
Graduate	60	51	9

Scheduled Castes (Dominant):

Mala, Relli, Madiga, Generic Castes etc.
Beda Jangam etc.

For their cultural identity please see Appendix-I

Villages without Scheduled Castes: There is 1 village without any scheduled caste population.

Scheduled Tribes: Out of the total population of 58191 persons, 432 persons (0.74%) belong to Scheduled Tribes.

The villages having less than 10% ST population are Chintada, Pavada, Jagaram, Thanavaram, Vizinigiri Thandrangi, Jannivalasa, Venne, Sasanapalle, Jami Lakshmipuram, Ramabhadrapuram, Kalagada, Mamidipalle Sirikipalem, Alamanda, Kirla, Jaddetivalasa Godikommu, Godikommu Singavaram, Lotlapalle Bheemasingi, Somayajulapalem, Attada, Kumaram Mokhasa Kothavalasa, Annamrajupeta.

The villages having more than 50% ST population are None.

Sex ratio of Scheduled tribe population is 486.

Scheduled Tribes Literates and Illiterates by Sex:

	Persons	Males	Females
Literate	144	101	43
Illiterate	288	121	167
Literacy rate	38.4	52.1	23.8
Graduate	1	1	0

Scheduled Tribes (Dominant):

Yerukulas, Konda Dhoras, Gadabas, Konda Kapus Bagata

For their cultural identity please see Appendix-II

Villages without Scheduled Tribes: There are 15 villages without any scheduled tribe population.

Literates and Illiterates by Sex (Total Population):

	Persons	Males	Females
Literate	25,919	16,075	9,844
Illiterate	32,272	13,097	19,175
Literacy rate	50	62	38
Graduate	1,064	879	185

Agriculture: ***Distribution of villages according to land use:*** Out of 28 villages, Total area (in hectare) is 14153, out of that 66.22 percent is cultivable and 65.59 percent of the cultivable area is irrigated.

Sources of Irrigation (Hectares): Government Canal 2686.31, Private Canal 0, Well without Electricity 50.56, Well with Electricity 97.92, Tubewell without Electricity 0, Tubewell with Electricity 277.2, Tank 3034.73, River 0, Lake 0, Waterfall 0, Others 0.

Villages with population of 5000 to 9999:
Alamanda.

Villages with population of 10000 and above:
Jami.

Distribution of Workers:

	Persons	Males	Females	WPR
Cultivators	11,936	7,121	4,815	36.15
Agricultural Labour	12,568	5,024	7,544	38.07
Household Industry	1,128	649	479	3.42
Other Workers	7,382	5,389	1,993	22.36
Main Workers	22,942	15,023	7,919	69.49
Marginal Workers	10,072	3,160	6,912	30.51
Total Workers	33,014	18,183	14,831	

Religion: Major Religious Communities:

	Persons	Males	Females	Sex Ratio
Hindu (98.91%)	57,558	28,869	28,689	994
Muslim (0.6%)	352	166	186	1,120

Christian (0.27%)	158	73	85	1,164
Sikh (0.01%)	5	4	1	250
Buddhists (0%)	-	-	-	-
Jain (0%)	-	-	-	-

Agewise Data:

	Persons	Males	Females	Sex Ratio
All ages	58,191	29,172	29,019	995
0-14	16,490	8,418	8,072	959
15-44	27,753	13,995	13,758	983
45-79	13,585	6,567	7,018	1069
80+	245	121	124	1025

Age not stated	118	71	47	662

Languages (Dominant):
Telugu, Oriya, Tamil, Urdu, Hindi

Disabled Population:

	Persons	Males	Females	%
Total Disabled	1,743	990	753	
In Seeing	1,052	604	448	60.36
In Speech	125	62	63	7.17
In Hearing	108	47	61	6.2
In Movement	350	222	128	20.08
Mentally	108	55	53	6.2

JAMMALAMADUGU

Jammalamadugu C.D. Block lies in the north-western part of Cuddapah district. It is a part of Moragudi tehsil. The Block is located at a distance of 80 kms. from district headquarters (Cuddapah). There are 19 villages in the block with the total population of 22,926 persons. Area of the C.D. Block is 250.13 sq. kms. It is bounded in the north by Mandals Mylavaram and Peddamudium, in the south by Mandal Muddanur, in the east by Mandals Yerraguntla and Proddatur, and in the west by Mandal Kondapuram.

Headquarters: Moragudi.

Communications:

Roadways : NH: Direction- Koilakuntla to Proddatur. Nearest Villages- Goriganur, Dharmapuram, Danavulapadu, Devagudi, Poorvapu Sugumanchipalle. State Highway (S.H.): Direction- Muddanur to Koilakuntla. Nearest Villages- Salevariuppalapadu, Vemaguntapalle, Kothaguntapalle, Gudemcheruvu, Ambavaram.

River: Penneru Nadi- Nearest Villages- Goriganur, Dharmapuram, Danavulapadu, Devagudi, Poorvapu Sugumancipalle, Ponnathota, Diguvapatnam, Gandikota, Thugutlapalle, Sunnapurallapalle, Peddandlur, Sirigepalle, Gudemcheruvu, Ambavaram.

It receives Backward Region Grants, and is identified as a drought-prone area as well

Integrated Child Development Scheme (ICDS) Project: Jammalamadugu, Total Anganwadi Centres: 112

Annual Rainfall: Average Rainfall 668 mm

Ground Water: Availability of the Ground Water in the Basin is 2086 H.A.M.and the utilization is 635 H.A. M.It belongs to Safe category. Depth to water level varies from 5 to 10 meter below the ground. Most of the wells go down in summer months, according to the Ground Water Estimation Committee.

Natural Division : Rayalaseema Region

Administration:

Division: Rayala Seema. Parliamentary Constituency: 38 Kadapa. District: Cuddapah.

Mandal: Jammalamadugu. Assembly Constituency: 250 Jammalamadugu. Gram Panchayat: 14.

Fairs and Festivals:

Agastheswaraswamy Festival : It is celebrated during the whole of Kartikam (November-December) for four weeks on four Mondays in particular and occasionally for five weeks when there occur five Mondays. Cocoanuts, camphor and naivedyam are offered. Devotees take bath in sacred pools in Agasthya kona (valley). The festival is of ancient origin and widely known. Not only the local Hindus but those from far at places also congregate. Pujari is a Brahmin. Prasadam is distributed to all. There is free feeding to all, irrespective of caste or creed, on the last Monday in Kartikam.

Villages: 19 **Inhabited:** 16 **Uninhabited:** 3

Ranking	District	State	National
Area	21	315	3395
Population	48	1081	6178
Sex Ratio	3	244	1166
Child Sex Ratio	30	810	3519
Literacy Rate	37	382	3374
Density	18	546	6183
Work Participation Rate	47	1070	1452

Gram Panchayats:

Ambavaram, Devagudi, Dharmapuram, Gandikota Goriganur, Gudemcheruvu, Moragudi, P.Bommepalli P.Sugumanchipalli, Peddadandluru, Ponnathota S.Uppalapadu, Seshareddypalli, Sunnapurallapalli.

Amenities:

Education: Primary School in 16 villages, Middle school in 4 villages, Matriculation or Secondary School in 2 villages, namely Salevariuppalapadu, Devagudi.

Higher Secondary or Pre University Courses or Intermediate or Junior College in 0 village of the CD Block, College in 0 village, Adult Literacy Center in 0 village.

Medical: Hospital in 0 village, Dispensary in 0 village, Health Center in 0 village, Sub Center in 4 villages, Maternity and Child Welfare Center in 0 village, Community health workers in 0 village.

Drinking Water: Tap water in 16 villages, Tank water in

16 villages, Well water in 16 villages, Tubewell in 16 villages and more than one source in 16 villages.

Bank: None.

Credit Society in 2 villages Agricultural Credit Society in 1 Non-Agricultural Credit Society in 2 villages.

Others: Power supply in 16 villages, Cinema hall in 0 village, sport club in 0 village, Stadium or Auditorium or Community Hall in 0 village, Post Office in 11 villages.

There are 15 villages having bus facilities.

Village with most of facilities: None.

Villages without Amenities (Education): None..

Scheduled Castes: Out of the total population of 22933 persons, 5344 persons (23.3%) belong to Scheduled Castes. The villages having less than 10% SC population are Gandikota, Poorva Bommepalle, Vemaguntapalle Kothaguntapalle, Dharmapuram, Sirigepalle.

The villages having more than 50% SC population are None.

Sex ratio of Scheduled Caste population is 502.

Scheduled Castes Literates and Illiterates by Sex:

	Persons	Males	Females
Literate	2,606	1,596	1,010
Illiterate	2,738	1,063	1,675
Literacy rate	56.5	69.9	43.4
Graduate	48	43	5

Scheduled Castes (Dominant):

Mala, Madiga

For their cultural identity please see Appendix-I

Villages without Scheduled Castes: There are 4 villages without any scheduled caste population.

Scheduled Tribes: Out of the total population of 22933 persons, 1086 persons (4.74%) belong to Scheduled Tribes. The villages having less than 10% ST population are Salevariuppalapadu, Gudemcheruvu, Ponnathota Gandikota, Vemaguntapalle, Kothaguntapalle Goriganur, Dharmapuram, Danavulapadu Sunnapurallapalle, Peddandlur, Devagudi Poorvapu Sugumanchipalle.

The villages having more than 50% ST population are None.

Sex ratio of Scheduled tribe population is 496.

Scheduled Tribes Literates and Illiterates by Sex:

	Persons	Males	Females
Literate	298	189	109
Illiterate	788	358	430
Literacy rate	33.3	41.8	24.6
Graduate	5	5	0

Scheduled Tribes (Dominant):

Sugalis etc., Yenadis, Yerukulas, Kammara

For their cultural identity please see Appendix-II

Villages without Scheduled Tribes: There are 9 villages without any scheduled tribe population.

Literates and Illiterates by Sex (Total Population):

	Persons	Males	Females
Literate	11,310	6,961	4,349
Illiterate	11,623	4,508	7,115
Literacy rate	57	70	43
Graduate	354	317	37

Agriculture: ***Distribution of villages according to land use:*** Out of 19 villages, Total area (in hectare) is 24883, out of that 34.33 percent is cultivable and 20.23 percent of the cultivable area is irrigated.

Sources of Irrigation (Hectares): Government Canal 8.1, Private Canal 0, Well without Electricity 186.96, Well with Electricity 218.92, Tubewell without Electricity 0, Tubewell with Electricity 926.13, Tank 388.04, River 0, Lake 0, Waterfall 0, Others 0.

Villages with population of 5000 to 9999: None

Villages with population of 10000 and above: None

Distribution of Workers:

	Persons	Males	Females	WPR
Cultivators	3,290	2,484	806	27.17
Agricultural Labour	5,901	2,323	3,578	48.73
Household Industry	98	67	31	0.81
Other Workers	2,820	2,179	641	23.29
Main Workers	8,892	6,324	2,568	73.43
Marginal Workers	3,217	729	2,488	26.57
Total Workers	12,109	7,053	5,056	

Religion: Major Religious Communities:

	Persons	Males	Females	Sex Ratio
Hindu (96.48%)	22,126	11,055	11,071	1,001
Muslim (2.92%)	670	342	328	959
Christian (0.52%)	120	65	55	846
Sikh (0%)	-	-	-	-
Buddhists (0%)	-	-	-	-
Jain (0%)	-	-	-	-

Agewise Data:

	Persons	Males	Females	Sex Ratio
All ages	22,933	11,469	11,464	1000
0-14	6,924	3,497	3,427	980
15-44	11,275	5,673	5,602	987
45-79	4,604	2,236	2,368	1059
80+	110	54	56	1037
Age not stated	20	9	11	1222

Languages (Dominant):

Telugu, Urdu, Hindi, Tamil, Gondi

Disabled Population:

	Persons	Males	Females	%
Total Disabled	626	288	338	
In Seeing	361	151	210	57.67

In Speech	47	25	22	7.51
In Hearing	48	24	24	7.67

In Movement	118	62	56	18.85
Mentally	52	26	26	8.31

JAMMIKUNTA

Jammikunta C.D. Block lies in the south-east part of Karimnagar district. The Block is located at a distance of 54 kms. from district headquarters (Karimnagar). There are 19 villages in the block with the total population of 93,501 persons. Area of the C.D. Block is 222.85 sq. kms. It is bounded by Odela Mandal on north, Warangal district on east, Kamalapur Mandal on south, Huzurabad Mandal on south-west, and Veenavanka Mandal on west.

Communications :

Roadways : State Highway (S.H.): Direction- Karimnagar to Thangula. Nearest Villages- Vilasagar,Vavilala, Korepalle, Thangula.

Railway Station: Bijigirsharief, Jammikunta

River: Manner Nadi- Nearest Villages- Vilasagar,Vavilala, Korepalle, Thangula.

Backwards Region Grants Fund: It receives Backward Region Grants.

Annual Rainfall: Average Rainfall 914 mm

Ground Water: Availability of the Ground Water in the Basin is 5910 H.A.M. and the utilization is 2572 H. A.M. It belongs to Safe category. Depth to water level varies from more than 10 meter below the ground. Most of the wells go down in summer months. The well density in the entire block is 30 wells per sq. km. Total no. of the wells in the block are enumerated as 6707, according to the Ground Water Estimation Committee.

Natural Division : Godavari Depression Region

Administration:

Division: Telangana. Parliamentary Constituency: 3 Karimnagar. District: Karimnagar. Mandal: Jammikunta. Assembly Constituency: 31 Huzurabad. Gram Panchayat: 33

Villages: 19 **Inhabited:** 19 **Uninhabited:** 0

Ranking	District	State	National
Area	14	425	3804
Population	1	8	3675
Sex Ratio	43	495	1842
Child Sex Ratio	20	379	1383
Literacy Rate	4	335	3113
Density	50	802	2621
Work Participation Rate	3	167	2392

Gram Panchayats:

Ankushapoor, Bizigirisharif, Bogampad, Buzunoor Chinna Komati Pally, Dharmaram, Ellanthakunta Gandrapally, Jaggaiahpally, Jammikunta, Kanagarthy Korapally, Kothapally, Lakmagipally, Machannapally Madipally, Mallial, Marrivanipally, Nagaram Patharlapally, Peddampally, Rachapalli, Ramannapally Saidabad, Seethampeta, Shayampeta, Sirsaid Sriramula Pally, Tekurthy, Thanugula, Vanthadupula Vavilala, Vilasagar.

Amenities:

Education: Primary School in 19 villages, Middle school in 14 villages, Matriculation or Secondary School in 10 villages, namely Thangula, Vavilala, Bijigirsharief, Korepalle, Jammikunta, Dharmaram (P.B), Madipalle, Ellanthakunta, Bujunoor, Sirsedu.

Higher Secondary or Pre University Courses or Intermediate or Junior College in 1 village of the CD Block,, namely Jammikunta.

College in 1 village, Adult Literacy Center in 19 villages., College is in village, namely Jammikunta.

Medical: Hospital in 0 village, Dispensary in 1 village, Health Center in 2 villages, Sub Center in 11 villages, Maternity and Child Welfare Center in 0 village, Community health workers in 0 village.

The Village having Hospital or Dispensary or Health Center is Vavilala.

Drinking Water: Tap water in 19 villages, Tank water in 18 villages, Well water in 19 villages, Tubewell in 18 villages and more than one source in 19 villages.

Bank: Banking facility in 3 villages, namely, Vavilala, Jammikunta, Bujunoor.

Credit Society in 18 villages Agricultural Credit Society in 12 Non-Agricultural Credit Society in 17 villages.

Others: Power supply in 19 villages, Cinema hall in 2 villages, sport club in 0 village, Stadium or Auditorium or Community Hall in 0 village, Post Office in 15 villages.

There are 17 villages having bus facilities.

Villages with most of facilities: Vavilala Jammikunta, Bujunoor.

Villages without Amenities (Education): None..

Scheduled Castes: Out of the total population of 93501 persons, 20787 persons (22.23%) belong to Scheduled Castes.

The villages having less than 10% SC population are None..

The villages having more than 50% SC population are None.

Sex ratio of Scheduled Caste population is 492.

Scheduled Castes Literates and Illiterates by Sex:

	Persons	Males	Females
Literate	8,560	5,279	3,281
Illiterate	12,227	5,285	6,942
Literacy rate	48.5	59.1	37.7
Graduate	196	163	33

Scheduled Castes (Dominant):
Madiga, Mala, Mala Sale etc., Beda Jangam etc. Pambada etc.

For their cultural identity please see Appendix-I

Villages without Scheduled Castes: There are 0 village without any scheduled caste population.

Scheduled Tribes: Out of the total population of 93501 persons, 785 persons (0.84%) belong to Scheduled Tribes. The villages having less than 10% ST population are Vilasagar, Thangula, Vavilala, Vanthadupula Rachapalle, Bijigirsharief, Korepalle, Saidabad Jammikunta, Dharmaram (P.B), Madipalle, Kanagarthi Mallial, Ellanthakunta, Chinnakomatipalle, Tekurthi Bujunoor, Sirsedu, Patharlapalle.

The villages having more than 50% ST population are None.

Sex ratio of Scheduled tribe population is 520.

Scheduled Tribes Literates and Illiterates by Sex:

	Persons	Males	Females
Literate	210	136	74
Illiterate	575	241	334
Literacy rate	33.1	43.2	23.2
Graduate	8	7	1

Scheduled Tribes (Dominant):
Yerukulas, Sugalis etc., Koya etc., Gond etc. Savaras etc.

For their cultural identity please see Appendix-II

Villages without Scheduled Tribes: There are 3 villages without any scheduled tribe population.

Literates and Illiterates by Sex (Total Population):

	Persons	Males	Females
Literate	46,660	28,435	18,225
Illiterate	46,841	18,692	28,149
Literacy rate	58	70	46
Graduate	2,314	1,955	359

Agriculture: ***Distribution of villages according to land use:***
Out of 19 villages, Total area (in hectare) is 22286, out of that 74.97 percent is cultivable and 58.86 percent of the cultivable area is irrigated.

Sources of Irrigation (Hectares): Government Canal 4542.73, Private Canal 0, Well without Electricity 502, Well with Electricity 3206.82, Tubewell without Electricity 226.63, Tubewell with Electricity 0, Tank 1356, River 0, Lake 0, Waterfall 0, Others 0.

Villages with population of 5000 to 9999:
Vavilala, Bijigirsharief, Ellanthakunta.

Villages with population of 10000 and above:
Jammikunta, Dharmaram (P.B).

Distribution of Workers:

	Persons	Males	Females	WPR
Cultivators	11,646	6,796	4,850	25.61
Agricultural Labour	19,022	7,252	11,770	41.84
Household Industry	1,446	932	514	3.18
Other Workers	13,352	11,305	2,047	29.37
Main Workers	37,025	23,887	13,138	81.43
Marginal Workers	8,441	2,398	6,043	18.57
Total Workers	45,466	26,285	19,181	

Religion: Major Religious Communities:

	Persons	Males	Females	Sex Ratio
Hindu (95.42%)	89,221	44,983	44,238	983
Muslim (4.13%)	3,861	1,930	1,931	1,001
Christian (0.36%)	338	173	165	954
Sikh (0.01%)	9	5	4	800
Buddhists (0%)	-	-	-	-
Jain (0%)	-	-	-	-

Agewise Data:

	Persons	Males	Females	Sex Ratio
All ages	93,501	47,127	46,374	984
0-14	28,971	14,607	14,364	983
15-44	44,563	22,764	21,799	958
45-79	18,994	9,264	9,730	1050
80+	778	378	400	1058
Age not stated	195	114	81	711

Languages (Dominant):
Telugu, Urdu, Hindi, Marathi, Tamil

Disabled Population:

	Persons	Males	Females	%
Total Disabled	1,609	931	678	
In Seeing	729	422	307	45.31
In Speech	167	80	87	10.38
In Hearing	85	42	43	5.28
In Movement	435	285	150	27.04
Mentally	193	102	91	12

JANAKAVARAMPANGULURU

Janakavaram Panguluru C.D. Block lies in the north-east ern part of Prakasam district. The Block is located at a distance of 45 kms. from district headquarters (Ongole). There are 15 villages in the block with the total population of 44,753 persons. Area of the C.D. Block is 168.82 sq. kms. It is bounded in the north by Mandals Martur and Inkollu, in the south by Mandal Korisapadu, in the east by Mandal Inkollu, and in the west by Mandal Addanki.

Communications:

Roadways : NH- 5: Direction- Ongole to Guntur. Nearest Villages- Konda Manjulur, Bytamanjulur, Muppavaram, Kondamur, Reningavaram, Kasyapuram, Alavalapadu.

Hills: Nearest Village- Ramakuru.

The Block is identified as a drought-prone area.

Annual Rainfall: Average Rainfall 806.6 mm

Ground Water: Availability of the Ground Water in the Basin is 8.00 MCM and the utilization is 3.67 MCM It belongs to Safe category. Depth to water level varies from 2 to 5 meter below the ground. Most of the wells go down in summer months., according to the Ground Water Estimation Committee.

Administration:

Division: Coastal Andhra. Parliamentary Constituency: 32 Baptala (SC). District: Prakasam. Mandal: Janakavara mpanguluru. Assembly Constituency: 224 Addanki. Gram Panchayat: 21.

Places of Tourist Interest:

Chandalur: Situated 30 kms. towards the north of Ongole, is one of the ancient and most famous villages. The two copper plate inscriptions of the village known as Chandalur Sasanamulu found references to it in the history of Andhra. These inscriptions date back to about 644 A.D. and 673 A.D., the former issued by the Chalukya King Kumara Vishnu II from Kanchipuram, while the latter was issued by King Vijayasiddhi alias Sarval okasraya Maharaj alias Mangi Yuvaraju, son of Maharaja Kumara Vishnu II. Prominent references to Kamma rashtra find place in these two inscriptions. A stone name plate with the writing the Chendaloor Talook Cutchery Anno domino, 1856, could be seen even now above the door-frame of the government Office, Addanki.

Villages: 15 **Inhabited:** 15 **Uninhabited:** 0

Ranking	District	State	National
Area	44	719	4723
Population	27	671	5522
Sex Ratio	7	252	1186
Child Sex Ratio	24	691	2862
Literacy Rate	17	307	2982
Density	7	135	3912
Work Participation Rate	17	487	398

Gram Panchayats:

Alavalapadu, Arikatlavaripalem, Bhagavanrajupalem Budawada, Bytamanjuluru, Chandaluru, Chinamallavaram Jagarlamudivaripalem, Janakavaram, Kallamvaripalem Kasyapuram, Kondamanjuluru, Kondamuru, Kotapadu Muppavaram, Nujellapalli, Panguluru, Ramakuru Renangivaram, T.Kopperapadu, T.Takkellapadu.

Amenities:

Education: Primary School in 15 villages, Middle school in 11 villages, Matriculation or Secondary School in 5 villages, namely Konda Manjulur, Muppavaram, Budavada, Janakavaram Panguluru, Chandalur.

Higher Secondary or Pre University Courses or Intermediate or Junior College in 1 village of the CD Block,, namely Janakavaram Panguluru.

College in 0 village, Adult Literacy Center in 15 villages.

Medical: Hospital in 0 village, Dispensary in 1 village, Health Center in 1 village, Sub Center in 8 villages, Maternity and Child Welfare Center in 0 village, Community health workers in 0 village.

The Village having Hospital or Dispensary or Health Center is Alavalapadu.

Drinking Water: Tap water in 15 villages, Tank water in 15 villages, Well water in 15 villages, Tubewell in 15 villages and more than one source in 15 villages.

Bank: Banking facility in 3 villages, namely, Muppavaram, Janakavaram Panguluru, Chandalur.

Credit Society in 9 villages Agricultural Credit Society in 8 Non-Agricultural Credit Society in 6 villages.

Others: Power supply in 15 villages, Cinema hall in 1 village, sport club in 0 village, Stadium or Auditorium or Community Hall in 0 village, Post Office in 14 villages.

There are 15 villages having bus facilities.

Villages with most of facilities: Muppavaram Janakavaram Panguluru, Chandalur.

Villages without Amenities (Education): None..

Scheduled Castes: Out of the total population of 44753 persons, 11401 persons (25.48%) belong to Scheduled Castes.

The villages having less than 10% SC population are None..

The villages having more than 50% SC population are None.

Sex ratio of Scheduled Caste population is 488.

Scheduled Castes Literates and Illiterates by Sex:

	Persons	Males	Females
Literate	5,012	3,174	1,838
Illiterate	6,389	2,663	3,726
Literacy rate	51.3	63.3	38.6
Graduate	128	101	27

Scheduled Castes (Dominant):

Madiga, Mala, Ellamalawar etc.

For their cultural identity please see Appendix-I

Villages without Scheduled Castes: There are 0 village without any scheduled caste population.

Scheduled Tribes: Out of the total population of 44753 persons, 1668 persons (3.73%) belong to Scheduled Tribes.

The villages having less than 10% ST population are Ramakuru, Konda Manjulur, Bytamanjulur, Muppavaram Kondamur, Kotapadu, Budavada, Janakavaram Panguluru Reningavaram, Kasyapuram, Alavalapadu Thurpu Thakkella Padu, Thurpu Koppera Padu Chandalur, Nuzendla Palle.

The villages having more than 50% ST population are None.

Sex ratio of Scheduled tribe population is 481.

Scheduled Tribes Literates and Illiterates by Sex:

	Persons	Males	Females
Literate	569	349	220
Illiterate	1,099	517	582
Literacy rate	40.1	47.5	32.1
Graduate	4	4	0

Scheduled Tribes (Dominant):
Yenadis, Yerukulas, Sugalis etc.
For their cultural identity please see Appendix-II
Villages without Scheduled Tribes: There is 1 village without any scheduled tribe population.

Literates and Illiterates by Sex (Total Population):

	Persons	Males	Females
Literate	23,295	13,701	9,594
Illiterate	21,458	8,683	12,775
Literacy rate	59	69	48
Graduate	988	796	192

Agriculture: ***Distribution of villages according to land use:*** Out of 15 villages, Total area (in hectare) is 16882, out of that 83.36 percent is cultivable and 40.82 percent of the cultivable area is irrigated.

Sources of Irrigation (Hectares): Government Canal 5676.51, Private Canal 0, Well without Electricity 0, Well with Electricity 0, Tubewell without Electricity 0, Tubewell with Electricity 68, Tank 0, River 0, Lake 0, Waterfall 0, Others 0.

Villages with population of 5000 to 9999:
Konda Manjulur, Janakavaram Panguluru.
Villages with population of 10000 and above: None

Distribution of Workers:

	Persons	Males	Females	WPR
Cultivators	7,331	4,358	2,973	27.87
Agricultural Labour	14,979	6,852	8,127	56.95
Household Industry	363	214	149	1.38
Other Workers	3,628	2,476	1,152	13.79
Main Workers	23,327	13,058	10,269	88.69
Marginal Workers	2,974	842	2,132	11.31
Total Workers	26,301	13,900	12,401	

Religion: Major Religious Communities:

	Persons	Males	Females	Sex Ratio
Hindu (93.84%)	41,994	21,017	20,977	998
Muslim (5.66%)	2,534	1,255	1,279	1,019
Christian (0.41%)	185	96	89	927
Sikh (0.01%)	3	2	1	500
Buddhists (0%)	-	-	-	-
Jain (0%)	-	-	-	-

Agewise Data:

	Persons	Males	Females	Sex Ratio
All ages	44,753	22,384	22,369	999
0-14	12,261	6,254	6,007	961
15-44	21,401	10,678	10,723	1004
45-79	10,357	5,091	5,266	1034
80+	586	260	326	1254
Age not stated	148	101	47	465

Languages (Dominant):
Telugu, Urdu, Gondi, Tamil, Hindi

Disabled Population:

	Persons	Males	Females	%
Total Disabled	691	380	311	
In Seeing	232	121	111	33.57
In Speech	100	55	45	14.47
In Hearing	32	15	17	4.63
In Movement	222	129	93	32.13
Mentally	105	60	45	15.2

JANGAON

Jangaon C.D. Block lies in the south-western part of Warangal district. It is a part of Jangaon Mandal. The Block is located at a distance of 54 kms. from district headquarters (Warangal). There are 19 villages in the block with the total population of 39,482 persons. Area of the C.D. Block is 174.37 sq. kms. It is bounded in the north by Narmetta and Raghunathpalle Mandals, in the south by Nalgonda district and Lingalaghanpur Mandal, in the east by Raghunathpalle Mandal, and in the west by Bachannapet Mandal.

Communications:
Roadways : NH- 202: Direction- Hyderabad to Warangal. Nearest Villages- Yellamla, Pembarthy, Cheetakodur, Yeswanthapur. State Highway (S.H): Direction- Siddipet to Suryapet. Nearest Villages- Oblakeshvapur, Pasarmadla, Shamirpet.
Railway Station: Pembarthy, Yeswanthapur.
Backwards Region Grants Fund: It receives Backward Region Grants.
Integrated Child Development Scheme (ICDS) Project: Janagaon, Total Anganwadi Centres: 196
Annual Rainfall: Average Rainfall 816 mm
Ground Water: Availability of the Ground Water in the Basin is 1681 H.A.M.and the utilization is 2523 H.A. M. It belongs to OE category. Depth to water level varies from 10 to 20 meter below the ground. Most of the wells go down in summer months. The well density in the entire block is 24 wells per sq. km. Total no. of the wells in the block are enumerated as 4591, according to the Ground Water Estimation Committee.
Natural Division : Godavari Depression Region
Administration:
Division: Telangana. Parliamentary Constituency. District: Warangal. Mandal: Jangaon.
Assembly Constituency: 09 Jangaon. Gram Panchayat: 18

Villages: 19 **Inhabited:** 19 **Uninhabited:** 0

Ranking	District	State	National
Area	35	694	4619
Population	40	834	5751
Sex Ratio	3	228	1121
Child Sex Ratio	19	476	1770
Literacy Rate	15	498	3831
Density	34	562	4358
Work Participation Rate	36	619	1488

Gram Panchayats:

Advikeshavapur, Cheetakoduru, Chowdaram, Gangupahad Goparajupalle, Marigidi, Obulakeshvapur, Pasarmadla Peddapahad, Peddaramancherla, Pembarthy, Shameerpet Siddenki, Vadlakonda, Venkriyala, Yellamula Yerragollapad, Yeswanthapur.

Amenities:

Education: Primary School in 18 villages, Middle school in 14 villages, Matriculation or Secondary School in 8 villages, namely Peddapahad, Venkriyala, Gangupahad, Wadlakonda, Oblakeshvapur, Siddenki, Pembarthy, Shamirpet.

Higher Secondary or Pre University Courses or Intermediate or Junior College in 0 village of the CD Block, College in 0 village, Adult Literacy Center in 15 villages.

Medical: Hospital in 1 village, Dispensary in 1 village, Health Center in 1 village, Sub Center in 10 villages, Maternity and Child Welfare Center in 0 village, Community health workers in 0 village.

The Villages having Hospital or Dispensary or Health Center are Pembarthy, Yeswanthapur.

Drinking Water: Tap water in 19 villages, Tank water in 19 villages, Well water in 19 villages, Tubewell in 19 villages and more than one source in 19 villages.

Bank: None.

Credit Society in 19 villages Agricultural Credit Society in 3 Non-Agricultural Credit Society in 19 villages.

Others: Power supply in 19 villages, Cinema hall in 1 village, sport club in 0 village, Stadium or Auditorium or Community Hall in 0 village, Post Office in 16 villages.

There are 17 villages having bus facilities.

Village with most of facilities: None.

Villages without amenities (Education):

Chowdarpalle..

Scheduled Castes: Out of the total population of 39570 persons, 7843 persons (19.82%) belong to Scheduled Castes.

The villages having less than 10% SC population are None..

The villages having more than 50% SC population are None.

Sex ratio of Scheduled Caste population is 500.

Scheduled Castes Literates and Illiterates by Sex:

	Persons	Males	Females
Literate	3,465	2,186	1,279
Illiterate	4,378	1,738	2,640
Literacy rate	51.6	64.9	38.2
Graduate	44	41	3

Scheduled Castes (Dominant):

Madiga, Mala, Beda Jangam etc., Sindhollu etc. Bindla

For their cultural identity please see Appendix-I

Villages without Scheduled Castes: There are 0 village without any scheduled caste population.

Scheduled Tribes: Out of the total population of 39570 persons, 2730 persons (6.9%) belong to Scheduled Tribes.

The villages having less than 10% ST population are Goparajpalle, Venkriyala, Gangupahad, Wadlakonda Oblakeshvapur, Peddaramancherla, Chowdarpalle Siddenki, Pasarmadla, Yellamla, Pembarthy, Shamirpet Cheetakodur, Chowdaram, Yeswanthapur.

The villages having more than 50% ST population are None.

Sex ratio of Scheduled tribe population is 484.

Scheduled Tribes Literates and Illiterates by Sex:

	Persons	Males	Females
Literate	756	515	241
Illiterate	1,974	894	1,080
Literacy rate	34.6	45.2	23.0
Graduate	7	7	0

Scheduled Tribes (Dominant):

Sugalis etc., Yerukulas, Chenchu etc.

For their cultural identity please see Appendix-II

Villages without Scheduled Tribes: There are 8 villages without any scheduled tribe population.

Literates and Illiterates by Sex (Total Population):

	Persons	Males	Females
Literate	18,237	11,292	6,945
Illiterate	21,333	8,488	12,845
Literacy rate	54	67	41
Graduate	375	325	50

Agriculture: ***Distribution of villages according to land use:***

Out of 19 villages, Total area (in hectare) is 17499, out of that 82.33 percent is cultivable and 21.25 percent of the cultivable area is irrigated.

Sources of Irrigation (Hectares): Government Canal 0, Private Canal 0, Well without Electricity 0, Well with Electricity 2438, Tubewell without Electricity 0, Tubewell with Electricity 390, Tank 234, River 0, Lake 0, Waterfall 0, Others 0.

Villages with population of 5000 to 9999: None

Villages with population of 10000 and above: None

Distribution of Workers:

	Persons	Males	Females	WPR
Cultivators	6,902	4,351	2,551	33.73
Agricultural Labour	7,857	2,510	5,347	38.39
Household Industry	1,081	580	501	5.28
Other Workers	4,625	3,628	997	22.6
Main Workers	16,018	9,631	6,387	78.27
Marginal Workers	4,447	1,438	3,009	21.73
Total Workers	20,465	11,069	9,396	

Religion: Major Religious Communities:

	Persons	Males	Females	Sex Ratio
Hindu (97.26%)	38,486	19,237	19,249	1,001
Muslim (1.81%)	717	371	346	933
Christian (0.6%)	239	104	135	1,298
Sikh (0%)	1	1	-	-
Buddhists (0%)	-	-	-	-
Jain (0%)	-	-	-	-

Agewise Data:

	Persons	Males	Females	Sex Ratio
All ages	39,570	19,780	19,790	1001
0-14	13,364	6,768	6,596	975
15-44	17,254	8,571	8,683	1013
45-79	8,472	4,215	4,257	1010
80+	395	179	216	1207
Age not stated	85	47	38	809

Languages (Dominant):

Telugu, Hindi, Urdu, Gondi, Tamil

Disabled Population:

	Persons	Males	Females	%
Total Disabled	1,046	649	397	
In Seeing	611	404	207	58.41
In Speech	66	29	37	6.31
In Hearing	51	22	29	4.88
In Movement	240	142	98	22.94
Mentally	78	52	26	7.46

JANGAREDDIGUDEM

Jangareddigudem C.D. Block lies in the northern part of West Godavari district. The Block is located at a distance of 67 kms. from district headquarters (Eluru). There are 22 villages in the block with the total population of 95,251 persons. Area of the C.D. Block is 217.91 sq. kms. It is bounded in the north by Mandals Jeelugumilli and Buttayagudem, in the south by Mandal Dwarka Tirumala, in the east by Mandal Koyyalagudem, and in the west by Mandals T. Narasapuram and Kamavara pukota.

Communications :

Roadways : State Highway (S.H.): Direction- Jeelugumilli to Bayyanagudem. and Kamavarapukota to Jangareddigudem. Nearest Villages- Ayyavaripolavaram, Taduvai, Vegavaram, Jangareddigudem, Ramacharlagudem, Devulapalle, Gurava igudem.

Backwards Region Grants Fund: It receives Backward Region Grants.

Annaul Rainfall: Average Rainfall 1005 mm

Ground Water: Availability of the Ground Water in the Basin is (Information not avavible) H.A.M .and the utilization is (Information not avavible) H.A.M. It belongs to (Information not avavible) category. Depth to water level varies from 3 to 10 meter below the ground. Most of the wells go down in summer months.

Natural Division : Godavari Delta Region

Administration:

Division: Coastal Andhra. Parliamentary Constituency: 17 Eluru. District: West Godavari. Mandal: Jangareddigu dem. Assembly Constituency: 187 Chintalapudi (SC). Gram Panchayat: 21.

Villages: 22 **Inhabited:** 20 **Uninhabited:** 2

Ranking	District	State	National
Area	6	446	3884
Population	1	7	3621
Sex Ratio	23	477	1817
Child Sex Ratio	29	586	2376
Literacy Rate	30	106	1528
Density	31	954	2512
Work Participation Rate	26	152	3416

Gram Panchayats:

A.Polavaram, Akkampeta, Ammapalem, Chakradevarapalle Devulapalle, Guruvaigudem, Jangareddigudem Kethavaram, Lakkavaram, Mysannagudem, Nagulagudem Nimmalagudem, Pangidigudem, Pattenapalem, Perampeta Putlagatlagudem, Sreenivasapuram, Taduvai Tekkinavarigudem, Tirumalapuram, Vegavaram.

Amenities:

Education: Primary School in 19 villages, Middle school in 6 villages, Matriculation or Secondary School in 4 villages, namely Taduvai, Jangareddigudem, Lakkavaram, Pangidigudem.

Higher Secondary or Pre University Courses or Intermediate or Junior College in 2 villages of the CD Block,, namely Jangareddigudem, Pangidigudem.

College in 1 village, Adult Literacy Center in 14 villages., College is in village, namely Jangareddigudem.

Medical: Hospital in 1 village, Dispensary in 0 village, Health Center in 1 village, Sub Center in 10 villages, Maternity and Child Welfare Center in 0 village, Community health workers in 0 village.

The Village having Hospital or Dispensary or Health Center is Jangareddigudem.

Drinking Water: Tap water in 20 villages, Tank water in

20 villages, Well water in 20 villages, Tubewell in 20 villages and more than one source in 20 villages.

Bank: Banking facility in 3 villages, namely, Taduvai, Jangareddigudem, Lakkavaram.

Credit Society in 9 villages Agricultural Credit Society in 8 Non-Agricultural Credit Society in 2 villages.

Others: Power supply in 20 villages, Cinema hall in 3 villages, sport club in 0 village, Stadium or Auditorium or Community Hall in 0 village, Post Office in 16 villages.

There are 17 villages having bus facilities.

Villages with most of facilities: Taduvai Jangareddigudem, Lakkavaram.

Villages without amenities (Education): Ramacharlagudem..

Scheduled Castes: Out of the total population of 95251 persons, 20131 persons (21.13%) belong to Scheduled Castes.

The villages having less than 10% SC population are None..

The villages having more than 50% SC population are None.

Sex ratio of Scheduled Caste population is 496.

Scheduled Castes Literates and Illiterates by Sex:

	Persons	Males	Females
Literate	9,753	5,262	4,491
Illiterate	10,378	4,875	5,503
Literacy rate	56.4	60.8	52.1
Graduate	390	277	113

Scheduled Castes (Dominant):

Madiga, Mala, Adi Andhra, Generic Castes etc. Mala Dasu

For their cultural identity please see Appendix-I

Villages without Scheduled Castes: There are 2 villages without any scheduled caste population.

Scheduled Tribes: Out of the total population of 95251 persons, 1870 persons (1.96%) belong to Scheduled Tribes.

The villages having less than 10% ST population are Ayyavaripolavaram, Taduvai, Mathanagudem, Vegavaram Mysanagudem, Pullepudi, Akkampeta, Sreenivasapuram Jangareddigudem, Ramacharlagudem, Devulapalle Ammapalem, Nimmalagudem, Lakkavaram, Guravaigudem Tirumalapuram, Kethavaram, Pangidigudem.

The villages having more than 50% ST population are None.

Sex ratio of Scheduled tribe population is 466.

Scheduled Tribes Literates and Illiterates by Sex:

	Persons	Males	Females
Literate	1,023	594	429
Illiterate	847	405	442
Literacy rate	63.3	70.2	55.6
Graduate	55	42	13

Scheduled Tribes (Dominant):

Yerukulas, Koya etc., Sugalis etc., Yenadis Savaras etc.

For their cultural identity please see Appendix-II

Villages without Scheduled Tribes: There are 9 villages without any scheduled tribe population.

Literates and Illiterates by Sex (Total Population):

	Persons	Males	Females
Literate	56,177	30,256	25,921
Illiterate	39,074	17,734	21,340
Literacy rate	68	72	63
Graduate	3,357	2,433	924

Agriculture: ***Distribution of villages according to land use:*** Out of 22 villages, Total area (in hectare) is 21792, out of that 77.47 percent is cultivable and 85.98 percent of the cultivable area is irrigated.

Sources of Irrigation (Hectares): Government Canal 516.29, Private Canal 64.78, Well without Electricity 109.66, Well with Electricity 3532.75, Tubewell without Electricity 14.8, Tubewell with Electricity 8665.79, Tank 1610.88, River 0, Lake 0, Waterfall 0, Others 0.

Villages with population of 5000 to 9999: Taduvai, Lakkavaram.

Villages with population of 10000 and above: Jangareddigudem.

Distribution of Workers:

	Persons	Males	Females	WPR
Cultivators	6,061	5,137	924	14.07
Agricultural Labour	22,222	11,946	10,276	51.58
Household Industry	1,106	638	468	2.57
Other Workers	13,691	11,452	2,239	31.78
Main Workers	39,075	27,716	11,359	90.7
Marginal Workers	4,005	1,457	2,548	9.3
Total Workers	43,080	29,173	13,907	

Religion: Major Religious Communities:

	Persons	Males	Females	Sex Ratio
Hindu (95.09%)	90,576	45,712	44,864	981
Muslim (3.45%)	3,290	1,625	1,665	1,025
Christian (1.41%)	1,343	628	715	1,139
Sikh (0.01%)	6	4	2	500
Buddhists (0%)	-	-	-	-
Jain (0%)	-	-	-	-

Agewise Data:

	Persons	Males	Females	Sex Ratio
All ages	95,251	47,990	47,261	985
0-14	29,834	15,083	14,751	978
15-44	48,302	24,202	24,100	996
45-79	16,559	8,415	8,144	968
80+	486	251	235	936
Age not stated	70	39	31	795

Languages (Dominant):
Telugu, Urdu, Hindi, Tamil, Gondi

Disabled Population:

	Persons	Males	Females	%
Total Disabled	1,408	729	679	
In Seeing	470	220	250	33.38
In Speech	148	72	76	10.51
In Hearing	99	42	57	7.03
In Movement	456	281	175	32.39
Mentally	235	114	121	16.69

JANNARAM

Jannaram C.D. Block lies in the south-west part of Adilabad district. The Block is located at a distance of 150 kms. from district headquarters (Adilabad). There are 26 villages in the block with the total popul ation of 49,464 persons. Area of the C.D. Block is 321. 70 sq. kms. It is bounded by Kaddam (Peddur) Mandal on south-west, west and north, Sirpur Mandal on north and north-east, Tiryani Mandal on east and south-east, Dandapalle Mandal on south-east and south, Karimnagar district on south-west, Kaddam (Peddur) Mandal on south -west, west and north-west.

Communications :

Roadways : State Highway (S.H.): Direction- Nirmal to Luxettipet. Nearest Villages- Indhanpalle, Kamanpalle, Raindlaguda, Marriguda, Ponakal, Jannaram, Paidpalle, Dongapalle, Bommena, Dharmaram, Chintaguda, Malyal.

River: Godavari Nadi- Naerest Villages- Kalmadagu, Badampalle, Puttiguda, Thimmapur, Rampur, Dharmaram, Chintaguda, Malyal.

Backwards Region Grants Fund: It receives Backward Region Grants.

Annual Rainfall: Average Rainfall 1257 mm

Ground Water: Availability of the Ground Water in the Basin is 5334 H.A.M.and the utilization is 1029 H.A. M. It belongs to Safe category. Depth to water level varies from 10 to 20 meter below the ground. Most of the wells go down in summer months, according to the Ground Water Estimation Committee.

Natural Division : Telangana Plateau Region

Administration:

Division: Telangana. Parliamentary Constituency: 1 Adilabad (ST). District: Adilabad. Mandal: Jannaram. Assembly Constituency: 6 Khanapur (ST). Gram Panchayat: 19

Villages: 26 **Inhabited:** 26 **Uninhabited:** 0

Ranking	District	State	National
Area	16	140	2653
Population	5	532	5310
Sex Ratio	24	290	1305
Child Sex Ratio	35	554	2129
Literacy Rate	28	817	4945
Density	37	659	5431
Work Participation Rate	15	875	1809

Gram Panchayats:

Badampalle, Chintalguda, Deveniguda, Dharmaram Indhanpalle, Jannaram, Kalmadugu, Kamanpalle, Kawal Kishtapur, Malyal, Marriguda, Murrimadugu, Ponkal Raindlaguda, Rampur, Routuguda, Singaraipet Thimmapur.

Amenities:

Education: Primary School in 26 villages, Middle school in 11 villages, Matriculation or Secondary School in 8 villages, namely Indhanpalle, Kawal, Kishtapur, Kalmadagu, Ponakal, Jannaram, Chintaguda, Singaraipet.

Higher Secondary or Pre University Courses or Intermediate or Junior College in 1 village of the CD Block,, namely Jannaram.

College in 1 village, Adult Literacy Center in 24 villages., College is in village, namely Jannaram.

Medical: Hospital in 0 village, Dispensary in 3 villages, Health Center in 2 villages, Sub Center in 9 villages, Maternity and Child Welfare Center in 3 villages, Community health workers in 0 village.

The Villages having Hospital or Dispensary or Health Center are Ponakal, Jannaram, Singaraipet.

Drinking Water: Tap water in 26 villages, Tank water in 26 villages, Well water in 26 villages, Tubewell in 26 villages and more than one source in 26 villages.

Bank: Banking facility in 2 villages, namely, Ponakal, Jannaram.

Credit Society in 15 villages Agricultural Credit Society in 12 Non-Agricultural Credit Society in 12 villages.

Others: Power supply in 26 villages, Cinema hall in 2 villages, sport club in 0 village, Stadium or Auditorium or Community Hall in 0 village, Post Office in 12 villages.

There are 16 villages having bus facilities.

Villages with most of facilities: Ponakal Jannaram.

Villages without Amenities (Education): None..

Scheduled Castes: Out of the total population of 49464 persons, 12107 persons (24.48%) belong to Scheduled Castes. The villages having less than 10% SC population are Narsingapur, Juviguda, Paidpalle, Dongapalle Bommena, Papammaguda, Malyal.

The villages having more than 50% SC population are None.

Sex ratio of Scheduled Caste population is 496.

Scheduled Castes Literates and Illiterates by Sex:

	Persons	Males	Females
Literate	4,198	2,804	1,394

Illiterate	7,909	3,295	4,614
Literacy rate	40.7	54.1	27.1
Graduate	77	69	8

Scheduled Castes (Dominant):

Mala Sale etc., Mala, Madiga, Generic Castes etc.
Gosangi

For their cultural identity please see Appendix-I

Villages without Scheduled Castes: There are 6 villages without any scheduled caste population.

Scheduled Tribes: Out of the total population of 49464 persons, 7242 persons (14.64%) belong to Scheduled Tribes. The villages having less than 10% ST population are Indhanpalle, Kamanpalle, Raindlaguda, Venkatapur Badampalle, Ponakal, Papammaguda, Chintaguda Singaraipet, Rampur.

The villages having more than 50% ST population are Kothapet, Narsingapur, Puttiguda, Juviguda Paidpalle, Dongapalle, Bommena, Malyal.

Sex ratio of Scheduled tribe population is 500.

Scheduled Tribes Literates and Illiterates by Sex:

	Persons	Males	Females
Literate	2,424	1,594	830
Illiterate	4,818	2,024	2,794
Literacy rate	39.5	52.0	27.0
Graduate	45	44	1

Scheduled Tribes (Dominant):

Sugalis etc., Gond etc., Pardhan, Kolam etc., Thoti

For their cultural identity please see Appendix-II

Villages without Scheduled Tribes: There are 0 village without any scheduled tribe population.

Literates and Illiterates by Sex (Total Population):

	Persons	Males	Females
Literate	19,979	12,822	7,157
Illiterate	29,485	11,960	17,525
Literacy rate	47	61	34
Graduate	599	532	67

Agriculture: ***Distribution of villages according to land use:*** Out of 26 villages, Total area (in hectare) is 31196, out of that 31.19 percent is cultivable and 68.85 percent of the cultivable area is irrigated.

Sources of Irrigation (Hectares): Government Canal 3444.97, Private Canal 0, Well without Electricity 53.42, Well with Electricity 337.86, Tubewell without Electricity 56.64, Tubewell with Electricity 2.02, Tank 458.66, River 0, Lake 0, Waterfall 0, Others 2345.79.

Villages with population of 5000 to 9999: Ponakal, Chintaguda.

Villages with population of 10000 and above: None

Distribution of Workers:

	Persons	Males	Females	WPR
Cultivators	5,483	4,028	1,455	21.84
Agricultural Labour	11,693	4,829	6,864	46.57
Household Industry	1,925	736	1,189	7.67
Other Workers	6,010	4,402	1,608	23.93
Main Workers	17,870	11,394	6,476	71.16
Marginal Workers	7,241	2,601	4,640	28.84
Total Workers	25,111	13,995	11,116	

Religion: Major Religious Communities:

	Persons	Males	Females	Sex Ratio
Hindu (94.45%)	46,721	23,377	23,344	999
Muslim (4.95%)	2,446	1,262	1,184	938
Christian (0.42%)	209	106	103	972
Sikh (0%)	-	-	-	-
Buddhists (0%)	-	-	-	-
Jain (0%)	-	-	-	-

Agewise Data:

	Persons	Males	Females	Sex Ratio
All ages	49,464	24,782	24,682	996
0-14	16,803	8,559	8,244	963
15-44	23,336	11,631	11,705	1006
45-79	8,917	4,406	4,511	1024
80+	355	145	210	1448
Age not stated	53	41	12	293

Languages (Dominant):

Telugu, Hindi, Gondi, Urdu, Marathi

Disabled Population:

	Persons	Males	Females	%
Total Disabled	635	365	270	
In Seeing	225	122	103	35.43
In Speech	70	30	40	11.02
In Hearing	13	9	4	2.05
In Movement	252	160	92	39.69
Mentally	75	44	31	11.81

JEELUGU MILLI

Jeelugumilli C.D. Block lies in the northern part of West Godavari district. The Block is located at a dista nce of 92 kms. from district headquarters (Eluru). There are 29 villages in the block with the total population of 28,501 persons. Area of the C.D. Block is 149.41 sq. kms. It is bounded in the north by district Khammam, in the south by Mandals T. Narasapuram and Jangareddig udem, in the east by Mandals Jangareddigudem and Buttaya gudem, and in the west by T. Narasapuram Mandal.

Communications :

Roadways : State Highway (S.H.): Direction- Aswaraopeta to Jangaeddigudem. Nearest Villages- Tatiyakulagudem, Jeelugu Milli, Vankavarigudem, Barrinkalapadu, Khandri kapadu, Ramannapalem, Darbhagudem.

Backwards Region Grants Fund: It receives Backward Region Grants.

ANDHRA PRADESH

Annaul Rainfall: Average Rainfall 1005 mm

Ground Water: Availability of the Ground Water in the Basin is (Information not avavible) H.A.M .and the utilization is (Information not avavible) H.A.M. It belongs to (Information not avavible) category. Depth to water level varies from 3 to 10 meter below the ground. Most of the wells go down in summer months.

Forest and Reserved **Forest:** (Reserved Forest): Nearest Villages- Ankampalem, Nersu Gudem, Danamvarigudem. (Bedadanuru)- Nearest Villages- Rachannagudem, Jagannad hapuram, Puchikapadu, Ankanna Gudem, Veerampalem, Thatir amudu Gudem, Gopalapuram, Lankalapalle, Jillellagudem, Bothappa Gudem, Kamayya Palem, Parimpudi Narayanapuram Rowthugudem. (Illagumilli)- Nearest Villages- Tatiyaku lagudem, Jeelugu Milli, Vankavarigudem, Palacherla Rajav aram. (Dabhagudem)- Nearest Villages- Barrinkalapadu, Madakamvarigudem, Khandrikapadu, Datlavarigudem, Raman napalem, Darbhagudem.

Administration:

Division: Coastal Andhra. Parliamentary Constituency: 27 Eluru. District: West Godavari. Mandal: Jeelugu Milli.Assembly Constituency: 186 Polavaram (ST). Gram Panchayat: 12.

Villages: 29 **Inhabited:** 26 **Uninhabited:** 3

Ranking	District	State	National
Area	21	825	5048
Population	46	1044	6089
Sex Ratio	29	549	1927
Child Sex Ratio	3	34	94
Literacy Rate	44	211	2343
Density	1	458	4870
Work Participation Rate	45	750	1147

Gram Panchayats:

Ankannagudem, Darbhagudem, Ganganngudem Jeelugu Milli, Kammaiah Palem, Mulagalampalle P.Ankam Palem, Palacherlarajavaram, Rachanna Gudem Swarnavarigudem, Tatikayala Gudem, Vankavari Gudem.

Amenities:

Education: Primary School in 24 villages, Middle school in 5 villages, Matriculation or Secondary School in 4 villages, namely Kamayya Palem, Jeelugu Milli, Mulagalampalle, Darbhagudem.

Higher Secondary or Pre University Courses or Intermediate or Junior College in 0 village of the CD Block, College in 0 village, Adult Literacy Center in 15 villages.

Medical: Hospital in 0 village, Dispensary in 1 village, Health Center in 1 village, Sub Center in 14 villages, Maternity and Child Welfare Center in 0 village, Community health workers in 0 village.

The Village having Hospital or Dispensary or Health Center is Darbhagudem.

Drinking Water: Tap water in 26 villages, Tank water in 26 villages, Well water in 26 villages, Tubewell in 26 villages and more than one source in 26 villages.

Bank: Banking facility in 2 villages, namely, Kamayya Palem, Darbhagudem.

Credit Society in 4 villages Agricultural Credit Society in 3 Non-Agricultural Credit Society in 3 villages.

Others: Power supply in 26 villages, Cinema hall in 2 villages, sport club in 0 village, Stadium or Auditorium or Community Hall in 0 village, Post Office in 12 villages.

There are 22 villages having bus facilities.

Villages with most of facilities: Kamayya Palem Darbhagudem.

Villages without amenities (Education):

Gopalapuram, Nersu Gudem..

Scheduled Castes: Out of the total population of 28501 persons, 5962 persons (20.92%) belong to Scheduled Castes.

The villages having less than 10% SC population are Jagannadhapuram, Ankanna Gudem, Thatiramudu Gudem Gopalapuram, Lankalapalle, Jillellagudem Bothappa Gudem, Kamayya Palem, Vankavarigudem Parimpudi Narayanapuram, Gangannagudem Madakamvarigudem, Datlavarigudem.

The villages having more than 50% SC population are None.

Sex ratio of Scheduled Caste population is 486.

Scheduled Castes Literates and Illiterates by Sex:

	Persons	Males	Females
Literate	3,228	1,818	1,410
Illiterate	2,734	1,248	1,486
Literacy rate	62.4	67.8	56.6
Graduate	100	77	23

Scheduled Castes (Dominant):

Mala, Madiga, Mala Dasari, Adi Andhra, Mala Dasu

For their cultural identity please see Appendix-I

Villages without Scheduled Castes: There are 7 villages without any scheduled caste population.

Scheduled Tribes: Out of the total population of 28501 persons, 8217 persons (28.83%) belong to Scheduled Tribes.

The villages having less than 10% ST population are Puchikapadu, Ankampalem, Tatiyakulagudem Mulagalampalle, Palacherla Rajavaram.

The villages having more than 50% ST population are Jagannadhapuram, Ankanna Gudem, Thatiramudu Gudem Lankalapalle, Jillellagudem, Bothappa Gudem Barrinkalapadu, Gangannagudem, Madakamvarigudem Datlavarigudem, Ramannapalem.

Sex ratio of Scheduled tribe population is 502.

Scheduled Tribes Literates and Illiterates by Sex:

	Persons	Males	Females
Literate	3,497	1,946	1,551
Illiterate	4,720	2,142	2,578
Literacy rate	49.7	55.2	44.1
Graduate	30	22	8

Scheduled Tribes (Dominant):

Koya etc., Nayaks, Sugalis etc., Yerukulas Kondareddis

For their cultural identity please see Appendix-II

Villages without Scheduled Tribes: There are 3 villages without any scheduled tribe population.

Literates and Illiterates by Sex (Total Population):

	Persons	Males	Females
Literate	15,572	8,579	6,993
Illiterate	12,929	5,802	7,127
Literacy rate	63	68	57
Graduate	362	279	83

Agriculture: ***Distribution of villages according to land use:*** Out of 29 villages, Total area (in hectare) is 14941, out of that 61.87 percent is cultivable and 37.04 percent of the cultivable area is irrigated.

Sources of Irrigation (Hectares): Government Canal 192.31, Private Canal 0, Well without Electricity 0, Well with Electricity 0, Tubewell without Electricity 0, Tubewell with Electricity 2427.96, Tank 803.64, River 0, Lake 0, Waterfall 0, Others 0.

Villages with population of 5000 to 9999: None

Villages with population of 10000 and above: None

Distribution of Workers:

	Persons	Males	Females	WPR
Cultivators	3,391	2,527	864	21.93
Agricultural Labour	9,645	4,690	4,955	62.38
Household Industry	154	80	74	1
Other Workers	2,272	1,502	770	14.69
Main Workers	9,239	6,351	2,888	59.75
Marginal Workers	6,223	2,448	3,775	40.25
Total Workers	15,462	8,799	6,663	

Religion: Major Religious Communities:

	Persons	Males	Females	Sex Ratio
Hindu (96.82%)	27,595	13,934	13,661	980
Muslim (2.35%)	671	321	350	1,090
Christian (0.74%)	212	112	100	893
Sikh (0%)	-	-	-	-
Buddhists (0%)	-	-	-	-
Jain (0%)	-	-	-	-

Agewise Data:

	Persons	Males	Females	Sex Ratio
All ages	28,501	14,381	14,120	982
0-14	9,705	4,956	4,749	958
15-44	13,795	6,938	6,857	988
45-79	4,808	2,387	2,421	1014
80+	130	63	67	1063
Age not stated	63	37	26	703

Languages (Dominant):

Telugu, Koya, Urdu, Konda, Oriya

Disabled Population:

	Persons	Males	Females	%
Total Disabled	451	224	227	
In Seeing	145	72	73	32.15
In Speech	58	30	28	12.86
In Hearing	26	16	10	5.76
In Movement	154	75	79	34.15
Mentally	68	31	37	15.08

JHARASANGAM

Jharasangam C.D. Block lies in the north-west part of Medak district. The Block is located at a distance of 72 kms. from district headquarters (Sangareddy). There are 35 villages in the block with the total population of 40,660 persons. Area of the C.D. Block is 210.67 sq. kms. It is bounded by Raikode Mandal on north, Munpalle Mandal on east, Kohir Mandal on south, Zahirabad Mandal on south-west, and Nyalkal Mandal on east.

Communications :

Roadways : Metalled Roads: Nearest Villages- Kamalpalle, Bardipur, Kuppanagar, Bopanpalle, Boregaon, Pyarawaram, Medpalle, Machnoor.

Backwards Region Grants Fund: It receives Backward Region Grants.

Annual Rainfall: Average Rainfall 900 mm

Ground Water: Availability of the Ground Water in the Basin is 1065 H.A.M. and the utilization is 804 H.A. M. It belongs to Semi Critical category. Depth to water level varies from 5 meter below the ground. Most of the wells go down in summer months. The well density in the entire block is 7 wells per sq. km. Total no. of the wells in the block are enumerated as 1438, according to the Ground Water Estimation Committee.

Natural Division : Telangana Plateau Region

Administration:

Division: Telanagana. Parliamentary Constituency: 5 Zahirabad. District: Medak. Mandal: Jharasangam. Assemb ly Constituency: 38 Zahirabad (SC). Gram Panchayat: 28

Villages: 35 **Inhabited:** 34 **Uninhabited:** 1

Ranking	District	State	National
Area	22	486	4003
Population	33	806	5711
Sex Ratio	43	1036	3852
Child Sex Ratio	38	925	4098

Literacy Rate	20	811	4922
Density	30	692	4827
Work Participation Rate	40	742	1961

Gram Panchayats:

Bardipur, Bidekanna, Bopanpalle, Boregaon Chilemamidi, Chilepalle, Chilkepalle, Devarampalle Edulapalle, Giniayarpalle, Guntamarpally Jeerlapalle, Jharsangam, Junegaon, Kakkerwada Kamalpalle, Kollur, Krishnapur, Kuppanagar, Machnoor Medpalle, Narsapur, Potpalle, Siddapur, Tummanpalli Vanampalle, Yedakulapalle, Yelgoi.

Amenities:

Education: Primary School in 34 villages, Middle school in 8 villages, Matriculation or Secondary School in 2 villages, namely Kuppanagar, Jharasangam.

Higher Secondary or Pre University Courses or Intermediate or Junior College in 0 village of the CD Block, College in 0 village, Adult Literacy Center in 12 villages.

Medical: Hospital in 0 village, Dispensary in 1 village, Health Center in 0 village, Sub Center in 3 villages, Maternity and Child Welfare Center in 0 village, Community health workers in 0 village.

The Village having Hospital or Dispensary or Health Center is Jharasangam.

Drinking Water: Tap water in 34 villages, Tank water in 34 villages, Well water in 34 villages, Tubewell in 34 villages and more than one source in 34 villages.

Bank: Banking facility in 3 villages, namely, Bardipur, Jharasangam, Jeerlapalle.

Credit Society in 6 villages Agricultural Credit Society in 3 Non-Agricultural Credit Society in 5 villages.

Others: Power supply in 34 villages, Cinema hall in 0 village, sport club in 0 village, Stadium or Auditorium or Community Hall in 0 village, Post Office in 11 villages.

There are 32 villages having bus facilities.

Village with most of facilities: Jharasangam.

Villages without Amenities (Education): None..

Scheduled Castes: Out of the total population of 40660 persons, 11163 persons (27.45%) belong to Scheduled Castes.

The villages having less than 10% SC population are None..

The villages having more than 50% SC population are None.

Sex ratio of Scheduled Caste population is 485.

Scheduled Castes Literates and Illiterates by Sex:

	Persons	Males	Females
Literate	3,649	2,309	1,340
Illiterate	7,514	3,436	4,078
Literacy rate	38.7	47.4	29.4
Graduate	41	36	5

Scheduled Castes (Dominant):

Madiga, Mala, Byagara, Generic Castes etc.

Beda Jangam etc.

For their cultural identity please see Appendix-I

Villages without Scheduled Castes: There is 1 village without any scheduled caste population.

Scheduled Tribes: Out of the total population of 40660 persons, 1109 persons (2.73%) belong to Scheduled Tribes.

The villages having less than 10% ST population are Siddapur, Gangapur, Kollur, Tummanpalle, Kappad Kamalpalle, Narsapur, Sangam [Khurd], Kakkerwada Yelgoi, Potpalle, Bardipur, Kuppanagar, Jharasangam Bopanpalle, Boregaon, Guntamarpalle, Jeerlapalle Junegaon, Islampur, Edakulapalle, Chilemamidi Devarampalle, Pyarawaram, Medpalle, Machnoor Krishnapur, Bidekanna, Edulapalle, Giniyarpalle Chilkepalle, Ananthasagar.

The villages having more than 50% ST population are None.

Sex ratio of Scheduled tribe population is 491.

Scheduled Tribes Literates and Illiterates by Sex:

	Persons	Males	Females
Literate	185	142	43
Illiterate	924	422	502
Literacy rate	22.5	34.1	10.6
Graduate	2	2	0

Scheduled Tribes (Dominant):

Sugalis etc., Yerukulas

For their cultural identity please see Appendix-II

Villages without Scheduled Tribes: There are 24 villages without any scheduled tribe population.

Literates and Illiterates by Sex (Total Population):

	Persons	Males	Females
Literate	16,183	10,485	5,698
Illiterate	24,477	10,443	14,034
Literacy rate	47	60	34
Graduate	280	251	29

Agriculture: ***Distribution of villages according to land use:*** Out of 35 villages, Total area (in hectare) is 21066, out of that 75.13 percent is cultivable and 11.66 percent of the cultivable area is irrigated.

Sources of Irrigation (Hectares): Government Canal 2.81, Private Canal 0, Well without Electricity 10, Well with Electricity 996.72, Tubewell without Electricity 0, Tubewell with Electricity 392.56, Tank 344.54, River 0, Lake 0, Waterfall 0, Others 98.4.

Villages with population of 5000 to 9999: None

Villages with population of 10000 and above: None

Distribution of Workers:

	Persons	Males	Females	WPR

Cultivators	5,744	3,920	1,824	28.67
Agricultural Labour	11,088	5,154	5,934	55.34
Household Industry	255	131	124	1.27
Other Workers	2,949	2,498	451	14.72
Main Workers	16,728	10,464	6,264	83.49
Marginal Workers	3,308	1,239	2,069	16.51
Total Workers	20,036	11,703	8,333	

Religion: Major Religious Communities:

	Persons	Males	Females	Sex Ratio
Hindu (80.65%)	32,792	16,890	15,902	942
Muslim (16.86%)	6,855	3,521	3,334	947
Christian (2.09%)	850	437	413	945
Sikh (0%)	-	-	-	-
Buddhists (0%)	-	-	-	-
Jain (0.01%)	5	2	3	1,500

Agewise Data:

	Persons	Males	Females	Sex Ratio
All ages	40,660	20,928	19,732	943
0-14	15,551	8,060	7,491	929
15-44	17,504	9,209	8,295	901
45-79	7,233	3,500	3,733	1067
80+	331	138	193	1399
Age not stated	41	21	20	952

Languages (Dominant):

Telugu, Urdu, Hindi, Kannada, Marathi

Disabled Population:

	Persons	Males	Females	%
Total Disabled	553	311	242	
In Seeing	198	117	81	35.8
In Speech	48	27	21	8.68
In Hearing	33	11	22	5.97
In Movement	204	127	77	36.89
Mentally	70	29	41	12.66

JINNARAM

Jinnaram C.D. Block lies in the south-east part of Medak district. It is a part of Jinnaram Mandal. The Block is located at a distance of 40 kms. from district headquarters (Sangareddy). There are 28 villages in the block with the total population of 56,115 persons. Area of the C.D. Block is 193.57 sq. kms. It is bounded by Narsapur and Shivampet Mandals on north, Tupran Mandal on north-east, Rangareddy district on east, Patancheru Mandal on south, Sangareddy Mandal on west, and Hathnoora Mandal on north-west.

Communications :

Roadways : State Highway (S.H.): Direction- Narsapur to Hyderabad. Nearest Villages- Lakshmapur, Pyaranagar, Mambapur, Gummadidala, Bonthapalle, Domadugu, Annaram, Gaddipotharam.

Backwards Region Grants Fund: It receives Backward Region Grants.

Annual Rainfall: Average Rainfall 952 mm

Ground Water: Availability of the Ground Water in the Basin is 1720 H.A.M. and the utilization is 1651 H. A.M. It belongs to Critical category. Depth to water level varies from 5 meter below the ground. Most of the wells go down in summer months. The well density in the entire block is 12 wells per sq. km. Total no. of the wells in the block are enumerated as 2596, according to the Ground Water Estimation Committee.

Natural Division : Telangana Plateau Region

Administration:

Division: Telangana. Parliamentary Constituency: 6 Medak. District: Medak. Mandal: Jinnaramm. Assembly Constituency: 40 Patancheru. Gram Panchayat: 23.

Villages: 28 **Inhabited:** 27 **Uninhabited:** 1

Ranking	**District**	**State**	**National**
Area	30	598	4301
Population	13	338	4996
Sex Ratio	44	1076	4412
Child Sex Ratio	33	758	3288
Literacy Rate	6	472	3730
Density	29	640	3636
Work Participation Rate	7	394	1749

Gram Panchayats:

Amdoor, Annaram, Antharam, Bollaram, Bonthapalle Dacharam, Domadugu, Gaddapotharam, Gummadidala Jinnaram, Kanukunta, Khazipalle, Kodakanchi Kothapalle, Madharam, Mambapur, Mangampet Nallavalli, Nalthur, Ootla, Shivanagar, Solakpalle Wailal.

Amenities:

Education: Primary School in 27 villages, Middle school in 16 villages, Matriculation or Secondary School in 7 villages, namely Kankunta, Gummadidala, Bonthapalle, Vailal, Jinnaram, Mangampet, Sivanagar.

Higher Secondary or Pre University Courses or Intermediate or Junior College in 1 village of the CD Block,, namely Jinnaram.

College in 0 village, Adult Literacy Center in 3 villages.

Medical: Hospital in 0 village, Dispensary in 1 village, Health Center in 3 villages, Sub Center in 10 villages, Maternity and Child Welfare Center in 0 village, Community health workers in 0 village.

The Villages having Hospital or Dispensary or Health Center are Kothapalle, Kankunta.

Drinking Water: Tap water in 27 villages, Tank water in 27 villages, Well water in 27 villages, Tubewell in 27 villages and more than one source in 27 villages.

Bank: Banking facility in 2 villages, namely,

Gummadidala, Jinnaram.

Credit Society in 11 villages Agricultural Credit Society in 4 Non-Agricultural Credit Society in 11 villages.

Others: Power supply in 27 villages, Cinema hall in 2 villages, sport club in 0 village, Stadium or Auditorium or Community Hall in 0 village, Post Office in 13 villages.

There are 22 villages having bus facilities.

Villages with most of facilities: Gummadidala Jinnaram.

Villages without Amenities (Education): None..

Scheduled Castes: Out of the total population of 56177 persons, 8075 persons (14.37%) belong to Scheduled Castes.

The villages having less than 10% SC population are Lakshmapur, Pyaranagar, Bonthapalle, Annaram Mangampet, Sivanagar, Kodakanchi, Chetlapotharam Gaddipotharam.

The villages having more than 50% SC population are None.

Sex ratio of Scheduled Caste population is 491.

Scheduled Castes Literates and Illiterates by Sex:

	Persons	Males	Females
Literate	3,099	2,093	1,006
Illiterate	4,976	2,016	2,960
Literacy rate	44.6	59.1	29.5
Graduate	28	21	7

Scheduled Castes (Dominant):

Madiga, Mala, Beda Jangam etc., Generic Castes etc. Bindla

For their cultural identity please see Appendix-I

Villages without Scheduled Castes: There are 4 villages without any scheduled caste population.

Scheduled Tribes: Out of the total population of 56177 persons, 1231 persons (2.19%) belong to Scheduled Tribes.

The villages having less than 10% ST population are Kothapalle, Nallapalle, Mambapur, Antharam, Kankunta Dacharam, Gummadidala, Bonthapalle, Domadugu Annaram, Vailal, Jinnaram, Mangampet, Gotla Solakpalle, Amdoor, Sivanagar, Kodakanchi, Puttaguda Nalthur, Madharam, Khazipalle, Kistaipalle Chetlapotharam, Gaddipotharam.

The villages having more than 50% ST population are None.

Sex ratio of Scheduled tribe population is 489.

Scheduled Tribes Literates and Illiterates by Sex:

	Persons	Males	Females
Literate	300	204	96
Illiterate	931	425	506
Literacy rate	30.8	40.6	20.4
Graduate	2	2	0

Scheduled Tribes (Dominant):

Sugalis etc., Yerukulas, Generic Tribes etc.

Koya etc., Gond etc.

For their cultural identity please see Appendix-II

Villages without Scheduled Tribes: There are 9 villages without any scheduled tribe population.

Literates and Illiterates by Sex (Total Population):

	Persons	Males	Females
Literate	26,179	16,827	9,352
Illiterate	29,998	12,264	17,734
Literacy rate	55	68	41
Graduate	707	587	120

Agriculture: ***Distribution of villages according to land use:*** Out of 28 villages, Total area (in hectare) is 19357, out of that 53.06 percent is cultivable and 36.87 percent of the cultivable area is irrigated.

Sources of Irrigation (Hectares): Government Canal 0, Private Canal 0, Well without Electricity 0, Well with Electricity 9, Tubewell without Electricity 0, Tubewell with Electricity 1052, Tank 2726, River 0, Lake 0, Waterfall 0, Others 0.

Villages with population of 5000 to 9999: Kankunta, Gummadidala, Bonthapalle, Annaram.

Villages with population of 10000 and above: None

Distribution of Workers:

	Persons	Males	Females	WPR
Cultivators	6,708	4,479	2,229	23.52
Agricultural Labour	9,867	3,853	6,014	34.59
Household Industry	1,092	588	504	3.83
Other Workers	10,859	8,497	2,362	38.07
Main Workers	22,071	15,022	7,049	77.37
Marginal Workers	6,455	2,395	4,060	22.63
Total Workers	28,526	17,417	11,109	

Religion: Major Religious Communities:

	Persons	Males	Females	Sex Ratio
Hindu (92.08%)	51,726	26,695	25,031	938
Muslim (6.48%)	3,641	1,975	1,666	844
Christian (1.22%)	684	354	330	932
Sikh (0.03%)	17	10	7	700
Buddhists (0.11%)	60	31	29	935
Jain (0%)	-	-	-	-

Agewise Data:

	Persons	Males	Females	Sex Ratio
All ages	56,177	29,091	27,086	931
0-14	18,846	9,590	9,256	965
15-44	27,744	14,817	12,927	872
45-79	9,199	4,534	4,665	1029
80+	339	128	211	1648
Age not stated	49	22	27	1227

Languages (Dominant):

Telugu, Urdu, Oriya, Hindi, Marathi

Disabled Population:

	Persons	Males	Females	%
Total Disabled	734	440	294	
In Seeing	284	165	119	38.69
In Speech	74	43	31	10.08
In Hearing	47	21	26	6.4
In Movement	229	151	78	31.2
Mentally	100	60	40	13.62

JIYYAMMAVALASA

Jiyyammavalasa C.D. Block lies in the northern part of Vizianagaram district. The Block is located at a distance of 131 kms. from district headquarters (Vizian agaram). There are 58 villages in the block with the total population of 53,810 persons. Area of the C.D. Block is 151.44 sq. kms. It is bounded in the north by Mandal Kurupam, in the south by Mandal Garugubilli and Srikakulam district, in the east by Mandal Kurupam, and in the west by Mandals Komarada and Garugubilli.

Communications :

Roadways : Metalled Roads: Nearest Villages- Batlabhadra, Subadramma Valasa, Jogirajupeta, Kannapudora Valasa, Mokhasaharipuram.

Railway Station: Pedatolumanda.

River: Nagavalli Nadi- Nearest Villages- Bitrapadu, Basangi, Sivaramarajapuram, Gadabavalasa. Vegavati Nadi- Nearest Villages- Lovagangarajapuram, Maruwada, Sikhabadi, Bommika Jagannadhapuram, Geddatiruvada, Bommika, Ankavaram, Chinabuddidi, Pedabuddidi, Gadisin gupuram.

Backwards Region Grants Fund: It receives Backward Region Grants.

Annaul Rainfall: Average Rainfall 886.7 mm

Ground Water: Availability of the Ground Water in the Basin is (Information not avavible) H.A.M .and the utilization is (Information not avavible) H.A.M. It belongs to (Information not avavible) category. Depth to water level varies from 3 to 10 meter below the ground. Most of the wells go down in summer months.

Administration:

Division: Coastal Andhra. Parliamentary Constituency: 18 Araku (ST). District: Vizianagram. Mandal: Jiyyammav alasa. Assembly Constituency: 130 Kurupam (ST) Gram Panchayat: 31.

Villages: 58 **Inhabited:** 56 **Uninhabited:** 2

Ranking	District	State	National
Area	17	819	5027
Population	14	400	5100
Sex Ratio	17	177	953
Child Sex Ratio	31	649	2595
Literacy Rate	7	676	4459
Density	28	493	3057
Work Participation Rate	23	260	1277

Gram Panchayats:

Alamanda, Ankavaram, Arnada, B.J.Puram, Basangi Bittarapadu, Bommika, Chinamerangi, Chintalabelagam Dangabadra, Gavarammapeta, Gedasingipuram Geddatiruvada, Itika, Jiyyammavalasa, Joguladumma Kannapudoravalasa, Kondachilakam, Kudama Kundaratiruvada, M.Alluvada, P.T.Manda, Parajapadu Pedabuddidi, Pedamerangi, Pippalabadra, Sikhabedi T.K.Jammu, T.N.Valasa, Talladumma, Tumbali.

Amenities:

Education: Primary School in 52 villages, Middle school in 15 villages, Matriculation or Secondary School in 5 villages, namely Maruwada, Jiyyammavalasa, Bommika Jagannadhapuram, Pippalabadra, Pedabuddidi. Higher Secondary or Pre University Courses or Intermediate or Junior College in 1 village of the CD Block,, namely Chinamerangi.

College in 1 village, Adult Literacy Center in 30 villages., College is in village, namely Chinamerangi.

Medical: Hospital in 2 villages, Dispensary in 2 villages, Health Center in 2 villages, Sub Center in 15 villages, Maternity and Child Welfare Center in 2 villages, Community health workers in 0 village.

The Villages having Hospital or Dispensary or Health Center are Jiyyammavalasa, Itika, Pedabuddidi.

Drinking Water: Tap water in 56 villages, Tank water in 56 villages, Well water in 56 villages, Tubewell in 56 villages and more than one source in 56 villages.

Bank: Banking facility in 4 villages, namely, Chinamerangi, Jiyyammavalasa, Alamanda, Chinabuddidi. Credit Society in 10 villages Agricultural Credit Society in 3 Non-Agricultural Credit Society in 7 villages.

Others: Power supply in 56 villages, Cinema hall in 1 village, sport club in 0 village, Stadium or Auditorium or Community Hall in 0 village, Post Office in 19 villages.

There are 25 villages having bus facilities.

Villages with most of facilities: Chinamerangi Jiyyammavalasa.

Villages without amenities (Education): Surapudoravalasa, Akkandoravalasa, Mokhasaharipuram..

Scheduled Castes: Out of the total population of 53810 persons, 5056 persons (9.4%) belong to Scheduled Castes. The villages having less than 10% SC population are Batlabhadra, Subadramma Valasa, Talladumma Chandrasekharajapuram, Mokasualluwada Lovagangarajapuram, Tumbali, Kondanidagallu Kidigesu, Balleru, Kondachilakam, Chinadodija Dakshini, Pedatolumanda, Pedadodija Tamarikandijammu, Gorli, Kutampandrasingi, Arnada

Jiyyammavalasa, Joguladumma
Lakshmipuram (Near) Parajapadu, Tummalavalasa
Surapudoravalasa, Gavarampeta, Basangi, Singanapuram
Kudama, Gowripuram, Gadabavalasa, Itika, Parajapadu
Geddatiruvada, Dangabadra (Near) Arnada, Ankavaram
Pedabuddidi.

The villages having more than 50% SC population are None.

Sex ratio of Scheduled Caste population is 498.

Scheduled Castes Literates and Illiterates by Sex:

	Persons	Males	Females
Literate	1,921	1,222	699
Illiterate	3,135	1,314	1,821
Literacy rate	44.9	57.5	32.5
Graduate	67	63	4

Scheduled Castes (Dominant):

Dom etc., Mala, Relli, Pamidi, Madiga

For their cultural identity please see Appendix-I

Villages without Scheduled Castes: There are 16 villages without any scheduled caste population.

Scheduled Tribes: Out of the total population of 53810 persons, 11054 persons (20.54%) belong to Scheduled Tribes.

The villages having less than 10% ST population are
Bitrapadu, Batlabhadra, Subadramma Valasa
Jogirajupeta, Kannapudora Valasa, Pedamerangi
Chinamerangi, Talladumma, Sikhabadi
Bommika Jagannadhapuram, Joguladumma
Lakshmipuram (Near) Parajapadu, Rajayyapeta
Mokhasaharipuram, Basangi, Chintalabelagam
Singanapuram, Gowripuram, Turakanaiduvalasa
Kundaratiruvada, Pippalabadra, Bommika, Ankavaram
Pedabuddidi.

The villages having more than 50% ST population are
Lovagangarajapuram, Ravada, Maruwada, Kondanidagallu
Kidigesu, Balleru, Kondachilakam, Chinadodija
Dakshini, Pedatolumanda, Pedadodija
Tamarikandijammu, Gorli, Kutampandrasingi, Arnada
Alamanda, Surapudoravalasa, Gadabavalasa.

Sex ratio of Scheduled tribe population is 492.

Scheduled Tribes Literates and Illiterates by Sex:

	Persons	Males	Females
Literate	3,985	2,692	1,293
Illiterate	7,069	2,923	4,146
Literacy rate	42.3	56.1	27.9
Graduate	21	18	3

Scheduled Tribes (Dominant):

Jatapus, Gadabas, Savaras etc., Konda Dhoras
Yerukulas

For their cultural identity please see Appendix-II

Villages without Scheduled Tribes: There are 7 villages without any scheduled tribe population.

Literates and Illiterates by Sex (Total Population):

	Persons	Males	Females
Literate	23,504	14,826	8,678
Illiterate	30,306	11,990	18,316
Literacy rate	50	64	37
Graduate	770	705	65

Agriculture: ***Distribution of villages according to land use:*** Out of 58 villages, Total area (in hectare) is 15143, out of that 78.32 percent is cultivable and 55.5 percent of the cultivable area is irrigated.

Sources of Irrigation (Hectares): Government Canal 4327.77, Private Canal 0, Well without Electricity 1.39, Well with Electricity 15.1, Tubewell without Electricity 0, Tubewell with Electricity 42.48, Tank 1506.44, River 171.78, Lake 0, Waterfall 177.61, Others 340.02.

Villages with population of 5000 to 9999: None

Villages with population of 10000 and above: None

Distribution of Workers:

	Persons	Males	Females	WPR
Cultivators	8,828	5,491	3,337	30.78
Agricultural Labour	14,962	6,602	8,360	52.17
Household Industry	1,008	574	434	3.51
Other Workers	3,884	2,880	1,004	13.54
Main Workers	19,939	12,264	7,675	69.52
Marginal Workers	8,743	3,283	5,460	30.48
Total Workers	28,682	15,547	13,135	

Religion: Major Religious Communities:

	Persons	Males	Females	Sex Ratio
Hindu (99.46%)	53,518	26,688	26,830	1,005
Muslim (0.13%)	70	29	41	1,414
Christian (0.22%)	117	50	67	1,340
Sikh (0%)	-	-	-	-
Buddhists (0%)	-	-	-	-
Jain (0%)	-	-	-	-

Agewise Data:

	Persons	Males	Females	Sex Ratio
All ages	53,810	26,816	26,994	1007
0-14	16,998	8,761	8,237	940
15-44	25,304	12,512	12,792	1022
45-79	11,172	5,385	5,787	1075
80+	259	126	133	1056
Age not stated	77	32	45	1406

Languages (Dominant):

Telugu, Savara, Oriya, Urdu, Gondi

Disabled Population:

	Persons	Males	Females	%
Total Disabled	1,240	694	546	
In Seeing	579	320	259	46.69
In Speech	96	56	40	7.74

In Hearing	77	37	40	6.21
In Movement	384	226	158	30.97
Mentally	104	55	49	8.39

JUKKAL

Jukkal C.D. Block lies in the western part of Nizamabad district. The Block is located at a distance of 100 kms. from district headquarters (Nizamabad). There are 35 villages in the block with the total population of 45,568 persons. Area of the C.D. Block is 238.78 sq. kms. It is bounded by Madnur Mandal on north and north-east, Bichkunda Mandal on north-east, east and south-east, and Medak district on south and south-west, and it has common boundary with the state of Karnataka on south-west and with the state of Maharashtra on south-west, west and north-west,

Communications :

Roadways : State Highway (S.H.): Direction- Madnoor to Bichkunda. Nearest Villages Khemraja Kallali, Kowlas, Shivapur.

Backwards Region Grants Fund: It receives Backward Region Grants.

Annual Rainfall: Average Rainfall 892 mm

Ground Water: Availability of the Ground Water in the Basin is 2177 H.A.M. and the utilization is 831 H.A. M. It belongs to Safe category. Depth to water level varies from 10 to 20 meter below the ground. Most of the wells go down in summer months, according to the Ground Water Estimation Committee.

Natural Division : Telangana Plateau Region

Administration:

Division: Telangana. Parliamentary Constituency: 5 Zahirabad. District: Nizamabad. Mandal: Jukkal. Assembly Constituency: 13 Jukkal (SC). Gram Panchayat: 22.

Border Villages: (Maharashtra)- Nearest Villages- Chand egaon, Madhapur, Hangarga, Kathalwadi, Chinna Ghulla Gundoor, Siddapur, Sopur, Dongaon.

Border Villages: (Karnataka)- Nearest Villages- Sopur, Dongaon, Babulgaon.

Places of Tourist Interest:

Kowlas: It is situated at a distance of about 16 kms. from Madnur and 45 kms. from Bodhan railway station. Kowlas is a village of historical importance. Many battles were fought between the Bahmanis and Musunuri Chiefs in this village. There are the ruins of an ancie nt fort at the place and a number of caves in the nearby hills. Anantagiri temple, Kalyan Ramadas Mandir and Shankaracharya Mandir are some of the places of Hindu worship.

Villages: 35 **Inhabited:** 33 **Uninhabited:** 2

Ranking	District	State	National
Area	12	348	3522
Population	23	651	5498
Sex Ratio	36	923	3158
Child Sex Ratio	28	825	3595
Literacy Rate	32	990	5644
Density	28	702	4893
Work Participation Rate	30	754	1985

Gram Panchayats:

Babalgaon, Baswapur, Bijjalwadi, Chandegaon Chinna Edgi, Dongaon, Gulla Big, Gundur, Hangarga Jukkal, Kandebellur, Kantali, Kemrajkallali, Kowlas Ladegaon, Mohmadabad, Nagulgaon, Padampalliy Pedda Edgi, Shivvapur, Vittalwadi, Wazrakhandi.

Amenities:

Education: Primary School in 33 villages, Middle school in 6 villages, Matriculation or Secondary School in 3 villages, namely Jukkal, Kowlas, Khandeballoor.

Higher Secondary or Pre University Courses or Intermediate or Junior College in 0 village of the CD Block, College in 0 village, Adult Literacy Center in 15 villages.

Medical: Hospital in 0 village, Dispensary in 1 village, Health Center in 1 village, Sub Center in 9 villages, Maternity and Child Welfare Center in 0 village, Community health workers in 0 village.

The Village having Hospital or Dispensary or Health Center is Jukkal.

Drinking Water: Tap water in 33 villages, Tank water in 33 villages, Well water in 33 villages, Tubewell in 33 villages and more than one source in 33 villages.

Bank: Banking facility in 1 villages, namely, Jukkal.

Credit Society in 2 villages Agricultural Credit Society in 2 Non-Agricultural Credit Society in 0 village.

Others: Power supply in 33 villages, Cinema hall in 0 village, sport club in 0 village, Stadium or Auditorium or Community Hall in 0 village, Post Office in 9 villages.

There are 28 villages having bus facilities.

Village with most of facilities: Jukkal.

Villages without Amenities (Education): None..

Scheduled Castes: Out of the total population of 45168 persons, 8626 persons (19.1%) belong to Scheduled Castes.

The villages having less than 10% SC population are None..

The villages having more than 50% SC population are None.

Sex ratio of Scheduled Caste population is 479.

Scheduled Castes Literates and Illiterates by Sex:

	Persons	Males	Females
Literate	2,269	1,482	787
Illiterate	6,357	3,014	3,343

Literacy rate	31.4	39.4	22.7
Graduate	30	28	2

Scheduled Castes (Dominant):

Madiga, Mala, Generic Castes etc., Mang, Chamar etc.

For their cultural identity ple~se see Appendix-I

Villages without Scheduled Castes: There are 2 villages without any scheduled caste population.

Scheduled Tribes: Out of the total population of 45168 persons, 3671 persons (8.13%) belong to Scheduled Tribes. The villages having less than 10% ST population are Chandegaon, Madhapur, Hangarga, Kathalwadi Bijjalwadi, Padampalle, Nagalgaon, Chinna Edgi Pedda Edgi, Longaon, Kanthali, Chinna Ghulla Gundoor, Jukkal, Ladegaon, Khemraja Kallali, Kowlas Khandeballoor, Baswapur, Bangarpalle, Sopur Wajrakhandi, Babulgaon, Mailar.

The villages having more than 50% ST population are None.

Sex ratio of Scheduled tribe population is 475.

Scheduled Tribes Literates and Illiterates by Sex:

	Persons	Males	Females
Literate	774	562	212
Illiterate	2,897	1,367	1,530
Literacy rate	27.2	37.1	15.9
Graduate	15	15	0

Scheduled Tribes (Dominant):

Sugalis etc., Generic Tribes etc., Yerukulas Kammara, Bagata

For their cultural identity please see Appendix-II

Villages without Scheduled Tribes: There are 16 villages without any scheduled tribe population.

Literates and Illiterates by Sex (Total Population):

	Persons	Males	Females
Literate	15,359	9,899	5,460
Illiterate	29,809	13,177	16,632
Literacy rate	41	52	30
Graduate	294	267	27

Agriculture: ***Distribution of villages according to land use:*** Out of 35 villages, Total area (in hectare) is 23879, out of that 83.79 percent is cultivable and 4.35 percent of the cultivable area is irrigated.

Sources of Irrigation (Hectares): Government Canal 0, Private Canal 0, Well without Electricity 0, Well with Electricity 1.21, Tubewell without Electricity 0, Tubewell with Electricity 811.28, Tank 50.57, River 0, Lake 0, Waterfall 0, Others 8.09.

Villages with population of 5000 to 9999: None

Villages with population of 10000 and above: None

Distribution of Workers:

	Persons	Males	Females	WPR
Cultivators	8,713	5,792	2,921	39.67
Agricultural Labour	9,935	4,369	5,566	45.24
Household Industry	783	482	301	3.57
Other Workers	2,530	1,976	554	11.52
Main Workers	18,142	11,055	7,087	82.61
Marginal Workers	3,819	1,564	2,255	17.39
Total Workers	21,961	12,619	9,342	

Religion: Major Religious Communities:

	Persons	Males	Females	Sex Ratio
Hindu (91.24%)	41,210	21,099	20,111	953
Muslim (8.73%)	3,943	1,973	1,970	998
Christian (0.02%)	7	1	6	6,000
Sikh (0%)	-	-	-	-
Buddhists (0%)	-	-	-	-
Jain (0%)	-	-	-	-

Agewise Data:

	Persons	Males	Females	Sex Ratio
All ages	45,168	23,076	22,092	957
0-14	18,090	9,383	8,707	928
15-44	19,024	9,775	9,249	946
45-79	7,706	3,751	3,955	1054
80+	298	140	158	1129
Age not stated	50	27	23	852

Languages (Dominant):

Telugu, Marathi, Kannada, Hindi, Urdu

Disabled Population:

	Persons	Males	Females	%
Total Disabled	825	458	367	
In Seeing	452	254	198	54.79
In Speech	61	32	29	7.39
In Hearing	29	17	12	3.52
In Movement	209	117	92	25.33
Mentally	74	38	36	8.97

JULAPALLE

Julapalle C.D. Block lies in the eastern part of Karimn agar district. The Block is located at a distance of 30 kms. from district headquarters (Karimnagar). There are 15 villages in the block with the total population of 45,094 persons. Area of the C.D. Block is 173.57 sq. kms. It is bounded by Dharmaram Mandal on north, Peddapalle Mandal on north-east, Sultanabad Mandal on east and south, and Choppadandi Mandal on west.

Communications :

Roadways : State Highway (S.H.): Direction- Sultanabad to Peddapalle. Nearest Villages- Burhanmiyapet, Sivapal le,

Backwards Region Grants Fund: It receives Backward Region Grants.

Annual Rainfall: Average Rainfall 915 mm

Ground Water: Availability of the Ground Water in the

Basin is 1616 H.A.M. and the utilization is 474 H.A. M. It belongs to Safe category. Depth to water level varies from more than 5 to 10 meter below the ground. Most of the wells go down in summer months. The well density in the entire block is 5 wells per sq. km. Total no. of the wells in the block are enumerated as 928, according to the Ground Water Estimation Committee.

Natural Division : Godavari Depression Region

Administration:

Division: Telangana. Parliamentary Constituency: 2 Peddapalle (SC). District: Karimnagar. Mandal: Julapalle. Assembly Constituency: 25 Peddapalle. Gram Panchayat: 8

Villages: 15 **Inhabited:** 15 **Uninhabited:** 0

Ranking	District	State	National
Area	34	700	4643
Population	33	656	5504
Sex Ratio	30	263	1227
Child Sex Ratio	16	283	924
Literacy Rate	31	763	4778
Density	42	646	3967
Work Participation Rate	34	503	1764

Gram Panchayats:

Julapally, Kachapur, Kummarikunta, Nagulapalli Peddapur, Telikunta, Venkatraopalli, Wadkapur.

Amenities:

Education: Primary School in 15 villages, Middle school in 12 villages, Matriculation or Secondary School in 6 villages, namely Julapalle, Wadkapur, Doolikatta, Telukunta, Elgaid, Sultanpur.

Higher Secondary or Pre University Courses or Intermediate or Junior College in 0 village of the CD Block, College in 0 village, Adult Literacy Center in 15 villages.

Medical: Hospital in 0 village, Dispensary in 2 villages, Health Center in 2 villages, Sub Center in 8 villages, Maternity and Child Welfare Center in 1 village, Community health workers in 0 village.

The Villages having Hospital or Dispensary or Health Center are Wadkapur, Elgaid.

Drinking Water: Tap water in 15 villages, Tank water in 15 villages, Well water in 15 villages, Tubewell in 14 villages and more than one source in 15 villages.

Bank: Banking facility in 4 villages, namely, Julapalle, Wadkapur, Doolikatta, Elgaid.

Credit Society in 14 villages Agricultural Credit Society in 3 Non-Agricultural Credit Society in 14 villages.

Others: Power supply in 15 villages, Cinema hall in 0 village, sport club in 0 village, Stadium or Auditorium or Community Hall in 0 village, Post Office in 13 villages.

There are 13 villages having bus facilities.

Villages with most of facilities: Julapalle Wadkapur, Doolikatta, Elgaid.

Villages without Amenities (Education): None..

Scheduled Castes: Out of the total population of 45094 persons, 10446 persons (23.16%) belong to Scheduled Castes.

The villages having less than 10% SC population are None..

The villages having more than 50% SC population are None.

Sex ratio of Scheduled Caste population is 496.

Scheduled Castes Literates and Illiterates by Sex:

	Persons	Males	Females
Literate	3,729	2,347	1,382
Illiterate	6,717	2,920	3,797
Literacy rate	41.8	52.3	31.3
Graduate	52	48	4

Scheduled Castes (Dominant):

Madiga, Mala, Mala Sale etc., Manne, Bindla

For their cultural identity please see Appendix-I

Villages without Scheduled Castes: There are 0 village without any scheduled caste population.

Scheduled Tribes: Out of the total population of 45094 persons, 283 persons (0.63%) belong to Scheduled Tribes.

The villages having less than 10% ST population are Peddapur, Julapalle, Kummarikunta, Kachapur Wadkapur, Lokapeta, Muppirithota, Doolikatta Telukunta, Elgaid, Sultanpur, Burhanmiyapet Sivapalle, Narsapur, Raikaldevapalle.

The villages having more than 50% ST population are None.

Sex ratio of Scheduled tribe population is 537.

Scheduled Tribes Literates and Illiterates by Sex:

	Persons	Males	Females
Literate	86	58	28
Illiterate	197	73	124
Literacy rate	36.6	52.3	22.6
Graduate	1	0	1

Scheduled Tribes (Dominant):

Yerukulas, Gond etc., Sugalis etc., Chenchu etc.

For their cultural identity please see Appendix-II

Villages without Scheduled Tribes: There are 2 villages without any scheduled tribe population.

Literates and Illiterates by Sex (Total Population):

	Persons	Males	Females
Literate	18,789	11,784	7,005
Illiterate	26,305	10,791	15,514
Literacy rate	48	61	36
Graduate	445	400	45

Agriculture: ***Distribution of villages according to land use:***

Out of 15 villages, Total area (in hectare) is 17357, out of that 75.4 percent is cultivable and 69.07 percent of the cultivable area is irrigated.

Sources of Irrigation (Hectares): Government Canal 5120, Private Canal 0, Well without Electricity 0, Well with Electricity 1873, Tubewell without Electricity 0, Tubewell with Electricity 0, Tank 1834, River 0, Lake 0, Waterfall 0, Others 212.

Villages with population of 5000 to 9999: Julapalle, Wadkapur, Elgaid.

Villages with population of 10000 and above: None

Distribution of Workers:

	Persons	Males	Females	WPR
Cultivators	7,142	4,655	2,487	31
Agricultural Labour	10,634	4,215	6,419	46.15
Household Industry	909	556	353	3.95
Other Workers	4,355	3,510	845	18.9
Main Workers	19,876	12,054	7,822	86.27
Marginal Workers	3,164	882	2,282	13.73
Total Workers	23,040	12,936	10,104	

Religion: Major Religious Communities:

	Persons	Males	Females	Sex Ratio
Hindu (97.15%)	43,809	21,935	21,874	997
Muslim (2.24%)	1,012	503	509	1,012
Christian (0.47%)	212	108	104	963
Sikh (0%)	-	-	-	-
Buddhists (0%)	-	-	-	-
Jain (0%)	-	-	-	-

Agewise Data:

	Persons	Males	Females	Sex Ratio
All ages	45,094	22,575	22,519	998
0-14	13,909	6,997	6,912	988
15-44	20,358	10,257	10,101	985
45-79	10,357	5,089	5,268	1035
80+	445	220	225	1023
Age not stated	25	12	13	1083

Languages (Dominant):

Telugu, Urdu, Hindi, Tamil, Marathi

Disabled Population:

	Persons	Males	Females	%
Total Disabled	721	416	305	
In Seeing	298	196	102	41.33
In Speech	84	42	42	11.65
In Hearing	42	23	19	5.83
In Movement	197	107	90	27.32
Mentally	100	48	52	13.87

JULURPAD

Julurpad C.D. Block lies in the south-western part of Khammam district. The Block is located at a distance of 60 kms. from district headquarters (Khammam). There are 08 villages in the block with the total population of 31,739 persons. Area of the C.D. Block is 255.41 sq. kms. It is bounded in the north by Mandals Yellandu and Kothagudem, in the south by Mandal Kallur, in the east by Mandals Penuballi, Chandrugonda and Kothagudem, and in the west by Mandals Singareni and Enkuru.

Communications:

Roadways : State Highway (S.H.): Direction- Enkuru to Kothagudem. Nearest Villages- Julurpad, Padamata Narsap uram, Karivarigudem, Machinenipeta, Kakarla.

Backwards Region Grants Fund: It receives Backward Region Grants.

Annual Rainfall: Average Rainfall 1013 mm

Ground Water: Availability of the Ground Water in the Basin is 3075 H.A.M.and the utilization is 244 H.A. M. It belongs to safe category. Depth to water level varies from 5 to 20 meter below the ground. Most of the wells go down in summer months. The well density in the entire block is 6 wells per sq. km. Total no. of the wells in the block are enumerated as 1311, according to the Ground Water Estimation Committee.

Forest and Reserved **Forest:** (Gubbagurthi R.F.)- Nearest Villages- Gundepudi, Nallabandabodu.

Natural Division : Godavari Depression Region

Administration:

Division: Telangana Parliamentary Constituency: 17 Kham.mam. District: Khammam.

Mandal: Julurpad. Assembly Constituency: 115 Wyra (ST). Gram Panchayat: 12.

Villages: 8 **Inhabited:** 8 **Uninhabited:** 0

Ranking	District	State	National
Area	20	289	3314
Population	37	997	6010
Sex Ratio	17	562	1958
Child Sex Ratio	18	327	1147
Literacy Rate	38	855	5089
Density	10	184	5899
Work Participation Rate	34	987	525

Gram Panchayats:

Anantharam, Bethalampadu, Gundepudi, Julurpad Kakarla, Karivarigudem, Kommugudem, Machinenipeta Machinenipeta Thanda, Padamati Narsapuram, Papakollu Vinobha Nagar.

Amenities:

Education: Primary School in 8 villages, Middle school in 6 villages, Matriculation or Secondary School in 3 villages, namely Papakollu, Julurpad, Kakarla.

Higher Secondary or Pre University Courses or Intermediate or Junior College in 0 village of the CD Block, College in 0 village, Adult Literacy Center in 7 villages.

Medical: Hospital in 0 village, Dispensary in 1 village,

Health Center in 1 village, Sub Center in 6 villages, Maternity and Child Welfare Center in 0 village, Community health workers in 0 village.
The Village having Hospital or Dispensary or Health Center is Papakollu.
Drinking Water: Tap water in 8 villages, Tank water in 8 villages, Well water in 8 villages, Tubewell in 8 villages and more than one source in 8 villages.
Bank: Banking facility in 1 villages, namely, Julurpad.
Credit Society in 6 villages Agricultural Credit Society in 2 Non-Agricultural Credit Society in 4 villages.
Others: Power supply in 8 villages, Cinema hall in 0 village, sport club in 0 village, Stadium or Auditorium or Community Hall in 0 village, Post Office in 6 villages.
There are 7 villages having bus facilities.
Village with most of facilities: Julurpad.
Villages without Amenities (Education): None..
Scheduled Castes: Out of the total population of 31739 persons, 3146 persons (9.91%) belong to Scheduled Castes.
The villages having less than 10% SC population are Papakollu, Padamata Narsapuram, Karivarigudem Machinenipeta, Kakarla, Nallabandabodu.
The villages having more than 50% SC population are None.
Sex ratio of Scheduled Caste population is 478.
Scheduled Castes Literates and Illiterates by Sex:

	Persons	Males	Females
Literate	1,167	748	419
Illiterate	1,979	895	1,084
Literacy rate	43.8	53.9	32.8
Graduate	21	17	4

Scheduled Castes (Dominant):
Madiga, Mala, Mala Dasari
For their cultural identity please see Appendix-I
Villages without Scheduled Castes: There is 1 village without any scheduled caste population.
Scheduled Tribes: Out of the total population of 31739 persons, 15600 persons (49.15%) belong to Scheduled Tribes.
The villages having less than 10% ST population are None..
The villages having more than 50% ST population are Papakollu, Karivarigudem, Machinenipeta Nallabandabodu.
Sex ratio of Scheduled tribe population is 497.
Scheduled Tribes Literates and Illiterates by Sex:

	Persons	Males	Females
Literate	4,591	3,071	1,520
Illiterate	11,009	4,770	6,239
Literacy rate	35.9	47.9	23.8
Graduate	49	45	4

Scheduled Tribes (Dominant):
Sugalis etc., Koya etc., Nayaks, Yerukulas Gond etc.
For their cultural identity please see Appendix-II
Villages without Scheduled Tribes: There are 0 village without any scheduled tribe population.
Literates and Illiterates by Sex (Total Population):

	Persons	Males	Females
Literate	12,311	7,645	4,666
Illiterate	19,428	8,375	11,053
Literacy rate	46	57	35
Graduate	291	251	40

Agriculture: ***Distribution of villages according to land use:*** Out of 8 villages, Total area (in hectare) is 25542, out of that 36.45 percent is cultivable and 26.78 percent of the cultivable area is irrigated.
Sources of Irrigation (Hectares): Government Canal 0, Private Canal 0, Well without Electricity 1429.35, Well with Electricity 490.89, Tubewell without Electricity 0, Tubewell with Electricity 0, Tank 567.78, River 0, Lake 0, Waterfall 0, Others 5.26.
Villages with population of 5000 to 9999: None
Villages with population of 10000 and above: Papakollu.
Distribution of Workers:

	Persons	Males	Females	WPR
Cultivators	6,094	3,758	2,336	34.79
Agricultural Labour	9,565	4,143	5,422	54.6
Household Industry	248	168	80	1.42
Other Workers	1,612	1,332	280	9.2
Main Workers	14,358	8,530	5,828	81.96
Marginal Workers	3,161	871	2,290	18.04
Total Workers	17,519	9,401	8,118	

Religion: Major Religious Communities:

	Persons	Males	Females	Sex Ratio
Hindu (97.22%)	30,856	15,605	15,251	977
Muslim (2.22%)	704	334	370	1,108
Christian (0.55%)	173	78	95	1,218
Sikh (0%)	-	-	-	-
Buddhists (0%)	-	-	-	-
Jain (0%)	-	-	-	-

Agewise Data:

	Persons	Males	Females	Sex Ratio
All ages	31,739	16,020	15,719	981
0-14	11,589	5,801	5,788	998
15-44	14,740	7,458	7,282	976
45-79	5,113	2,599	2,514	967
80+	270	144	126	875
Age not stated	27	18	9	500

Languages (Dominant):
Telugu, Hindi, Urdu, Koya, Tamil
Disabled Population:

	Persons	Males	Females	%
Total Disabled	863	506	357	
In Seeing	425	251	174	49.25
In Speech	78	46	32	9.04
In Hearing	47	21	26	5.45
In Movement	219	133	86	25.38
Mentally	94	55	39	10.89

JUPADU BUNGALOW

Japadu Banglow C.D. Block lies in the north-eastern part of Kurnool district. The Block is located at a distance of 40 kms. from district headquarters (Kurnool). There are 11 villages in the block with the total population of 34,193 persons. Area of the C.D. Block is 225.75 sq. kms. It is bounded in the north by Mandals Pagidyala and Kothapalle, in the south by Mandals Midthur and Pamulapadu, in the east by Mandal Pamulapadu, and in the west by Mandal Nandikotkur.

Communications:
Roadways : State Highway (S.H.): Direction- Kurnool to Atmakur. Nearest Villages- Mandlem, Tartur, Tangadan cha, Bannur.
River: Bhavanasi Nadi- Nearest Village- Ganapuram.
It is identified as a drought-prone area.
Annual Rainfall: Average Rainfall 743 mm
Ground Water: Availability of the Ground Water in the Basin is 2622 H.A.M. and the utilization is 947 H.A. M. It belongs to Safe category. Depth to water level varies from 5 meter to more than 10 meter below the ground. Most of the wells go down in summer months. The well density in the entire block is 5 wells per sq. km. Total no. of the wells in the block are enumera ted as 1058, according to the Ground Water Estimation Committee.
Natural Division : Rayalaseema Region
Administration:
Division: Rayala Seema. Parliamentary Constituency: 34 Nandayal. District: Kurnool. Mandal: Jupadu Bungalow. Assembly Constituency: 255 Nandikotkur (SC). Gram Panchayat: 12.
Villages: 11 **Inhabited:** 10 **Uninhabited:** 1

Ranking	District	State	National
Area	34	406	3731
Population	46	948	5932
Sex Ratio	12	620	2097
Child Sex Ratio	11	297	1031
Literacy Rate	5	346	3175
Density	40	461	5538
Work Participation Rate	37	901	1157

Gram Panchayats:
80 Bannur, Bhaskarapuram, Jupadu Bungalow, Mandiem P.Gangapuram, P.Lingapuram, Parumanchala Tangadancha, Tarigopula, Tartur, Tatipadu Thudicherla.

Amenities:
Education: Primary School in 10 villages, Middle school in 5 villages, Matriculation or Secondary School in 3 villages, namely Bannur, Parumanchala, Thudicherla.
Higher Secondary or Pre University Courses or Intermediate or Junior College in 0 village of the CD Block, College in 0 village, Adult Literacy Center in 10 villages.
Medical: Hospital in 0 village, Dispensary in 0 village, Health Center in 2 villages, Sub Center in 7 villages, Maternity and Child Welfare Center in 1 village, Community health workers in 0 village.
Drinking Water: Tap water in 10 villages, Tank water in 10 villages, Well water in 10 villages, Tubewell in 10 villages and more than one source in 10 villages.
Bank: Banking facility in 2 villages, namely, Bannur, Parumanchala.
Credit Society in 10 villages Agricultural Credit Society in 3 Non-Agricultural Credit Society in 10 villages.
Others: Power supply in 10 villages, Cinema hall in 1 village, sport club in 0 village, Stadium or Auditorium or Community Hall in 0 village, Post Office in 10 villages.
There are 10 villages having bus facilities.
Villages with most of facilities: Bannur Parumanchala.
Villages without Amenities (Education): None..
Scheduled Castes: Out of the total population of 34193 persons, 9325 persons (27.27%) belong to Scheduled Castes.
The villages having less than 10% SC population are None..
The villages having more than 50% SC population are None.
Sex ratio of Scheduled Caste population is 492.
Scheduled Castes Literates and Illiterates by Sex:

	Persons	Males	Females
Literate	4,223	2,691	1,532
Illiterate	5,102	2,045	3,057
Literacy rate	52.6	66.1	38.7
Graduate	102	89	13

Scheduled Castes (Dominant):
Madiga, Mala, Chachati
For their cultural identity please see Appendix-I
Villages without Scheduled Castes: There is 1 village without any scheduled caste population.
Scheduled Tribes: Out of the total population of 34193 persons, 292 persons (0.85%) belong to Scheduled Tribes.

The villages having less than 10% ST population are Mandlem, Tartur, Tangadancha, Tatipadu, Ganapuram Bannur, Tarigopula, Lingapuram, Parumanchala Thudicherla.

The villages having more than 50% ST population are None.

Sex ratio of Scheduled tribe population is 524.

Scheduled Tribes Literates and Illiterates by Sex:

	Persons	Males	Females
Literate	115	71	44
Illiterate	177	68	109
Literacy rate	48.5	62.8	35.5
Graduate	1	1	0

Scheduled Tribes (Dominant):

Yerukulas, Sugalis etc., Chenchu etc., Yenadis

For their cultural identity please see Appendix-II

Villages without Scheduled Tribes: There are 4 villages without any scheduled tribe population.

Literates and Illiterates by Sex (Total Population):

	Persons	Males	Females
Literate	17,086	10,540	6,546
Illiterate	17,107	6,748	10,359
Literacy rate	58	71	45
Graduate	549	474	75

Agriculture: ***Distribution of villages according to land use:*** Out of 11 villages, Total area (in hectare) is 22575, out of that 57.69 percent is cultivable and 15.08 percent of the cultivable area is irrigated.

Sources of Irrigation (Hectares): Government Canal 1380.05, Private Canal 0, Well without Electricity 0, Well with Electricity 381.66, Tubewell without Electricity 0, Tubewell with Electricity 61.3, Tank 141, River 0, Lake 0, Waterfall 0, Others 0.

Villages with population of 5000 to 9999:

Bannur.

Villages with population of 10000 and above: None

Distribution of Workers:

	Persons	Males	Females	WPR
Cultivators	3,085	2,466	619	16.84
Agricultural Labour	12,531	5,753	6,778	68.4
Household Industry	436	248	188	2.38
Other Workers	2,267	1,795	472	12.38
Main Workers	15,395	9,413	5,982	84.04
Marginal Workers	2,924	849	2,075	15.96
Total Workers	18,319	10,262	8,057	

Religion: Major Religious Communities:

	Persons	Males	Females	Sex Ratio
Hindu (81.22%)	27,770	14,042	13,728	978
Muslim (18.71%)	6,399	3,233	3,166	979
Christian (0.02%)	8	4	4	1,000
Sikh (0%)	-	-	-	-
Buddhists (0%)	-	-	-	-
Jain (0%)	-	-	-	-

Agewise Data:

	Persons	Males	Females	Sex Ratio
All ages	34,193	17,288	16,905	978
0-14	11,454	5,809	5,645	972
15-44	15,999	8,263	7,736	936
45-79	6,481	3,118	3,363	1079
80+	232	83	149	1795
Age not stated	27	15	12	800

Languages (Dominant):

Telugu, Urdu, Marathi, Gondi, Hindi

Disabled Population:

	Persons	Males	Females	%
Total Disabled	798	377	421	
In Seeing	453	186	267	56.77
In Speech	59	36	23	7.39
In Hearing	36	14	22	4.51
In Movement	192	113	79	24.06
Mentally	58	28	30	7.27

SURVEY OF RURAL INDIA

List of Volumes

SOUTH ZONE

Vol. 1 : Andhra Pradesh (A-J)
Vol. 2 : Andhra Pradesh (K-P)
Vol. 3 : Andhra Pradesh (Q-Z)
Vol. 4 : Karnataka
Vol. 5 : Kerala, Lekshdweep
Vol. 6 : Tamil Nadu (A-P)
Vol. 7 : Tamil Nadu (Q-Z), Pondicherry, Andaman & Nicobar Islands.

WEST ZONE

Vol. 8 : Gujrat, Dadra & Nagara and Haveli, Daman & Diu
Vol. 9 : Maharashtra
Vol. 10 : Maharashtra, Goa
Vol. 11 : Rajasthan

CENTRAL ZONE

Vol. 12 : Chhattisgarh
Vol. 13 : Madhya Pradesh
Vol. 14 : Madhra Pradesh
Vol. 15 : Uttar Pradesh
Vol. 16 : Uttar Pradesh
Vol. 17 : Uttar Pradesh

NORTH ZONE

Vol. 18 : Haryana, Delhi.
Vol. 19 : Himachal Pradesh, Jammu & Kashmir Uttarakhand
Vol. 20 : Punjab, Chandigarh.

EAST ZONE

Vol. 21 : Bihar
Vol. 22 : Bihar
Vol. 23 : Jharkhand
Vol. 24 : Orrisa
Vol. 25 : West Bangal.

NORTH EAST ZONE

Vol. 26 : Assam, Sikkim
Vol. 27 : Arunachal Pradesh, Manipur, Meghalaya, Mizoram, Nagaland, Tripura.

SURVEY OF RURAL INDIA

A Comprehensive Study of Gram Panchayat and Community Development Block

In 27 Volumes

Volume 6
Tamil Nadu
(A – P)

Editor

Dr. N. Seshagiri

GYAN

Survey of Rural India
Tamil Nadu (A – P)

ISBN : 978-81-212-1100-0 (Set)
ISBN : 978-81-212-1106-2 [Vol. 6 Tamil Nadu (A – P)]

Published in 2013 in India by
Gyan Publishing House
23, Main Ansari Road, Daryaganj,
New Delhi - 110002
Phones : 0091-011-23282060, 23261060
Fax : (011) 23285914
E-mail: books@gyanbooks.com
website: gyanbooks.com

Laser Type Setting : Rajender Vashist, Delhi
Printed at : G. Print Process, Delhi

Contents

List of Photographs (A – P)

1. Tea, C.D. Block : Coonoor
(District : The Nilgiris).

2. Betel Leaf, C.D.Block : Tiruttani
(District :Thiruvallur).

3. Coffee, C.D. Block: Gudalur
(District : The Nilgiris).

4. Cotton, C.D. Block : Uthiramerur
(District : Kancheepuram).

5. Jalagamparai, Waterfall C.D. Block : Jolarpet (District : Vellore).

6. Mettur Dam, C.D. Block: Kolathur (District : Salem)

7. Mudumalai Wildlife Sanctuary, C.D.Block : Gudalur (District : The Nilgiris).

8. Kodaikanal Lake, C.D. Block : Kodaikanal (District : Dindigul).

9. Kanniyakumari Beach, C.D. Block : Agastheeswaram (District : Kanniyakumari).

10. Rameshwaram Beach, C.D. Block : Kadaladi (District : Ramanathapuram).

Preface

The Community Development Block in India is a demarcated rural area for administration and development. The area is administered by a Block Development Officer. A Community Development block covers several gram panchayats, which are local administrative unit at the village level. It was launched on a pilot basis in 1952 to provide for substantial streamlining of the country's agricultural sector, and for sustained improvements in systems of rural health and hygiene, rural education and communication among others. By the end of the First Five Year Plan period, there were 248 blocks which rapidly increased to around 3,000 blocks covering about seventy percent of the rural population in the country by the end of the Second Five Year Plan period. By 1964 there were 6,312 blocks covering the entire country.

India has travelled a considerable distance on the road to development since independence and has made significant progress in various sectors. However, new challenging demands have emerged calling for more integrated rural information. Acute shortage of basic facilities such as drinking water, medical support, education infrastructure is still felt in the face of over 27 per cent of rural population who are still facing poverty and essential sustenance. The Block Development Offices face daunting job of having to accelerate the development process and correct imbalances in tune with the wishes and aspirations of the rural people. Progressive policies and huge investments are being inducted by the Ministry of Rural Development at the Centre towards this, while State Governments are continuously upgrading their implementation machinery.

In addition, new paradigms like rural marketing by a host of retail and manufacturing enterprises as well as expanding technological infrastructure for telecommunication, IT, Transport and Energy among others are posing demands of new types of information on rural India.

Agriculture is a mainstay of the Indian economy. Agriculture and allied sectors contribute nearly 18 per cent of Gross Domestic Product (GDP) of India. Total area coverage under food grains has been reported as 123.22 million hectares. Out of 328.7 million hectares of geographical area of India about 142 million hectares is the net cultivated area. Of this, about 57 million hectare (40%) is irrigated and the remaining is rain fed. This area poses numerous problems for bringing about intensive agricultural production. Information on the four main river systems of India, feeding much of the irrigation schemes- The Himalayan Rivers, The Brahmaputra–centric Rivers, The Deccan Rivers and The Inland Rivers – has to be accurate enough to facilitate efficient irrigation planning.

The government has started focusing on the development of rural heath infrastructure. In the rural areas, services are provided through a network of integrated health and family welfare delivery system. An extensive network of about 3,500 Community Health Centers, 25,000 Primary Health Centers and 1,37,311 Sub-Centers have been set up to provide primary health care at the grassroots level. One sub-centre manned by one female and one male multipurpose worker covers a population of 5000 in plain areas and 3,000 in hilly, tribal, backward and difficult terrain areas. One Primary Health Centre covers a population of 30,000 in the plain areas and 20,000 in tribal and terrain areas. One Community Health Centre covers 80,000 to 1,20,000 Population.

Universalisation of Elementary Education (UEE) has been accepted as a national goal. The Ninth Five year plan envisages UEE to mean universal access, universal retention and universal achievement. As a result of the efforts made by the central and state governments, 94 per cent of country's rural population has primary schools within 1 Km. At the upper primary stage, 84 per cent of the rural population have a school within a distance of three kilometers.

The social milieu of India is not only vast but also diverse. We have tried to capture a representative sample of this diversity. Economic and social development of Scheduled Castes and Scheduled Tribes, who together comprise 24 per cent of the population, and other disadvantaged sections of our society, has called for special efforts, as provided for in the Constitution, of an unprecedented magnitude not faced by any other country in the world.

With deep satisfaction and a sense of accomplishment the book 'SURVEY OF RURAL INDIA (A COMPREHENSIVE STUDY OF GRAM PANCHAYAT AND COMMUNITY DEVELOPMENT BLOCK)' is presented to the readers in 27 Volumes. Such a massive work on Rural India has been commissioned in support of rural-oriented initiatives, containing a wide spectrum of information brought out in a single coherent publication.

All facts and figures have been diligently collected and very little has been left to chance or conjecture by meticulously adhering to documentation and professional standards. We cherish the hope that the twenty-seven volumes presented here will prove to be an invaluable companion to all researchers, scholars, planners, administrators, corporate investors, libraries, NGOs and all those who want to know about any of our Community Development Blocks.

Every detail of the information collected, collated and formatted has gone through meticulous validation checks and rechecks. In line with the constant evolution of the rural scenario, this encyclopedia too will have to be updated and improved in successive editions. A country as vast and complex as India is, there will always be scope for improving the work through suggestions, omissions and additions pointed out. We request the beneficiaries of this encyclopedia to so participate in its evolution.

We sincerely thank the Ministries/Departments of Agriculture, Rural Development, Textiles, Mines, Energy, Finance, Railways, Labour, Human Resource Development, Health and Family Welfare, Culture, Environment and Forest, Minority Affairs, Panchayti Raj, Parliamentary Affairs, Rural Development, Statistics, Tribal affairs, Water Resources, Women and Child Development, University Grants Commission, Law, Justice and Company Affairs, Tourism, Information and Broadcasting, Road Transport and Highways, Home Affairs, Social Justice and Empowerment, Science and Technology, Publication Division, Meteorological Department, Census Commissioner, Backward Classes Commission, Election Commission, Central Statistical Organisation, National Sample Survey Organisation, Anthropological Survey of India, Directorate General of Health Services, Archaeological Survey of India, Central Board of Irrigation and Power, State Statistical Officers, State Editors and gazetteers, State Librarians, Directors of State Information Centers and other connected with the government for the valuable material they have made available to us. We have studied the contents of a large number of published works and drawn from them. We owe a debt of gratitude to all such publishers, authors, editors and compilers. The credit for producing and furnishing authentic data actually goes to them. We have only weaved, consolidated and formatted the content of the information collected by them.

Gyan Publishing House went far beyond the normal call of publishers to give background support to the preparation of these volumes.

DISCLAIMER

This publication contains the collected, collated, formatted and validated information on Community Development Blocks (CD Block) of India on a best and sincere effort basis for presentation in a single encyclopedic work. This work does not constitute an advisory for research, analysis or investment planning, nor, in general, any professional advice. The reader should seek the services of appropriate specialists for such advice.

The information presented here is to be regarded as a first information service on any CDB. The reader should make his/her own deeper investigation of the information on any particular CDB, or state before making any decision or investment of any kind. The Editorial Board or the Publishers cannot be held responsible for loss, if any, incurred as result of specific planning or decision or investments made by the reader in pursuance of this work.

Dr. N. Seshagiri

Introduction

Location

Tamil Nadu is situated on the eastern side of the Indian sub-continent. Geographically, it is situated on the eastern side of the Indian peninsula between the northern latitude of 8 degree 5' and 13 degree 35' and the eastern longitude of 76 degree 15' and 80 degree 20'. The state is bounded by Karnataka and Andhra Pradesh in the north and Kerala in the west. The eastern and western tips of the state are defined by the Point Calimere and Mudumalai wildlife sanctuaries while the northern extreme is Pulicat lake and the southernmost tip is Kanyakumari, the land's end. The Indian Ocean forms a picturesque boundary on its southern side, giving Tamil Nadu an enviable coastline of 1,000 km.

Area

With an area of 130,058 sq. km. and population over 55 million, Tamil Nadu is the 11th largest state in India. The Union Territory of Pondicherry is a small enclave in the district of South Arcot.

Coastal Plain

The coastal eastern and southern boundaries are lapped by the waters of the Bay of Bengal and the Indian Ocean respectively. The eastern and western tips of the state are defined by the Point Calimere and Mudumalai wildlife sanctuaries while the northern extreme is Pulicat lake and the southernmost tip is Cape Comorin or Kanyakumari - the Land's End of India.

Hills

Cradling on the south eastern side of Indian territory, the wonderful and culturally affluent state of Tamil Nadu houses some of the charming hill stations in south India. Invigorating climate, lush greenery, undulating slopes and rejuvenating atmosphere have made Tamilnadu hill stations an ideal destination for visitors to spend their vacations. Away from noisy cities, the hill stations of Tamil Nadu are paradise for nature lovers. The scenic beauty of floating clouds, grassy meadows, waterfalls cascading from great height, shimmering water streams, misty valleys and pristine lakes leaves the vacationers mesmerized. Wrapped in lush greenery, Ooty on Niligiri hills and Ooty on the Nilgiri's and Kodaikanal on Palani hills are real summer retreat for the vacationers. Yercaud also referred as 'Ooty of Poor', enchants the visitors for the orange groves and aromatic coffee plantations. Salubrious climate of Coonoor, Yelagiri, Velliangiri hills and Kotagiri makes them other most preferred summer resorts of Tamil Nadu.

Major Hill Stations

Ooty : Ootacamund, also referred to as Udhagamandalam is a precious and glittering jewel in the crown of Tamilnadu hill stations list. It has also earned itself the sobriquet of 'the queen of the hill stations of South India'. It sits comfortably at an altitude of 2240 metres on the Nilgiri hills, just like a crown. Ooty is known for its picture postcard scenic beauty and plesant climate round the year that make the green Udhagamandalam or Ooty the most popular hill station in the South India.

Yercaud : In contrast to Ooty or other popular summer resorts of Tamilnadu, Yercaud is less explored. It is a hidden treasure amongst hill stations in south India just for those who crave for a tranquil and uncrowded holiday, Yercaud is replete with a number of natural attractions that are incomaparable in their respective way.

Yelagiri : Another hill station in Tamil Nadu that is just adorable for adventure buffs, specially for trekkers. Yelagiri is a charming hill resort in Tamil Nadu endowed with salubrious weather all through the year. Yelagiri is an excellent place to rejuvenate oneself amidst placid beauty of Mother Nature.'

Kodaikanal : Perched at a height of 2100 meters above sea level and 120 kms from the sprightly town of Madurai, Kodaikanal is a perfect holiday spot for enjoying peace and tranquility. Refresh yourself with every breath you take here.

Coonoor : The spectacular hill station of Coonoor nestles in the laps of the Nilgiri Hills at a height of 1800 m. Coonoor is perhaps the best hill station in Tamil Nadu to enjoy trekking.

Kotagiri :In the peaceful surroundings of the Nilgiri

Hills and merely an hour's drive from Ooty, Kotagiri is a modest town amidst the green tea estates. The beauty of this hill station is simply adorable.

Velliangiri Hills : Apart from being a a hill station, Velliangiri is also a pilgrimage destination. Amongst all the mountain shrines in Kongunadu, the Siva temple of Velliangiri is deemed to be the most popular and sacred. Also known by other names as Rajathagiri, Velliangiri, Dakshin Kailash or Bhoolok Kailash, this holy destination is the place where Siva performed his cosmic dance to fulfil the request of his partner Umadevi.

Rivers

The rivers of the state flow eastward from the western ghats and are entirely rain-fed. The major rivers flowing through the state are the Cauvery, Vaigai, Tamaraparani and the west flowing river Periyar. The perennial river fed by both the monsoons is the Cauvery which flows across Tamil Nadu cutting the state in to two halves. The perennial rivers are:- Palar, Cheyyar, Ponnaiyar Kaveri, Meyar, Bhavan, Amaravati, Vaigai, Chittar and Tamaraparni. The non-perennial rivers are the Vellur, Noyal, Suruli, Gundar, Vaipar, Valparai and Varshali. The 760 km. long Cauveri is the largest river of the state.

Annual Rainfall

Tamil Nadu has an equatorial, tropical climate in the inlands and an equatorial, maritime climate in its coastal regions. In the inlands the temperature may go to extremes in some places while it tends to be moderate in the coastal areas. By and large, the average temperature for most parts of the state range between 28 to 40 degree Centigrade. In the summer and between 18 to 26 degree C. in the short-lived winter season. In the more hilly terrains, the maximum temperature may be as low as 26 degree C. and the minimum temperature may go down to 0.3 degree. Actual rainfall is 1133.8 mm.

Ground Water

Annual Replenishable Ground water Resource 23.07 Billon Cubic Meter (BCM), Net Annual Ground water Availability 20.76 Billion Cubic Meter (BCM), Annual Ground water Draft 17.65 Billon Cubic Meter (BCM). There are 142 C.D. Blocks reported over exploited, 33 C. D. Blocks found critical and 57 C.D. Blocks fell in the category of semi-critical.

Forest and Wildlife

The state receives abundant rainfall and the scenic valleys of Cumbum and Pollachi are dotted with plantations of tea, coffee and spices. However, the upper reaches of the Eastern ghats are not without their share of beauty and Yercaud in the Shevaroy hills is famous for its fruit orchards and banana and coffee plantations. Tamil Nadu has a wealth of flora and fauna and some of its major wildlife sanctuaries like Mudumalai and Anaimalai (Indira Gandhi W.S) are situated in the hills of the Western ghats which is the habitat of elephants, tigers, bisons and a variety of monkey and deer. Of the 3000 and more plant species found in Tamil Nadu, a majority are found in the mixed deciduous forests of this region. One of the most noteworthy flowers is the Kurinji of Kodaikkanal which blooms once in 12 years.

Wild life Sanctuaries, Bird Sanctuaries and National Parks : Mudumalai Wildlife Sanctuary, *Area*- 217 sq.kms. *District*- The Nilgiris. Indira Gandhi Wildlife Sanctuary, Area- 841 sq.kms. District- Coimbatore. Munadanthurai Wildlife Sanctuary, *Area*- 582 sq.kms. District-Tirunelveli. Kalakad Wildlife Sanctuary, *Area*- 223 sq.kms. District- Tirunelveli. Gurizzled Giant Squirrel Wildlife Sanctuary, *Area*- 485 sq.kms. District-Virudhunagar. Point Calimere Wildlife Sanctuary, *Area*-172 sq.kms. District- Nagapattinam. Vallanadu Balck Buck Sanctuary, *Area*- 1641 sq.kms. District- Tuticorin. Kanyakumari Wildlife Sanctuary, *Area*- 457 sq.kms. District- Kanyakumari. Vedanthangal Birds Sanctuary, *Area*- 30 sq.kms. District- Kancheepuram. Karikili Birds Sanctuary, Area- 61 sq.kms. District- Kancheepuram. Pulicat lake Birds Sanctuary, *Area*- 153 sq.kms. District-Tiruvallur. Vettangudi Birds Sanctuary, *Area*- 38 sq.kms. District- Sivangangai. Kanjirankulam Birds Sanctuary, *Area*- 104 sq.kms. District- Ramananthapuram. Chitrangudi Birds Sanctuary, *Area*- 47 sq.kms. District-Ramananthapuram. Udayamarthandpuram Birds Sanctuary, *Area*- 45 sq.kms. District- Tiruvarur. Vaduvoor Birds Sanctuary, *Area*- 128 sq.kms. District- Tiruvarur. Koonthankulam-Kadankulam Birds Sanctuary, Area-129 sq.kms. District- Tirunelveli. Karaivetti Birds Sanctuary, *Area*- 453 sq.kms. District- Permbalur. Vellode Birds Sanctuary, *Area*- 77 sq.kms. District- Erode. Melaselvanur-Kilaselvanur Birds Sanctuary, *Area*- 593 sq.kms. District- Ramanathapuram. Madumalai National Park, Area- 103 sq.kms. District- The Nilgiris. Indira Gandhi National Park, *Area*- 117 sq.kms. District-Coimbatore. Mukurthi National Park, *Area*- 784 sq.kms. District- The Nilgiris. Guindy National Park, *Area*- 282 sq.kms. District- Chennai. Gulf of Manner Marine National Park (21 Islands), *Area*- 526 sq.kms. District-

Ramanathapuram.

Communication

As on 30 March 2010, Tamil Nadu's road network is widespread with a total road length of 1,99,040 km. Tamil Nadu has about 14257 km of Highways network which is designated as *National Highways* and *State Highways* on the basis of traffic intensity and connectivity. The various types of roads and their lengths are ; National highways/expressways 4873 kms., State highways 9384.

National Highways

Road stretches which have heavy traffic intensity of more than 30,000 Passenger Car Units (PCUs) connecting different state capitals, Major ports, large industrial areas and tourist centers are designated / declared as *National Highway* by government of India. In Tamilnadu, "National Highways Wing" of Highways & Minor Ports Department was established in the year 1971 to look after the works of improving, maintaining and renewing of National Highways laid down by National Highways Authority of India (NHAI). National Highways wing exercises central government funds from Ministry of Road Transport and Highways for improvement works. Out of 25 National Highways in Tamil Nadu, 12 NH's runs inside the Tamil Nadu. NH 47, NH 49, NH 208, NH 220 connects Tamil Nadu with Kerala. NH 67, NH 207, NH 209 connects Tamil Nadu with Karnataka. NH 205, NH 219 and NH 234 connects Tamil Nadu with Andhra Pradesh. NH 4 connects Tamil Nadu with Maharashtra, Karnataka, and Andhra Pradesh. NH 5 connects Tamil Nadu with Orissa and Andhra Pradesh. NH 7 connects Tamil Nadu with Uttar Pradesh, Madhya Pradesh, Maharashtra, Andhra Pradesh, and Karnataka. NH 66 connects Tamil Nadu with Karnataka and Pondicherry. National Highways plying through Tamil Nadu are: NH- 4 : From Andhra Pradesh Border - Thiruvalam - Walajepet - Kancheepuram - Sriperumbdur - Poonamallee - Chennai Length 123 km, NH- 5 : From Andhra Pradesh Border - elaur - Gummidipundi – Kavarapettai - Chennai Length 45 km, NH- 7 : From Karnataka Border - Hosur - Krishnagiri - Dharmapuri - Salem - Namakkal - Karur - Dindigul - Madurai - Virudunagar - Sattur - Kovilpatti - Tirunelveli - Nanguneri - Vattakottai up to Kanniya Kumari Length 627 km, NH :7A : Palayan Kottai - Vagaikulam - Tuticorin Length 51 km, NH- 47 : Salem - Erode - Coimbatore - Palakkad - Thrissur - Kochi - Kollam - Trivandrum - Nagercoil - Kanniya Kumari Length 363 km, NH- 45 : Chennai - Tambaram - Chengalpattu - Madurantakam - Tindivanam - Viluppuram - Ulundurpettai - Trichy - Manapparai - Dindigul - Theni Length 550 km, NH- 45A: Villuppuram - Pondicherry - Cuddalore - Chidambaram - Karaikal - Nagappattinam Length 147 km, NH- 45 B: Trichy - Viralimalai - Thuvarankurichchi - Melur - Madurai - Aruppukottai - Pandalgudi - Ettaiyapuram - Tuticorin Length 257 km, NH- 45 C: Thanjavur - Kumbakonam - Sethiathope - Vadalur - Neyveli Township - Panruti and terminates near Vikravandi on NH-45.Lenght 159 km, NH- 46 : Krishnagiri - Vaniyambadi - Vellore - Ranipet Length 132 km, NH- 47 : It re-enters Tamil Nadu border at Kaliyakkavilai - Kuzhithurai - Marthandam - Thuckalay - Nagercoil - Suchindrum - Kanyakumari Length 224 km, NH- 47 B : The highway starting from the junction of NH 47 near Nagercoil connecting Aralvaymozhi and terminating at its junction with NH7 near Kavalkinaru length 45 km, NH-49 : From Kerala Border - Bodinayakkanur - Teni - Usilampatti - Madurai - Manamadurai - Paramakkudi - Ramanathapuram - Mandapam - Rameswaram Length 290 km, NH- 66 : Krishnagiri - Uthangarai - Chengam - Tiruvannamalai - Gingee - Tindivanam - Pondicherry Length 208 km, NH- 67 : Nagappattinam - Thiruvarur - Thanjavur - Trichy- Karur - Kangeyam - Coimbatore - Ooty – Gudalur - Teppakadu up to Karnataka Border Length 505 km, NH- 68 : Salem - Valapadi - Attur - Chinnasalem - Kallakkurichchi - Ulundurpettai Length 134 km, NH- 205 : From Andhra Pradesh Border - Tiruttani - Tiruvallur - Ambathur - Chennai Length 82 km, NH- 207 : Hosur up to Karnataka Border Length 20 km, NH- 208 : From Kerala Border - Sengottai - Tenkasi - Sivagiri - Srivilliputtur - T.Kallupati - Thirumangalam Length 125 km, NH- 209 : Dindigul - Palani - Udumalaippettai - Pollachi - Coimbatore - Annur - Satyamangalam - Hasanur up to Karnataka Border Length 286 km, NH- 210 : Trichy - Pudukkottai - Tirumayam - Karaikkudi - Devakottai - Devipattinam - Ramanathapuram Length 160 km, NH- 219 : From Andhra Pradesh Border - Krishnagiri Length 22 km, NH-220 : From Kerala Border - Gudalur - Cumbum - Uthamapalayam - Theni Length 55 km, NH- 226 : Thanjavur - Gandharvakottai - Pudukkottai - Thirumayam - Kilasevalpatti - Tirupattur - Madagupatti - Sivaganga - Manamadurai Length 144 km, NH- 227 : Trichy - Lalgudi - Kallakudi - Kizhapalur - Udaiarpalayam - Jayamkondam - Gangaikondacholapuram - Kattumannarkoil - Lalpet - Kumaratchi - Chidambaram Length 135 km, NH- 234 : From Andhra Pradesh Border - Peranampattu - Gudiyatham - Katpadi - Vellore - Polur - Tiruvanamalai

- Villupuram Length 234 km.

State Highways

SH- 4 : Arcot - Arni - Gingee - Villupuram Road. Length 114.6 km. SH- 5 : Arcot - Thiruvettipuram - Vandavasi - Tindivanam Road. Length 94.6 km. SH-6A : Arcot - Thiruvettipuram - Vandavasi - Tindivanam Road. Length 80.0 km. SH- 7 : Villupuram - Mambalapattu - Tirukkovilur Road. Length 35.0. SH- 8 : Vikkiravandy - Panruti - Neyveli Township - Kumbakonam - Thanjavur Road (converted as NH-45C). length 159.2. SH- 9 : Cuddalore - Nellikuppam - Panruti - Thiruvamur - Madapattu - Thirukovilur - Tiruvannamalai - Polur - Vellore - Katpadi - Chittoor Road (Katpadi - Vellore - Thiruvannamalai. This part has been converted as NH 234). Length 203 km. SH- 10 : Cuddalore - Vridhachalam - Salem Road. Length 93.2. SH- 15 : Ooty - Kothagiri - Mettupalayam - Sathyamangalam - Gobichettipalayam – Erode. Length 161.6. SH- 17 : Malur - Hosur - Adiyamancottah Road. Length 101.8 km. SH- 18 : Salem - Thirupathur - Vaniyambadi Road. Length 125 km. SH- 19 : Avinashi - Tirupur - Palladam - Pollachi - Cochin Road. Length 99.6 km. SH- 20 : Thoppur - Mecheri - Mettur Dam - Bhavani (Erode) - Erode Road. Length 94.0 km. SH- 21 : Pollachi - Dharapuram - Mulanur - Karur Road. Length 120.0 km. SH- 22 : Grand Anaicut - Cauveripattinam Road. Length 100 km. SH- 23 : Mayiladuthurai - Thiruthuraipoondi Road. Length 68.2 km. SH- 24 : Trichy - Chidambaram Road (converted as NH-227). Length 135.4 km. SH-25 : Trichy - Musiri -Namakkal-Thiruchencode Road. Length 120 km. SH- 26 : Trichy - Pudukottai - Aranthangi - Mimisal Road. Length 119 km. SH- 27 : Perambalur - Manamadurai Road (converted to NH-226). Length 228 km. SH- 28 : Thanjavur - Pattukkottai - Aranthangi - Karaikudi - Kallal - Kalayarkoil - Maravamangalam - Elayankudi - Paramakudi - Muthukulathur – Sayalkudi. Length 284 km. SH- 30: Musiri - Thuraiyur - Athur Road. Length 61 km. SH- 32 : Madurai - Turicorin Road (upgraded as a part of NH-45B). length 120 km. SH- 33 : Madurai - Thondi Road. Length 96 km. SH- 34 : Ramanathapuram - Nainarkoil - Andakudi - Ilaiyangudi - Sivagangai - Melur Road. Length 94 km. SH- 35 : Dindigul - Natham - Singampunari - Tiruppattur - Karaikudi Road. Length 94 km. SH- 36 : Dindigul - Vathalagundu - Theni (added to NH-45) - Cumbum - Kumuli Road (added to NH-220). Length 73 km. SH- 37 : Mettur - Palakkanuthu - Oddanchatram - Palani - Dharapuram - Kangeyam - Arachalur - Erode Road. Length 158 km. SH- 38 : Aruppukottai - Perunali - Sayalgudi - Kaduguchandai - Maniyur – Valinokkam. Length 79. SH- 39 : Tirunelveli - Shencottai - Quilon Road. Length 73. SH- 40 : Tiruchendur - Palayamkottai - Ambasamudram - Tenkasi - Courtallam - Shencottah Road. Length 130 km. SH- 41 : Rajapalayam - Sankarankoil - Tirunelveli Road. Length 85 km. SH- 42 : Srivilliputhur - Sivakasi - Virudhunagar - Aruppukottai - Tiruchuli - Narikudi - Parthibanoor Road. Length 197 km. SH- 43 : Tenkasi - Madurai Road (upgraded as a part of NH - 208). Length 137 km. SH- 44 : Paruvakudi - Kovilpatti - Ettayapuram - Vilathikulam - Vembar Road. Length 95 km. SH- 45 : Aralvoimozhi - Nedumangadu Road. Length 49 km. SH- 46 : Aralvoimozhi - Nagercoil - Rajakkamangalam - Colachel Road. Length 42 km. SH- 47 : Parthibanur - Kamuthi - Aruppukottai Road. Length 41. SH- 48 : Tambaram - Medavakkam - Velachery Road. Length 41 km. SH- 49 : Thiruvanmiyur - Mahabalipuram - Markanam - Pondicherry Road. Length 15 km. SH- 50 : Thirumazhisai - Sathyavedu Road. Length 147 km. SH- 51 : Korathalaiyar bridge - Puthur Road. Length 32 km. SH- 52 : Kavarapettai - Sathiavedu Road. Length 20 km. SH-54 : Chittoor - Thiruthani Road. Length 49. SH- 55 : Thomas Mount - Poonamallee - Avadi Road. Length 20 km. SH- 56 : Thiruvathiyur - Ponneri - Panchetty Road. Length 27 km. SH- 57 : Singaperumalkoil - Sriperumbadur - Thiruvallur - Redhills Road. Length 77 km. SH- 58 : Sadras - Chengalpattu - Kancheepuram - Arakonam - Thiruthani Road. Length 107 km. SH- 59 : Thiruvallam - Katpadi - Vengadagirikottai Road. Length 69 km. SH- 60 : Hogenakkal - Pennagaram - Dharmapuri - Thirupathur Road. Length 96 km. SH- 60A : Dharmapuri - Harur Road. Length 39 km. SH- 61 : Walajah - Sholinghur - Arakonam Road. Length 51 km. SH- 62 : Trichy - Thuraiyur Road. Length 31 km. SH- 63 : Thanjavur - Mannargudy - Thiruthuraipoondi - Vedaranyam - Kodiakkarai Road. Length 106 km. SH- 64 : Kumbakonam - Sirkali Road. Length 53 km. SH- 65 : Thiruvarur - Kodavasal - Kumbakonam Road. Length 37 km. SH- 66 : Kumbakonam - Mannargudi - Athirampattinam Road. Length 75 km. SH- 67 : Nagore - Nannilam - Nachiyar koil Road. Length 40 km. SH- 68 : Cuddalore - Palur - Panruti - Arasur - Tirukkovilur - Sankarapuram Road. Length 104 km. SH- 69 : Virdhachalam - Ulundurpet - Villupuram Road. Length 50 km. SH- 70 : Vridhachallam - Kammapuram - Bhuvanagiri - Parangipettai Road . length 50 km. SH- 71 : Musiri - Kulithalai - Manapparai - Pudukottai - Alangudi - Peravoorani - Sethubavachatram Road. Length 156 km. SH- 72 : Madurai - Natham Road.

Length 35 km. SH- 73 : Thirumangalam - Pallapatti Road. Length 37 km. SH- 74 : Dindigul - Guziliamparai - Karur Road. Length 80 km. SH- 75 : Palayamkottai - Kurukkuchalai - Kolathur - Vilathikulam - Nagalapuram - panthalkudi - Aruppukottai Road. Length 108 km. SH- 76 : Puliankudi - Sankarankoil - Kalugumalai - Nalatinputhur Road. Length 49 km. SH- 77 : Puliankudi - Sankarankoil - Kalugumalai - Nalatinputhur Road. Length 76 km. SH- 78 : Pollachi - Valaparai Road. Length 64 km. SH- 79 : Athur - Mallikkarai - Rasipuram - Tiruchengode - Erode Road. Length 98 km. SH- 79A : Sankagiri - Pallipalayam (Erode) Road. Length 15 km. SH- 80 : Avinashi - Annur - Mettupalayam Road. Length 42 km. SH- 81 : Gobichettipalayam - Uthukuli - Kangeyam – Dharapuram. Length 56 km. SH- 82 : Sathyamangalam - Athani - Aapakoodal - Bhavani Road. Length 52 km. SH- 83 : Palani - Dharapuram Road. Length 30 km. SH- 83A : Swastik Circle - Surampatti 4 Roads - Junction - Bullfight Circle - Old Railway Station Road. Length 4 km. SH- 84 : Erode - Unjalur - Kodumudi - Karur Road. Length 60 km. SH- 84A : Erode (Solar) - Modakurichi - Sivagiri (Vilakethi) - Muthur - Velakoil - Mulanur Road. Length 68 km. SH- 84B : Sivagiri (Vilakethi) - Anjur - Karvazhii - Chinna Dharapuram - Aravakurichi - Pallapatti - Vedasandur - Dindigul Road. Length 84 km. SH- 85 : Rayakottai (Rayakottah)- Athipalli Road. Length 35 km. SH- 86 : Omalur - Sankari - Tiruchengode - Paramathy Road. Length 81 km. SH- 86A : Ariyanoor (Salem) - Mallasamudram – Tiruchengode. Length 33 km. SH- 87 : Udumalpet - Dharapuram Road. Length 19 km. SH- 88 : Chittoor - Gudiyatham Road. Length 21 km. SH- 89 : Nanguneri - Bharathar Ovari Road. Length 35 km. SH-90 : Marthandam - Pechiparai Road. Length 20 km. SH- 91 : Parasery - Monday Market - Pudukkadai Road. Length 25 km. SH-92 : Nanguneri - Eruvadi - Valliyoor - Vijayapathi Road. Length 41 km. SH- 93 : Alwarthirunagari - Nazareth - Sathankulam - Ittamozhi - Valliyoor Road. Length 60 km. SH- 94 : Tiruchengode - Namakkal Road. Length 30 km. SH-95 : Mohanur - Namakkal - Sendamangalam - Rasipuram Road. Length 54 km. SH- 96 : Erode - Perundurai - Chennimalai - Kangeyam Road. Length 51 km. SH- 97 : Udumalpet - Palladam Road. Length 45. SH- 99 : Thirukattupalli - Sengipatti - Pattukkottai Road. Length 71 km. SH- 100 : Palayam - Bodi Road. Length 31 km. SH- 101 : Vaigai dam - Varusanadu Road. Length 35 km. SH- 102 : Palayam - Surulipatti Road. Length 20 km. SH- 104 : Chennai - Pulicat Road. Length 25 km. SH- 105 : Kanagamma Chathiram - Thakkolam Road. Length 18 km. SH- 106 : Thiruthani - Podatturpet - Pallipet Road. Length 30 km. SH- 107 : Minjur - Kattur - Thirupalaivanam Road. Length 17 km. SH- 108 : R.K.Pet - Pallipet Road. Length 16 km. SH- 109 : Pallavaram - Thuraipakkam Road. Length 10 km. SH- 110 : Tambaram - Mudichur - Sriperumbudur Road. Length 23 km. SH- 111 : Madavaram - Redhills Road. Length 9 km. SH- 112 : Thirumangalam - Mugappair Road. Length 2 km. SH- 113 : Kodambakkam - Sriperumbudur Road. Length 28 km. SH- 114 : Chennai - Ennore Road. Length 10 km. SH- 115 : Cheyyur - Vandawasi - Polur Road. Length 105 km. SH- 116 : Kanchipuram - Vandavasi Road. Length 39 km. SH- 117 : Madurantakam - Vennangupet Road. Length 37 km. SH- 118 : Bukkathurai - Uthiramerur Road. Length 31 km. SH- 119 : Km.11/8 of.C.K.A.T to Pudupattinam Road (v) Vitalapuram. Length 17 km. SH- 120 : Walajabad - Sunguvarchathiram - Keelachery Road. Length 27 km. SH- 121 : Vandalur - Mambakkam - Kelambakkam Road. Length 18 km. SH-122 : Abdullapuram - Asanampattu - Alangayam - Thirupathur Road. Length 79 km. SH- 123 : Kalavai - Valapandal Road. Length 21 km. SH-124: Ponnanai - Thiruvalam Road. Length 16 km. SH-125 : Panamadangi - Poosarivalasai Road. Length 19 km. SH- 126 : Arakkonam - Ocheri Road. Length 32 km. SH-127 : Pallikoda - Palamaneri Road. Length 28 km. SH- 128 : Sholinghur - Kaveripakkam Road. Length 30 km. SH- 129 : Arcot - Kannamangalam Road. Length 25 km. SH- 130 : Gudiyatham - Gadambur - Kailasagiri - Vanniyambadi Road. Length 41 km. SH- 131 : Barghur - Thirupathur Road. Length 24 km. SH- 132 : Kannamangalam - Arni Road. Length 17 km. SH- 133 : Polur - Chengam Road. Length 47 km. SH- 134 : Tindivanam - Marakkanam Road. Length 34 km. SH- 135 : Villupuram - Tiruvannamalai Road. Length 54 km. SH- 136 : Mailam - Pondicherry Road. Length 26 km. SH- 137 : Tirukoilur - Asanur Road. Length 39 km. SH- 138 : Jail Hills - Vellakarai - Kumalankulam Road. Length 18 km. SH- 139 : Ariyalur - Muttuvancheri - Govindaputhur Road. Length 35 km. SH- 140 : Km. 6/8 of Vridhachalam - Tholudur Road to Madhanathur Road (via) Jayakondam. Length 48 km. SH- 141 : Vridhachalam - Tholudur Road. Length 44 km. SH- 142 : Thuraiyur - Perambalur Road. Length 39 km. SH- 143 : Mathur - Thittakudi Road. Length 26 km. SH- 144 : Kodukkur - Kaduvetti Road. Length 30. SH- 145 : Aranthangi - Kattumavadi Road. Length 25 km. SH- 146 : Mannargudi - Pattukkottai - Sethubhavachatram Road. Length 51 km. SH- 147 : Kumbakonam - Karaikal Road. Length 42 km. SH- 148 : Nagore - Vettar Road.

Length 28. SH- 149 : Sembanarkoil - Nalladai Road. Length 11 km. SH- 150 : Vaitheeswarankoil - Lower Anaicut Road. Length 32 km. SH- 151 : Kilvelur - Katchanam Road. Length 20 km. SH-152 : Vadamadurai – Oddanchatram. Length 42 km. SH- 153 : Palani - Dharapuram Road (via) Alangiyam. Length 32 km. SH-154 : Vathalagundu - Peraiyur - T.Kallupatti Road. Length 58 km. SH- 155 : Ammaiyanaickanur - Vathalagundu Road. Length 18 km. SH- 156 : Kodai Ghat Road. Length 52 km. SH-157 : Perambalur - Athur Road. Length 26 km. SH- 158 : Salem Thermal Power Plant Road (via) Thangamapuripattinam. Length 5 km. SH- 159 : Pallapatti - Suramangalam Road. Length 2 km. SH- 160 : Ayothiyapattinam - Belur - Kilakkadu Road. Length 54 km. SH- 161 : Namakkal - Kanannur Road. Length 45 km. SH-162 : North Coimbatore Junction - Ramanathapûram Road - Chettipalayam Road (via) Lakshmi Mills Junction. Length 18 km. SH- 163 : Palladam - Cochin Frontier Road. Length 54 km. SH-164 : Coimbatore(Gandhipark) - Aanaikatti Road. Length 29 km. SH- 165 : Kamanaikenpalayam - Somanur - Karumathampatti - Annur. Length 38 km. SH- 166 : Palladam - Avinashi Road. Length 22 km. SH-167 : North Coimbatore Junction - Maruthamalai Road. Length 11 km. SH- 168 : Karamadai - Kariyampalayam Road. Length 15 km. SH-169 : Tirupur - Somanur Road. Length 19 km. SH-170 : Nellipalayam - Sirumugai Road. Length 17 km. SH-171 : Kovilvalli - Karappalayam Road. Length 17 km. SH- 172 : Tirupur - Padiyur(Kangeyam) Road. Length 15 km. SH- 173 : Erode - Kokarayanpet - Solasiramani - Paramathi - Velur Road. Length 50 km. SH-174 : Dharapuram - Tirupur Road. Length 44 km. SH- 175 : Bhavani - Anthiyur - Bargur - Kollegal Road. Length 69 km. SH-176 : Thoothukudi - Tiruchendur - Kanyakumari Road. Length 119 km. SH- 177 : Cheranmahadevi - Panagudi Road. Length 43 km. SH-178 : Ambasamudram - Papanasam - Upper Dam Road. Length 43 km. SH-179 : Kanyakumari - Pazhaya - Uchakadai Road. Length 71 km. SH- 180 : Colachel - Thiruvattar Road. Length 23 km. SH-181 : Marthandam - Panachamoodu Road. Length 14 km. SH-182 : Watrap - Maharajapuram - Alagapuri - Virudhunagar Road. Length 37 km. SH- 183 : Sivakasi - Alangulam Road. Length 15 km. SH-184 : Virudhunagar - Krishnapuram Road. Length 23 km. SH- 185 : Viswanatham - Venkatachalapuram Road. Length 16 km. SH- 186 : Rajapalayam - Vembakottai Road. Length 29 km. SH-187 : Sattur - Sivakasi - Kalukumalai Road, Length 38 km. SH- 188 : Salem - Yercaud Road. Length 30 km. SH-189 : Kangeyam - Muthur - Kodumudi Road. Length 39 km. SH-190 : Karumandampalayam (Erode) - Vellotamparappu - Thamaraipalayam - Othakadai - Thennilai Road. Length 43 km.

Natural Division

Traditionally, the land of Tamils has been divided into 5 major physiographic divisions - the Kurinji or mountainous region, the Mullai or forest region, the Palai or arid region, the Marudham or the fertile plains and the Neidhal or coastal region.

Administration

The Governor is the *constitutional head of the state* while the Chief minister is the *head of the government* and heads the council of ministers. The Chief Justice of the Madras High Court is the *head of the judiciary*. Tamil Nadu State has a population of 7,21,38,95 as per Census 2011 and covers an area of 130,058 km². The major administrative units of the state constitutes 32 Districts, 76 Revenue divisions, 220 Taluks, 10 Municipal corporations, 125 Municipalities, 385 Panchayat unions (Blocks), 529 Town panchayats and 12,524 Village panchayats. The total number of seats in the House of the people to be allocated to the State of Tamil Nadu as Thirty Nine (39): of which, seven (7) seats, shall be reserved for the Scheduled Castes and total number of seats to be assigned to the Legislative Assembly of the State as Two Hundred Thirty Four (234)': of which, Forty four (44) seats shall be reserved for the Scheduled Castes and Two (2) seats for the Scheduled Tribes.

Gram panchayat

Panchayati Raj is a system of governance in which gram (village) panchayats are the basic units of administration. It has three levels: village, block and district. Mahatma Gandhi advocated *Panchayati Raj*, a decentralized form of Government where each village is responsible for its own affairs, as the foundation of India's political system. State governments adopted this during 1950s and 60s as laws were passed to establish Panchayats in various states. Through the 73rd Amendment in 1992 on April 23, 1993 the Institution of Panchayati Raj was accorded the Constitutional status. There are 12617 Gram Panchayat in the state.

Education

Education in Tamilnadu now a days is vey has been gradually decreasing its effect day-by-day. Rural means living in or characteristic of farming or country life. The literacy rate in Tamilnadu is very decent compared to other states of India. As per 2001 census we stand at 11th position with a literacy rate of 77.13. Education in Tamilnadu rural areas is rarely considered as an asset in the state. In order to provide a good quality of education in rural areas, public schools in Tamilnadu have to be established not only establishment but also proper functioning of school. Government of TN has to appoint a particular officer only to supervise the functioning of the school. There are about 30,120 pre-primary and primary schools, 5,608 middle schools, 3,203 high schools, and 2,165 higher secondary school (junior colleges) in the state.

Medical

Tamil Nadu is very aware of the seriousness of making proper medical care available for its people and has taken several steps to ensure 'Health for All'. The medical care offered can be grouped under government provided facilities and private facilities including alternative Indian medicine. There are 425 special hospitals, 1,797 primary health centres, 542 dispensaries and special hospitals, and 8,681 sub-health centers in the state. List of important Hospitals : Adiparasakthi Hospital; Advanced Nuclear Medicine Research Institute, Chennai; Agarwal Eye Hospital - Ophthalmic Care and Research Center ; Apollo Speciality Hospitals, Chennai ; Appasamy Hospitals, Chennai ; Aravind Eye Hospital ; Aravind Hospitals ; Arun Hospital, Pollachi ; Asian Regional Center For Hip Resurfacing ; Billroth Hospital ; Chellamuthu Trust ; Chennai Hospitals ; Chettinad Health City, Kelambakkam, Tamilnadu ; Christian Medical College & Hospital, Vellore ; Coimbatore Cancer Foundation; CSR Memorial Hospital ; Dr. Mohan's Diabetes Specialities Centre, Chennai, vellore & Coimbatore ; Devadoss Multispeciality Hospitals, Madurai ; Department of Orthopaedic Surgery, Malar Hospitals ; Dr. Gautham's Neuro Centre ; Dr. Jeyasekharan Medical Trust and Nursing Home ; Eljay-All About Hearing, Purasawakkam, Chennai ; Ess Vee Hospital, Ambattur, Chennai; Eye Foundation ; Fortis Malar Hospital ; Frontier Lifeline & Dr. K.M. Cherian Heart Foundation ; Galaxy Hospital, Tirunelveli ; Ganga Hospital ; GEM Hospital ; Getwell Hospital, Tirunelveli ; Girishwari Hospitals Pvt Ltd, Theynampet ; GKNM Hospital ; Global Hospitals & Health City - Tertiary Care Centre ; Global Hospitals Group Global Hospitals & Health City, Chennai ; Global Hospitals Group, Perumbakkam, Chennai, Tamilnadu ; Grace Speech and Hearing, Chennai, Tamilnadu ; Grace Speech and Hearing, Mandaveli, Chennai ; Gynaecologists Chennai ; Hande Hospital - Plastic and Cosmetic Surgery Centre ; Harvey Heart Hospital - Cardiac Surgery and Ancillary Services ; Hearing Centre, Duraiswamy Reddy St, Near Deepam Hospital, Tambaram, Chennai ; Hearing Centre, Opp. Sidney Hospital, Nanganallur, Chennai ; Institute of Cardio-Vascular Diseases, The Madras Medical Mission ; Iswarya Fertility Centre ; Jayasakthi Nursing Home, Naduveerapatu, Cuddalore District ; Jebe Hospital, Tirunelveli ; Jeyan hospital – madurai ; Jeyalakshmi Heart Centre ; Kartheek Hospital, Tirunelveli ; Kaveri Medical Center ; KG Hospital ; Kongunadu Hospital ; Kovai Medical Center and Hospital (KMCH) ; Krishna Hospital ; Krishna Hospital, Tirunelveli ; Lasik Centre ; Lifeline Hospitals, Perungudi, Chennai ; Lotus Eye Hospital ; Madras Medical Mission ; Madurai Eye Hospital ; Malgudi Rural Hospital, Palani ; Meenakshi Mission Hospital and Research Centre Madurai ; Mohan Rau Memorial Hospital ; MV Hospital ; Navodhaya Siddha Hospital ; NG Hospital ; Nilgiri Ayurvedic Resort ; Nirmala Hospital, Karungal, Kanyakumari District ; NM Hospital ; Parvathy Hospital Chromepet Chennai ; Prakash Ayurvedic Nethralaya & Panchakarma Kendra ; PSG Hospitals ; Pushpalatha Hospital, Tirunelveli ; Rex Ortho Hospital ; Richmond Hospital ; RVS Hospital, Sulur ; Sankara Eye Society ; Sankara Nethralaya, Chennai ; Sankara Netralaya ; Shifa Hospital, Tirunelveli ; Sir Ivan Stedeford Hospital, Ambattur, Chennai ; SIVA Meds, Pollachi ; Sooriya Hospital - Vadapalani-Chennai ; Sri Devi Hospital - Anna Nagar ; Sri Devi Speciality – Koyambedu ; Sri Ramachandra Medical College and Research Institute ; Sri Ramakrishna Hospital ; SriRam Hospital ; Sri Saran Medical Center, Tirupur ; SRM General Hospital-Potheri-Tamil Nadu ; Stanley Hospital, Chennai ; Swami Sivananda Charitable Hospital ; Tarun Clinic, Mettur Dam ; The Madras Medical Mission ; Thyroid Clinic ; Trauma Care Consortium ; Tuberculosis Research Center ; Vallalar Hospital ; Vasan Eye Care - Tamil Nadu ; VeeCare Hospital, Chennai, Tamilnadu ; Vijaya Hospital, Chennai ; Vinayaka Mission Hospital ;YRG Care.

Bank

There are nearly 5,000 commercial bank offices in the state. Of these more than one third of the offices are in rural areas with the remaining offices being in semi-urban and urban metropolitan areas. State Bank of India 545, Associates of State Bank of India 103, Nationalized Banks 2541, Foreign Banks 11, Regional Rural Banks 208, Other Schedule Banks 876.

Scheduled Castes

The total population of Tamil Nadu, as per the 2001

Census is 62,405,679. Of this, 11,857,504 (19 per cent) are Scheduled Castes (SCs). The SC population constitutes 7.1 per cent of the country's SC population. Seventy-six (76) SCs have been notified in Tamil Nadu by the Scheduled Castes and Scheduled Tribes Order (Amendment) Act, 1976. Of these, fifteen SCs namely, Ayyanavar, Bharatar, Kakkalan, Kavara, Kootan, Mannan, Padannan, Panan, Paravan, Pathiyan, Thandan, Vannan, Vetan and Vettuvan have been notified with area restriction in Kanniyakumari district and Shencottah taluk of Tirunelveli district. Kanakkan have been notified in Nilgiri district only. Out of 76 SCs, two SCs i.e., Kakkalan and Padannan have not reported population in 2001 Census.

The growth rate of SC population in the decade 1991-2001 at 10.7 per cent is lower in comparison to the overall growth rate of 11.7 per cent of the state. Among major SCs, Paraiyan have recorded the highest growth rate of 38.6 per cent, followed by Arunthathiyar (33.2 per cent) and Pallan (18.5 per cent) during 1991-2001.

Population- Size and Distribution (SC)

Out of 76 SCs, five SCs Adi Dravida, Pallan, Paraiyan, Chakkiliyan and Arunthathiyar together constitute 93.5 per cent of the SC population of the state. Adi Dravida are numerically the largest SCs with a population of 5,402,755, constituting 45.6 per cent of the state SC population. They are followed by Pallan 2,272,265 (19.2 per cent), Paraiyan 1,860,519 (15.7 per cent), Chakkiliyan 777,139 (6.6 per cent) and Arunthathiyar 771,659 (6.5 per cent). Thirty five (35) SCs have reported population below one thousand. Among the districts Thiruvarur has the highest proportion of SC population to its total population (32.4 per cent) while Kanyakumari has the lowest (4 per cent).

As per 2001 Census, 70.1 per cent of them are living in the rural areas and 29.9 per cent in the urban areas of the state. Among the major SCs, Pallan have the highest (76 per cent) rural population, followed by Paraiyan (73.1 per cent), Adi Darvida (69.4 per cent), Chakkiliyan (67.9 per cent) and Arunthathiyar (64.4 per cent).

Sex ratio (SC)

The overall sex ratio of the SC population in Tamil Nadu is 999 females per 1000 males, which is higher than the national average of 936 for the SC population in 2001. The sex ratio of SC population has registered improvement over 978 reported in 1991 Census. Among the districts the highest sex ratio (1059), is recorded in Tirunelveli district and the lowest in Salem district (947). At the individual caste level, all the major SCs, except Pallan and Paraiyan, have registered overall lower sex ratio as compared to the state average. The Statement below shows sex ratio and child sex ratio (0-6) of the SC population at the national, state and the numerically largest five SCs in 2001 Census:

Sex Ratio

Age Groups	*All SCs (India)*	*All SCs (Tamil Nadu)*	*Adi Dravida*	Pallan	Paraiyan	Chakkiliyan	Arunthathiyar
All Ages	936	999	992	1013	1015	987	972
0-6	938	959	962	952	969	954	928

As may be seen from the Statement above, the child sex ratio (0-6) among SC population of Tamil Nadu is also higher than the national SC population in the corresponding age group. In case of child sex ratio, the position of Paraiyan and Adi Dravida is even better than the rest of state SC population. However, Arunthathiyar, which is comparatively an urbanized SC community, has recorded a lower child sex ratio of 928.

Literacy and educational level (SC)

Literacy and level of education are two basic indicators of the level of development achieved by a group/ society. Literacy results in more awareness besides contributing to the overall improvement of health, hygiene and other social conditions. According to 2001 Census, percentage of SC literate persons (those who can read and write with understanding) aged 7 years and above is 63.2 per cent, which is lower than 73.5 per cent reported for the state as a whole. The literacy data show that the SC population of the state has made significant improvement during the decade 1991-2001. The literacy rate, which was 46.7 per cent in 1991, has increased by 16.5 percentage points in 2001.

Among the major SCs, Paraiyan are reported to have the highest literacy rate of 65.9 per cent, followed by Adi Dravida (65.3 per cent), Pallan (65 per cent), Arunthathiyar (53.7 per cent) and Chakkiliyan (50.9 per cent). The female literacy rate of 53 per cent among SC population is lower as compared to 64.4 per cent among females of the state. As in literacy rate, the highest and lowest female literacy rate of 55.4 per cent and 40.8 per cent have also been recorded among Adi Dravida and Chakkiliyan.

Educational levels attained by major SCs

Name of SC	Literate without educational level	Below primary	Primary	Middle	Matric/ Secondary/ Higher Secondary Intermediate etc.	Technical & Non-technical diploma	Graduate & above
All SCs	9.1	19.9	31.9	18.4	17.4	0.6	2.7
Adi Dravida	6.6	19.0	31.7	19.8	19.2	0.6	3.0
Pallan	10.7	19.3	31.9	17.7	16.5	0.7	3.0
Paraiyan	11.2	19.4	31.3	18.0	16.8	0.6	2.8
Chakkiliyan	12.7	25.7	34.1	15.5	10.8	0.3	0.9
Arunthathiyar	10.5	23.6	34.0	16.1	13.5	0.5	0.7

Out of the total literates, 29 per cent are literates either without any educational level or have attained below Primary level. The literates, who have attained education up to Primary and Middle levels, constitute 31.9 per cent and 18.4 per cent respectively. 17.4 per cent are having educational level up to Matric/Higher Secondary etc. levels, implying that every 6th SC literate is a Matriculate. Literates with educational level of Graduation and above are 2.7 per cent. Individually, Adi Dravida and Pallan (3 per cent each) have highest percentage of Graduation and above educational levels.

From the educational level table, it also emerges that the drop out starts after the Primarily level and it increases with each subsequent level of education.

Population in the age group 5-14 years are the potential students. 83.1 per cent of the SC population in this age group is attending various educational institutions. At the individual caste level, Adi Dravida, Pallan and Paraiyan have more percentage of school going children than the overall state SC population.

Economic activity

Work Participation Rate (WPR) (SC)

The work participation rate (WPR) is the percentage of workers to the total population. The WPR among SC population is 48.1 per cent in 2001, which is higher than 44.7 per cent for the state population as a whole. The WPR of SC population however, has declined marginally, if compared to 48.4 per cent reported in 1991 Census. The male WPR has been 55.8 per cent and female WPR 40.3 per cent at 2001 Census.

At individual caste level, the WPR varies from the highest 55.4 per cent among Chakkiliyan to the lowest 44.4 per cent among Adi Dravida. Adi Dravida has also recorded the lowest female WPR of 35.1 per cent.

Category of Workers (SC)

There has been a decline in the SC main workers from 94.7 per cent in 1991 to 79.0 per cent in 2001 Census. This, in turn, has resulted in corresponding increase in the marginal workers from 5.3 per cent in 1991 to 21 per cent in 2001. Out of total workers, 'agricultural labourers' constitute 58.5 per cent, which is higher than 12.9 percentage points when compared to 45.6 per cent registered at national level for SC population. 'Other workers' account for 29 per cent. Only 10.2 per cent workers have been returned as 'cultivators'; remaining 2.3 per cent are workers in 'household industry'. Thus, there is a structural change in the category of workers among SC population; the workers engaged in agricultural activities (cultivators and agricultural labourers) constitute 68.7 per cent of the total work force against 79.7 per cent recorded in 1991 Census.

At the individual caste level, except Adi Dravida (56.7 per cent), other SCs have a higher percentage of workers in the category of 'agricultural labourers' than recorded for SC population at the state level (58.5 per cent).

Marital status (SC)

Marital status is one of the important determinants of fertility and growth of a population. The 2001 Census data on marital status shows that 47.2 per cent persons among the SCs of Tamil Nadu are 'never married'. The 'currently married' constitute 46.7 per cent while 5.5 per cent are 'widowed'. Only 0.5 per cent are 'divorced and separated'.

Majority of girls and boys among SCs in Tamil Nadu are getting married after attaining the legal age of marriage. Marriages of SC girls below 18 years (1.9 per cent) are lower than that recorded among SC population at national level (2.8 per cent). Similarly, the incidence of marriage of boys below 21 years at 1.4 per cent is significantly lower than 3.1 per cent aggregated at national level for SC population.

The mean number of children ever born per ever married SC women of all ages as well as 45-49 years age group are 2.5 and 3.2 respectively, which are lower than the corresponding figures of 3.2 and 4.2 for SC population aggregated at national level.

Religion (SC)

The SCs of the state are predominantly Hindus. Out of total 11,857,504 SC population of the state, only 840 are Buddhists and 837 are Sikhs, the remaining are all Hindus as per 2001 Census.

Scheduled Tribes

The total population of Tamil Nadu, as per the 2001 Census is 62,405,679. Of this, 651,321 (1 per cent) are Scheduled Tribes (STs). Thirty six (36) STs have been notified in Tamil Nadu by the Scheduled Castes and Scheduled Tribes Order (Amendment) Act, 1976. Of the STs, six have been notified with area restriction. These are Malayali, Kurumbas, Kanikaran, Kammara, Kota and Toda. Malayali have been notified in Dharmapuri, Vellore, Tiruvannamalai, Pudukkottai, Salem, Namakkal, Villupuram, Cuddalore, Tiruchirappalli, Karur and Perambalur districts, Kurumbas in Nilgiri district, Kanikaran in Kanniyakumari district and Shencottah taluk of Tirunelveli district. Kammara, Kota and Toda have been notified through out the state except Kanniyakumari district and Shencottah taluk of Tirunelveli district.

The growth rate of ST population in the decade 1991-2001 at 13.4 per cent is higher than the overall growth rate of 11.7 per cent of the state. As per the 2001 Census, among the numerically large STs, Kurumans have reported the highest growth rate of 43 per cent, followed by Malayali (24.2 per cent), Irular (12.1 per cent) and Kattunayakan (5.8 per cent).

Population- Size and Distribution (ST)

Of the STs, Malayali, Irular, Kattunayakan, Kurumans and Kondareddis together constitute 85.3 per cent of the ST population of the state. Malayali are the largest ST with a population of 310,042, constituting 47.6 per cent of the state ST population. They are followed by Irular, numbering 155,606 (23.9 per cent), Kattunayakan 45,227 (6.9 per cent), Kurumans 24,963 (3.8 per cent) and Kondareddis 19,653 (3 per cent). Fourteen (14) STs have returned population below one thousand in 2001 Census.

Expectedly STs are primarily residing in the rural areas and only 15.4 per cent are in the urban areas of the state. Among major STs, Malayali have the highest (98.3 per cent) rural population, followed by Irular (87 per cent), Kurumans (78.9 per cent) and Kondareddis (71.7 per cent). On the other hand, Kattunayakan, the third largest ST population have reported as much as 61.6 per cent urban population. Salem, Tiruvannamalai, Viluppuram, Vellore, Dharmapuri and Namakkal are major ST populated districts of the state as these six districts account for 64 per cent of the ST population of the state.

Sex ratio (ST)

The overall sex ratio of the ST population in Tamil Nadu is 980 females per 1000 males, which has recorded improvement from 960 in 1991 Census. Among the district, Thanavur has recorded the highest sex ratio of the ST population (1054) and Perambalur the lowest (936). The Statement below shows sex ratio and child sex ratio (0-6) of the ST population at the national, state and numerically the largest five STs in 2001 Census:

Sex Ratio (ST)

Age Groups	*All STs (India)*	*All*	*STs (Tamil Nadu)*	*Malayali*	*Irular Kattunayakan*	*Kurumans*	*Kondareddis*
All Ages	978	980	966	996	1012	953	984
0-6	973	945	932	984	923	872	859

As may be seen from the Statement, the overall sex ratio of ST population in Tamil Nadu is almost equal to the sex ratio of ST population of the country. But in case of child sex ratio (0-6), it is less by 28 points than that of ST population aggregated at the national level. At the individual tribe level, all major STs, except Irular, have lower sex ratio in 0-6 age-group populations, as compared to the state ST population. Among these Kondareddis and Kurumans child sex ratio is alarmingly low. Literacy and educational level

Literacy and level of education are two basic indicators of the level of development achieved by a group/ society as literacy results in more awareness besides contributing to the overall improvement of health, hygiene and other social conditions. According to 2001 Census, percentage of ST literate (those who can read and write with understanding) persons aged 7 years and above is 41.5 per cent in the state, which is lower than 73.5 per cent reported for the state as a whole. The literacy rate (41.5 per cent) has however increased from 27.9 per cent recorded in 1991 Census.

Among the major STs, Kondareddis are reported to have the highest 78.2 per cent literacy rate, followed by Kurumans (61.4 per cent), Kattunayakan (54.7 per cent), Malayali (37.4 per cent) and Irular (34.3 per cent). The female literacy rate of 32.8 per cent among ST population is lower than 64.4 per cent registered among total female population of the state. As in literacy rate, the highest and lowest female literacy rate of 68.9 per cent and 27.1 per cent are also recorded among Kondareddis and Irular.

Educational levels attained by Major STs

Name of ST	*Literate without educational level*	*Below primary*	*Primary*	*Middle*	*Matric/ Secondary/ Higher Secondary Intermediate etc.*	*Technical & Non-technical diploma*	*Graduate & above*
All STs 10.3	26.3	33.3	14.7	14.7	12.8	0.6	1.8
Malayali	10.6	27.6	35.2	14.2	10.8	0.5	0.9
Irular	12.5	31.4	33.5	13.6	8.1	0.3	0.5
Kattunayakan	10.6	23.9	31.0	16.5	14.7	0.6	2.6
Kurumans	6.1	19.3	31.7	17.7	20.1	1.5	3.6
Kondareddis	3.9	13.0	28.1	16.4	28.2	2.1	8.3

Out of the total literates, 36.6 per cent are either literates without any educational level or have attained below Primary level. The literates, who have attained education up to Primary and Middle levels, constitute 33.3 per cent and 14.7 per cent respectively. 12.8 per cent are having educational level up to Matric/Higher Secondary levels, implying that every 8th ST literate is a Matriculate. Literates with educational level of Graduation and above are 1.8 per cent. Individually, Kondareddis (8.3 per cent) have the highest percentage of Graduation and above educational level.

From the educational level table, it also emerges that the drop out starts after the Primarily level and it increases with each subsequent level of education.

Population in the age group 5-14 years are the potential students. 61.7 per cent of the ST population in this age group is attending various educational institutions Economic activity Work Participation Rate (WPR)

Work Participation Rate (WPR) (ST)

The work participation rate (WPR) is the percentage of workers to the total population. The WPR among the ST population at 2001 Census is 54.9 per cent, which is higher than that for state population as a whole (44.7 per cent) as well as the state SC population (48.1 per cent). The WPR of ST population has increased if compared to 52.1 per cent recorded at 1991 Census.The WPR at 60.1 per cent for ST males is higher than 49.5 per cent reported among ST females at 2001 Census.

At individual tribe level, the WPR varies from 59.5 per cent among Malayali to 40.5 per cent among Kattunayakan. The trend is same in case of female WPR. Malayali have the highest 57.7 per cent female WPR.

Category of Workers (ST)

There has been a decline in the ST main workers from 94.2 per cent at 1991 Census to 81.3 per cent at 2001 Census. This, in turn, has resulted in corresponding increase in the marginal workers from 5.8 per cent in 1991 to 18.7 percent in 2001. Out of total workers, 'agricultural labourers' constitute 37.8 per cent, which is similar to the national average of 36.9 per cent for ST population. 'Cultivators' account for 36.3 per cent and only 23.6 per cent has been returned as 'other workers'. Remaining 2.4 per cent have been workers in 'household industry'. Thus, there is a change in agriculture related economic activities; the workers engaged in agricultural activities (cultivators and agricultural labourers) constitute 74.1 per cent of the total workers against 81.8 per cent recorded at 1991 Census.

At the individual tribe level, the highest percentage of 'agricultural labourers' (58.2 per cent) is recorded among Irular; 'cultivators' (58.8 per cent) among

Malayali, 'other workers' (68.1 per cent) among Kattunayakan and 'household industry' (7.4 per cent) among Kondareddis.

Marital status (ST)

Marital status is one of the important determinants of fertility and growth of a population. The 2001 Census data on marital status show that 44.6 per cent persons among the STs of Tamil Nadu are 'never married'. The 'currently married' constitute 50.1 per cent while 4.8 per cent are 'widowed'. Only 0.5 per cent are 'divorced and separated'.

Majority of girls and boys among STs in Tamil Nadu are getting married after attaining the legal age of marriage. Marriages of ST girls below 18 years (2.7 per cent) are higher than that recorded among ST population at national level (2.1 per cent). On the other hand, the incidence of marriage of boys below 21 years at 2.6 per cent is almost equal to 2.8 per cent aggregated at national level for ST population.

The mean number of children ever born per ever married ST women of all ages as well as 45-49 years age group are 2.2 and 2.8 respectively, which are lower than that of 3.2 and 4.1 for ST population at national level.

Religion (ST)

Majority of the ST population of the state are Hindus (99.2 per cent). There are only 3,497 (0.5 per cent) Christians and 453 (0.1 per cent) Muslims ST populations in the state.

Agriculture

Agriculture is the major occupation in Tamilnadu. The total cultivated area in the State was 58.15 lakhs hectares in 2007-08. The principal food crops include paddy, millets and pulses. Commercial crops include sugarcane, cotton, sunflower, coconut, cashew, chillies, gingelly and groundnut. Plantation crops are tea, coffee, cardamom and rubber. Major forest produces are timber, sandalwood, pulp wood and fuel wood. Tamilnadu occupies a premier position in the production and extensive application of bio-fertilizers. Efforts are on to improve farming technologies so as to increase yields in the low rainfall areas of the State. Annual foodgrains production in the year 2007-08 was 65.81 lakhs Mt.

Irrigation

Important irrigation schemes and modernization of existing Periyar Vaigai System, Palar Basin System and Parambikhulam - Aliyar System besides the minor system in Vellar, Pennayar, Araniyar Amaravathi, Chithar basins totalling, an extent of six lakh acres of existing ayacut in Tamil Nadu have been benefited by implementing the 'System Improvement and Farmers Turnover Projects' executed with assistance from World Bank. The World Bank has also approved Rs 2,547 crores for the Irrigated Agriculture Modernisation and Water Bodies Restoration Management Project. The project covers about 6,17 lakh ha. In 63 selected sub-basins throughout the state. Nine irrigation projects which were just started and going on a slow progress have been speeded up with adequate found and guidance for early completion. The major irrigation system covering one-third of irrigated extent in Tamil Nadu, namely tank irrigation system has been given due regard for development under WRCP and 620 tanks maintained by public workers Department falling under Palar, viligai and Tamaraparani Basins have been taken up for rehabilitation and improvement. This project is nearing completion to the maximum satisfaction of the farmers. This State has become the pioneer State to implement the system of 'River basin management' by an individual body consisting of officials and farmers besides various representatives of the basin.

Religion

Distribution of Religion by Sex with Percentage of Total Population (State)

Religion	*T/R/U*	*Persons*	*Males*	*Females*	*%age*
Total	Total	62,405,679	31,400,909	31,004,770	100.00
Population	Rural	34,921,681	17,531,494	17,390,187	100.00
	Urban	27,483,998	13,869,415	13,614,583	100.00
Hindu	Total	54,937,144	27,705,978	27,231,166	88.03
	Rural	32,255,815	16,227,352	16,028,463	92.37
	Urban	22,681,329	11,478,626	11,202,703	82.53
Muslim	Total	3,466,380	1,716,402	1,749,978	5.55
	Rural	944,034	454,683	489,351	2.70
	Urban	2,522,346	1,261,719	1,260,627	9.18
Christian	Total	3,780,981	1,861,981	1,919,000	6.06
	Rural	1,648,185	810,754	837,431	4.72
	Urban	2,132,796	1,051,227	1,081,569	7.76
Sikh	Total	50,325	28,033	22,292	0.08
	Rural	20,635	11,337	9,298	0.06
	Urban	29,690	16,696	12,994	0.11
Buddhist	Total	21,787	11,368	10,419	0.03
	Rural	7,894	4,157	3,737	0.02
	Urban	13,893	7,211	6,682	0.05

Religion	T/R/U	Persons	Males	Females	%age
Jain	Total	82,970	42,914	40,056	0.13
	Rural	10,908	5,464	5,444	0.03
	Urban	72,062	37,450	34,612	0.26
Other	Total	7,249	3,851	3,398	0.01
Religions	Rural	1,924	1,065	859	0.01
	Urban	5,325	2,786	2,539	0.02
Religion	Total	58,843	30,382	28,461	0.09
Not Stated	Rural	32,286	16,682	15,604	0.09
	Urban	26,557	13,700	12,857	0.10

Language and Literature

Tamil Nadu is an ancient Dravidian civilization, with its own traditions of history and culture. The official language spoken in the state is Tamil, a language great influenced by its rich and colourful past.

Tamil is the oldest living language in the world (over 2000 years old). It has a wealth of literature and recorded history in Tamil. Tamil language has a history which can be traced back to the age of the Tolkapiyam, the Tamil Grammar text generally ascribed to 500 B.C. Sangam literature of the Tamils dates back to500 B.C. The Tamils have always been a hospitable race, known for their generous nature.

Concerted efforts have been made over the last decade or so to preserve the purity and identity of the Tamil language. More recently, there has been a steady stream of people migrating into the state from all parts of India, particularly to the State's urban centers, making Tamil Nadu truly cosmopolitan in its composition. Today one can hear several languages such as Telgu, Malayalam, Hindi and other Indian languages being spoken in the state. Above all, the foreign visitor need have no fear of not being understood as English is spoken with considerable fluency in most parts of the state.

Tamil Literature

The period of the three academies of Tamil covering a period of roughly 1700 years upto 250 A.D. This is considered to be the Golden Age of Tamil Literature. The literature, predominantly poetry is fresh, born out of fertile imagination takes the briefest of forms to present a picturesque panorama of the lives and times. War and love happen to be the subject matter. The serenity and chastity in love amply match nobility and greatness in war. What begins as a supreme effort of the most civilized people proceeds through steady progress to be mercilessly ended by the heartless sides of the rising oceanswhich are reported to have swallowed thousands of miles of the abode of this great people. However zealous kings and patriotic poets have preserved whatever was possible to the benefit of the succeeding generations.

Sangam Maruvia Kaalam

This period witnesses the growth of Buddhism and Jainism in the now shrinked Tamil country. Consequently the Northern concepts and ways of life start stamping their imprints on the Tamil Community. The origin charm of the early Tamil Literature starts wearing Puram costumes. First long poem 'Sillpathi Karam'. This epic is to remain unparalled and unexcelled in conception and grandeur till the advent of the Kamba Ramayana in the 9th century A.D. Besides this, Thirukkural which is certainly more ancient than silappadigaram and some of the other works on ethical way of life were written during this period.

The Dark age or the Kalabhra Interregnum The Dark age or the Kalabhra Interregnum

While the march of the mighty oceans have destroyed the early Tamils and their way of life, the Kalabhra invasion during 250 A.D. decidely alters the shape of Tamil literature and Tamil way of life. Kalabharas, having been the sons of the Kannada soil did not have the necessary love of Tamil to ensure its growth. Instead the pronounced Jainest fanatism of these rulers have more or less destroyed the acts and literature of the Tamil people to the point of extinction.

However various treatises on Poetics began to be written along with some of the ethical works which are grouped in Pathinenkil Kanakku. The most illustrious flower of the Dark Ages is probably the 'Muthollayiram' 900 songs each on the Chera, Chola and the Pandya Kings.

Bakthi or The Pallava Period

The severe austerity in matters practised by the Kalabrahs a band of alien waranders who overran the Pandiya Kingdom in the 3rd century have suppressed all vestiges of Tamil act art and letters. The valuable contributions like music, dance and drama of the Sangham period were suppressed. This strangling sway had practically obliterated the Tamil way of life of the legendary past. Most of the literary works of the Sangaham period might have been destroyed.

The supuression of the alien Kalabhra clan by Pandiyan Kadumkon by the end of the 6th century had helped a revival of the ancient orthodox religions of the land. Great spiritual preception both in Saivism and Vaishnavism towed the entire Tamil country, sanchtifying the temples by their songs, and directing the people, the masses and the elite, towards a higher and godly way of life. The sway of these preceptions held sway for about 13 centuries. This is called the Bakthi movement. The literature of this period reflects the ennobling qualities which have come to characterise the arts, architecture etc. The simplesongs of the Bakthi movement in elegant musical Tamil won over all the people high and low.

Chola period or the Epic Period

The culmination of the Bakthi Movement can be found in the materialisation of the Chola Empire. A new golden era of political supremacy which was synonynous with religous culture and temple buildings was thus ushered in.

Greatest of Tamil Epics Kamba Ramayanam was born in this period. The quintessance of the entire Tamil culture of the preceding years, the broad span of literary excellence which have been evolving through the millenia, the peak of religious fevour which has been embracing people in all their walks of life and all that is noble in the land and life of the Tamil as a people find their happy fusion and exemplary delineation in Kamba Ramayanam. Other epics preceding and following this great poet's pale into insignificance by compassion.

Another noble off spring of this period is Periapuranam. The work is in a sense a national epic of the Tamil people, because it treats of the lives of the Saints who lived in all the different parts of Tamilnadu, and belonged to all classes of society, men and women, high and low, educated an uneducated. We have among the saints princes from all the ruling dynasties of the land, as well as men from the harijan classes; but they are all equal in the devotion and service to God and godlymen. Sekkilar transcends the limits of time and space and comprises within the fold of his spiritual democracy even people who lived earlier and who will be living later, in all the distant climes. New literary forms begin to take shape during this period which were going to keep the literary tradition alive for many more centuries to come.

Nayakkar Period

The History of Tamil Literature during the Chola period has recorded glorious achievements. The Pandya period which follows does not exhibit such literary excellence mainly because of the political instability. The end of the 13th and the begining of the 14th century witness the capturing of power by the Mohammedians. For about the next two hundred years, until the spread of the Vijayanagara empire in the deep south practically there was no literary creations but for a few commentaries on Sangam literature including Silappadhikaram and Thirukkural. Philosophical treatises on Saiva Religion were also written in poetry. These were known as the 'Sithantha Sastirangal'.

Although 'epic' literature of the grand scale did not appear in the literary horizon several glittering stars started apearing and adorning the field of Tamil Literature, known as 'Small Prabandas' or 'Sitrilakkiyangal'. These new literary works varied in their content and structure from the earlier works. Some scholars opine that the literature of this period reflects the lives of thecommon people much more than those of the previous periods. The love of Tamil language in an alien political atmosphere can be very much seen in some excellent poets whose metre and rhythm have enriched our language. In fact the grand old musical tradition can be said to have been carefuly guarded, and be said to have been carefully guarded, and handed over to the succeeding generation by them. Mention must be made of Arunagirinathar and his Thiruppugazh (The Diving greatnes) and of Kumaragurupara Swamigal whose musical stanzas are still being sung in Temples with vigour and devotion.

The range and variety of the Prabandas of the period covering nearly 350 years are quite extensive and astounding. Though same repetitions mar the guarded literary landscape, much of trendsetting literature is born during this long period. Common people and their way of life including their harmless pursuits and their exemplary contentedness find happy expression in these works. The simple lives and the special featuers of the hill tribes (Kuraver) are recorded in the lovely lyrics of the Kuravanji literature.

The common features of the agravian society are found in the delightful pages of Pallu literature. March of war and deeds of valour form the basis of the Bharani Literature which contains myths and the supernatural elegantly interwoven in musical and rhythmic verses. A variety of verses speaking of war, love, humour, valour, season, charm etc. are cleverly compiled in Kalambagam poetry. The stages of a child's growth upto 3 years forms the subject matter of 'Pillai thamil' poetry which generally adopts God and greatmen as the 'children' to be sung. The puranic fevour, religious charms and astounding imagination found in these poems are unmatched by any poetry of the world literature. A damsel sending even an inanimate object to present her case to her lover forms the subject matter of 'Thoudhu'. It is quite common to see even birds and animals praised to dizzy heights in these resounding verses which succeed in portraying the lyrical longings of the love born lady. The different emotions stirred at the sight of a Grand Procession taken in honour of an Exemplary individual are beautifully presented in ULA. Seven stages of a girl's growth into womanhood and the corresponding feelings of awe, infactuation, unfulfilled love and longing associated with their behavioural patterns are studied in minute detail in the Ulas.

Distribution of Language

		Persons	*Males*	*Females*
Assamese	Total	509	365	144
	Rural	99	74	25
	Urban	410	291	119
Bengali	Total	5,574	3,291	2,283
	Rural	1,051	682	369
	Urban	4,523	2,609	1,914
Gujarati	Total	244,921	124,207	120,714
	Rural	24,006	12,168	11,838
	Urban	220,915	112,039	108,876
Hindi	Total	159,948	87,691	72,257
	Rural	22,625	13,059	9,566
	Urban	137,323	74,632	62,691
Kannada	Total	1,208,296	611,200	597,096
	Rural	818,957	414,007	404,950
	Urban	389,339	197,193	192,146
Kashmiri	Total	193	118	75
	Rural	15	11	4
	Urban	178	107	71
Konkani	Total	6,303	3,127	3,176
	Rural	409	211	198
	Urban	5,894	2,916	2,978
Malayalam	Total	661,137	343,671	317,466
	Rural	221,403	111,648	109,755
	Urban	439,734	232,023	207,711
Manipuri	Total	156	126	30
	Rural	70	56	14
	Urban	86	70	16
Marathi	Total	70,045	35,931	34,114
	Rural	19,788	10,011	9,777
	Urban	50,257	25,920	24,337
Nepali	Total	3,627	2,324	1,303
	Rural	977	650	327
	Urban	2,650	1,674	976
Oriya	Total	2,660	2,073	587
	Rural	581	433	148
	Urban	2,079	1,640	439
Punjabi	Total	5,536	3,005	2,531
	Rural	637	376	261
	Urban	4,899	2,629	2,270
Sanskrit	Total	169	94	75
	Rural	65	37	28
	Urban	104	57	47
Sindhi	Total	8,257	4,154	4,103
	Rural	43	24	19
	Urban	8,214	4,130	4,084
Tamil	Total	48,434,744	24,520,782	23,913,962
	Rural	32,972,931	16,639,834	16,333,097
	Urban	15,461,813	7,880,948	7,580,865
Telugu	Total	3,975,561	2,013,473	1,962,088
	Rural	2,406,206	1,216,647	1,189,559
	Urban	1,569,355	796,826	772,529
Urdu	Total	1,036,660	525,499	511,161
	Rural	285,039	144,306	140,733
	Urban	751,621	381,193	370,428
Angami	Total	7	7	-
	Rural	1	1	-
	Urban	6	6	-
Ao	Total	4	3	1
	Rural	2	1	1
	Urban	2	2	-
Arabic/Arbi	Total	1,056	571	485
	Rural	535	279	256
	Urban	521	292	229
Bhili/Bhilodi	Total	28	16	12
	Rural	2	2	-
	Urban	26	14	12
Coorgi/Kodagu	Total	224	123	101
	Rural	63	40	23
	Urban	161	83	78
Dogri	Total	94	52	42
	Rural	17	11	6
	Urban	77	41	36

		Persons	Males	Females
English	Total	22,724	11,341	11,383
	Rural	1,130	598	532
	Urban	21,594	10,743	10,851
Garo	Total	1	1	-
	Rural	-	-	-
	Urban	1	1	-
Gondi	Total	310	150	160
	Rural	-	-	-
	Urban	310	150	160
Hmar	Total	16	13	3
	Rural	-	-	-
	Urban	16	13	3
Kharia	Total	2	1	1
	Rural	-	-	-
	Urban	2	1	1
Khasi	Total	11	5	6
	Rural	2	-	2
	Urban	9	5	4
Konda	Total	1	1	-
	Rural	-	-	-
	Urban	1	1	-
Korku	Total	5	1	4
	Rural	-	-	-
	Urban	5	1	4
Korwa	Total	54	21	33
	Rural	-	-	-
	Urban	54	21	33
Koya	Total	1	1	-
	Rural	1	1	-
	Urban	-	-	-
Kuki	Total	3	1	2
	Rural	-	-	-
	Urban	3	1	2
Kurukh/Oraon	Total	10	6	4
	Rural	-	-	-
	Urban	10	6	4
Lahauli	Total	19	10	9
	Rural	7	4	3
	Urban	12	6	6

		Persons	Males	Females
Lahnda	Total	1	1	-
	Rural	-	-	-
	Urban	1	1	-
Liangmei	Total	1	1	-
	Rural	1	1	-
	Urban	-	-	-
Lushai/Mizo	Total	28	17	11
	Rural	8	4	4
	Urban	20	13	7
Munda	Total	1	1	-
	Rural	-	-	-
	Urban	1	1	-
Mundari	Total	3	1	2
	Rural	-	-	-
	Urban	3	1	2
Nicobarese	Total	2	1	1
	Rural	-	-	-
	Urban	2	1	1
Nocte	Total	4	4	-
	Rural	-	-	-
	Urban	4	4	-
Santali	Total	9	6	3
	Rural	9	6	3
	Urban	-	-	-
Sema	Total	19	12	7
	Rural	12	10	2
	Urban	7	2	5
Tangkhul	Total	3	3	-
	Rural	-	-	-
	Urban	3	3	-
Tibetan	Total	139	72	67
	Rural	-	-	-
	Urban	139	72	67
Total Of Other	Total	6,500	3,668	2,832
Languages	Rural	3,797	2,086	1,711
	Urban	2,703	1,582	1,121
Tulu	Total	3,370	1,733	1,637

Age wise Data

	Age distribution (in %)								
	0 - 4 years			5 - 9 years			10 - 14 years		
	P	M	F	P	M	F	P	M	F
Total	9.4	9.5	9.2	10.7	10.7	10.6	10.8	10.9	10.7
Rural	9.7	9.9	9.6	11.0	11.1	10.8	10.9	11.1	10.7
Urban	8.6	8.6	8.6	10.2	10.1	10.2	10.5	10.4	10.6
	15 - 44 years			*45 - 59 years*			*60 years and above*		
Total	48.3	47.6	49.1	13.1	13.4	12.8	7.5	7.6	7.3
Rural	46.7	45.6	47.7	13.6	13.8	13.4	7.8	8.2	7.4
Urban	51.6	51.3	51.8	12.0	12.4	11.6	6.9	6.7	6.9

Disabled

Distribution of Disabled Persons by Type of Disabilty and Residence (in %)

India/ States/ Union	*T/R/U*	*Total disabled population*	*In seeing*	*In speech*	*In hearing*	*In movement*	*Mental*
Tamil Nadu	T	1642497	58.7	7.6	4.4	21.5	7.8
	R	945019	58.6	8.0	4.7	21.7	7.1
	U	697478	58.9	7.1	4.1	21.4	8.6
Thiruvallur	T	69045	50.7	8.9	6.1	26.4	7.9
	R	34037	50.7	8.6	7.0	26.6	7.1
	U	35008	50.7	9.1	5.3	26.1	8.7
Chennai	T	96440	53.3	7.0	4.5	22.6	12.5
	R	0	0.0	0.0	0.0	0.0	0.0
	U	96440	53.3	7.0	4.5	22.6	12.5
Kancheepuram	T	71231	49.4	9.0	6.9	26.6	8.0
	R	35630	48.8	9.3	7.7	26.9	7.2
	U	35601	50.1	8.6	6.2	26.2	8.9
Vellore	T	84576	51.1	8.7	5.1	26.0	9.0
	R	50977	46.8	9.5	5.9	28.5	9.3
	U	33599	57.7	7.4	4.0	22.3	8.7
Dharmapuri	T	81448	67.6	6.6	3.0	17.7	5.0
	R	69794	68.2	6.6	3.1	17.3	4.8
	U	11654	63.8	6.9	2.7	20.2	6.4
Tiruvannamalai	T	49036	44.3	10.1	7.8	28.6	9.1
	R	42059	46.0	10.2	7.8	27.4	8.6
	U	6977	34.1	9.7	8.0	36.0	12.2
Viluppuram	T	66071	49.5	9.1	5.9	28.1	7.5
	R	58030	50.5	9.2	5.9	27.3	7.1
	U	8041	42.1	8.4	5.8	33.6	10.1
Salem	T	49560	45.4	9.8	4.8	30.3	9.6
	R	25397	42.9	10.7	5.3	31.6	9.5
	U	24163	48.0	8.8	4.4	29.0	9.8
Namakkal *	T	29696	52.5	8.5	5.2	25.3	8.5
	R	18438	51.7	8.9	5.8	24.8	8.8
	U	11258	53.8	7.8	4.4	26.0	8.0
Erode	T	66695	64.4	6.6	4.0	18.1	6.9
	R	35422	63.1	7.1	4.4	18.0	7.4
	U	31273	65.8	6.1	3.5	18.2	6.5
The Nilgiris	T	21456	61.5	5.7	4.9	20.9	7.0
	R	8939	59.5	6.2	4.7	22.3	7.2
	U	12517	62.8	5.4	5.1	19.8	6.8
Coimbatore	T	115738	67.1	6.1	3.4	15.7	7.6
	R	42019	65.6	6.3	3.9	16.7	7.5
	U	73719	67.9	6.0	3.1	15.2	7.7
Dindigul	T	63535	69.4	6.0	3.0	15.1	6.5
	R	43423	71.6	5.9	2.8	13.8	5.9
	U	20112	64.8	6.3	3.2	18.0	7.8
Karur *	T	15342	39.3	11.5	6.9	32.3	10.1
	R	10537	40.2	11.9	6.7	31.8	9.4
	U	4805	37.2	10.5	7.2	33.5	11.7
Tiruchirappalli	T	76445	63.5	8.3	4.0	18.1	6.2
	R	40650	64.3	8.2	4.0	17.9	5.6
	U	35795	62.5	8.3	4.0	18.4	6.8
Perambalur *	T	12820	59.9	9.7	4.2	20.2	5.9
	R	10510	57.7	10.8	4.3	21.0	6.1
	U	2310	69.8	4.7	3.8	16.6	5.1
Ariyalur *	T	21352	59.8	9.0	4.7	21.4	5.2
	R	19245	60.2	9.0	4.7	20.9	5.1
	U	2107	56.7	8.3	3.8	25.4	5.8
Cuddalore	T	64426	61.3	6.9	5.1	20.5	6.2
	R	44519	60.4	7.4	5.5	20.6	6.0
	U	19907	63.3	5.8	4.1	20.2	6.6
Nagapattinam*	T	50958	66.4	6.0	3.5	17.0	7.0
	R	37345	64.8	6.7	3.6	17.6	7.3
	U	13613	70.8	4.2	3.4	15.4	6.2
Thiruvarur	T	37371	64.3	7.2	4.1	18.4	6.1
	R	29682	63.8	7.2	4.1	18.8	6.2
	U	7689	66.2	7.3	4.1	16.8	5.6

India/ States/ Union	T/R/U	Total disabled population	In seeing	In speech	In hearing	In movement	Mental
Thanjavur	T	59468	54.3	9.2	5.2	23.4	7.9
	R	40867	55.5	9.2	5.1	23.2	7.0
	U	18601	51.8	9.0	5.3	24.0	9.9
Pudukkottai	T	40289	61.6	8.2	4.5	19.1	6.6
	R	33339	62.3	8.1	4.3	18.9	6.4
	U	6950	57.8	8.6	5.5	20.2	7.8
Sivaganga	T	39119	66.2	6.0	3.8	16.8	7.2
	R	29010	66.5	6.0	4.0	16.5	7.0
	U	10109	65.0	6.0	3.2	17.9	7.9
Madurai	T	70256	62.8	6.3	3.4	18.7	8.8
	R	32988	63.9	6.6	3.8	18.1	7.6
	U	37268	61.7	6.0	3.0	19.3	9.9
Theni *	T	30752	63.6	7.1	2.9	18.8	7.6
	R	15304	65.4	6.9	2.9	18.1	6.7
	U	15448	61.8	7.2	2.9	19.5	8.6
Virudhunagar	T	43277	58.5	7.7	3.6	21.9	8.4
	R	23952	57.1	8.6	3.6	21.9	8.8
	U	19325	60.2	6.7	3.5	21.8	7.8
Ramanathapuram	T	35524	59.3	8.3	3.5	20.2	8.7
	R	27022	58.0	8.9	3.8	20.4	9.0
	U	8502	63.6	6.4	2.6	19.7	7.7
Thoothukkudi	T	45845	58.7	6.6	3.9	22.2	8.6
	R	26248	56.8	7.1	4.1	23.0	8.9
	U	19597	61.3	5.9	3.5	21.2	8.1
Tirunelveli	T	74087	57.9	7.8	4.0	23.2	7.1
	R	39268	58.4	7.8	3.5	23.2	7.0
	U	34819	57.3	7.8	4.5	23.2	7.2
Kanniyakumari	T	60639	63.5	5.5	2.7	21.4	6.9
	R	20368	62.0	5.0	2.7	23.4	6.9
	U	40271	64.3	5.7	2.7	20.4	6.9

Drinking water

Distribution of Household by Sources of Drinking Water

		Total	Rural	Urban
Tap	Total	8,862,863	5,004,897	3,857,966
	Within Premises	2,663,884	604,454	2,059,430
	Near Premises	5,596,353	4,050,963	1,545,390
	Away	602,626	349,480	253,146
Hand-pump	Total	2,527,922	1,679,140	848,782
	Within Premises	476,658	178,453	298,205
	Near Premises	1,642,408	1,199,338	443,070
	Away	408,856	301,349	107,507
Tubewell	Total	734,826	373,612	361,214
	Within Premises	335,378	99,936	235,442
	Near Premises	307,122	217,004	90,118
	Away	92,326	56,672	35,654
Well	Total	1,505,004	938,285	566,719
	Within Premises	343,010	101,939	241,071
	Near Premises	806,122	584,256	221,866
	Away	355,872	252,090	103,782
Tank, Pond, etc.	Total	147,160	135,791	11,369
	Within Premises	1,905	1,125	780
	Near Premises	67,504	62,605	4,899
	Away	77,751	72,061	5,690
River, Canal	Total	48,907	33,731	15,176
	Within Premises	0	0	0
	Near Premises	26,275	16,032	10,243
	Away	22,632	17,699	4,933
Spring	Total	62,929	38,134	24,795
	Within Premises	0	0	0
	Near Premises	36,160	19,488	16,672
	Away	26,769	18,646	8,123
Any other	Total	284,015	71,200	212,815
	Within Premises	14,482	3,268	11,214
	Near Premises	138,527	33,363	105,164
	Away	131,006	34,569	96,437

Electricity

The total installed capacity for electricity in the State is 10,214 MW as on 31.03.2009. The installed capacity of State Sectors is 5,690 MW and that of Private Sector is 1,180 MW. Apart from this 2825 MW is available as share from Central Sector, 305 MW is obtained from external assistance and 214 MW from Captive Power Plants. Apart form this wind mills from the private sector provide 4270 MW and 466.10 MW is received from co-generation plants and 109.55 MW from Bio- mass plants.

As on 31.03.2009, there are 1259 sub stations,1.64 lakh ckt kms of Extra High Tension/ High Tension lines, 5.26 lakh kms of low tension lines, 1.86 distribution transformers and 203.87 lakh service connections.

Distribution of workers

Work Participation Rate

	Total main worker (in '000s)	Total marginal worker (in '000s)	Total non-worker (in '000s)	Per cent main worker engaged in Culti-vation	Agri-cul-tural	Livestock, Fore-stry, etc.
Persons	22,799	1,395	31,665	24.8	34.6	2.0
Males	15,875	83	12,342	26.6	26.3	2.1
Females	6,925	1,312	19,323	20.9	53.8	1.9

Total Population, Total Workers, Main Workers, Marginal Workers and Non-Workers–India, States and Union Territories

India/State/ Union territory*	Total Rural Urban	Persons Males Females	Total Population	Total Workers	Main Workers	Marginal Workers	Non-Workers
INDIA	Total	Persons	1,025,251,059	402,512,190	313,173,394	89,338,796	622,738,869
		Males	530,422,415	275,463,736	240,520,672	34,943,064	254,958,679
		Females	494,828,644	127,048,454	72,652,722	54,395,732	367,780,190
	Rural	Persons	740,255,371	310,655,339	229,672,348	80,982,991	429,600,032
		Males	380,438,194	199,199,602	169,333,233	29,866,369	181,238,592
		Females	359,817,177	111,455,737	60,339,115	51,116,622	248,361,440
	Urban	Persons	284,995,688	91,856,851	83,501,046	8,355,805	193,138,837
		Males	149,984,221	76,264,134	71,187,439	5,076,695	73,720,087
		Females	135,011,467	15,592,717	12,313,607	3,279,110	119,418,750
TamilNadu	Total	Persons	62,110,839	27,811,647	23,684,611	4,127,036	34,299,192
		Males	31,268,654	18,153,275	16,346,879	1,806,396	13,115,379
		Females	30,842,185	9,658,372	7,337,732	2,320,640	21,183,813
	Rural	Persons	34,869,286	17,572,083	14,290,211	3,281,872	17,297,203
		Males	17,508,985	10,396,912	9,067,457	1,329,455	7,112,073
		Females	17,360,301	7,175,171	5,222,754	1,952,417	10,185,130
	Urban	Persons	27,241,553	10,239,564	9,394,400	845,164	17,001,989
		Males	13,759,669	7,756,363	7,279,422	476,941	6,003,306
		Females	13,481,884	2,483,201	2,114,978	368,223	10,998,683

Total Workers (Main + Marginal) and their Categories–India, States and Union Territories

India/State/ Union territory*	Total Rural Urban	Persons Males Females	Total Workers (Main Marginal)
INDIA	Total	Persons	402,512,190
		Males	275,463,736
		Females	127,048,454
	Rural	Persons	310,655,339
		Males	199,199,602
		Females	111,455,737
	Urban	Persons	91,856,851
	Males	76,264,134	2,281,803
		Females	15,592,717
Tamil Nadu	Total	Persons	27,811,647
		Males	18,153,275
		Females	9,658,372
	Rural	Persons	17,572,083
		Males	10,396,912
		Females	7,175,171
	Urban	Persons	10,239,564
		Males	7,756,363
		Females	2,483,201

Cultivators	*Agricultural Labourers*	*House-hold Industry workers*	*Other wrrkers*
127,628,287	107,447,725	16,395,870	151,040,308
86,328,447	57,354,281	8,312,191	123,468,817
41,299,840	50,093,444	8,083,679	27,571,491
124,682,055	103,122,189	11,709,533	71,141,562
84,046,644	54,749,291	5,642,112	54,761,555
40,635,411	48,372,898	6,067,421	16,380,007
2,946,232	4,325,536	4,686,337	79,898,746
2,604,990	2,670,079	68,707,262	
664,429	1,720,546	2,016,258	11,191,484
5,114,384	8,665,020	1,458,546	12,573,697
3,305,413	4,277,140	619,096	9,951,626
1,808,971	4,387,880	839,450	2,622,071
4,725,890	7,565,439	815,009	4,465,745
3,028,113	3,667,853	324,381	3,376,565
1,697,777	3,897,586	490,628	1,089,180
388,494	1,099,581	643,537	8,107,952
277,300	609,287	294,715	6,575,061
111,194	490,294	348,822	1,532,891

Fair and Festivals

Adi Puram Festival : A Hindu festival named Adi-Puram is celebrated in all Hindu temples in Tamil Nadu in the month of Adi or *Ashada* (July-August), when the asterism 'Puram' (*Delta Leonis*) is in the ascendancy. The festival is one intended to propitiate the Goddess Sakti Devi who is said to have come into this world on this occasion to bless the people.

Bharani Deepam : It is true that the lighting of lamps in the month of Kartik is called 'Karthikai' Deepam. The lighting of the lamps during the asterism of Bharani has also a distinct significance. One should spin three hundred and sixty cotton wicks and all the wicks should be joined together and an oil lamp is lit with the name of Lord Shiva on the lips. This is a prelude to the lighting of the big lamp at Tiruvannamalai which is called 'Annamalai Deepam'.

Chitra—Pournami Festival : A Hindu festival by the name of Chitra Pournami is observed on the fullmoon day in the month of *Chithirai* or *chaitra* (April-May), when the asterism Chitra (*virgins*) holds sway. It is a festival observed to propitiate "Chitra-Gupta" the chief accountant of Yama, who is believed to record the commissions and omissions of the people to punish or reward them after their death.

Deepavali Pandigai Festival : Deepavali Pandigai goes by another name Naraka-Chaturdasi-Snanam, perhaps from a bath before daybreak on the fourteenth day of the dark fortnight in the month of *Arpisi* (Septemper-October). An asura named Narakasura is said to have been destroyed by Sri-Krishna on this day and the festival is intended to commemorate the incident.

Garudotsavam Festival : Garudotsavam or Garuda Sevai forms part of the annual Brahmotsavam of every Vaishnavite shrine in South India. This festival falls usually on the third day of the Brahmotsavam when the Lord gives darsan to his numerous devotees assembled on the occasion, seated on his favourite vahanam of "Garuda". Though a part of a festival, the importance and significance attached to this item is so much that it has almost assumed the significance of a great festival by itself.

Hayagriva festival : This is the 60th temple festival and an observance. The divine descent of Hayagriva occurred in Adi (Ashada July-Aug) Lord Vishnu with a horse's head appeared on the full moon day and even though it is a period of non-recitation, Veda and other Scriptures are taught and recited. But the worship is offered to Vyasa rather than to Lord Vishnu.Hayagriva festival : This is the 60th temple festival and an observance. The divine descent of Hayagriva occurred in Adi (Ashada July-Aug) Lord Vishnu with a horse's head appeared on the full moon day and even though it is a period of non-recitation, Veda and other Scriptures are taught and recited. But the worship is offered to Vyasa rather than to Lord Vishnu.

Jain Festivals : While Diwali is celebrated all over the south, it is also the Parinirvana day of Bhagavan Mahavir. Vardamana. Centres of Jainism are common all over Tamil Nadu especially on hillocks. In the various districts of Tamil Nadu there are nearly eighty hillocks which have an intimate and close association with Jainism. As the Jain community constitutes a negligible minority, the festivals organized by them have not been properly advertised. There was one, Jeeva Bhandu Sripal who had done yeoman service in the Jain cause and it is due to his efforts, something is known about the severe austerities practised by saints from time immemorial down to the present day.Jain Festivals : While Diwali is celebrated all over the south, it is also the Parinirvana day of Bhagavan Mahavir. Vardamana.

Centres of Jainism are common all over Tamil Nadu especially on hillocks. In the various districts of Tamil Nadu there are nearly eighty hillocks which have an intimate and close association with Jainism. As the Jain community constitutes a negligible minority, the festivals organized by them have not been properly advertised. There was one, Jeeva Bhandu Sripal who had done yeoman service in the Jain cause and it is due to his efforts, something is known about the severe austerities practised by saints from time immemorial down to the present day.

Kalashtami : This observance is done either in Aippasi or Kartik month as the case may be according to the calendar in which it is specified. This Kala is also called Kalabhairav and perhaps corresponds to the Bhairon Prasad located in the Vaishno Devi hills in Kashmir. He is deemed to have been born in an Ashtami thithi and hence the observance is performed in that Thithi. A small image of Bhairav either in gold or silver should be consecrated in brass metal pot filled with water and worship offered as for Lord Shiva, duly accompanied by the usual courtesies and prayers of praises! The Pandits giving support to this observances should be honoured generously. This practice is in vogue from time memorial.

Kalashtami : This observance is done either in Aippasi or Kartik month as the case may be according to the calendar in which it is specified. This Kala is also called Kalabhairav and perhaps corresponds to the Bhairon Prasad located in the Vaishno Devi hills in Kashmir. He is deemed to have been born in an Ashtami thithi and hence the observance is performed in that Thithi. A small image of Bhairav either in gold or silver should be consecrated in brass metal pot filled with water and worship offered as for Lord Shiva, duly accompanied by the usual courtesies and prayers of praises! The Pandits giving support to this observances should be honoured generously. This practice is in vogue from time memorial.

Madurai Cattlefair : The famous "Chithirai" festival of Madurai, has also an interesting cattle fair associated with it. It is held in April at Tallakulam and lasts for a fortnight. About 70,000 cattle are assembled here from various parts of the State, and most of them are sold during the period of the fair.

Nava Tiruppathis Festival : In the month of *Vaikasi* (May-June) a grand festival is celebrated for 10 days in Alwar Tirunagari. The most important day of the festival is the fifth day being the day of the Visakham star which is the birth day of Nammalwar, the great Vaishnavite saint.

Nava Tiruppathis Festival : In the month of *Vaikasi* (May-June) a grand festival is celebrated for 10 days in Alwar Tirunagari. The most important day of the festival is the fifth day being the day of the Visakham star which is the birth day of Nammalwar, the great Vaishnavite saint.

Panguni Uttiram Festival : Panguni Uttiram festival falls on the full-moon day in the month of *'Phalguna'* (March-April). The moon is then in the asterism Uttira *(Beta Leonis)*. Hence the day is considered to be specially favourable for the worship of Siva and consequently is dedicated for that purpose.

Saint Quadar Wali Urs : Nagore, a railway terminus of the Tanjavur Nagore branch line of the Southern Railway, is a suburb of the town of Nagapattinam in Tanjavur district and is famous for the shrine (Dargah) of Saint Hazareth Saiyed Shahul Hamid Quadar Wali who is believed to confer profusely on his worshippers blessings without any distinction of religion, caste, creed or colour. The devotion and respect for the saint has resulted in his elevation to Godhood with the result that the saint is famous among the Hindu community as Nagore Andavar or the God of Nagore. The anniversary of this saint is celebrated at Nagore during the first fourteen days of the month of Jamadiul Akhir (September) which is the ninth month of the Muslim calendar.

Saint Quadar Wali Urs : Nagore, a railway terminus of the Tanjavur Nagore branch line of the Southern Railway, is a suburb of the town of Nagapattinam in Tanjavur district and is famous for the shrine (Dargah) of Saint Hazareth Saiyed Shahul Hamid Quadar Wali who is believed to confer profusely on his worshippers blessings without any distinction of religion, caste, creed or colour. The devotion and respect for the saint has resulted in his elevation to Godhood with the result that the saint is famous among the Hindu community as Nagore Andavar or the God of Nagore. The anniversary of this saint is celebrated at Nagore during the first fourteen days of the month of Jamadiul Akhir (September) which is the ninth month of the Muslim calendar.

The Golden Car Feast of Our Lady of Snows : The Golden Car Feast of our Lady of Snows, is a very important festival for all inhabitants of Tuticorin and surrounding villages irrespective of caste or creed, and to all members of the Bharathar community all over India and Sri Lanka. The flag-hoisting for the feast commences on 26th July every year when the preparatory Novena begins. This lasts for nine days, and daily a number of Holy Masses are said by priests from 5 am., to 8 am. The final High Mass is sung at 8 am.

Uma Maheshwara Vratham : This also falls in the month of Avani (September - October) Full moon day is specially important for Shiva and Shakti Puja. Uma Maheshwara Vratha is observed for 15 years continuously when the image of Uma Maheshwara is consecrated in fifteen water filled metal-pots along with fifteen holy threads and fifteen sweet offerings! The sacred thread so consecrated should be worn by the performer with solemn devotion.

Uma Maheshwara Vratham : This also falls in the month of Avani (September - October) Full moon day is specially important for Shiva and Shakti Puja. Uma Maheshwara Vratha is observed for 15 years continuously when the image of Uma Maheshwara is consecrated in fifteen water filled metal-pots along with fifteen holy threads and fifteen sweet offerings! The sacred thread so consecrated should be worn by the performer with solemn devotion.

Vaikasi Visaka Festival : The festival Vaikasi Visaka is observed on the day when the asterism Visaka (*Libra*) rules in the month of *Vaikasi*, called also *Vaisaka* (May-June). It is the full-moon day of the month and the celebration of the festival consists of offering worship to Dharmraja, the God of death. The day is also said to be the one on which God Subrahmanya incarnated in this world when this asterism Visaka was in the ascendant. Hence this festive occasion is said to be doubly important and meritorious.

Yagnavalkya Jayanthi : Rishi Yagnavalkya was born in the month of Aippasi (October-November) partly an Avathar of the Sun-God 'Surya'. Rishis, who do not present themselves on certain occasions before the Creator Brahma will be affected by 'Brahmahathi Dosha'.

Abbreviations

BCM	: Billion Cubic Meter	NA	: Not Available
C	: Flood Control	NH	: National Highway
C.D. Block	: Community Development Block	O.G	: Outgrowth
CB	: Buttress	PG	: Gravity
ER	: Rockfill	R	: Purposes
GP	: Gram Panchayat	S	: Water Supply Recreational
GDP	: Gross Domestic Product	SC	: Scheduled Caste
H	: Hydro-electric	SH	: State Highway
HAM	: Hectare Meter	Sqs. Kms	: Square Kilometers
HQ	: Headquarters	ST	: Scheduled Tribes
I	: Irrigation	TE	: Earth
L	: Uncontrolled Spillway	UC	: Under Construction
MCM	: Million Cubic Meter	UE	: Universalisation of Elementary Education
MM	: Millimeter	VA	: Arch
MV	: Multi Arch	V	: Controlled Spillway
N	: Navigation	WRP	: Work Participation Rate

ACHARAPAKKAM

Acharapakkam C.D. Block lies in the south-westren part of Kancheepuram district. It is a part of Maduranthakam taluk. The Block is located at a distance of 75 kms. from district headquarters (Kancheepuram). There are 93 villages in the block with the total population of 93,334 persons. Area of the C.D. Block is 346.83 sq. kms. It is bounded in the north by CD Blocks Maduranthakam and Uthiramerur, in the south by Viluppuram district, in the east by CD Blocks Chithamur and Maduranthakam, and in the west by Tiruvannamalai district.

Communications:

Roadways : N.H.-45: Direction- Tindivanam to Maduranthakam, Nearest Villages- Unamalai, Sirungalur, Pallipettai, Perumbairkandigai, Kadamalaiputhur, Veliambakkam, Edayalam, Thozhuppedu, Athur.

Railway Station: Karasangal, Thozhuppedu.

Annual Rainfall: Average Rainfall 1105 mm.

Ground Water: Availability of the ground water in the Basin is 8355.48 H.A.M. and the utilization is 6136.39 H.A.M. It belongs to Over Expoited category. Depth to water level varies from 2 to 10 meter below the ground. Most of the wells go down in summer months, according to the Ground Water Estimation Committee.

Natural Division: Tondai Nadu.

Administration

Revenue **Division:** Madurnthakham. Parliamentary Constituency: 6 Kancheepuram (SC). District: Kancheepuram. Taluk: Maduranthakam. Assembly Constituency: 35 Madurantakam (SC). Gram Panchayat: 59.

Villages: 93 **Inhabited:** 93 **Uninhabited:** 0

Ranking	District	State	National
Area	4	120	2305
Population	10	163	3679
Sex Ratio	6	217	1537
Child Sex Ratio	10	147	2605
Literacy Rate	11	271	2328
Density	3	222	3873
Work Participation Rate	13	262	2365

Gram Panchayats:

Agili , Alapakkam, Anaikunnam, Anathamangalam , Annangal , Athivakkam, Athur, Baburayanpettai, Edayalam, Elapakkam , Gudalur, Guddalur , Kadamalaiputhur, Kadambur , Kalathur, Karasangal, Karikilli , Karikkilli , Kattugudalur, Kattugudalur , Kattukkaranai, Keezhamur , Kilathivakkam, Kiliyanagar, Kongaraimambattu, Kozhiyalam , L.Endathur , Madhur, Mathur , Minnal Chithamur, Mogalvadi, Morapakkam , Murungai , Nedungal, Orathur, Orathy, Padiri, Pallipettai, Pappanallur, Pasuvankaranai, Perumbairkandigai, Perumbakkam , Perumbakkam, Poragal, Porpanankaranai, Seethapuram, Semppondi, Sirudamur , Sirudamur , Sirumagalur, Sirupairpandi, Thandaraipuducheri , Theetalam, Thimmapuram, Thinnalur , Thozhuppedu, Tinnalur, Tirumukkadu, Unamalai, Vadamanipakkam, Vedantghangal , Vedanthangal , Vedanthangal , Velamur, Veliambakkam, Vellaputhur, Vilangadu , Vilangagu, Vinnampoondi.

Amenities:

Education: Primary School in 69 villages, Middle school in 20 villages, Matriculation or Secondary School in 8 villages, namely Vedanthangal, L Endathur, Morappakkam, Kattukkaranai, Elappakkam, Orathy, Anathamangalam, Thozhuppedu.

Higher Secondary or Pre University Courses or Intermediate or Junior College in 6 villages of the CD Block,, namely L Endathur, Morappakkam, Elappakkam, Orathy, Anathamangalam, Thozhuppedu.

College in 0 village, Adult Literacy Center in 0 village.

Medical: Hospital in 0 village, Dispensary in 3 villages, Health Center in 3 villages, Sub Center in 15 villages, Maternity and Child Welfare Center in 0 village, Community health workers in 93 villages.

The Villages having Hospital or Dispensary or Health Center are Padiri, Orathy, Kadamalaiputhur.

Drinking Water: Tap water in 93 villages, Tank water in 68 villages, Well water in 93 villages, Tubewell in 93 villages and more than one source in 93 villages.

Bank: Banking facility in 9 villages, namely, L Endathur, Kiliyanagar, Muniyanthangal, Sendivakkam Sirungalur, Orathy, Anathamangalam, Kongaraimambattu Kadamalaiputhur.

Credit Society in 9 villages Agricultural Credit Society in 7 Non-Agricultural Credit Society in 1 village.

Others: Power supply in 93 villages, Cinema hall in 0 village, sport club in 0 village, Stadium or Auditorium or Community Hall in 0 village, Post Office in 28 villages.

There are 66 villages having bus facilities.

Villages with most of facilities: L Endathur Kiliyanagar, Sirungalur, Orathy, Anathamangalam Kongaraimambattu, Kadamalaiputhur.

Villages without amenities (Education): Chithamur, Kolathur, Thuraiyur, Nellai, Valayaputhur, Madurai, Ladakaranai, Kalanipakkam, Karunagaravilagam, Muniyanthangal, Padiri, Agili, Chinthamani, Nemam, Pinnampoondi, Porpanankaranai A,B/B, Gunankaranai, Annangal, Vadakkuputhur (Na), Siruvangunam, Poragal, Allanur, Kilpattu, Munnakulam..

Scheduled Castes: Out of the total population of 93334 persons, 35098 persons (37.6%) belong to Scheduled Castes. The villages having less than 10% SC population are

Pappanallur, Pambayambattu, Nellai, Ladakaranai Pasuvankaranai, Karunagaravilagam, Sendivakkam Athivakkam, Madhur, Pinnampoondi, Annangal Sirudamur, Sirupairpandi, Minnal Chithamur.

The villages having more than 50% SC population are Kolathur, Karikkili, Vinayaganallur, Thuraiyur Chithathur, Theetalam, Vedanthangal, Puducheri Madurai, Perumbakkam, Vaippanai, L Endathur Thandalam, Kalanipakkam, Guddalur, Muniyanthangal Kattugudalur, Chinthamani, Sirungalur, Nemam Thimmapuram, Kottakayapakkam, Vadakkuputhur (Na) Senayaneri, Poragal, Baburayampettai, Vilangadu Thirumukkadu, Kilpattu, Thozhuppedu, Athur.

Sex ratio of Scheduled Caste population is 496.

Scheduled Castes Literates and Illiterates by Sex:

	Persons	Males	Females
Literate	16,922	9,949	6,973
Illiterate	18,176	7,729	10,447
Literacy rate	55.4	64.7	46.0
Graduate	146	119	27

Scheduled Castes (Dominant):

Adi Dravida, Arunthathiyar, Valluvan, Paraiyan etc.
Generic Castes etc.

For their cultural identity please see Appendix-I

Villages without Scheduled Castes: There are 7 villages without any scheduled caste population.

Scheduled Tribes: Out of the total population of 93334 persons, 1930 persons (2.07%) belong to Scheduled Tribes.

The villages having less than 10% ST population are Chithamur, Kolathur, Karikkili, Vinayaganallur Vellaputhur, Thuraiyur, Chithathur, Pappanallur Pambayambattu, Nellai, Kadambur, Theetalam Kozhiyalam, Valayaputhur, Vedanthangal, Thandarai Puducheri, Madurai, Perumbakkam, L Endathur Alapakkam, Kiliyanagar, Pasuvankaranai, Semppondi Thandalam, Kalanipakkam, Morappakkam Karunagaravilagam, Guddalur, Muniyanthangal, Orathur Keezhamur, Padiri, Velamur, Mogalvadi, Kattukkaranai Kattugudalur, Sendivakkam, Mathur, Agili Chinthamani, Unamalai, Sirungalur, Nemam, Athivakkam Thimmapuram, Kottakayapakkam, Madhur, Pinnampoondi Elappakkam, Porpanankaranai A,B/B, Rajapalayam Gunankaranai, Annangal, Orathy, Vadakkuputhur (Na) Vadamanipakkam, Thinnalur, Vinnampoondi Siruvangunam, Anathamangalam, Senayaneri, Sirudamur Kongaraimambattu, Kalathur, Poragal, Kilathivakkam Baburayampettai, Sirupairpandi, Allanur, Vilangadu Seethapuram, Uthamanallur, Thirumukkadu, Pallipettai Perumbairkandigai, Kadamalaiputhur, Minalkilminnal Minnal Chithamur, Nedungal, Munnakulam, Murungai Allur, Karasangal, Veliambakkam, Edayalam Thozhuppedu, Athur.

The villages having more than 50% ST population are None.

Sex ratio of Scheduled tribe population is 498.

Scheduled Tribes Literates and Illiterates by Sex:

	Persons	Males	Females
Literate	449	270	179
Illiterate	1,481	698	783
Literacy rate	28.1	33.7	22.5
Graduate	3	3	0

Scheduled Tribes (Dominant):

Irular, Kattunayakan, Malai Vedan
Generic Tribes etc.

For their cultural identity please see Appendix-II

Villages without Scheduled Tribes: There are 43 villages without any scheduled tribe population.

Literates and Illiterates by Sex (Total Population):

	Persons	Males	Females
Literate	51,625	30,281	21,344
Illiterate	41,709	16,603	25,106
Literacy rate	63	73	52
Graduate	665	506	159

Agriculture: ***Distribution of villages according to land use:*** Out of 93 villages, Total area (in hectare) is 34683.36, out of that 56.03 percent is cultivable and 68.73 percent of the cultivable area is irrigated.

Sources of Irrigation (Hectares): Government Canal 0, Private Canal 0, Well without Electricity 1391.55, Well with Electricity 5765.74, Tubewell without Electricity 50.28, Tubewell with Electricity 158.53, Tank 657.08, River 0, Lake 4689.18, Waterfall 0, Others 645.21.

Villages with population of 5000 to 9999: None

Villages with population of 10000 and above: None

Distribution of Workers:

	Persons	Males	Females	WPR
Cultivators	13,478	9,105	4,373	28.78
Agricultural Labour	25,111	11,959	13,152	53.61
Household Industry	1,406	693	713	3
Other Workers	6,843	5,413	1,430	14.61
Main Workers	33,355	21,354	12,001	71.21
Marginal Workers	13,483	5,816	7,667	28.79
Total Workers	46,838	27,170	19,668	

Religion: Major Religious Communities:

	Persons	Males	Females	Sex Ratio
Hindu (95.11%)	88,771	44,563	44,208	992
Muslim (1.45%)	1,354	695	659	948
Christian (3.41%)	3,183	1,612	1,571	975
Sikh (0%)	-	-	-	-
Buddhists (0%)	1	-	1	-

Jain (0%)	-	-	-	-

Agewise Data:

	Persons	Males	Females	Sex Ratio
All ages	93,334	46,884	46,450	991
0-14	27,329	13,880	13,449	969
15-44	43,705	21,567	22,138	1026
45-79	21,159	10,830	10,329	954
80+	928	502	426	849
Age not stated	213	105	108	1029

Languages (Dominant): Tamil, Telugu, Urdu, Kannada, Hindi

Disabled Population:

	Persons	Males	Females	%
Total Disabled	2,587	1,418	1,169	
In Seeing	1,164	618	546	44.99
In Speech	270	143	127	10.44
In Hearing	235	121	114	9.08
In Movement	739	448	291	28.57
Mentally	179	88	91	6.92

AGASTHEESWARAM

Agastheeswaram C.D. Block lies in the south-western part of Kanniyakumari district. It is a part of Agasthee swaram taluk. The Block is located at a distance of NA. kms. from district headquarters (Kanniyakumari). There are 12 villages in the block with the total population of 39,494 persons. Area of the C.D. Block is 138.30 sq. kms. It is bounded in the north by CD Block Thovala, in the south by Sea Arabian, in the east by the Gulf of Mannar and district Tirunelveli, and in the west by CD Block Rajakkamangalam.

Communications:

Roadways : N.H.-7: Direction- Kanniyakumari to Nagarkoil, Nearest Village- Kanniyakumari. N.H.-47: Direction- Tiruvanamthapuram to Kanniyakumari, Nearest Villages- Kulasekarapuram, Suchindram, Vadiveeswaram, Thamaraikulam, Agastheeswaram, Kanniyakumari. S.H.-46: Direction- Nagarkoil to Vellamadam, Nearest Village- Nagerkoil. **River:** Pazhayar Nadi- Nearest Villages- Nagerkoil, Suchindram, Thamaraikulam, Thengamputhoor.

Annual Rainfall: Average Rainfall 1448 mm.

Ground Water: Availability of the ground water in the Basin is 40.84 MCM and the utilization is 6.09 MCM. It belongs to Safe category. Depth to water level varies from 2 to 10 meter below the ground. Most of the wells go down in summer months, according to the Ground Water Estimation Committee.

Coastal Villages- (Arabian Sea)- Nearest Villages- Agastheeswaram, Kanniyakumari.

Forest and Reserved Forest: (Thekkumalai RF)- Nearest Villa ge- Therkkumalai RF W&E.

Natural Division: NA

Administration

Revenue **Division:** Nagarcoil. Parliamentary Constituency: 39 Kanniyakumari. District: Kanniyakumari. Taluk: Agast heeswaram. Assembly Constituency: 230 Nagerkoil, 229 Kanniyakumari. Gram Panchayat: 13.

Villages: 12 **Inhabited:** 11 **Uninhabited:** 1

Ranking	District	State	National
Area	4	350	5211
Population	9	372	5756
Sex Ratio	2	66	542
Child Sex Ratio	3	90	1823
Literacy Rate	2	2	138
Density	5	379	3689
Work Participation Rate	7	242	5641

Gram Panchayats:

Eravipudur, Kariamanicapuram, Karumpattur, Gandipuram, Kulasekarapuram, Leepuram, Manakudi, Nallur, North Tamaraikulam, Panchalingapuram, Ramapuram, Swamithope, Therekalpudur.

Amenities:

Education: Primary School in 8 villages, Middle school in 6 villages, Matriculation or Secondary School in 4 villages, namely Theroor, Eraviputhur, Thamaraikulam, Kanniyakumari.

Higher Secondary or Pre University Courses or Intermediate or Junior College in 1 village of the CD Block,, namely Kanniyakumari.

College in 1 village, Adult Literacy Center in 0 village., College is in village, namely Nagercoil.

Medical: Hospital in 0 village, Dispensary in 0 village, Health Center in 1 village, Sub Center in 5 villages, Maternity and Child Welfare Center in 3 villages, Community health workers in 1 village.

The Village having Hospital or Dispensary or Health Center is Agastheeswaram.

Drinking Water: Tap water in 11 villages, Tank water in 0 villages, Well water in 11 villages, Tubewell in 11 villages and more than one source in 11 villages.

Bank: Banking facility in 3 villages, namely, Marungoor, Vadiveeswaram, Kanniyakumari.

Credit Society in 3 villages Agricultural Credit Society in 2 Non-Agricultural Credit Society in 2 villages.

Others: Power supply in 11 villages, Cinema hall in 1 village, sport club in 0 village, Stadium or Auditorium or Community Hall in 0 village, Post Office in 7 villages.

There are 11 villages having bus facilities.

Villages with most of facilities: Vadiveeswaram Kanniyakumari.

Villages without amenities (Education): Marungoor,

Suchindram, Alagappapuram..

Scheduled Castes: Out of the total population of 39494 persons, 5380 persons (13.62%) belong to Scheduled Castes.

The villages having less than 10% SC population are None..

The villages having more than 50% SC population are None.

Sex ratio of Scheduled Caste population is 505.

Scheduled Castes Literates and Illiterates by Sex:

	Persons	Males	Females
Literate	4,258	2,186	2,072
Illiterate	1,122	475	647
Literacy rate	88.4	92.1	84.8
Graduate	97	49	48

Scheduled Castes (Dominant):

Paraiyan etc., Adi Dravida, Vannan, Bharatar, Samban

For their cultural identity please see Appendix-I

Villages without Scheduled Castes: There is 1 village without any scheduled caste population.

Scheduled Tribes: Out of the total population of 39494 persons, 155 persons (0.39%) belong to Scheduled Tribes.

The villages having less than 10% ST population are Nagercoil, Theroor, Marungoor, Kulasekarapuram Eraviputhur, Suchindram, Vadiveeswaram Thamaraikulam, Agastheeswaram, Alagappapuram Kanniyakumari.

The villages having more than 50% ST population are None.

Sex ratio of Scheduled tribe population is 510.

Scheduled Tribes Literates and Illiterates by Sex:

	Persons	Males	Females
Literate	60	33	27
Illiterate	95	43	52
Literacy rate	49.2	56.9	42.2
Graduate	0	0	0

Scheduled Tribes (Dominant):

Kattunayakan, Malakkuravan

For their cultural identity please see Appendix-II

Villages without Scheduled Tribes: There are 4 villages without any scheduled tribe population.

Literates and Illiterates by Sex (Total Population):

	Persons	Males	Females
Literate	31,197	15,807	15,390
Illiterate	8,297	3,677	4,620
Literacy rate	88	91	86
Graduate	1,145	651	494

Agriculture: ***Distribution of villages according to land use:***

Out of 12 villages, Total area (in hectare) is 13830, out of that 61.14 percent is cultivable and 65.48 percent of the cultivable area is irrigated.

Sources of Irrigation (Hectares): Government Canal 1972.17, Private Canal 0, Well without Electricity 0, Well with Electricity 21, Tubewell without Electricity 0, Tubewell with Electricity 0, Tank 3542.92, River 0, Lake 0, Waterfall 0, Others 0.

Villages with population of 5000 to 9999:

Vadiveeswaram, Kanniyakumari.

Villages with population of 10000 and above:

Thamaraikulam.

Distribution of Workers:

	Persons	Males	Females	WPR
Cultivators	785	649	136	5.87
Agricultural Labour	4,462	3,392	1,070	33.38
Household Industry	546	162	384	4.08
Other Workers	7,576	6,341	1,235	56.67
Main Workers	11,181	9,196	1,985	83.63
Marginal Workers	2,188	1,348	840	16.37
Total Workers	13,369	10,544	2,825	

Religion: Major Religious Communities:

	Persons	Males	Females	Sex Ratio
Hindu (71.54%)	28,255	14,030	14,225	1,014
Muslim (1.94%)	768	354	414	1,169
Christian (35.59%)	14,054	6,899	7,155	1,037
Sikh (0%)	1	-	1	-
Buddhists (0%)	1	-	1	-
Jain (0%)	1	1	-	-

Agewise Data:

	Persons	Males	Females	Sex Ratio
All ages	43,093	21,290	21,803	1024
0-14	10,768	5,464	5,304	971
15-44	21,110	10,256	10,854	1058
45-79	10,638	5,323	5,315	998
80+	478	203	275	1355
Age not stated	99	44	55	1250

Languages (Dominant):

Tamil, Telugu, Malayalam, Kannada, Konkani

Disabled Population:

	Persons	Males	Females	%
Total Disabled	1,925	792	1,133	
In Seeing	1,234	369	865	64.1
In Speech	91	51	40	4.73
In Hearing	56	31	25	2.91
In Movement	422	266	156	21.92
Mentally	122	75	47	6.34

ALANGANALLUR

Alanganallur C.D. Block lies in the northern part of Madurai district. It is a part of Vadipatti taluk. The Block is located at distance of 18 kms. from district headquarters (Madurai).

There are 46 villages in the block with the total population of 82,376 persons. Area of the C.D. Block is 270.56 sq. kms. It is bounded in the north by district Dindigul, in the south by CD

Blocks Vadipatti and Maduai West, in the east by CD Block Madurai West and district Dindigul, and in the west by CD Block Vadipatti.

Communications:

Roadways : N.H.-7: Direction- Dindigul to Madurai, Nearest Village- Thanichiyam.

Annual Rainfall: Average Rainfall 857 mm.

Ground Water: Availability of the ground water in the Basin is 3854.48 H.A.M. and the utilization is 3853. 67 H.A.M. It belongs to Critical category. Depth to water level varies from 2 to 10 meter below the ground. Most of the wells go down in summer months, according to the Ground Water Estimation Committee.

Forest and Reserved Forest: (Erakkalamalai RF)- Nearest Villages- Sirumalai RF, Erakkalanmalai RF, Valayapatty. (Perumalai)- Nearest Villages- Perumalai RF, Mettupatty, Senthamangalam, Chatravellalapatty, Valayapatty. (Katchiakatti)- Nearest Village- Thethoor. (Vaguthumalai)- Nearest Villages- Thethoor, Vaigashipatty, Vaguthumalai RF, Thanichiyam, Kondayampatti, Kolivelipatti, Keelakarai, Periyailanthaikulam, Kuttimaikipatty, Kovilpatty. (Krishnapuram)- Nearest Villages- Rajakkalpatti, Krishnapuram, Manickampatty. (Sukkampatti)- Nearest Villages- Muduvarpatty, Sukkampatti, Kovilpatty, Keelacinnarampattoorseri. (Sembathi)- Nearest Villages- Sempatti RF, Ramagoundanpatty, Valayapatty, Rajakkalpatti, Sempatti, Vaigashipatty.

Natural Division: NA

Administration

Revenue **Division:** Madurai. Parliamentary Constituency: 33 Theni. District: Madurai. Taluk: Vadipatti. Assembly Constituency: 190 Samayanallur (SC). Gram Panchayat: 37.

Villages: 46 **Inhabited:** 38 **Uninhabited:** 8

Ranking	District	State	National
Area	5	205	3099
Population	8	228	4027
Sex Ratio	7	255	1889
Child Sex Ratio	5	272	4517
Literacy Rate	7	167	1606
Density	7	181	3486
Work Participation Rate	8	218	1828

Gram Panchayats:

66.Mettupatti, Achampatti, Adanur, Alagapuri, Ayyankottai, Ayyur, B.mettupatti, Chatravellalapatti, Chinnailandaikulam, Errampatti, Kallanai, Kalvelipatti, Keelachinnanamapatti, Kodangipatti, Kondayampatti, Kottaimedu, Kovilpatti, Kuthimelkipatti, Manianji, Manickampatti, Melachinnampatti, Muduvarpatti, Pannaikudi, Paraipatti, Peria ilandaikulam, Rajakkalpatti, Senthamangalam, T.Mettupatti, Tandalai, Thanichayam, Thethoor, Thevaseri, Urseri, Vadugapatti, Valayapatti, Vavidamaruttur, Vellaiyampatti, .

Amenities:

Education: Primary School in 35 villages, Middle school in 16 villages, Matriculation or Secondary School in 5 villages, namely Thethoor, Kondayampatti, Vavidamaruthur, Achampatty, Manianji.

Higher Secondary or Pre University Courses or Intermediate or Junior College in 1 village of the CD Block,, namely Vavidamaruthur.

College in 0 village, Adult Literacy Center in 0 village.

Medical: Hospital in 0 village, Dispensary in 0 village, Health Center in 1 village, Sub Center in 31 villages, Maternity and Child Welfare Center in 34 villages, Community health workers in 35 villages.

Drinking Water: Tap water in 38 villages, Tank water in 1 villages, Well water in 38 villages, Tubewell in 38 villages and more than one source in 38 villages.

Bank: Banking facility in 10 villages, namely, Chatravellalapatty, Muduvarpatty, Thanichiyam Kondayampatti, Vavidamaruthur, Alagapuri Chinnailanthaikulam, Kallanai, Achampatty, Manianji.

Credit Society in 23 villages Agricultural Credit Society in 8 Non-Agricultural Credit Society in 2 villages.

Others: Power supply in 38 villages, Cinema hall in 6 villages, sport club in 1 village, Stadium or Auditorium or Community Hall in 7 villages, Post Office in 38 villages.

There are 35 villages having bus facilities.

Villages with most of facilities: Chatravellalapatty Muduvarpatty, Thanichiyam, Kondayampatti Vavidamaruthur, Alagapuri, Chinnailanthaikulam Kallanai, Achampatty, Manianji.

Villages without amenities (Education): Sempatti, Keelakarai, Kumaram..

Scheduled Castes: Out of the total population of 82376 persons, 17274 persons (20.97%) belong to Scheduled Castes.

The villages having less than 10% SC population are Sirumalai Rf, Senthamangalam, Chatravellalapatty Valayapatty, Ramagoundanpatty, Sempatti, Paraippatty Saranthangy, Periyailanthaikulam, Keelakarai.

The villages having more than 50% SC population are None.

Sex ratio of Scheduled Caste population is 502.

Scheduled Castes Literates and Illiterates by Sex:

	Persons	Males	Females
Literate	8,948	5,292	3,656
Illiterate	8,326	3,302	5,024
Literacy rate	60.6	72.4	49.1
Graduate	169	120	49

Scheduled Castes (Dominant):
Paraiyan etc., Pallan, Chakkiliyan, Kuravan etc. Valluvan

For their cultural identity please see Appendix-I

Villages without Scheduled Castes: There are 12 villages without any scheduled caste population.

Scheduled Tribes: Out of the total population of 82376 persons, 720 persons (0.87%) belong to Scheduled Tribes. The villages having less than 10% ST population are Sirumalai Rf, Senthamangalam, Mettupatty Chatravellalapatty, Valayapatty, Ramagoundanpatty Thethoor, Sempatti, Rajakkalpatti, Manickampatty Vellayampatty, Kodangipatty, Paraippatty Saranthangy, Usilampatti, Muduvarpatty, Errampatty Vaigashipatty, Thanichiyam, Kondayampatti Kolivelipatti, Periyailanthaikulam, Kuttimaikipatty Keelakarai, Kovilpatty, Keelacinnarampatty, Oorseri Aathanoor, Vavidamaruthur, Alagapuri Chinnailanthaikulam, Sambakulam, Kallanai Achampatty, Pannaikudi, Thandalai, Manianji, Kumaram. The villages having more than 50% ST population are None.

Sex ratio of Scheduled tribe population is 468.

Scheduled Tribes Literates and Illiterates by Sex:

	Persons	Males	Females
Literate	436	257	179
Illiterate	284	126	158
Literacy rate	66.9	74.5	58.3
Graduate	8	8	0

Scheduled Tribes (Dominant):
Malai Vedan, Malai Pandaram

For their cultural identity please see Appendix-II

Villages without Scheduled Tribes: There are 41 villages without any scheduled tribe population.

Literates and Illiterates by Sex (Total Population):

	Persons	Males	Females
Literate	48,147	28,109	20,038
Illiterate	34,229	13,433	20,796
Literacy rate	67	78	56
Graduate	1,244	888	356

Agriculture: *Distribution of villages according to land use:* Out of 46 villages, Total area (in hectare) is 27056.99, out of that 37.72 percent is cultivable and 60.89 percent of the cultivable area is irrigated.

Sources of Irrigation (Hectares): Government Canal 2600.55, Private Canal 0, Well without Electricity 216.76, Well with Electricity 2467.21, Tubewell without Electricity 203.79, Tubewell with Electricity 43.87, Tank 682.49, River 0, Lake 0, Waterfall 0, Others 0.

Villages with population of 5000 to 9999: Thethoor, Thanichiyam, Urseri, Kallanai.

Villages with population of 10000 and above: None

Distribution of Workers:

	Persons	Males	Females	WPR
Cultivators	6,330	4,179	2,151	14.91
Agricultural Labour	27,021	14,187	12,834	63.64
Household Industry	670	226	444	1.58
Other Workers	8,436	6,687	1,749	19.87
Main Workers	36,518	22,688	13,830	86.01
Marginal Workers	5,939	2,591	3,348	13.99
Total Workers	42,457	25,279	17,178	

Religion: Major Religious Communities:

	Persons	Males	Females	Sex Ratio
Hindu (98.29%)	80,970	40,843	40,127	982
Muslim (0.85%)	704	356	348	978
Christian (0.8%)	660	325	335	1,031
Sikh (0%)	-	-	-	-
Buddhists (0%)	-	-	-	-
Jain (0%)	1	-	1	-

Agewise Data:

	Persons	Males	Females	Sex Ratio
All ages	82,376	41,542	40,834	983
0-14	23,493	12,034	11,459	952
15-44	40,330	20,128	20,202	1004
45-79	17,501	8,850	8,651	978
80+	583	275	308	1120
Age not stated	469	255	214	839

Languages (Dominant):
Tamil, Telugu, Kannada, English, Hindi

Disabled Population:

	Persons	Males	Females	%
Total Disabled	2,273	1,123	1,150	
In Seeing	1,329	601	728	58.47
In Speech	161	92	69	7.08
In Hearing	132	60	72	5.81
In Movement	484	276	208	21.29
Mentally	167	94	73	7.35

ALANGAYAM

Alangayam C.D. Block lies in the south-western part of Vellore district. It is a part of Vaniyambadi and Tirupathur taluk. The Block is located at a distance of 83 kms. from district headquarters (Vellore). There are 32 villages in the block with the total population of 96,559 persons. Area of the C.D. Block is 397.93 sq. kms. It is bounded in the north by CD Blocks Natrampalli and Madhanur, in the south by CD Blocks Jolarpet and Tirupathur, in the east by district Tiruvannamalai, and in the west by CD Block Natrampalli. CD Block Alangayam falls in taluk Vaniyambadi by 27 villages, and in taluk Tirupathur by 05 villages.

Communications:

Roadways : N.H.-46: Direction- Krishnagiri to Ambur, Nearest Villages- Valayambattu, Girisamudram, Kelendra, Amburpettai. S.H.-18: Direction- Tirupacheri to Vaniyabadi, Nearest Villages- Kelendra, Govindapuram.

River: Polar Nadi- Nearest Villages- Valayambattu, Girisamudram, Kelendra

Annual Rainfall: Average Rainfall 949 mm.

Ground Water: Availability of the ground water in the Basin is 4449.90 H.A.M. and the utilization is 6313.84 H.A.M. It belongs to Over Expoited category. Depth to water level varies from 5 to 10 meter below the ground. Most of the wells go down in summer months, according to the Ground Water Estimation Committee.

Forest and Reserved Forest: (Kalrapatti RF)- Nearest Villages- Narasingapuram, Kalrapatti RF. (Madakadappa)- Nearest Villages- Elayanagaram, Madakadappa (RF), Velathigamani penta, Chinthagampenta, Madanancheri. (Mambakkam)- Nearest Villages- Pungampattunadu, Pudur Nadu, Mambakkam RF, Innesjavadu RF. (Narsingapuram)- Nearest Villages- Nimmiyampatti, Reddiyur, Narasimgapuram, Narasingapuram. (Singarapet)- Nearest Villages- Pungampattunadu. (Kalrapatti)- Nearest Villages- Narasingapuram, Kalrapatti RF. (Vellakuttai)- Nearest Villages- Vellakuttai Extn RF, Vellakuttai RF, Alangayam RF, Nimmiyampatti, Vallakutti, Narasingapuram, Naickanoor, Beemakullam. (Poongulam)- Nearest Villages- Naickanoor, Beemakullam, Poongulam RF.

Natural Division: Tondai Nadu.

Administration

Revenue **Division:** Tirupatahur. Parliamentary Constituency: 8 Vellore, 11 Tiruvannamalai. District: Vellore. Taluk: Vaniyambadi, Tirupathur. Assembly Constituency: 47 Vaniyambadi, 48 Ambur (SC), 50 Tiruppattur. Gram Pancha yat: 29.

Border Villages- (Andhra Pradesh)- Nearest Villages- Madakadappa (RF), Velathigamanipenta, Chinthagambenta.

Villages: 32 **Inhabited:** 26 **Uninhabited:** 6

Ranking	District	State	National
Area	4	76	1941
Population	13	144	3566
Sex Ratio	19	325	2843
Child Sex Ratio	19	332	5467
Literacy Rate	20	349	3354
Density	4	242	4179
Work Participation Rate	19	290	2600

Gram Panchayats:

Bheemakulam, Chettiappanur, Devasthanam, Echangal, Elayanagaram, Girisamudram, Govindapuram, Kalendra , Kothakottai, Madanancheri, Melkuppam, Naickanoor, Narasingapuram, Neknamalai, Nimmiyambattu, Pallipattu, Peddaveppambattu, Periakurumbatheru, Pudurnadu, Pungampattunadu, Reddiyur, Sammandikuppam, Valayambattu, Vallipattu, Velathigamanibenta, Vellakuttai, Vizilapuram, , .

Amenities:

Education: Primary School in 22 villages, Middle school in 9 villages, Matriculation or Secondary School in 8 villages, namely Nimmiyampatti, Vallakutti, Kothakottai, Girisamudram, Kelendra, Vallipattu, Beemakullam, Pudur Nadu.

Higher Secondary or Pre University Courses or Intermediate or Junior College in 4 villages of the CD Block,, namely Nimmiyampatti, Vallakutti, Kelendra, Pudur Nadu.

College in 0 village, Adult Literacy Center in 0 village.

Medical: Hospital in 2 villages, Dispensary in 1 village, Health Center in 2 villages, Sub Center in 5 villages, Maternity and Child Welfare Center in 9 villages, Community health workers in 22 villages.

The Villages having Hospital or Dispensary or Health Center are Nimmiyampatti, Valayambattu, Pudur Nadu.

Drinking Water: Tap water in 22 villages, Tank water in 4 villages, Well water in 13 villages, Tubewell in 1 village and more than one source in 22 villages.

Bank: Banking facility in 1 villages, namely, Vaniyambadi,Jaffrabad.

Credit Society in 9 villages Agricultural Credit Society in 9 Non-Agricultural Credit Society in 4 villages.

Others: Power supply in 22 villages, Cinema hall in 1 village, sport club in 0 village, Stadium or Auditorium or Community Hall in 0 village, Post Office in 19 villages.

There are 18 villages having bus facilities.

Villages with most of facilities: Vaniyambadi,Jaffrabad.

Villages without amenities (Education):

Alangayam Rf, Amburpettai, Innesjavadu Rf, Mambakkam Rf..

Scheduled Castes: Out of the total population of 96559 persons, 14406 persons (14.92%) belong to Scheduled Castes.

The villages having less than 10% SC population are Velathigamanipenta, Kothakottai, Govindapuram Amburpettai, Vallipattu, Reddiyur, Narasingapuram Naickanoor, Pungampattunadu, Innesjavadu Rf Pudur Nadu, Mambakkam Rf, Nellivasalnadu.

The villages having more than 50% SC population are None.

Sex ratio of Scheduled Caste population is 495.

Scheduled Castes Literates and Illiterates by Sex:

	Persons	Males	Females
Literate	7,789	4,544	3,245
Illiterate	6,617	2,729	3,888

Literacy rate	63.2	73.0	53.2
Graduate	110	90	20

Scheduled Castes (Dominant):
Adi Dravida, Arunthathiyar, Kuravan etc., Kudumban Puthirai Vannan

For their cultural identity please see Appendix-I

Villages without Scheduled Castes: There are 8 villages without any scheduled caste population.

Scheduled Tribes: Out of the total population of 96559 persons, 17301 persons (17.92%) belong to Scheduled Tribes. The villages having less than 10% ST population are Elayanagaram, Velathigamanipenta, Chinthagampenta Madanancheri, Nekkanamalai, Alangayam Rf Nimmiyampatti, Vallakutti, Valayambattu Girisamudram, Vaniyambadi,Jaffrabad, Devanthanam Kelendra, Govindapuram, Amburpettai, Vallipattu Reddiyur, Naickanoor.

The villages having more than 50% ST population are Pungampattunadu, Innesjavadu Rf, Pudur Nadu Mambakkam Rf, Nellivasalnadu.

Sex ratio of Scheduled tribe population is 483.

Scheduled Tribes Literates and Illiterates by Sex:

	Persons	Males	Females
Literate	6,055	3,971	2,084
Illiterate	11,246	4,969	6,277
Literacy rate	42.0	53.4	29.8
Graduate	67	62	5

Scheduled Tribes (Dominant):
Malayali, Kurumans, Irular, Malakkuravan Kattunayakan

For their cultural identity please see Appendix-II

Villages without Scheduled Tribes: There are 18 villages without any scheduled tribe population.

Literates and Illiterates by Sex (Total Population):

	Persons	Males	Females
Literate	46,841	28,139	18,702
Illiterate	49,718	21,045	28,673
Literacy rate	57	67	46
Graduate	639	495	144

Agriculture: ***Distribution of villages according to land use:*** Out of 32 villages, Total area (in hectare) is 39793.13, out of that 35.54 percent is cultivable and 6.77 percent of the cultivable area is irrigated.

Sources of Irrigation (Hectares): Government Canal 0, Private Canal 0, Well without Electricity 0, Well with Electricity 957.1, Tubewell without Electricity 0, Tubewell with Electricity 0, Tank 0, River 0, Lake 0, Waterfall 0, Others 0.

Villages with population of 5000 to 9999:
Madanancheri, Nimmiyambattu, Vellakuttai Kothakottai, Valayambattu, Kalendira Pungampattunadu.

Villages with population of 10000 and above: None

Distribution of Workers:

	Persons	Males	Females	WPR
Cultivators	18,185	11,588	6,597	39.49
Agricultural Labour	11,670	4,634	7,036	25.34
Household Industry	2,762	1,091	1,671	6
Other Workers	13,430	10,515	2,915	29.17
Main Workers	36,378	24,130	12,248	79
Marginal Workers	9,669	3,698	5,971	21
Total Workers	46,047	27,828	18,219	

Religion: Major Religious Communities:

	Persons	Males	Females	Sex Ratio
Hindu (97.47%)	94,116	47,981	46,135	962
Muslim (1.81%)	1,745	873	872	999
Christian (0.64%)	619	298	321	1,077
Sikh (0%)	1	1	-	-
Buddhists (0.01%)	5	2	3	1,500
Jain (0%)	2	1	1	1,000

Agewise Data:

	Persons	Males	Females	Sex Ratio
All ages	96,559	49,184	47,375	963
0-14	32,142	16,791	15,351	914
15-44	44,693	22,425	22,268	993
45-79	18,140	9,139	9,001	985
80+	847	453	394	870
Age not stated	737	376	361	960

Languages (Dominant):
Tamil, Telugu, Kannada, Urdu, Marathi

Disabled Population:

	Persons	Males	Females	%
Total Disabled	2,196	1,255	941	
In Seeing	1,154	652	502	52.55
In Speech	161	82	79	7.33
In Hearing	107	50	57	4.87
In Movement	616	380	236	28.05
Mentally	158	91	67	7.19

ALANGULAM

Alangulam C.D. Block lies in the central part of Tirunel veli district. It is a part of Veerakeralamputhur and Alangulam taluks. The Block is located at a distance of 35 kms. from district headquarters (Tirunelveli). There are 32 villages in the block with the total popul ation of 99,058 persons. Area of the C.D. Block is 342. 00 sq. kms. It is bounded in the north by CD Block Melaneelithallur, in the south by CD Block Pappakudi, in the east by CD Blocks Melaneelithanallur and Manur, in the west by CD Blocks Kadiyanallur and Keelapavoor.

CD Block Alangulam falls in taluk Veerakeralamputhur by 16 villages, and in taluk Alangulam by 16 villages.

Communications:

Roadways : S.H.-40: Direction- Alangulam to Tirunelveli, Nearest Villages- Sivacarkulam, Marandai. S.H.-41: Direction- Sankarankoil to Tirunelveli, Nearest Village- Marukkalankulam.

River: Chittar Nadi- Nearest Villages- Agaram, Mayaman Kurichi, Kadanganeri, Kaduvatty, Subbayapuram, Nettur I, Naranapuram, Veeranam.

Annual Rainfall: Average Rainfall 879 mm.

Ground Water: Availability of the ground water in the Basin is 46.92 MCM and the utilization is 36.98 MCM. It belongs to Semi Critical category. Depth to water level varies from 2 to 10 meter below the ground. Most of the wells go down in summer months, according to the Ground Water Estimation Committee.

Forest and Reserved Forest: (Kavalkutti RF)- Nearest Villages- Sivacarkulam, Kavalakutti Parambai RF, Marandai. (Kottamalai)- Nearest Villages- Subbayapuram, Nettur I - II Bit, Ayyanarkulam, Sivacarkulam, Kottamalai RF. (Mayamankurichi)- Nearest Villages- Mayaman Kurichi, Kaluneerkulam, Mayaman Kurichi RF. (Uthumalai)- Nearest Villages- Balabadraramapuram, Marukkalankulam, Uthumalai, Melamarudappapuram, Uthumalai, Muthammalpuram, Vadakku Kavalakurichi. (Vellakalparam)- Nearest Village- Veeranam.

Natural Division: NA

Administration

Revenue **Division:** Tenkasi. Parliamentary Constituency: 37 Tenkasi, 38 Tirunelveli. District: Tirunelveli. Taluk: Veerakeralamputhur, Alangulam. Assembly Constituency: 222 Tenkasi, 223 Alangulam. Gram Panchayat: 28.

Villages: 32 **Inhabited:** 27 **Uninhabited:** 5

Ranking	District	State	National
Area	8	126	2348
Population	3	132	3495
Sex Ratio	7	20	216
Child Sex Ratio	10	192	3232
Literacy Rate	13	156	1539
Density	1	52	3643
Work Participation Rate	9	239	476

Gram Panchayats:

Achankuttam, Ayyanarkulam, Balabhadraramapuram, Kadanganeri, Kaduvetti, Karuvantha, Kavalakurichi, Keelakkalangal, Keelaveerananam, Kidarankulam, Kurichampatti, Kurippankulam, Marandai, Marukkalangulam, Mayamankurichi, Melakalangal, Melamarudappapuram, Melaveeranam, Nallur, Naranapuram, Navaneethakrishnapuram, Nettur, Seevalasamudramkaradiudaippu, Sivalarkulam, Subbiahpuram, Uthumalai, Vadakkukavalakurichi, Vadi.

Amenities:

Education: Primary School in 25 villages, Middle school in 16 villages, Matriculation or Secondary School in 10 villages, namely Keelakalangal, Melamarudappapuram, Uthumalai, Vadi, Veeranam, Mayaman Kurichi, Kadanganeri, Naranapuram, Sivacarkulam, Marandai.

Higher Secondary or Pre University Courses or Intermediate or Junior College in 5 villages of the CD Block,, namely Melamarudappapuram, Uthumalai, Kadanganeri, Naranapuram, Sivacarkulam.

College in 1 village, Adult Literacy Center in 0 village., College is in village, namely Sivacarkulam.

Medical: Hospital in 2 villages, Dispensary in 1 village, Health Center in 2 villages, Sub Center in 13 villages, Maternity and Child Welfare Center in 8 villages, Community health workers in 23 villages.

The Villages having Hospital or Dispensary or Health Center are Navaneethakrishnapuram, Uthumalai, Mayaman Kurichi, Kadanganeri.

Drinking Water: Tap water in 27 villages, Tank water in 3 villages, Well water in 21 villages, Tubewell in 5 villages and more than one source in 24 villages.

Bank: Banking facility in 7 villages, namely, Uthumalai, Vadi, Veeranam, Kidarakulam, Kadanganeri Sivacarkulam, Marandai.

Credit Society in 6 villages Agricultural Credit Society in 2 Non-Agricultural Credit Society in 5 villages.

Others: Power supply in 25 villages, Cinema hall in 0 village, sport club in 0 village, Stadium or Auditorium or Community Hall in 0 village, Post Office in 23 villages.

There are 25 villages having bus facilities.

Villages with most of facilities: Uthumalai, Vadi Veeranam, Kidarakulam, Kadanganeri, Sivacarkulam.

Villages without amenities (Education):

Nettur I - Ii Bit (Uni), Nettur I..

Scheduled Castes: Out of the total population of 99058 persons, 14811 persons (14.95%) belong to Scheduled Castes.

The villages having less than 10% SC population are Marukkalankulam, Karuvanda, Achankuttam, Vadi Veeranam, Agaram, Nettur I - Ii Bit (Uni) Nettur I, Ayyanarkulam, Sivacarkulam.

The villages having more than 50% SC population are None.

Sex ratio of Scheduled Caste population is 522.

Scheduled Castes Literates and Illiterates by Sex:

	Persons	Males	Females
Literate	7,725	4,380	3,345
Illiterate	7,086	2,696	4,390
Literacy rate	60.0	72.3	49.1
Graduate	58	43	15

Scheduled Castes (Dominant):

Pallan, Paraiyan etc., Chakkiliyan, Arunthathiyar Puthirai Vannan

For their cultural identity please see Appendix-I

Villages without Scheduled Castes: There are 6 villages without any scheduled caste population.

Scheduled Tribes: Out of the total population of 99058 persons, 19 persons (0.02%) belong to Scheduled Tribes. The villages having less than 10% ST population are Keelakalangal, Balabadraramapuram, Marukkalankulam Melamarudappapuram, Navaneethakrishnapuram Melakkalangal, Kurichanipatti, Uthumalai Muthammalpuram, Vadakku Kavalakurichi, Karuvanda Achankuttam, Vadi, Veeranam, Agaram, Mayaman Kurichi Kidarakulam, Kavalakurichi Village, Kadanganeri Kaduvatty, Subbayapuram, Nettur I - Ii Bit (Uni) Nettur I, Naranapuram, Ayyanarkulam, Sivacarkulam Marandai.

The villages having more than 50% ST population are None.

Sex ratio of Scheduled tribe population is 368.

Scheduled Tribes Literates and Illiterates by Sex:

	Persons	Males	Females
Literate	9	6	3
Illiterate	10	6	4
Literacy rate	56.3	60.0	50.0
Graduate	0	0	0

Scheduled Tribes (Dominant):

Kattunayakan, Malakkuravan

For their cultural identity please see Appendix-II

Villages without Scheduled Tribes: There are 29 villages without any scheduled tribe population.

Literates and Illiterates by Sex (Total Population):

	Persons	Males	Females
Literate	58,338	33,017	25,321
Illiterate	40,720	14,986	25,734
Literacy rate	67	79	56
Graduate	748	476	272

Agriculture: *Distribution of villages according to land use:* Out of 32 villages, Total area (in hectare) is 34200.06, out of that 35.86 percent is cultivable and 49.96 percent of the cultivable area is irrigated.

Sources of Irrigation (Hectares): Government Canal 80.74, Private Canal 16.78, Well without Electricity 1520.88, Well with Electricity 2588.08, Tubewell without Electricity 73.56, Tubewell with Electricity 92.99, Tank 1715.56, River 3.53, Lake 35.77, Waterfall 0, Others 0.

Villages with population of 5000 to 9999: Uthumalai, Karuvanda, Veeranam, Mayamankurichi Kadanganeri, Sivalarkulam.

Villages with population of 10000 and above: None

Distribution of Workers:

	Persons	Males	Females	WPR
Cultivators	12,852	9,027	3,825	22.52
Agricultural Labour	15,705	8,986	6,719	27.52
Household Industry	18,189	1,371	16,818	31.88
Other Workers	10,313	8,421	1,892	18.07
Main Workers	53,320	26,377	26,943	93.45
Marginal Workers	3,739	1,428	2,311	6.55
Total Workers	57,059	27,805	29,254	

Religion: Major Religious Communities:

	Persons	Males	Females	Sex Ratio
Hindu (84.83%)	84,026	40,762	43,264	1,061
Muslim (3.09%)	3,064	1,475	1,589	1,077
Christian (12.04%)	11,929	5,745	6,184	1,076
Sikh (0%)	-	-	-	-
Buddhists (0%)	1	-	1	-
Jain (0%)	3	2	1	500

Agewise Data:

	Persons	Males	Females	Sex Ratio
All ages	99,058	48,003	51,055	1064
0-14	28,769	14,668	14,101	961
15-44	46,321	22,022	24,299	1103
45-79	22,702	10,722	11,980	1117
80+	1,048	470	578	1230
Age not stated	218	121	97	802

Languages (Dominant):

Tamil, Telugu, Malayalam, Hindi, Kannada

Disabled Population:

	Persons	Males	Females	%
Total Disabled	2,912	1,218	1,694	
In Seeing	1,856	623	1,233	63.74
In Speech	204	97	107	7.01
In Hearing	88	38	50	3.02
In Movement	588	358	230	20.19
Mentally	176	102	74	6.04

ALATHUR

Alathur C.D. Block lies in the southern part of Perambalur district. It is a part of Kunnam taluk. The Block is located at a distance of NA. kms. from district headquarters (Perambalur). There are 41 villages in the block with the total population of 96,585 persons. Area of the C.D. Block is 418.38 sq. kms. It is bounded in the north by CD Blocks Perambalur and Veppur, in the south by districts Tiruchirappali and Ariyalur, in the east by Ariyalur district, and in the west by district Tiruchirappalli.

Communications:

Roadways : N.H.-45: Direction- Tiruchirappalli to Ulundurpettai, Nearest Villages- Naranamangalam, Irur, Padalur (W), Padalur (E). S.H.-27: Direction- Kunnam to Ariyalur, Nearest Villages- Alagiripalayam, Melamathur, Thondapadi.

Railway Station: Sillakudi (N).

River: Anaippadi Nadi- Nearest Villages- Kolakkanatham, Kolathur (W), Kolathur (E), Grudalur, Nochikulam, Karai (E), Thirani, Aiyinapuram. Marudayar Nadi- Nearest Villages- Koothur, Bujangaranallur, Athur, Adhanur (S), Ariyalur (N), Kottarai, Grudalur, Adhanur (N).

Annual Rainfall: Average Rainfall 876 mm.

Ground Water: Availability of the ground water in the Basin is 4484.74 H.A.M. and the utilization is 4737.95 H.A.M. It belongs to Over Expoited category. Depth to water level varies from 2 to 10 meter below the ground. Most of the wells go down in summer months, according to the Ground Water Estimation Committee.

Forest and Reserved Forest: (Elandalapatti RF)- Nearest Villages- Elandalapatti RF, Elandalapatti. (Nekkaselam)- Nearest Villages- Siruvayalur, Nekkasalem RF, Nekkasalem.

Natural Division: Chola Nadu.

Administration

Revenue **Division:** Perambalur. Parliamentary Constituency: 25 Perambalur. District: Perambalur. Taluk: Kunnam. Assembly Constituency: 147 Perambalur (SC), 148 Kunnam. Gram Panchayat: 39.

Villages: 41 **Inhabited:** 39 **Uninhabited:** 2

Ranking	District	State	National
Area	3	59	1836
Population	3	143	3562
Sex Ratio	2	95	755
Child Sex Ratio	3	264	4362
Literacy Rate	3	242	2150
Density	1	45	4313
Work Participation Rate	3	302	391

Gram Panchayats:

Adhanur, Aiyinapuram, Alagiripalayam , Athur, Bhujangarayanallur , Chettikulam , Elandalapatti, Gudalur, Irur, Kannapady, Karai , Keelamathur, Kolakkanatham, Kolathur , Koothur, Kottarai, Kurambapalayam, Kurur, Mavilingai, Melamathur , Nakkaselam , Naranamangalam, Nattarmangalam, Nekkaselam, Nochikulam, Nochikulam, Padalur , Padalur , Peraiyur, Pilinisai, Sathanur, Sillakudi , Siruvayalur , T.Kalathur , Thenur , Thimmur, Thirani, Thondappadi , Varagupadi.

Amenities:

Education: Primary School in 38 villages, Middle school in 22 villages, Matriculation or Secondary School in 9 villages, namely Koothur, Karai (E), Chettikulam, Nekkasalem, T.Kalathur, Irur, Padalur (W), Kolakkanatham, Kolathur (E).

Higher Secondary or Pre University Courses or Intermediate or Junior College in 4 villages of the CD Block,, namely Koothur, Chettikulam, Padalur (W), Kolakkanatham.

College in 0 village, Adult Literacy Center in 0 village.

Medical: Hospital in 1 village, Dispensary in 5 villages, Health Center in 6 villages, Sub Center in 20 villages, Maternity and Child Welfare Center in 6 villages, Community health workers in 9 villages.

The Villages having Hospital or Dispensary or Health Center are Alagiripalayam, T.Kalathur, Thenur, Irur, Kolakkanatham.

Drinking Water: Tap water in 39 villages, Tank water in 1 villages, Well water in 39 villages, Tubewell in 39 villages and more than one source in 39 villages.

Bank: Banking facility in 13 villages, namely, Alagiripalayam, Melamathur, Koothur, Sathanur Sirukanpur [E], Sirukanpur [W], Chettikulam Nekkasalem, T.Kalathur, Irur, Padalur (W) Kolakkanatham, Sillakudi (N).

Credit Society in 21 villages Agricultural Credit Society in 17 Non-Agricultural Credit Society in 1 village.

Others: Power supply in 39 villages, Cinema hall in 3 villages, sport club in 0 village, Stadium or Auditorium or Community Hall in 0 village, Post Office in 36 villages.

There are 39 villages having bus facilities.

Villages with most of facilities: Alagiripalayam Melamathur, Koothur, Sirukanpur [E], Sirukanpur [W] Chettikulam, Nekkasalem, T.Kalathur, Irur Padalur (W), Kolakkanatham, Sillakudi (N).

Villages without amenities (Education):

Kolathur (W)..

Scheduled Castes: Out of the total population of 96585 persons, 25819 persons (26.73%) belong to Scheduled Castes.

The villages having less than 10% SC population are None..

The villages having more than 50% SC population are None.

Sex ratio of Scheduled Caste population is 509.

Scheduled Castes Literates and Illiterates by Sex:

	Persons	Males	Females
Literate	13,926	8,126	5,800
Illiterate	11,893	4,549	7,344
Literacy rate	61.6	73.4	50.3
Graduate	368	279	89

Scheduled Castes (Dominant):

Paraiyan etc., Pallan, Chakkiliyan, Arunthathiyar Adi Dravida

For their cultural identity please see Appendix-I

Villages without Scheduled Castes: There are 4 villages without any scheduled caste population.

Scheduled Tribes: Out of the total population of 96585

persons, 933 persons (0.97%) belong to Scheduled Tribes. The villages having less than 10% ST population are Alagiripalayam, Melamathur, Thondapadi, Koothur Adhanur [S], Ariyalur [N], Kottarai, Sathanur Sirukanpur [E], Sirukanpur [W], Varagupadi Karai (E), Karai (W), Naranamangalam Nattaramangalam, Chettikulam, Siruvayalur Nekkasalem, Elandalapatti, Puduammapalyam, Kannapady Thenur, Irur, Padalur (W), Padalur (E), Thirani Aiyinapuram, Kolakkanatham, Kolathur (W) Kolathur (E), Thimmur, Grudalur, Bujangaranallur Nochikulam, Athur, Sillakudi (N), Sillakudi (S).

The villages having more than 50% ST population are None.

Sex ratio of Scheduled tribe population is 494.

Scheduled Tribes Literates and Illiterates by Sex:

	Persons	Males	Females
Literate	677	365	312
Illiterate	256	107	149
Literacy rate	82.1	88.0	76.1
Graduate	57	40	17

Scheduled Tribes (Dominant):

Kondareddis, Uraly, Malakkuravan, Irular Kattunayakan

For their cultural identity please see Appendix-II

Villages without Scheduled Tribes: There are 31 villages without any scheduled tribe population.

Literates and Illiterates by Sex (Total Population):

	Persons	Males	Females
Literate	54,096	31,900	22,196
Illiterate	42,489	16,039	26,450
Literacy rate	64	76	52
Graduate	1,487	1,102	385

Agriculture: ***Distribution of villages according to land use:*** Out of 41 villages, Total area (in hectare) is 41838, out of that 65.95 percent is cultivable and 24.55 percent of the cultivable area is irrigated.

Sources of Irrigation (Hectares): Government Canal 490.93, Private Canal 6.21, Well without Electricity 1379.94, Well with Electricity 3545.86, Tubewell without Electricity 47.59, Tubewell with Electricity 146.09, Tank 506.32, River 0, Lake 370.11, Waterfall 0, Others 280.5.

Villages with population of 5000 to 9999:

Chettikulam , Siruvayalur , Padalur (West).

Villages with population of 10000 and above: None

Distribution of Workers:

	Persons	Males	Females	WPR
Cultivators	29,477	16,307	13,170	52.18
Agricultural Labour	18,671	7,287	11,384	33.05
Household Industry	994	443	551	1.76
Other Workers	7,347	5,415	1,932	13.01
Main Workers	49,101	27,045	22,056	86.92
Marginal Workers	7,388	2,407	4,981	13.08
Total Workers	56,489	29,452	27,037	

Religion: Major Religious Communities:

	Persons	Males	Females	Sex Ratio
Hindu (98.5%)	95,136	47,241	47,895	1,014
Muslim (1.05%)	1,013	490	523	1,067
Christian (0.38%)	363	169	194	1,148
Sikh (0%)	1	-	1	-
Buddhists (0%)	1	1	-	-
Jain (0%)	2	1	1	1,000

Agewise Data:

	Persons	Males	Females	Sex Ratio
All ages	96,585	47,939	48,646	1015
0-14	26,356	13,593	12,763	939
15-44	45,689	22,089	23,600	1068
45-79	23,492	11,713	11,779	1006
80+	831	430	401	933
Age not stated	217	114	103	904

Languages (Dominant):

Tamil, Telugu, Urdu, Hindi, Malayalam

Disabled Population:

	Persons	Males	Females	%
Total Disabled	2,413	1,109	1,304	
In Seeing	1,320	468	852	54.7
In Speech	328	182	146	13.59
In Hearing	94	46	48	3.9
In Movement	505	317	188	20.93
Mentally	166	96	70	6.88

ALWARTHIRUNAGIRI

Alwarthirunagiri C.D. Block lies in the southern part of Thoothukkudi district. It is a part of Tiruchendur and Sathankulam taluks. The Block is located at a distance of 32 kms. from district headquarters (Thoothukkudi). There are 30 villages in the block with the total population of 77,926 persons. Area of the C.D. Block is 181.18 sq. kms. It is bounded in the north by CD Block Srivaikuntam and Karunkulam, in the south by Blocks Sathankulam and Udangudi, in the east by the Gulf of Mannar and CD Block Tiruchendur, and in the west by district Tirunelveli.

CD Block Alwarthirunagiri falls in taluk Tiruchendur by 23 villages, and in taluk Sathankulam by 07 villages.

Communications:

Roadways : S.H.-40: Direction- Tirunelveli to Arumuganeri, Nearest Villages- Athinathapuram, Tirukkalur, T.Kurukat hur, Rajapathy, Angamangalam, Puriyoor, Alagiamanavalapuram, Nalumavadi.

Railway Station: Kachannavilai, Nalumavadi.

River: Tambraparani Nadi- Nearest Villages- Athinathapur am, Tirukkalur, Mavadippannai, Rajapathy, Sathukkuvaithan.

Suganthalai, Punnaikayal.

Annual Rainfall: Average Rainfall 661 mm.

Ground Water: Availability of the ground water in the Basin is 33.64 MCM and the utilization is 2.19 MCM. It belongs to Safe category. Depth to water level varies from 0 to 10 meter below the ground. Most of the wells go down in summer months, according to the Ground Water Estimation Committee.

Coastal Villages- (Gulf of Mannar)- Village- Punnaikayal.

Forest and Reserved Forest: (Kuthiraimoli RF)- Nearest Villages- Mukkuperi, Kachannavilai, Nalumavadi.

Natural Division: NA

Administration

Revenue **Division:** Tiruchendur. Parliamentary Constituenc y: 36 Thoothukkudi. District: Thoothukkudi. Taluk: Tiruc hendur, Sathankulam. Assembly Constituency. Gram Panchaya t: 30.

Villages: 30 **Inhabited:** 29 **Uninhabited:** 1

Ranking	District	State	National
Area	11	309	4523
Population	6	253	4173
Sex Ratio	3	4	74
Child Sex Ratio	9	257	4311
Literacy Rate	5	14	190
Density	9	350	2561
Work Participation Rate	2	95	4376

Gram Panchayats:

Alagiamanavalapuram, Angamangalam, Athinathapuram, Cambalcabad, Kadayanodai, Karungadal, Katchinavilai, Kattarimangalam, Kurangani, Kurippankulam, Kurukattur, Malavarayanatham, Meerankulam , Mela Authoor, Mukkuperi, Nalumavadi, Punnakayal, Puraiyoor, Rajapathi, Senthamangalam, Sethukkuvaithan, Srivenkateshwarapuram, Suganthalai , Themankulam, Thirukalore, Udayarkulam, Varandiavel, Vellamadam.

Amenities:

Education: Primary School in 27 villages, Middle school in 20 villages, Matriculation or Secondary School in 4 villages, namely Punnaikayal, Mukkuperi, Nalumavadi, Srivenkateswarapuram.

Higher Secondary or Pre University Courses or Intermediate or Junior College in 2 villages of the CD Block,, namely Mukkuperi, Srivenkateswarapuram.

College in 1 village, Adult Literacy Center in 0 village., College is in villages, namely Vellamadam.

Medical: Hospital in 2 villages, Dispensary in 0 village, Health Center in 3 villages, Sub Center in 15 villages, Maternity and Child Welfare Center in 1 village, Community health workers in 28 villages.

The Villages having Hospital or Dispensary or Health Center are Rajapathy, Punnaikayal, Nalumavadi.

Drinking Water: Tap water in 29 villages, Tank water in 3 villages, Well water in 29 villages, Tubewell in 29 villages and more than one source in 29 villages.

Bank: Banking facility in 7 villages, namely, Sathukkuvaithan, Mela Autoor, Punnaikayal Angamangalam, Mukkuperi, Kattarimangalam Srivenkateswarapuram.

Credit Society in 3 villages Agricultural Credit Society in 2 Non-Agricultural Credit Society in 1 village.

Others: Power supply in 27 villages, Cinema hall in 3 villages, sport club in 0 village, Stadium or Auditorium or Community Hall in 0 village, Post Office in 26 villages.

There are 28 villages having bus facilities.

Villages with most of facilities: Sathukkuvaithan Mela Autoor, Punnaikayal, Angamangalam, Mukkuperi Kattarimangalam, Srivenkateswarapuram.

Villages without amenities (Education):

Thirunavakailayapuram, Pirandakulam..

Scheduled Castes: Out of the total population of 77926 persons, 14506 persons (18.62%) belong to Scheduled Castes.

The villages having less than 10% SC population are Mavadippannai, Punnaikayal, Suganthalai Kurippankulam, Mukkuperi, Meerankulam, Karungadal Srivenkateswarapuram.

The villages having more than 50% SC population are Athinathapuram, T.Kurukathur, Rajapathy Thirunavakailayapuram, Alagiamanavalapuram.

Sex ratio of Scheduled Caste population is 513.

Scheduled Castes Literates and Illiterates by Sex:

	Persons	Males	Females
Literate	9,901	5,243	4,658
Illiterate	4,605	1,821	2,784
Literacy rate	77.7	85.2	70.7
Graduate	237	144	93

Scheduled Castes (Dominant):

Pallan, Paraiyan etc., Chakkiliyan, Puthirai Vannan Arunthathiyar

For their cultural identity please see Appendix-I

Villages without Scheduled Castes: There is 1 village without any scheduled caste population.

Scheduled Tribes: Out of the total population of 77926 persons, 40 persons (0.05%) belong to Scheduled Tribes.

The villages having less than 10% ST population are Malavarayanatham, Athinathapuram, Tirukkalur Mavadippannai, T.Kurukathur, Rajapathy Sathukkuvaithan, Mela Autoor, Sernthamangalam Punnaikayal, Suganthalai, Angamangalam, Puriyoor Kadaiyanodai, Themankulam, Thirunavakailayapuram

Alagiamanavalapuram, Udaiyarkulam, Kurippankulam Vellamadam, Mukkuperi, Kachannavilai, Nalumavadi Meerankulam, Meerankulam, Karungadal Kattarimangalam, Srivenkateswarapuram, Pirandakulam.

The villages having more than 50% ST population are None.

Sex ratio of Scheduled tribe population is 450.

Scheduled Tribes Literates and Illiterates by Sex:

	Persons	Males	Females
Literate	14	11	3
Illiterate	26	11	15
Literacy rate	41.2	57.9	20.0
Graduate	0	0	0

Scheduled Tribes (Dominant):

Kattunayakan, Kaniyan etc., Kadar, Kurumans Malakkuravan

For their cultural identity please see Appendix-II

Villages without Scheduled Tribes: There are 22 villages without any scheduled tribe population.

Literates and Illiterates by Sex (Total Population):

	Persons	Males	Females
Literate	57,140	28,171	28,969
Illiterate	20,786	8,608	12,178
Literacy rate	83	88	79
Graduate	1,422	795	627

Agriculture: ***Distribution of villages according to land use:*** Out of 30 villages, Total area (in hectare) is 18118.54, out of that 32.49 percent is cultivable and 66.37 percent of the cultivable area is irrigated.

Sources of Irrigation (Hectares): Government Canal 516.7, Private Canal 0, Well without Electricity 27.22, Well with Electricity 488.06, Tubewell without Electricity 3.48, Tubewell with Electricity 15.31, Tank 2856.59, River 0, Lake 0, Waterfall 0, Others 0.

Villages with population of 5000 to 9999: Mela Authoor, Punnakayal, Karungadal.

Villages with population of 10000 and above: None

Distribution of Workers:

	Persons	Males	Females	WPR
Cultivators	3,584	2,605	979	11.25
Agricultural Labour	12,289	6,462	5,827	38.58
Household Industry	2,928	652	2,276	9.19
Other Workers	13,055	9,979	3,076	40.98
Main Workers	27,025	17,553	9,472	84.83
Marginal Workers	4,831	2,145	2,686	15.17
Total Workers	31,856	19,698	12,158	

Religion: Major Religious Communities:

	Persons	Males	Females	Sex Ratio
Hindu (61.69%)	48,073	22,756	25,317	1,113
Muslim (4.52%)	3,520	1,520	2,000	1,316
Christian (31.89%)	24,849	11,830	13,019	1,101
Sikh (0%)	1	1	-	-
Buddhists (0%)	-	-	-	-
Jain (0.01%)	7	2	5	2,500

Agewise Data:

	Persons	Males	Females	Sex Ratio
All ages	76,474	36,121	40,353	1117
0-14	22,409	11,421	10,988	962
15-44	34,447	15,676	18,771	1197
45-79	18,665	8,557	10,108	1181
80+	826	390	436	1118
Age not stated	127	77	50	649

Languages (Dominant):

Tamil, Telugu, Malayalam, Kannada, Urdu

Disabled Population:

	Persons	Males	Females	%
Total Disabled	2,119	969	1,150	
In Seeing	1,048	391	657	49.46
In Speech	143	74	69	6.75
In Hearing	99	37	62	4.67
In Movement	598	345	253	28.22
Mentally	231	122	109	10.9

AMBASAMUDRAM

Ambasamudram C.D. Block lies in the south-western part of Tirunelveli district. It is a part of Ambasamudram taluk. The Block is located at a distance of 36 kms. from district headquarters (Tirunelveli). There are 15 villages in the block with the total population of 34,707 persons. Area of the C.D. Block is 663.60 sq. kms. It is bounded in the north by CD Block Tenkasi, in the south by district Kanniyakumari and CD Block Kalakkadu, in the east by CD Blocks Kadayam, Papakudi and Cheranma devi, and in the west it has common boundary with the state of Kerala.

Communications:

Roadways : S.H.-40: Direction- Tenkasi to Kallakurichi, Nearest Villages- Mannarkoil, Vagaikulam, Vellamguli, Vairavikulam, Therku Viravanallur.

River: Tambraparani Nadi- Nearest Villages- Adayakarunku lam, Ekambarapuram, Kodarankulam, Pappankulam, Ayansingampatti, Vairavikulam, Singampatti, Papanasam RF.

Annual Rainfall: Average Rainfall 879 mm.

Ground Water: Availability of the ground water in the Basin is 38.30 MCM and the utilization is 4.49 MCM. It belongs to Safe category. Depth to water level varies from 0 to 10 meter below the ground. Most of the wells go down in summer months, according to the Ground Water Estimation Committee.

Forest and Reserved Forest: (Papanasam RF)- Nearest Village s- Papanasam. (Singampatti)- Nearest Villages- Pappankulam, Singampatti, Singampatti Zamindar Forest.

Natural Division: NA

Administration

Revenue **Division:** Cheranmadevi. Parliamentary Constituen cy: 38 Tirunelveli. District: Tirunelveli. Taluk: Ambasa mudram. Assembly Constituency: 227 Nanguneri, 225 Ambasamudram. Gram Panchayat: 12.

Border Villages- (Kerala)- Nearest Village- Papanasam.

Villages: 15 **Inhabited:** 14 **Uninhabited:** 1

Ranking	District	State	National
Area	1	14	1006
Population	17	377	5918
Sex Ratio	12	48	421
Child Sex Ratio	1	1	48
Literacy Rate	5	36	525
Density	10	165	6305
Work Participation Rate	19	385	1637

Gram Panchayats:

Adaiyakarungulam, Ayansingampatti, Ayanthiruvaleswaram, Brahmadesam, Kedarangulam , Mannarkovil, Therkupappankulam, Vagaikulam, Vairavikulam, Vellanguli , Zaminsingampatti, .

Amenities:

Education: Primary School in 12 villages, Middle school in 7 villages, Matriculation or Secondary School in 4 villages, namely Papanasam, Mannarkoil, Vellamguli, Ayansingampatti.

Higher Secondary or Pre University Courses or Intermediate or Junior College in 1 village of the CD Block,, namely Mannarkoil.

College in 0 village, Adult Literacy Center in 0 village.

Medical: Hospital in 0 village, Dispensary in 0 village, Health Center in 4 villages, Sub Center in 8 villages, Maternity and Child Welfare Center in 2 villages, Community health workers in 7 villages.

Drinking Water: Tap water in 14 villages, Tank water in 4 villages, Well water in 2 villages, Tubewell in 1 village and more than one source in 13 villages.

Bank: Banking facility in 3 villages, namely, Brahmadesam, Vellamguli, Ayansingampatti.

Credit Society in 3 villages Agricultural Credit Society in 2 Non-Agricultural Credit Society in 1 village.

Others: Power supply in 13 villages, Cinema hall in 0 village, sport club in 0 village, Stadium or Auditorium or Community Hall in 0 village, Post Office in 11 villages.

There are 11 villages having bus facilities.

Villages with most of facilities: Brahmadesam Vellamguli, Ayansingampatti.

Villages without amenities (Education):

Ekambarapuram, Singampatti Zamindar Forest..

Scheduled Castes: Out of the total population of 34707 persons, 7786 persons (22.43%) belong to Scheduled Castes.

The villages having less than 10% SC population are None..

The villages having more than 50% SC population are None.

Sex ratio of Scheduled Caste population is 523.

Scheduled Castes Literates and Illiterates by Sex:

	Persons	Males	Females
Literate	4,498	2,498	2,000
Illiterate	3,288	1,216	2,072
Literacy rate	65.9	76.7	56.1
Graduate	42	30	12

Scheduled Castes (Dominant):

Paraiyan etc., Pallan, Chakkiliyan, Arunthathiyar Puthirai Vannan

For their cultural identity please see Appendix-I

Villages without Scheduled Castes: There is 1 village without any scheduled caste population.

Scheduled Tribes: Out of the total population of 34707 persons, 33 persons (0.1%) belong to Scheduled Tribes.

The villages having less than 10% ST population are Papanasam, Ayan Thiruvaleeshvaran, Mannarkoil Brahmadesam, Vagaikulam, Adayakarunkulam Ekambarapuram, Kodarankulam, Vellamguli, Pappankulam Ayansingampatti, Vairavikulam, Singampatti Singampatti Zamindar Forest.

The villages having more than 50% ST population are None.

Sex ratio of Scheduled tribe population is 394.

Scheduled Tribes Literates and Illiterates by Sex:

	Persons	Males	Females
Literate	21	14	7
Illiterate	12	6	6
Literacy rate	70.0	77.8	58.3
Graduate	1	0	1

Scheduled Tribes (Dominant):

Kaniyan etc., Kattunayakan, Irular, Paniyan

For their cultural identity please see Appendix-II

Villages without Scheduled Tribes: There are 11 villages without any scheduled tribe population.

Literates and Illiterates by Sex (Total Population):

	Persons	Males	Females
Literate	23,616	13,035	10,581
Illiterate	11,091	4,021	7,070
Literacy rate	77	86	68
Graduate	569	389	180

Agriculture: ***Distribution of villages according to land use:*** Out of 15 villages, Total area (in hectare) is 66360.78, out of that 3.78 percent is cultivable and 83.73 percent of the cultivable area is irrigated.

Sources of Irrigation (Hectares): Government Canal 1064.76, Private Canal 0, Well without Electricity 25.18, Well with Electricity 52.08, Tubewell without Electricity 0, Tubewell with Electricity 0, Tank 956.74, River 0, Lake 0, Waterfall 0, Others 0.

Villages with population of 5000 to 9999: Brahmadesam.

Villages with population of 10000 and above: None

Distribution of Workers:

	Persons	Males	Females	WPR
Cultivators	2,312	1,859	453	12.53
Agricultural Labour	5,497	3,390	2,107	29.79
Household Industry	5,111	598	4,513	27.7
Other Workers	5,530	4,272	1,258	29.97
Main Workers	13,982	7,909	6,073	75.78
Marginal Workers	4,468	2,210	2,258	24.22
Total Workers	18,450	10,119	8,331	

Religion: Major Religious Communities:

	Persons	Males	Females	Sex Ratio
Hindu (92.59%)	32,136	15,795	16,341	1,035
Muslim (2.1%)	728	365	363	995
Christian (5.21%)	1,809	875	934	1,067
Sikh (0.01%)	2	2	-	-
Buddhists (0%)	1	1	-	-
Jain (0.01%)	2	1	1	1,000

Agewise Data:

	Persons	Males	Females	Sex Ratio
All ages	34,707	17,056	17,651	1035
0-14	9,129	4,621	4,508	976
15-44	16,706	8,087	8,619	1066
45-79	8,193	4,003	4,190	1047
80+	341	168	173	1030
Age not stated	338	177	161	910

Languages (Dominant):

Tamil, Telugu, Malayalam, Urdu, Kannada

Disabled Population:

	Persons	Males	Females	%
Total Disabled	1,009	541	468	
In Seeing	482	253	229	47.77
In Speech	124	69	55	12.29
In Hearing	65	23	42	6.44
In Movement	259	159	100	25.67
Mentally	79	37	42	7.83

AMMAPET

Ammapet C.D. Block lies in the north-eastern part of Erode district. It is a part of Bhavani taluk. The Block is located at a distance of 45 kms. from district headquarters (Erode). There are 19 villages in the block with the total population of 97,786 persons. Area of the C.D. Block is 202.88 sq. kms. It is bounded in the north and east by district Salem, in the south by C.D. Block Bhavani, and in the west by C.D. Block Anthiyur.

Communications:

Roadways : S.H.-20: Direction- Bhavani to Mettur, Nearest Villages- Kurichi, Singampettai, Padavalkalvai, Kadappanalloor, Kesarimangalam.

River: Bhavani Nadi- Nearest Village- Mathur. Cauvery Nadi- Nearest Villages- Padavalkalvai, Kadappanalloor, Kesarimangalam.

Annual Rainfall: Average Rainfall 789 mm.

Ground Water: Availability of the ground water in the Basin is 5718.46 H.A.M. and the utilization is 6638.23 H.A.M. It belongs to Over Expoited category. Depth to water level varies from 2 to 20 meter below the ground. Most of the wells go down in summer months, according to the Ground Water Estimation Committee.

Forest and Reserved Forest: (Burgur RF)- Nearest Villages- Komarayanur.

Natural Division: Kongu Nadu.

Administration

Revenue **Division:** Gobichettipalayam. Parliamentary Constituency: 18 Gobichettipalayam. District: Erode. Taluk: Bhavani. Assembly Constituency: 105 Anthiyur, 104 Bhavani. Gram Panchayat: 20.

Villages: 19 **Inhabited:** 19 **Uninhabited:** 0

Ranking	District	State	National
Area	13	282	4129
Population	2	138	3528
Sex Ratio	20	366	4598
Child Sex Ratio	20	365	6090
Literacy Rate	17	365	3938
Density	8	11	2298
Work Participation Rate	4	63	100

Gram Panchayats:

Attavanaipudur, Boothapadi, Chennampatti, Guruvareddiyur, Kadappanallur, Kalbavi, Kannapalli, Kesarimangalam, Komarayanur, Kurichi , Manickampalayam, Mathur, Mukasipudur, Oddapalayam, Padavalkalvai, Patlur, Poonachi, Pudur, Singampettai, Vellithiruppur.

Amenities:

Education: Primary School in 19 villages, Middle school in 10 villages, Matriculation or Secondary School in 8 villages, namely Channampettai, Vellithiruppur, Illipili, Kurichi, Poonachi, Boodhapadi, Singampettai, Kesarimangalam.

Higher Secondary or Pre University Courses or Intermediate or Junior College in 4 villages of the CD Block,, namely Channampettai, Illipili, Poonachi, Singampettai.

College in 0 village, Adult Literacy Center in 0 village.
Medical: Hospital in 3 villages, Dispensary in 1 village, Health Center in 1 village, Sub Center in 16 villages, Maternity and Child Welfare Center in 8 villages, Community health workers in 7 villages.
The Villages having Hospital or Dispensary or Health Center are Illipili, Patloor, Boodhapadi.
Drinking Water: Tap water in 19 villages, Tank water in 0 villages, Well water in 19 villages, Tubewell in 19 villages and more than one source in 19 villages.
Bank: Banking facility in 8 villages, namely, Channampettai, Vellithiruppur, Illipili Attavanaipudur, Patloor, Singampettai, Padavalkalvai Kesarimangalam.
Credit Society in 11 villages Agricultural Credit Society in 10 Non-Agricultural Credit Society in 2 villages.
Others: Power supply in 19 villages, Cinema hall in 4 villages, sport club in 0 village, Stadium or Auditorium or Community Hall in 1 village, Post Office in 15 villages.
There are 15 villages having bus facilities.
Villages with most of facilities: Channampettai Vellithiruppur, Illipili, Attavanaipudur, Patloor Singampettai, Kesarimangalam.
Villages without Amenities (Education): None..
Scheduled Castes: Out of the total population of 97786 persons, 18756 persons (19.18%) belong to Scheduled Castes.
The villages having less than 10% SC population are None..
The villages having more than 50% SC population are None.
Sex ratio of Scheduled Caste population is 485.
Scheduled Castes Literates and Illiterates by Sex:

	Persons	Males	Females
Literate	7,018	4,464	2,554
Illiterate	11,738	5,202	6,536
Literacy rate	42.4	52.6	31.6
Graduate	125	103	22

Scheduled Castes (Dominant):
Chakkiliyan, Adi Dravida, Arunthathiyar Paraiyan etc., Kuravan etc.
For their cultural identity please see Appendix-I
Villages without Scheduled Castes: There is 0 village without any scheduled caste population.
Scheduled Tribes: Out of the total population of 97786 persons, 2404 persons (2.46%) belong to Scheduled Tribes.
The villages having less than 10% ST population are Komarayanur, Pudur, Channampettai, Mathur Vellithiruppur, Illipili, Kannappalli, Mukusipudur Oddapalayam, Kalbavi, Kurichi, Poonachi, Boodhapadi Singampettai, Padavalkalvai, Kadappanalloor Kesarimangalam.
The villages having more than 50% ST population are None.
Sex ratio of Scheduled tribe population is 493.
Scheduled Tribes Literates and Illiterates by Sex:

	Persons	Males	Females
Literate	1,667	942	725
Illiterate	737	277	460
Literacy rate	75.4	84.8	65.9
Graduate	76	50	26

Scheduled Tribes (Dominant):
Kondareddis, Kochu Velan, Uraly, Kattunayakan Malai Pandaram
For their cultural identity please see Appendix-II
Villages without Scheduled Tribes: There are 4 villages without any scheduled tribe population.
Literates and Illiterates by Sex (Total Population):

	Persons	Males	Females
Literate	46,950	29,554	17,396
Illiterate	50,836	21,229	29,607
Literacy rate	54	65	41
Graduate	1,192	920	272

Agriculture: ***Distribution of villages according to land use:***
Out of 19 villages, Total area (in hectare) is 20288.79, out of that 73.12 percent is cultivable and 48.15 percent of the cultivable area is irrigated.
Sources of Irrigation (Hectares): Government Canal 2235.92, Private Canal 0, Well without Electricity 287.24, Well with Electricity 4513.64, Tubewell without Electricity 0, Tubewell with Electricity 0, Tank 0, River 105.72, Lake 0, Waterfall 0, Others 0.
Villages with population of 5000 to 9999:
Chennampatti, Mathur, Vellithiruppur, Illippili Kannapalli, Patlur, Kesarimangalam.
Villages with population of 10000 and above:
Kurichi.
Distribution of Workers:

	Persons	Males	Females	WPR
Cultivators	17,402	9,827	7,575	27.75
Agricultural Labour	32,638	15,516	17,122	52.05
Household Industry	1,687	747	940	2.69
Other Workers	10,981	7,995	2,986	17.51
Main Workers	55,268	31,587	23,681	88.14
Marginal Workers	7,440	2,498	4,942	11.86
Total Workers	62,708	34,085	28,623	

Religion: Major Religious Communities:

	Persons	Males	Females	Sex Ratio
Hindu (98.77%)	96,585	50,192	46,393	924
Muslim (0.45%)	440	216	224	1,037
Christian (0.71%)	699	346	353	1,020

Sikh (0%)	2	1	1	1,000
Buddhists (0%)	1	-	1	-
Jain (0%)	2	-	2	-

Agewise Data:

	Persons	Males	Females	Sex Ratio
All ages	97,786	50,783	47,003	926
0-14	22,702	12,296	10,406	846
15-44	47,545	24,323	23,222	955
45-79	26,290	13,473	12,817	951
80+	1,085	606	479	790
Age not stated	164	85	79	929

Languages (Dominant):
Tamil, Telugu, Kannada, Hindi, Urdu

Disabled Population:

	Persons	Males	Females	%
Total Disabled	1,953	926	1,027	
In Seeing	973	355	618	49.82
In Speech	171	96	75	8.76
In Hearing	79	35	44	4.05
In Movement	552	339	213	28.26
Mentally	178	101	77	9.11

AMMAPETTAI

Ammapettai C.D. Block lies in the north-eastern part of Thanjavur district. It is a part of Papanasam taluk. The Block is located at a distance of 22 kms. from district headquarters (Thanjavur). There are 68 villages in the block with the total population of 93,138 persons. Area of the C.D. Block is 220.09 sq. kms. It is bounded in the north by C.D. Block Papanasam, in the south by CD Block Orathanadu and district Thiruvarur, in the east by district Thiruvarur, and in the west by CD Block Thanjavur.

Communications:
Roadways : N.H.-67: Direction- Thanjavur to Needamangalam, Nearest Villages- Palliyor, Vadapathi, Kelakovilpathu, Saliyamangalam, Poondi I, Kumilakudi, Pulavarnatham, Alangudi Bit, Bavaniambalpuram, Arulmozhipettai, Raramuthirakkottai, Nallavaiyan, Thirubavanam.
Railway Station: Neidalur, Saliyamangalam, Kumilakudi.
River: Vettar Nadi- Nearest Villages- Surikayur, Neidalur, Onbathuveli, Thirukkarugavur, Kavalur, Annappanpettai, Kattukkurichi, Vilithiyur, Agaramangudi. Vennar Nadi- Nearest Villages- Vilithiyur, Milattur V Sethy, Melattur IV Sethi, Kothangudi, Edakkudi, Utharamangalam Thottam, Authur Thottam, Melakkalukudi, Edavakudy, Kalanchery, Palliyor, Neikkunnam, Deebambalpuram, Mahimalai, Neduvasal, Karaimudukku, Ukkadai, Nellithoppu, Alangudi.
Annual Rainfall: Average Rainfall 1147 mm.
Ground Water: Availability of the ground water in the Basin is 6353.49 H.A.M. and the utilization is 6033. 05 H.A.M. It belongs to Critical category. Depth to water level varies from 2 to 20 meter below the ground. Most of the wells go down in summer months, according to the Ground Water Estimation Committee.
Natural Division: Chola Nadu.

Administration
Revenue **Division:** Kumbakonam. Parliamentary Constituency: 29 Thanjavur. District: Thanjavur. Taluk: Papanasam. Assembly Constituency: 172 Papanasam. Gram Panchayat: 46.
Villages: 68 **Inhabited:** 64 **Uninhabited:** 4

Ranking	District	State	National
Area	6	261	3855
Population	8	164	3685
Sex Ratio	11	154	1083
Child Sex Ratio	12	202	3315
Literacy Rate	12	164	1598
Density	7	300	2596
Work Participation Rate	7	100	3404

Gram Panchayats:
Agaramangudi, Alangudi, Annappanpettai, Arumalaikottai, Arundavapuram , Devaryampettai, Edaiyiruppu, Edavakkudi, Irumbuthalai, Jambugapuri, Kalancheri, Kambayanatham, Karuppumudaliyur kottai, Kathirinatham, Kavalur, Keelakoil Pathu , Kothangudi, Kovathagudi, Kumilakudi, Mahimalai, Melakalakudi, Melasemmangudi, Nallavanniyankudikadu, Neduvasal , Neikunnam, Nellithope, Ombathuveli, Palliyur, Perumakkanallur, Poondi, Poondi , Pulavarnatham, Puliyakudi , Pulvarnatham, Raramuthirakkottai, Saliyamangalam, Serumakkanallur, Sooliyakottai, Suraikkayur, Thirubuvanam, Thirukkarugavur, Thiruvaiyathukudi, Ukkadai, Vadakkumangudi, Vadapathy , Vaiyacheri, Vembukudi, Viluthiyur.

Amenities:
Education: Primary School in 58 villages, Middle school in 21 villages, Matriculation or Secondary School in 4 villages, namely Thirukkarugavur, Palliyor, Saliyamangalam, Poondi I.
Higher Secondary or Pre University Courses or Intermediate or Junior College in 1 village of the CD Block,, namely Palliyor.
College in 1 village, Adult Literacy Center in 0 village., College is in village, namely Poondi I.
Medical: Hospital in 0 village, Dispensary in 5 villages, Health Center in 3 villages, Sub Center in 12 villages, Maternity and Child Welfare Center in 0 village, Community health workers in 64 villages.
The Villages having Hospital or Dispensary or Health Center are Thiruvaiyathukudi, Vadakku Mangudi,

Thirukkarugavur, Milattur V Sethy, Arundavapuram.

Drinking Water: Tap water in 64 villages, Tank water in 1 villages, Well water in 64 villages, Tubewell in 64 villages and more than one source in 64 villages.

Bank: Banking facility in 6 villages, namely, Vadakku Mangudi, Perumakkanallur, Thirukkarugavur Kalanchery, Saliyamangalam, Poondi I.

Credit Society in 11 villages Agricultural Credit Society in 11 Non-Agricultural Credit Society in 1 village.

Others: Power supply in 64 villages, Cinema hall in 3 villages, sport club in 0 village, Stadium or Auditorium or Community Hall in 0 village, Post Office in 35 villages.

There are 54 villages having bus facilities.

Villages with most of facilities: Vadakku Mangudi Thirukkarugavur, Kalanchery, Saliyamangalam Poondi I.

Villages without amenities (Education): Pulimangalam, Ponmeinthanallur, Mahimalai Bit, Poondi Ii, Bavaniambalpuram..

Scheduled Castes: Out of the total population of 93138 persons, 32592 persons (34.99%) belong to Scheduled Castes. The villages having less than 10% SC population are Venukudi Thottam, Bavaniambalpuram, Arulmozhipettai Katharinatham, Thirubavanam, Puliyakkudi.

The villages having more than 50% SC population are Thiruvaiyathukudi, Purakkudi, Perumakkanallur Vembukudi, Edaiyiruppu, Kavalur, Neidalur Kattukkurichi, Milattur V Sethy, Kothangudi Edakkudi, Utharamangalam, Authur Thottam Melakkalukudi, Edavakudy, Kandavanam, Palliyor Mahimalai, Alangudi.

Sex ratio of Scheduled Caste population is 502.

Scheduled Castes Literates and Illiterates by Sex:

	Persons	Males	Females
Literate	16,192	9,609	6,583
Illiterate	16,400	6,611	9,789
Literacy rate	58.1	69.6	46.9
Graduate	197	169	28

Scheduled Castes (Dominant):

Pallan, Paraiyan etc., Adi Dravida, Valluvan Chakkiliyan

For their cultural identity please see Appendix-I

Villages without Scheduled Castes: There are 7 villages without any scheduled caste population.

Scheduled Tribes: Out of the total population of 93138 persons, 143 persons (0.15%) belong to Scheduled Tribes. The villages having less than 10% ST population are Thiruvaiyathukudi, Devarayampet, Pulimangalam Melasemmangudi, Ponmeinthanallur, Vadakku Mangudi Serumakkanallur, Vaiyacheri, Purakkudi Perumakkanallur, Vembukudi, Agaramangudi, Surikayur Onbathuveli, Thirukkarugavur, Edaiyiruppu, Kavalur Neidalur, Annappanpettai, Kattukkurichi, Vilithiyur Milattur V Sethy, Melattur Iv Sethi, Kothangudi Venukudi Thottam, Edakkudi, Utharamangalam Authur Thottam, Melakkalukudi, Edavakudy, Kandavanam Kalanchery, Palliyor, Neikkunnam, Deebambalpuram Mahimalai, Neduvasal, Mahimalai Bit, Ukkadai Puliyakkudi, Vadapathi, Kelakovilpathu Saliyamangalam, Poondi Ii, Poondi I, Kumilakudi Nellithoppu, Pulavarnatham, Alangudi Bavaniambalpuram, Arulmozhipettai, Thalavaipalayam Katharinatham, Raramuthirakkottai, Nallavaiyan Thirubavanam, Sooziyakkottai, Arunthavapuram Puliyakkudi, Arundavapuram, Kammpayanatham Jembagambalpuram, Jembagapuram, Jembugambalpuram Ii.

The villages having more than 50% ST population are None.

Sex ratio of Scheduled tribe population is 455.

Scheduled Tribes Literates and Illiterates by Sex:

	Persons	Males	Females
Literate	54	36	18
Illiterate	89	42	47
Literacy rate	48.7	62.1	34.0
Graduate	0	0	0

Scheduled Tribes (Dominant):

Kattunayakan, Adiyan, Paniyan, Palleyan

For their cultural identity please see Appendix-II

Villages without Scheduled Tribes: There are 62 villages without any scheduled tribe population.

Literates and Illiterates by Sex (Total Population):

	Persons	Males	Females
Literate	54,768	31,262	23,506
Illiterate	38,370	15,230	23,140
Literacy rate	67	77	57
Graduate	727	577	150

Agriculture: ***Distribution of villages according to land use:*** Out of 68 villages, Total area (in hectare) is 22009.68, out of that 74.28 percent is cultivable and 90.97 percent of the cultivable area is irrigated.

Sources of Irrigation (Hectares): Government Canal 13822.41, Private Canal 0, Well without Electricity 0, Well with Electricity 0, Tubewell without Electricity 259.98, Tubewell with Electricity 697.68, Tank 0, River 0, Lake 93.14, Waterfall 0, Others 0.

Villages with population of 5000 to 9999: None

Villages with population of 10000 and above: None

Distribution of Workers:

	Persons	Males	Females	WPR
Cultivators	5,724	4,710	1,014	13.53

Agricultural Labour	30,296	16,691	13,605	71.64
Household Industry	584	275	309	1.38
Other Workers	5,688	4,759	929	13.45
Main Workers	32,584	22,662	9,922	77.05
Marginal Workers	9,708	3,773	5,935	22.95
Total Workers	42,292	26,435	15,857	

Religion: Major Religious Communities:

	Persons	Males	Females	Sex Ratio
Hindu (91.37%)	85,104	42,556	42,548	1,000
Muslim (3.83%)	3,568	1,726	1,842	1,067
Christian (4.76%)	4,437	2,193	2,244	1,023
Sikh (0%)	-	-	-	-
Buddhists (0%)	-	-	-	-
Jain (0%)	3	1	2	2,000

Agewise Data:

	Persons	Males	Females	Sex Ratio
All ages	93,138	46,492	46,646	1003
0-14	27,236	13,829	13,407	969
15-44	45,349	22,253	23,096	1038
45-79	19,954	10,089	9,865	978
80+	504	267	237	888
Age not stated	95	54	41	759

Languages (Dominant):

Tamil, English, Telugu, Malayalam, Urdu

Disabled Population:

	Persons	Males	Females	%
Total Disabled	2,534	1,212	1,322	
In Seeing	1,569	628	941	61.92
In Speech	263	161	102	10.38
In Hearing	77	31	46	3.04
In Movement	467	301	166	18.43
Mentally	158	91	67	6.24

ANAICUT

Anaicut C.D. Block lies in the central part of Vellore district. It is a part of Vellore taluk. The taluk is located at a distance of 00 kms. from district headquarters (Vellore). There are 58 villages in the block with the total population of 116,052 persons. Area of the C.D. Block is 414.51 sq. kms. It is bounded in the north by CD Block K.V.Kuppam, in the south by Tiruvannamalai district, in the east by CD Block Vellore and district Tiruvananamalai, and in the west by CD Block Madhanur.

Communications:

Roadways : N.H.-46: Direction- Vaniyambadi to Vellore, Nearest Villages- Kandaneri, Kalanipakkam, Eraiyankadu, Okkanapuram, Virinjipuram, Sathiyamangalam, Poigai, Seduvalai.

River: Polar Nadi- Nearest Villages- Eraiyankadu, Virin jipuram, Sathiyamangalam, Poigai. Puniyathirtha Nadi- Nearest Villages- Bramanamangalam, Kilkrishnapuram, Karungali, Mahamadapuram, Kandaneri, Kalanipakkam, Madaiyapattu, Serpadi, Katharikuppam, Gengasainikuppam, Vannanthangal, Melarasampattu, Umayampattu.

Annual Rainfall: Average Rainfall 949 mm.

Ground Water: Availability of the ground water in the Basin is 5430.50 H.A.M. and the utilization is 7710.34 H.A.M. It belongs to Over Expoited category. Depth to water level varies from 5 to 15 meter below the ground. Most of the wells go down in summer months, according to the Ground Water Estimation Committee.

Forest and Reserved Forest: (Appupal RF)- Nearest Villages- Elavmbadi, Ganganallur, Appukkal (RF), Appukkal. (Arasam pattu)- Nearest Villages- Varadalampet, Arasampattu (RF), Keelkothur. (Athiyur)- Nearest Village- Athiyur (RF). (Paravamalai)- Nearest Villages- Karadigudi, Davicettikuppam, Mahamadapuram, Paravamalai (RF), Paravamalai (RF), Lungapadi, Keelkothur, Pinnathurai, Gengasinikuppam, Paravamalai (RF), Pasavamalai, Serpadi. (Karuthamalai)- Nearest Villages- Athikuppam, Madaiyapattu, Vannanthangal, Melarasampattu, Umayampattu. (Puthur)- Nearest Villages- Pudukuppam, Peenjamandai, Gengasainikuppam, Periyapanapparai, Umayampattu, Mulluvadi, Puthur (RF). (Nallimalai)- Nearest Villages- Vaniyambadi, Appukkal, Mallaimalai (RF), Lungapadi. (Pallikonda)- Nearest Villages- Kandaneri, Kalanipakkam, Unai, Pallikonda (RF), Othiyathur, Vaniyambadi. (Thellai)- Nearest Villages- Alleri, Yelluparai, Peenjamandai, Pelampattu, Jardankollai. Pelampattu, Jardankollai, Yelluparai, Alleri.

Natural Division: Tondai Nadu.

Administration

Revenue **Division:** Vellore. Parliamentary Constituency: 8 Vellore. District: Vellore. Taluk: Vellore. Assembly Constituency: 44 Anaikattu. Gram Panchayat: 38.

Villages: 58 **Inhabited:** 47 **Uninhabited:** 11

Ranking	**District**	**State**	**National**
Area	3	60	1855
Population	9	75	2971
Sex Ratio	9	153	1081
Child Sex Ratio	12	245	4012
Literacy Rate	15	230	2083
Density	6	264	3750
Work Participation Rate	18	253	2882

Gram Panchayats:

Anaikattu, Appukal, Athikuppam, Brahmanamangalam, Devichettikuppam, Elavambadi, Erayangadu, Genganallore, Jarthankollai, Kalanipakkam, Kandaneri, Karadikudi, Karunkali, Kilkothur, Kilkrishnapuram, Madayapattu, Mahammadapuram, Maruthavallipalayam, Melarasampattu, Nemandapuram, Odiyathur, Ongapadi, Palampattu, Peenjamandai, Pinnanthurai, Poigai, Puthur, Sathiyamangalam, Seduvalai , Serpadi,

Tippasamudram, Unai, Unai Vallandaraman, Vallandaraman, Vannanthangal, Varadalampattu, Vasanthanadai, Virinchipuram.

Amenities:

Education: Primary School in 45 villages, Middle school in 21 villages, Matriculation or Secondary School in 8 villages, namely Okkanapuram, Virinjipuram, Poigai, Elavmbadi, Anaicut, Thippasamudaram, Davicettikuppam, Keelkothur.

Higher Secondary or Pre University Courses or Intermediate or Junior College in 4 villages of the CD Block,, namely Okkanapuram, Virinjipuram, Poigai, Anaicut. College in 0 village, Adult Literacy Center in 0 village.

Medical: Hospital in 2 villages, Dispensary in 1 village, Health Center in 6 villages, Sub Center in 6 villages, Maternity and Child Welfare Center in 7 villages, Community health workers in 44 villages.

The Villages having Hospital or Dispensary or Health Center are Puthur, Vallandaramam, Karungali, Mahamadapuram.

Drinking Water: Tap water in 42 villages, Tank water in 11 villages, Well water in 27 villages, Tubewell in 24 villages and more than one source in 44 villages.

Bank: Banking facility in 7 villages, namely, Virinjipuram, Seduvalai, Poigai, Anaicut Kommalankuttai, Bramanamangalam, Appukkal.

Credit Society in 12 villages Agricultural Credit Society in 6 Non-Agricultural Credit Society in 7 villages.

Others: Power supply in 43 villages, Cinema hall in 3 villages, sport club in 0 village, Stadium or Auditorium or Community Hall in 0 village, Post Office in 32 villages.

There are 33 villages having bus facilities.

Villages with most of facilities: Virinjipuram Seduvalai, Poigai, Anaicut, Kommalankuttai Bramanamangalam, Appukkal.

Villages without amenities (Education): Pudukuppam, Periyapanapparai..

Scheduled Castes: Out of the total population of 116052 persons, 24853 persons (21.42%) belong to Scheduled Castes.

The villages having less than 10% SC population are Kandaneri, Elavmbadi, Alleri, Yelluparai Pinnathurai, Serpadi, Pudukuppam, Peenjamandai Vannanthangal, Mulluvadi, Periyapanapparai Pelampattu, Jardankollai.

The villages having more than 50% SC population are Bramanamangalam, Kilkrishnapuram, Mahamadapuram Athikuppam.

Sex ratio of Scheduled Caste population is 503.

Scheduled Castes Literates and Illiterates by Sex:

	Persons	Males	Females
Literate	15,151	8,505	6,646
Illiterate	9,702	3,840	5,862
Literacy rate	70.0	79.6	60.7
Graduate	335	235	100

Scheduled Castes (Dominant):

Adi Dravida, Arunthathiyar, Valluvan, Kuravan etc. Domban

For their cultural identity please see Appendix-I

Villages without Scheduled Castes: There are 19 villages without any scheduled caste population.

Scheduled Tribes: Out of the total population of 116052 persons, 10757 persons (9.27%) belong to Scheduled Tribes.

The villages having less than 10% ST population are Kandaneri, Kalanipakkam, Eraiyankadu, Okkanapuram Virinjipuram, Seduvalai, Sathiyamangalam, Poigai Puthur, Elavmbadi, Vallandaramam, Vasandhanadai Anaicut, Unai, Kommalankuttai, Bramanamangalam Kilkrishnapuram, Thippasamudaram, Othiyathur Vaniyambadi, Ganganallur, Appukkal, Karadigudi Davicettikuppam, Karungali, Mahamadapuram, Lungapadi Varadalampet, Keelkothur, Pinnathurai, Nemandapuram Athikuppam, Madaiyapattu, Serpadi, Katharikuppam Gengasainikuppam, Vannanthangal, Melarasampattu Umayampattu.

The villages having more than 50% ST population are Alleri, Yelluparai, Pudukuppam, Peenjamandai Mulluvadi, Periyapanapparai, Pelampattu. Jardankollai.

Sex ratio of Scheduled tribe population is 504.

Scheduled Tribes Literates and Illiterates by Sex:

	Persons	Males	Females
Literate	1,222	899	323
Illiterate	9,535	4,432	5,103
Literacy rate	14.0	20.7	7.4
Graduate	4	4	0

Scheduled Tribes (Dominant):

Malayali, Irular, Koraga, Generic Tribes etc.

For their cultural identity please see Appendix-II

Villages without Scheduled Tribes: There are 31 villages without any scheduled tribe population.

Literates and Illiterates by Sex (Total Population):

	Persons	Males	Females
Literate	64,875	37,735	27,140
Illiterate	51,177	20,218	30,959
Literacy rate	64	75	53
Graduate	1,129	844	285

Agriculture: ***Distribution of villages according to land use:***

Out of 58 villages, Total area (in hectare) is 41451.48, out of that 33.36 percent is cultivable and 28.96 percent of the cultivable area is irrigated.

Sources of Irrigation (Hectares): Government Canal 0, Private Canal 0, Well without Electricity 622.82, Well with Electricity 2706.8, Tubewell without Electricity 58.5, Tubewell with Electricity 605.31, Tank 0, River 2.5, Lake 9.4, Waterfall 0, Others 0.

Villages with population of 5000 to 9999:
Virinchipuram, Seduvalai , Poigai.

Villages with population of 10000 and above: None

Distribution of Workers:

	Persons	Males	Females	WPR
Cultivators	21,238	12,979	8,259	38.49
Agricultural Labour	19,216	9,347	9,869	34.83
Household Industry	4,310	2,305	2,005	7.81
Other Workers	10,413	8,347	2,066	18.87
Main Workers	42,953	27,894	15,059	77.85
Marginal Workers	12,224	5,084	7,140	22.15
Total Workers	55,177	32,978	22,199	

Religion: Major Religious Communities:

	Persons	Males	Females	Sex Ratio
Hindu (95.87%)	111,261	55,524	55,737	1,004
Muslim (3.46%)	4,014	2,029	1,985	978
Christian (0.56%)	648	335	313	934
Sikh (0%)	1	-	1	-
Buddhists (0%)	-	-	-	-
Jain (0.02%)	29	15	14	933

Agewise Data:

	Persons	Males	Females	Sex Ratio
All ages	116,052	57,953	58,099	1003
0-14	35,039	17,994	17,045	947
15-44	54,177	26,787	27,390	1023
45-79	24,775	12,199	12,576	1031
80+	1,269	610	659	1080
Age not stated	792	363	429	1182

Languages (Dominant):
Tamil, Telugu, Urdu, Kannada, Others

Disabled Population:

	Persons	Males	Females	%
Total Disabled	2,442	1,365	1,077	
In Seeing	1,145	625	520	46.89
In Speech	232	107	125	9.5
In Hearing	171	83	88	7
In Movement	640	397	243	26.21
Mentally	254	153	101	10.4

ANAIMALAI

Anamalai C.D. Block lies in the south-western part of Coimbatore district. It is a part of Pollachi and taluk. The Block is located at à distance of 55 kms. from district headquarters (Coimbatore). There are 15 villages in the block with the total population of 67,638 persons. Area of the C.D. Block is 203.48 sq. kms. It is bounded in the north by C.D. Blocks Pollachi North and Pollachi South, in the east by taluk Udumalaipettai, and it has common boundary with the state of Kerala on south and west.

Communications:

Roadways : S.H.-19: Direction- Palghat to Zamin Uthukuli, Nearest Village- Marchinaickanpalayam.

Railway Station: Marchinaickanpalayam.

River: Aliyar Nadi- Nearest Villages- Aththupollachi, Marchinaickanpalayam, Pethanicknur, Pillchinnampalayam, Somandurai, Thenchitoor, Kariyanchettipalayam, Kambalapatti, Arthanaripalayam, Jallipatti, Thoriyur, Angalakurichi.

Annual Rainfall: Average Rainfall 550 mm.

Ground Water: Availability of the ground water in the Basin is 12330.05 H.A.M. and the utilization is 6326. 53 H.A.M. It belongs to Safe category. Depth to water level varies from 2 to 10 meter below the ground. Most of the wells go down in summer months, according to the Ground Water Estimation Committee.

Natural Division: Kongu Nadu.

Administration

Revenue **Division:** Pollachi. Parliamentary Constituency: 21 Pollachi. District: Coimbatore. Taluk: Pollachi. Assembly Constituency: 124 Anaimalai. Gram Panchayat: 19.

Border Villages- (Kerala)- Nearest Villages- Aththupoll achi, Marchinaickanpalayam, Periyapodu.

Villages: 15 **Inhabited:** 15 **Uninhabited:** 0

Ranking	District	State	National
Area	13	281	4122
Population	12	301	4576
Sex Ratio	5	240	1656
Child Sex Ratio	19	323	5349
Literacy Rate	14	258	2257
Density	10	143	3251
Work Participation Rate	6	180	1412

Gram Panchayats:
Angalakurichi, Arthanaripalayam, Athupollachi, Divansapudur, Jallipatti, Kaliyapuram, Kambalapatti, Kariyanchettipalayam, Marappa goundenpudur, Periapodu, Pethanaickanur, Pillchinnampalayam, Ramanamudali pudur, Somandurai, Subbegoundanpudur, Thathur, Thensangampalayam, Thensithur, Vazhaikombunagore.

Amenities:

Education: Primary School in 13 villages, Middle school in 10 villages, Matriculation or Secondary School in 4 villages, namely Marchinaickanpalayam, Somandurai, Kaliyapuram, Kambalapatti.

Higher Secondary or Pre University Courses or Intermediate or Junior College in 2 villages of the CD Block,,

namely Kaliyapuram, Kambalapatti.
College in 1 village, Adult Literacy Center in 0 village., College is in village, namely Angalakurichi.
Medical: Hospital in 3 villages, Dispensary in 0 village, Health Center in 5 villages, Sub Center in 13 villages, Maternity and Child Welfare Center in 2 villages, Community health workers in 1 village.
The Villages having Hospital or Dispensary or Health Center are Aththupollachi, Kambalapatti, Thoriyur.
Drinking Water: Tap water in 15 villages, Tank water in 0 villages, Well water in 15 villages, Tubewell in 15 villages and more than one source in 15 villages.
Bank: Banking facility in 6 villages, namely, Marchinaickanpalayam, Somandurai, Thenchitoor Kaliyapuram, Kambalapatti, Angalakurichi.
Credit Society in 6 villages Agricultural Credit Society in 6 Non-Agricultural Credit Society in 1 village.
Others: Power supply in 15 villages, Cinema hall in 1 village, sport club in 0 village, Stadium or Auditorium or Community Hall in 0 village, Post Office in 15 villages.
There are 15 villages having bus facilities.
Villages with most of facilities: Marchinaickanpalayam Somandurai, Kaliyapuram, Kambalapatti, Angalakurichi.
Villages without amenities (Education):
Aththupollachi, Thenchitoor..
Scheduled Castes: Out of the total population of 67638 persons, 14877 persons (22%) belong to Scheduled Castes.
The villages having less than 10% SC population are None..
The villages having more than 50% SC population are None.
Sex ratio of Scheduled Caste population is 501.
Scheduled Castes Literates and Illiterates by Sex:

	Persons	Males	Females
Literate	5,879	3,475	2,404
Illiterate	8,998	3,948	5,050
Literacy rate	45.2	54.1	36.5
Graduate	28	22	6

Scheduled Castes (Dominant):
Arunthathiyar, Madari, Kudumban, Adi Dravida Chakkiliyan
For their cultural identity please see Appendix-I
Villages without Scheduled Castes: There is 1 village without any scheduled caste population.
Scheduled Tribes: Out of the total population of 67638 persons, 2491 persons (3.68%) belong to Scheduled Tribes.
The villages having less than 10% ST population are Aththupollachi, Marchinaickanpalayam, Pethanaicknur Pillchinnampalayam, Somandurai, Thenchitoor Periyapodu, Thensangampalayam, Kariyanchettipalayam Kambalapatti, Arthanaripalayam, Jallipatti, Thoriyur Angalakurichi.
The villages having more than 50% ST population are None.
Sex ratio of Scheduled tribe population is 499.
Scheduled Tribes Literates and Illiterates by Sex:

	Persons	Males	Females
Literate	547	323	224
Illiterate	1,944	924	1,020
Literacy rate	25.3	29.8	20.8
Graduate	0	0	0

Scheduled Tribes (Dominant):
Malasar, Eravallan, Mudugar etc., Kurumans, Kadar
For their cultural identity please see Appendix-II
Villages without Scheduled Tribes: There are 8 villages without any scheduled tribe population.
Literates and Illiterates by Sex (Total Population):

	Persons	Males	Females
Literate	38,107	21,947	16,160
Illiterate	29,531	12,069	17,462
Literacy rate	63	73	54
Graduate	453	304	149

Agriculture: ***Distribution of villages according to land use:***
Out of 15 villages, Total area (in hectare) is 20348.41, out of that 89.74 percent is cultivable and 54.81 percent of the cultivable area is irrigated.
Sources of Irrigation (Hectares): Government Canal 3577.42, Private Canal 0, Well without Electricity 0, Well with Electricity 5958.95, Tubewell without Electricity 0, Tubewell with Electricity 0, Tank 0, River 472.09, Lake 0, Waterfall 0, Others 0.
Villages with population of 5000 to 9999:
Somandurai, Periapodu, Kambalapatti Angalakurichi.
Villages with population of 10000 and above:
Marchinaickenpalayam.
Distribution of Workers:

	Persons	Males	Females	WPR
Cultivators	4,462	3,158	1,304	12.12
Agricultural Labour	22,051	11,174	10,877	59.88
Household Industry	964	592	372	2.62
Other Workers	9,349	6,997	2,352	25.39
Main Workers	32,064	20,033	12,031	87.07
Marginal Workers	4,762	1,888	2,874	12.93
Total Workers	36,826	21,921	14,905	

Religion: Major Religious Communities:

	Persons	Males	Females	Sex Ratio
Hindu (97.17%)	65,721	33,057	32,664	988
Muslim (1.81%)	1,227	617	610	989
Christian (0.93%)	628	312	316	1,013

Sikh (0%)	2	1	1	1,000
Buddhists (0%)	-	-	-	-
Jain (0%)	-	-	-	-

Agewise Data:

	Persons	Males	Females	Sex Ratio
All ages	67,638	34,016	33,622	988
0-14	15,872	8,267	7,605	920
15-44	33,317	16,415	16,902	1030
45-79	17,098	8,630	8,468	981
80+	710	354	356	1006
Age not stated	641	350	291	831

Languages (Dominant):
Tamil, Telugu, Kannada, Malayalam, Urdu

Disabled Population:

	Persons	Males	Females	%
Total Disabled	1,783	903	880	
In Seeing	1,030	450	580	57.77
In Speech	111	64	47	6.23
In Hearing	96	50	46	5.38
In Movement	406	262	144	22.77
Mentally	140	77	63	7.85

ANAKAVUR

Anakkavur C.D. Block lies in the north-eastern part of Tiruvannamalai district. It is a part of Cheyyar taluk. The taluk headquarters is located at a distance of 110 kms. from district headquarters (Tiruvannamalai). There are 61 villages in the block with the total population of 75,475 persons. Area of the C.D. Block is 259.55 sq. kms. It is bounded in the north by C.D. Blocks Vembakkam and Cheyyar, in the south by CD Blocks Peranamallur and Vandavasi, in the east by district Kancheepuram, and in the west by C.D. Block Cheyyar.

Communications:
Roadways : S.H.-4: Direction- Tiruvethipuram to Vandavasi, Nearest Villages- Kilmattai, Anakkavur, Erumaivetti,
River: Cheyyar Nadi- Nearest Villages- Madippakkam, Akkur, Ukkal, Kilnethapakkam, Kilathoor, Vellai, Kilmattai, Athi, Anakkavur, Annapathur, Vadaalappirandan, Kilneerkundram, Cheyyatraivendran.
Backwards Region Grants Fund: It receives Backward Region Grants.
Annual Rainfall: Average Rainfall 1019 mm.
Ground Water: Availability of the ground water in the Basin is (Information not available) H.A.M. and the utili zation is 160.44 H.A.M. It belongs to Over Expoited categ ory. Depth to water level varies from 2 to 5 meter below the ground. Most of the wells go down in summer months, according to the Ground Water Estimation Committee.
Natural Division: Tondai Nadu.

Administration
Revenue **Division:** Cheyyar. Parliamentary Constituency: 12 Arani. District: Tiruvannamalai. Taluk: Cheyyar. Assembly Constituency: 68 Cheyyar. Gram Panchayat: 55.
Villages: 61 **Inhabited:** 61 **Uninhabited:** 0

Ranking	District	State	National
Area	12	218	3255
Population	16	267	4267
Sex Ratio	8	187	1261
Child Sex Ratio	4	124	2288
Literacy Rate	9	172	1636
Density	12	205	3630
Work Participation Rate	13	237	2140

Gram Panchayats:
Akkur, Alathur, Alathurai, Anakkavoor, Anapathur, Arasur, Athi, Cheyyatraivendran, Chithamur, Echur, Enimaivetti& Kalamandai, Erumaivetti, Ilaneerkundram, Irungal, Karanai, Kil Nethapakkam, Kilathur, Kilkolathur, Kilneerkundram, Koolamandal, Kottagaram, Kovilur, Kunnavakkam, Kurumbur, Madipakkam, Mahajanambakkam, Mel Kolathur, Mel Nemili, Melma, Mulagiripattu, Nallalam, Narmapallam, Nedungal, Nelvoy, Palanjur, payyur, Payyur, Perumpalai, Purisai, Sengadu, Soundaryapuram, Tavasi, Then Mavandal, Thenelapakkam, Thenilluppai, Thenkalpakkam, Thenthandalam, Thethurai, Thirumpoondi, Ukkal, Vachanur, Vada Alapirandan, Vada Thinallur, Vadanangur, Veerambakkam, Vellai, Venkodu, Vilaripattu.

Amenities:
Education: Primary School in 57 villages, Middle school in 15 villages, Matriculation or Secondary School in 8 villages, namely Akkur, Ukkal, Cheyyatraivendran, Anakkavur, Annapathur, Thethurai, Purisai, Kovilur.
Higher Secondary or Pre University Courses or Intermediate or Junior College in 2 villages of the CD Block,, namely Thavasi, Kovilur.
College in 0 village, Adult Literacy Center in 0 village.
Medical: Hospital in 1 village, Dispensary in 0 village, Health Center in 7 villages, Sub Center in 4 villages, Maternity and Child Welfare Center in 24 villages, Community health workers in 55 villages.
The Villages having Hospital or Dispensary or Health Center are Nedungal, Thenmavathul.
Drinking Water: Tap water in 61 villages, Tank water in 16 villages, Well water in 61 villages, Tubewell in 61 villages and more than one source in 61 villages.
Bank: Banking facility in 2 villages, namely, Purisai, Alathur.
Credit Society in 7 villages Agricultural Credit Society in 6 Non-Agricultural Credit Society in 3 villages.
Others: Power supply in 57 villages, Cinema hall in 0 village,

sport club in 0 village, Stadium or Auditorium or Community Hall in 0 village, Post Office in 28 villages.

There are 47 villages having bus facilities.

Villages with most of facilities: Purisai, Alathur.

Villages without amenities (Education): Eadavel, Nelvoy, Thenmavathul, Ayyavadi..

Scheduled Castes: Out of the total population of 75475 persons, 20162 persons (26.71%) belong to Scheduled Castes. The villages having less than 10% SC population are Kozamandal, Vellai, Annapathur, Athi, Kurumboor Narmapallam, Vilaripattu, Nelvoy, Mulagripattu Thenmavathul, Chitamoor, Ayyavadi, Melnarma Vadanandakar, Kottagaram, Palanjur, Then Elappakkam. The villages having more than 50% SC population are Kunnawakkam, Karani, Madippakkam, Eadavel, Kilmattai Arasur.

Sex ratio of Scheduled Caste population is 495.

Scheduled Castes Literates and Illiterates by Sex:

	Persons	Males	Females
Literate	11,284	6,734	4,550
Illiterate	8,878	3,457	5,421
Literacy rate	63.5	75.3	51.5
Graduate	175	146	29

Scheduled Castes (Dominant):

Adi Dravida, Arunthathiyar, Pallan, Valluvan Kuravan etc.

For their cultural identity please see Appendix-I

Villages without Scheduled Castes: There are 12 villages without any scheduled caste population.

Scheduled Tribes: Out of the total population of 75475 persons, 1206 persons (1.6%) belong to Scheduled Tribes. The villages having less than 10% ST population are Mahajampakkam, Kunnawakkam, Karani, Pandiyambakkam Madippakkam, Eadavel, Akkur, Kozamandal, Ukkal Kilnethapakkam, Kilathoor, Cheyyatraivendran, Vellai Kilmattai, Anakkavur, Annapathur, Vadaalappirandan Athi, Elaneerkundram, Kilneerkundram, Nedungal Thethurai, Kurumboor, Narmapallam, Kilkolathur Erumaivetti, Thenthandalam, Perumpalai, Vilaripattu Thavasi, Nelvoy, Irungal, Mulagripattu, Thenmavathul Chitamoor, Arasur, Purisai, Tneneluppai, Veerabakkam Melma, Ayyavadi, Vachanoor, Melnarma, Soundraiapuram Vadanandakar, Thirumpoondi, Nallalam, Kovilur Sengadu, Melkolathur, Vadathinnalur, Malenemeli Kottagaram, Palanjur, Echur, Then Elappakkam Thenkalpakkam, Paiyur, Alaturai, Alathur, Vengodu. The villages having more than 50% ST population are None.

Sex ratio of Scheduled tribe population is 514.

Scheduled Tribes Literates and Illiterates by Sex:

	Persons	Males	Females
Literate	263	156	107
Illiterate	943	430	513
Literacy rate	26.8	32.4	21.4
Graduate	0	0	0

Scheduled Tribes (Dominant):

Irular, Palliyar, Uraly, Malakkuravan, Kattunayakan

For their cultural identity please see Appendix-II

Villages without Scheduled Tribes: There are 18 villages without any scheduled tribe population.

Literates and Illiterates by Sex (Total Population):

	Persons	Males	Females
Literate	44,859	26,815	18,044
Illiterate	30,616	10,988	19,628
Literacy rate	67	80	54
Graduate	771	623	148

Agriculture: ***Distribution of villages according to land use:*** Out of 61 villages, Total area (in hectare) is 25955.46, out of that 62.27 percent is cultivable and 51.68 percent of the cultivable area is irrigated.

Sources of Irrigation (Hectares): Government Canal 13.29, Private Canal 0, Well without Electricity 925.25, Well with Electricity 3861.83, Tubewell without Electricity 0, Tubewell with Electricity 0, Tank 1694.2, River 0, Lake 840.71, Waterfall 0, Others 704.82.

Villages with population of 5000 to 9999: None

Villages with population of 10000 and above: None

Distribution of Workers:

	Persons	Males	Females	WPR
Cultivators	14,365	10,071	4,294	37.05
Agricultural Labour	17,295	6,702	10,593	44.61
Household Industry	1,294	815	479	3.34
Other Workers	5,817	4,766	1,051	15
Main Workers	30,329	19,585	10,744	78.23
Marginal Workers	8,442	2,769	5,673	21.77
Total Workers	38,771	22,354	16,417	

Religion: Major Religious Communities:

	Persons	Males	Females	Sex Ratio
Hindu (97.84%)	73,843	36,980	36,863	997
Muslim (1.35%)	1,020	514	506	984
Christian (0.59%)	448	227	221	974
Sikh (0%)	3	3	-	-
Buddhists (0%)	-	-	-	-
Jain (0.02%)	18	12	6	500

Agewise Data:

	Persons	Males	Females	Sex Ratio
All ages	75,475	37,803	37,672	997
0-14	20,934	10,760	10,174	946
15-44	34,996	17,398	17,598	1011
45-79	18,704	9,191	9,513	1035

80+	772	416	356	856
Age not stated	69	38	31	816

Languages (Dominant):

Tamil, Telugu, Urdu, English, Nepali

Disabled Population:

	Persons	Males	Females	%
Total Disabled	1,871	1,091	780	
In Seeing	702	401	301	37.52
In Speech	228	129	99	12.19
In Hearing	236	118	118	12.61
In Movement	546	351	195	29.18
Mentally	159	92	67	8.5

ANDANALLUR

Andanallur C.D. Block lies in the south-western part of Tiruchirappalli district. It is a part of Srirangam taluk. The taluk is located at a distance of 25 kms. from district headquarters (Tiruchirappalli). There are 25 villages in the block with the total population of 79,982 persons. Area of the C.D. Block is 104.31 sq. kms. It is bounded in the north by CD Blocks Musiri and Manachanallur, in the south by C.D. Blocks Manikandam and Thiruvembur, in the east by CD Block Lalgudi, and in the west by district Karur.

Communications:

Roadways : N.H.-67: Direction- Kulithalai to Tiruchirappalli, Nearest Villages- Kulumani, Marudhandakurichi, Perur, Koppu North, Kodiyalam, Peeiyakaruppur, Malliampathu, Kumara Vayalur. S.H.-6: Direction- Kulatittalai to Tiruchirappalli, Nearest Villages- Pettavaithalai, Perugamani, Thirupparaithurai, Andanallur, Thiruchendurai, Allur, Palur, Kadiyakkurichi, Mutharasanallur, Kambarasampettai.

Railway Station: Perugamani, Thirupparaithurai, Thiruchendurai, Mutharasanallur.

River: Cauvery Nadi- Nearest Villages- Perugamani, Thirupparaithurai, Andanallur, Thiruchendurai, Allur, Palur, Kadiyakkurichi, Mutharasanallur, Kambarasampettai, Panayapuram, Uthamaseri, Kilikkoodu. Kollidam Nadi- Nearest Villages- Panayapuram, Uthamaseri, Kilikkoodu. Uyyakondan Nadi- Nearest Villages- Kodiyalam, Kulumani, Perugamani, Mullikkarumpur, Koppu North.

Annual Rainfall: Average Rainfall 841 mm.

Ground Water: Availability of the ground water in the Basin is 4218.50 H.A.M. and the utilization is 1733.15 H.A.M. It belongs to Safe category. Depth to water level varies from 2 to 5 meter below the ground. Most of the wells go down in summer months, according to the Ground Water Estimation Committee.

Natural Division: Chola Nadu.

Administration

Revenue **Division:** Tiruchirappalli. Parliamentary Constit uency: 24 Tiruchirappalli. District: Tiruchirappalli. Taluk: Srirangam. Assembly Constituency: 144 Manachanallur, 139 Srirangam, 142. Thiruverumbur. Gram Panchayat: 25.

Villages: 25 **Inhabited:** 25 **Uninhabited:** 0

Ranking	District	State	National
Area	14	368	5671
Population	11	243	4107
Sex Ratio	13	239	1672
Child Sex Ratio	3	65	1381
Literacy Rate	3	33	492
Density	12	301	1284
Work Participation Rate	1	17	3408

Gram Panchayats:

Allur, Andanallur, Ettarai, Kambarasanpettai, Kilikudu, Kodiyalem, Koppu, Kulumani, Malliampathu, Marudhandakurichi, Mekkudi, Mullikarumbur, Mutharasanallur, Palur, Panayapuram, Periyakaruppur, Perugamani, Perur, Pettavaithalai, Podavur, Posampatti, Puliyur, Thiruchendurai, Thirupparaithurai, Uthamar.

Amenities:

Education: Primary School in 25 villages, Middle school in 17 villages, Matriculation or Secondary School in 6 villages, namely Thirupparaithurai, Andanallur, Kodiyalam, Thiruchendurai, Allur, Koppu North.

Higher Secondary or Pre University Courses or Intermediate or Junior College in 2 villages of the CD Block,, namely Thirupparaithurai, Kodiyalam.

College in 0 village, Adult Literacy Center in 0 village.

Medical: Hospital in 2 villages, Dispensary in 6 villages, Health Center in 4 villages, Sub Center in 2 villages, Maternity and Child Welfare Center in 0 village, Community health workers in 1 village.

The Villages having Hospital or Dispensary or Health Center are Pettavaithalai, Perugamani, Thirupparaithurai, Andanallur, Allur, Mutharasanallur.

Drinking Water: Tap water in 25 villages, Tank water in 4 villages, Well water in 25 villages, Tubewell in 25 villages and more than one source in 25 villages.

Bank: Banking facility in 7 villages, namely, Pettavaithalai, Perugamani, Thirupparaithurai Andanallur, Kulumani, Allur, Mutharasanallur.

Credit Society in 8 villages Agricultural Credit Society in 7 Non-Agricultural Credit Society in 1 village.

Others: Power supply in 25 villages, Cinema hall in 1 village, sport club in 0 village, Stadium or Auditorium or Community Hall in 0 village, Post Office in 14 villages.

There are 23 villages having bus facilities.

Villages with most of facilities: Pettavaithalai Perugamani, Thirupparaithurai, Andanallur, Kulumani Allur, Mutharasanallur.

Villages without Amenities (Education): None..

Scheduled Castes: Out of the total population of 79982 persons, 21262 persons (26.58%) belong to Scheduled Castes.

The villages having less than 10% SC population are None..

The villages having more than 50% SC population are None.

Sex ratio of Scheduled Caste population is 507.

Scheduled Castes Literates and Illiterates by Sex:

	Persons	Males	Females
Literate	13,404	7,624	5,780
Illiterate	7,858	2,851	5,007
Literacy rate	72.8	84.6	61.4
Graduate	572	417	155

Scheduled Castes (Dominant):

Pallan, Paraiyan etc., Adi Dravida, Chakkiliyan Kuravan etc.

For their cultural identity please see Appendix-I

Villages without Scheduled Castes: There is 0 village without any scheduled caste population.

Scheduled Tribes: Out of the total population of 79982 persons, 45 persons (0.06%) belong to Scheduled Tribes.

The villages having less than 10% ST population are Pettavaithalai, Perugamani, Thirupparaithurai Andanallur, Kodiyalam, Kulumani, Peeiyakaruppur Thiruchendurai, Kadiyakkurichi, Mekkudi, Allur Palur, Mutharasanallur, Kambarasampettai Panayapuram, Uthamaseri, Kilikkoodu, Malliampathu Marudhandakurichi, Perur, Mullikkarumpur Koppu North, Koppu South, Padavoor, Puliyur.

The villages having more than 50% ST population are None.

Sex ratio of Scheduled tribe population is 556.

Scheduled Tribes Literates and Illiterates by Sex:

	Persons	Males	Females
Literate	12	7	5
Illiterate	33	13	20
Literacy rate	31.6	38.9	25.0
Graduate	0	0	0

Scheduled Tribes (Dominant):

Kattunayakan, Malayali, Malakkuravan, Irular Kurumans

For their cultural identity please see Appendix-II

Villages without Scheduled Tribes: There are 18 villages without any scheduled tribe population.

Literates and Illiterates by Sex (Total Population):

	Persons	Males	Females
Literate	54,534	30,966	23,568
Illiterate	25,448	9,267	16,181
Literacy rate	77	87	67
Graduate	2,963	2,066	897

Agriculture: ***Distribution of villages according to land use:*** Out of 25 villages, Total area (in hectare) is 10431.46, out of that 58.33 percent is cultivable and 85.24 percent of the cultivable area is irrigated.

Sources of Irrigation (Hectares): Government Canal 5009.79, Private Canal 0, Well without Electricity 42.02, Well with Electricity 104.81, Tubewell without Electricity 20.54, Tubewell with Electricity 9.35, Tank 0, River 0, Lake 0, Waterfall 0, Others 0.

Villages with population of 5000 to 9999: Pettavathalai , Koppu North.

Villages with population of 10000 and above: None

Distribution of Workers:

	Persons	Males	Females	WPR
Cultivators	5,115	3,713	1,402	13.98
Agricultural Labour	19,742	9,849	9,893	53.97
Household Industry	812	415	397	2.22
Other Workers	10,909	8,830	2,079	29.82
Main Workers	32,907	21,056	11,851	89.96
Marginal Workers	3,671	1,751	1,920	10.04
Total Workers	36,578	22,807	13,771	

Religion: Major Religious Communities:

	Persons	Males	Females	Sex Ratio
Hindu (96.84%)	77,453	38,993	38,460	986
Muslim (1.77%)	1,416	677	739	1,092
Christian (1.35%)	1,080	546	534	978
Sikh (0%)	-	-	-	-
Buddhists (0.01%)	5	1	4	4,000
Jain (0%)	1	1	-	-

Agewise Data:

	Persons	Males	Females	Sex Ratio
All ages	79,982	40,233	39,749	988
0-14	22,408	11,750	10,658	907
15-44	38,882	19,437	19,445	1000
45-79	17,939	8,682	9,257	1066
80+	647	305	342	1121
Age not stated	106	59	47	797

Languages (Dominant):

Tamil, Telugu, Urdu, Kannada, Marathi

Disabled Population:

	Persons	Males	Females	%
Total Disabled	2,164	1,073	1,091	
In Seeing	1,139	499	640	52.63
In Speech	162	89	73	7.49
In Hearing	160	77	83	7.39
In Movement	561	336	225	25.92
Mentally	142	72	70	6.56

ANDIMADAM

Andimadam C.D. Block lies in the north-eastern part of Ariyalur district. It is a part of Udayarpalayam taluk. The taluk is located at a distance of 30 kms. from district headquarters (Ariyalur). There are 37 villages in the block with the total population of 103,999 persons. Area of the C.D. Block is 280.47 sq. kms. It is bounded in the north by district Cuddalore, in the south by C.D. Block Jayankondan, in the east by C.D. Block Jayankondan and district Cuddalore, and in the west by CD Block Sendurai.

Communications:

Roadways : Information not Available.

Annual Rainfall: Average Rainfall 876 mm.

Ground Water: Availability of the ground water in the Basin is 6014.55 H.A.M. and the utilization is 3226.29 H.A.M. It belongs to Safe category. Depth to water level varies from 2 to 10 meter below the ground. Most of the wells go down in summer months, according to the Ground Water Estimation Committee.

Forest and Reserved Forest: (Ayur Kanguli RF)- Nearest Villages- Akigapuram, Silambur, Mudukulam RF, Ayyur RF, Ayyur, Ayyur Kanguli RF, Andimadam. (Mudukulam)- Nearest Villages- Silambur, Edaiyakurichy, Mudukulam RF. (Koovathur)- Nearest Villages- Annikkuthichan (N), Anikkudichan (S), Koovathur RF, Koovathur (N), Koovathur (S). (Kuvagam)- Nearest Villages- Kattathur (S), Kuvagam, Variyem Kaval, Devanur, Kuvagam RF, Melur, Elaiyur. (Melur Devanur)- Nearest Villages- Devanur, Melurdevanur RF, Elaiyur, Udayarpalayam. (Thanimarathukau)- Nearest Villages- Thanimarathukadu RF, Elaiyur, Melur. (Siluvaicheri)- Nearest Villages- Rangiam, Siluvaichery RF, Siluvaichery, Akigapuram, Vilandai (N).

Natural Division: Chola Nadu.

Administration

Revenue **Division:** Udayapalayam. Parliamentary Constituency: 25 Perambalur. District: Ariyalur. Taluk: Udayarpalayam. Assembly Constituency: 150 Jayankondam. Gram Panchayat: 30.

Villages: 37 **Inhabited:** 29 **Uninhabited:** 8

Ranking	District	State	National
Area	6	197	2997
Population	3	117	3340
Sex Ratio	4	167	1170
Child Sex Ratio	5	263	4368
Literacy Rate	1	229	2077
Density	4	192	2945
Work Participation Rate	1	136	1944

Gram Panchayats:

Alagapuram , Andimadam, Anikudichan , Ayyur, Devanur, Edaiyakurichi, Ellaiyur, Karukkai, Kattathur, Kavarapalayam, Kodukkur, Koilvalkkai, Koovathur , Kulathur, Kuvagam, Marudur, Melur, Nagambandal, Olaiyur, Periyakrishanapuram, Periyathukurichi, Pudukudi, Rangiam, Silumbur , Sriraman, Thirukalappur, Vallam, Variyankavel, Vilandai, Vizhudhudayan.

Amenities:

Education: Primary School in 29 villages, Middle school in 21 villages, Matriculation or Secondary School in 11 villages, namely Olaiyur, Siluvaichery, Akigapuram, Ayyur, Vilandai (N), Anikkudichan (S), Koovathur (S), Kuvagam, Kodukkur, Marudur, Udayarpalayam. Higher Secondary or Pre University Courses or Intermediate or Junior College in 3 villages of the CD Block,, namely Edaiyakurichy, Andimadam, Anikkudichan (S). College in 0 village, Adult Literacy Center in 0 village.

Medical: Hospital in 1 village, Dispensary in 1 village, Health Center in 3 villages, Sub Center in 12 villages, Maternity and Child Welfare Center in 7 villages, Community health workers in 0 village. The Villages having Hospital or Dispensary or Health Center are Andimadam, Anikkudichan (S).

Drinking Water: Tap water in 29 villages, Tank water in 0 villages, Well water in 29 villages, Tubewell in 29 villages and more than one source in 29 villages.

Bank: Banking facility in 13 villages, namely, Athukurichi, Akigapuram, Edaiyakurichy, Andimadam Vilanthai, Periyakrishnapuram, Thirukkalapur Koovathur (N), Kuvagam, Kodukkur, Marudur Variyem Kaval, Udayarpalayam.

Credit Society in 10 villages Agricultural Credit Society in 10 Non-Agricultural Credit Society in 0 village.

Others: Power supply in 29 villages, Cinema hall in 4 villages, sport club in 29 villages, Stadium or Auditorium or Communit Hall in 29 villages, Post Office in 27 villages.

There are 28 villages having bus facilities.

Villages with most of facilities: Athukurichi Akigapuram, Edaiyakurichy, Andimadam, Vilanthai Thirukkalapur, Koovathur (N), Kuvagam, Marudur Variyem Kaval, Udayarpalayam.

Villages without Amenities (Education): None..

Scheduled Castes: Out of the total population of 103999 persons, 19127 persons (18.39%) belong to Scheduled Castes. The villages having less than 10% SC population are Vilandai (N), Koovathur (N), Kuvagam, Marudur Devanur, Melur, Udayarpalayam.

The villages having more than 50% SC population are None.

Sex ratio of Scheduled Caste population is 497.

Scheduled Castes Literates and Illiterates by Sex:

	Persons	Males	Females
Literate	8,390	5,292	3,098
Illiterate	10,737	4,325	6,412

Literacy rate	52.3	65.7	38.7
Graduate	186	155	31

Scheduled Castes (Dominant):
Paraiyan etc., Adi Dravida, Arunthathiyar Chakkiliyan, Domban

For their cultural identity please see Appendix-I

Villages without Scheduled Castes: There are 8 villages without any scheduled caste population.

Scheduled Tribes: Out of the total population of 103999 persons, 1938 persons (1.86%) belong to Scheduled Tribes.
The villages having less than 10% ST population are Athukurichi, Sriraman, Rangiam, Akigapuram Silambur (N), Silambur, Edaiyakurichy, Ayyur Andimadam, Vilandai (N), Vilanthai Periyakrishnapuram, Thirukkalapur Annikkuthichan (N), Anikkudichan (S), Koovathur (N) Koovathur (S), Kattathur, Kattathur (S), Kuvagam Kodukkur, Marudur, Variyem Kaval, Devanur, Melur Udayarpalayam, Elaiyur.
The villages having more than 50% ST population are None.
Sex ratio of Scheduled tribe population is 493.

Scheduled Tribes Literates and Illiterates by Sex:

	Persons	Males	Females
Literate	631	414	217
Illiterate	1,307	569	738
Literacy rate	40.1	52.3	27.8
Graduate	1	1	0

Scheduled Tribes (Dominant):
Irular, Malakkuravan, Generic Tribes etc.

For their cultural identity please see Appendix-II

Villages without Scheduled Tribes: There are 23 villages without any scheduled tribe population.

Literates and Illiterates by Sex (Total Population):

	Persons	Males	Females
Literate	58,015	34,797	23,218
Illiterate	45,984	17,197	28,787
Literacy rate	64	77	51
Graduate	1,957	1,472	485

Agriculture: ***Distribution of villages according to land use:*** Out of 37 villages, Total area (in hectare) is 28047, out of that 77.38 percent is cultivable and 13.05 percent of the cultivable area is irrigated.

Sources of Irrigation (Hectares): Government Canal 22.6, Private Canal 0, Well without Electricity 660.6, Well with Electricity 271.91, Tubewell without Electricity 129.16, Tubewell with Electricity 1364.71, Tank 275.28, River 0, Lake 128.03, Waterfall 0, Others 0.

Villages with population of 5000 to 9999:
Authukurichi, Alagapuram, Andimadam Vilandai (South), Periakrishnapuram, Kuvagam Marudur, Elaiyur (East).

Villages with population of 10000 and above: None

Distribution of Workers:

	Persons	Males	Females	WPR
Cultivators	17,858	12,215	5,643	33.73
Agricultural Labour	24,332	10,555	13,777	45.96
Household Industry	4,728	2,368	2,360	8.93
Other Workers	6,022	4,556	1,466	11.38
Main Workers	33,842	22,951	10,891	63.93
Marginal Workers	19,098	6,743	12,355	36.07
Total Workers	52,940	29,694	23,246	

Religion: Major Religious Communities:

	Persons	Males	Females	Sex Ratio
Hindu (90.65%)	94,275	47,180	47,095	998
Muslim (0.44%)	462	227	235	1,035
Christian (8.85%)	9,206	4,555	4,651	1,021
Sikh (0%)	2	2	-	-
Buddhists (0%)	1	1	-	-
Jain (0%)	4	2	2	1,000

Agewise Data:

	Persons	Males	Females	Sex Ratio
All ages	103,999	51,994	52,005	1000
0-14	30,483	15,612	14,871	953
15-44	49,944	24,552	25,392	1034
45-79	22,478	11,231	11,247	1001
80+	817	454	363	800
Age not stated	277	145	132	910

Languages (Dominant):
Tamil, Telugu, Urdu, Malayalam, Kannada

Disabled Population:

	Persons	Males	Females	%
Total Disabled	3,305	1,350	1,955	
In Seeing	1,888	536	1,352	57.13
In Speech	428	224	204	12.95
In Hearing	155	70	85	4.69
In Movement	670	435	235	20.27
Mentally	164	85	79	4.96

ANDIPATTI

Andipatti C.D. Block lies in the eastern part of Theni district. It is a part of Andipatti taluk. The Block is located at a distance of 18 kms. from district headquarters (Theni Allinagaram). There are 20 villages in the block with the total population of 95,705 persons. Area of the C.D. Block is 345.13 sq. kms. It is bounded in the north by CD Block Periyakulam, in the south by CD Block K. Myladumparai, in the east by districts Dindigul and Madurai, and in the west by CD Blocks Theni and Periyakulam.

Communications:

Roadways : N.H.-49: Direction- Bodinayakkanur to Madurai, Nearest Villages- Thimmarasanayakkanur, Kovilpatty,

Sanmugasundarapuram, Kunnur.

River: Vaigai Nadi- Nearest Villages- Pulimancombai, Kovilpatty, Sanmugasundarapuram, Kunnur.

Annual Rainfall: Average Rainfall 709 mm.

Ground Water: Availability of the ground water in the Basin is 5649.04 H.A.M. and the utilization is 5892. 26 H.A.M. It belongs to Over Expoited category. Depth to water level varies from 2 to 10 meter below the ground. Most of the wells go down in summer months, according to the Ground Water Estimation Committee.

Forest and Reserved Forest: (Andipatti Northern RF)- Nearest Villages- Pulimancombai, Andipatti Northen Block RF, Thimmarasanayakkanur. (Andipatti Southern Slope)- Nearest Villages- Thimmarasanayakkanur, Anndipatti, Andipatty Soutrn Block RF. (Gandamanur)- Nearest Villages- Kunnur, Thekkampatti, G. Usilampatti, Kottapatti, Kothaluthu, Palayakottai, Rajathani, Chittarpathi, Theppampatti, Ramakirshnapuram, Palacombai.

Natural Division: NA

Administration

Revenue **Division:** Periyakulam. Parliamentary Constituency: 33 Theni. District: Theni. Taluk: Andipatti. Assembly Constituency: 198 Andipatti. Gram Panchayat: 30.

Villages: 20 **Inhabited:** 18 **Uninhabited:** 2

Ranking	District	State	National
Area	3	122	2319
Population	1	150	3605
Sex Ratio	3	261	1959
Child Sex Ratio	4	339	5585
Literacy Rate	5	186	1727
Density	2	60	3781
Work Participation Rate	4	256	526

Gram Panchayats:

Ammaichiyapuram, Anuppapatty, Bodithasanpatty, Chittarpatti, Ethakovil, G. Usilampatti, Kanniappapillaipatty, Kathir Narasingapuram, Kodaluthu, Kottapatti , Kovilpatti , Kunnur , Marikkundu, Mottanuthu, Okkaraipatty, Palacombai, Palayakottai, Pitchampatty, Pulimancombai, Rajadhani, Rajagopalanpatty, Rajakkalpatty, Ramakrishnapuram, Rangasamudram, Shanmugasundarapuram , T.subbalapuram, Tekkampatti, Theppampatti , Thirumalapuram, Timmarasanayakkanur .

Amenities:

Education: Primary School in 18 villages, Middle school in 15 villages, Matriculation or Secondary School in 10 villages, namely Thimmarasanayakkanur, Kovilpatty, Sanmugasundarapuram, Kunnur, G. Usilampatti, Mottanuthu, Kottapatti, Anndipatti, Rajathani, Theppampatti.

Higher Secondary or Pre University Courses or Intermediate or Junior College in 2 villages of the CD Block,, namely Mottanuthu, Rajathani.

College in 0 village, Adult Literacy Center in 0 village.

Medical: Hospital in 0 village, Dispensary in 1 village, Health Center in 5 villages, Sub Center in 15 villages, Maternity and Child Welfare Center in 5 villages, Community health workers in 6 villages.

The Villages having Hospital or Dispensary or Health Center are Palayakottai , Theppampatti, Ramakirshnapuram, Palacombai.

Drinking Water: Tap water in 18 villages, Tank water in 18 villages, Well water in 18 villages, Tubewell in 18 villages and more than one source in 18 villages.

Bank: Banking facility in 7 villages, namely, Thimmarasanayakkanur, Kovilpatty, Marikundu G. Usilampatti, Kottapatti, Anndipatti, Rajathani.

Credit Society in 3 villages Agricultural Credit Society in 2 Non-Agricultural Credit Society in 0 village.

Others: Power supply in 18 villages, Cinema hall in 2 villages, sport club in 0 village, Stadium or Auditorium or Community Hall in 0 village, Post Office in 17 villages.

There are 18 villages having bus facilities.

Villages with most of facilities: Thimmarasanayakkanur Kovilpatty, Marikundu, G. Usilampatti, Kottapatti Anndipatti, Rajathani.

Villages without Amenities (Education): None..

Scheduled Castes: Out of the total population of 95705 persons, 26030 persons (27.2%) belong to Scheduled Castes. The villages having less than 10% SC population are G. Usilampatti, Kothaluthu, Palayakottai Chittarpathi, Palacombai.

The villages having more than 50% SC population are None.

Sex ratio of Scheduled Caste population is 495.

Scheduled Castes Literates and Illiterates by Sex:

	Persons	Males	Females
Literate	13,851	8,227	5,624
Illiterate	12,179	4,931	7,248
Literacy rate	61.3	72.5	50.0
Graduate	123	91	32

Scheduled Castes (Dominant):

Pallan, Chakkiliyan, Paraiyan etc., Madari Arunthathiyar

For their cultural identity please see Appendix-I

Villages without Scheduled Castes: There are 3 villages without any scheduled caste population.

Scheduled Tribes: Out of the total population of 95705 persons, 7 persons (0.01%) belong to Scheduled Tribes. The villages having less than 10% ST population are

Pulimancombai, Thimmarasanayakkanur, Kovilpatty Sanmugasundarapuram, Kunnur, Marikundu, Thekkampatti G. Usilampatti, Mottanuthu, Kottapatti, Kothaluthu Anndipatti, Palayakottai , Rajathani, Chittarpathi Theppampatti, Ramakirshnapuram, Palacombai.

The villages having more than 50% ST population are None.

Sex ratio of Scheduled tribe population is 429.

Scheduled Tribes Literates and Illiterates by Sex:

	Persons	Males	Females
Literate	5	3	2
Illiterate	2	1	1
Literacy rate	71.4	75.0	66.7
Graduate	0	0	0

Scheduled Tribes (Dominant):

Palliyan

For their cultural identity please see Appendix-II

Villages without Scheduled Tribes: There are 19 villages without any scheduled tribe population.

Literates and Illiterates by Sex (Total Population):

	Persons	Males	Females
Literate	55,789	33,282	22,507
Illiterate	39,916	15,020	24,896
Literacy rate	66	79	54
Graduate	481	380	101

Agriculture: ***Distribution of villages according to land use:*** Out of 20 villages, Total area (in hectare) is 34513.17, out of that 50.6 percent is cultivable and 50.83 percent of the cultivable area is irrigated.

Sources of Irrigation (Hectares): Government Canal 0, Private Canal 0, Well without Electricity 32.45, Well with Electricity 8375, Tubewell without Electricity 0, Tubewell with Electricity 0, Tank 402.72, River 67.31, Lake 0, Waterfall 0, Others 0.

Villages with population of 5000 to 9999:

Kovilpatti , Shanmugasundarapuram , Mottanuthu.

Villages with population of 10000 and above:

Timmarasanayakkanur , Andipatti.

Distribution of Workers:

	Persons	Males	Females	WPR
Cultivators	10,908	6,137	4,771	19.76
Agricultural Labour	30,811	13,913	16,898	55.83
Household Industry	2,259	1,004	1,255	4.09
Other Workers	11,213	8,121	3,092	20.32
Main Workers	50,692	27,419	23,273	91.85
Marginal Workers	4,499	1,756	2,743	8.15
Total Workers	55,191	29,175	26,016	

Religion: Major Religious Communities:

	Persons	Males	Females	Sex Ratio
Hindu (98.18%)	93,967	47,434	46,533	981
Muslim (0.07%)	71	34	37	1,088
Christian (1.68%)	1,605	802	803	1,001
Sikh (0%)	-	-	-	-
Buddhists (0%)	-	-	-	-
Jain (0%)	2	2	-	-

Agewise Data:

	Persons	Males	Females	Sex Ratio
All ages	95,705	48,302	47,403	981
0-14	27,654	14,535	13,119	903
15-44	45,178	22,512	22,666	1007
45-79	21,081	10,296	10,785	1047
80+	876	446	430	964
Age not stated	916	513	403	786

Languages (Dominant):

Tamil, Telugu, Kannada, Urdu, Malayalam

Disabled Population:

	Persons	Males	Females	%
Total Disabled	2,302	1,184	1,118	
In Seeing	1,323	622	701	57.47
In Speech	198	119	79	8.6
In Hearing	82	33	49	3.56
In Movement	509	297	212	22.11
Mentally	190	113	77	8.25

ANNAGRAMAM

Annagramam C.D. Block lies in the northern part of Cuddalore district. It is a part of Panruti taluk. The taluk is located at a distance of 25 kms. from district headquarters (Cuddalore). There are 45 villages in the block with the total population of 115,072 persons. Area of the C.D. Block is 137.10 sq. kms. It is bounded in the north by district Viluppuram, in the south by C.D. Blocks Panruti and Cuddalore, in the east by CD Block Cuddalore, and in the west by district Viluppuram.

Communications:

Roadways : S.H.-8: Direction- Panruti to Kaliyanur, Nearest Villages- Kandarakottai, Pulavanoor, Maligaimedu, Kanisapakkam. S.H.-9: Direction- Triukkoyilur to Cuddalore, Nearest Villages- Palur, Sanniyasipettai, Sundaravandhi, Keelarungunam, Pallavarayanatham, Elumedu, Kottampakkam.

Railway Station: Akkadavalli, Poondi, Perumalnaichenpalayam.

Local Streams: Nearest Villages- Paithambadi, Kavanoor, Ulunthampattu, Enadirimangalam, Akkadavalli, Pagandai, Kandarakottai, Pulavanoor, Melkumanamangalam, Kongarayanur.

Backwards Region Grants Fund: It receives Backward Region Grants.

Annual Rainfall: Average Rainfall 1050 mm.

Ground Water: Availability of the ground water in the Basin is 15376.64 MCM and the utilization is 13581.10

MCM. It belongs to Semi Critical category. Depth to water level varies from 5 to 10 meter below the ground. Most of the wells go down in summer months, according to the Ground Water Estimation Committee.

Forest and Reserved Forest: (Karunbur RF)- Nearest Villages- Enadirimangalam, Korathi, Akkadavalli, Kayapakkam, Karumbur, Karumbur RF, Avianur, Alagaperumalkuppam. (Kayapakkam)- Nearest Villages- Thiruthuraiyur, Kayapakkam (RF), Kayapakkam, Oraiyur. (Oraiyur)- Nearest Villages- Karumbur, Oraiyur, Oriyur (RF). (Thiruthuraiyur)- Nearest Villages- Thiruthuraiyur (RF), Thiruthuraiyur, Varinjipakkam.

Natural Division: Tondai Nadu.

Administration

Revenue **Division:** Cuddalore. Parliamentary Constituency: 26 Cuddalore (SC). District: Cuddalore. Taluk: Panruti. Assembly Constituency: 154 Panruti. Gram Panchayat: 42.

Villages: 45 **Inhabited:** 41 **Uninhabited:** 4

Ranking	District	State	National
Area	13	351	5233
Population	7	77	2996
Sex Ratio	7	258	1936
Child Sex Ratio	12	195	3253
Literacy Rate	8	219	2015
Density	4	214	1086
Work Participation Rate	1	9	2291

Gram Panchayats:

Agaram, Akkadavalli, Alagapperumalkuppam, Aviyanur, Chinnaprttai, Chittarasur, Eidanur, Elumedu, Enadirimangalam, Kallipattu, Kandarakottai , Kanisapakkam, Karumbur, Kavanur, Kilarungunam, Kilkavarapattu, Kongarayanur, Korathi, Kotlampakkam, Kozhipakkam, Maligamedu, Melkavarapattu, Melkumaramangalam (North), Melkumaramangalam (North), Narimedu, Natham, Oraiyur, Pagandai, Paithambadi, Pallavarayanatham, Palur , Panapakkam, Pandarakkottai, Perumalnaickenpalayam, Poondi , Pulavanur, Sanniyasipettai , Sathipattu, Sundaravandi, Thattampalayam, Thirasu, Thiruthuraiyur , Varinjipakkam.

Amenities:

Education: Primary School in 37 villages, Middle school in 15 villages, Matriculation or Secondary School in 6 villages, namely Kandarakottai, Thiruthuraiyur, Oraiyur, Kilkavarapattu, Palur, Sathipattu.

Higher Secondary or Pre University Courses or Intermediate or Junior College in 2 villages of the CD Block,, namely Thiruthuraiyur, Kilkavarapattu.

College in 0 village, Adult Literacy Center in 0 village.

Medical: Hospital in 1 village, Dispensary in 0 village, Health Center in 5 villages, Sub Center in 20 villages, Maternity and Child Welfare Center in 5 villages, Community health workers in 7 villages.

The Villages having Hospital or Dispensary or Health Center are Thiruthuraiyur, Arigirundamangalam.

Drinking Water: Tap water in 41 villages, Tank water in 0 villages, Well water in 41 villages, Tubewell in 41 villages and more than one source in 41 villages.

Bank: Banking facility in 9 villages, namely, Paithambadi, Kandarakottai, Melkumanamangalam Avianur, Oraiyur, Perumalnaichenpalayam, Palur Elumedu, Sathipattu.

Credit Society in 8 villages Agricultural Credit Society in 8 Non-Agricultural Credit Society in 0 village.

Others: Power supply in 41 villages, Cinema hall in 0 village, sport club in 0 village, Stadium or Auditorium or Community Hall in 0 village, Post Office in 41 villages.

There are 37 villages having bus facilities.

Villages with most of facilities: Paithambadi Kandarakottai, Avianur, Oraiyur Perumalnaichenpalayam, Palur, Elumedu, Sathipattu.

Villages without amenities (Education): Kavanoor, Eaithanoor, Arigirundamangalam, Sirunangaivadi..

Scheduled Castes: Out of the total population of 115072 persons, 37850 persons (32.89%) belong to Scheduled Castes.

The villages having less than 10% SC population are Kavanoor, Ulunthampattu, Korathi, Pagandai, Poondi Avianur, Varinjipakkam, Sathipattu.

The villages having more than 50% SC population are Kongarayanur, Thirasu, Kayapakkam Alagaperumalkuppam, Perumalnaichenpalayam Chittarasur, Kanisapakkam, Eaithanoor Arigirundamangalam.

Sex ratio of Scheduled Caste population is 497.

Scheduled Castes Literates and Illiterates by Sex:

	Persons	Males	Females
Literate	17,286	10,612	6,674
Illiterate	20,564	8,415	12,149
Literacy rate	54.2	66.3	42.0
Graduate	295	226	69

Scheduled Castes (Dominant):

Adi Dravida, Arunthathiyar, Valluvan, Chakkiliyan Adi Andhra

For their cultural identity please see Appendix-I

Villages without Scheduled Castes: There are 7 villages without any scheduled caste population.

Scheduled Tribes: Out of the total population of 115072 persons, 375 persons (0.33%) belong to Scheduled Tribes.

The villages having less than 10% ST population are Paithambadi, Kavanoor, Ulunthampattu

Enadirimangalam, Korathi, Akkadavalli, Kandarakottai Pulavanoor, Melkumanamangalam, Pagandai Kongarayanur, Kozhipakkam, Maligaimedu, Thirasu Poondi, Thiruthuraiyur, Kayapakkam, Karumbur Avianur, Alagaperumalkuppam, Oraiyur, Varinjipakkam Panapakkam, Melkavarapattu, Kilkavarapattu Perumalnaichenpalayam, Chittarasur, Palur, Elumedu Kanisapakkam, Kotlampakkam, Pandarakottai Sanniyasipettai, Eaithanoor, Arigirundamangalam Sundaravandhi, Keelarungunam, Pallavarayanatham Palapattu, Sirunangaivadi, Sathipattu.

The villages having more than 50% ST population are None.

Sex ratio of Scheduled tribe population is 507.

Scheduled Tribes Literates and Illiterates by Sex:

	Persons	Males	Females
Literate	127	76	51
Illiterate	248	109	139
Literacy rate	39.3	50.3	29.7
Graduate	0	0	0

Scheduled Tribes (Dominant):

Irular, Malakkuravan, Kattunayakan

For their cultural identity please see Appendix-II

Villages without Scheduled Tribes: There are 37 villages without any scheduled tribe population.

Literates and Illiterates by Sex (Total Population):

	Persons	Males	Females
Literate	64,693	38,687	26,006
Illiterate	50,379	19,366	31,013
Literacy rate	65	77	52
Graduate	1,561	1,152	409

Agriculture: ***Distribution of villages according to land use:*** Out of 45 villages, Total area (in hectare) is 13710.11, out of that 73.24 percent is cultivable and 88.84 percent of the cultivable area is irrigated.

Sources of Irrigation (Hectares): Government Canal 189.38, Private Canal 0, Well without Electricity 0, Well with Electricity 79.84, Tubewell without Electricity 50, Tubewell with Electricity 8090.45, Tank 485.45, River 0, Lake 26.43, Waterfall 0, Others 0.

Villages with population of 5000 to 9999: Melkumaramangalam (South), Maligamedu, Oraiyur Kilkavarapattu, Perumalnaickenpalayam.

Villages with population of 10000 and above: None

Distribution of Workers:

	Persons	Males	Females	WPR
Cultivators	9,021	6,864	2,157	15.76
Agricultural Labour	38,191	19,854	18,337	66.72
Household Industry	1,329	750	579	2.32
Other Workers	8,696	7,019	1,677	15.19
Main Workers	46,851	30,179	16,672	81.85
Marginal Workers	10,386	4,308	6,078	18.15
Total Workers	57,237	34,487	22,750	

Religion: Major Religious Communities:

	Persons	Males	Females	Sex Ratio
Hindu (96.27%)	110,785	55,958	54,827	980
Muslim (1.44%)	1,658	786	872	1,109
Christian (2.25%)	2,584	1,289	1,295	1,005
Sikh (0%)	1	1	-	-
Buddhists (0%)	-	-	-	-
Jain (0%)	5	2	3	1,500

Agewise Data:

	Persons	Males	Females	Sex Ratio
All ages	115,072	58,053	57,019	982
0-14	33,180	16,898	16,282	964
15-44	57,583	28,799	28,784	999
45-79	23,349	11,845	11,504	971
80+	777	419	358	854
Age not stated	183	92	91	989

Languages (Dominant):

Tamil, Telugu, Urdu, Kannada, English

Disabled Population:

	Persons	Males	Females	%
Total Disabled	2,994	1,478	1,516	
In Seeing	1,566	634	932	52.3
In Speech	237	125	112	7.92
In Hearing	220	114	106	7.35
In Movement	739	474	265	24.68
Mentally	232	131	101	7.75

ANNAVASAL

Annavasal C.D. Block lies in the western part of Pudukkottai district. It is a part of Iluppur and Kulathur taluks. The Block is located at a distance of 18 kms. from district headquarters (Pudukkottai). There are 57 villages in the block with the total population of 109,783 persons. Area of the C.D. Block is 413.56 sq. kms. It is bounded in the north by C.D. Blocks Viralimalai and Kunnandarkvoil, in the south by CD Blocks Ponnamaravathi and Thirumayam, in the east by CD Block Pudukkottai, in the west by C.D. Blocks Viralimalai and Ponnamaravathi, and district Tiruchirappalli. CD Block Annavasal falls in taluk Iluppur by 47 villages, and in taluk Kulathur by 10 villages.

Communications:

Roadways : N.H.-210: Direction- Keeranaur to Karaikudi, Nearest Villages- Narthamalai, Ammachathiram, Sathyamangalam, Melur, Vellam.

Railway Station: Narthamalai.

River: Vellar Nadi- Nearest Villages- Kadavampatty, Gudalore, Vannarappatti, Kilikkudi, Mampatti, Parambur, Parambur R.F., Pulvayal, Sundarappatti, Kurukkapatti,

Kothandaramapuram.

Annual Rainfall: Average Rainfall 910 mm.

Ground Water: Availability of the ground water in the Basin is 6702.93 H.A.M. and the utilization is 1710. 24 H.A.M. It belongs to Safe category. Depth to water level varies from 2 to 5 meter below the ground. Most of the wells go down in summer months, according to the Ground Water Estimation Committee.

Forest and Reserved Forest: (Kudumiyamalai RF)- Nearest Villages- Pudur, Vayalogam, Kudumiyanmalai, Kudumiyanmalai R.F., Visalur, Pulvayal. (Perambur)- Nearest Villages- Veerappatti, Kadambarayapatti, Parambur, Parambur R.F., Pudur, Kudumiyanmalai, Pinnangudi.

Natural Division: Chola Nadu.

Administration

Revenue **Division:** Pudukottai. Parliamentary Constituency: 30 Pudukottai. District: 30 Pudukottai. Taluk: Iluppur, Kulathur. Assembly Constituency: 179 Kukathur, 178 Gandaruvakottai (SC). Gram Panchayat: 43.

Villages: 57 **Inhabited:** 56 **Uninhabited:** 1

Ranking	District	State	National
Area	2	63	1859
Population	4	95	3160
Sex Ratio	6	74	599
Child Sex Ratio	12	219	3511
Literacy Rate	11	252	2182
Density	5	200	3906
Work Participation Rate	7	267	2071

Gram Panchayats:

Alathur, Ammachatram, Ariyur, Chittannavasal, Easwarankoil, Ennai, Idaiyapatti, Irumbali, Irundirapatti, Kadavampatti, Kattakudi, Keelakurichi, Kilikkudi, Kothandaramapuram, Kothirappatti, Kudumiyanmalai, Mangudi, Mannavelampatti, Mathiyanallur, Melur, Muckannamalaipatti, Muthukkadu, Narthamalai, Panampatti, Parambur, Perumanadu, Poongudi, Pudur, Pulvayal, Punginipatti, Rapposal, Sathiamangalam, Thalinji, Thatchampatti, Thiruvengaivasal, Thudaiyur, Tirunallur, Vayalogam, Veerapatti, Vellanjar, Vellanur, Vettukadu, Vilathupatti.

Amenities:

Education: Primary School in 53 villages, Middle school in 24 villages, Matriculation or Secondary School in 11 villages, namely Thirunallur, Irundirappatti, Kotthirappatti, Rappusal, Keelakurichi, Veerappatti, Parambur, Vayalogam, Kudumiyanmalai R.F., Sathyamangalam, Muthukkadu.

Higher Secondary or Pre University Courses or Intermediate or Junior College in 1 village of the CD Block,, namely Muthukkadu.

College in 1 village, Adult Literacy Center in 0 village., College is in village, namely Kudumiyanmalai R.F..

Medical: Hospital in 1 village, Dispensary in 2 villages, Health Center in 2 villages, Sub Center in 15 villages, Maternity and Child Welfare Center in 1 village, Community health workers in 43 villages.

The Villages having Hospital or Dispensary or Health Center are Easwarankoil, Parambur, Vayalogam.

Drinking Water: Tap water in 55 villages, Tank water in 27 villages, Well water in 55 villages, Tubewell in 55 villages and more than one source in 55 villages.

Bank: Banking facility in 5 villages, namely, Veerappatti, Parambur, Kudumiyanmalai, Ammachathiram Muthukkadu.

Credit Society in 3 villages Agricultural Credit Society in 3 Non-Agricultural Credit Society in 0 village.

Others: Power supply in 55 villages, Cinema hall in 1 village, sport club in 0 village, Stadium or Auditorium or Community Hall in 0 village, Post Office in 26 villages.

There are 50 villages having bus facilities.

Villages with most of facilities: Veerappatti Parambur, Kudumiyanmalai, Ammachathiram, Muthukkadu.

Villages without amenities (Education):

Thiruvengaivasal, Kurukkapatti, Venkaivayal..

Scheduled Castes: Out of the total population of 109783 persons, 25618 persons (23.34%) belong to Scheduled Castes.

The villages having less than 10% SC population are Veerappatti, Panangudy, Ayingudy, Kurukkapatti Kothandaramapuram, Irumbali.

The villages having more than 50% SC population are None.

Sex ratio of Scheduled Caste population is 503.

Scheduled Castes Literates and Illiterates by Sex:

	Persons	Males	Females
Literate	13,128	7,821	5,307
Illiterate	12,490	4,905	7,585
Literacy rate	59.8	72.3	47.7
Graduate	133	99	34

Scheduled Castes (Dominant):

Pallan, Paraiyan etc., Chakkiliyan, Kuravan etc.

Adi Dravida

For their cultural identity please see Appendix-I

Villages without Scheduled Castes: There are 3 villages without any scheduled caste population.

Scheduled Tribes: Out of the total population of 109783 persons, 107 persons (0.1%) belong to Scheduled Tribes.

The villages having less than 10% ST population are Thirunallur, Kattakudi, Irundirappatti, Easwarankoil Kotthirappatti, Ennai, Puniginipatty, Vellanjar

Vettukadu, Rappusal, Keelakurichi, Vilathupatti Chithannavasal, Veerappatti, Kadambarayapatti Edayapatti, Alathur, Thalingi, Kadavampatty Gudalore, Peyal, Vannarappatti, Pinnangudi Kilikkudi, Mampatti, Parambur, Pudur, Thachampatti Panangudy, Athiyanallur, Panampatty Thiruvengaivasal, Perunjunai, Ariyur, Mangudy Vayalogam, Kudumiyanmalai, Kudumiyanmalai R.F. Visalur, Pulvayal, Marayappatti, Ayingudy Perumanadu, Sundarappatti, Kurukkapatti Kothandaramapuram, Narthamalai, Ammachathiram Thudaiyur, Sathyamangalam, Irumbali, Melur, Vellam Muthukkadu, Venkaivayal, Poongudi.

The villages having more than 50% ST population are None.

Sex ratio of Scheduled tribe population is 561.

Scheduled Tribes Literates and Illiterates by Sex:

	Persons	Males	Females
Literate	25	16	9
Illiterate	82	31	51
Literacy rate	33.3	53.3	20.0
Graduate	0	0	0

Scheduled Tribes (Dominant):

Palliyar, Kattunayakan, Koraga, Kurumans

For their cultural identity please see Appendix-II

Villages without Scheduled Tribes: There are 52 villages without any scheduled tribe population.

Literates and Illiterates by Sex (Total Population):

	Persons	Males	Females
Literate	60,383	35,637	24,746
Illiterate	49,400	18,618	30,782
Literacy rate	64	76	51
Graduate	502	365	137

Agriculture: ***Distribution of villages according to land use:*** Out of 57 villages, Total area (in hectare) is 41356.3, out of that 35.78 percent is cultivable and 51.33 percent of the cultivable area is irrigated.

Sources of Irrigation (Hectares): Government Canal 0, Private Canal 0, Well without Electricity 453.88, Well with Electricity 2405.96, Tubewell without Electricity 0, Tubewell with Electricity 67.7, Tank 4867.28, River 0, Lake 0, Waterfall 0, Others 0.

Villages with population of 5000 to 9999: Ennai, Veerapatti.

Villages with population of 10000 and above: None

Distribution of Workers:

	Persons	Males	Females	WPR
Cultivators	20,778	12,703	8,075	37.71
Agricultural Labour	18,795	7,856	10,939	34.11
Household Industry	2,545	1,345	1,200	4.62
Other Workers	12,987	9,594	3,393	23.57
Main Workers	44,847	27,780	17,067	81.38
Marginal Workers	10,258	3,718	6,540	18.62
Total Workers	55,105	31,498	23,607	

Religion: Major Religious Communities:

	Persons	Males	Females	Sex Ratio
Hindu (92.15%)	101,168	50,031	51,137	1,022
Muslim (4.69%)	5,152	2,489	2,663	1,070
Christian (2.94%)	3,229	1,611	1,618	1,004
Sikh (0%)	-	-	-	-
Buddhists (0%)	1	-	1	-
Jain (0%)	1	1	-	-

Agewise Data:

	Persons	Males	Females	Sex Ratio
All ages	109,783	54,255	55,528	1023
0-14	33,952	17,278	16,674	965
15-44	52,626	25,268	27,358	1083
45-79	22,353	11,272	11,081	983
80+	664	342	322	942
Age not stated	188	95	93	979

Languages (Dominant):

Tamil, Urdu, Gujarati, Telugu, Malayalam

Disabled Population:

	Persons	Males	Females	%
Total Disabled	3,200	1,409	1,791	
In Seeing	1,943	688	1,255	60.72
In Speech	323	186	137	10.09
In Hearing	174	83	91	5.44
In Movement	583	349	234	18.22
Mentally	177	103	74	5.53

ANNUR

Annur C.D. Block lies in the northern part of Coimbatore district. It is a part of Avanashi taluk. The Block is located at a distance of 33 kms. from district headquarters (Coimbatore). There are 21 villages in the block with the total population of 83,016 persons. Area of the C.D. Block is 270.61 sq. kms. It is bounded is bound ed in the north by CD Blocks Karamadai and Avanashi, in the south by CD Blocks Sarcarsamakulam and Sulur, in the east by CD Blocks Avanashi, and Sulur, in the west by CD Blocks Karamadai and Periyanayakkanpalayam.

Communications:

Roadways : N.H.-209: Direction- Coimbatore to Sathyamangalam, Nearest Villages- Kanuvakkarai, Pasur, Annur Mettupalayam, Odder Palayam, Kariampalayam, Karegoundampalayam, Kattampatti, Kunnathur, Masagoundan Chetti Palayam.

Annual Rainfall: Average Rainfall 550 mm.

Ground Water: Availability of the ground water in the Basin is 3413.10 H.A.M. and the utilization is 5909.62 H.A.M. It belongs to Semi Critical category. Depth to

water level varies from 0 to 20 meter below the ground. Most of the wells go down in summer months, according to the Ground Water Estimation Committee.

Natural Division: Kongu Nadu.

Administration

Revenue **Division:** Trippur. Parliamentary Constituency: 19 Nilgiris. District: Coimbatore. Taluk: Avanashi. Assembly Constituency: 112 Avanashi (SC). Gram Panchayat: 21.

Villages: 21 **Inhabited:** 21 **Uninhabited:** 0

Ranking	District	State	National
Area	9	204	3098
Population	8	220	4004
Sex Ratio	9	276	2157
Child Sex Ratio	6	60	1204
Literacy Rate	17	279	2368
Density	8	133	3465
Work Participation Rate	10	216	1332

Gram Panchayats:

Akkaraisengapalli, Allapalayam, Ambodi, Annur Mettupalayam, Kanjappalli, Kanuvakkarai, Karegoundenpalayam, Kariampalayam, Kattampatti, Kunnathur, Kuppanur, Kuppepalayam, Masagoundenchettipalayam, Naranapuram, Odderpalayam, Pachapalayam, Pasur, Pillaiappampalayam, Pogalur, Vadakkalur, Vadavalli.

Amenities:

Education: Primary School in 21 villages, Middle school in 16 villages, Matriculation or Secondary School in 4 villages, namely Vadakkalur, Kuppanur, Kattampatti, Masagoundan Chetti Palayam.

Higher Secondary or Pre University Courses or Intermediate or Junior College in 0 village of the CD Block, College in 1 village, Adult Literacy Center in 0 village., College is in village, namely Ambothi.

Medical: Hospital in 0 village, Dispensary in 0 village, Health Center in 2 villages, Sub Center in 18 villages, Maternity and Child Welfare Center in 3 villages, Community health workers in 2 villages.

The Village having Hospital or Dispensary or Health Center is Pachapalayam.

Drinking Water: Tap water in 21 villages, Tank water in 1 villages, Well water in 21 villages, Tubewell in 21 villages and more than one source in 21 villages.

Bank: Banking facility in 6 villages, namely, Pasur, Vadakkalur, Kuppanur, Pogalur, Kattampatti Masagoundan Chetti Palayam.

Credit Society in 14 villages Agricultural Credit Society in 13 Non-Agricultural Credit Society in 8 villages.

Others: Power supply in 21 villages, Cinema hall in 4 villages, sport club in 1 village, Stadium or Auditorium or Community Hall in 1 village, Post Office in 21 villages.

There are 21 villages having bus facilities.

Villages with most of facilities: Pasur Vadakkalur, Kuppanur, Pogalur, Kattampatti Masagoundan Chetti Palayam.

Villages without Amenities (Education): None..

Scheduled Castes: Out of the total population of 83016 persons, 22442 persons (27.03%) belong to Scheduled Castes. The villages having less than 10% SC population are None..

The villages having more than 50% SC population are None.

Sex ratio of Scheduled Caste population is 495.

Scheduled Castes Literates and Illiterates by Sex:

	Persons	Males	Females
Literate	8,010	4,790	3,220
Illiterate	14,432	6,548	7,884
Literacy rate	41.1	48.5	33.4
Graduate	31	23	8

Scheduled Castes (Dominant):

Chakkiliyan, Arunthathiyar, Pallan, Adi Dravida Madari

For their cultural identity please see Appendix-I

Villages without Scheduled Castes: There is 0 village without any scheduled caste population.

Scheduled Tribes: Out of the total population of 83016 persons, 471 persons (0.57%) belong to Scheduled Tribes. The villages having less than 10% ST population are Akkarai Sangappalli, Kanuvakkarai, Ambothi, Pasur Annur Mettupalayam, Vadakkalur, Odder Palayam Kuppanur, Pogalur, Vadavalli, Karegoundampalayam Kanchappalli, Pilliappampalayam, Kariampalayam Kuppepalayam, Kattampatti, Kunnathur Masagoundan Chetti Palayam, Pachapalayam Naranapuram.

The villages having more than 50% ST population are None.

Sex ratio of Scheduled tribe population is 471.

Scheduled Tribes Literates and Illiterates by Sex:

	Persons	Males	Females
Literate	303	189	114
Illiterate	168	60	108
Literacy rate	69.0	80.4	55.9
Graduate	22	14	8

Scheduled Tribes (Dominant):

Kondareddis, Irular

For their cultural identity please see Appendix-II

Villages without Scheduled Tribes: There are 17 villages without any scheduled tribe population.

Literates and Illiterates by Sex (Total Population):

	Persons	Males	Females
Literate	46,534	27,543	18,991
Illiterate	36,482	14,457	22,025
Literacy rate	62	73	52
Graduate	753	504	249

Agriculture: ***Distribution of villages according to land use:*** Out of 21 villages, Total area (in hectare) is 27061.17, out of that 88.27 percent is cultivable and 22.35 percent of the cultivable area is irrigated.

Sources of Irrigation (Hectares): Government Canal 0, Private Canal 0, Well without Electricity 35.84, Well with Electricity 3534.21, Tubewell without Electricity 0, Tubewell with Electricity 1767.95, Tank 0, River 0, Lake 0, Waterfall 0, Others 0.

Villages with population of 5000 to 9999: Vadakkalur, Odderpalayam, Karegoundenpalayam Masagoundenchettipalayam.

Villages with population of 10000 and above: None

Distribution of Workers:

	Persons	Males	Females	WPR
Cultivators	10,915	6,692	4,223	23.85
Agricultural Labour	18,106	9,297	8,809	39.56
Household Industry	2,313	1,402	911	5.05
Other Workers	14,429	10,987	3,442	31.53
Main Workers	40,736	26,314	14,422	89.02
Marginal Workers	5,027	2,064	2,963	10.98
Total Workers	45,763	28,378	17,385	

Religion: Major Religious Communities:

	Persons	Males	Females	Sex Ratio
Hindu (98.85%)	82,061	41,515	40,546	977
Muslim (0.33%)	274	158	116	734
Christian (0.78%)	650	312	338	1,083
Sikh (0%)	2	1	1	1,000
Buddhists (0.01%)	5	2	3	1,500
Jain (0%)	1	-	1	-

Agewise Data:

	Persons	Males	Females	Sex Ratio
All ages	83,016	42,000	41,016	977
0-14	18,269	9,290	8,979	967
15-44	39,808	20,088	19,720	982
45-79	22,904	11,551	11,353	983
80+	1,399	728	671	922
Age not stated	636	343	293	854

Languages (Dominant): Tamil, Telugu, Kannada, Urdu, Malayalam

Disabled Population:

	Persons	Males	Females	%
Total Disabled	3,045	1,137	1,908	
In Seeing	2,212	641	1,571	72.64
In Speech	157	89	68	5.16
In Hearing	77	40	37	2.53
In Movement	426	263	163	13.99
Mentally	173	104	69	5.68

ANTHIYUR

Anthiyur C.D. Block lies in the north-eastern part of Erode district. It is a part of Bhavani taluk. The Block is located at a distance of 36 kms. from district headquarters (Erode). There are 18 villages in the block with the total population of 96,469 persons. Area of the C.D. Block is 100.38 sq. kms. It is bounded in the south by CD Blocks Bhavani and Gobichettipalayam, in the east by district Salem and C.D. Block Ammapet, in the west by CD Block TN Palaiyam, and it has common boundary with the state of Karnataka on north and west.

Communications:

Roadways : Information not Available.

River: Bhavani Nadi- Nearest Villages- Kuppandampalayam, Keezhvani, Koothampoondi. Palar Nadi- Nearest Villages- Burgur North RF, Thamaraikkarai RF, Moongolpatti.

Annual Rainfall: Average Rainfall 789 mm.

Ground Water: Availability of the ground water in the basin is 6964.60 H.A.M. and the utilization is 7435.33 H.A.M. It belongs to Over Expoited category. Depth to water level varies from 5 to 10 meter below the ground. Most of the wells go down in summer months, according to the Ground Water Estimation Committee.

Forest and Reserved Forest: (Burgur RF)- Nearest Villages- Burgur South RF, Burgur, Ennamangalam RF, Channampettai, Ennamangalam, Sankarapalayam, Anthiyur, Nagalur RF, Nagalur, Burgur North RF. (Thamaraikkarai)- Nearest Villages- Burgur, Thamaraikkarai RF.

Natural Division: Kongu Nadu.

Administration

Revenue **Division:** Gobichettipalayam. Parliamentary Constituency: 18 Gobichettipalayam. District: Erode. Taluk: Bhavani. Assembly Constituency: 105 Anthiyur. Gram Panchayat: 14.

Border Villages- (Karnataka)- Nearest Village- Burgur North RF, Burgur.

Villages: 18 **Inhabited:** 13 **Uninhabited:** 5

Ranking	District	State	National
Area	2	4	434
Population	4	146	3571
Sex Ratio	19	353	3844
Child Sex Ratio	12	277	4587
Literacy Rate	19	379	4501
Density	11	27	6164
Work Participation Rate	18	380	223

Gram Panchayats:

Brammadesam, Burgur, Chinnathambipalayam, Ennamangalam, Gettisamudram, Kilwani, Kuppandampalayam, Kuthampoondi, Michaelpalayam, Moongilpatti, Nagalur, Pachampalayam, Sankarapalayam, Vembathi.

Amenities:

Education: Primary School in 13 villages, Middle school in 11 villages, Matriculation or Secondary School in 7 villages, namely Burgur, Nagalur, Kuppandampalayam, Bramadesam, Pachampalayam, Vempathi, Moongolpatti.

Higher Secondary or Pre University Courses or Intermediate or Junior College in 3 villages of the CD Block,, namely Kuppandampalayam, Bramadesam, Pachampalayam. College in 0 village, Adult Literacy Center in 0 village.

Medical: Hospital in 1 village, Dispensary in 0 village, Health Center in 4 villages, Sub Center in 4 villages, Maternity and Child Welfare Center in 1 village, Community health workers in 8 villages.

The Village having Hospital or Dispensary or Health Center is Sankarapalayam.

Drinking Water: Tap water in 13 villages, Tank water in 0 villages, Well water in 13 villages, Tubewell in 13 villages and more than one source in 13 villages.

Bank: Banking facility in 3 villages, namely, Ennamangalam, Kuppandampalayam, Bramadesam.

Credit Society in 8 villages Agricultural Credit Society in 5 Non-Agricultural Credit Society in 2 villages.

Others: Power supply in 13 villages, Cinema hall in 0 village, sport club in 0 village, Stadium or Auditorium or Community Hall in 1 village, Post Office in 13 villages.

There are 13 villages having bus facilities.

Villages with most of facilities: Ennamangalam Kuppandampalayam, Bramadesam.

Villages without Amenities (Education): None..

Scheduled Castes: Out of the total population of 96469 persons, 15155 persons (15.71%) belong to Scheduled Castes.

The villages having less than 10% SC population are None..

The villages having more than 50% SC population are None.

Sex ratio of Scheduled Caste population is 491.

Scheduled Castes Literates and Illiterates by Sex:

	Persons	Males	Females
Literate	6,377	3,892	2,485
Illiterate	8,778	3,823	4,955
Literacy rate	47.3	56.7	37.5
Graduate	98	75	23

Scheduled Castes (Dominant):

Chakkiliyan, Arunthathiyar, Adi Dravida, Pallan Paraiyan etc.

For their cultural identity please see Appendix-I

Villages without Scheduled Castes: There are 5 villages without any scheduled caste population.

Scheduled Tribes: Out of the total population of 96469 persons, 1845 persons (1.91%) belong to Scheduled Tribes.

The villages having less than 10% ST population are Burgur, Ennamangalam, Sankarapalayam, Anthiyur Nagalur, Kuppandampalayam, Bramadesam, Pachampalayam Gettisamudram, Vempathi, Moongolpatti, Keezhvani Koothampoondi.

The villages having more than 50% ST population are None.

Sex ratio of Scheduled tribe population is 495.

Scheduled Tribes Literates and Illiterates by Sex:

	Persons	Males	Females
Literate	552	336	216
Illiterate	1,293	595	698
Literacy rate	35.0	42.4	27.5
Graduate	28	20	8

Scheduled Tribes (Dominant):

Sholaga, Uraly, Kondareddis, Paniyan, Irular

For their cultural identity please see Appendix-II

Villages without Scheduled Tribes: There are 10 villages without any scheduled tribe population.

Literates and Illiterates by Sex (Total Population):

	Persons	Males	Females
Literate	42,948	26,957	15,991
Illiterate	53,521	22,680	30,841
Literacy rate	50	61	38
Graduate	1,079	809	270

Agriculture: ***Distribution of villages according to land use:*** Out of 18 villages, Total area (in hectare) is 100384.43, out of that 15.28 percent is cultivable and 41.4 percent of the cultivable area is irrigated.

Sources of Irrigation (Hectares): Government Canal 79.3, Private Canal 0, Well without Electricity 43.4, Well with Electricity 5686.61, Tubewell without Electricity 0, Tubewell with Electricity 0, Tank 0, River 541.14, Lake 0, Waterfall 0, Others 0.

Villages with population of 5000 to 9999: Ennamangalam, Nagalur, Kuppandampalayam Pachampalayam, Gettisamudram.

Villages with population of 10000 and above: Burgur, Anthiyur , Brammadesam, Vembathi.

Distribution of Workers:

	Persons	Males	Females	WPR
Cultivators	17,570	10,553	7,017	30.03
Agricultural Labour	27,856	13,697	14,159	47.61
Household Industry	2,905	1,291	1,614	4.97
Other Workers	10,176	7,284	2,892	17.39

Main Workers	53,100	31,538	21,562	90.76
Marginal Workers	5,407	1,287	4,120	9.24
Total Workers	58,507	32,825	25,682	

Religion: Major Religious Communities:

	Persons	Males	Females	Sex Ratio
Hindu (97.05%)	93,622	48,194	45,428	943
Muslim (0.33%)	319	172	147	855
Christian (2.19%)	2,111	1,052	1,059	1,007
Sikh (0.01%)	7	3	4	1,333
Buddhists (0.01%)	7	7	-	-
Jain (0%)	1	1	-	-

Agewise Data:

	Persons	Males	Females	Sex Ratio
All ages	96,469	49,637	46,832	943
0-14	24,814	12,901	11,913	923
15-44	46,840	23,806	23,034	968
45-79	23,468	12,220	11,248	920
80+	1,089	560	529	945
Age not stated	258	150	108	720

Languages (Dominant):

Tamil, Kannada, Telugu, Urdu, English

Disabled Population:

	Persons	Males	Females	%
Total Disabled	2,438	900	1,538	
In Seeing	1,619	448	1,171	66.41
In Speech	154	77	77	6.32
In Hearing	94	48	46	3.86
In Movement	424	247	177	17.39
Mentally	147	80	67	6.03

ARAKONAM

Arakkonam C.D. Block lies in the north-eastern part of Vellore district. It is a part of Arakkonam taluk. The Block is located at a distance of 80 kms. from district headquarters (Vellore). There are 29 villages in the block with the total population of 61,910 persons. Area of the C.D. Block is 173.24 sq. kms. It is bounded in the north by Thiruvallur District, in the south by CD Block Nemili and district Kancheepuram, in the east by district Thiruvallur, in the west by CD Blocks Kaveripakkam and Nemili.

Communications:

Roadways : Information not Available.

Local Streams: Nearest Villages- Vriyur, Anaikattaputhur, Pudukesavaran Village, Ananthapuram, Athur.

Annual Rainfall: Average Rainfall 949 mm.

Ground Water: Availability of the ground water in the Basin is 5074.82 H.A.M. and the utilization is 3844.57 H.A.M. It belongs to Semi Critical category. Depth to water level varies from 2 to 10 meter below the ground. Most of the wells go down in summer months, according to the Ground Water Estimation Committee.

Natural Division: Tondai Nadu.

Administration

Revenue **Division:** Arakonam. Parliamentary Constituency: 7 Arakkonam. District: Vellore. Taluk: Arakonam. Assembly Constituency: 38 Arakkonam (SC). Gram Panchayat: 26.

Villages: 29 **Inhabited:** 26 **Uninhabited:** 3

Ranking	District	State	National
Area	17	326	4652
Population	20	329	4797
Sex Ratio	20	327	2855
Child Sex Ratio	13	249	4086
Literacy Rate	6	112	1170
Density	18	348	3039
Work Participation Rate	15	148	4366

Gram Panchayats:

Amarishipuram, Ammanur , Anaikattaputhur, Anaipakkam, Ananthapuram, Athur, Kavanur, Kilandur, Kilkuppam, Kilpakkam, Konalam, Krishnapuram, Mosur, Mudur, Mulvoy, Perungalathur, Polur, Pudukesavaram, Puliyamangalam , Seyyur, Uliambakkam, Uriyur, Valarpuram, Velur.

Amenities:

Education: Primary School in 26 villages, Middle school in 11 villages, Matriculation or Secondary School in 5 villages, namely Polur, Valarpuram Village, Mudur, Kilpakkam, Mosur.

Higher Secondary or Pre University Courses or Intermediate or Junior College in 1 village of the CD Block,, namely Valarpuram Village.

College in 0 village, Adult Literacy Center in 0 village.

Medical: Hospital in 1 village, Dispensary in 0 village, Health Center in 2 villages, Sub Center in 1 village, Maternity and Child Welfare Center in 3 villages, Community health workers in 26 villages.

The Village having Hospital or Dispensary or Health Center is Athur.

Drinking Water: Tap water in 25 villages, Tank water in 6 villages, Well water in 10 villages, Tubewell in 15 villages and more than one source in 26 villages.

Bank: Banking facility in 2 villages, namely, Valarpuram Village, Mosur.

Credit Society in 7 villages Agricultural Credit Society in 7 Non-Agricultural Credit Society in 0 village.

Others: Power supply in 25 villages, Cinema hall in 0 village, sport club in 0 village, Stadium or Auditorium or Community Hall in 0 village, Post Office in 19 villages.

There are 24 villages having bus facilities.

Villages with most of facilities: Valarpuram Village Mosur.

Villages without Amenities (Education): None..

Scheduled Castes: Out of the total population of 61910 persons, 15637 persons (25.26%) belong to Scheduled Castes.
The villages having less than 10% SC population are None..
The villages having more than 50% SC population are None.
Sex ratio of Scheduled Caste population is 498.

Scheduled Castes Literates and Illiterates by Sex:

	Persons	Males	Females
Literate	9,445	5,467	3,978
Illiterate	6,192	2,381	3,811
Literacy rate	69.3	79.9	58.6
Graduate	184	135	49

Scheduled Castes (Dominant):
Adi Dravida, Arunthathiyar, Generic Castes etc.
Valluvan, Kuravan etc.
For their cultural identity please see Appendix-I
Villages without Scheduled Castes: There are 4 villages without any scheduled caste population.
Scheduled Tribes: Out of the total population of 61910 persons, 1306 persons (2.11%) belong to Scheduled Tribes.
The villages having less than 10% ST population are
Polur, Ulliyampakkam, Kilandur, Perungalahur
Krishnapuram, Valarpuram Village, Mudur, Valur
Konalam, Anaipakkam, Mulvoy, Kilpakkam, Kavanoor
Kilkuppam, Ammanoor, Puliamangalam, Ambarishipuram
Mosur, Chyuoor, Nagirikuppam, Vriyur
Anaikattaputhur, Pudukesavaran Village, Ananthapuram
Athur, Poyyapakkam.
The villages having more than 50% ST population are None.
Sex ratio of Scheduled tribe population is 495.

Scheduled Tribes Literates and Illiterates by Sex:

	Persons	Males	Females
Literate	280	181	99
Illiterate	1,026	478	548
Literacy rate	26.3	34.1	18.6
Graduate	1	1	0

Scheduled Tribes (Dominant):
Irular, Malayali, Kattunayakan, Generic Tribes etc.
Kurumans
For their cultural identity please see Appendix-II
Villages without Scheduled Tribes: There are 10 villages without any scheduled tribe population.

Literates and Illiterates by Sex (Total Population):

	Persons	Males	Females
Literate	38,168	22,648	15,520
Illiterate	23,742	8,887	14,855
Literacy rate	70	82	58
Graduate	1,296	1,010	286

Agriculture: ***Distribution of villages according to land use:***
Out of 29 villages, Total area (in hectare) is 17324.87, out of that 55.11 percent is cultivable and 41.22 percent of the cultivable area is irrigated.
Sources of Irrigation (Hectares): Government Canal 0, Private Canal 0, Well without Electricity 291.68, Well with Electricity 3350.24, Tubewell without Electricity 0, Tubewell with Electricity 117.87, Tank 55.6, River 0, Lake 120.08, Waterfall 0, Others 0.
Villages with population of 5000 to 9999:
Polur, Mosur.
Villages with population of 10000 and above: None
Distribution of Workers:

	Persons	Males	Females	WPR
Cultivators	3,812	2,811	1,001	15.06
Agricultural Labour	10,580	5,764	4,816	41.8
Household Industry	1,406	816	590	5.55
Other Workers	9,515	8,026	1,489	37.59
Main Workers	17,413	13,035	4,378	68.79
Marginal Workers	7,900	4,382	3,518	31.21
Total Workers	25,313	17,417	7,896	

Religion: Major Religious Communities:

	Persons	Males	Females	Sex Ratio
Hindu (88.41%)	54,734	27,871	26,863	964
Muslim (1.71%)	1,058	554	504	910
Christian (9.69%)	5,999	3,028	2,971	981
Sikh (0.08%)	49	37	12	324
Buddhists (0.01%)	9	6	3	500
Jain (0%)	-	-	-	-

Agewise Data:

	Persons	Males	Females	Sex Ratio
All ages	61,910	31,535	30,375	963
0-14	17,320	8,883	8,437	950
15-44	31,087	16,046	15,041	937
45-79	12,731	6,224	6,507	1045
80+	481	220	261	1186
Age not stated	291	162	129	796

Languages (Dominant):
Tamil, Telugu, Urdu, Hindi, Malayalam
Disabled Population:

	Persons	Males	Females	%
Total Disabled	1,180	669	511	
In Seeing	435	228	207	36.86
In Speech	120	63	57	10.17
In Hearing	101	55	46	8.56
In Movement	404	260	144	34.24
Mentally	120	63	57	10.17

ARANI

Arani C.D. Block lies in the northern part of Tiruvannamalai district. It is a part of Arani taluk. The Block is located at a distance of 66 kms. from district headquarters (Tiruvannamalai). There are 26 villages in the block with the total population of 98,409 persons. Area of the C.D. Block is 212.43 sq. kms. It is bounded in the north and east by district Vellore, in the south by C.D. Blocks Cheyyar and Arani West, in the west by district Vellore and C.D. Block Arani West.

Communications:

Roadways : S.H.-4: Direction- Chetpet to Arcot, Nearest Villages- Velleri, Irumbenu, Adanoor, Paiyur, Velapadi, Nesal.

River: Kamandala Nadi- Nearest Villages- Sevoor, Irumbenu, Mamandur, Kalpoondi, Paiyur.

Backwards Region Grants Fund: It receives Backward Region Grants.

Annual Rainfall: Average Rainfall 1019 mm.

Ground Water: Availability of the ground water in the Basin is (Information not available) H.A.M. and the utili zation is 160.44 H.A.M. It belongs to Over Expoited categ ory. Depth to water level varies from 2 to 5 meter below the ground. Most of the wells go down in summer months, according to the Ground Water Estimation Committee.

Forest and Reserved Forest: (Reserved Forest)- Nearest Villages- Mullandram, Poosimalaikuppam, Sirumoor, Putthur, Morappanthangal, Vettyanthuvam, Meyyer, Adayapuram, Agarapalayam, Ariyappaddy.

Natural Division: Tondai Nadu.

Administration

Revenue **Division:** Cheyyar. Parliamentary Constituency: 12 Arani. District: Tiruvannamalai. Taluk: Arani. Assembly Constituency: 67 Arani. Gram Panchayat: 38.

Villages: 26 **Inhabited:** 26 **Uninhabited:** 0

Ranking	District	State	National
Area	16	268	3970
Population	9	136	3509
Sex Ratio	7	168	1171
Child Sex Ratio	12	238	3945
Literacy Rate	1	102	1128
Density	16	227	2383
Work Participation Rate	2	75	2464

Gram Panchayats:

Adanur, Adayapalayam, Agarapalayam, Ariyapadi, chitheri, Irumbedu, Kalleripattu, Kalpoondi , Kanigiluppai, Katteri, Ladapadi, Ladavaram, Mamandur , Mattathari, Meyyur, Molugampoondi, Morrappanthangal, Mullandram , Nesal, Nethapakkum, Paiyur, Panaiyur, Poosimalaikuppam, pudupattu, Puthur, Randam Korattur, Rattinamanagalam, Sangeethavadi, Sevur, Sirumur , Srinivasa udayanavanam, Vedajipuram, Vedugasathu, velleri , Vettiyantholuvam, vilai.

Amenities:

Education: Primary School in 26 villages, Middle school in 21 villages, Matriculation or Secondary School in 7 villages, namely Sirumoor, Mullandram, Agarapalayam, Sevoor, Irumbenu, Adanoor, S.V.Nagaram.

Higher Secondary or Pre University Courses or Intermediate or Junior College in 1 village of the CD Block,, namely S.V.Nagaram.

College in 0 village, Adult Literacy Center in 0 village.

Medical: Hospital in 0 village, Dispensary in 0 village, Health Center in 3 villages, Sub Center in 7 villages, Maternity and Child Welfare Center in 4 villages, Community health workers in 25 villages.

Drinking Water: Tap water in 26 villages, Tank water in 0 villages, Well water in 26 villages, Tubewell in 26 villages and more than one source in 26 villages.

Bank: Banking facility in 5 villages, namely, Mullandram, Agarapalayam, Irumbenu, Adanoor S.V.Nagaram.

Credit Society in 15 villages Agricultural Credit Society in 4 Non-Agricultural Credit Society in 13 villages.

Others: Power supply in 26 villages, Cinema hall in 0 village, sport club in 0 village, Stadium or Auditorium or Community Hall in 0 village, Post Office in 20 villages.

There are 26 villages having bus facilities.

Villages with most of facilities: Mullandram Agarapalayam, Irumbenu, S.V.Nagaram.

Villages without Amenities (Education): None..

Scheduled Castes: Out of the total population of 98409 persons, 21330 persons (21.67%) belong to Scheduled Castes.

The villages having less than 10% SC population are Poosimalaikuppam, Mullandram, Sevoor Rattinamangalam.

The villages having more than 50% SC population are None.

Sex ratio of Scheduled Caste population is 503.

Scheduled Castes Literates and Illiterates by Sex:

	Persons	Males	Females
Literate	12,613	7,347	5,266
Illiterate	8,717	3,261	5,456
Literacy rate	68.2	80.2	56.5
Graduate	33	24	9

Scheduled Castes (Dominant):

Adi Dravida, Arunthathiyar, Valluvan, Pannadi Kuravan etc.

For their cultural identity please see Appendix-I

Villages without Scheduled Castes: There is 0 village without any scheduled caste population.

Scheduled Tribes: Out of the total population of 98409 persons, 224 persons (0.23%) belong to Scheduled Tribes.

The villages having less than 10% ST population are

Sirumoor, Poosimalaikuppam, Mullandram, Putthur Morappanthangal, Velleri, Meyyer, Vettyanthuvam Adayapulam, Agarapalayam, Ariyappaddy, Sevoor Rattinamangalam, Irumbenu, Adanoor, Mattathari Rantham Koratoor, Panaiyur, Ogaiyoor, S.V.Nagaram Mamandur, Kalpoondi, Paiyur, Vadagasathu, Velapadi Nesal.

The villages having more than 50% ST population are None.

Sex ratio of Scheduled tribe population is 513.

Scheduled Tribes Literates and Illiterates by Sex:

	Persons	Males	Females
Literate	57	32	25
Illiterate	167	77	90
Literacy rate	32.8	37.2	28.4
Graduate	0	0	0

Scheduled Tribes (Dominant):

Irular, Kattunayakan, Malai Pandaram, Kondareddis Generic Tribes etc.

For their cultural identity please see Appendix-II

Villages without Scheduled Tribes: There are 12 villages without any scheduled tribe population.

Literates and Illiterates by Sex (Total Population):

	Persons	Males	Females
Literate	60,907	35,684	25,223
Illiterate	37,502	13,519	23,983
Literacy rate	71	83	58
Graduate	172	123	49

Agriculture: ***Distribution of villages according to land use:*** Out of 26 villages, Total area (in hectare) is 21243.82, out of that 62.85 percent is cultivable and 47.44 percent of the cultivable area is irrigated.

Sources of Irrigation (Hectares): Government Canal 0, Private Canal 0, Well without Electricity 264.85, Well with Electricity 4204.95, Tubewell without Electricity 0, Tubewell with Electricity 14.5, Tank 395.9, River 0, Lake 658.58, Waterfall 0, Others 795.76.

Villages with population of 5000 to 9999: Ariyapadi, Sevur, Irumbedu, Paiyur, Velapadi.

Villages with population of 10000 and above: None

Distribution of Workers:

	Persons	Males	Females	WPR
Cultivators	10,525	7,391	3,134	21.59
Agricultural Labour	20,800	8,640	12,160	42.67
Household Industry	5,189	3,232	1,957	10.64
Other Workers	12,232	9,613	2,619	25.09
Main Workers	34,985	23,833	11,152	71.77
Marginal Workers	13,761	5,043	8,718	28.23
Total Workers	48,746	28,876	19,870	

Religion: Major Religious Communities:

	Persons	Males	Females	Sex Ratio
Hindu (96.89%)	95,348	47,681	47,667	1,000
Muslim (1.41%)	1,386	687	699	1,017
Christian (1.17%)	1,154	561	593	1,057
Sikh (0.01%)	6	3	3	1,000
Buddhists (0%)	2	-	2	-
Jain (0.44%)	435	235	200	851

Agewise Data:

	Persons	Males	Females	Sex Ratio
All ages	98,409	49,203	49,206	1000
0-14	28,561	14,609	13,952	955
15-44	46,893	23,427	23,466	1002
45-79	21,489	10,421	11,068	1062
80+	788	373	415	1113
Age not stated	678	373	305	818

Languages (Dominant):

Tamil, Telugu, Urdu, Kannada, Gujarati

Disabled Population:

	Persons	Males	Females	%
Total Disabled	2,348	1,322	1,026	
In Seeing	1,093	567	526	46.55
In Speech	247	139	108	10.52
In Hearing	202	106	96	8.6
In Movement	627	400	227	26.7
Mentally	179	110	69	7.62

ARANTHANGI

Aranthangi C.D. Block lies in the south-eastern part of Pudukkottai district. It is a part of Aranthangi taluk. The Block is located at a distance of 34 kms. from district headquarters (Pudukkottai). There are 94 villages in the block with the total population of 136,046 persons. Area of the C.D. Block is 399.62 sq. kms. It is bounded in the north by CD Block Thiruvarankulam, in the south by CD Blocks Arimalam, Avudayarkovil and Manamelkudi, in the east by district Thanjavur and CD Block Manamelkudi, in the west by CD Block Arimalam and district Sivaganga.

Communications:

Roadways : S.H.-26: Direction- Pudukkottai to Mimisal and Manamelkudi, Nearest Villages- Kurumbur, Narpavalakkudi, Silattur, Aliyanilai, Alappiranthan, Mookkudi, Rathnakottai, Chidambaraviduthi, Memangalam, Kovilvayal, Kummakkadu, Melapattu, Thedakki, Karavayal, Nagudi, Ariyamaraikkadu, Kalakkudi, Kilkudi, Eganivayal, Egapperumalur, Attani (N), Thiruvappadi, Nemmalikkadu, Urvani, Seenamangalam, kalakkamangalam, Pallathivayal. S.H.-29: Direction- Sakkottai to Pattukkottai, Nearest Villages- Avanathankottai, Erukkalakkottai, Rajendirapuram, Alangudi, Edayar, Puduvakottai, Darmarajanvayal, Kammangadu, Ulagalandanvasal, Rathnakottai.

Railway Station: Ayingudi, Vallavari.

River: Vellar Nadi- Nearest Villages- Aliyanilai, Alappiranthan, Alangudi, Edayar, Puduvakottai, Panjathi, Amangi, Serunhanvayal, Chidambaraviduthi, Narpavalakkudi, Sengamari, Gongudi.

Annual Rainfall: Average Rainfall 910 mm.

Ground Water: Availability of the ground water in the Basin is 5969.89 H.A.M. and the utilization is 1425. 90 H.A.M. It belongs to Safe category. Depth to water level varies from 0 to 10 meter below the ground. Most of the wells go down in summer months, according to the Ground Water Estimation Committee.

Natural Division: Chola Nadu.

Administration

Revenue **Division:** Pudukottai. Parliamentary Constituency: 31 Sivaganga. District: Pudukottai. Taluk: Arantangi. Assembly Constituency: 182 Alangudi, 183 Arantangi. Gram Panchayat: 52.

Villages: 94 **Inhabited:** 89 **Uninhabited:** 5

Ranking	District	State	National
Area	3	74	1930
Population	2	34	2301
Sex Ratio	4	56	500
Child Sex Ratio	6	134	2434
Literacy Rate	4	78	909
Density	8	233	3187
Work Participation Rate	3	172	2516

Gram Panchayats:

Alapirandan, Aliyanilai, Amanji, Amarasimmendra puram, Arasarkulam Keelpathi, Arasarkulam Thenpathi, Arasarkulam Vadapathi, Athani, Avanathankottai, Ayingudi, Edaiyar, Eganivayal, Ekaperumalur, Kammangadu, Keelakidiammanjakki, Kodivayal, Kongudi, Koohanoor subramaniyapuram, Kulathur, Kurumbur, Mangalanadu, Mangudi, Mannakudi, Maramadakki, Melapattu, Melpanaikadu, Memangalam, Mukkudi, Nakkudi, Narpavalakudi, Nattumangalam, Neyvattalai, Panjatti, Paravakottai, Periyalur, Perungadu, Puvathakudi, Rajendrapuram, Ramasamipuram, Retnakottai, Silathur, Sittangadu, Sunaiyakkadu, Thanthani, Thirunallur, Tholuvankadu, Uruani, Vallavarai, Vembangudi East, Vembangudi West, Vettivayal, Vijayapuram.

Amenities:

Education: Primary School in 71 villages, Middle school in 35 villages, Matriculation or Secondary School in 11 villages, namely Thirunaloor, Chidambaraviduthi, Thanthani, Poovathagudi, Periyalur, Merpanaikkadu, Silattur, Arasakkkulam, Subramaniyapuram, Kalakkudi, Attani (N).

Higher Secondary or Pre University Courses or Intermediate or Junior College in 7 villages of the CD Block,, namely Maramadukky, Chidambaraviduthi, Thanthani, Poovathagudi, Silattur, Subramaniyapuram, Kalakkudi. College in 1 village, Adult Literacy Center in 0 village., College is in village, namely Rajendirapuram.

Medical: Hospital in 1 village, Dispensary in 1 village, Health Center in 12 villages, Sub Center in 20 villages, Maternity and Child Welfare Center in 0 village, Community health workers in 64 villages.

The Villages having Hospital or Dispensary or Health Center are Subramaniyapuram, Omakanvayal.

Drinking Water: Tap water in 89 villages, Tank water in 6 villages, Well water in 89 villages, Tubewell in 89 villages and more than one source in 89 villages.

Bank: Banking facility in 7 villages, namely, Avanathankottai, Vembangudi, Silattur, Arasakkkulam Vijayapuram, Attani (N), Kandichamkadu.

Credit Society in 16 villages Agricultural Credit Society in 16 Non-Agricultural Credit Society in 0 village.

Others: Power supply in 89 villages, Cinema hall in 5 villages, sport club in 0 village, Stadium or Auditorium or Community Hall in 1 village, Post Office in 28 villages.

There are 74 villages having bus facilities.

Villages with most of facilities: Avanathankottai Silattur, Arasakkkulam, Vijayapuram, Attani (N).

Villages without amenities (Education):

Sathanenthal, Neyvalinathapuram, Mathur, Ambalpuram, Chidamparapuram, Urvani, Darmarajanvayal, Amangi, Seenamangalam, Arunachalapuram, Manivilanvayal, Nagudi, Kilkudi, Karaikadu, Omakanvayal, Kandichamkadu, Biramanvayal, Ammanjaki..

Scheduled Castes: Out of the total population of 136046 persons, 14609 persons (10.74%) belong to Scheduled Castes. The villages having less than 10% SC population are Maramadukky, Thirunaloor, Paravakkottai, Kurumbur Serunahanvayal, Chidambaraviduthi, Chettikadu Avanathankottai, Erukkalakkottai, Sathanenthal Neyvalinathapuram, Merpanaikkadu, Balakrishnapuram Mathur, Ayingudi, Vallavari, Mangudi, Rajendirapuram Ettiathali, Arasakkkulam, Arasarkulam East Mangalanadu, Ambalpuram, Kodivayal, Chittakanni Vijayapuram, Pidarikkadu, Memangalam Darmarajanvayal, Vengoor, Seenamangalam Arunachalapuram, Kookanoor, Manivilanvayal Rayanvayal, Thedakki, Karavayal, Ariyamaraikkadu Kilkudi, Egapperumalur, Adalaikalabairavapuram Thiruvappadi, Omakanvayal, Nemmalikkadu Vellathumangalam, Biramanvayal, Ammanjaki, Myvayal. The villages having more than 50% SC population are None.

Sex ratio of Scheduled Caste population is 507.

Scheduled Castes Literates and Illiterates by Sex:

	Persons	Males	Females
Literate	9,107	5,205	3,902
Illiterate	5,502	2,003	3,499
Literacy rate	70.8	82.1	59.9
Graduate	154	111	43

Scheduled Castes (Dominant):

Paraiyan etc., Pallan, Adi Dravida, Kuravan etc. Chakkiliyan

For their cultural identity please see Appendix-I

Villages without Scheduled Castes: There are 25 villages without any scheduled caste population.

Scheduled Tribes: Out of the total population of 136046 persons, 17 persons (0.01%) belong to Scheduled Tribes. The villages having less than 10% ST population are Maramadukky, Thirunaloor, Paravakkottai, Kurumbur Serunahanvayal, Sengamari, Narpavalakkudi Chidambaraviduthi, Thanthani, Chettikadu Avanathankottai, Erukkalakkottai, Poovathagudi Periyalur, Neyvathali, Sathanenthal Neyvalinathapuram, Merpanaikkadu, Vembangudi Balakrishnapuram, Ramasamipuram, Mathur, Ayingudi Vallavari, Mangudi, Maruthankudi, Rajendirapuram Silattur, Aliyanilai, Gongudi, Alappiranthan Mookkudi, Rathnakottai, Thothakudy, Ettiathali Arasakkkulam, Arasarkulam East, Mangalanadu Amarasimmendrapuram, Ambalpuram, Kodivayal Chittakanni, Vijayapuram, Subramaniyapuram Chidamparapuram, Pidarikkadu, Memangalam, Kovilvayal Melapattu, Pallathivayal, Urvani, Alangudi, Edayar Kulathur, Puduvakottai, Darmarajanvayal, Kammangadu Ulagalandanvasal, Panjathi, Amangi, Allarimelvayal Vengoor, Seenamangalam, Arunachalapuram, Mannakudy Kookanoor, Manivilanvayal, Rayanvayal, Thedakki Karavayal, Nagudi, Ariyamaraikkadu, Kalakkudi Kilkudi, Eganivayal, Egapperumalur Adalaikalabairavapuram, Karaikadu, Attani (N) Kalakkamangalam, Thiruvappadi, Omakanvayal Nemmalikkadu, Vellathumangalam, Kandichamkadu Biramanvayal, Ammanjaki, Manavanallur, Myvayal. The villages having more than 50% ST population are None.

Sex ratio of Scheduled tribe population is 294.

Scheduled Tribes Literates and Illiterates by Sex:

	Persons	Males	Females
Literate	7	7	0
Illiterate	10	5	5
Literacy rate	43.8	58.3	-
Graduate	0	0	0

Scheduled Tribes (Dominant):

Kattunayakan, Malai Pandaram

For their cultural identity please see Appendix-II

Villages without Scheduled Tribes: There are 91 villages without any scheduled tribe population.

Literates and Illiterates by Sex (Total Population):

	Persons	Males	Females
Literate	86,812	49,592	37,220
Illiterate	49,234	17,438	31,796
Literacy rate	73	84	61
Graduate	1,177	867	310

Agriculture: ***Distribution of villages according to land use:*** Out of 94 villages, Total area (in hectare) is 39962.96, out of that 66.18 percent is cultivable and 68.01 percent of the cultivable area is irrigated.

Sources of Irrigation (Hectares): Government Canal 5712.44, Private Canal 0, Well without Electricity 139.62, Well with Electricity 122.6, Tubewell without Electricity 2.72, Tubewell with Electricity 451.61, Tank 11558.7, River 0, Lake 0, Waterfall 0, Others 0.

Villages with population of 5000 to 9999: Melpanaikkadu, Arasarkulam Melpathi.

Villages with population of 10000 and above: None

Distribution of Workers:

	Persons	Males	Females	WPR
Cultivators	25,311	16,965	8,346	37.62
Agricultural Labour	30,232	14,805	15,427	44.93
Household Industry	1,203	605	598	1.79
Other Workers	10,536	8,326	2,210	15.66
Main Workers	50,070	33,571	16,499	74.42
Marginal Workers	17,212	7,130	10,082	25.58
Total Workers	67,282	40,701	26,581	

Religion: Major Religious Communities:

	Persons	Males	Females	Sex Ratio
Hindu (93.13%)	126,701	62,511	64,190	1,027
Muslim (5.34%)	7,266	3,485	3,781	1,085
Christian (1.25%)	1,706	842	864	1,026
Sikh (0%)	2	-	2	-
Buddhists (0%)	-	-	-	-
Jain (0%)	4	2	2	1,000

Agewise Data:

	Persons	Males	Females	Sex Ratio
All ages	135,876	66,946	68,930	1030
0-14	36,173	18,439	17,734	962
15-44	67,209	32,305	34,904	1080
45-79	30,740	15,226	15,514	1019
80+	1,105	573	532	928
Age not stated	649	403	246	610

Languages (Dominant):

Tamil, Telugu, Marathi, Kannada, Malayalam

Disabled Population:

	Persons	Males	Females	%
Total Disabled	3,585	1,492	2,093	
In Seeing	2,320	775	1,545	64.71
In Speech	214	112	102	5.97
In Hearing	134	66	68	3.74
In Movement	671	405	266	18.72
Mentally	246	134	112	6.86

ARAVAKURICHI

Aravakurichi C.D. Block lies in the south-western part of Karur district. It is a part of Aravakurichi taluk. The Block is located at a distance of 30 kms. from district headquarters (Karur). There are 21 villages in the block with the total population of 55,584 persons. Area of the C.D. Block is 404.69 sq. kms. It is bounded in the north by district Erode and C.D. Block K. Paramathi, in the south by district Dindigul, in the east by CD Block Thanthoni and district Dindigul, and in the west by district Erode.

Communications:

Roadways : N.H.-7: Direction- Karur to Dindigul, Nearest Villages- Nagampalli, Kodaiyur, Pungambadi (West), Velambadi, Thethupatti, Alamarathupatti, Periyamanjuveli, Pugambadi East.

Rivers: Kodavanar Nadi- Nearest Villages- Nagampalli, Kodaiyur, Venjamangudalur (West), Pugambadi (East), Anjagoundenpatty, Erumarpatti, Periyamanjuveli, Ammapatty, Esanatham. Nanganji Nadi- Nearest Villages- Nagampalli, Pungambadi (West), Senthamangalam (West), Velambadi, Sendamangalam (East).

Annual Rainfall: Average Rainfall 635 mm.

Ground Water: Availability of the ground water in the Basin is 2637.91 H.A.M. and the utilization is 2198.07 H.A.M. It belongs to Semi Critical category. Depth to water level varies from 5 to 10 meter below the ground. Most of the wells go down in summer months, according to the Ground Water Estimation Committee.

Natural Division: NA

Administration

Revenue **Division:** Karur. Parliamentary Constituency: 23 Karur. District: Karur. Taluk: Aravakurichi Assembly Constituency: 134 Aravakurichi. Gram Panchayat: 20.

Villages: 21 **Inhabited:** 21 **Uninhabited:** 0

Ranking	District	State	National
Area	3	70	1907
Population	7	344	5030
Sex Ratio	3	101	774
Child Sex Ratio	2	177	3004
Literacy Rate	5	294	2479
Density	3	40	5749
Work Participation Rate	8	367	352

Gram Panchayats:

Alamarathampatti, Ammapatti, Esannatham, Eurumarpatti, Inanganur, Kodaiyur, Lingamanickampatti, Modakkur (East), Modakkur (West), Nagamballi, Periyamanjuvalli, Pungambadi (West), Santhapadi, Sendamangalam (East), Sendamangalam (West), Thethupatti, Velambadi, Venjamangudalur (East).

Amenities:

Education: Primary School in 21 villages, Middle school in 11 villages, Matriculation or Secondary School in 7 villages, namely Nagampalli, Modakkur (West), Velambadi, Sendamangalam (East), Lingamanayakkanpatty, Eganatham, Alamarathupatti.

Higher Secondary or Pre University Courses or Intermediate or Junior College in 2 villages of the CD Block,, namely Nagampalli, Lingamanayakkanpatty.

College in 0 village, Adult Literacy Center in 0 village.

Medical: Hospital in 1 village, Dispensary in 2 villages, Health Center in 5 villages, Sub Center in 2 villages, Maternity and Child Welfare Center in 7 villages, Community health workers in 4 villages.

The Villages having Hospital or Dispensary or Health Center are Nagampalli, Lingamanayakkanpatty, Erumarpatti, Periyamanjuveli.

Drinking Water: Tap water in 21 villages, Tank water in 5 villages, Well water in 21 villages, Tubewell in 21 villages and more than one source in 21 villages.

Bank: Banking facility in 6 villages, namely, Nagampalli, Venjamangudalur (East), Modakkur (West) Sendamangalam (East), Eganatham, Alamarathupatti.

Credit Society in 11 villages Agricultural Credit Society in 10 Non-Agricultural Credit Society in 1 village.

Others: Power supply in 21 villages, Cinema hall in 1 village, sport club in 0 village, Stadium or Auditorium or Community Hall in 0 village, Post Office in 18 villages.

There are 20 villages having bus facilities.

Villages with most of facilities: Nagampalli Modakkur (West), Sendamangalam (East), Eganatham Alamarathupatti.

Villages without Amenities (Education): None..

Scheduled Castes: Out of the total population of 55584 persons, 13794 persons (24.82%) belong to Scheduled Castes.

The villages having less than 10% SC population are None..

The villages having more than 50% SC population are None.

Sex ratio of Scheduled Caste population is 499.

Scheduled Castes Literates and Illiterates by Sex:

	Persons	Males	Females
Literate	6,866	4,150	2,716

Illiterate	6,928	2,762	4,166
Literacy rate	55.4	66.6	44.1
Graduate	109	83	26

Scheduled Castes (Dominant):

Chakkiliyan, Paraiyan etc., Pallan, Madari

Adi Dravida

For their cultural identity please see Appendix-I

Villages without Scheduled Castes: There is 0 village without any scheduled caste population.

Scheduled Tribes: Out of the total population of 55584 persons, 14 persons (0.03%) belong to Scheduled Tribes. The villages having less than 10% ST population are Nagampalli, Kodaiyur, Venjamangudalur (East) Venjamangudalur (West), Pugambadi (East) Pungambadi (West), Santhappadi, Modakkur (West) Modakkur (East), Inunganur, Senthamangalam (West) Velambadi, Sendamangalam (East) Lingamanayakkanpatty, Thethupatti, Anjagoundenpatty Eganatham, Erumarpatti, Alamarathupatti Periyamanjuveli, Ammapatty.

The villages having more than 50% ST population are None.

Sex ratio of Scheduled tribe population is 429.

Scheduled Tribes Literates and Illiterates by Sex:

	Persons	Males	Females
Literate	6	5	1
Illiterate	8	3	5
Literacy rate	46.2	71.4	16.7
Graduate	0	0	0

Scheduled Tribes (Dominant):

Generic Tribes etc., Malai Pandaram, Palleyan

For their cultural identity please see Appendix-II

Villages without Scheduled Tribes: There are 18 villages without any scheduled tribe population.

Literates and Illiterates by Sex (Total Population):

	Persons	Males	Females
Literate	31,520	18,985	12,535
Illiterate	24,064	8,610	15,454
Literacy rate	62	75	49
Graduate	705	491	214

Agriculture: ***Distribution of villages according to land use:*** Out of 21 villages, Total area (in hectare) is 40469, out of that 30.46 percent is cultivable and 42.2 percent of the cultivable area is irrigated.

Sources of Irrigation (Hectares): Government Canal 373.28, Private Canal 0, Well without Electricity 76.45, Well with Electricity 4312.58, Tubewell without Electricity 17.03, Tubewell with Electricity 158.15, Tank 20, River 0, Lake 0, Waterfall 0, Others 0.

Villages with population of 5000 to 9999:

Nagamballi, Velambadi.

Villages with population of 10000 and above: None

Distribution of Workers:

	Persons	Males	Females	WPR
Cultivators	11,821	6,630	5,191	34.65
Agricultural Labour	14,234	6,510	7,724	41.73
Household Industry	407	211	196	1.19
Other Workers	7,650	5,642	2,008	22.43
Main Workers	31,473	17,897	13,576	92.26
Marginal Workers	2,639	1,096	1,543	7.74
Total Workers	34,112	18,993	15,119	

Religion: Major Religious Communities:

	Persons	Males	Females	Sex Ratio
Hindu (95.54%)	53,104	26,483	26,621	1,005
Muslim (3.32%)	1,846	791	1,055	1,334
Christian (1.09%)	604	308	296	961
Sikh (0.01%)	4	2	2	1,000
Buddhists (0%)	-	-	-	-
Jain (0%)	1	-	1	-

Agewise Data:

	Persons	Males	Females	Sex Ratio
All ages	55,584	27,595	27,989	1014
0-14	11,159	5,712	5,447	954
15-44	24,887	12,003	12,884	1073
45-79	18,642	9,398	9,244	984
80+	822	436	386	885
Age not stated	74	46	28	609

Languages (Dominant):

Tamil, Telugu, Kannada, Urdu, Hindi

Disabled Population:

	Persons	Males	Females	%
Total Disabled	788	410	378	
In Seeing	334	168	166	42.39
In Speech	105	54	51	13.32
In Hearing	59	35	24	7.49
In Movement	190	101	89	24.11
Mentally	100	52	48	12.69

ARCOT

Arcot C.D. Block lies in the north-eastern part of Vellore district. It is a part of Wallajah and Arcot taluks. The Block is located at a distance of 24 kms. from district headquarters (Vellore). There are 44 villages in the block with the total population of 92,265 persons. Area of the C.D. Block is 193.65 sq. kms. It is bounded in the north by CD Blocks Wallajah and Kaveripakkam, in the south by CD Block Timiri, in the east by district Tiruvannamalai and CD Block Kaveripakkam, in the west by CD Blocks Timiri and Wallajah. CD Block Arcot falls in Wallajah by 14 villages, and in taluk Arcot by 30 villages.

Communications:

Roadways : N.H.-46: Direction- Vellore to Arcot, Nearest

Villages- Kilminnal, Arapakkam, Nandiyalam, Veppur. S.H.-4: Direction- Timri to Chennai, Nearest Villages- Sathur, Tajpura. S.H.-5: Direction- Arcot to Cheyyar, Nearest Villages- Muppaduvetti, Poongodu, Manga du, Pudupadi, Kilambadi, Chakkaramallur, Kadappanthangal, Papperi, Kukkundi, Keerambadi, Mulluvadi, Mecheri, Karikanthangal, Kilanthangal.

River: Polar Nadi- Nearest Villages- Nandiyalam, Veppur, Arapakkam, Kilminnal RF, Kilminnal, Muppaduvetti, Poongadu, Mangadu, Puduppadi, Kilambadi, Sakkiremallur, Perungalmedu, Valavanur.

Annual Rainfall: Average Rainfall 949 mm.

Ground Water: Availability of the ground water in the Basin is 4811.50 H.A.M. and the utilization is 5511.91 H.A.M. It belongs to Over Expoited category. Depth to water level varies from 5 to 15 meter below the ground. Most of the wells go down in summer months, according to the Ground Water Estimation Committee.

Forest and Reserved Forest: (Kilminnal RF)- Nearest Villages- Kilminnal (RF), Kilminnal. (Punganur)- Nearest Villages- Kilminnal, Arapakkam, Punganur (RF), Melakuppam, T.C.Kuppam.

Natural Division: Tondai Nadu.

Administration

Revenue **Division:** Arakonam. Parliamentary Constituency: 7 Arakkonam. District: Vellore. Taluk: Wallajah, Arcot. Assembly Constituency: 42 Arcot, 41 Ranipettai. Gram Panchayat: 39.

Villages: 44 **Inhabited:** 42 **Uninhabited:** 2

Ranking	**District**	**State**	**National**
Area	15	295	4299
Population	15	170	3709
Sex Ratio	4	105	841
Child Sex Ratio	6	167	2937
Literacy Rate	7	114	1197
Density	11	309	2322
Work Participation Rate	6	65	3573

Gram Panchayats:

Annanthangal, Arapakkam, Arumpakkam , Arunkundram , Athithangal, Ayilam, Chakkiremallur, Esayanur , Karivedu, Kathiavadi, Kilambadi, Kilkuppam, Killanthangal, Kilminnal , KirambadiKadappanthangal, Koorambadi, Kukkundi, Ladavaram, Mangadu, Mecheri, Melakuppam, Mullavadi, Muppaduvetti Poongodu, Nandiyalam, Papperi, Poottuthakku, Puderi, Puduppadi, Punnappadi, Sambasivapuram, Saravanthangal, Sathur, Sembedu, Tajpura , Thalanur, Uppupettai, Valavanur, Velur, Veppur

Amenities:

Education: Primary School in 38 villages, Middle school in 19 villages, Matriculation or Secondary School in 12 villages, namely Arapakkam, Melakuppam, Kathiyavadi, Ayilam, Sathur, Mangadu, Chakkaramallur, Easyanoor, K.Velur, Mulluvadi, Mecheri, Sembedu.

Higher Secondary or Pre University Courses or Intermediate or Junior College in 3 villages of the CD Block,, namely Arapakkam, Chakkaramallur, K.Velur.

College in 1 village, Adult Literacy Center in 0 village., College is in village, namely Mulluvadi.

Medical: Hospital in 2 villages, Dispensary in 2 villages, Health Center in 6 villages, Sub Center in 5 villages, Maternity and Child Welfare Center in 10 villages, Community health workers in 39 villages.

The Villages having Hospital or Dispensary or Health Center are Kilminnal, Tajpura, Ladavaram.

Drinking Water: Tap water in 41 villages, Tank water in 7 villages, Well water in 16 villages, Tubewell in 20 villages and more than one source in 40 villages.

Bank: Banking facility in 5 villages, namely, Kilminnal, Arapakkam, Ayilam, Pudupadi Chakkaramallur.

Credit Society in 12 villages Agricultural Credit Society in 9 Non-Agricultural Credit Society in 6 villages.

Others: Power supply in 40 villages, Cinema hall in 5 villages, sport club in 0 village, Stadium or Auditorium or Community Hall in 0 village, Post Office in 36 villages.

There are 38 villages having bus facilities.

Villages with most of facilities: Kilminnal Arapakkam, Ayilam, Pudupadi, Chakkaramallur.

Villages without amenities (Education): Kilkuppam, Poongodu, Kunjavappanthangal..

Scheduled Castes: Out of the total population of 92265 persons, 21830 persons (23.66%) belong to Scheduled Castes.

The villages having less than 10% SC population are Melakuppam, Arungundrum, Easyanoor, Gurumudi Thangal Kukkundi, Sarvanthangal, Kunjavappanthangal Punnapadi, Karikanthangal.

The villages having more than 50% SC population are None.

Sex ratio of Scheduled Caste population is 504.

Scheduled Castes Literates and Illiterates by Sex:

	Persons	Males	Females
Literate	13,615	7,754	5,861
Illiterate	8,215	3,066	5,149
Literacy rate	71.5	82.2	61.0
Graduate	180	131	49

Scheduled Castes (Dominant):

Adi Dravida, Arunthathiyar, Valluvan, Pambada Kuravan etc.

For their cultural identity please see Appendix-I

Villages without Scheduled Castes: There are 5 villages without any scheduled caste population.

Scheduled Tribes: Out of the total population of 92265 persons, 520 persons (0.56%) belong to Scheduled Tribes. The villages having less than 10% ST population are Kilminnal, Arapakkam, Melakuppam, T.C.Kuppam Nandiyalam, Veppur, Thazhanur, Kathiyavadi, Ayilam Arungundrum, Kilkuppam, Koorambadi, Sathur, Tajpura Muppaduvetti, Poongodu, Mangadu, Pudupadi, Kilambadi Chakkaramallur, Perungalmadu, Valavanoor, Easyanoor Aharumbkkam, Gurumudi Thangal, Kadappanthangal Papperi, Kukkundi, Ladavaram, Sarvanthangal Kunjavappanthangal, Punnapadi, Athithangal, Karivedu K.Velur, Keerambadi, Mulluvadi, Mecheri Karikanthangal, Kilanthangal, Sembedu, Ozhalai.

The villages having more than 50% ST population are None.

Sex ratio of Scheduled tribe population is 529.

Scheduled Tribes Literates and Illiterates by Sex:

	Persons	Males	Females
Literate	125	73	52
Illiterate	395	172	223
Literacy rate	28.3	34.8	22.4
Graduate	0	0	0

Scheduled Tribes (Dominant):

Irular, Kattunayakan, Kurumans

For their cultural identity please see Appendix-II

Villages without Scheduled Tribes: There are 17 villages without any scheduled tribe population.

Literates and Illiterates by Sex (Total Population):

	Persons	Males	Females
Literate	56,653	32,984	23,669
Illiterate	35,612	12,876	22,736
Literacy rate	70	82	58
Graduate	881	636	245

Agriculture: ***Distribution of villages according to land use:*** Out of 44 villages, Total area (in hectare) is 19365.02, out of that 64.45 percent is cultivable and 42.47 percent of the cultivable area is irrigated.

Sources of Irrigation (Hectares): Government Canal 44.04, Private Canal 0, Well without Electricity 230.54, Well with Electricity 4163.22, Tubewell without Electricity 102.73, Tubewell with Electricity 75.9, Tank 358.45, River 0, Lake 326.03, Waterfall 0, Others 0.

Villages with population of 5000 to 9999:
Kilminnal , Nandiyalam, Tajpura.

Villages with population of 10000 and above: None

Distribution of Workers:

	Persons	Males	Females	WPR
Cultivators	9,741	6,687	3,054	23.57
Agricultural Labour	14,858	6,880	7,978	35.95
Household Industry	3,544	1,956	1,588	8.58
Other Workers	13,185	10,643	2,542	31.9
Main Workers	33,901	23,352	10,549	82.03
Marginal Workers	7,427	2,814	4,613	17.97
Total Workers	41,328	26,166	15,162	

Religion: Major Religious Communities:

	Persons	Males	Females	Sex Ratio
Hindu (95.57%)	88,182	43,895	44,287	1,009
Muslim (3.26%)	3,009	1,422	1,587	1,116
Christian (1.05%)	972	488	484	992
Sikh (0.03%)	24	15	9	600
Buddhists (0.02%)	16	6	10	1,667
Jain (0%)	3	-	3	-

Agewise Data:

	Persons	Males	Females	Sex Ratio
All ages	92,265	45,860	46,405	1012
0-14	26,643	13,511	13,132	972
15-44	44,347	22,134	22,213	1004
45-79	20,121	9,660	10,461	1083
80+	876	409	467	1142
Age not stated	278	146	132	904

Languages (Dominant):

Tamil, Telugu, Urdu, Marathi, Kannada

Disabled Population:

	Persons	Males	Females	%
Total Disabled	1,945	1,069	876	
In Seeing	789	382	407	40.57
In Speech	189	104	85	9.72
In Hearing	168	90	78	8.64
In Movement	604	375	229	31.05
Mentally	195	118	77	10.03

ARIMALAM

Arimalam C.D. Block lies in the southern part of Pudukkottai district. It is a part of Thirumayam and Avudayarkoil taluks. The Block is located at a distance of 19 kms. from district headquarters (Pudukkottai). There are 53 villages in the block with the total population of 70,673 persons. Area of the C.D. Block is 322.26 sq. kms. It is bounded in the north by CD Blocks Pudukkottai and Thiruvarankulam, in the south by district Sivaganga, in the east by CD Blocks Thiruvarankulam and Aranthangi, in the west by C.D. Block Thirumayam and district Sivagana. CD Block Arimalam falls in taluk Avudayarkoil by 17 villages, and taluk Thirumayam by 36 villages.

Communications:

Roadways : N.H.-210: Direction- Thirumayam to Pudukkottai, Nearest Village- Thekkatur.

Railway Station: Valara Mankkam, Thekkatur.

Annual Rainfall: Average Rainfall 910 mm.

Ground Water: Availability of the ground water in the Basin is 6969.76 H.A.M. and the utilization is 500.80

H.A.M. It belongs to Safe category. Depth to water level varies from 0 to 10 meter below the ground. Most of the wells go down in summer months, according to the Ground Water Estimation Committee.

Forest and Reserved Forest: (Sengirai RF)- Nearest Villages- Sengirai, Sengirai (RF), Keelapanaiyur, Melanilaivayal, Kummankudi, Perungudi, Mirattunilai, Sirayampatti, Rayaragunathasamuthiram, Nedungudi.

Natural Division: Chola Nadu.

Administration

Revenue Division: Pudukottai. Parliamentary Constituency: 31 Sivaganga. District: Pudukottai. Taluk: Avudayarko il, Thirumayam. Assembly Constituency: 181 Thirumayam, 183 Arantangi. Gram Panchayat: 32.

Villages: 53 **Inhabited:** 52 **Uninhabited:** 1

Ranking	District	State	National
Area	8	145	2539
Population	13	284	4438
Sex Ratio	2	25	240
Child Sex Ratio	11	188	3153
Literacy Rate	6	159	1568
Density	10	274	4448
Work Participation Rate	11	307	2984

Gram Panchayats:

Ayingudi, Embal, Irumbanadu, K.Chettiar Patti, K.Rayapuram, Kadayakudi, Kadiyapatti, Kaikulanvayal, Kallur, Kannankarakudi, Karamangalam, Keelapanaiyur, Kummangudi, Kurungalur, Madagam, Melanilaivayal, Mirattanilai, Munasandai, Nallambal Samudram, Nedungudi, Onangudi, Perungudi, Pillavayal, Pudunilaivayal, Rayavaram, Samudram, Sengirai, Thekkattur, Thiruvakudi, Thuraiyur, Valarmanickem, Vanniyampatti.

Amenities:

Education: Primary School in 38 villages, Middle school in 15 villages, Matriculation or Secondary School in 13 villages, namely Rayavaram, Samudram, Keelapanaiyur, Panangudi, Karamangalam, Pudunilaivayal, K.Rajapuram, Piliyavayal, Thekkatur, Perungudi, Mirattunilai, Rayaragunathasamuthiram, Yembal.

Higher Secondary or Pre University Courses or Intermediate or Junior College in 4 villages of the CD Block,, namely Panangudi, Karamangalam, Pudunilaivayal, Yembal.

College in 1 village, Adult Literacy Center in 0 village., College is in village, namely Thekkatur.

Medical: Hospital in 0 village, Dispensary in 1 village, Health Center in 3 villages, Sub Center in 4 villages, Maternity and Child Welfare Center in 0 village, Community health workers in 44 villages.

The Village having Hospital or Dispensary or Health Center is Nallambal Samudram.

Drinking Water: Tap water in 52 villages, Tank water in 0 villages, Well water in 52 villages, Tubewell in 52 villages and more than one source in 52 villages.

Bank: Banking facility in 6 villages, namely, Rayavaram, Panangudi, Pudunilaivayal, Kaikulam Vayal Agavayal, Yembal.

Credit Society in 9 villages Agricultural Credit Society in 9 Non-Agricultural Credit Society in 0 village.

Others: Power supply in 52 villages, Cinema hall in 2 villages, sport club in 0 village, Stadium or Auditorium or Community Hall in 0 village, Post Office in 19 villages.

There are 35 villages having bus facilities.

Villages with most of facilities: Rayavaram Panangudi, Pudunilaivayal, Kaikulam Vayal, Agavayal Yembal.

Villages without amenities (Education): Melivayal, Agavayal, Allan Vayal, Anikini, Chittampatti, Velavayal, Kurichi, Marudangudi, Thiruvakkudi, Sathirapatti, (Madagam) Arasur, Thillavayal, Seppavayal, Thirapidangi..

Scheduled Castes: Out of the total population of 70673 persons, 12325 persons (17.44%) belong to Scheduled Castes. The villages having less than 10% SC population are Melivayal, Agavayal, Keelapanaiyur, Nedungudi Melanilaivayal, Kummankudi, Thalayathivayal Kaikulam Vayal, Agavayal, Allan Vayal, Anikini Chittampatti, Velavayal, Valara Mankkam, Kurichi Thekkatur, Valayampatti, Rayaragunathasamuthiram Marudangudi, Sathirapatti, (Madagam) Arasur Thillavayal.

The villages having more than 50% SC population are None.

Sex ratio of Scheduled Caste population is 505.

Scheduled Castes Literates and Illiterates by Sex:

	Persons	Males	Females
Literate	7,121	4,187	2,934
Illiterate	5,204	1,914	3,290
Literacy rate	65.1	77.7	52.9
Graduate	136	104	32

Scheduled Castes (Dominant):

Pallan, Paraiyan etc., Adi Dravida, Kuravan etc. Valluvan

For their cultural identity please see Appendix-I

Villages without Scheduled Castes: There are 11 villages without any scheduled caste population.

Scheduled Tribes: Out of the total population of 70673 persons, 20 persons (0.03%) belong to Scheduled Tribes. The villages having less than 10% ST population are

Rayavaram, Sengirai, Melivayal, Samandavayal Agavayal, Samudram, Keelapanaiyur, Panangudi Kannan Karakudi, Nedungudi, Melanilaivayal Kummankudi, Thuraiyur, Karamangalam, Thalayathivayal Pudunilaivayal, K.Rajapuram, Nallambal Samudram Piliyavayal, Kaikulam Vayal, Agavayal, Allan Vayal Anikini, Chittampatti, Velavayal, Valara Mankkam Edayan Vayal, Kurichi, Thekkatur, Valayampatti Perungudi, Poovampatti, Mirattunilai, Sirayampatti Rayaragunathasamuthiram, Thonnakudi, Marudangudi Thiruvakkudi, Vellalavayal, Sathirapatti, Arasur (Madagam) Arasur, Irumbanadu, Kurungalur Thillavayal, Seppavayal, Madagam, Echikottai Thirapidangi, Yenengam, Thaniukadu, Yembal.

The villages having more than 50% ST population are None.

Sex ratio of Scheduled tribe population is 450.

Scheduled Tribes Literates and Illiterates by Sex:

	Persons	Males	Females
Literate	0	0	0
Illiterate	20	11	9
Literacy rate	-	-	-
Graduate	0	0	0

Scheduled Tribes (Dominant):

Malakkuravan

For their cultural identity please see Appendix-II

Villages without Scheduled Tribes: There are 52 villages without any scheduled tribe population.

Literates and Illiterates by Sex (Total Population):

	Persons	Males	Females
Literate	41,962	24,053	17,909
Illiterate	28,711	10,240	18,471
Literacy rate	67	80	55
Graduate	886	568	318

Agriculture: ***Distribution of villages according to land use:*** Out of 53 villages, Total area (in hectare) is 32226.5, out of that 22.45 percent is cultivable and 88.96 percent of the cultivable area is irrigated.

Sources of Irrigation (Hectares): Government Canal 0, Private Canal 0, Well without Electricity 11.34, Well with Electricity 130.29, Tubewell without Electricity 0, Tubewell with Electricity 142.99, Tank 6114.34, River 0, Lake 0, Waterfall 0, Others 0.

Villages with population of 5000 to 9999: Thekkattur, Perungudi , Panangudi.

Villages with population of 10000 and above: None

Distribution of Workers:

	Persons	Males	Females	WPR
Cultivators	12,278	7,774	4,504	36.38
Agricultural Labour	13,590	6,002	7,588	40.27
Household Industry	884	397	487	2.62
Other Workers	6,997	5,448	1,549	20.73
Main Workers	19,362	13,095	6,267	57.37
Marginal Workers	14,387	6,526	7,861	42.63
Total Workers	33,749	19,621	14,128	

Religion: Major Religious Communities:

	Persons	Males	Females	Sex Ratio
Hindu (94.9%)	67,066	32,482	34,584	1,065
Muslim (1.91%)	1,352	658	694	1,055
Christian (3.12%)	2,208	1,131	1,077	952
Sikh (0%)	1	-	1	-
Buddhists (0%)	-	-	-	-
Jain (0%)	-	-	-	-

Agewise Data:

	Persons	Males	Females	Sex Ratio
All ages	70,673	34,293	36,380	1061
0-14	19,084	9,632	9,452	981
15-44	34,030	16,081	17,949	1116
45-79	16,640	8,107	8,533	1053
80+	722	368	354	962
Age not stated	197	105	92	876

Languages (Dominant):

Tamil, Telugu, Marathi, Malayalam, Kannada

Disabled Population:

	Persons	Males	Females	%
Total Disabled	2,375	923	1,452	
In Seeing	1,565	474	1,091	65.89
In Speech	154	82	72	6.48
In Hearing	103	42	61	4.34
In Movement	403	235	168	16.97
Mentally	150	90	60	6.32

ARIYALUR

Ariyalur C.D. Block lies in the south-western part of Ariyalur district. It is a part of Ariyalur taluk. The Block is located at a distance of (00) kms. from district headquarters (Ariyalur). There are 31 villages in the block with the total population of 93,906 persons. Area of the C.D. Block is 331.89 sq. kms. It is bounded in the north by CD Block Sendurai and district Perambalur, in the south by CD Block Thirumanur, in the east by CD Block T. Palur, in the west by district Perambalur and C.D. Block Thirumanur.

Communications:

Roadways : S.H.-24: Direction- Lalgudi to Jayankondam, Nearest Villages- Kavanur, Vilangudi, Thelur, Siruvalur, Pudupalayam, Reddipalayam, Edaiyathankudi, Karuppur Larapaty, Arungal.

Railway Station: Pottaveli, Chakoil.

River: Marudayar Nadi- Nearest Villages- Mallur, Siruvalur, Karuppur Larapaty, Edaiyathankudi, Pudupalayam, Periyathirukkonam, Alanduraiyarkattalai, Andipattakkadu,

Punganguli.

Annual Rainfall: Average Rainfall 876 mm.

Ground Water: Availability of the ground water in the Basin is 3539.60 H.A.M. and the utilization is 1959.35 H.A.M. It belongs to Safe category. Depth to water level varies from 2 to 10 meter below the ground. Most of the wells go down in summer months, according to the Ground Water Estimation Committee.

Natural Division: Chola Nadu.

Administration

Revenue Division: Ariyalur. Parliamentary Constituency: 25 Perambalur. District: Ariyalur. Taluk: Ariyalur. Assembly Constituency: 149 Ariyalur. Gram Panchayat: 37.

Villages: 31 **Inhabited:** 31 **Uninhabited:** 0

Ranking	District	State	National
Area	2	133	2446
Population	6	160	3661
Sex Ratio	3	126	934
Child Sex Ratio	4	216	3454
Literacy Rate	6	345	3186
Density	2	153	3717
Work Participation Rate	6	249	1520

Gram Panchayats:

Alanduraiyarkattalai, Andipattakadu, Arungal, Edayathankudi, Eruthukaranpatti , Govindapuram, Hasthinapuram, Iluppaiyur, Kadugur , Kallankurichi, Karuppilakattalai, Kavanur, Kayarlabath, Manakkal, Manakudi, Melakaruppur, Nagamangalam, Ottakoil, Periyanagalur, Periyathirukonam, Pottaveli, Pudhupalayam, Punganku zhi , Rayampuram, Pudhupalayam, Sennivanam, Siruvalur, Srinivasapuram, Subburayapuram , Sundagudi, Thamaraikulam, Thelur, Usenabath, Valajanagaram , Venkitakrishnapuram, Vilangudi.

Amenities:

Education: Primary School in 31 villages, Middle school in 20 villages, Matriculation or Secondary School in 6 villages, namely Eluppaiyur, Kallangurichi, Kairulabad, Reddipalayam, Periyathirukkonam, Andipattakkadu. Higher Secondary or Pre University Courses or Intermediate or Junior College in 2 villages of the CD Block,, namely Kairulabad, Periyathirukkonam.

College in 0 village, Adult Literacy Center in 0 village.

Medical: Hospital in 3 villages, Dispensary in 3 villages, Health Center in 6 villages, Sub Center in 14 villages, Maternity and Child Welfare Center in 10 villages, Community health workers in 0 village.

The Villages having Hospital or Dispensary or Health Center are Govindapuram, Perianagalur, Ameenabad, Kairulabad, Nagamagalur.

Drinking Water: Tap water in 31 villages, Tank water in 0 villages, Well water in 31 villages, Tubewell in 31 villages and more than one source in 31 villages.

Bank: Banking facility in 9 villages, namely, Rayampuram, Govindapuram, Ayan Athur, Vilangudi Thelur, Perianagalur, Reddipalayam Periyathirukkonam, Punganguli.

Credit Society in 8 villages Agricultural Credit Society in 8 Non-Agricultural Credit Society in 0 village.

Others: Power supply in 31 villages, Cinema hall in 3 villages, sport club in 31 villages, Stadium or Auditorium or Communit Hall in 31 villages, Post Office in 28 villages.

There are 31 villages having bus facilities.

Villages with most of facilities: Rayampuram Govindapuram, Vilangudi, Thelur, Perianagalur Reddipalayam, Periyathirukkonam, Punganguli.

Villages without Amenities (Education): None..

Scheduled Castes: Out of the total population of 93906 persons, 21923 persons (23.35%) belong to Scheduled Castes. The villages having less than 10% SC population are None..

The villages having more than 50% SC population are None.

Sex ratio of Scheduled Caste population is 509.

Scheduled Castes Literates and Illiterates by Sex:

	Persons	Males	Females
Literate	9,376	5,733	3,643
Illiterate	12,547	5,026	7,521
Literacy rate	50.8	63.8	38.5
Graduate	221	180	41

Scheduled Castes (Dominant):

Paraiyan etc., Adi Dravida, Chakkiliyan

Generic Castes etc., Arunthathiyar

For their cultural identity please see Appendix-I

Villages without Scheduled Castes: There is 1 village without any scheduled caste population.

Scheduled Tribes: Out of the total population of 93906 persons, 671 persons (0.71%) belong to Scheduled Tribes. The villages having less than 10% ST population are Pottaveli, Rayampuram, Sennivanam, Eluppaiyur Chakoil, Govindapuram, Kallangurichi, Kadugoor Ayan Athur, Kavanur, Vilangudi, Thelur, Perianagalur Ameenabad, Kairulabad, Ariyalur (N), Valajanagaram Mallur, Siruvalur, Pudupalayam, Reddipalayam Nagamagalur, Periyathirukkonam, Edaiyathankudi Karuppur Larapaty, Arungal, Karupillaikkattalai Alanduraiyarkattalai, Andipattakkadu, Punganguli Oriyur.

The villages having more than 50% ST population are None.

Sex ratio of Scheduled tribe population is 501.

Scheduled Tribes Literates and Illiterates by Sex:

	Persons	Males	Females
Literate	159	105	54
Illiterate	512	230	282
Literacy rate	27.8	36.0	19.3
Graduate	0	0	0

Scheduled Tribes (Dominant):

Irular, Malakkuravan, Malai Pandaram, Kattunayakan

For their cultural identity please see Appendix-II

Villages without Scheduled Tribes: There are 23 villages without any scheduled tribe population.

Literates and Illiterates by Sex (Total Population):

	Persons	Males	Females
Literate	47,067	29,261	17,806
Illiterate	46,839	17,503	29,336
Literacy rate	58	73	43
Graduate	1,568	1,062	506

Agriculture: ***Distribution of villages according to land use:*** Out of 31 villages, Total area (in hectare) is 33189, out of that 62.33 percent is cultivable and 14.85 percent of the cultivable area is irrigated.

Sources of Irrigation (Hectares): Government Canal 449, Private Canal 55, Well without Electricity 171.73, Well with Electricity 550.34, Tubewell without Electricity 206.48, Tubewell with Electricity 610.02, Tank 373.85, River 0, Lake 631.33, Waterfall 25, Others 0.

Villages with population of 5000 to 9999: Valajanagaram.

Villages with population of 10000 and above: None

Distribution of Workers:

	Persons	Males	Females	WPR
Cultivators	18,048	12,422	5,626	36.65
Agricultural Labour	22,970	8,903	14,067	46.64
Household Industry	1,014	453	561	2.06
Other Workers	7,217	5,579	1,638	14.65
Main Workers	36,728	22,677	14,051	74.58
Marginal Workers	12,521	4,680	7,841	25.42
Total Workers	49,249	27,357	21,892	

Religion: Major Religious Communities:

	Persons	Males	Females	Sex Ratio
Hindu (98.99%)	92,959	46,311	46,648	1,007
Muslim (0.47%)	444	232	212	914
Christian (0.56%)	526	233	293	1,258
Sikh (0%)	-	-	-	-
Buddhists (0%)	-	-	-	-
Jain (0%)	-	-	-	-

Agewise Data:

	Persons	Males	Females	Sex Ratio
All ages	94,062	46,849	47,213	1008
0-14	27,605	14,257	13,348	936
15-44	44,145	21,224	22,921	1080
45-79	21,546	10,951	10,595	967
80+	677	369	308	835
Age not stated	89	48	41	854

Languages (Dominant):

Tamil, Telugu, Hindi, Malayalam, Urdu

Disabled Population:

	Persons	Males	Females	%
Total Disabled	3,058	1,215	1,843	
In Seeing	2,037	600	1,437	66.61
In Speech	172	90	82	5.62
In Hearing	127	61	66	4.15
In Movement	558	368	190	18.25
Mentally	164	96	68	5.36

ARUPPUKKOTTAI

Aruppukkottai C.D. Block lies in the south-eastern part of Virudhunagar district. It is a part of Aruppukkottai taluk. The Block is located at a distance of 18 kms. from district headquarters (Virudhunagar). There are 39 villages in the block with the total population of 88,591 persons. Area of the C.D. Block is 322.06 sq. kms. It is bounded in the north by CD Block Kariapatti and district Madurai, in the south by district Thoothkkudi, in the east by CD Block Tiruchuli, in the west by CD Blocks Virudhunagar and Sattur.

Communications:

Roadways : N.H.-7: Direction- Sattur to Virudhunagar, Nearest Villages- Sulakkarai, Kalmarpatti. N.H.-45 B: Direction- Kariapatti to Ettayapuram, Nearest Villages- Gopalapuram, Kovilangulam, Kattangudi, Palayampatti, Kanjanaiakanpatti, Aruppukottai, Chettikuruchi, T.Koppuchittampatti, Pondalgudi, Chettipatti, Velayuthapuram, Melapandagudi. S.H.-38: Direction- Aruppokkottai to Perunalli, Nearest Villages-. Kanjanaiakanpatti, Kattakanjampatti, Athipatti. S.H.-42: Direction- Virudunagar to Aruppokkottai, Nearest Villages- Villipathiri, Kullursandai, Palavanatham, Periyapulianpatti, Kanjanaiakanpatti, Kattakanjampatti, Athipatti.

Annual Rainfall: Average Rainfall 799 mm.

Ground Water: Availability of the ground water in the Basin is 26.33 H.A.M. and the utilization is 10.43 H. A.M. It belongs to Safe category. Depth to water level varies from 2 to 10 meter below the ground. Most of the wells go down in summer months, according to the Ground Water Estimation Committee.

Natural Division: NA

Administration

Revenue **Division:** Aruppukottai. Parliamentary Constituency: 34 Sivakasi. District: Virudhunagar. Taluk: Aruppukottai. Assembly Constituency: 207 Aruppukottai.

Gram Panchayat: 32.

Villages: 39 **Inhabited:** 33 **Uninhabited:** 6

Ranking	**District**	**State**	**National**
Area	10	147	2542
Population	6	190	3830
Sex Ratio	5	80	638
Child Sex Ratio	1	12	469
Literacy Rate	1	53	717
Density	11	218	3809
Work Participation Rate	4	258	2318

Gram Panchayats:

Amanakkunatham, Athipatti, Chettikurichi, Chettipatti, Chidambarapuram, Gopalapuram, Kanjanaiyakkanpatti, Kattangudi, Koppuchithampatti, Kovilangulam, Kullursendai, Kurundamadam, Malaipatti, Palavanatham, Palayampatti, Pandalkudi, Periavallikulam, Periyanayagipuram, Podampatti, Puliyuran, Ramanujapuram, Sambatti, Sembatti, Sethurajapuram, Soolakkarai, Sukkilanatham, T.Meenakshipuram, Thummakundu, Tiruvirunthalpuram, Vaduvarpatti, Velayuthapuram, Vellayapuram, Villipathiri.

Amenities:

Education: Primary School in 30 villages, Middle school in 15 villages, Matriculation or Secondary School in 11 villages, namely Sulakkarai, Kullursandai, Palavanatham, Gopalapuram, Kovilangulam, Athipatti, Amanakunathan, Koothiparai, Chettikuruchi, Vadhuvarpatti, Velayuthapuram.

Higher Secondary or Pre University Courses or Intermediate or Junior College in 3 villages of the CD Block,, namely Kullursandai, Palavanatham, Koothiparai.

College in 1 village, Adult Literacy Center in 0 village., College is in village, namely Chettikuruchi.

Medical: Hospital in 0 village, Dispensary in 1 village, Health Center in 6 villages, Sub Center in 2 villages, Maternity and Child Welfare Center in 2 villages, Community health workers in 1 village.

The Village having Hospital or Dispensary or Health Center is Chettikuruchi.

Drinking Water: Tap water in 33 villages, Tank water in 0 villages, Well water in 33 villages, Tubewell in 33 villages and more than one source in 33 villages.

Bank: Banking facility in 11 villages, namely, Kullursandai, Palavanatham, Gopalapuram Kovilangulam, Palayampatti, Puliyuran T.Meenatchipuram, Amanakunathan, Koothiparai Chettikuruchi, Chettipatti.

Credit Society in 7 villages Agricultural Credit Society in 6 Non-Agricultural Credit Society in 1 village.

Others: Power supply in 32 villages, Cinema hall in 0 village, sport club in 0 village, Stadium or Auditorium or Community Hall in 6 villages, Post Office in 30 villages.

There are 29 villages having bus facilities.

Villages with most of facilities: Kullursandai Palavanatham, Gopalapuram, Kovilangulam, Puliyuran Koothiparai, Chettikuruchi.

Villages without amenities (Education):
Kalmarpatti, Kuranjakulam, V.Koppuchithampatti..

Scheduled Castes: Out of the total population of 88591 persons, 11888 persons (13.42%) belong to Scheduled Castes.

The villages having less than 10% SC population are Villipathiri, Kattangudi, Palayampatti, Poyyankulam Kuranjakulam, Sempatty, Mettuthotiyankulam Kattakanjampatti, Athipatti, Thiruvirundalpuram V.Koppuchithampatti, T.Koppuchittampatti, Pondalgudi Thummakundu, Velayuthapuram.

The villages having more than 50% SC population are None.

Sex ratio of Scheduled Caste population is 503.

Scheduled Castes Literates and Illiterates by Sex:

	Persons	Males	Females
Literate	6,731	3,975	2,756
Illiterate	5,157	1,929	3,228
Literacy rate	64.9	76.7	53.1
Graduate	176	130	46

Scheduled Castes (Dominant):

Pallan, Chakkiliyan, Paraiyan etc., Pagadai Kudumban

For their cultural identity please see Appendix-I

Villages without Scheduled Castes: There are 9 villages without any scheduled caste population.

Scheduled Tribes: Out of the total population of 88591 persons, 55 persons (0.06%) belong to Scheduled Tribes.

The villages having less than 10% ST population are Villipathiri, Sulakkarai, Kalmarpatti, Kullursandai Palavanatham, Gopalapuram, Kovilangulam, Kattangudi Palayampatti, Poyyankulam, Kuranjakulam, Puliyuran Sempatty, Mettuthotiyankulam, Kanjanaiakanpatti Kattakanjampatti, Athipatti, Sukilanatham Thiruvirundalpuram, T.Meenatchipuram, Amanakunathan Koothiparai, Kurundamadam, Podampatti, Chettikuruchi V.Koppuchithampatti, T.Koppuchittampatti, Pondalgudi Chettipatti, Vadhuvarpatti, Thummakundu, P.Andipatti Velayuthapuram.

The villages having more than 50% ST population are None.

Sex ratio of Scheduled tribe population is 509.

Scheduled Tribes Literates and Illiterates by Sex:

	Persons	Males	Females

Literate	24	15	9
Illiterate	31	12	19
Literacy rate	50.0	62.5	37.5
Graduate	3	0	3

Scheduled Tribes (Dominant):
Kattunayakan, Kondareddis, Kaniyan etc.
Mudugar etc., Palleyan

For their cultural identity please see Appendix-II

Villages without Scheduled Tribes: There are 35 villages without any scheduled tribe population.

Literates and Illiterates by Sex (Total Population):

	Persons	Males	Females
Literate	58,118	32,889	25,229
Illiterate	30,473	10,951	19,522
Literacy rate	74	85	64
Graduate	1,941	1,234	707

Agriculture: ***Distribution of villages according to land use:*** Out of 39 villages, Total area (in hectare) is 32206.82, out of that 0 percent is cultivable and 0 percent of the cultivable area is irrigated.

Sources of Irrigation (Hectares): Government Canal 0, Private Canal 0, Well without Electricity 0, Well with Electricity 0, Tubewell without Electricity 0, Tubewell with Electricity 0, Tank 981.12, River 0, Lake 0, Waterfall 291.94, Others 0.

Villages with population of 5000 to 9999:
Palavanatham, Chettikurichi , Pandalkudi.

Villages with population of 10000 and above:
Palayampatti.

Distribution of Workers:

	Persons	Males	Females	WPR
Cultivators	6,483	3,423	3,060	14.54
Agricultural Labour	14,956	6,454	8,502	33.55
Household Industry	1,946	761	1,185	4.37
Other Workers	21,196	15,097	6,099	47.54
Main Workers	40,189	24,137	16,052	90.15
Marginal Workers	4,392	1,598	2,794	9.85
Total Workers	44,581	25,735	18,846	

Religion: Major Religious Communities:

	Persons	Males	Females	Sex Ratio
Hindu (96.94%)	85,880	42,511	43,369	1,020
Muslim (0.64%)	570	264	306	1,159
Christian (2.38%)	2,112	1,054	1,058	1,004
Sikh (0%)	-	-	-	-
Buddhists (0%)	2	2	-	-
Jain (0.01%)	5	1	4	4,000

Agewise Data:

	Persons	Males	Females	Sex Ratio
All ages	88,591	43,840	44,751	1021
0-14	23,781	11,994	11,787	983
15-44	43,655	21,540	22,115	1027
45-79	19,967	9,738	10,229	1050
80+	841	374	467	1249
Age not stated	347	194	153	789

Languages (Dominant):
Tamil, Telugu, Kannada, Urdu, Malayalam

Disabled Population:

	Persons	Males	Females	%
Total Disabled	2,407	928	1,479	
In Seeing	1,471	372	1,099	61.11
In Speech	140	83	57	5.82
In Hearing	65	27	38	2.7
In Movement	553	351	202	22.97
Mentally	178	95	83	7.4

ATTUR

Attur C.D. Block lies in the eastern part of Salem district. It is a part of Attur taluk. The Block is located at a distance of 55 kms. from district headquarters (Salem). There are 23 villages in the block with the total population of 81,557 persons. Area of the C.D. Block is 256.21 sq. kms. It is bounded in the north by C.D. Block Peddaniackenpalayam, in the south by CD Block Gangavalli, in the east by C.D. Block Talavasal, and in the west by district Namakkal.

Communications:

Roadways : N.H.-68: Direction- Ethapur to Kallakurichi, Nearest Villages- Ammampalayam, Kalpaganoor, Alagapuram, Appamma Samudram, Ramanaikanpalayam, Attavanai Kjothampadi, Thulukkanoor, Thennangudipalayam. S.H.-30: Direction- Keeripatti to Narasingapuram, Nearest Villages- Chokkanadapuram, Eachampatti, Thandavarayapuram, Seeliyampatti, Malliyakarai, Arasanatham.

River: Vasista Nadi- Nearest Villages- Ammampalayam, Thulukkanoor, Kalpaganoor, Attavanai Kjothampadi, Alagapuram, Ramanaikanpalayam, Appamma Samudram, Thennangudipalayam.

Annual Rainfall: Average Rainfall 540 mm.

Ground Water: Availability of the ground water in the Basin is 7543.47 H.A.M. and the utilization is 14696. 64 H.A.M. It belongs to Safe category. Depth to water level varies from 2 to 20 meter below the ground. Most of the wells go down in summer months, according to the Ground Water Estimation Committee.

Forest and Reserved Forest: (Mannur RF)- Nearest Village- Ramanaikanpalayam. (Nagalur)- Nearest Villages- Appamma Samudram, Ramanaikanpalayam. (Paithur)- Nearest Villages- Paithur, Paithur RF, Eachampatti, Thandavarayapuram, Seeliyampatti. (Pattimedu Extn)- Nearest Villages- Muttal, Kallanatham. (Jadayagoundan Slopes)- Nearest Village- Muttal.

Natural Division: Kongu Nadu.

Administration

Revenue **Division:** Attur. Parliamentary Constituency: 14 Kallakurichi (SC). District: Salem. Taluk: Attur. Assembly Constituency: 82 Attur. Gram Panchayat: 20.

Villages: 23 **Inhabited:** 22 **Uninhabited:** 1

Ranking	District	State	National
Area	7	224	3303
Population	8	233	4056
Sex Ratio	6	328	2878
Child Sex Ratio	6	325	5374
Literacy Rate	1	213	1953
Density	7	58	3365
Work Participation Rate	16	200	496

Gram Panchayats:

Akkichettipalayam, Ammampalayam, Appamasamudram, Arasanatham, Chokkanathapuram, Eachampatty, Kallanatham, Kalpaganoor, Koolamedu, Kothampadi, Malliakkarai, MalliakKarai, Manjini, Paithur, Pungavadi, Ramanaickenpalayam, Seeliampatty, Thandavarayapuram, Thenangudipalayam, Thulukkanoor, Valayamadevi.

Amenities:

Education: Primary School in 21 villages, Middle school in 9 villages, Matriculation or Secondary School in 7 villages, namely Ammampalayam, Manjini, Kalpaganoor, Appamma Samudram, Malliyakarai, Chokkanadapuram, Velayamadevi.

Higher Secondary or Pre University Courses or Intermediate or Junior College in 4 villages of the CD Block,, namely Ammampalayam, Manjini, Appamma Samudram, Malliyakarai.

College in 0 village, Adult Literacy Center in 1 village.

Medical: Hospital in 0 village, Dispensary in 1 village, Health Center in 6 villages, Sub Center in 13 villages, Maternity and Child Welfare Center in 1 village, Community health workers in 0 village.

The Village having Hospital or Dispensary or Health Center is Arasanatham.

Drinking Water: Tap water in 22 villages, Tank water in 0 villages, Well water in 22 villages, Tubewell in 22 villages and more than one source in 22 villages.

Bank: Banking facility in 5 villages, namely, Ammampalayam, Manjini, Arasanatham, Malliyakarai Velayamadevi.

Credit Society in 17 villages Agricultural Credit Society in 13 Non-Agricultural Credit Society in 14 villages.

Others: Power supply in 22 villages, Cinema hall in 1 village, sport club in 0 village, Stadium or Auditorium or Community Hall in 0 village, Post Office in 14 villages.

There are 21 villages having bus facilities.

Villages with most of facilities: Ammampalayam Manjini, Arasanatham, Malliyakarai, Velayamadevi.

Villages without amenities (Education):

Jarikothampadi..

Scheduled Castes: Out of the total population of 81557 persons, 19623 persons (24.06%) belong to Scheduled Castes.

The villages having less than 10% SC population are None..

The villages having more than 50% SC population are None.

Sex ratio of Scheduled Caste population is 487.

Scheduled Castes Literates and Illiterates by Sex:

	Persons	Males	Females
Literate	9,890	6,006	3,884
Illiterate	9,733	4,062	5,671
Literacy rate	57.4	68.1	46.2
Graduate	251	204	47

Scheduled Castes (Dominant):

Paraiyan etc., Adi Dravida, Arunthathiyar, Pallan Valluvan

For their cultural identity please see Appendix-I

Villages without Scheduled Castes: There is 1 village without any scheduled caste population.

Scheduled Tribes: Out of the total population of 81557 persons, 3129 persons (3.84%) belong to Scheduled Tribes.

The villages having less than 10% ST population are Ammampalayam, Muttal, Manjini, Jarikothampadi Arasanatham, Kalpaganoor, Alagapuram Appamma Samudram, Akkichetti Palayam, Malliyakarai Ramanaikanpalayam, Attavanai Kjothampadi Chokkanadapuram, Velayamadevi, Kallanatham Thulukkanoor, Eachampatti, Thennangudipalayam Thandavarayapuram, Pungavadi, Seeliyampatti.

The villages having more than 50% ST population are None.

Sex ratio of Scheduled tribe population is 488.

Scheduled Tribes Literates and Illiterates by Sex:

	Persons	Males	Females
Literate	1,458	937	521
Illiterate	1,671	666	1,005
Literacy rate	51.1	63.9	37.6
Graduate	29	28	1

Scheduled Tribes (Dominant):

Malayali, Generic Tribes etc., Malakkuravan, Uraly

For their cultural identity please see Appendix-II

Villages without Scheduled Tribes: There are 15 villages without any scheduled tribe population.

Literates and Illiterates by Sex (Total Population):

	Persons	Males	Females
Literate	47,016	27,744	19,272
Illiterate	34,541	13,827	20,714

Literacy rate	65	76	54
Graduate	1,440	1,127	313

Agriculture: ***Distribution of villages according to land use:*** Out of 23 villages, Total area (in hectare) is 25621.27, out of that 60.46 percent is cultivable and 39.6 percent of the cultivable area is irrigated.

Sources of Irrigation (Hectares): Government Canal 0, Private Canal 0, Well without Electricity 750.75, Well with Electricity 4104.85, Tubewell without Electricity 54, Tubewell with Electricity 862.12, Tank 363.29, River 0, Lake 0, Waterfall 0, Others 0.

Villages with population of 5000 to 9999: Ramanayakkampalayam, Kalpaganur, Ammampalayam Paithur, Arasanatham.

Villages with population of 10000 and above: None

Distribution of Workers:

	Persons	Males	Females	WPR
Cultivators	18,698	10,687	8,011	39.23
Agricultural Labour	21,772	10,109	11,663	45.68
Household Industry	772	308	464	1.62
Other Workers	6,418	5,094	1,324	13.47
Main Workers	37,575	22,204	15,371	78.84
Marginal Workers	10,085	3,994	6,091	21.16
Total Workers	47,660	26,198	21,462	

Religion: Major Religious Communities:

	Persons	Males	Females	Sex Ratio
Hindu (98.53%)	80,358	40,976	39,382	961
Muslim (0.83%)	677	328	349	1,064
Christian (0.48%)	392	200	192	960
Sikh (0%)	1	1	-	-
Buddhists (0%)	-	-	-	-
Jain (0%)	1	1	-	-

Agewise Data:

	Persons	Males	Females	Sex Ratio
All ages	81,557	41,571	39,986	962
0-14	21,633	11,397	10,236	898
15-44	40,391	20,257	20,134	994
45-79	18,671	9,457	9,214	974
80+	602	336	266	792
Age not stated	260	124	136	1097

Languages (Dominant):

Tamil, Telugu, Urdu, Malayalam, Others

Disabled Population:

	Persons	Males	Females	%
Total Disabled	1,312	724	588	
In Seeing	516	255	261	39.33
In Speech	139	78	61	10.59
In Hearing	110	55	55	8.38
In Movement	420	270	150	32.01
Mentally	127	66	61	9.68

ATTUR

Attur C.D. Block lies in the southern part of Dindigul district. It is a part of Dindigul taluk. The taluk is located at a distance of 00 kms. from district headquarters (Dindigul). There are 20 villages in the block with the total population of 98,526 persons. Area of the C.D. Block is 227.57 sq. kms. It is bounded in the north by C.D. Block Reddiyarchatram, in the south by CD Blocks Kodaikanal, Vattalkundu and Nilakkottai, in the east by C.D. Block Dindigul, and in the west by CD Block Kodaikanal.

Communications:

Roadways : N.H.-7: Direction- Madurai to Dindigul, Nearest Villages- Kalikampatti, Thampampatti, Ambathurai.

Backwards Region Grants Fund: It receives Backward Region Grants.

Annual Rainfall: Average Rainfall 813 mm.

Ground Water: Availability of the ground water in the Basin is 3698.57 H.A.M. and the utilization is 5156.40 H.A.M. It belongs to Over Expoited category. Depth to water level varies from 5 to 20 meter below the ground. Most of the wells go down in summer months, according to the Ground Water Estimation Committee.

Forest and Reserved Forest: (Sirumalai RF)- Nearest Villages- Kilakottai, Thompampatti, Ambathurai.

Natural Division: NA

Administration

Revenue **Division:** Dindigul. Parliamentary Constituency: 22 Dindigul. District: Dindigul. Taluk: Dindigul. Assembly Constituency: 129 Attur, 131 Natham. Gram Panchayat: 22.

Villages: 20 **Inhabited:** 20 **Uninhabited:** 0

Ranking	District	State	National
Area	12	254	3697
Population	6	134	3507
Sex Ratio	3	145	1049
Child Sex Ratio	13	344	5695
Literacy Rate	2	101	1125
Density	13	239	2545
Work Participation Rate	2	92	2578

Gram Panchayats:

AkkaraiPatti, Alamarathupatti, Ambathurai, Athoor, Ayyankottai, Bodikamanvadi , Chettiyapatti, Devarappanpatti, Gandhigram, Kalikkampatti , Manalur, Munnilaikottai, N.Panjampatti , Palayankottai , Paraipatti, Pillayarnatham, Pithalaipatti, Seevalsaragu, Sitharevu, Toppampatti, Vakkampatti, Virakkal.

Amenities:

Education: Primary School in 20 villages, Middle school in 12 villages, Matriculation or Secondary School in 6 villages, namely N. Panjanpatti, Manalur, Athoor, Kilakottai, Sitharevu, Ayyampalayam.

Higher Secondary or Pre University Courses or Intermediate or Junior College in 4 villages of the CD Block,, namely N. Panjanpatti, Athoor, Kilakottai, Ayyampalayam.

College in 2 villages, Adult Literacy Center in 0 village., Colleges are in villages, namely Manalur, Kilakottai.

Medical: Hospital in 1 village, Dispensary in 3 villages, Health Center in 5 villages, Sub Center in 18 villages, Maternity and Child Welfare Center in 12 villages, Community health workers in 4 villages.

The Villages having Hospital or Dispensary or Health Center are N. Panjanpatti, Athoor, Seeval Saragu, Kilakottai.

Drinking Water: Tap water in 20 villages, Tank water in 13 villages, Well water in 20 villages, Tubewell in 20 villages and more than one source in 20 villages.

Bank: Banking facility in 3 villages, namely, N. Panjanpatti, Athoor, Kilakottai.

Credit Society in 7 villages Agricultural Credit Society in 6 Non-Agricultural Credit Society in 2 villages.

Others: Power supply in 20 villages, Cinema hall in 6 villages, sport club in 0 village, Stadium or Auditorium or Community Hall in 1 village, Post Office in 20 villages.

There are 18 villages having bus facilities.

Villages with most of facilities: N. Panjanpatti Athoor, Kilakottai.

Villages without Amenities (Education): None..

Scheduled Castes: Out of the total population of 98526 persons, 22969 persons (23.31%) belong to Scheduled Castes.

The villages having less than 10% SC population are None..

The villages having more than 50% SC population are None.

Sex ratio of Scheduled Caste population is 500.

Scheduled Castes Literates and Illiterates by Sex:

	Persons	Males	Females
Literate	12,628	7,412	5,216
Illiterate	10,341	4,071	6,270
Literacy rate	62.6	73.9	51.5
Graduate	428	258	170

Scheduled Castes (Dominant):

Pallan, Chakkiliyan, Paraiyan etc., Kuravan etc. Madari

For their cultural identity please see Appendix-I

Villages without Scheduled Castes: There is 0 village without any scheduled caste population.

Scheduled Tribes: Out of the total population of 98526 persons, 64 persons (0.06%) belong to Scheduled Tribes.

The villages having less than 10% ST population are Virakkal, Kummampatty, Pithlapatty, Pillayarnatham Alamarathupatty, Vakkampatty, Munnilakottai N. Panjanpatti, Paraipatti, Manalur, Athoor Seeval Saragu, Kalikampatti, Kilakottai Thampampatti, Ambathurai, Palayankottai Bodikamanvadi, Sitharevu, Ayyampalayam.

The villages having more than 50% ST population are None.

Sex ratio of Scheduled tribe population is 562.

Scheduled Tribes Literates and Illiterates by Sex:

	Persons	Males	Females
Literate	41	20	21
Illiterate	23	8	15
Literacy rate	71.9	80.0	65.6
Graduate	5	4	1

Scheduled Tribes (Dominant):

Kattunayakan, Palleyan, Generic Tribes etc. Palliyar, Palliyan

For their cultural identity please see Appendix-II

Villages without Scheduled Tribes: There are 15 villages without any scheduled tribe population.

Literates and Illiterates by Sex (Total Population):

	Persons	Males	Females
Literate	61,693	34,972	26,721
Illiterate	36,833	14,199	22,634
Literacy rate	71	81	60
Graduate	2,257	1,297	960

Agriculture: ***Distribution of villages according to land use:***

Out of 20 villages, Total area (in hectare) is 22757.92, out of that 63.89 percent is cultivable and 51.82 percent of the cultivable area is irrigated.

Sources of Irrigation (Hectares): Government Canal 378.18, Private Canal 0, Well without Electricity 1749.83, Well with Electricity 3927.96, Tubewell without Electricity 5.85, Tubewell with Electricity 65.21, Tank 1300.1, River 108.48, Lake 0, Waterfall 0, Others 0.

Villages with population of 5000 to 9999:

Virakkal, Panjanpatti (N), Paraipatti, Attur Kilakottai, Ambathurai, Aiyampalayam.

Villages with population of 10000 and above:

Sitharevu.

Distribution of Workers:

	Persons	Males	Females	WPR
Cultivators	6,498	4,132	2,366	13.28
Agricultural Labour	28,771	14,144	14,627	58.79
Household Industry	1,257	599	658	2.57
Other Workers	12,413	9,258	3,155	25.36
Main Workers	41,620	25,327	16,293	85.04
Marginal Workers	7,319	2,806	4,513	14.96
Total Workers	48,939	28,133	20,806	

Religion: Major Religious Communities:

	Persons	Males	Females	Sex Ratio
Hindu (82.68%)	81,466	40,821	40,645	996
Muslim (2.7%)	2,661	1,341	1,320	984
Christian (14.48%)	14,270	6,941	7,329	1,056
Sikh (0.03%)	27	15	12	800
Buddhists (0.01%)	5	1	4	4,000
Jain (0%)	4	3	1	333

Agewise Data:

	Persons	Males	Females	Sex Ratio
All ages	98,526	49,171	49,355	1004
0-14	26,545	13,924	12,621	906
15-44	48,587	23,742	24,845	1046
45-79	22,082	10,857	11,225	1034
80+	863	425	438	1031
Age not stated	449	223	226	1013

Languages (Dominant):

Tamil, Kannada, Telugu, Urdu, Malayalam

Disabled Population:

	Persons	Males	Females	%
Total Disabled	3,104	1,300	1,804	
In Seeing	2,055	745	1,310	66.2
In Speech	207	98	109	6.67
In Hearing	99	43	56	3.19
In Movement	536	303	233	17.27
Mentally	207	111	96	6.67

AVANASHI

Avanashi C.D. Block lies in the northern part of Coimbatore district. It is a part of Avanashi taluk. The Block is located at a distance of 40 kms. from district headquarters (Coimbatore). There are 31 villages in the block with the total population of 110,792 persons. Area of the C.D. Block is 352.15 sq. kms. It is bounded in the north by Erode District, in the south by Palladam taluk, in the east by Tiruppur taluk, and in the west by Annur C.D. Block.

Communications:

Roadways : N.H.-47: Direction- Coimbatore to Bhavani, Nearest Villages- Sembianallur, Thekkalur, Puduppalayam, Velayathampalayam, Palangarai. N.H.-209: Direction- Annur to Satyamangalam, Nearest Villages- Pongalur, Alathur,

Railway Station: Puduppalayam.

River: Noyil Nadi- Nearest Villages- Thekkalur, Puduppal ayam.

Annual Rainfall: Average Rainfall 550 mm.

Ground Water: Availability of the ground water in the Basin is 3489.59 H.A.M. and the utilization is 4457.60 H.A.M. It belongs to Semi Critical category. Depth to water level varies from 0 to 20 meter below the ground. Most of the wells go down in summer months, according to the Ground Water Estimation Committee.

Natural Division: Kongu Nadu.

Administration

Revenue **Division:** Trippur. Parliamentary Constituency: 19 Nilgiris. District: Coimbatore. Taluk: Avanashi. Assembly Constituency: 112 Avanashi (SC). Gram Panchayat: 31.

Villages: 31 **Inhabited:** 31 **Uninhabited:** 0

Ranking	District	State	National
Area	3	112	2262
Population	3	91	3135
Sex Ratio	11	302	2480
Child Sex Ratio	9	83	1623
Literacy Rate	19	306	2588
Density	4	92	3400
Work Participation Rate	9	208	957

Gram Panchayats:

Alathur, Ayyampalayam, Kaniampundi, Kanur, Karumapalalayam, Karuvalur, Kuppandampalayam, Kuttagam, Mangarasavalayapalayam, Muriandampalayam, Naduvacheri, Nambiampalayam, Palangarai , Papankulam, Pongalur, Pothampalayam, Pudupalayam, Pulipar, Punjaithamaraikulam, Ramanathapuram, Sembianallur, Sevur, Sinnaripalayam, Thandukkarampalayam, Thathanur, Thekkalur, Thulukkamuthur, Uppilipalayam, Vadugapalayam, Velayudampalayam, Vettuvapalayam.

Amenities:

Education: Primary School in 31 villages, Middle school in 16 villages, Matriculation or Secondary School in 7 villages, namely Pappankulam, Sevur, Kannur, Sembianallur, Karuvalur, Thekkalur, Palangarai.

Higher Secondary or Pre University Courses or Intermediate or Junior College in 3 villages of the CD Block,, namely Sevur, Karuvalur, Thekkalur.

College in 3 villages, Adult Literacy Center in 0 village., Colleges are in villages, namely Alathur, Kuppandampalayam, Palangarai.

Medical: Hospital in 2 villages, Dispensary in 0 village, Health Center in 5 villages, Sub Center in 20 villages, Maternity and Child Welfare Center in 3 villages, Community health workers in 1 village.

The Villages having Hospital or Dispensary or Health Center are Ayyampalayam, Palangarai.

Drinking Water: Tap water in 31 villages, Tank water in 1 villages, Well water in 31 villages, Tubewell in 31 villages and more than one source in 31 villages.

Bank: Banking facility in 7 villages, namely, Kaniam Poondi, Alathur, Kuttagam, Sevur, Naduvachery Vadugapalayam, Palangarai.

Credit Society in 22 villages Agricultural Credit Society in 21 Non-Agricultural Credit Society in 6 villages.

Others: Power supply in 31 villages, Cinema hall in 5 villages, sport club in 0 village, Stadium or Auditorium or Community

Hall in 0 village, Post Office in 30 villages.
There are 30 villages having bus facilities.

Villages with most of facilities: Alathur Kuttagam, Sevur, Naduvachery, Vadugapalayam Palangarai.

Villages without Amenities (Education): None.

Scheduled Castes: Out of the total population of 110792 persons, 27128 persons (24.49%) belong to Scheduled Castes.

The villages having less than 10% SC population are None..

The villages having more than 50% SC population are None.

Sex ratio of Scheduled Caste population is 495.

Scheduled Castes Literates and Illiterates by Sex:

	Persons	Males	Females
Literate	9,394	5,620	3,774
Illiterate	17,734	8,089	9,645
Literacy rate	39.7	46.9	32.3
Graduate	26	18	8

Scheduled Castes (Dominant):

Chakkiliyan, Madari, Pallan, Adi Dravida Paraiyan etc.

For their cultural identity please see Appendix-I

Villages without Scheduled Castes: There is 0 village without any scheduled caste population.

Scheduled Tribes: Out of the total population of 110792 persons, 36 persons (0.03%) belong to Scheduled Tribes.

The villages having less than 10% ST population are Kaniam Poondi, Pongalur, Alathur Mangarsavalayapalayam, Kuttagam, Pothampalayam Pulippar, Thathanur, Punjai Tamarai Kulam Pappankulam, Sevur, Thandukkaram Palayam, Kannur Ramanathapuram, Murigadapalayam, Vettuvapalayam Karumapalayam, Naduvachery, Vadugapalayam Ayyampalayam, Thulukkamauthur, Kuppandampalayam Chinneripalayam, Sembianallur, Nambiampalayam Karuvalur, Uppalipalayam, Thekkalur, Puduppalayam Velayathampalayam, Palangarai.

The villages having more than 50% ST population are None.

Sex ratio of Scheduled tribe population is 333.

Scheduled Tribes Literates and Illiterates by Sex:

	Persons	Males	Females
Literate	22	17	5
Illiterate	14	7	7
Literacy rate	75.9	85.0	55.6
Graduate	0	0	0

Scheduled Tribes (Dominant):

Kurumans, Irular, Kammara, Kattunayakan, Kochu Velan

For their cultural identity please see Appendix-II

Villages without Scheduled Tribes: There are 27 villages without any scheduled tribe population.

Literates and Illiterates by Sex (Total Population):

	Persons	Males	Females
Literate	60,569	36,267	24,302
Illiterate	50,223	19,962	30,261
Literacy rate	61	72	50
Graduate	517	356	161

Agriculture: ***Distribution of villages according to land use:*** Out of 31 villages, Total area (in hectare) is 35215.56, out of that 89.63 percent is cultivable and 16.03 percent of the cultivable area is irrigated.

Sources of Irrigation (Hectares): Government Canal 0, Private Canal 0, Well without Electricity 84.96, Well with Electricity 2783.64, Tubewell without Electricity 0, Tubewell with Electricity 2190.59, Tank 0, River 0, Lake 0, Waterfall 0, Others 0.

Villages with population of 5000 to 9999: Sevur, Thekkalur, Pudupalayam, Velayudampalayam Palangarai.

Villages with population of 10000 and above: None

Distribution of Workers:

	Persons	Males	Females	WPR
Cultivators	14,369	8,886	5,483	23.01
Agricultural Labour	18,204	9,023	9,181	29.15
Household Industry	3,374	1,626	1,748	5.4
Other Workers	26,498	19,354	7,144	42.43
Main Workers	55,984	36,359	19,625	89.65
Marginal Workers	6,461	2,530	3,931	10.35
Total Workers	62,445	38,889	23,556	

Religion: Major Religious Communities:

	Persons	Males	Females	Sex Ratio
Hindu (97.85%)	108,409	55,022	53,387	970
Muslim (0.48%)	532	288	244	847
Christian (1.54%)	1,708	849	859	1,012
Sikh (0%)	1	1	-	-
Buddhists (0.01%)	8	5	3	600
Jain (0%)	1	-	1	-

Agewise Data:

	Persons	Males	Females	Sex Ratio
All ages	110,792	56,229	54,563	970
0-14	25,183	12,782	12,401	970
15-44	54,303	27,306	26,997	989
45-79	29,217	15,032	14,185	944
80+	1,648	901	747	829
Age not stated	441	208	233	1120

Languages (Dominant):

Tamil, Telugu, Kannada, Malayalam, Urdu

Disabled Population:

	Persons	Males	Females	%

Total Disabled	3,073	1,253	1,820	
In Seeing	2,064	668	1,396	67.17
In Speech	182	92	90	5.92

In Hearing	129	68	61	4.2
In Movement	474	306	168	15.42
Mentally	224	119	105	7.29

AVUDAYARKOIL

Avudayarkoil C.D. Block lies in the southern part of Pudukkottai district. It is a part of taluks Aranthangi and Avudayarkoil. The Block is located at a distance of NA. kms. from district headquarters (Pudukkottai). There are 86 villages in the block with the total population of 80,067 persons. Area of the C.D. Block is 390.66 sq. kms. It is bounded in the north by C.D. Blocks Aranthangi and Manamelkudi, in the south by district Ramanathapuram, in the east by the Palk Strait, in the west by CD Block Arimalam, and districts Sivaganga and Ramanathapuram. CD Block Avudayarkoil falls in taluk Arantagi by 08 villages, and in taluk Avudayarkoil by 78 villages.

Communications:

Roadways : S.H-26: Direction- Aranthangi to Tondi, Nearest Villages- Pilluyalasai, Avudayakoil, Esamangalam, Elunuttimangalam, Piranthani, Poovalur, Amaratakki, Veliyathur, Kanoor, Thalanur, Nariyanendal, Alathur, Veelimangalam, Palakulam, Kadavakkottai, Thiruppuravasal, Sirvkadavakkottai, Vezhimar, Veelimangalam.

River: Vellar Nadi- Nearest Villages- Avudayakoil, Keelkudi, Perunavloor, Piranthani, Sirumarudur, Vatathur, Sathakudi, P.V.Vadavayal, Veeramangalam.

Annual Rainfall: Average Rainfall 910 mm.

Ground Water: Availability of the ground water in the Basin is 11757.79 H.A.M. and the utilization is 168. 58 H.A.M. It belongs to Safe category. Depth to water level varies from 0 to 10 meter below the ground. Most of the wells go down in summer months, according to the Ground Water Estimation Committee.

Coastal Villages- (Palk Strait)- Nearest Villages- Nattani Puranakudi, Alathur, Mimsal Chatrampattinam, Palankulam, Sirvkadavakkottai, Vezhimar.

Natural Division: Chola Nadu.

Administration

Revenue **Division:** Pudukottai. Parliamentary Constituency: 31 Sivaganga. District: Pudukottai. Taluk: Arantangi, Avudayarkoil. Assembly Constituency: 183 Arantangi. Gram Panchayat: 35.

Villages: 86 **Inhabited:** 81 **Uninhabited:** 5

Ranking	District	State	National
Area	4	80	1993
Population	8	242	4105
Sex Ratio	3	54	481
Child Sex Ratio	5	126	2354
Literacy Rate	3	77	908
Density	9	249	4662
Work Participation Rate	12	322	2660

Gram Panchayats:

Amaradakki, Kalabam, Karur, Kathiramangalam, Kavathukudi, Keelkudivattathur, Kunnur, Mimisal, Okkur, Palavarasan, Pandipattinam, Ponbethi, Ponnamangalam, Poovalur, Punniavayal, Purasakudi, Puthambur, Satti,akudi, Senganam, Sirumaruthur, Thalanur, Theeyathur, Theeyur, Thiruperunthurai, Thirupunavasal, Thondamanandal, Thunjanur, Velivayal, Velvarai, Vettivayal, Vilanur, Keelacheri, Kundagavayal, Perunavalur, Veeramangalam, Vettanur.

Amenities:

Education: Primary School in 57 villages, Middle school in 14 villages, Matriculation or Secondary School in 8 villages, namely Avudayakoil, Piranthani, Okkur, Amaratakki, Karur, Ponbethi, Nattani Puranakudi, Mimsal Chatrampattinam.

Higher Secondary or Pre University Courses or Intermediate or Junior College in 3 villages of the CD Block,, namely Avudayakoil, Okkur, Mimsal Chatrampattinam. College in 0 village, Adult Literacy Center in 0 village.

Medical: Hospital in 1 village, Dispensary in 1 village, Health Center in 3 villages, Sub Center in 8 villages, Maternity and Child Welfare Center in 0 village, Community health workers in 65 villages.

The Village having Hospital or Dispensary or Health Center is Avudayakoil.

Drinking Water: Tap water in 81 villages, Tank water in 6 villages, Well water in 81 villages, Tubewell in 81 villages and more than one source in 81 villages.

Bank: Banking facility in 4 villages, namely, Avudayakoil, Karur, Mimsal Chatrampattinam Thiruppuravasal.

Credit Society in 9 villages Agricultural Credit Society in 9 Non-Agricultural Credit Society in 2 villages.

Others: Power supply in 81 villages, Cinema hall in 1 village, sport club in 0 village, Stadium or Auditorium or Community Hall in 0 village, Post Office in 18 villages.

There are 50 villages having bus facilities.

Villages with most of facilities: Avudayakoil Karur, Mimsal Chatrampattinam, Thiruppuravasal.

Villages without amenities (Education):

Sivanthankadu, Munnoothamvayal, Paagayathangudi, Vettinivayal, Muduvalarkudi, Kandayankottai, Kasavayal, Seluvanandal, Kudikkadu, Vatathur, P.V.Subramaniapuram, Pattamudaiyan, P.V.Vadavayal, Poovalur, Perunthamarai, Velur, Vettivayal, Kanoor, Siruveli, Nariyanendal, Theeyur, Kovinikkedangu,

Kulathur, Vezhimar..

Scheduled Castes: Out of the total population of 80067 persons, 14560 persons (18.18%) belong to Scheduled Castes.

The villages having less than 10% SC population are Kundagavayal, Puduvakkadu, Vettinivayal, Palavarasan Kandayankottai, Velivayal, Magaliyendal Seluvanandal, Vatathur, Keelkudi, Sanannanthàl Velur, Vettivayal, Kanoor, Soundaranayakipuram Siruveli, Ponbethi, Nariyanendal, Kathiramangalam Kovinikkedangu, Theeyathur, Velivayal Mimsal Chatrampattinam, Palankulam, Kadavakkottai Kannamangalam, Thiruppuravasal, Vezhimar.

The villages having more than 50% SC population are Munnoothamvayal, P.V.Subramaniapuram, Kallakathan Perunthamarai, Kavathukudi.

Sex ratio of Scheduled Caste population is 508.

Scheduled Castes Literates and Illiterates by Sex:

	Persons	Males	Females
Literate	8,000	4,695	3,305
Illiterate	6,560	2,471	4,089
Literacy rate	63.6	75.9	51.7
Graduate	82	67	15

Scheduled Castes (Dominant):

Pallan, Paraiyan etc., Kadaiyan, Adi Dravida Kuravan etc.

For their cultural identity please see Appendix-I

Villages without Scheduled Castes: There are 18 villages without any scheduled caste population.

Scheduled Tribes: Out of the total population of 80067 persons, 49 persons (0.06%) belong to Scheduled Tribes.

The villages having less than 10% ST population are Pilluyalasai, Avudayakoil, Ponniyavayal Veeramangalam, Perunavloor, Kundagavayal, Keelacheri Sivanthankadu, Munnoothamvayal, Paagayathangudi Vettanur, Kidangivayal, Puduvakkadu, Vettinivayal Muduvalarkudi, Esamangalam, Palavarasan Kandayankottai, Kasavayal, Velivayal, Magaliyendal Seluvanandal, Kudikkadu, Elunuttimangalam Piranthani, Sirumarudur, Vatathur, Keelkudi P.V.Subramaniapuram, Pattamudaiyan, Sathakudi Kallakathan, P.V.Vadavayal, Poovalur, Veelimangalam Sattiakudi, Pallivayal, Alathivayal, Perunthamarai Okkur, Sithakkur, Sanannanthal, Thunjanoor, Kumulur Narasingapuram, Velur, Vettivayal, Amaratakki Veliyathur, Kanoor, Soundaranayakipuram, Siruveli Kuneriyendal, Karur, Thanikondon, Kavathukudi Ponbethi, Thalanur, Nariyanendal, Veelvarai Nattani Puranakudi, Peranoor, Kathiramangalam Sathiyadi, Theeyur, Kalabam, Kovinikkedangu Senganam, Thennamari, Kulathur, Theeyathur Velivayal, Alathur, Mimsal Chatrampattinam Palankulam, Kadavakkottai, Parayathur, Kannamangalam Thiruppuravasal, Sirvkadavakkottai, Vezhimar.

The villages having more than 50% ST population are None.

Sex ratio of Scheduled tribe population is 571.

Scheduled Tribes Literates and Illiterates by Sex:

	Persons	Males	Females
Literate	14	10	4
Illiterate	35	11	24
Literacy rate	38.9	62.5	20.0
Graduate	0	0	0

Scheduled Tribes (Dominant):

Adiyan, Malakkuravan, Kammara, Palliyar

For their cultural identity please see Appendix-II

Villages without Scheduled Tribes: There are 83 villages without any scheduled tribe population.

Literates and Illiterates by Sex (Total Population):

	Persons	Males	Females
Literate	50,715	28,760	21,955
Illiterate	29,352	10,665	18,687
Literacy rate	73	84	62
Graduate	771	571	200

Agriculture: ***Distribution of villages according to land use:*** Out of 86 villages, Total area (in hectare) is 39066.87, out of that 42.42 percent is cultivable and 79.96 percent of the cultivable area is irrigated.

Sources of Irrigation (Hectares): Government Canal 395.28, Private Canal 0, Well without Electricity 0.51, Well with Electricity 0, Tubewell without Electricity 0, Tubewell with Electricity 0.58, Tank 12885.09, River 0, Lake 0, Waterfall 0, Others 0.

Villages with population of 5000 to 9999:
Avadaiyar Kovil, Nattanipurasakudi.

Villages with population of 10000 and above: None

Distribution of Workers:

	Persons	Males	Females	WPR
Cultivators	20,823	13,082	7,741	53.57
Agricultural Labour	10,961	4,032	6,929	28.2
Household Industry	417	159	258	1.07
Other Workers	6,672	5,675	997	17.16
Main Workers	29,241	19,918	9,323	75.22
Marginal Workers	9,632	3,030	6,602	24.78
Total Workers	38,873	22,948	15,925	

Religion: Major Religious Communities:

	Persons	Males	Females	Sex Ratio
Hindu (78.55%)	62,892	31,198	31,694	1,016
Muslim (12.55%)	10,046	4,694	5,352	1,140
Christian (9.15%)	7,328	3,634	3,694	1,017
Sikh (0%)	1	1	-	-

Buddhists (0%)	1	-	1	-
Jain (0%)	-	-	-	-

Agewise Data:

	Persons	Males	Females	Sex Ratio
All ages	80,280	39,533	40,747	1031
0-14	23,251	11,899	11,352	954
15-44	38,783	18,531	20,252	1093
45-79	17,579	8,737	8,842	1012
80+	496	267	229	858
Age not stated	171	99	72	727

Languages (Dominant):
Tamil, Telugu, Marathi, Malayalam, Kannada

Disabled Population:

	Persons	Males	Females	%
Total Disabled	2,080	804	1,276	
In Seeing	1,368	389	979	65.77
In Speech	168	104	64	8.08
In Hearing	56	22	34	2.69
In Movement	353	210	143	16.97
Mentally	135	79	56	6.49

AYODHIAPATTINAM

Ayodhyapattinam C.D. Block lies in the central part of Salem district. It is a part of Salem and Vazhappadi taluks. The Block is located at a distance of 09 kms. from district headquarters (Salem). There are 52 villages in the block with the total population of 127,331 persons. Area of the C.D. Block is 251.40 sq. kms. It is bounded in the north by and C.D. Block Yercaud in the south by C.D. Blocks Panamarathupatti and Vazhappadi, in the east by C.D. Block Vazhappadi, and in the west by C.D. Block Salem. CD Block Ayodhyapattinam falls in taluk Salem by 24 Villages and in taluk vazhapadi by 28 Villages.

Communications:

Roadways : N.H.-68: Direction- Salem to Vazhappadi, Nearest Villages- Adikarapatti, Agraharanattamangalam, Karipatti, Perumalapalayam, Karumapuram, Masinaickenpatti, Minnampalli, Mettuppatti. S.H.-18: Direction- Ayodhyapattinam to Harur, Nearest Villages- Kullampatty, Achnaguttapatty Pudur, Aramanoor, Achanguttapatty, Kathripatty, Mookkanoor, Kuppanur, Thathanur, Sukkampatty, Valasaiyur, Mettupattythanoor.

Railway Station: Karipatti.

Annual Rainfall: Average Rainfall 540 mm.

Ground Water: Availability of the ground water in the Basin is 3146.30 H.A.M. and the utilization is 5222.51 H.A.M. It belongs to Safe category. Depth to water level varies from 5 to 10 meter below the ground. Most of the wells go down in summer months, according to the Ground Water Estimation Committee.

Forest and Reserved Forest: (Gudamalai RF)- Nearest Villages- S.Nattamangalam, Koottathupatty, Perumalapalayam, Anuppoor. (Kurichi)- Nearest Villages- Kurichi RF, Pallikadu, Pelapadi. (Mathikuttai)- Nearest Village- Mandhikottai (RF). (Palapaddi)- Nearest Villages- Chinavelampatti,Chirumalai, Aranuthymalai, Pallikadu, Pelapadi RF,Pelapadi, Aledipetti, Periyavelanpetti. (Vaiermpatti)-Nearest Villages- Chinavelampatti, Vallapatti (RF),Chirumalai, Aranuthymalai, Pallikadu, Aledipetti, Vilampatty, Anuppoor. (Vellalakundam)- Nearest Village- Vellalagundam.

Natural Division: Kongu Nadu.

Administration

Revenue **Division:** Salem. Parliamentary Constituency: 14 Kallakurichi (SC). District: Salem. Taluk: Salem, Vazhapadi. Assembly Constituency: 83 Vazhappadi (SC). Gram Panchayat: 32.

Villages: 52 **Inhabited:** 48 **Uninhabited:** 4

Ranking	District	State	National
Area	8	232	3365
Population	2	45	2608
Sex Ratio	5	312	2605
Child Sex Ratio	2	293	4938
Literacy Rate	2	256	2206
Density	17	213	2191
Work Participation Rate	7	57	2284

Gram Panchayats:

Achankuttapatti, Adikarapatti, Chinnanur, D.Perumapalayam, Dasanaickenpatti, Korathupatti, Kuppanur, M.Palapatti, Mettupattithathanur, Pallipatti, Poovanur, Sukkampatti, Tailanur, Udayapatti, Valaiyakkaranur, Valasaiyur, Veeranam, Agrahara Nattarmangalam, AgraharaNattamangalam, Aladipatty, Anuppur, Chinnakavundapuram, Karipatti, Karumapuram, Kullampatty, Masinaickenpatty, Mettupatti, Minnampalli, Periyakavundapuram, Perumalpalayam, Sarkar Nattarmangalam, Vellalakundam.

Amenities:

Education: Primary School in 42 villages, Middle school in 13 villages, Matriculation or Secondary School in 10 villages, namely Vellalagundam, Adikarapatti, Valasaiyur, Sukkampatty, Achanguttapatty, Kuppanur, Koottathupatty, Karipatti, Minnampalli, Mettuppatti. Higher Secondary or Pre University Courses or Intermediate or Junior College in 6 villages of the CD Block,, namely Vellalagundam, Adikarapatti, Valasaiyur, Sukkampatty, Minnampalli, Mettuppatti.
College in 2 villages, Adult Literacy Center in 0 village., Colleges are in villages, namely Chinnagoundapuram, Masinaickenpatti.

Medical: Hospital in 1 village, Dispensary in 0 village, Health Center in 9 villages, Sub Center in 21 villages,

Maternity and Child Welfare Center in 11 villages, Community health workers in 4 villages.
The Village having Hospital or Dispensary or Health Center is Agraharanattamangalam.

Drinking Water: Tap water in 48 villages, Tank water in 0 villages, Well water in 48 villages, Tubewell in 48 villages and more than one source in 48 villages.

Bank: Banking facility in 10 villages, namely, Vellalagundam, Agraharanattamangalam, Kullampatty Valasaiyur, Sukkampatty, Udayapatti, Koottathupatty Karipatti, Masinaickenpatti, Periagoundapuram.
Credit Society in 25 villages Agricultural Credit Society in 16 Non-Agricultural Credit Society in 19 villages.

Others: Power supply in 47 villages, Cinema hall in 2 villages, sport club in 5 villages, Stadium or Auditorium or Community Hall in 0 village, Post Office in 36 villages.
There are 39 villages having bus facilities.

Villages with most of facilities: Vellalagundam Agraharanattamangalam, Kullampatty, Valasaiyur Sukkampatty, Udayapatti, Koottathupatty, Karipatti Masinaickenpatti, Periagoundapuram.

Villages without amenities (Education):
Valayakaranoor, Vellayampatty, Karpakam, Pallikadu, Mookkanoor, Palapatty..

Scheduled Castes: Out of the total population of 127331 persons, 34804 persons (27.33%) belong to Scheduled Castes.
The villages having less than 10% SC population are Chinavelampatti, Valayakaranoor Achnaguttapatty Pudur, Aramanoor, Thailanur Chirumalai, Aranuthymalai, Kathripatty, Pallikadu Vedapatty, Pelapadi, Mookkanoor, Aledipetti Periyavelanpetti, Mettupattythathanoor Dasanaicenpatty, Mettuppatti, Chinnanur.
The villages having more than 50% SC population are Korathupatti, Adikarapatti, Achanguttapatty Koottathupatty, Karipatti, Perumalapalayam.
Sex ratio of Scheduled Caste population is 494.

Scheduled Castes Literates and Illiterates by Sex:

	Persons	Males	Females
Literate	17,327	10,374	6,953
Illiterate	17,477	7,221	10,256
Literacy rate	58.0	68.9	46.9
Graduate	363	307	56

Scheduled Castes (Dominant):
Adi Dravida, Arunthathiyar, Paraiyan etc.
Kuravan etc., Valluvan

For their cultural identity please see Appendix-I

Villages without Scheduled Castes: There are 11 villages without any scheduled caste population.

Scheduled Tribes: Out of the total population of 127331 persons, 8283 persons (6.51%) belong to Scheduled Tribes.
The villages having less than 10% ST population are Vellalagundam, Valayakaranoor, Korathupatti Vellayampatty, Karpakam, Thailanur, Adikarapatti Vedapatty, Chinnagoundapuram, Agraharanattamangalam Kullampatty, Valasaiyur, Sukkampatty, Palapatty Udayapatti, Achanguttapatty, Kuppanur, Pallipatty D.Perumapalayam, Yeripudhur, S.Nattamangalam Mettupattythathanoor, Koottathupatty, Vilampatty Karipatti, Perumalapalayam, J.Veeranam, Karumapuram M.Palapatty, Dasanaicenpatty, Masinaickenpatti Minnampalli, Mettuppatti, Anuppoor, Chinnanur.
The villages having more than 50% ST population are Chinavelampatti, Achnaguttapatty Pudur, Chirumalai Aranuthymalai, Kathripatty, Pallikadu, Pelapadi Aledipetti, Periyavelanpetti.
Sex ratio of Scheduled tribe population is 503.

Scheduled Tribes Literates and Illiterates by Sex:

	Persons	Males	Females
Literate	3,043	1,832	1,211
Illiterate	5,240	2,286	2,954
Literacy rate	41.9	51.1	32.9
Graduate	25	16	9

Scheduled Tribes (Dominant):
Malayali, Kurumans, Irular, Malakkuravan
Generic Tribes etc.

For their cultural identity please see Appendix-II

Villages without Scheduled Tribes: There are 22 villages without any scheduled tribe population.

Literates and Illiterates by Sex (Total Population):

	Persons	Males	Females
Literate	70,550	41,412	29,138
Illiterate	56,781	23,302	33,479
Literacy rate	63	73	53
Graduate	2,389	1,812	577

Agriculture: ***Distribution of villages according to land use:*** Out of 52 villages, Total area (in hectare) is 25140.57, out of that 55.06 percent is cultivable and 33.4 percent of the cultivable area is irrigated.

Sources of Irrigation (Hectares): Government Canal 10.48, Private Canal 0, Well without Electricity 437.3, Well with Electricity 3572.06, Tubewell without Electricity 95.16, Tubewell with Electricity 496.33, Tank 0, River 0, Lake 12.15, Waterfall 0, Others 0.

Villages with population of 5000 to 9999:
Mettupattithathanur, J.Veeranam, Udayapatti Minnampalli, Masinayakkampatti, Vellalakundam.

Villages with population of 10000 and above: None

Distribution of Workers:

	Persons	Males	Females	WPR

Cultivators	16,183	9,557	6,626	25.42
Agricultural Labour	23,187	11,187	12,000	36.43
Household Industry	2,719	1,157	1,562	4.27
Other Workers	21,564	17,528	4,036	33.88
Main Workers	54,151	36,233	17,918	85.07
Marginal Workers	9,502	3,196	6,306	14.93
Total Workers	63,653	39,429	24,224	

Religion: Major Religious Communities:

	Persons	Males	Females	Sex Ratio
Hindu (97.86%)	124,606	63,366	61,240	966
Muslim (0.28%)	357	181	176	972
Christian (1.76%)	2,245	1,106	1,139	1,030
Sikh (0%)	5	3	2	667
Buddhists (0%)	2	-	2	-
Jain (0%)	-	-	-	-

Agewise Data:

	Persons	Males	Females	Sex Ratio
All ages	127,331	64,714	62,617	968
0-14	35,998	18,848	17,150	910
15-44	63,047	31,602	31,445	995
45-79	26,756	13,397	13,359	997
80+	1,152	583	569	976
Age not stated	378	284	94	331

Languages (Dominant):
Tamil, Telugu, Urdu, Kannada, Gujarati

Disabled Population:

	Persons	Males	Females	%
Total Disabled	2,167	1,232	935	
In Seeing	970	523	447	44.76
In Speech	233	121	112	10.75
In Hearing	109	50	59	5.03
In Movement	653	413	240	30.13
Mentally	202	125	77	9.32

BARGUR

Bargur C.D. Block lies in the eastern part of Dharmapuri, district. It is a part of Krishnagiri and Pochampalli taluks. The Block is located at a distance of 44 kms. from district headquarters (Dharmapuri). There are 44 villages in the block with the total population of 167,965 persons. Area of the C.D. Block is 527.75 sq. kms. It is bounded in the north by the common boundary with the state of Andhra Pradesh, in the south by district Dharmapuri, in the east by C.D. Block Mathur and district Vellore, in the west by C.D. Blocks Krishnagiri and Kaveripattinam. CD Block Bargur falls in taluk Krishnagiri by 30 villages, and in taluk Pochampalli by 14 villages.

Communications:

Roadways : N.H.-46: Direction- Krishnagiri to Vaniyambadi, Nearest Villages- Guruvinayanapalli, Maganurpalli, Salinayanapalli, V Mathepalli, Mallapadi, Balinayanapalli, Orappam, Oppathavadi. N.H.-66: Direction- Krishnagiri to Uttangarai, Nearest Villages- Nadibanda (RF) Uni, Soolamalai, Chendrapalli, Jagadevipalayam, Puligunta, Thogarapalli RF UNI, Modikuppam. N.H.-219: Direction- Krishnagiri to Kuppam, Nearest Villages- Chinnamattarapalli, Varathampalli, Palepalli.

Annual Rainfall: Average Rainfall 760 mm.

Ground Water: Availability of the ground water in the Basin is (Information not available) H.A.M. and the utili zation is 160.44 H.A.M. It belongs to Over Expoited categ ory. Depth to water level varies from 2 to 5 meter below the ground. Most of the wells go down in summer months, according to the Ground Water Estimation Committee.

Forest and Reserved Forest: (Bargur RF)- Nearest Villages- Oppathavadi, Bargur R.F. Uni, Mallapadi. (Kottur)- Nearest Villages- Oppathavadi, Kottur (RF) Uni. (Nandibanda)- Nearest Villages- Oppathavadi, Nadibanda (RF) Uni. (Neralakotta)- Nearest Villages- Guruvinayanapalli, Neeralakottai (RF) G256 Uni, Oppathavadi, Salinayanapalli, Chinnamattarapalli, Varathampalli. (Varatanaballi)- Nearest Villages- Salinayanapalli, Varathampalli (RF) Uni, Chinnamattarapalli, Varathampalli, Palepalli, V Mathepalli. (Magarajaakadi)- Nearest Villages- Guruvinayanapalli, Varathampalli. (Thegarapalli)- Nearest Villages- Jagadevipalayam, Puligunta, Thogarapalli (RF) Uni, Ikondam Kothapalli.

Natural Division: Baramahal.

Administration

Revenue **Division:** Krishnagiri. Parliamentary Constituency: 9 Krishnagiri. District: Dharmapuri. Taluk: Krishnagiri, Pochampalli. Assembly Constituency: 51 Uthangarai (SC), 52 Bargur. Gram Panchayat: 36.

Border Villages- (Andhra Pradesh)- Nearest Villages- Guruvinayanapalli, Neeralakottai (RF) G256 Uni, Oppathavadi Kottur (RF) Uni.

Villages: 44 **Inhabited:** 38 **Uninhabited:** 6

Ranking	District	State	National
Area	6	31	1392
Population	2	3	1326
Sex Ratio	3	324	2829
Child Sex Ratio	8	322	5353
Literacy Rate	2	241	2151
Density	11	163	3366
Work Participation Rate	8	201	1596

Gram Panchayats:

Achamangalam, Anchoor , Balinayanapalli, Bandaseemanur, Batlapalli, Belavarathi, Belethottam, Chinnamatarapalli, Guruvinayanalli, Guttur, Ikondamkothapalli, Jagadevipalayam, Jinkalkadirampatti, Kandikuppam, Karakuppam, Kattagaram, Kondeppanayanapalli, Kullampatti , Mahadevagollahalli, Majethgollahalli, Malapadi,

Mathepalli, Oppathavadi, Orappam, Palepalli, Parandapalli, Perugopanapalli, Pochampalli, Puliyanpatti, Sigarapalli, Soolamalai, Thadampatti, Thogarapalli, Valasagundanoor, Varatanapalli , Veppalampatti, .

Amenities:

Education: Primary School in 36 villages, Middle school in 28 villages, Matriculation or Secondary School in 22 villages, namely Guruvinayanapalli, Oppathavadi, Salinayanapalli, Chinnamattarapalli, Varathampalli, Chinnathimminayanapalli, Palepalli, V Mathepalli, Mallapadi, Sigaralapalli, Kondappanayanapalli, Orappam, Chendrapalli, Guttur, Puligunta, Ikondam Kothapalli, Modikuppam, Kattagaram, Veppalampatti, Vadamalampatti, Jambukuttapatti, Beleethottam.

Higher Secondary or Pre University Courses or Intermediate or Junior College in 10 villages of the CD Block,, namely Varathampalli, Palepalli, V Mathepalli, Sigaralapalli, Orappam, Chendrapalli, Puligunta, Kattagaram, Vadamalampatti, Jambukuttapatti.

College in 2 villages, Adult Literacy Center in 0 village., Colleges are in villages, namely Oppathavadi, V Mathepalli.

Medical: Hospital in 0 village, Dispensary in 1 village, Health Center in 6 villages, Sub Center in 24 villages, Maternity and Child Welfare Center in 1 village, Community health workers in 27 villages.

The Village having Hospital or Dispensary or Health Center is Soolamalai.

Drinking Water: Tap water in 38 villages, Tank water in 1 villages, Well water in 38 villages, Tubewell in 38 villages and more than one source in 38 villages.

Bank: Banking facility in 11 villages, namely, Oppathavadi, Salinayanapalli, Varathampalli Palepalli, Mallapadi, Sigaralapalli, Jagadevipalayam Puligunta, Kattagaram, Vadamalampatti Jambukuttapatti.

Credit Society in 17 villages Agricultural Credit Society in 8 Non-Agricultural Credit Society in 7 villages.

Others: Power supply in 38 villages, Cinema hall in 2 villages, sport club in 0 village, Stadium or Auditorium or Community Hall in 0 village, Post Office in 38 villages.

There are 38 villages having bus facilities.

Villages with most of facilities: Oppathavadi Salinayanapalli, Varathampalli, Palepalli, Mallapadi Sigaralapalli, Jagadevipalayam, Puligunta Kattagaram, Vadamalampatti, Jambukuttapatti.

Villages without amenities (Education): Pedeepampatti, Mathenakeyanpalli..

Scheduled Castes: Out of the total population of 167965 persons, 22191 persons (13.21%) belong to Scheduled Castes.

The villages having less than 10% SC population are Guruvinayanapalli, Oppathavadi, Varathampalli Mallapadi, Kondappanayanapalli, Ikondam Kothapalli Mazidgollahalli, Modikuppam, Mahadavagollahalli Kadapasanthampatti, Kattagaram, Veppalampatti Pedeepampatti, Alerahalli, Mathenakeyanpalli Vadamalampatti, Thimminaickkanpatti.

The villages having more than 50% SC population are None.

Sex ratio of Scheduled Caste population is 498.

Scheduled Castes Literates and Illiterates by Sex:

	Persons	Males	Females
Literate	12,198	7,040	5,158
Illiterate	9,993	4,095	5,898
Literacy rate	63.8	73.4	54.1
Graduate	274	205	69

Scheduled Castes (Dominant):

Adi Dravida, Arunthathiyar, Valluvan, Panniandi Kuravan etc.

For their cultural identity please see Appendix-I

Villages without Scheduled Castes: There are 8 villages without any scheduled caste population.

Scheduled Tribes: Out of the total population of 167965 persons, 2005 persons (1.19%) belong to Scheduled Tribes.

The villages having less than 10% ST population are Guruvinayanapalli, Oppathavadi, Salinayanapalli Chinnamattarapalli, Varathampalli Chinnathimminayanapalli, Palepalli, V Mathepalli Mallapadi, Sigaralapalli, Kondappanayanapalli Achamangalam, Balinayanapalli, Orappam, Soolamalai Chendrapalli, Jagadevipalayam, Pasinayanapalli Batlapalli, Guttur, Puligunta, Ikondam Kothapalli Mazidgollahalli, Modikuppam, Mahadavagollahalli Kadapasanthampatti, Kattagaram, Veppalampatti Pedeepampatti, Alerahalli, Mathenakeyanpalli Vadamalampatti, Thimminaickkanpatti, Jambukuttapatti Beleethottam, Parandapalli, Thathampatty Jingalkathivampatti.

The villages having more than 50% ST population are None.

Sex ratio of Scheduled tribe population is 497.

Scheduled Tribes Literates and Illiterates by Sex:

	Persons	Males	Females
Literate	626	376	250
Illiterate	1,379	632	747
Literacy rate	38.4	45.4	31.3
Graduate	5	4	1

Scheduled Tribes (Dominant):

Irular, Kurumans, Malai Pandaram, Malayali

For their cultural identity please see Appendix-II

Villages without Scheduled Tribes: There are 22 villages without any scheduled tribe population.

Literates and Illiterates by Sex (Total Population):

	Persons	Males	Females
Literate	93,299	54,671	38,628
Illiterate	74,666	30,902	43,764
Literacy rate	64	74	54
Graduate	2,405	1,647	758

Agriculture: ***Distribution of villages according to land use:*** Out of 44 villages, Total area (in hectare) is 52775.1, out of that 66.19 percent is cultivable and 23.13 percent of the cultivable area is irrigated.

Sources of Irrigation (Hectares): Government Canal 0, Private Canal 0, Well without Electricity 2432, Well with Electricity 4360, Tubewell without Electricity 0, Tubewell with Electricity 0, Tank 1281, River 0, Lake 0, Waterfall 0, Others 7.3.

Villages with population of 5000 to 9999: Oppathavadi, Salinayanapalli, Varatanapalli Palepalle, Madepalli, Mallapadi, Siganalapalli Orappam, Chendrapalli, Jagadevipalayam, Puligunta Mahadevagollahalli, Kadappasandampatti, Kattagaram Vadamalampatti, Jambukuttapatti.

Villages with population of 10000 and above: None

Distribution of Workers:

	Persons	Males	Females	WPR
Cultivators	31,959	19,436	12,523	36.28
Agricultural Labour	35,915	15,727	20,188	40.77
Household Industry	1,691	621	1,070	1.92
Other Workers	18,522	14,414	4,108	21.03
Main Workers	71,371	44,351	27,020	81.02
Marginal Workers	16,716	5,847	10,869	18.98
Total Workers	88,087	50,198	37,889	

Religion: Major Religious Communities:

	Persons	Males	Females	Sex Ratio
Hindu (93.31%)	156,732	79,855	76,877	963
Muslim (3.34%)	5,612	2,860	2,752	962
Christian (3.26%)	5,482	2,779	2,703	973
Sikh (0.01%)	12	5	7	1,400
Buddhists (0%)	-	-	-	-
Jain (0.01%)	11	6	5	833

Agewise Data:

	Persons	Males	Females	Sex Ratio
All ages	167,965	85,573	82,392	963
0-14	51,975	27,079	24,896	919
15-44	80,344	40,203	40,141	998
45-79	33,805	17,307	16,498	953
80+	1,514	789	725	919
Age not stated	327	195	132	677

Languages (Dominant):

Tamil, Telugu, Kannada, Urdu, Hindi

Disabled Population:

	Persons	Males	Females	%
Total Disabled	4,586	1,651	2,935	
In Seeing	2,733	583	2,150	59.59
In Speech	339	171	168	7.39
In Hearing	151	83	68	3.29
In Movement	1,134	691	443	24.73
Mentally	229	123	106	4.99

BATLAGUNDU

Vattalakundu C.D. Block lies in the southern part of Dindigul district. It is a part of Nilakkottai taluk. The Block is located at at a distance of 38 kms. from district headquarters (Dindigul). There are 16 villages in the block with the total population of 64,717 persons. Area of the C.D. Block is 185.09 sq. kms. It is bounded in the north by CD Block Attur, in the south by district Madurai, in the east by C.D. Block Nilakkottai, in the west by CD Blcok Kodaikanal and district Theni.

Communications:

Roadway: S.H.-36: Direction- Pariyakulam to Nilakottai, Nearest Villages- Vatlagundu, Komnbaipatti, Mallanampatti.

River: Vaigai Nadi- Nearest Villages- Kunnuvarankottai, Pannaipatti, Viralipatti, Rengappanaickanpatti, Sandaiyur, Sokkapatti, Nadakottai.

Backwards Region Grants Fund: It receives Backward Region Grants.

Annual Rainfall: Average Rainfall 813 mm.

Ground Water: Availability of the ground water in the Basin is 2789.69 H.A.M. and the utilization is 4267.05 H.A.M. It belongs to Over Expoited category. Depth to water level varies from 5 to 20 meter below the ground. Most of the wells go down in summer months, according to the Ground Water Estimation Committee.

Natural Division: NA

Administration

Revenue **Division:** Dindigul. Parliamentary Constituency: 22 Dindigul. District: Dindigul. Taluk: Nilakkottai. Assembly Constituency: 130 Nilakkottai (SC). Gram Panchayat: 17.

Villages: 16 **Inhabited:** 14 **Uninhabited:** 2

Ranking	District	State	National
Area	14	303	4435
Population	13	319	4700
Sex Ratio	14	348	3546
Child Sex Ratio	14	348	5839
Literacy Rate	11	316	2697
Density	12	199	3109
Work Participation Rate	3	160	2059

Gram Panchayats:

G.Thummalapatti, Kanavaipatti , Kattakamanpatti, Kombaipatti, Kottaipatti, Kunnuvarankottai, Mallanampatti, Nadakottai, Old Vathalagundu, Pannaipatti-Viralipatti, Rengappanaickanpatti, Sandaiyur, Sekkapatti, Sengattampatti, Viralimayanpatti, Viralipatti, Viruveedu.

Amenities:

Education: Primary School in 14 villages, Middle school in 11 villages, Matriculation or Secondary School in 4 villages, namely Vatlagundu, Mallanampatti, Sokkapatti, Viruveedu.

Higher Secondary or Pre University Courses or Intermediate or Junior College in 1 village of the CD Block,, namely Vatlagundu.

College in 0 village, Adult Literacy Center in 0 village.

Medical: Hospital in 3 villages, Dispensary in 4 villages, Health Center in 5 villages, Sub Center in 10 villages, Maternity and Child Welfare Center in 3 villages, Community health workers in 4 villages.

The Villages having Hospital or Dispensary or Health Center are Kanavaipatti, Vatlagundu, Kunnuvarankottai , Viralipatti, Sokkapatti.

Drinking Water: Tap water in 14 villages, Tank water in 9 villages, Well water in 14 villages, Tubewell in 14 villages and more than one source in 14 villages.

Bank: Banking facility in 5 villages, namely, Kanavaipatti, Vatlagundu, Kunnuvarankottai Viralipatti, Viruveedu.

Credit Society in 5 villages Agricultural Credit Society in 5 Non-Agricultural Credit Society in 1 village.

Others: Power supply in 14 villages, Cinema hall in 2 villages, sport club in 1 village, Stadium or Auditorium or Community Hall in 3 villages, Post Office in 11 villages.

There are 12 villages having bus facilities.

Villages with most of facilities: Kanavaipatti Vatlagundu, Kunnuvarankottai, Viralipatti, Viruveedu.

Villages without Amenities (Education): None..

Scheduled Castes: Out of the total population of 64717 persons, 17620 persons (27.23%) belong to Scheduled Castes.

The villages having less than 10% SC population are None..

The villages having more than 50% SC population are None.

Sex ratio of Scheduled Caste population is 479.

Scheduled Castes Literates and Illiterates by Sex:

	Persons	Males	Females
Literate	8,360	5,155	3,205
Illiterate	9,260	4,023	5,237
Literacy rate	54.6	64.7	43.6
Graduate	215	135	80

Scheduled Castes (Dominant):

Pallan, Chakkiliyan, Paraiyan etc., Madari Arunthathiyar

For their cultural identity please see Appendix-I

Villages without Scheduled Castes: There are 3 villages without any scheduled caste population.

Scheduled Tribes: Out of the total population of 64717 persons, 510 persons (0.79%) belong to Scheduled Tribes.

The villages having less than 10% ST population are Sengattampatti, Kanavaipatti, Vatlagundu Komnbaipatti, Mallanampatti, Kunnuvarankottai Pannaipatti, Viralipatti, Rengappanaickanpatti Sandaiyur, Sokkapatti, Nadakottai, Viralimayanpatti Viruveedu.

The villages having more than 50% ST population are None.

Sex ratio of Scheduled tribe population is 469.

Scheduled Tribes Literates and Illiterates by Sex:

	Persons	Males	Females
Literate	281	168	113
Illiterate	229	103	126
Literacy rate	63.7	72.1	54.3
Graduate	1	1	0

Scheduled Tribes (Dominant):

Malai Vedan, Kattunayakan, Palliyan, Palleyan

For their cultural identity please see Appendix-II

Villages without Scheduled Tribes: There are 11 villages without any scheduled tribe population.

Literates and Illiterates by Sex (Total Population):

	Persons	Males	Females
Literate	34,337	20,461	13,876
Illiterate	30,380	12,736	17,644
Literacy rate	60	71	50
Graduate	733	525	208

Agriculture: ***Distribution of villages according to land use:*** Out of 16 villages, Total area (in hectare) is 18509.48, out of that 47.8 percent is cultivable and 61.58 percent of the cultivable area is irrigated.

Sources of Irrigation (Hectares): Government Canal 175.35, Private Canal 0, Well without Electricity 1241.52, Well with Electricity 3134.3, Tubewell without Electricity 75.6, Tubewell with Electricity 181.37, Tank 517.97, River 121.85, Lake 0, Waterfall 0, Others 0.

Villages with population of 5000 to 9999: Kanavoipatti , Kombaipatti, Viralipatti, Viruveedu.

Villages with population of 10000 and above: Vattalagundu.

Distribution of Workers:

	Persons	Males	Females	WPR
Cultivators	8,241	5,089	3,152	24.99

Agricultural Labour	19,005	9,761	9,244	57.64
Household Industry	700	371	329	2.12
Other Workers	5,026	3,890	1,136	15.24
Main Workers	24,650	15,037	9,613	74.76
Marginal Workers	8,322	4,074	4,248	25.24
Total Workers	32,972	19,111	13,861	

Religion: Major Religious Communities:

	Persons	Males	Females	Sex Ratio
Hindu (96.82%)	62,662	32,172	30,490	948
Muslim (0.65%)	420	212	208	981
Christian (2.4%)	1,552	773	779	1,008
Sikh (0.05%)	34	21	13	619
Buddhists (0.03%)	20	7	13	1,857
Jain (0%)	3	2	1	500

Agewise Data:

	Persons	Males	Females	Sex Ratio
All ages	64,717	33,197	31,520	949
0-14	18,993	10,176	8,817	866
15-44	31,282	15,813	15,469	978
45-79	13,639	6,790	6,849	1009
80+	558	284	274	965
Age not stated	245	134	111	828

Languages (Dominant):

Tamil, Telugu, Kannada, English, Urdu

Disabled Population:

	Persons	Males	Females	%
Total Disabled	1,800	778	1,022	
In Seeing	1,243	452	791	69.06
In Speech	141	81	60	7.83
In Hearing	49	26	23	2.72
In Movement	276	167	109	15.33
Mentally	91	52	39	5.06

BHAVANI

Bhavani C.D. Block lies in the northern part of Erode district. It is a part of Bhavani taluk. The Block is located at a distance of 15 kms. from district headquarters (Erode). There are 17 villages in the block with the total population of 97,392 persons. Area of the C.D. Block is 158.12 sq. kms. It is bounded in the north by C.D. Block Ammapet, in the south by CD Blocks Perundurai and Erode, in the east by District Namakkal, in the west by C.D. Blocks Anthiyur and Gobichettipalayam.

Communications:

Roadways : S.H.-15: Direction- Gobichettipalayam to Erode, Nearest Villages- Kavandapadi, Odathurai, Periyapuliyur, Chettipalayam. S.H.-20: Direction- Bhavani to Ammapettai, Neraest Villages- Varadhanullar, Thalakulam, Bhavani, Urachikottai.

River: Cauvery Nadi- Nearest Villages- Sanyasipatti, Varadhanullar, Bhavani, Andikulam, Urachikottai. Bhavani Nadi- Nearest Villages- Bhavani, Oricheri, Vairamangalam, Andikulam, Chinnapuliyur.

Annual Rainfall: Average Rainfall 789 mm.

Ground Water: Availability of the ground water in the Basin is 6210.36 H.A.M. and the utilization is 3595.98 H.A.M. It belongs to Safe category. Depth to water level varies from 2 to 10 meter below the ground. Most of the wells go down in summer months, according to the Ground Water Estimation Committee.

Natural Division: Kongu Nadu.

Administration

Revenue **Division:** Gobichettipalayam. Parliamentary Constituency: 18 Gobichettipalayam. District: Erode. Taluk: Bhavani. Assembly Constituency: 104 Bhavani. Gram Panchayat: 15.

Villages: 17 **Inhabited:** 17 **Uninhabited:** 0

Ranking	District	State	National
Area	17	336	4913
Population	3	139	3539
Sex Ratio	15	331	2982
Child Sex Ratio	11	270	4473
Literacy Rate	10	331	2867
Density	18	106	1762
Work Participation Rate	2	34	1057

Gram Panchayats:

Alathur, Andikulam, Chinnapuliyur, Kavandapadi, Mylambadi, Odathurai, Oricheri, Paruvachi, Periyapuliyur, Punnam, Sanyasipatti, Thottipalayam, Urachikottai, Varadanallur, Vyramangalam.

Amenities:

Education: Primary School in 16 villages, Middle school in 12 villages, Matriculation or Secondary School in 7 villages, namely Paruvachi, Mylambadi, Oricheri, Kavandapadi, Odathurai, Urachikottai, Periyapuliyur.

Higher Secondary or Pre University Courses or Intermediate or Junior College in 5 villages of the CD Block,, namely Paruvachi, Mylambadi, Oricheri, Kavandapadi, Urachikottai.

College in 1 village, Adult Literacy Center in 0 village., College in village, namely Periyapuliyur.

Medical: Hospital in 2 villages, Dispensary in 1 village, Health Center in 4 villages, Sub Center in 10 villages, Maternity and Child Welfare Center in 1 village, Community health workers in 14 villages.

The Villages having Hospital or Dispensary or Health Center are Paruvachi, Kavandapadi, Odathurai.

Drinking Water: Tap water in 17 villages, Tank water in 0 villages, Well water in 17 villages, Tubewell in 17 villages and more than one source in 17 villages.

Bank: Banking facility in 4 villages, namely, Paruvachi, Bhavani, Kavandapadi, Odathurai.

Credit Society in 8 villages Agricultural Credit Society in 8 Non-Agricultural Credit Society in 1 village.

Others: Power supply in 17 villages, Cinema hall in 2 villages, sport club in 0 village, Stadium or Auditorium or Community Hall in 1 village, Post Office in 16 villages.

There are 17 villages having bus facilities.

Villages with most of facilities: Paruvachi Bhavani, Kavandapadi, Odathurai.

Villages without amenities (Education): Thalakulam..

Scheduled Castes: Out of the total population of 97392 persons, 14163 persons (14.54%) belong to Scheduled Castes.

The villages having less than 10% SC population are None..

The villages having more than 50% SC population are None.

Sex ratio of Scheduled Caste population is 497.

Scheduled Castes Literates and Illiterates by Sex:

	Persons	Males	Females
Literate	5,581	3,350	2,231
Illiterate	8,582	3,777	4,805
Literacy rate	44.5	52.8	36.0
Graduate	110	70	40

Scheduled Castes (Dominant):

Chakkiliyan, Arunthathiyar, Adi Dravida Paraiyan etc., Madari

For their cultural identity please see Appendix-I

Villages without Scheduled Castes: There is 0 village without any scheduled caste population.

Scheduled Tribes: Out of the total population of 97392 persons, 421 persons (0.43%) belong to Scheduled Tribes.

The villages having less than 10% ST population are Paruvachi, Punnam, Mylambadi, Sanyasipatti Varadhanullar, Thalakulam, Bhavani, Oricheri Vairamangalam, Alathur, Kavandapadi, Odathurai Andikulam, Urachikottai, Chinnapuliyur Periyapuliyur, Chettipalayam.

The villages having more than 50% ST population are None.

Sex ratio of Scheduled tribe population is 515.

Scheduled Tribes Literates and Illiterates by Sex:

	Persons	Males	Females
Literate	324	158	166
Illiterate	97	46	51
Literacy rate	84.6	88.3	81.4
Graduate	30	21	9

Scheduled Tribes (Dominant):

Kondareddis, Malai Pandaram, Irular, Kurumans Konda Kapus

For their cultural identity please see Appendix-II

Villages without Scheduled Tribes: There are 12 villages without any scheduled tribe population.

Literates and Illiterates by Sex (Total Population):

	Persons	Males	Females
Literate	52,188	31,236	20,952
Illiterate	45,204	18,445	26,759
Literacy rate	60	70	49
Graduate	2,505	1,700	805

Agriculture: ***Distribution of villages according to land use:*** Out of 17 villages, Total area (in hectare) is 15812.28, out of that 71.8 percent is cultivable and 73.36 percent of the cultivable area is irrigated.

Sources of Irrigation (Hectares): Government Canal 5849.6, Private Canal 0, Well without Electricity 0, Well with Electricity 1929.94, Tubewell without Electricity 0, Tubewell with Electricity 0, Tank 28.19, River 504.35, Lake 0, Waterfall 0, Others 16.71.

Villages with population of 5000 to 9999: Paruvachi, Punnam, Mylambadi, Oricheri, Odathurai Urachikottai, Periyapuliyur.

Villages with population of 10000 and above: Bhavani , Kavandapadi.

Distribution of Workers:

	Persons	Males	Females	WPR
Cultivators	10,258	6,158	4,100	18.71
Agricultural Labour	22,822	11,376	11,446	41.62
Household Industry	6,208	3,001	3,207	11.32
Other Workers	15,552	11,955	3,597	28.36
Main Workers	51,651	31,457	20,194	94.18
Marginal Workers	3,189	1,033	2,156	5.82
Total Workers	54,840	32,490	22,350	

Religion: Major Religious Communities:

	Persons	Males	Females	Sex Ratio
Hindu (97.71%)	95,161	48,585	46,576	959
Muslim (0.88%)	859	439	420	957
Christian (1.3%)	1,264	602	662	1,100
Sikh (0.01%)	12	10	2	200
Buddhists (0%)	2	-	2	-
Jain (0%)	3	-	3	-

Agewise Data:

	Persons	Males	Females	Sex Ratio
All ages	97,392	49,681	47,711	960
0-14	21,917	11,543	10,374	899
15-44	47,778	23,966	23,812	994
45-79	26,352	13,484	12,868	954
80+	1,156	575	581	1010
Age not stated	189	113	76	673

Languages (Dominant):

Tamil, Telugu, Kannada, Urdu, Malayalam

Disabled Population:

	Persons	Males	Females	%
Total Disabled	2,356	861	1,495	
In Seeing	1,510	378	1,132	64.09
In Speech	139	68	71	5.9
In Hearing	96	40	56	4.07
In Movement	459	290	169	19.48
Mentally	152	85	67	6.45

BHAVANISAGAR

Bhavanisagar C.D. Block lies in the northern part of Erode district. It is a part of Sathyamangalam taluk. The Block is located at a distance of 80 kms. from district headquarters (Erode). There are 27 villages in the block with the total population of 76,022 persons. Area of the C.D. Block is 221.74 sq. kms. It is bounded in the north by C.D. Blocks Talavadi and Sathyamangalam, in the south by district Coimatore and CD Block Nambiyur, in the east by C.D. Block Sathyamangalam, in the west by C.D. Block Talavadi and district Coimbatore.

Communications:

Roadways : N.H.-209: Direction- Chamrajanagar to Avanashi, Nearest Villages- Vinnappalli, Pungampalli, Thatchuperumalpuram, Nallur, Kurumbapalayam, Sungakkaranpalayam. S.H.-15: Direction- Mettuppalayam to Ariyappampalayam, Nearest Villages- Periakallipatti, Panayampalli, Velamundi RF, Ayyampalayam, Karidaddampalayam, Akkaraithathappalli, Boosaripalayam.

River: Bhavani Nadi- Nearest Villages- Pungar, Kothamangalam, Thoppampalayam, Ikkarai Thatha, Palli, Bagutham Palayam, Akkaraithathappalli, Dhoddampalayam, Mudukkanthurai, Boosaripalayam.

Canal: (Bhavani)- Nearest Villages- Boosaripalayam, Akkaraithathappalli, Dhoddampalayam, Thoppampalayam, Karidaddampalayam.

Annual Rainfall: Average Rainfall 789 mm.

Ground Water: Availability of the ground water in the Basin is 3069.02 H.A.M. and the utilization is 2892.72 H.A.M. It belongs to Critical category. Depth to water level varies from 2 to 10 meter below the ground. Most of the wells go down in summer months, according to the Ground Water Estimation Committee.

Forest and Reserved Forest: (Talamalai RF)- Nearest Villages- Pungar, Kothamangalam, Ikkarai Thatha Palli, Thoppampalayam, Velamundi RF, Ayyampalayam, Periakallipatti, Panayampalli.

Natural Division: Kongu Nadu.

Administration

Revenue **Division:** Gobichettipalayam. Parliamentary Constituency: 18 Gobichettipalayam. District: Erode. Taluk: Sathyamangalam. Assembly Constituency: 107 Sathyamangalam (SC), 106 Gobichettipalayam. Gram Panchayat: 15.

Villages: 27 **Inhabited:** 26 **Uninhabited:** 1

Ranking	**District**	**State**	**National**
Area	11	260	3829
Population	7	263	4252
Sex Ratio	18	350	3685
Child Sex Ratio	6	152	2733
Literacy Rate	11	337	2927
Density	16	84	3164
Work Participation Rate	9	167	803

Gram Panchayats:

Desipalayam, Karapadi, Kavilipalayam, Kothamangalam, Madampalayam, Mudukkanthurai , Nallur, Nochikuttai, Panayampalli, Periyakallipatti, Pungur , Thoppampalayam, Uthandiyur, Varapalayam, Vinnappalli.

Amenities:

Education: Primary School in 25 villages, Middle school in 8 villages, Matriculation or Secondary School in 5 villages, namely Dhoddampalayam, Vinnappalli, Panayampalli, Nallur, Kavilipalayam.

Higher Secondary or Pre University Courses or Intermediate or Junior College in 2 villages of the CD Block,, namely Nallur, Kavilipalayam.

College in 0 village, Adult Literacy Center in 1 village.

Medical: Hospital in 5 villages, Dispensary in 1 village, Health Center in 2 villages, Sub Center in 20 villages, Maternity and Child Welfare Center in 4 villages, Community health workers in 8 villages.

The Villages having Hospital or Dispensary or Health Center are Pungar, Kothamangalam, Dhoddampalayam, Periakallipatti, Nallur, Kavilipalayam.

Drinking Water: Tap water in 26 villages, Tank water in 0 villages, Well water in 26 villages, Tubewell in 26 villages and more than one source in 26 villages.

Bank: Banking facility in 4 villages, namely, Boosaripalayam, Dhoddampalayam, Panayampalli Kavilipalayam.

Credit Society in 8 villages Agricultural Credit Society in 8 Non-Agricultural Credit Society in 0 village.

Others: Power supply in 26 villages, Cinema hall in 1 village, sport club in 0 village, Stadium or Auditorium or Community Hall in 0 village, Post Office in 25 villages.

There are 25 villages having bus facilities.

Villages with most of facilities: Boosaripalayam Dhoddampalayam, Panayampalli, Kavilipalayam.

Villages without amenities (Education): Sellappampalayam..

Scheduled Castes: Out of the total population of 76022 persons, 15771 persons (20.75%) belong to Scheduled Castes.

The villages having less than 10% SC population are None..

The villages having more than 50% SC population are None.

Sex ratio of Scheduled Caste population is 487.

Scheduled Castes Literates and Illiterates by Sex:

	Persons	Males	Females
Literate	5,405	3,339	2,066
Illiterate	10,366	4,754	5,612
Literacy rate	38.6	46.5	30.3
Graduate	31	27	4

Scheduled Castes (Dominant):

Chakkiliyan, Arunthathiyar, Adi Dravida, Pallan Kuravan etc.

For their cultural identity please see Appendix-I

Villages without Scheduled Castes: There is 1 village without any scheduled caste population.

Scheduled Tribes: Out of the total population of 76022 persons, 141 persons (0.19%) belong to Scheduled Tribes.

The villages having less than 10% ST population are Pungar, Kothamangalam, Ikkarai Thatha Palli Bagutham Palayam, Boosaripalayam Akkaraithathappalli, Dhoddampalayam, Mudukkanthurai Thoppampalayam, Karidaddampalayam, Vinnappalli Kurumbapalayam, Ayyampalayam, Periakallipatti Panayampalli, Sungakkaranpalayam, Pungampalli Thatchuperumalpuram, Sellappampalayam, Nallur Marayeepalayam, Madampalayam, P. Puliyampatti Karapadi, Kavilipalayam, Varapalayam.

The villages having more than 50% ST population are None.

Sex ratio of Scheduled tribe population is 504.

Scheduled Tribes Literates and Illiterates by Sex:

	Persons	Males	Females
Literate	68	43	25
Illiterate	73	27	46
Literacy rate	54.4	68.3	40.3
Graduate	1	0	1

Scheduled Tribes (Dominant):

Mudugar etc., Irular, Kurumans, Malakkuravan Malai Pandaram

For their cultural identity please see Appendix-II

Villages without Scheduled Tribes: There are 18 villages without any scheduled tribe population.

Literates and Illiterates by Sex (Total Population):

	Persons	Males	Females
Literate	40,542	24,438	16,104
Illiterate	35,480	14,635	20,845
Literacy rate	59	69	48
Graduate	863	567	296

Agriculture: *Distribution of villages according to land use:*

Out of 27 villages, Total area (in hectare) is 22174.63, out of that 48.07 percent is cultivable and 32.83 percent of the cultivable area is irrigated.

Sources of Irrigation (Hectares): Government Canal 596.16, Private Canal 0, Well without Electricity 223.37, Well with Electricity 2593.77, Tubewell without Electricity 0, Tubewell with Electricity 0, Tank 0, River 86.51, Lake 0, Waterfall 0, Others 0.

Villages with population of 5000 to 9999:

Nallur.

Villages with population of 10000 and above: None

Distribution of Workers:

	Persons	Males	Females	WPR
Cultivators	10,189	6,210	3,979	23.33
Agricultural Labour	14,977	7,745	7,232	34.29
Household Industry	3,496	2,013	1,483	8
Other Workers	15,017	10,624	4,393	34.38
Main Workers	40,555	25,810	14,745	92.85
Marginal Workers	3,124	782	2,342	7.15
Total Workers	43,679	26,592	17,087	

Religion: Major Religious Communities:

	Persons	Males	Females	Sex Ratio
Hindu (96.6%)	73,439	37,700	35,739	948
Muslim (0.48%)	365	203	162	798
Christian (2.82%)	2,142	1,117	1,025	918
Sikh (0.03%)	26	23	3	130
Buddhists (0%)	2	2	-	-
Jain (0%)	2	2	-	-

Agewise Data:

	Persons	Males	Females	Sex Ratio
All ages	76,022	39,073	36,949	946
0-14	17,095	8,761	8,334	951
15-44	37,314	18,995	18,319	964
45-79	20,192	10,597	9,595	905
80+	1,089	553	536	969
Age not stated	332	167	165	988

Languages (Dominant):

Tamil, Telugu, Kannada, Hindi, Urdu

Disabled Population:

	Persons	Males	Females	%
Total Disabled	2,489	1,037	1,452	
In Seeing	1,535	503	1,032	61.67
In Speech	184	92	92	7.39
In Hearing	147	67	80	5.91
In Movement	477	303	174	19.16
Mentally	146	72	74	5.87

BHUVANAGIRI

Bhuvanagiri C.D. Block lies in the east central part of Cuddalore district. It is a part of Chidambaram taluk. The

Block is located at a distance of 42 kms. from district headquarters (Cuddalore). There are 50 villages in the block with the total population of 77,980 persons. Area of the C.D. Block is 163.66 sq. kms. It is bounded in the north by CD Blocks Kaumapuram and Kurinjipadi, in the south by CD Blocks Kattumannakoil, Komarathi and Keerapalayam, in the east by C.D. Blocks Keerapalayam and Parangipettai, and in the west by CD Block Kammapuram.

Communications:

Roadways : S.H.-8: Direction- Sethiyathope to Neyvali, Nearest Villages- Pinnalur, Anaiwari, Miralur.

River: Vellar Nadi- Nearest Villages- Agaraalambadi, B.Adhanoor, Periyanarkunam, Veeramudiyanatham, Vatharayanthethu, Kilavadinatham, Azhicikudi, Vandurayanpattu, Melamoongiladi, Kezhamoongiladi, Miralur.

Backwards Region Grants Fund: It receives Backward Region Grants.

Annual Rainfall: Average Rainfall 1050 mm.

Ground Water: Availability of the ground water in the Basin is 9703.62 MCM and the utilization is 5392.64 MCM. It belongs to Semi Critical category. Depth to water level varies from 2 to 10 meter below the ground. Most of the wells go down in summer months, according to the Ground Water Estimation Committee.

Natural Division: Tondai Nadu.

Administration

Revenue **Division:** Chidambaram. Parliamentary Constituency: 27 Chidambaram (SC). District: Cuddalore. Taluk: Chidambaram. Assembly Constituency: 157 Bahuvanagiri, 158 Chidambaram. Gram Panchayat: 47.

Villages: 50 **Inhabited:** 50 **Uninhabited:** 0

Ranking	District	State	National
Area	12	333	4813
Population	13	252	4170
Sex Ratio	6	254	1859
Child Sex Ratio	5	123	2297
Literacy Rate	5	137	1432
Density	11	306	2323
Work Participation Rate	5	66	3500

Gram Panchayats:

Agara Alambadi, Alambadi(Kaspa), Ambapuram, Anaivari, Azhichikudi, B.Udaiyur, Beetharayanpettai, C.Mutlur , Chinna Nerkunam, Chokkankollai, Ellaikudi, Erumbur, Jayankondam, Karaimedu, Kathazhai, Kezhamoongiladi, Krishnapuram , Krishnapuram, Kulakudi, Kumudimoolai, Lalpuram, Manjakollai, Marudur, Melanuvampattu, Melmanakudi, Melmoongiladi, Miralur, Nathamedu, Nellikollai, Periya Nerkunam, Pinnalur, Prasannaramapuram, Sathapadi, Sitheri, Thalaikulam (Then), Thalaikulam (Vada) , Therkuthittai, Thethampalayam, Thillainayakapuram, Thurinjikollai, Uluthur, Vadakkuthittai, Valayamadevi kizhpathi, Valayamadevi Melpathi, Vatharayanthethu, Veeramudaiyanatham.

Amenities:

Education: Primary School in 46 villages, Middle school in 15 villages, Matriculation or Secondary School in 8 villages, namely Vallayamadhevi, Pinnalur, Vadakrishnapuram, Erumbore, Valayamadeer(Mel), Manjakollai, Thenthalaikkulam, C.Mutlur.

Higher Secondary or Pre University Courses or Intermediate or Junior College in 2 villages of the CD Block,, namely Valayamadeer(Mel), C.Mutlur.

College in 0 village, Adult Literacy Center in 0 village.

Medical: Hospital in 1 village, Dispensary in 2 villages, Health Center in 5 villages, Sub Center in 13 villages, Maternity and Child Welfare Center in 3 villages, Community health workers in 20 villages.

The Villages having Hospital or Dispensary or Health Center are Thenthalaikkulam, Melenuvanpattu.

Drinking Water: Tap water in 50 villages, Tank water in 1 villages, Well water in 50 villages, Tubewell in 50 villages and more than one source in 50 villages.

Bank: Banking facility in 7 villages, namely, Vallayamadhevi, Pinnalur, Uluthur, Thenthalaikkulam Thenkrishnapuram, C.Mutlur, B.Odaiyur.

Credit Society in 10 villages Agricultural Credit Society in 8 Non-Agricultural Credit Society in 2 villages.

Others: Power supply in 50 villages, Cinema hall in 0 village, sport club in 0 village, Stadium or Auditorium or Community Hall in 0 village, Post Office in 48 villages.

There are 46 villages having bus facilities.

Villages with most of facilities: Vallayamadhevi Pinnalur, Uluthur, Thenthalaikkulam, C.Mutlur B.Odaiyur.

Villages without amenities (Education): Prasannaramapuram, Seeyapadi, Vandurayanpattu, Melasokkamethapettai..

Scheduled Castes: Out of the total population of 77980 persons, 27831 persons (35.69%) belong to Scheduled Castes. The villages having less than 10% SC population are Prasannaramapuram, Valayamadeer(Mel), Anaiwari Thenthalaikkulam, Thenkrishnapuram, Paluthanari.

The villages having more than 50% SC population are Pinnalur, Jayankondan, Nathamedu, Marudhur, Miralur Kasba Alambadi, B.Odaiyur, Kilavadinatham Melasokkamethapettai, Thilaynayagapuram.

Sex ratio of Scheduled Caste population is 497.

Scheduled Castes Literates and Illiterates by Sex:

	Persons	Males	Females
Literate	14,706	8,704	6,002
Illiterate	13,125	5,284	7,841
Literacy rate	61.3	72.3	50.3
Graduate	370	279	91

Scheduled Castes (Dominant):
Adi Dravida, Arunthathiyar, Generic Castes etc. Valluvan, Kuravan etc.

For their cultural identity please see Appendix-I

Villages without Scheduled Castes: There is 1 village without any scheduled caste population.

Scheduled Tribes: Out of the total population of 77980 persons, 614 persons (0.79%) belong to Scheduled Tribes. The villages having less than 10% ST population are Kathazhai, Vallayamadhevi, Thurinjikollai, Pinnalur B.Kolakkudi, Ellaikudi, Kumudimoolai, Jayankondan Nathamedu, Chockangollai, Sathappadi, Vadakkuthettai Vadakrishnapuram, Marudhur, Vadathalaikulam Prasannaramapuram, Ambapuram, Nellikollai, Erumbore Valayamadeer(Mel), Agaraalambadi, B.Adhanoor Periyanarkunam, Chinnanarakunam, Veeramudiyanatham Anaiwari, Miralur, Manjakollai, Uluthur Thenthalaikkulam, Thenkrishnapuram, Melamanakudi C.Mutlur, B.Sitheri, Therkuthittai Bhodhavarayanpettai, Kasba Alambadi, B.Odaiyur Seeyapadi, Vatharayanthethu, Kilavadinatham Azhicikudi, Vandurayanpattu, Melamoongiladi Kezhamoongiladi, Melenuvanpattu Melasokkamethapettai, Lalpuram, Thilaynayagapuram. The villages having more than 50% ST population are None.

Sex ratio of Scheduled tribe population is 482.

Scheduled Tribes Literates and Illiterates by Sex:

	Persons	Males	Females
Literate	142	100	42
Illiterate	472	218	254
Literacy rate	28.6	39.4	17.4
Graduate	0	0	0

Scheduled Tribes (Dominant):
Kattunayakan, Irular, Malakkuravan Generic Tribes etc.

For their cultural identity please see Appendix-II

Villages without Scheduled Tribes: There are 33 villages without any scheduled tribe population.

Literates and Illiterates by Sex (Total Population):

	Persons	Males	Females
Literate	46,706	27,609	19,097
Illiterate	31,274	11,694	19,580
Literacy rate	68	80	56
Graduate	1,358	1,042	316

Agriculture: ***Distribution of villages according to land use:*** Out of 50 villages, Total area (in hectare) is 16366.98, out of that 80.57 percent is cultivable and 83.89 percent of the cultivable area is irrigated.

Sources of Irrigation (Hectares): Government Canal 6586.64, Private Canal 0, Well without Electricity 12.76, Well with Electricity 18.36, Tubewell without Electricity 1184.94, Tubewell with Electricity 2794.43, Tank 364.26, River 0, Lake 0, Waterfall 0, Others 0.

Villages with population of 5000 to 9999: None

Villages with population of 10000 and above: None

Distribution of Workers:

	Persons	Males	Females	WPR
Cultivators	7,108	5,678	1,430	20.18
Agricultural Labour	21,778	12,107	9,671	61.84
Household Industry	848	370	478	2.41
Other Workers	5,481	4,492	989	15.56
Main Workers	23,923	17,268	6,655	67.93
Marginal Workers	11,292	5,379	5,913	32.07
Total Workers	35,215	22,647	12,568	

Religion: Major Religious Communities:

	Persons	Males	Females	Sex Ratio
Hindu (96.11%)	74,946	37,774	37,172	984
Muslim (0.59%)	457	221	236	1,068
Christian (3.27%)	2,553	1,293	1,260	974
Sikh (0.01%)	5	4	1	250
Buddhists (0%)	2	-	2	-
Jain (0%)	1	1	-	-

Agewise Data:

	Persons	Males	Females	Sex Ratio
All ages	77,980	39,303	38,677	984
0-14	21,565	10,910	10,655	977
15-44	37,626	18,677	18,949	1015
45-79	17,834	9,194	8,640	940
80+	671	375	296	789
Age not stated	284	147	137	932

Languages (Dominant):
Tamil, Telugu, Urdu, Malayalam, Kannada

Disabled Population:

	Persons	Males	Females	%
Total Disabled	1,888	986	902	
In Seeing	1,022	473	549	54.13
In Speech	148	89	59	7.84
In Hearing	123	54	69	6.51
In Movement	465	299	166	24.63
Mentally	130	71	59	6.89

BODINAYAKANUR

Bodinayakanur C.D. Block lies in the north-western part of Theni district. It is a part of Bodinayakanur taluk. The Block is located at a distance of 16 kms. from district headquarters (Theni-Allinagaram). There are 12 villages in the block with the total population of 65,789 persons. Area of the C.D. Block is 446.47 sq. kms. It is bounded in the north by district Dindigul and CD Block Periyakulam, in the south by CD Blocks Uthamapalayam, Chinnamunur and Theni, in the east by CD Blocks Theni and Periyakulam. It has common boundary with the state of Kerala on north-west and west.

Communications:

Roadways : N.H.-49: Direction- Bodimethu to Theni, Nearest Villages- Kodangipatty, Bodinayakanur. N.H.-220: Direction- Kuchanur to Virappandi, Nearest Villages- Uppukkottai, Koolayanur.

River: Theni Nadi- Nearest Villages- Kodangipatty, B.Meenachipuram. Surilli Nadi- Nearest Villages- Uppukkottai, Koolayanur.

Annual Rainfall: Average Rainfall 709 mm.

Ground Water: Availability of the ground water in the Basin is 4743.99 H.A.M. and the utilization is 4464. 07 H.A.M. It belongs to Critical category. Depth to water level varies from 0 to 10 meter below the ground. Most of the wells go down in summer months, according to the Ground Water Estimation Committee.

Natural Division: NA

Administration

Revenue **Division:** Uthampalayam. Parliamentary Constituency: 33 Theni. District: Theni. Taluk: Bodinayakanur. Assembly Constituency: 200 Bodinayankanur. Gram Panchayat: 15.

Border Villages- (Kerala)- Nearest Village- Kottagudi.

Villages: 12 **Inhabited:** 12 **Uninhabited:** 0

Ranking	District	State	National
Area	2	45	1691
Population	4	309	4651
Sex Ratio	5	285	2242
Child Sex Ratio	2	335	5510
Literacy Rate	7	249	2172
Density	4	85	5600
Work Participation Rate	6	364	824

Gram Panchayats:

Ahamalai, Ammapatti , Anaikaraipatti, Dombucheri, Kamarajapuram, Kodangipatti , Kottagudi, Kulaiyanur, Maniampatti, Manjinaickenpatti, Nagalapuram, Rasingapuram , Silamalai, Sillamarathupatti, Uppukottai

Amenities:

Education: Primary School in 11 villages, Middle school in 7 villages, Matriculation or Secondary School in 6 villages, namely B.Meenachipuram, Silamalai, Ammapatty, Dombuchery, Uppukkottai, Rasingapuram.

Higher Secondary or Pre University Courses or Intermediate or Junior College in 1 village of the CD Block,, namely Ammapatty.

College in 1 village, Adult Literacy Center in 0 village., Colleges are in villages, namely Ammapatty.

Medical: Hospital in 3 villages, Dispensary in 3 villages, Health Center in 4 villages, Sub Center in 11 villages, Maternity and Child Welfare Center in 7 villages, Community health workers in 3 villages.

The Villages having Hospital or Dispensary or Health Center are Kottagudi, Kodangipatty, Silamalai, Ammapatty, Dombuchery, Rasingapuram.

Drinking Water: Tap water in 12 villages, Tank water in 8 villages, Well water in 12 villages, Tubewell in 12 villages and more than one source in 12 villages.

Bank: Banking facility in 1 villages, namely, Rasingapuram.

Credit Society in 6 villages Agricultural Credit Society in 6 Non-Agricultural Credit Society in 1 village.

Others: Power supply in 12 villages, Cinema hall in 2 villages, sport club in 0 village, Stadium or Auditorium or Community Hall in 1 village, Post Office in 12 villages.

There are 11 villages having bus facilities.

Villages with most of facilities: Rasingapuram.

Villages without amenities (Education): Bodinorthhills..

Scheduled Castes: Out of the total population of 65786 persons, 11662 persons (17.73%) belong to Scheduled Castes. The villages having less than 10% SC population are None..

The villages having more than 50% SC population are None.

Sex ratio of Scheduled Caste population is 487.

Scheduled Castes Literates and Illiterates by Sex:

	Persons	Males	Females
Literate	5,828	3,604	2,224
Illiterate	5,834	2,381	3,453
Literacy rate	57.3	69.6	44.5
Graduate	50	42	8

Scheduled Castes (Dominant):

Pallan, Chakkiliyan, Paraiyan etc., Pulayan etc. Mala

For their cultural identity please see Appendix-I

Villages without Scheduled Castes: There is 0 village without any scheduled caste population.

Scheduled Tribes: Out of the total population of 65786 persons, 686 persons (1.04%) belong to Scheduled Tribes. The villages having less than 10% ST population are Kottagudi, Bodinorthhills, Agamalai, Kodangipatty B.Meenachipuram, Silamalai, Ammapatty, Dombuchery Uppukkottai, Koolayanur, Rasingapuram.

The villages having more than 50% ST population are

None.

Sex ratio of Scheduled tribe population is 507.

Scheduled Tribes Literates and Illiterates by Sex:

	Persons	Males	Females
Literate	139	90	49
Illiterate	547	248	299
Literacy rate	24.1	31.6	16.7
Graduate	0	0	0

Scheduled Tribes (Dominant):

Palliyar, Mudugar etc., Palliyan, Paniyan, Muthuvan

For their cultural identity please see Appendix-II

Villages without Scheduled Tribes: There are 6 villages without any scheduled tribe population.

Literates and Illiterates by Sex (Total Population):

	Persons	Males	Females
Literate	37,182	22,396	14,786
Illiterate	28,604	10,915	17,689
Literacy rate	64	76	51
Graduate	282	218	64

Agriculture: ***Distribution of villages according to land use:*** Out of 12 villages, Total area (in hectare) is 44647.69, out of that 37.54 percent is cultivable and 46.22 percent of the cultivable area is irrigated.

Sources of Irrigation (Hectares): Government Canal 1386.43, Private Canal 0, Well without Electricity 52.5, Well with Electricity 2848.68, Tubewell without Electricity 100, Tubewell with Electricity 919.5, Tank 1073.36, River 988.66, Lake 0, Waterfall 0, Others 80.

Villages with population of 5000 to 9999:

Silamalai, Dombucheri, Uppukottai , Rasingapuram.

Villages with population of 10000 and above:

Kodangipatti , Ammapatti (Bodi).

Distribution of Workers:

	Persons	Males	Females	WPR
Cultivators	3,916	2,504	1,412	10.52
Agricultural Labour	23,650	11,486	12,164	63.56
Household Industry	709	367	342	1.91
Other Workers	8,935	6,175	2,760	24.01
Main Workers	36,093	20,176	15,917	97
Marginal Workers	1,117	356	761	3
Total Workers	37,210	20,532	16,678	

Religion: Major Religious Communities:

	Persons	Males	Females	Sex Ratio
Hindu (98.66%)	64,904	32,868	32,036	975
Muslim (0.23%)	153	68	85	1,250
Christian (0.96%)	630	324	306	944
Sikh (0.01%)	8	5	3	600
Buddhists (0.01%)	5	5	-	-
Jain (0%)	1	-	1	-

Agewise Data:

	Persons	Males	Females	Sex Ratio
All ages	65,786	33,311	32,475	975
0-14	17,127	9,005	8,122	902
15-44	32,364	16,257	16,107	991
45-79	15,379	7,591	7,788	1026
80+	588	285	303	1063
Age not stated	328	173	155	896

Languages (Dominant):

Tamil, Kannada, Telugu, Urdu, Malayalam

Disabled Population:

	Persons	Males	Females	%
Total Disabled	1,962	941	1,021	
In Seeing	1,301	573	728	66.31
In Speech	132	78	54	6.73
In Hearing	38	15	23	1.94
In Movement	382	214	168	19.47
Mentally	109	61	48	5.56

BOGALUR

Bogalur C.D. Block lies in the central east part of Ramanathauram district. It is a part of Paramakudi taluk. The taluk is located at a distance of 38 kms. from district headquarters (Ramanathauram). There are 23 villages in the block with the total population of 39,246 persons. Area of the C.D. Block is 177.12 sq. kms. It is bounded in the north by CD Block Nainarkoil, in the south by CD Blocks Mudukulathur and Tiruppullani, in the east by CD Block Ramanathapuram, in the west by CD Blocks Mudukulathur and Paramakudi.

Communications:

Roadways : S.H.-34: Direction- Ilayangudi to Ramanathauram, Nearest Villages- Nagachi, Muthalur. N.H.-49: Direction- Paramukudi to Ramanathauram, Nearest Villages- Manjoor, Pandikanmai, Kumukottai, Keelakottai, Ariyaku di, Theeyanur, Ettivayal.

Railway Station: Manjoor, Bogaloor.

River: Vaigai Nadi- Nearest Villages- Manjakollai, Kakkandal, Mennenthi, Nagachi, Sevoor, Muthalur, Kamankottai.

Annual Rainfall: Average Rainfall 827 mm.

Ground Water: Availability of the ground water in the Basin is 2114.28 H.A.M. and the utilization is 233.36 H.A.M. It belongs to Safe category. Depth to water level varies from 2 to 10 meter below the ground. Most of the wells go down in summer months, according to the Ground Water Estimation Committee.

Natural Division: NA

Administration

Revenue **Division:** Paramkudi. Parliamentary Constituency: 35 Ramanathapuram. District: Ramanathapuram. Taluk: Paramakudi. Assembly Constituency: 209 Paramakudi (SC). Gram Panchayat: 26.

Villages: 23 **Inhabited:** 23 **Uninhabited:** 0

Ranking	District	State	National
Area	11	318	4581
Population	11	373	5769
Sex Ratio	8	63	507
Child Sex Ratio	1	24	644
Literacy Rate	5	149	1505
Density	2	48	4426
Work Participation Rate	5	306	426

Gram Panchayats:
Ariyakudiputhur , Bogalur , K.Karungulam , Kalaiyur , Kamankottai , Karuthanendal, Kavithaikudi, Keelambal , Kodikulam, Kummukottai, Manjakollai, Manjur, Mennendhinagachi , Mudalur, Muthuvayal , Pandikanmoi , Semanur, Sevvoor, T.Karungulam, Theeyanur, Theivendranallur, Urathur , Vairavanendal, Veeravanur.

Amenities:

Education: Primary School in 21 villages, Middle school in 9 villages, Matriculation or Secondary School in 1 village, namely Kamankottai.

Higher Secondary or Pre University Courses or Intermediate or Junior College in 0 village of the CD Block, College in 0 village, Adult Literacy Center in 0 village.

Medical: Hospital in 1 village, Dispensary in 0 village, Health Center in 3 villages, Sub Center in 4 villages, Maternity and Child Welfare Center in 3 villages, Community health workers in 0 village.

The Villages having Hospital or Dispensary or Health Center are Manjoor, Mennenthi.

Drinking Water: Tap water in 23 villages, Tank water in 4 villages, Well water in 23 villages, Tubewell in 23 villages and more than one source in 23 villages.

Bank: Banking facility in 5 villages, namely, Manjoor, Kamankottai, Nagachi, Bogaloor, Koraikulam.

Credit Society in 9 villages Agricultural Credit Society in 9 Non-Agricultural Credit Society in 0 village.

Others: Power supply in 23 villages, Cinema hall in 1 village, sport club in 0 village, Stadium or Auditorium or Community Hall in 0 village, Post Office in 8 villages.

There are 19 villages having bus facilities.

Villages with most of facilities: Manjoor Bogaloor.

Villages without amenities (Education):
Vallakulam..

Scheduled Castes: Out of the total population of 39246 persons, 16217 persons (41.32%) belong to Scheduled Castes.

The villages having less than 10% SC population are None..

The villages having more than 50% SC population are Manjoor, Kakkandal, Kamankottai, Mennenthi Vallakulam, Theeyanur, Seyyalur, Urathur, Koraikulam.

Sex ratio of Scheduled Caste population is 500.

Scheduled Castes Literates and Illiterates by Sex:

	Persons	Males	Females
Literate	9,058	5,451	3,607
Illiterate	7,159	2,662	4,497
Literacy rate	64.0	76.9	51.1
Graduate	371	282	89

Scheduled Castes (Dominant):
Pallan, Paraiyan etc., Chakkiliyan, Kuravan etc. Puthirai Vannan

For their cultural identity please see Appendix-I

Villages without Scheduled Castes: There is 0 village without any scheduled caste population.

Scheduled Tribes: Out of the total population of 39246 persons, 5 persons (0.01%) belong to Scheduled Tribes.

The villages having less than 10% ST population are Manjakollai, Manjoor, Pandikanmai, Kumukottai Kakkandal, Kamankottai, Mennenthi, Nagachi, Sevoor Muthalur, Veeravanoor, Bogaloor, Vallakulam Keelakottai, Ariyakudi, A. Puttur, Theeyanur Ettivayal, Seyyalur, Semanur, S. Kodikkulam, Urathur Koraikulam.

The villages having more than 50% ST population are None.

Sex ratio of Scheduled tribe population is 600.

Scheduled Tribes Literates and Illiterates by Sex:

	Persons	Males	Females
Literate	5	2	3
Illiterate	0	0	0
Literacy rate	100.0	100.0	100.0
Graduate	0	0	0

Scheduled Tribes (Dominant):
Kattunayakan, Kondareddis, Kurumans, Palliyar

For their cultural identity please see Appendix-II

Villages without Scheduled Tribes: There are 22 villages without any scheduled tribe population.

Literates and Illiterates by Sex (Total Population):

	Persons	Males	Females
Literate	23,500	13,871	9,629
Illiterate	15,746	5,468	10,278
Literacy rate	68	81	55
Graduate	682	511	171

Agriculture: ***Distribution of villages according to land use:*** Out of 23 villages, Total area (in hectare) is 17712, out of that 78.94 percent is cultivable and 26.71 percent of the cultivable area is irrigated.

Sources of Irrigation (Hectares): Government Canal 212.64, Private Canal 0, Well without Electricity 0, Well with

Electricity 0, Tubewell without Electricity 0, Tubewell with Electricity 0, Tank 3521.32, River 0, Lake 0, Waterfall 0, Others 0.

Villages with population of 5000 to 9999: None

Villages with population of 10000 and above: None

Distribution of Workers:

	Persons	Males	Females	WPR
Cultivators	10,122	5,586	4,536	43.95
Agricultural Labour	8,874	3,217	5,657	38.53
Household Industry	456	134	322	1.98
Other Workers	3,579	2,761	818	15.54
Main Workers	18,774	10,297	8,477	81.52
Marginal Workers	4,257	1,401	2,856	18.48
Total Workers	23,031	11,698	11,333	

Religion: Major Religious Communities:

	Persons	Males	Females	Sex Ratio
Hindu (86.78%)	34,059	16,859	17,200	1,020
Muslim (4.43%)	1,740	823	917	1,114
Christian (2.76%)	1,083	551	532	966
Sikh (0%)	-	-	-	-
Buddhists (0%)	-	-	-	-
Jain (0%)	-	-	-	-

Agewise Data:

	Persons	Males	Females	Sex Ratio
All ages	36,916	18,250	18,666	1023
0-14	10,043	5,045	4,998	991
15-44	17,586	8,652	8,934	1033
45-79	8,897	4,362	4,535	1040
80+	302	142	160	1127
Age not stated	88	49	39	796

Languages (Dominant):
Tamil, Urdu, Telugu, Malayalam, Hindi

Disabled Population:

	Persons	Males	Females	%
Total Disabled	1,234	546	688	
In Seeing	798	305	493	64.67
In Speech	103	52	51	8.35
In Hearing	50	20	30	4.05
In Movement	209	128	81	16.94
Mentally	74	41	33	6

BUDALUR

Budalur C.D. Block lies in the north-western part of Thanjavur district. It is a part of Thiruvaiyaru and Thanjavur taluks. The Block is located at a distance of NA kms. from district headquarters (Thanjavur). There are 50 villages in the block block with the total population of 84,852 persons. Area of the C.D. Block is 283.25 sq. kms. It is bounded in the north and west by district Tiruchirappalli, in the south by district Pudukkottai, in the east by C.D. Blocks Thiruvaiyaru and Thanjavur. CD Block Budalur falls in taluk Thiruvaiyaru by 24 villages, and in taluk Thanjavur by 26 villages.

Communications:

Roadways : N.H.-67: Direction- Tiruchirappalli to Vallam, Nearest Villages- Rayamundanpatti, Pudukkudi North, Manaiyeripatti, Samrappathi, Pudupatti, Sengipatti. S.H.-22: Direction- Koviladi to Thiruvaiyaru, Nearest Villages- Koothur, Vittalapuram, Pavanamangalam, Alamelupuram, Vishnampattai, Thiruchinampoondi, Kovilady, Palamannary, Thogur.

Railway Station: Budalur, Nandhavanappatti.

River: Cauvery Nadi- Nearest Villages- Koothur, Pavanamangalam, Vishnampattai, Thogur, Kovilady, Pathirakkudi, Onbathuveli, Palamannary, Nemam, Thiruchinampoondi, Agarpettai. Kollidam Nadi- Nearest Villages- Vittalapuram, Alamelupuram, Kovilady, Vishnampattai, Thiruchinampoondi, Thogur. Vennar Nadi- Nearest Villages- Thogur, Unjini, Arkot, Pathirakkudi, Mahadevapuram, Kachamangalam, Orathur, Meggelathur, Nathamangalam, Indalore, Kadampangudi, Mananeri, Kangeyampatti, Thondarayanbadi, Budalur, Kovilpathu. Kudamurittiyar Nadi- Nearest Villages- Onbathuveli, Michaelpattti, Palamannary, Nemam, Rajagiri, Agarapettai, Pathirakkudi, Mahadevapuram, Thogur.

Annual Rainfall: Average Rainfall 1147 mm.

Ground Water: Availability of the ground water in the Basin is 7081.58 H.A.M. and the utilization is 1280. 53 H.A.M. It belongs to Safe category. Depth to water level varies from 2 to 10 meter below the ground. Most of the wells go down in summer months, according to the Ground Water Estimation Committee.

Natural Division: Chola Nadu.

Administration

Revenue Division: Thanjavur. Parliamentary Constituency: 29 Thanjavur. District: Thanjavur. Taluk: Thiruvaiyalur, Thanjavur. Assembly Constituency: 173 Thiruvaiyaru. Gram Panchayat: 42.

Villages: 50 **Inhabited:** 49 **Uninhabited:** 1

Ranking	District	State	National
Area	4	194	2959
Population	11	208	3936
Sex Ratio	9	107	866
Child Sex Ratio	10	173	3005
Literacy Rate	6	97	1094
Density	·8	324	3527
Work Participation Rate	14	228	3886

Gram Panchayats:

Achampatti, Agarapettai, Alamelupuram , Alamelupuram, Arcadu, Avarampatti, Budalur, Deekshasamudram, Indalur, Kadambangudi, Kangeyampatti, Katchamangalam, Koothur, Koviladi, Kovilpathu, Maikkelpatti, Manaiyeripatti, Maraneri, Megalathur,

Muthuveerakandiampatti, Nandavanapatti, Nemam, Orathur, Padirakudi, Palaiyapatti , Palamaneri, Pavanamangalam, Pudukudi , Pudupatti, Rajagiri, Ranganathapuram, Sanoorapatti, Sellappanpettai, Sengipatti, Sholagampatti, Thogur, Thondarayampadi, Tiruchinampoondi, Veeramarasanpettai, Vendayampatti, Vishnampettai, Vitalapuram.

Amenities:

Education: Primary School in 47 villages, Middle school in 23 villages, Matriculation or Secondary School in 11 villages, namely Alamelupuram, Kovilady, Agarapettai, Rajagiri, Michaelpattti, Budalur, Muthuveerakandian Patti, Pudukkudi North, Manaiyeripatti, Pudupatti, Sengipatti.

Higher Secondary or Pre University Courses or Intermediate or Junior College in 3 villages of the CD Block,, namely Michaelpattti, Budalur, Sengipatti.

College in 0 village, Adult Literacy Center in 0 village.

Medical: Hospital in 1 village, Dispensary in 1 village, Health Center in 3 villages, Sub Center in 14 villages, Maternity and Child Welfare Center in 1 village, Community health workers in 49 villages.

The Villages having Hospital or Dispensary or Health Center are Alamelupuram, Meggelathur.

Drinking Water: Tap water in 49 villages, Tank water in 1 villages, Well water in 49 villages, Tubewell in 49 villages and more than one source in 49 villages.

Bank: Banking facility in 6 villages, namely, Thogur, Kadampangudi, Mananeri, Budalur, Samrappathi Sengipatti.

Credit Society in 18 villages Agricultural Credit Society in 18 Non-Agricultural Credit Society in 0 village.

Others: Power supply in 49 villages, Cinema hall in 2 villages, sport club in 0 village, Stadium or Auditorium or Community Hall in 0 village, Post Office in 31 villages.

There are 49 villages having bus facilities.

Villages with most of facilities: Thogur Kadampangudi, Mananeri, Budalur, Samrappathi Sengipatti.

Villages without amenities (Education):

Mahadevapuram, Unjini..

Scheduled Castes: Out of the total population of 84852 persons, 23368 persons (27.54%) belong to Scheduled Castes.

The villages having less than 10% SC population are Pavanamangalam, Palamannary, Michaelpattti, Unjini Kadampangudi, Chellappanpettai, Pudupatti.

The villages having more than 50% SC population are None.

Sex ratio of Scheduled Caste population is 503.

Scheduled Castes Literates and Illiterates by Sex:

	Persons	Males	Females
Literate	12,995	7,455	5,540
Illiterate	10,373	4,167	6,206
Literacy rate	65.0	75.1	55.0
Graduate	232	162	70

Scheduled Castes (Dominant):

Pallan, Paraiyan etc., Adi Dravida, Kuravan etc. Chakkiliyan

For their cultural identity please see Appendix-I

Villages without Scheduled Castes: There are 3 villages without any scheduled caste population.

Scheduled Tribes: Out of the total population of 84852 persons, 100 persons (0.12%) belong to Scheduled Tribes.

The villages having less than 10% ST population are Koothur, Vittalapuram, Pavanamangalam, Alamelupuram Vishnampattai, Thiruchinampoondi, Kovilady, Thogur Pathirakkudi, Mahadevapuram, Kachamangalam Agarapettai, Rajagiri, Renganathapuram, Nemam Palamannary, Michaelpattti, Deeshasamudram, Unjini Meggelathur, Orathur, Nathamangalam, Arkot, Indalore Kadampangudi, Solagampatti, Mananeri, Kangeyampatti Kottarapatti, Thondarayanbadi, Budalur, Kovilpathu Chellappanpettai, Veeramarasan Pettai, Avaram Patti Nandhavanappatti, Muthuveerakandian Patti Vendayanpatti, Sorrakudipatti, Rayamundanpatti Pudukkudi North, Manaiyeripatti, Samrappathi Pudupatti, Sengipatti, Palayapatti South Palayapatti North, Pudukkudi Souty, Achampatti.

The villages having more than 50% ST population are None.

Sex ratio of Scheduled tribe population is 520.

Scheduled Tribes Literates and Illiterates by Sex:

	Persons	Males	Females
Literate	23	12	11
Illiterate	77	36	41
Literacy rate	28.8	34.3	24.4
Graduate	0	0	0

Scheduled Tribes (Dominant):

Malakkuravan, Irular, Malai Pandaram, Kattunayakan

For their cultural identity please see Appendix-II

Villages without Scheduled Tribes: There are 44 villages without any scheduled tribe population.

Literates and Illiterates by Sex (Total Population):

	Persons	Males	Females
Literate	52,374	29,237	23,137
Illiterate	32,478	12,965	19,513
Literacy rate	71	80	62
Graduate	939	671	268

Agriculture: ***Distribution of villages according to land use:*** Out of 50 villages, Total area (in hectare) is 28325.9, out of

that 66.04 percent is cultivable and 57.45 percent of the cultivable area is irrigated.

Sources of Irrigation (Hectares): Government Canal 9854.81, Private Canal 0, Well without Electricity 0, Well with Electricity 0, Tubewell without Electricity 0, Tubewell with Electricity 201.44, Tank 0, River 0, Lake 690.93, Waterfall 0, Others 0.

Villages with population of 5000 to 9999: Budalur.

Villages with population of 10000 and above: None

Distribution of Workers:

	Persons	Males	Females	WPR
Cultivators	7,528	6,141	1,387	20.64
Agricultural Labour	21,389	11,937	9,452	58.64
Household Industry	952	508	444	2.61
Other Workers	6,603	5,241	1,362	18.1
Main Workers	25,315	17,744	7,571	69.41
Marginal Workers	11,157	6,083	5,074	30.59
Total Workers	36,472	23,827	12,645	

Religion: Major Religious Communities:

	Persons	Males	Females	Sex Ratio
Hindu (80.5%)	68,310	33,979	34,331	1,010
Muslim (1.77%)	1,500	769	731	951
Christian (17.6%)	14,931	7,393	7,538	1,020
Sikh (0%)	3	3	-	-
Buddhists (0%)	-	-	-	-
Jain (0%)	4	1	3	3,000

Agewise Data:

	Persons	Males	Females	Sex Ratio
All ages	84,852	42,202	42,650	1011
0-14	24,205	12,308	11,897	967
15-44	41,578	20,515	21,063	1027
45-79	18,316	8,976	9,340	1041
80+	560	298	262	879
Age not stated	193	105	88	838

Languages (Dominant):

Tamil, Telugu, Kannada, Urdu, Gujarati

Disabled Population:

	Persons	Males	Females	%
Total Disabled	2,819	1,315	1,504	
In Seeing	1,552	569	983	55.05
In Speech	258	134	124	9.15
In Hearing	140	65	75	4.97
In Movement	699	447	252	24.8
Mentally	170	100	70	6.03

CHELLAMPATTI

Chellampatti C.D. Block lies in the north-western part of Madurai district. It is a part of Usilampatti taluk. The taluk is located at a distance of 38 kms. from district headquarters (Madurai). There are 36 villages in the block with the total population of 84,725 persons. Area of the C.D. Block is 217.40 sq. kms. It is bounded in the north by CD Blocks Vadipatti and Usilampatti, in the south by CD Blocks Sedapatti and Thirumangalam, in the east by CD Block Vadipatti and Thirumangalam, and in the west by CDBlock Usilampatti.

Communications:

Roadways : N.H.-45: Direction- Usilampatti to Madurai, Nearest Villages- Valandur, Kovilangulam, Pullaneri, Karumathur, Nattamangalam, Ariyapatti, Pottulupatty.

Annual Rainfall: Average Rainfall 857 mm.

Ground Water: Availability of the ground water in the Basin is 5792.15 H.A.M. and the utilization is 6055. 12 H.A.M. It belongs to Over Expoited category. Depth to water level varies from 2 to 5 meter below the ground. Most of the wells go down in summer months, according to the Ground Water Estimation Committee.

Forest and Reserved Forest: (Kodimangalam RF)- Nearest Villages- Vikkiramangalam, Muthalaikulam, Panniyam. (Mannadi Mangalam)- Nearest Villages- Nagamalai RF, Ponamooppanpatti, Eravarpatti, Sakkarappanayakanur, Vikkiramangalam RF, Poppapatti, Boduvarpatti, Ayyanarkulam, Vikkiramangalam.

Natural Division: NA

Administration

Revenue **Division:** Usilampatti. Parliamentary Constituency: 33 Theni. District: Madurai. Taluk: Usilampatti. Assembly Constituency: 190 Samayanallur (SC) , 197 Usilampatti. Gram Panchayat: 29.

Villages: 36 **Inhabited:** 34 **Uninhabited:** 2

Ranking	District	State	National
Area	9	263	3890
Population	7	210	3943
Sex Ratio	13	372	5175
Child Sex Ratio	13	373	6209
Literacy Rate	9	218	2003
Density	2	43	2801
Work Participation Rate	5	119	381

Gram Panchayats:

Anaiyur Pudupatti, Ariyapatti, Ayyanarkulam, Boothipuram, Eravarpatti, Kannanur, Karumathur, Kattakaruppanpatti, Kodikulam, Kovilankulam, Kuruvakudi, Mudalaikulam, Nattarmangalam, Panamoopanpatti, Panniyan, Pappapatti, Poduvarpatti, Poruppumettupatti, Pottulupatti, Pullaneri, Sadachipatti, Sakkarappanaickanur, Sempatti, Sindupatti, Thidian, Thummakundu, Valandur, Veppanuthu, Vikkiramangalam.

Amenities:

Education: Primary School in 34 villages, Middle school in 14 villages, Matriculation or Secondary School in 7 villages,

namely Poppapatti, Vikkiramangalam, Kovilangulam, Karumathur, Nattamangalam, Thummakundu, Veppanoothu.
Higher Secondary or Pre University Courses or Intermediate or Junior College in 4 villages of the CD Block,, namely Poppapatti, Karumathur, Nattamangalam, Thummakundu.
College in 1 village, Adult Literacy Center in 0 village., College is in village, namely Kovilangulam.
Medical: Hospital in 2 villages, Dispensary in 2 villages, Health Center in 4 villages, Sub Center in 29 villages, Maternity and Child Welfare Center in 32 villages, Community health workers in 0 village.
The Villages having Hospital or Dispensary or Health Center are Vikkiramangalam, Karumathur, Pottulupatty, Thummakundu.
Drinking Water: Tap water in 34 villages, Tank water in 23 villages, Well water in 34 villages, Tubewell in 34 villages and more than one source in 34 villages.
Bank: Banking facility in 7 villages, namely, Vikkiramangalam, Valandur, Kovilangulam, Pullaneri Perumalpatti, Thummakundu, Sindupatti.
Credit Society in 24 villages Agricultural Credit Society in 11 Non-Agricultural Credit Society in 0 village.
Others: Power supply in 34 villages, Cinema hall in 3 villages, sport club in 0 village, Stadium or Auditorium or Community Hall in 8 villages, Post Office in 31 villages.
There are 32 villages having bus facilities.
Villages with most of facilities: Vikkiramangalam Valandur, Kovilangulam, Thummakundu, Sindupatti.
Villages without Amenities (Education): None..
Scheduled Castes: Out of the total population of 84725 persons, 13815 persons (16.31%) belong to Scheduled Castes.
The villages having less than 10% SC population are Ponamooppanpatti, Eravarpatti, Sakkarappanayakanur Ayyanarkulam, Sirupatti, A.Krishnapuram Kattakaruppanpatty, Sindupatti.
The villages having more than 50% SC population are None.
Sex ratio of Scheduled Caste population is 482.

Scheduled Castes Literates and Illiterates by Sex:

	Persons	Males	Females
Literate	6,463	4,095	2,368
Illiterate	7,352	3,063	4,289
Literacy rate	53.5	65.6	40.6
Graduate	86	78	8

Scheduled Castes (Dominant):
Paraiyan etc., Pallan, Chakkiliyan, Madari Generic Castes etc.
For their cultural identity please see Appendix-I
Villages without Scheduled Castes: There are 4 villages without any scheduled caste population.
Scheduled Tribes: Out of the total population of 84725 persons, 5 persons (0.01%) belong to Scheduled Tribes.
The villages having less than 10% ST population are Ponamooppanpatti, Eravarpatti, Sakkarappanayakanur Poppapatti, Boduvarpatti, Ayyanarkulam Vikkiramangalam, Muthalaikulam, Panniyam, Kannanur Kodikulam, Vinnakudi, Kuravakudi, Sadachipatty Pudupatti, Sirupatti, Boothipuram, A.Krishnapuram Kattakaruppanpatty, Valandur, Jothimanigam Kovilangulam, Pullaneri, Karumathur, Nattamangalam Ariyapatti, Pottulupatty, Sempatti, Thidiyan Poruppumettupatti, Perumalpatti, Thummakundu Sindupatti, Veppanoothu.
The villages having more than 50% ST population are None.
Sex ratio of Scheduled tribe population is 400.

Scheduled Tribes Literates and Illiterates by Sex:

	Persons	Males	Females
Literate	1	0	1
Illiterate	4	3	1
Literacy rate	25.0	-	50.0
Graduate	0	0	0

Scheduled Tribes (Dominant):
Irular, Malai Pandaram
For their cultural identity please see Appendix-II
Villages without Scheduled Tribes: There are 34 villages without any scheduled tribe population.

Literates and Illiterates by Sex (Total Population):

	Persons	Males	Females
Literate	48,387	30,041	18,346
Illiterate	36,338	14,463	21,875
Literacy rate	65	77	51
Graduate	1,363	1,124	239

Agriculture: ***Distribution of villages according to land use:*** Out of 36 villages, Total area (in hectare) is 21740.68, out of that 51.21 percent is cultivable and 74.1 percent of the cultivable area is irrigated.
Sources of Irrigation (Hectares): Government Canal 1940.16, Private Canal 0, Well without Electricity 284.64, Well with Electricity 4596.79, Tubewell without Electricity 10, Tubewell with Electricity 49.84, Tank 1407.61, River 0, Lake 0, Waterfall 0, Others 0.
Villages with population of 5000 to 9999: Vikkiramangalam, Kovilankulam, Karumathur.
Villages with population of 10000 and above: None

Distribution of Workers:

	Persons	Males	Females	WPR
Cultivators	16,982	9,795	7,187	34.06
Agricultural Labour	25,155	11,632	13,523	50.45

Household Industry	987	503	484	1.98
Other Workers	6,741	4,903	1,838	13.52
Main Workers	38,261	21,833	16,428	76.73
Marginal Workers	11,604	5,000	6,604	23.27
Total Workers	49,865	26,833	23,032	

Religion: Major Religious Communities:

	Persons	Males	Females	Sex Ratio
Hindu (98.7%)	83,621	43,786	39,835	910
Muslim (0.15%)	124	73	51	699
Christian (0.98%)	830	556	274	493
Sikh (0.07%)	63	34	29	853
Buddhists (0.01%)	5	3	2	667
Jain (0%)	4	2	2	1,000

Agewise Data:

	Persons	Males	Females	Sex Ratio
All ages	84,725	44,504	40,221	904
0-14	22,916	12,797	10,119	791
15-44	39,335	20,500	18,835	919
45-79	19,376	9,502	9,874	1039
80+	836	456	380	833
Age not stated	2,262	1,249	1,013	811

Languages (Dominant):

Tamil, Telugu, Malayalam, Urdu, Kannada

Disabled Population:

	Persons	Males	Females	%
Total Disabled	2,569	1,382	1,187	
In Seeing	1,705	863	842	66.37
In Speech	182	101	81	7.08
In Hearing	66	34	32	2.57
In Movement	464	290	174	18.06
Mentally	152	94	58	5.92

CHENGAM

Chengam C.D. Block lies in the south-western part of Tiruvannamalai district. It is a part of Chengam taluk. The Block is located at a distance of 35 kms. from district headquarters (Tiruvannamalai). There are 69 villages in the block with the total population of 123,642 persons. Area of the C.D. Block is 615.58 sq. kms. It is bounded in the north by C.D. Block Pudupalayam, in the south by C.D. Block Thandrampet and district Dharmapuri, in the east by Tiruvannamalai CD Block, in the west by district Dharmapuri and CD Block Jawadhu Hills.

Communications:

Roadways : N.H.-66: Direction- Uthangarai to Tiruvannamalai, Nearest Villages- Nachipattu, Kayampattu, Pakkaripalayam, Melchengam, Melchengam R.F, Melpulithiyoor, Perumpattam, Manmalai, Karaiyamangalam, Anandavadi, Melpennathur, Uchimalaikuppam, Vinnavanur, Pachal, Nallur, Kannakurukkai, Chinnakolapadi, Paliyapattu, Aswanagasurni, Anthanoor, Anandavadi RF, Periakolapadi.

River: Cheyyar Nadi- Nearest Villages- Kuppanatham, Paramanadal, Theethandapattu, Vazhampattu, Nachipattu, Manmalai, Karaiyamangalam.

Backwards Region Grants Fund: It receives Backward Region Grants.

Annual Rainfall: Average Rainfall 1019 mm.

Ground Water: Availability of the ground water in the Basin is (Information not available) H.A.M. and the utilization is 160.44 H.A.M. It belongs to Over Expoited category. Depth to water level varies from 2 to 5 meter below the ground. Most of the wells go down in summer months, according to the Ground Water Estimation Committee.

Forest and Reserved Forest: (Chennasamudram RF)- Nearest Villages- Paramanadal, Theethandapattu, Chennasamudram RF, Vazhampattu, Chennasamudram, Pakkaripalayam. (Eraiyurmalai)- Nearest Villages- Melpennathur, Uchimalaikuppam, Vinnavanur, Pachal, Nallur. (Uchimalai)- Nearest Villages- Melpennathur, Uchimalaikuppam, Vinnavanur, Beemanandal, Uchimalai RF, Uchimalai RF, Uchimalaikuppam. (Madanai)- Nearest Villages- Quilam, Anwarabath. (Paramanandal)- Nearest Villages- Paramanadal, Pudupet, Alaputhur, Quilam, Paramanandal RF, (Pinjur)- Nearest Villages- Anthanoor, Melpulithiyoor, Perumpattam, Karaiyamangalam, Pinjur RF, Rinjur RF, Pinjur, Pinjur RF, Vedankuppam, Porasapattu, Arattavadi, Ariyakunjur, Sorapanandal, Melpennathur. (Ponnaiyur)- Nearest Villages- Andipatti, Thambunaickenpatti, Mannandipatti, Porasapattu, Thalayouthu, Arattavadi, Ariyakunjur, Sorapanandal, Ponnaiyur RF, Elangunni, Kurumapatti, Manickal, Puliyampatti, Karungalipadi Patti. (Radhapuram)- Nearest Villages- Aswanagasurni, Periakolapadi, Beemanandal, Si Agaram, Perupakkam, Seranthangal. (Ravandavadi)- Nearest Villages- Kattamadu, Naradapattu, Melravandavadi, Karimalaipadi, Thambunaickenpatti, Ravanthavadi RF, Neepathurai, Vellalanpatti, Elangunni, Kalladavi, Puliyampatti, Karungalipadi Patti. (Thenmalai Hills)- Nearest Villages- Kuppanatham, Pinjur RF. (Kavuthimalai)- Nearest Villages- Nallur, Kannakurkkai, Chinakolapadi, Pahiapattu.

Natural Division: Tondai Nadu.

Administration

Revenue **Division:** Tiruvannamalai. Parliamentary Constituency: 11 Tiruvannamalai. District: Tiruvannamalai. Taluk: Chengam. Assembly Constituency: 62 Chengam (SC). Gram Panchayat: 44.

Villages: 69 **Inhabited:** 60 **Uninhabited:** 9

Ranking	District	State	National
Area	1	17	1117
Population	3	58	2749
Sex Ratio	17	304	2544
Child Sex Ratio	10	221	3590

Literacy Rate	15	329	2861
Density	4	130	4722
Work Participation Rate	17	328	1310

Gram Panchayats:

Agaram , Alaputhur, Andanur, Andipatti, Anwarabath, Arattavadi, Ariyakunjur, Aswanagasuranai, Beemanandal, Chennasamudram, Chinnakolapadi, Elangunni, Kannakurkkai, Kariyamangalam, Kattamaduvu, Kayampattu, Kottavoor, Kuppanatham, Manmalai, Melchangam, Melchengam, Melpallipattu, Melpennathur, Melpulidiyur, Melravanthavadi, Melvanakkambadi, Neepathurai, Pachal, Pakkiripalayam, Paliapattu, Paramanandal , Periakolapadi, Perumbakkam, Pinjur, Porasapattu, Pudupattu, Puliyampatti, Quilam, Se.Nachipattu, Sorapanandal, Thalayouthu, Theethandapattu, Uchimalaikuppam, Valayampattu, Vinnavanur,

Amenities:

Education: Primary School in 55 villages, Middle school in 22 villages, Matriculation or Secondary School in 7 villages, namely Paramanadal, Anthanoor, Melravandavadi, Arattavadi, Sorapanandal, Periakolapadi, Elangunni.

Higher Secondary or Pre University Courses or Intermediate or Junior College in 5 villages of the CD Block,, namely Paramanadal, Melpallipattu, Sorapanandal, Beemanandal, Elangunni.

College in 1 village, Adult Literacy Center in 0 village., College is in village, namely Vazhampattu.

Medical: Hospital in 0 village, Dispensary in 0 village, Health Center in 12 villages, Sub Center in 5 villages, Maternity and Child Welfare Center in 6 villages, Community health workers in 57 villages.

The Villages having Hospital or Dispensary or Health Center are Pinjur, Melravandavadi.

Drinking Water: Tap water in 60 villages, Tank water in 6 villages, Well water in 60 villages, Tubewell in 60 villages and more than one source in 60 villages.

Bank: Banking facility in 8 villages, namely, Quilam, Manmalai, Karaiyamangalam, Melpallipattu Melravandavadi, Arattavadi, Sorapanandal Neepathurai.

Credit Society in 37 villages Agricultural Credit Society in 10 Non-Agricultural Credit Society in 33 villages.

Others: Power supply in 58 villages, Cinema hall in 3 villages, sport club in 0 village, Stadium or Auditorium or Community Hall in 0 village, Post Office in 48 villages.

There are 51 villages having bus facilities.

Villages with most of facilities: Manmalai Karaiyamangalam, Melpallipattu, Melravandavadi Arattavadi, Sorapanandal, Neepathurai.

Villages without amenities (Education): Melchengam R F, Vedankuppam, Anandavadi R F, Naradapattu, Thambunaickenpatti..

Scheduled Castes: Out of the total population of 123642 persons, 41372 persons (33.46%) belong to Scheduled Castes. The villages having less than 10% SC population are Melchengam, Melchengam R F, Perumpattam Anandavadi R F, Anandavadi, Naradapattu Karimalaipadi, Mannandipatti, Nallur, Kurumapatti Kalladavi, Manickal, Karungalipadi Patti Seranthangal.

The villages having more than 50% SC population are Vazhampattu, Alaputhur, Quilam, Anwarabath Vedankuppam, Melravandavadi, Thambunaickenpatti Ariyakunjur.

Sex ratio of Scheduled Caste population is 496.

Scheduled Castes Literates and Illiterates by Sex:

	Persons	Males	Females
Literate	19,193	11,482	7,711
Illiterate	22,179	9,389	12,790
Literacy rate	54.3	64.4	44.0
Graduate	171	141	30

Scheduled Castes (Dominant):

Adi Dravida, Arunthathiyar, Adi Andhra, Kuravan etc. Valluvan

For their cultural identity please see Appendix-I

Villages without Scheduled Castes: There are 15 villages without any scheduled caste population.

Scheduled Tribes: Out of the total population of 123642 persons, 1562 persons (1.26%) belong to Scheduled Tribes. The villages having less than 10% ST population are Kuppanatham, Paramanadal, Theethandapattu Vazhampattu, Pudupet, Alaputhur, Quilam, Anwarabath Nachipattu, Kayampattu, Chennasamudram Pakkaripalayam, Arasankanni, Melchengam Melchengam R F, Anthanoor, Melpulithiyoor Perumpattam, Manmalai, Karaiyamangalam, Pinjur Vedankuppam, Melpallipattu, Melvanakkambadi Anandavadi R F, Melravandavadi, Karimalaipadi Andipatti, Thambunaickenpatti, Porasapattu Thalayouthu, Arattavadi, Ariyakunjur, Sorapanandal Melpennathur, Uchimalaikuppam, Vinnavanur, Pachal Nallur, Kannakurukkai, Chinnakolapadi, Paliyapattu Aswanagasurni, Periakolapadi, Beemanandal Neepathurai, Elangunni, Kurumapatti, Kalladavi Manickal, Puliyampatti, Si Agaram, Perupakkam Seranthangal.

The villages having more than 50% ST population are None.

Sex ratio of Scheduled tribe population is 513.

Scheduled Tribes Literates and Illiterates by Sex:

	Persons	Males	Females
Literate	348	199	149
Illiterate	1,214	562	652
Literacy rate	27.2	32.1	22.5
Graduate	0	0	0

Scheduled Tribes (Dominant):
Irular, Malayali, Kondareddis, Malai Pandaram Malakkuravan

For their cultural identity please see Appendix-II

Villages without Scheduled Tribes: There are 45 villages without any scheduled tribe population.

Literates and Illiterates by Sex (Total Population):

	Persons	Males	Females
Literate	63,975	38,332	25,643
Illiterate	59,667	24,459	35,208
Literacy rate	60	70	48
Graduate	508	393	115

Agriculture: ***Distribution of villages according to land use:*** Out of 69 villages, Total area (in hectare) is 61558.44, out of that 30.28 percent is cultivable and 49.79 percent of the cultivable area is irrigated.

Sources of Irrigation (Hectares): Government Canal 0, Private Canal 0, Well without Electricity 556.2, Well with Electricity 3328.03, Tubewell without Electricity 483.76, Tubewell with Electricity 377.82, Tank 1075.61, River 0, Lake 325.4, Waterfall 0, Others 438.35.

Villages with population of 5000 to 9999: Paramanandal , Pakkiripalayam, Kariyamangalam.

Villages with population of 10000 and above: None

Distribution of Workers:

	Persons	Males	Females	WPR
Cultivators	28,912	18,216	10,696	43.82
Agricultural Labour	27,600	12,531	15,069	41.83
Household Industry	1,140	543	597	1.73
Other Workers	8,333	6,301	2,032	12.63
Main Workers	52,899	32,501	20,398	80.17
Marginal Workers	13,086	5,090	7,996	19.83
Total Workers	65,985	37,591	28,394	

Religion: Major Religious Communities:

	Persons	Males	Females	Sex Ratio
Hindu (97.17%)	120,138	61,041	59,097	968
Muslim (2.27%)	2,812	1,412	1,400	992
Christian (0.51%)	631	304	327	1,076
Sikh (0%)	2	1	1	1,000
Buddhists (0%)	3	2	1	500
Jain (0.01%)	9	5	4	800

Agewise Data:

	Persons	Males	Females	Sex Ratio
All ages	123,642	62,791	60,851	969
0-14	37,453	19,140	18,313	957
15-44	59,278	29,811	29,467	988
45-79	24,978	12,836	12,142	946
80+	973	528	445	843
Age not stated	960	476	484	1017

Languages (Dominant):
Tamil, Telugu, Urdu, Kannada, Hindi

Disabled Population:

	Persons	Males	Females	%
Total Disabled	2,931	1,735	1,196	
In Seeing	1,692	998	694	57.73
In Speech	250	134	116	8.53
In Hearing	132	68	64	4.5
In Movement	624	408	216	21.29
Mentally	233	127	106	7.95

CHENNIMALAI

Chennimalai C.D. Block lies in the central-western part of Erode district. It is a part of Perundurai taluk. The Block is located at a distance of 30 kms. from district headquarters (Erode). There are 23 villages in the block with the total population of 61,920 persons. Area of the C.D. Block is 259.56 sq. kms. It is bounded in the north by C.D. Blocks Perundurai and Erode, in the south by district Dindigul, in the east by CD Blocks Uthukuli and Kodumudi, and in the west by district Coimbatore.

Communications:

Roadways : Information not Available.

Railway Station: Vadamugam Vellode.

River: Noyal Nadi- Nearest Villages- Kodumanal, Orathupa alyam, Ellaigramam, Ekkattampalayam, Pasuvapatti.

Annual Rainfall: Average Rainfall 789 mm.

Ground Water: Availability of the ground water in the Basin is 3392.59 H.A.M. and the utilization is 1613.78 H.A.M. It belongs to Safe category. Depth to water level varies from 2 to 20 meter below the ground. Most of the wells go down in summer months, according to the Ground Water Estimation Committee.

Forest and Reserved Forest: (Chennimalai RF)- Nearest Villages- Chennimalai, Chennimalai RF, Puduppalayam, Punjaipalatholuvu, Ekkattampalayam, Pasuvapatti.

Natural Division: Kongu Nadu.

Administration

Revenue **Division:** Erode. Parliamentary Constituency: 17 Erode, 18 Gobichettipalayam. District: Erode. Taluk: Perundurai. Assembly Constituency: 99 Erode (West), 103 Perundurai, 102 Kangayam. Gram Panchayat: 22.

Villages: 23 **Inhabited:** 22 **Uninhabited:** 1

Ranking	**District**	**State**	**National**
Area	9	217	3254
Population	13	328	4796

Sex Ratio	17	349	3533
Child Sex Ratio	14	282	4751
Literacy Rate	4	277	2360
Density	10	25	4224
Work Participation Rate	12	294	217

Gram Panchayats:
Basuvapatti, Ekkattampalayam, Ellaigramam, Ingur, Kavundachipalayam, Kodumanal, Kumaravalasu, Kuppuchipalayam, Kuthampalayam, Kuttapalayam, Mukasi Pulavapalayam, Murugatholuvu, Paniampalli, Pudupalayam ., Pungampadi, Punja: Palatholuvu, Sirukkalanchi, Vadamugam Vellode , Varapalayam, Voipadi.

Amenities:
Education: Primary School in 19 villages, Middle school in 8 villages, Matriculation or Secondary School in 3 villages, namely Vadamugam Vellode, Thenmugam Vellode, Ekkattampalayam.
Higher Secondary or Pre University Courses or Intermediate or Junior College in 2 villages of the CD Block,, namely Vadamugam Vellode, Thenmugam Vellode.
College in 2 villages, Adult Literacy Center in 1 village., Colleges are in villages, namely Vadamugam Vellode, Murungatholuvu.
Medical: Hospital in 1 village, Dispensary in 0 village, Health Center in 3 villages, Sub Center in 9 villages, Maternity and Child Welfare Center in 0 village, Community health workers in 1 village.
The Village having Hospital or Dispensary or Health Center is Murungatholuvu.
Drinking Water: Tap water in 22 villages, Tank water in 0 villages, Well water in 22 villages, Tubewell in 22 villages and more than one source in 22 villages.
Bank: Banking facility in 3 villages, namely, Vadamugam Vellode, Thenmugam Vellode, Ingur.
Credit Society in 9 villages Agricultural Credit Society in 6 Non-Agricultural Credit Society in 5 villages.
Others: Power supply in 22 villages, Cinema hall in 0 village, sport club in 3 villages, Stadium or Auditorium or Community Hall in 1 village, Post Office in 20 villages.
There are 20 villages having bus facilities.
Villages with most of facilities: Vadamugam Vellode Thenmugam Vellode.
Villages without amenities (Education):
Chennimalai, Nanjaipalatholuvu, Orathupalalyam..
Scheduled Castes: Out of the total population of 61920 persons, 12131 persons (19.59%) belong to Scheduled Castes.
The villages having less than 10% SC population are None..
The villages having more than 50% SC population are None.
Sex ratio of Scheduled Caste population is 489.

Scheduled Castes Literates and Illiterates by Sex:

	Persons	Males	Females
Literate	5,143	3,178	1,965
Illiterate	6,988	3,022	3,966
Literacy rate	48.0	58.1	37.5
Graduate	84	59	25

Scheduled Castes (Dominant):
Chakkiliyan, Arunthathiyar, Adi Dravida, Pallan Madari
For their cultural identity please see Appendix-I
Villages without Scheduled Castes: There is 1 village without any scheduled caste population.
Scheduled Tribes: Out of the total population of 61920 persons, 5 persons (0.01%) belong to Scheduled Tribes.
The villages having less than 10% ST population are Vadamugam Vellode, Pungampadi, Kaudachipalayam Thenmugam Vellode, Mugasipalavam Palayam, Ingur Varappalayam, Kongampalayam, Sirukalanji Koothampalayam, Voipadi, Chennimalai, Murungatholuvu Puduppalayam, Nanjaipalatholuvu, Punjaipalatholuvu Kodumanal, Orathupalalyam, Ellaigramam Ekkattampalayam, Pasuvapatti, Kuppichipalayam.
The villages having more than 50% ST population are None.
Sex ratio of Scheduled tribe population is 400.

Scheduled Tribes Literates and Illiterates by Sex:

	Persons	Males	Females
Literate	4	3	1
Illiterate	1	0	1
Literacy rate	80.0	100.0	50.0
Graduate	0	0	0

Scheduled Tribes (Dominant):
Kattunayakan, Kurumans
For their cultural identity please see Appendix-II
Villages without Scheduled Tribes: There are 21 villages without any scheduled tribe population.

Literates and Illiterates by Sex (Total Population):

	Persons	Males	Females
Literate	35,133	21,706	13,427
Illiterate	26,787	10,063	16,724
Literacy rate	62	75	49
Graduate	1,318	922	396

Agriculture: ***Distribution of villages according to land use:*** Out of 23 villages, Total area (in hectare) is 25956.68, out of that 70.04 percent is cultivable and 26.18 percent of the cultivable area is irrigated.
Sources of Irrigation (Hectares): Government Canal 3070.62, Private Canal 0, Well without Electricity 138.08, Well with

Electricity 1337.45, Tubewell without Electricity 0, Tubewell with Electricity 212.88, Tank 0, River 0, Lake 0, Waterfall 0, Others 0.

Villages with population of 5000 to 9999: Vadamugam Vellode , Kavundachipalayam Thenmugam Vellode, Ingur, Murugatholuvu.

Villages with population of 10000 and above: None

Distribution of Workers:

	Persons	Males	Females	WPR
Cultivators	10,159	5,413	4,746	26.33
Agricultural Labour	12,454	5,577	6,877	32.28
Household Industry	2,256	1,127	1,129	5.85
Other Workers	13,711	9,443	4,268	35.54
Main Workers	36,504	20,940	15,564	94.62
Marginal Workers	2,076	620	1,456	5.38
Total Workers	38,580	21,560	17,020	

Religion: Major Religious Communities:

	Persons	Males	Females	Sex Ratio
Hindu (97.65%)	60,462	31,041	29,421	948
Muslim (0.31%)	193	104	89	856
Christian (1.98%)	1,226	602	624	1,037
Sikh (0%)	3	2	1	500
Buddhists (0%)	-	-	-	-
Jain (0%)	-	-	-	-

Agewise Data:

	Persons	Males	Females	Sex Ratio
All ages	61,920	31,769	30,151	949
0-14	12,729	6,637	6,092	918
15-44	29,758	15,384	14,374	934
45-79	18,335	9,151	9,184	1004
80+	997	532	465	874
Age not stated	101	65	36	554

Languages (Dominant):

Tamil, Telugu, Kannada, Hindi, Urdu

Disabled Population:

	Persons	Males	Females	%
Total Disabled	1,243	590	653	
In Seeing	641	232	409	51.57
In Speech	119	70	49	9.57
In Hearing	70	36	34	5.63
In Movement	315	198	117	25.34
Mentally	98	54	44	7.88

CHERANMADEVI

Cheranmadevi C.D. Block lies in the southern part of Tirunelveli district. It is a part of Ambasamudram taluk. The Block is located at a distance of 20 kms. from district headquarters (Tirunelveli). There are 17 villag es in the block with the total population of 29,256 persons. Area of the C.D. Block is 124.97 sq. kms. It is bounded in the north by CD Blocks Pappakudi and Manur, in the south by CD Block Kalakkadu, in the east by CD Blocks Kalakkadu and Palayamkottai, and in the west by CD Block Ambasamudram.

Communications:

Roadways : S.H.-40: Direction- Kallakurichi to Tirunelveli, Nearest Villages- Vadakukarunkurichi, Kuniyur, Pudhukku di.

Railway Station: Pudhukkudi, Therkku Kallidaikurich I.

River: Tambraparani Nadi- Nearest Villages- Therku Ariya nayahipuram, Udaya Marthandapuram, Kuniyur.

Annual Rainfall: Average Rainfall 879 mm.

Ground Water: Availability of the ground water in the Basin is 45.01 MCM and the utilization is 14.03 MCM. It belongs to safe category. Depth to water level varies from 2 to 20 meter below the ground. Most of the wells go down in summer months, according to the Ground Water Estimation Committee.

Forest and Reserved Forest: (Kolendumamal RF)- Nearest Villages- Kolendumamalai RF, Pudhukkudi, Therk ku Karaikurichi, Thiruviruthan Palli. (Mampothai)- Nearest Villages- South Veeravanallur-I, Mampothai RF. (Singampatti Zamindar)- Nearest Villages- Therkku Kallidaikurich I, Malaiyankulam. (Therkuveera Vanallur)- Nearest Villages- South Veeravanallur-I, Malaiyankulam, Therkku Viravanallur RF, Therkku Karaikurichi.

Natural Division: NA

Administration

Revenue **Division:** Cheranmadevi. Parliamentary Constituen cy: 38 Tirunelveli. District: Tirunelveli. Taluk: Ambasa mudram. Assembly Constituency: 225 Ambasamudram. Gram Panchayat: 12.

Villages: 17 **Inhabited:** 13 **Uninhabited:** 4

Ranking	District	State	National
Area	18	358	5390
Population	18	380	6070
Sex Ratio	6	19	204
Child Sex Ratio	16	232	3811
Literacy Rate	6	45	638
Density	12	173	4272
Work Participation Rate	12	298	1736

Gram Panchayats:

Karisalpatti, Kuniyur, Malaiyankulam, Moolachi, Pottal, Pudukudi, Therku Ariyanayakipuram, Therkuveeravanallur , Thiruviruthanpuli, Ulagankulam, Vadakkukaraikuruchi, Venkattarengapuram.

Amenities:

Education: Primary School in 12 villages, Middle school in 3 villages, Matriculation or Secondary School in 2 villages, namely Therkku Kallidaikurich I, Thiruviruthan Palli.

Higher Secondary or Pre University Courses or Intermediate or Junior College in 1 village of the CD Block,, namely Thiruviruthan Palli.

College in 1 village, Adult Literacy Center in 0 village., College is in village, namely Karisalpatti.

Medical: Hospital in 0 village, Dispensary in 2 villages, Health Center in 2 villages, Sub Center in 3 villages, Maternity and Child Welfare Center in 1 village, Community health workers in 11 villages.

The Villages having Hospital or Dispensary or Health Center are Therkku Kallidaikurich I, Thiruviruthan Palli.

Drinking Water: Tap water in 13 villages, Tank water in 1 villages, Well water in 7 villages, Tubewell in 3 villages and more than one source in 12 villages.

Bank: Banking facility in 2 villages, namely, Vadakukarunkurichi, Thiruviruthan Palli.

Credit Society in 3 villages Agricultural Credit Society in 1 Non-Agricultural Credit Society in 1 village.

Others: Power supply in 13 villages, Cinema hall in 2 villages, sport club in 1 village, Stadium or Auditorium or Community Hall in 0 village, Post Office in 11 villages.

There are 11 villages having bus facilities.

Villages with most of facilities: Vadakukarunkurichi Thiruviruthan Palli.

Villages without amenities (Education):

Udaya Marthandapuram..

Scheduled Castes: Out of the total population of 29256 persons, 6522 persons (22.29%) belong to Scheduled Castes.

The villages having less than 10% SC population are Pudhukkudi, Thiruviruthan Palli, Poongudaiyarkulam Karisalpatti, Ulagankulam.

The villages having more than 50% SC population are None.

Sex ratio of Scheduled Caste population is 519.

Scheduled Castes Literates and Illiterates by Sex:

	Persons	Males	Females
Literate	3,596	1,995	1,601
Illiterate	2,926	1,145	1,781
Literacy rate	64.0	74.6	54.3
Graduate	45	29	16

Scheduled Castes (Dominant):

Pallan, Paraiyan etc., Kuravan etc., Chakkiliyan Arunthathiyar

For their cultural identity please see Appendix-I

Villages without Scheduled Castes: There are 5 villages without any scheduled caste population.

Scheduled Tribes: Out of the total population of 29256 persons, 221 persons (0.76%) belong to Scheduled Tribes.

The villages having less than 10% ST population are Therku Ariyanayahipuram, Udaya Marthandapuram Vadakukarunkurichi, Kuniyur, Pudhukkudi South Veeravanallur-I, Therkku Kallidaikurich I Malaiyankulam, Thiruviruthan Palli Poongudaiyarkulam, Karisalpatti, Ulagankulam Venkatarengapuram.

The villages having more than 50% ST population are None.

Sex ratio of Scheduled tribe population is 480.

Scheduled Tribes Literates and Illiterates by Sex:

	Persons	Males	Females
Literate	65	48	17
Illiterate	156	67	89
Literacy rate	38.2	55.8	20.2
Graduate	0	0	0

Scheduled Tribes (Dominant):

Kattunayakan, Kaniyan etc.

For their cultural identity please see Appendix-II

Villages without Scheduled Tribes: There are 12 villages without any scheduled tribe population.

Literates and Illiterates by Sex (Total Population):

	Persons	Males	Females
Literate	19,284	10,235	9,049
Illiterate	9,972	3,914	6,058
Literacy rate	75	83	68
Graduate	556	360	196

Agriculture: ***Distribution of villages according to land use:***

Out of 17 villages, Total area (in hectare) is 12497.41, out of that 24.7 percent is cultivable and 94.99 percent of the cultivable area is irrigated.

Sources of Irrigation (Hectares): Government Canal 620.99, Private Canal 0, Well without Electricity 11.83, Well with Electricity 643.64, Tubewell without Electricity 58.2, Tubewell with Electricity 43.2, Tank 1554.98, River 0, Lake 0, Waterfall 0, Others 0.

Villages with population of 5000 to 9999:

Therku Kallidaikurichi.

Villages with population of 10000 and above: None

Distribution of Workers:

	Persons	Males	Females	WPR
Cultivators	1,659	1,252	407	10.87
Agricultural Labour	4,688	2,899	1,789	30.72
Household Industry	4,558	647	3,911	29.87
Other Workers	4,354	3,116	1,238	28.53
Main Workers	12,241	6,593	5,648	80.22
Marginal Workers	3,018	1,321	1,697	19.78
Total Workers	15,259	7,914	7,345	

Religion: Major Religious Communities:

	Persons	Males	Females	Sex Ratio
Hindu (80.96%)	23,687	11,510	12,177	1,058

Muslim (1.82%)	531	244	287	1,176
Christian (17.17%)	5,022	2,385	2,637	1,106
Sikh (0%)	-	-	-	-
Buddhists (0%)	-	-	-	-
Jain (0%)	-	-	-	-

Agewise Data:

	Persons	Males	Females	Sex Ratio
All ages	29,256	14,149	15,107	1068
0-14	8,370	4,275	4,095	958
15-44	13,859	6,449	7,410	1149
45-79	6,613	3,214	3,399	1058
80+	261	125	136	1088
Age not stated	153	86	67	779

Languages (Dominant):
Tamil, Gujarati, Telugu, Others, Malayalam

Disabled Population:

	Persons	Males	Females	%
Total Disabled	720	394	326	
In Seeing	295	158	137	40.97
In Speech	124	62	62	17.22
In Hearing	37	16	21	5.14
In Movement	197	125	72	27.36
Mentally	67	33	34	9.31

CHETPET

Chetpet C.D. Block lies in the north-western part of Tiruvannamalai district. It is a part of Polur taluk. The taluk is located at a distance of 40 kms. from district headquarters (Tiruvannamalai). There are 62 villages in the block with the total population of 84,859 persons. Area of the C.D. Block is 263.06 sq. kms. It is bounded in the north by C.D. Blocks Polur and Arani West, in the south by Viluppuram district and CD Block Thurinjapuram, in the east by CD Block Peranamallur, in the west by CD Blocks Polur and Kalasapakkam.

Communications:
Roadways : S.H.-4: Direction- Arani to Gingee, Nearest Villages- Ettivadu, Karikathur, Kilkarikathur, Vambalur, Indiravanam, Manickavalli. S.H.-9: Direction- Nearest Villages- Ettivadu, Vadamathimangalam.
River: Cheyyar Nadi- Nearest Villages- Ariyathur, Ogoor, Karikathur, Vambalur, Odanagaram, Arumbaloor, Eyakolathur, Mandakolathur, Sarikkavady, Karaipoondi, Othalavadi.
Backwards Region Grants Fund: It receives Backward Region Grants.
Annual Rainfall: Average Rainfall 1019 mm.
Ground Water: Availability of the ground water in the Basin is (Information not available) H.A.M. and the utilization is 160.44 H.A.M. It belongs to Over Expoited category. Depth to water level varies from 2 to 5 meter below the ground. Most of the wells go down in summer months, according to the Ground Water Estimation Committee.
Forest and Reserved Forest: (Alliyalamang RF)- Nearest Villages- Modaiyur, Mattappriyar, Alliyalamangalam, Kovilur, Authurai, Thachambady, Devimangalam, Cheyyanandal, Srithathurai, Pernambakkam, Randham, Mansurabad, Alliyalamangalam RF, Savarapoondi. (Kelur)- Nearest Village- Ettivadu, Alampoondi, Tirumalai, Karikathur, Ogoor.
Natural Division: Tondai Nadu.
Administration
Revenue **Division:** Tiruvannamalai. Parliamentary Constituency: 12 Arani. District: Tiruvannamalai. Taluk: Polur. Assembly Constituency: 66 Polur. Gram Panchayat: 49.
Villages: 62 **Inhabited:** 59 **Uninhabited:** 3

Ranking	District	State	National
Area	11	214	3207
Population	14	207	3935
Sex Ratio	3	97	763
Child Sex Ratio	5	131	2359
Literacy Rate	11	194	1786
Density	10	187	3335
Work Participation Rate	10	194	1905

Gram Panchayats:
Alampoondy, Alliyalmangalam, Appedu, Ariyathur, Arumbulore, Athurai, Cheyyanandal, Chittathurai, Devimangalam, Edyankulathur, Ettivady, Eyakolathur, Gangasoodamani , Gudalore, Indiravanam, Indravanam, Karapoondy, Karikathur, Kilpattu, Kolakaravady, Kolavoor, Koralpakkam, Kothandavady, Madavilagam, Mandakolathur, Mansurabad, Maruthuvambady, Mattapiraur, Mattapirayur, Modaiyur, Nambedu, Narasingapuram, Ogur, Olagampattu, Othalavady, Pelasur, Peranambakkam, Rajamapuram, Randam, Saduperi, Sanikkavady, Semmiyamangalam, Sevarapoondi, Thachambady, Thathanur, Thirumalai, Thumbur, Uthur, Vadamathimangalam, Vambalore, Vilapakkam.

Amenities:
Education: Primary School in 56 villages, Middle school in 23 villages, Matriculation or Secondary School in 12 villages, namely Vadamathimangalam, Gudaloor, Tirumalai, Othalavadi, Ulagampet, Mandakolathur, Karaipoondi, Nambadu, Pernambakkam, Randham, Mansurabad, Savarapoondi.
Higher Secondary or Pre University Courses or Intermediate or Junior College in 2 villages of the CD Block,, namely Vadamathimangalam, Othalavadi.
College in 0 village, Adult Literacy Center in 0 village.
Medical: Hospital in 0 village, Dispensary in 0 village, Health Center in 2 villages, Sub Center in 9 villages, Maternity and Child Welfare Center in 5 villages, Community health workers in 59 villages.
The Village having Hospital or Dispensary or Health

Center is Ettivadu.

Drinking Water: Tap water in 59 villages, Tank water in 6 villages, Well water in 59 villages, Tubewell in 59 villages and more than one source in 59 villages.

Bank: Banking facility in 5 villages, namely, Vadamathimangalam, Modaiyur, Mandakolathur, Authurai Srithathurai.

Credit Society in 27 villages Agricultural Credit Society in 6 Non-Agricultural Credit Society in 27 villages.

Others: Power supply in 59 villages, Cinema hall in 0 village, sport club in 0 village, Stadium or Auditorium or Community Hall in 0 village, Post Office in 35 villages.

There are 58 villages having bus facilities.

Villages with most of facilities: Vadamathimangalam Modaiyur, Mandakolathur, Authurai, Srithathurai.

Villages without amenities (Education):
Othiyanthangal, Odanagaram, Otteri..

Scheduled Castes: Out of the total population of 84859 persons, 9388 persons (11.06%) belong to Scheduled Castes. The villages having less than 10% SC population are Ettivadu, Alampoondi, Othiyanthangal, Rayankuppam Saduperipalayam, Madavilagam, Jumbukonnampattu Ogoor, Kilkarikathur, Vambalur, Uthoor, Othalavadi Modanapalayam, Indiravanam, Ulagampet Narasingapuram, Odanagaram, Manickavalli Mandakolathur, Pulivananyhal, Otteri, Kolavoor Koralpakkam, Sothukkanny, Semmiyamangalam, Authurai Thachambady, Cheyyanandal, Pelasur, Mansurabad Idayankollathur, Maruthambody, Gengasudamani.

The villages having more than 50% SC population are None.

Sex ratio of Scheduled Caste population is 510.

Scheduled Castes Literates and Illiterates by Sex:

	Persons	Males	Females
Literate	5,249	3,049	2,200
Illiterate	4,139	1,551	2,588
Literacy rate	63.4	75.5	52.0
Graduate	28	26	2

Scheduled Castes (Dominant):
Adi Dravida, Arunthathiyar, Kuravan etc., Valluvan Domban

For their cultural identity please see Appendix-I

Villages without Scheduled Castes: There are 17 villages without any scheduled caste population.

Scheduled Tribes: Out of the total population of 84859 persons, 297 persons (0.35%) belong to Scheduled Tribes. The villages having less than 10% ST population are Kilpet, Vadamathimangalam, Ettivadu, Alampoondi Othiyanthangal, Rayankuppam, Gudaloor Saduperipalayam, Saduperi, Madavilagam Jumbukonnampattu, Ariyathur, Tirumalai, Ogoor Karikathur, Kilkarikathur, Vambalur, Uthoor Othalavadi, Veerasampanur, Modanapalayam, Thumpur Indiravanam, Appedu, Ulagampet, Kothanthavadi Kolakaravadi, Narasingapuram, Modaiyur, Odanagaram Arumbaloor, Manickavalli, Mandakolathur, Eyakolathur Sarikkavady, Karaipoondi, Pulivananyhal, Otteri Mattappriyar, Kolavoor, Koralpakkam, Sothukkanny Semmiyamangalam, Alliyalamangalam, Authurai Thachambady, Nambadu, Devimangalam, Cheyyanandal Srithathurai, Pernambakkam, Randham, Velapakkam Pelasur, Mansurabad, Savarapoondi, Idayankollathur Maruthambody, Gengasudamani.

The villages having more than 50% ST population are None.

Sex ratio of Scheduled tribe population is 495.

Scheduled Tribes Literates and Illiterates by Sex:

	Persons	Males	Females
Literate	56	35	21
Illiterate	241	115	126
Literacy rate	22.7	26.9	18.0
Graduate	0	0	0

Scheduled Tribes (Dominant):
Irular, Malai Pandaram, Malayali

For their cultural identity please see Appendix-II

Villages without Scheduled Tribes: There are 47 villages without any scheduled tribe population.

Literates and Illiterates by Sex (Total Population):

	Persons	Males	Females
Literate	49,576	29,662	19,914
Illiterate	35,283	12,443	22,840
Literacy rate	66	80	52
Graduate	473	373	100

Agriculture: ***Distribution of villages according to land use:*** Out of 62 villages, Total area (in hectare) is 26306.84, out of that 53.99 percent is cultivable and 45.69 percent of the cultivable area is irrigated.

Sources of Irrigation (Hectares): Government Canal 0, Private Canal 0, Well without Electricity 406.93, Well with Electricity 4177.93, Tubewell without Electricity 0, Tubewell with Electricity 0, Tank 1091.1, River 23.63, Lake 317.1, Waterfall 184.28, Others 137.02.

Villages with population of 5000 to 9999: Vadamathimangalam.

Villages with population of 10000 and above: None

Distribution of Workers:

	Persons	Males	Females	WPR
Cultivators	18,583	11,872	6,711	42.01
Agricultural Labour	16,828	6,691	10,137	38.04
Household Industry	2,105	1,089	1,016	4.76

Other Workers	6,722	5,078	1,644	15.2
Main Workers	34,472	20,720	13,752	77.92
Marginal Workers	9,766	4,010	5,756	22.08
Total Workers	44,238	24,730	19,508	

Religion: Major Religious Communities:

	Persons	Males	Females	Sex Ratio
Hindu (92.41%)	78,420	38,942	39,478	1,014
Muslim (1.24%)	1,055	548	507	925
Christian (5.74%)	4,867	2,344	2,523	1,076
Sikh (0%)	1	-	1	-
Buddhists (0%)	1	-	1	-
Jain (0.51%)	437	230	207	900

Agewise Data:

	Persons	Males	Females	Sex Ratio
All ages	84,859	42,105	42,754	1015
0-14	24,679	12,551	12,128	966
15-44	39,010	19,184	19,826	1033
45-79	20,255	9,882	10,373	1050
80+	744	387	357	922
Age not stated	171	101	70	693

Languages (Dominant):
Tamil, Telugu, Urdu, Malayalam, Hindi

Disabled Population:

	Persons	Males	Females	%
Total Disabled	1,666	921	745	
In Seeing	637	343	294	38.24
In Speech	227	121	106	13.63
In Hearing	159	81	78	9.54
In Movement	500	290	210	30.01
Mentally	143	86	57	8.58

CHEYYAR

Cheyyar C.D. Block lies in the north-eastern part of Tiruvannamalai district. It is a part of Cheyyar taluk. The taluk headquarters is located at a distance of 110 kms. from district headquarters (Tiruvannamalai). There are 67 villages in the block with the total population of 87,618 persons. Area of the C.D. Block is 243.40 sq. kms. It is bounded in the north by C.D. Block Vembakkam, in the south by CD Blocks Arani west and Pernamallur, in the east by C.D. Blocks Purnamallur and Anakkavur, in the west by CD Blocks Arani and Arani West, and district Vellore.

Communications:

Roadways : S.H.-4: Direction- Arcot to Tiruvethipuram, Nearest Villages- Sirugattoor, Pappanthangal, Duli, Kizhpudupakkam, Painkinar, Arugavoor.

River: Cheyyar Nadi- Nearest Villages- Velianallur, Kaliyar, Vadathandalam, Arugavoor, Perumalpallam, Thandari, Sarampattu, Thoyupedu, Eriyyur, Kilpalandai, Kaduganoor, Malenagarampeedu, Korukkathur, Munugappattu, Meiseshamangalam.

Backwards Region Grants Fund: It receives Backward Region Grants.

Annual Rainfall: Average Rainfall 1019 mm.

Ground Water: Availability of the ground water in the Basin is (Information not available) H.A.M. and the utili zation is 160.44 H.A.M. It belongs to Over Expoited categ ory. Depth to water level varies from 2 to 5 meter below the ground. Most of the wells go down in summer months, according to the Ground Water Estimation Committee.

Natural Division: Tondai Nadu.

Administration

Revenue **Division:** Cheyyar. Parliamentary Constituency: 12 Arani. District: Tiruvannamalai. Taluk: Cheyyar. Assembly Constituency: 67 Arani, 68 Cheyyar. Gram Panchayat: 53.

Villages: 67 **Inhabited:** 67 **Uninhabited:** 0

Ranking	District	State	National
Area	14	238	3469
Population	12	195	3862
Sex Ratio	5	143	1023
Child Sex Ratio	2	33	798
Literacy Rate	10	181	1718
Density	13	209	3016
Work Participation Rate	4	144	2226

Gram Panchayats:

Aradrivelur, Arugavoor, Arumparuthi, Duli, Enadavadi, Eraiyur, Kaduganur, Kalaniapakkam, Kaliyur, Kilapalandai, Kilpudupakkam, Korkkai, Korukkathur, Kunnathur, kunnathur, Madurai, malaigaipattu, Maligaipattu, Mariyanallur, Mel Seeshamangalam, Melnagarambedu, Melseesamangalam, Mukkur, Munugapattu, Murukkathampoondi, Naval, Navalpakkam, Nedumparai, Painkinar, Palli, Pappanthangal, Parasur, Perumpallam, Perungalathur, Pillandi, Pudukottai, Puliyarambakkam, Ramakrishnapuram, Sengathankundil, Siruvelianalloore, Sundivakkam, Talarapadi, Thandarai, Thenpoondipattu, Thirumani, Thozhupedu, Thumbai, Vadangampattu, Vadapoondipattu, Vadathandalam, Vadugapattu, Vakkadai, Velianallore, Vinnamanalam, Vinnavadi.

Amenities:

Education: Primary School in 60 villages, Middle school in 19 villages, Matriculation or Secondary School in 8 villages, namely Palli, Nedumbri, Vadanganpattu, Siruveliyanallore, Koorkai, Vinnamangalam, Valkadai, Munugappattu.

Higher Secondary or Pre University Courses or Intermediate or Junior College in 1 village of the CD Block,, namely Munugappattu.

College in 1 village, Adult Literacy Center in 1 village., College is in village, namely Perungalathur.

Medical: Hospital in 1 village, Dispensary in 2 villages,

Health Center in 10 villages, Sub Center in 3 villages, **Maternity** and Child Welfare Center in 11 villages, Community health workers in 59 villages.
The Villages having Hospital or Dispensary or Health Center are Vadanganpattu, Thandari, Thirumani.
Drinking Water: Tap water in 67 villages, Tank water in 18 villages, Well water in 67 villages, Tubewell in 67 villages and more than one source in 67 villages.
Bank: Banking facility in 8 villages, namely, Palli, Puliyarambakkam, Painkinar, Arugavoor Koorkai, Valkadai, Navalpakkam, Thirumani.
Credit Society in 18 villages Agricultural Credit Society in 12 Non-Agricultural Credit Society in 9 villages.
Others: Power supply in 66 villages, Cinema hall in 0 village, sport club in 0 village, Stadium or Auditorium or Community Hall in 0 village, Post Office in 36 villages.
There are 54 villages having bus facilities.
Villages with most of facilities: Puliyarambakkam Painkinar, Arugavoor, Koorkai, Valkadai, Navalpakkam Thirumani.
Villages without amenities (Education):
Perumpandi, Murugathanpoondi, Malamattai, Agaltheripattu, Melkovalavedu..
Scheduled Castes: Out of the total population of 87618 persons, 23689 persons (27.04%) belong to Scheduled Castes.
The villages having less than 10% SC population are Arathivellore, Marianallur, Perumpandi Barathanthangal, Ramakrishnapuram, Arumbarathi Vinnavadi, Vadaellappakkam, Vadanganpattu Siruveliyanallore, Vadathandalam, Murugathanpoondi Sarampattu, Malamattai, Maligaipattu, Melkovalavedu Korukkathur, Devanathur.
The villages having more than 50% SC population are Thalarapadi, Vadapoondipattu, Sirugattoor Puliyarambakkam, Sundivakkam, Thandari Vinnamangalam, Agaltheripattu, Puthukottai.
Sex ratio of Scheduled Caste population is 499.
Scheduled Castes Literates and Illiterates by Sex:

	Persons	Males	Females
Literate	12,808	7,624	5,184
Illiterate	10,881	4,245	6,636
Literacy rate	61.6	73.1	50.0
Graduate	310	252	58

Scheduled Castes (Dominant):
Adi Dravida, Arunthathiyar, Valluvan, Kuravan etc. Domban
For their cultural identity please see Appendix-I
Villages without Scheduled Castes: There are 11 villages without any scheduled caste population.
Scheduled Tribes: Out of the total population of 87618 persons, 1103 persons (1.26%) belong to Scheduled Tribes.
The villages having less than 10% ST population are Thalarapadi, Pullanthi, Arathivellore, Kunnathur Palli, Mangalam, Vadapoondipattu, Nedumbri, Jaderi Thenpoondipattu, Barathanthangal, Ramakrishnapuram Sirugattoor, Arumbarathi, Enaathavadi Sankattankundil, Pappanthangal, Duli, Periyakoil Vinnavadi, Perungalathur, Thumbai, Vadaellappakkam Vadanganpattu, Siruveliyanallore, Velianallur Kaliyar, Puliyarambakkam, Kizhpudupakkam, Painkinar Vadathandalam, Arugavoor, Perumalpallam, Sundivakkam Thandari, Murugathanpoondi, Vadugapattu, Sarampattu Thoyupedu, Eriyyur, Parasur, Madurai, Mukkur Koorkai, Kilpalandai, Kaduganoor, Malenagarampeedu Malamattai, Vinnamangalam, Agaltheripattu, Valkadai Kalanipakkam, Naval, Maligaipattu, Velleripattu Puthukottai, Navalpakkam, Korukkathur, Munugappattu Meiseshamangalam, Thirumani, Melputhur, Devanathur Pillanthi.
The villages having more than 50% ST population are None.
Sex ratio of Scheduled tribe population is 488.
Scheduled Tribes Literates and Illiterates by Sex:

	Persons	Males	Females
Literate	332	217	115
Illiterate	771	348	423
Literacy rate	36.8	47.3	26.0
Graduate	4	3	1

Scheduled Tribes (Dominant):
Irular, Malakkuravan, Kattunayakan, Malai Pandaram
For their cultural identity please see Appendix-II
Villages without Scheduled Tribes: There are 23 villages without any scheduled tribe population.
Literates and Illiterates by Sex (Total Population):

	Persons	Males	Females
Literate	51,289	30,504	20,785
Illiterate	36,329	13,198	23,131
Literacy rate	66	79	54
Graduate	1,442	1,109	333

Agriculture: ***Distribution of villages according to land use:***
Out of 67 villages, Total area (in hectare) is 24340.76, out of that 63.74 percent is cultivable and 45.27 percent of the cultivable area is irrigated.
Sources of Irrigation (Hectares): Government Canal 0, Private Canal 0, Well without Electricity 645.91, Well with Electricity 1433.28, Tubewell without Electricity 0, Tubewell with Electricity 16.17, Tank 2008.682, River 0, Lake 716.83, Waterfall 0, Others 331.68.
Villages with population of 5000 to 9999:
Kilpudupakkam, Mel Seeshamangalam.

Villages with population of 10000 and above: None

Distribution of Workers:

	Persons	Males	Females	WPR
Cultivators	12,585	8,245	4,340	28.36
Agricultural Labour	17,382	7,061	10,321	39.17
Household Industry	5,404	3,308	2,096	12.18
Other Workers	9,001	7,025	1,976	20.29
Main Workers	34,463	22,293	12,170	77.67
Marginal Workers	9,909	3,346	6,563	22.33
Total Workers	44,372	25,639	18,733	

Religion: Major Religious Communities:

	Persons	Males	Females	Sex Ratio
Hindu (98.44%)	86,250	43,006	43,244	1,006
Muslim (0.77%)	671	351	320	912
Christian (0.42%)	372	181	191	1,055
Sikh (0%)	1	-	1	-
Buddhists (0%)	-	-	-	-
Jain (0.22%)	193	97	96	990

Agewise Data:

	Persons	Males	Females	Sex Ratio
All ages	87,618	43,702	43,916	1005
0-14	24,822	12,619	12,203	967
15-44	41,038	20,388	20,650	1013
45-79	20,925	10,272	10,653	1037
80+	734	367	367	1000
Age not stated	99	56	43	768

Languages (Dominant):

Tamil, Telugu, Urdu, Hindi, Malayalam

Disabled Population:

	Persons	Males	Females	%
Total Disabled	1,991	1,110	881	
In Seeing	720	387	333	36.16
In Speech	209	118	91	10.5
In Hearing	164	78	86	8.24
In Movement	690	415	275	34.66
Mentally	208	112	96	10.45

CHINNA SALEM

Chinna Salem C.D. Block lies in the southern part of Viluppuram district. It is a part of Kallakurichi taluk. The Block is located at a distance of 89 kms. from district headquarters (Viluppuram). There are 63 villages in the block with the total population of 115,408 persons. Area of the C.D. Block is 392.78 sq. kms. It is bounded in the north by C.D. Block Kallakurichi, in the south by districts Perambalur and Cuddalore, in the east by C.D. Block Kallakurichi and district Cuddalore, in the west by district Salem and CD Block Kalreyan Hills.

Communications:

Roadways : N.H.-68: Direction- Attur to Chinnasalem, Neare st Villages- Ulagankathan, Bangaram, Kaniyamur, Rayappanur, A.Vasudevanur, Ammaiyagaram, Poondi.

Railway Station: Melnariyappanur.

River: Gomikar Nadi- Nearest Villages- Sadayampattu, Earvoipattinam, Mattigaikurichi. Vellor Nadi- Nearest Villages- Pakkambadi, Koogaiyur, V.Mamandur.

Backwards Region Grants Fund: It receives Backward Region Grants.

Annual Rainfall: Average Rainfall 1119 mm.

Ground Water: Availability of the ground water in the Basin is 8044.08 H.A.M. and the utilization is 7201.39 H.A.M. It belongs to Semi Critical category. Depth to water level varies from 5 to 10 meter below the ground. Most of the wells go down in summer months, according to the Ground Water Estimation Committee.

Forest and Reserved Forest: (Krishanpuram RF)- Nearest Villages- Eriyur, V.Krishnapuram R.F., Karunguzhi, Sembakurichi. (Poosappadi)- Nearest Villages- Elavadi, Poosapadi, Poosapadi R.F, Thenponparappi. (Thagarai)- Nearest Villages- Kadathur, Padarampallam, Thengiyanatham, Thagarai R.F, Thagarai, Paithanthurai. (Thottapadi)- Nearest Villages- Thottapadi, Thottapadi R.F, Thensiruv alur, Esanthai, Nainarpalayam.

Natural Division: Tondai Nadu.

Administration

Revenue **Division:** Kallkurichi. Parliamentary Constituenc y: 14 Kallakurichi (SC). District: Villupuram. Taluk: Kallakkurichi. Assembly Constituency: 80 Kallakurichi (SC), 79 Chinnasalem. Gram Panchayat: 50.

Villages: 63 **Inhabited:** 59 **Uninhabited:** 4

Ranking	District	State	National
Area	3	79	1977
Population	13	76	2993
Sex Ratio	9	228	1611
Child Sex Ratio	18	198	3246
Literacy Rate	14	333	2885
Density	1	26	3594
Work Participation Rate	21	231	221

Gram Panchayats:

Alambalam (Vridhachalam), Ammaiyagaram, Ammakalathur, Anumanandal, Bangaram, Elavadi, Eliyathur, Eriyur, Eruvaipattanam, Esandai, Kadathur, Kalasamudram, Kallanatham, Kaniyamur, Karanur, Karunguli, Karunthalakurichi, Koogaiyur, Kudiraichandal, Kural, Mattigaikurichi, Melnariyappanur, Moongilpadi, Nagakuppam, Nainarpalaiyam, Nallathur, Namasivayapuram, Paithanth, Pakkampadi, Pandiyankuppam , Pethanur, Pethasamudram, Poondi, Rayappanur, Rayarpalayam, Sadaiyampattu, Sembakurichi, Thagamtheerthapuram, Thagarai, Thenchettiyandal, Thengiyanatham, Thensiruvalur,

Thottapadi, Thottiyam, Timmapuram, Ulagamkathan, Ulagiyanallur, V. Mamandur, Vasudevanur, Vettiperumalagaram.

Amenities:

Education: Primary School in 56 villages, Middle school in 25 villages, Matriculation or Secondary School in 15 villages, namely Paithanthurai, Kudiraichandal, Karanur, Ulagankathan, Kaniyamur, Thenponparappi, Melnariyappanur, Ammaiyagaram, Olagiyanallur, Nainarpalayam, Thathathiripuram, Thagamtheerthapuram, Karunthalakurichi, Pakkambadi, Koogaiyur.

Higher Secondary or Pre University Courses or Intermediate or Junior College in 9 villages of the CD Block,, namely Ulagankathan, Thottiyam, Kaniyamur, Thenponparappi, Melnariyappanur, Nainarpalayam, Thagamtheerthapuram, Pakkambadi, Koogaiyur.

College in 0 village, Adult Literacy Center in 0 village.

Medical: Hospital in 0 village, Dispensary in 0 village, Health Center in 3 villages, Sub Center in 24 villages, Maternity and Child Welfare Center in 55 villages, Community health workers in 6 villages.

The Village having Hospital or Dispensary or Health Center is Pethanur.

Drinking Water: Tap water in 59 villages, Tank water in 13 villages, Well water in 59 villages, Tubewell in 59 villages and more than one source in 59 villages.

Bank: Banking facility in 8 villages, namely, Thottiyam, Bangaram, Rayappanur, Ammaiyagaram Poondi, Karunguzhi, Nainarpalayam, Kural.

Credit Society in 51 villages Agricultural Credit Society in 8 Non-Agricultural Credit Society in 2 villages.

Others: Power supply in 59 villages, Cinema hall in 42 villages, sport club in 0 village, Stadium or Auditorium or Community Hall in 0 village, Post Office in 57 villages.

There are 42 villages having bus facilities.

Villages with most of facilities: Thottiyam Bangaram, Rayappanur, Nainarpalayam, Kural.

Villages without amenities (Education):

Padarampallam, Maravanattham, Anumanandal..

Scheduled Castes: Out of the total population of 115408 persons, 40941 persons (35.48%) belong to Scheduled Castes.

The villages having less than 10% SC population are Padarampallam, Nallasavipuram, Thathathiripuram Thagamtheerthapuram, Veerapayangaram.

The villages having more than 50% SC population are Mattigaikurichi, Namasivayapuram, Thenponparappi A.Vasudevanur, Rayarpalayam, Esanthai, V.Mamandur.

Sex ratio of Scheduled Caste population is 497.

Scheduled Castes Literates and Illiterates by Sex:

	Persons	Males	Females
Literate	18,390	11,536	6,854
Illiterate	22,551	9,054	13,497
Literacy rate	52.0	65.0	38.9
Graduate	331	288	43

Scheduled Castes (Dominant):

Adi Dravida, Arunthathiyar, Valluvan, Pallan Kuravan etc.

For their cultural identity please see Appendix-I

Villages without Scheduled Castes: There are 5 villages without any scheduled caste population.

Scheduled Tribes: Out of the total population of 115408 persons, 108 persons (0.09%) belong to Scheduled Tribes.

The villages having less than 10% ST population are Sadayampattu, Earvoipattinam, Mattigaikurichi Kadathur, Padarampallam, Thengiyanatham, Thagarai Paithanthurai, Eliyathur, Nallathur, Kudiraichandal Karanur, Ulagankathan, Thottiyam, Thenchettiyandal Kallanatham, Thimmapuram, Pandiankuppam Maravanattham, Vettiperumalagaram, Namasivayapuram Bangaram, Kaniyamur, Moongilpady, Elavadi, Poosapadi Thenponparappi, Melnariyappanur, Rayappanur A.Vasudevanur, Ammaiyagaram, Poondi, Thottapadi Rayarpalayam, Pethanur, Nallasavipuram, Eriyur Karunguzhi, Ammakalathur, Olagiyanallur Nattarmangalam, Thensiruvalur, Esanthai Nainarpalayam, Pethosamuthiram, Thathathiripuram Kalasamudram, Thagamtheerthapuram, Kural V.Alambalam, Krishnapuram, Kilkuppam, Anumanandal Sembakurichi, Karunthalakurichi, Veerapayangaram Pakkambadi, Koogaiyur, V.Mamandur.

The villages having more than 50% ST population are None.

Sex ratio of Scheduled tribe population is 509.

Scheduled Tribes Literates and Illiterates by Sex:

	Persons	Males	Females
Literate	33	24	9
Illiterate	75	29	46
Literacy rate	37.1	53.3	20.5
Graduate	1	1	0

Scheduled Tribes (Dominant):

Malakkuravan, Adiyan, Malai Pandaram, Malayali

For their cultural identity please see Appendix-II

Villages without Scheduled Tribes: There are 55 villages without any scheduled tribe population.

Literates and Illiterates by Sex (Total Population):

	Persons	Males	Females
Literate	60,158	36,837	23,321
Illiterate	55,250	21,182	34,068
Literacy rate	59	73	46
Graduate	1,200	944	256

Agriculture: ***Distribution of villages according to land use:*** Out of 63 villages, Total area (in hectare) is 39278.25, out of that 63.75 percent is cultivable and 63.03 percent of the cultivable area is irrigated.

Sources of Irrigation (Hectares): Government Canal 134, Private Canal 0, Well without Electricity 4513, Well with Electricity 9162, Tubewell without Electricity 100, Tubewell with Electricity 0, Tank 36, River 0, Lake 1837, Waterfall 0, Others 0.

Villages with population of 5000 to 9999: Nainarpalaiyam.

Villages with population of 10000 and above: None

Distribution of Workers:

	Persons	Males	Females	WPR
Cultivators	29,732	16,386	13,346	42.89
Agricultural Labour	32,170	14,314	17,856	46.41
Household Industry	1,300	583	717	1.88
Other Workers	6,120	4,638	1,482	8.83
Main Workers	60,423	33,018	27,405	87.16
Marginal Workers	8,899	2,903	5,996	12.84
Total Workers	69,322	35,921	33,401	

Religion: Major Religious Communities:

	Persons	Males	Females	Sex Ratio
Hindu (98.33%)	113,486	57,091	56,395	988
Muslim (0.75%)	864	413	451	1,092
Christian (0.86%)	991	479	512	1,069
Sikh (0%)	3	2	1	500
Buddhists (0%)	-	-	-	-
Jain (0%)	-	-	-	-

Agewise Data:

	Persons	Males	Females	Sex Ratio
All ages	115,408	58,019	57,389	989
0-14	33,343	17,284	16,059	929
15-44	55,533	27,356	28,177	1030
45-79	24,830	12,499	12,331	987
80+	784	428	356	832
Age not stated	918	452	466	1031

Languages (Dominant):

Tamil, Telugu, Urdu, Kannada, Malayalam

Disabled Population:

	Persons	Males	Females	%
Total Disabled	1,792	1,041	751	
In Seeing	776	418	358	43.3
In Speech	166	100	66	9.26
In Hearing	92	56	36	5.13
In Movement	598	374	224	33.37
Mentally	160	93	67	8.93

CHINNAMANUR

Chinnamanur C.D. Block lies in the Central south part of Theni district. It is a part of Uthampalayam taluk. The Block is located at a distance of 19 kms. from district headquarters (Theni Allinagaram). There are 13 villages in the block with the total population of 49,601 persons. Area of the C.D. Block is 230.21 sq. kms. It is bounded in the north by CD Blocks Bodinayakkanur and Theni, in the south by CD Block Kambam, in the east by CD Block K. Myladumparai, and in the west by CD Block Uthamapalayam.

Communications:

Roadways : N.H.-220: Direction- Uthamapalayam to Theni, Nearest Village- Poolananthapuram.

River: Surilli Nadi- Nearest Village- Poolananthapuram.

Annual Rainfall: Average Rainfall 709 mm.

Ground Water: Availability of the ground water in the Basin is 4255.24 H.A.M. and the utilization is 4930.65 H.A.M. It belongs to Over Expoited category. Depth to water level varies from 2 to 10 meter below the ground. Most of the wells go down in summer months, according to the Ground Water Estimation Committee.

Forest and Reserved Forest: (Koothanatchiyar RF)- Nearest Village- Erasakanayakanur Hills.

Natural Division: NA

Administration

Revenue **Division:** Uthampalayam. Parliamentary Constituency: 33 Theni. District: Theni. Taluk: Uthampalayam. Assembly Constituency: 200 Bondinayakannur. Gram Panchayat: 14.

Villages: 13 **Inhabited:** 13 **Uninhabited:** 0

Ranking	**District**	**State**	**National**
Area	5	250	3659
Population	7	360	5302
Sex Ratio	6	299	2437
Child Sex Ratio	7	355	5931
Literacy Rate	3	175	1661
Density	5	102	4507
Work Participation Rate	5	312	1011

Gram Panchayats:

Alagapuri, Ayyampatty, Chinnaovalapuram, Erasakkanayackanur, Errananpatti, Kamatchipuram, Kanniservaipatti, Muthulapuram, Pottipuram , Pulanandapuram, Pulikkuthi, Sankarapuram, Seepalakottai , Veppampatti.

Amenities:

Education: Primary School in 12 villages, Middle school in 10 villages, Matriculation or Secondary School in 5 villages, namely Pottipuram, Seepulakottai, Pulikuthi, Erasakanayakanur, Kanniservaipatty.

Higher Secondary or Pre University Courses or Intermediate or Junior College in 1 village of the CD Block,, namely Seepulakottai.

College in 0 village, Adult Literacy Center in 0 village.

Medical: Hospital in 1 village, Dispensary in 0 village, Health Center in 4 villages, Sub Center in 12 villages, Maternity and Child Welfare Center in 1 village, Community health workers in 4 villages.
The Villages having Hospital or Dispensary or Health Center are Sangarapuram, Erasakanayakanur.
Drinking Water: Tap water in 13 villages, Tank water in 11 villages, Well water in 13 villages, Tubewell in 13 villages and more than one source in 13 villages.
Bank: Banking facility in 4 villages, namely, Pottipuram, Seepulakottai, Muthulapuram Erasakanayakanur.
Credit Society in 3 villages Agricultural Credit Society in 3 Non-Agricultural Credit Society in 0 village.
Others: Power supply in 13 villages, Cinema hall in 1 village, sport club in 0 village, Stadium or Auditorium or Community Hall in 0 village, Post Office in 13 villages.
There are 12 villages having bus facilities.
Villages with most of facilities: Pottipuram Seepulakottai, Muthulapuram, Erasakanayakanur.
Villages without amenities (Education):
Erasakanayakanur Hills..
Scheduled Castes: Out of the total population of 49601 persons, 12537 persons (25.28%) belong to Scheduled Castes.
The villages having less than 10% SC population are Veppampatty, Markayankottai, Pulikuthi Erasakanayakanur Hills.
The villages having more than 50% SC population are None.
Sex ratio of Scheduled Caste population is 498.
Scheduled Castes Literates and Illiterates by Sex:

	Persons	Males	Females
Literate	6,528	3,965	2,563
Illiterate	6,009	2,333	3,676
Literacy rate	59.8	72.6	47.0
Graduate	75	65	10

Scheduled Castes (Dominant):
Pallan, Paraiyan etc., Chakkiliyan, Arunthathiyar Madari
For their cultural identity please see Appendix-I
Villages without Scheduled Castes: There is 1 village without any scheduled caste population.
Scheduled Tribes: Out of the total population of 49601 persons, 0 persons (0%) belong to Scheduled Tribes.
The villages having less than 10% ST population are Pottipuram, Sangarapuram, Veppampatty, Seepulakottai Poolananthapuram, Markayankottai, Pulikuthi Alagapuri, Muthulapuram, Chinnaovulapuram Erasakanayakanur, Kanniservaipatty Erasakanayakanur Hills.
The villages having more than 50% ST population are None.
Villages without Scheduled Tribes: There are 13 villages without any scheduled tribe population.
Literates and Illiterates by Sex (Total Population):

	Persons	Males	Females
Literate	29,206	17,400	11,806
Illiterate	20,395	7,769	12,626
Literacy rate	67	79	54
Graduate	639	492	147

Agriculture: ***Distribution of villages according to land use:***
Out of 13 villages, Total area (in hectare) is 23021.22, out of that 35.08 percent is cultivable and 58.36 percent of the cultivable area is irrigated.
Sources of Irrigation (Hectares): Government Canal 213.12, Private Canal 0, Well without Electricity 403.43, Well with Electricity 2607.68, Tubewell without Electricity 678.5, Tubewell with Electricity 711.09, Tank 98.13, River 0, Lake 0, Waterfall 0, Others 0.
Villages with population of 5000 to 9999:
Pottipuram , Seepalakottai, Muthulapuram Erasakkanayackanur.
Villages with population of 10000 and above: None
Distribution of Workers:

	Persons	Males	Females	WPR
Cultivators	2,686	1,767	919	9.77
Agricultural Labour	20,539	9,943	10,596	74.67
Household Industry	571	255	316	2.08
Other Workers	3,710	2,746	964	13.49
Main Workers	23,155	12,833	10,322	84.18
Marginal Workers	4,351	1,878	2,473	15.82
Total Workers	27,506	14,711	12,795	

Religion: Major Religious Communities:

	Persons	Males	Females	Sex Ratio
Hindu (98%)	48,607	24,687	23,920	969
Muslim (1.13%)	560	274	286	1,044
Christian (0.85%)	420	200	220	1,100
Sikh (0.01%)	5	3	2	667
Buddhists (0%)	1	-	1	-
Jain (0.01%)	4	3	1	333

Agewise Data:

	Persons	Males	Females	Sex Ratio
All ages	49,601	25,169	24,432	971
0-14	13,565	7,286	6,279	862
15-44	23,730	11,852	11,878	1002
45-79	11,542	5,639	5,903	1047
80+	528	245	283	1155
Age not stated	236	147	89	605

Languages (Dominant):
Tamil, Telugu, Kannada, Malayalam, Urdu

Disabled Population:

	Persons	Males	Females	%
Total Disabled	1,684	783	901	
In Seeing	1,055	439	616	62.65
In Speech	130	65	65	7.72
In Hearing	54	26	28	3.21
In Movement	304	181	123	18.05
Mentally	141	72	69	8.37

CHITHAMUR

Chithamur C.D. Block lies in the south-eastern part of Kancheepuram district. It is a part of Cheyyur taluk. The taluk is located at a distance of 63 kms. from district headquarters (Kancheepuram). There are 59 villages in the block with the total population of 82,398 persons. Area of the C.D. Block is 293.70 sq. kms. It is bounded in the north by CD Blocks Maduranthakam and Lathur, in the south by Viluppuram district, in the east by the Bay of Bengal, and in the west by CD Block Acharapakkam.

Communications:

Roadways : N.H.-45: Direction- Viluppuram to Maduranthakam, Nearest Villages- Sothupakkam, Melmaruvathur, Keelmaruvathur, Thenpakkam.

Railway Station: Melmaruvathur.

Annual Rainfall: Average Rainfall 1105 mm.

Ground Water: Availability of the ground water in the Basin is 10967.37 H.A.M. and the utilization is 10850. 84 H.A.M. It belongs to Critical category. Depth to water level varies from 2 to 10 meter below the ground. Most of the wells go down in summer months, according to the Ground Water Estimation Committee.

Natural Division: Tondai Nadu.

Administration

Revenue **Division:** Madurnthakham. Parliamentary Constituency: 6 Kancheepuram (SC). District: Kancheepuram. Taluk: Cheyyur. Assembly Constituency: 34 Cheyyur (SC). Gram Panchayat: 43.

Villages: 59 **Inhabited:** 59 **Uninhabited:** 0

Ranking	**District**	**State**	**National**
Area	8	180	2854
Population	11	227	4026
Sex Ratio	7	218	1533
Child Sex Ratio	11	197	3244
Literacy Rate	13	326	2849
Density	1	196	3746
Work Participation Rate	10	251	2000

Gram Panchayats:

19. Kolathur , 289. kolathur, Agaram , Amandankaranai, Ammanambakkam, Arappedu, Chinnakayapakkam, Chinnakayapakkam , Chithamur, Chithamur , Chitharkadu, Chunampet , Easur , Indalur , Kumbili, Kadukalur, Kalpattu, Keelmaruvathur, Magundagiri, Maluvankaranai, Mambakkam , Melmaruvathur , Nerkunam , Nugumbal, Parukkal , Perambakkam, Periyakalakadi, Periyakayapakkam, Perukkaranai, Polambakkam , Pondur , Poongunam , Poraiyur, Porur, Puliyani , Puthirankottai, Puthur, Sirumailur , Sirunagar, Sothupakkam, Thandalam, Thenpakkam, Vannianallur , Vedal, Vilangadu .

Amenities:

Education: Primary School in 46 villages, Middle school in 16 villages, Matriculation or Secondary School in 7 villages, namely Polambakkam, Melmaruvathur, Indalur, Kayapakkam A,B/B, Kottaikadu B/B, Chunampet, Andarkuppam.

Higher Secondary or Pre University Courses or Intermediate or Junior College in 5 villages of the CD Block,, namely Polambakkam, Melmaruvathur, Indalur, Chunampet, Andarkuppam.

College in 0 village, Adult Literacy Center in 0 village.

Medical: Hospital in 2 villages, Dispensary in 2 villages, Health Center in 5 villages, Sub Center in 18 villages, Maternity and Child Welfare Center in 0 village, Community health workers in 59 villages.

The Villages having Hospital or Dispensary or Health Center are Poraiyur, Melmaruvathur, Chunampet.

Drinking Water: Tap water in 59 villages, Tank water in 45 villages, Well water in 59 villages, Tubewell in 59 villages and more than one source in 59 villages.

Bank: Banking facility in 9 villages, namely, Chithamur, Sothupakkam, Melmaruvathur, Indalur Kayapakkam A,B/B, Puthirankottai, Kottaikadu B/B Chunampet, Agaram.

Credit Society in 15 villages Agricultural Credit Society in 13 Non-Agricultural Credit Society in 7 villages.

Others: Power supply in 59 villages, Cinema hall in 0 village, sport club in 0 village, Stadium or Auditorium or Community Hall in 0 village, Post Office in 22 villages.

There are 48 villages having bus facilities.

Villages with most of facilities: Chithamur Sothupakkam, Melmaruvathur, Indalur Kayapakkam A,B/B, Puthirankottai, Kottaikadu B/B Chunampet, Agaram.

Villages without amenities (Education): Kannimangalam, Kurambarai, Kesavarayanpettai, Perambakkam, Vettamperumbakkam, Thuthuvilampattu, Voyalur, Illedu A,B/B, Kadappari, Siruvilambakkam, Venmalagaram, Vennandal, Vilambattu..

Scheduled Castes: Out of the total population of 82398 persons, 41707 persons (50.62%) belong to Scheduled Castes. The villages having less than 10% SC population are None..

The villages having more than 50% SC population are Chitharkadu, Kokkaranthangal A,B,C/C, Pondur Vilangadu, Porur, Poongunam A,B/B, Pazhuvur A,B/B Kannimangalam, Kurambarai, Poraiyur, Irumbili Parukkal, Thandalam, Vettamperumbakkam, Indalur Ammanambakkam, Kolathur, Ayakunnam, Thuthuvilampattu Puliyani, Voyalur, Attupattukottaipunji Puthirankottai, Panayadivakkam A,B,C/C Kottaikadu B/B, Kadukkalur A/B, Othivilagam Illedu A,B/B, Agaram, Sirunagar A,B/B Siruvilambakkam, Easur, Vennandal, Vilambattu Pudupattu, Vellankondagaram.

Sex ratio of Scheduled Caste population is 500.

Scheduled Castes Literates and Illiterates by Sex:

	Persons	Males	Females
Literate	19,475	11,443	8,032
Illiterate	22,232	9,408	12,824
Literacy rate	54.0	63.5	44.5
Graduate	328	271	57

Scheduled Castes (Dominant):

Adi Dravida, Arunthathiyar, Kuravan etc., Valluvan Moger

For their cultural identity please see Appendix-I

Villages without Scheduled Castes: There are 2 villages without any scheduled caste population.

Scheduled Tribes: Out of the total population of 82398 persons, 1040 persons (1.26%) belong to Scheduled Tribes. The villages having less than 10% ST population are Chitharkadu, Kokkaranthangal A,B,C/C, Pondur Vilangadu, Porur, Poongunam A,B/B, Pazhuvur A,B/B Kannimangalam, Polambakkam, Kurambarai Maluvankaranai, Poraiyur, Sothupakkam Kesavarayanpettai, Melmaruvathur, Keelmaruvathur Irumbili, Perambakkam, Magundagiri Perukkaranai A,B/B, Parukkal, Thandalam Vettamperumbakkam, Indalur, Ammanambakkam Thenpakkam, Arappedu, Kolathur, Ayakunnam Thuthuvilampattu, Puliyani, Voyalur Nerkunampattu A,B/B, Attupattukottaipunji Kayapakkam A,B/B, Periakalakadi, Puthirankottai Panayadivakkam A,B,C/C, Vedal, Kottaikadu B/B Kadukkalur A/B, Othivilagam, Chunampet, Illedu A,B/B Agaram, Sirunagar A,B/B, Sirumailur A,B/B Siruvilambakkam, Venmalagaram, Easur, Arasur A,B,C/C Vennandal, Andarkuppam, Vannianallur, Vilambattu Pudupattu, Vellankondagaram.

The villages having more than 50% ST population are None.

Sex ratio of Scheduled tribe population is 495.

Scheduled Tribes Literates and Illiterates by Sex:

	Persons	Males	Females
Literate	262	169	93
Illiterate	778	356	422
Literacy rate	30.1	39.2	21.1
Graduate	2	0	2

Scheduled Tribes (Dominant):

Irular, Kattunayakan, Malai Pandaram, Kondareddis Malakkuravan

For their cultural identity please see Appendix-II

Villages without Scheduled Tribes: There are 26 villages without any scheduled tribe population.

Literates and Illiterates by Sex (Total Population):

	Persons	Males	Females
Literate	43,129	25,498	17,631
Illiterate	39,269	15,877	23,392
Literacy rate	60	70	49
Graduate	1,065	811	254

Agriculture: ***Distribution of villages according to land use:*** Out of 59 villages, Total area (in hectare) is 29370.16, out of that 60.86 percent is cultivable and 73.22 percent of the cultivable area is irrigated.

Sources of Irrigation (Hectares): Government Canal 31.88, Private Canal 0, Well without Electricity 1091.49, Well with Electricity 5945.91, Tubewell without Electricity 2.02, Tubewell with Electricity 995.08, Tank 218.51, River 0, Lake 4603.61, Waterfall 0, Others 198.55.

Villages with population of 5000 to 9999: Chunampet.

Villages with population of 10000 and above: None

Distribution of Workers:

	Persons	Males	Females	WPR
Cultivators	8,286	5,759	2,527	19.65
Agricultural Labour	26,929	12,881	14,048	63.86
Household Industry	1,417	737	680	3.36
Other Workers	5,539	4,324	1,215	13.1
Main Workers	17,276	11,905	5,371	40.9
Marginal Workers	24,895	11,796	13,099	59.0
Total Workers	42,171	23,701	18,470	

Religion: Major Religious Communities:

	Persons	Males	Females	Sex Ratio
Hindu (98.57%)	81,219	40,796	40,423	991
Muslim (0.51%)	420	195	225	1,154
Christian (0.83%)	680	342	338	988
Sikh (0%)	-	-	-	-
Buddhists (0%)	-	-	-	-
Jain (0.01%)	8	4	4	1,000

Agewise Data:

	Persons	Males	Females	Sex Ratio
All ages	82,398	41,375	41,023	99
0-14	25,181	12,870	12,311	95

15-44	39,009	19,357	19,652	1015
45-79	17,398	8,714	8,684	997
80+	622	342	280	819
Age not stated	188	92	96	1043

Languages (Dominant):

Tamil, Telugu, Urdu, Hindi, Marathi

Disabled Population:

	Persons	Males	Females	%
Total Disabled	1,993	1,083	910	
In Seeing	852	422	430	42.75
In Speech	183	102	81	9.18
In Hearing	175	82	93	8.78
In Movement	627	396	231	31.46
Mentally	156	81	75	7.83

COONOOR

Coonoor C.D. Block lies in the southern part of Nilgiris district. It is a part of Coonoor taluk. The Block is located at a distance of 18 kms. from district headquarters (Uthagamandalam). There are 04 villages in the block with the total population of 30,663 persons. Area of the C.D. Block is 86.36 sq. kms. It is bounded in the north by CD Block Uthagamangalam and Kotagiri, in the south by district Coimbatore, in the east by CD Block Kotagiri and district Coimbatore, and in the west by CD Block Uthagamandalam.

Communications:

Roadways : S.H.-31: Direction- Uthagamandalam to Mettuppalayam, Nearest Villages- Burliar, Coonoor.

Railway Station: Burliar.

Annual Rainfall: Average Rainfall 1920 mm.

Ground Water: Availability of the ground water in the Basin is 1839.36 H.A.M. and the utilization is 84.93 H.A.M. It belongs to Safe category. Depth to water level varies from 0 to 10 meter below the ground. Most of the wells go down in summer months, according to the Ground Water Estimation Committee.

Forest and Reserved Forest: (Halakarai RF)- Nearest Villages- Yadappalli, Burliar, Coonoor. (Mellur Slopes)- Nearest Village- Melur. (Hadathoral)- Nearest Villages- Burliar, Coonoor. (Kulakambai)- Nearest Village- Melur.

Natural Division: NA

Administration

Revenue **Division:** Coonoor. Parliamentary Constituency: 19 Nilgiris. District: The Nilgiris. Taluk: Coonoor. Assembly Constituency: 110 Coonoor. Gram Panchayat: 06.

Villages: 4 **Inhabited:** 4 **Uninhabited:** 0

Ranking	District	State	National
Area	4	373	5825
Population	4	379	6043
Sex Ratio	2	49	447
Child Sex Ratio	4	178	3087
Literacy Rate	1	25	370
Density	3	215	3061
Work Participation Rate	1	151	2294

Gram Panchayats:

Bandishola, Berhatty, Burliyar, Melur, Yedappalli .

Amenities:

Education: Primary School in 4 villages, Middle school in 3 villages, Matriculation or Secondary School in 3 villages, namely Yadappalli, Coonoor, Melur.

Higher Secondary or Pre University Courses or Intermediate or Junior College in 3 villages of the CD Block,, namely Yadappalli, Coonoor, Melur.

College in 0 village, Adult Literacy Center in 0 village.

Medical: Hospital in 0 village, Dispensary in 0 village, Health Center in 2 villages, Sub Center in 2 villages, Maternity and Child Welfare Center in 0 village, Community health workers in 0 village.

Drinking Water: Tap water in 4 villages, Tank water in 0 villages, Well water in 4 villages, Tubewell in 4 villages and more than one source in 4 villages.

Bank: Banking facility in 2 villages, namely, Coonoor, Melur.

Credit Society in 2 villages Agricultural Credit Society in 2 Non-Agricultural Credit Society in 0 village.

Others: Power supply in 4 villages, Cinema hall in 1 village, sport club in 3 villages, Stadium or Auditorium or Community Hall in 0 village, Post Office in 4 villages.

There are 4 villages having bus facilities.

Villages with most of facilities: Coonoor, Melur.

Villages without Amenities (Education): None..

Scheduled Castes: Out of the total population of 30663 persons, 13540 persons (44.16%) belong to Scheduled Castes. The villages having less than 10% SC population are None..

The villages having more than 50% SC population are None.

Sex ratio of Scheduled Caste population is 504.

Scheduled Castes Literates and Illiterates by Sex:

	Persons	Males	Females
Literate	9,253	5,185	4,068
Illiterate	4,287	1,530	2,757
Literacy rate	76.9	87.4	66.7
Graduate	128	98	30

Scheduled Castes (Dominant):

Pallan, Paraiyan etc., Adi Dravida, Chakkiliyan Arunthathiyar

For their cultural identity please see Appendix-I

Villages without Scheduled Castes: There is 0 village without any scheduled caste population.

Scheduled Tribes: Out of the total population of 30663 persons, 956 persons (3.12%) belong to Scheduled Tribes.

The villages having less than 10% ST population are None..

The villages having more than 50% ST population are None.

Sex ratio of Scheduled tribe population is 482.

Scheduled Tribes Literates and Illiterates by Sex:

	Persons	Males	Females
Literate	328	215	113
Illiterate	628	280	348
Literacy rate	40.0	49.4	29.3
Graduate	1	1	0

Scheduled Tribes (Dominant):

Kurumbas, Irular, Kurumans, Malai Pandaram, Paniyan

For their cultural identity please see Appendix-II

Villages without Scheduled Tribes: There Villages without Sche 0 village without any scheduled tribe population.

Literates and Illiterates by Sex (Total Population):

	Persons	Males	Females
Literate	21,678	12,005	9,673
Illiterate	8,985	3,076	5,909
Literacy rate	79	89	69
Graduate	976	707	269

Agriculture: *Distribution of villages according to land use:* Out of 4 villages, Total area (in hectare) is 8636, out of that 59.18 percent is cultivable and 1.1 percent of the cultivable area is irrigated.

Sources of Irrigation (Hectares): Government Canal 0, Private Canal 0, Well without Electricity 0, Well with Electricity 56, Tubewell without Electricity 0, Tubewell with Electricity 0, Tank 0, River 0, Lake 0, Waterfall 0, Others 0.

Villages with population of 5000 to 9999:

Yedappalli, Coonoor.

Villages with population of 10000 and above:

Melur.

Distribution of Workers:

	Persons	Males	Females	WPR
Cultivators	271	138	133	1.73
Agricultural Labour	455	205	250	2.9
Household Industry	49	34	15	0.31
Other Workers	14,901	7,969	6,932	95.06
Main Workers	15,256	8,169	7,087	97.32
Marginal Workers	420	177	243	2.68
Total Workers	15,676	8,346	7,330	

Religion: Major Religious Communities:

	Persons	Males	Females	Sex Ratio
Hindu (87.4%)	26,798	13,179	13,619	1,033
Muslim (2.53%)	775	389	386	992
Christian (10.04%)	3,078	1,507	1,571	1,042
Sikh (0%)	-	-	-	-
Buddhists (0%)	1	1	-	-
Jain (0.01%)	2	1	1	1,000

Agewise Data:

	Persons	Males	Females	Sex Ratio
All ages	30,663	15,081	15,582	1033
0-14	7,310	3,721	3,589	965
15-44	16,253	7,883	8,370	1062
45-79	6,902	3,392	3,510	1035
80+	179	74	105	1419
Age not stated	19	11	8	727

Languages (Dominant):

Tamil, Kannada, Telugu, Malayalam, Others

Disabled Population:

	Persons	Males	Females	%
Total Disabled	873	497	376	
In Seeing	529	303	226	60.6
In Speech	53	26	27	6.07
In Hearing	50	21	29	5.73
In Movement	184	115	69	21.08
Mentally	57	32	25	6.53

CUDDALORE

Cuddalore C.D. Block lies in the north-eastern part of Cuddalore district. It is a part of Cuddalore taluk. The Block is located at a distance of (00) kms. from district headquarters (Cuddalore). There are 64 villages in the block with the total population of 170,292 persons. Area of the C.D. Block is 229.04 sq. kms. It is bounded in the south by CD Block Kurinjipadi, in the east by the Bay of Bengal, in the west by CD Blocks Panruti and Annagramam, and district Viluppuram, and it has common boundary with Union Territory of Pondicherry on north and east.

Communications:

Roadways : N.H.-45A: Direction- Pandurikuppam to Chidambaram, Nearest Villages- Pachaikuppam, Kudikadu, Karaikadu, Sedapalayam, Semmankuppam. N.H.-66: Direction- Pudirikuppam to Pondicherry, Nearest Villages- Chinnakanganabkuppam, Periyakanganankuppam. N.H-68: Direction- Kurinjipadi to Pondicherry, Nearest Villages- Pachaikuppam, Karaikadu, Annavalli, Sedapalayam. S.H.-9: Direction- Panruti to Cuddalore, Nearest Villages- Velisemmandalam, Kondur, Thottapatttu, Senjikumarapuram Varakkalpattu, Karamanikuppam, Gunamangalam, Pillali.

Railway Station: Varakkalpattu, Karaikadu.

Rivers: Baraha Nadi- Nearest Villages- Alagiyanatham, Erandayiravillagam, Vellapakkam, Marudadu, Nathapattu, Velisemmandalam, Subavappalavadi, Gunduuppalavadi, Uchimedu, Periyakanganankuppam. Ponnaiyar Nadi- Neares Villages- C N Palayam, Naduveerappattu, Vanamadevi, Vilangalpattu, Thirumanikuzhi, Otteri, Thiruuandipuram, Pillali, Thottapatttu, Kondur.

Backwards Region Grants Fund: It receives Backward Region

Grants.

Annual Rainfall: Average Rainfall 1050 mm.

Ground Water: Availability of the ground water in the Basin is 18107.29 MCM and the utilization is 16199.43 MCM. It belongs to Semi Critical category. Depth to water level varies from 2 to 10 meter below the ground. Most of the wells go down in summer months, according to the Ground Water Estimation Committee.

Coastal Villages- (Bay of Bengal)- Nearest Villages- Madalapattu, Subavappalavadi, Gunduuppalavadi, Pachaikuppam, Kudikadu.

Natural Division: Tondai Nadu.

Administration

Revenue **Division:** Cuddalore. Parliamentary Constituency: 26 Cuddalore (SC). District: Cuddalore. Taluk: Cuddalore. Assembly Constituency: 155 Cuddalore, 156 Kurinjipadi. Gram Panchayat: 51.

Border Villages- (U.T. of Pondicherry)- Nearest Villages- Melakuppam, Nallathur, Thookkanampakkam, Thennampakkam, Chellancherry, Pudukadai, Vadapuramkeelpathi, Killingikuppam, Singirigudi, Madalapattu, Keelalingipattu, Nagapanoor, Melingippattu, Odalappattu, Keelkumaramangalam, Karanappattu, Malayaperumalagaram, Ulleripattu, Karaimedu, Thiruppanampakkam, Kalaiyur, Alagiyanatham, Erandayiravillagam, Vellapakkam, Marudadu, Nathapattu, Velisemmandalam, Chinnakanganabkuppam, Subavappalavadi, Gunduuppalavadi, Uchimedu, Periyakangananakuppam.

Villages: 64 **Inhabited:** 64 **Uninhabited:** 0

Ranking	District	State	National
Area	7	251	3675
Population	1	1	1277
Sex Ratio	11	300	2514
Child Sex Ratio	8	144	2626
Literacy Rate	7	195	1792
Density	13	338	1354
Work Participation Rate	2	19	4127

Gram Panchayats:

Annavalli, Arisipperiyankuppam, Azhagiyanatham, Chellancheri, Chennappanayakkanpalayam, Cuddalore Port , Gunduuppalavadi , Kadukkampalayam, karaikkadu, Karaimedu, Karaiyeravittakuppam, Karamanikuppam, Karanaparttu, Kil Alinjipattu, Kilinjikuppam, Kilkumaramangalam, Konamangalam, Kondur, Kudikkadu, Kumalankulam, Madalapattu, Malaiaperumal Agaram, Marudadu, Melalinjippattu, Naduvirappattu , Nallathur, Nanamedu, Nattapattu, Pachayankuppam, Pallipattu, Periyakangananakuppam, Pillali, Pudukkadai, Ramapuram, Sedappalayam, Sembankuppam, Singirikkudi, Tennambakkam, Thukkanampakkam, Tirumanikkuli, Tiruppanambakkam, Tiruvandipuram, Tottappattu, Uchimedu, Ulleripattu, Vanamadevi, Varakalpattu, Vellakarai, Vellapakkam, Vilangalpattu.

Amenities:

Education: Primary School in 54 villages, Middle school in 22 villages, Matriculation or Secondary School in 9 villages, namely Thookkanampakkam, Pallipattu, Velisemmandalam, Varakkalpattu, Thiruuandipuram, Naduveerappattu, C N Palayam, Vellakkarai, Ramapuram.

Higher Secondary or Pre University Courses or Intermediate or Junior College in 5 villages of the CD Block,, namely Thookkanampakkam, Pallipattu, Velisemmandalam, Naduveerappattu, Vellakkarai.

College in 0 village, Adult Literacy Center in 0 village.

Medical: Hospital in 1 village, Dispensary in 0 village, Health Center in 6 villages, Sub Center in 26 villages, Maternity and Child Welfare Center in 0 village, Community health workers in 24 villages.

The Village having Hospital or Dispensary or Health Center is Uchimedu.

Drinking Water: Tap water in 64 villages, Tank water in 0 villages, Well water in 64 villages, Tubewell in 64 villages and more than one source in 64 villages.

Bank: Banking facility in 4 villages, namely, Thookkanampakkam, Naduveerappattu, Kudikadu Karaikadu.

Credit Society in 18 villages Agricultural Credit Society in 17 Non-Agricultural Credit Society in 0 village.

Others: Power supply in 64 villages, Cinema hall in 2 villages, sport club in 0 village, Stadium or Auditorium or Community Hall in 0 village, Post Office in 64 villages.

There are 62 villages having bus facilities.

Villages with most of facilities: Thookkanampakkam Naduveerappattu, Karaikadu.

Villages without amenities (Education): Vadapuramkeelpathi, Nagapanoor, Senjikumarapuram, Karuppadithundu, Kumarapettai, Mavadipalayam, Vettukkulam, Ponniyankuppam, Gangamanayakkam Kuppam

Scheduled Castes: Out of the total population of 170292 persons, 48609 persons (28.54%) belong to Scheduled Castes. The villages having less than 10% SC population are Melakuppam, Vadapuramkeelpathi, Odalappattu Chinnakanganabkuppam, Subavappalavadi Karuppadithundu, Arisiperiankuppam, Kumarapettai Mavadipalayam, Karaiyerattakuppam, Ponniyankuppam Pachaikuppam.

The villages having more than 50% SC population are Pudukadai, Madalapattu, Nagapanoor, Melingippattu

Malayaperumalagaram, Ulleripattu, Thiruppanampakkam Kalaiyur, Alagiyanatham, Erandayiravillagam Vellapakkam, Marudadu, Periyakanganankuppam Gunamangalam, Otteri, Gangamanayakkam Kuppam.

Sex ratio of Scheduled Caste population is 498.

Scheduled Castes Literates and Illiterates by Sex:

	Persons	Males	Females
Literate	23,331	13,751	9,580
Illiterate	25,278	10,658	14,620
Literacy rate	56.4	66.3	46.4
Graduate	487	371	116

Scheduled Castes (Dominant):

Adi Dravida, Arunthathiyar, Valluvan, Paraiyan etc. Generic Castes etc.

For their cultural identity please see Appendix-I

Villages without Scheduled Castes: There are 9 villages without any scheduled caste population.

Scheduled Tribes: Out of the total population of 170292 persons, 336 persons (0.2%) belong to Scheduled Tribes.

The villages having less than 10% ST population are Melakuppam, Nallathur, Thookkanampakkam Thennampakkam, Chellancherry, Pudukadai Vadapuramkeelpathi, Killingikuppam, Singirigudi Madalapattu, Keelalingipattu, Nagapanoor Melingippattu, Odalappattu, Keelkumaramangalam Karanappattu, Pallipattu, Malayaperumalagaram Ulleripattu, Karaimedu, Thiruppanampakkam, Kalaiyur Alagiyanatham, Erandayiravillagam, Vellapakkam Marudadu, Nathapattu, Velisemmandalam Chinnakanganabkuppam, Subavappalavadi Gunduuppalavadi, Uchimedu, Periyakanganankuppam Kondur, Thottapatttu, Senjikumarapuram Varakkalpattu, Karamanikuppam, Gunamangalam, Pillali Thiruuandipuram, Karuppadithundu, Arisiperiankuppam Kumarapettai, Otteri, Thirumanikuzhi, Vanamadevi Vilangalpattu, Naduveerappattu, C N Palayam Vellakkarai, Ramapuram, Mavadipalayam Karaiyerattakuppam, Vettukkulam, Cuddalore Ponniyankuppam, Pachaikuppam, Kudikadu, Karaikadu Annavalli, Gangamanayakkam Kuppam, Sedapalayam Semmankuppam.

The villages having more than 50% ST population are None.

Sex ratio of Scheduled tribe population is 497.

Scheduled Tribes Literates and Illiterates by Sex:

	Persons	Males	Females
Literate	95	50	45
Illiterate	241	119	122
Literacy rate	35.1	37.6	32.6
Graduate	7	5	2

Scheduled Tribes (Dominant):

Kattunayakan, Irular, Malakkuravan, Malai Pandaram Koraga

For their cultural identity please see Appendix-II

Villages without Scheduled Tribes: There are 51 villages without any scheduled tribe population.

Literates and Illiterates by Sex (Total Population):

	Persons	Males	Females
Literate	98,047	57,581	40,466
Illiterate	72,245	28,843	43,402
Literacy rate	66	76	55
Graduate	3,780	2,701	1,079

Agriculture: ***Distribution of villages according to land use:***

Out of 64 villages, Total area (in hectare) is 22904.23, out of that 76.28 percent is cultivable and 67.63 percent of the cultivable area is irrigated.

Sources of Irrigation (Hectares): Government Canal 0, Private Canal 0, Well without Electricity 0, Well with Electricity 35, Tubewell without Electricity 0, Tubewell with Electricity 11781.18, Tank 0, River 0, Lake 0, Waterfall 0, Others 0.

Villages with population of 5000 to 9999:

Kilinjikuppam, Gunduuppalavadi , Kondur Tiruvandipuram, Naduvirappattu Chennappanayakkanpalayam, Vellakarai , Ramapuram Cuddalore Port, Pachchyankuppam, karaikkadu.

Villages with population of 10000 and above: None

Distribution of Workers:

	Persons	Males	Females	WPR
Cultivators	10,271	7,502	2,769	14.4
Agricultural Labour	37,107	20,945	16,162	52.03
Household Industry	3,327	1,993	1,334	4.66
Other Workers	20,614	17,500	3,114	28.9
Main Workers	51,669	38,030	13,639	72.45
Marginal Workers	19,650	9,910	9,740	27.55
Total Workers	71,319	47,940	23,379	

Religion: Major Religious Communities:

	Persons	Males	Females	Sex Ratio
Hindu (98.05%)	166,975	84,701	82,274	971
Muslim (1.08%)	1,837	945	892	944
Christian (0.79%)	1,337	704	633	899
Sikh (0%)	4	3	1	333
Buddhists (0%)	3	2	1	500
Jain (0%)	8	4	4	1,000

Agewise Data:

	Persons	Males	Females	Sex Ratio
All ages	170,292	86,424	83,868	970
0-14	48,839	24,714	24,125	976
15-44	87,059	44,263	42,796	967
45-79	32,964	16,678	16,286	976

80+	1,176	637	539	846
Age not stated	254	132	122	924

Languages (Dominant):

Tamil, Telugu, Urdu, Malayalam, Hindi

Disabled Population:

	Persons	Males	Females	%
Total Disabled	5,034	2,228	2,806	
In Seeing	2,986	1,006	1,980	59.32
In Speech	359	191	168	7.13
In Hearing	289	147	142	5.74
In Movement	1,120	724	396	22.25
Mentally	280	160	120	5.56

DEVAKOTTAI

Devakottai C.D. Block lies in the eastern part of Sivagana district. It is a part of Devakottai taluk. The Block is located at a distance of 60 kms. from district headquarters (Sivaganga). There are 44 villages in the block with the total population of 68,687 persons. Area of the C.D. Block is 377.35 sq. kms. It is bounded in the north by CD Blocks Kannankkudi, Sakkottai and Kallal, in the south by district Ramanathapuram, in the east by CD Block Kannankudi and district Ramanathapuram, in the west by CD Blocks Kallal and Kalayarkoil.

Communications:

Roadways : N.H.-210: Direction- Karaikkudi to Tiruvadanai, Nearest Villages- Aravayal, Sirumaruthur, Kannankottai, Thenneervayal, Udayachi, Sathikkottai, Thalakkavayal, Maviduthikkottai, Kadagampatti, Thiruppakkotai, Kodikkottai, Pagayani, Thidakkottai, Karkkalathur, Melasemponmari. S.H.-33: Direction- Sivaganga to Tiruvadanai, Nearest Villages- Nedodai, Saruvanendal, Kodikulam, Mararisaruguni, Anthagudi, Orasoor, Ponnalikkottai, Thiruvagampet, Muppaiyur, Karkkalathur, Kurunthanakkottai.

River: Manimuttar Nadi- Nearest Villages- Kannankottai, Thenneervayal, Eluvankottai, Ekaraikottavayal, Udayachi, Nallankudi, Sathikkottai.

Backwards Region Grants Fund: It receives Backward Region Grants.

Annual Rainfall: Average Rainfall 904 mm.

Ground Water: Availability of the ground water in the Basin is 6727.62 H.A.M. and the utilization is 235.55 H.A.M. It belongs to Safe category. Depth to water level varies from 2 to 10 meter below the ground. Most of the wells go down in summer months, according to the Ground Water Estimation Committee.

Natural Division: NA

Administration

Revenue **Division:** Devakottai. Parliamentary Constituency: 31 Sivaganga. District: Sivaganga. Taluk: Devakottai. Assembly Constituency: 184 Karaikudi. Gram Panchayat: 42.

Villages: 67 **Inhabited:** 67 **Uninhabited:** 0

Ranking	**District**	**State**	**National**
Area	5	89	2075
Population	8	292	4525
Sex Ratio	1	5	85
Child Sex Ratio	9	201	3303
Literacy Rate	1	94	1076
Density	5	184	5007
Work Participation Rate	10	341	1870

Gram Panchayats:

Aravayal, Eluvankottai, Kallangudi , Kandadevi, Kannankottai , Karai, Karkalathur, Kiliyoor, Kurunthanakottai, Maviduthikottai, Muppaiyur, Kalipuli, Nagadi, Panangulam, Pudukiruchi, Tiruppakottai, Puliyal, Sakkanthi, Selugai, Shanmuganathapuram, Thalakkavayal, Thallakkavayal, Thanavayal, Theneervayal, Thidakkottai, Thirumanavayal, Thoonugudi, Tirumanavayal, Veerai, Vettivayal.

Amenities:

Education: Primary School in 47 villages, Middle school in 17 villages, Matriculation or Secondary School in 8 villages, namely Perattukkottai, Karai, Thalakkavayal, Nedodai, Mararisaruguni, Thidakkottai, Minnittakudi, Thiruvagampet.

Higher Secondary or Pre University Courses or Intermediate or Junior College in 5 villages of the CD Block,, namely Kallangudi, Thalakkavayal, Nedodai, Minnittakudi, Thiruvagampet.

College in 1 village, Adult Literacy Center in 0 village., College is in village, namely Mararisaruguni.

Medical: Hospital in 7 villages, Dispensary in 4 villages, Health Center in 5 villages, Sub Center in 21 villages, Maternity and Child Welfare Center in 6 villages, Community health workers in 62 villages.

The Villages having Hospital or Dispensary or Health Center are Eluvankottai, Vettiyalangaulam, Thiruppakkotai, Mararisaruguni, Kumani, Thidakkottai, Orumaniyandal, Thiruvagampet, Sirunallur, Edaiyagudi.

Drinking Water: Tap water in 67 villages, Tank water in 51 villages, Well water in 67 villages, Tubewell in 67 villages and more than one source in 67 villages.

Bank: Banking facility in 5 villages, namely, Perattukkottai, Karai, Vellikatti, Nedodai Thidakkottai.

Credit Society in 12 villages Agricultural Credit Society in 10 Non-Agricultural Credit Society in 0 village.

Others: Power supply in 67 villages, Cinema hall in 0 village, sport club in 0 village, Stadium or Auditorium or Community Hall in 25 villages, Post Office in 66 villages.

There are 56 villages having bus facilities.

Villages with most of facilities: Perattukkottai Karai, Vellikatti, Nedodai, Thidakkottai.

Villages without amenities (Education): Kandadevi, Elakkanivayal, Thazhayoor, Udayachi, Nallankudi, Sathikkottai, Thachanvayal, Kadagampatti, Kodikkottai, Thalanendal, Vasanthani, Saruvanendal, Kodikulam, Kumani, Seluvathi, Paraiyanenthel, Irumpuvayal, Virisoor, Edaiyagudi, Kumani..

Scheduled Castes: Out of the total population of 68687 persons, 16271 persons (23.69%) belong to Scheduled Castes. The villages having less than 10% SC population are Kannankottai, Thalanendal, Thirani, Nagamathi Seluvathi, Paraiyanenthel, Orasoor, Edaiyagudi Kumani, Selugai, Vadinanniyur.

The villages having more than 50% SC population are Sirumaruthur, Elakkanivayal, Nallankudi Sathikkottai, Thachanvayal, Maviduthikkottai Kadagampatti, Saruvanendal, Kodikulam, Irumpuvayal.

Sex ratio of Scheduled Caste population is 526.

Scheduled Castes Literates and Illiterates by Sex:

	Persons	Males	Females
Literate	9,431	5,199	4,232
Illiterate	6,840	2,516	4,324
Literacy rate	65.4	77.2	55.1
Graduate	135	89	46

Scheduled Castes (Dominant):

Pallan, Paraiyan etc., Chakkiliyan, Kadaiyan Valluvan

For their cultural identity please see Appendix-I

Villages without Scheduled Castes: There are 5 villages without any scheduled caste population.

Scheduled Tribes: Out of the total population of 68687 persons, 0 persons (0%) belong to Scheduled Tribes. The villages having less than 10% ST population are Kandadevi, Perattukkottai, Aravayal, Melasemponmari Sirumaruthur, Elakkanivayal, Thazhayoor Kannankottai, Thenneervayal, Eluvankottai Nachangulam, Ekaraikottavayal, Udayachi, Nallankudi Sathikkottai, Thachanvayal, Pudukottai, Kallangudi Nedungulam, Vettiyalangaulam, Vagaikudi, Karai Kottur, Thirumanavayal, Thalakkavayal Maviduthikkottai, Kadagampatti, Thiruppakkotai Kodikkottai, Thalanendal, Manjani, Vasanthani Sruvathi, Vejayapuram, Vellikatti, Thirani, Nedodai Saruvanendal, Kodikulam, Mararisaruguni, Nagamathi Kumani, Seluvathi, Panangulam, Sakkanthi, Pagayani Thidakkottai, Paraiyanenthel, Anthagudi, Orasoor Ponnalikkottai, Irumpuvayal, Uruvatti, N.Manakkudi Orumaniyandal, Minnittakudi, Virisoor, Thiruvagampet Muppaiyur, Karkkalathur, Kurunthanakkottai Sirunallur, Edaiyagudi, Kumani, Selugai, Vedimar Vadinanniyur.

The villages having more than 50% ST population are None.

Villages without Scheduled Tribes: There are 67 villages without any scheduled tribe population.

Literates and Illiterates by Sex (Total Population):

	Persons	Males	Females
Literate	43,604	24,094	19,510
Illiterate	25,083	8,417	16,666
Literacy rate	71	84	60
Graduate	911	588	323

Agriculture: ***Distribution of villages according to land use:*** Out of 67 villages, Total area (in hectare) is 37735.16, out of that 53.08 percent is cultivable and 44.66 percent of the cultivable area is irrigated.

Sources of Irrigation (Hectares): Government Canal 0, Private Canal 0, Well without Electricity 71.81, Well with Electricity 39.17, Tubewell without Electricity 2.25, Tubewell with Electricity 246.35, Tank 8586.03, River 0, Lake 0, Waterfall 0, Others 0.

Villages with population of 5000 to 9999: None

Villages with population of 10000 and above: None

Distribution of Workers:

	Persons	Males	Females	WPR
Cultivators	21,092	11,503	9,589	58.18
Agricultural Labour	10,391	3,946	6,445	28.66
Household Industry	522	207	315	1.44
Other Workers	4,248	3,318	930	11.72
Main Workers	30,379	17,261	13,118	83.8
Marginal Workers	5,874	1,713	4,161	16.2
Total Workers	36,253	18,974	17,279	

Religion: Major Religious Communities:

	Persons	Males	Females	Sex Ratio
Hindu (82.77%)	56,851	26,935	29,916	1,111
Muslim (1.43%)	984	442	542	1,226
Christian (15.79%)	10,844	5,067	5,777	1,140
Sikh (0%)	1	-	1	-
Buddhists (0%)	-	-	-	-
Jain (0.01%)	5	1	4	4,000

Agewise Data:

	Persons	Males	Females	Sex Ratio
All ages	68,740	32,472	36,268	1117
0-14	17,691	8,921	8,770	983
15-44	31,038	13,924	17,114	1229
45-79	19,078	9,162	9,916	1082
80+	830	407	423	1039
Age not stated	103	58	45	776

Languages (Dominant):

Tamil, Telugu, Malayalam, Others

Disabled Population:

	Persons	Males	Females	%
Total Disabled	2,058	940	1,118	
In Seeing	1,267	493	774	61.56
In Speech	157	90	67	7.63
In Hearing	88	33	55	4.28
In Movement	390	237	153	18.95
Mentally	156	87	69	7.58

DHARAPURAM

Dharapuram C.D. Block lies in the southern part of Erode district. It is a part of Dharapuram taluk. The Block is located at a distance of 80 kms. from district headquarters (Erode). There are 23 villages in the block with the total population of 63,020 persons. Area of the C.D. Block is 355.52 sq. kms. It is bounded in the north by C.D. Block Kundadam, in the south by district Dindigul, in the east by CD Block Malanur and district Dingigul, and in the west by district Coimbatore.

Communications:

Roadways : S.H.-21: Direction- Pallachi to Malanur, Neraest Villages- Ponnapuram, Naranapuram, Chinnaputhur, Govindapuram, Chittrauthanpalayam, Dharapuram (South), Kolinjivadi, Dhalavaipattinam. S.H.-37: Direction- Kangeyam to Dharapuram, Nearest Villages- Chittrauthanpalayam, Nangaipalayam, Dharapuram, Varapalayam.

River: Sanmukha Nadi- Nearest Villages- Mambadi, Dharapuram, Dharapuram (South), Kolinjivadi, Veeratchima ngalam, Manakkadavu, Dhalavaipattinam, Alagiyam, Kongur, Bommanallur. Uppar Nadi- Nearest Villages- Varapalayam, Thoppampatti, Madathupalayam, Nangaipalayam, Dharapuram.

Annual Rainfall: Average Rainfall 789 mm.

Ground Water: Availability of the ground water in the Basin is 6800.80 H.A.M. and the utilization is 4128.21 H.A.M. It belongs to Safe category. Depth to water level varies from 2 to 10 meter below the ground. Most of the wells go down in summer months, according to the Ground Water Estimation Committee.

Forest and Reserved Forest: (Ganapathi RF)- Nearest Villages- Govindapuram, Uthupalayam. (Dalavoipattinam)- Nearest Village- Uthupalayam. (Chinnakkam Palayam)- Nearest Villages- Uthupalayam, Dhalavaipattinam.

Natural Division: Kongu Nadu.

Administration

Revenue **Division:** Dharapuram. Parliamentary Constituency: 17 Erode. District: Erode. Taluk: Dharapuram. Assembly Constituency: 101 Dharapuram (SC). Gram Panchayat: 16.

Villages: 23 **Inhabited:** 23 **Uninhabited:** 0

Ranking	District	State	National
Area	5	107	2231
Population	12	325	4757
Sex Ratio	5	251	1740
Child Sex Ratio	8	237	3877
Literacy Rate	9	330	2866
Density	7	10	5099

Work Participation Rate	14	347	93

Gram Panchayats:

Alangiyam, Bommanallur, Chinnaputhur, Dalavoipattinam, Govindapuram, Kavundachipudur, Kongur, Mambadi, Manakadavu, Nallampalayam, Nanjiyampalayam, Nathampalayam, Ponnapuram, Pottikkampalayam, Thoppampatti, Verajimangalam.

Amenities:

Education: Primary School in 21 villages, Middle school in 10 villages, Matriculation or Secondary School in 4 villages, namely Govindapuram, Nangaipalayam, Dhalavaipattinam, Alagiyam.

Higher Secondary or Pre University Courses or Intermediate or Junior College in 1 village of the CD Block,, namely Govindapuram.

College in 1 village, Adult Literacy Center in 0 village., College is in village, namely Nangaipalayam.

Medical: Hospital in 0 village, Dispensary in 0 village, Health Center in 3 villages, Sub Center in 20 villages, Maternity and Child Welfare Center in 13 villages, Community health workers in 5 villages.

Drinking Water: Tap water in 23 villages, Tank water in 0 villages, Well water in 23 villages, Tubewell in 23 villages and more than one source in 23 villages.

Bank: Banking facility in 4 villages, namely, Govindapuram, Nangaipalayam, Dhalavaipattinam Alagiyam.

Credit Society in 11 villages Agricultural Credit Society in 9 Non-Agricultural Credit Society in 2 villages.

Others: Power supply in 23 villages, Cinema hall in 0 village, sport club in 0 village, Stadium or Auditorium or Community Hall in 2 villages, Post Office in 21 villages.

There are 21 villages having bus facilities.

Villages with most of facilities: Govindapuram Nangaipalayam, Dhalavaipattinam, Alagiyam.

Villages without amenities (Education):

Dharapuram (South), Kolinjivadi..

Scheduled Castes: Out of the total population of 63020 persons, 17643 persons (28%) belong to Scheduled Castes.

The villages having less than 10% SC population are None..

The villages having more than 50% SC population are None.

Sex ratio of Scheduled Caste population is 497.

Scheduled Castes Literates and Illiterates by Sex:

	Persons	Males	Females

Literate	7,309	4,468	2,841
Illiterate	10,334	4,402	5,932
Literacy rate	46.7	57.0	36.4
Graduate	110	82	28

Scheduled Castes (Dominant):

Madari, Kudumban, Arunthathiyar, Pallan Paraiyan etc.

For their cultural identity please see Appendix-I

Villages without Scheduled Castes: There is 0 village without any scheduled caste population.

Scheduled Tribes: Out of the total population of 63020 persons, 264 persons (0.42%) belong to Scheduled Tribes. The villages having less than 10% ST population are Mambadi, Nathampalayam, Varapalayam, Thoppampatti Madathupalayam, Munduvelampatti, Ponnapuram Naranapuram, Chinnaputhur, Govindapuram Chittrauthanpalayam, Nangaipalayam, Dharapuram Dharapuram (South), Kolinjivadi, Veeratchimangalam Nallampalayam, Manakkadavu, Dhalavaipattinam Uthupalayam, Alagiyam, Kongur, Bommanallur. The villages having more than 50% ST population are None.

Sex ratio of Scheduled tribe population is 500.

Scheduled Tribes Literates and Illiterates by Sex:

	Persons	Males	Females
Literate	92	66	26
Illiterate	172	66	106
Literacy rate	39.5	56.9	22.2
Graduate	5	4	1

Scheduled Tribes (Dominant):

Kurumans, Malai Pandaram, Kattunayakan

For their cultural identity please see Appendix-II

Villages without Scheduled Tribes: There are 20 villages without any scheduled tribe population.

Literates and Illiterates by Sex (Total Population):

	Persons	Males	Females
Literate	34,021	20,643	13,378
Illiterate	28,999	11,086	17,913
Literacy rate	60	72	47
Graduate	869	584	285

Agriculture: ***Distribution of villages according to land use:*** Out of 23 villages, Total area (in hectare) is 35598.18, out of that 41.58 percent is cultivable and 75.6 percent of the cultivable area is irrigated.

Sources of Irrigation (Hectares): Government Canal 5799.82, Private Canal 0, Well without Electricity 568.95, Well with Electricity 4292, Tubewell without Electricity 0, Tubewell with Electricity 0, Tank 36.21, River 551.19, Lake 0, Waterfall 0, Others 0.

Villages with population of 5000 to 9999: Dalavoipattinam, Alangiyam.

Villages with population of 10000 and above: None

Distribution of Workers:

	Persons	Males	Females	WPR
Cultivators	12,460	7,081	5,379	30.44
Agricultural Labour	20,024	9,334	10,690	48.91
Household Industry	1,361	678	683	3.32
Other Workers	7,092	5,066	2,026	17.32
Main Workers	33,275	19,324	13,951	81.28
Marginal Workers	7,662	2,835	4,827	18.72
Total Workers	40,937	22,159	18,778	

Religion: Major Religious Communities:

	Persons	Males	Females	Sex Ratio
Hindu (95.83%)	60,391	30,447	29,944	983
Muslim (2.87%)	1,807	873	934	1,070
Christian (1.16%)	731	363	368	1,014
Sikh (0.01%)	5	3	2	667
Buddhists (0%)	-	-	-	-
Jain (0%)	3	1	2	2,000

Agewise Data:

	Persons	Males	Females	Sex Ratio
All ages	63,020	31,729	31,291	986
0-14	13,173	6,787	6,386	941
15-44	30,331	15,100	15,231	1009
45-79	18,454	9,288	9,166	987
80+	894	468	426	910
Age not stated	168	86	82	953

Languages (Dominant):

Tamil, Telugu, Kannada, Urdu, Malayalam

Disabled Population:

	Persons	Males	Females	%
Total Disabled	1,460	646	814	
In Seeing	845	286	559	57.88
In Speech	106	64	42	7.26
In Hearing	81	30	51	5.55
In Movement	276	174	102	18.9
Mentally	152	92	60	10.41

DHARMAPURI

Dharmapuri C.D. Block lies in the south-westhern part of Dharmapuri district. It is a part of Dharmapuri taluk. The Block is located at a distance of 5 kms. from district headquarters (Dharmapuri). There are 31 villages in the block with the total population of 149,279 persons. Area of the C.D. Block is 321.39 sq. kms. It is bounded in the north by CD Blocks Palakkodu, Karimangalam and Morappur, in the south by Salem district, in the east by CD Blocks Morappur and Pappireddipatti, and in the west by C.D. Block Nalampalli.

Communications:

Roadways : N.H.-7: Direction- Salem to Krishnagiri, Nearest Villages- Nallanahalli, Konanginaickaha, Hale Dharmapuri,

Virupatchipuram. S.H.-17: Direction- Pappireddipatti to Dharmapuri, Nearest Villages- Kadagathur, K. Naduhalli, Hale Dharmapuri, Amani Reddihalli.

Railway Station: V. Muthampatti, Kukkalmalai.

River: Topai Nadi- Nearest Villages- V. Muthampatti, Kondagavahalli, Kukkalmalai.

Annual Rainfall: Average Rainfall 760 mm.

Ground Water: Availability of the ground water in the Basin is 5434.10 H.A.M. and the utilization is 6957.60 H.A.M. It belongs to Over Expoited category. Depth to water level varies from 2 to 5 meter below the ground. Most of the wells go down in summer months, according to the Ground Water Estimation Committee.

Forest and Reserved Forest: (Neonahalli RF)- Nearest Villages- Akkamanahalli, Mookakanoor, Vellalai, Nulahalli, Mukkalnaickenhalli, Vathalmali, Thippireddihally, Neonahalli (RF) Uni, V. Muthampatti, Kondagavahalli.

Natural Division: Baramahal.

Administration

Revenue **Division:** Dharmapuri. Parliamentary Constituency: 10 Dharmapuri. District: Dharmapuri. Taluk: Dharmapuri. Assembly Constituency: 59 Dharmapuri, 60 Pappireddippatti. Gram Panchayat: 28.

Villages: 31 **Inhabited:** 30 **Uninhabited:** 1

Ranking	**District**	**State**	**National**
Area	16	149	2551
Population	6	16	1892
Sex Ratio	13	364	4579
Child Sex Ratio	13	367	6113
Literacy Rate	4	280	2372
Density	17	247	2374
Work Participation Rate	2	73	2646

Gram Panchayats:

A. Gollahalli, Adagapadi, Akkanahalli, Andihalli, Hale-Dharmapuri, Kadagathur, Koduhalli, Konankinaickanahalli, Kondagarahalli , Kondampatti, Krishnapuram, Kuppur, Lakkiampatti , Mookanur, Mukkalnaickanahalli, Naduhalli, Naickanahalli, Nallasenahalli, Noolahalli, Pulithikarai, Semandakuppam , Settikarai , Sogathur , Thippireddihalli , Thippiredihalli , Ungaranahalli, Vellalapatti, Vellolai, Veppilaimuthampatti.

Amenities:

Education: Primary School in 30 villages, Middle school in 25 villages, Matriculation or Secondary School in 13 villages, namely Kadagathur, Nallanahalli, Konanginaickaha Halli, Krishnapuram, Hale Dharmapuri, Amani Reddihalli, Adagapadi, Virupatchipuram, Naikkanahalli, Mookakanoor, Nulahalli, Mukkalnaickenhalli, V. Muthampatti. Higher Secondary or Pre University Courses or Intermediate or Junior College in 9 villages of the CD Block,, namely Kadagathur, Konanginaickaha Halli, Krishnapuram, Hale Dharmapuri, Amani Reddihalli, Virupatchipuram, Naikkanahalli, Nulahalli, Mukkalnaickenhalli.

College in 0 village, Adult Literacy Center in 0 village.

Medical: Hospital in 1 village, Dispensary in 3 villages, Health Center in 2 villages, Sub Center in 16 villages, Maternity and Child Welfare Center in 1 village, Community health workers in 27 villages.

The Villages having Hospital or Dispensary or Health Center are Vellalapatti, Kuppur, Annasagaram, V. Muthampatti.

Drinking Water: Tap water in 30 villages, Tank water in 0 villages, Well water in 30 villages, Tubewell in 30 villages and more than one source in 30 villages.

Bank: Banking facility in 11 villages, namely, Kadagathur, Konanginaickaha Halli, Vellalapatti Krishnapuram, Puluthikarai, Kuppur, Adagapadi Virupatchipuram, Settikarai, Nulahalli V. Muthampatti.

Credit Society in 13 villages Agricultural Credit Society in 5 Non-Agricultural Credit Society in 5 villages.

Others: Power supply in 30 villages, Cinema hall in 1 village, sport club in 0 village, Stadium or Auditorium or Community Hall in 0 village, Post Office in 30 villages.

There are 29 villages having bus facilities.

Villages with most of facilities: Kadagathur Konanginaickaha Halli, Vellalapatti, Krishnapuram Puluthikarai, Kuppur, Adagapadi, Virupatchipuram Settikarai, Nulahalli, V. Muthampatti.

Villages without Amenities (Education): None..

Scheduled Castes: Out of the total population of 149279 persons, 14978 persons (10.03%) belong to Scheduled Castes. The villages having less than 10% SC population are Kadagathur, K. Naduhalli, Nallanahalli, Andihalli Krishnapuram, Hale Dharmapuri, Pappinaickanahalli Adagapadi, Settikarai, Naikkanahalli, Akkamanahalli Annasagaram, Unguranahalli, Nulahalli Mukkalnaickenhalli, Vathalmali, Thippireddihally Kukkalmalai.

The villages having more than 50% SC population are None.

Sex ratio of Scheduled Caste population is 487.

Scheduled Castes Literates and Illiterates by Sex:

	Persons	Males	Females
Literate	8,626	5,113	3,513
Illiterate	6,352	2,572	3,780
Literacy rate	67.0	78.0	55.6

Graduate	575	412	163

Scheduled Castes (Dominant):

Adi Dravida, Arunthathiyar, Panniandi, Paraiyan etc. Pallan

For their cultural identity please see Appendix-I

Villages without Scheduled Castes: There are 2 villages without any scheduled caste population.

Scheduled Tribes: Out of the total population of 149279 persons, 1541 persons (1.03%) belong to Scheduled Tribes. The villages having less than 10% ST population are Kadagathur, K. Naduhalli, Nallanahalli Konanginaickaha Halli, Vellalapatti, Andihalli Krishnapuram, Puluthikarai, Kondampatti, Kuppur Hale Dharmapuri, Amani Reddihalli Pappinaickanahalli, Adagapadi, Virupatchipuram Vellalgoundanpalayam, Settikarai, Naikkanahalli Akkamanahalli, Mookakanoor, Vellalai, Annasagaram Unguranahalli, Nulahalli, Mukkalnaickenhalli Thippireddihally, V. Muthampatti, Kondagavahalli Kukkalmalai.

The villages having more than 50% ST population are None.

Sex ratio of Scheduled tribe population is 494.

Scheduled Tribes Literates and Illiterates by Sex:

	Persons	Males	Females
Literate	361	229	132
Illiterate	1,180	551	629
Literacy rate	28.0	34.8	20.9
Graduate	20	14	6

Scheduled Tribes (Dominant):

Malayali, Kurumans, Generic Tribes etc., Irular Kattunayakan

For their cultural identity please see Appendix-II

Villages without Scheduled Tribes: There are 22 villages without any scheduled tribe population.

Literates and Illiterates by Sex (Total Population):

	Persons	Males	Females
Literate	80,603	48,339	32,264
Illiterate	68,676	29,120	39,556
Literacy rate	62	73	51
Graduate	4,513	3,044	1,469

Agriculture: ***Distribution of villages according to land use:*** Out of 31 villages, Total area (in hectare) is 32139.4, out of that 60.79 percent is cultivable and 37.6 percent of the cultivable area is irrigated.

Sources of Irrigation (Hectares): Government Canal 11.73, Private Canal 0, Well without Electricity 1687.11, Well with Electricity 4130.45, Tubewell without Electricity 0, Tubewell with Electricity 0, Tank 1511.68, River 0, Lake 0, Waterfall 0, Others 5.73.

Villages with population of 5000 to 9999:
Kuppur, Adagapadi, Settikarai, Naickanahalli Ungaranhalli, Noolahalli , Mukkalnaickanahalli Veppilaimuthempatti.

Villages with population of 10000 and above:
Virupatchipuram , Vellegoundan Palayam.

Distribution of Workers:

	Persons	Males	Females	WPR
Cultivators	22,708	14,626	8,082	31.58
Agricultural Labour	22,694	9,448	13,246	31.56
Household Industry	1,974	653	1,321	2.75
Other Workers	24,526	18,941	5,585	34.11
Main Workers	59,905	39,161	20,744	83.31
Marginal Workers	11,997	4,507	7,490	16.69
Total Workers	71,902	43,668	28,234	

Religion: Major Religious Communities:

	Persons	Males	Females	Sex Ratio
Hindu (97.16%)	145,034	75,310	69,724	926
Muslim (1.87%)	2,795	1,424	1,371	963
Christian (0.91%)	1,353	667	686	1,028
Sikh (0.02%)	26	19	7	368
Buddhists (0%)	4	3	1	333
Jain (0.01%)	9	4	5	1,250

Agewise Data:

	Persons	Males	Females	Sex Ratio
All ages	149,279	77,459	71,820	927
0-14	46,139	24,999	21,140	846
15-44	74,187	37,739	36,448	966
45-79	27,605	14,067	13,538	962
80+	1,184	575	609	1059
Age not stated	164	79	85	1076

Languages (Dominant):
Tamil, Telugu, Urdu, Kannada, Hindi

Disabled Population:

	Persons	Males	Females	%
Total Disabled	4,943	1,633	3,310	
In Seeing	3,425	706	2,719	69.29
In Speech	259	152	107	5.24
In Hearing	91	46	45	1.84
In Movement	953	598	355	19.28
Mentally	215	131	84	4.35

DINDIGUL

Dindigul C.D. Block lies in the east central part of Dindigul district. It is a part of Dindigul taluk. The Block is located at a distance of (00) kms. from district headquarters (Dindigul). There are 18 villages in the block with the total population of 90,914 persons. Area of the C.D. Block is 362.15 sq. kms. It is bounded in the north by CD Blocks Vedasandur and Vadanvadurai, in the south by CD Blocks Nilakottai and Shanarpatti, in the east by CD Blocks Vadamadurai and

Shanarpatti, in the west by CD Blocks Raddiyarchatram and Attur.

Communications:

Roadways : N.H.-7: Direction- Madurai to Thadiccombu, Nearest Villages- Chettinaickenpatti, Kurumbapatti, Adiyanuthu, A.Vellodu, Erukalamalai RF. N.H.-45: Direct ion- Dindigul to Tiruchirappalli, Nearest Villages- Seela padi, Mullipadi, Ammakulathupatti, Tamaraipadi. N.H.-209: Direction- Palani to Pallapatti, Nearest Villages- Kurum bapatti, Anaipatti. S.H.-35: Direction- Dindigul to Natham, Nearest Villages- Tottanuthu, Adiyanuthu, Sirumalai RF.

Railway Station: Tamaraipadi.

Backwards Region Grants Fund: It receives Backward Region Grants.

Annual Rainfall: Average Rainfall 813 mm.

Ground Water: Availability of the ground water in the Basin is 3230.63 H.A.M. and the utilization is 3385.06 H.A.M. It belongs to Over Expoited category. Depth to water level varies from 0 to 10 meter below the ground. Most of the wells go down in summer months, according to the Ground Water Estimation Committee.

Forest and Reserved Forest: (A.Vellodu RF)- Nearest Villages- Adiyanuthu, A.Vellodu, A.Vellodu RF. (Sirumalai)- Nearest Villages- Sirumalai RF , Sirumalai RF, Tavasimadai, Sirumalai, Adiyanuthu. (Erukkalmalai)- Nearest Village- Erukalamalai RF.

Natural Division: NA

Administration

Revenue **Division:** Dindigul. Parliamentary Constituency: 22 Dindigul. District: Dindigul. Taluk: Dindigul. Assembly Constituency: 132 Dindigul, 131 Natham. Gram Panchayat: 14.

Villages: 18 **Inhabited:** 14 **Uninhabited:** 4

Ranking	District	State	National
Area	5	99	2189
Population	8	180	3757
Sex Ratio	6	226	1600
Child Sex Ratio	5	243	4018
Literacy Rate	1	95	1088
Density	14	337	4064
Work Participation Rate	9	282	4124

Gram Panchayats:

A.Vellodu, Adiyanuthu , Anaipatti, Chettinaickenpatti , Kovilur, Kurumbapatti, Mullipadi, Periyakottai, Seelapadi, Sirumalai, Tamaraipadi, Tottanuthu.

Amenities:

Education: Primary School in 13 villages, Middle school in 10 villages, Matriculation or Secondary School in 8 villages, namely Chettinaickenpatti, Seelapadi, Mullipadi, Kovilur, Periakottai, Tottanuthu, Adiyanuthu, A.Vellodu.

Higher Secondary or Pre University Courses or Intermediate or Junior College in 4 villages of the CD Block,, namely Chettinaickenpatti, Seelapadi, Kovilur, Adiyanuthu.

College in 3 villages, Adult Literacy Center in 0 village., Colleges are in villages, namely Seelapadi, Kurumbapatti, Tottanuthu.

Medical: Hospital in 1 village, Dispensary in 0 village, Health Center in 5 villages, Sub Center in 7 villages, Maternity and Child Welfare Center in 6 villages, Community health workers in 4 villages.

The Villages having Hospital or Dispensary or Health Center are Seelapadi, Ammakulathupatti.

Drinking Water: Tap water in 14 villages, Tank water in 12 villages, Well water in 14 villages, Tubewell in 14 villages and more than one source in 14 villages.

Bank: Banking facility in 7 villages, namely, Chettinaickenpatti, Seelapadi, Tamaraipadi, Kovilur Tottanuthu, A.Vellodu, Sirumalai.

Credit Society in 5 villages Agricultural Credit Society in 5 Non-Agricultural Credit Society in 2 villages.

Others: Power supply in 14 villages, Cinema hall in 6 villages, sport club in 0 village, Stadium or Auditorium or Community Hall in 1 village, Post Office in 12 villages.

There are 13 villages having bus facilities.

Villages with most of facilities: Chettinaickenpatti Seelapadi, Tamaraipadi, Kovilur, Tottanuthu A.Vellodu, Sirumalai.

Villages without amenities (Education):

Ammakulathupatti..

Scheduled Castes: Out of the total population of 90914 persons, 21772 persons (23.95%) belong to Scheduled Castes.

The villages having less than 10% SC population are None..

The villages having more than 50% SC population are None.

Sex ratio of Scheduled Caste population is 499.

Scheduled Castes Literates and Illiterates by Sex:

	Persons	Males	Females
Literate	11,687	7,021	4,666
Illiterate	10,085	3,877	6,208
Literacy rate	61.7	74.5	49.0
Graduate	314	214	100

Scheduled Castes (Dominant):

Pallan, Paraiyan etc., Chakkiliyan, Madari Kuravan etc.

For their cultural identity please see Appendix-I

Villages without Scheduled Castes: There are 5 villages without any scheduled caste population.

Scheduled Tribes: Out of the total population of 90914 persons, 139 persons (0.15%) belong to Scheduled Tribes. The villages having less than 10% ST population are Chettinaickenpatti, Alakkuvarpatti, Seelapadi Mullipadi, Ammakulathupatti, Tamaraipadi, Kovilur Periakottai, Kurumbapatti, Anaipatti, Tottanuthu Adiyanuthu, A.Vellodu, Sirumalai.
The villages having more than 50% ST population are None.
Sex ratio of Scheduled tribe population is 547.

Scheduled Tribes Literates and Illiterates by Sex:

	Persons	Males	Females
Literate	64	31	33
Illiterate	75	32	43
Literacy rate	52.5	54.4	50.8
Graduate	3	1	2

Scheduled Tribes (Dominant):
Palliyar, Kattunayakan, Kurumans, Malakkuravan Malai Vedan

For their cultural identity please see Appendix-II

Villages without Scheduled Tribes: There are 11 villages without any scheduled tribe population.

Literates and Illiterates by Sex (Total Population):

	Persons	Males	Females
Literate	56,732	32,161	24,571
Illiterate	34,182	13,528	20,654
Literacy rate	71	80	61
Graduate	2,629	1,645	984

Agriculture: ***Distribution of villages according to land use:*** Out of 18 villages, Total area (in hectare) is 36215.22, out of that 22.87 percent is cultivable and 32.63 percent of the cultivable area is irrigated.

Sources of Irrigation (Hectares): Government Canal 8.5, Private Canal 0, Well without Electricity 638.31, Well with Electricity 1373.12, Tubewell without Electricity 79.52, Tubewell with Electricity 210.58, Tank 385.91, River 7.09, Lake 0, Waterfall 0, Others 0.

Villages with population of 5000 to 9999:
Mullipadi, Periyakottai, Tottanuthu, Sirumalai.

Villages with population of 10000 and above:
Settinaickenpatti , Silapadi, Adiyanuthu A.Vellodu.

Distribution of Workers:

	Persons	Males	Females	WPR
Cultivators	3,798	2,613	1,185	9.9
Agricultural Labour	10,842	5,277	5,565	28.25
Household Industry	1,328	764	564	3.46
Other Workers	22,406	16,999	5,407	58.39
Main Workers	30,485	21,770	8,715	79.44
Marginal Workers	7,889	3,883	4,006	20.56
Total Workers	38,374	25,653	12,721	

Religion: Major Religious Communities:

	Persons	Males	Females	Sex Ratio
Hindu (79.46%)	72,238	36,431	35,807	983
Muslim (2.53%)	2,299	1,170	1,129	965
Christian (17.89%)	16,269	8,030	8,239	1,026
Sikh (0.03%)	23	15	8	533
Buddhists (0.02%)	21	7	14	2,000
Jain (0%)	4	1	3	3,000

Agewise Data:

	Persons	Males	Females	Sex Ratio
All ages	90,914	45,689	45,225	990
0-14	24,853	12,776	12,077	945
15-44	46,018	22,831	23,187	1016
45-79	18,681	9,414	9,267	984
80+	717	345	372	1078
Age not stated	645	323	322	997

Languages (Dominant):
Tamil, Telugu, Kannada, Urdu, Malayalam

Disabled Population:

	Persons	Males	Females	%
Total Disabled	3,495	1,348	2,147	
In Seeing	2,381	697	1,684	68.13
In Speech	235	144	91	6.72
In Hearing	94	40	54	2.69
In Movement	582	350	232	16.65
Mentally	203	117	86	5.81

EDAPPADI

Edappadi C.D. Block lies in the western part of Salem district. It is a part of Edappadi taluk. The Block is located at a distance of 40 kms. from district headquarters (Salem). There are 11 villages in the block with the total population of 69,346 persons. Area of the C.D. Block is 169.98 sq. kms. It is bounded in the north by CD Block Nangavalli, in the south by CD Block Sankari, in the east by C.D. Block Konganapuram, in the west by district Erode and CD Block Kolathur.

Communications:

Roadways : Information not Available.

River: Cauvery Nadi- Nearest Villages- Nedungulam, Pakkanadu.

Annual Rainfall: Average Rainfall 1002 mm.

Ground Water: Availability of the ground water in the Basin is 4332.96 H.A.M. and the utilization is 2506.10 H.A.M. It belongs to Safe category. Depth to water level varies from 2 to 20 meter below the ground. Most of the wells go down in summer months, according to the Ground Water Estimation Committee.

Natural Division: Kongu Nadu.

Administration

Revenue **Division:** Sankari. Parliamentary Constituency:

15 Salem. District: Salem. Taluk: Edappadi. Assembly Constituency: 86 Edappadi. Gram Panchayat: 10.

Villages: 11 **Inhabited:** 11 **Uninhabited:** 0

Ranking	**District**	**State**	**National**
Area	13	328	4703
Population	12	288	4488
Sex Ratio	18	382	6047
Child Sex Ratio	21	385	6338
Literacy Rate	21	383	5000
Density	2	22	2692
Work Participation Rate	10	109	183

Gram Panchayats:
Adaiyur, Avaniperur East, Chettimankurichi, Chittur, Dadapuram, Irupali, Nedungulam, Pakkanadu, Vellarivalli, Vembaneri, .

Amenities:
Education: Primary School in 10 villages, Middle school in 7 villages, Matriculation or Secondary School in 6 villages, namely Adaiyur, Chettimankurichi, Nedungulam, Vellarivelli, Chittoor, Dadapuram.
Higher Secondary or Pre University Courses or Intermediate or Junior College in 4 villages of the CD Block,, namely Chettimankurichi, Nedungulam, Vellarivelli, Vembaneri.
College in 0 village, Adult Literacy Center in 0 village.
Medical: Hospital in 0 village, Dispensary in 0 village, Health Center in 2 villages, Sub Center in 7 villages, Maternity and Child Welfare Center in 0 village, Community health workers in 0 village.
Drinking Water: Tap water in 11 villages, Tank water in 0 villages, Well water in 11 villages, Tubewell in 11 villages and more than one source in 11 villages.
Bank: Banking facility in 1 villages, namely, Nedungulam.
Credit Society in 9 villages Agricultural Credit Society in 8 Non-Agricultural Credit Society in 6 villages.
Others: Power supply in 10 villages, Cinema hall in 1 village, sport club in 0 village, Stadium or Auditorium or Community Hall in 0 village, Post Office in 10 villages.
There are 10 villages having bus facilities.
Villages with most of facilities: Nedungulam.
Villages without amenities (Education): Pakkanadu..
Scheduled Castes: Out of the total population of 69346 persons, 6186 persons (8.92%) belong to Scheduled Castes.
The villages having less than 10% SC population are Chettimankurichi, Nedungulam, Pakkanadu, Grippali Chittoor, Vembaneri, Dadapuram, Avaniperur (E).
The villages having more than 50% SC population are None.
Sex ratio of Scheduled Caste population is 461.

Scheduled Castes Literates and Illiterates by Sex:

	Persons	Males	Females
Literate	2,428	1,617	811
Illiterate	3,758	1,715	2,043
Literacy rate	44.2	55.3	31.5
Graduate	62	54	8

Scheduled Castes (Dominant):
Arunthathiyar, Adi Dravida, Madari, Paraiyan etc.
Chakkiliyan
For their cultural identity please see Appendix-I
Villages without Scheduled Castes: There is 1 village without any scheduled caste population.
Scheduled Tribes: Out of the total population of 69346 persons, 7 persons (0.01%) belong to Scheduled Tribes.
The villages having less than 10% ST population are Adaiyur, Chettimankurichi, Nedungulam, Pakkanadu Grippali, Vellarivelli, Chittoor, Pakkanadu Vembaneri, Dadapuram, Avaniperur (E).
The villages having more than 50% ST population are None.
Sex ratio of Scheduled tribe population is 429.

Scheduled Tribes Literates and Illiterates by Sex:

	Persons	Males	Females
Literate	4	3	1
Illiterate	3	1	2
Literacy rate	66.7	100.0	33.3
Graduate	1	1	0

Scheduled Tribes (Dominant):
Kondareddis
For their cultural identity please see Appendix-II
Villages without Scheduled Tribes: There are 10 villages without any scheduled tribe population.

Literates and Illiterates by Sex (Total Population):

	Persons	Males	Females
Literate	28,605	19,032	9,573
Illiterate	40,741	18,459	22,282
Literacy rate	47	58	33
Graduate	744	609	135

Agriculture: ***Distribution of villages according to land use:*** Out of 11 villages, Total area (in hectare) is 16998.4, out of that 76.05 percent is cultivable and 27.67 percent of the cultivable area is irrigated.
Sources of Irrigation (Hectares): Government Canal 856.59, Private Canal 0, Well without Electricity 0, Well with Electricity 1833.1, Tubewell without Electricity 0, Tubewell with Electricity 858.21, Tank 0, River 0, Lake 28.76, Waterfall 0, Others 0.
Villages with population of 5000 to 9999:
Avaniperur(East) , Chettimankurichi.
Villages with population of 10000 and above:

Idupali, Chittur, Vellarivalli.

Distribution of Workers:

	Persons	Males	Females	WPR
Cultivators	12,673	7,110	5,563	29.88
Agricultural Labour	20,119	9,695	10,424	47.43
Household Industry	2,860	1,831	1,029	6.74
Other Workers	6,765	5,402	1,363	15.95
Main Workers	39,893	23,184	16,709	94.05
Marginal Workers	2,524	854	1,670	5.95
Total Workers	42,417	24,038	18,379	

Religion: Major Religious Communities:

	Persons	Males	Females	Sex Ratio
Hindu (98.73%)	68,465	37,037	31,428	849
Muslim (0.48%)	330	169	161	953
Christian (0.68%)	473	241	232	963
Sikh (0.03%)	19	9	10	1,111
Buddhists (0.02%)	13	7	6	857
Jain (0%)	2	-	2	-

Agewise Data:

	Persons	Males	Females	Sex Ratio
All ages	69,346	37,491	31,855	850
0-14	17,780	10,696	7,084	662
15-44	33,578	17,676	15,902	900
45-79	17,077	8,608	8,469	984
80+	795	440	355	807
Age not stated	116	71	45	634

Languages (Dominant):

Tamil, Telugu, Kannada, Urdu, Others

Disabled Population:

	Persons	Males	Females	%
Total Disabled	915	594	321	
In Seeing	431	279	152	47.1
In Speech	99	57	42	10.82
In Hearing	28	17	11	3.06
In Movement	279	190	89	30.49
Mentally	78	51	27	8.52

ELAICHIPALAYAM

Elachipalaiyam C.D. Block lies in the northern part of Namakkal district. It is a part of Tiruchengode taluk. The taluk is located at a distance of 36 kms. from district headquarters (Namakkal). There are 29 villages in the block with the total population of 73,710 persons. Area of the C.D. Block is 245.14 sq. kms. It is bounded in the north by C.D. Blocks Tiruchengode, Puduchatram and Mallasamudram, in the south by CD Blocks Paramathi and Namakkal, in the east by Puduchatram, and in the west by C.D. Block Tiruchengode.

Communications:

Roadways : Information not Available.

Annual Rainfall: Average Rainfall 650 mm.

Ground Water: Availability of the ground water in the Basin is 2032.64 H.A.M. and the utilization is 653.30 H.A.M. It belongs to Safe category. Depth to water level varies from 2 to 10 meter below the ground. Most of the wells go down in summer months, according to the Ground Water Estimation Committee.

Natural Division: Kongu Nadu.

Administration

Revenue **Division:** Tiruchengode. Parliamentary Constituency. District: Namakkal. Taluk: Tiruchengode. Assembly Constituency: 95 Palamathi – Velur, 96 Tiruchengodu. Gram Panchayat: 29.

Villages: 29 **Inhabited:** 29 **Uninhabited:** 0

Ranking	District	State	National
Area	3	236	3442
Population	6	272	4331
Sex Ratio	1	131	947
Child Sex Ratio	7	337	5546
Literacy Rate	4	210	1931
Density	9	33	3512
Work Participation Rate	9	223	254

Gram Panchayats:

Agaram, Bommanpatti, Chinnamanali, Elanagar, Illuppili, Kavundampalayam, Kavundampalayam , Kilapalayam, Kokkalai, Komaramangalam, Konnayar, Kuppandapalayam, Kuthampoondi , Kuttampundi, Lattivadi, Malukkalampatti, Manathi , Mandagapalayam, Marukkalempatti, Mavureddipatti, Molipalli, Musiri, Nallipalayam, Periyamanali , Pokkampalayam, Pullakkavundanpatti, Punjaipudupalayam, Sathinayakkanpalayam, Thondipatti, Unjanai.

Amenities:

Education: Primary School in 26 villages, Middle school in 10 villages, Matriculation or Secondary School in 8 villages, namely Oduvampalayam, Konnaiyar, Periyamanali, Unjanai, Kuttampundi, Thondipatti, Puthur East, Bommanpatti.

Higher Secondary or Pre University Courses or Intermediate or Junior College in 5 villages of the CD Block,, namely Konnaiyar, Unjanai, Kuttampundi, Thondipatti, Puthur East.

College in 0 village, Adult Literacy Center in 0 village.

Medical: Hospital in 1 village, Dispensary in 0 village, Health Center in 4 villages, Sub Center in 10 villages, Maternity and Child Welfare Center in 0 village, Community health workers in 0 village.

The Village having Hospital or Dispensary or Health Center is Elaiyampalayam.

Drinking Water: Tap water in 29 villages, Tank water in 0 villages, Well water in 29 villages, Tubewell in 29 villages and more than one source in 29 villages.

Bank: Banking facility in 6 villages, namely,

Elaiyampalayam, Agraharam, Periyamanali, Unjanai Kuttampundi, Puthur East.

Credit Society in 27 villages Agricultural Credit Society in 11 Non-Agricultural Credit Society in 25 villages.

Others: Power supply in 29 villages, Cinema hall in 0 village, sport club in 0 village, Stadium or Auditorium or Community Hall in 0 village, Post Office in 29 villages.

There are 29 villages having bus facilities.

Villages with most of facilities: Elaiyampalayam Agraharam, Periyamanali, Unjanai, Kuttampundi Puthur East.

Villages without amenities (Education):
Kuppandapalayam, Kovilpalayam, Kuthampoondi Aga..

Scheduled Castes: Out of the total population of 73710 persons, 18854 persons (25.58%) belong to Scheduled Castes.

The villages having less than 10% SC population are Kuppandapalayam, Oduvampalayam, Kilapalayam Pullakkavundampatti.

The villages having more than 50% SC population are None.

Sex ratio of Scheduled Caste population is 493.

Scheduled Castes Literates and Illiterates by Sex:

	Persons	Males	Females
Literate	9,097	5,519	3,578
Illiterate	9,757	4,039	5,718
Literacy rate	54.2	65.0	43.1
Graduate	327	246	81

Scheduled Castes (Dominant):
Arunthathiyar, Adi Dravida, Pallan, Chakkiliyan Devendrakulathan

For their cultural identity please see Appendix-I

Villages without Scheduled Castes: There are 2 villages without any scheduled caste population.

Scheduled Tribes: Out of the total population of 73710 persons, 35 persons (0.05%) belong to Scheduled Tribes.

The villages having less than 10% ST population are Andarapatti, Kavundampalayam, Sathinayakkanpalyam Kuppandapalayam, Oduvampalayam, Kovilpalayam Elaiyampalayam, Kavundampalayam, Agraharam Konnaiyar, Periyamanali, Kokkali, Illupuli Kilapalayam, Molipalli, Unjanai, Pokkampalayam Nallipalayam, Punjaipudupalayam, Kuthampoondi Aga Pullakkavundampatti, Kuttampundi, Lattivadi, Manathi Mavureddipatti, Thondipatti, Musiri, Puthur East Bommanpatti.

The villages having more than 50% ST population are None.

Sex ratio of Scheduled tribe population is 514.

Scheduled Tribes Literates and Illiterates by Sex:

	Persons	Males	Females
Literate	13	10	3
Illiterate	22	7	15
Literacy rate	41.9	66.7	18.8
Graduate	0	0	0

Scheduled Tribes (Dominant):
Malai Pandaram, Kurumans, Malayali

For their cultural identity please see Appendix-II

Villages without Scheduled Tribes: There are 24 villages without any scheduled tribe population.

Literates and Illiterates by Sex (Total Population):

	Persons	Males	Females
Literate	43,472	25,438	18,034
Illiterate	30,238	11,294	18,944
Literacy rate	65	77	53
Graduate	2,204	1,354	850

Agriculture: ***Distribution of villages according to land use:***
Out of 29 villages, Total area (in hectare) is 24514.01, out of that 91.49 percent is cultivable and 9.6 percent of the cultivable area is irrigated.

Sources of Irrigation (Hectares): Government Canal 84.52, Private Canal 0, Well without Electricity 157.8, Well with Electricity 720.16, Tubewell without Electricity 0, Tubewell with Electricity 251.34, Tank 10, River 0, Lake 169.43, Waterfall 0, Others 760.86.

Villages with population of 5000 to 9999:
Kavundampalayam , Periyamanali.

Villages with population of 10000 and above: None

Distribution of Workers:

	Persons	Males	Females	WPR
Cultivators	12,563	6,527	6,036	27.67
Agricultural Labour	15,231	6,263	8,968	33.55
Household Industry	1,831	773	1,058	4.03
Other Workers	15,775	10,896	4,879	34.75
Main Workers	39,607	22,529	17,078	87.24
Marginal Workers	5,793	1,930	3,863	12.76
Total Workers	45,400	24,459	20,941	

Religion: Major Religious Communities:

	Persons	Males	Females	Sex Ratio
Hindu (98.41%)	72,539	36,383	36,156	994
Muslim (0.54%)	396	175	221	1,263
Christian (0.9%)	662	110	552	5,018
Sikh (0%)	3	1	2	2,000
Buddhists (0%)	1	-	1	-
Jain (0.01%)	4	2	2	1,000

Agewise Data:

	Persons	Males	Females	Sex Ratio
All ages	73,710	36,732	36,978	1007
0-14	15,606	8,325	7,281	875
15-44	35,026	17,113	17,913	1047
45-79	20,528	9,990	10,538	1055

80+	1,048	525	523	996
Age not stated	1,502	779	723	928

Languages (Dominant):
Tamil, Telugu, Kannada, Malayalam, Urdu

Disabled Population:

	Persons	Males	Females	%
Total Disabled	1,278	713	565	
In Seeing	561	304	257	43.9
In Speech	135	68	67	10.56
In Hearing	67	32	35	5.24
In Movement	377	235	142	29.5
Mentally	138	74	64	10.8

ELLAPURAM

Ellapuram C.D. taluk lies in the northerrn part of Thiruvallur district. It is a part of Uttukkottai taluk. The taluk is located at a distance of 24 kms. from district headquarters (Thiruvallur). There are 73 villages in the block with the total population of 101,160 persons. Area of the C.D. Block is 255.36 sq. kms. It is bounded in the north by CD Blocks Gummidipoondi and Sholavaram, in the south by CD Blocks Villivakkam and Thiruvallur, in the east by CD Block Sholavaram, in the west by CD Block poondi. It has common boundary with the state of Andhra Pradesh on north-west. of the CD Block Ellapuram, the part under taluk Uttukkottai consists of 59 villages, and another under taluk Thiruvallur of 14 villages.

Communications:
Roadways : Information not Avaiable.
River: Arani Nadi- Nearest Villages- Rallapadi, Ellapuram, Ariapakkam, Athupakkam, Perandur, Tharatchi, Sennanka ranai, Tholavedu, Paruthimerikuppam, Thumbakkam, Chittrai pakkam (Ui), Moongilpattu (Ui), Periyapalayam, Vadam adurai, Enambakkam, Kalpattu, Melandur, Panapakkam, Melmaligaipattu. Korattalaiyar Nadi- Nearest Villages- Kottakuppam, Alinjivakkam, Athan jikavarur, Panapakkam, Pagalamedu, Kadarvedu, Poochiathipattu, Thirukkandalam, Madavilagam, Sembedu, Ammanambakkam, Agaram, Sethupakkam, Guruvoyal, Arkampattu, Singlikuppam, Ayalcheri, Pudukuppam, Perumudivakkam.
Annual Rainfall: Average Rainfall 1152 mm.
Ground Water: Availability of the ground water in the Basin is 114.68 MCM and the utilization is 160.44 MCM. It belongs to Over Expoited category. Depth to water level varies from 2 to 10 meter below the ground. Most of the wells go down in summer months, according to the Ground Water Estimation Committee.
Forest and Reserved Forest: (Palavakkam RF)- Nearest Villages- Senjiagaram, Palavakkam RF (Ui), Palavakkam, Sirunai (Ui), Sengarai, Damaraikuppam, Tharatchi. (Meyyur RF)- Nearest Villages- Kalpattu, Melandur.
Natural Division: Tondai Nadu.
Administration
Revenue **Division:** Ponneri. Parliamentary Constituency: 1 Thiruvallur (SC), 5 Sriperumbadur. District: Thiruvallur. Taluk: Uttukkottai, Thiruvallur. Assembly Constituency: 1 Gummidipoondi, 5 Thiruvallur. Gram Panchayat: 53.
Border Villages- (Andhra Pradesh)- Nearest Village- Damaraikuppam.

Villages: 73 **Inhabited:** 69 **Uninhabited:** 4

Ranking	**District**	**State**	**National**
Area	5	227	3315
Population	3	125	3429
Sex Ratio	1	121	916
Child Sex Ratio	7	137	2438
Literacy Rate	11	292	2471
Density	1	245	2758
Work Participation Rate	8	115	2636

Gram Panchayats:
Akkarapakkam, Alapakkam , Alinjivakkam, Amindanallur, Athanjikavanur, Athivakkam, Athupakkam , Ayalacheri , Boochiathipattu, Enambakkam , Guruvoyal, Guruvoyal , Kakkavakkam, Kalpattu, Kannigaipair, Kannigapuram, Kilambakkam , Koduveli , Komakkambedu, Kumarapettai, Lachivakkam, Maduravayal, Magaral, Malandur, Mamballam , Sembedu, Manjakaranai , Neiveli , Pagalamedu, Palavakkam , Panapakkam, Panapakkam , Panayancheri, Perandur, Periapalayam, Perumudivakkam, Poorivakkam , Punnapakkam , Sembedu, Sengarai, Senjiagram, Sennankaranai, Sethupakkam , Soolaimani , Tamaraipakkam , Thamaraikuppam, Thandalam, Tharatchi, Thirukkandalam , Thirunilai, Tholavedu, Thumbakkam , Vadamadurai , Vannankuppam, Vengal.

Amenities:
Education: Primary School in 64 villages, Middle school in 19 villages, Matriculation or Secondary School in 7 villages, namely Palavakkam, Ellapuram, Thandalam, Thirukkandalam, Madavilagam, Vengal, Guruvoyal.
Higher Secondary or Pre University Courses or Intermediate or Junior College in 1 village of the CD Block,, namely Ellapuram.
College in 1 village, Adult Literacy Center in 0 village., College is in village, namely Magaral.
Medical: Hospital in 2 villages, Dispensary in 3 villages, Health Center in 14 villages, Sub Center in 17 villages, Maternity and Child Welfare Center in 2 villages, Community health workers in 66 villages.
The Villages having Hospital or Dispensary or Health Center are Rallapadi, Ellapuram, Lachivakkam, Thirunilai.
Drinking Water: Tap water in 69 villages, Tank water in 69 villages, Well water in 69 villages, Tubewell in 69

villages and more than one source in 69 villages.
Bank: Banking facility in 7 villages, namely,
Palavakkam, Kakkavakkam, Periyapalayam, Akkarapakkam Kannigaipair, Poochiathipattu, Vengal.
Credit Society in 9 villages Agricultural Credit Society in 9 Non-Agricultural Credit Society in 0 village.
Others: Power supply in 69 villages, Cinema hall in 5 villages, sport club in 0 village, Stadium or Auditorium or Community Hall in 0 village, Post Office in 22 villages.
There are 48 villages having bus facilities.
Villages with most of facilities: Palavakkam Kakkavakkam, Periyapalayam, Kannigaipair Poochiathipattu.
Villages without amenities (Education):
Thandareddykuppam, Kaiyadi, Seeyancheri, Koorambakkam..
Scheduled Castes: Out of the total population of 101160 persons, 35705 persons (35.3%) belong to Scheduled Castes.
The villages having less than 10% SC population are Damaraikuppam, Athupakkam, Sennankaranai Paruthimerikuppam, Thumbakkam, Valapakkam Seeyancheri, Enambakkam, Melandur, Perumudivakkam Panapakkam, Kadarvedu, Poochiathipattu Thirukkandalam, Sethupakkam, Guruvoyal, Arkampattu Ayalcheri, Pudukuppam.
The villages having more than 50% SC population are Ellapuram, Kaiyadi, Tholavedu, Kakkavakkam Amindanallur, Akkarapakkam, Vadamadurai Melmaligaipattu, Mampattu, Kannigaipair Koorambakkam, Kottakuppam, Alinjivakkam Athanjikavarur, Pagalamedu, Madavilagam, Vengal Agaram, Karanai.
Sex ratio of Scheduled Caste population is 502.
Scheduled Castes Literates and Illiterates by Sex:

	Persons	Males	Females
Literate	17,116	10,143	6,973
Illiterate	18,589	7,624	10,965
Literacy rate	55.7	66.6	44.9
Graduate	344	285	59

Scheduled Castes (Dominant):
Adi Dravida, Arunthathiyar, Chakkiliyan, Domban Generic Castes etc.
For their cultural identity please see Appendix-I
Villages without Scheduled Castes: There are 13 villages without any scheduled caste population.
Scheduled Tribes: Out of the total population of 101160 persons, 1848 persons (1.83%) belong to Scheduled Tribes.
The villages having less than 10% ST population are Palavakkam, Sengarai, Rallapadi, Ellapuram Ariapakkam, Athupakkam, Vannankuppam Thandareddykuppam, Kaiyadi, Kilakarmanur, Soolaimani Lachivakkam, Perandur, Tharatchi, Panapakkam Sennankaranai, Tholavedu, Kakkavakkam Paruthimerikuppam, Thumbakkam, Thandalam Periyapalayam, Valapakkam, Seeyancheri, Panayancheri Thirunilai, Amindanallur, Akkarapakkam, Maduravayal Panapakkam, Vadamadurai, Melmaligaipattu, Enambakkam Kalpattu, Melandur, Mamballam, Mampattu, Alapakkam Kannigaipair, Koorambakkam, Manjankaranai Kottakuppam, Annadanakkavakkam, Neiveli Alinjivakkam, Athanjikavarur, Panapakkam, Pagalamedu Kadarvedu, Poochiathipattu, Thirukkandalam Madavilagam, Sembedu, Vengal, Ammanambakkam, Agaram Sethupakkam, Guruvoyal, Arkampattu, Singlikuppam Ayalcheri, Pudukuppam, Koduvalli, Karanai, Magaral Thamaraipakkam.
The villages having more than 50% ST population are None.
Sex ratio of Scheduled tribe population is 511.
Scheduled Tribes Literates and Illiterates by Sex:

	Persons	Males	Females
Literate	488	302	186
Illiterate	1,360	601	759
Literacy rate	31.7	39.8	23.9
Graduate	2	2	0

Scheduled Tribes (Dominant):
Irular, Kattunayakan, Generic Tribes etc.
Kondareddis, Malai Pandaram
For their cultural identity please see Appendix-II
Villages without Scheduled Tribes: There are 41 villages without any scheduled tribe population.
Literates and Illiterates by Sex (Total Population):

	Persons	Males	Females
Literate	54,570	32,015	22,555
Illiterate	46,590	18,344	28,246
Literacy rate	62	73	51
Graduate	1,511	1,205	306

Agriculture: ***Distribution of villages according to land use:***
Out of 73 villages, Total area (in hectare) is 25536.01, out of that 58.48 percent is cultivable and 85.82 percent of the cultivable area is irrigated.
Sources of Irrigation (Hectares): Government Canal 2.8, Private Canal 39.45, Well without Electricity 481.36, Well with Electricity 1948.06, Tubewell without Electricity 543.01, Tubewell with Electricity 7906.24, Tank 541.92, River 0, Lake 1239.2, Waterfall 0, Others 114.2.
Villages with population of 5000 to 9999:
Periyapalayam, Vadamadurai.
Villages with population of 10000 and above: None
Distribution of Workers:

	Persons	Males	Females	WPR
Cultivators	8,331	6,123	2,208	16.94
Agricultural Labour	30,982	16,116	14,866	62.99
Household Industry	1,847	1,204	643	3.76
Other Workers	8,026	6,651	1,375	16.32
Main Workers	41,917	26,881	15,036	85.22
Marginal Workers	7,269	3,213	4,056	14.78
Total Workers	49,186	30,094	19,092	

Religion: Major Religious Communities:

	Persons	Males	Females	Sex Ratio
Hindu (96.81%)	97,934	48,758	49,176	1,009
Muslim (1.4%)	1,418	712	706	992
Christian (1.7%)	1,717	839	878	1,046
Sikh (0%)	-	-	-	-
Buddhists (0.01%)	6	5	1	200
Jain (0.02%)	22	13	9	692

Agewise Data:

	Persons	Males	Females	Sex Ratio
All ages	101,160	50,359	50,801	1009
0-14	29,198	14,868	14,330	964
15-44	50,249	25,027	25,222	1008
45-79	20,808	10,012	10,796	1078
80+	678	332	346	1042
Age not stated	227	120	107	892

Languages (Dominant):
Tamil, Telugu, Urdu, Hindi, Malayalam

Disabled Population:

	Persons	Males	Females	%
Total Disabled	2,766	1,469	1,297	
In Seeing	1,475	736	739	53.33
In Speech	232	122	110	8.39
In Hearing	200	91	109	7.23
In Movement	699	434	265	25.27
Mentally	160	86	74	5.78

ERODE

Erode C.D. Block lies in the central eastern part of Erode district. It is a part of Erode taluk. The Block is located at a distance of (00) kms. from district headquarters (Erode). There are 20 villages in the block with the total population of 55,773 persons. Area of the C.D. Block is 71.77 sq. kms. It is bounded in the north by CD Block Bhavani, in the south by CD Blocks Chennimalai and Uthukuli, in the east by district Namakkal, in the west by CD Blocks Perundurai and Bhavani.

Communications:
Roadways : N.H.-47: Direction- Perundurai to Bhavani, Nearest Villages- Mettunasuvampalayam, Nochipalayam, Gangapuram, Kurapalayam. S.H.-15: Direction- Gobichettipalayam to Erode, Nearest Villages- Perode, Gangapuram. S.H.-20: Direction- Suriyampalayam to Erode, Nearest Villages- Karaiellapalayam, Elavamalai, Mettunasuvampalayam.
River: Cauvery Nadi- Nearest Village- Mettunasuvampalayam.
Annual Rainfall: Average Rainfall 789 mm.
Ground Water: Availability of the ground water in the Basin is 4300.32 H.A.M. and the utilization is 997.27 H.A.M. It belongs to Safe category. Depth to water level varies from 2 to 10 meter below the ground. Most of the wells go down in summer months, according to the Ground Water Estimation Committee.
Natural Division: Kongu Nadu.
Administration
Revenue **Division:** Erode. Parliamentary Constituency: 17 Erode. District: Erode. Taluk: Erode. Assembly Constituency: 99 Erode (West). Gram Panchayat: 11.
Villages: 20 **Inhabited:** 20 **Uninhabited:** 0

Ranking	District	State	National
Area	20	378	5937
Population	15	343	5019
Sex Ratio	6	256	1898
Child Sex Ratio	16	310	5193
Literacy Rate	1	108	1159
Density	20	250	1253
Work Participation Rate	1	14	2661

Gram Panchayats:
Elavamalai, Ellapalayam, Gangapuram, Kadirampatti, Koorapalayam, Mettunasuvanpalayam, Muthampalayam, Perodu, Pitchandampalayam, Pudur, Thindal , Villarasampatti.

Amenities:
Education: Primary School in 14 villages, Middle school in 5 villages, Matriculation or Secondary School in 4 villages, namely Elavamalai, Ellappalayam, Thindal (Mel), Thindal(Kil).
Higher Secondary or Pre University Courses or Intermediate or Junior College in 3 villages of the CD Block,, namely Ellappalayam, Thindal (Mel), Thindal(Kil).
College in 2 villages, Adult Literacy Center in 0 village., Colleges are in villages, namely Thottani, Nanjanapuram.
Medical: Hospital in 2 villages, Dispensary in 0 village, Health Center in 1 village, Sub Center in 11 villages, Maternity and Child Welfare Center in 1 village, Community health workers in 4 villages.
The Villages having Hospital or Dispensary or Health Center are Mettunasuvampalayam, Thindal(Kil).
Drinking Water: Tap water in 20 villages, Tank water in 0 villages, Well water in 20 villages, Tubewell in 20 villages and more than one source in 20 villages.
Bank: Banking facility in 5 villages, namely, Mettunasuvampalayam, Ellappalayam, Villarasampatti

Thindal (Mel), Pudurpuduppalayam.
Credit Society in 3 villages Agricultural Credit Society in 1 Non-Agricultural Credit Society in 2 villages.
Others: Power supply in 20 villages, Cinema hall in 0 village, sport club in 1 village, Stadium or Auditorium or Community Hall in 1 village, Post Office in 18 villages.
There are 18 villages having bus facilities.
Villages with most of facilities: Mettunasuvampalayam Ellappalayam, Villarasampatti, Thindal (Mel) Pudurpuduppalayam.
Villages without amenities (Education):
Karaiellapalayam, Nochipalayam, Rajapalayam, Kurapalayam, Pagalanthanpalayam..
Scheduled Castes: Out of the total population of 55773 persons, 9946 persons (17.83%) belong to Scheduled Castes.
The villages having less than 10% SC population are None..
The villages having more than 50% SC population are None.
Sex ratio of Scheduled Caste population is 488.
Scheduled Castes Literates and Illiterates by Sex:

	Persons	Males	Females
Literate	4,421	2,670	1,751
Illiterate	5,525	2,418	3,107
Literacy rate	51.2	60.3	41.6
Graduate	58	40	18

Scheduled Castes (Dominant):
Arunthathiyar, Chakkiliyan, Adi Dravida, Madari Pallan
For their cultural identity please see Appendix-I
Villages without Scheduled Castes: There is 1 village without any scheduled caste population.
Scheduled Tribes: Out of the total population of 55773 persons, 32 persons (0.06%) belong to Scheduled Tribes.
The villages having less than 10% ST population are Karaiellapalayam, Elavamalai, Mettunasuvampalayam Perode, Nochipalayam, Gangapuram, Ellappalayam Villarasampatti, Thindal (Mel), Thindal(Kil) Kadirampatti, Rajapalayam, Mulakkarai, Kurapalayam Thottani, Pudurpuduppalayam, Nanjanapuram Pagalanthanpalayam, Veppempalayam, Muthampalayam.
The villages having more than 50% ST population are None.
Sex ratio of Scheduled tribe population is 500.
Scheduled Tribes Literates and Illiterates by Sex:

	Persons	Males	Females
Literate	26	13	13
Illiterate	6	3	3
Literacy rate	89.7	86.7	92.9
Graduate	7	4	3

Scheduled Tribes (Dominant):
Kondareddis, Kattunayakan
For their cultural identity please see Appendix-II
Villages without Scheduled Tribes: There are 17 villages without any scheduled tribe population.
Literates and Illiterates by Sex (Total Population):

	Persons	Males	Females
Literate	35,158	19,710	15,448
Illiterate	20,615	8,418	12,197
Literacy rate	70	78	62
Graduate	1,941	1,108	833

Agriculture: ***Distribution of villages according to land use:***
Out of 20 villages, Total area (in hectare) is 7177.7, out of that 82.44 percent is cultivable and 62.14 percent of the cultivable area is irrigated.
Sources of Irrigation (Hectares): Government Canal 2970.89, Private Canal 0, Well without Electricity 97.06, Well with Electricity 459.05, Tubewell without Electricity 0, Tubewell with Electricity 42.37, Tank 0, River 107.79, Lake 0, Waterfall 0, Others 0.
Villages with population of 5000 to 9999:
Elavamalai, Thindal (Kil).
Villages with population of 10000 and above:
Mettunasuvanpalayam.
Distribution of Workers:

	Persons	Males	Females	WPR
Cultivators	5,083	3,072	2,011	18.27
Agricultural Labour	7,879	3,736	4,143	28.33
Household Industry	572	198	374	2.06
Other Workers	14,281	10,741	3,540	51.34
Main Workers	26,624	17,425	9,199	95.72
Marginal Workers	1,191	322	869	4.28
Total Workers	27,815	17,747	10,068	

Religion: Major Religious Communities:

	Persons	Males	Females	Sex Ratio
Hindu (97.15%)	54,181	27,317	26,864	983
Muslim (1.32%)	738	390	348	892
Christian (1.49%)	832	412	420	1,019
Sikh (0%)	-	-	-	-
Buddhists (0%)	-	-	-	-
Jain (0%)	1	-	1	-

Agewise Data:

	Persons	Males	Females	Sex Ratio
All ages	55,773	28,128	27,645	983
0-14	13,325	7,026	6,299	897
15-44	28,700	14,029	14,671	1046
45-79	13,045	6,725	6,320	940
80+	588	288	300	1042
Age not stated	115	60	55	917

Languages (Dominant):

TAMILNADU

Tamil, Telugu, Kannada, English, Urdu

Disabled Population:

	Persons	Males	Females	%
Total Disabled	1,531	674	857	
In Seeing	1,039	359	680	67.86
In Speech	73	45	28	4.77
In Hearing	29	13	16	1.89
In Movement	221	137	84	14.44
Mentally	169	120	49	11.04

ERUMAIPATTI

Erumaipatti C.D. Block lies in the south-eastern part of Namakkal district. It is a part of Namakkal taluk. The Block is located at a distance of 16 kms. from district headquarters (Namakkal). There are 23 villages in the block with the total population of 80,229 persons. Area of the C.D. Block is 231.09 sq. kms. It is bounded in the north by C.D. Blocks Sendamanglam and Kolli Hills, in the south and east by district Tiruchirappalli, in the west by C.D. Blocks Namakkal and Mohanur.

Communications:

Roadways : S.H.-6: Direction- Namakkal to Musiri, Nearest Villages- Reddipatti, Tipramahadevi, Agraharavalavanthi, Mettupatti.

Annual Rainfall: Average Rainfall 650 mm.

Ground Water: Availability of the ground water in the Basin is 3504.73 H.A.M. and the utilization is 4794.54 H.A.M. It belongs to Safe category. Depth to water level varies from 5 to 10 meter below the ground. Most of the wells go down in summer months, according to the Ground Water Estimation Committee.

Forest and Reserved Forest: (Jambuthu RF)- Neaerst Village- Puducombai. (Sellur Extn.)- Nearest Villages- Gajacombai, Thottamudayampatti. (Sellur)- Nearest Village- Thottamudayampatti.

Natural Division: Kongu Nadu

Administration

Revenue **Division:** Namakkal. Parliamentary Constituency. District: Namakkal. Taluk: Namakkal. Assembly Constituency: 93 Senthamangalm (ST). Gram Panchayat: 24.

Villages: 23 **Inhabited:** 22 **Uninhabited:** 1

Ranking	District	State	National
Area	5	248	3643
Population	3	241	4100
Sex Ratio	4	264	2015
Child Sex Ratio	3	308	5165
Literacy Rate	2	126	1298
Density	11	77	3123
Work Participation Rate	6	162	745

Gram Panchayats:

Agrahara valavanthi, Alanganatham, Bodinayakkanpatti, Devarayapuram, Kavakkrampatti, Puducombai, Konangipatti, Mettupatti, Muthugapatti, Muttanchetti, Pavithiram, Pavithiram pudur, Perumapatti, Pottireddipatti, Pottireddipatty , Pudukkottai, Reddipatti, Sarkarpalayapalayam, Sevindipatti, Sivanayakanpatti, Sevianupalayam, Vadavathur, Varadarajapuram, Varagur .

Amenities:

Education: Primary School in 21 villages, Middle school in 7 villages, Matriculation or Secondary School in 6 villages, namely Sarkarpalayapalayam, Muthugapatti, Reddipatti, Pottireddipatti, Pavithiram, Sevindipatti.

Higher Secondary or Pre University Courses or Intermediate or Junior College in 3 villages of the CD Block,, namely Muthugapatti, Reddipatti, Pottireddipatti.

College in 1 village, Adult Literacy Center in 1 village., College is in village, namely Varagur.

Medical: Hospital in 0 village, Dispensary in 0 village, Health Center in 4 villages, Sub Center in 11 villages, Maternity and Child Welfare Center in 0 village, Community health workers in 1 village.

Drinking Water: Tap water in 22 villages, Tank water in 0 villages, Well water in 22 villages, Tubewell in 22 villages and more than one source in 22 villages.

Bank: Banking facility in 4 villages, namely, Muthugapatti, Pottireddipatti, Pavithiram, Varagur.

Credit Society in 17 villages Agricultural Credit Society in 9 Non-Agricultural Credit Society in 15 villages.

Others: Power supply in 22 villages, Cinema hall in 2 villages, sport club in 0 village, Stadium or Auditorium or Community Hall in 0 village, Post Office in 20 villages.

There are 22 villages having bus facilities.

Villages with most of facilities: Muthugapatti Pottireddipatti, Pavithiram, Varagur.

Villages without amenities (Education): Thottamudayampatti..

Scheduled Castes: Out of the total population of 80229 persons, 22747 persons (28.35%) belong to Scheduled Castes.

The villages having less than 10% SC population are None..

The villages having more than 50% SC population are None.

Sex ratio of Scheduled Caste population is 501.

Scheduled Castes Literates and Illiterates by Sex:

	Persons	Males	Females
Literate	13,522	7,822	5,700
Illiterate	9,225	3,523	5,702
Literacy rate	66.9	77.6	56.2
Graduate	479	342	137

Scheduled Castes (Dominant):

Pallan, Arunthathiyar, Paraiyan etc., Chakkiliyan Adi Dravida

For their cultural identity please see Appendix-I

Villages without Scheduled Castes: There is 1 village without any scheduled caste population.

Scheduled Tribes: Out of the total population of 80229 persons, 244 persons (0.3%) belong to Scheduled Tribes. The villages having less than 10% ST population are Puducombai, Gajacombai, Bodinaickenpatti Sarkarpalayapalayam, Muthugapatti, Reddipatti Perumapatti, Thusur, Pottireddipatti Thottamudayampatti, Pavithiram, Varagur, Ponnari Pudukkottai, Tipramahadevi, Kavakkarampatti Mutanchetti, Varadarajapuram, Sevindipatti Vadavathur, Agraharavalavanthi, Mettupatti.
The villages having more than 50% ST population are None.

Sex ratio of Scheduled tribe population is 480.

Scheduled Tribes Literates and Illiterates by Sex:

	Persons	Males	Females
Literate	159	90	69
Illiterate	85	37	48
Literacy rate	72.6	79.7	65.1
Graduate	11	10	1

Scheduled Tribes (Dominant):
Kondareddis, Malayali, Malakkuravan, Malai Pandaram Generic Tribes etc.

For their cultural identity please see Appendix-II

Villages without Scheduled Tribes: There are 12 villages without any scheduled tribe population.

Literates and Illiterates by Sex (Total Population):

	Persons	Males	Females
Literate	49,642	28,716	20,926
Illiterate	30,587	11,795	18,792
Literacy rate	69	80	59
Graduate	1,945	1,341	604

Agriculture: ***Distribution of villages according to land use:*** Out of 23 villages, Total area (in hectare) is 23109.31, out of that 52.57 percent is cultivable and 36.63 percent of the cultivable area is irrigated.

Sources of Irrigation (Hectares): Government Canal 0, Private Canal 0, Well without Electricity 0, Well with Electricity 4027.58, Tubewell without Electricity 0, Tubewell with Electricity 55.2, Tank 284.49, River 0, Lake 82.37, Waterfall 0, Others 0.

Villages with population of 5000 to 9999:
Muthugapatti , Reddipatti, Pottireddipatty Pavithiram , Varagur.

Villages with population of 10000 and above: None

Distribution of Workers:

	Persons	Males	Females	WPR
Cultivators	12,532	7,198	5,334	27.25
Agricultural Labour	22,135	9,421	12,714	48.14
Household Industry	778	387	391	1.69
Other Workers	10,537	8,630	1,907	22.92
Main Workers	39,735	23,309	16,426	86.41
Marginal Workers	6,247	2,327	3,920	13.59
Total Workers	45,982	25,636	20,346	

Religion: Major Religious Communities:

	Persons	Males	Females	Sex Ratio
Hindu (100.44%)	80,580	40,703	39,877	980
Muslim (1.16%)	933	439	494	1,125
Christian (0.2%)	163	83	80	964
Sikh (0%)	4	4	-	-
Buddhists (0%)	-	-	-	-
Jain (0%)	3	2	1	500

Agewise Data:

	Persons	Males	Females	Sex Ratio
All ages	81,763	41,275	40,488	981
0-14	19,869	10,366	9,503	917
15-44	38,863	19,278	19,585	1016
45-79	20,955	10,568	10,387	983
80+	875	477	398	834
Age not stated	1,201	586	615	1049

Languages (Dominant):
Tamil, Telugu, Kannada, Urdu, Malayalam

Disabled Population:

	Persons	Males	Females	%
Total Disabled	2,014	1,111	903	
In Seeing	1,112	602	510	55.21
In Speech	156	85	71	7.75
In Hearing	106	51	55	5.26
In Movement	458	269	189	22.74
Mentally	182	104	78	9.04

GANDARVAKKOTTAI

Gandarvakottai C.D. Block lies in the north-eastern part of Pudukkottai district. It is a part of Gandarvakottai taluk. The Block is located at a distance of NA kms. from district headquarters (Pudukkottai). There are 35 villages in the block with the total population of 76,930 persons. Area of the C.D. Block is 320.37 sq. kms. It is bounded in the north by district Thanjavur, in the south by CD Block Karambakudi, in the east by CD Block Karambakudi and district Thanjavur, in the west by CD Blocks Kunnandarkvoil and Pudukkottai.

Communications:

Roadways : S.H.-27: Direction- Pudukkottai to Thanjavur, Nearest Villages- Manjappettai, Ariyanipatti, Punalkulam, Pudunagar, Palayagandhrvakottai, Koveelur, Pisanathur.

Annual Rainfall: Average Rainfall 910 mm.

Ground Water: Availability of the ground water in the Basin is 7225.92 H.A.M. and the utilization is 1974.

39 H.A.M. It belongs to Safe category. Depth to water level varies from 2 to 10 meter below the ground. Most of the wells go down in summer months, according to the Ground Water Estimation Committee.

Natural Division: Chola Nadu.

Administration

Revenue **Division:** Pudukottai. Parliamentary Constituency: 30 Pudukottai. District: Pudukottai. Taluk: Gandarvakottai, Pudukottai. Assembly Constituency: 178 Gandarvakottai (SC). Gram Panchayat: 36.

Villages: 35 **Inhabited:** 35 **Uninhabited:** 0

Ranking	District	State	National
Area	9	151	2561
Population	10	256	4214
Sex Ratio	11	175	1193
Child Sex Ratio	13	240	3946
Literacy Rate	10	246	2161
Density	3	170	4202
Work Participation Rate	10	292	1689

Gram Panchayats:

Akachipatty, Andanur, Aravanpatti, Ariyanipatty, Athankarai Viduthy, Gandharvakottai, Kallakottai, Kattunaval, Komapuram, Kulathur, Kurumpoondi, Manganoor, Manjapettai, Mattangal, Muthukulam, Nadupatty, Namburanpatti, Nathammadipatti, Neppugai, Nodiyur, Palayagandarvakottai, Pallavarampatti, Periakottai, Pisanathur, Pudunagar, Pudupatti, Punakulam, Sangamviduthi, Sundampatti, Thachankurichi, Thurusupatti, Thuvar, Vadugapatti, Veeradipatty, Vellalaviduthy, Viralipatti.

Amenities:

Education: Primary School in 34 villages, Middle school in 14 villages, Matriculation or Secondary School in 4 villages, namely Komapuram, Pudunagar, Koveelur, Kallakottai. Higher Secondary or Pre University Courses or Intermediate or Junior College in 1 village of the CD Block,, namely Koveelur.

College in 0 village, Adult Literacy Center in 0 village.

Medical: Hospital in 1 village, Dispensary in 1 village, Health Center in 3 villages, Sub Center in 11 villages, Maternity and Child Welfare Center in 1 village, Community health workers in 21 villages.

The Villages having Hospital or Dispensary or Health Center are Koveelur, Sundampatti.

Drinking Water: Tap water in 35 villages, Tank water in 0 villages, Well water in 35 villages, Tubewell in 35 villages and more than one source in 35 villages.

Bank: Banking facility in 5 villages, namely, Andanur, Thachankurichi, Pudunagar, Koveelur Kallakottai.

Credit Society in 12 villages Agricultural Credit Society in 12 Non-Agricultural Credit Society in 1 village.

Others: Power supply in 35 villages, Cinema hall in 2 villages, sport club in 0 village, Stadium or Auditorium or Community Hall in 0 village, Post Office in 17 villages.

There are 32 villages having bus facilities.

Villages with most of facilities: Andanur Thachankurichi, Pudunagar, Koveelur, Kallakottai.

Villages without amenities (Education): Malayapatti..

Scheduled Castes: Out of the total population of 76930 persons, 21036 persons (27.34%) belong to Scheduled Castes.

The villages having less than 10% SC population are None..

The villages having more than 50% SC population are None.

Sex ratio of Scheduled Caste population is 503.

Scheduled Castes Literates and Illiterates by Sex:

	Persons	Males	Females
Literate	11,250	6,795	4,455
Illiterate	9,786	3,655	6,131
Literacy rate	62.8	76.9	49.0
Graduate	263	195	68

Scheduled Castes (Dominant):

Paraiyan etc., Pallan, Adi Dravida, Kuravan etc. Valluvan

For their cultural identity please see Appendix-I

Villages without Scheduled Castes: There is 0 village without any scheduled caste population.

Scheduled Tribes: Out of the total population of 76930 persons, 25 persons (0.03%) belong to Scheduled Tribes.

The villages having less than 10% ST population are Andanur, Athangaraividuthi, Malayapatti, Nodiyur Viralippatti, Thachankurichi, Kurumpoondi Manjappettai, Komapuram, Manganoor, Vadugappatty Meikkudipatti, Ariyanipatti, Punalkulam, Pudunagar Palayagandhrvakottai, Aravampatty, Koveelur Pisanathur, Veeradipatty, Mudukulam, Xavierkudikadu Kulathur Nayakarpatti, Naduppatti, Namburanpatti Periakottai, Pudupatti, Mattangal, Kattunaval Sundampatti, Neppugai, Sengamuiduthi, Kallakottai Vellalaviduthi, Thovar.

The villages having more than 50% ST population are None.

Sex ratio of Scheduled tribe population is 440.

Scheduled Tribes Literates and Illiterates by Sex:

	Persons	Males	Females
Literate	14	11	3
Illiterate	11	3	8
Literacy rate	66.7	84.6	37.5

Graduate	1	1	0

Scheduled Tribes (Dominant):
Malakkuravan, Uraly

For their cultural identity please see Appendix-II

Villages without Scheduled Tribes: There are 34 villages without any scheduled tribe population.

Literates and Illiterates by Sex (Total Population):

	Persons	Males	Females
Literate	42,245	25,227	17,018
Illiterate	34,685	13,261	21,424
Literacy rate	64	76	51
Graduate	944	697	247

Agriculture: ***Distribution of villages according to land use:*** Out of 35 villages, Total area (in hectare) is 32037.04, out of that 49.45 percent is cultivable and 24.88 percent of the cultivable area is irrigated.

Sources of Irrigation (Hectares): Government Canal 155.55, Private Canal 0, Well without Electricity 279.41, Well with Electricity 419.4, Tubewell without Electricity 288.6, Tubewell with Electricity 697.13, Tank 2234.22, River 0, Lake 0, Waterfall 0, Others 0.

Villages with population of 5000 to 9999:
Kovilur.

Villages with population of 10000 and above: None

Distribution of Workers:

	Persons	Males	Females	WPR
Cultivators	14,748	9,855	4,893	37.23
Agricultural Labour	18,742	8,183	10,559	47.31
Household Industry	588	335	253	1.48
Other Workers	5,540	4,260	1,280	13.98
Main Workers	29,471	19,033	10,438	74.39
Marginal Workers	10,147	3,600	6,547	25.61
Total Workers	39,618	22,633	16,985	

Religion: Major Religious Communities:

	Persons	Males	Females	Sex Ratio
Hindu (95.62%)	73,562	36,814	36,748	998
Muslim (2.15%)	1,653	819	834	1,018
Christian (2.18%)	1,676	833	843	1,012
Sikh (0%)	-	-	-	-
Buddhists (0%)	-	-	-	-
Jain (0%)	-	-	-	-

Agewise Data:

	Persons	Males	Females	Sex Ratio
All ages	76,930	38,488	38,442	999
0-14	22,652	11,687	10,965	938
15-44	37,143	18,346	18,797	1025
45-79	16,541	8,152	8,389	1029
80+	538	273	265	971
Age not stated	56	30	26	867

Languages (Dominant):
Tamil, Telugu, Malayalam, Urdu, Hindi

Disabled Population:

	Persons	Males	Females	%
Total Disabled	2,798	1,008	1,790	
In Seeing	1,778	407	1,371	63.55
In Speech	186	98	88	6.65
In Hearing	115	44	71	4.11
In Movement	572	368	204	20.44
Mentally	147	91	56	5.25

GANGAVALLI

Gangavalli C.D. Block lies in the south-eastern part of Salem district. It is a part of Gangavalli taluk. The Block is located at a distance of 63 kms. from district headquarters (Salem). There are 31 villages in the block with the total population of 64,272 persons. Area of the C.D. Block is 310.92 sq. kms. It is bounded in the north by CD Block Attur, and district Namakkal, in the south by district, Namakkal and Tiruchirappalli, in the east by CD Block Talavasal and district Perambalur, and in the west by district Namakkal.

Communications:

Roadways : S.H.-30: Direction- Musiri to Arasamatham, Nearest Villages- Jangamasamuudram, Nagiampatti, Manmalai, Mudakkuppati.

River: Suratha Nadi- Nearest Villages- Kondayampalli, Ulipuram, Goodamalai, Manmalai, Jangamasamuudram, Krishnapuram, Anayampatti.

Annual Rainfall: Average Rainfall 540 mm.

Ground Water: Availability of the ground water in the Basin is 9482.49 H.A.M. and the utilization is 20948. 85 H.A.M. It belongs to Safe category. Depth to water level varies from 2 to 10 meter below the ground. Most of the wells go down in summer months, according to the Ground Water Estimation Committee.

Forest and Reserved Forest: (Attu Manmalai RF)- Nearest Villages- Belur, Attur Manalai RF, Manmalai, Goodamalai. (Belur)- Nearest Villages- Goodamalai, Manmalai, Belur R.F., Belur. (Gangavalli)- Nearest Villages- Gangavalli Rf, Udumbiam RF (Ui), Veppadai, Valasakkalpatti, Veppanthattai, Belur, Krishnapuram. (Nagoor)- Nearest Villages- Veppadai, Nagoor R.F., Pachamalai, Veppadi. (Periyasolai)- Nearest Villages- Pachamalai, Periyasolai R.F. (Vanjarai)- Nearest Villages- Vanjarai R.F., Pachamalai. (Vengamudi)- Nearest Villages- Pachamalai, Vengamudi R.F.

Natural Division: Kongu Nadu.

Administration

Revenue **Division:** Attur. Parliamentary Constituency: 14 Kallakurichi (SC). District: Salem. Taluk: Gangavalli. Assembly Constituency: 81 Gangavalli (SC). Gram Panchayat: 14.

Villages: 31 **Inhabited:** 23 **Uninhabited:** 8

Ranking	District	State	National
Area	6	160	2669
Population	14	321	4715
Sex Ratio	2	298	2431
Child Sex Ratio	5	324	5351
Literacy Rate	5	305	2562
Density	9	72	4633
Work Participation Rate	18	319	669

Gram Panchayats:

Anaiyampatty, Belur, Goodamalai , Jangama Samudram, Kadambur, Kondayampalli , Krishnapuram, Manmalai, Naduvalur, Nagiampatty, Othiyathur, Pachamalai, Thagarappudur, Ulipuram, .

Amenities:

Education: Primary School in 18 villages, Middle school in 8 villages, Matriculation or Secondary School in 4 villages, namely Kondayampalli, Kadambur, Ulipuram, Goodamalai. Higher Secondary or Pre University Courses or Intermediate or Junior College in 0 village of the CD Block, College in 0 village, Adult Literacy Center in 0 village.

Medical: Hospital in 0 village, Dispensary in 0 village, Health Center in 1 village, Sub Center in 9 villages, Maternity and Child Welfare Center in 2 villages, Community health workers in 0 village.

Drinking Water: Tap water in 23 villages, Tank water in 0 villages, Well water in 23 villages, Tubewell in 23 villages and more than one source in 23 villages.

Bank: Banking facility in 4 villages, namely, Kondayampalli, Ulipuram, Goodamalai, Othiyathur.

Credit Society in 14 villages Agricultural Credit Society in 7 Non-Agricultural Credit Society in 14 villages.

Others: Power supply in 23 villages, Cinema hall in 1 village, sport club in 0 village, Stadium or Auditorium or Community Hall in 0 village, Post Office in 15 villages.

There are 16 villages having bus facilities.

Villages with most of facilities: Kondayampalli Ulipuram, Goodamalai, Othiyathur.

Villages without amenities (Education): Veppadai, Veppanthattai, Kallipatti, Seeradimoolai, Pillaiyarmathi..

Scheduled Castes: Out of the total population of 64272 persons, 11736 persons (18.26%) belong to Scheduled Castes.

The villages having less than 10% SC population are Kondayampalli, Veppadai , Valasakkalpatti Pachamalai, Veppanthattai, Kallipatti, Belur Veppadi, Mudakkuppati, Seeradimoolai, Pillaiyarmathi.

The villages having more than 50% SC population are None.

Sex ratio of Scheduled Caste population is 488.

Scheduled Castes Literates and Illiterates by Sex:

	Persons	Males	Females
Literate	5,765	3,493	2,272
Illiterate	5,971	2,513	3,458
Literacy rate	56.0	66.9	44.8
Graduate	159	133	26

Scheduled Castes (Dominant):

Paraiyan etc., Adi Dravida, Arunthathiyar, Pallan Chakkiliyan

For their cultural identity please see Appendix-I

Villages without Scheduled Castes: There are 13 villages without any scheduled caste population.

Scheduled Tribes: Out of the total population of 64272 persons, 9745 persons (15.16%) belong to Scheduled Tribes.

The villages having less than 10% ST population are Kondayampalli, Nagiampatti, Kadambur, Naduvalur Goodamalai, Jangamasamuudram, Mudakkuppati Krishnapuram, Othiyathur, Anayampatti.

The villages having more than 50% ST population are Valasakkalpatti, Pachamalai, Veppanthattai Kallipatti, Belur, Veppadi, Seeradimoolai Pillaiyarmathi.

Sex ratio of Scheduled tribe population is 491.

Scheduled Tribes Literates and Illiterates by Sex:

	Persons	Males	Females
Literate	4,240	2,533	1,707
Illiterate	5,505	2,426	3,079
Literacy rate	48.7	57.4	39.8
Graduate	39	32	7

Scheduled Tribes (Dominant):

Malayali, Irular, Malakkuravan, Uraly Generic Tribes etc.

For their cultural identity please see Appendix-II

Villages without Scheduled Tribes: There are 11 villages without any scheduled tribe population.

Literates and Illiterates by Sex (Total Population):

	Persons	Males	Females
Literate	34,941	20,686	14,255
Illiterate	29,331	11,917	17,414
Literacy rate	61	72	50
Graduate	960	712	248

Agriculture: ***Distribution of villages according to land use:*** Out of 31 villages, Total area (in hectare) is 31092.38, out of that 49.72 percent is cultivable and 65.06 percent of the cultivable area is irrigated.

Sources of Irrigation (Hectares): Government Canal 0, Private Canal 0, Well without Electricity 825.01, Well with Electricity 8523.59, Tubewell without Electricity 0, Tubewell with Electricity 67, Tank 59.45, River 0, Lake 0, Waterfall 0, Others 0.

Villages with population of 5000 to 9999:

Naduvalur, Anaiyampatty, Kadambur, Ulipuram Nagiampatty, Kondayampalli , Goodamalai , Pachamalai.

Villages with population of 10000 and above: None

Distribution of Workers:

	Persons	Males	Females	WPR
Cultivators	15,264	9,205	6,059	41.41
Agricultural Labour	16,418	7,528	8,890	44.54
Household Industry	587	333	254	1.59
Other Workers	4,589	3,398	1,191	12.45
Main Workers	30,255	17,948	12,307	82.09
Marginal Workers	6,603	2,516	4,087	17.91
Total Workers	36,858	20,464	16,394	

Religion: Major Religious Communities:

	Persons	Males	Females	Sex Ratio
Hindu (98.13%)	63,072	32,026	31,046	969
Muslim (0.99%)	637	309	328	1,061
Christian (0.8%)	514	241	273	1,133
Sikh (0%)	-	-	-	-
Buddhists (0%)	3	2	1	500
Jain (0%)	1	1	-	-

Agewise Data:

	Persons	Males	Females	Sex Ratio
All ages	64,272	32,603	31,669	971
0-14	16,934	8,911	8,023	900
15-44	31,521	15,630	15,891	1017
45-79	15,059	7,633	7,426	973
80+	445	247	198	802
Age not stated	313	182	131	720

Languages (Dominant):

Tamil, Telugu, Urdu, Malayalam, Kannada

Disabled Population:

	Persons	Males	Females	%
Total Disabled	1,149	665	484	
In Seeing	571	328	243	49.7
In Speech	99	60	39	8.62
In Hearing	87	36	51	7.57
In Movement	311	189	122	27.07
Mentally	81	52	29	7.05

GINGEE

Gingee C.D. Block lies in the northern part of Viluppuram district. It is a part of Gingee taluk. The Block is located at a distance of 38 kms. from district headquarters (Viluppuram). There are 82 villages in the block with the total population of 123,431 persons. Area of the C.D. Block is 390.03 sq. kms. It is bounded in the north by C.D. Block Melmalayanur, in the south by CD Blocks Kanai, Magaiyur and Vikravandi, in the east by C.D. Block Vallam, and in the west by district Tiruvannamalai.

Communications:

Roadways : N.H-66: Direction- Tiruvannamalai to Tindivanam, Nearest Villages- Alampundi, Melpappampady, Semmedu, Viramanallur, Satyamangalam, Baharatantangal, Perungappur, Uranitangal, Anjancheri, Ponpatti. S.H-4: Direction- Arani to Vilupuram, Nearest Villages- Singavaram, Ponpatti, Jayankondan, Narasingarayapettai, Sittampundi, Appampattu, Kavarai, Kadagampundi, Mavattambadi, Palappattu, Mathur Thirukkai, Hampettu, Thiruvathikunram, Mattapparai.

River: Varahanadi- Nearest Villages- Alampundi, Ponpatti, Singavaram, Uranitangal, Anjancheri, Idayalam.

Backwards Region Grants Fund: It receives Backward Region Grants.

Annual Rainfall: Average Rainfall 1119 mm.

Ground Water: Availability of the ground water in the Basin is 7029.87 H.A.M. and the utilization is 9936.07 H.A.M. It belongs to Over Expoited category. Depth to water level varies from 2 to 5 meter below the ground. Most of the wells go down in summer months, according to the Ground Water Estimation Committee.

Forest and Reserved Forest: (Adukkam RF)- Nearest Villages- Adukkam R.F, Malavantangal. (Gangavaram)- Nearest Villages- Palavalam, Malarasankuppam, Malavantangal, Gangavaram R.F, Gangavaram, Kanakkankuppam. (Muttakadu)- Nearest Villages- Perungappur, Muttakadu R.F, Narasingarayapettai, Konai, Odiyathur, Chinnaponnampundi. (Padippallam)- Nearest Villages- Konai, Sennalur, Odiyathur, Manalapadi, Periyamur, Devadanampettai, Padipallam, Padipallam R.F, Tachampattu, Sittampundi, Sirunampundi, Karai RF, Attiyur. (Pakkamalai)- Nearest Villages- Nayampadi, Manalapadi, Periyamur, Pakkamalai R.F, Pudupalayam, Sorattupperiyamkuppam, Pakkam, Nallanpillaipetral, Settavarai, Tadagam, Pothuvoy, Palavalam, Gangavaram, Tandavasamudram. (Thandavasamudram)- Nearest Villages- Tandavasamudram, Mullur, Thandavasamudram R.F, Tuttipattu, Konalur. (Pulinjimalai)- Nearest Villages- Malarasankuppam, Pulinjimalai R.F, Malavantangal. (Siruvadi)- Nearest Villages- Alampundi, Perungappur, Singavaram. (Thurinjikdu)- Nearest Villages- Malavantangal, Thurinjikadu R.F.

Natural Division: Tondai Nadu.

Administration

Revenue **Division:** Tindivanam. Parliamentary Constituency: 12 Arani. District: Villupuram. Taluk: Gingee. Assembly Constituency: 70 Gingee. Gram Panchayat: 60.

Villages: 82 **Inhabited:** 76 **Uninhabited:** 6

Ranking	District	State	National
Area	4	81	1996
Population	9	59	2759
Sex Ratio	4	184	1264
Child Sex Ratio	7	56	1133
Literacy Rate	12	288	2444

Density	13	219	3377
Work Participation Rate	17	202	2324

Gram Panchayats:
Alampundi, Anaiyeri, Attiyur, Bharatantangal, Chinnaponnampundi, Devadanampettai, Gangavaram, Idayalam (Mel), Jambodi, Jayankondan, Kamagaram, Kanakkankuppam, Karai, Kattuchittamur, Kavarai, Konai, Konalur, Madappundi, Malavantangal, Manalapadi, MatturTirukkai, Mavattambadi, Melarungunam, Minamur, Nagalampattu, Nallampillaipetral, Narasingarayanpettai, Nayampadi , Oddambattu, Odiyathur, Paddippallam, Padippallam, Pakkam, Palaiyambattu, Palappattu, Palavalam, Pappambadi (Mel), Perungappur, Ponnankuppam, Ponpatti, Pothuvoy, Pudupalayam, Pullipattu, Puttagaram, Reddipalayam, Satyamangalam, Semmedu, Semmedu , Sepettai, Settavarai, Singavaram, Sirunampundi, Sittampundi, Sorattupperiyankuppam, Tachchampattu, Tadagam, Tandavasamudram, Tenpuduppattu, Thiruvadikunnam, Uranitangal, Varikkal, Velanthangal, .

Amenities:

Education: Primary School in 67 villages, Middle school in 24 villages, Matriculation or Secondary School in 8 villages, namely Alampundi, Satyamangalam, Devadanampettai, Nallanpillaipetral, Malavantangal, Kanakkankuppam, Kavarai, Anaiyeri.

Higher Secondary or Pre University Courses or Intermediate or Junior College in 2 villages of the CD Block,, namely Alampundi, Konai.

College in 0 village, Adult Literacy Center in 0 village.

Medical: Hospital in 1 village, Dispensary in 2 villages, Health Center in 4 villages, Sub Center in 24 villages, Maternity and Child Welfare Center in 66 villages, Community health workers in 0 village.

The Village having Hospital or Dispensary or Health Center is Alampundi, Sennalur.

Drinking Water: Tap water in 76 villages, Tank water in 17 villages, Well water in 76 villages, Tubewell in 76 villages and more than one source in 76 villages.

Bank: Banking facility in 5 villages, namely, Alampundi, Satyamangalam, Nallanpillaipetral Malavantangal, Appampattu.

Credit Society in 14 villages Agricultural Credit Society in 13 Non-Agricultural Credit Society in 0 village.

Others: Power supply in 76 villages, Cinema hall in 0 village, sport club in 0 village, Stadium or Auditorium or Community Hall in 0 village, Post Office in 70 villages.

There are 69 villages having bus facilities.

Villages with most of facilities: Alampundi Satyamangalam, Nallanpillaipetral, Malavantangal Appampattu.

Villages without amenities (Education):
Viramanallur, Muttakadu R.F, Tadanguppam, Kanjur, Uliyampattu, Kadagampundi, Karai R.F, Mullur, Thandavasamudram R.F..

Scheduled Castes: Out of the total population of 123431 persons, 25873 persons (20.96%) belong to Scheduled Castes.

The villages having less than 10% SC population are Alampundi, Semmedu, Satyamangalam, Nayampadi Baharatantangal, Pasumalaitangal, Muttakadu R.F Singavaram, Uranitangal, Anjancheri, Konai Chinnaponnampundi, Pullipattu, Pudupalayam Puttagaram, Kamagaram, Tadanguppam, Nagalampattu Uliyampattu, Tadagam, Malarasankuppam, Gangavaram Kanakkankuppam, Tandavasamudram, Kommedu Tenpuduppattu, Karai R.F, Tuttipattu, Ponnankuppam Thiruvathikunram.

The villages having more than 50% SC population are Viramanallur, Pakkam, Kadagampundi, Minamur, Mullur Thandavasamudram R.F.

Sex ratio of Scheduled Caste population is 496.

Scheduled Castes Literates and Illiterates by Sex:

	Persons	Males	Females
Literate	12,229	7,333	4,896
Illiterate	13,644	5,707	7,937
Literacy rate	54.7	65.1	44.1
Graduate	145	119	26

Scheduled Castes (Dominant):
Adi Dravida, Arunthathiyar, Domban, Dom etc.
Adi Andhra

For their cultural identity please see Appendix-I

Villages without Scheduled Castes: There are 19 villages without any scheduled caste population.

Scheduled Tribes: Out of the total population of 123431 persons, 2792 persons (2.26%) belong to Scheduled Tribes.

The villages having less than 10% ST population are Alampundi, Melpappampady, Semmedu, Viramanallur Satyamangalam, Nayampadi, Baharatantangal Pasumalaitangal, Perungappur, Singavaram Uranitangal, Anjancheri, Idayalam, Ponpatti Jayankondan, Narasingarayapettai, Konai, Odiyathur Chinnaponnampundi, Manalapadi, Periyamur Devadanampettai, Sorattupperiyamkuppam, Pullipattu Pudupalayam, Pakkam, Pettai (Gingee), Puttagaram Kamagaram, Tadanguppam, Kattuchittamur, Madappundi Kanjur, Nagalampattu, Nallanpillaipetral, Settavarai Tadagam, Pothuvoy, Palavalam, Malarasankuppam Malavantangal, Gangavaram, Kanakkankuppam Tandavasamudram, Padipallam, Tachampattu, Attiyur

Sittampundi, Sirunampundi, Appampattu, Kavarai Kadagampundi, Minamur, Jambodi, Kommedu Tenpuduppattu, Mavattambadi, Palappattu, Karai R.F Karai, Varikkal, Melarungunam, Mullur Thandavasamudram R.F, Tuttipattu, Ponnankuppam Konalur, Anaiyeri, Pulivandi, Mathur Thirukkai Hampettu, Mattapparai.

The villages having more than 50% ST population are None.

Sex ratio of Scheduled tribe population is 502.

Scheduled Tribes Literates and Illiterates by Sex:

	Persons	Males	Females
Literate	839	515	324
Illiterate	1,953	875	1,078
Literacy rate	35.2	43.6	27.0
Graduate	2	1	1

Scheduled Tribes (Dominant):
Irular, Adiyan, Malakkuravan, Kattunayakan Generic Tribes etc.

For their cultural identity please see Appendix-II

Villages without Scheduled Tribes: There are 29 villages without any scheduled tribe population.

Literates and Illiterates by Sex (Total Population):

	Persons	Males	Females
Literate	67,260	39,952	27,308
Illiterate	56,171	21,861	34,310
Literacy rate	62	74	50
Graduate	1,255	952	303

Agriculture: ***Distribution of villages according to land use:*** Out of 82 villages, Total area (in hectare) is 39003.2, out of that 50.81 percent is cultivable and 50.9 percent of the cultivable area is irrigated.

Sources of Irrigation (Hectares): Government Canal 0, Private Canal 0, Well without Electricity 2448.638, Well with Electricity 4815.16, Tubewell without Electricity 0, Tubewell with Electricity 0, Tank 0, River 0, Lake 2817.66, Waterfall 0, Others 6.59.

Villages with population of 5000 to 9999: None

Villages with population of 10000 and above: None

Distribution of Workers:

	Persons	Males	Females	WPR
Cultivators	23,101	15,079	8,022	37.35
Agricultural Labour	29,887	13,064	16,823	48.32
Household Industry	1,416	690	726	2.29
Other Workers	7,450	5,793	1,657	12.04
Main Workers	41,417	26,241	15,176	66.96
Marginal Workers	20,437	8,385	12,052	33.04
Total Workers	61,854	34,626	27,228	

Religion: Major Religious Communities:

	Persons	Males	Females	Sex Ratio
Hindu (87.77%)	108,330	54,354	53,976	993
Muslim (3.24%)	4,003	2,024	1,979	978
Christian (8.85%)	10,919	5,345	5,574	1,043
Sikh (0%)	1	1	-	-
Buddhists (0.01%)	13	9	4	444
Jain (0.05%)	62	25	37	1,480

Agewise Data:

	Persons	Males	Females	Sex Ratio
All ages	123,431	61,813	61,618	997
0-14	36,773	18,658	18,115	971
15-44	56,628	27,889	28,739	1030
45-79	28,307	14,318	13,989	977
80+	1,348	750	598	797
Age not stated	375	198	177	894

Languages (Dominant):
Tamil, Urdu, Telugu, Hindi, Gujarati

Disabled Population:

	Persons	Males	Females	%
Total Disabled	3,157	1,670	1,487	
In Seeing	1,465	748	717	46.4
In Speech	302	151	151	9.57
In Hearing	192	79	113	6.08
In Movement	936	547	389	29.65
Mentally	262	145	117	8.3

GOBICHETTIPALAYAM

Gobichettipalayam C.D. Block lies in the northern part of Erode district. It is a part of Gobichettipalayam taluk. The Block is located at a distance of 38 kms. from district headquarters (Erode). There are 26 villages in the block with the total population of 91,122 persons. Area of the C.D. Block is 201.01 sq. kms. It is bounded in the north by C.D. Blocks Thoockanaickenpalaiyam and Anthiyur, in the south by C.D. Blocks Nambiyur and Perundurai, in the east by CD Blocks Bhavani and Perundurai, in the west by C.D. Blocks Sathyamangalam and Thoockanaickenpalaiyam.

Communications:

Roadways : S.H.-15: Direction- Kasipalayam to Kuhalur, Nearest Villages- Alukkuli, Vellalapalayam, Pulavakalipalayam, Kullampalayam, Bodichinnampalayam, Cholamadevikarai, Kalingiam.

River: Bhavani Nadi- Nearest Villages- Savandapure, Ammapalayam, Mevani, Perunthalaiyur, Pudukkarai, Bodichinnampalayam, Palayapariyurkarai, Akrakarakarai.

Annual Rainfall: Average Rainfall 789 mm.

Ground Water: Availability of the ground water in the Basin is 9816.75 H.A.M. and the utilization is 5935.22 H.A.M. It belongs to Safe category. Depth to water level varies from 2 to 20 meter below the ground. Most of the wells go down in summer months, according to the Ground Water Estimation Committee.

Natural Division: Kongu Nadu.

Administration

Revenue **Division:** Gobichettipalayam. Parliamentary Constituency: 18 Gobichettipalayam. District: Erode. Taluk: Gobichettipalayam. Assembly Constituency: 105 Anthiyur, 106 Gobichettipalayam. Gram Panchayat: 21.

Villages: 26 **Inhabited:** 22 **Uninhabited:** 4

Ranking	**District**	**State**	**National**
Area	15	285	4158
Population	5	177	3749
Sex Ratio	9	283	2236
Child Sex Ratio	10	267	4420
Literacy Rate	13	339	3039
Density	14	47	2436
Work Participation Rate	5	81	418

Gram Panchayats:

Alukuli, Ammapalayam, Ayalur, Bommanaickanpalayam, Chandrapuram, Kadukkampalayam, Kalingiam, Kottupullampalayam, Kullampalayam, Mevani, Modachur, Nagadevampalayam, Nanjaigopi, Nathipalayam, Pariyur, Perundalaiyur, Pulavakalipalayam, Savandapur, Siruvalur, Vellalapalayam, Vellankovil.

Amenities:

Education: Primary School in 21 villages, Middle school in 14 villages, Matriculation or Secondary School in 4 villages, namely Vellalapalayam, Pulavakalipalayam, Kullampalayam, Vellalankovil.

Higher Secondary or Pre University Courses or Intermediate or Junior College in 2 villages of the CD Block,, namely Vellalapalayam, Pulavakalipalayam.

College in 1 village, Adult Literacy Center in 0 village., College is in village, namely Pariyurgramam.

Medical: Hospital in 1 village, Dispensary in 0 village, Health Center in 3 villages, Sub Center in 16 villages, Maternity and Child Welfare Center in 3 villages, Community health workers in 0 village.

The Village having Hospital or Dispensary or Health Center is Alukkuli.

Drinking Water: Tap water in 22 villages, Tank water in 0 villages, Well water in 22 villages, Tubewell in 22 villages and more than one source in 22 villages.

Bank: Banking facility in 4 villages, namely, Savandapure, Mevani, Chandrapuram, Vellalankovil.

Credit Society in 18 villages Agricultural Credit Society in 12 Non-Agricultural Credit Society in 15 villages.

Others: Power supply in 22 villages, Cinema hall in 2 villages, sport club in 1 village, Stadium or Auditorium or Community Hall in 0 village, Post Office in 21 villages.

There are 21 villages having bus facilities.

Villages with most of facilities: Savandapure Mevani, Chandrapuram, Vellalankovil.

Villages without Amenities (Education): None..

Scheduled Castes: Out of the total population of 91122 persons, 17756 persons (19.49%) belong to Scheduled Castes.

The villages having less than 10% SC population are Pudukkarai, Vellalapalayam, Kullampalayam Chandrapuram.

The villages having more than 50% SC population are None.

Sex ratio of Scheduled Caste population is 492.

Scheduled Castes Literates and Illiterates by Sex:

	Persons	Males	Females
Literate	6,455	3,838	2,617
Illiterate	11,301	5,190	6,111
Literacy rate	40.8	47.7	33.6
Graduate	139	106	33

Scheduled Castes (Dominant):

Chakkiliyan, Arunthathiyar, Pallan, Adi Dravida Madari

For their cultural identity please see Appendix-I

Villages without Scheduled Castes: There are 4 villages without any scheduled caste population.

Scheduled Tribes: Out of the total population of 91122 persons, 7 persons (0.01%) belong to Scheduled Tribes.

The villages having less than 10% ST population are Savandapure, Ammapalayam, Mevani, Perunthalaiyur Kugalur, Pudukkarai, Alukkuli, Pariyurgramam Vellalapalayam, Nanjaigobi, Pulavakalipalayam Kullampalayam, Naathipalayam, Modachur, Kalingiam Kottupullampalayam, Ayalur, Negadevampalayam Kadukkampalayam, Chandrapuram, Vellalankovil Siruvalur.

The villages having more than 50% ST population are None.

Sex ratio of Scheduled tribe population is 429.

Scheduled Tribes Literates and Illiterates by Sex:

	Persons	Males	Females
Literate	6	4	2
Illiterate	1	0	1
Literacy rate	85.7	100.0	66.7
Graduate	2	1	1

Scheduled Tribes (Dominant):

Kattunayakan, Kondareddis

For their cultural identity please see Appendix-II

Villages without Scheduled Tribes: There are 24 villages without any scheduled tribe population.

Literates and Illiterates by Sex (Total Population):

	Persons	Males	Females
Literate	48,359	28,895	19,464
Illiterate	42,763	17,246	25,517
Literacy rate	59	69	48

Graduate	1,878	1,281	597

Agriculture: ***Distribution of villages according to land use:*** Out of 26 villages, Total area (in hectare) is 20101.23, out of that 75.9 percent is cultivable and 77.88 percent of the cultivable area is irrigated.

Sources of Irrigation (Hectares): Government Canal 7333.13, Private Canal 0, Well without Electricity 718.24, Well with Electricity 3203.79, Tubewell without Electricity 0, Tubewell with Electricity 558.96, Tank 29.51, River 39.28, Lake 0, Waterfall 0, Others 0.

Villages with population of 5000 to 9999: Kugalur , Alukuli, Modachur, Kalingiam Kottupullampalayam, Ayalur, Vellankovil, Siruvalur.

Villages with population of 10000 and above: None

Distribution of Workers:

	Persons	Males	Females	WPR
Cultivators	12,403	7,396	5,007	22.64
Agricultural Labour	27,236	13,581	13,655	49.72
Household Industry	2,458	1,128	1,330	4.49
Other Workers	12,685	9,530	3,155	23.16
Main Workers	51,343	30,769	20,574	93.72
Marginal Workers	3,439	866	2,573	6.28
Total Workers	54,782	31,635	23,147	

Religion: Major Religious Communities:

	Persons	Males	Females	Sex Ratio
Hindu (98.19%)	89,471	45,347	44,124	973
Muslim (0.77%)	704	343	361	1,052
Christian (0.91%)	831	396	435	1,098
Sikh (0.02%)	15	8	7	875
Buddhists (0%)	3	1	2	2,000
Jain (0.01%)	7	3	4	1,333

Agewise Data:

	Persons	Males	Females	Sex Ratio
All ages	91,122	46,141	44,981	975
0-14	19,229	9,957	9,272	931
15-44	43,650	21,789	21,861	1003
45-79	26,712	13,591	13,121	965
80+	1,375	717	658	918
Age not stated	156	87	69	793

Languages (Dominant):

Tamil, Telugu, Urdu, Kannada, Malayalam

Disabled Population:

	Persons	Males	Females	%
Total Disabled	2,794	1,040	1,754	
In Seeing	1,847	537	1,310	66.11
In Speech	209	117	92	7.48
In Hearing	151	65	86	5.4
In Movement	399	234	165	14.28
Mentally	188	87	101	6.73

GUDALUR

Gudalur C.D. Block lies in the north-western part of Nilgiris district. It is a part of Panthalur, Gudalur and Uthagamandalam taluks. The Block is located at a distance of 50 kms. from district headquarters (Uthagamandalam). There are 08 villages in the block with the total population of 91,056 persons. Area of the C.D. Block is 545.01 sq. kms. It is bounded in the east and south by C.D. Block Uthagamandalam, and it has common boundary with the state of Karnataka on north, and with the state of Kerala on south, north and west. CD Block Gadalur falls in taluk Panthalur by 04 villages, in taluk Gudalur by 03 villages, and in taluk Uthagamandalam by 01 village.

Communications:

Roadways : S.H.-12: Direction- Vythiri to Gudalur, Nearest Villages- Erumad, Cherangode. S.H.-31: Direction- Uthagamandalam to Mysore, Nearest Village- Mudumalai.

River: Moyar Nadi- Nearest Village- Masinagudi. Sigur Nadi- Nearest Village- Masinagudi.

Annual Rainfall: Average Rainfall 1920 mm.

Ground Water: Availability of the ground water in the Basin is 6308.76 H.A.M. and the utilization is 161.10 H.A.M. It belongs to Safe category. Depth to water level varies from 2 to 10 meter below the ground. Most of the wells go down in summer months, according to the Ground Water Estimation Committee.

Forest and Reserved Forest: (Mudumalai RF)- Nearest Villages- Nellakotta, Mudumalai, Srimadurai, Masinagudi.

Natural Division: NA

Administration

Revenue **Division:** Gudalur. Parliamentary Constituency: 19 Nilgiris. District: The Nilgiris. Taluk: Uthagamandalam, Panthalur, Gudalur. Assembly Constituency: 109 Gudalur (SC). Gram Panchayat: 05.

Border Villages- (Kerala)- Nearest Village- Nellakotta. (Karnataka)- Nearest Village- Masinagudi.

Villages: 8 **Inhabited:** 8 **Uninhabited:** 0

Ranking	District	State	National
Area	2	27	1335
Population	2	178	3752
Sex Ratio	4	137	1000
Child Sex Ratio	3	84	1674
Literacy Rate	2	32	483
Density	4	313	5282
Work Participation Rate	3	351	3679

Gram Panchayats:

Cherangode, Cherankodu , Masinagudi , Mudumalai , Nellakkottai, Nellakotta, Sreemadurai.

Amenities:

Education: Primary School in 8 villages, Middle school in 6 villages, Matriculation or Secondary School in 6 villages,

namely Erumad, Moonanad, Nelliyalam, Cherangode, Srimadurai, Masinagudi.

Higher Secondary or Pre University Courses or Intermediate or Junior College in 3 villages of the CD Block,, namely Erumad, Nelliyalam, Masinagudi.

College in 0 village, Adult Literacy Center in 1 village.

Medical: Hospital in 1 village, Dispensary in 1 village, Health Center in 6 villages, Sub Center in 7 villages, Maternity and Child Welfare Center in 0 village, Community health workers in 0 village.

The Villages having Hospital or Dispensary or Health Center are Erumad, Nelliyalam.

Drinking Water: Tap water in 8 villages, Tank water in 0 villages, Well water in 8 villages, Tubewell in 8 villages and more than one source in 8 villages.

Bank: Banking facility in 4 villages, namely, Erumad, Cherangode, Srimadurai, Masinagudi.

Credit Society in 7 villages Agricultural Credit Society in 4 Non-Agricultural Credit Society in 5 villages.

Others: Power supply in 8 villages, Cinema hall in 1 village, sport club in 3 villages, Stadium or Auditorium or Community Hall in 0 village, Post Office in 7 villages.

There are 8 villages having bus facilities.

Villages with most of facilities: Erumad Cherangode, Srimadurai, Masinagudi.

Villages without Amenities (Education): None..

Scheduled Castes: Out of the total population of 91056 persons, 23891 persons (26.24%) belong to Scheduled Castes.

The villages having less than 10% SC population are None..

The villages having more than 50% SC population are None.

Sex ratio of Scheduled Caste population is 503.

Scheduled Castes Literates and Illiterates by Sex:

	Persons	Males	Females
Literate	16,006	8,907	7,099
Illiterate	7,885	2,957	4,928
Literacy rate	77.7	87.6	68.0
Graduate	162	123	39

Scheduled Castes (Dominant):

Paraiyan etc., Pallan, Adi Karnataka, Adi Dravida Chakkiliyan

For their cultural identity please see Appendix-I

Villages without Scheduled Castes: There is 1 village without any scheduled caste population.

Scheduled Tribes: Out of the total population of 91056 persons, 10338 persons (11.35%) belong to Scheduled Tribes.

The villages having less than 10% ST population are None..

The villages having more than 50% ST population are None.

Sex ratio of Scheduled tribe population is 505.

Scheduled Tribes Literates and Illiterates by Sex:

	Persons	Males	Females
Literate	3,484	2,029	1,455
Illiterate	6,854	3,091	3,763
Literacy rate	39.9	47.2	32.8
Graduate	18	8	10

Scheduled Tribes (Dominant):

Paniyan, Kurumbas, Kattunayakan, Irular, Kurumans

For their cultural identity please see Appendix-II

Villages without Scheduled Tribes: There is 0 village without any scheduled tribe population.

Literates and Illiterates by Sex (Total Population):

	Persons	Males	Females
Literate	60,940	33,196	27,744
Illiterate	30,116	12,198	17,918
Literacy rate	77	85	70
Graduate	1,650	1,049	601

Agriculture: ***Distribution of villages according to land use:***
Out of 8 villages, Total area (in hectare) is 54501.02, out of that 21.24 percent is cultivable and 0.01 percent of the cultivable area is irrigated.

Sources of Irrigation (Hectares): Government Canal 0, Private Canal 0, Well without Electricity 0, Well with Electricity 1.5, Tubewell without Electricity 0, Tubewell with Electricity 0, Tank 0, River 0, Lake 0, Waterfall 0, Others 0.

Villages with population of 5000 to 9999:
Munnanad, Srimadurai, Masinagudi.

Villages with population of 10000 and above:
Erumad, Nelliyalam , Cherangode.

Distribution of Workers:

	Persons	Males	Females	WPR
Cultivators	2,960	2,110	850	7.45
Agricultural Labour	6,323	3,511	2,812	15.92
Household Industry	507	238	269	1.28
Other Workers	29,917	18,625	11,292	75.34
Main Workers	33,021	21,199	11,822	83.16
Marginal Workers	6,686	3,285	3,401	16.84
Total Workers	39,707	24,484	15,223	

Religion: Major Religious Communities:

	Persons	Males	Females	Sex Ratio
Hindu (69.51%)	63,297	31,657	31,640	999
Muslim (16.54%)	15,060	7,328	7,732	1,055
Christian (13.82%)	12,585	6,353	6,232	981
Sikh (0%)	2	1	1	1,000
Buddhists (0.02%)	16	8	8	1,000
Jain (0.01%)	5	2	3	1,500

Agewise Data:

	Persons	Males	Females	Sex Ratio
All ages	91,056	45,394	45,662	1006
0-14	26,344	13,330	13,014	976
15-44	46,636	22,832	23,804	1043
45-79	17,365	8,883	8,482	955
80+	563	253	310	1225
Age not stated	148	96	52	542

Languages (Dominant):
Malayalam, Tamil, Kannada, Telugu, Bhili/Bhilodi

Disabled Population:

	Persons	Males	Females	%
Total Disabled	2,411	1,363	1,048	
In Seeing	1,504	848	656	62.38
In Speech	157	67	90	6.51
In Hearing	72	40	32	2.99
In Movement	502	323	179	20.82
Mentally	176	85	91	7.3

GUDIMANGALAM

Gudimangalam C.D. Block lies in the south-western part of Coimbatore district. It is a part of Udumalaipettai taluk. The taluk is located at a distance of 66 kms. from district headquarters (Coimbatore). There are 24 villages in the block with the total population of 74,134 persons. Area of the C.D. Block is 309.70 sq. kms. It is bounded in the north by taluk Palladam and district Erode, in the south by C.D. Blocks Udumalaipettai and Madathukulam, in the east by CD Block Madathukulam and district Erode, and in the west by taluk Pollachi.

Communications:
Roadways : S.H.-21: Direction- Pollachi to Dharapuram, Nearest Villages- Gudimangalam, Somauara Patti, Vadugampalayam, Kottamangalam, Kongalnagaram, Pudupalayam.

Annual Rainfall: Average Rainfall 550 mm.

Ground Water: Availability of the ground water in the Basin is 4965.37 H.A.M. and the utilization is 4576.01 H.A.M. It belongs to Safe category. Depth to water level varies from 2 to 20 meter below the ground. Most of the wells go down in summer months, according to the Ground Water Estimation Committee.

Natural Division: Kongu Nadu.

Administration
Revenue **Division:** Udumalaipettai. Parliamentary Constituency: 21 Pollachi. District: Coimbatore. Taluk: Udumalaipettai. Assembly Constituency: 125 Udumalaipettai. Gram Panchayat: 23.

Villages: 24 **Inhabited:** 24 **Uninhabited:** 0

Ranking	District	State	National
Area	7	162	2681
Population	10	269	4316
Sex Ratio	3	170	1156
Child Sex Ratio	11	132	2366
Literacy Rate	16	267	2296
Density	2	57	4214
Work Participation Rate	14	293	491

Gram Panchayats:
Amandakadavu, Anikkadavu, Athukinathupatti, Dhoddampatti, Gudimangalam, Iluppanagaram, Kondampatti, Kongalnagaram, Kosavampalayam, Kottamangalam, Kuppampalayam, Moongiltholuvu, Pannaikinar, Periapatti, Ponneri, Poolavadi, Pudupalayam, Pukkulam, Somavarapatti, Vadugapalayam, Vagatholuvu, Veedampatti, Virugalpatti.

Amenities:
Education: Primary School in 23 villages, Middle school in 12 villages, Matriculation or Secondary School in 6 villages, namely Poolavadi, Gudimangalam, Anikkadavu, Vagathozhuvu, Somauara Patti, Kongalnagaram.
Higher Secondary or Pre University Courses or Intermediate or Junior College in 2 villages of the CD Block,, namely Poolavadi, Somauara Patti.
College in 0 village, Adult Literacy Center in 0 village.
Medical: Hospital in 2 villages, Dispensary in 0 village, Health Center in 5 villages, Sub Center in 17 villages, Maternity and Child Welfare Center in 6 villages, Community health workers in 9 villages.
The Villages having Hospital or Dispensary or Health Center are Kosarampalayam, Ammandakadavu, Poolavadi.
Drinking Water: Tap water in 24 villages, Tank water in 0 villages, Well water in 24 villages, Tubewell in 24 villages and more than one source in 24 villages.
Bank: Banking facility in 9 villages, namely, Poolavadi, Athukinathupatty, Kondampatty Gudimangalam, Anikkadavu, Somauara Patti Kottamangalam, Ponneri, Pukkulam.
Credit Society in 20 villages Agricultural Credit Society in 18 Non-Agricultural Credit Society in 8 villages.
Others: Power supply in 24 villages, Cinema hall in 2 villages, sport club in 0 village, Stadium or Auditorium or Community Hall in 0 village, Post Office in 19 villages.
There are 17 villages having bus facilities.

Villages with most of facilities: Poolavadi Kondampatty, Gudimangalam, Kottamangalam, Pukkulam.

Villages without amenities (Education):
Mukkuduzallipeti..

Scheduled Castes: Out of the total population of 74134 persons, 17626 persons (23.78%) belong to Scheduled Castes.
The villages having less than 10% SC population are None..
The villages having more than 50% SC population are

None.

Sex ratio of Scheduled Caste population is 497.

Scheduled Castes Literates and Illiterates by Sex:

	Persons	Males	Females
Literate	6,328	3,842	2,486
Illiterate	11,298	5,022	6,276
Literacy rate	41.3	49.9	32.6
Graduate	45	38	7

Scheduled Castes (Dominant):

Madari, Chakkiliyan, Arunthathiyar, Adi Dravida Paraiyan etc.

For their cultural identity please see Appendix-I

Villages without Scheduled Castes: There is 0 village without any scheduled caste population.

Scheduled Tribes: Out of the total population of 74134 persons, 14 persons (0.02%) belong to Scheduled Tribes. The villages having less than 10% ST population are Kosarampalayam, Moongiltholuvu, Ammandakadavu Kuppampalayam, Periapatti, Poolavadi Athukinathupatty, Kondampatty, Gudimangalam Elluppanagaram, Anikkadavu, Vagathozhuvu Veedampatti, Virugalpatti, Somauara Patti Vadugampalayam, Kottamangalam, Ponneri, Pukkulam Doddam Patti, Kongalnagaram, Pudupalayam Pannaikkinar, Mukkuduzallipeti.

The villages having more than 50% ST population are None.

Sex ratio of Scheduled tribe population is 429.

Scheduled Tribes Literates and Illiterates by Sex:

	Persons	Males	Females
Literate	5	2	3
Illiterate	9	6	3
Literacy rate	41.7	33.3	50.0
Graduate	0	0	0

Scheduled Tribes (Dominant):

Malakkuravan, Muthuvan

For their cultural identity please see Appendix-II

Villages without Scheduled Tribes: There are 22 villages without any scheduled tribe population.

Literates and Illiterates by Sex (Total Population):

	Persons	Males	Females
Literate	41,881	24,460	17,421
Illiterate	32,253	12,600	19,653
Literacy rate	63	74	52
Graduate	987	623	364

Agriculture: ***Distribution of villages according to land use:***

Out of 24 villages, Total area (in hectare) is 30970.37, out of that 87.23 percent is cultivable and 46.72 percent of the cultivable area is irrigated.

Sources of Irrigation (Hectares): Government Canal 2219.4, Private Canal 0, Well without Electricity 725.98, Well with Electricity 9622.35, Tubewell without Electricity 0, Tubewell with Electricity 0, Tank 53.36, River 0, Lake 0, Waterfall 0, Others 0.

Villages with population of 5000 to 9999:

Somavarapatti, Kottamangalam.

Villages with population of 10000 and above: None

Distribution of Workers:

	Persons	Males	Females	WPR
Cultivators	11,292	6,867	4,425	25.72
Agricultural Labour	22,114	10,386	11,728	50.38
Household Industry	1,045	670	375	2.38
Other Workers	9,447	7,004	2,443	21.52
Main Workers	40,311	23,730	16,581	91.83
Marginal Workers	3,587	1,197	2,390	8.17
Total Workers	43,898	24,927	18,971	

Religion: Major Religious Communities:

	Persons	Males	Females	Sex Ratio
Hindu (98.73%)	73,192	36,601	36,591	1,000
Muslim (0.19%)	141	69	72	1,043
Christian (1%)	744	363	381	1,050
Sikh (0%)	2	1	1	1,000
Buddhists (0%)	-	-	-	-
Jain (0.01%)	7	4	3	750

Agewise Data:

	Persons	Males	Females	Sex Ratio
All ages	74,134	37,060	37,074	1000
0-14	16,496	8,339	8,157	978
15-44	36,087	17,873	18,214	1019
45-79	20,408	10,237	10,171	994
80+	898	470	428	911
Age not stated	245	141	104	738

Languages (Dominant):

Tamil, Telugu, Kannada, Urdu, Malayalam

Disabled Population:

	Persons	Males	Females	%
Total Disabled	1,660	786	874	
In Seeing	926	373	553	55.78
In Speech	143	69	74	8.61
In Hearing	103	45	58	6.2
In Movement	360	221	139	21.69
Mentally	128	78	50	7.71

GUDIYATHAM

Gudiyatham C.D. Block lies in the north-western part of Vellore district. It is a part of Gudiyatham taluk. The Block is located at a distance of 32 kms. from district headquarters (Vellore). There are 57 villages in the block with the total population of 152,223 persons. Area of the C.D. Block is 366. 55 sq. kms. It is bounded in the south by river Palar and CD Block Madhanur, in the east by CD Block K.V. Kuppam, in the west by Block Peranampattu, and it has common boundary with the state of Andhra Pradesh on north and north-east.

Communications:

Roadways : Information not Available.

Railway Station: Melalathur, Ulli.

Rivers: Kaundinya Nadi- Nearest Villages- Perumbadi, Agraharam, Rangasamuthiram, Semballi, Jittapalli, Thattaparai, Moongapattu, Neloorpet, Thalayatham, Sedukkarai, Melalathur, Pattu, Olakasi. Palar Nadi- Nearest Villages- Kulithigai, Chinnathotalam, Valathur, Vlli, Annaganalore, Kothakuppam, Pattv, Olakasi.

Annual Rainfall: Average Rainfall 949 mm.

Ground Water: Availability of the ground water in the Basin is 5152.47 H.A.M. and the utilization is 10136. 09 H.A.M. It belongs to Over Expoited category. Depth to water level varies from 5 to 15 meter below the ground. Most of the wells go down in summer months, according to the Ground Water Estimation Committee.

Forest and Reserved Forest: (Gundallapalli)- Nearest Villages- Sempalli, Agraharam, Erthangal, Jittapalli. (Kallapadi)- Nearest Villages- Sempalli, Agraharam, Erthangal, Veerachiti Palli, Ramalai,Thattimanapalli, Kallappadi, Kallappadi (Rrf), Pichanoor Village. (Pallalakuppam)- Nearest Villages- Erthangal, Pangarishi Kuppam, Rajakuppam, Sembedu, Kilpatti, Valathur. (Paradarami)- Nearest Villages- Paradarami (Rf), Paradarami Village, Puttavar Palli, Veerasettipalli (Rf), Veerachiti Palli, Paradarami Extn (Rf), Ramalai, Thattimanapalli, Kallappadi. (Syanagunta)- Nearest Villages- Syanagunta (Rf), Dhanakondapalli Village, Sengundram, Modikuppam, Syanagunda (Rf), Thattaparai.

Natural Division: Tondai Nadu.

Administration

Revenue **Division:** Vellore. Parliamentary Constituency: 8 Vellore. District: Vellore. Taluk: Gudiyatham. Assembly Constituency: 45 Kavanur (SC). Gram Panchayat: 44.

Border Villages- (Andhra Pradesh)- Nearest Villages- Syanagunta (RF), Paradarami (RF), Veezuthoneepalayam, D.P. Palayam, Rangasamudram, Paradarami Village, Puttav ar Palli, Veerasettipalli (RF), Varatharedi Palli, Paradarami Extn. (RF), Kallapadi.

Villages: 57 **Inhabited:** 51 **Uninhabited:** 6

Ranking	District	State	National
Area	5	97	2154
Population	1	12	1796
Sex Ratio	11	181	1271
Child Sex Ratio	10	233	3815
Literacy Rate	10	135	1409
Density	7	265	2652
Work Participation Rate	13	106	2885

Gram Panchayats:

Agraharam, Ananganallore, Bojanapuram, Chengundram, Chettikuppam, Chinnalapalli, Chinnathattalam, Dakshinapathapalayam, Danakondapali, Erthangal, Goodanagaram, Kallapadi, Karuneekasamudram, Kilpatti, Kondasamudram , Kothakkuppam, Kulidikai, Melalathur, Melumuttukur, Modikuppam, Moongapattu, Mukkundram, Nellorepettai, Olakasi, Pakkam, Paradarami, Pattu, Perumbadi, Puttavaraipalli, Rajakuppam, Ramalai, Sembedu, Sempali, Seruvangi, Singalpadi, Thalaiyatham, Thattaparai, Thattimanapalli, Ulli, Valathur, Varadhareddipalli, Veerichettipalli, Viludonapaliam, .

Amenities:

Education: Primary School in 48 villages, Middle school in 26 villages, Matriculation or Secondary School in 9 villages, namely Paradarami Village, Modikuppam, Sempalli, Thattaparai, Kallappadi, Agraharam, Erthangal, Valathur, Goodanagaram.

Higher Secondary or Pre University Courses or Intermediate or Junior College in 1 village of the CD Block,, namely Paradarami Village.

College in 0 village, Adult Literacy Center in 0 village.

Medical: Hospital in 1 village, Dispensary in 1 village, Health Center in 5 villages, Sub Center in 12 villages, Maternity and Child Welfare Center in 4 villages, Community health workers in 49 villages.

The Villages having Hospital or Dispensary or Health Center are Paradarami Village, Sempalli, Pangarishi Kuppam, Kilpatti, Valathur.

Drinking Water: Tap water in 50 villages, Tank water in 0 villages, Well water in 6 villages, Tubewell in 23 villages and more than one source in 49 villages.

Bank: Banking facility in 4 villages, namely, Paradarami Village, Sengundram, Melalathur, Valathur. Credit Society in 10 villages Agricultural Credit Society in 6 Non-Agricultural Credit Society in 5 villages.

Others: Power supply in 49 villages, Cinema hall in 0 village, sport club in 0 village, Stadium or Auditorium or Community Hall in 0 village, Post Office in 39 villages.

There are 41 villages having bus facilities.

Villages with most of facilities: Paradarami Village Sengundram, Melalathur, Valathur.

Villages without amenities (Education):

Veerasettipalli (Rf), Chithathur..

Scheduled Castes: Out of the total population of 152223 persons, 43814 persons (28.78%) belong to Scheduled Castes. The villages having less than 10% SC population are Rangasamudram, Chinnalapalli, Pichanoor Village Agraharam, Singlepadi.

The villages having more than 50% SC population are Veerasettipalli (Rf), Mukkundram, Seruvangi

Sembedu, Chinnathotalam, Kothakuppam, Pattv.

Sex ratio of Scheduled Caste population is 501.

Scheduled Castes Literates and Illiterates by Sex:

	Persons	Males	Females
Literate	26,399	15,017	11,382
Illiterate	17,415	6,867	10,548
Literacy rate	69.6	79.8	59.6
Graduate	588	398	190

Scheduled Castes (Dominant):

Adi Dravida, Arunthathiyar, Valluvan, Kuravan etc. Chakkiliyan

For their cultural identity please see Appendix-I

Villages without Scheduled Castes: There are 7 villages without any scheduled caste population.

Scheduled Tribes: Out of the total population of 152223 persons, 994 persons (0.65%) belong to Scheduled Tribes. The villages having less than 10% ST population are Veezuthoneepalayam, D.P. Palayam, Rangasamudram Paradarami Village, Puttavar Palli Veerasettipalli (Rf), Veerachiti Palli Varatharedi Palli, Sengundram, Modikuppam, Sempalli Thattaparai, Chinnalapalli, Mukkundram, Pakkam Ramalai, Thattimanapalli, Kallappadi Kondasamuthiram, Pichanoor Village, Kaathaarikuppam Moongapatty, Perumpadi, Agraharam, Rangasamuthiram Erthangal, Rajakuppam, Neloorpet, Seruvangi Thalayatham, Sedukkarai, Melalathur, Mell Muttur Chettikuppam, Bojanapuram, Sembedu Pangarishi Kuppam, Kilpatti, Kulithigai Chinnathotalam, Valathur, Karuneegasamudram, Vlli Singlepadi, Goodanagaram, Annaganalore, Kothakuppam Pattv, Olakasi, Chithathur.

The villages having more than 50% ST population are None.

Sex ratio of Scheduled tribe population is 487.

Scheduled Tribes Literates and Illiterates by Sex:

	Persons	Males	Females
Literate	337	214	123
Illiterate	657	296	361
Literacy rate	39.5	50.2	28.8
Graduate	2	1	1

Scheduled Tribes (Dominant):

Irular, Kurumans, Kattunayakan, Malayali Malai Pandaram

For their cultural identity please see Appendix-II

Villages without Scheduled Tribes: There are 41 villages without any scheduled tribe population.

Literates and Illiterates by Sex (Total Population):

	Persons	Males	Females
Literate	90,719	52,379	38,340
Illiterate	61,504	23,848	37,656
Literacy rate	68	79	58
Graduate	2,319	1,630	689

Agriculture: ***Distribution of villages according to land use:*** Out of 57 villages, Total area (in hectare) is 36655.17, out of that 43.82 percent is cultivable and 15.5 percent of the cultivable area is irrigated.

Sources of Irrigation (Hectares): Government Canal 0, Private Canal 0, Well without Electricity 233.28, Well with Electricity 2184.37, Tubewell without Electricity 0, Tubewell with Electricity 71.32, Tank 0, River 0, Lake 0, Waterfall 0, Others 0.

Villages with population of 5000 to 9999: Paradarami, Modikuppam, Semballi, Ramalai, Kallapadi Kondasamudram , Pichanur , Erthangal, Valathur Goodanagaram.

Villages with population of 10000 and above: None

Distribution of Workers:

	Persons	Males	Females	WPR
Cultivators	11,615	8,170	3,445	16.06
Agricultural Labour	26,612	13,310	13,302	36.79
Household Industry	9,941	4,136	5,805	13.74
Other Workers	24,162	18,659	5,503	33.41
Main Workers	58,281	38,831	19,450	80.58
Marginal Workers	14,049	5,444	8,605	19.42
Total Workers	72,330	44,275	28,055	

Religion: Major Religious Communities:

	Persons	Males	Females	Sex Ratio
Hindu (92.41%)	140,673	70,457	70,216	997
Muslim (5.47%)	8,327	4,184	4,143	990
Christian (2.01%)	3,058	1,506	1,552	1,031
Sikh (0.01%)	18	10	8	800
Buddhists (0%)	5	4	1	250
Jain (0.01%)	12	4	8	2,000

Agewise Data:

	Persons	Males	Females	Sex Ratio
All ages	152,223	76,227	75,996	997
0-14	45,053	23,035	22,018	956
15-44	72,728	36,336	36,392	1002
45-79	32,610	15,991	16,619	1039
80+	1,543	723	820	1134
Age not stated	289	142	147	1035

Languages (Dominant):

Tamil, Telugu, Urdu, Others, Kannada

Disabled Population:

	Persons	Males	Females	%
Total Disabled	4,242	2,321	1,921	
In Seeing	1,809	908	901	42.64
In Speech	378	203	175	8.91
In Hearing	320	146	174	7.54

In Movement	1,285	830	455	30.29

Mentally	450	234	216	10.61

GUMMIDIPOONDI

Gummidipoondi C.D. Block lies in the northern part of Thiruvallur district. It is a part of Gummidipoondi taluk. The Block is located at a distance of 55 kms. from district headquarters (Thiruvallur). There are 80 villages in the block with the total population of 142,679 persons. Area of the C.D. Block is 408.04 sq. kms. It is bounded in the south by CD Blocks Ellapuram and Sholavaram, in the east by CD Block Minjur, and it has common boundary with the state of Andhra Pradesh on north and west.

Communications:

Roadways : N.H.- 5: Direction- Gudur (AP) to Chennai, Nearest Villages- Arambakkam, Elavur, Thurappalam, Chinna Obulapuram, Pethikuppam, Thervali, Paleswarankandigai, Nangapallam, Verkadu, Keelmudalambedu, Puduvoyal.

Railway Station: Arambakkam, Thurappalam.

River: Arani Nadi- Nearest Villages- Paleswaram, Karani, Pudupalayam, Mangalam, Palavakkam, Annapanayakan-kuppam, Melmutalempadu, Keelmudalambedu, Puduvoyal.

Annual Rainfall: Average Rainfall 1152 mm.

Ground Water: Availability of the ground water in the Basin is 169.05 MCM and the utilization is 86.82 MCM. It belongs to Safe category. Depth to water level varies from 5 to 10 meter below the ground. Most of the wells go down in summer months, according to the Ground Water Estimation Committee.

Natural Division: Tondai Nadu.

Administration

Revenue **Division:** Ponneri. Parliamentary Constituency: 1 Thiruvallur (SC). District: Thiruvallur. Taluk: Gummi dipoondi. Assembly Constituency: 1 Gummidipoondi. Gram Panchayat: 61.

Border Villages- (Andhra Pradesh)- Nearest Villages- Poovalai, Edoor, Egumadurai, Naidupet, Arambakkam, Medhi palayam, Sunnambukalam, Obasamudram, Elavur, Poondavakkam, Sedilpakkam, Namallur, Budur, Dharkasth Kandigai (Ui), Vanrasikuppam, Kannankottai, Karadiputtur, Kannampakkam.

Villages: 81 **Inhabited:** 79 **Uninhabited:** 2

Ranking	District	State	National
Area	2	68	1883
Population	2	26	2099
Sex Ratio	8	199	1453
Child Sex Ratio	5	88	1773
Literacy Rate	10	291	2470
Density	7	317	3107
Work Participation Rate	11	159	3791

Gram Panchayats:

Annappanaickenkuppam, Arambakkam, Athupakkam, Ayanallur, Budur , Chedilpakkam, Edur, Egumadurai , Eguvarpalayam , Elavur, Enadimelpakkam , Erukkuvoy , Getnamallee, Guruvarajakandigai, Kannambakkam, Kannankottai , Karadipudur, Karani, Kilmudalambedu, Kollanur , Kuruvattucheri , Madharbakkam, Manellore, Mangalam, Mangavaram, Mangavaram, Medhipalayam, Melakalani , Melmudalambedu, Mukkarambakkam , Narasingapuram, Natham, Nelvoy , Nemalur, Obasamudram, Palavakkam , Pallavada, Panapakkam, Pathapalayam, Peddikuppam, Peria Obulapuram , Periapuliyur , Peruvoyal, Podihivedu, Pondavakkam, Poovalai, Poovalambedu , Pudugummidipundi , Pudupalayam, Puduvoyal, Rettambedu , Sanaputhur, Sidharajakandigai, Sirupulalpettai, Siruvada, Soorapundi, Sunnambukkulam, Thandalacheri, Theruali, Thervoy, Thokkamur, Vazhuthalambedu.

Amenities:

Education: Primary School in 72 villages, Middle school in 27 villages, Matriculation or Secondary School in 13 villages, namely Arambakkam, Sunnambukalam, Elavur, Eguvarapalayam, Madanpakkam, Mamellore, Poondavakkam, Budur, Kannankottai, Pappankuppam, Theruali, Thervoy Kondigai, Keelmudalambedu.

Higher Secondary or Pre University Courses or Intermediate or Junior College in 4 villages of the CD Block,, namely Sunnambukalam, Mamellore, Pappankuppam, Keelmudalambedu.

College in 0 village, Adult Literacy Center in 0 village.

Medical: Hospital in 2 villages, Dispensary in 2 villages, Health Center in 11 villages, Sub Center in 26 villages, Maternity and Child Welfare Center in 1 village, Community health workers in 79 villages.

The Villages having Hospital or Dispensary or Health Center are Eguvarapalayam, Pappankuppam, Paleswarankandigai, Kollanur.

Drinking Water: Tap water in 79 villages, Tank water in 79 villages, Well water in 79 villages, Tubewell in 79 villages and more than one source in 79 villages.

Bank: Banking facility in 6 villages, namely, Arambakkam, Thurappalam, Eguvarapalayam, Madanpakkam Poovalambedu, Thervoy Kondigai.

Credit Society in 7 villages Agricultural Credit Society in 6 Non-Agricultural Credit Society in 0 village.

Others: Power supply in 79 villages, Cinema hall in 3 villages, sport club in 0 village, Stadium or Auditorium or Community Hall in 0 village, Post Office in 22 villages.

There are 56 villages having bus facilities.

Villages with most of facilities: Arambakkam Thurappalam, Eguvarapalayam, Madanpakkam Poovalambedu, Thervoy Kondigai.

Villages without amenities (Education):

Nangapallam, Sinthalakuppam, Amirthamangalam, Paleswaram, Venkuzhi, Serpedu..

Scheduled Castes: Out of the total population of 142679 persons, 37867 persons (26.54%) belong to Scheduled Castes.

The villages having less than 10% SC population are Medhipalayam, Sunnambukalam, Obasamudram, Appavaram Chennavaram, Nathem, Narasingapuram, Thurappalam Thervali, Chinna Sozhiambakkam, Paleswarankandigai Guruvatcheri, Verkadu, New Gummidipoondi Chinnapuliyur, Kollanur, Nelvoy, Venkuzhi, Karani Gettanamallee.

The villages having more than 50% SC population are Egumadurai, Kannampakkam, Sanaputhur, Poondavakkam Budur, Kannankottai, Seruvada, Vaniyamalee Poovalambedu, Kuruviagaram, Ayanallur Periya Choliambakkam, Sinthalakuppam, Periyapuliyur Thervoy Kondigai, Serpedu, Palavakkam Melmutalempadu.

Sex ratio of Scheduled Caste population is 500.

Scheduled Castes Literates and Illiterates by Sex:

	Persons	Males	Females
Literate	17,838	10,626	7,212
Illiterate	20,029	8,316	11,713
Literacy rate	54.7	65.5	44.0
Graduate	479	385	94

Scheduled Castes (Dominant):

Adi Dravida, Mala, Adi Andhra, Arunthathiyar Chakkiliyan

For their cultural identity please see Appendix-I

Villages without Scheduled Castes: There are 7 villages without any scheduled caste population.

Scheduled Tribes: Out of the total population of 142679 persons, 3434 persons (2.41%) belong to Scheduled Tribes.

The villages having less than 10% ST population are Egumadurai, Naidupet, Arambakkam, Poovalai Kannampakkam, Pallavada, Sanaputhur, Edoor Medhipalayam, Sunnambukalam, Obasamudram Melakazhani, Appavaram, Chennavaram, Nathem, Elavur Narasingapuram, Thurappalam, Periya Obulapuram Eguvarapalayam, Soorapoondi, Madanpakkam Poondavakkam, Sedilpakkam, Namallur, Budur Kannankottai, Seruvada, Panchali, Vaniyamalee Poovalambedu, Chittur Natham, Pappankuppam Chinna Obulapuram, Pethikuppam, Thervali, Theruali Mangavaram, Vazhuthalampedu, Rottampedu Kuruviagaram, Chinna Sozhiambakkam, Ayanallur Enathimelpakkam, Periya Choliambakkam Paleswarankandigai, Nangapallam, Guruvatcheri Verkadu, New Gummidipoondi, Karumbukuppam Sinthalakuppam, Sirupuzhalalpettai, Amirthamangalam Chinnapuliyur, Periyapuliyur, Kollanur Thervoy Kondigai, Karadiputtur, Nelvoy, Paleswaram Venkuzhi, Serpedu, Manali, Erukavai, Pudupalayam Mangalam, Palavakkam, Gettanamallee, Thandalcherry Annapanayakankuppam, Melmutalempadu, Keelmudalambed Puduvoyal.

The villages having more than 50% ST population are None.

Sex ratio of Scheduled tribe population is 515.

Scheduled Tribes Literates and Illiterates by Sex:

	Persons	Males	Females
Literate	783	459	324
Illiterate	2,651	1,207	1,444
Literacy rate	27.9	33.5	22.6
Graduate	3	2	1

Scheduled Tribes (Dominant):

Irular, Kattunayakan, Kaniyan etc., Malakkuravan Malai Arayan

For their cultural identity please see Appendix-II

Villages without Scheduled Tribes: There are 39 villages without any scheduled tribe population.

Literates and Illiterates by Sex (Total Population):

	Persons	Males	Females
Literate	77,033	45,592	31,441
Illiterate	65,646	26,013	39,633
Literacy rate	62	73	51
Graduate	2,329	1,797	532

Agriculture: ***Distribution of villages according to land use:***

Out of 81 villages, Total area (in hectare) is 40804.09, out of that 62.26 percent is cultivable and 70.64 percent of the cultivable area is irrigated.

Sources of Irrigation (Hectares): Government Canal 376.28, Private Canal 122.55, Well without Electricity 675.93, Well with Electricity 1433.79, Tubewell without Electricity 5.27, Tubewell with Electricity 2185.59, Tank 551.38, River 0, Lake 7022.8, Waterfall 0, Others 5572.62.

Villages with population of 5000 to 9999:

Arambakkam , Madaharpakkam , Peddikuppam, Theruali Kilmudalambedu.

Villages with population of 10000 and above: None

Distribution of Workers:

	Persons	Males	Females	WPR
Cultivators	11,606	8,749	2,857	18.69
Agricultural Labour	28,287	15,426	12,861	45.56
Household Industry	3,322	1,806	1,516	5.35
Other Workers	18,875	15,502	3,373	30.4
Main Workers	46,552	34,378	12,174	74.98
Marginal Workers	15,538	7,105	8,433	25.02
Total Workers	62,090	41,483	20,607	

Religion: Major Religious Communities:

	Persons	Males	Females	Sex Ratio
Hindu (94.75%)	135,190	67,856	67,334	992
Muslim (1.99%)	2,835	1,439	1,396	970
Christian (3.59%)	5,116	2,536	2,580	1,017
Sikh (0.03%)	39	26	13	500
Buddhists (0%)	2	2	-	-
Jain (0.02%)	24	15	9	600

Agewise Data:

	Persons	Males	Females	Sex Ratio
All ages	143,402	71,979	71,423	992
0-14	41,954	21,189	20,765	980
15-44	73,813	37,391	36,422	974
45-79	26,099	12,658	13,441	1062
80+	851	409	442	1081
Age not stated	685	332	353	1063

Languages (Dominant):
Tamil, Telugu, Urdu, Hindi, Oriya

Disabled Population:

	Persons	Males	Females	%
Total Disabled	3,589	1,992	1,597	
In Seeing	1,783	908	875	49.68
In Speech	325	180	145	9.06
In Hearing	275	136	139	7.66
In Movement	989	638	351	27.56
Mentally	217	130	87	6.05

GUZILIAMPARAI

Guziliamparai C.D. Block lies in the north-eastern part of Dindigul district. It is a part of Vedasandur taluk. The taluk is located at a distance of 22 kms. from district headquarters (Dindigul). There are 19 villages in the block with the total population of 72,849 persons. Area of the C.D. Block is 359.41 sq. kms. It is bounded in the north by district Karur, in the south by CD Blocks Vedasandur and Vadamadurai, in the east by district Tiruchirappalli, in the west by CD Blcok Vedasandur and district Karur.

Communications:

Roadways : Information not Available.

Railway Station: Karikali.

River: Kadagal Nadi- Nearest Village- Koombur.

Backwards Region Grants Fund: It receives Backward Region Grants.

Annual Rainfall: Average Rainfall 813 mm.

Ground Water: Availability of the ground water in the Basin is 3811.04 H.A.M. and the utilization is 5240.63 H.A.M. It belongs to Over Expoited category. Depth to water level varies from 2 to 10 meter below the ground. Most of the wells go down in summer months, according to the Ground Water Estimation Committee.

Forest and Reserved Forest: (Thoppasamymalai RF)- Nearest Villages- Thoppasamyamalai RF, R. Kombai.

Natural Division: NA

Administration

Revenue **Division:** Palani. Parliamentary Constituency: 23 Karur. District: Dindigul. Taluk: Vedasandur. Assembly Constituency: 133 Vedasandur. Gram Panchayat: 17.

Villages: 19 **Inhabited:** 18 **Uninhabited:** 1

Ranking	District	State	National
Area	6	102	2207
Population	11	274	4362
Sex Ratio	8	234	1610
Child Sex Ratio	4	235	3818
Literacy Rate	14	332	2871
Density	1	13	4699
Work Participation Rate	11	326	118

Gram Panchayats:
Alambadi, Chinnaluppai, Dholipatti, Gudalur, Karikali, Karungal, Koombur, Kottanatham, Landakottai, Mallapuram, R.Kombai , R.Pudukottai, R.Vellodu , Thirukoornam, Ulliyakottai, Vadugambadi, Vanikarai.

Amenities:

Education: Primary School in 18 villages, Middle school in 13 villages, Matriculation or Secondary School in 4 villages, namely R.Vellodu, Alambady, D.Gudalur, Landakottai. Higher Secondary or Pre University Courses or Intermediate or Junior College in 2 villages of the CD Block,, namely D.Gudalur, Landakottai.

College in 0 village, Adult Literacy Center in 0 village.

Medical: Hospital in 1 village, Dispensary in 1 village, Health Center in 8 villages, Sub Center in 14 villages, Maternity and Child Welfare Center in 16 villages, Community health workers in 0 village.

The Villages having Hospital or Dispensary or Health Center are Thirukoornam, Alambady, Karungal, Mallapuram, Koombur, Vanikarai.

Drinking Water: Tap water in 18 villages, Tank water in 8 villages, Well water in 18 villages, Tubewell in 18 villages and more than one source in 18 villages.

Bank: Banking facility in 8 villages, namely, R.Vellodu, Kottanatham, Karungal, Karikali Mallapuram, Vadugambadi, R.Paudukkottai, Vanikarai.

Credit Society in 11 villages Agricultural Credit Society in 11 Non-Agricultural Credit Society in 2 villages.

Others: Power supply in 18 villages, Cinema hall in 2 villages, sport club in 2 villages, Stadium or Auditorium or Community Hall in 2 villages, Post Office in 16 villages.

There are 14 villages having bus facilities.

Villages with most of facilities: R.Vellodu Karungal, Karikali, Mallapuram, Vadugambadi R.Paudukkottai, Vanikarai.

Villages without Amenities (Education): None..

Scheduled Castes: Out of the total population of 72849 persons, 16567 persons (22.74%) belong to Scheduled Castes.

The villages having less than 10% SC population are None..

The villages having more than 50% SC population are None.

Sex ratio of Scheduled Caste population is 497.

Scheduled Castes Literates and Illiterates by Sex:

	Persons	Males	Females
Literate	7,794	4,840	2,954
Illiterate	8,773	3,499	5,274
Literacy rate	52.9	65.5	40.3
Graduate	124	105	19

Scheduled Castes (Dominant):

Chakkiliyan, Paraiyan etc., Pallan, Madari, Valluvan

For their cultural identity please see Appendix-I

Villages without Scheduled Castes: There is 1 village without any scheduled caste population.

Scheduled Tribes: Out of the total population of 72849 persons, 164 persons (0.23%) belong to Scheduled Tribes.

The villages having less than 10% ST population are Thirukoornam, R.Vellodu, Alambady, Kottanatham D.Gudalur, Landakottai, Theendakkal, Karungal Dholipatti, Karikali, Mallapuram, Koombur Ulliyakottai, Chinnaluppai, R.Kombai, Vadugambadi R.Paudukkottai, Vanikarai.

The villages having more than 50% ST population are None.

Sex ratio of Scheduled tribe population is 537.

Scheduled Tribes Literates and Illiterates by Sex:

	Persons	Males	Females
Literate	79	45	34
Illiterate	85	31	54
Literacy rate	53.7	65.2	43.6
Graduate	2	2	0

Scheduled Tribes (Dominant):

Malai Vedan, Malai Pandaram, Irular, Kadar

For their cultural identity please see Appendix-II

Villages without Scheduled Tribes: There are 16 villages without any scheduled tribe population.

Literates and Illiterates by Sex (Total Population):

	Persons	Males	Females
Literate	39,048	23,817	15,231
Illiterate	33,801	12,806	20,995
Literacy rate	59	72	47
Graduate	816	589	227

Agriculture: ***Distribution of villages according to land use:***

Out of 19 villages, Total area (in hectare) is 35941.87, out of that 52.89 percent is cultivable and 55.88 percent of the cultivable area is irrigated.

Sources of Irrigation (Hectares): Government Canal 99.18, Private Canal 60.31, Well without Electricity 4303.3, Well with Electricity 3346.42, Tubewell without Electricity 554, Tubewell with Electricity 999.44, Tank 332.59, River 0, Lake 0, Waterfall 313.2, Others 612.57.

Villages with population of 5000 to 9999:

Alambadi, Kottanatham, Gudalur, Landakottai Mallapuram, Kombai (R), Vadugambadi, Pudukottai (R).

Villages with population of 10000 and above: None

Distribution of Workers:

	Persons	Males	Females	WPR
Cultivators	13,749	8,179	5,570	29.62
Agricultural Labour	22,358	8,776	13,582	48.16
Household Industry	938	396	542	2.02
Other Workers	9,377	7,100	2,277	20.2
Main Workers	36,402	21,175	15,227	78.42
Marginal Workers	10,020	3,276	6,744	21.58
Total Workers	46,422	24,451	21,971	

Religion: Major Religious Communities:

	Persons	Males	Females	Sex Ratio
Hindu (97.8%)	71,244	35,863	35,381	987
Muslim (1.91%)	1,390	642	748	1,165
Christian (0.2%)	143	75	68	907
Sikh (0%)	2	2	-	-
Buddhists (0%)	-	-	-	-
Jain (0%)	1	-	1	-

Agewise Data:

	Persons	Males	Females	Sex Ratio
All ages	72,849	36,623	36,226	989
0-14	17,070	8,789	8,281	942
15-44	34,659	17,149	17,510	1021
45-79	19,377	9,836	9,541	970
80+	748	401	347	865
Age not stated	995	448	547	1221

Languages (Dominant):

Tamil, Telugu, Kannada, Malayalam, Oriya

Disabled Population:

	Persons	Males	Females	%
Total Disabled	2,228	976	1,252	
In Seeing	1,555	590	965	69.79
In Speech	142	71	71	6.37
In Hearing	82	47	35	3.68
In Movement	318	190	128	14.27
Mentally	131	78	53	5.88

HARUR

Harur C.D. Block lies in the north-eastern part of Dharmapuri district. It is a part of Harur and Pappireddipatti taluks. The Block is located at a distance of 42 kms. from district headquarters (Dharmapuri). There are 148 villages in the block with the total population of 144,213 persons. Area of the C.D. Block is 752.17 sq. kms. It is bounded in the north by Krishnagiri and Tiruvannamalai districts, in the south by C.D. Block Pappireddipatti and districts Salem and Tiruvannamalai, in the east by district Tiruvannamalai, and in the west by C.D. Block Morappur. CD Block Harur falls in taluk Harur by 132 villages, and in taluk Pappireddipatti by 16 villages.

Communications:

Roadways : S.H.-18: Direction- Pappireddipatti to Uthangarai, Nearest Villages- Karuthampatti, Kongavembu, Ilaiyampatti, Papinayakkanvalasai, Kumarampatti, Ittalapatti, Mampatty, Sakkilipatti, K.Vetrapatti, Vadugapatti, Kurampatti, Eachambadi, Chekkampatti, Kodamandupatti, Naveripatty, Soriyampatty, Thandakuppamm Moberi Patty, H. Doddampatty, Nachanampatty, Nambipatty, Chinnankuppam, Parayapattipudur, Devaajapalayam, Puludiyur, Kokkarapatty, Erumiyampatti, Vadhappatty.

River: Vaniyar Nadi- Nearest Villages- Chandarapurm, Mathiyampatti, Chinnapannimuduer, Periyapannimuduru, Vadhappatty, Kothampatti, Poyyapatti, Nambipatty, Chinn ankuppam, Parayapattipudur, Devaajapalayam, Puludiyur, Kokkarapatty, Naranapuram, Melanur, Keelanoor, Veppanatham, Kavoipatty, Chekkampatti, Nachanampatty, Chellampatti, Kalladipatti, Peathathampatti, Erumiyampatti.

Annual Rainfall: Average Rainfall 760 mm.

Ground Water: Availability of the ground water in the Basin is 7366.46 H.A.M. and the utili zation is 9699.12 H.A.M. It belongs to Over Expoited cateory. Depth to water level varies from 2 to 5 meter below the ground. Most of the wells go down in summer months, according to the Ground Water Estimation Committee.

Forest and Reserved Forest: (Kottapatti RF)- Nearest Villages- Sikkalur, Vedapatty, Kottapatti RF Uni, Naripalli, Kottapatty, Sengandipatti, Aandipatty, Mangalapatty, Jadiyam Kombai, Kottapatti (Extn.RF) Uni, Chetikuttai, Ammapet Uni, Sooranatham, Sittilingi, Kolumthambinatham, Thekkanampatty, Aavaloor, Selambai, Malathangi. (Stittilingi)- Nearest Villages- Sooranatham, Tariasal R.F. Uni, Sittilingi, Velanur, Sittilingi (Extn.RF) Uni. Baiyanaickampatti. (Thambal Extention)- Nearest Villages- Peathathampatti, Vachathi, (Theerthamalai)- Nearest Villages- Periyapatti, Thanipadi, Theerthamalai R.F. Uni, Keelchengapadi, Mondukuli, Andiyur, Theerthamalai, Palayam, Veerappanaickanpatti, Sendrayam Patti, Baiyanaickampatti. (Veppampatti)- Nearest Villages- Veerappanaickanpatti, Veppampatti R.F. Uni, Mambadi, Veeppampatti, Ponneri, Kelapparai, Pudur, Veppampatti (Extn. RF) Uni, Kambalai, Karapadi, Samanattam, Thathara-valasai, Samanatham, Kathiripatti. (Kottapatti Extn.)- Nearest Villages-Kottapatti RF Uni, Mangalapatty, Kathiripatti,

Natural Division: Baramahal.

Administration

Revenue **Division:** Krishnagiri. Parliamentary Constituency: 10 Dharmapuri. District: Dharmapuri. Taluk: Harur, Pappireddipatti. Assembly Constituency: 60 Pappireddipatti, 61 Hasur (SC). Gram Panchayat: 28.

Villages: 148 **Inhabited:** 138 **Uninhabited:** 10

Ranking	District	State	National
Area	3	8	827
Population	9	24	2050
Sex Ratio	10	359	4095
Child Sex Ratio	9	349	5855
Literacy Rate	11	355	3469
Density	1	76	4853
Work Participation Rate	15	334	744

Gram Panchayats:

Achallvadi , Agraharam , Bainaickampatti , Chellampatti , Chinnankuppam , Doddampatti , Ellappudayampatti , Gopalapuram , Gopinathampatti, Jammanahalli , Keeraipatti , Kilmorappur , Kokkarapatti , Kolagampatti , Kongavembu , Kottapatti , Mahiyampatti , Mampatty , Marudipalli, Mobiripatti , Naripalli , Parayapatti , Periyapatti , Pethathampatti , Ponneri , Setrapatti , Sittilingi , Theerthamalai , Vadugapatti , Vedakadamaduvu , Veerappanaickanpatti , Velampatti , Veppampatti, Veppampatti , Vetrapatti .

Amenities:

Education: Primary School in 103 villages, Middle school in 28 villages, Matriculation or Secondary School in 16 villages, namely Keealmorappur, Parayappatti, Ganapathipatti, Mampatty, K.Vetrapatti, Maruthipatti, Theerthamalai, Velampatty, Naripalli, Mambadi, Keeraipatti, Kottapatty, Nambipatty, Peathathampatti, Jammanahalli, Parayapattipudur.

Higher Secondary or Pre University Courses or Inter-mediate or Junior College in 4 villages of the CD Block,, namely Theerthamalai, Nambipatty, Jammanahalli, Parayapattipudur.

College in 0 village, Adult Literacy Center in 0 village.

Medical: Hospital in 1 village, Dispensary in 2 villages, Health Center in 5 villages, Sub Center in 25 villages, Maternity and Child Welfare Center in 2 villages, Community health workers in 120 villages.

The Villages having Hospital or Dispensary or Health Center are Moberi Patty, Kottapatty, Sittilingi.

Drinking Water: Tap water in 138 villages, Tank water in 3 villages, Well water in 138 villages, Tubewell in 138 villages and more than one source in 138 villages.

Bank: Banking facility in 15 villages, namely, Vadugapatti, Eachambadi, Theerthamalai, Ettiyampatty

Veerappanaickanpatti, Naripalli, Mambadi Keeraipatti, Kottapatty, Kolaganpatti, Jammanahalli Parayapattipudur, Kokkarapatty, Naranapuram Gopalapuram.

Credit Society in 45 villages Agricultural Credit Society in 13 Non-Agricultural Credit Society in 14 villages.

Others: Power supply in 137 villages, Cinema hall in 1 village, sport club in 0 village, Stadium or Auditorium or Community Hall in 0 village, Post Office in 137 villages.

There are 114 villages having bus facilities.

Villages with most of facilities: Eachambadi Theerthamalai, Ettiyampatty, Veerappanaickanpatti Naripalli, Mambadi, Keeraipatti, Kottapatty Jammanahalli, Parayapattipudur, Kokkarapatty.

Villages without amenities (Education):

Singiripatti, Thippampatti, Kurumpatti, Ittalapatti, Nariyampatti, Chinnapannimuduer, Kondampatti, Mathiampatti, Mettuvalasai, Kurampatti, Kuttipatti, Kothampatti, Valedupu, Kavoipatty, Kodamandupatti, Naveripatty, Thathampatti, Sundamgipatty, Morasapatti, Konam Patti, Vengiyam Patti, Vedapatty, Pachanampatty, Pudur, Sengandipatti, Aandipatty, Mangalapatty, Kambalai, Karapadi, Samanatham, Jadiyam Kombai, Chetikuttai, Kolumthambinatham, Selambai, Malagappadi..

Scheduled Castes: Out of the total population of 144213 persons, 45300 persons (31.41%) belong to Scheduled Castes. The villages having less than 10% SC population are Thippampatti, Thamaleripatti, Kurumpatti Karuthampatti, Kongavembu, Ilaiyampatti Papinayakkanvalasai, Ittalapatti, Chandarapurm Mampatty, Mettuvalasai, Velampatti, Kalladipatti Thoorarampatti, Kurampatti, Eachambadi, Alambadi Manthikulampatti, Ranganvalasai, Thanipadi, Valedupu Kodamandupatti, Naveripatty, Sundamgipatty Thambichettipatty, Appiyampatti, Panamarathu Patti Setrapatti, Vengiyam Patti, M. Thathampatti Pachanampatty, Nachanampatty, Keeraipatti, Pudur Aandipatty, Mangalapatty, Kathiripatti, Kambalai Karapadi, Thatharavalasai, Samanatham, Achalvadi Velimadurai, Jadiyam Kombai, Sooranatham Kolumthambinatham, Thekkanampatty, Aavaloor Selambai, Sittilingi, Malathangi, Velanur Kolaganpatti, Annamalaipatti, Devaajapalayam Puludiyur, Malagappadi, Vachathi, Erumiyampatti Naranapuram, Gopalapuram.

The villages having more than 50% SC population are Singiripatti, Kuttapatti, Parayappatti, Kumarampatti Mathiyampatti, Periyapannimuduru, Vadhappatty Sakkilipatti, Kondampatti, K.Vetrapatti Mathiampatti, Maruthipatti, Neruppandakuppam Veppanatham, Melanur, Keelanoor, Poyyapatti Vedakattamatuv, Sikkalur, Mondukuli, Melchengapadi Palayam, Soriyampatty, Morasapatti, Jangalvadi Ettiyampatty, Ponneri, S. Thathampatti Peathathampatti, Kokkarapatty.

Sex ratio of Scheduled Caste population is 488.

Scheduled Castes Literates and Illiterates by Sex:

	Persons	Males	Females
Literate	21,327	13,087	8,240
Illiterate	23,973	10,126	13,847
Literacy rate	55.0	66.3	43.3
Graduate	989	846	143

Scheduled Castes (Dominant):

Adi Dravida, Arunthathiyar, Kuravan etc., Valluvan Pallan

For their cultural identity please see Appendix-I

Villages without Scheduled Castes: There are 43 villages without any scheduled caste population.

Scheduled Tribes: Out of the total population of 144213 persons, 13200 persons (9.15%) belong to Scheduled Tribes. The villages having less than 10% ST population are Singiripatti, Kuttapatti, Keealmorappur Thippampatti, Thamaleripatti, Parayappatti Kurumpatti, Ganapathipatti, Karuthampatti Kongavembu, Ilaiyampatti, Papinayakkanvalasai Kumarampatti, Ittalapatti, Nariyampatti Chandarapurm, Thambal, Chinnapannimuduer Periyapannimuduru, Vadhappatty, Mampatty Sakkilipatti, Kondampatti, K.Vetrapatti Mathiampatti, Thamarakoliyampatti, Mettuvalasai Maruthipatti, Velampatti, Pallipatti, Kalladipatti Neruppandakuppam, Thoorarampatti, Vadugapatti Kurampatti, Eachambadi, Kuttipatti, Veppanatham Melanur, Keelanoor, Poyyapatti, Kattavadichampatti Vedakattamatuv, Alambadi, Periyapatti Manthikulampatti, Sikkalur, Ranganvalasai, Mondukuli Melchengapadi, Theerthamalai, Palayam, Gudalur Valedupu, Sellampatty, Kavoipatty, Chekkampatti Kodamandupatti, Naveripatty, Soriyampatty Thathampatti, Agraharam, Velampatty, Sundamgipatty Thambichettipatty, Appiyampatti, Morasapatti Panamarathu Patti, Setrapatti, Thandakuppam Moberi Patty, Konam Patti, Jangalvadi Vengiyam Patti, Ettiyampatty, Boothinatham Sendrayam Patti, Vedapatty, Veeppampatti, Ponneri M. Thathampatti, Kammalam Patti, Ellapudaiyam Patty Pachanampatty, H. Doddampatty, Nachanampatty Keeraipatti, Kelapparai, Pudur, Kuduimiyampatti Achalvadi, Chetikuttai, Andipatti, Kolaganpatti

Nambipatty, Peathathampatti, Chinnankuppam Annamalaipatti, Jammanahalli, Parayapattipudur Devaajapalayam, Puludiyur, Kokkarapatty Erumiyampatti, Naranapuram, Gopalapuram.

The villages having more than 50% ST population are Thanipadi, Aandipatty, Kambalai, Karapadi Thatharavalasai, Velimadurai, Jadiyam Kombai Kolumthambinatham, Thekkanampatty, Aavaloor Selambai, Sittilingi, Malathangi, Velanur Malagappadi, Vachathi.

Sex ratio of Scheduled tribe population is 489.

Scheduled Tribes Literates and Illiterates by Sex:

	Persons	Males	Females
Literate	4,063	2,542	1,521
Illiterate	9,137	4,203	4,934
Literacy rate	36.1	44.3	27.5
Graduate	55	39	16

Scheduled Tribes (Dominant):

Malayali, Irular, Malakkuravan, Kurumans, Malasar

For their cultural identity please see Appendix-II

Villages without Scheduled Tribes: There are 89 villages without any scheduled tribe population.

Literates and Illiterates by Sex (Total Population):

	Persons	Males	Females
Literate	70,592	42,904	27,688
Illiterate	73,621	31,499	42,122
Literacy rate	56	67	45
Graduate	2,648	2,104	544

Agriculture: ***Distribution of villages according to land use:*** Out of 148 villages, Total area (in hectare) is 75217.6, out of that 47.92 percent is cultivable and 27.37 percent of the cultivable area is irrigated.

Sources of Irrigation (Hectares): Government Canal 99.28, Private Canal 186.1, Well without Electricity 4555.69, Well with Electricity 4058.93, Tubewell without Electricity 104.46, Tubewell with Electricity 30.69, Tank 787.61, River 0, Lake 0, Waterfall 0, Others 43.23.

Villages with population of 5000 to 9999: None

Villages with population of 10000 and above: None

Distribution of Workers:

	Persons	Males	Females	WPR
Cultivators	35,229	19,954	15,275	43.74
Agricultural Labour	31,172	14,334	16,838	38.71
Household Industry	1,101	509	592	1.37
Other Workers	13,033	9,853	3,180	16.18
Main Workers	68,958	40,790	28,168	85.62
Marginal Workers	11,577	3,860	7,717	14.38
Total Workers	80,535	44,650	35,885	

Religion: Major Religious Communities:

	Persons	Males	Females	Sex Ratio
Hindu (98.33%)	141,808	73,188	68,620	938
Muslim (1.22%)	1,763	888	875	985
Christian (0.39%)	557	278	279	1,004
Sikh (0%)	-	-	-	-
Buddhists (0%)	-	-	-	-
Jain (0%)	-	-	-	-

Agewise Data:

	Persons	Males	Females	Sex Ratio
All ages	144,213	74,403	69,810	938
0-14	42,651	22,562	20,089	890
15-44	72,063	36,450	35,613	977
45-79	28,037	14,604	13,433	920
80+	1,023	552	471	853
Age not stated	439	235	204	868

Languages (Dominant):

Tamil, Telugu, Urdu, Hindi, Kannada

Disabled Population:

	Persons	Males	Females	%
Total Disabled	4,277	1,302	2,975	
In Seeing	3,028	535	2,493	70.8
In Speech	275	164	111	6.43
In Hearing	116	60	56	2.71
In Movement	681	450	231	15.92
Mentally	177	93	84	4.14

HOSUR

Hosur C.D. Block lies in the north-western part of Dharmapuri district. It is a part of Hosur taluk. The Block is located at a distance of 110 kms. from district headquarters (Dharmapuri). There are 83 villages in the block with the total population of 148,019 persons. Area of the C.D. Block is 342.52 sq. kms. It is bounded in the south by CD Blocks Thally, Kelamangalam and Shoolagiri, in the east by C.D. Block Shoolagiri, in the west by CD Block Thally, and it has common boundary with the state of Karnataka on north, east and west.

Communications:

Roadways : N.H.-7: Direction- Bangalore to Krishnagiri, Nearest Villages- Zuzuvadi, Motham Agraharam, Chennathur, Gollapalli, Mookondapalli. N.H.-207: Direction- Sajjapuram to Hosur, Nearest Villages- Sevaganapalli, Kogganoor, Chokkarasanapally, Bagalur, Kodiyalam, Kothapally, Eachangur, Oddapallidinna Uni, Jeemangalam, Nallur, Viswanathapuram, Eluvapally, Chennasandiram, Kalasthipuram, Avalapalli. S.H.-17: Direction- Hosur to Rayakottah, Nearest Villages- Nalikabetta Agraharam, Chennathur, Gollapalli, Thorapalli Agraharam, Onnalvadi, Nalikabetta Agraharam, Thiyagarsanapalli, Chennathur, Onnalvadi, Dinnapalli, Bagalur, Belattur, Bobbalapuram.

River: Ponnaiyar Nadi- Nearest Villages- Chokkarasanapally, Singaradevapalli, Belattur, Dinnapalli, Bagalur, Kodiyalam, Moorthiganadinna, Lingapuram, Thummanapalli, Badathepalli, Nanjapuram, Kempasandram, Kannimangalam,

Chennasandiram, Kallipuram Uni , Siddanapally, Thattaga napally, Pathamuthali, Peddakullu, Chinnakullu, Kelavarapally, Avalapalli, Gollapalli, Thorapalli Agraharam.

Annual Rainfall: Average Rainfall 760 mm.

Ground Water: Availability of the ground water in the Basin is 7366.46 H.A.M. and the utilization is 9699.12 H.A.M. It belongs to Over Expoited category. Depth to water level varies from 2 to 10 meter below the ground. Most of the wells go down in summer months, according to the Ground Water Estimation Committee.

Forest and Reserved Forest: (Sanamavoo RF)- Nearest Villages- Thorapalli, Agraharam.

Natural Division: Baramahal.

Administration

Revenue **Division:** Hosur. Parliamentary Constituency: 9 Krishnagiri. District: Dharmapuri. Taluk: Hosur. Assembly Constituency: Hosur. Gram Panchayat: 34.

Border Villages- (Karnataka)- Nearest Villages- Sevagana palli, Kogganoor, Chokkarasanapally, Singaradevapalli, Belattur, Bobbalapuram, Deveeripalli, Balignapalli, Puram, Edipalli, Magalapalli, Vathiripalli, Alur, Koosthanapalli, Anumepalli, Zuzuvadi, Mookondapalli, Motham Agraharam, Kothakondapalli, Poonapally, Begeppali, Santhapuram.

Villages: 83 **Inhabited:** 76 **Uninhabited:** 7

Ranking	District	State	National
Area	13	123	2341
Population	8	18	1926
Sex Ratio	18	379	5818
Child Sex Ratio	1	174	3074
Literacy Rate	1	110	1163
Density	18	321	2551
Work Participation Rate	3	94	3852

Gram Panchayats:

Achettipalli , Alasapalli Bathavarapalli, Alasapalli Bathavarapalli , Avalapalli, Badathapalli , Bagalur , Baliganapalli, Baliganapalli , Begapalli , Belathur , Chenathur, Chennasandiram , Gopanapalli, Ichangoor, Ichangoor , Kelavarapalli , Koladasapuram, Kothakandapalli, Masinaickenpalli, Mookandapalli , Mugalur, Muthali , Muthuganapalli, Nagondapalli, Nallur, Nandhimangalam, Onnalvadi, Palavanapalli , Poonapalli, Sevaganapalli , Thorapalli Agraharam , Thumanapalli , Zuzavadi , Zuzuvadi .

Amenities:

Education: Primary School in 56 villages, Middle school in 19 villages, Matriculation or Secondary School in 8 villages, namely Dinnapalli, Bagalur, Kothapally, Jeemangalam, Nallur, Mookondapalli, Onnalvadi, Mugalur.

Higher Secondary or Pre University Courses or Intermediate or Junior College in 3 villages of the CD Block,, namely Dinnapalli, Mookondapalli, Onnalvadi.

College in 1 village, Adult Literacy Center in 0 village., College is in village, namely Mookondapalli.

Medical: Hospital in 1 village, Dispensary in 0 village, Health Center in 4 villages, Sub Center in 14 villages, Maternity and Child Welfare Center in 0 village, Community health workers in 62 villages.

The Village having Hospital or Dispensary or Health Center is Mookondapalli.

Drinking Water: Tap water in 76 villages, Tank water in 5 villages, Well water in 76 villages, Tubewell in 76 villages and more than one source in 76 villages.

Bank: Banking facility in 8 villages, namely, Kogganoor, Bagalur, Mookondapalli, Kothakondapalli Thorapalli Agraharam, Achettipalli, Muthuganapalli Mugalur.

Credit Society in 7 villages Agricultural Credit Society in 5 Non-Agricultural Credit Society in 3 villages.

Others: Power supply in 75 villages, Cinema hall in 1 village, sport club in 0 village, Stadium or Auditorium or Community Hall in 0 village, Post Office in 68 villages.

There are 54 villages having bus facilities.

Villages with most of facilities: Kogganoor Bagalur, Mookondapalli, Achettipalli, Muthuganapalli Mugalur.

Villages without amenities (Education):

Bobbalapuram, Edipalli, Vathiripalli, Oddapalli, Lingapuram, Batavarapalli, Aduvanapalli, Sudagondapalli, Nanjapuram, Kempasandram, Anumepalli, Viswanathapuram, Eluvapally, Kalasthipuram, Karupally, Pathamuthali, Athur, Chinnakullu, Kelavarapally, Nalikabetta Agraharam..

Scheduled Castes: Out of the total population of 148019 persons, 26604 persons (17.97%) belong to Scheduled Castes. The villages having less than 10% SC population are Belattur, Bobbalapuram, Deveeripalli Moorthiganadinna, Badathepalli, Kempasandram Anumepalli, Govinda Agreharam, Santhapuram Siddanapally, Karupally, Pathamuthali, Desapally Mookondapalli, Motham Agraharam, Chennathur Gollapalli.

The villages having more than 50% SC population are None.

Sex ratio of Scheduled Caste population is 488.

Scheduled Castes Literates and Illiterates by Sex:

	Persons	Males	Females
Literate	11,945	7,174	4,771
Illiterate	14,659	6,440	8,219
Literacy rate	53.3	62.5	43.7
Graduate	136	106	30

Scheduled Castes (Dominant):
Adi Dravida, Adi Karnataka, Adi Andhra, Mala, Madiga
For their cultural identity please see Appendix-I
Villages without Scheduled Castes: There are 8 villages without any scheduled caste population.
Scheduled Tribes: Out of the total population of 148019 persons, 242 persons (0.16%) belong to Scheduled Tribes. The villages having less than 10% ST population are Sevaganapalli, Kogganoor, Chokkarasanapally Singaradevapalli, Belattur, Bobbalapuram Deveeripalli, Balignapalli, Edipalli, Magalapalli Vathiripalli, Alur, Oddapalli, Alasapalli Muduganapalli, Dinnapalli, Bagalur, Kodiyalam Kothapally, Koosthanapalli, Chookkanathapuram Eachangur, Moorthiganadinna, Lingapuram Batavarapalli, Mallasandram, Thummanapalli Koladasapuram, Aduvanapalli, Alenatham Sudagondapalli, Palavanapalli, Nandhimangalam, Attur Badathepalli, Nanjapuram, Kempasandram Kannimangalam, Jeemangalam, Nallur, Begepalli Anumepalli, Govinda Agreharam, Zuzuvadi, Santhapuram Viswanathapuram, Eluvapally, Chennasandiram Kalasthipuram, Siddanapally, Thattaganapally Karupally, Pathamuthali, Muthali, Athur, Desapally Peddakullu, Chinnakullu, Kelavarapally, Punugandoddi Avalapalli, Mookondapalli, Motham Agraharam Kothakondapalli, Poonapally, Nalikabetta Agraharam Chennathur, Gollapalli, Thorapalli Agraharam Onnalvadi, Achettipalli, Nagondapali, Muthuganapalli Gopanapalli, Mugalur, Panchakshipuram.
The villages having more than 50% ST population are None.
Sex ratio of Scheduled tribe population is 521.
Scheduled Tribes Literates and Illiterates by Sex:

	Persons	Males	Females
Literate	116	67	49
Illiterate	126	49	77
Literacy rate	61.4	71.3	51.6
Graduate	3	2	1

Scheduled Tribes (Dominant):
Sholaga, Kurumans, Kattunayakan, Malayali, Irular
For their cultural identity please see Appendix-II
Villages without Scheduled Tribes: There are 71 villages without any scheduled tribe population.
Literates and Illiterates by Sex (Total Population):

	Persons	Males	Females
Literate	89,374	54,312	35,062
Illiterate	58,645	24,921	33,724
Literacy rate	70	79	60
Graduate	4,222	2,742	1,480

Agriculture: ***Distribution of villages according to land use:***
Out of 83 villages, Total area (in hectare) is 34252.12, out of that 75.92 percent is cultivable and 13.88 percent of the cultivable area is irrigated.
Sources of Irrigation (Hectares): Government Canal 58.39, Private Canal 0, Well without Electricity 362.01, Well with Electricity 1573.03, Tubewell without Electricity 2.8, Tubewell with Electricity 0, Tank 1382.29, River 0, Lake 23.1, Waterfall 33.79, Others 180.05.
Villages with population of 5000 to 9999:
Bagalur, Zuzuvadi, Chenathur.
Villages with population of 10000 and above:
Anumepali, Avalapalli, Mookondapalli.
Distribution of Workers:

	Persons	Males	Females	WPR
Cultivators	15,755	12,374	3,381	25.02
Agricultural Labour	13,228	7,245	5,983	21
Household Industry	1,202	626	576	1.91
Other Workers	32,796	27,914	4,882	52.07
Main Workers	56,227	44,920	11,307	89.28
Marginal Workers	6,754	3,239	3,515	10.72
Total Workers	62,981	48,159	14,822	

Religion: Major Religious Communities:

	Persons	Males	Females	Sex Ratio
Hindu (94.74%)	140,234	75,056	65,178	868
Muslim (2.81%)	4,158	2,207	1,951	884
Christian (2.29%)	3,388	1,849	1,539	832
Sikh (0.03%)	42	23	19	826
Buddhists (0%)	2	1	1	1,000
Jain (0.01%)	21	13	8	615

Agewise Data:

	Persons	Males	Females	Sex Ratio
All ages	148,019	79,233	68,786	868
0-14	45,390	23,139	22,251	962
15-44	77,631	42,676	34,955	819
45-79	23,592	12,672	10,920	862
80+	1,233	641	592	924
Age not stated	173	105	68	648

Languages (Dominant):
Tamil, Telugu, Kannada, Urdu, Hindi
Disabled Population:

	Persons	Males	Females	%
Total Disabled	3,758	1,358	2,400	
In Seeing	2,561	657	1,904	68.15
In Speech	273	158	115	7.26
In Hearing	122	47	75	3.25
In Movement	526	334	192	14
Mentally	276	162	114	7.34

ILAYANGUDI

Ilayangudi C.D. Block lies in the south-western part of Sivagamga district. It is a part of Ilayangudi and

Manamadurai taluks. The Block is located at a distance of 35 kms. from district headquarters (Sivaganga). There are 54 villages in the block with the total population of 82,345 persons. Area of the C.D. Block is 439.44 sq. kms. It is bounded in the north by CD Block Kalayarkoil and district Ramanathapuram, in the south and east by district Ramanathapuram, in the west by CD Blocks Manamadurai and Kalayarkoil. CD Block Ilayangudi falls in taluk Ilayangudi by 52 villages, and in taluk Manamadurai by 02 villages.

Communications:

Roadways : S.H.-29: Direction- Paramakudi to Kaliyarkoil, Nearest Villages- Melathuraiyur, Kannamangalam, Devathagudi, Thiruvallur, A.Thiruvudayharpuram, Nagarakudi, Kumarakurichi. S.H.-34: Direction- Sivaganga to Ramanathapuram, Nearest Villages- Thadiyamangalam, Uthamanur, Nagamugunthangudi, Thiruvallur, South Ilayangudi, A.Thiruvudayharpuram, Sirupalai, North Andakudi, Kottaiyoor, Nagarakudi.

River: Vaigai Nadi- Nearest Villages- Katenathanallur, Perumpacheri.

Backwards Region Grants Fund: It receives Backward Region Grants.

Annual Rainfall: Average Rainfall 904 mm.

Ground Water: Availability of the ground water in the Basin is 8588.48 H.A.M. and the utilization is 263.49 H.A.M. It belongs to Safe category. Depth to water level varies from 2 to 10 meter below the ground. Most of the wells go down in summer months, according to the Ground Water Estimation Committee.

Natural Division: NA

Administration

Revenue **Division:** Sivaganga. Parliamentary Constituency. District: Sivaganga. Taluk: Manamadurai, Ilayangudi. Assembly Constituency: 186 Sivaganga, 187 Manamadurai (SC). Gram Panchayat: 55.

Villages: 55 **Inhabited:** 54 **Uninhabited:** 1

Ranking	District	State	National
Area	2	51	1728
Population	3	230	4030
Sex Ratio	5	15	165
Child Sex Ratio	3	30	750
Literacy Rate	10	206	1888
Density	3	145	4920
Work Participation Rate	9	335	1446

Gram Panchayats:

A.Nedunkulam, Adavidangan, Akkavayal, Alimadurai, Aranaiyur, Aranmanaikarai, Ariyaandipuram, Athikarai Meyyanendal, Biramanakurichi, Ilamanur , Kilapidavu, Kalaikulam, Kalanganthankottai, Kalladithidal, Kannamangalam , Karaikulam, Karunchutti, Katchathanallur , Kattanur, Keelanettur, Keelayakudi, Kongampatti Idayavalasai, Kottaiyur, Kottaiyur , Kumarakurichi, Kurichi, Maruthunganallore, Melayur, Munaivendri, Muthur, N.Andakkudi , Nagarakudi, Nagarakudi , Nenjathur, Perumbacheri , Poolangudi, Pudukkottai, Periyakannanur, Puliyur, S.Karaikudi, Salaigramam, Samudram, Sembanur, Sathani, Sathanur , Seevalathi, Sooranam, Thaerkkukeeranur, Thayamangalam, Thugavoor, Tiruvallur , Udayanoor, Vadakkukeeranur, Vandal, Vani, Vijayangudi, Visavanoor , Nagamugunthankudi, Tandiyamangalam.

Amenities:

Education: Primary School in 51 villages, Middle school in 21 villages, Matriculation or Secondary School in 10 villages, namely Suranam, Visavanur, Aladidangan, Sothukudi, Thiruvallur, Salaigramam, North Ilayangudi, South Ilayangudi, Munaivendry, Sivalathi.

Higher Secondary or Pre University Courses or Intermediate or Junior College in 2 villages of the CD Block,, namely Suranam, North Ilayangudi.

College in 1 village, Adult Literacy Center in 0 village., College is in village, namely South Ilayangudi.

Medical: Hospital in 5 villages, Dispensary in 10 villages, Health Center in 4 villages, Sub Center in 11 villages, Maternity and Child Welfare Center in 3 villages, Community health workers in 37 villages.

The Villages having Hospital or Dispensary or Health Center are Suranam, Visavanur, Sothukudi, Thayamangalam, Kattanoor, Salaigramam, North Keeranur, North Ilayangudi, South Ilayangudi, Munaivendry, Kottaiyoor.

Drinking Water: Tap water in 54 villages, Tank water in 34 villages, Well water in 54 villages, Tubewell in 54 villages and more than one source in 54 villages.

Bank: Banking facility in 10 villages, namely, Vadakkucandanoor, Suranam, Visavanur, Sothukudi Kannamangalam, Salaigramam, North Ilayangudi South Ilayangudi, Munaivendry, Ilamanur.

Credit Society in 25 villages Agricultural Credit Society in 21 Non-Agricultural Credit Society in 3 villages.

Others: Power supply in 54 villages, Cinema hall in 1 village, sport club in 2 villages, Stadium or Auditorium or Community Hall in 12 villages, Post Office in 46 villages.

There are 54 villages having bus facilities.

Villages with most of facilities: Suranam Visavanur, Sothukudi, Kannamangalam, Salaigramam North Ilayangudi, South Ilayangudi, Munaivendry Ilamanur.

Villages without amenities (Education):

Aranmanaikarai, Devathagudi, A.Thiruvudayharpuram..

Scheduled Castes: Out of the total population of 82345 persons, 18581 persons (22.56%) belong to Scheduled Castes. The villages having less than 10% SC population are Vadakkucandanoor, Aranmanaikarai, Sothukudi, Vandal North Keeranur, Pudukkottai, Sathanoor North Andakudi, Kumarakurichi, Perumpacheri.

The villages having more than 50% SC population are None.

Sex ratio of Scheduled Caste population is 510.

Scheduled Castes Literates and Illiterates by Sex:

	Persons	Males	Females
Literate	9,341	5,508	3,833
Illiterate	9,240	3,605	5,635
Literacy rate	57.2	69.2	45.9
Graduate	252	204	48

Scheduled Castes (Dominant):

Pallan, Paraiyan etc., Chakkiliyan, Kuravan etc. Devendrakulathan

For their cultural identity please see Appendix-I

Villages without Scheduled Castes: There are 3 villages without any scheduled caste population.

Scheduled Tribes: Out of the total population of 82345 persons, 15 persons (0.02%) belong to Scheduled Tribes. The villages having less than 10% ST population are Thadiyamangalam, Vadakkucandanoor, S.Kanikkudi Kalaikulam, Melathuraiyur, Kaaraikulam, Suranam Akkavayal, Visavanur, Aladidangan, Udayanur Kalankathankottai, Aranmanaikarai, Vallakkulam Nengathur, Sothukudi, Kannamangalam, Devathagudi Thayamangalam, Uthamanur, Vijayangudi Nagamugunthangudi, Thiruvallur, Aranaiyur, Thugavoor Virayathakandan, Kattanoor, Vandal, Muthur Samuthiram, Salaigramam, North Keeranur Valayanendal, Karunchuthi, North Ilayangudi South Ilayangudi, Keelayoor, Melayur, Keelanettur Kurichi, Munaivendry, A.Thiruvudayharpuram Sirupalai, Pudukkottai, Sivalathi, Sathanoor North Andakudi, Kottaiyoor, Nagarakudi Kumarakurichi, Mulliyarendal, Katenathanallur Ilamanur, Perumpacheri.

The villages having more than 50% ST population are None.

Sex ratio of Scheduled tribe population is 467.

Scheduled Tribes Literates and Illiterates by Sex:

	Persons	Males	Females
Literate	12	8	4
Illiterate	3	0	3
Literacy rate	80.0	100.0	57.1
Graduate	0	0	0

Scheduled Tribes (Dominant):

Malai Pandaram

For their cultural identity please see Appendix-II

Villages without Scheduled Tribes: There are 54 villages without any scheduled tribe population.

Literates and Illiterates by Sex (Total Population):

	Persons	Males	Females
Literate	47,990	27,700	20,290
Illiterate	34,355	11,952	22,403
Literacy rate	65	79	53
Graduate	1,368	1,040	328

Agriculture: ***Distribution of villages according to land use:*** Out of 55 villages, Total area (in hectare) is 43944.82, out of that 55.97 percent is cultivable and 39.82 percent of the cultivable area is irrigated.

Sources of Irrigation (Hectares): Government Canal 0, Private Canal 0, Well without Electricity 105.2, Well with Electricity 724.95, Tubewell without Electricity 87.76, Tubewell with Electricity 31.65, Tank 8810.3, River 0, Lake 0, Waterfall 0, Others 33.31.

Villages with population of 5000 to 9999: Salaigramam.

Villages with population of 10000 and above: None

Distribution of Workers:

	Persons	Males	Females	WPR
Cultivators	26,113	13,931	12,182	58.51
Agricultural Labour	12,781	5,165	7,616	28.64
Household Industry	996	501	495	2.23
Other Workers	4,737	3,637	1,100	10.61
Main Workers	35,775	20,261	15,514	80.16
Marginal Workers	8,852	2,973	5,879	19.84
Total Workers	44,627	23,234	21,393	

Religion: Major Religious Communities:

	Persons	Males	Females	Sex Ratio
Hindu (83.46%)	68,727	33,325	35,402	1,062
Muslim (2.35%)	1,938	860	1,078	1,253
Christian (15.61%)	12,858	6,099	6,759	1,108
Sikh (0%)	1	1	-	-
Buddhists (0%)	1	-	1	-
Jain (0.01%)	9	3	6	2,000

Agewise Data:

	Persons	Males	Females	Sex Ratio
All ages	83,605	40,319	43,286	1074
0-14	22,028	10,997	11,031	1003
15-44	37,425	17,285	20,140	1165
45-79	22,919	11,409	11,510	1009
80+	945	480	465	969
Age not stated	288	148	140	946

Languages (Dominant):

Tamil, Gujarati, Telugu, Kannada, Malayalam

Disabled Population:

	Persons	Males	Females	%
Total Disabled	3,943	1,557	2,386	
In Seeing	2,787	900	1,887	70.68
In Speech	226	132	94	5.73
In Hearing	95	50	45	2.41
In Movement	608	361	247	15.42
Mentally	227	114	113	5.76

JAWATHU HILLS

Jawathu Hills C.D. Block lies in the north-western part of Tiruvannamalai district. It is a part of Polur & Chengam taluks. The taluk (Chengam) is located at a distance of 35 kms. from district headquarters (Tiruvannamalai). There are 38 villages in the block with the total population of 40,904 persons. Area of the C.D. Block is 181.98 sq. kms. It is bounded in the north by district Vellore, in the south by CD Blocks Chengam, Pudupalayam and Kalasapakkam, in the east by CD Block Polur and district Vellore, in the west by districts Dharmapuri and Vellore. CD Block Jawathu Hills Falls in taluk Polur by 17 Villages, and in taluk Chengam by 21 Villages.

Communications:

Roadways : Information not Available.

River: Cheyyar Nadi- Nearest Villages- Bandirev, Oorgoun danoor, Kilaiyur, Kallathur.

Backwards Region Grants Fund: It receives Backward Region Grants.

Annual Rainfall: Average Rainfall 1019 mm.

Ground Water: Availability of the ground water in the Basin is (Information not available) H.A.M. and the utilization is 160.44 H.A.M. It belongs to Over Expoited category. Depth to water level varies from 2 to 5 meter below the ground. Most of the wells go down in summer months, according to the Ground Water Estimation Committee.

Forest and Reserved Forest: (Mulakkadu RF)- Nearest Villages- Sengadu, Kuttakarai, Kovilur, Pattaraikadu, Melcheppili, Odamangalam. (Nallapathur)- Nearest Villages- Palamarathur, Nallaputhur RF, Melsilambadi, Kilthatttappattu, Melthattiappattu. (Thenmalai Hills)- Nearest Villages- Kilthatttappattu, Thenmalai Hills, Melthattiappattu, Puliyur, Oorgoundanoor, Kilaiyur, Kallathur, Nellyvoy, Athippettu, Perumuttam, Kallathur, Melpattu, Erukkampatti, Chinnakilpattu, Kilpattu, Bandirev. (Sandavasal)- Nearest Villages- Kanamalai, Erriyur, Kilkanavayur, Puliyankuppam, Sengadu. (Parvathiamalai)- Nearest Villages- Kovilur, Erumyanur, Kilthatiyaoattu. (Palamarathur)- Nearest Villages- Palamarathur RF, Palamarathur, Vannankuttai, Padapanjamarathur, Melsilambadi. (Pattarikadu)- Nearest Villages- Kovilur, Erumyanur. (Melaiyalam)- Nearest Villages- Amirthi, Kanamalai. (Veerapanur)- Nearest Villages- Mandaparai, Veerappanoor, Pudupattu, Erriyur, Kovilur, Namiyambattu.

Natural Division: Tondai Nadu.

Administration

Revenue **Division:** Tiruvannamalai. Parliamentary Constituency: 11 Tiruvannamalai. District: Tiruvannamalai. Taluk: Polur, Chengam. Assembly Constituency: 62 Chengam, 65 Kalasapakkam (ST). Gram Panchayat: 11.

Villages: 38 **Inhabited:** 35 **Uninhabited:** 3

Ranking	District	State	National
Area	18	307	4507
Population	18	370	5696
Sex Ratio	18	358	4036
Child Sex Ratio	17	303	5120
Literacy Rate	18	384	5855
Density	2	105	4376
Work Participation Rate	16	305	1042

Gram Panchayats:

Athipattu, Kallathur, Kanamalai, Kanamalai, Kovilur, Kuttakarai, Melsilambadi, Nammiyambut, Nammiyampattu, Palamaruthur , Puliyur, Urgoundanur, Veerappanur.

Amenities:

Education: Primary School in 22 villages, Middle school in 5 villages, Matriculation or Secondary School in 2 villages, namely Namiyambattu, Kovilur.

Higher Secondary or Pre University Courses or Intermediate or Junior College in 1 village of the CD Block,, namely Kovilur.

College in 0 village, Adult Literacy Center in 0 village.

Medical: Hospital in 0 village, Dispensary in 0 village, Health Center in 3 villages, Sub Center in 0 village, Maternity and Child Welfare Center in 4 villages, Community health workers in 35 villages.

Drinking Water: Tap water in 35 villages, Tank water in 14 villages, Well water in 35 villages, Tubewell in 35 villages and more than one source in 35 villages.

Bank: Banking facility in 1 villages, namely, Kovilur.

Credit Society in 2 villages Agricultural Credit Society in 2 Non-Agricultural Credit Society in 1 village.

Others: Power supply in 34 villages, Cinema hall in 0 village, sport club in 0 village, Stadium or Auditorium or Community Hall in 0 village, Post Office in 11 villages.

There are 14 villages having bus facilities.

Villages with most of facilities: Kovilur.

Villages without amenities (Education): Erriyur, Odamangalam, Melcheppili, Erumyanur, Kilthatiyaoattu, Vannankuttai, Kilthatttappattu, Melthattiappattu, Erukkampatti, Nellyvoy, Athippettu, Perumuttam, Chinnakilpattu..

Scheduled Castes: Out of the total population of 40904 persons, 903 persons (2.21%) belong to Scheduled Castes.

The villages having less than 10% SC population are Amirthi, Kanamalai, Namiyambattu, Mandaparai Veerappanoor, Pudupattu, Erriyur, Kilkanavayur Puliyankuppam, Sengadu, Kuttakarai, Odamangalam Kovilur, Pattaraikadu, Melcheppili, Erumyanur Kilthatiyaoattu, Palamarathur, Vannankuttai Bandirev, Padapanjamarathur, Melsilambadi Kilthatttappattu, Melthattiappattu, Puliyur Oorgoundanoor, Erukkampatti, Nellyvoy, Athippettu Perumuttam, Kallathur, Melpattu, Chinnakilpattu Kilpattu.

The villages having more than 50% SC population are None.

Sex ratio of Scheduled Caste population is 507.

Scheduled Castes Literates and Illiterates by Sex:

	Persons	Males	Females
Literate	443	235	208
Illiterate	460	210	250
Literacy rate	58.4	63.9	53.3
Graduate	10	5	5

Scheduled Castes (Dominant):

Adi Dravida, Arunthathiyar, Pallan, Adi Andhra Kuravan etc.

For their cultural identity please see Appendix-I

Villages without Scheduled Castes: There are 29 villages without any scheduled caste population.

Scheduled Tribes: Out of the total population of 40904 persons, 36847 persons (90.08%) belong to Scheduled Tribes.

The villages having less than 10% ST population are None..

The villages having more than 50% ST population are Kanamalai, Namiyambattu, Mandaparai, Veerappanoor Pudupattu, Erriyur, Kilkanavayur, Puliyankuppam Sengadu, Kuttakarai, Odamangalam, Kovilur Pattaraikadu, Melcheppili, Erumyanur Kilthatiyaoattu, Palamarathur, Vannankuttai Bandirev, Padapanjamarathur, Melsilambadi Kilthatttappattu, Melthattiappattu, Puliyur Oorgoundanoor, Kilaiyur, Erukkampatti, Nellyvoy Athippettu, Perumuttam, Kallathur, Melpattu Chinnakilpattu, Kilpattu.

Sex ratio of Scheduled tribe population is 484.

Scheduled Tribes Literates and Illiterates by Sex:

	Persons	Males	Females
Literate	10,329	7,110	3,219
Illiterate	26,518	11,896	14,622
Literacy rate	34.0	45.6	21.8
Graduate	30	28	2

Scheduled Tribes (Dominant):

Malayali, Irular, Generic Tribes etc.

For their cultural identity please see Appendix-II

Villages without Scheduled Tribes: There are 3 villages without any scheduled tribe population.

Literates and Illiterates by Sex (Total Population):

	Persons	Males	Females
Literate	12,721	8,496	4,225
Illiterate	28,183	12,603	15,580
Literacy rate	38	49	26
Graduate	97	66	31

Agriculture: ***Distribution of villages according to land use:***
Out of 38 villages, Total area (in hectare) is 18198.35, out of that 34.18 percent is cultivable and 12.66 percent of the cultivable area is irrigated.

Sources of Irrigation (Hectares): Government Canal 0, Private Canal 0, Well without Electricity 10.22, Well with Electricity 125.19, Tubewell without Electricity 0, Tubewell with Electricity 0, Tank 4, River 0, Lake 0, Waterfall 0, Others 0.

Villages with population of 5000 to 9999: None

Villages with population of 10000 and above:
Kovilur.

Distribution of Workers:

	Persons	Males	Females	WPR
Cultivators	13,968	8,318	5,650	65.83
Agricultural Labour	5,793	2,255	3,538	27.3
Household Industry	127	66	61	0.6
Other Workers	1,330	942	388	6.27
Main Workers	17,531	10,249	7,282	82.62
Marginal Workers	3,687	1,332	2,355	17.38
Total Workers	21,218	11,581	9,637	

Religion: Major Religious Communities:

	Persons	Males	Females	Sex Ratio
Hindu (98.51%)	40,295	20,790	19,505	938
Muslim (1.09%)	446	233	213	914
Christian (0.36%)	146	70	76	1,086
Sikh (0%)	-	-	-	-
Buddhists (0%)	-	-	-	-
Jain (0.01%)	4	3	1	333

Agewise Data:

	Persons	Males	Females	Sex Ratio
All ages	40,904	21,099	19,805	939
0-14	15,139	8,176	6,963	852
15-44	19,253	9,586	9,667	1008
45-79	6,195	3,180	3,015	948
80+	136	72	64	889
Age not stated	181	85	96	1129

Languages (Dominant):

Tamil, Telugu, Urdu, Marathi, Malayalam

Disabled Population:

	Persons	Males	Females	%

Total Disabled	535	343	192	
In Seeing	242	163	79	45.23
In Speech	67	33	34	12.52
In Hearing	25	15	10	4.67
In Movement	145	97	48	27.1
Mentally	56	35	21	10.47

JAYANKONDAM

Jayankondam C.D. Block lies in the eastern part of Ariyalur district. It is a part of Udayarpalayam taluk. The Block is located at a distance of 36 kms. from district headquarters (Ariyalur). There are 36 villages in the block with the total population of 108,365 persons. Area of the C.D. Block is 299.93 sq. kms. It is bounded in the north by C.D. Block Andimadam and district Cuddalore, in the south by C.D. Block T.Padur and district Cuddalore, in the east by district Cuddalore, in the west by C.D. Blocks Andimadam and Sendurai.

Communications:

Roadways : S.H.-8: Direction- Settiathope to Tiruppanandal, Nearest Villages- Pappakudi (N), Pappakudi (S), Kundavedli, Kundaveli, Muthuseruvamadam, Kuruvalapparkovil, Thazhuthathai. S.H.-24: Direction- Kilapalur to Chidambaram, Nearest Villages- Kundaveli, Muthuseruvamadam, Thathanur, Amannakkanthandi, Suriamanal, Kuruvalapparkovil, Thathanur (W).

Local Streams: Nearest Villages- Kattagaram(S), Muthuser uvamadam, Thazhuthathai.

Annual Rainfall: Average Rainfall 876 mm.

Ground Water: Availability of the ground water in the Basin is 8268.83 H.A.M. and the utilization is 4054.56 H.A.M. It belongs to Safe category. Depth to water level varies from 2 to 10 meter below the ground. Most of the wells go down in summer months, according to the Ground Water Estimation Committee.

Forest and Reserved Forest: (Periyavalayam RF)- Nearest Villages- Periyavalayam RF, Periyavalayam, Ulkottai (N), Amannakkanthandi. (Sooriyamanai)- Nearest Villages- Suriamanal RF, Suriamanal. (Thanimarathukau)- Nearest Village- Keelakudieruppu. (Udayarpalayam)- Nearest Villages- Udayarpalayam RF, Thathanur (W). (Managethi)- Nearest Villages- Thathanur (W). (Vethiyarvettu)- Nearest Villages- Vethiyarvettu RF, Vethiyarvettu, Pichanur, Piranchery.

Natural Division: Chola Nadu.

Administration

Revenue **Division:** Udayapalayam. Parliamentary Constituency: 25 Perambalur. District: Ariyalur. Taluk: Udayarpalayam. Assembly Constituency: 148 Konnam, 150 Jayankondam, 149 Ariyalur. Gram Panchayat: 35.

Villages: 36 **Inhabited:** 32 **Uninhabited:** 4

Ranking	**District**	**State**	**National**
Area	5	170	2789
Population	2	98	3198
Sex Ratio	5	177	1231
Child Sex Ratio	1	82	1003
Literacy Rate	3	232	2089
Density	6	230	3006
Work Participation Rate	2	143	2491

Gram Panchayats:

Alathipallam, Amanakkanthondi, Angarayanallur, Ayyappannaickenpettai, Devamangalam, Edayar, Elayaperumalnallur, Eravankudi, Gangaikondasholapuram, Guruvalapparkovil, Kachipperumal, Kallathur, Kaluvanthondi, Nagalkuzhi, Kattagaram, Kazhumangalam, Kundaveli, Melanikuzhi, Muthuservamadam, Padanilai, Pappakudi , Periyavalayam , Pichanoor, Pillapalayam , Pillichikuzhi, Pirancheri, Saluppai, T. Sholankurichi, Thaluthalaimedu, Thandalai, Thathanur , Thuvarankurichi, Ulkottai , Vanathirayanpattinam, Vangudi, Vethiyarvettu .

Amenities:

Education: Primary School in 31 villages, Middle school in 18 villages, Matriculation or Secondary School in 10 villages, namely Pappakudi (S), Eravangudi, Thandalai, Vethiyarvettu, Kundaveli, Suriamanal, Kuruvalapparkovil, Vanathiragapattinam, Thathanur, Thathanur (W).

Higher Secondary or Pre University Courses or Intermediate or Junior College in 4 villages of the CD Block,, namely Pappakudi (S), Kundaveli, Suriamanal, Thathanur (W).

College in 0 village, Adult Literacy Center in 0 village.

Medical: Hospital in 4 villages, Dispensary in 1 village, Health Center in 5 villages, Sub Center in 5 villages, Maternity and Child Welfare Center in 15 villages, Community health workers in 2 villages.

The Villages having Hospital or Dispensary or Health Center are Thandalai, Keelakudieruppu, Vethiyarvettu, Kundavedli, Kuruvalapparkovil.

Drinking Water: Tap water in 31 villages, Tank water in 0 villages, Well water in 31 villages, Tubewell in 31 villages and more than one source in 31 villages.

Bank: Banking facility in 10 villages, namely, Pappakudi (S), Eravangudi, Thandalai, Kundaveli Muthuseruvamadam, Devamangalam, Ulkottai (N) Kuruvalapparkovil, Thazhuthathai, Thathanur (W).

Credit Society in 12 villages Agricultural Credit Society in 10 Non-Agricultural Credit Society in 1 village.

Others: Power supply in 31 villages, Cinema hall in 3 villages, sport club in 31 villages, Stadium or Auditorium or Community Hall in 31 villages, Post Office in 28 villages. There are 30 villages having bus facilities.

Villages with most of facilities: Pappakudi (S) Eravangudi, Thandalai, Kundaveli, Devamangalam Ulkottai (N), Kuruvalapparkovil, Thazhuthathai Thathanur (W).

Villages without amenities (Education): Kulothunganallur..

Scheduled Castes: Out of the total population of 108365 persons, 28147 persons (25.97%) belong to Scheduled Castes.

The villages having less than 10% SC population are None..

The villages having more than 50% SC population are None.

Sex ratio of Scheduled Caste population is 500.

Scheduled Castes Literates and Illiterates by Sex:

	Persons	Males	Females
Literate	13,080	8,018	5,062
Illiterate	15,067	6,062	9,005
Literacy rate	54.6	66.8	42.3
Graduate	339	278	61

Scheduled Castes (Dominant):

Paraiyan etc., Adi Dravida, Pallan, Arunthathiyar Valluvan

For their cultural identity please see Appendix-I

Villages without Scheduled Castes: There are 4 villages without any scheduled caste population.

Scheduled Tribes: Out of the total population of 108365 persons, 2421 persons (2.23%) belong to Scheduled Tribes.

The villages having less than 10% ST population are Nagalkuzhi, Vangudi, Pappakudi (N), Pappakudi (S) Eravangudi, Thandalai, Keelakudieruppu, Piranchery Vethiyarvettu, Kundavedli, Kundaveli, Kattakaram(N) Kattagaram(S), Muthuseruvamadam, Elayaperumalnallur Amannakkanthandi, Periyavalayam, Suriamanal, Edayar Angarayanallur (E), Devamangalam, Ulkottai (N) Kuruvalapparkovil, Kulothunganallur, Thazhuthathai Vanathiragapattinam, Pilichikuzhy, T. Chozhankurichy Thathanur, Thathanur (W).

The villages having more than 50% ST population are None.

Sex ratio of Scheduled tribe population is 506.

Scheduled Tribes Literates and Illiterates by Sex:

	Persons	Males	Females
Literate	705	446	259
Illiterate	1,716	749	967
Literacy rate	34.5	44.3	25.0
Graduate	2	2	0

Scheduled Tribes (Dominant):

Irular, Malakkuravan, Malai Arayan

For their cultural identity please see Appendix-II

Villages without Scheduled Tribes: There are 12 villages without any scheduled tribe population.

Literates and Illiterates by Sex (Total Population):

	Persons	Males	Females
Literate	60,727	36,490	24,237
Illiterate	47,638	17,755	29,883
Literacy rate	64	77	51
Graduate	1,924	1,512	412

Agriculture: *Distribution of villages according to land use:* Out of 36 villages, Total area (in hectare) is 29993, out of that 75.4 percent is cultivable and 10.23 percent of the cultivable area is irrigated.

Sources of Irrigation (Hectares): Government Canal 445.14, Private Canal 0, Well without Electricity 202.46, Well with Electricity 217.77, Tubewell without Electricity 142.44, Tubewell with Electricity 319.45, Tank 249.58, River 0, Lake 736.69, Waterfall 0, Others 0.

Villages with population of 5000 to 9999: Thandalai, Kundaveli (East), Ulkottai (North) Guruvalapparkovil.

Villages with population of 10000 and above: None

Distribution of Workers:

	Persons	Males	Females	WPR
Cultivators	16,411	10,839	5,572	30.78
Agricultural Labour	25,743	13,685	12,058	48.29
Household Industry	4,468	2,569	1,899	8.38
Other Workers	6,688	5,109	1,579	12.55
Main Workers	40,933	27,351	13,582	76.78
Marginal Workers	12,377	4,851	7,526	23.22
Total Workers	53,310	32,202	21,108	

Religion: Major Religious Communities:

	Persons	Males	Females	Sex Ratio
Hindu (97.32%)	105,462	52,785	52,677	998
Muslim (0.35%)	382	177	205	1,158
Christian (3.43%)	3,722	1,875	1,847	985
Sikh (0%)	1	1	-	-
Buddhists (0%)	-	-	-	-
Jain (0%)	1	-	1	-

Agewise Data:

	Persons	Males	Females	Sex Ratio
All ages	109,664	54,893	54,771	998
0-14	30,962	15,762	15,200	964
15-44	53,470	26,404	27,066	1025
45-79	24,064	12,095	11,969	990
80+	947	517	430	832
Age not stated	221	115	106	922

Languages (Dominant):

Tamil, Telugu, Kannada, Urdu, Malayalam

Disabled Population:

	Persons	Males	Females	%
Total Disabled	2,654	1,361	1,293	

In Seeing	1,353	574	779	50.98
In Speech	318	193	125	11.98
In Hearing	160	85	75	6.03

In Movement	687	433	254	25.89
Mentally	136	76	60	5.12

JOLARPET

Jolarpet C.D. Block lies in the south-western part of Vellore district. It is a part of Vaniyambadi and Tirupathur taluks. The Block is located at a distance of 81 kms. from district headquarters (Vellore). There are 31 villages in the block with the total population of 142,159 persons. Area of the C.D. is 278.38 sq. kms. It is bounded in the north by CD Blocks Natrampalli and Alangayam, in the south by CD Blocks Kandili and Tiruppattur, in the east by CD Blocks Alangayam and Tiruppattur, and in the west by district Dharmapuri. CD Block Jolarpet falls in taluk Vaniyambadi by 03 villages, and in taluk Tirupathur by 28 villages.

Communications:

Roadways : N.H.-46: Direction- Krishnagiri to Vaniyambadi, Nearest Villages- Chinnavepan Patti, Kethandappatti, Nandibenda RF, Biyanappalli, Vellakkal Natham, Mallappalli. S.H.-18: Direction- Tiruppattur to Vaniyambadi, Nearest Villages- Chinnaveppam Pattu, Chinnavepan Patti, Chinnamottur, Mandalavadi, Ponneri, Elagiri Gramam, Katteri, Damalerimuthur, Pachal.

Railway Station: Kethandappattu, Vettappattu.

Annual Rainfall: Average Rainfall 949 mm.

Ground Water: Availability of the ground water in the Basin is 3697.90 H.A.M. and the utilization is 7024.20 H.A.M. It belongs to Over Expoited category. Depth to water level varies from 5 to 15 meter below the ground. Most of the wells go down in summer months, according to the Ground Water Estimation Committee.

Forest and Reserved Forest: (Jolarpet RF)- Nearest Villages- Mandalavadi, Jolarpettai RF, Yelagiri Hills, Vellakkal Natham, Nandibenda RF, Nagalathur Extn, Ponneri. (Momgalam)- Nearest Villages- Mangalam RF, Mangalam Extn, Yelagiri Hills. (Nagaluthu)- Nearest Villages- Yelagiri Hills, Nagalathur, Nagalathur Extn. (Natrampalli)- Nearest Village- Biyanappalli.

Natural Division: Tondai Nadu.

Administration

Revenue **Division:** Tirupatahur. Parliamentary Constituency: 11 Tiruvannamalai, 8 Vellore. District: Vellore. Taluk: Vaniyambadi, Tirupatahur. Assembly Constituency: 49 Jolarpet, 47 Vaniyambadi. Gram Panchayat: 36.

Villages: 31 **Inhabited:** 31 **Uninhabited:** 0

Ranking	District	State	National
Area	10	200	3020
Population	4	28	2111
Sex Ratio	17	296	2454
Child Sex Ratio	17	326	5372
Literacy Rate	19	257	2208
Density	10	289	2165
Work Participation Rate	4	54	3187

Gram Panchayats:

Agraharam, Ammanankoil, Ammayappanagar, Chandrapuram ChinnaKallupalli, Chinnakanniyampatti, Chinnamookanur, Chinnaveppambattu , Damalerimuthur, Elagiri , Kalnarasampatti, Katteri , Kaveripatti, Kethandapatty , Konapattur, Koothandakuppam, Kudiyanakuppam , Mallapalli, Mandalavadi, Mangalam Extension, Mookanur , Nekkundi, Oddapatti, Pachal , Paniyandapalli, Peddakallupalli , PeriaKanniampattu, Periamottur, Ponneri , Pullaneri, Puthagaram , Reddiyur, Somanaickenpatti, Thiriyalam , Velakalnatham, Vettapattu, .

Amenities:

Education: Primary School in 24 villages, Middle school in 18 villages, Matriculation or Secondary School in 11 villages, namely Kethandappatti, Chinnamottur, Mandalavadi, Yelagiri Hills, Thiriyalam, Vellakkal Natham, Paniyandapalli, Agaragaram, Ammanankoil, Damalerimuthur, Chandrapuram.

Higher Secondary or Pre University Courses or Intermediate or Junior College in 7 villages of the CD Block,, namely Kethandappatti, Chinnamottur, Mandalavadi, Yelagiri Hills, Mallappalli, Ammanankoil, Mookanur. College in 1 village, Adult Literacy Center in 0 village., College is in village, namely Chinnaveppam Pattu.

Medical: Hospital in 1 village, Dispensary in 0 village, Health Center in 8 villages, Sub Center in 5 villages, Maternity and Child Welfare Center in 5 villages, Community health workers in 23 villages. The Villages having Hospital or Dispensary or Health Center are Chinnamottur, Mallappalli, Agaragaram, Ammanankoil.

Drinking Water: Tap water in 24 villages, Tank water in 7 villages, Well water in 18 villages, Tubewell in 8 villages and more than one source in 24 villages.

Bank: Banking facility in 6 villages, namely, Kethandappatti, Yelagiri Hills, Elagiri Gramam Vellakkal Natham, Ammanankoil, Pachal.

Credit Society in 12 villages Agricultural Credit Society in 10 Non-Agricultural Credit Society in 4 villages.

Others: Power supply in 25 villages, Cinema hall in 2 villages sport club in 1 village, Stadium or Auditorium or Community Hall in 1 village, Post Office in 22 villages.

There are 23 villages having bus facilities.

Villages with most of facilities: Kethandappatti Yelagiri Hills, Elagiri Gramam, Vellakkal Natham

Ammanankoil, Pachal.

Villages without amenities (Education):
Jolarpettai Rf, Mangalam Rf, Mangalam Extn, Nagalathur, Nagalathur Extn, Nandibenda Rf, Virupakshipuram..

Scheduled Castes: Out of the total population of 142159 persons, 15837 persons (11.14%) belong to Scheduled Castes.
The villages having less than 10% SC population are Mandalavadi, Jolarpettai Rf, Mangalam Rf Mangalam Extn, Yelagiri Hills, Nagalathur Nagalathur Extn, Ponneri, Vettappattu Vellakkal Natham, Nandibenda Rf, Gollankuttai Paniyandapalli, Mallappalli, Agaragaram, Ammanankoil Mookanur, Damalerimuthur, Virupakshipuram.
The villages having more than 50% SC population are None.
Sex ratio of Scheduled Caste population is 501.

Scheduled Castes Literates and Illiterates by Sex:

	Persons	Males	Females
Literate	9,276	5,361	3,915
Illiterate	6,561	2,548	4,013
Literacy rate	67.9	78.8	57.1
Graduate	277	195	82

Scheduled Castes (Dominant):
Adi Dravida, Arunthathiyar, Kuravan etc., Adi Andhra Generic Castes etc.

For their cultural identity please see Appendix-I

Villages without Scheduled Castes: There are 3 villages without any scheduled caste population.

Scheduled Tribes: Out of the total population of 142159 persons, 5148 persons (3.62%) belong to Scheduled Tribes.
The villages having less than 10% ST population are Chinnaveppam Pattu, Chinnavepan Patti Kethandappatti, Kudiyanakuppam, Chinnamottur Mandalavadi, Ponneri, Elagiri Gramam, Katteri Thiriyalam, Vettappattu, Biyanappalli Vellakkal Natham, Nandibenda Rf, Gollankuttai Paniyandapalli, Mallappalli, Agaragaram, Ammanankoil Mookanur, Damalerimuthur, Pachal, Puthagaram Chandrapuram, Virupakshipuram.
The villages having more than 50% ST population are Jolarpettai Rf, Mangalam Rf, Mangalam Extn Yelagiri Hills, Nagalathur , Nagalathur Extn.
Sex ratio of Scheduled tribe population is 502.

Scheduled Tribes Literates and Illiterates by Sex:

	Persons	Males	Females
Literate	2,416	1,464	952
Illiterate	2,732	1,098	1,634
Literacy rate	53.0	64.4	41.6
Graduate	61	48	13

Scheduled Tribes (Dominant):
Malayali, Kurumans, Generic Tribes etc., Irular Kurichchan

For their cultural identity please see Appendix-II

Villages without Scheduled Tribes: There are 14 villages without any scheduled tribe population.

Literates and Illiterates by Sex (Total Population):

	Persons	Males	Females
Literate	77,968	45,773	32,195
Illiterate	64,191	26,342	37,849
Literacy rate	63	74	53
Graduate	2,069	1,459	610

Agriculture: ***Distribution of villages according to land use:***
Out of 31 villages, Total area (in hectare) is 27838.71, out of that 44.52 percent is cultivable and 27.5 percent of the cultivable area is irrigated.

Sources of Irrigation (Hectares): Government Canal 0, Private Canal 0, Well without Electricity 10.95, Well with Electricity 2732.56, Tubewell without Electricity 0, Tubewell with Electricity 214.85, Tank 156.09, River 0, Lake 294.24, Waterfall 0, Others 0.

Villages with population of 5000 to 9999:
Peddakallupalli , Kethandapatty , Mandalavadi Ponneri , Katteri , Thiriyalam , Vettapattu Velakalnatham, Paniyandapalli, Mallapalli, Agraharam Ammanankoil, Mookanur , Puthagaram.

Villages with population of 10000 and above:
Pachchal.

Distribution of Workers:

	Persons	Males	Females	WPR
Cultivators	13,999	9,477	4,522	21.47
Agricultural Labour	14,107	6,662	7,445	21.64
Household Industry	19,785	9,249	10,536	30.35
Other Workers	17,299	13,856	3,443	26.54
Main Workers	50,544	33,046	17,498	77.53
Marginal Workers	14,646	6,198	8,448	22.47
Total Workers	65,190	39,244	25,946	

Religion: Major Religious Communities:

	Persons	Males	Females	Sex Ratio
Hindu (95.48%)	135,727	68,823	66,904	972
Muslim (3.07%)	4,368	2,201	2,167	985
Christian (1.37%)	1,947	1,030	917	890
Sikh (0%)	4	2	2	1,000
Buddhists (0%)	-	-	-	-
Jain (0%)	2	1	1	1,000

Agewise Data:

	Persons	Males	Females	Sex Ratio
All ages	142,159	72,115	70,044	971
0-14	44,433	23,152	21,281	919
15-44	67,281	33,663	33,618	999

TAMILNADU

45-79	28,419	14,331	14,088	983
80+	1,440	638	802	1257
Age not stated	586	331	255	770

Languages (Dominant):
Tamil, Telugu, Urdu, Kannada, Others

Disabled Population:

	Persons	Males	Females	%
Total Disabled	3,326	1,869	1,457	
In Seeing	1,561	864	697	46.93
In Speech	306	165	141	9.2
In Hearing	156	70	86	4.69
In Movement	971	597	374	29.19
Mentally	332	173	159	9.98

K.PARAMATHY

K. Paramathi C.D. Block lies in the north-western part of Karur district. It is a part of Aravakurichi taluk. The taluk is located at a distance of 30 kms. from district headquarters (Karur). There are 35 villages in the block with the total population of 82,754 persons. Area of the C.D. Block is 534.87 sq. kms. It is bounded in the north by district Erode and CD Block Karur, in in the north by district Erode and CD Block Karur, the south by district Erode and C.D. Block Aravakurichi, in the east by CD Blocks Karur and Thanthoni, and in the west by district Erode.

Communications:
Roadways : N.H.-67: Direction- Kangeyam to Karur, Nearest Villages- Thennilai East, Munnur, K. Paramathy, Thennilai (South), Thennilai (West), Monjanur (West), E. R. Puram, Nedungur, Karudampalayam, Pavithram. S.H.-21: Direction- Dharapuram to Karur, Nearest Villages- Gudalur (West), Viswanthapuri, Thumbivadi, P.Anaipalayam, Soodamani, Thennilivenkatapuram, Chinnadharapuram, Kalakurichipunjai, Nanjaikkallakurichi, Gudalur (East).
Rivers: Amaravathi Nadi- Nearest Villages- Kodanthur (South), Gudalur (West), Chinnadharapuram, Thokkupatti, Rajapuram, Kalakurichipunjai, Nanjai-kallakurichi, P. Anaipalayam, Thumbivadi. Cauvery Nadi- Nearest Villages- Anjur, Thukkachi, Thennilai East, Athipalayam.
Annual Rainfall: Average Rainfall 635 mm.
Ground Water: Availability of the ground water in the Basin is 5258.25 H.A.M. and the utilization is 1198.64 H.A.M. It belongs to Safe category. Depth to water level varies from 2 to 10 meter below the ground. Most of the wells go down in summer months, according to the Ground Water Estimation Committee.
Natural Division: NA
Administration
Revenue **Division:** Karur. Parliamentary Constituency: 23 Karur. District: Karur. Taluk: Aravakurichi. Assembly Constituency: 134 Aravakurichi. Gram Panchayat: 30.
Villages: 35 **Inhabited:** 35 **Uninhabited:** 0

Ranking	District	State	National
Area	1	30	1366
Population	4	224	4010
Sex Ratio	4	108	849
Child Sex Ratio	8	342	5663
Literacy Rate	4	265	2291
Density	2	32	5488

Work Participation Rate	7	358	241

Gram Panchayats:
Anjur , Ariyur, Athipalayam, Chinnadarapuram, Elavanur, Gudalur (East), Gudalur (West), K.Paramathi, Kalakurichi Nanjai, Kalakurichi Punjai, Karavazhi, Karudayampalayam, Kodanthur, Kuppam, Monjanur, Munnur, Nadanthai, Nedungur, P. Anaipalayam, Pavithiram, Punnam, Rajapuram, Soodamani, Thennilai (West), Thennilai(East), Thennilai(South), Thokkupatti, Thukkachi, Thumbivadi, Viswanathapuri.

Amenities:
Education: Primary School in 34 villages, Middle school in 19 villages, Matriculation or Secondary School in 6 villages, namely Karvazhi, Ponnam, K. Paramathy, Thennilai (South), Thennilivenkatapuram, Elavanur. Higher Secondary or Pre University Courses or Intermediate or Junior College in 3 villages of the CD Block,, namely Ponnam, K. Paramathy, Thennilivenkatapuram. College in 0 village, Adult Literacy Center in 0 village.
Medical: Hospital in 0 village, Dispensary in 3 villages, Health Center in 6 villages, Sub Center in 3 villages, Maternity and Child Welfare Center in 8 villages, Community health workers in 5 villages.
The Villages having Hospital or Dispensary or Health Center are Anjur, Gudalur, P.Anaipalayam, Thennilivenkatapuram.
Drinking Water: Tap water in 35 villages, Tank water in 9 villages, Well water in 35 villages, Tubewell in 35 villages and more than one source in 35 villages.
Bank: Banking facility in 5 villages, namely, Anjur, Karvazhi, K. Paramathy, Thennilai (South) Chinnadharapuram.
Credit Society in 16 villages Agricultural Credit Society in 16 Non-Agricultural Credit Society in 6 villages.
Others: Power supply in 35 villages, Cinema hall in 3 villages, sport club in 1 village, Stadium or Auditorium or Community Hall in 0 village, Post Office in 30 villages.
There are 35 villages having bus facilities.
Villages with most of facilities: Anjur, Karvazhi K. Paramathy, Thennilai (South).
Villages without amenities (Education):
E. R. Puram..

Scheduled Castes: Out of the total population of 82754 persons, 21046 persons (25.43%) belong to Scheduled Castes.
The villages having less than 10% SC population are None..
The villages having more than 50% SC population are None.
Sex ratio of Scheduled Caste population is 499.

Scheduled Castes Literates and Illiterates by Sex:

	Persons	Males	Females
Literate	10,665	6,406	4,259
Illiterate	10,381	4,133	6,248
Literacy rate	56.4	67.8	45.0
Graduate	296	214	82

Scheduled Castes (Dominant):
Chakkiliyan, Pallan, Paraiyan etc., Madari Kuravan etc.

For their cultural identity please see Appendix-I

Villages without Scheduled Castes: There is 0 village without any scheduled caste population.

Scheduled Tribes: Out of the total population of 82754 persons, 9 persons (0.01%) belong to Scheduled Tribes.
The villages having less than 10% ST population are Anjur, Karvazhi, Thukkachi, Thennilai East Athipalayam, Ponnam, Kuppam, Munnur, K. Paramathy Thennilai (South), Thennilai (West), Monjanur (East) Monjanur (West), E. R. Puram, Kodanthur (North) Kodanthur (South), Gudalur (West), Gudalur Nadanthai South, Nadanthainorth, Nedungur Karudampalayam, Pavithram, Viswanthapuri, Thumbivadi P.Anaipalayam, Ariyur, Soodamani Thennilivenkatapuram, Chinnadharapuram, Elavanur Thokkupatti, Rajapuram, Kalakurichipunjai Nanjaikkallakurichi.
The villages having more than 50% ST population are None.
Sex ratio of Scheduled tribe population is 667.

Scheduled Tribes Literates and Illiterates by Sex:

	Persons	Males	Females
Literate	1	1	0
Illiterate	8	2	6
Literacy rate	14.3	33.3	-
Graduate	0	0	0

Scheduled Tribes (Dominant):
Malai Pandaram, Kurumans, Aranadan

For their cultural identity please see Appendix-II

Villages without Scheduled Tribes: There are 32 villages without any scheduled tribe population.

Literates and Illiterates by Sex (Total Population):

	Persons	Males	Females
Literate	47,657	28,739	18,918
Illiterate	35,097	12,414	22,683
Literacy rate	63	77	49
Graduate	1,537	1,090	447

Agriculture: ***Distribution of villages according to land use:***
Out of 35 villages, Total area (in hectare) is 53487, out of that 41.25 percent is cultivable and 27.27 percent of the cultivable area is irrigated.

Sources of Irrigation (Hectares): Government Canal 3015.38, Private Canal 0, Well without Electricity 636.73, Well with Electricity 2298.14, Tubewell without Electricity 0, Tubewell with Electricity 73.02, Tank 0, River 27.67, Lake 0, Waterfall 0, Others 0.33.

Villages with population of 5000 to 9999:
Pavithiram, Chinnadarapuram.

Villages with population of 10000 and above: None

Distribution of Workers:

	Persons	Males	Females	WPR
Cultivators	16,446	9,130	7,316	31.85
Agricultural Labour	16,919	7,323	9,596	32.77
Household Industry	2,987	1,519	1,468	5.79
Other Workers	15,280	10,798	4,482	29.59
Main Workers	47,911	27,606	20,305	92.79
Marginal Workers	3,721	1,164	2,557	7.21
Total Workers	51,632	28,770	22,862	

Religion: Major Religious Communities:

	Persons	Males	Females	Sex Ratio
Hindu (97%)	80,273	39,957	40,316	1,009
Muslim (1.54%)	1,275	596	679	1,139
Christian (1.2%)	994	490	504	1,029
Sikh (0%)	-	-	-	-
Buddhists (0%)	1	-	1	-
Jain (0%)	2	1	1	1,000

Agewise Data:

	Persons	Males	Females	Sex Ratio
All ages	82,754	41,153	41,601	1011
0-14	15,598	8,168	7,430	910
15-44	37,884	18,631	19,253	1033
45-79	27,698	13,549	14,149	1044
80+	1,487	751	736	980
Age not stated	87	54	33	611

Languages (Dominant):
Tamil, Telugu, Kannada, Malayalam, Urdu

Disabled Population:

	Persons	Males	Females	%
Total Disabled	1,716	972	744	
In Seeing	785	432	353	45.75
In Speech	187	107	80	10.9
In Hearing	129	61	68	7.52
In Movement	460	291	169	26.81
Mentally	155	81	74	9.03

K.V. KUPPAM

K.V. Kuppam C.D. Block lies in the northern part of Vellore district. It is a part of Katpadi taluk. The taluk is located at a distance of 10 kms. from district headquarters (Vellore). There are 53 villages in the block with the total population of 118, 712 persons. Area of the C.D. Block is 228.44 sq. kms. It is bounded in the south by CD Block Anaicut and river Palar, in the east by CD Block Katpadi, in the west by Gudiyatham, and it has common boundary with the state of Andhra Pradesh on north.

Communications:

Roadways : Information not Available.

Railway Station: Latheir, Veppur, Vaduganthangal.

River: Palar Nadi- Nearest Villages- Ammanan Kuppam, Veppur, Pasumathur, Kavanur, Melur, Kilur, Mudinambattu, Valvankundram, Vadaviringhipuram, Virinjipuram Plantat ion, Kothamangalam, Ammundi (RF), Thirumani, Cholamur.

Annual Rainfall: Average Rainfall 949 mm.

Ground Water: Availability of the ground water in the Basin is 4614.25 H.A.M. and the utilization is 8008.27 H.A.M. It belongs to Over Expoited category. Depth to water level varies from 5 to 15 meter below the ground. Most of the wells go down in summer months, according to the Ground Water Estimation Committee.

Forest and Reserved Forest: (Ammundi RF)- Nearest Villages- Ammundi (RF), Thirumani. (Bomminayakkanpalayam)- Nearest Villages- Bomminayakanpalayam (RF), Kalampattu, Bomminay akanpalayam, Angarangkullam. (Chenji)- Nearest Villages- Thondan Thalasi, Senji, Senji (RF), Panamadangi. (Panama dagi)- Nearest Villages- Panamadangi, Maliyapattu, Panama dangi (RF), Melmail, Kilmuttukur. (Vikramachi)- Nearest Villages- Vikkarancachi, Vikkarancachi (RF), Velampattu. (Virinjipuram Plantation)- Nearest Villages- Mudinambat tu, Valvankundram, Vadaviringhipuram, Virinjipuram Plant ation.

Natural Division: Tondai Nadu.

Administration

Revenue **Division:** Vellore. Parliamentary Constituency: 8 Vellore. District: Vellore. Taluk: Katpadi. Assembly Constituency: 45 Kavanur (SC). Gram Panchayat: 39.

Border Villages- (Andhra Pradesh)- Nearest Villages- Thondan Thalasi, Senji (RF), Panamadangi.

Villages: 53 **Inhabited:** 47 **Uninhabited:** 6

Ranking	District	State	National
Area	12	253	3684
Population	8	68	2905
Sex Ratio	7	128	967
Child Sex Ratio	11	242	4011
Literacy Rate	5	81	920
Density	17	346	2117
Work Participation Rate	3	49	4346

Gram Panchayats:

Alanganeri, Ammanankuppam, Ankarankuppam, Annankudi, Arumbakkam, Bomminayakanpalayam, Chennankuppam, Cholamur, Devarishikuppam, Kalampattu, Kankuppam, Kavanur, Kavasampattu, Kilalathur, Kilmuttukur, Kilvazhithunaiankuppam, Kosavanpudur, Kothamangalam, Latheri, Machanur, Maliyapattu, Melmoil, Mudinampattu, Murukkampattu, Nagal, Netteri, Panamadangi, Pasumathur, Pazhayakrishnapuram, Pillanthipattu, Senji, Sethuvandai, Thirumani, Thondanthulasi, Vaduganthangal, Velampattu, Veppanganeri, Veppur, Vizhunthaggal.

Amenities:

Education: Primary School in 45 villages, Middle school in 24 villages, Matriculation or Secondary School in 14 villages, namely Senji, Malmankuppam, Melmail, Kalampattu, Latheir, Alanganeri, Sethuvandai, Veppur, Pasumathur, Machanoor, Kil Vaithinang Kuppam, Veppangaveri, Melur, Vaduganthangal.

Higher Secondary or Pre University Courses or Intermediate or Junior College in 8 villages of the CD Block,, namely Senji, Malmankuppam, Melmail, Kalampattu, Sethuvandai, Pasumathur, Veppangaveri, Vaduganthangal.

College in 0 village, Adult Literacy Center in 0 village.

Medical: Hospital in 0 village, Dispensary in 0 village, Health Center in 6 villages, Sub Center in 7 villages, Maternity and Child Welfare Center in 6 villages, Community health workers in 47 villages.

The Village having Hospital or Dispensary or Health Center is Kilmuttukur.

Drinking Water: Tap water in 46 villages, Tank water in 9 villages, Well water in 12 villages, Tubewell in 18 villages and more than one source in 47 villages.

Bank: Banking facility in 5 villages, namely, Latheir, Keela Alathur, Pasumathur Kil Vaithinang Kuppam, Vaduganthangal.

Credit Society in 11 villages Agricultural Credit Society in 8 Non-Agricultural Credit Society in 4 villages.

Others: Power supply in 47 villages, Cinema hall in 3 villages, sport club in 0 village, Stadium or Auditorium or Community Hall in 0 village, Post Office in 44 villages.

There are 41 villages having bus facilities.

Villages with most of facilities: Latheir Keela Alathur, Pasumathur, Kil Vaithinang Kuppam Vaduganthangal.

Villages without amenities (Education): Ozhayathur, Malvilachur..

Scheduled Castes: Out of the total population of 118712 persons, 30351 persons (25.57%) belong to Scheduled Castes.

The villages having less than 10% SC population are Malmankuppam, Villundakkal, Machanoor, P.K.Puram Malvilachur, Melur, Kilvilachur, Vikkarancachi.

The villages having more than 50% SC population are None.

Sex ratio of Scheduled Caste population is 505.

Scheduled Castes Literates and Illiterates by Sex:

	Persons	Males	Females
Literate	19,340	10,706	8,634
Illiterate	11,011	4,322	6,689
Literacy rate	72.6	81.8	63.6
Graduate	418	303	115

Scheduled Castes (Dominant):

Adi Dravida, Arunthathiyar, Valluvan, Adi Andhra Pannadi

For their cultural identity please see Appendix-I

Villages without Scheduled Castes: There are 9 villages without any scheduled caste population.

Scheduled Tribes: Out of the total population of 118712 persons, 1070 persons (0.9%) belong to Scheduled Tribes.

The villages having less than 10% ST population are Senji, Panamadangi, Maliyapattu, Malmankuppam Melmail, Kilmuttukur, Kalampattu, Arumbakkam Latheir, Villundakkal, Ozhayathur, Anangudi Bomminayakanpalayam, Angarangkullam, Alanganeri Murukampattu, Kangkuppam, Devarishikuppam, Nagal Keela Alathur, Sethuvandai, Ammanan Kuppam, Veppur Netteri, Pasumathur, Chennan Kuppam, Machanoor P.K.Puram, Kavanur, Kil Vaithinang Kuppam Veppangaveri, Thuthi Thangal, Malvilachur Pillanthipattu, Melur, Kilur, Mudinambattu Kilvilachur, Vaduganthangal, Vikkarancachi Velampattu, Valvankundram, Vadaviringhipuram Kothamangalam, Sholamur, Thirumani.

The villages having more than 50% ST population are None.

Sex ratio of Scheduled tribe population is 502.

Scheduled Tribes Literates and Illiterates by Sex:

	Persons	Males	Females
Literate	563	316	247
Illiterate	507	217	290
Literacy rate	62.5	70.5	54.5
Graduate	10	9	1

Scheduled Tribes (Dominant):

Irular, Kondareddis, Malakkuravan, Kattunayakan Generic Tribes etc.

For their cultural identity please see Appendix-II

Villages without Scheduled Tribes: There are 34 villages without any scheduled tribe population.

Literates and Illiterates by Sex (Total Population):

	Persons	Males	Females
Literate	75,857	43,103	32,754
Illiterate	42,855	16,050	26,805
Literacy rate	72	83	62
Graduate	2,174	1,580	594

Agriculture: ***Distribution of villages according to land use:*** Out of 53 villages, Total area (in hectare) is 22844.47, out of that 59.34 percent is cultivable and 21.74 percent of the cultivable area is irrigated.

Sources of Irrigation (Hectares): Government Canal 0, Private Canal 0, Well without Electricity 0, Well with Electricity 2928.59, Tubewell without Electricity 0, Tubewell with Electricity 18.06, Tank 0, River 0, Lake 0, Waterfall 0, Others 0.

Villages with population of 5000 to 9999: Latteri, Pasumathur.

Villages with population of 10000 and above: None

Distribution of Workers:

	Persons	Males	Females	WPR
Cultivators	10,242	8,370	1,872	20.96
Agricultural Labour	18,944	9,841	9,103	38.77
Household Industry	5,844	3,117	2,727	11.96
Other Workers	13,828	11,250	2,578	28.3
Main Workers	36,108	26,905	9,203	73.9
Marginal Workers	12,750	5,673	7,077	26.1
Total Workers	48,858	32,578	16,280	

Religion: Major Religious Communities:

	Persons	Males	Females	Sex Ratio
Hindu (97.4%)	115,621	57,634	57,987	1,006
Muslim (1.59%)	1,892	943	949	1,006
Christian (0.92%)	1,096	515	581	1,128
Sikh (0.01%)	10	4	6	1,500
Buddhists (0%)	3	3	-	-
Jain (0.02%)	26	14	12	857

Agewise Data:

	Persons	Males	Females	Sex Ratio
All ages	118,712	59,153	59,559	1007
0-14	32,944	16,768	16,176	965
15-44	56,541	28,047	28,494	1016
45-79	27,506	13,549	13,957	1030
80+	1,565	709	856	1207
Age not stated	156	80	76	950

Languages (Dominant):

Tamil, Telugu, Urdu, Marathi, Hindi

Disabled Population:

	Persons	Males	Females	%
Total Disabled	2,834	1,516	1,318	
In Seeing	1,277	641	636	45.06
In Speech	317	160	157	11.19
In Hearing	191	100	91	6.74

In Movement	765	460	305	26.99	Mentally	284	155	129	10.02

KABILAMALAI

Kabilamalai C.D. Block lies in the south-western part of Namakkal district. It is a part of Paramathi-Velur taluk. The taluk is located at a distance of 25 kms. from district headquarters (Namakkal). There are 25 villages in the block with the total population of 53,882 persons. Area of the C.D. Block is 193.89 sq. kms. It is bounded in the north by CD Block Tiruchengode, in the south by districts Erode and Karur, in the east by C.D. Blocks Paramathi and Mohanur, in the west by CD Block Tiruchengode and district Erode.

Communications:

Roadways : Information not Available.

River: Cauvery Nadi- Nearest Villages- Solaisiramani, Ellampalli, Kuttambalamahadevi, Kottamangalam, Vadagarai Attur, Agraharakunnathur, Anangur, M.Kunnathur, Selur, Agrahara Bommalapalayam, S.Kondalam, Agrahara Kondalam.

Annual Rainfall: Average Rainfall 650 mm.

Ground Water: Availability of the ground water in the Basin is 6091.86 H.A.M. and the utilization is 4976.79 H.A.M. It belongs to Safe category. Depth to water level varies from 2 to 5 meter below the ground. Most of the wells go down in summer months, according to the Ground Water Estimation Committee.

Natural Division: Kongu Nadu

Administration

Revenue Division: Tiruvhengodu. Parliamentary Constituency. District: Namakkal. Taluk : Paramathi-Velur. Assembly Constituency: 95 Paramathi–Velur. Gram Panchayat: 20.

Villages: 25 **Inhabited:** 25 **Uninhabited:** 0

Ranking	District	State	National
Area	10	293	4293
Population	10	345	5096
Sex Ratio	3	198	1373
Child Sex Ratio	2	299	5051
Literacy Rate	13	334	2892
Density	3	9	3776
Work Participation Rate	12	255	71

Gram Panchayats:

Agraharakunnathur, Anangur , Ellampalli, Gopanampalayam, Irukkur, Kabilakkurichi, Kottamangalam, Kuppirikapalayam, Kurumbalamahadevi, Periasolipalayam, Perunkurichi, Pillikalpalayam, S.Kondalam, Selur, Sirunallikoil, Solasiramani, Sullipalayam, T.Kavundampalayam, Tidumal, Vadagarai Attur.

Amenities:

Education: Primary School in 24 villages, Middle school in 10 villages, Matriculation or Secondary School in 6 villages, namely Solaisiramani, Ellampalli, Vadagarai Attur, Kabilakkurichi, Pilikkalpalayam, S.Kondalam.
Higher Secondary or Pre University Courses or Intermediate or Junior College in 2 villages of the CD Block,, namely Solaisiramani, Vadagarai Attur.
College in 0 village, Adult Literacy Center in 0 village.

Medical: Hospital in 0 village, Dispensary in 0 village, Health Center in 4 villages, Sub Center in 9 villages, Maternity and Child Welfare Center in 0 village, Community health workers in 0 village.

Drinking Water: Tap water in 25 villages, Tank water in 0 villages, Well water in 25 villages, Tubewell in 25 villages and more than one source in 25 villages.

Bank: Banking facility in 4 villages, namely, Solaisiramani, Vadagarai Attur, Kabilakkurichi Pilikkalpalayam.
Credit Society in 15 villages Agricultural Credit Society in 9 Non-Agricultural Credit Society in 12 villages.

Others: Power supply in 25 villages, Cinema hall in 2 villages, sport club in 0 village, Stadium or Auditorium or Community Hall in 0 village, Post Office in 24 villages.
There are 23 villages having bus facilities.

Villages with most of facilities: Solaisiramani Vadagarai Attur, Kabilakkurichi, Pilikkalpalayam.

Villages without amenities (Education): M.Kunnathur..

Scheduled Castes: Out of the total population of 53882 persons, 10556 persons (19.59%) belong to Scheduled Castes.
The villages having less than 10% SC population are None..
The villages having more than 50% SC population are None.
Sex ratio of Scheduled Caste population is 498.

Scheduled Castes Literates and Illiterates by Sex:

	Persons	Males	Females
Literate	4,475	2,673	1,802
Illiterate	6,081	2,626	3,455
Literacy rate	48.1	57.4	38.8
Graduate	83	61	22

Scheduled Castes (Dominant):
Arunthathiyar, Chakkiliyan, Adi Dravida Paraiyan etc., Pallan

For their cultural identity please see Appendix-I

Villages without Scheduled Castes: There is 0 village without any scheduled caste population.

Scheduled Tribes: Out of the total population of 53882 persons, 16 persons (0.03%) belong to Scheduled Tribes.
The villages having less than 10% ST population are

Kuppirikapalayam, Perunkurichi, Devanampalayam
Sullipalayam, Solaisiramani, Ellampalli
Nallagoundampalayam, T.Kavundampalayam, Tidumal
Sirunallikoil, Kuttambalamahadevi, Kottamangalam
Vadagarai Attur, Periyasolaipalayam, Kabilakkurichi
Irukkur, Gopanampalayam, Agraharakunnathur, Anangur
M.Kunnathur, Pilikkalpalayam, Selur
Agrahara Bommalapalayam, S.Kondalam
Agrahara Kondalam.

The villages having more than 50% ST population are None.

Sex ratio of Scheduled tribe population is 375.

Scheduled Tribes Literates and Illiterates by Sex:

	Persons	Males	Females
Literate	6	4	2
Illiterate	10	6	4
Literacy rate	46.2	57.1	33.3
Graduate	2	0	2

Scheduled Tribes (Dominant):

Malayali, Malai Pandaram, Generic Tribes etc.

For their cultural identity please see Appendix-II

Villages without Scheduled Tribes: There are 22 villages without any scheduled tribe population.

Literates and Illiterates by Sex (Total Population):

	Persons	Males	Females
Literate	28,986	17,251	11,735
Illiterate	24,896	9,769	15,127
Literacy rate	59	71	48
Graduate	1,201	861	340

Agriculture: ***Distribution of villages according to land use:*** Out of 25 villages, Total area (in hectare) is 19389.59, out of that 88.73 percent is cultivable and 35.13 percent of the cultivable area is irrigated.

Sources of Irrigation (Hectares): Government Canal 2764.21, Private Canal 0, Well without Electricity 0, Well with Electricity 2763.42, Tubewell without Electricity 0, Tubewell with Electricity 37.13, Tank 0, River 0, Lake 0, Waterfall 0, Others 478.77.

Villages with population of 5000 to 9999:
Vadagarai Attur.

Villages with population of 10000 and above: None

Distribution of Workers:

	Persons	Males	Females	WPR
Cultivators	9,605	5,594	4,011	27.16
Agricultural Labour	18,564	8,203	10,361	52.5
Household Industry	1,630	729	901	4.61
Other Workers	5,561	4,018	1,543	15.73
Main Workers	32,404	17,584	14,820	91.64
Marginal Workers	2,956	960	1,996	8.36
Total Workers	35,360	18,544	16,816	

Religion: Major Religious Communities:

	Persons	Males	Females	Sex Ratio
Hindu (99.28%)	53,493	26,815	26,678	995
Muslim (0.12%)	63	34	29	853
Christian (0.4%)	216	112	104	929
Sikh (0.01%)	7	4	3	750
Buddhists (0%)	2	1	1	1,000
Jain (0%)	2	1	1	1,000

Agewise Data:

	Persons	Males	Females	Sex Ratio
All ages	53,882	27,020	26,862	994
0-14	11,734	6,132	5,602	914
15-44	25,810	12,703	13,107	1032
45-79	15,095	7,528	7,567	1005
80+	708	377	331	878
Age not stated	535	280	255	911

Languages (Dominant):

Tamil, Telugu, Kannada, Hindi, Urdu

Disabled Population:

	Persons	Males	Females	%
Total Disabled	931	492	439	
In Seeing	467	244	223	50.16
In Speech	87	45	42	9.34
In Hearing	60	26	34	6.44
In Movement	237	131	106	25.46
Mentally	80	46	34	8.59

KADALADI

Kadaladi C.D. Block lies in the south-western part of Ramanathapuram district. It is a part of Kadaladi and Mudukulathur taluks. The Block is located at a distance of NA kms. from district headquarters (Ramanathauram). There are 52 villages in the block with the total population of 126,636 persons. Area of the C.D. Block is 677.55 sq. kms. It is bounded in the north by CD Blocks Mudukulathur and kamuthi, in the south by the Gulf of Mannar, in the east by CD. Block Tiruppullani, and in the west by district Thoothukkudi. CD Block Kadaladi falls in taluk Mudukulathur by 08 villages, and in taluk Kadaladi by 44 villages.

Communications:

Roadways : S.H.-29: Direction- Sayalgudi to Mudukulathur, Nearest Villages- Kandilan, Ilanchembur, Apunavasal, Meenangudi, Kadaladi, Kadugusanthai. S.H.-38: Direction- Aruppukkottai to Kuruchchikulam, Nearest Villages- Keelakidaram, Melakidaram, Keelaselvanur, Avathandai, T. Veppankulam, A. Nedungulam, S.Vakaikulam, Iruveli, Mookkaiyur, Periyakulam, Thanichiyam, Valiokkam, Kuruuchikulam.

River: Gundar Nadi- Nearest Villages- Appanoor, Kadaladi, K.Veppangulam, M.Karisalkulam, A.Ucilangulam, Kadugusanthai, Mookkaiyur, Periyakulam.

Annual Rainfall: Average Rainfall 827 mm.

Ground Water: Availability of the ground water in the Basin is 3149.58 H.A.M. and the utilization is 541.10 H.A.M. It belongs to Safe category. Depth to water level varies from 2 to 10 meter below the ground. Most of the wells go down in summer months, according to the Ground Water Estimation Committee.

Coastal Villages- (Gulf of Mannar)- Nearest Villages- Kannirajapuram, Narippaiyur, Kudiraimozhi, Mookkaiyur, Periyakulam, Valinokkam, Ervadi, S. Tharaikudi.

Natural Division: NA

Administration

Revenue **Division:** Paramakudi. Parliamentary Constituency: 35 Ramanathapuram. District: Ramanathapuram. Taluk: Mudukulathur, Kadaladi. Assembly Constituency: 212 Mudukulathur. Gram Panchayat: 60.

Villages: 52 **Inhabited:** 48 **Uninhabited:** 4

Ranking	District	State	National
Area	1	12	971
Population	1	46	2629
Sex Ratio	9	64	523
Child Sex Ratio	11	190	3156
Literacy Rate	10	221	2034
Density	7	268	4933
Work Participation Rate	7	337	2896

Gram Panchayats:

A.Punnavasal , A.Usilankulam , Appanur , Avathandai , Chitirangudi, Elamjambur , Enathi, Erwadi, Ethambadal, Ilanjembur , Kadaladi, Kadukusanthai, Kandilam , Kandilan , Kanjikoor, Kannirajapuram, Karunkulam , Kathakulam, Keelasakkulam , Keelaselvanur , Keelaselvanur , Keelasirupothu, Keelkidaram, Kidathirukkai, Pagangulam , Kokkarasankottai , Kondunallanpatti, Koothankudi , M.Karisalkulam , Mangulam , Marandai , Mariyur , Meenangudi, Melaselvanur , Melasirupattu, Melkidaram , Mookaiyur , Narippaiyur, Oppilan, Orivayal, Oruvanendal , P.Keerathi , Pannanthai, Pannivasal , Peikulam , Periyakulam, Pillayarkulam , Pothikulam , S.Keeerandai , S.Tharaikudi, S.Vagaikulam , Senjadainathapuram , Sethurajapuram, Sevalpatti, Sikkal , Siraikulam , Sokkanai , Sonnaipiriyankottai, T.Karisalkulam , T.Veppankulam , Thanichayam, Thirumalgoundankottai, Uchinatham, Valinockarai , .

Amenities:

Education: Primary School in 42 villages, Middle school in 16 villages, Matriculation or Secondary School in 11 villages, namely Chithirangudi, Kandilan, Keelasioupothu, Sikkal, Melakidaram, Kadaladi, Thirumaluganthankottai, Kokkaramkottai, Kannirajapuram, Periyakulam, Ervadi. Higher Secondary or Pre University Courses or Intermediate or Junior College in 3 villages of the CD Block,, namely Chithirangudi, Kandilan, Keelasioupothu.
College in 3 villages, Adult Literacy Center in 3 villages., Colleges are in villages, namely Chithirangudi, Kandilan, Keelasioupothu.

Medical: Hospital in 2 villages, Dispensary in 0 village, Health Center in 4 villages, Sub Center in 2 villages, Maternity and Child Welfare Center in 10 villages, Community health workers in 0 village.
The Villages having Hospital or Dispensary or Health Center are Marandai, Kadaladi, T.Mariyur, Ervadi.

Drinking Water: Tap water in 48 villages, Tank water in 19 villages, Well water in 47 villages, Tubewell in 47 villages and more than one source in 47 villages.

Bank: Banking facility in 10 villages, namely, Keelasioupothu, Panivasal, Sikkal, Orivayal Kadaladi, S.Vakaikulam, Melaselvanoor, S.Tharaikudi Narippaiyur, Ervadi.
Credit Society in 17 villages Agricultural Credit Society in 17 Non-Agricultural Credit Society in 2 villages.

Others: Power supply in 35 villages, Cinema hall in 2 villages, sport club in 0 village, Stadium or Auditorium or Community Hall in 0 village, Post Office in 22 villages.
There are 38 villages having bus facilities.

Villages with most of facilities: Kadaladi S.Tharaikudi, Ervadi.

Villages without amenities (Education): Ilanchembur, Senthaneri, Melasirupothu, Valinokkam..

Scheduled Castes: Out of the total population of 126636 persons, 19118 persons (15.1%) belong to Scheduled Castes.
The villages having less than 10% SC population are Ilanchembur, Apunavasal, Seraikulam, Kadaladi K.Veppangulam, M.Karisalkulam Thirumaluganthankottai, T.Karisalkulam Konduallanpatti, Kadugusanthai, Melaselvanoor Iruveli, Kannirajapuram, Narippaiyur, Kudiraimozhi Periyakulam, T.Mariyur, Valinokkam, Ervadi.
The villages having more than 50% SC population are None.
Sex ratio of Scheduled Caste population is 502.

Scheduled Castes Literates and Illiterates by Sex:

	Persons	Males	Females
Literate	8,559	5,157	3,402
Illiterate	10,559	4,359	6,200
Literacy rate	52.0	63.3	41.0
Graduate	175	150	25

Scheduled Castes (Dominant):

Pallan, Chakkiliyan, Paraiyan etc., Puthirai Vannan Arunthathiyar

For their cultural identity please see Appendix-I

Villages without Scheduled Castes: There are 6 villages without any scheduled caste population.

Scheduled Tribes: Out of the total population of 126636 persons, 10 persons (0.01%) belong to Scheduled Tribes. The villages having less than 10% ST population are Chithirangudi, Solai Priyankottai, Enathi, Kandilan Keelasioupothu, Ilanchembur, Senthaneri Melasirupothu, Appanoor, Oruvanendal, Apunavasal Marandai, Keeranthai, Peikullam, Panivasal, Sikkal Idambadal, Seraikulam, Keelakidaram, Melakidaram Keelaselvanur, Orivayal, Meenangudi, Kadaladi K.Veppangulam, M.Karisalkulam, Avathandai T.Veppankulam, Thirumaluganthankottai T.Karisalkulam, Kokkaramkottai, Konduallanpatti A.Nedungulam, S.Vakaikulam, A.Ucilangulam Kadugusanthai, Melaselvanoor, Iruveli, S.Tharaikudi Kannirajapuram, Narippaiyur, Kudiraimozhi Mookkaiyur, Periyakulam, T.Mariyur, Thanichiyam Valinokkam, Ervadi.

The villages having more than 50% ST population are None.

Sex ratio of Scheduled tribe population is 500.

Scheduled Tribes Literates and Illiterates by Sex:

	Persons	Males	Females
Literate	0	0	0
Illiterate	10	5	5
Literacy rate	-	-	-
Graduate	0	0	0

Scheduled Tribes (Dominant):

Kattunayakan

For their cultural identity please see Appendix-II

Villages without Scheduled Tribes: There are 51 villages without any scheduled tribe population.

Literates and Illiterates by Sex (Total Population):

	Persons	Males	Females
Literate	70,700	40,893	29,807
Illiterate	55,936	21,557	34,379
Literacy rate	64	76	53
Graduate	1,367	1,063	304

Agriculture: *Distribution of villages according to land use:* Out of 52 villages, Total area (in hectare) is 67755.65, out of that 74.38 percent is cultivable and 17.16 percent of the cultivable area is irrigated.

Sources of Irrigation (Hectares): Government Canal 247.07, Private Canal 0, Well without Electricity 27.18, Well with Electricity 85, Tubewell without Electricity 0, Tubewell with Electricity 0, Tank 10728.45, River 0, Lake 0, Waterfall 0, Others 0.

Villages with population of 5000 to 9999: Narippaiyur, Periakulam.

Villages with population of 10000 and above: Ervadi.

Distribution of Workers:

	Persons	Males	Females	WPR
Cultivators	23,373	13,731	9,642	39.12
Agricultural Labour	18,222	7,130	11,092	30.5
Household Industry	1,080	343	737	1.81
Other Workers	17,077	13,092	3,985	28.58
Main Workers	44,569	28,985	15,584	74.59
Marginal Workers	15,183	5,311	9,872	25.41
Total Workers	59,752	34,296	25,456	

Religion: Major Religious Communities:

	Persons	Males	Females	Sex Ratio
Hindu (77.87%)	98,616	48,907	49,709	1,016
Muslim (14.79%)	18,732	8,864	9,868	1,113
Christian (7.81%)	9,885	4,967	4,918	990
Sikh (0%)	4	2	2	1,000
Buddhists (0%)	3	1	2	2,000
Jain (0%)	1	-	1	-

Agewise Data:

	Persons	Males	Females	Sex Ratio
All ages	127,292	62,769	64,523	1028
0-14	39,212	20,073	19,139	953
15-44	59,825	28,752	31,073	1081
45-79	26,893	13,251	13,642	1030
80+	1,070	511	559	1094
Age not stated	292	182	110	604

Languages (Dominant):

Tamil, Telugu, Malayalam, Urdu, Kannada

Disabled Population:

	Persons	Males	Females	%
Total Disabled	4,002	1,966	2,036	
In Seeing	1,913	743	1,170	47.8
In Speech	314	165	149	7.85
In Hearing	165	58	107	4.12
In Movement	786	423	363	19.64
Mentally	824	577	247	20.59

KADAMALAIKUNDRU-MYLADUMPARAI

Kadamalaikundru-Myladumparai C.D. Block lies in the south-eastern part of Theni district. It is a part of Andipatti taluk. The taluk is located at a distance of 18 kms. from district headquarters (Theni Allinagaram). There are 04 villages in the block with the total population of 67,863 persons. Area of the C.D. Block is 620.67 sq. kms. It is bounded in the north by CD Block Andipatti, in the south by district Virudhunagar, in the east by district Madurai, in the west by CD Blocks Kambam and Chinnamanur. It has common boundary with the state of Kerala on south-west.

Communications:

Roadways : Information not Available.

River: Vaigai Nadi- Nearest Villages- Kadamalaigundu, Myladuparai, Megamalai, Gandamanur.
Annual Rainfall: Average Rainfall 709 mm.
Ground Water: Availability of the ground water in the Basin is 4609.23 H.A.M. and the utilization is 5496. 06 H.A.M. It belongs to Over Expoited category. Depth to water level varies from 5 to 20 meter below the ground. Most of the wells go down in summer months, according to the Ground Water Estimation Committee.
Forest and Reserved Forest: (Gandamanur RF)- Nearest Villages- Gandamanur, Kadamalaigundu, Megamalai.
Natural Division: NA
Administration
Revenue **Division:** Periyakulam. Parliamentary Constituency: 33 Theni. District: Theni. Taluk: Andipatti. Assembly Constituency: 198 Andipatti. Gram Panchayat: 18.
Border Villages- (Kerala)- Nearest Village- Megamalai.
Villages: 4 **Inhabited:** 4 **Uninhabited:** 0

Ranking	District	State	National
Area	1	16	1107
Population	3	297	4562
Sex Ratio	8	368	4787
Child Sex Ratio	8	371	6200
Literacy Rate	8	317	2710
Density	1	37	6056
Work Participation Rate	8	377	296

Gram Panchayats:
Athangaraipatty, Duraichamypuram, Ettapparajapuram, Gandamanur , Kadamalaikundu, Kumanan Tholu, Manthisunaimoolakadai, Megamalai, Murukkodai, Muthalampuram, Myladumparai, Nariyoothu, Paloothu, Ponnanpadugai, Singarajapuram, Thangammalpuram, Thummakkundu, Varushanadu.
Amenities:
Education: Primary School in 4 villages, Middle school in 4 villages, Matriculation or Secondary School in 3 villages, namely Gandamanur, Kadamalaigundu, Myladuparai. Higher Secondary or Pre University Courses or Intermediate or Junior College in 3 villages of the CD Block,, namely Gandamanur, Kadamalaigundu, Myladuparai. College in 0 village, Adult Literacy Center in 0 village.
Medical: Hospital in 1 village, Dispensary in 2 villages, Health Center in 4 villages, Sub Center in 4 villages, Maternity and Child Welfare Center in 4 villages, Community health workers in 4 villages.
The Villages having Hospital or Dispensary or Health Center are Gandamanur, Myladuparai.
Drinking Water: Tap water in 4 villages, Tank water in 4 villages, Well water in 4 villages, Tubewell in 4 villages and more than one source in 4 villages.
Bank: Banking facility in 3 villages, namely, Gandamanur, Kadamalaigundu, Myladuparai.
Credit Society in 2 villages Agricultural Credit Society in 2 Non-Agricultural Credit Society in 2 villages.
Others: Power supply in 4 villages, Cinema hall in 2 villages, sport club in 0 village, Stadium or Auditorium or Community Hall in 0 village, Post Office in 4 villages.
There are 4 villages having bus facilities.
Villages with most of facilities: Gandamanur Kadamalaigundu, Myladuparai.
Villages without Amenities (Education): None..
Scheduled Castes: Out of the total population of 67863 persons, 15388 persons (22.68%) belong to Scheduled Castes.
The villages having less than 10% SC population are None..
The villages having more than 50% SC population are None.
Sex ratio of Scheduled Caste population is 487.
Scheduled Castes Literates and Illiterates by Sex:

	Persons	Males	Females
Literate	7,137	4,370	2,767
Illiterate	8,251	3,523	4,728
Literacy rate	53.3	64.1	42.1
Graduate	51	45	6

Scheduled Castes (Dominant):
Pallan, Chakkiliyan, Paraiyan etc., Puthirai Vannan Kuravan etc.
For their cultural identity please see Appendix-I
Villages without Scheduled Castes: There is 0 village without any scheduled caste population.
Scheduled Tribes: Out of the total population of 67863 persons, 153 persons (0.23%) belong to Scheduled Tribes.
The villages having less than 10% ST population are None..
The villages having more than 50% ST population are None.
Sex ratio of Scheduled tribe population is 444.
Scheduled Tribes Literates and Illiterates by Sex:

	Persons	Males	Females
Literate	10	8	2
Illiterate	143	77	66
Literacy rate	8.6	12.1	3.9
Graduate	0	0	0

Scheduled Tribes (Dominant):
Palliyan, Paniyan, Malakkuravan, Palliyar
For their cultural identity please see Appendix-II
Villages without Scheduled Tribes: There are 2 villages without any scheduled tribe population.
Literates and Illiterates by Sex (Total Population):

	Persons	Males	Females

Literate	35,887	22,191	13,696
Illiterate	31,976	13,153	18,823
Literacy rate	60	72	48
Graduate	262	207	55

Agriculture: ***Distribution of villages according to land use:*** Out of 4 villages, Total area (in hectare) is 62067.97, out of that 25.88 percent is cultivable and 39.3 percent of the cultivable area is irrigated.

Sources of Irrigation (Hectares): Government Canal 41.45, Private Canal 0, Well-without Electricity 343.75, Well with Electricity 3530.78, Tubewell without Electricity 0, Tubewell with Electricity 495.51, Tank 115, River 87.07, Lake 9.15, Waterfall 0, Others 1690.55.

Villages with population of 5000 to 9999:
Megamalai.

Villages with population of 10000 and above:
Gandamanur , Kadamalaikundu, Myaladumparai.

Distribution of Workers:

	Persons	Males	Females	WPR
Cultivators	8,557	4,682	3,875	21.35
Agricultural Labour	25,297	12,200	13,097	63.13
Household Industry	340	183	157	0.85
Other Workers	5,880	4,238	1,642	14.67
Main Workers	33,875	18,652	15,223	84.53
Marginal Workers	6,199	2,651	3,548	15.47
Total Workers	40,074	21,303	18,771	

Religion: Major Religious Communities:

	Persons	Males	Females	Sex Ratio
Hindu (98.73%)	67,001	34,916	32,085	919
Muslim (0.74%)	501	257	244	949
Christian (0.45%)	303	145	158	1,090
Sikh (0%)	-	-	-	-
Buddhists (0%)	2	-	2	-
Jain (0%)	3	-	3	-

Agewise Data:

	Persons	Males	Females	Sex Ratio
All ages	67,863	35,344	32,519	920
0-14	20,754	11,413	9,341	818
15-44	33,686	17,255	16,431	952
45-79	12,543	6,243	6,300	1009
80+	453	217	236	1088
Age not stated	427	216	211	977

Languages (Dominant):
Tamil, Telugu, Kannada, English, Malayalam

Disabled Population:

	Persons	Males	Females	%
Total Disabled	2,211	1,134	1,077	
In Seeing	1,541	734	807	69.7
In Speech	133	82	51	6.02
In Hearing	46	25	21	2.08
In Movement	406	249	157	18.36
Mentally	85	44	41	3.84

KADAMBATTUR

Kadambathur C.D. Block lies in the south central part of Thiruvallur district. It is a part of Thiruvallur taluk. The taluk is located at a distance of 00 kms. from district headquarters (Thiruvallur). There are 52 villages in the block with the total population of 90,036 persons. Area of the C.D. Block is 240.60 sq. kms. It is bounded in the north by CD Blocks Poondi and Thiruvallur, in the south by district Kancheepuram, in the east by district Kancheepuram and CD Block Poonamalle, in the west by CD Block Thiruvelangadu and district Kancheepuram.

Communications:

Roadways : Information not Available.

Railway Station: Kadambathur, Egattur.

Annual Rainfall: Average Rainfall 1152 mm.

Ground Water: Availability of the ground water in the Basin is 88.03 MCM and the utilization is 81.88 MCM. It belongs to Critical category. Depth to water level varies from 2 to 10 meter below the ground. Most of the wells go down in summer months, according to the Ground Water Estimation Committee.

Natural Division: Tondai Nadu.

Administration

Revenue **Division:** Thiruvallur. Parliamentary Constituency: 1 Thiruvallur (SC). District: Thiruvallur. Taluk: Thiruvallur. Assembly Constituency: 4 Thiruvalangadu (SC). Gram Panchayat: 53.

Villages: 52 **Inhabited:** 50 **Uninhabited:** 2

Ranking	District	State	National
Area	6	241	3500
Population	7	182	3779
Sex Ratio	2	129	965
Child Sex Ratio	3	49	1070
Literacy Rate	5	116	1218
Density	8	320	2918
Work Participation Rate	10	133	3840

Gram Panchayats:
Adigathur, Aranvoyal , Chitrambakkam, Egattur, Erayamangalam, Iluppur, Irulanjeri, Kadambattur , Kallambedu , Kannur , Kavankolathur, Keelanallathur, Kilacheri, Kodanjeri, Koovam, Koppur, Kottaiyur, Kumaracheri, Mappedu, Melanallathur, Mudugur, Narasingaparam, Nungambakkam, Papparampakkam, Perambakkam, Pinjivakkam, Pirayankuppam, Polivakkam, Pudumavilangai, Pudupattu, Puduvallur, Ramankoil, Satharai, Senji, Thandalam, Thirumanikuppam, Thodukadu, Tirupandiyur , Ulundai , Valasaivettikadu, Vellerithungal, Vidaiyur, Voyalur , Keelanallathur.

Amenities:

Education: Primary School in 46 villages, Middle school in 26 villages, Matriculation or Secondary School in 12 villages, namely Vedaiyur, Kadambathur, Melnallathur, Koppur, Kasavanallathur, Kilacheri, Perumbakkam, Irulanjeri, Koovam, Pillaiyarkuppam, Ulundai, Thirupandiyur.
Higher Secondary or Pre University Courses or Intermediate or Junior College in 5 villages of the CD Block,, namely Kadambathur, Melnallathur, Kilacheri, Perumbakkam, Thirupandiyur.
College in 1 village, Adult Literacy Center in 0 village., College is in village, namely Vayalur.

Medical: Hospital in 0 village, Dispensary in 1 village, Health Center in 4 villages, Sub Center in 16 villages, Maternity and Child Welfare Center in 2 villages, Community health workers in 50 villages.
The Village having Hospital or Dispensary or Health Center is Melnallathur.

Drinking Water: Tap water in 50 villages, Tank water in 50 villages, Well water in 50 villages, Tubewell in 50 villages and more than one source in 50 villages.

Bank: Banking facility in 6 villages, namely, Kadambathur, Kasavanallathur, Kilacheri, Perumbakkam Koovam, Thirupandiyur.
Credit Society in 12 villages Agricultural Credit Society in 10 Non-Agricultural Credit Society in 2 villages.

Others: Power supply in 50 villages, Cinema hall in 2 villages, sport club in 0 village, Stadium or Auditorium or Community Hall in 0 village, Post Office in 23 villages.
There are 40 villages having bus facilities.

Villages with most of facilities: Kadambathur Kasavanallathur, Kilacheri, Perumbakkam Thirupandiyur.

Villages without amenities (Education):
Chitrambakkam, Kumarachery, Govindamedu, Karanai..

Scheduled Castes: Out of the total population of 90036 persons, 31571 persons (35.06%) belong to Scheduled Castes.
The villages having less than 10% SC population are None..
The villages having more than 50% SC population are Periyakuppam, Palliyaraikuppam, Venmanambudur Nayapakkam, Agaram, Panampakkam, Ramankoil Thenkaranai, Chitrambakkam, Mappedu, Irulanjeri Koovam, Pillaiyarkuppam.
Sex ratio of Scheduled Caste population is 500.

Scheduled Castes Literates and Illiterates by Sex:

	Persons	Males	Females
Literate	17,934	10,415	7,519
Illiterate	13,637	5,379	8,258
Literacy rate	66.1	77.0	55.2
Graduate	449	346	103

Scheduled Castes (Dominant):
Adi Dravida, Arunthathiyar, Paraiyan etc., Valluvan Generic Castes etc.

For their cultural identity please see Appendix-I

Villages without Scheduled Castes: There are 4 villages without any scheduled caste population.

Scheduled Tribes: Out of the total population of 90036 persons, 2088 persons (2.32%) belong to Scheduled Tribes.
The villages having less than 10% ST population are Periyakuppam, Palliyaraikuppam, Karani, Attupakkam Vedaiyur, Venmanambudur, Kadambathur, Egattur Melnallathur, Koppur, Nayapakkam, Papparambakkam Valasaivettikadu, Iluppur, Polivakkam, Nungambakkam Pinjivakkam, Agaram, Panampakkam, Ramankoil Madathukuppam, Senji, Thenkaranai, Chitrambakkam Kavankolathur, Pudumavilangai, Satharai Eriyamangalam, Alinjivakkam, Mappedu, Kilacheri Kondancheri, Perumbakkam, Narasingapuram, Irulanjeri Kumarachery, Koovam, Pillaiyarkuppam, Govindamedu Ulundai, Thodukadu, Vayalur, Kottaiur, Karanai Kallambadu, Uthirambakkam, Kannur, Pudupattu Thirupandiyur.
The villages having more than 50% ST population are None.
Sex ratio of Scheduled tribe population is 491.

Scheduled Tribes Literates and Illiterates by Sex:

	Persons	Males	Females
Literate	682	425	257
Illiterate	1,406	637	769
Literacy rate	39.2	48.5	29.8
Graduate	9	7	2

Scheduled Tribes (Dominant):
Irular, Kurumans, Kattunayakan, Palliyar Generic Tribes etc.

For their cultural identity please see Appendix-II

Villages without Scheduled Tribes: There are 14 villages without any scheduled tribe population.

Literates and Illiterates by Sex (Total Population):

	Persons	Males	Females
Literate	54,847	31,519	23,328
Illiterate	35,189	13,338	21,851
Literacy rate	70	81	59
Graduate	1,824	1,308	516

Agriculture: ***Distribution of villages according to land use:*** Out of 52 villages, Total area (in hectare) is 24060.57, out of that 45.06 percent is cultivable and 62.49 percent of the cultivable area is irrigated.

Sources of Irrigation (Hectares): Government Canal 23.1, Private Canal 0, Well without Electricity 232.17, Well with Electricity 659.58, Tubewell without Electricity 0,

Tubewell with Electricity 1759.69, Tank 925.02, River 0, Lake 2784.27, Waterfall 0, Others 390.91.

Villages with population of 5000 to 9999: Perambakkam, Tirupandiyur.

Villages with population of 10000 and above: None

Distribution of Workers:

	Persons	Males	Females	WPR
Cultivators	4,032	3,228	804	10.35
Agricultural Labour	19,414	10,188	9,226	49.84
Household Industry	3,729	2,158	1,571	9.57
Other Workers	11,781	9,366	2,415	30.24
Main Workers	25,233	17,802	7,431	64.77
Marginal Workers	13,723	7,138	6,585	35.23
Total Workers	38,956	24,940	14,016	

Religion: Major Religious Communities:

	Persons	Males	Females	Sex Ratio
Hindu (89.6%)	80,676	40,208	40,468	1,006
Muslim (1.54%)	1,388	693	695	1,003
Christian (9.07%)	8,169	4,035	4,134	1,025
Sikh (0.01%)	9	7	2	286
Buddhists (0.04%)	35	19	16	842
Jain (0.18%)	159	83	76	916

Agewise Data:

	Persons	Males	Females	Sex Ratio
All ages	90,481	45,076	45,405	1007
0-14	26,462	13,390	13,072	976
15-44	44,535	22,337	22,198	994
45-79	18,551	8,899	9,652	1085
80+	695	331	364	1100
Age not stated	238	119	119	1000

Languages (Dominant):
Tamil, Telugu, Urdu, Hindi, Malayalam

Disabled Population:

	Persons	Males	Females	%
Total Disabled	2,459	1,387	1,072	
In Seeing	1,207	645	562	49.08
In Speech	180	101	79	7.32
In Hearing	190	82	108	7.73
In Movement	702	459	243	28.55
Mentally	180	100	80	7.32

KADAVUR

Kadavur C.D. Block lies in the eastern part of Karur district. It is a part of Kulithalai taluk. The taluk is located at a distance of 42 kms. from district headquarters (Karur). There are 20 villages in the block with the total population of 82,870 persons. Area of the C.D. Block is 427.02 sq. kms. It is bounded in the north by CD Block Krishnarayapurm, in the south by districts Dindigul and Tiruchirappalli, in the east by CD Block Thogaimalai and district Tiruchirappalli, and in the west by district Dindingul.

Communications:

Roadways : Information not Available.

Annual Rainfall: Average Rainfall 635 mm.

Ground Water: Availability of the ground water in the Basin is 3642.16 H.A.M. and the utilization is 4503.59 H.A.M. It belongs to Over Expoited category. Depth to water level varies from 2 to 10 meter below the ground. Most of the wells go down in summer months, according to the Ground Water Estimation Committee.

Natural Division: NA

Administration

Revenue **Division:** Kulithalai. Parliamentary Constituency: 23 Karur. District: Karur. Taluk: Kutlithalai Assembly Constituency: 136 Krishnarayapuram (SC).

Gram Panchayat: 20.

Villages: 20 **Inhabited:** 20 **Uninhabited:** 0

Ranking	District	State	National
Area	2	55	1788
Population	3	221	4007
Sex Ratio	6	144	1006
Child Sex Ratio	3	199	3242
Literacy Rate	8	353	3440
Density	1	16	4813
Work Participation Rate	6	331	133

Gram Panchayats:

Adhanur, Devarmalai, Kadavur, Kalayapatti, Keelappaguthi, Keeranur, Manjanaickenpatti, Mavathur, Melappaguthi, Mullipadi, Palaviduthi, Pannapatti, Pappayambadi, Sembianatham, Thennilai, Vadavambadi, Valvarmangalam, Varavanai, Vellapatty.

Amenities:

Education: Primary School in 20 villages, Middle school in 13 villages, Matriculation or Secondary School in 7 villages, namely Manjanaickenpatti, Pannapatty, Thennelai, Devarmalai, Idayapatti, Balavuduthi, Keelappaguthy. Higher Secondary or Pre University Courses or Intermediate or Junior College in 3 villages of the CD Block,, namely Manjanaickenpatti, Pannapatty, Keelappaguthy. College in 0 village, Adult Literacy Center in 1 village.

Medical: Hospital in 1 village, Dispensary in 3 villages, Health Center in 3 villages, Sub Center in 1 village, Maternity and Child Welfare Center in 3 villages, Community health workers in 1 village.

The Villages having Hospital or Dispensary or Health Center are Pannapatty, Sembianatham, Idayapatti, Keelappaguthy.

Drinking Water: Tap water in 20 villages, Tank water in 1 villages, Well water in 20 villages, Tubewell in 20 villages and more than one source in 20 villages.

Bank: Banking facility in 5 villages, namely, Manjanaickenpatti, Devarmalai, Idayapatti

Balavuduthi, Keelappaguthy.
Credit Society in 6 villages Agricultural Credit Society in 4 Non-Agricultural Credit Society in 1 village.

Others: Power supply in 20 villages, Cinema hall in 4 villages, sport club in 0 village, Stadium or Auditorium or Community Hall in 0 village, Post Office in 17 villages.
There are 20 villages having bus facilities.

Villages with most of facilities: Manjanaickenpatti Idayapatti, Balavuduthi, Keelappaguthy.

Villages without Amenities (Education): None..

Scheduled Castes: Out of the total population of 82870 persons, 15335 persons (18.5%) belong to Scheduled Castes.
The villages having less than 10% SC population are None..
The villages having more than 50% SC population are None.
Sex ratio of Scheduled Caste population is 501.

Scheduled Castes Literates and Illiterates by Sex:

	Persons	Males	Females
Literate	6,859	4,225	2,634
Illiterate	8,476	3,424	5,052
Literacy rate	51.7	64.5	39.2
Graduate	116	102	14

Scheduled Castes (Dominant):
Paraiyan etc., Chakkiliyan, Pallan, Madari Kuravan etc.

For their cultural identity please see Appendix-I

Villages without Scheduled Castes: There is 0 village without any scheduled caste population.

Scheduled Tribes: Out of the total population of 82870 persons, 85 persons (0.1%) belong to Scheduled Tribes.
The villages having less than 10% ST population are Pappayambadi, Vadambadi, Manjanaickenpatti Pannapatty, Vellapatty, Keeranur, Thennelai Varavanai, Malapugathi, Kalayapatty, Devarmalai Adanur, Sembianatham, Idayapatti, Idayapatti Balavuduthi, Mullipadi, Mavathur, Keelappaguthy Valvarmangalam.
The villages having more than 50% ST population are None.
Sex ratio of Scheduled tribe population is 471.

Scheduled Tribes Literates and Illiterates by Sex:

	Persons	Males	Females
Literate	50	33	17
Illiterate	35	12	23
Literacy rate	63.3	80.5	44.7
Graduate	0	0	0

Scheduled Tribes (Dominant):
Uraly, Kattunayakan, Aranadan

For their cultural identity please see Appendix-II

Villages without Scheduled Tribes: There are 17 villages without any scheduled tribe population.

Literates and Illiterates by Sex (Total Population):

	Persons	Males	Females
Literate	40,823	25,191	15,632
Illiterate	42,047	16,141	25,906
Literacy rate	56	70	43
Graduate	794	609	185

Agriculture: ***Distribution of villages according to land use:***
Out of 20 villages, Total area (in hectare) is 42702, out of that 38.58 percent is cultivable and 40.91 percent of the cultivable area is irrigated.

Sources of Irrigation (Hectares): Government Canal 91.66, Private Canal 0, Well without Electricity 665.11, Well with Electricity 5664.84, Tubewell without Electricity 54.6, Tubewell with Electricity 84.55, Tank 179.46, River 0, Lake 0, Waterfall 0, Others 0.

Villages with population of 5000 to 9999:
Sembianatham , D.Edayapatti(West)
D.Edayapatti (East), Palaviduthi , Mavathur
Keelappaguthi.

Villages with population of 10000 and above: None

Distribution of Workers:

	Persons	Males	Females	WPR
Cultivators	19,188	11,395	7,793	37.72
Agricultural Labour	24,954	9,187	15,767	49.06
Household Industry	627	377	250	1.23
Other Workers	6,096	4,821	1,275	11.98
Main Workers	46,013	24,727	21,286	90.46
Marginal Workers	4,852	1,053	3,799	9.54
Total Workers	50,865	25,780	25,085	

Religion: Major Religious Communities:

	Persons	Males	Females	Sex Ratio
Hindu (95.44%)	79,091	39,433	39,658	1,006
Muslim (2.29%)	1,896	954	942	987
Christian (2.1%)	1,741	868	873	1,006
Sikh (0.01%)	8	5	3	600
Buddhists (0.01%)	6	3	3	1,000
Jain (0%)	1	1	-	-

Agewise Data:

	Persons	Males	Females	Sex Ratio
All ages	82,870	41,332	41,538	1005
0-14	23,587	12,226	11,361	929
15-44	37,866	18,555	19,311	1041
45-79	20,517	10,101	10,416	1031
80+	744	346	398	1150
Age not stated	156	104	52	500

Languages (Dominant):
Tamil, Telugu, Kannada, Marathi, Malayalam

Disabled Population:

	Persons	Males	Females	%
Total Disabled	1,301	721	580	
In Seeing	513	259	254	39.43
In Speech	201	110	91	15.45
In Hearing	74	32	42	5.69
In Movement	397	249	148	30.51
Mentally	116	71	45	8.92

KADAYAM

Kadayam C.D. Block lies in the south-western part of Tirunelveli district. It is a part of Alangulam and Ambasamudram taluks. The Block is located at a distance of NA kms. from district headquarters (Tirunelveli). There are 21 villages in the block with the total popul ation of 88,269 persons. Area of the C.D. Block is 181. 28 sq. kms. It is bounded in the north by CD Block Keela pavoor, in the south and west by CD Block Ambasamudram, and in the east by CD Block Pappakudi. CD Block Kadayam falls in taluk Alangulam by 06 villages, and in taluk Ambasamudram by 15 villages.

Communications:

Roadways : S.H.-40: Direction- Tenkasi to Ambasamudram, Nearest Villages- Kadavam Perum Pathu-I, Keelakadayam, Pattalpudur, Therkukadayam, Veerasamut hram, Pappankulam, Kizha Ambur, Mela Ambur.

Local Stream: Nearest Villages- Sivasailam, Pappankulam, Adaichari, Kizha Ambur, Mela Ambur.

Railway Station: Veerasamuthram.

Annual Rainfall: Average Rainfall 879 mm.

Ground Water: Availability of the ground water in the Basin is 43.47 MCM and the utilization is 15.44 MCM. It belongs to Safe category. Depth to water level varies from 0 to 5 meter below the ground. Most of the wells go down in summer months, according to the Ground Water Estimation Committee.

Forest and Reserved Forest: (Papanasam RF)- Nearest Village s- Kadavam Perum Pathu-I, Meela Kadayam, Govindap peri, Dharmapuramadam, Sivasailam, Mela Ambur.

Natural Division: NA

Administration

Revenue **Division:** Tenkasi, Cheranmadevi. Parliamentary Constituency: 38 Tirunelveli. District: Tirunelveli.

Taluk: Alangulam, Ambasamudram. Assembly Constituency: 223 Alangulam. Gram Panchayat: 23.

Villages: 21 **Inhabited:** 20 **Uninhabited:** 1

Ranking	District	State	National
Area	14	308	4520
Population	9	191	3842
Sex Ratio	5	18	199
Child Sex Ratio	7	96	1961
Literacy Rate	8	60	771
Density	8	136	2272
Work Participation Rate	2	60	1347

Gram Panchayats:

Adaichani, Anajaperumalnadanoor, Anjankatalai, Dharmapuramadam, Govindaperi, kadayam , Kadayam Perumpathu, Kila Ambur, Kilakadayam, Madathoor, Manthiyoor, Mela Ambur, Mudaliarpatti, Pappankulam, Pottalpudur, Ravanasamudram, Servaikaranpatti, Sivasailam, Therkukadayam , Therkumadathur, Thirumalaiappapuram, Thuppakudi, Vengadampatti, Virasamudram.

Amenities:

Education: Primary School in 20 villages, Middle school in 10 villages, Matriculation or Secondary School in 5 villages, namely Venkadampatti, Kadavam Perum Pathu-I, Therkukadayam, Sivasailam, Mela Ambur.

Higher Secondary or Pre University Courses or Intermediate or Junior College in 2 villages of the CD Block,, namely Venkadampatti, Therkukadayam.

College in 1 village, Adult Literacy Center in 0 village., College is in village, namely Dharmapuramadam.

Medical: Hospital in 1 village, Dispensary in 4 villages, Health Center in 6 villages, Sub Center in 5 villages, Maternity and Child Welfare Center in 4 villages, Community health workers in 16 villages.

The Villages having Hospital or Dispensary or Health Center are Anitha Perumal Nadannur, Inthan Kattalai, Keelakadayam, Pattalpudur, Therkukadayam, Dharmapuramadam, Pappankulam.

Drinking Water: Tap water in 20 villages, Tank water in 5 villages, Well water in 13 villages, Tubewell in 6 villages and more than one source in 20 villages.

Bank: Banking facility in 6 villages, namely, Venkadampatti, Kadavam Perum Pathu-I, Keelakadayam Pattalpudur, Therkukadayam, Ravanasamuthiram.

Credit Society in 6 villages Agricultural Credit Society in 3 Non-Agricultural Credit Society in 2 villages.

Others: Power supply in 20 villages, Cinema hall in 1 village, sport club in 1 village, Stadium or Auditorium or Community Hall in 1 village, Post Office in 19 villages.

There are 18 villages having bus facilities.

Villages with most of facilities: Venkadampatti Kadavam Perum Pathu-I, Keelakadayam, Pattalpudur Therkukadayam, Ravanasamuthiram.

Villages without Amenities (Education): None..

Scheduled Castes: Out of the total population of 88269 persons, 13783 persons (15.61%) belong to Scheduled Castes. The villages having less than 10% SC population are Venkadampatti, Anitha Perumal Nadannur Roovoothaperi, Inthan Kattalai

Kadavam Perum Pathu-I, Therkkumadathur, Mela Ambur.
The villages having more than 50% SC population are None.

Sex ratio of Scheduled Caste population is 518.

Scheduled Castes Literates and Illiterates by Sex:

	Persons	Males	Females
Literate	7,235	4,156	3,079
Illiterate	6,548	2,487	4,061
Literacy rate	60.4	72.4	49.3
Graduate	93	66	27

Scheduled Castes (Dominant):

Pallan, Paraiyan etc., Arunthathiyar, Adi Dravida Chakkiliyan

For their cultural identity please see Appendix-I

Villages without Scheduled Castes: There are 2 villages without any scheduled caste population.

Scheduled Tribes: Out of the total population of 88269 persons, 85 persons (0.1%) belong to Scheduled Tribes.
The villages having less than 10% ST population are Venkadampatti, Madathoor, Anitha Perumal Nadannur Thuppakuddy, Roovoothaperi, Inthan Kattalai Kadavam Perum Pathu-I, Keelakadayam, Therkkumadathur Pattalpudur, Therkukadayam, Ravanasamuthiram Govindapperi, Dharmapuramadam, Sivasailam Veerasamuthram, Pappankulam, Adaichari, Kizha Ambur Mela Ambur.

The villages having more than 50% ST population are None.

Sex ratio of Scheduled tribe population is 482.

Scheduled Tribes Literates and Illiterates by Sex:

	Persons	Males	Females
Literate	38	25	13
Illiterate	47	19	28
Literacy rate	55.1	67.6	40.6
Graduate	1	1	0

Scheduled Tribes (Dominant):

Sholaga, Kattunayakan, Kaniyan etc., Malai Arayan

For their cultural identity please see Appendix-II

Villages without Scheduled Tribes: There are 16 villages without any scheduled tribe population.

Literates and Illiterates by Sex (Total Population):

	Persons	Males	Females
Literate	57,153	30,977	26,176
Illiterate	31,116	11,676	19,440
Literacy rate	74	83	65
Graduate	1,383	937	446

Agriculture: ***Distribution of villages according to land use:*** Out of 21 villages, Total area (in hectare) is 18128.26, out of that 38.19 percent is cultivable and 70.81 percent of the cultivable area is irrigated.

Sources of Irrigation (Hectares): Government Canal 1286.63, Private Canal 0, Well without Electricity 528.72, Well with Electricity 1222.34, Tubewell without Electricity 2, Tubewell with Electricity 104.05, Tank 1745.22, River 11.34, Lake 0, Waterfall 0, Others 2.

Villages with population of 5000 to 9999:
Vengadampatti, Kadayam Perumpattu, Potta Pudur(I) Therku Kadayam , Ravanasamudram , Kila Ambur.

Villages with population of 10000 and above:
Kilakadayam.

Distribution of Workers:

	Persons	Males	Females	WPR
Cultivators	4,472	3,774	698	9.4
Agricultural Labour	11,882	8,295	3,587	25.0
Household Industry	17,867	921	16,946	37.6
Other Workers	13,201	10,916	2,285	27.8
Main Workers	39,180	19,358	19,822	82.6
Marginal Workers	8,242	4,548	3,694	17.3
Total Workers	47,422	23,906	23,516	

Religion: Major Religious Communities:

	Persons	Males	Females	Sex Ratio
Hindu (77.01%)	67,979	33,319	34,660	1,040
Muslim (11.8%)	10,420	4,549	5,871	1,291
Christian (11.14%)	9,833	4,764	5,069	1,064
Sikh (0%)	2	2	-	-
Buddhists (0%)	-	-	-	-
Jain (0%)	1	1	-	-

Agewise Data:

	Persons	Males	Females	Sex Ratio
All ages	88,269	42,653	45,616	106
0-14	24,965	12,819	12,146	94
15-44	41,440	19,341	22,099	114
45-79	20,834	10,042	10,792	107
80+	898	371	527	142
Age not stated	132	80	52	65

Languages (Dominant):
Tamil, Telugu, Malayalam, Urdu, Kannada

Disabled Population:

	Persons	Males	Females	%
Total Disabled	2,618	1,246	1,372	
In Seeing	1,405	552	853	53.6
In Speech	320	190	130	12.2
In Hearing	101	41	60	3.8
In Movement	628	366	262	23.9
Mentally	164	97	67	6.2

KADAYAMPATTI

Kadaiyampatti C.D. Block lies in the northern part of Salem district. It is a part of Omalur taluk. The Block is located at a distance of 32 kms. from district headquarters (Salem). There are 30 villages in the block with the total population of

108,017 persons. Area of the C.D. Block is 317.09 sq. kms. It is bounded in the north by district Dharmapuri, in the south by C.D. Blocks Yercaud and Omalur, in the east by district Dharmapuri and CD Block Yercaud, and in the west by CD Block Mecheri.

Communications:

Roadways : N.H.-7: Direction- Omalur to Dharmapuri, Nearest Villages- Dasasamudram, Poosaripatty, Sekkarappatty, Dharapuram, Deevathippatti, Pannapatti, Naduppatty, Elathur.

Railway Station: Kookuttapatty, Marakottai, Sekkarappatty, Semmandappatti, Kanavaipudur, Danishpet.

Annual Rainfall: Average Rainfall 540 mm.

Ground Water: Availability of the ground water in the Basin is 4291.40 H.A.M. and the utilization is 4161.55 H.A.M. It belongs to Safe category. Depth to water level varies from 2 to 10 meter below the ground. Most of the wells go down in summer months, according to the Ground Water Estimation Committee.

Forest and Reserved Forest: (Bommiyampatti RF)- Nearest Villages- Kadayampatty South, Pelappalli Kombai, Bommiyampatti (RF). (Manakondamalai)- Nearest Villages- Manakondanmalai (RF), Gundukkal, Kadayampatty South, Veppillai, Sekkarappatty, Naduppatty, Elathur. (Elathur)- Nearest Villages- Gundukkal, Elathur (RF), Mookanur, Elathur. (Gundukkal)- Nearest Villages- Gundukkal, Kongupatty North, Sekkarappatty, Ramanamimalai (RF). (Ramasamimalai)- Nearest Village- Kongupatty North. (Kanavaipudur)- Nearest Villages- Kamavaipudhr (RF), Kanavaipudur. (Lokkur)- Nearest Villages- Veppillai, Lokkur, Kanavaipudur. (Yerimalai)- Nearest Villages- Yerimalai (RF), K.N. Pudur, Kanavaipudur. (Karuvattuparai)- Nearest Villages- Danishpet, Karuvattuperai, Kookuttapatty.

Natural Division: Kongu Nadu.

Administration

Revenue **Division:** Mettur. Parliamentary Constituency: 15 Salem. District: Salem. Taluk: Omalur. Assembly Constituency: 84 Omalur. Gram Panchayat: 17.

Villages: 30 **Inhabited:** 24 **Uninhabited:** 6

Ranking	District	State	National
Area	5	156	2603
Population	4	102	3210
Sex Ratio	13	376	5540
Child Sex Ratio	14	377	6284
Literacy Rate	12	357	3511
Density	19	238	3185
Work Participation Rate	13	171	2570

Gram Panchayats:

Bommiampatty, Deevattipatti, Denispet, Dharapuram, Gundukkal, Kanavaipudur, Kanjanaickenpatty, Karuvalli, Kongupatty, Kookuttapatty, Mookanur, Naduppatty, Pannapatty, Poosaripatty, Semmandapatty, Umblicampatty, Veppilai, .

Amenities:

Education: Primary School in 20 villages, Middle school in 16 villages, Matriculation or Secondary School in 10 villages, namely Kanjanaickanpatty, K.N.Pudur, Kongupatty North, Kanavaipudur, Danishpet, Dharapuram, Deevathippatti, Pannapatti, Naduppatty, Semmandappatti.

Higher Secondary or Pre University Courses or Intermediate or Junior College in 4 villages of the CD Block,, namely K.N.Pudur, Kanavaipudur, Dharapuram, Naduppatty.

College in 0 village, Adult Literacy Center in 0 village.

Medical: Hospital in 2 villages, Dispensary in 1 village, Health Center in 3 villages, Sub Center in 12 villages, Maternity and Child Welfare Center in 6 villages, Community health workers in 0 village.

The Villages having Hospital or Dispensary or Health Center are Danishpet, Poosaripatty, Deevathippatti.

Drinking Water: Tap water in 24 villages, Tank water in 0 villages, Well water in 24 villages, Tubewell in 24 villages and more than one source in 24 villages.

Bank: Banking facility in 3 villages, namely, Kadayampatty South, Marakottai, Deevathippatti.

Credit Society in 16 villages Agricultural Credit Society in 16 Non-Agricultural Credit Society in 10 villages.

Others: Power supply in 23 villages, Cinema hall in 1 village, sport club in 0 village, Stadium or Auditorium or Community Hall in 0 village, Post Office in 17 villages.

There are 20 villages having bus facilities.

Villages with most of facilities: Kadayampatty South Marakottai, Deevathippatti.

Villages without amenities (Education):

Yerimalai (Rf), Lokkur, Karuvattuperai, Pelappalli Kombai..

Scheduled Castes: Out of the total population of 108017 persons, 20042 persons (18.55%) belong to Scheduled Castes.

The villages having less than 10% SC population are Yerimalai (Rf), Marakottai, Veppillai, Poosaripatty Karuvattuperai , Sekkarappatty, Dharapuram Pelappalli Kombai.

The villages having more than 50% SC population are None.

Sex ratio of Scheduled Caste population is 470.

Scheduled Castes Literates and Illiterates by Sex:

	Persons	Males	Females
Literate	8,583	5,594	2,989
Illiterate	11,459	5,032	6,427

Literacy rate	50.6	62.9	37.0
Graduate	190	164	26

Scheduled Castes (Dominant):

Adi Dravida, Arunthathiyar, Paraiyan etc., Pallan Kuravan etc.

For their cultural identity please see Appendix-I

Villages without Scheduled Castes: There are 6 villages without any scheduled caste population.

Scheduled Tribes: Out of the total population of 108017 persons, 4365 persons (4.04%) belong to Scheduled Tribes. The villages having less than 10% ST population are Yerimalai (Rf), Gundukkal, Kanjanaickanpatty Kadayampatty South, Marakottai, Veppillai, K.N.Pudur Kongupatty North, Dasasamudram, Danishpet Poosaripatty, Karuvattuperai , Mookanur, Dharapuram Deevathippatti, Pannapatti, Naduppatty, Elathur Semmandappatti.

The villages having more than 50% ST population are None.

Sex ratio of Scheduled tribe population is 474.

Scheduled Tribes Literates and Illiterates by Sex:

	Persons	Males	Females
Literate	1,344	875	469
Illiterate	3,021	1,420	1,601
Literacy rate	35.2	44.0	25.6
Graduate	16	9	7

Scheduled Tribes (Dominant):

Malayali, Kurumans, Irular, Kattunayakan Generic Tribes etc.

For their cultural identity please see Appendix-II

Villages without Scheduled Tribes: There are 14 villages without any scheduled tribe population.

Literates and Illiterates by Sex (Total Population):

	Persons	Males	Females
Literate	52,723	33,357	19,366
Illiterate	55,294	24,017	31,277
Literacy rate	56	67	43
Graduate	1,345	1,036	309

Agriculture: ***Distribution of villages according to land use:*** Out of 30 villages, Total area (in hectare) is 31709.94, out of that 48.73 percent is cultivable and 23.01 percent of the cultivable area is irrigated.

Sources of Irrigation (Hectares): Government Canal 0, Private Canal 0, Well without Electricity 0, Well with Electricity 3401.46, Tubewell without Electricity 0, Tubewell with Electricity 154.49, Tank 0, River 0, Lake 0, Waterfall 0, Others 0.

Villages with population of 5000 to 9999:

Kodunaickenpatty pudur, Kanavoipudur, Gundikkal Kongupatti, Danishpet, Marakkottai, Pannapatti Semmandapatti.

Villages with population of 10000 and above:

Kanjanayachanpatti.

Distribution of Workers:

	Persons	Males	Females	WPR
Cultivators	16,092	10,638	5,454	30.49
Agricultural Labour	21,489	10,877	10,612	40.72
Household Industry	2,041	1,209	832	3.87
Other Workers	13,151	10,276	2,875	24.92
Main Workers	43,702	29,490	14,212	82.81
Marginal Workers	9,071	3,510	5,561	17.19
Total Workers	52,773	33,000	19,773	

Religion: Major Religious Communities:

	Persons	Males	Females	Sex Ratio
Hindu (97.97%)	105,823	56,263	49,560	881
Muslim (0.65%)	698	358	340	950
Christian (1.26%)	1,361	688	673	978
Sikh (0.01%)	14	9	5	556
Buddhists (0%)	-	-	-	-
Jain (0%)	5	3	2	667

Agewise Data:

	Persons	Males	Females	Sex Ratio
All ages	108,017	57,374	50,643	883
0-14	31,583	17,920	13,663	762
15-44	50,790	26,119	24,671	945
45-79	23,541	12,202	11,339	929
80+	1,424	744	680	914
Age not stated	679	389	290	746

Languages (Dominant):

Tamil, Telugu, Kannada, Hindi, Urdu

Disabled Population:

	Persons	Males	Females	%
Total Disabled	1,826	1,059	767	
In Seeing	817	432	385	44.74
In Speech	239	143	96	13.09
In Hearing	93	46	47	5.09
In Movement	476	321	155	26.07
Mentally	201	117	84	11.01

KADAYANALLUR

Kadaiyanallur C.D. Block lies in the north-western part of Tirunelveli district. It is a part of Veerakeralamput hur, Tenkasi and Shenkottai taluks. The Block is located at a distance of 72 kms. from district headquarters (Tirunelveli). There are 16 villages in the block with the total population of 65,321 persons. Area of the C. D. Block is 206.69 sq. kms. It is bounded in the north by CD Blocks Vasudevanallur, Sankarankoil and Melaneelithanallur, in the south by CD Blocks Shenkottai, Tenkasi and Keelapavoor, in the east by CD Block Alangulam, and it has common boundary with the state of Kerala on west.

CD Block Kadaiyanallur falls in taluks Veerakeralamputhur by 02, Tenkasi by 13, and Shenkottai by 01 villages.

Communications:

Roadways : N.H.-208: Direction- Elanji to Rajapalayam, Nearest Villages- Chokkampatti, Kambaneri Puthukudi, Nainaragaram, Idaikal, Kodikkurichi.

Railway Station: Boganallur.

Annual Rainfall: Average Rainfall 879 mm.

Ground Water: Availability of the ground water in the Basin is 51.45 MCM and the utilization is 22.29 MCM. It belongs to Safe category. Depth to water level varies from 2 to 10 meter below the ground. Most of the wells go down in summer months, according to the Ground Water Estimation Committee.

Forest and Reserved Forest: (Kadayanallur Upper Slopes RF)- Nearest Villages- Kandayanallur Upper Slopes, Kambaneri Puthukudi, Idaikal. (Krishnapuram)- Nearest Villages- Krishnapuram, Chokkampatti. (Vairavaniku lam)- Nearest Village- Vairavankulam. (Puliyarai)- Nearest Villages- Puliyarai RF.

Natural Division: NA

Administration

Revenue **Division:** Tenkasi, Tirunelveli. Parliamentary Constituency: 37 Tenkasi. District: Tirunelveli. Taluk: Veerakeralamputhur, Tenkasi, Shenkottai. Assembly Consti tuency: 222 Tenkasi, 221 Kadayanallur. Gram Panchayat: 16.

Border Villages- (Kerala)- Nearest Villages- Krishnapuram, Vairavankulam, Kandayanallur , Upper Slopes.

Villages: 16 **Inhabited:** 13 **Uninhabited:** 3

Ranking	District	State	National
Area	13	274	4064
Population	13	314	4676
Sex Ratio	14	55	478
Child Sex Ratio	5	81	1586
Literacy Rate	17	223	2041
Density	7	135	3381
Work Participation Rate	6	203	1343

Gram Panchayats:

Anaikulam, Boganallur, Chokkampatti, Idaikal, Kambaneri , Kasidarnam, Kasidarrnam, Kodilkuruchi, Kulayaneri, Nainaragaram, Neduvayal, Poigai, Pudukudi, Punnaiahpuram, Thirukudapuram, Urmelalagiyan, Velayudapuram.

Amenities:

Education: Primary School in 13 villages, Middle school in 11 villages, Matriculation or Secondary School in 5 villages, namely Anailulam, Kambaneri Puthukudi, Ormellagiyan, Idaikal, Neduvayal.

Higher Secondary or Pre University Courses or Intermediate or Junior College in 1 village of the CD Block,, namely Idaikal.

College in 1 village, Adult Literacy Center in 1 village., College is in village, namely Kodikkurichi.

Medical: Hospital in 3 villages, Dispensary in 0 village, Health Center in 4 villages, Sub Center in 5 villages, Maternity and Child Welfare Center in 2 villages, Community health workers in 11 villages.

The Villages having Hospital or Dispensary or Health Center are Kulaiyaneri, Chokkampatti, Nainaragaram.

Drinking Water: Tap water in 13 villages, Tank water in 1 villages, Well water in 9 villages, Tubewell in 0 village and more than one source in 12 villages.

Bank: Banking facility in 4 villages, namely, Kulaiyaneri, Chokkampatti, Ormellagiyan, Idaikal.

Credit Society in 1 village Agricultural Credit Society in 1 Non-Agricultural Credit Society in 0 village.

Others: Power supply in 13 villages, Cinema hall in 1 village, sport club in 0 village, Stadium or Auditorium or Community Hall in 0 village, Post Office in 11 villages.

There are 13 villages having bus facilities.

Villages with most of facilities: Kulaiyaneri Chokkampatti, Ormellagiyan, Idaikal.

Villages without Amenities (Education): None..

Scheduled Castes: Out of the total population of 65321 persons, 17663 persons (27.04%) belong to Scheduled Castes.

The villages having less than 10% SC population are None..

The villages having more than 50% SC population are None.

Sex ratio of Scheduled Caste population is 505.

Scheduled Castes Literates and Illiterates by Sex:

	Persons	Males	Females
Literate	8,898	5,329	3,569
Illiterate	8,765	3,412	5,353
Literacy rate	57.6	70.1	45.5
Graduate	240	161	79

Scheduled Castes (Dominant):

Pallan, Paraiyan etc., Chakkiliyan, Arunthathiyar Kuravan etc.

For their cultural identity please see Appendix-I

Villages without Scheduled Castes: There are 3 villages without any scheduled caste population.

Scheduled Tribes: Out of the total population of 65321 persons, 47 persons (0.07%) belong to Scheduled Tribes.

The villages having less than 10% ST population are Kulaiyaneri, Anailulam, Chokkampatti, Boganallur Kambaneri Puthukudi, Kangasabapathperi, Tenkasi Ormellagiyan, Nainaragaram, Idaikal, Kasitharamam Kodikkurichi, Neduvayal.

The villages having more than 50% ST population are None.

Sex ratio of Scheduled tribe population is 511.

Scheduled Tribes Literates and Illiterates by Sex:

	Persons	Males	Females
Literate	6	4	2
Illiterate	41	19	22
Literacy rate	15.4	21.1	10.0
Graduate	0	0	0

Scheduled Tribes (Dominant):

Kattunayakan

For their cultural identity please see Appendix-II

Villages without Scheduled Tribes: There are 14 villages without any scheduled tribe population.

Literates and Illiterates by Sex (Total Population):

	Persons	Males	Females
Literate	36,896	21,695	15,201
Illiterate	28,425	10,469	17,956
Literacy rate	64	77	52
Graduate	845	558	287

Agriculture: ***Distribution of villages according to land use:*** Out of 16 villages, Total area (in hectare) is 20669, out of that 31.28 percent is cultivable and 67.09 percent of the cultivable area is irrigated.

Sources of Irrigation (Hectares): Government Canal 65.06, Private Canal 0, Well without Electricity 222, Well with Electricity 1972.09, Tubewell without Electricity 111.22, Tubewell with Electricity 8.55, Tank 1958.06, River 0, Lake 0, Waterfall 0, Others 0.

Villages with population of 5000 to 9999:

Kambaneri Pudukudi , Nainaragaram.

Villages with population of 10000 and above:

Chockampatti.

Distribution of Workers:

	Persons	Males	Females	WPR
Cultivators	6,309	4,313	1,996	17.99
Agricultural Labour	15,526	8,423	7,103	44.28
Household Industry	6,067	455	5,612	17.3
Other Workers	7,162	5,583	1,579	20.43
Main Workers	30,772	17,085	13,687	87.76
Marginal Workers	4,292	1,689	2,603	12.24
Total Workers	35,064	18,774	16,290	

Religion: Major Religious Communities:

	Persons	Males	Females	Sex Ratio
Hindu (92.91%)	60,692	29,987	30,705	1,024
Muslim (4.37%)	2,853	1,295	1,558	1,203
Christian (2.67%)	1,747	868	879	1,013
Sikh (0%)	-	-	-	-
Buddhists (0%)	-	-	-	-
Jain (0%)	3	3	-	-

Agewise Data:

	Persons	Males	Females	Sex Ratio
All ages	65,321	32,164	33,157	1031
0-14	18,149	9,289	8,860	954
15-44	31,710	15,473	16,237	1049
45-79	14,702	7,065	7,637	1081
80+	570	230	340	1478
Age not stated	190	107	83	776

Languages (Dominant):

Tamil, Telugu, Malayalam, Urdu, Hindi

Disabled Population:

	Persons	Males	Females	%
Total Disabled	1,989	819	1,170	
In Seeing	1,318	444	874	66.26
In Speech	134	75	59	6.74
In Hearing	57	25	32	2.87
In Movement	354	206	148	17.8
Mentally	126	69	57	6.33

KALAKKAD

Kalakkadu C.D. Block lies in the south-western part of Tirunelveli district. It is a part of Nanguneri taluk. The Block is located at a distance of 40 kms. from district headquarters (Tirunelveli). There are 27 villag es in the block with the total population of 47,680 persons. Area of the C.D. Block is 408.14 sq. kms. It is bounded in the north by taluks Ambasamudram and Palayamkottai, in the south by CD Block Valliyoor and district Kanniyakumari, in the east by CD Block Nanguneri, and in the west by district Kanniyakumari.

Communications:

Roadways : Information not Available.

River: Panchiyar Nadi- Nearest Villages- Melkarai, Thenneer-kulam, Singikulam New, Singikulam (Old), Keelakaduvetti, Devanallur, Padmaneri, Vadakarai, Keelakaruvelankulam. Nambiyur Nadi- Nearest Villages- Shengalakurchi, N.T.Pattayam.

Annual Rainfall: Average Rainfall 879 mm.

Ground Water: Availability of the ground water in the Basin is 41.36 MCM and the utilization is 18.10 MCM. It belongs to Safe category. Depth to water level varies from 2 to 5 meter below the ground. Most of the wells go down in summer months, according to the Ground Water Estimation Committee.

Forest and Reserved Forest: (Kalakadu RF)- Nearest Villages- Idayankulam, Vadakarai, Kalakadu RF, Seevalaperi, Kovilammalpuram, Shengalakurchi, Padmaneri.

Natural Division: NA

Administration

Revenue **Division:** Cherammadevi. Parliamentary Cons.: 38 Tirunelveli. District: Tirunelveli. Taluk: Nanguneri. Assem-bly Constituency: 227 Nanguneri. Gram Panchayat: 17.

Villages: 27 **Inhabited:** 27 **Uninhabited:** 0

Ranking	District	State	National
Area	7	67	1882
Population	16	365	5399
Sex Ratio	4	16	167
Child Sex Ratio	18	254	4195
Literacy Rate	4	23	346
Density	16	280	5996
Work Participation Rate	18	375	3048

Gram Panchayats:
Devanallur, Idaiyankulam, Kadamboduvalvu, Kallikulam, Keelakaduvetti, Keelakaruvelankulam, Kovilammalpuram, Malayadipudur , Padalaiyarkulam, Padmaneri , Puliyoorkurichi , Seevalaperi, Shenkalakuruchi, Singikulam , Soorankudi, Thavlavaipuram, Vadukachimathil , Vadukatchimathil , .

Amenities:

Education: Primary School in 22 villages, Middle school in 11 villages, Matriculation or Secondary School in 4 villages, namely Kallikulam, Idayankulam, Padmaneri, Puliyurkuruchi.

Higher Secondary or Pre University Courses or Intermediate or Junior College in 0 village of the CD Block, College in 0 village, Adult Literacy Center in 0 village.

Medical: Hospital in 1 village, Dispensary in 3 villages, Health Center in 3 villages, Sub Center in 12 villages, Maternity and Child Welfare Center in 2 villages, Community health workers in 22 villages.

The Villages having Hospital or Dispensary or Health Center are Keelakaruvelankulam, Padaleyarkulam, Seevalaperi, Shengalakurchi, Puliyurkuruchi.

Drinking Water: Tap water in 27 villages, Tank water in 1 villages, Well water in 19 villages, Tubewell in 4 villages and more than one source in 26 villages.

Bank: Banking facility in 4 villages, namely, Keelakaduvetti, Idayankulam, Vadakarai Puliyurkuruchi.

Credit Society in 4 villages Agricultural Credit Society in 3 Non-Agricultural Credit Society in 0 village.

Others: Power supply in 27 villages, Cinema hall in 0 village, sport club in 0 village, Stadium or Auditorium or Community Hall in 0 village, Post Office in 21 villages.

There are 20 villages having bus facilities.

Villages with most of facilities: Keelakaduvetti Idayankulam, Vadakarai, Puliyurkuruchi.

Villages without amenities (Education):
Inam Idaiyankulam, Kalakadu R.F., Seevalaperi, Alankulam+F2, Melamaliyaneri..

Scheduled Castes: Out of the total population of 47680 persons, 6637 persons (13.92%) belong to Scheduled Castes.

The villages having less than 10% SC population are Melkarai, Kallikulam, Keelakaduvetti Inam Idaiyankulam, Devanallur, Kalakadu R.F. Seevalaperi, Kadambodubalbu, Surankudi, Alankulam+F2 Melamaliyaneri, Malaiyadipudur.

The villages having more than 50% SC population are None.

Sex ratio of Scheduled Caste population is 528.

Scheduled Castes Literates and Illiterates by Sex:

	Persons	Males	Females
Literate	4,326	2,289	2,037
Illiterate	2,311	846	1,465
Literacy rate	74.8	85.3	65.7
Graduate	87	50	37

Scheduled Castes (Dominant):
Paraiyan etc., Adi Dravida, Pallan, Valluvan Kuravan etc.

For their cultural identity please see Appendix-I

Villages without Scheduled Castes: There is 1 village without any scheduled caste population.

Scheduled Tribes: Out of the total population of 47680 persons, 82 persons (0.17%) belong to Scheduled Tribes.

The villages having less than 10% ST population are Melkarai, Thenneerkulam, Singikulam New Singikulam (Old), Kallikulam, Keelakaduvetti Inam Idaiyankulam, Devanallur, Idayankulam Padmaneri, Vadakarai, Kalakadu R.F. Keelakaruvelankulam, Padaleyarkulam, Seevalaperi Kovilammalpuram, Uchikulam, Kadambodubalbu Surankudi, Alankulam+F2, Vadukachimathil Melamaliyaneri, Malaiyadipudur, Shengalakurchi N.T.Pattayam, Puliyurkuruchi, Madamalankulam.

The villages having more than 50% ST population are None.

Sex ratio of Scheduled tribe population is 463.

Scheduled Tribes Literates and Illiterates by Sex:

	Persons	Males	Females
Literate	31	21	10
Illiterate	51	23	28
Literacy rate	49.2	61.8	34.5
Graduate	0	0	0

Scheduled Tribes (Dominant):
Kattunayakan, Uraly, Malai Pandaram

For their cultural identity please see Appendix-II

Villages without Scheduled Tribes: There are 23 villages without any scheduled tribe population.

Literates and Illiterates by Sex (Total Population):

	Persons	Males	Females
Literate	33,013	17,268	15,74[illegible]
Illiterate	14,667	5,693	8,974

Literacy rate	79	87	72
Graduate	758	459	299

Agriculture: ***Distribution of villages according to land use:*** Out of 27 villages, Total area (in hectare) is 40814.73, out of that 18.71 percent is cultivable and 62.67 percent of the cultivable area is irrigated.

Sources of Irrigation (Hectares): Government Canal 142.88, Private Canal 0, Well without Electricity 251.25, Well with Electricity 882.31, Tubewell without Electricity 1, Tubewell with Electricity 24.19, Tank 3485.06, River 0, Lake 0, Waterfall 0, Others 0.

Villages with population of 5000 to 9999: None

Villages with population of 10000 and above: None

Distribution of Workers:

	Persons	Males	Females	WPR
Cultivators	4,445	3,473	972	19.85
Agricultural Labour	8,196	5,049	3,147	36.6
Household Industry	4,365	376	3,989	19.49
Other Workers	5,387	3,551	1,836	24.06
Main Workers	19,047	11,034	8,013	85.06
Marginal Workers	3,346	1,415	1,931	14.94
Total Workers	22,393	12,449	9,944	

Religion: Major Religious Communities:

	Persons	Males	Females	Sex Ratio
Hindu (76.79%)	36,614	17,740	18,874	1,064
Muslim (1.14%)	543	226	317	1,403
Christian (22.01%)	10,494	4,983	5,511	1,106
Sikh (0%)	-	-	-	-
Buddhists (0%)	-	-	-	-
Jain (0.01%)	3	2	1	500

Agewise Data:

	Persons	Males	Females	Sex Ratio
All ages	47,680	22,961	24,719	1077
0-14	13,974	7,205	6,769	939
15-44	22,008	10,334	11,674	1130
45-79	11,050	5,135	5,915	1152
80+	465	195	270	1385
Age not stated	183	92	91	989

Languages (Dominant):

Tamil, Telugu, Malayalam, Kannada, Hindi

Disabled Population:

	Persons	Males	Females	%
Total Disabled	1,221	518	703	
In Seeing	795	278	517	65.11
In Speech	71	31	40	5.81
In Hearing	30	12	18	2.46
In Movement	256	156	100	20.97
Mentally	69	41	28	5.65

KALASAPAKKAM

Kalasapakkam C.D. taluk lies in the north-western part of Tiruvannamalai district. It is a part of Polur taluk. The taluk is located at a distance of 30 kms. from district headquarters (Tiruvannamalai). There are 51 villages in the block with the total population of 107,943 persons. Area of the C.D. Block is 307.41 sq. kms. It is bounded in the north by C.D. Blocks Polur and Chetpet, in the south by CD Blocks Pudupalayam and Thurinjapuram, in the east by C.D. Blocks Chetpet and Thurinjapuram, in the west by CD Blocks Jawadhu Hills and Pudupalayam.

Communications:

Roadways : S.H.-9: Direction- Tiruvannamalai to Polur, Nearest Villages- Solapuram, Poondi, Pullur, Kalasapakkam, Thenpallipet, Vinuvampattu, Kalur.

River: Cheyyar Nadi- Nearest Villages- Anaivadi, Kadaladi, Thenmathimangalam, Banampattu, Solapuram, Kilpotharai, Palankoil, Elathur, Priyampattu, Poondi, Pullur, Thenpallipet, Kalasapakkam, Vinuvampattu, Kalur.

Backwards Region Grants Fund: It receives Backward Region Grants.

Annual Rainfall: Average Rainfall 1019 mm.

Ground Water: Availability of the ground water in the Basin is (Information not available) H.A.M. and the utilization is 160.44 H.A.M. It belongs to Over Expoited category. Depth to water level varies from 2 to 5 meter below the ground. Most of the wells go down in summer months, according to the Ground Water Estimation Committee.

Forest and Reserved Forest: (Alliyalamang RF)- Nearest Villages- Padagam, Seetempattu, Padiamputtur, Alangaramangalam. (Mulakkadu)- Nearest Villages- Kidampalayam, Gangavram. (Parvathiamalai)- Nearest Villages- Vadakarai Nammiyandal, Seenandal, Arunagirimangalam, Gangalamagadevi, Nallanpillai Petral, Parvathiagaram RF , Mattavettu, Melpallur, Keelpallur, Kilthathiyapattu, Erumaiyanur, Kadaladi , Thenmathimangalam. (Pattarikadu)- Nearest Villages- Gangavram, Melsolankuppam, Veeralur.

Natural Division: Tondai Nadu.

Administration

Revenue **Division:** Tiruvannamalai. Parliamentary Constituency: 11 Tiruvannamalai, 12 Arani. District: Tiruvannamalai. Taluk: Polur. Assembly Constituency: 65 Kalasapakkam (ST), 66 Polur. Gram Panchayat: 45.

Villages: 51 **Inhabited:** 49 **Uninhabited:** 2

Ranking	District	State	National
Area	7	164	2704
Population	7	105	3216
Sex Ratio	12	231	1630
Child Sex Ratio	15	286	4820
Literacy Rate	14	269	2315
Density	7	178	3095
Work Participation Rate	8	156	1775

Gram Panchayats:
Adamangalam, Alangaramangalam, Anaivady, Aniyalai, Arunagirimangalam, Deverayanpalayam, Elathur, Eranamangalam, Ernamangalam, Gangalamahadevi, Gangavaram, Kadalady, Kalasapakkam, Kalur, Kambut, Kanthapalayam, Kappalur, Kettavarampalayam, Kidampalayam, Kil palur, Kilkuppam, Kilpotharai, Koilmathingalam, Ladavaram, Mattavettu, Mel palur, Mela Arani, Melsholankuppam, Melvilvarayanallur, Mottur, Padagam, Palan koil, Pathiyavady, Pattiyandal, Pillur, Poondi, Seethambattu, Sengaputheri, Sholavaram, Singaravadi, Siruvallur, Thenmathimangalam, Thenpalliput, Vanniyanur, Veeralur, Venkidampalayam.

Amenities:

Education: Primary School in 45 villages, Middle school in 18 villages, Matriculation or Secondary School in 7 villages, namely Kidampalayam, Melsolankuppam, Adamangalam, Melvilvarayanallur, Kadaladi, Kalasapakkam, Ladavaram.

Higher Secondary or Pre University Courses or Intermediate or Junior College in 4 villages of the CD Block,, namely Adamangalam, Melvilvarayanallur, Kadaladi, Kalasapakkam.

College in 1 village, Adult Literacy Center in 0 village., College is in village, namely Kidampalayam.

Medical: Hospital in 1 village, Dispensary in 1 village, Health Center in 7 villages, Sub Center in 7 villages, Maternity and Child Welfare Center in 12 villages, Community health workers in 47 villages.

The Villages having Hospital or Dispensary or Health Center are Davarayanpalayam, Adamangalam.

Drinking Water: Tap water in 49 villages, Tank water in 7 villages, Well water in 49 villages, Tubewell in 49 villages and more than one source in 49 villages.

Bank: Banking facility in 7 villages, namely, Davarayanpalayam, Adamangalam, Melvilvarayanallur Ernamangalam, Kadaladi, Kalasapakkam, Ladavaram.

Credit Society in 19 villages Agricultural Credit Society in 7 Non-Agricultural Credit Society in 17 villages.

Others: Power supply in 49 villages, Cinema hall in 2 villages, sport club in 0 village, Stadium or Auditorium or Community Hall in 0 village, Post Office in 32 villages.

There are 42 villages having bus facilities.

Villages with most of facilities: Melvilvarayanallur Ernamangalam, Kadaladi, Kalasapakkam, Ladavaram.

Villages without amenities (Education):
Kanthapalayam, Katcherimangalam, Priyampattu, Ganganallur..

Scheduled Castes: Out of the total population of 107943 persons, 26124 persons (24.2%) belong to Scheduled Castes.

The villages having less than 10% SC population are Kidampalayam, Melsolankuppam, Vanniyanur Katcherimangalam, Gangalamagadevi, Thenmathimangalam Priyampattu, Kalasapakkam, Kambattu, Ladavaram Alangaramangalam.

The villages having more than 50% SC population are Seenandal, Nallanpillai Petral, Vinuvampattu Seetempattu.

Sex ratio of Scheduled Caste population is 494.

Scheduled Castes Literates and Illiterates by Sex:

	Persons	Males	Females
Literate	12,851	7,827	5,024
Illiterate	13,273	5,384	7,889
Literacy rate	56.9	68.9	44.7
Graduate	194	154	40

Scheduled Castes (Dominant):
Adi Dravida, Arunthathiyar, Valluvan, Kuravan etc. Domban

For their cultural identity please see Appendix-I

Villages without Scheduled Castes: There are 7 villages without any scheduled caste population.

Scheduled Tribes: Out of the total population of 107943 persons, 839 persons (0.78%) belong to Scheduled Tribes.

The villages having less than 10% ST population are Kidampalayam, Gangavram, Melsolankuppam Vadakarai Nammiyandal, Seenandal, Davarayanpalayam Kanthapalayam, Adamangalam, Kettavarampalayam Sengaputtreri, Melarni, Anaivadi, Kappalur Vanniyanur, Katcherimangalam, Melvilvarayanallur Ernamangalam, Siruvanur, Arunagirimangalam Gangalamagadevi, Nallanpillai Petral, Veeralur Mattavettu, Melpallur, Keelpallur, Kadaladi Thenmathimangalam, Banampattu, Solapuram Kilpotharai, Thennnagaram, Palankoil, Elathur Poondi, Pullur, Kalasapakkam, Thenpallipet Vinuvampattu, Kalur, Pathiyavadi, Kambattu Aniayalai, Ladavaram, Ganganallur, Alangaramangalam Padagam, Seetempattu, Padiamputtur.

The villages having more than 50% ST population are None.

Sex ratio of Scheduled tribe population is 485.

Scheduled Tribes Literates and Illiterates by Sex:

	Persons	Males	Females
Literate	107	64	43
Illiterate	732	368	364
Literacy rate	15.6	18.6	12.7
Graduate	2	2	0

Scheduled Tribes (Dominant):
Irular, Malayali, Malakkuravan, Kattunayakan

For their cultural identity please see Appendix-II

Villages without Scheduled Tribes: There are 33 villages without any scheduled tribe population.

Literates and Illiterates by Sex (Total Population):

	Persons	Males	Females
Literate	59,573	36,220	23,353
Illiterate	48,370	18,041	30,329
Literacy rate	63	76	49
Graduate	1,232	990	242

Agriculture: ***Distribution of villages according to land use:*** Out of 51 villages, Total area (in hectare) is 30741.08, out of that 48.08 percent is cultivable and 45.01 percent of the cultivable area is irrigated.

Sources of Irrigation (Hectares): Government Canal 0, Private Canal 0, Well without Electricity 269.25, Well with Electricity 3600.43, Tubewell without Electricity 33.37, Tubewell with Electricity 0, Tank 760.87, River 71.82, Lake 1094.84, Waterfall 0, Others 45.98.

Villages with population of 5000 to 9999: Kettavarampalayam, Viralur, Kadalady.

Villages with population of 10000 and above: None

Distribution of Workers:

	Persons	Males	Females	WPR
Cultivators	21,669	13,839	7,830	38.44
Agricultural Labour	26,155	11,738	14,417	46.4
Household Industry	1,550	891	659	2.75
Other Workers	6,990	5,390	1,600	12.4
Main Workers	42,940	26,944	15,996	76.18
Marginal Workers	13,424	4,914	8,510	23.82
Total Workers	56,364	31,858	24,506	

Religion: Major Religious Communities:

	Persons	Males	Females	Sex Ratio
Hindu (97.56%)	105,314	52,950	52,364	989
Muslim (1.48%)	1,597	802	795	991
Christian (0.85%)	915	446	469	1,052
Sikh (0%)	2	2	-	-
Buddhists (0%)	3	2	1	500
Jain (0.07%)	75	42	33	786

Agewise Data:

	Persons	Males	Females	Sex Ratio
All ages	107,943	54,261	53,682	989
0-14	31,581	16,281	15,300	940
15-44	50,917	25,432	25,485	1002
45-79	24,142	11,862	12,280	1035
80+	1,059	553	506	915
Age not stated	244	133	111	835

Languages (Dominant): Tamil, Telugu, Urdu, Marathi, Kannada

Disabled Population:

	Persons	Males	Females	%
Total Disabled	2,353	1,430	923	
In Seeing	1,078	699	379	45.81
In Speech	267	136	131	11.35
In Hearing	125	65	60	5.31
In Movement	678	406	272	28.81
Mentally	205	124	81	8.71

KALAYARKOIL

Kalayarkoil C.D. Block lies in the central part of Sivaganga district. It is a part of Tirupathur, Karaikkudi and Sivaganga taluks. The Block is located at a distance of NA kms. from district headquarters (Sivaganga). There are 74 villages in the block with the total population of 94,282 persons. Area of the C.D. Block is 593.39 sq. kms. It is bounded in the north by CD Blocks Singampunari, Tirupathur and Kallal, in the south by CD Block Ilayangudi, in the east by CD Block Devakottai and district Ramanathapuram, in the west by CD Blocks Sivaganga and Manamadurai. CD Block Kalayarkoil falls in taluks: Tirupathur by 02, Karaikkudi by 01, and Sivaganga by 71 villages.

Communications:

Roadways : S.H.-27: Direction- Manamadurai to Tirupathur, Nearest Villages- Silanthagudi, Nariyangudi, Nagarampatti, Paruththikanmai, Purusadiudaippu, Palkulam, Siruganaperi, Sethambal, Somanathamangalam. S.H.-33: Direction- Madurai to Tiruvadanai, Nearest Villages- Nedungulam, Kollangudi, Usilanendal, Nattarasankottai, Pallivayal, Somanathamangalam, Mongankanmai, Sennelgudi, Pirandaikulam. S.H.-34: Direction- Melur to Iiayangudi, Nearest Villages- Poovali, Mallal, Sembanoor, M. Velangulam.

Backwards Region Grants Fund: It receives Backward Region Grants.

Annual Rainfall: Average Rainfall 904 mm.

Ground Water: Availability of the ground water in the Basin is 11615.78 H.A.M. and the utilization is 671. 43 H.A.M. It belongs to Safe category. Depth to water level varies from 2 to 10 meter below the ground. Most of the wells go down in summer months, according to the Ground Water Estimation Committee.

Natural Division: NA

Administration

Revenue **Division:** Devakottai, Sivaganga. Parliamentary Constituency: Sivaganga. District: Sivaganga. Taluk: Tirupathur, Karaikkudi, Sivaganga. Assembly Constituency: 186 Sivaganga. Gram Panchayat: 43.

Villages: 72 **Inhabited:** 69 **Uninhabited:** 3

Ranking	District	State	National
Area	1	19	1194
Population	1	157	3649
Sex Ratio	4	14	166
Child Sex Ratio	1	22	573
Literacy Rate	4	134	1390

Density	8	246	5427
Work Participation Rate	11	356	2644

Gram Panchayats:
A.velangulam, Adappadakki, A.kurangulam, Allor , Ammanpatti, Chockanathapuram, Erivayal, Gowripatti , Ilandakarai, Kadaneri, Kalakanmai, Kalaikulam, Kalayarkoil, Kanjipatti, Kattandal Sukkanoorani, Karaikulam, Keelamangalam, Kollangudi, Kottagudi, Kuruthangudi, Mallal , Marakkathur, Marandai, Marandai , Maravamamgalam, Melamangalam, Melamarungoor, Melamarungur, Mudikkarai, Mudikkarani, Nariyangudi, Okkurpudur, Nadamangalam, Nagarampatti, Paganeri, Pallithamban, Paruthikanmai , Periyakannanur, Puliyadithammam, Sedambal , Sembanur, Sembanur , Sengulam, Silukkupatti, Silukkupatti , Siramam, Sirraman, Soorakkulam, Surakkulam, Surakkulam , Thenmavali, Udakulam, Usilangulam, Velarendal, Vittaneri .

Amenities:

Education: Primary School in 62 villages, Middle school in 27 villages, Matriculation or Secondary School in 11 villages, namely Paganeri, Soorakkulam, Gowripatti, Nedungulam, Kollangudi, Vittaneri, Pallivayal, Palkulam, Mallal, Sethambal, Sakkoor.

Higher Secondary or Pre University Courses or Intermediate or Junior College in 8 villages of the CD Block,, namely Paganeri, Soorakkulam, Gowripatti, Nedungulam, Kollangudi, Pallivayal, Palkulam, Mallal.

College in 1 village, Adult Literacy Center in 0 village., College is in village, namely Keelakottai.

Medical: Hospital in 0 village, Dispensary in 6 villages, Health Center in 8 villages, Sub Center in 21 villages, Maternity and Child Welfare Center in 9 villages, Community health workers in 4 villages.

The Villages having Hospital or Dispensary or Health Center are Keelamangalan, Vaniangudi, Nedungulam, Vittaneri, Somanathamangalam, Mallal, Purasupatty Udayarenthal.

Drinking Water: Tap water in 69 villages, Tank water in 45 villages, Well water in 69 villages, Tubewell in 69 villages and more than one source in 69 villages.

Bank: Banking facility in 9 villages, namely, Kathappattu, Paganeri, Somanathamangalam Mongankanmai, Purusadiudaippu, Athappadakki Palkulam, Mallal, Sethambal.

Credit Society in 12 villages Agricultural Credit Society in 12 Non-Agricultural Credit Society in 1 village.

Others: Power supply in 69 villages, Cinema hall in 1 village, sport club in 1 village, Stadium or Auditorium or Community Hall in 8 villages, Post Office in 51 villages.

There are 58 villages having bus facilities.

Villages with most of facilities: Kathappattu Paganeri, Somanathamangalam, Mongankanmai Athappadakki, Mallal.

Villages without amenities (Education): Kottappati, Mangattendhal, Usilanendal, Pirandaikulam, Cholavandan, Vettikkulam, Nadamangalam..

Scheduled Castes: Out of the total population of 94282 persons, 16150 persons (17.13%) belong to Scheduled Castes. The villages having less than 10% SC population are Kathappattu, Nariyangudi, Keelakottai, Mangattendhal Vaniangudi, Maththukanmai, Kodikadukadampurani Sevavoorani, Usilanendal, Sennelgudi, Pirandaikulam Allur, Vittaneri, Somanathamangalam, Mongankanmai Cholavandan, Kanjippatti, Settur Village, Marandai. The villages having more than 50% SC population are None.

Sex ratio of Scheduled Caste population is 516.

Scheduled Castes Literates and Illiterates by Sex:

	Persons	Males	Females
Literate	8,461	4,885	3,576
Illiterate	7,689	2,933	4,756
Literacy rate	59.9	71.6	48.9
Graduate	206	149	57

Scheduled Castes (Dominant):
Pallan, Paraiyan etc., Chakkiliyan, Adi Dravida Kuravan etc.

For their cultural identity please see Appendix-I

Villages without Scheduled Castes: There are 8 villages without any scheduled caste population.

Scheduled Tribes: Out of the total population of 94282 persons, 7 persons (0.01%) belong to Scheduled Tribes. The villages having less than 10% ST population are Silanthagudi, Kathappattu, Nariyangudi, Keelakottai Kottappati, Nagarampatti, Ammanpatti, Kadaneri Paganeri, Mangattendhal, Keelamangalan, Soorakkulam Karungalakudi, Gowripatti, Vaniangudi, Muthur Maththukanmai, Kodikadukadampurani, Nedungulam Sevavoorani, Kollangudi, Usilanendal, Sennelgudi Pirandaikulam, Allur, Panangadi, Vittaneri Somanathamangalam, Pallivayal, Mongankanmai Moorarkanmai, Mangulam, Kurithanivariendal Paruththikanmai, Pudukhizhuvachi, Oyyavandan Poovali, Cholavandan, Kanjippatti, Purusadiudaippu Marakkathur, Maraathur, Siramam, Mudikkarai Vettikkulam, Nadamangalam, Vembangudi, Athappadakki Palkulam, Nellenthal, Silukkapatti, Vannikkudi Siriyoor, Pulavanvayal, Allpattaviduthi, Mallal Purasupatty Udayarenthal, Sembanoor, Periyakannanoor

Semban, Siruganaperi, Sethambal, Kakkulam, Vallanai Kanjiram, Sakkoor, Kolandi, Settur Village, Marandai.

The villages having more than 50% ST population are None.

Sex ratio of Scheduled tribe population is 429.

Scheduled Tribes Literates and Illiterates by Sex:

	Persons	Males	Females
Literate	4	3	1
Illiterate	3	1	2
Literacy rate	57.1	75.0	33.3
Graduate	0	0	0

Scheduled Tribes (Dominant):

Kattunayakan, Irular, Malakkuravan

For their cultural identity please see Appendix-II

Villages without Scheduled Tribes: There are 68 villages without any scheduled tribe population.

Literates and Illiterates by Sex (Total Population):

	Persons	Males	Females
Literate	57,459	32,415	25,044
Illiterate	36,823	12,969	23,854
Literacy rate	69	81	57
Graduate	1,578	1,061	517

Agriculture: ***Distribution of villages according to land use:*** Out of 72 villages, Total area (in hectare) is 59339.67, out of that 49.86 percent is cultivable and 50.23 percent of the cultivable area is irrigated.

Sources of Irrigation (Hectares): Government Canal 2.97, Private Canal 0, Well without Electricity 929.08, Well with Electricity 1222.98, Tubewell without Electricity 23.56, Tubewell with Electricity 47.62, Tank 12291.54, River 0, Lake 0, Waterfall 0, Others 343.01.

Villages with population of 5000 to 9999: Somanathamangalam.

Villages with population of 10000 and above: None

Distribution of Workers:

	Persons	Males	Females	WPR
Cultivators	27,053	15,251	11,802	58.04
Agricultural Labour	12,272	5,100	7,172	26.33
Household Industry	952	428	524	2.04
Other Workers	6,330	5,012	1,318	13.58
Main Workers	36,364	22,201	14,163	78.02
Marginal Workers	10,243	3,590	6,653	21.98
Total Workers	46,607	25,791	20,816	

Religion: Major Religious Communities:

	Persons	Males	Females	Sex Ratio
Hindu (79.93%)	75,362	36,442	38,920	1,068
Muslim (1.86%)	1,754	869	885	1,018
Christian (14.67%)	13,829	6,475	7,354	1,136
Sikh (0%)	2	2	-	-
Buddhists (0%)	2	2	-	-
Jain (0.01%)	5	2	3	1,500

Agewise Data:

	Persons	Males	Females	Sex Ratio
All ages	91,023	43,824	47,199	1077
0-14	24,500	12,184	12,316	1011
15-44	41,965	19,333	22,632	1171
45-79	22,663	11,296	11,367	1006
80+	1,042	571	471	825
Age not stated	853	440	413	939

Languages (Dominant):

Tamil, Telugu, English, Malayalam, Oriya

Disabled Population:

	Persons	Males	Females	%
Total Disabled	2,927	1,338	1,589	
In Seeing	1,796	721	1,075	61.36
In Speech	166	95	71	5.67
In Hearing	155	59	96	5.3
In Movement	583	344	239	19.92
Mentally	227	119	108	7.76

KALLAKKURICHI

Kallakurichi C.D. Block lies in the southern part of Viluppuram district. It is a part of Kallakurichi taluk. The Block is located at a distance of 89 kms. from district headquarters (Viluppuram). There are 54 villages in the block with the total population of 126,234 persons. Area of the C.D. Block is 303.86 sq. kms. It is bounded in the north by CD Block Sankarapuram, in the south by C.D. Block Chinnasalem, in the east by C.D. Blocks Thyagadurgam and Rishivandiam, in the west by C. D. Blocks Kalrayan Hills and Chinnasalam.

Communications:

Roadways : N.H.-68: Direction- Kallakurichi to Thyagadurgam, Nearest Villages- Peruvangur, Neelamangalam, Madur, Veeracholapuram, Thenkeeranur, Thatchur, Indili, Porpad akurichi. S.H.-6: Direction- Sankarapuram to Vridddhachalam, Nearest Villages- Siruvangur, k. Mamanandal, Neelamangalam, Niraimathi.

Railway Station: Siruvathur, Pukkiravari.

River: Gomikar Nadi- Nearest Villages- Siruvangur, K. Mamanandal, Neelamangalam, Veeracholapuram, Thenkeeranur, Malaikottalam.

Backwards Region Grants Fund: It receives Backward Region Grants.

Annual Rainfall: Average Rainfall 1119 mm.

Ground Water: Availability of the ground water in the Basin is 9275.16 H.A.M. and the utilization is 8871.00 H.A.M. It belongs to Critical category. Depth to water level varies from 2 to 10 meter below the ground. Most of the wells go down in summer months, according to the Ground Water Estimation Committee.

Forest and Reserved Forest: (Karai RF)- Nearest Villages- Karai R.F, Eluthavanatham. (Kottalammalai)- Nearest Villages- Malaikottalam, Kothalamalai R.F., Vanavareddi, Thenthorasaloor. (Magarur)- Nearest Village- Keelanriy appanur. (Parigam)- Nearest Villages- Eluthavanatham, Parigam R.F, Parigram.

Natural Division: Tondai Nadu.

Administration

Revenue **Division:** Kallkurichi. Parliamentary Constituency: 14 Kallakurichi (SC).District: Villupuram. Taluk: Kallakkurichi. Assembly Constituency:
79 Chinnasalem , 80 Kallakurichi (SC). Gram Panchayat: 46.

Villages: 54 **Inhabited:** 50 **Uninhabited:** 4

Ranking	District	State	National
Area	11	167	2742
Population	7	47	2643
Sex Ratio	22	335	3089
Child Sex Ratio	22	312	5198
Literacy Rate	18	356	3510
Density	5	69	2648
Work Participation Rate	8	105	620

Gram Panchayats:

Agarakottalam, Alambalam (Kallakurichi), Alathur, Ariyaperumanur , Eduthavoinatham, Eravar, Indili, Ka. Mamanandal, Ka.Allambalam, Ka.sellampatu, Karadichittur , Kattananthal, Madavachcheri, Madur, Malaikottalam, Manmalai, Mathur, Melur, Mohur, Neelamangalam, Niraimathi, Palrampattu, Paramanatham, Parigam, Perumangalam, Peruvangur, Porpadakurichi, Pukkiravari, Renganathapuram, Sembadakurichi, Sirumangalam, Siruvangur, Siruvathur, Somandarkudi, Thachur, Thandalai, Thavadippattu, Thenkiranur, Thenthorasalur, V.palayam, Vanavaretti, Vaniyanthal, Vannanjur, Varadappanur, Veeracholapuram , Vilambur, Vinaitheerthapuram.

Amenities:

Education: Primary School in 48 villages, Middle school in 28 villages, Matriculation or Secondary School in 7 villages, namely Somandargudi, Mohur, Alambalam, Karadichittur, Eluthavanatham, Veeracholapuram, Siruvathur.

Higher Secondary or Pre University Courses or Intermediate or Junior College in 2 villages of the CD Block,, namely Alambalam, Siruvathur.

College in 2 villages, Adult Literacy Center in 0 village., Colleges are in villages, namely Thatchur, Indili.

Medical: Hospital in 1 village, Dispensary in 3 villages, Health Center in 4 villages, Sub Center in 6 villages, Maternity and Child Welfare Center in 36 villages, Community health workers in 15 villages.

The Villages having Hospital or Dispensary or Health Center are Alambalam, Parigram, Melur, Pukkiravari.

Drinking Water: Tap water in 50 villages, Tank water in 16 villages, Well water in 50 villages, Tubewell in 50 villages and more than one source in 50 villages.

Bank: Banking facility in 4 villages, namely, Alathur, Somandargudi, Madur, Melur.

Credit Society in 23 villages Agricultural Credit Society in 9 Non-Agricultural Credit Society in 3 villages.

Others: Power supply in 50 villages, Cinema hall in 22 villages sport club in 0 village, Stadium or Auditorium or Community Hall in 0 village, Post Office in 46 villages.

There are 39 villages having bus facilities.

Villages with most of facilities: Alathur Somandargudi, Madur.

Villages without amenities (Education):
Keezh Poondi..

Scheduled Castes: Out of the total population of 126234 persons, 45127 persons (35.75%) belong to Scheduled Castes.
The villages having less than 10% SC population are Kallerikuppam, Pombarapattu, Agarakottalam Somandargudi, Eluthavanatham, Madhavacheri Latchiyam, Vinaitheerthapuram.

The villages having more than 50% SC population are Paramanatham, Anaikaraikottalam, Vannanjur, Mohur Alambalam, Sambadakurichi, Parigram, Mathur Peruvangur, Thenkeeranur, Indili, Perumangalam.

Sex ratio of Scheduled Caste population is 489.

Scheduled Castes Literates and Illiterates by Sex:

	Persons	Males	Females
Literate	19,764	12,712	7,052
Illiterate	25,363	10,334	15,029
Literacy rate	50.4	63.7	36.6
Graduate	208	178	30

Scheduled Castes (Dominant):

Adi Dravida, Arunthathiyar, Pallan, Domban, Valluvan

For their cultural identity please see Appendix-I

Villages without Scheduled Castes: There are 9 villages without any scheduled caste population.

Scheduled Tribes: Out of the total population of 126234 persons, 61 persons (0.05%) belong to Scheduled Tribes.
The villages having less than 10% ST population are Kallerikuppam, Paramanatham, Tirukkanangur Pombarapattu, Alathur, Agarakottalam Anaikaraikottalam, Thandalai , Vaniyandal Ariyaperumanur, Vannanjur, Somandargudi, Mohur Alambalam, Sambadakurichi, Karadichittur, Manmalai Eluthavanatham, Parigram, Mathur, Palrampattu Thavadipattu, Madhavacheri , Siruvangur K. Mamanandal, Peruvangur, Neelamangalam, Madur Veeracholapuram, Niraimathi, Thenkeeranur, Thatchur

Indili, Porpadakurichi, Vilambur, Malaikottalam Vanavareddi, Thenthorasaloor, Kattanandal, Latchiyam Eravar, Melur, Keezh Poondi, Vinaitheerthapuram Siruvathur, Varadappanur, Pukkiravari, Sirumangalam Keelanriyappanur, Perumangalam.

The villages having more than 50% ST population are None.

Sex ratio of Scheduled tribe population is 492.

Scheduled Tribes Literates and Illiterates by Sex:

	Persons	Males	Females
Literate	16	9	7
Illiterate	45	22	23
Literacy rate	31.4	34.6	28.0
Graduate	0	0	0

Scheduled Tribes (Dominant):

Malakkuravan, Malayali, Malai Pandaram, Kattunayakan

For their cultural identity please see Appendix-II

Villages without Scheduled Tribes: There are 49 villages without any scheduled tribe population.

Literates and Illiterates by Sex (Total Population):

	Persons	Males	Females
Literate	61,672	38,724	22,948
Illiterate	64,562	25,759	38,803
Literacy rate	56	69	42
Graduate	777	611	166

Agriculture: ***Distribution of villages according to land use:*** Out of 54 villages, Total area (in hectare) is 30386.73, out of that 61.03 percent is cultivable and 83.41 percent of the cultivable area is irrigated.

Sources of Irrigation (Hectares): Government Canal 988, Private Canal 130, Well without Electricity 4138, Well with Electricity 8002, Tubewell without Electricity 0, Tubewell with Electricity 47, Tank 0, River 0, Lake 2144.47, Waterfall 11.3, Others 8.

Villages with population of 5000 to 9999: Karadichittur, Eduthavoinatham, Siruvangur.

Villages with population of 10000 and above: None

Distribution of Workers:

	Persons	Males	Females	WPR
Cultivators	27,535	16,689	10,846	38.41
Agricultural Labour	36,684	17,387	19,297	51.17
Household Industry	1,341	724	617	1.87
Other Workers	6,136	4,744	1,392	8.56
Main Workers	59,678	35,093	24,585	83.24
Marginal Workers	12,018	4,451	7,567	16.76
Total Workers	71,696	39,544	32,152	

Religion: Major Religious Communities:

	Persons	Males	Females	Sex Ratio
Hindu (96.6%)	121,938	62,312	59,626	957
Muslim (1.37%)	1,735	863	872	1,010
Christian (1.95%)	2,459	1,252	1,207	964
Sikh (0%)	-	-	-	-
Buddhists (0%)	1	1	-	-
Jain (0%)	1	-	1	-

Agewise Data:

	Persons	Males	Females	Sex Ratio
All ages	126,234	64,483	61,751	958
0-14	36,953	19,270	17,683	918
15-44	62,064	31,370	30,694	978
45-79	26,127	13,253	12,874	971
80+	762	413	349	845
Age not stated	328	177	151	853

Languages (Dominant):

Tamil, Telugu, Urdu, Kannada, Malayalam

Disabled Population:

	Persons	Males	Females	%
Total Disabled	2,212	1,237	975	
In Seeing	938	493	445	42.41
In Speech	234	141	93	10.58
In Hearing	146	67	79	6.6
In Movement	731	449	282	33.05
Mentally	163	87	76	7.37

KALLAL

Kallal C.D. Block lies in the northern part of Sivaganga district. It is a part of Tirupathur, Karaikkudi and Sivaganga taluks. The Block is located at a distance of NA kms. from district headquarters (Sivaganga). There are 42 villages in the block with the total population of 79,650 persons. Area of the C.D. Block is 385.76 sq. kms. It is bounded in the north by C.D. Blocks Tirupathur and Sakkottai, in the south by C.D. Block Kalayarkoil, in the east by C.D. Blocks Sakkottai and Devakottai, in the west by C.D. Blocks Kalayarkoil and Tirupathur. CD Block Kallal falls in taluks : Tirupathur by 16, Karaikkudi by 26, and Sivaganga by 01 villages.

Communications:

Roadways : N.H.-210: Direction- Karaikkudi to Devakottai, Nearest Village- Kalluppatti. S.H.-27: Direction- Tirupathur to Pudukkottai, Nearest village- K. Athangudi. S.H.-29: Direction-Kalayarkoil to Karaikkudi, Nearest Villages- Koviloor, Managiri Sukkanendal, Keeranipatti, Devapattu, Kallal, Aranmanai Siruvayal, Malaikandan,Vetriyur, Kurundmpattu, Keelapoongudi. S.H.-35: Direction- Tirupathur to Karaikkudi, Nearest Villages- Kunnakudi, Thattati, Siravayal, Thenkarai.

Railway Station: Aranmanai Siruvayal, Panangudi.

Backwards Region Grants Fund: It receives Backward Region Grants.

Annual Rainfall: Average Rainfall 904 mm.

Ground Water: Availability of the ground water in the Basin is 9018.48 H.A.M. and the utilization is 1583. 69 H.A.M. It belongs to Safe category. Depth to water level varies from 2 to 10 meter below the ground. Most of the wells go down in summer months, according to the Ground Water Estimation Committee.

Natural Division: NA

Administration

Revenue **Division:** Devakottai. Parliamentary Constituency: 31 Sivaganga. District: Sivaganga. Taluk: Tirupathur, Karaikkudi, Sivaganga. Assembly Constituency: 185 Tirupathur, 184 Karaikudi, 186 Sivaganga.

Gram Panchayat: 44.

Villages: 43 **Inhabited:** 43 **Uninhabited:** 0

Ranking	District	State	National
Area	4	84	2023
Population	5	245	4117
Sex Ratio	2	7	121
Child Sex Ratio	12	271	4508
Literacy Rate	2	98	1103
Density	10	291	4638
Work Participation Rate	7	320	3221

Gram Panchayats:

A.Karungulam, Eluvankottai, Alampattu, Alangudi, Ammanapatti, Aramanaipatti, Aranmanaipatti, Aranmanaisiruvayal , Arcot Velur, Devapattu , Ilangudi, K.Athankudi , Kalipuli, Kallal , Nemam, Kalluppatti, Oyyakundan Siruvayal, Kandarmanickam, Keelapattamangalam , Kottakudi, Keelapongudi , Koothalur, Koothalur , Kovilur , Kunnakudi , Kurundampattu , Malaikandan, Melapattamangalam, Nachiyapuram, Naduvikottai Keelaiyur, Veerai, Naduvikottai Melaiyur, Natarajapuram, P.Nerpugapatti, Palavangudi, Panangudi, Patharakudi, Poyyalur, Salayankottai, Sambanur, Sethuregunathapattinam , Severakottai, Siravayal , Siruvayal, Thalakkavoor, Thalakkavoor, Thattati , Thenkarai , Veliyathur , Veppankulam, Vetriym, .

Amenities:

Education: Primary School in 41 villages, Middle school in 23 villages, Matriculation or Secondary School in 14 villages, namely Kunnakudi, Siravayal, Thenkarai, Kambanur, Veliyathoor, Keelappattamangalam, Alangudi, Koothalur, Devapattu, Kallal, Sembanur, Kurundmpattu, Panangudi, Vetriyur.

Higher Secondary or Pre University Courses or Intermediate or Junior College in 3 villages of the CD Block,, namely Kunnakudi, Devapattu, Kallal.

College in 0 village, Adult Literacy Center in 0 village.

Medical: Hospital in 2 villages, Dispensary in 6 villages, Health Center in 5 villages, Sub Center in 13 villages, Maternity and Child Welfare Center in 3 villages, Community health workers in 19 villages.

The Villages having Hospital or Dispensary or Health Center are Veliyathoor, Keelappattamangalam, Aranmanaipatti, Koviloor, Sethuragunathapattanam, Kallal, Panangudi, Vetriyur.

Drinking Water: Tap water in 43 villages, Tank water in 38 villages, Well water in 43 villages, Tubewell in 43 villages and more than one source in 43 villages.

Bank: Banking facility in 9 villages, namely, Kunnakudi, Siravayal, Veliyathoor, Aranmanaipatti Koothalur, Kalluppatti, Kallal, Aranmanai Siruvayal Alampattu.

Credit Society in 7 villages Agricultural Credit Society in 7 Non-Agricultural Credit Society in 1 village.

Others: Power supply in 43 villages, Cinema hall in 1 village, sport club in 0 village, Stadium or Auditorium or Community Hall in 10 villages, Post Office in 36 villages.

There are 39 villages having bus facilities.

Villages with most of facilities: Kunnakudi Siravayal, Veliyathoor, Aranmanaipatti, Koothalur Kalluppatti, Kallal, Aranmanai Siruvayal, Alampattu.

Villages without amenities (Education): Karaikudi R. F., Thiruthipatti..

Scheduled Castes: Out of the total population of 79650 persons, 13226 persons (16.61%) belong to Scheduled Castes. The villages having less than 10% SC population are Melapattamangalam, Perchikovil, Koviloor Keeranipatti, Aranmanai Siruvayal, Thiruthipatti Mummudichanpatti, Malaikandan.

The villages having more than 50% SC population are None.

Sex ratio of Scheduled Caste population is 532.

Scheduled Castes Literates and Illiterates by Sex:

	Persons	Males	Females
Literate	8,239	4,442	3,797
Illiterate	4,987	1,752	3,235
Literacy rate	70.3	81.5	60.5
Graduate	222	130	92

Scheduled Castes (Dominant):

Paraiyan etc., Pallan, Kuravan etc., Adi Dravida Chakkiliyan

For their cultural identity please see Appendix-I

Villages without Scheduled Castes: There are 2 villages without any scheduled caste population.

Scheduled Tribes: Out of the total population of 79650 persons, 42 persons (0.05%) belong to Scheduled Tribes. The villages having less than 10% ST population are K. Athangudi, Kunnakudi, Thattati, Siravayal Thenkarai, Ilangudi, Kambanur, Veliyathoor Melapattamangalam, Keelappattamangalam, N.Melaiyur Alangudi, Naduvikottai Keelaiyur, Perchikovil

Kallipattu, Sevarakottai, Aranmanaipatti, Koviloor Managiri Sukkanendal, Karaikudi R. F., Keeranipatti Koothalur, Varivayal, Sethuragunathapattanam Kalluppatti, Pilar, Devapattu, Kallal, Sembanur Aranmanai Siruvayal, Kurundmpattu, Sannavanam Veppangulam, Vilavadiyandal, Alampattu Keelapoongudi, Thiruthipatti, Panangudi Elanthamangalm, Mummudichanpatti, Malaikandan Vetriyur, Usilangulam.

The villages having more than 50% ST population are None.

Sex ratio of Scheduled tribe population is 548.

Scheduled Tribes Literates and Illiterates by Sex:

	Persons	Males	Females
Literate	30	17	13
Illiterate	12	2	10
Literacy rate	79.0	94.4	65.0
Graduate	2	0	2

Scheduled Tribes (Dominant):

Malai Vedan, Malakkuravan, Palleyan

For their cultural identity please see Appendix-II

Villages without Scheduled Tribes: There are 36 villages without any scheduled tribe population.

Literates and Illiterates by Sex (Total Population):

	Persons	Males	Females
Literate	50,108	27,518	22,590
Illiterate	29,542	10,461	19,081
Literacy rate	71	82	60
Graduate	1,489	914	575

Agriculture: ***Distribution of villages according to land use:*** Out of 43 villages, Total area (in hectare) is 38576.14, out of that 44.6 percent is cultivable and 44.14 percent of the cultivable area is irrigated.

Sources of Irrigation (Hectares): Government Canal 0, Private Canal 0, Well without Electricity 52.255, Well with Electricity 352.52, Tubewell without Electricity 0, Tubewell with Electricity 96.23, Tank 6859.99, River 0, Lake 0, Waterfall 0, Others 233.28.

Villages with population of 5000 to 9999:

Veliyathur , Kallal.

Villages with population of 10000 and above: None

Distribution of Workers:

	Persons	Males	Females	WPR
Cultivators	12,534	6,981	5,553	33.52
Agricultural Labour	12,926	5,723	7,203	34.57
Household Industry	1,153	477	676	3.08
Other Workers	10,778	8,368	2,410	28.83
Main Workers	25,269	16,590	8,679	67.58
Marginal Workers	12,122	4,959	7,163	32.42
Total Workers	37,391	21,549	15,842	

Religion: Major Religious Communities:

	Persons	Males	Females	Sex Ratio
Hindu (90.82%)	72,340	34,591	37,749	1,091
Muslim (1.76%)	1,403	665	738	1,110
Christian (6.9%)	5,496	2,530	2,966	1,172
Sikh (0%)	-	-	-	-
Buddhists (0%)	1	-	1	-
Jain (0.01%)	4	2	2	1,000

Agewise Data:

	Persons	Males	Females	Sex Ratio
All ages	79,322	37,824	41,498	1097
0-14	20,444	10,454	9,990	956
15-44	36,413	16,790	19,623	1169
45-79	21,113	9,894	11,219	1134
80+	1,040	524	516	985
Age not stated	312	162	150	926

Languages (Dominant):

Tamil, Telugu, Gujarati, Malayalam, Kannada

Disabled Population:

	Persons	Males	Females	%
Total Disabled	2,637	1,052	1,585	
In Seeing	1,621	506	1,115	61.47
In Speech	159	75	84	6.03
In Hearing	176	74	102	6.67
In Movement	447	274	173	16.95
Mentally	234	123	111	8.87

KALLIKUDI

Kallikudi C.D. Block lies in the southern part of Madurai district. It is a part of Thirumangalam taluk. The taluk is located at a distance of 20 kms. from district headquarters (Madurai). There are 42 villages in the block with the total population of 68,263 persons. Area of the C.D. Block is 256.82 sq. kms. It is bounded in the north by CD Block Thirumangalam, in the south by district Virudhunagar, in the east by CD Block Thirparakundram and district Virudhunagar, and in the west by CD Block T. Kallupatti.

Communications:

Roadways : N.H.-7: Direction- Sattur to Thirumangalam, Nearest Villages- Karisalkalampatti, Keelanasanary, Sivarakkottai, K.Vellakulam, Kallikudi, Kokkalanchery, Nallamanakkanpatti.

Railway Station: K.Vellakulam, Kallikudi.

River: Therku Nadi- Nearest Villages- Idaiyanatham, Sennampatti, Kurayur, Karisalkalampatti, Sivarakkottai, T.Arasapatti, Melanasanary, Keelanasanary. Vaigai Nadi- Nearest Village- S.P.Natham.

Annual Rainfall: Average Rainfall 857 mm.

Ground Water: Availability of the ground water in the Basin is 3428.95 H.A.M. and the utilization is 1613. 52 H.A.M. It belongs to Safe category. Depth to water level varies from 2 to 5 meter below the ground. Most of the wells go down in summer months, according to the Ground Water Estimation Committee.

Natural Division: NA

Administration

Revenue **Division:** Usilampatti. Parliamentary Constituency: 34 Sivakasi. District: Madurai. Taluk: Thirumangalam. Assembly Constituency: 196 Thirumangalam. Gram Panchayat: 36.

Villages: 42 **Inhabited:** 42 **Uninhabited:** 0

Ranking	District	State	National
Area	6	223	3290
Population	10	293	4538
Sex Ratio	2	83	628
Child Sex Ratio	4	268	4453
Literacy Rate	8	196	1796
Density	1	36	3901
Work Participation Rate	10	266	293

Gram Panchayats:

Arasapatti , Avalsorrampatti, Chennampatti, Chittoor, K.Vellakulam , Kallanai, Kalligudi, Karisalkalampatti, Kokkulam (Thirumal), Koodakoil, Kurayur, M.Pothanathi, M.Pudupatti, Maittanpatti, Maravapatti, Maruthangudi, Melauppilikundu, Nallamanaikenpatti, Nedunkulam, Nesaneri, Odaippatti, Peikulam, Puliankulam , S.Vellakulam , Saluppapillayarnatham, Sengapadai, Sivarakottai, Swamimallampatti, Thennamanallur, Thirumal, Thoombakulam, Ulagani, Ullagani, Unnipatti, Valayankulam, Veeraperumalpuram, Veppankulam, Villur

Amenities:

Education: Primary School in 37 villages, Middle school in 12 villages, Matriculation or Secondary School in 11 villages, namely Sengappadai, T.Arasapatti, Koodakovil, Melaupplikundu, Kokkulam, Thirumal, Paraikulam, Kallikudi, Villur, Chittoor, M.Puliangulam.

Higher Secondary or Pre University Courses or Intermediate or Junior College in 4 villages of the CD Block,, namely Melanasanary, Sengappadai, Idaiyanatham, Chittoor.

College in 2 villages, Adult Literacy Center in 0 village., Colleges are in villages, namely K.Vellakulam, Chittoor.

Medical: Hospital in 1 village, Dispensary in 7 villages, Health Center in 2 villages, Sub Center in 16 villages, Maternity and Child Welfare Center in 4 villages, Community health workers in 0 village.

The Villages having Hospital or Dispensary or Health Center are Sengappadai, Sivarakkottai, Koodakovil, Melaupplikundu, Kokkulam, Thirumal, Paraikulam, Kallikudi.

Drinking Water: Tap water in 42 villages, Tank water in 18 villages, Well water in 42 villages, Tubewell in 42 villages and more than one source in 42 villages.

Bank: Banking facility in 7 villages, namely, Sengappadai, Koodakovil, K.Vellakulam, Kallikudi Villur, Kurayur, Kokkalanchery.

Credit Society in 16 villages Agricultural Credit Society in 14 Non-Agricultural Credit Society in 2 villages.

Others: Power supply in 42 villages, Cinema hall in 1 village, sport club in 0 village, Stadium or Auditorium or Community Hall in 3 villages, Post Office in 36 villages.

There are 35 villages having bus facilities.

Villages with most of facilities: Sengappadai Koodakovil, K.Vellakulam, Kallikudi, Villur, Kurayur Kokkalanchery.

Villages without amenities (Education): Achankulam, Pudukkulam, Odaipatti, Karukkuvaipatti..

Scheduled Castes: Out of the total population of 68263 persons, 11505 persons (16.85%) belong to Scheduled Castes. The villages having less than 10% SC population are Ulagani, Swamimallampatti, Karisalkalampatti Keelanasanary, Sivarakkottai, T.Arasapatti Valaiankulam, Nedunkulam, Chinnaulagam, Kallanai Achankulam, Melaupplikundu, Thumbagulam, Thirumal Paraikulam, Idaiyanatham, S.Vellakulam Karukkuvaipatti, Sundarangundu, Peikulam.

The villages having more than 50% SC population are None.

Sex ratio of Scheduled Caste population is 507.

Scheduled Castes Literates and Illiterates by Sex:

	Persons	Males	Females
Literate	5,944	3,549	2,395
Illiterate	5,561	2,126	3,435
Literacy rate	58.9	72.3	46.3
Graduate	40	30	10

Scheduled Castes (Dominant):

Pallan, Chakkiliyan, Paraiyan etc., Pagadai, Samban

For their cultural identity please see Appendix-I

Villages without Scheduled Castes: There is 1 village without any scheduled caste population.

Scheduled Tribes: Out of the total population of 68263 persons, 26 persons (0.04%) belong to Scheduled Tribes. The villages having less than 10% ST population are Ulagani, Melanasanary, Sengappadai, Swamimallampatti Karisalkalampatti, Keelanasanary, Sivarakkottai T.Arasapatti, Valaiankulam, Nedunkulam, Chinnaulagam Kallanai, Achankulam, Koodakovil, Melaupplikundu Thumbagulam, Kokkulam, Thirumal, Paraikulam S.P.Natham, K.Vellakulam, Kallikudi, Pudukkulam Villur, Kasipuram, Thennamanallur, Odaipatti

Idaiyanatham, Sennampatti, Kurayur, Maruthankudi S.Vellakulam, Karukkuvaipatti, Sundarangundu Veppankulam, Ilupakulam, Peikulam, Kokkalanchery Nallamanakkanpatti, Miattanpatti, Chittoor M.Puliangulam.

The villages having more than 50% ST population are None.

Sex ratio of Scheduled tribe population is 500.

Scheduled Tribes Literates and Illiterates by Sex:

	Persons	Males	Females
Literate	13	9	4
Illiterate	13	4	9
Literacy rate	56.5	69.2	40.0
Graduate	0	0	0

Scheduled Tribes (Dominant):

Malai Pandaram, Kattunayakan, Palliyar Generic Tribes etc.

For their cultural identity please see Appendix-II

Villages without Scheduled Tribes: There are 37 villages without any scheduled tribe population.

Literates and Illiterates by Sex (Total Population):

	Persons	Males	Females
Literate	39,848	23,985	15,863
Illiterate	28,415	9,789	18,626
Literacy rate	66	81	52
Graduate	374	288	86

Agriculture: ***Distribution of villages according to land use:*** Out of 42 villages, Total area (in hectare) is 25682.03, out of that 55.3 percent is cultivable and 24.25 percent of the cultivable area is irrigated.

Sources of Irrigation (Hectares): Government Canal 0.1, Private Canal 0, Well without Electricity 132.57, Well with Electricity 1351.34, Tubewell without Electricity 0, Tubewell with Electricity 2, Tank 1938.11, River 20, Lake 0, Waterfall 0, Others 0.

Villages with population of 5000 to 9999:
Vellakulam (K), Villur , Kurayur.

Villages with population of 10000 and above: None

Distribution of Workers:

	Persons	Males	Females	WPR
Cultivators	9,540	5,294	4,246	23.36
Agricultural Labour	21,776	9,019	12,757	53.33
Household Industry	716	307	409	1.75
Other Workers	8,799	6,166	2,633	21.55
Main Workers	36,511	19,125	17,386	89.42
Marginal Workers	4,320	1,661	2,659	10.58
Total Workers	40,831	20,786	20,045	

Religion: Major Religious Communities:

	Persons	Males	Females	Sex Ratio
Hindu (98.67%)	67,357	33,346	34,011	1,020
Muslim (0.58%)	396	190	206	1,084
Christian (0.62%)	424	192	232	1,208
Sikh (0.01%)	4	2	2	1,000
Buddhists (0%)	2	1	1	1,000
Jain (0.01%)	5	3	2	667

Agewise Data:

	Persons	Males	Females	Sex Ratio
All ages	68,263	33,774	34,489	1021
0-14	18,976	9,692	9,284	958
15-44	31,961	15,763	16,198	1028
45-79	16,233	7,784	8,449	1085
80+	604	281	323	1149
Age not stated	489	254	235	925

Languages (Dominant):

Tamil, Telugu, Kannada, Urdu, English

Disabled Population:

	Persons	Males	Females	%
Total Disabled	2,236	1,225	1,011	
In Seeing	1,417	762	655	63.37
In Speech	189	97	92	8.45
In Hearing	78	38	40	3.49
In Movement	366	233	133	16.37
Mentally	186	95	91	8.32

KALRAYAN HILLS

Kalrayan Hills C.D. Block lies in the western part of Viluppuram district. It is a part of Sankarapuram taluk. The taluk is located at a distance of 97 kms. from district headquarters (Viluppuram). There are 50 villages in the block with the total population of 49,081 persons. Area of the C.D. Block is 546.63 sq. kms. It is bounded in the north by district Tiruvannamalai, in the south by district Salem, in the east by C.D. Blocks Chinnasalem, Kallakkurichi and Sankarapuram, in the west by district, Dharmapuri and Salem.

Communications:

Roadways : Information not Available.

River: Manimuktha Nadi- Nearest Villages- Kilakkadu, Kalliparai, Villvathy, Melpacheri, Perumbur, Pudupalapa ttu, Vellarikkadu, Vengodu.

Backwards Region Grants Fund: It receives Backward Region Grants.

Annual Rainfall: Average Rainfall 1119 mm.

Ground Water: Availability of the ground water in the Basin is 3958.86 H.A.M. and the utilization is 1485.49 H.A.M. It belongs to Safe category. Depth to water level varies from 5 to 10 meter below the ground. Most of the wells go down in summer months, according to the Ground Water Estimation Committee.

Forest and Reserved Forest: (Rangappanur RF)- Nearest Villa Moolakkadu. (Pavunjipattu)- Nearest Village- Moolakkadu.

(Mallapuram)- Nearest Villgages- Melpacheri, Pudupalapattu.
Natural Division: Tondai Nadu.

Administration

Revenue **Division:** Kallkurichi. Parliamentary Constituenc y: 14 Kallakurichi (SC). District: Villupuram. Taluk: Sankarapuram. Assembly Constituency: 79 Chinnasalem. Gram Panchayat: 15.

Villages: 50 **Inhabited:** 50 **Uninhabited:** 0

Ranking	District	State	National
Area	1	26	1331
Population	22	361	5328
Sex Ratio	20	319	2627
Child Sex Ratio	19	222	3591
Literacy Rate	22	385	6227
Density	2	31	6198
Work Participation Rate	22	381	240

Gram Panchayats:

Alannur, Arampundi, Aravankadu, Erukkambattu, Erukkambattu (P), Ezhuthur, Gudaram, Innadu (P), Kalliparai, Kallipattu, Kandikkal, Kariyalur (P), Karuvelampadi (P), Keelathukkili, Keelnilavur, Kilakkadu (P), Kondiyanatham, Kurumbalur, Malliampadi, Maniyarpalayam , Mapadipattu, Melathukkuli, Melnilavur, Moolakkadu, Mozhipattu, Mundiyur, Nochchimedu (P), Pacheri, Pacheri (Mel), Pannippadi (P), Perumanatham (P), Perumbur, Pottiyam (P), Pudupalapattu, Serapattu, Sirukkalur , Thoradipattu (P), Thorangur, Uppur (P), Vandagappadi (P), Vanjikkuli (P), Vanniyur, Varam (P), Vazhakuli, Vellarikkadu, Vellimalai, Vengodu (P), Vezhappadi.T., Vilvathi.

Amenities:

Education: Primary School in 38 villages, Middle school in 15 villages, Matriculation or Secondary School in 5 villages, namely Serappattu, Mavadipattu, Kariyalur, Vellimalai, Ezhuthur.

Higher Secondary or Pre University Courses or Intermediate or Junior College in 2 villages of the CD Block,, namely Serappattu, Kariyalur.

College in 0 village, Adult Literacy Center in 0 village.
Medical: Hospital in 2 villages, Dispensary in 1 village, Health Center in 2 villages, Sub Center in 15 villages, Maternity and Child Welfare Center in 1 village, Community health workers in 19 villages.

The Villages having Hospital or Dispensary or Health Center are Serappattu, Melpacheri, Mavadipattu.

Drinking Water: Tap water in 50 villages, Tank water in 15 villages, Well water in 50 villages, Tubewell in 50 villages and more than one source in 50 villages.
Bank: Banking facility in 2 villages, namely, Melpacheri, Vellimalai.

Credit Society in 4 villages Agricultural Credit Society in 2 Non-Agricultural Credit Society in 0 village.

Others: Power supply in 40 villages, Cinema hall in 0 village, sport club in 0 village, Stadium or Auditorium or Community Hall in 0 village, Post Office in 50 villages.

There are 25 villages having bus facilities.

Villages with most of facilities: Melpacheri Vellimalai.

Villages without amenities (Education): Koodaram, Vashakuli, Sirukkalur, Perumanatham, Villvathy, Vengodu, Aravankadu, Melathukkuli, Erukkampattu, Vanniyur, Uppur, Erukkambattu..

Scheduled Castes: Out of the total population of 49081 persons, 1723 persons (3.51%) belong to Scheduled Castes. The villages having less than 10% SC population are Koodaram, Alanur, Kurumbalur, Moolakkadu, Vashakuli Vanjikkuli, Sirukkalur, Serappattu, Perumanatham Kilakkadu, Kalliparai, Villvathy, Melpacheri Perumbur, Vellarikkadu, Vengodu, Keelnilavur Melnilavur, Aravankadu, Maniyarpalayam Keelathukkuli, Melathukkuli, Innadu, Erukkampattu Panrapadi, Karuvelambadi, Nochimedu, Mavadipattu Kariyalur, Mozhipattu, Vellimalai, Vazhappadi Kendiyanatham, Malliampadi, Kandikkal, Vanniyur Arampundi, Uppur, Erukkambattu, Vandagappadi Theradipattu, Mundiyur, Pethiyam, Naranampatti Pacheri, Ezhuthur, Thorangur, Varan.

The villages having more than 50% SC population are None.

Sex ratio of Scheduled Caste population is 470.

Scheduled Castes Literates and Illiterates by Sex:

	Persons	Males	Females
Literate	679	428	251
Illiterate	1,044	486	558
Literacy rate	45.6	54.0	36.1
Graduate	17	13	4

Scheduled Castes (Dominant):

Adi Dravida, Arunthathiyar, Paraiyan etc., Valluvan Kuravan etc.

For their cultural identity please see Appendix-I

Villages without Scheduled Castes: There are 28 villages without any scheduled caste population.

Scheduled Tribes: Out of the total population of 49081 persons, 39943 persons (81.38%) belong to Scheduled Tribes. The villages having less than 10% ST population are None..

The villages having more than 50% ST population are Koodaram, Alanur, Kurumbalur, Moolakkadu, Vashakuli Vanjikkuli, Sirukkalur, Serappattu, Perumanatham

Kilakkadu, Kalliparai, Villvathy, Melpacheri Perumbur, Vellarikkadu, Vengodu, Keelnilavur Melnilavur, Aravankadu, Maniyarpalayam Keelathukkuli, Melathukkuli, Innadu, Erukkampattu Panrapadi, Karuvelambadi, Nochimedu, Mavadipattu Kariyalur, Mozhipattu, Vellimalai, Vazhappadi Kendiyanatham, Malliampadi, Kandikkal, Vanniyur Arampundi, Uppur, Erukkambattu, Vandagappadi Theradipattu, Mundiyur, Pethiyam, Naranampatti Pacheri, Ezhuthur, Thorangur, Varan.

Sex ratio of Scheduled tribe population is 492.

Scheduled Tribes Literates and Illiterates by Sex:

	Persons	Males	Females
Literate	7,774	4,985	2,789
Illiterate	32,169	15,318	16,851
Literacy rate	23.2	29.4	16.9
Graduate	23	21	2

Scheduled Tribes (Dominant):
Malayali, Malayekandi, Malakkuravan Generic Tribes etc.

For their cultural identity please see Appendix-II

Villages without Scheduled Tribes: There is 0 village without any scheduled tribe population.

Literates and Illiterates by Sex (Total Population):

	Persons	Males	Females
Literate	11,892	7,500	4,392
Illiterate	37,189	17,457	19,732
Literacy rate	29	36	22
Graduate	126	90	36

Agriculture: ***Distribution of villages according to land use:*** Out of 50 villages, Total area (in hectare) is 54663.54, out of that 26.25 percent is cultivable and 16.56 percent of the cultivable area is irrigated.

Sources of Irrigation (Hectares): Government Canal 0, Private Canal 0, Well without Electricity 602.68, Well with Electricity 1217.87, Tubewell without Electricity 0, Tubewell with Electricity 0, Tank 0, River 0, Lake 0, Waterfall 0, Others 555.57.

Villages with population of 5000 to 9999: None

Villages with population of 10000 and above: None

Distribution of Workers:

	Persons	Males	Females	WPR
Cultivators	14,614	8,986	5,628	51.74
Agricultural Labour	11,727	4,645	7,082	41.52
Household Industry	561	259	302	1.99
Other Workers	1,345	881	464	4.76
Main Workers	19,123	11,743	7,380	67.7
Marginal Workers	9,124	3,028	6,096	32.3
Total Workers	28,247	14,771	13,476	

Religion: Major Religious Communities:

	Persons	Males	Females	Sex Ratio
Hindu (97.41%)	47,810	24,347	23,463	964
Muslim (1.59%)	782	380	402	1,058
Christian (0.9%)	442	213	229	1,075
Sikh (0.03%)	15	5	10	2,000
Buddhists (0.01%)	4	-	4	-
Jain (0.01%)	5	1	4	4,000

Agewise Data:

	Persons	Males	Females	Sex Ratio
All ages	49,081	24,957	24,124	967
0-14	18,233	9,520	8,713	915
15-44	22,977	11,329	11,648	1028
45-79	7,464	3,896	3,568	916
80+	205	117	88	752
Age not stated	202	95	107	1126

Languages (Dominant):
Tamil, Urdu, Telugu, Kannada, Malayalam

Disabled Population:

	Persons	Males	Females	%
Total Disabled	752	431	321	
In Seeing	468	273	195	62.23
In Speech	47	21	26	6.25
In Hearing	31	17	14	4.12
In Movement	159	96	63	21.14
Mentally	47	24	23	6.25

KAMBAM

Kambam C.D. Block lies in the south western part of Theni district. It is a part of Uthamapalayam taluk. The Block is located at a distance of 40 kms. from district headquarters (Theni Allinagaram). There are 10 villages in the block with the total population of 22,229 persons. Area of the C.D. Block is 198.94 sq. kms. It is bounded in the north by CD Blocks Uthamapalayam and Chinnamanur, in the east by CD Block K. Myladumparai and, It has common boundary with the state of Kerala on south and west.

Communications:

Roadways : N.H.-220: Direction- Thekkaddi to Uthamapalayam, Neraest Village- Keelagudalur.

River: Suralli Nadi- Nearest Villages- Keelagudalur, Narayanathevanpatti.

Annual Rainfall: Average Rainfall 709 mm.

Ground Water: Availability of the ground water in the Basin is 5262.80 H.A.M. and the utilization is 4953. 91 H.A.M. It belongs to Critical category. Depth to water level varies from 5 to 20 meter below the ground. Most of the wells go down in summer months, according to the Ground Water Estimation Committee.

Forest and Reserved Forest: (Suranganur RF)- Nearest Villages- Suranganar RF, Melagudalur RF, Vannathiparai RF. (Pandarathurai)- Nearest Villages- Keelagudalur,

Narayanathevanpatti, Pandarathurai RF, Vannathiparai RF. (Koothanatchiyar)- Nearest Village- Koothanachayar RF. (Pandarathurai)- Nearest Villages- Keelagudalur, Narayanathevanpatti, Pandarathurai RF, Vannathiparai RF. (Perumal Koilkarudu)- Nearest Villages- Perumalkoil Karadu RF, Keelagudalur. (Suruli)- Nearest Villages- Suruli RF, Narayanathevanpatti.

Natural Division: NA

Administration

Revenue **Division:** Uthampalayam. Parliamentary Constituency: 33 Theni. District: Theni. Taluk: Uthampalayam. Assembly Constituency: 198 Andipatti. Gram Panchayat: 05.

Border Villages- (Kerala)- Nearest Villages- Suranganar RF, Melagudalur RF, Vannathiparai RF.

Villages: 10 **Inhabited:** 3 **Uninhabited:** 7

Ranking	District	State	National
Area	6	288	4199
Population	8	385	6187
Sex Ratio	1	188	1254
Child Sex Ratio	1	304	5137
Literacy Rate	6	203	1851
Density	3	83	6040
Work Participation Rate	7	376	799

Gram Panchayats:

Angoorpalayam, Karunaganuthanpatti, Kullappagoundenpatty, Narayanathevanpatti , Surulipatty.

Amenities:

Education: Primary School in 3 villages, Middle school in 2 villages, Matriculation or Secondary School in 2 villages, namely Keelagudalur, Narayanathevanpatti.

Higher Secondary or Pre University Courses or Intermediate or Junior College in 1 village of the CD Block,, namely Narayanathevanpatti.

College in 0 village, Adult Literacy Center in 0 village.

Medical: Hospital in 1 village, Dispensary in 1 village, Health Center in 2 villages, Sub Center in 3 villages, Maternity and Child Welfare Center in 1 village, Community health workers in 1 village.

The Villages having Hospital or Dispensary or Health Center are Keelagudalur, Narayanathevanpatti.

Drinking Water: Tap water in 3 villages, Tank water in 2 villages, Well water in 3 villages, Tubewell in 3 villages and more than one source in 3 villages.

Bank: Banking facility in 1 villages, namely, Narayanathevanpatti.

Credit Society in 0 village Agricultural Credit Society in 0 Non-Agricultural Credit Society in 0 village.

Others: Power supply in 3 villages, Cinema hall in 1 village, sport club in 0 village, Stadium or Auditorium or Community Hall in 0 village, Post Office in 3 villages.

There are 3 villages having bus facilities.

Villages with most of facilities: Narayanathevanpatti.

Villages without Amenities (Education): None..

Scheduled Castes: Out of the total population of 22229 persons, 2392 persons (10.76%) belong to Scheduled Castes.

The villages having less than 10% SC population are None..

The villages having more than 50% SC population are None.

Sex ratio of Scheduled Caste population is 505.

Scheduled Castes Literates and Illiterates by Sex:

	Persons	Males	Females
Literate	1,194	698	496
Illiterate	1,198	485	713
Literacy rate	57.8	69.5	46.8
Graduate	3	3	0

Scheduled Castes (Dominant):

Paraiyan etc., Pallan, Chakkiliyan, Valluvan Puthirai Vannan

For their cultural identity please see Appendix-I

Villages without Scheduled Castes: There are 7 villages without any scheduled caste population.

Scheduled Tribes: Out of the total population of 22229 persons, 6 persons (0.03%) belong to Scheduled Tribes.

The villages having less than 10% ST population are None..

The villages having more than 50% ST population are None.

Sex ratio of Scheduled tribe population is 667.

Scheduled Tribes Literates and Illiterates by Sex:

	Persons	Males	Females
Literate	4	2	2
Illiterate	2	0	2
Literacy rate	66.7	100.0	50.0
Graduate	0	0	0

Scheduled Tribes (Dominant):

Malakkuravan

For their cultural identity please see Appendix-II

Villages without Scheduled Tribes: There are 9 villages without any scheduled tribe population.

Literates and Illiterates by Sex (Total Population):

	Persons	Males	Females
Literate	12,854	7,524	5,330
Illiterate	9,375	3,608	5,767
Literacy rate	66	77	54
Graduate	108	87	21

Agriculture: ***Distribution of villages according to land use:*** Out of 10 villages, Total area (in hectare) is 19894.21, out of that 19.33 percent is cultivable and 60.06 percent of the

cultivable area is irrigated.

Sources of Irrigation (Hectares): Government Canal 1155.82, Private Canal 0, Well without Electricity 0, Well with Electricity 881.15, Tubewell without Electricity 0, Tubewell with Electricity 273.26, Tank 0, River 0, Lake 0, Waterfall 0, Others 0.

Villages with population of 5000 to 9999: Keelagudalur.

Villages with population of 10000 and above: Narayanathevanpatti.

Distribution of Workers:

	Persons	Males	Females	WPR
Cultivators	1,089	719	370	8.71
Agricultural Labour	9,230	4,609	4,621	73.78
Household Industry	181	77	104	1.45
Other Workers	2,010	1,410	600	16.07
Main Workers	12,272	6,723	5,549	98.1
Marginal Workers	238	92	146	1.9
Total Workers	12,510	6,815	5,695	

Religion: Major Religious Communities:

	Persons	Males	Females	Sex Ratio
Hindu (95.65%)	21,261	10,654	10,607	996
Muslim (0.52%)	116	57	59	1,035
Christian (3.79%)	843	416	427	1,026
Sikh (0.01%)	2	1	1	1,000
Buddhists (0%)	1	1	-	-
Jain (0.01%)	2	-	2	-

Agewise Data:

	Persons	Males	Females	Sex Ratio
All ages	22,229	11,132	11,097	997
0-14	6,012	3,198	2,814	880
15-44	10,982	5,428	5,554	1023
45-79	4,940	2,359	2,581	1094
80+	152	71	81	1141
Age not stated	143	76	67	882

Languages (Dominant):

Tamil, Kannada, Telugu, Urdu, Malayalam

Disabled Population:

	Persons	Males	Females	%
Total Disabled	733	366	367	
In Seeing	508	230	278	69.3
In Speech	48	32	16	6.55
In Hearing	16	3	13	2.18
In Movement	116	74	42	15.83
Mentally	45	27	18	6.14

KAMMAPURAM

Kammapuram C.D. Block lies in the central-west part of Cuddalore district. It is a part of Virudhachalam taluk. The Block is located at a distance of NA kms. from district headquarters (Cuddalore). There are 68 villages in the block with the total population of 131,345 persons. Area of the C.D. Block is 328.75 sq. kms. It is bounded in the north by district Vilupuram, in the south by CD Blocks Bhuvanagiri and Kattumannarkoil, in the east by CD Blocks Panruti and Kurinjipachi, and in the west by C.D. Block Virudhachalam.

Communications:

Roadways : S.H.-10: Direction- Virudhachalam to Kurinjipadi, Nearest Villages- Ponneri, V.Sathamangalam, Arasakuzhi, V.Agaram, Uthangal, Umangalam, Vadakkuvellore, Seplanatham, Periyakurichi.

Railway Station: Umangalam.

River: Manimukta Nadi- Nearest Villages- Karkudai, Kammapuram, Keeranur, Gopalapuram, Kumaramagalam, Ko.Adhanur, Sottavanam, Karmangudi, Valliyam, Melapalaiyur, Thozhur, Keezhapalaiyur, Devengudi, K.Puthur, Siruvarappur, Kottumulai, Kavanur, Keeramangalam, Perundurai, T.Parazhangudi, Ottimedu. Vellar Nadi- Nearest Villages- Karmangudi, Sakkaramangalam, Keeranur, Marungur, Kavanur, Keeramangalam, T.Parazhangudi. Backwards Region Grants Fund: It receives Backward Region Grants.

Annual Rainfall: Average Rainfall 1050 mm.

Ground Water: Availability of the ground water in the Basin is 13178.43 MCM and the utilization is 11070.75 MCM. It belongs to Semi Critical category. Depth to water level varies from 2 to 10 meter below the ground. Most of the wells go down in summer months, according to the Ground Water Estimation Committee.

Forest and Reserved Forest: (Semakottai RF)- Nearest Villages- Semmakottai (RF), Ammeri (RF), Mudangi, Irulakurchi, Periyakappankulam, Iruppu. (Ammeri)- Nearest Villages- Kolliruppu, Ammeri, Ammeri (RF), Mudangi, Periyakappankulam. (Narimanam)- Nearest Villages- Mudangi, V. Agaram. (Velangulam)- Nearest Villages- Iruppu Velangulam, Periyakappankulam.

Natural Division: Tondai Nadu.

Administration

Revenue **Division:** Virudhachalam. Parliamentary Constituency: 26 Cuddalore (SC), 27 Chidambaram. District: Cuddalore. Taluk: Virudhachalam. Assembly Constituency: 1 Virddhachalam, 157 Bhuvanagiri. Gram Panchayat: 53.

Villages: 68 **Inhabited:** 64 **Uninhabited:** 4

Ranking	District	State	National
Area	3	137	2472
Population	4	39	2459
Sex Ratio	13	311	2609
Child Sex Ratio	11	189	3177
Literacy Rate	6	188	1750
Density	8	286	2730
Work Participation Rate	10	113	3147

Gram Panchayats:
Ammeri , Devangudi, Gopalapuram, Irulakkurichi, Iruppu, Iruppukurichi, Kammapuram, Karkudal, Karmangudi, Kavanur, Keelapalaiyur, Keeranur, Kilpathi, Ko.Adhanur, Kolliruppu , Kottagam, Kotteri, Kottumulai, Kumaramangalam, Kunankurichi , Manakkollai, Marungur, Mavadandal, Melapalaiyur, Melpathi , Mudanai, Mudappuli, Mummudicholagan, Nadiyapattu, Neyveli , Palaiyapattinam, Palakkollai, Pavalangudi, Pavalangudi (Devangudi), Periyakappankulam, Perundurai, Peruvarappur, Peryakurichi, Sathamangalam, Sattapadi, Sepalanatham (North), Sepalanatham (South), Siruvappur, Tharmanallur, Tholur, U.Adhanur, U.Agaram , U.Kulapakkam, U.Mangalam , Uthangal, Uyyakondaravi, Vadakkuvellur , Valliyam, Veppankurichi .

Amenities:

Education: Primary School in 63 villages, Middle school in 29 villages, Matriculation or Secondary School in 11 villages, namely Iruppu, Ammeri, Mudangi, V.Agaram, Kunankurichi, Seplanatham, Kammapuram, Ko.Adhanur, Keeranur, Tharmanallur, Ottimedu.

Higher Secondary or Pre University Courses or Intermediate or Junior College in 5 villages of the CD Block,, namely Mudangi, V.Agaram, Seplanatham, Keeranur, Tharmanallur.

College in 0 village, Adult Literacy Center in 0 village.

Medical: Hospital in 0 village, Dispensary in 0 village, Health Center in 4 villages, Sub Center in 18 villages, Maternity and Child Welfare Center in 0 village, Community health workers in 47 villages.

Drinking Water: Tap water in 64 villages, Tank water in 1 villages, Well water in 64 villages, Tubewell in 64 villages and more than one source in 64 villages.

Bank: Banking facility in 11 villages, namely, Palakollai, Mudangi, V.Sathamangalam, Uyyakondarai Kammapuram, Kumaramagalam, Karmangudi, Devengudi Siruvarappur, Sathappady, Kavanur.

Credit Society in 11 villages Agricultural Credit Society in 10 Non-Agricultural Credit Society in 1 village.

Others: Power supply in 64 villages, Cinema hall in 1 village, sport club in 0 village, Stadium or Auditorium or Community Hall in 0 village, Post Office in 64 villages.

There are 59 villages having bus facilities.

Villages with most of facilities: Palakollai Mudangi, V.Sathamangalam, Uyyakondarai, Kammapuram Kumaramagalam, Karmangudi, Devengudi, Siruvarappur Sathappady, Kavanur.

Villages without amenities (Education): Sakkaramangalam..

Scheduled Castes: Out of the total population of 131345 persons, 34568 persons (26.32%) belong to Scheduled Castes.

The villages having less than 10% SC population are Chinnakappankulam, Arasakuzhi, Kunankurichi Melpappanapattu, Veppankurichi, K.Puthur.

The villages having more than 50% SC population are Manakkollai, Umangalam, Uyyakondarai, Managathi Karmangudi, U.Adhanur, Tharmanallur, Peruvarappur.

Sex ratio of Scheduled Caste population is 492.

Scheduled Castes Literates and Illiterates by Sex:

	Persons	Males	Females
Literate	16,858	10,506	6,352
Illiterate	17,710	7,065	10,645
Literacy rate	57.4	70.3	44.0
Graduate	285	223	62

Scheduled Castes (Dominant):

Adi Dravida, Arunthathiyar, Paraiyan etc., Domban Valluvan

For their cultural identity please see Appendix-I

Villages without Scheduled Castes: There are 7 villages without any scheduled caste population.

Scheduled Tribes: Out of the total population of 131345 persons, 1000 persons (0.76%) belong to Scheduled Tribes.

The villages having less than 10% ST population are Palakollai, Nadiyapattu, Mudapuli, Iruppu Irulakurchi, Manakkollai, Palayapattinam, Kottery Periyakappankulam, Chinnakappankulam, Kolliruppu Ammeri, Mudangi, Ponneri, Karkudai, Mavaidandal U.Kulapakkam, V.Agaram, Uthangal, Kunankurichi Umangalam, Vadakkuvellore, Periyakurichi Seplanatham, Kottagam, Uyyakondarai, Keezhpathi Managathi, Melpathi, Melpappanapattu, Neyveli Veppankurichi, Mummudechozhahan, Kammapuram Keeranur, Gopalapuram, Kumaramagalam, Ko.Adhanur Sottavanam, Karmangudi, Sakkaramangalam, Valliyam Melapalaiyur, Keeranur, Marungur, Thozhur, Kodumanur Keezhapalaiyur, Devengudi, K.Puthur, Siruvarappur Sathappady, U.Adhanur, Tharmanallur, Vilakkapadi Peruvarappur, Kottumulai, Kavanur, Keeramangalam Perundurai, T.Parazhangudi, Ottimedu.

The villages having more than 50% ST population are None.

Sex ratio of Scheduled tribe population is 524.

Scheduled Tribes Literates and Illiterates by Sex:

	Persons	Males	Females
Literate	361	205	156
Illiterate	639	271	368
Literacy rate	43.1	51.9	35.2
Graduate	1	1	0

Scheduled Tribes (Dominant):
Irular, Malakkuravan, Kattunayakan
Generic Tribes etc., Malai Pandaram
For their cultural identity please see Appendix-II
Villages without Scheduled Tribes: There are 51 villages without any scheduled tribe population.
Literates and Illiterates by Sex (Total Population):

	Persons	Males	Females
Literate	75,678	46,602	29,076
Illiterate	55,667	20,132	35,535
Literacy rate	66	80	52
Graduate	2,092	1,599	493

Agriculture: ***Distribution of villages according to land use:*** Out of 68 villages, Total area (in hectare) is 32875.01, out of that 49.61 percent is cultivable and 61.18 percent of the cultivable area is irrigated.
Sources of Irrigation (Hectares): Government Canal 287.78, Private Canal 0, Well without Electricity 296.5, Well with Electricity 532.46, Tubewell without Electricity 415.9, Tubewell with Electricity 8317.08, Tank 127, River 0, Lake 0, Waterfall 0, Others 0.
Villages with population of 5000 to 9999:
Iruppu, Ammeri, Mudanai, Periyakurichi, Sepalanatham.
Villages with population of 10000 and above: None
Distribution of Workers:

	Persons	Males	Females	WPR
Cultivators	15,772	11,084	4,688	25.9
Agricultural Labour	33,065	16,188	16,877	54.3
Household Industry	1,283	672	611	2.11
Other Workers	10,777	9,138	1,639	17.7
Main Workers	42,664	30,052	12,612	70.06
Marginal Workers	18,233	7,030	11,203	29.94
Total Workers	60,897	37,082	23,815	

Religion: Major Religious Communities:

	Persons	Males	Females	Sex Ratio
Hindu (94.63%)	124,298	63,115	61,183	969
Muslim (0.82%)	1,075	508	567	1,116
Christian (4.43%)	5,823	3,032	2,791	921
Sikh (0%)	3	1	2	2,000
Buddhists (0%)	-	-	-	-
Jain (0%)	6	2	4	2,000

Agewise Data:

	Persons	Males	Females	Sex Ratio
All ages	131,345	66,734	64,611	968
0-14	39,584	20,484	19,100	932
15-44	64,255	32,145	32,110	999
45-79	26,041	13,320	12,721	955
80+	830	462	368	797
Age not stated	635	323	312	966

Languages (Dominant):
Tamil, Telugu, Malayalam, Urdu, Hindi
Disabled Population:

	Persons	Males	Females	%
Total Disabled	3,357	1,551	1,806	
In Seeing	1,892	681	1,211	56.36
In Speech	322	176	146	9.59
In Hearing	174	93	81	5.18
In Movement	802	506	296	23.89
Mentally	167	95	72	4.97

KAMUTHI

Kamuthi C.D. Block lies in the western part of Ramanathauram district. It is a part of Kumuthi taluk. The Block is located at a distance of 80 kms. from district headquarters (Ramanathauram). There are 49 villages in the block with the total population of 93,748 persons. Area of the C.D. Block is 582.29 sq. kms. It is bounded in the north CD Block Paramakkudi and district Virudhunagar, in the south by CD Block Kadaladi, in the east by CD Blocks Madnkulathur, Paramakkudi and Kadaladi, in the west by districts Thoothukkudi and Virudhunagar.
Communications:
Roadways : S.H.-38: Direction- Aruppukkottai to Sayalgudi, Nearest Villages- Thimmanathapuram, Perunazhi, T.Valasubramaniapuram, Kadamangalam.
Railway Station: Kamuthi.
River: Gundar Nadi- Nearest Villages- Pulverikulam, Koodakulam, Kakkudi, Kamuthi, Maraikulam, Mandalamanickam, Pakkuvetti, Sangapadai, Pudhukottai, Peraiyur, Kallikulam, O. Karisalkulam, Kovilangulam, Komboothi.
Annual Rainfall: Average Rainfall 827 mm.
Ground Water: Availability of the ground water in the Basin is 3262.04 H.A.M. and the utilization is 850.45 H.A.M. It belongs to Safe category. Depth to water level varies from 5to 10 meter below the ground. Most of the wells go down in summer months, according to the Ground Water Estimation Committee.
Natural Division: NA
Administration
Revenue **Division:** Paramakudi. Parliamentary Constituency: 35 Ramanathapuram. District: Ramanathapuram. Taluk: Kamuthi. Assembly Constituency: 212 Kadaladi, 209 Paramakudi (SC). Gram Panchayat: 53.
Villages: 49 **Inhabited:** 49 **Uninhabited:** 0

Ranking	District	State	National
Area	2	21	1222
Population	4	161	3666
Sex Ratio	11	174	1191
Child Sex Ratio	8	148	2698
Literacy Rate	8	160	1570

Density	4	86	5396
Work Participation Rate	11	355	877

Gram Panchayats:

A.Tharakudi , Aanaiyoor , Achagankulam , Achankulam , Ariyamangalam, Athikulam , Eluvanoor, Erumaikulam , Idayankulam, Keelakanjiramkulam, Idivilagi , Ilandaikulam , K.Nedunkulam, K.Veppankulam , Kadamangalam, Kakkudi , Kathanendal, Kavadipatti, Keelakodumalur , Keelamudimankottai , Keelaramanathi, Komboothi , Koodakukam, Kovilangulam , M.Pudukulam , Mandalmanickam , Maraikulam, Mavilangai , Melamudimannarkottai, Melaramathi, Mudalnadu , Musthakurichi, N.Karisalkulam, Pulvoikulam , Nagaratharkurichi , Narayanapuram , Natham, Neeravi , O.Karisalkulam, Pakkuvetti, Pammanendal , Pappanam, Pappankulam , Pappurediyapatti, Pasumpon, Perunali, Ponthampuli, Pudukottai , Ramasamypatti, Sadayanendal , Sengabadai, T.Punavasal , T.Valasubramaniapuram, Thimmanathapuram, Udayanathapuram, Valayalookulam, Vallandai , Vangarupuram .

Amenities:

Education: Primary School in 47 villages, Middle school in 15 villages, Matriculation or Secondary School in 8 villages, namely Pulverikulam, Kamuthi, Mandalamanickam, Neeravi, Peraiyur, Pammanandal, Kovilangulam, Perunazhi.

Higher Secondary or Pre University Courses or Intermediate or Junior College in 2 villages of the CD Block,, namely Pulverikulam, Neeravi.

College in 3 villages, Adult Literacy Center in 1 village., Colleges are in villages, namely Pulverikulam, Kamuthi, Thavasikurichi.

Medical: Hospital in 6 villages, Dispensary in 5 villages, Health Center in 11 villages, Sub Center in 7 villages, Maternity and Child Welfare Center in 26 villages, Community health workers in 11 villages.

The Villages having Hospital or Dispensary or Health Center are Pulverikulam, Kamuthy, Vallanthai, Kamuthi, Kamuthi, Neeravi, Melaramanathi, Mustakurichi, Kovilangulam, Perunazhi.

Drinking Water: Tap water in 49 villages, Tank water in 28 villages, Well water in 49 villages, Tubewell in 49 villages and more than one source in 49 villages.

Bank: Banking facility in 10 villages, namely, Koodakulam, Abiramam, Kamuthi, Mandalamanickam Neeravi, Neeravi Karisalkulam, Melaramanathi Mudalnadu, Peraiyur, Perunazhi.

Credit Society in 32 villages Agricultural Credit Society in 32 Non-Agricultural Credit Society in 1 village.

Others: Power supply in 47 villages, Cinema hall in 2 villages, sport club in 0 village, Stadium or Auditorium or Community Hall in 0 village, Post Office in 28 villages.

There are 44 villages having bus facilities.

Villages with most of facilities: Koodakulam Kamuthi, Neeravi, Melaramanathi, Peraiyur, Perunazhi.

Villages without amenities (Education):

Vallanthai, Kakkudi..

Scheduled Castes: Out of the total population of 93748 persons, 21200 persons (22.61%) belong to Scheduled Castes.

The villages having less than 10% SC population are Kamuthi, Maraikulam, Mudimannarkottai Neeravi Karisalkulam, Melaramanathi, Keelaramanathi Seemanandal, Pudhukottai, Kallikulam, K. Vepankulam Pammanandal, Mavilangai, Komboothi, K. Villanendal Idivilagi, Panthampali, Thimmanathapuram T.Valasubramania Puram, Muthuramalingapuram.

The villages having more than 50% SC population are Vangarupuram, Vallanthai, Koodakulam, Kamuthi Abiramam, Peraiyur.

Sex ratio of Scheduled Caste population is 502.

Scheduled Castes Literates and Illiterates by Sex:

	Persons	Males	Females
Literate	11,119	6,739	4,380
Illiterate	10,081	3,825	6,256
Literacy rate	60.5	73.7	47.4
Graduate	341	276	65

Scheduled Castes (Dominant):

Pallan, Chakkiliyan, Paraiyan etc., Adi Dravida Puthirai Vannan

For their cultural identity please see Appendix-I

Villages without Scheduled Castes: There are 3 villages without any scheduled caste population.

Scheduled Tribes: Out of the total population of 93748 persons, 1 persons (0%) belong to Scheduled Tribes.

The villages having less than 10% ST population are Pulverikulam, Kamuthy, Vangarupuram, Kamuthi A. Thoraikkudi, Vallanthai, Eluvanoor, Koodakulam Kakkudi, Kamuthi, Abiramam, Kamuthi, Sadayanendal Sambakulam, Kamuthi, Maraikulam, Mandalamanickam Mudimannarkottai, Neeravi, Neeravi Karisalkulam Melaramanathi, Keelaramanathi, K. Nedungulam Thavasikurichi, Anaiyur, Pakkuvetti, Sangapadai Mudalnadu, Mustakurichi, Seemanandal, Pudhukottai Peraiyur, Kallikulam, O. Karisalkulam, K. Vepankulam Pammanandal, Mavilangai, Ariyamangalam, Kovilangulam Komboothi, K. Villanendal, M. Pudukulam, Idivilagi Panthampali, Thimmanathapuram T.Valasubramania Puram, Muthuramalingapuram Perunazhi, Kadamangalam.

The villages having more than 50% ST population are None.

Sex ratio of Scheduled tribe population is 1000.

Scheduled Tribes Literates and Illiterates by Sex:

	Persons	Males	Females
Literate	0	0	0
Illiterate	1	0	1
Literacy rate	-	-	-
Graduate	0	0	0

Scheduled Tribes (Dominant):

Palliyan

For their cultural identity please see Appendix-II

Villages without Scheduled Tribes: There are 48 villages without any scheduled tribe population.

Literates and Illiterates by Sex (Total Population):

	Persons	Males	Females
Literate	54,775	33,068	21,707
Illiterate	38,973	13,834	25,139
Literacy rate	67	81	53
Graduate	1,519	1,143	376

Agriculture: ***Distribution of villages according to land use:*** Out of 49 villages, Total area (in hectare) is 58229, out of that 69.27 percent is cultivable and 18.94 percent of the cultivable area is irrigated.

Sources of Irrigation (Hectares): Government Canal 202.15, Private Canal 0, Well without Electricity 1492.63, Well with Electricity 13084.61, Tubewell without Electricity 39.45, Tubewell with Electricity 878.83, Tank 5327.24, River 10.16, Lake 0, Waterfall 228.86, Others 0.

Villages with population of 5000 to 9999:
Natham, Peraiyur.

Villages with population of 10000 and above: None

Distribution of Workers:

	Persons	Males	Females	WPR
Cultivators	20,158	11,381	8,777	39.04
Agricultural Labour	22,374	9,394	12,980	43.33
Household Industry	918	321	597	1.78
Other Workers	8,188	6,157	2,031	15.86
Main Workers	43,445	24,575	18,870	84.13
Marginal Workers	8,193	2,678	5,515	15.87
Total Workers	51,638	27,253	24,385	

Religion: Major Religious Communities:

	Persons	Males	Females	Sex Ratio
Hindu (93.15%)	87,326	43,762	43,564	995
Muslim (3.14%)	2,941	1,384	1,557	1,125
Christian (4.4%)	4,124	2,009	2,115	1,053
Sikh (0%)	1	1	-	-
Buddhists (0%)	1	-	1	-
Jain (0%)	1	1	-	-

Agewise Data:

	Persons	Males	Females	Sex Ratio
All ages	94,755	47,360	47,395	1001
0-14	28,933	14,994	13,939	930
15-44	44,002	21,620	22,382	1035
45-79	20,835	10,294	10,541	1024
80+	734	348	336	1109
Age not stated	251	104	147	1413

Languages (Dominant):
Tamil, Telugu, Kannada, Bengali, Urdu

Disabled Population:

	Persons	Males	Females	%
Total Disabled	2,396	1,155	1,241	
In Seeing	1,358	548	810	56.68
In Speech	266	168	98	11.1
In Hearing	101	44	57	4.22
In Movement	509	307	202	21.24
Mentally	162	88	74	6.76

KANAI

Kanai C.D. Block lies in the eastern part of Viluppuram district. It is a part of Viluppuram taluk. The taluk is located at a distance of 00 kms. from district headquarters (Viluppuram). There are 64 villages in the block with the total population of 124,998 persons. Area of the C.D. Block is 257.95 sq. kms. It is bounded in the north by CD Block Gingee and Vikravandi, in the south by CD Blocks Thiruvennainallur and Koliyanur, in the east by C.D. Blocks Vikravandi and Koliyanur, and in the west by CD Block Mugaiyur.

Communications:

Roadways : S.H.-7: Direction- Tirukkoyilur to Viluppuram, Nearest Villages- Kangiyanur, Kuppam, Mamnalapattu, Karingali, Pattu, Kanai, Vailamur, Perumbakkam, Venkatesapuram.

Railway Station: Mamnalapattu, Theli.

River: Ponnaiyar Nadi- Nearest Villages- Kalpattu, Siruvakkur, Theli.

Backwards Region Grants Fund: It receives Backward Region Grants.

Annual Rainfall: Average Rainfall 1119 mm.

Ground Water: Availability of the ground water in the Basin is 7186.83 H.A.M. and the utilization is 6066.83 H.A.M. It belongs to Semi Critical category. Depth to water level varies from 2 to 10 meter below the ground. Most of the wells go down in summer months, according to the Ground Water Estimation Committee.

Forest and Reserved Forest: (Gangavaram RF)- Nearest Villages- Nallapalayam, Kadayam, Gangavaram R.F, Karuvatchi. (Kadayam)- Nearest Villages- Nallapalayam, Kadayam R.F, Kadayam. (Thirunjikadu)- Nearest Villages- Thurinji kadu R.F, Nallapalayam. (Udaiyanatham)- Nearest Villages- Kadayam, Karuvatchi, Udaiyanatham R.F, Kulirsunai,

Udayanatham.

Natural Division: Tondai Nadu.

Administration

Revenue **Division:** Villupuram. Parliamentary Constituency: 13 Villupuram (SC). District: Villupuram. Taluk: Villu puram. Assembly Constituency: 75 Vikravandi, 74 Villupuram. Gram Panchayat: 51.

Villages: 64 **Inhabited:** 59 **Uninhabited:** 5

Ranking	District	State	National
Area	18	220	3275
Population	8	56	2691
Sex Ratio	17	286	2307
Child Sex Ratio	20	228	3706
Literacy Rate	6	227	2073
Density	14	220	2286
Work Participation Rate	4	62	2336

Gram Panchayats:

Adanur, Agaram Chittamur, Anniyur, Ariyalur (Thirukkai) , Ariyur, Attiyur Thirukkai, Chennappanayakkanpalayam, Elusembon, Hanumanthapuram, Kadayam, Kakkanur, Kaliyanampundi, Kalpattu, Kanai, Kangiyanur, Kanjanur, Karingalippattu, Karuvakshi, Kedar, Kolippattu, Konur, Kottammangalam, Kuppam, Malligappattu, Mambalapattu, Melkaranai, Nallapalayam, Nangathur, Palliyandur, Panamalai, Perumbakkam, Perunkalapundi, Porur, Salavanur, Sangitamanagalam, Semmedu, Senji kunnathur, Siruvakkur, Siruvalai, Sitheri, Surappattu, Tat Nagar, Teli, Thirukkunam, Udaiyanatham, Valappattu, Vellayaimbattu, Vengamur, Vengandur, Venmaniyathur, Viramur.

Amenities:

Education: Primary School in 54 villages, Middle school in 27 villages, Matriculation or Secondary School in 13 villages, namely Karuvatchi, Sangithamangalam, Nangathur, Udayanatham, Anniyur, Athiyur Thirukkai, Kanjanur, Kakkanur, Kedar, Mamnalapattu, Kanai, Konur, Venkatesapuram.

Higher Secondary or Pre University Courses or Intermediate or Junior College in 5 villages of the CD Block,, namely Sangithamangalam, Anniyur, Surapattu, Kedar, Mamnalapattu.

College in 0 village, Adult Literacy Center in 0 village.

Medical: Hospital in 2 villages, Dispensary in 2 villages, Health Center in 4 villages, Sub Center in 2 villages, Maternity and Child Welfare Center in 15 villages, Community health workers in 20 villages.

The Villages having Hospital or Dispensary or Health Center are Elusembon, Kakkanur, Kalpattu, Perumbakkam.

Drinking Water: Tap water in 59 villages, Tank water in 33 villages, Well water in 59 villages, Tubewell in 59 villages and more than one source in 59 villages.

Bank: Banking facility in 9 villages, namely, Anniyur, Siruvalai, Ariyalur Thurukkai, Viramur Kuppam, Mamnalapattu, Kalpattu, Kanai, Perumbakkam.

Credit Society in 14 villages Agricultural Credit Society in 8 Non-Agricultural Credit Society in 6 villages.

Others: Power supply in 59 villages, Cinema hall in 1 village, sport club in 1 village, Stadium or Auditorium or Community Hall in 0 village, Post Office in 51 villages.

There are 56 villages having bus facilities.

Villages with most of facilities: Anniyur Siruvalai, Ariyalur Thurukkai, Viramur, Mamnalapattu Kalpattu, Kanai.

Villages without amenities (Education):

Kulirsunai, Venkayakuppam, Kuppam, Perumbakkam..

Scheduled Castes: Out of the total population of 124998 persons, 29193 persons (23.35%) belong to Scheduled Castes.

The villages having less than 10% SC population are Nangathur, Udayanatham, Hanumanthapuram, Porur Velleripattu, Sitheri, Venkayakuppam S.Kunnathurthangal, Semmedu, Kakkanur, Andanur Malligaipattu, Perumbakkam, Theli.

The villages having more than 50% SC population are Kulirsunai, Perunkalapundi, Koralur, Kanjanur Kuppam, Karingali Pattu, Kothamangalam Venkatesapuram.

Sex ratio of Scheduled Caste population is 496.

Scheduled Castes Literates and Illiterates by Sex:

	Persons	Males	Females
Literate	13,742	8,176	5,566
Illiterate	15,451	6,527	8,924
Literacy rate	55.5	65.9	45.0
Graduate	121	95	26

Scheduled Castes (Dominant):

Adi Dravida, Arunthathiyar, Generic Castes etc. Valluvan, Kuravan etc.

For their cultural identity please see Appendix-I

Villages without Scheduled Castes: There are 14 villages without any scheduled caste population.

Scheduled Tribes: Out of the total population of 124998 persons, 2478 persons (1.98%) belong to Scheduled Tribes.

The villages having less than 10% ST population are Nallapalayam, Kadayam, Karuvatchi, C.N. Palayam Panamalai, Sangithamangalam, Nangathur Senji Kunnathur, Salavanur, Vellaiyampattu Kulirsunai, Udayanatham, Vengamur, Hanumanthapuram Tirukkunam, Anniyur, Perunkalapundi, Kannathal Kalyanampoondi, Melkaranai, Porur, Velleripattu

Sitheri, Elusembon, Venkayakuppam, Kanjanur S.Kunnathurthangal, Siruvalai, Semmedu, Kakkanur Ariyalur Thurukkai, Viramur, Arumbuli, Andanur Surapattu, Valappattu, Kedar, Palliyandur Kozhipattu, Malligaipattu, Kangiyanur Agaramsithamur, Vengandur, Ariyur, Kuppam Mamnalapattu, Kalpattu, Siruvakkur, Karingali Pattu Kanai, Vailamur, Perumbakkam, Konur, Theli Venmaniyathur, Venkatesapuram.

The villages having more than 50% ST population are None.

Sex ratio of Scheduled tribe population is 496.

Scheduled Tribes Literates and Illiterates by Sex:

	Persons	Males	Females
Literate	802	484	318
Illiterate	1,676	765	911
Literacy rate	37.8	45.5	30.0
Graduate	1	1	0

Scheduled Tribes (Dominant):

Irular, Malayali, Kattunayakan, Malakkuravan Malai Vedan

For their cultural identity please see Appendix-II

Villages without Scheduled Tribes: There are 35 villages without any scheduled tribe population.

Literates and Illiterates by Sex (Total Population):

	Persons	Males	Females
Literate	70,083	41,822	28,261
Illiterate	54,915	21,499	33,416
Literacy rate	64	76	52
Graduate	1,062	815	247

Agriculture: ***Distribution of villages according to land use:*** Out of 64 villages, Total area (in hectare) is 25795.78, out of that 57.7 percent is cultivable and 53.5 percent of the cultivable area is irrigated.

Sources of Irrigation (Hectares): Government Canal 0, Private Canal 0, Well without Electricity 965.98, Well with Electricity 4121.59, Tubewell without Electricity 197.91, Tubewell with Electricity 725.21, Tank 0, River 0, Lake 1949.19, Waterfall 0, Others 2.81.

Villages with population of 5000 to 9999: Kedar.

Villages with population of 10000 and above: None

Distribution of Workers:

	Persons	Males	Females	WPR
Cultivators	16,446	11,434	5,012	26.48
Agricultural Labour	35,339	16,686	18,653	56.91
Household Industry	1,600	980	620	2.58
Other Workers	8,712	6,669	2,043	14.03
Main Workers	43,319	28,514	14,805	69.76
Marginal Workers	18,778	7,255	11,523	30.24
Total Workers	62,097	35,769	26,328	

Religion: Major Religious Communities:

	Persons	Males	Females	Sex Ratio
Hindu (91.62%)	114,527	58,104	56,423	971
Muslim (0.82%)	1,028	504	524	1,040
Christian (7.52%)	9,402	4,690	4,712	1,005
Sikh (0%)	-	-	-	-
Buddhists (0%)	1	1	-	-
Jain (0%)	2	1	1	1,000

Agewise Data:

	Persons	Males	Females	Sex Ratio
All ages	124,998	63,321	61,677	974
0-14	38,409	19,717	18,692	948
15-44	59,233	29,514	29,719	1007
45-79	25,949	13,322	12,627	948
80+	919	532	387	727
Age not stated	488	236	252	1068

Languages (Dominant):

Tamil, Telugu, Urdu, Kannada, Hindi

Disabled Population:

	Persons	Males	Females	%
Total Disabled	2,360	1,367	993	
In Seeing	961	521	440	40.72
In Speech	267	149	118	11.31
In Hearing	159	78	81	6.74
In Movement	762	487	275	32.29
Mentally	211	132	79	8.94

KANCHEEPURAM

Kancheepuram C.D. Block lies in the northern-western part of Kancheepuram district. It is a part of Kancheepuram taluk. The Block is located at a distance of (00) kms. from district headquarters (Kancheepuram). There are 69 villages in the block with the total population of 107958 persons. Area of the C.D. Block is 252.20 sq. kms. It is bounded in the north by district Vellore and CD Block Walajabad, in the south by CD Block Uthiram erur and disctrict Tiruvannamalai, in the east by CD Block Walajabad, in the west by districts Tiruvannamalai and Vellore.

Communications:

Roadways : N.H.-4: Direction- Walajabad to Sriperumbudur and Kancheepuram, Nearest Villages- Chitterimedu, Thuluk kanthandalam, Damal, Thiruppukuzhi, Melambi, Kilambi, Thimmasamudram, Pappankuzhi (UI), Sirukaveripakkam, Netteri, Achukattu, Karuppadithatadai.

River: Palar Nadi- Nearest Villages- Perumbakkam, Mutha vedu, Pitchavadi, Vishar, Alavandarmedu, Vippedu, Chinnai yankulam, Orikkai, Kolivakkam, Punjarasanthangal, Valatho ttam, Kamugampallam, Kuruvimalai, Vitchanthangal, Kalur, Avalur, Angambakkam, Musaravakkam, Asur.Cheyyar Nadi- Nearest Villages- Angambakkam, Thammanur, Magaral,

Kavanthandalam, Kambarajapuram, Elayanarvelur, Chithathur.

Annual Rainfall: Average Rainfall 1105 mm.

Ground Water: Availability of the ground water in the Basin is 9996.49 H.A.M. and the utilization is 4083.10 H.A.M. It belongs to Safe category. Depth to water level varies from 5 to 10 meter below the ground. Most of the wells go down in summer months, according to the Ground Water Estimation Committee.

Natural Division: Tondai Nadu.

Administration

Revenue **Division:** Kancheepuram. Parliamentary Constituency: 6 Kancheepuram (SC). District: Kancheepuram. Taluk: Kancheepuram. Assembly Constituency: 36 Uthiramerur, 37 Kancheepuram. Gram Panchayat: 43.

Villages: 69 **Inhabited:** 67 **Uninhabited:** 2

Ranking	District	State	National
Area	11	229	3350
Population	6	103	3213
Sex Ratio	2	172	1201
Child Sex Ratio	8	128	2368
Literacy Rate	6	180	1714
Density	4	232	2571
Work Participation Rate	3	96	2510

Gram Panchayats:

Angambakkam, Arapakkam , Ariyaperumbakkam , Ariyaperumbakkam , Avalur, Damal , Elayanarvelur , Iyangarkulam, Kalakattur , Kalakkattur , Kalur , Kambarajapuram, Karuppadithattadai , Kavanthandalam, Kilambi , Kilar, Kilkadirpoor, Kilperumanallur , Kolivakkam, Konerikuppam , Kuram, Magaral, Melkadirpoor , Melottivakkam, Musaravakkam, Muthavedu , Muttavakkam , Narapakkam , Olakkalpattu , Olakkolpattu , Orikkai , Perumbakkam, Punjarasanthangal, Putheri, Sirukaveripakkam, Sirukaveripakkam , Sirunaiperugal, Thammanur, Thimmasamudram, Thimmasamudram , Thiruparithikundram, Thiruppukuzhi, Valathottam , Vippedu , Vishar .

Amenities:

Education: Primary School in 51 villages, Middle school in 21 villages, Matriculation or Secondary School in 6 villages, namely Thiruppukuzhi, Musaravakkam, Vishar, Iyangarkulam, Avalur, Arpakkam.

Higher Secondary or Pre University Courses or Intermediate or Junior College in 3 villages of the CD Block,, namely Thiruppukuzhi, Iyangarkulam, Arpakkam.

College in 1 village, Adult Literacy Center in 0 village., . College is in village, namely Kilambi.

Medical: Hospital in 1 village, Dispensary in 3 villages, Health Center in 14 villages, Sub Center in 24 villages, Maternity and Child Welfare Center in 3 villages, Community health workers in 67 villages.

The Villages having Hospital or Dispensary or Health Center are Kuram, Ariyaperumbakkam, Sirunaiperugal, Iyangarkulam, Kalakattur.

Drinking Water: Tap water in 67 villages, Tank water in 38 villages, Well water in 67 villages, Tubewell in 67 villages and more than one source in 67 villages.

Bank: Banking facility in 14 villages, namely, Kuram, Damal, Kilar, Thiruppukuzhi, Netteri Kilkadirpoor A,B/B, Narapakkam, Vippedu, Valathottam Kalur A,B/B, Kalakattur, Thalaiyillaperumbakkam Magaral, Kavanthandalam.

Credit Society in 14 villages Agricultural Credit Society in 13 Non-Agricultural Credit Society in 2 villages.

Others: Power supply in 67 villages, Cinema hall in 0 village, sport club in 1 village, Stadium or Auditorium or Community Hall in 0 village, Post Office in 22 villages.

There are 58 villages having bus facilities.

Villages with most of facilities: Kuram, Damal Kilar, Thiruppukuzhi, Kilkadirpoor A,B/B, Narapakkam Vippedu, Valathottam, Kalakattur Thalaiyillaperumbakkam, Magaral, Kavanthandalam.

Villages without amenities (Education):

Chitterimedu, Melambi, Netteri, Achukattu, Karuppadithatadai, Putheri, Pitchavadi, Alavandarmedu, Kottakkaval, Velinkapatadai, Punjarasanthangal, Kamugampallam, Vitchanthangal, Melputhur, Kolathur, Nelveli..

Scheduled Castes: Out of the total population of 107958 persons, 33932 persons (31.43%) belong to Scheduled Castes.

The villages having less than 10% SC population are Melbangaram, Vathiyur, Thulukkanthandalam, Netteri Achukattu, Arappanacheri A/B, Mettukuppam, Vishar Velinkapatadai, Kamugampallam, Kuruvimalai, Avalur Perumanallur, Vedal, Kalakattur Thalaiyillaperumbakkam, Kilputhur, Chithaathur.

The villages having more than 50% SC population are Sembarambakkam, Melambi, Karuppadithatadai Konerikuppam A/B, Putheri, Melottivakkam Sadathangal, Narapakkam, Alavandarmedu, Kottakkaval Asoor, Angambakkam, Melputhur, Kolathur, Arpakkam Magaral, Nelveli.

Sex ratio of Scheduled Caste population is 498.

Scheduled Castes Literates and Illiterates by Sex:

	Persons	Males	Females
Literate	18,963	11,050	7,913
Illiterate	14,969	5,971	8,998
Literacy rate	64.6	75.3	53.9
Graduate	180	141	39

Scheduled Castes (Dominant):

Adi Dravida, Arunthathiyar, Kuravan etc., Valluvan Pallan

For their cultural identity please see Appendix-I

Villages without Scheduled Castes: There are 12 villages without any scheduled caste population.

Scheduled Tribes: Out of the total population of 107958 persons, 1748 persons (1.62%) belong to Scheduled Tribes. The villages having less than 10% ST population are Olakkalpattu, Thaipakkam, Melbangaram, Vathiyur Kuram, Sembarambakkam, Chitterimedu Thulukkanthandalam, Ariyaperumbakkam, Sirunaiperugal Muttavakkam, Damal, Kilar, Thiruppukuzhi, Kilambi Sirukaveripakkam, Thimmasamudram, Netteri, Achukattu Karuppadithatadai, Konerikuppam A/B Arappanacheri A/B, Putheri, Kilkadirpoor A,B/B Melkadirpoor, Mettukuppam, Melottivakkam Musaravakkam, Perumbakkam, Muthavedu, Pitchavadi Vishar, Sadathangal, Narapakkam, Alavandarmedu Vippedu, Chinnaiyankulam, Kottakkaval Velinkapatadai, Orikkai, Kolivakkam, Iyangarkulam Punjarasanthangal, Valathottam, Kuruvimalai Vitchanthangal, Kalur A,B/B, Asoor, Avalur Angambakkam, Thammanur, Melputhur, Kolathur Perumanallur, Vedal, Kalakattur, Arpakkam, Magaral Kavanthandalam, Nelveli, Kilputhur, Kambarajapuram Elayanarvelur, Chithaathur.

The villages having more than 50% ST population are None.

Sex ratio of Scheduled tribe population is 487.

Scheduled Tribes Literates and Illiterates by Sex:

	Persons	Males	Females
Literate	293	192	101
Illiterate	1,455	705	750
Literacy rate	20.6	26.4	14.5
Graduate	0	0	0

Scheduled Tribes (Dominant):

Irular, Malakkuravan, Kattunayakan, Malai Vedan Malai Pandaram

For their cultural identity please see Appendix-II

Villages without Scheduled Tribes: There are 30 villages without any scheduled tribe population.

Literates and Illiterates by Sex (Total Population):

	Persons	Males	Females
Literate	62,477	36,305	26,172
Illiterate	45,481	17,705	27,776
Literacy rate	66	77	55
Graduate	577	445	132

Agriculture: ***Distribution of villages according to land use:*** Out of 69 villages, Total area (in hectare) is 25220.15, out of that 56.43 percent is cultivable and 66.57 percent of the cultivable area is irrigated.

Sources of Irrigation (Hectares): Government Canal 124.29, Private Canal 20, Well without Electricity 160.18, Well with Electricity 3332.99, Tubewell without Electricity 10.04, Tubewell with Electricity 2165.77, Tank 669.09, River 150.84, Lake 2512.66, Waterfall 0, Others 327.76.

Villages with population of 5000 to 9999: Damal, Musaravakkam.

Villages with population of 10000 and above: None

Distribution of Workers:

	Persons	Males	Females	WPR
Cultivators	8,187	5,889	2,298	15.46
Agricultural Labour	24,962	11,264	13,698	47.14
Household Industry	6,532	4,342	2,190	12.34
Other Workers	13,268	10,602	2,666	25.06
Main Workers	46,264	30,067	16,197	87.37
Marginal Workers	6,685	2,030	4,655	12.63
Total Workers	52,949	32,097	20,852	

Religion: Major Religious Communities:

	Persons	Males	Females	Sex Ratio
Hindu (96.89%)	104,598	52,358	52,240	998
Muslim (1.5%)	1,618	808	810	1,002
Christian (1.44%)	1,550	752	798	1,061
Sikh (0%)	1	1	-	-
Buddhists (0.03%)	34	15	19	1,267
Jain (0.04%)	44	25	19	760

Agewise Data:

	Persons	Males	Females	Sex Ratio
All ages	107,958	54,010	53,948	999
0-14	31,288	15,823	15,465	977
15-44	53,652	26,778	26,874	1004
45-79	21,994	10,882	11,112	1021
80+	797	413	384	930
Age not stated	227	114	113	991

Languages (Dominant):

Tamil, Telugu, Urdu, Kannada, Gujarati

Disabled Population:

	Persons	Males	Females	%
Total Disabled	4,189	2,257	1,932	
In Seeing	2,914	1,511	1,403	69.56
In Speech	256	146	110	6.11
In Hearing	168	76	92	4.01
In Movement	632	402	230	15.09
Mentally	219	122	97	5.23

KANDAMANGALAM

Kandamangalam C.D. Block lies in the eastern part of Viluppuram district. It is a part of Viluppuram taluk. The taluk is located at a distance of 00 kms. from district headquarters (Viluppuram). There are 53 villages in the block with the total population of 129,398 persons. Area of the C.D. Block is 199.92 sq. kms. It is bounded in the north by CD Block Vanur, in the south by district Cuddalore, in the east by taluk Cuddalore, in the west by C.D. Blocks Vikravandi and Kolianur. It has common boundary with the Union Territory of Pondicherry on north and east.

Communications:

Roadways : N.H.-45 A: Direction- Valavanur to Pondicherry, Nearest Villages- Malrasankuppam, Gangarampalayam, Chinnababusamudiram, Pallithennal, Navamalkapper, Kandam angalam, Aliyur, Navamalmarudur.

Railway Station: Chinnababusamudiram.

River: Varahanadi- Nearest Villages- Kodukkur, Kalingamalai, Pakkiripalayam, V.Nerkunam, Mutrampattu, Ammanankuppam, Chinnababusamudiram, Pallithennal, Kalithirampattu. Ponnaiyar Nadi- Nearest Villages- Parasureddipalayam, Poovarasankuppam, Vadavambalam, Sornavourmeelpathy, Kalingikuppam, Sornavourkeelpathy, Perichampakkam, Kondur, Mittamandagapattu, Chokkampattu, Kongampattu, Parasureddipalayam, Poovarasankuppam, Panchanadevi, Vengatadri Agaram.

Backwards Region Grants Fund: It receives Backward Region Grants.

Annual Rainfall: Average Rainfall 1119 mm.

Ground Water: Availability of the ground water in the Basin is 10447.06 H.A.M. and the utilization is 15591. 55 H.A.M. It belongs to Over Expoited category. Depth to water level varies from 5 to 10 meter below the ground. Most of the wells go down in summer months, according to the Ground Water Estimation Committee.

Natural Division: Tondai Nadu.

Administration

Revenue **Division:** Villupuram. Parliamentary Constituency: 13 Villupuram (SC). District: Villupuram. Taluk: Villu puram. Assembly Constituency: 73 Vanur (SC), 74 Villupuram, 75 Vikramandi. Gram Panchayat: 45.

Villages: 53 **Inhabited:** 53 **Uninhabited:** 0

Ranking	District	State	National
Area	21	287	4183
Population	5	43	2531
Sex Ratio	14	262	2033
Child Sex Ratio	16	175	3023
Literacy Rate	2	139	1461
Density	15	228	1645
Work Participation Rate	2	27	2480

Gram Panchayats:

Aliyur, Arpisampalaiyam, Chinnababusamudram, Chittalambattu, Gangarampalaiyam, Kalanjukuppam, Kalittirambattu, Kallippattu, Kandamangalam, Kodukkur, Kondur, Kongambattu, Kottambakkam, Krishnapuram, Kumulam, Mandagappattu (Mitta), Mathur, Mokshakulam, Muttarampattu, Navamal Marudur, Navamalkapper, Nerkunam, Pakkam, Pakkiripalayam, Pallineriyanur, Pallippuduppattu, Pallittennal, Panchamadevi, Parasureddipalaiyam, Periyababusamudram, Puvarasamkuppam, Rampakkam, Seshanganur, Sheshangaanur, Siruvandadu, Sorappur, Sornavur (Kilpadi), Sornavur (Melpadi), Thadavamoorthykuppam, Tirumangalam, V.Pudur, Vadanur, Vadavambalam, Valudavur, Vengatadriagaram, Viranam.

Amenities:

Education: Primary School in 48 villages, Middle school in 14 villages, Matriculation or Secondary School in 10 villages, namely Chithalampatti, Pakkiripalayam, Chinnababusamudiram, Kandamangalam, Siruvanthadu, Mittamandagapattu, Rambakkam, Sornavourkeelpathy, Sornavourmeelpathy, Kalingikuppam.

Higher Secondary or Pre University Courses or Intermediate or Junior College in 7 villages of the CD Block,, namely Kodukkur, Chithalampatti, Pakkiripalayam, Chinnababusamudiram, Kandamangalam, Siruvanthadu, Sornavourkeelpathy.

College in 0 village, Adult Literacy Center in 0 village.

Medical: Hospital in 4 villages, Dispensary in 0 village, Health Center in 5 villages, Sub Center in 6 villages, Maternity and Child Welfare Center in 4 villages, Community health workers in 4 villages.

The Villages having Hospital or Dispensary or Health Center are Vengatadri Agaram, Siruvanthadu, Mittamandagapattu, C. Kallipattu, Vadavambalam.

Drinking Water: Tap water in 53 villages, Tank water in 36 villages, Well water in 53 villages, Tubewell in 53 villages and more than one source in 53 villages.

Bank: Banking facility in 10 villages, namely, Thirumangalam, Mutrampattu, Valudhavur, Vadhanur Kandamangalam, Vengatadri Agaram, Mittamandagapattu Mokshakulam, Pakkam, Rambakkam.

Credit Society in 14 villages Agricultural Credit Society in 14 Non-Agricultural Credit Society in 2 villages.

Others: Power supply in 52 villages, Cinema hall in 1 village, sport club in 4 villages, Stadium or Auditorium or Community Hall in 1 village, Post Office in 32 villages.

There are 48 villages having bus facilities.

Villages with most of facilities: Thirumangalam Valudhavur, Vadhanur, Kandamangalam Vengatadri Agaram, Mittamandagapattu, Rambakkam.

Villages without amenities (Education): Mudaliarkuppam, Manakuppam, Malrąsankuppam, Chokkampattu, Perichampakkam..

Scheduled Castes: Out of the total population of 129398 persons, 44067 persons (34.06%) belong to Scheduled Castes.

The villages having less than 10% SC population are Kalingamalai, Pakkiripalayam, Mudaliarkuppam Malrasankuppam, Poovarasankuppam, Sornavourmeelpathy Perichampakkam.

The villages having more than 50% SC population are Kodukkur, Mutrampattu, V.Nerkunam, Pallineliyanur Kothambakkam, Navamalmarudur, Chokkampattu Parasureddipalayam, Pakkam, Krishnapuram Sornavourkeelpathy.

Sex ratio of Scheduled Caste population is 501.

Scheduled Castes Literates and Illiterates by Sex:

	Persons	Males	Females
Literate	21,791	12,845	8,946
Illiterate	22,276	9,124	13,152
Literacy rate	57.9	68.6	47.2
Graduate	346	282	64

Scheduled Castes (Dominant):

Adi Dravida, Valluvan, Adi Andhra, Chakkiliyan Arunthathiyar

For their cultural identity please see Appendix-I

Villages without Scheduled Castes: There are 3 villages without any scheduled caste population.

Scheduled Tribes: Out of the total population of 129398 persons, 51 persons (0.04%) belong to Scheduled Tribes.

The villages having less than 10% ST population are Kodukkur, Chithalampatti, Thirumangalam, Mutrampattu Kalingamalai, Valudhavur, Pakkiripalayam, V.Nerkunam Kurampalayam, Vadhanur, V. Mathur, V.Pudur Mudaliarkuppam, Kumulam, Sashanganur Kalithirampattu, Ammanankuppam, Periyababusamudiram Manakuppam, Malrasankuppam, Gangarampalayam Chinnababusamudiram, Pallithennal, Navamalkapper Kandamangalam, Aliyur, Pallineliyanur, Kothambakkam Pallicherri, Arpisampalayam, Vengatadri Agaram Panchanadevi, Siruvanthadu, Pallipudupattu Mittamandagapattu, Navamalmarudur, Kondur Chokkampattu, Mokshakulam, Parasureddipalayam Poovarasankuppam, C. Kallipattu, Vadavambalam Kongampattu, Sorappur, Veeranam, Pakkam Krishnapuram, Rambakkam, Sornavourkeelpathy Sornavourmeelpathy, Kalingikuppam, Perichampakkam.

The villages having more than 50% ST population are None.

Sex ratio of Scheduled tribe population is 510.

Scheduled Tribes Literates and Illiterates by Sex:

	Persons	Males	Females
Literate	18	9	9
Illiterate	33	16	17
Literacy rate	40.0	42.9	37.5
Graduate	0	0	0

Scheduled Tribes (Dominant):

Malakkuravan, Kattunayakan, Irular, Malai Arayan Generic Tribes etc.

For their cultural identity please see Appendix-II

Villages without Scheduled Tribes: There are 48 villages without any scheduled tribe population.

Literates and Illiterates by Sex (Total Population):

	Persons	Males	Females
Literate	77,097	45,027	32,070
Illiterate	52,301	20,338	31,963
Literacy rate	68	79	57
Graduate	1,725	1,289	436

Agriculture: ***Distribution of villages according to land use:*** Out of 53 villages, Total area (in hectare) is 19992.85, out of that 69.11 percent is cultivable and 91.82 percent of the cultivable area is irrigated.

Sources of Irrigation (Hectares): Government Canal 0, Private Canal 0, Well without Electricity 0, Well with Electricity 0, Tubewell without Electricity 752, Tubewell with Electricity 11864.101, Tank 70.26, River 0, Lake 0, Waterfall 0, Others 0.

Villages with population of 5000 to 9999: Tirumangalam, Vengatadriagaram, Viranam.

Villages with population of 10000 and above: None

Distribution of Workers:

	Persons	Males	Females	WPR
Cultivators	9,685	7,238	2,447	15.16
Agricultural Labour	41,035	21,273	19,762	64.24
Household Industry	2,217	1,295	922	3.47
Other Workers	10,938	8,957	1,981	17.12
Main Workers	50,193	32,816	17,377	78.58
Marginal Workers	13,682	5,947	7,735	21.42
Total Workers	63,875	38,763	25,112	

Religion: Major Religious Communities:

	Persons	Males	Females	Sex Ratio
Hindu (98.23%)	127,110	64,231	62,879	979
Muslim (1.52%)	1,970	984	986	1,002
Christian (0.2%)	262	126	136	1,079
Sikh (0%)	4	2	2	1,000
Buddhists (0%)	-	-	-	-
Jain (0%)	2	1	1	1,000

Agewise Data:

	Persons	Males	Females	Sex Ratio
All ages	129,398	65,365	64,033	980
0-14	36,190	18,506	17,684	956
15-44	65,034	32,685	32,349	990
45-79	26,658	13,338	13,320	999
80+	954	532	422	793
Age not stated	562	304	258	849

Languages (Dominant):

Tamil, Telugu, Urdu, Kannada, Malayalam

Disabled Population:

	Persons	Males	Females	%
Total Disabled	2,904	1,645	1,259	
In Seeing	1,326	686	640	45.66
In Speech	278	155	123	9.57
In Hearing	239	121	118	8.23
In Movement	869	574	295	29.92
Mentally	192	109	83	6.61

KANDILI

Kandili C.D. Block lies in the south-westren part of Vellore district. It is a part of Tirupathur taluk. The taluk is located at a distance of 82 kms. from district headquarters (Vellore). There are 42 villages in the block with the total population of 132,846 persons. Area of the C.D. Block is 287.77 sq. kms. It is bounded in the north by CD Blocks Jolarpettai and Tirupattur, in the south and west by district Dharamapuri, in the east by CD Block Alangayam and district Tiruvannamalai.

Communications:

Roadways : S.H.-18: Direction- Uttangarai to Tirupatur, Nearest Villages- Adiyur, Koratti, Elavampatti, Chinnar ampatti.

Railway Station: Molagarampatti, Sevvathur.

River: Pambar Nadi- Nearest Villages- Udayamuthur, Chinn arampatti, Perampattu, Vishamangalam, Matrapalli.

Annual Rainfall: Average Rainfall 949 mm.

Ground Water: Availability of the ground water in the Basin is 5175.17 H.A.M. and the utilization is 8739.41 H.A.M. It belongs to Over Expoited category. Depth to water level varies from 5 to 15 meter below the ground. Most of the wells go down in summer months, according to the Ground Water Estimation Committee.

Forest and Reserved Forest: (Govindpuram RF)- Nearest Villages- Simmanapudur, Govindapuram. (Singarapet)- Nearest Villages- Singarpet, Singarpet Extn. (Mambakkam)- Nearest Villages- Simmanapudur, Kurumberi, Matrapalli.

Natural Division: Tondai Nadu.

Administration

Revenue **Division:** Tirupatahur. Parliamentary Constituenc y: 11 Tiruvannamalai. District: Vellore. Taluk: Tirupathur. Assembly Constituency: 50 Tiruppattur, 49 Jolarpet. Gram Panchayat: 39.

Villages: 41 **Inhabited:** 41 **Uninhabited:** 0

Ranking	District	State	National
Area	8	185	2905
Population	6	38	2409
Sex Ratio	18	322	2739
Child Sex Ratio	20	352	5885
Literacy Rate	18	254	2190
Density	3	234	2394
Work Participation Rate	7	77	2528

Gram Panchayats:

Adiyur, Avalnayakkampalli, Chinnakandhili, Chinnakasinaickenpatti, Chinnarampatti, East.Badanavadi, Elavampatti, Errampatti, Ganganayakanpatti, Gummidigampatti, Kakangarai, Kandili, Kasinayagampatti, Koratti, Kurichi, Kurumberi, Lakkinayakkampatti, Manavalli, Mandalanayanagunda, Matrapalli, Mottur, Narasampatti, Nariyaneri , Natham, Nellivasalnadu, Odayamuthur, Pallthoor, Paradesipatti, Paramithampatti, Perampatti, Periagaram, Periyakannalampatti, Sevvathur, Simmanapudur, Sundarampalli, Sundarampatti, SuPallipattu, Thokkiyam , Thoranampatti, Vengalapuram, Vishamangalam, .

Amenities:

Education: Primary School in 32 villages, Middle school in 21 villages, Matriculation or Secondary School in 13 villages, namely Peeiyagaram, Thokkiyam, Kandili, Karinakanpatti, Pallipattu, Matrapalli, Koratti, Kunichi, Sundarampalli, Natham, Perampattu, Vishamangalam, Kurumberi.

Higher Secondary or Pre University Courses or Intermediate or Junior College in 7 villages of the CD Block,, namely Thokkiyam, Pallipattu, Koratti, Kunichi, Sundarampalli, Perampattu, Kurumberi.

College in 1 village, Adult Literacy Center in 0 village., College is in village, namely Kurumberi.

Medical: Hospital in 2 villages, Dispensary in 1 village, Health Center in 5 villages, Sub Center in 2 villages, Maternity and Child Welfare Center in 7 villages, Community health workers in 36 villages.

The Villages having Hospital or Dispensary or Health Center are Kandili, Gummidiganpatti, Badanavadi, Vengalapuram, Kunichi.

Drinking Water: Tap water in 39 villages, Tank water in 8 villages, Well water in 16 villages, Tubewell in 10 villages and more than one source in 37 villages.

Bank: Banking facility in 10 villages, namely, Peeiyagaram, Thokkiyam, Kandili, Karinakanpatti Koratti, Kunichi, Avalnayakkanpatty, Sundarampalli Perampattu, Vishamangalam.

Credit Society in 7 villages Agricultural Credit Society in 7 Non-Agricultural Credit Society in 1 village.

Others: Power supply in 37 villages, Cinema hall in 3 villages, sport club in 0 village, Stadium or Auditorium or Community Hall in 0 village, Post Office in 33 villages.

There are 35 villages having bus facilities.

Villages with most of facilities: Peeiyagaram Thokkiyam, Kandili, Karinakanpatti, Koratti, Kunichi

Avalnayakkanpatty, Sundarampalli, Perampattu Vishamangalam.

Villages without amenities (Education): Mandalanayanagunda, Karungalipatti, Naravindampatti, Sokkalampatti, Ganganayakanpatti, Govindapuram, Singarpet, Singarpet Extn..

Scheduled Castes: Out of the total population of 132846 persons, 22073 persons (16.62%) belong to Scheduled Castes.

The villages having less than 10% SC population are Mandalanayanagunda, Chinnakandili, Gummidiganpatti Badanavadi, Nariyaneri, Pallipattu, Udayamuthur Molagarampatti, Chinnakannalapatti Periyakannalampatti, Errampatti, Avalnayakkanpatty Karungalipatti, Naravindampatti, Govindapuram Singarpet, Singarpet Extn.

The villages having more than 50% SC population are None.

Sex ratio of Scheduled Caste population is 494.

Scheduled Castes Literates and Illiterates by Sex:

	Persons	Males	Females
Literate	12,152	7,095	5,057
Illiterate	9,921	4,063	5,858
Literacy rate	64.0	74.2	53.6
Graduate	200	133	67

Scheduled Castes (Dominant):

Adi Dravida, Arunthathiyar, Kuravan etc., Valluvan Paraiyan etc.

For their cultural identity please see Appendix-I

Villages without Scheduled Castes: There are 6 villages without any scheduled caste population.

Scheduled Tribes: Out of the total population of 132846 persons, 4317 persons (3.25%) belong to Scheduled Tribes.

The villages having less than 10% ST population are Mandalanayanagunda, Peeiyagaram, Thokkiyam, Kandili Chinnakandili, Gummidiganpatti, Badanavadi Nariyaneri, Lakkinaiekenpatty, Karinakanpatti Pallipattu, Adiyur, Vengalapuram, Matrapalli Udayamuthur, Koratti, Kunichi, Chinnakannalapatti Periyakannalampatti, Errampatti, Avalnayakkanpatty Krishnapuram, Sundarampalli, Pudupatty, Natham Karungalipatti, Naravindampatti, Sokkalampatti Ganganayakanpatti, Kakangarai, Sevvathur Chinnarampatti, Perampattu, Vishamangalam Simmanapudur.

The villages having more than 50% ST population are None.

Sex ratio of Scheduled tribe population is 499.

Scheduled Tribes Literates and Illiterates by Sex:

	Persons	Males	Females
Literate	1,488	898	590
Illiterate	2,829	1,263	1,566
Literacy rate	41.7	50.5	32.9
Graduate	14	12	2

Scheduled Tribes (Dominant):

Malayali, Kurumans, Irular, Generic Tribes etc. Malakkuravan

For their cultural identity please see Appendix-II

Villages without Scheduled Tribes: There are 24 villages without any scheduled tribe population.

Literates and Illiterates by Sex (Total Population):

	Persons	Males	Females
Literate	73,027	42,983	30,044
Illiterate	59,819	24,624	35,195
Literacy rate	64	74	53
Graduate	1,496	1,082	414

Agriculture: ***Distribution of villages according to land use:*** Out of 41 villages, Total area (in hectare) is 28777.22, out of that 61.46 percent is cultivable and 25.1 percent of the cultivable area is irrigated.

Sources of Irrigation (Hectares): Government Canal 7, Private Canal 0, Well without Electricity 303.21, Well with Electricity 4005.21, Tubewell without Electricity 2.3, Tubewell with Electricity 80.99, Tank 40.9, River 0, Lake 0, Waterfall 0, Others 0.

Villages with population of 5000 to 9999: Thokkiyam , Nariyaneri , Kasinayagampatti, Adiyur Matrapalli, Kurichi, Sevvathur, Vishamangalam Kurumberi.

Villages with population of 10000 and above: None

Distribution of Workers:

	Persons	Males	Females	WPR
Cultivators	18,158	11,842	6,316	28.12
Agricultural Labour	23,269	10,998	12,271	36.04
Household Industry	6,087	2,040	4,047	9.43
Other Workers	17,057	13,198	3,859	26.42
Main Workers	49,129	31,942	17,187	76.09
Marginal Workers	15,442	6,136	9,306	23.91
Total Workers	64,571	38,078	26,493	

Religion: Major Religious Communities:

	Persons	Males	Females	Sex Ratio
Hindu (97.53%)	129,564	65,954	63,610	964
Muslim (2.17%)	2,887	1,458	1,429	980
Christian (0.22%)	289	138	151	1,094
Sikh (0%)	1	1	-	-
Buddhists (0%)	-	-	-	-
Jain (0%)	2	1	1	1,000

Agewise Data:

	Persons	Males	Females	Sex Ratio
All ages	132,846	67,607	65,239	965
0-14	42,014	22,218	19,796	891

15-44	63,263	31,595	31,668	1002
45-79	25,955	12,989	12,966	998
80+	1,104	535	569	1064
Age not stated	510	270	240	889

Languages (Dominant):
Tamil, Telugu, Kannada, Urdu, Malayalam
Disabled Population:

	Persons	Males	Females	%
Total Disabled	2,981	1,626	1,355	
In Seeing	1,547	766	781	51.9
In Speech	285	161	124	9.56
In Hearing	130	74	56	4.36
In Movement	783	485	298	26.27
Mentally	236	140	96	7.92

KANGEYAM

Kangeyam C.D. Block lies in the north-eastern part of Erode district. It is a part of Kangeyam taluk. The Block is located at a distance of 40 kms. from district headquarters (Erode). There are 19 villages in the block with the total population of 57,033 persons. Area of the C.D. Block is 327.31 sq. kms. It is bounded in the north by taluks Perundurai and Erode, in the south by C.D. Block Kundadam, in the east by C.D. Block Vellakoil, and in the west by district Coimbatore.

Communications:
Roadways : N.H.-67 A: Direction- Palladam to Vellakoil, Nearest Villages- Kadaiyur, Veranampalayam. S.H.-37: Direction- Kangeyam to Erode, Nearest Villages- Parnchervaly, Nathakkadaiyur, Mullipuram, Palayakottai, Kuttapalayam, Pappini, Vattamali,. Veranampalayam.
River: Noyal Nadi- Nearest Villages- Kathaikanni, Ganapathypalayam, Tammareddipalayam, Maravapalayam, Nallroad, Manideerai, Kuttapalayam, Nathakkadaiyur.
Annual Rainfall: Average Rainfall 789 mm.
Ground Water: Availability of the ground water in the Basin is 3326.36 H.A.M. and the utilization is 2019.34 H.A.M. It belongs to Safe category. Depth to water level varies from 2 to 10 meter below the ground. Most of the wells go down in summer months, according to the Ground Water Estimation Committee.
Natural Division: Kongu Nadu.

Administration
Revenue **Division:** Dharapuram. Parliamentary Constituency: 17 Erode. District: Erode. Taluk: Kangeyam. Assembly Constituency: 102 Kangayam .Gram Panchayat: 15
Villages: 19 **Inhabited:** 19 **Uninhabited:** 0

Ranking	District	State	National
Area	7	139	2489
Population	14	339	4964
Sex Ratio	10	289	2280
Child Sex Ratio	13	279	4633
Literacy Rate	12	338	3016
Density	6	8	5158
Work Participation Rate	15	349	66

Gram Panchayats:
Alambadi, Balasamudrampudur, Ganapathipalayam, Keeranur, Maravapalayam, Marudurai, Nathakadaiyur, Padiyur, Palayakottai, Pappini, Peranjervali, Pothiapalayam, Sivanmalai, Thammareddipalayam, Veeranampalayam.

Amenities:
Education: Primary School in 19 villages, Middle school in 12 villages, Matriculation or Secondary School in 4 villages, namely Nathakkadaiyur, Pappini, Padiyur, Kadaiyur.
Higher Secondary or Pre University Courses or Intermediate or Junior College in 1 village of the CD Block,, namely Nathakkadaiyur.
College in 0 village, Adult Literacy Center in 0 village.
Medical: Hospital in 0 village, Dispensary in 1 village, Health Center in 4 villages, Sub Center in 11 villages, Maternity and Child Welfare Center in 1 village, Community health workers in 0 village.
The Village having Hospital or Dispensary or Health Center is Nathakkadaiyur.
Drinking Water: Tap water in 19 villages, Tank water in 0 villages, Well water in 19 villages, Tubewell in 19 villages and more than one source in 19 villages.
Bank: Banking facility in 6 villages, namely, Maravapalayam, Nathakkadaiyur, Pappini, Sivanmalai Padiyur, Kadaiyur.
Credit Society in 5 villages Agricultural Credit Society in 5 Non-Agricultural Credit Society in 0 village.
Others: Power supply in 19 villages, Cinema hall in 1 village, sport club in 0 village, Stadium or Auditorium or Community Hall in 0 village, Post Office in 17 villages.
There are 17 villages having bus facilities.
Villages with most of facilities: Nathakkadaiyur Pappini, Sivanmalai, Padiyur, Kadaiyur.
Villages without Amenities (Education): None..
Scheduled Castes: Out of the total population of 57033 persons, 12581 persons (22.06%) belong to Scheduled Castes. The villages having less than 10% SC population are None..
The villages having more than 50% SC population are None.
Sex ratio of Scheduled Caste population is 495.
Scheduled Castes Literates and Illiterates by Sex:

	Persons	Males	Females
Literate	5,211	3,066	2,145
Illiterate	7,370	3,283	4,087
Literacy rate	46.9	54.5	39.1
Graduate	32	22	10

Scheduled Castes (Dominant):
Madari, Chakkiliyan, Adi Dravida, Arunthathiyar Pallan

For their cultural identity please see Appendix-I

Villages without Scheduled Castes: There is 0 village without any scheduled caste population.

Scheduled Tribes: Out of the total population of 57033 persons, 22 persons (0.04%) belong to Scheduled Tribes. The villages having less than 10% ST population are Kathaikanni, Ganapathypalayam, Tammareddipalayam Maravapalayam, Parnchervaly, Nallroad, Manideerai Nathakkadaiyur, Mullipuram, Palayakottai Kuttapalayam, Pappini, Alambadi, Keeranur Sivanmalai, Padiyur, Kadaiyur, Vattamali Veranampalayam.

The villages having more than 50% ST population are None.

Sex ratio of Scheduled tribe population is 545.

Scheduled Tribes Literates and Illiterates by Sex:

	Persons	Males	Females
Literate	15	8	7
Illiterate	7	2	5
Literacy rate	75.0	80.0	70.0
Graduate	0	0	0

Scheduled Tribes (Dominant):
Malai Pandaram, Kurumans, Kondareddis, Irular

For their cultural identity please see Appendix-II

Villages without Scheduled Tribes: There are 16 villages without any scheduled tribe population.

Literates and Illiterates by Sex (Total Population):

	Persons	Males	Females
Literate	30,457	18,482	11,975
Illiterate	26,576	10,404	16,172
Literacy rate	59	71	47
Graduate	460	324	136

Agriculture: ***Distribution of villages according to land use:*** Out of 19 villages, Total area (in hectare) is 32731.93, out of that 36.66 percent is cultivable and 59.42 percent of the cultivable area is irrigated.

Sources of Irrigation (Hectares): Government Canal 2734.85, Private Canal 0, Well without Electricity 538.77, Well with Electricity 3855.58, Tubewell without Electricity 0, Tubewell with Electricity 0, Tank 0, River 0, Lake 0, Waterfall 0, Others 0.

Villages with population of 5000 to 9999:
Nathakadaiyur, Sivanmalai.

Villages with population of 10000 and above: None

Distribution of Workers:

	Persons	Males	Females	WPR
Cultivators	12,839	6,909	5,930	34.03
Agricultural Labour	11,432	5,138	6,294	30.3
Household Industry	2,300	995	1,305	6.1
Other Workers	11,162	7,585	3,577	29.58
Main Workers	34,036	19,348	14,688	90.2
Marginal Workers	3,697	1,279	2,418	9.8
Total Workers	37,733	20,627	17,106	

Religion: Major Religious Communities:

	Persons	Males	Females	Sex Ratio
Hindu (97.95%)	55,865	28,301	27,564	974
Muslim (0.26%)	146	81	65	802
Christian (1.63%)	932	463	469	1,013
Sikh (0%)	2	1	1	1,000
Buddhists (0%)	-	-	-	-
Jain (0.01%)	4	1	3	3,000

Agewise Data:

	Persons	Males	Females	Sex Ratio
All ages	57,033	28,886	28,147	974
0-14	11,274	5,897	5,377	912
15-44	26,922	13,413	13,509	1007
45-79	17,479	8,873	8,606	970
80+	1,159	572	587	1026
Age not stated	199	131	68	519

Languages (Dominant):
Tamil, Telugu, Kannada, Urdu, Malayalam

Disabled Population:

	Persons	Males	Females	%
Total Disabled	1,395	674	721	
In Seeing	734	318	416	52.62
In Speech	103	51	52	7.38
In Hearing	105	45	60	7.53
In Movement	317	188	129	22.72
Mentally	136	72	64	9.75

KANIYAMBADI

Kaniyambadi C.D. Block lies in the central part of Vellore district. It is a part of Vellore taluk. The taluk is located at a distance of 00 kms. from district headquarters (Vellore). There are 31 villages in the block with the total population of 72,694 persons. Area of the C.D. Block is 168.12 sq. kms. It is bounded in the north by CD Block Vellore, in the south and west by Tiruvannamalai district, and in the east by CD Block Timiri.

Communications:

Roadways : S.H.-9: Direction- Vellore to Viluppuram, Neare st Villages- Edaiyansathu, Adukkamparai, Thuthipet, Nelvoy, Sathumadurai, Kaniyambadi, Singerikoil, Vallam, Kilpal lipattu.

Railway Station: Kaniyambadi.

Annual Rainfall: Average Rainfall 949 mm.

Ground Water: Availability of the ground water in the Basin is 3332.39 H.A.M. and the utilization is 5786.26 H.A.M. It belongs to Over Expoited category. Depth to

water level varies from 2 to 10 meter below the ground. Most of the wells go down in summer months, according to the Ground Water Estimation Committee.

Forest and Reserved Forest: (Athiyur RF)- Nearest Villages- Chozhavaram, Thuthikadu, Thellai. (Kathalampattu)- Nearest Villages- Thuthikadu, Thellai, Kathala, Pattu (RF), Kilarasampattu, Palathuvannan. (Kailasagiri)- Nearest Villages- Katuputhur, Kailasagiri (RF). (Kaniyambadi)- Nearest Villages- Kaniyambadi, Singerikoil, Vallam, Kamiambadi (RF), Mottupalayam. (Palamadai)- Nearest Villages- Adukkamparai, Munjurpet.

Natural Division: Tondai Nadu.

Administration

Revenue **Division:** Vellore. Parliamentary Constituency: 7 Arakkonam,8 Vellore. District: Vellore. Taluk: Vellore. Assembly Constituency: 42 Arcot, 44 Anaikattu. Gram Panchayat: 27.

Villages: 31 **Inhabited:** 27 **Uninhabited:** 4

Ranking	District	State	National
Area	18	330	4741
Population	17	276	4367
Sex Ratio	2	77	622
Child Sex Ratio	16	290	4899
Literacy Rate	1	48	660
Density	15	334	2550
Work Participation Rate	10	93	4054

Gram Panchayats:

Adukkamparai, Edayansathu, Kammasamudram , Kammavanprttai, Kanikkaniyan, Kaniyambadi, Kathalampattu , Kattuputhur, Kil Arasampattu, Kilpallipattu, Mothakkal, Mottupalayam, Munjurpattu, Nanjukondapuram, Nelvoy, Palampakkam, Palathuvannan, Sathapalaiyam, Sathumadurai, Selamanatham, Sholavaram, Thuttikadu, Thuttipattu, Vallam, Veppampattu.

Amenities:

Education: Primary School in 27 villages, Middle school in 9 villages, Matriculation or Secondary School in 6 villages, namely Edaiyansathu, Adukkamparai, Chozhavaram, Munjurpet, Kaniyambadi, Kilarasampattu.

Higher Secondary or Pre University Courses or Intermediate or Junior College in 0 village of the CD Block, College in 1 village, Adult Literacy Center in 0 village., College is in village, namely Edaiyansathu.

Medical: Hospital in 0 village, Dispensary in 2 villages, Health Center in 2 villages, Sub Center in 0 village, Maternity and Child Welfare Center in 1 village, Community health workers in 26 villages.

The Villages having Hospital or Dispensary or Health Center are Sathupalayam, Kaniyambadi.

Drinking Water: Tap water in 27 villages, Tank water in 9 villages, Well water in 14 villages, Tubewell in 11 villages and more than one source in 27 villages.

Bank: Banking facility in 4 villages, namely, Chozhavaram, Sathumadurai, Munjurpet, Kaniyambadi. Credit Society in 4 villages Agricultural Credit Society in 4 Non-Agricultural Credit Society in 2 villages.

Others: Power supply in 27 villages, Cinema hall in 0 village, sport club in 0 village, Stadium or Auditorium or Community Hall in 0 village, Post Office in 21 villages.

There are 23 villages having bus facilities.

Villages with most of facilities: Chozhavaram Sathumadurai, Munjurpet, Kaniyambadi.

Villages without Amenities (Education): None..

Scheduled Castes: Out of the total population of 72694 persons, 13472 persons (18.53%) belong to Scheduled Castes.

The villages having less than 10% SC population are Sathumadurai, Pongalathan, Kanikiniyan, Thuthikadu Thellai, Kilarasampattu, Palathuvannan, Singerikoil Motthakkal.

The villages having more than 50% SC population are None.

Sex ratio of Scheduled Caste population is 516.

Scheduled Castes Literates and Illiterates by Sex:

	Persons	Males	Females
Literate	9,242	5,034	4,208
Illiterate	4,230	1,486	2,744
Literacy rate	78.3	88.6	68.7
Graduate	179	130	49

Scheduled Castes (Dominant):

Adi Dravida, Arunthathiyar, Valluvan, Kuravan etc. Puthirai Vannan

For their cultural identity please see Appendix-I

Villages without Scheduled Castes: There are 5 villages without any scheduled caste population.

Scheduled Tribes: Out of the total population of 72694 persons, 462 persons (0.64%) belong to Scheduled Tribes.

The villages having less than 10% ST population are Edaiyansathu, Adukkamparai, Thuthipet, Sirukalambur Katuputhur, Chozhavaram, Sathupalayam, Nelvoy Sathumadurai, Munjurpet, Pongalathan, Selamanatham Kaniyambadi, Veppampattu, Kanikiniyan, Palampakkam Thuthikadu, Thellai, Kilarasampattu, Kattazampattu Palathuvannan, Singerikoil, Vallam, Kilpallipattu Mottupalayam, Kammasamudram, Motthakkal.

The villages having more than 50% ST population are None.

Sex ratio of Scheduled tribe population is 450.

Scheduled Tribes Literates and Illiterates by Sex:

	Persons	Males	Females

Literate	167	112	55
Illiterate	295	142	153
Literacy rate	45.8	57.7	32.2
Graduate	2	2	0

Scheduled Tribes (Dominant):
Irular, Generic Tribes etc., Malayali, Malakkuravan Kurumans

For their cultural identity please see Appendix-II

Villages without Scheduled Tribes: There are 19 villages without any scheduled tribe population.

Literates and Illiterates by Sex (Total Population):

	Persons	Males	Females
Literate	47,980	27,201	20,779
Illiterate	24,714	8,745	15,969
Literacy rate	75	87	64
Graduate	1,231	887	344

Agriculture: ***Distribution of villages according to land use:*** Out of 31 villages, Total area (in hectare) is 16812.84, out of that 44.58 percent is cultivable and 23.72 percent of the cultivable area is irrigated.

Sources of Irrigation (Hectares): Government Canal 0, Private Canal 0, Well without Electricity 294.65, Well with Electricity 1483.3, Tubewell without Electricity 0, Tubewell with Electricity 0, Tank 0, River 0, Lake 0, Waterfall 0, Others 0.

Villages with population of 5000 to 9999:
Munjurpattu, Kaniyambadi, Kathalampattu Kammasamudram.

Villages with population of 10000 and above: None

Distribution of Workers:

	Persons	Males	Females	WPR
Cultivators	8,222	5,452	2,770	26.61
Agricultural Labour	9,706	3,961	5,745	31.41
Household Industry	1,951	1,071	880	6.31
Other Workers	11,024	9,029	1,995	35.67
Main Workers	23,516	16,311	7,205	76.1
Marginal Workers	7,387	3,202	4,185	23.9
Total Workers	30,903	19,513	11,390	

Religion: Major Religious Communities:

	Persons	Males	Females	Sex Ratio
Hindu (94.99%)	69,051	34,141	34,910	1,023
Muslim (1.99%)	1,447	733	714	974
Christian (2.91%)	2,112	1,027	1,085	1,056
Sikh (0%)	2	1	1	1,000
Buddhists (0.01%)	4	2	2	1,000
Jain (0%)	1	1	-	-

Agewise Data:

	Persons	Males	Females	Sex Ratio
All ages	72,694	35,946	36,748	1022
0-14	20,543	10,488	10,055	959
15-44	34,238	16,725	17,513	1047
45-79	16,809	8,229	8,580	1043
80+	994	450	544	1209
Age not stated	110	54	56	1037

Languages (Dominant):
Tamil, Telugu, Urdu, Marathi, Kannada

Disabled Population:

	Persons	Males	Females	%
Total Disabled	1,748	961	787	
In Seeing	708	358	350	40.5
In Speech	179	94	85	10.24
In Hearing	113	61	52	6.46
In Movement	543	341	202	31.06
Mentally	205	107	98	11.73

KANNANKUDI

Kannankudi C.D. Block lies in the eastern part of Sivaganga district. It is a part of Devakottai taluk. The taluk is located at a distance of 60 kms. from district headquarters (Sivaganga). There are 25 villages in the block with the total population of 28,839 persons. Area of the C.D. Block is 212.67 sq. kms. It is bounded in the north by CD Blocks Sakkottai and Pudukkottai, in the south by district Ramanathapuram, in the east by districts Ramanathapuram and Pudukkottai, in the west by CD Blocks Sakkottai and Devakottai.

Communications:

Roadways : N.H.-210: Direction- Devakottai to Tiruvadanai, Nearest Village- Hanaumanthakudi.

River: Manimuttar Nadi- Nearest Villages- Iravuseri, Chiththanoor, Hanaumanthakudi.

Backwards Region Grants Fund: It receives Backward Region Grants.

Annual Rainfall: Average Rainfall 904 mm.

Ground Water: Availability of the ground water in the Basin is 4767.27 H.A.M. and the utilization is 275.61 H.A.M. It belongs to Safe category. Depth to water level varies from 2 to 10 meter below the ground. Most of the wells go down in summer months, according to the Ground Water Estimation Committee.

Natural Division: NA

Administration

Revenue **Division:** Devakottai. Parliamentary Constituency: 31 Sivaganga. District: Sivaganga. Taluk: Devakottai. Assembly Constituency: 184 Karaikudi. Gram Panchayat: 17.

Villages: 25 **Inhabited:** 25 **Uninhabited:** 0

Ranking	District	State	National
Area	11	267	3967
Population	12	381	6081
Sex Ratio	3	11	144
Child Sex Ratio	5	70	1434
Literacy Rate	6	155	1538
Density	1	44	5769

Work Participation Rate	12	368	385

Gram Panchayats:
Chittanur, Hanumanthagudi, K.siruvanoor, Kalathur , Kallivayal, Kallivayal, I..Mathur , Kandiyur , Kangani, Kannangudi, Kannangudi , Koduvoor, Pusalagudi, Puthurani, Siruvachi, Thattani, Theralappur, Unjanai , Vengalore , Thallakkavayal.

Amenities:

Education: Primary School in 19 villages, Middle school in 6 villages, Matriculation or Secondary School in 3 villages, namely Unjanai, Vannangudi, Hanaumanthakudi.
Higher Secondary or Pre University Courses or Intermediate or Junior College in 1 village of the CD Block,, namely Hanaumanthakudi.
College in 0 village, Adult Literacy Center in 0 village.

Medical: Hospital in 0 village, Dispensary in 1 village, Health Center in 1 village, Sub Center in 9 villages, Maternity and Child Welfare Center in 1 village, Community health workers in 24 villages.
The Village having Hospital or Dispensary or Health Center is Kappalur.

Drinking Water: Tap water in 25 villages, Tank water in 20 villages, Well water in 25 villages, Tubewell in 25 villages and more than one source in 25 villages.

Bank: Banking facility in 1 villages, namely, Kandiyur.
Credit Society in 3 villages Agricultural Credit Society in 3 Non-Agricultural Credit Society in 0 village.

Others: Power supply in 25 villages, Cinema hall in 0 village, sport club in 0 village, Stadium or Auditorium or Community Hall in 12 villages, Post Office in 25 villages.
There are 23 villages having bus facilities.

Villages with most of facilities: Kandiyur.

Villages without amenities (Education): Kodadudi, Nagamangalam, Iravuseri, Thangankudi, Kalapangudi, Poolangudi..

Scheduled Castes: Out of the total population of 28839 persons, 10992 persons (38.12%) belong to Scheduled Castes.
The villages having less than 10% SC population are None..
The villages having more than 50% SC population are Unjanai, Siruganoor, Medakottai, Iravuseri Chiththanoor, Theralapur, Puthurani, Borkudi.
Sex ratio of Scheduled Caste population is 513.

Scheduled Castes Literates and Illiterates by Sex:

	Persons	Males	Females
Literate	6,245	3,589	2,656
Illiterate	4,747	1,759	2,988
Literacy rate	64.9	77.4	53.3
Graduate	70	47	23

Scheduled Castes (Dominant):
Pallan, Paraiyan etc., Adi Dravida, Chakkiliyan Generic Castes etc.

For their cultural identity please see Appendix-I

Villages without Scheduled Castes: There are 2 villages without any scheduled caste population.

Scheduled Tribes: Out of the total population of 28839 persons, 23 persons (0.08%) belong to Scheduled Tribes.
The villages having less than 10% ST population are Mathur, Unjanai, Iruvinivayal, Vengalore Poosalagudi, Kalathur, Kilamalai, Siruganoor Naranamangalam, Kandiyur, Kappalur, Kodadudi Medakottai, Nagamangalam, Iravuseri, Chiththanoor Theralapur, Puthurani, Thangankudi, Kalapangudi Poolangudi, Vannangudi, Sadayanmangalam, Borkudi Hanaumanthakudi.
The villages having more than 50% ST population are None.
Sex ratio of Scheduled tribe population is 435.

Scheduled Tribes Literates and Illiterates by Sex:

	Persons	Males	Females
Literate	19	11	8
Illiterate	4	2	2
Literacy rate	90.5	91.7	88.9
Graduate	1	1	0

Scheduled Tribes (Dominant):
Malai Pandaram

For their cultural identity please see Appendix-II

Villages without Scheduled Tribes: There are 24 villages without any scheduled tribe population.

Literates and Illiterates by Sex (Total Population):

	Persons	Males	Females
Literate	17,397	9,808	7,589
Illiterate	11,442	4,013	7,429
Literacy rate	67	80	56
Graduate	279	186	93

Agriculture: ***Distribution of villages according to land use:***
Out of 25 villages, Total area (in hectare) is 21267.22, out of that 34.59 percent is cultivable and 65.74 percent of the cultivable area is irrigated.

Sources of Irrigation (Hectares): Government Canal 0, Private Canal 0, Well without Electricity 0, Well with Electricity 44.44, Tubewell without Electricity 0, Tubewell with Electricity 55.5, Tank 4736.25, River 0, Lake 0, Waterfall 0, Others 0.

Villages with population of 5000 to 9999: None

Villages with population of 10000 and above: None

Distribution of Workers:

	Persons	Males	Females	WPR
Cultivators	12,214	6,316	5,898	71.1

Agricultural Labour	3,496	1,412	2,084	20.35
Household Industry	242	65	177	1.41
Other Workers	1,227	1,004	223	7.14
Main Workers	15,644	8,305	7,339	91.06
Marginal Workers	1,535	492	1,043	8.94
Total Workers	17,179	8,797	8,382	

Religion: Major Religious Communities:

	Persons	Males	Females	Sex Ratio
Hindu (90.84%)	26,196	12,655	13,541	1,070
Muslim (1.7%)	490	227	263	1,159
Christian (6.64%)	1,916	899	1,017	1,131
Sikh (0.01%)	2	2	-	-
Buddhists (0%)	-	-	-	-
Jain (0.01%)	2	1	1	1,000

Agewise Data:

	Persons	Males	Females	Sex Ratio
All ages	28,609	13,786	14,823	1075
0-14	7,297	3,643	3,654	1003
15-44	13,232	6,188	7,044	1138
45-79	7,769	3,773	3,996	1059
80+	266	155	111	716
Age not stated	45	27	18	667

Languages (Dominant):
Tamil, Telugu, Kannada, Malayalam, Urdu

Disabled Population:

	Persons	Males	Females	%
Total Disabled	1,177	390	787	
In Seeing	960	263	697	81.56
In Speech	42	18	24	3.57
In Hearing	22	10	12	1.87
In Movement	121	83	38	10.28
Mentally	32	16	16	2.72

KARAMADAI

Karamadai C.D. Block lies in the northern part of Coimbatore district. It is a part of Mettupalayam taluk. The Block is located at a distance of 29 kms. from district headquarters (Coimbatore). There are 30 villages in the block with the total population of 124,010 persons. Area of the C.D. Block is 664.12 sq. kms. It is bounded in the north by districts Nilgiri and Erode, in the south by CD Block Periyanayakkanpalayam, in the east by taluk Anavashi and CD Block Annur, and it has common boundary with the state of Kerala on west.

Communications:

Roadways : S.H.-31: Direction- Coonoor to Coimbatore, Nearest Villages- Odanthurai, Chikkadasampalayam, Marudur, Chikkarampalayam.

Railway Station: Odanthurai.

River: Bhavani Nadi- Nearest Villages- Nellithurai, Thekkampatti, Odanthurai, Gopaneri RF, Mellur Slope RF, Nellithurai & Sundapatti RF, Nilagiri Eastern Slope RF, Pillurslope RF, Kandiyar RF, Nellithurai RF, Medurpethikuttai Forest. Coonoor Nadi- Nearest Villages- Odanthurai, Kallar RF, Hulical Drug RF.

Annual Rainfall: Average Rainfall 550 mm.

Ground Water: Availability of the ground water in the Basin is 4136.26 H.A.M. and the utilization is 3979.92 H.A.M. It belongs to Safe category. Depth to water level varies from 2 to 20 meter below the ground. Most of the wells go down in summer months, according to the Ground Water Estimation Committee.

Forest and Reserved Forest: (Anaikatti RF)- Nearest Villages- Anaikatti North RF, Tholampalayam. (Gopanari)- Nearest Villages- Gopaneri RF, Tholampalayam, Velliangadu. (Nilgiri Eastern Slope)- Nearest Villages- Nilagiri Eastern Slope RF, Velliangadu, Kemmarampalayam. (Hulical Drug)- Nearest Vilages- Odanthurai, Hulical Drug RF, Nellithurai. (Kallar)- Nearest Villages- Odanthurai, Kallar RF. (Jaganarai Slopes)- Nearest Villages- Jaganarai Slope RF, Odanthurai. (Kandiyur)- Nearest Villages- Thekkampatti, Kandiyar RF, Kemmarampalayam. (Madur Pethikuttai)- Nearest Villages- Medurpethikuttai Forest, Irumbarai. (Nillithurai & Sundapatti)- Nearest Village- Nellithurai & Sundapatti RF. (Odabthurai)- Nearest Villages- Odathurai RF, Chikkadasampalayam. (Pillurslope)- Nearest Village- Pillurslope RF. (Mellur Slope)- Village- Melur Slope RF.

Natural Division: Kongu Nadu.

Administration

Revenue **Division:** Coimbatore. Parliamentary Constituency: 19 Nilgiris. District: Coimbatore. Taluk: Mettupalayam. Assembly Constituency: 111 Mettupalayam. Gram Panchayat: 17.

Border Villages- (Kerala)- Nearest Villages- Melur Slope RF, Gopaneri RF, Tholampalayam.

Villages: 30 **Inhabited:** 23 **Uninhabited:** 7

Ranking	District	State	National
Area	2	13	1004
Population	2	57	2728
Sex Ratio	13	315	2647
Child Sex Ratio	10	116	2229
Literacy Rate	11	233	2097
Density	13	201	4936
Work Participation Rate	17	338	2072

Gram Panchayats:

Belladhi, Bellapalayam, Chickadasampalayam , Chikkarampalayam , Chinnakallipatti, Illuppanatham, Irumborai, Jadayampalayam, Kalampalayam, Kemmarampalayam, Marudur, Muduthurai, Nellithurai, Odanthurai , Thekkampatti, Tholampalayam, Velliangadu.

Amenities:

Education: Primary School in 18 villages, Middle school in

15 villages, Matriculation or Secondary School in 8 villages, namely Irumbarai, Bellapalayam, Jadayampalayam, Chikkadasampalayam, Velliangadu, Kemmarampalayam, Kalampalayam, Chikkarampalayam.

Higher Secondary or Pre University Courses or Intermediate or Junior College in 4 villages of the CD Block,, namely Irumbarai, Chikkadasampalayam, Kemmarampalayam, Kalampalayam.

College in 0 village, Adult Literacy Center in 0 village.

Medical: Hospital in 1 village, Dispensary in 0 village, Health Center in 4 villages, Sub Center in 13 villages, Maternity and Child Welfare Center in 5 villages, Community health workers in 0 village.

The Village having Hospital or Dispensary or Health Center is Tholampalayam.

Drinking Water: Tap water in 23 villages, Tank water in 0 villages, Well water in 23 villages, Tubewell in 23 villages and more than one source in 23 villages.

Bank: Banking facility in 6 villages, namely, Odanthurai, Irumbarai, Illuppanatham Kemmarampalayam, Kalampalayam, Belladhi.

Credit Society in 15 villages Agricultural Credit Society in 13 Non-Agricultural Credit Society in 1 village.

Others: Power supply in 23 villages, Cinema hall in 3 villages, sport club in 0 village, Stadium or Auditorium or Community Hall in 0 village, Post Office in 18 villages.

There are 16 villages having bus facilities.

Villages with most of facilities: Odanthurai Irumbarai, Illuppanatham, Kemmarampalayam Kalampalayam, Belladhi.

Villages without amenities (Education): Nellithurai & Sundapatti Rf, Melur Slope Rf, Nilagiri Eastern Slope Rf, Gopaneri Rf, Anaikatti North Rf..

Scheduled Castes: Out of the total population of 124010 persons, 22615 persons (18.24%) belong to Scheduled Castes.

The villages having less than 10% SC population are Nellithurai, Pillurslope Rf Nellithurai & Sundapatti Rf, Melur Slope Rf Nilagiri Eastern Slope Rf , Gopaneri Rf Anaikatti North Rf, Velliangadu.

The villages having more than 50% SC population are None.

Sex ratio of Scheduled Caste population is 497.

Scheduled Castes Literates and Illiterates by Sex:

	Persons	Males	Females
Literate	9,152	5,510	3,642
Illiterate	13,463	5,874	7,589
Literacy rate	46.3	55.1	37.2
Graduate	37	28	9

Scheduled Castes (Dominant):

Chakkiliyan, Arunthathiyar, Pallan, Adi Dravida Kuravan etc.

For their cultural identity please see Appendix-I

Villages without Scheduled Castes: There are 12 villages without any scheduled caste population.

Scheduled Tribes: Out of the total population of 124010 persons, 7406 persons (5.97%) belong to Scheduled Tribes.

The villages having less than 10% ST population are Chinnakallipatti, Thekkampatti, Muduthurai Irumbarai, Illuppanatham, Bellapalayam Jadayampalayam, Chikkadasampalayam, Kemmarampalayam Kalampalayam, Marudur, Belladhi, Chikkarampalayam.

The villages having more than 50% ST population are Pillurslope Rf, Nellithurai & Sundapatti Rf Melur Slope Rf , Nilagiri Eastern Slope Rf Gopaneri Rf, Anaikatti North Rf.

Sex ratio of Scheduled tribe population is 493.

Scheduled Tribes Literates and Illiterates by Sex:

	Persons	Males	Females
Literate	2,836	1,705	1,131
Illiterate	4,570	2,051	2,519
Literacy rate	43.6	51.8	35.2
Graduate	1	1	0

Scheduled Tribes (Dominant):

Irular, Generic Tribes etc., Kattunayakan, Kurumans Malai Pandaram

For their cultural identity please see Appendix-II

Villages without Scheduled Tribes: There are 12 villages without any scheduled tribe population.

Literates and Illiterates by Sex (Total Population):

	Persons	Males	Females
Literate	71,340	41,704	29,636
Illiterate	52,670	21,340	31,330
Literacy rate	64	74	54
Graduate	1,237	735	502

Agriculture: ***Distribution of villages according to land use:*** Out of 30 villages, Total area (in hectare) is 66412.51, out of that 38.47 percent is cultivable and 26.63 percent of the cultivable area is irrigated.

Sources of Irrigation (Hectares): Government Canal 74.35, Private Canal 0, Well without Electricity 55.65, Well with Electricity 5347.8, Tubewell without Electricity 0, Tubewell with Electricity 678.82, Tank 0, River 163.5, Lake 0, Waterfall 0, Others 482.88.

Villages with population of 5000 to 9999: Irumborai, Illuppanatham, Bellapalayam Jadayampalayam, Tholampalayam, Velliangadu Kemmarampalayam, Kalampalayam, Marudur, Belladhi Chikkarampalayam.

Villages with population of 10000 and above:
Chickadasampalayam , Thekkampatti.

Distribution of Workers:

	Persons	Males	Females	WPR
Cultivators	13,740	8,794	4,946	21.28
Agricultural Labour	25,893	14,199	11,694	40.1
Household Industry	3,537	1,928	1,609	5.48
Other Workers	21,396	16,105	5,291	33.14
Main Workers	59,049	39,346	19,703	91.46
Marginal Workers	5,517	1,680	3,837	8.54
Total Workers	64,566	41,026	23,540	

Religion: Major Religious Communities:

	Persons	Males	Females	Sex Ratio
Hindu (95.66%)	118,624	60,331	58,293	966
Muslim (1.93%)	2,398	1,218	1,180	969
Christian (2.05%)	2,544	1,285	1,259	980
Sikh (0.01%)	11	5	6	1,200
Buddhists (0%)	1	-	1	-
Jain (0.01%)	10	5	5	1,000

Agewise Data:

	Persons	Males	Females	Sex Ratio
All ages	124,010	63,044	60,966	967
0-14	28,781	14,873	13,908	935
15-44	61,519	30,768	30,751	999
45-79	31,628	16,376	15,252	931
80+	1,679	825	854	1035
Age not stated	403	202	201	995

Languages (Dominant):
Tamil, Kannada, Telugu, Malayalam, Urdu

Disabled Population:

	Persons	Males	Females	%
Total Disabled	3,705	1,596	2,109	
In Seeing	2,201	732	1,469	59.41
In Speech	250	124	126	6.75
In Hearing	150	77	73	4.05
In Movement	752	472	280	20.3
Mentally	352	191	161	9.5

KARAMBAKKUDI

Karambakudi C.D. Block lies in the south-eastern part of Pudukkottai district. It is a part of Alangudi taluk. The Block is located at a distance of 44 kms. from district headquarters (Pudukkottai). There are 49 villages in the block with the total population of 88,849 persons. Area of the C.D. Block is 260.31 sq. kms. It is bounded in the north by CD Block Gandarvakottai and district Thanjavur, in the south by C.D. Block Thiruvarankulam, in the east by district Thanjavur, and in the west by CD Block Pudukkottai.

Communications:
Roadways : Information not Available.

Annual Rainfall: Average Rainfall 910 mm.

Ground Water: Availability of the ground water in the Basin is 7319.02 H.A.M. and the utilization is 3465. 22 H.A.M. It belongs to Safe category. Depth to water level varies from 5 to 10 meter below the ground. Most of the wells go down in summer months, according to the Ground Water Estimation Committee.

Natural Division: Chola Nadu.

Administration
Revenue **Division:** Pudukottai. Parliamentary Constituency: 30 Pudukottai, 31 Sivaganga. District: Pudukottai. Taluk: Alangudi. Assembly Constituency: 178 Gandarvakottai (SC), 180 Pudukottai, 182 Alangudi. Gram Panchayat: 39.

Villages: 49 **Inhabited:** 48 **Uninhabited:** 1

Ranking	District	State	National
Area	12	216	3244
Population	5	189	3816
Sex Ratio	7	122	911
Child Sex Ratio	7	136	2437
Literacy Rate	9	228	2072
Density	2	140	3179
Work Participation Rate	2	170	1383

Gram Panchayats:
Adiranviduthy, Ambukovil, Bhanduvakottai, Elaikadividuthy, K.Mudalipatti, K.Therkutheru, Kalabam, Kaliyaran Viduthy, Kanakkankadu, Karambaviduthy, Karukeelatheru, Karupattipatti, Kattathi, Keerathur, Kulanthiranpatti, M.Therkutheru, Mailankonpatti, Malaiyur, Mangottai, Maruthankanviduthi, Mullankurichi, Odappaviduthy, Pallavarayan Pathai, Pappapatti, Pattathikadu, Pilaviduthy, Ponnanviduthy, Puduviduthy, Rangian Viduthy, Regunathapuram, Sengamedu, Theethanipatty, Theethanviduthy, Thirumanancheri, Vadatheru, Valankondan Viduthy, Vanakkankadu, Vandanviduthy, Vellalaviduthy.

Amenities:
Education: Primary School in 48 villages, Middle school in 22 villages, Matriculation or Secondary School in 6 villages, namely Puduviduthi, Kaliyaranvidothy, Banduvakkottai, Mullangurichi (N), Kanakkankadu, Malaiyur.
Higher Secondary or Pre University Courses or Intermediate or Junior College in 3 villages of the CD Block,, namely Puduviduthi, Kaliyaranvidothy, Mullangurichi (N).
College in 0 village, Adult Literacy Center in 0 village.
Medical: Hospital in 0 village, Dispensary in 1 village, Health Center in 4 villages, Sub Center in 12 villages, Maternity and Child Welfare Center in 1 village, Community health workers in 20 villages.
The Village having Hospital or Dispensary or Health

Center is Theethanvidutty.

Drinking Water: Tap water in 48 villages, Tank water in 0 villages, Well water in 48 villages, Tubewell in 48 villages and more than one source in 48 villages.

Bank: Banking facility in 6 villages, namely, Regunatha Puram, Malaiyur, M.Therukutheru Theethanipatti, Ponnanveduthi, Mangkottai.

Credit Society in 8 villages Agricultural Credit Society in 8 Non-Agricultural Credit Society in 0 village.

Others: Power supply in 48 villages, Cinema hall in 1 village, sport club in 0 village, Stadium or Auditorium or Community Hall in 0 village, Post Office in 20 villages.

There are 41 villages having bus facilities.

Villages with most of facilities: Regunatha Puram Malaiyur, Mangkottai.

Villages without Amenities (Education): None..

Scheduled Castes: Out of the total population of 88849 persons, 24386 persons (27.45%) belong to Scheduled Castes.

The villages having less than 10% SC population are Kilangadu, Kallumadai, Thiruppakkovil Banduvakkottai, Ponnanveduthi.

The villages having more than 50% SC population are None.

Sex ratio of Scheduled Caste population is 504.

Scheduled Castes Literates and Illiterates by Sex:

	Persons	Males	Females
Literate	14,157	8,292	5,865
Illiterate	10,229	3,812	6,417
Literacy rate	67.3	79.4	55.4
Graduate	420	337	83

Scheduled Castes (Dominant):

Paraiyan etc., Adi Dravida, Pallan, Kuravan etc. Chakkiliyan

For their cultural identity please see Appendix-I

Villages without Scheduled Castes: There are 5 villages without any scheduled caste population.

Scheduled Tribes: Out of the total population of 88849 persons, 3 persons (0%) belong to Scheduled Tribes.

The villages having less than 10% ST population are Thattamanaipatti, Keerathur, Kilangadu, Mudalipatti Sengamedu, Kallumadai, Pappapatti, Regunatha Puram Puduviduthi, Peyadippatty, Thiruppakkovil Odappaviduthi, Kaliyaranvidothy, Kattathi Chinnamgonviduthi, Vandanviduthy, Banduvakkottai Maruthangonviduthy, Mylangonpatti, Korambavidutti Ambukkovil, Pilaviduthy, Theethanvidutty Kulandivanpattu, Rangianviduthy, Pallavaranpattai Elaikadividutti, Thirumanajery, Pattathikkadu Kurumbivayal, Karukkakkurichi-Keelatheru K.Therkkutheru, Vadatheru, Vanakkankadu Mullangurichi (S), Mullangurichi (N), Kanakkankadu Karuppattipatti, Ayippatti, Valankondanviduthi Vellalaviduthi, Adhiranviduthi, Malaiyur M.Therukutheru, Theethanipatti, Ponnanveduthi Mangkottai, Kalabam.

The villages having more than 50% ST population are None.

Sex ratio of Scheduled tribe population is 667.

Scheduled Tribes Literates and Illiterates by Sex:

	Persons	Males	Females
Literate	2	0	2
Illiterate	1	1	0
Literacy rate	66.7		100.0
Graduate	0	0	0

Scheduled Tribes (Dominant):

Irular

For their cultural identity please see Appendix-II

Villages without Scheduled Tribes: There are 48 villages without any scheduled tribe population.

Literates and Illiterates by Sex (Total Population):

	Persons	Males	Females
Literate	49,088	29,252	19,836
Illiterate	39,761	14,980	24,781
Literacy rate	64	77	51
Graduate	956	758	198

Agriculture: ***Distribution of villages according to land use:*** Out of 49 villages, Total area (in hectare) is 26031.12, out of that 48.73 percent is cultivable and 55.39 percent of the cultivable area is irrigated.

Sources of Irrigation (Hectares): Government Canal 1138.83, Private Canal 0, Well without Electricity 352.68, Well with Electricity 267.5, Tubewell without Electricity 0, Tubewell with Electricity 2235.4, Tank 2845.93, River 0, Lake 0, Waterfall 0, Others 0.

Villages with population of 5000 to 9999: Pallavarayanpathai, Mangottai.

Villages with population of 10000 and above: None

Distribution of Workers:

	Persons	Males	Females	WPR
Cultivators	19,978	12,604	7,374	42.82
Agricultural Labour	21,242	9,070	12,172	45.53
Household Industry	1,032	401	631	2.21
Other Workers	4,408	3,374	1,034	9.45
Main Workers	31,687	20,727	10,960	67.91
Marginal Workers	14,973	4,722	10,251	32.09
Total Workers	46,660	25,449	21,211	

Religion: Major Religious Communities:

	Persons	Males	Females	Sex Ratio
Hindu (92.98%)	82,612	41,087	41,525	1,011
Muslim (2.59%)	2,302	1,112	1,190	1,070

Christian (4.4%)	3,905	2,019	1,886	934
Sikh (0%)	1	-	1	-
Buddhists (0%)	-	-	-	-
Jain (0%)	1	-	1	-

Agewise Data:

	Persons	Males	Females	Sex Ratio
All ages	88,849	44,232	44,617	1009
0-14	27,357	13,899	13,458	968
15-44	42,751	21,078	21,673	1028
45-79	17,929	8,840	9,089	1028
80+	603	293	310	1058

Age not stated	209	122	87	713

Languages (Dominant):
Tamil, Telugu, Kannada, Marathi, Others

Disabled Population:

	Persons	Males	Females	%
Total Disabled	2,422	1,050	1,372	
In Seeing	1,414	501	913	58.38
In Speech	309	162	147	12.76
In Hearing	86	47	39	3.55
In Movement	483	274	209	19.94
Mentally	130	66	64	5.37

KARIAPATTI

Kariapatti C.D. Block lies in the north-eastern part of Virudhunagar district. It is a part of Kariapatti and Tiruchuli taluks. The Block is located at a distance of 20 kms. from district headquarters (Virudhunagar). There are 102 villages in the block with the total population of 65,794 persons. Area of the C.D. Block is 366.40 sq. kms. It is bounded in the north by districts Sivaganga and Madurai, in the south by CD Blocks Aruppukkottai and Tiruchuli, in the east by CD Block Narikudi, in the west by district Madurai and CD Block Aruppukkottai. CD Block Kariapatti falls in taluk Kariapatti by 100 villages, and in taluk Tiruchuli by 02 villages.

Communications:

Roadways : N.H.-45 B: Direction- Aruppukkottai to Madurai, Nearest Villages- Mangulam, Aviyur, D.Kadambangulam, Kambikudi, S.Kallupatti, Kaluvanacherry, Karianenthal, Vakkanaugundy, Thonugal, Kalkurichi, Johilpatty.

River: Terku Nadi- Nearest Villages- Viyampatti, Pisindi, Achangulam, Vadakarai, Karianenthal, Vakkanaugundy, Thonugal, Kalkurichi, Johilpatty, Kanakkanenthal, Melapuram.

Annual Rainfall: Average Rainfall 799 mm.

Ground Water: Availability of the ground water in the Basin is 50.36 MCM and the utilization is 27.84 H.A. M. It belongs to MCM category. Depth to water level varies from 5 to 20 meter below the ground. Most of the wells go down in summer months, according to the Ground Water Estimation Committee.

Natural Division: NA

Administration

Revenue **Division:** Aruppukottai. Parliamentary Constituency: 35 Ramanathapuram. District: Virudhunagar. Taluk: Kariapatti, Tiruchuli. Assembly Constituency: 208 Tiruchuli. Gram Panchayat: 36.

Villages: 102 **Inhabited:** 75 **Uninhabited:** 27

Ranking	District	State	National
Area	6	98	2157
Population	9	308	4650
Sex Ratio	9	132	950
Child Sex Ratio	8	230	3763
Literacy Rate	10	251	2178
Density	4	74	5058
Work Participation Rate	9	345	733

Gram Panchayats:
Alagianallur, Alagianallur, Allalaperi, Arasakulam, Aviyoor, Chartapuliyankulam, D.kadambakulam, Johilpatti, Kalkurichi, Kambikudi, Keepilingampatti, Kilavaneri, Kurandi, Mangalam, Manthoppu, Melakalangulam, Mudukkakulam, Mudukkangulam, Mudukkankulam, Mustakurichi, Nandikundu, P.Pudupatti, Pambatti, Pampatti, Pandanendal, Pannikurippu, Pannikuruppu, Pappanam, Pisindi, S.kallupatti, S.Maraikulam, Sooranoor, T.Chettikulam, T.Veppankulam, Thandiyanendal, Thonugal, Thoppur, Thulukkangulam, Thulukkankulam, V.Nangoor, Vakkanangundu, Valukkalotti, Varaletti, Varalotti.

Amenities:

Education: Primary School in 65 villages, Middle school in 15 villages, Matriculation or Secondary School in 6 villages, namely Aviyur, Mustakuruchi, Alagianallur, Johilpatty, S.Maraikulam, P.Pudupatti.

Higher Secondary or Pre University Courses or Intermediate or Junior College in 1 village of the CD Block,, namely Johilpatty.

College in 1 village, Adult Literacy Center in 0 village., College is in village, namely D.Kadambangulam.

Medical: Hospital in 0 village, Dispensary in 0 village, Health Center in 1 village, Sub Center in 7 villages, Maternity and Child Welfare Center in 6 villages, Community health workers in 0 village.

Drinking Water: Tap water in 75 villages, Tank water in 0 villages, Well water in 75 villages, Tubewell in 75 villages and more than one source in 75 villages.

Bank: Banking facility in 9 villages, namely, Thotiyankulam, T.Veepankulam, Viyampatti, Manthoppu Mudukkankulam, Alagianallur, Valukkalotty Kalkurichi, S.Maraikulam.

Credit Society in 16 villages Agricultural Credit Society in 15 Non-Agricultural Credit Society in 2 villages.

Others: Power supply in 73 villages, Cinema hall in 2 villages, sport club in 0 village, Stadium or Auditorium or Community Hall in 0 village, Post Office in 42 villages.

There are 53 villages having bus facilities.

Villages with most of facilities: Viyampatti Manthoppu, Alagianallur, Kalkurichi, S.Maraikulam.

Villages without amenities (Education): Ariyanandal, Vadakarai, Chinna Alangulam, Karungulam Nedungulam, Vellangulam, Kovilankulam, Manaviyendal, Karianenthal, Koovarkulam, Thenoor..

Scheduled Castes: Out of the total population of 65794 persons, 15069 persons (22.9%) belong to Scheduled Castes.

The villages having less than 10% SC population are Melakallankulam, S.Kallupatti, N.Nedungulam M.Elupaikulam, Pampatti, Manthoppu, Achangulam Allalaperi, Periya Alangulam, Chinna Alangulam Vellangulam, Karianenthal, Thonugal Vaddakkupulliampatti, Chandrankulam Malakancharankulam, Thenoor, Thamaraikulam Panikurippu, Chokkampatti.

The villages having more than 50% SC population are Amaiperuki, Panchar, Vadakarai, Sirukulam Karungulam Nedungulam, Kovilankulam, Manaviyendal Kurangakkulan, Esalimadai, Koovarkulam, Kundukulam Karaikkulam, Kambali.

Sex ratio of Scheduled Caste population is 498.

Scheduled Castes Literates and Illiterates by Sex:

	Persons	Males	Females
Literate	6,930	4,312	2,618
Illiterate	8,139	3,247	4,892
Literacy rate	53.7	66.8	40.6
Graduate	60	46	14

Scheduled Castes (Dominant):

Pallan, Paraiyan etc., Chakkiliyan, Kudumban Pagadai

For their cultural identity please see Appendix-I

Villages without Scheduled Castes: There are 34 villages without any scheduled caste population.

Scheduled Tribes: Out of the total population of 65794 persons, 0 persons (0%) belong to Scheduled Tribes.

The villages having less than 10% ST population are Mangulam, Kurandi, Aviyur, D.Kadambangulam Arasakulam, Mustakuruchi, Melakallankulam, V.Nangor Pappanam, Kambikudi, S.Kallupatti, Ariyanandal Amaiperuki, Thotiyankulam, N.Nedungulam M.Elupaikulam, T.Veepankulam, Pampatti, Panchar Viyampatti, Manthoppu, Achangulam, Pisindi Vadakarai, Kaluvanacherry, Thoppur Chathirampuliyangulam, Allalaperi, Mudukkankulam Sirukulam, Chockkanandal, Periya Alangulam Chithanandal, Chinna Alangulam Karungulam Nedungulam, Vellangulam, Kovilankulam Manaviyendal, Vetrilai Muriyanpatti, Kilavaneri Chithemoondradaippu, Allikulam, Karianenthal Vakkanaugundy, Thonugal, Vaddakkupulliampatti Nanthikundu, Alagianallur, Varolotte, Valukkalotty Chandrankulam, Kalkurichi, Johilpatty Kanakkanenthal, Athikulam, Malakancharankulam T.Chettikulam, Kurangakkulan, Esalimadai, Sooranoor Koovarkulam, Thenoor, S.Maraikulam, Manangathan Thamaraikulam, Kilakancharankulam, Pandanendal Panikurippu, Thullukkangulam, Kundukulam Karaikkulam, Kambali, Kilidayangulam, P.Pudupatti Chokkampatti.

The villages having more than 50% ST population are None.

Villages without Scheduled Tribes: There are 102 villages without any scheduled tribe population.

Literates and Illiterates by Sex (Total Population):

	Persons	Males	Females
Literate	36,425	22,047	14,378
Illiterate	29,369	10,728	18,641
Literacy rate	64	78	50
Graduate	417	315	102

Agriculture: ***Distribution of villages according to land use:*** Out of 102 villages, Total area (in hectare) is 36640.74, out of that 0 percent is cultivable and 0 percent of the cultivable area is irrigated.

Sources of Irrigation (Hectares): Government Canal 0, Private Canal 0, Well without Electricity 0, Well with Electricity 0, Tubewell without Electricity 0, Tubewell with Electricity 2.6, Tank 1808.31, River 0, Lake 0, Waterfall 765.72, Others 0.

Villages with population of 5000 to 9999: None

Villages with population of 10000 and above: None

Distribution of Workers:

	Persons	Males	Females	WPR
Cultivators	10,454	5,866	4,588	28.42
Agricultural Labour	15,235	6,397	8,838	41.42
Household Industry	697	326	371	1.89
Other Workers	10,397	6,902	3,495	28.27
Main Workers	30,513	17,073	13,440	82.95
Marginal Workers	6,270	2,418	3,852	17.05
Total Workers	36,783	19,491	17,292	

Religion: Major Religious Communities:

	Persons	Males	Females	Sex Ratio
Hindu (97.37%)	64,065	31,965	32,100	1,004
Muslim (0.78%)	514	221	293	1,326
Christian (1.83%)	1,202	581	621	1,069
Sikh (0%)	1	1	-	-

Buddhists (0%)	2	-	2	-
Jain (0%)	3	3	-	-

Agewise Data:

	Persons	Males	Females	Sex Ratio
All ages	65,794	32,775	33,019	1007
0-14	19,783	10,177	9,606	944
15-44	31,219	15,307	15,912	1040
45-79	14,009	6,904	7,105	1029
80+	426	200	226	1130
Age not stated	357	187	170	909

Languages (Dominant):
Tamil, Telugu, Kannada, Urdu, Malayalam

Disabled Population:

	Persons	Males	Females	%
Total Disabled	1,794	808	986	
In Seeing	1,125	442	683	62.71
In Speech	158	93	65	8.81
In Hearing	73	33	40	4.07
In Movement	324	179	145	18.06
Mentally	114	61	53	6.35

KARIMANGALAM

Karimangalam C.D. Block lies in the north-western part of Dharmapuri district. It is a part of Palakkodu taluk. The Block is located at a distance of 30 kms. from district headquarters (Dharmapuri). There are 40 villages in the block with the total population of 125,240 persons. Area of the C.D. Block is 338. 52 sq. kms. It is bounded in the north by taluk Krishnagiri, in the south by CD Blocks Dharmapuri and Nallampalli, in the east by CD Block Morappur and district Krishnagiri, and in the west by C.D. Block Palakkodu.

Communications:

Roadways : N.H.-7: Direction- Dharmapuri to Krishnagiri, Nearest Villages- Kumbarahalli, Kerikodahalli, Karimang alam, Naganampatti, Periyanahalli, Adilam, Donnenahalli, Baisuhalli, Kalappana Hally. S.H.-17: Direction- Hosur to Palakkodu, Nearest Villages- Jittanchahalli, Mahanathramangalam, Thimarayahalli, Karukkanahalli, Jakkasamudhiram, Giddanahalli, Velakalahalli.

Annual Rainfall: Average Rainfall 760 mm.

Ground Water: Availability of the ground water in the Basin is 4771.41 H.A.M. and the utilization is 6739.63 H.A.M. It belongs to Over Expoited category. Depth to water level varies from 5 to 20 meter below the ground. Most of the wells go down in summer months, according to the Ground Water Estimation Committee.

Natural Division: Baramahal.

Administration

Revenue **Division:** Dharmapuri. Parliamentary Constituency: 10 Dharmapuri. District: Dharmapuri. Taluk: Palakkodu. Assembly Constituency: 57 Palakodu. Gram Panchayat: 30.

Villages: 39 **Inhabited:** 39 **Uninhabited:** 0

Ranking	District	State	National
Area	14	129	2382
Population	12	54	2686
Sex Ratio	14	365	4603
Child Sex Ratio	16	372	6199
Literacy Rate	14	369	4004
Density	4	112	2951
Work Participation Rate	4	138	1142

Gram Panchayats:

Adilam, Annamalaihalli, Baisuhalli, Bandarahalli , Begarahalli, Bikkanahalli , Bommahalli , Dinidal , Elumichanahalli , Erraseegalahalli, Gandiganahalli, Golasanahalli , Hanumanthapuram , Indamangalam, Jakkasamudram , Jittandahalli , Jittandahalli, Kalappanahalli, Kattanahalli , Kerakondahalli , Kovilur , Kumbarahalli , Mahendramangalam , Mallikuttai, Mottalur, Mukulam, Murukkampatti, Naganampatty, Periyampatty, Pulikkal, Pumandahalli, Thumbalahalli .

Amenities:

Education: Primary School in 35 villages, Middle school in 23 villages, Matriculation or Secondary School in 8 villages, namely Thimarayahalli, Jakkasamudhiram, Hanumanthapuram, Periyanahalli, Bandarahalli, Indamangalam, Baisuhalli, Begarahalli.

Higher Secondary or Pre University Courses or Intermediate or Junior College in 7 villages of the CD Block,, namely Thimarayahalli, Jakkasamudhiram, Hanumanthapuram, Periyanahalli, Indamangalam, Baisuhalli, Begarahalli.

College in 1 village, Adult Literacy Center in 0 village., College is in village, namely Periyanahalli.

Medical: Hospital in 0 village, Dispensary in 1 village, Health Center in 6 villages, Sub Center in 16 villages, Maternity and Child Welfare Center in 3 villages, Community health workers in 31 villages.

The Village having Hospital or Dispensary or Health Center is Narinaganahalli.

Drinking Water: Tap water in 39 villages, Tank water in 0 villages, Well water in 39 villages, Tubewell in 39 villages and more than one source in 39 villages.

Bank: Banking facility in 10 villages, namely, Thimarayahalli, Jakkasamudhiram, Hanumanthapuram Kerikodahalli, Narinaganahalli, Periyanahalli Bandarahalli, Baisuhalli, Kalappana Hally Begarahalli.

Credit Society in 23 villages Agricultural Credit Society in 11 Non-Agricultural Credit Society in 6 villages.

Others: Power supply in 39 villages, Cinema hall in 1 village, sport club in 0 village, Stadium or Auditorium or Community

Hall in 0 village, Post Office in 39 villages.

There are 37 villages having bus facilities.

Villages with most of facilities: Thimarayahalli Jakkasamudhiram, Hanumanthapuram, Kerikodahalli Narinaganahalli, Periyanahalli, Bandarahalli Baisuhalli, Kalappana Hally, Begarahalli.

Villages without amenities (Education): Jittanchahalli, Pachikamapalli, Karimangalam, Donnenahalli..

Scheduled Castes: Out of the total population of 125240 persons, 13829 persons (11.04%) belong to Scheduled Castes.

The villages having less than 10% SC population are Giddanahalli, Mukkulam, Kumbarahalli, Pachikamapalli Kerikodahalli, Karimangalam, Bommahalli Narinaganahalli, Pulikkal, Kondachamanahalli Naganampatti, Periyanahalli, Adilam, Thindal Indamangalam, Poonathanhalli, Chennanaraganahalli Donnenahalli, Begarahalli, Boomandahelli Malliayakuttai.

The villages having more than 50% SC population are None.

Sex ratio of Scheduled Caste population is 492.

Scheduled Castes Literates and Illiterates by Sex:

	Persons	Males	Females
Literate	6,253	3,823	2,430
Illiterate	7,576	3,207	4,369
Literacy rate	53.6	65.1	42.0
Graduate	83	70	13

Scheduled Castes (Dominant):

Adi Dravida, Arunthathiyar, Panniandi, Kuravan etc. Pallan

For their cultural identity please see Appendix-I

Villages without Scheduled Castes: There are 5 villages without any scheduled caste population.

Scheduled Tribes: Out of the total population of 125240 persons, 403 persons (0.32%) belong to Scheduled Tribes.

The villages having less than 10% ST population are Jittanchahalli, Mahanathramangalam, Thimarayahalli Murukkalanatham, Bikkamahalli, Karukkanahalli Jakkasamudhiram, Giddanahalli, Annamalaihalli Hanumanthapuram, Elumichainahalli, Mukkulam Kumbarahalli, Pachikamapalli, Kerikodahalli Karimangalam, Bommahalli, Narinaganahalli, Pulikkal Kondachamanahalli, Kottumaranahalli, Naganampatti Periyanahalli, Adilam, Thindal, Bandarahalli Bandarahalli, Murakkampatty, Indamangalam Poonathanhalli, Poonathanhalli, Chennanaraganahalli Donnenahalli, Baisuhalli, Kalappana Hally Begarahalli, Boomandahelli, Malliayakuttai.

The villages having more than 50% ST population are None.

Sex ratio of Scheduled tribe population is 491.

Scheduled Tribes Literates and Illiterates by Sex:

	Persons	Males	Females
Literate	39	26	13
Illiterate	364	179	185
Literacy rate	11.9	15.7	8.1
Graduate	3	3	0

Scheduled Tribes (Dominant):

Irular, Malayali, Kurumans, Kattunayakan Malai Arayan

For their cultural identity please see Appendix-II

Villages without Scheduled Tribes: There are 30 villages without any scheduled tribe population.

Literates and Illiterates by Sex (Total Population):

	Persons	Males	Females
Literate	57,064	35,633	21,431
Illiterate	68,176	29,394	38,782
Literacy rate	53	65	41
Graduate	1,008	809	199

Agriculture: ***Distribution of villages according to land use:*** Out of 39 villages, Total area (in hectare) is 33852.08, out of that 74.5 percent is cultivable and 40.1 percent of the cultivable area is irrigated.

Sources of Irrigation (Hectares): Government Canal 224.93, Private Canal 0, Well without Electricity 1656.82, Well with Electricity 6881.63, Tubewell without Electricity 0, Tubewell with Electricity 0, Tank 1345.94, River 0, Lake 0, Waterfall 0, Others 3.36.

Villages with population of 5000 to 9999: Jittandahalli , Themmarayanahalli, Elumichanahalli Periyanahalli, Adilam, Baisuhalli, Begarahalli.

Villages with population of 10000 and above: None

Distribution of Workers:

	Persons	Males	Females	WPR
Cultivators	31,426	18,268	13,158	47.12
Agricultural Labour	25,337	11,314	14,023	37.99
Household Industry	1,108	531	577	1.66
Other Workers	8,828	6,954	1,874	13.24
Main Workers	55,435	33,073	22,362	83.11
Marginal Workers	11,264	3,994	7,270	16.89
Total Workers	66,699	37,067	29,632	

Religion: Major Religious Communities:

	Persons	Males	Females	Sex Ratio
Hindu (97.6%)	122,232	63,507	58,725	925
Muslim (1.14%)	1,431	723	708	979
Christian (0.85%)	1,068	543	525	967
Sikh (0%)	-	-	-	-
Buddhists (0%)	1	1	-	-
Jain (0%)	2	-	2	-

Agewise Data:

	Persons	Males	Females	Sex Ratio
All ages	124,751	64,784	59,967	926
0-14	40,571	22,283	18,288	821
15-44	60,170	30,328	29,842	984
45-79	22,803	11,548	11,255	975
80+	1,009	513	496	967
Age not stated	198	112	86	768

Languages (Dominant):

Tamil, Telugu, Kannada, Urdu, Marathi

Disabled Population:

	Persons	Males	Females	%
Total Disabled	3,185	1,075	2,110	
In Seeing	2,171	458	1,713	68.16
In Speech	226	133	93	7.1
In Hearing	87	40	47	2.73
In Movement	571	370	201	17.93
Mentally	130	74	56	4.08

KARUNKULAM

Karunkulam C.D. Block lies in the south-western part of Thoothukkudi district. It is a part of Srivaikuntam taluk. The taluk is located at a distance of 40 kms. from district headquarters (Thoothukkudi). There are 34 villages in the block with the total population of 79,443 persons. Area of the C.D. Block is 352.88 sq. kms. It is bounded in the north by CD Block Ottapidaram, in the south by CD Block Alwarthirunagiri, in the east by CD Blocks Thoothukkudi, Srivaikuntam and Alwarthirunagiri, and the west by district Tirunelveli.

Communications:

Roadways : N.H.-7 A: Direction- Tirunelveli to Thoothukkudi, Nearest Villages- Vadavallanadu, Keelavallanad, Deivachailpuram, Ellinayakanpattai, Chettimallanpatti, Vallanad Kasba, Keelaputhaneri, Vasappapuram, Vallandu RF, Murappanaduputhugramam. S.H.-40: Direction- Tirunelveli to Tiruchendur, Nearest Villages- Vittilapuram, Vittilapuram Kovilpattu, Kongarayarkurichi, Karungulam, Seydunganallur.

Railway Station: Seydunganallur.

River: Tambraparani Nadi- Nearest Villages- Kaliyavur, Murappanadu Kovilpattu, Vadavallanadu, Vallanad Kasba, Keelaputhaneri, Aligudi, Murappanaduputhugramam, Nanalkadu, Manakkarai, Muthalangurichi, Arampannai, Kongarayarkurichi, Karungulam, Seydunganallur.

Annual Rainfall: Average Rainfall 661 mm.

Ground Water: Availability of the ground water in the Basin is 28.70 MCM and the utilization is 24.25 MCM. It belongs to Semi Critical category. Depth to water level varies from 0 to 10 meter below the ground. Most of the wells go down in summer months, according to the Ground Water Estimation Committee.

Natural Division: NA

Administration

Revenue **Division:** Thoothukkudi. Parliamentary Constituency: 36 Thoothukkudi. District: Thoothukkudi. Taluk: Srivaikuntam. Assembly Constituency: 217 Ottapidaram (SC), 216 Srivaikuntam. Gram Panchayat: 31.

Villages: 34 **Inhabited:** 33 **Uninhabited:** 1

Ranking	District	State	National
Area	6	110	2256
Population	4	247	4126
Sex Ratio	7	30	275
Child Sex Ratio	11	315	5264
Literacy Rate	8	47	657
Density	6	262	4371
Work Participation Rate	8	304	2840

Gram Panchayats:

Alanda, Alikkudi, Alwarkarkulam, Anavarathanallur, Arampannai, Cherakulam , Ellainayakkanpatti, Kaliyavur, Kalvay, Karungulam, Kilavallanadu, Kilputhaneri, Kongarayankurichi, Manakkarai, Murappanadu Pudugramam, Muruppanadukovilpattu, Muthulangurichi, Nanalkadu, Poovani, Ramanujampudur, Sekkarakkudi, Seydunganallur, Singathakurichi, Terkukariseri, Thathankulam, Vadakkukariseri, Vadavallanadu, Vallakulam, Vallanadu (Kasba), Vasavappapuram, Vitthalapuram, Vitthalapuram Kovilpattu.

Amenities:

Education: Primary School in 32 villages, Middle school in 18 villages, Matriculation or Secondary School in 7 villages, namely Alanda, Poouani, Sekkarakudi, Vallanad Kasba, Kongarayarkurichi, Karungulam, Serakolam.

Higher Secondary or Pre University Courses or Intermediate or Junior College in 3 villages of the CD Block,, namely Alanda, Vallanad Kasba, Karungulam.

College in 1 village, Adult Literacy Center in 1 village., College is in village, namely Manakkarai.

Medical: Hospital in 1 village, Dispensary in 1 village, Health Center in 5 villages, Sub Center in 12 villages, Maternity and Child Welfare Center in 1 village, Community health workers in 31 villages.

The Villages having Hospital or Dispensary or Health Center are Sekkarakudi, Arampannai, Serakolam.

Drinking Water: Tap water in 33 villages, Tank water in 1 villages, Well water in 33 villages, Tubewell in 33 villages and more than one source in 33 villages.

Bank: Banking facility in 11 villages, namely, Poouani, Meenachipuram, Sekkarakudi, Singathakurichi Vallanad Kasba, Aligudi, Kongarayarkurichi Alwarkarkulam, Karungulam, Seydunganallur, Serakolam.

Credit Society in 4 villages Agricultural Credit Society in 1 Non-Agricultural Credit Society in 4 villages.

Others: Power supply in 33 villages, Cinema hall in 1 village, sport club in 0 village, Stadium or Auditorium or Community Hall in 0 village, Post Office in 33 villages.

There are 31 villages having bus facilities.

Villages with most of facilities: Poouani Meenachipuram, Sekkarakudi, Singathakurichi Vallanad Kasba, Aligudi, Kongarayarkurichi Alwarkarkulam, Karungulam, Seydunganallur, Serakolam.

Villages without amenities (Education): Vittilapuram Kovilpattu..

Scheduled Castes: Out of the total population of 79443 persons, 21359 persons (26.89%) belong to Scheduled Castes.

The villages having less than 10% SC population are Meenachipuram, Kaliyavur, Ellinayakanpattai Nanalkadu, Arampannai, Kongarayarkurichi, Serakolam Kalvoay.

The villages having more than 50% SC population are Alanda, Poouani, Ulagudi, Keelavallanad Alwarkarkulam.

Sex ratio of Scheduled Caste population is 508.

Scheduled Castes Literates and Illiterates by Sex:

	Persons	Males	Females
Literate	12,947	7,324	5,623
Illiterate	8,412	3,176	5,236
Literacy rate	69.0	79.9	58.7
Graduate	247	167	80

Scheduled Castes (Dominant):

Pallan, Paraiyan etc., Adi Dravida, Chakkiliyan Arunthathiyar

For their cultural identity please see Appendix-I

Villages without Scheduled Castes: There are 2 villages without any scheduled caste population.

Scheduled Tribes: Out of the total population of 79443 persons, 100 persons (0.13%) belong to Scheduled Tribes.

The villages having less than 10% ST population are Alanda, Poouani, Meenachipuram, Sekkarakudi Vadakkukaraseri, Singathakurichi, Ulagudi, Kaliyavur Murappanadu Kovilpattu, Vadavallanadu, Keelavallanad Deivachailpuram, Ellinayakanpattai Chettimallanpatti, Vallanad Kasba, Keelaputhaneri Vasappapuram, Aligudi, Murappanaduputhugramam Nanalkadu, Manakkarai, Vittilapuram, Muthalangurichi Vittilapuram Kovilpattu, Arampannai Kongarayarkurichi, Alwarkarkulam, Karungulam Seydunganallur, Therkkukaraseri, Serakolam Vallakkulam, Kalvoay.

The villages having more than 50% ST population are None.

Sex ratio of Scheduled tribe population is 590.

Scheduled Tribes Literates and Illiterates by Sex:

	Persons	Males	Females
Literate	13	8	5
Illiterate	87	33	54
Literacy rate	15.7	22.9	10.4
Graduate	0	0	0

Scheduled Tribes (Dominant):

Kattunayakan, Malakkuravan

For their cultural identity please see Appendix-II

Villages without Scheduled Tribes: There are 30 villages without any scheduled tribe population.

Literates and Illiterates by Sex (Total Population):

	Persons	Males	Females
Literate	52,326	28,571	23,755
Illiterate	27,117	10,102	17,015
Literacy rate	75	85	66
Graduate	914	659	255

Agriculture: ***Distribution of villages according to land use:*** Out of 34 villages, Total area (in hectare) is 35288.95, out of that 26.59 percent is cultivable and 43.41 percent of the cultivable area is irrigated.

Sources of Irrigation (Hectares): Government Canal 1587.41, Private Canal 4.1, Well without Electricity 13.07, Well with Electricity 653.55, Tubewell without Electricity 10.6, Tubewell with Electricity 340.06, Tank 1464.6, River 0, Lake 0, Waterfall 0, Others 0.

Villages with population of 5000 to 9999: Sekkarakkudi, Vallanadu (Kasba), Karungulam Seydunganallur.

Villages with population of 10000 and above: None

Distribution of Workers:

	Persons	Males	Females	WPR
Cultivators	6,675	4,452	2,223	17.48
Agricultural Labour	16,496	7,912	8,584	43.19
Household Industry	3,549	645	2,904	9.29
Other Workers	11,476	8,930	2,546	30.05
Main Workers	31,341	19,144	12,197	82.05
Marginal Workers	6,855	2,795	4,060	17.95
Total Workers	38,196	21,939	16,257	

Religion: Major Religious Communities:

	Persons	Males	Females	Sex Ratio
Hindu (86.66%)	68,843	33,735	35,108	1,041
Muslim (7.43%)	5,901	2,688	3,213	1,195
Christian (5.85%)	4,647	2,224	2,423	1,089
Sikh (0.01%)	6	3	3	1,000
Buddhists (0%)	-	-	-	-
Jain (0%)	3	1	2	2,000

Agewise Data:

	Persons	Males	Females	Sex Ratio
All ages	79,443	38,673	40,770	1054
0-14	22,299	11,538	10,761	933

15-44	36,776	17,513	19,263	1100
45-79	18,769	8,842	9,927	1123
80+	826	391	435	1113
Age not stated	773	389	384	987

Languages (Dominant):
Tamil, Telugu, Malayalam, Hindi, Others

Disabled Population:

	Persons	Males	Females	%
Total Disabled	2,105	1,051	1,054	
In Seeing	1,175	482	693	55.82
In Speech	149	87	62	7.08
In Hearing	88	34	54	4.18
In Movement	534	355	179	25.37
Mentally	159	93	66	7.55

KARUR

Karur C.D. Block lies in the northern part of Karur district. It is a part of Karur taluk. The Block is located at a distance of (00) kms. from district headquarters (Karur). There are 19 villages in the block with the total population of 73,259 persons. Area of the C.D. Block is 187.06 sq. kms. It is bounded in the north by district Namakkal, in the south by C.D. Blocks Thanthoni and K.Paramathi, in the east by district Namakkal and CD Block Krishnarayapuram, in the west by district Erode and CD Block K.Paramathy.

Communications:

Roadways : N.H.-7: Direction- Namakkal to Karur, Nearest Villages- N. Pugalur, Punjai Kadambakurichi, Manmangalam, Athur, Kathapparai.

Railway Station: Vattamangalam(West), Kuppichipalayam, Vangal, Athur.

River: Amaravathi Nadi- Nearest Villages- Achamapuram, Somur, Panjamadevi, Nerur (South). Cauvery Nadi- Nearest Villages- Vattamangalam(West), Vettamangalalm (East), Thirukattuthurai, N. Pugalur, Nanjai Kadambankurichi, Punjai Kadambakurichi, Nanniyur, Vangal, Nerur North, Nerur (South), Achamapuram.

Annual Rainfall: Average Rainfall 635 mm.

Ground Water: Availability of the ground water in the Basin is 3598.31 H.A.M. and the utilization is 2284.85 H.A.M. It belongs to Safe category. Depth to water level varies from 0 to 10 meter below the ground. Most of the wells go down in summer months, according to the Ground Water Estimation Committee.

Natural Division: NA

Administration

Revenue **Division:** Karur. Parliamentary Constituency: 23 Karur. District: Karur. Taluk: Karur. Assembly Constituency: 134 Aravakurichi, 135 Karur. Gram Panchayat: 14.

Villages: 19 **Inhabited:** 19 **Uninhabited:** 0

Ranking	District	State	National
Area	7	302	4400
Population	6	273	4346
Sex Ratio	1	67	548
Child Sex Ratio	1	115	2201
Literacy Rate	2	193	1772
Density	5	79	2788
Work Participation Rate	2	117	755

Gram Panchayats:

Athur Poolampalayam, Kadambankurichi punjai, Kadaparai, Kumbupalayam, Manmangalam, Minampalli-Pachamadevi, Nanjaipugalur , Nanniyur, Nerur (North), Nerur (South), Somur, Thirukkattuthurai, Vangal Kuppuchipalayam, Vettamangalam .

Amenities:

Education: Primary School in 18 villages, Middle school in 13 villages, Matriculation or Secondary School in 8 villages, namely Vattamangalam(West), Kombupalayam, Thirukattuthurai, Nanniyur, Kuppichipalayam, Nerur (South), Manmangalam, Kathapparai.

Higher Secondary or Pre University Courses or Intermediate or Junior College in 3 villages of the CD Block,, namely Vattamangalam(West), Kombupalayam, Kuppichipalayam.

College in 0 village, Adult Literacy Center in 0 village.

Medical: Hospital in 1 village, Dispensary in 3 villages, Health Center in 4 villages, Sub Center in 2 villages, Maternity and Child Welfare Center in 8 villages, Community health workers in 0 village.

The Villages having Hospital or Dispensary or Health Center are Kombupalayam, Kuppichipalayam, Nerur North, Manmangalam.

Drinking Water: Tap water in 19 villages, Tank water in 13 villages, Well water in 19 villages, Tubewell in 19 villages and more than one source in 19 villages.

Bank: Banking facility in 8 villages, namely, Vattamangalam(West), Thirukattuthurai Kuppichipalayam, Vangal, Nerur North, Panjamadevi Athur, Kathapparai.

Credit Society in 11 villages Agricultural Credit Society in 10 Non-Agricultural Credit Society in 2 villages.

Others: Power supply in 19 villages, Cinema hall in 1 village, sport club in 0 village, Stadium or Auditorium or Community Hall in 0 village, Post Office in 16 villages.

There are 17 villages having bus facilities.

Villages with most of facilities: Vattamangalam(West) Kuppichipalayam, Vangal, Nerur North, Panjamadevi Athur.

Villages without amenities (Education):
Nanjai Kadambankurichi..

Scheduled Castes: Out of the total population of 73259

persons, 16707 persons (22.81%) belong to Scheduled Castes. The villages having less than 10% SC population are None..

The villages having more than 50% SC population are None.

Sex ratio of Scheduled Caste population is 508.

Scheduled Castes Literates and Illiterates by Sex:

	Persons	Males	Females
Literate	8,532	5,144	3,388
Illiterate	8,175	3,069	5,106
Literacy rate	58.1	71.8	45.1
Graduate	325	232	93

Scheduled Castes (Dominant):

Chakkiliyan, Pallan, Paraiyan etc., Valluvan Kuravan etc.

For their cultural identity please see Appendix-I

Villages without Scheduled Castes: There is 0 village without any scheduled caste population.

Scheduled Tribes: Out of the total population of 73259 persons, 73 persons (0.1%) belong to Scheduled Tribes. The villages having less than 10% ST population are Vattamangalam(West), Vettamangalalm (East) Kombupalayam, Thirukattuthurai, N. Pugalur Nanjai Kadambankurichi, Punjai Kadambakurichi Nanniyur, Kuppichipalayam, Vangal, Nerur North Nerur (South), Achamapuram, Somur, Panjamadevi Minnampalli, Manmangalam, Athur, Kathapparai.

The villages having more than 50% ST population are None.

Sex ratio of Scheduled tribe population is 466.

Scheduled Tribes Literates and Illiterates by Sex:

	Persons	Males	Females
Literate	17	10	7
Illiterate	56	29	27
Literacy rate	28.3	33.3	23.3
Graduate	0	0	0

Scheduled Tribes (Dominant):

Malakkuravan, Mudugar etc., Kudiya etc., Kurichchan Palliyan

For their cultural identity please see Appendix-II

Villages without Scheduled Tribes: There are 15 villages without any scheduled tribe population.

Literates and Illiterates by Sex (Total Population):

	Persons	Males	Females
Literate	43,395	25,848	17,547
Illiterate	29,864	10,306	19,558
Literacy rate	66	80	52
Graduate	2,045	1,489	556

Agriculture: ***Distribution of villages according to land use:*** Out of 19 villages, Total area (in hectare) is 18706, out of that 53.49 percent is cultivable and 59.81 percent of the cultivable area is irrigated.

Sources of Irrigation (Hectares): Government Canal 3714.37, Private Canal 130.15, Well without Electricity 386.01, Well witl Electricity 1705.84, Tubewell without Electricity 0, Tubewell with Electricity 48.91, Tank 0, River 0, Lake 0, Waterfall 0, Others 0.

Villages with population of 5000 to 9999: Kuppuchipalayam, Nerur North, Panchamadevi Manmangalam, Kadaparai.

Villages with population of 10000 and above: None

Distribution of Workers:

	Persons	Males	Females	WPR
Cultivators	7,065	4,076	2,989	16.77
Agricultural Labour	16,514	6,974	9,540	39.21
Household Industry	2,180	953	1,227	5.18
Other Workers	16,362	11,695	4,667	38.85
Main Workers	38,560	22,470	16,090	91.55
Marginal Workers	3,561	1,228	2,333	8.45
Total Workers	42,121	23,698	18,423	

Religion: Major Religious Communities:

	Persons	Males	Females	Sex Ratio
Hindu (97.87%)	71,699	35,413	36,286	1,025
Muslim (1.4%)	1,026	486	540	1,111
Christian (0.66%)	486	232	254	1,095
Sikh (0%)	1	1	-	-
Buddhists (0%)	1	1	-	-
Jain (0%)	-	-	-	-

Agewise Data:

	Persons	Males	Females	Sex Ratio
All ages	73,259	36,154	37,105	1026
0-14	16,457	8,461	7,996	945
15-44	35,833	17,604	18,229	1036
45-79	20,171	9,686	10,485	1082
80+	744	377	367	973
Age not stated	54	26	28	1077

Languages (Dominant):

Tamil, Telugu, Urdu, Kannada, Malayalam

Disabled Population:

	Persons	Males	Females	%
Total Disabled	1,204	656	548	
In Seeing	380	184	196	31.56
In Speech	145	77	68	12.04
In Hearing	105	49	56	8.72
In Movement	442	271	171	36.71
Mentally	132	75	57	10.96

KATPADI

katpadi C.D. Block lies in the northern part of Vellore district. It is a part of Katpadi taluk. The Block is located at a distance of 10 kms. from district headquarters (Vellore). There are 26 villages in the block with the total population of 67,745 persons. Area of the C.D. Block is 118.21 sq. kms. It is bounded in the north by CD Block Sholinghur, in the south by by CD Block Sholinghur, in the south by river palar, CD Blocks Vellore and Walajapet, in the east by CD Block Wallajapet, in the west by CD Block K.V. Kuppam, and it has common boundary with the state of Andhra Pradesh on north.

Communications:

Roadways : N.H.-4: Direction- Chittoor to Ranipettai, Nearest Villages- Eranthangal, Serkadu, Sembarayanallur. S.H.-9: Direction- Chittoor to Vellore, Nearest Villages- Vandranthangal, Virudampattu, Darapadavedu.

River: Palar Nadi- Nearest Villages- Thiruvalam-Platation RF. Unnamalai Samudram, Thalayarampattu, Thandalam Krishnapuram, Virudampattu, Brahmapuram, Kugaiyanallore, Sevur, Arumparuthy, Karnambut, Ammundi.

Annual Rainfall: Average Rainfall 949 mm.

Ground Water: Availability of the ground water in the Basin is 2782.47 H.A.M. and the utilization is 3896.97 H.A.M. It belongs to Over Expoited category. Depth to water level varies from 10 to 15 meter below the ground. Most of the wells go down in summer months, according to the Ground Water Estimation Committee.

Forest and Reserved Forest: (Kunjanur RF)- Nearest Villages- Kunjanur (RF), Karigiri, Darapadavedu. (Senur)- Nearest Villages- Senur (RF), Jafrapettai. (Thiruvalam Plantatio n)- Nearest Villages- Ammundi, Thiruvalam Plantation (RF). (Ammundi)- Nearest Villages- Unnamalai Samudram, Thalayarampattu.

Natural Division: Tondai Nadu.

Administration

Revenue **Division:** Vellore. Parliamentary Constituency: 7 Arakkonam, 8 Vellore. District: Vellore. Taluk: Katpa di. Assembly Constituency: 40 Katpadi, 45 Kavanur (SC). Gram Panchayat: 23.

Border Villages- (Andhra Pradesh)- Nearest Villages- Kunjanur (RF), Karigiri, Darapadavedu, Vandaranthangal, Oddanthangal.

Villages: 26 **Inhabited:** 22 **Uninhabited:** 4

Ranking	District	State	National
Area	20	362	5510
Population	18	299	4567
Sex Ratio	1	75	606
Child Sex Ratio	3	72	1507
Literacy Rate	2	54	724
Density	20	367	1931
Work Participation Rate	2	38	4692

Gram Panchayats:

Ammundi , Animuthumottur, Arumparuthi, Bramapuram, Eranthangal, Gugaiyanallur, Jabbrapet, Kandipedu, Karasamangalam, Karigiri, Karnampattu, Knadipedu, Kuppathamottur, Mettukulam, Puddur, Sembarayanallore, Serkadu, Sevur, Thandalamkrishnapuram, Vandaranthangal, Vanjur, Virudampattu.

Amenities:

Education: Primary School in 21 villages, Middle school in 12 villages, Matriculation or Secondary School in 6 villages, namely Serkadu, Karigiri, Vanjur, Darapadavedu, Brahmapuram, Karnambut.

Higher Secondary or Pre University Courses or Intermediate or Junior College in 3 villages of the CD Block,, namely Serkadu, Karigiri, Darapadavedu.

College in 0 village, Adult Literacy Center in 0 village.

Medical: Hospital in 0 village, Dispensary in 0 village, Health Center in 1 village, Sub Center in 5 villages, Maternity and Child Welfare Center in 4 villages, Community health workers in 22 villages.

Drinking Water: Tap water in 22 villages, Tank water in 3 villages, Well water in 2 villages, Tubewell in 9 villages and more than one source in 22 villages.

Bank: Banking facility in 7 villages, namely, Oddanthangal, Vandranthangal, Karigiri, Kandipedu Darapadavedu, Sevur, Ammundi.

Credit Society in 6 villages Agricultural Credit Society in 3 Non-Agricultural Credit Society in 3 villages.

Others: Power supply in 22 villages, Cinema hall in 2 villages, sport club in 0 village, Stadium or Auditorium or Community Hall in 0 village, Post Office in 20 villages.

There are 20 villages having bus facilities.

Villages with most of facilities: Oddanthangal Vandranthangal, Karigiri, Kandipedu, Darapadavedu Sevur, Ammundi.

Villages without amenities (Education):

Thalayarampattu..

Scheduled Castes: Out of the total population of 67745 persons, 12030 persons (17.76%) belong to Scheduled Castes. The villages having less than 10% SC population are Serkadu, Puthur, Unnamalai Samudram, Thalayarampattu Ammundi.

The villages having more than 50% SC population are None.

Sex ratio of Scheduled Caste population is 504.

Scheduled Castes Literates and Illiterates by Sex:

	Persons	Males	Females
Literate	8,245	4,518	3,727
Illiterate	3,785	1,451	2,334
Literacy rate	77.9	86.5	69.5
Graduate	220	148	72

Scheduled Castes (Dominant):

Adi Dravida, Arunthathiyar, Baira, Valluvan Kuravan etc.

For their cultural identity please see Appendix-I

Villages without Scheduled Castes: There are 4 villages without any scheduled caste population.

Scheduled Tribes: Out of the total population of 67745 persons, 377 persons (0.56%) belong to Scheduled Tribes. The villages having less than 10% ST population are Kugaiyanallore, Eranthangal, Serkadu, Oddanthangal Vandranthangal, Karasamangalam, Jafrapettai Karigiri, Kandipedu, Puthur, Sembarayanallur, Vanjur Unnamalai Samudram, Thalayarampattu Thandalam Krishnapuram, Virudampattu, Darapadavedu Brahmapuram, Sevur, Arumparuthy, Karnambut, Ammundi. The villages having more than 50% ST population are None.

Sex ratio of Scheduled tribe population is 512.

Scheduled Tribes Literates and Illiterates by Sex:

	Persons	Males	Females
Literate	138	81	57
Illiterate	239	103	136
Literacy rate	43.5	52.3	35.2
Graduate	1	1	0

Scheduled Tribes (Dominant):

Irular, Malakkuravan, Palliyan

For their cultural identity please see Appendix-II

Villages without Scheduled Tribes: There are 15 villages without any scheduled tribe population.

Literates and Illiterates by Sex (Total Population):

	Persons	Males	Females
Literate	44,354	24,847	19,507
Illiterate	23,391	8,643	14,748
Literacy rate	74	84	64
Graduate	1,187	784	403

Agriculture: ***Distribution of villages according to land use:*** Out of 26 villages, Total area (in hectare) is 11821.65, out of that 61.09 percent is cultivable and 26.21 percent of the cultivable area is irrigated.

Sources of Irrigation (Hectares): Government Canal 0, Private Canal 0, Well without Electricity 2.4, Well with Electricity 1030.89, Tubewell without Electricity 0, Tubewell with Electricity 708.63, Tank 151.18, River 0, Lake 0, Waterfall 0, Others 0.

Villages with population of 5000 to 9999: Vandaranthangal, Virudampattu, Brahmapuram, Ammundi.

Villages with population of 10000 and above: None

Distribution of Workers:

	Persons	Males	Females	WPR
Cultivators	4,247	3,259	988	16.04
Agricultural Labour	7,082	3,590	3,492	26.74
Household Industry	4,656	2,524	2,132	17.58
Other Workers	10,496	8,605	1,891	39.64
Main Workers	22,477	15,980	6,497	84.88
Marginal Workers	4,004	1,998	2,006	15.12
Total Workers	26,481	17,978	8,503	

Religion: Major Religious Communities:

	Persons	Males	Females	Sex Ratio
Hindu (87.28%)	59,125	29,350	29,775	1,014
Muslim (3.45%)	2,336	1,149	1,187	1,033
Christian (9.13%)	6,184	2,946	3,238	1,099
Sikh (0%)	3	2	1	500
Buddhists (0.02%)	14	5	9	1,800
Jain (0%)	-	-	-	-

Agewise Data:

	Persons	Males	Females	Sex Ratio
All ages	67,745	33,490	34,255	1023
0-14	19,480	9,783	9,697	991
15-44	32,802	16,086	16,716	1039
45-79	14,607	7,218	7,389	1024
80+	659	299	360	1204
Age not stated	197	104	93	894

Languages (Dominant):

Tamil, Telugu, Urdu, Malayalam, Others

Disabled Population:

	Persons	Males	Females	%
Total Disabled	1,605	851	754	
In Seeing	728	360	368	45.36
In Speech	165	97	68	10.28
In Hearing	107	43	64	6.67
In Movement	448	260	188	27.91
Mentally	157	91	66	9.78

KATTANKOLATTUR

Kattankolattur C.D. Block lies in the eastern part of Kancheepuram district. It is a part of Chengalpattu taluk. The taluk is located at a distance of 40 kms. from district headquarters (Kancheepuram). There are 78 villages in the block with the total population of 95,585 persons. Area of the C.D. Block is 274.92 sq. kms. It is bounded in the north by CD Blocks Kunnathur and St. Thomas Mount, in the south by CD Block Tirukkalukunram, in the east by CD Block St. Thomas Mount and Thirupporur, in the west by CD Block Walajabad and Uthiramerur.

Communications:

Roadways : N.H.-45: Direction- Madurant to Chennai, Nearest Villages- Thirutheri RF (Ui), Paranur, Ideeyankodumanthangal (Ui), Pulipakkam, Rajakulipettai, Hanumanthaputheri RF (Ui), Kammalampattu.

River: Palar Nadi- Nearest Villages- Melmanapakkam, Palur,Villiambakkam, Athur, Pazhaveli, Kammalampattu, Ozhalur.

Annual Rainfall: Average Rainfall 1105 mm.

Ground Water: Availability of the ground water in the Basin is 7506.20 H.A.M. and the utilization is 4850.54 H.A.M. It belongs to Safe category. Depth to water level varies from 2 to 10 meter below the ground. Most of the wells go down in summer months, according to the Ground Water Estimation Committee.

Forest and Reserved Forest: (Anjur RF)- Nearest Villages- Echankaranai, Pattarvakkam, Karunilam, Karambur, Sengundram (Ui), Kachadimangalam, Kondamangalam, Anjur RF (Ui), Anjur, Thenmelpakkam. (Thirutheri)- Nearest Villages- Chettipunyam, Thirutheri RF (Ui), Kachadimangalam, Thenmelpakkam, Veerapuram, Paranur. (Appur)- Nearest Villages- Appur RF, Perumalthangal, Appur, Thalimangalam (Ui), Dasarikunnathur, Vembakkam. Chettipunyam, Kolathur,. (Parnanur)- Nearest Villages- Chettipunyam, Paranur, Paranur RF, Kanthalur, Ideeyankodumanthangal (Ui), Pulipakkam, Rajakulipettai. (Gudalore)- Nearest Villages- Gudalore RF, Kayarambedu, Karambur. (Hanumanthaputheri)- Nearest Villages- Hanumanthaputheri RF (Ui), Pazhaveli, Kammalampattu. (Kalvoy)- Nearest Village- Kalvoy, Kalvoy RF (Ui). (Kattankolathr)- Nearest Village- Kattankolathur RF (Ui). (Kumuzhi)- Nearest Villages- Arungal, Kumuzhi RF (Ui), Keerappakkam, Kumizhi, Othivakkam, Kannivakkam. (Mambakkam)- Nearest Village- Murugamangalam. (Othivakkam)- Nearest Villages- Hasthinapuram, Othivakkam, Othivakkam RF (Ui). (Unamancheri)- Nearest Villages- Unamancheri, Rattinamangalam, Nallambakkam, Unamancheri RF (Ui), Arungal. (Vallam)- Nearest Villages- Thiruvadisoolam, Kovilanthangal (Ui), Thenur, Ammman ambakkam, Vallam, Vallam RF (Ui), Porunthavakkam. (Vandal ur)- Nearest Villages- Vandalur RF (Ui), Nedungundram,

Natural Division: Tondai Nadu.

Administration

Revenue **Division:** Chengalpattu. Parliamentary Constituen cy: 6 Kancheepuram (SC). District: Kancheepuram. Taluk: Chengalpattu. Assembly Constituency: 32 Chengalpattu, 33 Thiruporur. Gram Panchayat: 39.

Villages: 78 **Inhabited:** 62 **Uninhabited:** 16

Ranking	District	State	National
Area	10	201	3047
Population	8	152	3609
Sex Ratio	9	243	1733
Child Sex Ratio	5	109	2140
Literacy Rate	4	133	1384
Density	11	354	3119
Work Participation Rate	5	161	4463

Gram Panchayats:

Anjur, Appur , Athur, Chettipunyam, Guruvanmedu , Kalvoy, Karanaipuducheri, Karunilam , Kayarambedu, Keerapakkam , Keerappakkam , Kolathur , Kondamangalam, Kumizhi , Kunnavakkam , Mannivakkam, Nallambakkam, Nedungundram , Ozhalur, Palur , Pattaravakkam , Pazhaveli , Periaputheri , Periyaputheri , Perumathunallur, Perumattunallur , Pulipakkam , Reddipalayam, Thenmalpakkam , Thimmavaram, Thiruvadisoolam , Unamancheri, Vallam, Vallam , Veerapuram , Vengadamangalam , Venkatapuram , Villiambakkam, .

Amenities:

Education: Primary School in 46 villages, Middle school in 16 villages, Matriculation or Secondary School in 5 villages, namely Mannivakkam, Nedungundram, Kayarambedu, Anjur, Athur A,B/B.

Higher Secondary or Pre University Courses or Intermediate or Junior College in 2 villages of the CD Block,, namely Mannivakkam, Athur A,B/B.

College in 1 village, Adult Literacy Center in 0 village., Colleges is in village, namely Athur A,B/B.

Medical: Hospital in 1 village, Dispensary in 3 villages, Health Center in 7 villages, Sub Center in 21 villages, Maternity and Child Welfare Center in 2 villages, Community health workers in 60 villages.

The Villages having Hospital or Dispensary or Health Center are Mannivakkam, Nedungundram, Palur A/B, B/B, Veerapuram.

Drinking Water: Tap water in 62 villages, Tank water in 50 villages, Well water in 62 villages, Tubewell in 62 villages and more than one source in 62 villages.

Bank: Banking facility in 7 villages, namely, Nallambakkam, Palur A/B, B/B, Thenmelpakkam Athur A,B/B, Senneri, Ozhalur, Vallam.

Credit Society in 9 villages Agricultural Credit Society in 9 Non-Agricultural Credit Society in 0 village.

Others: Power supply in 61 villages, Cinema hall in 1 village, sport club in 0 village, Stadium or Auditorium or Community Hall in 0 village, Post Office in 26 villages.

There are 49 villages having bus facilities.

Villages with most of facilities: Nallambakkam Palur A/B, B/B, Thenmelpakkam, Athur A,B/B, Ozhalur Vallam.

Villages without amenities (Education): Puthur, Gudalore Rf, Murugamangalam, Appur Rf, Senthamangalam, Karambur, Dasarikunnathur, Melmanapakkam, Sasthirambakkam, Kachadimangalam, Paranur Rf, Kanthalur, Rajakulipettai, Thenur, Kammalampattu, Porunthavakkam..

Scheduled Castes: Out of the total population of 95585 persons, 35069 persons (36.69%) belong to Scheduled Castes. The villages having less than 10% SC population are Unamancheri, Gudalore Rf, Ammanambakkam, Appur Karambur, Dasarikunnathur, Villiambakkam Kondamangalam, Paranur, Paranur Rf, Kunnavakkam Senneri, Thenur.

The villages having more than 50% SC population are Puthur, Perumathanallur, Kumizhi, Othivakkam Appur Rf, Melmanapakkam, Palur A/B, B/B Venkatapuram, Kachadimangalam, Thenmelpakkam Kanthalur, Echankaranai, Ammmanambakkam, Pazhaveli Kammalampattu, Ozhalur.

Sex ratio of Scheduled Caste population is 498.

Scheduled Castes Literates and Illiterates by Sex:

	Persons	Males	Females
Literate	20,124	11,441	8,683
Illiterate	14,945	6,150	8,795
Literacy rate	65.8	74.7	56.8
Graduate	354	239	115

Scheduled Castes (Dominant):

Adi Dravida, Arunthathiyar, Generic Castes etc. Pambada, Baira

For their cultural identity please see Appendix-I

Villages without Scheduled Castes: There are 23 villages without any scheduled caste population.

Scheduled Tribes: Out of the total population of 95585 persons, 1652 persons (1.73%) belong to Scheduled Tribes.

The villages having less than 10% ST population are Mannivakkam, Nedungundram, Puthur, Kolapakam Unamancheri, Rattinamangalam, Vengadamangalam Nallambakkam, Arungal, Karanaipuducheri, Gudalore Rf Kayarambedu, Perumathanallur, Keerappakkam Murugamangalam, Ammanambakkam, Kumizhi, Othivakkam Kannivakkam, Appur Rf, Senthamangalam, Appur Hasthinapuram, Karunilam, Karambur, Kolathur Dasarikunnathur, Guruvanmedu, Melmanapakkam Palur A/B, B/B, Villiambakkam, Sasthirambakkam Vembakkam, Venkatapuram, Chettipunyam Kachadimangalam, Kondamangalam, Anjur , Thenmelpakkam Veerapuram, Paranur, Paranur Rf, Kanthalur Athur A,B/B, Pulipakkam, Rajakulipettai, Hanumanthai Kunnavakkam, Echankaranai, Pattaravakkam Periyaputheri, Thiruvadisoolam, Thenur Ammmanambakkam, Pazhaveli, Kammalampattu, Ozhalur Vallam, Porunthavakkam.

The villages having more than 50% ST population are None.

Sex ratio of Scheduled tribe population is 502.

Scheduled Tribes Literates and Illiterates by Sex:

	Persons	Males	Females
Literate	500	293	207
Illiterate	1,152	529	623
Literacy rate	36.2	42.8	29.7
Graduate	4	4	0

Scheduled Tribes (Dominant):

Irular, Malakkuravan, Generic Tribes etc., Kurumans Kondareddis

For their cultural identity please see Appendix-II

Villages without Scheduled Tribes: There are 40 villages without any scheduled tribe population.

Literates and Illiterates by Sex (Total Population):

	Persons	Males	Females
Literate	57,603	32,801	24,802
Illiterate	37,982	15,303	22,679
Literacy rate	69	78	59
Graduate	1,352	904	448

Agriculture: ***Distribution of villages according to land use:*** Out of 78 villages, Total area (in hectare) is 27492.98, out of that 38.43 percent is cultivable and 61.05 percent of the cultivable area is irrigated.

Sources of Irrigation (Hectares): Government Canal 248.11, Private Canal 0, Well without Electricity 331.9, Well with Electricity 1760.42, Tubewell without Electricity 0, Tubewell with Electricity 278.79, Tank 160.37, River 0, Lake 3636.58, Waterfall 0, Others 35.18.

Villages with population of 5000 to 9999: Mannivakkam, Nedungundram, Palur , Athur , Vallam.

Villages with population of 10000 and above: None

Distribution of Workers:

	Persons	Males	Females	WPR
Cultivators	7,422	5,061	2,361	19.27
Agricultural Labour	10,303	5,735	4,568	26.74
Household Industry	1,766	806	960	4.58
Other Workers	19,034	14,600	4,434	49.41
Main Workers	28,069	20,922	7,147	72.86
Marginal Workers	10,456	5,280	5,176	27.14
Total Workers	38,525	26,202	12,323	

Religion: Major Religious Communities:

	Persons	Males	Females	Sex Ratio
Hindu (93.88%)	89,734	45,164	44,570	987
Muslim (1.47%)	1,406	720	686	953
Christian (4.46%)	4,259	2,119	2,140	1,010
Sikh (0.01%)	6	4	2	500
Buddhists (0.01%)	10	6	4	667
Jain (0.01%)	6	4	2	500

Agewise Data:

	Persons	Males	Females	Sex Ratio
All ages	95,585	48,104	47,481	987
0-14	27,931	14,089	13,842	982
15-44	48,073	24,014	24,059	1002
45-79	18,122	9,239	8,883	961
80+	776	413	363	879
Age not stated	683	349	334	957

Languages (Dominant):

Tamil, Telugu, Urdu, Malayalam, Kannada

Disabled Population:

	Persons	Males	Females	%
Total Disabled	2,323	1,337	986	
In Seeing	856	459	397	36.85
In Speech	190	111	79	8.18
In Hearing	191	96	95	8.22
In Movement	921	571	350	39.65
Mentally	165	100	65	7.1

KATTUMANNARKOIL

Kattumannarkoil C.D. Block lies in the southern part of Cuddalore district. It is a part of Kattumannarkoil taluk. The Block is located at a distance of 75 kms. from district headquarters (Cuddalore). There are 67 villages in the block with the total population of 94,527 persons. Area of the C.D. C.D. Block is 214.51 sq. kms. It is bounded in the north by CD Block Komaratchi, in the south by districts Thanjavur and Nagapattinam, in the east by C.D. Block Komaratchi, and in the west by district Ariyalur.

Communications:

Roadways : Information not Available.

River: Vellar Nadi- Nearest Villages- Ananthakudy, Kokaranpettai, Madakalirmanikkam, Gunamangalam, Kallippadi, Sriputhur, Srineduncheri, T. Arulmozhidevan. Kollidam Nadi- Nearest Villages- Sirukattur, Kanjankollai, Achalpuram, Eyyalur, Keelpuliyampattu, Adhanur, Kunavasal, Omampuliyur, Muttam, Kunjamedu, Karupperi, Veerasolapuram, Alanganatham, T. Arulmozhidevan.

Backwards Region Grants Fund: It receives Backward Region Grants.

Annual Rainfall: Average Rainfall 1050 mm.

Ground Water: Availability of the ground water in the Basin is 10942.42 MCM and the utilization is 5408.81 MCM. It belongs to Safe category. Depth to water level varies from 2 to 10 meter below the ground. Most of the wells go down in summer months, according to the Ground Water Estimation Committee.

Natural Division: Tondai Nadu.

Administration

Revenue **Division:** Chidambaram. Parliamentary Constituency: 27 Chidambaram (SC). District: Cuddalore. Taluk: Kattumannarkoil. Assembly Constituency: 159 Kattumannarkoil (SC). Gram Panchayat: 54.

Villages: 67 **Inhabited:** 67 **Uninhabited:** 0

Ranking	District	State	National
Area	8	264	3940
Population	11	154	3639
Sex Ratio	9	279	2207
Child Sex Ratio	3	114	2224
Literacy Rate	2	72	888
Density	5	221	2501
Work Participation Rate	9	86	2344

Gram Panchayats:

Achalpuram, Adhanur (Mannargudi), Adivaraganallur (Srimushnam), Agaraputhur, Alanganatham, Alinjamangalam, Arantangi, Arulmozhidevan, Ayangudi, Chettithangal , Eachampoondi, Esanur, Kallippadi, Kanattampuliyur, Kandamangalam, Kandiyankuppam, Kanjankollai, Karunakaranallur, Keelakadambur, Keelpuliyampattu, Kokkarasanpettai, Kollumedu, Kondasamudram, Kozhai, Kunamangalam, Kunavasal, Kunjamedu, Kuppunkuli Poovilandanallur, Kurungudi, Madhalirmanickam, Mamangalam, Maniyam Adur, Melakadambur, Melpuliyangudi, Melradhambur, Movur, Muttam, Nagarappadi, Nathamalai, Nattarmangalam, Palanchanallur, Rayanallur, Reddiyur, Shandan, Sirukattur, Sithamalli, Srineduncheri, Sriputhur, Thethambattu, Thorappu, Tiruchinnapuram, Uttamasolagan(Mannargudi), Vanamadevi, Veerananallur, Veeranandapuram.

Amenities:

Education: Primary School in 58 villages, Middle school in 26 villages, Matriculation or Secondary School in 10 villages, namely Srineduncheri, Mamangalam, Rayanallur, Karunakanallur, Nattarmangalam, Kurungudi, Chettithangal, Ayangudi, Roddiyur, Karupperi.

Higher Secondary or Pre University Courses or Intermediate or Junior College in 2 villages of the CD Block,, namely Nattarmangalam, Roddiyur.

College in 2 villages, Adult Literacy Center in 0 village., Colleges are in villages, namely Thethambattu, Kozhai.

Medical: Hospital in 0 village, Dispensary in 2 villages, Health Center in 6 villages, Sub Center in 14 villages, Maternity and Child Welfare Center in 5 villages, Community health workers in 59 villages.

The Villages having Hospital or Dispensary or Health Center are Shandan, Kanjankollai, Roddiyur.

Drinking Water: Tap water in 67 villages, Tank water in 1 villages, Well water in 67 villages, Tubewell in 67 villages and more than one source in 67 villages.

Bank: Banking facility in 6 villages, namely, Mamangalam, Rayanallur, Nathamalai, Chettithangal Ayangudi, Eyyalur.

Credit Society in 6 villages Agricultural Credit Society in 6 Non-Agricultural Credit Society in 0 village.

Others: Power supply in 67 villages, Cinema hall in 0 village, sport club in 0 village, Stadium or Auditorium or Community Hall in 0 village, Post Office in 65 villages.

There are 61 villages having bus facilities.

Villages with most of facilities: Mamangalam

Nathamalai, Chettithangal, Ayangudi, Eyyalur.

Villages without amenities (Education): Ayankeezhpulyamgudi, Kilpuliyangudi, Thoranguppam, Velapoondi, Periyakottagam, Keezharadhambur, Thondamanatham, Palvaikandan, Alanganatham..

Scheduled Castes: Out of the total population of 94527 persons, 37327 persons (39.49%) belong to Scheduled Castes.

The villages having less than 10% SC population are Ayankeezhpulyamgudi, Thoranguppam, Movur Melapakkathurai.

The villages having more than 50% SC population are Gunamangalam, Nagarapadi, Kilpuliyangudi Kondasamuthiram, Vanamadevi, Nattarmangalam Thiruchinnapuram, Veerananallur, Thorappu Velapoondi, Melakadambur, Keelakadampur Poovizganthanallur, Periyakottagam, Melarahamboor Keezharadhambur, Thondamanatham, Azhinjamangalam Kuchur, Palvaikandan, Echampoondi, Sirukattur Achalpuram, Eyyalur, Roddiyur, Keelpuliyampattu Adhanur, Kanattampuliyur, Karupperi, Veerasolapuram.

Sex ratio of Scheduled Caste population is 495.

Scheduled Castes Literates and Illiterates by Sex:

	Persons	Males	Females
Literate	21,170	12,446	8,724
Illiterate	16,157	6,413	9,744
Literacy rate	65.9	76.5	55.0
Graduate	389	326	63

Scheduled Castes (Dominant):

Adi Dravida, Valluvan, Arunthathiyar, Chakkiliyan Kuravan etc.

For their cultural identity please see Appendix-I

Villages without Scheduled Castes: There are 3 villages without any scheduled caste population.

Scheduled Tribes: Out of the total population of 94527 persons, 606 persons (0.64%) belong to Scheduled Tribes.

The villages having less than 10% ST population are Ananthakudy, Madakalirmanikkam, Srisathamangalam Gunamangalam, Kallippadi, Ayankeezhpulyamgudi Sriputhur, Srineduncheri, Santhavattam, Thethambattu Nagarapadi, Kilpuliyangudi, Melpuliyangudi Thoranguppam, Adivaranganallur, Kozhai Kondasamuthiram, Mamangalam, Vanamadevi, Rayanallur Uythamacholagan, Maniamadoor, Nathamalai, Sithamalli Akaraputhur, Karunakanallur, Palaujanullur Nattarmangalam, Thiruchinnapuram, Kurungudi Veerananallur, Chettithangal, Veerananthapuram Thorappu, Velapoondi, Melakadambur, Keelakadampur Poovizganthanallur, Periyakottagam, Melarahamboor Keezharadhambur, Thondamanatham, Azhinjamangalam Movur, Kuchur, Ayangudi, Melapakkathurai, Shandan Palvaikandan, Echampoondi, Sirukattur, Kanjankollai Achalpuram, Eyyalur, T.Arulmozhidevan, Roddiyur Keelpuliyampattu, Adhanur, Kunavasal, Omampuliyur Muttam, Kunjamedu, Kanattampuliyur, Karupperi Veerasolapuram, Alanganatham.

The villages having more than 50% ST population are None.

Sex ratio of Scheduled tribe population is 472.

Scheduled Tribes Literates and Illiterates by Sex:

	Persons	Males	Females
Literate	247	170	77
Illiterate	359	150	209
Literacy rate	48.7	63.9	32.0
Graduate	2	2	0

Scheduled Tribes (Dominant):

Irular, Malakkuravan, Kattunayakan Generic Tribes etc., Kurumans

For their cultural identity please see Appendix-II

Villages without Scheduled Tribes: There are 48 villages without any scheduled tribe population.

Literates and Illiterates by Sex (Total Population):

	Persons	Males	Females
Literate	60,300	34,940	25,360
Illiterate	34,227	12,902	21,325
Literacy rate	73	83	62
Graduate	1,488	1,188	300

Agriculture: ***Distribution of villages according to land use:*** Out of 67 villages, Total area (in hectare) is 21451.09, out of that 74.82 percent is cultivable and 64.66 percent of the cultivable area is irrigated.

Sources of Irrigation (Hectares): Government Canal 5832.7, Private Canal 0, Well without Electricity 0, Well with Electricity 0, Tubewell without Electricity 696.38, Tubewell with Electricity 3848.6, Tank 0, River 0, Lake 0, Waterfall 0, Others 0.

Villages with population of 5000 to 9999: None

Villages with population of 10000 and above: None

Distribution of Workers:

	Persons	Males	Females	WPR
Cultivators	10,024	7,391	2,633	21.24
Agricultural Labour	30,510	16,137	14,373	64.65
Household Industry	1,660	577	1,083	3.52
Other Workers	4,995	3,735	1,260	10.59
Main Workers	28,173	19,245	8,928	59.7
Marginal Workers	19,016	8,595	10,421	40.3
Total Workers	47,189	27,840	19,349	

Religion: Major Religious Communities:

	Persons	Males	Females	Sex Ratio
Hindu (89%)	84,126	42,550	41,576	977
Muslim (5.65%)	5,345	2,740	2,605	951

Christian (5.23%)	4,942	2,488	2,454	986
Sikh (0%)	-	-	-	-
Buddhists (0%)	-	-	-	-
Jain (0%)	3	3	-	-

Agewise Data:

	Persons	Males	Females	Sex Ratio
All ages	94,527	47,842	46,685	976
0-14	26,614	13,574	13,040	961
15-44	46,303	23,140	23,163	1001
45-79	20,660	10,617	10,043	946
80+	701	386	315	816

Age not stated	249	125	124	992

Languages (Dominant):
Tamil, Urdu, Telugu, Kannada, Malayalam

Disabled Population:

	Persons	Males	Females	%
Total Disabled	3,060	1,436	1,624	
In Seeing	2,045	835	1,210	66.83
In Speech	194	109	85	6.34
In Hearing	131	64	67	4.28
In Movement	522	335	187	17.06
Mentally	168	93	75	5.49

KAVERIPAKKAM

Kaveripakkam C.D. Block lies in the north-eastern part of Vellore district. It is a part of Arakonam taluk. The Block is located at a distance of 45 kms. from district headquarters (Vellore). There are 56 villages in the block with the total population of 147,126 persons. Area of the C.D. Block is 332. 43 sq. kms. It is bounded in the north by Thiruvallur district, in the south by CD Block Arcot and Thiruvannamalai district, in the east by CD Blocks Arakkonam and Nemili, in the west by CD Blocks Sholinghur and Wallajah, and district Thiruvallur.

Communications:

Roadways : N.H.-4: Direction- Wallajah to Chennai, Nearest Villages- Eralacherri, Karivedu, Ocheri, Sirukarumbur, Athipattu, Aryarpadi.

Railway Station: Vadamambakkam, Anavarthikan Pettai, Banavaram, Koothampakkam.

Local Streams: Nearest Villages- Vedal, Minnal, Vailamba di, Thupoór, Kunnathur, Anavarthikan Pettai, Asamanbur, Peruvaliyam, Duraiperumpakkam, Eralacherri, Uthirampatti.

Annual Rainfall: Average Rainfall 949 mm.

Ground Water: Availability of the ground water in the Basin is 7366.77 H.A.M. and the utilization is 6793.49 H.A.M. It belongs to Over Expoited category. Depth to water level varies from 2 to 10 meter below the ground. Most of the wells go down in summer months, according to the Ground Water Estimation Committee.

Forest and Reserved Forest: (Banavaram RF)- Nearest Villages- Palipakkam Village, Pazhayapalayam, Banavaram (RF), Banavaram, Koothampakkam.

Natural Division: Tondai Nadu.

Administration

Revenue **Division:** Arakonam. Parliamentary Constituency: 7 Arakkonam. District: Vellore. Taluk: Arakonam. Assembly Constituency: 38 Arakkonam (SC), 39 Sholingur. Gram Panchayat: 55.

Villages: 56 **Inhabited:** 55 **Uninhabited:** 1

Ranking	District	State	National
Area	6	132	2439
Population	3	21	1957
Sex Ratio	12	182	1275
Child Sex Ratio	4	74	1515
Literacy Rate	12	165	1601
Density	9	288	2489
Work Participation Rate	8	85	3171

Gram Panchayats:

Akkachikuppam, Alapakkam, Anverthikanpettai, Athipattu, Ayal, Ayarpadi, Aypedu, Banavaram, Cheri, Chithambadi, Cuddalore, Dharmaneedhi, Eralacheri, Itchiputhur, Kainoor, Karikkal, Karivedu, Karnavoor, Kattalai, Keezveeranam, Kilvanam, Koothampakkam, Kunnathur, Maganipatty, Mamandur, Mangalam, Minnal, Mittapet, Nandhimangalam, Nandiveduthangal, Ocheri, Palayapalayam, Panniyur, Paranji, Paravathur, Perumalrajapet, Peruvalayam, Polipakkam, Pudupattu, Pudur, Sembedu, Sirukarumbur, Siruvalayam, Soorai, Thalikkal, Thandalam, Thappur, Thuraiperumbakkam, Uthirampattu, Vadampakkam, Vailambadi, Vedal, Vegamangalam, Vengapattu.

Amenities:

Education: Primary School in 54 villages, Middle school in 29 villages, Matriculation or Secondary School in 11 villages, namely Paravathur, Sembedu, Thandalam, Minnal, Cuddalore, Palipakkam Village, Anavarthikan Pettai, Banavaram, Koothampakkam, Cheri, Sirukarumbur.

Higher Secondary or Pre University Courses or Intermediate or Junior College in 2 villages of the CD Block,, namely Minnal, Banavaram.

College in 2 villages, Adult Literacy Center in 0 village., Colleges are in villages, namely Ichiputtur, Thandalam.

Medical: Hospital in 1 village, Dispensary in 1 village, Health Center in 6 villages, Sub Center in 7 villages, Maternity and Child Welfare Center in 11 villages, Community health workers in 53 villages.

The Villages having Hospital or Dispensary or Health Center are Paravathur, Sembedu.

Drinking Water: Tap water in 55 villages, Tank water in 5 villages, Well water in 1 village, Tubewell in 26 villages and more than one source in 54 villages.

Bank: Banking facility in 11 villages, namely, Paranji, Sembedu, Minnal, Palipakkam Village Anavarthikan Pettai, Banavaram, Mangalam Koothampakkam, Siruvalayam, Ocheri, Sirukarumbur. Credit Society in 17 villages Agricultural Credit Society in 12 Non-Agricultural Credit Society in 10 villages.

Others: Power supply in 55 villages, Cinema hall in 1 village, sport club in 0 village, Stadium or Auditorium or Community Hall in 0 village, Post Office in 49 villages.

There are 51 villages having bus facilities.

Villages with most of facilities: Sembedu, Minnal Palipakkam Village, Anavarthikan Pettai, Banavaram Mangalam, Koothampakkam, Ocheri, Sirukarumbur.

Villages without amenities (Education): Panniyur..

Scheduled Castes: Out of the total population of 147126 persons, 41113 persons (27.94%) belong to Scheduled Castes.

The villages having less than 10% SC population are Perumal Raje Pettai, Vailambadi, Nandhimangalam Palipakkam Village, Pazhayapalayam, Karnaoor, Pudur Pudupattu.

The villages having more than 50% SC population are Chithambadi, Ayal, Asamanbur, Maganipattur Eralacherri, Uthirampatti, Dharumaneedhi, Karivedu Vegamangalam, Mamandur.

Sex ratio of Scheduled Caste population is 500.

Scheduled Castes Literates and Illiterates by Sex:

	Persons	Males	Females
Literate	24,229	13,970	10,259
Illiterate	16,884	6,588	10,296
Literacy rate	67.4	78.0	56.9
Graduate	425	333	92

Scheduled Castes (Dominant):

Adi Dravida, Arunthathiyar, Valluvan, Baira Adi Andhra

For their cultural identity please see Appendix-I

Villages without Scheduled Castes: There are 2 villages without any scheduled caste population.

Scheduled Tribes: Out of the total population of 147126 persons, 1962 persons (1.33%) belong to Scheduled Tribes.

The villages having less than 10% ST population are Vengupattu, Paravathur, Akkachikuppam, Paranji Nandiveduthangal, Sembedu, Chithambadi, Ichiputtur Kilavanam, Vadamambakkam, Kainoor, Thandalam, Vedal Minnal, Vailambadi, Cuddalore, Thalikkal, Ayppedu Ariyur, Karikkal, Nandhimangalam, Soorai, Ayal Palipakkam Village, Thup00R, Pazhayapalayam Kunnathur, Anavarthikan Pettai, Asamanbur, Banavaram Mangalam, Koothampakkam, Karnaoor, Pudur Keezveeranam, Panniyur, Pudupattu, Siruvalayam Peruvaliyam, Alappakkam, Duraiperumpakkam Maganipattur, Cheri, Kattalai, Eralacherri Uthirampatti, Dharumaneedhi, Karivedu, Ayarpadi Ocheri, Sirukarumbur, Athipattu, Vegamangalam Mamandur.

The villages having more than 50% ST population are None.

Sex ratio of Scheduled tribe population is 501.

Scheduled Tribes Literates and Illiterates by Sex:

	Persons	Males	Females
Literate	579	351	228
Illiterate	1,383	628	755
Literacy rate	34.7	42.1	27.2
Graduate	3	3	0

Scheduled Tribes (Dominant):

Irular, Kattunayakan, Malayali, Malakkuravan Paniyan

For their cultural identity please see Appendix-II

Villages without Scheduled Tribes: There are 19 villages without any scheduled tribe population.

Literates and Illiterates by Sex (Total Population):

	Persons	Males	Females
Literate	86,315	51,116	35,199
Illiterate	60,811	22,564	38,247
Literacy rate	67	79	55
Graduate	1,701	1,342	359

Agriculture: ***Distribution of villages according to land use:*** Out of 56 villages, Total area (in hectare) is 33243.51, out of that 57.64 percent is cultivable and 37.18 percent of the cultivable area is irrigated.

Sources of Irrigation (Hectares): Government Canai 0, Private Canal 0, Well without Electricity 0, Well with Electricity 7046.35, Tubewell without Electricity 0, Tubewell with Electricity 0, Tank 76.64, River 0, Lake 0, Waterfall 0, Others 0.

Villages with population of 5000 to 9999: Itchiputhur, Minnal , Anverthikanpettai, Banavaram.

Villages with population of 10000 and above: Sembedu.

Distribution of Workers:

	Persons	Males	Females	WPR
Cultivators	16,914	11,576	5,338	24.78
Agricultural Labour	33,722	16,744	16,978	49.4
Household Industry	4,887	2,873	2,014	7.16
Other Workers	12,741	10,375	2,366	18.66
Main Workers	50,026	34,335	15,691	73.28
Marginal Workers	18,238	7,233	11,005	26.72
Total Workers	68,264	41,568	26,696	

Religion: Major Religious Communities:

	Persons	Males	Females	Sex Ratio
Hindu (96.57%)	142,086	71,143	70,943	997

Muslim (1.72%)	2,534	1,275	1,259	987
Christian (1.62%)	2,385	1,202	1,183	984
Sikh (0%)	3	2	1	500
Buddhists (0.01%)	13	8	5	625
Jain (0.01%)	10	4	6	1,500

Agewise Data:

	Persons	Males	Females	Sex Ratio
All ages	147,126	73,680	73,446	997
0-14	44,112	22,553	21,559	956
15-44	70,042	35,146	34,896	993
45-79	31,050	14,996	16,054	1071
80+	1,138	552	586	1062
Age not stated	784	433	351	811

Languages (Dominant):

Tamil, Telugu, Urdu, Marathi, Hindi

Disabled Population:

	Persons	Males	Females	%
Total Disabled	3,167	1,826	1,341	
In Seeing	1,314	717	597	41.49
In Speech	355	183	172	11.21
In Hearing	207	113	94	6.54
In Movement	983	635	348	31.04
Mentally	308	178	130	9.73

KAVERIPATTINAM

Kaveripattinam C.D. Block lies in the south-eastern part of Dharmapuri district. It is a part of Krishnagiri and Pochampalli taluks. The Block is located at a distance of 34 kms. from district headquarters (Dharmapuri). There are 33 villages in the block with the total population of 148,325 persons. Area of the C.D. Block is 291.15 sq. kms. It is bounded in the north by C.D. Blocks Krishnagiri and Bargur, in the south and west by district Dharmapuri, and in the east by C.D. Block Bargur. CD Block Kaveripattinam falls in taluk Krishnagiri by 19 villages, and in taluk Pochampalli by 14 villages.

Communications:

Roadways : N.H.-7: Direction- Dharmapuri to Krishnagiri, Nearest Villages- Sendekuppam, Thimmapuram, Errahalli, Kaveripattinam, Paiyur, Jagadap, Karadihalli, Chowttahalli, Gundalapatty.

River: Ponnaiyar Nadi- Nearest Villages- Chowttahalli, Sendekuppam, Thimmapuram, Katheri, Gundalapatty, Kaveri pattinam, Thalihalli, Marichettihalli, Mottur, Penneswara madam, Maruderi, Kudimanahalli, Velagamudi, Barur, Sellag uddapatti, Pannandur, Vadamangalam, Bendrahalli, Kottappatti.

Annual Rainfall: Average Rainfall 760 mm.

Ground Water: Availability of the ground water in the Basin is (Information not available) H.A.M. and the utili zation is 160.44 H.A.M. It belongs to Over Expoited categ ory. Depth to water level varies from 2 to 5 meter below the ground. Most of the wells go down in summer months, according to the Ground Water Estimation Committee.

Natural Division: Baramahal.

Administration

Revenue **Division:** Krishnagiri. Parliamentary Constituency: 9 Krishnagiri. District: Dharmapuri. Taluk: Krishnagiri, Pochampalli. Assembly Constituency: 52 Bargur, 53 Krishnagiri. Gram Panchayat: 36.

Villages: 33 **Inhabited:** 32 **Uninhabited:** 1

Ranking	District	State	National
Area	17	184	2880
Population	7	17	1920
Sex Ratio	4	329	2941
Child Sex Ratio	14	368	6135
Literacy Rate	6	285	2433
Density	8	127	2172
Work Participation Rate	1	55	1296

Gram Panchayats:

Agaram, Arasampatti, Avathavadi, Balekuli, Bannihalli, Barur, Chaparthi, Chellakuttapatti, Chowttahalli, Damodarhalli, Eramampatti, Errahalli, Gundalapatti, Jagadab, Karadihalli, Katteri, Keelkuppam, Kottapatti, Kudimenahalli, Malayandahalli, Marichettihalli, Maruderi, Mittahalli, Nadugal, Paiyur, Pannandur, Panneswaramadam, Papparapatti, Sandekuppam, Santhapuram, Sundekuppam, Talihalli, Thatrahalli, Timmapuram, Vadamangalam, Veeramalai, Vilangamudi.

Amenities:

Education: Primary School in 32 villages, Middle school in 23 villages, Matriculation or Secondary School in 15 villages, namely Baleguli, Chowttahalli, Thimmapuram, Chaparthi, Errahalli, Mottur, Paiyur, Jagadap, Thatrahalli, Kudimanahalli, Velagamudi, Barur, Pannandur, Puliyampatty, Bendrahalli.

Higher Secondary or Pre University Courses or Intermediate or Junior College in 6 villages of the CD Block,, namely Errahalli, Kudimanahalli, Barur, Pannandur, Puliyampatty, Bendrahalli.

College in 0 village, Adult Literacy Center in 0 village.

Medical: Hospital in 1 village, Dispensary in 2 villages, Health Center in 3 villages, Sub Center in 18 villages, Maternity and Child Welfare Center in 0 village, Community health workers in 30 villages.

The Villages having Hospital or Dispensary or Health Center are Errahalli, Barur, Pannandur.

Drinking Water: Tap water in 32 villages, Tank water in 0 villages, Well water in 32 villages, Tubewell in 32 villages and more than one source in 32 villages.

Bank: Banking facility in 10 villages, namely,

Baleguli, Thimmapuram, Gundalapatty, Chaparthi Paiyur, Kudimanahalli, Barur, Pannandur, Bendrahalli Kottappatti.

Credit Society in 14 villages Agricultural Credit Society in 11 Non-Agricultural Credit Society in 3 villages.

Others: Power supply in 32 villages, Cinema hall in 3 villages, sport club in 0 village, Stadium or Auditorium or Community Hall in 0 village, Post Office in 32 villages.

There are 31 villages having bus facilities.

Villages with most of facilities: Baleguli Thimmapuram, Gundalapatty, Chaparthi, Paiyur Kudimanahalli, Barur, Pannandur, Bendrahalli Kottappatti.

Villages without Amenities (Education): None..

Scheduled Castes: Out of the total population of 148325 persons, 11877 persons (8.01%) belong to Scheduled Castes.

The villages having less than 10% SC population are Baleguli, Chowttahalli, Sendekuppam, Katheri Gundalapatty, Bannihalli, Mittahalli, Errahalli Kaveripattinam, Thalihalli, Marichettihalli, Mottur Penneswaramadam, Jagadap, Karadihalli, Velagamudi Keelkuppam, Sellaguddapatti, Damodarahalli Puliyampatty.

The villages having more than 50% SC population are None.

Sex ratio of Scheduled Caste population is 507.

Scheduled Castes Literates and Illiterates by Sex:

	Persons	Males	Females
Literate	6,540	3,823	2,717
Illiterate	5,337	2,034	3,303
Literacy rate	63.9	76.3	52.0
Graduate	152	116	36

Scheduled Castes (Dominant):

Adi Dravida, Arunthathiyar, Kuravan etc., Panniandi Valluvan

For their cultural identity please see Appendix-I

Villages without Scheduled Castes: There is 1 village without any scheduled caste population.

Scheduled Tribes: Out of the total population of 148325 persons, 283 persons (0.19%) belong to Scheduled Tribes.

The villages having less than 10% ST population are Baleguli, Chowttahalli, Sendekuppam, Thimmapuram Katheri, Gundalapatty, Chaparthi, Bannihalli Mittahalli, Errahalli, Kaveripattinam, Thalihalli Marichettihalli, Mottur, Penneswaramadam, Paiyur Jagadap, Karadihalli, Thatrahalli, Veeramalai Maruderi, Kudimanahalli, Velagamudi, Keelkuppam Barur, Sellaguddapatti, Pannandur, Damodarahalli Puliyampatty, Vadamangalam, Bendrahalli, Kottappatti.

The villages having more than 50% ST population are None.

Sex ratio of Scheduled tribe population is 530.

Scheduled Tribes Literates and Illiterates by Sex:

	Persons	Males	Females
Literate	60	39	21
Illiterate	223	94	129
Literacy rate	26.8	36.1	18.1
Graduate	0	0	0

Scheduled Tribes (Dominant):

Irular, Kurumans, Kattunayakan, Malai Vedan

For their cultural identity please see Appendix-II

Villages without Scheduled Tribes: There are 27 villages without any scheduled tribe population.

Literates and Illiterates by Sex (Total Population):

	Persons	Males	Females
Literate	80,793	48,585	32,208
Illiterate	67,532	27,063	40,469
Literacy rate	62	74	50
Graduate	2,270	1,657	613

Agriculture: ***Distribution of villages according to land use:***

Out of 33 villages, Total area (in hectare) is 29115.23, out of that 81.08 percent is cultivable and 39.33 percent of the cultivable area is irrigated.

Sources of Irrigation (Hectares): Government Canal 3869, Private Canal 15, Well without Electricity 2276.58, Well with Electricity 1717.42, Tubewell without Electricity 0, Tubewell with Electricity 0, Tank 1326, River 0, Lake 0, Waterfall 0, Others 81.

Villages with population of 5000 to 9999:

Balekuli, Chowttahalli, Sundekuppam, Timmapuram Gundalapatti, Bannihalli, Mittahalli, Errahalli Kaveripattinam, Mottur, Paiyur, Kudimenahalli Bendarahalli.

Villages with population of 10000 and above: None

Distribution of Workers:

	Persons	Males	Females	WPR
Cultivators	32,384	19,869	12,515	40.41
Agricultural Labour	30,710	12,026	18,684	38.32
Household Industry	1,357	520	837	1.69
Other Workers	15,683	12,333	3,350	19.57
Main Workers	61,159	38,511	22,648	76.32
Marginal Workers	18,975	6,237	12,738	23.68
Total Workers	80,134	44,748	35,386	

Religion: Major Religious Communities:

	Persons	Males	Females	Sex Ratio
Hindu (97.6%)	144,768	73,818	70,950	961
Muslim (2.1%)	3,118	1,605	1,513	943
Christian (0.22%)	333	163	170	1,043
Sikh (0%)	1	-	1	-
Buddhists (0%)	-	-	-	-

Jain (0%)	-	-	-	-

Agewise Data:

	Persons	Males	Females	Sex Ratio
All ages	148,325	75,648	72,677	961
0-14	43,354	23,405	19,949	852
15-44	73,119	36,390	36,729	1009
45-79	30,446	15,116	15,330	1014
80+	1,212	608	604	993
Age not stated	194	129	65	504

Languages (Dominant): Tamil, Telugu, Kannada, Urdu, Hindi

Disabled Population:

	Persons	Males	Females	%
Total Disabled	5,028	1,581	3,447	
In Seeing	3,427	638	2,789	68.16
In Speech	297	156	141	5.91
In Hearing	158	87	71	3.14
In Movement	938	588	350	18.66
Mentally	208	112	96	4.14

KAYATHARU

Kayathar C.D. Block lies in the north-western part of Thoothukkudi district. It is a part of Kovilpatti, Ettayapuram and Ottapidaram taluks. The Block is located at a distance of 60 kms. from district headquarters (Thoothukkudi). There are 53 villages in the block with the total population of 76,875 persons. Area of the C.D. Block is 520.91 sq. kms. It is bounded in the north by district Tirunelveli and CD Block Kovilpatti in the south and west by district Tiruneleveli, by CD Blocks Ottapiduram and Vilathikulam in the east. CD Block Kayathar falls in taluks: Kovilpatti by 48, Ettayapuram by 04 and Ottapidaram by 01 village.

Communications:

Roadways : N.H.-7: Direction- Tiruneleveli to Kovilpatti, Nearest Villages- Sevalaperi, Asoor, Akilandapuram, Vadaku Ilandaikulam, Therku Ilandaikulam, Rajaputhukudi, Sannathupudukudi. N.H.-45 B: Direction- Ettayapuram to Thoothukkudi, Nearest Village- Cholapuram. S.H.-44: Direction-Kalugumala to Kovilpatti, Nearest Villages- Kumaraettaya Puram, Venaramutti, Kalankaraipatti, Therku Kalugumalai.

River: Uppodai Nadi- Nearest Villages- Kalampatti, Kattarankulam, Chidambarampatti, Vellalan Kottai, Sevalaperi, Akilandapuram, Vadaku, Ilandaikulam, Therku Ilandaikulam, Rajaputhukudi, Sannathupudukudi, Saravanapuram, Terku Mylodai.

Annual Rainfall: Average Rainfall 661 mm.

Ground Water: Availability of the ground water in the Basin is 26.04 MCM and the utilization is 33.80 MCM. It belongs to Over Expoited category. Depth to water level varies from 2 to 5 meter below the ground. Most of the wells go down in summer months, according to the Ground Water Estimation Committee.

Natural Division: NA

Administration

Revenue **Division:** Kovilpatti. Parliamentary Constituency: 36 Thoothukkudi. District: Thoothukkudi. Taluk: Kovilpatti, Ettayapuram, Ottapidaram. Assembly Constituency: 218 Kovilpatti, 213 Vilathikulam. Gram Panchayat: 45.

Villages: 53 **Inhabited:** 52 **Uninhabited:** 1

Ranking	District	State	National
Area	3	32	1409
Population	7	257	4218
Sex Ratio	5	17	181
Child Sex Ratio	5	146	2584
Literacy Rate	12	224	2051
Density	2	68	5596
Work Participation Rate	10	363	595

Gram Panchayats:

Achankulam, Ahilandapuram, Asoor, Ayyanaruthu, Chettikurichi, Chidambarampatti, Cholapuram, K.Chidambarapuram, K.Durasamypuram, K.Subramaniapuram, K.Venkateswarapuram , Kalampatti, Kalangaraipatti, Kamanaickenpatti, Kannakkattai, Kappulingampatti, Karadikulam, Kattarankulam, Koppampatti, Kumara Ettayapuram, Kuppanapuram, Kurumalai, Kuruvinatham, Mudakkalankulam, Panikkarkulam, Panneerkulam, Podupatti, Podupatti, Pungavarnatham, Rajapudukudi, Sannadhuputhukudi, Sevalaperi, Sivagnanapuram, Terku Ilandaikulam, Theethampatti, Therkkukalugumalai, Therku Kalugumalai, Therku Mylodai, Therku Vandanam, Thirumalaipuram, Thirumangalakuruchi, Tottampatti, Usilankulam, Vadakku Ilandaikulam, Vadakku Vandanam, Vanaramutti, Vellalankottai.

Amenities:

Education: Primary School in 52 villages, Middle school in 15 villages, Matriculation or Secondary School in 8 villages, namely Kumaraettaya Puram, Venaramutti, Kalampatti, Chettikurachy, Sivagnanapuram, Kamanaicken Patti, Akilandapuram, Cholapuram.

Higher Secondary or Pre University Courses or Intermediate or Junior College in 2 villages of the CD Block,, namely Karadaikulam, Vadakkuvandanam.

College in 1 village, Adult Literacy Center in 0 village., College is in village, namely Chidambarapuram.

Medical: Hospital in 2 villages, Dispensary in 0 village, Health Center in 4 villages, Sub Center in 15 villages, Maternity and Child Welfare Center in 3 villages, Community health workers in 45 villages.

The Villages having Hospital or Dispensary or Health

Center are Kalankaraipatti, Pannekar Kulam.

Drinking Water: Tap water in 52 villages, Tank water in 1 villages, Well water in 52 villages, Tubewell in 52 villages and more than one source in 52 villages.

Bank: Banking facility in 12 villages, namely, Venaramutti, Kalampatti, Subramaniyapuram Chettikurachy, Thirumangalakuruchi, Sivagnanapuram Kamanaicken Patti, Theethampatti, Therkuvandanam Chidambarapuram, Akilandapuram, Cholapuram.

Credit Society in 11 villages Agricultural Credit Society in 9 Non-Agricultural Credit Society in 2 villages.

Others: Power supply in 52 villages, Cinema hall in 1 village, sport club in 0 village, Stadium or Auditorium or Community Hall in 0 village, Post Office in 43 villages.

There are 35 villages having bus facilities.

Villages with most of facilities: Venaramutti Subramaniyapuram, Chettikurachy, Kamanaicken Patti Theethampatti, Therkuvandanam, Akilandapuram Cholapuram.

Villages without Amenities (Education): None..

Scheduled Castes: Out of the total population of 76875 persons, 21535 persons (28.01%) belong to Scheduled Castes.

The villages having less than 10% SC population are Therku Kalugumalai, Subramaniyapuram, Sevalaperi Asoor, Melaparaipatti, Kamanaicken Patti Therkuvandanam, Kumarapuram, Kuppanapuram Vadaku Ilandaikulam, Pannekar Kulam, Usilangulam Ayyanaroothu, Pannikulam, Podupatti.

The villages having more than 50% SC population are Mudukkalamkulam, Achankulam, Thottampatti Govindampatti, Ottudanpatti, Terku Mylodai Rajaputhukudi.

Sex ratio of Scheduled Caste population is 512.

Scheduled Castes Literates and Illiterates by Sex:

	Persons	Males	Females
Literate	11,731	6,797	4,934
Illiterate	9,804	3,711	6,093
Literacy rate	61.6	73.5	50.4
Graduate	134	109	25

Scheduled Castes (Dominant):

Pallan, Paraiyan etc., Chakkiliyan, Arunthathiyar Puthirai Vannan

For their cultural identity please see Appendix-I

Villages without Scheduled Castes: There are 4 villages without any scheduled caste population.

Scheduled Tribes: Out of the total population of 76875 persons, 20 persons (0.03%) belong to Scheduled Tribes.

The villages having less than 10% ST population are Venkateswarapuram, Kumaraettaya Puram, Venaramutti Kalampatti, Kalankaraipatti, Therku Kalugumalai Kattalampatty, Karadaikulam, Subramaniyapuram Saravanapuram, Kattarankulam, Mudukkalamkulam Kurumalai, Chidambarampatti, Chettikurachy Thirumangalakuruchi, Vellalan Kottai, Sevalaperi Asoor, Sivagnanapuram, Melaparaipatti Sundareswarapuram, Koppampatti, Kuruvinatham Kamanaicken Patti, Achankulam, Thottampatti Theethampatti, Govindampatti, Vadakkuvandanam Therkuvandanam, Kumarapuram, Kuppanapuram Ottudanpatti, Chidambarapuram, Kappulingampatti Thirumalapuram, Akilandapuram, Vadaku Ilandaikulam Pannekar Kulam, Usilangulam, Ayyanaroothu Therku Ilandaikulam, Pannikulam, Terku Mylodai Rajaputhukudi, Sannathupudukudi, Podupatti Pungavaranattam, Cholapuram, Kannakattai Muthuramalingapuram.

The villages having more than 50% ST population are None.

Sex ratio of Scheduled tribe population is 500.

Scheduled Tribes Literates and Illiterates by Sex:

	Persons	Males	Females
Literate	20	10	10
Illiterate	0	0	0
Literacy rate	100.0	100.0	100.0
Graduate	1	0	1

Scheduled Tribes (Dominant):

Kattunayakan, Kondareddis, Kaniyan etc., Uraly

For their cultural identity please see Appendix-II

Villages without Scheduled Tribes: There are 50 villages without any scheduled tribe population.

Literates and Illiterates by Sex (Total Population):

	Persons	Males	Females
Literate	43,909	24,992	18,917
Illiterate	32,966	12,101	20,865
Literacy rate	64	76	53
Graduate	552	384	168

Agriculture: ***Distribution of villages according to land use:*** Out of 53 villages, Total area (in hectare) is 52091.56, out of that 24 percent is cultivable and 18.96 percent of the cultivable area is irrigated.

Sources of Irrigation (Hectares): Government Canal 0, Private Canal 0, Well without Electricity 278.35, Well with Electricity 1870.05, Tubewell without Electricity 0, Tubewell with Electricity 0, Tank 222.06, River 0, Lake 0, Waterfall 0, Others 0.

Villages with population of 5000 to 9999: Vanaramutti.

Villages with population of 10000 and above: None

Distribution of Workers:

	Persons	Males	Females	WPR

Cultivators	9,482	5,744	3,738	21.32
Agricultural Labour	19,538	8,939	10,599	43.94
Household Industry	1,440	336	1,104	3.24
Other Workers	14,010	7,502	6,508	31.5
Main Workers	37,934	20,150	17,784	85.3
Marginal Workers	6,536	2,371	4,165	14.7
Total Workers	44,470	22,521	21,949	

Religion: Major Religious Communities:

	Persons	Males	Females	Sex Ratio
Hindu (88.11%)	67,731	32,685	35,046	1,072
Muslim (2.14%)	1,645	727	918	1,263
Christian (8.55%)	6,574	3,219	3,355	1,042
Sikh (0%)	2	-	2	-
Buddhists (0%)	1	1	-	-
Jain (0.01%)	9	4	5	1,250

Agewise Data:

	Persons	Males	Females	Sex Ratio
All ages	76,041	36,675	39,366	1073
0-14	21,100	10,667	10,433	978
15-44	35,776	16,857	18,919	1122
45-79	17,939	8,561	9,378	1095
80+	790	370	420	1135
Age not stated	436	220	216	982

Languages (Dominant):

Tamil, Telugu, Kannada, Malayalam, Others

Disabled Population:

	Persons	Males	Females	%
Total Disabled	1,705	774	931	
In Seeing	1,005	391	614	58.94
In Speech	141	73	68	8.27
In Hearing	51	27	24	2.99
In Movement	348	193	155	20.41
Mentally	160	90	70	9.38

KEELAIYUR

Keelaiyur C.D. Block lies in the south-western part of Nagapattinam district. It is a part of Kilvelur and Thirukkuvalai taluks.It is located at a distance of NA kms. from district headquarters (Nagapattinam). There are 28 villages in the block with the total population of 68,721 persons. Area of the C.D. Block is 178.15 sq. kms. It is boumded in the north by C.D. Blocks Kilvelur and Nagapattinam, in the south by C.D. Block Thalainayar, in the east by the Bay of Bengal, in the west by C.D. Blocks Kilvelur and Thalainayar. CD Block Keelaiyur falls in taluk Kilvelur by 19 villages, and in taluk Thirukkuvalai by 09 villages.

Communications:

Roadways : Information not Available.

Railway Station: Thirukkuvalai.

Backwards Region Grants Fund: It receives Backward Region Grants.

Annual Rainfall: Average Rainfall 1230 mm.

Ground Water: Availability of the ground water in the Basin is (Information not available) H.A.M. and the utilization is (Information not available) H.A.M. It belongs to (Information not available) category. Depth to water level varies from 2 to 5 meter below the ground. Most of the wells go down in summer months, according to the Ground Water Estimation Committee.

Natural Division: Chola Nadu.

Administration

Revenue **Division:** Nagapattinam. Parliamentary Constituency: 28 Nagapattinam (SC). District: Nagapattinam. Taluk: Thirukkuvalai, Kilvelur. Assembly Constituency: 164 Kilvelur (SC). Gram Panchayat: 27.

Villages: 28 **Inhabited:** 28 **Uninhabited:** 0

Ranking	**District**	**State**	**National**
Area	7	313	4568
Population	9	291	4524
Sex Ratio	1	53	464
Child Sex Ratio	5	34	831
Literacy Rate	9	66	820
Density	3	308	2838
Work Participation Rate	10	126	3567

Gram Panchayats:

Chinathumboor, Cholavidyapuram, Eraiyangudi, Esanur, Ettugudi, Karappidakai North, Karappidakai South, Karumguni, Keelaiyur, Keelappidakai, Madapuram, Meenamallur, Melavalakarai, Palakkuruchi, Prathabaramapuram, Puthuppalli, Thalayamazhai, Thanilappadi, thirukkuvalai, Thirupoondi East, Thirupoondi West, Thiruvaimur, Vazhakarai, Venmanacherry, Veppancheri, Vettaikaraniruppu, Vizhunthamavadi.

Amenities:

Education: Primary School in 27 villages, Middle school in 15 villages, Matriculation or Secondary School in 10 villages, namely Prathabaranapuram, Ottathattai, Palaguruchy, Karunkkanni, Thirupoondi, Keelaiyur, Vimandamavadi, Vehaikaraniruppu, Thirukkuvalai, Ettukudy.

Higher Secondary or Pre University Courses or Intermediate or Junior College in 5 villages of the CD Block,, namely Prathabaranapuram, Thirupoondi, Keelaiyur, Vimandamavadi, Thirukkuvalai.

College in 0 village, Adult Literacy Center in 0 village.

Medical: Hospital in 1 village, Dispensary in 1 village, Health Center in 6 villages, Sub Center in 11 villages, Maternity and Child Welfare Center in 0 village, Community health workers in 26 villages.

The Villages having Hospital or Dispensary or Health Center are Prathabaranapuram, Thirukkuvalai.

Drinking Water: Tap water in 28 villages, Tank water in 2 villages, Well water in 28 villages, Tubewell in 28 villages and more than one source in 28 villages.

Bank: Banking facility in 4 villages, namely, Palaguruchy, Thirupoondi, Vimandamavadi Thirukkuvalai.

Credit Society in 7 villages Agricultural Credit Society in 7 Non-Agricultural Credit Society in 0 village.

Others: Power supply in 27 villages, Cinema hall in 1 village, sport club in 0 village, Stadium or Auditorium or Community Hall in 0 village, Post Office in 19 villages.

There are 25 villages having bus facilities.

Villages with most of facilities: Palaguruchy Thirupoondi, Vimandamavadi, Thirukkuvalai.

Villages without amenities (Education): Valakkarai..

Scheduled Castes: Out of the total population of 68721 persons, 23687 persons (34.47%) belong to Scheduled Castes. The villages having less than 10% SC population are None..

The villages having more than 50% SC population are Erayangudi, Thannilapadi, Chinnathumboor Ottathattai, Palaguruchy, Venmanacheri, Karapidagai Melavalakkari, Valakkarai, Thiruvaimoor, Vallam.

Sex ratio of Scheduled Caste population is 504.

Scheduled Castes Literates and Illiterates by Sex:

	Persons	Males	Females
Literate	12,720	7,367	5,353
Illiterate	10,967	4,392	6,575
Literacy rate	63.3	74.2	52.7
Graduate	127	100	27

Scheduled Castes (Dominant):

Paraiyan etc., Pallan, Koliyan, Adi Dravida Valluvan

For their cultural identity please see Appendix-I

Villages without Scheduled Castes: There is 1 village without any scheduled caste population.

Scheduled Tribes: Out of the total population of 68721 persons, 0 persons (0%) belong to Scheduled Tribes.

The villages having less than 10% ST population are Erayangudi, Vepanchary, Thannilapadi, Chinnathumboor Prathabaranapuram, Thalaiyamazai, Ottathattai Palaguruchy, Solavidyapuram, Karunkkanni Thirupoondi, Thirupoondi, Keelapidagai, Keelaiyur Venmanacheri, Karapidagai, Vimandamavadi Karapidagai, Vehaikaraniruppu, Thirukkuvalai Melavalakkari, Madapuram, Meanamanallur, Valakkarai Esanur, Thiruvaimoor, Ettukudy, Vallam.

The villages having more than 50% ST population are None.

Villages without Scheduled Tribes: There are 28 villages without any scheduled tribe population.

Literates and Illiterates by Sex (Total Population):

	Persons	Males	Females
Literate	43,680	24,303	19,377
Illiterate	25,041	9,517	15,524
Literacy rate	73	83	64
Graduate	389	285	104

Agriculture: ***Distribution of villages according to land use:*** Out of 28 villages, Total area (in hectare) is 17815.33, out of that 71.62 percent is cultivable and 73.8 percent of the cultivable area is irrigated.

Sources of Irrigation (Hectares): Government Canal 9413.46, Private Canal 0.49, Well without Electricity 2.14, Well with Electricity 0, Tubewell without Electricity 0, Tubewell with Electricity 0, Tank 0, River 0, Lake 0, Waterfall 0, Others 0.

Villages with population of 5000 to 9999: Prathabaramapuram, Vizhunthamavadi Vettaikkaraniruppu.

Villages with population of 10000 and above: None

Distribution of Workers:

	Persons	Males	Females	WPR
Cultivators	4,565	3,625	940	15
Agricultural Labour	18,936	10,041	8,895	62.22
Household Industry	487	220	267	1.6
Other Workers	6,446	5,326	1,120	21.18
Main Workers	25,589	17,265	8,324	84.08
Marginal Workers	4,845	1,947	2,898	15.92
Total Workers	30,434	19,212	11,222	

Religion: Major Religious Communities:

	Persons	Males	Females	Sex Ratio
Hindu (91.54%)	62,908	31,061	31,847	1,025
Muslim (3.77%)	2,591	1,186	1,405	1,185
Christian (4.64%)	3,191	1,559	1,632	1,047
Sikh (0%)	1	-	1	-
Buddhists (0%)	3	2	1	500
Jain (0.01%)	4	4	-	-

Agewise Data:

	Persons	Males	Females	Sex Ratio
All ages	68,721	33,820	34,901	1032
0-14	20,060	10,070	9,990	992
15-44	33,002	15,802	17,200	1088
45-79	14,677	7,415	7,262	979
80+	611	344	267	776
Age not stated	371	189	182	963

Languages (Dominant):

Tamil, Telugu, Malayalam, Kannada, Urdu

Disabled Population:

	Persons	Males	Females	%

Total Disabled	2,958	1,054	1,904	
In Seeing	1,977	488	1,489	66.84
In Speech	164	90	74	5.54
In Hearing	139	74	65	4.7
In Movement	483	295	188	16.33
Mentally	195	107	88	6.59

KEERAPALAYAM

Keerapalayam C.D. Block lies in the south-eastern part of Cuddalore district. It is a part of Chidambaram and Kattumannarkoil taluks. The Block is located at a distance of NA kms. from district headquarters (Cuddalore). There are 73 villages in the block with the total population of 107,374 persons. Area of the C.D. Block is 205.51 sq. kms. It is bounded in the north by C.D. Blocks Bhuvanagiri and Parangipettai, in the south by C.D. Block Komaratchi and district Nagapattinam, in the east by C.D. Block Parangipettai, and in the west by C.D. Block Komaratchi. CD Block Keerapalayam falls in taluk Chidambaram by 51 villages, and in taluk Kattumannarkoil 22 by villages.

Communications:

Roadways : S.H.-8: Direction- Sethiya Thope to Lalpettai, Nearest Villages- Boothangudi, Veyyalore, Vazhaikollai,

River: Vellar Nadi- Nearest Villages- C.Sathamangalam, Keerappalayam, Thirupaninatham, Vadagriraja Puram, Thathanpetti, Ayipettai, Kiliyanur, Orathur, Paradur, Boothangudi, Sakkangudi.

Backwards Region Grants Fund: It receives Backward Region Grants.

Annual Rainfall: Average Rainfall 1050 mm.

Ground Water: Availability of the ground water in the Basin is 11625.21 MCM and the utilization is 5567.26 MCM. It belongs to Safe category. Depth to water level varies from 0 to 10 meter below the ground. Most of the wells go down in summer months, according to the Ground Water Estimation Committee.

Natural Division: Tondai Nadu.

Administration

Revenue **Division:** Chidambaram. Parliamentary Constituency: 27 Chidambaram (SC). District: Cuddalore. Taluk: Chidambaram, Kattumannarkoil. Assembly Constituency: 157 Bhuvanagiri, 159 Kattumannarkoil (SC). Gram Panchayat: 63.

Villages: 73 **Inhabited:** 73 **Uninhabited:** 0

Ranking	District	State	National
Area	9	275	4084
Population	8	109	3238
Sex Ratio	5	248	1769
Child Sex Ratio	7	143	2612
Literacy Rate	4	111	1162
Density	7	271	2105
Work Participation Rate	4	48	2973

Gram Panchayats:

Ayeepettai, Ayyanurakkaramangalam, Beethangudi, C.Melvanniyur, C.Veerasozhagan, Devangudi, Edayanpalcheri, Ennanagaram, Gudalaiyathur, K.Adoor, Kaliayamalai, Kandakumaran, Kannangudi, Kanur, Kavalagudi, Keelappadi, Keerapalayam, Kezhnatham, Kiliyanur, Kothandavilagam, Kumarakudi, Malavarayanallur, Mathuranthaganallur, Mudikandanallur, Mugaiyur, Nandeeswaramangalam, Nangudi, Odakkanallur, Orathur, Palayancherthangudi, Palayankottai(Kilpathi), Palayankottai(Melpathi), Pannapattu, Paradur, Perungalur, Perur, Poonthottam, Poorthangudi, Pudaiyur, Ramapuram, Sakkangudi, Sathamangalam, Sengalmedu, Sethiyur, Sirugalur, Solatharam, T.Manalur, T.Neduncheri, Tharasur, Then Harirajapuram, Therkkuviruthangan, Therkuviruthangan, Thunisiramedu, Vada Harirajapuram, Vadakkupalayam, Vadappakkam, Vakkur, Valasakkadu, Vattathur, Vayalur, Vazhakollai, Velliyakudi, Veyyalur, Vilagam.

Amenities:

Education: Primary School in 66 villages, Middle school in 32 villages, Matriculation or Secondary School in 10 villages, namely Keerappalayam, Thirupaninatham, Orathur, Maduranthaganallur, T.Neduncheri, Mazhavarayanallur, Kanoor, Palayankottaikilpathi, Sozhatharam, Vadukkupalayam.

Higher Secondary or Pre University Courses or Intermediate or Junior College in 4 villages of the CD Block,, namely Orathur, Maduranthaganallur, Sozhatharam, Vadukkupalayam.

College in 1 village, Adult Literacy Center in 0 village., College is in village, namely Thunisiramedu.

Medical: Hospital in 0 village, Dispensary in 0 village, Health Center in 4 villages, Sub Center in 16 villages, Maternity and Child Welfare Center in 0 village, Community health workers in 33 villages.

Drinking Water: Tap water in 73 villages, Tank water in 3 villages, Well water in 73 villages, Tubewell in 73 villages and more than one source in 73 villages.

Bank: Banking facility in 7 villages, namely, Orathur, Vilagam, T.Neduncheri, Mudikandanallur Perur, Kanoor, Palayankottaikilpathi.

Credit Society in 14 villages Agricultural Credit Society in 13 Non-Agricultural Credit Society in 1 village.

Others: Power supply in 73 villages, Cinema hall in 1 village, sport club in 0 village, Stadium or Auditorium or Community Hall in 0 village, Post Office in 73 villages.

There are 70 villages having bus facilities.

Villages with most of facilities: Orathur, Vilagam

T.Neduncheri, Mudikandanallur, Perur, Kanoor Palayankottaikilpathi.

Villages without amenities (Education):
Thathanpetti, Palayamcherthangudi, Manakudiyaniruppam, Vadakkuvirudhangan, Madapuram, Easanai, Kothandavilagam..

Scheduled Castes: Out of the total population of 107374 persons, 43016 persons (40.06%) belong to Scheduled Castes.
The villages having less than 10% SC population are Vayalur, Orathur, Ramapuram, Palayankottaimalepathy Palayankottaikilpathi, Kurinjikudi.
The villages having more than 50% SC population are C.Sathamangalam, Kiliyanur, Paradur, Veeliyagudi Palayamcherthangudi, Puliangudi, Ennanagaram Edaianpalcheri, Maduranthaganallur, Vakkur, Tharasur Devangudi, K. Adoor, Poongudi, Pannapattu Ayyanrakkaramangalam, Manakudiyaniruppam, Vilagam Sediyur, Vadakkuvirudhangan, Manalur, Madapuram Sirukalur, Easanai, Kodiyalam, Mugaiyur, Perunkalur Mudikandanallur, Kumarakkudi, Kaliyamalai.
Sex ratio of Scheduled Caste population is 498.

Scheduled Castes Literates and Illiterates by Sex:

	Persons	Males	Females
Literate	23,713	13,900	9,813
Illiterate	19,303	7,703	11,600
Literacy rate	64.7	75.6	53.7
Graduate	725	556	169

Scheduled Castes (Dominant):
Adi Dravida, Arunthathiyar, Kuravan etc.
Chakkiliyan, Valluvan

For their cultural identity please see Appendix-I

Villages without Scheduled Castes: There are 2 villages without any scheduled caste population.

Scheduled Tribes: Out of the total population of 107374 persons, 606 persons (0.56%) belong to Scheduled Tribes.
The villages having less than 10% ST population are C.Sathamangalam, Vayalur, Keerappalayam Thirupaninatham, Vadagriraja Puram, Thathanpetti Ayipettai, Kiliyanur, Orathur, Paradur, Boothangudi Veeliyagudi, Palayamcherthangudi, Sakkangudi Puliangudi, Thenharirajapuram, Melavanniyur Ennanagaram, Kannangudi, Kezhnatam, Edaianpalcheri Maduranthaganallur, Poonthottam, Vakkur, Vadappakam Veyyalore, Vazhaikollai, Odakkanallur, Tharasur Devangudi, K. Adoor, C. Veeracholagan, Thunisiramedu Poongudi, Pannapattu, Ayyanrakkaramangalam Manakudiyaniruppam, Vilagam, Sediyur, Koolapadi Vadakkuvirudhangan, Manalur, Therkkuviruthangan Madapuram, Sirukalur, Easanai, Chenkalmedu Kodiyalam, Mugaiyur, Perunkalur, T.Neduncheri Koodalaiathur, Kavalagudi, Mudikandanallur Mazhavarayanallur, Kumarakkudi, Kothandavilagam Nangudi, Perur, Kanoor, Ramapuram Palayankottaimalepathy, Palayankottaikilpathi Valasakkadu, Kurinjikudi, Nandeeswaramangalm Vattathur, Pudaiyur, Sozhatharam, Vadukkupalayam Kandakumaran, Kaliyamalai, Poorthangudi.
The villages having more than 50% ST population are None.
Sex ratio of Scheduled tribe population is 520.

Scheduled Tribes Literates and Illiterates by Sex:

	Persons	Males	Females
Literate	201	121	80
Illiterate	405	170	235
Literacy rate	39.3	49.0	30.2
Graduate	1	1	0

Scheduled Tribes (Dominant):
Irular, Kattunayakan, Malakkuravan
Generic Tribes etc.

For their cultural identity please see Appendix-II

Villages without Scheduled Tribes: There are 43 villages without any scheduled tribe population.

Literates and Illiterates by Sex (Total Population):

	Persons	Males	Females
Literate	65,839	38,240	27,599
Illiterate	41,535	15,821	25,714
Literacy rate	70	81	59
Graduate	2,224	1,706	518

Agriculture: ***Distribution of villages according to land use:***
Out of 73 villages, Total area (in hectare) is 20551.23, out of that 81.87 percent is cultivable and 92.83 percent of the cultivable area is irrigated.

Sources of Irrigation (Hectares): Government Canal 15615.21, Private Canal 0, Well without Electricity 0, Well with Electricity 4.71, Tubewell without Electricity 0, Tubewell with Electricity 0, Tank 0, River 0, Lake 0, Waterfall 0, Others 0.

Villages with population of 5000 to 9999: None

Villages with population of 10000 and above: None

Distribution of Workers:

	Persons	Males	Females	WPR
Cultivators	9,905	7,256	2,649	19.51
Agricultural Labour	32,705	17,441	15,264	64.41
Household Industry	1,013	376	637	2
Other Workers	7,153	5,716	1,437	14.09
Main Workers	35,018	23,858	11,160	68.97
Marginal Workers	15,758	6,931	8,827	31.03
Total Workers	50,776	30,789	19,987	

Religion: Major Religious Communities:

	Persons	Males	Females	Sex Ratio

Religion	Persons	Males	Females	Sex Ratio
Hindu (90.92%)	97,627	49,116	48,511	988
Muslim (1.46%)	1,573	755	818	1,083
Christian (7.5%)	8,058	4,130	3,928	951
Sikh (0%)	3	-	3	-
Buddhists (0%)	1	1	-	-
Jain (0%)	4	1	3	3,000

Agewise Data:

	Persons	Males	Females	Sex Ratio
All ages	107,374	54,061	53,313	986
0-14	30,588	15,508	15,080	972
15-44	51,019	25,207	25,812	1024
45-79	24,662	12,739	11,923	936
80+	853	480	373	777
Age not stated	252	127	125	984

Languages (Dominant):

Tamil, Telugu, Urdu, Malayalam, Hindi

Disabled Population:

	Persons	Males	Females	%
Total Disabled	3,078	1,457	1,621	
In Seeing	1,868	740	1,128	60.69
In Speech	203	118	85	6.6
In Hearing	191	98	93	6.21
In Movement	635	400	235	20.63
Mentally	181	101	80	5.88

KEEZHAPAVUR

Keelapavoor C.D. Block lies in the north-western part of Tirunelveli district. It is a part of Veerakeralamputhur, Tenkasi and Alangulam taluks. The Block is located at a distance of 45 kms. from district headquarters (Tirunelveli). There are 15 villages in the block with the total population of 113,063 persons. Area of the C.D. Block is 135.14 sq. kms. It is bounded in the north by CD Block Kadaiyanallur, in the south by CD Block Kadayam, in the east by CD Block Alangulam, and in the west by CD Block Tenkasi.

CD Block Keelapavoor falls in taluks: Alangulam by 05, Tenkasi by 06, and Veerakeralamputhur by 04 villages.

Communications:

Roadways : S.H.-40: Direction- Tenkasi to Alangulam, Nearest Villages- Kulasekarapatti, Gunaramanaloor, Kalunearkulam, Andipatti, Poolankulam, Pethanadarpatti, Thippanam Patti. S.H.-43: Direction- Tenkasi to Tirunelveli, Nearest Villages- Kulasekarapatti, Gunaramanaloor, Kallurani.

Railway Station: Kulasekarapatti, Thippanam Patti, Avoodaiyanoor.

River: Chittar Nadi- Nearest Villages- Rajagopalaperi, Vellakal, Veerakeralampudur, Melupavoor, Kulasekarapatti, Gunaramanaloor.

Annual Rainfall: Average Rainfall 879 mm.

Ground Water: Availability of the ground water in the Basin is 43.58 MCM and the utilization is 26.54 MCM. It belongs to Safe category. Depth to water level varies from 2 to 10 meter below the ground. Most of the wells go down in summer months, according to the Ground Water Estimation Committee.

Forest and Reserved Forest: (Vellakalparam RF)- Nearest Village- Vellakalparambu.

Natural Division: NA

Administration

Revenue **Division:** Tenkasi. Parliamentary Constituency: 37 Tenkasi, 38 Tirunelveli.District: Tirunelveli. Taluk: Veerakeralamputhur, Tenkasi, Alangulam. Assembly Constituency: 222 Tenkasi, 223 Alangulam. Gram Panchayat: 21.

Villages: 15 **Inhabited:** 14 **Uninhabited:** 1

Ranking	District	State	National
Area	16	352	5257
Population	1	84	3064
Sex Ratio	17	76	612
Child Sex Ratio	2	20	576
Literacy Rate	10	69	843
Density	2	62	1100
Work Participation Rate	1	10	551

Gram Panchayats:

Andipatti, Ariyappapuram , Avudaiyanoor, Gunaramanallur, Idaiyarthavanai, Inamvellakal , Kallurani, Kaluneerkualam, Keelavellakkal , Kulasekarapatti, Melakrishnaperi, Melappavur, Nagalkulam, Pethanadarpatti, Poolankulam, Rajagopalaperi, Rajapandi, Sivanadanoor, Thuthikulam, Tippampatti, Veerakeralampudur.

Amenities:

Education: Primary School in 14 villages, Middle school in 12 villages, Matriculation or Secondary School in 7 villages, namely Veerakeralampudur, Melupavoor, Gunaramanaloor, Kallurani, Avoodaiyanoor, Kalunearkulam, Poolankulam. Higher Secondary or Pre University Courses or Intermediate or Junior College in 4 villages of the CD Block,, namely Veerakeralampudur, Kallurani, Avoodaiyanoor, Kalunearkulam.

College in 1 village, Adult Literacy Center in 0 village., College is in village, namely Poolankulam.

Medical: Hospital in 0 village, Dispensary in 1 village, Health Center in 3 villages, Sub Center in 7 villages, Maternity and Child Welfare Center in 4 villages, Community health workers in 10 villages.

The Village having Hospital or Dispensary or Health Center is Kallurani.

Drinking Water: Tap water in 14 villages, Tank water in 1 villages, Well water in 14 villages, Tubewell in 2 villages and more than one source in 14 villages.

Bank: Banking facility in 6 villages, namely,

Veerakeralampudur, Melupavoor, Kulasekarapatti Thippanam Patti, Avoodaiyanoor, Pethanadarpatti.
Credit Society in 5 villages Agricultural Credit Society in 3 Non-Agricultural Credit Society in 4 villages.
Others: Power supply in 14 villages, Cinema hall in 3 villages, sport club in 0 village, Stadium or Auditorium or Community Hall in 0 village, Post Office in 13 villages.
There are 13 villages having bus facilities.
Villages with most of facilities: Veerakeralampudur Melupavoor, Kulasekarapatti, Thippanam Patti Avoodaiyanoor, Pethanadarpatti.
Villages without Amenities (Education): None..
Scheduled Castes: Out of the total population of 113063 persons, 10382 persons (9.18%) belong to Scheduled Castes.
The villages having less than 10% SC population are Veerakeralampudur, Kulasekarapatti, Kallurani Thippanam Patti, Avoodaiyanoor, Kalunearkulam Thuthikulam, Andipatti, Poolankulam, Pethanadarpatti.
The villages having more than 50% SC population are None.
Sex ratio of Scheduled Caste population is 518.
Scheduled Castes Literates and Illiterates by Sex:

	Persons	Males	Females
Literate	5,418	3,093	2,325
Illiterate	4,964	1,907	3,057
Literacy rate	60.5	72.1	49.8
Graduate	65	43	22

Scheduled Castes (Dominant):
Pallan, Paraiyan etc., Chakkiliyan, Arunthathiyar Valluvan
For their cultural identity please see Appendix-I
Villages without Scheduled Castes: There is 1 village without any scheduled caste population.
Scheduled Tribes: Out of the total population of 113063 persons, 43 persons (0.04%) belong to Scheduled Tribes.
The villages having less than 10% ST population are Rajagopalaperi, Vellakal, Veerakeralampudur Melupavoor, Kulasekarapatti, Gunaramanaloor Kallurani, Thippanam Patti, Avoodaiyanoor Kalunearkulam, Thuthikulam, Andipatti, Poolankulam Pethanadarpatti.
The villages having more than 50% ST population are None.
Sex ratio of Scheduled tribe population is 535.
Scheduled Tribes Literates and Illiterates by Sex:

	Persons	Males	Females
Literate	12	6	6
Illiterate	31	14	17
Literacy rate	34.3	35.3	33.3
Graduate	0	0	0

Scheduled Tribes (Dominant):
Kattunayakan, Sholaga
For their cultural identity please see Appendix-II
Villages without Scheduled Tribes: There are 11 villages without any scheduled tribe population.
Literates and Illiterates by Sex (Total Population):

	Persons	Males	Females
Literate	71,794	40,445	31,349
Illiterate	41,269	15,458	25,811
Literacy rate	73	83	63
Graduate	1,748	1,020	728

Agriculture: ***Distribution of villages according to land use:***
Out of 15 villages, Total area (in hectare) is 13514.37, out of that 34.67 percent is cultivable and 70.42 percent of the cultivable area is irrigated.
Sources of Irrigation (Hectares): Government Canal 341.5, Private Canal 0, Well without Electricity 831.43, Well with Electricity 678.85, Tubewell without Electricity 167.88, Tubewell with Electricity 42.35, Tank 1237.17, River 0, Lake 0, Waterfall 0, Others 0.
Villages with population of 5000 to 9999:
Vellakal , Veerakeralampudur, Kaluneerkulam Poolankulam.
Villages with population of 10000 and above:
Kulasekarapatti , Gunaramanallur, Kallurani Thippampatti , Avudaiyanoor , Pethanadarpatti.
Distribution of Workers:

	Persons	Males	Females	WPR
Cultivators	9,882	7,955	1,927	15.36
Agricultural Labour	14,843	10,911	3,932	23.08
Household Industry	25,506	1,360	24,146	39.65
Other Workers	14,094	12,194	1,900	21.91
Main Workers	59,735	29,867	29,868	92.86
Marginal Workers	4,590	2,553	2,037	7.14
Total Workers	64,325	32,420	31,905	

Religion: Major Religious Communities:

	Persons	Males	Females	Sex Ratio
Hindu (89%)	100,631	49,725	50,906	1,024
Muslim (1.64%)	1,857	927	930	1,003
Christian (9.31%)	10,526	5,227	5,299	1,014
Sikh (0%)	1	-	1	-
Buddhists (0%)	-	-	-	-
Jain (0%)	5	4	1	250

Agewise Data:

	Persons	Males	Females	Sex Ratio
All ages	113,063	55,903	57,160	1022
0-14	32,920	16,605	16,315	983
15-44	53,249	26,191	27,058	1033
45-79	25,542	12,482	13,060	1046
80+	1,020	433	587	1356

Age not stated	332	192	140	729

Languages (Dominant):
Tamil, Telugu, Malayalam, Urdu, Kannada

Disabled Population:

	Persons	Males	Females	%
Total Disabled	2,934	1,363	1,571	
In Seeing	1,691	689	1,002	57.63
In Speech	260	130	130	8.86
In Hearing	96	30	66	3.27
In Movement	692	410	282	23.59
Mentally	195	104	91	6.65

KELAMANGALAM

Kelamangalam C.D. Block lies in the south-western part of Dharmapuri district. It is a part of Denkanikottai taluk. The Block is located at a distance of 74 kms. from district headquarters (Dharmapuri). There are 43 villages in the block with the total population of 114,898 persons. Area of the C.D. Block is 692.16 sq. kms. It is bounded in the north by CD Block Shoopgiri and Hosur, in the south by C.D. Block Thally and district Dharmapuri, in the east by district Dharmapuri and CD Block Krishnagiri, in the west by C.D. Blocks Hosur and Thally.

Communications:
Roadways : S.H.-17: Direction- Hosur to Palakkodu, Nearest Villages- Muthanahalli, T.Gollahalli, Karukanalli, Royakottai, Pillari Agraharam, Nellur, Echanahalli, Odyandahalli (RF) Uni, Odyandahalli.
River: Ponnaiyar Nadi- Nearest Villages- Karukanalli, Sengodachinnahulli, Sengodachinnahulli (RF) Uni, Soolig ounta.
Annual Rainfall: Average Rainfall 760 mm.
Ground Water: Availability of the ground water in the Basin is (Information not available) H.A.M. and the utili zation is 160.44 H.A.M. It belongs to Over Expoited categ ory. Depth to water level varies from 2 to 5 meter below the ground. Most of the wells go down in summer months, according to the Ground Water Estimation Committee.
Forest and Reserved Forest: (Ayyur RF)- Nearest Villages- Ayyur R.F. Uni, Battamugalalam. (Denkanikotta)- Nearest Villages- Pachappanatti, Bithireddy, Denkanikottai (RF) Uni, Bevvnatham,Sandanapally. (Noganoor)- Nearest Villages- Sandanapally, Thanavakarai, Erudukotta. (Galigattam)- Nearest Village- Galigattam (RF) Uni. (Gullaty)- Nearest Villages- Gullarhy R.F. Uni, Hanumanthapuram, Rathanagiri, Sandanapally, Erudukotta, Belalam, Battamugalalam. (Marandahalli)- Nearest Village- Manandahalhi (RF) Uni. (Odayandahalli)- Nearest Villages- Echanahalli, Odyandahalli (RF) Uni, Odyandahali. (Sengodachinnathali)- Nearest Villages- Sengodachinnahulli, Sengodachinnahulli (RF) Uni, Sooligounta. (Thuluvabetta)- Nearest Villages- Battamugalalam, Thuluvabetta (RF) Uni. (Udedurgam)- Nearest Villages- Nagamangalam, Udedurgam, Thinijepalli, Udedurgam (RF) Uni, Pachappanatti, Bevvnatham, Rathanagiri.
Natural Division: Baramahal.
Administration
Revenue **Division:** Hosur. Parliamentary Constituency: 9 Krishnagiri, 10 Dharmapuri. District: Dharmapuri. Taluk: Denkanikottai. Assembly Constituency: 54 Veppanahalli, 56 Thalli, 57 Palacodu. Gram Panchayat: 28.
Border Villages- (Karnataka)- Nearest Villages- Nagamangalam, Udedurgam.
Villages: 43 **Inhabited:** 33 **Uninhabited:** 10

Ranking	District	State	National
Area	4	11	933
Population	14	79	3001
Sex Ratio	7	347	3542
Child Sex Ratio	4	287	4827
Literacy Rate	18	380	4667
Density	12	166	5299
Work Participation Rate	16	352	1663

Gram Panchayats:
Anekollu, Bairamangalam, Battamugalalam, Bevunatham, Bithireddi, Bodichipalli, Bommathathunur, Doddametrai , Doddathimmanahalli , Erudukotta , H.Chettipalli, Hanumanthapuram, Jagir Karupalli, Jakkeri, Kandaganapalli, Karukkanahalli, Koppagarai , Kundumaranapalli, Madagraharam , Nagamangalam, Pillariagraharam , Rathnagiri, Rayakotta, Rayakotta , Santhanapalli, Thavarakkarai, Thimijapalli, Udedurgam, Ulimangalam.
Amenities:
Education: Primary School in 33 villages, Middle school in 18 villages, Matriculation or Secondary School in 7 villages, namely Kundumaranapalli, Bariamangalam, Nagamangalam, Thinijepalli, Royakottai, Ulimangalam, Erudukotta.
Higher Secondary or Pre University Courses or Intermediate or Junior College in 2 villages of the CD Block,, namely Royakottai, Ulimangalam.
College in 0 village, Adult Literacy Center in 0 village.
Medical: Hospital in 0 village, Dispensary in 0 village, Health Center in 0 village, Sub Center in 19 villages, Maternity and Child Welfare Center in 1 village, Community health workers in 29 villages.
Drinking Water: Tap water in 33 villages, Tank water in 0 villages, Well water in 33 villages, Tubewell in 33 villages and more than one source in 33 villages.
Bank: Banking facility in 2 villages, namely, Nagamangalam, Battamugalalam.
Credit Society in 9 villages Agricultural Credit Society in 8 Non-Agricultural Credit Society in 1 village.

Others: Power supply in 33 villages, Cinema hall in 0 village, sport club in 0 village, Stadium or Auditorium or Community Hall in 0 village, Post Office in 33 villages.
There are 31 villages having bus facilities.
Villages with most of facilities: Nagamangalam Battamugalalam.
Villages without Amenities (Education): None..
Scheduled Castes: Out of the total population of 114898 persons, 15554 persons (13.54%) belong to Scheduled Castes.
The villages having less than 10% SC population are Jageer Karupalli, Nagappan Agraharam, Bodichipalli Karukanalli, Sengodachinnahulli, Sooligounta Pillari Agraharam, Nellur, Anekollu, Bevvnatham Echanahalli, Battamugalalam, Thanavakarai.
The villages having more than 50% SC population are None.
Sex ratio of Scheduled Caste population is 492.
Scheduled Castes Literates and Illiterates by Sex:

	Persons	Males	Females
Literate	6,015	3,698	2,317
Illiterate	9,539	4,198	5,341
Literacy rate	46.5	56.3	36.4
Graduate	37	34	3

Scheduled Castes (Dominant):
Adi Dravida, Arunthathiyar, Paraiyan etc.
Kuravan etc., Madiga
For their cultural identity please see Appendix-I
Villages without Scheduled Castes: There are 11 villages without any scheduled caste population.
Scheduled Tribes: Out of the total population of 114898 persons, 4660 persons (4.06%) belong to Scheduled Tribes.
The villages having less than 10% ST population are Jageer Karupalli, Nagappan Agraharam, Hosapuram Kundumaranapalli, Bariamangalam, Bodichipalli Nagamangalam, Udedurgam, Thinijepalli, T.Gollahalli Karukanalli, Sengodachinnahulli, Sooligounta Royakottai, Pillari Agraharam, Nellur, Pachappanatti Jakkei, Anekollu, Ulimangalam, Bithireddy Bevvnatham, Echanahalli, Odyandahalli Hanumanthapuram, Rathanagiri, Sandanapally Thanavakarai, Kottur, Erudukotta, Belalam.
The villages having more than 50% ST population are None.
Sex ratio of Scheduled tribe population is 486.
Scheduled Tribes Literates and Illiterates by Sex:

	Persons	Males	Females
Literate	1,029	651	378
Illiterate	3,631	1,742	1,889
Literacy rate	27.2	33.5	20.6
Graduate	6	6	0

Scheduled Tribes (Dominant):
Irular, Kurumans, Kurichchan, Sholaga, Kondareddis
For their cultural identity please see Appendix-II
Villages without Scheduled Tribes: There are 24 villages without any scheduled tribe population.
Literates and Illiterates by Sex (Total Population):

	Persons	Males	Females
Literate	47,763	29,771	17,992
Illiterate	67,135	29,187	37,948
Literacy rate	49	60	38
Graduate	575	424	151

Agriculture: ***Distribution of villages according to land use:*** Out of 43 villages, Total area (in hectare) is 69216.27, out of that 42.28 percent is cultivable and 12.41 percent of the cultivable area is irrigated.
Sources of Irrigation (Hectares): Government Canal 15.46, Private Canal 0, Well without Electricity 284.99, Well with Electricity 2220.72, Tubewell without Electricity 34.5, Tubewell with Electricity 0, Tank 0, River 0, Lake 953.75, Waterfall 0, Others 122.04.
Villages with population of 5000 to 9999: Sengodachinnahalli, Rayakotta, Battamugulalam Santhanapalli, Erudukotta.
Villages with population of 10000 and above: None
Distribution of Workers:

	Persons	Males	Females	WPR
Cultivators	31,024	20,666	10,358	53.52
Agricultural Labour	16,137	6,992	9,145	27.84
Household Industry	2,150	618	1,532	3.71
Other Workers	8,661	6,199	2,462	14.94
Main Workers	45,913	30,287	15,626	79.2
Marginal Workers	12,059	4,188	7,871	20.8
Total Workers	57,972	34,475	23,497	

Religion: Major Religious Communities:

	Persons	Males	Females	Sex Ratio
Hindu (96.67%)	111,075	56,953	54,122	950
Muslim (2.8%)	3,216	1,669	1,547	927
Christian (0.46%)	526	291	235	808
Sikh (0%)	1	-	1	-
Buddhists (0%)	-	-	-	-
Jain (0%)	2	2	-	-

Agewise Data:

	Persons	Males	Females	Sex Ratio
All ages	114,898	58,958	55,940	949
0-14	39,725	20,507	19,218	937
15-44	51,645	26,041	25,604	983
45-79	22,274	11,720	10,554	901
80+	1,064	600	464	773
Age not stated	190	90	100	1111

Languages (Dominant):

Tamil, Telugu, Kannada, Urdu, Marathi

Disabled Population:

	Persons	Males	Females	%
Total Disabled	3,392	961	2,431	
In Seeing	2,552	457	2,095	75.24
In Speech	190	94	96	5.6
In Hearing	89	50	39	2.62
In Movement	425	290	135	12.53
Mentally	136	70	66	4.01

KILLIYUR

Killiyur C.D. Block lies in the southern part of Kanniya kumari district. It is a part of Vilavancode taluk. The Block is located at a distance of NA kms. from district headquarters (Nagarkoil). There are 05 villages in the block with the total population of 50,936 persons. Area of the C.D. Block is 63.80 sq. kms. It is bounded in the north by CD Block Thakkalay, in the south by the CD Block Kurunthancode, in the east by CD Blocks Kurunthancode and Thakkalay, and in the west by CD Block Munchira.

Communications:

Roadways : Information not Available.

Annual Rainfall: Average Rainfall 1448 mm.

Ground Water: Availability of the ground water in the Basin is 16.58 MCM and the utilization is 3.45 MCM. It belongs to Safe category. Depth to water level varies from more than 10 meter below the ground. Most of the wells go down in summer months, according to the Ground Water Estimation Committee.

Coastal Villages- (Arabian Sea)- Nearest Villages- Keezhkulam, Medalam. **Natural Division:** NA

Administration

Revenue **Division:** Padmanabhapuram. Parliamentary Constit uency: 39 Kanniyakumari. District: Kanniyakumari. Taluk: Vilavancode. Assembly Constituency: 233 Vilavancode, 234 Killiyur. Gram Panchayat: 08.

Villages: 5 **Inhabited:** 5 **Uninhabited:** 0

Ranking	**District**	**State**	**National**
Area	8	380	5995
Population	6	355	5232
Sex Ratio	9	273	2135
Child Sex Ratio	7	154	2790
Literacy Rate	5	6	156
Density	2	376	1175
Work Participation Rate	4	12	5504

Gram Panchayats:

Enayamputham thurai, Kollanchy, Mathicode, Midalam, Mullaginavilai, Nattalam, Paloor, Thipramalai.

Amenities:

Education: Primary School in 5 villages, Middle school in 4 villages, Matriculation or Secondary School in 4 villages, namely Nattalam, Keezhkulam, Paloor, Medalam.

Higher Secondary or Pre University Courses or Intermediate or Junior College in 4 villages of the CD Block,, namely Nattalam, Keezhkulam, Paloor, Medalam.

College in 1 village, Adult Literacy Center in 0 village., College is in village, namely Paloor.

Medical: Hospital in 2 villages, Dispensary in 1 village, Health Center in 1 village, Sub Center in 5 villages, Maternity and Child Welfare Center in 2 villages, Community health workers in 0 village.

The Villages having Hospital or Dispensary or Health Center are Keezhkulam, Medalam.

Drinking Water: Tap water in 5 villages, Tank water in 0 villages, Well water in 5 villages, Tubewell in 5 villages and more than one source in 5 villages.

Bank: Banking facility in 2 villages, namely, Nattalam, Keezhkulam.

Credit Society in 4 villages Agricultural Credit Society in 3 Non-Agricultural Credit Society in 2 villages.

Others: Power supply in 5 villages, Cinema hall in 0 village, sport club in 0 village, Stadium or Auditorium or Community Hall in 0 village, Post Office in 4 villages.

There are 5 villages having bus facilities.

Villages with most of facilities: Nattalam Keezhkulam.

Villages without Amenities (Education): None..

Scheduled Castes: Out of the total population of 50936 persons, 881 persons (1.73%) belong to Scheduled Castes.

The villages having less than 10% SC population are None..

The villages having more than 50% SC population are None.

Sex ratio of Scheduled Caste population is 511.

Scheduled Castes Literates and Illiterates by Sex:

	Persons	Males	Females
Literate	643	331	312
Illiterate	238	100	138
Literacy rate	81.6	86.2	77.2
Graduate	18	8	10

Scheduled Castes (Dominant):

Paraiyan etc., Samban, Paravan, Samagara, Pallan

For their cultural identity please see Appendix-I

Villages without Scheduled Castes: There are 2 villages without any scheduled caste population.

Scheduled Tribes: Out of the total population of 50936 persons, 4 persons (0.01%) belong to Scheduled Tribes.

The villages having less than 10% ST population are None..

The villages having more than 50% ST population are None.

Sex ratio of Scheduled tribe population is 500.

Scheduled Tribes Literates and Illiterates by Sex:

	Persons	Males	Females
Literate	4	2	2
Illiterate	0	0	0
Literacy rate	100.0	100.0	100.0
Graduate	0	0	0

Scheduled Tribes (Dominant):

Kadar

For their cultural identity please see Appendix-II

Villages without Scheduled Tribes: There are 4 villages without any scheduled tribe population.

Literates and Illiterates by Sex (Total Population):

	Persons	Males	Females
Literate	38,974	19,979	18,995
Illiterate	11,962	5,776	6,186
Literacy rate	86	87	85
Graduate	1,390	659	731

Agriculture: ***Distribution of villages according to land use:*** Out of 5 villages, Total area (in hectare) is 6380.5, out of that 78.93 percent is cultivable and 22.76 percent of the cultivable area is irrigated.

Sources of Irrigation (Hectares): Government Canal 323.12, Private Canal 0, Well without Electricity 0, Well with Electricity 0, Tubewell without Electricity 0, Tubewell with Electricity 0, Tank 823.33, River 0, Lake 0, Waterfall 0, Others 0.

Villages with population of 5000 to 9999:

Paloor.

Villages with population of 10000 and above:

Nattalam, Keezhkulam, Midalam.

Distribution of Workers:

	Persons	Males	Females	WPR
Cultivators	402	289	113	2.29
Agricultural Labour	1,467	1,335	132	8.37
Household Industry	1,127	380	747	6.43
Other Workers	14,534	12,304	2,230	82.91
Main Workers	15,364	12,992	2,372	87.64
Marginal Workers	2,166	1,316	850	12.36
Total Workers	17,530	14,308	3,222	

Religion: Major Religious Communities:

	Persons	Males	Females	Sex Ratio
Hindu (26.66%)	13,581	6,915	6,666	964
Muslim (0.78%)	396	186	210	1,129
Christian (72.55%)	36,955	18,651	18,304	981
Sikh (0%)	-	-	-	-
Buddhists (0%)	-	-	-	-
Jain (0%)	1	1	-	-

Agewise Data:

	Persons	Males	Females	Sex Ratio
All ages	50,936	25,755	25,181	978
0-14	13,135	6,660	6,475	972
15-44	25,977	13,080	12,897	986
45-79	11,375	5,774	5,601	970
80+	424	230	194	843
Age not stated	25	11	14	1273

Languages (Dominant):

Tamil, Malayalam, Telugu, English, Kannada

Disabled Population:

	Persons	Males	Females	%
Total Disabled	1,435	654	781	
In Seeing	836	283	553	58.26
In Speech	85	43	42	5.92
In Hearing	27	14	13	1.88
In Movement	377	238	139	26.27
Mentally	110	76	34	7.67

KILPERNNATHUR

Kilpennathur C.D. Block lies in the southern part of Tiruvannamalai district. It is a part of Tiruvannamalai taluk. The Block is located at a distance of 16 kms. from district headquarters (Tiruvannamalai). There are 63 villages in the block with the total population of 85,212 persons. Area of the C.D. Block is 237.96 sq. kms. It is bounded in the north by C.D. Block Thirunjapuram and district Viluppuram, in the south and east by district Viluppuram, and in the east by C.D. Block Tiruvannamalai.

Communications:

Roadways : N.H.-66: Direction- Tiruvannamalai to Gingee, Nearest Villages- Nariyamangalam, Sirunathur, Somasipadi, Sirukothan, Sambandanur.

Railway Station: Vallannathal.

Backwards Region Grants Fund: It receives Backward Region Grants.

Annual Rainfall: Average Rainfall 1019 mm.

Ground Water: Availability of the ground water in the Basin is (Information not available) H.A.M. and the utilization is 160.44 H.A.M. It belongs to Over Expoited category. Depth to water level varies from 2 to 5 meter below the ground. Most of the wells go down in summer months, according to the Ground Water Estimation Committee.

Forest and Reserved Forest: (Tippakodu RF)- Nearest Villages Keeranur, Vallannathal, Neykuppam, Chyallari, Chellankuppam. RF. (Poomjimalai RF)- Nearest Villages- Ponnamedu, Poornijimalai .

Natural Division: Tondai Nadu.

Administration

Division. Parliamentary Constituency: 11 Tiruvannamalai. District: Tiruvannamalai. Taluk: Tiruvannamalai. Assembly Constituency: 64 Kilpennathur. Gram Panchayat: 45.

Villages: 63 **Inhabited:** 62 **Uninhabited:** 1

Ranking	District	State	National

Area	15	244	3541
Population	13	204	3918
Sex Ratio	2	86	656
Child Sex Ratio	11	229	3761
Literacy Rate	7	169	1628
Density	6	171	3034
Work Participation Rate	6	146	1715

Gram Panchayats:
Agaram, Angunam, Anukkumalai, Aranji, Arumbakkam, Avoor, Chellancuppam, Ganabapuram, Ganalapadi, Gengapattu(Na), Gudalur (Z) , Iyengunam, Kadambai, Kalingaleri, Kallayyee, Kalpoondi, Kaniampundi, Karikilambadi, Kathalambattu, Kattumalayanur, Kazhikulam, Keekalur, Keeranur, Kolathur, Konalur, Mekkalore, Nadalaganandal, Nammiandal(SO), Nariyamangalam, Neelanthangal, Neivanatham, Olaipadi, Panniyur, Rajanthangal, Rayampettai, Sanippundi, Sevarapundi, Sirunathur, Somasipadi, Su. Polakunam, Vaipur, Valuthalangulam, Vayalur, Vedanatham, Velananandal.

Amenities:
Education: Primary School in 49 villages, Middle school in 23 villages, Matriculation or Secondary School in 6 villages, namely Iyengunam, Somasipadi, Karikalambady, Vedanatham, Rajanthangal, Gengapattu.
Higher Secondary or Pre University Courses or Intermediate or Junior College in 3 villages of the CD Block,, namely Somasipadi, Kaniyampoondi, Angunam.
College in 0 village, Adult Literacy Center in 2 villages.
Medical: Hospital in 0 village, Dispensary in 0 village, Health Center in 7 villages, Sub Center in 4 villages, Maternity and Child Welfare Center in 12 villages, Community health workers in 49 villages.
Drinking Water: Tap water in 62 villages, Tank water in 10 villages, Well water in 62 villages, Tubewell in 62 villages and more than one source in 62 villages.
Bank: Banking facility in 6 villages, namely, Kazhikulam, Sirunathur, Somasipadi, Nadazgaganadal Avoor, Venniyandal.
Credit Society in 10 villages Agricultural Credit Society in 7 Non-Agricultural Credit Society in 6 villages.
Others: Power supply in 62 villages, Cinema hall in 1 village, sport club in 0 village, Stadium or Auditorium or Community Hall in 0 village, Post Office in 29 villages.
There are 55 villages having bus facilities.
Villages with most of facilities: Kazhikulam Sirunathur, Somasipadi, Nadazgaganadal, Avoor Venniyandal.
Villages without amenities (Education): Mekkalore, Uthapoondi, Kumarakudi, Kalitheri, Sirukothan, Andalur, Kattuvelanthal, Polakunam, Neykuppam, Elupanthangal..

Scheduled Castes: Out of the total population of 85212 persons, 20263 persons (23.78%) belong to Scheduled Castes.
The villages having less than 10% SC population are Ganabapuram, Uthapoondi, Vattaraputhur Nariyamangalam, Sonamiyandal, Ananji, Kalitheri Sirukothan, Kunnakuppam, Rayampeattai, Andalur Mannavaram, Kaniyampoondi, Kalingaleri, Sorpanadal Vallannathal, Neykuppam, Nadazgaganadal, Eirpakkam Guddalore, Avoor, Rajanthangal, Gengapattu Chyallari, Anukkumalai, Ponnamedu, Kallayee.
The villages having more than 50% SC population are Karanampoondi, Kalpoondi, Kadambai, Keeranur Elupanthangal, Panniyur.
Sex ratio of Scheduled Caste population is 508.

Scheduled Castes Literates and Illiterates by Sex:

	Persons	Males	Females
Literate	10,699	6,202	4,497
Illiterate	9,564	3,761	5,803
Literacy rate	61.1	72.7	50.1
Graduate	67	55	12

Scheduled Castes (Dominant):
Adi Dravida, Valluvan, Arunthathiyar, Chakkiliyan Kuravan etc.
For their cultural identity please see Appendix-I
Villages without Scheduled Castes: There are 17 villages without any scheduled caste population.
Scheduled Tribes: Out of the total population of 85212 persons, 2360 persons (2.77%) belong to Scheduled Tribes.
The villages having less than 10% ST population are Ganalapadi, Savarappoondi, Keekkalur, Katthalampattu Mekkalore, Vazuthalankulam, Ganabapuram, Kazhikulam Uthapoondi, Vattaraputhur, Iyengunam, Karanampoondi Nariyamangalam, Kalpoondi, Sirunathur, Somasipadi Sonamiyandal, Kumarakudi, Ananji, Kalitheri Sirukothan, Kadambai, Kunnakuppam, Rayampeattai Andalur, Mannavaram, Karikalambady, Kaniyampoondi Vedanatham, Kolathur, Kattumalayanur, Kattuvelanthal Polakunam, Keeranur, Arumbakkam, Vallannathal Neykuppam, Konalur, Nadazgaganadal, Sanipoondi Eirpakkam, Guddalore, Avoor, Rajanthangal Elupanthangal, Gengapattu, Chyallari, Chellankuppam Venniyandal, Olaippadi, Anukkumalai, Kallayee Sorathur, Vaipur, Agaram, Panniyur, Angunam.
The villages having more than 50% ST population are None.
Sex ratio of Scheduled tribe population is 513.

Scheduled Tribes Literates and Illiterates by Sex:

	Persons	Males	Females

Literate	976	586	390
Illiterate	1,384	563	821
Literacy rate	47.5	58.2	37.2
Graduate	1	1	0

Scheduled Tribes (Dominant):
Irular, Kattunayakan, Kurumans, Malai Pandaram Palleyan

For their cultural identity please see Appendix-II

Villages without Scheduled Tribes: There are 31 villages without any scheduled tribe population.

Literates and Illiterates by Sex (Total Population):

	Persons	Males	Females
Literate	50,055	29,211	20,844
Illiterate	35,157	12,983	22,174
Literacy rate	67	79	55
Graduate	369	282	87

Agriculture: ***Distribution of villages according to land use:*** Out of 63 villages, Total area (in hectare) is 23796.84, out of that 68.39 percent is cultivable and 44.01 percent of the cultivable area is irrigated.

Sources of Irrigation (Hectares): Government Canal 0, Private Canal 0, Well without Electricity 802.8, Well with Electricity 3578.46, Tubewell without Electricity 0, Tubewell with Electricity 0, Tank 1936.79, River 2.57, Lake 120.97, Waterfall 0, Others 0.

Villages with population of 5000 to 9999: None

Villages with population of 10000 and above: None

Distribution of Workers:

	Persons	Males	Females	WPR
Cultivators	17,336	10,922	6,414	38.87
Agricultural Labour	20,467	8,515	11,952	45.89
Household Industry	1,295	621	674	2.9
Other Workers	5,501	4,400	1,101	12.33
Main Workers	33,972	20,666	13,306	76.17
Marginal Workers	10,627	3,792	6,835	23.83
Total Workers	44,599	24,458	20,141	

Religion: Major Religious Communities:

	Persons	Males	Females	Sex Ratio
Hindu (89.29%)	76,084	37,891	38,193	1,008
Muslim (3.75%)	3,198	1,513	1,685	1,114
Christian (6.38%)	5,436	2,554	2,882	1,128
Sikh (0%)	3	2	1	500
Buddhists (0%)	2	1	1	1,000
Jain (0.47%)	404	193	211	1,093

Agewise Data:

	Persons	Males	Females	Sex Ratio
All ages	85,212	42,194	43,018	1020
0-14	25,592	13,020	12,572	966
15-44	38,347	18,493	19,854	1074
45-79	19,834	9,919	9,915	1000
80+	897	487	410	842
Age not stated	542	275	267	971

Languages (Dominant):
Tamil, Urdu, Telugu, Kannada, Hindi

Disabled Population:

	Persons	Males	Females	%
Total Disabled	2,222	1,277	945	
In Seeing	1,054	620	434	47.43
In Speech	205	108	97	9.23
In Hearing	154	80	74	6.93
In Movement	584	356	228	26.28
Mentally	225	113	112	10.13

KILVELUR

Kilvelur C.D. Block lies in the south-western part of Nagapattinam district. It is a part of Kilvelur and Thirukkuvalai taluks. The Block is located at a distance of 11 kms. from district headquarters (Nagapattinam). There are 42 villages in the block with the total population of 66,173 persons. Area of the C.D. Block is 151.63 sq. kms. It is bounded in the north by CD Block Thirumarugal, in the south by C.D. Blocks Thalanayar and Keelaiyur, in the east by CD Blocks Nagapattinam and Keelaiyur, and in the west by district Thiruvarur. CD Block Kilvelur falls in taluk Kilvelur by 34 villages, and in taluk Thirukkuvalai by 08 villages.

Communications:

Roadways : N.H.-67: Direction- Thanjavur to Nagore, Nearest Villages- Agarakadambanur, Kurukkathi, Atthippuliyur.

Railway Station: Koothur.

River: Vellar Nadi- Nearest Villages- Okkur, Vadakarai, Kohur, Anaimangalam, Vengidangal.

Backwards Region Grants Fund: It receives Backward Region Grants.

Annual Rainfall: Average Rainfall 1230 mm.

Ground Water: Availability of the ground water in the Basin is (Information not available) H.A.M. and the utilization is (Information not available) H.A.M. It belongs to (Information not available) category. Depth to water level varies from 2 to 5 meter below the ground. Most of the wells go down in summer months, according to the Ground Water Estimation Committee.

Natural Division: Chola Nadu.

Administration

Revenue **Division:** Nagapattinam. Parliamentary Constituency: 28 Nagapattinam (SC). District: Nagapattinam. Taluk: Kilvelur, Thirukkuvalai. Assembly Constituency: 164 Kilvelur (SC). Gram Panchayat: 38.

Villages: 42 **Inhabited:** 42 **Uninhabited:** 0

Ranking	District	State	National
Area	10	343	5023
Population	10	306	4634

Sex Ratio	2	60	502
Child Sex Ratio	2	15	491
Literacy Rate	6	52	703
Density	2	273	2517
Work Participation Rate	8	89	2981

Gram Panchayats:
Aanaimangalam, Adhamangalam, Agarakkadambanur, Anagudi, Anakkudi, Ananthagudi, Athipuliyur, Eravancherry, Illuppur, Irukkai, Kakkalani, Killugudi, Kodiyalathur, Kohur, Koorathangudi, Kovilkanapoor, Kurukkathi, Kurumanangudi, Kuthur, Manallur, Manaloor, Mohanur, Okkur, Pattamangalam, Rathamangalam, Sattiyakudi, Serunallur, Sigar, Therkkupanaiyur, Thevur, Thirukannangudi, Vadakalathur, Vadakarai, Vadakkupanaiyur, Valivalam, Vandaloor, Vengidangal, Venmani.

Amenities:
Education: Primary School in 41 villages, Middle school in 14 villages, Matriculation or Secondary School in 3 villages, namely Kurukkathi, Thevur, Kilukudi.
Higher Secondary or Pre University Courses or Intermediate or Junior College in 1 village of the CD Block,, namely Thevur.
College in 0 village, Adult Literacy Center in 0 village.
Medical: Hospital in 0 village, Dispensary in 2 villages, Health Center in 1 village, Sub Center in 12 villages, Maternity and Child Welfare Center in 0 village, Community health workers in 41 villages.
The Villages having Hospital or Dispensary or Health Center are Atthippuliyur, Kodiyalathur.
Drinking Water: Tap water in 42 villages, Tank water in 5 villages, Well water in 42 villages, Tubewell in 42 villages and more than one source in 42 villages.
Bank: Banking facility in 4 villages, namely, Koothur, Thevur, Vadakkayanar, Kodiyalathur.
Credit Society in 13 villages Agricultural Credit Society in 13 Non-Agricultural Credit Society in 0 village.
Others: Power supply in 42 villages, Cinema hall in 2 villages, sport club in 0 village, Stadium or Auditorium or Community Hall in 0 village, Post Office in 25 villages.
There are 39 villages having bus facilities.
Villages with most of facilities: Koothur, Thevur Kodiyalathur.
Villages without amenities (Education):
Thenmardur..
Scheduled Castes: Out of the total population of 66173 persons, 34631 persons (52.33%) belong to Scheduled Castes.
The villages having less than 10% SC population are None..
The villages having more than 50% SC population are Vengidangal, Okkur, Vadakarai, Kohur, Kurumanangudi Eravanchery, Agarakadambanur, Vadakkuveli Thirukkannangudi Agaram, Pattamangalam, Serunallure Radhamangalam, Irukkai, Venmani, Manalur, Anakudi Vandalur, Moganur, Kilukudi, Sattiyakudi, Thenmardur Adhamangalam, Anagudi, Vadakkayanar, Terkupanaiur Kodiyalathur, Kargudi.
Sex ratio of Scheduled Caste population is 509.
Scheduled Castes Literates and Illiterates by Sex:

	Persons	Males	Females
Literate	19,067	10,968	8,099
Illiterate	15,564	6,050	9,514
Literacy rate	64.9	76.2	54.1
Graduate	136	111	25

Scheduled Castes (Dominant):
Pallan, Paraiyan etc., Kuravan etc., Chakkiliyan Generic Castes etc.
For their cultural identity please see Appendix-I
Villages without Scheduled Castes: There is 0 village without any scheduled caste population.
Scheduled Tribes: Out of the total population of 66173 persons, 50 persons (0.08%) belong to Scheduled Tribes.
The villages having less than 10% ST population are Vengidangal, Okkur, Vadakarai, Kohur, Anaimangalam Kurumanangudi, Eravanchery, Agarakadambanur Vadakkuveli, Thirukkannangudi Thirukkannangudi Agaram, Kurukkathi, Atthippuliyur Koothur, Pattamangalam, Vadakalathur, Illuppur Serunallure, Kakkalani, Thevur, Radhamangalam Irukkai, Venmani, Manalur, Anthakudi, Sikar Koorathangudi, Manalur, Anakudi, Vandalur, Moganur Kilukudi, Koilkannapur, Sattiyakudi, Thenmardur Adhamangalam, Anagudi, Vadakkayanar, Terkupanaiur Valivalam, Kodiyalathur, Kargudi.
The villages having more than 50% ST population are None.
Sex ratio of Scheduled tribe population is 520.
Scheduled Tribes Literates and Illiterates by Sex:

	Persons	Males	Females
Literate	20	8	12
Illiterate	30	16	14
Literacy rate	45.5	38.1	52.2
Graduate	0	0	0

Scheduled Tribes (Dominant):
Irular, Kaniyan etc., Sholaga, Palleyan
For their cultural identity please see Appendix-II
Villages without Scheduled Tribes: There are 38 villages without any scheduled tribe population.
Literates and Illiterates by Sex (Total Population):

	Persons	Males	Females

Literate	42,749	23,700	19,049
Illiterate	23,424	8,898	14,526
Literacy rate	74	84	65
Graduate	518	370	148

Agriculture: ***Distribution of villages according to land use:*** Out of 42 villages, Total area (in hectare) is 15163.6, out of that 78.23 percent is cultivable and 97.26 percent of the cultivable area is irrigated.

Sources of Irrigation (Hectares): Government Canal 11514.39, Private Canal 0, Well without Electricity 17.03, Well with Electricity 0, Tubewell without Electricity 0, Tubewell with Electricity 6.15, Tank 0, River 0, Lake 0, Waterfall 0, Others 0.

Villages with population of 5000 to 9999: None

Villages with population of 10000 and above: None

Distribution of Workers:

	Persons	Males	Females	WPR
Cultivators	3,465	2,634	831	11.15
Agricultural Labour	21,577	11,249	10,328	69.44
Household Industry	569	351	218	1.83
Other Workers	5,464	4,528	936	17.58
Main Workers	28,158	17,473	10,685	90.61
Marginal Workers	2,917	1,289	1,628	9.39
Total Workers	31,075	18,762	12,313	

Religion: Major Religious Communities:

	Persons	Males	Females	Sex Ratio
Hindu (94.95%)	62,830	31,074	31,756	1,022
Muslim (4.02%)	2,658	1,186	1,472	1,241
Christian (1.01%)	669	328	341	1,040
Sikh (0%)	-	-	-	-
Buddhists (0%)	-	-	-	-
Jain (0%)	-	-	-	-

Agewise Data:

	Persons	Males	Females	Sex Ratio
All ages	66,173	32,598	33,575	1030
0-14	19,244	9,612	9,632	1002
15-44	31,817	15,217	16,600	1091
45-79	13,921	7,221	6,700	928
80+	428	213	215	1009
Age not stated	763	335	428	1278

Languages (Dominant):

Tamil, Telugu, Malayalam, Kannada, Urdu

Disabled Population:

	Persons	Males	Females	%
Total Disabled	2,454	777	1,677	
In Seeing	1,745	363	1,382	71.11
In Speech	133	75	58	5.42
In Hearing	79	44	35	3.22
In Movement	361	219	142	14.71
Mentally	136	76	60	5.54

KINATHUKADAVU

Kinathukadavu C.D. Block lies in the south-western part of Coimbatore district. It is a part of Pallachi taluk. The Block is located at a distance of 42 kms. from district headquarters (Coimbatore). There are 34 villages in the block with the total population of 91,531 persons. Area of the C.D. Block is 317.56 sq. kms. It is bounded in the north by CD Blocks Mudukkarai and Sultanpet, in the south by C.D. Block Pollachi North, in the east by CD Block Sultanpet and taluk Udumalaipettai, and in the west it has common boundary with the state of Kerala.

Communications:

Roadways : N.H.-209: Direction- Pollachi to Coimbatore, Nearest Villages- Solavampalayam, Vadapudur, Kodangipal ayam, Nallattipalayam, Devarayapuram, Mettuppalayam, Mullipadi, Solanur. S.H.-19: Direction- Pollachi to Palladam, Nearest Villages- Periakalandai, Kottampatti, Kappalankarai, Sirukkalandai, Varadanur.

Railway Station: Solavampalayam, Vadapudur, Nallattipalayam.

Annual Rainfall: Average Rainfall 550 mm.

Ground Water: Availability of the ground water in the Basin is 4283.47 H.A.M. and the utilization is 4934.70 H.A.M. It belongs to Semi Critical category. Depth to water level varies from 2 to 20 meter below the ground. Most of the wells go down in summer months, according to the Ground Water Estimation Committee.

Natural Division: Kongu Nadu.

Administration

Revenue **Division:** Pollachi. Parliamentary Constituency: 21 Pollachi. District: Coimbatoe. Taluk: Pollachi.

Assembly Constituency: 123 Pollachi, 122 Kinathukadavu.

Gram Panchayat: 34.

Border Villages- (Kerala)- Nearest Village- Chokkanur.

Villages: 34 **Inhabited:** 33 **Uninhabited:** 1

Ranking	District	State	National
Area	5	154	2596
Population	4	173	3736
Sex Ratio	1	90	720
Child Sex Ratio	3	8	314
Literacy Rate	10	220	2027
Density	7	119	3656
Work Participation Rate	12	241	1212

Gram Panchayats:

Andipalayam, Arasampalayam, Chettiakkapalayam, Devanampalayam , Devarayapuram, Govindapuram, Kakkadavu, Kaniyalampalayam, Kappalankarai, Kattampatti, Kodangipalayam, Koil palayam, Kolathu palayam, Kondampatty, Kothavadi, Kurunallipalayam, Kuthiraialampalayam, Manrampalayam, Mettubavi, Mettupalayam , Mullipadi, Muthur, Nallattipalayam, Panappatti, Periakalandai,

Pottaiyandiporambu, Sholanur, Sirukkalandai, Sokkanur, Solavampalayam, Sulakkal, Vadaputhur, Vadasithur , Varadanur.

Amenities:

Education: Primary School in 33 villages, Middle school in 15 villages, Matriculation or Secondary School in 7 villages, namely Vadasithur, Chokkanur, Andipalayam, Mettuppalayam, Devanampalayam, Sirukkalandai, Varadanur.

Higher Secondary or Pre University Courses or Intermediate or Junior College in 2 villages of the CD Block,, namely Vadasithur, Andipalayam.

College in 0 village, Adult Literacy Center in 1 village.

Medical: Hospital in 1 village, Dispensary in 1 village, Health Center in 3 villages, Sub Center in 21 villages, Maternity and Child Welfare Center in 1 village, Community health workers in 5 villages.

The Villages having Hospital or Dispensary or Health Center are Vadapudur, Mettuppalayam.

Drinking Water: Tap water in 33 villages, Tank water in 1 villages, Well water in 33 villages, Tubewell in 33 villages and more than one source in 33 villages.

Bank: Banking facility in 6 villages, namely, Arasampalayam, Chokkanur, Kottampatti, Mettuppalayam Devanampalayam, Kappalankarai.

Credit Society in 13 villages Agricultural Credit Society in 11 Non-Agricultural Credit Society in 3 villages.

Others: Power supply in 33 villages, Cinema hall in 1 village, sport club in 0 village, Stadium or Auditorium or Community Hall in 0 village, Post Office in 31 villages.

There are 31 villages having bus facilities.

Villages with most of facilities: Arasampalayam Chokkanur, Kottampatti, Mettuppalayam Devanampalayam, Kappalankarai.

Villages without Amenities (Education): None..

Scheduled Castes: Out of the total population of 91531 persons, 18207 persons (19.89%) belong to Scheduled Castes.

The villages having less than 10% SC population are None..

The villages having more than 50% SC population are None.

Sex ratio of Scheduled Caste population is 511.

Scheduled Castes Literates and Illiterates by Sex:

	Persons	Males	Females
Literate	6,815	3,862	2,953
Illiterate	11,392	5,038	6,354
Literacy rate	43.4	50.2	36.8
Graduate	36	32	4

Scheduled Castes (Dominant):

Madari, Chakkiliyan, Arunthathiyar, Adi Dravida Kuravan etc.

For their cultural identity please see Appendix-I

Villages without Scheduled Castes: There is 1 village without any scheduled caste population.

Scheduled Tribes: Out of the total population of 91531 persons, 726 persons (0.79%) belong to Scheduled Tribes.

The villages having less than 10% ST population are Arasampalayam, Panapatti, Mettubavi, Vadasithur Kondampatti, Solavampalayam, Vadapudur Kuthiraiyampalayam, Pottaiyandipurambur, Chokkanur Sangarayapuram, Muthur, Kodangipalayam, Kothavadi Kurunallipalayam, Periakalandai, Kottampatti Andipalayam, Chettiakkapalayam, Nallattipalayam Devarayapuram, Govindhapuram, Sulakkal Mettuppalayam, Mullipadi, Kaniyalam Palayam Devanampalayam, Kappalankarai, Sirukkalandai Vagotham Palayam, Kakkadavu, Solanur, Varadanur.

The villages having more than 50% ST population are None.

Sex ratio of Scheduled tribe population is 489.

Scheduled Tribes Literates and Illiterates by Sex:

	Persons	Males	Females
Literate	167	95	72
Illiterate	559	276	283
Literacy rate	26.8	30.3	23.3
Graduate	0	0	0

Scheduled Tribes (Dominant):

Malasar, Kattunayakan, Maha Malasar, Mudugar etc. Irular

For their cultural identity please see Appendix-II

Villages without Scheduled Tribes: There are 22 villages without any scheduled tribe population.

Literates and Illiterates by Sex (Total Population):

	Persons	Males	Females
Literate	52,829	30,271	22,558
Illiterate	38,702	15,109	23,593
Literacy rate	65	75	55
Graduate	1,124	698	426

Agriculture: ***Distribution of villages according to land use:*** Out of 34 villages, Total area (in hectare) is 31756.8, out of that 91.96 percent is cultivable and 44.38 percent of the cultivable area is irrigated.

Sources of Irrigation (Hectares): Government Canal 1517.98, Private Canal 0, Well without Electricity 0, Well with Electricity 11350.08, Tubewell without Electricity 0, Tubewell with Electricity 0, Tank 0, River 81.92, Lake 0, Waterfall 0, Others 11.89.

Villages with population of 5000 to 9999:

Vadasithur , Solavampalayam, Sokkanur, Mettupalayam Kappalankarai.

Villages with population of 10000 and above: None

Distribution of Workers:

	Persons	Males	Females	WPR
Cultivators	13,140	8,048	5,092	25.93
Agricultural Labour	20,346	9,754	10,592	40.16
Household Industry	1,553	947	606	3.07
Other Workers	15,629	11,608	4,021	30.85
Main Workers	46,280	28,711	17,569	91.34
Marginal Workers	4,388	1,646	2,742	8.66
Total Workers	50,668	30,357	20,311	

Religion: Major Religious Communities:

	Persons	Males	Females	Sex Ratio
Hindu (97.48%)	89,227	44,295	44,932	1,014
Muslim (1.57%)	1,434	689	745	1,081
Christian (0.85%)	779	350	429	1,226
Sikh (0%)	3	2	1	500
Buddhists (0%)	2	1	1	1,000
Jain (0.01%)	7	3	4	1,333

Agewise Data:

	Persons	Males	Females	Sex Ratio
All ages	91,531	45,380	46,151	1017
0-14	20,931	10,292	10,639	1034
15-44	44,065	21,721	22,344	1029
45-79	24,107	12,111	11,996	991
80+	1,212	632	580	918
Age not stated	1,216	624	592	949

Languages (Dominant):

Tamil, Telugu, Kannada, Malayalam, Urdu

Disabled Population:

	Persons	Males	Females	%
Total Disabled	1,998	920	1,078	
In Seeing	1,073	399	674	53.7
In Speech	159	88	71	7.96
In Hearing	125	60	65	6.26
In Movement	465	274	191	23.27
Mentally	176	99	77	8.81

KODAIKANAL

Kodaikanal C.D. Block lies in the south-western part of Dindigul district. It is a part of Kodaikanal taluk. The Block is located at a distance of 105 kms. from district headquarters (Dindigul). There are 15 villages in the block with the total population of 58,203 persons. Area of the C.D. Block is 407.76 sq. kms. It is bounded in the north by CD Block Palani, in the south by district Theni, in the east by CD Blocks Palani, Reddiyarchatram, Attur and Vattalkundu, in the west by district Coimbatore, and it has common boundary with the state of Kerala on west.

Communications:

Roadways : Information not Available.

Backwards Region Grants Fund: It receives Backward Region Grants.

Annual Rainfall: Average Rainfall 813 mm.

Ground Water: Availability of the ground water in the Basin is 5326.35 H.A.M. and the utilization is 67.00 H.A.M. It belongs to Safe category. Depth to water level varies from 0 to 10 meter below the ground. Most of the wells go down in summer months, according to the Ground Water Estimation Committee.

Forest and Reserved Forest: (Palani Hills Northen Slope East RF)- Nearest Villages- Vadagounchi, Pachalur, Periyur, Thandigudi, Kamanur, Kilakkuchettipatti. (Palani Hills Northern Slope, West)- Nearest Villages- Kookal, Vilpatti. (Palani Hills Southern Slope, West)- Nearest Villages- Vilpatti, Thandigudi, Kodaikanal, Poombarai, Mannavanur, Poondi, Vellagavi, Adukkam, Kamanur, Poolathur.

Natural Division: NA.

Administration

Revenue **Division:** Kodaikanal. Parliamentary Constituency: 22 Dindigul. District: Dindigul. Taluk: Kodaikanal. Assembly Constituency: 127 Palani. Gram Panchayat: 15.

Border Villages- (Kerala)- Nearest Villages- Mannavanur, Poondi.

Villages: 15 **Inhabited:** 15 **Uninhabited:** 0

Ranking	District	State	National
Area	4	69	1885
Population	14	333	4919
Sex Ratio	13	342	3186
Child Sex Ratio	2	80	1635
Literacy Rate	3	146	1498
Density	4	29	5661
Work Participation Rate	14	365	237

Gram Panchayats:

Adukkam, Kamanur, Kilakkuchettipatti, Kookkal, Kumbaraiyur, Mannavanur, Pachalur, Periyur, Poolathur , Poombarai, Poondi, Thandigudi, Vadagounchi, Vellagavi, Vilpatti .

Amenities:

Education: Primary School in 15 villages, Middle school in 12 villages, Matriculation or Secondary School in 5 villages, namely Vilpatti, Thandigudi, Poombarai, Adukkam, Poolathur.

Higher Secondary or Pre University Courses or Intermediate or Junior College in 1 village of the CD Block,, namely Vilpatti.

College in 0 village, Adult Literacy Center in 0 village.

Medical: Hospital in 2 villages, Dispensary in 3 villages, Health Center in 5 villages, Sub Center in 10 villages, Maternity and Child Welfare Center in 4 villages, Community health workers in 14 villages.

The Villages having Hospital or Dispensary or Health Center are Thandigudi, Adukkam, Poolathur.

Drinking Water: Tap water in 15 villages, Tank water in 9 villages, Well water in 15 villages, Tubewell in 15 villages and more than one source in 15 villages.

Bank: Banking facility in 11 villages, namely, Kookal, Vilpatti, Vadagounchi, Pachalur, Thandigudi Poombarai, Mannavanur, Adukkam, Kamanur Kilakkuchettipatti, Poolathur.

Credit Society in 11 villages Agricultural Credit Society in 11 Non-Agricultural Credit Society in 0 village.

Others: Power supply in 15 villages, Cinema hall in 0 village, sport club in 1 village, Stadium or Auditorium or Community Hall in 4 villages, Post Office in 15 villages.

There are 14 villages having bus facilities.

Villages with most of facilities: Kookal, Vilpatti Vadagounchi, Pachalur, Thandigudi, Poombarai Mannavanur, Adukkam, Kamanur, Kilakkuchettipatti Poolathur.

Villages without Amenities (Education): None..

Scheduled Castes: Out of the total population of 58203 persons, 9863 persons (16.95%) belong to Scheduled Castes.

The villages having less than 10% SC population are None..

The villages having more than 50% SC population are None.

Sex ratio of Scheduled Caste population is 495.

Scheduled Castes Literates and Illiterates by Sex:

	Persons	Males	Females
Literate	4,624	2,814	1,810
Illiterate	5,239	2,166	3,073
Literacy rate	54.5	65.5	43.2
Graduate	31	22	9

Scheduled Castes (Dominant):

Chakkiliyan, Paraiyan etc., Pulayan etc., Pallan Madari

For their cultural identity please see Appendix-I

Villages without Scheduled Castes: There is 1 village without any scheduled caste population.

Scheduled Tribes: Out of the total population of 58203 persons, 1528 persons (2.63%) belong to Scheduled Tribes.

The villages having less than 10% ST population are Kookal, Vilpatti, Vadagounchi, Pachalur, Periyur Thandigudi, Kodaikanal, Poombarai, Mannavanur Poondi, Kamanur, Kilakkuchettipatti, Poolathur.

The villages having more than 50% ST population are None.

Sex ratio of Scheduled tribe population is 486.

Scheduled Tribes Literates and Illiterates by Sex:

	Persons	Males	Females
Literate	333	197	136
Illiterate	1,195	588	607
Literacy rate	26.4	30.6	22.0
Graduate	0	0	0

Scheduled Tribes (Dominant):

Palliyar, Palliyan, Paniyan, Palleyan Generic Tribes etc.

For their cultural identity please see Appendix-II

Villages without Scheduled Tribes: There are 2 villages without any scheduled tribe population.

Literates and Illiterates by Sex (Total Population):

	Persons	Males	Females
Literate	34,522	20,565	13,957
Illiterate	23,681	9,187	14,494
Literacy rate	68	79	56
Graduate	599	425	174

Agriculture: ***Distribution of villages according to land use:*** Out of 15 villages, Total area (in hectare) is 40776.69, out of that 42.76 percent is cultivable and 10.37 percent of the cultivable area is irrigated.

Sources of Irrigation (Hectares): Government Canal 665.83, Private Canal 0, Well without Electricity 0, Well with Electricity 12.3, Tubewell without Electricity 0, Tubewell with Electricity 0, Tank 0, River 96.85, Lake 0, Waterfall 0.95, Others 1033.08.

Villages with population of 5000 to 9999: Kookkal, Vilpatti , Mannavanur.

Villages with population of 10000 and above: None

Distribution of Workers:

	Persons	Males	Females	WPR
Cultivators	10,315	6,152	4,163	29.69
Agricultural Labour	16,152	8,040	8,112	46.49
Household Industry	647	274	373	1.86
Other Workers	7,627	4,776	2,851	21.95
Main Workers	32,114	18,329	13,785	92.44
Marginal Workers	2,627	913	1,714	7.56
Total Workers	34,741	19,242	15,499	

Religion: Major Religious Communities:

	Persons	Males	Females	Sex Ratio
Hindu (91.37%)	53,178	27,123	26,055	961
Muslim (1.56%)	908	461	447	970
Christian (6.19%)	3,603	1,836	1,767	962
Sikh (0%)	1	-	1	-
Buddhists (0%)	1	1	-	-
Jain (0.01%)	4	1	3	3,000

Agewise Data:

	Persons	Males	Females	Sex Ratio
All ages	58,203	29,752	28,451	956
0-14	16,418	8,288	8,130	981
15-44	29,383	14,659	14,724	1004
45-79	11,716	6,410	5,306	828
80+	354	196	158	806

Age not stated	332	199	133	668

Languages (Dominant):
Tamil, Telugu, Kannada, Malayalam, Urdu

Disabled Population:

	Persons	Males	Females	%
Total Disabled	1,648	753	895	
In Seeing	1,102	425	677	66.87
In Speech	79	48	31	4.79
In Hearing	82	39	43	4.98
In Movement	274	176	98	16.63
Mentally	111	65	46	6.74

KODAVASAL

Kodavasal C.D. Block lies in the northern part of Thiruvarur district. It is a part of Kodavasal and Nannilam taluks. The Block is located at a distance of 22 kms. from district headquarters (Thiruvarur). There are 57 villages in the block with the total population of 91,388 persons. Area of the C.D. Block is 176.25 sq. kms. It is bounded in the north by district Nagapattinam, in the south by C.D. Block Koradacherry, in the east by C.D. Blocks Nannilam and Thiruvarur, in the west by district Thanjavur and CD Block Valangaiman. CD Block Kodavasal falls in taluk Kodavasal by 50 villages, and in taluk Nannilam by 07 villages.

Communications:
Roadways : S.H.-23: Direction- Thiruvarar to Mayiladuthurai, Nearest Village- Kuthanoor.

River: Arasalar Nadi- Nearest Villages- Vadugakkudi, Vilagam, Thiruvezhimizhalai, Kadalangudi, Sarguneswarapuram, Vishnupuram, Sarabojiraja Puram, Tethiyur, Manavala Nallur, Maruthuvakkudi, Koonthalur, Puthukudi, Kadagakudy, Ayyampettai, Marudavancheri, Kuthanoor. Thirumalairajan Nadi- Nearest Villages- Marudavancheri, Kuthanoor, Nemmeli, Adambar, Adambar, Kandiramanickam, Prathaparamapuram, Melaramansethi, Seethakkmangalam, Koonthalur, Tethiyur, Manavala Nallur.

Annual Rainfall: Average Rainfall 1184 mm.

Ground Water: Availability of the ground water in the Basin is 3708.71 H.A.M. and the utilization is 3625.
25 H.A.M. It belongs to Critical category. Depth to water level varies from 2 to 10 meter below the ground. Most of the wells go down in summer months, according to the Ground Water Estimation Committee.

Natural Division: Chola Nadu.

Administration
Revenue **Division:** Thiruvarur. Parliamentary Constituency: 29 Thanjavur. District: Thiruvarur. Taluk: Kodavasal, Nannilam. Assembly Constituency: 169 Nannilam. Gram Panchayat: 49.

Villages: 57 **Inhabited:** 56 **Uninhabited:** 1

Ranking	District	State	National
Area	8	321	4599
Population	5	174	3741
Sex Ratio	10	206	1456
Child Sex Ratio	1	17	549
Literacy Rate	3	34	510
Density	8	336	2122
Work Participation Rate	3	51	4103

Gram Panchayats:
Adambar , Adip[puilyur, Alathur, Annavasal , Anniyur , Ayyampaettai, Kadagagudi, Kadalangdudi, Kandiramanickam, Kangayanagaram, Killiyur, Koonthalur, Koothanoor, Manapparavai, Manavalanallur, Manjakkudi, Maruthuvakkudi, Maruthuvancheri, Melapalaiyur, Naranamangalam, Neduncheri, Neikuppai, Nemmeli, Paravakkarai, Paruthiyur, Perulmpannaiyur, Prathalbaramapuram, Pudukkudi, Sarabojirajapuram , Sarguneswarapuram, Seethakkamangalam , Sengalipuram, Serugalathur , Serugudi, Sethinipuram, Simizhi, Suraikkayur , Thettiyur , Thilruppampuram, Thilruvizhimizhalai, Thirukkudi, Thiruvidacheri, Vadavursd, Vadugakkudi , Vayalur , Vikkirapandilyam , Vilagam, Vishnupuram.

Amenities:
Education: Primary School in 54 villages, Middle school in 19 villages, Matriculation or Secondary School in 7 villages, namely Vadamattam, Suraikkayur, Manavala Nallur, Sengalipuram, Manjakkudi, Ayyampettai, Adambar. Higher Secondary or Pre University Courses or Intermediate or Junior College in 2 villages of the CD Block,, namely Kandiramanickam, Manjakkudi.
College in 1 village, Adult Literacy Center in 0 village., College is in village, namely Manjakkudi.

Medical: Hospital in 2 villages, Dispensary in 3 villages, Health Center in 6 villages, Sub Center in 12 villages, Maternity and Child Welfare Center in 1 village, Community health workers in 55 villages.
The Villages having Hospital or Dispensary or Health Center are Thiruvezhimizhalai, Prathaparamapuram, Seethakkmangalam, Serukalathur.

Drinking Water: Tap water in 56 villages, Tank water in 9 villages, Well water in 56 villages, Tubewell in 56 villages and more than one source in 56 villages.

Bank: Banking facility in 3 villages, namely, Manavala Nallur, Thiruvidacheri, Sengalipuram.
Credit Society in 12 villages Agricultural Credit Society in 12 Non-Agricultural Credit Society in 0 village.

Others: Power supply in 56 villages, Cinema hall in 0 village, sport club in 0 village, Stadium or Auditorium or Community Hall in 0 village, Post Office in 35 villages.
There are 46 villages having bus facilities.

Villages with most of facilities: Manavala Nallur Thiruvidacheri, Sengalipuram.

Villages without amenities (Education): Annavasal, Thirukkudi..

Scheduled Castes: Out of the total population of 91388 persons, 21431 persons (23.45%) belong to Scheduled Castes. The villages having less than 10% SC population are Kadalangudi, Vishnupuram, Manavala Nallur Puliyancheri, Serukalathur, Vadaver, Simizhi.

The villages having more than 50% SC population are None.

Sex ratio of Scheduled Caste population is 497.

Scheduled Castes Literates and Illiterates by Sex:

	Persons	Males	Females
Literate	12,088	6,983	5,105
Illiterate	9,343	3,789	5,554
Literacy rate	65.9	75.8	55.9
Graduate	129	105	24

Scheduled Castes (Dominant):

Paraiyan etc., Adi Dravida, Pallan
Generic Castes etc., Chakkiliyan

For their cultural identity please see Appendix-I

Villages without Scheduled Castes: There is 1 village without any scheduled caste population.

Scheduled Tribes: Out of the total population of 91388 persons, 67 persons (0.07%) belong to Scheduled Tribes. The villages having less than 10% ST population are Vayalur, Vadamattam, Anniyur, Serukudi Thirupampuram, Suraikkayur, Alathur, Killiyur Vadugakkudi, Vilagam, Thiruvezhimizhalai Panavakarai, Kadalangudi, Sarguneswarapuram Vishnupuram, Sarabojiraja Puram, Vallaiadambar Tethiyur, Manavala Nallur, Maruthuvakkudi Koonthalur, Puthukudi, Kandiramanickam Prathaparamapuram, Melaramansethi, Seethakkmangalam Sethinipuram, Vikkirapandiyam, Puliyancheri Parithiyur, Sithadi, Adipuliyur, Serukalathur Vadaver, Thiruvidacheri, Naranamangalam, Nedunchery Neikkuppai, Perumpannaiyur, Sengalipuram Perumangalam, Annavasal, Manapparavai, Aladikaruppur Melapalaiyur, Thirukkudi, Manjakkudi, Pudukkudi Simizhi, Kadagakudy, Ayyampettai, Marudavancheri Kuthanoor, Nemmeli, Adambar, Adambar.

The villages having more than 50% ST population are None.

Sex ratio of Scheduled tribe population is 478.

Scheduled Tribes Literates and Illiterates by Sex:

	Persons	Males	Females
Literate	33	17	16
Illiterate	34	18	16
Literacy rate	62.3	65.4	59.3
Graduate	0	0	0

Scheduled Tribes (Dominant):

Malakkuravan, Malai Vedan, Irular

For their cultural identity please see Appendix-II

Villages without Scheduled Tribes: There are 52 villages without any scheduled tribe population.

Literates and Illiterates by Sex (Total Population):

	Persons	Males	Females
Literate	62,116	34,824	27,292
Illiterate	29,272	11,019	18,253
Literacy rate	77	86	68
Graduate	981	741	240

Agriculture: ***Distribution of villages according to land use:*** Out of 57 villages, Total area (in hectare) is 17625.83, out of that 78.95 percent is cultivable and 90.78 percent of the cultivable area is irrigated.

Sources of Irrigation (Hectares): Government Canal 12633.63, Private Canal 0, Well without Electricity 0, Well with Electricity 0, Tubewell without Electricity 0, Tubewell with Electricity 0, Tank 0, River 0, Lake 0, Waterfall 0, Others 0.

Villages with population of 5000 to 9999: None

Villages with population of 10000 and above: None

Distribution of Workers:

	Persons	Males	Females	WPR
Cultivators	6,001	5,029	972	15.49
Agricultural Labour	25,805	16,344	9,461	66.62
Household Industry	780	512	268	2.01
Other Workers	6,150	5,202	948	15.88
Main Workers	26,623	20,675	5,948	68.73
Marginal Workers	12,113	6,412	5,701	31.27
Total Workers	38,736	27,087	11,649	

Religion: Major Religious Communities:

	Persons	Males	Females	Sex Ratio
Hindu (87.8%)	80,237	40,447	39,790	984
Muslim (4.97%)	4,542	2,103	2,439	1,160
Christian (7.16%)	6,543	3,254	3,289	1,011
Sikh (0%)	2	1	1	1,000
Buddhists (0%)	4	2	2	1,000
Jain (0%)	1	1	-	-

Agewise Data:

	Persons	Males	Females	Sex Ratio
All ages	91,388	45,843	45,545	993
0-14	25,660	12,910	12,750	988
15-44	44,127	21,741	22,386	1030
45-79	20,226	10,481	9,745	930
80+	847	427	420	984
Age not stated	528	284	244	859

Languages (Dominant):

Tamil, Telugu, Others, Malayalam, Kannada

Disabled Population:

	Persons	Males	Females	%
Total Disabled	2,274	1,120	1,154	
In Seeing	1,286	541	745	56.55
In Speech	230	120	110	10.11
In Hearing	81	41	40	3.56
In Movement	539	347	192	23.7
Mentally	138	71	67	6.07

KODUMUDI

Kodumudi C.D. Block lies in the Central eastern part of Erode district. It is a part of Erode taluk. The Block is located at a distance of 40 kms. from district headquarters (Erode). There are 14 villages in the block with the total population of 31,480 persons. Area of the C.D. Block is 103.60 sq. kms. It is bounded in the north by district Namakkal and C.D. Block Modakurichi in the south by district Dindigul, in the east by district Karur, and in the west by CD Block Chennimalai.

Communications:

Roadways : S.H-37: Direction- Kangeyam to Arachalur, Nearest Village- Kongudayam Palayam.

Railway Station: Nanjaikolanalli.

River: Cauvery Nadi- Nearest Villages- Nanjaikolanalli, Nagamanaickenpalayam.

Annual Rainfall: Average Rainfall 789 mm.

Ground Water: Availability of the ground water in the Basin is 5943.88 H.A.M. and the utilization is 2380.38 H.A.M. It belongs to Safe category. Depth to water level varies from 2 to 5 meter below the ground. Most of the wells go down in summer months, according to the Ground Water Estimation Committee.

Natural Division: Kongu Nadu.

Administration

Revenue **Division:** Erode. Parliamentary Constituency: 17 Erode. District: Erode. Taluk: Erode. Assembly Constituency: 100 Modakkurichi. Gram Panchayat: 10.

Villages: 14 **Inhabited:** 14 **Uninhabited:** 0

Ranking	District	State	National
Area	18	369	5678
Population	20	378	6018
Sex Ratio	4	222	1508
Child Sex Ratio	19	338	5576
Literacy Rate	2	244	2152
Density	5	6	3492
Work Participation Rate	11	220	47

Gram Panchayats:

Anjur, Avudayaparai, Ayyampalayam, Elunoothimangalam, Ichipalayam, Kolathupalayam, Kondalam, Kongudayampalayam, Nanjaikolanalli, Vallipuram.

Amenities:

Education: Primary School in 13 villages, Middle school in 4 villages, Matriculation or Secondary School in 1 village, namely Ichipalayam.

Higher Secondary or Pre University Courses or Intermediate or Junior College in 1 village of the CD Block,, namely Ichipalayam.

College in 0 village, Adult Literacy Center in 0 village.

Medical: Hospital in 0 village, Dispensary in 0 village, Health Center in 2 villages, Sub Center in 6 villages, Maternity and Child Welfare Center in 1 village, Community health workers in 0 village.

Drinking Water: Tap water in 14 villages, Tank water in 0 villages, Well water in 14 villages, Tubewell in 14 villages and more than one source in 14 villages.

Bank: Banking facility in 2 villages, namely, Kolathupalayan, Ichipalayam.

Credit Society in 3 villages Agricultural Credit Society in 3 Non-Agricultural Credit Society in 0 village.

Others: Power supply in 14 villages, Cinema hall in 2 villages, sport club in 0 village, Stadium or Auditorium or Community Hall in 0 village, Post Office in 14 villages.

There are 12 villages having bus facilities.

Villages with most of facilities: Kolathupalayan Ichipalayam.

Villages without amenities (Education): Devakiammapuram..

Scheduled Castes: Out of the total population of 31480 persons, 6463 persons (20.53%) belong to Scheduled Castes. The villages having less than 10% SC population are Murungiyampalayam, Vallipuram, Ayyampalayam Devakiammapuram.

The villages having more than 50% SC population are None.

Sex ratio of Scheduled Caste population is 492.

Scheduled Castes Literates and Illiterates by Sex:

	Persons	Males	Females
Literate	3,080	1,885	1,195
Illiterate	3,383	1,399	1,984
Literacy rate	53.3	64.9	41.6
Graduate	57	41	16

Scheduled Castes (Dominant):

Chakkiliyan, Paraiyan etc., Pallan, Adi Dravida Madari

For their cultural identity please see Appendix-I

Villages without Scheduled Castes: There is 0 village without any scheduled caste population.

Scheduled Tribes: Out of the total population of 31480 persons, 24 persons (0.08%) belong to Scheduled Tribes. The villages having less than 10% ST population are Nanjaikolanalli, Kolathupalayan, Kondalam

Kongudaiyanpalayam, Murungiyampalayam, Anjur Vallipuram, Ichipalayam, Vadivullamangalam Ayyampalayam, Elumoothimangalam, Devakiammapuram Avadayaparai, Nagamanaickenpalayam.

The villages having more than 50% ST population are None.

Sex ratio of Scheduled tribe population is 667.

Scheduled Tribes Literates and Illiterates by Sex:

	Persons	Males	Females
Literate	7	2	5
Illiterate	17	6	11
Literacy rate	33.3	28.6	35.7
Graduate	0	0	0

Scheduled Tribes (Dominant):

Uraly, Irular, Kadar, Toda, Kurumans

For their cultural identity please see Appendix-II

Villages without Scheduled Tribes: There are 11 villages without any scheduled tribe population.

Literates and Illiterates by Sex (Total Population):

	Persons	Males	Females
Literate	18,356	11,025	7,331
Illiterate	13,124	4,788	8,336
Literacy rate	64	77	51
Graduate	575	424	151

Agriculture: ***Distribution of villages according to land use:*** Out of 14 villages, Total area (in hectare) is 10360.29, out of that 88.38 percent is cultivable and 61.23 percent of the cultivable area is irrigated.

Sources of Irrigation (Hectares): Government Canal 5028.15, Private Canal 0, Well without Electricity 92.93, Well with Electricity 485.35, Tubewell without Electricity 0, Tubewell with Electricity 0, Tank 0, River 0, Lake 0, Waterfall 0, Others 0.

Villages with population of 5000 to 9999: Kolathupalayam, Ichipalayam.

Villages with population of 10000 and above: None

Distribution of Workers:

	Persons	Males	Females	WPR
Cultivators	7,766	4,168	3,598	36.63
Agricultural Labour	9,976	4,525	5,451	47.05
Household Industry	483	249	234	2.28
Other Workers	2,977	2,151	826	14.04
Main Workers	20,674	10,943	9,731	97.51
Marginal Workers	528	150	378	2.49
Total Workers	21,202	11,093	10,109	

Religion: Major Religious Communities:

	Persons	Males	Females	Sex Ratio
Hindu (98.93%)	31,143	15,652	15,491	990
Muslim (0.44%)	139	62	77	1,242
Christian (0.56%)	175	88	87	989
Sikh (0%)	-	-	-	-
Buddhists (0%)	-	-	-	-
Jain (0%)	1	1	-	-

Agewise Data:

	Persons	Males	Females	Sex Ratio
All ages	31,480	15,813	15,667	991
0-14	6,130	3,230	2,900	898
15-44	14,859	7,351	7,508	1021
45-79	9,953	4,943	5,010	1014
80+	482	254	228	898
Age not stated	56	35	21	600

Languages (Dominant):

Tamil, Telugu, Kannada, Urdu, Malayalam

Disabled Population:

	Persons	Males	Females	%
Total Disabled	1,009	502	507	
In Seeing	695	314	381	68.88
In Speech	55	31	24	5.45
In Hearing	24	11	13	2.38
In Movement	163	106	57	16.15
Mentally	72	40	32	7.14

KOLATHUR

Kolathur C.D. Block lies in the north-western part of Salem district. It is a part of Mettur taluk. The Block is located at a distance of 65 kms. from district headquarters (Salem). There are 13 villages in the block with the total population of 68,836 persons. Area of the C.D. Block is 357.21 sq. kms. It is bounded in the north by district Dharmapuri, in the south and west by district Erode, in the east by C.D. Blocks Mecheri and Nangavalli.

Communications:

Roadways : S.H.-20: Direction- Bhavani to Mettur, Nearest Villages- Navappatti, Kolnaickanpatty.

River: Cauvery Nadi- Nearest Villages- Navappatti, Kolnaickanpatty, Moolakkadu, Sampalli, Palamalai, Dhinnapatty, Singirippatti, Kaveripuram.

Annual Rainfall: Average Rainfall 540 mm.

Ground Water: Availability of the ground water in the Basin is 3994.43 H.A.M. and the utilization is 3206.71 H.A.M. It belongs to Safe category. Depth to water level varies from 2 to 10 meter below the ground. Most of the wells go down in summer months, according to the Ground Water Estimation Committee.

Forest and Reserved Forest: (Palamalai RF)- Nearest Villages- Palamalai, Palamalai RF. (Pochapalli)- Nearest Villages- Pachapatti (RF), Lakkampatty, Alamarathuppatti, Kaveripuram. (Vandavasi)- Nearest Village- Kolnaickanpatty.

Natural Division: Kongu Nadu.

Administration

Revenue **Division:** Mettur. Parliamentary Constituency:

10 Dharmapuri. District: Salam. Taluk: Mettur. Assembly Constituency: 85 Mettur. Gram Panchayat: 14.

Villages: 13 **Inhabited:** 11 **Uninhabited:** 2

Ranking	**District**	**State**	**National**
Area	4	105	2225
Population	13	290	4516
Sex Ratio	14	377	5600
Child Sex Ratio	16	379	6315
Literacy Rate	17	371	4059
Density	12	100	4835
Work Participation Rate	19	332	1008

Gram Panchayats:
Alamarathupatti , Chittarapattipudur, Dinnappatti , Kannamoochi, Karungallur, Kaveripuram , Kolnaickenpatti, Lakkampatti, Moolakadu, Navappatti , Palamalai, Pannvadi, Sampalli , Singiripatti.

Amenities:

Education: Primary School in 11 villages, Middle school in 7 villages, Matriculation or Secondary School in 2 villages, namely Kolnaickanpatty, Lakkampatty.

Higher Secondary or Pre University Courses or Intermediate or Junior College in 1 village of the CD Block,, namely Kaveripuram.

College in 0 village, Adult Literacy Center in 0 village.

Medical: Hospital in 0 village, Dispensary in 0 village, Health Center in 1 village, Sub Center in 5 villages, Maternity and Child Welfare Center in 2 villages, Community health workers in 0 village.

Drinking Water: Tap water in 11 villages, Tank water in 0 villages, Well water in 11 villages, Tubewell in 11 villages and more than one source in 11 villages.

Bank: None.

Credit Society in 5 villages Agricultural Credit Society in 3 Non-Agricultural Credit Society in 5 villages.

Others: Power supply in 11 villages, Cinema hall in 0 village, sport club in 0 village, Stadium or Auditorium or Community Hall in 0 village, Post Office in 11 villages.

There are 9 villages having bus facilities.

Villages with most of facilities: None.

Villages without Amenities (Education): None..

Scheduled Castes: Out of the total population of 68836 persons, 9864 persons (14.33%) belong to Scheduled Castes.

The villages having less than 10% SC population are None..

The villages having more than 50% SC population are None.

Sex ratio of Scheduled Caste population is 484.

Scheduled Castes Literates and Illiterates by Sex:

	Persons	Males	Females
Literate	4,074	2,550	1,524
Illiterate	5,790	2,543	3,247
Literacy rate	46.4	56.4	35.8
Graduate	56	44	12

Scheduled Castes (Dominant):
Chakkiliyan, Arunthathiyar, Adi Dravida Paraiyan etc., Kuravan etc.

For their cultural identity please see Appendix-I

Villages without Scheduled Castes: There are 2 villages without any scheduled caste population.

Scheduled Tribes: Out of the total population of 68836 persons, 8359 persons (12.14%) belong to Scheduled Tribes.

The villages having less than 10% ST population are Navappatti, Kolnaickanpatty, Moolakkadu Singirippatti, Kaveripuram.

The villages having more than 50% ST population are None.

Sex ratio of Scheduled tribe population is 478.

Scheduled Tribes Literates and Illiterates by Sex:

	Persons	Males	Females
Literate	3,275	2,108	1,167
Illiterate	5,084	2,252	2,832
Literacy rate	44.2	54.7	32.8
Graduate	51	36	15

Scheduled Tribes (Dominant):
Malayali, Kondareddis, Kurumans, Sholaga Generic Tribes etc.

For their cultural identity please see Appendix-II

Villages without Scheduled Tribes: There are 2 villages without any scheduled tribe population.

Literates and Illiterates by Sex (Total Population):

	Persons	Males	Females
Literate	32,525	20,715	11,810
Illiterate	36,311	15,892	20,419
Literacy rate	53	64	41
Graduate	762	601	161

Agriculture: ***Distribution of villages according to land use:***
Out of 13 villages, Total area (in hectare) is 35721.44, out of that 32.11 percent is cultivable and 27.95 percent of the cultivable area is irrigated.

Sources of Irrigation (Hectares): Government Canal 531, Private Canal 0, Well without Electricity 58, Well with Electricity 1954.28, Tubewell without Electricity 0, Tubewell with Electricity 392, Tank 270, River 0, Lake 0, Waterfall 0, Others 0.

Villages with population of 5000 to 9999:
Dinnappatti , Alamarathupatti , Lakkampatti Navappatti.

Villages with population of 10000 and above:
Kaveripuram.

Distribution of Workers:

	Persons	Males	Females	WPR
Cultivators	13,882	8,187	5,695	35.91
Agricultural Labour	17,822	9,350	8,472	46.11
Household Industry	623	393	230	1.61
Other Workers	6,326	5,097	1,229	16.37
Main Workers	35,219	21,698	13,521	91.12
Marginal Workers	3,434	1,329	2,105	8.88
Total Workers	38,653	23,027	15,626	

Religion: Major Religious Communities:

	Persons	Males	Females	Sex Ratio
Hindu (97.03%)	66,791	35,559	31,232	878
Muslim (0.17%)	115	55	60	1,091
Christian (2.57%)	1,769	907	862	950
Sikh (0.05%)	36	25	11	440
Buddhists (0.01%)	10	6	4	667
Jain (0.01%)	5	2	3	1,500

Agewise Data:

	Persons	Males	Females	Sex Ratio
All ages	68,836	36,607	32,229	880
0-14	16,967	9,674	7,293	754
15-44	34,044	17,684	16,360	925
45-79	16,280	8,450	7,830	927
80+	748	379	369	974
Age not stated	797	420	377	898

Languages (Dominant):

Tamil, Telugu, Kannada, Marathi, Hindi

Disabled Population:

	Persons	Males	Females	%
Total Disabled	958	556	402	
In Seeing	398	210	188	41.54
In Speech	112	63	49	11.69
In Hearing	54	27	27	5.64
In Movement	293	194	99	30.58
Mentally	101	62	39	10.54

KOLIYANUR

Koliyanur C.D. Block lies in the eastern part of Viluppu ram district. It is a part of Viluppuram taluk. The taluk is located at a distance of 00 kms. from district headq uarters (Viluppuram). There are 62 villages in the block with the total population of 130,133 persons. Area of the C.D. Block is 188.52 sq. kms. It is bounded in the north by C.D. Blocks Kanai and Vikravandi, in the south by CD Blocks Thiruvennainallur and Kandamgagalam, and district Cuddalore, in the east by C.D. Block Kandamanga lam, and in the west by C.D. Block Kanai.

Communications:

Roadways : N.H .-45: Direction- Ulundurpettai to Vikravandi, Nearest Villages- Ayyankovilpatti, Thieuvamathur, Kakup pam, Poonthottam, Valudareddi, Salamedu, Kandamanadi, Kandambakkam, Pidagam, Athiyur Thiruvathy. N.H.-45 A: Direction- Viluppuram to Valavanur, Neraest Villages-Erum-ananthangal, Salaiagaram, Koliyanur, Kudumiyankuppam, Naraiyur, Panankuppam, Todandanur, Panampattu. S.H.-7: Direction- Tirukkoyilur to Viluppuram, Nearest Villages- Verattikuppam, Viluppuram, Nannadu, Thokavadi, Kondangi, Valudareddi.

Railway Station: Orukodi, Thokavadi, Kandambakkam, Sernt hanur.

River: Ponnaiyar Nadi- Nearest Villages- Kongarakontan, Thalavanur, Thiruppachanur, Sernthanur, Arasamanglam, Kappur, Maragathapuram. Pidagam, Athiyur Thiruvathy, Sittattur Tirukki, Veliyampakkam, Kavanippakkam, Pillur, Sernthanur, Thiruppachanur, Thalavanur, Kongarakontan, Arasamanglam, Thenkucchipalayam.

Backwards Region Grants Fund: It receives Backward Region Grants.

Annual Rainfall: Average Rainfall 1119 mm.

Ground Water: Availability of the ground water in the Basin is 8388.33 H.A.M. and the utilization is 10714. 94 H.A.M. It belongs to Over Expoited category. Depth to water level varies from 5 to 10 meter below the ground. Most of the wells go down in summer months, according to the Ground Water Estimation Committee.

Natural Division: Tondai Nadu.

Administration

Revenue **Division:** Villupuram. Parliamentary Constituency: 13 Villupuram (SC). District: Villupuram. Taluk: Villu puram. Assembly Constituency: 74 Villupuram, 75 Vikravandi, 73 Vanur (SC). Gram Panchayat: 48.

Villages: 62 **Inhabited:** 62 **Uninhabited:** 0

Ranking	**District**	**State**	**National**
Area	22	301	4377
Population	4	42	2499
Sex Ratio	5	209	1499
Child Sex Ratio	5	45	1026
Literacy Rate	1	120	1244
Density	22	307	1515
Work Participation Rate	1	23	3503

Gram Panchayats:

Alathur, Anangur, Arasamangalam, Ariyalur (Villupuram), Asarakuppam, Athiyur (Tiruvadi), Ayyankovilpattu, Cholaganur, Cholampundi, Dalavanur (Tiruvadi), Elangadu, Erumanthangal, Ezangadu, Kakuppam (I), Kallappattu, Kandamanadi, Kandambakkam, Kappur, Kavanippakkam, Koliyanur, Kondangi, Kuchipalaiyam (Ten), Kulathur, Malavarayanur, Maragathapuram, Melpadi, Mettupalaiyam, Nannadu, Naraiyur, Panampattu , Pananguppam, Pedagam, Pillur, Poyyapakkam, Sahadevanpettai, Salaiagaram, Salamedu, Salayampalayam , Sattipattu, Sengadu, Serndanur,

Tennamadevi, Thiruvamattur, Tiruppachchanur, Todandanur, Tokavadi, Valudureddi, Veliyambakkam, Virattikuppam.

Amenities:

Education: Primary School in 55 villages, Middle school in 23 villages, Matriculation or Secondary School in 13 villages, namely Ayyankovilpatti, Idappalayam, Verattikuppam, Salaiagaram, Koliyanur, Todandanur, V.Marudur, Valudareddi, Salamedu, Pillur, Kandamanadi, Kappur, Maragathapurm.

Higher Secondary or Pre University Courses or Intermediate or Junior College in 3 villages of the CD Block,, namely Ayyankovilpatti, Salaiagaram, Todandanur.

College in 1 village, Adult Literacy Center in 1 village., College is in village, namely Salamedu.

Medical: Hospital in 6 villages, Dispensary in 3 villages, Health Center in 5 villages, Sub Center in 7 villages, Maternity and Child Welfare Center in 9 villages, Community health workers in 9 villages.

The Villages having Hospital or Dispensary or Health Center are Thieuvamathur, Koliyanur, Panampattu, V.Marudur, Poonthottam, Sathipattu, Orukodi, Salayampalayam.

Drinking Water: Tap water in 62 villages, Tank water in 18 villages, Well water in 62 villages, Tubewell in 62 villages and more than one source in 62 villages.

Bank: Banking facility in 8 villages, namely, Koliyanur, V.Marudur, Poonthottam, Salamedu Kandamanadi, Kappur, Maragathapurm, Thiruppachanur.

Credit Society in 11 villages Agricultural Credit Society in 10 Non-Agricultural Credit Society in 4 villages.

Others: Power supply in 62 villages, Cinema hall in 1 village, sport club in 1 village, Stadium or Auditorium or Community Hall in 0 village, Post Office in 35 villages.

There are 60 villages having bus facilities.

Villages with most of facilities: Koliyanur V.Marudur, Poonthottam, Salamedu, Kappur Maragathapurm, Thiruppachanur.

Villages without amenities (Education): Alathur, Viluppuram, Pedhureddikuppam, Mazhavarayanur, Ariyalur, Sittattur Tirukki, Kongarakontan..

Scheduled Castes: Out of the total population of 130133 persons, 33809 persons (25.98%) belong to Scheduled Castes.

The villages having less than 10% SC population are Ayyankovilpatti, Idappalayam, Alathur, Kakuppam Vaduganathan Kuppam, Erumananthangal, Salaiagaram Koliyanur, Pedhureddikuppam, Todandanur, V.Marudur Poonthottam, Salamedu, Kandiyamadai Athiyur Thiruvathy, Kongarakontan, Thenkucchipalayam Mettupalayam.

The villages having more than 50% SC population are Madhirimangalam, Vedampattu, Sathipattu, Orukodi Thokavadi, Kondangi, Mazhavarayanur Sittattur Tirukki.

Sex ratio of Scheduled Caste population is 503.

Scheduled Castes Literates and Illiterates by Sex:

	Persons	Males	Females
Literate	17,656	10,308	7,348
Illiterate	16,153	6,479	9,674
Literacy rate	61.6	72.5	50.8
Graduate	474	345	129

Scheduled Castes (Dominant):

Adi Dravida, Arunthathiyar, Valluvan Generic Castes etc., Pallan

For their cultural identity please see Appendix-I

Villages without Scheduled Castes: There are 5 villages without any scheduled caste population.

Scheduled Tribes: Out of the total population of 130133 persons, 448 persons (0.34%) belong to Scheduled Tribes.

The villages having less than 10% ST population are Asarakuppam, Cholaganur, Thennamadevi Ayyankovilpatti, Thieuvamathur, Cholam Poondi Idappalayam, Alathur, Verattikuppam, Viluppuram Kakuppam, Payyapakkam, Madhirimangalam, Sengadu Vaduganathan Kuppam, Melpatti, Maharajapuram Erumananthangal, Salaiagaram, Koliyanur, Kallapattu Pedhureddikuppam, Illangadu, Kudumiyankuppam Naraiyur, Panankuppam, Todandanur, Panampattu V.Marudur, Poonthottam, Nannadu, Vedampattu Sathipattu, Orukodi, Thokavadi, Kondangi Valudareddi, Salamedu, Anangur, Nannattampalayam Mazhavarayanur, Salayampalayam, Pillur Kavanippakkam, Kolathur, Kandamanadi, Kandambakkam Kappur, Maragathapurm, Kandiyamadai, Pidagam Ariyalur, Sittattur Tirukki, Athiyur Thiruvathy Veliyampakkam, Kongarakontan, Thalavanur Thiruppachanur, Sernthanur, Arasamanglam Thenkucchipalayam, Mettupalayam.

The villages having more than 50% ST population are None.

Sex ratio of Scheduled tribe population is 487.

Scheduled Tribes Literates and Illiterates by Sex:

	Persons	Males	Females
Literate	172	99	73
Illiterate	276	131	145
Literacy rate	47.3	54.4	40.1
Graduate	0	0	0

Scheduled Tribes (Dominant):

Irular, Kattunayakan, Malakkuravan, Sholaga Generic Tribes etc.

For their cultural identity please see Appendix-II

Villages without Scheduled Tribes: There are 43 villages without any scheduled tribe population.

Literates and Illiterates by Sex (Total Population):

	Persons	Males	Females
Literate	79,269	45,844	33,425
Illiterate	50,864	19,497	31,367
Literacy rate	70	80	59
Graduate	2,968	2,028	940

Agriculture: ***Distribution of villages according to land use:*** Out of 62 villages, Total area (in hectare) is 18852.72, out of that 58.97 percent is cultivable and 79.58 percent of the cultivable area is irrigated.

Sources of Irrigation (Hectares): Government Canal 0, Private Canal 0, Well without Electricity 156.37, Well with Electricity 664.04, Tubewell without Electricity 503.12, Tubewell with Electricity 6213.49, Tank 266.76, River 0, Lake 995.08, Waterfall 48.2, Others 0.

Villages with population of 5000 to 9999: Koliyanur, Panampattu, Salamedu Salayampalayam (East).

Villages with population of 10000 and above: None

Distribution of Workers:

	Persons	Males	Females	WPR
Cultivators	9,760	7,475	2,285	16.66
Agricultural Labour	32,112	16,119	15,993	54.83
Household Industry	1,332	743	589	2.27
Other Workers	15,366	12,677	2,689	26.24
Main Workers	40,541	29,313	11,228	69.22
Marginal Workers	18,029	7,701	10,328	30.78
Total Workers	58,570	37,014	21,556	

Religion: Major Religious Communities:

	Persons	Males	Females	Sex Ratio
Hindu (96.4%)	125,449	62,970	62,479	992
Muslim (1.53%)	1,994	1,005	989	984
Christian (1.96%)	2,556	1,296	1,260	972
Sikh (0%)	3	2	1	500
Buddhists (0%)	5	3	2	667
Jain (0.06%)	74	35	39	1,114

Agewise Data:

	Persons	Males	Females	Sex Ratio
All ages	130,133	65,341	64,792	992
0-14	37,762	19,095	18,667	978
15-44	64,649	32,028	32,621	1019
45-79	26,103	13,355	12,748	955
80+	925	503	422	839
Age not stated	694	360	334	928

Languages (Dominant):
Tamil, Telugu, Urdu, Kannada, Hindi

Disabled Population:

	Persons	Males	Females	%
Total Disabled	2,930	1,696	1,234	
In Seeing	1,116	607	509	38.09
In Speech	269	140	129	9.18
In Hearing	262	136	126	8.94
In Movement	991	641	350	33.82
Mentally	292	172	120	9.97

KOLLI HILLS

Kolli Hills C.D. Block lies in the north-eastern part of Namakkal district. It is a part of Rasipuram taluk. The Block is located at a distance of 28 kms. from district headquarters Namakkal). There are 29 villages in the block with the total population of 36,852 persons. Area of the C.D. Block is 516.71 sq. kms. It is bounded in the north by C.D. Block Namagiripettai and district Salem, in the south by C.D. Block Erumaipatti, in the east by district Tiruchirappali, and in the west by C.D. Blocks Namagiripettai, Sendamangalam and Erumaipatti. CD Block Kolli Hills falls in taluk Rasipuram by 16 villages, and in taluk Namakkal by 13 villages.

Communications:

Roadways : Information not Available.

Annual Rainfall: Average Rainfall 650 mm.

Ground Water: Availability of the ground water in the Basin is 2501.90 H.A.M. and the utilization is 15.02 H.A.M. It belongs to Safe category. Depth to water level varies from 2 to 20 meter below the ground. Most of the wells go down in summer months, according to the Ground Water Estimation Committee.

Forest and Reserved Forest: (Ariyursolai RF)- Nearest Villages- Ariyursolai RF, Gundurnadu, Ariyurnadu. (Gundur)- Nearest Villages- Gundurnadu, Gundur RF. (Bailnadu North)- Nearest Villages- Bailnadu RF North, Peraikkarainadu, Bailnadu, Chitthurnadu. (Nayakkan Kombai)- Nearest Villages- Chitthurnadu, Nayakkankombai RF, Edappulinadu, Thirupulinadu. (Bailnadu)- Nearest Village- Bailnadu (R.F.) North. (Bellnadu South)- Nearest Villages- Bailandu South R.F., Peraikkarainadu, Bailnadu. (Jambuthu)- Nearest Villages- Valavanthinadu, Jambuthu RF, Thinnanurnadu, Selurnadu. (Karavallicombai)- Nearest Villages- Ariyurnadu, Valavanthinadu. (Perumalmalai)- Nearest Villages- Thirupulinadu, Perumalmalai RF, Pelappadinadu, Alathurnadu, Gunduni. (Puliansolai)- Nearest Villages- Puliansolai RF, Valappur Nadu, Devanurnadu, Selurnadu. (Sellur)- Nearest Villages- Selur, Selur Extn. RF. (Sellur Extn.)- Nearest Villages- Sellur Extn. RF, Selurnadu, Devanurnadu. (Varkur)- RF Extn. Nearest Villages- Varkur RF, Chitthurnadu, Varakkur.

Natural Division: Kongu Nadu.

Administration

Revenue **Division:** Namakkal. Parliamentary Constituency:

16 Namakkal. District: Namakkal. Taluk: Rasipuram, Namakkal. Assembly Constituency: 93 Senthamangala (ST), 92 Rasipuram (SC). Gram Panchayat: 14.

Villages: 29 **Inhabited:** 17 **Uninhabited:** 12

Ranking	**District**	**State**	**National**
Area	1	33	1431
Population	14	376	5855
Sex Ratio	7	290	2278
Child Sex Ratio	1	296	4934
Literacy Rate	14	382	4954
Density	1	1	6263
Work Participation Rate	14	383	21

Gram Panchayats:

Alathurnadu, Bailnadu, Chithurnadu, Edappulinadu, Gundaninadu, Peraikkarinadu, Thiruppulinadu, Ariyurnadu, Devanurnadu, Gundurnadu, Selurnadu, Thinnanurnadu, Valappurnadu, Valavanthinadu, .

Amenities:

Education: Primary School in 15 villages, Middle school in 5 villages, Matriculation or Secondary School in 2 villages, namely Edappulinadu, Valavanthinadu.

Higher Secondary or Pre University Courses or Intermediate or Junior College in 1 village of the CD Block,, namely Valavanthinadu.

College in 0 village, Adult Literacy Center in 0 village.

Medical: Hospital in 0 village, Dispensary in 0 village, Health Center in 2 villages, Sub Center in 1 village, Maternity and Child Welfare Center in 0 village, Community health workers in 0 village.

The Village having Hospital or Dispensary or Health Center is Edappulinadu.

Drinking Water: Tap water in 17 villages, Tank water in 0 villages, Well water in 17 villages, Tubewell in 17 villages and more than one source in 17 villages.

Bank: Banking facility in 1 villages, namely, Valavanthinadu.

Credit Society in 4 villages Agricultural Credit Society in 2 Non-Agricultural Credit Society in 3 villages.

Others: Power supply in 16 villages, Cinema hall in 0 village, sport club in 0 village, Stadium or Auditorium or Community Hall in 0 village, Post Office in 16 villages.

There are 12 villages having bus facilities.

Villages with most of facilities: Valavanthinadu.

Villages without amenities (Education):

Adakkampudukombai, Selur..

Scheduled Castes: Out of the total population of 36852 persons, 672 persons (1.82%) belong to Scheduled Castes.

The villages having less than 10% SC population are Peraikkarainadu, Bailnadu, Chitthurnadu Edappulinadu, Thirupulinadu, Pelappadinadu Alathurnadu, Gunduni, Adakkampudukombai, Gundurnadu Valappur Nadu, Ariyurnadu, Valavanthinadu Thinnanurnadu, Devanurnadu, Selur.

The villages having more than 50% SC population are None.

Sex ratio of Scheduled Caste population is 484.

Scheduled Castes Literates and Illiterates by Sex:

	Persons	Males	Females
Literate	296	187	109
Illiterate	376	160	216
Literacy rate	50.3	61.3	38.4
Graduate	12	9	3

Scheduled Castes (Dominant):

Adi Dravida, Pallan, Paraiyan etc., Arunthathiyar Kuravan etc.

For their cultural identity please see Appendix-I

Villages without Scheduled Castes: There are 21 villages without any scheduled caste population.

Scheduled Tribes: Out of the total population of 36852 persons, 35173 persons (95.44%) belong to Scheduled Tribes.

The villages having less than 10% ST population are None..

The villages having more than 50% ST population are Peraikkarainadu, Bailnadu, Chitthurnadu Edappulinadu, Thirupulinadu, Pelappadinadu Alathurnadu, Gunduni, Adakkampudukombai, Gundurnadu Valappur Nadu, Ariyurnadu, Valavanthinadu Thinnanurnadu, Devanurnadu, Selurnadu, Selur.

Sex ratio of Scheduled tribe population is 494.

Scheduled Tribes Literates and Illiterates by Sex:

	Persons	Males	Females
Literate	14,220	8,796	5,424
Illiterate	20,953	9,004	11,949
Literacy rate	46.3	56.8	35.6
Graduate	103	85	18

Scheduled Tribes (Dominant):

Malayali, Kondareddis

For their cultural identity please see Appendix-II

Villages without Scheduled Tribes: There are 12 villages without any scheduled tribe population.

Literates and Illiterates by Sex (Total Population):

	Persons	Males	Females
Literate	15,162	9,365	5,797
Illiterate	21,690	9,307	12,383
Literacy rate	47	58	36
Graduate	156	123	33

Agriculture: ***Distribution of villages according to land use:*** Out of 29 villages, Total area (in hectare) is 51671.59, out of that 31.89 percent is cultivable and 6.1 percent of the cultivable area is irrigated.

Sources of Irrigation (Hectares): Government Canal 0, Private Canal 0, Well without Electricity 0, Well with Electricity 42, Tubewell without Electricity 0, Tubewell with Electricity 0, Tank 0, River 0, Lake 0, Waterfall 0, Others 963.

Villages with population of 5000 to 9999: None

Villages with population of 10000 and above: None

Distribution of Workers:

	Persons	Males	Females	WPR
Cultivators	18,130	9,706	8,424	73.59
Agricultural Labour	5,018	1,880	3,138	20.37
Household Industry	275	142	133	1.12
Other Workers	1,214	721	493	4.93
Main Workers	23,736	12,124	11,612	96.34
Marginal Workers	901	325	576	3.66
Total Workers	24,637	12,449	12,188	

Religion: Major Religious Communities:

	Persons	Males	Females	Sex Ratio
Hindu (99.46%)	36,652	18,567	18,085	974
Muslim (0.05%)	17	7	10	1,429
Christian (0.49%)	180	97	83	856
Sikh (0%)	-	-	-	-
Buddhists (0%)	-	-	-	-
Jain (0%)	-	-	-	-

Agewise Data:

	Persons	Males	Females	Sex Ratio
All ages	36,852	18,672	18,180	974
0-14	11,030	5,682	5,348	941
15-44	17,887	8,726	9,161	1050
45-79	7,455	4,006	3,449	861
80+	236	136	100	735
Age not stated	244	122	122	1000

Languages (Dominant):

Tamil, Telugu, Malayalam, Others, Hindi

Disabled Population:

	Persons	Males	Females	%
Total Disabled	411	248	163	
In Seeing	156	91	65	37.96
In Speech	60	34	26	14.6
In Hearing	37	19	18	9
In Movement	120	81	39	29.2
Mentally	38	23	15	9.25

KOLLIDAM

Kollidam C.D. Block lies in the northern part of Nagapattinam district. It is a part of Sirkali taluk. The taluk is located at a distance of 72 kms. from district headquarters (Nagapattinam). There are 43 villages in the block with the total population of 125,367 persons. Area of the C.D. Block is 236.05 sq. kms. It is bounded in the north by district Cuddalore, in the south by C.D. Block Sirkali, in the east by the Bay of Bengal, in the west by district Cuddalore and CD Block Mayiladuthurai.

Communications:

Roadways : N.H.-45A: Direction- Chidambaram to Sirkali, Nearest Villages- Thirumailadi, Gopalasamuthiram, Puthur, Erukkur, Arasur, Olayamputhur.

Railway Station: Thirumailadi.

River: Kollidam Nadi- Nearest Villages- Alakkudi, Mahendrapalli, Kattur, Mudhalaimedu, Gopalasamuthiram, Sothiyakudi, Madhirvelur, Vadarengam, Agaraelathur.

Backwards Region Grants Fund: It receives Backward Region Grants.

Annual Rainfall: Average Rainfall 1230 mm.

Ground Water: Availability of the ground water in the Basin is 3239.28 H.A.M. and the utilization is 4145.34 H.A.M. It belongs to Over Exploited category. Depth to water level varies from 2 to 5 meter below the ground. Most of the wells go down in summer months, according to the Ground Water Estimation Committee.

Coastal Villages- (Bay of Bengal)- Nearest Villages- Kattur, Thirumullaivasal, Pudhupattinam, Thandavankulam, Vettangudi.

Natural Division: Chola Nadu.

Administration

Revenue **Division:** Mayiladuthurai. Parliamentary Constituency: 27 Chidambaram (SC). District: Nagapattinam. Taluk: Sirkali. Assembly Constituency: 160 Sirkazhi (SC). Gram Panchayat: 42.

Villages: 43 **Inhabited:** 43 **Uninhabited:** 0

Ranking	District	State	National
Area	4	245	3566
Population	5	53	2679
Sex Ratio	8	151	1087
Child Sex Ratio	9	187	3163
Literacy Rate	10	103	1134
Density	10	360	2075
Work Participation Rate	6	45	4575

Gram Panchayats:

Achalpuram, Agara elathur, Agaravattaram, Alakkudi, Alalasundaram, Alangadu, Anaikkaranchattaram, Arapakkam, Arapallam, Arasur, Edamanal, Erukkur, Gopalasamudram, Kadavasal, Kattur, Keelamathur, Kodiyampalayam, Koothiyampettai, Kunnam, Madhanam, Madhiravelur, Maharajapuram, Mahendrapalli, Mudhalaimedu, Nallanayakpuram, Odhavandhangudi, Olayamputhur, Pachaiperumal nallur, Palayapalayam, Panangudi, Pudhupattinam, Puliyanthurai, Puthur, Seeyalam, Sothiyakudi, Thandavankulam, Thirukarugavur, Thirumullaivasal, Umayalpathy, Vadarengam, Varisaipathu vadagal, Vettangudi.

Amenities:

Education: Primary School in 41 villages, Middle school in 20 villages, Matriculation or Secondary School in 5 villages, namely Pudhupattinam, Thirumailadi, Madhirvelur, Thirumullaivasal, V. Vadagal.

Higher Secondary or Pre University Courses or Intermediate or Junior College in 3 villages of the CD Block,, namely Pudhupattinam, Thirumailadi, Thirumullaivasal.

College in 0 village, Adult Literacy Center in 0 village.

Medical: Hospital in 2 villages, Dispensary in 6 villages, Health Center in 3 villages, Sub Center in 24 villages, Maternity and Child Welfare Center in 5 villages, Community health workers in 43 villages.

The Villages having Hospital or Dispensary or Health Center are Thirumailadi, Gopalasamuthiram, Puthur, Erukkur, Edamanal, Kadavasal, Arppakkam.

Drinking Water: Tap water in 43 villages, Tank water in 2 villages, Well water in 43 villages, Tubewell in 43 villages and more than one source in 43 villages.

Bank: Banking facility in 8 villages, namely, Pudhupattinam, Achalpuram, Thirumailadi Gopalasamuthiram, Puthur, Thirumullaivasal Agaraelathur, Thirukkarukavur.

Credit Society in 12 villages Agricultural Credit Society in 12 Non-Agricultural Credit Society in 1 village.

Others: Power supply in 43 villages, Cinema hall in 5 villages, sport club in 0 village, Stadium or Auditorium or Community Hall in 0 village, Post Office in 31 villages.

There are 41 villages having bus facilities.

Villages with most of facilities: Pudhupattinam Achalpuram, Thirumailadi, Gopalasamuthiram, Puthur Thirumullaivasal, Agaraelathur, Thirukkarukavur.

Villages without amenities (Education): Madhanam, Serugudi..

Scheduled Castes: Out of the total population of 125367 persons, 44855 persons (35.78%) belong to Scheduled Castes.

The villages having less than 10% SC population are None..

The villages having more than 50% SC population are Kattur, Puliyanthurai, Arappallam, Alalasundaram Agaravattaram, Kannapirandi, Pannankudi Othavanthangudi, Arasur, Pachaiperumanallur Maharajapuram, Edamanal, Umayalpathi, Arppakkam.

Sex ratio of Scheduled Caste population is 501.

Scheduled Castes Literates and Illiterates by Sex:

	Persons	Males	Females
Literate	24,108	13,788	10,320
Illiterate	20,747	8,612	12,135
Literacy rate	63.1	72.6	53.8
Graduate	326	233	93

Scheduled Castes (Dominant):

Adi Dravida, Pallan, Valluvan, Kuravan etc.

Adi Andhra

For their cultural identity please see Appendix-I

Villages without Scheduled Castes: There is 0 village without any scheduled caste population.

Scheduled Tribes: Out of the total population of 125367 persons, 413 persons (0.33%) belong to Scheduled Tribes.

The villages having less than 10% ST population are Alakkudi, Mahendrapalli, Kattur, Pudhupattinam Puliyanthurai, Arappallam, Mudhalaimedu, Achalpuram Thirumailadi, Nallanayakipuram, Alalasundaram Palayapalayam, Thandavankulam, Vettangudi Agaravattaram, Madhanam, Serugudi, Kannapirandi Pannankudi, Othavanthangudi, Koothiyempettai Gopalasamuthiram, Sothiyakudi, Madhirvelur Vadarengam, Kunnam, Puthur, Erukkur, Arasur Pachaiperumanallur, Maharajapuram, Alangadu Thirumullaivasal, Radhanallur, Edamanal, V. Vadagal Kadavasal, Umayalpathi, Arppakkam, Olayamputhur Keelmathur, Agaraelathur, Thirukkarukavur.

The villages having more than 50% ST population are None.

Sex ratio of Scheduled tribe population is 494.

Scheduled Tribes Literates and Illiterates by Sex:

	Persons	Males	Females
Literate	102	54	48
Illiterate	311	155	156
Literacy rate	31.1	31.4	30.8
Graduate	3	1	2

Scheduled Tribes (Dominant):

Irular, Adiyan, Kattunayakan, Malakkuravan Generic Tribes etc.

For their cultural identity please see Appendix-II

Villages without Scheduled Tribes: There are 33 villages without any scheduled tribe population.

Literates and Illiterates by Sex (Total Population):

	Persons	Males	Females
Literate	76,757	42,994	33,763
Illiterate	48,610	19,589	29,021
Literacy rate	70	79	62
Graduate	1,172	832	340

Agriculture: ***Distribution of villages according to land use:*** Out of 43 villages, Total area (in hectare) is 23605.3, out of that 61.17 percent is cultivable and 80.24 percent of the cultivable area is irrigated.

Sources of Irrigation (Hectares): Government Canal 11585.81, Private Canal 0, Well without Electricity 0, Well with Electricity 0, Tubewell without Electricity 0, Tubewell with Electricity 0, Tank 0, River 0, Lake 0, Waterfall 0, Others 0.

Villages with population of 5000 to 9999:
Pudupattinam , Gopalasamuthiram.

Villages with population of 10000 and above:
Thirumailadi, Thirumullaivasal.

Distribution of Workers:

	Persons	Males	Females	WPR
Cultivators	5,277	4,359	918	10.72
Agricultural Labour	30,052	18,781	11,271	61.07
Household Industry	1,187	735	452	2.41
Other Workers	12,696	10,954	1,742	25.8
Main Workers	35,482	27,029	8,453	72.1
Marginal Workers	13,730	7,800	5,930	27.9
Total Workers	49,212	34,829	14,383	

Religion: Major Religious Communities:

	Persons	Males	Females	Sex Ratio
Hindu (90.86%)	113,909	57,205	56,704	991
Muslim (7.31%)	9,163	4,252	4,911	1,155
Christian (1.76%)	2,211	1,083	1,128	1,042
Sikh (0%)	1	-	1	-
Buddhists (0%)	2	1	1	1,000
Jain (0.01%)	17	10	7	700

Agewise Data:

	Persons	Males	Females	Sex Ratio
All ages	125,367	62,583	62,784	1003
0-14	36,300	18,370	17,930	976
15-44	60,305	29,365	30,940	1054
45-79	26,889	13,890	12,999	936
80+	1,008	512	496	969
Age not stated	865	446	419	939

Languages (Dominant):
Tamil, Telugu, Kannada, Urdu, Malayalam

Disabled Population:

	Persons	Males	Females	%
Total Disabled	4,372	1,884	2,488	
In Seeing	3,015	1,051	1,964	68.96
In Speech	264	149	115	6.04
In Hearing	159	76	83	3.64
In Movement	607	410	197	13.88
Mentally	327	198	129	7.48

KOMARATCHI

Komaratchi C.D. Block lies in the south-eastern part of Cuddalore district. It is a part of Chidambaram and Kathumannarkoil taluks. The Block is located at a distance of NA kms. from district headquarters (Cuddalore). There are 84 villages in the block with the total population of 104,485 persons. Area of the C.D. Block is 176. 85 sq. kms. It is bounded in the north by C.D. Block Bhuvanagiri and Keerapalayam, in the south by CD Block Kattumannarkoil and district Nagapattinam, in the east by C.D. Block Keerapalayam and district Nagapattinam, in the west by C.D. Block Kattumannarkoil and district Ariyalur. CD Block Komaratchi falls in taluk Chidambaram by 25 villages, and in taluk Kathumannarkoil by 59 villages.

Communications:

Roadways : N.H.-45 A: Direction- Cuddalore to Sirkali, Nearest Villages- Usupoor, Chidambaram, Kadavacheri, Saliyanthope, Vallampadugai, Kezhkundalapadi, Perampatty. S.H.-24: Direction- Komarakshi to Chidambaram, Nearest Villages- Thandeswaranallur, Chidambaram, Nanjalur, Chettimuttu,Vakkaramari, Sivayam, Poolamadu, Davarthampatu.

Railway Station: Vallampadugai.

River: Kollidam Nadi- Nearest Villages- Perampatty, Janangondapattinam, Vallampadugai, Kezhkundalapadi, Erukankattupadugai, Karuppur, Nelamputtur, Mullangudi, Keezhaparuthikudi, Kanjivay, Malaparuthigudi, Elanganbur, Puliyangudi, Mannargudi (Arasur), Velloor, Chidambara Arasur.

Backwards Region Grants Fund: It receives Backward Region Grants.

Annual Rainfall: Average Rainfall 1050 mm.

Ground Water: Availability of the ground water in the Basin is 10092.92 MCM and the utilization is 2219.07 MCM. It belongs to Safe category. Depth to water level varies from 2 to 10 meter below the ground. Most of the wells go down in summer months, according to the Ground Water Estimation Committee.

Natural Division: Tondai Nadu.

Administration

Revenue **Division:** Chidambaram. Parliamentary Constituency: 27 Chidambaram (SC). District: Cuddalore. Taluk: Chidambaram, Kattumannarkoil. Assembly Constituency: 158 Chidambaram, 157 Bhuvanagiri, 159 Kattumannarkoil (SC). Gram Panchayat: 57.

Villages: 84 **Inhabited:** 84 **Uninhabited:** 0

Ranking	**District**	**State**	**National**
Area	11	320	4587
Population	9	116	3325
Sex Ratio	12	306	2567
Child Sex Ratio	1	7	304
Literacy Rate	1	30	479
Density	12	322	1866
Work Participation Rate	3	37	3878

Gram Panchayats:
Agaranallur, Alkondanatham, Athipattu, C.Thandeswaranallur, C.Vakkaramari, Chettikkattalai, Chidambara Arasur, Chidambaram (Nm), Edaiyur, Elanangoore, Elleri, Jayangkondapattanam, Kadavacheri, Karuppur, Kattukudalur, Keelparuthigudi, Keezadhangudi, Kezhakundalapadi, Komaratchi,

Koothankoil, Kuduveli Chavadi, Madarsudamani, Madarsudamani-Puliyangudi, Mannargudi (Arasur), Mannarkulakudi, Melaparuthigudi, Meyyathur, Mullangudi, Nalamputhur, Nandimangalam, Nanjalur, Nedumbur, Neyvasal, Odaiyur (Mannargudi), Parivilagam, Perampattu, Poolamedu, Puliyangudi (Mannargudi), Puthur (Therku nadu), Rudrasolai, Saliyanthoppu, Sarvarajanpettai, Sivapuri, Sivayam, Solakkur, Suravilandur, Thandesweraranallur, Thavarthampattu, Themmur, Therkumangudi, Thirunaraiyur, Usuppur , Vadakkumangudi, Vadamur, Vaiyur, Vallampadugai, Varagur, Vellur, Vennaiyur.

Amenities:

Education: Primary School in 70 villages, Middle school in 25 villages, Matriculation or Secondary School in 7 villages, namely Chidambaram, Vallampadugai, Parivilagam, Karuppur, Melavanniyur, Komarachi (West), Velloor. Higher Secondary or Pre University Courses or Intermediate or Junior College in 4 villages of the CD Block,, namely Chidambaram, Vallampadugai, Melavanniyur, Komarachi (West).

College in 0 village, Adult Literacy Center in 0 village.

Medical: Hospital in 0 village, Dispensary in 0 village, Health Center in 4 villages, Sub Center in 8 villages, Maternity and Child Welfare Center in 2 villages, Community health workers in 53 villages.

Drinking Water: Tap water in 84 villages, Tank water in 0 villages, Well water in 84 villages, Tubewell in 84 villages and more than one source in 84 villages.

Bank: Banking facility in 12 villages, namely, Usupoor, Vallampadugai, Parivilagam, Kooduveli Meiyathur, Atthipattu, Elleri, Thiruraraiyur Komarachi (West), Vennaiyur, Elanganbur Matharsoodamani.

Credit Society in 11 villages Agricultural Credit Society in 11 Non-Agricultural Credit Society in 0 village.

Others: Power supply in 84 villages, Cinema hall in 0 village, sport club in 0 village, Stadium or Auditorium or Community Hall in 0 village, Post Office in 83 villages.

There are 80 villages having bus facilities.

Villages with most of facilities: Usupoor Vallampadugai, Kooduveli, Meiyathur, Atthipattu Elleri, Thiruraraiyur, Komarachi (West), Vennaiyur Elanganbur, Matharsoodamani.

Villages without amenities (Education): Parameswaranallur, Varagur, Vakkaramari, Lakshmigudy, Sivakkam, Radhanallur, Oblangemedu, Kalikandanthan, Thorukkuzhi, Lalpet, Vanathirayanpettai, Vetchiyur, Vovval Thoppu, Kuthur..

Scheduled Castes: Out of the total population of 104485 persons, 42798 persons (40.96%) belong to Scheduled Castes. The villages having less than 10% SC population are Parameswaranallur, Janangondapattinam, Koothankoil Kezhkundalapadi, Meiyathur, Keezhaparuthikudi Lalpet, Malaparuthigudi.

The villages having more than 50% SC population are Chettimuttu, Varagur, Vakkaramari, Kattukudalore Kothangudi, Lakshmigudy, Alkondanatham, Sivakkam Radhanallur, Kothavasal, Parivilagam, Vadamur Kooduveli, Themmur, Oblangemedu, Nandhimangalam Therkumangudi, Keelavanniyur, Melavanniyur Keezhanedumboor, Melnedumbur, Kalikandanthan Neyvasal, Thorukkuzhi, Sozhakkur, Viranatham M.Kolakkudi, Thiruraraiyur, Suravilandur, Kanjivay Vetchiyur, Keelathangudi, Vovval Thoppu Pillaiyarthangal, M.Odaiyur, Kuthur Chidambara Arasur.

Sex ratio of Scheduled Caste population is 493.

Scheduled Castes Literates and Illiterates by Sex:

	Persons	Males	Females
Literate	25,923	14,988	10,935
Illiterate	16,875	6,731	10,144
Literacy rate	71.1	80.7	61.1
Graduate	1,009	715	294

Scheduled Castes (Dominant):

Adi Dravida, Paraiyan etc., Valluvan, Arunthathiyar Generic Castes etc.

For their cultural identity please see Appendix-I

Villages without Scheduled Castes: There are 3 villages without any scheduled caste population.

Scheduled Tribes: Out of the total population of 104485 persons, 675 persons (0.65%) belong to Scheduled Tribes. The villages having less than 10% ST population are Parameswaranallur, Thandeswaranallur, Usupoor Chidambaram, Nanjalur, Chettimuttu, Kadavacheri Sivapuri, Varagur, Janangondapattinam, Perampatty Saliyanthope, Koothankoil, Elanangoor, Vakkaramari Sivayam, Poolamadu, Davarthampatu, Kattukudalore Vaiyur, Agaranallur, Vallampadugai, Kezhkundalapadi Erukankattupadugai, T.Puthur, Kothangudi Lakshmigudy, Chethikattalai, Alkondanatham, Sivakkam Radhanallur, Kothavasal, Parivilagam, Vadamur Kooduveli, Themmur, Oblangemedu, Meiyathur Nandhimangalam, Atthipattu, Therkumangudi Vadakkumangudi, Karuppur, Nelamputtur, Mullangudi Keezhaparuthikudi, Keelakarai, Keelavanniyur Melavanniyur, Keezhanedumboor, Melnedumbur Kalikandanthan, Neyvasal, Thorukkuzhi, Sozhakkur Vilathur, Viranatham, Elleri, Lalpet, M.Kolakkudi

Vadakkukolagudi, Sarvarajanpettai, Thiruraraiyur Suravilandur, Komarachi (West), Kanjivay Malaparuthigudi, Vennaiyur, Elanganbur, Vetchiyur Keelathangudi, Naduthittu, Vovval Thoppu Pillaiyarthangal, Edaiyar, M.Odaiyur Matharsoodamani, Kuthur, Puliyangudi Mannargudi (Arasur), Velloor, Chidambara Arasur.

The villages having more than 50% ST population are None.

Sex ratio of Scheduled tribe population is 480.

Scheduled Tribes Literates and Illiterates by Sex:

	Persons	Males	Females
Literate	223	149	74
Illiterate	452	202	250
Literacy rate	40.3	51.9	27.8
Graduate	1	1	0

Scheduled Tribes (Dominant):

Irular, Malakkuravan, Adiyan, Kattunayakan Generic Tribes etc.

For their cultural identity please see Appendix-II

Villages without Scheduled Tribes: There are 64 villages without any scheduled tribe population.

Literates and Illiterates by Sex (Total Population):

	Persons	Males	Females
Literate	70,450	40,042	30,408
Illiterate	34,035	13,027	21,008
Literacy rate	77	86	68
Graduate	3,918	2,724	1,194

Agriculture: ***Distribution of villages according to land use:*** Out of 84 villages, Total area (in hectare) is 17685.2, out of that 78.59 percent is cultivable and 84.15 percent of the cultivable area is irrigated.

Sources of Irrigation (Hectares): Government Canal 11351.02, Private Canal 0, Well without Electricity 0, Well with Electricity 0, Tubewell without Electricity 41.74, Tubewell with Electricity 302.85, Tank 0, River 0, Lake 0, Waterfall 0, Others 0.

Villages with population of 5000 to 9999: Usuppur , Chidambaram.

Villages with population of 10000 and above: None

Distribution of Workers:

	Persons	Males	Females	WPR
Cultivators	5,957	4,968	989	13.26
Agricultural Labour	27,954	16,070	11,884	62.22
Household Industry	1,247	637	610	2.78
Other Workers	9,767	8,012	1,755	21.74
Main Workers	29,978	21,812	8,166	66.73
Marginal Workers	14,947	7,875	7,072	33.27
Total Workers	44,925	29,687	15,238	

Religion: Major Religious Communities:

	Persons	Males	Females	Sex Ratio
Hindu (94.09%)	98,314	50,022	48,292	965
Muslim (4.21%)	4,402	2,138	2,264	1,059
Christian (1.47%)	1,540	785	755	962
Sikh (0%)	-	-	-	-
Buddhists (0%)	1	1	-	-
Jain (0%)	3	-	3	-

Agewise Data:

	Persons	Males	Females	Sex Ratio
All ages	104,485	53,069	51,416	969
0-14	29,845	15,109	14,736	975
15-44	50,734	25,544	25,190	986
45-79	22,826	11,828	10,998	930
80+	831	449	382	851
Age not stated	249	139	110	791

Languages (Dominant):

Tamil, Telugu, Urdu, Malayalam, Kannada

Disabled Population:

	Persons	Males	Females	%
Total Disabled	2,903	1,296	1,607	
In Seeing	1,872	696	1,176	64.49
In Speech	206	103	103	7.1
In Hearing	110	39	71	3.79
In Movement	513	344	169	17.67
Mentally	202	114	88	6.96

KONGANAPURAM

Konganapuram C.D. Block lies in the western part of Salem district. It is a part of Edappadi taluk. The Block is located at a distance of 35 kms. from district headquarters (Salem). There are 09 villages in the block with the total population of 58,118 persons. Area of the C.D. Block is 110.43 sq. kms. It is bounded in the north by CD Block Taramangalam, in the south by CD Block Sankari, in the east by CD Block Macdonald Choultry, in the west by CD Blocks Sankari and Edappadi.

Communications:

Roadways : Information not Available.

Annual Rainfall: Average Rainfall 540 mm.

Ground Water: Availability of the ground water in the Basin is 1504.64 H.A.M. and the utilization is 2128.37 H.A.M. It belongs to Safe category. Depth to water level varies from 2 to 5 meter below the ground. Most of the wells go down in summer months, according to the Ground Water Estimation Committee.

Natural Division: Kongu Nadu.

Administration

Revenue **Division:** Sankari. Parliamentary Constituency: 15 Salem. District: Salem Taluk: Edappadi. Assembly Constituency: 86 Edappadi. Gram Panchayat: 09.

Villages: 9 **Inhabited:** 9 **Uninhabited:** 0

Ranking	District	State	National

Area	18	364	5602
Population	16	334	4923
Sex Ratio	19	383	6078
Child Sex Ratio	20	384	6337
Literacy Rate	20	375	4242
Density	8	70	2089
Work Participation Rate	6	47	643

Gram Panchayats:
Erumaipatti, Kachipalli, Konasamudram, Koranampatti, Kurumbapatti, Pudupalayam, Samudram, Thangayur, Vellalapuram.

Amenities:
Education: Primary School in 9 villages, Middle school in 7 villages, Matriculation or Secondary School in 3 villages, namely Erumaipatti, Vellalapuram, Konganapuram.
Higher Secondary or Pre University Courses or Intermediate or Junior College in 1 village of the CD Block,, namely Konganapuram.
College in 0 village, Adult Literacy Center in 0 village.
Medical: Hospital in 0 village, Dispensary in 0 village, Health Center in 2 villages, Sub Center in 4 villages, Maternity and Child Welfare Center in 0 village, Community health workers in 0 village.
Drinking Water: Tap water in 9 villages, Tank water in 0 villages, Well water in 9 villages, Tubewell in 9 villages and more than one source in 9 villages.
Bank: None.
Credit Society in 6 villages Agricultural Credit Society in 4 Non-Agricultural Credit Society in 5 villages.
Others: Power supply in 9 villages, Cinema hall in 0 village, sport club in 0 village, Stadium or Auditorium or Community Hall in 0 village, Post Office in 9 villages.
There are 9 villages having bus facilities.
Villages with most of facilities: None.
Villages without Amenities (Education): None..
Scheduled Castes: Out of the total population of 58118 persons, 5149 persons (8.86%) belong to Scheduled Castes.
The villages having less than 10% SC population are Vellalapuram, Koranampetti, Katchupalli, Konasandram Pudupalayam, Konganapuram.
The villages having more than 50% SC population are None.
Sex ratio of Scheduled Caste population is 467.

Scheduled Castes Literates and Illiterates by Sex:

	Persons	Males	Females
Literate	2,362	1,538	824
Illiterate	2,787	1,207	1,580
Literacy rate	51.5	63.2	38.3
Graduate	100	81	19

Scheduled Castes (Dominant):
Arunthathiyar, Adi Dravida, Pallan
Generic Castes etc., Kuravan etc.
For their cultural identity please see Appendix-I
Villages without Scheduled Castes: There is 0 village without any scheduled caste population.
Scheduled Tribes: Out of the total population of 58118 persons, 0 persons (0%) belong to Scheduled Tribes.
The villages having less than 10% ST population are Erumaipatti, Kurumbapatti, Vellalapuram Koranampetti, Katchupalli, Thangayur, Konasandram Pudupalayam, Konganapuram.
The villages having more than 50% ST population are None.
Villages without Scheduled Tribes: There are 9 villages without any scheduled tribe population.

Literates and Illiterates by Sex (Total Population):

	Persons	Males	Females
Literate	26,587	17,759	8,828
Illiterate	31,531	13,688	17,843
Literacy rate	52	65	37
Graduate	729	573	156

Agriculture: ***Distribution of villages according to land use:***
Out of 9 villages, Total area (in hectare) is 11043.41, out of that 92.83 percent is cultivable and 15.92 percent of the cultivable area is irrigated.
Sources of Irrigation (Hectares): Government Canal 0, Private Canal 0, Well without Electricity 175, Well with Electricity 982, Tubewell without Electricity 0, Tubewell with Electricity 289.6, Tank 0, River 0, Lake 185.9, Waterfall 0, Others 0.
Villages with population of 5000 to 9999:
Kachchippalli, Koranampatti, Kurubapatti Erumaipatti, Tangayur.
Villages with population of 10000 and above:
Vellalapuram.

Distribution of Workers:

	Persons	Males	Females	WPR
Cultivators	9,301	5,438	3,863	27.95
Agricultural Labour	12,943	5,536	7,407	38.89
Household Industry	2,320	1,476	844	6.97
Other Workers	8,716	7,138	1,578	26.19
Main Workers	28,245	17,928	10,317	84.87
Marginal Workers	5,035	1,660	3,375	15.13
Total Workers	33,280	19,588	13,692	

Religion: Major Religious Communities:

	Persons	Males	Females	Sex Ratio
Hindu (99.54%)	57,851	31,301	26,550	848
Muslim (0.17%)	97	52	45	865
Christian (0.17%)	96	47	49	1,043
Sikh (0.05%)	29	21	8	381

Buddhists (0.01%)	8	5	3	600
Jain (0%)	1	1	-	-

Agewise Data:

	Persons	Males	Females	Sex Ratio
All ages	58,118	31,447	26,671	848
0-14	14,900	8,906	5,994	673
15-44	27,718	14,720	12,998	883
45-79	14,348	7,204	7,144	992
80+	766	411	355	864
Age not stated	386	206	180	874

Languages (Dominant):
Tamil, Telugu, Urdu, Kannada, Oriya

Disabled Population:

	Persons	Males	Females	%
Total Disabled	870	565	305	
In Seeing	399	232	167	45.86
In Speech	95	71	24	10.92
In Hearing	52	38	14	5.98
In Movement	258	178	80	29.66
Mentally	66	46	20	7.59

KORADACHERI

Koradacherry C.D. Block lies in the northern part of Thiruvarur district. It is a part of Kodavasal and Nannilam taluks. The Block is located at a distance of 17 kms. from district headquarters (Thiruvarur). There are 57 villages in the block with the total population of 95,675 persons. Area of the C.D. Block is 173.54 sq. kms. It is bounded in the north by C.D. Blocks Kodavasal and Thiruvarur, in the south by CD Blocks Needamangalam and Mannargudi, in the east by CD Block Mannargudi, and in the west by CD Block Valangiman. CD Block Koradacheri falls in taluk Kodavasal by 52 villages, and taluk Nannilam by 05 villages.

Communications:

Roadways : N.H.-67: Direction- Thanjavur to Thiruvarur, Neaerest Villages- Engan, Karaiyapalaiyur, Arpar, Ayikkudi, Ammaiyappan, Agarathirunallur, Kattur, Elavangargudi, Anaivadapathi, Kavanoor, Oorgudi, Keelapalaiyur, Pathur, Viswanathapuram. S.H.-23: Direction- Nannilam to Thiruvarur, Nearest Villages- Neelakkudi,Perumpugalur, Vandampalai.

Railway Station: Melathirumathikkunnam, Kullikarai, Peruntharagudi.

River: Vettar Nadi- Nearest Villages- Pulavanallur, Manakkal, Engan, Karaiyapalaiyur, Thirukkalambur, Sellur, Arpar, Ammaiyappan, Keelapalaiyur, Pathur, Abivirutheeswaram, Kamugakudi, Viswanathapuram, Nagakkudi, Vandampalai, Vadakandam, Ayikkudi, Oorgudi, Thirukkannamangai, Agarathirunallur, Kattur. Vennar Nadi- Nearest Villages- Perumalagaram, Nalilonru, Erukkattur, Kankoduthavanitham, Melaradhanallur, Thittanimuttam, Vidayapuram, Musiriyam, Tiruvidavasal, Kalathur, Kamalapuram.

Annual Rainfall: Average Rainfall 1184 mm.

Ground Water: Availability of the ground water in the Basin is 3774.74 H.A.M. and the utilization is 2306. 95 H.A.M. It belongs to Safe category. Depth to water level varies from 2 to 10 meter below the ground. Most of the wells go down in summer months, according to the Ground Water Estimation Committee.

Natural Division: Chola Nadu.

Administration

Revenue **Division:** Thiruvarar. Parliamentary Constituency: 29 Thanjavur, 28 Nagapattinam (SC). District: Thiruvarur. Taluk: Kodavasal, Nannilam. Assembly Constituency: 169 Nannilam, 168 Thiruvarur. Gram Panchayat: 44.

Villages: 57 **Inhabited:** 57 **Uninhabited:** 0

Ranking	**District**	**State**	**National**
Area	9	324	4645
Population	4	151	3607
Sex Ratio	6	115	893
Child Sex Ratio	4	43	1011
Literacy Rate	4	42	594
Density	9	341	2017
Work Participation Rate	2	41	4168

Gram Panchayats:

Abivirutheeswaram , Agarathilrunallur, Ammaiyppan , Arasavanangadu, Athicholamangalam, Athilkkadai, Ayikukkudi, Devarkandanallur, Elaiyur, Elavangargudi, Engan, Erakattur, Kalathur, Kamalapuram, Kamukakudi, Kankoduthavanitham, Kappanamangalam, Karaiyappalaiyur , Karanur , Kattur, Keerangudi, Manakkal , Melaradhanallur, Melathilrumadhikunnam, Musiriyam , Nagagudi, Neikuppai, Paruthiyur, Pathur, Perumalagaram , Perumpugaloor , Peruntharakkudi , Sellur, Semmangudi , Thilrukkalambur, Thirukkannamangai, Thiruvidavasal, Thiyagarajapuram, Urkudi, Uthirangudi , Vadakandam, Vandampalai , Vidayapuram, Viswanathapuram.

Amenities:

Education: Primary School in 55 villages, Middle school in 22 villages, Matriculation or Secondary School in 6 villages, namely Sembangudi, Manakkal, Ammaiyappan, Kattur, Kullikarai, Peruntharagudi.

Higher Secondary or Pre University Courses or Intermediate or Junior College in 2 villages of the CD Block,, namely Sembangudi, Ammaiyappan.

College in 0 village, Adult Literacy Center in 0 village.

Medical: Hospital in 0 village, Dispensary in 0 village, Health Center in 7 villages, Sub Center in 15 villages, Maternity and Child Welfare Center in 0 village, Community health workers in 57 villages.

Drinking Water: Tap water in 57 villages, Tank water in

2 villages, Well water in 57 villages, Tubewell in 57 villages and more than one source in 57 villages.

Bank: Banking facility in 6 villages, namely, Manakkal, Elavangargudi, Kullikarai, Peruntharagudi Erukkattur, Kankoduthavanitham.

Credit Society in 13 villages Agricultural Credit Society in 13 Non-Agricultural Credit Society in 1 village.

Others: Power supply in 57 villages, Cinema hall in 2 villages, sport club in 1 village, Stadium or Auditorium or Community Hall in 0 village, Post Office in 26 villages.

There are 39 villages having bus facilities.

Villages with most of facilities: Manakkal Elavangargudi, Kullikarai, Peruntharagudi Erukkattur, Kankoduthavanitham.

Villages without amenities (Education): Deebangudi, Vidayapuram..

Scheduled Castes: Out of the total population of 95675 persons, 40003 persons (41.81%) belong to Scheduled Castes.

The villages having less than 10% SC population are None..

The villages having more than 50% SC population are Deebangudi, Keerangudi, Karaiyapalaiyur, Uttirangudi Melaadichamangalam, Anaivadapathi, Nattuvakkudi Athisolamangalam, Kamugakudi, Perumalagaram Nalilonru, Melathirumathikkunnam, Thiyagarajapuram Kamalapuram, Paruthiyur, Melaradhanallur Thittanimuttam, Vidayapuram, Nagakkudi, Neelakkudi Perumpugalur, Vandampalai, Thirupallimukkudal.

Sex ratio of Scheduled Caste population is 500.

Scheduled Castes Literates and Illiterates by Sex:

	Persons	Males	Females
Literate	21,391	12,532	8,859
Illiterate	18,612	7,482	11,130
Literacy rate	63.0	74.0	52.1
Graduate	184	153	31

Scheduled Castes (Dominant):

Paraiyan etc., Pallan, Adi Dravida, Kuravan etc. Valluvan

For their cultural identity please see Appendix-I

Villages without Scheduled Castes: There is 1 village without any scheduled caste population.

Scheduled Tribes: Out of the total population of 95675 persons, 26 persons (0.03%) belong to Scheduled Tribes.

The villages having less than 10% ST population are Sembangudi, Kappanamangalam, Arasavanangadu Deebangudi, Keerangudi, Pulavanallur, Vadakandam Manakkal, Engan, Karaiyapalaiyur, Neikuppai Keelapalaiyur, Uttirangudi, Elaiyur, Thirukkalambur Sellur, Melaadichamangalam, Arpar, Ayikkudi Ammaiyappan, Thirukkannamangai, Agarathirunallur Kattur, Elavangargudi, Anaivadapathi, Kavanoor Nattuvakkudi, Athisolamangalam, Krishnankottagam Oorgudi, Keelapalaiyur, Pathur, Abivirutheeswaram Kamugakudi, Viswanathapuram, Perumalagaram Nalilonru, Melathirumathikkunnam, Thiyagarajapuram Kullikarai, Peruntharagudi, Devarkandanallur Kamalapuram, Erukkattur, Paruthiyur Kankoduthavanitham, Melaradhanallur, Thittanimuttam Vidayapuram, Musiriyam, Tiruvidavasal, Kalathur Nagakkudi, Neelakkudi, Perumpugalur, Vandampalai Thirupallimukkudal.

The villages having more than 50% ST population are None.

Sex ratio of Scheduled tribe population is 154.

Scheduled Tribes Literates and Illiterates by Sex:

	Persons	Males	Females
Literate	6	5	1
Illiterate	20	17	3
Literacy rate	27.3	23.8	100.0
Graduate	0	0	0

Scheduled Tribes (Dominant):

Generic Tribes etc., Kattunayakan, Palleyan

For their cultural identity please see Appendix-II

Villages without Scheduled Tribes: There are 54 villages without any scheduled tribe population.

Literates and Illiterates by Sex (Total Population):

	Persons	Males	Females
Literate	63,312	35,059	28,253
Illiterate	32,363	12,548	19,815
Literacy rate	76	85	67
Graduate	1,120	833	287

Agriculture: ***Distribution of villages according to land use:*** Out of 57 villages, Total area (in hectare) is 17354.41, out of that 71.66 percent is cultivable and 95.5 percent of the cultivable area is irrigated.

Sources of Irrigation (Hectares): Government Canal 11876.38, Private Canal 0, Well without Electricity 0, Well with Electricity 0, Tubewell without Electricity 0, Tubewell with Electricity 0, Tank 0, River 0, Lake 0, Waterfall 0, Others 0.

Villages with population of 5000 to 9999: Thiruvidavasal.

Villages with population of 10000 and above: None

Distribution of Workers:

	Persons	Males	Females	WPR
Cultivators	3,946	3,302	644	9.92
Agricultural Labour	25,066	14,507	10,559	63.04
Household Industry	1,237	736	501	3.11
Other Workers	9,514	8,373	1,141	23.93
Main Workers	31,432	22,888	8,544	79.05

Marginal Workers	8,331	4,030	4,301	20.95
Total Workers	39,763	26,918	12,845	

Religion: Major Religious Communities:

	Persons	Males	Females	Sex Ratio
Hindu (89.67%)	85,796	42,862	42,934	1,002
Muslim (7.67%)	7,338	3,474	3,864	1,112
Christian (2.58%)	2,467	1,227	1,240	1,011
Sikh (0%)	4	4	-	-
Buddhists (0%)	1	-	1	-
Jain (0.05%)	50	30	20	667

Agewise Data:

	Persons	Males	Females	Sex Ratio
All ages	95,675	47,607	48,068	1010
0-14	27,331	13,786	13,545	983
15-44	46,761	22,690	24,071	1061
45-79	20,667	10,646	10,021	941
80+	723	383	340	888
Age not stated	193	102	91	892

Languages (Dominant):

Tamil, Gujarati, Telugu, Hindi, English

Disabled Population:

	Persons	Males	Females	%
Total Disabled	2,768	1,380	1,388	
In Seeing	1,425	602	823	51.48
In Speech	343	176	167	12.39
In Hearing	177	86	91	6.39
In Movement	653	428	225	23.59
Mentally	170	88	82	6.14

KOTAGIRI

Kotagiri C.D. Block lies in the north-eastern part of Nilgiris district. It is a part of Kotagiri taluk. The Block is located at a distance of 27 kms. from district headquarters (Uthagamandalam). There are 15 villages in the block with the total population of 69,728 persons. Area of the C.D. Block is 359.15 sq. kms. It is bounded in the north by district Erode, in the south by CD Block Coonoor and district Coimbatore, in the east by district Erode, and in the west by CD Block Uthagamandalam.

Communications:

Roadways : S.H.-15: Direction- Uthagamandalam to Mettuppalayam, Nearest Villages- Konavakorai, Naduhatty, Kotagiri, Jackanarai.

River: Moyar Nadi- Nearest Villages- Nilgiri Eastern Slopes RF, Hallimayar, Kallampalayam.

Annual Rainfall: Average Rainfall 1920 mm.

Ground Water: Availability of the ground water in the Basin is 2826.76 H.A.M. and the utilization is 85.95 H.A.M. It belongs to Safe category. Depth to water level varies from 0 to 10 meter below the ground. Most of the wells go down in summer months, according to the Ground Water Estimation Committee.

Forest and Reserved Forest: (Nilgiri Eastern Slope RF)- Nearest Villages- Nilgiri Eastern Slopes, Hallimayar, Jackanarai, Kallampalayam, Kodanad, Neduoula, Denad, Nandipuram, Aracode, Kadinamala, Kengarai, Konavakorai, Naduhatty, Jackanarai.

Natural Division: NA.

Administration

Revenue **Division:** Coonoor. Parliamentary Constituency: 19 Nilgiris. District: The Nilgiris. Taluk: Kotagiri. Assembly Constituency: 110 Coonoor. Gram Panchayat: 11.

Villages: 15 **Inhabited:** 15 **Uninhabited:** 0

Ranking	District	State	National
Area	3	103	2210
Population	3	287	4475
Sex Ratio	1	46	417
Child Sex Ratio	1	69	1438
Literacy Rate	3	75	905
Density	1	95	4809
Work Participation Rate	2	330	977

Gram Panchayats:

Aracode , Denad, Jackanarai, Kadinamala, Kengarai, Kodanad, Konavakkorai, Kunjupannai, Naduhatty, Nedugula, Thengamarahada .

Amenities:

Education: Primary School in 12 villages, Middle school in 9 villages, Matriculation or Secondary School in 7 villages, namely Neduoula, Denad, Kengarai, Konavakorai, Naduhatty, Kotagiri, Jackanarai.

Higher Secondary or Pre University Courses or Intermediate or Junior College in 3 villages of the CD Block,, namely Neduoula, Denad, Jackanarai.

College in 0 village, Adult Literacy Center in 2 villages.

Medical: Hospital in 2 villages, Dispensary in 0 village, Health Center in 7 villages, Sub Center in 8 villages, Maternity and Child Welfare Center in 0 village, Community health workers in 0 village.

The Villages having Hospital or Dispensary or Health Center are Kengarai, Jackanarai.

Drinking Water: Tap water in 15 villages, Tank water in 0 villages, Well water in 15 villages, Tubewell in 15 villages and more than one source in 15 villages.

Bank: Banking facility in 7 villages, namely, Kodanad, Neduoula, Denad, Kengarai, Konavakorai Naduhatty, Kotagiri.

Credit Society in 8 villages Agricultural Credit Society in 6 Non-Agricultural Credit Society in 5 villages.

Others: Power supply in 15 villages, Cinema hall in 1 village, sport club in 0 village, Stadium or Auditorium or Community Hall in 0 village, Post Office in 14 villages.

There are 11 villages having bus facilities.

Villages with most of facilities: Kodanad Neduoula, Denad, Kengarai, Konavakorai, Naduhatty Kotagiri.

Villages without amenities (Education): Nilgiri Eastern Slopes, Kokkode..

Scheduled Castes: Out of the total population of 69728 persons, 18561 persons (26.62%) belong to Scheduled Castes. The villages having less than 10% SC population are Hallimayar, Kallampalayam, Nandipuram, Aracode Kokkode.

The villages having more than 50% SC population are None.

Sex ratio of Scheduled Caste population is 505.

Scheduled Castes Literates and Illiterates by Sex:

	Persons	Males	Females
Literate	11,750	6,746	5,004
Illiterate	6,811	2,439	4,372
Literacy rate	71.3	82.9	60.0
Graduate	135	98	37

Scheduled Castes (Dominant):

Paraiyan etc., Pallan, Adi Dravida, Chakkiliyan Arunthathiyar

For their cultural identity please see Appendix-I

Villages without Scheduled Castes: There are 3 villages without any scheduled caste population.

Scheduled Tribes: Out of the total population of 69728 persons, 5939 persons (8.52%) belong to Scheduled Tribes. The villages having less than 10% ST population are Kodanad, Neduoula, Denad, Kengarai, Naduhatty Kotagiri.

The villages having more than 50% ST population are Hallimayar, Kallampalayam, Nandipuram, Aracode Kokkode, Kadinamala.

Sex ratio of Scheduled tribe population is 503.

Scheduled Tribes Literates and Illiterates by Sex:

	Persons	Males	Females
Literate	2,672	1,619	1,053
Illiterate	3,267	1,335	1,932
Literacy rate	51.8	63.4	40.4
Graduate	14	13	1

Scheduled Tribes (Dominant):

Irular, Kurumbas, Kota, Kurumans, Toda

For their cultural identity please see Appendix-II

Villages without Scheduled Tribes: There is 0 village without any scheduled tribe population.

Literates and Illiterates by Sex (Total Population):

	Persons	Males	Females
Literate	45,409	25,986	19,423
Illiterate	24,319	8,271	16,048
Literacy rate	73	85	61
Graduate	1,774	1,310	464

Agriculture: ***Distribution of villages according to land use:*** Out of 15 villages, Total area (in hectare) is 35915.15, out of that 29.12 percent is cultivable and 0.23 percent of the cultivable area is irrigated.

Sources of Irrigation (Hectares): Government Canal 24, Private Canal 0, Well without Electricity 0, Well with Electricity 0, Tubewell without Electricity 0, Tubewell with Electricity 0, Tank 0, River 0, Lake 0, Waterfall 0, Others 0.

Villages with population of 5000 to 9999: Denad, Kengarai, Konakarai, Naduhatty.

Villages with population of 10000 and above: Nedugula, Kotagiri.

Distribution of Workers:

	Persons	Males	Females	WPR
Cultivators	934	534	400	2.37
Agricultural Labour	2,056	985	1,071	5.22
Household Industry	174	87	87	0.44
Other Workers	36,221	18,935	17,286	91.97
Main Workers	37,396	19,670	17,726	94.95
Marginal Workers	1,989	871	1,118	5.05
Total Workers	39,385	20,541	18,844	

Religion: Major Religious Communities:

	Persons	Males	Females	Sex Ratio
Hindu (94.9%)	66,171	32,489	33,682	1,037
Muslim (0.93%)	650	320	330	1,031
Christian (4.09%)	2,853	1,418	1,435	1,012
Sikh (0.02%)	17	11	6	545
Buddhists (0.01%)	7	3	4	1,333
Jain (0%)	2	-	2	-

Agewise Data:

	Persons	Males	Females	Sex Ratio
All ages	69,728	34,257	35,471	1035
0-14	16,555	8,430	8,125	964
15-44	36,993	17,776	19,217	1081
45-79	15,719	7,831	7,888	1007
80+	372	162	210	1296
Age not stated	89	58	31	534

Languages (Dominant):

Tamil, Kannada, Telugu, Malayalam, Others

Disabled Population:

	Persons	Males	Females	%
Total Disabled	1,793	1,031	762	
In Seeing	1,013	581	432	56.5
In Speech	131	75	56	7.31
In Hearing	86	42	44	4.8
In Movement	425	261	164	23.7
Mentally	138	72	66	7.7

KOTTAMPATTI

Kottampatti C.D. Block lies in the north-eastern part of Madurai district. It is a part of Melur taluk. The taluk is located at a distance of 30 kms. from district headquarters (Madurai). There are 35 villages in the block with the total population of 98,022 persons. Area of the C.D. Block is 302.84 sq. kms. It is bounded in the north by district Tiruchirappalli, in the south by CD Block Melur, in the east by CD Block Melur and district Sivaganga, and in the west by district Dindigul.

Communications:

Roadways : N.H.-45 B: Direction- Melur to Tiruchirappalli, Nearest Villages- Soorapatti, Pallapatti, Kottampatty, Valaicheripatti, Pandangudi, Chockalingapuram, Ayanpandankudi, Ayyapatty, Thiruchunai, Karungalakudi, Vanjinagaram, Katchirayanpatty, Thumbaipatty.

Annual Rainfall: Average Rainfall 857 mm.

Ground Water: Availability of the ground water in the Basin is 5673.63 H.A.M. and the utilization is 1234. 79 H.A.M. It belongs to Safe category. Depth to water level varies from 2 to 10 meter below the ground. Most of the wells go down in summer months, according to the Ground Water Estimation Committee.

Natural Division: NA

Administration

Revenue **Division:** Madurai. Parliamentary Constituency: 32 Madurai. District: Madurai. Taluk: Melur. Assembly Constituency: 188 Melur. Gram Panchayat: 27.

Villages: 35 **Inhabited:** 32 **Uninhabited:** 3

Ranking	District	State	National
Area	3	168	2749
Population	3	137	3521
Sex Ratio	1	51	463
Child Sex Ratio	1	112	2115
Literacy Rate	12	268	2298
Density	9	203	3322
Work Participation Rate	7	192	2093

Gram Panchayats:

Attappatti, Ayyapatti, Boodamangalam, Chokkalingapuram, Chokkampatti, Ettimangalam, Kachirayanpatti, Kambur, Karungalakudi, Kesampatti, Kodukkampatti, Kottampatti, Kunnarampatti, Manappacheri, Melavalavu, Pallapatti, Pandankudi, Pattur, Pottapatti, Sekkipatti, Sennagarampatti, Sukkampatti, Surappatti, Thumbaipatti, Tonthilingapuram, Valaicharippatti, Vanjinagaram.

Amenities:

Education: Primary School in 30 villages, Middle school in 14 villages, Matriculation or Secondary School in 8 villages, namely Pottapatti, Kottampatty, Chockalingapuram, Kunnarampatty, Sekkipatty, Karungalakudi, Melavalavu, Thumbaipatty.

Higher Secondary or Pre University Courses or Intermediate or Junior College in 2 villages of the CD Block,, namely Kottampatty, Karungalakudi.

College in 0 village, Adult Literacy Center in 0 village.

Medical: Hospital in 0 village, Dispensary in 0 village, Health Center in 4 villages, Sub Center in 15 villages, Maternity and Child Welfare Center in 1 village, Community health workers in 28 villages.

Drinking Water: Tap water in 32 villages, Tank water in 29 villages, Well water in 32 villages, Tubewell in 32 villages and more than one source in 32 villages.

Bank: Banking facility in 14 villages, namely, Pallapatti, Kottampatty, Manappachery Chockalingapuram, Kunnarampatty, Sekkipatty Kesampatti, Karungalakudi, Vanjinagaram Katchirayanpatty, Boothamangalam, Thumbaipatty Sennagarampatty, Ettimangalam.

Credit Society in 27 villages Agricultural Credit Society in 6 Non-Agricultural Credit Society in 1 village.

Others: Power supply in 32 villages, Cinema hall in 3 villages, sport club in 14 villages, Stadium or Auditorium or Community Hall in 23 villages, Post Office in 31 villages. There are 29 villages having bus facilities.

Villages with most of facilities: Pallapatti Kottampatty, Manappachery, Chockalingapuram Kunnarampatty, Sekkipatty, Kesampatti, Karungalakudi Vanjinagaram, Katchirayanpatty, Boothamangalam Thumbaipatty, Sennagarampatty, Ettimangalam.

Villages without amenities (Education):
Dhargakudi, Ayanpandankudi..

Scheduled Castes: Out of the total population of 98022 persons, 13304 persons (13.57%) belong to Scheduled Castes. The villages having less than 10% SC population are Silambakkonepatti, Pandangudi, Chockalingapuram Ayyapatty, Kesampatti, Kambur, Thiruchunai Sukkampatty, Vanjinagaram, Pattoor.

The villages having more than 50% SC population are None.

Sex ratio of Scheduled Caste population is 501.

Scheduled Castes Literates and Illiterates by Sex:

	Persons	Males	Females
Literate	6,702	4,026	2,676
Illiterate	6,602	2,611	3,991
Literacy rate	57.7	69.7	45.9
Graduate	86	74	12

Scheduled Castes (Dominant):

Paraiyan etc., Pallan, Adi Dravida, Chakkiliyan Kuravan etc.

For their cultural identity please see Appendix-I

Villages without Scheduled Castes: There are

4 villages without any scheduled caste population.

Scheduled Tribes: Out of the total population of 98022 persons, 0 persons (0%) belong to Scheduled Tribes.

The villages having less than 10% ST population are Soorapatti, Pottapatti, Thonthilingapuram Pallapatti, Silambakkonepatti, Kottampatty Valaicheripatti, Chokkampatty, Manappachery Dhargakudi, Pandangudi, Chockalingapuram Ayanpandankudi, Ayyapatty, Kunnarampatty, Sekkipatty Kesampatti, Kambur, Thiruchunai, Karungalakudi Sukkampatty, Vanjinagaram, Katchirayanpatty, Pattoor Melavalavu, Boothamangalam, Koddukampatty, Attapatty Thumbaipatty, Sennagarampatty, Ettimangalam Kavatayampatty.

The villages having more than 50% ST population are None.

Villages without Scheduled Tribes: There are 35 villages without any scheduled tribe population.

Literates and Illiterates by Sex (Total Population):

	Persons	Males	Females
Literate	53,961	32,022	21,939
Illiterate	44,061	16,226	27,835
Literacy rate	63	76	50
Graduate	729	571	158

Agriculture: ***Distribution of villages according to land use:*** Out of 35 villages, Total area (in hectare) is 30284.68, out of that 44.6 percent is cultivable and 38.85 percent of the cultivable area is irrigated.

Sources of Irrigation (Hectares): Government Canal 900.93, Private Canal 0, Well without Electricity 205.16, Well with Electricity 562.08, Tubewell without Electricity 0, Tubewell with Electricity 8.62, Tank 3571.42, River 0, Lake 0, Waterfall 0, Others 0.

Villages with population of 5000 to 9999: Chokkalingapuram, Kambur, Karungalakudi Kachirayanpatti, Thumbaipatti.

Villages with population of 10000 and above: None

Distribution of Workers:

	Persons	Males	Females	WPR
Cultivators	14,193	8,528	5,665	28.52
Agricultural Labour	24,579	12,178	12,401	49.39
Household Industry	1,551	620	931	3.12
Other Workers	9,442	7,026	2,416	18.97
Main Workers	38,012	23,135	14,877	76.38
Marginal Workers	11,753	5,217	6,536	23.62
Total Workers	49,765	28,352	21,413	

Religion: Major Religious Communities:

	Persons	Males	Females	Sex Ratio
Hindu (91.16%)	89,356	44,051	45,305	1,028
Muslim (8.52%)	8,351	4,052	4,299	1,061
Christian (0.24%)	233	107	126	1,178
Sikh (0%)	3	1	2	2,000
Buddhists (0%)	-	-	-	-
Jain (0.01%)	11	4	7	1,750

Agewise Data:

	Persons	Males	Females	Sex Ratio
All ages	98,022	48,248	49,774	1032
0-14	27,787	14,058	13,729	977
15-44	46,047	22,109	23,938	1083
45-79	22,092	11,023	11,069	1004
80+	749	374	375	1003
Age not stated	1,347	684	663	969

Languages (Dominant):
Tamil, Telugu, Hindi, Kannada, Urdu

Disabled Population:

	Persons	Males	Females	%
Total Disabled	2,708	1,374	1,334	
In Seeing	1,845	879	966	68.13
In Speech	180	99	81	6.65
In Hearing	81	35	46	2.99
In Movement	387	226	161	14.29
Mentally	215	135	80	7.94

KOTTUR

Kottur C.D. Block lies in the central east part of Thiruvarur district. It is a part of Needamangalam and Mannargudi taluks. The Block is located at a distance of NA kms. from district headquarters (Thiruvarur). There are 56 villages in the block with the total population of 103,867 persons. Area of the C.D. Block is 267.48 sq. kms. It is bounded in the north by C.D. Block Mannargudi, in the south by CD Block Muttupet, in the east by CD Blocks Muttupet and Thiruthuraipoondi, and in the west by district Thanjavur. CD Block Kottur falls Needamangalam by 05 villages, and in taluk Mannargudi by 51 villages.

Communications:

Roadways : Information not Available.

Railway Station: Marangudi.

Annual Rainfall: Average Rainfall 1184 mm.

Ground Water: Availability of the ground water in the Basin is 3943.16 H.A.M. and the utilization is 1669. 57 H.A.M. It belongs to Safe category. Depth to water level varies from 2 to 10 meter below the ground. Most of the wells go down in summer months, according to the Ground Water Estimation Committee.

Natural Division: Chola Nadu.

Administration

Revenue **Division:** Mannargudi. Parliamentary Constituency: 28 Nagapattinam (SC). District: Thiruvarur. Taluk: Nedamangalam, Mannargudi. Assembly Constituency: 168 Thiruvarur, 166 Thiruthuraipoondi, 167 Mannargudi. Gram Panchayat: 49.

Villages: 56 **Inhabited:** 56 **Uninhabited:** 0

Ranking	District	State	National
Area	2	211	3139
Population	3	118	3342
Sex Ratio	3	72	583
Child Sex Ratio	3	37	916
Literacy Rate	5	56	745
Density	1	240	2811
Work Participation Rate	9	122	2580

Gram Panchayats:

Adichapuram, Akkaraikottagam, Alathur, Cheri, Devadanam, Elavanur, Irulneeki, Kalappal , Karuupukilai, Keluvather , Kottar, Kottuthottam, Kulamanickam, Kulamanickam , Kummaththidal, Kunniyur, Kuruchi, Kuruchimoolai, Mannukkumundam , Mavattukkudo, Mazhavaranellur , Melanatham, Nallur, Nemmeli, Nochiyur, Orathur, Paingattur, Palaiyusdr, Palayakottaiparaapuram, Pallivarthy, Panaiyur , Perungavalandan , Puzhuthikudi, Radhanarasimmapuram, Renganathapuram, Sendamangalam, Sendangudi, Serugalathur, Seruvamani, Sithamalli, Thenparai, Therkuunallur, Thirukkalar, Thirumakkottai , Thiruvellikkaval, Vallur, Vattar, Vikrapandian, Vsenkathangudi.

Amenities:

Education: Primary School in 54 villages, Middle school in 24 villages, Matriculation or Secondary School in 11 villages, namely Kottur, Radhavarshnapuram, Thirumakkottai, Thirumakkottai Ii, Melanatham, Thenpari, Palaiyur, Perugavazhndhan I, Perugavalndan Ii, Sithamalli, Puthagaram.

Higher Secondary or Pre University Courses or Intermediate or Junior College in 5 villages of the CD Block,, namely Kottur, Thirumakkottai, Thirumakkottai Ii, Melanatham, Perugavazhndhan I.

College in 0 village, Adult Literacy Center in 0 village.

Medical: Hospital in 0 village, Dispensary in 1 village, Health Center in 4 villages, Sub Center in 15 villages, Maternity and Child Welfare Center in 3 villages, Community health workers in 56 villages.

The Village having Hospital or Dispensary or Health Center is Naruvalikalappal.

Drinking Water: Tap water in 56 villages, Tank water in 1 villages, Well water in 56 villages, Tubewell in 56 villages and more than one source in 56 villages.

Bank: Banking facility in 13 villages, namely, Marangudi, Malavaraya Nallur, Adichapuram, Kottur Vattar, Thirumakkottai, Thirumakkottai Ii Melanatham, Kurichimoolai Ii, Palaiyur Naruvalikalappal, Perugavazhndhan I Perugavalndan Ii.

Credit Society in 27 villages Agricultural Credit Society in 26 Non-Agricultural Credit Society in 3 villages.

Others: Power supply in 56 villages, Cinema hall in 3 villages, sport club in 0 village, Stadium or Auditorium or Community Hall in 0 village, Post Office in 45 villages.

There are 54 villages having bus facilities.

Villages with most of facilities: Marangudi Malavaraya Nallur, Adichapuram, Kottur, Vattar Thirumakkottai, Thirumakkottai Ii, Melanatham Kurichimoolai Ii, Palaiyur, Naruvalikalappal Perugavazhndhan I, Perugavalndan Ii.

Villages without amenities (Education): Nokkaunkkadam, Kotturthottam..

Scheduled Castes: Out of the total population of 103867 persons, 46098 persons (44.38%) belong to Scheduled Castes. The villages having less than 10% SC population are Kotturthottam, Radhavarshnapuram, Thirumakkottai Ii Thenpari.

The villages having more than 50% SC population are Kulamanikam, Mavattagudi, Malavaraya Nallur Kunniyur, Pallivarthy, Sendamangalam, Nemeli Kandamangalam, Panaiyur, Nokkaunkkadam, Erulneeki Puluthukudi, Alathur, Vattar, Paingathur, Orathur Akkaraikottagam, Thilrukkalar, Kurichimoolai I Narayanapuram Kalappal, Venkathangudi, Keluvathur Manangathan Kottagam, Therkkunanalur Naruvalikalappal, Kulamanickam, Serūgalathur Sithamalli.

Sex ratio of Scheduled Caste population is 504.

Scheduled Castes Literates and Illiterates by Sex:

	Persons	Males	Females
Literate	26,013	14,871	11,142
Illiterate	20,085	7,972	12,113
Literacy rate	65.6	76.0	55.5
Graduate	264	209	55

Scheduled Castes (Dominant):

Pallan, Paraiyan etc., Kuravan etc., Koliyan, Domban

For their cultural identity please see Appendix-I

Villages without Scheduled Castes: There is 0 village without any scheduled caste population.

Scheduled Tribes: Out of the total population of 103867 persons, 253 persons (0.24%) belong to Scheduled Tribes. The villages having less than 10% ST population are Senthangudi, Kulamanikam, Mavattagudi, Seruvamani Marangudi, Malavaraya Nallur, Kunniyur, Pallivarthy Vikkirapandiyam, Sendamangalam, Nemeli, Adichapuram Kandamangalam, Renganathapuram, Panaiyur Nokkaunkkadam, Kottur, Erulneeki, Puluthukudi Alathur, Karuppukilar, Vattar, Paingathur, Kuruchi

Radhavarshnapuram, Vallur, Thirumakkottai
Thirumakkottai Ii, Melanatham, Thenpari, Orathur
Nallur, Akkaraikottagam, Thilrukkalar
Kurichimoolai I, Kurichimoolai Ii
Narayanapuram Kalappal, Venkathangudi, Keluvathur
Manangathan Kottagam, Palaiyur
Palayakottai Parasapuram, Elavanur
Peruvidaimarudhur, Therkkunanalur, Naruvalikalappal
Kulamanickam, Devadhanam, Mannukkumundan
Perugavazhndhan I, Perugavalndan Ii, Serugalathur
Sithamalli, Nochiyur, Puthagaram.

The villages having more than 50% ST population are None.

Sex ratio of Scheduled tribe population is 514.

Scheduled Tribes Literates and Illiterates by Sex:

	Persons	Males	Females
Literate	67	37	30
Illiterate	186	86	100
Literacy rate	32.1	36.6	27.8
Graduate	0	0	0

Scheduled Tribes (Dominant):

Adiyan, Malakkuravan, Malai Vedan, Kattunayakan Generic Tribes etc.

For their cultural identity please see Appendix-II

Villages without Scheduled Tribes: There are 47 villages without any scheduled tribe population.

Literates and Illiterates by Sex (Total Population):

	Persons	Males	Females
Literate	67,768	37,712	30,056
Illiterate	36,099	13,615	22,484
Literacy rate	74	84	65
Graduate	798	588	210

Agriculture: ***Distribution of villages according to land use:*** Out of 56 villages, Total area (in hectare) is 26748.01, out of that 78.61 percent is cultivable and 88.42 percent of the cultivable area is irrigated.

Sources of Irrigation (Hectares): Government Canal 17856.64, Private Canal 0, Well without Electricity 0, Well with Electricity 0, Tubewell without Electricity 0, Tubewell with Electricity 735.36, Tank 0, River 0, Lake 0, Waterfall 0, Others 0.

Villages with population of 5000 to 9999: None

Villages with population of 10000 and above: None

Distribution of Workers:

	Persons	Males	Females	WPR
Cultivators	8,685	6,488	2,197	16.96
Agricultural Labour	34,631	17,928	16,703	67.61
Household Industry	849	429	420	1.66
Other Workers	7,055	5,729	1,326	13.77
Main Workers	42,381	27,197	15,184	82.74
Marginal Workers	8,839	3,377	5,462	17.26
Total Workers	51,220	30,574	20,646	

Religion: Major Religious Communities:

	Persons	Males	Females	Sex Ratio
Hindu (94.42%)	98,073	48,511	49,562	1,022
Muslim (1.74%)	1,805	875	930	1,063
Christian (3.76%)	3,903	1,900	2,003	1,054
Sikh (0%)	-	-	-	-
Buddhists (0%)	-	-	-	-
Jain (0%)	-	-	-	-

Agewise Data:

	Persons	Males	Females	Sex Ratio
All ages	103,867	51,327	52,540	1024
0-14	28,278	14,211	14,067	990
15-44	51,261	24,753	26,508	1071
45-79	23,437	11,919	11,518	966
80+	788	391	397	1015
Age not stated	103	53	50	943

Languages (Dominant):

Tamil, Telugu, Marathi, Hindi, Malayalam

Disabled Population:

	Persons	Males	Females	%
Total Disabled	3,021	1,346	1,675	
In Seeing	1,935	718	1,217	64.05
In Speech	193	106	87	6.39
In Hearing	131	69	62	4.34
In Movement	562	336	226	18.6
Mentally	200	117	83	6.62

KOVILPATTI

Kovilpatti C.D. Block lies in the northern part of Thoothukkudi district. It is a part of Kovilpatti and Ettayapuram taluks. The Block is located at a distance of 60 kms. from district headquarters (Thuthookkudi). There are 43 villages in the block with the total population of 92,392 persons. Area of the C.D. Block is 396.16 sq. kms. It is bounded in the north by districts Virudhunagar and Tirunelveli, in the south and west by CD Block Kayathar, in the east by CD Blocks Pudur and Vilathikulam. CD Block Kovilpatti falls in taluk Kovilpatti by 19 villages, and in taluk Ettayapuram by 24 villages.

Communications:

Roadways : N.H.-7: Direction- Kayathar to Kovilpatti, Nearest Villages- Alampatti, Inam Maniyachi, Manthithoppu, Nallathenputhur, Idaiseval, Villiseri.
N.H.-45 B: Direction- Aruppukkottai to Thoothukkudi, Nearest Villages- Sindalakkarai, Melae
ral, Keelaeral, Manjayanayakkanpatti, Ethilappanaickenpatti,
S.H.-44: Direction- Kalugumalai to Vilattikulam, Nearest Villages- Thittankulam, Nallathenputhur, Chidambarapuram, Mudukkummendanpatti, Kumarakiri, Ilambuvanam, Nakkala Kaltai.

Railway Station: Kovilpatti.

Annual Rainfall: Average Rainfall 661 mm.

Ground Water: Availability of the ground water in the Basin is 14.02 MCM and the utilization is 16.82 MCM. It belongs to Over Expoited category. Depth to water level varies from 2 to 10 meter below the ground. Most of the wells go down in summer months, according to the Ground Water Estimation Committee.

Natural Division: NA

Administration

Revenue **Division:** Kovilpatti. Parliamentary Constituency: 36 Thoothukkudi. District: Thoothukkudi. Taluk: Kovilp atti, Ettayapuram. Assembly Constituency: 218 Kovilpatti, 213 Vilathikulam. Gram Panchayat: 38.

Villages: 43 **Inhabited:** 43 **Uninhabited:** 0

Ranking	District	State	National
Area	5	77	1952
Population	3	169	3708
Sex Ratio	9	39	393
Child Sex Ratio	4	76	1583
Literacy Rate	9	59	761
Density	4	169	4282
Work Participation Rate	6	299	1682

Gram Panchayats:

Avalnatham, Ayyakottaiyur, Chattrapatti, Chidambarapuram, Chinnamalai kundru, Chinnamalaikundru, Duraiyoor , Idaiseval , Ilambuvanam, Inam Maniyachi, Irachi, Kadalaiyur, Kila Eral, Kilalipatti, Kodukkamparai, Kulasekarapuram, Lingampatti , Manjanaickenpatti, Manthithoppu, Meenakshipuram, Mela Eral, Mooppanpatti, Mudukkumeendanpatti, Nalattinputhur, Pandavarmangalam, Semmaputhur, Sindalakkarai , Sivandipatti, Suraikkaipatti, T.Shanmugapuram, Thonugal, Tittangulam, Urulaikudi, Utthupatti, Varadampatti, Villiseri.

Amenities:

Education: Primary School in 41 villages, Middle school in 17 villages, Matriculation or Secondary School in 8 villages, namely Inam Maniyachi, Pandavarmangalm, Nallathenputhur, Mudukkummendanpatti, Kadalaiyur, Kumarakiri, Ilambuvanam, Erachi.

Higher Secondary or Pre University Courses or Intermediate or Junior College in 3 villages of the CD Block,, namely Pandavarmangalm, Mudukkummendanpatti, Kumarakiri.

College in 2 villages, Adult Literacy Center in 0 village., Colleges are in villages, namely Alampatti, Nallathenputhur.

Medical: Hospital in 0 village, Dispensary in 2 villages, Health Center in 2 villages, Sub Center in 17 villages, Maternity and Child Welfare Center in 7 villages, Community health workers in 35 villages.

The Villages having Hospital or Dispensary or Health Center are Manthithoppu, Chinnamalai Kundu, Keelaeral.

Drinking Water: Tap water in 43 villages, Tank water in 2 villages, Well water in 42 villages, Tubewell in 42 villages and more than one source in 43 villages.

Bank: Banking facility in 15 villages, namely, Inam Maniyachi, Avelnetham, Lingampatti Nallathenputhur, Mudukkummendanpatti, Idaiseval Uthupatti, Duraiyoor, Kadalaiyur, Meenachipuram Sindalakkarai, Ilambuvanam, Erachi, T.Shunmugapuram Keelaeral.

Credit Society in 7 villages Agricultural Credit Society in 5 Non-Agricultural Credit Society in 2 villages.

Others: Power supply in 42 villages, Cinema hall in 0 village, sport club in 0 village, Stadium or Auditorium or Community Hall in 2 villages, Post Office in 40 villages.

There are 38 villages having bus facilities.

Villages with most of facilities: Inam Maniyachi Avelnetham, Lingampatti, Mudukkummendanpatti Idaiseval, Uthupatti, Duraiyoor, Kadalaiyur Meenachipuram, Sindalakkarai, Ilambuvanam, Erachi T.Shunmugapuram, Keelaeral.

Villages without amenities (Education):

Kangankulam, Ranasooraettunaickan Patti..

Scheduled Castes: Out of the total population of 92392 persons, 21945 persons (23.75%) belong to Scheduled Castes.

The villages having less than 10% SC population are Inam Maniyachi, Kovilpatti, Kadalaiyur, Kumarakiri Nakkala Kaltai, Suraikkarpatti, Arunachalapuram.

The villages having more than 50% SC population are Urulaikudi, Chidambarapuram Ranasooraettunaickan Patti, Valampathi, Melaeral Athikeenar.

Sex ratio of Scheduled Caste population is 512.

Scheduled Castes Literates and Illiterates by Sex:

	Persons	Males	Females
Literate	12,842	7,371	5,471
Illiterate	9,103	3,333	5,770
Literacy rate	66.0	78.0	54.7
Graduate	389	264	125

Scheduled Castes (Dominant):

Pallan, Paraiyan etc., Chakkiliyan, Arunthathiyar Kudumban

For their cultural identity please see Appendix-I

Villages without Scheduled Castes: There are 2 villages without any scheduled caste population.

Scheduled Tribes: Out of the total population of 92392

persons, 278 persons (0.3%) belong to Scheduled Tribes. The villages having less than 10% ST population are Thonugal, Kangankulam, Alampatti, Inam Maniyachi Kovilpatti, Avelnetham, Lingampatti, Thittankulam Pandavarmangalm, Manthithoppu, Nallathenputhur Mudukkummendanpatti, Idaiseval, Uthupatti Kilaipatti, Sivanthipatti, Koddukombarai, Duraiyoor Villiseri, Ayyakkottaiyur, Urulaikudi Kattaramanpatti, Kadalaiyur, Meenachipuram Sindalakkarai, Navalakkampatti, Chinnamalai Kundu Chidambarapuram, Kumarakiri, Ilambuvanam Nakkala Kaltai, Suraikkarpatti Ranasooraettunaickan Patti, Erachi, Semmapudur T.Shunmugapuram, Valampathi, Melaeral, Keelaeral Arunachalapuram, Manjayanayakkanpatti, Athikeenar Ethilappanaickenpatti.

The villages having more than 50% ST population are None.

Sex ratio of Scheduled tribe population is 518.

Scheduled Tribes Literates and Illiterates by Sex:

	Persons	Males	Females
Literate	84	57	27
Illiterate	194	77	117
Literacy rate	37.2	51.8	23.3
Graduate	0	0	0

Scheduled Tribes (Dominant):

Kattunayakan, Malai Vedan, Kondareddis Malai Pandaram

For their cultural identity please see Appendix-II

Villages without Scheduled Tribes: There are 39 villages without any scheduled tribe population.

Literates and Illiterates by Sex (Total Population):

	Persons	Males	Females
Literate	61,176	33,962	27,214
Illiterate	31,216	11,365	19,851
Literacy rate	74	84	64
Graduate	2,761	1,699	1,062

Agriculture: ***Distribution of villages according to land use:*** Out of 43 villages, Total area (in hectare) is 39616.78, out of that 42.54 percent is cultivable and 9.43 percent of the cultivable area is irrigated.

Sources of Irrigation (Hectares): Government Canal 0, Private Canal 0, Well without Electricity 303.29, Well with Electricity 1027.2, Tubewell without Electricity 12.13, Tubewell with Electricity 60.11, Tank 182.2, River 0, Lake 0, Waterfall 0, Others 0.

Villages with population of 5000 to 9999:

Tittangulam.

Villages with population of 10000 and above:

Inam Maniyachi, Pandavarmangalam.

Distribution of Workers:

	Persons	Males	Females	WPR
Cultivators	6,678	4,129	2,549	13.5
Agricultural Labour	12,795	6,010	6,785	25.86
Household Industry	3,184	564	2,620	6.44
Other Workers	26,816	15,969	10,847	54.2
Main Workers	42,448	24,096	18,352	85.8
Marginal Workers	7,025	2,576	4,449	14.2
Total Workers	49,473	26,672	22,801	

Religion: Major Religious Communities:

	Persons	Males	Females	Sex Ratio
Hindu (93.53%)	86,410	42,457	43,953	1,035
Muslim (0.78%)	721	354	367	1,037
Christian (5.65%)	5,217	2,494	2,723	1,092
Sikh (0.01%)	5	3	2	667
Buddhists (0%)	1	-	1	-
Jain (0.01%)	12	5	7	1,400

Agewise Data:

	Persons	Males	Females	Sex Ratio
All ages	92,392	45,327	47,065	1038
0-14	23,393	11,992	11,401	951
15-44	46,234	22,085	24,149	1093
45-79	21,558	10,653	10,905	1024
80+	892	425	467	1099
Age not stated	315	172	143	831

Languages (Dominant):

Tamil, Telugu, Kannada, Urdu, Marathi

Disabled Population:

	Persons	Males	Females	%
Total Disabled	2,690	1,224	1,466	
In Seeing	1,656	606	1,050	61.56
In Speech	179	103	76	6.65
In Hearing	96	47	49	3.57
In Movement	541	337	204	20.11
Mentally	218	131	87	8.1

KRISHNAGIRI

Krishnagiri C.D. Block lies in the northern part of Dharampuri district. It is a part of Krishnagiri taluk. The Block is located at a distance of 46 kms. from district headquarters (Dharmapuri). There are 29 villages in the block with the total population of 108,325 persons. Area of the C.D. Block is 375.82 sq. kms. It is bounded in the north by the common boundary with the state of Andhra Pradesh, in the south by district Dharmapuri and C.D. Block Kaveripattinam, in the east by C.D. Block Bargur, in the west by C.D. Blocks Veppanapalli, Shoolagiri and Kelamangalam.

Communications:

Roadways : N.H.-7: Direction- Hosur to Kaveripattinam, Nearest Villages- Junjupalli, Bayanapalli, Raginampalli, Kothapatta, Periyamuthur, Devasamuthiram, Agasipalli.

tion- Krishnagiri to Vaniyambadi, Nearest Villages- Kathi to Nayanapalli, Boganapalli. N.H.-66: Direction- Krishnagiri Uthangarai, Nearest Villages- Boganapalli, Devasamuthiram. N.H.-219: Direction- Krishnagiri to Kuppam, Nearest Villages- Kathinayanapalli, Kammampalli, Boganapalli.

River: Ponnaiyar Nadi- Nearest Villages- Gangaleri, Sembadamuthur, Gooliyam, Marigampalli, Bellarampalli, Periyamuthur, Raginamapalli.

Annual Rainfall: Average Rainfall 760 mm.

Ground Water: Availability of the ground water in the Basin is (Information not available) H.A.M. and the utili zation is 160.44 H.A.M. It belongs to Over Expoited categ ory. Depth to water level varies from 2 to 5 meter below the ground. Most of the wells go down in summer months, according to the Ground Water Estimation Committee.

Forest and Reserved Forest: (Magarajaajadi RF)- Nearest Villages- Naralapalli, Maharasakkadi R.F. Uni, Kothigutalapalli. (Naralapalli)- Nearest Villages- Uni, Naralapalli, Kothigutalapalli, Peddatanapalli, Kallukurkki.

Natural Division: Baramahal.

Administration

Revenue **Division:** Krishnagiri. Parliamentary Constituency: 9 Krishnagiri. District: Dharmapuri. Taluk: Krishnagiri. Assembly Constituency: 53 Krishnagiri. Gram Panchayat: 30.

Border Villages- (Andhra Pradesh)- Nearest Villages- Naralapalli, Maharasakkadi R.F. Uni.

Villages: 29 **Inhabited:** 27 **Uninhabited:** 2

Ranking	District	State	National
Area	12	90	2090
Population	15	100	3200
Sex Ratio	1	242	1714
Child Sex Ratio	5	294	4931
Literacy Rate	10	327	2853
Density	16	208	3655
Work Participation Rate	10	240	2201

Gram Panchayats:

Agaram, Agasipalli, Bayanapalli, Bellarapalli, Chikkapoovathi , Devasamudiram, Gengaleri , Gooliam, Janjupalli, Kallukurikki, Kamamanpalli, Kathinayanapalli, Kondapalli, Malinayapalli, Mechakalachannampalli, Moramadagu, Naralapalli, Pachiganapalli, Peddampatti, Peddatalapalli, Periamuthur, Periyakottapalli, Sembadamuthur, Sokkadi, Thippanapalli , Velakalahalli, Venkatapuram .

Amenities:

Education: Primary School in 26 villages, Middle school in 19 villages, Matriculation or Secondary School in 13 villages, namely Kothigutalapalli, Peddatanapalli, Kallukurkki, Kammampalli, Peddatalapalli, Gangaleri, Chikkapoovathi, Alapatty, Agaram, Bellarampalli, N.H.-46: Direc Periyamuthur, Agasipalli, Sokkadi.

Higher Secondary or Pre University Courses or Intermediate or Junior College in 6 villages of the CD Block,, namely Kothigutalapalli, Kammampalli, Peddatalapalli, Alapatty, Periyamuthur, Agasipalli.

College in 1 village, Adult Literacy Center in 0 village., College is in village, namely Boganapalli.

Medical: Hospital in 0 village, Dispensary in 1 village, Health Center in 2 villages, Sub Center in 11 villages, Maternity and Child Welfare Center in 0 village, Community health workers in 17 villages.

The Village having Hospital or Dispensary or Health Center is Agaram.

Drinking Water: Tap water in 27 villages, Tank water in 0 villages, Well water in 27 villages, Tubewell in 27 villages and more than one source in 27 villages.

Bank: Banking facility in 3 villages, namely, Naralapalli, Alapatty, Periyamuthur.

Credit Society in 6 villages Agricultural Credit Society in 4 Non-Agricultural Credit Society in 3 villages.

Others: Power supply in 27 villages, Cinema hall in 0 village, sport club in 0 village, Stadium or Auditorium or Community Hall in 0 village, Post Office in 27 villages.

There are 26 villages having bus facilities.

Villages with most of facilities: Naralapalli Alapatty, Periyamuthur.

Villages without amenities (Education): Kompalli..

Scheduled Castes: Out of the total population of 108325 persons, 15918 persons (14.69%) belong to Scheduled Castes.

The villages having less than 10% SC population are Peddatanapalli, Kothapatta, Kammampalli, Gangaleri Kondepalli, Kompalli, Sembadamuthur, Gooliyam Sokkadi.

The villages having more than 50% SC population are None.

Sex ratio of Scheduled Caste population is 497.

Scheduled Castes Literates and Illiterates by Sex:

	Persons	Males	Females
Literate	8,549	5,027	3,522
Illiterate	7,369	2,982	4,387
Literacy rate	62.9	73.6	52.0
Graduate	243	198	45

Scheduled Castes (Dominant):

Adi Dravida, Arunthathiyar, Kuravan etc., Panniandi Generic Castes etc.

For their cultural identity please see Appendix-I

Villages without Scheduled Castes: There are 3 villages without any scheduled caste population.

Scheduled Tribes: Out of the total population of 108325 persons, 736 persons (0.68%) belong to Scheduled Tribes.

The villages having less than 10% ST population are Naralapalli, Kothigutalapalli, Peddatanapalli Kallukurkki, Junjupalli, Bayanapalli, Kothapatta Kathinayanapalli, Kammampalli, Boganapalli Peddatalapalli, Gangaleri, Kondepalli, Kompalli Sembadamuthur, Gooliyam, Tandegoundarahalli Alapatty, Agaram, Marigampalli, Bellarampalli Periyamuthur, Devasamuthiram, Agasipalli, Sokkadi Velakalahalli.

The villages having more than 50% ST population are None.

Sex ratio of Scheduled tribe population is 484.

Scheduled Tribes Literates and Illiterates by Sex:

	Persons	Males	Females
Literate	125	75	50
Illiterate	611	305	306
Literacy rate	20.8	24.4	17.1
Graduate	2	1	1

Scheduled Tribes (Dominant):

Irular, Kurumans, Malakkuravan, Kurichchan, Malayali

For their cultural identity please see Appendix-II

Villages without Scheduled Tribes: There are 16 villages without any scheduled tribe population.

Literates and Illiterates by Sex (Total Population):

	Persons	Males	Females
Literate	55,425	32,870	22,555
Illiterate	52,900	21,637	31,263
Literacy rate	60	71	49
Graduate	1,188	835	353

Agriculture: ***Distribution of villages according to land use:*** Out of 29 villages, Total area (in hectare) is 37582.74, out of that 45.76 percent is cultivable and 32.06 percent of the cultivable area is irrigated.

Sources of Irrigation (Hectares): Government Canal 842.57, Private Canal 0, Well without Electricity 148.59, Well with Electricity 2201.97, Tubewell without Electricity 104.72, Tubewell with Electricity 1448.9, Tank 765.87, River 0, Lake 0, Waterfall 0, Others 0.

Villages with population of 5000 to 9999:

Naralapalli, Kallukurikki, Kammaampalli, Boganapalli Peddatalapalli, Periamuthu.

Villages with population of 10000 and above:

Agasipalli.

Distribution of Workers:

	Persons	Males	Females	WPR
Cultivators	21,073	12,711	8,362	39.41
Agricultural Labour	18,194	7,856	10,338	34.02
Household Industry	1,678	628	1,050	3.14
Other Workers	12,530	9,994	2,536	23.43
Main Workers	42,038	26,824	15,214	78.61
Marginal Workers	11,437	4,365	7,072	21.39
Total Workers	53,475	31,189	22,286	

Religion: Major Religious Communities:

	Persons	Males	Females	Sex Ratio
Hindu (94.39%)	102,244	51,404	50,840	989
Muslim (3.71%)	4,023	2,094	1,929	921
Christian (0.52%)	566	277	289	1,043
Sikh (0%)	3	1	2	2,000
Buddhists (0%)	-	-	-	-
Jain (0%)	-	-	-	-

Agewise Data:

	Persons	Males	Females	Sex Ratio
All ages	106,884	53,802	53,082	987
0-14	34,957	17,946	17,011	948
15-44	51,180	25,240	25,940	1028
45-79	19,608	10,002	9,606	960
80+	944	494	450	911
Age not stated	195	120	75	625

Languages (Dominant):

Tamil, Telugu, Kannada, Urdu, Marathi

Disabled Population:

	Persons	Males	Females	%
Total Disabled	2,685	996	1,689	
In Seeing	1,695	433	1,262	63.13
In Speech	236	120	116	8.79
In Hearing	74	36	38	2.76
In Movement	546	331	215	20.34
Mentally	134	76	58	4.99

KRISHNARAYAPURAM

Krishnarayapuram C.D. Block lies in the north-eastern part of Karur district. It is a part of Krishnarayapuram taluk. The Block is located at a distance of 24 kms. from district headquarters (Karur). There are 25 villages in the block with the total population of 107,526 persons. Area of the C.D. Block is 349.80 sq. kms. It is bounded in the north by district Tiruchirappalli, in the south by CD Blocks Kadavur and Thogaimalai, in the east by CD Blocks Kulithalai and Thogaimalai, in the west by CD Blocks Karur and Thanthoni.

Communications:

Roadways : N.H.-67: Direction- Erode to Tiruchirappalli, Nearest Villages- Balarajapuram, Renganathapuram South, Mayanur, Thirukampuliyur, Kammanallur, Mahadhanapuram North, Chinthalavadi, Kallappalli, Manavasi.

Railway Station: Balarajapuram, Mayanur, Manavasi, Mahadhanapuram North, Chinthalavadi, Kallappalli.

River: Cauvery Nadi- Nearest Villages- Renganathapuram North, Mayanur, Thirukampuliyur, Kammanallur, Mahadhanapuram North, Chinthalavadi, Kallappalli, Balarajapuram.

Annual Rainfall: Average Rainfall 635 mm.

Ground Water: Availability of the ground water in the

Basin is 4978.99 H.A.M. and the utilization is 4287.49 H.A.M. It belongs to Semi Critical category. Depth to water level varies from 2 to 10 meter below the ground. Most of the wells go down in summer months, according to the Ground Water Estimation Committee.

Natural Division: NA

Administration

Revenue **Division:** Kulithalai. Parliamentary Constituency: 23 Karur. District: Karur. Taluk: Krishnarayapuram. Assembly Constituency: 136 Krishnarayapuram (SC), 137 Kulithalai. Gram Panchayat: 23.

Villages: 25 **Inhabited:** 25 **Uninhabited:** 0

Ranking	District	State	National
Area	4	117	2286
Population	1	108	3230
Sex Ratio	8	204	1438
Child Sex Ratio	6	274	4516
Literacy Rate	6	304	2555
Density	6	113	3458
Work Participation Rate	4	215	1149

Gram Panchayats:

Balarajapuram, Chinathalavadi, Kallapalli, Kammanallur, Karupathur , Kosur, Mahadhanapuram , Manavasi, Mathagiri, Mayanur, Muthurengampatti, Panjapatti, Pappakkapatti, Pillapalayam, Pothuravuthanapatti, Renganathapuram , Sengal, Sithalavai, Sivayam , Thirukkampuliyur, Thondamanginam, Vayalur, Veeriyapalayam.

Amenities:

Education: Primary School in 25 villages, Middle school in 14 villages, Matriculation or Secondary School in 6 villages, namely Balarajapuram, Renganathapuram North, Mayanur, Thirukampuliyur, Karuppathur, Panjapatti.

Higher Secondary or Pre University Courses or Intermediate or Junior College in 1 village of the CD Block,, namely Panjapatti.

College in 0 village, Adult Literacy Center in 2 villages.

Medical: Hospital in 3 villages, Dispensary in 6 villages, Health Center in 5 villages, Sub Center in 3 villages, Maternity and Child Welfare Center in 7 villages, Community health workers in 7 villages.

The Villages having Hospital or Dispensary or Health Center are Balarajapuram, Renganathapuram North, Mayanur, Kallappalli, Sengal, Panjapatti, Kosur.

Drinking Water: Tap water in 25 villages, Tank water in 5 villages, Well water in 25 villages, Tubewell in 25 villages and more than one source in 25 villages.

Bank: Banking facility in 6 villages, namely, Balarajapuram, Mayanur, Mahadhanapuram North Kallappalli, Sengal, Panjapatti.

Credit Society in 12 villages Agricultural Credit Society in 10 Non-Agricultural Credit Society in 3 villages.

Others: Power supply in 25 villages, Cinema hall in 3 villages, sport club in 0 village, Stadium or Auditorium or Community Hall in 0 village, Post Office in 21 villages.

There are 25 villages having bus facilities.

Villages with most of facilities: Balarajapuram Mayanur, Mahadhanapuram North, Kallappalli, Sengal Panjapatti.

Villages without Amenities (Education): None..

Scheduled Castes: Out of the total population of 107526 persons, 26526 persons (24.67%) belong to Scheduled Castes.

The villages having less than 10% SC population are None..

The villages having more than 50% SC population are None.

Sex ratio of Scheduled Caste population is 504.

Scheduled Castes Literates and Illiterates by Sex:

	Persons	Males	Females
Literate	13,601	8,223	5,378
Illiterate	12,925	4,924	8,001
Literacy rate	58.9	72.2	46.0
Graduate	501	364	137

Scheduled Castes (Dominant):

Pallan, Paraiyan etc., Chakkiliyan, Kuravan etc. Mavilan

For their cultural identity please see Appendix-I

Villages without Scheduled Castes: There is 0 village without any scheduled caste population.

Scheduled Tribes: Out of the total population of 107526 persons, 369 persons (0.34%) belong to Scheduled Tribes.

The villages having less than 10% ST population are Balarajapuram, Renganathapuram North Renganathapuram South, Mayanur, Thirukampuliyur Manavasi, Sithalavai, Kammanallur Mahadhanapuram North, Chinthalavadi, Pillappalayam Kallappalli, Karuppathur, Vayalur, Veeriyapalayam Sengal, Muthurengampatti, Panjapatti Pothuravuthanpatti, Pappakkapatti, Sivayam North Sivayam (South), Kosur, Mathagiri, Thandamanginam.

The villages having more than 50% ST population are None.

Sex ratio of Scheduled tribe population is 526.

Scheduled Tribes Literates and Illiterates by Sex:

	Persons	Males	Females
Literate	235	143	92
Illiterate	134	32	102
Literacy rate	72.1	91.1	54.4
Graduate	14	11	3

Scheduled Tribes (Dominant):

Kattunayakan, Paniyan, Uraly, Malakkuravan, Irular

For their cultural identity please see Appendix-II

Villages without Scheduled Tribes: There are 17 villages without any scheduled tribe population.

Literates and Illiterates by Sex (Total Population):

	Persons	Males	Females
Literate	57,752	34,799	22,953
Illiterate	49,774	19,144	30,630
Literacy rate	61	74	49
Graduate	1,763	1,274	489

Agriculture: ***Distribution of villages according to land use:*** Out of 25 villages, Total area (in hectare) is 34980, out of that 54.73 percent is cultivable and 40.96 percent of the cultivable area is irrigated.

Sources of Irrigation (Hectares): Government Canal 2570.03, Private Canal 0, Well without Electricity 678.88, Well with Electricity 4433.3, Tubewell without Electricity 4, Tubewell with Electricity 12.07, Tank 246.06, River 0, Lake 0, Waterfall 0, Others 0.

Villages with population of 5000 to 9999: Balarajapuram, Thirukkampuliyur Mahadhanapuram(North), Chinthalavadi, Kallapalli Karuppathur R.F., Pothuravuthanpatti, Pappakkapatti Sivayam (North), Kosur.

Villages with population of 10000 and above: None

Distribution of Workers:

	Persons	Males	Females	WPR
Cultivators	14,778	9,725	5,053	25.26
Agricultural Labour	32,292	14,745	17,547	55.19
Household Industry	1,073	641	432	1.83
Other Workers	10,368	8,007	2,361	17.72
Main Workers	52,044	31,030	21,014	88.95
Marginal Workers	6,467	2,088	4,379	11.05
Total Workers	58,511	33,118	25,393	

Religion: Major Religious Communities:

	Persons	Males	Females	Sex Ratio
Hindu (98.65%)	106,078	53,219	52,859	993
Muslim (0.55%)	593	307	286	932
Christian (0.71%)	762	368	394	1,071
Sikh (0%)	1	-	1	-
Buddhists (0%)	2	1	1	1,000
Jain (0%)	1	1	-	-

Agewise Data:

	Persons	Males	Females	Sex Ratio
All ages	107,526	53,943	53,583	993
0-14	29,531	15,324	14,207	927
15-44	51,888	25,705	26,183	1019
45-79	25,124	12,386	12,738	1028
80+	858	448	410	915
Age not stated	125	80	45	563

Languages (Dominant):

Tamil, Telugu, Urdu, Kannada, Malayalam

Disabled Population:

	Persons	Males	Females	%
Total Disabled	1,809	1,004	805	
In Seeing	703	368	335	38.86
In Speech	197	105	92	10.89
In Hearing	113	58	55	6.25
In Movement	634	386	248	35.05
Mentally	162	87	75	8.96

KULITHALAI

Kulithalai C.D. Block lies in the north-eastern part of Karur district. It is a part of Kulithalai taluk. The Block is located at a distance of 42 kms. from district headquarters (Karur). There are 15 villages in the block with the total population of 53,082 persons. Area of the C.D. Block is 121.30 sq. kms. It is bounded in the north and east by district Tiruchirappalli, in the south by C.D. Block Thogaimalai, and in the west by CD Block Krishnarayapuram.

Communications:

Roadways : N.H.-67: Direction- Karur to Tiruchirapalli, Nearest Villages- Karuvappanaicken Pettai, Vathiam, Kulithalai RF, Rajendram (North), Kumaramangalam.

Railway Station: Karuvappanaicken Pettai.

River: Cauvery Nadi- Nearest Villages- Karuvappanaicken Pettai, Vathiam, Kulithalai RF, Rajendram (North), Kumaramangalam.

Annual Rainfall: Average Rainfall 635 mm.

Ground Water: Availability of the ground water in the Basin is 5062.39 H.A.M. and the utilization is 1550.25 H.A.M. It belongs to Safe category. Depth to water level varies from 2 to 5 meter below the ground. Most of the wells go down in summer months, according to the Ground Water Estimation Committee.

Natural Division: NA

Administration

Revenue **Division:** Kulithalai. Parliamentary Constituency: 23 Karur. District: Karur. Taluk: Kulthalai. Assembly Constituency: 137 Kulithalai. Gram Panchayat: 13.

Villages: 15 **Inhabited:** 14 **Uninhabited:** 1

Ranking	District	State	National
Area	8	361	5455
Population	8	348	5130
Sex Ratio	2	92	721
Child Sex Ratio	5	255	4258
Literacy Rate	3	202	1843
Density	8	144	2511
Work Participation Rate	1	88	1443

Gram Panchayats:

Hiranyamangalam, Inungur, Karuvappanaickenpettai, Kumaramangalam, Manathattai, Nallur, Poyyamani,

Rajendram , Sathiyamangalam, Sooriyanur, Timmampatti, Vadhiyan, Vaiganallur .

Amenities:

Education: Primary School in 14 villages, Middle school in 8 villages, Matriculation or Secondary School in 3 villages, namely Vighnallur, Inungur, Sathyamangalam.

Higher Secondary or Pre University Courses or Intermediate or Junior College in 0 village of the CD Block, College in 0 village, Adult Literacy Center in 1 village.

Medical: Hospital in 0 village, Dispensary in 2 villages, Health Center in 4 villages, Sub Center in 2 villages, Maternity and Child Welfare Center in 1 village, Community health workers in 1 village.

The Villages having Hospital or Dispensary or Health Center are Poyyamani, Hiranyamangalam.

Drinking Water: Tap water in 14 villages, Tank water in 2 villages, Well water in 14 villages, Tubewell in 14 villages and more than one source in 14 villages.

Bank: Banking facility in 3 villages, namely, Karuvappanaicken Pettai, Rajendram (North) Rajendiram (South).

Credit Society in 6 villages Agricultural Credit Society in 6 Non-Agricultural Credit Society in 0 village.

Others: Power supply in 14 villages, Cinema hall in 1 village, sport club in 0 village, Stadium or Auditorium or Community Hall in 0 village, Post Office in 13 villages.

There are 14 villages having bus facilities.

Villages with most of facilities: None.

Villages without Amenities (Education): None..

Scheduled Castes: Out of the total population of 53082 persons, 14549 persons (27.41%) belong to Scheduled Castes.

The villages having less than 10% SC population are None..

The villages having more than 50% SC population are None.

Sex ratio of Scheduled Caste population is 518.

Scheduled Castes Literates and Illiterates by Sex:

	Persons	Males	Females
Literate	7,443	4,294	3,149
Illiterate	7,106	2,720	4,386
Literacy rate	59.3	71.4	48.1
Graduate	312	228	84

Scheduled Castes (Dominant):

Pallan, Paraiyan etc., Chakkiliyan, Pagadai Valluvan

For their cultural identity please see Appendix-I

Villages without Scheduled Castes: There is 1 village without any scheduled caste population.

Scheduled Tribes: Out of the total population of 53082 persons, 413 persons (0.78%) belong to Scheduled Tribes.

The villages having less than 10% ST population are Karuvappanaicken Pettai, Vathiam, Manathottai Vighnallur, Vaiganallur South, Rajendram (North) Rajendiram (South), Kumaramangalam, Poyyamani Suriyanoor, Inungur, Nallur, Hiranyamangalam Sathyamangalam.

The villages having more than 50% ST population are None.

Sex ratio of Scheduled tribe population is 501.

Scheduled Tribes Literates and Illiterates by Sex:

	Persons	Males	Females
Literate	275	158	117
Illiterate	138	48	90
Literacy rate	73.1	85.4	61.3
Graduate	12	10	2

Scheduled Tribes (Dominant):

Kattunayakan, Kaniyan etc., Malakkuravan Malai Vedan

For their cultural identity please see Appendix-II

Villages without Scheduled Tribes: There are 11 villages without any scheduled tribe population.

Literates and Illiterates by Sex (Total Population):

	Persons	Males	Females
Literate	30,556	17,639	12,917
Illiterate	22,526	8,672	13,854
Literacy rate	66	77	55
Graduate	973	738	235

Agriculture: ***Distribution of villages according to land use:*** Out of 15 villages, Total area (in hectare) is 12130, out of that 55.18 percent is cultivable and 69.88 percent of the cultivable area is irrigated.

Sources of Irrigation (Hectares): Government Canal 3567.1, Private Canal 19.21, Well without Electricity 358.1, Well with Electricity 625.04, Tubewell without Electricity 42.4, Tubewell with Electricity 10, Tank 23.51, River 0, Lake 0, Waterfall 0, Others 32.

Villages with population of 5000 to 9999: Vaiganallur(South), Poyyamani, Inungur Sathiyamangalam.

Villages with population of 10000 and above: None

Distribution of Workers:

	Persons	Males	Females	WPR
Cultivators	4,817	3,446	1,371	17
Agricultural Labour	18,251	8,767	9,484	64.43
Household Industry	1,077	624	453	3.8
Other Workers	4,182	3,213	969	14.76
Main Workers	25,440	14,831	10,609	89.81
Marginal Workers	2,887	1,219	1,668	10.19
Total Workers	28,327	16,050	12,277	

Religion: Major Religious Communities:

	Persons	Males	Females	Sex Ratio
Hindu (98.99%)	52,544	26,028	26,516	1,019
Muslim (0.63%)	333	178	155	871
Christian (0.34%)	180	96	84	875
Sikh (0%)	-	-	-	-
Buddhists (0%)	-	-	-	-
Jain (0%)	2	1	1	1,000

Agewise Data:

	Persons	Males	Females	Sex Ratio
All ages	53,082	26,311	26,771	1017
0-14	14,380	7,359	7,021	954
15-44	25,615	12,542	13,073	1042
45-79	12,590	6,162	6,428	1043
80+	422	205	217	1059
Age not stated	75	43	32	744

Languages (Dominant):

Tamil, Telugu, Urdu, Malayalam, Kannada

Disabled Population:

	Persons	Males	Females	%
Total Disabled	970	538	432	
In Seeing	441	255	186	45.46
In Speech	69	33	36	7.11
In Hearing	54	24	30	5.57
In Movement	331	189	142	34.12
Mentally	75	37	38	7.73

KUMBAKONAM

Kumbakonam C.D. Block lies in the north-eastern part of Thanjavur district. It is a part of Thiruvaidaumarudur and Kumbakonam taluks. The Block is located at a distance of 36 kms. from district headquarters (Thanjavur). There are 73 villages in the block with the total population of 145,807 persons. Area of the C.D. Block is 167.16 sq. kms. It is bounded in the north by CD Block Thiruppanandal and district Ariyalur, in the south by district Thiruvarur, in the east by C.D. Blocks Thiruppanandal and Thiruvidaimarudur, and in the west by CD Block Papanasam. CD Block Kumbakonam falls in taluk Thiruvidaimarudur by 06 villages, and in taluk Kumbakonam by 67 villages.

Communications:

Roadways : S.H.-8: Direction- Perumandi to Thiruppananda, Nearest Villages- Vilanthagandam, Kovilacherry, Kallur, Kallapuliyar, K.Karuppur, Agarathur, Manambadi, Senganur. S.H.-22: Direction- Thiruvidaimarudur to Papanasam, Nearest Villages- Darasuram, Thiruvalanzuli, Sundara.

Railway Station: Thiruvalanzuli, Vellalapillayam Petti, Thiruvalanjulithattimal.

River: Kollidam Nadi- Nearest Villages- Neerathanallur, Athiyur, Kotthangudi, Maharajapuram. Cauvery Nadi- Nearest Villages- Vellalapillayam Petti, Darasuram, Thiruvalanjulithattimal, Thiruvalanzuli, Thirumaignanam, Annalagrahram, Thiruvalanjuli Thattimal, Marutadi, Sarangapanipettai-Maruthadi, Agarathur, Kallapuliyar, Valayapattai, Madavapuram, Thimmagudi. Thirumalairajanar Nadi- Nearest Villages- Thenampadugai, Udaiyalur, Thenampadugai, Patteeswaram, Umamaheswarapuram, Cholanmaligai, Ariyapadaiveedu, Melakkorukkai, Maruthanallur.

Annual Rainfall: Average Rainfall 1147 mm.

Ground Water: Availability of the ground water in the Basin is 5894.90 H.A.M. and the utilization is 5924. 44 H.A.M. It belongs to Over Expoited category. Depth to water level varies from 2 to 10 meter below the ground. Most of the wells go down in summer months, according to the Ground Water Estimation Committee.

Natural Division: Chola Nadu.

Administration

Revenue **Division:** Kumbakunam. Parliamentary Constituency: 29 Thanjavur. District: Thanjavur. Taluk: Thiruvidaimarudur, Kumbakonam. Assembly Constituency: 170 Thiruvidaimarudur (SC), 171 Kumbakonam, 172 Papanasam. Gram Panchayat: 47.

Villages: 73 **Inhabited:** 66 **Uninhabited:** 7

Ranking	**District**	**State**	**National**
Area	10	331	4758
Population	3	22	1999
Sex Ratio	14	183	1281
Child Sex Ratio	3	40	978
Literacy Rate	5	85	987
Density	13	363	1006
Work Participation Rate	1	7	4648

Gram Panchayats:

Agarathur, Ammachatram, Anakudi, Annalagraharam, Ariyapadaiveedu, Asur, Asur, Athiyur, Bapurasapuram , Devanancheri, Eraharam , Innambur, Kadichambadi, Kallapuliyur, Kallur, keelapalaiyur, Koranattu Karuppur, Koranattu Karuppur , Korukkai, Kothangudi, Kovilacheri, Kumarankudi, Maharajapuram, Mambadi, Marudanallur, Nagagudi, Neerathanallur, Palavathankattalai , Patteeswaram, Puthur, Sakkottai, Senganur, Seshambadi, Sholamaligai, Sundaraperumalkoil , Thenampadugai, ThenamPadugai , Thenampadugai , Thillaiyambur, Thippirajapuram, Thirunallur, Thiruppurambiyam, Thiruvalanjuli , Udaiyalur, Umamahaswarapuram, Umamahesharapuram, Uthamadani, Valaiyapettai , Valapuram, Valayapettai, Vilandakandam.

Amenities:

Education: Primary School in 48 villages, Middle school in 13 villages, Matriculation or Secondary School in 4 villages, namely Vilanthagandam, Thiruppirambiyam,

Patteeswaram, Melakkorukkai.

Higher Secondary or Pre University Courses or Intermediate or Junior College in 2 villages of the CD Block,, namely Vilanthagandam, Patteeswaram.

College in 1 village, Adult Literacy Center in 0 village., College is in village, namely Miruthanpadaiveedu.

Medical: Hospital in 2 villages, Dispensary in 3 villages, Health Center in 3 villages, Sub Center in 25 villages, Maternity and Child Welfare Center in 1 village, Community health workers in 63 villages.

The Villages having Hospital or Dispensary or Health Center are Thiruppirambiyam, Melakkorukkai, Keelakorukkai, Sakkottai, Karuppur.

Drinking Water: Tap water in 66 villages, Tank water in 0 villages, Well water in 66 villages, Tubewell in 66 villages and more than one source in 66 villages.

Bank: Banking facility in 3 villages, namely, Thiruppirambiyam, Koranaru Karuppur, Thippirajapuram.

Credit Society in 12 villages Agricultural Credit Society in 12 Non-Agricultural Credit Society in 1 village.

Others: Power supply in 65 villages, Cinema hall in 0 village, sport club in 0 village, Stadium or Auditorium or Community Hall in 0 village, Post Office in 39 villages.

There are 61 villages having bus facilities.

Villages with most of facilities: Thiruppirambiyam Koranaru Karuppur, Thippirajapuram.

Villages without amenities (Education):

K.Karuppur, Inam Asoor, Marutadi, Moopakoil, Malacavery, Madavapuram, Thimmagudi, Ammathottam, Mathi, Chidambaranadha Mudalithottam, Darasuram, Sundara Perumal Koil Tenpathi, Thenampadugai, Vellalapillayam Petti, Thiruvalanjulithattimal, Vanian Karambai, Palayanallur..

Scheduled Castes: Out of the total population of 145807 persons, 41068 persons (28.17%) belong to Scheduled Castes.

The villages having less than 10% SC population are Koranaru Karuppur, Marutadi, Ammachatram, Malacavery Madavapuram, Nagakkudi, Ammathottam, Thirumaignanam Darasuram, Sundara Perumal Koil Tenpathi Vellalapillayam Petti, Thiruvalanjulithattimal Vanian Karambai, Palayanallur, Karuppur.

The villages having more than 50% SC population are Vilanthagandam, Kovilacherry, Kumarangudi K.Karuppur, Maruthanallur, Anakudy.

Sex ratio of Scheduled Caste population is 499.

Scheduled Castes Literates and Illiterates by Sex:

	Persons	Males	Females
Literate	20,384	12,158	8,226
Illiterate	20,684	8,416	12,268
Literacy rate	58.4	69.6	47.2
Graduate	288	213	75

Scheduled Castes (Dominant):

Paraiyan etc., Adi Dravida, Pallan, Valluvan Arunthathiyar

For their cultural identity please see Appendix-I

Villages without Scheduled Castes: There are 14 villages without any scheduled caste population.

Scheduled Tribes: Out of the total population of 145807 persons, 73 persons (0.05%) belong to Scheduled Tribes.

The villages having less than 10% ST population are Athiyur, Vilanthagandam, Kovilacherry, Kumarangudi Uthamathani, Devananjeri, Neerathanallur Kotthangudi, Kothangudithattimal, Tirunallur, Kallur Kallapuliyar, K.Karuppur, Agarathur, Kadichambadi Valapuram, Thiruppirambiyam, Innambur, Eragaram Asoor, Inam Asoor, Koranaru Karuppur Sarangapanipettai-Maruthadi, Marutadi, Ammachatram Moopakoil, Malacavery, Baburajapuram, Madavapuram Thimmagudi, Nagakkudi, Valayapattai Palavathankattalai, Miruthanpadaiveedu, Ammathottam Mathi, Chidambaranadha Mudalithottam, Thirumaignanam Annalagraharam, Darasuram, Thiruvalanzuli Sundara Perumal Koil Tenpathi, Thenampadugai Vellalapillayam Petti, Thiruvalanjulithattimal Patteeswaram, Vanian Karambai, Cholanmaligai Ariyapadaiveedu, Melakkorukkai, Keelakorukkai Palayanallur, Sakkottai, Karuppur, Maruthanallur Shesambadi, Thenampadugai, Udaiyalur, Thillaiyambur Thippirajapuram, Maharajapuram, Manambadi, Puthur Senganur, Anakudy, Umamaheswarapuram.

The villages having more than 50% ST population are None.

Sex ratio of Scheduled tribe population is 452.

Scheduled Tribes Literates and Illiterates by Sex:

	Persons	Males	Females
Literate	22	11	11
Illiterate	51	29	22
Literacy rate	40.0	36.7	44.0
Graduate	0	0	0

Scheduled Tribes (Dominant):

Kurumans, Irular, Malai Pandaram, Malakkuravan Kattunayakan

For their cultural identity please see Appendix-II

Villages without Scheduled Tribes: There are 66 villages without any scheduled tribe population.

Literates and Illiterates by Sex (Total Population):

	Persons	Males	Females
Literate	91,803	51,952	39,851
Illiterate	54,004	21,074	32,930
Literacy rate	72	81	62

Graduate	2,063	1,349	714

Agriculture: ***Distribution of villages according to land use:*** Out of 73 villages, Total area (in hectare) is 16716.29, out of that 68.33 percent is cultivable and 80.62 percent of the cultivable area is irrigated.

Sources of Irrigation (Hectares): Government Canal 8452.43, Private Canal 0, Well without Electricity 14.36, Well with Electricity 19.35, Tubewell without Electricity 142.85, Tubewell with Electricity 510.27, Tank 69.11, River 0, Lake 0, Waterfall 0, Others 0.

Villages with population of 5000 to 9999: Thiruppurambiyam, Koranattu Karuppur II Palavathankattalai , Annalagraharam, Patteeswaram.

Villages with population of 10000 and above: Thiruvalanjuli.

Distribution of Workers:

	Persons	Males	Females	WPR
Cultivators	6,210	5,222	988	10.86
Agricultural Labour	29,481	19,022	10,459	51.54
Household Industry	2,689	1,765	924	4.7
Other Workers	18,825	16,033	2,792	32.91
Main Workers	49,804	38,853	10,951	87.06
Marginal Workers	7,401	3,189	4,212	12.94
Total Workers	57,205	42,042	15,163	

Religion: Major Religious Communities:

	Persons	Males	Females	Sex Ratio
Hindu (93.72%)	136,644	68,630	68,014	991
Muslim (3.76%)	5,478	2,575	2,903	1,127
Christian (2.43%)	3,546	1,740	1,806	1,038
Sikh (0%)	7	5	2	400
Buddhists (0.01%)	8	6	2	333
Jain (0.01%)	9	4	5	1,250

Agewise Data:

	Persons	Males	Females	Sex Ratio
All ages	145,807	73,026	72,781	997
0-14	40,871	20,749	20,122	970
15-44	71,857	35,260	36,597	1038
45-79	31,787	16,366	15,421	942
80+	1,031	520	511	983
Age not stated	261	131	130	992

Languages (Dominant): Tamil, Telugu, Gujarati, Malayalam, English

Disabled Population:

	Persons	Males	Females	%
Total Disabled	4,477	2,232	2,245	
In Seeing	2,373	986	1,387	53
In Speech	357	208	149	7.97
In Hearing	259	116	143	5.79
In Movement	1,192	759	433	26.62
Mentally	296	163	133	6.61

KUNDADAM

Kundadam C.D. Block lies in the south-western part of Erode district. It is a part of Kangeyam and Dharapuram taluks. The Block is located at a distance of NA kms. from district headquarters (Erode). There are 29 villages in the block with the total population of 70,371 persons. Area of the C.D. Block is 536.36 sq. kms. It is bounded in the north by C.D. Block Kangeyam, in the south by CD Block Dharapuram, in the east by CD Blocks Vellakoil and Mulanur, and in the west by district Coimbatore. CD Block Kundadam falls in taluk Kangeyam by 08 villages, and in taluk Dharapuram by 21 villages.

Communications:

Roadways : N.H.-67 A: Direction- Palladam to Kangeyam, Nearest Village- Kangayampalayam. S.H.-37: Direction- Kangeyam to Dharapuram, Nearest Villages- Mudalipalayam, Uthiyur, Sirukinar, Vadugapalayam, Kannankoil.

River: Uppar Nadi- Nearest Villages- Vadugapalayam, Kannankoil, Velayuthampalayam, Periyakumarapalayam, Navanari, Bellampatti, Marudur, Molarapatti, Gelthelrev. Amaravathi Nadi- Nearest Villages- Pungandurai, Sirukinar.

Annual Rainfall: Average Rainfall 789 mm.

Ground Water: Availability of the ground water in the Basin is 3836.64 H.A.M. and the utilization is 2106.14 H.A.M. It belongs to Safe category. Depth to water level varies from 2 to 10 meter below the ground. Most of the wells go down in summer months, according to the Ground Water Estimation Committee.

Natural Division: Kongu Nadu.

Administration

Division. Parliamentary Constituency: 17 Erode. District: Erode. Taluk: Dharapuram, Kangayam. Assembly Constituency: 101 Dharapuram (SC), 102 Kangayam. Gram Panchayat: 24.

Villages: 29 **Inhabited:** 29 **Uninhabited:** 0

Ranking	District	State	National
Area	4	29	1359
Population	9	285	4452
Sex Ratio	11	297	2427
Child Sex Ratio	15	292	4907
Literacy Rate	14	346	3195
Density	3	4	5820
Work Participation Rate	16	371	41

Gram Panchayats:

Aratholuvu, Bellampatti, Ellapalayampudur, Gathelrev, Jothiampatti, Kannankoil, Kokkampalayam, Kolumanguli, Kurukkapalayam, Marudur, Molarapatti, Muthiampatti, Nandavanampalayam, Navanari, Periyakumarapalayam, Perumalpalayam, Punganthurai, Sadayapalayam, Sankarandampalayam, Sengodampalayam, Sirukinar, Surianallur, Vadasinnaripalayam, Velayudhampalayam.

Amenities:

Education: Primary School in 29 villages, Middle school in 11 villages, Matriculation or Secondary School in 5 villages, namely Mudalipalayam, Uthiyur, Sankarandampalayam, Manurpalayam, Bellampatti.

Higher Secondary or Pre University Courses or Intermediate or Junior College in 2 villages of the CD Block,, namely Mudalipalayam, Uthiyur.

College in 0 village, Adult Literacy Center in 0 village.

Medical: Hospital in 2 villages, Dispensary in 1 village, Health Center in 3 villages, Sub Center in 8 villages, Maternity and Child Welfare Center in 18 villages, Community health workers in 0 village.

The Villages having Hospital or Dispensary or Health Center are Mudalipalayam, Sankarandampalayam, Gelthelrev.

Drinking Water: Tap water in 29 villages, Tank water in 0 villages, Well water in 29 villages, Tubewell in 29 villages and more than one source in 29 villages.

Bank: Banking facility in 5 villages, namely, Uthiyur, Nilali, Sankarandampalayam, Manurpalayam Navanari.

Credit Society in 8 villages Agricultural Credit Society in 7 Non-Agricultural Credit Society in 1 village.

Others: Power supply in 29 villages, Cinema hall in 0 village, sport club in 0 village, Stadium or Auditorium or Community Hall in 0 village, Post Office in 24 villages.

There are 29 villages having bus facilities.

Villages with most of facilities: Uthiyur Sankarandampalayam, Manurpalayam, Navanari.

Villages without Amenities (Education): None..

Scheduled Castes: Out of the total population of 70371 persons, 16417 persons (23.33%) belong to Scheduled Castes.

The villages having less than 10% SC population are None..

The villages having more than 50% SC population are None.

Sex ratio of Scheduled Caste population is 491.

Scheduled Castes Literates and Illiterates by Sex:

	Persons	Males	Females
Literate	6,193	3,783	2,410
Illiterate	10,224	4,574	5,650
Literacy rate	43.0	51.6	34.1
Graduate	38	31	7

Scheduled Castes (Dominant):

Madari, Chakkiliyan, Pallan, Arunthathiyar Adi Dravida

For their cultural identity please see Appendix-I

Villages without Scheduled Castes: There is 1 village without any scheduled caste population.

Scheduled Tribes: Out of the total population of 70371 persons, 6 persons (0.01%) belong to Scheduled Tribes.

The villages having less than 10% ST population are Kangayampalayam, Vadasinnaripalayam Sambandhampalayam, Arutholugu, Mudalipalayam Uthiyur, Kurukkapalayam, Nilali, Kokkampalayam Jolliyampatti, Surianallur, Kolumanguli, Sirukinar Pungandurai, Sankarandampalayam, Vadugapalayam Kannankoil, Gelthelrev, Velayuthampalayam Eragampatti, Manurpalayam, Nandavanampalayam Kasilingampalayam, Muthiyampatti Periyakumarapalayam, Navanari, Bellampatti, Marudur Molarapatti.

The villages having more than 50% ST population are None.

Sex ratio of Scheduled tribe population is 500.

Scheduled Tribes Literates and Illiterates by Sex:

	Persons	Males	Females
Literate	4	3	1
Illiterate	2	0	2
Literacy rate	66.7	100.0	33.3
Graduate	0	0	0

Scheduled Tribes (Dominant):

Malai Pandaram

For their cultural identity please see Appendix-II

Villages without Scheduled Tribes: There are 28 villages without any scheduled tribe population.

Literates and Illiterates by Sex (Total Population):

	Persons	Males	Females
Literate	37,014	22,647	14,367
Illiterate	33,357	13,062	20,295
Literacy rate	58	70	45
Graduate	671	462	209

Agriculture: ***Distribution of villages according to land use:*** Out of 29 villages, Total area (in hectare) is 53636.62, out of that 29.98 percent is cultivable and 51.68 percent of the cultivable area is irrigated.

Sources of Irrigation (Hectares): Government Canal 2918.93, Private Canal 0, Well without Electricity 999.2, Well with Electricity 3929.13, Tubewell without Electricity 0, Tubewell with Electricity 206.95, Tank 0, River 93.6, Lake 0, Waterfall 0, Others 163.12.

Villages with population of 5000 to 9999: Nelali, Surianallur, Manurpalayam.

Villages with population of 10000 and above: None

Distribution of Workers:

	Persons	Males	Females	WPR
Cultivators	21,248	11,760	9,488	44.91
Agricultural Labour	18,314	8,483	9,831	38.71
Household Industry	1,397	721	676	2.95

Other Workers	6,354	4,510	1,844	13.43
Main Workers	43,843	24,262	19,581	92.67
Marginal Workers	3,470	1,212	2,258	7.33
Total Workers	47,313	25,474	21,839	

Religion: Major Religious Communities:

	Persons	Males	Females	Sex Ratio
Hindu (98.22%)	69,116	35,096	34,020	969
Muslim (0.11%)	74	41	33	805
Christian (1.6%)	1,128	548	580	1,058
Sikh (0%)	3	-	3	-
Buddhists (0%)	-	-	-	-
Jain (0%)	3	-	3	-

Agewise Data:

	Persons	Males	Females	Sex Ratio
All ages	70,371	35,709	34,662	971
0-14	14,061	7,238	6,823	943
15-44	32,727	16,323	16,404	1005
45-79	22,090	11,293	10,797	956
80+	1,227	719	508	707
Age not stated	266	136	130	956

Languages (Dominant):

Tamil, Telugu, Kannada, Urdu, Malayalam

Disabled Population:

	Persons	Males	Females	%
Total Disabled	1,313	588	725	
In Seeing	732	278	454	55.75
In Speech	117	61	56	8.91
In Hearing	49	21	28	3.73
In Movement	295	173	122	22.47
Mentally	120	55	65	9.14

KUNDRATHUR

Kunnathur C.D. Block lies in the northern part of Kancheepuram district. It is a part of Sriperumbudur taluk. The Block is located at a distance of 65 kms. from district headquarters (Kancheepuram). There are 85 villages in the block with the total population of 33,102 persons. Area of the C.D. Block is 231.06 sq. kms. It is bounded in the north by district Thiruvallur, in the south by CD Block Kattankolathur, in the east by CD Blocks Kattanklathur and St. Thomas Mount, in the west by CD Blocks Sriperumbudur and Walajabad.

Communications:

Roadways : N.H.-4: (Direction)- Sriperumbudur to Cheenai, Nearest Villages- Ayyapanthangal, Thelliaragaram.

Railway Station: Villiambakkam, Paranur, Paranur RF.

Annual Rainfall: Average Rainfall 1105 mm.

Ground Water: Availability of the ground water in the Basin is 7889.65 H.A.M. and the utilization is 4813.71 H.A.M. It belongs to Safe category. Depth to water level varies from 5 to 10 meter below the ground. Most of the wells go down in summer months, according to the Ground Water Estimation Committee.

Forest and Reserved Forest: (Kavanur RF)- Nearest Villages- Madambakkam, Kuthanur, Kavanur RF (Ui), Kavanur. (Nallur)- Nearest Villages- Nallur RF (Ui) (Na), Nallur, Nabdumbakkam, Somangalam, Poonthandalam. (Siruvanjur)- Nearest Villages- Valayakaranai, Umayalparamancheri, Nattarasampattu, Siruvanjur RF (Ui). (Vattambakkam)- Nearest Villages- ...anapakkam, Vattambakkam, Oragadam, Vadakkupattu RF, Padervadi, Valayakaranai, Umayalparamancheri.

Natural Division: Tondai Nadu.

Administration

Revenue Division: Kancheepuram. Parliamentary Constituency: 5 Sriperumbudur. District: Kancheepurm. Taluk: Sriperumbudur. Assembly Constituency: 28 Alandur, 29 Sriperumbudur (SC). Gram Panchayat: 44.

Villages: 85 **Inhabited:** 75 **Uninhabited:** 10

Ranking	District	State	National
Area	12	249	3646
Population	1	20	1945
Sex Ratio	10	270	2132
Child Sex Ratio	7	120	2302
Literacy Rate	2	43	616
Density	12	370	1677
Work Participation Rate	2	28	4720

Gram Panchayats:

Adhanur , Amarambedu, Ayyappanthangal , Erumaiyur, Ezhichur , Gerugambakkam, Irandankattalai, Karasangal , Kavanur, Kivur, Kolapakkam, Kollacheri, Kozhumanivakkam, Madambakkam , Malaipattu, Malayambakkam, Manimangalam, Mowlivakkam, Mugalivakkam , Naduveerapattu, Nandambakkam, Nattarasampattu , Orathur , Padappai , Paraniputhur, Paraniputhur , Pazhanthandalam, Periyapanicheri, Poonthandalam , Salamangalam , Sennakuppam , Serapanacheri, Serapanacheri , Sethupattu, Sirukalathur , Somangalam, Thandalam , Tharapakkam, Tharapakkam , Thirumudivakkam, Vadakkupattu , Vaipoor , Valayakaranai , Varadharajapuram, Vattambakkam , .

Amenities:

Education: Primary School in 62 villages, Middle school in 25 villages, Matriculation or Secondary School in 11 villages, namely Ayyapanthangal, Malayambakkam, Kollacheri, Kovur, Mowlivakkam, Madanandapuram, Somangalam, Pazhanthandalam, Padappai, Vadakkupattu Rf, Padervadi.

Higher Secondary or Pre University Courses or Intermediate or Junior College in 7 villages of the CD Block,, namely Malayambakkam, Kollacheri, Kovur, Mowlivakkam, Madanandapuram, Padappai, Padervadi.

College in 4 villages, Adult Literacy Center in 0 village., Colleges are in villages, namely Ayyapanthangal,

Kovur, Manimangalam, Venjuvancheri.

Medical: Hospital in 3 villages, Dispensary in 4 villages, Health Center in 9 villages, Sub Center in 23 villages, Maternity and Child Welfare Center in 3 villages, Community health workers in 75 villages.

The Villages having Hospital or Dispensary or Health Center are Ayyapanthangal, Kovur, Somangalam, Poonthandalam, Naduveerapattu, Padappai, Oragadam.

Drinking Water: Tap water in 75 villages, Tank water in 28 villages, Well water in 75 villages, Tubewell in 75 villages and more than one source in 75 villages.

Bank: Banking facility in 11 villages, namely, Ayyapanthangal, Kovur, Mowlivakkam, Mugalivakkam Kolapakkam, Thandalam A,B,C,D/D, Somangalam Pazhanthandalam, Manimangalam, Padappai, Oragadam.

Credit Society in 6 villages Agricultural Credit Society in 5 Non-Agricultural Credit Society in 0 village.

Others: Power supply in 75 villages, Cinema hall in 5 villages, sport club in 0 village, Stadium or Auditorium or Community Hall in 0 village, Post Office in 21 villages.

There are 46 villages having bus facilities.

Villages with most of facilities: Ayyapanthangal Kovur, Mowlivakkam, Mugalivakkam, Kolapakkam Thandalam A,B,C,D/D, Somangalam, Pazhanthandalam Manimangalam, Padappai, Oragadam.

Villages without amenities (Education):
Thelliaragaram, Kolathuvincheri, Kavanur, Malaipattu, Mahanyam (Rf), Varadharajapuram, Karanaithangal, Vellerithangal, Poondi, Erivakkam, Keelakalani, Kuthanur, Kattupakkam..

Scheduled Castes: Out of the total population of 147499 persons, 57372 persons (38.9%) belong to Scheduled Castes.

The villages having less than 10% SC population are Puducheri, Sethupattu, Nariyambakkam, Panapakkam Neelamangalam, Navalur, Valayakaranai, Kattupakkam.

The villages having more than 50% SC population are Kavanur, Kollacheri, Periyapanicheri, Kolapakkam Tharapakkam, Irandankattalai,A/B,B/B, Nallur Poonthandalam, Thirumudivakkam, Erumaiyur Naduveerapattu, Mahanyam (Rf), Sirumathur Kodangacheri, Serapanacheri, Karanaithangal Venjuvancheri, Vellerithangal, Arambakkam, Orathur Vattambakkam, Oragadam, Semakuppam, Panaiyyur Ezhichur, Poondi, Vadakkupattu Rf, Padervadi Kanchivakkam, Nattarasampattu, Siruvanjur Keelakalani, Kavanur.

Sex ratio of Scheduled Caste population is 500.

Scheduled Castes Literates and Illiterates by Sex:

	Persons	Males	Females
Literate	33,797	19,277	14,520
Illiterate	23,575	9,402	14,173
Literacy rate	68.4	78.1	58.6
Graduate	280	219	61

Scheduled Castes (Dominant):
Adi Dravida, Valluvan, Dom etc., Generic Castes etc. Arunthathiyar

For their cultural identity please see Appendix-I

Villages without Scheduled Castes: There are 14 villages without any scheduled caste population.

Scheduled Tribes: Out of the total population of 147499 persons, 1441 persons (0.98%) belong to Scheduled Tribes.

The villages having less than 10% ST population are Ayyapanthangal, Thelliaragaram, Kolathuvincheri Srinivasapuram, Kozhumanivakkam, Malayambakkam Sirukalathur, Kavanur, Kollacheri, Kovur Chinnapanicheri, Paraniputhur, Periyapanicheri Mowlivakkam, Madanandapuram, Mugalivakkam Kolapakkam, Gerugambakkam, Thandalam A,B,C,D/D Tharapakkam, Irandankattalai,A/B,B/B, Nandambakkam Nallur, Amarambedu, Somangalam, Poonthandalam Pazhanthandalam, Thirumudivakkam, Erumaiyur Naduveerapattu, Puducheri, Sethupattu, Malaipattu Mahanyam (Rf), Manimangalam, Varadharajapuram Kaasangal, Padappai, Sirumathur, Salamangalam Nariyambakkam, Kodangacheri, Serapanacheri Karanaithangal, Venjuvancheri, Vellerithangal Arambakkam, Athanancheri, Korukkanthangal, Adhanur Madambakkam, Neelamangalam, Orathur, Navalur Vattambakkam, Oragadam, Semakuppam, Panaiyyur Ezhichur, Poondi, Vadakkupattu Rf, Padervadi Valayakaranai, Umayalparamancheri, Kanchivakkam Nattarasampattu, Siruvanjur , Vadamelpakkam Erivakkam, Keelakalani, Kuthanur, Kavanur Kattupakkam.

The villages having more than 50% ST population are None.

Sex ratio of Scheduled tribe population is 516.

Scheduled Tribes Literates and Illiterates by Sex:

	Persons	Males	Females
Literate	411	239	172
Illiterate	1,030	458	572
Literacy rate	35.0	42.2	28.3
Graduate	3	2	1

Scheduled Tribes (Dominant):
Irular, Kattunayakan, Kurumans, Malakkuravan Malai Pandaram

For their cultural identity please see Appendix-II

Villages without Scheduled Tribes: There are 48 villages without any scheduled tribe population.

Literates and Illiterates by Sex (Total Population):

	Persons	Males	Females
Literate	97,071	54,384	42,687
Illiterate	50,428	20,170	30,258
Literacy rate	76	84	67
Graduate	1,766	1,219	547

Agriculture: ***Distribution of villages according to land use:*** Out of 85 villages, Total area (in hectare) is 23106.21, out of that 49.79 percent is cultivable and 54.14 percent of the cultivable area is irrigated.

Sources of Irrigation (Hectares): Government Canal 2.81, Private Canal 0, Well without Electricity 84.25, Well with Electricity 1009.62, Tubewell without Electricity 0, Tubewell with Electricity 325.66, Tank 401.56, River 0, Lake 4315.44, Waterfall 0, Others 89.21.

Villages with population of 5000 to 9999: Ayyappanthangal, Malayambakkam, Kovur, Mugalivakkam Gerugambakkam, Nandambakkam, Manimangalam, Padappai.

Villages with population of 10000 and above: None

Distribution of Workers:

	Persons	Males	Females	WPR
Cultivators	3,998	3,061	937	7.06
Agricultural Labour	16,660	9,902	6,758	29.41
Household Industry	2,043	1,261	782	3.61
Other Workers	33,956	26,919	7,037	59.93
Main Workers	42,130	32,251	9,879	74.36
Marginal Workers	14,527	8,892	5,635	25.64
Total Workers	56,657	41,143	15,514	

Religion: Major Religious Communities:

	Persons	Males	Females	Sex Ratio
Hindu (92.03%)	135,742	68,623	67,119	978
Muslim (2.81%)	4,144	2,084	2,060	988
Christian (4.85%)	7,155	3,617	3,538	978
Sikh (0.01%)	16	13	3	231
Buddhists (0%)	4	4	-	-
Jain (0.01%)	17	10	7	700

Agewise Data:

	Persons	Males	Females	Sex Ratio
All ages	147,237	74,426	72,811	978
0-14	43,180	22,078	21,102	956
15-44	75,913	38,416	37,497	976
45-79	26,692	13,225	13,467	1018
80+	964	454	510	1123
Age not stated	488	253	235	929

Languages (Dominant): Tamil, Telugu, Urdu, Kannada, Malayalam

Disabled Population:

	Persons	Males	Females	%
Total Disabled	3,405	1,931	1,474	
In Seeing	1,706	928	778	50.1
In Speech	345	183	162	10.13
In Hearing	212	118	94	6.23
In Movement	892	567	325	26.2
Mentally	250	135	115	7.34

KUNNANDARKOVIL

Kunnandarkovil C.D. Block lies in the northern part of Pudukkottai district. It is a part of Iluppur and Kulathur taluks. The Block is located at a distance of NA kms. from district headquarters (Pudukkottai). There are 49 villages in the block with the total population of 77,751 persons. Area of the C.D. Block is 382.41 sq. kms. It is bounded in the north by districts Tiruchirappalli and Thanjavur, in the south by C.D. Blocks Annavasal and Pudukkottai, in the east by CD Blocks Pudukkottai and Gandarvakottai, and in the west by C.D. Block Viralimalai. CD Block Kunnandarkovil falls in taluk Iluppur by 04 villages, and in taluk Kulathur by 45 villages.

Communications:

Roadways : N.H.-210: Direction- Tiruchirappalli to Karaikudi, Nearest Villages- Melapuduvayal, Keeranur, Kulathur.

Annual Rainfall: Average Rainfall 910 mm.

Ground Water: Availability of the ground water in the Basin is 5865.22 H.A.M. and the utilization is 1414. 56 H.A.M. It belongs to Safe category. Depth to water level varies from 2 to 10 meter below the ground. Most of the wells go down in summer months, according to the Ground Water Estimation Committee.

Natural Division: Chola Nadu.

Administration

Revenue **Division:** Pudukottai. Parliamentary Constituency: 30 Pudukottai. District: Pudokottai. Taluk: Iluppur, Kulathur. Assembly Constituency: 179 Kulathur, 178 Gandarvakottai (SC). Gram Panchayat: 37.

Villages: 49 **Inhabited:** 49 **Uninhabited:** 0

Ranking	District	State	National
Area	5	85	2039
Population	9	255	4182
Sex Ratio	12	196	1352
Child Sex Ratio	2	28	715
Literacy Rate	12	263	2281
Density	6	224	4690
Work Participation Rate	13	324	2373

Gram Panchayats:

Andakkulam, Chettipatti, Kannangudi, Killanur, Killukkottai, Killukulavai Patti, Koppampatti, Kulathur, Lekkanapatti, Mangathevanpatti, Melapuduvayal, Minnathur, Mootampatti, Nanjur, Odugampatti, Odukkur, Pallathu patti, Pappudaiyan Patti, Perambur, Periyathambiudayanpatti, Puliyur, Rakkathan Patti, Senayakkudi, Sengalur, Sonayakkudi, T.Keelaiyur, Thayinipatti, Themmavur,

Thenangudi, Udayalipatti, Upplikkudi, Vaithur, Valiampatti, Vathanakkurichi, Vathanakottai, Vazhamangalam, Veerakudi, Visalur.

Amenities:

Education: Primary School in 42 villages, Middle school in 18 villages, Matriculation or Secondary School in 9 villages, namely Sengalur, Killukkottai, Puliyur, Nanjur, Marudhur, Odugampathy, Uppiliyakkudi, Andakkulam, Vathanakurichi.

Higher Secondary or Pre University Courses or Intermediate or Junior College in 1 village of the CD Block,, namely Kannangudi.

College in 0 village, Adult Literacy Center in 0 village.

Medical: Hospital in 0 village, Dispensary in 1 village, Health Center in 4 villages, Sub Center in 15 villages, Maternity and Child Welfare Center in 0 village, Community health workers in 37 villages.

The Village having Hospital or Dispensary or Health Center is Udayaalipatti.

Drinking Water: Tap water in 49 villages, Tank water in 23 villages, Well water in 49 villages, Tubewell in 49 villages and more than one source in 49 villages.

Bank: Banking facility in 3 villages, namely, Killukkottai, Kulathur, Andakkulam.

Credit Society in 8 villages Agricultural Credit Society in 8 Non-Agricultural Credit Society in 0 village.

Others: Power supply in 49 villages, Cinema hall in 1 village, sport club in 0 village, Stadium or Auditorium or Community Hall in 0 village, Post Office in 21 villages.

There are 44 villages having bus facilities.

Villages with most of facilities: Killukkottai Kulathur, Andakkulam.

Villages without amenities (Education):
Pathipatti, Peruingudippattai, Kattukkottaipatti, T.Keelaiyur, Vadugapatty, Sathinippatti, Narangiyanpatti..

Scheduled Castes: Out of the total population of 77751 persons, 11041 persons (14.2%) belong to Scheduled Castes. The villages having less than 10% SC population are Lakkannapatti, Chettipatty, Sengalur Kattukkottaipatti, Rakkathampatti, Puliyur, Nanjur Marudhur, Udayaalipatti, Killanur, Kadambavayal Mangadevanpathy, Uppiliyakkudi, Vaithur Narangiyanpatti.

The villages having more than 50% SC population are None.

Sex ratio of Scheduled Caste population is 497.

Scheduled Castes Literates and Illiterates by Sex:

	Persons	Males	Females
Literate	5,967	3,608	2,359
Illiterate	5,074	1,947	3,127
Literacy rate	62.4	74.8	49.7
Graduate	120	95	25

Scheduled Castes (Dominant):
Paraiyan etc., Pallan, Adi Dravida, Valluvan Chakkiliyan

For their cultural identity please see Appendix-I

Villages without Scheduled Castes: There are 3 villages without any scheduled caste population.

Scheduled Tribes: Out of the total population of 77751 persons, 0 persons (0%) belong to Scheduled Tribes. The villages having less than 10% ST population are Lakkannapatti, Pathipatti, Peruingudippattai Thiyinippattai, Chettipatty, Vellaippilayarpatty Kannangudi, Sengalur, Kattukkottaipatti Killukkottai, Ulagankathanpatti, Killukulavaipatti Rakkathampatti, T.Keelaiyur, Visalur, Puliyur Vadugapatty, Melapuduvayal, Keeranur, Nanjur Marudhur, Valiyampatty, Odugampathy, Udayaalipatti Kunnandarkoil, Themmavoor, Minnathur, Vathanakkottai Perambur, Killanur, Veerakkudi, Kadambavayal Mangadevanpathy, Bragathambalpuram, Kulathur Odukkur, Uppiliyakkudi, Valamangalam, Seemanur Senayakkudi, Andakkulam, Sathinippatti, Vaithur Seerangampatti, Uchani, Thennangudi, Moodampatti Narangiyanpatti, Vathanakurichi.

The villages having more than 50% ST population are None.

Villages without Scheduled Tribes: There are 49 villages without any scheduled tribe population.

Literates and Illiterates by Sex (Total Population):

	Persons	Males	Females
Literate	42,505	25,515	16,990
Illiterate	35,246	13,466	21,780
Literacy rate	63	75	50
Graduate	626	483	143

Agriculture: ***Distribution of villages according to land use:*** Out of 49 villages, Total area (in hectare) is 38241.54, out of that 60.93 percent is cultivable and 28.06 percent of the cultivable area is irrigated.

Sources of Irrigation (Hectares): Government Canal 0, Private Canal 0, Well without Electricity 455.21, Well with Electricity 1869.28, Tubewell without Electricity 0, Tubewell with Electricity 143.59, Tank 4119.81, River 0, Lake 0, Waterfall 0, Others 0.

Villages with population of 5000 to 9999:
Andakkulam.

Villages with population of 10000 and above: None

Distribution of Workers:

	Persons	Males	Females	WPR

Cultivators	18,852	12,554	6,298	49.13
Agricultural Labour	13,451	6,147	7,304	35.06
Household Industry	739	408	331	1.93
Other Workers	5,326	4,326	1,000	13.88
Main Workers	31,652	21,142	10,510	82.5
Marginal Workers	6,716	2,293	4,423	17.5
Total Workers	38,368	23,435	14,933	

Religion: Major Religious Communities:

	Persons	Males	Females	Sex Ratio
Hindu (88.95%)	69,161	34,708	34,453	993
Muslim (2.77%)	2,154	1,059	1,095	1,034
Christian (8.25%)	6,412	3,201	3,211	1,003
Sikh (0%)	-	-	-	-
Buddhists (0%)	-	-	-	-
Jain (0%)	-	-	-	-

Agewise Data:

	Persons	Males	Females	Sex Ratio
All ages	77,751	38,981	38,770	995
0-14	22,656	11,585	11,071	956
15-44	37,849	18,815	19,034	1012
45-79	16,594	8,262	8,332	1008
80+	528	250	278	1112
Age not stated	124	69	55	797

Languages (Dominant):
Tamil, Telugu, Kannada, Urdu, Hindi

Disabled Population:

	Persons	Males	Females	%
Total Disabled	2,136	950	1,186	
In Seeing	1,246	454	792	58.33
In Speech	170	98	72	7.96
In Hearing	121	54	67	5.66
In Movement	452	275	177	21.16
Mentally	147	69	78	6.88

KURINJIPADI

Kurinjipadi C.D. Block lies in the eastern part of Cuddalore district. It is a part of Panruti and Cuddalore taluks. The Block is located at a distance of 32 kms. from district headquarters (Cuddalore). There are 59 villages in the block with the total population of 153,614 persons. Area of the C.D. Block is 326.69 sq. kms. It is bounded in the north by C.D. Blocks Panruti and Cuddalore, in the south by CD Blocks Bhuvanagiri and Parangipettai, in the east by the Bay of Bengal, and in the west by CD Blocks Kammapuram. CD Block Kuringipadi falls in taluk Panruti by 11 villages, and in taluk Cuddalore by 48 villages.

Communications:

Roadways : N.H.-45A: Direction- Chidambaram to Padirikuppam, Nearest Villages- Agaram, Anukkampattu, Kayalpattu, Allapakkam, Poovanikuppam (N), Adhinarayanapuram (W), Thiruchepuram, Andarmullipallam, Thanoor. N.H.-68: Direction- Pondicherry to Virudhachalam, Nearest Villages- Vazuthalampattu, Thondamanatham, Kothandaramapuram, Amabalavannapettai, Thopukollai, Kesavanarayanapuram, Tambipettai, Pethunaickkenkuppam, Thambipalayam, Ayikuppam, Kambalimedu, Kanjamanathanpettai, Thaiyalgunampattinam, Ranga Nathapuram, Rajakuppam. S.H.-8: Direction- Panruti to Settiya Tope, Nearest Villages- Vadakkuthu, Thenkuthu.

Railway Station: Vazuthalampattu, Amabalavannapettai, Kambalimedu.

Local Streams: Nearest Villages- Thiyagavalli, Thiruchopuram, Kambalimedu.

Backwards Region Grants Fund: It receives Backward Region Grants.

Annual Rainfall: Average Rainfall 1050 mm.

Ground Water: Availability of the ground water in the Basin is 17625.19 MCM and the utilization is 14095.26 MCM. It belongs to Semi Critical category. Depth to water level varies from 2 to 10 meter below the ground. Most of the wells go down in summer months, according to the Ground Water Estimation Committee.

Coastal Villages- (Bay of Bengal)- Nearest Villages- Thiyagavalli, Thiruchopuram, Kayalpattu, Andarmullipallam.

Natural Division: Tondai Nadu.

Administration

Revenue **Division:** Cuddalore. Parliamentary Constituency: 26 Cuddalore (SC). District: Cuddalore. Taluk: Cuddalore, Panruti. Assembly Constituency: 153 Neyveli, 156 Kurinjipadi. Gram Panchayat: 49.

Villages: 59 **Inhabited:** 59 **Uninhabited:** 0

Ranking	District	State	National
Area	4	140	2497
Population	2	10	1757
Sex Ratio	8	274	2171
Child Sex Ratio	13	246	4024
Literacy Rate	9	272	2335
Density	6	257	2351
Work Participation Rate	6	69	2796

Gram Panchayats:

Adinarayanapuram, Aduragaram, Agaram, Alappakkam, Ambalavanampettai, Andarmullipallam, Annadanampettai, Anukkambattu, Arangamangalam, Ayikuppam, Budampadi, Guruvappanpettai, Kalkunam, Kalliyan kuppam, Kannadi, Karunguli, Kayalpattu, Keelur, Kodandaramapuram, Kolakkudi, Koranapattu, Kothavacheri, Krishnankuppam, Kundiyamallur , Madanagopalapuram, Maruvay, Melapudupettai, Nayinakuppam, Peddunayakkankuppam, Puliyur, Puvanikuppam, Ranganathapuram, Samuttikuppam, Sirupalaiyur, Tambipettai, Tayilgunampattinam, Thambipalayam, Tirttanagari,

Tiruchchepuram, Tiyagavelli, Tondamanatham, Vadakkumelur, Vadakuthu , Valudambattu, Vanadirayapuram, Vandiyampallam, Varadarajanpettai, Vengadampettai, Virupakshi.

Amenities:

Education: Primary School in 54 villages, Middle school in 18 villages, Matriculation or Secondary School in 7 villages, namely Venkatampettai, Vazuthalampattu, Thondamanatham, Krishnakuppam, Thiruchopuram, Andarmullipallam, Viruppatchi.

Higher Secondary or Pre University Courses or Intermediate or Junior College in 0 village of the CD Block, College in 0 village, Adult Literacy Center in 0 village.

Medical: Hospital in 0 village, Dispensary in 0 village, Health Center in 10 villages, Sub Center in 22 villages, Maternity and Child Welfare Center in 1 village, Community health workers in 12 villages.

Drinking Water: Tap water in 59 villages, Tank water in 0 villages, Well water in 59 villages, Tubewell in 59 villages and more than one source in 59 villages.

Bank: Banking facility in 5 villages, namely, Amabalavannapettai, Thambipalayam, Poovanikuppam (N) Ranga Nathapuram, Theerthanagiri.

Credit Society in 18 villages Agricultural Credit Society in 18 Non-Agricultural Credit Society in 1 village.

Others: Power supply in 59 villages, Cinema hall in 2 villages, sport club in 0 village, Stadium or Auditorium or Community Hall in 0 village, Post Office in 59 villages.

There are 58 villages having bus facilities.

Villages with most of facilities: Amabalavannapettai Poovanikuppam (N), Ranga Nathapuram, Theerthanagiri.

Villages without amenities (Education):

Thopukollai, Idankondampattu, Kesavanarayanapuram, Adhinarayanapuram (W), Karuvepampady..

Scheduled Castes: Out of the total population of 153614 persons, 50967 persons (33.18%) belong to Scheduled Castes. The villages having less than 10% SC population are Mathanagopalapuram, Venkatampettai, Thenkuthu Thimmaravutham Kuppam, Krishnakuppam, Ayikuppam Karuvepampady, Kolakkudi, Nainarkuppam, Maruvai Arangamangalam, Kuruvappanpettai.

The villages having more than 50% SC population are Vanathirayapuram, Kothandaramapuram, Agaram Kambalimedu, Allapakkam, Poovanikuppam (N) Idankondampattu, Akgatimmapuram, Kesavanarayanapuram Theerthanagiri, Adhinarayanapuram (W), Kannadi Adoorkuppam, Rajakuppam, Melapudupattai.

Sex ratio of Scheduled Caste population is 496.

Scheduled Castes Literates and Illiterates by Sex:

	Persons	Males	Females
Literate	23,188	14,023	9,165
Illiterate	27,779	11,648	16,131
Literacy rate	53.8	64.8	42.7
Graduate	318	265	53

Scheduled Castes (Dominant):

Adi Dravida, Arunthathiyar, Valluvan

Generic Castes etc., Domban

For their cultural identity please see Appendix-I

Villages without Scheduled Castes: There are 6 villages without any scheduled caste population.

Scheduled Tribes: Out of the total population of 153614 persons, 495 persons (0.32%) belong to Scheduled Tribes. The villages having less than 10% ST population are Puliyur East, Koranapattu, Mathanagopalapuram Venkatampettai, Poiganatham, Annathanampettai Keelur, Vadakkuthu, Vadakkuthelur, Vanathirayapuram Thenkuthu, Vazuthalampattu, Thondamanatham Thiyagavalli, Kothandaramapuram, Amabalavannapettai Thopukollai, Thimmaravutham Kuppam, Krishnakuppam Thambipalayam, Ayikuppam, Agaram, Thiruchopuram Kayalpattu, Kambalimedu, Allapakkam Poovanikuppam (N), Idankondampattu, Akgatimmapuram Ranga Nathapuram, Kesavanarayanapuram, Tambipettai Pethunaickkenkuppam, Kanjamanathanpettai Thaiyalgunampattinam, Theerthanagiri Adhinarayanapuram (W), Thanoor, Andarmullipallam Sirupallaiyur (N), Karuvepampady, Kannadi Adoorkuppam, Viruppatchi, Rajakuppam, Karunkuzhi Kolakkudi, Nainarkuppam, Maruvai, Arangamangalam Kurinjipadi, Kalkunam, Kuruvappanpettai, Boothampadi Melapudupattai, Adooragaram, Kothavacherry Kundiyamallur (N).

The villages having more than 50% ST population are None.

Sex ratio of Scheduled tribe population is 481.

Scheduled Tribes Literates and Illiterates by Sex:

	Persons	Males	Females
Literate	157	102	55
Illiterate	338	155	183
Literacy rate	38.6	48.6	27.9
Graduate	1	1	0

Scheduled Tribes (Dominant):

Kattunayakan, Irular, Adiyan, Malakkuravan

For their cultural identity please see Appendix-II

Villages without Scheduled Tribes: There are 44 villages without any scheduled tribe population.

Literates and Illiterates by Sex (Total Population):

	Persons	Males	Females
Literate	83,328	50,232	33,096
Illiterate	70,286	27,481	42,805

Literacy rate	63	75	50
Graduate	1,932	1,488	444

Agriculture: ***Distribution of villages according to land use:*** Out of 59 villages, Total area (in hectare) is 32669.27, out of that 76 percent is cultivable and 52.08 percent of the cultivable area is irrigated.

Sources of Irrigation (Hectares): Government Canal 2266.81, Private Canal 0, Well without Electricity 78.5, Well with Electricity 593.01, Tubewell without Electricity 0, Tubewell with Electricity 9209.02, Tank 785.28, River 0, Lake 0, Waterfall 0, Others 0.

Villages with population of 5000 to 9999: Puliyur(west), Kilur, Vadakuthu , Valudambattu Tondamanatham, Tiyagavelli.

Villages with population of 10000 and above: None

Distribution of Workers:

	Persons	Males	Females	WPR
Cultivators	14,575	10,763	3,812	19.9
Agricultural Labour	44,108	22,706	21,402	60.23
Household Industry	2,922	1,344	1,578	3.99
Other Workers	11,626	9,466	2,160	15.88
Main Workers	47,643	33,094	14,549	65.06
Marginal Workers	25,588	11,185	14,403	34.94
Total Workers	73,231	44,279	28,952	

Religion: Major Religious Communities:

	Persons	Males	Females	Sex Ratio
Hindu (95.51%)	146,719	74,143	72,576	979
Muslim (0.61%)	937	514	423	823
Christian (3.59%)	5,522	2,824	2,698	955
Sikh (0%)	4	2	2	1,000
Buddhists (0%)	1	-	1	-
Jain (0%)	2	2	-	-

Agewise Data:

	Persons	Males	Females	Sex Ratio
All ages	153,614	77,713	75,901	977
0-14	45,386	23,178	22,208	958
15-44	76,584	38,377	38,207	996
45-79	30,156	15,361	14,795	963
80+	991	547	444	812
Age not stated	497	250	247	988

Languages (Dominant): Tamil, Telugu, Urdu, Hindi, Malayalam

Disabled Population:

	Persons	Males	Females	%
Total Disabled	4,669	2,076	2,593	
In Seeing	3,048	1,143	1,905	65.28
In Speech	325	166	159	6.96
In Hearing	253	135	118	5.42
In Movement	792	496	296	16.96
Mentally	251	136	115	5.38

KURIVIKULAM

Kuruvikulam C.D. Block lies in the north-eastern part of Tirunelveli district. It is a part of Sankarankoil taluk. The taluk is located at a distance of 56 kms. from district headquarters (Tirunelvali). There are 50 villages in the block with the total population of 101,415 persons. Area of the C.D. Block is 473.14 sq. kms. It is bounded in the north by district Virudhunagar, in the south by CD Blcok Melaneelithanallur and district Thoothukkudi, in the east by district Thoothukkudi, in the west by CD Blocks Sankarankoil and Melaneelithanallur.

Communications:

Roadways : S.H.-41: Direction- Rajapalayam to Alagiapandia puram, Nearest Village- Rengasamuthuram. S.H.-44: Direction- Sankarankovil to Koilpatti, Nearest Villages- Kalingapa tti, Subbiahpuram, Chatrapatti, Mukkuttumalai, Ilaiyarasa nendal, Ayyaneri, Nakkalamuthampatti, Naduvapatti, Maippa rai, Sangupatti, Kulasekaraperi, Karisathan, Vellakulam.

River: Nichibandhi Nadi- Nearest Villages- Kalingapatti, Chatrapatti, Karisathan, Vellakulam.

Annual Rainfall: Average Rainfall 879 mm.

Ground Water: Availability of the ground water in the Basin is 48.72 MCM and the utilization is 33.19 MCM. It belongs to Safe category. Depth to water level varies from 2 to 10 meter below the ground. Most of the wells go down in summer months, according to the Ground Water Estimation Committee.

Natural Division: NA

Administration

Revenue **Division:** Tirunelveli. Parliamentary Constituenc y: 37 Tenkasi. District: Tirunelveli. Taluk: Sankarankoil. Assembly Constituency: 219 Sankarankovil (SC). Gram Panchayat: 43.

Villages: 50 **Inhabited:** 48 **Uninhabited:** 2

Ranking	**District**	**State**	**National**
Area	2	38	1596
Population	2	124	3422
Sex Ratio	11	43	416
Child Sex Ratio	8	129	2353
Literacy Rate	15	183	1720
Density	3	80	4520
Work Participation Rate	14	315	761

Gram Panchayats:

A. Karisalkulam , Alagapuri , Alankulam, Appaneri, Athipatti, Ayyaneri, Chathrakondan, Chattrapatti , Chattrapatti, Chidambarapuram, Chitrampatti, Ilayarasanendal , K.Karisalkulam, Kalappalankulam, Kalingapatti, Karisathan , Kulakattakurichi, Kurunjaikulam, Kuruvikulam (north), Kuruvikulam (South), Mahendravadi, Maipparai, Malaiyankulam, Maruthankinar, Mukkutumalai,

Mukkutumalai , Nakkalamuthanpatti, Nalanthula, Palankottai, Perunkottur, Pillaiyarrnatham, Pitchaithalaivanpatti, Puliyankulam, Ramalingapuram, Sangupatti, Sayamalai, Sevalkulam, Sundaresapuram, Umayathalaivanpatty , Usilankulam, Usilankulam , Vadukkupatti, Vagaikulam , Varaganur, Vellakulam, Venkatachalapuram, Z. Devarkulam.

Amenities:

Education: Primary School in 46 villages, Middle school in 23 villages, Matriculation or Secondary School in 9 villages, namely Kalingapatti, Ilaiyarasanendal, Maipparai, Karisalkulam, Karisathan, Pillayarnatham, Thirugukuruvikulam, Pazhancottai, Sayamalai.

Higher Secondary or Pre University Courses or Intermediate or Junior College in 2 villages of the CD Block,, namely Kalingapatti, Thirugukuruvikulam.

College in 1 village, Adult Literacy Center in 0 village., College is in village, namely Appaneri.

Medical: Hospital in 2 villages, Dispensary in 3 villages, Health Center in 4 villages, Sub Center in 20 villages, Maternity and Child Welfare Center in 3 villages, Community health workers in 34 villages.

The Villages having Hospital or Dispensary or Health Center are Sangupatti, Karisalkulam, Vadakkukuruvikulam, Thirugukuruvikulam.

Drinking Water: Tap water in 48 villages, Tank water in 14 villages, Well water in 31 villages, Tubewell in 10 villages and more than one source in 37 villages.

Bank: Banking facility in 18 villages, namely, Kalingapatti, Ilaiyarasanendal, Chithirampatti Appaneri, Naduvapatti, Maipparai, Karisalkulam Sathirankondan, Alagapuri, Vadakkukuruvikulam Ramalingapuram, Thirugukuruvikulam, Sevalkulam Pazhancottai, K.Alangulam, Mahendravadi, Nalanthula Sayamalai.

Credit Society in 8 villages Agricultural Credit Society in 7 Non-Agricultural Credit Society in 2 villages.

Others: Power supply in 47 villages, Cinema hall in 0 village, sport club in 2 villages, Stadium or Auditorium or Community Hall in 0 village, Post Office in 34 villages.

There are 31 villages having bus facilities.

Villages with most of facilities: Kalingapatti Ilaiyarasanendal, Chithirampatti, Appaneri Maipparai, Karisalkulam, Sathirankondan, Alagapuri Vadakkukuruvikulam, Ramalingapuram, Sevalkulam Pazhancottai, Nalanthula, Sayamalai.

Villages without amenities (Education):

Subbiahpuram, Chettykulam..

Scheduled Castes: Out of the total population of 101415 persons, 32967 persons (32.51%) belong to Scheduled Castes.

The villages having less than 10% SC population are Rengasamuthuram, Mukkuttumalai, Karisalkulam Kulasekaraperi, Sundarasapuram, Kalappalankulam K.Karisalkulam.

The villages having more than 50% SC population are Subbiahpuram, Naduvapatti, Perunkottur Thirugukuruvikulam, Naluvasamkottai, Usinangulam Pazhancottai, K.Alangulam, Mahendravadi.

Sex ratio of Scheduled Caste population is 509.

Scheduled Castes Literates and Illiterates by Sex:

	Persons	Males	Females
Literate	17,623	10,495	7,128
Illiterate	15,344	5,696	9,648
Literacy rate	60.6	73.6	48.2
Graduate	231	175	56

Scheduled Castes (Dominant):

Pallan, Paraiyan etc., Chakkiliyan, Arunthathiyar Puthirai Vannan

For their cultural identity please see Appendix-I

Villages without Scheduled Castes: There are 3 villages without any scheduled caste population.

Scheduled Tribes: Out of the total population of 101415 persons, 87 persons (0.09%) belong to Scheduled Tribes.

The villages having less than 10% ST population are Rengasamuthuram, Kalingapatti, Subbiahpuram Chatrapatti, Varagahur, Mukkuttumalai Ilaiyarasanendal, Pulangulam, Chithirampatti Appaneri, Ayyaneri, Nakkalamuthampatti, Naduvapatti Maipparai, Sangupatti, Vellakulam, Karisalkulam Kulasekaraperi, Karisathan, Sathirankondan Perunkottur, Alagapuri, Madhurapuri Vadakkukuruvikulam, Kurunjakkulam, Sundarasapuram Kulakattakurichi, Vadakkupatti Pitchaithalaivanpatti, Pillayarnatham Zamin Devarkulam, Atthipatti, Ramalingapuram Thirugukuruvikulam, Vagaikulam, Naluvasamkottai Sevalkulam, Malayankulam, Usinangulam, Pazhancottai K.Alangulam, Chettykulam, Mahendravadi Kalappalankulam, Nalanthula, K.Karisalkulam Sayamalai, Maruthankinaru.

The villages having more than 50% ST population are None.

Sex ratio of Scheduled tribe population is 563.

Scheduled Tribes Literates and Illiterates by Sex:

	Persons	Males	Females
Literate	41	23	18
Illiterate	46	15	31
Literacy rate	55.4	67.7	45.0
Graduate	0	0	0

Scheduled Tribes (Dominant):

Kattunayakan

For their cultural identity please see Appendix-II

Villages without Scheduled Tribes: There are 45 villages without any scheduled tribe population.

Literates and Illiterates by Sex (Total Population):

	Persons	Males	Females
Literate	59,917	34,825	25,092
Illiterate	41,498	15,020	26,478
Literacy rate	66	79	54
Graduate	893	623	270

Agriculture: ***Distribution of villages according to land use:*** Out of 50 villages, Total area (in hectare) is 47314.1, out of that 38.75 percent is cultivable and 19.16 percent of the cultivable area is irrigated.

Sources of Irrigation (Hectares): Government Canal 0, Private Canal 0, Well without Electricity 877.44, Well with Electricity 1923.78, Tubewell without Electricity 0, Tubewell with Electricity 0, Tank 710.4, River 0, Lake 0, Waterfall 0, Others 0.

Villages with population of 5000 to 9999: Kalingappatti, Ilaiyarasanendal , Kuruvikulam (North) Palankottai.

Villages with population of 10000 and above: None

Distribution of Workers:

	Persons	Males	Females	WPR
Cultivators	9,548	5,808	3,740	16.51
Agricultural Labour	28,463	13,834	14,629	49.21
Household Industry	2,887	1,136	1,751	4.99
Other Workers	16,945	9,069	7,876	29.29
Main Workers	48,452	26,303	22,149	83.76
Marginal Workers	9,391	3,544	5,847	16.24
Total Workers	57,843	29,847	27,996	

Religion: Major Religious Communities:

	Persons	Males	Females	Sex Ratio
Hindu (93.16%)	94,478	46,458	48,020	1,034
Muslim (0.16%)	161	80	81	1,013
Christian (6.6%)	6,697	3,264	3,433	1,052
Sikh (0%)	5	3	2	667
Buddhists (0%)	-	-	-	-
Jain (0%)	-	-	-	-

Agewise Data:

	Persons	Males	Females	Sex Ratio
All ages	101,415	49,845	51,570	1035
0-14	26,151	13,366	12,785	957
15-44	49,840	24,282	25,558	1053
45-79	24,277	11,665	12,612	1081
80+	960	420	540	1286
Age not stated	187	112	75	670

Languages (Dominant): Tamil, Telugu, Kannada, Urdu, Malayalam

Disabled Population:

	Persons	Males	Females	%
Total Disabled	2,915	1,231	1,684	
In Seeing	1,856	642	1,214	63.67
In Speech	222	114	108	7.62
In Hearing	67	35	32	2.3
In Movement	598	344	254	20.51
Mentally	172	96	76	5.9

KURUNTHANCODE

Kurunthancode C.D. Block lies in the southern part of Kanniyakumari district. It is a part of Kalkulam taluk. The Block is located at a distance of NA kms. from district headquarters (Nagarkoil). There are 04 villages in the block with the total population of 50,353 persons. Area of the C.D. Block is 53.34 sq. kms. It is bounded in the north by CD Blocks Thakkalay, Killiyur and Thiruvattaru, in the south by the Arabian Sea, in the east by CD Block Rajakkamangalam, and in the west by CD Block Munchira.

Communications:

Roadways : S.H.-46: Direction- Kolachal to Rajakkamangalam, Nearest Village- Kadiapattanam.

Annual Rainfall: Average Rainfall 1448 mm.

Ground Water: Availability of the ground water in the Basin is 31.31 MCM and the utilization is 5.60 MCM. It belongs to Safe category. Depth to water level varies from 5 to 10 meter below the ground. Most of the wells go down in summer months, according to the Ground Water Estimation Committee.

Coastal Villages- (Arabian Sea)- Nearest Village- Colachel.

Natural Division: NA

Administration

Revenue **Division:** Padmanabhapuram. Parliamentary Constituency: 39 Kanniyakumari. District: Kanniyakumari. Taluk: Kalkulam. Assembly Constituency: 231 Colachal. Gram Panchayat: 09.

Villages: 4 **Inhabited:** 4 **Uninhabited:** 0

Ranking	District	State	National
Area	9	382	6043
Population	7	357	5264
Sex Ratio	7	148	1062
Child Sex Ratio	8	236	3872
Literacy Rate	9	12	184
Density	6	380	844
Work Participation Rate	2	6	5643

Gram Panchayats: Kakkottuthalai, Kattimancode, Kurunthancode, Muttam, Nettancode, Simoncolony, Thalakulam, Vellichandai.

Amenities:

Education: Primary School in 4 villages, Middle school in 4 villages, Matriculation or Secondary School in 4 villages,

namely Colachel, Thalakulam, Kurunthencode, Kadiapattanam.

Higher Secondary or Pre University Courses or Intermediate or Junior College in 3 villages of the CD Block,, namely Colachel, Kurunthencode, Kadiapattanam.

College in 0 village, Adult Literacy Center in 0 village.

Medical: Hospital in 1 village, Dispensary in 1 village, Health Center in 2 villages, Sub Center in 4 villages, Maternity and Child Welfare Center in 0 village, Community health workers in 0 village.

The Villages having Hospital or Dispensary or Health Center are Thalakulam, Kurunthencode.

Drinking Water: Tap water in 4 villages, Tank water in 0 villages, Well water in 4 villages, Tubewell in 4 villages and more than one source in 4 villages.

Bank: Banking facility in 4 villages, namely, Colachel, Thalakulam, Kurunthencode, Kadiapattanam.

Credit Society in 1 village Agricultural Credit Society in 1 Non-Agricultural Credit Society in 1 village.

Others: Power supply in 4 villages, Cinema hall in 2 villages, sport club in 0 village, Stadium or Auditorium or Community Hall in 0 village, Post Office in 4 villages.

There are 4 villages having bus facilities.

Villages with most of facilities: Colachel Thalakulam, Kurunthencode, Kadiapattanam.

Villages without Amenities (Education): None..

Scheduled Castes: Out of the total population of 50353 persons, 1144 persons (2.27%) belong to Scheduled Castes.

The villages having less than 10% SC population are None..

The villages having more than 50% SC population are None.

Sex ratio of Scheduled Caste population is 490.

Scheduled Castes Literates and Illiterates by Sex:

	Persons	Males	Females
Literate	850	442	408
Illiterate	294	141	153
Literacy rate	84.1	88.2	80.0
Graduate	19	9	10

Scheduled Castes (Dominant):

Paraiyan etc., Pallan, Adi Dravida, Vannan Pulayan etc.

For their cultural identity please see Appendix-I

Villages without Scheduled Castes: There is 0 village without any scheduled caste population.

Scheduled Tribes: Out of the total population of 50353 persons, 24 persons (0.05%) belong to Scheduled Tribes.

The villages having less than 10% ST population are None..

The villages having more than 50% ST population are None.

Sex ratio of Scheduled tribe population is 500.

Scheduled Tribes Literates and Illiterates by Sex:

	Persons	Males	Females
Literate	9	6	3
Illiterate	15	6	9
Literacy rate	56.3	66.7	42.9
Graduate	0	0	0

Scheduled Tribes (Dominant):

Kattunayakan

For their cultural identity please see Appendix-II

Villages without Scheduled Tribes: There are 2 villages without any scheduled tribe population.

Literates and Illiterates by Sex (Total Population):

	Persons	Males	Females
Literate	37,262	18,840	18,422
Illiterate	13,091	6,292	6,799
Literacy rate	84	85	82
Graduate	782	380	402

Agriculture: ***Distribution of villages according to land use:*** Out of 4 villages, Total area (in hectare) is 5334, out of that 79.42 percent is cultivable and 43.98 percent of the cultivable area is irrigated.

Sources of Irrigation (Hectares): Government Canal 875.76, Private Canal 0, Well without Electricity 0, Well with Electricity 108.92, Tubewell without Electricity 0, Tubewell with Electricity 0, Tank 874.24, River 0, Lake 0, Waterfall 0, Others 4.14.

Villages with population of 5000 to 9999: Thalakkulam.

Villages with population of 10000 and above: Colachel , Kurunthencode , Kadiapattinam.

Distribution of Workers:

	Persons	Males	Females	WPR
Cultivators	878	690	188	5.2
Agricultural Labour	1,837	1,681	156	10.89
Household Industry	1,752	288	1,464	10.38
Other Workers	12,405	11,044	1,361	73.52
Main Workers	14,379	12,041	2,338	85.22
Marginal Workers	2,493	1,662	831	14.78
Total Workers	16,872	13,703	3,169	

Religion: Major Religious Communities:

	Persons	Males	Females	Sex Ratio
Hindu (44.95%)	22,635	11,244	11,391	1,013
Muslim (0.45%)	228	117	111	949
Christian (50.98%)	25,671	12,907	12,764	989
Sikh (0%)	-	-	-	-
Buddhists (0%)	-	-	-	-
Jain (0%)	1	-	1	-

Agewise Data:

	Persons	Males	Females	Sex Ratio
All ages	48,552	24,280	24,272	1000
0-14	12,768	6,558	6,210	947
15-44	23,976	11,743	12,233	1042
45-79	11,106	5,566	5,540	995
80+	475	241	234	971
Age not stated	227	172	55	320

Languages (Dominant):
Tamil, Telugu, Malayalam, Kannada

Disabled Population:

	Persons	Males	Females	%
Total Disabled	1,931	901	1,030	
In Seeing	1,339	535	804	69.34
In Speech	76	43	33	3.94
In Hearing	37	19	18	1.92
In Movement	368	227	141	19.06
Mentally	111	77	34	5.75

KUTHALAM

Kuttalam C.D. Block lies in the northern part of Nagupattinam district. It is a part of Mayiladuthurai and Jharangambadi taluks. The Block is located at a distance of 84 kms. from district headquarters (Nagapattinam). There are 65 villages in the block with the total population of 125,387 persons. Area of the C.D. Block is 190.64 sq. kms. It is bounded in the north and east by C.D. Block Mayiladuthurai, in the south by district Thiruvaur, and in the west by district Thanjavur. CD Block Kuttalam falls in taluk Mayilaluthurai by 56 villages, and in taluk Tharangambadi by 09 villages.

Communications:

Roadways : S.H.-22: Direction- Kumbakonam to Mayiladuthurai, Nearest Villages- Thirumananchery, Vanathivajapuram, Kadalangudy, Villiyanallur, Valuvoor, Thirunalkondacheri, Arivalur, Peruncheri, Kazhanivasal, Thathangudy, Manganallur, Pandaravadi. S.H.-23: Direction- Mayiladuthurai to Nannilam, Thirunalkondacheri, Peruncheri, Kazhanivasal, Thathangudy, Pandaravadai, Manganallur, Kappur.

Railway Station: Thirunalkondacheri, Manganallur.

Backwards Region Grants Fund: It receives Backward Region Grants.

Annual Rainfall: Average Rainfall 1230 mm.

Ground Water: Availability of the ground water in the Basin is 4167.34 H.A.M. and the utilization is 7556. 73 H.A.M. It belongs to Over Exploited category. Depth to water level varies from 2 to 5 meter below the ground. Most of the wells go down in summer months, according to the Ground Water Estimation Committee.

Natural Division: Chola Nadu.

Administration

Revenue **Division:** Mayiladuthurai. Parliamentary Constituency: 27 Chidambaram (SC). District: Nagapattinam. Taluk: Mayiladuthurai, Tharangambadi. Assembly Constituency: 161 Mayiladuthurai, 162 Poompuhar. Gram Panchayat: 51

Villages: 65 **Inhabited:** 64 **Uninhabited:** 1

Ranking	District	State	National
Area	5	298	4340
Population	4	52	2677
Sex Ratio	3	78	643
Child Sex Ratio	7	159	2855
Literacy Rate	3	41	592
Density	9	357	1613
Work Participation Rate	2	26	4479

Gram Panchayats:

Alangudi, Anathanallur, Arivalur, Asikkadu, Edakkudi, Elumagalur, Gangatharapuram, Kadakkam, Kadalangudi, Kanjivoy, Kappur, Karuppur, Kazhanivasal, Keelaiyur, Killiyanur, Kodaivilagam, Kodimangalam, Kokkur, Komal, Konerirajapuram, Kothangudi, Kozhaiyur, Madhirimangalam, Mandai, Manganallur, Maruthur, Mekkirimangalam, Melaiyur, Muthur, Nakkambadi, Palayagudalure, Palayur, Pandaravadai, Paruthikudi, Perambur, Peravur, Perumalkoil, Peruncheri, Porumbur, Senniayanallur, Sethur, Shetirapalapuram, Sivanaragaram, Thathangudi, Thirumanancheri, Tholuthalangudi, Tiruvaduthurai, Tiruvlangadu, Valuvur, Vanadirajapuram, Villiyanallur.

Amenities:

Education: Primary School in 59 villages, Middle school in 27 villages, Matriculation or Secondary School in 10 villages, namely Thiruvavaduthurai, Theraizhandur, Thirunalkondacheri, Manganallur, Ananthanallur, Peravoor, Gangadarapuram, Elumagalur, Kiliyanoor, Perambur.

Higher Secondary or Pre University Courses or Intermediate or Junior College in 3 villages of the CD Block,, namely Peravoor, Gangadarapuram, Elumagalur.

College in 0 village, Adult Literacy Center in 0 village.

Medical: Hospital in 3 villages, Dispensary in 4 villages, Health Center in 5 villages, Sub Center in 23 villages, Maternity and Child Welfare Center in 1 village, Community health workers in 63 villages.

The Villages having Hospital or Dispensary or Health Center are Thozhuthalangudi, Thulasendhirapuram, Inamsenniya Nallur, Thiruvalangadu, Perumalkoil, Theraizhandur, Peruncheri.

Drinking Water: Tap water in 64 villages, Tank water in 2 villages, Well water in 64 villages, Tubewell in 64 villages and more than one source in 64 villages.

Bank: Banking facility in 12 villages, namely,

Thozhuthalangudi, Thulasendhirapuram
Inam Thiruvalangadu, Thiruvavaduthurai
Theraizhandur, Thirunalkondacheri, Arivalur
Thathangudy, Kanjivoy, Nakkambadi
Konerirajapuram Ii, Kiliyanoor.
Credit Society in 19 villages Agricultural Credit Society in 18 Non-Agricultural Credit Society in 5 villages.

Others: Power supply in 64 villages, Cinema hall in 4 villages, sport club in 0 village, Stadium or Auditorium or Community Hall in 1 village, Post Office in 30 villages.

There are 59 villages having bus facilities.

Villages with most of facilities: Thozhuthalangudi Thulasendhirapuram, Inam Thiruvalangadu Thiruvavaduthurai, Theraizhandur, Thirunalkondacheri Arivalur, Thathangudy, Kanjivoy, Nakkambadi Konerirajapuram Ii, Kiliyanoor.

Villages without amenities (Education): Manthai, Keelaparuthikudy, Kodimangalam, Melaagalangan, Agaravallam..

Scheduled Castes: Out of the total population of 125387 persons, 39814 persons (31.75%) belong to Scheduled Castes.

The villages having less than 10% SC population are Inamsenniya Nallur, Inam Thiruvalangadu Konerirajapuram Ii.

The villages having more than 50% SC population are Kadalangudy, Senniyanallur, Mekkirimangalam, Kokkur Sengudi, Kappur, Kozilayur, Ananthanallur, Kanjivoy Kothangudy, Nalavoor, Kodavilagam, Edakkudy, Sethur.

Sex ratio of Scheduled Caste population is 500.

Scheduled Castes Literates and Illiterates by Sex:

	Persons	Males	Females
Literate	22,881	13,071	9,810
Illiterate	16,933	6,832	10,101
Literacy rate	67.2	76.9	57.6
Graduate	255	181	74

Scheduled Castes (Dominant):

Adi Dravida, Paraiyan etc., Generic Castes etc. Valluvan, Pallan

For their cultural identity please see Appendix-I

Villages without Scheduled Castes: There are 2 villages without any scheduled caste population.

Scheduled Tribes: Out of the total population of 125387 persons, 76 persons (0.06%) belong to Scheduled Tribes.

The villages having less than 10% ST population are Alangudi, Thirumananchery, Vanathivajapuram Kadalangudy, Villiyanallur, Setherapalapuram Asikkadu, Thozhuthalangudi, Thulasendhirapuram Melaiyur, Senniyanallur, Inamsenniya Nallur Mekkirimangalam, Mathrimangalam, Thiruvalangadu Inam Thiruvalangadu, Thiruvavaduthurai Palayacudalore, Kokkur, Maruthur, Perumalkoil Theraizhandur, Sengudi, Valuvoor, Thirunalkondacheri Arivalur, Peruncheri, Kazhanivasal, Thathangudy Pandaravadai, Manganallur, Kappur, Kozilayur Ananthanallur, Komal East, Komal West, Peravoor Karuppur, Kanjivoy, Palaiyur, Srikandapuram Kothangudy, Gangadarapuram, Porumbur, Elumagalur Nakkambadi, Manthai, Keelaparuthikudy Melaparuthikudy, Nalavoor, Kodimangalam Melaagalangan, Konerirajapuram, Sivanaragaram Konerirajapuram Ii, Kiliyanoor, Kadakkam Agaraathanur, Muthur, Kodavilagam, Agaravallam Edakkudy, Perambur, Sethur.

The villages having more than 50% ST population are None.

Sex ratio of Scheduled tribe population is 461.

Scheduled Tribes Literates and Illiterates by Sex:

	Persons	Males	Females
Literate	30	19	11
Illiterate	46	22	24
Literacy rate	50.9	57.6	42.3
Graduate	0	0	0

Scheduled Tribes (Dominant):

Malakkuravan, Paniyan, Kurumans

For their cultural identity please see Appendix-II

Villages without Scheduled Tribes: There are 60 villages without any scheduled tribe population.

Literates and Illiterates by Sex (Total Population):

	Persons	Males	Females
Literate	83,716	45,858	37,858
Illiterate	41,671	16,183	25,488
Literacy rate	76	84	68
Graduate	1,506	1,083	423

Agriculture: ***Distribution of villages according to land use:*** Out of 65 villages, Total area (in hectare) is 19064.49, out of that 80.45 percent is cultivable and 89.5 percent of the cultivable area is irrigated.

Sources of Irrigation (Hectares): Government Canal 13430.16, Private Canal 0, Well without Electricity 5.01, Well with Electricity 0, Tubewell without Electricity 60.8, Tubewell with Electricity 230.62, Tank 0, River 0, Lake 0, Waterfall 0, Others 0.

Villages with population of 5000 to 9999: Tiruvaduthurai.

Villages with population of 10000 and above: None

Distribution of Workers:

	Persons	Males	Females	WPR
Cultivators	6,507	5,503	1,004	12.89
Agricultural Labour	32,785	20,100	12,685	64.97
Household Industry	1,031	540	491	2.04

Other Workers	10,139	8,742	1,397	20.09
Main Workers	40,992	29,977	11,015	81.23
Marginal Workers	9,470	4,908	4,562	18.77
Total Workers	50,462	34,885	15,577	

Religion: Major Religious Communities:

	Persons	Males	Females	Sex Ratio
Hindu (86.01%)	107,841	53,898	53,943	1,001
Muslim (9.57%)	11,999	5,280	6,719	1,273
Christian (4.29%)	5,385	2,780	2,605	937
Sikh (0.01%)	8	5	3	600
Buddhists (0%)	4	1	3	3,000
Jain (0.01%)	14	7	7	1,000

Agewise Data:

	Persons	Males	Females	Sex Ratio
All ages	125,387	62,041	63,346	1021
0-14	36,537	18,382	18,155	988
15-44	59,772	28,958	30,814	1064
45-79	26,918	13,626	13,292	975
80+	1,031	506	525	1038
Age not stated	1,129	569	560	984

Languages (Dominant):

Tamil, Telugu, Urdu, Malayalam, English

Disabled Population:

	Persons	Males	Females	%
Total Disabled	3,445	1,779	1,666	
In Seeing	2,213	1,044	1,169	64.24
In Speech	245	143	102	7.11
In Hearing	104	57	47	3.02
In Movement	642	395	247	18.64
Mentally	241	140	101	7

LALGUDI

Lalgudi C.D. Block lies in the north-eastern part of Tiruchirappalli district. It is a part of Lalgudi taluk. The Block is located at a distance of 25 kms. from district headquarters (Tiruchirappalli). There are 53 villages in the block with the total population of 111,143 persons. Area of the C.D. Block is 213.92 sq. kms. It is bounded in the north by C.D. Blocks Manachanallur and Pullambadi, in the south by CD Block Thiruverumbur and district Thanjavur, in the east by CD Block Pullambadi and district Thanjavur, in the west by CD Blocks Manachanallur and Andanallur.

Communications:

Roadways : S.H.-24: Direction- Tiruchirappalli to Pullampadi, Nearest Villages- Peruvalanallur, Peruvalanallur West, Angarai, Pambaramsuthi, Nerujalakkudi, Valadi, Pudukkudi, Thalakudi, Appadurai, Therkuchatiram, Easanakorai, T. Valavanur, Thirumanamedu (W).

Railway Station: V.Thuraiyur, Sirumayankudi (W), Keeramangalam.

River: Kollidam Nadi- Nearest Villages- Alangudimahajan am, Nathamangudi, Thalakudi, Appadurai, Easanakorai, Thirumanamedu (W), Thirumanamedu East, Jevanithinathapuram, Edaiyathumangalam, Koohur, Sathamangalam, Mangammalpuram, Keelanbil, Ariyur. Kulaiyar Nadi- Nearest Villages- Nagar, Kallikadi, Alangudimahajan, Thirumangalam, Keelamari, Mangalam, Neikkuppai (S), R.Valavanur, Marudur, Sirumayankudi (W), Sirumayankudi (E), Thinniyam, Metupatti, Athikudi, Keelanbil, Nathamangudi, Ariyur. Upparnandiyar Nadi- Nearest Villages- Nathamangudi, Alangudimahajanam, Neikkuppai (S), Alangudimahajan, Kallikadi.

Annual Rainfall: Average Rainfall 841 mm.

Ground Water: Availability of the ground water in the Basin is 8580.45 H.A.M. and the utilization is 2919.22 H.A.M. It belongs to Safe category. Depth to water level varies from 2 to 5 meter below the ground. Most of the wells go down in summer months, according to the Ground Water Estimation Committee.

Natural Division: Chola Nadu.

Administration

Revenue **Division:** Lalgudi. Parliamentary Constituency: 24 Tiruchirappalli. District: Tiruchirappalli. Taluk: Lalgudi. Assembly Constituency: 143 Lalgudi. Gram Panchayat: 35.

Villages: 53 **Inhabited:** 50 **Uninhabited:** 3

Ranking	District	State	National
Area	11	265	3950
Population	2	90	3129
Sex Ratio	2	94	767
Child Sex Ratio	9	260	4363
Literacy Rate	2	24	364
Density	13	314	2118
Work Participation Rate	2	50	3688

Gram Panchayats:

Aangarai, Alanganallur, Alankudi Mahajanam, Appathurai, Ariyur, Athikudi, Esanaikkorai, Idaiyathumangalam, Jangamarajapuram, Jevanthinathapuram, Keelanbil, Kilaperungavur, Koahur, Komakudi, Madakkudi, Magizhampadi, Manakkal, Mangammalpuram, Mangudi, Marudur, Mettuppatti, Nagar, Natham, Neikuppai, T.Kallikudi, Pallapuram, Pambaramchutti, Peruvalanallur, Pudhukudi, Pudur Uttamanur, R.Valavanur, Sathamangalam, Sembarai, Sirumaruthur, Sirumayangudi, T.Kallikudi, T.Valavanur, Thalakudi, Thatchankurichi, Thinniyam, Thirumanamedu, Thirumangalam, Vaaladi.

Amenities:

Education: Primary School in 48 villages, Middle school in 24 villages, Matriculation or Secondary School in 7 villages, namely Peruvalanallur, Nagar, Sembarai, Jengamarajapuram, Thalakudi, Mangammalpuram, Keelanbil.

Higher Secondary or Pre University Courses or Intermediate or Junior College in 0 village of the CD Block, College in 0 village, Adult Literacy Center in 1 village.
Medical: Hospital in 2 villages, Dispensary in 7 villages, Health Center in 4 villages, Sub Center in 4 villages, Maternity and Child Welfare Center in 4 villages, Community health workers in 0 village.
The Villages having Hospital or Dispensary or Health Center are Sirumayankudi (W), Sembarai, Angarai, Nerujalakkudi, Valadi, Thalakudi, Appadurai, Thirumanamedu East, Mangammalpuram.
Drinking Water: Tap water in 50 villages, Tank water in 20 villages, Well water in 50 villages, Tubewell in 50 villages and more than one source in 50 villages.
Bank: Banking facility in 10 villages, namely, Peruvalanallur, Marudur, Nagar, Sirumayankudi (W) Manakkal (E), Nerujalakkudi, Valadi, Mangammalpuram Keelanbil, Ariyur.
Credit Society in 12 villages Agricultural Credit Society in 11 Non-Agricultural Credit Society in 0 village.
Others: Power supply in 50 villages, Cinema hall in 2 villages, sport club in 0 village, Stadium or Auditorium or Community Hall in 0 village, Post Office in 34 villages.
There are 45 villages having bus facilities.
Villages with most of facilities: Peruvalanallur Nagar, Sirumayankudi (W), Nerujalakkudi, Valadi Mangammalpuram, Keelanbil.
Villages without amenities (Education):
Keelamari Mangalam, Pudukkudi..
Scheduled Castes: Out of the total population of 111143 persons, 28691 persons (25.81%) belong to Scheduled Castes.
The villages having less than 10% SC population are Mahilambadi, Peruvalanallur West, Komakudy Manakkal (E), Easanakorai.
The villages having more than 50% SC population are V.Thuraiyur, Keelaperungavur, Pudukkudi Therkuchatiram.
Sex ratio of Scheduled Caste population is 511.
Scheduled Castes Literates and Illiterates by Sex:

	Persons	Males	Females
Literate	18,448	10,251	8,197
Illiterate	10,243	3,786	6,457
Literacy rate	74.2	84.8	64.1
Graduate	821	575	246

Scheduled Castes (Dominant):
Pallan, Paraiyan etc., Chakkiliyan, Arunthathiyar Domban
For their cultural identity please see Appendix-I
Villages without Scheduled Castes: There are 4 villages without any scheduled caste population.

Scheduled Tribes: Out of the total population of 111143 persons, 201 persons (0.18%) belong to Scheduled Tribes.
The villages having less than 10% ST population are Thatchankurichi, Mahilambadi, Pudur Uthamanur Alangudimahajanam, Kallikadi, Peruvalanallur Peruvalanallur West, Thirumangalam Keelamari Mangalam, Neikkuppai (N), Neikkuppai (S) R.Valavanur, Madakudi, V.Thuraiyur, Marudur Keelaperungavur, Nagar, Sirumayankudi (W) Sirumayankudi (E), Komakudy, Sembarai, Nathamangudi Thinniyam, Metupatti, Jengamarajapuram, Athikudi Manakkal (E), Manakkal, Angarai, Pambaramsuthi Nerujalakkudi, Valadi, Sirumarudhar, Pudukkudi Keeramangalam, Thalakudi, Appadurai, Therkuchatiram Easanakorai, T. Valavanur, Thirumanamedu (W) Thirumanamedu East, Jevanithinathapuram Sesasamuthiram, Edaiyathumangalam, Koohur Sathamangalam, Mangammalpuram, Keelanbil, Ariyur.
The villages having more than 50% ST population are None.
Sex ratio of Scheduled tribe population is 498.
Scheduled Tribes Literates and Illiterates by Sex:

	Persons	Males	Females
Literate	92	52	40
Illiterate	109	49	60
Literacy rate	54.1	63.4	45.5
Graduate	3	2	1

Scheduled Tribes (Dominant):
Irular, Malai Arayan, Malai Pandaram, Kattunayakan Kaniyan etc.
For their cultural identity please see Appendix-II
Villages without Scheduled Tribes: There are 42 villages without any scheduled tribe population.
Literates and Illiterates by Sex (Total Population):

	Persons	Males	Females
Literate	77,643	42,769	34,874
Illiterate	33,500	12,376	21,124
Literacy rate	79	88	70
Graduate	4,104	2,750	1,354

Agriculture: ***Distribution of villages according to land use:*** Out of 53 villages, Total area (in hectare) is 21392.66, out of that 54.01 percent is cultivable and 89.17 percent of the cultivable area is irrigated.
Sources of Irrigation (Hectares): Government Canal 8896.76, Private Canal 145.1, Well without Electricity 116.82, Well with Electricity 131.7, Tubewell without Electricity 330.2, Tubewell with Electricity 682.69, Tank 0, River 0, Lake 0, Waterfall 0, Others 0.
Villages with population of 5000 to 9999: None
Villages with population of 10000 and above: None

Distribution of Workers:

	Persons	Males	Females	WPR
Cultivators	8,894	6,584	2,310	17.98
Agricultural Labour	26,746	13,656	13,090	54.06
Household Industry	1,679	685	994	3.39
Other Workers	12,159	9,635	2,524	24.57
Main Workers	40,277	26,627	13,650	81.4
Marginal Workers	9,201	3,933	5,268	18.6
Total Workers	49,478	30,560	18,918	

Religion: Major Religious Communities:

	Persons	Males	Females	Sex Ratio
Hindu (78.63%)	87,396	43,343	44,053	1,016
Muslim (3.02%)	3,362	1,666	1,696	1,018
Christian (18.26%)	20,296	10,090	10,206	1,011
Sikh (0%)	-	-	-	-
Buddhists (0%)	2	2	-	-
Jain (0%)	3	1	2	2,000

Agewise Data:

	Persons	Males	Females	Sex Ratio
All ages	111,143	55,145	55,998	1015
0-14	30,588	15,635	14,953	956
15-44	53,877	26,571	27,306	1028
45-79	25,362	12,262	13,100	1068
80+	868	449	419	933
Age not stated	448	228	220	965

Languages (Dominant):

Tamil, Telugu, Urdu, Malayalam, Kannada

Disabled Population:

	Persons	Males	Females	%
Total Disabled	3,847	1,616	2,231	
In Seeing	2,592	906	1,686	67.38
In Speech	214	114	100	5.56
In Hearing	159	78	81	4.13
In Movement	662	398	264	17.21
Mentally	220	120	100	5.72

LATHUR

Lathur C.D. Block lies in the south-eastern part of Kancheepuram district. It is a part of cheyyur taluk. The taluk is located at a distance of 63 kms. from district headquarters (Kancheepuram). There are 59 villa ges in the block with the total population of 78,090 persons. Area of the C.D. Block is 278.76 sq. kms. It is bounded in the north by CD Blocks Maduranthakam and Tirukalukunram, in the south by CD Block Chithamur, in the east by the Bay of Bengal, and in the west by CD Block Maduranthakam.

Communications:

Roadways : Information not Available.

River: Palar Nadi- Nearest Villages- Neelamangalam, Nelvoy, Karuppur, Sevur, Madavilagam, Thandarai, Poigana llur, Poranjeri, Parameswaramangalam, Veppancheri, Kadalur.

Annual Rainfall: Average Rainfall 1105 mm.

Ground Water: Availability of the ground water in the Basin is 8744.55 H.A.M. and the utilization is 9573.83 H.A.M. It belongs to Over Expoited category. Depth to water level varies from 2 to 10 meter below the ground. Most of the wells go down in summer months, according to the Ground Water Estimation Committee.

Coastal Villages: Nearest Villages- (Bay of Bengal)- Kadalur, Kilarkollai, Kanathur, Vadapattinam, Mugaiyur, Paramankeni.

Natural Division: Tondai Nadu.

Administration

Revenue Division: Madurnthakham. Parliamentary Constituency: 6 Kancheepuram (SC). District: Kancheepuram. Taluk: Cheyyur. Assembly Constituency : 34 Cheyyur (SC). Gram Panchayat: 41.

Villages: 59 **Inhabited:** 59 **Uninhabited:** 0

Ranking	District	State	National
Area	9	199	3016
Population	12	251	4167
Sex Ratio	4	195	1356
Child Sex Ratio	6	117	2214
Literacy Rate	12	286	2440
Density	7	293	3749
Work Participation Rate	11	252	3262

Gram Panchayats:

Adayalacheri, Akkinambattu, Ammanur, Anaicut, Cheyyur, Iranyasidhi, Kadalur , Kadugupattu, Kalkulam , Kalkulam, Kalkulam , Kanathur , Keelacheri, Kodur , Kodur, Koovathur , Lathur , Mugaiyur , Mugaiyur, Nedumaram, Neelamangalam, Nelvoy , Nelvoy, Nelvoypalayam , Nemanadam, Nemandam , Nemandam , Nerkunampattu, Pachambakkam, Pachambakkam , Paramankeni, Parameswaramangalam, Pavunjur , Periyavelikadu , Perumbakkam , Perumbakkam , Seekinamkuppam , Seevadi , Sembur , sengathur , Sengathur , Siruvangunam, Thandarai, Thandarai , Thandarai , Thattambattu, Thenpattinam, Thiruvadur , Thondamanallur, Vadakkuvayaloor, Vadapattinam, Veerabogam , Vettakarakuppam.

Amenities:

Education: Primary School in 45 villages, Middle school in 30 villages, Matriculation or Secondary School in 6 villages, namely Parameswaramangalam A,B,C/C, Koovathur, Pavunjur A,B/B, Thiruvadur, Sathiamangalam, Cheyyur. Higher Secondary or Pre University Courses or Intermediate or Junior College in 2 villages of the CD Block,, namely Koovathur, Cheyyur.

College in 0 village, Adult Literacy Center in 0 village.

Medical: Hospital in 3 villages, Dispensary in 0 village, Health Center in 5 villages, Sub Center in 19 villages, Maternity and Child Welfare Center in 0 village, Community health workers in 59 villages.

The Villages having Hospital or Dispensary or Health Center are Koovathur, Pavunjur A,B/B, Cheyyur.

Drinking Water: Tap water in 59 villages, Tank water in 48 villages, Well water in 59 villages, Tubewell in 59 villages and more than one source in 59 villages.

Bank: Banking facility in 7 villages, namely, Parameswaramangalam A,B,C/C, Koovathur Pavunjur A,B/B, Nelvoypalayam, Kodur, Madayambakkam Cheyyur.

Credit Society in 7 villages Agricultural Credit Society in 7 Non-Agricultural Credit Society in 2 villages.

Others: Power supply in 58 villages, Cinema hall in 1 village, sport club in 1 village, Stadium or Auditorium or Community Hall in 0 village, Post Office in 19 villages.

There are 36 villages having bus facilities.

Villages with most of facilities: Parameswaramangalam A,B,C/C Koovathur, Pavunjur A,B/B, Nelvoypalayam, Kodur Cheyyur.

Villages without amenities (Education): Karuppur, Madavilagam, Parasanallur, Poranjeri, Sathamangalam, Perumalcheri, Malrajakuppam, Murukkanthangal, Kodapattinam, Pudupattu, Pakkavancheri, Thirupurakoil, Maruderi..

Scheduled Castes: Out of the total population of 78090 persons, 33549 persons (42.96%) belong to Scheduled Castes.

The villages having less than 10% SC population are Sembur, Punnamai, Murukkanthangal, Kodapattinam Nemandam, Thirupurakoil, Madayambakkam, Maruderi.

The villages having more than 50% SC population are Neelamangalam, Karuppur, Madavilagam, Poiganallur Veppancheri, Kilarkollai, Koovathur, Manicuppam Thondamanallur A,B,C/C, Vadakkuvayaloor, Pekkaranai Seevadi, Lathur, Periavelikadu, Thiruvadur, Palur Malrajakuppam, Vadapattinam, Kodur, Pudupattu Atchivilagam.

Sex ratio of Scheduled Caste population is 499.

Scheduled Castes Literates and Illiterates by Sex:

	Persons	Males	Females
Literate	16,518	9,627	6,891
Illiterate	17,031	7,179	9,852
Literacy rate	56.6	65.9	47.4
Graduate	223	164	59

Scheduled Castes (Dominant):

Adi Dravida, Arunthathiyar, Paraiyan etc., Valluvan Chakkiliyan

For their cultural identity please see Appendix-I

Villages without Scheduled Castes: There are 6 villages without any scheduled caste population.

Scheduled Tribes: Out of the total population of 78090 persons, 633 persons (0.81%) belong to Scheduled Tribes.

The villages having less than 10% ST population are Neelamangalam, Nelvoy, Karuppur, Sevur, Madavilagam Sembur, Thandarai, Parasanallur, Poiganallur Poranjeri, Parameswaramangalam A,B,C/C, Veppancheri Kadalur, Kilarkollai, Koovathur, Nerkunampattu A,B/B Manicuppam, Thondamanallur A,B,C/C, Kalkulam Vadakkuvayaloor, Sathamangalam, Pekkaranai, Seevadi Punnamai, Lathur, Pachambakkam, Pavunjur A,B/B Uludamangalam, Periavelikadu, Chinnavelikadu A,B/B Thiruvadur, Kadugupattu, Palur, Nelvoypalayam Perumalcheri, Malrajakuppam, Nedumaram, Kodapattinam Kanathur, Vadapattinam, Mugaiyur A,B/B, Kodur Sathiamangalam, Akkinambattu A,B,C/C Perumbakkam A,B/B, Pudupattu, Iranyasidhi, Nemandam Pakkavancheri, Sengattur, Thirupurakoil Madayambakkam, Atchivilagam, Paramankeni A,B,C/C Pakkur A,B/B, Cheyyur, Ammanur A,B,C/C.

The villages having more than 50% ST population are None.

Sex ratio of Scheduled tribe population is 498.

Scheduled Tribes Literates and Illiterates by Sex:

	Persons	Males	Females
Literate	127	78	49
Illiterate	506	240	266
Literacy rate	24.1	29.8	18.4
Graduate	0	0	0

Scheduled Tribes (Dominant):

Irular, Kattunayakan, Malakkuravan Generic Tribes etc.

For their cultural identity please see Appendix-II

Villages without Scheduled Tribes: There are 32 villages without any scheduled tribe population.

Literates and Illiterates by Sex (Total Population):

	Persons	Males	Females
Literate	42,506	24,539	17,967
Illiterate	35,584	14,598	20,986
Literacy rate	62	72	52
Graduate	550	387	163

Agriculture: ***Distribution of villages according to land use:*** Out of 59 villages, Total area (in hectare) is 27876.82, out of that 63 percent is cultivable and 57.63 percent of the cultivable area is irrigated.

Sources of Irrigation (Hectares): Government Canal 0, Private Canal 0, Well without Electricity 417.63, Well with Electricity 3357.86, Tubewell without Electricity 178.96, Tubewell with Electricity 463.88, Tank 448.75, River 0,

Lake 5113.1, Waterfall 0, Others 140.66.

Villages with population of 5000 to 9999:

Kadalur.

Villages with population of 10000 and above:

Cheyyur.

Distribution of Workers:

	Persons	Males	Females	WPR
Cultivators	6,193	4,606	1,587	17.16
Agricultural Labour	22,923	12,249	10,674	63.52
Household Industry	898	431	467	2.49
Other Workers	6,074	4,483	1,591	16.83
Main Workers	21,709	14,929	6,780	60.16
Marginal Workers	14,379	6,840	7,539	39.84
Total Workers	36,088	21,769	14,319	

Religion: Major Religious Communities:

	Persons	Males	Females	Sex Ratio
Hindu (94.76%)	73,995	37,126	36,869	993
Muslim (1.02%)	799	400	399	998
Christian (4.17%)	3,254	1,592	1,662	1,044
Sikh (0%)	1	-	1	-
Buddhists (0%)	1	1	-	-
Jain (0%)	1	-	1	-

Agewise Data:

	Persons	Males	Females	Sex Ratio
All ages	78,090	39,137	38,953	995
0-14	23,221	11,823	11,398	964
15-44	37,614	18,686	18,928	1013
45-79	16,368	8,162	8,206	1005
80+	685	368	317	861
Age not stated	202	98	104	1061

Languages (Dominant):

Tamil, Telugu, Urdu, Kannada, Malayalam

Disabled Population:

	Persons	Males	Females	%
Total Disabled	2,094	1,157	937	
In Seeing	1,041	572	469	49.71
In Speech	187	99	88	8.93
In Hearing	169	92	77	8.07
In Movement	565	337	228	26.98
Mentally	132	57	75	6.3

MADATHUKULAM

Madathukulam C.D. Block lies in the southern part of Coimbatore district. It is a part of Udumalaipettai taluk. The Block is located at a distance of 87 kms. from district headquarters (Coimbatore). There are 11 villages in the block with the total population of 48,295 persons. Area of the C.D. Block is 150.43 sq. kms. It is bounded in the north by CD block Gudimangalam and district Erode, in the south and east by district Dindigul, in the west by C.D. Blocks Gudimangalam and Udamalaipettai.

Communications:

Roadways : N.H.-209: Direction- Udumalaipettai to Palani, Nearest Village- Myvadi.

Railway Station: Myvadi.

River: Amaravathi Nadi- Nearest Villages- Jothampatu, Kadathur, Karatholuvu, Solamadevi, Kolumam.

Canal: Amravathi River Canal- Nearest Villages- Metrathi, Karatholuvu, Thungavi, Myvadi, Jothampatu, Pappankulam.

Annual Rainfall: Average Rainfall 550 mm.

Ground Water: Availability of the ground water in the Basin is 6307.51 H.A.M. and the utilization is 3560.38 H.A.M. It belongs to Safe category. Depth to water level varies from 2 to 10 meter below the ground. Most of the wells go down in summer months, according to the Ground Water Estimation Committee.

Natural Division: Kongu Nadu.

Administration

Revenue **Division:** Udumalaipettai. Parliamentary Constituency: 21 Pollachi. District: Coimbatore. Taluk: Udumalaipettai. Assembly Constituency: 125 Udumalaipettai, 126 Valparai (SC). Gram Panchayat: 11.

Villages: 11 **Inhabited:** 11 **Uninhabited:** 0

Ranking	District	State	National
Area	16	345	5038
Population	17	364	5373
Sex Ratio	8	257	1883
Child Sex Ratio	12	149	2715
Literacy Rate	13	236	2121
Density	6	114	3345
Work Participation Rate	8	196	1156

Gram Panchayats:

Jothampatti, Kadathur, Karatholuvu, Kolumam, Metrathi, Myvadi, Pappankulam, Sholamadevi, Thanthoni, Thungavi, Vedappatti.

Amenities:

Education: Primary School in 11 villages, Middle school in 7 villages, Matriculation or Secondary School in 0 village Higher Secondary or Pre University Courses or Intermediate or Junior College in 0 village of the CD Block, College in 0 village, Adult Literacy Center in 0 village.

Medical: Hospital in 1 village, Dispensary in 0 village, Health Center in 2 villages, Sub Center in 10 villages, Maternity and Child Welfare Center in 1 village, Community health workers in 1 village.

The Village having Hospital or Dispensary or Health Center is Solamadevi.

Drinking Water: Tap water in 11 villages, Tank water in 0 villages, Well water in 11 villages, Tubewell in 11 villages and more than one source in 11 villages.

Bank: Banking facility in 4 villages, namely, Karatholuvu, Thungavi, Pappankulam, Kolumam.

Credit Society in 6 villages Agricultural Credit Society in 5 Non-Agricultural Credit Society in 3 villages.

Others: Power supply in 11 villages, Cinema hall in 1 village, sport club in 0 village, Stadium or Auditorium or Community Hall in 0 village, Post Office in 11 villages.

There are 10 villages having bus facilities.

Villages with most of facilities: Karatholuvu Pappankulam, Kolumam.

Villages without Amenities (Education): None..

Scheduled Castes: Out of the total population of 48295 persons, 9808 persons (20.31%) belong to Scheduled Castes.

The villages having less than 10% SC population are None..

The villages having more than 50% SC population are None.

Sex ratio of Scheduled Caste population is 501.

Scheduled Castes Literates and Illiterates by Sex:

	Persons	Males	Females
Literate	3,764	2,220	1,544
Illiterate	6,044	2,674	3,370
Literacy rate	44.4	52.3	36.5
Graduate	18	16	2

Scheduled Castes (Dominant):

Madari, Paraiyan etc., Samban, Valluvan, Kudumban

For their cultural identity please see Appendix-I

Villages without Scheduled Castes: There is 0 village without any scheduled caste population.

Scheduled Tribes: Out of the total population of 48295 persons, 27 persons (0.06%) belong to Scheduled Tribes.

The villages having less than 10% ST population are Metrathi, Karatholuvu, Thungavi, Thanthoni, Myvadi Jothampatu, Kadathur, Solamadevi, Vedapatti Pappankulam, Kolumam.

The villages having more than 50% ST population are None.

Sex ratio of Scheduled tribe population is 481.

Scheduled Tribes Literates and Illiterates by Sex:

	Persons	Males	Females
Literate	19	12	7
Illiterate	8	2	6
Literacy rate	82.6	100.0	63.6
Graduate	0	0	0

Scheduled Tribes (Dominant):

Malai Vedan

For their cultural identity please see Appendix-II

Villages without Scheduled Tribes: There are 10 villages without any scheduled tribe population.

Literates and Illiterates by Sex (Total Population):

	Persons	Males	Females
Literate	27,493	16,002	11,491
Illiterate	20,802	8,352	12,450
Literacy rate	64	74	54
Graduate	354	255	99

Agriculture: ***Distribution of villages according to land use:*** Out of 11 villages, Total area (in hectare) is 15043.27, out of that 86.15 percent is cultivable and 50.75 percent of the cultivable area is irrigated.

Sources of Irrigation (Hectares): Government Canal 3739.82, Private Canal 0, Well without Electricity 437.5, Well with Electricity 2247.33, Tubewell without Electricity 0, Tubewell with Electricity 0, Tank 152.75, River 0, Lake 0, Waterfall 0, Others 0.

Villages with population of 5000 to 9999:

Thungavi, Myvadi, Jothampatti, Pappankulam.

Villages with population of 10000 and above: None

Distribution of Workers:

	Persons	Males	Females	WPR
Cultivators	5,201	3,671	1,530	19.49
Agricultural Labour	13,952	7,187	6,765	52.28
Household Industry	837	450	387	3.14
Other Workers	6,695	4,903	1,792	25.09
Main Workers	24,009	15,221	8,788	89.97
Marginal Workers	2,676	990	1,686	10.03
Total Workers	26,685	16,211	10,474	

Religion: Major Religious Communities:

	Persons	Males	Females	Sex Ratio
Hindu (92%)	44,430	22,390	22,040	984
Muslim (7.38%)	3,563	1,816	1,747	962
Christian (0.61%)	296	144	152	1,056
Sikh (0%)	-	-	-	-
Buddhists (0%)	-	-	-	-
Jain (0%)	-	-	-	-

Agewise Data:

	Persons	Males	Females	Sex Ratio
All ages	48,295	24,354	23,941	983
0-14	11,723	5,980	5,743	960
15-44	24,206	12,091	12,115	1002
45-79	11,868	6,007	5,861	976
80+	368	189	179	947
Age not stated	130	87	43	494

Languages (Dominant):

Tamil, Telugu, Kannada, Urdu, Malayalam

Disabled Population:

	Persons	Males	Females	%
Total Disabled	1,945	692	1,253	
In Seeing	1,590	498	1,092	81.75
In Speech	74	35	39	3.8
In Hearing	41	17	24	2.11
In Movement	177	108	69	9.1
Mentally	63	34	29	3.24

Madhanur C.D. Block lies in the west central part of Vellore district. It is a part of Vellore and Vaniyambadi taluks. The taluk (Vaniyambadi) is located at a distance of 70 kms. from district headquarters (Vellore). There are 62 villages in the block with the total population of 93,997 persons. Area of the C.D. Block is 722.96 sq. kms. It is bounded in the north by CD Block Peranampattu and Gudiyatham, in the south by CD Block Alangayam, in the east by CD Block Anaicut, in the west by CD Blocks Alangayam, in the east by CD Block, and in the west by CD Blocks Alangayam Natrampalli and Pernampattu. CD Block Madhanur falls in taluk Vellore by 32 villages, and in taluk by Vaniyambadi 30 villages.

Communications:

Roadways : N.H.-46: Direction- Vaniyambadi to Pallikonda, Nearest Villages- Madanur, Vadapudupet, Kilmurungai, Sanakuppam, Vengili, Kulithigai, Thottalam, Kutrambakkam, Agramcheri, Gollamangalam, Komaswaram, Somalapuram, Periyankuppam, Solur, Alankuppam, Kannadikuppam, Vinnamangalam, Minnur, Sengilikuppam.

River: Puniyathirtha Nadi- Nearest Villages- Agraharam, Jhollappalli, Guruvarajapalayam, Agaram, Arjathy, Kuppampattu, Veppankuppam, Palappadi. Palar Nadi- Nearest Villages- Kulithigai, Thottalam, Madanur, Kutrambakkam, Agramcheri, Somalapuram, Komaswaram, Sengilikuppam, Minnur, Vinnamangalam, Kannadikuppam, Alankuppam, Solur.

Annual Rainfall: Average Rainfall 949 mm.

Ground Water: Availability of the ground water in the Basin is 5449.84 H.A.M. and the utilization is 9451.49 H.A.M. It belongs to Over Expoited category. Depth to water level varies from 5 to 15 meter below the ground. Most of the wells go down in summer months, according to the Ground Water Estimation Committee.

Forest and Reserved Forest: (Ambur Fuel RF)- Nearest Villages- Kammiyambattu, Ambur Tuel (RF), Nacharkuppam, Vinnamangalam, Vellakkal RF, Vellakkal. (Ambur Plantation)- Nearest Villages- Ambur (RF), Naickaneri. (Ambur)- Nearest Villages- Nedumipalayam, Ambur (RF), Arimalai, Ambur (RF), Periyankuppam, Kuppampalayam, Ambur, Ambur, Ambur, Pakkampalayam, Chinnapallikuppam, Melpallipattu, Ambur, Ambur, Asanambut, Thenpudupattu, Anankuppam. (Karuthamalai)- Nearest Villages- Pakkam, Kasnthamalai, Kasnthamalai, Melpallipattu, Asanambut, Thenpudupattu, Kasuthamalai, Kallaparai, Kasuthamalai. (Paravamalai)- Nearest Villages- Guruvarajapalayam, Agaram, Veppankuppam. (Sanankuppam)- Nearest Villages- Agaram, Arjathy, Palappadi, Sasnankuppam (RF), Sasnankuppam (RF), Nedumipalayam, Ramanayanikuppam, Vadapudupet, Vengili, Kulithigai, Thottalam, Madanur, Kutrambakkam, Agramcheri, Pallikuppam, Palur, Tirumalaikuppam, Sanankuppam, Komaswaram. (Vellakuttai Extn RF)- Nearest Villages- Vinnamangalam.

Natural Division: Tondai Nadu.

Administration

Revenue **Division:** Vellore, Tirupatahur. Parliamentary Constituency: 8 Vellore. District: Vellore. Taluk: Vellore, Vaniyambadi. Assembly Constituency: 48 Ambur, 44 Anaikattu. Gram Panchayat: 36.

Villages: 62 **Inhabited:** 44 **Uninhabited:** 18

Ranking	District	State	National
Area	1	10	878
Population	14	159	3656
Sex Ratio	6	116	892
Child Sex Ratio	9	210	3383
Literacy Rate	8	123	1279
Density	13	329	5834
Work Participation Rate	20	372	3983

Gram Panchayats:

Agaram, Agaramcheri , Agraharam, Alankuppam, Arimalai, Asanampattu, Chengilikuppam, Chinnacheri, Chinnapallukuppam, Gollamangalam, Guruvarajapalayam, Kannadikuppam, Kilmurungai, Koothambakkam, Kulithigai, Kuppambattu, Kuppampalayam, Madanur, Melpallipattu, Minnur, Nacharkuppam, Nayakkaneri, Pakkampalayam, Pallikuppam, Palur, Periyankuppam, Ramanayanikuppam, Solur, Somalapuram, Thirumalaikuppam, Thollapalli, Thottalam, Vadapudupattu, Vengili, Veppankuppam, Vinnamangalam.

Amenities:

Education: Primary School in 42 villages, Middle school in 17 villages, Matriculation or Secondary School in 7 villages, namely Agaram, Veppankuppam, Chinnapallikuppam, Asanambut, Madanur, Agramcheri, Periyankuppam.

Higher Secondary or Pre University Courses or Intermediate or Junior College in 1 village of the CD Block,, namely Madanur.

College in 0 village, Adult Literacy Center in 0 village.

Medical: Hospital in 1 village, Dispensary in 0 village, Health Center in 3 villages, Sub Center in 3 villages, Maternity and Child Welfare Center in 12 villages, Community health workers in 41 villages.

The Villages having Hospital or Dispensary or Health Center are Thottalam, Kutrambakkam, Vellakkal.

Drinking Water: Tap water in 44 villages, Tank water in 3 villages, Well water in 37 villages, Tubewell in 3 villages and more than one source in 44 villages.

Bank: Banking facility in 6 villages, namely, Agaram, Nedumipalayam, Arimalai, Madanur, Alankuppam Vinnamangalam.

Credit Society in 13 villages Agricultural Credit Society in 12

Non-Agricultural Credit Society in 3 villages.

Others: Power supply in 44 villages, Cinema hall in 5 villages, sport club in 0 village, Stadium or Auditorium or Community Hall in 0 village, Post Office in 37 villages.

There are 39 villages having bus facilities.

Villages with most of facilities: Agaram, Arimalai Madanur, Alankuppam, Vinnamangalam.

Villages without amenities (Education):
Nacharkuppam..

Scheduled Castes: Out of the total population of 93997 persons, 32282 persons (34.34%) belong to Scheduled Castes.
The villages having less than 10% SC population are None..
The villages having more than 50% SC population are Ramanayanikuppam, Pakkampalayam, Somalapuram Kannadikuppam, Kammiyambattu, Nacharkuppam.
Sex ratio of Scheduled Caste population is 503.

Scheduled Castes Literates and Illiterates by Sex:

	Persons	Males	Females
Literate	18,917	10,625	8,292
Illiterate	13,365	5,404	7,961
Literacy rate	67.6	76.9	58.6
Graduate	408	306	102

Scheduled Castes (Dominant):
Adi Dravida, Arunthathiyar, Kuravan etc., Valluvan Puthirai Vannan

For their cultural identity please see Appendix-I

Villages without Scheduled Castes: There are 19 villages without any scheduled caste population.

Scheduled Tribes: Out of the total population of 93997 persons, 4253 persons (4.52%) belong to Scheduled Tribes.
The villages having less than 10% ST population are Agraharam, Jhollappalli, Guruvarajapalayam, Agaram Arjathy, Palappadi, Nedumipalayam, Arimalai Ramanayanikuppam, Kuppampattu, Veppankuppam Kuppampalayam, Chinnapallikuppam, Melpallipattu Thenpudupattu, Kallaparai, Vadapudupet, Kilmurungai Vengili, Kulithigai, Thottalam, Madanur Kutrambakkam, Agramcheri, Gollamangalam, Pallikuppam Palur, Tirumalaikuppam, Komaswaram, Somalapuram Periyankuppam, Solur, Alankuppam, Kannadikuppam Kammiyambattu, Nacharkuppam, Vinnamangalam, Minnur Sengilikuppam, Vellakkal.
The villages having more than 50% ST population are None.
Sex ratio of Scheduled tribe population is 499.

Scheduled Tribes Literates and Illiterates by Sex:

	Persons	Males	Females
Literate	1,140	723	417
Illiterate	3,113	1,407	1,706
Literacy rate	32.1	40.5	23.6
Graduate	1	0	1

Scheduled Tribes (Dominant):
Malayali, Irular, Kurumans, Malakkuravan Generic Tribes etc.

For their cultural identity piease see Appendix-II

Villages without Scheduled Tribes: There are 40 villages without any scheduled tribe population.

Literates and Illiterates by Sex (Total Population):

	Persons	Males	Females
Literate	56,747	31,989	24,758
Illiterate	37,250	14,776	22,474
Literacy rate	69	79	60
Graduate	1,506	1,101	405

Agriculture: ***Distribution of villages according to land use:*** Out of 62 villages, Total area (in hectare) is 72296.41, out of that 14.2 percent is cultivable and 30.3 percent of the cultivable area is irrigated.

Sources of Irrigation (Hectares): Government Canal 0, Private Canal 0, Well without Electricity 95.21, Well with Electricity 2752.246, Tubewell without Electricity 82.88, Tubewell with Electricity 37.51, Tank 81.44, River 0, Lake 60.45, Waterfall 0, Others 0.

Villages with population of 5000 to 9999:
Agaram, Agaramcheri , Periyankuppam.

Villages with population of 10000 and above: None

Distribution of Workers:

	Persons	Males	Females	WPR
Cultivators	5,839	4,661	1,178	14.66
Agricultural Labour	16,443	9,105	7,338	41.27
Household Industry	1,402	726	676	3.52
Other Workers	16,159	11,692	4,467	40.56
Main Workers	31,499	21,893	9,606	79.06
Marginal Workers	8,344	4,291	4,053	20.94
Total Workers	39,843	26,184	13,659	

Religion: Major Religious Communities:

	Persons	Males	Females	Sex Ratio
Hindu (92.64%)	87,081	43,352	43,729	1,009
Muslim (4.2%)	3,952	1,952	2,000	1,025
Christian (3.02%)	2,841	1,401	1,440	1,028
Sikh (0.02%)	19	9	10	1,111
Buddhists (0.01%)	13	6	7	1,167
Jain (0.02%)	23	11	12	1,091

Agewise Data:

	Persons	Males	Females	Sex Ratio
All ages	93,997	46,765	47,232	1010
0-14	27,934	14,183	13,751	970
15-44	44,921	22,245	22,676	1019
45-79	20,077	9,877	10,200	1033
80+	913	387	526	1359

Age not stated	152	73	79	1082

Languages (Dominant):
Tamil, Telugu, Urdu, Kannada, Marathi

Disabled Population:

	Persons	Males	Females	%
Total Disabled	2,333	1,321	1,012	
In Seeing	1,210	646	564	51.86
In Speech	209	116	93	8.96
In Hearing	105	43	62	4.5
In Movement	610	386	224	26.15
Mentally	199	130	69	8.53

MADUKKARAI

Madukkarai C.D. Block lies in the northern part of Coimbatore district. It is a part of Coimbatore South taluk. The Block is located at a distance of 15 kms. from district headquarters (Coimbatore). There are 13 villages in the block with the total population of 37,846 persons. Area of the C.D. Block is 125.92 sq. kms. It is bounded in the north by CD Blocks Periyanaickenpalayam and Sarcarsamakulam, in the south by CD Block Kinathukadavu, in the east by CD Blocks Sulur and Sultanpet, in the west by C.D. Block Thondamuthur, and it has common boundary with the state of Kerala on south-west.

Communications:

Roadways : N.H.-47: Direction- Palghat to Coimbatore, Nearest Villages- Mavuthampatty, Pichanur. N.H.-209: Direction- Coimbatore to Pallachi, Nearest Villages- Seerapalayam, Malumachanpatti, Myleripalayam, Arisipalalyam.

River: Noyil Nadi- Nearest Village- Ettimadai Extn. RF.

Annual Rainfall: Average Rainfall 550 mm.

Ground Water: Availability of the ground water in the Basin is 2294.21 H.A.M. and the utilization is 4060.47 H.A.M. It belongs to Semi Critical category. Depth to water level varies from 5 to 20 meter below the ground. Most of the wells go down in summer months, according to the Ground Water Estimation Committee.

Forest and Reserved Forest: (Ettimadai RF)- Nearest Villages- Ettimadai Extn. RF, Ettimadai Extn. RF, Perurchettipalayam. (Booluvampatti Extn.)- Nearest Villages- Mavuthampatty, Pichanur. (Solakarai)- Nearest Villages- Mavuthampatty, Pichanur.

Natural Division: Kongu Nadu.

Administration

Revenue **Division:** Coimbatore. Parliamentary Constituency: 21 Pollachi. District: Coimbatore. Taluk: Coimbatore South. Assembly Constituency: 122 Kinathukadavu. Gram Panchayat: 09.

Border Villages- (Kerala)- Nearest Villages- Mavuthampatty. Pichanur.

Villages: 13 **Inhabited:** 11 **Uninhabited:** 2

Ranking	District	State	National
Area	18	356	5379
Population	18	375	5828
Sex Ratio	16	344	3205
Child Sex Ratio	5	38	943
Literacy Rate	7	176	1666
Density	16	241	3517
Work Participation Rate	11	227	2590

Gram Panchayats:
Arisippalayam, Malumichampatti, Mavuthampathi, Myleripalayam, Nachippalayam, Palathurai, Pichanur, Seerappalayam, Valukkupparai.

Amenities:

Education: Primary School in 9 villages, Middle school in 6 villages, Matriculation or Secondary School in 4 villages, namely Pichanur, Malumachanpatti, Arisipalalyam, Valukkuparai.

Higher Secondary or Pre University Courses or Intermediate or Junior College in 1 village of the CD Block,, namely Arisipalalyam.

College in 2 villages, Adult Literacy Center in 0 village., Colleges are in villages, namely Seerapalayam, Malumachanpatti.

Medical: Hospital in 0 village, Dispensary in 1 village, Health Center in 4 villages, Sub Center in 11 villages, Maternity and Child Welfare Center in 1 village, Community health workers in 0 village.

The Village having Hospital or Dispensary or Health Center is Valukkuparai.

Drinking Water: Tap water in 11 villages, Tank water in 0 villages, Well water in 11 villages, Tubewell in 11 villages and more than one source in 11 villages.

Bank: Banking facility in 2 villages, namely, Palathurai, Nachipalayam.

Credit Society in 3 villages Agricultural Credit Society in 2 Non-Agricultural Credit Society in 1 village.

Others: Power supply in 11 villages, Cinema hall in 0 village, sport club in 1 village, Stadium or Auditorium or Community Hall in 0 village, Post Office in 10 villages.

There are 10 villages having bus facilities.

Villages with most of facilities: Palathurai Nachipalayam.

Villages without amenities (Education):
Thambagoundampalayam, Karunchamigounderpalayam..

Scheduled Castes: Out of the total population of 37846 persons, 9204 persons (24.32%) belong to Scheduled Castes.

The villages having less than 10% SC population are None..

The villages having more than 50% SC population are None.

Sex ratio of Scheduled Caste population is 501.

Scheduled Castes Literates and Illiterates by Sex:

	Persons	Males	Females
Literate	3,828	2,227	1,601
Illiterate	5,376	2,363	3,013
Literacy rate	48.0	55.7	40.2
Graduate	31	24	7

Scheduled Castes (Dominant):

Arunthathiyar, Madari, Adi Dravida, Paraiyan etc. Pallan

For their cultural identity please see Appendix-I

Villages without Scheduled Castes: There are 3 villages without any scheduled caste population.

Scheduled Tribes: Out of the total population of 37846 persons, 798 persons (2.11%) belong to Scheduled Tribes. The villages having less than 10% ST population are Pichanur, Palathurai, Thambagoundampalayam Karunchamigounderpalayam, Seerapalayam Malumachanpatti, Myleripalayam, Nachipalayam Arisipalalyam, Valukkuparai.

The villages having more than 50% ST population are None.

Sex ratio of Scheduled tribe population is 508.

Scheduled Tribes Literates and Illiterates by Sex:

	Persons	Males	Females
Literate	242	143	99
Illiterate	556	250	306
Literacy rate	34.9	41.6	28.4
Graduate	2	1	1

Scheduled Tribes (Dominant):

Irular, Malasar, Mudugar etc., Generic Tribes etc.

For their cultural identity please see Appendix-II

Villages without Scheduled Tribes: There are 9 villages without any scheduled tribe population.

Literates and Illiterates by Sex (Total Population):

	Persons	Males	Females
Literate	22,516	13,114	9,402
Illiterate	15,330	6,232	9,098
Literacy rate	67	76	57
Graduate	645	459	186

Agriculture: ***Distribution of villages according to land use:*** Out of 13 villages, Total area (in hectare) is 12592.86, out of that 78.94 percent is cultivable and 31.41 percent of the cultivable area is irrigated.

Sources of Irrigation (Hectares): Government Canal 0, Private Canal 0, Well without Electricity 339.44, Well with Electricity 2105.28, Tubewell without Electricity 0, Tubewell with Electricity 677.57, Tank 0, River 0, Lake 0, Waterfall 0, Others 0.

Villages with population of 5000 to 9999: Pichanur, Malumichampatti.

Villages with population of 10000 and above: None

Distribution of Workers:

	Persons	Males	Females	WPR
Cultivators	3,813	2,439	1,374	20.17
Agricultural Labour	7,284	3,638	3,646	38.53
Household Industry	324	195	129	1.71
Other Workers	7,486	5,981	1,505	39.59
Main Workers	17,543	11,680	5,863	92.79
Marginal Workers	1,364	573	791	7.21
Total Workers	18,907	12,253	6,654	

Religion: Major Religious Communities:

	Persons	Males	Females	Sex Ratio
Hindu (96.4%)	36,485	18,586	17,899	963
Muslim (0.51%)	193	106	87	821
Christian (3.03%)	1,148	639	509	797
Sikh (0%)	-	-	-	-
Buddhists (0%)	1	-	1	-
Jain (0.01%)	4	3	1	333

Agewise Data:

	Persons	Males	Females	Sex Ratio
All ages	37,846	19,346	18,500	956
0-14	8,978	4,647	4,331	932
15-44	19,105	9,684	9,421	973
45-79	9,089	4,680	4,409	942
80+	478	241	237	983
Age not stated	196	94	102	1085

Languages (Dominant):

Tamil, Telugu, Kannada, Malayalam, Urdu

Disabled Population:

	Persons	Males	Females	%
Total Disabled	698	420	278	
In Seeing	267	145	122	38.25
In Speech	78	39	39	11.17
In Hearing	29	17	12	4.15
In Movement	180	119	61	25.79
Mentally	144	100	44	20.63

MADUKKUR

Madukkur C.D. Block lies in the south-eastern part of Thanjavur district. It is a part of Pattukkottai taluk. The Block is located at a distance of 61 kms. from district headquarters (Thanjavur). There are 46 villages in the block with the total population of 66,761 persons. Area of the C.D. Block is 171.43 sq. kms. It is bounded in the north by CD Block Orathanadu and district Thiruvarur, in the south by C.D. Block Pattukkottai, in the east by district Thiruvarur, in the west by CD Blocks Orattanadur and Pattukkottai.

Communications:

Roadways : Information not Available.

River: Kannanar Nadi- Nearest Villages- Nemmeli,

Keelakurichi, Keelakurichi East, Kanniyakurichi, Olyiaankkunnam, Mottoor, Andamy, Madukkur, Gopala, Samudram, Periyakkottai, Chokkanavur, Pulaiyakudi, Kadathangudi, MadurabashaniPuram, Elangadu, Karappankadu, Siramelkudi, Reguramasamudram.

Annual Rainfall: Average Rainfall 1147 mm.

Ground Water: Availability of the ground water in the Basin is 3787.28 H.A.M. and the utilization is 3169. 82 H.A.M. It belongs to Semi Critical category. Depth to water level varies from 2 to 10 meter below the ground. Most of the wells go down in summer months, according to the Ground Water Estimation Committee.

Natural Division: Chola Nadu.

Administration

Revenue **Division:** Pattukottai. Parliamentary Constituency: 30 Pudukottai. District: Thanjavur. Taluk: Pattukottai. Assembly Constituency: 176 Pottukkottai, 177 Peravurani. Gram Panchayat: 33.

Villages: 46 **Inhabited:** 45 **Uninhabited:** 1

Ranking	District	State	National
Area	9	327	4675
Population	14	304	4609
Sex Ratio	1	26	241
Child Sex Ratio	2	21	575
Literacy Rate	9	104	1135
Density	6	276	2802
Work Participation Rate	9	120	2990

Gram Panchayats:

Alampallam, Alathur, Andami, Athivetti , Avikkottai, Bavajikkottai, Chokkanavur, Elangadu, Kadathankudi, Kalyanaodai, Kaniyakurichi, Karappankadu, Karuppur, Kasangadu, Keelakurichi, Keelakurichi , Madukkur North, Madurabashanipuram, Mannankadu, Mohur, Moothakurichi, Nemmeli, Olayakunnam, Palaverikadu, Periyakkottai, Pulavanji, Puliyakudi, Siramelkudi, Sirankudi, Talikkottai, Vattakudi , Vattakudi Ukkadai, Veppankulam, Vikkiramam.

Amenities:

Education: Primary School in 36 villages, Middle school in 24 villages, Matriculation or Secondary School in 9 villages, namely Keelakurichi East, Kanniyakurichi, Alathur, Thalikkottai, Periyakkottai, Moothakurichi, Kasangadu, Vattagudi, Siramelkudi.

Higher Secondary or Pre University Courses or Intermediate or Junior College in 3 villages of the CD Block,, namely Alathur, Moothakurichi, Kasangadu.

College in 0 village, Adult Literacy Center in 0 village.

Medical: Hospital in 0 village, Dispensary in 0 village, Health Center in 3 villages, Sub Center in 13 villages, Maternity and Child Welfare Center in 0 village, Community health workers in 44 villages.

Drinking Water: Tap water in 45 villages, Tank water in 2 villages, Well water in 45 villages, Tubewell in 45 villages and more than one source in 45 villages.

Bank: Banking facility in 5 villages, namely, Keelakurichi East, Alathur, Vikramam, Kasangadu Siramelkudi.

Credit Society in 13 villages Agricultural Credit Society in 13 Non-Agricultural Credit Society in 1 village.

Others: Power supply in 45 villages, Cinema hall in 1 village, sport club in 0 village, Stadium or Auditorium or Community Hall in 0 village, Post Office in 24 villages.

There are 37 villages having bus facilities.

Villages with most of facilities: Keelakurichi East Alathur, Vikramam, Kasangadu, Siramelkudi.

Villages without amenities (Education): Nemmeli, Keelakurichi, Balaji Regunatha Samudram, Mahadevapuram, Gopala Samudram, Regunathapuram, Vattagudi Ukkadai, Reguramasamudram, Palayee Agraharam..

Scheduled Castes: Out of the total population of 66761 persons, 8613 persons (12.9%) belong to Scheduled Castes. The villages having less than 10% SC population are Keelakurichi East, Balaji Regunatha Samudram Kalichankottai, Mahadevapuram, Musiri, Alathur Vadugankuthakai, Thalikkottai, Veppankulam Periyakkottai, Kadathangudi, Kasangadu, Ponnangundu Karappankadu, Reguramasamudram, Palayee Agraharam Kaliyanaodai, Mannankadu.

The villages having more than 50% SC population are None.

Sex ratio of Scheduled Caste population is 511.

Scheduled Castes Literates and Illiterates by Sex:

	Persons	Males	Females
Literate	4,548	2,607	1,941
Illiterate	4,065	1,602	2,463
Literacy rate	60.9	72.2	50.3
Graduate	37	27	10

Scheduled Castes (Dominant):

Paraiyan etc., Adi Dravida, Pallan, Koliyan, Samban

For their cultural identity please see Appendix-I

Villages without Scheduled Castes: There are 7 villages without any scheduled caste population.

Scheduled Tribes: Out of the total population of 66761 persons, 39 persons (0.06%) belong to Scheduled Tribes. The villages having less than 10% ST population are Nemmeli, Keelakurichi, Keelakurichi East, Avikkottai Balajikkottai, Balaji Regunatha Samudram Kalichankottai, Kanniyakurichi, Olyiaankkunnam Mottoor, Andamy, Karuppur, Pulavanji, Mahadevapuram

Musiri, Alathur, Vadugankuthakai, Thalikkottai Alampallam, Veppankulam, Madukkur, Gopala Samudram Periyakkottai, Chokkanavur, Pulaiyakudi Kadathangudi, Madurabashani Puram, Vikramam Vadiakkadu, Moothakurichi, Kasangadu, Regunathapuram Vattagudi Ukkadai, Vattagudi, Athivetti West Athivetti East, Ponnangundu, Elangadu, Karappankadu Siramelkudi, Reguramasamudram, Palayee Agraharam Kaliyanaodai, Pazaverikkadu, Mannankadu.

The villages having more than 50% ST population are None.

Sex ratio of Scheduled tribe population is 513.

Scheduled Tribes Literates and Illiterates by Sex:

	Persons	Males	Females
Literate	13	6	7
Illiterate	26	13	13
Literacy rate	39.4	40.0	38.9
Graduate	0	0	0

Scheduled Tribes (Dominant):

Kattunayakan, Malakkuravan, Koraga, Kurumans

For their cultural identity please see Appendix-II

Villages without Scheduled Tribes: There are 42 villages without any scheduled tribe population.

Literates and Illiterates by Sex (Total Population):

	Persons	Males	Females
Literate	41,637	23,262	18,375
Illiterate	25,124	9,152	15,972
Literacy rate	70	81	60
Graduate	993	707	286

Agriculture: ***Distribution of villages according to land use:*** Out of 46 villages, Total area (in hectare) is 17143.53, out of that 69.87 percent is cultivable and 74.93 percent of the cultivable area is irrigated.

Sources of Irrigation (Hectares): Government Canal 7553.56, Private Canal 0, Well without Electricity 0, Well with Electricity 252.2, Tubewell without Electricity 0, Tubewell with Electricity 710.2, Tank 458.54, River 0, Lake 0, Waterfall 0, Others 0.

Villages with population of 5000 to 9999: Alathur, Madukkur.

Villages with population of 10000 and above: None

Distribution of Workers:

	Persons	Males	Females	WPR
Cultivators	9,628	7,069	2,559	30.11
Agricultural Labour	18,290	9,543	8,747	57.21
Household Industry	395	225	170	1.24
Other Workers	3,659	2,628	1,031	11.44
Main Workers	26,731	17,267	9,464	83.61
Marginal Workers	5,241	2,198	3,043	16.39
Total Workers	31,972	19,465	12,507	

Religion: Major Religious Communities:

	Persons	Males	Females	Sex Ratio
Hindu (97.87%)	65,337	31,692	33,645	1,062
Muslim (0.17%)	113	65	48	738
Christian (1.92%)	1,280	645	635	984
Sikh (0%)	-	-	-	-
Buddhists (0%)	-	-	-	-
Jain (0%)	1	-	1	-

Agewise Data:

	Persons	Males	Females	Sex Ratio
All ages	66,761	32,414	34,347	1060
0-14	16,932	8,568	8,364	976
15-44	32,747	15,615	17,132	1097
45-79	16,312	7,836	8,476	1082
80+	625	307	318	1036
Age not stated	145	88	57	648

Languages (Dominant):

Tamil, Telugu, Malayalam, Kannada, Urdu

Disabled Population:

	Persons	Males	Females	%
Total Disabled	1,744	1,012	732	
In Seeing	895	509	386	51.32
In Speech	143	76	67	8.2
In Hearing	121	60	61	6.94
In Movement	418	269	149	23.97
Mentally	167	98	69	9.58

MADURAI EAST

Madurai East C.D. Block lies in the eastern part of Madurai district. It is a part of Madurai North taluk. The Block is located at a distance of NA kms. from district headquarters (Madurai). There are 88 villages in the block with the total population of 95,420 persons. Area of the C.D. Block is 205.36 sq. kms. It is bounded in the north by CD Blocks Melur and Madurai West, in the south by district Sivaganga, in the east by CD Block Melur, in the west by CD Blocks Madurai West and Thiruparankundram.

Communications:

Roadways : N.H.-45 B: Direction- Maduri to Melur, Nearest Villages- Nayakkanpatti, Poyyakkarai Patty, Kallandirı, Pappankulam, Savalakkaraiyan, Poovakkudi, Kollangulam, Velliyankundram, Appan Thiruppathi, Mathur, Thuyaneri, Arumbanoor, Kada, Kinaru, K.Pappankulam, Narasingam, Mangalakudi, Uthangudi. S.H.-33: Direction- Madurai to Sivaganga, Nearest Villages- Sakkudi, Ananjiur, Angadimangalam.

River: Vaigai Nadi- Nearest Villages- Andarkutarasm, Kondabethan, Karuppapillaiendhal, Sakkimangalam.

Annual Rainfall: Average Rainfall 857 mm.

Ground Water: Availability of the ground water in the Basin is 7195.13 H.A.M. and the utilization is 1037. 99 H.A.M. It belongs to Safe category. Depth to water level varies from 5 to 10 meter below the ground. Most of the wells go down in summer months, according to the Ground Water Estimation Committee.

Natural Division: NA

Administration

Revenue **Division:** Madurai. Parliamentary Constituency: 32 Madurai. District: Madurai. Taluk: Madurai North. Assembly Constituency: 189 Madurai East.

Gram Panchayat: 39.

Villages: 88 **Inhabited:** 77 **Uninhabited:** 11

Ranking	District	State	National
Area	11	276	4090
Population	4	153	3617
Sex Ratio	9	308	2558
Child Sex Ratio	7	316	5270
Literacy Rate	5	132	1336
Density	10	261	2372
Work Participation Rate	2	72	2836

Gram Panchayats:

Andarkottaram, Angadimangalam, Arumbanur, Ayilangudi, Chinnamangalam, Elangiyendal, Idayapatti, Ilamanur, Isalani, Kadhakinaru, Kalimangalam, Kallanthiri, Karseri, Karuppayurani, Kodikulam , Kunnathur, Kuruthur, Mangulam, Mathur, Meenakshipuram, Narasingam , Panaikulam, Poolampatti, Porusupatti, Poyyakaraipatti, Pudupatti, Puduthamaraipatti, Rajakkur, Sakkimangalam , Sakkudi, Thamaraipatti Thindiyur, Thirumohur, Uthangudi, Varichiyur, Velliyankundram.

Amenities:

Education: Primary School in 54 villages, Middle school in 15 villages, Matriculation or Secondary School in 8 villages, namely Mangulam, Meenakshipuram, Mathur, Kodikkulam, Mangalakudi, Kalikappan, Elamanur, Kalimangalam. Higher Secondary or Pre University Courses or Intermediate or Junior College in 4 villages of the CD Block,, namely Kodikkulam, Mangalakudi, Elamanur, Kpzhikudi. College in 1 village, Adult Literacy Center in 0 village., College is in village, namely Kodikkulam.

Medical: Hospital in 2 villages, Dispensary in 1 village, Health Center in 2 villages, Sub Center in 25 villages, Maternity and Child Welfare Center in 4 villages, Community health workers in 10 villages.

The Villages having Hospital or Dispensary or Health Center are Kallandiri, Kalikappan, Andarkutarasm.

Drinking Water: Tap water in 77 villages, Tank water in 49 villages, Well water in 77 villages, Tubewell in 77 villages and more than one source in 77 villages.

Bank: Banking facility in 11 villages, namely, Mangulam, Meenakshipuram, Mathur, Chettikulam Kodikkulam, Poolampatty, Narasingam, Kalikappan Varichiyur, Sakkimangalam, Kalimangalam.

Credit Society in 16 villages Agricultural Credit Society in 15 Non-Agricultural Credit Society in 2 villages.

Others: Power supply in 77 villages, Cinema hall in 3 villages, sport club in 0 village, Stadium or Auditorium or Community Hall in 4 villages, Post Office in 77 villages.

There are 58 villages having bus facilities.

Villages with most of facilities: Mangulam Meenakshipuram, Mathur, Chettikulam, Kodikkulam Narasingam, Kalikappan, Varichiyur, Sakkimangalam Kalimangalam.

Villages without amenities (Education):

Savalakkaraiyan, Thuyaneri, Perakoor, Podasapatty, S.Nedunkulam, Vallakuppam, Varakaneri, Nattarmangalam, Mundanayagam, Thathankulam, Poolangulam, Kathavanenthal, Veerapanjan, Vellakulam, Edayapatti, Seegankulam,, Vallakundu, Parayankulam, Aalavanthan, Karuppapillaiendhal, Udangundu, Oovalur..

Scheduled Castes: Out of the total population of 95420 persons, 23617 persons (24.75%) belong to Scheduled Castes. The villages having less than 10% SC population are Nayakkanpatti, Savalakkaraiyan, Appan Thiruppathi Kollangulam, Jothiyapatti, Sembinayendhal Mangalakudi, Isalani, Karuppukkal, Varichiyur Seegankulam,, Pottapaniyur, Vallakundu, Kondabethan Karuppapillaiendhal.

The villages having more than 50% SC population are Meenakshipuram, Chettikulam, Kuruthur, Thuyaneri Ayilangudi, Kada Kinaru, Perakoor, Podasapatty Varakaneri, Nattarmangalam, Mundanayagam, Vellakulam Parayankulam, Oovalur, Ananjiur.

Sex ratio of Scheduled Caste population is 490.

Scheduled Castes Literates and Illiterates by Sex:

	Persons	Males	Females
Literate	12,499	7,482	5,017
Illiterate	11,118	4,567	6,551
Literacy rate	61.9	73.1	50.5
Graduate	215	157	58

Scheduled Castes (Dominant):

Pallan, Paraiyan etc., Chakkiliyan, Adi Dravida Kuravan etc.

For their cultural identity please see Appendix-I

Villages without Scheduled Castes: There are 16 villages without any scheduled caste population.

Scheduled Tribes: Out of the total population of 95420 persons, 120 persons (0.13%) belong to Scheduled Tribes. The villages having less than 10% ST population are Nayakkanpatti, Poyyakkarai Patty, Kallandiri Mangulam, Meenakshipuram, Savalakkaraiyan

Velliyankundram, Appan Thiruppathi, Andaman, Mathur Pilluchery, Porusuppatti, Chettikulam, Kollangulam Kuruthur, Jothiyapatti, Thuyaneri, Arumbanoor Ayilangudi, Kada Kinaru, Pudupatty, Sembinayendhal Kodikkulam, Thamarappatti, Poolampatty, Valachikulam Thirukkanai, Perakoor, Podasapatty, Narasingam Mangalakudi, Uthangudi, Milakaranai, Thirumohur Elagiendal, Sithakoor, Pannikulam, S.Nedunkulam Vallakuppam, Varakaneri, Nattarmangalam, Rajakkoor Mundanayagam, Maylangundu, Thidiyur, Thathankulam Kalikappan, Poolangulam, Kathavanenthal, Veerapanjan Vilathur, Vellakulam, Edayapatti, Isalani Thatchanendal, Karuppukkal, Varichiyur, Seegankulam, Andarkutarasm, Elamanur, Pottapaniyur, Vallakundu Parayankulam, Aalavanthan, Unnathur, Kpzhikudi Kondabethan, Karuppapillaiendhal, Sakkimangalam Udangundu, Oovalur, Senkottai, Kalimangalam, Karseri Sakkudi, Ananjiur, Angadimangalam.

The villages having more than 50% ST population are None.

Sex ratio of Scheduled tribe population is 508.

Scheduled Tribes Literates and Illiterates by Sex:

	Persons	Males	Females
Literate	9	5	4
Illiterate	111	54	57
Literacy rate	10.1	10.6	9.5
Graduate	0	0	0

Scheduled Tribes (Dominant):

Sholaga, Adiyan, Kattunayakan

For their cultural identity please see Appendix-II

Villages without Scheduled Tribes: There are 85 villages without any scheduled tribe population.

Literates and Illiterates by Sex (Total Population):

	Persons	Males	Females
Literate	57,220	33,212	24,008
Illiterate	38,200	15,254	22,946
Literacy rate	69	79	59
Graduate	1,473	1,042	431

Agriculture: ***Distribution of villages according to land use:*** Out of 88 villages, Total area (in hectare) is 20536.96, out of that 58.14 percent is cultivable and 94.48 percent of the cultivable area is irrigated.

Sources of Irrigation (Hectares): Government Canal 6003.2, Private Canal 25.19, Well without Electricity 188.13, Well with Electricity 351.07, Tubewell without Electricity 6.14, Tubewell with Electricity 12.09, Tank 4592.45, River 0, Lake 0, Waterfall 0, Others 3.

Villages with population of 5000 to 9999:

Kallandhiri, Kodikulam , Narasingam , Sakkimangalam.

Villages with population of 10000 and above: None

Distribution of Workers:

	Persons	Males	Females	WPR
Cultivators	4,901	3,281	1,620	10.79
Agricultural Labour	24,177	12,558	11,619	53.22
Household Industry	1,739	930	809	3.83
Other Workers	14,612	11,169	3,443	32.16
Main Workers	33,023	21,607	11,416	72.69
Marginal Workers	12,406	6,331	6,075	27.31
Total Workers	45,429	27,938	17,491	

Religion: Major Religious Communities:

	Persons	Males	Females	Sex Ratio
Hindu (92.42%)	88,183	44,822	43,361	967
Muslim (6.24%)	5,955	3,012	2,943	977
Christian (1.25%)	1,190	582	608	1,045
Sikh (0.01%)	8	6	2	333
Buddhists (0%)	2	2	-	-
Jain (0.01%)	6	3	3	1,000

Agewise Data:

	Persons	Males	Females	Sex Ratio
All ages	95,420	48,466	46,954	969
0-14	27,527	14,366	13,161	916
15-44	46,030	23,007	23,023	1001
45-79	17,923	9,000	8,923	991
80+	574	285	289	1014
Age not stated	3,366	1,808	1,558	862

Languages (Dominant):

Tamil, Telugu, Gujarati, Malayalam, Urdu

Disabled Population:

	Persons	Males	Females	%
Total Disabled	2,666	1,431	1,235	
In Seeing	1,707	873	834	64.03
In Speech	183	98	85	6.86
In Hearing	68	29	39	2.55
In Movement	469	289	180	17.59
Mentally	239	142	97	8.96

MADURAI WEST

Madurai West C.D. Block lies in the central north part of Madurai district. It is a part of Madurai North taluk. The Block is located at a distance of NA kms. from district headquarters (Madurai). There are 56 villages in the block with the total population of 80,704 persons. Area of the C.D. Block is 191.68 sq. kms. It is bounded in the north by CD Block Alamganallur and district Dindigul, in the south by CD Blocks Thiruparankundram and Madurai East, in the east by CD Blocks Madurai East and Melur, and in the west by CD Block Alanganallur.

Communications:

Roadways : N.H.-7: Direction- Dindigul to Madurai, Nearest Villages- Kovilappangudi, Thenur, Samayanallur. N.H.-45B: Direction- Madurai to Melur, Nearest Village- Iraniyam.

Railway Station: Samayanallur.
River: Vaigai Nadi- Nearest Villages- Thenur, Samayanallur.
Annual Rainfall: Average Rainfall 857 mm.
Ground Water: Availability of the ground water in the Basin is 4822.32 H.A.M. and the utilization is 1479. 86 H.A.M. It belongs to Safe category. Depth to water level varies from 2 to 10 meter below the ground. Most of the wells go down in summer months, according to the Ground Water Estimation Committee.
Natural Division: NA
Administration
Revenue **Division:** Madurai. Parliamentary Constituency: 32 Madurai, 33 Theni. District: Madurai. Taluk: Madurai North. Assembly Constituency: 189 Madurai East, 190 Samayanallur (SC), 194 Madurai West. Gram Panchayat: 32.
Villages: 56 **Inhabited:** 53 **Uninhabited:** 3

Ranking	District	State	National
Area	12	297	4327
Population	9	237	4081
Sex Ratio	5	220	1554
Child Sex Ratio	3	220	3579
Literacy Rate	1	39	572
Density	13	323	2610
Work Participation Rate	4	103	3882

Gram Panchayats:
Adalai, Alathur, Ambalathadi, Ariyur, Boothagudi, Chatrapatti, Chettikulam, Chinnapatti, Iraniyam, Karuvanur, Kavanur, Kodimangalam, Kovilapappankudi, Kulamangalam, Malaipatti, Manjampatti, Pechikulam, Periyapatti, Podumbu, Samayanallur, Siruvalai, Thenur, Thiruppalai, Thodaneri, Usilampatti, Vagaikulam, Vairavanatham, Vayalur, Veerapandi, Velichianatham.
Amenities:
Education: Primary School in 46 villages, Middle school in 12 villages, Matriculation or Secondary School in 8 villages, namely Manjampatti, Chattrapatti, Periyapatti, Kulamangalam, Samayanallur, Keelanedunkulam, Iraniyam, Tiruppalai.
Higher Secondary or Pre University Courses or Intermediate or Junior College in 6 villages of the CD Block,, namely Chattrapatti, Periyapatti, Samayanallur, Keelanedunkulam, Iraniyam, Tiruppalai.
College in 2 villages, Adult Literacy Center in 0 village., Colleges are in villages, namely Kadavoor, Tiruppalai.
Medical: Hospital in 5 villages, Dispensary in 2 villages, Health Center in 3 villages, Sub Center in 26 villages, Maternity and Child Welfare Center in 3 villages, Community health workers in 3 villages.
The Villages having Hospital or Dispensary or Health Center are Manjampatti, Thodaneri, Samayanallur, Kallikudi, Podhumpu, Kovilpappakudi.
Drinking Water: Tap water in 53 villages, Tank water in 38 villages, Well water in 53 villages, Tubewell in 53 villages and more than one source in 53 villages.
Bank: Banking facility in 5 villages, namely, Chattrapatti, Karuvanur, Thenur, Samayanallur Tiruppalai.
Credit Society in 9 villages Agricultural Credit Society in 9 Non-Agricultural Credit Society in 0 village.
Others: Power supply in 53 villages, Cinema hall in 3 villages, sport club in 1 village, Stadium or Auditorium or Community Hall in 8 villages, Post Office in 53 villages.
There are 43 villages having bus facilities.
Villages with most of facilities: Chattrapatti Karuvanur, Thenur, Samayanallur, Tiruppalai.
Villages without amenities (Education):
Veppangulam, Eluppakudi, Kannikudi, Vagaikulam, Pattakkurichi, Kurunthan Kulam, Keelappanangudi..
Scheduled Castes: Out of the total population of 80704 persons, 19888 persons (24.64%) belong to Scheduled Castes.
The villages having less than 10% SC population are Chinnapatti, Periyapatti, Vittankulam, Sambakkulam Keelanedunkulam, Veppangulam, Kannikudi Keelappanangudi.
The villages having more than 50% SC population are Ambalathadi, Karuvanur, Erukkalainathan, Usilampatti Pillayar Natham, Moolakurichi, Pattakkurichi.
Sex ratio of Scheduled Caste population is 507.
Scheduled Castes Literates and Illiterates by Sex:

	Persons	Males	Females
Literate	11,061	6,370	4,691
Illiterate	8,827	3,434	5,393
Literacy rate	65.0	75.9	54.3
Graduate	225	163	62

Scheduled Castes (Dominant):
Paraiyan etc., Pallan, Chakkiliyan, Kuravan etc. Puthirai Vannan
For their cultural identity please see Appendix-I
Villages without Scheduled Castes: There are 7 villages without any scheduled caste population.
Scheduled Tribes: Out of the total population of 80704 persons, 117 persons (0.14%) belong to Scheduled Tribes.
The villages having less than 10% ST population are Kadavoor, Manjampatti, Chattrapatti, Malaipatty Poolampatti, Velchinatham, Chinnapatti, Periyapatti Kavanur, Therkupetampatti, Siruvalai Chellanagowendanpatti, Ariyur, Ambalathadi Vittankulam, Vairavanatham, Vayalur, Kulamangalam

Karuvanur, Mandikulam, Paraipatty, Erukkalainathan Usilampatti, Kodimangalam, Keelapandi, Veerapandi Vadugapatty, Sambakkulam, Pillayar Natham Moolakurichi, Thodaneri, Thenur, Samayanallur Kallikudi, Keelanedunkulam, Boothagudy, Veppangulam Chettikulam, Maranivariyen, Eluppakudi, Iraniyam Kannikudi, Alathur, Petchikulam, Vagaikulam Podhumpu, Athalai, Pattakkurichi, Kurunthan Kulam Kovilpappakudi, Melapannangudi, Keelappanangudi Tiruppalai.

The villages having more than 50% ST population are None.

Sex ratio of Scheduled tribe population is 496.

Scheduled Tribes Literates and Illiterates by Sex:

	Persons	Males	Females
Literate	85	43	42
Illiterate	32	16	16
Literacy rate	82.5	81.1	84.0
Graduate	0	0	0

Scheduled Tribes (Dominant):

Malai Vedan, Malai Pandaram, Kattunayakan

For their cultural identity please see Appendix-II

Villages without Scheduled Tribes: There are 52 villages without any scheduled tribe population.

Literates and Illiterates by Sex (Total Population):

	Persons	Males	Females
Literate	53,999	30,225	23,774
Illiterate	26,705	10,310	16,395
Literacy rate	76	85	67
Graduate	2,218	1,502	716

Agriculture: ***Distribution of villages according to land use:*** Out of 56 villages, Total area (in hectare) is 19168.09, out of that 39.68 percent is cultivable and 86.97 percent of the cultivable area is irrigated.

Sources of Irrigation (Hectares): Government Canal 4908.55, Private Canal 0, Well without Electricity 28.67, Well with Electricity 57.03, Tubewell without Electricity 5.72, Tubewell with Electricity 5.67, Tank 1609.43, River 0, Lake 0, Waterfall 0, Others 0.

Villages with population of 5000 to 9999:

Thenur, Samayanallur, Thiruppalai.

Villages with population of 10000 and above: None

Distribution of Workers:

	Persons	Males	Females	WPR
Cultivators	3,762	2,635	1,127	10.75
Agricultural Labour	17,413	9,469	7,944	49.76
Household Industry	1,054	435	619	3.01
Other Workers	12,765	10,178	2,587	36.48
Main Workers	24,554	17,665	6,889	70.17
Marginal Workers	10,440	5,052	5,388	29.83
Total Workers	34,994	22,717	12,277	

Religion: Major Religious Communities:

	Persons	Males	Females	Sex Ratio
Hindu (93.92%)	75,799	38,169	37,630	986
Muslim (3.15%)	2,542	1,198	1,344	1,122
Christian (2.62%)	2,113	1,037	1,076	1,038
Sikh (0%)	1	1	-	-
Buddhists (0%)	3	1	2	2,000
Jain (0.08%)	64	35	29	829

Agewise Data:

	Persons	Males	Females	Sex Ratio
All ages	80,704	40,535	40,169	991
0-14	22,377	11,396	10,981	964
15-44	39,158	19,339	19,819	1025
45-79	16,016	8,087	7,929	980
80+	579	293	286	976
Age not stated	2,574	1,420	1,154	813

Languages (Dominant):

Tamil, Telugu, Kannada, Gujarati, Malayalam

Disabled Population:

	Persons	Males	Females	%
Total Disabled	2,449	1,280	1,169	
In Seeing	1,513	759	754	61.78
In Speech	146	74	72	5.96
In Hearing	128	59	69	5.23
In Movement	461	279	182	18.82
Mentally	201	109	92	8.21

MADURANTHAKAM

Maduranthakam C.D. Block lies in the south western part of Kancheepuram district. It is a part of Maduranthakam taluk. The Block is located at a distance of 60 kms. from district headquarters (Kancheepuram). There are 96 villages in the block with the total population of 112,057 persons. Area of the C.D. Block is 368.20 sq. kms. It is bounded in the north by CD Blocks Tirukkaluk unram and Uthiramerur, in the south by CD Block Chittamur, in the east by CD Blocks Tirukalukunram and Lathur, in the west by CD Block Acharapakkam and Uthiramerur.

Communications:

Roadways : N.H.-45: Direction- Tindivanam to Chengalpattu, Nearest Villages- Maiyur, Mamandur, Pazhamathur, Bukkat hurai, Moosivakkam, Palayanur, Arayapakkam, Janak ipuram (Sanur), Athimanam, Kallabiranpuram, Thottanaval, Silavattam, Pakkam.

Railway Station: Padalam, Pakkam.

River: Palar River: Nearest Villages- Pilappur, Palayanur, Padalam, Pulipurakoil, Lakshminarayanapuram, Budur, Isur, Maiyur, Mamandur, Pazhamathur.

Annual Rainfall: Average Rainfall 1105 mm.

Ground Water: Availability of the ground water in the

Basin is 10385.78 H.A.M. and the utilization is 6541. 34 H.A.M. It belongs to Safe category. Depth to water level varies from 5 to 10 meter below the ground. Most of the wells go down in summer months, according to the Ground Water Estimation Committee.

Natural Division: Tondai Nadu.

Administration

Revenue **Division:** Maduranthakham. Parliamentary Constituency: 6 Kancheepuram (SC). District: Kancheepuram. Taluk: Maduranthakam. Assembly Constituency: 35 Madurantakam (SC). Gram Panchayat: 58.

Villages: 95 **Inhabited:** 95 **Uninhabited:** 0

Ranking	District	State	National
Area	3	95	2141
Population	5	87	3097
Sex Ratio	3	176	1234
Child Sex Ratio	1	50	1072
Literacy Rate	9	215	1980
Density	6	284	3488
Work Participation Rate	8	219	3114

Gram Panchayats:

Andavakkam , Arayapakkam, Ariyanur, Arungunam , Athivakkam, Avirimedu , Budur , Bukkathurai, Chinnavenmani, Devadur, Erumbedu, Gendracheri, Janakipuram (Sanur), Kallabiranpuram , Karunakaracheri , Kattudevadur , Kavadur , Keelakandai , Keelavalam, Kinar , Kumaravadi, Kunnathur, Laxminarayanapuram , Maiyur, Mamdandur, Mangalam , Munnithikuppam , Munnuthikuppam , munnuthikuppam , Murukkambakkam, Nallamur, Nallur , Neerpair , Nelli , Nellli , Nelvoy, Nesapakkam, Nethapakkam , Netrambakkam , Netrambakkam, Netrambakkam , Onambakkam, Padalam , Pakkam, Palayanur, Pazhamathur, Periyavenmani , Peruveli, Pilappur, Pudupattu , Puliaranankottai , Saravambakkam, Silavattam, Sirunallur, Sithandi , sithandi , Sithandi , Soorai , Thondadu, Vaiyavur , Veeranakunnam, Vettur , Vilvarayanallur, Viralur , Z.Budur, Z.Endathur .

Amenities:

Education: Primary School in 77 villages, Middle school in 22 villages, Matriculation or Secondary School in 9 villages, namely Sithandi, Bukkathurai, Padalam, Budur, Veeranakunnam, Z Endathur A,B/B, Kattudevadur A,B,C/C, Erumbedu A,B/B, Neerpair A,B/B. Higher Secondary or Pre University Courses or Intermediate or Junior College in 3 villages of the CD Block,, namely Padalam, Budur, Neerpair A,B/B.

College in 1 village, Adult Literacy Center in 0 village., Colleges is in village, namely Mamandur.

Medical: Hospital in 2 villages, Dispensary in 1 village, Health Center in 9 villages, Sub Center in 19 villages, Maternity and Child Welfare Center in 4 villages, Community health workers in 95 villages.

The Villages having Hospital or Dispensary or Health Center are Mamandur, Palligaram, Irusumanallur, Erumbedu A,B/B.

Drinking Water: Tap water in 95 villages, Tank water in 70 villages, Well water in 95 villages, Tubewell in 95 villages and more than one source in 95 villages.

Bank: Banking facility in 12 villages, namely, Maiyur, Mamandur, Pazhamathur, Bukkathurai, Nelvoy Padalam, Vedavakkam A,B,C/C, Veeranakunnam, Pakkam Z Endathur A,B/B, Nesapakkam, Erumbedu A,B/B.

Credit Society in 18 villages Agricultural Credit Society in 18 Non-Agricultural Credit Society in 0 village.

Others: Power supply in 95 villages, Cinema hall in 0 village, sport club in 0 village, Stadium or Auditorium or Community Hall in 0 village, Post Office in 31 villages.

There are 67 villages having bus facilities.

Villages with most of facilities: Maiyur, Mamandur Pazhamathur, Bukkathurai, Nelvoy, Padalam Vedavakkam A,B,C/C, Veeranakunnam, Pakkam Z Endathur A,B/B, Erumbedu A,B/B.

Villages without amenities (Education): Athiyur. Sampathinallur, Kodithandalam, Mambattu, Moosivakkam, Kunnavakkam, Pillanthikuppam, Eruvakkam, Murukkancheri, Irusumanallur, Uludamangalam, Vilagam, Sholamthangal, Pulikkoradu, Amayambattu, Viralur, Poondi, Vellarai..

Scheduled Castes: Out of the total population of 112057 persons, 54794 persons (48.9%) belong to Scheduled Castes. The villages having less than 10% SC population are Pilappur, Kunnakolathur, Arayapakkam, Kunnavakkam Pillanthikuppam, Irusumanallur, Vilagam, Amayambattu Poondi.

The villages having more than 50% SC population are Sithandi, Sampathinallur, Mamandur, Pazhamathur Bukkathurai, Kodithandalam, Karunagaracheri Palligaram, Vaiyavur, Moosivakkam, Padalam Pulipurakoil, Pathur, Janakipuram (Sanur), Athimanam Pasumbur, Pudupatu, Thottanaval, Eruvakkam, Budur Isur, Murukkancheri, Uludamangalam, Kathiricheri Munuthikuppam, Mulli, Kavadur, Murukkambakkam Devadur, Sholamthangal, Vilvarayanallur, Pulikkoradu Vasanthavadi, Nethapakkam, Puliyaranankottai Z Endathur A,B/B, Melakandai, Athivakkam, Nesapakkam Venmari, Ozhavetti, Netrambakkam, Peruveli A,B/B Nallamur Keelakaranai A,B,C/C, Vellarai Erumbedu A,B/B, Kilvasalai A,B/B.

Sex ratio of Scheduled Caste population is 497.

Scheduled Castes Literates and Illiterates by Sex:

	Persons	Males	Females
Literate	28,923	16,821	12,102
Illiterate	25,871	10,734	15,137
Literacy rate	61.0	70.8	51.2
Graduate	569	463	106

Scheduled Castes (Dominant):

Adi Dravida, Valluvan, Paraiyan etc., Arunthathiyar Adi Andhra

For their cultural identity please see Appendix-I

Villages without Scheduled Castes: There are 6 villages without any scheduled caste population.

Scheduled Tribes: Out of the total population of 112057 persons, 1289 persons (1.15%) belong to Scheduled Tribes. The villages having less than 10% ST population are Pilappur, Sithandi, Athiyur, Sampathinallur, Maiyur Mamandur, Pazhamathur, Bukkathurai, Kodithandalam Kumaravadi, Karunagaracheri, Palligaram, Nelli Mangalam, Nelvoy, Puzhuthivakkam, Kunnakolathur Mambattu, Vaiyavur, Moosivakkam, Palayanur A,B,C/C Padalam, Pulipurakoil, Lakshminarayanapuram, Pathur Arayapakkam, Janakipuram (Sanur), Athimanam Kallabiranpuram, Vedavakkam A,B,C/C, Soorai Chithalamangalam, Andavakkam, Kunnavakkam, Pasumbur Pudupatu, Thottanaval, Keelavalam, Eruvakkam, Budur Isur, Kunnathur, Veeranakunnam, Murukkancheri Irusumanallur, Kinar, Uludamangalam, Kathiricheri Munuthikuppam, Mulli, Valarbirai, Kavadur Murukkambakkam, Mariputhur, Devadur, Sholamthangal Genracheri, Vilvarayanallur, Silavattam, Pakkam Pulikkoradu, Amayambattu, Vasanthavadi, Nethapakkam Sirunallur, Avirimedu, Chitravadi, Puliyaranankottai Z Endathur A,B/B, Melakandai, Athivakkam Dharmapuram, Nesapakkam, Ariyanur, Venmari Chinnavenmani, Ozhavetti, Netrambakkam Peruveli A,B/B, Nallamur Keelakaranai A,B,C/C Chitamur, Kattudevadur A,B,C/C, Viralur, Poondi Devanur, Vellarai, Nallur, Erumbedu A,B/B Z Budur A,B/B, Kilvasalai A,B/B, Neerpair A,B/B.

The villages having more than 50% ST population are None.

Sex ratio of Scheduled tribe population is 488.

Scheduled Tribes Literates and Illiterates by Sex:

	Persons	Males	Females
Literate	293	176	117
Illiterate	996	484	512
Literacy rate	26.8	31.4	22.0
Graduate	1	1	0

Scheduled Tribes (Dominant):

Irular, Kattunayakan, Malakkuravan, Kurumans Generic Tribes etc.

For their cultural identity please see Appendix-II

Villages without Scheduled Tribes: There are 47 villages without any scheduled tribe population.

Literates and Illiterates by Sex (Total Population):

	Persons	Males	Females
Literate	63,657	36,672	26,985
Illiterate	48,400	19,418	28,982
Literacy rate	65	75	55
Graduate	1,449	1,089	360

Agriculture: ***Distribution of villages according to land use:*** Out of 95 villages, Total area (in hectare) is 36820.4, out of that 62.65 percent is cultivable and 63.25 percent of the cultivable area is irrigated.

Sources of Irrigation (Hectares): Government Canal 309.26, Private Canal 252.7, Well without Electricity 758.67, Well with Electricity 4705.02, Tubewell without Electricity 70.98, Tubewell with Electricity 1813.28, Tank 1653.566, River 11.11, Lake 4859.728, Waterfall 0, Others 157.02.

Villages with population of 5000 to 9999: None

Villages with population of 10000 and above: None

Distribution of Workers:

	Persons	Males	Females	WPR
Cultivators	11,549	8,012	3,537	22.01
Agricultural Labour	30,274	15,464	14,810	57.7
Household Industry	1,145	566	579	2.18
Other Workers	9,498	7,578	1,920	18.1
Main Workers	41,080	26,928	14,152	78.3
Marginal Workers	11,386	4,692	6,694	21.7
Total Workers	52,466	31,620	20,846	

Religion: Major Religious Communities:

	Persons	Males	Females	Sex Ratio
Hindu (94.15%)	105,507	52,829	52,678	997
Muslim (0.64%)	722	376	346	920
Christian (5.13%)	5,744	2,844	2,900	1,020
Sikh (0.01%)	10	5	5	1,000
Buddhists (0%)	1	1	-	-
Jain (0%)	3	1	2	2,000

Agewise Data:

	Persons	Males	Females	Sex Ratio
All ages	112,057	56,090	55,967	998
0-14	33,679	16,999	16,680	981
15-44	53,937	26,803	27,134	1012
45-79	23,449	11,752	11,697	995
80+	866	474	392	827
Age not stated	126	62	64	1032

Languages (Dominant):

Tamil, Telugu, Urdu, Gujarati, Hindi

Disabled Population:

	Persons	Males	Females	%
Total Disabled	2,640	1,469	1,171	
In Seeing	1,006	517	489	38.11
In Speech	280	154	126	10.61
In Hearing	280	157	123	10.61
In Movement	854	529	325	32.35
Mentally	220	112	108	8.33

MAILAM

Mailam C.D. Block lies in the north-eastern part of Viluppuram district. It is a part of Tindivanam taluk. The taluk is located at a distance of 38 kms. from district headquarters (Viluppuram). There are 59 villages in the block with the total population of 110,083 persons. Area of the C.D. Block is 284.52 sq. kms. It is bounded in the north by C.D. Block Olakkur, in the south by CD Blocks Vikramvandi and Vanur, in the east by C.D. Blocks Marakkanam and Vanur, in the west by CD Blocks Vallam and Vikravandi.

Communications:

Roadways : N.H.-45: Direction- Viluppuram to Tindivanam, Nearest Villages- T. Kenipattu, Chinnanerkunam, Kutteripattu, Chinnavalavanur, Chendur, Vilangampadi, Padirapuliyur, Palapattu, Perani, Chittani. N.H.-66: Direction- Gingee to Tindivanam, Nearest Villages- Pelakuppam, Vilukkam, Deevanur, Kilperadikuppam, Salai, Kollar, Vempoondi.

Railway Station: Kutteripattu, Chinnavalavanur, Perani.

River: Tondi Nadi- Nearest Villages- Alagrammam, Nedumozhianur, Chendur, Padirapuliyur, Athikuppam, Veedur. Varahanadi Nadi- Nearest Villages- Kothamangalam, Perani, Sndiyampakkam, Palapattu, Athikuppam, Nedumozhianur, Chittani, Ganaphathipattu, Anganikuppam, Ezhaoi.

Backwards Region Grants Fund: It receives Backward Region Grants.

Annual Rainfall: Average Rainfall 1119 mm.

Ground Water: Availability of the ground water in the Basin is 6588.55 H.A.M. and the utilization is 6836.24 H.A.M. It belongs to Over Expoited category. Depth to water level varies from 2 to 5 meter below the ground. Most of the wells go down in summer months, according to the Ground Water Estimation Committee.

Natural Division: Tondai Nadu.

Administration

Revenue **Division:** Tindivanam. Parliamentary Constituency: 12 Arani, 13 Villupuram (SC).District: Villupuram. Taluk: Tindivanam. Asembly Constituency: 71 Mailam, 72 Tindivanam (SC). Gram Panchayat: 47.

Villages: 59 **Inhabited:** 59 **Uninhabited:** 0

Ranking	District	State	National
Area	15	192	2947
Population	14	93	3153
Sex Ratio	7	215	1547
Child Sex Ratio	6	51	1075
Literacy Rate	7	235	2116
Density	19	253	2828

Work Participation Rate	10	125	2743

Gram Panchayats:

Agoor, Alagrammam, Asur, Avayakuppam, Chendur, Chinnanerkunam, Chittani, Deevanur, Ganapathipattu, Ilamangalam, Kallakolathur, Kanniyam, Kattusiviri, Kenipattu, Kodima, Kollar, Kolliyankunam, Konamangalam, Kutteripattu, Mailam, Muppuli, Naduvanandal, Nallamur, Nedumozhianur, Padirapuliyur, Palakuppam, Palapattu, Pampundi, Peradikuppam (Mel), Peramandur, Perani, Periathatchur, Puliyanur, Rettanai, Salai, Se-kothamangalam, Sendiyampakkam, Taludali, Taniyal, Tennalapakkam, Thenkulapakkam, V. Nallalam, V.Nallalam, Velangampadi, Veliyanur, Vengandur, Vidur, Vilukkam.

Amenities:

Education: Primary School in 57 villages, Middle school in 24 villages, Matriculation or Secondary School in 12 villages, namely Agoor, Kollar, Rettanai (East), Kolliyenkunam, Alagrammam, Nedumozhianur, Mailam, Taludali, Padirapuliyur, Perani, Periathatchur, Veedur.

Higher Secondary or Pre University Courses or Intermediate or Junior College in 5 villages of the CD Block,, namely Rettanai (East), Alagrammam, Taludali, Kanniyam, Periathatchur.

College in 1 village, Adult Literacy Center in 0 village., College is in village, namely Mailam.

Medical: Hospital in 0 village, Dispensary in 0 village, Health Center in 6 villages, Sub Center in 19 villages, Maternity and Child Welfare Center in 58 villages, Community health workers in 58 villages.

Drinking Water: Tap water in 59 villages, Tank water in 19 villages, Well water in 59 villages, Tubewell in 59 villages and more than one source in 59 villages.

Bank: Banking facility in 11 villages, namely, Naduvananthal, Vilukkam, Deevanur, Agoor, Kollar Rettanai (East), Kallakolathur, Kutteripattu, Mailam Periathatchur, Veedur.

Credit Society in 14 villages Agricultural Credit Society in 11 Non-Agricultural Credit Society in 0 village.

Others: Power supply in 59 villages, Cinema hall in 2 villages, sport club in 0 village, Stadium or Auditorium or Community Hall in 0 village, Post Office in 31 villages.

There are 58 villages having bus facilities.

Villages with most of facilities: Naduvananthal Vilukkam, Deevanur, Agoor, Kollar, Rettanai (East) Kutteripattu, Mailam, Periathatchur, Veedur.

Villages without amenities (Education):
Ariyankuppam, Anganikuppam..

Scheduled Castes: Out of the total population of 110083 persons, 36929 persons (33.55%) belong to Scheduled Castes.
The villages having less than 10% SC population are Kattuseveri, Muppuli, Kodima, Ariyankuppam Soliachokkulam, Anganikuppam.
The villages having more than 50% SC population are Taniyal, Pelakuppam, Kollar, Vempoondi Pandamangalam, Kallakolathur, Kolliyenkunam Chinnavalavanur, Tennalapakkam, Padirapuliyur Konamangalam.
Sex ratio of Scheduled Caste population is 497.

Scheduled Castes Literates and Illiterates by Sex:

	Persons	Males	Females
Literate	18,853	11,206	7,647
Illiterate	18,076	7,353	10,723
Literacy rate	59.1	70.0	48.1
Graduate	447	372	75

Scheduled Castes (Dominant):
Adi Dravida, Valluvan, Arunthathiyar, Domban Kuravan etc.

For their cultural identity please see Appendix-I

Villages without Scheduled Castes: There are 5 villages without any scheduled caste population.

Scheduled Tribes: Out of the total population of 110083 persons, 1578 persons (1.43%) belong to Scheduled Tribes.
The villages having less than 10% ST population are Taniyal, Puliyanur, Pelakuppam, Kattuseveri Pampundi, Naduvananthal, Mannampoondi, Elamangalam Vilukkam, Deevanur, Agoor, Kilperadikuppam, Salai Kollar, Vempoondi, Muttiyur, Peramandur, Asur Vengandur, Rettanai (East), Avayakuppam, Muppuli Kodima, Pandamangalam, T. Kenipattu, Ariyankuppam Veliyanur, Kallakolathur, Nallamur, Chinnanerkunam Kutteripattu, Chinnavalavanur, Soliachokkulam Alagrammam, Nedumozhianur, Se Kothamangalam V. Nallalam, V. Panchalam, Sndiyampakkam, Chendur Vilangampadi, Mailam, Thenkulapakkam, Taludali Kanniyam, Tennalapakkam, Kuralur, Padirapuliyur Palapattu, Perani, Periathatchur, Chittani, Ezhaoi Athikuppam, Anganikuppam, Veedur, Konamangalam Ganaphathipattu.
The villages having more than 50% ST population are None.
Sex ratio of Scheduled tribe population is 504.

Scheduled Tribes Literates and Illiterates by Sex:

	Persons	Males	Females
Literate	416	255	161
Illiterate	1,162	528	634
Literacy rate	31.3	38.7	24.1
Graduate	2	0	2

Scheduled Tribes (Dominant):
Irular, Malai Pandaram, Generic Tribes etc.
Kattunayakan

For their cultural identity please see Appendix-II

Villages without Scheduled Tribes: There are 24 villages without any scheduled tribe population.

Literates and Illiterates by Sex (Total Population):

	Persons	Males	Females
Literate	61,828	36,740	25,088
Illiterate	48,255	18,553	29,702
Literacy rate	64	76	52
Graduate	1,423	1,126	297

Agriculture: ***Distribution of villages according to land use:*** Out of 59 villages, Total area (in hectare) is 28452.27, out of that 65.19 percent is cultivable and 42.73 percent of the cultivable area is irrigated.

Sources of Irrigation (Hectares): Government Canal 159, Private Canal 65.37, Well without Electricity 1056.59, Well with Electricity 2243.94, Tubewell without Electricity 0, Tubewell with Electricity 296.09, Tank 0, River 0, Lake 4105.07, Waterfall 0, Others 0.

Villages with population of 5000 to 9999:
Rettanai.

Villages with population of 10000 and above: None

Distribution of Workers:

	Persons	Males	Females	WPR
Cultivators	17,541	11,863	5,678	32.86
Agricultural Labour	26,560	12,780	13,780	49.75
Household Industry	1,018	665	353	1.91
Other Workers	8,266	6,647	1,619	15.48
Main Workers	46,763	29,547	17,216	87.6
Marginal Workers	6,622	2,408	4,214	12.4
Total Workers	53,385	31,955	21,430	

Religion: Major Religious Communities:

	Persons	Males	Females	Sex Ratio
Hindu (96.83%)	106,588	53,566	53,022	990
Muslim (0.89%)	984	486	498	1,025
Christian (1.45%)	1,600	792	808	1,020
Sikh (0%)	1	-	1	-
Buddhists (0%)	-	-	-	-
Jain (0.72%)	796	395	401	1,015

Agewise Data:

	Persons	Males	Females	Sex Ratio
All ages	110,083	55,293	54,790	991
0-14	32,353	16,315	16,038	983
15-44	51,756	25,886	25,870	999
45-79	24,203	12,129	12,074	995
80+	968	554	414	747

Age not stated	803	409	394	963

Languages (Dominant):

Tamil, Telugu, Urdu, Kannada, Hindi

Disabled Population:

	Persons	Males	Females	%
Total Disabled	2,690	1,459	1,231	
In Seeing	1,399	700	699	52.01
In Speech	248	143	105	9.22
In Hearing	154	78	76	5.72
In Movement	710	439	271	26.39
Mentally	179	99	80	6.65

MALLASAMUDRAM

Mallasamudram C.D. Block lies in the north-western part of Namakkal district. It is a part of Tiruchengode taluk. The Block is located at a distance of 70 kms. from district headquarters (Namakkal). There are 26 villages in the block with the total population of 48580 persons. Area of the C.D. Block is 146.45 sq. kms. It is bounded in the north by district Salem, in the south by C.D. Block Elachipalaiyam, in the east by CD Blocks Rasipuram, Puduchatram and Vennandur, in the west by C.D. Block Tiruchengode and district Salem.

Communications:

Roadways : Information not Available.

Annual Rainfall: Average Rainfall 540 mm.

Ground Water: Availability of the ground water in the Basin is 1788.35 H.A.M. and the utilization is 1765.00 H.A.M. It belongs to Safe category. Depth to water level varies from 2 to 10 meter below the ground. Most of the wells go down in summer months, according to the Ground Water Estimation Committee.

Natural Division: Kongu Nadu.

Administration

Revenue **Division:** Sankari. Parliamentary Constituency: 15 Salem. Districts: Salem, Namakkal. Taluk: Tiruchengode. Assembly Constituency: 87 Sankari. Gram Panchayat: 27.

Villages: 27 **Inhabited:** 27 **Uninhabited:** 0

Ranking	District	State	National
Area	15	346	5095
Population	20	362	5358
Sex Ratio	9	361	4192
Child Sex Ratio	10	364	6088
Literacy Rate	8	341	3061
Density	1	15	3255
Work Participation Rate	14	181	128

Gram Panchayats:

Avanasipatti, Ballakkuli Agraharam , Ballakuli , Kallupalayam, Karumanur, Karungalpatti, Kolankondai, Koothanatham, Kottaipalayam, Kuppuchipalayam, Mallasamudram (West), Mamundi, Mamundi Agraharam , Mangalam, Marapparai, Minnampalli,Mettupalayam, Morangam, Munjanur , Nagarpalayam, Palamedu, Paruttipalli, Pillanatham, Ramapuram, Sanbagamahadevi, Seppayapuram, Vandinatham.

Amenities:

Education: Primary School in 26 villages, Middle school in 9 villages, Matriculation or Secondary School in 5 villages Higher Secondary or Pre University Courses or Intermediate or Junior College in 1 village of the CD Block, College in 0 village, Adult Literacy Center in 0 village.

Medical: Hospital in 0 village, Dispensary in 0 village, Health Center in 4 villages, Sub Center in 9 villages, Maternity and Child Welfare Center in 0 village, Community health workers in 0 village.

Drinking Water: Tap water in 27 villages, Tank water in 0 villages, Well water in 27 villages, Tubewell in 27 villages and more than one source in 27 villages.

Credit Society in 22 villages Agricultural Credit Society in 9 Non-Agricultural Credit Society in 21 villages.

Others: Power supply in 27 villages, Cinema hall in 0 village, sport club in 0 village, Stadium or Auditorium or Community Hall in 0 village, Post Office in 27 villages.

There are 27 villages having bus facilities.

Scheduled Castes: Out of the total population of 48580 persons, 13153 persons (27.07%) belong to Scheduled Castes.

Scheduled Castes Literates and Illiterates by Sex:

	Persons	Males	Females
Literate	5,488	3,413	2,075
Illiterate	7,665	3,379	4,286
Literacy rate	47.4	57.5	36.9
Graduate	2	1	1

Scheduled Castes (Dominant):

Arunthathiyar, Adi Dravida, Pallan, Chakkiliyan Paraiyan etc.

For their cultural identity please see Appendix-I

Villages without Scheduled Castes: There is 0 village without any scheduled caste population.

Scheduled Tribes: Out of the total population of 48580 persons, 35 persons (0.07%) belong to Scheduled Tribes.

Scheduled Tribes Literates and Illiterates by Sex:

	Persons	Males	Females
Literate	19	11	8
Illiterate	16	7	9
Literacy rate	67.9	73.3	61.5
Graduate	0	0	0

Scheduled Tribes (Dominant):

Generic Tribes etc., Malayali

For their cultural identity please see Appendix-II

Villages without Scheduled Tribes: There are

24 villages without any scheduled tribe population.

Literates and Illiterates by Sex (Total Population):

	Persons	Males	Females
Literate	25,576	15,711	9,865
Illiterate	23,004	9,380	13,624
Literacy rate	58	70	46
Graduate	16	12	4

Agriculture: ***Distribution of villages according to land use:*** Out of 27 villages, Total area (in hectare) is 14645.51, out of that 93.46 percent is cultivable and 15.13 percent of the cultivable area is irrigated.

Sources of Irrigation (Hectares): Government Canal 0, Private Canal 0, Well without Electricity 0, Well with Electricity 1894.63, Tubewell without Electricity 0, Tubewell with Electricity 176.25, Tank 0, River 0, Lake 0, Waterfall 0, Others 0.

Villages with population of 5000 to 9999: Mallasamudram (West).

Villages with population of 10000 and above: None

Distribution of Workers:

	Persons	Males	Females	WPR
Cultivators	9,561	5,114	4,447	30.99
Agricultural Labour	12,960	5,589	7,371	42.01
Household Industry	1,381	690	691	4.48
Other Workers	6,946	5,063	1,883	22.52
Main Workers	25,246	14,099	11,147	81.84
Marginal Workers	5,602	2,357	3,245	18.16
Total Workers	30,848	16,456	14,392	

Religion: Major Religious Communities:

	Persons	Males	Females	Sex Ratio
Hindu (99.15%)	48,166	24,858	23,308	938
Muslim (0.26%)	127	69	58	841
Christian (0.45%)	220	130	90	692
Sikh (0.01%)	4	3	1	333
Buddhists (0%)	1	-	1	-
Jain (0.01%)	3	2	1	500

Agewise Data:

	Persons	Males	Females	Sex Ratio
All ages	48,580	25,091	23,489	936
0-14	10,938	5,993	4,945	825
15-44	22,171	11,507	10,664	927
45-79	13,464	6,533	6,931	1061
80+	718	390	328	841
Age not stated	1,289	668	621	930

Languages (Dominant):

Tamil, Telugu, Malayalam, Urdu, Kannada

Disabled Population:

	Persons	Males	Females	%
Total Disabled	933	567	366	
In Seeing	462	292	170	49.52
In Speech	97	56	41	10.4
In Hearing	55	23	32	5.89
In Movement	229	144	85	24.54
Mentally	90	52	38	9.65

MANACHANALLUR

Manachanallur C.D. Block lies in the northern part of Tiruchirappalli district. It is a part of Manachanallur taluk. The Block is located at a distance of 12 kms. from district headquarters (Tiruchirappalli). There are 41 villages in the block with the total population of 125,720 persons. Area of the C.D. Block is 356.48 sq. kms. It is bounded in the north by district Perambalur, in the south by CD Block Andanallur, in the east by CD Blocks Pullambadi and Lalgudi, in the west by CD Block Musiri and district Perambalur.

Communications:

Roadways : N.H.-45: Direction- Tiruchirappalli to Perambalur, Nearest Villages- Shanamangalam, Siruganur, Konalai, Irungalur, Samayapuram, Vegangudi, Koothur, Pichandar Koil. S.H.-25: Direction- Musiri to Lalgudi, Nearest Villages- Kariyamanickam (W), Kariyamanickam (E), Kiliya nallur (S), Melpathu, Thiruvasi, Mathavaperumal Koil, Pichandar Koil.

Railway Station: Pichandar Koil.

Rivers: Uppar Nadi- Nearest Villages- Omandur, Sirugudi, Siruppathur, Thathamangalam, Ayyampalayam, Ayiakudi, Irungalur, Samayapuram. Kollidam Nadi- Nearest Villages- Kariyamanickam (W), Kariyamanickam (E), Kiliyanallur (S), Melpathu, Thiruvasi, Mathavaperumal Koil, Pichandar Koil.

Annual Rainfall: Average Rainfall 841 mm.

Ground Water: Availability of the ground water in the Basin is 5374.31 H.A.M. and the utilization is 3109.03 H.A.M. It belongs to Safe category. Depth to water level varies from 2 to 10 meter below the ground. Most of the wells go down in summer months, according to the Ground Water Estimation Committee.

Natural Division: Chola Nadu.

Administration

Revenue **Division:** Lalgudi. Parliamentary Constituency: 24 Tiruchirappalli. District: Tiruchirappalli. Taluk: Manachanallur. Assembly Constituency: 144 Manachanallur. Gram Panchayat: 35.

Villages: 41 **Inhabited:** 40 **Uninhabited:** 1

Ranking	**District**	**State**	**National**
Area	4	106	2229
Population	1	50	2666
Sex Ratio	3	104	835
Child Sex Ratio	1	32	796
Literacy Rate	4	64	801
Density	10	180	3083
Work Participation Rate	5	154	1789

Gram Panchayats:

Alagiyamanavalam, Ayikudi, Ayyampalayam, Edumalai, Irungalur, Kalapalayam, Kariamanikam, Kariyamanickam, Kariyamanickam , Killiyanallur , Konalai, Koothur, Kovathakudi, Madavarperumalkovil, Maramareddipalayam, Melapathu, Omandur, Palaiyur, Perakambi, Pichandarkovil, Poonampalayam, Rajampalayam, Samayapuram, Seedavimangalam, Shanamangalam, Siruganur, Sirugudi, Siruppathur, Thathamangalam, Theevampalayam, Thiruppangali , Thiruppattur, Thiruvallarai, Thiruvasi, Valaiyur, Vazhaiyur, Vengangudi.

Amenities:

Education: Primary School in 39 villages, Middle school in 24 villages, Matriculation or Secondary School in 9 villages, namely Shanamangalam, Omandur, Siruganur, Kariyamanickam, Thiruvellachi, Ayyampalayam, Irungalur, Kariyamanickam (E), Pichandar Koil.

Higher Secondary or Pre University Courses or Intermediate or Junior College in 5 villages of the CD Block,, namely Thiruvellachi, Irungalur, Kariyamanickam (W), Kariyamanickam (E), Pichandar Koil.

College in 1 village, Adult Literacy Center in 1 village., College is in village, namely Siruganur.

Medical: Hospital in 3 villages, Dispensary in 13 villages, Health Center in 7 villages, Sub Center in 5 villages, Maternity and Child Welfare Center in 2 villages, Community health workers in 10 villages.

The Villages having Hospital or Dispensary or Health Center are Omandur, Palaiyur, Siruganur, Konalai, Thiruvellachi, Ayyampalayam, Ayiakudi, Thiruppangali(N), Thiruppangali (S), Kariyamanickam (E), Koothur, Mathavaperumal Koil, Pichandar Koil.

Drinking Water: Tap water in 40 villages, Tank water in 0 villages, Well water in 40 villages, Tubewell in 40 villages and more than one source in 40 villages.

Bank: Banking facility in 9 villages, namely, Edumalai, Omandur, Siruganur, Kariyamanickam Irungalur, Thiruppangali(N), Kariyamanickam (E) Mathavaperumal Koil, Pichandar Koil.

Credit Society in 9 villages Agricultural Credit Society in 8 Non-Agricultural Credit Society in 2 villages.

Others: Power supply in 40 villages, Cinema hall in 4 villages, sport club in 0 village, Stadium or Auditorium or Community Hall in 0 village, Post Office in 28 villages.

There are 40 villages having bus facilities.

Villages with most of facilities: Edumalai Omandur, Siruganur, Kariyamanickam, Irungalur Thiruppangali(N), Kariyamanickam (E) Mathavaperumal Koil, Pichandar Koil.

Villages without amenities (Education): Rajampalayam..

Scheduled Castes: Out of the total population of 125720 persons, 24237 persons (19.28%) belong to Scheduled Castes. The villages having less than 10% SC population are Seedevimangalam(North), Valaiyur, Konalai Siruppathur, Ayyampalayam, Rajampalayam Theerampalayam, Thiruppangali(N), Thiruppangali (S). The villages having more than 50% SC population are None.

Sex ratio of Scheduled Caste population is 508.

Scheduled Castes Literates and Illiterates by Sex:

	Persons	Males	Females
Literate	15,151	8,602	6,549
Illiterate	9,086	3,319	5,767
Literacy rate	71.3	82.0	60.8
Graduate	671	481	190

Scheduled Castes (Dominant):

Pallan, Paraiyan etc., Chakkiliyan, Adi Dravida Arunthathiyar

For their cultural identity please see Appendix-I

Villages without Scheduled Castes: There are 3 villages without any scheduled caste population.

Scheduled Tribes: Out of the total population of 125720 persons, 229 persons (0.18%) belong to Scheduled Tribes. The villages having less than 10% ST population are Perakambi, Seedevimangalam(North) Seedevimangalam (South), Shanamangalam, Vazhaiyur Edumalai, Omandur, Sirugudi, Valaiyur, Palaiyur Thiruppattur, Siruganur, Konalai, Kariyamanickam Thathamangalam, Siruppathur, Thiruvellachi Ayyampalayam, Ayiakudi, Irungalur, Samayapuram Kalpalayam, Rajampalayam, Ponnampalayam Theerampalayam, Thiruppangali(N), Thiruppangali (S) Solanganallur, Kariyamanickam (W) Kariyamanickam (E), Killiyanallur (N) Kiliyanallur (S), Melpathu, Thiruvasi, Kovatakudi Azaniyamanavalam, Vegangudi, Koothur Mathavaperumal Koil, Pichandar Koil.

The villages having more than 50% ST population are None.

Sex ratio of Scheduled tribe population is 489.

Scheduled Tribes Literates and Illiterates by Sex:

	Persons	Males	Females
Literate	150	86	64
Illiterate	79	31	48
Literacy rate	71.8	81.9	61.5
Graduate	19	12	7

Scheduled Tribes (Dominant):

Generic Tribes etc., Kondareddis, Malayali

Kattunayakan, Uraly

For their cultural identity please see Appendix-II

Villages without Scheduled Tribes: There are 35 villages without any scheduled tribe population.

Literates and Illiterates by Sex (Total Population):

	Persons	Males	Females
Literate	81,316	46,065	35,251
Illiterate	44,404	16,425	27,979
Literacy rate	73	84	63
Graduate	3,747	2,567	1,180

Agriculture: ***Distribution of villages according to land use:*** Out of 41 villages, Total area (in hectare) is 35648.42, out of that 43.71 percent is cultivable and 34.16 percent of the cultivable area is irrigated.

Sources of Irrigation (Hectares): Government Canal 2015.46, Private Canal 0, Well without Electricity 485.89, Well with Electricity 2631.99, Tubewell without Electricity 14.94, Tubewell with Electricity 49.73, Tank 123.95, River 0, Lake 0, Waterfall 1, Others 0.

Villages with population of 5000 to 9999: Ayyampalayam, Irungalur, Thiruppangali (North).

Villages with population of 10000 and above: Pichandarkovil.

Distribution of Workers:

	Persons	Males	Females	WPR
Cultivators	16,487	9,837	6,650	25.12
Agricultural Labour	23,549	10,174	13,375	35.88
Household Industry	4,686	2,345	2,341	7.14
Other Workers	20,902	14,598	6,304	31.85
Main Workers	53,994	32,220	21,774	82.28
Marginal Workers	11,630	4,734	6,896	17.72
Total Workers	65,624	36,954	28,670	.

Religion: Major Religious Communities:

	Persons	Males	Females	Sex Ratio
Hindu (90.25%)	113,466	56,549	56,917	1,007
Muslim (2.68%)	3,371	1,656	1,715	1,036
Christian (7.01%)	8,811	4,250	4,561	1,073
Sikh (0%)	-	-	-	-
Buddhists (0%)	-	-	-	-
Jain (0%)	2	1	1	1,000

Agewise Data:

	Persons	Males	Females	Sex Ratio
All ages	125,720	62,490	63,230	1012
0-14	34,433	17,497	16,936	968
15-44	60,509	29,844	30,665	1028
45-79	29,377	14,445	14,932	1034
80+	1,068	525	543	1034
Age not stated	333	179	154	860

Languages (Dominant):
Tamil, Telugu, Urdu, Kannada, Malayalam

Disabled Population:

	Persons	Males	Females	%
Total Disabled	4,558	1,905	2,653	
In Seeing	2,876	960	1,916	63.1
In Speech	417	233	184	9.15
In Hearing	172	81	91	3.77
In Movement	837	504	333	18.36
Mentally	256	127	129	5.62

MANAMADURAI

Manamadurai C.D. Block lies in the southern part of Sivaganga district. It is a part of Sivaganga and Manamadurai taluks. The Block is located at a distance of 18 kms. from district headquarters (Sivaganga). There are 43 villages in the block with the total population of 70,794 persons. Area of the C.D. Block is 346.63 sq. kms. It is bounded in the north by CD Blocks Tiruppuvanam and Sivaganga, in the south by districts Virudhunagar and Ramanathapuram, in the east by CD Blocks Kalayarkoil and Ilayangudi, and in the west by district Virudhunagar. CD Block Manamadurai falls in taluk Sivaganga by 06 villages, and in taluk Manamadurai by 37 villages.

Communications:

Roadways : N.H.-49: Direction- Tiruppuvanam to Paramakkudi, Nearest Villages- Vellikkuruchi, Vagudi, Perumpatcheri, Kirukakottai, Krishna Thavoo, Seikalathur, Kalpravu, Rajakambiram, Killankattur, Arasanendal, Keelapasalai, M.Karisalkulam. S.H.-27: Direction- Sivagana to Manamadurai, Nearest Villages- Manampakki, Katturani, Thuvakulam, Krishna Thavoo, Seikalathur.

Railway Station: Thuvakulam, Rajakambiram.

River: Vaigai Nadi- Nearest Villages- Idaikkattur, Perumpatcheri, Kirukakottai, Krishna Thavoo, Seikalathur, Kalpravu, Rajakambiram, Arasanendal, Mangulam, Vediyarandal, Keelapasalai, Vagudi, Sirangudi.

Backwards Region Grants Fund: It receives Backward Region Grants.

Annual Rainfall: Average Rainfall 904 mm.

Ground Water: Availability of the ground water in the Basin is 6587.13 H.A.M. and the utilization is 1486. 04 H.A.M. It belongs to Safe category. Depth to water level varies from 2 to 10 meter below the ground. Most of the wells go down in summer months, according to the Ground Water Estimation Committee.

Natural Division: NA

Administration

Revenue **Division:** Sivaganga. Parliamentary Constituency. District: Sivaganga. Taluk: Sivaganga, Ilayangudi, Manamadurai. Assembly Constituency: 186 Sivaganga. Gram Panchayat: 39.

Villages: 43 **Inhabited:** 43 **Uninhabited:** 0

Ranking	**District**	**State**	**National**
Area	6	121	2309

Population	6	283	4432
Sex Ratio	11	221	1553
Child Sex Ratio	7	110	2133
Literacy Rate	5	148	1501
Density	11	319	4674
Work Participation Rate	8	323	3838

Gram Panchayats:

Annavasal, Arasakulam, Chinnakkannanur, Idaikattur , Kalkurichi, Kalpiravu, Kattikulam, Keelamalkudi, Keelapasalai, Keelapasalai , Kilpidavur, Kuvalaiveli, Manambakki, Mangulam, Maramvetti karisalkulam, Melanettur , Melapasalai, Melapidavoor, Milaganoor, Muthaneadhal, Pacheri, Pathinettankottai, Periya Aravangadu, Periyakottai, Perumbacheri , Rajagambiram , Sannathipudukulam, Seikalathur , Sirugudi, Soorakkulam pillaruthan, Soorakulam Pillaruthau, Sullangudi , T.Pudukottai, Thanjakoor, Theethampettai, Therkuchandanur, Vagudi , Valuthani Pudukkulam , Vellikurichi, Vembathur , Vilathur, Veeranendhal , Keelanattur.

Amenities:

Education: Primary School in 40 villages, Middle school in 17 villages, Matriculation or Secondary School in 11 villages, namely Vempathur, Valuthanipudukkulam, Idaikkattur, Vellikkuruchi, Krishna Thavoo, Rajakambiram, Theethanpettai, Kattikulam, Milaganoor, Chinnakannanoor, Melanettur.

Higher Secondary or Pre University Courses or Intermediate or Junior College in 5 villages of the CD Block,, namely Vempathur, Krishna Thavoo, Seikalathur, Rajakambiram, Theethanpettai.

College in 1 village, Adult Literacy Center in 0 village., College is in village, namely Killankattur.

Medical: Hospital in 4 villages, Dispensary in 4 villages, Health Center in 5 villages, Sub Center in 19 villages, Maternity and Child Welfare Center in 4 villages, Community health workers in 0 village.

The Villages having Hospital or Dispensary or Health Center are Valuthanipudukkulam, Idaikkattur, Vagudi, Melapidavoor, Krishna Thavoo, Seikalathur, Theethanpettai, Milaganoor.

Drinking Water: Tap water in 43 villages, Tank water in 9 villages, Well water in 43 villages, Tubewell in 43 villages and more than one source in 43 villages.

Bank: Banking facility in 8 villages, namely, Valuthanipudukkulam, Idaikkattur, Maranadu, Vagudi Thuvakulam, Krishna Thavoo, Theethanpettai Milaganoor.

Credit Society in 14 villages Agricultural Credit Society in 14 Non-Agricultural Credit Society in 2 villages.

Others: Power supply in 43 villages, Cinema hall in 0 village, sport club in 2 villages, Stadium or Auditorium or Community Hall in 8 villages, Post Office in 38 villages.

There are 42 villages having bus facilities.

Villages with most of facilities: Valuthanipudukkulam Idaikkattur, Maranadu, Vagudi, Thuvakulam Krishna Thavoo, Theethanpettai, Milaganoor.

Villages without amenities (Education): Katturani, Ezuthutrimangalam, P.Alangkulam..

Scheduled Castes: Out of the total population of 70794 persons, 16746 persons (23.65%) belong to Scheduled Castes.

The villages having less than 10% SC population are Puliyankulam, K Perunkarai, Sullangudi, Melapidavoor Vilathoor, Mangulam, P.Alangkulam.

The villages having more than 50% SC population are None.

Sex ratio of Scheduled Caste population is 498.

Scheduled Castes Literates and Illiterates by Sex:

	Persons	Males	Females
Literate	8,975	5,523	3,452
Illiterate	7,771	2,884	4,887
Literacy rate	61.1	74.9	47.2
Graduate	285	222	63

Scheduled Castes (Dominant):

Pallan, Paraiyan etc., Chakkiliyan, Kuravan etc.
Puthirai Vannan

For their cultural identity please see Appendix-I

Villages without Scheduled Castes: There is 1 village without any scheduled caste population.

Scheduled Tribes: Out of the total population of 70794 persons, 102 persons (0.14%) belong to Scheduled Tribes.

The villages having less than 10% ST population are Vempathur, Valuthanipudukkulam, Idaikkattur Puliyankulam, K Perunkarai, Keelappidavoor, Maranadu Sullangudi, Vellikkuruchi, Vagudi, Perumpatcheri Kirukakottai, Sirangudi, Manampakki, Katturani Thuvakulam, Melapidavoor, Krishna Thavoo Seikalathur, Kalpravu, Rajakambiram, Theethanpettai Kattikulam, Kuvalaiveli, Vilathoor, Thamaraikudi Senthattiyendal, K.Pudukulam, Milaganoor, Annavasal Killankattur, Arasanendal, Mangulam Ezuthutrimangalam, Therkuchandanur, Vediyarandal Keelapasalai, Arimandapam, Chinnakannanoor M.Karisalkulam, T.Pudukkottai, P.Alangkulam Melanettur.

The villages having more than 50% ST population are None.

Sex ratio of Scheduled tribe population is 539.

Scheduled Tribes Literates and Illiterates by Sex:

	Persons	Males	Females

Literate	63	33	30
Illiterate	39	14	25
Literacy rate	69.2	80.5	60.0
Graduate	2	1	1

Scheduled Tribes (Dominant):

Palliyar, Kaniyan etc., Palleyan, Malai Pandaram

For their cultural identity please see Appendix-II

Villages without Scheduled Tribes: There are 39 villages without any scheduled tribe population.

Literates and Illiterates by Sex (Total Population):

	Persons	Males	Females
Literate	42,445	25,381	17,064
Illiterate	28,349	10,180	18,169
Literacy rate	68	81	55
Graduate	1,164	857	307

Agriculture: ***Distribution of villages according to land use:*** Out of 43 villages, Total area (in hectare) is 34663.81, out of that 60.73 percent is cultivable and 57.03 percent of the cultivable area is irrigated.

Sources of Irrigation (Hectares): Government Canal 154.69, Private Canal 0, Well without Electricity 384.14, Well with Electricity 1178.35, Tubewell without Electricity 2.9, Tubewell with Electricity 579.05, Tank 8472.57, River 59.05, Lake 0, Waterfall 0, Others 1176.44.

Villages with population of 5000 to 9999:

Vembathur.

Villages with population of 10000 and above: None

Distribution of Workers:

	Persons	Males	Females	WPR
Cultivators	13,110	9,239	3,871	42.22
Agricultural Labour	11,291	5,195	6,096	36.36
Household Industry	772	364	408	2.49
Other Workers	5,881	4,434	1,447	18.94
Main Workers	22,631	15,595	7,036	72.88
Marginal Workers	8,423	3,637	4,786	27.12
Total Workers	31,054	19,232	11,822	

Religion: Major Religious Communities:

	Persons	Males	Females	Sex Ratio
Hindu (92.8%)	65,696	33,002	32,694	991
Muslim (2.7%)	1,912	931	981	1,054
Christian (4.75%)	3,362	1,690	1,672	989
Sikh (0.01%)	9	4	5	1,250
Buddhists (0.01%)	5	2	3	1,500
Jain (0%)	3	2	1	500

Agewise Data:

	Persons	Males	Females	Sex Ratio
All ages	71,079	35,674	35,405	992
0-14	19,652	10,083	9,569	949
15-44	33,534	16,622	16,912	1017
45-79	16,790	8,375	8,415	1005
80+	586	327	259	792
Age not stated	517	267	250	936

Languages (Dominant):

Tamil, Telugu, Gujarati, English, Kannada

Disabled Population:

	Persons	Males	Females	%
Total Disabled	2,722	1,247	1,475	
In Seeing	1,802	714	1,088	66.2
In Speech	167	84	83	6.14
In Hearing	131	72	59	4.81
In Movement	439	272	167	16.13
Mentally	183	105	78	6.72

MANAMELKUDI

Manamelkudi C.D. Block lies in the south-eastern part of Pudukkottai district. It is a part of Manamelkudi taluk. The Block is located at a distance of NA kms. from district headquarters (Pudukkottai). There are 72 villages in the block with the total population of 82,369 persons. Area of the C.D. Block is 250.76 sq. kms. It is bounded in the north by CD Block Aranthangi and district Thanjavur, in the south by CD Block Avudayarkoil and the Palk Strait, in the east by the Palk Strait, and in the west by CD Block Avudayarkoil.

Communications:

Roadways : Information not Available.

River: Vellar Nadi- Nearest Villages- Vellur Siruvarai, Chellappankottai, Panavayal, Mumbalai, Kallakurichi, Thandalai.

Annual Rainfall: Average Rainfall 910 mm.

Ground Water: Availability of the ground water in the Basin is 3901.37 H.A.M. and the utilization is 85.21 H.A.M. It belongs to Safe category. Depth to water level varies from 0 to 5 meter below the ground. Most of the wells go down in summer months, according to the Ground Water Estimation Committee.

Coastal Villages- (Palk Strait)- Nearest Villages- Alanganvayal, Enathi, Rowthanvayal, Karakkottai, Subramaniapuram, Pillaiyarthidal, Melasthanam, Mumbalai, Thandalai, Manamelkudi, Avidayarpattinam, Vichoor, Kodikulam, Keelamanjakkudi, Periyamadaipaissal, Seyyanam.

Natural Division: Chola Nadu.

Administration

Revenue **Division:** Pudukottai. Parliamentary Constituency: 31 Sivaganga. District: Pudukottai. Taluk: Manamelkudi. Assembly Constituency: 183 Arantangi. Gram Panchayat: 28.

Villages: 72 **Inhabited:** 72 **Uninhabited:** 0

Ranking	District	State	National
Area	13	234	3375
Population	7	229	4028
Sex Ratio	8	139	1001
Child Sex Ratio	4	104	2057
Literacy Rate	1	35	514

Density	13	330	3285
Work Participation Rate	4	187	3996

Gram Panchayats:
Ammapattinam, Bhramanavayal, Edaiyathimangalam, Edayathur, Kanadu, Karakathikottai, Karakkottai, Kattumavadi, Keelamanjakudi, Kolendram, Kottaipattinam, Krishnajipathnam, Manalur, Manamelkudi, Poovalur, Mimisal, Minnamozhi, Mumbalai, Neikuppai, Nelveli, Nilayur, Perumarudhur, Sattiyadi, Seyyanam, Tandalai, Thinayakudi, Vellur, Vettivayal, Vichur.

Amenities:
Education: Primary School in 43 villages, Middle school in 18 villages, Matriculation or Secondary School in 8 villages, namely Alanganvayal, Karakkottai, Gopalapuram, Perumarudur, Manamelkudi, Vichoor, Kodikulam, Ko. Palankulam.
Higher Secondary or Pre University Courses or Intermediate or Junior College in 2 villages of the CD Block,, namely Manamelkudi, Kodikulam.
College in 0 village, Adult Literacy Center in 0 village.
Medical: Hospital in 1 village, Dispensary in 2 villages, Health Center in 3 villages, Sub Center in 7 villages, Maternity and Child Welfare Center in 0 village, Community health workers in 48 villages.
The Villages having Hospital or Dispensary or Health Center are Subramaniapuram, Manamelkudi, Ko. Palankulam.
Drinking Water: Tap water in 72 villages, Tank water in 2 villages, Well water in 72 villages, Tubewell in 72 villages and more than one source in 72 villages.
Bank: Banking facility in 3 villages, namely, Subramaniapuram, Manamelkudi, Kodikulam.
Credit Society in 9 villages Agricultural Credit Society in 8 Non-Agricultural Credit Society in 3 villages.
Others: Power supply in 72 villages, Cinema hall in 2 villages, sport club in 0 village, Stadium or Auditorium or Community Hall in 0 village, Post Office in 14 villages.
There are 55 villages having bus facilities.
Villages with most of facilities: Subramaniapuram Manamelkudi, Kodikulam.
Villages without amenities (Education):
Mavilankanenthal, Kokumuttai, Silathani, Solani, Kamparkovil, Enathi, Rowthanvayal, Pallargudi Pitchanendal, Singavanam, Thinaiyagudi, Brahmanavayal, Tharmarajanvayal, Pettivoyal, Thalikottai, Vinaitheertha Gopalapuram, Nemmelivayal, Pillaiyarthidal, Kolluthidal, Koothangudi, Pillangudi, Sodalaivayal, Neikuppai, Kandanivayal, Kallakurichi, Melapappanoor, Keelapappanuri, Avidayarpattinam, Vettivayal, Palayavettivayal..

Scheduled Castes: Out of the total population of 82369 persons, 10645 persons (12.92%) belong to Scheduled Castes.
The villages having less than 10% SC population are Thirunellivayal, Mavilankanenthal, Kokumuttai Eadayathur, Silathani, Solani, Gopalapuram Neervilangulam, Tharmarajanvayal, Pettivoyal Thalikottai, Subramaniapuram, Koothangudi Pillangudi, Minnamozhi, Kandanivayal, Mumbalai Keelapappanuri, Manamelkudi, Avidayarpattinam Kolendram, Kavanoor, Keelamanjakkudi Periyamadaipaissal, Kilaravayal.
The villages having more than 50% SC population are Kadaiedaiyathur, Rowthanvayal Pallargudi Pitchanendal, Nemmelivayal Pillaiyarthidal, Kolluthidal, Vellur Siruvarai.
Sex ratio of Scheduled Caste population is 508.

Scheduled Castes Literates and Illiterates by Sex:

	Persons	Males	Females
Literate	6,189	3,472	2,717
Illiterate	4,456	1,763	2,693
Literacy rate	67.0	76.9	57.6
Graduate	61	44	17

Scheduled Castes (Dominant):
Paraiyan etc., Pallan, Chakkiliyan, Kuravan etc.
Adi Dravida
For their cultural identity please see Appendix-I
Villages without Scheduled Castes: There are 15 villages without any scheduled caste population.
Scheduled Tribes: Out of the total population of 82369 persons, 99 persons (0.12%) belong to Scheduled Tribes.
The villages having less than 10% ST population are Koomballam, Thirunellivayal, Mavilankanenthal Kannakur, Kadaiedaiyathur, Kokumuttai, Eadayathur Silathani, Solani, Kamparkovil, Alanganvayal, Enathi Rowthanvayal, Pallargudi Pitchanendal, Karakkottai Singavanam, Thinaiyagudi, Gopalapuram Neervilangulam, Koothanoor, Nilaiyur, Brahmanavayal Tharmarajanvayal, Pettivoyal, Thalikottai Vinaitheertha Gopalapuram, Nemmelivayal Subramaniapuram, Pillaiyarthidal, Kolluthidal Koothangudi, Pillangudi, Ollanur, Sodalaivayal Vellur Siruvarai, Perumarudur, Minnamozhi, Neikuppai Karkamalam, Chellappankottai, Panavayal Idaiyathimangalam, Melasthanam, Kandanivayal Mumbalai, Kallakurichi, Thandalai, Vellur, Manalur Nelveli, Melapappanoor, Keelapappanuri, Manthangudi Manamelkudi, Avidayarpattinam, Vichoor Karakathikkottai, Rettaiyalam, Moovanoor Ukkadai Sathiyadi, Kolendram, Kanadu, Kavanoor, Vettivayal

Manchakudi, Kodikulam, Keelamanjakkudi Periyamadaipaissal, Kilaravayal, Palayavettivayal Seyyanam, Ko. Palankulam.

The villages having more than 50% ST population are None.

Sex ratio of Scheduled tribe population is 535.

Scheduled Tribes Literates and Illiterates by Sex:

	Persons	Males	Females
Literate	15	5	10
Illiterate	84	41	43
Literacy rate	22.1	14.7	29.4
Graduate	0	0	0

Scheduled Tribes (Dominant):

Adiyan, Malai Pandaram, Koraga

For their cultural identity please see Appendix-II

Villages without Scheduled Tribes: There are 68 villages without any scheduled tribe population.

Literates and Illiterates by Sex (Total Population):

	Persons	Males	Females
Literate	54,634	30,579	24,055
Illiterate	27,735	10,479	17,256
Literacy rate	77	87	67
Graduate	605	476	129

Agriculture: *Distribution of villages according to land use:* Out of 72 villages, Total area (in hectare) is 25076.88, out of that 47.62 percent is cultivable and 79.52 percent of the cultivable area is irrigated.

Sources of Irrigation (Hectares): Government Canal 1986.21, Private Canal 0, Well without Electricity 0, Well with Electricity 0, Tubewell without Electricity 0, Tubewell with Electricity 0, Tank 7701.49, River 0, Lake 0, Waterfall 0, Others 0.

Villages with population of 5000 to 9999: None

Villages with population of 10000 and above: Manamelkudi , Kodikulam.

Distribution of Workers:

	Persons	Males	Females	WPR
Cultivators	9,815	6,437	3,378	28.4
Agricultural Labour	11,565	5,688	5,877	33.47
Household Industry	585	266	319	1.69
Other Workers	12,590	11,432	1,158	36.43
Main Workers	24,918	19,719	5,199	72.11
Marginal Workers	9,637	4,104	5,533	27.89
Total Workers	34,555	23,823	10,732	

Religion: Major Religious Communities:

	Persons	Males	Females	Sex Ratio
Hindu (67.59%)	55,671	28,049	27,622	985
Muslim (23.93%)	19,714	9,494	10,220	1,076
Christian (8.34%)	6,870	3,447	3,423	993
Sikh (0%)	1	1	-	-
Buddhists (0%)	4	3	1	333
Jain (0%)	-	-	-	-

Agewise Data:

	Persons	Males	Females	Sex Ratio
All ages	82,326	41,034	41,292	1006
0-14	24,803	12,535	12,268	979
15-44	40,520	19,940	20,580	1032
45-79	16,361	8,224	8,137	989
80+	494	242	252	1041
Age not stated	148	93	55	591

Languages (Dominant):

Tamil, Telugu, English, Kannada, Urdu

Disabled Population:

	Persons	Males	Females	%
Total Disabled	2,216	873	1,343	
In Seeing	1,489	448	1,041	67.19
In Speech	130	67	63	5.87
In Hearing	59	35	24	2.66
In Movement	402	249	153	18.14
Mentally	136	74	62	6.14

MANAPPARAI

Manapparai C.D. Block lies in the southern part of Tiruchirappalli district. It is a part of Manapparai taluk. The Block is located at a distance of 38 kms. from district headquarters (Tiruchirappalli). There are 31 villages in the block with the total population of 94,409 persons. Area of the C.D. Block is 287.76 sq. kms. It is bounded in the north by district Karur, in the south by C.D. Blocks Marungapuri and Vaiyampatti, in the east by district Pudukkottai and CD Block Manikandam, and in the west by C.D. Block Vaiyampatti.

Communications:

Roadways : N.H.-45: Direction- Dindigul to Tiruchirappalli, Nearest Villages- Chithanatham, K Periapatti South, Sathirapatti, Kannudayanpatti, Kalingapatti, Vadugapatti, Vengaikurichi, Chettiapatti, Malayadipatty, Madampatti.

Railway Station: Samudram, Chettiapatti.

Annual Rainfall: Average Rainfall 841 mm.

Ground Water: Availability of the ground water in the Basin is 3563.96 H.A.M. and the utilization is 3641.42 H.A.M. It belongs to Over Expoited category. Depth to water level varies from 2 to 10 meter below the ground. Most of the wells go down in summer months, according to the Ground Water Estimation Committee.

Forest and Reserved Forest: (Karuppur Reddiapatti RF)- Nearest Villages- Pannappatty East, Pannapatti West, Karuppur, Karuppurpatti RF, Puthanatham. (Puthanatham)- Nearest Villages- Pannappatty East, Puthanatham. (Poigaimalai)- Nearest Villages- Poigaimalai RF, Vadugapatti, Poigaipatty. (Veeramalai)- NearesT Villages- Pannapatti West, Chettichatram, Edayapatti, Chithanatham, (Mohavanur)- Nearest Villages- Puthanatham, Puthanatham RF, Thatanoor.

Natural Division: Chola Nadu.

Administration

Revenue **Division:** Tiruchirappalli. Parliamentary Constituency: 23 Karur, 24 Tiruchirappalli. District: Tiruchirappalli. Taluk: Manapparai. Assembly Constituency: 139 Srirangam, 138 Marungapuri. Gram Panchayat: 21.

Villages: 31 **Inhabited:** 29 **Uninhabited:** 2

Ranking	District	State	National
Area	9	186	2906
Population	7	156	3643
Sex Ratio	10	179	1220
Child Sex Ratio	7	213	3388
Literacy Rate	11	177	1674
Density	8	142	3290
Work Participation Rate	6	188	1400

Gram Panchayats:

Chettiapatti, Chithanatham, F.Keelaiyar, K.Periapatti, Kalingapatti, Kannudaiyanpatti , Karuppur, Malayadipatti, Mondipatti, Poigaipatti, Putha Natham, Sampatti, Samudram, Seegampatti, Soolaipatti, Thoppampatti, Usilampatti, Vadugapatti, Venkaikurichi, , Pannapatti , Podangupatti, Thathanur.

Amenities:

Education: Primary School in 25 villages, Middle school in 17 villages, Matriculation or Secondary School in 6 villages, namely Usilampatti, Chettiapatti, Malayadipatty, Poigaipatty, Pannappatty East, Puthanatham.

Higher Secondary or Pre University Courses or Intermediate or Junior College in 2 villages of the CD Block,, namely Usilampatti, Vadugapatti.

College in 2 villages, Adult Literacy Center in 0 village., Colleges are in villages, namely Chithanatham, Vengaikurichi.

Medical: Hospital in 5 villages, Dispensary in 6 villages, Health Center in 4 villages, Sub Center in 4 villages, Maternity and Child Welfare Center in 13 villages, Community health workers in 14 villages.

The Villages having Hospital or Dispensary or Health Center are Toppampatti, Periapatti North, Chettichatram, Chithanatham, Samudram, Kannudayanpatti, Vadugapatti, Chettiapatti, Pannappatty East, Karuppur, Puthanatham.

Drinking Water: Tap water in 29 villages, Tank water in 3 villages, Well water in 29 villages, Tubewell in 29 villages and more than one source in 29 villages.

Bank: Banking facility in 3 villages, namely, K Periapatti South, Pannappatty East, Puthanatham.

Credit Society in 18 villages Agricultural Credit Society in 13 Non-Agricultural Credit Society in 5 villages.

Others: Power supply in 29 villages, Cinema hall in 1 village, sport club in 0 village, Stadium or Auditorium or Community Hall in 0 village, Post Office in 16 villages.

There are 23 villages having bus facilities.

Villages with most of facilities: Pannappatty East Puthanatham.

Villages without amenities (Education):

Edayapatti, Madampatti, Poigaimalai R F, Adampatty..

Scheduled Castes: Out of the total population of 94409 persons, 16024 persons (16.97%) belong to Scheduled Castes.

The villages having less than 10% SC population are None..

The villages having more than 50% SC population are None.

Sex ratio of Scheduled Caste population is 505.

Scheduled Castes Literates and Illiterates by Sex:

	Persons	Males	Females
Literate	8,339	5,106	3,233
Illiterate	7,685	2,822	4,863
Literacy rate	60.9	75.9	46.4
Graduate	203	164	39

Scheduled Castes (Dominant):

Paraiyan etc., Pallan, Chakkiliyan, Kuravan etc. Adi Dravida

For their cultural identity please see Appendix-I

Villages without Scheduled Castes: There are 2 villages without any scheduled caste population.

Scheduled Tribes: Out of the total population of 94409 persons, 345 persons (0.37%) belong to Scheduled Tribes.

The villages having less than 10% ST population are Toppampatti, Mandipatti, Periapatti North Edayapatti, Chettichatram, Chithanatham K Periapatti South, Samudram, Sathirapatti Kannudayanpatti, Kalingapatti, Madampatti Seegampatti, Usilampatti, Poigaimalai R F Vadugapatti, Vengaikurichi, Chettiapatti Malayadipatty, Poigaipatty, Samppatti, Suliyapatti Adampatty, Pannappatty East, Pannapatti West F Keelaiyur, Karuppur, Puthanatham, Thatanoor.

The villages having more than 50% ST population are None.

Sex ratio of Scheduled tribe population is 475.

Scheduled Tribes Literates and Illiterates by Sex:

	Persons	Males	Females
Literate	185	118	67
Illiterate	160	63	97
Literacy rate	63.8	77.6	48.6
Graduate	6	5	1

Scheduled Tribes (Dominant):

Kattunayakan, Uraly, Toda, Malai Pandaram, Palleyan

For their cultural identity please see Appendix-II

Villages without Scheduled Tribes: There are 23 villages without any scheduled tribe population.

Literates and Illiterates by Sex (Total Population):

	Persons	Males	Females
Literate	54,460	32,736	21,724
Illiterate	39,949	14,510	25,439
Literacy rate	67	80	53
Graduate	1,361	995	366

Agriculture: ***Distribution of villages according to land use:*** Out of 31 villages, Total area (in hectare) is 28776.66, out of that 37.16 percent is cultivable and 50.39 percent of the cultivable area is irrigated.

Sources of Irrigation (Hectares): Government Canal 0, Private Canal 0, Well without Electricity 272.38, Well with Electricity 4301.94, Tubewell without Electricity 0, Tubewell with Electricity 4.1, Tank 809.9, River 0, Lake 0, Waterfall 0, Others 0.

Villages with population of 5000 to 9999: Kannudayanpatti, Poigaipatti, Pannapatti (East) Karuppur, Puthanatham.

Villages with population of 10000 and above: None

Distribution of Workers:

	Persons	Males	Females	WPR
Cultivators	16,308	9,359	6,949	32.69
Agricultural Labour	18,196	7,021	11,175	36.47
Household Industry	1,921	1,020	901	3.85
Other Workers	13,465	10,442	3,023	26.99
Main Workers	44,096	25,993	18,103	88.39
Marginal Workers	5,794	1,849	3,945	11.61
Total Workers	49,890	27,842	22,048	

Religion: Major Religious Communities:

	Persons	Males	Females	Sex Ratio
Hindu (83.92%)	79,226	39,676	39,550	997
Muslim (4.44%)	4,188	2,133	2,055	963
Christian (12.31%)	11,620	5,725	5,895	1,030
Sikh (0%)	-	-	-	-
Buddhists (0.01%)	6	6	-	-
Jain (0%)	2	1	1	1,000

Agewise Data:

	Persons	Males	Females	Sex Ratio
All ages	95,399	47,723	47,676	999
0-14	28,388	14,496	13,892	958
15-44	45,906	22,680	23,226	1024
45-79	20,243	10,077	10,166	1009
80+	677	350	327	934
Age not stated	185	120	65	542

Languages (Dominant):
Tamil, Telugu, Urdu, Malayalam, Nepali

Disabled Population:

	Persons	Males	Females	%
Total Disabled	3,369	1,566	1,803	
In Seeing	2,185	882	1,303	64.86
In Speech	310	167	143	9.2
In Hearing	89	52	37	2.64
In Movement	597	355	242	17.72
Mentally	188	110	78	5.58

MANDAPAM

Mandapam C.D. Block lies in the south-eastern part of Ramanathapuram district. It is a part of Ramanathapuram and Rameswaram taluks. The Block is located at a distance of 40 kms. from district headquarters (Ramanathapuram). There are 18 villages in the block with the total population of 126,185 persons. Area of the C.D. Block is 238.19 sq. kms. It is bounded in the north by the Palk Strait, in the south and east by the Gulf of Mannar, in the west by CD Blocks Ramanathapuram and Tiruppallani. CD Block Mandapam falls in taluk Ramanathapuram by 17 villages, and in taluk Rameswarm by 01 village.

Communications:

Roadways : N.H.-49: Direction- Ramanathapuram to Rameswaram, Nearest Villages- Pattinamkathan, Azhangulam, Atthankarai, Perungulam, Valantharavai, Kusavankudi, Nagachi, Enmanamkondan, Pirappanvalasi, Sathakonvalasai, Mandapam, Noochiyoorani.

Railway Station: Valantharavai, Enmanamkondan, Mandapam, Pamban.

River: Vaigai Nadi- Nearest Villages- Therbogi, Azhangul, Valantharavai.

Annual Rainfall: Average Rainfall 827 mm.

Ground Water: Availability of the ground water in the Basin is 4727.58 H.A.M. and the utilization is 4053.15 H.A.M. It belongs to Semi Critical category. Depth to water level varies from 0 to 5 meter below the ground. Most of the wells go down in summer months, according to the Ground Water Estimation Committee.

Coastal Villages- (Palk Strait and Gulf of Mannar)- Nearest Villages- Therbogi, Azhangulam, Atthankarai, Rettaiyurani, Nagachi, Enmanamkondan, Pirappanvalasi, Sathakonvalasai, Mandapam, Noochiyoorani, Pudhumadam, Karan.

Natural Division: NA

Administration

Revenue **Division:** Ramanathapuram. Parliamentary Constituency: 35 Ramanathapuram. District: Ramanathapuram. Taluk: Ramanathapuram, Rameswaram. Assembly Constituency: 210 Tiruvadanai, 211 Ramanathapuram. Gram Panchayat: 28.

Villages: 18 **Inhabited:** 18 **Uninhabited:** 0

Ranking	District	State	National
Area	10	243	3535

Population	2	48	2644
Sex Ratio	6	38	395
Child Sex Ratio	7	119	2279
Literacy Rate	1	28	458
Density	11	375	2078
Work Participation Rate	1	46	5497

Gram Panchayats:
Alagangulam, Attarangarai, Enmanamkondam, Irumeni, Karan, Keelanagatchi, Koravalli, Kumbaram, Kusavankudi, Manankudi, Marayakarpattinam, Nochioorani , Pamban, Panaikulam, Perungulam, Pirappanvalasai , Pudumadam, Puduvalasai, Rettaioorani , Sambadaiyarkulam, Sathakonevalasai, Tamaraikulam, Thangachimadam, Valantharavai, Vallarioodai, Vedalai, Vallarioodai.

Amenities:

Education: Primary School in 16 villages, Middle school in 8 villages, Matriculation or Secondary School in 6 villages, namely Azhangulam, Kumbaram, Rettaiyurani, Enmanamkondan, Mandapam, Pamban.

Higher Secondary or Pre University Courses or Intermediate or Junior College in 3 villages of the CD Block,, namely Azhangulam, Mandapam, Pudhumadam.

College in 0 village, Adult Literacy Center in 0 village.

Medical: Hospital in 3 villages, Dispensary in 2 villages, Health Center in 5 villages, Sub Center in 0 village, Maternity and Child Welfare Center in 3 villages, Community health workers in 1 village.

The Villages having Hospital or Dispensary or Health Center are Azhangulam, Enmanamkondan, Mandapam, Pudhumadam, Pamban.

Drinking Water: Tap water in 18 villages, Tank water in 4 villages, Well water in 18 villages, Tubewell in 18 villages and more than one source in 18 villages.

Bank: Banking facility in 9 villages, namely, Azhangulam, Perungulam, Kusavankudi, Rettaiyurani Enmanamkondan, Pirappanvalasi, Mandapam, Pudhumadam Pamban.

Credit Society in 9 villages Agricultural Credit Society in 6 Non-Agricultural Credit Society in 2 villages.

Others: Power supply in 13 villages, Cinema hall in 2 villages, sport club in 0 village, Stadium or Auditorium or Community Hall in 0 village, Post Office in 14 villages.

There are 18 villages having bus facilities.

Villages with most of facilities: Azhangulam Enmanamkondan, Pirappanvalasi, Mandapam, Pudhumadam Pamban.

Villages without amenities (Education):
Kusavankudi..

Scheduled Castes: Out of the total population of 126185 persons, 6199 persons (4.91%) belong to Scheduled Castes.

The villages having less than 10% SC population are Therbogi, Azhangulam, Atthankarai, Perungulam Kumbaram, Rettaiyurani, Nagachi, Enmanamkondan Pirappanvalasi, Sathakonvalasai, Mandapam Noochiyoorani, Pudhumadam, Karan, Pamban.

The villages having more than 50% SC population are None.

Sex ratio of Scheduled Caste population is 512.

Scheduled Castes Literates and Illiterates by Sex:

	Persons	Males	Females
Literate	3,797	2,118	1,679
Illiterate	2,402	908	1,494
Literacy rate	71.0	81.0	61.5
Graduate	207	128	79

Scheduled Castes (Dominant):
Pallan, Chakkiliyan, Paraiyan etc., Arunthathiyar Kuravan etc.

For their cultural identity please see Appendix-I

Villages without Scheduled Castes: There are 2 villages without any scheduled caste population.

Scheduled Tribes: Out of the total population of 126185 persons, 28 persons (0.02%) belong to Scheduled Tribes.

The villages having less than 10% ST population are Pattinamkathan, Therbogi, Azhangulam, Atthankarai Perungulam, Valantharavai, Kusavankudi, Kumbaram Rettaiyurani, Nagachi, Enmanamkondan, Pirappanvalasi Sathakonvalasai, Mandapam, Noochiyoorani, Pudhumadam Karan, Pamban.

The villages having more than 50% ST population are None.

Sex ratio of Scheduled tribe population is 500.

Scheduled Tribes Literates and Illiterates by Sex:

	Persons	Males	Females
Literate	14	8	6
Illiterate	14	6	8
Literacy rate	60.9	66.7	54.6
Graduate	2	1	1

Scheduled Tribes (Dominant):
Kattunayakan, Malai Pandaram, Palliyan

For their cultural identity please see Appendix-II

Villages without Scheduled Tribes: There are 14 villages without any scheduled tribe population.

Literates and Illiterates by Sex (Total Population):

	Persons	Males	Females
Literate	84,754	44,680	40,074
Illiterate	41,431	17,245	24,186
Literacy rate	78	84	72
Graduate	2,439	1,658	781

Agriculture: ***Distribution of villages according to land use:***

Out of 18 villages, Total area (in hectare) is 23819, out of that 32.25 percent is cultivable and 8.63 percent of the cultivable area is irrigated.

Sources of Irrigation (Hectares): Government Canal 0, Private Canal 0, Well without Electricity 614.19, Well with Electricity 288.96, Tubewell without Electricity 0, Tubewell with Electricity 0, Tank 96.96, River 0, Lake 0, Waterfall 0, Others 0.

Villages with population of 5000 to 9999: Perungulam, Valantaravai, Rettaiyurani Enmanamkondan, Mandapam , Pudumadam.

Villages with population of 10000 and above: Pattinamkattan , Alagankulam , Pamban.

Distribution of Workers:

	Persons	Males	Females	WPR
Cultivators	2,529	1,800	729	5.98
Agricultural Labour	6,935	4,578	2,357	16.41
Household Industry	5,070	504	4,566	11.99
Other Workers	27,739	24,145	3,594	65.62
Main Workers	33,252	27,749	5,503	78.66
Marginal Workers	9,021	3,278	5,743	21.34
Total Workers	42,273	31,027	11,246	

Religion: Major Religious Communities:

	Persons	Males	Females	Sex Ratio
Hindu (65.49%)	82,642	41,315	41,327	1,000
Muslim (22.96%)	28,968	13,057	15,911	1,219
Christian (13.61%)	17,176	8,918	8,258	926
Sikh (0.01%)	9	5	4	800
Buddhists (0%)	-	-	-	-
Jain (0%)	-	-	-	-

Agewise Data:

	Persons	Males	Females	Sex Ratio
All ages	128,878	63,334	65,544	1035
0-14	40,286	20,497	19,789	965
15-44	64,539	31,040	33,499	1079
45-79	22,965	11,275	11,690	1037
80+	927	430	497	1156
Age not stated	161	92	69	750

Languages (Dominant):
Tamil, Urdu, Telugu, Marathi, Hindi

Disabled Population:

	Persons	Males	Females	%
Total Disabled	4,168	1,971	2,197	
In Seeing	2,516	1,046	1,470	60.36
In Speech	341	177	164	8.18
In Hearing	114	39	75	2.74
In Movement	851	514	337	20.42
Mentally	346	195	151	8.3

MANGALUR

Mangalur C.D. Block lies in the western part of Cuddalore district. It is a part of Tittakudi taluk. The taluk is located at a distance of 95 kms. from district headquarters (Cuddalore). There are 86 villages in the block with the total population of 125,923 persons. Area of the C.D. Block is 443.85 sq. kms. It is bounded in the north by district Viluppuram, in the south by districts Perambalur and Ariyalur, in the east by C.D. Block Nallur, and in the west by district Perambalur.

Communications:

Roadways : N.H.-45: Direction- Perambalur to Ulundurpettai, Nearest Villages- Kaludur, Thondankurichi, Pasar, Kallur, Avatti, Pudaiyur Ma, Ramanatham, Eluthur, Venkanur, Adharnatham. S.H.-31: Direction- Attur to Virudhachalam, Nearest Villages- Arasankudi, Sirupakkam, Rettakurichi, Adari, Mangulam.

River: Vellar Nadi- Nearest Villages- Lakshmanapuram, Korakkavadi, Vadakarampoondi, Melakaipoondi, Kelkalpoondi, Chithur Va, Alathur, Tholudur, Ramanatham, Peramgiyam, Arangur, Vagaiyur, Aakkanur, Edaicheruvi, Kilseruvai, Pattur, Neivasai.

Backwards Region Grants Fund: It receives Backward Region Grants.

Annual Rainfall: Average Rainfall 1050 mm.

Ground Water: Availability of the ground water in the Basin is 9380.53 MCM and the utilization is 7156.90 MCM. It belongs to Semi Critical category. Depth to water level varies from 2 to 10 meter below the ground. Most of the wells go down in summer months, according to the Ground Water Estimation Committee.

Forest and Reserved Forest: (Kil Orathur RF)- Nearest Villages- Kilorathur RF, Kilorathur. (Lakkur)- Nearest Villages- Pudur Ma, Lakkur, Lakkur (RF). (Nangur)- Nearest Villages- Pulikarambalur, Lakkur, Nangur (RF), Nangur, Kothanur Ma. (Thachur)- Nearest Villages- Thatchur (RF), Nangur, Thatchur. (Rettakurichi)- Nearest Villages- Rettakurichi (RF), Rettakurichi, Mangulam. (Sirupakkam)- Nearest Villages- Sirupakkam, Sirupakkam (RF), Mangulam.

Natural Division: Tondai Nadu.

Administration

Revenue **Division:** Virudhachalam. Parliamentary Constituency: 14 Kallakurichi (SC). District: Cuddalore. Taluk: Tittakudi. Assembly Constituency: 151 Tittakudi (SC). Gram Panchayat: 66.

Villages: 86 **Inhabited:** 83 **Uninhabited:** 3

Ranking	**District**	**State**	**National**
Area	1	49	1706
Population	5	49	2657
Sex Ratio	1	61	510
Child Sex Ratio	6	133	2355
Literacy Rate	13	361	3741
Density	2	117	3706
Work Participation Rate	13	247	1194

Gram Panchayats:
Adari, Akkanur, Alambadi, Alathur, Arangur, Arasankudi, Avatti, Avinangudi, Chitheri, E. Keeranur, E. Keeranur , Edacheruvi, Eluthur, Endal T., Endal .Ja, Ivanur, Kallur, Kaludur, Kanchirankulam, Kandamathan, Keelacheruvai, Kil orathur, Kilakalpoondi, Kodangudi, Korakkai, Korakkavadi, Kothanur.Ma, Lakkur, Ma. Pudaiyur , Malayanur, Mangalore, Mangulam, Meladhanur, Melakalpoondi, Navalur, Nedunkulam, Nidhinatham, Orangur, Panaiyandur, Pasar, Pattakurichi, Pattur, Perumulai, Pothirumangalam, Poyanapadi, Pudhur.Ma, Pulikarambalur, Pulivalam, Pullur, Ramanatham, Rettakurichi, S. Naraiyur , S. Pudur, Sevveri, Sirukarambalur, Sirumulai, Sirupakkam, Thatchur, Tholudur, Thondankurichi, Vadakarampoondi, Vadapathy, Vagaiyur, Vaiyangudi, Vallimarudham, Venkanur, Vinayaganandhal, .

Amenities:
Education: Primary School in 79 villages, Middle school in 22 villages, Matriculation or Secondary School in 9 villages, namely Sirupakkam, Adari, Mangalore, Kaludur, Keeranur.E., Pudaiyur.Ma, Kelkalpoondi, Tholudur, Avinangudi.
Higher Secondary or Pre University Courses or Intermediate or Junior College in 4 villages of the CD Block,, namely Sirupakkam, Pudaiyur.Ma, Tholudur, Avinangudi. College in 0 village, Adult Literacy Center in 0 village.
Medical: Hospital in 0 village, Dispensary in 0 village, Health Center in 8 villages, Sub Center in 6 villages, Maternity and Child Welfare Center in 1 village, Community health workers in 41 villages.
Drinking Water: Tap water in 83 villages, Tank water in 0 villages, Well water in 83 villages, Tubewell in 83 villages and more than one source in 83 villages.
Bank: Banking facility in 11 villages, namely, Sirupakkam, Adari, Vadapathy, Kandamathan, Mangalore Kaludur, Keeranur.E., Lakkur, Kelkalpoondi, Tholudur Avinangudi.
Credit Society in 14 villages Agricultural Credit Society in 11 Non-Agricultural Credit Society in 0 village.
Others: Power supply in 82 villages, Cinema hall in 0 village, sport club in 0 village, Stadium or Auditorium or Community Hall in 0 village, Post Office in 82 villages.
There are 82 villages having bus facilities.
Villages with most of facilities: Sirupakkam Adari, Vadapathy, Kandamathan, Mangalore, Kaludur Keeranur.E., Tholudur, Avinangudi.
Villages without amenities (Education): Lakshmanapuram, Keeladhanur, Lakkur (Rf), Nangur (Rf)..

Scheduled Castes: Out of the total population of 125923 persons, 51881 persons (41.2%) belong to Scheduled Castes.
The villages having less than 10% SC population are Kumarai, Pudhukulam, Lakkur (Rf), Nangur (Rf) Konagambadi.
The villages having more than 50% SC population are Naraiyur, Sirupakkam, Rettakurichi, Kolavai, Orangur Panaiyandur, Pattakurichi, Kanjirangulam Nidhinatham, Navalur, Nadunkulam, Keeladhanur, Pasar Kallur, Nangur, Vadakarampoondi, Kelkalpoondi Alathur, Peramgiyam, Ivanur, Sirumulai, Kodangudi Elumathur, Avinangudi.
Sex ratio of Scheduled Caste population is 503.

Scheduled Castes Literates and Illiterates by Sex:

	Persons	Males	Females
Literate	21,733	13,823	7,910
Illiterate	30,148	11,973	18,175
Literacy rate	49.0	62.8	35.4
Graduate	444	389	55

Scheduled Castes (Dominant):
Adi Dravida, Arunthathiyar, Paraiyan etc.
Kuravan etc., Valluvan
For their cultural identity please see Appendix-I
Villages without Scheduled Castes: There are 6 villages without any scheduled caste population.
Scheduled Tribes: Out of the total population of 125923 persons, 176 persons (0.14%) belong to Scheduled Tribes.
The villages having less than 10% ST population are Naraiyur, Arasankudi, Sirupakkam, Sirupakkam (Rf) Rettakurichi, Kolavai, Kilorathur, Edal Ja, Kalathur Adari, Mangulam, Malaiyanur, Orangur, Vadapathy Chitheri, Panaiyandur, Lakshmanapuram, Korakkavadi Vallimarudham, Pattakurichi, Kandamathan Pulikarambalur, Kothanur.Ma, Pudur.Ma, Mangalore Kachimailur, Vinayaganandal, Poyanapadi Kanjirangulam, Sirukarambalur, Kaludur Thondankurichi, Pullur, Nidhinatham, Navalur Kumarai, Pudhukulam, Nadunkulam, Sevveri Keeranur.E., Keeladhanur, Meladhanur, Avatti, Pasar Kallur, Pudaiyur.Ma, Lakkur, Lakkur (Rf) Nangur (Rf), Nangur, Vadakarampoondi, Melakaipoondi Kelkalpoondi, Chithur.Va, Alathur, Vaidhanathapuram Thatchur, Tholudur, Ramanatham, Peramgiyam, Eluthur Venkanur, Adharnatham, T.Endal, Arangur, Vagaiyur Aakkanur, Edaicheruvi, Korakkai, Alambadi Konagambadi, Ivanur, Kilseruvai, Pulivalam Perumulai, Sirumulai, Vaiyangudi, Pothirumangalam Kodangudi, Elumathur, Pattur, Avinangudi, Neivasai.
The villages having more than 50% ST population are

None.

Sex ratio of Scheduled tribe population is 449.

Scheduled Tribes Literates and Illiterates by Sex:

	Persons	Males	Females
Literate	32	27	5
Illiterate	144	70	74
Literacy rate	22.7	35.5	7.7
Graduate	0	0	0

Scheduled Tribes (Dominant):

Adiyan, Kurumans, Malakkuravan, Kattunayakan

For their cultural identity please see Appendix-II

Villages without Scheduled Tribes: There are 80 villages without any scheduled tribe population.

Literates and Illiterates by Sex (Total Population):

	Persons	Males	Females
Literate	59,848	37,009	22,839
Illiterate	66,075	25,051	41,024
Literacy rate	55	69	41
Graduate	1,199	979	220

Agriculture: ***Distribution of villages according to land use:*** Out of 86 villages, Total area (in hectare) is 44385.68, out of that 74.49 percent is cultivable and 25.07 percent of the cultivable area is irrigated.

Sources of Irrigation (Hectares): Government Canal 653.37, Private Canal 0, Well without Electricity 1635.5, Well with Electricity 3621.78, Tubewell without Electricity 177.1, Tubewell with Electricity 1764.33, Tank 297.13, River 0, Lake 0, Waterfall 0, Others 141.

Villages with population of 5000 to 9999: Sirupakkam.

Villages with population of 10000 and above: None

Distribution of Workers:

	Persons	Males	Females	WPR
Cultivators	28,400	16,726	11,674	41.79
Agricultural Labour	32,521	14,211	18,310	47.85
Household Industry	894	436	458	1.32
Other Workers	6,151	4,468	1,683	9.05
Main Workers	53,986	30,806	23,180	79.43
Marginal Workers	13,980	5,035	8,945	20.57
Total Workers	67,966	35,841	32,125	

Religion: Major Religious Communities:

	Persons	Males	Females	Sex Ratio
Hindu (98.11%)	123,548	60,914	62,634	1,028
Muslim (1.47%)	1,847	900	947	1,052
Christian (0.34%)	432	200	232	1,160
Sikh (0%)	3	1	2	2,000
Buddhists (0%)	-	-	-	-
Jain (0%)	2	-	2	-

Agewise Data:

	Persons	Males	Females	Sex Ratio
All ages	125,923	62,060	63,863	1029
0-14	37,563	19,402	18,161	936
15-44	59,097	27,757	31,340	1129
45-79	28,148	14,273	13,875	972
80+	756	437	319	730
Age not stated	359	191	168	880

Languages (Dominant):

Tamil, Telugu, Urdu, Malayalam, Others

Disabled Population:

	Persons	Males	Females	%
Total Disabled	3,428	1,653	1,775	
In Seeing	1,925	807	1,118	56.16
In Speech	272	158	114	7.93
In Hearing	207	99	108	6.04
In Movement	816	485	331	23.8
Mentally	208	104	104	6.07

MANIKANDAM

Manikandam C.D. Block lies in the south-western part of Tiruchirappalli district. It is a part of Srirangam taluk. The taluk is located at a distance of 25 kms. from district headquarters (Tiruchirappalli). There are 26 villages in the block with the total population of 84,713 persons. Area of the C.D. Block is 176.94 sq. kms. It is bounded in the north by C.D. Block Andanallur, in the south by district Pudukkottai, in the east by CD Block Thiruverumbur, in the west by CD Block Manapparai and district Karur.

Communications:

Roadways : N.H.-45: Direction- Dindigul to Tiruchirappalli, Nearest Villages- Sholaganallur, K.Kallikudi North, Thayanur, Navalur Kottappattu, Ariyavoor, Periyanayakichathiram, Ammapettai, Kulathur, Mathur.

Railway Station: Kulathur.

River: Koraiyar Nadi- Nearest Villages- Kolukkattugudy, Thirumalai Samudram, Olaiyur, Madikandam, Thoraikudi.

Annual Rainfall: Average Rainfall 841 mm.

Ground Water: Availability of the ground water in the Basin is 4709.60 H.A.M. and the utilization is 1565.86 H.A.M. It belongs to Safe category. Depth to water level varies from 2 to 5 meter below the ground. Most of the wells go down in summer months, according to the Ground Water Estimation Committee.

Natural Division: Chola Nadu.

Administration

Revenue **Division:** Tiruchirappalli. Parliamentary Constituency: 24 Tiruchirappalli. District: Tiruchirappalli. Taluk: Srirangam. Assembly Constituency: 139 Sriranga. Gram Panchayat: 22.

Villages: 26 **Inhabited:** 26 **Uninhabited:** 0

Ranking	District	State	National
Area	13	319	4585
Population	9	211	3944

Sex Ratio	4	106	839
Child Sex Ratio	2	48	1068
Literacy Rate	5	93	1075
Density	11	294	2312
Work Participation Rate	3	64	3290

Gram Panchayats:
Adhavathur, Allithurai, Alundur, Ammapettai, Ariyavur, Kallikudi, Kulathur, Kumaravayalur, Mathur, Mekkudi, Mudikandam, Nachikurichi, Nagamangalam, Navalurkottapattu, Paganur, Pariyanayaki Chatram, Punganur, Sethurapatti, Somarasanpettai, Thayanur, Thorakudi, Tirumalaisamudram.

Amenities:

Education: Primary School in 26 villages, Middle school in 9 villages, Matriculation or Secondary School in 5 villages, namely Somarasampettai, K.Kallikudi North, Kulathur, Allandur, Nagamangalam.

Higher Secondary or Pre University Courses or Intermediate or Junior College in 4 villages of the CD Block,, namely Somarasampettai, Adavathur East, Kulathur, Allandur.

College in 1 village, Adult Literacy Center in 0 village., College is in village, namely Ammapettai.

Medical: Hospital in 2 villages, Dispensary in 5 villages, Health Center in 3 villages, Sub Center in 3 villages, Maternity and Child Welfare Center in 4 villages, Community health workers in 0 village.

The Villages having Hospital or Dispensary or Health Center are Somarasampettai, Kumaravayalur, Kallikudi South, Thayanur, Kulathur, Nagamangalam.

Drinking Water: Tap water in 26 villages, Tank water in 7 villages, Well water in 26 villages, Tubewell in 26 villages and more than one source in 26 villages.

Bank: Banking facility in 5 villages, namely, Somarasampettai, Navalur Kottappattu Periyanayakichathiram, Kulathur, Sethurapatti.

Credit Society in 5 villages Agricultural Credit Society in 5 Non-Agricultural Credit Society in 0 village.

Others: Power supply in 26 villages, Cinema hall in 2 villages, sport club in 0 village, Stadium or Auditorium or Community Hall in 0 village, Post Office in 10 villages.

There are 21 villages having bus facilities.

Villages with most of facilities: Somarasampettai Kulathur.

Villages without Amenities (Education): None..

Scheduled Castes: Out of the total population of 84713 persons, 15150 persons (17.88%) belong to Scheduled Castes. The villages having less than 10% SC population are None..

The villages having more than 50% SC population are None.

Sex ratio of Scheduled Caste population is 511.

Scheduled Castes Literates and Illiterates by Sex:

	Persons	Males	Females
Literate	8,421	4,872	3,549
Illiterate	6,729	2,530	4,199
Literacy rate	64.2	76.2	52.9
Graduate	343	241	102

Scheduled Castes (Dominant):
Pallan, Paraiyan etc., Chakkiliyan, Adi Dravida Kuravan etc.

For their cultural identity please see Appendix-I

Villages without Scheduled Castes: There is 0 village without any scheduled caste population.

Scheduled Tribes: Out of the total population of 84713 persons, 339 persons (0.4%) belong to Scheduled Tribes. The villages having less than 10% ST population are Somarasampettai, Kumaravayalur, Adavathur West Adavathur East, Nachi Kurichi, Sholaganallur K.Kallikudi North, Kallikudi South, Thayanur Navalur Kottappattu, Ariyavoor Periyanayakichathiram, Ammapettai, Kulathur, Mathur Sethurapatti, Allandur, Paganur, Nagamangalam Kottappattu, Mekkudi, Madikandam, Kolukkattugudy Thoraikudi, Thirumalai Samudram, Olaiyur.

The villages having more than 50% ST population are None.

Sex ratio of Scheduled tribe population is 481.

Scheduled Tribes Literates and Illiterates by Sex:

	Persons	Males	Females
Literate	58	34	24
Illiterate	281	142	139
Literacy rate	21.7	24.5	18.8
Graduate	3	2	1

Scheduled Tribes (Dominant):
Adiyan, Generic Tribes etc., Kattunayakan Malai Pandaram, Malakkuravan

For their cultural identity please see Appendix-II

Villages without Scheduled Tribes: There are 19 villages without any scheduled tribe population.

Literates and Illiterates by Sex (Total Population):

	Persons	Males	Females
Literate	52,460	29,726	22,734
Illiterate	32,253	12,379	19,874
Literacy rate	71	81	61
Graduate	2,442	1,573	869

Agriculture: ***Distribution of villages according to land use:*** Out of 26 villages, Total area (in hectare) is 17694.76, out of that 42.79 percent is cultivable and 71.61 percent of the cultivable area is irrigated.

Sources of Irrigation (Hectares): Government Canal 3292.43, Private Canal 0, Well without Electricity 122.41, Well with Electricity 900.26, Tubewell without Electricity 31.5, Tubewell with Electricity 407.56, Tank 561.31, River 0, Lake 105.75, Waterfall 0, Others 0.

Villages with population of 5000 to 9999: Somarasampettai, Adavathur (West), Thayanur Kulathur.

Villages with population of 10000 and above: None

Distribution of Workers:

	Persons	Males	Females	WPR
Cultivators	7,214	4,681	2,533	18.59
Agricultural Labour	14,136	6,543	7,593	36.43
Household Industry	1,784	638	1,146	4.6
Other Workers	15,668	12,228	3,440	40.38
Main Workers	32,625	21,723	10,902	84.08
Marginal Workers	6,177	2,367	3,810	15.92
Total Workers	38,802	24,090	14,712	

Religion: Major Religious Communities:

	Persons	Males	Females	Sex Ratio
Hindu (81.03%)	68,642	34,107	34,535	1,013
Muslim (7.11%)	6,024	2,990	3,034	1,015
Christian (11.82%)	10,017	4,995	5,022	1,005
Sikh (0%)	1	-	1	-
Buddhists (0%)	-	-	-	-
Jain (0%)	2	-	2	-

Agewise Data:

	Persons	Males	Females	Sex Ratio
All ages	84,713	42,105	42,608	1012
0-14	24,211	12,199	12,012	985
15-44	42,630	21,092	21,538	1021
45-79	17,176	8,467	8,709	1029
80+	574	283	291	1028
Age not stated	122	64	58	906

Languages (Dominant):
Tamil, Telugu, Urdu, Malayalam, Kannada

Disabled Population:

	Persons	Males	Females	%
Total Disabled	3,037	1,412	1,625	
In Seeing	1,960	765	1,195	64.54
In Speech	235	128	107	7.74
In Hearing	122	76	46	4.02
In Movement	549	349	200	18.08
Mentally	171	94	77	5.63

MANNARGUDI

Mannargudi C.D. Block lies in the central south part of Thiruvarur district. It is a part of Needamangalam and Mannargudi taluks. The Block is located at a distance of 28 kms. from district headquarters (Thiruvarur). There are 69 villages in the block with the total population of 118,867 persons. Area of the C.D. Block is 256.85 sq. kms. It is bounded in the north by C.D. Blocks Needamaugalam, Koradacherry and Thiruvarur, and district Nagapattinam, in the south by CD Blocks Kottur and Thirutturaipoondi, and district Thanjavur, in the east by district Nagapattinam, in the west by C.D. Block Needamangalam and district Thanjavur. CD Block Mannargudi falls in taluk Needamangalam by 16 villages, and in taluk Mannargudi by 43 villages.

Communications:

Roadways : Information not Available.

Railway Station: Chithraiyur.

Annual Rainfall: Average Rainfall 1184 mm.

Ground Water: Availability of the ground water in the Basin is 5571.44 H.A.M. and the utilization is 3084. 98 H.A.M. It belongs to Safe category. Depth to water level varies from 2 to 10 meter below the ground. Most of the wells go down in summer months, according to the Ground Water Estimation Committee.

Natural Division: Chola Nadu.

Administration

Revenue **Division:** Mannargudi. Parliamentary Constituency: 28 Nagapattenam (SC). District: Thiruvarur. Taluk: Nedamangalam, Mannargudi. Assembly Constituency: 168 Thirvuvarur, 167 Mannargudi. Gram Panchayat: 51.

Villages: 69 **Inhabited:** 69 **Uninhabited:** 0

Ranking	District	State	National
Area	3	222	3289
Population	1	67	2901
Sex Ratio	9	200	1451
Child Sex Ratio	10	179	3095
Literacy Rate	7	80	917
Density	5	315	2387
Work Participation Rate	5	76	3710

Gram Panchayats:

Aesham , Bharathlimoolangudi , Chithraiyur, Edaiyaramethi, Edaiyaramethi , Edayarnatham, Ethangudi, Harichandrapuram, Kamavur , Kandithampettai, Karikottai, Keelathiruppalkudi , Kelamanali, Koopachikkottai, Kothangudi, Mahadevapattinam , Manakkarai, Manchanavadi Thirurameswaram , Maravakkadu, Melathiruppalakudi, Melavasal , Moonam sethi , Moovanallur , Neduvakottai, Nemmeli, Ohaiperaiyur, Overcheri , Painganadu, Palaiyanur , Palkurichi, Paravakkottai , Paruthkikottai, Perikothur, Poonthalankudi, Pullamangalam, Ramapuram , Savala karan, Seramangalam , Sithanagudi, Sundarakkottai, Thalayamangalam, Thengavanur, Thenpathi, Thulasendarapuram, Ullikkottai, Vadagavanur, Vadapathimangalam , Vadapthi, Velukudi, Vettathidal.

Amenities:

Education: Primary School in 61 villages, Middle school in 30 villages, Matriculation or Secondary School in 10 villages, namely Pullamangalam, Savalakkaran, Moovanallur, Muthalsethi, Mahadevapparinam, Ullikottai Ii, Paravakkottai Ii, Paikaladu, Thulasendrapuram, Thalayamangalam.

Higher Secondary or Pre University Courses or Intermediate or Junior College in 6 villages of the CD Block,, namely Pullamangalam, Muthalsethi, Mahadevapparinam, Ullikottai Ii, Paravakkottai Ii, Thalayamangalam.

College in 1 village, Adult Literacy Center in 0 village., College is in village, namely Edayarnatham.

Medical: Hospital in 0 village, Dispensary in 5 villages, Health Center in 8 villages, Sub Center in 18 villages, Maternity and Child Welfare Center in 0 village, Community health workers in 69 villages.

The Villages having Hospital or Dispensary or Health Center are Pullamangalam, Paruthikottai, Thirupalakudi I, Mahadevappattinam Ii, Paravakkottai Ii, Thalayamangalam.

Drinking Water: Tap water in 69 villages, Tank water in 2 villages, Well water in 69 villages, Tubewell in 69 villages and more than one source in 69 villages.

Bank: Banking facility in 10 villages, namely, Vakranallur, Vengaramperaiyur, Palayanur Vadapathimangalam, Harichandrapuram, Periyakothur Neduvakkottai, Serangulam, Ullikottai I Paravakkottai Ii.

Credit Society in 25 villages Agricultural Credit Society in 25 Non-Agricultural Credit Society in 0 village.

Others: Power supply in 69 villages, Cinema hall in 4 villages, sport club in 0 village, Stadium or Auditorium or Community Hall in 0 village, Post Office in 40 villages.

There are 62 villages having bus facilities.

Villages with most of facilities: Vakranallur Vengaramperaiyur, Palayanur, Vadapathimangalam Harichandrapuram, Periyakothur, Neduvakkottai Serangulam, Ullikottai I, Paravakkottai Ii.

Villages without amenities (Education): Overcheri, Kakkaiyadi, Kiliyanur, Kallarempette, Kumarapuram, Rajasambalpuram, Paravakkottai I..

Scheduled Castes: Out of the total population of 118867 persons, 39540 persons (33.26%) belong to Scheduled Castes.

The villages having less than 10% SC population are Paruthikottai, Rajalikudikadu, Kallarempette Kumarapuram, Neduvakkottai, Gopiralayam, Asesam Thirupalakudi I, Mahadevapparinam, Ullikottai I Ullikottai Ii, Paravakkottai I, Paravakkottai Ii.

The villages having more than 50% SC population are Sithanakudi, Vengaramperaiyur, Punavasal Poothazangudi, Keelamanali, Onaiperaiyur Agravelugudi, Thengovanur, Thirurameswaram Manjanavadi, Overcheri, Kakkaiyadi Vadapathimangalam, Kiliyanur, Periyakothur Chithraiyur, Pamani, Karnavur, Savalakkaran Aravathur, Ramapuram, Kailasanatherkovil Muthalsethi, Moonamsethi, Nalamchethi, Vadapathi Ethakkodi.

Sex ratio of Scheduled Caste population is 498.

Scheduled Castes Literates and Illiterates by Sex:

	Persons	Males	Females
Literate	21,285	12,493	8,792
Illiterate	18,255	7,375	10,880
Literacy rate	63.0	73.7	52.2
Graduate	257	204	53

Scheduled Castes (Dominant):

Pallan, Paraiyan etc., Koliyan, Adi Dravida Generic Castes etc.

For their cultural identity please see Appendix-I

Villages without Scheduled Castes: There are 4 villages without any scheduled caste population.

Scheduled Tribes: Out of the total population of 118867 persons, 37 persons (0.03%) belong to Scheduled Tribes.

The villages having less than 10% ST population are Vakranallur, Sithanakudi, Vengaramperaiyur Punavasal, Poothazangudi, Keelamanali, Onaiperaiyur Agravelugudi, Palayanur, Kothangudi, Vadagovanur Thengovanur, Thirurameswaram, Manjanavadi, Overcheri Verkudi, Sathanur, Kakkaiyadi, Vadapathimangalam Harichandrapuram, Pullamangalam, Kiliyanur Periyakothur, Mannakkari, Palakurichi, Chithraiyur Paruthikottai, Pamani, Karnavur, Savalakkaran Aravathur, Rajalikudikadu, Moovanallur Kallarempette, Edayar Empetti, Melavasal Kumarapuram, Karrikkottai, Neduvakkottai Gopiralayam, Ramapuram, Kailasanatherkovil Muthalsethi, Moonamsethi, Nalamchethi, Nammeli Maravakkadu, Serangulam, Asesam, Thirupalakudi I Thiruppalakkudi Ii, Thiruppalakkudi Iii, Nammeli Mahadevapparinam, Mahadevappattinam Ii, Ullikottai I Ullikottai Ii, Koopachikkottai, Rajasambalpuram Paravakkottai I, Paravakkottai Ii, Paikaladu Thulasendrapuram, Sundarakottai, Edayarnatham Thenpathy, Vadapathi, Ethakkodi, Thalayamangalam.

The villages having more than 50% ST population are None.

Sex ratio of Scheduled tribe population is 486.

Scheduled Tribes Literates and Illiterates by Sex:

	Persons	Males	Females

Literate	18	11	7
Illiterate	19	8	11
Literacy rate	58.1	73.3	43.8
Graduate	0	0	0

Scheduled Tribes (Dominant):

Kattunayakan, Malai Pandaram, Palliyan

For their cultural identity please see Appendix-II

Villages without Scheduled Tribes: There are 63 villages without any scheduled tribe population.

Literates and Illiterates by Sex (Total Population):

	Persons	Males	Females
Literate	75,920	43,171	32,749
Illiterate	42,947	16,461	26,486
Literacy rate	72	82	62
Graduate	1,621	1,223	398

Agriculture: ***Distribution of villages according to land use:*** Out of 69 villages, Total area (in hectare) is 25685.99, out of that 70.59 percent is cultivable and 94.25 percent of the cultivable area is irrigated.

Sources of Irrigation (Hectares): Government Canal 13744.72, Private Canal 0, Well without Electricity 2.1, Well with Electricity 0, Tubewell without Electricity 101.32, Tubewell with Electricity 3241.22, Tank 0, River 0, Lake 0, Waterfall 0, Others 0.

Villages with population of 5000 to 9999:

Paravakkottai-I.

Villages with population of 10000 and above: None

Distribution of Workers:

	Persons	Males	Females	WPR
Cultivators	11,514	9,278	2,236	21.87
Agricultural Labour	32,573	18,016	14,557	61.86
Household Industry	791	501	290	1.5
Other Workers	7,774	6,477	1,297	14.76
Main Workers	43,056	30,284	12,772	81.77
Marginal Workers	9,596	3,988	5,608	18.23
Total Workers	52,652	34,272	18,380	

Religion: Major Religious Communities:

	Persons	Males	Females	Sex Ratio
Hindu (95.35%)	113,336	56,954	56,382	990
Muslim (3.36%)	3,996	1,904	2,092	1,099
Christian (1.08%)	1,283	655	628	959
Sikh (0%)	1	1	-	-
Buddhists (0%)	-	-	-	-
Jain (0%)	-	-	-	-

Agewise Data:

	Persons	Males	Females	Sex Ratio
All ages	118,867	59,632	59,235	993
0-14	32,407	16,458	15,949	969
15-44	59,138	29,199	29,939	1025
45-79	26,315	13,451	12,864	956
80+	774	399	375	940
Age not stated	233	125	108	864

Languages (Dominant):

Tamil, Telugu, Urdu, Kannada, Gujarati

Disabled Population:

	Persons	Males	Females	%
Total Disabled	3,786	1,587	2,199	
In Seeing	2,567	886	1,681	67.8
In Speech	229	113	116	6.05
In Hearing	141	57	84	3.72
In Movement	615	403	212	16.24
Mentally	234	128	106	6.18

MANUR

Manur C.D. Block lies in the eastern part of Tirunelveli district. It is a part of Tirunelveli taluk. The taluk is located at a distance of 00 kms. from district headq uarters (Tirunelveli). There are 57 villages in the block with the total population of 96,533 persons. Area of the C.D. Block is 470.30 sq. kms. It is bounded in the north by CD Block Melaneelithanallur and district Thoothukkudi, in the south by CD Blocks Cheranmadevi and Palayamkottai, in the east by CD Block Palayamkottai, in the west by CD Blocks Alangulam and Pappakudi.

Communications:

Roadways : N.H.-7: Direction- Tirunelveli to Kovilpatti, Nearest Villages- Chitharsathiram, Gangaikondan, Tazhai yuthu. S.H.-39: Direction- Tenkasi to Tirunelveli, Nearest Villages- Pudur, Karuvanallur, Vallavankottai, Sirrukkankurchi, Thlukkarkulam, Srithaparppanallur, Thirupanikarisalkulam. S.H.-41: Direction- Samkaramkoil to Tirunelveli, Nearest Villages- Azhagiapandiapuram, Kanarpatti, Manur, Mavadi, Madavakuruchi, Setturayanpudur.

Rivers: Chittar Nadi- Nearest Villages- Kattarankulam, Shelliy anallur, Pirancheri, Chitharsathiram, Gangaikondan, Pathi nalamperi, Kuppakurichi, Vakaikulam, Azhagiapandiapuram, Kanarpatti, Sivagurunathan Tiruthu, Pillarkulam. Tambraparnani Nadi- Nearest Villages- Kuppakurichi, Kalkurichi, Suthamalli, Karukadu, Thenpathu.

Annual Rainfall: Average Rainfall 879 mm.

Ground Water: Availability of the ground water in the Basin is 69.80 MCM and the utilization is 22.58 MCM. It belongs to Safe category. Depth to water level varies from 2 to 10 meter below the ground. Most of the wells go down in summer months, according to the Ground Water Estimation Committee.

Forest and Reserved Forest: (Reserved Forest)- Nearest Villages- Pirancheri, Gangaikondan, Pallikottai, Tazhaiy uthu, Thenkulam, Alankaraperi. (Puliyarai)- Nearest Villa ge- Thenkulam.

Natural Division: NA

Administration

Revenue **Division:** Tirunelveli. Parliamentary Constituenc y: 38 Tirunelveli. District: Tirunelveli. Taluk: Tirunel veli. Assembly Constituency: 224 Tirunelveli. Gram Pancha yat: 41.

Villages: 57 **Inhabited:** 54 **Uninhabited:** 3

Ranking	District	State	National
Area	3	39	1604
Population	6	145	3568
Sex Ratio	8	21	224
Child Sex Ratio	13	212	3374
Literacy Rate	14	174	1651
Density	13	188	4657
Work Participation Rate	15	321	1910

Gram Panchayats:
Alagiapandiapuram, Alangaraperi , Chezhianallur, Chitharchatram, Ettankulam, Gangaikondan, Kalakudi, Kanarpatti, Karungadu, Katttarankulam, Kodaganallur, Kondanagaram, Kuppakurichi, Kurichikulam, Madhavakurichi, Manur, Mavadi, Melakkallur, Nanjankulam, Narasinganallur, Palamadai , Palavoor, Pallikottai, Pettairural, Pillaiyarkulam, Pirancheri, Plamadai , Pudhur , Sanganthiradu, Seethaparpanallur , Sethurayanpudur, Suthamalli, T.P.Karisalkulam , Thalaiyuthu, Thenkalam, Thenpathu, Therkuupatti, Thulukkarkulam , Ukkirankottai, Vagaikulam, Vallankottai , Vellalankulam.

Amenities:

Education: Primary School in 50 villages, Middle school in 22 villages, Matriculation or Secondary School in 11 villages, namely Ukkirankottai, Shelliyanallur, Gangaikondan, Kalakkudi, Tirukupatti, Manur, Pallikottai, Thenkulam, Palamadai, Kodaganallur, Thenpathu.
Higher Secondary or Pre University Courses or Intermediate or Junior College in 7 villages of the CD Block,, namely Ukkirankottai, Gangaikondan, Kalakkudi, Tirukupatti, Pallikottai, Thenkulam, Kodaganallur.
College in 0 village, Adult Literacy Center in 0 village.

Medical: Hospital in 0 village, Dispensary in 1 village, Health Center in 7 villages, Sub Center in 15 villages, Maternity and Child Welfare Center in 9 villages, Community health workers in 19 villages.
The Villages having Hospital or Dispensary or Health Center are Manur, Kodaganallur.

Drinking Water: Tap water in 54 villages, Tank water in 2 villages, Well water in 27 villages, Tubewell in 3 villages and more than one source in 38 villages.

Bank: Banking facility in 10 villages, namely, Ukkirankottai, Vakaikulam, Gangaikondan, Manur Tazhaiyuthu, Thenkulam, Seethaparppanallur Kalkurichi, Suthamalli, Pettai Ii.

Credit Society in 4 villages Agricultural Credit Society in 3 Non-Agricultural Credit Society in 0 village.

Others: Power supply in 53 villages, Cinema hall in 0 village, sport club in 1 village, Stadium or Auditorium or Community Hall in 0 village, Post Office in 41 villages.
There are 51 villages having bus facilities.

Villages with most of facilities: Ukkirankottai Vakaikulam, Gangaikondan, Manur, Tazhaiyuthu Thenkulam, Seethaparppanallur, Kalkurichi Suthamalli.

Villages without amenities (Education): Kottampuli, Udayaneri, Sivaniyarkulam, Thuvarasi..

Scheduled Castes: Out of the total population of 96533 persons, 30111 persons (31.19%) belong to Scheduled Castes.
The villages having less than 10% SC population are Kanarpatti, Kurichikulam, Tirukupatti Sirrukkankurchi, Sivaniyarkulam, Sankanthiradu.
The villages having more than 50% SC population are Chitharsathiram, Thenkulam, Nanjankulam Madavakuruchi, Ugandanpatti, Karuvanallur Vallavankottai, Thulukkarpatti, Setturayanpudur Kottampuli, Kalkurichi, Thuvarasi, Kodaganallur Thenpathu.
Sex ratio of Scheduled Caste population is 518.

Scheduled Castes Literates and Illiterates by Sex:

	Persons	Males	Females
Literate	17,287	9,615	7,672
Illiterate	12,824	4,901	7,923
Literacy rate	65.3	76.1	55.4
Graduate	244	152	92

Scheduled Castes (Dominant):
Pallan, Paraiyan etc., Arunthathiyar
Puthirai Vannan, Adi Dravida

For their cultural identity please see Appendix-I

Villages without Scheduled Castes: There are 5 villages without any scheduled caste population.

Scheduled Tribes: Out of the total population of 96533 persons, 84 persons (0.09%) belong to Scheduled Tribes.
The villages having less than 10% ST population are Ukkirankottai, Vakaikulam, Azhagiapandiapuram Kattarankulam, Shelliyanallur, Pirancheri Chitharsathiram, Gangaikondan, Pillarkulam Kanarpatti, Ettankulam, Kalakkudi, Kurichikulam Tirukupatti, Manur, Pallikottai, Tazhaiyuthu Thenkulam, Nanjankulam, Mavadi, Madavakuruchi Ugandanpatti, Pudur, Karuvanallur Seethaparppanallur, Vallavankottai, Thulukkarpatti Setturayanpudur, Palamadai, Alankaraperi Kuppakurichi, Katalaiudyaneri, Kottampuli, Udayaneri Kalkurichi, Sirrukkankurchi, Vettuvankulam

Velarkulam, Sivaniyarkulam, Thlukkarkulam Thirupanikarisalkulam, Thuvarasi, Vaduganpatti Sankanthiradu, Mellakulore, Kodaganallur, Palavoor Kondanagaram, Suthamalli, Karukadu, Narasinganallur Pettai Ii, Thenpathu.

The villages having more than 50% ST population are None.

Sex ratio of Scheduled tribe population is 548.

Scheduled Tribes Literates and Illiterates by Sex:

	Persons	Males	Females
Literate	48	23	25
Illiterate	36	15	21
Literacy rate	73.9	79.3	69.4
Graduate	0	0	0

Scheduled Tribes (Dominant):

Kondareddis, Kattunayakan, Malai Pandaram, Palleyan Palliyar

For their cultural identity please see Appendix-II

Villages without Scheduled Tribes: There are 49 villages without any scheduled tribe population.

Literates and Illiterates by Sex (Total Population):

	Persons	Males	Females
Literate	56,665	31,517	25,148
Illiterate	39,868	15,273	24,595
Literacy rate	67	77	57
Graduate	716	462	254

Agriculture: ***Distribution of villages according to land use:*** Out of 57 villages, Total area (in hectare) is 47030.56, out of that 22.09 percent is cultivable and 55.24 percent of the cultivable area is irrigated.

Sources of Irrigation (Hectares): Government Canal 1618.96, Private Canal 0, Well without Electricity 473.71, Well with Electricity 1380.22, Tubewell without Electricity 0, Tubewell with Electricity 105.29, Tank 2160.155, River 0, Lake 0, Waterfall 0, Others 0.

Villages with population of 5000 to 9999: Gangaikondan , Suttamalli.

Villages with population of 10000 and above: None

Distribution of Workers:

	Persons	Males	Females	WPR
Cultivators	8,423	5,575	2,848	16.87
Agricultural Labour	19,144	10,283	8,861	38.34
Household Industry	8,988	797	8,191	18
Other Workers	13,376	10,090	3,286	26.79
Main Workers	42,425	23,701	18,724	84.97
Marginal Workers	7,506	3,044	4,462	15.03
Total Workers	49,931	26,745	23,186	

Religion: Major Religious Communities:

	Persons	Males	Females	Sex Ratio
Hindu (82.9%)	80,025	38,888	41,137	1,058
Muslim (4.77%)	4,604	2,150	2,454	1,141
Christian (12.24%)	11,813	5,706	6,107	1,070
Sikh (0%)	-	-	-	-
Buddhists (0%)	-	-	-	-
Jain (0%)	3	2	1	500

Agewise Data:

	Persons	Males	Females	Sex Ratio
All ages	96,533	46,790	49,743	1063
0-14	27,073	13,722	13,351	973
15-44	45,849	21,906	23,943	1093
45-79	22,432	10,631	11,801	1110
80+	969	415	554	1335
Age not stated	210	116	94	810

Languages (Dominant):

Tamil, Telugu, Kannada, Hindi, Malayalam

Disabled Population:

	Persons	Males	Females	%
Total Disabled	2,797	1,239	1,558	
In Seeing	1,636	569	1,067	58.49
In Speech	183	96	87	6.54
In Hearing	113	52	61	4.04
In Movement	667	429	238	23.85
Mentally	198	93	105	7.08

MARAKKANAM

Marakkanam C.D. Block lies in the north-eastern part of Viluppuram district. It is a part of Tindivanam taluk. The Block is located at a distance of 75 kms. from district headquarters (Viluppuram). There are 85 villages in the block with the total population of 132,903 persons. Area of the C.D. Block is 371. 61 sq. kms. It is bounded in the north by C.D. Block Olakkur and district Kancheepuram, in the south by C.D. Blocks Mailam and Vanur, in the east by the Bay of Bengal, in the west by C.D. Block Mailam and the Union Territory of Pondicherry.

Communications:

Roadways : N.H.-45: Direction- Viluppuram to Madurantakam, Nearest Villages- Salavadi, Jaggampettai, Singanur, Thenpasiyar, Avanampattu, Kiledayalam. S.H.-2: Direction- Tindivanam to Pondicherry, Nearest Villages- Molasur, Omamandur, Varaguppattu, Iraiyanur.

Railway Station: Sorappattu.

Backwards Region Grants Fund: It receives Backward Region Grants.

Annual Rainfall: Average Rainfall 1119 mm.

Ground Water: Availability of the ground water in the Basin is 9118.67 H.A.M. and the utilization is 10843. 20 H.A.M. It belongs to Over Expoited category. Depth to water level varies from 2 to 5 meter below the ground. Most of the wells go down in summer months, according to the Ground Water Estimation Committee.

Coastal Villages: (Bay of Bengal)- Nearest Villages-

Vadaalapakkam, Atchikadu, Panchichamedu, Kilpettai, Anumandai, Chettikuppam, Koonimedu, Kilputhupattu.

Forest and Reserved Forest: (Agarma Vadal RF)- Nearest Villages- Vadaagaram R.F, Vadagram. (Kilseyur)- Nearest Villages- Kattalai, Perumukkal, Keel Arungunam, Vadakulapakkam. (Kuramparam)- Nearest Villages- Assappur, Kandadu, Kurumbaram. (Marakkanam)- Nearest Village- Marakkanam R.F.

Natural Division: Tondai Nadu.

Administration

Revenue Division: Tindivanam. Parliamentary Constituency: 12 Arani, 13 Villupuram (SC).District: Villupuram. Taluk: Tindivanam. Assembly Constituency: 72 Tindivanam (SC), 71 Mailam.Gram Panchayat: 56

Villages: 85 **Inhabited:** 82 **Uninhabited:** 3

Ranking	District	State	National
Area	5	91	2119
Population	3	37	2405
Sex Ratio	8	227	1636
Child Sex Ratio	12	125	2292
Literacy Rate	10	270	2319
Density	20	266	3036
Work Participation Rate	11	147	2886

Gram Panchayats:

Adasal, Adavallikuttam, Alanguppam, Alapakkam, Alapakkam (Vada), Alathur, Annamputhur, Anumandai, Asappur, Attur, Bramaddesam, Chettikuppam, Endiyur, Endur, Iraiyanur, Jaggampettai, Kalavay (Then), Kandadu, Kattalai, Keelarungunam, Kilarungunam, Kiledayalam, Kilpettai, Kilpudupattu, Kilsithamur, Kilsiviri, Kodipakkam (Vada), Koonimedu, Kovadi, Kulathur, Nagalpakkam, Manur, Molasur, Munnur, Nadukuppam, Nagalpakkam, Nagar, Nallur, Nalmukkal, Nerkunam (Vada), Omipper, Ommandur, Panichamedu, Pasiyar (Then), Perumukkal, Pudupakkam, Salavadi, Seyyankuppam, Singanur, Siruvadi, T.Nallalam, Thennerkunam, Urani, Vaidapakkam, Vanniper, Vengai, Vittalapuram, .

Amenities:

Education: Primary School in 72 villages, Middle school in 22 villages, Matriculation or Secondary School in 9 villages, namely Nagar, Endiur, Vepperi, Nadukuppam, Anumandai, Kilsiviri, Omamandur, Singanur, Koonimedu.

Higher Secondary or Pre University Courses or Intermediate or Junior College in 6 villages of the CD Block,, namely Endiur, Vepperi, Anumandai, Singanur, Kilperidikuppam, Kilputhupattu.

College in 0 village, Adult Literacy Center in 0 village.

Medical: Hospital in 3 villages, Dispensary in 5 villages, Health Center in 8 villages, Sub Center in 0 village, Maternity and Child Welfare Center in 23 villages, Community health workers in 35 villages.

The Villages having Hospital or Dispensary or Health Center are Siruvadi, Perumukkal, Nadukuppam, Vadaalapakkam, Bramaddesam, Alagaipakkam, T. Nallalam, Omamandur, Koonimedu.

Drinking Water: Tap water in 82 villages, Tank water in 39 villages, Well water in 82 villages, Tubewell in 82 villages and more than one source in 82 villages.

Bank: Banking facility in 12 villages, namely, Kandadu, Siruvadi, Endiur, Guruvammapettai, Vepperi Nadukuppam, Anumandai, Aalnguppam, Bramaddesam Omamandur, Jaggampettai, Kilputhupattu.

Credit Society in 13 villages Agricultural Credit Society in 12 Non-Agricultural Credit Society in 1 village.

Others: Power supply in 79 villages, Cinema hall in 2 villages, sport club in 2 villages, Stadium or Auditorium or Community Hall in 1 village, Post Office in 42 villages.

There are 62 villages having bus facilities.

Villages with most of facilities: Kandadu Siruvadi, Endiur, Guruvammapettai, Nadukuppam Anumandai, Bramaddesam, Omamandur, Jaggampettai Kilputhupattu.

Villages without amenities (Education):

Kurumbaram R.F, Alapakkam, Perumukkal, Murukeri, Keesavanayakkampalayam, Singanandai, Aviyathangal, Alagaipakkam, T. Nallalam, Palamukkal..

Scheduled Castes: Out of the total population of 132903 persons, 42986 persons (32.34%) belong to Scheduled Castes.

The villages having less than 10% SC population are Kurumbaram, Endiur, Madaventangal, Murukeri Tirukanur, Panchichamedu, Anumandai, Adasal Adavallikuttam, Alagaipakkam, Palamukkal Varaguppattu, Seyyankuppam.

The villages having more than 50% SC population are Vittalapuram, Kurumbaram R.F, Vadakodipakkam Molasur, Keel Arungunam, Vadakulapakkam, Endur Vepperi, Kulathur, Atchikadu, Aviyathangal T. Nallalam, Elavalappakkam, Annamputhur Jaggampettai, Singanur, Avanampattu, Vengai Kilsithamur, Kilperidikuppam, Kiledayalam.

Sex ratio of Scheduled Caste population is 500.

Scheduled Castes Literates and Illiterates by Sex:

	Persons	Males	Females
Literate	21,093	12,424	8,669
Illiterate	21,893	9,088	12,805
Literacy rate	56.8	66.9	46.7
Graduate	622	497	125

Scheduled Castes (Dominant):

Adi Dravida, Arunthathiyar, Valluvan

Generic Castes etc., Palluvan

For their cultural identity please see Appendix-I

Villages without Scheduled Castes: There are 8 villages without any scheduled caste population.

Scheduled Tribes: Out of the total population of 132903 persons, 1407 persons (1.06%) belong to Scheduled Tribes. The villages having less than 10% ST population are Salavadi, Vittalapuram, Nallur, Panthadu Nagalpakkam, Rayanallur, Nagar, Assappur Kurumbaram R.F, Kandadu , Vadagram, Pudupakkam Alathur, Vadakodipakkam, Siruvadi, Vaidapakkam Vadanerkunam, Kattalai, Endiur, Authur, Alapakkam Manur, Molasur, Guruvammapettai, Janagipettai Perumukkal, Keel Arungunam, Vadakulapakkam Madaventangal, Endur, Kurur, Murukeri, Kulathur Nadukuppam, Keesavanayakkampalayam, Tirukanur, Urani Vadaalapakkam, Atchikadu, Panchichamedu, Kilpettai Anumandai, Omipper, Adasal, Adavallikuttam Sathamangalam, Singanandai, Aalnguppam, Mannur Vanniper, Bramaddesam, Aviyathangal, Chokkantangal Nalmukkal, Alagaipakkam, T. Nallalam, Kilsiviri Palamukkal, Elavalappakkam, Thennerkulam, Kovadi Omamandur, Annamputhur, Varaguppattu, Iraiyanur Karnavoor, Jaggampettai, Singanur, Thenpasiyar Avanampattu, Thenkalavai, Vengai, Kilsithamur Sorappattu, Seyyankuppam, Chettikuppam, Koonimedu Kilperidikuppam, Kiledayalam, Kilputhupattu.

The villages having more than 50% ST population are None.

Sex ratio of Scheduled tribe population is 502.

Scheduled Tribes Literates and Illiterates by Sex:

	Persons	Males	Females
Literate	461	264	197
Illiterate	946	436	510
Literacy rate	38.8	44.7	32.9
Graduate	3	3	0

Scheduled Tribes (Dominant):

Irular, Kattunayakan, Generic Tribes etc.
Malakkuravan, Malai Pandaram

For their cultural identity please see Appendix-II

Villages without Scheduled Tribes: There are 52 villages without any scheduled tribe population.

Literates and Illiterates by Sex (Total Population):

	Persons	Males	Females
Literate	72,961	43,037	29,924
Illiterate	59,942	23,772	36,170
Literacy rate	63	74	52
Graduate	1,817	1,397	420

Agriculture: ***Distribution of villages according to land use:*** Out of 85 villages, Total area (in hectare) is 37161.66, out of that 57.82 percent is cultivable and 41.22 percent of the cultivable area is irrigated.

Sources of Irrigation (Hectares): Government Canal 0, Private Canal 0, Well without Electricity 1562.33, Well with Electricity 2629.41, Tubewell without Electricity 217.15, Tubewell with Electricity 519.88, Tank 113.87, River 0, Lake 3711.18, Waterfall 102.41, Others 0.

Villages with population of 5000 to 9999: Nadukuppam, Anumandai, Koonimedu, Kilpudupatti.

Villages with population of 10000 and above: None

Distribution of Workers:

	Persons	Males	Females	WPR
Cultivators	20,174	13,379	6,795	31.76
Agricultural Labour	29,952	14,208	15,744	47.16
Household Industry	1,197	552	645	1.88
Other Workers	12,194	9,339	2,855	19.2
Main Workers	53,042	33,706	19,336	83.51
Marginal Workers	10,475	3,772	6,703	16.49
Total Workers	63,517	37,478	26,039	

Religion: Major Religious Communities:

	Persons	Males	Females	Sex Ratio
Hindu (95.19%)	126,512	63,792	62,720	983
Muslim (3.34%)	4,444	2,090	2,354	1,126
Christian (1.4%)	1,866	886	980	1,106
Sikh (0%)	2	1	1	1,000
Buddhists (0%)	1	1	-	-
Jain (0.02%)	25	11	14	1,273

Agewise Data:

	Persons	Males	Females	Sex Ratio
All ages	132,903	66,809	66,094	989
0-14	40,329	20,433	19,896	974
15-44	62,453	31,400	31,053	989
45-79	27,493	13,627	13,866	1018
80+	1,016	531	485	913
Age not stated	1,612	818	794	971

Languages (Dominant):

Tamil, Urdu, Telugu, Kannada, Marathi

Disabled Population:

	Persons	Males	Females	%
Total Disabled	3,797	2,063	1,734	
In Seeing	2,282	1,150	1,132	60.1
In Speech	271	156	115	7.14
In Hearing	193	90	103	5.08
In Movement	845	542	303	22.25
Mentally	206	125	81	5.43

MARUNGAPURI

Marungapuri C.D. Block lies in the southern part of Tiruchirappalli district. It is a part of Manapparai taluk. The taluk is located at a distance of 38 kms. from district headquarters (Tiruchirappalli). There are 44 villages in the block with the total population of 104,717 persons. Area of the C.D. Block is 424.52 sq. kms. It is bounded in the north by C.D. Blocks Vaiyampatti and Manapparai, and district Pudukkottai, in the south by districts Madurai and Sivaganga, in the east by district Pudukkottai, in the west by district Dindigul and C.D. Block Vaiyampatti.

Communications:

Roadways : Information not Available.

Annual Rainfall: Average Rainfall 841 mm.

Ground Water: Availability of the ground water in the Basin is 6691.77 H.A.M. and the utilization is 3400.92 H.A.M. It belongs to Safe category. Depth to water level varies from 2 to 10 meter below the ground. Most of the wells go down in summer months, according to the Ground Water Estimation Committee.

Forest and Reserved Forest: (Kumarikatti Hills RF)- Nearest Villages- Kannuthu, Kamarikatti Hills RF, Ammachatram, Endapuli. (Puthanatham)- Nearest Villages- Tirunellipatti, Muthalvarpatti, Karumalai.

Natural Division: Chola Nadu.

Administration

Revenue **Division:** Tiruchirappalli. Parliamentary Constituency: 23 Karur. District: Tiruchirappalli. Taluk: Manapparai. Assembly Constituency: 138 Marungapuri. Gram Panchayat: 49.

Villages: 44 **Inhabited:** 44 **Uninhabited:** 0

Ranking	District	State	National
Area	1	57	1805
Population	3	114	3315
Sex Ratio	5	120	906
Child Sex Ratio	8	253	4135
Literacy Rate	13	275	2351
Density	4	81	4121
Work Participation Rate	12	286	765

Gram Panchayats:

Adaikkampatti, Alampatti , Amanakkampatti, Ammachathiram, Athikaram , Athikarampatti , Ayanporuvai, Ayanpudupatti, Endapuli, Ikkaraikasukuruchi, Kalingapatti , Kallakkanpatti, Kanjanaickenpatti, Kannivadugapatti, Kannukuli, Kannuthu, Karadipatti , Karaipatti , Karumalai, Kavandampatti , Kodumbapatty , M.Idayapatti, Maniankuruchi, Manikkur, Manikurichi, Marungapuri, Muthalvarpatti, Nallur, Nattarapatti , Nattarpatti , Palakurichy, Palayapalayam , Palayepalayam , Paluvanji, Pidarapatti, Pirampatti , Sevalpatti, T.Edayapatti, Thazhampadi, Thenur, Thethanur, Thirunallipatti, Thottiapatti, Unaiyur, Unaiyur , Usilampatti, Uthukuli, V.Edaiyapatti, Vaguthalvarpatti, Vairampatti, Valanadu, Vembanur, .

Amenities:

Education: Primary School in 43 villages, Middle school in 25 villages, Matriculation or Secondary School in 11 villages, namely Thottiapatti, Amanakkampatty, Tirunellipatti, Uthukuli, Palakkurichi, Valanadu, Marungapuri, T.Idayapatti, Karippatti, Sevalpatti, Thethur.

Higher Secondary or Pre University Courses or Intermediate or Junior College in 4 villages of the CD Block,, namely Thottiapatti, Tirunellipatti, Palakkurichi, Karippatti.

College in 0 village, Adult Literacy Center in 0 village.

Medical: Hospital in 0 village, Dispensary in 7 villages, Health Center in 2 villages, Sub Center in 2 villages, Maternity and Child Welfare Center in 19 villages, Community health workers in 7 villages.

The Villages having Hospital or Dispensary or Health Center are Vellaiyakkonpatti, Pirampatti South, Thenur, Palakkurichi, Valanadu, Karumalai, T.Idayapatti.

Drinking Water: Tap water in 44 villages, Tank water in 10 villages, Well water in 44 villages, Tubewell in 44 villages and more than one source in 44 villages.

Bank: Banking facility in 5 villages, namely, Thottiapatti, Palakkurichi, Paluvanji East Marungapuri, Karippatti.

Credit Society in 15 villages Agricultural Credit Society in 7 Non-Agricultural Credit Society in 7 villages.

Others: Power supply in 43 villages, Cinema hall in 0 village, sport club in 0 village, Stadium or Auditorium or Community Hall in 0 village, Post Office in 31 villages.

There are 33 villages having bus facilities.

Villages with most of facilities: Palakkurichi Marungapuri.

Villages without amenities (Education):

Kamarikatti Hills R F..

Scheduled Castes: Out of the total population of 104717 persons, 21173 persons (20.22%) belong to Scheduled Castes.

The villages having less than 10% SC population are Kannuthu, Uthukuli, Ayan Poruvai, Endapuli Kanjanaickenpatti, Velakkurichi, Marungapuri Ikkaraikosakurichi, Thethur.

The villages having more than 50% SC population are None.

Sex ratio of Scheduled Caste population is 505.

Scheduled Castes Literates and Illiterates by Sex:

	Persons	Males	Females
Literate	10,212	6,309	3,903
Illiterate	10,961	4,164	6,797
Literacy rate	57.3	72.1	43.0
Graduate	159	125	34

Scheduled Castes (Dominant):

Pallan, Paraiyan etc., Chakkiliyan, Kuravan etc.
Puthirai Vannan

For their cultural identity please see Appendix-I

Villages without Scheduled Castes: There is 1 village without any scheduled caste population.

Scheduled Tribes: Out of the total population of 104717 persons, 38 persons (0.04%) belong to Scheduled Tribes. The villages having less than 10% ST population are Thottiapatti, Amanakkampatty, Kannivadugapatti Kannuthu, Kamarikatti Hills R F, Tirunellipatti Vellaiyakkonpatti, Pirampatti North Pirampatti South, Thenur, Ayanpudupatti, Uthukuli Vembanur, Kannukuzhi, Kavinaripatti, Puthakudi Kappakudi, Kodumbapatti, Palakkurichi Kalingapatti East, Kalingapatti West, Ayan Poruvai Valanadu, Paluvanji East, Paluvanji West Muthalvarpatti, Karumalai, Ammachatram, Endapuli Kanjanaickenpatti, Velakkurichi, Venkatanaickenpatti Marungapuri, T.Idayapatti, Yagapuram, Nallur Karippatti, Sevalpatti, Ikkaraikosakurichi Akkiyampatti, Alagapuri, Lekkanayakanpatti, Thethur Sevanthapatti.

The villages having more than 50% ST population are None.

Sex ratio of Scheduled tribe population is 500.

Scheduled Tribes Literates and Illiterates by Sex:

	Persons	Males	Females
Literate	16	11	5
Illiterate	22	8	14
Literacy rate	53.3	68.8	35.7
Graduate	1	1	0

Scheduled Tribes (Dominant):

Malai Pandaram, Uraly, Kattunayakan

For their cultural identity please see Appendix-II

Villages without Scheduled Tribes: There are 41 villages without any scheduled tribe population.

Literates and Illiterates by Sex (Total Population):

	Persons	Males	Females
Literate	56,280	34,695	21,585
Illiterate	48,437	17,437	31,000
Literacy rate	62	78	. 47
Graduate	1,032	755	277

Agriculture: ***Distribution of villages according to land use:*** Out of 44 villages, Total area (in hectare) is 42452.98, out of that 36.56 percent is cultivable and 45.56 percent of the cultivable area is irrigated.

Sources of Irrigation (Hectares): Government Canal 2.82, Private Canal 0, Well without Electricity 1093.56, Well with Electricity 3283.24, Tubewell without Electricity 9.1, Tubewell with Electricity 201.41, Tank 2433.99, River 0, Lake 0, Waterfall 0, Others 48.17.

Villages with population of 5000 to 9999: None

Villages with population of 10000 and above: None

Distribution of Workers:

	Persons	Males	Females	WPR
Cultivators	23,892	14,090	9,802	41.44
Agricultural Labour	24,976	10,317	14,659	43.32
Household Industry	1,108	562	546	1.92
Other Workers	7,678	5,965	1,713	13.32
Main Workers	46,642	26,555	20,087	80.9
Marginal Workers	11,012	4,379	6,633	19.1
Total Workers	57,654	30,934	26,720	

Religion: Major Religious Communities:

	Persons	Males	Females	Sex Ratio
Hindu (96.01%)	100,537	50,032	50,505	1,009
Muslim (1.24%)	1,296	658	638	970
Christian (1.74%)	1,817	922	895	971
Sikh (0%)	1	1	-	-
Buddhists (0%)	1	-	1	-
Jain (0%)	2	2	-	-

Agewise Data:

	Persons	Males	Females	Sex Ratio
All ages	103,727	51,655	52,072	1008
0-14	31,962	16,516	15,446	935
15-44	48,727	23,584	25,143	1066
45-79	21,691	10,876	10,815	994
80+	640	332	308	928
Age not stated	707	347	360	1037

Languages (Dominant):

Tamil, Telugu, Urdu, Kannada, English

Disabled Population:

	Persons	Males	Females	%
Total Disabled	3,719	1,586	2,133	
In Seeing	2,692	1,012	1,680	72.39
In Speech	202	116	86	5.43
In Hearing	129	68	61	3.47
In Movement	532	298	234	14.3
Mentally	164	92	72	4.41

MATHUR

Mathur C.D. Block lies in the central-east part of Dharmapuri district. It is a part of Pochampalli and Uthangarai taluk. The taluk (Uthangarai) is located at a distance of 57 kms. from district headquarters (Dharmapuri). There are 58 villages in the block with the total population of 91,001 persons. Area of the C.D. Block is 250.86 sq. kms. It is bounded in the north by CD Block Bargur and District Vellore, in the south and east by Uthangarai CD Block, and in the west by Bargur CD Block. CD Block Mathur falls in taluk Pochampalli by 12 villages, and in taluk Uthangarai by 46 villages.

Communications:

Roadways : N.H.-66: Direction- Krishnagiri to Uthangarai, Nearest Villages- Kannandahalli, Nagampatti, Pichukondanahalli, Bathrahalli, Sonarahalli, Kondireddipatti, Gandiganampatti, Marappanaickenpatti, Samalpatti, Kannichi, Oddapatti, Kursampatti, Kanganur, Nagalpatti.

Railway Station: Kunnathur.

River: Mattur Nadi- Nearest Villages- Sonarahalli, Nagampatti, Rangampatti, Kondireddipatti, Mookkampatti, Marappanaickenpatti, Kunnathur, Savadiyur, Bathrahalli, Kullampatti, Ramakrishnampathy, Papparapatti, Kamatchipatti, Mukkarampalli. Ponnaiyar Nadi- Nearest Village- Anandhur.

Annual Rainfall: Average Rainfall 760 mm.

Ground Water: Availability of the ground water in the Basin is (Information not available) H.A.M. and the utili zation is 160.44 H.A.M. It belongs to Over Expoited categ ory. Depth to water level varies from 2 to 5 meter below the ground. Most of the wells go down in summer months, according to the Ground Water Estimation Committee.

Natural Division: Baramahal.

Administration

Revenue **Division:** Krishnagiri. Parliamentary Constituency: 9 Krishnagiri. District: Dharmapuri. Taluk: Pochampalli, Uthangarai. Assembly Constituency: 51 Uthangarai (SC). Gram Panchayat: 24.

Villages: 58 **Inhabited:** 58 **Uninhabited:** 0

Ranking	District	State	National
Area	18	233	3373
Population	16	179	3755
Sex Ratio	8	354	3853
Child Sex Ratio	12	363	6087
Literacy Rate	7	293	2476
Density	14	195	3002
Work Participation Rate	5	142	1991

Gram Panchayats:

Anandur, Antheripatti, Bommepalli, Gerigepalli, Gerigepalli , Inamkattupatti, K.Ethipatti , K.Papparapatty , Kalarpathi, Kannandahalli, Kavanthanur, Kodamandapatti, Kunnathur, Mathur, Nagampatti , Naralapalli, Naralapalli , Oddapatti, Ramakrishnapathi , Salamarathapatti , Samalpatti , Sevampatti, Soolagarai , Valipatti, Vanipathi, Veerachikuppam .

Amenities:

Education: Primary School in 43 villages, Middle school in 20 villages, Matriculation or Secondary School in 14 villages, namely Kannandahalli, Sivampatti, Nagampatti, Bathrahalli, Sonarahalli, Rangampatti, Gandiganampatti, Mookkampatti, Marappanaickenpatti, Kunnathur, Samalpatti, Pasanthi, Kanjanoor, Anandhur. Higher Secondary or Pre University Courses or Intermediate or Junior College in 7 villages of the CD Block,, namely Kannandahalli, Sivampatti, Bathrahalli, Kunnathur, Samalpatti, Kanjanoor, Anandhur.

College in 0 village, Adult Literacy Center in 0 village.

Medical: Hospital in 1 village, Dispensary in 0 village, Health Center in 3 villages, Sub Center in 14 villages, Maternity and Child Welfare Center in 0 village, Community health workers in 55 villages.

The Village having Hospital or Dispensary or Health Center is Bathrahalli.

Drinking Water: Tap water in 58 villages, Tank water in 0 villages, Well water in 58 villages, Tubewell in 58 villages and more than one source in 58 villages.

Bank: Banking facility in 8 villages, namely, Kannandahalli, Nagampatti, Bathrahalli, Rangampatti Marappanaickenpatti, Samalpatti, Salamarathupatty Anandhur.

Credit Society in 16 villages Agricultural Credit Society in 6 Non-Agricultural Credit Society in 10 villages.

Others: Power supply in 58 villages, Cinema hall in 0 village, sport club in 0 village, Stadium or Auditorium or Community Hall in 0 village, Post Office in 58 villages.

There are 47 villages having bus facilities.

Villages with most of facilities: Kannandahalli Nagampatti, Bathrahalli, Rangampatti Marappanaickenpatti, Samalpatti, Salamarathupatty Anandhur.

Villages without amenities (Education): Kullampatti, Mukkarampalli, Kunnampatti, Parasanoor, Kannichi, Oddapatti, Badadasampatti, Kursampatti, Kanganur, Gerigepalli, Mallapuram, Boorgalapalli, Kurugapatti, Botharajanpatty, Obilinaickkampatty..

Scheduled Castes: Out of the total population of 91001 persons, 13060 persons (14.35%) belong to Scheduled Castes.

The villages having less than 10% SC population are Kannandahalli, Poommappalli, Kondireddipatti Kottapathy, Ramakrishnampathy, Papparapatti Kullampatti, Mukkarampalli, Kunnampatti, Vadukanoor Savadiyur, Parasanoor, Kumarampatti, Ettipatti Oddapatti, Naralappalli, Kullaganappalli, Kanganur Mottur, Pasanthi, Kullampatti, Kollampatti Badavanur, Olaippatty, Mallapuram, Boorgalapalli Kurugapatti, Veerachikuppam, Papparapatti Reddipatty, Thathinnaickampatti, Botharajanpatty Obilinaickkampatty.

The villages having more than 50% SC population are Kamatchipatti, Athiveeriampatti, Podar, Oannagarai Kanjanoor, Soolagarai.

Sex ratio of Scheduled Caste population is 491.

Scheduled Castes Literates and Illiterates by Sex:

	Persons	Males	Females
Literate	6,588	3,960	2,628
Illiterate	6,472	2,691	3,781
Literacy rate	57.9	68.4	47.1
Graduate	167	137	30

Scheduled Castes (Dominant):
Adi Dravida, Arunthathiyar, Kuravan etc.
Chamar etc., Valluvan
For their cultural identity please see Appendix-I
Villages without Scheduled Castes: There are 13 villages without any scheduled caste population.
Scheduled Tribes: Out of the total population of 91001 persons, 175 persons (0.19%) belong to Scheduled Tribes.
The villages having less than 10% ST population are Kannandahalli, Poommappalli, Sivampatti, Nagampatti Pichukondanahalli, Bathrahalli, Sonarahalli Rangampatti, Kondireddipatti, Gandiganampatti Mookkampatti, Marappanaickenpatti, Kottapathy Ramakrishnampathy, Papparapatti, Kullampatti Kamatchipatti, Mukkarampalli, Kunnampatti, Kunnathur Vadukanoor, Savadiyur, Parasanoor, Kumarampatti Ettipatti, Samalpatti, Kannichi, Oddapatti Naralappalli, Kullaganappalli, Badadasampatti Kursampatti, Kanganur, Mottur, Pasanthi, Nagalpatti Kullampatti, Kollampatti, Athiveeriampatti Gerigepalli, Badavanur, Podar, Salamarathupatty Olaippatty, Mallapuram, Oannagarai, Boorgalapalli Kanjanoor, Kurugapatti, Veerachikuppam, Papparapatti Kattuppatti, Soolagarai, Reddipatty, Anandhur Thathinnaickampatti, Botharajanpatty Obilinaickkampatty.
The villages having more than 50% ST population are None.
Sex ratio of Scheduled tribe population is 451.

Scheduled Tribes Literates and Illiterates by Sex:

	Persons	Males	Females
Literate	41	30	11
Illiterate	134	66	68
Literacy rate	31.3	42.9	18.0
Graduate	0	0	0

Scheduled Tribes (Dominant):
Irular, Kurumans
For their cultural identity please see Appendix-II
Villages without Scheduled Tribes: There are 53 villages without any scheduled tribe population.

Literates and Illiterates by Sex (Total Population):

	Persons	Males	Females
Literate	49,064	29,507	19,557
Illiterate	41,937	17,328	24,609
Literacy rate	62	73	50
Graduate	909	702	207

Agriculture: ***Distribution of villages according to land use:*** Out of 58 villages, Total area (in hectare) is 25086.92, out of that 80.46 percent is cultivable and 27.39 percent of the cultivable area is irrigated.
Sources of Irrigation (Hectares): Government Canal 0, Private Canal 0, Well without Electricity 2643.81, Well with Electricity 2191.6, Tubewell without Electricity 12.16, Tubewell with Electricity 18.36, Tank 662.82, River 0, Lake 0, Waterfall 0, Others 0.
Villages with population of 5000 to 9999:
Kannandahalli, Batrahalli, Rengampatti Gendigampatti.
Villages with population of 10000 and above: None

Distribution of Workers:

	Persons	Males	Females	WPR
Cultivators	16,638	9,984	6,654	35.89
Agricultural Labour	19,175	9,072	10,103	41.36
Household Industry	1,037	361	676	2.24
Other Workers	9,510	7,677	1,833	20.51
Main Workers	40,092	24,790	15,302	86.48
Marginal Workers	6,268	2,304	3,964	13.52
Total Workers	46,360	27,094	19,266	

Religion: Major Religious Communities:

	Persons	Males	Females	Sex Ratio
Hindu (95.4%)	86,814	44,684	42,130	943
Muslim (4.39%)	3,994	2,053	1,941	945
Christian (0.17%)	152	77	75	974
Sikh (0%)	2	2	-	-
Buddhists (0%)	4	3	1	333
Jain (0%)	1	1	-	-

Agewise Data:

	Persons	Males	Females	Sex Ratio
All ages	91,001	46,835	44,166	943
0-14	28,073	15,026	13,047	868
15-44	44,732	22,608	22,124	979
45-79	17,298	8,702	8,596	988
80+	741	390	351	900
Age not stated	157	109	48	440

Languages (Dominant):
Tamil, Telugu, Urdu, Kannada, Hindi

Disabled Population:

	Persons	Males	Females	%
Total Disabled	3,004	1,045	1,959	
In Seeing	2,126	529	1,597	70.77
In Speech	175	90	85	5.83
In Hearing	73	38	35	2.43
In Movement	518	331	187	17.24
Mentally	112	57	55	3.73

MAYILADUTHURAI

Mayiladuthurai C.D. Block lies in the north-western part of Nagapattinam district. It is a part of Mayiladuthurai taluk. The Block is located at a distance of 60 kms. from district headquarters (Nagapattinam). There are 59 villages in the block with the total population of 150,694 persons. Area of the C.D. Block is 239.08 sq. kms. It is bounded in the north by district Cuddalore, in the south by district Thiruvarur, in the east by CD Blocks Sirkazhi, Kollidam and Sembanarkoil, in the west by district Thanjavur and CD Block Kuttalam.

Communications:

Roadways : S.H.-22: Direction- Kumbakonam to Kaveripatnam, Nearest Villages- Thirindalur, Mannakudi, Vellalagaram, Mappadugai, Cholampettai, Pattamangalam, Mannanpandal, Agarakirangudy, Kovangudi. S.H.-23: Direction- Nannilam to Mayiladuthurai, Nearest Villages- Pattamangalam, Myiladuthurai, Agarakirangudy.

Railway Station: Anathandapuram, Nidur, Anaimelagaram, Sithankadu.

River: Kollidam Nadi- Nearest Villages- Mayiladuthurai, Kurichchi, Kadakkam, Mudikandanallur, Thiruchitrambalam. Backwards Region Grants Fund: It receives Backward Region Grants.

Annual Rainfall: Average Rainfall 1230 mm.

Ground Water: Availability of the ground water in the Basin is 3943.26 H.A.M. and the utilization is 3443. 30 H.A.M. It belongs to Semi Critical category. Depth to water level varies from 2 to 10 meter below the ground. Most of the wells go down in summer months, according to the Ground Water Estimation Committee.

Natural Division: Chola Nadu.

Administration

Revenue **Division:** Mayiladuthurai. Parliamentary Constituency: 27 Chidambaram (SC). District: Nagapattinam. Taluk: Mayiladuthurai. Assembly Constituency: 161 Mayiladuthurai. Gram Panchayat : 54.

Villages: 59 **Inhabited:** 59 **Uninhabited:** 0

Ranking	District	State	National
Area	3	242	3517
Population	2	14	1842
Sex Ratio	10	171	1210
Child Sex Ratio	4	31	801
Literacy Rate	7	55	726
Density	7	353	1701
Work Participation Rate	3	29	4447

Gram Panchayats:

Agarakirangudi, Anai Melagaram, Anathandavapuram, Arulmolithevan, Aruvappadi, Attur, Boothangudi, Dharmadanapuram, Elanthoppu, Ivanallur, Kadakkam, Kadalangudi, Kaduvangudi, Kali, Kanganamputhur, Keelamarudandanallur, Kesingan, Kiloy, Kodangudi, Korukkai, Kulichar, Kurichi, Maharajapuram, Manakkudi, Mannampandal, Maraiyur, Mayiladuthurai, Melamallur, Mozhaiyur, mudikandanallur, Murugamangalam, Muvalur, Nallathukudi, Namasivayapuram, Nidur, Pandaravadai mappadugai, Pandur, Pattamangalam, Pattavarthi, Ponnur, Serudiyur, Sethur, Sholampettai, Siddamalli, Sitharkadu, Talainayar, Thalancheri, Thiruindalur, Thirumangalam, Tiruchitrambalam, Uluthukuppai, Varadampattu, Vellalaragaram, Villianallur.

Amenities:

Education: Primary School in 58 villages, Middle school in 28 villages, Matriculation or Secondary School in 6 villages, namely Thiruchitrambalam, Koruikkai, Nidur, Thirumangalam, Sithankadu, Mannanpandal.

Higher Secondary or Pre University Courses or Intermediate or Junior College in 1 village of the CD Block,, namely Thiruchitrambalam.

College in 2 villages, Adult Literacy Center in 0 village., Colleges are in villages, namely Sithankadu, Mannanpandal.

Medical: Hospital in 1 village, Dispensary in 8 villages, Health Center in 3 villages, Sub Center in 23 villages, Maternity and Child Welfare Center in 0 village, Community health workers in 59 villages.

The Villages having Hospital or Dispensary or Health Center are Tiruvalaputtur, Varadampattu, Thalainayar, Aruvappadi, Anathandapuram, Nidur, Thirumangalam, Murugamangalam, Uluthukkupai.

Drinking Water: Tap water in 59 villages, Tank water in 0 villages, Well water in 59 villages, Tubewell in 59 villages and more than one source in 59 villages.

Bank: Banking facility in 8 villages, namely, Thalaignayuru, Kali, Anathandapuram, Nidur Thirumangalam, Anaimelagaram, Mannanpandal, Kulichar. Credit Society in 15 villages Agricultural Credit Society in 12 Non-Agricultural Credit Society in 4 villages.

Others: Power supply in 59 villages, Cinema hall in 3 villages, sport club in 0 village, Stadium or Auditorium or Community Hall in 0 village, Post Office in 38 villages.

There are 52 villages having bus facilities.

Villages with most of facilities: Kali Anathandapuram, Nidur, Thirumangalam, Anaimelagaram Mannanpandal.

Villages without amenities (Education): Maharajapuram..

Scheduled Castes: Out of the total population of 150694 persons, 59402 persons (39.42%) belong to Scheduled Castes. The villages having less than 10% SC population are None..

The villages having more than 50% SC population are Kurichchi, Thiruchitrambalam, Kesingan Tiruvalaputtur, Sethur, Ponmasanallur, Melanallur Thazhanchery, Namasivayapuram, Boothangudy, Kali Kilatharudanda Nallur, Dharmathanapuram Arulmozhithevan, Myiladuthurai, Agarakirangudy Kovangudi.

Sex ratio of Scheduled Caste population is 498.

Scheduled Castes Literates and Illiterates by Sex:

	Persons	Males	Females
Literate	34,166	19,550	14,616
Illiterate	25,236	10,256	14,980
Literacy rate	67.2	76.7	57.6
Graduate	657	462	195

Scheduled Castes (Dominant):

Adi Dravida, Pallan, Valluvan, Generic Castes etc. Kuravan etc.

For their cultural identity please see Appendix-I

Villages without Scheduled Castes: There is 0 village without any scheduled caste population.

Scheduled Tribes: Out of the total population of 150694 persons, 272 persons (0.18%) belong to Scheduled Tribes.

The villages having less than 10% ST population are Mayiladuthurai, Kurichchi, Kaduvangudi, Elanthope Pattavarthy, Kadakkam, Mudikandanallur Thiruchitrambalam, Kadalangudi, Authur, Kesingan Kizhai, Tiruvalaputtur, Varadampattu, Thalainayar Thalaignayuru, Sethur, Ponmasanallur, Melanallur Villianallur, Thazhanchery, Namasivayapuram Boothangudy, Kali, Kali, Ivanallur, Koruikkai Aruvappadi, Kilatharudanda Nallur, Dharmathanapuram Mozhilayur, Anathandapuram, Nidur, Kanganamputhur Arulmozhithevan, Pandur, Thirumangalam Murugamangalam, Ponnur, Maharajapuram, Thirindalur Uluthukkupai, Mannakudi, Vellalagaram, Mappadugai Cholampettai, Anaimelagaram, Moovalur, Sithankadu Pattamangalam, Myiladuthurai, Nallathukudi Serithiyur, Mannanpandal, Kulichar, Kodangudi Agarakirangudy, Kovangudi, Mariyur.

The villages having more than 50% ST population are None.

Sex ratio of Scheduled tribe population is 533.

Scheduled Tribes Literates and Illiterates by Sex:

	Persons	Males	Females
Literate	131	67	64
Illiterate	141	60	81
Literacy rate	55.3	60.9	50.4
Graduate	3	3	0

Scheduled Tribes (Dominant):

Malakkuravan, Kattunayakan, Malai Pandaram, Adiyan

For their cultural identity please see Appendix-II

Villages without Scheduled Tribes: There are 46 villages without any scheduled tribe population.

Literates and Illiterates by Sex (Total Population):

	Persons	Males	Females
Literate	98,084	54,805	43,279
Illiterate	52,610	20,569	32,041
Literacy rate	74	83	65
Graduate	3,185	2,165	1,020

Agriculture: ***Distribution of villages according to land use:*** Out of 59 villages, Total area (in hectare) is 23908.53, out of that 79.71 percent is cultivable and 76.41 percent of the cultivable area is irrigated.

Sources of Irrigation (Hectares): Government Canal 14561.11, Private Canal 0, Well without Electricity 0, Well with Electricity 0, Tubewell without Electricity 0, Tubewell with Electricity 0, Tank 0, River 0, Lake 0, Waterfall 0, Others 0.

Villages with population of 5000 to 9999:

Nidur, Thiruindalur , Mannampandal.

Villages with population of 10000 and above: None

Distribution of Workers:

	Persons	Males	Females	WPR
Cultivators	7,861	6,355	1,506	12.93
Agricultural Labour	36,652	22,209	14,443	60.28
Household Industry	1,273	562	711	2.09
Other Workers	15,012	12,778	2,234	24.69
Main Workers	50,572	36,529	14,043	83.18
Marginal Workers	10,226	5,375	4,851	16.82
Total Workers	60,798	41,904	18,894	

Religion: Major Religious Communities:

	Persons	Males	Females	Sex Ratio
Hindu (92.12%)	138,814	69,827	68,987	988
Muslim (5.52%)	8,314	3,797	4,517	1,190
Christian (2.21%)	3,328	1,622	1,706	1,052
Sikh (0.01%)	12	7	5	714
Buddhists (0%)	5	2	3	1,500
Jain (0.01%)	14	10	4	400

Agewise Data:

	Persons	Males	Females	Sex Ratio
All ages	150,694	75,374	75,320	999
0-14	44,026	22,263	21,763	978
15-44	71,773	35,084	36,689	1046
45-79	32,992	17,003	15,989	940
80+	1,272	669	603	901
Age not stated	631	355	276	777

Languages (Dominant):

Tamil, Telugu, Marathi, Urdu, Malayalam

Disabled Population:

	Persons	Males	Females	%

Total Disabled	4,369	2,269	2,100	
In Seeing	2,692	1,306	1,386	61.62
In Speech	344	176	168	7.87
In Hearing	170	84	86	3.89
In Movement	785	493	292	17.97
Mentally	378	210	168	8.65

MC. DONALD CHOULTRY

Mac. Donald Choultry C.D. Block lies in the south-western part of Salem district. It is a part of Sankari taluk. The taluk is located at a distance of 35 kms. from district headquarters (Salem). There are 13 villages in the block with the total population of 64,084 persons. Area of the C.D. Block is 102.94 sq. kms. It is bounded in the north by CD Block Taramangalam, in the south by district Namakkal and CD Block Sankari, in the east by CD Block Veerapandi, and in the west by CD Block Konganapuram.

Communications:

Roadways : N.H.-47: Direction- Sankari to Salem, Nearest Villages- Vaikuntham, Kanagagiri, Agrahara Thalaiyur, Gudalur, Kalingoundapalayam.

Railway Station: Ernapuram.

Annual Rainfall: Average Rainfall 540 mm.

Ground Water: Availability of the ground water in the Basin is 2951.83 H.A.M. and the utilization is 3699.19 H.A.M. It belongs to Safe category. Depth to water level varies from 2 to 10 meter below the ground. Most of the wells go down in summer months, according to the Ground Water Estimation Committee.

Natural Division: Kongu Nadu.

Administration

Revenue **Division:** Sankari. Parliamentary Constituency: 15 Salem. District: Salem. Taluk: Sankari. Assembly Constituency: 87 Sankari. Gram Panchayat: 12.

Villages: 13 **Inhabited:** 13 **Uninhabited:** 0

Ranking	District	State	National
Area	20	370	5686
Population	15	322	4726
Sex Ratio	16	380	5849
Child Sex Ratio	17	381	6333
Literacy Rate	11	351	3363
Density	14	157	1730
Work Participation Rate	5	31	1554

Gram Panchayats:

Agraharam Thalaiyur, Egapuram, Ernapuram, Gudalur, Kaligoundampalayam, Kanagagiri, Kandarkulamanickam, Kannanderi, Naduvaneri, Pudur, Thappakuttai, Vaikuntham.

Amenities:

Education: Primary School in 13 villages, Middle school in 7 villages, Matriculation or Secondary School in 3 villages, namely Ernapuram, Vaikuntham, Pudur.

Higher Secondary or Pre University Courses or Intermediate or Junior College in 0 village of the CD Block, College in 0 village, Adult Literacy Center in 0 village.

Medical: Hospital in 2 villages, Dispensary in 0 village, Health Center in 2 villages, Sub Center in 8 villages, Maternity and Child Welfare Center in 1 village, Community health workers in 0 village.

The Villages having Hospital or Dispensary or Health Center are Ernapuram, Vaikuntham.

Drinking Water: Tap water in 13 villages, Tank water in 0 villages, Well water in 13 villages, Tubewell in 13 villages and more than one source in 13 villages.

Bank: Banking facility in 3 villages, namely, Ernapuram, Vaikuntham, Egapuram.

Credit Society in 9 villages Agricultural Credit Society in 4 Non-Agricultural Credit Society in 8 villages.

Others: Power supply in 13 villages, Cinema hall in 1 village, sport club in 0 village, Stadium or Auditorium or Community Hall in 0 village, Post Office in 12 villages.

There are 13 villages having bus facilities.

Villages with most of facilities: Ernapuram Vaikuntham, Egapuram.

Villages without Amenities (Education): None..

Scheduled Castes: Out of the total population of 64084 persons, 5762 persons (8.99%) belong to Scheduled Castes.

The villages having less than 10% SC population are Ernapuram, Gedikaval, Agrahara Thalaiyur, Egapuram Theppakuttai, Pudur, Kalingoundapalayam.

The villages having more than 50% SC population are None.

Sex ratio of Scheduled Caste population is 479.

Scheduled Castes Literates and Illiterates by Sex:

	Persons	Males	Females
Literate	2,309	1,417	892
Illiterate	3,453	1,583	1,870
Literacy rate	46.2	55.1	36.8
Graduate	84	66	18

Scheduled Castes (Dominant):

Arunthathiyar, Adi Dravida, Pallan, Chakkiliyan Panniandi

For their cultural identity please see Appendix-I

Villages without Scheduled Castes: There is 0 village without any scheduled caste population.

Scheduled Tribes: Out of the total population of 64084 persons, 603 persons (0.94%) belong to Scheduled Tribes.

The villages having less than 10% ST population are Ernapuram, Vaikuntham, Kanagagiri, Gedikaval Agrahara Thalaiyur, Kandarkulamanickam, Naduvaneri Egapuram, Theppakuttai, Kannaderi, Pudur, Gudalur Kalingoundapalayam.

The villages having more than 50% ST population are None.

Sex ratio of Scheduled tribe population is 483.

Scheduled Tribes Literates and Illiterates by Sex:

	Persons	Males	Females
Literate	383	225	158
Illiterate	220	87	133
Literacy rate	72.8	83.0	62.0
Graduate	8	6	2

Scheduled Tribes (Dominant):

Kondareddis, Kattunayakan, Malakkuravan

For their cultural identity please see Appendix-II

Villages without Scheduled Tribes: There are 8 villages without any scheduled tribe population.

Literates and Illiterates by Sex (Total Population):

	Persons	Males	Females
Literate	32,208	20,517	11,691
Illiterate	31,876	13,829	18,047
Literacy rate	57	68	44
Graduate	1,099	819	280

Agriculture: ***Distribution of villages according to land use:*** Out of 13 villages, Total area (in hectare) is 10294.36, out of that 68.36 percent is cultivable and 33.68 percent of the cultivable area is irrigated.

Sources of Irrigation (Hectares): Government Canal 0, Private Canal 0, Well without Electricity 0, Well with Electricity 1602.834, Tubewell without Electricity 0, Tubewell with Electricity 751.76, Tank 15.72, River 0, Lake 0, Waterfall 0, Others 0.

Villages with population of 5000 to 9999:

Teppakkutai, Naduvaneri, Pudur, Eranapuram, Gudalur Vaikuntam.

Villages with population of 10000 and above: None

Distribution of Workers:

	Persons	Males	Females	WPR
Cultivators	6,653	3,939	2,714	19.44
Agricultural Labour	·8,129	3,556	4,573	23.76
Household Industry	5,658	3,591	2,067	16.54
Other Workers	13,775	10,769	3,006	40.26
Main Workers	29,365	19,916	9,449	85.82
Marginal Workers	4,850	1,939	2,911	14.18
Total Workers	34,215	21,855	12,360	

Religion: Major Religious Communities:

	Persons	Males	Females	Sex Ratio
Hindu (99.16%)	63,543	34,055	29,488	866
Muslim (0.52%)	331	173	158	913
Christian (0.22%)	142	82	60	732
Sikh (0.01%)	4	2	2	1,000
Buddhists (0%)	2	1	1	1,000
Jain (0%)	2	1	1	1,000

Agewise Data:

	Persons	Males	Females	Sex Ratio
All ages	64,084	34,346	29,738	866
0-14	16,402	9,510	6,892	725
15-44	31,232	16,508	14,724	892
45-79	15,280	7,716	7,564	980
80+	840	430	410	953
Age not stated	330	182	148	813

Languages (Dominant):

Tamil, Telugu, Kannada, Urdu, Malayalam

Disabled Population:

	Persons	Males	Females	%
Total Disabled	1,120	701	419	
In Seeing	569	356	213	50.8
In Speech	88	50	38	7.86
In Hearing	52	17	35	4.64
In Movement	299	207	92	26.7
Mentally	112	71	41	10

MECHERI

Mecheri C.D. Block lies in the northern part of Salem district. It is a part of Mettur taluk. The Block is located at a distance of 35 kms. from district headquarters (Salem). There are 19 villages in the block with the total population of 88,245 persons. Area of the C.D. Block is 176.14 sq. kms. It is bounded in the north by district Dharmapuri, in the south by C.D. Blocks Nangavalli, Taramangalam and Omalur, in the east by CD Blocks Kadaiyampatty and Omalur, in the west by C.D. Blocks Kolathur and Nangavalli.

Communications:

Roadways : S.H.-20: Direction- Mettur to Dharmapuri, Nearest Villages- Amaram, Thethugivipatty, Virudasampatty, Pottaneri, M.Kalipatty, Vellar.

Railway Station: M.Kalipatty.

River: Cavery Nadi- Nearest Village- Koonandiyur.

Annual Rainfall: Average Rainfall 540 mm.

Ground Water: Availability of the ground water in the Basin is 2160.74 H.A.M. and the utilization is 2451.46 H.A.M. It belongs to Safe category. Depth to water level varies from 2 to 10 meter below the ground. Most of the wells go down in summer months, according to the Ground Water Estimation Committee.

Natural Division: Kongu Nadu.

Administration

Revenue **Division:** Mettur. Parliamentary Constituency: 10 Dharmapuri. District: Salem. Taluk: Mettur. Assembly Constituency : 85 Mettur. Gram Panchayat: 17.

Villages: 19 **Inhabited:** 19 **Uninhabited:** 0

Ranking	**District**	**State**	**National**
Area	12	322	4602
Population	6	192	3844
Sex Ratio	20	384	6093

Child Sex Ratio	18	382	6334
Literacy Rate	6	324	2823
Density	11	90	2213
Work Participation Rate	8	59	952

Gram Panchayats:

Amaram, Aranganur, Banapuram, Bukkampatti, Guttapatti, Koonandiyur, Koppampatti, M.Kalipatti, Mallikundam, Manathal Nallagoundampatti, Olaipatti, Pallipatti, Pottaneri, Sathapadi, Thethigiripatti, Vellar, Virudasampatti.

Amenities:

Education: Primary School in 18 villages, Middle school in 10 villages, Matriculation or Secondary School in 6 villages, namely M.N.Patty, Olaipatty, Pottaneri, Vellar, Kuttapatti, Mallikuntham.

Higher Secondary or Pre University Courses or Intermediate or Junior College in 1 village of the CD Block,, namely Mallikuntham.

College in 0 village, Adult Literacy Center in 0 village.

Medical: Hospital in 0 village, Dispensary in 0 village, Health Center in 2 villages, Sub Center in 8 villages, Maternity and Child Welfare Center in 2 villages, Community health workers in 0 village.

Drinking Water: Tap water in 19 villages, Tank water in 0 villages, Well water in 19 villages, Tubewell in 19 villages and more than one source in 19 villages.

Bank: Banking facility in 1 villages, namely, Vellar.

Credit Society in 12 villages Agricultural Credit Society in 10 Non-Agricultural Credit Society in 7 villages.

Others: Power supply in 19 villages, Cinema hall in 1 village, sport club in 0 village, Stadium or Auditorium or Community Hall in 0 village, Post Office in 16 villages.

There are 19 villages having bus facilities.

Villages with most of facilities: Vellar.

Villages without amenities (Education):

Chinna Sathappady..

Scheduled Castes: Out of the total population of 88245 persons, 12277 persons (13.91%) belong to Scheduled Castes.

The villages having less than 10% SC population are Koppampatty, Koppam, Amaram, Banapuram Thethugivipatty, Koonandiyur, Virudasampatty Pottaneri, M.Kalipatty, Pallipatty.

The villages having more than 50% SC population are None.

Sex ratio of Scheduled Caste population is 468.

Scheduled Castes Literates and Illiterates by Sex:

	Persons	Males	Females
Literate	5,280	3,399	1,881
Illiterate	6,997	3,127	3,870
Literacy rate	50.6	61.9	38.1
Graduate	92	81	11

Scheduled Castes (Dominant):

Adi Dravida, Arunthathiyar, Paraiyan etc., Valluvan Chakkiliyan

For their cultural identity please see Appendix-I

Villages without Scheduled Castes: There are 2 villages without any scheduled caste population.

Scheduled Tribes: Out of the total population of 88245 persons, 36 persons (0.04%) belong to Scheduled Tribes.

The villages having less than 10% ST population are Koppampatty, Koppam, M.N.Patty, Amaram Periya Sathappady, Chinna Sathappady, Banapuram Thethugivipatty, Bukkampatty, Koonandiyur, Olaipatty Virudasampatty, Pottaneri, M.Kalipatty, Arayaoor Vellar, Pallipatty, Kuttapatti, Mallikuntham.

The villages having more than 50% ST population are None.

Sex ratio of Scheduled tribe population is 528.

Scheduled Tribes Literates and Illiterates by Sex:

	Persons	Males	Females
Literate	11	4	7
Illiterate	25	13	12
Literacy rate	37.9	33.3	41.2
Graduate	0	0	0

Scheduled Tribes (Dominant):

Irular, Malai Pandaram

For their cultural identity please see Appendix-II

Villages without Scheduled Tribes: There are 17 villages without any scheduled tribe population.

Literates and Illiterates by Sex (Total Population):

	Persons	Males	Females
Literate	46,229	29,343	16,886
Illiterate	42,016	18,422	23,594
Literacy rate	60	71	47
Graduate	1,307	986	321

Agriculture: ***Distribution of villages according to land use:*** Out of 19 villages, Total area (in hectare) is 17614.04, out of that 76.98 percent is cultivable and 16.4 percent of the cultivable area is irrigated.

Sources of Irrigation (Hectares): Government Canal 101.02, Private Canal 0, Well without Electricity 132.63, Well with Electricity 1630.71, Tubewell without Electricity 0, Tubewell with Electricity 359, Tank 0, River 0, Lake 0, Waterfall 0, Others 0.

Villages with population of 5000 to 9999:

Pallipatti, Mallikudam, Vellar, M.Kallipatti Pottaneri, Virudasampatti, Guttapatti, Aranganur Olaipatti.

Villages with population of 10000 and above: None

Distribution of Workers:

	Persons	Males	Females	WPR
Cultivators	15,381	8,832	6,549	31.55
Agricultural Labour	15,643	6,435	9,208	32.09
Household Industry	4,248	2,389	1,859	8.71
Other Workers	13,474	10,968	2,506	27.64
Main Workers	38,035	24,579	13,456	78.03
Marginal Workers	10,711	4,045	6,666	21.97
Total Workers	48,746	28,624	20,122	

Religion: Major Religious Communities:

	Persons	Males	Females	Sex Ratio
Hindu (99.66%)	87,946	47,589	40,357	848
Muslim (0.09%)	81	43	38	884
Christian (0.12%)	106	62	44	710
Sikh (0.03%)	28	23	5	217
Buddhists (0.02%)	19	14	5	357
Jain (0%)	2	-	2	-

Agewise Data:

	Persons	Males	Females	Sex Ratio
All ages	88,245	47,765	40,480	847
0-14	24,813	14,458	10,355	716
15-44	42,177	22,432	19,745	880
45-79	19 746	10,074	9,672	960
80+	1,144	587	557	949
Age not stated	365	214	151	706

Languages (Dominant):

Tamil, Telugu, Kannada, Urdu, Hindi

Disabled Population:

	Persons	Males	Females	%
Total Disabled	1,375	839	536	
In Seeing	518	285	233	37.67
In Speech	175	104	71	12.73
In Hearing	85	45	40	6.18
In Movement	457	320	137	33.24
Mentally	140	85	55	10.18

MELANEELITHANALLUR

Melaneelithanallur C.D. Block lies in the north-eastern part of Tirunelveli district. It is a part of Sankaranko il taluk. The taluk is located at a distance of 56 kms. from district headquarters (Tirunelveli). There are 24 villages in the block with the total population of 87,168 persons. Area of the C.D. Block is 318.76 sq. kms. It is bounded in the north by CD Blocks Sankarankoil and Kuruvikulam, in the south by CD Blocks Kadaiyanallur, Alangalam and Manur, in the east by district Thoothukkudi, and in the west by CD Block Kadaiyanallur.

Communications:

Roadways : S.H.-41: Direction- Sankarankoil to Alagiapandi apuram, Nearest Villages- Ko.Maruthappapuram, Keelaneelid anallur, Melaneelathanallur, Kurukkalpatti, Vadakku Panav adali, Narikudi, Vannikonendal, Devarkulam, Sundankurichi, Mela Ilandaikulam, Periya Kovilangulam.

Annual Rainfall: Average Rainfall 879 mm.

Ground Water: Availability of the ground water in the Basin is 36.29 MCM and the utilization is 37.55 MCM. It belongs to Over Expoited category. Depth to water level varies from 5 to 10 meter below the ground. Most of the wells go down in summer months, according to the Ground Water Estimation Committee.

Natural Division: NA

Administration

Revenue **Division:** Tirunelveli. Parliamentary Constituenc y: 37 Temlaso. District: Tirunelveli. Taluk: Sankarankoil. Assembly Constituency: 219 Sankarankovil (SC). Gram Panchayat: 25.

Villages: 24 **Inhabited:** 24 **Uninhabited:** 0

Ranking	**District**	**State**	**National**
Area	10	153	2579
Population	10	197	3876
Sex Ratio	15	57	498
Child Sex Ratio	12	204	3307
Literacy Rate	19	284	2415
Density	5	111	3826
Work Participation Rate	11	259	1133

Gram Panchayats:

Achampatti, Chinnakovilankulam, Devarkulam, Echanda, Ilandaikulam, Keelaneelithanallur, Ko.Maruthappapuram, Kulasekaramangalam, Kurukkalpatti, Mela ilandaikulam, Melaneelithanallur, Moovirunthalai, Naduvakuruchi (Major), Naduvakuruchi (Minor), Narikudi, Pattadailkatti, Periyakovilankulam, Sendamangalam (kaspa) , Sendamangalam (Major), Sundankuruchi, Thadiampatti, Vadakkupanavadali, Vanniconendhal, Vellalankulam, Vellapaneri.

Amenities:

Education: Primary School in 24 villages, Middle school in 19 villages, Matriculation or Secondary School in 7 villages, namely Periya Kovilangulam, Naduvakkurichi Major, Sendamangalam, Vellaiankulam, Vadakku Panavadali, Vannikonendal, Mela Ilandaikulam.

Higher Secondary or Pre University Courses or Intermediate or Junior College in 3 villages of the CD Block,, namely Sendamangalam, Vellaiankulam, Vadakku Panavadali.

College in 1 village, Adult Literacy Center in 1 village., College is in village, namely Melaneelathanallur.

Medical: Hospital in 2 villages, Dispensary in 0 village, Health Center in 3 villages, Sub Center in 11 villages, Maternity and Child Welfare Center in 5 villages,

Community health workers in 16 villages.

The Villages having Hospital or Dispensary or Health Center are Kurukkalpatti, Sendamangalam.

Drinking Water: Tap water in 24 villages, Tank water in 4 villages, Well water in 21 villages, Tubewell in 4 villages and more than one source in 23 villages.

Bank: Banking facility in 7 villages, namely, Keelaneelidanallur, Kurukkalpatti, Sendamangalam Echchanda, Vadakku Panavadali, Devarkulam Mela Ilandaikulam.

Credit Society in 8 villages Agricultural Credit Society in 7 Non-Agricultural Credit Society in 1 village.

Others: Power supply in 24 villages, Cinema hall in 0 village, sport club in 1 village, Stadium or Auditorium or Community Hall in 1 village, Post Office in 22 villages.

There are 19 villages having bus facilities.

Villages with most of facilities: Keelaneelidanallur Kurukkalpatti, Sendamangalam, Echchanda, Devarkulam Mela Ilandaikulam.

Villages without Amenities (Education): None..

Scheduled Castes: Out of the total population of 87168 persons, 13168 persons (15.11%) belong to Scheduled Castes.

The villages having less than 10% SC population are Pattadaikatti, Sendamangalam, Vadakku Panavadali Narikudi, Achampatti.

The villages having more than 50% SC population are None.

Sex ratio of Scheduled Caste population is 514.

Scheduled Castes Literates and Illiterates by Sex:

	Persons	Males	Females
Literate	6,435	3,712	2,723
Illiterate	6,733	2,682	4,051
Literacy rate	55.4	66.5	45.2
Graduate	129	104	25

Scheduled Castes (Dominant):

Pallan, Chakkiliyan, Paraiyan etc., Arunthathiyar Puthirai Vannan

For their cultural identity please see Appendix-I

Villages without Scheduled Castes: There is 0 village without any scheduled caste population.

Scheduled Tribes: Out of the total population of 87168 persons, 13 persons (0.01%) belong to Scheduled Tribes.

The villages having less than 10% ST population are Periya Kovilangulam, Ko.Maruthappapuram Ilandaikulam, Keelaneelidanallur, Melaneelathanallur Kurukkalpatti, Chinnakovilangulam Naduvakkuruchiminor, Naduvakkurichi Major Pattadaikatti, Kulasekaramangalam, Sendamangalam Vellaiankulam, Echchanda, Vadakku Panavadali Narikudi, Achampatti, Vellappaneri, Thadiyampatti Muvirunthali, Vannikonendal, Devarkulam Sundankurichi, Mela Ilandaikulam.

The villages having more than 50% ST population are None.

Sex ratio of Scheduled tribe population is 462.

Scheduled Tribes Literates and Illiterates by Sex:

	Persons	Males	Females
Literate	4	3	1
Illiterate	9	4	5
Literacy rate	33.3	50.0	16.7
Graduate	0	0	0

Scheduled Tribes (Dominant):

Kattunayakan, Malai Pandaram, Sholaga

For their cultural identity please see Appendix-II

Villages without Scheduled Tribes: There are 21 villages without any scheduled tribe population.

Literates and Illiterates by Sex (Total Population):

	Persons	Males	Females
Literate	47,909	27,924	19,985
Illiterate	39,259	15,019	24,240
Literacy rate	62	74	51
Graduate	1,197	829	368

Agriculture: ***Distribution of villages according to land use:*** Out of 24 villages, Total area (in hectare) is 31876.62, out of that 19.61 percent is cultivable and 51.64 percent of the cultivable area is irrigated.

Sources of Irrigation (Hectares): Government Canal 0, Private Canal 0, Well without Electricity 563.44, Well with Electricity 1975.65, Tubewell without Electricity 0, Tubewell with Electricity 0, Tank 688.26, River 0, Lake 0, Waterfall 0, Others 0.

Villages with population of 5000 to 9999: Keelaneelidanallur, Kulasekaramangalam Vadakkuppanaivadali, Achchampatti, Vanniconendal.

Villages with population of 10000 and above: Sendamangalam.

Distribution of Workers:

	Persons	Males	Females	WPR
Cultivators	10,813	6,838	3,975	22.57
Agricultural Labour	21,344	11,111	10,233	44.54
Household Industry	7,016	831	6,185	14.64
Other Workers	8,743	6,257	2,486	18.25
Main Workers	43,102	23,270	19,832	89.95
Marginal Workers	4,814	1,767	3,047	10.05
Total Workers	47,916	25,037	22,879	

Religion: Major Religious Communities:

	Persons	Males	Females	Sex Ratio
Hindu (90.8%)	79,150	39,000	40,150	1,029
Muslim (0.14%)	119	65	54	831
Christian (8.98%)	7,828	3,839	3,989	1,039

Sikh (0%)	-	-	-	-
Buddhists (0%)	-	-	-	-
Jain (0%)	-	-	-	-

Agewise Data:

	Persons	Males	Females	Sex Ratio
All ages	87,168	42,943	44,225	1030
0-14	24,122	12,331	11,791	956
15-44	42,464	20,825	21,639	1039
45-79	19,596	9,364	10,232	1093
80+	781	326	455	1396
Age not stated	205	97	108	1113

Languages (Dominant):
Tamil, Telugu, Malayalam, Kannada, Hindi

Disabled Population:

	Persons	Males	Females	%
Total Disabled	1,935	902	1,033	
In Seeing	1,130	438	692	58.4
In Speech	116	62	54	5.99
In Hearing	75	29	46	3.88
In Movement	485	296	189	25.06
Mentally	129	77	52	6.67

MELMALAYANUR

Melmalayanur C.D. Block lies in the northern part of Viluppuram district. It is a part of Gingee taluk. The taluk is located at a distance of 38 kms. from district headquarters (Viluppuram). There are 80 villages in the block with the total population of 122,448 persons. Area of the C.D. Block is 355. 37 sq. kms. It is bounded in the north by district Tiruvannamalai, in the south by C.D. Block Gingee, in the east by C.D. Block Vallam, and in the west by district Tiruvannamalai.

Communications:

Roadways : S.H.-4: Direction- Gingee to Arani, Nearest Villages- Periyanolambai, Pinnanur, Marakkonam, Melnemili, Kuduvampoondi, Vadavetti, Arukkampoondi, Vallathi, Devanur, Annamangalam, Kannalam, Kadali, Mavanandal, Vanakkambadi.

River: Varahanadi Nadi- Nearest Villages- Porkunam, Kadali, Mavanandal, Melacheri, Sevalapurai, Thenpalai, Vadapalai, Vanakkambadi.

Backwards Region Grants Fund: It receives Backward Region Grants.

Annual Rainfall: Average Rainfall 1119 mm.

Ground Water: Availability of the ground water in the Basin is 8212.07 H.A.M. and the utilization is 9974.88 H.A.M. It belongs to Over Expoited category. Depth to water level varies from 2 to 5 meter below the ground. Most of the wells go down in summer months, according to the Ground Water Estimation Committee.

Forest and Reserved Forest: (Siruvadi RF)- Nearest Villages- Melacheri, Sevalapurai, Sevalapurai.

Natural Division: Tondai Nadu.

Administration

Revenue **Division:** Tindivanam. Parliamentary Constituency: 12 Arani. District: Villupuram. Taluk: Gingee. Assembly Constituency: 70 Gingee. Gram Panchayat: 55.

Villages: 80 **Inhabited:** 80 **Uninhabited:** 0

Ranking	District	State	National
Area	7	108	2237
Population	10	60	2795
Sex Ratio	2	152	1072
Child Sex Ratio	10	111	2126
Literacy Rate	8	259	2261
Density	9	148	3150
Work Participation Rate	12	166	1482

Gram Panchayats:

Annamangalam, Athipattu, Avalurpet, Chitteri, Chokkanandal, Devandavadi, Devanur, Edapattu, Eyyakunnam, Eyyal, Gangapuram, Guduvampoondi, Kadali, Kadapanandal, Kalathambattu, Kannalam, Kappalambadi, Kodambadi, Kodukankuppam, Kottaipoondi, Kovilporaiyur, Kuduvampoondi, Kundalampattu, Malaiyanur (Mel), Manandal, Marakonam, Markonam, Mel Sevalambadi, Melacheri, Melarangunam, Naranamangalam, Nemili (Mel), Nochaloor, Paraiyanpattu, Paraiyantangal, Paruttipuram, Periyanolambai, Peruvalur, Puduppattu (Mel), Sangilikkuppam, Sathambadi, Sathanandal, Sevalapurai, Sindipattu, Sirudalaipoondi, Talankunram, Tayanur, Tenpalai, Teppirampattu, Torappadi, Turinjippundi, Vadapalai, Vadavetti, Vaduganpoondi, Vailamur (Mel), Valathi, .

Amenities:

Education: Primary School in 76 villages, Middle school in 24 villages, Matriculation or Secondary School in 13 villages, namely Teppirampattu, Peruvalur, Melnemili, Sevalambai[Mel], Kappalambadi, Kottaipoondi, Avalurpet, Melmalaiyanur, Vallathi, Devanur, Annamangalam, Turinjipoondy, Kadali.

Higher Secondary or Pre University Courses or Intermediate or Junior College in 7 villages of the CD Block,, namely Peruvalur, Kilavampoondi, Avalurpet, Melmalaiyanur, Vallathi, Devanur, Annamangalam. College in 0 village, Adult Literacy Center in 0 village.

Medical: Hospital in 1 village, Dispensary in 6 villages, Health Center in 2 villages, Sub Center in 25 villages, Maternity and Child Welfare Center in 21 villages, Community health workers in 1 village.

The Villages having Hospital or Dispensary or Health Center are Eyyal, Avalurpet, Vallathi, Devanur,

Melmampattu, Turinjipoondy.

Drinking Water: Tap water in 80 villages, Tank water in 32 villages, Well water in 80 villages, Tubewell in 80 villages and more than one source in 80 villages.

Bank: Banking facility in 8 villages, namely, Modipattu, Peruvalur, Eyyal, Sathambadi, Avalurpet Melmalaiyanur, Vallathi, Kannalam.

Credit Society in 10 villages Agricultural Credit Society in 10 Non-Agricultural Credit Society in 2 villages.

Others: Power supply in 79 villages, Cinema hall in 2 villages, sport club in 6 villages, Stadium or Auditorium or Community Hall in 1 village, Post Office in 53 villages.

There are 72 villages having bus facilities.

Villages with most of facilities: Modipattu Peruvalur, Eyyal, Sathambadi, Avalurpet Melmalaiyanur, Vallathi.

Villages without amenities (Education): Pappantangal, Chokkapalam, Mavanandal, Sevalapurai..

Scheduled Castes: Out of the total population of 122448 persons, 19358 persons (15.81%) belong to Scheduled Castes.

The villages having less than 10% SC population are Ethapattu, Melvailanur, Teppirampattu, Paruthipuram Periyanolambai, Pinnanur, Kammanthangal, Melnemili Chinnanolambai, Paraiyanpattu, Sangilikuppam Palampoondi, Pappantangal, Chokkapalam Kilsevalambadi, Siruthalaipoondi, Kodukkankuppam Kundalampattu, Kodapananadal, Avalurpet, Chittari Samathankuppam, Sathanandal, Melmampattu, Siyappundi Melpudupattu, Eyyakunnam, Embalam, Melmannur Porkunam, Vanakkambadi, Sevalapurai, Chokkanandal.

The villages having more than 50% SC population are None.

Sex ratio of Scheduled Caste population is 501.

Scheduled Castes Literates and Illiterates by Sex:

	Persons	Males	Females
Literate	9,751	5,726	4,025
Illiterate	9,607	3,927	5,680
Literacy rate	57.7	68.2	47.4
Graduate	92	84	8

Scheduled Castes (Dominant):

Adi Dravida, Arunthathiyar, Valluvan, Kuravan etc. Panniandi

For their cultural identity please see Appendix-I

Villages without Scheduled Castes: There are 16 villages without any scheduled caste population.

Scheduled Tribes: Out of the total population of 122448 persons, 2030 persons (1.66%) belong to Scheduled Tribes.

The villages having less than 10% ST population are Ethapattu, Melvailanur, Teppirampattu, Nandipuram Paruthipuram, Periyanolambai, Kammanthangal Devandavadi, Kaividantangal, Modipattu, Peruvalur Marakkonam, Melnemili, Chinnanolambai, Eyyal Sevalambai[Mel], Unnamanandal, Naranamangalam Talankunram, Paraiyanpattu, Kappalambadi Kottaipoondi, Sangilikuppam, Paraiyantangal Palampoondi, Sindagampoondi, Kilavampoondi Kuduvampoondi, Pappantangal, Chokkapalam Kilsevalambadi, Melkaranai, Vadavetti, Arukkampoondi Siruthalaipoondi, Kodukkankuppam, Sindipattu Nochalur, Kundalampattu, Kodambadi, Vaduganpoondy Kodapananadal, Avalurpet, Kovilporaiyur, Thayanur Melmalaiyanur, Vallathi, Devanur, Gangapuram Chittari, Samathankuppam, Annamangalam, Sathanandal Kannalam, Sathaputhur, Melmampattu, Thorappadi Siyappundi, Manandal, Melpudupattu, Vadapalai Eyyakunnam, Embalam, Turinjipoondy, Melmannur Porkunam, Kadali, Mavanandal, Vanakkambadi Melacheri, Sevalapurai, Sevalapurai, Thenpalai Chokkanandal, Kalathampattu, Melarangunam, Athipattu Kuzhapalur.

The villages having more than 50% ST population are None.

Sex ratio of Scheduled tribe population is 513.

Scheduled Tribes Literates and Illiterates by Sex:

	Persons	Males	Females
Literate	576	343	233
Illiterate	1,454	646	808
Literacy rate	33.0	40.3	26.0
Graduate	0	0	0

Scheduled Tribes (Dominant):

Irular, Kattunayakan, Generic Tribes etc. Malai Vedan

For their cultural identity please see Appendix-II

Villages without Scheduled Tribes: There are 34 villages without any scheduled tribe population.

Literates and Illiterates by Sex (Total Population):

	Persons	Males	Females
Literate	68,408	40,652	27,756
Illiterate	54,040	20,467	33,573
Literacy rate	63	75	51
Graduate	876	703	173

Agriculture: ***Distribution of villages according to land use:*** Out of 80 villages, Total area (in hectare) is 35537, out of that 70.08 percent is cultivable and 39.69 percent of the cultivable area is irrigated.

Sources of Irrigation (Hectares): Government Canal 0, Private Canal 0, Well without Electricity 2660, Well with Electricity 5328.86, Tubewell without Electricity 0, Tubewell with Electricity 6.42, Tank 0, River 9.27, Lake 1879.45, Waterfall 0, Others 0.

Villages with population of 5000 to 9999:
Avalurpet, Malaiyanur (Mel.).

Villages with population of 10000 and above: None

Distribution of Workers:

	Persons	Males	Females	WPR
Cultivators	30,533	19,360	11,173	46.38
Agricultural Labour	24,013	10,008	14,005	36.47
Household Industry	2,469	1,026	1,443	3.75
Other Workers	8,820	6,389	2,431	13.4
Main Workers	51,430	31,523	19,907	78.12
Marginal Workers	14,405	5,260	9,145	21.88
Total Workers	65,835	36,783	29,052	

Religion: Major Religious Communities:

	Persons	Males	Females	Sex Ratio
Hindu (95.23%)	116,611	58,233	58,378	1,002
Muslim (2.72%)	3,325	1,670	1,655	991
Christian (1.55%)	1,896	913	983	1,077
Sikh (0%)	4	1	3	3,000
Buddhists (0%)	4	2	2	1,000
Jain (0.41%)	497	243	254	1,045

Agewise Data:

	Persons	Males	Females	Sex Ratio
All ages	122,448	61,119	61,329	1003
0-14	33,886	17,073	16,813	985
15-44	55,105	27,173	27,932	1028
45-79	29,365	14,724	14,641	994
80+	1,517	835	682	817
Age not stated	2,575	1,314	1,261	960

Languages (Dominant):
Tamil, Telugu, Urdu, Kannada, Hindi

Disabled Population:

	Persons	Males	Females	%
Total Disabled	3,062	1,674	1,388	
In Seeing	1,580	778	802	51.6
In Speech	305	168	137	9.96
In Hearing	159	86	73	5.19
In Movement	796	510	286	26
Mentally	222	132	90	7.25

MELPURAM

Melapuram C.D. Block lies in the north-western part of Kanniyakumari district. It is a part of Vilavancode taluk. The Block is located at a distance of NA kms. from district headquarters (Nagarkoil). There are 08 villages in the block with the total population of 68,050 persons. Area of the C.D. Block is 177.44 sq. kms. It is bounded in the north by district Tirunelveli, in the south by CD Block Munchira, in the east by CD Block Thiruvattaru, and in the west it has common boundary with the state of Kerala.

Communications:
Roadways : S.H.-45: Direction- Nedumangadu to Kulasekharam, Nearest Village- Moncode.

River: Tambraparani Nadi- Nearest Village- Vellancode.

Annual Rainfall: Average Rainfall 1448 mm.

Ground Water: Availability of the ground water in the Basin is 22.15 MCM and the utilization is 3.18 MCM. It belongs to Safe category. Depth to water level varies from 5 to 10 meter below the ground. Most of the wells go down in summer months, according to the Ground Water Estimation Committee.

Forest and Reserved Forest: (Kilmalai RF)- Nearest Village- Kilamalai RF.

Natural Division: NA

Administration
Revenue **Division:** Padmanabhapuram. Parliamentary Constit uency: 39 Kanniyakumari. District: Kanniyakumari. Taluk: Vilavancode. Assembly Constituency: 233 Vilavancode. Gram Panchayat: 10.

Border Villages- (Kerala)- Nearest Villages- Kilamalai RF, Moncode, Edaicode, Palugal, Vilavancode.

Villages: 8 **Inhabited:** 8 **Uninhabited:** 0

Ranking	District	State	National
Area	3	316	4576
Population	3	295	4557
Sex Ratio	1	41	411
Child Sex Ratio	1	3	157
Literacy Rate	7	8	159
Density	4	378	2855
Work Participation Rate	6	127	5559

Gram Panchayats:
Devicode, Malayadi, Manjalumoodu, Maruthancode, Moncode, Muzhucode, Puliyoorsalai, Vanniyoor, Vellancode, Vilavancode, .

Amenities:
Education: Primary School in 8 villages, Middle school in 7 villages, Matriculation or Secondary School in 7 villages, namely Moncode, Arumanai, Vellancode, Edaicode, Palugal, Vilavancode, Pacode.

Higher Secondary or Pre University Courses or Intermediate or Junior College in 3 villages of the CD Block,, namely Edaicode, Palugal, Pacode.

College in 0 village, Adult Literacy Center in 0 village.

Medical: Hospital in 2 villages, Dispensary in 2 villages, Health Center in 0 village, Sub Center in 7 villages, Maternity and Child Welfare Center in 1 village, Community health workers in 0 village.

The Villages having Hospital or Dispensary or Health Center are Moncode, Arumanai, Vellancode, Vilavancode.

Drinking Water: Tap water in 8 villages, Tank water in 0 villages, Well water in 8 villages, Tubewell in 8

villages and more than one source in 8 villages.

Bank: Banking facility in 3 villages, namely, Moncode, Arumanai, Palugal.

Credit Society in 4 villages Agricultural Credit Society in 3 Non-Agricultural Credit Society in 1 village.

Others: Power supply in 8 villages, Cinema hall in 1 village, sport club in 0 village, Stadium or Auditorium or Community Hall in 0 village, Post Office in 7 villages.

There are 8 villages having bus facilities.

Villages with most of facilities: Moncode Arumanai, Palugal.

Villages without Amenities (Education): None..

Scheduled Castes: Out of the total population of 68050 persons, 1789 persons (2.63%) belong to Scheduled Castes.

The villages having less than 10% SC population are Kilamalai R.F., Moncode, Arumanai, Vellancode Edaicode, Palugal, Vilavancode, Pacode.

The villages having more than 50% SC population are None.

Sex ratio of Scheduled Caste population is 529.

Scheduled Castes Literates and Illiterates by Sex:

	Persons	Males	Females
Literate	1,390	680	710
Illiterate	399	163	236
Literacy rate	87.4	92.1	83.3
Graduate	33	14	19

Scheduled Castes (Dominant):

Paraiyan etc., Pulayan etc., Cheruman, Vannan Mannan

For their cultural identity please see Appendix-I

Villages without Scheduled Castes: There is 1 village without any scheduled caste population.

Scheduled Tribes: Out of the total population of 68050 persons, 209 persons (0.31%) belong to Scheduled Tribes.

The villages having less than 10% ST population are Moncode, Arumanai, Vellancode, Edaicode, Palugal Vilavancode, Pacode.

The villages having more than 50% ST population are None.

Sex ratio of Scheduled tribe population is 507.

Scheduled Tribes Literates and Illiterates by Sex:

	Persons	Males	Females
Literate	151	81	70
Illiterate	58	22	36
Literacy rate	80.3	84.4	76.1
Graduate	22	8	14

Scheduled Tribes (Dominant):

Kanikaran etc., Kaniyan etc., Mannan, Malai Pandaram

For their cultural identity please see Appendix-II

Villages without Scheduled Tribes: There are 4 villages without any scheduled tribe population.

Literates and Illiterates by Sex (Total Population):

	Persons	Males	Females
Literate	51,712	26,495	25,217
Illiterate	16,338	6,928	9,410
Literacy rate	86	90	82
Graduate	1,777	866	911

Agriculture: ***Distribution of villages according to land use:*** Out of 8 villages, Total area (in hectare) is 17744, out of that 47.37 percent is cultivable and 13.38 percent of the cultivable area is irrigated.

Sources of Irrigation (Hectares): Government Canal 369.02, Private Canal 0, Well without Electricity 0, Well with Electricity 0, Tubewell without Electricity 0, Tubewell with Electricity 0, Tank 755.18, River 0, Lake 0, Waterfall 0, Others 0.

Villages with population of 5000 to 9999:

Arumanai , Edaicode, Palugal , Pacode.

Villages with population of 10000 and above:

Mancode , Vellomcode , Vilavancode.

Distribution of Workers:

	Persons	Males	Females	WPR
Cultivators	700	542	158	3.04
Agricultural Labour	4,914	4,446	468	21.31
Household Industry	2,111	941	1,170	9.15
Other Workers	15,338	11,889	3,449	66.5
Main Workers	16,034	12,488	3,546	69.52
Marginal Workers	7,029	5,330	1,699	30.48
Total Workers	23,063	17,818	5,245	

Religion: Major Religious Communities:

	Persons	Males	Females	Sex Ratio
Hindu (44.78%)	30,472	15,057	15,415	1,024
Muslim (1.16%)	788	358	430	1,201
Christian (53.99%)	36,743	17,984	18,759	1,043
Sikh (0%)	1	-	1	-
Buddhists (0.01%)	8	4	4	1,000
Jain (0%)	2	-	2	-

Agewise Data:

	Persons	Males	Females	Sex Ratio
All ages	68,050	33,423	34,627	1036
0-14	17,253	8,564	8,689	1015
15-44	34,912	17,049	17,863	1048
45-79	15,156	7,475	7,681	1028
80+	661	301	360	1196
Age not stated	68	34	34	1000

Languages (Dominant):

Tamil, Malayalam, Telugu, Urdu, Kannada

Disabled Population:

	Persons	Males	Females	%
Total Disabled	2,690	1,019	1,671	

In Seeing	1,805	489	1,316	67.1
In Speech	147	74	73	5.46
In Hearing	77	44	33	2.86
In Movement	474	313	161	17.62
Mentally	187	99	88	6.95

MELUR

Melur C.D. Block lies in the north-eastern part of Madurai district. It is a part of Melur taluk. The Block is located at a distance of 30 kms. from district headquarters (Madurai). There are 49 villages in the block with the total population of 112,928 persons. Area of the C.D. Block is 339.23 sq. kms. It is bounded in the north by CD Block Kottampatti, and districts Dindigul and Sivaganga, in the south and east by district Sivaganga, in the west by CD Blocks Madurai East and West.

Communications:

Roadways : N.H.-45 B: Direction- Madurai to Tirnchirappalli, Nearest Villages- Pudusukkampatti, Navinipatti, Soorakkundu, Kallampatti, Uduppaikulam, Narasingampatti, Therkutheru, Perumalmalai Forest. S.H.-34: Direction- Melur to Sivaganga, Nearest Villages- Navinipatti, Attukulam, Vannanparaipatti, Vellalur, Amblakaranpatty, Sathamangalam, Thaniyamangalam.

Annual Rainfall: Average Rainfall 857 mm.

Ground Water: Availability of the ground water in the Basin is 11288.27 H.A.M. and the utilization is 997. 88 H.A.M. It belongs to Safe category. Depth to water level varies from 5 to 10 meter below the ground. Most of the wells go down in summer months, according to the Ground Water Estimation Committee.

Natural Division: NA

Administration

Revenue **Division:** Madurai. Parliamentary Constituency: 32 Madurai. District: Madurai. Taluk: Melur. Assembly Constituency: 188 Melur. Gram Panchayat: 36.

Villages: 49 **Inhabited:** 47 **Uninhabited:** 2

Ranking	District	State	National
Area	2	128	2371
Population	2	85	3070
Sex Ratio	4	203	1445
Child Sex Ratio	8	321	5348
Literacy Rate	4	127	1311
Density	8	183	3248
Work Participation Rate	6	179	1844

Gram Panchayats:

A.Valayapatti, Ambalakaranpatti, Amoor, Arasappanpatti, Arittapatti, Attukulam, Kallampatti, Keelaiyur, Keelavalavu, Keeranur, Kidaripatti, Kongampatti, Kottakudi, Kottanathampatti, Kottangudi, Kurichipatti, Malampatti, Narasingampatti, Navinipatti, Panangudi, Pathinettankudi, Poonjuthi, Pudusukkampatti, Pulipattii, Saruguvalayapatti, Sathamangalam, Semminipatti, Surakkundu, T.Vellalapatti, Thaniamangalam, Therkkutheru, Thiruvadavur, Uranganpatti, Vannamparaipatti, Vellalore, Vellaripatti, Veppadappu.

Amenities:

Education: Primary School in 39 villages, Middle school in 16 villages, Matriculation or Secondary School in 11 villages, namely Malampatty, Ayuthapatti, Valayapatti, Navinipatti, Sarugu Valaiyapatty, Thaniyamangalam, Therkutheru, Vellalur, Uranganpatti, Amblakaranpatty, Tiruvadavur.

Higher Secondary or Pre University Courses or Intermediate or Junior College in 4 villages of the CD Block,, namely Ayuthapatti, Navinipatti, Vellalur, Tiruvadavur.

College in 2 villages, Adult Literacy Center in 0 village., Colleges are in villages, namely Kidaripatti, Navinipatti.

Medical: Hospital in 1 village, Dispensary in 2 villages, Health Center in 4 villages, Sub Center in 13 villages, Maternity and Child Welfare Center in 3 villages, Community health workers in 46 villages.

The Villages having Hospital or Dispensary or Health Center are Navinipatti, Narasingampatti, Therkutheru, Panangadi.

Drinking Water: Tap water in 47 villages, Tank water in 34 villages, Well water in 47 villages, Tubewell in 47 villages and more than one source in 47 villages.

Bank: Banking facility in 15 villages, namely, Kongampatti, Kidaripatti, Navinipatti, Keelaiyur Keelavalavu, Sarugu Valaiyapatty, Thaniyamangalam Soorakkundu, Kallampatti, Therkutheru, Vellalur Uranganpatti, Amblakaranpatty, Kottakudi Tiruvadavur.

Credit Society in 34 villages Agricultural Credit Society in 3 Non-Agricultural Credit Society in 3 villages.

Others: Power supply in 47 villages, Cinema hall in 2 villages, sport club in 27 villages, Stadium or Auditorium or Communit Hall in 30 villages, Post Office in 47 villages.

There are 43 villages having bus facilities.

Villages with most of facilities: Kongampatti Kidaripatti, Navinipatti, Keelaiyur, Keelavalavu Sarugu Valaiyapatty, Thaniyamangalam, Soorakkundu Kallampatti, Therkutheru, Vellalur, Uranganpatti Amblakaranpatty, Kottakudi, Tiruvadavur.

Villages without amenities (Education): Uduppaikulam, Perungalakudi, Valayangulam, Marudoor, Unukal Puliyankulam, Kilavikulam, Sorugulipatti,

Mukkampatty..

Scheduled Castes: Out of the total population of 112928 persons, 21590 persons (19.12%) belong to Scheduled Castes.

The villages having less than 10% SC population are Malampatty, Ayuthapatti, Valayapatti Pudusukkampatti, Sarugu Valaiyapatty, Sathamangalam Kurichipatti, Amblakaranpatty, Kottakudi Valayangulam, Kilavikulam, Sorugulipatti Arasappanpatti, Panangadi.

The villages having more than 50% SC population are None.

Sex ratio of Scheduled Caste population is 499.

Scheduled Castes Literates and Illiterates by Sex:

	Persons	Males	Females
Literate	11,059	6,669	4,390
Illiterate	10,531	4,158	6,373
Literacy rate	59.8	72.1	47.5
Graduate	209	172	37

Scheduled Castes (Dominant):

Paraiyan etc., Pallan, Chakkiliyan, Kuravan etc.

Adi Dravida

For their cultural identity please see Appendix-I

Villages without Scheduled Castes: There are 3 villages without any scheduled caste population.

Scheduled Tribes: Out of the total population of 112928 persons, 23 persons (0.02%) belong to Scheduled Tribes.

The villages having less than 10% ST population are Kongampatti, Malampatty, Pulipatti, Kidaripatti Ayuthapatti, Valayapatti, Pudusukkampatti Navinipatti, Keelaiyur, Keelavalavu Sarugu Valaiyapatty, Thaniyamangalam, Sathamangalam Soorakkundu, Kallampatti, Arittapatty Chadurmadangan, Uduppaikulam, Narasingampatti Therkutheru, Pathinettangudi, Attukulam Vannanparaipatti, Vellalur, Uranganpatti Kurichipatti, Amblakaranpatty, Kottakudi Perungalakudi, Valayangulam, Manickampatti Vellalapatty, Marudoor, Unukal Puliyankulam Kilavikulam, Amoor, Sorugulipatti, Mukkampatty Tiruvadavur, Nalukulam, Arasappanpatti, Panangadi Kovilpatti, Veppadappu, Poonjuthi, Thuvarangulam Keeranur.

The villages having more than 50% ST population are None.

Sex ratio of Scheduled tribe population is 435.

Scheduled Tribes Literates and Illiterates by Sex:

	Persons	Males	Females
Literate	14	10	4
Illiterate	9	3	6
Literacy rate	70.0	90.9	44.4
Graduate	0	0	0

Scheduled Tribes (Dominant):

Malai Pandaram, Kurumans

For their cultural identity please see Appendix-II

Villages without Scheduled Tribes: There are 47 villages without any scheduled tribe population.

Literates and Illiterates by Sex (Total Population):

	Persons	Males	Females
Literate	68,083	39,768	28,315
Illiterate	44,845	16,891	27,954
Literacy rate	69	81	57
Graduate	1,698	1,341	357

Agriculture: ***Distribution of villages according to land use:*** Out of 49 villages, Total area (in hectare) is 33923.04, out of that 47.91 percent is cultivable and 92.23 percent of the cultivable area is irrigated.

Sources of Irrigation (Hectares): Government Canal 10487.88, Private Canal 0, Well without Electricity 4.82, Well with Electricity 576.86, Tubewell without Electricity 0, Tubewell with Electricity 72.54, Tank 3847.43, River 0, Lake 0, Waterfall 0, Others 0.

Villages with population of 5000 to 9999: Navinipatti, Keelaiyur, Keelavalavu Saruguvalayapatti, Narasingampatti, Therkutheru Vellalur, Uranganpatti, Ambalakaranpatti Thiruvadavur.

Villages with population of 10000 and above: None

Distribution of Workers:

	Persons	Males	Females	WPR
Cultivators	15,905	9,635	6,270	27.34
Agricultural Labour	32,607	16,268	16,339	56.04
Household Industry	1,090	474	616	1.87
Other Workers	8,581	6,767	1,814	14.75
Main Workers	42,110	25,794	16,316	72.38
Marginal Workers	16,073	7,350	8,723	27.62
Total Workers	58,183	33,144	25,039	

Religion: Major Religious Communities:

	Persons	Males	Females	Sex Ratio
Hindu (95.69%)	108,058	54,205	53,853	994
Muslim (3.48%)	3,934	1,981	1,953	986
Christian (0.72%)	813	411	402	978
Sikh (0.01%)	16	5	11	2,200
Buddhists (0.02%)	18	10	8	800
Jain (0%)	3	-	3	-

Agewise Data:

	Persons	Males	Females	Sex Ratio
All ages	112,928	56,659	56,269	993
0-14	32,280	16,872	15,408	913
15-44	54,549	26,888	27,661	1029
45-79	24,739	12,180	12,559	1031

80+	805	424	381	899
Age not stated	555	295	260	881

Languages (Dominant):

Tamil, Telugu, Urdu, Gujarati, Kannada

Disabled Population:

	Persons	Males	Females	%
Total Disabled	3,841	2,044	1,797	
In Seeing	2,676	1,368	1,308	69.67
In Speech	196	98	98	5.1
In Hearing	122	59	63	3.18
In Movement	555	340	215	14.45
Mentally	292	179	113	7.6

MINJUR

Minjur C.D. Block lies in the north-eastern part of Thiruvallur district. It is a part of Ponneri taluk. The Block is located at a distance of 75 kms. from district headquarters (Thiruvallur). There are 87 villages in the block with the total population of 145,635 persons. Area of the C.D. Block is 454.28 sq. kms. It is bounded in the south by CD Blocks Sholavaram and Puzhal, in the east by the Bay of Bengal, in the west by CD Block Sholavaram and Goomidipoondi, and it has common boundary with the state of Andhra Pradesh on north. CD Block Minjur falls in taluk Gummidipoondi by a village, Ayanallur.

Communications:

Roadways : Information not Available.

Railway Station: Nandiambakkam.

River: Arani Nadi- Nearest Villages- Vanjivakkam, Peril ayambakkam, Andarmadam, Ernakuracheri (Ui), Perumbedui, Chinnakavanam, Ealiyambedu, Aladu, Thangalperumbalam, Siripazhaverkadu, Kadapakkam, Thathamanji, Lingapayampettai, Somanjeri. Korattalaiyar Nadi- Nearest Village- Edayaanchavady, Nalur, Vannipakkam, Vallur. Canal: (Buckingham)- Nearest Villages- Pazhaverkadu, Thangalperumbalam, Karungali, Kalanj, Kattupallai, Puzhidivakkam, Ennore (Ui), Valliur.

Annual Rainfall: Average Rainfall 1152 mm.

Ground Water: Availability of the ground water in the Basin is 111.35 MCM and the utilization is 149.07 MCM. It belongs to Over Expoited category. Depth to water level varies from 2 to 5 meter below the ground. Most of the wells go down in summer months, according to the Ground Water Estimation Committee.

Coastal Villages: (Bay of Bengal)- Nearest Villages- Annamalaichari, Pazhaverkadu, Thangalperumbalam, Karungali, Kalanj, Kattupallai, Puzhidivakkam, Ennore (Ui), Valliur, Edayaanchavady, Karimanal (UI).

Natural Division: Tondai Nadu.

Administration

Revenue **Division:** Ponneri. Parliamentary Constituency: 1 Thiruvallur (SC). District: Thiruvallur. Taluk: Gummi dipoondi, Ponneri. Assembly Constituency: 2 Ponneri (SC). Gram Panchayat: 56.

Border Villages- (Andhra Pradesh)- Nearest Villages- Mangadu, Keerapakkam, Kallur, Karimanal (Ui), Annamalai chari, Poongulam.

Villages: 87 **Inhabited:** 82 **Uninhabited:** 5

Ranking	District	State	National
Area	1	44	1661
Population	1	23	2006
Sex Ratio	4	159	1138
Child Sex Ratio	2	23	615
Literacy Rate	7	158	1558
Density	9	351	3349
Work Participation Rate	12	197	4405

Gram Panchayats:

Agaram , Aladu , Anuppampattu , Arasur , Avoor , Avurivakkam , Devathanam , Edyanchavadi, Elaimbedu , Erusivan, Guduvanjeri , Kadapakkam , Kallur , Kalpakkam , Kammarpalayam , Kaniampakkam, Kattavur , Kattoor , Kattupalli , Killikodi , Kodur, Kolur , Kondakarai, Kottaikuppam, Lighthouse kuppam, Medur , Melur, Meratoor , Nalur, Nandiambakkam, Neithavayal, Palaiyambakkam, Panapakkam , Periakarambur , Perumbedu , Poongulam , Pulicut, Reddipalayam , Seliambedu , Senganyan , Sirulapakkam , Siruvakkam, Subbareddipalayam, Thadaperumbakkam, Thangalperumbulam, Thathamanji , Thirupalaivanam, Thiruvellavoyal, Vallur, Vanjivakkam , Vannipakkam , Velur , Voyalur .

Amenities:

Education: Primary School in 69 villages, Middle school in 25 villages, Matriculation or Secondary School in 11 villages, namely Kallur, Kolur, Medur, Pazhaverkadu, Perumbedui, Kattur, Vayaloor, Nalur, Nandiambakkam, Valliur, Edayaanchavady.

Higher Secondary or Pre University Courses or Intermediate or Junior College in 3 villages of the CD Block,, namely Pazhaverkadu, Vayaloor, Edayaanchavady.

College in 0 village, Adult Literacy Center in 0 village.

Medical: Hospital in 1 village, Dispensary in 0 village, Health Center in 7 villages, Sub Center in 23 villages, Maternity and Child Welfare Center in 0 village, Community health workers in 82 villages.

The Village having Hospital or Dispensary or Health Center is Pazhaverkadu.

Drinking Water: Tap water in 82 villages, Tank water in 82 villages, Well water in 82 villages, Tubewell in 82 villages and more than one source in 82 villages.

Bank: Banking facility in 8 villages, namely, Kallur, Panapakkam, Tirupalaivanam, Kilikodi, Medur Pazhaverkadu, Kattur, Edayaanchavady.

Credit Society in 10 villages Agricultural Credit Society in 9 Non-Agricultural Credit Society in 1 village.

Others: Power supply in 82 villages, Cinema hall in 2 villages, sport club in 0 village, Stadium or Auditorium or Community Hall in 0 village, Post Office in 23 villages.

There are 60 villages having bus facilities.

Villages with most of facilities: Kallur Panapakkam, Tirupalaivanam, Medur, Pazhaverkadu Kattur, Edayaanchavady.

Villages without amenities (Education): Enjur, Kanganimedu, Mumipedu, Kanavanthirai, Appalapuram, Andavayal, Andarmadam, Thiruper, Kalanj, Eripillaikuppam, Thinaipakkam, Thottakadu, Puzhidivakkam..

Scheduled Castes: Out of the total population of 145635 persons, 52865 persons (36.3%) belong to Scheduled Castes.

The villages having less than 10% SC population are Mangadu, Keerapakkam, Annamalaichari, Sirulapakkam Kanavanthirai, Arasoor, Kanagavallipuram Lingapayampettai, Kalanj, Kalpakkam.

The villages having more than 50% SC population are Kallur, Periyaveppathur, Uppunelvoyal, Mumipedu Periakarumbur, Panapakkam, Kumarancherry, Pakkam Poovami, Avoor, Kattavoor, Medur, Asanupudur Vanjivakkam, Andarmadam, Siripazhaverkadu Kadapakkam, Somanjer, Sirulapooncheri, Kattur Kattupallai, Eripillaikuppam, Velur, Kaniyambakkam Kadamanjeri, Thinaipakkam, Merattur, Thottakadu Neithavoyal, Vannipakkam, Valliur.

Sex ratio of Scheduled Caste population is 499.

Scheduled Castes Literates and Illiterates by Sex:

	Persons	Males	Females
Literate	28,044	16,437	11,607
Illiterate	24,821	10,028	14,793
Literacy rate	61.2	71.9	50.5
Graduate	618	486	132

Scheduled Castes (Dominant):

Adi Dravida, Paraiyan etc., Generic Castes etc. Chakkiliyan, Adi Karnataka

For their cultural identity please see Appendix-I

Villages without Scheduled Castes: There are 11 villages without any scheduled caste population.

Scheduled Tribes: Out of the total population of 145635 persons, 3008 persons (2.07%) belong to Scheduled Tribes.

The villages having less than 10% ST population are Poongulam, Enjur, Seliyambedu, Mangadu, Keerapakkam Kallur, Annamalaichari, Periyaveppathur Uppunelvoyal, Agaram, Devampattu, Kanganimedu Mumipedu, Senganyam, Periakarumbur, Panapakkam Kumarancherry, Illupakkam, Kolur, Sirulapakkam Auriwakkam, Pakkam, Tirupalaivanam, Poovami, Vembedu Avoor, Vidathandalam, Arasoor, Appalapuram Andavayal, Sompathu, Paranambedu, Kilikodi Kattavoor, Medur, Asanupudur, Vanjivakkam Perilayambakkam, Andarmadam, Pazhaverkadu Thangalperumbalam, Siripazhaverkadu, Kadapakkam Thathamanji, Perumbedui, Chinnakavanam, Guduvancheri Thiruper, Ealiyambedu, Lingapayampettai, Somanjer Athamanjeri, Sirulapooncheri, Kattur, Karungali Kalanj, Kattupallai, Vayaloor, Thiruvellavayal Eripillaikuppam, Velur, Aladu, Kumarasiralapakkam Kaniyambakkam, Thinaipakkam, Merattur, Devadanam Thadaperumbakkam, Anuppampattu, Vellambakkam Thottakadu, Kalpakkam, Neithavoyal, Nalur Vannipakkam, Nandiambakkam, Puzhidivakkam, Valliur Edayaanchavady.

The villages having more than 50% ST population are None.

Sex ratio of Scheduled tribe population is 500.

Scheduled Tribes Literates and Illiterates by Sex:

	Persons	Males	Females
Literate	644	406	238
Illiterate	2,364	1,098	1,266
Literacy rate	26.4	33.6	19.3
Graduate	3	2	1

Scheduled Tribes (Dominant):

Irular, Kattunayakan, Kurumans, Generic Tribes etc. Malai Pandaram

For their cultural identity please see Appendix-II

Villages without Scheduled Tribes: There are 46 villages without any scheduled tribe population.

Literates and Illiterates by Sex (Total Population):

	Persons	Males	Females
Literate	85,853	48,894	36,959
Illiterate	59,782	23,894	35,888
Literacy rate	67	77	58
Graduate	3,309	2,338	971

Agriculture: ***Distribution of villages according to land use:*** Out of 87 villages, Total area (in hectare) is 45428.37, out of that 43.13 percent is cultivable and 68.19 percent of the cultivable area is irrigated.

Sources of Irrigation (Hectares): Government Canal 24.91, Private Canal 0, Well without Electricity 120.99, Well with Electricity 663.14, Tubewell without Electricity 197.53, Tubewell with Electricity 6347.12, Tank 800.68, River 195.3, Lake 4457.55, Waterfall 0, Others 554.44.

Villages with population of 5000 to 9999:
Voyalur, Thadaperumbakkam, Anuppampattu , Nalur Edayanchavadi.

Villages with population of 10000 and above:

Pulicut, Vallur.

Distribution of Workers:

	Persons	Males	Females	WPR
Cultivators	6,759	5,237	1,522	11.45
Agricultural Labour	28,176	16,327	11,849	47.73
Household Industry	1,199	581	618	2.03
Other Workers	22,900	19,456	3,444	38.79
Main Workers	44,678	33,816	10,862	75.68
Marginal Workers	14,356	7,785	6,571	24.32
Total Workers	59,034	41,601	17,433	

Religion: Major Religious Communities:

	Persons	Males	Females	Sex Ratio
Hindu (92.64%)	134,910	67,450	67,460	1,000
Muslim (3.44%)	5,003	2,491	2,512	1,008
Christian (2.78%)	4,046	1,993	2,053	1,030
Sikh (0%)	-	-	-	-
Buddhists (0%)	5	3	2	667
Jain (0%)	1	-	1	-

Agewise Data:

	Persons	Males	Females	Sex Ratio
All ages	144,091	71,999	72,092	1001
0-14	41,402	20,858	20,544	985
15-44	74,276	37,030	37,246	1006
45-79	27,100	13,463	13,637	1013
80+	866	422	444	1052
Age not stated	447	226	221	978

Languages (Dominant):

Tamil, Telugu, Urdu, Malayalam, Hindi

Disabled Population:

	Persons	Males	Females	%
Total Disabled	3,542	1,902	1,640	
In Seeing	1,775	899	876	50.11
In Speech	339	179	160	9.57
In Hearing	246	117	129	6.95
In Movement	946	581	365	26.71
Mentally	236	126	110	6.66

MODAKURICHI

Modakurichi C.D. Block lies in the central-eastern part of Erode district. It is a part of Erode taluk. The Block is located at a distance of 14 kms. from district headquarters (Erode). There are 25 villages in the block with the total population of 100,523 persons. Area of the C.D. Block is 244.07 sq. kms. It is bounded in the north by district Namakkal and C.D. Block Erode, in the south and east by C.D. Block Kodumudi, and in the west by CD Block Chennimalai.

Communications:

Roadways : S.H.-37: Direction- Kanagayam to Kasipalayam, Nearest Villages- Thoyampoondurai, Avalpoondurai, Modavandi Sathiyamangalam, Mukasihanumanpalli, Attavanai Hanumanpalli, Pudur.

Railway Station: Nanjai Uthukuli.

River: Cauvery Nadi- Nearest Villages- Nanjailakkapuram Kangayampalayam, Sathampoor, Nanjaikdamangalam.

Annual Rainfall: Average Rainfall 789 mm.

Ground Water: Availability of the ground water in the Basin is 8606.76 H.A.M. and the utilization is 2290.71 H.A.M. It belongs to Safe category. Depth to water level varies from 2 to 10 meter below the ground. Most of the wells go down in summer months, according to the Ground Water Estimation Committee.

Natural Division: Kongu Nadu.

Administration

Revenue **Division:** Erode. Parliamentary Constituency: 17 Erode. District: Erode. Taluk: Erode. Assembly Constituency: 100 Modakkurichi. Gram Panchayat: 23.

Villages: 25 **Inhabited:** 23 **Uninhabited:** 2

Ranking	**District**	**State**	**National**
Area	10	237	3455
Population	1	128	3450
Sex Ratio	12	307	2534
Child Sex Ratio	17	328	5399
Literacy Rate	3	245	2154
Density	15	67	2671
Work Participation Rate	6	108	591

Gram Panchayats:

Annandampalayam, Attavanai Hanuman Palli, Elumathur, Ganapathipalayam, Injampalli , Kagam, Kanagapuram, Kandikattuvalsu, Kulavilakku, Kulur, Lakkapuram, Modavandi Sathyamangalam, Mukasi Hanuman Palli, Muthugounderpalayam, Nanjaikalamangalam, Nanjaiuthukuli , Palamangalam, Pudur, Punduraisemur, Punjai Kalamangalam , Thuyyampoondurai, Velampalayam, Vilakethi.

Amenities:

Education: Primary School in 21 villages, Middle school in 12 villages, Matriculation or Secondary School in 5 villages, namely Punjailakkapuram, Nanjai Uthukuli, Punjaikalamangalam, Mukasihanumanpalli, Palamangalam. Higher Secondary or Pre University Courses or Intermediate or Junior College in 3 villages of the CD Block,, namely Nanjai Uthukuli, Punjaikalamangalam, Mukasihanumanpalli.

College in 0 village, Adult Literacy Center in 1 village.

Medical: Hospital in 1 village, Dispensary in 1 village, Health Center in 3 villages, Sub Center in 20 villages, Maternity and Child Welfare Center in 4 villages, Community health workers in 0 village.

The Villages having Hospital or Dispensary or Health Center are Thoyampoondurai, Punjaikalamangalam.

Drinking Water: Tap water in 23 villages, Tank water in 0 villages, Well water in 23 villages, Tubewell in 23

villages and more than one source in 23 villages.

Bank: Banking facility in 9 villages, namely, Punjailakkapuram, Pudur, Avalpoondurai Modavandi Sathiyamangalam, Nanjai Uthukuli Punjaikalamangalam, Enjampalli, Elumathur Mukasihanumanpalli.

Credit Society in 13 villages Agricultural Credit Society in 10 Non-Agricultural Credit Society in 3 villages.

Others: Power supply in 23 villages, Cinema hall in 0 village, sport club in 0 village, Stadium or Auditorium or Community Hall in 1 village, Post Office in 23 villages.

There are 21 villages having bus facilities.

Villages with most of facilities: Punjailakkapuram Pudur, Avalpoondurai, Modavandi Sathiyamangalam Nanjai Uthukuli, Punjaikalamangalam, Enjampalli Elumathur, Mukasihanumanpalli.

Villages without amenities (Education):
Velampalayam, Thanathampalayam..

Scheduled Castes: Out of the total population of 100523 persons, 18325 persons (18.23%) belong to Scheduled Castes.

The villages having less than 10% SC population are None..

The villages having more than 50% SC population are None.

Sex ratio of Scheduled Caste population is 494.

Scheduled Castes Literates and Illiterates by Sex:

	Persons	Males	Females
Literate	7,809	4,730	3,079
Illiterate	10,516	4,542	5,974
Literacy rate	48.3	58.0	38.4
Graduate	138	111	27

Scheduled Castes (Dominant):
Chakkiliyan, Arunthathiyar, Adi Dravida, Pallan Paraiyan etc.

For their cultural identity please see Appendix-I

Villages without Scheduled Castes: There are 3 villages without any scheduled caste population.

Scheduled Tribes: Out of the total population of 100523 persons, 157 persons (0.16%) belong to Scheduled Tribes.

The villages having less than 10% ST population are Punjailakkapuram, Pudur, Thoyampoondurai Kanagapuram, Velampalayam, Poondurai Semur Avalpoondurai, Modavandi Sathiyamangalam Nanjai Uthukuli, Kangayampalayam, Nanjaikdamangalam Punjaikalamangalam, Enjampalli, Thanathampalayam Elumathur, Velampalayam, Mukasihanumanpalli Attavanai Hanumanpalli, Kagam, Kulavilakku Palamangalam, Ellaikadu, Vilakkethi.

The villages having more than 50% ST population are None.

Sex ratio of Scheduled tribe population is 478.

Scheduled Tribes Literates and Illiterates by Sex:

	Persons	Males	Females
Literate	84	51	33
Illiterate	73	31	42
Literacy rate	62.2	73.9	50.0
Graduate	7	6	1

Scheduled Tribes (Dominant):
Generic Tribes etc., Irular, Kurumans, Uraly Kammara

For their cultural identity please see Appendix-II

Villages without Scheduled Tribes: There are 18 villages without any scheduled tribe population.

Literates and Illiterates by Sex (Total Population):

	Persons	Males	Females
Literate	57,929	34,391	23,538
Illiterate	42,594	16,673	25,921
Literacy rate	64	75	52
Graduate	2,847	1,973	874

Agriculture: ***Distribution of villages according to land use:***
Out of 25 villages, Total area (in hectare) is 24407.4, out of that 84.87 percent is cultivable and 67.39 percent of the cultivable area is irrigated.

Sources of Irrigation (Hectares): Government Canal 11876.69, Private Canal 0, Well without Electricity 229.39, Well with Electricity 1355.23, Tubewell without Electricity 0, Tubewell with Electricity 0, Tank 0, River 0, Lake 0, Waterfall 0, Others 498.71.

Villages with population of 5000 to 9999:
Punjailakkapuram, Pudur, Modavandi Sathyamangalam Punjai Kalamangalam , Elumathur.

Villages with population of 10000 and above:
Thuyyampoondurai , Nanjaiuthukuli.

Distribution of Workers:

	Persons	Males	Females	WPR
Cultivators	15,998	9,375	6,623	26.98
Agricultural Labour	24,298	11,089	13,209	40.98
Household Industry	1,408	732	676	2.37
Other Workers	17,590	13,377	4,213	29.67
Main Workers	55,409	33,321	22,088	93.45
Marginal Workers	3,885	1,252	2,633	6.55
Total Workers	59,294	34,573	24,721	

Religion: Major Religious Communities:

	Persons	Males	Females	Sex Ratio
Hindu (97.78%)	98,295	49,963	48,332	967
Muslim (0.96%)	967	473	494	1,044
Christian (1.15%)	1,153	569	584	1,026
Sikh (0.01%)	8	6	2	333
Buddhists (0%)	1	1	-	-
Jain (0%)	5	3	2	667

Agewise Data:

	Persons	Males	Females	Sex Ratio
All ages	100,523	51,064	49,459	969
0-14	21,317	11,153	10,164	911
15-44	48,849	24,634	24,215	983
45-79	28,452	14,300	14,152	990
80+	1,448	730	718	984
Age not stated	457	247	210	850

Languages (Dominant):

Tamil, Telugu, Kannada, Urdu, Malayalam

Disabled Population:

	Persons	Males	Females	%
Total Disabled	2,998	1,354	1,644	
In Seeing	1,930	775	1,155	64.38
In Speech	222	115	107	7.4
In Hearing	129	46	83	4.3
In Movement	491	286	205	16.38
Mentally	226	132	94	7.54

MOHANUR

Mohanur C.D. Block lies in the southern part of Namakkal district. It is a part of Namakkal and Paramathi-Velur taluks. The Block is located at a distance of 19 kms. from district headquarters (Namakkal). There are 27 villages in the block with the total population of 77,787 persons. Area of the C.D. Block is 252.40 sq. kms. It is bounded in the north by C.D. Block Namakkal, in the south by districts Karur and Tiruchirappalli, in the east by C.D. Blocks Erumaipatti, and in the west by C.D. Block Kabilamalai. CD Block Mohanur falls in taluk Namakkal by 14 villages, and in taluk Paramathi-Velur by 13 villages.

Communications:

Roadways : S.H.-6: Direction- Namakkal to Musiri, Nearest Villages- N.Puduppatti, Valaiyapatti.

River: Cauvery Nadi- Nearest Villages- Pettaipalayam, Oruvandur, Ponjai Idiyar, Keelmugam, Nanjai Edayar, Kumarapalayam, Sarkar Manappalli, Agrahara Manappalli.

Annual Rainfall: Average Rainfall 650 mm.

Ground Water: Availability of the ground water in the Basin is 4776.78 H.A.M. and the utilization is 3782.44 H.A.M. It belongs to Safe category. Depth to water level varies from 2 to 10 meter below the ground. Most of the wells go down in summer months, according to the Ground Water Estimation Committee.

Natural Division: Kongu Nadu

Administration

Revenue **Division:** Namakkal, Tiruchengode.

Parliamentary Constituency. District: Namakkal. Taluk: Namakkal, Paramathi-Velur. Assembly Constituency: 95 Paramathi – Velur, 93 Senthamangalam (ST), 94 Namakkal.

Gram Panchayat: 25.

Villages: 27 **Inhabited:** 27 **Uninhabited:** 0

Ranking	District	State	National
Area	2	228	3348
Population	4	254	4178
Sex Ratio	2	191	1289
Child Sex Ratio	8	343	5670
Literacy Rate	3	199	1811
Density	5	14	3448
Work Participation Rate	8	211	124

Gram Panchayats:

Andapuram, Aniyapuram , Arasanatham, Ariyur, Arur, Chinnapethampatti, Kumaripalayam, Laddivadi, N.Puduppatti, Oruvandur, Parali, Pettaipalayam, Rasipalayam , Tholur, Valaiyapatti, K. pudupalayam, Kalipalayam, Kumarapalayam, Madagasampatty, Manappalli, Nanjai Edayar, Olapalayam, Perumandampalayam, Sengapalli, Sircarvalavandhi.

Amenities:

Education: Primary School in 26 villages, Middle school in 8 villages, Matriculation or Secondary School in 5 villages, namely N.Puduppatti, Aniyapuram, Valaiyapatti, Andapuram, Sengapalli.

Higher Secondary or Pre University Courses or Intermediate or Junior College in 4 villages of the CD Block,, namely Aniyapuram, Valaiyapatti, Pettaipalayam, Sengapalli.

College in 1 village, Adult Literacy Center in 1 village., College is in village, namely Laddivadi.

Medical: Hospital in 1 village, Dispensary in 1 village, Health Center in 5 villages, Sub Center in 12 villages, Maternity and Child Welfare Center in 0 village, Community health workers in 0 village.

The Villages having Hospital or Dispensary or Health Center are Valaiyapatti, Sengapalli.

Drinking Water: Tap water in 27 villages, Tank water in 0 villages, Well water in 27 villages, Tubewell in 27 villages and more than one source in 27 villages.

Bank: Banking facility in 7 villages, namely, Laddivadi, Valaiyapatti, Arur, Kumaripalayam Pettaipalayam, Oruvandur, Sengapalli.

Credit Society in 21 villages Agricultural Credit Society in 17 Non-Agricultural Credit Society in 17 villages.

Others: Power supply in 27 villages, Cinema hall in 0 village, sport club in 0 village, Stadium or Auditorium or Community Hall in 0 village, Post Office in 25 villages.

There are 27 villages having bus facilities.

Villages with most of facilities: Laddivadi Valaiyapatti, Arur, Kumaripalayam, Pettaipalayam Oruvandur, Sengapalli.

Villages without amenities (Education):

Agrahara Manappalli..

Scheduled Castes: Out of the total population of 77787 persons, 14784 persons (19.01%) belong to Scheduled Castes.
The villages having less than 10% SC population are K.Puliampatti, Sengapalli, Idumbankulam Nanjai Edayar, Agrahara Manappalli.
The villages having more than 50% SC population are None.
Sex ratio of Scheduled Caste population is 498.

Scheduled Castes Literates and Illiterates by Sex:

	Persons	Males	Females
Literate	7,642	4,611	3,031
Illiterate	7,142	2,809	4,333
Literacy rate	58.7	70.8	46.5
Graduate	203	161	42

Scheduled Castes (Dominant):
Arunthathiyar, Pallan, Paraiyan etc., Adi Dravida Chakkiliyan

For their cultural identity please see Appendix-I

Villages without Scheduled Castes: There is 1 village without any scheduled caste population.

Scheduled Tribes: Out of the total population of 77787 persons, 22 persons (0.03%) belong to Scheduled Tribes.
The villages having less than 10% ST population are N.Puduppatti, Laddivadi, Tholur, Aniyapuram, Parali Valaiyapatti, Arur, Andapuram, Arasanatham Kumaripalayam, Ariyur, Pettaipalayam, Rasipalayam Oruvandur, Kalipalayam, Kuttamparai, K.Puliampatti Madagasampatty, Perumandampalayam, Sircarvalavandhi Sengapalli, Ponjai Idiyar Keelmugam, Idumbankulam Nanjai Edayar, Kumarapalayam, Sarkar Manappalli Agrahara Manappalli.
The villages having more than 50% ST population are None.
Sex ratio of Scheduled tribe population is 409.

Scheduled Tribes Literates and Illiterates by Sex:

	Persons	Males	Females
Literate	11	8	3
Illiterate	11	5	6
Literacy rate	64.7	80.0	42.9
Graduate	0	0	0

Scheduled Tribes (Dominant):
Malakkuravan, Malayali, Paniyan

For their cultural identity please see Appendix-II

Villages without Scheduled Tribes: There are 22 villages without any scheduled tribe population.

Literates and Illiterates by Sex (Total Population):

	Persons	Males	Females
Literate	45,981	27,114	18,867
Illiterate	31,806	11,848	19,958
Literacy rate	66	78	54
Graduate	2,020	1,399	621

Agriculture: ***Distribution of villages according to land use:*** Out of 27 villages, Total area (in hectare) is 25240.56, out of that 71.66 percent is cultivable and 38.4 percent of the cultivable area is irrigated.

Sources of Irrigation (Hectares): Government Canal 2232, Private Canal 0, Well without Electricity 0, Well with Electricity 4137.82, Tubewell without Electricity 0, Tubewell with Electricity 27.1, Tank 94.11, River 0, Lake 0, Waterfall 0, Others 454.63.

Villages with population of 5000 to 9999: N.Puduppatti, Valaiyapatti, Oruvandur.

Villages with population of 10000 and above: None

Distribution of Workers:

	Persons	Males	Females	WPR
Cultivators	13,794	7,479	6,315	27.95
Agricultural Labour	22,596	9,640	12,956	45.78
Household Industry	1,327	482	845	2.69
Other Workers	11,640	8,611	3,029	23.58
Main Workers	45,546	25,105	20,441	92.28
Marginal Workers	3,811	1,107	2,704	7.72
Total Workers	49,357	26,212	23,145	

Religion: Major Religious Communities:

	Persons	Males	Females	Sex Ratio
Hindu (98.61%)	76,709	38,422	38,287	996
Muslim (0.73%)	567	273	294	1,077
Christian (0.56%)	432	221	211	955
Sikh (0.02%)	17	9	8	889
Buddhists (0.02%)	13	13	-	-
Jain (0.01%)	5	3	2	667

Agewise Data:

	Persons	Males	Females	Sex Ratio
All ages	77,787	38,962	38,825	996
0-14	17,695	9,256	8,439	912
15-44	37,153	18,399	18,754	1019
45-79	21,430	10,543	10,887	1033
80+	873	440	433	984
Age not stated	636	324	312	963

Languages (Dominant):
Tamil, Telugu, Kannada, Urdu, Malayalam

Disabled Population:

	Persons	Males	Females	%
Total Disabled	1,370	765	605	
In Seeing	576	313	263	42.04
In Speech	151	88	63	11.02
In Hearing	83	35	48	6.06
In Movement	422	257	165	30.8
Mentally	138	72	66	10.07

MORAPPUR

Morappur C.D. Block lies in the north-eastern part of Dharmapuri district. It is a part of Harur and Pappireddipatti taluks. The taluk (Pappireddipatti) is located at a distance of 52 kms. from district headquarters (Dharmapuri). There are 83 villages in the block with the total population of 133,983 persons. Area of the C.D. Block is 469.34 sq. kms. It is bounded in the north by district Krishnagiri, in the south by Pappireddipatti C.D. Block, in the east by C.D. Block Harur, in the west by CD Blocks Dharmapuri and Karimangalam. CD Block Morappur falls in taluk Harur by 45 villages, and in taluk Pappireddipatti by 38 villages.

Communications:

Roadways : Information not Available.

Railway Station: Samandahalli, Rasalampatti, Chinthalpadi, Buddireddipatti.

River: Ponnaiyar Nadi- Nearest Villages- Irumathur, Kongarapatti.

Annual Rainfall: Average Rainfall 760 mm.

Ground Water: Availability of the ground water in the Basin is 7047.62 H.A.M. and the utilization is 12524. 75 H.A.M. It belongs to Over Expoited category. Depth to water level varies from 2 to 10 meter below the ground. Most of the wells go down in summer months, according to the Ground Water Estimation Committee.

Forest and Reserved Forest: (Kavaramalai RF)- Nearest Villages- Kavaramalai (Extn .RF) Uni, Mekalanaickenhally, Obilinaickenhally, Thalanatham, Kethureddipatti, Kavaramalai R.F. Uni.

Natural Division: Baramahal.

Administration

Revenue **Division:** Harur. Parliamentary Constituency: 10 Dharmapuri. District: Dharmapuri. Taluk: Hasur, Pappireddippatti. Assembly Constituency: 60 Paddireddippatti, 61 Hasur (SC). Gram Panchayat: 43.

Villages: 83 **Inhabited:** 81 **Uninhabited:** 2

Ranking	District	State	National
Area	7	40	1607
Population	11	36	2374
Sex Ratio	11	362	4239
Child Sex Ratio	10	356	5958
Literacy Rate	5	282	2406
Density	9	147	3690
Work Participation Rate	11	243	1477

Gram Panchayats:

Bannikulam , Basuvapuram, Buddireddipatti, Chintalpadi, Dasirihalli , Gobinathampatti , Gopichettipalayam , Gurubarahalli , Ichambadi , Irumathur, Jakkupatti, Kadirnaickanhalli, Karthanur, Kelavalli, Kerakodahalli, Kethureddipatti, Konkarapatty, Kosapatty , Linginaickenahalli, Madathahalli, Maniyambadi, Morappur , Mottankurichi, Nallagudlahalli, Navalai , Obilinayakkanahalli , Osahalli, Palayampalli, Poliyampatti , Rameyanahalli , Ranimookkanur, Regadahalli, Samandahalli, Sandapatti , Sillarahalli, Sunkarahalli , Thadhanur, Thalanatham, Thenkaraikottai, Thoppampatti , Vagurappampatti , Vaguthupatti, Venkatadarahalli.

Amenities:

Education: Primary School in 64 villages, Middle school in 28 villages, Matriculation or Secondary School in 18 villages, namely Irumathur, K.Eachambadi, Samandahalli, Navalai, Vagurappampatti, Obilinaickenpatty, Rasalampatti, Sennampatty, Gobinathampatti, Surapatti, Maniyambadi, Kerakodahalli, Chinthalpadi, Kadathur, Buddireddipatti, Basuvapuram, Ramiyanahally, Mottankurichi.

Higher Secondary or Pre University Courses or Intermediate or Junior College in 9 villages of the CD Block,, namely Samandahalli, Vagurappampatti, Rasalampatti, Gobinathampatti, Kerakodahalli, Chinthalpadi, Kadathur, Basuvapuram, Ramiyanahally.

College in 0 village, Adult Literacy Center in 0 village.

Medical: Hospital in 3 villages, Dispensary in 2 villages, Health Center in 3 villages, Sub Center in 23 villages, Maternity and Child Welfare Center in 0 village, Community health workers in 56 villages.

The Villages having Hospital or Dispensary or Health Center are K.Eachambadi, Chinthalpadi, Ramiyanahally, Thalanatham, Mekalanaickenhally.

Drinking Water: Tap water in 81 villages, Tank water in 2 villages, Well water in 81 villages, Tubewell in 81 villages and more than one source in 81 villages.

Bank: Banking facility in 8 villages, namely, Nainagoundampatty, Rasalampatti, Singrihalli Kadathur, Buddireddipatti, Ramiyanahally Thalanatham, Sunkarahalli.

Credit Society in 36 villages Agricultural Credit Society in 12 Non-Agricultural Credit Society in 16 villages.

Others: Power supply in 81 villages, Cinema hall in 1 village, sport club in 0 village, Stadium or Auditorium or Community Hall in 0 village, Post Office in 79 villages.

There are 66 villages having bus facilities.

Villages with most of facilities: Rasalampatti Singrihalli, Kadathur, Buddireddipatti Ramiyanahally, Thalanatham, Sunkarahalli.

Villages without amenities (Education): Ettipatti, Andipatti, Kosapatti, Vengiyampatti, Nainagoundampatty, Mottiayampatti, Morappur, Kondayampatti, Veppachennampatty, Bodinaickanpatty, Avalampatti, Kattur, Vanakkampadi, Kadavanampatti, Obilinaickenhally, Mekalanaickenhally..

Scheduled Castes: Out of the total population of 133983

persons, 35285 persons (26.34%) belong to Scheduled Castes. The villages having less than 10% SC population are Bannikulam, Kongarapatti, Kelavalli, Gettupatti Palayam, Chinnagoundampalli, Andipatti, Kosapatti Vetrapatty, Kondayampatti, Sennampatty Veppachennampatty, Reddipatty, Kurumbapatty Nadupatti, Nachinam Patti, Kottarapatty Vanakkampadi, Santhapatty, Mookkanoor Patty Singrihalli, Nallakudlahalli, Kadakarahalli Kadathur, Thinnahalli, Sikkampatti Gopichettipalayam, Thurinjihalli, Ramiyanahally Obilinaickenhally, Mottankurichi, Vattalamalai.

The villages having more than 50% SC population are Elavadai, Navalai, Palaiyampalli, Thoppampatti Morappur, Bodinaickanpatty, Surapatti, Madathahalli Balasamudram, Peddur, Pippichettipatti, Allalapatty.

Sex ratio of Scheduled Caste population is 486.

Scheduled Castes Literates and Illiterates by Sex:

	Persons	Males	Females
Literate	18,383	11,300	7,083
Illiterate	16,902	6,840	10,062
Literacy rate	60.5	72.5	47.9
Graduate	875	725	150

Scheduled Castes (Dominant):

Adi Dravida, Arunthathiyar, Kuravan etc., Gosangi Adi Andhra

For their cultural identity please see Appendix-I

Villages without Scheduled Castes: There are 15 villages without any scheduled caste population.

Scheduled Tribes: Out of the total population of 133983 persons, 1390 persons (1.04%) belong to Scheduled Tribes. The villages having less than 10% ST population are Bannikulam, Irumathur, Kongarapatti, Kelavalli K.Eachambadi, K.Agraharam, Ettipatti, Gettupatti Samandahalli, Palayam, Elavadai, Navalai Chinnagoundampalli, Vagurappampatti, Pallipatti Jukkupatti, Bathalahalli, Palaiyampalli, Andipatti Thoppampatti, Kosapatti, Vengiyampatti Obilinaickenpatty, Nainagoundampatty, Mottiayampatti Vetrapatty, Rasalampatti, Morappur, Kondayampatti Sennampatty, Veppachennampatty, Gobinathampatti Dasirahalli, Reddipatty, Bodinaickanpatty Kurumbapatty, Nadupatti, Avalampatti, Nachinam Patti Kattur, Kottarapatty, Vanakkampadi, Santhapatty Mookkanoor Patty, Surapatti, Maniyambadi Singrihalli, Kerakodahalli, Chinthalpadi Linganaikkanahalli, Bosinaiyakanahalli Nallakudlahalli, Kadakarahalli, Kadathur Madathahalli, Buddireddipatti, Basuvapuram Gurubarahalli, Thinnahalli, Balasamudram, Peddur Sikkampatti, Gopichettipalayam, Pippichettipatti Annamalaipatti, Allalapatty, Kadavanampatti Thengaraikottai, Ramiyanahally, Pethasamudram Obilinaickenhally, Thalanatham, Kethureddipatti Mottankurichi, Sunkarahalli, Unisinihalli Regadahalli, Mekalanaickenhally.

The villages having more than 50% ST population are None.

Sex ratio of Scheduled tribe population is 481.

Scheduled Tribes Literates and Illiterates by Sex:

	Persons	Males	Females
Literate	466	290	176
Illiterate	924	432	492
Literacy rate	39.6	47.2	31.3
Graduate	7	6	1

Scheduled Tribes (Dominant):

Malayali, Irular, Kurumans, Malakkuravan, Palliyar

For their cultural identity please see Appendix-II

Villages without Scheduled Tribes: There are 61 villages without any scheduled tribe population.

Literates and Illiterates by Sex (Total Population):

	Persons	Males	Females
Literate	72,760	44,069	28,691
Illiterate	61,223	25,167	36,056
Literacy rate	62	73	50
Graduate	2,543	2,045	498

Agriculture: ***Distribution of villages according to land use:*** Out of 83 villages, Total area (in hectare) is 46934.1, out of that 72.3 percent is cultivable and 32.97 percent of the cultivable area is irrigated.

Sources of Irrigation (Hectares): Government Canal 92.94, Private Canal 0, Well without Electricity 2640.12, Well with Electricity 7138.48, Tubewell without Electricity 0, Tubewell with Electricity 80.38, Tank 1172.98, River 0, Lake 0, Waterfall 0, Others 61.45.

Villages with population of 5000 to 9999: Maniyabadi, Chintalpadi , Kettureddipatty Unisenahalli.

Villages with population of 10000 and above: None

Distribution of Workers:

	Persons	Males	Females	WPR
Cultivators	29,952	17,740	12,212	42.19
Agricultural Labour	28,068	12,460	15,608	39.54
Household Industry	1,323	614	709	1.86
Other Workers	11,647	9,110	2,537	16.41
Main Workers	58,050	35,212	22,838	81.77
Marginal Workers	12,940	4,712	8,228	18.23
Total Workers	70,990	39,924	31,066	

Religion: Major Religious Communities:

	Persons	Males	Females	Sex Ratio

Hindu (97.54%)	130,681	67,584	63,097	934
Muslim (1.51%)	2,027	1,039	988	951
Christian (0.79%)	1,056	505	551	1,091
Sikh (0%)	-	-	-	-
Buddhists (0%)	-	-	-	-
Jain (0%)	3	1	2	2,000

Agewise Data:

	Persons	Males	Females	Sex Ratio
All ages	133,983	69,236	64,747	935
0-14	39,719	21,214	18,505	872
15-44	65,503	33,296	32,207	967
45-79	27,478	14,058	13,420	955
80+	1,096	566	530	936
Age not stated	187	102	85	833

Languages (Dominant):

Tamil, Telugu, Kannada, Urdu, Malayalam

Disabled Population:

	Persons	Males	Females	%
Total Disabled	4,103	1,252	2,851	
In Seeing	2,808	484	2,324	68.44
In Speech	261	148	113	6.36
In Hearing	130	75	55	3.17
In Movement	715	448	267	17.43
Mentally	189	97	92	4.61

MUDUKULATHUR

Mudukulathur C.D. Block lies in the central part of Ramanathauram district. It is a part of Mudukulathur and Kamuthi taluks. The Block is located at a distance of 47 kms. from district headquarters (Ramanathauram). There are 37 villages in the block with the total population of 74,096 persons. Area of the C.D. Block is 413.62 sq. kms. It is bounded in the north by CD Blocks Bogalur and Paramakudi, in the south by CD Block Kadaladi, in the east by CD Block Tiruppullani, and in the west by CD Block Kamuthi. CD Block Mudukulathur falls in taluk Mudukulathur by 36 villages, and in taluk Kamuthi by 01 village.

Communications:

Roadways : S.H.-29: Direction- Paramakkudi to Kadaladi, Nearest Villages- Sathanoor, Manjakottai, Sellur, Vilangulathur, Kelelathooval, Vengalakurichi.

River: Gundar Nadi- Nearest Villages- Nallur, Keeranur, Melamudukulathur, Valanadu, Ilankakkoor, Karumal, Kakkoor, Pooseri, Thaliyarendal, Melakodmalur, Thattanendal, Merkkukottakudi, Melakkulam, Manaloor, Pulvoikulam.

Annual Rainfall: Average Rainfall 827 mm.

Ground Water: Availability of the ground water in the Basin is 4070.82 H.A.M. and the utilization is 546.00 H.A.M. It belongs to Safe category. Depth to water level varies from 2 to 10 meter below the ground. Most of the wells go down in summer months, according to the Ground Water Estimation Committee.

Natural Division: NA

Administration

Revenue **Division:** Paramakudi. Parliamentary Constituency: 35 Ramanathapuram. District: Ramanthapuram. Taluk: Mudukulathur, Kamuthi. Assembly Constituency: 212 Kadaladi. Gram Panchayat: 46.

Villages: 37 **Inhabited:** 35 **Uninhabited:** 2

Ranking	District	State	National
Area	4	62	1858
Population	6	270	4318
Sex Ratio	7	45	415
Child Sex Ratio	9	158	2759
Literacy Rate	11	239	2128
Density	3	73	5065
Work Participation Rate	9	346	701

Gram Panchayats:

Alanganur , Anaiseri, Arapothu , Athanakurichi , Athankothangudi , Athikulam , Kakkur, Karumal , Keelakodumalar , Keelakodumalar , Keelakulam , Keelathooval , Keeranur , Kolundurai , Kumarakurichi, Mahindi , Manalur, Melakanniseri , Melekodumalar , Michaelpattinam, Nallukurichi, Nallur, Periaelai, Pirabakalur, Ponnakkaneri , Melakodumalar , Pooseri , Posukudi , Pulithikulam , Puliyangudi , Puliyankudi , Sambakulam , Sathanur , Sellur, Selvanayagapuram, Sembongudi, Sirugudi , Siruthalai , Theririveli , Theriruveli , Tiruvarangam, Ulaiyar , Valanedu , Vengalakurichi , Vikkiramapandiapuram, Vikkiramapandiapuram , Vilakanendal , Vilangulathur , Vangarupuram .

Amenities:

Education: Primary School in 25 villages, Middle school in 17 villages, Matriculation or Secondary School in 12 villages, namely Keelalulam, Keelathooval, Kolundurai, Swathan, Vengalakurichi, Vilangulathur, Melathooval, Manaloor, Nallur, Melamudukulathur, Karumal, Athankothankudi. Higher Secondary or Pre University Courses or Intermediate or Junior College in 12 villages of the CD Block,, namely Keelalulam, Keelathooval, Kolundurai, Vengalakurichi, Vilangulathur, Melathooval, Manaloor, Nallur, Melamudukulathur, Pirabakkalur, Karumal, Athankothankudi.

College in 11 villages, Adult Literacy Center in 12 villages., Colleges are in villages, namely Kolundurai, Swathan, Vengalakurichi, Vilangulathur, Melathooval, Manaloor, Nallur, Melamudukulathur, Pirabakkalur, Karumal, Athankothankudi.

Medical: Hospital in 10 villages, Dispensary in 8 villages, Health Center in 9 villages, Sub Center in 9 villages,

Maternity and Child Welfare Center in 8 villages, Community health workers in 7 villages.

The Villages having Hospital or Dispensary or Health Center are Swathan, Vengalakurichi, Vilangulathur, Anaiseri, Manaloor, Nallur, Melamudukulathur, Puliyangudi, Pirabakkalur, Karumal.

Drinking Water: Tap water in 35 villages, Tank water in 20 villages, Well water in 35 villages, Tubewell in 35 villages and more than one source in 35 villages.

Bank: Banking facility in 14 villages, namely, Sellur, Swathan, Vengalakurichi, Vilangulathur Melathooval, Anaiseri, Manaloor, Nallur Melamudukulathur, Pirabakkalur, Valanadu, Karumal Kakkoor, Theriruveli.

Credit Society in 18 villages Agricultural Credit Society in 17 Non-Agricultural Credit Society in 14 villages.

Others: Power supply in 34 villages, Cinema hall in 10 villages, sport club in 10 villages, Stadium or Auditorium or Community Hall in 10 villages, Post Office in 16 villages.

There are 28 villages having bus facilities.

Villages with most of facilities: Swathan Vengalakurichi, Karumal.

Villages without amenities (Education): Thattanendal, Sellur, Thiruvarangam, Puliyangudi, Posukkudi, Ulaiyur, Kumarakurichi..

Scheduled Castes: Out of the total population of 74096 persons, 22040 persons (29.75%) belong to Scheduled Castes.

The villages having less than 10% SC population are Thattanendal, Sathanoor, Merkkukottakudi Melathooval, Manaloor, Nallur, Melamudukulathur Puliyangudi, Thaliyarendal, Peranaikulam.

The villages having more than 50% SC population are Melakodumalur, Keelakodumaloor, Swathan, Karumal Athankothankudi.

Sex ratio of Scheduled Caste population is 499.

Scheduled Castes Literates and Illiterates by Sex:

	Persons	Males	Females
Literate	11,190	6,821	4,369
Illiterate	10,850	4,228	6,622
Literacy rate	58.2	71.1	45.4
Graduate	334	272	62

Scheduled Castes (Dominant):

Pallan, Chakkiliyan, Paraiyan etc., Puthirai Vannan Arunthathiyar

For their cultural identity please see Appendix-I

Villages without Scheduled Castes: There are 5 villages without any scheduled caste population.

Scheduled Tribes: Out of the total population of 74096 persons, 0 persons (0%) belong to Scheduled Tribes.

The villages having less than 10% ST population are Melakodumalur, Thattanendal, Keelakodumaloor Vikkiramapandiyapuram, Sathanoor, Merkkukottakudi Melakkulam, Keelalulam, Keelathooval, Sellur Kolundurai, Thiruvarangam, Swathan, Vengalakurichi Vilangulathur, Melathooval, Anaiseri, Manaloor Nallur, Keeranur, Melamudukulathur, Puliyangudi Posukkudi, Pirabakkalur, Ulaiyur, Valanadu Ilankakkoor, Karumal, Kakkoor, Kumarakurichi Theriruveli, Pooseri, Thaliyarendal, Athankothankudi Peranaikulam.

The villages having more than 50% ST population are None.

Villages without Scheduled Tribes: There are 37 villages without any scheduled tribe population.

Literates and Illiterates by Sex (Total Population):

	Persons	Males	Females
Literate	41,906	24,776	17,130
Illiterate	32,190	11,633	20,557
Literacy rate	64	77	51
Graduate	1,073	839	234

Agriculture: ***Distribution of villages according to land use:*** Out of 37 villages, Total area (in hectare) is 41362, out of that 147.59 percent is cultivable and 62.97 percent of the cultivable area is irrigated.

Sources of Irrigation (Hectares): Government Canal 0, Private Canal 0, Well without Electricity 2580.3, Well with Electricity 24604.36, Tubewell without Electricity 15100.03, Tubewell with Electricity 293.58, Tank 5885.58, River 0, Lake 0, Waterfall 0, Others 0.

Villages with population of 5000 to 9999: None

Villages with population of 10000 and above: None

Distribution of Workers:

	Persons	Males	Females	WPR
Cultivators	25,861	13,667	12,194	61.19
Agricultural Labour	12,147	4,602	7,545	28.74
Household Industry	377	165	212	0.89
Other Workers	3,880	2,912	968	9.18
Main Workers	37,934	20,057	17,877	89.75
Marginal Workers	4,331	1,289	3,042	10.25
Total Workers	42,265	21,346	20,919	

Religion: Major Religious Communities:

	Persons	Males	Females	Sex Ratio
Hindu (86.92%)	64,406	31,808	32,598	1,025
Muslim (3.53%)	2,616	1,168	1,448	1,240
Christian (7.62%)	5,649	2,775	2,874	1,036
Sikh (0%)	-	-	-	-
Buddhists (0%)	2	-	2	-
Jain (0%)	1	-	1	-

Agewise Data:

	Persons	Males	Females	Sex Ratio

All ages	72,709	35,772	36,937	1033
0-14	20,348	10,448	9,900	948
15-44	33,779	16,149	17,630	1092
45-79	17,717	8,736	8,981	1028
80+	631	304	327	1076
Age not stated	234	135	99	733

Languages (Dominant):
Tamil, Telugu, Urdu, Hindi, Kannada

Disabled Population:

	Persons	Males	Females	%
Total Disabled	2,210	930	1,280	
In Seeing	1,355	426	929	61.31
In Speech	162	98	64	7.33
In Hearing	107	47	60	4.84
In Movement	463	286	177	20.95
Mentally	123	73	50	5.57

MUGAIYUR

Mugaiyur C.D. Block lies in the central part of Viluppuram district. It is a part of Tirukkoyilur taluk. The taluk is located at a distance of 38 kms. from district headquarters (Viluppuram). There are 90 villages in the block with the total population of 166,607 persons. Area of the C.D. Block is 352.77 sq. kms. It is bounded in the north by district Tiruvannamalai, and CD Blocks Gingee and Kanai, in the south by C.D. Blocks Tirukkoyilur, Kanai and Tiruvennainallur, in the east by CD Block Kanai, in the west by district Tiruvannamalai, and CD Blocks Sankarapuram and Rishivandiam.

Communications:

Roadways : S.H-7: Direction- Vilupuram to Arakandanallur, Nearest Villages- Vadagarithayanur, S. Kollur, Kadaganur, V. Sithamur, Alambadi, Sathiyakandanur, Perichanur, Sennakunam, Ayandur, Mugaiyur, Paranur. S.H.-9: Direction- Tiruvannamalai to Arakandanallur, Nearest Villages- Athipakkam, Adurkolappakkam, Puthagaram U. I., Sadaikkatti, Velanthi, Kuladeepamangalam, Kudumuratti, Manampoondi, T. Devanur.

Railway Station: Adhichanur, Ayandur, Mugaiyur.

River: Ponnaiyar Nadi- Nearest Villages- Melandal, Kangiyanoor, Pallichandal, Jambai, Kottagam, Kalumalam, Velanthi, Kuladeepamangalam, Kudumuratti, Manampoondi, Andili, Nerkumam, Emapper, Arumalai, Paranur, Keelakondur, Veerashozhapuram, Arkadu, Paiyur, T. Devanur, Arulavadi, Konagarayanur, Marangiyur.

Backwards Region Grants Fund: It receives Backward Region Grants.

Annual Rainfall: Average Rainfall 1119 mm.

Ground Water: Availability of the ground water in the Basin is 8306.60 H.A.M. and the utilization is 9778.39 H.A.M. It belongs to Over Expoited category. Depth to water level varies from 2 to 10 meter below the ground. Most of the wells go down in summer months, according to the Ground Water Estimation Committee.

Forest and Reserved Forest: (Adukkam RF)- Nearest Villages- Arunapuram, Ottampattu, Thandarai, Adukkam R.F, Adukkam, Thurinjikadu R.F, Veerangipuram, Pudupalayam, Appanandal. (Nayanur)- Nearest Villages- Pulikkal, Kallandal, Nayanur R.F, Thirumalaipattu, Vellamputhur, Nayanoor, Vadagarithayanur. (Odaiyanatham)- Nearest Villages- Kandachipuram, Odaiyar Matham R.F. (T.Athipakkam)- Nearest Villages- Chitapattinam, T.Athipakkam R.F, Athipakkam, Kolundriampattu, Sooriyapattu, Nedungampattu. (Thachampattu)- Nearest Villages- Murukkambadi, Konganamoor, Thachampattu R.F.

Natural Division: Tondai Nadu.

Administration

Revenue **Division:** Tirukkoyilur. Parliamentary Constituency: 13 Villupuram (SC). District: Villupuram. Taluk: Tirukkoyilur. Assembly Constituency: 76 Mugaiyur, 78 Rishivandiyam. Gram Panchayat: 63.

Villages: 90 **Inhabited:** 84 **Uninhabited:** 6

Ranking	District	State	National
Area	8	111	2257
Population	1	4	1372
Sex Ratio	15	269	2112
Child Sex Ratio	13	150	2716
Literacy Rate	9	266	2297
Density	17	243	2341
Work Participation Rate	6	68	2614

Gram Panchayats:

A. Gudalur, Adhichanur, Adoor Kolapakkam, Adukkam, Alambadi, Andili, Arcadu, Arulavadi, Arumalai, Arunapuram, Athiyandal, Ayandur, Chithapattinam, Devanur, Devaradiarkuppam, Emapper, Jambai, Kadaganur, Kallandal, Kalumalam, Kandachipuram, Kangaiyanur, Kasbakaranai, Keelakondur, Kodukkapattu, Kodungal, Kollur, Kolundriampattu, Kongarayanur, Kottamarudur, Kuladipamangalam, Manampoondi, Marangiyur, Melakondur, Melendal, Melvalai, Mugaiyur, Murukkambadi, Nayanur, Nedungampattu, Nerkunam, Oddampattu, Othiyathur, Paiyur, Paranur, Pilrampattu, Sadaikatti, Sathiyakandanur, Sennakunam, Sithathur, Sorayapattu, T. Athipakkam, Thandarai, Thanikelampattu, V.Chithamur, V.Puthur, Vadagaraithayanur, Vasanthkrishnapuram, Veerangipuram, Veerapandi, Veerashozhapuram, Vellamputhur, Vilandai, .

Amenities:

Education: Primary School in 77 villages, Middle school in 25 villages, Matriculation or Secondary School in 10 villages, namely Athipakkam, Veerapandi, Kandachipuram,

Othiyathur, Velanthi, V. Puttur, Alambadi, Kasbakaranai, Mugaiyur, Arkadu.

Higher Secondary or Pre University Courses or Intermediate or Junior College in 2 villages of the CD Block,, namely Kandachipuram, Mugaiyur.

College in 0 village, Adult Literacy Center in 0 village.

Medical: Hospital in 2 villages, Dispensary in 3 villages, Health Center in 7 villages, Sub Center in 30 villages, Maternity and Child Welfare Center in 5 villages, Community health workers in 2 villages.

The Villages having Hospital or Dispensary or Health Center are Athipakkam, Othiyathur, Melakondur, Kodungal, Mugaiyur, Marangiyur.

Drinking Water: Tap water in 84 villages, Tank water in 71 villages, Well water in 84 villages, Tubewell in 84 villages and more than one source in 84 villages.

Bank: Banking facility in 10 villages, namely, Veerapandi, Kandachipuram, Sithathur, Kalumalam Agastyarmoolai, Kuladeepamangalam, Manampoondi V. Puttur, Mugaiyur, Arkadu.

Credit Society in 19 villages Agricultural Credit Society in 14 Non-Agricultural Credit Society in 4 villages.

Others: Power supply in 83 villages, Cinema hall in 4 villages, sport club in 3 villages, Stadium or Auditorium or Community Hall in 1 village, Post Office in 83 villages.

There are 82 villages having bus facilities.

Villages with most of facilities: Veerapandi Kandachipuram, Manampoondi, V. Puttur, Mugaiyur Arkadu.

Villages without amenities (Education):
Thurinjikadu R.F, Madavilagam, Appanandal, Su.Pulrampattu, Agastyarmoolai, Kingilivady..

Scheduled Castes: Out of the total population of 166607 persons, 48121 persons (28.88%) belong to Scheduled Castes.

The villages having less than 10% SC population are Pallichandal, Athipakkam, Kodukkapattu, Adhichanur Thandarai, Thurinjikadu R.F, Kilvalai, Othiyathur Sithathur, Arasankuppam, Sadaikkatti, Nedungampattu Kolundriampattu, Kalumalam, Agastyarmoolai Kudumuratti, Arumalai, Kingilivady, Sathiyakandanur Perichanur, Ayandur, Mugaiyur.

The villages having more than 50% SC population are Konganamoor, Velakulam, Vasanthakrishnapuram Sengamedu, Vedalam, Thirumalaipattu, Adurkolappakkam Kottagam, S. Kollur, Andili, Nerkumam, Kasbakaranai Sitheripattu, A.Gudalur, Keelakondur, Marangiyur.

Sex ratio of Scheduled Caste population is 492.

Scheduled Castes Literates and Illiterates by Sex:

	Persons	Males	Females
Literate	22,229	13,715	8,514
Illiterate	25,892	10,752	15,140
Literacy rate	54.6	66.3	42.5
Graduate	196	160	36

Scheduled Castes (Dominant):
Adi Dravida, Arunthathiyar, Dombán, Chakkiliyan Kuravan etc.

For their cultural identity please see Appendix-I

Villages without Scheduled Castes: There are 20 villages without any scheduled caste population.

Scheduled Tribes: Out of the total population of 166607 persons, 1760 persons (1.06%) belong to Scheduled Tribes.

The villages having less than 10% ST population are Melandal, Kangiyanoor, Pallichandal, Jambai Athiyandal, Murukkambadi, Konganamoor Devaradiyarkuppam, Sellanguppam, Chitapattinam Athipakkam, Kodukkapattu, Velakulam Vasanthakrishnapuram, Adhichanur, Veerapandi Pulikkal, Kallandal, Arunapuram, Ottampattu, Adukkam Thurinjikadu R.F, Veerangipuram, Kandachipuram Melvalai, Kilvalai, Othiyathur, Oduvankuppam Sithathur, Sengamedu, Madavilagam, Pudupalayam Vedalam, Appanandal, Thirumalaipattu, Vellamputhur Arasankuppam, Nayanoor, Kottamaruthur Adurkolappakkam, Sadaikkatti, Nedungampattu Kolundriampattu, Sooriyapattu, Kottagam, Kalumalam Velanthi, Agastyarmoolai, Kuladeepamangalam Kudumuratti, Manampoondi, T. Devanur Vadagarithayanur, S. Kollur, Andili, Nerkumam Emapper, Arumalai, Melakondur, V. Puttur, Kadaganur Kingilivady, V. Sithamur, Thanikalampattu, Alambadi Sathiyakandanur, Kasbakaranai, Perichanur Sennakunam, A.Gudalur, Ayandur, Kodungal, Mugaiyur Paranur, Keelakondur, Veerashozhapuram, Arkadu Arulavadi, Konagarayanur, Paiyur, Marangiyur.

The villages having more than 50% ST population are None.

Sex ratio of Scheduled tribe population is 494.

Scheduled Tribes Literates and Illiterates by Sex:

	Persons	Males	Females
Literate	571	365	206
Illiterate	1,189	526	663
Literacy rate	37.3	47.2	27.3
Graduate	5	2	3

Scheduled Tribes (Dominant):
Irular, Kattunayakan, Malakkuravan, Adiyan, Paniyan

For their cultural identity please see Appendix-II

Villages without Scheduled Tribes: There are 61 villages without any scheduled tribe population.

Literates and Illiterates by Sex (Total Population):

	Persons	Males	Females

Literate	90,769	54,400	36,369
Illiterate	75,838	29,823	46,015
Literacy rate	63	75	51
Graduate	1,696	1,252	444

Agriculture: ***Distribution of villages according to land use:*** Out of 90 villages, Total area (in hectare) is 35277.49, out of that 69.33 percent is cultivable and 47.31 percent of the cultivable area is irrigated.

Sources of Irrigation (Hectares): Government Canal 3640.31, Private Canal 0, Well without Electricity 1839.65, Well with Electricity 3131.42, Tubewell without Electricity 242.14, Tubewell with Electricity 596.17, Tank 96.14, River 0, Lake 2024.1, Waterfall 0, Others 0.

Villages with population of 5000 to 9999: Veerapandi, Kandachipuram, Arcadu.

Villages with population of 10000 and above: None

Distribution of Workers:

	Persons	Males	Females	WPR
Cultivators	23,079	17,056	6,023	28.63
Agricultural Labour	43,264	19,884	23,380	53.67
Household Industry	3,177	1,792	1,385	3.94
Other Workers	11,098	8,780	2,318	13.77
Main Workers	53,549	37,181	16,368	66.42
Marginal Workers	27,069	10,331	16,738	33.58
Total Workers	80,618	47,512	33,106	

Religion: Major Religious Communities:

	Persons	Males	Females	Sex Ratio
Hindu (89.4%)	148,951	75,472	73,479	974
Muslim (0.96%)	1,593	788	805	1,022
Christian (9.61%)	16,010	7,934	8,076	1,018
Sikh (0%)	1	1	-	-
Buddhists (0%)	3	3	-	-
Jain (0%)	6	1	5	5,000

Agewise Data:

	Persons	Males	Females	Sex Ratio
All ages	166,607	84,223	82,384	978
0-14	52,840	26,851	25,989	968
15-44	77,893	39,127	38,766	991
45-79	34,184	17,265	16,919	980
80+	1,211	737	474	643
Age not stated	479	243	236	971

Languages (Dominant):
Tamil, Telugu, Urdu, Kannada, Malayalam

Disabled Population:

	Persons	Males	Females	%
Total Disabled	5,133	2,806	2,327	
In Seeing	3,344	1,773	1,571	65.15
In Speech	328	181	147	6.39
In Hearing	203	98	105	3.95
In Movement	1,011	630	381	19.7
Mentally	247	124	123	4.81

MULANUR

Mulanur C.D. Block lies in the south-eastern part of Erode district. It is a part of Dharapuram taluk. The Block is located at a distance of 75 kms. from district headquarters. There are 17 villages in the block with the total population of 45,697 persons. Area of the C.D. Block is 353.52 sq. kms. It is bounded in the north by C.D. Block Vellakoil and district Karur, in the south by district Dindigul, in the east by district Karur, in the west by C.D. Blocks Kundadam and Dharapuram.

Communications:

Roadways : S.H.-21: Direction- Dharapuram to Karur, Nearest Villages- Thattaravalasu, Punjiyhalayur, Velampoondi, Edakkalpadi. S.H.-37: Direction- Dharapuram to Dindigul, Nearest Village- Ponnivadi.

River: Amaravathi Nadi- Nearest Villages- Thurampadi, Mulaiampoondi, Erasinampalayam, Punjiyhalayur, Senapathypalayam, Nanjaithalaiyur.

Annual Rainfall: Average Rainfall 789 mm.

Ground Water: Availability of the ground water in the Basin is 3323.95 H.A.M. and the utilization is 2105.48 H.A.M. It belongs to Safe category. Depth to water level varies from 2 to 10 meter below the ground. Most of the wells go down in summer months, according to the Ground Water Estimation Committee.

Natural Division: Kongu Nadu.

Administration

Revenue **Division:** Dharapuram. Parliamentary Constituency: 17 Erode. District: Erode. Taluk: Dharapuram. Assembly Constituency: 101 Dharapuram (SC). Gram Panchayat: 12.

Villages: 17 **Inhabited:** 17 **Uninhabited:** 0

Ranking	District	State	National
Area	6	109	2252
Population	19	366	5477
Sex Ratio	1	118	874
Child Sex Ratio	18	331	5418
Literacy Rate	5	309	2614
Density	1	2	5846
Work Participation Rate	17	373	22

Gram Panchayats:
Edakkalpadi, Erasinampalayam, Kalipalayam, Karuppanvalasu, Kilangudal, Komarapalayam, Kottamarudur, Peramium, Ponnivadi, Punjaithalaiyur, Senapathypalayam, Thurambadi, Velampoondi.

Amenities:

Education: Primary School in 17 villages, Middle school in 10 villages, Matriculation or Secondary School in 5 villages, namely Punjiyhalayur, Komarapalayam, Kilangundal,

Peramiam, Ponnivadi.

Higher Secondary or Pre University Courses or Intermediate or Junior College in 0 village of the CD Block, College in 0 village, Adult Literacy Center in 0 village.

Medical: Hospital in 0 village, Dispensary in 0 village, Health Center in 0 village, Sub Center in 15 villages, Maternity and Child Welfare Center in 8 villages, Community health workers in 0 village.

Drinking Water: Tap water in 17 villages, Tank water in 0 villages, Well water in 17 villages, Tubewell in 17 villages and more than one source in 17 villages.

Bank: Banking facility in 3 villages, namely, Arikkaranvalasu, Edakkalpadi, Ponnivadi.

Credit Society in 8 villages Agricultural Credit Society in 7 Non-Agricultural Credit Society in 3 villages.

Others: Power supply in 17 villages, Cinema hall in 0 village, sport club in 0 village, Stadium or Auditorium or Community Hall in 0 village, Post Office in 16 villages.

There are 17 villages having bus facilities.

Villages with most of facilities: Arikkaranvalasu Edakkalpadi, Ponnivadi.

Villages without Amenities (Education): None..

Scheduled Castes: Out of the total population of 45697 persons, 10881 persons (23.81%) belong to Scheduled Castes.

The villages having less than 10% SC population are None..

The villages having more than 50% SC population are None.

Sex ratio of Scheduled Caste population is 495.

Scheduled Castes Literates and Illiterates by Sex:

	Persons	Males	Females
Literate	5,188	3,144	2,044
Illiterate	5,693	2,349	3,344
Literacy rate	53.0	63.8	42.1
Graduate	48	39	9

Scheduled Castes (Dominant):

Madari, Chakkiliyan, Adi Dravida, Pallan Paraiyan etc.

For their cultural identity please see Appendix-I

Villages without Scheduled Castes: There is 1 village without any scheduled caste population.

Scheduled Tribes: Out of the total population of 45697 persons, 7 persons (0.02%) belong to Scheduled Tribes.

The villages having less than 10% ST population are Thurampadi, Mulaiampoondi, Erasinampalayam Thattaravalasu, Punjiyhalayur, Senapathypalayam Nanjaithalaiyur, Sundakkampalayam, Velampoondi Arikkaranvalasu, Edakkalpadi, Chinnamarudur Komarapalayam, Kilangundal, Kalipalayam, Peramiam Ponnivadi.

The villages having more than 50% ST population are None.

Sex ratio of Scheduled tribe population is 429.

Scheduled Tribes Literates and Illiterates by Sex:

	Persons	Males	Females
Literate	4	3	1
Illiterate	3	1	2
Literacy rate	66.7	100.0	33.3
Graduate	0	0	0

Scheduled Tribes (Dominant):

Generic Tribes etc., Malai Pandaram

For their cultural identity please see Appendix-II

Villages without Scheduled Tribes: There are 16 villages without any scheduled tribe population.

Literates and Illiterates by Sex (Total Population):

	Persons	Males	Females
Literate	25,840	15,980	9,860
Illiterate	19,857	6,751	13,106
Literacy rate	61	76	46
Graduate	529	373	156

Agriculture: ***Distribution of villages according to land use:*** Out of 17 villages, Total area (in hectare) is 35352.51, out of that 27.76 percent is cultivable and 44.59 percent of the cultivable area is irrigated.

Sources of Irrigation (Hectares): Government Canal 272.43, Private Canal 0, Well without Electricity 254.71, Well with Electricity 3347.74, Tubewell without Electricity 0, Tubewell with Electricity 0, Tank 0, River 500.6, Lake 0, Waterfall 0, Others 0.

Villages with population of 5000 to 9999: Kilangudal, Ponnivadi.

Villages with population of 10000 and above: None

Distribution of Workers:

	Persons	Males	Females	WPR
Cultivators	13,971	7,302	6,669	43.18
Agricultural Labour	12,718	5,417	7,301	39.31
Household Industry	710	392	318	2.19
Other Workers	4,954	3,614	1,340	15.31
Main Workers	30,712	16,218	14,494	94.93
Marginal Workers	1,641	507	1,134	5.07
Total Workers	32,353	16,725	15,628	

Religion: Major Religious Communities:

	Persons	Males	Females	Sex Ratio
Hindu (98.52%)	45,020	22,409	22,611	1,009
Muslim (0.46%)	212	102	110	1,078
Christian (0.86%)	395	184	211	1,147
Sikh (0.01%)	5	2	3	1,500
Buddhists (0%)	1	-	1	-
Jain (0%)	1	1	-	-

Agewise Data:

	Persons	Males	Females	Sex Ratio
All ages	45,697	22,731	22,966	1010
0-14	7,617	3,966	3,651	921
15-44	19,589	9,537	10,052	1054
45-79	17,405	8,634	8,771	1016
80+	1,027	560	467	834
Age not stated	59	34	25	735

Languages (Dominant):
Tamil, Telugu, Kannada, Gujarati, Urdu

Disabled Population:

	Persons	Males	Females	%
Total Disabled	1,384	528	856	
In Seeing	875	239	636	63.22
In Speech	116	60	56	8.38
In Hearing	84	37	47	6.07
In Movement	209	139	70	15.1
Mentally	100	53	47	7.23

MUNCHIRA

Munchira C.D. Block lies in the south-western part of Kanniyakumari district. It is a part of Vilavancode taluk. The Block is located at a distance of NA kms. from district headquarters (Nagarkoil). There are 07 villages in the block with the total population of 115,022 persons. Area of the C.D. Block is 72.03 sq. kms. It is bounded in the north by CD Block Melapuram, in the south by the Arabian Sea, in the east by CD Blocks Killiyur, Thiruvattaru, Thakkalay and Kurunthancode. It has common boundary with the state of Kerala on west and north-west.

Communications:

Roadways : N.H.-47: Direction- Thiruvananthapuram to Nager koil, Nearest Village- Kulappuram.

River: Tambraparani Nadi- Nearest Villages- Kunnathoor, Kulappuram, Arudesam, Poinkulam.

Annual Rainfall: Average Rainfall 1448 mm.

Ground Water: Availability of the ground water in the Basin is 13.71 MCM and the utilization is 3.58 MCM. It belongs to Safe category. Depth to water level varies from 5 to 10 meter below the ground. Most of the wells go down in summer months, according to the Ground Water Estimation Committee.

Coastal Villages- (Arabian Sea)- Nearest Villages- Ezhudesam, Poinkulam.

Natural Division: NA

Administration

Revenue **Division:** Padmanabhapuram. Parliamentary Constit uency: 39 Kanniyakumari. District: Kanniyakumari. Taluk: Vilavancode. Assembly Constituency: 234 Killiyur. Gram Panchayat: 11.

Border Villages- (Kerala)- Nearest Villages- Kulappuram, Methukummal, Kollemcode.

Villages: 7 **Inhabited:** 7 **Uninhabited:** 0

Ranking	District	State	National
Area	7	377	5931
Population	1	78	2998
Sex Ratio	8	201	1461
Child Sex Ratio	6	140	2599
Literacy Rate	8	10	167
Density	7	382	310
Work Participation Rate	1	1	5718

Gram Panchayats:
Kullapuram, Mancode, Munchirai, Thoothoor, Vallathurai, Vavarai, Nadaikavu, Thoothoor, Choozhai, Methukummal, Nadaikavu, Painkulam, Thoothoor.

Amenities:

Education: Primary School in 7 villages, Middle school in 7 villages, Matriculation or Secondary School in 7 villages, namely Kunnathoor, Kulappuram, Methukummal, Kollemcode, Ezhudesam, Arudesam, Poinkulam.
Higher Secondary or Pre University Courses or Intermediate or Junior College in 4 villages of the CD Block,, namely Kulappuram, Ezhudesam, Arudesam, Poinkulam. College in 0 village, Adult Literacy Center in 0 village.

Medical: Hospital in 1 village, Dispensary in 3 villages, Health Center in 3 villages, Sub Center in 7 villages, Maternity and Child Welfare Center in 2 villages, Community health workers in 0 village.
The Villages having Hospital or Dispensary or Health Center are Kunnathoor, Kulappuram, Arudesam, Poinkulam.

Drinking Water: Tap water in 7 villages, Tank water in 0 villages, Well water in 7 villages, Tubewell in 7 villages and more than one source in 7 villages.

Bank: Banking facility in 5 villages, namely, Kunnathoor, Kulappuram, Kollemcode, Arudesam Poinkulam.
Credit Society in 6 villages Agricultural Credit Society in 5 Non-Agricultural Credit Society in 4 villages.

Others: Power supply in 7 villages, Cinema hall in 1 village, sport club in 1 village, Stadium or Auditorium or Community Hall in 0 village, Post Office in 7 villages.
There are 7 villages having bus facilities.

Villages with most of facilities: Kunnathoor Kulappuram, Kollemcode, Arudesam, Poinkulam.

Villages without Amenities (Education): None..

Scheduled Castes: Out of the total population of 115022 persons, 2045 persons (1.78%) belong to Scheduled Castes. The villages having less than 10% SC population are Kunnathoor, Kulappuram, Methukummal, Kollemcode Ezhudesam, Arudesam, Poinkulam.
The villages having more than 50% SC population are

None.

Sex ratio of Scheduled Caste population is 517.

Scheduled Castes Literates and Illiterates by Sex:

	Persons	Males	Females
Literate	1,543	786	757
Illiterate	502	201	301
Literacy rate	85.2	89.1	81.4
Graduate	64	33	31

Scheduled Castes (Dominant):

Ayyanavar, Paraiyan etc., Thandan, Pulayan etc. Kavara

For their cultural identity please see Appendix-I

Villages without Scheduled Castes: There is 0 village without any scheduled caste population.

Scheduled Tribes: Out of the total population of 115022 persons, 118 persons (0.1%) belong to Scheduled Tribes. The villages having less than 10% ST population are Kunnathoor, Kulappuram, Methukummal, Kollemcode Ezhudesam, Arudesam, Poinkulam.

The villages having more than 50% ST population are None.

Sex ratio of Scheduled tribe population is 492.

Scheduled Tribes Literates and Illiterates by Sex:

	Persons	Males	Females
Literate	84	45	39
Illiterate	34	15	19
Literacy rate	84.9	91.8	78.0
Graduate	0	0	0

Scheduled Tribes (Dominant):

Malai Pandaram, Kaniyan etc.

For their cultural identity please see Appendix-II

Villages without Scheduled Tribes: There are 5 villages without any scheduled tribe population.

Literates and Illiterates by Sex (Total Population):

	Persons	Males	Females
Literate	85,701	44,520	41,181
Illiterate	29,321	13,192	16,129
Literacy rate	84	88	81
Graduate	4,270	2,068	2,202

Agriculture: ***Distribution of villages according to land use:*** Out of 7 villages, Total area (in hectare) is 7203, out of that 82.64 percent is cultivable and 16.77 percent of the cultivable area is irrigated.

Sources of Irrigation (Hectares): Government Canal 270.65, Private Canal 0, Well without Electricity 0, Well with Electricity 79.29, Tubewell without Electricity 0, Tubewell with Electricity 43.23, Tank 615.89, River 0, Lake 0, Waterfall 0, Others 32.62.

Villages with population of 5000 to 9999:

Kollencode.

Villages with population of 10000 and above:

Kunnathoor, Kulappuram, Methukummal, Ezhudesam Arudesam, Painkulam.

Distribution of Workers:

	Persons	Males	Females	WPR
Cultivators	1,111	883	228	2.94
Agricultural Labour	3,841	3,396	445	10.16
Household Industry	1,710	822	888	4.52
Other Workers	31,156	24,978	6,178	82.38
Main Workers	29,151	23,644	5,507	77.08
Marginal Workers	8,667	6,435	2,232	22.92
Total Workers	37,818	30,079	7,739	

Religion: Major Religious Communities:

	Persons	Males	Females	Sex Ratio
Hindu (42.06%)	48,373	24,353	24,020	986
Muslim (3.83%)	4,401	2,145	2,256	1,052
Christian (54.08%)	62,209	31,189	31,020	995
Sikh (0%)	1	1	-	-
Buddhists (0%)	-	-	-	-
Jain (0%)	1	1	-	-

Agewise Data:

	Persons	Males	Females	Sex Ratio
All ages	115,022	57,712	57,310	993
0-14	29,758	15,027	14,731	980
15-44	59,310	29,553	29,757	1007
45-79	24,646	12,477	12,169	975
80+	1,069	523	546	1044
Age not stated	239	132	107	811

Languages (Dominant):

Tamil, Malayalam, Telugu, Kannada, Urdu

Disabled Population:

	Persons	Males	Females	%
Total Disabled	3,997	1,661	2,336	
In Seeing	2,433	699	1,734	60.87
In Speech	207	122	85	5.18
In Hearing	109	55	54	2.73
In Movement	990	635	355	24.77
Mentally	258	150	108	6.45

MUSIRI

Musiri C.D. Block lies in the northern part of Tiruchirappalli district. It is a part of Musiri taluk. The Block is located at a distance of 40 kms. from district headquarters (Tiruchirappalli). There are 32 villages in the block with the total population of 96,461 persons. Area of the C.D. Block is 331.23 sq. kms. It is bounded in the north by CD Block Thuraiyur, in the south by district Karur and CD Block Andanallur, in the east by district Perambalur and CD Block Manachanallur, in the west by CD Blocks Thottiyam and Thathaiyangarpettai.

Communications:

Roadways : S.H.-25: Direction- Thottiyam to Tiruchirappalli,

Nearest Villages- Sevanthalingapuram, Umayalpuram, Vellur, Ayyampalayam, Evoor, Amoor, Gunaseelam. S.H.-30: Direction- Musiri to Thuraiyur, Nearest Villages- Perur, Thiruthaliyur.

River: Cauvery Nadi- Nearest Villages- Sevanthalingapuram, Umayalpuram, Vellur, Ayyampalayam, Evoor, Gunaseelam. Amoor.

Annual Rainfall: Average Rainfall 841 mm.

Ground Water: Availability of the ground water in the Basin is 4626.74 H.A.M. and the utilization is 4544.24 H.A.M. It belongs to Critical category. Depth to water level varies from 2 to 10 meter below the ground. Most of the wells go down in summer months, according to the Ground Water Estimation Committee.

Natural Division: Chola Nadu.

Administration

Revenue **Division:** Musiri. Parliamentary Constituency: 25 Perambalur, 24 Tiruchirappalli. District: Tiruchirappalli. Taluk: Musiri. Assembly Constituency: 145 Musiri, 146 Thuraiyur (SC), 144 Manachanallur. Gram Panchayat: 33.

Villages: 32 **Inhabited:** 32 **Uninhabited:** 0

Ranking	District	State	National
Area	6	134	2453
Population	6	147	3572
Sex Ratio	6	125	932
Child Sex Ratio	4	79	1598
Literacy Rate	7	124	1280
Density	9	149	3624
Work Participation Rate	7	236	1486

Gram Panchayats:

Abinimangalam, Amoor, Ayyampalayam, Evoor, Kamatchipatti, Jeyankondan, Karattampatti, Kattukulam, Kodunthurai, Komangalam, Kottathur, Manparai, Moovanur, Neyveli, Peramangalam, Perur, Pulivalam, Puthanampatti, Sathanur, Thandalaiputhur, Sithambur, Sukkampatty, T.Pudupatti, Thandalaiputhur, Thinnakkonam, Thinnanur, Thiruthalaiyur, Thiruthiyamalai, Veliyanur, Vellakkalpatti, Vellore, Vellore , Vengaimandalam.

Amenities:

Education: Primary School in 32 villages, Middle school in 21 villages, Matriculation or Secondary School in 11 villages, namely Thiruthaliyur, Thinanur, Kottathur, Puthanampatty, Abinimangalam, Pulivalam, T.Putthur, Moovaanur, Vellur, Ayyampalayam, Amoor.

Higher Secondary or Pre University Courses or Intermediate or Junior College in 4 villages of the CD Block,, namely Thiruthaliyur, Abinimangalam, Pulivalam, T.Putthur.

College in 0 village, Adult Literacy Center in 0 village.

Medical: Hospital in 1 village, Dispensary in 6 villages, Health Center in 5 villages, Sub Center in 3 villages, Maternity and Child Welfare Center in 3 villages, Community health workers in 12 villages.

The Villages having Hospital or Dispensary or Health Center are Kottathur, Pulivalam, T.Putthur, Komangalam, Naiveli, Thinnakonam, Sithambur.

Drinking Water: Tap water in 32 villages, Tank water in 5 villages, Well water in 32 villages, Tubewell in 32 villages and more than one source in 32 villages.

Bank: Banking facility in 3 villages, namely, Puthanampatty, Pulivalam, Amoor.

Credit Society in 10 villages Agricultural Credit Society in 10 Non-Agricultural Credit Society in 0 village.

Others: Power supply in 31 villages, Cinema hall in 0 village, sport club in 0 village, Stadium or Auditorium or Community Hall in 0 village, Post Office in 27 villages.

There are 31 villages having bus facilities.

Villages with most of facilities: Puthanampatty Pulivalam, Amoor.

Villages without Amenities (Education): None..

Scheduled Castes: Out of the total population of 96461 persons, 22464 persons (23.29%) belong to Scheduled Castes. The villages having less than 10% SC population are T.Pudupatti, Jayankondan, Kamachipatty Thiruthiyamalai, Vengaimandalam, Moovaanur Komangalam, Thinnakonam.

The villages having more than 50% SC population are None.

Sex ratio of Scheduled Caste population is 510.

Scheduled Castes Literates and Illiterates by Sex:

	Persons	Males	Females
Literate	13,252	7,653	5,599
Illiterate	9,212	3,363	5,849
Literacy rate	67.0	79.0	55.5
Graduate	648	482	166

Scheduled Castes (Dominant):

Pallan, Paraiyan etc., Chakkiliyan, Adi Dravida Arunthathiyar

For their cultural identity please see Appendix-I

Villages without Scheduled Castes: There is 0 village without any scheduled caste population.

Scheduled Tribes: Out of the total population of 96461 persons, 285 persons (0.3%) belong to Scheduled Tribes. The villages having less than 10% ST population are Thiruthaliyur, T.Pudupatti, Karattampatti, Thinanur Kottathur, Puthanampatty, Abinimangalam, Pulivalam Manaparai, Sukkampatti, Jayankondan, Perur Kamachipatty, T.Putthur, Thiruthiyamalai Vengaimandalam, Moovaanur, Peramangalam, Kattukulam

Komangalam, Naiveli, Thinnakonam, Mooveli Sevanthalingapuram, Umayalpuram, Vellur Ayyampalayam, Evoor, Kodunduri, Sithambur, Amoor Gunaseelam.

The villages having more than 50% ST population are None.

Sex ratio of Scheduled tribe population is 481.

Scheduled Tribes Literates and Illiterates by Sex:

	Persons	Males	Females
Literate	230	123	107
Illiterate	55	25	30
Literacy rate	90.6	95.4	85.6
Graduate	15	8	7

Scheduled Tribes (Dominant):

Kondareddis, Malakkuravan, Malai Pandaram Kattunayakan, Kurumans

For their cultural identity please see Appendix-II

Villages without Scheduled Tribes: There are 27 villages without any scheduled tribe population.

Literates and Illiterates by Sex (Total Population):

	Persons	Males	Females
Literate	59,543	34,458	25,085
Illiterate	36,918	13,572	23,346
Literacy rate	69	81	58
Graduate	2,306	1,685	621

Agriculture: ***Distribution of villages according to land use:*** Out of 32 villages, Total area (in hectare) is 33123.51, out of that 51.73 percent is cultivable and 39.82 percent of the cultivable area is irrigated.

Sources of Irrigation (Hectares): Government Canal 1960.94, Private Canal 0, Well without Electricity 652.41, Well with Electricity 4054.18, Tubewell without Electricity 68.71, Tubewell with Electricity 77.77, Tank 8.58, River 0, Lake 0, Waterfall 0, Others 0.

Villages with population of 5000 to 9999: Perur, Ayyampalayam.

Villages with population of 10000 and above: None

Distribution of Workers:

	Persons	Males	Females	WPR
Cultivators	16,943	10,709	6,234	32.55
Agricultural Labour	22,490	10,017	12,473	43.21
Household Industry	2,423	1,123	1,300	4.66
Other Workers	10,194	7,584	2,610	19.59
Main Workers	45,551	27,406	18,145	87.51
Marginal Workers	6,499	2,027	4,472	12.49
Total Workers	52,050	29,433	22,617	

Religion: Major Religious Communities:

	Persons	Males	Females	Sex Ratio
Hindu (97.9%)	94,439	47,081	47,358	1,006
Muslim (1.7%)	1,641	766	875	1,142
Christian (0.2%)	190	91	99	1,088
Sikh (0%)	1	-	1	-
Buddhists (0%)	-	-	-	-
Jain (0%)	-	-	-	-

Agewise Data:

	Persons	Males	Females	Sex Ratio
All ages	96,461	48,030	48,431	1008
0-14	24,934	12,752	12,182	955
15-44	46,384	22,691	23,693	1044
45-79	24,155	12,049	12,106	1005
80+	878	476	402	845
Age not stated	110	62	48	774

Languages (Dominant):

Tamil, Telugu, Urdu, Kannada, Malayalam

Disabled Population:

	Persons	Males	Females	%
Total Disabled	2,627	1,160	1,467	
In Seeing	1,576	546	1,030	59.99
In Speech	197	106	91	7.5
In Hearing	142	74	68	5.41
In Movement	538	353	185	20.48
Mentally	174	81	93	6.62

MUTHUPET

Muttupet C.D. Block lies in the southern part of Thiruvarur district. It is a part of Thirthuraipoondi taluk. The Block is located at a distance of 58 kms. from district headquarters (Thiruvarur). There are 37 villages in the block with the total population of 75,721 persons. Area of the C.D. Block is 351.69 sq. kms. It is bounded in the north by C.D. Blocks Kottur and Thiruthuraipoondi, in the south by the Palk Strait, in the east by district Nagappatinam, and in the west by district Thanjavur.

Communications:

Roadways : Information not Available.

Railway Station: Udayamarthandapuram, Muthupettai.

River: Palampandiyar Nadi- Nearest Villages- Ariyalur, Maruthavanam, Mangudi, Vanganagar, Ovarur, Edaiyur, Keelaperumalai, Udayamarthandapuram, Melaperumalai, Idumbavanam, Thillaiviagam, Thondiakkadu, Saltswampmuthupet RF. Korayar Nadi- Nearest Villages- Thol Pinnathur, Uppur, Alangadu, Jambuvandai, Veeranvayal, Thillaiviagam, Kaluvankadu, Duraikkadu RF. Valavanar Nadi- Nearest Villages- Kunnalur, Vilangadu, Muthupet RF.

Annual Rainfall: Average Rainfall 1184 mm.

Ground Water: Availability of the ground water in the Basin is (Information not available) H.A.M. and the utilization is (Information not available) H.A.M. It belongs to (Information not available) category. Depth to water level varies from 2 to 10 meter below the ground. Most of the wells go down in summer months, according to the Ground Water Estimation Committee.

Coastal Villages- (Palk Strait)- Villages- Duraikkadu RF, Thillaiviagam, Salt Swamp Muthupet RF, Muthupet RF.
Forest and Reserved Forest: (Muthupet RF)- Nearest Village- Muthupet RF. (Salt Swamp Muthupet)- Nearest Villages- Thillaiviagam, Thondiakkadu, Karppaganathar Kulam, Salt Swamp Muthupet RF. (Thuraikkadu)- Nearest Villages- Duraikkadu RF, Jambuvandai, Thillaiviagam.
Natural Division: Chola Nadu.

Administration

Revenue **Division:** Mannargudi. Parliamentary Constituency: 28 Nagapattinam (SC). District: Thiruvarur. Taluk: Thiruthuraipoondi. Assembly Constituency: 166 Thiruthuraipoondi (SC). Gram Panchayat: 29.

Villages: 37 **Inhabited:** 34 **Uninhabited:** 3

Ranking	District	State	National
Area	1	114	2267
Population	10	266	4265
Sex Ratio	1	40	394
Child Sex Ratio	9	180	3085
Literacy Rate	8	86	1005
Density	3	290	4510
Work Participation Rate	10	313	3207

Gram Panchayats:

Alangadu, Ariyalur, Edaiyur, Idumbavanam, Jamlbuvanodai , Karpaganatharkulam, Keelakadu, Keelanammankurichi , Keelapandivenpencheri, Keelaperumazhai, Kullikudy, Kunnalur , Mangudi, Maruthuvanam, Melammankurichi, Melapermazhai, Milangadu, Ovarur, Pandy, Pinnathur, Sanganthi, Thillaivilagam , Tholi, Thondiyakkadu, Udayamurthandapuram, Uppur, Vadakadu, Vadasanganthi, Vanganagar.

Amenities:

Education: Primary School in 33 villages, Middle school in 12 villages, Matriculation or Secondary School in 5 villages, namely Edaiyur, Udayamarthandapuram, Idumbavanam, Muthupettai, Thillaiviagam.

Higher Secondary or Pre University Courses or Intermediate or Junior College in 4 villages of the CD Block,, namely Edaiyur, Idumbavanam, Muthupettai, Thillaiviagam.

College in 0 village, Adult Literacy Center in 0 village.

Medical: Hospital in 0 village, Dispensary in 4 villages, Health Center in 7 villages, Sub Center in 13 villages, Maternity and Child Welfare Center in 0 village, Community health workers in 34 villages.

The Villages having Hospital or Dispensary or Health Center are Keelaperumalai, Muthupettai, Thillaiviagam, Karppaganathar Kulam.

Drinking Water: Tap water in 34 villages, Tank water in 3 villages, Well water in 34 villages, Tubewell in 34 villages and more than one source in 34 villages.

Bank: Banking facility in 5 villages, namely, Udayamarthandapuram, Idumbavanam, Muthupettai Jambuvandai, Thillaiviagam.

Credit Society in 15 villages Agricultural Credit Society in 15 Non-Agricultural Credit Society in 1 village.

Others: Power supply in 34 villages, Cinema hall in 1 village, sport club in 0 village, Stadium or Auditorium or Community Hall in 0 village, Post Office in 22 villages.

There are 29 villages having bus facilities.

Villages with most of facilities: Udayamarthandapuram Idumbavanam, Muthupettai, Thillaiviagam.

Villages without amenities (Education): Kaluvankadu..

Scheduled Castes: Out of the total population of 75721 persons, 23600 persons (31.17%) belong to Scheduled Castes.

The villages having less than 10% SC population are Vilangadu, Uppur, Alangadu, Kaluvankadu Thondiakkadu, Karppaganathar Kulam.

The villages having more than 50% SC population are Maruthavanam, Mangudi, Vanganagar, Pandi, Kallikkudi Tholi, Ekkal, Kunnalur, Muthupettai Keelanammankuruchi.

Sex ratio of Scheduled Caste population is 506.

Scheduled Castes Literates and Illiterates by Sex:

	Persons	Males	Females
Literate	12,917	7,413	5,504
Illiterate	10,683	4,238	6,445
Literacy rate	63.6	74.6	53.0
Graduate	195	153	42

Scheduled Castes (Dominant):

Pallan, Paraiyan etc., Koliyan, Kuravan etc. Vettiyan

For their cultural identity please see Appendix-I

Villages without Scheduled Castes: There are 5 villages without any scheduled caste population.

Scheduled Tribes: Out of the total population of 75721 persons, 118 persons (0.16%) belong to Scheduled Tribes.

The villages having less than 10% ST population are Maruthavanam, Mangudi, Vanganagar, Pandi, Kallikkudi Ovarur, Ariyalur, Tholi, Vadasanganthi, Sanganthi Edaiyur, Kilapandi, Ekkal, Kunnalur, Keelaperumalai Pinnathur, Udayamarthandapuram, Melaperumalai Vilangadu, Idumbavanam, Uppur, Alangadu, Vadakadu Muthupettai, Melanammankuruchi, Keelanammankuruchi Mangal, Duraikkadu, Jambuvandai, Veeranvayal Thillaiviagam, Kaluvankadu, Thondiakkadu Karppaganathar Kulam.

The villages having more than 50% ST population are

None.

Sex ratio of Scheduled tribe population is 508.

Scheduled Tribes Literates and Illiterates by Sex:

	Persons	Males	Females
Literate	31	17	14
Illiterate	87	41	46
Literacy rate	33.3	37.8	29.2
Graduate	0	0	0

Scheduled Tribes (Dominant):

Kondareddis, Kattunayakan, Adiyan

For their cultural identity please see Appendix-II

Villages without Scheduled Tribes: There are 30 villages without any scheduled tribe population.

Literates and Illiterates by Sex (Total Population):

	Persons	Males	Females
Literate	47,743	27,002	20,741
Illiterate	27,978	10,148	17,830
Literacy rate	72	83	61
Graduate	664	525	139

Agriculture: ***Distribution of villages according to land use:*** Out of 37 villages, Total area (in hectare) is 35169.89, out of that 41.22 percent is cultivable and 82.75 percent of the cultivable area is irrigated.

Sources of Irrigation (Hectares): Government Canal 11972.25, Private Canal 0, Well without Electricity 0, Well with Electricity 0, Tubewell without Electricity 0, Tubewell with Electricity 24.12, Tank 0, River 0, Lake 0, Waterfall 0, Others 0.

Villages with population of 5000 to 9999: Udayamarthandapuram, Idumbavanam, Thillaivilagam.

Villages with population of 10000 and above: None

Distribution of Workers:

	Persons	Males	Females	WPR
Cultivators	7,317	5,605	1,712	20.75
Agricultural Labour	21,767	11,181	10,586	61.73
Household Industry	616	301	315	1.75
Other Workers	5,563	4,852	711	15.78
Main Workers	26,055	18,460	7,595	73.89
Marginal Workers	9,208	3,479	5,729	26.11
Total Workers	35,263	21,939	13,324	

Religion: Major Religious Communities:

	Persons	Males	Females	Sex Ratio
Hindu (96.26%)	72,892	35,825	37,067	1,035
Muslim (2.69%)	2,038	929	1,109	1,194
Christian (0.96%)	727	365	362	992
Sikh (0%)	-	-	-	-
Buddhists (0%)	-	-	-	-
Jain (0%)	1	-	1	-

Agewise Data:

	Persons	Males	Females	Sex Ratio
All ages	75,721	37,150	38,571	1038
0-14	19,762	10,083	9,679	960
15-44	36,869	17,660	19,209	1088
45-79	18,384	9,042	9,342	1033
80+	627	330	297	900
Age not stated	79	35	44	1257

Languages (Dominant):

Tamil, Telugu, Kannada, Hindi, Urdu

Disabled Population:

	Persons	Males	Females	%
Total Disabled	2,620	1,215	1,405	
In Seeing	1,459	543	916	55.69
In Speech	223	129	94	8.51
In Hearing	115	54	61	4.39
In Movement	538	346	192	20.53
Mentally	285	143	142	10.88

NAGAPATTINAM

Nagapattinam C.D. Block lies in the south-eastern part of Nagapattinam district. It is a part of Nagapattinam taluk. The Block is located at a distance of (00) kms. from district headquarters (Nagapattinam). There are 31 villages in the block with the total population of 76,374 persons. Area of the C.D. Block is 105.06 sq. kms. It is bounded in the north by C.D. Block Thirumarugal, in the south by CD Block Keelaiyur, in the east by the Bay of Bengal, in the west by CD Blocks Thirumarugal and Kilvelur.

Communications:

Roadways : N.H.-67: Direction- Thiruvanur to Nagapattinam, Nearest Villages- Themangalam, Ivanallur, Andanapettai, Poravacheri, Sikkal, Nagore-Muttam, Thetthi, Nagappattinam.

Railway Station: Nagore - Muttam, Andanapettai, Sikkal.

Backwards Region Grants Fund: It receives Backward Region Grants.

Annual Rainfall: Average Rainfall 1230 mm.

Ground Water: Availability of the ground water in the Basin is (Information not available) H.A.M. and the utilization is (Information not available) H.A.M. It belongs to (Information not available) category. Depth to water level varies from 2 to 5 meter below the ground. Most of the wells go down in summer months, according to the Ground Water Estimation Committee.

Coastal Villages- (Bay of Bengal)- Nearest Villages- Nagore - Muttam, Vadakkupoygainallur, South Poigainallur.

Natural Division: Chola Nadu.

Administration

Revenue **Division:** Nagapattinam. Parliamentary Constituency: 28 Nagapattinam (SC). District: Nagapattinam. Taluk: Nagapattinam. Assembly Constituency: 163 Nagapattinam, 164 Kilvelur (SC). Gram Panchayat: 29.

Villages: 31 **Inhabited:** 30 **Uninhabited:** 1

Ranking	District	State	National
Area	11	367	5661
Population	8	262	4234
Sex Ratio	7	123	921
Child Sex Ratio	1	11	422
Literacy Rate	1	27	434
Density	8	355	1409
Work Participation Rate	1	21	4467

Gram Panchayats:

Agalangan, Agaraorathur, Akkaraipettai, Alangudi, Aliyur, Andanapettai, Avarani, Ivanallur, Karuvelangadai, Kuruchi, Mahadanam, Manjakollai, Muttam, Orathur, Palaiyur, Pappakovil, Perungadambanur, Poravacheri, Puduchery, Sembiyanmahadevi, Sengamangalam, Sikkal, Themangalam, Therkupoigainallur, Thethi, Vadakkupoigainallur, Vadakudi, Vadavoor, Vadugachery.

Amenities:

Education: Primary School in 28 villages, Middle school in 15 villages, Matriculation or Secondary School in 8 villages, namely Nagore - Muttam, Themangalam, Andanapettai, Sikkal, Vadakkupoygainallur, Orathur, Puduchery, Kurichi.

Higher Secondary or Pre University Courses or Intermediate or Junior College in 2 villages of the CD Block,, namely Andanapettai, Sikkal.

College in 1 village, Adult Literacy Center in 0 village., College is in village, namely Thetthi.

Medical: Hospital in 5 villages, Dispensary in 2 villages, Health Center in 2 villages, Sub Center in 12 villages, Maternity and Child Welfare Center in 0 village, Community health workers in 30 villages.

The Villages having Hospital or Dispensary or Health Center are Nagore - Muttam, Sirangudipuliyur, Andanapettai, Sikkal, Mahadanam, Vadavoor, Sembianmahadevi.

Drinking Water: Tap water in 30 villages, Tank water in 6 villages, Well water in 30 villages, Tubewell in 30 villages and more than one source in 30 villages.

Bank: Banking facility in 5 villages, namely, Nagore - Muttam, Themangalam, Sikkal, Kurichi Sembianmahadevi.

Credit Society in 4 villages Agricultural Credit Society in 4 Non-Agricultural Credit Society in 0 village.

Others: Power supply in 30 villages, Cinema hall in 1 village, sport club in 0 village, Stadium or Auditorium or Community Hall in 0 village, Post Office in 17 villages.

There are 29 villages having bus facilities.

Villages with most of facilities: Nagore - Muttam Themangalam, Sikkal, Kurichi, Sembianmahadevi.

Villages without amenities (Education): Sellur, Ponveli..

Scheduled Castes: Out of the total population of 76374 persons, 26281 persons (34.41%) belong to Scheduled Castes. The villages having less than 10% SC population are None..

The villages having more than 50% SC population are Perungadambanur, Vadagudi, Thetthi, Sangamangalam Sellur, Ivanallur, Abaranadari, Ponveli, Pappakovil Karuvelankadai, Orathur, Agaraorathur, Puduchery Alangudi, Vadugachery, Mahadanam, Agalangan.

Sex ratio of Scheduled Caste population is 503.

Scheduled Castes Literates and Illiterates by Sex:

	Persons	Males	Females
Literate	15,198	8,811	6,387
Illiterate	11,083	4,258	6,825
Literacy rate	68.7	80.0	57.5
Graduate	198	150	48

Scheduled Castes (Dominant):

Paraiyan etc., Pallan, Adi Dravida, Valluvan, Domban

For their cultural identity please see Appendix-I

Villages without Scheduled Castes: There is 1 village without any scheduled caste population.

Scheduled Tribes: Out of the total population of 76374 persons, 78 persons (0.1%) belong to Scheduled Tribes. The villages having less than 10% ST population are Perungadambanur, Vadagudi, Nagore - Muttam, Thetthi Palaiyur, Elangadambanoor, Themangalam Sirangudipuliyur, Sangamangalam, Sellur, Ivanallur Andanapettai, Poravacheri, Sikkal, Abaranadari Ponveli, Pappakovil, Vadakkupoygainallur Karuvelankadai, Orathur, Agaraorathur, Puduchery Alangudi, Vadugachery, Mahadanam, Vadavoor South Poigainallur, Kurichi, Agalangan Sembianmahadevi.

The villages having more than 50% ST population are None.

Sex ratio of Scheduled tribe population is 462.

Scheduled Tribes Literates and Illiterates by Sex:

	Persons	Males	Females
Literate	54	33	21
Illiterate	24	9	15
Literacy rate	79.4	86.8	70.0
Graduate	1	1	0

Scheduled Tribes (Dominant):

Malakkuravan, Kattunayakan, Malai Pandaram, Palliyar

For their cultural identity please see Appendix-II

Villages without Scheduled Tribes: There are 24 villages without any scheduled tribe population.

Literates and Illiterates by Sex (Total Population):

	Persons	Males	Females
Literate	51,613	28,713	22,900
Illiterate	24,761	9,308	15,453
Literacy rate	78	87	69
Graduate	1,205	875	330

Agriculture: ***Distribution of villages according to land use:*** Out of 31 villages, Total area (in hectare) is 10506.14, out of that 72.32 percent is cultivable and 88.1 percent of the cultivable area is irrigated.

Sources of Irrigation (Hectares): Government Canal 6694.14, Private Canal 0, Well without Electricity 0, Well with Electricity 0, Tubewell without Electricity 0, Tubewell with Electricity 0, Tank 0, River 0, Lake 0, Waterfall 0, Others 0.

Villages with population of 5000 to 9999:
Andanapettai , Sikkal.

Villages with population of 10000 and above:
Vadakkupoigainallur.

Distribution of Workers:

	Persons	Males	Females	WPR
Cultivators	2,588	2,053	535	8.53
Agricultural Labour	15,815	8,735	7,080	52.12
Household Industry	479	287	192	1.58
Other Workers	11,464	9,948	1,516	37.78
Main Workers	24,416	18,060	6,356	80.46
Marginal Workers	5,930	2,963	2,967	19.54
Total Workers	30,346	21,023	9,323	

Religion: Major Religious Communities:

	Persons	Males	Females	Sex Ratio
Hindu (90.82%)	69,364	34,678	34,686	1,000
Muslim (7.48%)	5,716	2,689	3,027	1,126
Christian (1.65%)	1,262	636	626	984
Sikh (0%)	1	-	1	-
Buddhists (0%)	3	2	1	500
Jain (0%)	3	1	2	2,000

Agewise Data:

	Persons	Males	Females	Sex Ratio
All ages	76,374	38,021	38,353	1009
0-14	23,061	11,636	11,425	982
15-44	37,299	18,453	18,846	1021
45-79	14,916	7,428	7,488	1008
80+	529	231	298	1290
Age not stated	569	273	296	1084

Languages (Dominant):
Tamil, Telugu, Malayalam, Hindi, Kannada

Disabled Population:

	Persons	Males	Females	%
Total Disabled	2,252	973	1,279	
In Seeing	1,419	457	962	63.01
In Speech	149	83	66	6.62
In Hearing	75	35	40	3.33
In Movement	433	288	145	19.23
Mentally	176	110	66	7.82

NAINARKOIL

Nainarkoil C.D. Block lies in the northern part of Ramanathapuram district. It is a part of Paramakudi taluk. The taluk is located at a distance of 38 kms. from district headquarters (Ramanathapuram). There are 36 villages in the block with the total population of 45,279 persons. Area of the C.D. Block is 241.95 sq. kms. It is bounded in the north by district Sivaganga, in the south by CD Blocks Bogalur and Ramanathapuram, in the east by CD Blocks R.S. Mangalam and Ramanathapuram, in the west by district Sivaganga and CD Block Paramakudi.

Communications:

Roadways : S.H.-34: Direction- Ilayangudi to Ramanathapuram, Nearest Villages- Rathapuli, Thalaiyadikottai, Vaniyavallam, Vallam, Sirakikottai, Gangaikondan, Thethangal, Kulathur, Pandiyoor.

River: Vaigai Nadi- Nearest Villages- Sirakikottai, Gangaikondan, Kulathur.

Annual Rainfall: Average Rainfall 827 mm.

Ground Water: Availability of the ground water in the Basin is 5508.94 H.A.M. and the utilization is 902.20 H.A.M. It belongs to Safe category. Depth to water level varies from 2 to 10 meter below the ground. Most of the wells go down in summer months, according to the Ground Water Estimation Committee.

Natural Division: NA

Administration

Revenue **Division:** Paramakudi. Parliamentary Constituency: 35 Ramanathapuram. District: Ramanathapuram. Taluk: Paramakudi. Assembly Constituency: 209 Paramakudi (SC). Gram Panchayat: 37.

Villages: 36 **Inhabited:** 36 **Uninhabited:** 0

Ranking	District	State	National
Area	9	239	3482
Population	10	367	5492
Sex Ratio	2	12	156
Child Sex Ratio	4	62	1297
Literacy Rate	9	192	1762
Density	1	38	4927
Work Participation Rate	6	336	308

Gram Panchayats:

A.Panaiyur, Akkirameri, Anjamadai, Araganur, Ariyankottai, Arumbur , Attangudi, Gangaikondam, Kalliyadiyendal, Karadarthakudi, Keelakavaloor, Kiliyur, Koluvur, Kottagudi , Kulathur, Manakudi, Mumudisathan, Nagaram, Kottakudi , Nagaramangalam, Melapaniyur , Nainarkoil, P.Kodikulam, Pagaivenri,

Pandiyur, Panthappanendal, Perungalur, Pottagavayal, Radhapuli , Sathurvedamangalam, Sirakikottai, Siruvayal, Thalayadikottai, Thavaikulam, Thethangal, Thiyagavanseri, Vadavaneri , Vallam, Vanavayal, Vaniyavallam.

Amenities:

Education: Primary School in 28 villages, Middle school in 11 villages, Matriculation or Secondary School in 6 villages, namely Karadarnthakudi, Vaniyavallam, Pottagavayal, Siruvayal, Kiliyur, Kulathur.

Higher Secondary or Pre University Courses or Intermediate or Junior College in 0 village of the CD Block, College in 0 village, Adult Literacy Center in 0 village.

Medical: Hospital in 0 village, Dispensary in 0 village, Health Center in 0 village, Sub Center in 5 villages, Maternity and Child Welfare Center in 1 village, Community health workers in 0 village.

Drinking Water: Tap water in 36 villages, Tank water in 14 villages, Well water in 36 villages, Tubewell in 36 villages and more than one source in 36 villages.

Bank: Banking facility in 4 villages, namely, Vadavaneri, Vaniyavallam, Kottakudi, Pottagavayal.

Credit Society in 7 villages Agricultural Credit Society in 6 Non-Agricultural Credit Society in 1 village.

Others: Power supply in 36 villages, Cinema hall in 0 village, sport club in 0 village, Stadium or Auditorium or Community Hall in 0 village, Post Office in 15 villages.

There are 33 villages having bus facilities.

Villages with most of facilities: None.

Villages without amenities (Education): Sethukal, Koluvoor, Gangaikondan, Perungalur..

Scheduled Castes: Out of the total population of 45279 persons, 10154 persons (22.43%) belong to Scheduled Castes.

The villages having less than 10% SC population are Nagaram, Thalaiyadikottai, Manakkudi, Sethukal Panthappananthal, Sirakikottai, P. Kodikulam.

The villages having more than 50% SC population are None.

Sex ratio of Scheduled Caste population is 508.

Scheduled Castes Literates and Illiterates by Sex:

	Persons	Males	Females
Literate	5,492	3,238	2,254
Illiterate	4,662	1,756	2,906
Literacy rate	61.9	74.4	49.8
Graduate	103	82	21

Scheduled Castes (Dominant):

Pallan, Paraiyan etc., Chakkiliyan, Puthirai Vannan Valluvan

For their cultural identity please see Appendix-I

Villages without Scheduled Castes: There is 1 village without any scheduled caste population.

Scheduled Tribes: Out of the total population of 45279 persons, 4 persons (0.01%) belong to Scheduled Tribes.

The villages having less than 10% ST population are Rathapuli, Karadarnthakudi, Vadavaneri, Ariyankottai Attangudi, Nagaram, Nagaramangalam, Thalaiyadikottai Vaniyavallam, A. Katchan, Thavalaikulam, Kottakudi Manakkudi, Vagavayal, Pottagavayal, Sethukal Koluvoor, Panthappananthal, Periyannthal, Akkiramesi Vallam, Sirakikottai, Chithananthal, S.V. Mangalam P. Kodikulam, Arasanur, Siruvayal, Paniyur, Kiliyur Thiyagavanseri, Mummudisathan, Pandiyoor Gangaikondan, Thethangal, Kulathur, Perungalur.

The villages having more than 50% ST population are None.

Sex ratio of Scheduled tribe population is 250.

Scheduled Tribes Literates and Illiterates by Sex:

	Persons	Males	Females
Literate	4	3	1
Illiterate	0	0	0
Literacy rate	100.0	100.0	100.0
Graduate	0	0	0

Scheduled Tribes (Dominant):

Malai Pandaram

For their cultural identity please see Appendix-II

Villages without Scheduled Tribes: There are 35 villages without any scheduled tribe population.

Literates and Illiterates by Sex (Total Population):

	Persons	Males	Females
Literate	26,525	15,329	11,196
Illiterate	18,754	6,438	12,316
Literacy rate	66	80	53
Graduate	430	337	93

Agriculture: ***Distribution of villages according to land use:*** Out of 36 villages, Total area (in hectare) is 24195, out of that 79.91 percent is cultivable and 26.5 percent of the cultivable area is irrigated.

Sources of Irrigation (Hectares): Government Canal 5.4, Private Canal 0, Well without Electricity 86.74, Well with Electricity 54.65, Tubewell without Electricity 0, Tubewell with Electricity 0, Tank 4757.65, River 0, Lake 0, Waterfall 0, Others 0.

Villages with population of 5000 to 9999: None

Villages with population of 10000 and above: None

Distribution of Workers:

	Persons	Males	Females	WPR
Cultivators	16,367	8,480	7,887	60.57
Agricultural Labour	7,714	2,681	5,033	28.55
Household Industry	215	116	99	0.8
Other Workers	2,725	2,189	536	10.08

Main Workers	22,771	12,212	10,559	84.27
Marginal Workers	4,250	1,254	2,996	15.73
Total Workers	27,021	13,466	13,555	

Religion: Major Religious Communities:

	Persons	Males	Females	Sex Ratio
Hindu (97.77%)	44,271	21,288	22,983	1,080
Muslim (4.09%)	1,854	834	1,020	1,223
Christian (2.17%)	983	478	505	1,056
Sikh (0%)	-	-	-	-
Buddhists (0%)	-	-	-	-
Jain (0%)	-	-	-	-

Agewise Data:

	Persons	Males	Females	Sex Ratio
All ages	47,165	22,629	24,536	1084
0-14	12,505	6,288	6,217	989
15-44	21,128	9,699	11,429	1178
45-79	12,918	6,300	6,618	1050
80+	419	237	182	768
Age not stated	195	105	90	857

Languages (Dominant):

Tamil, Telugu, Kannada, Malayalam, Hindi

Disabled Population:

	Persons	Males	Females	%
Total Disabled	1,480	692	788	
In Seeing	823	319	504	55.61
In Speech	170	102	68	11.49
In Hearing	56	27	29	3.78
In Movement	325	191	134	21.96
Mentally	106	53	53	7.16

NALLAMPALLI

Nalampalli C.D. Block lies in the south-western part of Dharmapuri district. It is a part of Dharmapuri taluk. The taluk is located at a distance of 5 kms. from district headquarters (Dharmapuri). There are 33 villages in the block with the total population of 161,347 persons.Area of the C.D. Block is 465.46 sq. kms. It is bounded in the north and west by CD Block Pennagaram, in the south by district Salem, in the east by C.D. Blocks Dharmapuri and Palakkodu.

Communications:

Roadways : N.H.-7: Direction- Dharmapuri to Salem, Nearest Villages- Thadangam, A. Jettihalli, Adiyamankottai, Pagalahalli, Nallampalli, Palayam, Dokkubothanalli, Maniyadhahalli, Thoppur Kanikarahalli, K. Thoppur RF.

Railway Station: Sivadi Village, Thoppur Kanikarahalli.

River: Toppai Nadi- Nearest Villages- Kammampatti, Thoppur Kanikarahalli, K. Thoppur RF.

Annual Rainfall: Average Rainfall 760 mm.

Ground Water: Availability of the ground water in the Basin is 5657.18 H.A.M. and the utilization is 7459.83 H.A.M. It belongs to Over Expoited category. Depth to water level varies from 2 to 10 meter below the ground. Most of the wells go down in summer months, according to the Ground Water Estimation Committee.

Forest and Reserved Forest: (Neonahalli RF)- Nearest Villages- M. Dhinnahalli, Mittareddihalli, Boothanahalli, Laligam. (Parigam)- Nearest Villages- Maniyadhahalli, Barigam (RF) Uni, Kammampatti. (Thoppur)- Nearest Villages- K.Thoppur (RF), Boothanahalli, Dokkubothanalli, Sivadi Village, Thoppur Kanikarahalli, Palayam.

Natural Division: Baramahal.

Administration

Revenue **Division:** Dharmapuri. Parliamentary Constituency: 10 Dharmapuri. District: Dharmapuri. Taluk: Dharmapuri. Assembly Constituency: 59 Dharmapuri, 58 Pennagaram. Gram Panchayat: 32.

Villages: 34 **Inhabited:** 33 **Uninhabited:** 1

Ranking	District	State	National
Area	8	42	1622
Population	4	6	1523
Sex Ratio	16	369	4905
Child Sex Ratio	17	374	6222
Literacy Rate	9	318	2715
Density	10	158	3129
Work Participation Rate	6	164	1561

Gram Panchayats:

A. Jettihalli, Athiyamankottai, Balajangamanahalli, Bandahalli, Bedrahalli, Bommasamudram, Boothanahalli, Dhalavaihalli, Dhinnahalli, Dokkubothanahalli, Echanahalli, Elagiri, Errahiyanahalli , K. Thoppur, Kammampatti, Konangihalli, Laligam, Mademangalam, Manithahalli, Mittareddihalli, Nadhathahalli, Nagarkoodal , Nallampalli, Narthampatti, Pagalahalli, Palavadi , Palayampudur, Pangunatham, Samichettipatti, Sivadi, Somenahalli, Thadangam, Thoppur.

Amenities:

Education: Primary School in 31 villages, Middle school in 21 villages, Matriculation or Secondary School in 14 villages, namely Dalawai Halli, Pangunatham, Konangi Halli, Thadangam, A. Jettihalli, Adiyamankottai, Errabaiyanahalli, Elagiri, Nallampalli, Laligam, Madhamanglam, Palayam, Maniyadhahalli, Thoppur Kanikarahalli.

Higher Secondary or Pre University Courses or Intermediate or Junior College in 11 villages of the CD Block,, namely Dalawai Halli, Pangunatham, Konangi Halli, Thadangam, A. Jettihalli, Adiyamankottai, Elagiri, Nallampalli, Laligam, Palayam, Thoppur Kanikarahalli.

College in 1 village, Adult Literacy Center in 0 village., College is in village, namely Thadangam.

Medical: Hospital in 0 village, Dispensary in 3 villages, Health Center in 5 villages, Sub Center in 21 villages, Maternity and Child Welfare Center in 0 village, Community health workers in 25 villages.

The Villages having Hospital or Dispensary or Health Center are Adiyamankottai, Maniyadhahalli, Kammampatti.

Drinking Water: Tap water in 33 villages, Tank water in 0 villages, Well water in 33 villages, Tubewell in 33 villages and more than one source in 33 villages.

Bank: Banking facility in 12 villages, namely, Thadangam, Adiyamankottai, Balajangumanahalli Pagalahalli, Nallampalli, Laligam, Madhamanglam Palayam, Bolanahalli, Maniyadhahalli, Kammampatti Thoppur Kanikarahalli.

Credit Society in 11 villages Agricultural Credit Society in 2 Non-Agricultural Credit Society in 7 villages.

Others: Power supply in 32 villages, Cinema hall in 0 village, sport club in 0 village, Stadium or Auditorium or Community Hall in 0 village, Post Office in 31 villages.

There are 30 villages having bus facilities.

Villages with most of facilities: Thadangam Adiyamankottai, Balajangumanahalli, Pagalahalli Nallampalli, Laligam, Madhamanglam, Palayam Bolanahalli, Maniyadhahalli, Kammampatti Thoppur Kanikarahalli.

Villages without amenities (Education):

K.Thoppur (Rf), Barigam (Rf)..

Scheduled Castes: Out of the total population of 161347 persons, 17843 persons (11.06%) belong to Scheduled Castes.

The villages having less than 10% SC population are Mookanahalli, Dalawai Halli, Pangunatham Kumbalapadi, A. Jettihalli, Balajangumanahalli Nagarkodal, Elagiri, Laligam, M. Dhinnahalli Boothanahalli, Palayam, Dokkubothanalli, Bolanahalli Barigam (Rf).

The villages having more than 50% SC population are None.

Sex ratio of Scheduled Caste population is 487.

Scheduled Castes Literates and Illiterates by Sex:

	Persons	Males	Females
Literate	9,354	5,685	3,669
Illiterate	8,489	3,461	5,028
Literacy rate	61.5	73.3	49.3
Graduate	389	303	86

Scheduled Castes (Dominant):

Adi Dravida, Arunthathiyar, Valluvan, Paraiyan etc. Adi Karnataka

For their cultural identity please see Appendix-I

Villages without Scheduled Castes: There are 3 villages without any scheduled caste population.

Scheduled Tribes: Out of the total population of 161347 persons, 1579 persons (0.98%) belong to Scheduled Tribes.

The villages having less than 10% ST population are Mookanahalli, Pallavadi, Dalawai Halli, Somenahalli Pangunatham, Konangi Halli, Kumbalapadi Nathatha Halli, Thadangam, A. Jettihalli Adiyamankottai, Balajangumanahalli, Nagarkodal Nekkundhi, Errabaiyanahalli, Echanahalli, Elagiri Pagalahalli, Nallampalli, Laligam, Madhamanglam M. Dhinnahalli, Mittareddihalli, Boothanahalli Sivadi Village, Palayam, Dokkubothanalli Bolanahalli, Maniyadhahalli, Kammampatti Thoppur Kanikarahalli, K.Thoppur (Rf) Barigam (Rf).

The villages having more than 50% ST population are None.

Sex ratio of Scheduled tribe population is 477.

Scheduled Tribes Literates and Illiterates by Sex:

	Persons	Males	Females
Literate	674	411	263
Illiterate	905	415	490
Literacy rate	50.6	60.0	40.7
Graduate	43	33	10

Scheduled Tribes (Dominant):

Kurumans, Irular, Kondareddis, Malakkuravan Malayali

For their cultural identity please see Appendix-II

Villages without Scheduled Tribes: There are 16 villages without any scheduled tribe population.

Literates and Illiterates by Sex (Total Population):

	Persons	Males	Females
Literate	84,549	51,822	32,727
Illiterate	76,798	32,382	44,416
Literacy rate	60	72	48
Graduate	3,336	2,453	883

Agriculture: ***Distribution of villages according to land use:*** Out of 34 villages, Total area (in hectare) is 46546.91, out of that 59.25 percent is cultivable and 27.64 percent of the cultivable area is irrigated.

Sources of Irrigation (Hectares): Government Canal 96.65, Private Canal 0, Well without Electricity 2305.79, Well with Electricity 4010.39, Tubewell without Electricity 0, Tubewell with Electricity 98.34, Tank 1069.2, River 0, Lake 0, Waterfall 0, Others 43.62.

Villages with population of 5000 to 9999:

Dhalavaihalli , Pangunatham , Konangihalli Nathathahalli, Thadangam, A.Jettihalli Adiyamankottai, Pagalahalli, Nallampalli, Laligam Dhinnahalli, Palayam, Dokkubodanahalli, Kammampatti

Thoppur T.Kanigarahalli.

Villages with population of 10000 and above:
Maniathahalli.

Distribution of Workers:

	Persons	Males	Females	WPR
Cultivators	35,105	20,716	14,389	41.58
Agricultural Labour	25,537	9,871	15,666	30.25
Household Industry	2,150	1,042	1,108	2.55
Other Workers	21,628	16,102	5,526	25.62
Main Workers	68,372	43,150	25,222	80.99
Marginal Workers	16,048	4,581	11,467	19.01
Total Workers	84,420	47,731	36,689	

Religion: Major Religious Communities:

	Persons	Males	Females	Sex Ratio
Hindu (98%)	158,119	82,577	75,542	915
Muslim (0.65%)	1,045	530	515	972
Christian (1.27%)	2,054	1,031	1,023	992
Sikh (0%)	5	5	-	-
Buddhists (0%)	1	-	1	-
Jain (0%)	8	5	3	600

Agewise Data:

	Persons	Males	Females	Sex Ratio
All ages	161,347	84,204	77,143	916
0-14	50,747	28,045	22,702	809
15-44	77,013	39,239	37,774	963
45-79	31,807	15,980	15,827	990
80+	1,576	836	740	885
Age not stated	204	104	100	962

Languages (Dominant):
Tamil, Telugu, Kannada, Urdu, Hindi

Disabled Population:

	Persons	Males	Females	%
Total Disabled	4,442	1,537	2,905	
In Seeing	2,873	596	2,277	64.68
In Speech	320	182	138	7.2
In Hearing	144	76	68	3.24
In Movement	889	564	325	20.01
Mentally	216	119	97	4.86

NALLUR

Nallur C.D. Block lies in the western part of Cuddalore district. It is a part of Virudhachalam and Tittakudi taluks. The Block is located at a distance of NA kms. from district headquarters (Cuddalore). There are 76 villages in the block with the total population of 116,729 persons. Area of the C.D. Block is 347.92 sq. kms. It is bounded in the north by district Viluppuram, in the south by district Ariyalur, in the east by CD Blocks Virudhachalam and Kattumannarkoil, in the west by district Viluppuram and C.D. Block Mangalur. CD Block Nallur falls in taluk Virudhachalam by 34 villages, and in taluk Tittakudi by 42 villages.

Communications:

Roadways : N.H.-45: Direction- Tiruchirappalli to Ulundurpettai, Nearest Villages- Kulapakkam (Eranji), Aivadugudi, Seppakkam, Sirunesalur, Veppur. S.H.-10: Direction- Kilkuppam to Virudhachalam, Nearest Villages- Seppakkam, Kattumailur, Periyanesalur, Sirunesalur, Veppur, N.Naraiyur, Thiruppayur, Ko. Kotthanoor, A. Chittur, Sathiyam.

Railway Station: Pe. Ponneri.

River: Manimukta Nadi- Nearest Villages- Adhiyur, Kulapakkam (Eranji), Aivadugudi, Elangiyanur, Memathur, Vannathur, Nallur, Nagar, Seppakkam, Kattumailur, Sathiyam, Varanjaram (RF), A. Marur, Kothanur (Pandavanpattu), Maligaimedu, Melakurichi, Kelakurichi. Vellar Nadi- Nearest Villages- Venkarumbur, Mosattai, Kilimangalam, Murugankudi, Murugankudi, Kosapallam, Thiruvattathurai, Guddalore, Eraiyur, Pe. Ponneri, Soundaracholapuram, Irulampattu.

Backwards Region Grants Fund: It receives Backward Region Grants.

Annual Rainfall: Average Rainfall 1050 mm.

Ground Water: Availability of the ground water in the Basin is 11633.89 MCM and the utilization is 10457.63 MCM. It belongs to Semi Critical category. Depth to water level varies from 2 to 10 meter below the ground. Most of the wells go down in summer months, according to the Ground Water Estimation Committee.

Forest and Reserved Forest: (Kattumayilur RF)- Nearest Villages- Melakurichi, Kelakurichi, Kattumailur, Periyanesalur.

Natural Division: Tondai Nadu.

Administration

Revenue **Division:** Virudhachalam. Parliamentary Constituency: 26 Cuddalore (SC), 14 Kallakurichi (SC). District: Cuddalore. Taluk: Virudhachalam, Tittakudi. Assembly Constituency: 152 Vriddhachalam, 151 Tittakudi (SC). Gram Panchayat: 64.

Villages: 76 **Inhabited:** 74 **Uninhabited:** 2

Ranking	District	State	National
Area	2	118	2301
Population	6	72	2953
Sex Ratio	3	210	1481
Child Sex Ratio	9	171	2944
Literacy Rate	12	322	2759
Density	1	116	3229
Work Participation Rate	12	176	1175

Gram Panchayats:

A. Agaram, A. Marur, Adhamangalam, Adiyur, Aivadugudi, Arugeri, Chittur, Dheevalur, Eraiyur, Erappavur, Ganapathi Kurichi, Guddalore, Ilangiyuanur, Karaiyur, Kattumayilur, Keelakurichi, Kilimangalam, Ko.kothanur, Kodikkalam, Konur, Kosapallam, Kothanur (Pandavanpattu), Kothattai,

Kovilur, Kurukkathancheri, Madhuravalli, Maligaikottam, Maligaimedu, Mannampadi, Marudhathur, Melur, Memathur, Murugankudi, Nagar, Nallur, Naraiyur, Narasingamangalam, Niramani, Pasikulam, Pe. Poovanur , Pe.Ponneri, Pelandurai , Periyanesalur, Pinjanur, Poolambadi, Sathiyam, Seppakkam, Setuvarayankuppam, Sevur, Sirumangalam, Sirunesalur, Soundaracholapuram, T. Poudaiyur, Thazhanallur, Thiruvattathurai, Tholar, Thoraiyur, Tiruppayur, Vadakarai, Valasai, Vannathur, Varambanur, Venkarumbur, Veppur.

Amenities:

Education: Primary School in 71 villages, Middle school in 20 villages, Matriculation or Secondary School in 10 villages, namely Nallur, Seppakkam, Periyanesalur, Veppur, Poolambadi, Koviloor, Deevalur, Tholar, Eraiyur, Pelandurai.

Higher Secondary or Pre University Courses or Intermediate or Junior College in 4 villages of the CD Block,, namely Nallur, Seppakkam, Veppur, Eraiyur.

College in 0 village, Adult Literacy Center in 0 village.

Medical: Hospital in 0 village, Dispensary in 0 village, Health Center in 3 villages, Sub Center in 18 villages, Maternity and Child Welfare Center in 1 village, Community health workers in 56 villages.

Drinking Water: Tap water in 74 villages, Tank water in 0 villages, Well water in 74 villages, Tubewell in 74 villages and more than one source in 74 villages.

Bank: Banking facility in 8 villages, namely, Maligaimedu, Nallur, Seppakkam, Veppur, Sirumangalam Murugankudi, Guddalore, Eraiyur.

Credit Society in 13 villages Agricultural Credit Society in 9 Non-Agricultural Credit Society in 7 villages.

Others: Power supply in 74 villages, Cinema hall in 1 village, sport club in 0 village, Stadium or Auditorium or Community Hall in 0 village, Post Office in 73 villages.

There are 70 villages having bus facilities.

Villages with most of facilities: Maligaimedu Nallur, Seppakkam, Veppur, Sirumangalam, Murugankudi Eraiyur.

Villages without amenities (Education):

Melakurichi, T.Pudiyur, Keelnemili..

Scheduled Castes: Out of the total population of 116729 persons, 51053 persons (43.74%) belong to Scheduled Castes. The villages having less than 10% SC population are Valasai, Kaliyamedu, Murugankudi, Keelnemili Putheri, Melnemili, Kosapallam, Thiruvattathurai.

The villages having more than 50% SC population are Sethuvarayankuppam, A.Marur Kothanur (Pandavanpattu), Aivadugudi, Memathur Vannathur, Nagar, Seppakkam, Sirunesalur, N.Naraiyur Thiruppayur, Mannampady, T.Pudiyur, Poolambadi Sevoor, Sirumangalam, Koviloor, Erapavur Narasingamangalam, Deevalur, Kurukkathancheri Karaiyur, Arugeri, Keeranur. Kothattai, Kodikkalam Pe.Ponneri.

Sex ratio of Scheduled Caste population is 490.

Scheduled Castes Literates and Illiterates by Sex:

	Persons	Males	Females
Literate	24,423	15,533	8,890
Illiterate	26,630	10,504	16,126
Literacy rate	55.7	69.4	41.4
Graduate	604	506	98

Scheduled Castes (Dominant):

Adi Dravida, Arunthathiyar, Domban, Valluvan Kuravan etc.

For their cultural identity please see Appendix-I

Villages without Scheduled Castes: There are 7 villages without any scheduled caste population.

Scheduled Tribes: Out of the total population of 116729 persons, 688 persons (0.59%) belong to Scheduled Tribes.

The villages having less than 10% ST population are Sethuvarayankuppam, A.Marur, Maligaimedu Kothanur (Pandavanpattu), Adhiyur Kulapakkam (Eranji), Aivadugudi, Elangiyanur Valasai, Pinchanur, Memathur, Vannathur, Nallur Nagar, Seppakkam, Kattumailur, Kelakurichi Melakurichi, Periyanesalur, Sirunesalur, Veppur N.Naraiyur, Thiruppayur, Ko.Kotthanoor, A.Chittur Sathiyam, Mannampady, T.Pudiyur, Varambanoor Kaliyamedu, Poolambadi, Niramani, A.Agaram, Sevoor Maduravalli, Sirumangalam, Koviloor, Erapavur Narasingamangalam, Talanallur, Deevalur, Venkarumbur Mosattai, Kurukkathancheri, Kilimangalam Murugankudi, Murugankudi, Karaiyur, Poovanur.Pe. Konur, Vadakarai, Nandhimangalam, Keelnemili Arugeri, Marudhathur, Melur, Adhamangalam, Putheri Melnemili, Kollathankurichi, Keeranur, Ariyaravi Kosapallam, Maligaikottam, Kothattai, Tholar Kodikkalam, Thiruvattathurai, Guddalore, Eraiyur Pe.Ponneri, Soundaracholapuram, Irulampattu Pelandurai.

The villages having more than 50% ST population are None.

Sex ratio of Scheduled tribe population is 509.

Scheduled Tribes Literates and Illiterates by Sex:

	Persons	Males	Females
Literate	238	145	93
Illiterate	450	193	257
Literacy rate	40.2	49.8	30.9

Graduate	0	0	0

Scheduled Tribes (Dominant):

Irular, Kattunayakan, Malakkuravan

Generic Tribes etc., Malai Pandaram

For their cultural identity please see Appendix-II

Villages without Scheduled Tribes: There are 60 villages without any scheduled tribe population.

Literates and Illiterates by Sex (Total Population):

	Persons	Males	Females
Literate	61,457	38,013	23,444
Illiterate	55,272	20,582	34,690
Literacy rate	60	74	46
Graduate	1,587	1,281	306

Agriculture: ***Distribution of villages according to land use:*** Out of 76 villages, Total area (in hectare) is 34792.65, out of that 76.11 percent is cultivable and 34.02 percent of the cultivable area is irrigated.

Sources of Irrigation (Hectares): Government Canal 21.11, Private Canal 0, Well without Electricity 180.68, Well with Electricity 2362.38, Tubewell without Electricity 113.24, Tubewell with Electricity 6191.22, Tank 139.73, River 0, Lake 0, Waterfall 0, Others 0.

Villages with population of 5000 to 9999:

Tholar.

Villages with population of 10000 and above: None

Distribution of Workers:

	Persons	Males	Females	WPR
Cultivators	23,302	14,507	8,795	36.81
Agricultural Labour	32,491	14,092	18,399	51.33
Household Industry	1,147	529	618	1.81
Other Workers	6,359	4,719	1,640	10.05
Main Workers	45,478	27,518	17,960	71.85
Marginal Workers	17,821	6,329	11,492	28.15
Total Workers	63,299	33,847	29,452	

Religion: Major Religious Communities:

	Persons	Males	Females	Sex Ratio
Hindu (98.13%)	114,541	57,525	57,016	991
Muslim (1.16%)	1,357	650	707	1,088
Christian (0.57%)	662	336	326	970
Sikh (0%)	3	2	1	500
Buddhists (0%)	-	-	-	-
Jain (0%)	5	2	3	1,500

Agewise Data:

	Persons	Males	Females	Sex Ratio
All ages	116,729	58,595	58,134	992
0-14	34,424	17,752	16,672	939
15-44	55,199	26,970	28,229	1047
45-79	25,975	13,273	12,702	957
80+	773	413	360	872
Age not stated	358	187	171	914

Languages (Dominant):

Tamil, Telugu, Urdu, Malayalam, English

Disabled Population:

	Persons	Males	Females	%
Total Disabled	4,609	1,950	2,659	
In Seeing	3,140	1,083	2,057	68.13
In Speech	258	144	114	5.6
In Hearing	195	95	100	4.23
In Movement	821	512	309	17.81
Mentally	195	116	79	4.23

NAMAGIRIPETTAI

Namagiripettai C.D. Block lies in the north-eastern part of Namakkal district. It is a part of Rasipuram taluk. The Block is located at a distance of 32 kms. from district headquarters (Namakkal). There are 37 villages in the block with the total population of 64,849 persons. Area of the C.D. Block is 222.24 sq. kms. It is bounded in the north and east by district Salem, in the south by CD Blocks Sendamangalam and Kolli Hills, in the west by C.D. Blocks Vennandur and Rasipuram.

Communications:

Roadways : Information not Available.

Annual Rainfall: Average Rainfall 650 mm.

Ground Water: Availability of the ground water in the Basin is 4490.32 H.A.M. and the utilization is 6913.31 H.A.M. It belongs to Safe category. Depth to water level varies from 2 to 20 meter below the ground. Most of the wells go down in summer months, according to the Ground Water Estimation Committee.

Forest and Reserved Forest: (Bailnadu North RF)- Nearest Villages- Karkoodalpatti, Molakkadu, Kariampatty, Unanthangal, Varakur Kombai, Pachagoundampatti, Kolakkamedu. (Varkur)- Nearest Villages- Unanthangal, Periyakompai, Mulaikuruchi, Periyasekkadi, Chinnasekkadi, Varakur Kombai. (Mavar)- Nearest Villages- Mullukurichi, Periakurichi, Mavar RF, Mavar, Perappansolai, Periyakompai, Mulaikuruchi. (Nayakkan Kombai)- Nearest Villages- Periyakompai, Pudurpalapatti. (Perumalmalai)- Nearest Perappansolai, Periyakompai, Pudurpalapatti. (Pudupatti)- Nearest Villages- Pudupatti RF, Ayilpatti, Karkoodalpatti, Moolapallipatti. (Bailnadu)- Nearest Villages- Tho Jedarpalayam, Pachudaiampalayam.

Natural Division: Kongu Nadu.

Administration

Revenue **Division:** Namakkal. Parliamentary Constituency: 16 Namakkal. District: Namakkal. Taluk: Rasipuram. Assembly Constituency: 92 Rasipuram (SC). Gram Panchayat: 18

Villages: 37 **Inhabited:** 35 **Uninhabited:** 2

Ranking	District	State	National
Area	6	257	3816
Population	8	316	4693

Sex Ratio	11	336	3084
Child Sex Ratio	5	320	5307
Literacy Rate	12	325	2835
Density	4	12	3614
Work Participation Rate	10	235	111

Gram Panchayats:

Jedarpalayam, Ayilpatti, Eswaramurthipalayam, Jodarpalayam, Karkoodalpatti, Mangalapuram, Moolapallipatti, Mulaikurichi, Mullukurichi, Mulaikurichi, Muthuruttu, Naraikinar, Navalpatti, O Pachudaiyampalayam, Pachudaiampalayam, Perappansolai, Perumagoundampalayam, Thimmanaickenpatti, Thoppapatti, Unanthangal, Vadugam Muniappampalayam, .

Amenities:

Education: Primary School in 24 villages, Middle school in 7 villages, Matriculation or Secondary School in 6 villages, namely Ayilpatti, Mangalapuram, Thimmanaickenpatti, Karkoodalpatti, Mullukurichi, Tho.Jedarpalayam.

Higher Secondary or Pre University Courses or Intermediate or Junior College in 3 villages of the CD Block,, namely Mangalapuram, Mullukurichi, Tho.Jedarpalayam. College in 0 village, Adult Literacy Center in 0 village.

Medical: Hospital in 0 village, Dispensary in 1 village, Health Center in 2 villages, Sub Center in 10 villages, Maternity and Child Welfare Center in 0 village, Community health workers in 0 village.

The Village having Hospital or Dispensary or Health Center is Mangalapuram.

Drinking Water: Tap water in 35 villages, Tank water in 0 villages, Well water in 35 villages, Tubewell in 35 villages and more than one source in 35 villages.

Bank: Banking facility in 3 villages, namely, Mangalapuram, Mullukurichi, Tho.Jedarpalayam.

Credit Society in 21 villages Agricultural Credit Society in 9 Non-Agricultural Credit Society in 19 villages.

Others: Power supply in 35 villages, Cinema hall in 2 villages, sport club in 0 village, Stadium or Auditorium or Community Hall in 0 village, Post Office in 32 villages.

There are 31 villages having bus facilities.

Villages with most of facilities: Mangalapuram Mullukurichi.

Villages without amenities (Education):

Naraikinar Block, Ayilpatti, Naraikinar South, Molakkadu, Mavar, Pudurpalapatti, Periyasekkadi, Chinnasekkadi, Pachagoundampatti, Kolakkamedu, O.Jedarpalayam..

Scheduled Castes: Out of the total population of 64849 persons, 13048 persons (20.12%) belong to Scheduled Castes. The villages having less than 10% SC population are Eswaramurthipalayam, Naraikinar Block Naraikinar South , Molakkadu, Unanthangal Periakurichi, Mavar , Perappansolai, Periyakompai Pudurpalapatti, Mulaikuruchi, Periyasekkadi Chinnasekkadi, Varakur Kombai, Pachagoundampatti Kolakkamedu, O.Jedarpalayam, Chinnakkapalayam.

The villages having more than 50% SC population are None.

Sex ratio of Scheduled Caste population is 486.

Scheduled Castes Literates and Illiterates by Sex:

	Persons	Males	Females
Literate	5,849	3,566	2,283
Illiterate	7,199	3,146	4,053
Literacy rate	50.7	59.9	40.9
Graduate	165	128	37

Scheduled Castes (Dominant):

Arunthathiyar, Adi Dravida, Pallan, Paraiyan etc. Kuravan etc.

For their cultural identity please see Appendix-I

Villages without Scheduled Castes: There are 11 villages without any scheduled caste population.

Scheduled Tribes: Out of the total population of 64849 persons, 10845 persons (16.72%) belong to Scheduled Tribes. The villages having less than 10% ST population are Ayilpatti, Navalpatti, Mangalapuram Eswaramurthipalayam, Thimmanaickenpatti Naraikinar Block , Muthuruthu, Ayilpatti Vadugm Muniappampalayam, Pachudaiyampalayam O.Jedarpalayam, Perumagoundampalayam Chinnakkapalayam, Thoppapatty, Tho.Jedarpalayam Pachudaiamplayam.

The villages having more than 50% ST population are Naraikinar South , Molakkadu, Kariampatty Unanthangal, Periakurichi, Mavar , Perappansolai Periyakompai, Pudurpalapatti, Mulaikuruchi Periyasekkadi, Chinnasekkadi, Varakur Kombai Pachagoundampatti, Kolakkamedu.

Sex ratio of Scheduled tribe population is 493.

Scheduled Tribes Literates and Illiterates by Sex:

	Persons	Males	Females
Literate	4,896	3,002	1,894
Illiterate	5,949	2,499	3,450
Literacy rate	50.6	61.3	39.6
Graduate	57	49	8

Scheduled Tribes (Dominant):

Malayali, Irular, Malakkuravan, Kurumans Malayekandi

For their cultural identity please see Appendix-II

Villages without Scheduled Tribes: There are 8 villages without any scheduled tribe population.

Literates and Illiterates by Sex (Total Population):

	Persons	Males	Females
Literate	34,626	20,648	13,978
Illiterate	30,223	12,480	17,743
Literacy rate	60	70	49
Graduate	1,103	818	285

Agriculture: ***Distribution of villages according to land use:*** Out of 37 villages, Total area (in hectare) is 22224.04, out of that 51.8 percent is cultivable and 59.05 percent of the cultivable area is irrigated.

Sources of Irrigation (Hectares): Government Canal 75.89, Private Canal 0, Well without Electricity 730.83, Well with Electricity 4671.54, Tubewell without Electricity 113.36, Tubewell with Electricity 848.76, Tank 8, River 0, Lake 0, Waterfall 0, Others 0.

Villages with population of 5000 to 9999: None

Villages with population of 10000 and above: Mangalapuram, Karkoodalpatti.

Distribution of Workers:

	Persons	Males	Females	WPR
Cultivators	14,723	7,963	6,760	35.76
Agricultural Labour	21,329	9,756	11,573	51.8
Household Industry	898	481	417	2.18
Other Workers	4,225	3,258	967	10.26
Main Workers	38,208	20,358	17,850	92.79
Marginal Workers	2,967	1,100	1,867	7.21
Total Workers	41,175	21,458	19,717	

Religion: Major Religious Communities:

	Persons	Males	Females	Sex Ratio
Hindu (99.23%)	64,352	32,874	31,478	958
Muslim (0.36%)	232	122	110	902
Christian (0.3%)	194	97	97	1,000
Sikh (0.01%)	5	3	2	667
Buddhists (0%)	-	-	-	-
Jain (0.01%)	7	4	3	750

Agewise Data:

	Persons	Males	Females	Sex Ratio
All ages	64,849	33,128	31,721	958
0-14	16,344	8,844	7,500	848
15-44	31,479	15,677	15,802	1008
45-79	15,973	8,047	7,926	985
80+	674	370	304	822
Age not stated	379	190	189	995

Languages (Dominant):
Tamil, Telugu, Kannada, Urdu, Hindi

Disabled Population:

	Persons	Males	Females	%
Total Disabled	1,319	787	532	
In Seeing	716	427	289	54.28
In Speech	121	66	55	9.17
In Hearing	71	34	37	5.38
In Movement	302	205	97	22.9
Mentally	109	55	54	8.26

NAMAKKAL

Namakkal C.D. Block lies in the southern part of Namakkal district. It is a part of Namakkal taluk. The Block is located at a distance of (00) kms. from district headquarters (Namakkal). There are 23 villages in the block with the total population of 83,364 persons. Area of the C.D. Block is 204.94 sq. kms. It is bounded in the north by CD Blocks Elachipalaiyam and Puduchatram, in the south by C.D. Block Mohanur, in the east by C.D. Blocks Sendamangalam and Erumaipatti, and in the west by CD Block Paramathi.

Communications:

Roadways : N.H.-7: Direction- Paramathi to Salem, Neraest Villages- Nallipalayam, Keerambur, Periyapatti, Namakkal, Thottipatti, Rasampalayam, Konur, Kilsathambur, Vallipuram. S.H.-6: Direction- Namakkal to Musiri, Kondichettipatti, Vasanthapuram, Vagurampatti.

Annual Rainfall: Average Rainfall 650 mm.

Ground Water: Availability of the ground water in the Basin is 2258.51 H.A.M. and the utilization is 2348.59 H.A.M. It belongs to Safe category. Depth to water level varies from 0 to 10 meter below the ground. Most of the wells go down in summer months, according to the Ground Water Estimation Committee.

Natural Division: Kongu Nadu

Administration

Revenue **Division:** Namakkal. Parliamentary Constituency. District: Namakkal. Taluk: Namakkal. Assembly Constituency: 94 Namakkal. Gram Panchayat: 34.

Villages: 23 **Inhabited:** 23 **Uninhabited:** 0

Ranking	District	State	National
Area	7	277	4096
Population	2	215	3992
Sex Ratio	6	284	2255
Child Sex Ratio	6	330	5419
Literacy Rate	1	89	1031
Density	14	193	2698
Work Participation Rate	3	110	1947

Gram Panchayats:

Aniyar, Avalnaickenpatti, Ayyampalayam, Chinnamudalaipatti, Eranapuram , Kadappalli, Kavettipatti, Keerambur, Kondichettipatti, Konur, Kosavampatti, Marappanaickanpatti, Marurpatti , Mudalaipatti, Nallipalayam , Naravalur, Periyagoundampalayam, Rangappanaickenpalayam, Rasampalayam, Seiluvampatti , Singilipatti, Thaligai, Thindamangalam, Thottipatti, Thummankurichi , Vagurampatti, Vallipuram, Vasanthapuram, Veesanam ,

Vettampadi, Vittamanaickenpatti.

Amenities:

Education: Primary School in 23 villages, Middle school in 12 villages, Matriculation or Secondary School in 7 villages, namely Mururpatti, Vettampadi, Nallipalayam, Ernapuram, Periyapatti, Vagurampatti, Konur.

Higher Secondary or Pre University Courses or Intermediate or Junior College in 4 villages of the CD Block,, namely Nallipalayam, Ernapuram, Periyapatti, Vagurampatti.

College in 1 village, Adult Literacy Center in 0 village., College is in village, namely Vagurampatti.

Medical: Hospital in 1 village, Dispensary in 0 village, Health Center in 4 villages, Sub Center in 12 villages, Maternity and Child Welfare Center in 0 village, Community health workers in 0 village.

The Village having Hospital or Dispensary or Health Center is Periyapatti.

Drinking Water: Tap water in 23 villages, Tank water in 0 villages, Well water in 23 villages, Tubewell in 23 villages and more than one source in 23 villages.

Bank: Banking facility in 6 villages, namely, Nallipalayam, Thligai, Thindamangalam, Keerambur Periyapatti, Rasampalayam.

Credit Society in 22 villages Agricultural Credit Society in 12 Non-Agricultural Credit Society in 19 villages.

Others: Power supply in 23 villages, Cinema hall in 0 village, sport club in 0 village, Stadium or Auditorium or Community Hall in 0 village, Post Office in 23 villages.

There are 23 villages having bus facilities.

Villages with most of facilities: Nallipalayam Thligai, Thindamangalam, Keerambur, Periyapatti.

Villages without Amenities (Education): None..

Scheduled Castes: Out of the total population of 83364 persons, 21291 persons (25.54%) belong to Scheduled Castes.

The villages having less than 10% SC population are None..

The villages having more than 50% SC population are None.

Sex ratio of Scheduled Caste population is 495.

Scheduled Castes Literates and Illiterates by Sex:

	Persons	Males	Females
Literate	11,455	6,853	4,602
Illiterate	9,836	3,902	5,934
Literacy rate	61.4	72.5	50.0
Graduate	472	340	132

Scheduled Castes (Dominant):

Arunthathiyar, Pallan, Adi Dravida, Paraiyan etc. Chakkiliyan

For their cultural identity please see Appendix-I

Villages without Scheduled Castes: There is 0 village without any scheduled caste population.

Scheduled Tribes: Out of the total population of 83364 persons, 116 persons (0.14%) belong to Scheduled Tribes.

The villages having less than 10% ST population are Aniyar, Seiluvampatti, Kadappalli, Mururpatti Vettampadi, Veesanam, Nallipalayam, Thummankurichi Ernapuram, Thligai, Naravalur Thottipalayam Thindamangalam, Keerambur, Vallipuram, Periyapatti Kondichettipatti, Namakkal, Vasanthapuram Vagurampatti, Thottipatti, Rasampalayam, Konur Kilsathambur.

The villages having more than 50% ST population are None.

Sex ratio of Scheduled tribe population is 474.

Scheduled Tribes Literates and Illiterates by Sex:

	Persons	Males	Females
Literate	93	49	44
Illiterate	23	12	11
Literacy rate	86.9	89.1	84.6
Graduate	6	5	1

Scheduled Tribes (Dominant):

Malayali, Kondareddis, Malakkuravan, Irular Kurumans

For their cultural identity please see Appendix-II

Villages without Scheduled Tribes: There are 16 villages without any scheduled tribe population.

Literates and Illiterates by Sex (Total Population):

	Persons	Males	Females
Literate	53,275	31,019	22,256
Illiterate	30,089	11,185	18,904
Literacy rate	71	82	60
Graduate	3,905	2,565	1,340

Agriculture: ***Distribution of villages according to land use:*** Out of 23 villages, Total area (in hectare) is 20494.99, out of that 78.01 percent is cultivable and 24.78 percent of the cultivable area is irrigated.

Sources of Irrigation (Hectares): Government Canal 0, Private Canal 0, Well without Electricity 318.32, Well with Electricity 3165.42, Tubewell without Electricity 0, Tubewell with Electricity 224.85, Tank 183.54, River 0, Lake 4.1, Waterfall 0, Others 65.14.

Villages with population of 5000 to 9999: Nallipalayam , Kondichettipatti.

Villages with population of 10000 and above: Namakkal.

Distribution of Workers:

	Persons	Males	Females	WPR
Cultivators	9,091	4,942	4,149	20.78
Agricultural Labour	14,138	5,764	8,374	32.31

Household Industry	992	289	703	2.27
Other Workers	19,535	15,391	4,144	44.65
Main Workers	37,179	24,189	12,990	84.97
Marginal Workers	6,577	2,197	4,380	15.03
Total Workers	43,756	26,386	17,370	

Religion: Major Religious Communities:

	Persons	Males	Females	Sex Ratio
Hindu (96.06%)	80,081	40,538	39,543	975
Muslim (1.32%)	1,098	553	545	986
Christian (0.65%)	538	285	253	888
Sikh (0.02%)	15	9	6	667
Buddhists (0.01%)	5	4	1	250
Jain (0%)	3	2	1	500

Agewise Data:

	Persons	Males	Females	Sex Ratio
All ages	81,830	41,440	40,390	975
0-14	19,056	10,113	8,943	884
15-44	40,102	20,073	20,029	998
45-79	21,264	10,509	10,755	1023
80+	974	503	471	936
Age not stated	434	242	192	793

Languages (Dominant):
Tamil, Telugu, Urdu, Kannada, Malayalam

Disabled Population:

	Persons	Males	Females	%
Total Disabled	1,691	963	728	
In Seeing	933	517	416	55.17
In Speech	133	58	75	7.87
In Hearing	73	34	39	4.32
In Movement	399	261	138	23.6
Mentally	153	93	60	9.05

NAMBIYUR

Nambiyur C.D. Block lies in the north-western part of Erode district. It is a part of Gobichettipalayam taluk. The Block is located at a distance of 60 kms. from district headquarters (Erode). There are 21 villages in the block with the total population of 65,449 persons. Area of the C.D. Block is 202.38 sq. kms. It is bounded in the north by CD Blocks Sathyamangalam and Bobichettipalayam, in the south by district Coimbatore, in the east by C.D. Blocks Gobichettipalayam and Perundurai, in the west by CD Block Bhavanisagar and district Coimbatore.

Communications:

Roadways : Information not Available.

Annual Rainfall: Average Rainfall 789 mm.

Ground Water: Availability of the ground water in the Basin is 3782.41 H.A.M. and the utilization is 4061.04 H.A.M. It belongs to Over Expoited category. Depth to water level varies from 5 to 20 meter below the ground. Most of the wells go down in summer months, according to the Ground Water Estimation Committee.

Natural Division: Kongu Nadu.

Administration

Revenue **Division:** Gobichettipalayam. Parliamentary Constituency: 18 Gobichettipalayam. District: Erode. Taluk: Gobichettipalayam. Assembly Constituency: 106 Gobichettipalayam. Gram Panchayat: 15.

Villages: 21 **Inhabited:** 21 **Uninhabited:** 0

Ranking	**District**	**State**	**National**
Area	14	283	4138
Population	11	312	4672
Sex Ratio	7	266	2047
Child Sex Ratio	5	89	1781
Literacy Rate	16	360	3660
Density	4	5	3323
Work Participation Rate	10	193	43

Gram Panchayats:

Andipalayam, Anjanur, Emmampoondi, Gettichaviyur, Gudakkarai, Kadathur, Karattupalayam, Koshanam, Kurumandur, Lagampalayam, Olalakovil, Polavapalayam, Sundakkampalayam, Talguni, Vemandampalayam.

Amenities:

Education: Primary School in 20 villages, Middle school in 9 villages, Matriculation or Secondary School in 7 villages, namely Kadathur, Gudakkarai, Kuruandur, Vemandampalayam, Emmanpoondi, Ozhalakovil, Shanthipalayam.

Higher Secondary or Pre University Courses or Intermediate or Junior College in 3 villages of the CD Block,, namely Kuruandur, Ozhalakovil, Shanthipalayam.

College in 0 village, Adult Literacy Center in 0 village.

Medical: Hospital in 0 village, Dispensary in 1 village, Health Center in 2 villages, Sub Center in 14 villages, Maternity and Child Welfare Center in 0 village, Community health workers in 2 villages.

The Village having Hospital or Dispensary or Health Center is Shanthipalayam.

Drinking Water: Tap water in 21 villages, Tank water in 0 villages, Well water in 21 villages, Tubewell in 21 villages and more than one source in 21 villages.

Bank: Banking facility in 6 villages, namely, Kadathur, Kuruandur, Kosanam, Vemandampalayam Ozhalakovil, Shanthipalayam.

Credit Society in 14 villages Agricultural Credit Society in 10 Non-Agricultural Credit Society in 9 villages.

Others: Power supply in 21 villages, Cinema hall in 0 village, sport club in 0 village, Stadium or Auditorium or Community Hall in 0 village, Post Office in 18 villages.

There are 21 villages having bus facilities.

Villages with most of facilities: Kadathur

Kuruandur, Kosanam, Vemandampalayam, Ozhalakovil Shanthipalayam.

Villages without amenities (Education):
Kodasellipalayam..

Scheduled Castes: Out of the total population of 65449 persons, 12768 persons (19.51%) belong to Scheduled Castes.
The villages having less than 10% SC population are None..
The villages having more than 50% SC population are None.
Sex ratio of Scheduled Caste population is 498.

Scheduled Castes Literates and Illiterates by Sex:

	Persons	Males	Females
Literate	4,167	2,471	1,696
Illiterate	8,601	3,941	4,660
Literacy rate	36.4	42.9	29.7
Graduate	25	18	7

Scheduled Castes (Dominant):
Chakkiliyan, Madari, Kuravan etc., Paraiyan etc. Adi Dravida
For their cultural identity please see Appendix-I

Villages without Scheduled Castes: There is 0 village without any scheduled caste population.

Scheduled Tribes: Out of the total population of 65449 persons, 9 persons (0.01%) belong to Scheduled Tribes.
The villages having less than 10% ST population are Karattupalayam, Kadathur, Sundakkampalayam Gudakkarai, Andipalayam, Kuruandur, Talkuni, Kosanam Irugaloor, Anjanoor, Lagampalayam, Vemandampalayam Polavapalayam, Mottanam, Emmanpoondi, Ozhalakovil Kodasellipalayam, Chinnaripalayam, Shanthipalayam Avalampalayam, Nichampalayam.
The villages having more than 50% ST population are None.
Sex ratio of Scheduled tribe population is 556.

Scheduled Tribes Literates and Illiterates by Sex:

	Persons	Males	Females
Literate	4	2	2
Illiterate	5	2	3
Literacy rate	44.4	50.0	40.0
Graduate	0	0	0

Scheduled Tribes (Dominant):
Kondareddis, Malai Pandaram, Malai Vedan
For their cultural identity please see Appendix-II

Villages without Scheduled Tribes: There are 17 villages without any scheduled tribe population.

Literates and Illiterates by Sex (Total Population):

	Persons	Males	Females
Literate	32,563	19,932	12,631
Illiterate	32,886	13,145	19,741
Literacy rate	55	67	43
Graduate	442	311	131

Agriculture: ***Distribution of villages according to land use:***
Out of 21 villages, Total area (in hectare) is 20238.37, out of that 78.9 percent is cultivable and 30.11 percent of the cultivable area is irrigated.

Sources of Irrigation (Hectares): Government Canal 1387, Private Canal 0, Well without Electricity 82, Well with Electricity 3089.94, Tubewell without Electricity 0, Tubewell with Electricity 248.82, Tank 0, River 0, Lake 0, Waterfall 0, Others 0.

Villages with population of 5000 to 9999:
Karattupalayam, Koshanam, Emmampoondi.

Villages with population of 10000 and above: None

Distribution of Workers:

	Persons	Males	Females	WPR
Cultivators	13,282	7,775	5,507	30.47
Agricultural Labour	17,637	7,591	10,046	40.46
Household Industry	3,273	1,703	1,570	7.51
Other Workers	9,400	6,395	3,005	21.56
Main Workers	36,175	22,128	14,047	82.99
Marginal Workers	7,417	1,336	6,081	17.01
Total Workers	43,592	23,464	20,128	

Religion: Major Religious Communities:

	Persons	Males	Females	Sex Ratio
Hindu (98.98%)	64,783	32,746	32,037	978
Muslim (0.51%)	335	166	169	1,018
Christian (0.35%)	228	107	121	1,131
Sikh (0%)	2	1	1	1,000
Buddhists (0%)	-	-	-	-
Jain (0%)	-	-	-	-

Agewise Data:

	Persons	Males	Females	Sex Ratio
All ages	65,449	33,077	32,372	979
0-14	14,092	7,174	6,918	964
15-44	30,286	15,027	15,259	1015
45-79	19,885	10,223	9,662	945
80+	1,076	593	483	815
Age not stated	110	60	50	833

Languages (Dominant):
Tamil, Telugu, Kannada, Urdu, English

Disabled Population:

	Persons	Males	Females	%
Total Disabled	1,690	572	1,118	
In Seeing	1,137	261	876	67.28
In Speech	106	57	49	6.27
In Hearing	69	37	32	4.08
In Movement	274	164	110	16.21
Mentally	104	53	51	6.15

NANGAVALLI

Nangavalli C.D. Block lies in the north-western part of Salem district. It is a part of Mettur taluk. The Block is located at a distance of 36 kms. from district headquarters (Salem). There are 13 villages in the block with the total population of 57,650 persons. Area of the C.D. Block is 133.11 sq. kms. It is bounded bounded in the north by C.D. Block Mecheri, in the south by CD Block Edappadi, in the east by C.D. Blocks Mecheri, Taraman galam, Omalur, in the west by C.D. Block Kolathur.

Communications:

Roadways : S.H-20: Direction- Mettur to Mecheri, Nearest Village- Gonur (W).

River: Cauvery Nadi- Nearest Villages- Vanavasi (RF), Vanavasi, Solappadi (RF).

Annual Rainfall: Average Rainfall 540 mm.

Ground Water: Availability of the ground water in the Basin is 1910.71 H.A.M. and the utilization is 2272.70 H.A.M. It belongs to Safe category. Depth to water level varies from 2 to 20 meter below the ground. Most of the wells go down in summer months, according to the Ground Water Estimation Committee.

Forest and Reserved Forest: (Gonur RF)- Nearest Villages- Gonur (W), Genur (RF). (Solapadi)- Nearest Villages- Solappadi (RF), Gonur (W). (Vanavasi)- Nearest Villages- Veerakkal, Vanavasi, Vanavasi (RF).

Natural Division: Kongu Nadu.

Administration

Revenue **Division:** Mettur. Parliamentary Constituency: 10 Dharmapuri. District: Salem. Taluk: Mettur. Assembly Constituency: 86 Edappadi, 85 Mettur. Gram Panchayat: 9.

Villages: 13 **Inhabited:** 10 **Uninhabited:** 3

Ranking	District	State	National
Area	16	353	5279
Population	17	336	4938
Sex Ratio	21	385	6248
Child Sex Ratio	19	383	6336
Literacy Rate	15	368	3975
Density	18	229	2544
Work Participation Rate	9	91	2484

Gram Panchayats:

Chinnasoragai, Doramangalam , Gonur, Karikkapatti, Periyasoragai, Sanarapatti, Soorappalli, Veerakkal.

Amenities:

Education: Primary School in 9 villages, Middle school in 3 villages, Matriculation or Secondary School in 2 villages, namely Gonur (W), Vanavasi.

Higher Secondary or Pre University Courses or Intermediate or Junior College in 2 villages of the CD Block,, namely Soorappalli, Vanavasi.

College in 0 village, Adult Literacy Center in 0 village.

Medical: Hospital in 1 village, Dispensary in 0 village, Health Center in 1 village, Sub Center in 0 village, Maternity and Child Welfare Center in 1 village, Community health workers in 0 village.

The Village having Hospital or Dispensary or Health Center is Soorappalli.

Drinking Water: Tap water in 10 villages, Tank water in 0 villages, Well water in 10 villages, Tubewell in 10 villages and more than one source in 10 villages.

Bank: Banking facility in 2 villages, namely, Soorappalli, Thoramangalam.

Credit Society in 4 villages Agricultural Credit Society in 3 Non-Agricultural Credit Society in 4 villages.

Others: Power supply in 10 villages, Cinema hall in 3 villages, sport club in 0 village, Stadium or Auditorium or Community Hall in 1 village, Post Office in 8 villages.

There are 9 villages having bus facilities.

Villages with most of facilities: Soorappalli Thoramangalam.

Villages without amenities (Education):

Dasakappatti..

Scheduled Castes: Out of the total population of 57650 persons, 4477 persons (7.77%) belong to Scheduled Castes.

The villages having less than 10% SC population are Gonur (W), Periya Soragai, Dasakappatti, Soorappalli Karikkappatty, Chinna Soragai, Thoramangalam.

The villages having more than 50% SC population are None.

Sex ratio of Scheduled Caste population is 461.

Scheduled Castes Literates and Illiterates by Sex:

	Persons	Males	Females
Literate	1,867	1,183	684
Illiterate	2,610	1,232	1,378
Literacy rate	48.8	58.1	38.3
Graduate	19	14	5

Scheduled Castes (Dominant):

Adi Dravida, Arunthathiyar, Paraiyan etc.

Chakkiliyan, Madari

For their cultural identity please see Appendix-I

Villages without Scheduled Castes: There are 5 villages without any scheduled caste population.

Scheduled Tribes: Out of the total population of 57650 persons, 375 persons (0.65%) belong to Scheduled Tribes.

The villages having less than 10% ST population are Gonur (W), Periya Soragai, Veerakkal, Dasakappatti Soorappalli, Mullikuttappatti, Vanavasi Karikkappatty, Thoramangalam.

The villages having more than 50% ST population are None.

Sex ratio of Scheduled tribe population is 472.

Scheduled Tribes Literates and Illiterates by Sex:

	Persons	Males	Females
Literate	221	138	83
Illiterate	154	60	94
Literacy rate	66.6	79.8	52.2
Graduate	10	6	4

Scheduled Tribes (Dominant):
Kondareddis, Adiyan

For their cultural identity please see Appendix-II

Villages without Scheduled Tribes: There are 10 villages without any scheduled tribe population.

Literates and Illiterates by Sex (Total Population):

	Persons	Males	Females
Literate	26,692	17,148	9,544
Illiterate	30,958	14,386	16,572
Literacy rate	53	63	41
Graduate	607	466	141

Agriculture: ***Distribution of villages according to land use:*** Out of 13 villages, Total area (in hectare) is 13311.29, out of that 53.57 percent is cultivable and 27.31 percent of the cultivable area is irrigated.

Sources of Irrigation (Hectares): Government Canal 0, Private Canal 0, Well without Electricity 57, Well with Electricity 1510.49, Tubewell without Electricity 0, Tubewell with Electricity 318, Tank 62, River 0, Lake 0, Waterfall 0, Others 0.

Villages with population of 5000 to 9999:
Periyasoragai, Vanavasi.

Villages with population of 10000 and above:
Gonur, Surappalli.

Distribution of Workers:

	Persons	Males	Females	WPR
Cultivators	7,172	4,461	2,711	25.4
Agricultural Labour	7,066	3,457	3,609	25.03
Household Industry	2,768	2,014	754	9.8
Other Workers	11,228	8,935	2,293	39.77
Main Workers	24,477	17,539	6,938	86.69
Marginal Workers	3,757	1,328	2,429	13.31
Total Workers	28,234	18,867	9,367	

Religion: Major Religious Communities:

	Persons	Males	Females	Sex Ratio
Hindu (99.7%)	57,479	31,457	26,022	827
Muslim (0.07%)	43	18	25	1,389
Christian (0.15%)	88	36	52	1,444
Sikh (0.03%)	16	11	5	455
Buddhists (0%)	2	1	1	1,000
Jain (0.01%)	4	2	2	1,000

Agewise Data:

	Persons	Males	Females	Sex Ratio
All ages	57,650	31,534	26,116	828
0-14	17,077	10,111	6,966	689
15-44	27,444	14,588	12,856	881
45-79	12,162	6,304	5,858	929
80+	705	371	334	900
Age not stated	262	160	102	638

Languages (Dominant):
Tamil, Telugu, Kannada, Urdu, Malayalam

Disabled Population:

	Persons	Males	Females	%
Total Disabled	729	465	264	
In Seeing	275	161	114	37.72
In Speech	99	69	30	13.58
In Hearing	37	22	15	5.08
In Movement	245	176	69	33.61
Mentally	73	37	36	10.01

NANGUNERI

Nanguneri C.D. Block lies in the south-western part of Tirunelveli district. It is a part of Nanguneri taluk. The Block is located at a distance of 33 kms. from district headquarters (Tirunelveli). There are 32 villag es in the block with the total population of 89,481 persons. Area of the C.D. Block is 440.66 sq. kms. It is bounded in the north by CD Block palayamkottai, in the south by taluk Radhapuram, in the east by district Thoothukkudi, and in the west by CD Block Kalakkadu.

Communications:

Roadways : N.H.-7: Direction- Nagarkoil to Tirunelveli, Nearest Villages- Poolam, Thottakudi, Karanthaneri, Pambankulam, Terku Nanganeri, Rajakkalmangalam, Dalapat hi Samudram, Vilvarayankulam, Marugalkrchi.

River: Nambiyur Nadi- Nearest Villages- Rajakkalmangalam, Eraippuvari.

Annual Rainfall: Average Rainfall 879 mm.

Ground Water: Availability of the ground water in the Basin is 66.02 MCM and the utilization is 25.42 MCM. It belongs to Safe category. Depth to water level varies from 0 to 5 meter below the ground. Most of the wells go down in summer months, according to the Ground Water Estimation Committee.

Natural Division: NA

Administration

Revenue **Division:** Cherammadevi. Parliamentary Constituen cy: 38 Tirunelveli. District: Tirunelveli. Taluk: Nanguneri. Assembly Constituency: 227 Nanguneri. Gram Panchayat: 27.

Villages: 32 **Inhabited:** 32 **Uninhabited:** 0

Ranking	District	State	National
Area	6	50	1720
Population	8	185	3792
Sex Ratio	3	10	143
Child Sex Ratio	15	217	3503
Literacy Rate	3	19	259
Density	17	283	4693

Work Participation Rate	16	325	3108

Gram Panchayats:
A.Sathankulam, Alagappapuram, Alwaneri, Ariyakulam, Chinthamani, Dhalapathisamudram, Ilangulam, Iraippuvari, Ittamozhi, kadamkulamthirumalapuram, karanthaneri, Koonthankulam, Marukalkurichi, Marukalkuruchi , Munanchipatti, Pappankulam, Paruthipadu, Poolam , Rajakkalmanglam, Ramakrishnapuram, Sadayaneri(Venkatarayapuram), Sankanankulam, Shenbagaramanallur, Singaneri , Therkunanguneri, Thottakudi, Unnankulam, Vijayanarayanam.

Amenities:

Education: Primary School in 29 villages, Middle school in 20 villages, Matriculation or Secondary School in 8 villages, namely Thottakudi, Deivanayakaperi, Karanthaneri, Marugalkurchi, Muunanjipatti, Dalapathi Samudram, Ilangulam, Ittamozhi.
Higher Secondary or Pre University Courses or Intermediate or Junior College in 5 villages of the CD Block,, namely Thottakudi, Deivanayakaperi, Marugalkurchi, Ilangulam, Ittamozhi.
College in 2 villages, Adult Literacy Center in 0 village., Colleges are in villages, namely Thottakudi, Rajakkalmangalam.

Medical: Hospital in 1 village, Dispensary in 0 village, Health Center in 6 villages, Sub Center in 14 villages, Maternity and Child Welfare Center in 4 villages, Community health workers in 28 villages.
The Villages having Hospital or Dispensary or Health Center are Singaneri, Ilangulam, Vijayanarayanam.

Drinking Water: Tap water in 32 villages, Tank water in 4 villages, Well water in 27 villages, Tubewell in 9 villages and more than one source in 32 villages.

Bank: Banking facility in 11 villages, namely, Thottakudi, Paruthippadu, Unnangulam, Kadankulam Muunanjipatti, Ramakrishnapuram, Dalapathi Samudram Eraippuvari, Ilangulam, Vijayanarayanam, Ittamozhi.
Credit Society in 5 villages Agricultural Credit Society in 5 Non-Agricultural Credit Society in 0 village.

Others: Power supply in 32 villages, Cinema hall in 1 village, sport club in 1 village, Stadium or Auditorium or Community Hall in 0 village, Post Office in 28 villages.
There are 29 villages having bus facilities.

Villages with most of facilities: Thottakudi Paruthippadu, Unnangulam, Kadankulam, Muunanjipatti Ramakrishnapuram, Dalapathi Samudram, Eraippuvari Ilangulam, Vijayanarayanam, Ittamozhi.

Villages without amenities (Education):
Vilvarayankulam, Ilayankulam, Veppankulam..

Scheduled Castes: Out of the total population of 89481 persons, 15813 persons (17.67%) belong to Scheduled Castes.
The villages having less than 10% SC population are Alwaneri, Deivanayakaperi, Sivaramangaipuram Marugalkurchi, Karankadu, Veppankulam Dalapathi Samudram, Vijayanarayanam.
The villages having more than 50% SC population are None.
Sex ratio of Scheduled Caste population is 523.

Scheduled Castes Literates and Illiterates by Sex:

	Persons	Males	Females
Literate	10,232	5,480	4,752
Illiterate	5,581	2,058	3,523
Literacy rate	74.1	84.3	65.0
Graduate	133	84	49

Scheduled Castes (Dominant):
Pallan, Paraiyan etc., Adi Dravida, Chakkiliyan Vathiriyan

For their cultural identity please see Appendix-I

Villages without Scheduled Castes: There are 2 villages without any scheduled caste population.

Scheduled Tribes: Out of the total population of 89481 persons, 191 persons (0.21%) belong to Scheduled Tribes.
The villages having less than 10% ST population are Poolam, Thottakudi, A.Sathangulam, Alwaneri Paruthippadu, Chinthamani, Deivanayakaperi Unnangulam, Karanthaneri, Sivaramangaipuram Vilvarayankulam, Marugalkurchi, Ilayankulam Singaneri, Shenbaga Ramanallur, Ariyankulam Koondakulum, Kadankulam, Muunanjipatti, Sadayaneri Ramakrishnapuram, Pappankulam, Karankadu Pambankulam, Terku Nanganeri, Veppankulam Rajakkalmangalam, Dalapathi Samudram, Eraippuvari Ilangulam, Vijayanarayanam, Ittamozhi.
The villages having more than 50% ST population are None.
Sex ratio of Scheduled tribe population is 461.

Scheduled Tribes Literates and Illiterates by Sex:

	Persons	Males	Females
Literate	120	74	46
Illiterate	71	29	42
Literacy rate	75.0	85.1	63.0
Graduate	0	0	0

Scheduled Tribes (Dominant):
Sholaga, Kaniyan etc., Malakkuravan, Kattunayakan Malai Pandaram

For their cultural identity please see Appendix-II

Villages without Scheduled Tribes: There are 22 villages without any scheduled tribe population.

Literates and Illiterates by Sex (Total Population):

	Persons	Males	Females
Literate	63,462	32,772	30,690
Illiterate	26,019	10,082	15,937
Literacy rate	81	88	74
Graduate	1,462	829	633

Agriculture: ***Distribution of villages according to land use:*** Out of 32 villages, Total area (in hectare) is 44066.3, out of that 15.32 percent is cultivable and 63.77 percent of the cultivable area is irrigated.

Sources of Irrigation (Hectares): Government Canal 0, Private Canal 0, Well without Electricity 253.27, Well with Electricity 2321.36, Tubewell without Electricity 8.12, Tubewell with Electricity 11.78, Tank 1711.82, River 0, Lake 0, Waterfall 0, Others 0.

Villages with population of 5000 to 9999: Dalapathi Samudram, Ittamozhi.

Villages with population of 10000 and above: Vijayanarayanam.

Distribution of Workers:

	Persons	Males	Females	WPR
Cultivators	8,452	5,994	2,458	20.13
Agricultural Labour	16,948	9,078	7,870	40.37
Household Industry	5,227	732	4,495	12.45
Other Workers	11,356	8,137	3,219	27.05
Main Workers	32,662	20,034	12,628	77.8
Marginal Workers	9,321	3,907	5,414	22.2
Total Workers	41,983	23,941	18,042	

Religion: Major Religious Communities:

	Persons	Males	Females	Sex Ratio
Hindu (78.91%)	70,613	34,017	36,596	1,076
Muslim (0.19%)	172	82	90	1,098
Christian (20.79%)	18,604	8,711	9,893	1,136
Sikh (0.02%)	16	9	7	778
Buddhists (0%)	1	1	-	-
Jain (0%)	3	-	3	-

Agewise Data:

	Persons	Males	Females	Sex Ratio
All ages	89,481	42,854	46,627	1088
0-14	25,481	13,087	12,394	947
15-44	41,041	19,079	21,962	1151
45-79	21,728	10,112	11,616	1149
80+	971	445	526	1182
Age not stated	260	131	129	985

Languages (Dominant): Tamil, Telugu, Hindi, Malayalam, Kannada

Disabled Population:

	Persons	Males	Females	%
Total Disabled	2,436	1,122	1,314	
In Seeing	1,491	568	923	61.21
In Speech	155	88	67	6.36
In Hearing	65	28	37	2.67
In Movement	498	307	191	20.44
Mentally	227	131	96	9.32

NANNILAM

Nannilam C.D. Block lies in the north-eastern part of Thiruvarur district. It is a part of Nannilam taluk. The Block is located at a distance of 16 kms. from district headquarters (Thiruvarur). There are 58 villages in the block with the total population of 91,162 persons. Area of the C.D. Block is 193.97 sq. kms. It is bounded in the north by district Nagapattinam, in the south by CD Block Thiruvarur and district Nagapattinam, in the east by district Nagapattinam, and in the west by CD Block Kodavasal. It has common boundary with the U.T. of Pondicherry on east.

Communications:

Roadways : S.H.-23: Direction- Thiruvarur to Mayiladuthurai, Nearest Villages- Kollumangudi, Keeranoor, Agarathirumalam, Seruvalur, Mudikondan, Thirukkanpeswaram, Mahilancherry, Panangudi, Visalur, Kuvalaikkal, Moonkillkudi, Sorakkudi, Kaduvangudi, Thirumeyachoor, Maharajapuram.

Rivers: Arasalar Nadi- Nearest Villages- Koilthirumalam, Agarathirumalam, Maharajapuram, Kothavasal. Thirumalairajan Nadi- Nearest Villages- Mudikondan, Seruvalur.

Annual Rainfall: Average Rainfall 1184 mm.

Ground Water: Availability of the ground water in the Basin is 3172.02 H.A.M. and the utilization is 2683. 42 H.A.M. It belongs to Semi Critical category. Depth to water level varies from 2 to 5 meter below the ground. Most of the wells go down in summer months, according to the Ground Water Estimation Committee.

Natural Division: Chola Nadu.

Administration

Revenue **Division:** Thiruvarur. Parliamentary Constituency: 29 Thanjavur. District: Thiruvarur. Taluk: Kodavasal, Nannilam. Assembly Constituency: 169 Nannilam. Gram Panchayat: 48.

Border Villages: (Pondicherry)- Nearest Villages- Kollapuram, Kumarakkudi, Thirukottaram, Velangudi, Kadagam, Ubayavedanthapuram.

Villages: 58 **Inhabited:** 58 **Uninhabited:** 0

Ranking	District	State	National
Area	6	292	4290
Population	6	176	3748
Sex Ratio	8	165	1137
Child Sex Ratio	8	141	2597
Literacy Rate	2	26	422
Density	10	344	2352
Work Participation Rate	4	70	4328

Gram Panchayats:
Achuthanmangalam , Agarthirumalam, Alangudi , Anaikuppam , Annathanapuram , Kadagam, Kaduvangudi, Kaliyarkudi , Keelgudi, Keeranur, Kollapuram, Kothavasal, Kottur, Kovilthirumalam, Kurungulam, Kuvalikkal, Maharajapuram, Mahilanchieri, Menangudi , Moolangudi, Moongilgudi, Mudikondan, Nadagudi, Panangudi, Pandaravadai, Paruthiyur, Pavattagudi, Pillur , Pozagudi, Rettagudi, Saliperi, Sembianallur, Senganoor, Seruvaloor, Sirupuliyur, Soragudi, Srivanchiam, Thalaiyur , Thattathimoolai, Thirukandeeswaram , Thirukottaram , Thirumaichur, Ubayavethanapuram, Vadakudi, Vazhkai, Veethividangan , Velangudi , Visuloor.

Amenities:
Education: Primary School in 57 villages, Middle school in 17 villages, Matriculation or Secondary School in 8 villages, namely Nedungulam, Kaduvangudi, Agarathirumalam, Mudikondan, Srivanjiyam, Nannilam, Anaikuppam, Panangudi.
Higher Secondary or Pre University Courses or Intermediate or Junior College in 2 villages of the CD Block,, namely Nedungulam, Nannilam.
College in 0 village, Adult Literacy Center in 0 village.
Medical: Hospital in 5 villages, Dispensary in 5 villages, Health Center in 9 villages, Sub Center in 3 villages, Maternity and Child Welfare Center in 1 village, Community health workers in 57 villages.
The Villages having Hospital or Dispensary or Health Center are Keeranoor, Kaduvangudi, Kumarakkudi, Menangudi, Valkai, Srivanjiyam, Tattathimoolai, Salipperi, Anaikuppam, Panangudi, Sorakkudi.
Drinking Water: Tap water in 58 villages, Tank water in 1 villages, Well water in 58 villages, Tubewell in 58 villages and more than one source in 58 villages.
Bank: Banking facility in 6 villages, namely, Nedungulam, Thirukottaram, Kaduvangudi, Kollapuram Agarathirumalam, Moonkillkudi.
Credit Society in 11 villages Agricultural Credit Society in 11 Non-Agricultural Credit Society in 0 village.
Others: Power supply in 58 villages, Cinema hall in 2 villages, sport club in 0 village, Stadium or Auditorium or Community Hall in 0 village, Post Office in 35 villages.
There are 47 villages having bus facilities.
Villages with most of facilities: Nedungulam Thirukottaram, Kaduvangudi, Kollapuram Agarathirumalam, Moonkillkudi.
Villages without amenities (Education): Poongulam..
Scheduled Castes: Out of the total population of 91162 persons, 32853 persons (36.04%) belong to Scheduled Castes.
The villages having less than 10% SC population are None..
The villages having more than 50% SC population are Koothanoor, Nedungulam, Velangudi, Sirupuliyur Pantaravadi, Ubayavedanthapuram, Achudamangalam Paruthiyur, Moolamangalam, Visalur, Moolangudi Moonkillkudi, Sorakkudi.
Sex ratio of Scheduled Caste population is 496.

Scheduled Castes Literates and Illiterates by Sex:

	Persons	Males	Females
Literate	19,650	11,275	8,375
Illiterate	13,203	5,283	7,920
Literacy rate	69.8	79.6	59.8
Graduate	297	222	75

Scheduled Castes (Dominant):
Paraiyan etc., Adi Dravida, Pallan, Arunthathiyar Valluvan
For their cultural identity please see Appendix-I
Villages without Scheduled Castes: There is 1 village without any scheduled caste population.
Scheduled Tribes: Out of the total population of 91162 persons, 37 persons (0.04%) belong to Scheduled Tribes.
The villages having less than 10% ST population are Pillur, Kollumangudi, Keeranoor, Koothanoor Annadhanapuram, Kaliyakudy, Nedungulam, Mugundhanur Thirukottaram, Velangudi, Kadagam, Thalaiyur Pavattakudi, Sirupuliyur, Panagattangudi Kaduvangudi, Pozakudi, Thirumeyachoor, Pantaravadi Kottur, Kurungulam, Kollapuram, Kumarakkudi Menangudi, Ubayavedanthapuram, Rettakkudi Sembianallur, Koilthirumalam, Agarathirumalam Maharajapuram, Seruvalur, Kothavasal, Mudikondan Alangudi, Vadagudi, Valkai, Senganoor, Srivanjiyam Achudamangalam, Nallamankudy, Manavalampettai Thirukkanpeswaram, Nannilam, Kilgudal, Poongulam Vidividangan, Paruthiyur, Tattathimoolai, Salipperi Anaikuppam, Mahilancherry, Moolamangalam, Panangudi Visalur, Kuvalaikkal, Moolangudi, Moonkillkudi Sorakkudi.
The villages having more than 50% ST population are None.
Sex ratio of Scheduled tribe population is 541.

Scheduled Tribes Literates and Illiterates by Sex:

	Persons	Males	Females
Literate	18	6	12
Illiterate	19	11	8
Literacy rate	60.0	50.0	66.7
Graduate	0	0	0

Scheduled Tribes (Dominant):
Kattunayakan, Irular, Malakkuravan, Malai Pandaram

For their cultural identity please see Appendix-II

Villages without Scheduled Tribes: There are 52 villages without any scheduled tribe population.

Literates and Illiterates by Sex (Total Population):

	Persons	Males	Females
Literate	62,713	34,660	28,053
Illiterate	28,449	10,896	17,553
Literacy rate	78	87	70
Graduate	1,125	810	315

Agriculture: ***Distribution of villages according to land use:*** Out of 58 villages, Total area (in hectare) is 19397.32, out of that 76.62 percent is cultivable and 97.52 percent of the cultivable area is irrigated.

Sources of Irrigation (Hectares): Government Canal 13633.14, Private Canal 0, Well without Electricity 0, Well with Electricity 0, Tubewell without Electricity 26.81, Tubewell with Electricity 91.82, Tank 0, River 741.94, Lake 0, Waterfall 0, Others 0.

Villages with population of 5000 to 9999: None

Villages with population of 10000 and above: None

Distribution of Workers:

	Persons	Males	Females	WPR
Cultivators	5,166	4,199	967	13.79
Agricultural Labour	24,406	15,352	9,054	65.13
Household Industry	490	298	192	1.31
Other Workers	7,413	6,469	944	19.78
Main Workers	28,344	21,642	6,702	75.63
Marginal Workers	9,131	4,676	4,455	24.37
Total Workers	37,475	26,318	11,157	

Religion: Major Religious Communities:

	Persons	Males	Females	Sex Ratio
Hindu (93.56%)	85,293	42,909	42,384	988
Muslim (5.11%)	4,656	2,054	2,602	1,267
Christian (1.29%)	1,176	573	603	1,052
Sikh (0%)	1	1	-	-
Buddhists (0%)	1	-	1	-
Jain (0%)	2	-	2	-

Agewise Data:

	Persons	Males	Females	Sex Ratio
All ages	91,162	45,556	45,606	1001
0-14	25,553	12,920	12,633	978
15-44	44,821	21,934	22,887	1043
45-79	19,931	10,267	9,664	941
80+	751	379	372	982
Age not stated	106	56	50	893

Languages (Dominant):

Tamil, Telugu, Malayalam, Others, Marathi

Disabled Population:

	Persons	Males	Females	%
Total Disabled	3,606	1,234	2,372	
In Seeing	2,667	673	1,994	73.96
In Speech	171	113	58	4.74
In Hearing	103	56	47	2.86
In Movement	507	304	203	14.06
Mentally	158	88	70	4.38

NARIKUDI

Narikudi C.D. Block lies in the north-eastern part of Virudhunagar district. It is a part of Tiruchuli and Kariapatti taluks. The Block is located at a distance of NA kms. from district headquarters (Virudhunagar). There are 92 villages in the block with the total population of 65,163 persons. Area of the C.D. Block is 424.57 sq. kms. It is bounded in the north by district Sivaganga, in the south by district Ramanathapuram, in the east by district Ramanathapuram and Sivaganga, in the west by CD Blocks Kariapatti and Tihuchuli. CD Block Narikudi falls in taluk Tiruchuli by 91 villages, in taluk Kariapatti by 01 village.

Communications:

Roadways : S.H.-42: Direction- Aruppukkottai to Paramakudi, Nearest Villages- T.Velangudi, Mayaleri, Athitharudal, Kandukondammanickam, Veerakkudi, Sathiseri, Andiyendal.

River: Gridhamai Nadi- Nearest Villages- Vagaikulam, Katalur, Athikulam, Ulakkudi, Manur, Athitharudal, Varisaiyur, Melaparuthiyoor, Ottangulam, Veeranchozan.

Annual Rainfall: Average Rainfall 799 mm.

Ground Water: Availability of the ground water in the Basin is 59.86 MCM and the utilization is 27.62 MCM. It belongs to Safe category. Depth to water level varies from 5 to 10 meter below the ground. Most of the wells go down in summer months, according to the Ground Water Estimation Committee.

Natural Division: NA

Administration

Revenue **Division:** Aruppukottai. Parliamentary Constituency: 35 Ramanathapuram. District: Virudhunagar. Taluk: Kariapatti, Tiruchuli. Assembly Constituency: 208 Tiruchuli. Gram Panchayat: 44.

Villages: 92 **Inhabited:** 74 **Uninhabited:** 18

Ranking	District	State	National
Area	2	56	1802
Population	11	315	4682
Sex Ratio	2	42	406
Child Sex Ratio	3	57	1119
Literacy Rate	11	311	2623
Density	2	53	5506
Work Participation Rate	11	359	477

Gram Panchayats:

A.mukkulam, Agathakulam, Alagapuri, Alathur, Anaikulam, Andiandal, Eluvani, Illuppaiyur,

Irunjirai, Isali, Kallumadaipoolankulam, Kandukondamanickam, Karisalkulam, Kattanoor, Keelakondaraikulam, Kottaikatcheiendal, Manur, Maraiyur, Melaparithiyur, Minakulam, N.Mukulam, Nallukkurichi, Nallur, Narikudi, Nathakulam, Panaikudi, Pillaiyarkulam, Pillaiyarnatham, Pillayarnatham, Poomalapatti, Poombidagai, Pulvaikarai, Regunathamadai, Salaiilupaikulam, Salaiilupukulam, Sethupuram, T.Kadambankulam, T.Velangudi, Thimmapuram, Timmapuram, Tiruvidainallur, Ulakudi, Uluthamadai, Urduranikidakulam, V.Karisalkulam, Varisaiyur, Veeracholan, Velaneri, Velanoorani.

Amenities:

Education: Primary School in 67 villages, Middle school in 14 villages, Matriculation or Secondary School in 8 villages, namely Pillayarkulam, U Kidakulam, Katalur, Ulakkudi, Athitharudal, Veeranchozan, Annaikkulam, Iluppaiyur. Higher Secondary or Pre University Courses or Intermediate or Junior College in 3 villages of the CD Block,, namely Ulakkudi, Athitharudal, Veeranchozan. College in 0 village, Adult Literacy Center in 0 village.

Medical: Hospital in 0 village, Dispensary in 0 village, Health Center in 6 villages, Sub Center in 14 villages, Maternity and Child Welfare Center in 15 villages, Community health workers in 19 villages.

Drinking Water: Tap water in 74 villages, Tank water in 1 villages, Well water in 74 villages, Tubewell in 74 villages and more than one source in 74 villages.

Bank: Banking facility in 7 villages, namely, U Kidakulam, Athikulam, Naloor, Athitharudal Veeranchozan, Annaikkulam, Iluppaiyur.

Credit Society in 13 villages Agricultural Credit Society in 12 Non-Agricultural Credit Society in 2 villages.

Others: Power supply in 74 villages, Cinema hall in 0 village, sport club in 0 village, Stadium or Auditorium or Community Hall in 0 village, Post Office in 16 villages.

There are 41 villages having bus facilities.

Villages with most of facilities: U Kidakulam Naloor, Veeranchozan, Annaikkulam.

Villages without amenities (Education): Pulichchikulam, Keelasimboor, Kaladipapaangkulam, Kuruthankulam, Kongalakudi, Nambiyandal, 5Ellikulam..

Scheduled Castes: Out of the total population of 65163 persons, 14247 persons (21.86%) belong to Scheduled Castes. The villages having less than 10% SC population are Pillayarkulam, S Kallumadai, Erumaikkulam, Panaikudi Sorikulam, Isali, Melakumilangulam Kamalipuliangulam, Ottangulam, Veeranchozan Muthameri, Panaiyoor, Semponnerunji, Raguvathamadai Pappanagkulam, Minakulam, Nambiyandal, 5Ellikulam T.Karisalkulam, Pilliyar Natham, Iluppaiyur Kathanpatti, Velanoorani, Poomalaipatti.

The villages having more than 50% SC population are Kalathur, Usilangulam, Pulichchikulam Kuraiyaravasithan, Keelasimboor, Kaladipapaangkulam Pathankkurachi, Kuruthankulam, Nallukurchi.

Sex ratio of Scheduled Caste population is 504.

Scheduled Castes Literates and Illiterates by Sex:

	Persons	Males	Females
Literate	5,994	3,853	2,141
Illiterate	8,253	3,219	5,034
Literacy rate	49.5	64.4	35.0
Graduate	49	35	14

Scheduled Castes (Dominant):

Pallan, Chakkiliyan, Paraiyan etc., Kuravan etc. Devendrakulathan

For their cultural identity please see Appendix-I

Villages without Scheduled Castes: There are 28 villages without any scheduled caste population.

Scheduled Tribes: Out of the total population of 65163 persons, 0 persons (0%) belong to Scheduled Tribes. The villages having less than 10% ST population are Thimmapuram, Poombidagai, Karisalkulam, Kalathur Pillayarkulam, S Kallumadai, K Nedungulam Tiruvidanallur, Eluvani, Pulvoikarai, Erumaikkulam U Kidakulam, Kundukulam, Vagaikulam, Katalur Athikulam, Naloor, M Pudukulam, Panaikudi, Ulakkudi Irunjierai, Theli, Sorikulam, T.Velangudi, Mayaleri Manur, Salaiiluppaikulam, Isali, Melakumilangulam Sottamuri, Athitharudal, Velaneri, Sathiseri Andiyendal, Varisaiyur, Kandukondammanickam Veerakkudi, Usilangulam, Melaparuthiyoor Pulichchikulam, Kamalipuliangulam, Kuraiyaravasithan Ottangulam, Veeranchozan, Keelasimboor Kaladipapaangkulam, Pathankkurachi, Muthameri Agathakulam, Kuruthankulam, Panaiyoor, Semponnerunji Raguvathamadai, Nathakulan, Kongalakudi, Nallukurchi Pappanagkulam, Minakulam, Nambiyandal Veeraalangulam, Sullangudi, 5Ellikulam T.Karisalkulam, Pilliyar Natham, Sethupuram Naduvapacheri, Annaikkulam, Iluppaiyur, Seelanpatti Kathanpatti, Velanoorani, Thamotharaporam Poomalaipatti, Muthuramalingapuram.

The villages having more than 50% ST population are None.

Villages without Scheduled Tribes: There are 92 villages without any scheduled tribe population.

Literates and Illiterates by Sex (Total Population):

	Persons	Males	Females

Literate	34,333	21,010	13,323
Illiterate	30,830	10,989	19,841
Literacy rate	61	76	46
Graduate	366	278	88

Agriculture: ***Distribution of villages according to land use:*** Out of 92 villages, Total area (in hectare) is 42457.51, out of that 0 percent is cultivable and 0 percent of the cultivable area is irrigated.

Sources of Irrigation (Hectares): Government Canal 0, Private Canal 0, Well without Electricity 0, Well with Electricity 0, Tubewell without Electricity 0, Tubewell with Electricity 6.87, Tank 772.21, River 0, Lake 0, Waterfall 7762.91, Others 0.

Villages with population of 5000 to 9999: None

Villages with population of 10000 and above: None

Distribution of Workers:

	Persons	Males	Females	WPR
Cultivators	15,719	9,451	6,268	42.24
Agricultural Labour	15,650	5,939	9,711	42.06
Household Industry	563	253	310	1.51
Other Workers	5,280	4,023	1,257	14.19
Main Workers	27,845	17,197	10,648	74.83
Marginal Workers	9,367	2,469	6,898	25.17
Total Workers	37,212	19,666	17,546	

Religion: Major Religious Communities:

	Persons	Males	Females	Sex Ratio
Hindu (94.17%)	61,361	30,282	31,079	1,026
Muslim (4.96%)	3,229	1,446	1,783	1,233
Christian (0.84%)	546	260	286	1,100
Sikh (0%)	1	1	-	-
Buddhists (0%)	-	-	-	-
Jain (0%)	-	-	-	-

Agewise Data:

	Persons	Males	Females	Sex Ratio
All ages	65,163	31,999	33,164	1036
0-14	19,892	10,159	9,733	958
15-44	29,679	14,177	15,502	1093
45-79	15,104	7,416	7,688	1037
80+	349	171	178	1041
Age not stated	139	76	63	829

Languages (Dominant):

Tamil, Telugu, Kannada, Urdu, English

Disabled Population:

	Persons	Males	Females	%
Total Disabled	1,052	566	486	
In Seeing	453	236	217	43.06
In Speech	101	54	47	9.6
In Hearing	74	32	42	7.03
In Movement	335	199	136	31.84
Mentally	89	45	44	8.46

NATHAM

Natham C.D. Block lies in the south-eastern part of Dindigul district. It is a part of Natham taluk. The Block is located at a distance of 35 kms. from district headquarters (Dindigul). There are 41 villages in the block with the total population of 111,663 persons. Area of the C.D. Block is 581.22 sq. kms. It is bounded in the north by district Tiruchirappalli, in the south by district Madurai, in the east by district Madurai and Tiruchirappalli, in the west by CD Blocks Vadamadurai and Sanarpatti, and district Madurai.

Communications:

Roadways : S.H.-35: Direction- Dindigul to Kottampatti, Nearest Villages- Velampatty, Boothagudi, Samutrapatti, Uralipatti, Pannappatty, Pappanmalai RF, Poolamalai RF. Backwards Region Grants Fund: It receives Backward Region Grants.

Annual Rainfall: Average Rainfall 813 mm.

Ground Water: Availability of the ground water in the Basin is 4295.27 H.A.M. and the utilization is 2798.32 H.A.M. It belongs to Over Expoited category. Depth to water level varies from 2 to 10 meter below the ground. Most of the wells go down in summer months, according to the Ground Water Estimation Committee.

Forest and Reserved Forest: (Alagar Hills RF)- Nearest Villages- Reddiapatti, Lingavadi, Pudur, Alagar Hills RF. (Chembulimalai)- Nearest Villages- Saththambadi, Idayapatti, Chellappanaickenpatti, Chembulimalai RF, Reddiapatti. (Senamalai)- Nearest Villages- Lingavadi, Senamalai RF, Pudur. (Budagudi)- Nearest Villages- Sirugudi, Boothagudi, Boothagudi RF. (Nedunkuttu)- Nearest Villages- Sirugudi, Nedunkuttu RF, Nadumandalam. (Nadumalai)- Nearest Villages- Samutrapatti, Uralipatti, Nadumalai RF, Chellappanaickenpatti. (Perumalai)- Nearest Villages- Saththambadi, Mulaiyur, Perumalai RF, Reddiapatti, Lingavadi. (Chinnayanpattikaradu)- Nearest Villages- Sirangattupatti, Kottaiyur, Chinnayampatti Karadu RF, Seithur. (Kaluvadimalai)- Nearest Villages- Pillaiyarnatham, Kaluvadimalai RF, Sendurai. (Pillaiyarnattam)- Nearest Villages- Pillaiyarnatham RF, Pillaiyarnatham, Sendurai. (Karanthamalai)- Nearest Villages- Kudagipatti, Seithur, Karanthamalai RF, Nadumandalam, Pannappatty, Velampatty. (Pappanmalai)- Nearest Villages- Pannappatty, Pappanmalai RF, Mulaiyur. (Kodangikuttu)- Nearest Villages- Kodangikuttu RF, Kudagipatti. Sendurai. (Methugumalai)- Nearest Villages- Sirangattupatti, Kottaiyur, Seithur, Methugumalai RF, Sirugudi, Nadumandalam. (Mottamalai)- Nearest VIllages- Uralipatti, Mottamalai RF. (Poolamalai)- Nearest Villages- Avichipatti, Pannianmalai, Samutrapatti, Poolamalai RF, Uralipatti.

Natural Division: NA

Administration

Revenue **Division:** Dindigul. Parliamentary Constituency: 22 Dindigul. District: Dindigul. Taluk: Natham. Assembly Constituency: 131 Natham. Gram Panchayat: 23.

Villages: 41 **Inhabited:** 30 **Uninhabited:** 11

Ranking	District	State	National
Area	1	22	1227
Population	1	88	3113
Sex Ratio	7	229	1618
Child Sex Ratio	3	234	3819
Literacy Rate	12	319	2714
Density	8	94	4844
Work Participation Rate	12	333	974

Gram Panchayats:

Avichippatti, Budagudi, Chellappanaickenpatti, Kosukurichi, Kottaiyur, Kudagipatti, Kuttupatti, Lingavadi, Mulaiyur, Pannuvarpatti, Pillaiyarnatham, Pudupatti, Pudur, Punnapatti, Reddiapatti, Samutrapatti, Sathambadi, Seithur, Sendurai, Sirangattupatti, Sirugudi, Uralipatti, Velampatti,

Amenities:

Education: Primary School in 24 villages, Middle school in 15 villages, Matriculation or Secondary School in 3 villages, namely Sendurai, Kottaiyur, Sirugudi.

Higher Secondary or Pre University Courses or Intermediate or Junior College in 1 village of the CD Block,, namely Sendurai.

College in 0 village, Adult Literacy Center in 0 village.

Medical: Hospital in 0 village, Dispensary in 0 village, Health Center in 9 villages, Sub Center in 22 villages, Maternity and Child Welfare Center in 22 villages, Community health workers in 2 villages.

The Villages having Hospital or Dispensary or Health Center are Pillaiyarnatham, Sendurai, Pannappatty, Samutrapatti, Lingavadi, Pudur.

Drinking Water: Tap water in 30 villages, Tank water in 24 villages, Well water in 30 villages, Tubewell in 30 villages and more than one source in 30 villages.

Bank: Banking facility in 7 villages, namely, Sendurai, Sirugudi, Nadumandalam, Pannappatty Velampatty, Reddiapatti, Pudur.

Credit Society in 8 villages Agricultural Credit Society in 8 Non-Agricultural Credit Society in 1 village.

Others: Power supply in 30 villages, Cinema hall in 3 villages, sport club in 1 village, Stadium or Auditorium or Community Hall in 1 village, Post Office in 17 villages.

There are 23 villages having bus facilities.

Villages with most of facilities: Sendurai Sirugudi, Nadumandalam, Velampatty, Reddiapatti Pudur.

Villages without amenities (Education): Kodangikuttu R F, Karanthamalai R F, Methugumalai R F, Mottamalai R F, Nadumalai R F, Alagar Hills R F..

Scheduled Castes: Out of the total population of 111663 persons, 13110 persons (11.74%) belong to Scheduled Castes. The villages having less than 10% SC population are Pillaiyarnatham, Kodangikuttu R F, Kudagipatti Sirangattupatti, Kottaiyur, Seithur Karanthamalai R F, Methugumalai R F, Avichipatti Boothagudi, Mulaiyur, Idayapatti, Mottamalai R F Nadumalai R F, Lingavadi, Pudur, Alagar Hills R F. The villages having more than 50% SC population are None.

Sex ratio of Scheduled Caste population is 495.

Scheduled Castes Literates and Illiterates by Sex:

	Persons	Males	Females
Literate	6,429	3,991	2,438
Illiterate	6,681	2,631	4,050
Literacy rate	57.0	70.4	43.5
Graduate	74	61	13

Scheduled Castes (Dominant):

Paraiyan etc., Pallan, Chakkiliyan, Adi Dravida Puthirai Vannan

For their cultural identity please see Appendix-I

Villages without Scheduled Castes: There are 17 villages without any scheduled caste population.

Scheduled Tribes: Out of the total population of 111663 persons, 5 persons (0%) belong to Scheduled Tribes. The villages having less than 10% ST population are Pillaiyarnatham, Sendurai, Kodangikuttu R F Kudagipatti, Sirangattupatti, Kottaiyur, Seithur Karanthamalai R F, Methugumalai R F, Sirugudi Nadumandalam, Pannappatty, Velampatty, Avichipatti Pannianmalai, Boothagudi, Samutrapatti Pannuvarpatti, Palappanaickenpatti, Saththambadi Mulaiyur, Idayapatti, Uralipatti, Mottamalai R F Nadumalai R F, Chellappanaickenpatti, Reddiapatti Lingavadi, Pudur, Alagar Hills R F.

The villages having more than 50% ST population are None.

Sex ratio of Scheduled tribe population is 800.

Scheduled Tribes Literates and Illiterates by Sex:

	Persons	Males	Females
Literate	3	1	2
Illiterate	2	0	2
Literacy rate	75.0	100.0	66.7
Graduate	0	0	0

Scheduled Tribes (Dominant):

Malakkuravan

For their cultural identity please see Appendix-II

Villages without Scheduled Tribes: There are 40 villages without any scheduled tribe population.

Literates and Illiterates by Sex (Total Population):

	Persons	Males	Females
Literate	58,384	35,803	22,581
Illiterate	53,279	20,350	32,929
Literacy rate	60	74	47
Graduate	738	561	177

Agriculture: ***Distribution of villages according to land use:*** Out of 41 villages, Total area (in hectare) is 58122.18, out of that 36.86 percent is cultivable and 23.77 percent of the cultivable area is irrigated.

Sources of Irrigation (Hectares): Government Canal 0, Private Canal 0, Well without Electricity 735.5, Well with Electricity 1927.37, Tubewell without Electricity 112.76, Tubewell with Electricity 0, Tank 2263.78, River 52.47, Lake 0, Waterfall 0, Others 0.

Villages with population of 5000 to 9999: Sirangattupatti , Seithur, Sirugudi, Nadumandalam Punnapatti, Velanpatti, Sattambadi, Reddiapatti Lingavadi, Pudur.

Villages with population of 10000 and above: Sendurai.

Distribution of Workers:

	Persons	Males	Females	WPR
Cultivators	16,465	10,767	5,698	27.06
Agricultural Labour	35,262	16,498	18,764	57.96
Household Industry	1,202	388	814	1.98
Other Workers	7,912	6,135	1,777	13
Main Workers	47,710	29,288	18,422	78.42
Marginal Workers	13,131	4,500	8,631	21.58
Total Workers	60,841	33,788	27,053	

Religion: Major Religious Communities:

	Persons	Males	Females	Sex Ratio
Hindu (94.3%)	105,300	53,073	52,227	984
Muslim (4.14%)	4,620	2,205	2,415	1,095
Christian (1.49%)	1,660	827	833	1,007
Sikh (0%)	5	5	-	-
Buddhists (0%)	5	3	2	667
Jain (0%)	3	2	1	500

Agewise Data:

	Persons	Males	Females	Sex Ratio
All ages	111,663	56,153	55,510	989
0-14	34,571	17,845	16,726	937
15-44	53,560	26,414	27,146	1028
45-79	22,506	11,391	11,115	976
80+	690	343	347	1012
Age not stated	336	160	176	1100

Languages (Dominant):

Tamil, Telugu, Kannada, Urdu, Malayalam

Disabled Population:

	Persons	Males	Females	%
Total Disabled	2,895	1,201	1,694	
In Seeing	2,018	714	1,304	69.71
In Speech	196	94	102	6.77
In Hearing	124	69	55	4.28
In Movement	396	247	149	13.68
Mentally	161	77	84	5.56

NATRAMPALLI

Natrampalli C.D. Block lies in the south-western part of Vellore district. It is a part of Vaniyambadi and Tirupathur taluks. The Block is located at a distance of 95 kms. from district headquarters (Vellore). There are 28 villages in the block with the total population of 85,167 persons. Area of the C.D. Block is 200.98 sq. kms. It is bounded in the south by CD Block Jolarpettai, in the east by CD Blocks Alangayam, Madhanur and Peranampattu, in the west by district Dharmapuri, and it has common boundary with the state of Andhra Pardesh on north and west. CD Bolck Natrampalli falls in taluk Vaniyambadi by 19 villages, and in taluk Tirupathur by 09 Villages.

Communications:

Roadways : N.H.-46: Direction- Krishnagiri to Vaniyambadi, Nearest Villages- Kathari, Athukkuppam, Bandarapalli, Ambalur.

Railway Station: Vaddakkuppattu, Bandarapalli, Patchur.

River: Polar Nadi- Nearest Villages- Chikkanankuppam, Thimmampettai, Pullur, Ramanayakanpettai, Ambalur.

Annual Rainfall: Average Rainfall 949 mm.

Ground Water: Availability of the ground water in the Basin is 2880.98 H.A.M. and the utilization is 4848.94 H.A.M. It belongs to Over Expoited category. Depth to water level varies from 5 to 15 meter below the ground. Most of the wells go down in summer months, according to the Ground Water Estimation Committee.

Forest and Reserved Forest: (Natrampalli RF)- Nearest Villages- Kothur RF, Kothur, Patchur.

Natural Division: Tondai Nadu.

Administration

Revenue **Division:** Tirupatahur. Parliamentary Constituency: 11Tiruvannamalai, 8 Vellore. District: Vellore. Taluk: Vaniyambadi, Tirupathur. Assembly Constituency: 49 Jolarpet, 47 Vaniyambadi. Gram Panchayat: 26.

Border Villages- (Andhra Pardesh)- Nearest Villages- Thumberi, Chikkanankuppam, Thimmampettai, Pullur, Alasardapuram, Venkatarajapuram, Narayanapuram, Javadhiramasamuduram, Gollapalli, Gurubavani Gunda, Mallagunda, Kothur RF, Kothur, Sorakkayalnatham, Nayanacheruvu, Simugampattu.

Villages: 28 **Inhabited:** 27 **Uninhabited:** 1

Ranking	District	State	National
Area	14	286	4160
Population	16	205	3919
Sex Ratio	15	275	2165
Child Sex Ratio	14	273	4519
Literacy Rate	16	238	2126
Density	1	198	2594
Work Participation Rate	11	99	2017

Gram Panchayats:
Alasandapuram, Alinjikulam, Ambalur , Athurkuppam, Avarankuppam, Bandarapalli, Chiknankuppam, Eklaspuram, Kadayanchi, Katheri, Kothur , Mallagunta, Mallangunta, Mallankuppam, Narayanapuram, Nayanaseruvu, Pachoor, Pullur, Ramanaickenpettai, Sankarapuram, Sorakanatham, Thekkupattu, Thimmampettai, Thoppalagunda, Thumberi, Vadakkupattu ,

Amenities:

Education: Primary School in 24 villages, Middle school in 12 villages, Matriculation or Secondary School in 8 villages, namely Thumberi, Thimmampettai, Vaddakkuppattu, Ambalur, Mallagunda, Kothur, Athukkuppam, Bandarapalli.

Higher Secondary or Pre University Courses or Intermediate or Junior College in 2 villages of the CD Block,, namely Vaddakkuppattu, Ambalur.

College in 0 village, Adult Literacy Center in 0 village.

Medical: Hospital in 0 village, Dispensary in 0 village, Health Center in 2 villages, Sub Center in 3 villages, Maternity and Child Welfare Center in 4 villages, Community health workers in 26 villages.

The Village having Hospital or Dispensary or Health Center is Bandarapalli.

Drinking Water: Tap water in 26 villages, Tank water in 3 villages, Well water in 15 villages, Tubewell in 7 villages and more than one source in 26 villages.

Bank: Banking facility in 3 villages, namely, Ramanayakanpettai, Ambalur, Patchur.

Credit Society in 5 villages Agricultural Credit Society in 4 Non-Agricultural Credit Society in 2 villages.

Others: Power supply in 26 villages, Cinema hall in 1 village, sport club in 0 village, Stadium or Auditorium or Community Hall in 0 village, Post Office in 23 villages.

There are 25 villages having bus facilities.

Villages with most of facilities: Ramanayakanpettai Ambalur, Patchur.

Villages without amenities (Education):
Venkatarajapuram, Gollapalli, Kothur Rf..

Scheduled Castes: Out of the total population of 85167 persons, 12884 persons (15.13%) belong to Scheduled Castes.

The villages having less than 10% SC population are Venkatarajapuram, Javadhiramasamuduram, Tekkupattu Mallagunda, Kothur Rf, Kothur, Sorakkayalnatham Thoppulagunda, Kathari, Patchur.

The villages having more than 50% SC population are None.

Sex ratio of Scheduled Caste population is 498.

Scheduled Castes Literates and Illiterates by Sex:

	Persons	Males	Females
Literate	7,039	4,129	2,910
Illiterate	5,845	2,336	3,509
Literacy rate	63.6	74.4	52.7
Graduate	65	50	15

Scheduled Castes (Dominant):
Adi Dravida, Arunthathiyar, Kuravan etc.
Generic Castes etc., Valluvan

For their cultural identity please see Appendix-I

Villages without Scheduled Castes: There is 1 village without any scheduled caste population.

Scheduled Tribes: Out of the total population of 85167 persons, 95 persons (0.11%) belong to Scheduled Tribes.

The villages having less than 10% ST population are Thumberi, Chikkanankuppam, Thimmampettai, Pullur Semukkampattu, Alasandapuram, Venkatarajapuram Narayanapuram, Javadhiramasamuduram, Gollapalli Gurubavani Gunda, Ramanayakanpettai, Vaddakkuppattu Kawkapattu, Ambalur, Tekkupattu, Mallangkuppam Mallagunda, Kothur Rf, Kothur, Sorakkayalnatham Nayanacheruvu, Thoppulagunda, Kathari, Athukkuppam Bandarapalli, Patchur.

The villages having more than 50% ST population are None.

Sex ratio of Scheduled tribe population is 547.

Scheduled Tribes Literates and Illiterates by Sex:

	Persons	Males	Females
Literate	30	17	13
Illiterate	65	26	39
Literacy rate	40.5	53.1	31.0
Graduate	0	0	0

Scheduled Tribes (Dominant):
Irular, Kurumans, Malai Vedan

For their cultural identity please see Appendix-II

Villages without Scheduled Tribes: There are 23 villages without any scheduled tribe population.

Literates and Illiterates by Sex (Total Population):

	Persons	Males	Females
Literate	46,978	27,826	19,152
Illiterate	38,189	15,258	22,931
Literacy rate	64	75	52

Graduate	626	480	146

Agriculture: ***Distribution of villages according to land use:*** Out of 28 villages, Total area (in hectare) is 20098.87, out of that 56.8 percent is cultivable and 18.66 percent of the cultivable area is irrigated.

Sources of Irrigation (Hectares): Government Canal 0, Private Canal 0, Well without Electricity 0, Well with Electricity 2032.46, Tubewell without Electricity 9.98, Tubewell with Electricity 87.65, Tank 0, River 0, Lake 0, Waterfall 0, Others 0.

Villages with population of 5000 to 9999: Thumberi, Mallangunta, Kothur , Athurkuppam Bandarapalli, Pachoor.

Villages with population of 10000 and above: None

Distribution of Workers:

	Persons	Males	Females	WPR
Cultivators	14,785	9,167	5,618	34.52
Agricultural Labour	12,861	5,947	6,914	30.03
Household Industry	6,613	2,874	3,739	15.44
Other Workers	8,568	6,611	1,957	20.01
Main Workers	32,773	20,433	12,340	76.52
Marginal Workers	10,054	4,166	5,888	23.48
Total Workers	42,827	24,599	18,228	

Religion: Major Religious Communities:

	Persons	Males	Females	Sex Ratio
Hindu (98.82%)	84,162	42,592	41,570	976
Muslim (0.67%)	567	269	298	1,108
Christian (0.4%)	342	180	162	900
Sikh (0%)	1	-	1	-
Buddhists (0%)	2	1	1	1,000
Jain (0%)	3	2	1	500

Agewise Data:

	Persons	Males	Females	Sex Ratio
All ages	85,167	43,084	42,083	977
0-14	26,887	13,978	12,909	924
15-44	39,472	19,698	19,774	1004
45-79	17,405	8,783	8,622	982
80+	879	378	501	1325
Age not stated	524	247	277	1121

Languages (Dominant):
Tamil, Telugu, Kannada, Urdu, Hindi

Disabled Population:

	Persons	Males	Females	%
Total Disabled	1,996	1,120	876	
In Seeing	993	525	468	49.75
In Speech	177	94	83	8.87
In Hearing	98	59	39	4.91
In Movement	561	353	208	28.11
Mentally	167	89	78	8.37

NEEDAMANGALAM

Needamangalam C.D. Block lies in the western part of Thiruvarur district. It is a part of Needamangalam and Mannargudi taluks. The Block is located at a distance of 20 kms. from district headquarters (Thiruvarur). There are 58 villages in the block with the total population of 108,350 persons. Area of the C.D. Block is 241.86 sq. kms. It is bounded in the north by CD Blocks Valangaiman and Koradacherry, in the south and west by district Thanjavur, and in the east by C.D. Block Mannargudi. CD Block Needamangalam falls in taluk Needamangalam by 34 villages, and in taluk Mannargudi by 24 villages.

Communications:

Roadways : N.H.-67: Direction- Thanjavur to Thiruvarur, Nearest Villages- Kovilvenni, Sithamallimalpathi, Adanur, Kalacheri, Parappanamedu, Vaiyakalathur, Olimathi, Ottagudi, Pallagalathur, Hannumandapuram.

Railway Station: Kovilvenni.

Annual Rainfall: Average Rainfall 1184 mm.

Ground Water: Availability of the ground water in the Basin is 6149.41 H.A.M. and the utilization is 4460. 61 H.A.M. It belongs to Semi Critical category. Depth to water level varies from 5 to 10 meter below the ground. Most of the wells go down in summer months, according to the Ground Water Estimation Committee.

Natural Division: Chola Nadu.

Administration

Revenue **Division:** Mannargudi. Parliamentary Constituency: 28 Nagapattinam (SC). District: Thiruvarur. Taluk: Needamangalam, Mannargudi. Assembly Constituency 167 Mannargudi. Gram Panchayat: 44.

Villages: 58 **Inhabited:** 55 **Uninhabited:** 3

Ranking	District	State	National
Area	4	240	3484
Population	2	99	3199
Sex Ratio	2	68	575
Child Sex Ratio	5	77	1588
Literacy Rate	10	92	1067
Density	6	318	2465
Work Participation Rate	7	83	3798

Gram Panchayats:
Adhanur, Arichapuram, Athankudi, Ayikudi, Chettichatram Iyyampettai , Edamelaiyr Kandian Theru, Edamelaiyur Nadutheru, Edamelaiyur West, Hanumanthapuram , Kalacheri, Kanur Annavasal , Karakkottai, Karuvakurichi, Kattakudi , Kelavanthacheri, Kovilvenni, Melavanthacheri, Moovankkottai, Mukkulamsaathanur, Munnavalkottai, Nagar , Nallikkottai, Oimathi , Peraiyur , Perambur, Poovanur, Pothakudi, Pududevangudi, Pullavarayankudi , Pullavarayankudikadu, Rayapuram, Rishiyur,

Serumangalam , Sitamallimelpathi, Sithambur, Sonapettai , Thalikottai, Vadakkaravayal, Vadavur Agraharam, Vadavurhtenpathy , Vadhur vadapatti, Vellakkudi.

Amenities:

Education: Primary School in 50 villages, Middle school in 20 villages, Matriculation or Secondary School in 9 villages, namely Kovilvenni, Munnavalkottai, Pullavarayankudikadu, Rayapuram, Ayikudi, Vaduvur Agraharam, Edamelaiyur, Eda-Melaiyar Iii, Peraiyur I.

Higher Secondary or Pre University Courses or Intermediate or Junior College in 7 villages of the CD Block,, namely Sekari, Ayikudi, Vaduvur Agraharam, Edamelaiyur, Eda-Melaiyar Iii, Kallanjimedu, Peraiyur I.

College in 1 village, Adult Literacy Center in 0 village., College is in village, namely Kovilvenni.

Medical: Hospital in 1 village, Dispensary in 2 villages, Health Center in 7 villages, Sub Center in 19 villages, Maternity and Child Welfare Center in 0 village, Community health workers in 54 villages.

The Villages having Hospital or Dispensary or Health Center are Parappanamedu, Athangudi, Vellagudi.

Drinking Water: Tap water in 55 villages, Tank water in 1 villages, Well water in 55 villages, Tubewell in 55 villages and more than one source in 55 villages.

Bank: Banking facility in 6 villages, namely, Kovilvenni, Sithampoor, Sekari, Edamelaiyur Eda-Keelaiyur I, Peraiyur Iii.

Credit Society in 17 villages Agricultural Credit Society in 16 Non-Agricultural Credit Society in 3 villages.

Others: Power supply in 55 villages, Cinema hall in 0 village, sport club in 0 village, Stadium or Auditorium or Community Hall in 0 village, Post Office in 37 villages.

There are 50 villages having bus facilities.

Villages with most of facilities: Kovilvenni Sithampoor, Sekari, Edamelaiyur, Eda-Keelaiyur I Peraiyur Iii.

Villages without amenities (Education): Ottagudi, Pallagalathur, Annavasal Thenpathi, Edamelaiyur, Serumangalam Ii..

Scheduled Castes: Out of the total population of 108350 persons, 28045 persons (25.88%) belong to Scheduled Castes.

The villages having less than 10% SC population are Ponnimangalam, Munnavasalkottai, Vadulur Melpathy Vaduvur Agraharam, Edamelaiyur, Eda-Keelaiyur Ii Vaduvurthenpatai, Peraiyur Ii, Peraiyur Iii Attaikottai, Serumangalam I, Karuvakkurichi Karuvakkurichi.

The villages having more than 50% SC population are Nagar, Vaiyakalathur, Pallagalathur, Hannumandapuram Rishiyur, Vellagudi, Annavasal, Puduthevagudi Arichapuram, Sithampoor, Vadakarayayal.

Sex ratio of Scheduled Caste population is 501.

Scheduled Castes Literates and Illiterates by Sex:

	Persons	Males	Females
Literate	14,673	8,683	5,990
Illiterate	13,372	5,312	8,060
Literacy rate	61.0	72.7	49.5
Graduate	204	170	34

Scheduled Castes (Dominant):

Pallan, Paraiyan etc., Adi Dravida, Kuravan etc. Generic Castes etc.

For their cultural identity please see Appendix-I

Villages without Scheduled Castes: There are 6 villages without any scheduled caste population.

Scheduled Tribes: Out of the total population of 108350 persons, 48 persons (0.04%) belong to Scheduled Tribes.

The villages having less than 10% ST population are Kovilvenni, Nagar, Ponnimangalam, Sithamallimalpathi Adanur, Munnavalkottai, Munnavasalkottai Cheetichatram, Pullavarayankudikadu, Rayapuram Kalacheri, Parappanamedu, Poovanur, Vaiyakalathur Olimathi, Ottagudi, Pallagalathur, Hannumandapuram Perambur, Rishiyur, Athangudi, Vellagudi Keelalavanthacheri, Melalavanthan Cheri, Annavasal Annavasal Thenpathi, Puduthevagudi, Arichapuram Sithampoor, Sekari, Ayikudi, Moovarkottai Vadulur Melpathy, Vaduvur Agraharam Vaduvur Vadapathy, Edamelaiyur, Edamelaiyur Eda-Melaiyar Iii, Eda-Keelaiyur I, Eda-Keelaiyur Ii Kallanjimedu, Vadakarayayal, Vaduvurthenpatai Vaduvor Thenpathy Ii, Karakkottai, Peraiyur I Peraiyur Ii, Peraiyur Iii, Peraiyur Iv, Attaikottai Serumangalam I, Serumangalam Ii, Karuvakkurichi Karuvakkurichi, Thalikkottai.

The villages having more than 50% ST population are None.

Sex ratio of Scheduled tribe population is 417.

Scheduled Tribes Literates and Illiterates by Sex:

	Persons	Males	Females
Literate	32	17	15
Illiterate	16	11	5
Literacy rate	72.7	68.0	79.0
Graduate	0	0	0

Scheduled Tribes (Dominant):

Malakkuravan, Malai Pandaram, Toda, Kochu Velan Irular

For their cultural identity please see Appendix-II

Villages without Scheduled Tribes: There are 53 villages without any scheduled tribe population.

Literates and Illiterates by Sex (Total Population):

	Persons	Males	Females
Literate	67,895	38,274	29,621
Illiterate	40,455	15,245	25,210
Literacy rate	71	81	61
Graduate	1,616	1,256	360

Agriculture: ***Distribution of villages according to land use:*** Out of 58 villages, Total area (in hectare) is 24186.93, out of that 66.79 percent is cultivable and 95.85 percent of the cultivable area is irrigated.

Sources of Irrigation (Hectares): Government Canal 14428.27, Private Canal 0, Well without Electricity 0, Well with Electricity 0, Tubewell without Electricity 11.83, Tubewell with Electricity 1043.2, Tank 0, River 0, Lake 0, Waterfall 0, Others 0.

Villages with population of 5000 to 9999: Sekarai.

Villages with population of 10000 and above: None

Distribution of Workers:

	Persons	Males	Females	WPR
Cultivators	10,027	8,368	1,659	21.08
Agricultural Labour	29,827	16,244	13,583	62.7
Household Industry	1,075	534	541	2.26
Other Workers	6,644	5,374	1,270	13.97
Main Workers	36,408	25,601	10,807	76.53
Marginal Workers	11,165	4,919	6,246	23.47
Total Workers	47,573	30,520	17,053	

Religion: Major Religious Communities:

	Persons	Males	Females	Sex Ratio
Hindu (90.62%)	98,192	48,864	49,328	1,009
Muslim (6.22%)	6,740	2,940	3,800	1,293
Christian (3.11%)	3,366	1,688	1,678	994
Sikh (0%)	-	-	-	-
Buddhists (0%)	-	-	-	-
Jain (0%)	1	1	-	-

Agewise Data:

	Persons	Males	Females	Sex Ratio
All ages	108,350	53,519	54,831	1025
0-14	29,858	15,069	14,789	981
15-44	53,550	26,063	27,487	1055
45-79	23,930	11,867	12,063	1017
80+	774	393	381	969
Age not stated	238	127	111	874

Languages (Dominant):

Tamil, Telugu, Malayalam, Kannada, Hindi

Disabled Population:

	Persons	Males	Females	%
Total Disabled	3,996	1,668	2,328	
In Seeing	2,817	1,005	1,812	70.5
In Speech	236	115	121	5.91
In Hearing	129	69	60	3.23
In Movement	618	371	247	15.47
Mentally	196	108	88	4.9

NEMILI

Nemili C.D. Block lies in the north-eastren part of Vellore district. It is a part of Arakonam taluk. The Block is located at a distance of 49 kms. from district headquarters (Vellore). There are 54 villages in the block with the total population of 122, 445 persons. Area of the C.D. Block is 281.93 sq. kms. It is bounded in the north by CD Block Arakkonam, in the south by Thiruvannamalai district, in the east by district Kancheepuram, and in the west by CD Block Kaveripakkam.

Communications:

Roadways : N.H.-4: Direction- Kaveripakkam to Chennai, Nearest Villages- Poigainalloor, Perubulipakkam, Avalur.

Railway Station: Pallur.

Local Streams: Nearest Villages- Mangattucheri, Arigilab adi, Kilandurai, Ochalam, Arumbakkam, Silamandai, Elathur, Kilkalathur, Sirunamalli, Illupaithandalam, Kilvenkatap uram, Vettangulam, Asanallikuppam, Reddivalam, Agadalam, Nedumpuli, Nangamangalam, Vellianallur.

Annual Rainfall: Average Rainfall 949 mm.

Ground Water: Availability of the ground water in the Basin is 7858.40 H.A.M. and the utilization is 7170.61 H.A.M. It belongs to Critical category. Depth to water level varies from 5 to 10 meter below the ground. Most of the wells go down in summer months, according to the Ground Water Estimation Committee.

Forest and Reserved Forest: (Banavaram RF)- Nearest Village- Kattupakkam.

Natural Division: Tondai Nadu.

Administration

Revenue **Division:** Arakonam. Parliamentary Constituency: 7 Arakkonam. District: Vellore. Taluk: Arakonam. Assembly Constituency: 38 Arakkonam (SC), 39 Sholingur. Gram Panchayat: 52

Villages: 54 **Inhabited:** 54 **Uninhabited:** 0

Ranking	District	State	National
Area	9	195	2973
Population	7	61	2796
Sex Ratio	13	185	1273
Child Sex Ratio	7	176	3009
Literacy Rate	11	162	1593
Density	8	279	2534
Work Participation Rate	9	90	3037

Gram Panchayats:

Agavalam, Arigilapadi , Arumbakkam, Asanallikuppam, Attupakkam, Avalur, Chitheri, Chittoor, Elathur,

Ganapathipuram, Illupaithandalam, Kalathur, Kattupakkam, Kilakalathur, Kilandurai, Kilveedhi, Kilvenkatapuram, Kilvenpakkam, Kodambakkam, Mahendravadi, Mangattucheri(Kadambanallur), Melandurai, Melapulam, Meleri, Melkalathur, Melpakkam, Murangai, Nedumpuli, Negavedu, Nelvoy, Pallur, Parameswaramangalam, Parthiputhur, Perapperi, Perumpulipakkam, Pinnavaram, Poigainallur, Reddivalam, Sankaranpadi, Sayanavaram (Jagir), Selvamandai, Sirunamalli, Thandalam , Thirumadaiambakkam, Thirumalpur, Thuraiyur, Uliyanallur, Velianallur, Velithangipuram, Vepperi, Vettangulam.

Amenities:

Education: Primary School in 51 villages, Middle school in 27 villages, Matriculation or Secondary School in 10 villages, namely Melpakkam, Nagavedu, Arumbakkam, Elathur, Pinnavaram, Sayanavaram, Mahendravadi, Ganapathipuram, Thirumalperu, Melapuram.

Higher Secondary or Pre University Courses or Intermediate or Junior College in 5 villages of the CD Block,, namely Nagavedu, Sayanavaram, Thirumalperu, Thuraiur, Melapuram.

College in 0 village, Adult Literacy Center in 0 village.

Medical: Hospital in 3 villages, Dispensary in 0 village, Health Center in 6 villages, Sub Center in 5 villages, Maternity and Child Welfare Center in 5 villages, Community health workers in 54 villages.

The Villages having Hospital or Dispensary or Health Center are Agadalam, Perubulipakkam, Kalathur.

Drinking Water: Tap water in 53 villages, Tank water in 8 villages, Well water in 19 villages, Tubewell in 16 villages and more than one source in 50 villages.

Bank: Banking facility in 7 villages, namely, Nagavedu, Kattupakkam, Sayanavaram, Koddambakkam Pallur, Thirumalperu, Kalathur.

Credit Society in 8 villages Agricultural Credit Society in 7 Non-Agricultural Credit Society in 1 village.

Others: Power supply in 54 villages, Cinema hall in 0 village, sport club in 0 village, Stadium or Auditorium or Community Hall in 0 village, Post Office in 48 villages.

There are 51 villages having bus facilities.

Villages with most of facilities: Nagavedu Kattupakkam, Sayanavaram, Pallur, Thirumalperu Kalathur.

Villages without amenities (Education):
Melandurai, Koddambakkam..

Scheduled Castes: Out of the total population of 122445 persons, 33167 persons (27.09%) belong to Scheduled Castes. The villages having less than 10% SC population are Chitheri, Illupaithandalam, Perapperi, Vepperi Nelvoy, S.Kolathur, Nangamangalam, Perubulipakkam.

The villages having more than 50% SC population are Kilandurai, Silamandai, Murungai, Vettangulam Kalathur.

Sex ratio of Scheduled Caste population is 502.

Scheduled Castes Literates and Illiterates by Sex:

	Persons	Males	Females
Literate	19,261	11,164	8,097
Illiterate	13,906	5,348	8,558
Literacy rate	66.8	77.9	55.9
Graduate	231	203	28

Scheduled Castes (Dominant):

Adi Dravida, Arunthathiyar, Valluvan, Pannadi Kuravan etc.

For their cultural identity please see Appendix-I

Villages without Scheduled Castes: There are 2 villages without any scheduled caste population.

Scheduled Tribes: Out of the total population of 122445 persons, 1677 persons (1.37%) belong to Scheduled Tribes. The villages having less than 10% ST population are Chitheri, Parithiputhurvillage, Melpakkam Mangattucheri, Arigilabadi, Kilandurai, Melandurai Nagavedu, Ochalam, Arumbakkam, Silamandai Melkalathur, Kattupakkam, Velithangipuram, Meleri Elathur, Kilkalathur, Sirunamalli, Illupaithandalam Paramaswaramangalam, Murungai, Chithur, Pinnavaram Attupakkam, Sayanavaram, Kilvenkatapuram, Kilveedhi Koddambakkam, Mahendravadi, Perapperi, Vepperi Asanallikuppam, Pallur, Ganapathipuram, Thirumalperu Nelvoy, Reddivalam, Agadalam, Nedumpuli, Thuraiur Nangamangalam, Melapuram, Poigainalloor Vellianallur, Thandalam, Melvanbakkam, Kilvenbakkam Perubulipakkam, Avalur, Kalathur, Sankaranpadi.

The villages having more than 50% ST population are None.

Sex ratio of Scheduled tribe population is 500.

Scheduled Tribes Literates and Illiterates by Sex:

	Persons	Males	Females
Literate	392	232	160
Illiterate	1,285	606	679
Literacy rate	28.5	33.9	23.1
Graduate	0	0	0

Scheduled Tribes (Dominant):

Irular, Kattunayakan, Malakkuravan

For their cultural identity please see Appendix-II

Villages without Scheduled Tribes: There are 15 villages without any scheduled tribe population.

Literates and Illiterates by Sex (Total Population):

	Persons	Males	Females

Literate	72,068	42,604	29,464
Illiterate	50,377	18,697	31,680
Literacy rate	67	80	55
Graduate	1,018	796	222

Agriculture: ***Distribution of villages according to land use:*** Out of 54 villages, Total area (in hectare) is 28193.77, out of that 55.77 percent is cultivable and 48.19 percent of the cultivable area is irrigated.

Sources of Irrigation (Hectares): Government Canal 0, Private Canal 0, Well without Electricity 135.88, Well with Electricity 6434.69, Tubewell without Electricity 85.7, Tubewell with Electricity 60.48, Tank 133.27, River 0, Lake 475.52, Waterfall 251.11, Others 0.

Villages with population of 5000 to 9999: Kattupakkam, Sayanavaram (Jagir).

Villages with population of 10000 and above: None

Distribution of Workers:

	Persons	Males	Females	WPR
Cultivators	14,271	10,790	3,481	24.71
Agricultural Labour	28,593	13,562	15,031	49.51
Household Industry	4,329	2,673	1,656	7.5
Other Workers	10,561	8,778	1,783	18.29
Main Workers	40,361	29,361	11,000	69.88
Marginal Workers	17,393	6,442	10,951	30.12
Total Workers	57,754	35,803	21,951	

Religion: Major Religious Communities:

	Persons	Males	Females	Sex Ratio
Hindu (97.7%)	119,627	59,924	59,703	996
Muslim (1.26%)	1,538	766	772	1,008
Christian (0.95%)	1,167	553	614	1,110
Sikh (0%)	1	1	-	-
Buddhists (0%)	5	3	2	667
Jain (0.01%)	8	2	6	3,000

Agewise Data:

	Persons	Males	Females	Sex Ratio
All ages	122,445	61,301	61,144	997
0-14	35,028	17,806	17,222	967
15-44	59,239	29,879	29,360	983
45-79	26,560	12,808	13,752	1074
80+	880	442	438	991
Age not stated	738	366	372	1016

Languages (Dominant):

Tamil, Telugu, Urdu, Kannada, Malayalam

Disabled Population:

	Persons	Males	Females	%
Total Disabled	2,327	1,311	1,016	
In Seeing	876	437	439	37.65
In Speech	268	160	108	11.52
In Hearing	171	79	92	7.35
In Movement	777	500	277	33.39
Mentally	235	135	100	10.1

NILAKKOTTAI

Nilakkottai C.D. Block lies in the southern part of Dindigul district. It is a part of Nilakkottai taluk. The Block is located at a distance of 30 kms. from district headquarters (Dindigul). There are 26 villages in the block with the total population of 110,113 persons. Area of the C.D. Block is 219.36 sq. kms. It is bounded in the north by CD Blocks Attur and Dindigul, in the south by district Madurai, in the east by district Madurai and CD Block Shanarpatti, in the west by C.D. Blocks Vattalakundu and Attur.

Communications:

Roadways : N.H.-7: Direction- Madurai to Dindigul, Nearest Villages- Jambuduraikottai, Malayagoundapatti, Pallapatti, Kullalagunda, Mattaparai, Kalladipatti. S.H.-36: Direction- Nilakkottai to Oddanchatram, Nearest Villages- Kottur, Pachamalayankottai, Nuthulapuram, Bangalapatti.

River: Vaigai Nadi- Nearest Villages- Bodiyagokindanpatti, Sivagnanapuram, Kullichettipatti, Sithargalnatham, Pillayarnatham, Vilampatti.

Backwards Region Grants Fund: It receives Backward Region Grants.

Annual Rainfall: Average Rainfall 813 mm.

Ground Water: Availability of the ground water in the Basin is 6878.13 H.A.M. and the utilization is 6484.20 H.A.M. It belongs to Critical category. Depth to water level varies from 5 to 20 meter below the ground. Most of the wells go down in summer months, according to the Ground Water Estimation Committee.

Natural Division: NA

Administration

Revenue **Division:** Dindigul. Parliamentary Constituency: 22 Dindigul. District: Dindigul. Taluk: Nilakkottai. Assembly Constituency: Nilakottai (SC). Gram Panchayat: 23.

Villages: 26 **Inhabited:** 26 **Uninhabited:** 0

Ranking	District	State	National
Area	13	262	3866
Population	2	92	3152
Sex Ratio	12	305	2546
Child Sex Ratio	9	301	5089
Literacy Rate	5	189	1752
Density	10	155	2210
Work Participation Rate	1	58	1544

Gram Panchayats:

Ethilodu, Gullalagundu, Jambudurai Kottai, Kodanginaickan patti, Koovanuthu, Kottur, Kullichettipatti, Malayagoundanpatti , Mattapparai, Musuvanuthu, Nakkaloothu, Nariyoothu, Nuthulapuram, Pachamalayankottai, Pallapatti, Pillaiyarnatham, Ramarajapuram, S.mettupatti, Silukkuvarpatti,

Sithargalnatham , Sivagnanapuram, Veelinaickanpatti, Vilampatti.

Amenities:

Education: Primary School in 24 villages, Middle school in 13 villages, Matriculation or Secondary School in 6 villages, namely Pachamalayankottai, Jambuduraikottai, Kottur, Silukkuvarpatty, Pallapatti, Pillayarnatham.

Higher Secondary or Pre University Courses or Intermediate or Junior College in 1 village of the CD Block,, namely Jambuduraikottai.

College in 0 village, Adult Literacy Center in 0 village.

Medical: Hospital in 3 villages, Dispensary in 1 village, Health Center in 6 villages, Sub Center in 15 villages, Maternity and Child Welfare Center in 8 villages, Community health workers in 13 villages.

The Villages having Hospital or Dispensary or Health Center are Pallapatti, Koovanuthu, Kullichettipatti, Kalladipatti.

Drinking Water: Tap water in 26 villages, Tank water in 16 villages, Well water in 26 villages, Tubewell in 26 villages and more than one source in 26 villages.

Bank: Banking facility in 4 villages, namely, Pachamalayankottai, Silukkuvarpatty, Pallapatti Ethilodu.

Credit Society in 12 villages Agricultural Credit Society in 12 Non-Agricultural Credit Society in 0 village.

Others: Power supply in 26 villages, Cinema hall in 6 villages, sport club in 0 village, Stadium or Auditorium or Community Hall in 0 village, Post Office in 20 villages.

There are 23 villages having bus facilities.

Villages with most of facilities: Pachamalayankottai Silukkuvarpatty, Pallapatti, Ethilodu.

Villages without amenities (Education):

Bangalapatti, Mattaparai..

Scheduled Castes: Out of the total population of 110113 persons, 34075 persons (30.95%) belong to Scheduled Castes.

The villages having less than 10% SC population are None..

The villages having more than 50% SC population are None.

Sex ratio of Scheduled Caste population is 492.

Scheduled Castes Literates and Illiterates by Sex:

	Persons	Males	Females
Literate	17,953	10,606	7,347
Illiterate	16,122	6,700	9,422
Literacy rate	60.8	71.1	50.4
Graduate	344	241	103

Scheduled Castes (Dominant):

Pallan, Paraiyan etc., Chakkiliyan, Valluvan Kuravan etc.

For their cultural identity please see Appendix-I

Villages without Scheduled Castes: There is 0 village without any scheduled caste population.

Scheduled Tribes: Out of the total population of 110113 persons, 8 persons (0.01%) belong to Scheduled Tribes.

The villages having less than 10% ST population are Pachamalayankottai, Jambuduraikottai, Nariyaothu Kottur, Kodanginaickanpatti, Chinnamanaickenkottai Nuthulapuram, Bangalapatti, Veelinaickenpatti Nakkaloothu, Silukkuvarpatty, Malayagoundapatti Kullalagunda, Pallapatti, Ethilodu, Koovanuthu Musuvanuthu, Bodiyagokindanpatti, Sivagnanapuram Kullichettipatti, Sithargalnatham, Pillayarnatham Mattaparai, Kalladipatti, Ramarajapuram, Vilampatti.

The villages having more than 50% ST population are None.

Sex ratio of Scheduled tribe population is 375.

Scheduled Tribes Literates and Illiterates by Sex:

	Persons	Males	Females
Literate	6	5	1
Illiterate	2	0	2
Literacy rate	75.0	100.0	33.3
Graduate	0	0	0

Scheduled Tribes (Dominant):

Kammara, Kurumans, Malai Pandaram

For their cultural identity please see Appendix-II

Villages without Scheduled Tribes: There are 23 villages without any scheduled tribe population.

Literates and Illiterates by Sex (Total Population):

	Persons	Males	Females
Literate	63,729	37,402	26,327
Illiterate	46,384	18,530	27,854
Literacy rate	66	77	55
Graduate	1,268	843	425

Agriculture: ***Distribution of villages according to land use:*** Out of 26 villages, Total area (in hectare) is 21936.55, out of that 57.34 percent is cultivable and 56.42 percent of the cultivable area is irrigated.

Sources of Irrigation (Hectares): Government Canal 346.07, Private Canal 73.56, Well without Electricity 1439.31, Well with Electricity 2941.36, Tubewell without Electricity 147.34, Tubewell with Electricity 97, Tank 1025.55, River 341.3, Lake 0, Waterfall 0, Others 685.98.

Villages with population of 5000 to 9999:

Pachamalayankottai, Jambudurai Kottai, Kottur Malayagoundanpatti , Pallapatti, Ethilodu Sithargalnatham , Pillaiyarnatham.

Villages with population of 10000 and above:

Silukkuvarpatti.

Distribution of Workers:

	Persons	Males	Females	WPR
Cultivators	14,088	8,643	5,445	24.22
Agricultural Labour	31,477	15,969	15,508	54.11
Household Industry	2,481	1,055	1,426	4.26
Other Workers	10,127	7,498	2,629	17.41
Main Workers	45,538	27,482	18,056	78.28
Marginal Workers	12,635	5,683	6,952	21.72
Total Workers	58,173	33,165	25,008	

Religion: Major Religious Communities:

	Persons	Males	Females	Sex Ratio
Hindu (87.99%)	96,885	49,376	47,509	962
Muslim (2.08%)	2,288	1,140	1,148	1,007
Christian (9.67%)	10,645	5,302	5,343	1,008
Sikh (0.02%)	17	9	8	889
Buddhists (0.01%)	7	2	5	2,500
Jain (0.01%)	10	7	3	429

Agewise Data:

	Persons	Males	Females	Sex Ratio
All ages	110,113	55,932	54,181	969
0-14	31,573	16,751	14,822	885
15-44	53,296	26,605	26,691	1003
45-79	22,906	11,543	11,363	984
80+	870	433	437	1009
Age not stated	1,468	600	868	1447

Languages (Dominant):
Tamil, Telugu, Kannada, Urdu, English

Disabled Population:

	Persons	Males	Females	%
Total Disabled	3,138	1,444	1,694	
In Seeing	2,100	823	1,277	66.92
In Speech	191	111	80	6.09
In Hearing	57	30	27	1.82
In Movement	572	350	222	18.23
Mentally	218	130	88	6.95

ODDANCHATRAM

Oddanachatram C.D. Block lies in the Central North part of Dindigul district. It is a part of Oddanachatram taluk. The Block is located at a distance of 32 kms. from district headquarters (Dindigul). There are 38 villages in the block with the total population of 99,765 persons. Area of the C.D. Block is 465.03 sq. kms. It is bounded in the north by district Erode and Karur, in the south by CD Blocks Palani and Reddiyarchatiram, in the east by CD Block Vedasandur, and in the west by C.D. Block Thoppampatti.

Communications:

Roadways : N.H.-209: Direction- Palani to Dindigul, Nearest Villages- Chatrapatti, Lekkayankottai, Athikombai, Arasappapillaipatty, Virupatchi, Sindalavadampatty. S.H.-37: Direction- Dharapuram to Oddanachatram, Nearest Villages- Mandavadi, Ambilikkai, Kappiliapatty, Thangachiammapatti, Kollapatty.

Railway Station: Chatrapatti.

Backwards Region Grants Fund: It receives Backward Region Grants.

Annual Rainfall: Average Rainfall 813 mm.

Ground Water: Availability of the ground water in the Basin is 4773.53 H.A.M. and the utilization is 8155.91 H.A.M. It belongs to Over Expoited category. Depth to water level varies from 2 to 10 meter below the ground. Most of the wells go down in summer months, according to the Ground Water Estimation Committee.

Natural Division: **NA**

Administration

Revenue **Division:** Palani. Parliamentary Constituency: 22 Dindigul. District: Dindigul. Taluk: Oddanchatram. Assembly Constituency: 128 Oddanchatram.
Gram Panchayat: 35.

Villages: 38 **Inhabited:** 38 **Uninhabited:** 0

Ranking	District	State	National
Area	3	43	1624
Population	5	131	3472
Sex Ratio	2	142	1007
Child Sex Ratio	8	302	5080
Literacy Rate	8	262	2279
Density	3	20	4515
Work Participation Rate	10	314	161

Gram Panchayats:
Ambilikai, Arasappapillaipatti, Athicombai, Chatrapatti , Chinnakampatti, D.Pudukottai, Ellapatti, I.Vadipatti, Idayakottai, Javadupatti, Jogipatti, Kalanjipatti, Kappilliapatti, Kaveriyammapatti, Kethaiyurambu, Kollapatti, Kondaramgi Keeranur, Kuthiluppai, Lakkayankottai, Mandavadi, Markampatti, Odaipatti, Periyakottai, Puliyamarathukottai, Puliyurnatham, Reddiapatti, Sindalapatti, Sindalavadampatti, Thangachiammapatti, Vadagadu, Valayapatti, Veeralapatti, Velur Anuppapatti, Veriappur, Verupakshi.

Amenities:

Education: Primary School in 37 villages, Middle school in 18 villages, Matriculation or Secondary School in 10 villages, namely Markampatti, Odaipatti, Idayakottai, Kallupatti, Ambilikkai, Periakottai, Chatrapatti, Kappiliapatty, Puliyurnatham, Virupatchi.

Higher Secondary or Pre University Courses or Intermediate or Junior College in 4 villages of the CD Block,, namely Markampatti, Kallupatti, Ambilikkai, Chatrapatti.

College in 1 village, Adult Literacy Center in 0 village., College is in village, namely Ambilikkai.

Medical: Hospital in 4 villages, Dispensary in 4 villages,

Health Center in 14 villages, Sub Center in 22 villages, Maternity and Child Welfare Center in 23 villages, Community health workers in 17 villages.

The Villages having Hospital or Dispensary or Health Center are Markampatti, Odaipatti, Idayakottai, Kallupatti, Ambilikkai, Chatrapatti, Veeralapatty, Veriyapur, Virupatchi.

Drinking Water: Tap water in 38 villages, Tank water in 28 villages, Well water in 38 villages, Tubewell in 38 villages and more than one source in 38 villages.

Bank: Banking facility in 12 villages, namely, Markampatti, Kondarangi Keeranur, Odaipatti Idayakottai, Javadupatty, Ambilikkai, Kappiliapatty Thangachiammapatti, Puliyurnatham, Kethaiyurambu Virupatchi, Sindalavadampatty.

Credit Society in 17 villages Agricultural Credit Society in 15 Non-Agricultural Credit Society in 2 villages.

Others: Power supply in 38 villages, Cinema hall in 4 villages, sport club in 0 village, Stadium or Auditorium or Community Hall in 0 village, Post Office in 36 villages.

There are 36 villages having bus facilities.

Villages with most of facilities: Markampatti Kondarangi Keeranur, Odaipatti, Idayakottai Javadupatty, Ambilikkai, Kappiliapatty Thangachiammapatti, Puliyurnatham, Kethaiyurambu Virupatchi, Sindalavadampatty.

Villages without amenities (Education): Navakani..

Scheduled Castes: Out of the total population of 99765 persons, 20789 persons (20.84%) belong to Scheduled Castes.

The villages having less than 10% SC population are None..

The villages having more than 50% SC population are None.

Sex ratio of Scheduled Caste population is 501.

Scheduled Castes Literates and Illiterates by Sex:

	Persons	Males	Females
Literate	10,220	6,136	4,084
Illiterate	10,569	4,238	6,331
Literacy rate	55.1	66.8	43.7
Graduate	124	96	28

Scheduled Castes (Dominant):

Chakkiliyan, Madari, Pallan, Paraiyan etc.

Adi Dravida

For their cultural identity please see Appendix-I

Villages without Scheduled Castes: There is 1 village without any scheduled caste population.

Scheduled Tribes: Out of the total population of 99765 persons, 165 persons (0.17%) belong to Scheduled Tribes.

The villages having less than 10% ST population are M. Athappampatti, Markampatti, Ellapadi Chinnakkampatty, I. Vadipatty, Kondarangi Keeranur Mandavadi, Navakani, Odaipatti, Kuthiluppai Idayakottai, Valayapatti, Kallupatti, Jogipatti Javadupatty, Sindalapatti, Ambilikkai, Periakottai Chatrapatti, Veeralapatty, Reddiyapatti Kaveriammapatty, Kappiliapatty, Thangachiammapatti Kollapatty, Veriyapur, Puliyurnatham Puliyamarathukottai, Kethaiyurambu, Kalangipatty Lekkayankottai, Athikombai, Arasappapillaipatty Virupatchi, Dasaripatty, Pudukottai Sindalavadampatty, Vadakadu.

The villages having more than 50% ST population are None.

Sex ratio of Scheduled tribe population is 497.

Scheduled Tribes Literates and Illiterates by Sex:

	Persons	Males	Females
Literate	40	23	17
Illiterate	125	60	65
Literacy rate	28.4	32.4	24.3
Graduate	0	0	0

Scheduled Tribes (Dominant):

Palliyar, Palliyan, Generic Tribes etc., Paniyan Kattunayakan

For their cultural identity please see Appendix-II

Villages without Scheduled Tribes: There are 34 villages without any scheduled tribe population.

Literates and Illiterates by Sex (Total Population):

	Persons	Males	Females
Literate	57,072	34,466	22,606
Illiterate	42,693	15,287	27,406
Literacy rate	63	77	49
Graduate	1,245	866	379

Agriculture: ***Distribution of villages according to land use:*** Out of 38 villages, Total area (in hectare) is 46503.51, out of that 54.97 percent is cultivable and 52.49 percent of the cultivable area is irrigated.

Sources of Irrigation (Hectares): Government Canal 40.35, Private Canal 0, Well without Electricity 1638.57, Well with Electricity 10996.45, Tubewell without Electricity 0, Tubewell with Electricity 210.93, Tank 494.27, River 0, Lake 37.96, Waterfall 0, Others 0.

Villages with population of 5000 to 9999: Chatrapatti , Thangachiammapatti, Puliyurnatham Virupakshi, Vadagadu.

Villages with population of 10000 and above: None

Distribution of Workers:

	Persons	Males	Females	WPR
Cultivators	21,108	11,998	9,110	33.38
Agricultural Labour	28,939	12,114	16,825	45.76
Household Industry	1,515	665	850	2.4

Other Workers	11,680	9,163	2,517	18.47
Main Workers	56,050	31,360	24,690	88.63
Marginal Workers	7,192	2,580	4,612	11.37
Total Workers	63,242	33,940	29,302	

Religion: Major Religious Communities:

	Persons	Males	Females	Sex Ratio
Hindu (95.73%)	95,508	47,695	47,813	1,002
Muslim (2.84%)	2,831	1,334	1,497	1,122
Christian (1.28%)	1,276	653	623	954
Sikh (0%)	3	3	-	-
Buddhists (0%)	1	-	1	-
Jain (0.01%)	7	3	4	1,333

Agewise Data:

	Persons	Males	Females	Sex Ratio
All ages	99,765	49,753	50,012	1005
0-14	21,201	10,887	10,314	947
15-44	46,568	22,723	23,845	1049
45-79	29,998	15,085	14,913	989
80+	1,277	680	597	878
Age not stated	721	378	343	907

Languages (Dominant):

Tamil, Telugu, Kannada, Urdu, Malayalam

Disabled Population:

	Persons	Males	Females	%
Total Disabled	4,527	1,621	2,906	
In Seeing	3,521	1,043	2,478	77.78
In Speech	196	99	97	4.33
In Hearing	123	67	56	2.72
In Movement	427	263	164	9.43
Mentally	260	149	111	5.74

OLAKKUR

Olakkur C.D. Block lies in the north-eastern part of Viluppuram district. It is a part of Tindivanam taluk. The taluk is located at a distance of 38 kms. from district headquarters (Viluppuram). There are 79 villages in the block with the total population of 83,279 persons. Area of the C.D. Block is 270.30 sq. kms. It is bounded in the north by districts Tiruvannamalai and Kancheepuram, in the south by C.D. Blocks Marakkanam Mailam, in the east by district Kancheepuram and CD Block Marakkanam, in the west by C.D.Blocks Mailam and Vallam, and district Tiruvannamalai.

Communications:

Roadways : N.H.-45: Direction- Tindivanam to Madurantakam, Nearest Villages- Olakkur Kil, Padiri, Karikambattu, Ongur, Nangunam, Nallathur, Saram, Melpettai. N.H.-66: Direction- Gingee to Tindivanam, Nearest Village- Pattanam. S.H.-2: Direction- Tindivanam to Vandavasi, Nearest Villages- Puthananthal, Kilmavilangal, Mavilangai, Nagavaram, Vadampoondi, Perapari, Karuvambakkam, Ural, Pattanam.

Railway Station: Saram.

Backwards Region Grants Fund: It receives Backward Region Grants.

Annual Rainfall: Average Rainfall 1119 mm.

Ground Water: Availability of the ground water in the Basin is 5913.40 H.A.M. and the utilization is 8614.77 H.A.M. It belongs to Over Expoited category. Depth to water level varies from 2 to 10 meter below the ground. Most of the wells go down in summer months, according to the Ground Water Estimation Committee.

Forest and Reserved Forest: (Kilseyur RF)- Nearest Villages- Nolambur, Keelsevur, Kilsevur R.F.

Natural Division: Tondai Nadu.

Administration

Revenue **Division:** Tindivanam. Parliamentary Constituency: 12 Arani, 13 Villupuram (SC). District: Villupuram. Taluk: Tindivanam. Assembly Constituency: 71 Mailam, 72 Tindivanam (SC). Gram Panchayat: 52.

Villages: 79 **Inhabited:** 79 **Uninhabited:** 0

Ranking	District	State	National
Area	17	206	3102
Population	21	216	3996
Sex Ratio	3	180	1233
Child Sex Ratio	1	4	167
Literacy Rate	11	281	2395
Density	18	244	3449
Work Participation Rate	19	212	2620

Gram Panchayats:

Andapattu, Annambakkam, Atchipakkam, Attipakkam, Avanipur, Dadapuram, Eppakkam, Evalur, Kadavambakkam, Kambur, Karuvapakkam, Kiladanur, Kilbuderi, Kilgudalur, Killmannur, Kilmavilangai, Kilpasar, Kilsevur, Kirandipuram, Kodiam, Koochikolathur, Kunnappakkam, Mambakkam, Mangalam, Mavilangai (Mel), Meladhanur, Melmavilangai, Melpakkam, Melpettai, Melsiviri, Nallathur, Neykuppi, Nolambur, Olakkur , Ongur, Padiri, Pallipakkam, Panaiyur, Panchalam, Pangalathur, Pattanam, Purangarai, Saram, Sattanur, Sembakkam, Sendamangalam, Siruvalur (Vada), Ural, Vadakalavoi, Vadampundi, Vadasiruvallur, Vairapuram, Vellimedupettai, Venmaniyathur, .

Amenities:

Education: Primary School in 65 villages, Middle school in 17 villages, Matriculation or Secondary School in 9 villages, namely Puthananthal, Dhadapuram, Olakkurpadi, Avanippur, Saram, Karuvambakkam, Nolambur, Atchippakkam, Naramagani.

Higher Secondary or Pre University Courses or Intermediate or Junior College in 2 villages of the CD Block,, namely Puthananthal, Olakkurpadi.

College in 1 village, Adult Literacy Center in 0 village., College is in village, namely Melapakkam.

Medical: Hospital in 1 village, Dispensary in 0 village, Health Center in 7 villages, Sub Center in 0 village, Maternity and Child Welfare Center in 26 villages, Community health workers in 43 villages.
The Villages having Hospital or Dispensary or Health Center are Nallathur, Ural, T. Panchalam.
Drinking Water: Tap water in 79 villages, Tank water in 38 villages, Well water in 79 villages, Tubewell in 79 villages and more than one source in 79 villages.
Bank: Banking facility in 6 villages, namely, Puthananthal, Dhadapuram, Olakkurpadi, Avanippur Saram, Nolambur.
Credit Society in 9 villages Agricultural Credit Society in 9 Non-Agricultural Credit Society in 1 village.
Others: Power supply in 78 villages, Cinema hall in 2 villages, sport club in 0 village, Stadium or Auditorium or Community Hall in 0 village, Post Office in 40 villages.
There are 48 villages having bus facilities.
Villages with most of facilities: Puthananthal Dhadapuram, Olakkurpadi, Avanippur, Saram, Nolambur.
Villages without amenities (Education):
Thengapakkam, Olakkur Kil, Koochikolathur, Paniyur, Nangunam, Sitteripattu, Nagavaram, Kilnemeli, Vandarampundi, Kilmannur, Kilsevur R.F, Senalur, Kunnapakkam, Mandaperumpakkam..
Scheduled Castes: Out of the total population of 83279 persons, 31298 persons (37.58%) belong to Scheduled Castes.
The villages having less than 10% SC population are Mambakkam, Konalour, Vellimedu, Puthananthal Singanikuppam, Kilmalayanur, Karikambattu Sitteripattu, Vadasiruvalur, Ural, Pallipakkam Vandarampundi.
The villages having more than 50% SC population are Athipakkam, Nedunthondi, Ammanampakkam, Thengapakkam Kambur, Kadavampakkaam, Avanippur, Paniyur Pangolathur, Saram, Purankarai, Keelkaranai Sattanur, Neikuppi, Nagavaram, T. Panchalam Melpettai, Kilgudalur, Kiladanur, Kilpasar Naramagani, Kilnemeli, Keelsevur, Kilsevur R.F Senalur, Kunnapakkam, Thennampoondi.
Sex ratio of Scheduled Caste population is 500.

Scheduled Castes Literates and Illiterates by Sex:

	Persons	Males	Females
Literate	15,456	9,143	6,313
Illiterate	15,842	6,518	9,324
Literacy rate	56.6	66.7	46.4
Graduate	243	198	45

Scheduled Castes (Dominant):
Adi Dravida, Arunthathiyar, Valluvan, Kuravan etc. Adi Andhra
For their cultural identity please see Appendix-I
Villages without Scheduled Castes: There are 6 villages without any scheduled caste population.
Scheduled Tribes: Out of the total population of 83279 persons, 1573 persons (1.89%) belong to Scheduled Tribes.
The villages having less than 10% ST population are Mambakkam, Sembakkam, Konalour, Melsiviri Athipakkam, Nedunthondi, Vellimedu, Puthananthal Dhadapuram, Singanikuppam, Maleadhanoor Ammanampakkam, Thengapakkam, Olakkurpadi Olakkur Kil, Koochikolathur, Padiri, Kambur Karikambattu, Ongur, Annambakkam, Kattupunji Vadakalavai, Kadavampakkaam, Avanippur, Paniyur Pangolathur, Nangunam, Nallathur, S. Kadur, Saram Purankarai, Keelkaranai, Evaloor, Sattanur Sitteripattu, Melapakkam, Neikuppi, Puliyur, Kodiyam Kilmavilangal, Mavilangai, Nagavaram, Vadasiruvalur Kalpakkam, Kirandipuram, Vadampoondi, Perapari Karuvambakkam, Ural, Pattanam, T. Panchalam Melpettai, Kilgudalur, Inchcheri, Nolambur, Mangalam Kiladanur, Pallipakkam, Eppakkam, Andappattu Kilpasar, Atchippakkam, Naramagani, Sendamangalam Kilnemeli, Vandarampundi, Kilmannur, Karupur Keelsevur, Venmaniyathur, Senalur, Keelbuderi Kunnapakkam, Mandaperumpakkam.
The villages having more than 50% ST population are None.
Sex ratio of Scheduled tribe population is 507.

Scheduled Tribes Literates and Illiterates by Sex:

	Persons	Males	Females
Literate	434	252	182
Illiterate	1,139	524	615
Literacy rate	31.3	36.6	26.0
Graduate	1	1	0

Scheduled Tribes (Dominant):
Irular, Adiyan, Malai Pandaram, Kattunayakan Kammara
For their cultural identity please see Appendix-II
Villages without Scheduled Tribes: There are 42 villages without any scheduled tribe population.

Literates and Illiterates by Sex (Total Population):

	Persons	Males	Females
Literate	45,857	27,281	18,576
Illiterate	37,422	14,397	23,025
Literacy rate	62	74	50
Graduate	747	601	146

Agriculture: ***Distribution of villages according to land use:***
Out of 79 villages, Total area (in hectare) is 27030.83, out of that 58.88 percent is cultivable and 44.47 percent of the cultivable area is irrigated.

Sources of Irrigation (Hectares): Government Canal 0, Private Canal 0, Well without Electricity 1051.95, Well with Electricity 2097.99, Tubewell without Electricity 0, Tubewell with Electricity 195.6, Tank 0, River 53.71, Lake 3679.11, Waterfall 0, Others 0.

Villages with population of 5000 to 9999: None

Villages with population of 10000 and above: None

Distribution of Workers:

	Persons	Males	Females	WPR
Cultivators	13,985	9,480	4,505	34.02
Agricultural Labour	21,562	9,855	11,707	52.45
Household Industry	692	368	324	1.68
Other Workers	4,868	3,918	950	11.84
Main Workers	33,271	20,550	12,721	80.94
Marginal Workers	7,836	3,071	4,765	19.06
Total Workers	41,107	23,621	17,486	

Religion: Major Religious Communities:

	Persons	Males	Females	Sex Ratio
Hindu (98%)	81,615	40,841	40,774	998
Muslim (0.97%)	805	413	392	949
Christian (0.84%)	696	339	357	1,053
Sikh (0%)	2	2	-	-
Buddhists (0%)	3	1	2	2,000
Jain (0.13%)	108	56	52	929

Agewise Data:

	Persons	Males	Females	Sex Ratio
All ages	83,279	41,678	41,601	998
0-14	24,260	12,329	11,931	968
15-44	38,405	19,009	19,396	1020
45-79	19,045	9,518	9,527	1001
80+	799	432	367	850
Age not stated	770	390	380	974

Languages (Dominant):

Tamil, Telugu, Urdu, Kannada, Hindi

Disabled Population:

	Persons	Males	Females	%
Total Disabled	2,089	1,153	936	
In Seeing	943	524	419	45.14
In Speech	216	98	118	10.34
In Hearing	163	83	80	7.8
In Movement	621	365	256	29.73
Mentally	146	83	63	6.99

OMALUR

Omalur C.D. Block lies in the western part of Salem district. It is a part of Omalur taluk. The Block is located at a distance of 16 kms. from district headquarters (Salem). There are 49 villages in the block with the total population of 157,921 persons. Area of the C.D. Block is 204.15 sq. kms. It is bounded in the north by C.D. Block Kadaiyampatty, in the south by C.D. Blocks Veerapandi and Salem, in the east by CD Blocks Salem and Yercaud, in the west by C.D. Blocks Taramangalam and Mecheri.

Communications:

Roadways : N.H.-7: Direction- Salem to Kadayampatti, Nearest Villages- Puliampatti, Thumbipadi, Saminaikkanpatty, Mankuppai, Kottagoundampatty, Kullamanickenpatti, Kothamettupatty, Sikkanampatty, Balbakki, Anaigoundampatty, Naranampalayam, Kamalapuram.

Railway Station: Thumbipadi.

River: Sirabanga Nadi- Nearest Villages- Muthunaikkanpatty, Thathyanpatti, M.Chettipatti, Kothamettupatty, Sikkanampatty, Balbakki, Omalur, Kamalapuram, Darapuram.

Annual Rainfall: Average Rainfall 540 mm.

Ground Water: Availability of the ground water in the Basin is 3279.48 H.A.M. and the utilization is 5651.33 H.A.M. It belongs to Safe category. Depth to water level varies from 2 to 10 meter below the ground. Most of the wells go down in summer months, according to the Ground Water Estimation Committee.

Forest and Reserved Forest: (Karuvattuparai RF)- Nearest Village- Kaniyeri. (Pannikaradu)- Nearest Villages- Pannikaradu (RF), Kaniyeri, Sakkarachuttipatty, Thathiya ngarpatty. (Ramasamimalai)- Nearest Village- Pottipuram. (Kaduvampatti)- Nearest Villages- Thathiyangarpatty.

Natural Division: Kongu Nadu.

Administration

Revenue **Division:** Mettur. Parliamentary Constituency: 15 Salem. District: Salem. Taluk: Omalur. Assembly Constituency: 84 Omalur, 88 Salem (West). Gram Panchayat: 33.

Villages: 49 **Inhabited:** 47 **Uninhabited:** 2

Ranking	District	State	National
Area	11	280	4111
Population	1	8	1616
Sex Ratio	15	378	5695
Child Sex Ratio	11	370	6195
Literacy Rate	7	336	2896
Density	20	248	1266
Work Participation Rate	2	16	2659

Gram Panchayats:

Balbakki, Chellapillaikuttai , Ettikuttapatti, Gollappatty, Kamalapuram, Kottagoundampatty, Kottaimariammankoil, Kottamettupatty , M.Chettipatti, Mankuppai, Mungilpadi, Muthunaickenpatti , Nallagoundanpatti, Naranampalayam, Pachanampatty, Pagalpatti , Periyerippatty, Pottipuram, Puliyampatti, Sakkarachettipatty, Saminaikkanpatty, Sangithapatti, Semmankoodal, Sikkampatti, Sikkanampatti, Thekkampatti, Thekkampatty, Thethayampatty, Tholasampatti, Tindamangalam,

Tumbipadi, Umbilikamaramangalam, Vellakkalpatty, Vellalapatti, .

Amenities:

Education: Primary School in 40 villages, Middle school in 19 villages, Matriculation or Secondary School in 7 villages, namely Ettikuttapatti, Kothamettupatty, Periyaripatty, Vellalappatty, Omalur, Pachanampatti, Kamalapuram.

Higher Secondary or Pre University Courses or Intermediate or Junior College in 5 villages of the CD Block,, namely Tholasampatty, Mylappalayam, Kothamettupatty, Vellalappatty, Pachanampatti.

College in 1 village, Adult Literacy Center in 0 village., College is in village, namely Vellakkalpatty.

Medical: Hospital in 3 villages, Dispensary in 2 villages, Health Center in 7 villages, Sub Center in 20 villages, Maternity and Child Welfare Center in 13 villages, Community health workers in 2 villages.

The Villages having Hospital or Dispensary or Health Center are Sangithapatti, Poojikalipatty, Sikkanampatty, Vellalappatty, Omalur, Pagalpatty.

Drinking Water: Tap water in 47 villages, Tank water in 0 villages, Well water in 47 villages, Tubewell in 47 villages and more than one source in 47 villages.

Bank: Banking facility in 2 villages, namely, Jagothavampatty, Vellalappatty.

Credit Society in 20 villages Agricultural Credit Society in 17 Non-Agricultural Credit Society in 11 villages.

Others: Power supply in 47 villages, Cinema hall in 2 villages, sport club in 0 village, Stadium or Auditorium or Community Hall in 0 village, Post Office in 33 villages.

There are 39 villages having bus facilities.

Villages with most of facilities: Vellalappatty.

Villages without amenities (Education):

Sekkarapatti, Jagothavampatty, Kaniyeri, Veddapatty, Thundumaniyam, Kaminaikkanpatty..

Scheduled Castes: Out of the total population of 157921 persons, 36453 persons (23.08%) belong to Scheduled Castes.

The villages having less than 10% SC population are Muthunaikkanpatty, Tholasampatty, Veddapatty Golappatty, Poojikalipatty, Gobinathapuram Mungilpadi, Vellakkalpatty, Reddipatty Naranampalayam, Kathaperiyampatty.

The villages having more than 50% SC population are Karuppananpatty, Saminaikkanpatty, Mankuppai Thathyanpatti, Kottagoundampatty.

Sex ratio of Scheduled Caste population is 467.

Scheduled Castes Literates and Illiterates by Sex:

	Persons	Males	Females
Literate	17,615	11,344	6,271
Illiterate	18,838	8,086	10,752
Literacy rate	56.3	68.4	42.7
Graduate	515	388	127

Scheduled Castes (Dominant):

Adi Dravida, Arunthathiyar, Paraiyan etc., Valluvan Pallan

For their cultural identity please see Appendix-I

Villages without Scheduled Castes: There are 4 villages without any scheduled caste population.

Scheduled Tribes: Out of the total population of 157921 persons, 287 persons (0.18%) belong to Scheduled Tribes.

The villages having less than 10% ST population are Sekkarapatti, Muthunaikkanpatty, Jagothavampatty Tholasampatty, Puliampatti, Kaniyeri , Thumbipadi Veddapatty, Karuppananpatty, Saminaikkanpatty Mankuppai, Sangithapatti, Thekkampatti, Golappatty Poojikalipatty, Thathyanpatti, Ettikuttapatti Mylappalayam, Kottagoundampatty, Gobinathapuram V.Maramangalam, Mungilpadi, Kullamanickenpatti Sakkarachuttipatty, M.Chettipatti, Kothamettupatty Vellakkalpatty, Sikkanampatty, T.Maramangalam Periyaripatty, Pottipuram, Balbakki, Tindamangalam Vellalappatty, Sikkampatti, Reddipatty Anaigoundampatty, Omalur, Pachanampatti Naranampalayam, Thundumaniyam, Kamalapuram Pagalpatty, Kaminaikkanpatty, Kathaperiyampatty Chellapillaikuttai.

The villages having more than 50% ST population are None.

Sex ratio of Scheduled tribe population is 446.

Scheduled Tribes Literates and Illiterates by Sex:

	Persons	Males	Females
Literate	126	96	30
Illiterate	161	63	98
Literacy rate	47.2	65.3	25.0
Graduate	3	3	0

Scheduled Tribes (Dominant):

Malayali, Malai Pandaram, Generic Tribes etc. Malakkuravan

For their cultural identity please see Appendix-II

Villages without Scheduled Tribes: There are 38 villages without any scheduled tribe population.

Literates and Illiterates by Sex (Total Population):

	Persons	Males	Females
Literate	82,032	51,318	30,714
Illiterate	75,889	32,915	42,974
Literacy rate	59	70	47
Graduate	2,576	1,900	676

Agriculture: ***Distribution of villages according to land use:***

Out of 49 villages, Total area (in hectare) is 20415.75, out of

that 67.39 percent is cultivable and 28.66 percent of the cultivable area is irrigated.

Sources of Irrigation (Hectares): Government Canal 0, Private Canal 0, Well without Electricity 0, Well with Electricity 3626.73, Tubewell without Electricity 0, Tubewell with Electricity 276.19, Tank 0, River 0, Lake 39.25, Waterfall 0, Others 0.

Villages with population of 5000 to 9999: Pottipuram, Kamalapuram, Vellalapatti, Pachanampatti Omalur , Thenkkampatti, Chellapillaikuttai Pagalpatti.

Villages with population of 10000 and above: Tumbipadi, Muthunaickenpatti.

Distribution of Workers:

	Persons	Males	Females	WPR
Cultivators	15,703	9,781	5,922	20.44
Agricultural Labour	26,414	13,037	13,377	34.39
Household Industry	5,663	3,515	2,148	7.37
Other Workers	29,037	22,985	6,052	37.8
Main Workers	65,376	44,711	20,665	85.11
Marginal Workers	11,441	4,607	6,834	14.89
Total Workers	76,817	49,318	27,499	

Religion: Major Religious Communities:

	Persons	Males	Females	Sex Ratio
Hindu (97.31%)	153,675	81,964	71,711	875
Muslim (0.91%)	1,437	867	570	657
Christian (1.72%)	2,719	1,351	1,368	1,013
Sikh (0.01%)	8	4	4	1,000
Buddhists (0%)	1	-	1	-
Jain (0%)	4	4	-	-

Agewise Data:

	Persons	Males	Females	Sex Ratio
All ages	157,921	84,233	73,688	875
0-14	45,358	25,483	19,875	780
15-44	77,142	40,467	36,675	906
45-79	33,374	17,171	16,203	944
80+	1,583	859	724	843
Age not stated	464	253	211	834

Languages (Dominant):
Tamil, Telugu, Urdu, Kannada, Malayalam

Disabled Population:

	Persons	Males	Females	%
Total Disabled	2,159	1,293	866	
In Seeing	838	473	365	38.81
In Speech	245	140	105	11.35
In Hearing	94	52	42	4.35
In Movement	726	475	251	33.63
Mentally	256	153	103	11.86

ORATHANADU

Orathanadu C.D. Block lies in the central part of Thanjavur district. It is a part of Orathanadu taluk. The Block is located at a distance of 24 kms. from district headquarters (Thanjavur). There are 82 villages in the block with the total population of 155,294 persons. Area of the C.D. Block is 398.47 sq. kms. It is bounded in the north by CD Blocks Thanjavur and Ammapettai, in the south by CD Blocks Madukkur, Pattukkottai and Thiruvonam, in the east by district Thiruvarur, in the west by CD Block Thanjavur and district Pudukkottai.

Communications:

Roadways : S.H.-29: Direction- Thanjavur to Pattukkottai, Nearest Villages- Ulur West, Paruthikkottai, Kannanthangudi, Melaiyur, Thennamanadu (North), Thenamanadu, Palamuthur, Pudur, Pulavankadu, Thelungankudikkadu, Vellur, Vedavijayapuram, Ambalapattu, Andainallavijayapuram.

Railway Station: Ambalapattu Sivakollai.

Annual Rainfall: Average Rainfall 1147 mm.

Ground Water: Availability of the ground water in the Basin is 6126.95 H.A.M. and the utilization is 3533. 49 H.A.M. It belongs to (Information not available) category. Depth to water level varies from 2 to 20 meter below the ground. Most of the wells go down in summer months, according to the Ground Water Estimation Committee.

Natural Division: Chola Nadu.

Administration

Revenue **Division:** Thanjavur. Parliamentary Constituency: 30 Pudukoottai. District: Thanjavur. Taluk: Orathanadu. Assembly Constituency: 175 Orattanadu. Gram Panchayat: 58.

Villages: 82 **Inhabited:** 80 **Uninhabited:** 2

Ranking	District	State	National
Area	1	75	1937
Population	1	9	1706
Sex Ratio	4	37	373
Child Sex Ratio	14	278	4621
Literacy Rate	13	170	1629
Density	3	256	2800
Work Participation Rate	8	118	2779

Gram Panchayats:

Adanakottai, Alivoikkal , Ambalapattu North, Ambalapattu South, Arumulai, Avidanalla Vijayapuram, Ayangudi, Chinnaponnappur, Cholapuram, IChankottai, Ichankottai, Kakkarai, Kakkarakottai, Kannathangudi East, Kannathangudi West, Kannugudi West, Kannugudi West, Kannugudi East, Karaimeendarkottai, Karukadipatti, Kattukuruchi, Kavarapattu, Keelulur, Kelavannipet, Kovilur, Kulamangalam, Mandalakkottai, Melaulur, Moorthiambalpuram, Mullurpattikadu, Nadur, Neivasal South, Okkanadukeelayur, Okkanadukeelayur ,

Okkanadumelayur, Okkanadumelayur , Oratharayam kandikadu, Pachiyur, Palampudur, Panchanandhikottai, Paruthikottai, Peikarambankottai, Ponnappur (East), Ponnappur (West), Poovathur, Poovathur (Pudhunagar), Poyyunddarkottai, Pudur, Pulavankadu, Raghavambalpuram , Sethurayangudi Kadu, Thalayamangalam, Thekkur, Thelungan kudikadu , Thennamanadu, Thondarampet, Tirumangalakottai East, Tirumangalakottai West, Vadakkur North, Vadakkur South, Vadaseri , Vandayariruppu, Vellur.

Amenities:

Education: Primary School in 74 villages, Middle school in 42 villages, Matriculation or Secondary School in 21 villages, namely Ragavambalpuram, Panayakkottai, Ulur West, Ponnappur West, Okkanadu Keelaiyur, Kannanthankudi East Chief, Kannanthankudi West Additional, Thennamanadu (North), Thenamanadu, Eachankottai, Kakikarai, Pudhunagar, Thirumangalakottai Keelaiyur, Thirumangalakottai, Thelungankudikkadu, Thekkur, Pachiyur, Vellur, Kannugudi West Additional, Vadaseri North, Ambalapattu.

Higher Secondary or Pre University Courses or Intermediate or Junior College in 11 villages of the CD Block,, namely Vandayariruppu, Ulur West, Okkanadu Keelaiyur, Eachankottai, Pudhunagar, Thirumangalakottai Keelaiyur, Thelungankudikkadu, Thekkur, Kannugudi West Additional, Vadaseri North, Ambalapattu.

College in 0 village, Adult Literacy Center in 0 village.

Medical: Hospital in 1 village, Dispensary in 1 village, Health Center in 6 villages, Sub Center in 27 villages, Maternity and Child Welfare Center in 2 villages, Community health workers in 76 villages.

The Villages having Hospital or Dispensary or Health Center are Ulur West, Vadakkur North, Muthurpattukadu.

Drinking Water: Tap water in 80 villages, Tank water in 0 villages, Well water in 80 villages, Tubewell in 80 villages and more than one source in 80 villages.

Bank: Banking facility in 12 villages, namely, Ulur West, Naduvur, Pachanathi Kottai, Aliavaikkal Okkanadu Keelaiyur, Vadakkur North, Pudur Pudhunagar, Thondarampattu (W), Vadaseri North Vedavijayapuram, Andainallavijayapuram.

Credit Society in 41 villages Agricultural Credit Society in 41 Non-Agricultural Credit Society in 3 villages.

Others: Power supply in 80 villages, Cinema hall in 6 villages, sport club in 0 village, Stadium or Auditorium or Community Hall in 0 village, Post Office in 50 villages.

There are 78 villages having bus facilities.

Villages with most of facilities: Ulur West Naduvur, Pachanathi Kottai, Aliavaikkal Okkanadu Keelaiyur, Vadakkur North, Pudur Thondarampattu (W), Vadaseri North, Vedavijayapuram Andainallavijayapuram.

Villages without amenities (Education): Okkanadu Melaiyur, Kannugudi West Chief, Vadaseri (S), Muthurpattukadu..

Scheduled Castes: Out of the total population of 155294 persons, 21759 persons (14.01%) belong to Scheduled Castes.

The villages having less than 10% SC population are Moorthiyanpuram, Ponnappur East, Paruthiapparkovil Thalayamangalam, Kulamangalam, Okkanadu Keelaiyur Okkanadu Melaiyur, Kannanthankudi East Chief Kannanthankudi East, Kannanthangudi Melaiyur Thennamanadu (North), Pudur, Poovathur Keelavannipattu, Thirumangalakottai Keelaiyur Colony Thirumangalakottai, Thondarampattu (W) Kannugudi West Chief, Paravathur, Kannugudi (E) Andainallavijayapuram, Ambalapattu Sivakollai Gopalapuram, Ramapuram.

The villages having more than 50% SC population are None.

Sex ratio of Scheduled Caste population is 506.

Scheduled Castes Literates and Illiterates by Sex:

	Persons	Males	Females
Literate	11,685	7,025	4,660
Illiterate	10,074	3,725	6,349
Literacy rate	61.5	75.2	48.2
Graduate	122	96	26

Scheduled Castes (Dominant):

Paraiyan etc., Adi Dravida, Pallan, Kuravan etc. Valluvan

For their cultural identity please see Appendix-I

Villages without Scheduled Castes: There are 6 villages without any scheduled caste population.

Scheduled Tribes: Out of the total population of 155294 persons, 95 persons (0.06%) belong to Scheduled Tribes.

The villages having less than 10% ST population are Karimeendarkkottai, Vandayariruppu, Ragavambalpuram Sadiyarkovil, Moorthiyanpuram, Panayakkottai Arasapattu, Neivasal South, Ponnappur East Chinnaponnapur, Keelaulur, Ulur West, Kattukaruchi Naduvur, Karukkakottai, Pachanathi Kottai Aliavaikkal, Paruthikkottai, Paruthiapparkovil Ponnappur West, Thalayamangalam, Kulamangalam Kavarapattu, Okkanadu Keelaiyur Chief Okkanadu Keelaiyur, Okkanadu Melaiyur Samayakudikkadu, Kannanthankudi East Chief

Kannanthankudi East, Kannanthankudi West Additional Kannanthangudi Melaiyur, Thennamanadu (North) Thenamanadu, Eachankottai, Samipatti Poyyundarkottai, Palangandankudikadu, Vadakkur North Vadakkur South, Cholapuram, Vadakikottai, Ayangudi Mandalakottai, Kovilur, Pudur, Palamuthur, Kakikarai Poovathur, Pudhunagar, Keelavannipattu, Arumulai Thirumangalakottai Keelaiyur Thirumangalakottai Keelaiyur Colony Thirumangalakottai Maliyur, Thirumangalakottai Peikkarumbankottai, Pulavankadu, Thelungankudikkadu Kakkarai Kottai, Thekkur, Athanakkottai, Pachiyur Vellur, Thondarampattu (W), Thondarampattu (E) Kannugudi West Chief, Kannugudi West Additional Kodiyalam, Vadaseri North, Vadaseri (S), Paravathur Kannugudi (E), Vedavijayapuram Andainallavijayapuram, Ambalapattu, Ambalapattu Ambalapattu Sivakollai, Muthurpattukadu, Gopalapuram Ramapuram.

The villages having more than 50% ST population are None.

Sex ratio of Scheduled tribe population is 547.

Scheduled Tribes Literates and Illiterates by Sex:

	Persons	Males	Females
Literate	41	18	23
Illiterate	54	25	29
Literacy rate	49.4	52.9	46.9
Graduate	0	0	0

Scheduled Tribes (Dominant):

Kattunayakan, Malakkuravan, Malai Pandaram

For their cultural identity please see Appendix-II

Villages without Scheduled Tribes: There are 76 villages without any scheduled tribe population.

Literates and Illiterates by Sex (Total Population):

	Persons	Males	Females
Literate	92,650	53,323	39,327
Illiterate	62,644	22,799	39,845
Literacy rate	67	79	55
Graduate	1,123	803	320

Agriculture: ***Distribution of villages according to land use:*** Out of 82 villages, Total area (in hectare) is 39847.84, out of that 68.82 percent is cultivable and 79.97 percent of the cultivable area is irrigated.

Sources of Irrigation (Hectares): Government Canal 19606.07, Private Canal 0, Well without Electricity 160.05, Well with Electricity 0, Tubewell without Electricity 0, Tubewell with Electricity 2164.26, Tank 0, River 0, Lake 0, Waterfall 0, Others 0

Villages with population of 5000 to 9999: Thekkur.

Villages with population of 10000 and above: None

Distribution of Workers:

	Persons	Males	Females	WPR
Cultivators	25,557	18,488	7,069	33.49
Agricultural Labour	41,329	20,259	21,070	54.15
Household Industry	1,767	754	1,013	2.32
Other Workers	7,665	5,995	1,670	10.04
Main Workers	62,461	40,668	21,793	81.84
Marginal Workers	13,857	4,828	9,029	18.16
Total Workers	76,318	45,496	30,822	

Religion: Major Religious Communities:

	Persons	Males	Females	Sex Ratio
Hindu (98%)	152,188	74,583	77,605	1,041
Muslim (0.66%)	1,029	533	496	931
Christian (1.25%)	1,937	924	1,013	1,096
Sikh (0%)	-	-	-	-
Buddhists (0%)	-	-	-	-
Jain (0%)	3	2	1	500

Agewise Data:

	Persons	Males	Females	Sex Ratio
All ages	155,294	76,122	79,172	1040
0-14	39,133	20,057	19,076	951
15-44	76,469	36,922	39,547	1071
45-79	37,988	18,293	19,695	1077
80+	1,406	674	732	1086
Age not stated	298	176	122	693

Languages (Dominant):

Tamil, English, Marathi, Telugu, Malayalam

Disabled Population:

	Persons	Males	Females	%
Total Disabled	3,929	1,931	1,998	
In Seeing	2,090	909	1,181	53.19
In Speech	330	172	158	8.4
In Hearing	281	127	154	7.15
In Movement	933	559	374	23.75
Mentally	295	164	131	7.51

OTTAPIDARAM

Ottapidaram C.D. Block lies in the central part of Thoothukkudi district. It is a part of Ottapidaram taluk. The Block is located at a distance of NA kms. from district headquarters (Thoothukkudi). There are 62 villages in the block with the total population of 113,925 persons. Area of the C.D. Block is 748.22 sq. kms. It is bounded in the north by CD Blocks Kayathar and Vilathikulam, in the south by CD Blocks Karunkulam and Thoothukkudi, in the east by the Gulf of Mannar, in the west by district Tirunelveli and CD Block Kayathar.

Communications:

Roadways : N.H.-45 B: Direction- Ettayapuram to Thoothukkudi, Nearest Villages- Eppodhumvendran, Kattunayakkanpatti, Jegaveerapandiapuram, Melamarudur,

S. Kumarapuram, Mela Arasadi, Valasamudram, Sinthalakatai, Pudurpandiapuram.

Railway Station: Maruthanvalvoo Naraikinar, Kodiankulam, Melapandiapuram.

Annual Rainfall: Average Rainfall 661 mm.

Ground Water: Availability of the ground water in the Basin is 20.03 MCM and the utilization is 28.29 MCM. It belongs to Over Expoited category. Depth to water level varies from 0 to 10 meter below the ground. Most of the wells go down in summer months, according to the Ground Water Estimation Committee.

Coastal Villages- (Gulf of Mannar)- Nearest Villages- Veppalodai, Pattanamarudur, Thanuvaikulam, Keelaarasadi.

Natural Division: NA

Administration

Revenue **Division:** Kovilpatti. Parliamentary Constituency: 36 Thoothukkudi. District: Thoothukkudi. Taluk: Ottapidaram. Assembly Constituency: 217 Ottapidaram (SC), 213 Vilathikulam. Gram Panchayat: 61.

Villages: 62 **Inhabited:** 61 **Uninhabited:** 1

Ranking	District	State	National
Area	1	9	835
Population	1	82	3033
Sex Ratio	11	99	786
Child Sex Ratio	8	241	4008
Literacy Rate	7	44	632
Density	5	235	5523
Work Participation Rate	9	360	2543

Gram Panchayats:

Ackanaickenpatti, Adanur, Akilandapuram, Araikkulam, Chandragiri, Eppodumvendran, Gownagiri, Ilavelangal, Jagaveerapandiapuram, Jambulingapuram, K.Dalavaipuram, K.Shanmukapuram, Kalappaipatti, Kattunayakkanpatti, Keela Arasadi, Keela Mangalam, Keelakottai, Kila Mudiman, Kodiyankulam, Kollankinaru, Kollanparambu, Kottali, Kudiraikulam, Kulasekaranallur, Kumara Ettaiyapuram, Kurukkuchalai, Malaipatti, Podupatti, Marudanvalvenaraikinar, Mela Arasadi, Melapandiyapuram, Minakshipuram, Mullur Muthukumarapuram, Muramban, Nagampatti, Onamakulam, Ottainatham, Ottappidaram, P.Duraiswamipuram, Panchalamkurichi , Paraikuttam, Parivallikkottai, Passuvandanai , Pattanamarudur, Pudiyamputhur , Pudurpandiyapuram, Rajavinkoil, S.kailasapuram, Sangampatti, Sillanatham, Sillangulam, Swaminatham, Terku Kalmedu, Tharuvaikulam, Thennampatti, Therkkuveerapandiyapyram, Vadanatham, Valasamuthram, Vallinyakipuram, Vellaram, Veppalodai.

Amenities:

Education: Primary School in 61 villages, Middle school in 29 villages, Matriculation or Secondary School in 13 villages, namely Nagampatti, Kattunayakkanpatti, Keelamuduman, Sillankulam, Parivillikottai, Thanuvaikulam, Sinthalakatai, Ottapidaram, Kollankinur, Maruthanvalvoo Naraikinar, Keelakotai, Savarimangalam, Puthiamputhur.

Higher Secondary or Pre University Courses or Intermediate or Junior College in 5 villages of the CD Block,, namely Nagampatti, Pasuvanthanai, Sillankulam, Ottapidaram, Puthiamputhur.

College in 1 village, Adult Literacy Center in 0 village., College is in village, namely Govindapuram.

Medical: Hospital in 0 village, Dispensary in 1 village, Health Center in 11 villages, Sub Center in 26 villages, Maternity and Child Welfare Center in 10 villages, Community health workers in 60 villages.

The Village having Hospital or Dispensary or Health Center is Pasuvanthanai.

Drinking Water: Tap water in 61 villages, Tank water in 7 villages, Well water in 61 villages, Tubewell in 61 villages and more than one source in 61 villages.

Bank: Banking facility in 20 villages, namely, Nagampatti, Pasuvanthanai, Meenakshipuram Eppodhumvendran, Veppalodai, Vedanatham, Chandragiri Jegaveerapandiapuram, Vellaram, Keelamuduman Ilavelangal, Parivillikottai, Thanuvaikulam Sinthalakatai, Ottapidaram, Ottanatham Akkanayakkanpatti, Savarimangalam, Puthiamputhur Saminatham.

Credit Society in 12 villages Agricultural Credit Society in 10 Non-Agricultural Credit Society in 2 villages.

Others: Power supply in 61 villages, Cinema hall in 2 villages, sport club in 0 village, Stadium or Auditorium or Community Hall in 0 village, Post Office in 58 villages.

There are 57 villages having bus facilities.

Villages with most of facilities: Nagampatti Meenakshipuram, Eppodhumvendran, Veppalodai Vedanatham, Chandragiri, Jegaveerapandiapuram Vellaram, Keelamuduman, Ilavelangal, Parivillikottai Thanuvaikulam, Sinthalakatai, Ottapidaram Ottanatham, Savarimangalam, Puthiamputhur Saminatham.

Villages without Amenities (Education): None..

Scheduled Castes: Out of the total population of 113925 persons, 46491 persons (40.81%) belong to Scheduled Castes.

The villages having less than 10% SC population are Nagampatti, Kumarettaiyapuram, P. Duraisamypuram Valasamudram.

The villages having more than 50% SC population are

Eppodhumvendran, Chandragiri, Dhalavaipuram
Keelamangalam, Sillankulam, Malaipatti, Samgampatti
Araikkulam, K. Shanmugapuram, Mela Arasadi
Ottapidaram, Kulasekara Nallur, Murampan
Kollankinur, Maruthanvalvoo Naraikinar, Govindapuram
Ilalappaipatti, Keelakotai, Kodiankulam
Akkanayakkanpatti, Pudurpandiapuram.

Sex ratio of Scheduled Caste population is 496.

Scheduled Castes Literates and Illiterates by Sex:

	Persons	Males	Females
Literate	30,086	17,013	13,073
Illiterate	16,405	6,427	9,978
Literacy rate	73.3	82.4	64.0
Graduate	572	347	225

Scheduled Castes (Dominant):

Pallan, Paraiyan etc., Arunthathiyar, Chakkiliyan
Vathiriyan

For their cultural identity please see Appendix-I

Villages without Scheduled Castes: There are
3 villages without any scheduled caste population.

Scheduled Tribes: Out of the total population of 113925 persons, 88 persons (0.08%) belong to Scheduled Tribes.

The villages having less than 10% ST population are
Onamakulam, Kuthiraikulam, Nagampatti, Pasuvanthanai
Meenakshipuram, Kumarettaiyapuram, Eppodhumvendran
Kattunayakkanpatti, Athanoor
Mullur Muthukumarapuram, Veppalodai, Therkukalmedu
Vedanatham, Kollamparambu, Chandragiri
Jegaveerapandiapuram, Dhalavaipuram, Vellaram
P. Duraisamypuram, Keelamuduman, Keelamangalam
Sillankulam, Malaipatti, Ilavelangal, Thennampatti
Kothalai, Parivillikottai, Samgampatti, Araikkulam
Panchalamkurichi, S. Kumarapuram, K. Shanmugapuram
Melamarudur, D. Duraisamypuram, Pattanamarudur
Thanuvaikulam, Mela Arasadi, Valasamudram
Sinthalakatai, Ottapidaram, Kulasekara Nallur
Murampan, Ottanatham, Kollankinur
Maruthanvalvoo Naraikinar, Govindapuram
Ilalappaipatti, Keelakotai, Kodiankulam
Akkanayakkanpatti, Maniyachi, Paraikuttam
Melapandiapuram, Savarimangalam, Jambulingapuram
Puthiamputhur, Saminatham, Therkkuveerapandiyapuram
Sillanatham, Pudurpandiapuram, Keelaarasadi.

The villages having more than 50% ST population are None.

Sex ratio of Scheduled tribe population is 523.

Scheduled Tribes Literates and Illiterates by Sex:

	Persons	Males	Females
Literate	54	31	23
Illiterate	34	11	23
Literacy rate	70.1	83.8	57.5
Graduate	0	0	0

Scheduled Tribes (Dominant):

Kattunayakan, Kondareddis, Malai Pandaram

For their cultural identity please see Appendix-II

Villages without Scheduled Tribes: There are
55 villages without any scheduled tribe population.

Literates and Illiterates by Sex (Total Population):

	Persons	Males	Females
Literate	76,066	42,058	34,008
Illiterate	37,859	14,513	23,346
Literacy rate	75	84	67
Graduate	1,273	766	507

Agriculture: ***Distribution of villages according to land use:***
Out of 62 villages, Total area (in hectare) is 74822.5, out of that 40.05 percent is cultivable and 8.91 percent of the cultivable area is irrigated.

Sources of Irrigation (Hectares): Government Canal 0, Private Canal 0, Well without Electricity 76.73, Well with Electricity 1567.77, Tubewell without Electricity 81.45, Tubewell with Electricity 0, Tank 944.42, River 0, Lake 6, Waterfall 0, Others 0.

Villages with population of 5000 to 9999:
Sillangulam, Tharuvaikulam, Ottappidaram
Pudiyamputhur.

Villages with population of 10000 and above: None

Distribution of Workers:

	Persons	Males	Females	WPR
Cultivators	10,661	6,147	4,514	18.81
Agricultural Labour	24,680	10,691	13,989	43.54
Household Industry	2,486	1,322	1,164	4.39
Other Workers	18,852	14,027	4,825	33.26
Main Workers	43,563	27,166	16,397	76.86
Marginal Workers	13,116	5,021	8,095	23.14
Total Workers	56,679	32,187	24,492	

Religion: Major Religious Communities:

	Persons	Males	Females	Sex Ratio
Hindu (89.39%)	101,841	50,626	51,215	1,012
Muslim (0.57%)	651	311	340	1,093
Christian (10.71%)	12,198	6,020	6,178	1,026
Sikh (0%)	2	2	-	-
Buddhists (0%)	3	1	2	2,000
Jain (0%)	4	2	2	1,000

Agewise Data:

	Persons	Males	Females	Sex Ratio
All ages	114,759	56,989	57,770	1014
0-14	33,202	17,085	16,117	943
15-44	53,799	26,474	27,325	1032
45-79	25,655	12,369	13,286	1074
80+	1,061	531	530	998

Age not stated	1,042	530	512	966

Languages (Dominant):

Tamil, Telugu, Malayalam, Kannada, Urdu

Disabled Population:

	Persons	Males	Females	%
Total Disabled	2,929	1,295	1,634	
In Seeing	1,711	604	1,107	58.42
In Speech	238	131	107	8.13
In Hearing	104	45	59	3.55
In Movement	633	378	255	21.61
Mentally	243	137	106	8.3

PALAKKODU

Palakkodu C.D. Block lies in the north-western part of Dharmapuri district. It is a part of Palakkodu taluk. The Block is located at a distance of 26 kms. from district headquarters (Dharmapuri). There are 54 villages in the block with the total population of 135,461 persons. Area of the C.D. Block is 393.08 sq. kms. It is bounded in the north and west by district Krishnagiri, in the south by CD Blocks Pennagaram, Nallampalli and Dharmapuri, and in the east by C.D. Block Karimangalam.

Communications:

Roadways : S.H.-17: Direction- Hosur to Jettihalli, Nearest Villages- Sudanur, Gommanoor, Dandukaranahalli, Jarthalau, Erranahalli, Karagathahalli, K.Settiha lli, P Gollahalli, Pulikarai, Selliyampatty, Pappinayakkanahalli.

Railway Station: Chikkamarandahalli, Erranahalli.

River: Chinnar Nadi- Nearest Villages- Gujjarahalli, Kanavenahalli, Nallur, Budihalli, Beladaranahalli, Errakuhahalli, Boppidi, Upparahalli, Bevuhalli, Seeriyanhalli, Sirendapuram, Chikkadornabettam, Gendannahalli.

Annual Rainfall: Average Rainfall 760 mm.

Ground Water: Availability of the ground water in the Basin is 6207.44 H.A.M. and the utilization is 9718.32 H.A.M. It belongs to Over Expoited category. Depth to water level varies from 2 to 20 meter below the ground. Most of the wells go down in summer months, according to the Ground Water Estimation Committee.

Natural Division: Baramahal.

Administration

Revenue **Division:** Dharmapuri. Parliamentary Constituency: 10 Dharmapuri. District: Dharmapuri. Taluk: Palakkodu. Assembly Constituency: 58 Pennagaram, 57 Palacodu. Gram Panchayat: 32.

Villages: 55 **Inhabited:** 55 **Uninhabited:** 0

Ranking	**District**	**State**	**National**
Area	11	78	1972
Population	10	35	2325
Sex Ratio	15	367	4640
Child Sex Ratio	15	369	6168
Literacy Rate	13	366	3974
Density	5	118	3149
Work Participation Rate	7	165	1204

Gram Panchayats:

A. Mallapuram , Athimutlu, Belamaranahalli , Belarahalli, Bevuhalli , Booganahalli, Chikkadornabettam, Chikkamarandahalli, Chudanur, Dandukaranahalli, Erranahalli , Ganapathy, Gendanahalli, Gummanur , Gundalanhalli, Jertalav, Kammalapatti , Karagadahalli, Kattampatti, Koravandahalli, M. Settihalli , Modugulahalli , Nallur, Nallur , P.Gollahalli , P.Sethihalli, Padi, Panjapalli , Pulikkarai, Samanur, Sekkodi, Selliyampatti .

Amenities:

Education: Primary School in 48 villages, Middle school in 17 villages, Matriculation or Secondary School in 8 villages, namely Periyanur, Gommanoor, Gujjarahalli, Jarthalau, Bevuhalli, Palacode Town, Pulikarai, Selliyampatty. Higher Secondary or Pre University Courses or Intermediate or Junior College in 4 villages of the CD Block,, namely Gujjarahalli, Bevuhalli, Palacode Town, Selliyampatty.

College in 0 village, Adult Literacy Center in 0 village.

Medical: Hospital in 1 village, Dispensary in 1 village, Health Center in 4 villages, Sub Center in 21 villages, Maternity and Child Welfare Center in 0 village, Community health workers in 45 villages.

The Villages having Hospital or Dispensary or Health Center are Athimuttlu, Gujjarahalli.

Drinking Water: Tap water in 55 villages, Tank water in 0 villages, Well water in 55 villages, Tubewell in 55 villages and more than one source in 55 villages.

Bank: Banking facility in 5 villages, namely, Samanoor, Gujjarahalli, P. Settihalli, Jarthalau Pulikarai.

Credit Society in 26 villages Agricultural Credit Society in 11 Non-Agricultural Credit Society in 10 villages.

Others: Power supply in 55 villages, Cinema hall in 0 village, sport club in 0 village, Stadium or Auditorium or Community Hall in 0 village, Post Office in 55 villages,

There are 49 villages having bus facilities.

Villages with most of facilities: Samanoor Gujjarahalli, P. Settihalli, Jarthalau, Pulikarai.

Villages without amenities (Education):

Bodikuhalapalli, Chennanahalli, Upparahalli, Rengampatti, Budihalli, Sirendapuram, Pothalahalli..

Scheduled Castes: Out of the total population of 135461 persons, 11516 persons (8.5%) belong to Scheduled Castes. The villages having less than 10% SC population are

Chinnegoundanahalli, Bodikuhalapalli, Marandahalli
Chennanahalli, Chikkamarandahalli, Gujjarahalli
Upparahalli, Rengampatti, Sanganbasauvantalau
P. Settihalli, Chikkardahalli, Jarthalau
Kanavenahalli, Nallur, Budihalli, Sirendapuram
Errakuhahalli, Boppidi, Erudukuttahalli, Erranahalli
Palacode Town, Bolabhagundhanahalli, Sitiganahalli
Kattanahalli, Karukkanaranahalli, Modukulahalli
Demalahalli, Pappinayakkanahalli, P Gollahalli
Pulikarai, Naralamavudhanahalli, Battalahalli
Jagirburgur, Selliyampatty, Sekkodi.

The villages having more than 50% SC population are None.

Sex ratio of Scheduled Caste population is 486.

Scheduled Castes Literates and Illiterates by Sex:

	Persons	Males	Females
Literate	5,334	3,297	2,037
Illiterate	6,182	2,626	3,556
Literacy rate	54.2	65.7	42.3
Graduate	83	66	17

Scheduled Castes (Dominant):

Adi Dravida, Arunthathiyar, Kuravan etc.
Paraiyan etc., Valluvan

For their cultural identity please see Appendix-I

Villages without Scheduled Castes: There are 11 villages without any scheduled caste population.

Scheduled Tribes: Out of the total population of 135461 persons, 1009 persons (0.74%) belong to Scheduled Tribes.

The villages having less than 10% ST population are
Panjapalli, Periyanur, Namadahalli
Chinnegoundanahalli, Sudanur, Gommanoor
Velagalahalli, Chikkadornabettam, Samanoor
Bodikuhalapalli, Athimuttlu, Marandahalli
Chennanahalli, Chikkamarandahalli, Gujjarahalli
Upparahalli, Rengampatti, Sanganbasauvantalau
P. Settihalli, Dandukaranahalli, Chikkardahalli
Jarthalau, Kanavenahalli, Nallur, Budihalli
Beladaranahalli, Thirumalvadi, Bevuhalli
Seeriyanahalli, Sirendapuram, Errakuhahalli, Boppidi
Erudukuttahalli, Erranahalli, Karagathahalli
Palacode Town, Bolabhagundhanahalli, Sitiganahalli
Guthalahalli, Kattanahalli, Karukkanaranahalli
Modukulahalli, K.Settihalli, Demalahalli
Pappinayakkanahalli, P Gollahalli, Pulikarai
Naralamavudhanahalli, Battalahalli, Pothalahalli
Jagirburgur, Selliyampatty, Buganehalli, Sekkodi.

The villages having more than 50% ST population are None.

Sex ratio of Scheduled tribe population is 469.

Scheduled Tribes Literates and Illiterates by Sex:

	Persons	Males	Females
Literate	181	100	81
Illiterate	828	436	392
Literacy rate	22.2	23.7	20.6
Graduate	2	1	1

Scheduled Tribes (Dominant):

Irular, Kurumans, Kurichchan, Malakkuravan
Malai Vedan

For their cultural identity please see Appendix-II

Villages without Scheduled Tribes: There are 40 villages without any scheduled tribe population.

Literates and Illiterates by Sex (Total Population):

	Persons	Males	Females
Literate	62,111	38,336	23,775
Illiterate	73,350	32,029	41,321
Literacy rate	53	64	42
Graduate	1,361	1,043	318

Agriculture: ***Distribution of villages according to land use:*** Out of 55 villages, Total area (in hectare) is 39308.82, out of that 75.16 percent is cultivable and 38.13 percent of the cultivable area is irrigated.

Sources of Irrigation (Hectares): Government Canal 744.33, Private Canal 0, Well without Electricity 3275.02, Well with Electricity 5635.58, Tubewell without Electricity 0, Tubewell with Electricity 0, Tank 1339.42, River 0, Lake 0, Waterfall 0, Others 269.84.

Villages with population of 5000 to 9999:
Panjapalli, P.Settighalli, Jertalar, Erranahalli
Palacode.

Villages with population of 10000 and above: None

Distribution of Workers:

	Persons	Males	Females	WPR
Cultivators	31,464	19,517	11,947	43.6
Agricultural Labour	29,282	12,874	16,408	40.58
Household Industry	755	364	391	1.05
Other Workers	10,661	8,235	2,426	14.77
Main Workers	60,365	37,061	23,304	83.65
Marginal Workers	11,797	3,929	7,868	16.35
Total Workers	72,162	40,990	31,172	

Religion: Major Religious Communities:

	Persons	Males	Females	Sex Ratio
Hindu (98.14%)	132,945	69,081	63,864	924
Muslim (0.99%)	1,345	718	627	873
Christian (1.16%)	1,570	764	806	1,055
Sikh (0%)	-	-	-	-
Buddhists (0%)	1	-	1	-
Jain (0%)	3	1	2	2,000

Agewise Data:

	Persons	Males	Females	Sex Ratio
All ages	135,950	70,608	65,342	925

0-14	43,617	23,789	19,828	833
15-44	64,924	32,701	32,223	985
45-79	25,886	13,284	12,602	949
80+	1,179	619	560	905
Age not stated	344	215	129	600

Languages (Dominant):
Tamil, Kannada, Telugu, Urdu, Marathi

Disabled Population:

	Persons	Males	Females	%
Total Disabled	4,093	1,405	2,688	
In Seeing	2,792	638	2,154	68.21
In Speech	334	182	152	8.16
In Hearing	138	74	64	3.37
In Movement	654	410	244	15.98
Mentally	175	101	74	4.28

PALANI

Palani C.D. Block lies in the western part of Dindigul district. It is a part of Palani taluk. The Block is located at a distance of 57 kms. from district headquarters (Dindigul). There are 34 villages in the block with the total population of 86,551 persons. Area of the C.D. Block is 342.33 sq. kms. It is bounded in the north by C.D. Blocks Oddanchatram and Thoppampatti, in the south by CD Block Kodaikanal, in the east by CD Block Reddiyarchatiram, and in the west by district Coimbatore.

Communications:
Roadways : N.H.-209: Direction- Udumalaipettai to Oddanchatram, Nearest Villages- Chithiraikulam, Sukkamanaikenpatti, Eramanaickanpatty, Kanakkanpatti, Palani, Sivagiripatti, A.Kalayamputhur, Chinnakalayamputhur, Thamaraikulam.
Railway Station: Palani, Thattankulam.
River: Shanmuga Nadi- Nearest Villages- Pethanaickenpatti, Palani, A.Kalayamputhur, Periyammapatti, Thamaraikulam.
Backwards Region Grants Fund: It receives Backward Region Grants.
Annual Rainfall: Average Rainfall 813 mm.
Ground Water: Availability of the ground water in the Basin is 7664.22 H.A.M. and the utilization is 7053.22 H.A.M. It belongs to Critical category. Depth to water level varies from 0 to 10 meter below the ground. Most of the wells go down in summer months, according to the Ground Water Estimation Committee.
Forest and Reserved Forest: (Karadi Kuttu RF)- Nearest Village- Kavadikoottam RF. (Palani Hills Northern Slopes, West RF)- Nearest Villages- Andipatti, R. Vadipatty (South), Sitharevu, Iravimangalam, Periyamapatti.
Natural Division: NA
Administration
Revenue **Division:** Palani. Parliamentary Constituency: 22 Dindigul. District: Dindigul. Taluk: Palani. Assembly Constituency: 127 Palani, 128 Oddanchatram. Gram Panchayat: 20.
Villages: 34 **Inhabited:** 33 **Uninhabited:** 1

Ranking	District	State	National
Area	7	124	2343
Population	9	199	3888
Sex Ratio	4	190	1304
Child Sex Ratio	1	55	1135
Literacy Rate	4	184	1722
Density	11	160	4044
Work Participation Rate	8	281	1568

Gram Panchayats:
A-Kalayamputhur, Amarapoondi, Andipatti, Ayyampalayam, Chinnakalayamputhur, Eramanaickenpatti, Kalikkanaickenpatti, Kanakkanpatti, KaradiKoottam, Kavalapatti, Kothaimangalam, Melakottai, Pachalanaickenpatti, Pappampatti, Periyammapatti, Pethanaickenpatti, Sithraikulam, Sivagiripatti , Thamaraikulam, Thathanaickenpatti, Thathanaickenpatti .

Amenities:
Education: Primary School in 32 villages, Middle school in 13 villages, Matriculation or Secondary School in 4 villages, namely Kothaimangalam, Sivagiripatti, A.Kalayamputhur, Neikkarapatti.
Higher Secondary or Pre University Courses or Intermediate or Junior College in 3 villages of the CD Block,, namely Kothaimangalam, Palani, Neikkarapatti.
College in 1 village, Adult Literacy Center in 0 village., College is in village, namely Chinnakalayamputhur.
Medical: Hospital in 1 village, Dispensary in 1 village, Health Center in 7 villages, Sub Center in 6 villages, Maternity and Child Welfare Center in 8 villages, Community health workers in 4 villages.
The Villages having Hospital or Dispensary or Health Center are Kanakkanpatti, Palani.
Drinking Water: Tap water in 33 villages, Tank water in 24 villages, Well water in 33 villages, Tubewell in 33 villages and more than one source in 33 villages.
Bank: Banking facility in 7 villages, namely, Amarapoondi, Kanakkanpatti, Palani, Sivagiripatti Neikkarapatti, Pappampatti, Andipatti.
Credit Society in 12 villages Agricultural Credit Society in 10 Non-Agricultural Credit Society in 1 village.
Others: Power supply in 33 villages, Cinema hall in 5 villages, sport club in 1 village, Stadium or Auditorium or Community Hall in 0 village, Post Office in 32 villages.
There are 29 villages having bus facilities.
Villages with most of facilities: Amarapoondi

Kanakkanpatti, Palani, Sivagiripatti, Neikkarapatti Pappampatti, Andipatti.

Villages without amenities (Education):
Rettaiambadi..

Scheduled Castes: Out of the total population of 86551 persons, 26165 persons (30.23%) belong to Scheduled Castes.
The villages having less than 10% SC population are None..
The villages having more than 50% SC population are None.
Sex ratio of Scheduled Caste population is 498.

Scheduled Castes Literates and Illiterates by Sex:

	Persons	Males	Females
Literate	11,469	7,055	4,414
Illiterate	14,696	6,069	8,627
Literacy rate	50.6	62.2	39.0
Graduate	351	236	115

Scheduled Castes (Dominant):
Pallan, Paraiyan etc., Madari, Chakkiliyan Kuravan etc.

For their cultural identity please see Appendix-I

Villages without Scheduled Castes: There are 3 villages without any scheduled caste population.

Scheduled Tribes: Out of the total population of 86551 persons, 187 persons (0.22%) belong to Scheduled Tribes.
The villages having less than 10% ST population are Ayyampalayam, Thathanaickenpatti(North) Chithiraikulam, Sukkamanaikenpatti Pethanaickenpatti, Melakkottai, Amarapoondi Veppanvalasu, Eramanaickanpatty, Kanakkanpatti Pachalanaickenpatti, Kombaipatti Kalikkanayakkan Patti, Kothaimangalam, Palani Sivagiripatti, Thattankulam, A.Kalayamputhur Neikkarapatti, Chinnakalayamputhur R.Vadipatti(North), Pappampatti, Velusamudram Andipatti, Chinnammapatti, Rettaiambadi, Kavalapatti R.Vadipatty(South), Sitharevu, Thathanaickenpatti Iravimangalam, Periyammapatti, Thamaraikulam.
The villages having more than 50% ST population are None.
Sex ratio of Scheduled tribe population is 508.

Scheduled Tribes Literates and Illiterates by Sex:

	Persons	Males	Females
Literate	35	24	11
Illiterate	152	68	84
Literacy rate	20.8	27.6	13.6
Graduate	0	0	0

Scheduled Tribes (Dominant):
Palliyar, Malakkuravan, Kattunayakan, Paniyan Palliyan

For their cultural identity please see Appendix-II

Villages without Scheduled Tribes: There are 28 villages without any scheduled tribe population.

Literates and Illiterates by Sex (Total Population):

	Persons	Males	Females
Literate	50,857	29,448	21,409
Illiterate	35,694	13,920	21,774
Literacy rate	66	77	56
Graduate	2,285	1,479	806

Agriculture: ***Distribution of villages according to land use:***
Out of 34 villages, Total area (in hectare) is 34233.92, out of that 53.77 percent is cultivable and 49.1 percent of the cultivable area is irrigated.

Sources of Irrigation (Hectares): Government Canal 1709.17, Private Canal 25, Well without Electricity 276.33, Well with Electricity 4711.09, Tubewell without Electricity 0, Tubewell with Electricity 37.36, Tank 1916.03, River 308.96, Lake 0, Waterfall 45.14, Others 10.

Villages with population of 5000 to 9999:
Kodaimangalam, Sivagiripatti, A-Kalayamputhur Chinnakalayamputhur, Pappampatti, Periyammapatti.

Villages with population of 10000 and above: None

Distribution of Workers:

	Persons	Males	Females	WPR
Cultivators	8,528	5,154	3,374	18.44
Agricultural Labour	21,864	10,623	11,241	47.29
Household Industry	1,282	703	579	2.77
Other Workers	14,561	10,369	4,192	31.49
Main Workers	41,496	24,790	16,706	89.75
Marginal Workers	4,739	2,059	2,680	10.25
Total Workers	46,235	26,849	19,386	

Religion: Major Religious Communities:

	Persons	Males	Females	Sex Ratio
Hindu (96.56%)	83,576	41,883	41,693	995
Muslim (2.11%)	1,824	902	922	1,022
Christian (1.14%)	991	482	509	1,056
Sikh (0%)	1	1	-	-
Buddhists (0%)	-	-	-	-
Jain (0%)	4	3	1	333

Agewise Data:

	Persons	Males	Females	Sex Ratio
All ages	86,551	43,368	43,183	996
0-14	21,618	11,100	10,518	948
15-44	43,149	21,113	22,036	1044
45-79	20,251	10,365	9,886	954
80+	669	344	325	945
Age not stated	864	446	418	937

Languages (Dominant):
Tamil, Telugu, Kannada, Malayalam, Urdu

Disabled Population:

	Persons	Males	Females	%
Total Disabled	2,582	1,085	1,497	
In Seeing	1,773	620	1,153	68.67
In Speech	142	68	74	5.5
In Hearing	119	75	44	4.61
In Movement	389	235	154	15.07
Mentally	159	87	72	6.16

PALAYAMKOTTAI

Palayamkottai C.D. Block lies in the eastern part of Tirunelveli district. It is a part of Tirunelveli and Palayamkottai taluks. The Block is located at a distance of NA kms. from district headquarters (Tirunelveli). There are 48 villages in the block with the total popul ation of 76,664 persons. Area of the C.D. Block is 269. 60 sq. kms. It is bounded in the north by CD Block Manur, in the south by CD Blocks Kalakkadu and Nanguneri, in the east by district Thoothukkudi, in the west by CD Blocks Manur and Cheranamadevi. CD Block Palayamkottai falls in taluk Tirunelveli by 07 villages, and in taluk Palayamkottai by 41 villages.

Communications:

Roadways : N.H.-7: Direction- Tirunelveli to Nagarkoil, Nearest Villages- Tharuvai, Munnerpallam, Muthur, Reddiyapatti, Kongandanparai, Sengulam, Ponnaku di. S.H.-39: Direction- Tenkasi to Tirunelveli, Nearest Village- Abishakapatti. S.H.-40: Direction- Tirunelveli to Srivaikuntam, Nearest Village- Parpakulam. S.H.-41: Direction- Sankarankoil to Tirunelveli, Nearest Villages- Chatrampudukulam, Ramiyanpatti, Krishnapuram, Vappankulam, Mehamudaiyarkulam, Ramalinganeri.

Railway Station: Rajavallipuram, Sengulam.

River: Tambraparnani Nadi- Nearest Villages- Rajavallipu ram, Seevalaperi, Kansapuram, Keelapattam, Thirumalai Kolunthu Puram, Manappadaividu, Keelanatham, Maruthur, Melathiruvenkatanathapuram, Tharuvai, Keelath iruvenkatanathapuram, Munnerpallam. Chittar Nadi- Nearest Village- Seevalaperi.

Annual Rainfall: Average Rainfall 879 mm.

Ground Water: Availability of the ground water in the Basin is 56.66 MCM and the utilization is 18.09 MCM. It belongs to Safe category. Depth to water level varies from 2 to 20 meter below the ground. Most of the wells go down in summer months, according to the Ground Water Estimation Committee.

Natural Division: NA

Administration

Revenue **Division:** Tirunelveli. Parliamentary Constituenc y: 38 Tirunelveli. District: Tirunelveli. Taluk: Tirunel veli, Palayamkottai. Assembly Constituency: 224 Tirunelve li, 227 Nanguneri. Gram Panchayat: 30.

Villages: 48 **Inhabited:** 45 **Uninhabited:** 3

Ranking	District	State	National
Area	12	209	3112
Population	11	259	4224
Sex Ratio	16	70	574
Child Sex Ratio	14	209	3378
Literacy Rate	7	50	688
Density	15	263	3700
Work Participation Rate	10	244	2848

Gram Panchayats:

Ariyakulam , Itteri, Kansapuram, Keelanatham, Keelapattam , Konganthanparai, Kunnathur, Manappadaiveedu, Maruthur, Melapattam, Melaputhaneri , Melaputheri , Melathidiyoor , Munnirpallam, Muthur, Naduvakuruchi, Nochikulam , Palayamchettikulam, Ponnakudi, Puthukulam, Rajavalllipuram, Ramayanpatti, Ramayyampatti , Ramayyanpatti, Reddiarpatty , Seevalaperi, Sengulam, Sengulam , Sivanthipatti, Theruvai, Thidiyoor, Thirumalaikolunthupuram, Thiruvengadanathapuram, Udaiyarkulam .

Amenities:

Education: Primary School in 38 villages, Middle school in 14 villages, Matriculation or Secondary School in 7 villages, namely Seevalaperi, Keelanatham, Naduvakurichi, Ariyakulam, Uthamapandiankulam, Munnerpallam, Reddiyarpatty.

Higher Secondary or Pre University Courses or Intermediate or Junior College in 4 villages of the CD Block,, namely Keelanatham, Ariyakulam, Uthamapandiankulam, Reddiyarpatty.

College in 2 villages, Adult Literacy Center in 2 villages., Colleges are in villages, namely Ariyakulam, Melathidiyoor.

Medical: Hospital in 4 villages, Dispensary in 3 villages, Health Center in 8 villages, Sub Center in 14 villages, Maternity and Child Welfare Center in 3 villages, Community health workers in 36 villages.

The Villages having Hospital or Dispensary or Health Center are Seevalaperi, Thirumalai Kolunthu Puram, Melapattam, Naduvakurichi, Tharuvai, Reddiyarpatty, Thidiyur, Ponnakudi.

Drinking Water: Tap water in 45 villages, Tank water in 10 villages, Well water in 30 villages, Tubewell in 6 villages and more than one source in 40 villages.

Bank: Banking facility in 5 villages, namely, Abishakapatti, Seevalaperi, Munnerpallam Reddiyarpatty, Sivanthipatti.

Credit Society in 11 villages Agricultural Credit Society in 10 Non-Agricultural Credit Society in 2 villages.

Others: Power supply in 44 villages, Cinema hall in 0 village, sport club in 0 village, Stadium or Auditorium or Community Hall in 0 village, Post Office in 35 villages.
There are 37 villages having bus facilities.
Villages with most of facilities: Abishakapatti Seevalaperi, Munnerpallam, Reddiyarpatty Sivanthipatti.
Villages without amenities (Education): Vappankulam, Thiruthu, Udayarkulam, Muthur Reddiyapatti, Gangainadarkulam..
Scheduled Castes: Out of the total population of 76664 persons, 19440 persons (25.36%) belong to Scheduled Castes.
The villages having less than 10% SC population are Abishakapatti, Vagaikulam, Udayarkulam Uthamapandiankulam, Krishnapuram, Araikulam Muthur Reddiyapatti, Gangainadarkulam, Thidiyur Pudukulam, Sivanthipatti.
The villages having more than 50% SC population are Kansapuram, Paraikulam, Parpakulam, Kunnathur Melathiruvenkatanathapuram Keelathiruvenkatanathapuram, Muthoor.
Sex ratio of Scheduled Caste population is 512.

Scheduled Castes Literates and Illiterates by Sex:

	Persons	Males	Females
Literate	11,736	6,558	5,178
Illiterate	7,704	2,926	4,778
Literacy rate	69.6	80.1	59.7
Graduate	179	115	64

Scheduled Castes (Dominant):
Pallan, Paraiyan etc., Adi Dravida, Puthirai Vannan Chakkiliyan
For their cultural identity please see Appendix-I
Villages without Scheduled Castes: There are 6 villages without any scheduled caste population.
Scheduled Tribes: Out of the total population of 76664 persons, 114 persons (0.15%) belong to Scheduled Tribes.
The villages having less than 10% ST population are Rajavallipuram, Vappankulam, Ramiyanpatti Abishakapatti, Seevalaperi, Kansapuram, Keelapattam Thirumalai Kolunthu Puram, Manappadaividu Melapattam, Keelanatham, Palayamchettikulam Avanaperi, Thiruthu, Maruthur, Vagaikulam Udayarkulam, Naduvakurichi, Ariyakulam, Velankulam Melaputheneri, Paraikulam, Uthamapandiankulam Parpakulam, Nuchikulam, Krishnapuram, Kunnathur Melathiruvenkatanathapuram, Tharuvai Keelathiruvenkatanathapuram, Munnerpallam, Araikulam Reddiyarpatty, Muthur Reddiyapatti, Muthoor Kongandanparai, Kuravankulam, Melathidiyoor Gangainadarkulam, Thidiyur, Sengulam, Ponnakudi Pudukulam, Itteri, Sivanthipatti.
The villages having more than 50% ST population are None.
Sex ratio of Scheduled tribe population is 509.

Scheduled Tribes Literates and Illiterates by Sex:

	Persons	Males	Females
Literate	72	42	30
Illiterate	42	14	28
Literacy rate	67.3	76.4	57.7
Graduate	2	0	2

Scheduled Tribes (Dominant):
Kattunayakan, Malakkuravan, Malai Pandaram, Kammara Kaniyan etc.
For their cultural identity please see Appendix-II
Villages without Scheduled Tribes: There are 43 villages without any scheduled tribe population.

Literates and Illiterates by Sex (Total Population):

	Persons	Males	Females
Literate	50,203	27,550	22,653
Illiterate	26,461	10,306	16,155
Literacy rate	75	83	66
Graduate	1,030	677	353

Agriculture: ***Distribution of villages according to land use:*** Out of 48 villages, Total area (in hectare) is 26960.92, out of that 15.08 percent is cultivable and 90.15 percent of the cultivable area is irrigated.
Sources of Irrigation (Hectares): Government Canal 520.68, Private Canal 0, Well without Electricity 115.67, Well with Electricity 574.28, Tubewell without Electricity 6.23, Tubewell with Electricity 15.37, Tank 2363.02, River 69.71, Lake 0, Waterfall 0, Others 1.11.
Villages with population of 5000 to 9999: Munnirpallam.
Villages with population of 10000 and above: None

Distribution of Workers:

	Persons	Males	Females	WPR
Cultivators	5,153	3,781	1,372	14.01
Agricultural Labour	11,918	6,428	5,490	32.4
Household Industry	6,466	824	5,642	17.58
Other Workers	13,252	10,207	3,045	36.02
Main Workers	28,461	17,303	11,158	77.36
Marginal Workers	8,328	3,937	4,391	22.64
Total Workers	36,789	21,240	15,549	

Religion: Major Religious Communities:

	Persons	Males	Females	Sex Ratio
Hindu (83.56%)	64,061	31,628	32,433	1,025
Muslim (2.15%)	1,650	773	877	1,135
Christian (14.1%)	10,806	5,377	5,429	1,010
Sikh (0%)	2	1	1	1,000
Buddhists (0%)	1	-	1	-

Jain (0%)	1	1	-	-

Agewise Data:

	Persons	Males	Females	Sex Ratio
All ages	76,664	37,856	38,808	1025
0-14	21,760	11,335	10,425	920
15-44	36,550	17,783	18,767	1055
45-79	16,930	8,034	8,896	1107
80+	764	367	397	1082
Age not stated	660	337	323	958

Languages (Dominant):
Tamil, Gujarati, Telugu, Urdu, Kannada

Disabled Population:

	Persons	Males	Females	%
Total Disabled	2,485	1,212	1,273	
In Seeing	1,564	697	867	62.94
In Speech	114	67	47	4.59
In Hearing	98	43	55	3.94
In Movement	549	318	231	22.09
Mentally	160	87	73	6.44

PALLADAM

Palladam C.D. Block lies in the eastern part of Coimbatore district. It is a part of Palladam taluk. The Block is located at a distance of 40 kms. from district headquarters (Coimbatore). There are 19 villages in the block with the total population of 85,834 persons. Area of the C.D. Block is 262.42 sq. kms. in the north by CD Block Tiruppur, in the south by CD Blocks Sultanpet and Pongalur, in the east by C.D. Block Pongalur, in the west by CD Blocks Sulur and Sultanpet.

Communications:

Roadways : N.H.-67: Direction- Sulur to Palladam, Nearest Villages- Sukkampalayam, Kodangipalayalm. S.H.-19: Direction- Pollachi to Tiruppur, Nearest Villages- Naranapuram, Karaipudur, Panickampatty, P.Vadugapalayam, Anuppatti, K. Krishnapuram, Ganapathipalayam.

Annual Rainfall: Average Rainfall 550 mm.

Ground Water: Availability of the ground water in the Basin is 2745.61 H.A.M. and the utilization is 2681.78 H.A.M. It belongs to Safe category. Depth to water level varies from 5 to 20 meter below the ground. Most of the wells go down in summer months, according to the Ground Water Estimation Committee.

Natural Division: Kongu Nadu.

Administration

Revenue **Division:** Trippur. Parliamentary Constituency: 20 Coimbatore. District: Coimbatore. Taluk: Palladam. Assembly Constituency: 115 Palladam. Gram Panchayat: 20.

Villages: 19 **Inhabited:** 19 **Uninhabited:** 0

Ranking	District	State	National
Area	10	215	3214
Population	6	202	3907
Sex Ratio	17	345	3243
Child Sex Ratio	14	170	2966
Literacy Rate	5	145	1499
Density	11	161	3297
Work Participation Rate	7	189	1575

Gram Panchayats:

Anuppatti, Arumutham palayam, Chittambalam, Ganapathipalayam, Ichipatti, K. Ayyampalayam, K.Krishnapuram, Karadibavi, Karaipudur, Kodangipalayam, Mallegoundenpalayam, Manickapuram, Panickkampatti, Paruvai, Poomalur, Puliampatti, Sukkampalayam, Vadugapalayam , Velampalayam.

Amenities:

Education: Primary School in 19 villages, Middle school in 8 villages, Matriculation or Secondary School in 4 villages, namely Karaipudur, Ganapathipalayam, P.Vadugapalayam, Karadivavi.

Higher Secondary or Pre University Courses or Intermediate or Junior College in 3 villages of the CD Block,, namely Karaipudur, P.Vadugapalayam, Karadivavi.

College in 1 village, Adult Literacy Center in 0 village., College is in village, namely Karaipudur.

Medical: Hospital in 1 village, Dispensary in 0 village, Health Center in 2 villages, Sub Center in 15 villages, Maternity and Child Welfare Center in 2 villages, Community health workers in 3 villages.

The Villages having Hospital or Dispensary or Health Center are Kodangipalayalm.

Drinking Water: Tap water in 19 villages, Tank water in 0 villages, Well water in 19 villages, Tubewell in 19 villages and more than one source in 19 villages.

Bank: Banking facility in 2 villages, namely, Ganapathipalayam, Karadivavi.

Credit Society in 9 villages Agricultural Credit Society in 8 Non-Agricultural Credit Society in 3 villages.

Others: Power supply in 19 villages, Cinema hall in 2 villages, sport club in 0 village, Stadium or Auditorium or Community Hall in 0 village, Post Office in 18 villages.

There are 19 villages having bus facilities.

Villages with most of facilities: Ganapathipalayam Karadivavi.

Villages without Amenities (Education): None..

Scheduled Castes: Out of the total population of 85834 persons, 16914 persons (19.71%) belong to Scheduled Castes.

The villages having less than 10% SC population are None..

The villages having more than 50% SC population are None.

Sex ratio of Scheduled Caste population is 494.

Scheduled Castes Literates and Illiterates by Sex:

	Persons	Males	Females
Literate	6,665	4,008	2,657
Illiterate	10,249	4,557	5,692
Literacy rate	46.1	54.9	37.1
Graduate	5	3	2

Scheduled Castes (Dominant):
Madari, Arunthathiyar, Adi Dravida, Chakkiliyan Generic Castes etc.

For their cultural identity please see Appendix-I

Villages without Scheduled Castes: There is 0 village without any scheduled caste population.

Scheduled Tribes: Out of the total population of 85834 persons, 44 persons (0.05%) belong to Scheduled Tribes. The villages having less than 10% ST population are Pumalur, Vellampalayam, Naranapuram, Karaipudur Ganapathipalayam, Palladam, Sukkampalayam, Ichipatty Kodangipalayalm, Panickampatty, P.Vadugapalayam Chittampalam, Anuppatti, K.Ayyampalayam, Karadivavi Paruvai, Mallegoundenpalayam, Puliyampatti K. Krishnapuram.

The villages having more than 50% ST population are None.

Sex ratio of Scheduled tribe population is 455.

Scheduled Tribes Literates and Illiterates by Sex:

	Persons	Males	Females
Literate	26	16	10
Illiterate	18	8	10
Literacy rate	63.4	72.7	52.6
Graduate	0	0	0

Scheduled Tribes (Dominant):
Kochu Velan, Malai Pandaram, Irular, Toda Kondareddis

For their cultural identity please see Appendix-II

Villages without Scheduled Tribes: There are 14 villages without any scheduled tribe population.

Literates and Illiterates by Sex (Total Population):

	Persons	Males	Females
Literate	51,483	30,174	21,309
Illiterate	34,351	13,742	20,609
Literacy rate	68	78	57
Graduate	550	341	209

Agriculture: ***Distribution of villages according to land use:*** Out of 19 villages, Total area (in hectare) is 26242.55, out of that 90.68 percent is cultivable and 18.17 percent of the cultivable area is irrigated.

Sources of Irrigation (Hectares): Government Canal 1227.37, Private Canal 0, Well without Electricity 131.02, Well with Electricity 2215.63, Tubewell without Electricity 0, Tubewell with Electricity 749.6, Tank 0, River 0, Lake 0, Waterfall 0, Others 0.

Villages with population of 5000 to 9999:
Poomalur, Naranapuram , Ganapathipalayam Kodangipalayam.

Villages with population of 10000 and above:
Karaipudur.

Distribution of Workers:

	Persons	Males	Females	WPR
Cultivators	6,798	4,096	2,702	14.84
Agricultural Labour	9,533	4,448	5,085	20.81
Household Industry	3,815	2,409	1,406	8.33
Other Workers	25,661	18,841	6,820	56.02
Main Workers	40,883	27,634	13,249	89.25
Marginal Workers	4,924	2,160	2,764	10.75
Total Workers	45,807	29,794	16,013	

Religion: Major Religious Communities:

	Persons	Males	Females	Sex Ratio
Hindu (94.74%)	81,321	41,632	39,689	953
Muslim (2.04%)	1,752	865	887	1,025
Christian (3.1%)	2,665	1,369	1,296	947
Sikh (0%)	-	-	-	-
Buddhists (0%)	3	1	2	2,000
Jain (0.01%)	5	3	2	667

Agewise Data:

	Persons	Males	Females	Sex Ratio
All ages	85,834	43,916	41,918	955
0-14	20,633	10,545	10,088	957
15-44	44,336	22,592	21,744	962
45-79	19,407	10,023	9,384	936
80+	1,037	534	503	942
Age not stated	421	222	199	896

Languages (Dominant):
Tamil, Telugu, Kannada, Urdu, Malayalam

Disabled Population:

	Persons	Males	Females	%
Total Disabled	2,600	1,268	1,332	
In Seeing	1,614	701	913	62.08
In Speech	212	122	90	8.15
In Hearing	126	60	66	4.85
In Movement	433	263	170	16.65
Mentally	215	122	93	8.27

PALLIPALAYAM

Pallipalayam C.D. Block lies in the western part of Namakkal district. It is a part of Tiruchengode taluk. The Block is located at a distance of 55 kms. from district headquarters (Namakkal). There are 13 villages in the block with the total population of 85,871 persons. Area of the C.D. Block is 128.63 sq. kms. It is bounded in the north by district Salem, in the south and west by district Erode, and in the east by C.D. Block Tiruchengode.

Communications:

Roadways : N.H.-47: Direction- Bhavani to Sankari, Nearest Villages- Komarapalayam Amani, Pallakkapalayam.

River: Cauvery Nadi- Nearest Villages- Kumarapalayam Agraharam, Kalianur, Samayasangili Agraharam, Odapalli Agraharam, Pappaampalayam, Kokkarayanpettai.

Annual Rainfall: Average Rainfall 650 mm.

Ground Water: Availability of the ground water in the Basin is 4210.65 H.A.M. and the utilization is 4399.61 H.A.M. It belongs to Safe category. Depth to water level varies from 2 to 10 meter below the ground. Most of the wells go down in summer months, according to the Ground Water Estimation Committee.

Natural Division: Kongu Nadu.

Administration

Revenue **Division:** Tiruchengode. Parliamentary Constituency: 17 Erode. District: Namakkal. Taluk: Tiruchengode. Assembly Constituency: 97 Kumarapalayam. Gram Panchayat: 15.

Villages: 13 **Inhabited:** 13 **Uninhabited:** 0

Ranking	District	State	National
Area	12	354	5342
Population	1	201	3905
Sex Ratio	13	356	4038
Child Sex Ratio	10	347	5797
Literacy Rate	7	255	2199
Density	13	122	1583
Work Participation Rate	1	25	1225

Gram Panchayats:

Irugalur Pudupalayam, Ellandaikuttai, Kadachanallur, Kalaiyanur, Kalaiyanur Agraharam, Kokkarayanpettai, Kuppandapalayam, Odappalli Agraharam, Pallakkapalayam, Patharai, Pappampalayam, Samayasangili Agraharam, Savudapuram, Thathankuttai.

Amenities:

Education: Primary School in 13 villages, Middle school in 10 villages, Matriculation or Secondary School in 4 villages, namely Kumarapalayam Agraharam, Pallakkapalayam, Sowdhapuram, Kokkarayanpettai.

Higher Secondary or Pre University Courses or Intermediate or Junior College in 1 village of the CD Block,, namely Pallakkapalayam.

College in 1 village, Adult Literacy Center in 0 village., Colleges are in villages, namely Komarapalayam Amani.

Medical: Hospital in 0 village, Dispensary in 0 village, Health Center in 5 villages, Sub Center in 13 villages, Maternity and Child Welfare Center in 0 village, Community health workers in 0 village.

The Village having Hospital or Dispensary or Health Center is Sowdhapuram.

Drinking Water: Tap water in 13 villages, Tank water in 0 villages, Well water in 13 villages, Tubewell in 13 villages and more than one source in 13 villages.

Bank: Banking facility in 4 villages, namely, Elandaikuttai, Kalianur, Pallipalayam Agraharam Odapalli Agraharam.

Credit Society in 11 villages Agricultural Credit Society in 8 Non-Agricultural Credit Society in 10 villages.

Others: Power supply in 13 villages, Cinema hall in 1 village, sport club in 0 village, Stadium or Auditorium or Community Hall in 0 village, Post Office in 13 villages.

There are 13 villages having bus facilities.

Villages with most of facilities: Elandaikuttai Kalianur, Pallipalayam Agraharam, Odapalli Agraharam.

Villages without Amenities (Education): None..

Scheduled Castes: Out of the total population of 85871 persons, 12166 persons (14.17%) belong to Scheduled Castes.

The villages having less than 10% SC population are Komarapalayam Amani, Kaliyanur Agraharam Pappaampalayam.

The villages having more than 50% SC population are None.

Sex ratio of Scheduled Caste population is 486.

Scheduled Castes Literates and Illiterates by Sex:

	Persons	Males	Females
Literate	5,323	3,207	2,116
Illiterate	6,843	3,049	3,794
Literacy rate	49.9	58.6	40.7
Graduate	131	90	41

Scheduled Castes (Dominant):

Arunthathiyar, Adi Dravida, Chakkiliyan, Pannadi Paraiyan etc.

For their cultural identity please see Appendix-I

Villages without Scheduled Castes: There is 0 village without any scheduled caste population.

Scheduled Tribes: Out of the total population of 85871 persons, 72 persons (0.08%) belong to Scheduled Tribes.

The villages having less than 10% ST population are Kumarapalayam Agraharam, Komarapalayam Amani Pallakkapalayam, Sowdhapuram, Elandaikuttai Kalianur, Kaliyanur Agraharam Samayasangili Agraharam, Pallipalayam Agraharam Odapalli Agraharam, Kadachanallur, Pappaampalayam Kokkarayanpettai.

The villages having more than 50% ST population are None.

Sex ratio of Scheduled tribe population is 444.

Scheduled Tribes Literates and Illiterates by Sex:

	Persons	Males	Females
Literate	41	25	16

Illiterate	31	15	16
Literacy rate	68.3	75.8	59.3
Graduate	2	1	1

Scheduled Tribes (Dominant):

Malayali, Irular, Kaniyan etc., Generic Tribes etc. Kondareddis

For their cultural identity please see Appendix-II

Villages without Scheduled Tribes: There are 7 villages without any scheduled tribe population.

Literates and Illiterates by Sex (Total Population):

	Persons	Males	Females
Literate	48,696	28,775	19,921
Illiterate	37,175	15,510	21,665
Literacy rate	63	73	53
Graduate	2,433	1,602	831

Agriculture: ***Distribution of villages according to land use:*** Out of 13 villages, Total area (in hectare) is 12863.93, out of that 83.69 percent is cultivable and 43.69 percent of the cultivable area is irrigated.

Sources of Irrigation (Hectares): Government Canal 3136.82, Private Canal 0, Well without Electricity 0, Well with Electricity 597.05, Tubewell without Electricity 0, Tubewell with Electricity 111.22, Tank 2, River 0, Lake 0, Waterfall 0, Others 856.21.

Villages with population of 5000 to 9999:

Kalaiyanur, Kadachanallur, Kokkarayanpettai.

Villages with population of 10000 and above:

Kumarapalaiyam Agraharam , Komarapalayam Ellandaikuttai.

Distribution of Workers:

	Persons	Males	Females	WPR
Cultivators	8,104	4,901	3,203	17.07
Agricultural Labour	7,747	3,405	4,342	16.32
Household Industry	3,697	1,653	2,044	7.79
Other Workers	27,935	18,455	9,480	58.83
Main Workers	43,402	27,059	16,343	91.41
Marginal Workers	4,081	1,355	2,726	8.59
Total Workers	47,483	28,414	19,069	

Religion: Major Religious Communities:

	Persons	Males	Females	Sex Ratio
Hindu (94.7%)	81,317	41,987	39,330	937
Muslim (2.8%)	2,407	1,208	1,199	993
Christian (2.41%)	2,067	1,049	1,018	970
Sikh (0%)	3	3	-	-
Buddhists (0%)	2	1	1	1,000
Jain (0.01%)	8	2	6	3,000

Agewise Data:

	Persons	Males	Females	Sex Ratio
All ages	85,871	44,285	41,586	939
0-14	20,146	10,841	9,305	858
15-44	44,680	22,659	22,021	972
45-79	19,224	9,865	9,359	949
80+	692	364	328	901
Age not stated	1,129	556	573	1031

Languages (Dominant):

Tamil, Telugu, Urdu, Kannada, Malayalam

Disabled Population:

	Persons	Males	Females	%
Total Disabled	1,702	1,009	693	
In Seeing	1,139	687	452	66.92
In Speech	111	56	55	6.52
In Hearing	67	39	28	3.94
In Movement	285	169	116	16.75
Mentally	100	58	42	5.88

PALLIPATTU

Pallipattu C.D. Block lies in the western part of Thiruvallur district. It is a part of Pallipattu taluk. The Block is located at a distance of 65 kms. from district headquarters (Thiruvallur). There are 20 villages in the block with the total population of 66,193 persons. Area of the C.D. Block is 157.16 sq. kms. It is bounded in the south by CD Block R.K. pet, in the east by CD Block Tiruttani, and it has common boundary with the state of Andhra Pradesh on north, west and east.

Communications:

Roadways : Information not Available.

River: Nagarai Nadi- Nearest Villages- Venkatarajakuppam, Veliagaram, Perumanallur, Pallipattu, Kolathur, Nediyam, Karimbedu.

Annual Rainfall: Average Rainfall 1152 mm.

Ground Water: Availability of the ground water in the Basin is 46.93 MCM and the utilization is 73.78 MCM. It belongs to Over Expoited category. Depth to water level varies from 2 to 5 meter below the ground. Most of the wells go down in summer months, according to the Ground Water Estimation Committee.

Natural Division: Tondai Nadu.

Administration

Revenue **Division:** Tiruttani. Parliamentary Constituency: 7 Arakkonam. District: Thiruvallur. Taluk: Pallapattu. Assembly Constituency: 3 Tiruttani. Gram Panchayat: 33.

Border Villages- (Andhra Pradesh)- Nearest Villages- Venkatarajakuppam, Veliagaram, Perumanallur, Kolathur, Nediyam, Karimbedu, Kolalakuppam, Karlambakkam, Athimanjur, Kodivalasa, Nochili, Nedigalltur RF (Ui), Krishnamarajakuppam.

Villages: 20 **Inhabited:** 19 **Uninhabited:** 1

Ranking	District	State	National
Area	11	337	4923
Population	11	305	4632
Sex Ratio	9	207	1450
Child Sex Ratio	8	183	3094

Literacy Rate	14	302	2547
Density	6	311	2609
Work Participation Rate	7	102	3664

Gram Panchayats:
Athimanjeri, Gollalakuppam, Jangalapalli, Kakkalur, Karimbedu, Karlambakkam, Keechalam, Keelapudi, Kesavarajakuppam, Kodivalasa, Kolathur, Konasamudram, Koracuppam, Kumararajupattu, Melapudi, Nedigallu, Nediyam, Nochili, Pandravedu, Perumanallur, Pettaikandigai, Punniyam, Ramacharapuram , Ramapuram, Ramasamudram, Samanthawada, Srikaverirajulingaripet, Surarajapattadai , Thirumalrajpet, Vadakuppam, Veliagaram, Venkatarajakuppam .

Amenities:
Education: Primary School in 19 villages, Middle school in 13 villages, Matriculation or Secondary School in 6 villages, namely Veliagaram, Kolathur, Nediyam, Kodivalasa, Nochili, Keechalam.
Higher Secondary or Pre University Courses or Intermediate or Junior College in 1 village of the CD Block,, namely Kodivalasa.
College in 0 village, Adult Literacy Center in 0 village.
Medical: Hospital in 0 village, Dispensary in 0 village, Health Center in 10 villages, Sub Center in 11 villages, Maternity and Child Welfare Center in 0 village, Community health workers in 19 villages.
Drinking Water: Tap water in 19 villages, Tank water in 19 villages, Well water in 19 villages, Tubewell in 19 villages and more than one source in 19 villages.
Bank: Banking facility in 4 villages, namely, Pallipattu, Athimanjur, Nedugallur, Ramasamudram.
Credit Society in 7 villages Agricultural Credit Society in 7 Non-Agricultural Credit Society in 1 village.
Others: Power supply in 19 villages, Cinema hall in 2 villages, sport club in 0 village, Stadium or Auditorium or Community Hall in 0 village, Post Office in 17 villages.
There are 19 villages having bus facilities.
Villages with most of facilities: Pallipattu Athimanjur, Nedugallur, Ramasamudram.
Villages without Amenities (Education): None..
Scheduled Castes: Out of the total population of 66193 persons, 16970 persons (25.64%) belong to Scheduled Castes.
The villages having less than 10% SC population are None..
The villages having more than 50% SC population are None.
Sex ratio of Scheduled Caste population is 497.

Scheduled Castes Literates and Illiterates by Sex:

	Persons	Males	Females
Literate	7,949	4,809	3,140
Illiterate	9,021	3,735	5,286
Literacy rate	54.3	65.5	43.0
Graduate	231	210	21

Scheduled Castes (Dominant):
Adi Dravida, Adi Andhra, Arunthathiyar, Chakkiliyan Paraiyan etc.
For their cultural identity please see Appendix-I
Villages without Scheduled Castes: There is 1 village without any scheduled caste population.
Scheduled Tribes: Out of the total population of 66193 persons, 3546 persons (5.36%) belong to Scheduled Tribes.
The villages having less than 10% ST population are Venkatarajakuppam, Veliagaram, Pallipattu, Kolathur Karimbedu, Kolalakuppam, Konasamudram, Karlambakkam Athimanjur, Kodivalasa, Nochili, Pettaikanoikai Nedugallur, Keechalam, Ramasamudram Krishnamarajakuppam.
The villages having more than 50% ST population are None.
Sex ratio of Scheduled tribe population is 490.

Scheduled Tribes Literates and Illiterates by Sex:

	Persons	Males	Females
Literate	1,710	1,071	639
Illiterate	1,836	739	1,097
Literacy rate	56.0	69.4	42.3
Graduate	79	61	18

Scheduled Tribes (Dominant):
Kondareddis, Irular, Generic Tribes etc.
Konda Kapus, Kurumans
For their cultural identity please see Appendix-II
Villages without Scheduled Tribes: There are 3 villages without any scheduled tribe population.

Literates and Illiterates by Sex (Total Population):

	Persons	Males	Females
Literate	35,334	21,614	13,720
Illiterate	30,859	11,599	19,260
Literacy rate	61	75	48
Graduate	1,712	1,425	287

Agriculture: ***Distribution of villages according to land use:***
Out of 20 villages, Total area (in hectare) is 15716.52, out of that 54.19 percent is cultivable and 71.68 percent of the cultivable area is irrigated.
Sources of Irrigation (Hectares): Government Canal 548.4, Private Canal 64, Well without Electricity 156.47, Well with Electricity 2378.61, Tubewell without Electricity 530.65, Tubewell with Electricity 1494.8, Tank 256.1, River 26, Lake 500.77, Waterfall 0, Others 149.
Villages with population of 5000 to 9999: Kolathur, Kodivalasa.
Villages with population of 10000 and above: None

Distribution of Workers:

	Persons	Males	Females	WPR
Cultivators	5,816	4,312	1,504	19.99
Agricultural Labour	12,983	6,593	6,390	44.62
Household Industry	3,660	2,106	1,554	12.58
Other Workers	6,635	5,141	1,494	22.81
Main Workers	22,701	15,507	7,194	78.03
Marginal Workers	6,393	2,645	3,748	21.97
Total Workers	29,094	18,152	10,942	

Religion: Major Religious Communities:

	Persons	Males	Females	Sex Ratio
Hindu (96.43%)	63,827	32,019	31,808	993
Muslim (1.62%)	1,073	551	522	947
Christian (1.87%)	1,235	612	623	1,018
Sikh (0.02%)	15	8	7	875
Buddhists (0.01%)	9	7	2	286
Jain (0%)	1	-	1	-

Agewise Data:

	Persons	Males	Females	Sex Ratio
All ages	66,193	33,213	32,980	993
0-14	19,461	10,019	9,442	942
15-44	31,681	15,878	15,803	995
45-79	14,248	6,936	7,312	1054
80+	489	233	256	1099
Age not stated	314	147	167	1136

Languages (Dominant):
Tamil, Telugu, Urdu, Kannada, Malayalam

Disabled Population:

	Persons	Males	Females	%
Total Disabled	1,927	1,152	775	
In Seeing	1,023	600	423	53.09
In Speech	238	133	105	12.35
In Hearing	100	63	37	5.19
In Movement	456	288	168	23.66
Mentally	110	68	42	5.71

PANAIMARATHUPATTI

Panamarathupatti C.D. Block lies in the southern part of Salem district. It is a part of Salem taluk. The Block is located at a distance of 12 kms. from district headquarters (Salem). There are 29 villages in the block with the total population of 57,064 persons. Area of the C.D. Block is 155.06 sq. kms. It is bounded in the north by C.D. Blocks Salem and Ayodhyapattinam, in the south by district Namakkal, in the east by CD Block Ayodhyapattinam, and in the west by C.D. Block Veerapandi.

Communications:

Roadways : N.H.-7: Direction- Salem to Rasipuram, Nearest Villages- Ammapalayam, Sandiyur Attayampatti, Sandiyur, Gajalnaickenpatti, Nilavarapatti, Nallikkalpatti.

River: Varista Nadi- Nearest Village- Muthugoundanoor.

Annual Rainfall: Average Rainfall 540 mm.

Ground Water: Availability of the ground water in the Basin is 1994.98 H.A.M. and the utilization is 3760.44 H.A.M. It belongs to Safe category. Depth to water level varies from 2 to 10 meter below the ground. Most of the wells go down in summer months, according to the Ground Water Estimation Committee.

Forest and Reserved Forest: (Jalluthuppatti RF)- Nearest Villages- Jalluthupattti (RF), Kanamaduru, Kuralnatham, Jalluthupattti, Thumbalpatti, Kammalapatti. (Jerugumalai)- Nearest Villages- Jerugumalai, Jerugumalai (RF), Nilavarapatti.

Natural Division: Kongu Nadu.

Administration

Revenue **Division:** Salem. Parliamentary Constituency: 16 Nanakkal. District: Salem. Taluk: Salem. Assembly Constituency: 91 Veerapandi. Gram Panchayat: 20.

Villages: 29 **Inhabited:** 27 **Uninhabited:** 2

Ranking	**District**	**State**	**National**
Area	14	340	4959
Population	18	338	4961
Sex Ratio	8	357	4042
Child Sex Ratio	9	362	6055
Literacy Rate	10	348	3326
Density	15	159	2969
Work Participation Rate	11	140	1565

Gram Panchayats:

Ammapalayam, Dasanaickenpatti, Eruvadi Vaniyambadi, Gajalnaickenpatti, Kammalapatti, Kuralnatham, Mukkuthipalayam, Nallikkalpatti, Nilavarapatti, Pallitherupatti, Parapatti, Peramanur, Sandiyur, Sandiyur Attayampatti , Thammanaickenpatti, Thippampatti, Thumbalpatti, Valakuttapatti.

Amenities:

Education: Primary School in 24 villages, Middle school in 6 villages, Matriculation or Secondary School in 2 villages, namely Nilavarapatti, Thippampatti.

Higher Secondary or Pre University Courses or Intermediate or Junior College in 1 village of the CD Block,, namely Nilavarapatti.

College in 0 village, Adult Literacy Center in 0 village.

Medical: Hospital in 0 village, Dispensary in 0 village, Health Center in 1 village, Sub Center in 8 villages, Maternity and Child Welfare Center in 5 villages, Community health workers in 0 village.

Drinking Water: Tap water in 27 villages, Tank water in 0 villages, Well water in 27 villages, Tubewell in 27 villages and more than one source in 27 villages.

Bank: Banking facility in 4 villages, namely, Sandiyur Attayampatti, Kuralnatham Gajalnaickenpatti, Nilavarapatti.

Credit Society in 5 villages Agricultural Credit Society in 4 Non-Agricultural Credit Society in 2 villages.

Others: Power supply in 27 villages, Cinema hall in 0 village, sport club in 0 village, Stadium or Auditorium or Community Hall in 0 village, Post Office in 23 villages.

There are 25 villages having bus facilities.

Villages with most of facilities: Kuralnatham Gajalnaickenpatti, Nilavarapatti.

Villages without amenities (Education): Adimalaipatti, Nulathukombai, Vedapatti..

Scheduled Castes: Out of the total population of 57064 persons, 12215 persons (21.41%) belong to Scheduled Castes. The villages having less than 10% SC population are Pallitherupatti, Jerugumalai, Eruvadi Pathampatti Basuvanathampatti, Kanamaduru, Erachinampatti Valakkuttapatti, Adimalaipatti, Nulathukombai Vedapatti, Jalluthupattti, Sambakuttapatti.

The villages having more than 50% SC population are None.

Sex ratio of Scheduled Caste population is 489.

Scheduled Castes Literates and Illiterates by Sex:

	Persons	Males	Females
Literate	5,655	3,537	2,118
Illiterate	6,560	2,703	3,857
Literacy rate	53.9	66.3	41.1
Graduate	93	71	22

Scheduled Castes (Dominant):

Adi Dravida, Arunthathiyar, Paraiyan etc., Pallan Chakkiliyan

For their cultural identity please see Appendix-I

Villages without Scheduled Castes: There are 7 villages without any scheduled caste population.

Scheduled Tribes: Out of the total population of 57064 persons, 5597 persons (9.81%) belong to Scheduled Tribes. The villages having less than 10% ST population are Pallitherupatti, Eruvadi Pathampatti Basuvanathampatti, Ammapalayam, Erachinampatti Thammanaichenpatti, Valakkuttapatti Sandiyur Attayampatti, Vaniyampadi, Sandiyur Gajalnaickenpatti, Nilavarapatti, Parapatti Thippampatti, Nallikkalpatti, Mukkuthipalayam Erumainaicken Palayam.

The villages having more than 50% ST population are Jerugumalai, Kanamaduru, Adimalaipatti Nulathukombai, Vedapatti, Jalluthupattti Sambakuttapatti.

Sex ratio of Scheduled tribe population is 496.

Scheduled Tribes Literates and Illiterates by Sex:

	Persons	Males	Females
Literate	1,731	1,086	645
Illiterate	3,866	1,735	2,131
Literacy rate	34.9	43.7	26.1
Graduate	14	13	1

Scheduled Tribes (Dominant):

Malayali, Irular, Malakkuravan

For their cultural identity please see Appendix-II

Villages without Scheduled Tribes: There are 17 villages without any scheduled tribe population.

Literates and Illiterates by Sex (Total Population):

	Persons	Males	Females
Literate	28,502	17,488	11,014
Illiterate	28,562	11,945	16,617
Literacy rate	57	68	45
Graduate	973	706	267

Agriculture: ***Distribution of villages according to land use:*** Out of 29 villages, Total area (in hectare) is 15506.91, out of that 24.87 percent is cultivable and 71.02 percent of the cultivable area is irrigated.

Sources of Irrigation (Hectares): Government Canal 0, Private Canal 0, Well without Electricity 134.35, Well with Electricity 2354.59, Tubewell without Electricity 0, Tubewell with Electricity 174.67, Tank 74.17, River 0, Lake 0, Waterfall 0, Others 1.21.

Villages with population of 5000 to 9999: Nilavarapatti , Nallikkalpatti.

Villages with population of 10000 and above: None

Distribution of Workers:

	Persons	Males	Females	WPR
Cultivators	7,387	4,378	3,009	24.49
Agricultural Labour	10,502	4,599	5,903	34.82
Household Industry	2,058	1,374	684	6.82
Other Workers	10,215	7,935	2,280	33.87
Main Workers	24,409	15,756	8,653	80.93
Marginal Workers	5,753	2,530	3,223	19.07
Total Workers	30,162	18,286	11,876	

Religion: Major Religious Communities:

	Persons	Males	Females	Sex Ratio
Hindu (99.23%)	56,626	29,204	27,422	939
Muslim (0.46%)	262	137	125	912
Christian (0.29%)	165	88	77	875
Sikh (0.01%)	5	3	2	667
Buddhists (0%)	-	-	-	-
Jain (0%)	1	-	1	-

Agewise Data:

	Persons	Males	Females	Sex Ratio
All ages	57,064	29,433	27,631	939
0-14	15,552	8,520	7,032	825
15-44	28,111	14,271	13,840	970
45-79	12,848	6,355	6,493	1022
80+	477	238	239	1004

Age not stated	76	49	27	551

Languages (Dominant):

Tamil, Telugu, Kannada, Urdu, Malayalam

Disabled Population:

	Persons	Males	Females	%
Total Disabled	908	513	395	
In Seeing	344	176	168	37.89
In Speech	101	52	49	11.12
In Hearing	54	25	29	5.95
In Movement	330	202	128	36.34
Mentally	79	58	21	8.7

PANRUTI

Panruti C.D. Block lies in the northern part of Cuddalore district. It is a part of Panruti taluk. The Block is located at a distance of 25 kms. from district headquarters (Cuddalore). There are 50 villages in the block with the total population of 141,069 persons. Area of the C.D. Block is 307.80 sq. kms. It is bounded in the north by C.D. Block Annagramam and district Viluppuram, in the south by C.D. Block Kurinjipadi, in the east by C.D. Blocks Kurinjipadi and Cuddalore, in the west by district Viluppuram and CD Block Kammapuram.

Communications:

Roadways : S.H.-8: Direction- Neyveli to Kaliyanur, Nearest Villages- Poongunam, Lakshminarayanapuram, Panikankuppam, Kadampuliyur, Melmampattu, Marungur. S.H.-9: Direction- Tirukoyilur to Panruti, Nearest Villages- Manappakkam, Anguchettipalayam, Siruvathur, Elanthampattu, Semakottai, Kolappakkam, Veerapperumanallur, Thiruvamur.

Backwards Region Grants Fund: It receives Backward Region Grants.

Annual Rainfall: Average Rainfall 1050 mm.

Ground Water: Availability of the ground water in the Basin is 10240.26 MCM and the utilization is 8246.72 MCM. It belongs to Semi Critical category. Depth to water level varies from 5 to 10 meter below the ground. Most of the wells go down in summer months, according to the Ground Water Estimation Committee.

Forest and Reserved Forest: (Karukkai RF)- Nearest Villages- Karukkai (RF), Karukkai, Meliruppu. (Meliruppu)- Nearest Villages- Meliruppu, Meliruppu (RF), Keeliruppu. (Kattugudalur)- Nearest Villages- Veerasingankuppam, Kattugudalora (RF), Kattugudalore. (Kilkangeyankuppam)- Nearest Villages- Keelkangayenkuppam, Melkangeyamkuppam (RF), Malkangiyankuppam. (Melkangeyankuppam)- Nearest Villages- Meliruppu, Keelkangayenkuppam, Kilkangeyamkuppam (RF). (Perperiankuppam)- Nearest Villages- Vallam, Perperiyankuppam (RF), Perperiyankuppam, Keelkangayenkuppam. (Vallam)- Nearest Villages- Vallam, Vallam (RF). (Virasingankuppam)- Nearest Villages- Visur (RF), Perperiyankuppam, Veerasingankuppam, Veeralingamkuppam (RF), Kattugudalore. (Visur)- Nearest Villages- Vissor, Visur (RF). (Nadukuppam RF)- Nearest Villages- Nadukuppam, Nadukuppam RF.

Natural Division: Tondai Nadu.

Administration

Revenue **Division:** Cuddalore. Parliamentary Constituency: 26 Cuddalore (SC). District: Cuddalore. Taluk: Panruti. Assembly Constituency: 154 Panruti, 153 Neyveli. Gram Panchayat: 42.

Villages: 50 **Inhabited:** 40 **Uninhabited:** 10

Ranking	District	State	National
Area	5	163	2701
Population	3	29	2131
Sex Ratio	10	291	2360
Child Sex Ratio	4	118	2226
Literacy Rate	11	307	2604
Density	9	296	2413
Work Participation Rate	8	80	3368

Gram Panchayats:

Alagappasamudram, Anguchettipalayam, Arasadikuppam, Elandampattu, Kadampuliyur, Karukkai, Kattugudalur, Kilakuppam, Kiliruppu , Kilkangeyankuppam, Kilmambattu, Kolapakkam, Kudimian Kuppam, Lakshminarayanapuram, Maligampattu, Manamthavizhnthaputhur, Manappakkam, Marungur, Meliruppu, Melkangeyankuppam, Melmambattu, Nadukuppam, Natham, Panikkankuppam, Periyakattupalayam, Perperiyankuppam, Poongunam, Purangani, Rayarpalayam, Semakottai , Semmedu, Silambinathanpettai, Sirugramam, Siruvathur, Sorathur, Thalambattu, Tiruvamur, Vallam , Veerapperumanallur, Veerasingankuppam, Vegakollai , Visur.

Amenities:

Education: Primary School in 39 villages, Middle school in 21 villages, Matriculation or Secondary School in 11 villages, namely Poongunam, Sirugramam, Anguchettipalayam, Semakottai, Veerapperumanallur, Keeliruppu, Kadampuliyur, Azhagappasamuthiram, Silimbinethampatti, Perperiyankuppam, Malkangiyankuppam.

Higher Secondary or Pre University Courses or Intermediate or Junior College in 4 villages of the CD Block,, namely Sirugramam, Semakottai, Kadampuliyur, Perperiyankuppam.

College in 0 village, Adult Literacy Center in 0 village.

Medical: Hospital in 0 village, Dispensary in 1 village, Health Center in 5 villages, Sub Center in 19 villages,

Maternity and Child Welfare Center in 3 villages, Community health workers in 9 villages.
The Villages having Hospital or Dispensary or Health Center are Vissor, Kadampuliyur.
Drinking Water: Tap water in 40 villages, Tank water in 0 villages, Well water in 40 villages, Tubewell in 40 villages and more than one source in 40 villages.
Bank: Banking facility in 6 villages, namely, **Anguchettipalayam, Thiruvamur, Kadampuliyur** Marungur, Perperiyankuppam, Kattugudalore.
Credit Society in 13 villages Agricultural Credit Society in 13 Non-Agricultural Credit Society in 0 village.
Others: Power supply in 40 villages, Cinema hall in 0 village, sport club in 0 village, Stadium or Auditorium or Community Hall in 0 village, Post Office in 39 villages.
There are 40 villages having bus facilities.
Villages with most of facilities: Anguchettipalayam Thiruvamur, Kadampuliyur, Marungur, Perperiyankuppam Kattugudalore.
Villages without amenities (Education): Manamthavizhnthaputhur..
Scheduled Castes: Out of the total population of 141069 persons, 29330 persons (20.79%) belong to Scheduled Castes.
The villages having less than 10% SC population are Siruvathur, Kolappakkam, Melmampattu, Purangani Keelmampattu, Azhagappasamuthiram, Vegakottai Nadukuppam, Veerasingankuppam.
The villages having more than 50% SC population are None.
Sex ratio of Scheduled Caste population is 496.
Scheduled Castes Literates and Illiterates by Sex:

	Persons	Males	Females
Literate	12,188	7,711	4,477
Illiterate	17,142	7,060	10,082
Literacy rate	49.5	62.0	36.7
Graduate	203	158	45

Scheduled Castes (Dominant):
Adi Dravida, Arunthathiyar, Kuravan etc., Valluvan Generic Castes etc.
For their cultural identity please see Appendix-I
Villages without Scheduled Castes: There are 13 villages without any scheduled caste population.
Scheduled Tribes: Out of the total population of 141069 persons, 109 persons (0.08%) belong to Scheduled Tribes.
The villages having less than 10% ST population are Poongunam, Lakshminarayanapuram Manamthavizhnthaputhur, Sirugramam, Natham Melarungunam, Rayapalayam, Manappakkam Anguchettipalayam, Keelakuppam, Panikankuppam Maligampattu, Siruvathur, Elanthampattu, Semakottai Kolappakkam, Veerapperumanallur, Thiruvamur, Vissor Karukkai, Semmedu, Meliruppu, Keeliruppu Thalampattu, Kadampuliyur, Melmampattu, Purangani Keelmampattu, Azhagappasamuthiram Silimbinethampatti, Vegakottai, Marungur, Vallam Nadukuppam, Perperiyankuppam, Keelkangayenkuppam Malkangiyankuppam, Veerasingankuppam Kattugudalore, Sorathur.
The villages having more than 50% ST population are None.
Sex ratio of Scheduled tribe population is 514.
Scheduled Tribes Literates and Illiterates by Sex:

	Persons	Males	Females
Literate	42	27	15
Illiterate	67	26	41
Literacy rate	45.7	57.5	33.3
Graduate	1	1	0

Scheduled Tribes (Dominant):
Malakkuravan, Kattunayakan, Irular Generic Tribes etc., Kondareddis
For their cultural identity please see Appendix-II
Villages without Scheduled Tribes: There are 43 villages without any scheduled tribe population.
Literates and Illiterates by Sex (Total Population):

	Persons	Males	Females
Literate	74,339	47,005	27,334
Illiterate	66,730	24,487	42,243
Literacy rate	61	76	45
Graduate	2,318	1,848	470

Agriculture: ***Distribution of villages according to land use:*** Out of 50 villages, Total area (in hectare) is 30780.07, out of that 73.72 percent is cultivable and 27.12 percent of the cultivable area is irrigated.
Sources of Irrigation (Hectares): Government Canal 0, Private Canal 0, Well without Electricity 0, Well with Electricity 0, Tubewell without Electricity 0, Tubewell with Electricity 5986.21, Tank 0, River 0, Lake 167.08, Waterfall 0, Others 0.
Villages with population of 5000 to 9999: Lakshminarayanpuram, Anguchettipalayam, Siruvathur Veerapperumanallur , Kadampuliyur, Kilmambattu Silambinathanpettai, Vegakollai , Marungur Perperiyankuppam, Kattugudalur.
Villages with population of 10000 and above: None
Distribution of Workers:

	Persons	Males	Females	WPR
Cultivators	18,113	13,555	4,558	28.59
Agricultural Labour	29,624	14,870	14,754	46.76
Household Industry	3,100	988	2,112	4.89
Other Workers	12,514	10,036	2,478	19.75

Main Workers	41,235	30,244	10,991	65.09
Marginal Workers	22,116	9,205	12,911	34.91
Total Workers	63,351	39,449	23,902	

Religion: Major Religious Communities:

	Persons	Males	Females	Sex Ratio
Hindu (95.98%)	135,399	68,580	66,819	974
Muslim (0.8%)	1,132	579	553	955
Christian (3.16%)	4,451	2,284	2,167	949
Sikh (0%)	2	1	1	1,000
Buddhists (0%)	-	-	-	-
Jain (0%)	6	5	1	200

Agewise Data:

	Persons	Males	Females	Sex Ratio
All ages	141,069	71,492	69,577	973
0-14	43,663	22,107	21,556	975
15-44	70,043	35,356	34,687	981
45-79	26,114	13,357	12,757	955
80+	912	497	415	835
Age not stated	337	175	162	926

Languages (Dominant):

Tamil, Telugu, Urdu, Kannada, Marathi

Disabled Population:

	Persons	Males	Females	%
Total Disabled	3,642	1,716	1,926	
In Seeing	2,070	778	1,292	56.84
In Speech	309	174	135	8.48
In Hearing	225	128	97	6.18
In Movement	785	495	290	21.55
Mentally	253	141	112	6.95

PAPANASAM

Papanasam C.D. Block lies in the northern part of Thanjavur district. It is a part of Papanasam taluk. The Block is located at a distance of 27 kms. from district headquarters (Thanjavur). There are 39 villages in the block with the total population of 109,335 persons. Area of the C.D. Block is 127.65 sq. kms. It is bounded in the north by district Ariyalur, in the south by C.D. Block Ammapettai, in the east by CD Block Kumbakonam and district Thiruvarur, in the west by CD Blocks Thanjavur and Thiruvaiyaru.

Communications:

Roadways : S.H.-22: Direction- Thiruvaiyaru to Kumbakonam, Nearest Villages- Alavanthipuram, Sarukkai, Thyagasamudram, Umayalpuram (I), Ramanujapuram, Kabisthalam, Sathiyamangalam, Regunathapuram, Ullikkadai, Perumalkovil, Ganapathy Agraharam, Eluppakorai Bit, Ganapathy Agraharam I (Manalur), Echangudi.

Railway Station: Valuthoor, Pandaravadai.

River: Kollidam Nadi- Nearest Villages- Nadupadugai, Thiruvaigavur, Konthagai, Thirumandangudi, Sarukkai, Sathiyamangalam, Umbalapadi, Karuppur Padugai, Govindanattuchery, Ullikkadai, Ganapathy Agraharam, Veeramangudi. Cauvery Nadi- Nearest Villages- Eluppakorai Bit, Sarabojirajapuram, Regunathapuram, Pasupathikoil, Ullikkadai, Perumalkovil, Ganapathy, Agraharam, Ganapathy AgraharamI (Manalur), Sarukkai, Sathiyamangalam, Ramanujapuram, Kabisthalam, Umayalpuram (I), Rajagiri. Thirumalairajanar Nadi- Nearest Villages- Chaakkarappali, Sarabojirajapuram, Valuthoor, Regunathapuram, Pandaravadai, Rajagiri.

Annual Rainfall: Average Rainfall 1147 mm.

Ground Water: Availability of the ground water in the Basin is 4644.33 H.A.M. and the utilization is 2007. 66 H.A.M. It belongs to Safe category. Depth to water level varies from 0 to 10 meter below the ground. Most of the wells go down in summer months, according to the Ground Water Estimation Committee.

Natural Division: Chola Nadu.

Administration

Revenue **Division:** Kumbakunam. Parliamentary Constituency: 29 Thanjavur. District: Thanjavur. Taluk: Thiruvaiyaru. Assembly Constituency: 173 Thiruvaiyaru. Gram Panchayat: 34.

Villages: 39 **Inhabited:** 38 **Uninhabited:** 1

Ranking	District	State	National
Area	14	355	5356
Population	5	97	3174
Sex Ratio	2	35	349
Child Sex Ratio	8	165	2933
Literacy Rate	4	71	862
Density	12	362	1042
Work Participation Rate	2	8	4634

Gram Panchayats:

Adhanur, Alavandipuram, Chakkarapalli, Eachankudi , Ganapathiagraharam , Gopurajapuram, Govindanallucheri, Illuppakkorai, Kabisthalam, Konthagai, Koonancheri, Manalur, Melakabisthalam, Olaipadi, Pandaravadai, Pasupathikoil, Perumalkoil, Ragunathapuram, Rajagiri, Ramanujapuram, Sarapojirajapuram, Sarukkai, Sathiyamangalam, Someswarapuram, Soolamangalam , Thirumandangudi, Thiruvaigavur, Thiyagasamudram, Thurumbur, Ullikkadai, Umayalpuram , Umbalapadi, Valuthur, Veeramangudi.

Amenities:

Education: Primary School in 35 villages, Middle school in 18 villages, Matriculation or Secondary School in 6 villages, namely Umayalpuram (I), Ramanujapuram, Kabisthalam, Melakabistalam, Valuthoor, Pandaravadai.

Higher Secondary or Pre University Courses or Intermediate or Junior College in 3 villages of the CD Block,,

namely Kabisthalam, Melakabistalam, Valuthoor.
College in 0 village, Adult Literacy Center in 0 village.
Medical: Hospital in 1 village, Dispensary in 1 village, Health Center in 3 villages, Sub Center in 19 villages, Maternity and Child Welfare Center in 0 village, Community health workers in 36 villages.
The Villages having Hospital or Dispensary or Health Center are Thiruvaigavur, Rajagiri.
Drinking Water: Tap water in 38 villages, Tank water in 1 villages, Well water in 38 villages, Tubewell in 38 villages and more than one source in 38 villages.
Bank: Banking facility in 9 villages, namely, Umayalpuram (I), Kabisthalam, Melakabistalam Ganapathy Agraharam, Echangudi, Chaakkarapalli Sarabojirajapuram, Pandaravadai, Rajagiri.
Credit Society in 10 villages Agricultural Credit Society in 9 Non-Agricultural Credit Society in 1 village.
Others: Power supply in 38 villages, Cinema hall in 1 village, sport club in 0 village, Stadium or Auditorium or Community Hall in 0 village, Post Office in 27 villages.
There are 36 villages having bus facilities.
Villages with most of facilities: Umayalpuram (I) Kabisthalam, Melakabistalam, Ganapathy Agraharam Echangudi, Chaakkarapalli, Sarabojirajapuram Pandaravadai, Rajagiri.
Villages without amenities (Education):
Nadupadugai, Anumanallore, Karuppur Padugai..
Scheduled Castes: Out of the total population of 109335 persons, 23622 persons (21.61%) belong to Scheduled Castes.
The villages having less than 10% SC population are None..
The villages having more than 50% SC population are None.
Sex ratio of Scheduled Caste population is 503.
Scheduled Castes Literates and Illiterates by Sex:

	Persons	Males	Females
Literate	12,192	7,168	5,024
Illiterate	11,430	4,562	6,868
Literacy rate	60.4	71.9	49.2
Graduate	135	109	26

Scheduled Castes (Dominant):
Paraiyan etc., Pallan, Adi Dravida, Kuravan etc. Chakkiliyan
For their cultural identity please see Appendix-I
Villages without Scheduled Castes: There are 3 villages without any scheduled caste population.
Scheduled Tribes: Out of the total population of 109335 persons, 69 persons (0.06%) belong to Scheduled Tribes.
The villages having less than 10% ST population are Nadupadugai, Thiruvaigavur, Konthagai, Thirumbur Anumanallore, Adanoor, Oolaipadi, Maruthuvakudi Alavanthipuram, Thyagasamudram, Narasimmapuram Koonancherry, Umayalpuram (I), Thirumandangudi Sathiyamangalam, Ramanujapuram, Kabisthalam Melakabistalam, Umbalapadi, Karuppur Padugai Sarukkai, Govindanattuchery, Ullikkadai Perumalkovil, Ganapathy Agraharam Ganapathy Agraharam I (Manalur), Veeramangudi Echangudi, Eluppaikorai, Chaakkarapalli Sarabojirajapuram, Valuthoor, Regunathapuram Pandaravadai, Rajagiri, Gopurajapuram, Soolamangalam Pasupathikoil.
The villages having more than 50% ST population are None.
Sex ratio of Scheduled tribe population is 551.
Scheduled Tribes Literates and Illiterates by Sex:

	Persons	Males	Females
Literate	10	8	2
Illiterate	59	23	36
Literacy rate	17.2	27.6	6.9
Graduate	0	0	0

Scheduled Tribes (Dominant):
Malakkuravan, Irular, Kondareddis, Kattunayakan
For their cultural identity please see Appendix-II
Villages without Scheduled Tribes: There are 34 villages without any scheduled tribe population.
Literates and Illiterates by Sex (Total Population):

	Persons	Males	Females
Literate	69,956	38,284	31,672
Illiterate	39,379	15,232	24,147
Literacy rate	73	82	64
Graduate	1,407	1,030	377

Agriculture: ***Distribution of villages according to land use:*** Out of 39 villages, Total area (in hectare) is 12765.62, out of that 65.17 percent is cultivable and 85.57 percent of the cultivable area is irrigated.
Sources of Irrigation (Hectares): Government Canal 6466.29, Private Canal 0, Well without Electricity 0, Well with Electricity 0, Tubewell without Electricity 314.45, Tubewell with Electricity 304.98, Tank 0, River 0, Lake 0, Waterfall 0, Others 33.91.
Villages with population of 5000 to 9999:
Kabisthalam, Chakkarapalli, Valathur, Pandaravadai Rajagiri, Pasupathikoil.
Villages with population of 10000 and above: None
Distribution of Workers:

	Persons	Males	Females	WPR
Cultivators	5,974	5,187	787	13.89
Agricultural Labour	24,759	15,470	9,289	57.56
Household Industry	1,777	1,079	698	4.13

Other Workers	10,502	8,889	1,613	24.42
Main Workers	35,716	27,332	8,384	83.04
Marginal Workers	7,296	3,293	4,003	16.96
Total Workers	43,012	30,625	12,387	

Religion: Major Religious Communities:

	Persons	Males	Females	Sex Ratio
Hindu (75.97%)	83,058	41,532	41,526	1,000
Muslim (20.05%)	21,918	9,862	12,056	1,222
Christian (3.86%)	4,222	2,051	2,171	1,059
Sikh (0%)	-	-	-	-
Buddhists (0%)	-	-	-	-
Jain (0%)	3	2	1	500

Agewise Data:

	Persons	Males	Females	Sex Ratio
All ages	109,335	53,516	55,819	1043
0-14	30,840	15,599	15,241	977
15-44	53,882	25,763	28,119	1091
45-79	23,759	11,743	12,016	1023
80+	714	342	372	1088
Age not stated	140	69	71	1029

Languages (Dominant):

Tamil, Telugu, Urdu, Gujarati, Others

Disabled Population:

	Persons	Males	Females	%
Total Disabled	3,011	1,379	1,632	
In Seeing	1,796	635	1,161	59.65
In Speech	227	138	89	7.54
In Hearing	129	58	71	4.28
In Movement	639	417	222	21.22
Mentally	220	131	89	7.31

PAPPAKUDI

Pappakudi C.D. Block lies in the central south part of Tirunelveli district. It is a part of Alangulam and Ambasamudram taluks. The Block is located at a distance of 56 kms. from district headquarters (Tirunelveli). There are 23 villages in the block with the total population of 57,169 persons. Area of the C.D. Block is 153.27 sq. kms.
It is bounded in the north by CD Block Alangulam, in the south by CD Block Cheranmadevi, in the east by CD Block Manur, and in the west by CD Block Kadayam. CD Block Pappakudi falls in taluk Alangulam by 05 villages, and in taluk Ambasamduram by 18 villages.

Communications:

Roadways : S.H.-40: Direction- Ambasamudram to Tirunelveli, Nearest Village- Maradrampudur.

River: Tambraparani Nadi- Nearest Villages- Adakku Ariya nayakipuram, Poppakudi Part-I, Geriyanmal Puram, Thenthir uppuvanam, Manabaranalloor, Thirupudai Maruthur, Athala Nallur, Sathupattur, Manamangalam, Vellangali, Sattupattu.

Annual Rainfall: Average Rainfall 879 mm.

Ground Water: Availability of the ground water in the Basin is 35.94 MCM and the utilization is 18.79 MCM. It belongs to Safe category. Depth to water level varies from 0 to 5 meter below the ground. Most of the wells go down in summer months, according to the Ground Water Estimation Committee.

Natural Division: NA

Administration

Revenue **Division:** Tenkasi, Cheranmadevi. Parliamentary Constituency: 38 Tirunelveli. District: Tirunelveli. Taluk: Alangulam, Ambasamudram. Assembly Constituency: 223 Alangulam, 225 Ambasamudram. Gram Panchayat: 15.

Villages: 23 **Inhabited:** 20 **Uninhabited:** 3

Ranking	District	State	National
Area	15	341	4991
Population	14	337	4958
Sex Ratio	9	22	223
Child Sex Ratio	11	200	3305
Literacy Rate	9	67	833
Density	4	82	2928
Work Participation Rate	4	134	781

Gram Panchayats:

Athalanallur, Harikesavanallur , Idaikal, Kapaliparai , Kuthapanjan, Maruthamputhur, Mylappapuram, Odaimanichan, Pallakkal , Pappakudi, Pappakudi , Pudupatti, Rengasamudram, Sattupathu, Thirupudaimarudur, Vadakku Ariyanayakipuram .

Amenities:

Education: Primary School in 17 villages, Middle school in 11 villages, Matriculation or Secondary School in 2 villages, namely Maradrampudur, Rengasamudram.
Higher Secondary or Pre University Courses or Intermediate or Junior College in 0 village of the CD Block, College in 0 village, Adult Literacy Center in 0 village.

Medical: Hospital in 1 village, Dispensary in 4 villages, Health Center in 3 villages, Sub Center in 10 villages, Maternity and Child Welfare Center in 4 villages, Community health workers in 17 villages.
The Villages having Hospital or Dispensary or Health Center are Adakku Ariyanayakipuram, Poppakudi Part-I, Edaikal, Geriyanmal Puram, Harikesava Naloor.

Drinking Water: Tap water in 20 villages, Tank water in 5 villages, Well water in 14 villages, Tubewell in 4 villages and more than one source in 20 villages.

Bank: Banking facility in 3 villages, namely, Maradrampudur, Adakku Ariyanayakipuram Poppakudi Part-I.
Credit Society in 3 villages Agricultural Credit Society in 3 Non-Agricultural Credit Society in 0 village.

Others: Power supply in 20 villages, Cinema hall in 1 village,

sport club in 0 village, Stadium or Auditorium or Community Hall in 0 village, Post Office in 16 villages.

There are 18 villages having bus facilities.

Villages with most of facilities: Maradrampudur Adakku Ariyanayakipuram, Poppakudi Part-I.

Villages without amenities (Education):

Kasitharmam, Harikesava Naloor, Pananchadi..

Scheduled Castes: Out of the total population of 57169 persons, 8785 persons (15.37%) belong to Scheduled Castes.

The villages having less than 10% SC population are Maradrampudur, Odamarichan, Udayampuly, Kasitharmam Geriyanmal Puram, Manabaranalloor, Pananchadi.

The villages having more than 50% SC population are None.

Sex ratio of Scheduled Caste population is 515.

Scheduled Castes Literates and Illiterates by Sex:

	Persons	Males	Females
Literate	4,894	2,793	2,101
Illiterate	3,891	1,470	2,421
Literacy rate	64.7	76.6	53.7
Graduate	63	41	22

Scheduled Castes (Dominant):

Pallan, Paraiyan etc., Arunthathiyar, Adi Dravida Chakkiliyan

For their cultural identity please see Appendix-I

Villages without Scheduled Castes: There are 7 villages without any scheduled caste population.

Scheduled Tribes: Out of the total population of 57169 persons, 56 persons (0.1%) belong to Scheduled Tribes.

The villages having less than 10% ST population are Kutha Panchan, Pudupatti, Maradrampudur, Odamarichan Udayampuly, Adakku Ariyanayakipuram Poppakudi Part-I, Kasitharmam, Edaikal, Sengulam Geriyanmal Puram, Thenthiruppuvanam, Manabaranalloor Harikesava Naloor, Thirupudai Maruthur Athala Nallur, Sathupattur, Rengasamudram Pananchadi, Pallakkal.

The villages having more than 50% ST population are None.

Sex ratio of Scheduled tribe population is 518.

Scheduled Tribes Literates and Illiterates by Sex:

	Persons	Males	Females
Literate	19	8	11
Illiterate	37	19	18
Literacy rate	41.3	40.0	42.3
Graduate	0	0	0

Scheduled Tribes (Dominant):

Kattunayakan

For their cultural identity please see Appendix-II

Villages without Scheduled Tribes: There are 22 villages without any scheduled tribe population.

Literates and Illiterates by Sex (Total Population):

	Persons	Males	Females
Literate	36,321	19,852	16,469
Illiterate	20,848	7,863	12,985
Literacy rate	73	83	64
Graduate	578	429	149

Agriculture: ***Distribution of villages according to land use:***

Out of 23 villages, Total area (in hectare) is 15327.05, out of that 37.42 percent is cultivable and 63.1 percent of the cultivable area is irrigated.

Sources of Irrigation (Hectares): Government Canal 1235.02, Private Canal 0, Well without Electricity 277.82, Well with Electricity 734.54, Tubewell without Electricity 0, Tubewell with Electricity 0, Tank 1381.71, River 0, Lake 0, Waterfall 0, Others 0.

Villages with population of 5000 to 9999:

Kuthapanjan, Maruthamputhur Vadakku Ariyanayakipuram , Pappakudi, Idaikkal.

Villages with population of 10000 and above: None

Distribution of Workers:

	Persons	Males	Females	WPR
Cultivators	3,769	3,172	597	11.87
Agricultural Labour	7,855	5,617	2,238	24.74
Household Industry	13,614	1,430	12,184	42.89
Other Workers	6,507	5,446	1,061	20.5
Main Workers	25,871	12,833	13,038	81.5
Marginal Workers	5,874	2,832	3,042	18.5
Total Workers	31,745	15,665	16,080	

Religion: Major Religious Communities:

	Persons	Males	Females	Sex Ratio
Hindu (84.67%)	48,404	23,597	24,807	1,051
Muslim (3.04%)	1,739	831	908	1,093
Christian (11.99%)	6,856	3,233	3,623	1,121
Sikh (0.01%)	3	1	2	2,000
Buddhists (0%)	1	1	-	-
Jain (0%)	-	-	-	-

Agewise Data:

	Persons	Males	Females	Sex Ratio
All ages	57,169	27,715	29,454	1063
0-14	16,549	8,466	8,083	955
15-44	26,847	12,703	14,144	1113
45-79	13,116	6,264	6,852	1094
80+	494	202	292	1446
Age not stated	163	80	83	1038

Languages (Dominant):

Tamil, Telugu, Malayalam, Kannada, English

Disabled Population:

	Persons	Males	Females	%
Total Disabled	1,379	611	768	

In Seeing	800	290	510	58.01
In Speech	99	60	39	7.18
In Hearing	55	20	35	3.99

In Movement	337	200	137	24.44
Mentally	88	41	47	6.38

PAPPIREDDIPATTI

Pappireddipatti C.D. Block lies in the south-eastern part of Dharmapuri district. It is a part of Pappireddipatti taluk. The Block is located at a distance of 52 kms. from district headquarters (Dharmapuri). There are 48 villages in the block with the total population of 82,809 persons. Area of the C.D. Block is 410.03 sq. kms. It is bounded in the north by C.D. Blocks Morappur and Harur, in the south by district Salem, in the east by CD Block Harur and district salem, in the west by CD Block Dharmapuri and district Salem.

Communications:

Roadways : S.H.-18: Direction- Salem to Harur, Nearest Villages- Pappambadi, H.Pudupatti, Athikarappatti, Goundampatti, Mookkareddipatti, Irulapatti, Pallipatti, Kombur, Chinnamanjavadi, Manjavadi, Kallathupatti, Nonankanoor, Pattukonampatti, Nadupatty.

River: Vaniyar Nadi- Nearest Villages- H.Pudupatti, Alapuram, Venkatasamudram, Kolimekkanur, Goundampatti. Molaiyanoor.

Annual Rainfall: Average Rainfall 760 mm.

Ground Water: Availability of the ground water in the Basin is 7589.42 H.A.M. and the utilization is 15112. 30 H.A.M. It belongs to Over Expoited category. Depth to water level varies from 0 to 10 meter below the ground. Most of the wells go down in summer months, according to the Ground Water Estimation Committee.

Forest and Reserved Forest: (Kalnad Extention RF)- Nearest Villages- Sitheri, Mangade, Kaland (RF) Uni. (Karungal)- Nearest Villages- Kurungal (RF) Uni, Suriyakadai Uni, Sitheri. (Kavaramalai)- Nearest Villages- Menisi, Boothinatham, Gundalamaduvu, Kathiripuram, Kumbarahalli, Kavaramalai Extn.RF, Jangalahalli. (Nochikuttai)- Nearest Villages- Sitheri, Nachikatti (RF). (Sitheri Extn.)- Nearest Villages- Suriyakadai, Sitteri (RF) Uni, Sitheri. (Sitheri)- Nearest Village- Sitteri (RF) Uni. (Thambal Extention)- Nearest Villages- Thambal (Exrn.RF) Uni, Sitheri, Pallipatti (RF) Uni, Pappambadi, Mookkareddipatti, Irulapatti, Pallipatti, Kombur, Chinnamanjavadi, Manjavadi, Nadupatty, Elannthakottapatty, Pattukonampatti, Ammapalayam RF, Kullampatti.

Natural Division: Baramahal.

Administration

Revenue **Division:** Krishnagiri. Parliamentary Constituency: 10 Dharmapuri. District: Dharmapuri. Taluk: Pappireddipatti Assembly Constituency: 60 Pappireddippatti, 61 Hasur (SC). Gram Panchayat: 19.

Villages: 48 **Inhabited:** 39 **Uninhabited:** 9

Ranking	District	State	National
Area	10	65	1874
Population	17	222	4008
Sex Ratio	6	341	3191
Child Sex Ratio	7	317	5282
Literacy Rate	3	276	2357
Density	6	120	4709
Work Participation Rate	14	327	1219

Gram Panchayats:

A. Pallipatty, Adigarapatty, Alapuram , B. Pallipatti, B. Pallipatti , Bairanatham , Bommidi , Boothinatham , Bothakkadu, Irulapatty, Kavandampatty , Manjavadi , Menasi , Molayanur, Mookkareddipatty , Pappambadi , Pattukonampatti , Pudupatti, Sitteri , Venkatasamudram , .

Amenities:

Education: Primary School in 37 villages, Middle school in 14 villages, Matriculation or Secondary School in 12 villages, namely Sitheri, Alapuram, Menisi, Bommidi, Pallippatti, Bairnatham, Molaiyanoor, Venkatasamudram, Kolimekkanur, Athikarappatti, Mookkareddipatti, Nonankanoor.

Higher Secondary or Pre University Courses or Intermediate or Junior College in 7 villages of the CD Block,, namely Sitheri, Menisi, Bommidi, Bairnatham, Kolimekkanur, Mookkareddipatti, Nonankanoor.

College in 0 village, Adult Literacy Center in 0 village.

Medical: Hospital in 1 village, Dispensary in 1 village, Health Center in 5 villages, Sub Center in 11 villages, Maternity and Child Welfare Center in 4 villages, Community health workers in 25 villages.

The Village having Hospital or Dispensary or Health Center is Kumbarahalli.

Drinking Water: Tap water in 39 villages, Tank water in 1 villages, Well water in 39 villages, Tubewell in 39 villages and more than one source in 39 villages.

Bank: Banking facility in 1 villages, namely, Kolimekkanur.

Credit Society in 21 villages Agricultural Credit Society in 14 Non-Agricultural Credit Society in 3 villages.

Others: Power supply in 39 villages, Cinema hall in 2 villages, sport club in 0 village, Stadium or Auditorium or Community Hall in 0 village, Post Office in 39 villages.

There are 36 villages having bus facilities.

Villages with most of facilities: None.

Villages without amenities (Education): Sembiyanoor, Nachikatti (Rf)..

Scheduled Castes: Out of the total population of 82809 persons, 16965 persons (20.49%) belong to Scheduled Castes.

The villages having less than 10% SC population are Sitheri, Alapuram, Gundalamaduvu, Kathiripuram Kumbarahalli, Devaajapalayam, Irulapatti, Mangade Bothakadu, Sembiyanoor, Ajjampatti, Kombur Chinnamanjavadi, Kallathupatti, Nadupatty Nonankanoor, Nachikatti (Rf), S.Ammapalayam Kullampatti.

The villages having more than 50% SC population are None.

Sex ratio of Scheduled Caste population is 496.

Scheduled Castes Literates and Illiterates by Sex:

	Persons	Males	Females
Literate	9,223	5,527	3,696
Illiterate	7,742	3,029	4,713
Literacy rate	61.9	73.6	49.9
Graduate	513	419	94

Scheduled Castes (Dominant):

Adi Dravida, Arunthathiyar, Kuravan etc., Valluvan Adi Andhra

For their cultural identity please see Appendix-I

Villages without Scheduled Castes: There are 20 villages without any scheduled caste population.

Scheduled Tribes: Out of the total population of 82809 persons, 18917 persons (22.84%) belong to Scheduled Tribes.

The villages having less than 10% ST population are Pappambadi, H.Pudupatti, Alapuram, Menisi Boothinatham, Gundalamaduvu, Kathiripuram Kumbarahalli, Bommidi, Vellalappatti, Pallippatti Jangalahalli, Devaajapalayam, Venkatasamudram Kolimekkanur, Athikarappatti, K.Thathampatti Goundampatti, Mookkareddipatti, Sembiyanoor.

The villages having more than 50% ST population are Sitheri, Mangade, Bothakadu, Ajjampatti, Kombur Chinnamanjavadi, Kallathupatti, Nadupatty Nonankanoor, Elannthakottapatty, Pattukonampatti Nachikatti (Rf), Kullampatti.

Sex ratio of Scheduled tribe population is 491.

Scheduled Tribes Literates and Illiterates by Sex:

	Persons	Males	Females
Literate	7,731	4,777	2,954
Illiterate	11,186	4,848	6,338
Literacy rate	46.4	56.4	36.0
Graduate	80	68	12

Scheduled Tribes (Dominant):

Malayali, Kurumans, Irular, Malai Arayan

For their cultural identity please see Appendix-II

Villages without Scheduled Tribes: There are 14 villages without any scheduled tribe population.

Literates and Illiterates by Sex (Total Population):

	Persons	Males	Females
Literate	45,602	27,155	18,447
Illiterate	37,207	15,175	22,032
Literacy rate	62	73	51
Graduate	1,985	1,500	485

Agriculture: ***Distribution of villages according to land use:*** Out of 48 villages, Total area (in hectare) is 41003.82, out of that 30.41 percent is cultivable and 64.68 percent of the cultivable area is irrigated.

Sources of Irrigation (Hectares): Government Canal 175.17, Private Canal 0, Well without Electricity 2503.42, Well with Electricity 4649.72, Tubewell without Electricity 0, Tubewell with Electricity 37.65, Tank 560.59, River 0, Lake 0, Waterfall 0, Others 138.85.

Villages with population of 5000 to 9999: Menasi, Molayanur.

Villages with population of 10000 and above: None

Distribution of Workers:

	Persons	Males	Females	WPR
Cultivators	15,932	9,287	6,645	35.26
Agricultural Labour	19,458	8,965	10,493	43.07
Household Industry	1,169	567	602	2.59
Other Workers	8,621	6,665	1,956	19.08
Main Workers	39,293	23,579	15,714	86.97
Marginal Workers	5,887	1,905	3,982	13.03
Total Workers	45,180	25,484	19,696	

Religion: Major Religious Communities:

	Persons	Males	Females	Sex Ratio
Hindu (94.78%)	78,486	40,138	38,348	955
Muslim (3.15%)	2,610	1,338	1,272	951
Christian (2.03%)	1,684	841	843	1,002
Sikh (0%)	-	-	-	-
Buddhists (0%)	-	-	-	-
Jain (0.01%)	11	4	7	1,750

Agewise Data:

	Persons	Males	Females	Sex Ratio
All ages	82,809	42,330	40,479	956
0-14	23,135	12,155	10,980	903
15-44	41,203	20,644	20,559	996
45-79	17,710	9,122	8,588	941
80+	612	326	286	877
Age not stated	149	83	66	795

Languages (Dominant):

Tamil, Telugu, Urdu, Kannada, Malayalam

Disabled Population:

	Persons	Males	Females	%
Total Disabled	2,203	722	1,481	
In Seeing	1,439	269	1,170	65.32
In Speech	147	78	69	6.67
In Hearing	86	45	41	3.9
In Movement	428	276	152	19.43

Mentally	103	54	49	4.68

PARAMAKUDI

Parmakudi C.D. Block lies in the north-western part of Ramanathapuram district. It is a part of Parmakudi taluk. The Block is located at a distance of 38 kms. from district headquarters (Ramanathapuram). There are 34 villages in the block with the total population of 70,977 persons. Area of the C.D. Block is 436.80 sq. kms. It is bounded in the north by district Sivaganga, in the south by CD Blocks Kamuthi and Mudukulathur, in the east by CD Blocks Nainarkoil and Bogalur, in the west by districts Virudhunagar and Sivaganga.

Communications:

Roadways : N.H.-49: Direction- Manamadurai to Ramanathapuram Paramakudi, Nearest Villages- Paramakudi, Melaparthipanu, Soodiyoor, Perungarai, Kamuthakkudi, Kattupparamakudi, Eeneswaram, Vendoni, Kalaiyoor. S.H.-29: Direction- Madukulathur to Paramakudi, Nearest Villages- Kattupparamakudi, Melaykudi, Vendoni, S. Kavanoor, Thenpothuvakkudi, Pambur.

Railway Station: Soodiyoor.

River: Vaigai Nadi- Nearest Villages- Soodiyoor, Perungarai, Kamuthakkudi, Kattupparamakudi, Eeneswaram, Vendoni, Urappali.

Annual Rainfall: Average Rainfall 827 mm.

Ground Water: Availability of the ground water in the Basin is 2520.00 H.A.M. and the utilization is 577.59 H.A.M. It belongs to Safe category. Depth to water level varies from 5to 10 meter below the ground. Most of the wells go down in summer months, according to the Ground Water Estimation Committee.

Natural Division: NA

Administration

Revenue **Division:** Paramakudi. Parliamentary Constituency: 35 Ramanathapuram. District: Ramanathapuram. Taluk: Paramakudi. Assembly Constituency: 209 Paramakudi (SC). Gram Panchayat: 39.

Villages: 34 **Inhabited:** 34 **Uninhabited:** 0

Ranking	District	State	National
Area	3	52	1741
Population	8	282	4422
Sex Ratio	10	82	636
Child Sex Ratio	3	53	1124
Literacy Rate	6	150	1515
Density	6	152	5360
Work Participation Rate	10	354	1503

Gram Panchayats:

Ariyanendal, Enathikottai, K.Karungulam , Kalaiyur , Kallikudi, Kalliyur , Kamuthakudi, Kanjiyendal, Keelaparthibanur , Keelaparuthiyur, Kelparthibanur , Kulanthapuriarungulam, Madanthai , Melayakudi, Melkavanoor, Melparthibanur, Mosugudi , Nelmadur , Nenmeni, P.Puthur, Padugudi, Pamboor, Peerkankurichi , Perunkarai , Poduvakudi, S.Andakudi , S.Kavanoor, Soodiyur , Thelichathanallur , Thenpoduvakudi, Thinaikulam, Tholur , Urakkudi, Urapuli, Valangudi, Valimarichan, Vendoni , Vengalur, Venkatankurichi, Vilathoor.

Amenities:

Education: Primary School in 30 villages, Middle school in 10 villages, Matriculation or Secondary School in 2 villages, namely Melaparthipanu, Pambur.

Higher Secondary or Pre University Courses or Intermediate or Junior College in 0 village of the CD Block, College in 0 village, Adult Literacy Center in 0 village.

Medical: Hospital in 1 village, Dispensary in 1 village, Health Center in 3 villages, Sub Center in 1 village, Maternity and Child Welfare Center in 2 villages, Community health workers in 1 village.

The Village having Hospital or Dispensary or Health Center is Melaparthipanu.

Drinking Water: Tap water in 34 villages, Tank water in 11 villages, Well water in 34 villages, Tubewell in 34 villages and more than one source in 34 villages.

Bank: Banking facility in 5 villages, namely, Melaparthipanu, Thaduthalankottai, Ariyanendal Venkattankurichi, Vilathur.

Credit Society in 5 villages Agricultural Credit Society in 5 Non-Agricultural Credit Society in 0 village.

Others: Power supply in 32 villages, Cinema hall in 3 villages, sport club in 0 village, Stadium or Auditorium or Community Hall in 0 village, Post Office in 15 villages.

There are 28 villages having bus facilities.

Villages with most of facilities: Melaparthipanu Vilathur.

Villages without amenities (Education):

Venkattankurichi, N. Pethanandal, Karungulam..

Scheduled Castes: Out of the total population of 70977 persons, 22532 persons (31.75%) belong to Scheduled Castes.

The villages having less than 10% SC population are None..

The villages having more than 50% SC population are Paramakudi, S.Andakudi, Vengalur, Kalaiyoor Thenpothuvakkudi, N. Pethanandal.

Sex ratio of Scheduled Caste population is 502.

Scheduled Castes Literates and Illiterates by Sex:

	Persons	Males	Females
Literate	12,248	7,331	4,917
Illiterate	10,284	3,899	6,385
Literacy rate	62.5	75.2	49.9
Graduate	438	342	96

Scheduled Castes (Dominant):

Pallan, Chakkiliyan, Paraiyan etc., Kuravan etc. Puthirai Vannan

For their cultural identity please see Appendix-I

Villages without Scheduled Castes: There is 0 village without any scheduled caste population.

Scheduled Tribes: Out of the total population of 70977 persons, 6 persons (0.01%) belong to Scheduled Tribes. The villages having less than 10% ST population are Paramakudi, Melaparthipanu, Soodiyoor, Perungarai Pidariseri, Kothankulam, Kamuthakkudi, Poduvakudi Kattupparamakudi, Eeneswaram, S.Andakudi, Vengalur Kulanthapuri, Mosukudi, 6.Koonangulam, Veppankulam Thaduthalankottai, 9.Keelapparathiyur, Valimanicham Valankudi, Madanthai, Melaykudi, Vendoni, Urappali Kalaiyoor, Ariyanendal, Venkattankurichi S. Kavanoor, Vilathur, Thoulur, Thenpothuvakkudi Pambur, N. Pethanandal, Karungulam.

The villages having more than 50% ST population are None.

Sex ratio of Scheduled tribe population is 333.

Scheduled Tribes Literates and Illiterates by Sex:

	Persons	Males	Females
Literate	4	2	2
Illiterate	2	2	0
Literacy rate	80.0	66.7	100.0
Graduate	0	0	0

Scheduled Tribes (Dominant):

Malai Pandaram, Koraga

For their cultural identity please see Appendix-II

Villages without Scheduled Tribes: There are 32 villages without any scheduled tribe population.

Literates and Illiterates by Sex (Total Population):

	Persons	Males	Females
Literate	42,179	24,753	17,426
Illiterate	28,798	10,360	18,438
Literacy rate	68	80	55
Graduate	1,308	953	355

Agriculture: ***Distribution of villages according to land use:*** Out of 34 villages, Total area (in hectare) is 43680, out of that 103.48 percent is cultivable and 72.08 percent of the cultivable area is irrigated.

Sources of Irrigation (Hectares): Government Canal 0, Private Canal 0, Well without Electricity 20.93, Well with Electricity 149.34, Tubewell without Electricity 7.25, Tubewell with Electricity 559, Tank 6507.87, River 0, Lake 0, Waterfall 0, Others 0.

Villages with population of 5000 to 9999: Melaparthibanur , Kattuparmakudi.

Villages with population of 10000 and above: None

Distribution of Workers:

	Persons	Males	Females	WPR
Cultivators	17,665	9,711	7,954	46.75
Agricultural Labour	10,331	4,091	6,240	27.34
Household Industry	2,483	1,288	1,195	6.57
Other Workers	7,305	5,667	1,638	19.33
Main Workers	32,507	18,854	13,653	86.03
Marginal Workers	5,277	1,903	3,374	13.97
Total Workers	37,784	20,757	17,027	

Religion: Major Religious Communities:

	Persons	Males	Females	Sex Ratio
Hindu (91.9%)	65,230	32,412	32,818	1,013
Muslim (3.49%)	2,475	1,103	1,372	1,244
Christian (5.21%)	3,696	1,817	1,879	1,034
Sikh (0%)	-	-	-	-
Buddhists (0%)	-	-	-	-
Jain (0%)	1	-	1	-

Agewise Data:

	Persons	Males	Females	Sex Ratio
All ages	71,421	35,340	36,081	1021
0-14	20,254	10,218	10,036	982
15-44	34,042	16,609	17,433	1050
45-79	16,473	8,186	8,287	1012
80+	572	284	288	1014
Age not stated	80	43	37	860

Languages (Dominant):

Tamil, Gujarati, Telugu, Hindi, Kannada

Disabled Population:

	Persons	Males	Females	%
Total Disabled	2,234	970	1,264	
In Seeing	1,262	435	827	56.49
In Speech	253	130	123	11.32
In Hearing	86	37	49	3.85
In Movement	472	282	190	21.13
Mentally	161	86	75	7.21

PARAMATHI

Paramathi C.D. Block lies in the south-western part of Namakkal district. It is a part of Paramathi-Velur taluk. The Block is located at a distance of 25 kms. from district headquarters (Namakkal). There are 23 villages in the block with the total population of 43,743 persons. Area of the C.D. Block is 193.71 sq. kms. It is bounded in the north by CD Block Elachipalaiyam, in the south and west by CD Block Kabilamalai, and in the east by C.D. Block Namakkal.

Communications:

Roadways : N.H.-7: Direction- Karur to Namakkal, Nearest Villages- Villipalayam, Pillakalathur.

Local Stream: Nearest Villages- Kudatheri, Sungukarampatty, Villipalayam, Pillur, Pillakalathur, Iruttanai, Ariyurpatti.

Annual Rainfall: Average Rainfall 650 mm.

Ground Water: Availability of the ground water in the Basin is 5722.13 H.A.M. and the utilization is 5293.47 H.A.M. It belongs to Safe category. Depth to water level varies from 0 to 5 meter below the ground. Most of the wells go down in summer months, according to the Ground Water Estimation Committee.

Natural Division: Kongu Nadu

Administration

Revenue **Division:** Tiruvhengodu. Parliamentary Constituency. District: Namakkal. Taluk: Paramathi-Velur. Assembly Constituency: 95 Paramathi–Velur. Gram Panchayat: 20.

Villages: 23 **Inhabited:** 23 **Uninhabited:** 0

Ranking	District	State	National
Area	11	294	4296
Population	13	369	5576
Sex Ratio	5	268	2048
Child Sex Ratio	4	319	5302
Literacy Rate	10	313	2637
Density	2	7	4362
Work Participation Rate	13	303	62

Gram Panchayats:

Iruttanai, Kodur, Kolaram, Kudacheri, Kunnamalai, Manickanatham, Maniyanur, Melsathambur, Nadandai, Nallur, Pillur, Pirandagam, Ramadevam, Sarkarserukali, Sirapalli, Sittampoondi, Sungakarampatty, Villipalayam, Viranampalayam.

Amenities:

Education: Primary School in 22 villages, Middle school in 10 villages, Matriculation or Secondary School in 10 villages, namely Maniyanur, Kolaram, Sarkarserukali, Kodur, Nallur, Sittampoondi, Villipalayam, Pillur, Arthanaripalayam, Nadandai.

Higher Secondary or Pre University Courses or Intermediate or Junior College in 2 villages of the CD Block,, namely Maniyanur, Nallur.

College in 1 village, Adult Literacy Center in 0 village., Colleges are in villages, namely Pillakalathur.

Medical: Hospital in 0 village, Dispensary in 0 village, Health Center in 2 villages, Sub Center in 4 villages, Maternity and Child Welfare Center in 0 village, Community health workers in 0 village.

Drinking Water: Tap water in 23 villages, Tank water in 0 villages, Well water in 23 villages, Tubewell in 23 villages and more than one source in 23 villages.

Bank: Banking facility in 2 villages, namely, Nallur, Nadandai.

Credit Society in 18 villages Agricultural Credit Society in 10 Non-Agricultural Credit Society in 16 villages.

Others: Power supply in 23 villages, Cinema hall in 0 village, sport club in 0 village, Stadium or Auditorium or Community Hall in 0 village, Post Office in 20 villages.

There are 22 villages having bus facilities.

Villages with most of facilities: Nallur, Nadandai.

Villages without amenities (Education):

Kodur Agraharam..

Scheduled Castes: Out of the total population of 43743 persons, 11077 persons (25.32%) belong to Scheduled Castes.

The villages having less than 10% SC population are None..

The villages having more than 50% SC population are None.

Sex ratio of Scheduled Caste population is 497.

Scheduled Castes Literates and Illiterates by Sex:

	Persons	Males	Females
Literate	5,161	3,134	2,027
Illiterate	5,916	2,433	3,483
Literacy rate	52.3	63.4	41.2
Graduate	142	115	27

Scheduled Castes (Dominant):

Arunthathiyar, Adi Dravida, Pallan, Paraiyan etc. Chakkiliyan

For their cultural identity please see Appendix-I

Villages without Scheduled Castes: There is 0 village without any scheduled caste population.

Scheduled Tribes: Out of the total population of 43743 persons, 7 persons (0.02%) belong to Scheduled Tribes.

The villages having less than 10% ST population are Maniyanur, Kolaram, Sarkarserukali, Kodur Kodur Agraharam, Pirandagam, Iruttanai, Ariyurpatti Ramadevam, Nallur, Sittampoondi, Kunnamalai Melsathambur, Kudatheri, Sungukarampatty Villipalayam, Pillur, Pillakalathur Arthanaripalayam, Nadandai, Sirapalli, Manickanatham Viranampalayam.

The villages having more than 50% ST population are None.

Sex ratio of Scheduled tribe population is 571.

Scheduled Tribes Literates and Illiterates by Sex:

	Persons	Males	Females
Literate	4	2	2
Illiterate	3	1	2
Literacy rate	57.1	66.7	50.0
Graduate	0	0	0

Scheduled Tribes (Dominant):

Malayali, Malai Pandaram

For their cultural identity please see Appendix-II

Villages without Scheduled Tribes: There are 21 villages without any scheduled tribe population.

Literates and Illiterates by Sex (Total Population):

	Persons	Males	Females
Literate	24,151	14,859	9,292
Illiterate	19,592	7,243	12,349
Literacy rate	61	74	47
Graduate	1,262	910	352

Agriculture: ***Distribution of villages according to land use:*** Out of 23 villages, Total area (in hectare) is 19371.56, out of that 85.24 percent is cultivable and 11.06 percent of the cultivable area is irrigated.

Sources of Irrigation (Hectares): Government Canal 0, Private Canal 0, Well without Electricity 258.4, Well with Electricity 1330.97, Tubewell without Electricity 0, Tubewell with Electricity 220.26, Tank 15.76, River 0, Lake 0, Waterfall 0, Others 0.

Villages with population of 5000 to 9999: None

Villages with population of 10000 and above: None

Distribution of Workers:

	Persons	Males	Females	WPR
Cultivators	9,642	5,199	4,443	33.21
Agricultural Labour	10,804	4,284	6,520	37.21
Household Industry	1,489	541	948	5.13
Other Workers	7,100	5,033	2,067	24.45
Main Workers	26,346	14,337	12,009	90.74
Marginal Workers	2,689	720	1,969	9.26
Total Workers	29,035	15,057	13,978	

Religion: Major Religious Communities:

	Persons	Males	Females	Sex Ratio
Hindu (99.2%)	43,391	21,929	21,462	979
Muslim (0.39%)	172	82	90	1,098
Christian (0.28%)	123	58	65	1,121
Sikh (0.01%)	3	1	2	2,000
Buddhists (0%)	-	-	-	-
Jain (0%)	-	-	-	-

Agewise Data:

	Persons	Males	Females	Sex Ratio
All ages	43,743	22,102	21,641	979
0-14	8,860	4,757	4,103	863
15-44	19,960	10,042	9,918	988
45-79	13,625	6,617	7,008	1059
80+	710	368	342	929
Age not stated	588	318	270	849

Languages (Dominant):

Tamil, Telugu, Urdu, Malayalam, Hindi

Disabled Population:

	Persons	Males	Females	%
Total Disabled	775	449	326	
In Seeing	330	176	154	42.58
In Speech	56	26	30	7.23
In Hearing	52	25	27	6.71
In Movement	267	179	88	34.45
Mentally	70	43	27	9.03

PARANGIPETTAI

Parangipettai C.D. Block lies in the south-eastern part of Cuddalore district. It is a part of Chidambaram taluk. The Block is located at a distance of 38 kms. from district headquarters (Cuddalore). There are 51 villages in the block with the total population of 92,694 persons. Area of the C.D. Block is 198.63 sq. kms. It is bounded in the north by CD Block Kurinjipadi, in the south by C.D. Block Keerapalayam and district Nagapattinam, in the east by the Bay of Bengal, in the west by C.D. Blocks Bhuvanagiri and Komaratchi.

Communications:

Roadways : N.H.-45 A: Direction- Cuddalore to Chidambaram, Nearest Villages- Manikollai, Periyapattu, Silambimangalam, Villiyanallur, Kothattai, Chinnakomatti, Vellangipattu, Manjakuzhi, Periyakomatti, B. Mutlur, Pallipadi.

Railway Station: Keezhavanvanpattu.

River: Vellar Nadi- Nearest Villages- Nanjai Mahathu Valkai, B. Madhuvankarai, B. Mutlur, B. Adhivaraganallur, Aaipuram. Kollidam Nadi- Nearest Villages- T.S. Pettai, Kavarapatlu, Kizhathirukalipalai, Melathrikkalipalai.

Backwards Region Grants Fund: It receives Backward Region Grants.

Annual Rainfall: Average Rainfall 1050 mm.

Ground Water: Availability of the ground water in the Basin is 6329.05 MCM and the utilization is 644.61 MCM. It belongs to Safe category. Depth to water level varies from 2 to 5 meter below the ground. Most of the wells go down in summer months, according to the Ground Water Estimation Committee.

Coastal Villages- (Bay of Bengal)- Nearest Villages- Periyapattu, Silambimangalam, Villiyanallur, Kothattai, Ariyagosti, T.S. Pettai, Killai (RF), Pitchavaram RF, Pitchavaram Extn RF.

Forest and Reserved Forest: (Killai RF)- Nearest Village- Killai (RF). (Pichavaram Extn)- Nearest Villages- Pitchavaram Extn (RF), Pinnathur. (Pichavaram)- Nearest Villages- Pichavaram, T.S.Pettai.

Natural Division: Tondai Nadu.

Administration

Revenue **Division:** Chidambaram. Parliamentary Constituency: 27 Chidambaram (SC). District: Cuddalore. Taluk: Chidambaram. Assembly Constituency: 158 Chidambaram. Gram Panchayat: 41.

Villages: 51 **Inhabited:** 48 **Uninhabited:** 3

Ranking	**District**	**State**	**National**
Area	10	289	4203
Population	12	167	3697
Sex Ratio	2	146	1054

Child Sex Ratio	2	61	1308
Literacy Rate	3	88	1022
Density	10	305	2366
Work Participation Rate	7	71	3494

Gram Panchayats:

Ariyeekoshti , Ayyepuram, B.Adhivaraganallur, B.Arunmozhidevan, B.Maduvankarai, B.Mutlur, C.Kothangudi , Chinnakumatti, Kanakkarapattu, Kavarapattu, Kezhamanakudi, Kezhanuvampattu, Kezhaperambai, Kothattai, Kovilampoondi, Kumaramangalam, Kuriyamangalam, Manikollai, Manjakuzhi, Meethikudi, Nakkaravanthangudi, Nanjaimaghathuvazhkai, Pallipadai, Periyakumatti, Periyapattu, Pichavaram, Pinnathur, Puinathur, Puvalai, Sendirakillai, Silambimangalam, Thandavarayasozhaganpettai, Thatchakkadu, Thirukazhipalai(Kezh), Thirukazhippalai(Mel), Tillaividangan, Uthamasozhamangalam, Vasaputhur, Vayalamur, Velangipattu, Villiyanallur.

Amenities:

Education: Primary School in 48 villages, Middle school in 16 villages, Matriculation or Secondary School in 5 villages, namely Vellangipattu, B.Mutlur, Pinnathur, T.S.Pettai, Kavarapatlu.

Higher Secondary or Pre University Courses or Intermediate or Junior College in 1 village of the CD Block,, namely B.Mutlur.

College in 1 village, Adult Literacy Center in 0 village., Colleges are in villages, namely B.Mutlur.

Medical: Hospital in 0 village, Dispensary in 0 village, Health Center in 3 villages, Sub Center in 13 villages, Maternity and Child Welfare Center in 0 village, Community health workers in 5 villages.

Drinking Water: Tap water in 48 villages, Tank water in 3 villages, Well water in 48 villages, Tubewell in 48 villages and more than one source in 48 villages.

Bank: Banking facility in 4 villages, namely, Villiyanallur, B.Mutlur, Thillaividangan, Pinnathur.

Credit Society in 7 villages Agricultural Credit Society in 7 Non-Agricultural Credit Society in 0 village.

Others: Power supply in 48 villages, Cinema hall in 1 village, sport club in 0 village, Stadium or Auditorium or Community Hall in 0 village, Post Office in 48 villages.

There are 48 villages having bus facilities.

Villages with most of facilities: B.Mutlur Thillaividangan, Pinnathur.

Villages without Amenities (Education): None..

Scheduled Castes: Out of the total population of 92694 persons, 27802 persons (29.99%) belong to Scheduled Castes. The villages having less than 10% SC population are Kothattai, Periyakomatti, B.Adhivaraganallur Punjaimagathuvankai, Kodipallam, Pichavaram.

The villages having more than 50% SC population are Poovalai, Nanjai Mahathu Valkai, B.Madhuvankarai Thillaividangan, Pinnathur, Radhavilagam Uthamasolamangalam, Vasaputur, Keelaperambai Sithalapadi, Melathrikkalipalai, Ambikapuram.

Sex ratio of Scheduled Caste population is 501.

Scheduled Castes Literates and Illiterates by Sex:

	Persons	Males	Females
Literate	15,981	9,152	6,829
Illiterate	11,821	4,728	7,093
Literacy rate	67.3	77.2	57.4
Graduate	423	308	115

Scheduled Castes (Dominant):

Adi Dravida, Valluvan, Adi Andhra, Tiruvalluvar Arunthathiyar

For their cultural identity please see Appendix-I

Villages without Scheduled Castes: There are 5 villages without any scheduled caste population.

Scheduled Tribes: Out of the total population of 92694 persons, 526 persons (0.57%) belong to Scheduled Tribes. The villages having less than 10% ST population are Vayalamur, Poovalai, Palvathummam, Palathu Vannan Manikollai, Periyapattu, Silambimangalam Villiyanallur, Kothattai, Ariyagosti, Chinnakomatti Vellangipattu, Sendirakkillai, Keezhamanagudi Thachakadi, Manjakuzhi, Periyakomatti Nanjai Mahathu Valkai, B.Madhuvankarai, B.Mutlur B.Adhivaraganallur, Arunmozidevan, Aaipuram Kuriyamanagalam, Punjaimagathuvankai Thillaividangan, Pinnathur, Keezhavanvanpattu Kovilampoondi, Kodipallam, Radhavilagam Uthamasolamangalam, Pichavaram, T.S.Pettai Kanakkarapattu, Nakkaravanthangudi Chidambaranathanpatti, Meetaigudi, Pallipadi Kothangudi, Kumaramangalam, Vasaputur, Kavarapatlu Keelaperambai, Kizhathirukalipalai, Sithalapadi Melathrikkalipalai, Ambikapuram.

The villages having more than 50% ST population are None.

Sex ratio of Scheduled tribe population is 475.

Scheduled Tribes Literates and Illiterates by Sex:

	Persons	Males	Females
Literate	160	100	60
Illiterate	366	176	190
Literacy rate	37.6	44.4	29.9
Graduate	0	0	0

Scheduled Tribes (Dominant):

Irular, Malakkuravan, Kattunayakan

For their cultural identity please see Appendix-II

Villages without Scheduled Tribes: There are 36 villages without any scheduled tribe population.

Literates and Illiterates by Sex (Total Population):

	Persons	Males	Females
Literate	57,626	32,758	24,868
Illiterate	35,068	13,505	21,563
Literacy rate	71	82	61
Graduate	1,813	1,322	491

Agriculture: *Distribution of villages according to land use:* Out of 51 villages, Total area (in hectare) is 19863.05, out of that 70.29 percent is cultivable and 63.24 percent of the cultivable area is irrigated.

Sources of Irrigation (Hectares): Government Canal 7992.92, Private Canal 163.03, Well without Electricity 447.66, Well with Electricity 18.74, Tubewell without Electricity 109.25, Tubewell with Electricity 68.81, Tank 28.02, River 0, Lake 0, Waterfall 0, Others 0.

Villages with population of 5000 to 9999: Silambimangalam, Manjakuzhi.

Villages with population of 10000 and above: None

Distribution of Workers:

	Persons	Males	Females	WPR
Cultivators	6,339	4,667	1,672	15.27
Agricultural Labour	23,871	13,234	10,637	57.51
Household Industry	1,014	460	554	2.44
Other Workers	10,284	8,303	1,981	24.78
Main Workers	26,581	19,531	7,050	64.04
Marginal Workers	14,927	7,133	7,794	35.96
Total Workers	41,508	26,664	14,844	

Religion: Major Religious Communities:

	Persons	Males	Females	Sex Ratio
Hindu (90.52%)	83,910	42,054	41,856	995
Muslim (7.87%)	7,293	3,439	3,854	1,121
Christian (1.48%)	1,375	711	664	934
Sikh (0.02%)	22	11	11	1,000
Buddhists (0.01%)	11	5	6	1,200
Jain (0.01%)	7	3	4	1,333

Agewise Data:

	Persons	Males	Females	Sex Ratio
All ages	92,694	46,263	46,431	1004
0-14	26,700	13,386	13,314	995
15-44	45,292	22,295	22,997	1031
45-79	19,405	9,908	9,497	959
80+	806	429	377	879
Age not stated	491	245	246	1004

Languages (Dominant):
Tamil, Urdu, Telugu, Gujarati, Malayalam

Disabled Population:

	Persons	Males	Females	%
Total Disabled	2,830	1,370	1,460	
In Seeing	1,622	676	946	57.31
In Speech	241	131	110	8.52
In Hearing	177	86	91	6.25
In Movement	581	357	224	20.53
Mentally	209	120	89	7.39

PATTUKKOTTAI

Pattukkottai C.D. Block lies in the south-eastern part of Thanjavur district. It is a part of Pattukottai taluk. The Block is located at a distance of 50 kms. from district headquarters (Thanjavur). There are 56 villages in the block with the total population of 105,225 persons. Area of the C.D. Block is 284.82 sq. kms. It is bounded in the north by CD Blocks Orathanadu and Thiruvonam and Madukkur, in the south by the Palk Strait, in the east by district Thiruvarur, and in the west by C.D. Blocks Thiruvonam, Peravurani and Sethubhavachatram.

Communications:

Roadways : S.H.-29: Direction- Orathanadu to Pattukkottai, Nearest Villages- Karambayam, Aladikkumulai, Sukkiranpatty, Veerakkorichi, Kondikulam, Kazhugapulikkadu.

Railway Station: Thambikkottaivadakadu, Earipurakkari.

River: Maharajasamudram Nadi- Nearest Villages- Nambivayal, Enathi, Palamuthi, Sathankadu, Naduvikkottai, Paingattuvayal, Koothadivayal, Kargavayal, Nainankulam, Pallikondan, Sendakkottai, Thokkalikadu, Rajamadam, Mahilankottai, Chinna Avudayar Koil. Agniyar Nadi- Nearest Villages- Sendakkottai, Chinna Avudayar Koil, Kargavayal, Pannaivayal, Koothadivayal.

Annual Rainfall: Average Rainfall 1147 mm.

Ground Water: Availability of the ground water in the Basin is 7103.86 H.A.M. and the utilization is 4260. 88 H.A.M. It belongs to Safe category. Depth to water level varies from 5 to 10 meter below the ground. Most of the wells go down in summer months, according to the Ground Water Estimation Committee.

Coastal Villages- (Palk Strait)- Nearest Villages- Palanjur, Thamaraikottai South, Thambikkottai Maravakkadu, Thambikkottaivadakadu, Earipurakkari, Rajamadam.

Natural Division: Chola Nadu.

Administration

Revenue Division: Pattukottai. Parliamentary Constituency: 30 Pudukottai. District: Thanjavur. Taluk: Pattukottai. Assembly Constituency: 176 Pattukottai, 177 Peravurani. Gram Panchayat: 43.

Villages: 56 **Inhabited:** 56 **Uninhabited:** 0

Ranking	District	State	National
Area	3	190	2942
Population	6	112	3304
Sex Ratio	3	36	356
Child Sex Ratio	13	214	3450

Literacy Rate	7	99	1105
Density	5	275	2959
Work Participation Rate	13	139	2987

Gram Panchayats:

Aladikkumulai, Anaikkadu, Athikkottai, Enathi, Eripurakarai, Kalugapulikkadu, Karambayam, Kargavayal, Kondikulam, Mahilankottai, Malavernikadu, Maliakkadu, Mudalcheri, Naduvikkottai, Nambivayal, Narasingapuram, Nattuchalai, Othiyadikkadu, Palamuthi, Palanjur, Pallikondan, Pannavayal, Parakakalakottai, Ponnavarayankottai, Ponnavarayankottai , Pudukkottai Ullur, Rajamadam, Santhanakadu, Sembalur, Sendakkottai , Sendankadu, Soorapallam, Soundaranayakipuram, Thamarankottai North, Thamarankottai South, Thambikottai Maravakadu , Thambikottai Melakkadu, Thambikottai Vadakadu, Thittakudi, Thokkalikkadu, Thuvarankurichi , Veerakurichi, Vendakkottai, Veppankkadu, Veppankkadu .

Amenities:

Education: Primary School in 46 villages, Middle school in 24 villages, Matriculation or Secondary School in 13 villages, namely Nambivayal, Enathi, Aladikkumulai, Veerakkorichi, Soorapallam, Naduvikkottai, Anaikkadu, Thuvarankurichi North, Pallikondan, Pudukkottai Ullar, Thamarai Kottai North, Thambikkottai, Rajamadam.

Higher Secondary or Pre University Courses or Intermediate or Junior College in 5 villages of the CD Block,, namely Nambivayal, Nattuchalai, Pallikondan, Thamarai Kottai North, Rajamadam.

College in 3 villages, Adult Literacy Center in 0 village., Colleges are in villages, namely Karambayam, Enathi, Earipurakkari.

Medical: Hospital in 0 village, Dispensary in 2 villages, Health Center in 8 villages, Sub Center in 14 villages, Maternity and Child Welfare Center in 0 village, Community health workers in 55 villages.

The Villages having Hospital or Dispensary or Health Center are Kondikulam, Vendakkottai.

Drinking Water: Tap water in 56 villages, Tank water in 1 villages, Well water in 56 villages, Tubewell in 56 villages and more than one source in 56 villages.

Bank: Banking facility in 3 villages, namely, Karambayam, Nattuchalai, Thamarai Kottai North.

Credit Society in 17 villages Agricultural Credit Society in 17 Non-Agricultural Credit Society in 1 village.

Others: Power supply in 55 villages, Cinema hall in 0 village, sport club in 0 village, Stadium or Auditorium or Community Hall in 0 village, Post Office in 29 villages.

There are 53 villages having bus facilities.

Villages with most of facilities: Karambayam Nattuchalai, Thamarai Kottai North.

Villages without amenities (Education): Sukkiranpatty, Thuvaramadai, Paingattuvayal, Koothadivayal, Nainankulam, Ponnavarayankottai Ukkadai, Chatramthokkalikkadu, Sundaram, Pudukkottagam, Narasingapuram..

Scheduled Castes: Out of the total population of 105225 persons, 15621 persons (14.85%) belong to Scheduled Castes.

The villages having less than 10% SC population are Ettuppulikkadu, Veppangadu, Palamuthi, Sukkiranpatty Veerakkorichi, Thittakudi, Sathankadu, Kondikulam Thuvaramadai, Kazhugapulikkadu, Paingattuvayal Nainankulam, Ponnavarayankottai Ukkadai Vendakkottai, Thuvarankuruchi South, Pallikondan Sendakkottai, Chinna Avudayar Koil Chatramthokkalikkadu, Thokkalikadu, Adirampattinam Palanjur, Thamarai Kottai North, Thambikkottai Sundaram, Soundranagi Puram, Rajamadam.

The villages having more than 50% SC population are None.

Sex ratio of Scheduled Caste population is 509.

Scheduled Castes Literates and Illiterates by Sex:

	Persons	Males	Females
Literate	9,109	5,177	3,932
Illiterate	6,512	2,495	4,017
Literacy rate	67.3	78.3	56.7
Graduate	287	192	95

Scheduled Castes (Dominant):

Paraiyan etc., Pallan, Adi Dravida, Koliyan Valluvan

For their cultural identity please see Appendix-I

Villages without Scheduled Castes: There are 3 villages without any scheduled caste population.

Scheduled Tribes: Out of the total population of 105225 persons, 143 persons (0.14%) belong to Scheduled Tribes.

The villages having less than 10% ST population are Sembalur, Ettuppulikkadu, Karambayam Veppangadu Ukkadai, Veppangadu, Nambivayal, Enathi Palamuthi, Aladikkumulai, Sukkiranpatty Veerakkorichi, Sendangadu (I), Thittakudi Nattuchalai, Athikkottai, Soorapallam, Sathankadu Naduvikkottai, Kondikulam, Thuvaramadai Kazhugapulikkadu, Pillanguzhi, Pannaivayal Paingattuvayal, Koothadivayal, Kargavayal Nainankulam, Mudalcheri, Anaikkadu Ponnavarayanigottai, Ponnavarayankottai Ukkadai Vendakkottai, Thuvarankurichi North Thuvarankuruchi South, Pallikondan, Sendakkottai

Chinna Avudayar Koil, Mahilankottai
Chatramthokkalikkadu, Thokkalikadu
Pudukkottai Ullar, Adirampattinam, Palanjur
Thamarai Kottai North, Thamaraikottai South
Parakkalakottai, Krishnapuram, Thambikkottai
Thambikkottai Maravakkadu, Sundaram
Thambikkottaivadakadu, Pudukkottagam
Soundranagi Puram, Narasingapuram, Earipurakkari
Rajamadam.

The villages having more than 50% ST population are None.

Sex ratio of Scheduled tribe population is 497.

Scheduled Tribes Literates and Illiterates by Sex:

	Persons	Males	Females
Literate	60	39	21
Illiterate	83	33	50
Literacy rate	52.6	65.0	38.9
Graduate	0	0	0

Scheduled Tribes (Dominant):

Kondareddis, Adiyan, Kattunayakan, Malakkuravan Malai Pandaram

For their cultural identity please see Appendix-II

Villages without Scheduled Tribes: There are 47 villages without any scheduled tribe population.

Literates and Illiterates by Sex (Total Population):

	Persons	Males	Females
Literate	65,573	36,961	28,612
Illiterate	39,652	14,565	25,087
Literacy rate	71	82	60
Graduate	1,773	1,256	517

Agriculture: ***Distribution of villages according to land use:*** Out of 56 villages, Total area (in hectare) is 28482.74, out of that 55.27 percent is cultivable and 68.48 percent of the cultivable area is irrigated.

Sources of Irrigation (Hectares): Government Canal 10139.5, Private Canal 0, Well without Electricity 6.27, Well with Electricity 2.33, Tubewell without Electricity 36.4, Tubewell with Electricity 375.77, Tank 191.54, River 0, Lake 27.65, Waterfall 0, Others 0.

Villages with population of 5000 to 9999: Thamarankottai North.

Villages with population of 10000 and above: None

Distribution of Workers:

	Persons	Males	Females	WPR
Cultivators	12,714	9,061	3,653	25.35
Agricultural Labour	27,752	13,951	13,801	55.34
Household Industry	891	457	434	1.78
Other Workers	8,788	6,922	1,866	17.53
Main Workers	39,020	25,644	13,376	77.81
Marginal Workers	11,125	4,747	6,378	22.19
Total Workers	50,145	30,391	19,754	

Religion: Major Religious Communities:

	Persons	Males	Females	Sex Ratio
Hindu (93.26%)	98,131	48,058	50,073	1,042
Muslim (1.22%)	1,286	611	675	1,105
Christian (5.41%)	5,689	2,782	2,907	1,045
Sikh (0%)	-	-	-	-
Buddhists (0%)	1	-	1	-
Jain (0%)	-	-	-	-

Agewise Data:

	Persons	Males	Females	Sex Ratio
All ages	105,225	51,526	53,699	1042
0-14	27,604	14,016	13,588	969
15-44	52,082	25,155	26,927	1070
45-79	24,347	11,743	12,604	1073
80+	997	493	504	1022
Age not stated	195	119	76	639

Languages (Dominant):

Tamil, Telugu, English, Malayalam, Marathi

Disabled Population:

	Persons	Males	Females	%
Total Disabled	3,006	1,535	1,471	
In Seeing	1,336	626	710	44.44
In Speech	393	198	195	13.07
In Hearing	208	96	112	6.92
In Movement	823	478	345	27.38
Mentally	246	137	109	8.18

PENNAGARAM

Pennagaram C.D. Block lies in the south-western part of Dharmapuri district. It is a part of Pennagaram taluk. The Block is located at a distance of 30 kms. from district headquarters (Dharmapuri). There are 51 villages in the block with the total population of 168,296 persons. Area of the C.D. Block is 113.70 sq. kms. It is bounded in the north by CD Block Palakkodu, in the south by district Salem, in the east by CD Bloks Palakkodu and Nallampalli, in the west by district Krishnagiri, and it has common boundary with the state of Karnataka on west.

Communications:

Roadways : Information not Available.

River: Chinnar Nadi- Nearest Villages- Pikkili, Keserkuli RF, Keserkuli , Morappur RF, Gruthiyaram RF, Oddapatti RF, Rangapuram RF, Cauvery Nadi- Villages- Oddapatti (RF), Devanurmalai (RF), Ajjana Halli, Sunjal Natham, Badanavadi RF. Palar Nadi- Villages- Vattuvanahalli, Morappur (RF), Keserkuli (Extn RF) Uni, Arakasanahally, Chinnampalli, Kalapampadi, Perumbalai, Gendenahalli, Barigam RF.

Annual Rainfall: Average Rainfall 760 mm.

Ground Water: Availability of the ground water in the Basin is 5588.80 H.A.M. and the utilization is 5557.98

H.A.M. It belongs to Over Expoited category. Depth to water level varies from 5 to 10 meter below the ground. Most of the wells go down in summer months, according to the Ground Water Estimation Committee.

Forest and Reserved Forest: (Bavanurmalai RF)- Nearest Villages- Devanurmalai (RF), Ajjana Halli. (Singarahath)- Nearest Villages- Badanavadi RF, Sigralahalli (RF), Ajjana Halli, Badanavadi Extn RF, Sunjal Natham, Nagamarai. (Guthirayan)- Nearest Village- Gruthiyaram (RF). (Kalappambadi)- Nearest Villages- Kukuttamaruthahalli, Kadamadai, Kalapampadi, Kalappampad (RF), Dhonnakuttahalli. (Masakkal)- Nearest Villages- Senganur, Kodihalli, Ajjana Halli, Masakkal (RF) Uni, Kukuttamaruthahalli, Dhonnakuttahalli. (Kesarkuli)- Nearest Villages- Keserkuli (RF), Keserkuli (Extn RF), Pikkili,Papparapatty, Thithiyoppanahalli, Kodihalhi, Sigarala Halli, Anjehalli, Vattuvanahalli, Kattinakkanahalli. (Morrappur)- Nearest Villages-Vattuvanahalli, Morappur (RF). (Oddnpatti)- Nearest Village- Oddapatti (RF). (Pennagaram)- Nearest Villages- Rangapuram (RF), Paruvathanahalli, Koothapadi. (Perumbalai)- Nearest Villages- Dhonnakuttahalli, Ramakonda Halli, Perumbalai Uni, Manjarihalli, Perumbalai. (Baduvadi Extn.)- Nearest Village- Sunjal Natham,

Natural Division: Baramahal.

Administration

Revenue **Division:** Dharmapuri. Parliamentary Constituency: 10 Dharmapuri. District: Dharmapuri. Taluk: Pennagram. Assembly Constituency: 58 Pennagaram. Gram Panchayat: 33.

Border Villages: (Karnataka)- Nearest Villages- Oddapatti (RF), Devanurmalai (RF), Ajjana Halli, Sunjal Natham, Badanavadi, Sigralahalli (RF) UNI,

Villages: 50 **Inhabited:** 42 **Uninhabited:** 8

Ranking	District	State	National
Area	2	2	315
Population	1	2	1324
Sex Ratio	17	373	5249
Child Sex Ratio	18	380	6322
Literacy Rate	15	373	4161
Density	2	93	5586
Work Participation Rate	17	362	964

Gram Panchayats:

Acharahalli, Ajjanahalli, Anjehalli , Arakasanahalli, Badrahalli , Billiyanoor, Chinnampalli, Donnakuttahalli, Gendenahalli, Giddanahalli, Kalappambadi, Kodihalli, Koothapadi, Kukuttamaruthahalli, Madehalli, Manajarahalli , Mangarai , Manjinaickanahalli, Nagamarai, Onnappagoundanahalli, Pallipatti , Panaikulam, Paruvathanahalli , Perambalai , Pikkili, Ramakondahalli, Sathiyanathapuram, Senganur, Sunchalnatham, Thithiyoppanahalli, Vattuvanahalli, Velampatti, Veppalahalli, .

Amenities:

Education: Primary School in 37 villages, Middle school in 20 villages, Matriculation or Secondary School in 10 villages, namely Panaikulam, Sigarala Halli, Peyalmari, Koothapadi, Ajjana Halli, Kalapampadi, Sunjal Natham, Nagamarai, Manjarihalli, Perumbalai.

Higher Secondary or Pre University Courses or Intermediate or Junior College in 4 villages of the CD Block,, namely Sigarala Halli, Sunjal Natham, Nagamarai, Perumbalai.

College in 1 village, Adult Literacy Center in 0 village., Colleges are in villages, namely Sigarala Halli.

Medical: Hospital in 1 village, Dispensary in 0 village, Health Center in 9 villages, Sub Center in 14 villages, Maternity and Child Welfare Center in 0 village, Community health workers in 17 villages.

The Village having Hospital or Dispensary or Health Center is Paruvathanahalli.

Drinking Water: Tap water in 42 villages, Tank water in 2 villages, Well water in 42 villages, Tubewell in 42 villages and more than one source in 42 villages.

Bank: Banking facility in 3 villages, namely, Chinnampalli, Sunjal Natham, Perumbalai.

Credit Society in 12 villages Agricultural Credit Society in 10 Non-Agricultural Credit Society in 0 village.

Others: Power supply in 39 villages, Cinema hall in 2 villages, sport club in 0 village, Stadium or Auditorium or Community Hall in 0 village, Post Office in 37 villages.

There are 32 villages having bus facilities.

Villages with most of facilities: Chinnampalli Sunjal Natham, Perumbalai.

Villages without amenities (Education): Morappur (Rf), Oddapatti (Rf), Rangapuram (Rf), Devanurmalai (Rf), Badanavadi..

Scheduled Castes: Out of the total population of 168296 persons, 18533 persons (11.01%) belong to Scheduled Castes.

The villages having less than 10% SC population are Pikkili, Panaikulam, Madehalli, Andrahalli Pallipatty, Velampatti, Kariappanahalli Onnappagoundanahally, Papparapatty Thithiyoppanahalli, Sigarala Halli, Vattuvanahalli Morappur (Rf), Oddapatti (Rf) , Rangapuram (Rf) Kattinakkanahalli, Peyalmari, Sathiyanathapuram Devanurmalai (Rf), Ajjana Halli, Kukuttamaruthahalli Pudupatti, Arakasanahally, Badanavadi Jarimankuriahi, Manjarihalli, Perumbalai.

The villages having more than 50% SC population are None.

Sex ratio of Scheduled Caste population is 475.

Scheduled Castes Literates and Illiterates by Sex:

	Persons	Males	Females
Literate	8,102	5,143	2,959
Illiterate	10,431	4,594	5,837
Literacy rate	52.0	63.8	39.4
Graduate	127	106	21

Scheduled Castes (Dominant):
Adi Dravida, Arunthathiyar, Kuravan etc., Valluvan Generic Castes etc.

For their cultural identity please see Appendix-I

Villages without Scheduled Castes: There are 16 villages without any scheduled caste population.

Scheduled Tribes: Out of the total population of 168296 persons, 3380 persons (2.01%) belong to Scheduled Tribes. The villages having less than 10% ST population are Pikkili, Panaikulam, Madehalli, Andrahalli Pallipatty, Velampatti, Kariappanahalli Onnappagoundanahally, Papparapatty Thithiyoppanahalli, Sigarala Halli, Vattuvanahalli Paruvathanahalli, Kattinakkanahalli, Anjehalli Peyalmari, Manjanayakkanahalli, Sathiyanathapuram Senganur, Koothapadi, Devanurmalai (Rf) Ajjana Halli, Kukuttamaruthahalli, Kadamadai Pudupatti, Arakasanahally, Chinnampalli, Kalapampadi Dhonnakuttahalli, Sunjal Natham, Badanavadi Nagamarai, Ramakonda Halli, Jarimankuriahi Manjarihalli, Perumbalai, Bhadrahalli, Gendenahalli. The villages having more than 50% ST population are None.

Sex ratio of Scheduled tribe population is 480.

Scheduled Tribes Literates and Illiterates by Sex:

	Persons	Males	Females
Literate	1,445	888	557
Illiterate	1,935	868	1,067
Literacy rate	50.5	60.8	39.8
Graduate	46	32	14

Scheduled Tribes (Dominant):
Kurumans, Irular, Kondareddis, Kurichchan Malai Vedan

For their cultural identity please see Appendix-II

Villages without Scheduled Tribes: There are 25 villages without any scheduled tribe population.

Literates and Illiterates by Sex (Total Population):

	Persons	Males	Females
Literate	75,399	47,493	27,906
Illiterate	92,897	41,081	51,816
Literacy rate	52	63	40
Graduate	1,280	1,019	261

Agriculture: ***Distribution of villages according to land use:*** Out of 50 villages, Total area (in hectare) is 113707.27, out of that 30.57 percent is cultivable and 20.69 percent of the cultivable area is irrigated.

Sources of Irrigation (Hectares): Government Canal 3, Private Canal 0, Well without Electricity 2294.51, Well with Electricity 3893.22, Tubewell without Electricity 0, Tubewell with Electricity 0, Tank 470.75, River 0, Lake 0, Waterfall 0, Others 530.92.

Villages with population of 5000 to 9999:
Pikkili, Panaikulam, Thithiyoppanahalli Sigaralahalli, Vattuvanahalli, Anjehalli, Peyalmari Senganur, Koothapadi, Ajjanahalli, Bonnakuttahalli Sunchainatham, Nagamarai, Ramakondahalli Manjarahalli, Perumbalai.

Villages with population of 10000 and above: None

Distribution of Workers:

	Persons	Males	Females	WPR
Cultivators	45,439	26,111	19,328	50.05
Agricultural Labour	29,152	12,219	16,933	32.11
Household Industry	927	507	420	1.02
Other Workers	15,275	11,815	3,460	16.82
Main Workers	77,493	46,077	31,416	85.35
Marginal Workers	13,300	4,575	8,725	14.65
Total Workers	90,793	50,652	40,141	

Religion: Major Religious Communities:

	Persons	Males	Females	Sex Ratio
Hindu (99.65%)	167,700	88,293	79,407	899
Muslim (0.08%)	136	60	76	1,267
Christian (0.2%)	339	161	178	1,106
Sikh (0%)	1	1	-	-
Buddhists (0%)	-	-	-	-
Jain (0%)	-	-	-	-

Agewise Data:

	Persons	Males	Females	Sex Ratio
All ages	168,296	88,574	79,722	900
0-14	55,745	31,351	24,394	778
15-44	78,640	40,154	38,486	958
45-79	31,983	16,057	15,926	992
80+	1,654	865	789	912
Age not stated	274	147	127	864

Languages (Dominant):
Tamil, Telugu, Kannada, Hindi, Urdu

Disabled Population:

	Persons	Males	Females	%
Total Disabled	5,316	1,615	3,701	
In Seeing	3,694	645	3,049	69.49
In Speech	332	192	140	6.25
In Hearing	195	93	102	3.67
In Movement	852	537	315	16.03
Mentally	243	148	95	4.57

PERAMBALUR

Perambalur C.D. Block lies in the central west part of Perambalur district. It is a part of Perambalur taluk. The Block is located at a distance of (00) kms. from district headquarters (Perambalur). There are 29 villages in the block with the total population of 83,229 persons. Area of the C.D. Block is 284.34 sq. kms. It is bounded in the north by CD Block Veppanthattai, in the south by CD Block Alathur, in the east by CD Block Veppur, and in the west by district Tiruchirappalli.

Communications:

Roadways : N.H.-45: Direction- Tiruchirappalli to Ulundurpettai, Nearest Villages- Sengunam, Elambalur, Thoramangalam, Kalpadi (N), Siruvachur, Nochiyam. S.H.-27: Direction- Perambalur to Ariyalur, Nearest Villages- Sengunam, Elambalur, Thoramangalam.

River: Marudayar Nadi- Nearest Village- Thoramangalam, Kalpadi (N), Kalpadi (S), Nochiyam. Chinnar Nadi- Nearest Villages- Ladapuram (E), Aranarai (N), Perambalur, Keelakkarai, Elambalur.

Annual Rainfall: Average Rainfall 876 mm.

Ground Water: Availability of the ground water in the Basin is 5036.98 H.A.M. and the utilization is 7681.01 H.A.M. It belongs to Over Expoited category. Depth to water level varies from 2 to 10 meter below the ground. Most of the wells go down in summer months, according to the Ground Water Estimation Committee.

Forest and Reserved Forest: (Esanai RF)- Nearest Villages- Esanai RF, Esanai, Keelakkarai, Melapuliyur (E), Melapliyur (W) (Melapuliyur)- Nearest Villages- Melapliyur (W), Melapliyur RF, Ladapuram (W). (Kalarampatti)- Nearest Villages- Kalarampatti RF, Kalarampatti. (Keelakkarai)- Nearest Villages- Keelakkarai RF, Ammapalayam, Ladapuram RF, Aranarai (N). (Siruvayalur)- Nearest Villages- Velur, Siruvayalur RF, Chathiramanai.

Natural Division: Chola Nadu.

Administration

Revenue Division: Perambalur. Parliamentary Constituency: 25 Perambalur. District: Permbalur. Taluk: Perambalur. Assembly Constituency: 147 Perambalur (SC). Gram Panchayat: 20.

Villages: 29 **Inhabited:** 22 **Uninhabited:** 7

Ranking	**District**	**State**	**National**
Area	4	193	2948
Population	4	217	3997
Sex Ratio	4	309	2538
Child Sex Ratio	4	300	5088
Literacy Rate	1	182	1719
Density	3	78	3605
Work Participation Rate	1	234	753

Gram Panchayats:

Aiyilur, Alampady, Ammapalayam, Bommanappady, Chatramani , Elambalur, Esanai , Kalarampatti , Kalpadi , Kavulpalayam, Konaripalayam, Ladapuram , Melapuliyur, Nochiyam, Pudunaduvalur, Sengunam, Siruvacher , Vadukkumadevi, Velur .

Amenities:

Education: Primary School in 22 villages, Middle school in 14 villages, Matriculation or Secondary School in 9 villages, namely Esanai, Elambalur, Aranarai (N), Melapliyur (W), Ladapuram (E), Siruvachur, Ammapalayam, Kalarampatti, Chathiramanai.

Higher Secondary or Pre University Courses or Intermediate or Junior College in 1 village of the CD Block,, namely Ammapalayam.

College in 2 villages, Adult Literacy Center in 0 village., Colleges are in villages, namely Elambalur, Ammapalayam.

Medical: Hospital in 2 villages, Dispensary in 5 villages, Health Center in 3 villages, Sub Center in 20 villages, Maternity and Child Welfare Center in 3 villages, Community health workers in 2 villages.

The Villages having Hospital or Dispensary or Health Center are Melapliyur (W), Siruvachur, Velur, Ammapalayam, Chathiramanai.

Drinking Water: Tap water in 22 villages, Tank water in 0 villages, Well water in 22 villages, Tubewell in 22 villages and more than one source in 22 villages.

Bank: Banking facility in 5 villages, namely, Thoramangalam, Kalpadi (S), Siruvachur, Ammapalayam Bommanappady.

Credit Society in 4 villages Agricultural Credit Society in 2 Non-Agricultural Credit Society in 1 village.

Others: Power supply in 22 villages, Cinema hall in 0 village, sport club in 0 village, Stadium or Auditorium or Community Hall in 0 village, Post Office in 21 villages.

There are 22 villages having bus facilities.

Villages with most of facilities: Thoramangalam Kalpadi (S), Siruvachur, Ammapalayam, Bommanappady.

Villages without Amenities (Education): None..

Scheduled Castes: Out of the total population of 83229 persons, 27872 persons (33.49%) belong to Scheduled Castes.

The villages having less than 10% SC population are None..

The villages having more than 50% SC population are None.

Sex ratio of Scheduled Caste population is 502.

Scheduled Castes Literates and Illiterates by Sex:

	Persons	Males	Females
Literate	16,661	9,523	7,138
Illiterate	11,211	4,368	6,843
Literacy rate	67.7	77.9	57.7

Graduate	782	596	186

Scheduled Castes (Dominant):

Paraiyan etc., Pallan, Arunthathiyar, Chakkiliyan Adi Dravida

For their cultural identity please see Appendix-I

Villages without Scheduled Castes: There are 7 villages without any scheduled caste population.

Scheduled Tribes: Out of the total population of 83229 persons, 132 persons (0.16%) belong to Scheduled Tribes. The villages having less than 10% ST population are Esanai, Keelakkarai, Sengunam, Elambalur Perambular (N), Aranarai (N), Melapuliyur (E) Melapliyur (W), Ladapuram (W), Ladapuram (E) Thoramangalam, Kalpadi (N), Kalpadi (S), Ayilur Siruvachur, Nochiyam, Pudunaduvalur, Velur Ammapalayam, Kalarampatti, Chathiramanai Bommanappady.

The villages having more than 50% ST population are None.

Sex ratio of Scheduled tribe population is 470.

Scheduled Tribes Literates and Illiterates by Sex:

	Persons	Males	Females
Literate	72	47	25
Illiterate	60	23	37
Literacy rate	63.2	77.1	47.2
Graduate	1	1	0

Scheduled Tribes (Dominant):

Uraly, Irular, Malayali, Malakkuravan, Toda

For their cultural identity please see Appendix-II

Villages without Scheduled Tribes: There are 17 villages without any scheduled tribe population.

Literates and Illiterates by Sex (Total Population):

	Persons	Males	Females
Literate	48,732	28,650	20,082
Illiterate	34,497	13,610	20,887
Literacy rate	66	77	55
Graduate	1,715	1,315	400

Agriculture: ***Distribution of villages according to land use:*** Out of 29 villages, Total area (in hectare) is 28434, out of that 60.07 percent is cultivable and 39.04 percent of the cultivable area is irrigated.

Sources of Irrigation (Hectares): Government Canal 200.85, Private Canal 0, Well without Electricity 827.65, Well with Electricity 4569.06, Tubewell without Electricity 302.52, Tubewell with Electricity 10.9, Tank 514.56, River 0, Lake 238.34, Waterfall 0, Others 4.

Villages with population of 5000 to 9999: Esanai, Elambalur, Ladapuram (East), Ammapalayam.

Villages with population of 10000 and above: None

Distribution of Workers:

	Persons	Males	Females	WPR
Cultivators	22,677	12,364	10,313	48.18
Agricultural Labour	14,347	5,774	8,573	30.48
Household Industry	1,066	571	495	2.26
Other Workers	8,975	6,560	2,415	19.07
Main Workers	42,133	23,637	18,496	89.52
Marginal Workers	4,932	1,632	3,300	10.48
Total Workers	47,065	25,269	21,796	

Religion: Major Religious Communities:

	Persons	Males	Females	Sex Ratio
Hindu (97.48%)	81,135	41,236	39,899	968
Muslim (1.57%)	1,306	597	709	1,188
Christian (0.83%)	689	373	316	847
Sikh (0%)	-	-	-	-
Buddhists (0%)	-	-	-	-
Jain (0%)	1	1	-	-

Agewise Data:

	Persons	Males	Females	Sex Ratio
All ages	83,229	42,260	40,969	969
0-14	22,339	11,619	10,720	923
15-44	40,532	20,306	20,226	996
45-79	19,600	9,929	9,671	974
80+	621	327	294	899
Age not stated	137	79	58	734

Languages (Dominant):

Tamil, Telugu, Urdu, Malayalam, Kannada

Disabled Population:

	Persons	Males	Females	%
Total Disabled	1,840	772	1,068	
In Seeing	1,158	378	780	62.93
In Speech	161	84	77	8.75
In Hearing	80	35	45	4.35
In Movement	337	213	124	18.32
Mentally	104	62	42	5.65

PERANAMALLUR

Peranamallur C.D. Block lies in the eastern part of Tiruvannamalai district. It is a part of Vandavasi taluk. The Block is located at a distance of 60 kms. from district Hq. (Tiruvannamalai). There are 69 villages in the block with the total population of 80,490 persons. Area of the C.D. Block is 255.71 sq. kms. It is bounded in the north by CD Blocks Cheyyar and Anakkavur, south by CD Block Thellar and district Viluppuram, in the east by C.D. Blocks Vandavasi and Thellar, in the west by CD Blocks Arani West & Chetpet

Communications:

Roadways : S.H.-4: Direction- Arani to Gingee, Nearest Villages- Semmambadi, Kolappalur, Gengapuram,

River: Cheyyar Nadi- Nearest Villages- Anmarudai, Avaniyapuram, Melsathamangalam, Natiyambody, Virayagapuram, Konaiyur, Gengapuram, Kolappalur, Narayanamangalam.

Backwards Region Grants Fund: It receives Backward Region Grants.

Annual Rainfall: Average Rainfall 1019 mm.

Ground Water: Availability of the ground water in the Basin is (Information not available) H.A.M. and the utilization is 160.44 H.A.M. It belongs to Over Expoited category. Depth to water level varies from 2 to 5 meter below the ground. Most of the wells go down in summer months, according to the Ground Water Estimation Committee.

Forest and Reserved Forest: (Nambedu RF)- Nearest Villages- Nambedu RF, Namedu, Ariyapadi. (Nedungunam)- Nearest Villages- Katubakkam, Jaganathapuram, Arasampattu, Nedungunam, Veppambattu, Nedungunam RF, Melnandiyambadi, Nalladisenai, Vayalur. (Visamangalam)- Nearest Villages- Tavani, Tellrampet, Konammangalam, Melooondi, Visamangalam RF, Visamangalam, Thengappanthangal.

Natural Division: Tondai Nadu.

Administration

Revenue **Division:** Cheyyar. Parliamentary Constituency: 12 Arani. District: Tiruvannamalai. Taluk: Vanadavasi. Assembly Constituency: 66 Polur, 69 Vandavasi (SC). Gram Panchayat: 57.

Villages: 69 **Inhabited:** 66 **Uninhabited:** 3

Ranking	District	State	National
Area	13	226	3310
Population	15	238	4086
Sex Ratio	1	73	579
Child Sex Ratio	1	13	468
Literacy Rate	8	171	1633
Density	9	186	3398
Work Participation Rate	11	207	1884

Gram Panchayats:

Aliyur, Alliyandal, Anadimangalam, Anaibogi, Anmarudai, Arasampattu, Ariyapadi, Avaniyapuram, Ayalavadi, Chandirambadi, Endal, Erumbur, Gengapuram, Imapuram, Injimedu, Isakolathur, Jagannathapuram, Kalyanapuram, Kolappalur, Konaiyur, Konamangalam, Kottupakkam, kozhipuliyur, Kozhipuliyur, Madam, Mahadevimangalam, Marakkunam, Melanur, Melapoondi , melapoondi , Melathangal, Melnandiyambadi , Melsathamangalam, Melvillivalam, Morakkaniyanur, Mosavadi, Nalladisenai, Namathodu-Thellarampattu, Nambedu, Narayanamangalam, Nariyambadi, Nedungunam, Peranambakkam, Poongunam, Raghunathasamudram, Reddikuppam, Semmambadi, Septankulam, Solaiarugavur, Solavaram, Sudrakatteri, Thadinolambai, Thavani, Vallam, Vayaloor, Veppampattu, Vilanallur, Vinayagapuram, Visamangalam.

Amenities:

Education: Primary School in 65 villages, Middle school in 23 villages, Matriculation or Secondary School in 11 villages, namely Avaniyapuram, Ayalavadi, Vallam, Kolappalur, Alliyandal, Namathodu, Melathangal, Madam, Katubakkam, Melacheri, Vayalur.

Higher Secondary or Pre University Courses or Intermediate or Junior College in 1 village of the CD Block,, namely Kolappalur.

College in 0 village, Adult Literacy Center in 0 village.

Medical: Hospital in 0 village, Dispensary in 0 village, Health Center in 8 villages, Sub Center in 6 villages, Maternity and Child Welfare Center in 4 villages, Community health workers in 66 villages.

The Village having Hospital or Dispensary or Health Center is Madam.

Drinking Water: Tap water in 66 villages, Tank water in 7 villages, Well water in 66 villages, Tubewell in 66 villages and more than one source in 66 villages.

Bank: Banking facility in 7 villages, namely, Anmarudai, Vallam, Kolappalur, Mosavadi, Namathodu Melacheri, Nedungunam.

Credit Society in 16 villages Agricultural Credit Society in 4 Non-Agricultural Credit Society in 14 villages.

Others: Power supply in 66 villages, Cinema hall in 0 village, sport club in 0 village, Stadium or Auditorium or Community Hall in 0 village, Post Office in 49 villages.

There are 62 villages having bus facilities.

Villages with most of facilities: Anmarudai Vallam, Kolappalur, Mosavadi, Namathodu, Melacheri Nedungunam.

Villages without amenities (Education): Tellrampet..

Scheduled Castes: Out of the total population of 80490 persons, 16647 persons (20.68%) belong to Scheduled Castes.

The villages having less than 10% SC population are Melsembadu, Vedugamangalam, Chandranpadi Melsathamangalam, Natiyambody, Imapuram Narayanamangalam, Endal, Tellrampet, Semmambadi Konammangalam, Visamangalam, Melacheri Thengappanthangal, Pernampakkam, Melvillivalam Vayalur, Poongunam.

The villages having more than 50% SC population are None.

Sex ratio of Scheduled Caste population is 504.

Scheduled Castes Literates and Illiterates by Sex:

	Persons	Males	Females
Literate	9,438	5,580	3,858
Illiterate	7,209	2,680	4,529
Literacy rate	63.8	76.0	51.7
Graduate	144	122	22

Scheduled Castes (Dominant):
Adi Dravida, Arunthathiyar, Valluvan, Chakkiliyan Kuravan etc.

For their cultural identity please see Appendix-I

Villages without Scheduled Castes: There are 11 villages without any scheduled caste population.

Scheduled Tribes: Out of the total population of 80490 persons, 945 persons (1.17%) belong to Scheduled Tribes. The villages having less than 10% ST population are Melanoore, S.Katteri, Anmarudai, Avaniyapuram Sozhavaram, Namedu, Anaibogi, Villandure, Ayalavadi Erumbur, Tennalapranthan, Melsembadu, Vallam Vedugamangalam, Septangulam, Ariyapadi, Injimedu Chandranpadi, Kattamangalam, Melsathamangalam Natiyambody, Virayagapuram, Konaiyur, Gengapuram Kolappalur, Imapuram, Narayanamangalam, Maragunam Alliyandal, Mahadevimangalam, Mosavadi, Thadinolambi Endal, Manickamangalam, Reddikuppam Raghunathasamuthiram, Melpapayam, Tavani, Tellrampet Namathodu, Semmambadi, Anadimangalam, Konammangalam Melooondi, Visamangalam, Melathangal, Kozhipuliyoor Kalyanapuram, Solaiarugatur, Madam, Isakolathur Katubakkam, Melacheri, Jaganathapuram, Arasampattu Nedungunam, Thengappanthangal, Pernampakkam Morakkaniyanoor, Veppambattu, Melnandiyambadi Nalladisenai, Vayalur, Poongunam.

The villages having more than 50% ST population are None.

Sex ratio of Scheduled tribe population is 501.

Scheduled Tribes Literates and Illiterates by Sex:

	Persons	Males	Females
Literate	229	132	97
Illiterate	716	340	376
Literacy rate	29.7	35.3	24.4
Graduate	0	0	0

Scheduled Tribes (Dominant):
Irular, Malakkuravan, Kurumans

For their cultural identity please see Appendix-II

Villages without Scheduled Tribes: There are 30 villages without any scheduled tribe population.

Literates and Illiterates by Sex (Total Population):

	Persons	Males	Females
Literate	48,224	28,794	19,430
Illiterate	32,266	10,983	21,283
Literacy rate	67	81	53
Graduate	730	588	142

Agriculture: ***Distribution of villages according to land use:*** Out of 69 villages, Total area (in hectare) is 25571.21, out of that 65.77 percent is cultivable and 31.34 percent of the cultivable area is irrigated.

Sources of Irrigation (Hectares): Government Canal 0, Private Canal 0, Well without Electricity 216.35, Well with Electricity 1282.39, Tubewell without Electricity 0, Tubewell with Electricity 0, Tank 1794.7, River 24.61, Lake 427.39, Waterfall 0, Others 0.

Villages with population of 5000 to 9999: None

Villages with population of 10000 and above: None

Distribution of Workers:

	Persons	Males	Females	WPR
Cultivators	17,287	12,046	5,241	40.68
Agricultural Labour	18,173	6,597	11,576	42.76
Household Industry	2,096	1,421	675	4.93
Other Workers	4,941	3,791	1,150	11.63
Main Workers	33,689	21,486	12,203	79.27
Marginal Workers	8,808	2,369	6,439	20.73
Total Workers	42,497	23,855	18,642	

Religion: Major Religious Communities:

	Persons	Males	Females	Sex Ratio
Hindu (96.51%)	77,678	38,453	39,225	1,020
Muslim (0.61%)	488	237	251	1,059
Christian (2.01%)	1,620	738	882	1,195
Sikh (0%)	-	-	-	-
Buddhists (0%)	-	-	-	-
Jain (0.79%)	634	307	327	1,065

Agewise Data:

	Persons	Males	Females	Sex Ratio
All ages	80,490	39,777	40,713	1024
0-14	22,168	11,216	10,952	976
15-44	36,709	18,046	18,663	1034
45-79	20,446	9,912	10,534	1063
80+	865	437	428	979
Age not stated	302	166	136	819

Languages (Dominant):
Tamil, Telugu, Urdu, Kannada, English

Disabled Population:

	Persons	Males	Females	%
Total Disabled	1,930	1,119	811	
In Seeing	808	459	349	41.87
In Speech	207	126	81	10.73
In Hearing	137	65	72	7.1
In Movement	612	378	234	31.71
Mentally	166	91	75	8.6

PERAVURANI

Peravurani C.D. Block lies in the south-western part of Thanjavur district. It is a part of Pattukkottai and Peravurani taluks. The Block is located at a distance of 44 kms. from district headquarters (Thanjavur). There are 59 villages in the block with the total population of 84,319 persons. Area of the C.D. Block is 197.29 sq. kms. It is bounded in the north by C.D. Blocks Thiruvonam and Pattukkottai, in the south by district Pudukkottai and C.D. Block Sethubhavachatram, in the east by C.D. Blocks Pattukkottai and Sethubhavachatram, and in the west by district Pudukkottai. CD Block Peravurani falls in taluk Pattukkottai by 30 villages, and in taluk Peravurani by 29 villages.

Communications:

Roadways : S.H.-29: Direction- Karaikkudi to Thiruthuraipoondi, Nearest Villages- Thuravikkadu, Punavasal West, Punavasal East, Kurichi, Alivalam, Manauayal, Ottankadu, Thiruchitarmbalam West, Ottankkadu Ukkadai, Kalagam, Kalagam, Mavadukuruchi East, Mavadukuruchi West, Chittathikadu, Padappanarvayal, Sornakkadu, Pinnavasal.

River: Agniyar Nadi- Nearest Villages- Poovaloor, Valuthalaivattam, Vattathikkottai, Edaiyathi - North, Edaiyathy, Sooriyanarayanapuram, Seruraviduth Vadapati, Madathikkadu, Thuravikkadu, Punavasal East, Kurichi, Eduthanivayal, Madanpattavur, Punavasal West. Punakkutiyar Nadi- Nearest Village- Mavadukuruchi West, Palayanagaram. Ambuliar Nadi- Nearest Villages- Enathikrambai, Paingal, Sankkarai, Sengamangalam, Chittahikadu.

Annual Rainfall: Average Rainfall 1147 mm.

Ground Water: Availability of the ground water in the Basin is 2688.02 H.A.M. and the utilization is 1682. 77 H.A.M. It belongs to Safe category. Depth to water level varies from 2 to 10 meter below the ground. Most of the wells go down in summer months, according to the Ground Water Estimation Committee.

Natural Division: Chola Nadu.

Administration

Revenue **Division:** Pattukottai. Parliamentary Constituency: 30 Pudukottai. District: Thanjavur. Taluk: Pattukottai, Peravurani. Assembly Constituency: 177 Peravurani. Gram Panchayat: 26.

Villages: 59 **Inhabited:** 55 **Uninhabited:** 4

Ranking	District	State	National
Area	8	291	4230
Population	12	213	3962
Sex Ratio	6	58	501
Child Sex Ratio	6	122	2283
Literacy Rate	10	119	1237
Density	4	272	2574
Work Participation Rate	6	97	2976

Gram Panchayats:

Alivalam, Ammayandi, Edayathi , Kalagam, Kalathur, Kalluranikkadu, Kattaiyankadukkadai, Kurichi, Madathikkadu, Maduvakurichi, Maduvakurichi , Mavadukurichi , Ottankadu, Ottankadu , Paingal , Palathali, Palayanagaram, Periyanayagipuram, Pinnavasal, Poovalur, Punavasal , Sengamangalam, Seruvaviduthi South, Seruvaviduthi Vadapathi, Sornakkadu, Thennankudi, Thuravikkadu, Tiruchitrambalam , Valabramankadu, Vattathikkottai .

Amenities:

Education: Primary School in 44 villages, Middle school in 21 villages, Matriculation or Secondary School in 11 villages, namely Edaiyathi - North, Punavasal West, Kalathur West, Kalluranikkodu, Kalagam, Kalagam, Renganayakipuram, Avanam, Enathikrambai, Paingal, Pinnavasal.

Higher Secondary or Pre University Courses or Intermediate or Junior College in 5 villages of the CD Block,, namely Edaiyathi - North, Punavasal West, Thiruchitarmbalam West, Renganayakipuram, Avanam. College in 0 village, Adult Literacy Center in 0 village.

Medical: Hospital in 0 village, Dispensary in 0 village, Health Center in 5 villages, Sub Center in 17 villages, Maternity and Child Welfare Center in 0 village, Community health workers in 52 villages.

The Village having Hospital or Dispensary or Health Center is Kalathur East.

Drinking Water: Tap water in 55 villages, Tank water in 3 villages, Well water in 55 villages, Tubewell in 55 villages and more than one source in 55 villages.

Bank: Banking facility in 3 villages, namely, Thiruchitarmbalam West, Thiruchitrambalam East Avanam.

Credit Society in 19 villages Agricultural Credit Society in 19 Non-Agricultural Credit Society in 0 village.

Others: Power supply in 52 villages, Cinema hall in 1 village, sport club in 0 village, Stadium or Auditorium or Community Hall in 0 village, Post Office in 24 villages.

There are 45 villages having bus facilities.

Villages with most of facilities: Thiruchitarmbalam West Thiruchitrambalam East, Avanam.

Villages without amenities (Education): Valuthalaivattam, Bimapuram, Sooriyanarayanapuram, Seruvaviduthi South, Ennanivayal, Eduthanivayal, Kattayankadu, Arasalamkarambai, Thondupulikkadu, Panchanathipuram..

Scheduled Castes: Out of the total population of 84319 persons, 10829 persons (12.84%) belong to Scheduled Castes. The villages having less than 10% SC population are Valuthalaivattam, Vattathikkottai, Edaiyathy Krishnapuram, Madathikkadu, Thuravikkadu Punavasal West, Ananthesvarapuram, Palathali Eduthanivayal, Thiruchitarmbalam West, Kalathur West Arasalamkarambai, Thondupulikkadu, Kalagam, Kalagam Mavadukuruchi East, Mavadukuruchi West Panchanathipuram, Avanam, Sanakkarai, Sengamangalam

Chittathikadu, Andakkottai, Padappanarvayal Panancheri, Valapramanagadu.

The villages having more than 50% SC population are None.

Sex ratio of Scheduled Caste population is 515.

Scheduled Castes Literates and Illiterates by Sex:

	Persons	Males	Females
Literate	6,668	3,827	2,841
Illiterate	4,161	1,425	2,736
Literacy rate	69.7	82.8	57.5
Graduate	208	146	62

Scheduled Castes (Dominant):

Paraiyan etc., Pallan, Adi Dravida, Kuravan etc. Thoti

For their cultural identity please see Appendix-I

Villages without Scheduled Castes: There are 14 villages without any scheduled caste population.

Scheduled Tribes: Out of the total population of 84319 persons, 99 persons (0.12%) belong to Scheduled Tribes.

The villages having less than 10% ST population are Poovaloor, Valuthalaivattam, Vattathikkottai Bimapuram, Edaiyathi - North, Edaiyathy Sooriyanarayanapuram, Seruraviduth Vadapati Krishnapuram, Seruvaviduthi South, Madathikkadu Thuravikkadu, Punavasal West, Punavasal East Kurichi, Neivaviduthy, Ananthesvarapuram, Alivalam Manauayal, Palathali, Ennanivayal, Eduthanivayal Madanpattavur, Ottankadu, Thiruchitarmbalam West Thiruchitrambalam East, Kalathur West, Kalathur East Ottankkadu Ukkadai, Kattayankadu, Peraiyanayagipuram Arasalamkarambai, Palayanagaram, Thondupulikkadu Kalluranikkodu, Kalagam, Kalagam, Mavadukuruchi East Mavadukuruchi West, Thennangudi, Renganayakipuram Ammaiyandi, Panchanathipuram, Avanam, Enathikrambai Paingal, Sanakkarai, Sengamangalam, Chittathikadu Andakkottai, Padappanarvayal, Sornakkadu, Panancheri Valapramanagadu, Pinnavasal.

The villages having more than 50% ST population are None.

Sex ratio of Scheduled tribe population is 485.

Scheduled Tribes Literates and Illiterates by Sex:

	Persons	Males	Females
Literate	16	10	6
Illiterate	83	41	42
Literacy rate	19.8	25.0	14.6
Graduate	0	0	0

Scheduled Tribes (Dominant):

Adiyan, Kattunayakan, Malakkuravan

For their cultural identity please see Appendix-II

Villages without Scheduled Tribes: There are 55 villages without any scheduled tribe population.

Literates and Illiterates by Sex (Total Population):

	Persons	Males	Females
Literate	51,722	29,780	21,942
Illiterate	32,597	11,765	20,832
Literacy rate	70	82	58
Graduate	918	695	223

Agriculture: ***Distribution of villages according to land use:*** Out of 59 villages, Total area (in hectare) is 19729.43, out of that 66.89 percent is cultivable and 75.83 percent of the cultivable area is irrigated.

Sources of Irrigation (Hectares): Government Canal 9465.01, Private Canal 0, Well without Electricity 40.39, Well with Electricity 68.41, Tubewell without Electricity 79.91, Tubewell with Electricity 171.44, Tank 181.93, River 0, Lake 0, Waterfall 0, Others 0.

Villages with population of 5000 to 9999: None

Villages with population of 10000 and above: None

Distribution of Workers:

	Persons	Males	Females	WPR
Cultivators	12,286	8,676	3,610	30.54
Agricultural Labour	21,916	10,810	11,106	54.48
Household Industry	648	219	429	1.61
Other Workers	5,379	4,279	1,100	13.37
Main Workers	31,598	20,397	11,201	78.55
Marginal Workers	8,631	3,587	5,044	21.45
Total Workers	40,229	23,984	16,245	

Religion: Major Religious Communities:

	Persons	Males	Females	Sex Ratio
Hindu (94.82%)	79,949	39,397	40,552	1,029
Muslim (2.81%)	2,370	1,098	1,272	1,158
Christian (2.32%)	1,956	1,029	927	901
Sikh (0%)	-	-	-	-
Buddhists (0%)	-	-	-	-
Jain (0%)	-	-	-	-

Agewise Data:

	Persons	Males	Females	Sex Ratio
All ages	84,319	41,545	42,774	1030
0-14	22,834	11,720	11,114	948
15-44	41,802	20,245	21,557	1065
45-79	19,019	9,249	9,770	1056
80+	573	280	293	1046
Age not stated	91	51	40	784

Languages (Dominant):

Tamil, Telugu, Kannada, Malayalam, Urdu

Disabled Population:

	Persons	Males	Females	%
Total Disabled	2,251	1,082	1,169	
In Seeing	1,312	555	757	58.29
In Speech	193	89	104	8.57

In Hearing	112	57	55	4.98
In Movement	479	304	175	21.28

Mentally	155	77	78	6.89

PERIYAKULAM

Periyakulam C.D. Block lies in the north-eastern part of Theni district. It is a part of Periyakulam taluk. The Block is located at a distance of 15 kms. from district headquarters (Theni Allinayaram). There are 16 villages in the block with the total population of 87,634 persons. Area of the C.D. Block is 291.44 sq. kms. It is bounded in the north and east by district Dindigul, in the south by CD Block Andipatti, in the west by CD Blocks Bodinayak, Kanur and Theni.

Communications:

Roadways : N.H.-220: Direction- Theni to Vattalakundu, Nearest Villages- Keelavadakarai, Genguvarpatty Bit I, D.Vadipatty, Silvarpatty, Kamachipuram, Endappuli, Thamaraikulam Bit[I], Vadaveeranayakanpatty, Parambikaradu.

Annual Rainfall: Average Rainfall 709 mm.

Ground Water: Availability of the ground water in the Basin is 8942.36 H.A.M. and the utilization is 9691. 66 H.A.M. It belongs to Over Expoited category. Depth to water level varies from 2 to 10 meter below the ground. Most of the wells go down in summer months, according to the Ground Water Estimation Committee.

Forest and Reserved Forest: (Murugumalai RF)- Nearest Villages- Pudukkottai, Murugamalai R F, D.Vadipatty, Silvarpatty, Kamachipuram, Endappuli, Jayamangalam Bit[I]. (Parambikaredu)- Nearest Villages- Mullaikaradu RF, Parambikaradu RF.

Natural Division: NA

Administration

Revenue **Division:** Periyakulam. Parliamentary Constituenc y: 33 Theni. District: Theni. Taluk: Periyakulam. Assem bly Constituency: 199 Periyakulam (SC). Gram Panchayat: 17.

Villages: 16 **Inhabited:** 14 **Uninhabited:** 2

Ranking	District	State	National
Area	4	183	2876
Population	2	194	3860
Sex Ratio	7	337	3174
Child Sex Ratio	3	336	5548
Literacy Rate	4	185	1726
Density	8	292	3513
Work Participation Rate	2	224	3235

Gram Panchayats:

A.vadipatti, Alagarnaickenpatti, Bomminaickenpatti, D.Vadipatty, Endapuli, Erumalinackenpatti, G.kallupatty, Gullapuram , Jeyamangalam , Keelavadagarai , Lakshmipuram, Melmangalam , Mudalakkampatti, Sallipatti, Saruthipatti, Silvarpatty, Vadapudupatti, .

Amenities:

Education: Primary School in 13 villages, Middle school in 9 villages, Matriculation or Secondary School in 5 villages, namely Vadagarai, Genguvarpatty Bit I, Endapuli, Thamaraikulam Bit[I], Jayamangalam Bit[I].
Higher Secondary or Pre University Courses or Intermediate or Junior College in 3 villages of the CD Block,, namely Vadagarai, Genguvarpatty Bit I, Thamaraikulam Bit[I].
College in 2 villages, Adult Literacy Center in 0 village., Colleges are in villages, namely Kamachipuram, Vadaveeranayakanpatty.

Medical: Hospital in 4 villages, Dispensary in 7 villages, Health Center in 5 villages, Sub Center in 8 villages, Maternity and Child Welfare Center in 4 villages, Community health workers in 2 villages.
The Villages having Hospital or Dispensary or Health Center are Pudukkottai, Genguvarpatty Bit I, Silvarpatty, Endappuli, Thamaraikulam Bit[I], Melmangalam [I], Jayamangalam Bit[I], Vadaveeranayakanpatty.

Drinking Water: Tap water in 14 villages, Tank water in 11 villages, Well water in 14 villages, Tubewell in 14 villages and more than one source in 14 villages.

Bank: Banking facility in 6 villages, namely, Vadagarai, Genguvarpatty Bit I Thamaraikulam Bit[I], Jayamangalam Bit[I] Kullappuram, Vadaveeranayakanpatty.
Credit Society in 5 villages Agricultural Credit Society in 5 Non-Agricultural Credit Society in 0 village.

Others: Power supply in 14 villages, Cinema hall in 4 villages, sport club in 0 village, Stadium or Auditorium or Community Hall in 1 village, Post Office in 13 villages.
There are 13 villages having bus facilities.

Villages with most of facilities: Vadagarai Genguvarpatty Bit I, Thamaraikulam Bit[I] Jayamangalam Bit[I], Kullappuram Vadaveeranayakanpatty.

Villages without amenities (Education): Mullaikaradu R F..

Scheduled Castes: Out of the total population of 87634 persons, 20422 persons (23.3%) belong to Scheduled Castes.
The villages having less than 10% SC population are Keelavadakarai, Mullaikaradu R F, Kamachipuram Melmangalam [I].
The villages having more than 50% SC population are None.
Sex ratio of Scheduled Caste population is 482.

Scheduled Castes Literates and Illiterates by Sex:

	Persons	Males	Females
Literate	9,364	5,848	3,516
Illiterate	11,058	4,721	6,337
Literacy rate	53.1	64.5	41.0
Graduate	43	32	11

Scheduled Castes (Dominant):
Pallan, Paraiyan etc., Chakkiliyan, Madari Devendrakulathan

For their cultural identity please see Appendix-I

Villages without Scheduled Castes: There are 3 villages without any scheduled caste population.

Scheduled Tribes: Out of the total population of 87634 persons, 184 persons (0.21%) belong to Scheduled Tribes. The villages having less than 10% ST population are Vadagarai, Keelavadakarai, Pudukkottai Mullaikaradu R F, Genguvarpatty Bit I, D.Vadipatty Silvarpatty, Kamachipuram, Thamaraikulam Bit[I] Melmangalam [I], Jayamangalam Bit[I], Kullappuram Vadaveeranayakanpatty.

The villages having more than 50% ST population are None.

Sex ratio of Scheduled tribe population is 467.

Scheduled Tribes Literates and Illiterates by Sex:

	Persons	Males	Females
Literate	52	36	16
Illiterate	132	62	70
Literacy rate	34.4	44.4	22.9
Graduate	0	0	0

Scheduled Tribes (Dominant):
Kattunayakan, Paniyan, Palliyar, Kurumans Generic Tribes etc.

For their cultural identity please see Appendix-II

Villages without Scheduled Tribes: There are 11 villages without any scheduled tribe population.

Literates and Illiterates by Sex (Total Population):

	Persons	Males	Females
Literate	51,280	30,412	20,868
Illiterate	36,354	14,362	21,992
Literacy rate	66	77	55
Graduate	394	265	129

Agriculture: ***Distribution of villages according to land use:*** Out of 16 villages, Total area (in hectare) is 29144.83, out of that 46.03 percent is cultivable and 69.87 percent of the cultivable area is irrigated.

Sources of Irrigation (Hectares): Government Canal 1178.76, Private Canal 0, Well without Electricity 334.67, Well with Electricity 4787.16, Tubewell without Electricity 89.81, Tubewell with Electricity 395.14, Tank 754.79, River 436.91, Lake 0, Waterfall 504.61, Others 1227.81.

Villages with population of 5000 to 9999:
Vadagarai , Genguvarpatty , Silvarpatty Vadaveeranaickenpatty.

Villages with population of 10000 and above:
Thamarai Kulam , Melmangalam , Jeyamangalam Gullapuram.

Distribution of Workers:

	Persons	Males	Females	WPR
Cultivators	5,259	3,886	1,373	12.9
Agricultural Labour	24,665	13,723	10,942	60.5
Household Industry	606	290	316	1.49
Other Workers	10,240	7,951	2,289	25.12
Main Workers	37,273	24,556	12,717	91.42
Marginal Workers	3,497	1,294	2,203	8.58
Total Workers	40,770	25,850	14,920	

Religion: Major Religious Communities:

	Persons	Males	Females	Sex Ratio
Hindu (93.81%)	82,206	42,063	40,143	954
Muslim (4.23%)	3,710	1,876	1,834	978
Christian (1.92%)	1,681	810	871	1,075
Sikh (0.01%)	6	3	3	1,000
Buddhists (0%)	2	2	-	-
Jain (0.01%)	12	8	4	500

Agewise Data:

	Persons	Males	Females	Sex Ratio
All ages	87,634	44,774	42,860	957
0-14	24,246	12,863	11,383	885
15-44	43,119	21,723	21,396	985
45-79	18,696	9,381	9,315	993
80+	790	384	406	1057
Age not stated	783	423	360	851

Languages (Dominant):
Tamil, Telugu, Kannada, Gujarati, Malayalam

Disabled Population:

	Persons	Males	Females	%
Total Disabled	2,128	1,026	1,102	
In Seeing	1,243	517	726	58.41
In Speech	155	85	70	7.28
In Hearing	73	36	37	3.43
In Movement	468	280	188	21.99
Mentally	189	108	81	8.88

PERIYANAICKENPALAYAM

Perianaickenpalayam C.D. Block lies in the north-western part of Coimbatore district. It is a part of Coimbatore north taluk. The Block is located at a distance of 15 kms. from district headquarters (Coimbatore). There are 10 villages in the block with the total population of 58,044 persons. Area of the C.D. Block is 204.28 sq. kms. It is bounded in the north by CD Block Karamadai, in the south by CD Blocks Thondamathur and Mudukkarai, in the east by C.D. Blocks Annur and Sarcarsamakulam, and it has common boundary with the state of Kerala on west and south.

Communications:

Roadways : S.H.-31: Direction- Coimbatore to Mettupalayam, Nearest Village- Bilichi.

Annual Rainfall: Average Rainfall 550 mm.

Ground Water: Availability of the ground water in the Basin is 2311.71 H.A.M. and the utilization is 3482.00 H.A.M. It belongs to Semi Critical category. Depth to water level varies from 10 to 20 meter below the ground. Most of the wells go down in summer months, according to the Ground Water Estimation Committee.

Forest and Reserved Forest: (Thadagam RF)- Nearest Villages- Thadagam R.F., Anaikatti (North), Anaikatti (South), Naickenpalayam, Veerapandi, Chinnathadagam, Nanjundapuram, Pannimadai.

Natural Division: Kongu Nadu.

Administration

Revenue **Division:** Coimbatore. Parliamentary Constituency: 19 Nilgiris. District: Coimbatore. Taluk: Coimbatore. Assembly Constituency: 111 Mettupalayam, 117 Kavandampalayam. Gram Panchayat: 09.

Border Villages- (Kerala)- Nearest Villages- Anaikatti (North), Anaikatti (South), Veerapandi.

Villages: 10 **Inhabited:** 10 **Uninhabited:** 0

Ranking	District	State	National
Area	12	279	4106
Population	16	335	4927
Sex Ratio	10	295	2407
Child Sex Ratio	17	261	4383
Literacy Rate	6	166	1603
Density	17	255	3702
Work Participation Rate	13	245	2754

Gram Panchayats:

Bilichi, Chinnathadagam, Naickenpalayam, Nanjundapuram, Pannimadai, Somayampalayam, Veerapandi, .

Amenities:

Education: Primary School in 7 villages, Middle school in 5 villages, Matriculation or Secondary School in 5 villages, namely Naickenpalayam, Veerapandi, Chinnathadagam, Somayampalayam, Pannimadai.

Higher Secondary or Pre University Courses or Intermediate or Junior College in 4 villages of the CD Block,, namely Naickenpalayam, Chinnathadagam, Somayampalayam, Pannimadai.

College in 1 village, Adult Literacy Center in 0 village., Colleges are in villages, namely Nanjundapuram.

Medical: Hospital in 4 villages, Dispensary in 0 village, Health Center in 3 villages, Sub Center in 7 villages, Maternity and Child Welfare Center in 2 villages, Community health workers in 0 village.

The Villages having Hospital or Dispensary or Health Center are Bilichi, Naickenpalayam, Veerapandi, Chinnathadagam.

Drinking Water: Tap water in 10 villages, Tank water in 0 villages, Well water in 10 villages, Tubewell in 10 villages and more than one source in 10 villages.

Bank: Banking facility in 5 villages, namely, Bilichi, Naickenpalayam, Chinnathadagam Nanjundapuram, Somayampalayam.

Credit Society in 2 villages Agricultural Credit Society in 2 Non-Agricultural Credit Society in 0 village.

Others: Power supply in 10 villages, Cinema hall in 1 village, sport club in 1 village, Stadium or Auditorium or Community Hall in 0 village, Post Office in 7 villages.

There are 7 villages having bus facilities.

Villages with most of facilities: Bilichi Naickenpalayam, Chinnathadagam, Nanjundapuram Somayampalayam.

Villages without amenities (Education):

Thadagam R.F., Anaikatti (North), Anaikatti (South)..

Scheduled Castes: Out of the total population of 58044 persons, 9614 persons (16.56%) belong to Scheduled Castes. The villages having less than 10% SC population are None..

The villages having more than 50% SC population are None.

Sex ratio of Scheduled Caste population is 498.

Scheduled Castes Literates and Illiterates by Sex:

	Persons	Males	Females
Literate	4,339	2,579	1,760
Illiterate	5,275	2,246	3,029
Literacy rate	51.3	60.8	41.7
Graduate	19	15	4

Scheduled Castes (Dominant):

Chakkiliyan, Arunthathiyar, Generic Castes etc. Panniandi, Adi Dravida

For their cultural identity please see Appendix-I

Villages without Scheduled Castes: There is 0 village without any scheduled caste population.

Scheduled Tribes: Out of the total population of 58044 persons, 3675 persons (6.33%) belong to Scheduled Tribes. The villages having less than 10% ST population are Thadagam R.F., Bilichi, Veerapandi, Chinnathadagam Nanjundapuram, Somayampalayam, Pannimadai.

The villages having more than 50% ST population are None.

Sex ratio of Scheduled tribe population is 494.

Scheduled Tribes Literates and Illiterates by Sex:

	Persons	Males	Females
Literate	1,480	881	599

Illiterate	2,195	979	1,216
Literacy rate	44.8	52.9	36.6
Graduate	2	1	1

Scheduled Tribes (Dominant):
Irular, Malai Vedan, Malasar, Kurumans
For their cultural identity please see Appendix-II
Villages without Scheduled Tribes: There are 2 villages without any scheduled tribe population.
Literates and Illiterates by Sex (Total Population):

	Persons	Males	Females
Literate	34,858	19,980	14,878
Illiterate	23,186	9,453	13,733
Literacy rate	67	76	58
Graduate	874	512	362

Agriculture: ***Distribution of villages according to land use:*** Out of 10 villages, Total area (in hectare) is 20428.01, out of that 43.35 percent is cultivable and 18.82 percent of the cultivable area is irrigated.
Sources of Irrigation (Hectares): Government Canal 0, Private Canal 0, Well withoit Electricity 459.12, Well with Electricity 885.05, Tubewell without Electricity 0, Tubewell with Electricity 247.12, Tank 0, River 0, Lake 0, Waterfall 0, Others 0.
Villages with population of 5000 to 9999:
Bilichi, Naickenpalayam, Chinnathadagam Nanjundapuram, Somayampalayam.
Villages with population of 10000 and above:
Pannimadai.
Distribution of Workers:

	Persons	Males	Females	WPR
Cultivators	3,639	2,528	1,111	12.69
Agricultural Labour	6,832	3,548	3,284	23.83
Household Industry	847	496	351	2.95
Other Workers	17,357	12,027	5,330	60.53
Main Workers	25,542	16,989	8,553	89.07
Marginal Workers	3,133	1,610	1,523	10.93
Total Workers	28,675	18,599	10,076	

Religion: Major Religious Communities:

	Persons	Males	Females	Sex Ratio
Hindu (96.77%)	56,169	28,454	27,715	974
Muslim (1%)	583	329	254	772
Christian (2.02%)	1,170	582	588	1,010
Sikh (0%)	1	1	-	-
Buddhists (0%)	-	-	-	-
Jain (0.01%)	8	3	5	1,667

Agewise Data:

	Persons	Males	Females	Sex Ratio
All ages	58,044	29,433	28,611	972
0-14	13,747	7,100	6,647	936
15-44	29,273	14,580	14,693	1008
45-79	13,489	7,013	6,476	923
80+	775	363	412	1135
Age not stated	760	377	383	1016

Languages (Dominant):
Tamil, Kannada, Telugu, Malayalam, Urdu
Disabled Population:

	Persons	Males	Females	%
Total Disabled	1,884	797	1,087	
In Seeing	1,221	391	830	64.81
In Speech	120	60	60	6.37
In Hearing	69	38	31	3.66
In Movement	325	204	121	17.25
Mentally	149	104	45	7.91

PERNAMPATTU

Peranampattu C.D. Block lies in the north-western part of Vellore district. It is a part of Gudiyatham and Vaniyambadi Taluks. The Block is located at a distance of 60 kms. from district headquarters (Vellore). There are 81 villages in the block with the total population of 152,145 persons. Area of the the C.D. Block is 507.93 sq. kms. It is bounded in the south by CD Block Natrampalli and Madhanur, in the east by CD Blocks Gudiyatham and Madhanur, and it has common boundary with the state of Andhra Pradesh on north and west. CD Block Peranampattu falls in taluk Gudiyatham by 44 villages, and in taluk Vaniyambadi by 37 villages.
Communications:
Roadways : N.H.-46: Direction- Vaniyambadi to Vellore, Nearest Village- Kommeswaram.
Railway Station: Melpatti.
Rivers: Kaundiya Nadi- Nearest Villages- Mordana, Jagalapalli (RF), Gundalappali Extn (RF). Malattar Nadi- Nearest Villages- Vasanampalli, Reddimanku, Balur, Kailasagiri, Pallalakuppam (RF), Nariyambattu, Sathambakkam, Kommeswaram, Bavarthapattadai, Aiythampattu, Mayakkaneri (RF), Erukkampattu (RF), Nayakkaneri Extn (RF), Bathalapalli, Erukkampattu, Masigam, Kempasmudram (RF), Kempasamuthiram, Machampattu. Palar Nadi- Nearest Villages- Rajahhal, Reddimankuppam, Alinjikuppam, Melvaithanan Kuppam, Melpatti, Chinnapallikuppam, Veerankuppam, Kammakrishnapalli, Vellakuttai Extn RF, Parsanampalli, Karumbur, Devalapuram, Labbaimankuppam, Periyavarikkam, Aythampattu, Kommeswaram.
Annual Rainfall: Average Rainfall 949 mm.
Ground Water: Availability of the ground water in the Basin is 4828.50 H.A.M. and the utilization is 9691.35 H.A.M. It belongs to Over Expoited category. Depth to water level varies from 5 to 15 meter below the ground. Most of the wells go down in summer months, according to the Ground Water Estimation Committee.
Forest and Reserved Forest: (Ambur Durg RF)- Nearest

Village- Venkatasamuthiram. (Charakkal)- Nearest Villages- Chanakkal (RF), Bairapalli. (Gundalapalli)- Nearest Villages- Mordana, Gundalappali, Jagalapalli (RF), Morasapalli, Gundalappali Extn (RF), Rangam Pettai, Gundalapalli, Gundalappali (RF), Morasapalli, Pernambat. (Jangalapalli)- Nearest Village- Mordana. (Morddana)- Nearest Villages- Aravatla, Mordana (RF), Rangam Pettai, Gundalapalli. (Erukkampattu)- Nearest Villages- Erukkampattu (RF), Erukkampattu. (Karapattu)- Nearest Villages- Kasapattu (RF), Karapet. (Kempasamudram)- Nearest Villages- Masigam, Kembasmudram (RF), Sarakkal, Reddanakkanur Bathalapalli, (RF), Kempasamuthiram, Balur, Machampattu. (Nayakkaneri)- Nearest Villages- Mayakkaneri (RF), Nayakkaneri Extn (RF). (Pallalakuppam)- Nearest Villages- Erikuthi, T.T. Mottoor, Kothapalli, Melkothakuppam, Chinnadamancherubu, Pallalakuppam, Pallalakuppam (RF), Pogalur, Melvaithanan kuppam, K.Paravakkal, Pallalakuppam, Kothamarikuppam, Nariambattu, Pallalakuppam (RF), Karkoor, Vasanampall, Balur, Chokkarisi Kuppam, Chendathur, Melmuragai, Melpatti, Pallalakuppam (RF). (Peddur)- Nearest Villages- Ambur Drug (RF), Paddur (RF), Peddur (RF), Eachampattu.

Natural Division: Tondai Nadu.

Administration

Revenue **Division:** Vellore, Tirupatahur. Parliamentary Constituency: 8 Vellore., District: Vellore. Taluk: Gudiyatham, Vaniyambadi. Assembly Constituency: 46 Gudiy atham, 48 Ambur (SC). Gram Panchayat: 51.

Border Villages- (Andhra Pardesh)- Nearest Villages- Mayakkaneri (RF), Mordana (RF), Mordana, Jagalapalli (RF), Erukkampattu (RF), Nayakkaweri Extn (RF), Reddana kkanur (RF), Chanakkal (RF), Paddur (RF), Kasapattu (RF), Peddur (RF), Aravatla.

Villages: 81 **Inhabited:** 62 **Uninhabited:** 19

Ranking	District	State	National
Area	2	36	1468
Population	2	13	1802
Sex Ratio	8	150	1086
Child Sex Ratio	1	46	1017
Literacy Rate	14	187	1733
Density	14	333	3528
Work Participation Rate	17	229	4015

Gram Panchayats:

Alinjikuppam, Aravatla, Balur, Bathalapalli, Chendathur, Chinnadaman Cheruvu, Chokkarishikuppam, Erikuthi, Erukkampattu, Gundalapalli, Karkur, Kothapalli, Kothur, Machampattu, Mailpatti, Masigam, Melvaithinankuppam, Morasappalli, Mordana, Pallalakuppam, Paravakkal, Pogalur, Rajakkal, Sathkar, Thottithoraimottur, Aragaldurgam, Ayiathambattu, Bapanapalli, Chinnapallikuppam, Chinnavarikam, Devalapuram, Gollakuppam, Kadhavalam, Kailasagiri, Karumbur, Komeswaram, Kumaramangalam , Malayampattu, Melshanankuppam, Mittalam, Mothugapalli, Nariambattu, Parasanapalli, Periavarigam, Sathambakkam, Thennambattu, Vadacheri, Vadakarai, Veerankuppam, Vengatasamudram.

Amenities:

Education: Primary School in 58 villages, Middle school in 27 villages, Matriculation or Secondary School in 12 villages, namely T.T. Mottoor, Pernambat, Pallalakuppam, Machampattu, Alinjikuppam, Kailasagiri, Nariyampattu, Karapet, Karumbur, Devalapuram, Gollakuppam, Vadacheri.

Higher Secondary or Pre University Courses or Intermediate or Junior College in 4 villages of the CD Block,, namely Pernambat, Karumbur, Malayambut, Vadacheri. College in 0 village, Adult Literacy Center in 0 village.

Medical: Hospital in 1 village, Dispensary in 2 villages, Health Center in 6 villages, Sub Center in 7 villages, Maternity and Child Welfare Center in 13 villages, Community health workers in 61 villages.

The Villages having Hospital or Dispensary or Health Center are Pernambat, Pallalakuppam, Karkoor, Alinjikuppam.

Drinking Water: Tap water in 61 villages, Tank water in 8 villages, Well water in 19 villages, Tubewell in 15 villages and more than one source in 62 villages.

Bank: Banking facility in 12 villages, namely, Morasapalli, Pernambat, Melkothakuppam, Rajahhal Chendathur, Melpatti, Kailasagiri, Karapet, Karumbur Maniyarkuppam, Melsanakuppam, Vadacheri.

Credit Society in 15 villages Agricultural Credit Society in 14 Non-Agricultural Credit Society in 5 villages.

Others: Power supply in 62 villages, Cinema hall in 4 villages, sport club in 0 village, Stadium or Auditorium or Community Hall in 0 village, Post Office in 53 villages.

There are 55 villages having bus facilities.

Villages with most of facilities: Pernambat Melkothakuppam, Rajahhal, Chendathur, Melpatti Kailasagiri, Karapet, Karumbur, Maniyarkuppam Melsanakuppam, Vadacheri.

Villages without amenities (Education):

Rangam Pettai, Kothamarikuppam, Vasanampalli, Venkatasamuthiram..

Scheduled Castes: Out of the total population of 152145 persons, 55213 persons (36.29%) belong to Scheduled Castes.

The villages having less than 10% SC population are Gundalapalli, Melmuragai, Bairapalli Kammakrishnapalli, Thennambut.

The villages having more than 50% SC population are

Pernambat, Kothapalli, Masigam, Kothamarikuppam Karkoor, Bavarthapattadai, Aythampattu Periyavarikkam, Maniyarkuppam, Vadakarai Melsanakuppam.

Sex ratio of Scheduled Caste population is 506.

Scheduled Castes Literates and Illiterates by Sex:

	Persons	Males	Females
Literate	29,336	16,642	12,694
Illiterate	25,877	10,612	15,265
Literacy rate	61.8	71.1	52.8
Graduate	383	289	94

Scheduled Castes (Dominant):

Adi Dravida, Arunthathiyar, Valluvan, Kuravan etc. Adi Andhra

For their cultural identity please see Appendix-I

Villages without Scheduled Castes: There are 20 villages without any scheduled caste population.

Scheduled Tribes: Out of the total population of 152145 persons, 1794 persons (1.18%) belong to Scheduled Tribes. The villages having less than 10% ST population are Aravatla, Mordana, Rangam Pettai, Gundalapalli Bathalapalli, Erukkambut, Erikuthi, Morasapalli T.T. Mottoor, Pernambat, Kothapalli Chinnadamancherubu, Masigam, Sarakkal Kempasamuthiram, Pallalakuppam, Pogalur, Paravakkal Kothamarikuppam, Karkoor, Vasanampalli, Balur Machampattu, Melkothakuppam, Rajahhal Reddimankuppam, Chokkarisi Kuppam, Chendathur Melmuragai, Alinjikuppam, Melvaithanan Kuppam Melpatti, Bairapalli, Kailasagiri, Nariyampattu Sathambakkam, Kommeswaram, Bavarthapattadai Aythampattu, Chinnavarikkam, Mittalam Venkatasamuthiram, Karapet, Kadavalam, Parsanampalli Karumbur, Devalapuram, Labbaimankuppam Periyavarikkam, Kammakrishnapalli, Kumaramangalam Malayambut, Thennambut, Maniyarkuppam, Veerankuppam Vadakarai, Melsanakuppam, Chinnapallikuppam Eachampattu, Gollakuppam, Vadacheri, Papanapalli. The villages having more than 50% ST population are None.

Sex ratio of Scheduled tribe population is 512.

Scheduled Tribes Literates and Illiterates by Sex:

	Persons	Males	Females
Literate	521	306	215
Illiterate	1,273	570	703
Literacy rate	34.5	42.2	27.4
Graduate	2	2	0

Scheduled Tribes (Dominant):

Irular, Malakkuravan, Generic Tribes etc., Kurumans Adiyan

For their cultural identity please see Appendix-II

Villages without Scheduled Tribes: There are 50 villages without any scheduled tribe population.

Literates and Illiterates by Sex (Total Population):

	Persons	Males	Females
Literate	87,571	50,129	37,442
Illiterate	64,574	25,819	38,755
Literacy rate	66	76	56
Graduate	1,574	1,196	378

Agriculture: ***Distribution of villages according to land use:*** Out of 81 villages, Total area (in hectare) is 50793.67, out of that 36.59 percent is cultivable and 12.77 percent of the cultivable area is irrigated.

Sources of Irrigation (Hectares): Government Canal 0, Private Canal 0, Well without Electricity 151.44, Well with Electricity 2180.46, Tubewell without Electricity 0, Tubewell with Electricity 42.37, Tank 0, River 0, Lake 0, Waterfall 0, Others 0.

Villages with population of 5000 to 9999: Erikuthi, Pernambut , Balur, Kailasagiri Vengatasamudram.

Villages with population of 10000 and above: None

Distribution of Workers:

	Persons	Males	Females	WPR
Cultivators	8,243	6,653	1,590	12.85
Agricultural Labour	28,938	15,928	13,010	45.12
Household Industry	4,922	2,742	2,180	7.67
Other Workers	22,032	16,799	5,233	34.35
Main Workers	50,154	35,229	14,925	78.2
Marginal Workers	13,981	6,893	7,088	21.8
Total Workers	64,135	42,122	22,013	

Religion: Major Religious Communities:

	Persons	Males	Females	Sex Ratio
Hindu (90.14%)	137,148	68,187	68,961	1,011
Muslim (7.06%)	10,747	5,633	5,114	908
Christian (2.72%)	4,132	2,076	2,056	990
Sikh (0.03%)	39	17	22	1,294
Buddhists (0.01%)	8	4	4	1,000
Jain (0.01%)	17	9	8	889

Agewise Data:

	Persons	Males	Females	Sex Ratio
All ages	152,145	75,948	76,197	1003
0-14	47,254	23,893	23,361	978
15-44	72,718	36,220	36,498	1008
45-79	30,567	15,069	15,498	1028
80+	1,290	594	696	1172
Age not stated	316	172	144	837

Languages (Dominant):

Tamil, Telugu, Urdu, Kannada, Marathi

Disabled Population:

	Persons	Males	Females	%
Total Disabled	3,980	2,195	1,785	
In Seeing	2,331	1,217	1,114	58.57
In Speech	314	181	133	7.89
In Hearing	122	59	63	3.07
In Movement	895	576	319	22.49
Mentally	318	162	156	7.99

PERUNDURAI

Perundurai C.D. Block lies in the central western part of Erode district. It is a part of Perundurai taluk. The Block is located at a distance of 20 kms. from district headquarters (Erode). There are 39 villages in the block with the total population of 67,999 persons. Area of the C.D. Block is 177.66 sq. kms. It is bounded in the north by CD Block Bhavani, in the south by C.D. Block Chennimalai, in the east by CD Block Erode, in the west by CD Blocks Nambiur and Gobichettipalayam, and district Coimbatore.

Communications:

Roadways : N.H.-47: Direction- Vijayapuri to Erode, Nearest Villages- Kandampalayam, Periyavilamalai, Thiruvachi, Poovampalayam, Moongelpalayam, Ponmudi, Kampiliampatti.

Annual Rainfall: Average Rainfall 789 mm.

Ground Water: Availability of the ground water in the Basin is 4499.07 H.A.M. and the utilization is 4175.74 H.A.M. It belongs to Critical category. Depth to water level varies from 0 to 20 meter below the ground. Most of the wells go down in summer months, according to the Ground Water Estimation Committee.

Natural Division: Kongu Nadu.

Administration

Revenue **Division:** Erode. Parliamentary Constituency: 18 Gobichettipalayam. District: Erode. Taluk: Perundurai. Assembly Constituency: 103 Perundurai.

Gram Panchayat: 29.

Villages: 39 **Inhabited:** 39 **Uninhabited:** 0

Ranking	District	State	National
Area	16	314	4572
Population	10	296	4561
Sex Ratio	14	321	2672
Child Sex Ratio	9	250	4084
Literacy Rate	7	323	2762
Density	12	28	2859
Work Participation Rate	7	128	231

Gram Panchayats:

Kallakulam, Kambiliampatti, Kandampalayam, Karandipalayam, Karukkapalayam, Kullampalayam, Madathupalayam, Mettupudur, Moongilpalayam, Mullampatti, Nichampalayam, Pandiampalayam, Pappampalayam, Pattackarampalayam, Periyaveerasangili, Periyavilamalai, Polanaickampalayam, Ponmudi, Seenapuram, Sellappampalayam, Singanallur, Sinnavirasangili, Sullipalayam, Thingalur, Thiruvachi, Thoranavavi, Thuduppathi, Vettaiankinar.

Amenities:

Education: Primary School in 33 villages, Middle school in 7 villages, Matriculation or Secondary School in 5 villages, namely Thingalur, Pandiampalayam, Palakarai, Seenapuram, Ponmudi.

Higher Secondary or Pre University Courses or Intermediate or Junior College in 3 villages of the CD Block,, namely Thingalur, Palakarai, Ponmudi.

College in 2 villages, Adult Literacy Center in 0 village., Colleges are in villages, namely Palakarai, Thuduppathy.

Medical: Hospital in 2 villages, Dispensary in 2 villages, Health Center in 1 village, Sub Center in 19 villages, Maternity and Child Welfare Center in 4 villages, Community health workers in 2 villages.

The Villages having Hospital or Dispensary or Health Center are Thingalur, Nicham Palayam, Pandiampalayam, Seenapuram.

Drinking Water: Tap water in 39 villages, Tank water in 0 villages, Well water in 39 villages, Tubewell in 39 villages and more than one source in 39 villages.

Bank: Banking facility in 7 villages, namely, Thingalur, Karukkupalayam, Chinnamallam Palayam Karandhipalayam, Mettupudur, Thuduppathy Sullipalayam.

Credit Society in 10 villages Agricultural Credit Society in 9 Non-Agricultural Credit Society in 2 villages.

Others: Power supply in 39 villages, Cinema hall in 1 village, sport club in 0 village, Stadium or Auditorium or Community Hall in 1 village, Post Office in 29 villages.

There are 35 villages having bus facilities.

Villages with most of facilities: Thingalur Karukkupalayam, Thuduppathy, Sullipalayam.

Villages without amenities (Education): Sungagaranpalayam, Poovampalayam, Chinnamallam Palayam, Unjampalayam, Marappanaikam Palayam..

Scheduled Castes: Out of the total population of 67999 persons, 10978 persons (16.14%) belong to Scheduled Castes.

The villages having less than 10% SC population are Vettainkinar, Sungagaranpalayam, Kandampalayam Periyavilamalai, Sellappampalayam, Karandhipalayam Pappampalayam, Periaveerasangali, Mettupudur Ayeegoundanpalayam, Kullampalayam.

The villages having more than 50% SC population are

None.

Sex ratio of Scheduled Caste population is 495.

Scheduled Castes Literates and Illiterates by Sex:

	Persons	Males	Females
Literate	3,852	2,282	1,570
Illiterate	7,126	3,260	3,866
Literacy rate	39.9	46.5	33.0
Graduate	63	44	19

Scheduled Castes (Dominant):

Chakkiliyan, Arunthathiyar, Adi Dravida
Kuravan etc., Madari

For their cultural identity please see Appendix-I

Villages without Scheduled Castes: There are 2 villages without any scheduled caste population.

Scheduled Tribes: Out of the total population of 67999 persons, 0 persons (0%) belong to Scheduled Tribes.

The villages having less than 10% ST population are Doranavavi, Madathupalayam, Vettainkinar Sungagaranpalayam, Thingalur, Karukkupalayam Nicham Palayam, Pandiampalayam, Singanallur Olapalayam, Mullampatti, Kandampalayam Periyavilamalai, Chinnavilamalai, Thiruvachi Poovampalayam, Palakarai, Chinnamallam Palayam Namitipalayam, Unjampalayam, Kallakulam Sellappampalayam, Thalaiyampalayam Balanaicanpalayam, Karandhipalayam, Pappampalayam Chinnaveerasangali, Periaveerasangali Marappanaikam Palayam, Moongelpalayam, Mettupudur Ayeegoundanpalayam, Seenapuram, Thuduppathy Sullipalayam, Pattakaran Palayam, Kullampalayam Ponmudi, Kampiliampatti.

The villages having more than 50% ST population are None.

Scheduled Tribes Literates and Illiterates by Sex:

	Persons	Males	Females
Literate	0	0	0
Illiterate	0	0	0
Literacy rate	-	-	-
Graduate	0	0	0

Villages without Scheduled Tribes: There are 39 villages without any scheduled tribe population.

Literates and Illiterates by Sex (Total Population):

	Persons	Males	Females
Literate	36,911	22,153	14,758
Illiterate	31,088	12,436	18,652
Literacy rate	60	71	49
Graduate	1,225	851	374

Agriculture: *Distribution of villages according to land use:* Out of 39 villages, Total area (in hectare) is 17766.52, out of that 87.51 percent is cultivable and 20.61 percent of the cultivable area is irrigated.

Sources of Irrigation (Hectares): Government Canal 1309.56, Private Canal 0, Well without Electricity 103.53, Well with Electricity 1565.08, Tubewell without Electricity 0, Tubewell with Electricity 151.62, Tank 75.4, River 0, Lake 0, Waterfall 0, Others 0.

Villages with population of 5000 to 9999: None

Villages with population of 10000 and above: None

Distribution of Workers:

	Persons	Males	Females	WPR
Cultivators	11,163	6,453	4,710	26.68
Agricultural Labour	13,377	6,534	6,843	31.97
Household Industry	2,182	1,139	1,043	5.21
Other Workers	15,120	9,887	5,233	36.14
Main Workers	37,986	22,644	15,342	90.78
Marginal Workers	3,856	1,369	2,487	9.22
Total Workers	41,842	24,013	17,829	

Religion: Major Religious Communities:

	Persons	Males	Females	Sex Ratio
Hindu (97.24%)	66,121	33,672	32,449	964
Muslim (0.58%)	395	185	210	1,135
Christian (2.07%)	1,406	685	721	1,053
Sikh (0.03%)	18	13	5	385
Buddhists (0%)	2	2	-	-
Jain (0%)	1	-	1	-

Agewise Data:

	Persons	Males	Females	Sex Ratio
All ages	67,998	34,589	33,409	966
0-14	14,703	7,579	7,124	940
15-44	32,526	16,312	16,214	994
45-79	19,471	10,022	9,449	943
80+	978	505	473	937
Age not stated	320	171	149	871

Languages (Dominant):

Tamil, Telugu, Kannada, Urdu, Malayalam

Disabled Population:

	Persons	Males	Females	%
Total Disabled	1,181	471	710	
In Seeing	677	173	504	57.32
In Speech	117	62	55	9.91
In Hearing	71	38	33	6.01
In Movement	228	152	76	19.31
Mentally	88	46	42	7.45

PETHANAICKENPALAYAM

Pethanaickenpalayam C.D. Block lies in the eastern part of Salem district. It is a part of Attur taluk. The Block is located at a distance of 40 kms. from district headquarters (Salem). There are 49 villages in the block with the total Pop. of 92,581 persons. Area of it is 515.56 sq. kms. It is bounded in the north by districts Dharmapuri and Villuppuram, in the south by district Namakkal, and CD Blocks Attur and Talavasal, in the east by district Viluppuram, and in the west by CD Block Vazhapadi.

Communications:

Roadways : N.H.-68: Direction- Salem to Attur, Nearest Villages- Veeragoundanoor, Mettupalayam (Ui), Periyakrishnapuram, Puthirgoundanpalayam.

River: Vasista Nadi- Nearest Villages- Thumbal, Nayyamalai, Edaiyappatti, Penamadal, Sekkadipatti, Kumarapalayam, Puthirgoundanpalayam, Kalyanagiri, Kottavadi, Mettudayampalayam, Periyakrishnapuram, Chinna Krishnapuram, Vadugathampati, Thamayanoor, West Rajapalayam.

Railway Station: Puthirgoundanpalayam.

Annual Rainfall: Average Rainfall 540 mm.

Ground Water: Availability of the ground water in the Basin is 8208.99 H.A.M. and the utilization is 16361. 39 H.A.M. It belongs to Safe category. Depth to water level varies from 5 to 50 meter below the ground. Most of the wells go down in summer months, according to the Ground Water Estimation Committee.

Forest and Reserved Forest: (Aruna RF)- Nearest Villages- Malayalappatti, Chinnakalrayan Hills Therkunadu, Aruna. (Thumbal Extention)- Nearest Villages- Kariyakoilvalavu, Tumbal, Koilputhur, Malayalappatti, Chinnakalrayan Hills Therkunadu, Tumbal Extn. (Mannur)- Nearest Villages- Mannur, Penamadal, Tumbal, Koilputhur, Soolankurichi, Kellerippatti, Mannur, Kalyanagiri. (Nagalur)- Nearest Villages- Adiyanur, Soolankurichi, Nagalur RF. (Pattimedu)- Nearest Villages- Adiyanur, Pattimedu RF. (Pattimedu Extn)- Nearest Villages- Adiyanur, Kilavari, Pattimedu Extn. (Thirthagiri)- Nearest Villages- Chinnakalrayan Hills Vadakkunadu, Theerathagiri RF.

Natural Division: Kongu Nadu.

Administration

Division. Parliamentary Constituency: 14 Kallakurichi (SC). District Salem. Taluk: Attur. Assembly Constituency: 83 Vazhapadi (SC), 82 Attur. Gram Panchayat: 36.

Villages: 49 **Inhabited:** 46 **Uninhabited:** 3

Ranking	District	State	National
Area	1	34	1434
Population	5	168	3702
Sex Ratio	1	265	2054
Child Sex Ratio	3	298	4997
Literacy Rate	16	370	4051
Density	4	42	5057
Work Participation Rate	20	344	380

Gram Panchayats:

A. Kumarapalayam, Ariyapalayam, Belurkaradipatti, ChinnakalrayanHills Therkunadu, ChinnakalrayanHills Vadakkunadu, Chinnaksrishnapuram, Dalavaipatti, Dalavopatty, Edaiyappatti, Etapur Karadipatti, Gopalapuram, Kalarampatty, Kalleripatty, Kalyanagiri, Kottavadi, Mettudayampalayam, Muthagoundanur, Oddapatty, Olappadi, Palaniyapuri, Panamadal , Pappanaickenpatty, Periakriashnapuram, Periyakalarayanmalai keelanadu, Periyakalrayanmalaikeelnadu, Periyakalrayanmalaimelandu, Periyakriashnapuram, Puthiragoundampalayam , Sekkadipatti, Thamayanoor, Thandanoor, Thennampillaiyur, Thumbal, Umayalpuram, Vadugathampatti, Veeragoundanoor, Vellalapatti, Vidyagoundanpudur, West Rajapalayam, .

Amenities:

Education: Primary School in 38 villages, Middle school in 15 villages, Matriculation or Secondary School in 8 villages, namely Penamadal, Thumbal, Kottavadi, Ariyapalayam, Gopalapuram, Chinnakalrayan Hills Vadakkunadu, Periyakrishnapuram, Puthirgoundanpalayam.

Higher Secondary or Pre University Courses or Intermediate or Junior College in 2 villages of the CD Block,, namely Thumbal, Puthirgoundanpalayam.

College in 0 village, Adult Literacy Center in 0 village.

Medical: Hospital in 0 village, Dispensary in 0 village, Health Center in 6 villages, Sub Center in 13 villages, Maternity and Child Welfare Center in 0 village, Community health workers in 1 village.

Drinking Water: Tap water in 46 villages, Tank water in 0 villages, Well water in 46 villages, Tubewell in 46 villages and more than one source in 46 villages.

Bank: Banking facility in 9 villages, namely, Penamadal, Thumbal, Edaiyappatti, Belurkaradipatti Kumarapalayam, Chinnakalrayan Hills Vadakkunadu Periyakrishnapuram, Puthirgoundanpalayam, Oddappatti. Credit Society in 32 villages Agricultural Credit Society in 18 Non-Agricultural Credit Society in 27 villages.

Others: Power supply in 42 villages, Cinema hall in 3 villages, sport club in 0 village, Stadium or Auditorium or Community Hall in 0 village, Post Office in 31 villages.

There are 33 villages having bus facilities.

Villages with most of facilities: Penamadal Thumbal, Edaiyappatti, Kumarapalayam Chinnakalrayan Hills Vadakkunadu, Periyakrishnapuram Puthirgoundanpalayam.

Villages without amenities (Education): Mannur, Tumbal, Belurkaradipatti, Mettupalayam (Ui), Kilavari, Aruna, Tumbal Extn., Pattimedu Extn..

Scheduled Castes: Out of the total population of 92581 persons, 15558 persons (16.8%) belong to Scheduled Castes. The villages having less than 10% SC population are

Mannur , Adiyanur, Kariyakoilvalavu, Koilputhur
Chinna Krishnapuram, Soolankurichi, Belurkaradipatti
Malayalappatti, Rangappanaicken Palayam
Veeragoundanoor, Kottavadi, Mettupalayam (Ui)
Mannur, Chinnakalrayan Hills Therkunadu, Gopalapuram
Nayyamalai, Chinnakalrayan Hills Vadakkunadu
Kilavari, Aruna , Kalyanagiri, Kunnur
Pattimedu Extn.

The villages having more than 50% SC population are Mettudayampalayam, Tumbal Extn. Puthirgoundanpalayam.

Sex ratio of Scheduled Caste population is 497.

Scheduled Castes Literates and Illiterates by Sex:

	Persons	Males	Females
Literate	7,567	4,558	3,009
Illiterate	7,991	3,268	4,723
Literacy rate	55.9	67.3	44.5
Graduate	186	166	20

Scheduled Castes (Dominant):

Paraiyan etc., Arunthathiyar, Adi Dravida, Pallan Valluvan

For their cultural identity please see Appendix-I

Villages without Scheduled Castes: There are 13 villages without any scheduled caste population.

Scheduled Tribes: Out of the total population of 92581 persons, 28303 persons (30.57%) belong to Scheduled Tribes.

The villages having less than 10% ST population are Penamadal, Mettudayampalayam, Thumbal, Tumbal
Ethapur Karadippatti, Edaiyappatti, Palaniyapuri
Sekkadipatti, Chinna Krishnapuram, Belurkaradipatti
Rangappanaicken Palayam, Thamayanoor
Veeragoundanoor, Olappadi, Kelleripppatti, Kottavadi
Mettupalayam (Ui), Kumarapalayam, Thennam Pillaiyur
Dalavoipatti, Kalarampatti, Ariyapalayam
Gopalapuram, Vadugathampatti, Umaiyalpuram
Periyakrishnapuram, Kalyanagiri, Tumbal Extn.
Puthirgoundanpalayam, Oddappatti, West Rajapalayam
Muthugoundanoor.

The villages having more than 50% ST population are
Mannur , Adiyanur, Kariyakoilvalavu, Koilputhur
Soolankurichi, Malayalappatti, Mannur
Chinnakalrayan Hills Therkunadu, Nayyamalai
Chinnakalrayan Hills Vadakkunadu, Kilavari, Aruna
Kunnur, Pattimedu Extn.

Sex ratio of Scheduled tribe population is 495.

Scheduled Tribes Literates and Illiterates by Sex:

	Persons	Males	Females
Literate	5,383	3,436	1,947
Illiterate	22,920	10,850	12,070
Literacy rate	22.2	28.2	16.2
Graduate	38	34	4

Scheduled Tribes (Dominant):

Malayali, Generic Tribes etc., Kurumans
Malakkuravan, Irular

For their cultural identity please see Appendix-II

Villages without Scheduled Tribes: There are 20 villages without any scheduled tribe population.

Literates and Illiterates by Sex (Total Population):

	Persons	Males	Females
Literate	42,830	25,339	17,491
Illiterate	49,751	21,433	28,318
Literacy rate	53	62	43
Graduate	1,301	1,014	287

Agriculture: ***Distribution of villages according to land use:*** Out of 49 villages, Total area (in hectare) is 51556.53, out of that 45 percent is cultivable and 29.99 percent of the cultivable area is irrigated.

Sources of Irrigation (Hectares): Government Canal 310.72, Private Canal 0, Well without Electricity 230.25, Well with Electricity 5416.7, Tubewell without Electricity 111.78, Tubewell with Electricity 488.86, Tank 179.96, River 0, Lake 203.95, Waterfall 0, Others 15.35.

Villages with population of 5000 to 9999: Tumbal, ChinnakalrayanHillsvadakkunadu, Panaimadal Sekkadipatti.

Villages with population of 10000 and above: None

Distribution of Workers:

	Persons	Males	Females	WPR
Cultivators	27,017	15,187	11,830	50.01
Agricultural Labour	19,452	8,619	10,833	36.01
Household Industry	1,177	593	584	2.18
Other Workers	6,376	4,907	1,469	11.8
Main Workers	46,896	26,800	20,096	86.81
Marginal Workers	7,126	2,506	4,620	13.19
Total Workers	54,022	29,306	24,716	

Religion: Major Religious Communities:

	Persons	Males	Females	Sex Ratio
Hindu (98.39%)	91,091	46,051	45,040	978
Muslim (1.06%)	978	474	504	1,063
Christian (0.54%)	496	238	258	1,084
Sikh (0%)	1	1	-	-
Buddhists (0%)	-	-	-	-
Jain (0%)	1	1	-	-

Agewise Data:

	Persons	Males	Females	Sex Ratio
All ages	92,581	46,772	45,809	979
0-14	27,134	14,045	13,089	932
15-44	45,733	22,752	22,981	1010
45-79	18,930	9,545	9,385	983
80+	653	368	285	774

Age not stated	131	62	69	1113

Languages (Dominant):

Tamil, Telugu, Urdu, Malayalam, Others

Disabled Population:

	Persons	Males	Females	%
Total Disabled	1,232	694	538	
In Seeing	472	240	232	38.31
In Speech	122	66	56	9.9
In Hearing	107	50	57	8.69
In Movement	425	267	158	34.5
Mentally	106	71	35	8.6

POLLACHI NORTH

Pollachi North C.D. Block lies in the south-western part of Coimbatore district. It is a part of Pollachi taluk. The Block is located at a distance of 40 kms. from district headquarters (Coimbatore). There are 43 villages in the block with the total population of 89,227 persons. Area of the C.D. Block is 257.03 sq. kms. It is bounded in the north by C.D. Block Kinathukadau in the south by C.D. Blocks Pollachi South and Anamalai, in the east by taluk Udumalaipettai, and in the west it has common boundary with the state of Kerala.

Communications:

Roadways : N.H.-209: Direction- Kinathukadavu to Palani, Nearest Villages- Santhegounden Palayam, Okkilipalayam, Kurubapalayam, Kittasurampalayam, Thippampatty. S.H.-19: Direction- Palghat to Palladam, Nearest Villages- Chandrapuram, Kallippatti, Avalampatti, Vellalapalayam, Thoppampatti, Rosakkapalayam, Puliyampatti, Bodipalayam, Kullakapalayam, Kulathur. S.H.-21: Direction- Chinnampalayam to Dharapuram, Nearest Villages- Anupperpalayam, Poosaripatti, Boligoundenpalayam, Eripatti.

Railway Station: Thippampatty.

River: Aliyar Nadi- Nearest Villages- Mannur, Timmankuthu, Kulathur, Servakaranpalayam.

Annual Rainfall: Average Rainfall 550 mm.

Ground Water: Availability of the ground water in the Basin is 5818.92 H.A.M. and the utilization is 7059.93 H.A.M. It belongs to Semi Critical category. Depth to water level varies from 2 to 20 meter below the ground. Most of the wells go down in summer months, according to the Ground Water Estimation Committee.

Natural Division: Kongu Nadu.

Administration

Revenue **Division:** Pollachi. Parliamentary Constituency: 21 Pollachi. District: Coimbatore. Taluk: Pollachi. Assembly Constituency: 123 Pollachi. Gram Panchayat: 39.

Border Villages- (Kerala)- Nearest Villages- Servakaran Palayam, Ramapattinam, Mannur, Timmankuthu.

Villages: 43 **Inhabited:** 43 **Uninhabited:** 0

Ranking	District	State	National
Area	11	221	3287
Population	5	187	3802
Sex Ratio	4	214	1480
Child Sex Ratio	2	6	208
Literacy Rate	9	207	1900
Density	5	109	3124
Work Participation Rate	5	163	1117

Gram Panchayats:

A. Nagoor, Anupparpalayam, Avalappampatti, Ayyampalayam, Bodipalayam, Boligoundenpalayam, Chandrapuram, Chikkarayapuram, chinna Negamam, Devambadi, Eripatti, Gollapatti, Kabilipalayam, Kallipatti, Kittasurampalayam, Kondegoundenpalayam, Kullakkalpalayam, Kullichettipalayam, Kurumbapalayam, Mannur, Mulanur, Nalluthukuli, Okkilipalayam, Poosaripatti, Poravipalayam, Puliampatti, R. Ponnapuram, Ramapattanam, Rasakkapalayam, Rasichettipalayam, Santhegoundanpalayam, Servakaranpalayam, Thalakkarai , Thimmankuthu, Thippampatti, Vadakkipalayam, Vellalapalayam, Zamin Muthur.

Amenities:

Education: Primary School in 43 villages, Middle school in 18 villages, Matriculation or Secondary School in 6 villages, namely Poravipalayam, Devampady, Ramapattinam, Puliyampatti, Gollapatti, Nagoor.

Higher Secondary or Pre University Courses or Intermediate or Junior College in 1 village of the CD Block,, namely Nagoor.

College in 1 village, Adult Literacy Center in 0 village., Colleges are in villages, namely Thippampatty.

Medical: Hospital in 1 village, Dispensary in 0 village, Health Center in 2 villages, Sub Center in 26 villages, Maternity and Child Welfare Center in 4 villages, Community health workers in 4 villages.

The Village having Hospital or Dispensary or Health Center is Poosaripatti.

Drinking Water: Tap water in 43 villages, Tank water in 0 villages, Well water in 43 villages, Tubewell in 43 villages and more than one source in 43 villages.

Bank: Banking facility in 6 villages, namely, Vadakkipalayam, Ramapattinam, Avalampatti Puliyampatti, Kittasurampalayam, Poosaripatti.

Credit Society in 13 villages Agricultural Credit Society in 12 Non-Agricultural Credit Society in 1 village.

Others: Power supply in 43 villages, Cinema hall in 0 village, sport club in 0 village, Stadium or Auditorium or Community Hall in 1 village, Post Office in 35 villages.

There are 42 villages having bus facilities.

Villages with most of facilities: Vadakkipalayam Ramapattinam, Avalampatti, Puliyampatti Kittasurampalayam, Poosaripatti.

Villages without Amenities (Education): None..

Scheduled Castes: Out of the total population of 89227 persons, 19269 persons (21.6%) belong to Scheduled Castes.

The villages having less than 10% SC population are None..

The villages having more than 50% SC population are None.

Sex ratio of Scheduled Caste population is 501.

Scheduled Castes Literates and Illiterates by Sex:

	Persons	Males	Females
Literate	7,240	4,204	3,036
Illiterate	12,029	5,412	6,617
Literacy rate	43.4	50.1	36.5
Graduate	13	13	0

Scheduled Castes (Dominant):

Madari, Chakkiliyan, Arunthathiyar, Adi Dravida Kuravan etc.

For their cultural identity please see Appendix-I

Villages without Scheduled Castes: There is 1 village without any scheduled caste population.

Scheduled Tribes: Out of the total population of 89227 persons, 429 persons (0.48%) belong to Scheduled Tribes.

The villages having less than 10% ST population are Poravipalayam, Servakaran Palayam, Vadakkipalayam Chandrapuram, Chinnegamam, Santhegounden Palayam Kullichettipalayam, Poosanaickendhali, Devampady Ramapattinam, Thalakkarai, Chikkarayapuram Kavilipalayam, Okkilipalayam, Kurubapalayam Kullakapalayam, Kallippatti, Kondegounderpalayam Mulanur, Avalampatti, Vellalapalayam, Thoppampatti Rosakkapalayam, Puliyampatti, R.Ponnapuram Kittasurampalayam, Anupperpalayam, Gollapatti Nagoor, Poosaripatti, Boligoundenpalayam, Eripatti Zaminmuthur, Ayyampalayam, Nallathukuli Kumarapalayam, Mannur, Timmankuthu Rasichettypalayam, Bodipalayam, Thippampatty Kulathur, Servakaranpalayam.

The villages having more than 50% ST population are None.

Sex ratio of Scheduled tribe population is 508.

Scheduled Tribes Literates and Illiterates by Sex:

	Persons	Males	Females
Literate	75	43	32
Illiterate	354	168	186
Literacy rate	20.7	24.3	17.2
Graduate	0	0	0

Scheduled Tribes (Dominant):

Malasar, Eravallan, Malai Pandaram, Mudugar etc. Kurumans

For their cultural identity please see Appendix-II

Villages without Scheduled Tribes: There are 31 villages without any scheduled tribe population.

Literates and Illiterates by Sex (Total Population):

	Persons	Males	Females
Literate	52,045	30,102	21,943
Illiterate	37,182	14,698	22,484
Literacy rate	65	75	55
Graduate	642	412	230

Agriculture: ***Distribution of villages according to land use:*** Out of 43 villages, Total area (in hectare) is 25703.08, out of that 90.86 percent is cultivable and 54.28 percent of the cultivable area is irrigated.

Sources of Irrigation (Hectares): Government Canal 2580.43, Private Canal 0, Well without Electricity 94.77, Well with Electricity 10002.27, Tubewell without Electricity 0, Tubewell with Electricity 0, Tank 0, River 0, Lake 0, Waterfall 0, Others 0.

Villages with population of 5000 to 9999: Poravipalayam, Ramapatinam.

Villages with population of 10000 and above: None

Distribution of Workers:

	Persons	Males	Females	WPR
Cultivators	8,884	6,001	2,883	17.89
Agricultural Labour	23,043	11,146	11,897	46.41
Household Industry	2,100	1,312	788	4.23
Other Workers	15,626	11,657	3,969	31.47
Main Workers	44,522	28,320	16,202	89.67
Marginal Workers	5,131	1,796	3,335	10.33
Total Workers	49,653	30,116	19,537	

Religion: Major Religious Communities:

	Persons	Males	Females	Sex Ratio
Hindu (96.94%)	86,495	43,437	43,058	991
Muslim (2.23%)	1,990	998	992	994
Christian (0.68%)	609	303	306	1,010
Sikh (0%)	2	-	2	-
Buddhists (0%)	-	-	-	-
Jain (0%)	2	2	-	-

Agewise Data:

	Persons	Males	Females	Sex Ratio
All ages	89,227	44,800	44,427	992
0-14	20,317	10,151	10,166	1001
15-44	43,821	21,760	22,061	1014
45-79	23,233	11,906	11,327	951
80+	1,015	540	475	880
Age not stated	841	443	398	898

Languages (Dominant):

Tamil, Telugu, Kannada, Malayalam, Urdu

Disabled Population:

	Persons	Males	Females	%
Total Disabled	2,276	1,071	1,205	
In Seeing	1,424	571	853	62.57
In Speech	127	71	56	5.58
In Hearing	122	55	67	5.36
In Movement	412	267	145	18.1
Mentally	191	107	84	8.39

POLLACHI SOUTH

Pollachi South C.D. Block lies in the southern part of Coimbatore district. It is a part of Pollachi taluk. The Block is located at a distance of 40 kms. from district headquarters (Coimbatore). There are 25 villages in the block with the total population of 65,659 persons. Area of the C.D. Block is 177.38 sq. kms. It is bounded in the north by C.D. Block Pollachi north, in the south by C.D. Block Anamalai and taluk Udumalaipettai, in the east by taluk Udumalaipettai, and in the west by C.D. Block Anamalai.

Communications:

Roadways : N.H.-209: Direction- Pollachi to Palani, Nearest Villages- Unjavelampatti, Makkinampatti, Solapalayam, Nallampalli, Maliyandipattinam, Kolarpatti, Gomangalampudur. S.H.-19: Direction- Palghat to Pollachi, Nearest Village- Ambarampalayam. S.H.-21: Direction- Chinnampalayam to Dharapuram, Nearest Villages- Unjavelampatti, Seelakkampatti, Gomangalam.

Railway Station: Gomangalampudur.

River: Aliyar Nadi- Nearest Villages- Ambarampalayam, Singanallur, Vakkampalayam.

Annual Rainfall: Average Rainfall 550 mm.

Ground Water: Availability of the ground water in the Basin is 2868.52 H.A.M. and the utilization is 5492.74 H.A.M. It belongs to Safe category. Depth to water level varies from 0 to 5 meter below the ground. Most of the wells go down in summer months, according to the Ground Water Estimation Committee.

Natural Division: Kongu Nadu.

Administration

Revenue **Division:** Pollachi. Parliamentary Constituency: 21 Pollachi. District: Coimbatore. Taluk: Pollachi. Assembly Constituency: 124 Anaimalai. Gram Panchayat: 26.

Villages: 25 **Inhabited:** 25 **Uninhabited:** 0

Ranking	District	State	National
Area	15	317	4577
Population	13	310	4663
Sex Ratio	12	314	2600
Child Sex Ratio	13	157	2795
Literacy Rate	4	144	1497
Density	12	176	2949
Work Participation Rate	3	137	1761

Gram Panchayats:

Ambarampalayam, Dhalavaipalayam, Gomangalam, Gomangalampudur, Kanjampatti, Kolarpatti, Koolanaickenpatti, Makkinampatti, Naickenpalayam, Nallampalli, Nattukkalpalayam, Palayur, S. Malayandipattnam, S. Nallur, S. Ponnapuram, Seelakkampatti, Singanallur, Sinjuvadi, Solapalayam, Thenkumarapalayam, Thondamuthur, Unjavelampatti, Vakkampalayam, Veeralpatti, Zamin Kottampatti.

Amenities:

Education: Primary School in 25 villages, Middle school in 12 villages, Matriculation or Secondary School in 5 villages, namely Unjavelampatti, Kanjampatti, Gomangalampudur, S.Nallur, Thondamuthur.

Higher Secondary or Pre University Courses or Intermediate or Junior College in 1 village of the CD Block,, namely S.Nallur.

College in 0 village, Adult Literacy Center in 0 village.

Medical: Hospital in 1 village, Dispensary in 0 village, Health Center in 3 villages, Sub Center in 21 villages, Maternity and Child Welfare Center in 0 village, Community health workers in 3 villages.

The Village having Hospital or Dispensary or Health Center is Ambarampalayam.

Drinking Water: Tap water in 25 villages, Tank water in 0 villages, Well water in 25 villages, Tubewell in 25 villages and more than one source in 25 villages.

Bank: Banking facility in 6 villages, namely, Makkinampatti, Kanjampatti, Nattukalpalayam Singanallur, Gomangalampudur, S.Nallur.

Credit Society in 12 villages Agricultural Credit Society in 8 Non-Agricultural Credit Society in 5 villages.

Others: Power supply in 25 villages, Cinema hall in 0 village, sport club in 0 village, Stadium or Auditorium or Community Hall in 1 village, Post Office in 23 villages.

There are 25 villages having bus facilities.

Villages with most of facilities: Makkinampatti Kanjampatti, Singanallur, Gomangalampudur, S.Nallur.

Villages without Amenities (Education): None..

Scheduled Castes: Out of the total population of 65659 persons, 13355 persons (20.34%) belong to Scheduled Castes. The villages having less than 10% SC population are None..

The villages having more than 50% SC population are None.

Sex ratio of Scheduled Caste population is 492.

Scheduled Castes Literates and Illiterates by Sex:

	Persons	Males	Females
Literate	5,074	3,030	2,044
Illiterate	8,281	3,752	4,529
Literacy rate	43.9	51.8	35.8

Graduate	10	7	3

Scheduled Castes (Dominant):
Madari, Chakkiliyan, Arunthathiyar, Adi Dravida Paraiyan etc.

For their cultural identity please see Appendix-I

Villages without Scheduled Castes: There is 0 village without any scheduled caste population.

Scheduled Tribes: Out of the total population of 65659 persons, 117 persons (0.18%) belong to Scheduled Tribes. The villages having less than 10% ST population are Unjavelampatti, Makkinampatti, Solapalayam Nallampalli, Seelakkampatti, Gomangalam Maliyandipattinam, Kolarpatti, Kanjampatti Nattukalpalayam, Zaminkottompatti, Naikkampalayam Ambarampalayam, Singanallur, Vakkampalayam Ponnapuram, Palaiyoor, Thenkumarapalayam Koolanaickanpatti, Gomangalampudur, Sinjuvadi S.Nallur, Veeralpatti, Thalavaipalayam, Thondamuthur. The villages having more than 50% ST population are None.

Sex ratio of Scheduled tribe population is 556.

Scheduled Tribes Literates and Illiterates by Sex:

	Persons	Males	Females
Literate	59	32	27
Illiterate	58	20	38
Literacy rate	60.8	71.1	51.9
Graduate	0	0	0

Scheduled Tribes (Dominant):
Malai Vedan, Mudugar etc., Eravallan, Malasar Kattunayakan

For their cultural identity please see Appendix-II

Villages without Scheduled Tribes: There are 17 villages without any scheduled tribe population.

Literates and Illiterates by Sex (Total Population):

	Persons	Males	Females
Literate	40,014	23,181	16,833
Illiterate	25,645	10,183	15,462
Literacy rate	68	77	58
Graduate	430	269	161

Agriculture: ***Distribution of villages according to land use:*** Out of 25 villages, Total area (in hectare) is 17738.23, out of that 88.55 percent is cultivable and 54.84 percent of the cultivable area is irrigated.

Sources of Irrigation (Hectares): Government Canal 2523.58, Private Canal 0, Well without Electricity 292.24, Well with Electricity 5761.44, Tubewell without Electricity 0, Tubewell with Electricity 0, Tank 0, River 36.43, Lake 0, Waterfall 0, Others 0.

Villages with population of 5000 to 9999:
Makkinampatti, Z. Kottampatti.

Villages with population of 10000 and above: None

Distribution of Workers:

	Persons	Males	Females	WPR
Cultivators	7,456	4,797	2,659	21.24
Agricultural Labour	14,003	7,122	6,881	39.89
Household Industry	1,438	759	679	4.1
Other Workers	12,204	8,898	3,306	34.77
Main Workers	32,658	21,004	11,654	93.04
Marginal Workers	2,443	572	1,871	6.96
Total Workers	35,101	21,576	13,525	

Religion: Major Religious Communities:

	Persons	Males	Females	Sex Ratio
Hindu (95.88%)	62,953	31,987	30,966	968
Muslim (1.79%)	1,175	582	593	1,019
Christian (1.62%)	1,061	546	515	943
Sikh (0%)	2	2	-	-
Buddhists (0%)	1	1	-	-
Jain (0.02%)	10	4	6	1,500

Agewise Data:

	Persons	Males	Females	Sex Ratio
All ages	65,659	33,364	32,295	968
0-14	14,544	7,481	7,063	944
15-44	32,836	16,519	16,317	988
45-79	17,042	8,717	8,325	955
80+	747	402	345	858
Age not stated	490	245	245	1000

Languages (Dominant):
Tamil, Telugu, Kannada, Malayalam, Urdu

Disabled Population:

	Persons	Males	Females	%
Total Disabled	2,301	937	1,364	
In Seeing	1,639	566	1,073	71.23
In Speech	115	57	58	5
In Hearing	93	40	53	4.04
In Movement	312	198	114	13.56
Mentally	142	76	66	6.17

POLUR

Polur C.D. Block lies in the north-western part of Tiruvannamalai district. It is a part of Polur taluk. The Block is located at a distance of 30 kms. from district headquarters (Tiruvannamalai). There are 66 villages in the block with the total population of 120,559 persons. Area of the C.D. Block is 610.27 sq. kms. It is bounded in the north by district Vellore and CD Block Arani West, in the south by C.D. Block Kalasapakkam, in the east by CD Blocks Arani West and Chetpet, in the west by C.D. Blocks Kalasapakkam and Jawadhu Hills.

Communications:

Roadways : S.H.-9: Direction- Vellore to Tiruvannamalai, Neraest Villages- Velloor, Kangirananthal, Kalvasal, Munivanthangal, Santhavasal, Mukkurumbai, Thappamandal,

Palvarthivenram, Sengunam, Renderipattu, Kunnathur, Murugapadi, Papampadi, Vasur, Kuruvimalai, Kasthambadi, Kelur RF.

Railway Station: Setharampattu, Parvathiagaram, Aliyabad @ Kalambur.

River: Cheyyar Nadi- Nearest Villages- Venmani, Vasur, Kuruvimalai.

Backwards Region Grants Fund: It receives Backward Region Grants.

Annual Rainfall: Average Rainfall 1019 mm.

Ground Water: Availability of the ground water in the Basin is (Information not available) H.A.M. and the utilization is 160.44 H.A.M. It belongs to Over Expoited category. Depth to water level varies from 2 to 5 meter below the ground. Most of the wells go down in summer months, according to the Ground Water Estimation Committee.

Forest and Reserved Forest: (Kelur RF)- Nearest Villages- Kelur, Kuttupoondi, Kelur RF, Sengunam, Murugapadi. (Melaiyalam)- Nearest Villages- Neepalampattu, Amirdee, Kalpattu, Irumbili, Anantapuram, Melaiyalam RF, Padavedu. (Pattarikadu)- Nearest Village- Pattarikadu RF. (Periyamalai)- Nearest Villages- Thumbakkadu, Periyamalai RF, Athimoor, Jadatharikuppam, Edapirai, Somanthaputhoor, Vilankuppam. (Mulakkadu)- Nearest Village- Mulakkadu RF. (Sandavasal)- Nearest Villages- Melaiyalam RF, Padavedu, Santhavasal RF, Shenpagathoppu, Thuringikuppam, Vilankuppam, Santhavasal. (Vallimalai)- Nearest Villages- Vazhiyur, Anantapuram, Padavedu, Vallaimalai RF, Teluvapushpagiri. (Veerapanur)- Nearest Village- Veerappanoor RF. (Sandavasal Extn.)- Nearest Villages- Pushpagiri, Thuringikuppam, Sandavasal Extn. RF, Kalvasal, Santhavasal RF, Vilankuppam.

Natural Division: Tondai Nadu.

Administration

Revenue **Division:** Tiruvannamalai. Parliamentary Constituency: 12 Arani, 11 Tiruvannamalai. District: Tiruvannamalai. Taluk: Polur. Assembly Constituency: 66 Polur, 65 Kalasapakkam (ST). Gram Panchayat: 40.

Villages: 66 **Inhabited:** 57 **Uninhabited:** 9

Ranking	District	State	National
Area	2	18	1138
Population	4	63	2854
Sex Ratio	6	161	1125
Child Sex Ratio	16	288	4853
Literacy Rate	4	151	1520
Density	8	182	4762
Work Participation Rate	18	329	1830

Gram Panchayats:

Ananthapuram, Athuvambady, Kanamalai, kanamalai, Enduvambady, Erikuppam, Illupakunam, Kalasamudram, Kalkuppam, Kalpattu, Kalvasal, Kangiyanoor, Kasthambady, Kattipoondy, Kelur, krishnapuram, Kunnanthur, Kuppam, Kuruvimalai, Mambattu, Mukkurambai, Murugapady, Naranamangalam, Padavedu, Palvathuvendran, Perigaram, Potharai, Pudupalayam, Renderipattu, Sandhavasal, Santhavasal , Sedarampattu, Sengunam, Thindivanam, Thurinjikuppam, Tirusoor, Valiyur, Vasur, Vellur, Venmani, Vilankuppam, .

Amenities:

Education: Primary School in 54 villages, Middle school in 22 villages, Matriculation or Secondary School in 7 villages, namely Kuppam, Padavedu, Aliyabad @ Kalambur, Santhavasal, Kelur, Athimoor, Mambattu.

Higher Secondary or Pre University Courses or Intermediate or Junior College in 3 villages of the CD Block,, namely Anantapuram, Aliyabad @ Kalambur, Santhavasal. College in 0 village, Adult Literacy Center in 0 village.

Medical: Hospital in 0 village, Dispensary in 2 villages, Health Center in 7 villages, Sub Center in 2 villages, Maternity and Child Welfare Center in 8 villages, Community health workers in 56 villages.

The Villages having Hospital or Dispensary or Health Center are Kuppam, Santhavasal, Kasthambadi.

Drinking Water: Tap water in 57 villages, Tank water in 9 villages, Well water in 57 villages, Tubewell in 57 villages and more than one source in 57 villages.

Bank: Banking facility in 7 villages, namely, Padavedu, Aliyabad @ Kalambur, Pushpagiri Santhavasal, Kelur, Athimoor, Thindivanam.

Credit Society in 22 villages Agricultural Credit Society in 8 Non-Agricultural Credit Society in 18 villages.

Others: Power supply in 57 villages, Cinema hall in 3 villages, sport club in 0 village, Stadium or Auditorium or Community Hall in 0 village, Post Office in 39 villages.

There are 53 villages having bus facilities.

Villages with most of facilities: Padavedu Aliyabad @ Kalambur, Pushpagiri, Santhavasal, Kelur Athimoor.

Villages without amenities (Education): Chettri, Papampadi, Jadatharikuppam..

Scheduled Castes: Out of the total population of 120559 persons, 22393 persons (18.57%) belong to Scheduled Castes. The villages having less than 10% SC population are Neepalampattu, Kalpattu, Irumbili, Kalasamuddiram Anantapuram, Padavedu, Teluvapushpagiri Parvathiagaram, Aliyabad @ Kalambur, Shenpagathoppu Thumbakkadu, Thuringikuppam, Authuvambody Palvarthivenram, Periyakaram, Athimoor, Thindivanam Murugapadi, Mambattu, Edapirai.

The villages having more than 50% SC population are None.

Sex ratio of Scheduled Caste population is 504.

Scheduled Castes Literates and Illiterates by Sex:

	Persons	Males	Females
Literate	13,304	7,660	5,644
Illiterate	9,089	3,458	5,631
Literacy rate	67.3	78.8	56.2
Graduate	78	58	20

Scheduled Castes (Dominant):

Adi Dravida, Arunthathiyar, Valluvan, Kuravan etc. Domban

For their cultural identity please see Appendix-I

Villages without Scheduled Castes: There are 15 villages without any scheduled caste population.

Scheduled Tribes: Out of the total population of 120559 persons, 2271 persons (1.88%) belong to Scheduled Tribes. The villages having less than 10% ST population are Kalpattu, Irumbili, Kuppam, Kalkuppam, Vazhiyur Kalasamuddiram, Anantapuram, Padavedu Teluvapushpagiri, Velloor, Setharampattu Parvathiagaram, Aliyabad @ Kalambur, Iluppaguram Naranamangalam, Kangirananthal, Pushpagiri Thuringikuppam, Vilankuppam, Kalvasal Munivanthangal, Santhavasal, Kasthambadi Eaudhuvambadi, Mukkurumbai, Thappamandal, Chettri Kelur, Authuvambody, Kuttupoondi, Palvarthivenram Sengunam, Potharai, Periyakaram, Athimoor, Kaliyam Thindivanam, Renderipattu, Kunnathur, Murugapadi Venmani, Papampadi, Mambattu, Eluvambadi Jadatharikuppam, Somanthaputhoor, Edapirai, Tirusur Padiyanipet, Nammiyandal, Kangeyanoor, Puduppalayam Vasur, Kuruvimalai.

The villages having more than 50% ST population are None.

Sex ratio of Scheduled tribe population is 510.

Scheduled Tribes Literates and Illiterates by Sex:

	Persons	Males	Females
Literate	827	524	303
Illiterate	1,444	589	855
Literacy rate	43.3	56.2	31.0
Graduate	0	0	0

Scheduled Tribes (Dominant):

Malayali, Irular, Malakkuravan, Kattunayakan

For their cultural identity please see Appendix-II

Villages without Scheduled Tribes: There are 49 villages without any scheduled tribe population.

Literates and Illiterates by Sex (Total Population):

	Persons	Males	Females
Literate	72,031	42,531	29,500
Illiterate	48,528	17,718	30,810
Literacy rate	68	80	55
Graduate	445	340	105

Agriculture: ***Distribution of villages according to land use:***

Out of 66 villages, Total area (in hectare) is 61027.45, out of that 28.88 percent is cultivable and 41.33 percent of the cultivable area is irrigated.

Sources of Irrigation (Hectares): Government Canal 0, Private Canal 0, Well without Electricity 515.86, Well with Electricity 4315.07, Tubewell without Electricity 70.36, Tubewell with Electricity 0, Tank 1083.87, River 0, Lake 281.87, Waterfall 0, Others 0.

Villages with population of 5000 to 9999:

Ananthapuram, Kasthambady.

Villages with population of 10000 and above:

Padavedu.

Distribution of Workers:

	Persons	Males	Females	WPR
Cultivators	24,317	15,259	9,058	38.6
Agricultural Labour	28,719	12,936	15,783	45.58
Household Industry	2,005	1,305	700	3.18
Other Workers	7,960	6,362	1,598	12.63
Main Workers	47,387	29,213	18,174	75.22
Marginal Workers	15,614	6,649	8,965	24.78
Total Workers	63,001	35,862	27,139	

Religion: Major Religious Communities:

	Persons	Males	Females	Sex Ratio
Hindu (97.41%)	117,433	58,718	58,715	1,000
Muslim (1.21%)	1,457	707	750	1,061
Christian (1.21%)	1,455	722	733	1,015
Sikh (0%)	-	-	-	-
Buddhists (0%)	5	2	3	1,500
Jain (0.12%)	144	72	72	1,000

Agewise Data:

	Persons	Males	Females	Sex Ratio
All ages	120,559	60,249	60,310	1001
0-14	34,681	17,791	16,890	949
15-44	56,746	27,969	28,777	1029
45-79	27,582	13,680	13,902	1016
80+	1,072	558	514	921
Age not stated	478	251	227	904

Languages (Dominant):

Tamil, Telugu, Urdu, Kannada, Malayalam

Disabled Population:

	Persons	Males	Females	%
Total Disabled	2,476	1,443	1,033	
In Seeing	947	541	406	38.25
In Speech	326	192	134	13.17
In Hearing	198	105	93	8
In Movement	731	462	269	29.52
Mentally	274	143	131	11.07

PONGALUR

Pongalur C.D. Block lies in the north-eastern part of Coimbatore district. It is a part of Tiruppur taluk. The taluk is located at a distance of 58 kms. from district headquarters Coimbatore. There are 16 villages in the block with the total population of 76,655 persons. Area of the C.D. Block is 350.22 sq. kms. It is bounded in the north by C.D. Blocks Tiruppur and Palladam, and district Erode, in the south and east by District Erode, in the west by CD Blocks Palladam and Sultanpet.

Communications:

Roadways : N.H.-67: Direction- Polladam to Kangayam, Nearest Villages- Alangumalai, Kandian Kovil, South Avanashipalayam, Pongalur, Madapur.

Annual Rainfall: Average Rainfall 550 mm.

Ground Water: Availability of the ground water in the Basin is 3636.10 H.A.M. and the utilization is 2925.15 H.A.M. It belongs Safe category. Depth to water level varies from 5 to 10 meter below the ground. Most of the wells go down in summer months, according to the Ground Water Estimation Committee.

Natural Division: Kongu Nadu.

Administration

Revenue **Division:** Trippur. Parliamentary Constituency: 20 Combatore. District: Combatore. Taluk: Tiruppur. Assembly Constituency: 115 Palladam. Gram Panchayat: 16.

Villages: 16 **Inhabited:** 16 **Uninhabited:** 0

Ranking	District	State	National
Area	4	116	2279
Population	9	260	4225
Sex Ratio	14	320	2675
Child Sex Ratio	16	247	4030
Literacy Rate	18	299	2516
Density	3	71	4454
Work Participation Rate	16	308	647

Gram Panchayats:

Alagumalai, Elavanthi, Kandiankoil, Kattur, Kethanur, Madappur, Nachipalayam, North Avanashipalayam, Perunthokuvu, Pongalur, South Avanashipalayam, Thonguttipalayam, Ugayanur, Vavipalayam, Velarasikallipalayam, Velarasivadamalaipalayam.

Amenities:

Education: Primary School in 16 villages, Middle school in 12 villages, Matriculation or Secondary School in 5 villages, namely Perunthokuvu, Avinashipalayam, South Avanashipalayam, Pongalur, Keethanoor.

Higher Secondary or Pre University Courses or Intermediate or Junior College in 4 villages of the CD Block,, namely Perunthokuvu, Avinashipalayam, Pongalur, Keethanoor.

College in 0 village, Adult Literacy Center in 0 village.

Medical: Hospital in 2 villages, Dispensary in 0 village, Health Center in 4 villages, Sub Center in 15 villages, Maternity and Child Welfare Center in 2 villages, Community health workers in 0 village.

The Villages having Hospital or Dispensary or Health Center are South Avanashipalayam, Pongalur.

Drinking Water: Tap water in 16 villages, Tank water in 0 villages, Well water in 16 villages, Tubewell in 16 villages and more than one source in 16 villages.

Bank: Banking facility in 11 villages, namely, Kattur, Perunthokuvu, Thonguttipalayam Avinashipalayam, Kandian Kovil South Avanashipalayam, Pongalur, Madapur V.Kallipalayam, Keethanoor, Vavipalayam.

Credit Society in 13 villages Agricultural Credit Society in 11 Non-Agricultural Credit Society in 9 villages.

Others: Power supply in 15 villages, Cinema hall in 2 villages, sport club in 0 village, Stadium or Auditorium or Community Hall in 0 village, Post Office in 16 villages.

There are 16 villages having bus facilities.

Villages with most of facilities: Kattur Perunthokuvu, Thonguttipalayam, Avinashipalayam Kandian Kovil, South Avanashipalayam, Pongalur Madapur, V.Kallipalayam, Keethanoor, Vavipalayam.

Villages without Amenities (Education): None..

Scheduled Castes: Out of the total population of 76655 persons, 19326 persons (25.21%) belong to Scheduled Castes.

The villages having less than 10% SC population are None..

The villages having more than 50% SC population are None.

Sex ratio of Scheduled Caste population is 493.

Scheduled Castes Literates and Illiterates by Sex:

	Persons	Males	Females
Literate	7,227	4,184	3,043
Illiterate	12,099	5,621	6,478
Literacy rate	43.3	49.7	36.7
Graduate	35	26	9

Scheduled Castes (Dominant):

Madari, Chakkiliyan, Adi Dravida, Arunthathiyar Kuravan etc.

For their cultural identity please see Appendix-I

Villages without Scheduled Castes: There is 0 village without any scheduled caste population.

Scheduled Tribes: Out of the total population of 76655 persons, 4 persons (0.01%) belong to Scheduled Tribes.

The villages having less than 10% ST population are Alangumalai, Kattur, Elavanthi, Nachipalayam Perunthokuvu, Ugayanur, Thonguttipalayam Avinashipalayam, Kandian Kovil

South Avanashipalayam, Pongalur, Madapur V.Kallipalayam, Keethanoor, Vavipalayam Velarasi Vadamalapalayam.

The villages having more than 50% ST population are None.

Sex ratio of Scheduled tribe population is 750.

Scheduled Tribes Literates and Illiterates by Sex:

	Persons	Males	Females
Literate	4	1	3
Illiterate	0	0	0
Literacy rate	100.0	100.0	100.0
Graduate	0	0	0

Scheduled Tribes (Dominant):

Kattunayakan

For their cultural identity please see Appendix-II

Villages without Scheduled Tribes: There are 15 villages without any scheduled tribe population.

Literates and Illiterates by Sex (Total Population):

	Persons	Males	Females
Literate	42,037	24,606	17,431
Illiterate	34,618	14,387	20,231
Literacy rate	62	71	52
Graduate	939	545	394

Agriculture: ***Distribution of villages according to land use:***

Out of 16 villages, Total area (in hectare) is 35022.9, out of that 89.45 percent is cultivable and 24.12 percent of the cultivable area is irrigated.

Sources of Irrigation (Hectares): Government Canal 2022.98, Private Canal 0, Well without Electricity 1680.99, Well with Electricity 3851.49, Tubewell without Electricity 0, Tubewell with Electricity 0, Tank 0, River 0, Lake 0, Waterfall 0, Others 0.

Villages with population of 5000 to 9999:

Kandiankoil, South Avanashipalayam, Pongalur, Kattur Vavipalayam.

Villages with population of 10000 and above: None

Distribution of Workers:

	Persons	Males	Females	WPR
Cultivators	11,800	7,373	4,427	26.67
Agricultural Labour	18,717	9,241	9,476	42.3
Household Industry	1,126	616	510	2.54
Other Workers	12,608	9,238	3,370	28.49
Main Workers	40,146	25,062	15,084	90.72
Marginal Workers	4,105	1,406	2,699	9.28
Total Workers	44,251	26,468	17,783	

Religion: Major Religious Communities:

	Persons	Males	Females	Sex Ratio
Hindu (97.27%)	74,559	37,933	36,626	966
Muslim (0.31%)	235	121	114	942
Christian (2.28%)	1,751	882	869	985
Sikh (0.01%)	4	1	3	3,000
Buddhists (0%)	-	-	-	-
Jain (0.01%)	8	3	5	1,667

Agewise Data:

	Persons	Males	Females	Sex Ratio
All ages	76,655	38,993	37,662	966
0-14	17,883	9,114	8,769	962
15-44	37,077	18,711	18,366	982
45-79	19,660	10,067	9,593	953
80+	1,149	636	513	807
Age not stated	886	465	421	905

Languages (Dominant):

Tamil, Telugu, Kannada, Malayalam, Urdu

Disabled Population:

	Persons	Males	Females	%
Total Disabled	1,707	853	854	
In Seeing	1,022	471	551	59.87
In Speech	149	75	74	8.73
In Hearing	76	38	38	4.45
In Movement	314	190	124	18.39
Mentally	146	79	67	8.55

PONNAMARAVATHI

Ponnamaravathi C.D. Block lies in the western part of Pudukkottai district. It is a part of Thirumayam taluk. The Block is located at a distance of 40 kms. from district headquarters (Pudukkottai). There are 49 villages in the block with the total population of 84,337 persons. Area of the C.D. Block is 326.45 sq. kms. It is bounded in the north by district Tiruchirappalli and CD Block Annavasal, in the south by district Sivaganga, in the east by C.D. Blocks Thirumayam and Annavasal, in the west by districts Sivaganga and Tiruchirappalli.

Communications:

Roadways : Information not Available.

Annual Rainfall: Average Rainfall 910 mm.

Ground Water: Availability of the ground water in the Basin is 4071.06 H.A.M. and the utilization is 505.19 H.A.M. It belongs to Safe category. Depth to water level varies from 2 to 5 meter below the ground. Most of the wells go down in summer months, according to the Ground Water Estimation Committee.

Natural Division: Chola Nadu.

Administration

Revenue **Division:** Pudukottai. Parliamentary Constituency: 31 Sivaganga. District: Pudokottai. Taluk: Thirumayam. Assembly Constituency: 181 Thirumayam.Gram Panchayat: 42

Villages: 49 **Inhabited:** 49 **Uninhabited:** 0

Ranking	District	State	National
Area	7	141	2500
Population	6	212	3961

Sex Ratio	1	23	234
Child Sex Ratio	1	9	330
Literacy Rate	7	211	1928
Density	11	277	3981
Work Participation Rate	8	277	2996

Gram Panchayats:
Alampatti, Alavayal, Ammankurichi, Arasamalai, Bagavabdipatti, Edayathur, Enathi, Gudalur, Kallampatti, Kandiyanatham, Karaiyur, Kattupatti, Keelathaniam, Konaippatti, Konnaiyampatti, Koppanapatti, Kovanur, M.Usilampatti, Maravamadurai, Melamelanilai, Melasivapuri, Melathaniam, Mullipatti, Mylapore, Nagarappatti, Nallur, Nerinjikudi, Oliyamangalam, P.Usilampati, R.Palakurichi, Semboothi, Seranur, Sevalur, Sundaram, Thenur, Thirukkalambur, Thottiampatti, Thuthur, Valakurichi, Varpatti, Vegupatti, Vendanpattu.

Amenities:

Education: Primary School in 46 villages, Middle school in 13 villages, Matriculation or Secondary School in 8 villages, namely Ponnamaravathy (W), Varpatty, Mepathaniyam, Karaiyur, Magarappatti, Konnaiyur, Alavayal, Moolangudi.

Higher Secondary or Pre University Courses or Intermediate or Junior College in 5 villages of the CD Block,, namely Ponnamaravathy (W), Varpatty, Mepathaniyam, Maravamadurai, Thenur.

College in 1 village, Adult Literacy Center in 0 village., Colleges are in villages, namely Varpatty.

Medical: Hospital in 0 village, Dispensary in 0 village, Health Center in 4 villages, Sub Center in 16 villages, Maternity and Child Welfare Center in 0 village, Community health workers in 38 villages.

Drinking Water: Tap water in 49 villages, Tank water in 2 villages, Well water in 49 villages, Tubewell in 49 villages and more than one source in 49 villages.

Bank: Banking facility in 6 villages, namely, Ponnamaravathy(E), Varpatty, Mepathaniyam, Karaiyur Konnaiyur, Moolangudi.

Credit Society in 9 villages Agricultural Credit Society in 9 Non-Agricultural Credit Society in 0 village.

Others: Power supply in 49 villages, Cinema hall in 3 villages, sport club in 0 village, Stadium or Auditorium or Community Hall in 0 village, Post Office in 24 villages.

There are 47 villages having bus facilities.

Villages with most of facilities: Ponnamaravathy(E) Varpatty, Mepathaniyam, Karaiyur, Konnaiyur.

Villages without amenities (Education):
Soorappatty, Vellayagavandanpatty, Mekkinipatti..

Scheduled Castes: Out of the total population of 84337 persons, 13603 persons (16.13%) belong to Scheduled Castes.

The villages having less than 10% SC population are Thirukkalambur, Vadakkuppatty, Mepathaniyam Vellakkudi, Nullur, Mullippatty Vellayagavandanpatty, Magarappatti, Ammankurichi Semmalapatti, Mathiyani, Nathupatti, Alavayal Kandiyanatham.

The villages having more than 50% SC population are None.

Sex ratio of Scheduled Caste population is 512.

Scheduled Castes Literates and Illiterates by Sex:

	Persons	Males	Females
Literate	7,500	4,458	3,042
Illiterate	6,103	2,175	3,928
Literacy rate	62.8	76.9	49.5
Graduate	178	128	50

Scheduled Castes (Dominant):
Pallan, Paraiyan etc., Kuravan etc., Chakkiliyan Adi Dravida

For their cultural identity please see Appendix-I

Villages without Scheduled Castes: There are 5 villages without any scheduled caste population.

Scheduled Tribes: Out of the total population of 84337 persons, 10 persons (0.01%) belong to Scheduled Tribes.

The villages having less than 10% ST population are Ponnamaravathy(E), Ponnamaravathy (W), R.Palakavichy Varpatty, Keelakurichi Patti, Thirukkalambur Oliamangalam, Usilampatty, Soorappatty Vadakkuppatty, Mepathaniyam, Keelathaniyam Kalanivoipatti, Karnapatti, Vellakkudi, Seranur Nullur, Nerunjikkudi, Vellakkudi, Karaiyur Mullippatty, Avampatty, Vellayagavandanpatty Maravamadurai, Magarappatti, Kallampatti Ammankurichi, Edaiyathur, Semmalapatti, Thenur Sathanur, Arasamalai, Neiveli, Gudalur, Chithur Valakkurichi, Kovanur, Sundaram, Mathiyani Sempoothy, Konnaiyur, Nathupatti, Alavayal Kandiyanatham, Thoothur, Moolangudi, Melamelanilai Mekkinipatti, Sevalur.

The villages having more than 50% ST population are None.

Sex ratio of Scheduled tribe population is 400.

Scheduled Tribes Literates and Illiterates by Sex:

	Persons	Males	Females
Literate	7	5	2
Illiterate	3	1	2
Literacy rate	70.0	83.3	50.0
Graduate	0	0	0

Scheduled Tribes (Dominant):
Malakkuravan

For their cultural identity please see Appendix-II

Villages without Scheduled Tribes: There are 48 villages without any scheduled tribe population.

Literates and Illiterates by Sex (Total Population):

	Persons	Males	Females
Literate	48,058	28,379	19,679
Illiterate	36,279	12,513	23,766
Literacy rate	65	80	52
Graduate	801	561	240

Agriculture: ***Distribution of villages according to land use:*** Out of 49 villages, Total area (in hectare) is 32645.11, out of that 26.31 percent is cultivable and 58.29 percent of the cultivable area is irrigated.

Sources of Irrigation (Hectares): Government Canal 0, Private Canal 0, Well without Electricity 33.41, Well with Electricity 361.59, Tubewell without Electricity 0, Tubewell with Electricity 0, Tank 4629.99, River 0, Lake 0, Waterfall 0, Others 0.

Villages with population of 5000 to 9999: Karaiyur , Maravamadurai, Ponnamaravathi West Varpattu, Thirukulambur.

Villages with population of 10000 and above: None

Distribution of Workers:

	Persons	Males	Females	WPR
Cultivators	18,076	10,730	7,346	45.3
Agricultural Labour	12,907	5,780	7,127	32.35
Household Industry	843	463	380	2.11
Other Workers	8,074	6,518	1,556	20.24
Main Workers	31,585	19,991	11,594	79.16
Marginal Workers	8,315	3,500	4,815	20.84
Total Workers	39,900	23,491	16,409	

Religion: Major Religious Communities:

	Persons	Males	Females	Sex Ratio
Hindu (94.38%)	79,600	38,676	40,924	1,058
Muslim (4.83%)	4,071	1,899	2,172	1,144
Christian (0.71%)	603	289	314	1,087
Sikh (0%)	-	-	-	-
Buddhists (0%)	-	-	-	-
Jain (0%)	-	-	-	-

Agewise Data:

	Persons	Males	Females	Sex Ratio
All ages	84,337	40,892	43,445	1062
0-14	24,311	12,282	12,029	979
15-44	38,791	18,231	20,560	1128
45-79	20,338	9,907	10,431	1053
80+	751	398	353	887
Age not stated	146	74	72	973

Languages (Dominant):

Tamil, Telugu, Kannada, Urdu, Malayalam

Disabled Population:

	Persons	Males	Females	%
Total Disabled	1,935	797	1,138	
In Seeing	1,195	393	802	61.76
In Speech	143	66	77	7.39
In Hearing	109	48	61	5.63
In Movement	349	209	140	18.04
Mentally	139	81	58	7.18

POONAMALLEE

Poonamalle C.D. Block lies in the south-eastern part of Thirunallur district. It is a part of Poonamalle taluk. The Block is located at a distance of 30 kms. from district headquarters (Thirunallur). There are 37 villages in the block with the total population of 81,907 persons. Area of the C.D. Block is 105.83 sq. kms. It is bounded in the north by CD Blocks Thiruvallur and Villivakkam, in the south by district Kancheepuram, in the east by CD Block Villivakkam, in the west by CD Blocks Thiruvallur and Kadambathur.

Communications:

Roadways : N.H.-4: Direction- Sriperumbudur to Chennai, Nearest Villages- Senneerkuppam, Varadharajapuram, Kuthambakkam, Chembaambakkam, Nazarathpettai, Kattupakkam, Goparasnallur.

Railway Station: Thirunindravoor.

River: Coovum Nadi- Nearest Villages- Kannapalayam, Sorancherry, Amudurmedu, Karunakaracherry, Melpakkam, Agaragrammale, Thirunindravoor, Gudappakkam, Korattur, Senneerkuppam.

Annual Rainfall: Average Rainfall 1152 mm.

Ground Water: Availability of the ground water in the Basin is 64.81 MCM and the utilization is 60.27 MCM. It belongs to Critical category. Depth to water level varies from 2 to 10 meter below the ground. Most of the wells go down in summer months, according to the Ground Water Estimation Committee.

Forest and Reserved Forest: (Gudapakkam RF)- Nearest Villages- Meyyur RF (Ui), Gudappakkam, Meiyur. (Meyyur)- Villages- Gudapakkam RF (Ui), Gudappakkam, Meiyur.

Natural Division: Tondai Nadu.

Administration

Revenue **Division:** Thiruvallur. Parliamentary Constituency: 1 Thiruvallur (SC). District: Thiruvallur. Taluka: Poonamalle. Assembly Constituency: 4 Thiruvelangadu (SC), 5 Thiruvallur, 6 Avadi. Gram Panchayat: 28.

Villages: 37 **Inhabited:** 34 **Uninhabited:** 3

Ranking	District	State	National
Area	12	366	5649
Population	8	231	4044
Sex Ratio	10	233	1647
Child Sex Ratio	11	208	3394
Literacy Rate	2	37	529

Density	13	373	1263
Work Participation Rate	3	15	5014

Gram Panchayats:

Agaramel, Annambedu, Banaveduthottam, Chittukadu, Gudapakkam, Kannapalayam, Karunakaracheri, Kattupakkam, Kavalacheri, Kolappancheri, Kosavanpalayam, Kuthambakkam, Melmanambedu, Meppur, Nadukuthagai, Nazarathpettai, Nemam, Nemilicheri, Padur, Parivakkam, Sembarambakkam , Senneerkuppam, Soranjeri, Thirumanam, Varadarajapuram, Veduthottam, Vellavedu, Voyalanallur

Amenities:

Education: Primary School in 29 villages, Middle school in 12 villages, Matriculation or Secondary School in 5 villages, namely Thirunindravoor, Kolappancheri, Senneerkuppam, Nazarathpettai, Kattupakkam.

Higher Secondary or Pre University Courses or Intermediate or Junior College in 3 villages of the CD Block,, namely Thirunindravoor, Kolappancheri, Kattupakkam.

College in 5 villages, Adult Literacy Center in 0 village., Colleges are in villages, namely Nadukerthigai, Parivakkam, Varadharajapuram, Agarammel, Nazarathpettai.

Medical: Hospital in 2 villages, Dispensary in 1 village, Health Center in 6 villages, Sub Center in 5 villages, Maternity and Child Welfare Center in 0 village, Community health workers in 34 villages.

The Villages having Hospital or Dispensary or Health Center are Nemilichery, Vellavedu, Nazarathpettai.

Drinking Water: Tap water in 34 villages, Tank water in 34 villages, Well water in 34 villages, Tubewell in 34 villages and more than one source in 34 villages.

Bank: Banking facility in 5 villages, namely, Nadukerthigai, Thirunindravoor, Kezeehmanambedu Vellavedu, Nazarathpettai.

Credit Society in 3 villages Agricultural Credit Society in 3 Non-Agricultural Credit Society in 0 village.

Others: Power supply in 34 villages, Cinema hall in 1 village, sport club in 0 village, Stadium or Auditorium or Community Hall in 0 village, Post Office in 12 villages.

There are 25 villages having bus facilities.

Villages with most of facilities: Nadukerthigai Thirunindravoor, Kezeehmanambedu, Vellavedu Nazarathpettai.

Villages without amenities (Education):

Amudurmedu, Panaveduthottam, Nochimedu, Narasingapuram, Goparasnallur..

Scheduled Castes: Out of the total population of 81907 persons, 29723 persons (36.29%) belong to Scheduled Castes.

The villages having less than 10% SC population are Kannapalayam, Agaragrammale, Narasingapuram Agarammel.

The villages having more than 50% SC population are Melpakkam, Thirunindravoor, Gudappakkam, Korattur Vayalanallur, Panaveduthottam, Pedarithangal Koratoor, Nemam, Nochimedu, Padur, Parvadarajapuram Meppur, Goparasnallur.

Sex ratio of Scheduled Caste population is 502.

Scheduled Castes Literates and Illiterates by Sex:

	Persons	Males	Females
Literate	18,307	10,348	7,959
Illiterate	11,416	4,458	6,958
Literacy rate	71.7	81.7	61.8
Graduate	377	276	101

Scheduled Castes (Dominant):

Adi Dravida, Arunthathiyar, Generic Castes etc. Baira, Paraiyan etc.

For their cultural identity please see Appendix-I

Villages without Scheduled Castes: There are 4 villages without any scheduled caste population.

Scheduled Tribes: Out of the total population of 81907 persons, 887 persons (1.08%) belong to Scheduled Tribes.

The villages having less than 10% ST population are Nadukerthigai, Nemilichery, Kannapalayam, Melpakkam Sorancherry, Amudurmedu, Karunakaracherry Agaragrammale, Thirunindravoor, Gudappakkam Korattur, Vayalanallur, Kolappancheri Panaveduthottam, Pedarithangal, Parivakkam Senneerkuppam, Varadharajapuram, Koratoor Kezeehmanambedu, Vellavedu, Nemam, Nochimedu, Meiyur Padur, Kuthambakkam, Narasingapuram Parvadarajapuram, Chembaambakkam, Meppur, Agarammel Nazarathpettai, Kattupakkam, Goparasnallur.

The villages having more than 50% ST population are None.

Sex ratio of Scheduled tribe population is 485.

Scheduled Tribes Literates and Illiterates by Sex:

	Persons	Males	Females
Literate	394	232	162
Illiterate	493	225	268
Literacy rate	53.0	62.5	43.6
Graduate	10	7	3

Scheduled Tribes (Dominant):

Irular, Malai Vedan, Kammara, Kattunayakan Malai Arayan

For their cultural identity please see Appendix-II

Villages without Scheduled Tribes: There are 18 villages without any scheduled tribe population.

Literates and Illiterates by Sex (Total Population):

	Persons	Males	Females

Literate	54,767	30,397	24,370
Illiterate	27,140	10,775	16,365
Literacy rate	77	85	68
Graduate	2,223	1,450	773

Agriculture: ***Distribution of villages according to land use:*** Out of 37 villages, Total area (in hectare) is 10583.76, out of that 40.47 percent is cultivable and 76.2 percent of the cultivable area is irrigated.

Sources of Irrigation (Hectares): Government Canal 0, Private Canal 0, Well without Electricity 58, Well with Electricity 901.27, Tubewell without Electricity 30.9, Tubewell with Electricity 1995.26, Tank 55.81, River 0, Lake 222.94, Waterfall 0, Others 0.

Villages with population of 5000 to 9999: Nadukuthagai, Senneerkuppam, Nazarathpettai.

Villages with population of 10000 and above: None

Distribution of Workers:

	Persons	Males	Females	WPR
Cultivators	2,333	1,705	628	7.78
Agricultural Labour	6,365	3,959	2,406	21.22
Household Industry	742	421	321	2.47
Other Workers	20,561	16,410	4,151	68.53
Main Workers	23,995	18,910	5,085	79.98
Marginal Workers	6,006	3,585	2,421	20.02
Total Workers	30,001	22,495	7,506	

Religion: Major Religious Communities:

	Persons	Males	Females	Sex Ratio
Hindu (93%)	76,177	38,285	37,892	990
Muslim (1.34%)	1,094	556	538	968
Christian (5.43%)	4,450	2,215	2,235	1,009
Sikh (0.02%)	14	7	7	1,000
Buddhists (0%)	3	1	2	2,000
Jain (0.03%)	28	14	14	1,000

Agewise Data:

	Persons	Males	Females	Sex Ratio
All ages	81,907	41,172	40,735	989
0-14	23,548	12,072	11,476	951
15-44	42,899	21,582	21,317	988
45-79	14,615	7,096	7,519	1060
80+	558	277	281	1014
Age not stated	287	145	142	979

Languages (Dominant):
Tamil, Telugu, Urdu, Kannada, Malayalam

Disabled Population:

	Persons	Males	Females	%
Total Disabled	1,851	1,064	787	
In Seeing	815	456	359	44.03
In Speech	171	88	83	9.24
In Hearing	140	70	70	7.56
In Movement	527	342	185	28.47
Mentally	198	108	90	10.7

POONDI

Poondi C.D. Block lies in the northern part of Thiruvallur district. It is a part of Uttukkottai and Thiruvallur taluks. The taluk (Uttukkottai) is located at a distance of 24 kms. from district headquarters (Thiruvallur). There are 77 villages in the block with the total population of 91,322 persons. Area of the C.D. Block is 321.54 sq. kms. It is bounded in the south by CD Block kadambathur, in the east by CD Blocks Ellapuram, Kadambathur and Thiruvallur, in the west by CD Block Tiruvalangadu, and it has common boundary with the state of Andhra Pradesh on north and west. CD Block Poondi falls in taluk Uttukkottai by 40 villages, and in taluk Thiruvallur by 36 villages.

Communications:

Roadways : N.H.-205: Direction- Tiruttani to Thruvallur, Nearest Villages- Pondavakkam, Ramanjeri, Pattairaiperu mbudur, Kanagavallipuram, Pandur, Thirupachur.

River: Arani Nadi- Nearest Villages- Vadathillai, Ananderi, Puducheri, Pondavakkam, Perittivakkam, Mambakkam, Velagapuram. Korattalaiyar Nadi- Nearest Villages- Attrambakkam, Arumbakkam, Vembedu, Meyyur, Oddappai, Korakkanthandlam, Rangapuram, Krishnapuram, Poondi, Neiveli, Ramathandalam, Eraiyur, Monnavedu, Kattanur (UI), Ramanjeri, Karattanur, Thiruppair, Karanizampattu, Kunnavalam, Pattairaiperumbudur.

Annual Rainfall: Average Rainfall 1152 mm.

Ground Water: Availability of the ground water in the Basin is 115.04 MCM and the utilization is 80.30 MCM. It belongs to Safe category. Depth to water level varies from 2 to 10 meter below the ground. Most of the wells go down in summer months, according to the Ground Water Estimation Committee.

Forest and Reserved Forest: (Meyyur RF)- Nearest Villages- Gurugambakkam, Gurupuram, Meyyur RF (UI), Meyyur. (Mylapore RF)- Nearest Village- Gurugambakkam, Alapakkam,Adhilivakkam, Kalavai, Ammambakkam, Mylapore RF (UI),Sengunram, Devandavakkam, Mylapore, Kunjavam.(Nayapakkam)- Nearest Villages- Nayapakkam, Nayapakkam RF (UI).

Natural Division: Tondai Nadu.

Administration

Revenue **Division:** Thiruvallur. Parliamentary Constituency: 1 Thiruvallur (SC). District: Thiruvallur. Taluk: Uttukkottai, Thiruvallur. Assembly Constituency: 1 Gummidipoondi, 4 Thiruvallur (SC) 5 Thiruvallur. Gram Panchayat: 49.

Border Villages- (A P)- Nearest Villages- Avicheri, Melakaramanur, Pennalurpettai, Puducheri, Goonipalayam, Allikuzhi RF, Hudsonpuram, Placepalayam, Abragampuram RF (Ui), Hudsanagaram (Ui), Allikuzhi, Greenvelnatham,

Senrayanpalayam, Thomour, Chennakagavapuram.

Villages: 76 **Inhabited:** 68 **Uninhabited:** 8

Ranking	District	State	National
Area	3	148	2550
Population	6	175	3744
Sex Ratio	3	136	997
Child Sex Ratio	4	64	1307
Literacy Rate	12	296	2501
Density	3	278	3704
Work Participation Rate	14	246	3034

Gram Panchayats:

Allikuzhi, Ammambakkam, Ananderi, Ariyathur , Attrambakkam , Chithambakkam, Devandavakkam , Ellappanaidupettai, Eraiyur , Goonipalayam, Kaivandur, Kalavai , Karanisampattu, Katchur, Kunnavallam, Mamandur, Mambakkam, Melakaramanur , Meyyur , Monnavedu, Moovur , Nambakkam, Nandimangalam, Neiveli, Nelvoy , Nemiliagaram , Oddappai, Pandur, Pandur , Pattaraiperambudur, Pennalurpet , Perittivakkam , Perunjeri, Placepalayam , Pondavakkam, Poondi , Ramalingapuram, Ramanathapuram, Ramanjery, Ramathandalam, Sendrayanpalayam , Siruvanur , Somadevanampattu , Somadevanpatti , Thimmaboopalapuram, Thirupachur, Thiruppair , Thomur, Velagapuram, Velamandigai, Vellathukottai, Poondi , Ramathandalam.

Amenities:

Education: Primary School in 55 villages, Middle school in 17 villages, Matriculation or Secondary School in 11 villages, namely Pennalurpettai, Pondavakkam, Mambakkam, Goonipalayam, Ammambakkam, Meyyur, Rangapuram, Poondi, Ramanjeri, Pattairaiperumbudur, Thirupachur. Higher Secondary or Pre University Courses or Intermediate or Junior College in 4 villages of the CD Block,, namely Pennalurpettai, Poondi, Ramanjeri, Thirupachur.

College in 1 village, Adult Literacy Center in 0 village., Colleges are in villages, namely Thirupachur.

Medical: Hospital in 4 villages, Dispensary in 0 village, Health Center in 8 villages, Sub Center in 17 villages, Maternity and Child Welfare Center in 2 villages, Community health workers in 65 villages.

The Villages having Hospital or Dispensary or Health Center are Vadathillai, Chennakesavapuram, Sengunram, Kannammapettai.

Drinking Water: Tap water in 68 villages, Tank water in 68 villages, Well water in 68 villages, Tubewell in 68 villages and more than one source in 68 villages.

Bank: Banking facility in 5 villages, namely, Pennalurpettai, Pondavakkam, Krishnapuram, Poondi Pattairaiperumbudur.

Credit Society in 8 villages Agricultural Credit Society in 7 Non-Agricultural Credit Society in 1 village.

Others: Power supply in 67 villages, Cinema hall in 0 village, sport club in 0 village, Stadium or Auditorium or Community Hall in 0 village, Post Office in 23 villages.

There are 46 villages having bus facilities.

Villages with most of facilities: Pennalurpettai Pondavakkam, Poondi, Pattairaiperumbudur.

Villages without amenities (Education): Vadathillai, Melakaramanur, Chennakesavapuram, Puducheri, Adhilivakkam, Gurupuram, Ariapakkam, Nayapakkam, Hudsonpuram, Seeyamcheri, Pandur, Kezhvilagam, Melvilagam..

Scheduled Castes: Out of the total population of 91322 persons, 32362 persons (35.44%) belong to Scheduled Castes. The villages having less than 10% SC population are Chennakesavapuram, Gurupuram, Mylapore Govindarajakuppam, Nayapakkam, Thomour, Rangapuram Krishnapuram, Monur, Memiliagaram, Melvilagam.

The villages having more than 50% SC population are Vadathillai, Avicheri, Adhilivakkam, Edambedu Kalavai, Sengunram, Devandavakkam, Ariapakkam Korakkanthandlam, Neiveli, Ramathandalam, Monnavedu Cithambakkam, Karaninizampattu, Kezhvilagam.

Sex ratio of Scheduled Caste population is 501.

Scheduled Castes Literates and Illiterates by Sex:

	Persons	Males	Females
Literate	16,438	9,742	6,696
Illiterate	15,924	6,412	9,512
Literacy rate	59.1	70.3	47.9
Graduate	403	339	64

Scheduled Castes (Dominant):

Adi Dravida, Arunthathiyar, Samban, Tiruvalluvar Valluvan

For their cultural identity please see Appendix-I

Villages without Scheduled Castes: There are 13 villages without any scheduled caste population.

Scheduled Tribes: Out of the total population of 91322 persons, 3192 persons (3.5%) belong to Scheduled Tribes. The villages having less than 10% ST population are Vadathillai, Avicheri, Melakaramanur Chennakesavapuram, Pennalurpettai, Puducheri Pondavakkam, Mambakkam, Velagapuram, Adhilivakkam Edambedu, Alapakkam, Kalavai, Katchur, Goonipalayam Thimmaboopalapuram, Nelvoy, Ammambakkam, Sengunram Gurugambakkam, Vembedu, Meyyur, Devandavakkam Mylapore, Kunjavam, Nambakkam, Ariapakkam, Ariyathur Nayapakkam, Attrambakkam, Oddappai, Korakkanthandlam Hudsonpuram, Placepalayam, Gengulukandigai

Allikuzhi, Greenvelnatham, Senrayanpalayam, Thomour Arumbakkam, Rangapuram, Krishnapuram, Poondi Kannammapettai, Monur, Neiveli, Ramathandalam Eraiyur, Monnavedu, Cithambakkam, Ramanjeri Karaninizampattu, Kunnavalam, Pattairaiperumbudur Kanagavallipuram, Pandur, Thirupachur, Memiliagaram Melvilagam, Kaliyanur.

The villages having more than 50% ST population are None.

Sex ratio of Scheduled tribe population is 508.

Scheduled Tribes Literates and Illiterates by Sex:

	Persons	Males	Females
Literate	792	467	325
Illiterate	2,400	1,102	1,298
Literacy rate	29.9	36.1	24.0
Graduate	3	2	1

Scheduled Tribes (Dominant):

Irular, Kattunayakan, Palliyar, Malai Pandaram Generic Tribes etc.

For their cultural identity please see Appendix-II

Villages without Scheduled Tribes: There are 32 villages without any scheduled tribe population.

Literates and Illiterates by Sex (Total Population):

	Persons	Males	Females
Literate	49,155	29,130	20,025
Illiterate	42,167	16,401	25,766
Literacy rate	62	73	50
Graduate	1,377	1,099	278

Agriculture: ***Distribution of villages according to land use:*** Out of 76 villages, Total area (in hectare) is 32154.35, out of that 44.44 percent is cultivable and 60.34 percent of the cultivable area is irrigated.

Sources of Irrigation (Hectares): Government Canal 247, Private Canal 23.55, Well without Electricity 554.81, Well with Electricity 516.83, Tubewell without Electricity 0, Tubewell with Electricity 2911.4, Tank 1141.05, River 90.27, Lake 3072.13, Waterfall 0, Others 66.12.

Villages with population of 5000 to 9999: None

Villages with population of 10000 and above: Thirupachur.

Distribution of Workers:

	Persons	Males	Females	WPR
Cultivators	7,777	5,765	2,012	18.12
Agricultural Labour	25,440	12,843	12,597	59.26
Household Industry	1,420	781	639	3.31
Other Workers	8,291	6,741	1,550	19.31
Main Workers	31,469	20,744	10,725	73.31
Marginal Workers	11,459	5,386	6,073	26.69
Total Workers	42,928	26,130	16,798	

Religion: Major Religious Communities:

	Persons	Males	Females	Sex Ratio
Hindu (93.61%)	85,491	42,649	42,842	1,005
Muslim (0.67%)	613	298	315	1,057
Christian (5.21%)	4,760	2,359	2,401	1,018
Sikh (0.02%)	17	7	10	1,429
Buddhists (0%)	-	-	-	-
Jain (0%)	1	1	-	-

Agewise Data:

	Persons	Males	Females	Sex Ratio
All ages	90,962	45,350	45,612	1006
0-14	25,871	13,143	12,728	968
15-44	44,377	22,186	22,191	1000
45-79	19,771	9,557	10,214	1069
80+	659	320	339	1059
Age not stated	284	144	140	972

Languages (Dominant):

Tamil, Telugu, Urdu, Hindi, Malayalam

Disabled Population:

	Persons	Males	Females	%
Total Disabled	2,902	1,562	1,340	
In Seeing	1,664	859	805	57.34
In Speech	187	92	95	6.44
In Hearing	152	74	78	5.24
In Movement	712	438	274	24.53
Mentally	187	99	88	6.44

PUDUCHATRAM

Puduchatram C.D. Block lies in the northern part of Namakkal district. It is a part of Namakkal taluk. The taluk is located at a distance of 00 kms. from district headquarters (Namakkal). There are 31 villages in the block with the total population of 72,751 persons. Area of the C.D. Block is 204.88 sq. kms. It is bounded in the north by CD Blocks Rasipuram, in the south by C.D. Block Namakkal, in the east by C.D. Block Sendamangalam, and in the west by CD Blocks Elachipalaiyam and Mallasamudram.

Communications:

Roadways : N.H.-7: Direction- Namakkal to Salem, Nearest Villages- Kalyani, Anandakrishnanarayasamudram, Pachal, Pidaripatty, Thathaiyangarpatti, Navani, Kalangani, Karaikurichi, Minnampalli, Sellappampatty, Thalambady, Sarkar Uduppam.

Annual Rainfall: Average Rainfall 650 mm.

Ground Water: Availability of the ground water in the Basin is 2038.64 H.A.M. and the utilization is 2433.69 H.A.M. It belongs to Safe category. Depth to water level varies from 2 to 10 meter below the ground. Most of the wells go down in summer months, according to the Ground Water Estimation Committee.

Natural Division: Kongu Nadu

Administration

Revenue **Division:** Namakkal. Parliamentary Constituency. District: Namakkal. Taluk: Namakkal. Assembly Constitu ency: 94 Namakkal. Gram Panchayat: 21.

Villages: 31 **Inhabited:** 31 **Uninhabited:** 0

Ranking	District	State	National
Area	8	278	4098
Population	7	275	4365
Sex Ratio	9	326	2814
Child Sex Ratio	13	360	6049
Literacy Rate	8	274	2348
Density	8	24	3059
Work Participation Rate	4	150	215

Gram Panchayats:
Ananthakrishnarayasamudram, Dadhadripuram, Elur, Kadiranallur, Kalangani, Kalyani, Kannurpatti, Karadipatti, Karadipatti , Karadippatti, Karakurichipudur, Karakuruchi, Karakuruchi pudur, Lakkapuram, Minnampalli, Navanithottakurapatti, Pachal, Pappinayakkanpatti, Sarkar Uduppam, Sarkarnattamangalam, Sellappampatti, Tattayyangarpatti , Thalambadi, Thirumalaipatti.

Amenities:

Education: Primary School in 25 villages, Middle school in 10 villages, Matriculation or Secondary School in 7 villages, namely Pachal, Kathiranallur, Thirumalaipatty, Elur, Kalangani, Karaikurichi, Sellappampatty.
Higher Secondary or Pre University Courses or Inter-mediate or Junior College in 6 villages of the CD Block,, namely Kathiranallur, Thirumalaipatty, Elur, Kalangani, Karaikurichi, Sellappampatty.
College in 2 villages, Adult Literacy Center in 0 village., Colleges are in villages, namely Pachal, Pappinaickenpatti.

Medical: Hospital in 3 villages, Dispensary in 0 village, Health Center in 4 villages, Sub Center in 11 villages, Maternity and Child Welfare Center in 0 village, Community health workers in 0 village.
The Villages having Hospital or Dispensary or Health Center are Elur, Dadharipuram Karadipatti, Minnampalli.

Drinking Water: Tap water in 31 villages, Tank water in 0 villages, Well water in 31 villages, Tubewell in 31 villages and more than one source in 31 villages.

Bank: Banking facility in 7 villages, namely, S.Nattamangalam, Thirumalaipatty, Navani, Elur Dadharipuram, Karaikurichi, Sellappampatty.
Credit Society in 20 villages Agricultural Credit Society in 12 Non-Agricultural Credit Society in 18 villages.

Others: Power supply in 31 villages, Cinema hall in 0 village, sport club in 0 village, Stadium or Auditorium or Community Hall in 0 village, Post Office in 26 villages.
There are 28 villages having bus facilities.

Villages with most of facilities: S.Nattamangalam Thirumalaipatty, Navani, Elur, Dadharipuram Karaikurichi.

Villages without amenities (Education):
Agrahara Nattamangalam, Jekkalnayakkanpatty, Podangam, Dadharipuram Karadipatti, Karadipatti Thanathampatti, Illaiyapuram..

Scheduled Castes: Out of the total population of 72751 persons, 17929 persons (24.64%) belong to Scheduled Castes.
The villages having less than 10% SC population are Agrahara Nattamangalam, Anandakrishnanarayasamudram Jekkalnayakkanpatty, Kadendapatti, Ramanaickenpatti Kannoorpatti, Podangam, Dadharipuram Karadipatti Thanathampatti, Illaiyapuram.
The villages having more than 50% SC population are None.
Sex ratio of Scheduled Caste population is 488.

Scheduled Castes Literates and Illiterates by Sex:

	Persons	Males	Females
Literate	8,725	5,315	3,410
Illiterate	9,204	3,873	5,331
Literacy rate	54.7	65.4	43.6
Graduate	366	273	93

Scheduled Castes (Dominant):
Arunthathiyar, Adi Dravida, Pallan, Chakkiliyan Paraiyan etc.

For their cultural identity please see Appendix-I

Villages without Scheduled Castes: There are 4 villages without any scheduled caste population.

Scheduled Tribes: Out of the total population of 72751 persons, 98 persons (0.13%) belong to Scheduled Tribes.
The villages having less than 10% ST population are S.Nattamangalam, Agrahara Nattamangalam, Kalyani Anandakrishnanarayasamudram, Jekkalnayakkanpatty Pachal, Pidaripatty, Kadendapatti, Ramanaickenpatti Kathiranallur, Thirumalaipatty, Kannoorpatti Podangam, Thathaiyangarpatti, Navani, Lakkapuram Elur, Dadharipuram, Dadharipuram Karadipatti Karadipatti Thanathampatti, Karadipatti Thanathampatti, Agraharauduppam, Kalangani Karaikurichi, Minnampalli, Sellappampatty Thalambady, Sarkar Uduppam, Illaiyapuram Pappinaickenpatti.
The villages having more than 50% ST population are None.
Sex ratio of Scheduled tribe population is 510.

Scheduled Tribes Literates and Illiterates by Sex:

	Persons	Males	Females

Literate	25	16	9
Illiterate	73	32	41
Literacy rate	28.7	37.2	20.5
Graduate	0	0	0

Scheduled Tribes (Dominant):

Irular, Malayali, Generic Tribes etc.

For their cultural identity please see Appendix-II

Villages without Scheduled Tribes: There are 27 villages without any scheduled tribe population.

Literates and Illiterates by Sex (Total Population):

	Persons	Males	Females
Literate	41,037	24,611	16,426
Illiterate	31,714	12,454	19,260
Literacy rate	62	74	51
Graduate	2,590	1,927	663

Agriculture: ***Distribution of villages according to land use:*** Out of 31 villages, Total area (in hectare) is 20488.4, out of that 79.01 percent is cultivable and 18.54 percent of the cultivable area is irrigated.

Sources of Irrigation (Hectares): Government Canal 11.53, Private Canal 0, Well without Electricity 0, Well with Electricity 2339.32, Tubewell without Electricity 14.18, Tubewell with Electricity 193.05, Tank 400.36, River 0, Lake 0, Waterfall 0, Others 42.46.

Villages with population of 5000 to 9999: Thirumalaipatti, Navani, Elur, Karakuruchi Sellappampatti.

Villages with population of 10000 and above: None

Distribution of Workers:

	Persons	Males	Females	WPR
Cultivators	11,335	5,991	5,344	25.18
Agricultural Labour	18,581	7,961	10,620	41.27
Household Industry	3,287	1,638	1,649	7.3
Other Workers	11,820	8,697	3,123	26.25
Main Workers	41,593	23,059	18,534	92.38
Marginal Workers	3,430	1,228	2,202	7.62
Total Workers	45,023	24,287	20,736	

Religion: Major Religious Communities:

	Persons	Males	Females	Sex Ratio
Hindu (98.49%)	71,654	36,505	35,149	963
Muslim (0.59%)	426	205	221	1,078
Christian (0.88%)	637	336	301	896
Sikh (0%)	-	-	-	-
Buddhists (0%)	3	2	1	500
Jain (0.01%)	4	2	2	1,000

Agewise Data:

	Persons	Males	Females	Sex Ratio
All ages	72,751	37,065	35,686	963
0-14	16,445	8,841	7,604	860
15-44	34,685	17,605	17,080	970
45-79	20,054	9,808	10,246	1045
80+	948	485	463	955
Age not stated	619	326	293	899

Languages (Dominant):

Tamil, Telugu, Kannada, Urdu, Malayalam

Disabled Population:

	Persons	Males	Females	%
Total Disabled	1,436	798	638	
In Seeing	754	408	346	52.51
In Speech	119	59	60	8.29
In Hearing	80	31	49	5.57
In Movement	390	252	138	27.16
Mentally	93	48	45	6.48

PUDUKKOTTAI

Pudukkottai C.D. Block lies in the central north part of Pudukkottai district. It is a part of Pudukkottai and Gandarvakkottai taluks. The Block is located at a distance of 3 kms. from district headquarters (Pudukkottai). There are 42 villages in the block with the total population of 71,193 persons. Area of the C.D. Block is 266.24 sq. kms. It is bounded in the north by CD Blocks Kunandarkovil and Gandarvakottai, in the south by CD Blocks Thirumayam and Thiruvarankulam, in the east by CD Blocks Gandarvakottai, Karambakudi and Thiruvarankulam, and in the west by CD Block Annavasal. CD Block Pudukkottai falls in taluk Pudukkottai by 40 villages, and in taluk Gandarvakkotai by 02 villages.

Communications:

Roadways : N.H.-210: Direction- Kiranur to Thirumayam, Nearest Villages- Kanivadu - West, Kavinadu East, Purakarainatham Pannai. S.H.-27: Direction- Alangudi to Gandarvakottai, Nearest Villages- Valavanpatti, Mullur, Perungalur, Adanakkottai, Kallukkaranpatti, Vannarappatti, Manaviduthi, Perungondanviduthy, Ichadi, Ichadi Ii Bit, Vadavalam, Kuppaiyampatti, Nemmelipatti RF, Pudukottai RF, Thirumalairayapamuthiram.

Annual Rainfall: Average Rainfall 910 mm.

Ground Water: Availability of the ground water in the Basin is 5176.33 H.A.M. and the utilization is 2007. 16 H.A.M. It belongs to Safe category. Depth to water level varies from 2 to 10 meter below the ground. Most of the wells go down in summer months, according to the Ground Water Estimation Committee.

Forest and Reserved Forest: (Nemmelipatti RF)- Nearest Villages- Perungalur, Kuppaiyanpatti, Nemmelipatti R.F., Nemmelipatti. (Pudukkottai)- Nearest Villages- Vagavasal, Mullur, Vadavalam, Pudukottai R.F., Siruvayal, Ayyavayal. (Varappur)- Nearest Villages- Thondamanurani, Vannarappatti, Kuppaiyanpatti, Varappur R.F., Pulavankadu, Varappur.

Natural Division: Chola Nadu.

Administration

Revenue **Division:** Pudukottai. Parliamentary Constituency: 30 Pudukottai. District: Pudukottai. Taluk: Gandaruakottai, Pudukottai. Assembly Constituency: 178 Gandaruakottai (SC), 180 Pudukottai. Gram Panchayat: 28.

Villages: 42 **Inhabited:** 38 **Uninhabited:** 4

Ranking	District	State	National
Area	11	212	3159
Population	12	281	4411
Sex Ratio	9	140	988
Child Sex Ratio	8	135	2440
Literacy Rate	8	226	2068
Density	4	172	3885
Work Participation Rate	5	264	1730

Gram Panchayats:

Adanakottai, Ganapathipuram, Kallukarampatti, Karuppudayanpatti, Kavinad East, Kavinad West, Kulavaipatti, Kuppayampatti, Manaviduthi, Mangalathupatti, Mukkanpatti, Mullur, Nathampannai (Purakarai), Perungalur, Perungondanviduthi, Puthambur, Sembattur, Semmattividuthy, Sothupalai, Sothupalai, Thirumalrayasamudram, Thondamanurani, Vadavalam, Vagavasal, Valavanpatti, Vanarapatti, Varappur.

Amenities:

Education: Primary School in 33 villages, Middle school in 17 villages, Matriculation or Secondary School in 8 villages, namely Agavayal, Sembattur, Puthambur, Perungalur, Adanakkottai, Nemmelipatti, Kulavaipatti, Vadavalam. Higher Secondary or Pre University Courses or Intermediate or Junior College in 4 villages of the CD Block,, namely Ganapathipuram, Thondamanurani, Nemmelipatti, Purakarainathan Pannai.

College in 0 village, Adult Literacy Center in 0 village.

Medical: Hospital in 0 village, Dispensary in 1 village, Health Center in 5 villages, Sub Center in 10 villages, Maternity and Child Welfare Center in 0 village, Community health workers in 14 villages.

The Village having Hospital or Dispensary or Health Center is Varappur.

Drinking Water: Tap water in 38 villages, Tank water in 5 villages, Well water in 38 villages, Tubewell in 38 villages and more than one source in 38 villages.

Bank: Banking facility in 2 villages, namely, Perungalur, Adanakkottai.

Credit Society in 9 villages Agricultural Credit Society in 9 Non-Agricultural Credit Society in 0 village.

Others: Power supply in 38 villages, Cinema hall in 1 village, sport club in 0 village, Stadium or Auditorium or Community Hall in 0 village, Post Office in 17 villages.

There are 37 villages having bus facilities.

Villages with most of facilities: Perungalur Adanakkottai.

Villages without amenities (Education): Sanivayal, Kurinjippatti, Tatampatti, Ayyavayal, Ichadi..

Scheduled Castes: Out of the total population of 71193 persons, 16646 persons (23.38%) belong to Scheduled Castes.

The villages having less than 10% SC population are Agavayal, Sanivayal, Tatampatti, Ayyavayal Ichadi Ii Bit, Sellukudi.

The villages having more than 50% SC population are None.

Sex ratio of Scheduled Caste population is 505.

Scheduled Castes Literates and Illiterates by Sex:

	Persons	Males	Females
Literate	9,412	5,561	3,851
Illiterate	7,234	2,678	4,556
Literacy rate	65.4	78.7	52.6
Graduate	153	123	30

Scheduled Castes (Dominant):

Paraiyan etc., Pallan, Adi Dravida, Chakkiliyan Kuravan etc.

For their cultural identity please see Appendix-I

Villages without Scheduled Castes: There are 9 villages without any scheduled caste population.

Scheduled Tribes: Out of the total population of 71193 persons, 7 persons (0.01%) belong to Scheduled Tribes.

The villages having less than 10% ST population are Valavanpatti, Sothupalai, Agavayal, Sembattur Puthambur, Sanivayal, Kurinjippatti, Kedayapatti Tatampatti, Thennathirayanpatti, Vagavasal Ayyavayal, Mullur, Mangalathupatti, Perungalur Adanakkottai, Sokkanathapatti, Kallukkaranpatti Ganapathipuram, Thondamanurani, Vannarappatti Kuppaiyanpatti, Nemmelipatti, Pulavankadu, Varappur Manaviduthi, Sammattividuthi, Mookkampatti Kulavaipatti, Perungondanviduthy, Ichadi Ichadi Ii Bit, Vadavalam, Sellukudi Purakarainathan Pannai, Kanivadu - West Kavinadu East, Thirumalairayapamuthiram.

The villages having more than 50% ST population are None.

Sex ratio of Scheduled tribe population is 429.

Scheduled Tribes Literates and Illiterates by Sex:

	Persons	Males	Females
Literate	4	4	0
Illiterate	3	0	3
Literacy rate	66.7	100.0	-
Graduate	0	0	0

Scheduled Tribes (Dominant):

Malai Pandaram, Irular, Palliyan

For their cultural identity please see Appendix-II

Villages without Scheduled Tribes: There are 40 villages without any scheduled tribe population.

Literates and Illiterates by Sex (Total Population):

	Persons	Males	Females
Literate	39,741	23,773	15,968
Illiterate	31,452	11,716	19,736
Literacy rate	64	77	51
Graduate	600	455	145

Agriculture: ***Distribution of villages according to land use:*** Out of 42 villages, Total area (in hectare) is 26624.91, out of that 34.49 percent is cultivable and 46.93 percent of the cultivable area is irrigated.

Sources of Irrigation (Hectares): Government Canal 0, Private Canal 0, Well without Electricity 58, Well with Electricity 1278, Tubewell without Electricity 0, Tubewell with Electricity 33, Tank 2944, River 0, Lake 0, Waterfall 0, Others 0.

Villages with population of 5000 to 9999: Perungalur, Vadavalam.

Villages with population of 10000 and above: None

Distribution of Workers:

	Persons	Males	Females	WPR
Cultivators	15,750	10,055	5,695	42.79
Agricultural Labour	13,796	5,561	8,235	37.48
Household Industry	512	228	284	1.39
Other Workers	6,753	5,247	1,506	18.35
Main Workers	27,848	18,124	9,724	75.65
Marginal Workers	8,963	2,967	5,996	24.35
Total Workers	36,811	21,091	15,720	

Religion: Major Religious Communities:

	Persons	Males	Females	Sex Ratio
Hindu (95.38%)	67,905	33,863	34,042	1,005
Muslim (2.14%)	1,524	730	794	1,088
Christian (2.44%)	1,737	883	854	967
Sikh (0%)	3	1	2	2,000
Buddhists (0%)	1	-	1	-
Jain (0%)	2	2	-	-

Agewise Data:

	Persons	Males	Females	Sex Ratio
All ages	71,193	35,489	35,704	1006
0-14	20,683	10,495	10,188	971
15-44	34,874	17,121	17,753	1037
45-79	15,041	7,583	7,458	984
80+	528	255	273	1071
Age not stated	67	35	32	914

Languages (Dominant):

Tamil, Telugu, Kannada, Gujarati, English

Disabled Population:

	Persons	Males	Females	%
Total Disabled	2,075	888	1,187	
In Seeing	1,220	383	837	58.8
In Speech	195	110	85	9.4
In Hearing	134	71	63	6.46
In Movement	387	251	136	18.65
Mentally	139	73	66	6.7

PUDUPALAYAM

Pudupalayam C.D. Block lies in the western part of Tiruvannamalai district. It is a part of Chengam taluk. The Block is located at a distance of 50 kms. from district headquarters (Tiruvannamalai). There are 48 villages in the block with the total population of 72,374 persons. Area of the C.D. Block is 296.49 sq. kms. It is bounded in the north by CD Block Jawadhu Hills, in the south by C.D. Block Chengam, in the east by CD Block Thurinjapuram, in the west by C.D. Blocks Chengam and Jawadhu Hills, and in the north-east by CD Block Kalasapakkam.

Communications:

Roadways : N.H.-66: Direction- Chengam to Tiruvannamalai, Nearest Villages- Kottakulam, Eraiyur, Melmudiyanur.

River: Cheyyar Nadi- Nearest Villages- Korattampet, Kanji, Arithari Mangalam, Tamaraipakkam, Alathur, Oravandavadi, Kottakulam, Thorapadi, Narashinga, Nallur, Padi Agraharam, Alliyandal, Japthi Kariandal, Annandal, Vasudevampattu, Eraiyur, Melmudiyanur, Muthanur.

Backwards Region Grants Fund: It receives Backward Region Grants.

Annual Rainfall: Average Rainfall 1019 mm.

Ground Water: Availability of the ground water in the Basin is (Information not available) H.A.M. and the utilization is 160.44 H.A.M. It belongs to Over Expoited category. Depth to water level varies from 2 to 5 meter below the ground. Most of the wells go down in summer months, according to the Ground Water Estimation Committee.

Forest and Reserved Forest: (Dhamaraikkadu RF)- Nearest Villages- Thamaraikadu RF, Veerandal. (Eraiyurmalai)- Nearest Villages- Thorapadi, Melnachipattu, Senthamangalam, Annandal, Melapunjai, Vasudevampattu, Iraiyammalai RF, Eraiyur. (Madanai)- Nearest Villages- Madanai RF, Munniur Mangalam, Pudur Chengam, Unnamalaipalayam. (Munnurmangalam)- Nearest Villages- Munniur Mangalam, Pudur Chengam, Panaiolaipadi, Munnurmangalam, Periyeri, Munnurmangalam RF, Muthanur, Thorapadi, Narashinga Nallur, Padi Agraharam, Vaividanthangal, Melpadur, Gulal Pady, Nathavadi, Vadamathur, Melnachipattu, Gowthimalai RF. (Pinjur)- Nearest Village- Melmudiyanur.

Natural Division: Tondai Nadu.

Administration

Division Cheyyar. Parliamentary Constituency: 11

Tiruvannamalai. District: Tiruvannamalai. Taluk: Chengam. Assembly Constituency: 65 Kalasapakkam (ST), 62 Chengam (SC). Gram Panchayat: 37.

Villages: 48 **Inhabited:** 41, **Uninhabited:** 7

Ranking	District	State	National
Area	9	174	2823
Population	17	277	4378
Sex Ratio	16	280	2205
Child Sex Ratio	18	307	5141
Literacy Rate	16	335	2893
Density	15	212	4159
Work Participation Rate	15	289	2265

Gram Panchayats:

Alliandal, Amarnathapnoynr, Amarnathaputhere, Amarnathaputhur, Aridharimangalam, Davanandal, Dhamarapakkam, Eraiyur, Gengampattu, Gulalpadi, Japthikariyandal, Kallarpadi, Kanji, Karapattu , Kilpadur, Korattambattu, Kottakulam, Mashar, Melapunjai, Melmudiyanur, Melnachipattu, Melpadur, Munnurmangalam , Muthanur, Nagapadi, Nammiandal, Narasinganallur, Nayambadi, Oravanthavadi, Padiagraharam, Panaiolapadi , Perieri, Pudurchengam, Senthamangalam, Thorapadi, Unnamalaipalayam, Vadamathur, Vasudevanpattu, Veeranandal, Voividanthangal.

Amenities:

Education: Primary School in 39 villages, Middle school in 18 villages, Matriculation or Secondary School in 6 villages, namely Kanji, Panaiolaipadi, Thorapadi, Gengampattu, Eraiyur, Melmudiyanur.

Higher Secondary or Pre University Courses or Intermediate or Junior College in 4 villages of the CD Block,, namely Karapet, Kanji, Nandimangalam, Melmudiyanur. College in 0 village, Adult Literacy Center in 0 village.

Medical: Hospital in 0 village, Dispensary in 0 village, Health Center in 4 villages, Sub Center in 5 villages, Maternity and Child Welfare Center in 5 villages, Community health workers in 41 villages.

The Village having Hospital or Dispensary or Health Center is Karapet.

Drinking Water: Tap water in 41 villages, Tank water in 8 villages, Well water in 41 villages, Tubewell in 41 villages and more than one source in 41 villages.

Bank: Banking facility in 8 villages, namely, Karapet, Kanji, Arithari Mangalam, Panaiolaipadi Gengampattu, Vaividanthangal, Melpadur, Vadamathur. Credit Society in 9 villages Agricultural Credit Society in 5 Non-Agricultural Credit Society in 4 villages.

Others: Power supply in 41 villages, Cinema hall in 2 villages, sport club in 0 village, Stadium or Auditorium or Community Hall in 0 village, Post Office in 31 villages.

There are 37 villages having bus facilities.

Villages with most of facilities: Karapet, Kanji Arithari Mangalam, Panaiolaipadi, Gengampattu Vaividanthangal, Melpadur, Vadamathur.

Villages without amenities (Education): Mashar, Endal..

Scheduled Castes: Out of the total population of 72374 persons, 21110 persons (29.17%) belong to Scheduled Castes.

The villages having less than 10% SC population are None..

The villages having more than 50% SC population are Ko. Pudupet, Arithari Mangalam, Alliyandal Gulal Pady, Senthamangalam.

Sex ratio of Scheduled Caste population is 497.

Scheduled Castes Literates and Illiterates by Sex:

	Persons	Males	Females
Literate	9,421	5,776	3,645
Illiterate	11,689	4,832	6,857
Literacy rate	51.8	63.4	40.2
Graduate	61	56	5

Scheduled Castes (Dominant):

Adi Dravida, Arunthathiyar, Valluvan, Kuravan etc. Panniandi

For their cultural identity please see Appendix-I

Villages without Scheduled Castes: There are 7 villages without any scheduled caste population.

Scheduled Tribes: Out of the total population of 72374 persons, 379 persons (0.52%) belong to Scheduled Tribes.

The villages having less than 10% ST population are Veerandal, Munniur Mangalam, Pudur Chengam Unnamalaipalayam, Karapet, Ko. Pudupet, Korattampet Kanji, Arithari Mangalam, Tamaraipakkam, Nayambadi Mashar, Kallarappadi, Endal, Nammiyandal, Alathur Oravandavadi, Nandimangalam, Panaiolaipadi, Periyeri Kottakulam, Muthanur, Thorapadi, Narashinga Nallur Padi Agraharam, Alliyandal, Japthi Kariandal Gengampattu, Kilpadur, Vaividanthangal, Melpadur Gulal Pady, Vadamathur, Melnachipattu Senthamangalam, Annandal, Melapunjai, Vasudevampattu Eraiyur, Melmudiyanur.

The villages having more than 50% ST population are None.

Sex ratio of Scheduled tribe population is 504.

Scheduled Tribes Literates and Illiterates by Sex:

	Persons	Males	Females
Literate	118	71	47
Illiterate	261	117	144
Literacy rate	36.0	44.1	28.1
Graduate	0	0	0

Scheduled Tribes (Dominant):
Irular, Kattunayakan, Sholaga
For their cultural identity please see Appendix-II
Villages without Scheduled Tribes: There are 37 villages without any scheduled tribe population.

Literates and Illiterates by Sex (Total Population):

	Persons	Males	Females
Literate	37,613	22,860	14,753
Illiterate	34,761	13,765	20,996
Literacy rate	59	72	47
Graduate	359	296	63

Agriculture: *Distribution of villages according to land use:* Out of 48 villages, Total area (in hectare) is 29649.65, out of that 43.87 percent is cultivable and 64.5 percent of the cultivable area is irrigated.
Sources of Irrigation (Hectares): Government Canal 0, Private Canal 0, Well without Electricity 1971.05, Well with Electricity 3298.98, Tubewell without Electricity 0, Tubewell with Electricity 0.03, Tank 663.49, River 10, Lake 1201.57, Waterfall 0, Others 135.05.
Villages with population of 5000 to 9999:
Karapattu , Kanji.
Villages with population of 10000 and above: None
Distribution of Workers:

	Persons	Males	Females	WPR
Cultivators	13,090	9,212	3,878	36.1
Agricultural Labour	18,062	8,209	9,853	49.81
Household Industry	477	240	237	1.32
Other Workers	4,633	3,654	979	12.78
Main Workers	26,443	17,154	9,289	72.92
Marginal Workers	9,819	4,161	5,658	27.08
Total Workers	36,262	21,315	14,947	

Religion: Major Religious Communities:

	Persons	Males	Females	Sex Ratio
Hindu (93.7%)	67,811	34,400	33,411	971
Muslim (2.19%)	1,583	785	798	1,017
Christian (4.03%)	2,919	1,413	1,506	1,066
Sikh (0%)	-	-	-	-
Buddhists (0.01%)	7	3	4	1,333
Jain (0%)	1	1	-	-

Agewise Data:

	Persons	Males	Females	Sex Ratio
All ages	72,374	36,625	35,749	976
0-14	21,776	11,291	10,485	929
15-44	34,294	17,011	17,283	1016
45-79	15,311	7,785	7,526	967
80+	573	315	258	819
Age not stated	420	223	197	883

Languages (Dominant):
Tamil, Telugu, Urdu, Kannada, Malayalam
Disabled Population:

	Persons	Males	Females	%
Total Disabled	1,694	1,018	676	
In Seeing	928	604	324	54.78
In Speech	170	89	81	10.04
In Hearing	98	46	52	5.79
In Movement	380	221	159	22.43
Mentally	118	58	60	6.97

PUDUR

Pudur C.D. Block lies in the northern eastern part of Thoothukkudi district. It is a part of Ettayapuram and Vitathikulam taluks. The Block is located at a distance of 67 kms. from district headquarters (Thoothukkudi). There are 52 villages in the block with the total population of 63,171 persons. Area of the C.D. Block is 465. 90 sq. kms. It is bounded in the north by district Virudhunagar, in the south by CD Block Vilathikulam, in the east by districts Virudhunagar and Ramanathapuram, in the west by CD Block Kovilppati and district Virudhunagar. CD Block Pudur falls in taluk Ettayapuram by 19 villages, and in taluk Vilathikulam by 33 villages.

Communications:
Roadways : N.H.-45 B: Direction- Ettayapuram to Aruppukkottai, Nearest Villages- Kodangipatti, Vemboor, Melakkarandai, Thappathi, Keznattukuruchi, Muthulapuram.
River: Vaippar Nadi- Nearest Villages- Ayanrajapatti, Ayanvadamalapuram, Thappathi, Keznattukuruchi, Arunasalapuram, Tholmalaipatti, Muthulapuram, Nambipuram, Vedapatti.
Annual Rainfall: Average Rainfall 661 mm.

Ground Water: Availability of the ground water in the Basin is 7.58 MCM and the utilization is 7.20 MCM. It belongs to Critical category. Depth to water level varies from 0 to 10 meter below the ground. Most of the wells go down in summer months, according to the Ground Water Estimation Committee.
Natural Division: NA
Administration
Revenue **Division:** Kovilpatti. Parliamentary Constituency: 36 Thoothukkudi. District: Thoothukkudi. Taluk: Ettayapuram Vilathikulam. Assembly Constituency: 213 Vilathikulam.
Gram Panchayat: 44.
Villages: 52 **Inhabited:** 51 **Uninhabited:** 1

Ranking	District	State	National
Area	4	41	1618
Population	10	324	4753
Sex Ratio	10	65	530
Child Sex Ratio	1	52	1123
Literacy Rate	11	68	834
Density	1	30	5770
Work Participation Rate	11	369	239

Gram Panchayats:
Arunachalapuram, Ayan Karisalkulam , Boothalapuram, Chinnamaickenpatti, Chinnamanaickenpatti, Goundampatti, K.Duraisamipuram, Kadalgudi, Kandasamypuram, Karuppur, KeelaArunachalapuram, Keelakarandai, Keelnattukurichi, Lakshmipuram, Madalapuram, Maniakaranpatti, Mavilodai, Mavilpatti, MeelaArunachalapuram, Melakallurani, Melakarandai, Mettilpatti , Mittavadamalapuram, Muthiahpuram, Muthulapuram, Muthusamypuram, N.Jagaveerapuram, N.Vedapatti, Nagalapuram, Nambipuram, Nasarpatti, Pattithevanpatti, Rajapatti, Ramachandrapuram, Sennampatti, Shankaralingapuram , Shencottai, Sivalarpatti, Thappathi, Vadamalaipuram, Vathalakarai, Veerapatti, Vembur, Vowalthothi.

Amenities:
Education: Primary School in 50 villages, Middle school in 27 villages, Matriculation or Secondary School in 7 villages, namely Vemboor, Keznattukuruchi, Muthulapuram, Mettipatti, Senkottai, Goundanpatti, Nagalapuram. Higher Secondary or Pre University Courses or Intermediate or Junior College in 2 villages of the CD Block,, namely Goundanpatti, Nagalapuram.
College in 0 village, Adult Literacy Center in 0 village.
Medical: Hospital in 1 village, Dispensary in 2 villages, Health Center in 4 villages, Sub Center in 15 villages, Maternity and Child Welfare Center in 2 villages, Community health workers in 51 villages.
The Villages having Hospital or Dispensary or Health Center are Muthusamypuram, Nagalapuram, Vadalakkari.
Drinking Water: Tap water in 51 villages, Tank water in 11 villages, Well water in 51 villages, Tubewell in 51 villages and more than one source in 51 villages.
Bank: Banking facility in 21 villages, namely,
Vemboor, Nasarpatti, Keelakkarandai
Ayanvadamalapuram, Karupur, Muthulapuram, Nambipuram
Singilipatti, Mettipatti, Naddukattur, Sivalarpatti
Senkottai, Madalapuram, Jeegaveerapuram
Boothalapuram, Sankaralingapuram, Goundanpatti
Vowalthothi, Nagalapuram, Kadalkudi, Subaiahpuram.
Credit Society in 11 villages Agricultural Credit Society in 8 Non-Agricultural Credit Society in 4 villages.
Others: Power supply in 50 villages, Cinema hall in 0 village, sport club in 0 village, Stadium or Auditorium or Community Hall in 0 village, Post Office in 44 villages.
There are 43 villages having bus facilities.
Villages with most of facilities: Vemboor
Nasarpatti, Keelakkarandai, Ayanvadamalapuram
Karupur, Muthulapuram, Nambipuram, Singilipatti
Mettipatti, Naddukattur, Sivalarpatti, Senkottai
Madalapuram, Boothalapuram, Vowalthothi, Nagalapuram
Kadalkudi, Subaiahpuram.
Villages without amenities (Education):
Kumaralingapuram..
Scheduled Castes: Out of the total population of 63171 persons, 12303 persons (19.48%) belong to Scheduled Castes.
The villages having less than 10% SC population are
Kodangipatti, Arunasalapuram, Karupur, Vedapatti
Singilipatti, Mettipatti, Maniyakananpatti
Vannipatti, Chennampatti, Pattithevar Patti
Madalapuram, Kumaralingapuram, Jagaveerapuram
Kandasamypuram, Jeegaveerapuram, Melakkallarani
Kinnur, Maleeswarapuram, Ienamvadamalapuram
Sundarapachaiah Puram, Subaiahpuram.
The villages having more than 50% SC population are None.
Sex ratio of Scheduled Caste population is 507.

Scheduled Castes Literates and Illiterates by Sex:

	Persons	Males	Females
Literate	7,083	4,105	2,978
Illiterate	5,220	1,959	3,261
Literacy rate	66.2	78.4	54.5
Graduate	86	61	25

Scheduled Castes (Dominant):
Pallan, Paraiyan etc., Chakkiliyan, Pagadai
Arunthathiyar
For their cultural identity please see.Appendix-I
Villages without Scheduled Castes: There are 8 villages without any scheduled caste population.
Scheduled Tribes: Out of the total population of 63171 persons, 2 persons (0%) belong to Scheduled Tribes.
The villages having less than 10% ST population are
Ayankarisalkulam, Kodangipatti, Vemboor
Melakkarandai, Ayanrajapatti, Nasarpatti
Keelakkarandai, Ayanvadamalapuram, Thappathi
Chakliyapatti, Keznattukuruchi, Arunasalapuram
Karupur, Veerappatti, Tholmalaipatti, Muthulapuram
Nambipuram, Vedapatti, Singilipatti, Mettipatti
Muthusamypuram, Maniyakananpatti, Vannipatti
Naddukattur, Chennampatti, Sivalarpatti
Pattithevar Patti, Senkottai, Madalapuram
Kumaralingapuram, Jagaveerapuram, Kandasamypuram
Jeegaveerapuram, Boothalapuram, Melakkallarani
Sankaralingapuram, Goundanpatti, Vowalthothi
Nagalapuram, Duraichamypuram, Mavilodai, Kadalkudi
Kinnur, Maleeswarapuram, Lakshmipuram
Ienamvadamalapuram, Sundarapachaiah Puram
Subaiahpuram, Vadalakkari, Ramachandrapuram
Muthaiyapuram.
The villages having more than 50% ST population are

None.

Sex ratio of Scheduled tribe population is 500.

Scheduled Tribes Literates and Illiterates by Sex:

	Persons	Males	Females
Literate	0	0	0
Illiterate	2	1	1
Literacy rate	-	-	-
Graduate	0	0	0

Scheduled Tribes (Dominant):

Malai Pandaram

For their cultural identity please see Appendix-II

Villages without Scheduled Tribes: There are 51 villages without any scheduled tribe population.

Literates and Illiterates by Sex (Total Population):

	Persons	Males	Females
Literate	41,131	23,403	17,728
Illiterate	22,040	7,765	14,275
Literacy rate	73	85	62
Graduate	552	359	193

Agriculture: ***Distribution of villages according to land use:*** Out of 52 villages, Total area (in hectare) is 46590.92, out of that 57.56 percent is cultivable and 3.68 percent of the cultivable area is irrigated.

Sources of Irrigation (Hectares): Government Canal 0, Private Canal 0, Well without Electricity 46.66, Well with Electricity 654.78, Tubewell without Electricity 0, Tubewell with Electricity 37.68, Tank 248.42, River 0, Lake 0, Waterfall 0, Others 0.

Villages with population of 5000 to 9999: None

Villages with population of 10000 and above: None

Distribution of Workers:

	Persons	Males	Females	WPR
Cultivators	10,814	6,040	4,774	28.22
Agricultural Labour	15,833	7,012	8,821	41.32
Household Industry	1,626	293	1,333	4.24
Other Workers	10,047	6,454	3,593	26.22
Main Workers	29,196	16,207	12,989	76.19
Marginal Workers	9,124	3,592	5,532	23.81
Total Workers	38,320	19,799	18,521	

Religion: Major Religious Communities:

	Persons	Males	Females	Sex Ratio
Hindu (95.24%)	60,163	29,712	30,451	1,025
Muslim (0.52%)	328	159	169	1,063
Christian (4.12%)	2,604	1,260	1,344	1,067
Sikh (0%)	2	1	1	1,000
Buddhists (0%)	2	-	2	-
Jain (0.01%)	4	2	2	1,000

Agewise Data:

	Persons	Males	Females	Sex Ratio
All ages	63,171	31,168	32,003	1027
0-14	15,874	8,064	7,810	969
15-44	29,693	14,506	15,187	1047
45-79	16,636	8,116	8,520	1050
80+	693	350	343	980
Age not stated	275	132	143	1083

Languages (Dominant):

Tamil, Telugu, Kannada, Malayalam, Urdu

Disabled Population:

	Persons	Males	Females	%
Total Disabled	1,982	952	1,030	
In Seeing	1,288	552	736	64.98
In Speech	163	93	70	8.22
In Hearing	74	33	41	3.73
In Movement	349	208	141	17.61
Mentally	108	66	42	5.45

PULLAMPADI

Pullambadi C.D. Block lies in the north-eastern part of Tiruchirappalli district. It is a part of Lalgudi taluk. The Block is located at a distance of 31-kms. from district headquarters (Tiruchirappalli). There are 36 villages in the block with the total population of 79,538 persons. Area of the C.D. Block is 366.86 sq. kms. It is bounded in the north by district Perambalur, in the south by C.D. Block Lalgudi and district Thanjavur, in the east by districts Ariyalur and Perambalur, and in the west by CD Block Manachanallur.

Communications:

Roadways : N.H.-45: Direction- Tiruchirappalli to Perambalur, Nearest Villages- Neikulam, Periyakurukkai. S.H.-24: Direction- Puvalur to Kilabalurer, Nearest Villages- Melarasur, Keezharasur, Kallagam, Muthuvathur, Venkadachalapuram (N), Kouandakurichi, Vellanur, Nanjai Sangudhi, Edagimangalam, Punjaisangenthi.

Railway Station: Kallagam.

River: Upparnandiyar Nadi- Nearest Villages- Neikulam, Periyakurukkai, Peruvalappur, Vandalaikuddalur, Kannakudi, Punjaisangenthi, Vellanur. Kollidam Nadi- Nearest Villages- Veragalur, Alambadi. Nandiodai Nadi- Nearest Villages- Keezharasur, Sadurbagam, Muthuvathur, Kallagam, Malvoi.

Annual Rainfall: Average Rainfall 841 mm.

Ground Water: Availability of the ground water in the Basin is 4889.04 H.A.M. and the utilization is 2375.65 H.A.M. It belongs to Safe category. Depth to water level varies from 0 to 10 meter below the ground. Most of the wells go down in summer months, according to the Ground Water Estimation Committee.

Natural Division: Chola Nadu.

Administration

Revenue **Division:** Lalgudi. Parliamentary Constituency: 24 Tiruchirappalli. District: Tiruchirappalli. Taluk: Lalgudi. Assembly Constituency: 143 Lalgudi. Gram Panchayat: 33.

Villages: 36 **Inhabited:** 35 **Uninhabited:** 1

Ranking	District	State	National
Area	3	96	2150
Population	12	246	4121
Sex Ratio	1	89	698
Child Sex Ratio	10	284	4774
Literacy Rate	6	122	1276
Density	7	128	4485
Work Participation Rate	14	311	1303

Gram Panchayats:

Aalampakkam, Alampadi, Kallagam, Kanakkiliyanallur, Kannakudi, Karudamangalam, Kelarasur, Kovandakurichi, Kumalur, M.Kannanur, Malvoy, Melarasur, Muthuvathur, Nambukurichi, Nanchai sanganthi, Neikulam, Oottathur, Orathur, Peiryakurukkai, Peruvalappur, Pudurpalayam, Punchai Sankenthi, Reddymangudi, Saradamangalam, Sirukalappur, Thinnakulam, Thiranipalayam, Thoppai, Vandalai Gudalur, Varakuppai, Vellanur, Venkatachalapuram, Virakalur.

Amenities:

Education: Primary School in 33 villages, Middle school in 21 villages, Matriculation or Secondary School in 7 villages, namely Uttathur, Malvoi, Sirukalappur, Peruvalappur, Kallagam, Kouandakurichi, Pudurpalayam.

Higher Secondary or Pre University Courses or Intermediate or Junior College in 2 villages of the CD Block,, namely Kouandakurichi, Pudurpalayam.

College in 1 village, Adult Literacy Center in 0 village., Colleges are in villages, namely Kumulur.

Medical: Hospital in 1 village, Dispensary in 2 villages, Health Center in 5 villages, Sub Center in 5 villages, Maternity and Child Welfare Center in 3 villages, Community health workers in 0 village.

The Villages having Hospital or Dispensary or Health Center are Kouandakurichi, Alambakkam.

Drinking Water: Tap water in 35 villages, Tank water in 16 villages, Well water in 35 villages, Tubewell in 35 villages and more than one source in 35 villages.

Bank: Banking facility in 5 villages, namely, Karudamangalam (S), Malvoi, Peruvalappur, Kumulur Punjaisangenthi.

Credit Society in 8 villages Agricultural Credit Society in 7 Non-Agricultural Credit Society in 0 village.

Others: Power supply in 35 villages, Cinema hall in 0 village, sport club in 0 village, Stadium or Auditorium or Community Hall in 0 village, Post Office in 27 villages.

There are 32 villages having bus facilities.

Villages with most of facilities: Karudamangalam (S) Malvoi, Peruvalappur, Kumulur.

Villages without amenities (Education):

Sadurbagam, Venkadachalapuram (S)..

Scheduled Castes: Out of the total population of 79538 persons, 13809 persons (17.36%) belong to Scheduled Castes.

The villages having less than 10% SC population are Uttathur, Malvoi, Thappai, Vandalaikuddalur, Kumulur Punjaisangenthi, Venkadachalapuram (S) Kouandakurichi, Pudurpalayam, Nanjai Sangudhi Veragalur.

The villages having more than 50% SC population are None.

Sex ratio of Scheduled Caste population is 501.

Scheduled Castes Literates and Illiterates by Sex:

	Persons	Males	Females
Literate	7,737	4,549	3,188
Illiterate	6,072	2,342	3,730
Literacy rate	64.3	75.8	52.8
Graduate	147	121	26

Scheduled Castes (Dominant):

Paraiyan etc., Pallan, Chakkiliyan, Domban

Adi Dravida

For their cultural identity please see Appendix-I

Villages without Scheduled Castes: There are 2 villages without any scheduled caste population.

Scheduled Tribes: Out of the total population of 79538 persons, 127 persons (0.16%) belong to Scheduled Tribes.

The villages having less than 10% ST population are Neikulam, Uttathur, Theranipalaiyam Karudamangalam (N), Karudamangalam (S) Saradamangalam, Kannanur, Orathur, Sadurbagam Malvoi, Sirukalappur, Nambukuruchi, Periyakurukkai Reddimangudi, Peruvalappur, Kanakkiliyanallur Varakuppai, Melarasur, Keezharasur, Kallagam Muthuvathur, Thappai, Vandalaikuddalur, Kannakudi Kumulur, Punjaisangenthi, Venkadachalapuram (S) Kouandakurichi, Pudurpalayam, Alambakkam, Vellanur Nanjai Sangudhi, Edagimangalam, Veragalur, Alambadi.

The villages having more than 50% ST population are None.

Sex ratio of Scheduled tribe population is 504.

Scheduled Tribes Literates and Illiterates by Sex:

	Persons	Males	Females
Literate	36	21	15
Illiterate	91	42	49
Literacy rate	33.0	40.4	26.3
Graduate	0	0	0

Scheduled Tribes (Dominant):

Irular, Muthuvan

For their cultural identity please see Appendix-II

Villages without Scheduled Tribes: There are 31 villages without any scheduled tribe population.

Literates and Illiterates by Sex (Total Population):

	Persons	Males	Females
Literate	48,804	28,091	20,713
Illiterate	30,734	11,316	19,418
Literacy rate	69	81	58
Graduate	1,232	830	402

Agriculture: ***Distribution of villages according to land use:*** Out of 36 villages, Total area (in hectare) is 36686.05, out of that 55.27 percent is cultivable and 36.42 percent of the cultivable area is irrigated.

Sources of Irrigation (Hectares): Government Canal 3572.46, Private Canal 0, Well without Electricity 713.34, Well with Electricity 2398.06, Tubewell without Electricity 211.56, Tubewell with Electricity 333.86, Tank 155.41, River 0, Lake 0, Waterfall 0, Others 0.

Villages with population of 5000 to 9999: Kovandakurichi.

Villages with population of 10000 and above: None

Distribution of Workers:

	Persons	Males	Females	WPR
Cultivators	19,159	11,074	8,085	44.31
Agricultural Labour	17,528	7,835	9,693	40.54
Household Industry	765	356	409	1.77
Other Workers	5,784	4,481	1,303	13.38
Main Workers	30,660	18,023	12,637	70.91
Marginal Workers	12,576	5,723	6,853	29.09
Total Workers	43,236	23,746	19,490	

Religion: Major Religious Communities:

	Persons	Males	Females	Sex Ratio
Hindu (78.98%)	62,819	31,184	31,635	1,014
Muslim (1.5%)	1,197	583	614	1,053
Christian (19.36%)	15,401	7,575	7,826	1,033
Sikh (0%)	-	-	-	-
Buddhists (0%)	-	-	-	-
Jain (0%)	-	-	-	-

Agewise Data:

	Persons	Males	Females	Sex Ratio
All ages	79,538	39,407	40,131	1018
0-14	21,335	10,961	10,374	946
15-44	37,554	18,397	19,157	1041
45-79	19,542	9,528	10,014	1051
80+	598	300	298	993
Age not stated	509	221	288	1303

Languages (Dominant): Tamil, Telugu, Malayalam, Urdu, Hindi

Disabled Population:

	Persons	Males	Females	%
Total Disabled	2,394	1,111	1,283	
In Seeing	1,406	555	851	58.73
In Speech	237	134	103	9.9
In Hearing	131	68	63	5.47
In Movement	483	280	203	20.18
Mentally	137	74	63	5.72

PUZHAL

Puzhal C.D. Block lies in the eastern part of Thiruvallur district. It is a part of Ambattur taluk. The Block is located at a distance of 35 kms. from district headquarters (Thiruvallur). There are 22 villages in the block with the total population of 51,081 persons. Area of the C.D. Block is 46.69 sq. kms. It is bounded in the north by CD Blocks Minjur and Sholavaram, in the south by CD Block Villivakkam and district Chennai, in the east by the Bay of Bangal, and in the west by CD Block Villivakkam.

Communications:

Roadways : N.H.-5: Direction- Gummidipoondi to Chennai, Nearest Villages- Line Grant, Kadirvedu, Soorapattu, Puthagaram.

Canal: (Backingham)- Nearest Village- Sadayankuppam.

Annual Rainfall: Average Rainfall 1152 mm.

Ground Water: Availability of the ground water in the Basin is 31.39 MCM and the utilization is 17.53 MCM. It belongs to Critical category. Depth to water level varies from 2 to 10 meter below the ground. Most of the wells go down in summer months, according to the Ground Water Estimation Committee.

Natural Division: Tondai Nadu.

Administration Revenue **Division:** Ponneri. Parliamentary Constituency: 2 Chennai North. District: Thiruvallur. Taluk: Ambattur. Assembly Constituency: 9 Madavaram. Gram Panchayat: 15.

Villages: 22 **Inhabited:** 22 **Uninhabited:** 0

Ranking	District	State	National
Area	14	384	6064
Population	14	353	5219
Sex Ratio	14	318	2666
Child Sex Ratio	10	186	3179
Literacy Rate	1	20	264
Density	14	381	638
Work Participation Rate	1	3	5704

Gram Panchayats:

Alinjivakkam, Grant Lyon, Kadapakkam, Kadhirvedu, Lyon , Mathur, Puthagaram, Sadayankuppam, Sendrambakkam, Soorapattu, Theerthagiriyampattu, Theeyambakkam, Vadagarai, Vadaperumbakkam, Vilangadupakkam.

Amenities:

Education: Primary School in 17 villages, Middle school in 7 villages, Matriculation or Secondary School in 4 villages, namely Sadayankuppam, Vadakarai, Soorappattu, Kadirvedu.

Higher Secondary or Pre University Courses or Intermediate or Junior College in 4 villages of the CD Block,, namely Sadayankuppam, Vadakarai, Soorappattu, Kadirvedu.
College in 1 village, Adult Literacy Center in 0 village., Colleges are in villages, namely Soorappattu.
Medical: Hospital in 0 village, Dispensary in 0 village, Health Center in 7 villages, Sub Center in 4 villages, Maternity and Child Welfare Center in 0 village, Community health workers in 22 villages.
Drinking Water: Tap water in 22 villages, Tank water in 22 villages, Well water in 22 villages, Tubewell in 22 villages and more than one source in 22 villages.
Bank: None.
Credit Society in 0 village Agricultural Credit Society in 0 Non-Agricultural Credit Society in 0 village.
Others: Power supply in 21 villages, Cinema hall in 0 village, sport club in 0 village, Stadium or Auditorium or Community Hall in 0 village, Post Office in 7 villages.
There are 17 villages having bus facilities.
Villages with most of facilities: None.
Villages without amenities (Education):
Sisrugavoor, Elanthancheri, Chittimedu, Line Grant, Athivakkam..
Scheduled Castes: Out of the total population of 51081 persons, 15879 persons (31.09%) belong to Scheduled Castes.
The villages having less than 10% SC population are Palavoyal, Sisrugavoor, Manjampakkam, Kosappur Soorappattu, Puthagaram.
The villages having more than 50% SC population are Vilangadupakkam, Ariyalur, Vadaperumbakkam Payasambakkam, Athivakkam, Vadakarai.
Sex ratio of Scheduled Caste population is 502.
Scheduled Castes Literates and Illiterates by Sex:

	Persons	Males	Females
Literate	10,993	6,078	4,915
Illiterate	4,886	1,832	3,054
Literacy rate	78.8	88.2	69.6
Graduate	343	235	108

Scheduled Castes (Dominant):
Adi Dravida, Generic Castes etc., Pallan, Valluvan Paraiyan etc.
For their cultural identity please see Appendix-I
Villages without Scheduled Castes: There is 1 village without any scheduled caste population.
Scheduled Tribes: Out of the total population of 51081 persons, 516 persons (1.01%) belong to Scheduled Tribes.
The villages having less than 10% ST population are Theerthaniriampattu, Palavoyal, Vilangadupakkam Sisrugavoor, Ariyalur, Kadappakkam, Sadayankuppam Elanthancheri, Mathur, Manjampakkam, Kosappur Chittimedu, Vadaperumbakkam, Line Grant Payasambakkam, Grand Lyon, Alingavakkam, Athivakkam Vadakarai, Soorappattu, Kadirvedu, Puthagaram.
The villages having more than 50% ST population are None.
Sex ratio of Scheduled tribe population is 514.
Scheduled Tribes Literates and Illiterates by Sex:

	Persons	Males	Females
Literate	129	81	48
Illiterate	387	170	217
Literacy rate	31.5	39.1	23.7
Graduate	4	1	3

Scheduled Tribes (Dominant):
Irular, Kattunayakan, Generic Tribes etc., Kurumans Palliyar
For their cultural identity please see Appendix-II
Villages without Scheduled Tribes: There are 11 villages without any scheduled tribe population.
Literates and Illiterates by Sex (Total Population):

	Persons	Males	Females
Literate	36,204	20,177	16,027
Illiterate	14,877	5,787	9,090
Literacy rate	81	89	73
Graduate	1,575	991	584

Agriculture: ***Distribution of villages according to land use:***
Out of 22 villages, Total area (in hectare) is 4669.35, out of that 42.6 percent is cultivable and 65.57 percent of the cultivable area is irrigated.
Sources of Irrigation (Hectares): Government Canal 0, Private Canal 0, Well without Electricity 0, Well with Electricity 294.82, Tubewell without Electricity 14.72, Tubewell with Electricity 437.51, Tank 0, River 0, Lake 477.14, Waterfall 0, Others 80.25.
Villages with population of 5000 to 9999:
Mathur, Soorapattu, Puthagaram.
Villages with population of 10000 and above: None
Distribution of Workers:

	Persons	Males	Females	WPR
Cultivators	882	667	215	5.26
Agricultural Labour	1,545	1,033	512	9.22
Household Industry	765	386	379	4.56
Other Workers	13,574	11,459	2,115	80.96
Main Workers	12,291	10,349	1,942	73.31
Marginal Workers	4,475	3,196	1,279	26.69
Total Workers	16,766	13,545	3,221	

Religion: Major Religious Communities:

	Persons	Males	Females	Sex Ratio
Hindu (90.69%)	46,325	23,565	22,760	966
Muslim (2.35%)	1,201	578	623	1,078

Christian (6.69%)	3,418	1,724	1,694	983
Sikh (0.02%)	12	7	5	714
Buddhists (0.01%)	5	3	2	667
Jain (0.05%)	25	17	8	471

Agewise Data:

	Persons	Males	Females	Sex Ratio
All ages	51,081	25,964	25,117	967
0-14	14,360	7,369	6,991	949
15-44	27,288	13,834	13,454	973
45-79	8,753	4,441	4,312	971
80+	357	159	198	1245
Age not stated	323	161	162	1006

Languages (Dominant):

Tamil, Telugu, Urdu, Malayalam, Hindi

Disabled Population:

	Persons	Males	Females	%
Total Disabled	948	545	403	
In Seeing	283	161	122	29.85
In Speech	90	52	38	9.49
In Hearing	80	36	44	8.44
In Movement	332	204	128	35.02
Mentally	163	92	71	17.19